English Pronouncing Dictionary

CAMBRIDGE
UNIVERSITY PRESS

PUBLISHED BY THE PRESS SYNDICATE OF THE UNIVERSITY OF CAMBRIDGE
The Pitt Building, Trumpington Street, Cambridge CB2 1RP, United Kingdom

CAMBRIDGE UNIVERSITY PRESS
The Edinburgh Buiding, Cambridge CB2 2RU, United Kingdom
40 West 20th Street, New York, NY 10011–4211, USA
477 Williamstown Road, Port Melbourne, VIC 3207, Australia
Ruiz de Alarcón 13, 28014 Madrid, Spain
Dock House, The Waterfront, Cape Town 8001, South Africa

Visit our website at http://www.cup.cam.ac.uk/elt/reference
Email comments about this book to epd@cup.cam.ac.uk

First published by J. M. Dent & Sons Ltd 1917

First published by Cambridge University Press 1991
This edition published 2003

Printed in Italy by G. Canale & C. S.p.A

Typeface Times Phonetic IPA 7/9 pt. *System* QuarkXPress® [UPH]

A catalogue record for this book is available from the British Library

Library of Congress Cataloguing in Publication data applied for

ISBN 0 521 81693 9 hardback
ISBN 0 521 01712 2 paperback
ISBN 0 521 01713 0 paperback & CD-ROM
ISBN 3 12 539683 2 Klett paperback & CD-ROM
ISBN 3 12 539684 0 Klett paperback

Contents

Editors' preface to the 16th Edition

The *English Pronouncing Dictionary* was first published in 1917, perhaps the greatest work of the greatest of British phoneticians, Daniel Jones (born in 1881). Jones was Professor of Phonetics at University College London from 1921 until his retirement in 1949. He was still an occasional visitor to the Department in 1967 when Peter Roach was there as a postgraduate student of phonetics, though he died in December of that year. The dictionary was preceded by a now forgotten work by Michaelis and Jones (1913) in which the phonemic transcription was presented first and the corresponding spelling followed it. The last edition in which Jones was directly involved was the 12th, and the 13th was substantially revised by his successor as Professor of Phonetics at University College, A. C. Gimson. From the 13th edition, Gimson was assisted by Dr. Susan Ramsaran, and in her preface to the 14th edition she notes that they had been making plans for a 15th edition at the time of Gimson's death. After this, the publishing rights were acquired from the original publishers, J. M. Dent & Sons, by Cambridge University Press.

With the publication of the 15th Edition in 1997, the *English Pronouncing Dictionary* entered the computer age. The type-set text of the 14th Edition was converted into a computer database, and the task of editing was carried out by a team of phonetics experts who worked by transferring the data of the developing new edition in electronic form between universities in Reading, Leeds, Kansas and Hong Kong, and the University Press in Cambridge. Despite the complexity of this operation, the process of updating and adding to the previous edition has been made more efficient, and has enabled this 16th Edition to be prepared much more rapidly. Versions of the database are available electronically, and are currently being used by language researchers in both academic and commercial institutions. For details of licensing the database, see the Cambridge Dictionaries website: www.dictionaries.cambridge.org

The *English Pronouncing Dictionary* has been in use for over 80 years, and during that time it has become established as a classic work of reference, both for native speakers of English wanting an authoritative guide to pronunciation and for users of English as a foreign or second language all over the world.

Above all, the aim of the Dictionary is to include information which is relevant to the needs of contemporary users and which is presented in the clearest possible way. This aim has informed both the choice of vocabulary covered and the range of pronunciations shown. The 15th edition saw a massive injection of 18,000 new words. Large numbers of terms connected with science and technology were added, as were hundreds of people and places which had acquired fame or notoriety in recent years. The more cosmopolitan nature of modern life was reflected in the increase of geographical names as well as a significant number of items of international cuisine. Personal names, both first names and family names, were based on census reports and statistical analysis, and many subject areas such as literature and law were revised and updated. For the first time, U.S. spellings and vocabulary items were included.

This 16th edition builds on that work, its wordlist fully updated with items which have become current since 1997. Another major feature is the addition of over 150 information panels explaining phonetics terminology and discussing the relationship between spelling and pronunciation.

Perhaps the most significant development of the 16th edition, and the one which truly takes it into the 21st century, is that it is now available with a CD-ROM which contains spoken pronunciations of every headword. The CD-ROM gives both linguists and learners of English a wealth of other features, from advanced search options on both alphabetic and phonetic characters, the ability to record the user's own voice and compare it with the spoken pronunciation on the CD-ROM, and a large number of interactive exercises.

In the Preface to the 15th Edition we thanked the many people who had contributed to our work, and our debt to them remains. Above all, we are very grateful to Liz Walter, our Commissioning Editor at Cambridge University Press who oversaw the production of the 15th Edition and has continued to advise and encourage us through the work on the 16th.

PETER ROACH, University of Reading
JAMES HARTMAN, University of Kansas
JANE SETTER, University of Reading

Introduction

It is strongly recommended that users of this dictionary read the introduction, since a full understanding of the information in it will ensure the most effective use of the dictionary.

(PART 1) **'What is the English Pronouncing Dictionary?'**: The intended use of the dictionary, the principles of its design and the accents of English represented in it.

(PART 2) **'Principles of Transcription'**: The main characteristics of the British and American accents.

(PART 3) **'Explanatory Notes'**: How to interpret the information provided with the individual words in the dictionary.

Part 1: Introduction to the English Pronouncing Dictionary

1.1 What is the English Pronouncing Dictionary?

This dictionary is designed to provide information on the current pronunciation of approximately 80,000 English words and phrases. For each entry, a British and an American pronunciation is shown (see Section 1.2 below). The pronunciation is given in modified phonemic transcription, and you need to understand the principles of phonemic transcription in order to be able to make proper use of this information (see Section 2.1 below).

The Pronouncing Dictionary provides much essential information that is not available in a general dictionary, such as the pronunciation of proper names, the pronunciation of all inflected forms of each word, and a larger amount of detail about variant pronunciations than is usual in a general dictionary.

1.2 Whose pronunciation is represented?

A pronouncing dictionary must base its recommendations on one or more *models.* A pronunciation model is a carefully chosen and defined accent of a language. In the first edition of this dictionary (1917), Daniel Jones described the type of pronunciation recorded as "that most usually heard in everyday speech in the families of Southern English persons whose menfolk have been educated at the great public boarding-schools". Accordingly, he felt able to refer to his model as "Public School Pronunciation" (PSP). In later editions, e.g. that of 1937, he added the remark that boys in boarding-schools tend to lose their markedly local peculiarities, whereas this is not the case for those in day-schools. He had by 1926, however, abandoned the term PSP in favour of "Received Pronunciation" (RP). The type of speech he had in mind had for centuries been regarded as a kind of standard, having its base in the educated pronunciation of London and the Home Counties (the counties surrounding London). Its use was not restricted to this region, however, being characteristic by the nineteenth century of upper-class speech throughout the country. The Editor of the 14th Edition of this dictionary, A. C. Gimson, commented in 1977 "Such a definition of RP is hardly tenable today", and went on "If I have retained the traditional, though imprecise, term 'received pronunciation', it is because the label has such wide currency in books on present-day English and because it is a convenient name for an accent which remains generally acceptable and intelligible within Britain".

For this edition a more broadly-based and accessible model accent for British English is represented, and pronunciations for one broadly-conceived accent of American English have been added. The time has come to abandon the archaic name *Received Pronunciation.* The model used for British English is what is referred to as *BBC English*; this is the pronunciation of professional speakers employed by the BBC as newsreaders and announcers on BBC1 and BBC2 television, the World Service and BBC Radio 3 and 4, as well as many commercial broadcasting organisations such as ITN. Of course, one finds differences between such speakers – individual broadcasters all have their own personal characteristics, and an increasing number of broadcasters with Scottish, Welsh and Irish accents are employed. However, the accent described here is typical of broadcasters with an English accent, and there is a useful degree of consistency in the broadcast speech of these speakers. Their speech does not carry for most people the connotations of high social class and privilege that PSP and RP have had in the past. An additional advantage in concentrating on the accent of broadcasters is that it is easy to gain access to examples, and the sound quality is usually of a very high standard.

For American English, the selection also follows what is frequently heard from professional voices on national network news and information programmes. It is similar to what has been termed "General American", which refers to a geographically (largely non-coastal) and socially based set of pronunciation features. It is important to note that no single dialect – regional or social – has been singled out as an American standard. Even national media (radio, television, movies, CD-ROM, etc.), with professionally trained voices have speakers with regionally mixed features. However, "Network English", in its most colourless form, can be described as a relatively homogeneous dialect that reflects the ongoing development of progressive American dialects (Canadian English has several notable differences). This "dialect" itself contains some variant forms. The variants included within this targeted accent involve vowels before /r/, possible differences in words like 'cot' and 'caught' and some vowels before /l/. It is fully rhotic. These differences largely pass unnoticed by the audiences for Network English, and are also reflective of age differences. What are thought to be the more progressive (used by educated, socially mobile, and younger speakers) variants are listed first in each entry. The intent is to list the variety of pronunciations with the least amount of regional or social marking, while still being sensitive to the traits of the individual word.

1.3 How are the pronunciations chosen?

It is important to remember that the pronunciation of English words is not governed by a strict set of rules; most words have more than one pronunciation, and the speaker's choice of which to use depends on a wide range of factors. These include the degree of formality, the amount of background noise, the speed of utterance, the speaker's perception of the listener and the frequency with which the speaker uses the word. For example, the two words 'virtuous' and 'virtuoso' are closely similar in spelling and share a common origin. However, the former is more common than the latter, and for British English /ˈvɜː.tʃu.əs/ is given as the first pronunciation of the former but /ˈvɜː.tju.əʊ.səʊ/ for the latter (which in general is typical of more careful speech). If such variation did not exist, most of the work of compiling a pronouncing dictionary could be done easily by means of one of the available computer programs that convert English spelling into a phonemic transcription. Ultimately, however, the decisions about which pronunciation to recommend, which pronunciations have dropped out of use, and so on, have been based on the editors' intuitions as professional phoneticians and observers of the pronunciation of English (particularly broadcast English) over many years. The opinion of many colleagues and acquaintances has also been a valuable source of advice.

In general, a pronunciation typical of a more casual, informal style of speaking is given for common words, and a more careful pronunciation for uncommon words. In real life, speakers tend to articulate most carefully when listeners are likely to have difficulty in recognising the words they hear. When more than one pronunciation of a word is given, the order of the alternatives is important. The first pronunciation given is believed to be the most usual one although the distance between the alternatives may vary, with some alternant forms rivalling the first-given in perceived frequency while others may be a more distant second.

1.4 Regional Accents

A pronouncing dictionary that systematically presented the pronunciations of a range of regional accents would be very valuable, but it would be very much bigger than the present volume and the job of ensuring an adequate coverage which treated all accents as equally important would have taken many years. In the case of some place-names, information about local pronunciations has been retained or added as well as "official" broadcasting ones, but the other words are given only in the standard accents chosen for British and American English.

1.5 Pronunciation of foreign words

Many of the words in an English dictionary are of foreign origin, and in previous editions of this dictionary many such words have been given both in an Anglicised pronunciation used by most English speakers, and in a broad phonetic transcription of the "authentic" pronunciation in the original language. This edition does not give detailed phonetic transcriptions of foreign words; the primary aim of this dictionary is to list pronunciations likely to be used by educated speakers of English, and an authentic pronunciation would in some circumstances be quite inappropriate (pronouncing 'Paris' as /pærˈiː/, for example). In some cases the information is unnecessary (very few English speakers would attempt, or even recognise, an authentic pronunciation of a word from a non-European language), while in other cases it is difficult to establish the authentic original (many African place-names, for example, have reached us after being adapted by British, French or Portuguese colonists; place-names in Spain may be pronounced in different ways according to their regional affiliation, so that the name of Barcelona might be given a Catalan or a Castilian Spanish pronunciation, while other Spanish names are different according to whether they originate in Spain or South America). Words and names of foreign origin are therefore given in what is felt to be the pronunciation likely to be used among educated speakers of English.

In some cases it is possible to identify an alternative pronunciation which represents an attempt to pronounce in a manner closer to the supposed original. This is marked by first indicating the language which the speaker would be aiming at, then giving the pronunciation, using where necessary additional phonetic symbols not required for the phonemic transcription of English. For example, the word 'bolognese' is widely used to refer to a sauce served with pasta. This is given as /ˌbɒl.əˈneɪz/ for British English and as /ˌboʊ.ləˈniːz/ for American; for speakers of both groups, a pronunciation aimed at being nearer to the Italian original would be /ˌbɒl.əˈnjeɪ.zeɪ/ (though this would still be different from the pronunciation that would be produced by an Italian speaker). To indicate that this last pronunciation is aimed at sounding Italian, it is marked in the entry as: *as if Italian:* ˌbɒl.əˈnjeɪ.zeɪ. In a few cases it has been necessary to mark separate British and American pronunciations within this field, as the degree of Anglicisation of any given word may vary between British and American English.

1.6 Usage notes

Usage notes are included with some words. In some cases these are needed so that users of the dictionary can understand how alternative pronunciations are to be used. In some cases the rules needed for correct pronunciation are quite complex, most noticeably in the case of the so-called "weak-form words" such as 'there', 'her'. Explanations with examples are given in such cases.

1.7 Syllable divisions

Earlier editions of this dictionary regularly marked the division between syllables. This practice was largely abandoned in the 14th Edition, but the present edition gives syllable divisions in all cases, since it is felt that foreign learners will find the information useful. Syllable division is marked with the symbol . recommended by the International Phonetic Association. The decision on where to place a syllable division is not always easy, and the rules used in this work are explained later in this Introduction (Section 2.6).

Part 2: Principles of transcription

2.1 The phoneme principle

The basic principle of the transcription used is, as in all previous editions, *phonemic*. This means that a small set of symbols is used to represent the sounds that can be shown to be distinctive in English, so that replacing one phoneme by another can change the identity of a word. We do not usually add phonetic detail such as the presence of glottal stops, aspiration or vowel devoicing. It is usual to put slant brackets before and after symbols representing phonemes (e.g. the word 'cat' would be represented phonemically as /kæt/). When non-phonemic symbols are used, the convention is to use square brackets (e.g. the glottal stop will be represented as [ʔ]). In entries in the dictionary itself, however, we do not use these brackets, in order to keep the information simple; only in explanatory notes do we use slant or square brackets. For an explanation of the principle of the phoneme and some of the problems associated with it, see Roach (2000), Chapters 5 and 13. The use of phonemic transcription in works on pronunciation (including this one) has remained in the "realist" tradition established by Jones, while approaches to the phoneme by theoretical phonologists have changed radically during recent decades and become much more abstract. There are a few exceptions to our general use of the phoneme principle that should be mentioned here, however. One is the use, in American pronunciations, of the [̬] diacritic to indicate the voicing and "flapping" of /t/ in words such as 'getting' /ˈget̬.ɪŋ/, and 'better' /ˈbet̬.ɚ/. This is an important feature of American pronunciation, but speakers of British English find it difficult to apply the rule which determines when /t/ is voiced and/or flapped. Another is the use of the symbols [i] and [u] , the use of which is explained below (Section 2.9). Finally, it is necessary to use a number of special symbols which are not normally used for English phonemes. This set includes some nasalised vowels used particularly in some words taken from French, the [x] sound found in Scottish words such as 'loch', and some non-linguistic sounds used in certain exclamations and interjections (see Section 2.4).

2.2 Vowels and diphthongs

It is standard practice in phonetics to represent the quality of vowels and diphthongs by placing them on a four-sided figure usually known as the *Cardinal Vowel quadrilateral* (see Roach (2000), pp. 13–14). This device is used in the vowel descriptions in the following section.

(a) British English

British English (BBC accent) is generally described as having short vowels, long vowels and diphthongs. There are said to be seven short vowels, five long ones and eight diphthongs. At the end of this section some attention is also given to triphthongs.

- Short vowels:

pit	pet	pat	putt	pot	put	another	
ɪ	e	æ	ʌ	ɒ	ʊ	ə	ə

- Long vowels:

bean	barn	born	boon	burn
iː	ɑː	ɔː	uː	ɜː

- Diphthongs:

bay	buy	boy	no	now	peer	pair	poor
eɪ	aɪ	ɔɪ	əʊ	aʊ	ɪə	eə	ʊə

These vowels and diphthongs may be placed on the Cardinal Vowel quadrilateral as shown in Figs. 1 -3. It should be noted that though each vowel (or diphthong starting-point) is marked with a point (●), it is misleading to think of this as a precise target; the point represents the centre of an area within which the typical vowel pronunciation falls.

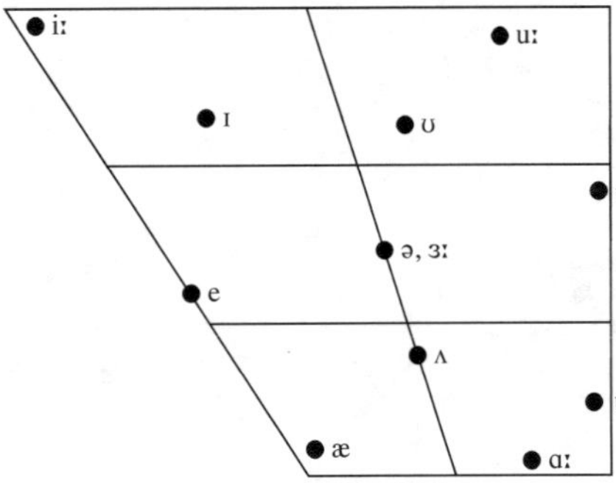

Fig. 1 BBC English pure vowels

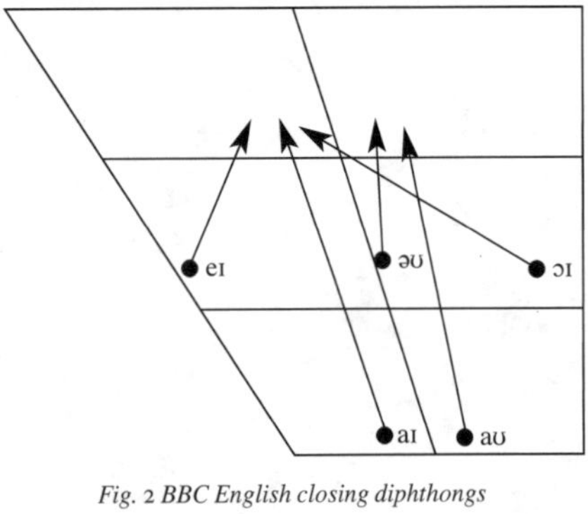

Fig. 2 BBC English closing diphthongs

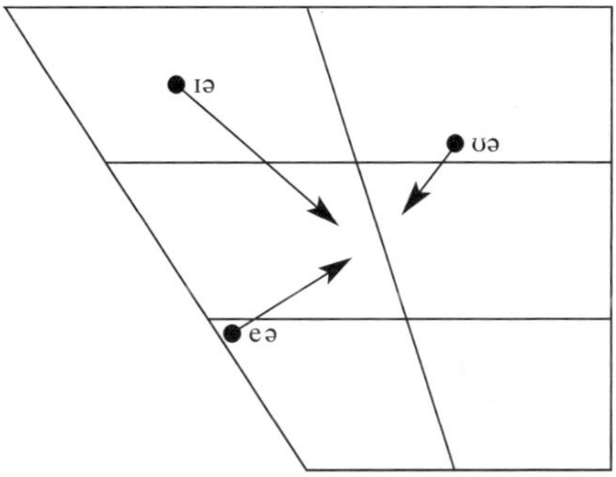

Fig. 3 BBC English centring diphthongs

A few comments on individual vowels and vowel symbols are needed. The pronunciation of any language is constantly changing, and a dictionary such as this one should reflect such changes. However, there is a general reluctance among users of phonemic transcription to change the symbols used too frequently, as this causes existing teaching materials and textbooks to become out of date. The following remarks apply chiefly to BBC pronunciation.

(a) The length of long vowels and diphthongs is very much reduced when they occur in syllables closed by the consonants / p, t, k, tʃ, f, θ, s, ʃ /. Thus /iː/ in 'beat' has only about half the length of /iː/ in 'bead' or 'bee'; similarly /eɪ/ in 'place' is much reduced in length compared with /eɪ/ in 'plays' or 'play'.

(b) The vowel /æ/, classified as a short vowel, is nevertheless generally lengthened before /b, d, g, dʒ, m, n/. Thus /æ/ in 'bag' is considerably longer than /æ/ in 'back'. The quality of this vowel is now more open than it used to be, and the symbol /a/ might one day be considered preferable. We have retained the /æ/ symbol partly because it is phonetically appropriate for the corresponding American vowel.

(c) The vowel /ʌ/ used to be a back vowel, and the symbol was chosen for this reason. This is no longer a back vowel, but a central one. Alternative symbols could be considered in the future.

(d) Among younger speakers, the /uː/ vowel has moved to a more front quality, with less lip-rounding, particularly when preceded by /j/ as in 'use'.

(e) Among the diphthongs, there seems to be a progressive decline in the use of /ʊə/, with /ɔː/ taking its place (e.g. the pronunciation of the word 'poor' as /pɔː/ is increasingly common).

(f) Triphthongs create some problems. These three-vowel sequences are generally held to be composed of one of the diphthongs /eɪ, aɪ, ɔɪ, əʊ, aʊ/ plus a schwa (e.g. 'layer' /leɪəʳ/; 'fire' /faɪəʳ/). In British English many of these triphthongs are pronounced with such slight movement in vowel quality that it is difficult for foreign learners to recognise them; for example, the name 'Ireland', which is generally transcribed /'aɪə.lənd/, frequently has an initial syllable which sounds virtually indistinguishable from /ɑː/. It seems reasonable in this case to treat these sounds as being monosyllabic (e.g. the word 'fire' is a single syllable), but in other words and names transcribed with the same symbols it seems necessary to insert a syllable division. This is usually done (i) when there is a morpheme boundary (e.g. 'buyer' /baɪ.əʳ/) and (ii) when the word is felt to be foreign (this includes many Biblical names originating from Hebrew, e.g. 'Messiah').

Another problem with triphthongs is that before an /r/ consonant at the beginning of a following syllable, the distinction between /aɪə/ and /aɪ/ seems to be neutralised – it seems to make no difference whether one represents 'Irish', 'irate' as /'aɪə.rɪʃ/, /aɪə'reɪt/ or as /'aɪ.rɪʃ/ , /aɪ'reɪt/, since there is no regular distinction made in pronunciation. In general, the practice of this edition is to transcribe such cases as /aɪə- /.

(b) American English

American English is commonly described as having lax vowels, tense vowels, and wide diphthongs. Generally speaking, lax vowels are lower and made with less oral tension; they do not usually end syllables. Vowel length in American English is generally considered to be conditioned by phonological environment, so the long/short distinction described for BBC English is not usually present, though we have retained the length mark on the tense vowels /iː, ɑː, ɔː, ɜː, uː/ in order to mark their relationship to the English long vowels. Since the diphthongal movement in /eɪ/ and /oʊ/ is small in American pronunciation, these are treated as tense vowels. Vowels preceding /r/ are notably influenced by rhotic colouring. Word spellings such as 'bird', 'word', 'curd', 'earth', 'jerk', which now rhyme with /ɝ/ in American English, at one time in history had differing vowels. The retroflexed vowels /ɝ/ and /ɚ/, stressed and unstressed, are among those features that noticeably distinguish

American English from BBC English. All vowels occurring before /r/ within a syllable are likely to become "r-coloured" to some extent.

- lax vowels: ɪ e æ ʌ ʊ ə
- tense vowels: iː ɑː ɔː ɜː uː eɪ oʊ
- wide diphthongs: aʊ aɪ ɔɪ
- retroflexed vowels ("r-coloured") ɚ ɝ

There is an issue in the symbolization of the diphthong in the word "home". This has for many years been represented as /əʊ/, but in earlier editions of this and others of Jones' works the symbolization /ou/ indicated a rounded initial vowel. This is still the preferred transcription for the American English diphthong. In order to preserve compatibility with other works, we have chosen to use /əʊ/ for BBC English and /oʊ/ for American, though it can be argued that the latter symbolization would be suitable for both.

The American /æ/ vowel is somewhat closer than BBC /æ/, and seems to be evolving into an even closer vowel in many speakers. It is used in the same words as BBC /æ/ and also in most of the words which in BBC have /ɑː/ when there is no letter r in the spelling, e.g. 'pass', 'ask'. The quality of American /ɑː/ is similar to the BBC /ɑː/ vowel; it is used in some of the words which have /ɑː/ in BBC when there is no letter r in the spelling (e.g. 'father', 'calm'). It also replaces the BBC short /ɒ/ vowel in many words (e.g. 'hot', 'top', 'bother'): 'bother' rhymes with 'father'. American /ɔː/ is more open in quality than BBC /ɔː/. It is used where BBC has /ɔː/ (e.g. 'cause', 'walk'), and also replaces BBC short /ɒ/ in many words, e.g. 'long', 'dog'. American /uː/ is similar to BBC /uː/, but is also used where BBC has /juː/ after alveolar consonants (e.g. 'new', 'duty').

2.3 Consonants
(a) British English (BBC)

- Plosives: p b t d k g
  pin **b**in **t**in **d**in **k**in **g**um
- Affricates: tʃ dʒ
  chain **J**ane
- Fricatives: f v θ ð s z
  fine **v**ine **th**ink **th**is **s**eal **z**eal
  ʃ ʒ h
  sheep mea**s**ure **h**ow
- Nasals: m n ŋ
  su**m** su**n** su**ng**
- Approximants: l r w j
  light **r**ight **w**et **y**et

These consonants can be arranged in table form as shown below. The layout of the symbols follows the principle that, where there are two consonants which differ only in voicing, they are placed side by side with the voiceless one to the left.

(a) Certain types of consonant have a distinction such as that between /t/ and /d/; this is commonly classed as a distinction between voiceless and voiced consonants, but the distinction is in fact much more complex. Consonants usually classed as voiceless are /p, t, k, f, θ, s, ʃ, h, tʃ/, with voiced partners /b, d, g, v, ð, z, ʒ, dʒ/. Since the presence or absence of voicing is often less important than some other phonetic features, it has been suggested that instead the terms *fortis* (equivalent to voiceless) and *lenis* (equivalent to voiced) should be used. These terms imply that the main distinguishing factor is the amount of energy used in the articulation (fortis consonants being made with greater energy than lenis). These terms

Table of English Consonants

	Bilabial	*Labio-dental*	*Dental*	*Alveolar*	*Post-alveolar*	*Palatal*	*Velar*	*Glottal*
Plosive	p b			t d			k g	
Affricate					tʃ dʒ			
Fricative		f v	θ ð	s z	ʃ ʒ		(x)	h
Nasal	m			n			ŋ	
Lateral approximant				l				
Approximant	w				r	j		

are not used in this dictionary, since the usefulness of this terminology is uncertain. Some of the characteristics of the two types of consonant are set out below.

(b) /p,t,k/ are typically accompanied by aspiration (i.e. an interval of breath before the following vowel onset), especially when initial in a stressed syllable. Thus, ‘pin’ is distinguished from ‘bin’ very largely by the aspiration accompanying /p/. However, in the syllable-initial sequences /sp-, st-, sk- /, /p, t, k/ lack such aspiration. When /l/, /j/, /w/ or /r/ immediately follow /p,t,k/, they are devoiced and are pronounced as fricatives. Another characteristic of /p,t,k/ that is not marked in transcriptions is glottalization; when one of these consonants is followed by another consonant it is now usual to find that a glottal closure precedes the /p/, /t/ or /k/, particularly if the syllable in which they occur is stressed. Thus the pronunciation of ‘captain’, ‘rightful’, ‘Yorkshire’, which are phonemically /ˈkæp.tɪn/, /ˈraɪt.f^{ə}l/, /ˈjɔːk.ʃə^{r}/, could be shown (using the symbol [ʔ] for glottal closure) as [ˈkæʔp.tɪn], [ˈraɪʔt.fl̩], [ˈjɔːʔk.ʃə^{r}]. Similarly, in American English ‘mountain’ has one pronunciation that could be represented as [maʊ̃.ʔn̩].

(c) Voiceless consonants have a shortening effect on sounds preceding them within a syllable. Thus in the words ‘right’ and ‘ride’ (/raɪt/ and /raɪd/) the diphthong is noticeably shorter in the first word than in the second; in the words ‘bent’ and ‘bend’ (/bent/ and /bend/), both the vowel /e/ and the nasal consonant /n/ are shorter in the first word. This length difference is not always easy to observe in connected speech.

(d) The consonant /l/ has two different allophones in BBC English, the so-called “clear” and “dark” allophones. The “clear” one (which has an /iː/-like quality) occurs before vowels, the “dark” one (which has an /uː/-like quality) before consonants or before a pause.

(e) The consonants /ʃ/, /ʒ/, /tʃ/, dʒ/, /r/ are usually accompanied by lip-rounding.

(b) American English

The consonants of the American English model, at the phonemic level, may be represented by the same broad scheme used for British English above. Similarly, many of the distinguishing phonetic traits discussed for British English hold for American English as well: initial /p,t,k/ are normally aspirated except when immediately preceded by /s/. Glottalization preceding and, at times, replacing the plosives occurs often in rapid speech. There are, of course, numerous phonetic and phonological differences between British and American English, as there are within regional and social varieties within the two political entities. Two differences receive sufficient attention and have attained sufficient generality within the two varieties that they are represented here. One is phonetic: the “flapped” medial /t/ (as in ‘butter’) is transcribed as /t̬/ (see Section 2.1 above); the other is phonological: the presence (in American English) of postvocalic /r/ (as in ‘farmer’ /ˈfɑːr.mɚ/). It should also be noted that the difference between “clear” and “dark” /l/ is much less marked in American than in the BBC accent, so that even prevocalic /l/ in American pronunciation sounds dark to English ears.

2.4 Non-English sounds

In addition to the phonemes of English described above, most English speakers are aware of, and often attempt to pronounce, some sounds of languages other than English. The number of such sounds is small, since most foreign words and names are Anglicised so that they are pronounced with English phonemes. We find the voiceless velar fricative [x] in the Gaelic languages of Scotland and Ireland in words such as ‘loch’ and names such as ‘Strachan’. The same sound is often used by English speakers for the German sound which is written ‘ch’ (e.g. ‘Bach’ [bɑːx]) and the Spanish sound spelt ‘j’ (e.g. ‘Badajoz’ [ˌbæd.əˈxɒθ]). The voiceless lateral fricative [ɬ] is found (always represented in spelling with ‘ll’) in Welsh words and names such as ‘Llanberis’; we give the pronunciation of this sound as *h*l to indicate that it may be pronounced as a voiceless [ɬ] (as many British English speakers do), but alternatively as a voiced one: thus /*h*lænˈber.ɪs/. The dictionary lists a few names with more than one of these sounds (e.g. Llanelli). Most non-Welsh speakers are unlikely to pronounce more than one [ɬ] sound in a word, so we give the pronunciation as /θl/ for ‘ll’ sounds after the initial one.

The other case which needs special attention is the pronunciation of French nasalised vowels. Many English speakers attempt to produce something similar to the French vowels /ɛ̃/, /ɑ̃/, /ɔ̃/, /œ̃/ in words such as ‘v**in** rouge’, ‘restaur**ant**’, ‘b**on** marché’, ‘Verd**un**’.

Although many speakers do not get close to the French vowels, the principle adopted here is to use symbols for English vowels, with added nasalisation. The equivalents are:

French	*English*
ɛ̃	æ̃
ɑ̃	ɑ̃ː
ɔ̃	ɔ̃ː
œ̃	ɜ̃ː

2.5 Stress

Stress patterns present one of the most difficult problems in a pronouncing dictionary. One reason for this is that many polysyllabic words have more than one possible stress pattern, and one must consider carefully which should be recommended. Secondly, the stress of many words changes in different contexts, and it is necessary to indicate how this happens. Thirdly, there is no straightforward way to decide on how many different levels of stress are recognisable.

(a) Where more than one stress pattern is possible, the preferred pronunciation is given first and then alternatives are listed. Many dictionaries use the convention of representing stress patterns using dashes to represent syllables: thus the two possible patterns for 'cigarette' (ˌciga'rette and 'cigarette) can be shown as ˌ--'- and '---. This convention, which is sometimes referred to (incorrectly) as "Morse Code", is used in this work for short words, since it is economical on space. However, in longer words users are likely to find it difficult to interpret. In the planning of this edition, an experiment was carried out to test this, and it was found that readers (both native speakers and non-native speakers of English) do indeed take less time to read word stress patterns when the whole word is given, rather than just a "dashes and dots" pattern (Stromberg and Roach, 1993). Consequently, words of more than three syllables are given in full when alternative stress patterns are being given.

(b) The most common case of variable stress placement caused by context is what is usually nowadays known as "stress-shift". As a general rule, when a word of several syllables has a stress near the end of the word, and is followed by another word with stress near its beginning, there is a tendency for the stress in the first word to move nearer the beginning if it contains a syllable that is capable of receiving stress. For example, the word 'academic' in isolation usually has the stress on the penultimate syllable /-dem-/. However, when the word 'year' follows, the stress is often found to move to the first syllable /æk-/. The whole phrase 'academic year' will have its primary stress on the word 'year', so the resulting stress pattern will be ˌacademic 'year (where ˌ represents secondary stress and ' represents primary stress). To make this process easier to understand, this dictionary now gives specific examples in each case where stress-shift is possible except where certain prefixes such as 'un-' produce hundreds of such cases. In general, this shift is not obligatory: it would not be a mispronunciation to say acaˌdemic 'year. However, it is undoubtedly widespread and in some cases is used almost without exception: for example, although the adjective 'compact' on its own is pronounced with the stress pattern -'-, in the phrase 'compact disc' it is virtually always pronounced with stress on the first syllable.

(c) It is necessary to decide how many levels of stress to mark. The minimum possible range is two: stressed and unstressed. This is inadequate for representing English words in a pronouncing dictionary: a word such as 'controversial' clearly has stress(es) on the first and third syllables, and equally clearly has stronger stress on the third syllable than on the first. It is therefore necessary to recognise an intermediate level of stress ("secondary"). The transcription of this word, therefore, is /ˌkɒn.trə'vɜː.ʃəl/. An argument can be made for recognising yet another level (tertiary stress): in a word such as 'indivisibility', for example, it can be claimed that the level of stress on the third syllable /vɪz/ is weaker than that on the first syllable /ɪn/, which has secondary stress (primary stress being placed on the penultimate syllable /bɪl/). However, introducing this extra level creates a degree of complexity that it is better to avoid. In EPD14 some long polysyllabic words were transcribed with two primary stress marks (e.g. 'cross-examination' was given as /'krɒsɪgˌzæmɪ'neɪʃn/): for the present edition only one primary stress may occur in a word or compound.

(d) Secondary stresses have only limited occurrence after a primary stress: such a secondary stress is only marked in closed or hyphenated compound words where the second element is polysyllabic (e.g. 'fishˌmonger).

(e) Stress assignment on prefixes:

(i) In words containing a prefix such as, for example, **con-**, **de-**, **im-**, **in-**, secondary stress is not applied to the prefix where the following (i.e., second) syllable is stressed. Examples include 'intoxicate' /ɪnˈtɒk.sɪ.keɪt (US) -ˈtɑːk-/.

(ii) Where the prefix is separable, however, as in **impossible**, a variant showing secondary stress on the prefix is listed, as follows: /ɪmˈpɒs.ə.bl̩ ,ˌɪm -/.

(iii) In all other cases, primary or secondary stress is applied to the prefix where appropriate.

(f) In the case of words which do not have a prefix but have a stressed second syllable preceded by a syllable with a full vowel (e.g. 'shampoo', 'Chinese') the first syllable is usually treated as unstressed, though in some cases capable of receiving primary stress through stress-shift.

2.6 Syllable divisions

The 14th Edition of EPD marked syllable division (using hyphens) only when it was important to distinguish between the affricate /tʃ/ and the phonemes /t/ and /ʃ/ at a syllable juncture (e.g. 'satchel' /ˈsætʃəl/ and 'nutshell' /ˈnʌt-ʃel/). However, although native speakers may well find no difficulty in dividing words into syllables, it seems that learners of English have trouble in doing so, and the divisions are therefore marked. Descriptions of stress and rhythm are usually expressed in terms of syllables, and so it is helpful to have polysyllabic words clearly broken up into their constituent syllables. The syllabified transcription of a polysyllabic word is easier to read and interpret than an undivided one. In addition, the dictionary is likely to be of interest to the field of speech and language technology, where syllable divisions can be useful in developing automatic speech and language analysis systems.

A dot . is used to divide syllables, in accordance with the current recommendations of the International Phonetic Association. These may be read in the *IPA Handbook* (International Phonetic Association 1999). However, this is not used where a stress mark ˈ or ˌ occurs, as these are effectively also syllable division markers.

No completely satisfactory scheme of syllable division can be produced – all sets of rules will throw up some cases which cannot be dealt with properly. The principles used in this edition are set out below. This requires some discussion of *phonotactics*, the study of permissible phoneme sequences.

(a) As far as possible, syllables should not be divided in a way that violates what is known of English syllable structure. The 'Maximal Onsets Principle', which is widely recognised in contemporary phonology, is followed as far as possible. This means that, where possible, syllables should be divided in such a way that as many consonants as possible are assigned to the beginning of the syllable to the right (if one thinks in terms of how they are written in transcription), rather than to the end of the syllable to the left. However, when this would result in a syllable ending with a stressed /ɪ/, /e/, /æ/, /ʌ/, /ɒ/ or /ʊ/, it is considered that this would constitute a violation of English phonotactics, and the first (or only) intervocalic consonant is assigned to the preceding syllable; thus the word 'better' is divided /ˈbet.əʳ/, whereas 'beater' is divided /ˈbiː.təʳ/. In the case of unstressed short vowels, /e/, /æ/, /ʌ/ and /ɒ/ are also prevented from appearing in syllable-final position; however, unstressed /ɪ/ and /ʊ/ are allowed the same "privilege of occurrence" as /ə/ when a consonant begins a following syllable, and may therefore occur in final position in unstressed syllables except pre-pausally. Thus in a word such as 'develop', the syllable division is /dɪˈvel.əp/.

(b) Notwithstanding the above, words in compounds should not be re-divided syllabically in a way that does not agree with perceived word boundaries. For example, 'hardware' could in theory be divided /ˈhɑː.dweəʳ/, but most readers would find this counter-intuitive and would prefer /ˈhɑːd.weəʳ/. This principle applies to open, closed and hyphenated compounds.

2.7 Assimilation

Assimilation is a process found in all languages which causes speech sounds to be modified in a way which makes them more similar to their neighbours. A well-known example is that of English alveolar consonants such as /t , d , n/, which, when they are followed by a consonant which does not have alveolar place of articulation, tend to adopt the place of articulation of the following consonant. Thus the /t/ at the end of 'foot' /fʊt/ changes to /p/ when followed by /b/ in the word 'football', giving the pronunciation /ˈfʊp.bɔːl/. A similar case is the assimilation of /s/ to a following /ʃ/ or /j/, resulting in the pronunciation of 'this ship' as /ðɪʃˈʃɪp/ and 'this year' as /ðɪʃˈjɪəʳ/. This assimilation can be considered to be optional.

The assimilation of /n/ is a rather special case: many English words begin with the prefixes 'in-'

and 'un-', and in a number of cases the /n/ of these prefixes is followed by a consonant which is not alveolar. In some cases it seems to be normal that the /n/ is regularly assimilated to the place of articulation of the following consonant (e.g. 'inquest' /ˈɪŋ.kwest/), while in others this assimilation is optional (e.g. 'incautious' may be /ɪnˈkɔː.ʃəs/ or /ɪŋˈkɔː.ʃəs/). Where it is clear that the prefix is attached to a word that exists independently, so that prefix and stem are easily separable, the assimilation is normally treated as optional. When it seems more like an integral part of the word, the assimilation is shown as obligatory. The occurrence of assimilation in British and American English may differ.

2.8 Treatment of /r/

The accent used for British English is classed as *non-rhotic* – the phoneme /r/ is not usually pronounced except when a vowel follows it. The American pronunciations, on the other hand, do show a rhotic accent, and in general in the accent described, /r/ is pronounced where the letter r is found in the spelling.

It is necessary to show, in British English entries, cases of *potential* pronunciation of /r/, mainly in word-final position; in other words, it is necessary to indicate, in a word such as 'car', that though the word when said in isolation does not have /r/ in the pronunciation (/kɑː/), there is a *potential* /r/ which is realised if a vowel follows (e.g. in 'car owner'). This is indicated by giving the transcription as /kɑːʳ/, where the superscript /ʳ/ indicates the potential for pronunciation. This is traditionally known as 'linking r'. A controversial question is that of so-called 'intrusive r', where the phoneme /r/ is pronounced when no 'r' is seen in the spelling. For example, the phrase 'china and glass' will often be pronounced with /r/ at the end of the word 'china'; although this type of pronunciation is widespread in the speech of native speakers of the accent described, it is still safer not to recommend it to foreign learners, and it is therefore avoided in this dictionary.

2.9 Use of /i/ and /u/

There are many places in present-day British and American English where the distinction between /ɪ/ and /iː/ is neutralised. For example, the final vowel of 'city' and 'seedy' seems to belong neither to the /ɪ/ phoneme nor to /iː/. The symbol /i/ is used in this case (though it is not, strictly speaking, a phoneme symbol; there is no obvious way to choose suitable brackets for this symbol, but phoneme brackets // will be used for simplicity). A parallel argument can be made for the distinction between /ʊ/ and /uː/ (with a corresponding 'neutralised' symbol /u/), though this is needed much less frequently. This issue, and the issues which follow, are discussed in detail in Roach (2000), pp. 84–86.

(a) In word-final position, /ɪ/ and /ʊ/ do not occur. Word-final, close vowels are transcribed with /i/ and /u/ if unstressed. Word-final /iː/ and /uː/ are possible both with stress ('grandee', 'bamboo') and without ('Hindi', 'argue'), although in the unstressed case it is often not possible to draw a clear line between /iː/ and /i/ , or between /uː/ and /u/.

(b) In compounds such as 'busybody' and names such as 'Merryweather', /i/ is permitted to occur word-medially, e.g. 'busybody' is transcribed /ˈbɪz.iˌbɒd.i ⓊⓈ ˈbɪz.i.bɑː.di/) and 'Merryweather' as /ˈmer.iˌweð.əʳ ⓊⓈ ˈmer.iˌ weð.ɚ/ . In all other cases word-medially, /ɪ/ is used when the vowel is unstressed, unless a vowel follows (see below).

(c) The vowel symbols /ɪ/ and /ʊ/ only occur in front of another vowel symbol if they form part of a composite (diphthong or triphthong) phoneme symbol (e.g. /ɪə, ʊə/). Otherwise /i/ or /u/ is used (e.g. 'scurrying' /ˈskʌr.i.ɪŋ/, 'influenza' /ˌɪn.fluˈen.zə/.

(d) A matter related to this decision concerns words ending in '-ier', '-eer', '-ia'. The usual transcription in the 14th Edition of the EPD was /ɪə/. However, 'reindeer' and 'windier' (comparative form of 'windy') do not have identical pronunciations in their final syllables in British English (BBC). In this edition, the alternative /-jə/ previously given for the latter type of word has been dropped; 'reindeer' is transcribed as /ˈreɪn.dɪəʳ/ and 'windier' as /ˈwɪn.di.əʳ/. The latter transcription, which indicates a different (closer) vowel quality in the second syllable of 'windier', and implies a pronunciation with three rather than two syllables, is felt to be accurate in terms of contemporary pronunciation.

The long vowels /iː/ and /uː/ may also occur before other vowels, but only when in a stressed syllable (e.g. 'skiing' /ˈskiː.ɪŋ/, 'canoeing' /kəˈnuː.ɪŋ/).

2.10 Syllabic consonants

Syllabic consonants are frequently found in English pronunciation: these are cases where instead of an expected vowel-plus-consonant sequence, the consonant alone (usually one of /m, n, ŋ, l, r/) is pronounced with the rhythmical value of a syllable. (See Roach, 2000, pp. 86–90.) In EPD14, syllabic consonants were only marked where there is ambiguity in the pronunciation of a word; for example, in a word such as ‘bottle’, the transcription /ˈbɒtl/ is said to imply unambiguously that the /l/ is syllabic, whereas in the derived form ‘bottling’ there may be two pronunciations, one with and one without a syllabic /l/. In this instance the EPD14 preferred pronunciation was /ˈbɒtl̩ɪŋ/, with /ˈbɒtlɪŋ/ given as an alternative.

(a) The main problem here is how to deal with optional and obligatory syllabicity and the permissibility of vowels. The most frequently found case is where an item may have (i) a schwa vowel followed by a non-syllabic consonant, (ii) a syllabic consonant not preceded by schwa or (iii) a non-syllabic consonant not preceded by schwa. For example, ‘lightening’ may be (i) /ˈlaɪ.tə.nɪŋ/, (ii) /ˈlaɪt.n̩.ɪŋ/ or (iii) /ˈlaɪt.nɪŋ/. Such items are transcribed as /ˈlaɪ.tᵊn̩.ɪŋ/ and /ˈlaɪt.nɪŋ/, the first representing cases (i) and (ii), in which there are three syllables, and the second representing only the disyllabic pronunciation, (iii). The use of superscript schwa in words such as /ˈlaɪ.tᵊn.ɪŋ/ should be interpreted as meaning that the schwa may be pronounced, or may be omitted while giving its syllabic character to the following consonant.

(b) The problem remaining is that of /l/ corresponding to the ‘-le’ spelling form, preceded by any plosive or homorganic fricative, as in ‘bottle’, ‘wrestle’. It is not felt to be acceptable in BBC pronunciation to pronounce this with a vowel in the second syllable, and therefore the superscript schwa convention is not used in such cases: rather, the /l/ is marked as syllabic, i.e. /l̩/. The entry for ‘bottle’ is /ˈbɒt.l̩/, and for ‘cycle’, /ˈsaɪ.kl̩/.

(c) Where a word such as the above carries a suffix with an initial vowel, as in ‘bottling’, ‘cycling’, speakers’ intuitions about the number of syllables are very divergent, so no single recommendation will be adequate. The entry for ‘bottle’ gives the syllabic /l̩/ (three-syllable) version of ‘bottling’ as the first recommendation, and it is therefore necessary to add for the -ing form the two-syllable alternative /ˈbɒt.lɪŋ/.

(d) Syllabic nasals are not usual where they would result in a nasal-plosive-syllabic consonant sequence (e.g. ‘London’, ‘abandon’ must contain a schwa vowel in the final syllable).

2.11 Optional sounds

The convention used in EPD14 of printing phoneme symbols in italics to indicate that they may be omitted is retained, though used more sparingly. It is not necessary to give alternative pronunciations that simply follow general rules of simplification that apply in rapid speech. For example, pointing out the possibility of omitting the [d] sound in ‘engine’ seems unnecessary, whereas it does seem worth recording the fact that some speakers pronounce words such as ‘lunch’ and ‘French’ with a final /ntʃ/ while others have final /nʃ/. There is a difference between the two cases: the former is a straightforward example of elision, and needs no special explanation that refers to a specific word or class of word, while the latter is a particular case of an insertion or deletion that is restricted to a particular phonological environment; speakers are usually consistent in using one or other of the alternative pronunciations in the latter case.

2.12 Elision

As mentioned in the preceding section, there are many cases where sounds which are produced in words pronounced on their own, or in slow, careful speech, are not found in a different style of speech. This is known as *elision*, and this dictionary normally does not show elisions in order to avoid adding a large number of additional pronunciations that are typical of casual speech. It is usual to explain elision in terms of the Principle of Least Effort – we try to avoid doing more work than is necessary. We find elision most commonly in the simplification of consonant clusters. A common example is the loss of /t/ and /d/ in combination with other consonants. Examples are:

‘act badly’ /ˌæktˈbæd.li/ (careful speech) /ˌækˈbæd.li/ (rapid speech)

‘strange person’ /ˌstreɪndʒˈpɜː.sᵊn (US) -ˈpɝː.sᵊn/ (careful speech) /ˌstreɪnʒˈpɜː.sᵊn (US) -ˈpɝː.sᵊn/ (rapid speech)

The fricative /θ/ is also frequently lost in clusters in rapid speech. Examples are:

‘sixth place’ /ˌsɪksθˈpleɪs/ (careful speech) /ˌsɪksˈpleɪs/ (rapid speech)

Elision of vowels is also found, and again this seems to be characteristic of rapid or casual speech. Examples are:

‘philosophy’ /fɪˈlɒs.ə.fi (US) -ˈlɑː.sə-/ (careful speech) /fəˈlɒs.fi (US) -ˈlɑːs.fi/ (rapid speech)

‘persuade’ /pəˈsweɪd (US) pɚˈ-/ (careful speech) /psweɪd/ (rapid speech)

Part 3: Explanatory notes

In order to explain the way in which the information in the dictionary is laid out, several entries are presented below with explanatory notes.

• Throughout the dictionary we use the convention of the cutback bar, a vertical line | which marks the place at which a word is divided so that alternative endings can be shown without having to print the entire word again.

• The brackets used for phonemic and phonetic transcriptions are not used in the entries in the dictionary, for the sake of clarity.

affectation ˌæf.ekˈteɪ.ʃ^{ə}n,-ɪkˈ- **-s** -z

Spelling of word. — Main pronunciation. — Variant pronunciation.

afar əˈfɑː^{r} (US) -ˈfɑːr

British pronunciation. — This sign indicates that an American pronunciation follows. If this sign is not shown, pronunciation is the same for British and American. — American pronunciation.

affected əˈfek.tɪd **-ly** -li **-ness** -nəs, -nɪs

Derived forms of the headword (affectedly & affectedness).

addl|e ˈæd.l̩ **-es** -z **-ing** -ɪŋ, ˈæd.lɪŋ **-ed** -d

Cutback bar. This shows where endings of inflected forms and derived forms are added to the word stem. — Inflections of the word. All inflected forms are shown for each word.

Adam ˈæd.əm ˌ**Adam's** ˈ**apple** (US) ˈ**Adam's** ˌ**apple**

American stress pattern for compound word.

Stress pattern for compound word, British pronunciation.

Aden *in the Yemen:* ˈeɪ.dᵊn (US) ˈɑː-, ˈeɪ- *in Grampian region:* ˈæd.ᵊn

Glosses indicate where pronunciations differ according to meaning.

---

addict (*n.*) ˈæd.ɪkt **-s** -s
addict (*v.*) əˈdɪkt **-s** -s **-ing** -ɪŋ

Labels indicate where pronunciation differs according to part of speech.

Adriatic ˌeɪ.driˈæt.ɪk (US) -ˈæt̬ - *stress shift:* ˌAdriatic ˈSea

Example of stress shift when the word is used before a noun.

---

advent (A) ˈæd.vent, -vənt **-s** -s

This indicates that the word can be spelled with a capital letter in some contexts.

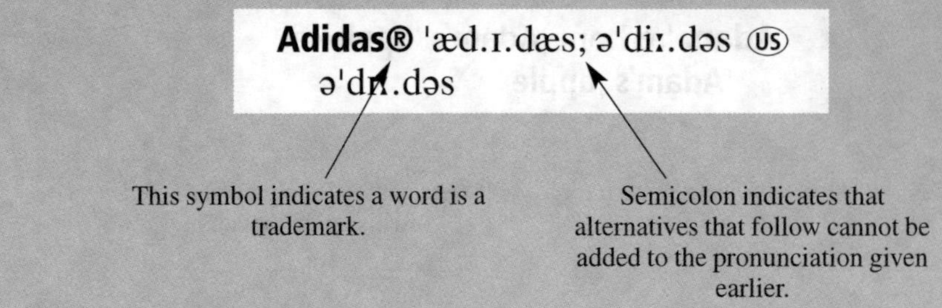

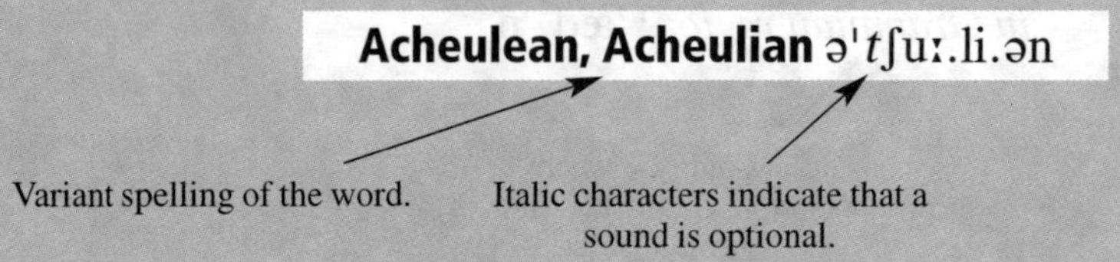

References in introduction

Roach, P. (2000) *English Phonetics and Phonology,* 3rd ed., Cambridge University Press.

Stromberg, K. and Roach, P. (1993) 'The representation of stress-patterns in pronunciation dictionaries: 'Morse-code' vs. orthographic marking', *Journal of the International Phonetic Association*, vol.23.3, pp. 55-58.

Michaelis, H., and Jones, D. (1913) *A Phonetic Dictionary of the English Language*, Carl Meyer (Gustav Prior), Hanover.

List of recommended reading

A. Works principally on British English

Brown, G. (1990) *Listening to Spoken English*, (2nd ed.), Longman.
An introductory book with many insights on connected speech.

Jones, D. (1960) *Outline of English Phonetics*, (9th ed.), Cambridge University Press.
The classic textbook written by the original author of the *English Pronouncing Dictionary*. First published in 1918, but still readable and informative.

Fudge, E. (1984) *English Word Stress*, Allen and Unwin.
A comprehensive and valuable treatment of stress.

Giegerich, H.J. (1992) *English Phonology*, Cambridge University Press.
A theoretical introduction to the phonology of English.

Gimson, A.C., revised by A.Cruttenden (2001) *The Pronunciation of English (6th Edition)*, Edward Arnold.
The best contemporary description of the phonetics of English, written by the person responsible for the 13th and 14th editions of the *English Pronouncing Dictionary*.

International Phonetic Association (1999) *Handbook of the International Phonetic Association*, Cambridge University Press.

Knowles, G.O., (1987) *Patterns of Spoken English*, Longman.
An introductory textbook on the phonetics of English.

Kreidler, C.W. (1989) *The Pronunciation of English*, Blackwell.
A modern treatment of the phonetics and phonology of English, with coverage of American as well as British English.

Roach, P. (2000) *English Phonetics and Phonology*, 3rd ed., Cambridge University Press.
An introductory textbook with practical exercises.

Roach. P. (2001) *Phonetics*, Oxford University Press.
A short introductory book.

Wells, J.C (1982) *Accents of English*, Cambridge University Press (3 vols).
A very detailed and comprehensive account of the different accents of English throughout the world.

Wells, J.C. (2000) *Longman Pronunciation Dictionary*, 2nd ed., Longman.
An alternative pronouncing dictionary to this one.

B. American English

Cassidy, F.G (ed.) (1985) *Dictionary of American Regional English*, Belknap Press, Harvard.
An ongoing publication, each entry listing pronunciations in designated regions.

Kenyon, J.S and Knott, T.A. (1953) *A Pronouncing Dictionary of American English*, G.&C. Merrian & Co.
One of the earlier pronouncing dictionaries for American English.

Lujan, B. (1999) *The American Accent*, Lingual Arts.

Wolfram, W. and Johnson, R. (1988) *Phonological Analysis: Focus on American English*, Prentice Hall.

Wolfram, W. and Schilling-Estes, N. (1998) 'American English: Dialects and Variation', *Language in Society*, vol. 25.

Van Riper, C. and Smith, D. (1992) *Introduction to General American Phonetics*, Waveland Press.
A practical workbook.

THE INTERNATIONAL PHONETIC ALPHABET (revised to 1993, updated 1996)

CONSONANTS (PULMONIC)

	Bilabial	Labiodental	Dental	Alveolar	Postalveolar	Retroflex	Palatal	Velar	Uvular	Pharyngeal	Glottal
Plosive	p b			t d		ʈ ɖ	c ɟ	k ɡ	q ɢ		ʔ
Nasal	m	ɱ		n		ɳ	ɲ	ŋ	ɴ		
Trill	ʙ			r					ʀ		
Tap or Flap				ɾ		ɽ					
Fricative	ɸ β	f v	θ ð	s z	ʃ ʒ	ʂ ʐ	ç ʝ	x ɣ	χ ʁ	ħ ʕ	h ɦ
Lateral fricative				ɬ ɮ							
Approximant		ʋ		ɹ		ɻ	j	ɰ			
Lateral approximant				l		ɭ	ʎ	ʟ			

Where symbols appear in pairs, the one to the right represents a voiced consonant. Shaded areas denote articulations judged impossible.

CONSONANTS (NON-PULMONIC)

Clicks		Voiced implosives		Ejectives	
ʘ	Bilabial	ɓ	Bilabial	ʼ	Examples:
ǀ	Dental	ɗ	Dental/alveolar	pʼ	Bilabial
ǃ	(Post)alveolar	ʄ	Palatal	tʼ	Dental/alveolar
ǂ	Palatoalveolar	ɠ	Velar	kʼ	Velar
ǁ	Alveolar lateral	ʛ	Uvular	sʼ	Alveolar fricative

VOWELS

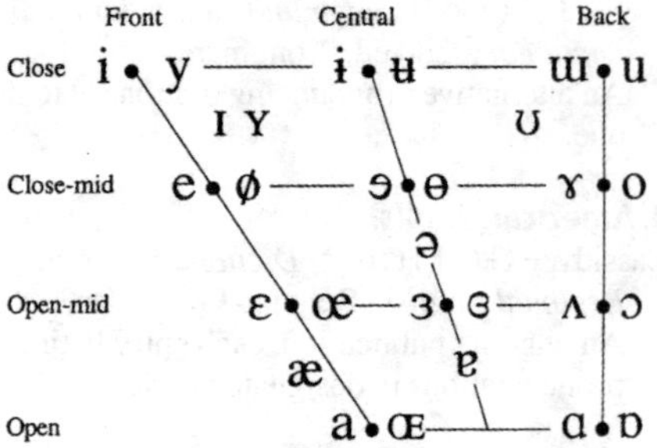

Where symbols appear in pairs, the one to the right represents a rounded vowel.

OTHER SYMBOLS

ʍ	Voiceless labial-velar fricative	ɕ ʑ	Alveolo-palatal fricatives
w	Voiced labial-velar approximant	ɺ	Alveolar lateral flap
ɥ	Voiced labial-palatal approximant	ɧ	Simultaneous ʃ and x
ʜ	Voiceless epiglottal fricative		
ʢ	Voiced epiglottal fricative		Affricates and double articulations can be represented by two symbols joined by a tie bar if necessary. k͡p t͜s
ʡ	Epiglottal plosive		

SUPRASEGMENTALS

ˈ	Primary stress
ˌ	Secondary stress ˌfoʊnəˈtɪʃən
ː	Long eː
ˑ	Half-long eˑ
˘	Extra-short ĕ
|	Minor (foot) group
‖	Major (intonation) group
.	Syllable break ɹi.ækt
‿	Linking (absence of a break)

DIACRITICS

Diacritics may be placed above a symbol with a descender, e.g. ŋ̊

̥	Voiceless	n̥ d̥	̤	Breathy voiced	b̤ a̤	̪	Dental	t̪ d̪
̬	Voiced	s̬ t̬	̰	Creaky voiced	b̰ a̰	̺	Apical	t̺ d̺
ʰ	Aspirated	tʰ dʰ	̼	Linguolabial	t̼ d̼	̻	Laminal	t̻ d̻
̹	More rounded	ɔ̹	ʷ	Labialized	tʷ dʷ	̃	Nasalized	ẽ
̜	Less rounded	ɔ̜	ʲ	Palatalized	tʲ dʲ	ⁿ	Nasal release	dⁿ
̟	Advanced	u̟	ˠ	Velarized	tˠ dˠ	ˡ	Lateral release	dˡ
̠	Retracted	e̠	ˤ	Pharyngealized	tˤ dˤ	̚	No audible release	d̚
̈	Centralized	ë	̴	Velarized or pharyngealized	ɫ			
̽	Mid-centralized	e̽	̝	Raised	e̝		(ɹ̝ = voiced alveolar fricative)	
̩	Syllabic	n̩	̞	Lowered	e̞		(β̞ = voiced bilabial approximant)	
̯	Non-syllabic	e̯	̘	Advanced Tongue Root	e̘			
˞	Rhoticity	ɚ a˞	̙	Retracted Tongue Root	e̙			

TONES AND WORD ACCENTS

LEVEL			CONTOUR		
e̋ or	˥	Extra high	ě or	˩˥	Rising
é	˦	High	ê	˥˩	Falling
ē	˧	Mid	e᷄	˦˥	High rising
è	˨	Low	e᷅	˩˨	Low rising
ȅ	˩	Extra low	e᷈	˧˦˧	Rising-falling
↓		Downstep	↗		Global rise
↑		Upstep	↘		Global fall

This chart is reproduced by courtesy of the International Phonetic Association

Index of Information Panels

Pronouncing the letter A

See also AE, AEO, AI/AY, AU/AW

The vowel letter **a** has two main strong pronunciations linked to spelling: a 'short' pronunciation /æ/ and a 'long' pronunciation /eɪ/. In the 'short' pronunciation, the **a** is usually followed by a consonant which closes the syllable, or a double consonant before another vowel, e.g.:

tap	/tæp/
tapping	/ˈtæp.ɪŋ/

The 'long' pronunciation usually means the **a** is followed by a single consonant and then a vowel, e.g.:

tape	/teɪp/
taping	/ˈteɪ.pɪŋ/

When there is an **r** in the spelling, the strong pronunciation is one of three possibilities: /ɑː (US) ɑːr/, /eə (US) er/ or /æ (US) e, æ/, e.g.:

car	/kɑːʳ/	(US) /kɑːr/
care	/keəʳ/	(US) /ker/
carry	/kær.i/	(US) /ker.i, kær.i/

In addition

There are other vowel sounds associated with the letter **a**, e.g.:

/ɑː/	father	/ˈfɑː.ðəʳ/	(US) /ˈfɑː.ðɚ/
/ɑː (US) æ/	bath	/bɑːθ/	(US) /bæθ/
/ɒ (US) ɑː/	swan	/swɒn/	(US) /swɑːn/
/ɔː (US) ɑː, ɔː/	walk	/wɔːk/	(US) /wɑːk/
	warm	/wɔːm/	(US) /wɔːrm/

And, in rare cases:

/e/	many	/ˈmen.i/

In weak syllables

The vowel letter **a** is realised with the vowels /ə/ and /ɪ/ in weak syllables, and may also not be pronounced at all in British English, due to compression, e.g.:

above	/əˈbʌv/	
village	/ˈvɪl.ɪdʒ/	
necessary	/ˈnes.ə.sri/	(US) /-ser.i/

a *indefinite article: strong form:* eɪ *weak form:* ə
Note: Weak form word. The strong form /eɪ/ is used mainly for contrast (e.g. 'This is *a* solution, but not the only one.'). The weak form only occurs before consonants, and is usually pronounced /ə/. In rapid speech, when /ə/ is preceded by a consonant, it may combine with a following /l/, /n/ or /r/ to produce a syllabic consonant (e.g. 'got a light' /ˌgɒt.l̩ˈaɪt (US) ˌgɑːt̬.əˈlaɪt/; 'get another' /ˌget.n̩ˈʌð.əʳ (US) -ɚ/).
a (A) *the letter:* eɪ **-'s** -z
A-1 ˌeɪˈwʌn *stress shift:* ˌA-1 conˈdition
A4 ˌeɪˈfɔːʳ (US) -ˈfɔːr *stress shift:* ˌA4 ˈpaper
AA ˌeɪˈeɪ *stress shift:* ˌAA patˈrol
Aachen ˈɑː.kən
aah ɑː
Aalborg ˈɑːl.bɔːg (US) ˈɑːl.bɔːrg, ˈɔːl-
aardvark ˈɑːd.vɑːk (US) ˈɑːrd.vɑːrk **-s** -s
aardwol|f ˈɑːd.wʊl|f (US) ˈɑːrd- **-ves** -vz
Aarhus ˈɑː.hʊs (US) ˈɑːr-, ˈɔːr-
Aaron ˈeə.rən (US) ˈer.ən, ˈær-
ab- æb-, əb-
Note: Prefix. Examples include **abnegate** /ˈæb.nɪ.geɪt/, in which it is stressed, and **abduct** /əbˈdʌkt/, where it is unstressed.
ab (A) æb
AB ˌeɪˈbiː
Abacha əˈbætʃ.ə (US) -bɑːtʃ-
aback əˈbæk
Abaco ˈæb.ə.kəʊ (US) -koʊ
abacus ˈæb.ə.kəs **-es** -ɪz
Abadan ˌæb.əˈdɑːn, -ˈdæn
Abaddon əˈbæd.ᵊn
abaft əˈbɑːft (US) -ˈbæft
abalone æb.əˈləʊ.ni (US) -ˈloʊ-
abandon əˈbæn.dən **-s** -z **-ing** -ɪŋ **-ed** -d **-ment** -mənt
à bas æˈbɑː (US) æ-, ɑː-
abas|e əˈbeɪs **-es** -ɪz **-ing** -ɪŋ **-ed** -t **-ement** -mənt
abash əˈbæʃ **-es** -ɪz **-ing** -ɪŋ **-ed** -t
abatab|le əˈbeɪ.tə.b|l̩ (US) -t̬ə- **-ly** -li
a|bate ə|ˈbeɪt **-bates** -ˈbeɪts **-bating** -ˈbeɪ.tɪŋ (US) -ˈbeɪ.t̬ɪŋ **-bated** -ˈbeɪ.tɪd (US) -ˈbeɪ.t̬ɪd **-batement/s** -ˈbeɪt.mənt/s
abat(t)is ˈæb.ə.tɪs, -tiː (US) -ə.t̬ɪs, əˈbæt̬.ɪs **-es** ˈæb.ə.tɪ.sɪz (US) -t̬ɪ-, əˈbæt̬.ɪ.sɪz *alternative plur.:* ˈæb.ə.tiːz (US) -t̬iːz, əˈbæt̬.iːz
abattoir ˈæb.ə.twɑːʳ (US) -twɑːr, -twɔːr **-s** -z
abaxial əˈbæk.si.əl, æbˈæk-
Abba ˈæb.ə
abbac|y ˈæb.ə.s|i **-ies** -iz
Abbado əˈbɑː.dəʊ (US) -oʊ
Abbas ˈæb.əs, əˈbæs
Abbassid, Abbasid əˈbæs.ɪd **-s** -z
abbé ˈæb.eɪ (US) ˈæb.eɪ, -ˈ- **-s** -z
abbess ˈæb.es, -ɪs (US) -əs **-es** -ɪz
Abbeville *in France:* ˈæb.viːl (US) ˌæbˈviːl *in US:* ˈæb.ɪ.vɪl
abbey (A) ˈæb.i **-s** -z
Abbie ˈæb.i
abbot (A) ˈæb.ət **-s** -s
Abbotsford ˈæb.əts.fəd (US) -fɚd
abbotship ˈæb.ət.ʃɪp **-s** -s
Abbott ˈæb.ət **-s** -s ˌ**Abbott and Cosˈtello**
abbrevi|ate əˈbriː.vi|.eɪt **-ates** -eɪts **-ating** -eɪ.tɪŋ (US) -eɪ.t̬ɪŋ **-ated** -eɪ.tɪd (US) -eɪ.t̬ɪd **-ator/s** -eɪ.təʳ/z (US) -eɪ.t̬ɚ/z
abbreviation əˌbriː.viˈeɪ.ʃᵊn **-s** -z
abbreviatory əˈbriː.vi.ə.tri, əˌbriː.viˈeɪ.tᵊr.i (US) əˈbriː.vi.ə.tɔːr.i
Abbs æbz
Abby ˈæb.i
abc, ABC ˌeɪ.biːˈsiː **-'s** -z
Abdera æbˈdɪə.rə (US) -ˈdɪr.ə
abdicant ˈæb.dɪ.kənt **-s** -s
abdi|cate ˈæb.dɪ|.keɪt **-cates** -keɪts **-cating** -keɪ.tɪŋ (US) -keɪ.t̬ɪŋ **-cated** -keɪ.tɪd (US) -keɪ.t̬ɪd **-cator/s** -keɪ.təʳ/z (US) -keɪ.t̬ɚ/z
abdication ˌæb.dɪˈkeɪ.ʃᵊn **-s** -z
Abdiel ˈæb.dɪəl (US) -di.əl
abdomen ˈæb.də.mən, -men; æbˈdəʊ.mən (US) ˈæb.də.mən, æbˈdoʊ- **-s** -z
abdominal æbˈdɒm.ɪ.nᵊl, əb-, -ˈdəʊ.mɪ- (US) -ˈdɑː.mə- **-ly** -i
abducent əbˈdjuː.sᵊnt, æb- (US) -ˈduː-, -ˈdjuː-
abduct əbˈdʌkt, æb- **-s** -s **-ing** -ɪŋ **-ed** -ɪd **-or/s** -əʳ/z (US) -ɚ/z
abduction əbˈdʌk.ʃᵊn, æb- **-s** -z
Abdul ˈæb.dʊl
Abdulla(h) æbˈdʌl.ə, əb-, -ˈdʊl-

Abbreviations

The pronunciation of individual abbreviations is not predictable and must be treated on a word-by-word basis.

Examples

Some good examples of abbreviations which are spoken in full are to be found in titles used for people, e.g.:

Mr	/ˈmɪs.təʳ/	(US) /-tɚ/
Mrs	/ˈmɪs.ɪz/	
Dr	/ˈdɒk.təʳ/	(US) /ˈdɑːk.tɚ/
Esq	/ɪsˈkwaɪəʳ/	(US) /ˈes.kwaɪɚ/

However, in some cases, an abbreviation may be pronounced the way it is written, e.g.:

Bros. (*Brothers*)	/ˈbrʌð.əz/, /brɒs/
	(US) /ˈbrʌð.ɚz/
des res (*desirable residence*)	/ˌdezˈrez/

Some words or phrases are abbreviated to initial letters. In this case, the item may be pronounced as the initial letters, or in full. This is not the same as an ACRONYM, in which the letters are pronounced as a word (see, for example, *NATO*), e.g.:

MS (*multiple sclerosis; manuscript*)	/ˌemˈes/
NBA (*National Basketball Association*)	/ˌen.biːˈeɪ/
UCLA (*University of California Los Angeles*)	/ˌjuː.siː.elˈeɪ/

Abbreviations derived from Latin words and phrases are common, but do not all follow the same pattern, some being pronounced in full, some as letters, and some as they are spelt, e.g.:

e.g. (*exempli gratia*)	/ˌiːˈdʒiː/	
et al (*et alia*)	/etˈæl/	(US) /-ˈɑːl/
etc. (*et cetera*)	/ɪtˈset.ər.ə/	(US) /-ˈset̬.ɚ-/
i.e. (*id est*)	/ˌaɪˈiː/	

Abe eɪb
abeam əˈbiːm
abecedarian ˌeɪ.biː.siːˈdeə.ri.ən (US) -ˈder.i-
à Becket əˈbek.ɪt
abed əˈbed
Abednego ˌæb.edˈniː.gəʊ, əˈbed.nɪ.gəʊ (US) -goʊ
Abel ˈeɪ.bᵊl
Abelard ˈæb.ə.lɑːd, ˈ-ɪ- (US) -lɑːrd
Abelmeholah ˌeɪ.bᵊl.miˈhəʊ.lə, -məˈ- (US) -ˈhoʊ-
Abenaki ˌæb.əˈnæk.i (US) ˌɑː.bəˈnɑː.ki, ˌæb.əˈ-, -ˈnæk.i **-s** -z
Aberavon ˌæb.əˈræv.ᵊn (US) -ɚˈæv-
Abercanaid ˌæb.əˈkæn.aɪd (US) ˌ-ɚ-
Abercarn ˌæb.əˈkɑːn (US) -ɚˈkɑːrn
Aberconway ˌæb.əˈkɒn.weɪ (US) -ɚˈkɑːn-
Aberconwy ˌæb.əˈkɒn.wi (US) -ɚˈkɑːn-
Abercorn ˈæb.ə.kɔːn (US) -ɚ.kɔːrn
Abercrombie, Abercromby ˈæb.ə.krɒm.bi, -krʌm-, ˌæb.əˈkrɒm.bi, -ˈkrʌm- (US) -ɚ.krɑːm-, -ɚˈkrɑːm-
Aberdare ˌæb.əˈdeəʳ (US) -ɚˈder
Aberdeen ˌæb.əˈdiːn (US) -ɚˈ- **-shire** -ʃəʳ, -ˌʃɪəʳ (US) -ʃɚ, -ˌʃɪr *stress shift:* ˌAberdeen ˈstation
Aberdonian ˌæb.əˈdəʊ.ni.ən (US) -ɚˈdoʊ- **-s** -z
Aberdour ˌæb.əˈdaʊəʳ (US) -ɚˈdaʊɚ
Aberdovey ˌæb.əˈdʌv.i (US) -ɚˈ-
Aberfan ˌæb.əˈvæn (US) -ɚˈ-
Abergavenny *place:* ˌæb.ə.gəˈven.i (US) -ɚˈ- *family name:* ˌæb.əˈgen.i (US) -ɚˈ-
Abergele ˌæb.əˈgel.i (US) -ɚˈ-
Aberkenfig ˌæb.əˈken.fɪg (US) -ɚˈ-
Abernathy ˌæb.əˈnæθ.i (US) ˈæb.ɚ.næθ-
Abernethy ˌæb.əˈneθ.i, -ˈniː.θi (US) ˈæb.ɚˈneθ.i
aberran|t æbˈer.ᵊn|t, əˈber-; ˈæb.ə.rᵊn|t **-ce** -*t*s **-cy** -*t*.si
aber|rate ˈæb.ə|.reɪt **-rates** -reɪts **-rating** -reɪ.tɪŋ (US) -reɪ.t̬ɪŋ **-rated** -reɪ.tɪd (US) -reɪ.t̬ɪd
aberration ˌæb.əˈreɪ.ʃᵊn **-s** -z
Abersychan ˌæb.əˈsɪk.ən (US) -ɚˈ-
Abert ˈeɪ.bɜːt, -bət (US) -bɝːt, -bɚt
Abertillery ˌæb.ə.tɪˈleə.ri, -təˈ- (US) -ɚ.təˈler.i
Abertridwr ˌæb.əˈtrɪd.ʊəʳ (US) -ʊr
Aberystwyth ˌæb.əˈrɪs.*t*wɪθ
a|bet ə|ˈbet **-bets** -ˈbets **-betting** -ˈbet.ɪŋ (US) -ˈbet̬.ɪŋ **-betted** -ˈbet.ɪd (US) -ˈbet̬.ɪd **-bettor/s** -ˈbet.əʳ/z (US) -ˈbet̬.ɚ/z **-betment** -ˈbet.mənt
abeyance əˈbeɪ.ən*t*s
abhor əbˈhɔːʳ, əˈbɔːʳ (US) æbˈhɔːr, əb- **-s** -z **-ring** -ɪŋ **-red** -d **-rer/s** -əʳ/z (US) -ɚ/z
abhorren|ce əbˈhɒr.ᵊn|*t*s, əˈbɒr- (US) æbˈhɔːr-, əb- **-t** -t
Abia *biblical name:* əˈbaɪ.ə *city:* ˈæb.i.ə
Abiathar əˈbaɪ.ə.θəʳ (US) -θɚ
abid|e əˈbaɪd **-es** -z **-ing** -ɪŋ **-ed** -ɪd **abode** əˈbəʊd (US) -ˈboʊd
Abidjan ˌæb.iːˈdʒɑːn, -ɪˈ-
abigail (A) ˈæb.ɪ.geɪl **-s** -z
Abilene *in Syria:* ˌæb.ɪˈliː.ni, -əˈ- *in US:* ˈæb.ə.liːn
abilit|y əˈbɪl.ə.t|i, -ɪ.t|i (US) -ə.t̬|i **-ies** -iz
-ability -əˈbɪl.ə.ti, -ɪ.ti (US) -ə.t̬i
Note: Suffix. Words containing **-ability** always exhibit primary stress as shown above, e.g. **capability** /ˌkeɪ.pəˈbɪl.ə.ti (US) -ə.t̬i/.
Abimelech əˈbɪm.ə.lek
Abingdon ˈæb.ɪŋ.dən
Abinger ˈæb.ɪn.dʒəʳ (US) -dʒɚ
Abington ˈæb.ɪŋ.tən
ab initio ˌæb.ɪˈnɪʃ.i.əʊ, -əˈ-, -ˈnɪs- (US) -oʊ
abiogenesis ˌeɪ.baɪ.əʊˈdʒen.ə.sɪs, ˈ-ɪ- (US) -oʊˈ-
Abiola ˌæb.iˈəʊ.lə (US) -ˈoʊ-
abiotic ˌeɪ.baɪˈɒt.ɪk (US) -ˈɑː.t̬ɪk
abject ˈæb.dʒekt (US) ˈæb.dʒekt, -ˈ- **-ly** -li **-ness** -nəs, -nɪs
abjection æbˈdʒek.ʃᵊn
abjudi|cate æbˈdʒuː.dɪ|.keɪt, əb- (US) -də- **-cates** -keɪts **-cating** -keɪ.tɪŋ (US) -keɪ.t̬ɪŋ **-cated** -keɪ.tɪd (US) -keɪ.t̬ɪd
abjuration ˌæb.dʒʊˈreɪ.ʃᵊn, -dʒəˈ-, -dʒʊəˈ- (US) -dʒəˈ-, -dʒʊˈ- **-s** -z
abjur|e əbˈdʒʊəʳ, æb-, -ˈdʒɔːʳ (US) -ˈdʒʊr **-es** -z **-ing** -ɪŋ **-ed** -d **-er/s** -əʳ/z (US) -ɚ/z
ablat|e əˈbleɪt, æbˈleɪt, ˌæbˈleɪt **-es** -s **-ing** -ɪŋ (US) ˌæbˈleɪ.t̬ɪŋ **-ed** -ɪd (US) ˌæbˈleɪ.t̬ɪd
ablation əˈbleɪ.ʃᵊn, æbˈleɪ- (US) ˌæb-
ablatival ˈæb.ləˈtaɪ.vᵊl
ablative ˈæb.lə.tɪv (US) -t̬ɪv **-s** -z
ablaut ˈæb.laʊt **-s** -s
ablaze əˈbleɪz
ab|le ˈeɪ.b|l̩ **-ler** -l̩.əʳ, -ləʳ (US) -l̩.ɚ, -lɚ **-lest** -l̩.əst, -ləst, -l̩.ɪst, -lɪst **-ly** -l̩.i, -li
-able -ə.bl̩
Note: Suffix. Does not normally affect stress patterning, e.g. **knowledge** /ˈnɒl.ɪdʒ (US) ˈnɑː.lɪdʒ/, **knowledgeable** /ˈnɒl.ɪ.dʒə.bl̩ (US) ˈnɑː.lɪ-/; **rely** /rɪˈlaɪ/, **reliable** /rɪˈlaɪ.ə.bl̩/. In some cases, however,

the stress patterning may change, e.g. **admire** /ədˈmaɪəʳ ⓤⓢ -ˈmaɪɚ/, **admirable** /ˈæd.mᵊr.ə.bl̩/.

able-bodied ˌeɪ.bl̩ˈbɒd.ɪd ⓤⓢ ˈeɪ.bl̩ˌbɑː.dɪd, ˌeɪ.bl̩ˈbɑː- *stress shift, British only:* ˌable-bodied ˈperson

Ablett ˈæb.lət, -lɪt

ablution əˈbluː.ʃᵊn **-s** -z

-ably -ə.bli

Note: Suffix. Behaves as **-able** above.

Abnaki æbˈnæk.i ⓤⓢ -ˈnɑː.ki **-s** -z

abneg|ate ˈæb.nɪ.g|eɪt, -neg|.eɪt, -nə.g|eɪt **-ates** -eɪts **-ating** -eɪ.tɪŋ ⓤⓢ -eɪ.t̬ɪŋ **-ated** -eɪ.tɪd ⓤⓢ -eɪ.t̬ɪd

abnegation ˌæb.nɪˈgeɪ.ʃᵊn, -negˈeɪ-, -nəˈgeɪ- **-s** -z

Abner ˈæb.nəʳ ⓤⓢ -nɚ

abnormal æbˈnɔː.mᵊl, əb- ⓤⓢ -ˈnɔːr- **-ly** -i

abnormalit|y ˌæb.nɔːˈmæl.ə.t|i, -ɪ.t|i ⓤⓢ -nɔːrˈmæl.ə.t̬|i **-ies** -iz

abnormit|y æbˈnɔː.mə.t|i, əb-, -mɪ- ⓤⓢ -ˈnɔːr.mə.t̬|i **-ies** -iz

abo ˈæb.əʊ ⓤⓢ -oʊ **-s** -z

ABO ˌeɪ.biːˈəʊ ⓤⓢ -ˈoʊ

aboard əˈbɔːd ⓤⓢ -ˈbɔːrd

abode əˈbəʊd ⓤⓢ -ˈboʊd **-s** -z

abolish əˈbɒl.ɪʃ ⓤⓢ -ˈbɑː.lɪʃ **-es** -ɪz **-ing** -ɪŋ **-ed** -t **-er/s** -əʳ/z ⓤⓢ -ɚ/z

abolition ˌæb.əˈlɪʃ.ᵊn **-s** -z

abolition|ism ˌæb.əˈlɪʃ.ᵊn|.ɪ.zᵊm **-ist/s** -ɪst/s

abomas|um ˌæb.əʊˈmeɪ.s|ᵊm ⓤⓢ -oʊˈ- **-a** -ə

A-bomb ˈeɪˌbɒm ⓤⓢ -ˌbɑːm **-s** -z

abominab|le əˈbɒm.ɪ.nə.b|l̩, -ᵊn.ə- ⓤⓢ -ˈbɑː.mɪ- **-ly** -li **-leness** -l̩.nəs, -nɪs

abomi|nate əˈbɒm.ɪ|.neɪt, ˈ-ə- ⓤⓢ -ˈbɑː.mɪ- **-nates** -neɪts **-nating** -neɪ.tɪŋ ⓤⓢ -neɪ.t̬ɪŋ **-nated** -neɪ.tɪd ⓤⓢ -neɪ.t̬ɪd

abomination əˌbɒm.ɪˈneɪ.ʃᵊn, -əˈ- ⓤⓢ -ˌbɑː.mɪˈ- **-s** -z

à bon marché æˌbɔ̃ː.mɑːˈʃeɪ, -ˌbɒn- ⓤⓢ -ˌbõʊn.mɑːrˈ-

aboriginal (A) ˌæb.əˈrɪdʒ.ᵊn.ᵊl, -ɪ.nᵊl **-s** -z **-ly** -i

aborigine (A) ˌæb.əˈrɪdʒ.ᵊn.i, -ɪ.ni **-s** -z

a|bort ə|ˈbɔːt ⓤⓢ -ˈbɔrt **-borts** -ˈbɔːts ⓤⓢ -ˈbɔːrts **-borting** -ˈbɔː.tɪŋ ⓤⓢ -ˈbɔːr.t̬ɪŋ **-borted** -ˈbɔː.tɪd ⓤⓢ -ˈbɔːr.t̬ɪd

aborticide əˈbɔː.tɪ.saɪd ⓤⓢ -ˈbɔːr.t̬ə-

abortifacient əˌbɔː.tɪˈfeɪ.ʃi.ənt, -ʃᵊnt ⓤⓢ -ˌbɔːr.t̬əˈ-

abortion əˈbɔː.ʃᵊn ⓤⓢ -ˈbɔːr- **-s** -z **-ist/s** -ɪst/s

abortive əˈbɔː.tɪv ⓤⓢ -ˈbɔːr.t̬ɪv **-ly** -li **-ness** -nəs, -nɪs

Aboukir ˌæb.uːˈkɪəʳ, -ʊˈ- ⓤⓢ -ˈkɪr

abound əˈbaʊnd **-s** -z **-ing** -ɪŋ **-ed** -ɪd

about əˈbaʊt

about-fac|e əˌbaʊtˈfeɪs **-es** -ɪz **-ing** -ɪŋ **-ed** -d

about-turn əˌbaʊtˈtɜːn ⓤⓢ -ˈtɝːn **-s** -z

above əˈbʌv

above-board əˌbʌvˈbɔːd ⓤⓢ əˈbʌv.bɔːrd

aboveground əˌbʌvˈgraʊnd ⓤⓢ əˈbʌv.graʊnd

above-mentioned əˌbʌvˈmen.*t*ʃᵊnd ⓤⓢ -ˈmen*t*.ʃᵊnd *stress shift:* aˌbove-mentioned ˈperson

ab ovo ˌæbˈəʊ.vəʊ ⓤⓢ -ˈoʊ.voʊ

abracadabra ˌæb.rə.kəˈdæb.rə **-s** -z

abrad|e əˈbreɪd **-es** -z **-ing** -ɪŋ **-ed** -ɪd

Abraham ˈeɪ.brə.hæm, -həm *as a biblical name in Britain often also:* ˈɑː-

Abrahams ˈeɪ.brə.hæmz

Abram ˈeɪ.brəm, -bræm *as a biblical name in Britain often also:* ˈɑː-

abranchi|al eɪˈbræŋ.ki|.əl, əˈbræŋ-, æbˈræŋ- **-ate** -eɪt, -ət

abrasion əˈbreɪ.ʒᵊn **-s** -z

abrasive əˈbreɪ.sɪv, -zɪv **-ly** -li **-s** -z

abreact ˌæb.riˈækt **-s** -s **-ing** -ɪŋ **-ed** -ɪd

abreaction ˌæb.riˈæk.ʃᵊn

abreast əˈbrest

abridg|e əˈbrɪdʒ **-es** -ɪz **-ing** -ɪŋ **-ed** -d

abridg(e)ment əˈbrɪdʒ.mənt **-s** -s

abroad əˈbrɔːd ⓤⓢ -ˈbrɑːd, -ˈbrɔːd

abro|gate ˈæb.rəʊ|.geɪt ⓤⓢ -rə- **-gates** -geɪts **-gating** -geɪ.tɪŋ ⓤⓢ -geɪ.t̬ɪŋ **-gated** -geɪ.tɪd ⓤⓢ -geɪ.t̬ɪd

abrogation ˌæb.rəʊˈgeɪ.ʃᵊn ⓤⓢ -rəˈ- **-s** -z

A'Brook əˈbrʊk

abrupt əˈbrʌpt **-er** -əʳ ⓤⓢ -ɚ **-est** -əst, -ɪst **-ly** -li **-ness** -nəs, -nɪs

abruption əˈbrʌp.ʃᵊn

Abruzzi əˈbrʊt.si, -bruːt-

Absalom ˈæb.sᵊl.əm

abscess ˈæb.ses, -sɪs **-es** -ɪz

abscis|e æbˈsaɪz, əb- **-es** -ɪz **-ing** -ɪŋ **-ed** -d

abscisin æbˈsɪs.ɪn

absciss|a æbˈsɪs|.ə, əb- **-ae** -i **-as** -əz

abscission æbˈsɪʃ.ᵊn, -ˈsɪʒ- **-s** -z

abscond æbˈskɒnd, əb- ⓤⓢ -ˈskɑːnd **-s** -z **-ing** -ɪŋ **-ed** -ɪd **-er/s** -əʳ/z ⓤⓢ -ɚ/z

Abse ˈæb.si, -zi

abseil ˈæb.seɪl, -saɪl **-s** -z **-ing** -ɪŋ **-ed** -d

absenc|e ˈæb.sᵊn*t*s **-es** -ɪz

absent (*adj.*) ˈæb.sᵊnt **-ly** -li ˌ**absent without ˈleave**

ab|sent (*v.*) æb|ˈsent, əb- **-sents** -ˈsents **-senting** -ˈsen.tɪŋ ⓤⓢ -ˈsen.t̬ɪŋ **-sented** -ˈsen.tɪd ⓤⓢ -ˈsen.t̬ɪd

absentee ˌæb.sᵊnˈtiː, -senˈ- **-s** -z **-ism** -ɪ.zᵊm *stress shift, see compounds:* ˌ**absentee ˈballot;** ˌ**absentee ˈlandlord**

absentia æbˈsen.ti.ə, -ɑː, -ˈsen*t*.ʃi- ⓤⓢ -ˈsen*t*.ʃə, ˈ-ʃi.ə

absent-minded ˌæb.sᵊntˈmaɪn.dɪd **-ly** -li **-ness** -nəs, -nɪs *stress shift:* ˌabsent-minded ˈperson

absinth(e) ˈæb.sæ̃θ, -sɪn*t*θ

absolut|e ˌæb.səˈluːt, -ljuːt, ˈæb.sᵊl.uːt, -juːt ⓤⓢ ˌæb.səˈluːt, ˈ--- **-es** -s **-est** -əst, -ɪst **-ness** -nəs, -nɪs

absolutely ˌæb.səˈluːt.li, -ˈljuːt- ⓤⓢ ˌæb.səˈluːt-, ˈæb.sə.luːt- *stress shift:* ˌabsolutely ˈfabulous

absolution ˌæb.səˈluː.ʃᵊn, -ˈljuː- ⓤⓢ -ˈluː- **-s** -z

absolut|ism ˈæb.sᵊl.uː.t|ɪ.zᵊm, -juː- ⓤⓢ -sə.luː.t̬|ɪ- **-ist/s** -ɪst/s

absolutive ˌæb.səˈluː.tɪv, -ˈljuː- ⓤⓢ -ˈluː.t̬ɪv

absolv|e əbˈzɒlv, -ˈsɒlv ⓤⓢ -ˈzɑː*l*v, -ˈsɑː*l*v, -ˈzɔː*l*v, -ˈsɔː*l*v **-es** -z **-ing** -ɪŋ **-ed** -d **-er/s** -əʳ/z ⓤⓢ -ɚ/z

absorb əbˈzɔːb, -ˈsɔːb ⓤⓢ -ˈsɔːrb, -ˈzɔːrb **-s** -z **-ed** -d **-edly** -ɪd.li, -əd.li **-able** -ə.bl̩

absorbency əbˈzɔː.bən*t*.si, -ˈsɔː- ⓤⓢ -ˈsɔːr-, -ˈzɔːr-

absorbent əbˈzɔː.bənt, -ˈsɔː- ⓤⓢ -ˈsɔːr-, -ˈzɔːr- **-ly** -li

absorbing əbˈzɔː.bɪŋ, -ˈsɔː- ⓤⓢ -ˈsɔːr-, -ˈzɔːr- **-ly** -li

absorbing əbˈzɔː.bɪŋ, -ˈsɔː- ⓤⓢ -ˈsɔːr-, -ˈzɔːr- **-ly** -li

absorption əbˈzɔːp.ʃᵊn, -ˈsɔːp- ⓤⓢ -ˈsɔːrp-, -ˈzɔːrp-

absorptive əbˈzɔːp.tɪv, -ˈsɔːp- ⓤⓢ -ˈsɔːrp-, -ˈzɔːrp-

abstain æbˈsteɪn, əb- **-s** -z **-ing** -ɪŋ **-ed** -d **-er/s** -əʳ/z ⓤⓢ -ɚ/z

abstemious æbˈstiː.mi.əs, əb- **-ly** -li **-ness** -nəs, -nɪs

abstention æbˈsten.*t*ʃᵊn, əb- ⓤⓢ -ˈsten*t*.ʃᵊn **-s** -z

abstergent æbˈstɜː.dʒᵊnt, əb- ⓤⓢ -ˈstɝː- **-s** -s

abstinen|ce ˈæb.stɪ.nən|*t*s, -stə- **-t** -t

abstract (*n. adj.*) ˈæb.strækt **-s** -s

abstract (*v.*) æbˈstrækt, əb- **-s** -s **-ing** -ɪŋ **-ed/ly** -ɪd/li

abstraction æbˈstræk.ʃᵊn, əb- **-s** -z

abstraction|ism æbˈstræk.ʃᵊn|.ɪ.zᵊm, əb- **-ist/s** -ɪst/s

abstract|ly ˈæb.strækt|.li, əbˈstræk*t*-, æbˈ- **-ness** -nəs, -nɪs

abstrict əbˈstrɪkt, æb- **-s** -s **-ing** -ɪŋ **-ed** -ɪd

abstriction əbˈstrɪk.ʃᵊn, æb-

abstruse æbˈstruːs, əb- **-ly** -li **-ness** -nəs, -nɪs

absurd əbˈzɜːd, -ˈsɜːd ⓤⓢ -ˈsɝːd, -ˈzɝːd **-est** -ɪst, -əst **-ly** -li **-ness** -nəs, -nɪs

absurd|ism əbˈzɜː.d|ɪ.zᵊm, -ˈsɜː- ⓤⓢ -ˈsɝː-, -ˈzɝː- **-ist** -ɪst

Accent

Accent may refer to prominence given to a syllable (see STRESS), or to a particular way of pronouncing. This panel concentrates on the latter definition.

Examples for English

Speakers may share the same grammar and vocabulary, but pronounce what they say with different accents. In Britain, for example, there are accents such as Scots, Cockney (in London), and Scouse (in Liverpool), and in the United States the New York accent differs considerably from that commonly heard in Texas. There are also different world standard English accents, such as British, American, Australian, Indian or Singaporean.

Major differences between British and US English include the vowel in words such as *glass*, the use of a flapped /t/ in words like *butter*, and the fact that US English is RHOTIC while British English is non-rhotic, that is, an *r* in the spelling is always pronounced in US English, but only where a vowel follows in British English, e.g.:

glass	/ɡlɑːs/	(US) /ɡlæs/
butter	/ˈbʌt.əʳ/	(US) /ˈbʌt̬.ɚ/
car	/kɑːʳ/	(US) /kɑːr/

More information on the accents chosen to represent British and American English is given on pp xx.

absurdit|y əbˈzɜː.də.t|i, -ˈsɜː-, -dɪ- (US) -ˈsɝː.də.t̬|i, -ˈzɝː- **-ies** -iz
ABTA ˈæb.tə
Abu ˈɑː.buː, ˈæb.uː
Abu Dhabi ˌæb.uːˈdɑː.bi, ˌɑː.buː-, -ˈdæb.i (US) ˌɑː.buːˈdɑː.bi
Abuja əˈbuː.dʒə
abulia əˈbuː.li.ə, eɪ-, -ˈbjuː-
abundance əˈbʌn.dən*t*s
abundant əˈbʌn.dənt **-ly** -li
Abu Nidal ˌæb.uː.niːˈdɑːl, ˌɑː.buː-, -ˈdæl (US) ˌɑː.buː-
Abury ˈeɪ.bᵊr.i (US) -ber-, -bɚ-
abus|e (*n.*) əˈbjuːs **-es** -ɪz
abus|e (*v.*) əˈbjuːz **-es** -ɪz **-ing** -ɪŋ **-ed** -d **-er/s** -əʳ/z (US) -ɚ/z
Abu Simbel ˌæb.uːˈsɪm.bᵊl, -bel (US) ˌɑː.buːˈ-
abusive əˈbjuː.sɪv, -zɪv **-ly** -li **-ness** -nəs, -nɪs
a|but ə|ˈbʌt **-buts** -ˈbʌts **-butting** -ˈbʌt.ɪŋ (US) -ˈbʌt̬.ɪŋ **-butted** -ˈbʌt.ɪd (US) -ˈbʌt̬.ɪd **-buttal** -ˈbʌt.ᵊl (US) -ˈbʌt̬.ᵊl
abutilon əˈbjuː.tɪ.lən, -lɒn (US) -t̬ə.lɑːn, -lən **-s** -z
abutment əˈbʌt.mənt **-s** -s
aabutter əˈbʌt.əʳ (US) -ˈbʌt̬.ɚ **-s** -z
abuzz əˈbʌz
Abydos əˈbaɪ.dɒs, -dəs; ˈæb.ɪ.dɒs (US) əˈbaɪ.dɑːs; ˈæb.ɪ-
abysm əˈbɪz.ᵊm **-s** -z
abysmal əˈbɪz.mᵊl **-ly** -i
abyss əˈbɪs **-es** -ɪz
abyssal əˈbɪs.ᵊl
Abyssini|a ˌæb.ɪˈsɪn.i|.ə, -əˈ- **-an/s** -ən/z
a/c (*abbrev. for* **account**) əˈkaʊnt
AC (*US abbrev. for* **air conditioning**), **a/c** ˌeɪˈsiː
-ac -æk, -ək
Note: Suffix. Does not normally affect stress patterning, e.g. **mania**, /ˈmeɪ.ni.ə/, **maniac** /ˈmeɪ.ni.æk/.
acacia əˈkeɪ.ʃə, ˈ-si.ə (US) ˈ-ʃə **-s** -z
academe (A) ˈæk.ə.diːm
academia ˌæk.əˈdiː.mi.ə
academic ˌæk.əˈdem.ɪk **-s** -s *stress shift, see compound:* ˌ**academic** ˈ**year**
academic|al ˌæk.əˈdem.ɪ.k|ᵊl **-als** -ᵊlz **-ally** -ᵊl.i, -li
academician əˌkæd.əˈmɪʃ.ᵊn, ˌæk.ə.dəˈ-, -dɪˈ- (US) ˌæk.ə-, əˌkæd- **-s** -z
academicism ˌæk.əˈdem.ɪ.sɪ.zᵊm, ˈ-ə-
academism əˈkæd.ə.mɪ.zᵊm
academ|y əˈkæd.ə.m|i **-ies** -iz
Aˌ**cademy A**ˈ**ward**
Acadi|a əˈkeɪ.di|.ə **-an/s** -ən/z
acajou ˈæk.ə.ʒuː **-s** -z
acanth|oid əˈkæn*t*.θ|ɔɪd **-ous** -əs
acanth|us əˈkæn*t*.θ|əs **-i** -aɪ **-uses** -ə.sɪz **-ine** -aɪn
a cap(p)ella ˌæ.kəˈpel.ə, -kæpˈel- (US) ˌɑː.kəˈpel-
Acapulco ˌæk.əˈpʊl.kəʊ (US) ˌæk.əˈpuːl.koʊ, ˌɑː.kəˈ-, -ˈpʊl-
acarid ˈæk.ᵊr.ɪd **-s** -z
acarolog|y ˌæk.əˈrɒl.ə.dʒ|i (US) -ˈrɑː.lə- **-ist/s** -ɪst/s
acarpel(l)ous ˌeɪˈkɑː.pᵊl.əs (US) -ˈkɑːr-
acarpous ˌeɪˈkɑː.pəs (US) -ˈkɑːr-
ACAS, Acas ˈeɪˌkæs
acatalectic ˌeɪ.kæt.əˈlek.tɪk, əˌkæt- (US) -kæt̬.əˈ- **-s** -s *stress shift:* ˌacatalectic ˈverse, aˌcatalectic ˈverse
acatalepsy ˌeɪˈkæt.ə.lep.si, əˈkæt- (US) -ˈkæt̬.ə-
acataleptic ˌeɪ.kæt.əˈlep.tɪk, əˌkæt- (US) -kæt̬.əˈ-
Accad ˈæk.æd
Accadi|a əˈkeɪ.di|.ə, ækˈeɪ- **-an/s** -ən/z
acced|e əkˈsiːd, æk- **-es** -z **-ing** -ɪŋ **-ed** -ɪd **-er/s** -əʳ/z (US) -ɚ/z
accelerando ækˌsel.əˈræn.dəʊ, ək-, əˌtʃel- (US) -ˈrɑːn.doʊ
accelerant əkˈsel.ə.rᵊnt, æk- (US) -ɚ.ənt **-s** -s
accele|rate əkˈsel.ə|.reɪt, æk- **-rates** -reɪts **-rating** -reɪ.tɪŋ (US) -reɪ.t̬ɪŋ **-rated** -reɪ.tɪd (US) -reɪ.t̬ɪd
acceleration əkˌsel.əˈreɪ.ʃᵊn, æk- **-s** -z
accelerative əkˈsel.ə.rə.tɪv, æk- (US) -ɚ.ə.t̬ɪv
accelerator əkˈsel.ə.reɪ.təʳ, æk- (US) -t̬ɚ **-s** -z
accelerometer əkˌsel.əˈrɒm.ɪ.təʳ, æk-, ˈ-ə- (US) -ˈrɑː.mə.t̬ɚ **-s** -z
accent (*n.*) ˈæk.sᵊnt (US) -sent **-s** -s
ac|cent (*v.*) ək|ˈsent, æk- (US) æk-, ək- **-cents** -ˈsents **-centing** -ˈsen.tɪŋ (US) -ˈsen.t̬ɪŋ **-cented** -ˈsen.tɪd (US) -ˈsen.t̬ɪd
accentual əkˈsen.tʃu.əl, æk-, -tju- **-ly** -i
accentu|ate əkˈsen.tʃu.eɪt, æk-, -tju- **-ates** -eɪts **-ating** -eɪ.tɪŋ (US) -eɪ.t̬ɪŋ **-ated** -eɪ.tɪd (US) -eɪ.t̬ɪd
accentuation əkˌsen.tʃuˈeɪ.ʃᵊn, æk-, -tjuˈ- **-s** -z
accept əkˈsept, æk- **-s** -s **-ing** -ɪŋ **-ed** -ɪd **-er/s** -əʳ/z (US) -ɚ/z **-or/s** -əʳ/z (US) -ɚ/z
acceptability əkˌsep.təˈbɪl.ə.ti, æk-, -ɪ.ti (US) -ə.t̬i
acceptab|le əkˈsep.tə.b|l̩, æk- **-ly** -li **-leness** -l̩.nəs, -nɪs
acceptanc|e əkˈsep.tən*t*s, æk- **-es** -ɪz
acceptant əkˈsep.tᵊnt, æk- **-s** -s
acceptation ˌæk.sepˈteɪ.ʃᵊn **-s** -z
access (A®) ˈæk.ses **-es** -ɪz **-ing** -ɪŋ **-ed** -t
accessar|y əkˈses.ᵊr|.i, æk- **-ies** -iz
accessibility əkˌses.əˈbɪl.ə.ti, æk-, -ɪˈ-, -ɪ.ti (US) -ə.t̬i
accessible əkˈses.ə.bl̩, æk-, ˈ-ɪ-
accession əkˈseʃ.ᵊn, æk- **-s** -z
accessit ækˈses.ɪt, ək- **-s** -s

accessoriz|e, -is|e ək'ses.ᵊr.aɪz ⓤⓢ -ə.raɪz **-es** -ɪz **-ing** -ɪŋ **-ed** -d
accessor|y ək'ses.ᵊr|.i, æk- **-ies** -iz
acciaccatur|a əˌtʃæk.ə'tʊə.r|ə ⓤⓢ ɑːˌtʃɑː.kə'tʊr|.ə **-as** -əz **-e** -eɪ, -iː
accidence 'æk.sɪ.dᵊnts, -sə-
accident 'æk.sɪ.dᵊnt, -sə- **-s** -s
'**accident-**ˌ**prone**
accidental ˌæk.sɪ'den.tᵊl, -sə'- ⓤⓢ -t̬ᵊl **-ly** -i
accidia æk'sɪd.i.ə
accidie 'æk.sɪ.di, -sə-
accipiter æk'sɪp.ɪ.təʳ, ək-, -ə.təʳ ⓤⓢ -ə.t̬ɚ **-s** -z
acclaim ə'kleɪm **-s** -z **-ing** -ɪŋ **-ed** -d
acclamation ˌæk.lə'meɪ.ʃᵊn **-s** -z
acclamatory ə'klæm.ə.tᵊr.i ⓤⓢ -ə.tɔːr.i
acclimatation əˌklaɪ.mə'teɪ.ʃᵊn
acclima|te 'æk.lɪ.meɪ|t, -lə-; ə'klaɪ.mə|t ⓤⓢ 'æk.lə.meɪ|t; ə'klaɪ.mə|t **-tes** -ts **-ting** -tɪŋ ⓤⓢ -t̬ɪŋ **-ted** -tɪd ⓤⓢ -t̬ɪd
acclimation ˌæk.lɪ'meɪ.ʃᵊn
acclimatization, -isa- əˌklaɪ.mə.taɪ'zeɪ.ʃᵊn, -tɪ'- ⓤⓢ -t̬ə'-
acclimatiz|e, -is|e ə'klaɪ.mə.taɪz, -mɪ- **-es** -ɪz **-ing** -ɪŋ **-ed** -d
acclivit|y ə'klɪv.ə.t|i, æk'lɪv-, -ɪt|i ⓤⓢ -t̬|i **-ies** -iz
accolade 'æk.ə.leɪd, ˌ--'- **-s** -z
accommo|date ə'kɒm.ə|.deɪt ⓤⓢ -'kɑː.mə- **-dates** -deɪts **-dated** -de.tɪd ⓤⓢ -deɪ.t̬ɪd **-dator/s** -deɪ.təʳ/z ⓤⓢ -deɪ.t̬ɚ/z **-dative/ly** -deɪ.tɪv/li ⓤⓢ -deɪ.t̬ɪv/li
accommodating ə'kɒm.ə.deɪ.tɪŋ ⓤⓢ ə'kɑː.mə.deɪ.t̬ɪŋ **-ly** -li
accommodation əˌkɒm.ə'deɪ.ʃᵊn ⓤⓢ əˌkɑː.mə'- **-s** -z
accompaniment ə'kʌm.pᵊn.ɪ.mənt **-s** -s
accompanist ə'kʌm.pə.nɪst **-s** -s
accompan|y ə'kʌm.pə.n|i **-ies** -iz **-ying** -i.ɪŋ **-ied** -id **-yist/s** -i.ɪsts **-ier/s** -i.əʳ/z ⓤⓢ -i.ɚ/z
accomplic|e ə'kʌm.plɪs, -'kɒm- ⓤⓢ -'kɑːm-, -'kʌm- **-es** -ɪz
accomplish ə'kʌm.plɪʃ, -'kɒm- ⓤⓢ -'kɑːm-, -'kʌm- **-es** -ɪz **-ing** -ɪŋ **-ed** -t
accomplishment ə'kʌm.plɪʃ.mənt, -'kɒm- ⓤⓢ -'kɑːm-, -'kʌm- **-s** -s
accord ə'kɔːd ⓤⓢ -'kɔːrd **-ed** -ɪd **-ing** -ɪŋ **-s** -z
accordan|ce ə'kɔː.dᵊn|*t*s ⓤⓢ -'kɔːr- **-t** -t
according ə'kɔː.dɪŋ ⓤⓢ -'kɔːr- **-ly** -li
accordion ə'kɔː.di.ən ⓤⓢ -'kɔːr- **-s** -z
accost ə'kɒst ⓤⓢ -'kɑːst **-s** -s **-ing** -ɪŋ **-ed** -ɪd
accouchement ə'kuːʃ.mɑ̃ː*ŋ* ⓤⓢ -mɑːnt, ˌæk.uːʃ'mɑ̃ː
accoucheur ˌæk.uː'ʃɜːʳ, ə'kuː.ʃɜːʳ ⓤⓢ ˌæk.uː'ʃɝː **-s** -z
accoucheus|e ˌæk.uː'ʃɜːz, ə'kuː.ʃɜːz ⓤⓢ ˌæk.uː'ʃɜːz **-es** -ɪz
ac|count ə|'kaʊnt **-counts** -'kaʊnts **-counting** -'kaʊn.tɪŋ ⓤⓢ -'kaʊn.t̬ɪŋ **-counted** -'kaʊn.tɪd ⓤⓢ -'kaʊn.t̬ɪd
a'ccount ˌ**book**
accountability əˌkaʊn.tə'bɪl.ə.ti, -ɪ.ti ⓤⓢ -t̬ə'bɪl.ə.t̬i
accountab|le ə'kaʊn.tə.b|l̩ ⓤⓢ -t̬ə- **-ly** -li **-leness** -l̩.nəs, -nɪs
accountancy ə'kaʊn.tən*t*.si ⓤⓢ -t̬ən*t*-
accountant ə'kaʊn.tənt **-s** -s
accout|er ə'kuː.t|əʳ ⓤⓢ -t̬|ɚ **-ers** -əz ⓤⓢ -ɚz **-ering** -ᵊr.ɪŋ **-ered** -əd ⓤⓢ -ɚd **-erment/s** -ə.mənt/s ⓤⓢ -ɚ-
accout|re ə'kuː.t|əʳ ⓤⓢ ə'kuː.t̬|ɚ **-res** -əz **-ring** -ᵊr.ɪŋ **-red** -əd ⓤⓢ -ɚd **-rement/s** -rə.mənt/s, -ə.mənt/s ⓤⓢ -ɚ.mənt/s
Accra ə'krɑː, æk'rɑː
accred|it ə'kred|.ɪt **-its** -ɪts **-iting** -ɪ.tɪŋ ⓤⓢ -ɪ.t̬ɪŋ **-ited** -ɪ.tɪd ⓤⓢ -ɪ.t̬ɪd
accreditation əˌkred.ɪ'teɪ.ʃᵊn ⓤⓢ -ə'-
accre|te ə'kriː|t, æk'riː|t **-tes** -ts **-ting** -tɪŋ ⓤⓢ -t̬ɪŋ **-ted** -tɪd ⓤⓢ -t̬ɪd
accretion ə'kriː.ʃᵊn, æk'riː- **-s** -z
accretive ə'kriː.tɪv, æk'riː- ⓤⓢ ə'kriː.t̬ɪv
Accrington 'æk.rɪŋ.tən
accrual ə'kruː.əl, -'krʊəl ⓤⓢ -'kruː.əl
accru|e ə'kruː **-es** -z **-ing** -ɪŋ **-ed** -d
accruement ə'kruː.mənt
acculturate ə'kʌl.tʃᵊr|.eɪt, æk'ʌl- ⓤⓢ -tʃə.r|eɪt **-ates** -eɪts **-ating** -eɪ.tɪŋ ⓤⓢ -eɪ.t̬ɪŋ **-ated** -eɪ.tɪd ⓤⓢ -eɪ.t̬ɪd
acculturation əˌkʌl.tʃᵊr'eɪ.ʃᵊn, ækˌʌl- ⓤⓢ -tʃə'reɪ-
accumben|t ə'kʌm.bən|t **-cy** -*t*.si
accumu|late ə'kjuː.mjə|.leɪt, -mjʊ- **-lates** -leɪts **-lating** -leɪ.tɪŋ ⓤⓢ -leɪ.t̬ɪŋ **-lated** -leɪ.tɪd ⓤⓢ -leɪ.t̬ɪd **-lator/s** -leɪ.təʳ/z ⓤⓢ -leɪ.t̬ɚ/z
accumulation əˌkjuː.mjə'leɪ.ʃᵊn, -mjʊ'- **-s** -z
accumulative ə'kjuː.mjə.lə.tɪv, -mjʊ- ⓤⓢ -t̬ɪv
accuracy 'æk.jə.rə.si, -jʊ- ⓤⓢ -jɚ.ə-, -jʊ.rə-
accurate 'æk.jə.rət, -jʊ-, -rɪt ⓤⓢ -jɚ.ət, -jʊ.rət, -rɪt **-ly** -li **-ness** -nəs, -nɪs
accursed ə'kɜː.sɪd, -'kɜːst ⓤⓢ ə'kɝːst, -'kɝː.səd, ə'kɜːst **-ly** -li
accusal ə'kjuː.zᵊl **-s** -z
accusation ˌæk.jʊ'zeɪ.ʃᵊn, -jə'- **-s** -z
accusatival əˌkjuː.zə'taɪ.vᵊl
accusative ə'kjuː.zə.tɪv ⓤⓢ -t̬ɪv **-s** -z
accusativity əˌkjuː.zə'tɪv.ə.ti, -ɪ.ti ⓤⓢ -ə.t̬i
accusatory ə'kjuː.zə.tᵊr.i, ˌæk.jʊ'zeɪ-, -jə'-, -tri ⓤⓢ ə'kjuː.zə.tɔːr.i
accus|e ə'kjuːz **-es** -ɪz **-ing/ly** -ɪŋ/li **-ed** -d **-er/s** -əʳ/z ⓤⓢ -ɚ/z
accustom ə'kʌs.təm **-s** -z **-ing** -ɪŋ **-ed/ness** -d/nəs, -nɪs
AC/DC ˌeɪ.siː'diː.siː
ac|e eɪs **-es** -ɪz
acedia ə'siː.di.ə
Aceldama ə'kel.də.mə, -'sel-; ˌæk.el'dɑː- ⓤⓢ ə'sel.də-
-aceous -'eɪ.ʃəs, -'eɪ.ʃi.əs
Note: Suffix. Words containing **-aceous** always exhibit primary stress as shown above, e.g. **herbaceous** /hɜː'beɪ.ʃəs ⓤⓢ hɚ-/.
acephalous ə'sef.ᵊl.əs, ˌeɪ-, -'kef- ⓤⓢ eɪ'sef-, ə-
acequia ə'seɪ.ki.ə, -'siː- **-s** -z
acer|bate 'æs.ə.|beɪt ⓤⓢ '-ɚ- **-bates** -beɪts **-bating** -beɪ.tɪŋ ⓤⓢ -beɪ.t̬ɪŋ **-bated** -beɪ.tɪd ⓤⓢ -beɪ.t̬ɪd
acerbic ə'sɜː.bɪk, æs'ɜː- ⓤⓢ ə'sɝː- **-ally** -ᵊl.i, -li
acerbity ə'sɜː.bə.ti, -bɪ- ⓤⓢ ə'sɝː.bə.t̬i
Acestes ə'ses.tiːz, -'kes-
acetabul|um ˌæs.ɪ'tæb.jə.l|əm, -jʊ- **-ums** -əmz **-a** -ə **-ar** -əʳ ⓤⓢ -ɚ
acetaldehyde ˌæs.ɪ'tæl.dɪ.haɪd, -də-
acetaminophen əˌsiː.tə'mɪn.ə.fən ⓤⓢ ˌæs.ɪ.t̬ə'-; əˌsiː.t̬ə'-, -ˌset̬.ə'-
acetate 'æs.ɪ.teɪt, '-ə- **-s** -s
acetic ə'siː.tɪk, æs'iː-, -'et.ɪk ⓤⓢ ə'siː.t̬ɪk **a**ˌ**cetic** '**acid**
acetif|y ə'siː.tɪ.f|aɪ, æs'iː-, -'set.ɪ- ⓤⓢ -'set̬.ə- **-ies** -aɪz **-ying** -aɪ.ɪŋ **-ied** -aɪd
acetin 'æs.ə.tɪn, '-ɪ- ⓤⓢ -t̬ɪn
acetone 'æs.ɪ.təʊn, '-ə- ⓤⓢ -t̬oʊn
acetose 'æs.ɪ.təʊs, '-ə-, -təʊz ⓤⓢ -toʊs
acetous 'æs.ɪ.təs, '-ə- ⓤⓢ 'æs.ɪ.t̬əs; ə'siː-
acetum ə'siː.təm ⓤⓢ -t̬əm
acetyl 'æs.ɪ.taɪl, '-ə-, -tɪl; ə'siː-, -taɪl ⓤⓢ 'æs.ə.t̬ᵊl, -t̬iːl; ə'siː.t̬ᵊl
acetyl|ate ə'set.ɪ.l|eɪt, -ᵊl|.eɪt ⓤⓢ -'set̬.ə.l|eɪt, -'siː.t̬ə- **-ates** -eɪts **-ating** -eɪ.tɪŋ ⓤⓢ -eɪ.t̬ɪŋ **-ated** -eɪ.tɪd ⓤⓢ -eɪ.t̬ɪd
acetylation əˌset.ɪ'leɪ.ʃᵊn, -ᵊl'eɪ- ⓤⓢ -ˌset̬.ə'leɪ-
acetylcholine ˌæs.ɪ.taɪl'kəʊ.liːn, ˌ-ə- ⓤⓢ əˌsiː.t̬ᵊl'koʊ-, -ˌset̬.ᵊl'-; ˌæs.ə.t̬ᵊl'-
acetylene ə'set.ɪ.liːn, -ᵊl.iːn ⓤⓢ -'set̬.ə.liːn
Achae|a ə'kiː|.ə **-an/s** -ən/z
Achaia ə'kaɪ.ə
Achates ə'keɪ.tiːz, -'kɑː- ⓤⓢ -t̬iːz
ach|e eɪk **-es** -s **-ing/ly** -ɪŋ/li **-ed** -t **-er/s** -əʳ/z ⓤⓢ -ɚ/z
Achebe ə'tʃeɪ.bi
Achernar 'eɪ.kə.nɑːʳ ⓤⓢ -kɚ.nɑːr
Acheron 'æk.ə.rɒn, -rᵊn ⓤⓢ -rɑːn
Acheson 'ætʃ.ɪ.sᵊn, '-ə-
Acheulean, Acheulian ə'*t*ʃuː.li.ən
à cheval ˌæ.ʃə'væl

achiev|e əˈtʃiːv **-es** -z **-ing** -ɪŋ **-ed** -d **-able** -ə.bl̩ **-er/s** -əʳ/z (US) -ɚ/z

achievement əˈtʃiːv.mənt **-s** -s

Achil(l) ˈæk.ɪl

Achilles əˈkɪl.iːz **Aˌchilles ˈheel** (US) **Aˈchilles ˌheel**

Achille Serre æʃ.ɪlˈseəʳ, -iːl- (US) -ˈser

Achin əˈtʃiːn

Achish ˈeɪ.kɪʃ

achondro|plasia əˌkɒn.drəʊ|ˈpleɪ.zi.ə, -ʒə (US) -ˌkɑːn.drə|ˈpleɪ.ʒi.ə, ˌeɪ- **-plastic** -ˈplæs.tɪk

Achray əˈkreɪ, əˈxreɪ

achromatic ˌæk.rəʊˈmæt.ɪk, ˌeɪ.krəʊ- (US) ˌæk.rəˈmæt̬- **-ally** -əl.i *stress shift:* ˌachromatic ˈlens

achromatism əˈkrəʊ.mə.tɪ.zəm, ˌeɪ- (US) -ˈkroʊ-

achromatiz|e, -is|e əˈkrəʊ.mə.taɪz, ˌeɪ- (US) -ˈkroʊ- **-es** -ɪz **-ing** -ɪŋ **-ed** -d

achromatous əˈkrəʊ.mə.təs, ˌeɪ- (US) -ˈkroʊ.mə.t̬əs

achtung ˈɑːx.tʊŋ, ˈæx- (US) ˈɑːx-, ˈɑːk-

achy ˈeɪ.ki

acicul|a əˈsɪk.jʊ.l|ə, -jə- **-ae** -i **-ar** -ə

acid ˈæs.ɪd **-s** -z **-ly** -li **-ness** -nəs, -nɪs ˈ**acid ˌdrop**; ˌ**acid ˈrain**; ˌ**acid ˈtest**, ˈ**acid ˌtest**

acidhead ˈæs.ɪd.hed **-s** -z

acidic əˈsɪd.ɪk

acidif|y əˈsɪd.ɪ.f|aɪ, æsˈɪd- **-ies** -aɪz **-ying** -aɪ.ɪŋ **-ied** -aɪd

acidity əˈsɪd.ə.ti, æsˈɪd-, -ɪ.ti (US) -ə.t̬i

acidiz|e, -is|e ˈæs.ɪ.daɪz **-es** -ɪz **-ing** -ɪŋ **-ed** -d

acidophilus ˌæs.ɪˈdɒf.ɪ.ləs, -əl.əs (US) -ˈdɑː.fəl-

acidosis ˌæs.ɪˈdəʊ.sɪs (US) -ˈdoʊ-

acidu|late əˈsɪd.jʊ|.leɪt, æsˈɪd-, -jə-, -ˈsɪdʒ.ʊ-, ˈ-ə- **-lates** -leɪts **-lating** -leɪ.tɪŋ (US) -leɪ.t̬ɪŋ **-lated** -leɪ.tɪd (US) -leɪ.t̬ɪd

acidulous əˈsɪd.jʊ.ləs, æsˈɪd-, -jə-, -ˈsɪdʒ.ʊ-, ˈ-ə-

acin|ose ˈæs.ɪ.n|əʊs, -n|əʊz (US) -n|oʊs, -n|oʊz **-ous** -əs

acin|us ˈæs.ɪ.n|əs **-i** -aɪ

Acis ˈeɪ.sɪs

ack-ack ˌækˈæk *stress shift:* ˌack-ack ˈgun

ackee ˈæk.i **-s** -z

Ackerley ˈæk.əl.i (US) -ɚ.li

Ackerman(n) ˈæk.ə.mən, -mæn (US) ˈ-ɚ-

Ackland ˈæk.lənd

acknowledg|e əkˈnɒl.ɪdʒ, æk- (US) -ˈnɑː.lɪdʒ **-es** -ɪz **-ing** -ɪŋ **-ed** -d **-eable** -ə.bl̩

acknowledg(e)ment əkˈnɒl.ɪdʒ.mənt, æk- (US) -ˈnɑː.lɪdʒ- **-s** -s

Ackroyd ˈæk.rɔɪd

Ackworth Moor Top ˌæk.wəθˌmɔːˈtɒp (US) -wɚθˌmʊrˈtɑːp

Acland ˈæk.lənd

ACLU ˌeɪ.siː.elˈjuː

acme ˈæk.mi **-s** -z

acne ˈæk.ni

acnode ˈæk.nəʊd (US) -noʊd **-s** -z

Acol *road in London, system of bridge playing:* ˈæk.əl *in Kent:* ˈeɪ.kɒl (US) -kɑːl

acolyte ˈæk.əl.aɪt (US) -ə.laɪt **-s** -s

Acomb ˈeɪ.kəm

Aconcagua ˌæk.ɒnˈkæg.wə, -ɒŋˈ- (US) ˌɑː.kənˈ-, -kəŋˈ-, -kɑː.gwə

aconite ˈæk.ə.naɪt **-s** -s

acorn ˈeɪ.kɔːn (US) -kɔrn **-s** -z ˈ**acorn ˌsquash**

acotyledon əˌkɒt.ɪˈliː.dən, ˌeɪ-, -əlˈiː- (US) -ˌkɑː.t̬əˈliː- **-s** -z

acouchi əˈkuː.ʃi (US) ɑːˈkuː.ʃi, ə-

acoustic əˈkuː.stɪk **-s** -s **-ally** -əl.i (US) -li

acoustician ˌæ.kuːˈstɪʃ.ən **-s** -z

acoustooptic əˌkuː.stəʊˈɒp.tɪk (US) -stoʊˈɑːp- **-s** -s **-al** -əl

ac|quaint ə|ˈkweɪnt **-quaints** -ˈkweɪnts **-quainting** -ˈkweɪn.tɪŋ (US) -ˈkweɪn.t̬ɪŋ **-quainted** -ˈkweɪn.tɪd (US) -ˈkweɪn.t̬ɪd

acquaintanc|e əˈkweɪn.tənts **-es** -ɪz

acquaintanceship əˈkweɪn.tənts.ʃɪp, -tənt.ʃɪp **-s** -s

acquest əˈkwest **-s** -s

acquiesc|e ˌæk.wiˈes **-es** -ɪz **-ing** -ɪŋ **-ed** -t **-ence** -ənts **-ent/ly** -ənt/li

acquir|e əˈkwaɪəʳ (US) -ˈkwaɪɚ **-es** -z **-ing** -ɪŋ **-ed** -d **-ement/s** -mənt/s **-able** -ə.bl̩

acquisition ˌæk.wɪˈzɪʃ.ən, -wə-, -z

acquisitive əˈkwɪz.ɪ.tɪv, ˈ-ə- (US) -ə.t̬ɪv **-ly** -li **-ness** -nəs, -nɪs

acquit əˈkwɪt **-s** -s **-ting** -ɪŋ (US) əˈkwɪt̬.ɪŋ **-ted** -ɪd (US) əˈkwɪt̬.ɪd

acquittal əˈkwɪt.əl (US) -ˈkwɪt̬- **-s** -z

acquittance əˈkwɪt.ənts

acre (A) ˈeɪ.kəʳ (US) -kɚ **-s** -z

acreag|e ˈeɪ.kər.ɪdʒ, ˈ-krɪdʒ **-es** -ɪz

acrid ˈæk.rɪd **-ly** -li **-ness** -nəs, -nɪs

acridine ˈæk.rɪ.diːn, -daɪn

acridity əˈkrɪd.ə.ti, ækˈrɪd-, -ɪ.ti (US) -ə.t̬i

Acrilan® ˈæk.rɪ.læn, -rə-

acrimonious ˌæk.rɪˈməʊ.ni.əs, -rəˈ- (US) -ˈmoʊ- **-ly** -li **-ness** -nəs, -nɪs

acrimon|y ˈæk.rɪ.mə.n|i, -rə- (US) -moʊ- **-ies** -iz

acritical ˌeɪˈkrɪt.ɪ.kəl, ˈ-ə- (US) -ˈkrɪt̬.ə-

acritude ˈæk.rɪ.tjuːd, -rə-, -tʃuːd (US) -tuːd, -tjuːd

acro- æk.rəʊ-; əˈkrɒ- (US) æk.rə-, -roʊ-; əˈkrɑː-

Note: Prefix. Either takes primary or secondary stress on the first syllable, e.g. **acrosome** /ˈæk.rəʊ.səʊm (US) -rə.soʊm/, **acrosomal** /ˌæk.rəʊˈsəʊ.məl (US) -rəˈsoʊ-/, or primary stress only on the second syllable, e.g. **acropolis** /əˈkrɒp.ə.lɪs (US) -ˈkrɑː.pə-/.

acrobat ˈæk.rə.bæt **-s** -s

acrobatic ˌæk.rəˈbæt.ɪk (US) -ˈbæt̬- **-s** -s **-ally** -əl.i, -li *stress shift:* ˌacrobatic ˈleap

acrobatism ˈæk.rə.bæt.ɪ.zəm, ˌæk.rəˈbæt- (US) ˈæk.rə.bæt̬-, ˌæk.rəˈbæt̬-

acrogen ˈæk.rəʊ.dʒən, -dʒen (US) -roʊ-, -rə- **-s** -z

acrolect ˈæk.rəʊ.lekt (US) -roʊ-, -rə- **-s** -s **-al** -əl

acrolith ˈæk.rəʊ.lɪθ (US) -roʊ-, -rə- **-s** -s

acromegalic ˌæk.rəʊ.mɪˈgæl.ɪk, -məˈ- (US) -roʊ-

acromegaly ˌæk.rəʊˈmeg.əl.i (US) -roʊˈ-

acromion əˈkrəʊ.mi.ən (US) -ˈkroʊ- **-s** -z

acronym ˈæk.rəʊ.nɪm (US) -rə- **-s** -z

acropetal əˈkrɒp.ɪ.təl (US) -ˈkrɑː.pə.t̬əl **-ly** -i

acrophob|ia ˌæk.rəʊˈfəʊ.b|i.ə (US) -rəˈfoʊ- **-ic** -ɪk

acropolis (A) əˈkrɒp.ə.lɪs (US) -ˈkrɑː.pə- **-es** -ɪz

acrosomal ˌæk.rəʊˈsəʊ.məl (US) -rəˈsoʊ-

acrosome ˈæk.rəʊ.səʊm (US) -rə.soʊm

across əˈkrɒs (US) -ˈkrɑːs

across-the-board əˌkrɒs.ðəˈbɔːd (US) -ˌkrɑːs.ðəˈbɔːrd

acrostic əˈkrɒs.tɪk (US) -ˈkrɑː.stɪk **-s** -s

Acrux ˈeɪ.krʌks

acrylic əˈkrɪl.ɪk, ækˈrɪl- **-s** -s

act ækt **-s** -s **-ing** -ɪŋ **-ed** -ɪd **get ˌin on the ˈact**; **ˌget one's ˈact together**

ACT ˌeɪ.siːˈtiː

acta ˈæk.tə

Actaeon ˈæk.ti.ən (US) ækˈtiː-

ACTH ˌeɪ.siː.tiːˈeɪtʃ, ækθ

actinic ækˈtɪn.ɪk **-ly** -li

actinide ˈæk.tɪn.aɪd **-s** -z

actinism ˈæk.tɪn.ɪz.əm

actinium ækˈtɪn.i.əm

action ˈæk.ʃən **-s** -z **-ing** -ɪŋ **-ed** -d ˈ**action ˌman**; ˈ**action ˌstations**

actionable ˈæk.ʃən.ə.bl̩

Actium ˈæk.ti.əm

activable ˈæk.tɪv.ə.bl̩

acti|vate ˈæk.tɪ|.veɪt **-vates** -veɪts **-vating** -veɪ.tɪŋ (US) -veɪ.t̬ɪŋ **-vated** -veɪ.tɪd (US) -veɪ.t̬ɪd **-vator/s** -veɪ.təʳ/z (US) -veɪ.t̬ɚ/z

activation ˌæk.tɪˈveɪ.ʃən

active ˈæk.tɪv **-ly** -li **-ness** -nəs, -nɪs

activ|ism ˈæk.tɪ.v|ɪ.zəm **-ist/s** -ɪst/s

activit|y ækˈtɪv.ə.t|i, -ɪ.t|i (US) -ə.t̬|i **-ies** -iz

activiz|e ˈæk.tɪ.vaɪz **-es** -ɪz **-ing** -ɪŋ **-ed** -d

Acton ˈæk.tən

Acronyms

Acronyms are words or phrases written in an abbreviated form, usually with their initial letters, and pronounced as if they were words, usually with the most obvious pronunciation. However, it is best to treat them on a word-by-word basis, since there are exceptions.

Examples

Many organisations, particularly those to do with government, charities and trade unions, use acronyms. Phrases can also be reduced to acronym form. Acronyms are usually written using capital letters, although there are exceptions. Where there is a letter *E* at the end of an acronym, it is usually pronounced /iː/, e.g.:

- ► NATFHE (*National Association of Teachers in Further and Higher Education*) /ˈnæt.fiː/
- ► NATO (*North Atlantic Treaty Organisation*) /ˈneɪ.təʊ/ (US) /-t̬oʊ/
- ► snafu (*situation normal, all fouled up*) /snæfˈuː/
- ► Tardis (*time and relative dimensions in space*) /ˈtɑː.dɪs/ (US) /ˈtɑːr-/

Some words or phrases are abbreviated to initial letters but do not become acronyms. See **ABBREVIATIONS**.

actor ˈæk.təʳ (US) -tɚ **-s** -z
actress ˈæk.trəs, -trɪs **-es** -ɪz
Acts ækts
actual ˈæk.tʃu.əl, -tju-, -tʃəl, -tʃʊl (US) -tʃu.əl, -tʃəl, -tʃʊl **-ly** -i
actualit|y ˌæk.tʃuˈæl.ə.t|i, -tju-, -ɪ.t|i (US) -tʃuˈæl.ə.t̬|i **-ies** -iz
actualiz|e, -is|e ˈæk.tʃu.ə.laɪz, -tju-, -ʃu- (US) -tʃu- **-es** -ɪz **-ing** -ɪŋ **-ed** -d
actuarial ˌæk.tʃuˈeə.ri.əl, -tju- (US) -tʃuˈer.i-
actuar|y ˈæk.tʃu.ə.r|i, -tju.er|i (US) -tʃu- **-ies** -iz
actu|ate ˈæk.tʃu|.eɪt, -tju- (US) -tʃu- **-ates** -eɪts **-ating** -eɪ.tɪŋ (US) -eɪ.t̬ɪŋ **-ated** -eɪ.tɪd (US) -eɪ.t̬ɪd
actuation ˌæk.tʃuˈeɪ.ʃən, -tjuˈ- (US) -tʃuˈ- **-s** -z
Act-Up ˌæktˈʌp
acuity əˈkjuː.ə.ti, -ɪt.i (US) -ə.t̬i
acumen ˈæk.jʊ.mən, -jə-, -men (US) əˈkjuː.mən, ˈæk.jə-
acupressure ˈæk.jʊ.preʃ.əʳ, -jə- (US) -ɚ
acupunctur|e ˈæk.jʊ.pʌŋk.tʃəʳ, -jə- (US) -tʃɚ **-ist/s** -ɪst/s
a|cute əˈkjuːt **-cuter** -ˈkjuː.təʳ (US) -ˈkjuː.t̬ɚ **-cutest** -ˈkjuː.tɪst, -təst (US) -ˈkjuː.t̬ɪst, -t̬əst **-cutely** -ˈkjuːt.li **-cuteness** -ˈkjuːt.nəs, -nɪs **aˌcute ˈangle**
acyl ˈæs.ɪl **-s** -z
ad- æd-, əd-
Note: Prefix. Examples include **adjective** /ˈædʒ.ɪk.tɪv/, in which it is stressed, and **admonish** /ədˈmɒn.ɪʃ (US) -ˈmɑː.nɪʃ/, where it is unstressed.
ad æd **-s** -z
AD *(abbrev. for* **Anno Domini***)* ˌeɪˈdiː, ˌæn.əʊˈdɒm.ɪ.naɪ (US) ˌeɪˈdiː, ˌæn.oʊˈdɑː.mə.niː, -ˈdoʊ-, -naɪ
ADA ˌeɪ.diːˈeɪ
Ada, ADA *woman's name, trademark, US town:* ˈeɪ.də
adactylous ˌeɪˈdæk.tɪ.ləs
adag|e ˈæd.ɪdʒ **-es** -ɪz
adagio əˈdɑː.dʒi.əʊ, ˈ-ʒi- (US) -ˈdɑː.dʒoʊ, -dʒi.oʊ **-s** -z
Adair əˈdeəʳ (US) -ˈder
Adalbert ˈæd.əl.bɜːt (US) -bɝːt
Adam ˈæd.əm **ˌAdam's ˈapple** (US) **ˈAdam's ˌapple**
adamant ˈæd.ə.mənt **-ly** -li
adamantine ˌæd.əˈmæn.taɪn (US) -tiːn, -taɪn, -tən
adamite (A) ˈæd.ə.maɪt **-s** -s
Adams ˈæd.əmz
adamsite ˈæd.əm.zaɪt
Adamson ˈæd.əm.sən
Adamthwaite ˈæd.əm.θweɪt
Adana ˈɑː.də.nə; əˈdɑː-
Adapazari ˌɑː.dəˈpɑː.zər.i (US) -ˌpɑː.zəˈriː
adapt əˈdæpt **-s** -s **-ing** -ɪŋ **-ed** -ɪd **-ive** -ɪv
adaptability əˌdæp.təˈbɪl.ə.ti, -ɪt.i (US) -ə.t̬i
adaptable əˈdæp.tə.bl̩ **-ness** -nəs, -nɪs
adaptation ˌæd.æpˈteɪ.ʃən, -əpˈ- **-s** -z
adapter əˈdæp.təʳ (US) -tɚ **-s** -z
adaption əˈdæp.ʃən, ædˈæp- **-s** -z
adaptive əˈdæp.tɪv, ædˈæp- **-ly** -li
adaptor əˈdæp.təʳ (US) -tɚ **-s** -z
Adare əˈdeəʳ (US) -ˈder
Adar Sheni ɑːˌdɑːˈʃeɪ.ni (US) -ˌdɑːrˈ-
ADC ˌeɪ.diːˈsiː
Adcock ˈæd.kɒk (US) -kɑːk
add æd **-s** -z **-ing** -ɪŋ **-ed** -ɪd
Addams ˈæd.əmz
addax ˈæd.æks **-es** -ɪz
addend əˈdend, ædˈend (US) ˈæd.end; əˈdend **-s** -z
addend|um əˈden.d|əm, ædˈen- **-a** -ə
adder ˈæd.əʳ (US) -ɚ **-s** -z **ˈadder's ˌtongue**
adderwort ˈæd.ə.wɜːt (US) -ɚ.wɝːt, -wɔːrt
addict *(n.)* ˈæd.ɪkt **-s** -s
addict *(v.)* əˈdɪkt **-s** -s **-ing** -ɪŋ **-ed/ness** -ɪd/nəs, -nɪs
addiction əˈdɪk.ʃən **-s** -z
addictive əˈdɪk.tɪv **-ly** -li **-ness** -nəs, -nɪs
Addington ˈæd.ɪŋ.tən
Addis ˈæd.ɪs
Addis Ababa ˌæd.ɪsˈæb.ə.bə, -ˈɑːb-
Addiscombe ˈæd.ɪ.skəm
Addison ˈæd.ɪ.sən
addition əˈdɪʃ.ən **-s** -z
additional əˈdɪʃ.ən.əl **-ly** -i
additive ˈæd.ə.tɪv, ˈ-ɪ- (US) -ə.t̬ɪv **-s** -z
addl|e ˈæd.l̩ **-es** -z **-ing** -ɪŋ, ˈæd.lɪŋ **-ed** -d
addleheaded ˌæd.l̩ˈhed.ɪd (US) ˈæd.l̩ˌhed- *stress shift, British only:* ˌaddleheaded ˈperson
Addlestone ˈæd.l̩.stən
add-on ˈæd.ɒn (US) -ɑːn **-s** -z
address *(n.)* əˈdres (US) ˈæd.res, əˈdres **-es** -ɪz **aˈddress ˌbook** (US) **ˈaddress ˌbook**
address *(v.)* əˈdres **-es** -ɪz **-ing** -ɪŋ **-ed** -t
addressable əˈdres.ə.bl̩
addressee ˌæd.resˈiː **-s** -z
Addressograph® əˈdres.əʊ.grɑːf, -græf (US) -ə.græf **-s** -s
adduc|e əˈdjuːs, ædˈjuːs (US) əˈduːs, -ˈdjuːs **-es** -ɪz **-ing** -ɪŋ **-ed** -t **-er/s** -əʳ/z (US) -ɚ/z **-ible** -ə.bl̩, -ɪ.bl̩
adducent əˈdjuː.sənt (US) -ˈduː-, -ˈdjuː-
adduct əˈdʌkt **-s** -s **-ing** -ɪŋ **-ed** -ɪd **-ive** -ɪv
adduction əˈdʌk.ʃən
adductor əˈdʌk.təʳ (US) -tɚ **-s** -z
Ade eɪd
-ade -eɪd, -ɑːd
Note: Suffix. Generally carries primary stress, e.g. **lemonade**

/ˌlem.əˈneɪd/, but see individual entries. For instance, **escapade** is also /ˈes.kə.peɪd/. In words derived from French it is often pronounced /-ɑːd/, e.g. **roulade** is /ruːˈlɑːd/.

Adeane əˈdiːn
Adel ˈæd.ᵊl
Adela *English name:* ˈæd.ɪ.lə, ˈ-ə- *foreign name:* əˈdeɪ.lə
Adelaide ˈæd.ᵊl.eɪd, -ɪ.leɪd (US) -ə.leɪd
Adele əˈdel
Adelina ˌæd.ɪˈliː.nə, -ᵊlˈiː- (US) -əˈliː-
Adeline ˈæd.ɪ.liːn, -ᵊl.iːn, -aɪn (US) -ə.laɪn, -liːn
Adelphi əˈdel.fi
ademption əˈdemp.ʃᵊn **-s** -z
Aden *in the Yemen:* ˈeɪ.dᵊn (US) ˈɑː-, ˈeɪ- *in Grampian region:* ˈæd.ᵊn
Adenauer ˈæd.ᵊn.aʊ.əʳ, ˈɑː.dᵊn- (US) -ɚ
adenoid ˈæd.ᵊ.nɔɪd, -ɪn.ɔɪd (US) -ᵊn.ɔɪd; ˈæd.nɔɪd **-s** -z
adenoidal ˌæd.ᵊˈnɔɪ.dᵊl, -ɪnˈɔɪ- (US) -ᵊnˈɔɪ-; ædˈnɔɪ-
adenoidectom|y ˌæd.ᵊ.nɔɪˈdek.tə.m|i, -ɪn.ɔɪˈ- (US) -ᵊn.ɔɪˈ-; ˌæd.nɔɪˈ- **-ies** -iz
adenoma ˌæd.ɪˈnəʊ.mə, -əˈ- (US) -ˈnoʊ- **-s** -z **-tous** -təs (US) -t̬əs
adenosine ædˈen.əʊ.siːn, əˈden-; ˌæd.ɪˈnəʊ- (US) əˈden.ə.siːn, -sᵊn
adept (*n.*) ˈæd.ept, əˈdept, ædˈept **-s** -s
adept (*adj.*) əˈdept, ædˈept; ˈæd.ept (US) əˈdept **-ly** -li
adequacy ˈæd.ɪ.kwə.si, ˈ-ə-
adequate ˈæd.ɪ.kwət, ˈ-ə-, -kwɪt **-ly** -li **-ness** -nəs, -nɪs
adessive əˈdes.ɪv, ædˈes-
à deux æˈdɜː
adher|e ədˈhɪəʳ, æd-; əˈdɪəʳ (US) ədˈhɪr, æd- **-es** -z **-ing** -ɪŋ **-ed** -d **-er/s** -əʳ/z (US) -ɚ/z
adheren|ce ədˈhɪə.rᵊn|ts, æd-, -ˈher.ᵊn|ts; əˈdɪə.rᵊn|ts (US) ədˈhɪr.ᵊn|ts, æd- **-t/s** -t/s
adhesion ədˈhiː.ʒən, æd-; **-s** -z
adhesive ədˈhiː.sɪv, æd-, -zɪv; -zɪv **-ly** -li **-ness** -nɪs, -nəs
ad hoc ˌædˈhɒk, -ˈhəʊk (US) -ˈhɑːk, -ˈhoʊk
ad hominem ˌædˈhɒm.ɪ.nəm, ˈ-ə-, -nem (US) -ˈhɑː.mə.nəm, -nem
adiabatic ˌeɪ.daɪəˈbæt.ɪk, ˌæd.aɪə- (US) ˌæd.ɪ.əˈbæt̬-; ˌeɪ.daɪəˈ- **-ally** -ᵊl.i, -li
Adidas® ˈæd.ɪ.dæs; əˈdiː.dəs (US) əˈdiː.dəs
Adie ˈeɪ.di
adieu əˈdjuː *as if French:* ædˈjɜː (US) əˈduː, -ˈdjuː
adieus, adieux əˈdjuː, -ˈdjuːz *as if French:* ædˈjɜː (US) əˈduːz, -ˈdjuːz
Adige ˈæd.ɪ.dʒeɪ (US) ˈɑː.di.dʒeɪ, -ə
ad infinitum ˌæd.ɪn.fɪˈnaɪ.təm (US) ˌæd.ɪn.fɪˈnaɪ.t̬əm, ˌɑːd-
adios ˈæd.i.ɒs, --ˈ- (US) ˌɑː.diˈoʊs, ˌæd.iˈ-
adipocere ˌæd.ɪ.pəʊˈsɪəʳ (US) ˈæd.ə.poʊ.sɪr, -pə-
adipose ˈæd.ɪ.pəʊs, -pəʊz (US) -ə.poʊs
adiposity ˌæd.ɪˈpɒs.ə.ti, -ɪ.ti (US) -əˈpɑː.sə.t̬i
Adirondack ˌæd.ɪˈrɒn.dæk, -əˈrɒn- (US) -rɑːn- **-s** -s
adit ˈæd.ɪt **-s** -s
adjacency əˈdʒeɪ.sᵊn*t*.si
adjacent əˈdʒeɪ.sᵊnt **-ly** -li
adjectival ˌædʒ.ɪkˈtaɪ.vᵊl, -ekˈ-, -əkˈ- **-ly** -i
adjective ˈædʒ.ɪk.tɪv, -ek-, -ək- **-s** -z
adjoin əˈdʒɔɪn **-s** -z **-ing** -ɪŋ **-ed** -d
adjourn əˈdʒɜːn (US) -ˈdʒɝːn **-s** -z **-ing** -ɪŋ **-ed** -d **-ment/s** -mənt/s
adjudg|e əˈdʒʌdʒ, ædʒˈʌdʒ (US) əˈdʒʌdʒ **-es** -ɪz **-ing** -ɪŋ **-ed** -d **-ment/s** -mənt/s
adjudi|cate əˈdʒuː.dɪ|.keɪt, -də- **-cates** -keɪts **-cating** -keɪ.tɪŋ (US) -keɪ.t̬ɪŋ **-cated** -keɪ.tɪd (US) -keɪ.t̬ɪd
adjudication əˌdʒuː.dɪˈkeɪ.ʃᵊn, -dəˈ- **-s** -z
adjudicator əˈdʒuː.dɪ.keɪ.təʳ, -də- (US) -t̬ɚ **-s** -z
adjunct ˈædʒ.ʌŋ*k*t **-s** -s **-ly** -li; əˈdʒʌŋ*k*t.li
adjunction əˈdʒʌŋ*k*.ʃᵊn, ædʒˈʌŋ*k*-
adjunctival ˌædʒ.ʌŋ*k*ˈtaɪ.vᵊl
adjuration ˌædʒ.əˈreɪ.ʃᵊn, -ʊəˈ-, -ɔːˈ- (US) -əˈ- **-s** -z
adjuratory əˈdʒʊə.rə.tᵊr.i, -ˈdʒɔː- (US) -ˈdʒʊr.ə.tɔːr-
adjur|e əˈdʒʊəʳ, -ɔːʳ (US) -dʒʊr **-es** -z **-ing** -ɪŋ **-ed** -d
adjust əˈdʒʌst **-s** -s **-ing** -ɪŋ **-ed** -ɪd **-able** -ə.bl̩ **-er/s** -əʳ/z (US) -ɚ/z
adjustment əˈdʒʌs*t*.mənt **-s** -s
adjutage ˈædʒ.ʊ.tɪdʒ; əˈdʒuː-
adjutan|cy ˈædʒ.ʊ.tᵊn|*t*.si, ˈ-ə- **-t/s** -t/s
Adkins ˈæd.kɪnz
Adkinson ˈæd.kɪn.sən
Adlai ˈæd.leɪ
Adler ˈæd.ləʳ, ˈɑːd.ləʳ (US) -lɚ
ad-lib ˌædˈlɪb **-s** -z **-bing** -ɪŋ **-bed** -d
Adlington ˈæd.lɪŋ.tən
ad|man ˈæd.mæn, -mən **-men** -men, -mən
admass ˈæd.mæs
admeasur|e ædˈmeʒ.əʳ, əd- (US) -ɚ, -ˈmeɪ.ʒɚ **-es** -z **-ing** -ɪŋ **-ed** -d **-ement/s** -mənt/s
Admetus ædˈmiː.təs (US) -t̬əs
admin ˈæd.mɪn
administer ədˈmɪn.ɪ.stəʳ, ˈ-ə- (US) -ɚ, æd- **-s** -z **-ing** -ɪŋ **-ed** -d
administr|able ədˈmɪn.ɪ.str|ə.bl̩, ˈ-ə- (US) əd-, æd- **-ant/s** -ᵊnt/s
admini|strate ədˈmɪn.ɪ|.streɪt, ˈ-ə- (US) əd-, æd- **-strates** -streɪts **-strating** -streɪ.tɪŋ (US) -streɪ.t̬ɪŋ **-strated** -streɪ.tɪd (US) -streɪ.t̬ɪd
administration ədˌmɪn.ɪˈstreɪ.ʃᵊn, -əˈ- (US) əd-, æd- **-s** -z
administrative ədˈmɪn.ɪ.strə.tɪv, ˈ-ə-, -streɪ- (US) əd-, æd- **-ly** -li
administrator ədˈmɪn.ɪ.streɪ.təʳ, ˈ-ə- (US) -t̬ɚ, æd- **-s** -z **-ship/s** -ʃɪp/s
administra|trix ədˈmɪn.ɪ.streɪ|.trɪks, ˈ-ə- (US) əd-, æd- **-trixes** -trɪk.sɪz **-trices** -trɪ.siːz
admirab|le ˈæd.mᵊr.ə.bl|̩ **-ly** -li **-leness** -l̩.nəs, -nɪs
admiral ˈæd.mᵊr.əl, -mɪ.rəl **-s** -z
admiralt|y (A) ˈæd.mᵊr.əl.t|i, -mɪ.rəl- (US) -t̬|i **-ies** -iz
admiration ˌæd.məˈreɪ.ʃᵊn, -mɪˈ-
admir|e ədˈmaɪəʳ (US) -ˈmaɪɚ, æd- **-es** -z **-ing/ly** -ɪŋ/li **-ed** -d **-er/s** -əʳ/z (US) -ɚ/z
admissibility ədˌmɪs.əˈbɪl.ə.ti, æd-, -ɪˈ-, -ɪ.ti (US) -ə.t̬i
admissibl|e ədˈmɪs.ə.bl|̩, æd-, -ɪ.bl|̩ **-y** -i
admission ədˈmɪʃ.ᵊn, æd- **-s** -z
ad|mit əd|ˈmɪt **-mits** -ˈmɪts **-mitting** -ˈmɪt.ɪŋ (US) -ˈmɪt̬.ɪŋ **-mitted/ly** -ˈmɪt.ɪd/li (US) -ˈmɪt̬.ɪd/li
admittanc|e ədˈmɪt.ᵊn*t*s **-es** -ɪz
admix ædˈmɪks, əd- **-es** -ɪz **-ing** -ɪŋ **-ed** -t
admixture ədˈmɪks.tʃəʳ, æd- **-s** -z
admonish ədˈmɒn.ɪʃ, æd- (US) -ˈmɑː.nɪʃ **-es** -ɪz **-ing/ly** -ɪŋ **-ed** -t **-ment/s** -mənt/s
admonition ˌæd.məˈnɪʃ.ᵊn **-s** -z
admonitory ədˈmɒn.ɪ.tᵊr.i, æd- (US) -ˈmɑː.nə.tɔːr-
Adnams ˈæd.nəmz
ad nauseam ˌædˈnɔː.zi.æm, -si-, -əm (US) -ˈnɑː-, -ˈnɔː-
adnominal ˌædˈnɒm.ɪn.ᵊl (US) -ˈnɑːm- **-s** -z
ado əˈduː
adobe əˈdəʊ.bi, ædˈəʊ- (US) -ˈdoʊ- **-s** -z
adolescence ˌæd.ᵊlˈes.ᵊn*t*s, -əʊˈles- (US) -əˈles-
adolescent ˌæd.ᵊlˈes.ᵊnt, -əʊˈles- (US) -əˈles- **-s** -s
Adolf ˈæd.ɒlf (US) ˈeɪ.dɑːlf, ˈæd.ɑːlf
Adolphus əˈdɒl.fəs (US) -ˈdɑːl-
Adonai ˈæd.əʊ.naɪ (US) ˌɑː.dəˈnaɪ, -doʊˈ-, -ˈnɔɪ
Adonais ˌæd.əʊˈneɪ.ɪs (US) -əˈ-
Adonijah ˌæd.əʊˈnaɪ.dʒə (US) -əˈ-
Adonis əˈdəʊ.nɪs, -ˈdɒn.ɪs (US) -ˈdɑː.nɪs, -ˈdoʊ-
adopt əˈdɒpt (US) -ˈdɑːpt **-s** -s **-ing** -ɪŋ **-ed** -ɪd **-ive** -ɪv **-er/s**
adoption əˈdɒp.ʃᵊn (US) -ˈdɑːp- **-s** -z
adoptionism əˈdɒp.ʃᵊn.ɪ.zᵊm (US) -ˈdɑːp-
adorab|le əˈdɔː.rə.bl|̩ (US) -ˈdɔːr.ə- **-ly** -li **-leness** -l̩.nəs, -nɪs

adoration ˌæd.əˈreɪ.ʃᵊn, -ɔːˈ- (US) -əˈreɪ- **-s** -z
ador|e əˈdɔːʳ (US) -ˈdɔːr **-es** -z **-ing/ly** -ɪŋ/li **-ed** -d **-er/s** -əʳ/z (US) -ɚ/z
adorn əˈdɔːn (US) -ˈdɔːrn **-s** -z **-ing** -ɪŋ **-ed** -d **-ment/s** -mənt/s
Adorno əˈdɔː.nəʊ (US) -ˈdɔːr.noʊ
ADP ˌeɪ.diːˈpiː
Adrastus əˈdræs.təs
adrenal əˈdriː.nᵊl **aˈdrenal ˌgland**
adrenalin(e) əˈdren.ᵊl.ɪn (US) -ə.lɪn
adrenocortical əˌdriː.nəʊˈkɔː.tɪ.kᵊl (US) -noʊˈkɔːr.t̬ɪ-, -ˌdren.oʊˈ-, -əˈ-
adrenocorticotroph|ic əˌdriː.nəʊˌkɔː.tɪ.kəʊˈtrɒf|.ɪk (US) -noʊˌkɔːr.t̬ɪ.koʊˈtroʊ.f|ɪk, -ˌdren.oʊˌ-, -əˌ-, -ˈtrɑː- **-in** -ɪn
Adria ˈeɪ.dri.ə
Adrian ˈeɪ.dri.ən
Adriana ˌeɪ.driˈɑː.nə, ˌæd.riˈ-
Adrianople ˌeɪ.dri.əˈnəʊ.pl̩, ˌæd.ri- (US) -ˈnoʊ-
Adrianopolis ˌeɪ.dri.əˈnɒp.ᵊl.ɪs, ˌæd.ri- (US) -ˈnɑː.pᵊl-
Adriatic ˌeɪ.driˈæt.ɪk (US) -ˈæt̬- *stress shift:* ˌAdriatic ˈSea
Adrienne ˌeɪ.driˈen, ˌæd.riˈ-; ˈeɪ.dri.ən, ˈæd.ri-
adrift əˈdrɪft
adroit əˈdrɔɪt **-est** -əst, -ɪst **-ly** -li **-ness** -nəs, -nɪs
adsorb ædˈzɔːb, əd-, -ˈsɔːb (US) -ˈsɔːrb, -ˈzɔːrb **-s** -z **-ing** -ɪŋ **-ed** -d
adsorbent ædˈzɔː.bᵊnt, ədˈ-, -ˈsɔː- (US) -ˈsɔːr-, -ˈzɔːr-
adsorption ædˈzɔːp.ʃᵊn, ədˈ-, -ˈsɔːp- (US) -ˈsɔːrp-, -ˈzɔːrp-
adsorptive ædˈzɔːp.tɪv, ədˈ-, -ˈsɔːp- (US) -ˈsɔːrp-, -ˈzɔːrp-
adsum ˈæd.sʌm, -sʊm, -səm
adularia ˌæd.jʊˈleə.ri.ə, -jəˈ-, ˌædʒ.ʊˈ- (US) ˌædʒ.ʊˈler.i-, ˌæd.jəˈ-
adu|late ˈæd.jʊ|.leɪt, -jə-, ˈædʒ.ʊ-, ˈ-ə- (US) ˈædʒ.ə-, ˈæd.jə-, ˈ-ə- **-lates** -leɪts **-lating** -leɪ.tɪŋ (US) -leɪ.t̬ɪŋ **-lated** -leɪ.tɪd (US) -leɪ.t̬ɪd
adulation ˌæd.jʊˈleɪ.ʃᵊn, -jəˈ-, ˌædʒ.ʊˈ-, -əˈ- (US) ˌædʒ.əˈ-, ˌæd.jəˈ-, -əˈ- **-s** -z
adulatory ˌæd.jʊˈleɪ.tᵊr.i, -jəˈ-, ˌædʒ.ʊˈ-, -əˈ-; ˈæd.jʊ.leɪ-, -jə-, ˈædʒ.ʊ-, ˈ-ə-, -tᵊr.i (US) ˈædʒ.ᵊl.ə.tɔːr-, ˈæd.jᵊl-, -ᵊl-
Adullam əˈdʌl.əm **-ite/s** -aɪt/s
adult ˈæd.ʌlt, əˈdʌlt (US) əˈdʌlt, ˈæd.ʌlt **-s** -s ˌ**adult eduˈcation**
adulterant əˈdʌl.tᵊr.ənt (US) -t̬ᵊr- **-s** -s
adulter|ate əˈdʌl.tᵊr|.eɪt (US) -t̬ə.r|eɪt **-ates** -eɪts **-ating** -eɪ.tɪŋ (US) -eɪ.t̬ɪŋ **-ated** -eɪ.tɪd (US) -eɪ.t̬ɪd **-ator/s** -eɪ.təʳ/z (US) -eɪ.t̬ɚ/z
adulteration əˌdʌl.tᵊrˈeɪ.ʃᵊn (US) -t̬əˈreɪ- **-s** -z
adulterer əˈdʌl.tᵊr.əʳ (US) -t̬ɚ.ɚ **-s** -z
adulteress əˈdʌl.tᵊr.es, -ɪs, -əs (US) -t̬ɚ-, ˈ-trɪs **-es** -ɪz
adulterous əˈdʌl.tᵊr.əs, ˈ-trəs (US) ˈ-t̬ɚ.əs, ˈ-trəs **-ly** -li
adulter|y əˈdʌl.tᵊr|.i, ˈ-tr|i (US) ˈ-t̬ɚ.i, ˈ-tri **-ies** -iz
adulthood ˈæd.ʌlt.hʊd, əˈdʌlt- (US) əˈdʌlt-
adum|brate ˈæd.ʌm|.breɪt, -əm- **-brates** -breɪts **-brating** -breɪ.tɪŋ (US) -breɪ.t̬ɪŋ **-brated** -breɪ.tɪd (US) -breɪ.t̬ɪd
adumbration ˌæd.ʌmˈbreɪ.ʃᵊn, -əm- **-s** -z
Adur ˈeɪ.dəʳ (US) -dɚ
ad valorem ˌæd.vəˈlɔː.rem, -vælˈɔː-, -rəm (US) -vəˈlɔːr.əm
advanc|e ədˈvɑːnts (US) -ˈvænts, æd- **-es** -ɪz **-ing** -ɪŋ **-ed** -t **-ement/s** -mənt/s **adˌvance ˈnotice; adˌvance ˈpayment; Adˈvanced ˌLevel**
advantag|e ədˈvɑːn.tɪdʒ (US) -ˈvæn.t̬ɪdʒ, æd- **-es** -ɪz
advantageous ˌæd.vənˈteɪ.dʒəs, -vɑːnˈ-, -vænˈ- (US) -vænˈ-, -vənˈ- **-ly** -li **-ness** -nəs, -nɪs
adven|e ædˈviːn, əd- **-es** -z **-ing** -ɪŋ **-ed** -d
advent (A) ˈæd.vent, -vənt **-s** -s ˈ**Advent ˌcalendar**
Adventism ˈæd.ven.tɪ.zᵊm, -vən- (US) -vən-
Adventist ˈæd.ven.tɪst, -vən- (US) -vən-; ədˈven-
adventitious ˌæd.vᵊnˈtɪʃ.əs, -ven- **-ly** -li
adventive ædˈven.tɪv (US) -t̬ɪv **-ly** -li
advent|ure ədˈven.tʃ|əʳ (US) -tʃ|ɚ, æd- **-ures** -əz, -ɚz **-uring** -ᵊr.ɪŋ **-ured** -əd, -ɚd **-urer/s** -ᵊr.əʳ/z (US) -ɚ.ɚ/z **-uress/es** -ᵊr.əs/ɪz, -ə.res/ɪz **adˌventure ˈplayground**
adventuresome ədˈven.tʃə.sᵊm (US) -tʃɚ-, æd-
adventurous ədˈven.tʃᵊr.əs (US) əd-, æd- **-ly** -li **-ness** -nəs, -nɪs
adverb ˈæd.vɜːb (US) -vɝːb **-s** -z
adverbial ədˈvɜː.bi.əl, æd- (US) -ˈvɝː- **-ly** -i
adversarial ˌæd.vəˈseə.ri.əl, -vɜːˈ- (US) -vɚˈser.i- **-ly** -i
adversar|y ˈæd.və.sᵊr|.i, ədˈvɜː- (US) ˈæd.vɚ.ser- **-ies** -iz
adversative ədˈvɜː.sə.tɪv, æd- (US) -ˈvɝː.sə.t̬ɪv
adverse ˈæd.vɜːs, -ˈ-, əd- (US) ædˈvɝːs, ˈ-- **-ly** -li

Pronouncing the letters AE

The vowel digraph **ae** is a fairly low-frequency spelling. In some cases, the American spelling of words containing **ae** omits the **a**, e.g. in *aesthetic*, which is spelt in American English as *esthetic*.

The pronunciation of the digraph in strong syllables depends on whether or not it is followed by an **r** in the spelling. If so, the pronunciation is /eə (US) er/, e.g:

aeroplane /ˈeə.rə.pleɪn/ (US) /ˈer.ə-/

When not followed by **r**, the pronunciation is most usually one of /iː/, /ɪ/ or /e/, the latter being most common in American English pronunciation, e.g.:

Caesar /ˈsiː.zəʳ/ (US) /-zɚ/
aesthetic /iːsˈθet.ɪk, ɪs-/ (US) /esˈθet̬-/

In addition

Other vowel sounds associated with the digraph **ae** include /æ/, for Old English names, e.g.:

Aethelstan /ˈæθ.ᵊl.stən/

In weak syllables

The vowel digraph is realised with the vowels /ə/ and /ɪ/ in weak syllables, e.g.:

gynaecology /ˌgaɪ.nəˈkɒl.ə.dʒi, -nɪˈ-/ (US) /-ˈkɑː.lə-/

Pronouncing the letters AEO

The vowel letter combination **aeo** is low frequency, and is often spelt **eo** in American English. It has two pronunciations associated with it:

/iˈɒ (US) iˈɑː/	archaeology	/ˌɑː.kiˈɒl.ə.dʒi/ (US) /ˌɑːr.kiˈɑː.lə-/
/iəʊ (US) ioʊ, iə/	palaeotype	/ˈpæl.i.əʊ.taɪp/ (US) /ˈpeɪ.li.oʊ-, -ə-/

adversit|y ədˈvɜː.sə.t|i, -sɪ- (US) -ˈvɝː.sə.t̬|i, æd- **-ies** -iz
advert (*n.*) ˈæd.vɜːt (US) -vɝːt **-s** -s
ad|vert (*v.*) əd|ˈvɜːt, æd- (US) -ˈvɝːt **-verts** -ˈvɜːts (US) -ˈvɝːts **-verting** -ˈvɜː.tɪŋ (US) -ˈvɝː.t̬ɪŋ **-verted** -ˈvɜː.tɪd (US) -ˈvɝː.t̬ɪd
advertenc|e ədˈvɜː.tᵊnts (US) -ˈvɝː-, æd- **-y** -i
advertent ədˈvɜː.tᵊnt (US) -ˈvɝː-, æd- **-ly** -li
advertis|e, -iz|e ˈæd.və.taɪz (US) -vɚ- **-es** -ɪz **-ing** -ɪŋ **-ed** -d **-er/s** -əʳ/z (US) -ɚ/z
advertisement, -ize- ədˈvɜː.tɪs.mənt, -tɪz-, -təs-, -təz- (US) ˌæd.vɚˈtaɪz.mənt; ədˈvɝː.t̬əs-, -t̬əz- **-s** -s
advertorial ˌæd.vəˈtɔː.ri.əl (US) -vɚˈtɔːr.i-
advic|e ədˈvaɪs (US) əd-, æd- **-es** -ɪz
advisability ədˌvaɪ.zəˈbɪl.ə.ti, -ɪ- (US) -ə.t̬i, æd-
advisab|le ədˈvaɪ.zə.bl̩ (US) əd-, æd- **-ly** -li **-leness** -l̩.nəs, -nɪs
advis|e ədˈvaɪz (US) əd-, æd- **-es** -ɪz **-ing** -ɪŋ **-ed** -d **-edly** -ɪd.li **-edness** -ɪd.nəs, -nɪs
adviser, advisor ədˈvaɪ.zəʳ (US) -zɚ, æd- **-s** -z
advisor|y ədˈvaɪ.zᵊr|.i (US) əd-, æd- **-ies** -iz **adˈvisory ˌbody**
advocaat ˈæd.vəʊ.kɑː, -kɑːt (US) -voʊ-
advocacy ˈæd.və.kə.si
advocate (*n.*) ˈæd.və.kət, -keɪt, -kɪt **-s** -s
advo|cate (*v.*) ˈæd.və|.keɪt **-cates** -keɪts **-cating** -keɪ.tɪŋ (US) -keɪ.t̬ɪŋ **-cated** -keɪ.tɪd (US) -keɪ.t̬ɪd **-cator/s** -keɪ.təʳ/z (US) -keɪ.t̬ɚ/z
advocation ˌæd.vəˈkeɪ.ʃᵊn
advowson ədˈvaʊ.zᵊn **-s** -z
Adwa ˈɑː.dwə
Adwick le Street ˌæd.wɪk.lɪˈstriːt
Adye ˈeɪ.di
adynamia ˌeɪ.daɪˈneɪ.mi.ə, ˌæd.ɪˈ-
adynamic ˌeɪ.daɪˈnæm.ɪk, ˌæd.aɪˈ-, -ɪˈ-
adz|e, adz ædz **-es** -ɪz **-ing** -ɪŋ **-ed** -d
adzuki ædˈzuː.ki **adˈzuki ˌbean**
Aeacus ˈiː.ə.kəs
aedile ˈiː.daɪl **-s** -z **-ship/s** -ʃɪp/s
Aeetes iːˈiː.tiːz
Aegean iːˈdʒiː.ən, ɪˈ-
Aegeus ˈiː.dʒi.əs (US) ˈiː.dʒi.əs, ˈiː.dʒuːs
Aegina iːˈdʒaɪ.nə, ɪˈdʒaɪ-
aegis ˈiː.dʒɪs
Aegisthus iːˈdʒɪs.θəs, ɪˈdʒɪs-
aegrotat ˈaɪ.grəʊ.tæt, ˈiː- (US) -groʊ- **-s** -s
Aegyptus iːˈdʒɪp.təs
Aelfric ˈæl.frɪk
Aemilius iːˈmɪl.i.əs, ɪˈmɪl-
Aeneas iːˈniː.əs, ɪˈniː-, -æs
Aeneid ˈiː.ni.ɪd, iːˈniː.ɪd, ɪˈ- **-s** -z
Aeneus ˈiː.ni.əs, iːˈniː-, ɪ-
Aeoli|a iːˈəʊ.li|.ə (US) -ˈoʊ- **-an/s** -ən/z
Aeolic iːˈɒl.ɪk, -ˈəʊ.lɪk (US) -ˈɑː.lɪk
Aeolus ˈiː.əʊ.ləs (US) ˈ-ə-
aeon ˈiː.ən, -ɒn (US) -ɑːn **-s** -z
aera|te eəˈreɪ|t, ˈ-- (US) erˈeɪ|t **-tes** -ts **-ting** -tɪŋ (US) -t̬ɪŋ **-ted** -tɪd (US) -t̬ɪd **-tor/s** -təʳ/z (US) -t̬ɚ/z
aeration eəˈreɪ.ʃᵊn (US) erˈeɪ-
aerial ˈeə.ri.əl (US) ˈer.i- **-s** -z **-ly** -i
aerie ˈɪə.ri, ˈeə- (US) ˈer.i, ˈɪr-, ˈeɪ.ri **-s** -z
aerif|y ˈeə.rɪ.faɪ (US) ˈer.ə- **-ies** -z **-ying** -ɪŋ **-ied** -aɪd
Aer Lingus® ˌeəˈlɪŋ.gəs (US) ˌer-
aero- eə.rəʊ-; eəˈrɒ- (US) er.oʊ-, er.ə-; erˈɑː-
Note: Prefix. Either takes primary or secondary stress on the first syllable, e.g. **aeronaut** /ˈeə.rə.nɔːt (US) ˈer.ə.nɑːt/ **aeronautic** /ˌeə.rəˈnɔː.tɪk (US) ˌer.əˈnɑː.t̬ɪk/, or primary stress on the second syllable, e.g. **aerology** /eəˈrɒl.ə.dʒi (US) erˈɑː.lə-/.
aero ˈeə.rəʊ (US) ˈer.oʊ
aeroballistics ˌeə.rəʊ.bəˈlɪs.tɪks (US) ˌer.oʊ-
aerobatic ˌeə.rəʊˈbæt.ɪk (US) ˌer.oʊˈbæt̬- **-s** -s **-ally** -ᵊl.i, -li
aerobe ˈeə.rəʊb (US) ˈer.oʊb **-s** -z
aerobic eəˈrəʊ.bɪk (US) erˈoʊ- **-s** -s
aerodrome ˈeə.rə.drəʊm (US) ˈer.ə.droʊm **-s** -z
aerodynamic ˌeə.rəʊ.daɪˈnæm.ɪk, -dɪˈ- (US) ˌer.oʊ- **-s** -s **-ally** -ᵊl.i, -li *stress shift:* ˌaerodynamic ˈfairing
aerodyne ˈeə.rəʊ.daɪn (US) ˈer.ə- **-s** -z
Aeroflot® ˈeə.rəʊ.flɒt (US) ˈer.ə.floʊt, -flɑːt
aerofoil ˈeə.rəʊ.fɔɪl (US) ˈer.oʊ- **-s** -z
aerogram, aerogramme ˈeə.rəʊ.græm (US) ˈer.ə- **-s** -z
aerolite ˈeə.rəʊ.laɪt (US) ˈer.ə- **-s** -s
aerolith ˈeə.rəʊ.lɪθ (US) ˈer.ə- **-s** -s
aerological ˌeə.rəʊˈlɒdʒ.ɪ.kᵊl (US) ˌer.oʊˈlɑː.dʒɪ-
aerologist eəˈrɒl.ə.dʒɪst (US) erˈɑːl.ə- **-s** -s
aerolog|y eəˈrɒl.ə.dʒ|i (US) erˈɑː.lə- **-ist/s** -ɪst/s
aeronaut ˈeə.rə.nɔːt (US) ˈer.ə.nɑːt, -nɔːt **-s** -s
aeronautic ˌeə.rəˈnɔː.tɪk (US) ˌer.əˈnɑː.t̬ɪk, -ˈnɔː- **-s** -s **-al** -ᵊl
aerophone ˈeə.rə.fəʊn (US) ˈer.ə.foʊn **-s** -z
aeroplane ˈeə.rə.pleɪn (US) ˈer- **-s** -z
Aerosmith ˈeə.rəʊ.smɪθ (US) ˈe.roʊ-
aerosol ˈeə.rə.sɒl (US) ˈer.ə.sɑːl **-s** -z
aerospace ˈeə.rəʊ.speɪs (US) ˈer.oʊ-
aerostat ˈeə.rəʊ.stæt (US) ˈer.oʊ- **-s** -s
Aertex® ˈeə.teks (US) ˈer-
aer|y (*n.*) ˈɪə.r|i, ˈeə- (US) ˈer|.i, ˈɪr-, ˈeɪ|.ri **-ies** -iz
aery (*adj.*) ˈeə.ri (US) ˈer.i, ˈeɪ.ə.ri
Aeschines ˈiː.skɪ.niːz, -skə.niːz (US) ˈes.kə-, ˈiː.skə-
Aeschylus ˈiː.skɪ.ləs, -skə.ləs (US) ˈes.kə-, ˈiː.skə-
Aesculapi|us ˌiː.skjʊˈleɪ.pi|.əs (US) ˌes.kjəˈ-, -kəˈ- **-an** -ən
Aesop ˈiː.sɒp (US) -sɑːp, -səp
aesthete ˈiːs.θiːt (US) ˈes- **-s** -s
aesthetic iːsˈθet.ɪk, ɪs-, es- (US) esˈθet̬-, ɪs- **-s** -s **-al** -ᵊl **-ally** -ᵊl.i, -li
aesthetic|ism iːsˈθet.ɪ.s|ɪ.zᵊm, ɪs-, es- (US) es-, ɪs- **-ist/s** -ɪst/s
aestival iːˈstaɪ.vᵊl (US) ˈes.tə-, esˈtaɪ-
Aethelstan ˈæθ.ᵊl.stən, -stæn
aether ˈiː.θəʳ (US) -θɚ
aetiolog|y ˌiː.tiˈɒl.ə.dʒ|i (US) -t̬iˈɑː.lə- **-ist/s** -ɪst/s
Aetna ˈet.nə
afar əˈfɑːʳ (US) -ˈfɑːr
afeard əˈfɪəd (US) -ˈfɪrd
affability ˌæf.əˈbɪl.ə.ti, -ɪ.ti (US) -ə.t̬i
affab|le ˈæf.ə.bl̩ **-ly** -li **-leness** -l̩.nəs, -nɪs
affair əˈfeəʳ (US) -ˈfer **-s** -z
affect (*v.*) əˈfekt **-s** -s **-ing/ly** -ɪŋ/li **-ed** -ɪd
affect (*n.*) *in psychology:* ˈæf.ekt **-s** -s
affectation ˌæf.ekˈteɪ.ʃᵊn, -ɪkˈ- **-s** -z
affected əˈfek.tɪd **-ly** -li **-ness** -nəs, -nɪs

Affricate

A type of consonant consisting of a PLOSIVE followed by a FRICATIVE with the same place of ARTICULATION.

Examples for English

Examples are the /tʃ/ and /dʒ/ sounds (sometimes symbolised /č/ /ǰ/ by American writers) at the beginning and end of the words *church* and *judge*, where the first of these sounds is voiceless and the second voiced (see VOICING), e.g.:

church	/tʃɜːtʃ/	(US) /tʃɝːtʃ/
judge	/dʒʌdʒ/	

It is often difficult to decide whether any particular combination of a plosive plus a fricative should be classed as a single affricate sound or as two separate sounds, and the question depends on whether these are to be regarded as separate PHONEMES or not. It is usual to regard /tʃ/ and /dʒ/ as affricate phonemes in English; /ts dz tr dr/ also occur in English but are not usually regarded as affricate phonemes, but are treated as clusters. The two phrases *why choose* and *white shoes* are said to show the difference between the /tʃ/ affricate (in the first example) and separate /t/ and /ʃ/ (in the second), e.g.:

why choose	/*h*waɪ tʃuːz/
white shoes	/*h*waɪt ʃuːz/

affection əˈfek.ʃᵊn **-s** -z
affectionate əˈfek.ʃᵊn.ət, -ɪt **-ly** -li **-ness** -nəs, -nɪs
affective əˈfek.tɪv, æfˈek-
affenpinscher ˈæf.ənˌpɪn.*t*ʃəʳ (US) -ˌpɪn*t*.ʃɚ **-s** -z
afferent ˈæf.ᵊr.ənt
affettuoso əˌfet.juˈəʊ.səʊ, æfˌet-, -zəʊ (US) əˌfet.juˈoʊ.soʊ, æfˌet-, -ˌetʃ.uˈ-
affianc|e əˈfaɪən*t*s **-es** -ɪz **-ing** -ɪŋ **-ed** -t
affiant əˈfaɪənt **-s** -s
affich|e æfˈiːʃ, əˈfiːʃ **-es** -ɪz
affidavit ˌæf.ɪˈdeɪ.vɪt, -əˈ- **-s** -s
affili|ate əˈfɪl.i|.eɪt **-ates** -eɪts **-ating** -eɪ.tɪŋ (US) -eɪ.t̬ɪŋ **-ated** -eɪ.tɪd (US) -eɪ.t̬ɪd
affiliation əˌfɪl.iˈeɪ.ʃᵊn **-s** -z
affinit|y əˈfɪn.ə.t|i, -ɪt|i (US) -ə.t̬|i **-ies** -iz
affirm əˈfɜːm (US) -ˈfɝːm **-s** -z **-ing** -ɪŋ **-ed** -d **-able** -ə.bl̩
affirmation ˌæf.əˈmeɪ.ʃᵊn (US) -ɚˈ- **-s** -z
affirmative əˈfɜː.mə.tɪv (US) -ˈfɝː.mə.t̬ɪv **-ly** -li **afˌfirmative ˈaction**
affirmatory əˈfɜː.mə.tᵊr.i (US) -ˈfɝː.mə.tɔːr-
affix (*n.*) ˈæf.ɪks **-es** -ɪz
affix (*v.*) əˈfɪks, ˈæf.ɪks **-es** -ɪz **-ing** -ɪŋ **-ed** -d
affixation ˌæf.ɪkˈseɪ.ʃᵊn
affixture æfˈɪks.tʃəʳ (US) -tʃɚ, æfˈɪks-
afflatus əˈfleɪ.təs (US) -t̬əs
Affleck ˈæf.lek
afflict əˈflɪkt **-s** -s **-ing** -ɪŋ **-ed** -ɪd **-ive** -ɪv
affliction əˈflɪk.ʃᵊn **-s** -z
affluence ˈæf.lu.ən*t*s
afflux ˈæf.lʌks **-es** -ɪz
afford əˈfɔːd (US) -ˈfɔːrd **-s** -z **-ing** -ɪŋ **-ed** -ɪd
affordab|le əˈfɔː.də.b|l̩ (US) -ˈfɔːr- **-ly** -li
afforest əˈfɒr.ɪst, æfˈɒr- (US) əˈfɔːr.əst **-s** -s **-ing** -ɪŋ **-ed** -ɪd
afforestation æfˌɒr.ɪˈsteɪ.ʃᵊn, əˌfɒr-, -əˈ- (US) əˌfɔːr.əˈ- **-s** -z
affranchis|e əˈfræn.*t*ʃaɪz, æfˈræn- (US) əˈfræn.tʃaɪz **-es** -ɪz **-ing** -ɪŋ **-ed** -d
affray əˈfreɪ **-s** -z
affricate ˈæf.rɪ.kət, -rə-, -kɪt, -keɪt (US) -kɪt **-s** -s
affricated ˈæf.rɪ.keɪ.tɪd, -rə- (US) -t̬ɪd
affrication ˌæf.rɪˈkeɪ.ʃᵊn, -rəˈ-
affricative æfˈrɪk.ə.tɪv, əˈfrɪk- (US) -t̬ɪv **-s** -z
af|fright əˈ|fraɪt **-frights** -ˈfraɪts **-frighting** -ˈfraɪ.tɪŋ (US) -ˈfraɪ.t̬ɪŋ **-frighted/ly** -ˈfraɪ.tɪd/li (US) -ˈfraɪ.t̬ɪd/li
af|front əˈ|frʌnt **-fronts** -ˈfrʌnts **-fronting** -ˈfrʌn.tɪŋ (US) -ˈfrʌn.t̬ɪŋ **-fronted** -ˈfrʌn.tɪd (US) -ˈfrʌn.t̬ɪd
Afghan ˈæf.gæn **-s** -z **ˌAfghan ˈhound**
afghani æfˈgæn.i, -ˈgɑː.ni **-s** -z
Afghanistan æfˈgæn.ɪ.stæn, ˈ-ə-, -stɑːn, æfˌgæn.ɪˈstɑːn, -əˈ-, -ˈstæn (US) æfˈgæn.ə.stæn, -stɑːn
aficionado əˌfɪʃ.i.ənˈɑː.dəʊ, -ˌfɪs- *as if Spanish:* æfˌɪθ.jəˈnɑː.dəʊ (US) əˌfɪʃ.i.əˈnɑː.doʊ, -ˌfɪs-, -ˌfiː.si- **-s** -z
afield əˈfiːld
afire əˈfaɪəʳ (US) -ˈfaɪɚ
aflame əˈfleɪm
aflatoxin ˌæf.ləˈtɒk.sɪn (US) -ˈtɑːk.sᵊn
AFL-CIO eɪ.efˌel.siː.aɪˈəʊ (US) -ˈoʊ
afloat əˈfləʊt (US) -ˈfloʊt
aflutter əˈflʌt.əʳ (US) -ˈflʌt̬.ɚ
afoot əˈfʊt
afore əˈfɔːʳ (US) -ˈfɔːr
aforementioned əˈfɔː.men.*t*ʃᵊnd, əˌfɔːˈmen- (US) əˈfɔːr.men*t*.ʃᵊnd
Note: In British English, the latter form is not used attributively.
aforesaid əˈfɔː.sed (US) -ˈfɔːr-
aforethought əˈfɔː.θɔːt (US) -ˈfɔːr.θɑːt, -θɔːt
aforetime əˈfɔː.taɪm (US) -ˈfɔːr-
a fortiori eɪˌfɔː.tiˈɔː.raɪ, ɑːˌ-, -ri (US) ˌeɪˌfɔːr.t̬iˈɔːr.i, -ʃiˈ-, -aɪ
afraid əˈfreɪd
afreet ˈæf.riːt, əˈfriːt **-s** -s
afresh əˈfreʃ
Afric ˈæf.rɪk
Afric|a ˈæf.rɪ.k|ə **-an/s** -ən/z
African-American ˌæf.rɪ.kən.əˈmer.ɪ.kən **-s** -z
Africander ˌæf.rɪˈkæn.dəʳ (US) -dɚ **-s** -z
Africanist ˈæf.rɪ.kə.nɪst **-s** -s
Africanization, -isa- ˌæf.rɪ.kə.naɪˈzeɪ.ʃᵊn, -rə-, -nɪˈ- (US) -nɪˈ-
Africaniz|e, -is|e ˈæf.rɪ.kə.naɪz **-es** -ɪz **-ing** -ɪŋ **-ed** -d
Africanus ˌæf.rɪˈkɑː.nəs, -ˈkeɪ-
Afridi æfˈriː.di, əˈfriː- **-s** -z
Afrikaans ˌæf.rɪˈkɑːn*t*s, -rəˈkɑːn*t*s, -rɪkˈɑːnz, -rəˈkɑːnz
Afrikaner ˌæf.rɪˈkɑː.nəʳ (US) -nɚ **-s** -z
afrit ˈæf.riːt, əˈfriːt **-s** -s
Afro- ˌæf.rəʊ- (US) ˌæf.roʊ-
Note: Prefix. Normally carries secondary stress on the first syllable, e.g. **Afro-American** /ˌæf.rəʊ.əˈmer.ɪ.kən (US) -roʊ-/.
Afro ˈæf.rəʊ (US) -roʊ **-s** -z
Afro-American ˌæf.rəʊ.əˈmer.ɪ.kən (US) -roʊ- **-s** -z
Afro-Asian ˌæf.rəʊˈeɪ.ʃᵊn, -ʒᵊn (US) -roʊˈeɪ.ʒᵊn, -ʃᵊn **-s** -z
Afro-Asiatic ˌæf.rəʊ.eɪ.ʃiˈæt.ɪk, -siˈ-, -ʒiˈ-, -ziˈ- (US) -roʊ.eɪ.ʒiˈ-, -ʃiˈ-
Afro-Caribbean ˌæf.rəʊ.kær.ɪˈbiː.ən (US) -roʊ.ker-, -kær-; -kəˈrɪb.i- **-s** -z
aft ɑːft (US) æft
after- ˈɑːf.tə- (US) ˈæf.tɚ-

Note: Prefix. Words containing **after-** usually carry primary stress on the first syllable, e.g. **afterglow** /ˈɑːf.tə.ɡləʊ (US) ˈæf.tɚ.ɡloʊ/, but there are exceptions, including **afternoon** /ˌɑːf.təˈnuːn (US) ˌæf.tɚ-/.

after ˈɑːf.təʳ (US) ˈæf.tɚ **ˌafter ˈall; ˌAfter ˈEights®**

afterbirth ˈɑːf.tə.bɜːθ (US) ˈæf.tɚ.bɝːθ **-s** -s

after-burner ˈɑːf.təˌbɜː.nəʳ (US) ˈæf.tɚˌbɝː.nɚ **-s** -z

aftercare ˈɑːf.tə.keəʳ (US) ˈæf.tɚ.ker

after-crop ˈɑːf.tə.krɒp (US) ˈæf.tɚ.krɑːp **-s** -s

aftereffect ˈɑːf.təʳ.ɪˌfekt, -əˌfekt (US) ˈæf.tɚ- **-s** -s

afterglow ˈɑːf.tə.ɡləʊ (US) ˈæf.tɚ.ɡloʊ **-s** -z

after-hours ˌɑːf.təʳˈaʊəz (US) ˈæf.tɚˌaʊɚz, ˌ--ˈ-

afterli|fe ˈɑːf.tə.laɪ|f (US) ˈæf.tɚ- **-ves** -vz

aftermath ˈɑːf.tə.mɑːθ, -mæθ (US) ˈæf.tɚ.mæθ **-s** -s

afternoon ˌɑːf.təˈnuːn (US) ˌæf.tɚˈ- **-s** -z
stress shift, see compounds: **ˌafternoon ˈtea; good ˌafterˈnoon**

afterpiec|e ˈɑːf.tə.piːs (US) ˈæf.tɚ- **-es** -ɪz

afters ˈɑːf.təz (US) ˈæf.tɚz

after-sales ˌɑːf.təˈseɪlz (US) ˌæf.tɚˈ-
stress shift: ˌafter-sales ˈservice

aftershave ˈɑːf.tə.ʃeɪv (US) ˈæf.tɚ- **-s** -z

aftershock ˈɑːf.tə.ʃɒk (US) ˈæf.tɚ.ʃɑːk **-s** -s

aftertaste ˈɑːf.tə.teɪst (US) ˈæf.tɚ- **-s** -s

afterthought ˈɑːf.tə.θɔːt (US) ˈæf.tɚ.θɑːt, -θɔːt **-s** -s

afterward ˈɑːf.tə.wəd (US) ˈæf.tɚ.wɚd **-s** -z

AFTRA ˈæf.trə

Aga® ˈɑː.ɡə

Agadir ˌæɡ.əˈdɪə (US) ˌɑː.ɡəˈdɪr, ˌæɡ.əˈ-

Agag ˈeɪ.ɡæɡ

again əˈɡen, -ˈɡeɪn (US) əˈɡen

against əˈɡentst, -ˈɡeɪntst (US) əˈɡentst

Aga Khan ˌɑː.ɡəˈkɑːn

Agamemnon ˌæɡ.əˈmem.nən, -nɒn (US) -nɑːn, -nən

agamete eɪˈɡæm.iːt, əˈ- (US) ˌæɡ.əˈmiːt **-s** -s

Agana ɑːˈɡɑː.nə, -njə (US) -njə

agape (*adj. adv.*) əˈɡeɪp

agape (*n.*) ˈæɡ.ə.pi, -peɪ (US) ɑːˈɡɑː.peɪ, ˈɑː.ɡə- **-s** -z

Agar *family name:* ˈeɪ.ɡəʳ, -ɡɑːʳ (US) -ɡɚ, -ɡɑːr

agar *jelly:* ˈeɪ.ɡɑːʳ, -əʳ (US) -ɡɑːr, ˈɑː-, -ɡɚ

agar-agar ˌeɪ.ɡəʳˈeɪ.ɡəʳ, -ɡɑːʳˈ-, -ɡɑːʳ (US) -ɡɚˈeɪ.ɡɚ, ˌɑː.ɡɚˈɑ-, -ɡɑːrˈ-, -ɡɑːr

agaric (*n.*) ˈæɡ.ə.rɪk; əˈɡær.ɪk (US) ˈæɡ.ɚ.ɪk, əˈɡer-; -ˈɡær- **-s** -s

agaric (*adj.*) æɡˈær.ɪk, əˈɡær-

Agassi ˈæɡ.ə.si

Agassiz ˌæɡ.əˈsiː (US) ˈæɡ.ə.si

Agassizhorn əˈɡæs.ɪ.hɔːn (US) -hɔːrn

agate *stone:* ˈæɡ.ət, -ɡɪt **-s** -s

Agate *surname:* ˈeɪ.ɡət, ˈæɡ.ət

Agatha ˈæɡ.ə.θə

Agathocles əˈɡæθ.əʊ.kliːz (US) ˈ-ə-

agave əˈɡeɪ.vi, -ˈɡɑː-, ˈæɡ.eɪ- (US) əˈɡɑː- **-s** -z

agaze əˈɡeɪz

ag|e eɪdʒ **-es** -ɪz **-(e)ing** -ɪŋ **-ed** -d **ˌage of conˈsent; ˈgolden ˌage**

-age -ɪdʒ, -ɑːʒ

Note: Suffix. Normally pronounced /-ɪdʒ/, e.g. **advantage** /ədˈvɑːn.tɪdʒ (US) -ˈvæn.t̬ɪdʒ/, which is unstressed, but in words of French origin it is often /-ɑːʒ/, which may be stress bearing; see for example, **corsage**, in which it has both stressed and unstressed variants.

aged (*adj.*) *old:* ˈeɪ.dʒɪd *of the age of:* eɪdʒd

agedness ˈeɪdʒ.ɪd.nəs, -nɪs

Agee ˈeɪ.dʒi

age|ism ˈeɪdʒ.|ɪ.zᵊm **-ist/s** -ɪst/s

ageless ˈeɪdʒ.ləs, -lɪs

agelong ˈeɪdʒ.lɒŋ (US) -lɑːŋ, -lɔːŋ

agenc|y ˈeɪ.dʒᵊnt.s|i **-ies** -iz

agenda əˈdʒen.də **-s** -z

agendum əˈdʒen.dəm **-s** -z

agene ˈeɪ.dʒiːn

agenesis ˌeɪˈdʒen.ə.sɪs, ˈ-ɪ-

agent ˈeɪ.dʒᵊnt **-s** -s **ˌAgent ˈOrange**

agentival ˌeɪ.dʒᵊnˈtaɪ.vᵊl

agentive ˈeɪ.dʒᵊn.tɪv

agent(s) provocateur(s) ˌæʒ.ɑ̃ː.prəˌvɒk.ə.tɜːʳ, ˌæʒ.ɒŋ- (US) ˌɑːʒ.ɑ̃ː.proʊˌvɑː.kəˈtɝː, -tʊr

age-old ˌeɪdʒˈəʊld (US) ˈeɪdʒ.oʊld
stress shift, British only: ˌage-old ˈcity

-ageous -ˈeɪ.dʒəs

Note: Suffix. Words containing **-ageous** are normally stressed on the penultimate syllable, e.g. **advantageous** /ˌæd.vənˈteɪ.dʒəs (US) -vænˈ-/.

Ager ˈeɪ.dʒəʳ (US) -dʒɚ

Agesilaus əˌdʒes.ɪˈleɪ.əs, ædʒˌes- (US) -əˈ-

Agfa® ˈæɡ.fə

aggie (A) ˈæɡ.i **-s** -z

aggiornamento əˌdʒɔː.nəˈmen.təʊ (US) -ˌdʒɔːr.nəˈmen.toʊ

agglomerate (*n. adj.*) əˈɡlɒm.ᵊr.ət, -ɪt (US) -ˈɡlɑː.mɚ- **-s** -s

agglomer|ate (*v.*) əˈɡlɒm.ᵊr|.eɪt (US) -ˈɡlɑː.mə.r|eɪt **-ates** -eɪts **-ating** -eɪ.tɪŋ (US) -eɪ.t̬ɪŋ **-ated** -eɪ.tɪd (US) -eɪ.t̬ɪd

agglomeration əˌɡlɒm.əˈreɪ.ʃᵊn (US) -ˌɡlɑː.məˈ- **-s** -z

agglutinate (*adj.*) əˈɡluː.tɪ.nət, -ɪt (US) -tᵊn.ət

agglutin|ate (*v.*) əˈɡluː.tɪ.n|eɪt (US) -tᵊn|.eɪt **-ates** -eɪts **-ating** -eɪ.tɪŋ (US) -eɪ.t̬ɪŋ **-ated** -eɪ.tɪd (US) -eɪ.t̬ɪd

agglutination əˌɡluː.tɪˈneɪ.ʃᵊn (US) -tᵊnˈeɪ- **-s** -z

agglutinative əˈɡluː.tɪ.nə.tɪv, -eɪ.tɪv (US) -tᵊn.eɪ.t̬ɪv

agglutinin əˈɡluː.tɪ.nɪn (US) -tᵊn.ɪn

agglutinogen ˌæɡ.lʊˈtɪn.ə.dʒᵊn (US) -luːˈ-

aggrandiz|e, -is|e əˈɡræn.daɪz **-es** -ɪz **-ing** -ɪŋ **-ed** -d

aggrandizement, -ise- əˈɡræn.dɪz.mənt (US) -dɪz-, -daɪz-

aggra|vate ˈæɡ.rə|.veɪt **-vates** -veɪts **-vating/ly** -veɪ.tɪŋ/li (US) -veɪ.t̬ɪŋ/li **-vated** -veɪ.tɪd (US) -veɪ.t̬ɪd

aggravation ˌæɡ.rəˈveɪ.ʃᵊn **-s** -z

aggregate (*n. adj.*) ˈæɡ.rɪ.ɡət, -rə.ɡət, -ɡɪt **-s** -s

aggre|gate (*v.*) ˈæɡ.rɪ|.ɡeɪt, -rə- **-gates** -ɡeɪts **-gating** -ɡeɪ.tɪŋ (US) -ɡeɪ.t̬ɪŋ **-gated** -ɡeɪ.tɪd (US) -ɡeɪ.t̬ɪd

aggregation ˌæɡ.rɪˈɡeɪ.ʃᵊn, -rəˈ- **-s** -z

aggregative ˈæɡ.rɪ.ɡə.tɪv, -rə-

aggress əˈɡres, æɡˈres **-es** -ɪz **-ing** -ɪŋ **-ed** -t

aggression əˈɡreʃ.ᵊn, æɡˈreʃ- **-s** -z

aggressive əˈɡres.ɪv, æɡˈres- **-ly** -li **-ness** -nəs, -nɪs

aggressor əˈɡres.əʳ, æɡˈres- (US) -ɚ **-s** -z

aggriev|e əˈɡriːv **-es** -z **-ing** -ɪŋ **-ed** -d

aggro ˈæɡ.rəʊ (US) -roʊ

aghast əˈɡɑːst (US) -ˈɡæst

agil|e ˈædʒ.aɪl (US) -ᵊl **-ist** -əst, -ɪst **-ely** -li

agility əˈdʒɪl.ə.ti, -ɪ.ti (US) -ə.t̬i

agin əˈɡɪn

Agincourt ˈædʒ.ɪn.kɔːʳ, -kɔːt, -kʊəʳ (US) -kɔːrt

agiotage ˈædʒ.ə.tɪdʒ, ˈædʒ.i.əʊ-, -tɑːʒ (US) ˈædʒ.i.ə.tɪdʒ; ˌæʒ.əˈtɑːʒ

ag|ism ˈeɪ.dʒ|ɪ.zᵊm **-ist/s** -ɪst/s

agi|tate ˈædʒ.ɪ|.teɪt, ˈ-ə- **-tates** -teɪts **-tating** -teɪ.tɪŋ (US) -teɪ.t̬ɪŋ **-tated** -teɪ.tɪd (US) -teɪ.t̬ɪd **-tator/s** -teɪ.təʳ/z (US) -teɪ.t̬ɚ/z

agitation ˌædʒ.ɪˈteɪ.ʃᵊn, -əˈ- **-s** -z

agitato ˌædʒ.ɪˈtɑː.təʊ (US) -t̬oʊ

agitprop ˈædʒ.ɪt.prɒp (US) -prɑːp

Aglaia əˈɡlaɪ.ə, -ˈɡleɪ-

aglow əˈɡləʊ (US) -ˈɡloʊ

AGM ˌeɪ.dʒiːˈem

agnail ˈæɡ.neɪl **-s** -z

agnate ˈæɡ.neɪt

agnation æɡˈneɪ.ʃᵊn

Agnes ˈæɡ.nəs, -nɪs

Agnew ˈæɡ.njuː (US) -nuː, -njuː

Agni ˈæɡ.ni

agnomen æg'nəʊ.men, -mən (US) -'noʊ- **-s** -z
agnostic æg'nɒs.tɪk, əg- (US) -'nɑː.stɪk **-s** -s
agnosticism æg'nɒs.tɪ.sɪ.zᵊm, əg-, -tə- (US) -'nɑː.stɪ-, -stə-
Agnus Dei ˌæg.nəs'deɪ.i, -nʊs-, -'diː.aɪ **-s** -z
ago ə'gəʊ (US) -'goʊ
agog ə'gɒg (US) -'gɑːg, -'gɔːg
-agogic -ə'gɒdʒ.ɪk, -'gɒg-, -'gəʊ.dʒɪk (US) -ə'gɑː.dʒɪk, -'goʊ-
Note: Suffix. Words containing **-agogic** are normally stressed on the penultimate syllable, e.g. **pedagogic** /ˌped.ə'gɒdʒ.ɪk (US) -'gɑː-/.
-agogue -ə.gɒg (US) -ə.gɑːg, -ə.gɔːg
Note: Suffix. Normally unstressed, e.g. **pedagogue** /'ped.ə.gɒg (US) -gɑːg/.
-agogy -ə.gɒdʒ.i, -gɒg-, -gəʊ.dʒi (US) -ə.gɑː.dʒi, -goʊ.gi
Note: Suffix. Normally unstressed, e.g. **pedagogy** /'ped.ə.gɒdʒ.i (US) -gɑː.dʒi/.
agone ə'gɒn (US) -'gɑːn
agonist 'æg.ə.nɪst **-s** -s
Agonistes ˌæg.əʊ'nɪs.tiːz (US) -ə'-
agonistic ˌæg.əʊ'nɪs.tɪk (US) -ə'- **-s** -s **-ally** -ᵊl.i
agoniz|e, -is|e 'æg.ə.naɪz **-es** -ɪz **-ing/ly** -ɪŋ/li **-ed** -d
agon|y 'æg.ə.n|i **-ies** -iz **'agony ˌaunt; 'agony ˌcolumn**
agor|a 'æg.ə.r|ə, -ɒr.ə, ˌæg.ə'rɑː (US) 'æg.ə.r|ə, -ɔːr.ə **-ae** -iː **-as** -əz
agoraphob|ia ˌæg.ᵊr.ə'fəʊ.b|i.ə, -ɔː.rə'- (US) -ɚ.ə'foʊ-; əˌgɔːr.ə'- **-ic/s** -ik
agouti ə'guː.ti (US) -t̬i **-s** -z
Agra 'ɑː.grə, 'æg.rə
agrarian ə'greə.ri.ən (US) -'grer.i- **-s** -z **-ism** -ɪ.zᵊm
agree ə'griː **-s** -z **-ing** -ɪŋ **-d** -d
agreeab|le ə'griː.ə.b|l̩ **-ly** -li **-leness** -l̩.nəs, -nɪs
agreement ə'griː.mənt **-s** -s
agribusiness 'æg.riˌbɪz.nɪs, -nəs **-es** -ɪz
Agricola ə'grɪk.əʊ.lə (US) -ᵊl.ə
agricultural ˌæg.rɪ'kʌl.tʃᵊr.ᵊl, -rə'- **-ist/s** -ɪst/s
agriculture 'æg.rɪ.kʌl.tʃəʳ, -rə- (US) -tʃɚ
agriculturist ˌæg.rɪ'kʌl.tʃᵊr.ɪst, -rə'- **-s** -s
Agrigento ˌæg.rɪ'dʒen.təʊ (US) -toʊ
agrimony 'æg.rɪ.mə.ni, -rə- (US) -moʊ-
Agrippa ə'grɪp.ə
Agrippina ˌæg.rɪ'piː.nə, -rə'-
agro- æg.rəʊ-; ə'grɒ- (US) æg.roʊ-, -rə-; ə'grɑː-
Note: Prefix. Either takes primary or secondary stress on the first syllable, e.g. **agronomics** /ˌæg.rə'nɒm.ɪks (US) -'nɑː.mɪks/, or primary stress on the second syllable, e.g. **agronomy** /ə'grɒn.ə.mi (US) -'grɑː.nə-/.
agrobiologic ˌæg.rəʊ.baɪə'lɒdʒ.ɪk (US) -roʊ.baɪə'lɑː.dʒɪk **-al** -ᵊl **-ally** -ᵊl.i, -li
agrobiology ˌæg.rəʊ.baɪ'ɒl.ə.dʒi (US) -roʊ.baɪ'ɑː.lə-
agrochemical ˌæg.rəʊ'kem.ɪ.kᵊl (US) -roʊ'- **-s** -z
agrolog|y ə'grɒl.ə.dʒ|i, æg'- (US) ə'grɑː.lə- **-ist/s** -ɪst/s
agronomics ˌæg.rə'nɒm.ɪks (US) -'nɑː.mɪks
agronom|y ə'grɒn.ə.m|i (US) -'grɑː.nə- **-ist/s** -ɪst/s
aground ə'graʊnd
Aguascalientes ˌæg.wɑːs.kæl.i'en.tes (US) ˌɑː.gwɑːs.kæl'jen.tes, -i'en-
ague 'eɪg.juː **-s** -z
Aguecheek 'eɪg.juː.tʃiːk
Agulhas ə'gʌl.əs
Agutter 'æg.ə.təʳ; ə'gʌt.əʳ (US) ə'gʌt̬.ɚ; 'æg.ə.t̬ɚ
ah ɑː
aha ɑː'hɑː, ə'hɑː
Ahab 'eɪ.hæb
Ahasuerus eɪˌhæz.ju'ɪə.rəs, əˌhæz- (US) -'ɪr.əs
Ahaz 'eɪ.hæz
Ahaziah ˌeɪ.hə'zaɪ.ə
ahead ə'hed
aheap ə'hiːp
ahem m'ʔm̩m, 'ʔm̩m, hm, ə'hem
Note: Interjection. The spelling attempts to represent a clearing of the throat to attract attention. The pronunciation /ə'hem/ represents the reading aloud of this word by someone who does not know what it stands for.
Ahenobarbus əˌhen.əʊ'bɑː.bəs (US) -oʊ'bɑːr-, -ˌhiː.noʊ'-
A'Hern 'eɪ.hɜːn (US) -hɝːn
Ahern(e) ə'hɜːn (US) -'hɝːn
Ahimsa ɑː'hɪm.sɑː (US) ə-
ahistorical ˌeɪ.hɪ'stɒr.ɪ.kᵊl (US) -'stɔːr-
Ahithophel ə'hɪθ.əʊ.fel (US) '-ə-
Ahmadabad 'ɑː.mə.də.bæd (US) -bɑːd
Ahmed 'ɑː.med
ahold ə'həʊld (US) -hoʊld
ahoy ə'hɔɪ
ahungered ə'hʌŋ.gəd (US) -gɚd
AI ˌeɪ'aɪ
ai 'ɑː.i, aɪ
Aicken 'eɪ.kᵊn
aid eɪd **-s** -z **-ing** -ɪŋ **-ed** -ɪd **-er/s** -əʳ/z (US) -ɚ/z **ˌaid and a'bet**
Aïda, Aida aɪ'iː.də, ɑː-
Aidan 'eɪ.dᵊn
aide eɪd **-s** -z
Aideed aɪ'diːd
aide(s)-de-camp ˌeɪd.də'kɑ̃ː (US) -'kæmp
aide(s)-mémoire ˌeɪd.mem'wɑː (US) -'wɑːr
aid|-man 'eid|.mən, -mæn **-men** -men, -mən
AIDS, Aids eɪdz
aigrette 'eɪ.gret, eɪ'gret **-s** -s
aiguille ˌeɪ'gwiː, -'gwiːl (US) ˌeɪ'gwiːl, '-- **-s** -z
Aiken 'eɪ.kᵊn
aikido ˌaɪ'kiː.dəʊ, 'aɪ.kɪ- (US) ˌaɪ'kiː.doʊ
Aikin 'eɪ.kɪn, -kᵊn
Aikman 'eɪk.mən
ail eɪl **-s** -z **-ing** -ɪŋ **-ed** -d
ailanthus ˌaɪ'lænt.θəs **-es** -ɪz
Aileen 'eɪ.liːn (US) aɪ'liːn
aileron 'eɪ.lᵊr.ɒn (US) -ə.rɑːn **-s** -z
Ailesbury 'eɪlz.bᵊr.i (US) -ber-
ailment 'eɪl.mənt **-s** -s
Ailred 'eɪl.red, 'aɪl-
Ailsa 'eɪl.sə
ailuro- aɪ'ljʊə.rəʊ-, eɪ-, 'aɪ.ljʊə.rəʊ- (US) aɪ'lʊr.ə-
ailurophile aɪ'ljʊə.rəʊ.faɪl, eɪ- (US) -'lʊr.ə- **-s** -z
ailurophobe aɪ'ljʊə.rəʊ.fəʊb, eɪ- (US) -'lʊr.ə.foʊb **-s** -z
ailurophobia aɪˌljʊə.rəʊ'fəʊ.bi.ə, eɪ- (US) -ˌlʊr.ə'foʊ-
aim eɪm **-s** -z **-ing** -ɪŋ **-ed** -d
aimless 'eɪm.ləs, -lɪs **-ly** -li **-ness** -nəs, -nɪs
Ainger 'eɪn.dʒəʳ (US) -dʒɚ
Ainsley, Ainslie 'eɪnz.li
Ainsworth 'eɪnz.wəθ, -wɜːθ (US) -wɚθ, -wɝːθ
ain't eɪnt
Aintree 'eɪn.triː
Ainu 'aɪ.nuː **-s** -z
aïoli, aioli aɪ'əʊ.li, eɪ'- (US) -'oʊ-
air eəʳ (US) er **-s** -z **-ing/s** -ɪŋ/z **-ed** -d **'air ˌforce; 'air hoˌstess; 'air ˌletter; 'air ˌpocket; 'air ˌraid; 'air ˌrifle; 'air ˌroute; 'air ˌterminal; ˌair traffic con'trol; ˌair traffic con'troller; ˌclear the 'air**
airbag 'eə.bæg (US) 'er- **-s** -z
airbase 'eə.beɪs (US) 'er- **-s** -ɪz
airbed 'eə.bed (US) 'er- **-s** -z
air-boat 'eə.bəʊt (US) 'er.boʊt **-s** -s
airborne 'eə.bɔːn (US) 'er.bɔːrn
airbrake 'eə.breɪk (US) 'er- **-s** -s
airbrick 'eə.brɪk, 'er-
airbridg|e 'eə.brɪdʒ (US) 'er- **-es** -ɪz
airbrush 'eə.brʌʃ (US) 'er- **-es** -ɪz **-ing** -ɪŋ **-ed** -d
air-burst 'eə.bɜːst (US) 'er.bɝːst **-s** -s
airbus (A®) 'eə.bʌs (US) 'er- **-es** -ɪz
air-check 'eə.tʃek (US) 'er- **-s** -s
air-condition 'eə.kənˌdɪʃ.ᵊn, ˌeə.kən'dɪʃ- (US) 'er.kənˌdɪʃ- **-s** -z **-ing** -ɪŋ **-ed** -d **-er/s** -əʳ/z (US) -ɚ/z

Pronouncing the letters AI, AY

The vowel letter digraphs **ai** and **ay** are similar in that their most common pronunciation is /eɪ/, e.g.:

day /deɪ/
daily /ˈdeɪ.li/

However, in days of the week, **ay** is also frequently pronounced /i/, e.g.:

Monday /ˈmʌn.di/

When followed by an **r** in the spelling, **ai** and **ay** are pronounced as /eə, (US) er/, e.g.:

air /eəʳ/ (US) /er/
Ayr /eəʳ/ (US) /er/

In addition

There are other vowel sounds associated with the digraphs **ai** and **ay**, e.g.:

/e/ said, says /sed, sez/
/æ/ plait /plæt/
/aɪ/ aisle /aɪl/

And, in rare cases:

/eɪ.ɪ/ archaic /ɑːˈkeɪ.ɪk/ (US) /ɑːr-/

In weak syllables

The vowel digraphs **ai** and **ay** are realised with the vowels /ɪ/ and /i/ in weak syllables respectively, and **ai** may also result in a schwa vowel or a syllabic consonant, e.g.:

bargain /ˈbɑː.gɪn/ (US) /ˈbɑːr-/
Murray /ˈmʌr.i/ (US) /ˈmɝː-/
Britain /ˈbrɪt.ᵊn/

air-cool ˈeə.kuːl (US) ˈer- **-s** -z **-ing** -ɪŋ **-ed** -d
aircraft ˈeə.krɑːft (US) ˈer.kræft
aircraft|man ˈeə.krɑːft|.mən (US) ˈer.kræft- **-men** -mən
aircraft|woman ˈeə.krɑːft|ˌwʊm.ən (US) ˈer.kræft- **-women** -ˌwɪm.ɪn
aircrew ˈeə.kruː (US) ˈer- **-s** -z
Aird eəd (US) erd
airdate ˈeə.deɪt (US) ˈer- **-s** -s
Airdrie ˈeə.dri (US) ˈer-
Airdrieonian ˌeə.driˈəʊ.ni.ən (US) ˌer.driˈoʊ- **-s** -z
airdrome ˈeə.drəʊm (US) ˈer.droʊm **-s** -z
air-drop ˈeə.drɒp (US) ˈer.drɑːp **-s** -s **-ping** -ɪŋ **-ped** -t
air-dr|y ˈeə.dr|aɪ (US) ˈer- **-ies** -z **-ing** -ɪŋ **-ied** -d
Aire eəʳ (US) er
Airedale ˈeə.deɪl (US) ˈer- **-s** -z
air-engine ˈeəʳ.en.dʒɪn (US) ˈer- **-s** -z
airer ˈeə.rəʳ (US) ˈer.ɚ **-s** -z
Airey ˈeə.ri (US) ˈer.i
airfare ˈeə.feəʳ (US) ˈer.fer **-s** -z
airfield ˈeə.fiːld (US) ˈer- **-s** -z
airfleet ˈeə.fliːt (US) ˈer-
airflow ˈeə.fləʊ (US) ˈer.floʊ **-s** -z
air-foil ˈeə.fɔɪl (US) ˈer- **-s** -z
airgraph ˈeə.grɑːf, -græf (US) ˈer.græf **-s** -s
airgun ˈeəˌgʌn (US) ˈer- **-s** -z
airhead ˈeə.hed (US) ˈer- **-s** -z
airi|ly ˈeə.rɪ|.li, -rᵊl|.i (US) ˈer- **-ness** -nəs, -nɪs
airing ˈeə.rɪŋ (US) ˈer.ɪŋ **-s** -z **ˈairing ˌcupboard**
airless ˈeə.ləs, -lɪs (US) ˈer-
Airlie ˈeə.li (US) ˈer-
airlift ˈeə.lɪft (US) ˈer- **-s** -s **-ing** -ɪŋ **-ed** -ɪd
airlin|e ˈeə.laɪn (US) ˈer- **-es** -z **-er/s** -əʳ/z (US) -ɚ/z
airlock ˈeə.lɒk (US) ˈer.lɑːk **-s** -s
airmail ˈeə.meɪl (US) ˈer- **-s** -z
air|man ˈeə|.mən, -mæn (US) ˈer- **-men** -mən, -men
airmarshal ˈeəˌmɑː.ʃᵊl (US) ˈerˌmɑːr-
airmobile ˈeə.məʊ.biːl (US) ˈerˌmoʊ.bᵊl
airplane ˈeə.pleɪn (US) ˈer- **-s** -z
airplay ˈeə.pleɪ (US) ˈer-
airport ˈeə.pɔːt (US) ˈer.pɔːrt **-s** -s
air-sea ˌeəˈsiː (US) ˌer- *stress shift, see compound:* **ˌair-sea ˈrescue**
airship ˈeə.ʃɪp (US) ˈer- **-s** -s
airshow ˈeə.ʃəʊ (US) ˈer.ʃoʊ **-s** -z
airsick ˈeə.sɪk (US) ˈer- **-ness** -nəs, -nɪs
airspace ˈeə.speɪs (US) ˈer-
airspeed ˈeə.spiːd (US) ˈer- **-s** -z
airstream ˈeə.striːm (US) ˈer-
airstrike ˈeə.straɪk (US) ˈer- **-s** -s
airstrip ˈeə.strɪp (US) ˈer- **-s** -s
airtight ˈeə.taɪt (US) ˈer-
airtime ˈeə.taɪm (US) ˈer-
air-to-air ˌeə.tuˈeəʳ (US) ˌer.t̬əˈer, -tuˈ- *stress shift:* ˌair-to-air ˈmissile
air-to-surface ˌeə.təˈsɜː.fɪs (US) ˌer.t̬əˈsɝː.fəs *stress shift:* ˌair-to-surface ˈmissile
Airtours® ˈeə.tɔːz, -tʊəz (US) ˈer.tʊrz
air traffic ˈeəˌtræf.ɪk (US) ˈer-
airwave ˈeə.weɪv (US) ˈer- **-s** -z
airway ˈeə.weɪ (US) ˈer- **-s** -z
air|woman ˈeə|ˌwʊm.ən (US) ˈer- **-women** -ˌwɪm.ɪn
airworth|y ˈeəˌwɜː.ð|i (US) ˈerˌwɝː- **-iness** -ɪ.nəs, -ɪ.nɪs
air|y (A) ˈeə.r|i (US) ˈer|.i **-ier** -i.əʳ (US) -i.ɚ **-iest** -i.əst, -i.ɪst **-ily** -ɪ.li, -ə.li **-iness** -ɪ.nəs, -ɪ.nɪs
airy-fairy ˌeə.riˈfeə.ri (US) ˌer.iˈfer.i *stress shift:* ˌairy-fairy ˈconcept
Aisha aɪˈiː.ʃə
Aislaby ˈeɪz.lə.bi *locally:* ˈeɪ.zᵊl.bi
aisle aɪl **-s** -z **-d** -d
aitch eɪtʃ **-es** -ɪz
aitchbone ˈeɪtʃ.bəʊn (US) -boʊn **-s** -z
Aitchison ˈeɪ.tʃɪ.sᵊn
Aith eɪθ
Aitken ˈeɪt.kɪn, -kən
Aix eɪks, eks
Aix-en-Provence ˌeɪks.ɑ̃ːm.prəˈvɑ̃ːns, ˌeks- (US) -ɑːn.proʊˈvɑ̃ːs
Aix-la-Chapelle ˌeɪks.lɑː.ʃæpˈel, ˌeks-, -ʃəˈpel (US) -ʃɑːˈpel
Aix-les-Bains ˌeɪks.leɪˈbæ̃ː, ˌeks-, -ˈbæŋ
Ajaccio əˈjætʃ.i.əʊ, əˈdʒæs.i.əʊ (US) ɑːˈjɑː.tʃoʊ, -tʃi.oʊ
ajar əˈdʒɑːʳ (US) -dʒɑːr
Ajax *cleaning substance* ® ˈeɪ.dʒæks *football team:* ˈaɪ.æks
ajutage ˈædʒ.ʊ.tɪdʒ, əˈdʒuːt- (US) ˈædʒ.ə.t̬ɪdʒ, əˈdʒuː-
AKA, aka ˌeɪ.keɪˈeɪ, ˈæk.ə
Akaba ˈæk.ə.bə
Akabusi ˌæk.əˈbuː.si
Akahito ˌæk.əˈhiː.təʊ (US) ˌɑː.kəˈhiː.toʊ
Akbar ˈæk.bɑːʳ (US) -bɑːr
akela ɑːˈkeɪ.lə
Akenside ˈeɪ.kən.saɪd, -kɪn-
Akerman ˈæk.ə.mən (US) ˈ-ɚ-
Akers ˈeɪ.kəz (US) -kɚz

Akhmatova əkˈmɑː.tə.və, ˌɑːk.məˈtəʊ- (US) ʌkˈmɑː.tə.və, ˌɑːk.məˈtoʊ-
Akihito ˌæk.iˈhiː.təʊ (US) ˌɑː.kiˈhiː.toʊ
akimbo əˈkɪm.bəʊ (US) -boʊ
akin əˈkɪn
Akkad ˈæk.æd (US) ˈæk.æd, ˈɑː.kɑːd
Akkadian əˈkeɪ.di.ən (US) -ˈkeɪ-, -ˈkɑː- **-s** -z
Akond of Swat *former title of the Wali of Swat territory in Pakistan:* əˌkuːnd.əvˈswɒt (US) -ˈswɑːt *name in poem by Edward Lear:* ˌæk.ənd.əvˈswɒt (US) -ˈswɑːt
Akron ˈæk.rɒn, -rən (US) -rən
Akrotiri ˈæk.rəʊˈtɪə.ri (US) ˌɑːk.roʊˈtɪr.i
Akroyd ˈæk.rɔɪd
al- əl-, æl-
Note: Prefix. Examples include **allocate** /ˈæl.ə.keɪt/, in which it is stressed, and **allure** /əˈljʊəʳ (US) -ˈlʊr/, where it is unstressed.
AL ˌeɪˈel
Al æl
-al -əl
Note: Suffix. When forming a noun, **-al** does not normally affect the stress pattern, e.g. **arouse** /əˈraʊz/, **arousal** /əˈraʊ.zᵊl/. In forming adjectives, however, the resulting item is usually either stressed one or two syllables before the suffix, e.g. **abdomen** becomes **abdominal** /æbˈdɒm.ɪ.nᵊl (US) -ˈdɑː.mə-/, **adjective** becomes **adjectival** /ˌædʒ.ɪkˈtaɪ.vᵊl/.
Ala. *(abbrev. for* **Alabama***)* ˌæl.əˈbæm.ə, -ˈbɑː.mə (US) -ˈbæm.ə
à la ˈæl.ɑː, ˈɑː.lɑː (US) ˈɑː.lɑː, ˈɑː.lə, ˈæl.ə
Alabama ˌæl.əˈbæm.ə, -ˈbɑː.mə (US) -ˈbæm.ə
alabaster (A) ˌæl.əˈbæs.təʳ, -ˈbɑː.stəʳ, ˈæl.ə.bæs.təʳ, -bɑː.stəʳ (US) ˈæl.ə.bæs.tɚ
à la carte ˌæl.əˈkɑːt, ˌɑː.lɑːˈ- (US) ˌɑː.ləˈkɑːrt, ˌæl.əˈ-
alack əˈlæk
alackaday əˈlæk.ə.deɪ, əˌlæk.əˈdeɪ
alacrity əˈlæk.rə.ti, -rɪ.ti (US) -t̬i
Aladdin əˈlæd.ɪn (US) -ᵊn **Aˌladdin's ˈcave**
Alagoas ˌæl.əˈɡəʊ.əs (US) -ˈɡoʊ-
à la grecque ˌæl.əˈɡrek, ˌɑː.lɑːˈ- (US) ˌɑː.ləˈ-, ˌæl.əˈ-
Alain *man's name:* ælˈæ̃ (US) ælˈẽn *woman's name:* əˈleɪn
Alain-Fournier ælˌæ̃ˈfɔː.ni.eɪ *as if French:* -fʊəˈnjeɪ (US) -ˌẽn.fɔːrˈnjeɪ
Alameda æl.əˈmiː.də, -ˈmeɪ-
Alamein ˈæl.ə.meɪn
Alamo ˈæl.ə.məʊ (US) -moʊ
à la mode ˌæl.əˈməʊd, ˌɑː.lɑː-, -ˈmɒd (US) ˌɑː.ləˈmoʊd, ˌæl.əˈ-
Alamogordo ˌæl.ə.məˈɡɔː.dəʊ (US) -ˈɡɔːr.doʊ
Alan ˈæl.ən
Alana əˈlɑː.nə, -ˈlæn.ə
Aland *islands:* ˈɑː.lənd, ˈɔː-
aland *(adv.)* əˈlænd
à l'anglaise ˌæl.ɑ̃ːŋˈɡleɪz, ˌɑː.lɑ̃ːŋˈ-, -ˈɡlez
alanine ˈæl.ə.naɪn, -niːn
alar ˈeɪ.ləʳ, -lɑːʳ (US) -lɚ
Alaric ˈæl.ə.rɪk
alarm əˈlɑːm (US) -ˈlɑːrm **-s** -z **-ing/ly** -ɪŋ/li **-ed** -d **aˈlarm ˌclock**
alarmist əˈlɑː.mɪst (US) -ˈlɑːr- **-s** -s
alarum əˈlær.əm, -ˈlɑː.rəm, -ˈleə- (US) -ˈler.əm, -ˈlɑːr- **-s** -z
alas əˈlæs, -ˈlɑːs (US) -ˈlæs
Alasdair ˈæl.ə.stəʳ, -steəʳ (US) -stɚ
Alask|a əˈlæs.k|ə **-an/s** -ən/z
Alastair ˈæl.ə.stəʳ, -steəʳ (US) -stɚ, -ster
Alastor əˈlæs.tɔːʳ, ælˈæs- (US) -tɔːr, -tɚ
alate ˈeɪ.leɪt **-s** -s
alb ælb **-s** -z
Alba ˈæl.bə
albacore ˈæl.bə.kɔː (US) -kɔːr **-s** -z
Alba Longa ˌæl.bəˈlɒŋ.ɡə (US) -ˈlɑːŋ.ɡə, -ˈlɔːŋ-
Alban ˈɔːl.bən, ˈɒl- (US) ˈɑːl-
Albani ælˈbɑː.ni (US) ɑːl-, ɔːl-
Albani|a ælˈbeɪ.ni|.ə, ɔːl- **-an/s** -ən/z
Albany *in London:* ˈɔːl.bə.ni, ˈɒl-, ˈæl- (US) ˈɑːl-, ˈɔːl- *in Australia:* ˈæl.bə.ni (US) ˈɑːl.bə-, ˈɔːl- *in US:* ˈɔːl.bə.ni, ˈɒl- (US) ˈɑːl-
Albarn ˈɔːl.bɑːn, ˈɒl- (US) ˈɑːl.bɑːrn
albatross ˈæl.bə.trɒs (US) -trɑːs, -trɔːs **-es** -ɪz
albedo ælˈbiː.dəʊ (US) -doʊ **-(e)s** -z
Albee ˈɔːl.biː, ˈæl- (US) ˈɑːl-, ˈɔːl-, ˈæl-
albeit ɔːlˈbiː.ɪt (US) ɔːl-, ɑːl-
Albemarle ˈæl.bə.mɑːl, -bɪ- (US) -mɑːrl
Alberic ˈæl.bə.rɪk
Alberich ˈæl.bə.rɪk, -rɪx (US) -rɪk
Albers ˈæl.bɜːz, ˈɔːl.bəz (US) ˈæl.bɝːz, ˈɑːl.bɚz
albert (A) ˈæl.bət (US) -bɚt **-s** -s **ˌAlbert ˈHall**
Alberta ælˈbɜː.tə (US) -ˈbɝː.t̬ə
albertite ˈæl.bə.taɪt (US) -bɚ-
Alberton ˈæl.bə.tən (US) -bɚ-
albescen|ce ælˈbes.ᵊn|*t*s **-t** -t
Albi ˈæl.bi
Albigenses ˌæl.bɪˈɡen*t*.siːz, -bɪˈdʒen*t*-
albinism ˈæl.bɪ.nɪ.zᵊm
albino ælˈbiː.nəʊ (US) -ˈbaɪ.noʊ **-s** -z
Albinoni ˌæl.bɪˈnəʊ.ni (US) -ˈnoʊ-
Albinus ælˈbiː.nəs
Albion ˈæl.bi.ən
Albrecht ˈæl.brekt, -brext (US) ˈɑːl.brekt
Albright ˈɔːl.braɪt, ˈɒl- (US) ˈɑːl-, ˈɔːl-
Albrighton ˈɔː.braɪ.tᵊn, ˈɔːl-, ˈɒl- (US) ˈɑːl-
Albrow ˈɔːl.braʊ (US) ˈɑːl-
Albufeira ˌæl.bʊˈfeə.rə (US) ˌɑːl.buːˈfeɪ.rə
Albula ˈæl.bjʊ.lə (US) ˈɑːl.buː-, -bjuː-
album ˈæl.bəm **-s** -z
albumen ˈæl.bjʊ.mən, -men, -mɪn (US) ælˈbjuː.mən
albumin ˈæl.bjʊ.mɪn, -bjə.mɪn (US) ælˈbjuː.mən
albuminoid ælˈbjuː.mɪ.nɔɪd **-s** -z
albuminous ælˈbjuː.mɪ.nəs
albuminuria ˌæl.bjuː.mɪˈnjʊə.ri.ə (US) -ˈnʊr.i-, -ˈnjʊr-
Albuquerque ˌæl.bəˈkɜː.ki, ˈæl.bəˌkɜː- (US) ˈæl.bəˌkɝː- *esp. for person:* ˌ--ˈ--
alburnum ælˈbɜː.nəm (US) -ˈbɝː- **-s** -z
Albury ˈɔːl.bᵊr.i, ˈɒl- (US) ˈɔːl-, ˈɑːl-
Alcaeus ælˈsiː.əs
alcaic (A) ælˈkeɪ.ɪk **-s** -s
alcalde ælˈkæl.deɪ, -di (US) -ˈkɑːl.di, -deɪ **-s** -z
Alcan® ˈæl.kæn
Alcatraz ˈæl.kə.træz, ˌ--ˈ-
Alcazar *Spanish palace:* ˌæl.kəˈzɑː (US) ˈæl.kə.zɑːr; ælˈkæz.ɚ *music hall:* ælˈkæz.əʳ (US) -ɚ
Alcester ˈɔːl.stəʳ, ˈɒl- (US) ˈɔːl.stɚ, ˈɑːl-
Alcestis ælˈses.tɪs
alchemic ælˈkem.ɪk **-al** -ᵊl
alchemist ˈæl.kə.mɪst, -kɪ- **-s** -s
alchemy ˈæl.kə.mi, -kɪ-
Alcibiades ˌæl.sɪˈbaɪ.ə.diːz
Alcinous ˌælˈsɪn.əʊ.əs (US) ˈ-oʊ-
Alcmene ælkˈmiː.niː
Alcock ˈæl.kɒk, ˈɔːl-, ˈɒl- (US) ˈæl.kɑːk, ˈɑːl-, ˈɔːl-
alcohol ˈæl.kə.hɒl (US) -hɑːl **-s** -z
alcoholic ˌæl.kəˈhɒl.ɪk (US) -ˈhɑː.lɪk **-s** -s *stress shift:* ˌalcoholic ˈdrink
alcoholism ˈæl.kə.hɒl.ɪ.zᵊm (US) -hɑː.lɪ-
Alconbury ˈɔːl.kən.bᵊr.i, ˈɔː-, ˈɒl-, -kəm-, -bri (US) ˈɔːl.kən.ber.i, ˈɑːl-, -bɚ-
alcopop ˈæl.kəʊ.pɒp (US) -koʊ.pɑːp **-s** -s
Alcott ˈɔːl.kət, ˈɒl-, -kɒt (US) ˈɑːl.kɑːt, ˈæl-, -kət
alcove ˈæl.kəʊv, ˈɒl- (US) ˈæl.koʊv **-s** -z **-d** -d
Alcuin ˈæl.kwɪn, ˈɒl- (US) ˈæl-
Alcyone ælˈsaɪə.ni
Aldborough ˈɔːl*d*.bᵊr.ə, ˈɒl- *locally:* ˈɔː.brə (US) ˈɔːld.bɚ.oʊ, ˈɑːld-
Aldbury ˈɔːld.bᵊr.i, ˈɒl- (US) ˈɔːld.ber-, ˈɑːld-, -bɚ-
Alde ɔːld (US) ɔːld, ɑːld
Aldebaran ælˈdeb.ə.rən, -ræn
Aldeburgh ˈɔːld.bᵊr.ə, ˈɒl- (US) ˈɔːld.bɚ.oʊ, ˈɑːld-
aldehyde ˈæl.dɪ.haɪd, -də- **-s** -z
Alden ˈɔːl.dᵊn, ˈɒl- (US) ˈɔːl-, ˈɑːl-
Aldenham ˈɔːld.ᵊn.əm, ˈɒl- (US) ˈɔːl-, ˈɑːl-

al dente æl'den.teɪ, ɑːl-
alder (A) 'ɔːl.dəʳ, 'ɒl- (US) 'ɔːl.dɚ, 'ɑːl- **-s** -z
Alderley Edge ˌɔːl.də.li'edʒ, ˌɒl- (US) ˌɔːl.dɚ-, ˌɑːl-
alder|man (A) 'ɔːl.də|.mən, 'ɒl- (US) 'ɔːl.dɚ-, 'ɑːl- **-men** -mən, -men
aldermanic ˌɔːl.də'mæn.ɪk, ˌɒl- (US) ˌɔːl.dɚ'-, ˌɑːl-
Aldermaston 'ɔːl.də.mɑː.stən (US) 'ɔːl.dɚ-, 'ɑːl-
aldern 'ɔːl.dən, 'ɒl-, -dɜːn (US) 'ɔːl.dɚn, 'ɑːl-
Alderney 'ɔːl.də.ni, 'ɒl- (US) 'ɔːl.dɚ-, 'ɑːl-
Aldersgate 'ɔːl.dəz.geɪt, 'ɒl-, -gɪt (US) 'ɔːl.dɚz-, 'ɑːl-
Aldershot 'ɔːl.də.ʃɒt, 'ɒl- (US) 'ɔːl.dɚ.ʃɑːt, 'ɑːl-
Alderson 'ɔːl.də.sᵊn, 'ɒl- (US) 'ɔːl.dɚ-, 'ɑːl-
Alderton 'ɔːl.də.tᵊn, 'ɒl- (US) 'ɔːl.dɚ-, 'ɑːl-
Aldgate 'ɔːl*d*.geɪt, 'ɒl-, -gɪt (US) 'ɔːl*d*-, 'ɑːl*d*-
Aldhelm 'ɔːld.helm, 'ɒl- (US) 'ɔːld-, 'ɑːld-
Aldi 'æl.di (US) 'ɑːl-
Aldine 'ɔːl.daɪn, ɒl-, -diːn (US) 'ɔːl-, 'ɑːl-
Aldington 'ɔːl.dɪŋ.tən, 'ɒl- (US) 'ɔːl-, 'ɑːl-
Aldis(s) 'ɔːl.dɪs, 'ɒl- (US) 'ɔːl-, 'ɑːl-
Aldous 'ɔːl.dəs, 'ɒl- (US) 'ɔːl.dəs, 'ɑːl-, 'æl-
Aldred 'ɔːl.drɪd, 'ɒl-, -dred (US) 'ɔːl-, 'ɑːl-
Aldrich 'ɔːl.drɪtʃ, 'ɒl-, -drɪdʒ (US) 'ɔːl-, 'ɑːl-
Aldridge 'ɔːl.drɪdʒ, 'ɒl- (US) 'ɔːl-, 'ɑːl-
Aldrin 'ɔːl.drɪn, 'ɒl- (US) 'ɔːl-, 'ɑːl-
Aldsworth 'ɔːldz.wəθ, 'ɒl-, -wɜːθ (US) 'ɔːldz.wɚθ, 'ɑːldz-, -wɝːθ
Aldus 'ɔːl.dəs, 'ɒl-, 'æl- (US) 'ɔːl-, 'ɑːl-
Aldwych 'ɔːld.wɪtʃ, 'ɒld- (US) 'ɔːld-, 'ɑːld-
ale (A) eɪl **-s** -z
aleatoric ˌæl.i.ə'tɒr.ɪk, ˌeɪ.li- (US) -'tɔːr-, -'tɑːr- **-ally** -ᵊl.i, -li
aleatory 'eɪ.li.ə.tᵊr.i, ˌæl.i'eɪ.tᵊr.i (US) 'eɪ.li.ə.tɔːr-
Alec(k) 'æl.ɪk, -lek
Alecto ə'lek.təʊ (US) -toʊ
Aled 'æl.ed, -ɪd
alehou|se 'eɪl.haʊ|s **-ses** -zɪz
Alemannic ˌæl.ɪ'mæn.ɪk, -ə'-
alembic ə'lem.bɪk **-s** -s
Alençon 'æl.æ̃n.sɔ̃ːŋ (US) ə'len.sən; ˌæl.ɑːn'soʊn
Aleppo ə'lep.əʊ, æl'ep- (US) -oʊ
a|lert ə|'lɜːt (US) -'lɝːt **-lerts** -'lɜːts (US) -'lɝːts **-lertly** -'lɜːt.li (US) -'lɝːt- **-lertness** -'lɜːt.nəs, -nɪs (US) -'lɝːt.nəs, -nɪs **-lerting** -'lɜː.tɪŋ (US) -'lɝː.t̬ɪŋ **-lerted** -'lɜː.tɪd (US) -'lɝː.t̬ɪd
Alessandria ˌæl.ɪ'sæn.dri.ə, -es'- (US) ˌɑː.lə'sɑːn-, ˌæl.ə'-, -'sæn-
Alessi ə'les.i
Alethea ˌæl.ə'θiː.ə; ə'liː.θi-; 'æl.ɪ.θi- (US) ˌæl.ɪ'θiː.ə; ə'liː.θi-
alethic æl'iː.θɪk, ə'liː-
Aletsch 'æl.ɪtʃ, 'ɑː.lɪtʃ, -letʃ (US) 'ɑː.letʃ
Aleut ə'ljuːt, -luːt; 'æl.juːt, -uːt (US) ə'luːt; 'æl.juːt, -i.uːt **-s** -s
Aleutian ə'ljuː.ʃən, -'luː- (US) -'luː-
A-level 'eɪ.lev.ᵊl **-s** -z
alewi|fe 'eɪl.waɪ|f **-ves** -vz
Alex 'æl.ɪks
Alexander ˌæl.ɪg'zɑːn.dəʳ, -eg'-, -'əg'-, -'zæn-, -ɪk'sɑːn- (US) -'zæn.dɚ **Alex'ander techˌnique**
Alexandra ˌæl.ɪg'zɑːn.drə, -eg'-, -əg'-, -'zæn-, -ɪk'sɑːn- (US) -'zæn-
Alexandria ˌæl.ɪg'zɑːn.dri.ə, -əg'-, -'zæn-, -ɪk'sɑːn-
alexandrian ˌæl.ɪg'zɑːn.dri.ən, -eg'-, -əg'-, -'zæn-, -ɪk'sɑːn- (US) -'zæn- **-s** -z
Alexandrina ˌæl.ɪg.zæn'driː.nə, -eg-, -əg'-, -zɑːn-, -ɪk.sɑːn'-
alexandrine ˌæl.ɪg'zæn.draɪn, -eg'-, -əg'-, -'zɑːn-, -ɪk'sɑːn- (US) -'zæn.drɪn, -'zæn.draɪn **-s** -z
alexia ˌeɪ'lek.si.ə, ə- (US) ə-
Alexis ə'lek.sɪs
Alf ælf
alfalfa ˌæl'fæl.fə
Alfa Romeo® ˌæl.fə.rəʊ'meɪ.əʊ (US) -roʊ'meɪ.oʊ
Alfie 'æl.fi
Alfonso æl'fɒn*t*.səʊ, -'fɒn.zəʊ (US) -'fɑːn*t*.soʊ, -'fɑːn.zoʊ
Alford 'ɔːl.fəd, 'ɒl- (US) 'ɔːl.fɚd, 'ɑːl-
Alfred 'æl.frɪd, -frəd
Alfreda æl'friː.də
Alfredian æl'friː.di.ən
alfresco, al fresco æl'fres.kəʊ (US) -koʊ
Alfreton 'ɔːl.frɪ.tᵊn, 'ɒl- (US) 'ɔːl.frɪ.tən, 'ɑːl-
Alfric 'æl.frɪk
Alfriston 'æl.frɪ.stən, 'ɔːl-
al|ga 'æl|.gə **-gae** -dʒiː, -dʒaɪ, -giː, -gaɪ
Algarve æl'gɑːv, 'æl.gɑːv (US) ɑːl'gɑːr.və
algebra 'æl.dʒɪ.brə, -dʒə- **-s** -z
algebraic ˌæl.dʒɪ'breɪ.ɪk, -dʒə'- **-al** -ᵊl **-ally** -ᵊl.i, -li *stress shift:* ˌalgebraic 'sum
algebraist ˌæl.dʒɪ'breɪ.ɪst, -dʒə'- **-s** -s
Algeciras ˌæl.dʒɪ'sɪə.rəs, -dʒə'-, -dʒes'ɪə-, -'sɪr.əs (US) -'sɪr-
Alger 'æl.dʒəʳ (US) -dʒɚ
Algeri|a æl'dʒɪə.ri|.ə (US) -'dʒɪr.i- **-an/s** -ən/z
Algerine ˌæl.dʒə'riːn
Algernon 'æl.dʒə.nən, -nɒn (US) -dʒɚ.nɑːn, -nən
Algiers æl'dʒɪəz (US) -'dʒɪrz
Algoa æl'gəʊ.ə (US) -'goʊ-
Algol, ALGOL 'æl.gɒl (US) -gɑːl
Algonquian æl'gɒŋ.kwi.ən, -ki.ən (US) -'gɑːŋ-, -'gɔːŋ-
Algonquin æl'gɒŋ.kwɪn, -kɪn (US) -'gɑːn-, -'gɔːŋ-
algorism 'æl.gᵊr.ɪ.zᵊm
algorithm 'æl.gᵊr.ɪ.ðᵊm **-s** -z
algorithmic ˌæl.gə'rɪð.mɪk *stress shift:* ˌalgorithmic de'sign
Algren 'ɔːl.grɪn, 'ɒl- (US) 'ɔːl-, 'ɑːl-
Algy 'æl.dʒi
Alhambra *in Spain:* æl'hæm.brə, əl-; ə'læm- *in California:* æl'hæm.brə
Ali *girl's name:* 'æl.i *boy's name and surname:* 'ɑː.li, ɑː'li
alias 'eɪ.li.əs, -æs **-es** -ɪz
Ali Baba ˌæl.i'bɑː.bə, ˌɑː.li-, -bɑː
alibi 'æl.ɪ.baɪ **-s** -z
Alicante ˌæl.ɪ'kæn.teɪ, -ti (US) -ti, -teɪ
Alice 'æl.ɪs **ˌAlice 'Springs; ˌAlice in 'Wonderland**
Alicia ə'lɪs.i.ə, -'lɪʃ.ə (US) -'lɪʃ.ə, -i.ə
Alick 'æl.ɪk
alien 'eɪ.li.ən **-s** -z **ing** -ɪŋ **-ed** -d **-age** -ɪdʒ
alienable 'eɪ.li.ə.nə.bl̩
alie|nate 'eɪ.li.ə|.neɪt **-nates** -neɪts **-nating** -neɪ.tɪŋ (US) -neɪ.t̬ɪŋ **-nated** -neɪ.tɪd (US) -neɪ.t̬ɪd **-nator/s** -neɪ.təʳ/z (US) -neɪ.t̬ɚ/z
alienation ˌeɪ.li.ə'neɪ.ʃᵊn **-s** -z
alien|ism 'eɪ.li.ə.nɪ|.zᵊm **-ist/s** -ɪst/s
a|light ə|'laɪt **-lights** -'laɪts **-lighting** -'laɪ.tɪŋ (US) -'laɪ.t̬ɪŋ **-lighted** -'laɪ.tɪd (US) -'laɪ.t̬ɪd
align ə'laɪn **-s** -z **-ing** -ɪŋ **-ed** -d
alignment ə'laɪn.mənt, -'laɪm- (US) -'laɪn- **-s** -s
alike ə'laɪk
aliment 'æl.ɪ.mənt **-s** -z
alimental ˌæl.ɪ'men.tᵊl (US) -t̬ᵊl
alimentary ˌæl.ɪ'men.tᵊr.i, '-tri (US) -t̬ᵊr.i, '-tri **aliˌmentary ca'nal** (US) **ali'mentary caˌnal**
alimentation ˌæl.ɪ.men'teɪ.ʃᵊn
alimon|y 'æl.ɪ.mə.n|i (US) -moʊ- **-ies** -iz
A-line 'eɪ.laɪn
Aline *woman's name:* æl'iːn, ə'liːn; 'æl.iːn
alin|e ə'laɪn **-es** -z **-ing** -ɪŋ **-ed** -d
alineation əˌlɪn.i'eɪ.ʃᵊn **-s** -z
Alington 'æl.ɪŋ.tən
Ali Pasha ˌæl.i'pɑː.ʃə, ˌɑː.li-, -'pæʃ.ə (US) ˌɑː.li'pɑː.ʃɑː, ˌæl.i'-
aliqu|ant 'æl.ɪ.kw|ənt **-ot** -ɒt (US) -ɑːt
Alisha ə'lɪʃ.ə
Alison 'æl.ɪ.sᵊn
Alissa ə'lɪs.ə
Alistair, Alister 'æl.ɪ.stəʳ (US) -stɚ

alit ə'lɪt
Alitalia® ˌæl.ɪ'tæl.i.ə, ˌɑː.li'tɑː.li- US -jə
alive ə'laɪv
Alix 'æl.ɪks
alizarin ə'lɪz.ə.rɪn
alkahest 'æl.kə.hest
alkalescen|ce ˌæl.kəl'es.ən|*ts* US -kə'les- **-cy** -*t*.si **-t** -t
alkali 'æl.kəl.aɪ US -kə.laɪ **-(e)s** -z
alkalic ˌæl'kæl.ɪk
alkalif|y æl'kæl.ɪ.f|aɪ **-ies** -aɪz **-ying** -aɪ.ɪŋ **-ied** -aɪd
alkaline 'æl.kəl.aɪn US -kə.laɪn
alkalinity ˌæl.kəl'ɪn.ə.ti, -ɪ.ti US -kə'lɪn.ə.ţi
alkalization, -isa- ˌæl.kəl.aɪ'zeɪ.ʃən, -ɪ'- US -ɪ'-
alkaliz|e, -is|e 'æl.kəl.aɪz US -kə.laɪz **-es** -ɪz **-ing** -ɪŋ **-ed** -d
alkaloid 'æl.kəl.ɔɪd US -kə.lɔɪd **-s** -z **-al** -əl
alkane 'æl.keɪn **-s** -z
Alka Seltzer® ˌæl.kə'selt.səʳ US 'æl.kəˌselt.sɚ
alkene 'æl.kiːn **-s** -z
Alkoran ˌæl.kɒr'ɑːn, -kɔː'rɑːn, -kə'rɑːn US -kɔːr'ɑːn, -kə'rɑːn, -'ræn
alk|y 'æl.k|i **-ies** -iz
alkyl 'æl.kɪl US -kəl **-s** -z
alkyne 'æl.kaɪn **-s** -z
all ɔːl US ɔːl, ɑːl **all 'fours**; **ˌall 'right**
alla breve ˌæl.ə'breɪ.veɪ, -vi US ˌɑː.lə'breɪ.vi, -veɪ
Allah 'æl.ə, -ɑː; ə'lɑː, æl'ɑː
Allahabad ˌæl.ə.hə'bɑːd, -'bæd
all-American ˌɔːl.ə'mer.ɪ.kən US ˌɔːl-, ˌɑːl-
Allan 'æl.ən
Allan-a-Dale ˌæl.ən.ə'deɪl
Allandale 'æl.ən.deɪl
allantois ə'læn.təʊ.ɪs US -toʊ-
allantoides əˌlæn'təʊ.ɪ.diːz US ˌæl.ən'toʊ.ə-
Allard 'æl.ɑːd, -əd US -ɑːrd, -ɚd
Allardice, Allardyce 'æl.ə.daɪs US '-ɚ-
allargando ˌæl.ɑː'gæn.dəʊ US ˌɑː.lɑːr'gɑːn.doʊ
allative 'æl.ə.tɪv US -ţɪv
allay ə'leɪ **-s** -z **-ing** -ɪŋ **-ed** -d
All-Bran® 'ɔːl.bræn US 'ɔːl-, 'ɑːl-
Allbright 'ɔːl.braɪt, 'ɒl- US 'ɔːl-, 'ɑːl-
all-clear ˌɔːl'klɪəʳ US ˌɔːl'klɪr, ˌɑːl-
Allcock 'ɔːl.kɒk US 'ɔːl.kɑːk, 'ɑːl-
Allcroft 'ɔːl.krɒft, 'ɒl- US 'ɔːl.krɑːft, 'ɑːl-
allegation ˌæl.ɪ'geɪ.ʃən, -ə'-, -eg'eɪ- **-s** -z
alleg|e ə'ledʒ **-es** -ɪz **-ing** -ɪŋ **-ed** -d
allegedly ə'ledʒ.ɪd.li, -əd-
Alleghany ˌæl.ɪ'geɪ.ni, -ə'- US -ə'-
Allegheny 'æl.ɪ.gen.i US ˌæl.ə'geɪ.ni
allegian|ce ə'liː.dʒən|*ts* **-ces** -sɪz **-t** -t
allegoric ˌæl.ɪ'gɒr.ɪk, -ə'gɒr- US -'gɔːr- **-al** -əl **-ally** -əl.i, -li
allegorist 'æl.ɪ.gə.rɪst, '-ə- US -gɔːr.ɪst **-s** -s
allegoriz|e, -is|e 'æl.ɪ.gə.raɪz, '-ə- US -gɔː-, -gə- **-es** -ɪz **-ing** -ɪŋ **-ed** -d
allegor|y 'æl.ɪ.gə.r|i, '-ə- US -gɔːr|.i **-ies** -iz
allegretto ˌæl.ɪ'gret.əʊ, -ə'- US -'greţ.oʊ **-s** -z
Allegri æl'eg.ri, -'eɪ.gri
allegro ə'leg.rəʊ, æl'eg-, -'eɪ.grəʊ US -'leg.roʊ, -'leɪ.groʊ **-s** -z
Allein(e) 'æl.ɪn
allele ə'liːl **-s** -z
allelic ə'liː.lɪk
allelism ə'liː.li.zəm
alleluia (A) ˌæl.ɪ'luː.jə, -ə'- **-s** -z
allemande 'æl.ə.mɑːnd, -mænd, -mɒnd US -mænd, -mɑːnd, -mæn, -mən **-s** -z
all-embracing ˌɔːl.ɪm'breɪ.sɪŋ, -em'- US ˌɔːl.em'-, ˌɑːl-, -ɪm'- *stress shift:* ˌall-embracing 'theory
Allen 'æl.ən, -ɪn **'Allen ˌkey**; **'Allen ˌwrench**
Allenby 'æl.ən.bi
Allendale 'æl.ən.deɪl, -ɪn-
Allende aɪ'end.i, -eɪ US ɑː'jen.deɪ, ɑːl-
Allentown 'æl.ən.taʊn, -ɪn-
allergen 'æl.ə.dʒen, -dʒən US '-ɚ- **-s** -z
allergenic ˌæl.ə'dʒen.ɪk US -ɚ'-
allergic ə'lɜː.dʒɪk US -'lɝː-
allergist 'æl.ə.dʒɪst US '-ɚ- **-s** -s
allerg|y 'æl.ə.dʒ|i US '-ɚ- **-ies** -iz
Allerton 'æl.ə.tən US '-ɚ.tən
allevi|ate ə'liː.vi|.eɪt **-ates** -eɪts **-ating** -eɪ.tɪŋ US -eɪ.ţɪŋ **-ated** -eɪ.tɪd US -eɪ.ţɪd **-ator/s** -eɪ.təʳ/z US -eɪ.ţɚ/z
alleviation əˌliː.vi'eɪ.ʃən
alley 'æl.i **-s** -z **'alley ˌcat**
Alleyn 'æl.ɪn
Alleyne æl'iːn, 'æl.ɪn, æl'eɪn
Alleynian ə'leɪ.ni.ən, æl'eɪ- **-s** -z
alleyway 'æl.i.weɪ **-s** -z
All Fools' Day ˌɔːl'fuːlz.deɪ US ˌɔːl-, ˌɑːl- **-s** -z
Allhallows ˌɔːl'hæl.əʊz US -oʊz, ˌɑːl-
allianc|e ə'laɪ.ən*t*s **-es** -ɪz
allicin 'æl.ə.sɪn, '-ɪ-
allied 'æl.aɪd
Allies 'æl.aɪz
alligator 'æl.ɪ.geɪ.təʳ US -ţɚ **-s** -z
all-important ˌɔːl.ɪm'pɔː.tənt US ɔːl.ɪm'pɔːr-, ɑːl- *stress shift:* ˌall-important 'meeting
all-in ˌɔːl'ɪn US ˌɔːl-, ˌɑːl- *stress shift:* ˌall-in 'wrestling
all-inclusive ˌɔːl.ɪŋ'kluː.sɪv US -ɪn'-, ˌɑːl-, -ɪŋ'-
allineation əˌlɪn.i'eɪ.ʃən, ælˌɪn- **-s** -z
Allingham 'æl.ɪŋ.əm
all-in-one ˌɔːl.ɪn'wʌn US ˌɔːl-, ˌɑːl- *stress shift:* ˌall-in-one sham'poo
Allison 'æl.ɪ.sən
alliter|ate ə'lɪt.ər|.eɪt, æl'ɪt- US ə'lɪţ.ə.r|eɪt **-ates** -eɪts **-ating** -eɪ.tɪŋ US -eɪ.ţɪŋ **-ated** -eɪ.tɪd US -eɪ.ţɪd
alliteration əˌlɪt.ə'reɪ.ʃən, ælˌɪt- US əˌlɪţ- **-s** -z
alliterative ə'lɪt.ər.ə.tɪv, æl'ɪt-, -eɪ- US ə'lɪţ.ər.ə.ţɪv, -ə.reɪ.ţɪv
Allman 'ɔːl.mən US 'ɔːl-, 'ɑːl-
all-nighter ˌɔːl'naɪ.təʳ US -ţɚ, ˌɑːl- **-s** -z
Alloa 'æl.əʊə US -oʊə
Allobroges ə'lɒb.rə.dʒiːz, æl'ɒb-, -rəʊ- US ə'lɑː.broʊ-
allo|cate 'æl.ə|.keɪt **-cates** -keɪts **-cating** -keɪ.tɪŋ US -keɪ.ţɪŋ **-cated** -keɪ.tɪd US -keɪ.ţɪd
allocation ˌæl.ə.keɪ.ʃən **-s** -z
allocution ˌæl.ə'kjuː.ʃən **-s** -z
allodi|al ə'ləʊ.di|.əl US -'loʊ- **-um** -əm
allogeneic ˌæl.əʊ.dʒə'niː.ɪk, -'neɪ- US ˌ-ə-, ˌ-oʊ- **-ally** -əl.i
allokine 'æl.əʊ.kaɪn US '-ə- **-s** -z
allomorph 'æl.əʊ.mɔːf US -ə.mɔːrf, -oʊ- **-s** -s
Allon 'æl.ən
allopath 'æl.əʊ.pæθ US '-ə-, '-oʊ- **-s** -s
allopathic ˌæl.əʊ'pæθ.ɪk US -ə'-, -oʊ'-
allopath|y ə'lɒp.ə.θ|i, æl'ɒp- US ə'lɑː.pə- **-ist/s** -ɪst/s
allophone 'æl.əʊ.fəʊn US -ə.foʊn, -oʊ- **-s** -z
allophonic ˌæl.əʊ'fɒn.ɪk US -ə'fɑː.nɪk *stress shift:* ˌallophonic 'variant
all-or-nothing ˌɔːl.ɔː'nʌθ.ɪŋ, -ə'- US -ɔːr'-, ˌɑːl-, -ɚ'- *stress shift:* ˌall-or-nothing 'gamble
alloseme 'æl.əʊ.siːm US '-ə- **-s** -z
al|lot ə'lɒt US -'lɑːt **-lots** -'lɒts US -'lɑːts **-lotting** -'lɒt.ɪŋ US -'lɑː.ţɪŋ **-lotted** -'lɒt.ɪd US -'lɑː.ţɪd
allotment ə'lɒt.mənt US -'lɑːt- **-s** -s
allotone 'æl.əʊ.təʊn US -ə.toʊn **-s** -z
allotrope 'æl.ə.trəʊp US -troʊp **-s** -s
allotropic ˌæl.ə'trɒp.ɪk US -'trɑː.pɪk
allotropy æl'ɒt.rə.pi, ə'lɒt- US ə'lɑː.trə-
all-out ˌɔːl'aʊt US ˌɔːl-, ˌɑːl- *stress shift:* ˌall-out 'effort
allow ə'laʊ **-s** -z **-ing** -ɪŋ **-ed** -d
allowab|le ə'laʊ.ə.b|l̩ **-ly** -li **-leness** -l̩.nəs, -nɪs
allowanc|e ə'laʊ.ən*t*s **-es** -ɪz **-ing** -ɪŋ **-ed** -t
Alloway 'æl.ə.weɪ
allowedly ə'laʊ.ɪd.li, -əd-
alloy (*n.*) 'æl.ɔɪ **-s** -z
alloy (*v.*) ə'lɔɪ **-s** -z **-ing** -ɪŋ **-ed** -d

Allophone

A variant of a phoneme.

Examples for English

Central to the concept of the PHONEME is the idea that it may be pronounced in many different ways. In English we take it for granted that the /r/ sound in *ray* and *tray* are "the same sound" (i.e. the same phoneme), but in reality the two sounds are very different – the /r/ in *ray* is voiced and non-fricative, while the /r/ sound in *tray* is voiceless and FRICATIVE. In phonemic transcription we use the same symbol /r/ for both (the slant brackets indicate that phonemic symbols are being used), but we know that the allophones of /r/ include the voiced non-fricative sound and the voiceless fricative one. Using the square brackets that indicate PHONETIC (allophonic) symbols, the former is [ɹ] and the latter [ɹ̥], e.g.:

ray	/reɪ/	[ɹeɪ]
tray	/treɪ/	[tɹ̥eɪ]

In theory a phoneme can have an infinite number of allophones, but in practice for descriptive purposes we tend to concentrate on the ones that occur most regularly and recognizably.

all-powerful ˌɔːl'paʊə.fᵊl, -fʊl ⓤⓢ -'paʊɚ-, ˌɑːl- *stress shift:* ˌall-powerful 'monarch
all-purpose ˌɔːl'pɜː.pəs ⓤⓢ ˌɔːl'pɝː-, ˌɑːl- *stress shift:* ˌall-purpose 'knife
all-round ˌɔːl'raʊnd ⓤⓢ ˌɔːl-, ˌɑːl- *stress shift:* ˌall-round 'athlete
all-rounder ˌɔːl'raʊn.dəʳ ⓤⓢ -dɚ, ˌɑːl- **-s** -z
All Saints' Day ˌɔːl'seɪnts ˌdeɪ ⓤⓢ ˌɔːl-, ˌɑːl- **-s** -z
Allsop(p) 'ɔːl.sɒp ⓤⓢ 'ɔːl.sɑːp, 'ɑːl-
allsorts 'ɔːl.sɔːts ⓤⓢ -sɔːrts, 'ɑːl-
All Souls' Day ˌɔːl'səʊlz ˌdeɪ ⓤⓢ ˌɔːl'soʊlz-, ˌɑːl- **-s** -z
allspice 'ɔːl.spaɪs ⓤⓢ 'ɔːl-, 'ɑːl-
all-star 'ɔːl.stɑːʳ ⓤⓢ 'ɔːl.stɑːr, 'ɑːl-
all-time ˌɔːl'taɪm ⓤⓢ 'ɔːl.taɪm, 'ɑːl- *stress shift, British only, see compound:* ˌ**all-time** '**greats**
allud|e ə'luːd, -'ljuːd ⓤⓢ -'luːd **-es** -z **-ing** -ɪŋ **-ed** -ɪd
Allum 'æl.əm
allur|e ə'ljʊəʳ, -'lʊəʳ, -'ljɔːʳ ⓤⓢ -'lʊr **-es** -z **-ing/ly** -ɪŋ/li **-ed** -d **-ement/s** -mənt/s
allusion ə'luː.ʒᵊn, ə'ljuː- ⓤⓢ -'luː- **-s** -z
allusive ə'luː.sɪv, -'ljuː- ⓤⓢ -'luː- **-ly** -li **-ness** -nəs, -nɪs
alluvi|al ə'luː.vi|.əl, -'ljuː- ⓤⓢ -'luː- **-a** -ə
alluvion ə'luː.vi.ən, -'ljuː- ⓤⓢ -'luː- **-s** -z
alluvi|um ə'luː.vi|.əm, -'ljuː- ⓤⓢ -'luː- **-ums** -əmz **-a** -ə
Allworth 'ɔːl.wəθ, -wɜːθ ⓤⓢ -wɚθ, 'ɑːl-, -wɝːθ
Allworthy 'ɔːlˌwɜː.ði ⓤⓢ -ˌwɝː-, ɑːl-
all|y (*n.*) 'æl.aɪ, ə'laɪ **-ies** -z
all|y (*v.*) ə'l|aɪ, æl|'aɪ; 'æl|.aɪ **-ies** -aɪz **-ying** -aɪ.ɪŋ **-ied** -aɪd
Note: **Allied** is usually pronounced /'æl.aɪd/ when attributive.
Ally 'æl.i
-ally -əl.i, -li
Note: Suffix. Words containing **-ally** are stressed in the same manner as adjectives containing **-al**. Where the word ends **-ically**, two forms are possible, e.g. **musically** is either /'mjuː.zɪ.kᵊl.i/ or /'mjuː.zɪ.kli/.
Allyson 'æl.ɪ.sᵊn
Alma 'æl.mə
Alma-Ata ˌæl.mɑː.ə'tɑː, ælˌmɑː-, ˌɑːl.mə'ɑː.tə
Almack 'ɔːl.mæk, 'ɒl- ⓤⓢ 'ɔːl-, 'ɑːl-
almagest 'æl.mə.dʒest **-s** -s
alma mater (A M) ˌæl.mə'mɑː.təʳ, -'meɪ.təʳ ⓤⓢ -'mɑː.t̬ɚ, ˌɑːl- **-s** -z
almanac(k) 'ɔːl.mə.næk, 'ɒl-, 'æl- ⓤⓢ 'ɔːl-, 'ɑːl-, 'æl- **-s** -s
almandine 'æl.mən.diːn, -dɪn **-s** -z
Almanzor æl'mæn.zɔːʳ, -zəʳ ⓤⓢ -zɔːr, -zɚ
Alma-Tadema ˌæl.mə'tæd.ɪ.mə
Almeida æl'miː.də, -'meɪ- ⓤⓢ -'meɪ-
Almeria ˌæl.mə'ri.ə
Almesbury 'ɑːmz.bᵊr.i ⓤⓢ -ber-, -bɚ-
almight|y (A) ɔːl'maɪ.t|i ⓤⓢ -t̬|i, ɑːl- **-ily** -ɪ.li, -ᵊl.i **-iness** -ɪ.nəs, -ɪ.nɪs
Almodovar ˌæl.mə'dəʊ.vɑːʳ, -'dɒ- ⓤⓢ -'doʊ.vɑːr
Almon 'æl.mən
almond (A) 'ɑː.mənd ⓤⓢ 'ɑː-, 'ɑːl-, 'æl- **-s** -z
Almondbury 'æl.mən*d*.bᵊr.i, 'ɑː-, 'ɔː- ⓤⓢ 'æl.mən*d*.ber.i, 'ɑː-, 'ɑːl-, -bɚ-
Almondsbury 'ɑː.mən*d*z.bᵊr.i *locally also:* 'eɪmz.bᵊr.i ⓤⓢ 'ɑː.mən*d*z.ber.i, 'ɑːl-, -bɚ-
almoner 'ɑː.mə.nəʳ, 'æl- ⓤⓢ 'æl.mə.nɚ, 'ɑː-, 'ɑːl- **-s** -z
almonr|y 'ɑː.mən.r|i, 'æl- ⓤⓢ 'æl-, 'ɑː-, 'ɑːl- **-ies** -iz
almost 'ɔːl.məʊst, -məst ⓤⓢ 'ɔːl.moʊst, 'ɑːl-
alms ɑːmz
almsgiv|er 'ɑːmz.gɪ.v|əʳ ⓤⓢ -v|ɚ **-ers** -əz ⓤⓢ -ɚz **-ing** -ɪŋ
almshou|se 'ɑːmz.haʊ|s **-ses** -zɪz
Alne ɔːn
Alness 'ɔːl.nɪs, 'æl-
Alnmouth 'æln.maʊθ, 'eɪl-
Alnwick 'æn.ɪk
aloe 'æl.əʊ ⓤⓢ -oʊ **-s** -z
aloe vera ˌæl.əʊ'vɪə.rə ⓤⓢ -oʊ'vɪr.ə
aloft ə'lɒft ⓤⓢ -'lɑːft
aloha ə'ləʊ.hə, æl'əʊ-, -hɑː, -ə ⓤⓢ ə'loʊ-
alone ə'ləʊn ⓤⓢ -'loʊn **-ness** -nəs, -nɪs
along ə'lɒŋ ⓤⓢ -'lɑːŋ, -'lɔːŋ
alongside əˌlɒŋ'saɪd ⓤⓢ ə'lɑːŋ.saɪd, -'lɔːŋ-, -ˌ-'-
Alonso ə'lɒn*t*.səʊ, -'lɒn.zəʊ ⓤⓢ -'lɑːn*t*.soʊ, -'lɑːn.zoʊ
aloof ə'luːf **-ness** -nəs, -nɪs
alopecia ˌæl.əʊ'piː.ʃə, '-ʃi.ə ⓤⓢ -ə'-, -oʊ'-
aloud ə'laʊd
Aloysius ˌæl.əʊ'ɪʃ.əs, -'ɪs.i.əs ⓤⓢ ˌæl.oʊ'ɪʃ-, -'ɪs.i.əs, -ə'wɪʃ.əs, -i.əs
alp (A) ælp **-s** -s
alpaca æl'pæk.ə **-s** -z
Alpen® 'æl.pən
alpenglow 'æl.pən.gləʊ ⓤⓢ -gloʊ
alpenhorn 'æl.pən.hɔːn, -pɪn- ⓤⓢ -hɔːrn **-s** -z
alpenstock 'æl.pən.stɒk, -pɪn- ⓤⓢ -stɑːk **-s** -s
Alperton 'æl.pə.tᵊn ⓤⓢ -pɚ-
alpha 'æl.fə **-s** -z '**alpha** ˌ**particle**; '**alpha** ˌ**ray**; '**alpha** ˌ**rhythm**; '**alpha** ˌ**wave**
alphabet 'æl.fə.bet **-s** -s
alphabetic ˌæl.fə'bet.ɪk ⓤⓢ -'bet̬- *stress shift:* ˌalphabetic 'writing
alphabetic|al ˌæl.fə'bet.ɪ.k|ᵊl ⓤⓢ -'bet̬- **-ally** -ᵊl.i, -li ˌ**alphabetical** '**order**, **alpha**ˌ**betical** '**order**
alphabeticiz|e, -is|e ˌæl.fə'bet.ɪ.saɪz ⓤⓢ -'bet̬.ə- **-es** -ɪz **-ing** -ɪŋ **-ed** -d
alphabetization, -isa- ˌæl.fə.bet.aɪ'zeɪ.ʃᵊn ⓤⓢ -bet̬.ɪ'-
alphabetiz|e, -is|e 'æl.fə.bet.aɪz, -bə.taɪz, -bɪ- ⓤⓢ -bə.taɪz **-es** -ɪz **-ing** -ɪŋ **-ed** -d

Alveolar

Alveolar sounds are made with a place of articulation behind the upper front teeth, against the hard, bony ridge called the alveolar ridge; the skin covering it is corrugated with transverse wrinkles.

Examples for English

The tongue comes into contact with the alveolar ridge in some of the consonants of English and many other languages; sounds such as [t], [d], [s], [z], [n], [l] are consonants with alveolar place of articulation. Some examples for English follow, e.g.:

tip	/tɪp/	zip	/zɪp/
dip	/dɪp/	nip	/nɪp/
sip	/sɪp/	lip	/lɪp/

Although /r/ is described as alveolar or post-alveolar in British English, in US English it is in fact nearer to RETROFLEX, e.g.:

rip /rɪp/ [ɹɪʔp] (US) [ɻɪʔp]

Alpha Centauri ˌæl.fə.sen'tɔː.ri, -ken'-, -'taʊ- (US) -sen'tɔːr.i
Alphaeus æl'fiː.əs
alphanumeric ˌæl.fə.njuː'mer.ɪk (US) -nuː'-, -njuː'- **-al** -ᵊl **-ally** -ᵊl.i, -li *stress shift:* ˌalphanumeric 'code
Alphonse æl'fɒnts, '-- (US) æl'fɑːnts, -'fɔːnts, '--
Alphonso æl'fɒnt.səʊ, -'fɒn.zəʊ (US) -'fɑːnt.soʊ, -'fɑːn.zoʊ
alpine (A) 'æl.paɪn
alpin|ism 'æl.pɪ.n|ɪ.zᵊm **-ist/s** -ɪst/s
Alps ælps
Al-Qaida, Al Qaeda ˌæl'kaɪ.də; ˌæl.kɑː'iː.də (US) ˌæl'keɪ.də, ˌɑːl-; ˌɑːl'kaɪ.ə.də
already ɔːl'red.i (US) ɔːl-, ɑːl- *stress shift:* ˌalready 'here
Alresford 'ɔːlz.fəd, 'ɔːls-, 'ɑːlz-, 'ɑːls- (US) -fɚd
alright ɔːl'raɪt (US) ɔːl-, ɑːl-
Alsace æl'sæs, -'zæs
Alsace-Lorraine ælˌsæs.lɒr'eɪn, -'zæs (US) -loʊ'reɪn, -ˌseɪs-, -lə'-
Alsager 'ɔːl.sɪ.dʒəʳ, -sə.dʒəʳ, ɔːl'seɪ.dʒəʳ (US) 'ɔːl.sə.dʒɚ, 'ɑːl-, ɔːl'seɪ.dʒɚ, ɑːl-
Alsatia æl'seɪ.ʃə, '-ʃi.ə
alsatian (A) æl'seɪ.ʃᵊn **-s** -z
also 'ɔːl.səʊ (US) 'ɔːl.soʊ, 'ɑːl-
Alsop(p) 'ɔːl.sɒp, 'ɒl-, -səp (US) 'ɔːl.sɑːp, 'ɑːl-
also-ran 'ɔːl.səʊˌræn (US) 'ɔːl.soʊ.ræn, 'ɑːl- **-s** -z
Alston 'ɔːl.stən, 'ɒl- (US) 'ɔːl-, 'ɑːl-
alt ælt, ɔːlt (US) ælt, ɑːlt
Altai ɑːl'taɪ
Altaic æl'teɪ.ɪk
Altair 'æl.teəʳ, -'- (US) æl'ter, -'tær, -'taɪr
altar 'ɔːl.təʳ, 'ɒl- (US) 'ɔːl.t̬ɚ, 'ɑːl- **-s** -z **'altar ˌboy; 'altar ˌrail**
altarpiec|e 'ɔːl.tə.piːs, 'ɒl- (US) 'ɔːl.t̬ɚ-, 'ɑːl- **-es** -ɪz
AltaVista® ˌæl.tə'vɪs.tə, ˌɔːl- (US) ˌɑːl-, ˌæl-
altazimuth æl'tæz.ɪ.məθ **-s** -s
Altdorf 'ælt.dɔːf (US) 'ɑːlt.dɔːrf, 'ælt-
alter 'ɔːl.təʳ, 'ɒl- (US) 'ɔːl.t̬ɚ, 'ɑːl- **-s** -z **-ing** -ɪŋ **-ed** -d **-able** -ə.bl̩ **-ant/s** -ᵊnt/s
alteration ˌɔːl.tᵊr'eɪ.ʃᵊn, ˌɒl- (US) ˌɔːl.t̬ə'reɪ-, ˌɑːl- **-s** -z
alterative 'ɔːl.tᵊr.ə.tɪv, 'ɒl-, -tᵊr.eɪ- (US) 'ɔːl.t̬ə.reɪ.t̬ɪv, 'ɑːl-, -t̬ɚ.ə-
alter|cate 'ɔːl.tə|.keɪt, 'ɒl- (US) 'ɔːl.t̬ɚ-, 'ɑːl- **-cates** -keɪts **-cating** -keɪ.tɪŋ (US) -keɪ.t̬ɪŋ **-cated** -keɪ.tɪd (US) -keɪ.t̬ɪd
altercation ˌɔːl.tə'keɪ.ʃᵊn, ˌɒl- (US) ˌɔːl.t̬ɚ'-, ˌɑːl- **-s** -z
alter ego ˌɔːl.təʳ'iː.gəʊ, ˌɒl-, ˌæl-, -'eg.əʊ (US) ˌɔːl.t̬ɚ'iː.goʊ, ˌɑːl- **-s** -z
alternanc|e ɔːl'tɜː.nənts, 'ɒl- (US) 'ɔːl.tɝː-, 'ɑːl- **-es** -ɪz
alternant ɔːl'tɜː.nənt, ɒl- (US) 'ɔːl.tɝː-, 'ɑːl- **-s** -s
alternate (*adj.*) ɔːl'tɜː.nət, ɒl-, -nɪt (US) ɔːl'tɝː-, ɑːl-; 'ɔːl.t̬ɚ-, 'ɑːl- **-ly** -li **-ness** -nəs, -nɪs
alter|nate (*v.*) 'ɔːl.tə|.neɪt, 'ɒl- (US) 'ɔːl.t̬ɚ-, 'ɑːl- **-nates** -neɪts **-nating** -neɪ.tɪŋ (US) -neɪ.t̬ɪŋ **-nated** -neɪ.tɪd (US) -neɪ.t̬ɪd
alternation ˌɔːl.tə'neɪ.ʃᵊn, ˌɒl- (US) ˌɔːl.t̬ɚ'-, ˌɑːl- **-s** -z
alternative ɔːl'tɜː.nə.tɪv, ɒl- (US) ɔːl'tɝː.nə.t̬ɪv, ɑːl- **-s** -z **-ly** -li **alˌternative 'medicine**
alternator 'ɔːl.tə.neɪ.təʳ (US) 'ɔːl.tɚ.neɪ.t̬ɚ, 'ɑːl-, 'æl- **-s** -z
Althea 'æl.θi.ə (US) æl'θiː-
Althorp 'ɔːl.θɔːp, 'ɒl-, -trəp (US) 'ɔːl.θɔːrp, 'ɑːl-
Note: Viscount Althorp pronounces /'ɔːl.trəp/.
although ɔːl'ðəʊ (US) ɔːl'ðoʊ, ɑːl-
Althusser ˌæl.tʊ'seə (US) ˌɑːl.tuː'ser
altimeter 'æl.tɪ.miː.təʳ, 'ɔːl-, 'ɒl-; æl'tɪm.ɪ- (US) æl'tɪm.ə.t̬ɚ, 'æl.t̬ə.miː- **-s** -z
altimetry æl'tɪm.ɪ.tri, ɔːl-, ɒl-, '-ə- (US) æl'tɪm.ə-
altissimo æl'tɪs.ɪ.məʊ (US) -moʊ, ɑːl-
altitude 'æl.tɪ.tjuːd, 'ɔːl-, 'ɒl-, -tʃuːd (US) 'æl.tə.tuːd, -tjuːd **-s** -z
Altman 'ɔːlt.mən (US) 'ɔːlt-, 'ɑːlt-
alto 'æl.təʊ, 'ɒl- (US) 'æl.toʊ **-s** -z
altogether ˌɔːl.tə'geð.əʳ (US) -ɚ, ˌɑːl- *stress shift:* ˌaltogether 'marvellous
Alton 'ɔːl.tᵊn, 'ɒl- (US) 'ɔːl-, 'ɑːl-
Altona 'æl.təʊ.nə (US) ɑːl'toʊ-
Altoona æl'təʊ.nə (US) -'tuː-
alto-relievo, alto-rilievo ˌæl.təʊ.rɪ'liː.vəʊ (US) -toʊ.rə'liː.voʊ, ˌɑːl-
Altrincham 'ɔːl.trɪŋ.əm, 'ɒl- (US) 'ɔːl-, 'ɑːl-
altru|ism 'æl.tru|.ɪ.zᵊm **-ist/s** -ɪst/s
altruistic ˌæl.tru'ɪs.tɪk **-ally** -ᵊl.i, -li *stress shift:* ˌaltruistic 'action
alum (A) 'æl.əm **-s** -z
alumina ə'luː.mɪ.nə, æl'uː-, -'ljuː- (US) ə'luː-
aluminium ˌæl.jə'mɪn.i.əm, -jʊ'-, -ə-, '-jəm *stress shift:* ˌaluminium 'foil
aluminiz|e, -is|e ə'ljuː.mɪ.naɪz, ə'luː- (US) -'luː- **-es** -ɪz **-ing** -ɪŋ **-ed** -d
aluminous ə'luː.mɪ.nəs, -'ljuː- (US) -'luː-
aluminum ə'luː.mɪ.nəm, -'ljuː- (US) -'luː-
alumn|a ə'lʌm.n|ə **-ae** -iː
alumn|us ə'lʌm.n|əs **-i** -aɪ
Alun 'æl.ɪn
Alva 'æl.və
Alvar 'æl.vɑːʳ, -vəʳ (US) -vɑːr, -vɚ
Alvarez æl'vɑː.rez; 'æl.və- (US) 'æl.və.rez; 'ɑːl.vɑː.reθ
Alvary 'æl.vᵊr.i
alveolar ˌæl.vi'əʊ.ləʳ; æl'viː.ə-; 'æl.vi- (US) æl'viː.ə.lɚ **-s** -z
alveolate æl'viː.ə.lət, -lɪt, -leɪt (US) -lɪt
alveole 'æl.vi.əʊl (US) -oʊl **-s** -z
alveol|us ˌæl.vi'əʊ.l|əs; æl'viː.ə-; 'æl.vi.ə- (US) æl'viː.ə- **-i** -aɪ, -iː
Alverstone 'ɔːl.və.stᵊn, 'ɒl- (US) 'ɔːl.vɚ-, 'ɑːl-
Alvescot 'æl.vɪ.skɒt, -skət *locally:* 'ɔːl.skət (US) -skɑːt

Alveston 'æl.vɪ.stən
Alvey 'æl.vi
Alvin 'æl.vɪn
alway 'ɔːl.weɪ, 'ɑːl-
always 'ɔːl.weɪz, -wəz, -wɪz ⓤⓢ 'ɔːl-, 'ɑːl-
Alwyn 'æl.wɪn, 'ɔːl-
Alyn 'æl.ɪn, -ən
Alyson 'æl.ɪ.sən
Alyssa æl'ɪs.ə
alyssum 'æl.ɪ.səm
Alzheimer 'ælts.haɪ.məʳ ⓤⓢ 'ɑːlts.haɪ.mɚ, 'ælts- **'Alzheimer's di,sease**
a.m., AM ,eɪ'em
am *strong form:* æm *weak forms:* əm, m
Note: Weak form word. The strong form /æm/ is used for emphasis (e.g. 'I **am** going to leave.'), for contrast (e.g. 'I know what I **am** and am **not** capable of.') and in final position (e.g. 'That's who I am.'). The weak form is usually /əm/ (e.g. 'How am I going to pay?' /,haʊ.əm.aɪ,gəʊ.ɪŋ.tə'peɪ ⓤⓢ -goʊ.ɪŋ.t̬ə'-/), but after 'I' /aɪ/ it is frequently shortened to /m/ (e.g. 'I am (I'm) here' /aɪm'hɪəʳ ⓤⓢ aɪm'hɪr/).
AMA ,eɪ.em'eɪ
Amabel 'æm.ə.bel
Amadeus ,æm.ə'deɪ.əs ⓤⓢ ,ɑː.mə'deɪ.ʊs, -əs
Amadis 'æm.ə.dɪs
amadou 'æm.ə.duː
amah 'ɑː.mə, 'æm.ɑː ⓤⓢ 'ɑː.mɑː **-s** -z
Amahl 'æm.ɑːl ⓤⓢ ə'mɑːl
amain ə'meɪn
Amalekite ə'mæl.ə.kaɪt, '-ɪ- ⓤⓢ ,æm.ə'lek.aɪt; ə'mæl.ə.kaɪt **-s** -s
Amalfi ə'mæl.fi, æm'æl- ⓤⓢ ə'mæl-, -'mɑːl
amalgam ə'mæl.gəm **-s** -z
amalga|mate ə'mæl.gəl.meɪt **-mates** -meɪts **-mating** -meɪ.tɪŋ ⓤⓢ -meɪ.t̬ɪŋ **-mated** -meɪ.tɪd ⓤⓢ -meɪ.t̬ɪd
amalgamation ə,mæl.gə'meɪ.ʃən **-s** -z
amalgamative ə'mæl.gə.mə.tɪv ⓤⓢ -t̬ɪv
Amalia ə'mɑː.li.ə, æm'ɑː- ⓤⓢ ə'meɪl.jə
Amalth(a)ea ,æm.əl'θiː.ə
Aman 'æm.ən ⓤⓢ 'eɪ.mən
Amanda ə'mæn.də
amandine ə'mæn.daɪn; ,ɑː.mən'diːn ⓤⓢ ,ɑː.mən'diːn, ,æm.ən'-
Amantia ə'mæn.ʃi.ə
amanuens|is ə,mæn.ju'ent.s|ɪs **-es** -iːz
Amara ə'mɑː.rə
amaranth 'æm.ər.æntθ ⓤⓢ -ə.ræntθ **-s** -s
amaranthine ,æm.ər'ænt.θaɪn ⓤⓢ -ə'rænt.θɪn, -θiːn, -θaɪn
amaretto (A) ,æm.ər'et.əʊ ⓤⓢ -ə'ret̬.oʊ
Amarillo ,æm.ər'ɪl.əʊ ⓤⓢ -ə'rɪl.oʊ
amaryllis (A) ,æm.ər'ɪl.ɪs ⓤⓢ -ə'rɪl- **-es** -ɪz
Amasis ə'meɪ.sɪs
amass ə'mæs **-es** -ɪz **-ing** -ɪŋ **-ed** -t
amateur 'æm.ə.təʳ, -tɜːʳ, -tjʊəʳ, -tjəʳ, -tʃəʳ; ,æm.ə'tɜːʳ ⓤⓢ 'æm.ə.tʃɚ, -tʃʊr, -t̬ɚ, -tɝː **-s** -z **,amateur dra'matics**
Note: The final British form is not used attributively.
amateurish 'æm.ə.tər.ɪʃ, -tɜː.rɪʃ, -tjʊə-, -tjɔː-, -tjər.ɪʃ, -tʃər- ⓤⓢ ,æm.ə'tɝː.ɪʃ, -'tʃʊr-, -'tjʊr- **-ly** -li **-ness** -nəs, -nɪs
amateurism 'æm.ə.tər.ɪ.zəm, -tɜː.rɪ-, -tjʊə-, -tjɔː-, -tjər.ɪ-, -tʃər- ⓤⓢ 'æm.ə.tʃɚ.ɪ-, -tʃʊ.rɪ-, -t̬ɚ.ɪ-
Amati ə'mɑː.ti, æm'ɑː- ⓤⓢ -t̬i **-s** -z
amatol 'æm.ə.tɒl ⓤⓢ -tɑːl
amatory 'æm.ə.tər.i ⓤⓢ -tɔːr-
amaurosis ,æm.ɔː'rəʊ.sɪs ⓤⓢ -'roʊ-
amaz|e ə'meɪz **-es** -ɪz **-ed** -d **-edly** -ɪd.li **-edness** -ɪd.nəs, -nɪs **-ement/s** -mənt/s
amazing ə'meɪ.zɪŋ **-ly** -li
amazon (A) 'æm.ə.zən ⓤⓢ -zɑːn **-s** -z
Amazonia ,æm.ə'zəʊ.ni.ə ⓤⓢ -'zoʊ-
amazonian (A) ,æm.ə'zəʊ.ni.ən ⓤⓢ -'zoʊ-
amazonite 'æm.ə.zə.naɪt **-s** -s
ambassador æm'bæs.ə.dəʳ ⓤⓢ -dɚ **-s** -z
ambassadorial æm,bæs.ə'dɔː.ri.əl, ,æm.bæs-
ambassadress æm'bæs.ə.drəs, -drɪs, -dres ⓤⓢ -drəs **-es** -ɪz
Ambato ɑːm'bɑː.təʊ, æm- ⓤⓢ -toʊ
amber (A) 'æm.bəʳ ⓤⓢ -bɚ
ambergris 'æm.bə.griːs, -bɚ.grɪs
amberjack 'æm.bə.dʒæk ⓤⓢ -bɚ- **-s** -s
ambi- æm.bɪ-, æm.bi-; æm'bi-
Note: Prefix. Normally either takes primary or secondary stress on the first syllable, e.g. **ambient** /'æm.bi.ənt/, **ambidextrous** /,æm.bɪ'dek.strəs/, or primary stress on the second syllable, e.g. **ambivalence** /æm'bɪv.əl.ənts/.
ambianc|e 'æm.bi.ənts, -ɑ̃ːnts ⓤⓢ 'æm.bi.ənts, ,ɑːm.bi'ɑːnts **-es** -ɪz
ambidexter ,æm.bɪ'dek.stəʳ ⓤⓢ -stɚ **-s** -z
ambidexterity ,æm.bɪ.dek'ster.ə.ti, -ɪ.ti ⓤⓢ -ə.t̬i
ambidextrous ,æm.bɪ'dek.strəs
ambienc|e 'æm.bi.ənts, -ɑ̃ːnts ⓤⓢ 'æm.bi.ənts, ,ɑːm.bi'ɑːnts **-es** -ɪz
ambient 'æm.bi.ənt
ambiguit|y ,æm.bɪ'gjuː.ə.t|i, -ɪ.t|i ⓤⓢ -bə'gjuː.ə.t̬|i **-ies** -iz
ambiguous æm'bɪg.ju.əs **-ly** -li **-ness** -nəs, -nɪs
Ambiorix æm'baɪ.ə.rɪks ⓤⓢ -ɚ.ɪks, -oʊ.rɪks
ambit 'æm.bɪt **-s** -s
ambition æm'bɪʃ.ən **-s** -z
ambitious æm'bɪʃ.əs **-ly** -li **-ness** -nəs, -nɪs
ambivalen|ce æm'bɪv.əl.ən|ts **-t/ly** -t/li
ambl|e (A) 'æm.bl̩ **-es** -z **-ing** -ɪŋ, 'æm.blɪŋ **-ed** -d **-er/s** -əʳ/z, '-bləʳ/z ⓤⓢ '-bl̩.ɚ/z, '-blɚ/z
Ambler 'æm.bləʳ, '-bl̩.əʳ ⓤⓢ '-blɚ, '-bl̩.ɚ
Ambleside 'æm.bl̩.saɪd
amboyna (A) æm'bɔɪ.nə
Ambree 'æm.bri
Ambridge 'æm.brɪdʒ
Ambrose 'æm.brəʊz, -brəʊs ⓤⓢ -broʊz
ambrosi|a æm'brəʊ.zi|.ə, -ʒ|ə ⓤⓢ -'broʊ.ʒ|ə **-al** -əl **-ally** -əl.i **-an** -ən
Ambrosius æm'brəʊ.zi.əs, -ʒəs ⓤⓢ -'broʊ.ʒəs
ambsace 'eɪm.zeɪs, 'æm-
ambulance 'æm.bjə.lənts, -bjʊ.lənts, -bə- **-s** -ɪz **-man** -mæn **-men** -men **-woman** -,wʊm.ən **-women** -,wɪm.ɪn
ambulance-chaser 'æm.bjə.lənts,tʃeɪ.səʳ, -bjʊ- ⓤⓢ -sɚ **-s** -z
ambulant 'æm.bjə.lənt, -bjʊ.lənt
ambu|late 'æm.bjəl.leɪt, -bjʊ- **-lates** -leɪts **-lating** -leɪ.tɪŋ ⓤⓢ -leɪ.t̬ɪŋ **-lated** -leɪ.tɪd ⓤⓢ -leɪ.t̬ɪd
ambulation ,æm.bjə'leɪ.ʃən, -bjʊ'- **-s** -z
ambulator|y ,æm.bjə'leɪ.tər|.i, -bjʊ-; 'æm.bjə.lə-, -bjʊ- ⓤⓢ 'æm.bjə.lə.tɔːr-, -bjʊ- **-ies** -iz
ambuscad|e ,æm.bə'skeɪd **-es** -z **-ing** -ɪŋ **-ed** -ɪd
ambush 'æm.bʊʃ **-es** -ɪz **-ing** -ɪŋ **-ed** -t
ameb|a ə'miː.b|ə **-as** -əz **-ae** -iː **-ic** -ɪk
Amelia ə'miː.li.ə ⓤⓢ -'miːl.jə, -'miː.li.ə
amelior|ate ə'miː.li.ər|.eɪt ⓤⓢ -'miː.li.ə.r|eɪt, -'miːl.jə- **-ates** -eɪts **-ating** -eɪ.tɪŋ ⓤⓢ -eɪ.t̬ɪŋ **-ated** -eɪ.tɪd ⓤⓢ -eɪ.t̬ɪd
amelioration ə,miː.li.ər'eɪ.ʃən ⓤⓢ -,miː.li.ə'reɪ-, -,miːl.jə'- **-s** -z
ameliorative ə'miː.li.ər.ə.tɪv, -eɪ- ⓤⓢ -'miː.li.ə.reɪ.t̬ɪv, -'miːl.jə-
amen ,ɑː'men, ,eɪ- **-s** -z
amenability ə,miː.nə'bɪl.ə.ti, -ɪ.ti ⓤⓢ -ə.t̬i
amenab|le ə'miː.nə.bl̩ ⓤⓢ -'miː.nə-, -'men.ə- **-ly** -li **-leness** -l̩.nəs, -nɪs
Amen Corner ,eɪ.men'kɔː.nəʳ ⓤⓢ -'kɔr.nɚ
amend ə'mend **-s** -z **-ing** -ɪŋ **-ed** -ɪd
amendatory ə'men.də.tər.i ⓤⓢ -tɔː.ri
amendment ə'mend.mənt **-s** -s
amenit|y ə'miː.nə.t|i, -'men.ə-, -ɪ.t|i ⓤⓢ ə'men.ə.t̬|i **-ies** -iz

amenorrh(o)ea ˌeɪ.men.əˈriː.ə, ˌæm.en- (US) ˌeɪ.men-
Amerasian ˌæm.əˈreɪ.ʃᵊn, -ʒᵊn (US) -əˈreɪ.ʒᵊn, -ʃᵊn **-s** -z
amerc|e əˈmɜːs (US) -ˈmɝːs **-es** -ɪz **-ing** -ɪŋ **-ed** -t **-ement/s** -mənt/s
America əˈmer.ɪ.kə **-s** -z
American əˈmer.ɪ.kən **-s** -z **-ist/s** -ɪst/s **AˌmericanEx'press®**
Americana əˌmer.ɪˈkɑː.nə (US) -ˈkæn.ə, -ˈkɑː.nə
Americanese əˌmer.ɪ.kəˈniːz (US) -ˈniːz, -ˈniːs
american|ism (A) əˈmer.ɪ.kə.n|ɪ.zᵊm **-isms** -ɪ.zᵊmz **-ist/s** -ɪst/s
americanization, -isa- (A) əˌmer.ɪ.kə.naɪˈzeɪ.ʃᵊn, -nɪˈ- (US) -nɪˈ-
americaniz|e, -is|e (A) əˈmer.ɪ.kə.naɪz **-es** -ɪz **-ing** -ɪŋ **-ed** -d
americium ˌæm.əˈrɪs.i.əm, -ˈrɪʃ-
Amerindian ˌæm.əˈrɪn.di.ən **-s** -z
Amersham ˈæm.ə.ʃᵊm (US) -ɚ-
Amery ˈeɪ.mᵊr.i
Ames eɪmz
Amesbury ˈeɪmz.bᵊr.i (US) -ber.i
Ameslan ˈæm.ɪ.slæn
amethyst ˈæm.ə.θɪst, -ɪ.θɪst **-s** -s
amethystine ˌæm.əˈθɪs.taɪn, -ɪˈ- (US) -tᵊn, -taɪn, -tɪn, -tiːn
Amex ˈæm.eks
AMF ˌeɪ.emˈef
Amharic æmˈhær.ɪk (US) -ˈhær-, -ˈhɑːr-
Amherst ˈæm.əst, -hɜːst (US) -ɚst, -hɝːst
amiability ˌeɪ.mi.əˈbɪl.ə.ti, -ɪ.ti (US) -ə.t̬i
amiab|le ˈeɪ.mi.ə.b|l̩ **-ly** -li **-leness** -l̩.nəs, -nɪs
amicability ˌæm.ɪ.kəˈbɪl.ə.ti, -ɪ.ti (US) -ə.t̬i
amicab|le ˈæm.ɪ.kə.b|l̩, əˈmɪk- **-ly** -li **-leness** -l̩.nəs, -nɪs
amic|e ˈæm.ɪs **-es** -ɪz
Amice ˈeɪ.mɪs
amid əˈmɪd
amide ˈæm.aɪd, ˈeɪ.maɪd (US) ˈæm.aɪd, -əd **-s** -z
amidships əˈmɪd.ʃɪps
amidst əˈmɪdst, -ˈmɪtst
Amiel ˈæm.i.əl, ˈeɪ.mi-
Amiens *French city:* ˈæm.jæ̃, -i.ɑ̃ː, -i.ɒŋ, -i.ənz *Shakespearean character:* ˈæm.i.ənz *street in Dublin:* ˈeɪ.mi.ənz
Amies ˈeɪ.miz
amiga (A®) əˈmiː.gə (US) əˈmiː.gə, ɑː- **-s** -z
amigo əˈmiː.gəʊ (US) -goʊ, ɑː- **-s** -z
Amin ɑːˈmiːn, æmˈiːn
amino əˈmiː.nəʊ, æmˈiː- (US) -noʊ **aˌmino ˈacid, aˈmino ˌacid**
amir əˈmɪəʳ (US) -ˈmɪr **-s** -z
Amis ˈeɪ.mɪs
Amish ˈɑː.mɪʃ, ˈæm.ɪʃ, ˈeɪ.mɪʃ (US) ˈɑːm-, ˈæm-
amiss əˈmɪs
amitosis ˌæm.ɪˈtəʊ.sɪs (US) -ˈtoʊ-
amitotic ˌæm.ɪˈtəʊ.tɪk (US) -ˈtoʊ-
amity ˈæm.ɪ.ti, -ə.ti (US) -ə.t̬i
Amlwch ˈæm.lʊk, -lʊx
Amman əˈmɑːn (US) ɑːˈmɑːn
Ammanford ˈæm.ən.fəd (US) -fɚd
ammeter ˈæm.iː.təʳ, -ɪ.təʳ (US) -t̬ɚ **-s** -z
ammo ˈæm.əʊ (US) -oʊ
Ammon ˈæm.ən, -ɒn (US) -ən
ammonia əˈməʊ.ni.ə (US) -ˈmoʊ.njə
ammoniac əˈməʊ.ni.æk (US) -ˈmoʊ-
ammoniacal ˌæm.əʊˈnaɪ.ə.kᵊl, -əˈ-
ammoniated əˈməʊ.ni.eɪ.tɪd (US) -ˈmoʊ.ni.eɪ.t̬ɪd
ammonification əˌməʊ.nɪ.fɪˈkeɪ.ʃᵊn, -nə- (US) -mɑː-, -moʊ-
ammonif|y əˈməʊ.nɪ|.faɪ, -nə- (US) -ˈmɑː-, -ˈmoʊ- **-ies** -aɪz **-ying** -aɪ.ɪŋ **-ied** -aɪd **-ier/s** -aɪ.əʳ/z (US) -aɪ.ɚ/z
ammonite (A) ˈæm.ə.naɪt **-s** -s
ammonium əˈməʊ.ni.əm (US) -ˈmoʊ-
Ammons ˈæm.ənz
ammunition ˌæm.jəˈnɪʃ.ᵊn, -jʊˈ- (US) -jəˈ-
amnesia æmˈniː.zi.ə, -ʒə (US) -ʒə
amnesiac æmˈniː.zi.æk (US) -ʒi- **-s** -s
amnesic æmˈniː.zɪk, -sɪk **-s** -s
amnest|y ˈæm.nə.st|i, -nɪ- **-ies** -iz **ˌAmnesty Interˈnational**
amniocentesis ˌæm.ni.əʊ.senˈtiː.sɪs, -sənˈ- (US) -oʊ-
amniotic ˌæm.niˈɒt.ɪk (US) -ˈɑː.t̬ɪk *stress shift:* ˌamniotic ˈmembrane
Amoco® ˈæm.ə.kəʊ; əˈməʊ- (US) ˈæm.ə-
amoeb|a əˈmiː.b|ə **-ae** -iː **-as** -əz **-ic** -ɪk
amoebiasis ˌæm.iːˈbaɪə.sɪs, -ɪˈ-
amok əˈmɒk, -ˈmʌk (US) -ˈmʌk, -ˈmɑːk
Amon ˈɑː.mən
among əˈmʌŋ
amongst əˈmʌŋst
Amon-Ra ˌɑː.mənˈrɑː
amontillado (A) əˌmɒn.tiˈjɑː.dəʊ, -tɪˈlɑː- (US) -ˌmɑːn.təˈlɑː.doʊ **-s** -z
amoral ˌeɪˈmɒr.əl, æmˈɒr- (US) ˌeɪˈmɔːr- **-ly** -li
Amoretti ˌæm.əˈret.i (US) -ˈret̬-, ˌɑː.məˈ-
amorett|o ˌæm.əˈret|.əʊ (US) -ˈret̬|.oʊ, ˌɑː.məˈ- **-i** -i
amorist ˈæm.ᵊr.ɪst **-s** -s
Amorite ˈæm.ᵊr.aɪt (US) -ə.raɪt **-s** -s
amorous ˈæm.ᵊr.əs **-ly** -li **-ness** -nəs, -nɪs
amorph|ism əˈmɔː.f|ɪ.zᵊm (US) -ˈmɔːr- **-ous** -əs
amortizable, -isa- əˈmɔː.taɪ.zə.bl̩ (US) ˌæm.ɔːrˈtaɪ-
amortization, -isa- əˌmɔː.tɪˈzeɪ.ʃᵊn, -təˈ- (US) æmˌɔːr.t̬əˈ- **-s** -z
amortiz|e, -is|e əˈmɔː.taɪz (US) æmˈɔːr- **-es** -ɪz **-ing** -ɪŋ **-ed** -d
amortizement, -ise- əˈmɔː.tɪz.mənt (US) ˈæm.ɚˈtaɪz.mənt, əˌmɔːr.t̬ɪz.mənt
Amory ˈeɪ.mᵊr.i
Amos ˈeɪ.mɒs (US) -məs
a|mount ə|ˈmaʊnt **-mounts** -ˈmaʊnts **-mounting** -ˈmaʊn.tɪŋ (US) -ˈmaʊn.t̬ɪŋ **-mounted** -ˈmaʊn.tɪd (US) -ˈmaʊn.t̬ɪd
amour əˈmʊəʳ, æmˈʊəʳ, əˈmɔːʳ, æmˈɔːʳ (US) əˈmʊr, æmˈʊr **-s** -z
amour-propre ˌæm.ʊəˈprɒp.rə (US) ˌɑː.mʊrˈproʊ.prə, ˌæm.ʊrˈ-
Amoy əˈmɔɪ, æmˈɔɪ
amp æmp **-s** -s
ampelopsis ˌæm.pɪˈlɒp.sɪs (US) -ˈlɑːp-
amperage ˈæm.pᵊr.ɪdʒ, -per-, -peə.rɪdʒ (US) ˈæm.prɪdʒ, -pɪ.rɪdʒ
ampère, ampere (A) ˈæm.peəʳ (US) -pɪr, -per **-s** -z
ampersand ˈæm.pə.sænd (US) -pɚ- **-s** -z
amphetamine æmˈfet.ə.miːn, -mɪn (US) -fet̬- **-s** -z
amphi- æmp.fɪ-; æmˈfɪ- (US) æmp.fɪ-, -fə-; æmˈfɪ-
Note: Prefix. Either takes primary or secondary stress on the first syllable, e.g. **amphora** /ˈæmp.fᵊr.ə/, **amphibiotic** /ˌæmp.fɪ.baɪˈɒt.ɪk (US) -ˈɑː.t̬ɪk/, or primary stress on the second syllable, e.g. **amphibian** /æmˈfɪb.i.ən/.
amphibi|a æmˈfɪb.i|ə **-ous** -əs
amphibian æmˈfɪb.i.ən **-s** -z
amphibiotic ˌæmp.fɪ.baɪˈɒt.ɪk (US) -ˈɑː.t̬ɪk
amphibole ˈæmp.fɪ.bəʊl (US) -boʊl
amphibology ˌæmp.fɪˈbɒl.ə.dʒi (US) -ˈbɑː.lə-
amphiboly æmˈfɪb.ə.l|i **-ies** -iz
amphibrach ˈæmp.fɪ.bræk **-s** -s
Amphictyon æmˈfɪk.ti.ən **-s** -z
amphictyonic æmˌfɪk.tiˈɒn.ɪk (US) -ˈɑː.nɪk
amphimacer æmˈfɪm.ɪ.səʳ (US) -ə.sɚ
Amphion æmˈfaɪən
Amphipolis æmˈfɪp.ə.lɪs
amphitheatre, amphitheater ˈæmp.fɪˌθɪə.təʳ (US) -fəˌθiː.ə.t̬ɚ **-s** -z
Amphitrite ˌæmp.fɪˈtraɪ.ti (US) -t̬i
Amphitryon æmˈfɪt.ri.ən
amphor|a ˈæmp.fᵊr|.ə **-ae** -iː **-as** -əz
amphoric æmˈfɒr.ɪk (US) -ˈfɔːr-
amphoteric ˌæmp.fəʊˈter.ɪk (US) -fəˈ-
ampicillin ˌæm.pɪˈsɪl.ɪn (US) -pəˈ-
amp|le ˈæm.p|l̩ **-ler** -ləʳ (US) -lɚ **-lest** -ləst, -lɪst **-ly** -li **-leness** -l̩.nəs, -nɪs
Ampleforth ˈæm.pl̩.fɔːθ, -fəθ
amplification ˌæm.plɪ.fɪˈkeɪ.ʃᵊn, -plə- **-s** -z
amplificatory ˌæm.plɪ.fɪˈkeɪ.tᵊr.i, -plə-, ˈ-tri (US) æmˈplɪf.ɪ.kə.tɔːr.i
amplifier ˈæm.plɪ.faɪ.əʳ (US) -ɚ **-s** -z

amplif|y ˈæm.plɪ.f|aɪ **-ies** -aɪz **-ying** -aɪ.ɪŋ **-ied** -aɪd
amplitude ˈæm.plɪ.tjuːd, -tʃuːd (US) -tuːd, -tjuːd **-s** -z
ampoule ˈæm.puːl **-s** -z
Amps æmps
Ampthill ˈæm*pt*.*h*ɪl
ampule ˈæm.pjuːl (US) -pjuːl, -puːl **-s** -z
ampull|a æmˈpʊl|.ə **-ae** -iː
ampu|tate ˈæm.pjə|.teɪt, ˈæm.pjʊ- **-tates** -teɪts **-tating** -teɪ.tɪŋ (US) -teɪ.t̬ɪŋ **-tated** -teɪ.tɪd (US) -teɪ.t̬ɪd
amputation ˌæm.pjəˈteɪ.ʃᵊn, ˌæm.pjʊˈ- **-s** -z
amputee ˌæm.pjəˈtiː, -pjʊˈ- **-s** -z
Amram ˈæm.ræm
Amritsar æmˈrɪt.səʳ, -sɑːʳ (US) -sɚ
Amsterdam ˌæm*p*.stəˈdæm, ˈ--ˌ- (US) ˈæm*p*.stɚ.dæm
Note: In British English, the latter form is used when attributive.
Amstrad® ˈæm.stræd
Amtrak® ˈæm.træk
amuck əˈmʌk
amulet ˈæm.jʊ.lət, -jə-, -let, -lɪt **-s** -s
Amundsen ˈɑː.mənd.sᵊn, -mʊnd-
Amur əˈmʊəʳ, æmˈʊəʳ, ˈæm.ʊəʳ (US) ɑːˈmʊr
amus|e əˈmjuːz **-es** -ɪz **-ing/ly** -ɪŋ/li **-ingness** -ɪŋ.nəs, -nɪs **-ed** -d
amusement əˈmjuːz.mənt **-s** -s **aˈmusement arˌcade**; **aˈmusement ˌpark**
Amway® ˈæm.weɪ
Amy ˈeɪ.mi
Amyas ˈeɪ.mi.əs
amygdalin əˈmɪg.də.lɪn, æmˈɪg-
amygdaloid əˈmɪg.də.lɔɪd
amyl ˈæm.ɪl, -əl **-s** -z
amylase ˈæm.ɪ.leɪz, ˈ-ə-, -leɪs
amylic æmˈɪl.ɪk, əˈmɪl-
amylopsin ˌæm.ɪˈlɒp.sɪn (US) -ˈlɑːp-
amytal ˈæm.ɪ.tæl (US) -tɑːl
an- æn-, ən-
Note: Prefix. When used as a negative prefix, **an-** is normally /æn-/, e.g. **anaerobic** /ˌæn.əˈrəʊ.bɪk (US) -erˈoʊ-/, but in some items it may be reduced, e.g. **anomaly** /əˈnɒm.ə.li (US) -ˈnɑː.mə-/. Otherwise, it contains /æ/ when stressed, e.g. **annular** /ˈænj.ə.ləʳ (US) -lɚ/, and /ə/ when unstressed, e.g. **annul** /əˈnʌl/.
an *strong form:* æn *weak form:* ᵊn
Note: Weak form word. The strong form /æn/ is used mainly for contrast (e.g. 'This is **an** ideal, but it's not **the** ideal.'). The weak form is usually /ən/ (e.g., 'make an excuse' /ˌmeɪk.ən.ɪkˈskjuːs/); in rapid speech, and particularly after an alveolar or palatoalveolar consonant, it may be pronounced as a syllabic /n̩/ (e.g. 'find an example' /ˌfaɪnd.n̩.ɪgˈzɑːm.pl̩ (US) -ˈzæm-/).
ana- æn.ə-, əˈnæ-
Note: Prefix. Either takes primary or secondary stress on the first syllable, e.g. **anagram** /ˈæn.ə.græm/, **anatomic** /ˌæn.əˈtɒm.ɪk/, or primary stress on the second syllable, e.g. **anachronism** /əˈnæk.rə.nɪ.zᵊm/.
ana (A) ˈɑː.nə
Anabapt|ism ˌæn.əˈbæp.t|ɪ.zᵊm **-ist/s** -ɪst/s
anabas|is əˈnæb.ə.s|ɪs **-es** -iːz
anabi|osis ˌæn.ə.baɪ|ˈəʊ.sɪs (US) -ˈoʊ- **-otic** -ˈɒt.ɪk (US) -ˈɑː.t̬ɪk
anabolic ˌæn.əˈbɒl.ɪk (US) -ˈbɑː.lɪk *stress shift, see compound:* **ˌanabolic ˈsteroid**
anabolism əˈnæb.əʊ.lɪ.zᵊm (US) -ᵊl.ɪ-
anachronism əˈnæk.rə.nɪ.zᵊm **-s** -z
anachronistic əˌnæk.rəˈnɪs.tɪk **-ally** -ᵊl.i, -li
anachronous əˈnæk.rə.nəs **-ly** -li
Anacin® ˈæn.ə.sɪn
anacoluth|on ˌæn.ə.kəʊˈluː.θ|ɒn, -ˈljuː-, -θ|ᵊn (US) -kəˈluː.θ|ᵊn **-a** -ə
anaconda ˌæn.əˈkɒn.də (US) -ˈkɑːn- **-s** -z
Anacreon əˈnæk.ri.ən (US) -ɑːn, -ən
anacrus|is ˌæn.əˈkruː.s|ɪs **-es** -iːz
Anadin® ˈæn.ə.dɪn
anadiplosis ˌæn.ə.dɪˈpləʊ.sɪs (US) -ˈploʊ-
anaemia əˈniː.mi.ə
anaemic əˈniː.mɪk
anaerobe ˈæn.ə.rəʊb, ˈæn.ɪ- (US) -roʊb **-s** -z
anaerobic ˌæn.əˈrəʊ.bɪk, -eəˈ- (US) -erˈoʊ-, -əˈroʊ-
anaesthesia ˌæn.əsˈθiː.zi.ə, -ɪsˈ-, -iːsˈ-, -ʒi-, ˈ-ʒə (US) ˌæn.əsˈθiː.ʒə
anaesthesiology ˌæn.əsˌθiː.ziˈɒl.ə.dʒi, -ɪsˌ-, -iːsˌ-, -ʒiˈ- (US) -ziˈɑː.lə-
anaesthetic ˌæn.əsˈθet.ɪk, -ɪsˈ-, -iːsˈ- (US) -ˈθet̬- **-s** -s **-ally** -ᵊl.i, -li *stress shift:* ˌanaesthetic ˈmask
anaesthetist əˈniːs.θə.tɪst, ænˈiːs-, -θɪ- (US) əˈnes.θə.t̬ɪst **-s** -s
anaesthetiz|e, -is|e əˈniːs.θə.taɪz, ænˈiːs-, -θɪ- (US) əˈnes- **-es** -ɪz **-ing** -ɪŋ **-ed** -d
anaglyph ˈæn.ə.glɪf **-s** -s
anagram ˈæn.ə.græm **-s** -z
anagrammatic ˌæn.ə.grəˈmæt.ɪk (US) -ˈmæt̬- **-al** -ᵊl **-ally** -ᵊl.i
Anaheim ˈæn.ə.haɪm
Anaïs ˌæn.aɪˈiːs
anal ˈeɪ.nᵊl **-ly** -i
analects ˈæn.ə.lekts
analeptic ˌæn.əˈlep.tɪk
analgesia ˌæn.əlˈdʒiː.zi.ə, -ælˈ-, -si- (US) ˈ-ʒə
analgesic ˌæn.əlˈdʒiː.zɪk, -ælˈ-, -sɪk
analog ˈæn.ə.lɒg (US) -lɑːg, -lɔːg **-s** -z
analogic ˌæn.əˈlɒdʒ.ɪk (US) -ˈlɑː.dʒɪk **-al** -ᵊl **-ally** -ᵊl.i, -li
analogist əˈnæl.ə.dʒɪst **-s** -s
analogous əˈnæl.ə.gəs **-ly** -li **-ness** -nəs, -nɪs
analogue ˈæn.ə.lɒg (US) -lɑːg, -lɔːg **-s** -z
analog|y əˈnæl.ə.dʒ|i **-ies** -iz
analphabetic ˌæn.æl.fəˈbet.ɪk (US) -ˈbet̬- **-al** -ᵊl **-ally** -ᵊl.i, -li
anal-retentive ˌeɪ.nᵊl.rɪˈten.tɪv (US) -t̬ɪv
analysable ˌæn.ᵊlˈaɪ.zə.bl̩ (US) -əˈlaɪ-, ˈæn.ə.laɪ-
analysand əˈnæl.ɪ.sænd, ˈ-ə- **-s** -z
analys|e, -yz|e ˈæn.ᵊl.aɪz, -ə.laɪz **-es** -ɪz **-ing** -ɪŋ **-ed** -d
analys|is əˈnæl.ə.s|ɪs, -ɪ.sɪs **-es** -iːz
analyst ˈæn.ᵊl.ɪst (US) -ə.lɪst **-s** -s
analytic ˌæn.ᵊlˈɪt.ɪk (US) -əˈlɪt̬- **-s** -s **-al** -ᵊl **-ally** -ᵊl.i, -li *stress shift:* ˌanalytic ˈmind
analyzable ˌæn.ᵊlˈaɪ.zə.bl̩ (US) -əˈlaɪ-, ˈæn.ə.laɪ-
analyz|e, -ys|e ˈæn.ᵊl.aɪz, -ə.laɪz **-es** -ɪz **-ing** -ɪŋ **-ed** -d
anamorphosis ˌæn.əˈmɔː.fə.sɪs; -mɔːˈfəʊ- (US) -ˈmɔːr.fə-; -mɔːrˈfoʊ-
Anand ˈɑː.nənd
Ananias ˌæn.əˈnaɪ.əs
anap(a)est ˈæn.ə.pest, -piːst (US) -pest **-s** -s
anap(a)estic ˌæn.əˈpes.tɪk, -ˈpiː.stɪk (US) -ˈpes.tɪk
anaphor ˈæn.ə.fɔːʳ, -fəʳ (US) -fɔːr **-s** -z
anaphora əˈnæf.ᵊr.ə **-s** -z
anaphoric ˌæn.əˈfɒr.ɪk (US) -ˈfɔːr- *stress shift:* ˌanaphoric ˈreference
anaphrodisiac ˌæn.æf.rəʊˈdɪz.i.æk (US) -roʊˈ- **-s** -s
anaptyctic ˌæn.əpˈtɪk.tɪk, -æpˈ-
anaptyxis ˌæn.əpˈtɪk.sɪs, -æpˈ-
Anapurna ˌæn.əˈpɜː.nə, -ˈpʊə- (US) -ˈpɝː-, -ˈpʊr-
anarch ˈæn.ɑːk (US) -ɑːrk **-s** -s
anarchic əˈnɑː.kɪk, ænˈɑː- (US) ænˈɑːr-, əˈnɑːr- **-al** -ᵊl **-ally** -ᵊl.i, -li
anarchism ˈæn.ə.kɪ.zᵊm, -ɑː- (US) -ɚ-, -ɑːr-
anarchist ˈæn.ə.kɪst, -ɑː- (US) -ɚ-, -ɑːr- **-s** -s
anarchistic ˌæn.əˈkɪs.tɪk, -ɑːˈ- (US) -ɚˈ-, -ɑːrˈ- *stress shift:* ˌanarchistic ˈviews
anarchy ˈæn.ə.ki, -ɑː- (US) -ɚ-, -ɑːr-
Anastasia *English Christian name:* ˌæn.əˈsteɪ.zi.ə, ˈ-ʒə (US) ˈ-ʒə *foreign name:* ˌæn.əˈstɑː.zi.ə (US) ˈ-ʒə
Anastasius ˌæn.əˈstɑː.zi.əs, -ˈsteɪ- (US) ˈ-ʒəs

anastigmat əˈnæs.tɪɡ.mæt, ænˈæs-; ˌæn.əˈstɪɡ- (US) əˈnæs.tɪɡ-; ˌæn.əˈstɪɡ- **-s** -s
anastigmatic ˌæn.ə.stɪɡˈmæt.ɪk; əˌnæs.tɪɡˈ- (US) əˌnæs.tɪɡˈmæt̬-; ˌæn.ə.stɪɡˈmæt̬-
anastomosis ˌæn.ə.stəˈməʊ.sɪs (US) -ˈmoʊ-
anastrophe əˈnæs.trə.fi, ænˈæs- **-s** -z
anathema əˈnæθ.ə.mə, ænˈ-, ˈ-ɪ- **-s** -z
anathematization, -isa- əˌnæθ.ə.mə.taɪˈzeɪ.ʃən, ænˈ-, ˌ-ɪ-, -tɪˈ- **-s** -z
anathematiz|e, -is|e əˈnæθ.ə.mə.taɪz, ænˈ-, ˈ-ɪ- **-es** -ɪz **-ing** -ɪŋ **-ed** -d
Anatole ˈæn.ə.təʊl (US) -toʊl
Anatoli|a ˌæn.əˈtəʊ.li|.ə (US) -ˈtoʊ- **-an/s** -ən/z
anatomic ˌæn.əˈtɒm.ɪk (US) -ˈtɑː.mɪk **-al** -əl **-ally** -əl.i, -li *stress shift:* ˌanatomic ˈdiagram
anatomist əˈnæt.ə.mɪst (US) -ˈnæt̬- **-s** -s
anatomiz|e, -is|e əˈnæt.ə.maɪz (US) -ˈnæt̬- **-es** -ɪz **-ing** -ɪŋ **-ed** -d
anatom|y əˈnæt.ə.m|i (US) -ˈnæt̬- **-ies** -iz
Anaxagoras ˌæn.ækˈsæɡ.ə.rəs, -ræs (US) -ɚ.əs
ANC ˌeɪ.enˈsiː
-ance -ənts
Note: Suffix. When attached to a free stem, **-ance** does not change the stress pattern of the word, e.g. **admit** /ədˈmɪt/, **admittance** /ədˈmɪt.ənts/. In other cases, the stress may be on the penultimate or antepenultimate syllable, e.g. **reluctance**/rɪˈlʌk.tənts/, **brilliance** /ˈbrɪl.i.ənts (US) ˈ-jənts/. There are exceptions; see individual entries.
ancestor ˈæn.ses.təʳ, -sɪ.stəʳ, -sə- (US) -ses.tɚ **-s** -z
ancestral ænˈses.trəl
ancestress ˈæn.ses.trəs; -sɪ.strəs, -ses.trɪs (US) -ses.trɪs **-es** -ɪz
ancestr|y ˈæn.ses.tr|i, -sɪ.str|i, -sə- (US) -ses.tr|i **-ies** -iz
Anchises ænˈkaɪ.siːz, æŋˈ-
anch|or ˈæŋ.k|əʳ (US) -k|ɚ **-ors** -əz (US) -ɚz **-oring** -ər.ɪŋ **-ored** -əd (US) -ɚd
anchorag|e (A) ˈæŋ.kər.ɪdʒ **-es** -ɪz
anchoress ˈæŋ.kər.ɪs, -es, -əs **-es** -ɪz
anchoret ˈæŋ.kər.et, -ɪt **-s** -s
anchorhold ˈæŋ.kə.həʊld (US) -kɚ.hoʊld **-s** -z
anchorite ˈæŋ.kər.aɪt (US) -kə.raɪt **-s** -s
anchor|man ˈæŋ.kə|.mæn, -mən (US) -kɚ- **-men** -men, -mən
anchorperson ˈæŋ.kəˌpɜː.sən (US) -kɚˌpɝː-
anchor|woman ˈæŋ.kə|ˌwʊm.ən (US) -kɚˌ- **-women** -ˌwɪm.ɪn
anchov|y ˈæn.tʃə.v|i, ænˈtʃəʊ- (US) ˈæn.tʃoʊ-, -ˈ-- **-ies** -iz
ancien(s)-régime(s) ˌɑ̃ːnt.si.æ̃n.reɪˈʒiːm, ˌɑːnt-, ɒntˌsjæn- (US) ˌɑːnt.si.æn-
ancient ˈeɪn.tʃənt (US) ˈeɪnt.ʃənt **-est** -əst, -ɪst **-ly** -li **-s** -s ˌ**ancient** ˈ**Greek**; ˌ**ancient** ˈ**history**
ancillar|y ænˈsɪl.ər|.i (US) ˈænt.sə.ler- **-ies** -iz
ancipit|al ænˈsɪp.ɪ.t|əl (US) -t̬|əl **-ous** -əs
Ancona æŋˈkəʊ.nə (US) ænˈ-, ɑːnˈ-, -ˈkoʊ-
Ancram ˈæŋ.krəm
Ancren Riwle ˌæŋ.krɪnˈri.ʊ.li, -krenˈ-, -krənˈ-, -lə
-ancy -ənt.si
Note: Suffix. Words containing **-ancy** are stressed in a similar way to those containing **-ance**; see above.
and *strong form:* ænd *weak forms:* ənd, ən, nd, n, m, ŋ
Note: Weak form word. The strong form /ænd/ is used for emphasis (e.g. 'The price included bed **and** breakfast.'), for contrast (e.g. 'It's not trick **and** treat, it's trick **or** treat.') or for citation (e.g. 'You should not begin a sentence with "and".').There are several weak pronunciations. In slow, careful speech the pronunciation may be /ənd/, but is more often /ən/ (e.g. 'Come and see.' /ˌkʌm.ənˈsiː/). In more rapid speech, when it occurs between consonants, the pronunciation may be a syllabic nasal consonant with a place of articulation assimilated to the neighbouring consonants (e.g. 'cut and dried' /ˌkʌt.n̩ˈdraɪd/; 'thick and creamy' /ˌθɪk.ŋ̍ˈkriː.mi/; 'up and back' /ˌʌp.m̩ˈbæk/).
Andalusi|a ˌæn.dəˈluː.si|.ə, -zi-, -lʊˈsiː|.ə (US) -ˈluː.ʒ|ə, ˈ-ʒi|.ə, -ʃi- **-an** -ən
Andaman ˈæn.də.mæn, -mən
andante ænˈdæn.teɪ, -ti (US) ɑːnˈdɑːn.teɪ, ænˈdæn.t̬i **-s** -z
andantino ˌæn.dænˈtiː.nəʊ (US) ˌɑːn.dɑːnˈtiː.noʊ, ˌæn.dænˈ-
Andean ænˈdiː.ən, ˈæn.di.ən
Anderlecht ˈæn.də.lekt (US) -dɚ-
Andersen, Anderson ˈæn.də.sən (US) -dɚ-
Anderton ˈæn.də.tən (US) -dɚ-
Andes ˈæn.diːz
Andhra Pradesh ˌæn.drə.prɑːˈdeʃ, -prəˈ-, ˌɑːn-, -ˈdeɪʃ
andiron ˈæn.daɪən (US) -daɪɚn **-s** -z
Andizhan ˈæn.dɪ.ʒæn (US) ˈɑːn.dɪ.ʒɑːn, ˈæn.dɪ.ʒæn
Andorra ænˈdɔː.rə, -ˈdɒr.ə (US) -ˈdɔːr.ə
Andorra la Vella ænˌdɔː.rə.ləˈveɪ.jə (US) -ˌdɔːr.ə.lɑːˈveɪl.jə
Andover ˈæn.dəʊ.vəʳ (US) -doʊ.vɚ
Andow ˈæn.daʊ
Andrade ˈæn.dreɪd, -drɑːd
Andrassy ænˈdræs.i
Andre, André ˈɑ̃ːn.dreɪ, ˈɑːn-, ˈæn- (US) ˈɑːn.dreɪ, ˈæn-, ˈɑ̃ː-
Andrea ˈæn.dri.ə; ænˈdreɪə (US) ˈæn.dri.ə, ˈɑːn-; ænˈdreɪə, ɑːn-
Andrea del Sarto ænˌdreɪə.delˈsɑː.təʊ (US) ɑːnˌdreɪə.delˈsɑːr.t̬oʊ, æn-
Andreas ˈæn.dri.əs, -dri.æs; ænˈdreɪəs (US) ɑːnˈdreɪəs, æn-
Andrei ˈɒnˌdreɪ, ˈæn- (US) ˈɑːn.dreɪ, ˈæn-, ˈa-˜
Andrew ˈæn.druː
Andrewatha *Cornish family:* ænˈdruː.θə *Plymouth family:* ænˈdruː.ə.θə, ˌæn.druˈɒθ.ə (US) -ˈɑː.θə
Andrews, Andrewes ˈæn.druːz
Andrex® ˈæn.dreks
Andria ˈæn.dri.ə (US) ˈæn-, ˈɑːn-
andro- æn.drəʊ-; ænˈdrɒ- (US) æn.drə-, -droʊ-; ænˈdrɑː-
Note: Prefix. Either takes primary or secondary stress on the first syllable, e.g. **androgen** /ˈæn.drəʊ.dʒən (US) -drə-/ **androgenic** /ˌæn.drəʊˈdʒen.ɪk (US) -drəˈ-/, or primary stress on the first syllable, e.g. **androgynous** /ænˈdrɒdʒ.ən.əs (US) -drɑː.dʒən.əs/.
androcentric ˌæn.drəʊˈsen.trɪk (US) -drəˈ-
Androcles ˈæn.drəʊ.kliːz (US) -drə-
Androclus ænˈdrɒk.ləs (US) -ˈdrɑː.kləs
androeci|um ænˈdriː.si|.əm (US) -ʃi-, -si- **-ia** -ə
androgen ˈæn.drəʊ.dʒən, -dʒen, -dʒɪn (US) -drə-, -droʊ- **-s** -z
androgenic ˌæn.drəʊˈdʒen.ɪk (US) -drəˈ-, -droʊˈ-
androgenous ænˈdrɒdʒ.ən.əs, ˈ-ɪ.nəs (US) -ˈdrɑː.dʒən.əs
androgynous ænˈdrɒdʒ.ɪ.nəs, -ən.əs (US) -ˈdrɑː.dʒən-
androgyny ænˈdrɒdʒ.ɪ.ni, -ən.i (US) -ˈdrɑː.dʒən-
android ˈæn.drɔɪd **-s** -z
Andromache ænˈdrɒm.ə.ki (US) -ˈdrɑː.mə-
Andromeda ænˈdrɒm.ɪ.də, -ə.də (US) -ˈdrɑː.mə-
Andronicus *Byzantine emperors and other figures in ancient history:* ˌæn.drəˈnaɪ.kəs, ænˈdrɒn.ɪ.kəs (US) -ˈdrɑː.nə- *in Shakespeare's* **Titus Andronicus**: ænˈdrɒn.ɪ.kəs (US) -ˈdrɑː.nɪ-

Andropov 'æn.drə.pɒf, æn'drɒp.ɒf, -əf (US) ɑːn'drɔː.pəf, -'droʊ-, -pɔːf
Andros 'æn.drɒs (US) -'drɑːs
Andvari æn'dwɑː.ri (US) ɑːn-
Andy 'æn.di
-ane -eɪn
Note: Suffix. Does not normally affect word stress, e.g. **alkane** /'æl.keɪn/.
anecdotage 'æn.ɪk.dəʊ.tɪdʒ, -ək- (US) -doʊ.t̬ɪdʒ
anecdotal ˌæn.ɪk'dəʊ.tᵊl, -ək- (US) -'doʊ.t̬ᵊl
anecdote 'æn.ɪk.dəʊt, -ək- (US) -doʊt **-s** -s
anecdotic ˌæn.ɪk'dəʊ.tɪk, -ek-, -ək-, -'dɒt- (US) -ɪk'dɑː.t̬ɪk **-al** -ᵊl **-ally** -ᵊl.i, -li
anechoic ˌæn.ɪ'kəʊ.ɪk, -ek'əʊ-, -ə'kəʊ- (US) -ə'koʊ-, -ɪ'-, -ek'oʊ- *stress shift:* ˌanechoic 'chamber
anelectric ˌæn.ɪ'lek.trɪk, -ə'lek- **-s** -s
anelectrode ˌæn.ɪ'lek.trəʊd, -ə'lek- (US) -troʊd **-s** -z
anemia ə'niː.mi.ə
anemic ə'niː.mɪk
anemometer ˌæn.ɪ'mɒm.ɪ.təʳ, -ə.təʳ (US) -'mɑː.mə.t̬ɚ **-s** -z
anemometric ˌæn.ɪ.məʊ'met.rɪk (US) -moʊ'-
anemometry ˌæn.ɪ'mɒm.ɪ.tri, -ə.tri (US) -'mɑː.mə-
anemone ə'nem.ə.ni **-s** -z
anemoscope ə'nem.ə.skəʊp (US) -skoʊp **-s** -s
anent ə'nent
aneroid 'æn.ə.rɔɪd, -ɪ.rɔɪd **-s** -z
anesthesia ˌæn.əs'θiː.zi.ə, -ɪs'-, -iːs'-, -ʒi-, '-ʒə (US) '-ʒə
anesthesiolog|y ˌæn.əsˌθiː.zi'ɒl.ə.dʒ|i, -ɪsˌ-, -iːsˌ-, -ʒi'- (US) -zi'ɑː.lə- **-ist/s** -ɪst/s
anesthetic ˌæn.əs'θet.ɪk, -ɪs'-, -iːs'- (US) -θet̬- **-s** -s **-ally** -ᵊl.i, -li *stress shift:* ˌanesthetic 'mask
anesthetist ə'niːs.θə.tɪst, æn'iːs-, -θɪ- (US) ə'nes.θə.t̬ɪst **-s** -s
anesthetiz|e, -is|e ə'niːs.θə.taɪz, æn'iːs-, -θɪ- (US) ə'nes.θə- **-es** -ɪz **-ing** -ɪŋ **-ed** -d
aneurin ə'njʊr.ɪn, -'njʊə.rɪn (US) 'æn.jɚ.ɪn, -jʊ.rɪn
Aneurin ə'naɪə.rɪn (US) -'naɪ-
aneurism 'æn.jʊə.rɪ.zᵊm (US) 'æn.jɚ.ɪ-, -jʊ.rɪ- **-s** -z
aneurismal ˌæn.jʊə'rɪz.məl (US) -jə'-, -jʊ'-
aneurysm 'æn.jʊə.rɪ.zᵊm (US) -jɚ.ɪ-, -jʊ.rɪ- **-s** -z
aneurysmal ˌæn.jʊə'rɪz.məl (US) -jə'-, -jʊ'-
anew ə'njuː (US) -'nuː, -'njuː
Anfield 'æn.fiːld
anfractuosity ˌæn.fræk.tju'ɒs.ə.ti, -ɪ.ti (US) -tʃu'ɑː.sə.t̬i
angel (A) 'eɪn.dʒᵊl **-s** -z 'angel ˌdust
Angela 'æn.dʒᵊl.ə, -dʒɪ.lə
Angeleno ˌæn.dʒᵊl'iː.nəʊ (US) -dʒə'liː.noʊ
Angeles 'æn.dʒᵊl.iːz, -dʒɪ.liːz, -liz, -lis (US) -dʒᵊl.əs, -dʒə.liːz
angelfish 'eɪn.dʒᵊl.fɪʃ **-es** -ɪz
angel-food cake ˌeɪn.dʒᵊl'fuːdˌkeɪk (US) 'eɪn.dʒᵊlˌfuːd-
angelic æn'dʒel.ɪk **-al** -ᵊl **-ally** -ᵊl.i, -li
angelica (A) æn'dʒel.ɪ.kə
Angelico æn'dʒel.ɪ.kəʊ (US) -koʊ
Angelina ˌæn.dʒᵊl'iː.nə, -dʒel'- (US) -dʒə'liː-, -dʒel'iː-
Angelo 'æn.dʒᵊl.əʊ, -dʒɪ.ləʊ (US) -dʒə.loʊ
Angelou 'æn.dʒᵊl.uː (US) -dʒə.luː, -loʊ
angelus (A) 'æn.dʒᵊl.əs, -dʒɪ.ləs **-es** -ɪz
angl|er 'æŋ.gl|əʳ (US) -gl|ɚ **-ers** -əz (US) -ɚz **-ering** -ᵊr.ɪŋ **-ered** -əd (US) -ɚd
Angers ɑ̃ːn'ʒeɪ
Angevin 'æn.dʒɪ.vɪn, -dʒə-
Angharad æŋ'hær.əd, æn-; 'æŋ.ᵊr- (US) æŋ'her-, æn- (US) -'hær-
Angie 'æn.dʒi
Angier 'æn.dʒɪəʳ
angina æn'dʒaɪ.nə **-s** -z
angiogram 'æn.dʒi.əʊ.græm (US) -ə-, -oʊ- **-s** -z
angiographic ˌæn.dʒi.əʊ'græf.ɪk (US) -ə'-, -oʊ'-
angiography ˌæn.dʒi'ɒg.rə.fi (US) -'ɑː.grə-
angioplasty 'æn.dʒi.əʊ.plæs.ti (US) -ə-, -oʊ-
angiosperm 'æn.dʒi.əʊ.spɜːm (US) -ə.spɝːm, -oʊ- **-s** -z
Angkor Thom ˌæŋ.kɔː'tɔːm (US) -kɔːr'tɑːm
angl|e (A) 'æŋ.gl̩ **-es** -z **-ing** -ɪŋ, '-glɪŋ **-ed** -d
Anglepoise® 'æŋ.gl̩.pɔɪz ˌ**Anglepoise 'lamp** (US) '**Anglepoise** ˌ**lamp**
angler 'æŋ.gləʳ, -gl̩.əʳ (US) '-glɚ, -gl̩.ɚ **-s** -z
Anglesea 'æŋ.gl̩.si, -siː
Anglesey 'æŋ.gl̩.si, -siː
Angli|a 'æŋ.gli|.ə **-an/s** -ən/z
Anglican 'æŋ.glɪ.kən **-s** -z **-ism** -ɪ.zᵊm
anglice 'æŋ.glɪ.si, -glə-
anglicism 'æŋ.glɪ.sɪ.zᵊm, -glə- **-s** -z
anglicist 'æŋ.glɪ.sɪst, -glə- **-s** -s
anglicization, -isa- ˌæŋ.glɪ.saɪ'zeɪ.ʃᵊn, -glə-, -ɪ'- (US) -ɪ'-
angliciz|e, -is|e 'æŋ.glɪ.saɪz, -glə- **-es** -ɪz **-ing** -ɪŋ **-ed** -d
angling 'æŋ.glɪŋ, -gl̩.ɪŋ
Anglo- æŋ.gləʊ- (US) æŋ.gloʊ-
Note: Prefix. Words containing **anglo-** normally carry either primary or secondary stress on the first syllable, e.g. **anglophobe** /'æŋ.gləʊ.fəʊb (US) -gloʊ.foʊb/, **anglophobia** /ˌæŋ.gləʊ'fəʊ.bi.ə (US) -gloʊ'foʊ-/. Where the prefix is used to mean "English and ...", it usually carries secondary stress, e.g. **Anglo-French** /ˌæŋ.gləʊ'frentʃ (US) -gloʊ'-/.
Anglo 'æŋ.gləʊ (US) -gloʊ **-s** -z
Anglo-American ˌæŋ.gləʊ.ə'mer.ɪ.kən (US) -gloʊ- **-s** -z
Anglo-French ˌæŋ.gləʊ'frentʃ (US) -gloʊ'-
Anglo-Irish ˌæŋ.gləʊ'aɪə.rɪʃ (US) -gloʊ'aɪ-
anglomania ˌæŋ.gləʊ'meɪ.ni.ə (US) -gloʊ'-
Anglo-Norman ˌæŋ.gləʊ'nɔː.mən (US) -gloʊ'nɔːr-
anglophile (A) 'æŋ.gləʊ.faɪl (US) -glə- **-s** -z
anglophilia ˌæŋ.gləʊ'fɪl.i.ə (US) -glə'-
anglophobe 'æŋ.gləʊ.fəʊb (US) -glə.foʊb **-s** -z
anglophobia ˌæŋ.gləʊ'fəʊ.bi.ə (US) -glə'foʊ-
anglophone 'æŋ.gləʊ.fəʊn (US) -glə.foʊn **-s** -z
Anglo-Saxon ˌæŋ.gləʊ'sæk.sᵊn (US) -gloʊ'- **-s** -z
Anglo-Saxondom ˌæŋ.gləʊ'sæk.sᵊn.dəm (US) -gloʊ'-
Anglo-Saxonism ˌæŋ.gləʊ'sæk.sᵊn.ɪ.zᵊm (US) -gloʊ'- **-s** -z
Angmering 'æŋ.mə.rɪŋ
Angol|a æŋ'gəʊ.l|ə (US) -'goʊ-, æn- **-an/s** -ən/z
angora (A) *cat, rabbit, cloth:* æŋ'gɔː.rə (US) -'gɔːr.ə, æn- **-s** -z
Angora *old form of* **Ankara** *in Turkey:* 'æŋ.gə.rə, æŋ'gɔː.rə (US) æŋ'gɔːr.ə, æn-
angostura (A) ˌæŋ.gə'stjʊə.rə, -gɒs'tjʊə-, -'stjɔː- (US) -gə'stʊr.ə, -'stjʊr- ˌ**Angostura 'bitters®**
Angoulême ɑ̃ːŋ.gʊ'lem
angr|y 'æŋ.gr|i **-ier** -i.əʳ (US) -i.ɚ **-iest** -i.əst, -i.ɪst **-ily** -ɪ.li, -ᵊl.i **-iness** -ɪ.nəs, -ɪ.nɪs ˌ**angry young 'man**
angst æŋkst (US) æŋkst, ɑːŋkst
angstrom 'æŋk.strəm **-s** -z
Anguill|a æŋ'gwɪl.ə **-an/s** -ən/z
anguine 'æŋ.gwɪn
anguish 'æŋ.gwɪʃ **-es** -ɪz **-ing** -ɪŋ **-ed** -t
angular 'æŋ.gjʊ.ləʳ, -gjə- (US) -lɚ **-ly** -li **-ness** -nəs, -nɪs
angularit|y ˌæŋ.gjʊ'lær.ə.t|i, -gjə-, -ɪ.t|i (US) -'ler.ə.t̬|i, -'lær- **-ies** -iz
angulate 'æn.gjʊ.leɪt, -gjə-, -lɪt, -lət
angulated 'æŋ.gjʊ.leɪ.tɪd, -gjə- (US) -t̬ɪd

Angus ˈæŋ.ɡəs
Angustura ˌæŋ.ɡəˈstjʊə.rə, -ˈstjɔː-, -ˈstʊr.ə (US) -ˈstʊr-, -ˈstjʊr-
anharmonic ˌæn.hɑːˈmɒn.ɪk (US) -hɑːrˈmɑː.nɪk *stress shift:* ˌanharmonic ˈsystem
anhungered ənˈhʌŋ.ɡəd, æn- (US) -ɡɚd
anhydride ænˈhaɪ.draɪd **-s** -z
anhydrite ænˈhaɪ.draɪt
anhydrous ænˈhaɪ.drəs
anil ˈæn.ɪl
anile ˈeɪ.naɪl, ˈæn.aɪl
aniline ˈæn.ɪ.liːn, -lɪn, -laɪn (US) -lɪn, -liːn, -laɪn
anility ænˈɪl.ə.ti, əˈnɪl-, -ɪ.ti (US) -ə.t̬i
anima ˈæn.ɪ.mə
animadversion ˌæn.ɪ.mædˈvɜː.ʃən, -mədˈ-, -ʒən (US) -ˈvɝː.ʒən, -ʃən **-s** -z
animad|vert ˌæn.ɪ.mædˈ|vɜːt, -mədˈ- (US) -ˈvɝːt **-verts** -ˈvɜːts (US) -ˈvɝːts **-verting** -ˈvɜː.tɪŋ (US) -ˈvɝː.t̬ɪŋ **-verted** -ˈvɜː.tɪd (US) -ˈvɝː.t̬ɪd
animal ˈæn.ɪ.məl, ˈ-ə- **-s** -z
animalcule ˌæn.ɪˈmæl.kjuːl **-s** -z
animalism ˈæn.ɪ.məl.ɪ.zəm
animalistic ˌæn.ɪ.məlˈɪs.tɪk (US) -məˈlɪs-, -məlˈ-
animate (*adj.*) ˈæn.ɪ.mət, -mɪt, -meɪt
ani|mate (*v.*) ˈæn.ɪ|.meɪt, ˈ-ə- **-mates** -meɪts **-mating** -meɪ.tɪŋ (US) -meɪ.t̬ɪŋ **-mated/ly** -meɪ.tɪd/li (US) -meɪ.t̬ɪd/li
animation ˌæn.ɪˈmeɪ.ʃən, -əˈ- **-s** -z
animator ˈæn.ɪ.meɪ.təʳ, ˈ-ə- (US) -t̬ɚ **-s** -z
animatronic ˌæn.ɪ.məˈtrɒn.ɪk, ˌ-ə- (US) -ˈtrɑː.nɪk **-s** -s
anim|ism ˈæn.ɪ.m|ɪ.zəm, ˈ-ə- **-ist/s** -ɪst/s
animosit|y ˌæn.ɪˈmɒs.ə.t|i, -əˈ-, -ɪ.t|i (US) -ˈmɑː.sə.t̬|i **-ies** -iz
animus ˈæn.ɪ.məs
anion ˈæn.aɪən **-s** -z
anis ˈæn.iːs, -i; ænˈiːs (US) ˈæn.iːs, ˈɑː.niːs, -i; ænˈiːs, ɑːˈniːs
anise ˈæn.ɪs, ænˈiːs
aniseed ˈæn.ɪ.siːd, ˈ-ə-
anisette ˌæn.ɪˈset, -əˈ-, -ˈzet
anisometric ænˌaɪ.səʊˈmet.rɪk (US) -soʊˈ-
anisotropic ˌæn.aɪ.səʊˈtrɒp.ɪk, -ˈtrəʊ.pɪk (US) -soʊˈtrɑː.pɪk, -ˈtroʊ- **-ally** -əl.i, -li
anisotropism ˌæn.aɪˈsɒt.rə.pɪ.zəm (US) -ˈsɑː.trə-
anisotropy ˌæn.aɪˈsɒt.rə.pi (US) -ˈsɑː.trə-
Aniston ˈæn.ɪ.stən
Anita əˈniː.tə (US) -t̬ə
Anjou ɑ̃ːnˈʒuː, ɑːnˈ-
Ankara ˈæŋ.kər.ə (US) ˈæŋ-, ˈɑːŋ-
ankerite ˈæŋ.kər.aɪt (US) -kə.raɪt
ankh ɑːŋk, æŋk **-s** -s
ankle ˈæŋ.kl̩ **-s** -z ˈ**ankle** ˌ**sock**
anklet ˈæŋ.klət, -klɪt **-s** -s
Ann æn
anna (A) ˈæn.ə **-s** -z
Annaba ænˈɑː.bə
Annabel ˈæn.ə.bel
Annabella ˌæn.əˈbel.ə
Annagh ænˈɑː, ˈæn.ɑː
Annakin ˈæn.ə.kɪn
annalist ˈæn.əl.ɪst **-s** -s
annals ˈæn.əlz
Annaly ˈæn.ə.li
Annam ænˈæm, ˈæn.æm
Annamese ˌæn.əˈmiːz
Annan ˈæn.ən
Annandale ˈæn.ən.deɪl
Annapolis əˈnæp.əl.ɪs, ænˈæp-
Annapurna ˌæn.əˈpɜː.nə, -ˈpʊə- (US) -ˈpɝː-, -ˈpʊr-
Ann Arbor ˌænˈɑː.bə (US) -ˈɑːr.bɚ
Annas ˈæn.æs, -əs
annatto əˈnæt.əʊ, ænˈæt- (US) əˈnɑː.toʊ, əˈnæt.oʊ
Anne æn
anneal əˈniːl **-s** -z **-ing** -ɪŋ **-ed** -d
Anneka ˈæn.ɪ.kə, -ə.kə
annelid ˈæn.ə.lɪd **-s** -z
Annesley ˈænz.li
Annett ˈæn.ɪt, -ət
Annette əˈnet, ænˈet (US) əˈnet
annex (*n.*) ˈæn.eks **-es** -ɪz
annex (*v.*) əˈneks, ænˈeks **-es** -ɪz **-ing** -ɪŋ **-ed** -t **-ment/s** -mənt/s
annexation ˌæn.ekˈseɪ.ʃən, -ɪkˈ- **-s** -z
annex|e ˈæn.eks **-es** -ɪz
Annfield Plain ˌæn.fiːldˈpleɪn
Annie ˈæn.i
Annigoni ˌæn.ɪˈɡəʊ.ni (US) -ˈɡoʊ-
annihi|late əˈnaɪ.ɪ|.leɪt, ˈ-ə- (US) ˈ-ə- **-lates** -leɪts **-lating** -leɪ.tɪŋ (US) -leɪ.t̬ɪŋ **-lated** -leɪ.tɪd (US) -leɪ.t̬ɪd **-lator/s** -leɪ.təʳ/z (US) -leɪ.t̬ɚ/z
annihilation əˌnaɪ.ɪˈleɪ.ʃən, -əˈ- (US) -əˈ- **-s** -z
Anning ˈæn.ɪŋ
Anniston ˈæn.ɪ.stən
anniversar|y ˌæn.ɪˈvɜː.sər|.i (US) -ˈvɝː- **-ies** -iz
anno Domini (A) ˌæn.əʊˈdɒm.ɪ.naɪ (US) -oʊˈdɑː.mə.niː, -ˈdoʊ-, -naɪ
anno|tate ˈæn.əʊ|.teɪt (US) ˈ-ə-, ˈ-oʊ- **-tates** -teɪts **-tating** -teɪ.tɪŋ (US) -teɪ.t̬ɪŋ **-tated** -teɪ.tɪd (US) -teɪ.t̬ɪd **-tator/s** -teɪ.təʳ/z (US) -teɪ.t̬ɚ/z **-tative** -teɪ.tɪv (US) -teɪ.t̬ɪv
annotation ˌæn.əʊˈteɪ.ʃən (US) -əˈ-, -oʊˈ- **-s** -z
announc|e əˈnaʊnts **-es** -ɪz **-ing** -ɪŋ **-ed** -t **-ement/s** -mənt/s
announcer əˈnaʊnt.səʳ (US) -sɚ **-s** -z
annoy əˈnɔɪ **-s** -z **-ing/ly** -ɪŋ/li **-ed** -d
annoyanc|e əˈnɔɪ.ənts **-es** -ɪz
annual ˈæn.ju.əl **-s** -z **-ly** -i
annualiz|e, -is|e ˈæn.ju.əl.aɪz (US) -ə.laɪz **annuali|ze** -julˈ- **-es** -ɪz **-ing** -ɪŋ **-ed** -d
annuit|y əˈnjuː.ə.t|i, -ɪ.t|i (US) -ˈnuː.ə.t̬|i, -ˈnjuː- **-ies** -iz **-ant/s** -ənt/s
annul əˈnʌl **-s** -z **-ling** -ɪŋ **-led** -d
annular ˈæn.jə.ləʳ, ˈ-jʊ- (US) -lɚ
annu|late ˈæn.jə|.leɪt, ˈ-jʊ- **-lated** -leɪ.tɪd (US) -leɪ.t̬ɪd
annulet ˈæn.jʊ.lət, ˈ-jə-, -lɪt **-s** -s
annulment əˈnʌl.mənt **-s** -s
annul|us æn.jə.l|əs, ˈ-jʊ- **-uses** -ə.sɪz **-i** -aɪ, -iː
annum ˈæn.əm
annunci|ate əˈnʌnt.si|.eɪt, -ʃi- **-ates** -eɪts **-ating** -eɪ.tɪŋ (US) -eɪ.t̬ɪŋ **-ated** -eɪ.tɪd (US) -eɪ.t̬ɪd
annunciation (A) əˌnʌnt.siˈeɪ.ʃən **-s** -z
annus mirabilis (A) ˌæn.əs.mɪˈrɑː.bəl.ɪs, -məˈ- (US) ˌɑː.nəs-, ˌæn.əs-
anode ˈæn.əʊd (US) -oʊd **-s** -z
anodiz|e, -ise ˈæn.əʊ.daɪz (US) ˈ-oʊ-, ˈ-ə- **-es** -ɪz **-ing** -ɪŋ **-ed** -d
anodyne ˈæn.əʊ.daɪn (US) ˈ-oʊ-, ˈ-ə- **-s** -z
a|noint ə|ˈnɔɪnt **-noints** -ˈnɔɪnts **-nointing** -ˈnɔɪn.tɪŋ (US) -ˈnɔɪn.t̬ɪŋ **-nointed** -ˈnɔɪn.tɪd (US) -ˈnɔɪn.t̬ɪd **-nointment/s** -ˈnɔɪnt.mənt/s
anomalous əˈnɒm.ə.ləs (US) -ˈnɑː.mə- **-ly** -li
anomal|y əˈnɒm.ə.l|i (US) -ˈnɑː.mə- **-ies** -iz
anon (A) əˈnɒn (US) -ˈnɑːn
anonym ˈæn.ə.nɪm, -ɒn.ɪm (US) -ə.nɪm **-s** -z
anonymity ˌæn.əˈnɪm.ə.ti, -ɒnˈɪm-, -ɪ.ti (US) -əˈnɪm.ə.t̬i
anonymiz|e, -is|e əˈnɒn.ɪ.maɪz, ˈ-ə- (US) -ˈnɑː.nə- **-es** -ɪz **-ing** -ɪŋ **-ed** -d
anonymous əˈnɒn.ɪ.məs, ˈ-ə- (US) -ˈnɑː.nə- **-ly** -li
anopheles əˈnɒf.ɪ.liːz, ˈ-ə- (US) -ˈnɑː.fə-
anorak ˈæn.ər.æk (US) -ə.ræk **-s** -s
anorectic ˌæn.ərˈek.tɪk (US) -əˈrek- **-s** -s
anorexia ˌæn.ərˈek.si.ə (US) -əˈrek- anoˌrexia nerˈvosa
anorexic ˌæn.ərˈek.sɪk (US) -əˈrek- **-s** -s
anosmia ænˈɒz.mi.ə, -ˈnɒs- (US) ænˈɑːz-, -ˈɑːs-
another əˈnʌð.əʳ (US) -ɚ
A N Other ˌeɪˌenˈʌð.əʳ (US) -ɚ
Anouilh ˈæn.uː.iː, ˌæn.uːˈiː (US) ɑːˈnuː.jə, ænˈuː-, -iː; ˌɑː.nuːˈiː, ˌæn.uːˈ-
anoxia ænˈɒk.si.ə, eɪˈnɒk- (US) ænˈɑːk-
ansaphone, ansafone (A®) ˈɑːnt.sə.fəʊn (US) ˈæn.sə.foʊn **-s** -z
anschauung (A) ˈæn.ʃaʊ.ʊŋ (US) ˈɑːn.ʃaʊ.əŋ
anschluss (A) ˈæn.ʃlʊs (US) ˈɑːn-, ˈæn-
Ansell ˈænt.səl
Anselm ˈænt.selm

anserine 'æn*t*.sə.raɪn, -riːn, -rɪn
Ansley 'ænz.li
Anson 'æn*t*.sən
Ansonia æn'səʊ.ni.ə US -'soʊ-, '-njə
Ansted 'æn*t*.sted, -stɪd
Anster 'æn*t*.stəʳ US -stɚ
Anstey 'æn*t*.sti
Anston 'æn*t*.stən
Anstruther 'æn*t*.strʌð.əʳ US -ɚ
answ|er 'ɑːn*t*.s|əʳ US 'æn*t*.s|ɚ **-ers** -əz US -ɚz **-ering** -ᵊr.ɪŋ **-ered** -əd US -ɚd **-erer/s** -ᵊr.əʳ/z US -ɚ.ɚ/z '**answering ma,chine**
answerability ,ɑːn*t*.sᵊr.ə'bɪl.ə.ti, -ɪ.ti US ,æn*t*.sɚ.ə'bɪl.ə.ţi
answerab|le 'ɑːn*t*.sᵊr.ə.b|l US 'æn*t*- **-ly** -li
answerphone 'ɑːn*t*.sə.fəʊn US 'æn*t*.sɚ.foʊn **-s** -z
ant- ænt-
Note: Prefix. Where **ant-** is attached to a free stem it often carries secondary stress, e.g. **antacid** /,æn'tæs.ɪd/. In other cases it may take primary, secondary or no stress at all, e.g. **antonym** /'æn.tə.nɪm US -tᵊn.ɪm/, **antonymic** /,æn.tə'nɪm.ɪk/, **antonymous** /æn'tɒn.ɪ.məs US -'tɑː.nə-/.
ant ænt **-s** -s '**ant ,lion**
-ant -ənt
Note: Suffix. Words containing **-ant** are stressed in a similar way to those containing **-ance**; see above.
Antabuse® 'æn.tə.bjuːs, -bjuːz
antacid ,æn'tæs.ɪd **-s** -z
Antaeus æn'tiː.əs, -'teɪ-
antagonism æn'tæg.ᵊn.ɪ.zᵊm **-s** -z
antagonist æn'tæg.ᵊn.ɪst **-s** -s
antagonistic æn,tæg.ᵊn'ɪs.tɪk, ,æn.tæg.ᵊn'- US -ə'nɪs- **-ally** -ᵊl.i, -li
antagoniz|e, -is|e æn'tæg.ᵊn.aɪz US -ə.naɪz **-es** -ɪz **-ing** -ɪŋ **-ed** -d
Antalya æn'tæl.jə US ,ɑːn.tᵊl'jɑː, ,æn-
Antananarivo ,æn.tə,næn.ə'riː.vəʊ US -voʊ
Antarctic æn'tɑːk.tɪk US -'tɑːrk-, -'tɑːr.ţɪk **Ant,arctic 'Circle; Ant,arctic 'Ocean**
Antarctica æn'tɑːk.tɪ.kə US -'tɑːrk-, -'tɑːr.ţɪ-
Antares æn'teə.riːz US -'ter.iːz
ant-bear 'ænt.beəʳ US -ber **-s** -z
ante- æn.tɪ- US -ţi-, -ţə-
Note: Prefix. Words containing **ante-** carry either primary or secondary stress on the first syllable, e.g. **antechamber** /'æn.tɪ,tʃeɪm.bəʳ US -ţɪ,tʃeɪm.bɚ/, **antenatal** /,æn.tɪ'neɪ.tᵊl US -ţᵊl/.
ante 'æn.ti US -ţi **-s** -z **-ing** -ɪŋ **-d** -d
anteater 'ænt,iː.təʳ US -ţɚ **-s** -z
antebellum ,æn.tɪ'bel.əm US -ţə'-
antecedence ,æn.tɪ'siː.dᵊn*t*s, 'æn.tɪ.siː- US ,æn.ţə'siː-
antecedent ,æn.tɪ'siː.dᵊnt, -ţə'- **-s** -s **-ly** -li
antechamber 'æn.tɪ,tʃeɪm.bəʳ US -ţɪ,tʃeɪm.bɚ **-s** -z
antechapel 'æn.tɪ,tʃæp.ᵊl US -ţɪ- **-s** -z
ante|date ,æn.tɪ|'deɪt US 'æn.ţɪ|.deɪt **-dates** -'deɪts US -deɪts **-dating** -'deɪ.tɪŋ US -deɪ.ţɪŋ **-dated** -'deɪ.tɪd US -deɪ.ţɪd
antediluvi|an ,æn.tɪ.dɪ'luː.vi|.ən, -də'-, -daɪ'-, -'ljuː- US -ţɪ.də'luː- **-ans** -ənz **-al** -ᵊl **-ally** -ᵊl.i
antelope 'æn.tɪ.ləʊp US -ţᵊl.oʊp **-s** -s
antemeridian ,æn.tɪ.mə'rɪd.i.ən US -ţɪ-
ante meridiem ,æn.tɪ.mə'rɪd.i.əm US -ţɪ-
antenatal ,æn.tɪ'neɪ.tᵊl US -ţɪ'neɪ.ţᵊl
antenn|a æn'ten|.ə **-ae** -iː **-as** -əz **-al** -ᵊl **-ary** -ᵊr.i
Antenor æn'tiː.nɔːʳ US -nɔːr
antenuptial ,æn.tɪ'nʌp.ʃᵊl, -tʃᵊl US -ţɪ'-
antepenult ,æn.tɪ.pɪ'nʌlt, -pen'ʌlt, -pə'nʌlt US ,æn.ţɪ'piː.nʌlt; -pɪ'nʌlt **-s** -s
antepenultimate ,æn.tɪ.pə'nʌl.tɪ.mət, -pɪ'nʌl-, -pen'ʌl-, -tə-, -mɪt US -ţɪ.pɪ'nʌl.ţə.mət **-s** -s
anteprandial ,æn.tɪ'præn.di.əl US -ţɪ'-
anterior æn'tɪə.ri.əʳ US -'tɪr.i.ɚ **-ly** -li
anteroom 'æn.tɪ.rʊm, -ruːm US -ţɪ.ruːm, -rʊm **-s** -z
Anthea 'æn*t*.θi.ə US æn'θiː-
ant-heap 'ænt.hiːp **-s** -s
antheli|on ænt'hiː.li|.ən, æn*t*'θiː- **-ons** -ənz **-a** -ə
anthelix ænt'hiː.lɪks, æn*t*'θiː- **-es** -ɪz
anthem 'æn*t*.θəm **-s** -z
anther 'æn*t*.θəʳ US -θɚ **-s** -z
anthill 'ænt.hɪl **-s** -z
anthological ,æn*t*.θə'lɒdʒ.ɪ.kᵊl US -'lɑː.dʒɪ-
anthologist æn'θɒl.ə.dʒɪst US -'θɑː.lə- **-s** -s
anthologiz|e, -is|e æn'θɒl.ə.dʒaɪz US -'θɑː.lə- **-es** -ɪz **-ing** -ɪŋ **-ed** -d
antholog|y æn'θɒl.ə.dʒ|i US -'θɑː.lə- **-ies** -iz
Anthon 'æn.tɒn US 'æn*t*.θən, 'æn.tɑːn
Anthony 'æn.tə.ni, 'æn*t*.θə.ni US 'æn.θə.ni, 'æn.tə.ni
anthracite 'æn*t*.θrə.saɪt
anthracitic ,æn*t*.θrə'sɪt.ɪk US -'sɪţ-
anthrax 'æn*t*.θræks
anthropic æn'θrɒp.ɪk US -'θrɑː.pɪk **-al** -ᵊl
anthropo- ,æn*t*.θrəʊ.pəʊ-; ,æn*t*.θrəʊ'pɒ- US ,æn*t*.θrə.pə-, -poʊ-; ,æn*t*.θrə'pɑː-
Note: Prefix. Words containing **anthropo-** normally exhibit secondary stress on the first syllable, e.g. **anthropomorphic** /,æn*t*.θrə.pəʊ'mɔː.fɪk US -pə'mɔːr-/, but may also have primary stress on the third syllable, e.g., **anthropology** /,æn*t*.θrə'pɒl.ə.dʒi US -'pɑː.lə-/.
anthropocentric ,æn*t*.θrəʊ.pəʊ'sen.trɪk US -θrə.pə'-, -poʊ'-
anthropocentrism ,æn.θrəʊ.pəʊ'sen.trɪ.zᵊm US -θrə.pə'-, -poʊ'-
anthropoid 'æn*t*.θrəʊ.pɔɪd US -θrə-, -θroʊ- **-s** -z
anthropoidal ,æn*t*.θrəʊ'pɔɪd.ᵊl US -θrə'-, -θroʊ'-
anthropological ,æn*t*.θrə.pə'lɒdʒ.ɪ.kᵊl US -'lɑː.dʒɪ- **-ly** -i
anthropologist ,æn*t*.θrə'pɒl.ə.dʒɪst US -'pɑː.lə- **-s** -s
anthropology ,æn*t*.θrə'pɒl.ə.dʒi US -'pɑː.lə-
anthropometric ,æn*t*.θrəʊ.pəʊ'met.rɪk US -θrə.pə'-
anthropometry ,æn.θrə'pɒm.ɪ.tri, '-ə- US -'pɑː.mə-
anthropomorph|ic ,æn*t*.θrə.pəʊ'mɔː.f|ɪk US -pə'mɔːr- **-ous** -əs
anthropomorph|ism ,æn*t*.θrə.pəʊ'mɔː.f|ɪ.zᵊm US -pə'mɔːr- **-ist/s** -ɪst/s
anthropomorphiz|e, -is|e ,æn*t*.θrə.pəʊ'mɔː.faɪz US -pə'mɔːr- **-es** -ɪz **-ing** -ɪŋ **-ed** -d
anthropomorphosis ,æn*t*.θrə.pəʊ.mɔː'fəʊ.sɪs US -pə.mɔːr'foʊ-
anthropopha|gus ,æn*t*.θrəʊ'pɒf.ə|.gəs US -θrə'pɑː.fə- **-gi** -dʒaɪ, -gaɪ US -dʒaɪ
anthropopha|gy ,æn*t*.θrəʊ'pɒf.ə|.dʒi US -θrə'pɑː.fə- **-gous** -gəs
anthroposoph|y ,æn*t*.θrəʊ'pɒs.ə.f|i US -θrə'pɑː.sə- **-ist/s** -ɪst/s
anti- æn.tɪ-, -ti-; æn'tɪ- US -ţɪ-, -ţi-, -taɪ-; æn'tɪ-
Note: Prefix. Numerous compounds may be formed by prefixing **anti-** to other words. Most often, these compounds carry primary or secondary stress on the first syllable, e.g. **antihero** /'æn.tɪ,hɪə.rəʊ US -ţɪ,hɪr.oʊ/, **anti-icer** /,æn.ti'aɪ.səʳ US -ţi'aɪ.sɚ/, but there are also cases in which the second syllable takes the primary stress, e.g. **antinomy** /æn'tɪn.ə.mi/.

anti 'æn.ti US -t̬i, -taɪ **-s** -z

antiabortion ˌæn.ti.ə'bɔː.ʃᵊn US -t̬i.ə'bɔːr-, -taɪ- **-ist/s** -ɪst/s

anti-aircraft ˌæn.ti'eə.krɑːft US -t̬i'er.kræft, -taɪ'-

antibacterial ˌæn.tɪ.bæk'tɪə.ri.əl US -t̬ɪ.bæk'tɪr.i-, -taɪ-

antiballistic ˌæn.tɪ.bə'lɪs.tɪk US -t̬ɪ-, -taɪ-

Antibes ɑːn'tiːb, æn-, ɒn'- US ɑːn'-

antibiosis ˌæn.tɪ.baɪ'əʊ.sɪs US -t̬ɪ.baɪ'oʊ-, -taɪ-

antibiotic ˌæn.tɪ.baɪ'ɒt.ɪk US -t̬ɪ.baɪ'ɑː.t̬ɪk, -taɪ- **-s** -s

antibod|y 'æn.tɪˌbɒd|.i US -t̬ɪˌbɑː.d|i, -taɪˌ- **-ies** -iz

antic 'æn.tɪk US -t̬ɪk **-s** -s

anticatholic ˌæn.tɪ'kæθ.ᵊl.ɪk US -t̬ɪ'-, -taɪ'- **-s** -s

anti-choice ˌæn.tɪ'tʃɔɪs US -t̬ɪ'-, -taɪ'-

antichrist (A) 'æn.tɪ.kraɪst US -t̬ɪ-, -taɪ- **-s** -s

antichristian *opposing Christianity:* ˌæn.tɪ'krɪs.tʃᵊn, -'krɪʃ- US -t̬ɪ'-, -taɪ'- **-s** -z *pertaining to Antichrist:* 'æn.tɪˌkrɪʃ.tʃᵊn US -t̬ɪˌ-, -taɪˌ- **-s** -z

anticipant æn'tɪs.ɪ.pənt, '-ə- **-s** -s

antici|pate æn'tɪs.ɪ|.peɪt, '-ə- US '-ə- **-pates** -peɪts **-pating** -peɪ.tɪŋ US -peɪ.t̬ɪŋ **-pated** -peɪ.tɪd US -peɪ.t̬ɪd **-pative/ly** -peɪ.tɪv/li US -peɪ.t̬ɪv/li

anticipation ænˌtɪs.ɪ'peɪ.ʃᵊn, -ə'-; ˌæn.tɪ.sɪ'-, -sə'- US ænˌtɪs.ə'- **-s** -z

anticipator|y ænˌtɪs.ɪ'peɪ.tᵊr|.i, -ə'-; ˌæn.tɪ.sɪ'-, -sə'- US æn'tɪs.ə.pə.tɔːr- **-ily** -ᵊl.i, -ɪ.li

anticiz|e, -is|e 'æn.tɪ.saɪz US -t̬ɪ-, -taɪ- **-es** -ɪz **-ing** -ɪŋ **-ed** -d

anticlerical ˌæn.tɪ'kler.ɪ.kᵊl US -t̬ɪ'-, -taɪ'- **-ism** -ɪ.zᵊm **-ist/s** -ɪst/s

anticlimactic ˌæn.tɪ.klaɪ'mæk.tɪk, -klɪ'- US -t̬ɪ.klaɪ'-, -taɪ- **-ally** -ᵊl.i, -li

anticlimatic ˌæn.tɪ.klaɪ'mæt.ɪk, -klɪ'- US -t̬ɪ.klaɪ'mæt̬-, -taɪ- **-al** -ᵊl **-ally** -ᵊl.i, -li

anticlimax ˌæn.tɪ'klaɪ.mæks, 'æn.tɪˌklaɪ- US ˌæn.t̬ɪ'klaɪ-, -taɪˌ- **-es** -ɪz

anticline 'æn.tɪ.klaɪn US -t̬ɪ- **-s** -z

anticlockwise ˌæn.tɪ'klɒk.waɪz US -t̬ɪ'klɑːk-, -taɪ'- *stress shift:* ˌanticlockwise 'action

anticoagulant ˌæn.tɪ.kəʊ'æg.jʊ.lənt, -jə- US -t̬ɪ.koʊ'æg.jə-, -taɪ- **-s** -s

anticonsumer|ism ˌæn.tɪ.kən'sjuː.mᵊr|.ɪ.zᵊm, -'suː- US -t̬ɪ.kən'suː- **-ist/s** -ɪst/s

anticonvulsant ˌæn.tɪ.kən'vʌl.sᵊnt US -t̬ɪ-, -taɪ- **-s** -s

anticonvulsive ˌæn.tɪ.kən'vʌl.sɪv US -t̬ɪ-, -taɪ- **-s** -z

anticyclone ˌæn.tɪ'saɪ.kləʊn, 'æn.tɪ.saɪ- US ˌæn.t̬ɪ'saɪ.kloʊn, -taɪ'- **-s** -z

anticyclonic ˌæn.tɪ.saɪ'klɒn.ɪk US -t̬ɪ.saɪ'klɑː.nɪk, -taɪ-

antidepressant ˌæn.tɪ.dɪ'pres.ᵊnt, -də'- US -t̬ɪ-, -taɪ- **-s** -s

antidotal ˌæn.tɪ'dəʊ.tᵊl, 'æn.tɪ.dəʊ- US 'æn.t̬ɪ.doʊ-

antidote 'æn.tɪ.dəʊt US -t̬ɪ.doʊt **-s** -s

Antietam æn'tiː.təm US -t̬əm

antifebrile ˌæn.tɪ'fiː.braɪl, -'feb.raɪl US -t̬ɪ'fiː.brɪl, -taɪ'-, -'feb.rɪl, -rəl

anti-federal ˌæn.tɪ'fed.ᵊr.ᵊl US -t̬ɪ'-, -taɪ'- **-ism** -ɪ.zᵊm **-ist/s** -ɪst/s

antifreeze 'æn.tɪ.friːz US -t̬ɪ-

antigen 'æn.tɪ.dʒən, -dʒen US -t̬ɪ- **-s** -z

Antigone æn'tɪg.ə.ni

Antigonus æn'tɪg.ə.nəs

Antigu|a æn'tiː.g|ə US -gw|ə, -g|ə, -'tɪg.w|ə, '-ə **-an/s** -ən/z

antihel|ix ˌæn.tɪ'hiː.l|ɪks US -t̬ɪ'-, -taɪ'- **-ixes** -ɪk.sɪz **-ices** -ɪ.siːz, -'hel.ɪs.iːz

antihero 'æn.tɪˌhɪə.rəʊ US -t̬ɪˌher.oʊ, -t̬i-, -taɪ-, -hiː.roʊ **-es** -z

antiheroic ˌæn.tɪ.hɪ'rəʊ.ɪk, -hə'-, -her'əʊ- US -t̬ɪ.hɪ'roʊ-, -t̬i-, -taɪ-

antiheroine 'æn.tɪˌher.əʊ.ɪn US -t̬ɪˌher.oʊ-, -taɪ- **-s** -z

antihistamine ˌæn.tɪ'hɪs.tə.miːn, -mɪn US -t̬ɪ'- **-s** -z

anti-icer ˌæn.ti'aɪ.səʳ US -t̬i'aɪ.sɚ **-s** -z

anti-inflammatory ˌæn.ti.ɪn'flæm.ə.tᵊr.i US -t̬i.ɪn'flæm.ə.tɔːr-, -taɪ-

Anti-Jacobin ˌæn.tɪ'dʒæk.ə.bɪn, -ɒb.ɪn US -t̬ɪ'dʒæk.ə.bɪn, -taɪ'-

antiknock ˌæn.tɪ'nɒk US 'æn.t̬ɪ'nɑːk, -t̬i'-, -taɪ'- **-ing** -ɪŋ

Antilles æn'tɪl.iːz

antilock ˌæn.tɪ'lɒk US -t̬ɪ'lɑːk, -t̬i'-, -taɪ'- *stress shift:* ˌantilock 'brakes

anti-locking ˌæn.tɪ'lɒk.ɪŋ US -t̬ɪ'lɑː.kɪŋ

antilog ˌæn.tɪ'lɒg US 'æn.t̬ɪ.lɑːg, -taɪ-, -lɔːg **-s** -z

antilogarithm ˌæn.tɪ'lɒg.ə.rɪ.ðᵊm, -θᵊm US -t̬ɪ'lɑː.gɚ.ɪ.ðᵊm, -taɪ'-, -'lɔː- **-s** -z

antilog|y æn'tɪl.ə.dʒ|i **-ies** -iz

antimacassar ˌæn.tɪ.mə'kæs.əʳ US -t̬ɪ.mə'kæs.ɚ **-s** -z

Antimachus æn'tɪm.ə.kəs

antimatter 'æn.tɪˌmæt.əʳ US -t̬ɪˌmæt̬.ɚ, -t̬iˌ-, -taɪˌ-

anti-missile ˌæn.tɪ'mɪs.aɪl US -t̬ɪ'mɪs.ᵊl, -t̬i'-, -taɪ'-

antimonarchical ˌæn.tɪ.mɒn'ɑː.kɪ.kᵊl, -mə'nɑː- US -t̬ɪ.mə'nɑːr-, -taɪ-

antimonarchist ˌæn.tɪ'mɒn.ə.kɪst US -t̬ɪ'mɑː.nɚ-, -taɪ'-, -nɑːr- **-s** -s

antimonial ˌæn.tɪ'məʊ.ni.əl US -t̬ɪ'moʊ- **-s** -z

antimonic ˌæn.tɪ'mɒn.ɪk US -t̬ɪ'mɑː.nɪk

antimony 'æn.tɪ.mə.ni, æn'tɪm.ə- US 'æn.t̬ə.moʊ-

antinode 'æn.tɪ.nəʊd US -t̬ɪ.noʊd

antinomian ˌæn.tɪ'nəʊ.mi.ən US -t̬ɪ'noʊ-, -taɪ'- **-s** -z

antinomic ˌæn.tɪ'nɒm.ɪk US -t̬ɪ'nɑː.mɪk **-al** -ᵊl **-ally** -ᵊl.i, -li

antinom|y æn'tɪn.ə.m|i **-ies** -iz

Antinous æn'tɪn.əʊ.əs US -oʊ-

antinovel 'æn.tɪˌnɒv.ᵊl US -t̬ɪˌnɑː.vᵊl, -t̬iˌ-, -taɪˌ- **-s** -z

antinuclear ˌæn.tɪ'njuː.kli.ə US -t̬ɪ'nuː-, -t̬i'-, -taɪ'-, -'njuː-

Antioch 'æn.ti.ɒk US -t̬i.ɑːk

Antiochus æn'taɪ.ə.kəs

Antioquia ˌæn.ti.əʊ'kiː.ə US -t̬i.ə'-; ɑːn'tjoʊ.kjɑː

antioxidant ˌæn.ti'ɒk.sɪ.dᵊnt US -t̬i'ɑːk-, -taɪ'- **-s** -s

Antipas 'æn.tɪ.pæs US -t̬ɪ-

antipasti ˌæn.tɪ'pæs.ti US ˌæn.t̬ɪ'pɑː.sti, ˌɑːn.t̬ɪ'-, -'pæs.ti

antipasto ˌæn.ti'pæs.təʊ US ˌæn.t̬i'pɑː.stoʊ, ˌɑːn-, -'pæs.toʊ **-s** -z

Antipater æn'tɪp.ə.təʳ US -t̬ɚ

antipathetic ˌæn.tɪ.pə'θet.ɪk, ænˌtɪp.ə'- US ˌæn.t̬ɪ.pə'θet̬.ɪk, ænˌtɪ.pə'- **-al** -ᵊl **-ally** -ᵊl.i, -li

antipath|y æn'tɪp.ə.θ|i **-ies** -iz

anti-personnel ˌæn.tɪˌpɜː.sᵊn'el US -t̬ɪˌpɝː-, -t̬iˌ-, -taɪˌ-

antiperspirant ˌæn.tɪ'pɜː.spᵊr.ənt, -spɪ.rənt US -t̬ɪ'pɝː.spɚ.ənt, -t̬i'-, -taɪ'- **-s** -s

Antipholus æn'tɪf.ə.ləs

antiphon 'æn.tɪ.fən, -fɒn US -t̬ə.fɑːn, -fən **-s** -z

antiphonal æn'tɪf.ə.nᵊl **-s** -z

antiphoner æn'tɪf.ᵊn.əʳ US -ɚ **-s** -z

antiphonic ˌæn.tɪ'fɒn.ɪk US -t̬ɪ'fɑː.nɪk **-al** -ᵊl **-ally** -ᵊl.i, -li

antiphon|y æn'tɪf.ə.n|i **-ies** -iz

antipodal æn'tɪp.ə.dᵊl

antipodean (A) ænˌtɪp.əʊ'diː.ən, ˌæn.tɪp- US -ə'-

antipodes æn'tɪp.ə.diːz

antipope 'æn.tɪ.pəʊp US -t̬ɪ.poʊp **-s** -s

antipyretic ˌæn.tɪ.paɪə'ret.ɪk, -pɪ'ret- US -t̬ɪ.paɪ'ret̬-, -t̬i-, -taɪ- **-s** -s

antipyrin ˌæn.tɪ'paɪə.rɪn, -riːn US -t̬ɪ'paɪ-, -taɪ'-

antiquarian ˌæn.tɪ'kweə.ri.ən US -t̬ə'kwer.i- **-s** -z **-ism** -ɪ.zᵊm

antiquar|y 'æn.tɪ.kwᵊr|.i US -t̬ə.kwer- **-ies** -iz

anti|quate 'æn.tɪ|.kweɪt US -t̬ə- **-quates** -kweɪts **-quating** -kweɪ.tɪŋ US -kweɪ.t̬ɪŋ **-quated** -kweɪ.tɪd US -kweɪ.t̬ɪd

antique æn'tiːk **-s** -s **-ly** -li **-ness** -nəs, -nɪs
antiquit|y æn'tɪk.wə.t|i, -wɪ- ⓤⓢ -wə.t̬|i **-ies** -iz
anti-racial|ism ˌæn.tɪ'reɪ.ʃəl|.ɪ.zəm, -ʃi.ə.l|ɪ- ⓤⓢ -t̬ɪ'reɪ.ʃəl|.ɪ-, -taɪ'- **-ist/s** -ɪst/s
anti-rac|ism ˌæn.tɪ'reɪ.s|ɪ.zəm ⓤⓢ -t̬ɪ'-, -taɪ'- **-ist/s** -ɪst/s
antirrhinum ˌæn.tɪ'raɪ.nəm, -tə'- ⓤⓢ -t̬ə'- **-s** -z
antiscorbutic ˌæn.tɪ.skɔː'bjuː.tɪk ⓤⓢ -t̬ɪ.skɔːr'bjuː.t̬ɪk, -taɪ- **-s** -s
anti-Semite ˌæn.tɪ'siː.maɪt, -'sem.aɪt ⓤⓢ -t̬ɪ'sem.aɪt, -t̬i'-, -taɪ'- **-s** -s
anti-Semitic ˌæn.tɪ.sɪ'mɪt.ɪk, -sə'- ⓤⓢ -t̬ɪ.sə'mɪt̬-, -t̬i-, -taɪ- *stress shift:* ˌanti-Semitic 'views
anti-Semitism ˌæn.tɪ'sem.ɪ.tɪ.zəm, '-ə- ⓤⓢ -t̬ɪ'sem.ə-, -t̬i'-, -taɪ'-
antisepsis ˌæn.tɪ'sep.sɪs ⓤⓢ -t̬ə'-
antiseptic ˌæn.tɪ'sep.tɪk ⓤⓢ -t̬ə'- **-s** -s **-ally** -əl.i, -li *stress shift:* ˌantiseptic 'lozenge
antiser|um ˌæn.tɪ'sɪə.r|əm ⓤⓢ -t̬ɪ'sɪr|.əm, -taɪ'- **-ums** -əmz **-a** -ə
antisocial ˌæn.tɪ'səʊ.ʃəl ⓤⓢ -t̬ɪ'soʊ-, -t̬i'-, -taɪ'- **-ly** -i
antisocialist ˌæn.tɪ'səʊ.ʃəl.ɪst ⓤⓢ -t̬ɪ'soʊ-, -t̬i'-, -taɪ'- **-s** -s
antistatic ˌæn.tɪ'stæt.ɪk ⓤⓢ -t̬ɪ'stæt̬-, -taɪ'- *stress shift:* ˌantistatic 'cloth
Antisthenes æn'tɪs.θə.niːz, -θɪ-
antistrophe æn'tɪs.trə.fi **-s** -z
antistrophic ˌæn.tɪ'strɒf.ɪk ⓤⓢ -t̬ə'strɑː.fɪk
anti-tank ˌæn.tɪ'tæŋk ⓤⓢ -t̬ɪ'-, -t̬i'-, -taɪ'-
antithes|is æn'tɪθ.ə.s|ɪs, '-ɪ- **-es** -iːz
antithetic ˌæn.tɪ'θet.ɪk ⓤⓢ -t̬ə'θet̬.ɪk **-al** -əl **-ally** -əl.i, -li
antitox|ic ˌæn.tɪ'tɒk.s|ɪk ⓤⓢ -t̬ɪ'tɑːk-, -taɪ'- **-in/s** -sɪn/z
antitrust ˌæn.tɪ'trʌst ⓤⓢ -t̬ɪ'-, -taɪ'-, -tiː-
antiviral ˌæn.tɪ'vaɪə.rəl ⓤⓢ -t̬ɪ'vaɪ-, -t̬i'-, -taɪ'-
anti-vivisection ˌæn.tɪˌvɪv.ɪ'sek.ʃən ⓤⓢ -t̬i'vɪv.ɪ.sek-, -taɪ'- **-ist/s** -ɪst/s
antler 'ænt.ləʳ ⓤⓢ -lɚ **-s** -z **-ed** -d
Antofagasta ˌæn.tə.fə'gæs.tə
Antoine ɑːn'twæn, ɒn'- ⓤⓢ 'æn.twɑːn; 'ɑːn-
Antoinette ˌæn.twɑː'net, ˌɑːn-, -twə'- ⓤⓢ ˌæn.twə'-, ˌɑːn-
Anton 'æn.tɒn ⓤⓢ -tɑːn
Antonia æn'təʊ.ni.ə ⓤⓢ -'toʊ-; ˌæn.toʊ'niː-
Antonine 'æn.tə.naɪn ⓤⓢ -t̬ə- **-s** -z
Antoninus ˌæn.təʊ'naɪ.nəs ⓤⓢ -t̬ə'-
Antonio æn'təʊ.ni.əʊ ⓤⓢ -'toʊ.ni.oʊ
Antonius æn'təʊ.ni.əs ⓤⓢ -'toʊ-
Antony 'æn.tə.ni ⓤⓢ -tən.i
antonym 'æn.tə.nɪm ⓤⓢ -tən.ɪm **-s** -z
antonymic ˌæn.tə'nɪm.ɪk ⓤⓢ -tən'ɪm-
antonymous æn'tɒn.ɪ.məs, '-ə- ⓤⓢ -'tɑː.nə-
antonymy æn'tɒn.ɪ.mi, '-ə- ⓤⓢ -'tɑː.nə-
Antrim 'æn.trɪm
Antrobus 'æn.trə.bəs
Antron 'æn.trɒn ⓤⓢ -trɑːn
antr|um 'æn.tr|əm **-ums** -əmz **-a** -ə
antsy 'ænt.si
Antwerp 'æn.twɜːp ⓤⓢ -twɝːp
ANU ˌeɪ.en'juː
Anubis ə'njuː.bɪs ⓤⓢ -'nuː-, -'njuː-
anuresis ˌæn.jʊə'riː.sɪs, -jə- ⓤⓢ -ju'-, -jə'-
anuria ˌæn'juː.ri.ə, -'jɔː- ⓤⓢ -'jʊr.i-
anus 'eɪ.nəs **-es** -ɪz
anvil 'æn.vɪl ⓤⓢ -vəl, -vɪl **-s** -z
Anwar 'æn.wɑːʳ ⓤⓢ 'ɑːn.wɑːr, 'æn-
Anwick 'æn.ɪk ⓤⓢ -wɪk
anxiet|y æŋ'zaɪ.ə.t|i, æŋg-, -ɪt|.i ⓤⓢ -ə.t̬|i **-ies** -iz
anxious 'æŋ*k*.ʃəs **-ly** -li **-ness** -nəs, -nɪs
any *normal form:* 'en.i *occasional weak form:* ə.ni *occasional weak form after t or d:* ən.i

Note: The usual pronunciation is /'en.i/, but when the word follows immediately after a strongly stressed word it may be weakened to /ə.ni/ (e.g. 'Have you got any change?' /hæv.juˌgɒt.ə.ni'tʃeɪndʒ ⓤⓢ -ˌgɑːt-/). In more rapid speech, and when preceded by an alveolar consonant, the first syllable may be reduced to syllabic /n̩/ (e.g. 'Got any more?' /ˌgɒt.n̩.i'mɔːʳ ⓤⓢ ˌgɑːt̬.n̩.i'mɔːr/).

anybody 'en.iˌbɒd.i, -bə.di ⓤⓢ -ˌbɑː.di
anyhow 'en.i.haʊ
anymore ˌen.i'mɔːʳ ⓤⓢ -'mɔːr
anyone 'en.i.wʌn, -wən
anyplace 'en.i.pleɪs
anyroad 'en.i.rəʊd ⓤⓢ -roʊd
anything 'en.i.θɪŋ
anytime 'en.i.taɪm
anyway 'en.i.weɪ **-s** -z
anywhere 'en.i.*h*weəʳ ⓤⓢ -*h*wer
anywise 'en.i.waɪz
Anzac 'æn.zæk **-s** -s **'Anzac ˌDay**
Anzio 'æn.zi.əʊ ⓤⓢ -oʊ
AOB ˌeɪ.əʊ'biː ⓤⓢ -oʊ'-
A-OK, A-Okay ˌeɪ.əʊ'keɪ ⓤⓢ -oʊ'-
AOL® ˌeɪ.əʊ'el ⓤⓢ -oʊ-
A-one ˌeɪ'wʌn *stress shift:* ˌA-one con'dition
Aoni|a eɪ'əʊ.ni|.ə ⓤⓢ -'oʊ- **-an/s** -ən/z
aorist 'eɪ.ə.rɪst, 'eə.rɪst ⓤⓢ 'eɪ.ə- **-s** -s
aort|a eɪ'ɔː.t|ə ⓤⓢ -'ɔːr.t̬|ə **-as** -əz **-ae** -iː **-al** -əl **-ic** -ɪk
Aosta ɑː'ɒs.tə ⓤⓢ -'ɔː.stə, -'oʊ-
Aouita aʊ'iː.tə ⓤⓢ -t̬ə
apace ə'peɪs
Apache ə'pætʃ.i **-s** -z
apart ə'pɑːt ⓤⓢ -'pɑːrt **-ness** -nəs, -nɪs
apartheid ə'pɑː.taɪt, -teɪd, -teɪt, -'pɑːt.heɪt, -heɪd, -haɪt ⓤⓢ -'pɑːr.teɪt, -taɪt
apartment ə'pɑːt.mənt ⓤⓢ -'pɑːrt- **-s** -s **a'partment ˌblock; a'partment ˌhouse**
apathetic ˌæp.ə'θet.ɪk ⓤⓢ -'θet̬- **-al** -əl **-ally** -əl.i, -li *stress shift:* ˌapathetic 'voters
apath|y 'æp.ə.θ|i **-ies** -iz
ap|e eɪp **-es** -s **-ing** -ɪŋ **-ed** -t
Apelles ə'pel.iːz
Apemantus æp.ɪ'mæn.təs ⓤⓢ -t̬əs
Apennines 'æp.ə.naɪnz, -en.aɪnz
aperçu ˌæp.ɜː'sjuː, -ə'-, -'suː ⓤⓢ -ɚ'suː, ˌɑː.pɚ'- **-s** -z
aperient ə'pɪə.ri.ənt ⓤⓢ -'pɪr.i- **-s** -s
aperiodic ˌeɪ.pɪə.ri'ɒd.ɪk ⓤⓢ -pɪr.i'ɑː.dɪk
aperiodicity ˌeɪ.pɪə.ri.ə'dɪs.ə.ti, -ɪ.ti ⓤⓢ -pɪr.i.ə'dɪs.ə.t̬i
aperitif əˌper.ə'tiːf, æpˌer-, -ɪ'-, ə'per.ə.tɪf ⓤⓢ ɑːˌper.ɪ'-, -ə'- **-s** -s
aperture 'æp.ə.tʃəʳ, -tjʊəʳ ⓤⓢ -ɚ.tʃʊr, -tʃɚ **-s** -z
aper|y 'eɪ.pə.r|i **-ies** -iz
apeshit 'eɪp.ʃɪt
apex, APEX (A) 'eɪ.peks **-es** -ɪz
aphaeresis æf'ɪə.rə.sɪs, ə'fɪə-, -rɪ- ⓤⓢ ə'fer.ə-
aphasia ə'feɪ.zi.ə, æf'eɪ-, eɪ'feɪ-, -ʒi.ə, -ʒə ⓤⓢ ə'feɪ.ʒə, -ʒi.ə
aphasic ə'feɪ.zɪk, æf'eɪ-, eɪ'feɪ- ⓤⓢ ə'feɪ-
apheli|on æf'iː.li.|ən **-a** -ə
apheresis æf'ɪə.rə.sɪs, ə'fɪə-, -rɪ- ⓤⓢ ə'fer.ə-
aphes|is 'æf.ə.s|ɪs, '-ɪ- **-es** -iːz
aphid 'eɪ.fɪd ⓤⓢ 'eɪ.fɪd, 'æf.ɪd, -əd **-s** -z
aphidian eɪ'fɪd.i.ən, æf'ɪd- **-s** -z
aph|is 'eɪ.f|ɪs, 'æf|.ɪs **-ides** -ɪ.diːz **-ises** -ɪ.sɪz
aphonia eɪ'fəʊ.ni.ə, æf'əʊ-, ə'fəʊ- ⓤⓢ eɪ'foʊ-
aphonic eɪ'fɒn.ɪk, æf'ɒn-, ə'fɒn- ⓤⓢ eɪ'fɑː.nɪk
aphony 'æf.ə.ni
aphorism 'æf.ər.ɪ.zəm, -ɒr- ⓤⓢ '-ɚ- **-s** -z
aphorist 'æf.ər.ɪst, -ɒr- ⓤⓢ '-ɚ- **-s** -s
aphoristic ˌæf.ər'ɪs.tɪk, -ɒr'- ⓤⓢ -ə'rɪs- **-ally** -əl.i, -li
aphoriz|e, -is|e 'æf.ər.aɪz, -ɒr- ⓤⓢ -ə.raɪz **-es** -ɪz **-ing** -ɪŋ **-ed** -d **-er/s** -əʳ/z ⓤⓢ -ɚ/z
Aphra 'æf.rə
aphrodisiac ˌæf.rəʊ'dɪz.i.æk ⓤⓢ -rə'-, -roʊ'-, -'diː.zi- **-s** -s
aphrodisian ˌæf.rəʊ'dɪz.i.ən

(US) -rəˈdiː.zi-, -roʊˈ-, -ˈdɪz.i-, -ˈdɪʒ.ən **-s** -z

Aphrodite ˌæf.rəʊˈdaɪ.ti (US) -rəˈdaɪ.t̬i, -roʊˈ-

aphtha ˈæf.θə

Apia ɑːˈpiː.ə

apian ˈeɪ.pi.ən

apiarian ˌeɪ.piˈeə.ri.ən (US) -ˈer.i- **-s** -z

apiarist ˈeɪ.pi.ə.rɪst **-s** -s

apiar|y ˈeɪ.pi.ə.r|i (US) -er|.i **-ies** -iz

apical ˈæp.ɪ.kᵊl, ˈeɪ.pɪ- **-ly** -i

apices *(alternative plur. of* **apex***)* ˈeɪ.pɪ.siːz, ˈæp.ɪ-

apiculture ˈeɪ.pɪ.kʌl.tʃəʳ (US) -tʃɚ

apiece əˈpiːs

apis ˈeɪ.pɪs

Apis ˈɑː.pɪs, ˈeɪ-

apish ˈeɪ.pɪʃ **-ly** -li **-ness** -nəs, -nɪs

aplenty əˈplen.ti (US) -t̬i

aplomb əˈplɒm, æpˈlɒm (US) əˈplɑːm, -ˈplʌm

apn(o)ea æpˈniː.ə, ˈæp.ni.ə

apn(o)eic æpˈniː.ɪk

apocalyps|e (A) əˈpɒk.ə.lɪps (US) -ˈpɑː.kə- **-es** -ɪz

apocalypt|ic əˌpɒk.əˈlɪp.t|ɪk (US) -ˌpɑː.kəˈ- **-ist/s** -ɪst/s **-ical** -ɪ.kᵊl *stress shift:* aˌpocalyptic ˈvision

apocope əˈpɒk.əʊ.pi (US) -ˈpɑː.kə- **-s** -z

apocryph|a (A) əˈpɒk.rɪ.f|ə, -rə- (US) -ˈpɑː.krə- **-al** -ᵊl

apocryphal əˈpɒk.rɪ.fəl, -rə- (US) -ˈpɑː.krə-

apodeictic ˌæp.əʊˈdaɪk.tɪk (US) -əˈ-, -oʊˈ- **-al** -ᵊl **-ally** -ᵊl.i, -li

apodictic ˌæp.əʊˈdɪk.tɪk (US) -əˈ-, -oʊˈ- **-al** -ᵊl **-ally** -ᵊl.i, -li

apodos|is əˈpɒd.ə.s|ɪs (US) -ˈpɑː.də- **-es** -iːz

apogee ˈæp.əʊ.dʒiː (US) -ə- **-s** -z

apolitical ˌeɪ.pəˈlɪt.ɪ.kᵊl, ˈ-ə- (US) -ˈlɪt̬.ə-

Apollinaire əˌpɒl.ɪˈneəʳ (US) -ˌpɑː.lɪˈner

Apollinaris əˌpɒl.ɪˈnɑː.rɪs, -ˈeə- (US) -pɑː.lɪˈner.ɪs

Apollo əˈpɒl.əʊ (US) -ˈpɑː.loʊ

Apollodorus əˌpɒl.əˈdɔː.rəs (US) -ˌpɑː.ləˈdɔːr.əs

Apolloni|a ˌæp.əˈləʊ.ni.|ə, -ɒlˈəʊ- (US) -əˈloʊ- **-an** -ən **-us** -əs

Apollos əˈpɒl.əs (US) -ˈpɑː.ləs

Apollyon əˈpɒl.i.ən (US) -ˈpɑː.li-

apologetic əˌpɒl.əˈdʒet.ɪk (US) -ˌpɑː.ləˈdʒet̬.ɪk **-al** -ᵊl **-ally** -ᵊl.i, -li **-s** -s

apologia ˌæp.əˈləʊ.dʒə, dʒi.ə (US) -ˈloʊ- **-s** -z

apologist əˈpɒl.ə.dʒɪst (US) -ˈpɑː.lə- **-s** -s

apologiz|e, -is|e əˈpɒl.ə.dʒaɪz (US) -ˈpɑː.lə- **-es** -ɪz **-ing** -ɪŋ **-ed** -d **-er/s** -əʳ/z, -ɚ/z

apologue ˈæp.əʊ.lɒg (US) -ə.lɑːg **-s** -z

apolog|y əˈpɒl.ə.dʒ|i (US) -ˈpɑː.lə- **-ies** -iz

apophthegm ˈæp.ə.θem **-s** -z

apoplectic ˌæp.əˈplek.tɪk **-al** -ᵊl **-ally** -ᵊl.i, -li

apoplex|y ˈæp.ə.plek.s|i **-ies** -iz

aposiopes|is ˌæp.ə.saɪ.əʊˈpiː.s|ɪs, əˌpɒs.i.əʊˈ- (US) ˌæp.oʊ.saɪ.oʊˈ-, -ə.saɪ.əˈ- **-es** -iːz

apostas|y əˈpɒs.tə.s|i (US) -ˈpɑː.stə- **-ies** -iz

apostate əˈpɒs.teɪt, -tɪt, -tət (US) -ˈpɑː.steɪt, -stɪt, -stət **-s** -s

apostatic ˌæp.əʊˈstæt.ɪk (US) -əˈstæt̬- **-al** -ᵊl

apostatiz|e, -is|e əˈpɒs.tə.taɪz (US) -ˈpɑː.stə- **-es** -ɪz **-ing** -ɪŋ **-ed** -d

a posteriori eɪ.pɒsˌter.iˈɔː.raɪ, ˌɑː-, -tɪə.ri- -riː- (US) eɪ.pɑːˌstɪr-

apostil əˈpɒs.tɪl (US) -ˈpɑː.stɪl **-s** -z

apostle əˈpɒs.l̩ (US) -ˈpɑː.sl̩ **-s** -z **-ship** -ʃɪp

apostolate əˈpɒs.tə.lət, -lɪt, -leɪt (US) -ˈpɑː.stə.lɪt, -leɪt **-s** -s

apostolic ˌæp.əˈstɒl.ɪk (US) -ˈstɑː.lɪk **-al** -ᵊl **-ally** -ᵊl.i

apostolicism ˌæp.əˈstɒl.ɪ.sɪ.zᵊm (US) -ˈstɑː.lɪ-

apostrophe əˈpɒs.trə.fi (US) -ˈpɑː.strə- **-s** -z

apostrophiz|e, -is|e əˈpɒs.trə.faɪz (US) -ˈpɑː.strə- **-es** -ɪz **-ing** -ɪŋ **-ed** -d

apothecar|y əˈpɒθ.ə.kᵊr.|i, ˈ-ɪ- (US) -ˈpɑː.θə- **-ies** -iz

apothegm ˈæp.ə.θem **-s** -z

apothegmatic ˌæp.ə.θegˈmæt.ɪk (US) -ˈmæt̬- **-al** -ᵊl

apotheos|is əˌpɒθ.iˈəʊ.s|ɪs, ˌæp.əʊ.θiˈ- (US) əˌpɑː.θiˈoʊ-, ˌæp.əˈθiː.ə- **-es** -iːz

apotheosiz|e, -is|e əˈpɒθ.i.əʊ.saɪz, ˌæp.əˈθiː.əʊ.saɪz (US) əˈpɑː.θi.oʊ-, ˌæp.əˈθiː.ə- **-es** -ɪz **-ing** -ɪŋ **-ed** -d

appal əˈpɔːl (US) -ˈpɔːl, -ˈpɑːl **-s** -z **-ling/ly** -ɪŋ/li **-led** -d

Appalachi|a ˌæp.əˈleɪ.ʃ|ə, -tʃ|ə, -ʃi|.ə (US) -ˈleɪ.tʃi-, -ˈlætʃ.i-, -ˈleɪ.tʃ|ə, -ˈlætʃ|.ə **-an/s** -ən/z

appall əˈpɔːl (US) -ˈpɔːl, -ˈpɑːl **-s** -z **-ing/ly** -ɪŋ/li **-ed** -d

Appaloosa ˌæp.əˈluː.sə

appanag|e ˈæp.ə.nɪdʒ **-es** -ɪz

apparat ˌæp.əˈrɑːt (US) ˌɑː.pəˈ-, ˈæp.ə.ræt **-s** -s

apparatchik ˌæp.əˈrætʃ.ɪk, -ˈræt.tʃɪk, -ˈrɑːt-, -ˈrɑː.tʃɪk (US) ˌɑː.pəˈrɑː.tʃɪk, -ˈrɑːt.tʃɪk **-s** -s **-i** -i

apparatus ˌæp.ᵊrˈeɪ.təs, -ˈæt.əs (US) -əˈræt̬- **-es** -ɪz

apparel əˈpær.ᵊl (US) -ˈper-, -ˈpær- **-s** -z **-ling** -ɪŋ **-led** -d

apparent əˈpær.ᵊnt, -ˈpeə.rᵊnt (US) -ˈper.ᵊnt, -ˈpær- **-ly** -li **-ness** -nəs, -nɪs

apparition ˌæp.ᵊrˈɪʃ.ᵊn (US) -əˈrɪʃ- **-s** -z

apparitor əˈpær.ɪ.təʳ (US) -ˈper.ɪ.t̬ɚ, -ˈpær- **-s** -z

appassionata əˌpæs.i.əˈnɑː.tə, -ˌpæs.jəˈ- (US) -ˌpɑː.si.əˈnɑː.t̬ə, -ˌpæs.i-

appeal əˈpiːl **-s** -z **-ing** -ɪŋ **-ed** -d **-er/s** -əʳ/z (US) -ɚ/z **Apˈpeal ˌCourt**

appealing əˈpiː.lɪŋ **-ly** -li **-ness** -nəs, -nɪs

appear əˈpɪəʳ (US) -ˈpɪr **-s** -z **-ing** -ɪŋ **-ed** -d **-er/s** -əʳ/z (US) -ɚ/z

appearanc|e əˈpɪə.rᵊnts (US) -ˈpɪr.ᵊnts **-es** -ɪz

appeas|e əˈpiːz **-es** -ɪz **-ing/ly** -ɪŋ/li **-ed** -d **-able** -ə.bl̩

appeasement əˈpiːz.mənt **-s** -s

appellant əˈpel.ənt **-s** -s

appellate əˈpel.ət, æpˈel-, -eɪt, -ɪt (US) -ɪt

appellation ˌæp.əˈleɪ.ʃᵊn, -ɪˈ-, -elˈeɪ- **-s** -z

appellation contrôlée *as if French:* æp.el.æsˌjɔ̃ːŋ.kɔ̃ːn.trəʊˈleɪ, æp.elˌæs.jɔ̃ːŋ-, -kɒnˈtrəʊ.leɪ (US) æp.elˌɑː.sjoʊn.kɑːn.troʊˈleɪ

appellative əˈpel.ə.tɪv, æpˈel- (US) -t̬ɪv **-ly** -li **-ness** -nəs, -nɪs

append əˈpend **-s** -z **-ing** -ɪŋ **-ed** -ɪd

appendag|e əˈpen.dɪdʒ **-es** -ɪz

appendant əˈpen.dənt **-s** -s

appendectom|y ˌæp.enˈdek.tə.m|i **-ies** -iz

appendicitis əˌpen.dɪˈsaɪ.tɪs, -dəˈ-

appendicular ˌæp.enˈdɪk.jʊ.ləʳ, -ənˈ-, -ɪnˈ-, -jə- (US) -ju.lɚ

append|ix əˈpen.d|ɪks **-ixes** -ɪk.sɪz **-ices** -ɪ.siːz

appercep|tion ˌæp.əˈsep.|ʃᵊn (US) -ɚˈ- **-tive** -tɪv

Apperley ˈæp.ə.li (US) -ɚ-

appertain ˌæp.əˈteɪn (US) -ɚˈ- **-s** -z **-ing** -ɪŋ **-ed** -d

appertinent əˈpɜː.tɪ.nənt, æpˈɜː- (US) əˈpɝː.tᵊn.ənt

appeten|ce ˈæp.ɪ.tᵊn|ts **-cy** -t.si **-t** -t

appetite ˈæp.ɪ.taɪt, ˈ-ə- (US) ˈ-ə- **-s** -s

appetizer, -iser ˈæp.ɪ.taɪ.zəʳ, ˈ-ə- (US) -ə.taɪ.zɚ **-s** -z

appetizing, -isi- ˈæp.ɪ.taɪ.zɪŋ, ˈ-ə- (US) ˈ-ə- **-ly** -li

Appi|an ˈæp.i|.ən **-us** -əs

applaud əˈplɔːd (US) -ˈplɑːd, -ˈplɔːd **-s** -z **-ing/ly** -ɪŋ/lɪ **-ed** -ɪd **-er/s** -əʳ/z, -ɚ/z

applause əˈplɔːz (US) -ˈplɑːz, -ˈplɔːz

apple ˈæp.l̩ **-s** -z **ˈapple ˌblossom; ˈapple ˌbutter; ˌapple ˈsauce;** (US) **ˈapple ˌsauce; ˈapple ˌtree; the ˌapple of one's ˈeye**

Appleby ˈæp.l̩.bi

apple-cart ˈæp.l̩.kɑːt (US) -kɑːrt

Appledore ˈæp.l̩.dɔːʳ (US) -dɔːr

Approximant

A phonetic term of comparatively recent origin, used to denote a consonant which makes very little obstruction to the airflow.

Examples for English

Traditionally approximants have been divided into two groups. Sounds in the first group are known as 'semivowels' such as the /w/ and /j/, which are very similar to 'close vowels' such as [u] and [i] but are produced as a rapid glide, e.g.:

wet /wet/
yet /jet/

'Liquids' are sounds which have an identifiable constriction of the airflow but not one that is sufficiently obstructive to produce fricative noise, compression or the diversion of airflow through another part of the vocal tract as in nasals. This category includes laterals such as /l/ and non-fricative /r/ (phonetically [ɹ] in British English and [ɻ] in US English), e.g.:

lead /liːd/
read /riːd/

Approximants therefore are never fricative and never contain interruptions to the flow of air.

Appleford 'æp.l̩.fəd US -fɚd
Applegate 'æp.l̩.geɪt, -gɪt
applejack 'æp.l̩.dʒæk
apple-pie ˌæp.l̩'paɪ **-s** -z *stress shift, see compounds:* **in** ˌ**apple-pie** '**order**; *British only:* ˌ**apple-pie** '**bed**
Appleseed 'æp.l̩.siːd
applet 'æp.lət **-s** -s
Appleton 'æp.l̩.tən US -t̬ən
appliable ə'plaɪ.ə.bl̩ **-ness** -nəs, -nɪs
applianc|e ə'plaɪ.ənts **-es** -ɪz
applicability ˌæp.lɪ.kə'bɪl.ə.ti, əˌplɪk-, -ɪ.ti US -ə.t̬i
applicab|le ə'plɪk.ə.bl|l̩, 'æp.lɪ- **-ly** -li **-leness** -l̩.nəs, -nɪs
applicant 'æp.lɪ.kənt, -lə- **-s** -s
applicate 'æp.lɪ.kət, -lə-, -kɪt, -keɪt
application ˌæp.lɪ'keɪ.ʃᵊn, -lə'- **-s** -z
applicator 'æp.lɪ.keɪ.təʳ, -lə- US -t̬ɚ **-s** -z
appliqué æp'liː.keɪ, ə'pliː-; 'æp.lɪ.keɪ US 'æp.lə.keɪ, -lɪ- **-s** -z **-ing** -ɪŋ, **-d** -d
appl|y ə'pl|aɪ **-ies** -aɪz **-ying** -aɪ.ɪŋ **-ied** -aɪd
appoggiatura əˌpɒdʒ.ə'tʊə.rə, -i.ə'-, -'tjʊə- US əˌpɑː.dʒə'tʊr.ə **-s** -z
ap|point ə|'pɔɪnt **-points** -'pɔɪnts **-pointing** -'pɔɪn.tɪŋ US -'pɔɪn.t̬ɪŋ **-pointed** -'pɔɪn.tɪd US -'pɔɪn.t̬ɪd
appointee əˌpɔɪn'tiː, ˌæp.ɔɪn'- **-s** -z
appointive ə'pɔɪn.tɪv US -t̬ɪv
appointment ə'pɔɪnt.mənt **-s** -s
Appomattox ˌæp.ə'mæt.əks US -'mæt̬-
ap|port ə|'pɔːt US -'pɔːrt **-ports** -'pɔːts US -'pɔːrts **-porting** -'pɔː.tɪŋ US -'pɔːr.t̬ɪŋ **-ported** -'pɔː.tɪd US -'pɔːr.t̬ɪd
apportion ə'pɔː.ʃᵊn US -'pɔːr- **-s** -z **-ing** -ɪŋ **-ed** -d **-ment/s** -mənt/s
appos|e ə'pəʊz, æp'əʊz US ə'poʊz **-es** -ɪz **-ing** -ɪŋ **-ed** -d
apposite 'æp.ə.zɪt, -zaɪt US -zɪt **-ly** -li **-ness** -nəs, -nɪs
apposition ˌæp.ə'zɪʃ.ᵊn **-s** -z
appositional ˌæp.ə'zɪʃ.ᵊn.ᵊl
appraisal ə'preɪ.zᵊl **-s** -z
apprais|e ə'preɪz **-es** -ɪz **-ing** -ɪŋ **-ed** -d **-er/s** -əʳ/z US -ɚ/s **-able** -ə.bl̩
appraisee ˌæp.reɪ'ziː, -'-- US ˌæ.preɪ'ziː, ˌə- **-s** -z
appraisement ə'preɪz.mənt **-s** -s
appreciab|le ə'priː.ʃə.bl|l̩, -ʃi.ə-, -si.ə- US '-ʃə-, '-ʃi.ə- **-ly** -li
appreci|ate ə'priː.ʃi|.eɪt, -si- US -ʃi- **-ates** -eɪts **-ating/ly** -eɪ.tɪŋ/li US -eɪ.t̬ɪŋ/li **-ated** -eɪ.tɪd US -eɪ.t̬ɪd **-ator/s** -eɪ.təʳ/z US -eɪ.t̬ɚ/z
appreciation əˌpriː.ʃi'eɪ.ʃᵊn, -si'- US -ʃi'- **-s** -z
appreciative ə'priː.ʃə.tɪv, '-ʃi.ə.tɪv US -'priː.ʃə.t̬ɪv, '-ʃi.ə-, -eɪ- **-ly** -li **-ness** -nəs, -nɪs
appreciatory ə'priː.ʃi.ə.tᵊr.i, -ʃi.eɪ-, -si.ə- US '-ʃə.tɔːr-, '-ʃi.ə-
apprehend ˌæp.rɪ'hend, -rə'- **-s** -z **-ing** -ɪŋ **-ed** -ɪd
apprehensibility ˌæp.rɪˌhent.sɪ'bɪl.ə.ti, -rə-, -sə'-, -ɪ.ti US -ə.t̬i
apprehensible ˌæp.rɪ'hent.sɪ.bl̩, -rə'-, -sə-
apprehension ˌæp.rɪ'hen.tʃᵊn, -rə'- US -'hent.ʃᵊn **-s** -z
apprehensive ˌæp.rɪ'hent.sɪv, -rə'- **-ly** -li **-ness** -nəs, -nɪs
apprentic|e ə'pren.tɪs US -t̬ɪs **-es** -ɪz **-ing** -ɪŋ **-ed** -t
apprenticeship ə'pren.tɪ.ʃɪp, -tɪs- US -t̬əs.ʃɪp, -t̬ə- **-s** -s
appris|e, -iz|e ə'praɪz **-es** -ɪz **-ing** -ɪŋ **-ed** -d **-er/s** -əʳ/z US -ɚ/z
appro 'æp.rəʊ US -roʊ
approach ə'prəʊtʃ US -'proʊtʃ **-es** -ɪz **-ing** -ɪŋ **-ed** -t
approachability əˌprəʊ.tʃə'bɪl.ə.ti, -ɪ.ti US -ˌproʊ.tʃə'bɪl.ə.t̬i
approachable ə'prəʊ.tʃə.bl̩ US -'proʊ-
appro|bate 'æp.rəʊ|.beɪt US -rə- **-bates** -beɪts **-bating** -beɪ.tɪŋ US -beɪ.t̬ɪŋ **-bated** -beɪ.tɪd US -beɪ.t̬ɪd **-bative** -beɪ.tɪv US -beɪ.t̬ɪv
approbation ˌæp.rəʊ'beɪ.ʃᵊn US -rə'-, -roʊ'- **-s** -z
approbatory ˌæp.rəʊ'beɪ.tᵊr.i US ə'proʊ.bə.tɔːr-
appropriate *(adj.)* ə'prəʊ.pri.ət, -ɪt US -'proʊ- **-ly** -li **-ness** -nəs, -nɪs
appropri|ate *(v.)* ə'prəʊ.pri|.eɪt US -'proʊ- **-ates** -eɪts **-ating** -eɪ.tɪŋ US -eɪ.t̬ɪŋ **-ated** -eɪ.tɪd US -eɪ.t̬ɪd **-ator/s** -eɪ.təʳ/z US -eɪ.t̬ɚ/z
appropriation əˌprəʊ.pri'eɪ.ʃᵊn US -ˌproʊ- **-s** -z
approval ə'pruː.vᵊl **-s** -z
approv|e ə'pruːv **-es** -z **-ing/ly** -ɪŋ/li **-ed** -d **-er/s** -əʳ/z US -ɚ/z **-able** -ə.bl̩
approx *(abbrev. for* **approximate/ly***)* ə'prɒk.sɪ.mət/li, -sə-, -mɪt/li US -'prɑːk-
approximant ə'prɒk.sɪ.mənt, -sə- US -'prɑːk- **-s** -s
approximate *(adj.)* ə'prɒk.sɪ.mət, -sə-, -mɪt US -'prɑːk- **-ly** -li
approxi|mate *(v.)* ə'prɒk.sɪ|.meɪt, -sə- US -'prɑːk- **-mates** -meɪts **-mating** -meɪ.tɪŋ US -meɪ.t̬ɪŋ **-mated** -meɪ.tɪd US -meɪ.t̬ɪd
approximation əˌprɒk.sɪ'meɪ.ʃᵊn, -sə'- US -ˌprɑːk- **-s** -z
approximative ə'prɒk.sɪ.mə.tɪv, -sə- US -'prɑːk.sə.mə.t̬ɪv
appui æp'wiː, ə'pwiː
appuls|e æp'ʌls, ə'pʌls, 'æp.ʌls **-es** -ɪz
appurtenan|ce ə'pɜː.tɪ.nən|ts, -tᵊn.ᵊn|ts US -'pɝː.tᵊn- **-ces** -t.sɪz **-t** -t
APR ˌeɪ.pi'ɑːʳ US -'ɑːr
Apr. *(abbrev. for* **April***)* 'eɪ.prᵊl, -prɪl
après 'æp.reɪ US ˌɑː'preɪ, ˌæp'reɪ
après-ski ˌæp.reɪ'skiː US ˌɑː.preɪ'-, ˌæp.reɪ'- *stress shift:* ˌapräs-ski 'drinks

apricot 'eɪ.prɪ.kɒt (US) -kɑːt, 'æp.rɪ- **-s** -s

April 'eɪ.prᵊl, -prɪl **-s** -z ˌ**April 'Fools' ˌDay**

a priori eɪ.praɪ'ɔː.raɪ, ˌɑː.priː'ɔː.ri (US) ˌɑː.priː'ɔːr.aɪ, ˌeɪ-, -i

apriority ˌeɪ.praɪ'ɒr.ə.ti, -ɪ.ti (US) -'ɔːr.ə.t̬i

apron 'eɪ.prən **-s** -z **-ed** -d **'apron ˌstrings**

apropos ˌæp.rə'pəʊ (US) -'poʊ

aps|e æps **-es** -ɪz

apsidal 'æp.sɪ.dᵊl

Apsley 'æp.sli

apt æpt **-er** -əʳ (US) -ɚ **-est** -əst, -ɪst **-ly** -li **-ness** -nəs, -nɪs

apter|al 'æp.tᵊr|.ᵊl **-ous** -əs

apteryx 'æp.tᵊr.ɪks **-es** -ɪz

aptitude 'æp.tɪ.tjuːd, -tə-, -tʃuːd (US) -tuːd, -tjuːd **-s** -z

aptitudinal ˌæp.tɪ'tjuː.dɪ.nᵊl, -tə'-, -'tʃuː- (US) -'tuː.dᵊn.ᵊl, -'tjuː- **-ly** -li

Apuli|a ə'pjuː.li|.ə **-an/s** -ən/z

apyretic ˌæp.aɪə'ret.ɪk, ˌeɪ.paɪə'-, -paɪ.ɪ'- (US) -paɪ'ret̬-

aqua 'æk.wə (US) 'ɑːk-

aquacultural ˌæk.wə'kʌl.tʃᵊr.ᵊl (US) ˌɑː.kwə'-, ˌæk.wə'-

aquaculture 'æk.wəˌkʌl.tʃəʳ (US) 'ɑː.kwəˌkʌl.tʃɚ, 'æk.wəˌ-

aqua fortis ˌæk.wə'fɔː.tɪs (US) ˌɑː.kwə'fɔːr.t̬ɪs, ˌæk.wə'-

aquamarine ˌæk.wə.mə'riːn, 'æk.wə.mə.riːn (US) ˌɑː.kwə.mə'riːn, ˌæk.wə- **-s** -z

aquaplan|e 'æk.wə.pleɪn (US) 'ɑː.kwə-, 'æk.wə- **-es** -z **-ing** -ɪŋ **-ed** -d

aqua regia ˌæk.wə'riː.dʒi.ə (US) ˌɑː.kwə'-, ˌæk.wə'-

aquarell|e ˌæk.wə'rel (US) ˌɑː.kwə'-, ˌæk.wə'- **-es** -z **-ist/s** -ɪst/s

aquarist 'æk.wə.rɪst (US) ə'kwer.ɪst **-s** -s

aquari|um ə'kweə.ri.|əm (US) -'kwer.i- **-ums** -əmz **-a** -ə

Aquari|us ə'kweə.ri.|əs (US) -'kwer.i- **-an/s** -ən/z

Aquascutum® ˌæk.wə'sk*j*uː.təm (US) ˌɑː.kwə'skuː.t̬əm, ˌæk.wə'-

aquatic ə'kwæt.ɪk, -'kwɒt- (US) -'kwæt̬-, -'kwɑː.t̬ɪk **-s** -s **-ally** -ᵊl.i, -li

aquatint 'æk.wə.tɪnt (US) 'ɑː.kwə-, 'æk.wə- **-s** -s

aquatube 'æk.wə.tjuːb, -tʃuːb (US) 'ɑː.kwə.tuːb, 'æk.wə-, -tjuːb **-s** -z

aquavit 'æk.wə.vɪt, -viːt (US) 'ɑː.kwə.viːt

aqua vitae ˌæk.wə'viː.taɪ, -'vaɪ.tiː (US) ˌɑː.kwə'vaɪ.t̬iː, ˌæk.wə'-

aqueduct 'æk.wɪ.dʌkt, -wə- **-s** -s

aqueous 'eɪ.kwi.əs, 'æk.wi- **-ly** -li

aquifer 'æk.wɪ.fəʳ, -wə.fəʳ (US) 'ɑː.kwə.fɚ, 'æk.wə- **-s** -z

Aquila 'æk.wɪ.lə, -wə-; ə'kwɪl.ə

aquilegia ˌæk.wɪ'liː.dʒi.ə, -wə-, -'liː.dʒə **-s** -z

aquiline 'æk.wɪ.laɪn, -wə- (US) -lən

Aquinas ə'kwaɪ.nəs, æk'waɪ-, -næs

Aquino ə'kiː.nəʊ (US) -noʊ

Aquitaine ˌæk.wɪ'teɪn, -wə'teɪn, '---

Aquitania ˌæk.wɪ'teɪ.ni.ə

aquiver ə'kwɪv.əʳ (US) -ɚ

ar- ə'r-; 'ær- (US) ə'r-; 'er-, 'ær-

Note: Prefix. Examples include **arrogate** /'ær.əʊ.geɪt (US) 'er.ə-/, in which it is stressed, and **array** /ə'reɪ/, where it is unstressed.

-ar -əʳ, -ɑːʳ (US) -ɚ, -ɑːr

Note: Suffix. Normally pronounced /-əʳ (US) -ɚ/, e.g. **molecular** /məʊ'lek.jə.ləʳ (US) moʊ'lek.juː.lɚ/, but in some cases /-ɑːʳ (US) -ɑːr/, e.g. **sonar** /'səʊ.nɑːʳ (US) 'soʊ.nɑːr/.

Arab 'ær.əb (US) 'er-, 'ær- **-s** -z

Arabella ˌær.ə'bel.ə (US) ˌer-, ˌær-

arabesque ˌær.ə'besk (US) ˌer-, ˌær- **-s** -s **-d** -t

Arabi|a ə'reɪ.bi|.ə **-an/s** -ən/z

Arabic *of Arabia:* 'ær.ə.bɪk (US) 'er-, 'ær- *name of ship:* 'ær.ə.bɪk; ə'ræb- (US) 'er.ə-, 'ær-; ə'ræb-

arabis 'ær.ə.bɪs (US) 'er-, 'ær-

Arabist 'ær.ə.bɪst (US) 'er-, 'ær- **-s** -s

arable 'ær.ə.bl̩ (US) 'er-, 'ær-

Araby 'ær.ə.bi (US) 'er-, 'ær-

Aracaju ˌær.ə.kæʒ'uː (US) ɑːˌrɑː.kə'ʒuː

Arachne ə'ræk.ni

arachnid ə'ræk.nɪd **-a** -ə **-s** -z

arachnoid ə'ræk.nɔɪd **-s** -z

arachnologist ˌær.æk'nɒl.ə.dʒɪst, -ək'- (US) ˌer.ək'nɑː.lə-, ˌær- **-s** -s

arachnopho|bia əˌræk.nəʊ'fəʊ.|bi.ə (US) -nə'foʊ-, -noʊ'- **-bic** -bɪk

Arafat 'ær.ə.fæt (US) 'er-, 'ær-

Arafura ˌær.ə'fʊə.rə (US) ˌɑːr.ə'fʊr.ə

Aragon 'ær.ə.gən (US) 'er.ə.gɑːn, 'ær-, -gən

aragonite ə'ræg.ᵊn.aɪt; 'ær.ə.gᵊn- (US) ə'ræg.ᵊn-; 'er.ə.gᵊn-, 'ær-

Aral 'ɑː.rəl, 'ær.əl, -æl (US) 'er.əl, 'ær-

Araldite® 'ær.ᵊl.daɪt (US) 'er-, 'ær-

Aram *biblical name:* 'eə.ræm, -rəm (US) 'er.æm, 'ær-, 'eɪ.rəm, 'ɑːr.əm *surname:* 'eə.rəm (US) 'er.əm, 'ær-

Aramaean ˌær.ə'miː.ən (US) ˌer-, ˌær-

Arama|ic ˌær.ə'meɪ|.ɪk (US) ˌer-, ˌær- **-ism** -ɪ.zᵊm

Aramean ˌær.ə'miː.ən (US) ˌer-, ˌær- **-s** -z

aramid 'ær.ə.mɪd (US) 'er-, 'ær- **-s** -z

Aramite 'ær.ə.maɪt (US) 'er-, 'ær- **-s** -s

Aran 'ær.ən (US) 'er-, 'ær-

Arapaho ə'ræp.ə.həʊ (US) -hoʊ

Ararat 'ær.ə.ræt (US) 'er-, 'ær-

Araucani|a ˌær.ɔː'keɪ.ni|.ə (US) ˌer-, ˌær-, -ɑː'-; əˌraʊ.kɑː'niː- **-an/s** -ən/z

araucaria ˌær.ɔː'keə.ri.ə (US) ˌer.ɔː'ker.i-, ˌær-, -ɑː'- **-s** -z

Arawak 'ær.ə.wæk, -wɑːk (US) 'ɑːr.ə.wɑːk; 'ær.ə.wæk, 'er- **-s** -s

Arber 'ɑː.bəʳ (US) 'ɑːr.bɚ

Arberry 'ɑː.bᵊr.i (US) 'ɑːr.ber-

Arbil 'ɑː.bɪl (US) 'ɑːr-

arbiter 'ɑː.bɪ.təʳ (US) 'ɑːr.bɪ.t̬ɚ **-s** -z

arbitrage *arbitration:* 'ɑː.bɪ.trɪdʒ (US) 'ɑːr- *of stocks, etc.:* ˌɑː.bɪ'trɑːʒ, 'ɑː.bɪ.trɪdʒ (US) 'ɑːr.bɪ.trɑːʒ

arbitrageur ˌɑː.bɪ.trɑː'ʒɜːʳ (US) 'ɑːr.bɪ.trɑː.ʒɚ **-s** -z

arbitrament ɑː'bɪt.rə.mənt (US) ɑːr- **-s** -s

arbitrarily ˌɑː.bɪ'treᵊ.rᵊl.i, 'ɑː.bɪ.trᵊr.ᵊl.i (US) ˌɑːr.bə'trer.ᵊl-

arbitrar|y 'ɑː.bɪ.trᵊr|.i (US) 'ɑːr.bə.trer- **-iness** -ɪ.nəs, -ɪ.nɪs

arbi|trate 'ɑː.bɪ|.treɪt (US) 'ɑːr.bə|.treɪt **-trates** -treɪts **-trating** -treɪ.tɪŋ (US) -treɪ.t̬ɪŋ **-trated** -treɪ.tɪd (US) -treɪ.t̬ɪd

arbitration ˌɑː.bɪ'treɪ.ʃᵊn (US) ˌɑːr.bə'- **-s** -z

arbitrator 'ɑː.bɪ.treɪ.təʳ (US) 'ɑːr.bə- **-s** -z

Arblay 'ɑː.bleɪ (US) 'ɑːr-

arbor *tree:* 'ɑː.bɔːʳ, -bəʳ (US) 'ɑːr.bɚ *axle, shaft:* 'ɑː.bəʳ (US) 'ɑːr.bɚ **-s** -z

Arbor 'ɑː.bəʳ (US) 'ɑːr.bɚ **'Arbor ˌDay**

arboraceous ˌɑː.bᵊr'eɪ.ʃəs, -bɔː'reɪ- (US) ˌɑːr.bə'reɪ-, -bɔː'-

arbore|al ɑː'bɔː.ri|.əl (US) ɑːr'bɔːr.i- **-ous** -əs

arborescen|ce ˌɑː.bᵊr'es.ᵊn|ts, -bɔː'res- (US) ˌɑːr.bə'res-, -bɔː'- **-t** -t

arbore|tum ˌɑː.bᵊr'iː.|təm, -bɔː'riː- (US) ˌɑːr.bə'riː-, -bɔː'- **-tums** -təmz (US) -t̬əmz **-ta** -tə (US) -t̬ə

arboriculture 'ɑː.bᵊr.ɪˌkʌl.tʃəʳ, -bɔː-; ɑː'bɒr.ɪˌ- (US) 'ɑːr.bɚ.ɪˌkʌl.tʃɚ; ɑːr'bɔːr-

arborization, -isa- ˌɑː.bᵊr.aɪ'zeɪ.ʃᵊn, -bɔː.raɪ'-, -rɪ'- (US) ˌɑːr.bɚ.ɪ'-, -bɔːr-

arboriz|e, -is|e 'ɑː.bᵊr.aɪz (US) 'ɑːr.bə.raɪz **-es** -ɪz **-ing** -ɪŋ **-ed** -d

arbor-vitae ˌɑː.bə'viː.taɪ, -bɔː-, -'vaɪ-, -tiː (US) ˌɑːr.bɚ'vaɪ.tiː, -'viː- **-s** -z

arbour 'ɑː.bəʳ (US) 'ɑːr.bɚ **-s** -z

Arbroath ɑː'brəʊθ (US) ɑːr'broʊθ

Arbus 'ɑː.bəs (US) 'ɑːr-

Arbuthnot(t) ɑː'bʌθ.nət, ə'bʌθ- (US) ɑːr-, -nɑːt

arbutus ɑː'bjuː.təs (US) ɑːr'bjuː.t̬əs **-es** -ɪz

arc (A) ɑːk (US) ɑːrk **-s** -s **-(k)ing** -ɪŋ **-(k)ed** -t **'arc ˌlamp; 'arc ˌlight**

arcade ɑː'keɪd (US) ɑːr- **-s** -z

Arcadi|a ɑːˈkeɪ.di|.ə US ɑːr- **-an/s** -ən/z
Arcady ˈɑː.kə.di US ˈɑːr-
arcane ɑːˈkeɪn US ɑːr-
arcan|um ɑːˈkeɪ.n|əm US ɑːr- **-a** -ə
arch- ɑːtʃ-, ɑːk- US ɑːrtʃ-, ɑːrk-
Note: Prefix. Words containing **arch-** normally carry secondary stress on the first syllable, e.g. **archbishop** /ˌɑːtʃˈbɪʃ.əp US ˌɑːrtʃ-/, with the obvious exception of **archangel**.
arch *(adj.)* ɑːtʃ US ɑːrtʃ **-est** -əst, -ɪst **-ly** -li **-ness** -nəs, -nɪs
arch *(n. v.)* ɑːtʃ US ɑːrtʃ **-es** -ɪz **-ing** -ɪŋ **-ed** -t
-arch -ɑːk, -ək US -ɑːrk, -ɚk
Note: Suffix. Normally /-ɑːk US -ɑːrk/, e.g. **oligarch** /ˈɒl.ɪ.gɑːk US ˈɑː.lɪ.gɑːrk/, but /-ək, -ɚk/ is preferred in some words, e.g. **monarch** /ˈmɒn.ək US ˈmɑː.nɚk -nɑːrk/.
archaean **(A)** ɑːˈkiː.ən US ɑːr-
archaeo- ˌɑː.ki.əʊ-; ˌɑː.kiˈɒ- US ˌɑːr.ki.oʊ-, -ə-; ˌɑːr.kiˈɑː-
Note: Prefix. Words containing **archaeo-** normally carry secondary stress on the first syllable, and in the items which follow have primary stress on the second syllable, e.g. **archaeology** /ˌɑː.kiˈɒl.ə.dʒi US ˌɑːr.kiˈɑː.lə-/, with the exception of **archaeological**.
archaeologic|al ˌɑː.ki.əˈlɒdʒ.ɪ.k|ᵊl US ˌɑːr.ki.əˈlɑː.dʒɪ- **-ally** -ᵊl.i, -li
archaeologist ˌɑː.kiˈɒl.ə.dʒɪst US ˌɑːr.kiˈɑː.lə- **-s** -s
archaeology ˌɑː.kiˈɒl.ə.dʒi US ˌɑːr.kiˈɑː.lə-
archaeopteryx ˌɑː.kiˈɒp.tᵊr.ɪks US ˌɑːr.kiˈɑːp- **-es** -ɪz
archaic ɑːˈkeɪ.ɪk US ɑːr- **-ally** -ᵊl.i, -li
archaism ɑːˈkeɪ.ɪ.zᵊm, ˈɑː.keɪ- US ˈɑːr.ki-, -keɪ- **-s** -z
archangel ɑːˈkeɪn.dʒᵊl, ˈɑː.keɪn- US ˈɑːr.keɪn- **-s** -z
Archangel ˈɑːˌkeɪn.dʒᵊl, ˌɑːˈkeɪn- US ˈɑːr.keɪn-
archbishop ˌɑːtʃˈbɪʃ.əp US ˌɑːrtʃ- **-s** -s *stress shift:* ˌArchbishop of ˈCanterbury
archbishopric ˌɑːtʃˈbɪʃ.ə.prɪk US ˌɑːrtʃ- **-s** -s
Archbold ˈɑːtʃ.bəʊld US ˈɑːrtʃ.boʊld
Archdale ˈɑːtʃ.deɪl US ˈɑːrtʃ-
archdeacon ˌɑːtʃˈdiː.kən US ˌɑːrtʃ- **-s** -z
archdeaconr|y ˌɑːtʃˈdiː.kᵊn.r|i US ˌɑːrtʃ- **-ies** -iz
archdioces|e ˌɑːtʃˈdaɪə.sɪs US ˌɑːrtʃ- **-es** -ɪz
archducal ˌɑːtʃˈdjuː.kᵊl US ˌɑːrtʃˈduː-, -ˈdjuː-
archduchess ˌɑːtʃˈdʌtʃ.ɪs, -əs US ˌɑːrtʃ- **-es** -ɪz
archduch|y ˌɑːtʃˈdʌtʃ.|i US ˌɑːrtʃ- **-ies** -iz
archduke ˌɑːtʃˈdjuːk US ˌɑːrtʃˈduːk, -ˈdjuːk **-s** -s *stress shift:* ˌArchduke ˈFerdinand
archdukedom ˌɑːtʃˈdjuːk.dəm US ˌɑːrtʃˈduːk-, -ˈdjuːk **-s** -z
Archelaus ˌɑː.kɪˈleɪ.əs, -kəˈ- US ˌɑːr-
archenem|y ˌɑːtʃˈen.ə.m|i, -ɪ.m|i US ˌɑːrtʃ- **-ies** -iz
archeo- ˌɑː.ki.əʊ-; ˌɑː.kiˈɒ- US ˌɑːr.ki.oʊ-, -ə-; ˌɑːr.kiˈɑː-
Note: Prefix. See **archaeo-**.
archeologic|al ˌɑː.ki.əˈlɒdʒ.ɪ.k|ᵊl US ˌɑr.ki.əˈlɑː.dʒɪ- **-ally** -ᵊl.i, -li
archeologist ˌɑː.kiˈɒl.ə.dʒɪst US ˌɑːr.kiˈɑː.lə- **-s** -s
archeology ˌɑː.kiˈɒl.ə.dʒi US ˌɑːr.kiˈɑː.lə-
archeopteryx ˌɑː.kiˈɒp.tə.rɪks US ˌɑːr.kiˈɑːp- **-es** -ɪz
archer **(A)** ˈɑː.tʃəʳ US ˈɑːr.tʃɚ **-s** -z
archeress ˈɑː.tʃᵊr.ɪs, -es US ˈɑːr.tʃɚ.əs **-es** -ɪz
archery ˈɑː.tʃᵊr.i US ˈɑːr-
archetypal ˌɑː.kɪˈtaɪ.pᵊl, ˈɑː.kɪˌtaɪ- US ˌɑːr.kɪˈtaɪ-
archetype ˈɑː.kɪ.taɪp US ˈɑːr- **-s** -s
archetypic|al ˌɑː.kɪˈtɪp.ɪ.k|ᵊl US ˌɑːr.kəˈ- **-ally** -ᵊl.i, -li *stress shift:* ˌarchetypical ˈincident
archfiend ˌɑːtʃˈfiːnd US ˌɑːrtʃ- **-s** -z
arch-heretic ˌɑːtʃˈher.ə.tɪk, ˈ-ɪ- US ˌɑːrtʃˈher.ə- **-s** -s
archi- ɑː.tʃi- US ɑːr.tʃi-
Archibald ˈɑː.tʃɪ.bɔːld, -bᵊld US ˈɑːr.tʃə.bɔːld, -bɑːld
-archic -ɑː.kɪk US -ɑːr.kɪk
Archie ˈɑː.tʃi US ˈɑːr-
Archilochus ɑːˈkɪl.ə.kəs US ɑːr-
archimandrite ˌɑː.kɪˈmæn.draɪt US ˌɑːr.kəˈ- **-s** -s
archimedean ˌɑː.kɪˈmiː.di.ən, -miːˈdiː.ən US ˌɑːr.kə- *stress shift:* ˌarchimedean ˈscrew
Archimedes ˌɑː.kɪˈmiː.diːz US ˌɑːr.kəˈ-
archipelago ˌɑː.kɪˈpel.əg.əʊ US ˌɑːr.kəˈpel.ə.goʊ **-(e)s** -z
archiphoneme ˌɑː.kɪˈfəʊ.niːm US ˈɑːr.kɪˌfoʊ-, ˌɑːr.kɪˈfo- **-s** -z
architect ˈɑː.kɪ.tekt US ˈɑːr.kə- **-s** -s
architectonic ˌɑː.kɪ.tekˈtɒn.ɪk US ˌɑːr.kə.tekˈtɑː.nɪk **-s** -s
architectural ˌɑː.kɪˈtek.tʃᵊr.ᵊl US ˌɑːr.kəˈ- **-ly** -i
architecture ˈɑː.kɪ.tek.tʃəʳ US ˈɑːr.kə.tek.tʃɚ
architrave ˈɑː.kɪ.treɪv US ˈɑːr.kə- **-s** -z **-d** -d
archival ˌɑːˈkaɪ.vᵊl US ˌɑːr-
archive ˈɑː.kaɪv US ˈɑːr- **-s** -z
archivist ˈɑː.kɪ.vɪst US ˈɑːr.kaɪ-, -kə- **-s** -s
archon ˈɑː.kən, -kɒn US ˈɑːr.kɑːn **-s** -z
arch-prelate ˌɑːtʃˈprel.ət, -ɪt US ˌɑːrtʃ- **-s** -s
arch-priest ˌɑːtʃˈpriːst US ˌɑːrtʃ- **-s** -s *stress shift:* ˌarch-priest's ˈceremony
arch-traitor ˌɑːtʃˈtreɪ.təʳ US ˌɑːrtʃˈtreɪ.t̬ɚ **-s** -z *stress shift:* ˌarch-traitor ˈclique
archway **(A)** ˈɑːtʃ.weɪ US ˈɑːrtʃ- **-s** -z
archwise ˈɑːtʃ.waɪz US ˈɑːrtʃ-
Archytas ɑːˈkaɪ.təs, -tæs US ɑːrˈkaɪ.t̬əs
Arcite ˈɑː.saɪt US ˈɑːr-
Arcot ˈɑː.kɒt US ˈɑːr.kɑːt
arctic **(A)** ˈɑːk.tɪk US ˈɑːrk-; ˈɑːr.t̬ɪk **ˌArctic ˈCircle**; **ˌArctic ˈOcean**
Arcturus ɑːkˈtjʊə.rəs US ɑːrkˈtʊr.əs
arcuate ˈɑː.kju.ət, -eɪt, -ɪt US ˈɑːr-
arcuated ˈɑː.kju.eɪ.tɪd US ˈɑːr.kju.eɪ.t̬ɪd
Arcy ˈɑː.si US ˈɑːr-
-ard -əd, -ɑːd US -ɚd, -ɑːrd
Note: Suffix. In frequently occurring words, normally /-əd US -ɚd/, e.g. **wizard** /ˈwɪz.əd US -ɚd/, but may also be /-ɑːd US -ɑːrd/, e.g. **dullard** /ˈdʌl.əd, -ɑːd US -ɚd/. See individual items.
Ardagh ˈɑː.də, -dɑː US ˈɑːr-
Ardèche ɑːˈdeʃ US ɑːr-
Ardee ɑːˈdiː US ɑːr-
Arden ˈɑː.dᵊn US ˈɑːr-
ardency ˈɑː.dᵊnt.si US ˈɑːr-
Ardennes ɑːˈden, -denz US ɑːr-
ardent ˈɑː.dᵊnt US ˈɑːr- **-ly** -li
Arding ˈɑː.dɪŋ US ˈɑːr-
Ardingly ˈɑː.dɪŋ.laɪ, ˌ--ˈ- US ˈɑːr.dɪŋ-, ˌ--ˈ-
Ardleigh, Ardley ˈɑːd.li US ˈɑːrd-
Ardoch ˈɑː.dɒk, -dɒx US ˈɑːr.dɑːk
ardo(u)r ˈɑː.dəʳ US ˈɑːr.dɚ
Ardrishaig ɑːˈdrɪʃ.ɪg, -eɪg US ɑːr-
Ardrossan ɑːˈdrɒs.ᵊn US ɑːrˈdrɑː.sᵊn
Ards ɑːdz US ɑːrdz
Arduin ˈɑː.dwɪn US ˈɑːr-
arduous ˈɑː.dju.əs, -dʒu- US ˈɑːr.dʒu- **-ly** -li **-ness** -nəs, -nɪs
Ardwick ˈɑː.dwɪk US ˈɑːr-
are *(from* **be***) strong form:* ɑːʳ US ɑːr *weak form:* əʳ US ɚ *occasional weak form before vowels:* r
Note: Weak form word. The strong form /ɑːʳ US ɑːr/ is used for emphasis (e.g. 'You **are** stupid.'), for contrast (e.g. 'You **are** rich, but you **aren't** handsome.') and in final position (e.g. 'Here you are.'). The weak form is usually /əʳ US ɚ/ (e.g. 'These are mine.' /ˌðiːz.əˈmaɪn

(US) -ɚˈ-/; 'These are old.' /ˌðiːz.əʳˈəʊld (US) -ɚˈoʊld/), but when the weak form precedes a vowel, as in the last example, it often happens that the word is pronounced as a syllabic /r̩/ (e.g. /ˌðiːz.r̩ˈəʊld (US) -ˈoʊld/).

are *surface measure:* ɑːʳ (US) ɑːr **-s** -z

area ˈeə.ri.ə (US) ˈer.i- **-s** -z ˈ**area** ˌ**code**

areca əˈriː.kə; ˈær.ɪ- (US) əˈriː.kə; ˈær.ɪ-, ˈer- **-s** -z

arena əˈriː.nə **-s** -z

Arendt ˈær.ənt, ˈɑː.rənt (US) ˈɑːr.ənt, ˈer-

aren't ɑːnt (US) ɑːrnt

areol|a əˈriː.əl|.ə, ærˈiː- **-as** -əz **-ae** -iː

areometer ˌær.iˈɒm.ɪ.təʳ, ˌeə.riˈ-, ˈ-ə- (US) ˌer.iˈɑː.mə.t̬ɚ, ˌær- **-s** -z

areometry ˌær.iˈɒm.ɪ.tri, ˌeə.riˈ-, ˈ-ə- (US) ˌer.iˈɑː.mə-, ˌær-

Areopagite ˌær.iˈɒp.ə.gaɪt, -dʒaɪt (US) ˌer.iˈɑː.pə-, ˌær- **-s** -s

Areopagitic ˌær.i.ɒp.əˈdʒɪt.ɪk (US) ˌer.iˌɑː.pəˈ-, ˌær- **-a** -ə

Areopagus ˌær.iˈɒp.ə.gəs (US) ˌer.iˈɑː.pə-, ˌær-

Arequipa ˌær.ɪˈkiː.pə, -ekˈiː- (US) ˌɑː.rəˈkiː-, ˌer.əˈ-, ˌær-

Ares ˈeə.riːz (US) ˈer.iːz

arête ærˈet, əˈret

Aretha əˈriː.θə

Arethusa ˌær.ɪˈθjuː.zə, -eθˈjuː- (US) ˌɑːr.əˈθuː-

Arezzo ærˈet.səʊ, əˈret- (US) ɑːˈret.soʊ

Arfon ˈɑː.vᵊn, -vɒn (US) ˈɑːr-, -fᵊn

Argand ˈɑː.gænd, -gənd (US) ˌɑːrˈgɑːnd, -ˈgænd **-s** -z *stress shift, US only, see compound:* ˌ**Argand** ˈ**diagram**

argent **(A)** ˈɑː.dʒᵊnt (US) ˈɑːr-

Argentina ˌɑː.dʒᵊnˈtiː.nə, -dʒenˈ- (US) ˌɑːr-

argentine **(A)** ˈɑː.dʒᵊn.taɪn (US) ˈɑːr.dʒᵊn.taɪn, -tiːn, -tɪn

Argentinian ˌɑː.dʒᵊnˈtɪn.i.ən (US) ˌɑːr- **-s** -z

argillaceous ˌɑː.dʒɪˈleɪ.ʃəs (US) ˌɑːr.dʒəˈ-

Argive ˈɑː.gaɪv (US) ˈɑːr- **-s** -z

Argo ˈɑː.gəʊ (US) ˈɑːr.goʊ

argol ˈɑː.gɒl, -gᵊl (US) ˈɑːr.gɑːl, -gᵊl

Argolis ˈɑː.gᵊl.ɪs (US) ˈɑːr-

argon ˈɑː.gɒn, -gən (US) ˈɑːr.gɑːn

Argonaut ˈɑː.gə.nɔːt (US) ˈɑːr.gə.nɑːt, -nɔːt **-s** -s

Argonautic ˌɑː.gəˈnɔː.tɪk (US) ˌɑːr.gəˈnɑː.t̬ɪk, -ˈnɔː-

Argos ˈɑː.gɒs (US) ˈɑːr.gɑːs, -gəs

argos|y ˈɑː.gə.s|i (US) ˈɑːr.gə.s|i **-ies** -iz

argot ˈɑː.gəʊ (US) ˈɑːr.goʊ, -gət **-s** -z

arguab|le ˈɑːg.ju.ə.b|l̩ (US) ˈɑːrg- **-ly** -li

argu|e ˈɑːg.juː (US) ˈɑːrg- **-es** -z **-ing** -ɪŋ **-ed** -d **-er/s** -əʳ/z (US) -ɚ/z

argument ˈɑːg.jə.mənt, -jʊ- (US) ˈɑːrg.jə-, -jʊ- **-s** -s

argumental ˌɑːg.jəˈmen.tᵊl, -jʊ- (US) ˌɑːrg.jəˈmen.t̬ᵊl, -jʊˈ-

argumentation ˌɑːg.jə.menˈteɪ.ʃᵊn, -jʊ-, -mən- (US) ˌɑːrg.jə-, -jʊ- **-s** -z

argumentative ˌɑːg.jəˈmen.tə.tɪv, -jʊ- (US) ˌɑːrg.jəˈmen.t̬ə.t̬ɪv, -jʊˈ- **-ly** -li **-ness** -nəs, -nɪs

argus **(A)** ˈɑː.gəs (US) ˈɑːr- **-es** -ɪz

argy-bargy ˌɑː.dʒiˈbɑː.dʒi (US) ˌɑːr.dʒiˈbɑːr-

Argyle ɑːˈgaɪl (US) ɑːr-, ˈ-- *stress shift:* ˌArgyle ˈtartan

Argyllshire ɑːˈgaɪl.ʃəʳ, -ˌʃɪəʳ (US) ɑːrˈgaɪl.ʃɚ, -ˌʃɪr

aria ˈɑː.ri.ə (US) ˈɑːr.i- **-s** -z

Ariadne ˌær.iˈæd.ni (US) ˌær-, ˌer-

Arian ˈeə.ri.ən (US) ˈer.i-, ˈær- **-s** -z **-ism** -ɪ.zᵊm

-arian -ˈeə.ri.ən (US) -ˈer.i-, -ˈær-

Note: Suffix. Always carries primary stress, e.g. **grammarian** /grəˈmeə.ri.ən (US) -ˈmer.i-/.

arid ˈær.ɪd (US) ˈer-, ˈær- **-ly** -li **-ness** -nəs, -nɪs

aridity ærˈɪd.ə.ti, əˈrɪd-, -ɪ.ti (US) erˈɪd.ə.t̬i, ær-

ariel **(A)** ˈeə.ri.əl (US) ˈer.i- **-s** -z

Aries ˈeə.riːz, -ri.iːz (US) ˈer.iːz

arietta ˌær.iˈet.ə, ˌɑː.riˈ- (US) ˌɑːr.iˈet̬-, ˌær.iˈ-, ˌer- **-s** -z

aright əˈraɪt

-arily -ᵊr.ə.li, -ɪ.li; -ˈer.ᵊl.i, -ɪ.li (US) -er.ə.li, -ær-

Note: Suffix. The stress pattern of words containing **-arily** in British English is either unaffected by the affix or primary stress moves to the antepenultimate syllable, in which case it contains a full vowel, e.g. **momentarily** /ˈməʊ.mən.tᵊr.ᵊl.i, -ɪ.li, ˌməʊ.mənˈter-/. In American English, **-arily** normally has a full vowel, but the antepenultimate syllable may or may not take primary stress, e.g. **momentarily** /ˈmoʊ.mən.ter.ᵊl.i, ˌmoʊ.mənˈter-/. See individual entries.

Arimathaea ˌær.ɪ.məˈθiː.ə (US) ˌer.ə-, ˌær-

Arion əˈraɪən, ærˈaɪən (US) əˈraɪən

arioso ˌɑː.riˈəʊ.səʊ, ˌær.iˈ-, -zəʊ (US) ˌɑːr.iˈoʊ.soʊ

Ariosto ˌær.iˈɒs.təʊ (US) ˌɑːr.iˈɑː.stoʊ, ˌer-, ˌær-, -ˈɔː-, -ˈoʊ-

aris|e əˈraɪz **-es** -ɪz **-ing** -ɪŋ

arisen əˈrɪz.ᵊn

Aristaeus ˌær.ɪˈstiː.əs, -əˈ- (US) ˌer.əˈ-, ˌær-

Aristarchus ˌær.ɪˈstɑː.kəs (US) ˌer.əˈstɑːr-, ˌær-

Aristide ˌær.ɪˈstiːd (US) ˌer-, ˌær-

Aristides ˌær.ɪˈstaɪ.diːz (US) ˌer.əˈ-, ˌær-

aristo əˈrɪs.təʊ (US) -toʊ **-s** -z

aristocrac|y ˌær.ɪˈstɒk.rə.s|i (US) ˌer.əˈstɑː.krə-, ˌær- **-ies** -iz

aristocrat ˈær.ɪ.stə.kræt; əˈrɪs.tə- (US) əˈrɪs-; ˈer.ə.stə-, ˈær- **-s** -s

aristocratic ˌær.ɪ.stəˈkræt.ɪk (US) əˌrɪs.təˈkræt̬.ɪk; ˌer.ə.stəˈ-, ˌær- **-al** -ᵊl **-ally** -ᵊl.i, -li *stress shift, British:* ˌaristocratic ˈairs *stress shift, US:* aˌristocratic ˈairs, ˌaristocratic ˈairs

aristocratism ˌær.ɪˈstɒk.rə.tɪ.zᵊm (US) ˌer.əˈstɑː.krə-, ˌær-

Aristophanes ˌær.ɪˈstɒf.ə.niːz (US) ˌer.əˈstɑː.fə-, ˌær-

aristophanic ˌær.ɪ.stəˈfæn.ɪk, -tɒfˈæn- (US) ˌer.ə.stəˈ-, ˌær-

aristotelian **(A)** ˌær.ɪ.stɒtˈiː.li.ən, -stəˈtiː- (US) ˌer.ə.stəˈtiː-, ˌær- **-s** -z

Aristotle ˈær.ɪ.stɒt.l̩ (US) ˈer.ə.stɑː.t̬l̩, ˈær-

Aristoxenus ˌær.ɪˈstɒk.sɪ.nəs, -sə.nəs (US) ˌer.əˈstɑːk.sə-, ˌær-

arithmetic *(n.)* əˈrɪθ.mə.tɪk, -mɪ- **-s** -s

arithmetic *(adj.)* ˌær.ɪθˈmet.ɪk (US) ˌer.ɪθˈmet̬-, ˌær- **-al** -ᵊl **-ally** -ᵊl.i, -li *stress shift:* ˌarithmetic ˈmean

arithmetician əˌrɪθ.məˈtɪʃ.ᵊn, -mɪˈ-; ˌær.ɪθ- (US) əˌrɪθ.məˈ- **-s** -z

-arium -ˈeə.ri.əm (US) -ˈer.i-

Note: Suffix. Always carries primary stress, e.g. **solarium** /səʊˈleə.ri.əm (US) soʊ-, sə-/.

Arius ˈeə.ri.əs; əˈraɪ- (US) ˈer.i-, ˈær-

Ariz. *(abbrev. for* **Arizona***)* ˌær.ɪˈzəʊ.nə (US) ˌer.ɪˈzoʊ-, ˌær-, -əˈ-

Arizona ˌær.ɪˈzəʊ.nə (US) ˌer.ɪˈzoʊ-, ˌær-, -əˈ-

Arjuna ɑːˈjuː.nə (US) ɑːr-, ɜː-

ark **(A)** ɑːk (US) ɑːrk **-s** -s

Ark. *(abbrev. for* **Arkansas***)* ˈɑː.kən.sɔː; ɑːˈkæn.zəs (US) ˈɑːr.kən.sɑː, -sɔː; ɑːrˈkæn.zəs

Arkan ˈɑː.kæn (US) ˈɑːr-

Arkansas *US state:* ˈɑː.kən.sɔː; (US) ˈɑːr.kən.sɑː, -sɔː; *river:* ɑːˈkæn.zəs (US) ɑːrˈkæn.zəs

Arkhangelsk ˌɑː.kæŋˈgelsk (US) ɑːrˈkɑːn.gelsk

Arklow ˈɑː.kləʊ (US) ˈɑːr.kloʊ

Arkwright ˈɑː.kraɪt (US) ˈɑːr-

Arlen ˈɑː.lən (US) ˈɑːr-

Arlene ˈɑː.liːn (US) ɑːrˈliːn

Arlington ˈɑː.lɪŋ.tən (US) ˈɑːr-

arm ɑːm (US) ɑːrm **-s** -z **-ing** -ɪŋ **-ed** -d
cost an ˌ**arm and a** ˈ**leg**; ˌ**keep someone at** ˌ**arm's** ˈ**length**; ˌ**armed to the** ˈ**teeth**

armada **(A)** ɑːˈmɑː.də (US) ɑːrˈ- **-s** -z

Armadale ˈɑː.mə.deɪl (US) ˈɑːr-

armadillo ˌɑː.məˈdɪl.əʊ (US) ˌɑːr.məˈdɪl.oʊ **-s** -z

Armado ɑːˈmɑː.dəʊ (US) ɑːrˈmɑː.doʊ

Armageddon ˌɑː.məˈɡed.ᵊn (US) ˌɑːr-

Armagh ˌɑːˈmɑː (US) ˌɑːr-

Armagnac ˈɑː.mə.njæk (US) ˈɑːr-, ˌ--ˈ-

Armah ˈɑː.mə (US) ˈɑːr-

Armalite® ˈɑː.mᵊl.aɪt (US) ˈɑːr.mə.laɪt

armament ˈɑː.mə.mənt (US) ˈɑːr- **-s** -s

Armani ˌɑːˈmɑː.ni (US) ˌɑːr-

Armatrading ˌɑː.məˈtreɪ.dɪŋ, ˈɑː.mə.treɪ- (US) ˈɑːr.mə.treɪ-, ˌɑːr.məˈtreɪ-

armature ˈɑː.mə.tʃəʳ, -tʃʊəʳ, -tjʊəʳ, -tjəʳ (US) ˈɑːr.mə.tʃɚ **-s** -z

armband ˈɑːm.bænd (US) ˈɑːrm- **-s** -z

armchair ˈɑːm.tʃeəʳ, -ˈ- (US) ˈɑːrm.tʃer **-s** -z

Note: The latter British form is used when attributive.

armed ɑːmd (US) ɑːrmd ˌ**armed** ˈ**robbery**

Armeni|a ɑːˈmiː.ni|.ə (US) ɑːr- **-an/s** -ən/z

Armfield ˈɑːm.fiːld (US) ˈɑːrm-

armful ˈɑːm.fʊl (US) ˈɑːrm- **-s** -z

armhole ˈɑːm.həʊl (US) ˈɑːrm.hoʊl **-s** -z

armiger (A) ˈɑː.mɪ.dʒəʳ (US) ˈɑːr.mɪ.dʒɚ **-s** -z

Armin ˈɑː.mɪn (US) ˈɑːr-

arm-in-arm ˌɑːm.ɪnˈɑːm (US) ˌɑːrm.ɪnˈɑːrm

Arminian ɑːˈmɪn.i.ən (US) ɑːr- **-s** -z

Armistead ˈɑː.mɪ.sted, -stɪd (US) ˈɑːr-

armistic|e ˈɑː.mɪ.stɪs (US) ˈɑːr.mə- **-es** -ɪz ˈ**Armistice** ˌ**Day**

Armitage ˈɑː.mɪ.tɪdʒ, -mə- (US) ˈɑːr.mə.t̬ɪdʒ

armless ˈɑːm.ləs, -lɪs (US) ˈɑːrm-

armlet ˈɑːm.lət, -lɪt (US) ˈɑːrm- **-s** -s

armload ˈɑːm.ləʊd (US) ˈɑːrm.loʊd **-s** -z

armlock ˈɑːm.lɒk (US) ˈɑːrm.lɑːk **-s** -s

arm|or ˈɑː.m|əʳ (US) ˈɑːr.m|ɚ **-ors** -əz (US) -ɚz **-oring** -ᵊr.ɪŋ **-ored** -əd (US) -ɚd ˌ**armored** ˈ**vehicle**

armorer ˈɑː.mᵊr.əʳ (US) ˈɑːr.mɚ.ɚ **-s** -z

armorial ɑːˈmɔː.ri.əl (US) ɑːrˈmɔːr.i-

Armoric ɑːˈmɒr.ɪk (US) ɑːrˈmɔːr-

Armoric|a ɑːˈmɒr.ɪ.k|ə (US) ɑːrˈmɔːr- **-an/s** -ən/z

armor-pla|te ˌɑː.məˈpleɪ|t, ˈ--- (US) ˈɑːr.mɚ.pleɪ|t **-tes** -ts **-ting** -tɪŋ (US) -t̬ɪŋ **-ted** -tɪd (US) -t̬ɪd

armor|y ˈɑː.mᵊr|.i (US) ˈɑːr- **-ies** -iz

arm|our (A) ˈɑː.m|əʳ (US) ˈɑːr.m|ɚ **-ours** -əz (US) -ɚz **-ouring** -ᵊr.ɪŋ **-oured** -əd (US) -ɚd ˌ**armoured** ˈ**vehicle**

armourer ˈɑː.mᵊr.əʳ (US) ˈɑːr.mɚ.ɚ **-s** -z

armour-pla|te ˌɑː.məˈpleɪ|t, ˈ--- (US) ˈɑːr.mɚ.pleɪ|t **-tes** -ts **-ting** -tɪŋ (US) -t̬ɪŋ **-ted** -tɪd (US) -t̬ɪd

Note: The latter British form is used attributively.

armour|y ˈɑː.mᵊr|.i (US) ˈɑːr- **-ies** -iz

armpit ˈɑːm.pɪt (US) ˈɑːrm- **-s** -s

armrest ˈɑːm.rest (US) ˈɑːrm- **-s** -s

arms ɑːmz (US) ɑːrmz ˈ**arms con**ˌ**trol**; ˈ**arms** ˌ**race**; ˌ**up in** ˈ**arms**

Armstead ˈɑːm.sted, -stɪd (US) ˈɑːrm-

Armstrong ˈɑːm.strɒŋ (US) ˈɑːrm.strɑːŋ, -strɔːŋ

Armthorpe ˈɑːm.θɔːp (US) ˈɑːrm.θɔːrp

arm|y ˈɑː.m|i (US) ˈɑːr- **-ies** -iz

army-corps *sing.:* ˈɑː.mi.kɔːʳ (US) ˈɑːr.mi.kɔːr *plur.:* -kɔːz (US) -kɔːrz

Arnald ˈɑː.nəld (US) ˈɑːr-

Arndale ˈɑːn.deɪl (US) ˈɑːrn-

Arne ɑːn (US) ɑːrn

Arnfield ˈɑːn.fiːld (US) ˈɑːrn-

Arnhem ˈɑː.nəm, ˈɑːn.həm (US) ˈɑːr.nəm, ˈɑːrn.hem

arnica ˈɑː.nɪ.kə (US) ˈɑːr-

Arno ˈɑː.nəʊ (US) ˈɑːr.noʊ

Arnold ˈɑː.nᵊld (US) ˈɑːr- **-son** -sᵊn

Arnot(t) ˈɑː.nət, -nɒt (US) ˈɑːr.nət, -nɑːt

Arolla əˈrɒl.ə (US) -ˈrɑː.lə

aroma əˈrəʊ.mə (US) -ˈroʊ- **-s** -z

aromatherap|y əˌrəʊ.məˈθer.ə.p|i (US) -ˌroʊ- **-ist/s** -ɪst/s

aromatic ˌær.əʊˈmæt.ɪk (US) ˌer.əˈmæt̬-, ˌær- **-s** -s *stress shift:* ˌaromatic ˈoils

arose *(from* **arise***)* əˈrəʊz (US) -ˈroʊz

around əˈraʊnd

arousal əˈraʊ.zᵊl **-s** -z

arous|e əˈraʊz **-es** -ɪz **-ing** -ɪŋ **-ed** -d

arpeggio ɑːˈpedʒ.i.əʊ, -ˈpedʒ.əʊ (US) ɑːrˈpedʒ.i.oʊ, -ˈpeʒ-, -ˈpedʒ.oʊ **-s** -z

arquebus ˈɑː.kwɪ.bəs, -kwə.bəs, -bʌs (US) ˈɑːr- **-es** -ɪz

Arquette ɑːˈket (US) ɑːr-

arr *(abbrev. for* **arranged by***)* əˈreɪndʒdˌbaɪ *(abbrev. for* **arrives, arrival***)* əˈraɪ|vz; -vᵊl

arrack ˈær.ək (US) ˈer-, ˈær-; əˈræk

arraign əˈreɪn **-s** -z **-ing** -ɪŋ **-ed** -d **-er/s** -əʳ/z (US) -ɚ/z **-ment/s** -mənt/s

Arran ˈær.ᵊn (US) ˈer-, ˈær-

arrang|e əˈreɪndʒ **-es** -ɪz **-ing** -ɪŋ **-ed** -d **-er/s** -əʳ/z (US) -ɚ/z

arrangement əˈreɪndʒ.mənt **-s** -s

arrant ˈær.ᵊnt (US) ˈer-, ˈær- **-ly** -li

arras ˈær.əs (US) ˈer-, ˈær- **-es** -ɪz

Arras *French town:* ˈær.əs, -æs (US) ˈer-, ˈær-

Arrau əˈraʊ; ˈær.aʊ (US) əˈraʊ

array əˈreɪ **-s** -z **-ing** -ɪŋ **-ed** -d

arrear əˈrɪəʳ (US) -ˈrɪr **-s** -z **-age** -ɪdʒ

arrest əˈrest **-s** -s **-ing** -ɪŋ **-ed** -ɪd **-ment/s** -mənt/s

arrestable əˈres.tə.bl̩

arrestation ˌær.esˈteɪ.ʃᵊn (US) ˌer-, ˌær-; əˌresˈ- **-s** -z

arrhythm|ia əˈrɪð.m|i.ə **-ic** -ɪk **-ical** -ɪ.kᵊl **-ically** -ɪ.kᵊl.i, -ɪ.kli

Arrian ˈær.i.ən (US) ˈer-, ˈær-

arrière-ban ˌær.i.eəˈbæn (US) -erˈbɑːn, -ˈbæn **-s** -z

arrière pensée ˌær.i.eəˈpɑ̃ː*nt*.seɪ, -pɑː*nt*ˈseɪ (US) -er.pɑː*n*ˈseɪ

arris ˈær.ɪs (US) ˈer-, ˈær- **-es** -ɪz

arrival əˈraɪ.vᵊl **-s** -z

arriv|e əˈraɪv **-es** -z **-ing** -ɪŋ **-ed** -d

arrivederci ˌær.i.vəˈdeə.tʃi (US) əˌriː.vəˈder-

arriviste ˌær.iːˈviːst (US) ˌer-, ˌær- **-s** -s

arroganc|e ˈær.ə.ɡən*t*s (US) ˈer-, ˈær- **-y** -i

arrogant ˈær.ə.ɡənt (US) ˈer-, ˈær- **-ly** -li

arro|gate ˈær.əʊ|.ɡeɪt (US) ˈer.ə-, ˈær- **-gates** -ɡeɪts **-gating** -ɡeɪ.tɪŋ (US) -ɡeɪ.t̬ɪŋ **-gated** -ɡeɪ.tɪd (US) -ɡeɪ.t̬ɪd

arrogation ˌær.əʊˈɡeɪ.ʃᵊn (US) ˌer.əˈ-, ˌær- **-s** -z

arrogative əˈrɒɡ.ə.tɪv (US) -ˈrɑː.ɡə.t̬ɪv

arrondissement ˌær.ɒnˈdiː.sᵊm.ɑ̃ː (US) erˌɑːn.diːsˈmɑːn, ær-; əˌrɑːn- **-s** -s

arrow ˈær.əʊ (US) ˈer.oʊ, ˈær- **-s** -z ˈ**arrow** ˌ**head**

arrowroot ˈær.əʊ.ruːt (US) ˈer.oʊ-, ˈær-

Arrowsmith ˈær.əʊ.smɪθ (US) ˈer.oʊ-, ˈær-

arrowwood ˈær.əʊ.wʊd (US) ˈer.oʊ-, ˈær-

arroyo əˈrɔɪ.əʊ (US) -oʊ **-s** -z

ars ɑːz (US) ɑːrz

ars|e ɑːs (US) ɑːrs **-es** -ɪz

Note: In US dictionaries, **arse** is usually listed as a variant of **ass**, which is pronounced /æs/. **Arse** is a British term.

arsehole ˈɑːs.həʊl (US) ˈɑːrs.hoʊl **-s** -z

arsenal (A) ˈɑː.sᵊn.ᵊl (US) ˈɑːr- **-s** -z

arsenate ˈɑː.sᵊn.eɪt, -sɪ.neɪt, -nɪt, -nət (US) ˈɑːr- **-s** -s

arsenic *(n.)* ˈɑː.sᵊn.ɪk (US) ˈɑːr-

arsenic *(adj.)* ɑːˈsen.ɪk (US) ɑːr- **-al** -ᵊl

arsenide ˈɑː.sᵊn.aɪd (US) ˈɑːr- **-s** -z

arsenite ˈɑː.sᵊn.aɪt, -sɪ.naɪt (US) ˈɑːr-

ars|is ˈɑː.s|ɪs (US) ˈɑːr- **-es** -iːz

arson ˈɑː.sᵊn (US) ˈɑːr-

arsonist ˈɑː.sᵊn.ɪst (US) ˈɑːr- **-s** -s

art *(n.)* ɑːt (US) ɑːrt **-s** -s ˈ**art** ˌ**gallery**; ˌ**arts and** ˈ**crafts**; ˈ**art** ˌ**school**

art *(from* **be***) (v.) normal form:* ɑːt (US) ɑːrt *occasional weak form:* ət (US) ɚt

Artaxerxes ˌɑː.təˈzɜːk.siːz, -tækˈsɜːk-, -təɡˈzɜːk-, ˈɑː.tə.zɜːk-, -tæk.sɜːk-, -təɡ.zɜːk- (US) ˌɑːr.t̬əˈzɝːk-

Art Deco ˌɑːtˈdek.əʊ (US) ˌɑːrt.deɪˈkoʊ, ˌɑːr-, -ˈdeɪ.koʊ

artefact ˈɑː.tɪ.fækt, -tə.fækt (US) ˈɑːr.t̬ə- **-s** -s

Artemis ˈɑː.tɪ.mɪs, -tə.mɪs (US) ˈɑːr.t̬ə-

Artemus ˈɑː.tɪ.məs, -tə.məs (US) ˈɑːr.t̬ɪ-

Articulation

The movement of the vocal organs to produce speech sounds. The vocal organs are often referred to as 'articulators', and these include the tongue, the lips, the hard palate, the soft palate, the teeth, the pharynx and the larynx. In classifying CONSONANTS, phoneticians note the 'place of articulation' (the point in the vocal tract where the obstruction to the airflow is made) and the 'manner of articulation' (the type of obstruction made by the articulators). Thus the sound [s] is classified as ALVEOLAR (because the place of articulation is at the alveolar ridge, just behind the upper front teeth) and FRICATIVE (because the obstruction is one which allows air to escape with difficulty, creating a hissing noise).

arterial ɑːˈtɪə.ri.əl ⓤⓢ ɑːrˈtɪr.i-
arteriolar ɑːˌtɪə.riˈəʊ.ləʳ ⓤⓢ ɑːrˌtɪr.iˈoʊ.lɚ
arteriol|e ɑːˈtɪə.ri.əʊl ⓤⓢ ɑːrˈtɪr.i.oʊl **-es** -z
arteriosclerosis ɑːˌtɪə.ri.əʊ.skləˈrəʊ.sɪs, -sklɪəˈ- ⓤⓢ ɑːrˌtɪr.i.oʊ.skləˈroʊ.səs
arteritis ˌɑː.tᵊrˈaɪ.tɪs, -tɪˈraɪ-, -təs ⓤⓢ ˌɑːr.t̬əˈraɪ.t̬ɪs
arter|y ˈɑː.tᵊr|.i ⓤⓢ ˈɑːr.t̬ɚ- **-ies** -iz
artesian ɑːˈtiː.zi.ən, -ʒi.ən, -ʒᵊn ⓤⓢ ɑːrˈtiː.ʒᵊn **arˌtesian ˈwell**
Artex® ˈɑː.teks ⓤⓢ ˈɑːr-
artful ˈɑːt.fᵊl, -fʊl ⓤⓢ ˈɑːrt- **-ly** -i **-ness** -nəs, -nɪs **ˌArtful ˈDodger**
arthouse ˈɑːtˌhaʊs ⓤⓢ ˈɑːrt-
arthritic ɑːˈθrɪt.ɪk ⓤⓢ ɑːrˈθrɪt̬.ɪk **-s** -s
arthritis ɑːˈθraɪ.tɪs, -təs ⓤⓢ ɑːrˈθraɪ.t̬ɪs
arthropod ˈɑː.θrə.pɒd ⓤⓢ ˈɑːr.θrə.pɑːd **-s** -z
arthroscope ˈɑː.θrə.skəʊp ⓤⓢ ˈɑːr.θrə.skoʊp **-s** -s
arthroscopic ˌɑː.θrəˈskɒp.ɪk ⓤⓢ ˌɑːr.θrəˈskɑː.pɪk
arthroscopy ɑːˈθrɒs.kə.pi ⓤⓢ ɑːrˈθrɑː.skə-
Arthur ˈɑː.θəʳ ⓤⓢ ˈɑːr.θɚ
Arthurian ɑːˈθjʊə.ri.ən, -ˈθʊə- ⓤⓢ ɑːrˈθʊr.i-, -ˈθɜː-
artichoke ˈɑː.tɪ.tʃəʊk ⓤⓢ ˈɑːr.t̬ə.tʃoʊk **-s** -s
articl|e ˈɑː.tɪ.kl̩ ⓤⓢ ˈɑːr.t̬ɪ- **-es** -z **-ing** -ɪŋ, -klɪŋ **-ed** -d
articular ɑːˈtɪk.jə.ləʳ, -jʊ- ⓤⓢ ɑːrˈtɪk.jə.lɚ
articulate (*adj.*) ɑːˈtɪk.jə.lət, -jʊ-, -lɪt ⓤⓢ ɑːrˈtɪk.jə.lət **-ly** -li **-ness** -nəs, -nɪs
articu|late (*v.*) ɑːˈtɪk.jə|.leɪt, -jʊ- ⓤⓢ ɑːrˈtɪk.jə- **-lates** -leɪts **-lating** -leɪ.tɪŋ ⓤⓢ -leɪ.t̬ɪŋ **-lated** -leɪ.tɪd ⓤⓢ -leɪ.t̬ɪd **-lator/s** -leɪ.təʳ/z ⓤⓢ -leɪ.t̬ɚ/s **arˌticulated ˈlorry**
articulation ɑːˌtɪk.jəˈleɪ.ʃᵊn, -jʊˈ- ⓤⓢ ɑːrˌtɪk.jəˈ- **-s** -z
articulatory ɑːˈtɪk.jə.lə.tᵊr.i, -jʊ-; ɑːˌtɪk.jəˈleɪ-, -jʊˈ- ⓤⓢ ɑːrˈtɪk.jə.lə.tɔːr-
artifact ˈɑː.tɪ.fækt ⓤⓢ ˈɑːr.t̬ə- **-s** -s
artific|e ˈɑː.tɪ.fɪs ⓤⓢ ˈɑːr.t̬ə- **-es** -ɪz
artificer ɑːˈtɪf.ɪ.səʳ ⓤⓢ ɑːrˈtɪf.ə.sɚ **-s** -z
artificial ˌɑː.tɪˈfɪʃ.ᵊl ⓤⓢ ˌɑːr.t̬əˈ- **-ly** -i **-ness** -nəs, -nɪs *stress shift, see compounds:* **ˌartificial insemiˈnation**; **ˌartificial inˈtelligence**; **ˌartificial respiˈration**
artificialit|y ˌɑː.tɪ.fɪʃ.iˈæl.ə.t|i, -ɪ.t|i ⓤⓢ ˌɑːr.t̬ə.fɪʃ.iˈæl.ə.t̬|i **-ies** -iz
artificializ|e, -is|e ˌɑː.tɪˈfɪʃ.ᵊl.aɪz ⓤⓢ ˌɑːr.t̬ə- **-es** -ɪz **-ing** -ɪŋ **-ed** -d
artiller|y ɑːˈtɪl.ᵊr|.i ⓤⓢ ɑːr- **-ies** -iz **-ist/s** -ɪst/s
artillery|-man ɑːˈtɪl.ᵊr.i|.mən, -mæn ⓤⓢ ɑːrˈ- **-men** -mən, -men
artisan ˌɑː.tɪˈzæn, -təˈzæn, ˈ--- ⓤⓢ ˈɑːr.t̬ə.zᵊn, -sᵊn **-s** -z
artist ˈɑː.tɪst ⓤⓢ ˈɑːr.t̬əst, -t̬ɪst **-s** -s
artiste ɑːˈtiːst ⓤⓢ ɑːr- **-s** -s
artistic ɑːˈtɪs.tɪk ⓤⓢ ɑːr- **-al** -ᵊl **-ally** -ᵊl.i, -li
artistry ˈɑː.tɪ.stri ⓤⓢ ˈɑːr.t̬ə-, -t̬ɪ-
artless ˈɑːt.ləs, -lɪs ⓤⓢ ˈɑːrt- **-ly** -li **-ness** -nəs, -nɪs
Art Nouveau ˌɑːt.nuːˈvəʊ, ˌɑː-, ˌ-ˈ-- ⓤⓢ ˌɑːrt.nuːˈvoʊ, ˌɑːr-
Artois ɑːˈtwɑː, ˈ-- ⓤⓢ ɑːr-
arts|man ˈɑːts|.mæn ⓤⓢ ˈɑːrts- **-men** -men
artsy ˈɑːt.si ⓤⓢ ˈɑːrt-
artwork ˈɑːt.wɜːk ⓤⓢ ˈɑːrt.wɝːk
arty ˈɑː.ti ⓤⓢ ˈɑːr.t̬i
arty-farty ˌɑː.tiˈfɑː.ti ⓤⓢ ˌɑːr.t̬iˈfɑːr.t̬i *stress shift:* ˌarty-farty ˈperson
Arub|a əˈruː.b|ə **-an/s** -ən/z
arugula əˈruː.gᵊl.ə, -gjʊ.lə, -gjᵊl.ə **-s** -z
arum ˈeə.rəm ⓤⓢ ˈer- **-s** -z
Arun ˈær.ᵊn ⓤⓢ ˈer-, ˈær-
Arundel ˈær.ᵊn.dᵊl; əˈrʌn- ⓤⓢ ˈer.ᵊn-, ˈær-; əˈrʌn-
Arundell ˈær.ᵊn.del, -dᵊl ⓤⓢ ˈer-, ˈær-
Arveragus ɑːˈver.ə.gəs ⓤⓢ ɑːr-
-ary -ᵊr.i ⓤⓢ -er.i, -ɚ.i
Note: Suffix. When added to a free stem, **-ary** does not normally affect the stress pattern, e.g. **imagine** /ɪˈmædʒ.ɪn/, **imaginary** /ɪˈmæʒd.ɪ.nᵊr.i ⓤⓢ -ə.ner-/. Otherwise words containing **-ary** normally carry stress one or two syllables before the suffix,e.g. **centenary** /senˈtiː.nᵊr.i, -ˈten.ᵊr- ⓤⓢ ˈsen.tᵊn.er-, senˈten.ᵊr-/, **culinary** /ˈkʌl.ɪ.nᵊr.i ⓤⓢ -ə.ner-/. There are exceptions; see individual entries.
Aryan ˈeə.ri.ən, ˈɑː- ⓤⓢ ˈer.i-, ˈær-, ˈɑːr- **-s** -z **-ism** -ɪ.zᵊm
arytenoid ˌær.ɪˈtiː.nɔɪd, -rəˈtiː-; ærˈɪt.ᵊn.ɔɪd ⓤⓢ əˈrɪt.ᵊn-; ˌer.ɪˈtiː.nɔɪd, ˌær- **-s** -z
as (conj.) *strong form:* æz *weak form:* əz
Note: Weak form word. The strong form /æz/ is used in contrastive or coordinative constructions (e.g. 'as and when it's ready'), and in sentence-final position (e.g. 'That's what I bought it as.'). Quite frequently the strong form is found when the word occurs in initial position in a sentence if the following word is not stressed (e.g. 'As I was saying, ...'). The weak form is /əz/ (e.g. 'as good as gold' /əz,gʊd.əzˈgəʊld ⓤⓢ -ˈgoʊld/).
as (*n.*) *coin:* æs **-es** -ɪz
AS (*abbrev. for* **airspeed** *or* **Anglo-Saxon** *or* **antisubmarine**) ˌeɪˈes
Asa *biblical name:* ˈeɪ.sə, ˈɑː.sə *as modern first name:* ˈeɪ.zə
asaf(o)etida ˌæs.əˈfet.ɪ.də, -ˈfiː.tɪ- ⓤⓢ -ˈfet̬.ə-
a.s.a.p., ASAP ˌeɪ.es.eɪˈpiː, ˈeɪ.sæp
Asaph ˈæs.əf
ASAT ˈeɪ.sæt
asbest|ic æsˈbes.t|ɪk, əs-, æz-, əz- **-ous** -əs
asbestos æsˈbes.tɒs, æz-, əs-, əz-, -təs ⓤⓢ -təs
asbestosis ˌæs.besˈtəʊ.sɪs, ˌæz-, -bɪs- ⓤⓢ -ˈtoʊ-
Ascalon ˈæs.kə.lɒn, -lən ⓤⓢ -lɑːn
Ascanius æsˈkeɪ.ni.əs
ascend əˈsend, æsˈend **-s** -z **-ing** -ɪŋ **-ed** -ɪd
ascendan|ce əˈsen.dən|ts, æsˈen- **-cy** -*t*.si **-t** -t

ascenden|ce ə'sen.dən|ts, æs'en- **-cy** -*t*.si **-t** -t
ascender ə'sen.dəʳ ⓤⓢ -dɚ **-s** -z
ascension (A) ə'sen.*t*ʃᵊn ⓤⓢ -'sen*t*.ʃᵊn **-s** -z **A'scension ˌDay**
ascensional ə'sen.*t*ʃᵊn.ᵊl ⓤⓢ -'sen*t*.ʃᵊn-
ascent ə'sent, æs'ent **-s** -s
ascertain ˌæs.ə'teɪn ⓤⓢ -ɚ'- **-s** -z **-ing** -ɪŋ **-ed** -d **-ment** -mənt **-able** -ə.bl̩
ascetic ə'set.ɪk, æs'et- ⓤⓢ ə'set̬.ɪk **-al** -ᵊl **-ally** -ᵊl.i, -li **-s** -s
asceticism ə'set.ɪ.sɪ.zᵊm, æs'et- ⓤⓢ ə'set̬.ə-
Asch æʃ
Ascham 'æs.kəm
ASCII 'æs.kiː, -ki
Asclepius ə'skliː.pi.əs, æs'kliː-
ascorbate ə'skɔː.beɪt, æs'kɔː- ⓤⓢ ə'skɔːr- **-s** -s
ascorbic ə'skɔː.bɪk, æs'kɔː- ⓤⓢ ə'skɔːr- **aˌscorbic 'acid**
Ascot *place in Berkshire:* 'æs.kət ⓤⓢ -kɑːt
ascot *item of clothing:* 'æs.kət ⓤⓢ -kɑːt, -kət **-s** -s
ascrib|e ə'skraɪb **-es** -z **-ing** -ɪŋ **-ed** -d **-able** -ə.bl̩
ascription ə'skrɪp.ʃᵊn, æs'krɪp-
ascriptive ə'skrɪp.tɪv
Asda® 'æz.də
asdic 'æz.dɪk **-s** -s
-ase -eɪz, -eɪs
Note: Suffix. Does not normally affect stress pattern, e.g. **amylase** /'æm.ɪ.leɪz/.
asepsis ˌeɪ'sep.sɪs, ə-, æs'ep-
aseptic ˌeɪ'sep.tɪk, ə-, æ'sep- **-s** -s
asexual ˌeɪ'sek.ʃʊəl, -ʃu.əl, -sjʊəl, -ʃᵊl ⓤⓢ -ʃu.əl **-ly** -i
asexuality ˌeɪ.sek.ʃu'æl.ə.ti, -sju'-, -ɪ.ti ⓤⓢ -ʃu'æl.ə.t̬i
Asgard 'æs.gɑːd, 'æz- ⓤⓢ -gɑːrd, 'ɑːs-, 'ɑːz-
Asgill 'æs.gɪl, 'æz-
ash (A) æʃ **-es** -ɪz **'ash ˌcan**; **ˌAsh 'Wednesday**
asham|ed ə'ʃeɪm|d **-edly** -ɪd.li **-edness** -ɪd.nəs, -nɪs
Ashanti ə'ʃæn.ti, æʃ'- ⓤⓢ ə'ʃæn-, -'ʃɑːn- **-s** -z
Ashbee 'æʃ.bi
Ashbery 'æʃ.bᵊr.i ⓤⓢ -ber-
Ashbourne 'æʃ.bɔːn ⓤⓢ -bɔːrn
Ashburne 'æʃ.bɜːn ⓤⓢ -bɝːn
Ashburnham æʃ'bɜː.nəm ⓤⓢ -'bɝː-
Ashburton æʃ'bɜː.tᵊn ⓤⓢ -'bɝː-
Ashbury 'æʃ.bᵊr.i ⓤⓢ -ber-, -bɚ-
Ashby 'æʃ.bi
Ashby-de-la-Zouch ˌæʃ.bi.də.lɑː'zuːʃ, -de.lə'-
ashcan 'æʃ.kæn **-s** -z
Ashcombe 'æʃ.kəm
Ashcroft 'æʃ.krɒft ⓤⓢ -krɑːft
Ashdod 'æʃ.dɒd ⓤⓢ -dɑːd
Ashdown 'æʃ.daʊn
Ashe æʃ
ashen 'æʃ.ᵊn
Asher 'æʃ.əʳ ⓤⓢ -ɚ
asher|y 'æʃ.ᵊr|.i **-ies** -iz
Ashfield 'æʃ.fiːld
Ashford 'æʃ.fəd ⓤⓢ -fɚd
Ashington 'æʃ.ɪŋ.tən
Ashkenazy, Ashkenazi ˌæʃ.kə'nɑː.zi, -kɪ'nɑː- ⓤⓢ ɑːʃ-
Ashkhabad ˌɑːʃ.kə'bɑːd ⓤⓢ ˌɑːʃ.kɑː'bɑːd
Ashland 'æʃ.lənd
ashlar 'æʃ.ləʳ, -lɑːʳ ⓤⓢ -lɚ
Ashley, Ashlee, Ashleigh 'æʃ.li
Ashman 'æʃ.mən
Ashmole 'æʃ.məʊl ⓤⓢ -moʊl
Ashmolean æʃ'məʊ.li.ən, æʃ.məʊ'liː.ən ⓤⓢ -'moʊ.li-
Ashmore 'æʃ.mɔːʳ ⓤⓢ -mɔːr
ashore ə'ʃɔːʳ ⓤⓢ -'ʃɔːr
Ashover 'æʃ.əʊ.vəʳ ⓤⓢ -oʊ.vɚ
ashpan 'æʃ.pæn **-s** -z
ashram 'æʃ.rəm, -ræm **-s** -z
Ashtaroth 'æʃ.tə.rɒθ ⓤⓢ -rɑːθ, -rɔːθ
Ashton 'æʃ.tᵊn
Ashton-in-Makerfield ˌæʃ.tᵊn.ɪn'meɪ.kə.fiːld ⓤⓢ -kɚ-
Ashton-under-Lyne ˌæʃ.tᵊn.ʌn.də'laɪn, -'ʌn.dəˌlaɪn ⓤⓢ -ʌn.dɚ'-, -'ʌn.dɚˌ-
Ashtoreth 'æʃ.tə.reθ, -tɒr.eθ ⓤⓢ -tə.reθ
ashtray 'æʃ.treɪ **-s** -z
Ashurbanipal ˌæʃ.ɜː'bɑː.nɪ.pæl, -pᵊl ⓤⓢ ˌɑː.ʃʊr'bɑː.nɪ.pɑːl
Ashwell 'æʃ.wel, -wᵊl
Ashworth 'æʃ.wəθ, -wɜːθ ⓤⓢ -wɚθ, -wɝːθ
ash|y 'æʃ|.i **-ier** -i.əʳ ⓤⓢ -i.ɚ **-iest** -i.əst, -i.ɪst **-iness** -ɪ.nəs, -ɪ.nɪs
Asia 'eɪ.ʒə, -ʃə ⓤⓢ 'eɪ.ʒə **ˌAsia 'Minor**
Asian 'eɪ.ʒᵊn, -ʃᵊn ⓤⓢ 'eɪ.ʒᵊn, -ʃᵊn **-s** -z **ˌAsian 'flu**
Asiatic ˌeɪ.zi'æt.ɪk, ˌeɪ.si-, ˌeɪ.ʒi-, ˌeɪ.ʃi- ⓤⓢ ˌeɪ.ʒi'æt̬.ɪk, -ʃi'- **-s** -s *stress shift:* ˌAsiatic 'origin
aside ə'saɪd **-s** -z
Asimov 'æz.ɪ.mɒf, 'æs-, '-ə-, -mɒv ⓤⓢ 'æz.ə.mɑːf, -mɑːv
asinine 'æs.ɪ.naɪn, -ə.naɪn
asininit|y ˌæs.ɪ'nɪn.ə.t|i, -ə'nɪn-, -ɪ.t|i ⓤⓢ -ə'nɪn.ə.t̬|i **-ies** -iz
ask (*v.*) ɑːsk ⓤⓢ æsk **-s** -s **-ing** -ɪŋ **-ed** -t
askance ə'skæn*t*s, -'skɑːn*t*s ⓤⓢ ə'skæn*t*s
askant ə'skænt
Aske æsk
Askelon 'æs.kɪ.lən, -kə.lən, -lɒn ⓤⓢ -kə.lɑːn
Askern 'æs.kɜːn, -kən ⓤⓢ -kɝːn, -kɚn
askew ə'skjuː
Askew 'æs.kjuː
Askey 'æs.ki
Askrigg 'æs.krɪg
Askwith 'æs.kwɪθ
Aslam 'æz.ləm
aslant ə'slɑːnt ⓤⓢ -'slænt
asleep ə'sliːp
ASLEF, Aslef 'æz.lef
Asmara æs'mɑː.rə, æz- ⓤⓢ -'mɑːr.ə
Asmodeus æs'məʊ.di.əs ⓤⓢ ˌæz.moʊ'diː-, ˌæs-, -mə'-
Note: For British English, the name must be pronounced /ˌæs.məʊ'diː.əs/ in Milton's 'Paradise Lost', iv, 168.
asocial ˌeɪ'səʊ.ʃᵊl ⓤⓢ -'soʊ-
Asoka ə'ʃəʊ.kə, ə'səʊ- ⓤⓢ -'soʊ-
asp æsp, ɑːsp ⓤⓢ æsp **-s** -s
asparagus ə'spær.ə.gəs ⓤⓢ -'sper-, -'spær-
aspartame ə'spɑː.teɪm; 'æs.pə- ⓤⓢ 'æs.pɚ-; ə'spɑːr-
Aspasia æs'peɪ.zi.ə, ə'speɪ-, -ʒə ⓤⓢ -ʒə
ASPCA ˌeɪ.es.piː.siː'eɪ
aspect 'æs.pekt **-s** -s
aspectable æs'pek.tə.bl̩
aspectual ə'spek.tʃu.əl, æs'pek-, -tju- ⓤⓢ -tʃu-
Aspel(l) 'æs.pᵊl
aspen (A) 'æs.pən **-s** -z
asper 'æs.pəʳ ⓤⓢ -pɚ
asperg|e ə'spɜːdʒ, æs'pɜːdʒ ⓤⓢ ə'spɝːdʒ **-es** -ɪz **-ing** -ɪŋ **-ed** -d
asperges (A) *religious service:* æs'pɜː.dʒiːz, ə'spɜː- ⓤⓢ ə'spɝː-
aspergill 'æs.pə.dʒɪl ⓤⓢ -pɚ- **-s** -z
asperit|y æs'per.ə.t|i, ə'sper-, -ɪ.t|i ⓤⓢ -ə.t̬|i **-ies** -iz
Aspern 'æs.pɜːn ⓤⓢ -pɝːn
aspers|e ə'spɜːs, æs'pɜːs ⓤⓢ ə'spɝːs **-es** -ɪz **-ing** -ɪŋ **-ed** -t
aspersion ə'spɜː.ʃᵊn, æs'pɜː- ⓤⓢ ə'spɝː.ʒᵊn, -ʃᵊn **-s** -z
asphalt (*n.*) 'æs.fælt, -fɔːlt, -fəlt ⓤⓢ -fɑːlt, -fɔːlt **-s** -s **ˌasphalt 'jungle**
asphal|t (*v.*) 'æs.fæl|t, æs'fæl|t ⓤⓢ 'æs.fɑːl|t, -fɔːl|t **-ts** -ts **-ting** -tɪŋ ⓤⓢ -t̬ɪŋ **-ted** -tɪd ⓤⓢ -t̬ɪd
asphaltic æs'fæl.tɪk ⓤⓢ -'fɑːl.t̬ɪk, -'fɔːl-
asphodel 'æs.fəʊ.del ⓤⓢ -fə- **-s** -z
asphyxia əs'fɪks.i.ə, æs-
asphyxiant əs'fɪk.si.ənt, æs'- **-s** -s
asphyxi|ate əs'fɪk.si|.eɪt, æs- **-ates** -s **-ating** -eɪ.tɪŋ ⓤⓢ -eɪ.t̬ɪŋ **-ated** -eɪ.tɪd ⓤⓢ -eɪ.t̬ɪd **-ator/s** -eɪ.təʳ/z ⓤⓢ -eɪ.t̬ɚ/z
asphyxiation əsˌfɪk.si'eɪ.ʃᵊn, æs- **-s** -z
asphyx|y æs'fɪk.s|i **-ies** -iz
aspic 'æs.pɪk

Aspiration

Noise made when the constriction of a plosive consonant is released and air is allowed to escape relatively freely.

Examples for English

English /p t k/ at the beginning of a syllable are aspirated in most accents. In words like *pea, tea, key*, there is a silent period during which the compressed air is prevented from escaping by the articulatory closure; this is followed by a sound similar to /h/ before the VOICING of the vowel begins, the result of the vocal folds being widely parted at the time of the articulatory release. Aspiration is an important factor in whether we perceive a sound to be /p t k/ or /b d g/ in syllable-initial position.

/p t k/ are aspirated at the beginning of a syllable containing a full vowel, e.g.:

pin	/pɪn/	[pʰĩn]
tick	/tɪk/	[tʰɪʔk]
kin	/kɪn/	[kʰĩn]
appease	/ə'piːz/	[ə'pʰiːz̥]
attain	/ə'teɪn/	[ə'tʰeĩn]
accord	/ə'kɔːd/	[ə'kʰɔːd̥] (US) /ə'kɔːrd/ [ə'kʰɔːɹd̥]

When followed by /l r w/ or /j/ in initial consonant clusters, the release of the PLOSIVE gives the following sound a voiceless quality, e.g.:

play	/pleɪ/	[pl̥eɪ]
tree	/triː/	[tɹ̥iː]
queue	/kjuː/	[kj̊ʉː]
twice	/twaɪs/	[tw̥aɪs]

It is noticeable that when /p t k/ are preceded by /s/ at the beginning of a syllable they are not aspirated. This makes them very similar to /b d g/, and is an example of NEUTRALISATION – the distinctive difference between /p t k/ and /b d g/ is lost when there is a preceding /s/, e.g.:

spin	/spɪn/	[spĩn]	(compare pɪn	[pʰĩn])
stick	/stɪk/	[stɪʔk]	(compare tɪk	[tʰɪʔk])
skin	/skɪn/	[skĩn]	(compare kɪn	[kʰĩn])

Word final /p t k/ may be aspirated or not, for stylistic reasons.

aspidistra ˌæs.pɪ'dɪs.trə (US) -pə'- **-s** -z
Aspinall 'æs.pɪ.nɔːl, -nᵊl
Aspinwall 'æs.pɪn.wɔːl (US) -wɔːl, -wɑːl
aspirant 'æs.pɪ.rᵊnt; ə'spaɪə- (US) 'æs.pɚ.ᵊnt, -pɪ.rᵊnt **-s** -s
aspirate (*n. adj.*) 'æs.pᵊr.ət, -pɪ.rət-, -rɪt **-s** -s
aspir|ate (*v.*) 'æs.pᵊr.leɪt, -pɪ.rleɪt (US) -pə.rleɪt, -pɪ- **-ates** -eɪts **-ating** -eɪ.tɪŋ (US) -eɪ.t̬ɪŋ **-ated** -eɪ.tɪd (US) -eɪ.t̬ɪd **-ator/s** -eɪ.təʳ/z (US) -eɪ.t̬ɚ/z
aspiration ˌæs.pᵊr'eɪ.ʃᵊn, -pɪ'reɪ- (US) -pə'reɪ-, -pɪ'- **-s** -z
aspirational ˌæs.pᵊr'eɪ.ʃᵊn.ᵊl, -pɪ'reɪ- (US) -pə'reɪ-, -pɪ'- **-ly** -i
aspir|e ə'spaɪəʳ (US) -spaɪɚ **-es** -z **-ing/ly** -ɪŋ/li **-ed** -d **-er/s** -əʳ/z (US) -ɚ/z
aspirin 'æs.pᵊr.ɪn, '-prɪn **-s** -z
aspirine 'æs.pᵊr.iːn, -pɪ.riːn (US) -pə.riːn, -pɪ- **-s** -z
asplenium æs'pliː.ni.əm, ə'spliː- **-s** -z
Asquith 'æs.kwɪθ
ass æs **-es** -ɪz
assaf(o)etida ˌæs.ə'fet.ɪ.də, -'fiː.tɪ- (US) -'fet̬.ə-
assagai 'æs.ə.gaɪ **-s** -z
assai æs'aɪ
assail ə'seɪl **-s** -z **-ing** -ɪŋ **-ed** -d **-able** -ə.bl̩ **-ant/s** -ənt/s
Assam æs'æm, 'æs.æm
Assamese ˌæs.ə'miːz, -æm'iːz (US) -ə'miːz, -'miːs
assassin ə'sæs.ɪn (US) -ən **-s** -z
assassi|nate ə'sæs.ɪ.l.neɪt, '-ə- **-nates** -neɪts **-nating** -neɪ.tɪŋ (US) -neɪ.t̬ɪŋ **-nated** -neɪ.tɪd (US) -neɪ.t̬ɪd **-nator/s** -neɪ.təʳ/z (US) -neɪ.t̬ɚ/z
assassination əˌsæs.ɪ'neɪ.ʃᵊn, -ə'- **-s** -z
assault ə'sɔːlt, -'sɒlt (US) -'sɔːlt, -'sɑːlt **-s** -s **-ing** -ɪŋ (US) ə'sɔːl.t̬ɪŋ **-ed** -ɪd (US) ə'sɔːl.t̬ɪd **-er/s** -əʳ/z (US) ə'sɔːl.t̬ɚ/z **asˌsault and 'battery; as'sault ˌcourse**
assay (*n.*) ə'seɪ; 'æs.eɪ (US) 'æs.eɪ; ə'seɪ **-s** -z
assay (*v.*) ə'seɪ, æs'eɪ **-s** -z **-ing** -ɪŋ **-ed** -d **-er/s** -əʳ/z (US) -ɚ/z
Assaye æs'eɪ
assegai 'æs.ə.gaɪ, '-ɪ- (US) '-ə- **-s** -z
assemblag|e ə'sem.blɪdʒ **-es** -ɪz
assembl|e ə'sem.bl̩ **-es** -z **-ing** -ɪŋ, '-blɪŋ **-ed** -d **-er/s** -əʳ/z, '-bləʳ/z (US) '-bl̩.ɚ/z, -blɚ/z
assembl|y ə'sem.bl|i **-ies** -iz **as'sembly ˌline; as'sembly ˌroom; as'sembly ˌlanguage**
assembly|man ə'sem.bli|.mæn, -mən **-men** -men, -mən
assen|t ə'sen|t, æs'en|t **-ts** -ts **-ting/ly** -tɪŋ/li (US) -t̬ɪŋ/li **-ted** -tɪd (US) -t̬ɪd
Asser 'æs.əʳ (US) -ɚ
as|sert ə|'sɜːt (US) -'sɝːt **-serts** -'sɜːts (US) -'sɝːts **-serting** -'sɜː.tɪŋ (US) -'sɝː.t̬ɪŋ **-serted** -'sɜː.tɪd (US) -'sɝː.t̬ɪd **-serter/s** -'sɜː.təʳ/z (US) -'sɝː.t̬ɚ/s **-sertor/s** -'sɜː.təʳ/z (US) -'sɝː.t̬ɚ/z **-sertable** -'sɜː.tə.bl̩ (US) -'sɝː.t̬ə.bl̩
assertion ə'sɜː.ʃᵊn (US) -'sɝː- **-s** -z
assertive ə'sɜː.tɪv (US) -sɝː.t̬ɪv **-ly** -li **-ness** -nəs, -nɪs **as'sertiveness ˌtraining**
assess ə'ses **-es** -ɪz **-ing** -ɪŋ **-ed** -t **-or/s** -əʳ/z (US) -ɚ/z **-able** -ə.bl̩
assessment ə'ses.mənt **-s** -s
asset 'æs.et, -ɪt **-s** -s
asset-stripp|ing 'æs.etˌstrɪp|.ɪŋ **-er/s** -əʳ/z (US) -ɚ/z
assev|er æs'ev|.əʳ, ə'sev- (US) -ɚ **-ers** -əz (US) -ɚs **-ering** -ᵊr.ɪŋ **-ered** -əd (US) -ɚd
assever|ate ə'sev.ᵊr|.eɪt, æs'ev- (US) -ə.r|eɪt **-ates** -eɪts **-ating** -eɪ.tɪŋ (US) -eɪ.t̬ɪŋ **-ated** -eɪ.tɪd (US) -eɪ.t̬ɪd
asseveration əˌsev.ə'reɪ.ʃᵊn, æsˌev- **-s** -z
asshole 'ɑːs.həʊl, 'æs- (US) 'æs.hoʊl **-s** -z
Note: Chiefly US; see note at **arse**.
assibi|late ə'sɪb.ɪ|.leɪt, æs'ɪb-, '-ə- **-lates** -leɪts **-lating** -leɪ.tɪŋ (US) -leɪ.t̬ɪŋ **-lated** -leɪ.tɪd (US) -leɪ.t̬ɪd
assibilation əˌsɪb.ɪ'leɪ.ʃᵊn, æsˌɪb-, -ə'- **-s** -z
assiduit|y ˌæs.ɪ'djuː.ə.t|i, -'dʒuː-, -ɪ.t|i (US) -'duː.ə.t̬|i, -'djuː- **-ies** -iz
assiduous ə'sɪd.ju.əs, -'sɪdʒ.u- (US) -'sɪdʒ.u- **-ly** -li **-ness** -nəs, -nɪs
assign ə'saɪn **-s** -z **-ing** -ɪŋ **-ed** -d **-er/s** -əʳ/z (US) -ɚ/z **-able** -ə.bl̩

Assimilation

Assimilation is what happens to a sound when it is influenced by one of its neighbours; essentially it becomes more similar to a neighbour.

Examples for English

Assimilation is said to be 'progressive' when a sound influences a following sound, or 'regressive' when a sound influences one which precedes it. The most familiar case of regressive assimilation in English is that of ALVEOLAR consonants (e.g. /t d s z n/) which are followed by non-alveolar consonants: assimilation results in a change of place of articulation from alveolar to a different place. For example, the word *this* has the sound /s/ at the end if it is pronounced on its own, but when followed by post-alveolar /ʃ/ in a word such as *shop* it often changes in rapid speech (through assimilation) to /ʃ/, giving the pronunciation /ðɪʃʃɒp/. The following examples occur especially in British English:

batman	/ˈbæt.mæn/	→	[ˈbæp.mæn]
fruitcake	/ˈfruːt.keɪk/	→	[ˈfruːk.keɪk]
handbag	/ˈhænd.bæg/	→	[ˈhæmb .bæg]

Progressive assimilation is exemplified by the behaviour of the 's' plural ending in English, which is pronounced with a voiced /z/ after a voiced consonant but with a voiceless /s/ after a voiceless consonant, e.g.:

dog	/dɒg/	+ plural →	/dɒgz/
	(US) /dɑːg/		(US) /dɑːgz/
cat	/kæt/	+ plural →	/kæts/

assignat *as if French:* ˌæs.ɪnˈjɑː, æs.ɪgˈnæt **-s** -z, -s
assignation ˌæs.ɪgˈneɪ.ʃᵊn **-s** -z
assignee ˌæs.aɪˈniː, -ɪˈniː (US) əˌsaɪˈniː, ˌæs.əˈ- **-s** -z
assignment əˈsaɪn.mənt, -ˈsaɪm- (US) -ˈsaɪn- **-s** -s
assimilable əˈsɪm.ᵊl.ə.bl̩, -ɪ.lə-
assimil|ate əˈsɪm.ɪ.l|eɪt, -ᵊl|.eɪt (US) -ə.l|eɪt **-ates** -eɪts **-ating** -eɪ.tɪŋ (US) -eɪ.t̬ɪŋ **-ated** -eɪ.tɪd (US) -eɪ.t̬ɪd
assimilation əˌsɪm.ɪˈleɪ.ʃᵊn, -ᵊlˈeɪ- (US) -əˈleɪ- **-s** -z
assimilative əˈsɪm.ɪ.lə.tɪv, -ᵊl.ə-, -ə.leɪ- (US) -ə.leɪ.t̬ɪv, -lə-
assimilatory əˈsɪm.ɪ.lə.tᵊr.i, -ᵊl.ə-; əˌsɪm.ɪˈleɪ-, -əˈ- (US) əˈsɪm.ᵊl.ə.tɔːr-
Assiniboine əˈsɪn.ɪ.bɔɪn, -ə.bɔɪn **-s** -z
Assisi əˈsiː.si, -zi, -ˈsɪs.i
assist əˈsɪst **-s** -s **-ing** -ɪŋ **-ed** -ɪd **-er/s** -əʳ/z (US) -ɚ/z
assistanc|e əˈsɪs.tᵊnts **-es** -ɪz
assistant əˈsɪs.tᵊnt **-s** -s
Assiut æsˈjuːt (US) ɑːˈsjuːt
assiz|e əˈsaɪz **-es** -ɪz **-er/s** -əʳ/z (US) -ɚ/z
assoc *(abbrev. for* **associated***)* əˈsəʊ.ʃi.eɪ.tɪd, -si- (US) -ˈsoʊ.ʃi.eɪ.t̬ɪd, -si-
associable əˈsəʊ.ʃi.ə.bl̩, -ʃə-, -si.ə- (US) -ˈsoʊ-
associate *(n.)* əˈsəʊ.ʃi.ət, -si.ət (US) -ˈsoʊ.ʃi.ɪt, -si-, -ət **-s** -s
associ|ate *(v.)* əˈsəʊ.ʃi|.eɪt, -si- (US) -ˈsoʊ- **-ates** -eɪts **-ating** -eɪ.tɪŋ (US) -eɪ.t̬ɪŋ **-ated** -eɪ.tɪd (US) -eɪ.t̬ɪd
association əˌsəʊ.ʃiˈeɪ.ʃᵊn, -siˈ- (US) -ˌsoʊ **-s** -z
associative əˈsəʊ.ʃi.ə.tɪv, -si- (US) -ˈsoʊ-
assonanc|e ˈæs.ᵊn.ənts **-es** -ɪz
assonant ˈæs.ᵊn.ənt **-s** -s
asson|ate ˈæs.ᵊn|.eɪt (US) -ə.n|eɪt **-ates** -eɪts **-ating** -eɪ.tɪŋ (US) -eɪ.t̬ɪŋ **-ated** -eɪ.tɪd (US) -eɪ.t̬ɪd
as|sort əˈsɔːt (US) -ˈsɔːrt **-sorts** -ˈsɔːts (US) -ˈsɔːrts **-sorting** -ˈsɔː.tɪŋ (US) -ˈsɔːr.t̬ɪŋ **-sorted** -ˈsɔː.tɪd (US) -ˈsɔːr.t̬ɪd
assortment əˈsɔːt.mənt (US) -ˈsɔːrt- **-s** -s
Assouan æsˈwæn, ɑːˈswæn, -ˈswɑːn (US) ˈæs.wɑːn, ˈɑː.swɑːn *stress shift, British only, see compound:* ˌ**Assouan ˈDam**
asst *(abbrev. for* **assistant***)* əˈsɪs.tᵊnt
assuag|e əˈsweɪdʒ **-es** -ɪz **-ing** -ɪŋ **-ed** -d **-ement** -mənt
assum|e əˈsjuːm, -suːm (US) -suːm **-es** -z **-ing/ly** -ɪŋ/li **-ed** -d **-edly** -ɪd.li, -əd- **-able** -ə.bl̩ **-ably** -ə.bli
assumpsit əˈsʌmp.sɪt
assumption (A) əˈsʌmp.ʃᵊn **-s** -z
assumptive əˈsʌmp.tɪv
assuranc|e əˈʃɔː.rᵊnts, -ˈʃʊə- (US) -ˈʃʊr.ᵊnts, -ˈʃɜː- **-es** -ɪz
assur|e əˈʃʊəʳ, -ʃɔːʳ (US) -ˈʃʊr, -ˈʃɜː **-es** -z **-ing** -ɪŋ **-ed** -d **-edly** -ɪd.li, -əd- **-edness** -d.nəs, -nɪs **-er/s** -əʳ/z (US) -ɚ/z
Assyri|a əˈsɪr.i|.ə **-an/s** -ən/z
assyriologist (A) əˌsɪr.iˈɒl.ə.dʒɪst (US) -ˈɑː.lə- **-s** -s
assyriology (A) əˌsɪr.iˈɒl.ə.dʒi (US) -ˈɑː.lə-
Astaire əˈsteəʳ (US) -ˈster
Astarte æsˈtɑː.ti (US) əˈstɑr.t̬i
astatine ˈæs.tə.tiːn, -tɪn
Astbury ˈæst.bᵊr.i (US) -ber-
aster ˈæs.təʳ (US) -tɚ **-s** -z
asterisk ˈæs.tᵊr.ɪsk **-s** -s **-ing** -ɪŋ **-ed** -t
asterism ˈæs.tᵊr.ɪ.zᵊm **-s** -z
Asterix ˈæs.tᵊr.ɪks
astern əˈstɜːn (US) -ˈstɝːn
asteroid ˈæs.tᵊr.ɔɪd (US) -tə.rɔɪd **-s** -z
asthenia æsˈθiː.ni.ə
asthenic æsˈθen.ɪk **-al** -ᵊl
asthma ˈæsθ.mə, ˈæs.mə (US) ˈæz.mə
asthmatic æsθˈmæt.ɪk, æsˈmæt.ɪk (US) æzˈmæt̬- **-al** -ᵊl **-ally** -ᵊl.i, -li **-s** -s
Asti ˈæs.ti, -tiː (US) ˈɑː.sti
astigmatic ˌæs.tɪgˈmæt.ɪk (US) -ˈmæt̬-
astigmatism əˈstɪg.mə.tɪ.zᵊm, æsˈtɪg-
astir əˈstɜːʳ (US) -ˈstɝː
Asti Spumante ˌæs.ti.spuˈmæn.ti, -teɪ (US) ˌɑː.sti.spuˈmɑːn-, ˌæs.ti-
Astle ˈæs.l̩, ˈæs.tl̩
Astley ˈæst.li
Aston ˈæs.tᵊn ˌ**Aston ˈMartin®**; ˌ**Aston ˈVilla**
astonish əˈstɒn.ɪʃ (US) -ˈstɑː.nɪʃ **-es** -ɪz **-ed/ly** -t/li
astonishing əˈstɒn.ɪ.ʃɪŋ (US) -ˈstɑː.nɪ- **-ly** -li
astonishment əˈstɒn.ɪʃ.mənt (US) -ˈstɑː.nɪʃ-
Astor ˈæs.təʳ, -tɔːʳ (US) -tɚ
Astoria əˈstɔː.ri.ə, æsˈtɔː- (US) əˈstɔːr.i-, æsˈtɔːr-
astound əˈstaʊnd **-s** -z **-ing/ly** -ɪŋ **-ed** -ɪd
Astra® ˈæs.trə
Astraea æsˈtriː.ə
astragal ˈæs.trə.gᵊl **-s** -z
astrakhan (A) ˌæs.trəˈkæn, -kɑːn
astral ˈæs.trᵊl **-ly** -i
astray əˈstreɪ
Astrid ˈæs.trɪd
astride əˈstraɪd
astring|e əˈstrɪndʒ **-es** -ɪz **-ing** -ɪŋ **-ed** -d
astringency əˈstrɪn.dʒənt.si
astringent əˈstrɪn.dʒənt **-s** -s **-ly** -li
astro- æs.trəʊ-; əˈstrɒ- (US) æs.troʊ-; əˈstrɑː-

Note: Prefix. Either takes primary or secondary stress on the first syllable, e.g. **astrolabe** /'æs.trəʊ.leɪb (US) -trə-/, **astronomic** /ˌæs.trə'nɒm.ɪk (US) -'nɑː.mɪk/, or primary stress on the second syllable, e.g. **astronomy** /ə'strɒn.ə.mi (US) ə'strɑː.nə-/.

astrobiology ˌæs.trəʊ.baɪ'ɒl.ə.dʒi (US) -troʊ.baɪ'ɑː.lə-, -trə-

astrodome 'æs.trəʊ.dəʊm (US) -trə.doʊm **-s** -z

astrolabe 'æs.trəʊ.leɪb (US) -trə- **-s** -z

astrologer ə'strɒl.ə.dʒəʳ, æs'- (US) ə'strɑː.lə.dʒɚ **-s** -z

astrologic ˌæs.trə'lɒdʒ.ɪk (US) -'lɑː.dʒɪk **-al** -ᵊl **-ally** -ᵊl.i

astrologist ə'strɒl.ə.dʒɪst, æs'- (US) ə'strɑː.lə- **-s** -s

astrology ə'strɒl.ə.dʒi, æs'- (US) ə'strɑː.lə-

astromet|er ə'strɒm.ɪ.t|əʳ, æs'trɒm-, -ə.təʳ (US) ə'strɑː.mə.t̬|ɚ **-ers** -əz (US) -ɚz **-ry** -ri

astronaut 'æs.trə.nɔːt (US) -nɑːt, -nɔːt **-s** -s

astronautic|al ˌæs.trəʊ'nɔː.tɪ.k|ᵊl (US) -trə'nɑː.t̬ɪ-, -'nɔː- **-s** -s

astronomer ə'strɒn.ə.məʳ, æs'- (US) ə'strɑː.nə.mɚ **-s** -z

astronomic ˌæs.trə'nɒm.ɪk (US) -'nɑː.mɪk **-al** -ᵊl **-ally** -ᵊl.i, -li *stress shift:* ˌastronomic 'increase

astronom|y ə'strɒn.ə.m|i, æs'- (US) ə'strɑː.nə- **-ies** -iz

Astrophil 'æs.trəʊ.fɪl (US) -trə-

astrophysical ˌæs.trəʊ'fɪz.ɪ.kᵊl (US) -troʊ'-, -trə'-

astrophysicist ˌæs.trəʊ'fɪz.ɪ.sɪst (US) -troʊ'-, -trə'- **-s** -s

astrophysics ˌæs.trəʊ'fɪz.ɪks (US) -troʊ'-

Astros 'æs.trəʊz (US) -troʊz

astroturf (A®) 'æs.trəʊ.tɜːf (US) -troʊ.tɝːf

Asturias æs'tʊə.ri.æs, ə'stʊə-, -stjʊə-, -əs (US) ə'stʊr.i-

astu|te ə'stjuː|t, æs'tjuː|t, -'tʃuː|t (US) ə'stuː|t, -'stjuː|t **-ter** -təʳ (US) -t̬ɚ **-test** -tɪst, -təst (US) -t̬ɪst, -t̬əst **-tely** -t.li **-teness** -t.nəs, -t.nɪs

Astyanax ə'staɪ.ə.næks, æs'taɪ-

astylar eɪ'staɪ.ləʳ, -lɑːʳ (US) -lɚ

Asunción əˌsʊnt.si'əʊn, 'ɒn (US) ɑːˌsuːnt.si'oʊn, ˌɑː.suːnt-

asunder ə'sʌn.dəʳ (US) -dɚ

Aswan æs'wæn, ɑː'swæn, -swɑːn (US) 'æs.wɑːn, 'ɑː.swɑːn *stress shift, British only, see compound:* ˌ**Aswan 'Dam**

asyllabic ˌeɪ.sɪ'læb.ɪk, -sə'- (US) -sɪ'- *stress shift:* ˌasyllabic 'vowel

asylum ə'saɪ.ləm **-s** -z **a'sylum ˌseeker**

asymmetric ˌeɪ.sɪ'met.rɪk, ˌæs.ɪ'-, -sə'- **-al** -ᵊl **-ally** -ᵊl.i, -li *stress shift:* ˌasymmetric 'bars

asymmetry eɪ'sɪm.ə.tri, æs'ɪm-, '-ɪ-

asymptote 'æs.ɪmp.təʊt (US) -toʊt **-s** -s

asymptotic ˌæs.ɪmp'tɒt.ɪk (US) -'tɑː.t̬ɪk **-al** -ᵊl **-ally** -ᵊl.i, -li *stress shift:* ˌasymptotic 'curve

asyndet|on æs'ɪn.dɪ.t|ən, ə'sɪn- (US) ə'sɪn.də.t|ɑːn, ˌeɪ- **-a** -ə

at- ət-, æt-

Note: Prefix. Examples include **attestation** /ˌæt.es'teɪ.ʃᵊn (US) æt̬-/, in which it is stressed, and **attest** /ə'test/, where it is unstressed.

at *(prep.) strong form:* æt *weak form:* ət

Note: Weak form word. The strong form is /æt/, and is used mainly in sentence-final position (e.g. 'What are you playing at?'). It may also be used in sentence-initial position. The weak form is /ət/ (e.g. 'She's at home.' /ʃiz.ət'həʊm (US) -'hoʊm/).

at *currency:* ɑːt, æt

Atalanta ˌæt.ə'læn.tə (US) ˌæt̬.ə'læn.t̬ə

Atall 'æt.ɔːl

Atari® ə'tɑː.ri (US) -'tɑːr.i

AT&T® ˌeɪ.tiː.ᵊnd'tiː

Atatürk 'æt.ə.tɜːk, ˌ--'- (US) 'æt̬.ə.tɝːk

atavism 'æt.ə.vɪ.zᵊm (US) 'æt̬-

atavistic ˌæt.ə'vɪs.tɪk (US) ˌæt̬.ə'- **-ally** -ᵊl.i, -li *stress shift:* ˌatavistic 'feelings

ataxia ə'tæk.si.ə, æt'æk-, eɪ'-

atax|y ə'tæk.s|i, eɪ- **-ies** -iz **-ic** -ɪk

Atbara æt'bɑː.rə (US) -'bɑːr.ə

ATC ˌeɪ.tiː'siː

Atchison 'ætʃ.ɪ.sᵊn, 'eɪ.tʃɪ- (US) 'ætʃ.ɪ-

Ate *(n.)* 'ɑː.ti, 'eɪ- (US) 'ɑː-

ate *(from* **eat***)* et, eɪt (US) eɪt

-ate -eɪt, -ət, -ɪt

Note: Suffix. When forming a verb, **-ate** is always pronounced with a full vowel, and the verb itself is usually stressed two syllables before the suffix, e.g. **demonstrate** /'dem.ən.streɪt/, unless it is a word containing two syllables, in which case the suffix normally carries primary stress in British English, e.g. **rotate** /rəʊ'teɪt (US) 'roʊ.teɪt, -'-/. In nouns, **-ate** is normally pronounced /-ət/ or /-ɪt/, e.g. **climate** /'klaɪ.mət, -mɪt/, but where the noun is a chemical term it generally has a full vowel, e.g. **nitrate** /'naɪ.treɪt, -trɪt (US) -treɪt/. There are numerous exceptions; see individual entries.

A-team 'eɪˌtiːm

atelic ə'tel.ɪk, æt'el.ɪk, -iː.lɪk (US) ˌeɪ'tiː.lɪk, ˌæt'iː-, -'el.ɪk

atelier ə'tel.i.eɪ, 'æt.el-, 'æt.ə.li-, -jeɪ (US) ə'tᵊl.jeɪ, æt'el-; ˌæt.el'jeɪ **-s** -z

Atfield 'æt.fiːld

Athabasca ˌæθ.ə'bæs.kə

Athaliah ˌæθ.ə'laɪ.ə

Athanasian ˌæθ.ə'neɪ.zi.ən, '-ʒən, -si.ən, -ʒi- (US) -ʒən

Athanasius ˌæθ.ə'neɪ.zi.əs, '-ʒəs, -si.əs, -ʒi- (US) -ʒəs

Athawes 'æt.hɔːz, 'æθ.ɔːz (US) 'æt̬.hɑːz, -hɔːz, 'æθ.ɑːz, -ɔːz

atheism 'eɪ.θi.ɪ.zᵊm

atheist 'eɪ.θi.ɪst **-s** -s

atheistic ˌeɪ.θi'ɪs.tɪk **-al** -ᵊl **-ally** -ᵊl.i, -li *stress shift:* ˌatheistic 'culture

atheling (A) 'æθ.ə.lɪŋ **-s** -z

Athelney 'æθ.ᵊl.ni

Athelstan 'æθ.ᵊl.stən *as if Old English:* 'æð.ᵊl.stɑːn

Athelston 'æθ.ᵊl.stən

Athena ə'θiː.nə

Athenaeum ˌæθ.ɪ'niː.əm, -ə'- **-s** -z

Athene ə'θiː.ni, -niː

Athenian ə'θiː.ni.ən **-s** -z

Athenry ˌæθ.ən'raɪ, -ɪn'-

Athens 'æθ.ᵊnz, -ɪnz

Atherley 'æθ.ə.li (US) '-ɚ-

atherosclerosis ˌæθ.ə.rəʊ.sklə'rəʊ.sɪs, -skler'əʊ-, sklɪr'- (US) -roʊ.sklə'roʊ.səs

atherosclerotic ˌæθ.ə.rəʊ.sklə'rɒt.ɪk, -skler'ɒt-, -sklɪr'- (US) -roʊ.sklə'rɑː.t̬ɪk

Atherston 'æθ.ə.stᵊn (US) '-ɚ-

Atherstone 'æθ.ə.stəʊn, -stᵊn (US) -ɚ.stoʊn, -stᵊn

Atherton 'æθ.ə.tᵊn (US) '-ɚ.t̬ən

athirst ə'θɜːst (US) -'θɝːst

Athlestaneford 'el.ʃən.fəd (US) -fɚd

athlete 'æθ.liːt **-s** -s ˌ**athlete's 'foot** (US) **'athlete's ˌfoot**

athletic æθ'let.ɪk, əθ- (US) -'let̬.ɪk **-al** -ᵊl **-ally** -ᵊl.i, -li **-s** -s

athleticism æθ'let.ɪ.sɪ.zᵊm, əθ-, '-ə- (US) -'let̬.ə-

Athlone æθ'ləʊn (US) -'loʊn *stress shift:* ˌAthlone 'Press

Athol 'æθ.ᵊl, -ɒl (US) -ɑːl, -ᵊl

Atholl, Athole 'æθ.ᵊl

Athos 'æθ.ɒs, 'eɪ.θɒs (US) 'æθ.ɑːs, 'eɪ.θɑːs; 'æθ.oʊs

athwart ə'θwɔːt (US) -'θwɔːrt

Athy ə'θaɪ

-ation -'eɪ.ʃᵊn

Note: Suffix. Always carries primary stress, e.g. **demonstration** /ˌdem.ən'streɪ.ʃᵊn/.

atishoo ə'tɪʃ.uː

-ative -ə.tɪv, -eɪ- (US) -ə.t̬ɪv, -eɪ-

Note: Suffix. Words containing **-ative** are normally stressed one or two syllables before the suffix, e.g.

ablative /ˈæb.lə.tɪv (US) -t̬ɪv/, **operative** /ˈɒp.ᵊr.ə.tɪv (US) ˈɑː.pɚ.ə.t̬ɪv/. See individual entries for exceptions.

Atkins ˈæt.kɪnz

Atkinson ˈæt.kɪn.sᵊn

Atlanta ətˈlæn.tə, æt- (US) -t̬ə

atlantean ˌæt.lænˈtiː.ən, -lənˈ-; ətˈlæn.ti-, æt- (US) ˌæt.lænˈtiː-, -lənˈ-

Atlantes *statues:* ətˈlæn.tiːz, æt- *in Ariosto's 'Orlando Furioso':* ətˈlæn.tes, æt-

Atlantic ətˈlæn.tɪk, æt- (US) -t̬ɪk
Atˌlantic ˈCity

Atlantis ətˈlæn.tɪs, æt- (US) -t̬ɪs

atlas (A) ˈæt.ləs **-es** -ɪz

ATM ˌeɪ.tiːˈem **-s** -z

atman (A) ˈɑːt.mən

atmometer ætˈmɒm.ɪ.təʳ, ˈ-ə- (US) -ˈmɑː.mə.t̬ɚ **-s** -z

atmosphere ˈæt.məs.fɪəʳ (US) -fɪr **-s** -z

atmospheric ˌæt.məsˈfer.ɪk (US) -ˈfer-, -ˈfɪr- **-s** -s **-al** -ᵊl **-ally** -ᵊl.i, -li *stress shift:* ˌatmospheric ˈpressure

atoll ˈæt.ɒl; əˈtɒl (US) ˈæt.ɑːl, ˈeɪ.tɑːl, -tɔːl **-s** -z

atom ˈæt.əm (US) ˈæt̬- **-s** -z

atomic əˈtɒm.ɪk (US) -ˈtɑː.mɪk **-s** -s **-ally** -ᵊl.i, -li **aˌtomic ˈenergy**

atom|ism ˈæt.ə.m|ɪ.zᵊm (US) ˈæt̬- **-ist/s** -ɪst/s

atomistic ˌæt.əˈmɪs.tɪk (US) ˌæt̬-

atomization, -isa- ˌæt.ə.maɪˈzeɪ.ʃᵊn (US) ˌæt̬.ə.mɪˈ-

atomiz|e, -is|e ˈæt.ə.maɪz (US) ˈæt̬- **-es** -ɪz **-ing** -ɪŋ **-ed** -d **-er/s** -əʳ/z (US) -ɚ/z

atonal eɪˈtəʊ.nᵊl, ə-, ætˈəʊ- (US) eɪˈtoʊ-, ætˈoʊ- **-ism** -ɪ.zᵊm **-ly** -i

atonality ˌeɪ.təʊˈnæl.ə.ti, ə-, ˌæt.əʊˈ-, -ɪ.ti (US) ˌeɪ.toʊˈnæl.ə.t̬i, ˌæt.oʊˈ-

aton|e əˈtəʊn (US) -ˈtoʊn **-es** -z **-ing/ly** -ɪŋ/li **-ed** -d **-er/s** -əʳ/z, -ɚ/z

atonement əˈtəʊn.mənt, -ˈtəʊm- (US) -ˈtoʊn- **-s** -s

atonic eɪˈtɒn.ɪk, ə-, ætˈɒn- (US) eɪˈtɑː.nɪk, ætˈɑː- **-s** -s

atony ˈæt.ᵊn.i (US) ˈæt̬-

atop əˈtɒp (US) -ˈtɑːp

-ator -ə.təʳ, -eɪ.təʳ (US) -ə.t̬ɚ, -eɪ.t̬ɚ

Note: Suffix. Words containing **-ator** behave similarly to verbs containing **-ate**, e.g. **demonstrator** /ˈdem.ən.streɪ.təʳ (US) -t̬ɚ/.

-atory -ə.tᵊr.i, -eɪ- (US) -ə.tɔːr.i

Note: Suffix. The pronunciation differs between British and American English. In British English, the penultimate syllable is always reduced, but the antepenultimate syllable may be stressed, and in either case may be pronounced with a full vowel, e.g. **articulatory** /ɑːˈtɪk.jə.lə.tᵊr.i, -jʊ-ˌɑːˌtɪk.jəˈleɪ-, -jʊˈ-/. In American English, the penultimate syllable is pronounced with a full vowel (but does not carry primary stress), e.g. **articulatory** /ɑːrˈtɪk.jə.lə.tɔːr.i/.

ATP ˌeɪ.tiːˈpiː

atrabilious ˌæt.rəˈbɪl.i.əs (US) ˈ-jəs

Atreus ˈeɪ.tri.əs, -tri.uːs, -truːs

atri|um ˈeɪ.tri.|əm, ˈæt.ri- (US) ˈeɪ.tri- **-a** -ə **-ums** -əmz

atrocious əˈtrəʊ.ʃəs (US) -ˈtroʊ- **-ly** -li **-ness** -nəs, -nɪs

atrocit|y əˈtrɒs.ə.t|i, -ɪ.t|i, -ˈtrɑː.sə.t̬|i **-ies** -iz

atrophic əˈtrɒf.ɪk, ætˈrɒf- (US) əˈtrɑː.fɪk

atroph|y ˈæt.rə.f|i **-ies** -iz **-ying** -i.ɪŋ **-ied** -id

atropine ˈæt.rə.pɪn, -piːn

Atropos ˈæt.rə.pɒs, -pəs (US) -pɑːs

attaboy ˈæt.ə.bɔɪ (US) ˈæt̬-

attach əˈtætʃ **-es** -ɪz **-ing** -ɪŋ **-ed** -t **-able** -ə.bl̩

attaché əˈtæʃ.eɪ, ætˈæʃ- (US) ˌæt̬.əˈʃeɪ, əˈtæʃ.eɪ **-s** -z **atˈtaché ˌcase** (US) **attaˈché ˌcase,** (US) **atˈtaché ˌcase**

attachment əˈtætʃ.mənt **-s** -s

attack əˈtæk **-s** -s **-ing** -ɪŋ **-ed** -t **-er/s** -əʳ/z, -ɚ/z

attain əˈteɪn **-s** -z **-ing** -ɪŋ **-ed** -d **-able** -ə.bl̩

attainability əˌteɪ.nəˈbɪl.ə.ti, -ɪ.ti (US) -ə.t̬i

attainder əˈteɪn.dəʳ (US) -dɚ **-s** -z

attainment əˈteɪn.mənt, -ˈteɪm- (US) -ˈteɪn- **-s** -s

at|taint ə|ˈteɪnt **-taints** -ˈteɪnts **-tainting** -ˈteɪn.tɪŋ (US) -ˈteɪn.t̬ɪŋ **-tainted** -ˈteɪn.tɪd (US) -ˈteɪn.t̬ɪd

attar ˈæt.əʳ (US) ˈæt̬.ɚ, -ɑːr

attempt əˈtempt **-s** -s **-ing** -ɪŋ **-ed** -ɪd **-er/s** -əʳ/z (US) -ɚ/z **-able** -ə.bl̩

Attenborough ˈæt.ᵊn.bᵊr.ə, -ᵊm-, -ˌbʌr.ə (US) -ᵊnˌbɝː.oʊ

attend əˈtend **-s** -z **-ing** -ɪŋ **-ed** -ɪd **-er/s** -əʳ/z (US) -ɚ/z

attendanc|e əˈten.dᵊnts **-es** -ɪz

attendant əˈten.dᵊnt **-s** -s

attendee ə.tenˈdiː, ˌæt.en- **-s** -z

attention əˈten.tʃᵊn **-s** -z

attentive əˈten.tɪv (US) -t̬ɪv **-ly** -li **-ness** -nəs, -nɪs

attenuate (*adj.*) əˈten.ju.ɪt, -ət, -eɪt

attenu|ate (*v.*) əˈten.ju|.eɪt **-ates** -eɪts **-ating** -eɪ.tɪŋ (US) -eɪ.t̬ɪŋ **-ated** -eɪ.tɪd (US) -eɪ.t̬ɪd

attenuation əˌten.juˈeɪ.ʃᵊn **-s** -z

attenuator əˈten.ju.eɪ.təʳ (US) -t̬ɚ **-s** -z

Atterbury ˈæt.ə.bᵊr.i (US) ˈæt̬.ɚ.ber.i, -bɚ-

Attercliffe ˈæt.ə.klɪf (US) ˈæt̬.ɚ-

attest əˈtest **-s** -s **-ing** -ɪŋ **-ed** -ɪd **-or/s** -əʳ/z (US) -ɚ/z **-able** -ə.bl̩

attestation ˌæt.esˈteɪ.ʃᵊn (US) ˌæt̬- **-s** -z

Attfield ˈæt.fiːld

attic ˈæt.ɪk (US) ˈæt̬- **-s** -s

Attica ˈæt.ɪ.kə (US) ˈæt̬-

atticism ˈæt.ɪ.sɪ.zᵊm (US) ˈæt̬- **-s** -z

atticiz|e, -is|e ˈæt.ɪ.saɪz (US) ˈæt̬- **-es** -ɪz **-ing** -ɪŋ **-ed** -d

Attila əˈtɪl.ə; ˈæt.ɪ.lə (US) əˈtɪl.ə; ˈæt̬.ɪ.lə

attir|e əˈtaɪəʳ (US) -ˈtaɪɚ **-es** -z **-ing** -ɪŋ **-ed** -d **-ement** -mənt

Attis ˈæt.ɪs (US) ˈæt̬-

attitude ˈæt.ɪ.tjuːd, -tʃuːd (US) ˈæt̬.ə.tuːd, -tjuːd **-s** -z

attitudinal ˌæt.ɪˈtjuː.dɪ.nᵊl, -ˈtʃuː- (US) ˌæt̬.əˈtuː.dᵊn.ᵊl, -ˈtjuː-

attitudinarian ˌæt.ɪ.tjuː.dɪˈneə.ri.ən, -tʃuː- (US) ˌæt̬.əˌtuː.dɪˈner.i-, -ˌtjuː- **-s** -z

attitudiniz|e, -is|e ˌæt.ɪˈtjuː.dɪ.naɪz, -ˈtʃuː- (US) ˌæt̬.əˈtuː.dᵊn.aɪz, -ˈtjuː- **-es** -ɪz **-ing** -ɪŋ **-ed** -d **-er/s** -əʳ/z, -ɚ/z

Attleborough ˈæt.ᵊl.bᵊr.ə, -ˌbʌr.ə (US) -ˌbɝː.oʊ

Attlee ˈæt.li

Attock əˈtɒk (US) -ˈtɑːk

attorn əˈtɜːn (US) -ˈtɝːn **-s** -z **-ing** -ɪŋ **-ed** -d

attorney əˈtɜː.ni (US) -ˈtɝː- **-s** -z **aˌttorney ˈgeneral**

attorney-at-law əˌtɜː.ni.ətˈlɔː (US) -ˌtɝː.ni.ətˈlɑː, -ˈlɔː **attorneys-at-law** əˌtɜː.niz.ətˈlɔː (US) -ˌtɝː.niz.ətˈlɑː, -ˈlɔː

attorneyship əˈtɜː.ni.ʃɪp (US) -ˈtɝː- **-s** -s

attract əˈtrækt **-s** -s **-ing/ly** -ɪŋ/li **-ed** -ɪd **-or/s** -əʳ/z (US) -ɚ/z **-able** -ə.bl̩

attractability əˌtræk.təˈbɪl.ə.ti, -ɪ.ti (US) -ə.t̬i

attraction əˈtræk.ʃᵊn **-s** -z

attractive əˈtræk.tɪv **-ly** -li **-ness** -nəs, -nɪs

attributable əˈtrɪb.jə.tə.bl̩, -jʊ- (US) -jə.t̬ə-

attribute (*n.*) ˈæt.rɪ.bjuːt **-s** -s

attri|bute (*v.*) əˈtrɪ|.bjuːt **-butes** -bjuːts **-buting** -bjʊ.tɪŋ (US) -bjə.t̬ɪŋ, -bjuː- **-buted** -bjʊ.tɪd (US) -bjə.t̬ɪd, -bjuː-

attribution ˌæt.rɪˈbjuː.ʃᵊn **-s** -z

attributive əˈtrɪb.jə.tɪv, -jʊ- (US) -jə.t̬ɪv **-ly** -li

attrition əˈtrɪʃ.ᵊn, ætˈrɪʃ-

attun|e əˈtjuːn, ætˈjuːn (US) əˈtuːn, -ˈtjuːn **-es** -z **-ing** -ɪŋ **-ed** -d

Attwell ˈæt.wel, -wəl

At(t)wood ˈæt.wʊd

ATV ˌeɪ.tiːˈviː **-s** -z

Atwater ˈæt.wɔː.təʳ (US) -wɑː.t̬ɚ, -wɔː-

atypical ˌeɪˈtɪp.ɪ.kᵊl

aubade əʊˈbɑːd (US) oʊ- **-s** -z

Pronouncing the letters AU, AW

The vowel letter combinations **au** and **aw** are similar in that their most common pronunciation is /ɔː Ⓤⓢ ɑː/, e.g.:

sauce	/sɔːs/	Ⓤⓢ /sɑːs/
saw	/sɔː/	Ⓤⓢ /sɑː/

However, there is more variation in the case of **au.** When followed by **gh** in the spelling realised as /f/, it is pronounced as /ɑː, Ⓤⓢ æ/, e.g.:

laugh	/lɑːf/	Ⓤⓢ /læf/

The combination **au** may also be pronounced as /ɒ Ⓤⓢ ɑː/, e.g.:

Australia	/ɒsˈtreɪ.li.ə/	Ⓤⓢ /ɑːˈstreɪ-/
because	/bɪˈkɒz/	Ⓤⓢ /-ˈkɑːz/

In addition

Other sounds associated with the combinations **au** are:

/əʊ Ⓤⓢ oʊ/	chauffeur	/ˈʃəʊ.fəʳ/	Ⓤⓢ /ʃoʊˈfɝː/

And, in rare cases:

/eɪ/	gauge	/geɪdʒ/

In weak syllables

The vowel combinations **au** and **aw** are realised with the vowel /ə/ in weak syllables, and **au** may also result in a syllabic consonant or an elided vowel, e.g.:

awry	/əˈraɪ/
restaurant	/ˈres.tᵊr.ɔ̃ːŋ, ˈ-trɔ̃ːŋ/ Ⓤⓢ /-tə.rɑːnt, ˈ-trɑːnt/

auberg|e əʊˈbeəʒ, -ˈbɜːʒ Ⓤⓢ oʊˈberʒ **-es** -ɪz
aubergine ˈəʊ.bə.ʒiːn, -dʒiːn, ˌ--ˈ- Ⓤⓢ ˈoʊ.bɚ- **-s** -z
Auberon ˈɔː.bə.rən, ˈəʊ-, -rɒn, ˌ--ˈ- Ⓤⓢ ˈɑː.bə.rɑːn, ˈɔː-
aubretia ɔːˈbriː.ʃə, -ʃi.ə Ⓤⓢ ɑː-, ɔː-
Aubrey ˈɔː.bri Ⓤⓢ ˈɑː-, ˈɔː-
aubrietia ɔːˈbriː.ʃə, -ʃi.ə Ⓤⓢ ɑː-, ɔː- **-s** -z
auburn (A) ˈɔː.bən, -bɜːn Ⓤⓢ ˈɑː.bɚn, ˈɔː-
Auchindachie ˌɔː.kɪnˈdæk.i, -xɪnˈdæx- Ⓤⓢ ˌɑː.kɪnˈdæk-, ˌɔː-
Auchinleck ˌɔː.kɪnˈlek, -xɪn-, ˈ--- Ⓤⓢ ˌɑː.kɪnˈlek, ˌɔː-, ˈ---
Auchmuty ɔːkˈmjuː.ti Ⓤⓢ ɑːk-, ɔːk-
Auchtermuchty ˌɔːk.təˈmʌk.ti, ˌɒk.tə-, ˌɔːx.təˈmʌx.ti, ˌɒx.tə- Ⓤⓢ ˌɑːk.tɚˈmʌk-, ˌɔːk-
Auckland ˈɔːk.lənd Ⓤⓢ ˈɑːk-, ˈɔːk-
au contraire ˌəʊ.kɒnˈtreəʳ Ⓤⓢ ˌoʊ.kɑːnˈtrer
au courant əʊˈkʊr.ɑ̃ːŋ Ⓤⓢ ˌoʊ.kuːˈrɑːn
auction ˈɔːk.ʃᵊn, ˈɒk- Ⓤⓢ ˈɑːk.ʃᵊn, ˈɔːk- **-s** -z **-ing** -ɪŋ **-ed** -d
auctionary ˈɔːk.ʃᵊn.ᵊr.i, ˈɒk- Ⓤⓢ ˈɑːk.ʃᵊn.er-, ˈɔːk-
auctioneer ˌɔːk.ʃᵊnˈɪəʳ, ˌɒk- Ⓤⓢ ˌɑːk.ʃəˈnɪr, ˌɔːk- **-s** -z **-ing** -ɪŋ **-ed** -d
audacious ɔːˈdeɪ.ʃəs Ⓤⓢ ɑː-, ɔː- **-ly** -li **-ness** -nəs, -nɪs
audacit|y ɔːˈdæs.ə.t|i, -ɪ.t|i Ⓤⓢ ɑːˈdæs.ə.t̬|i, ɔː- **-ies** -iz
Audelay ˈɔːd.leɪ Ⓤⓢ ˈɑːd-, ˈɔːd-
Auden ˈɔː.dᵊn Ⓤⓢ ˈɑː-, ˈɔː-
Audenshaw ˈɔː.dᵊn.ʃɔː Ⓤⓢ ˈɑː.dᵊn.ʃɑː, ˈɔː-, -ʃɔː
Audi® ˈaʊ.di Ⓤⓢ ˈaʊ-, ˈɑː-
audibility ˌɔː.dɪˈbɪl.ə.ti, -dəˈ-, -ɪ.ti Ⓤⓢ ˌɑː.dəˈbɪl.ə.t̬i, ˌɔː-
audib|le ˈɔː.də.b|l̩, ˈ-dɪ- Ⓤⓢ ˈɑː.də-, ˈɔː- **-ly** -li **-leness** -l̩.nəs, -nɪs
audienc|e ˈɔː.di.ən*t*s Ⓤⓢ ˈɑː-, ˈɔː- **-es** -ɪz
audio ˈɔː.di.əʊ Ⓤⓢ ˈɑː.di.oʊ, ˈɔː-
audiocassette ˌɔː.di.əʊ.kəˈset Ⓤⓢ ˌɑː.di.oʊ-, ˌɔː- **-s** -s
audiologist ˌɔː.diˈɒl.ə.dʒɪst Ⓤⓢ ˌɑː.diˈɑː.lə-, ˌɔː- **-s** -s
audiology ˌɔː.diˈɒl.ə.dʒi Ⓤⓢ ˌɑː.diˈɑː.lə-, ˌɔː-
audiometer ˌɔː.diˈɒm.ɪ.təʳ, -ə.təʳ Ⓤⓢ ˌɑː.diˈɑː.mə.t̬ɚ, ˌɔː- **-s** -z
audiometry ˌɔː.diˈɒm.ɪ.tri, ˈ-ə- Ⓤⓢ ˌɑː.diˈɑː.mə-, ˌɔː-
audiotape ˈɔː.di.əʊ.teɪp Ⓤⓢ ˈɑː.di.oʊ-, ˈɔː- **-s** -s
audio-typ|ing ˈɔː.di.əʊˌtaɪ.p|ɪŋ Ⓤⓢ ˈɑː.di.oʊ-, ˈɔː- **-ist/s** -ɪst/s
audio-visual ˌɔː.di.əʊˈvɪʒ.u.əl, -ˈvɪz.ju- Ⓤⓢ ˌɑː.di.oʊˈvɪʒ.ju-, ˌɔː-
audiphone ˈɔː.dɪ.fəʊn Ⓤⓢ ˈɑː.dɪ.foʊn, ˈɔː- **-s** -z
au|dit ˈɔː|.dɪt Ⓤⓢ ˈɑː-, ˈɔː- **-dits** -dɪts **-diting** -dɪ.tɪŋ Ⓤⓢ -də.t̬ɪŋ **-dited** -dɪ.tɪd Ⓤⓢ -də.t̬ɪd
audition ɔːˈdɪʃ.ᵊn Ⓤⓢ ɑː-, ɔː- **-s** -z **-ing** **-ed**
auditor ˈɔː.dɪt.əʳ Ⓤⓢ ˈɑː.də.t̬ɚ, ˈɔː- **-s** -z
auditori|um ˌɔː.dɪˈtɔː.ri|.əm Ⓤⓢ ˌɑː.dəˈtɔːr.i-, ˌɔː- **-ums** -əmz **-a** -ə
auditorship ˈɔː.dɪt.ə.ʃɪp Ⓤⓢ ˈɑː.də.t̬ɚ-, ˈɔː- **-s** -s
auditor|y ˈɔː.dɪ.tᵊr|.i Ⓤⓢ ˈɑː.də.tɔːr-, ˈɔː- **-ies** -iz
Audley ˈɔːd.li Ⓤⓢ ˈɑːd-, ˈɔːd-
Audrey ˈɔː.dri Ⓤⓢ ˈɑː-, ˈɔː-
Audubon ˈɔː.də.bɒn, -bən Ⓤⓢ ˈɑː.də.bɑːn, ˈɔː-, -bən
au fait ˌəʊˈfeɪ Ⓤⓢ ˌoʊ-
Aufidius ɔːˈfɪd.i.əs Ⓤⓢ ɑː-, ɔː-
Aufklärung ˈaʊf.kleə.rʊŋ Ⓤⓢ -kler.ʊŋ
Auf Wiedersehen ˌaʊfˈviː.də.zeɪ.ən, -zeɪn Ⓤⓢ -ˈviː.dɚ-
Aug. *(abbrev. for* **August***)* ˈɔː.gəst Ⓤⓢ ˈɑː-, ˈɔː-
Augean ɔːˈdʒiː.ən Ⓤⓢ ɑː-, ɔː-
Augeas ɔːˈdʒiː.æs Ⓤⓢ ɑː-, ɔː-
Augener ˈaʊ.gᵊn.əʳ Ⓤⓢ -ɚ
auger ˈɔː.gəʳ Ⓤⓢ ˈɑː.gɚ, ˈɔː- **-s** -z
Aughrim ˈɔː.grɪm Ⓤⓢ ˈɑː-, ˈɔː-
aught ɔːt Ⓤⓢ ɑːt, ɔːt
Aughton *Humberside, S. Yorks & Nr. Ormskirk, Lancashire:* ˈɔː.tᵊn Ⓤⓢ ˈɑː-, ˈɔː- *Nr. Lancaster, Lancashire:* ˈæf.tən
Augie ˈɔː.gi Ⓤⓢ ˈɑː-, ˈɔː-
augment *(n.)* ˈɔːg.mənt Ⓤⓢ ˈɑːg-, ˈɔːg- **-s** -s
aug|ment *(v.)* ɔːg|ˈment Ⓤⓢ ɑːg-, ɔːg- **-ments** -ˈments **-menting** -ˈmen.tɪŋ Ⓤⓢ -ˈmen.t̬ɪŋ **-mented** -ˈmen.tɪd Ⓤⓢ -ˈmen.t̬ɪd **-mentable** -ˈmen.tə.bl̩ Ⓤⓢ -ˈmen.t̬ə.bl̩
augmentation ˌɔːg.menˈteɪ.ʃᵊn, -mənˈ- Ⓤⓢ ˌɑːg-, ˌɔːg- **-s** -z
augmentative ɔːgˈmen.tə.tɪv Ⓤⓢ ɑːgˈmen.t̬ə.t̬ɪv, ɔːg-
au gratin ˌəʊˈgræt.æ̃ŋ Ⓤⓢ oʊˈgrɑː.tᵊn, -ˈgræt.ᵊn
Augsburg ˈaʊgz.bɜːg, ˈaʊks-, -bʊəg Ⓤⓢ ˈɑːgz.bɝːg, ˈɔːgz-, -bʊrg
aug|ur ˈɔː.g|əʳ Ⓤⓢ ˈɑː.g|ɚ, ˈɔː- **-urs** -əz Ⓤⓢ -ɚz **-uring** -ᵊr.ɪŋ **-ured** -əd Ⓤⓢ -ɚd
augural ˈɔːg.jʊ.rᵊl, -jᵊr.ᵊl Ⓤⓢ ˈɑːg.jɚ.ᵊl, ˈɔːg-
augur|y ˈɔːg.jʊ.r|i, -jᵊr.|i Ⓤⓢ ˈɑːg.jɚ|.i, ˈɔːg- **-ies** -iz
August *(n.)* ˈɔː.gəst Ⓤⓢ ˈɑː-, ˈɔː- **-s** -s ˌ**August Bank** ˈ**Holiday**
august *(adj.)* ɔːˈgʌst Ⓤⓢ ɑː-, ɔː-, ˈ-- **-est** -ɪst **-ly** -li **-ness** -nəs, -nɪs

August|a ɔːˈɡʌs.t|ə, ə- US əˈ-, ɑːˈ-, ɔːˈ- **-an** -ən
Augustine ɔːˈɡʌs.tɪn, ə- US ɑː-, ɔː-; ˈɑː.ɡə.stɪn, ˈɔː-
Augustinian ˌɔː.ɡəˈstɪn.i.ən US ˌɑː-, ˌɔː-
Augustus ɔːˈɡʌs.təs, ə- US ə-, ɑː-, ɔː-
auk ɔːk US ɑːk, ɔːk **-s** -s
aul|a ˈɔː.l|ə, ˈaʊ- US ˈɑː-, ˈɔː- **-ae** -iː, -aɪ, -eɪ
auld (A) ɔːld US ɑːld, ɔːld
auld lang syne ˌɔːld.læŋˈsaɪn, -zaɪn US ˌɑːld-, ˌɔːld-
Aumerle ɔːˈmɜːl US ɑːˈmɝːl, ɔː-
au naturel ˌəʊ.næt.jʊˈrel US ˌoʊ.nætʃ.əˈrel; -nɑː.tʊˈ-
Aungier ˈeɪn.dʒəʳ US -dʒɚ
aunt ɑːnt US ænt, ɑːnt **-s** -s
Note: Although **aunt** is generally /ænt/ in American English, regional and social subgroups have persistent /ɑːnt/.
auntie, aunty ˈɑːn.ti US ˈæn.t̬i, ˈɑːn- **-s** -z
au pair ˌəʊˈpeəʳ US oʊˈper
aura ˈɔː.rə US ˈɔːr.ə **-s** -z
aural ˈɔː.rəl, ˈaʊ- US ˈɔːr.əl **-ly** -i
aurate ˈɔː.reɪt, -rɪt US ˈɔːr.eɪt **-s** -s
aureate ˈɔː.ri.eɪt, -ət, -ɪt US ˈɔːr.i-
Aureli|a ɔːˈriː.li.|ə **-an** -ən **-us** -əs
aureola ɔːˈriː.ə.lə US ˌɔːr.iˈoʊ- **-s** -z
aureole ˈɔː.ri.əʊl US ˈɔːr.i.oʊl **-s** -z
aureomycin ˌɔː.ri.əʊˈmaɪ.sɪn US ˌɔːr.i-
au revoir ˌəʊ.rəvˈwɑːʳ, -rɪvˈ- US ˌoʊ.rəvˈwɑːr
auricle ˈɔː.rɪ.kl̩, ˈɒr.ɪ- US ˈɔːr.ɪ- **-s** -z
auricula ɔːˈrɪk.jʊ.lə, ɒrˈɪk-, -jə- US ɔːˈrɪk.jə- **-s** -z
auricular ɔːˈrɪk.jʊ.ləʳ, ɒrˈɪk-, -jə- US ɔːˈrɪk.jə.lɚ **-ly** -li
auricu|late ɔːˈrɪk.jʊ|.lət, -jə-, -lɪt, -leɪt US -jə- **-lated** -leɪ.tɪd US -leɪ.t̬ɪd
Auriel ˈɔː.ri.əl US ˈɔːr.i-
auriferous ɔːˈrɪf.ər.əs
Auriga ɔːˈraɪ.ɡə
Aurignacian ˌɔː.rɪɡˈneɪ.ʃən, -ʃi.ən US ˌɔːr.ɪɡ-
aurist ˈɔː.rɪst US ˈɔːr.ɪst **-s** -s
aurochs ˈɔː.rɒks, ˈaʊ- US ˈɔːr.ɑːks, ˈaʊ.rɑːks **-es** -ɪz
auror|a (A) ɔːˈrɔː.r|ə, ə- US -ˈrɔːr|.ə **-as** -əz **-al** -əl
aurora australis ɔːˌrɔː.rə.ɒsˈtreɪ.lɪs, ə-, -ˈtrɑː- US -ˌrɔːr.ə.ɔːˈstreɪ-
aurora borealis ɔːˌrɔː.rə.bɔːr.iˈeɪ.lɪs, ə-, -ˈɑː.lɪs US -ˌrɔːr.ə.bɔːr.iˈæl.ɪs, -ˈɑː.lɪs
Auschwitz ˈaʊʃ.wɪts *as if German:* -vɪts
auscul|tate ˈɔː.skəl|.teɪt, ˈɒs.kəl-, -kʌl- US ˈɑː.skəl-, ˈɔː- **-tates** -teɪts **-tating** -teɪ.tɪŋ US -teɪ.t̬ɪŋ **-tated** -teɪ.tɪd US -teɪ.t̬ɪd
auscultation ˌɔː.skəlˈteɪ.ʃən, ˌɒs.kəlˈ-, -kʌlˈ- US ˌɑː.skəl-, ˌɔː- **-s** -z
auscultator ˈɔː.skəl.teɪ.təʳ, ˈɒs.kəl-, -kʌl- US ˈɑː.skəl.teɪ.t̬ɚ, ˈɔː- **-s** -z
auspic|e ˈɔː.spɪs, ˈɒs.pɪs US ˈɑː.spɪs, ˈɔː- **-es** -ɪz
auspicious ɔːˈspɪʃ.əs, ɒsˈpɪʃ- US ɑːˈspɪʃ-, ɔː- **-ly** -li **-ness** -nəs, -nɪs
Aussie ˈɒz.i US ˈɑː.zi, ˈɔː-, -si **-s** -z
Austell ˈɔː.stəl, ˈɒs.təl *local Cornish pronunciation:* ˈɔː.səl US ˈɑː.stəl, ˈɔː-
Austen ˈɒs.tɪn, ˈɔː.stɪn US ˈɑː.stɪn, ˈɔː-
Auster ˈɔː.stəʳ, ˈɒs.təʳ US ˈɑː.stɚ, ˈɔː-
auster|e ɒsˈtɪəʳ, ɔːˈstɪəʳ US ɑːˈstɪr, ɔː- **-er** -əʳ, -ɚ **-est** -ɪst, -əst **-ely** -li **-eness** -nəs, -nɪs
austerit|y ɒsˈter.ə.t|i, ɔːˈster-, -ɪ.t|i US ˈɑː.ster.ə.t̬|i, ˈɔː- **-ies** -iz
Austerlitz ˈɔː.stə.lɪts, ˈaʊ- US ˈɑː.stɚ-, ˈɔː-
Austin ˈɒs.tɪn, ˈɔː.stɪn US ˈɑː.stɪn, ˈɔː- **-s** -z
austral ˈɒs.trəl, ˈɔː.strəl US ˈɑː.strəl, ˈɔː-
Australasi|a ˌɒs.trəˈleɪ.ʒ|ə, ˌɔː.strə-, -zi|.ə, -ʃi|.ə, -ʃ|ə US ˌɑː.strəˈ-, ˌɔː- **-an/z** -ən/z
Australi|a ɒsˈtreɪ.li|.ə, ɔːˈstreɪ- US ɑːˈstreɪl.jə, ɔː- **-an/s** -ən/z
australopithecus ˌɒs.trə.ləʊˈpɪθ.ɪ.kəs, ˌɔː.strə-, -ə.kəs US ˌɑː.strə.loʊˈ-, ˌɔː-
Austri|a ˈɒs.tri|.ə, ˈɔː.stri- US ˈɑː.stri-, ˈɔː- **-an/s** -ən/z
Austro- ɒs.trəʊ-, ɔː.strəʊ- US ɑː.stroʊ-, ɔː-
Note: Prefix. Behaves as **Anglo-**.
Austro-German ˌɒs.trəʊˈdʒɜː.mən, ˌɔː.strəʊˈ- US ˌɑː.stroʊˈdʒɝː-, ˌɔː-
Austro-Hungarian ˌɒs.trəʊ.hʌŋˈɡeə.ri.ən, ˌɔː.strəʊ- US ˌɑː.stroʊ.hʌŋˈɡer.i-, ˌɔː-
Austronesi|a ˌɒs.trəʊˈniː.ʒ|ə, ˌɔː.strəʊˈ-, -zi|.ə, -si|.ə, -ʃ|ə US ˌɑː.stroʊˈ-, ˌɔː- **-an/s** -ən/z
autarchic ɔːˈtɑː.kɪk US ɑːˈtɑːr-, ɔː- **-al** -əl
autarch|y ˈɔː.tɑː.k|i US ˈɑː.tɑːr-, ˈɔː- **-ies** -iz
autarkic ɔːˈtɑː.kɪk US ɑːˈtɑr-, ɔː- **-al** əl
Auteuil əʊˈtɜːj US oʊˈtʊj, -ˈtɜːj
authentic ɔːˈθen.tɪk US ɑːˈθen.t̬ɪk, ɔː- **-al** -əl **-ally** -əl.i, -li
authenti|cate ɔːˈθen.tɪ|.keɪt US ɑːˈθen.t̬ɪ-, ɔː- **-cates** -keɪts **-cating** -keɪ.tɪŋ US -keɪ.t̬ɪŋ **-cated** -keɪ.tɪd US -keɪ.t̬ɪd **-cator/s** -keɪ.təʳ/z US -keɪ.t̬ɚ/z
authentication ɔːˌθen.tɪˈkeɪ.ʃən US ɑːˌθen.t̬ɪˈ-, ɔː- **-s** -z
authenticit|y ˌɔː.θenˈtɪs.ə.t|i, -θənˈ-, -ɪ.t|i US ˌɑː.θenˈtɪs.ə.t̬|i, ˌɔː- **-ies** -iz
author ˈɔː.θəʳ US ˈɑː.θɚ, ˈɔː- **-s** -z **-ing** **-ed**
authoress ˈɔː.θər.es, -ɪs, -əs; ˌɔː.θərˈes US ˈɑː.θɚ.ɪs, ˈɔː-, -əs **-es** -ɪz
authorial ɔːˈθɔː.ri.əl US ɑːˈθɔːr.i-, ɔː-
authoritarian ˌɔː.θɒr.ɪˈteə.ri.ən, ɔːˌθɒr-, -əˈ- US əˌθɔːr.əˈter.i-, ɑː-, ɔː- **-s** -z
authoritarianism ɔːˌθɒr.ɪˈteə.ri.ə.nɪ.zəm, -əˈ- US əˌθɔːr.əˈter.i-, ɑː-, ɔː-
authoritative ɔːˈθɒr.ɪ.tə.tɪv, ə-, ˈ-ə-, -teɪ- US əˈθɔːr.ə.teɪ.t̬ɪv, ɑː-, ɔː- **-ly** -li **-ness** -nəs, -nɪs
authorit|y ɔːˈθɒr.ə.t|i, ə-, -ɪ.t|i US əˈθɔːr.ə.t̬|i, ɑː-, ɔː- **-ies** -iz
authorization, -isa- ˌɔː.θər.aɪˈzeɪ.ʃən, -ɪˈ- US ˌɑː.θɚ.ɪˈ-, ˌɔː- **-s** -z
authoriz|e, -is|e ˈɔː.θər.aɪz US ˈɑː-, ˈɔː- **-es** -ɪz **-ing** -ɪŋ **-ed** -d **-able** -ə.bl̩
authorship ˈɔː.θə.ʃɪp US ˈɑː.θɚ-, ˈɔː-
autism ˈɔː.tɪ.zəm US ˈɑː.tɪ-, ˈɔː-
autistic ɔːˈtɪs.tɪk US ɑː-, ɔː-
auto- ɔː.təʊ-; ɔːˈtɒ- US ɑː.t̬oʊ-, ɔː-; ɑːˈtɑː-, ɔː-
Note: Prefix. Either takes primary or secondary stress on the first syllable. e.g. **autocrat** /ˈɔː.tə.kræt US ˈɑː.t̬ə-, ɔː-/, **automatic** /ˌɔː.təˈmæt.ɪk US ˌɑː.t̬əˈmæt̬-, ɔː-/, or primary stress on the second syllable, e.g. **automaton** /ɔːˈtɒm.ə.tən US ɑːˈtɑː.mə-, ɔː-, -tɑːn/.
auto ˈɔː.təʊ US ˈɑː.t̬oʊ, ˈɔː- **-s** -z
autobahn ˈɔː.təʊ.bɑːn, ˈaʊ- US ˈɑː.t̬oʊ-, ˈɔː-, -t̬ə- **-s** -z
autobiographer ˌɔː.tə.baɪˈɒɡ.rə.fəʳ US ˌɑː.t̬ə.baɪˈɑː.ɡrə.fɚ, ˌɔː-, -t̬oʊ- **-s** -z
autobiographic ˌɔː.təˌbaɪ.əʊˈɡræf.ɪk US ˌɑː.t̬əˌbaɪ.əˈ-, ˌɔː-, -t̬oʊˌ- **-al** -əl **-ally** -əl.i, -li *stress shift:* ˌautobiographic ˈnovel
autobiograph|y ˌɔː.tə.baɪˈɒɡ.rə.f|i US ˌɑː.t̬ə.baɪˈɑː.ɡrə-, ˌɔː-, -t̬oʊ- **-ies** -iz
autocade ˈɔː.təʊ.keɪd US ˈɑː.t̬oʊ-, ˈɔː-
auto-car ˈɔː.təʊ.kɑːʳ US ˈɑː.t̬oʊ.kɑːr, ˈɔː- **-s** -z
autochthon ɔːˈtɒk.θən, -θɒn US ɑːˈtɑːk.θən, ɔː- **-s** -z
autochthonous ɔːˈtɒk.θən.əs US ɑːˈtɑːk-, ɔː-
autoclav|e ˈɔː.təʊ.kleɪv US ˈɑː.t̬oʊ-, ˈɔː- **-es** -z **-ing** -ɪŋ **-ed** -d
autocrac|y ɔːˈtɒk.rə.s|i US ɑːˈtɑː.krə-, ɔː- **-ies** -iz
autocrat ˈɔː.tə.kræt US ˈɑː.t̬ə-, ˈɔː- **-s** -s
autocratic ˌɔː.təˈkræt.ɪk US ˌɑː.t̬əˈkræt̬-, ˌɔː- **-al** -əl **-ally** -əl.i, -li *stress shift:* ˌautocratic ˈgovernment

autocross ˈɔː.təʊ.krɒs (US) ˈɑː.t̬oʊ.krɑːs, ˈɔː-
autocue (A®) ˈɔː.təʊ.kjuː (US) ˈɑː.t̬oʊ-, ˈɔː- **-s** -z
auto-da-fé ˌɔː.təʊ.dɑːˈfeɪ, ˌaʊ- (US) ˌɑː.t̬oʊ.də'-, ˌɔː- **-s** -z
autodestruct ˌɔː.təʊ.dɪˈstrʌkt, -dəˈ- (US) ˌɑː.t̬oʊ-, ˌɔː- **-s** -s **-ing** -ɪŋ **-ed** -ɪd
autodidact ˌɔː.təʊˈdaɪ.dækt (US) ˌɑː.t̬oʊ-, ˌɔː- **-s** -s
autodidactic ˌɔː.təʊ.daɪˈdæk.tɪk, -dɪˈ- (US) ˌɑː.t̬oʊ-, ˌɔː-
autoerotic ˌɔː.təʊ.ɪˈrɒt.ɪk, -əˈrɒt- (US) ˌɑː.t̬oʊ.ɪˈrɑː.t̬ɪk, ˌɔː- *stress shift:* ˌautoerotic ˈfantasy
autoerot|ism ˌɔː.təʊ.ɪˈrɒt|.ɪ.zᵊm; -ˈer.ə.t|ɪ- (US) ˌɑː.t̬oʊ.ɪˈrɑː.t̬|ɪ-, ˌɔː- **-icism** -ɪ.sɪ.zᵊm (US) -ə.sɪ.zᵊm
autogam|ous ɔːˈtɒg.ə.m|əs (US) ɑːˈtɑː.gə-, ɔː- **-y** -i
autogenesis ˌɔː.təʊˈdʒen.ə.sɪs, ˈ-ɪ- (US) ˌɑː.t̬oʊˈdʒen.ə-, ˌɔː-
autogenetic ˌɔː.təʊ.dʒᵊnˈet.ɪk (US) ˌɑː.t̬oʊ.dʒəˈnet̬-, ˌɔː-
autogenic ˌɔː.təʊˈdʒen.ɪk (US) ˌɑː.t̬oʊˈ-, ˌɔː-
autogenous ɔːˈtɒdʒ.ə.nəs (US) ɑːˈt̬ɑː.dʒə-, ɔː- **-ly** -li
autogiro ˌɔː.təʊˈdʒaɪə.rəʊ (US) ˌɑː.t̬oʊˈdʒaɪ.roʊ, ˌɔː- **-s** -z
autograph ˈɔː.tə.grɑːf, -græf (US) ˈɑː.t̬ə.græf, ˈɔː- **-s** -s **-ing** -ɪŋ **-ed** -d
autographic ˌɔː.təʊˈgræf.ɪk (US) ˌɑː.t̬əˈ-, ˌɔː- **-al** -ᵊl **-ally** -ᵊl.i
autography ɔːˈtɒg.rə.fi (US) ɑːˈtɑː.grə-, ɔː-
autogyro ˌɔː.təʊˈdʒaɪə.rəʊ (US) ˌɑː.t̬oʊˈdʒaɪ.roʊ, ˌɔː- **-s** -z
Autoharp® ˈɔː.təʊ.hɑːp (US) ˈɑː.t̬oʊ.hɑːrp, ˈɔː-
auto-immun|e ˌɔː.təʊ.ɪˈmjuːn (US) ˌɑː.t̬oʊ-, ˌɔː- **-ity** -ə.ti, -ɪ.ti (US) -ə.t̬i
autolexic|al ˌɔː.təʊˈlek.sɪ.k|ᵊl (US) ˌɑː.t̬oʊˈlek.sə-, ˌɔː- **-ally** -ᵊl.i, -li
autolock ˈɔː.təʊ.lɒk (US) ˈɑː.t̬oʊ.lɑːk, ˈɔː-
Autolycus ɔːˈtɒl.ɪ.kəs (US) ɑːˈtɑː.lɪ-, ɔː-
automaker ˈɔː.təʊˌmeɪ.kəʳ (US) ˈɑː.t̬oʊˌmeɪ.kɚ, ˈɔː- **-s** -z
automat (A®) ˈɔː.tə.mæt (US) ˈɑː.t̬ə-, ˈɔː-
auto|mate ˈɔː.tə|.meɪt (US) ˈɑː.t̬ə-, ˈɔː- **-mates** -meɪts **-mating** -meɪ.tɪŋ (US) -meɪ.t̬ɪŋ **-mated** -meɪ.tɪd (US) -meɪ.t̬ɪd
automatic ˌɔː.təˈmæt.ɪk (US) ˌɑː.t̬əˈmæt̬-, ˌɔː- **-al** -ᵊl **-ally** -ᵊl.i, -li *stress shift, see compound:* ˌ**automatic** ˈ**pilot**
automation ˌɔː.təˈmeɪ.ʃᵊn (US) ˌɑː.t̬əˈ-, ˌɔː-
automat|ism ɔːˈtɒm.ə.t|ɪ.zᵊm (US) ɑːˈtɑː.mə.t̬|ɪ-, ɔː- **-ist/s** -ɪst/s
automat|on ɔːˈtɒm.ə.t|ᵊn (US) ɑːˈtɑː.mə-, ɔː-, -t|ɑːn **-ons** -ᵊnz (US) -ᵊnz, -ɑːnz **-a** -ə
automobile ˈɔː.tə.məʊ.biːl, ˌɔː.tə.məʊˈbiːl (US) ˈɑː.t̬ə.moʊ.biːl, ˈɔː-, ˌɑː.t̬ə.moʊˈbiːl, ˌɔː-, ˌɑː.t̬əˈmoʊ-, ˈɔː- **-s** -z
automotive ˌɔː.təˈməʊ.tɪv (US) ˌɑː.t̬əˈmoʊ.t̬ɪv, ˌɔː-
autonomic ˌɔː.təˈnɒm.ɪk (US) ˌɑː.t̬əˈnɑː.mɪk, ˌɔː- *stress shift:* ˌautonomic ˈreflex
autonomous ɔːˈtɒn.ə.məs (US) ɑːˈtɑː.nə-, ɔː-
autonom|y ɔːˈtɒn.ə.m|i (US) ɑːˈtɑː.nə-, ɔː- **-ies** -iz
autonym ˈɔː.tə.nɪm (US) ˈɑː.t̬ə-, ˈɔː- **-s** -z
auto-pilot ˈɔː.təʊˌpaɪ.lət (US) ˈɑː.t̬oʊ-, ˈɔː- **-s** -s
autops|y ˈɔː.tɒp.s|i, -təp-, ɔːˈtɒp.s|i (US) ˈɑː.tɑːp-, ˈɔː-, -t̬əp- **-ies** -iz
autoroute ˈɔː.təʊ.ruːt (US) ˈɑː.t̬oʊ-, ˈɔː-, -raʊt **-s** -s
autosegment ˈɔː.təʊ.seg.mənt (US) ˈɑː.t̬oʊ-, ˈɔː- **-s** -s
autosegmental ˌɔː.təʊ.segˈmen.tᵊl (US) ˌɑː.t̬oʊ.segˈmen.t̬ᵊl, ˌɔː- **-ly** -i
autosug|gestion ˌɔː.təʊ.səlˈdʒes.tʃᵊn, -ˈdʒeʃ- (US) ˌɑː.t̬oʊ.səgˈ-, ˌɔː- **-gestive** -ˈdʒes.tɪv
autotroph ˈɔː.təʊ.trɒf (US) ˈɑː.t̬oʊ.trɑːf, ˈɔː-, -troʊf
autotyp|e ˈɔː.təʊ.taɪp (US) ˈɑː.t̬oʊ-, ˈɔː- **-es** -s **-ing** -ɪŋ **-ed** -t
autotypography ˌɔː.təʊ.taɪˈpɒg.rə.fi (US) ˌɑː.t̬oʊ.taɪˈpɑː.grə-, ˌɔː-
autoworker ˈɔː.təʊˌwɜː.kəʳ (US) ˈɑː.t̬oʊˌwɝː.kɚ, ˈɔː- **-s** -z
autumn (A) ˈɔː.təm (US) ˈɑː.t̬ᵊm, ˈɔː- **-s** -z
autumnal ɔːˈtʌm.nᵊl (US) ɑː-, ɔː- **-ly** -i
Auvergne əʊˈveən, -ˈvɜːn (US) oʊˈvern, -ˈvɝːn
auxiliar|y ɔːgˈzɪl.i.ᵊr|.i, ɔːkˈsɪl-, -jᵊr|.i (US) ɑːgˈzɪl.jᵊr-, ɔːg-, ˈ-i.er|.i **-ies** -iz
auxin ˈɔːk.sɪn (US) ˈɑːk-, ˈɔːk-
Ava ˈɑː.və, ˈeɪ.və (US) ˈeɪ-
avail əˈveɪl **-s** -z **-ing/ly** -ɪŋ/li **-ed** -d
availability əˌveɪ.ləˈbɪl.ə.ti, -ɪ.ti (US) -ə.t̬i
availab|le əˈveɪ.lə.b|l̩ **-ly** -li **-leness** -l̩.nəs, -nɪs
avalanch|e ˈæv.ᵊl.ɑːntʃ (US) -æntʃ **-es** -ɪz
Avalon ˈæv.ᵊl.ɒn (US) -ə.lɑːn
avant-courier ˌæv.ɑ̃ːŋˈkʊr.i.eɪ (US) ˌɑː.vɑːnt-, ˌæv.ɑːnt-; əˌvɑːnt- **-s** -z
avant-garde ˌæv.ɑ̃ːŋˈgɑːd (US) ˌɑː.vɑːntˈgɑːrd, ˌæv.ɑːnt-; əˌvɑːnt-
avarice ˈæv.ᵊr.ɪs
avaricious ˌæv.ᵊrˈɪʃ.əs (US) -əˈrɪʃ- **-ly** -li **-ness** -nəs, -nɪs
avast əˈvɑːst (US) əˈvæst
avatar ˌæv.əˈtɑːʳ, ˈ--- (US) ˈæv.ə.tɑːr **-s** -z
avaunt əˈvɔːnt (US) -ˈvɑːnt, -ˈvɔːnt
AVC ˌeɪ.viːˈsiː
ave *prayer:* ˈɑː.veɪ, -viː **-s** -z
Ave. *(abbrev. for* **avenue***)* æv, ˈæv.ə.njuː, ˈ-ɪ- (US) ˈæv.ə.nuː, ˈ-ɪ-, -njuː
Avebury ˈeɪv.bᵊr.i (US) -ber-, -bɚ-
Aveley ˈeɪv.li
Aveline ˈæv.ə.laɪn, -liːn
Aveling ˈeɪv.lɪŋ
Ave Maria ˌɑː.veɪ.məˈriː.ə, -viː- **-s** -z
Ave Maria Lane ˌɑː.vi.mə.riː.əˈleɪn *formerly:* ˌeɪ.vi.məˌraɪəˈleɪn
aveng|e əˈvendʒ **-es** -ɪz **-ing** -ɪŋ **-ed** -d **-er/s** -əʳ/z (US) -ɚ/z **-eful** -fʊl
avenue ˈæv.ə.njuː, ˈ-ɪ- (US) -nuː, -njuː **-s** -z
aver əˈvɜːʳ (US) -ˈvɝː **-s** -z **-ring** -ɪŋ **-red** -d **-ment/s** -mənt/s
averag|e ˈæv.ᵊr.ɪdʒ, ˈ-rɪdʒ **-es** -ɪz **-ing** -ɪŋ **-ed** -d **-ely** -li
averse əˈvɜːs (US) -ˈvɝːs **-ly** -li **-ness** -nəs, -nɪs
aversion əˈvɜː.ʃᵊn, -ʒᵊn (US) -ˈvɝː.ʒᵊn, -ʃᵊn **-s** -z
a|vert ə|ˈvɜːt (US) -ˈvɝːt **-verts** -ˈvɜːts (US) -ˈvɝːts **-verting** -ˈvɜː.tɪŋ (US) -ˈvɝː.t̬ɪŋ **-verted** -ˈvɜː.tɪd (US) -ˈvɝː.t̬ɪd **-vertible** -ˈvɜː.tə.bl̩, -tɪ- (US) -ˈvɝː.t̬ə.bl̩
Avery ˈeɪ.vᵊr.i, ˈeɪv.ri
Aves ˈeɪ.viːz
Avesta əˈves.tə
avgolemono ˌæv.gəʊˈlem.ə.nəʊ (US) ˌɑːv.goʊˈlem.ə.noʊ
Avia® ˈeɪ.vi.ə (US) əˈviː-
avian ˈeɪ.vi.ən **-s** -z
aviarist ˈeɪ.vi.ᵊr.ɪst **-s** -s
aviar|y ˈeɪ.vi.ᵊr|.i (US) -er- **-ies** -iz
aviation ˌeɪ.viˈeɪ.ʃᵊn
aviator ˈeɪ.vi.eɪ.təʳ (US) -t̬ɚ **-s** -z
Avice ˈeɪ.vɪs
Avicenna ˌæv.ɪˈsen.ə
aviculture ˈeɪ.vɪˌkʌl.tʃəʳ, ˈæv.ɪ- (US) -tʃɚ
avid ˈæv.ɪd **-ly** -li
avidity əˈvɪd.ə.ti, ævˈɪd-, -ɪ.ti (US) -ə.t̬i
Aviemore ˈæv.ɪ.mɔːʳ, ˌ--ˈ- (US) ˌæv.ɪˈmɔːr
Avignon ˈæv.i.njɔ̃ːŋ (US) ˌæv.iːˈnjõʊn, -ˈnjɑːn
avionic ˌeɪ.viˈɒn.ɪk (US) -ˈɑː.nɪk **-s** -s *stress shift:* ˌavionic ˈsystem
Avis® ˈeɪ.vɪs
Avoca əˈvəʊ.kə (US) -ˈvoʊ-
avocado ˌæv.əˈkɑː.dəʊ (US) -doʊ, ɑː.vəˈ- **-s** -z
avocation ˌæv.əʊˈkeɪ.ʃᵊn (US) -əˈ-, -oʊˈ- **-s** -z

avocet 'æv.əʊ.set US '-ə- **-s** -s
Avoch ɔːk, ɔːx
Avogadro ˌæv.əʊ'gæd.rəʊ, -'gɑː.drəʊ US -ə'gɑː.droʊ, ˌɑː.və'-, -'gæd.roʊ
avoid ə'vɔɪd **-s** -z **-ing** -ɪŋ **-ed** -ɪd
avoidab|le ə'vɔɪ.də.b|l̩ **-ly** -li
avoidanc|e ə'vɔɪ.dᵊn*t*s **-es** -ɪz
avoirdupois ˌæv.ə.də'pɔɪz, ˌæv.wɑː.dju'pwɑː US ˌæv.ɚ.də'pɔɪz, 'æv.ɚ.dəˌpɔɪz
Avon *in Avon:* 'eɪ.vᵊn US -vɑːn, -vᵊn, 'æv.ᵊn *in Devon:* 'æv.ᵊn *in the Grampian region:* ɑːn *trademark:* 'eɪ.vɒn US -vɑːn
Avondale 'eɪ.vᵊn.deɪl US 'eɪ.vᵊn-, 'æv.ᵊn-
Avonmouth 'eɪ.vᵊn.maʊθ, -vᵊm- US -vᵊn-
Avory 'eɪ.vᵊr.i US 'eɪv.ri
avow ə'vaʊ **-s** -z **-ing** -ɪŋ **-ed** -d **-edly** -ɪd.li, -əd-
avowal ə'vaʊ.əl **-s** -z
Avril 'æv.rɪl, -rəl
avuncular ə'vʌŋ.kjə.ləʳ, -kjʊ- US -lɚ **-ly** -li
AWACS 'eɪ.wæks
a|wait ə|'weɪt **-waits** -'weɪts **-waiting** -'weɪ.tɪŋ US -'weɪ.t̬ɪŋ **-waited** -'weɪ.tɪd US -'weɪ.t̬ɪd
awak|e ə'weɪk **-es** -s **-ing** -ɪŋ **-ed** -t **awoke** ə'wəʊk US -'woʊk
awaken ə'weɪ.kᵊn **-s** -z **-ing/s** -ɪŋ/z **-ed** -d **-ment/s** -mənt/s
awakening *(n.)* ə'weɪ.kᵊn.ɪŋ **-s** -z
award ə'wɔːd US -'wɔːrd **-s** -z **-ing** -ɪŋ **-ed** -ɪd **-able** -ə.bl̩
aware ə'weəʳ US -'wer **-ness** -nəs, -nɪs
awash ə'wɒʃ US -'wɑːʃ, -'wɔːʃ
away ə'weɪ
aw|e (A) ɔː US ɑː, ɔː **-es** -z **-(e)ing** -ɪŋ **-ed** -d
awe-inspiring 'ɔː.ɪn.spaɪə.rɪŋ US 'ɑː-, 'ɔː- **-ly** -li
aweless 'ɔː.ləs, -lɪs US 'ɑː-, 'ɔː- **-ness** -nəs, -nɪs
awesome 'ɔː.səm US 'ɑː-, 'ɔː- **-ly** -li **-ness** -nəs, -nɪs
awe-stricken 'ɔːˌstrɪk.ᵊn US 'ɑː-, 'ɔː-
awe-struck 'ɔː.strʌk US 'ɑː-, 'ɔː-
awful *terrible:* 'ɔː.fᵊl, -fʊl US 'ɑː-, 'ɔː- **-ness** -nəs, -nɪs *inspiring awe:* 'ɔː.fʊl US 'ɑː-, 'ɔː- **-ness** -nəs, -nɪs
awfully 'ɔː.fᵊl.i, -fʊl- US 'ɑː-, 'ɔː-
awhile ə'*h*waɪl
awkward 'ɔː.kwəd US 'ɑː.kwɚd, 'ɔː- **-est** -əst, -ɪst **-ly** -li **-ness** -nəs, -nɪs **-ish** -ɪʃ
awl ɔːl US ɔːl, ɑːl **-s** -z
awn ɔːn US ɑːn, ɔːn **-s** -z **-ed** -d
awning 'ɔː.nɪŋ US 'ɑː-, 'ɔː- **-s** -z
awoke *(from* **awake***)* ə'wəʊk US -'woʊk
awoken ə'wəʊ.kᵊn US -'woʊ-
AWOL, Awol 'eɪ.wɒl US -wɑːl
Awooner ə'wuː.nəʳ US -nɚ
awry ə'raɪ
Axa® 'æk.sə
ax|e, ax æks **-es** -ɪz **-ing** -ɪŋ **-ed** -t **have an 'axe to ˌgrind**
axel (A) 'æk.sᵊl **-s** -z
axes *(plur. of* **axis***)* 'æk.siːz
axes *(plur. of* **axe***)* 'æk.sɪz
Axholm(e) 'æks.*h*əʊm, -əm US -*h*oʊm
axial 'æk.si.əl **-ly** -i
axil 'æk.sɪl, -sᵊl **-s** -z
axill|a æk'sɪl.|ə **-ae** -iː **-as** -əz **-ar** -əʳ US -ɚ **-ary** -ᵊr.i
axiom 'æk.si.əm **-s** -z
axiomatic ˌæk.si.ə'mæt.ɪk US -'mæt̬- **-al** -ᵊl **-ally** -ᵊl.i, -li
ax|is 'æk.s|ɪs **-es** -iːz
axle 'æk.sl̩ **-s** -z **-d** -d
axle-tree 'æk.sl̩.triː **-s** -z
Axminster 'æks.mɪn.stəʳ US -stɚ **-s** -z
axolotl 'æk.sə.lɒt.l̩ US 'æk.sə.lɑː.tl̩ **-s** -z
axon 'æk.sɒn US -sɑːn **-s** -z
ay aɪ, eɪ **-es** -z
ayah 'aɪ.ə, 'ɑː.jə **-s** -z
ayatollah ˌaɪ.ə'tɒl.ə US -'toʊ.lə; -toʊ'lɑː **-s** -z
Ayckbourn 'eɪk.bɔːn US -bɔːrn
Aycliffe 'eɪ.klɪf
aye *ever:* eɪ *yes:* aɪ **-s** -z
aye-aye 'aɪ.aɪ **-s** -z
Ayenbite of Inwyt ˌeɪ.ən.baɪt.əv'ɪn.wɪt
Ayer eəʳ US er
Ayers eəz US erz ˌ**Ayers 'Rock**
Ayesha aɪ'iː.ʃə
Aylesbury 'eɪlz.bᵊr.i US -ber-, -bɚ-
Aylesford 'eɪlz.fəd, 'eɪls- US -fɚd
Ayling 'eɪ.lɪŋ
Aylmer 'eɪl.məʳ US -mɚ
Aylsham 'eɪl.ʃəm
Aylward 'eɪl.wəd US -wɚd
Aylwin 'eɪl.wɪn
Aymer 'eɪ.məʳ US -mɚ
Ayot 'eɪ.ət
Ayr eəʳ US er **-shire** -ʃəʳ, -ˌʃɪəʳ US -ʃɚ, -ˌʃɪr
Ayre eəʳ US er **-s** -z
Ayrton 'eə.tᵊn US 'er-
Ayscough 'æs.kə, 'æsk.juː, 'eɪ.skəf, 'eɪz.kɒf US 'æs.kjuː
Ayscue 'eɪ.skjuː US 'æs.kjuː
Ayton, Aytoun 'eɪ.tᵊn
ayurved|a aɪ.ʊə'veɪ.d|ə, ɑː-, -'viː- US ˌɑː.jʊr'veɪ- **-ic** -ɪk
A-Z ˌeɪ.tə'zed US -t̬ə'ziː
azalea ə'zeɪ.li.ə US -'zeɪl.jə **-s** -z
Azani|a ə'zeɪ.ni|.ə **-an/s** -ən/z
Azariah ˌæz.ə'raɪ.ə
Azerbaijan ˌæz.ə.baɪ'dʒɑːn, -'ʒɑːn US ˌɑː.zɚ-, ˌæz.ɚ- **-i/s** -i/z
azimuth 'æz.ɪ.məθ, '-ə- **-s** -s
Aziz ə'ziːz, -'zɪz
Aznavour 'æz.nə.vɔːʳ, -vʊəʳ US ˌ--'vɔːr, -'vʊr
azodye 'eɪ.zəʊ.daɪ, 'æz.əʊ- US -zoʊ- **-s** -z
azoic ə'zəʊ.ɪk, æz'əʊ-, eɪ'zəʊ- US ə'zoʊ-, eɪ-
Azores ə'zɔːz US 'eɪ.zɔːrz; ə'zɔːrz
Note: It is customary to pronounce /ə'zɔː.rɪz US -'zɔːr.ɪz/ (or /-'zɔː.rez US -'zɔːr.ez/) in reciting Tennyson's poem 'The Revenge'.
azote ə'zəʊt, æz'əʊt; 'æz.əʊt, 'eɪ.zəʊt US 'æz.oʊt, 'eɪ.zoʊt; ə'zoʊt
azotic ə'zɒt.ɪk, æz'ɒt-, eɪ'zɒt- US ə'zɑː.t̬ɪk
Azov 'ɑː.zɒv, 'eɪ-, 'æz.ɒv US 'ɑː.zɑːf, 'eɪ-, 'æz.ɑːf, -ɔːf
AZT® ˌeɪ.zed'tiː US -ziː'-
Aztec 'æz.tek **-s** -s
azure 'æz.jʊəʳ, 'eɪ.zjʊəʳ, 'æʒ.əʳ, 'eɪ.ʒəʳ, ə'zjʊəʳ, ə'zjʊəʳ US 'æʒ.ɚ, 'eɪ.ʒɚ
azygous ə'zaɪ.gəs, æz'aɪ-, ˌeɪ'zaɪ- US 'æz.ɪ-; ˌeɪ'zaɪ-

Pronouncing the letter B

The consonant **b** is most often realised as /b/, e.g.:

boy /bɔɪ/
grab /græb/

In addition

b can be silent, or have a zero realisation. There are two combinations in which this can occur: **bt** and **mb**.

bt is either word medial or word final, e.g.:

doubt /daʊt/
subtle /ˈsʌt.l̩/ (US) /ˈsʌt̬.l̩/

Words containing **mb** in which **b** is silent have the **mb** in word final position, except where an inflection is added, e.g.:

bomb /bɒm/ (US) /bɑːm/
bombing /ˈbɒm.ɪŋ/ (US) /ˈbɑː.mɪŋ/

However, the appearance of **bt** and **mb** does not necessarily indicate a silent **b**. In the case of **mb**, the **b** is pronounced if it occurs inside a morpheme or unit of meaning. Compare:

number = arithmetical value /ˈnʌm.bəʳ/ (US) /ˈnʌm.bɚ/
number = comparative of *numb* /ˈnʌm.əʳ/ (US) /ˈnʌm.ɚ/

For **bt**, the **b** is not silent if part of a prefix. Compare:

subtract /səbˈtrækt/
subtle /ˈsʌt.l̩/ (US) /ˈsʌt̬.l̩/

b **(B)** biː **-'s** -z
ba beɪ **-s** -z
BA ˌbiːˈeɪ
baa bɑː (US) bæ, bɑː **-s** -z **-ing** -ɪŋ **-ed** -d
Baader-Meinhof ˌbɑː.dəˈmaɪn.hɒf (US) -dɚˈmaɪn.hɑːf, -hoʊf
Baal ˈbeɪ.ᵊl *Jewish pronunciation:* bɑːl
BAAL bɑːl
baa-lamb ˈbɑː.læm (US) ˈbɑː-, ˈbæ- **-s** -z
Baalim ˈbeɪ.ᵊl.ɪm *Jewish pronunciation:* ˈbɑː.lɪm
baas *master:* bɑːs **-es** -ɪz
baas *(from* **baa***)* bɑːz (US) bæz, bɑːz
baaskaap ˈbɑːs.kæp (US) -kɑːp
Ba'ath bɑːθ (US) bɑːθ, bæθ **-ist/s** -ɪst/s
Bab bɑːb
baba ˈbɑː.bɑː, -bə **-s** -z
Babar ˈbɑː.bɑːʳ (US) bəˈbɑːr; ˈbæb.ɑːr, ˈbɑː.bɑːr
Babbage ˈbæb.ɪdʒ
babbit **(B)** ˈbæb.ɪt **-s** -s
babbl|e ˈbæb.l̩ **-es** -z **-ing** -ɪŋ, ˈbæb.lɪŋ **-ed** -d **-er/s** -əʳ/z, ˈ-ləʳ/z (US) ˈ-l̩.ɚ/z, ˈ-lɚ/z **-ement/s** -mənt/s
Babcock ˈbæb.kɒk (US) -kɑːk
babe beɪb **-s** -z
babel **(B)** ˈbeɪ.bᵊl (US) ˈbeɪ-, ˈbæb.ᵊl **-s** -z
Babington ˈbæb.ɪŋ.tən
Bab|ism ˈbɑː.b|ɪ.zᵊm **-ist/s** -ɪst/s **-ite** -aɪt
Babi Yar ˌbɑː.biˈjɑːʳ (US) -ˈjɑːr *stress shift:* ˌBabi Yar ˈmassacre
babka ˈbɑːb.kə **-s** -z
baboo **(B)** ˈbɑː.buː **-s** -z
baboon bəˈbuːn (US) bæbˈuːn, bəˈbuːn **-s** -z
babooner|y bəˈbuː.nᵊr|.i, bæbˈuː- **-ies** -iz
Babs bæbz
babu **(B)** ˈbɑː.buː **-s** -z
babushka bæbˈuːʃ.kə, bəˈbuːʃ-, -ˈbʊʃ- **-s** -z
bab|y **(B)** ˈbeɪ.b|i **-ies** -iz **-ying** -i.ɪŋ **-ied** -id **ˈbaby ˌboom; ˈbaby ˌboomer; ˌbaby ˈgrand; ˈbaby ˌtalk; ˈbaby ˌcarriage; throw the ˌbaby out with the ˈbath water**
Babycham® ˈbeɪ.bɪ.ʃæm
Babygro® ˈbeɪ.bɪ.grəʊ (US) -groʊ **-s** -z
babyhood ˈbeɪ.bi.hʊd
babyish ˈbeɪ.bi.ɪʃ **-ly** -li **-ness** -nəs, -nɪs
Babylon ˈbæb.ɪ.lɒn, -ə-, -lən (US) -lɑːn
Babyloni|a ˌbæb.ɪˈləʊ.ni|.ə, -əˈ- (US) -ˈloʊ- **-an/s** -ən/z
baby|sit ˈbeɪ.bɪ|.sɪt **-sitter/s** -ˌsɪt.əʳ/z (US) -ˌsɪt̬.ɚ/z **-sits** -sɪts **-sitting** -ˌsɪt.ɪŋ (US) -ˌsɪt̬.ɪŋ **-sat** -sæt
Bacall bəˈkɔːl (US) -ˈkɔːl, -ˈkɑːl
Bacardi® bəˈkɑː.di (US) -ˈkɑːr- **-s** -z
baccalaureate ˌbæk.əˈlɔː.ri.ət, -ɪt (US) -ˈlɔːr.i-, -ɪt **-s** -s
baccarat ˈbæk.ə.rɑː, ˌ--ˈ- (US) ˌbæk.əˈrɑː, ˌbɑː.kəˈ-, ˈ---
Bacchae ˈbæk.iː
bacchanal ˈbæk.ə.nᵊl; ˌbæk.əˈnæl (US) ˌbæk.əˈnæl **-s** -z
bacchanali|a ˌbæk.əˈneɪ.li|.ə (US) -jə **-an/s** -ən/z
bacchant ˈbæk.ənt **-s** -s
bacchante bəˈkæn.ti, bəˈkænt (US) -ˈkænt, -ˈkæn.ti, -ˈkɑːn- **-s** -z, -s
bacchic ˈbæk.ɪk
Bacchus ˈbæk.əs (US) ˈbæk.əs, ˈbɑː.kəs
Bacchylides bækˈɪl.ɪ.diːz, bəˈkɪl-
baccy ˈbæk.i
Bach *German composer:* bɑːk *as if German:* bɑːx (US) bɑːk *English surname:* beɪtʃ, bætʃ
bach *Welsh term of address:* bɑːk *as if Welsh:* bɑːx (US) bɑːk
Bacharach ˈbæk.ə.ræk
Bache beɪtʃ
bachelor **(B)** ˈbætʃ.ᵊl.əʳ, -ɪ.ləʳ (US) -ᵊl.ɚ **-s** -z **-hood** -hʊd **-ship** -ʃɪp **ˌBachelor of ˈArts; ˌBachelor of ˈScience; ˈbachelor ˌgirl**
baciliform bəˈsɪl.ɪ.fɔːm, bæsˈɪl- (US) bəˈsɪl.ə.fɔːrm
bacillary bəˈsɪl.ᵊr.i, bæsˈɪl- (US) bəˈsɪl-
bacill|us bəˈsɪl.|əs, bæsˈɪl- (US) bəˈsɪl- **-i** -aɪ, -iː
back **(B)** bæk **-s** -s **-ing** -ɪŋ **-ed** -t **ˈBack ˌBay; ˌback ˈdoor;** *stress shift:* ˌback door ˈdeal; **ˌback ˈgarden; ˌback of beˈyond; ˌback ˈseat; ˌback seat ˈdriver; ˈback ˌtalk; ˌback ˈyard** *stress shift:* ˌback yard ˈspecial; **have one's ˌback to the ˈwall; ˌput someone's ˈback up; ˌturn one's ˈback on someone/something**
backache ˈbæk.eɪk **-s** -s
backbeat ˈbæk.biːt
backbench ˌbækˈbentʃ **-es** -ɪz *stress shift:* ˌbackbench ˈspeaker
backbencher ˌbækˈben.tʃəʳ (US) -tʃɚ **-s** -z *stress shift:* ˌbackbencher ˈvote
backbi|ting ˈbækˌbaɪ|.tɪŋ (US) -t̬ɪŋ **-ter/s** -təʳ/z (US) -t̬ɚ/z
backboard ˈbæk.bɔːd (US) -bɔːrd **-s** -z
backbone ˈbæk.bəʊn (US) -boʊn **-s** -z
backbreaker ˈbækˌbreɪ.kəʳ (US) -kɚ **-s** -z
backbreaking ˈbækˌbreɪ.kɪŋ **-ly** -li
backchat ˈbæk.tʃæt
back|cloth ˈbæk|.klɒθ (US) -klɑːθ **-cloths** -klɒθs, -klɒðz (US) -klɑːθs, -klɑːðz
backcomb ˈbæk.kəʊm, ˌ-ˈ- (US) ˈbæk.koʊm **-s** -z **-ing** -ɪŋ **-ed** -d
back|date ˌbæk|ˈdeɪt (US) ˈbæk|.deɪt **-dates** -ˈdeɪts (US) -deɪts **-dating** -ˈdeɪ.tɪŋ (US) -deɪ.t̬ɪŋ **-dated** -ˈdeɪ.tɪd (US) -deɪ.t̬ɪd *stress shift:* ˌbackdated ˈcheque

backdrop ˈbæk.drɒp (US) -drɑːp **-s** -s
backer ˈbæk.əʳ (US) -ɚ **-s** -z
backfield ˈbæk.fiːld
backfill ˈbæk.fɪl **-s** -z **-ing** -ɪŋ **-ed** -d
backfir|e ˌbækˈfaɪəʳ, ˈ-- (US) ˌbækˈfaɪɚ, ˈ-- **-es** -z **-ing** -ɪŋ **-ed** -d
back-formation ˈbæk.fɔːˌmeɪ.ʃᵊn (US) -fɔːrˌ- **-s** -z
backgammon ˈbæk.gæm.ən, ˌ-ˈ--
background ˈbæk.graʊnd **-s** -z **ˈbackground ˌnoise, ˌbackground ˈnoise** (US) **ˈbackground ˌnoise**
backhand ˈbæk.hænd **-s** -z
backhanded ˌbækˈhænd.ɪd **-ly** -li **-ness** -nəs, -nɪs *stress shift, see compound:* **ˌbackhanded ˈcompliment**
backhander ˌbækˈhænd.əʳ (US) -ɚ **-z** -z
backhoe ˈbæk.həʊ (US) -hoʊ **-s** -z
Backhouse ˈbæk.haʊs
backing ˈbæk.ɪŋ **-s** -z
backlash ˈbæk.læʃ
backless ˈbæk.ləs, -lɪs
back|light ˈbæk|.laɪt **-lights** -laɪts **-lighting** -ˌlaɪ.tɪŋ (US) -ˌlaɪ.t̬ɪŋ **-lighted** -ˌlaɪ.tɪd (US) -ˌlaɪ.t̬ɪd **backlit** ˈbæk.lɪt
backlist ˈbæk.lɪst **-s** -s **-ing** -ɪŋ **-ed** -ɪd
backlog ˈbæk.lɒg (US) -lɑːg, -lɔːg **-s** -z
backpack ˈbæk.pæk **-s** -s **-ing** -ɪŋ **-ed** -d **-er/s** -əʳ/z (US) -ɚ/z
back-pedal ˌbækˈped.ᵊl, ˈ-ˌ-- (US) ˈbæk.ped- **-s** -z **-(l)ing** -ɪŋ **-(l)ed** -d
backrest ˈbæk.rest **-s** -s
backroom ˌbækˈrʊm, -ˈruːm, ˈ-- (US) ˌbækˈruːm, -ˈrʊm, ˈ-- **ˈbackroom ˌboy**
backscratcher ˈbækˌskrætʃ.əʳ (US) -ɚ **-s** -z
backsheesh, backshish ˌbækˈʃiːʃ, ˈ--
backside ˌbækˈsaɪd, ˈ-- (US) ˈ-- **-s** -z
backslap ˈbæk.slæp **-s** -s **-ping** -ɪŋ **-ped** -t **-per/s** -əʳ/z (US) -ɚ/z
backslash ˈbæk.slæʃ **-es** -ɪz
backslid|e ˈbæk.slaɪd **-es** -z **-ing** -ɪŋ **-er/s** -əʳ/z (US) -ɚ/z **backslid** ˈbæk.slɪd
backspac|e ˈbæk.speɪs **-es** -ɪz **-ing** -ɪŋ **-ed** -t
backspin ˈbæk.spɪn
backstage ˌbækˈsteɪdʒ *stress shift:* ˌbackstage ˈpass
backstairs ˌbækˈsteəz (US) ˌbækˈsterz *stress shift:* ˌbackstairs ˈgossip
backstay ˈbæk.steɪ **-s** -z
backstitch ˈbæk.stɪtʃ **-es** -ɪz **-ing** -ɪŋ **-ed** -t
backstop ˈbæk.stɒp (US) -stɑːp **-s** -s **-ping** -ɪŋ **-ped** -t
backstrap ˈbæk.stræp **-s** -s
backstreet ˈbæk.striːt **-s** -s
backstroke ˈbæk.strəʊk (US) -stroʊk
back-to-back ˌbæk.təˈbæk *stress shift:* ˌback-to-back ˈhouse
backtrack ˈbæk.træk **-s** -s **-ing** -ɪŋ **-ed** -t
backup ˈbæk.ʌp **-s** -s
backward ˈbæk.wəd (US) -wɚd **-ly** -li **-ness** -nəs, -nɪs **-s** -z **ˌbend over ˈbackwards**
backwash ˈbæk.wɒʃ (US) -wɑːʃ, -wɔːʃ **-es** -ɪz
backwater ˈbækˌwɔː.təʳ (US) -ˌwɑː.t̬ɚ, -ˌwɔː- **-s** -z
backwoods ˈbæk.wʊdz
backwoods|man ˌbækˈwʊdz|.mən, ˈ-ˌ-- **-men** -mən, -men
bacon (B) ˈbeɪ.kᵊn **ˌbring home the ˈbacon**
Baconian beɪˈkəʊ.ni.ən, bəˈkəʊ- (US) -ˈkoʊ- **-s** -z
bacteria bækˈtɪə.ri.ə (US) bækˈtɪr.i.ə
bacterial bækˈtɪə.ri.əl (US) bækˈtɪr.i.əl
bacteriological bækˌtɪə.ri.əˈlɒdʒ.ɪ.kᵊl (US) -ˌtɪr.i.əˈlɑː.dʒɪ-
bacteriolog|y bækˌtɪə.riˈɒl.ə.dʒ|i (US) -ˌtɪr.iˈɑː.lə- **-ist/s** -ɪst/s
bacteriophag|e bækˈtɪə.ri.əʊ.feɪdʒ (US) -ˈtɪr.i.ə- **-es** -ɪz
bacterium bækˈtɪə.ri.əm (US) bækˈtɪr.i.əm
Bactri|a ˈbæk.tri|.ə **-an/s** -ən/z
Bacup ˈbeɪ.kəp
bad bæd **ˌbad ˈblood; ˌbad ˈlanguage; ˌbad ˈnews; ˌbad ˈtemper; go from ˌbad to ˈworse**
Bad bæd, bɑːd (US) bɑːd
Badajoz ˌbæd.əˈhɒs *as if Spanish:* ˌbæd.əˈxɒθ (US) ˌbɑː.dɑːˈhoʊz, -ðɑːˈhoʊθ
badass ˈbæd.æs **-ed** -t
Badcock ˈbæd.kɒk (US) -kɑːk
Baddeley ˈbæd.ᵊl.i
baddie ˈbæd.i **-s** -z
Baddiel bəˈdɪəl, bædˈɪəl
baddish ˈbæd.ɪʃ
badd|y ˈbæd|.i **-ies** -iz
bade *(from **bid**)* bæd, beɪd
Badedas® ˈbæd.ɪ.dæs; bəˈdeɪ.dəs
Badel bəˈdel
Badely ˈbæd.ᵊl.i
Baden ˈbɑː.dᵊn
Baden-Powell ˌbeɪ.dᵊnˈpaʊəl, -ˈpəʊəl, -ˈpəʊ.ɪl, -ˈpəʊ.el (US) -ˈpoʊ.əl, -ˈpaʊəl
Baden-Württemberg ˌbɑː.dᵊnˈvɜː.tᵊm.bɜːg (US) -ˈvɝː.tᵊm.bɜːrg
Bader ˈbɑː.dəʳ, ˈbeɪ- (US) -dɚ
badg|e bædʒ **-es** -ɪz **-ing** -ɪŋ **-ed** -d
badg|er (B) ˈbædʒ|.əʳ (US) -ɚ **-ers** -əz (US) -ɚz **-ering** -ᵊr.ɪŋ **-ered** -əd (US) -ɚd
badger-baiting ˈbædʒ.əˌbeɪ.tɪŋ (US) -ɚˌbeɪ.t̬ɪŋ
badger-dog ˈbædʒ.ə.dɒg (US) -ɚ.dɑːg, -dɔːg **-s** -z
Bad Godesburg ˌbɑːdˈgəʊ.dəz.bɜːg, -ˈgəʊdz-, -beəg (US) -ˈgoʊ.dəz.bɝːg
Badham ˈbæd.əm
badinage ˈbæd.ɪ.nɑːʒ, -nɑːdʒ, ˌ--ˈ-
badlands ˈbæd.lændz
badly ˈbæd.li
badminton (B) ˈbæd.mɪn.tən
bad-mouth ˈbæd.maʊθ **-s** -z **-ing** -ɪŋ **-ed** -d
badness ˈbæd.nəs, -nɪs
Badoit® ˈbæd.wɑː, -ˈ- (US) bɑːˈdwɑː
bad-tempered ˌbædˈtem.pəd (US) ˈbædˌtem.pɚd **-ly** -li **-ness** -nəs, -nɪs *stress shift, British only:* ˌbad-tempered ˈperson
Baeda ˈbiː.də
Baedeker ˈbeɪ.dek.əʳ, ˈbaɪ-, -dɪ.kəʳ (US) ˈbeɪ.də.kɚ, ˈbaɪ- **-s** -z
Baez ˈbaɪ.ez, -ˈ-
Baffin ˈbæf.ɪn **ˌBaffin ˈBay; ˌBaffin ˈIsland**
baffl|e ˈbæf.l̩ **-es** -z **-ing/ly** -ɪŋ/li, ˈ-lɪŋ **-ed** -d **-er/s** -əʳ/z, ˈ-ləʳ/z (US) ˈ-l̩.ɚ/z, ˈ-lɚ/z **-ement** -mənt
BAFTA, Bafta ˈbæf.tə
bag bæg **-s** -z **-ging** -ɪŋ **-ged** -d **ˈbag ˌlady; ˌbag of ˈbones -ger/s** -gəʳ/z (US) -gɚ/z
bagatelle ˌbæg.əˈtel **-s** -z
Bagdad *in Iraq:* ˌbægˈdæd, ˈ-- (US) ˈbæg.dæd *in Tasmania, Florida:* ˈbæg.dæd
Bagehot ˈbædʒ.ət, ˈbæg-
bagel ˈbeɪ.gᵊl **-s** -z
bagful ˈbæg.fʊl **-s** -z
baggag|e ˈbæg.ɪdʒ **-es** -ɪz
Baggie® ˈbæg.i **-s** -z
bagg|y ˈbæg|.i **-ier** -i.əʳ (US) -i.ɚ **-iest** -i.ɪst, -i.əst **-ily** -ɪ.li, -ᵊl.i **-iness** -ɪ.nəs, -ɪ.nɪs
Baghdad bægˈdæd, ˈ-- (US) ˈbæg.dæd
Bagheera bægˈɪə.rə, bəˈgɪə- (US) bəˈgɪr.ə
Bagley ˈbæg.li
Bagnall ˈbæg.nəl, -nɔːl
Bagnell ˈbæg.nəl
bagnio ˈbæn.jəʊ, ˈbɑː.njəʊ (US) ˈbɑː.njoʊ, ˈbæn.joʊ **-s** -z
Bagnold ˈbæg.nəʊld (US) -noʊld
Bagot ˈbæg.ət
bagpip|e ˈbæg.paɪp **-es** -s **-er/s** -əʳ/z (US) -ɚ/z
bags bægz **-es** -ɪz **-ing** -ɪŋ **-ed** -d
Bagshaw(e) ˈbæg.ʃɔː (US) -ʃɑː, -ʃɔː
Bagshot ˈbæg.ʃɒt (US) -ʃɑːt
bags|y ˈbæg.z|i **-ies** -iz **-ing** -ɪŋ **-ied** -id
baguette, baguet bægˈet, bəˈget **-s** -s
Bagworthy ˈbædʒ.ᵊr.i
bah bɑː (US) bɑː, bæ
bahadur bəˈhɑː.dəʳ (US) -dɚ **-s** -z
Baha'i bəˈhaɪ, bɑː-, -ˈhɑː.i, -ˈhaɪ.i **-s** -z
Baha|ism bəˈhaɪ|.ɪ.zᵊm, bɑː-, -ˈhɑː- **-ist/s** -ɪst/s
Bahama bəˈhɑː.mə **-s** -z
Bahamian bəˈheɪ.mi.ən, -ˈhɑː- **-s** -z

Bahasa bə'hɑː.sə
Bahawalpur bɑː'hɑː.wəl.pʊəʳ, bə- (US) -pʊr
Bahia bə'hiː.ə
Bahrain, Bahrein bɑː'reɪn **-i** -i
baht bɑːt **-s** -s
baignoire 'beɪn.wɑːʳ (US) ben'wɑːr, beɪn- **-s** -z
Baikal 'baɪ.kæl, -kɑːl, -'-
bail beɪl **-s** -z **-ing** -ɪŋ **-ed** -d **-er/s** -əʳ/z (US) -ɚ/z
bailable 'beɪ.lə.bl̩
bail-bond 'beɪl.bɒnd, -'- (US) 'beɪl.bɑːnd **-s** -z
bail-bonds|man 'beɪl,bɒndz|.mən (US) -,bɑːndz- **-men** -mən
Baildon 'beɪl.dən
bailee ,beɪ'liː **-s** -z
bailey (B) 'beɪ.li
bailie (B) 'beɪ.li **-s** -z
bailiff 'beɪ.lɪf **-s** -s
bailiwick 'beɪ.lɪ.wɪk **-s** -s
Baille 'beɪ.li
Baillie 'beɪ.li
Baillieu 'beɪ.ljuː (US) 'beɪl.juː
Bailly 'beɪ.li
bailment 'beɪl.mənt **-s** -s
bailout 'beɪ.laʊt (US) 'beɪl.aʊt **-s** -s
Baily 'beɪ.li
Bain beɪn
Bainbridge 'beɪn.brɪdʒ, 'beɪm- (US) 'beɪn-
Baines beɪnz
bain-marie ,bæn.mə'riː *as if French:* bæ̃m- (US) ,bæn- **-s** -z
Baird beəd (US) berd
bairn beən (US) bern **-s** -z
Bairstow 'beə.stəʊ (US) 'ber.stoʊ
bait beɪt **-s** -s **-ing** -ɪŋ (US) 'beɪ.t̬ɪŋ **-ed** -ɪd (US) 'beɪ.t̬ɪd
bai|za 'baɪ|.zə (US) -zɑː **-zas** -zəz
baiz|e beɪz **-es** -ɪz
Baja California ,bɑː.hɑː.kæl.ɪ'fɔː.njə (US) -ə'fɔːr-
bak|e beɪk **-es** -s **-ing** -ɪŋ **-ed** -t **,baked A'laska; ,baked 'beans; 'baking ,powder; 'baking ,soda**
bakehou|se 'beɪk.haʊ|s **-ses** -zɪz
Bakelite® 'beɪ.kᵊl.aɪt (US) 'beɪ.kə.laɪt, 'beɪk.laɪt
baker (B) 'beɪ.kəʳ (US) -kɚ **-s** -z
Bakerloo ,beɪ.kᵊl'uː (US) -kɚ'luː
Bakersfield 'beɪ.kəz.fiːld (US) -kɚz-
baker|y 'beɪ.kᵊr|.i **-ies** -iz
Bakewell 'beɪk.wel, -wəl
Bakke 'bɑː.ki
baklava 'bæk.lə.vɑː, 'bɑː.klə- *as if Greek:* ,--'- **-s** -z
baksheesh ,bæk'ʃiːʃ, '--
Baku bæk'uː (US) bɑː'kuː
Bakunin bə'kuː.nɪn, bɑː- (US) bɑː'kuːn.jɪn, bə-
Bala 'bæl.ə
balaam (B) 'beɪ.læm, -ləm **-s** -z
balaclava (B) ,bæl.ə'klɑː.və, ,bɑː.lə'- **-s** -z
Balakirev bə'læk.ɪ.rev, -'lɑː.kɪ- (US) ,bɑː.lɑː'kɪr.jef
balalaika ,bæl.ə'laɪ.kə **-s** -z
balanc|e 'bæl.ənts **-es** -ɪz **-ing** -ɪŋ **-ed** -t **'balancing ,act; ,balance of 'payments; 'balance ,sheet**
Balanchine 'bæl.ən.tʃiːn, ,--'- (US) 'bæl.ənt.ʃiːn
Balatka bə'læt.kə (US) -kɑː, -'lɑːt-
Balaton bæl'æt.ən *as if Hungarian:* bɒl'ɒt- (US) 'bɑː.lɑː.tɑːn
Balboa bæl'bəʊ.ə (US) -'boʊ-
Balbriggan bæl'brɪg.ən
Balbus 'bæl.bəs
Balchin 'bɔːl.tʃɪn, 'bɒl- (US) 'bɔːl-, 'bɑːl-
balcon|y 'bæl.kə.n|i **-ies** -iz
bald bɔːld (US) bɔːld, bɑːld **-er** -əʳ (US) -ɚ **-est** -ɪst, -əst **-ing** -ɪŋ **-ish** -ɪʃ **-ly** -li **-ness** -nəs, -nɪs **,bald 'eagle**
baldachin, baldaquin 'bɔːl.də.kɪn (US) 'bɔːl-, 'bɑːl- **-s** -z
Balder 'bɔːl.dəʳ, 'bɒl- (US) 'bɔːl.dɚ, 'bɑːl-
balderdash 'bɔːl.də.dæʃ, 'bɒl- (US) 'bɔːl.dɚ-, 'bɑːl-
baldfaced ,bɔːld'feɪst (US) 'bɔːld.feɪst, 'bɑːld- *stress shift, British only:* ,baldfaced 'liar
bald-headed ,bɔːld'hed.ɪd (US) ,bɔːld-, ,bɑːld- *stress shift:* ,bald-headed 'man
Baldock 'bɔːl.dɒk (US) 'bɔːl.dɑːk, 'bɑːl-
baldric (B) 'bɔːl.drɪk, 'bɒl- (US) 'bɔːl-, 'bɑːl- **-s** -s
Baldry 'bɔːl.dri (US) 'bɔːl-, 'bɑːl-
Baldwin 'bɔːld.wɪn (US) 'bɔːld-, 'bɑːld-
bald|y 'bɔːl.d|i (US) 'bɔːl-, 'bɑːl- **-ies** -iz
bal|e (B) beɪl **-es** -z **-ing** -ɪŋ **-ed** -d
Bale, Bâle *in Switzerland:* bɑːl
Baleares ,bæl.i'ɑː.rɪz (US) ,bɑː.li'-, ,bæl.i'-
Balearic ,bæl.i'ær.ɪk (US) ,bɑː.li'-, ,bæl.i'-, -'er-
baleen bə'liːn, bæl'iːn **-s** -z
baleful 'beɪl.fᵊl, -fʊl **-ly** -i **-ness** -nəs, -nɪs
baler 'beɪ.ləʳ (US) -lɚ **-s** -z
Balfour 'bæl.fəʳ, -fɔːʳ (US) -fɚ, -fɔːr
Balguy 'bɔːl.gi (US) 'bɔːl-, 'bɑːl-
Balham 'bæl.əm
Bali 'bɑː.li (US) 'bɑː.li, 'bæl.i
Balinese ,bɑː.lɪ'niːz (US) ,bɑː.lə'-, ,bæl.ə'-
Baliol 'beɪ.li.əl
balk bɔːlk, bɔːk (US) bɔːk, bɑːk **-s** -s **-ing** -ɪŋ **-ed** -t
Balkan 'bɔːl.kən, bɒl- (US) 'bɔːl-, 'bɑːl- **-s** -z
Balkanization, -isa- ,bɔːl.kə.naɪ'zeɪ.ʃᵊn, ,bɒl-, -nɪ'- (US) ,bɔːl-, ,bɑːl-
Balkaniz|e, -is|e 'bɔːl.kə.naɪz, 'bɒl- (US) 'bɔːl-, 'bɑːl- **-es** -ɪz **-ing** -ɪŋ **-ed** -d
Balkhash bæl'kæʃ (US) bɑːl'kɑːʃ, bæl-, -'kæʃ
ball (B) bɔːl (US) bɔːl, bɑːl **-s** -z **,ball and 'chain; ,ball 'bearing; 'ball ,boy; 'ball ,game; 'ball ,girl; 'ball ,park; ,on the 'ball; ,set the ball 'rolling, ,set the 'ball ,rolling**
ballad 'bæl.əd **-s** -z
ballade bæl'ɑːd, bə'lɑːd **-s** -z
balladeer ,bæl.ə'dɪəʳ (US) -'dɪr **-s** -z
Ballantine, Ballantyne 'bæl.ən.taɪn
Ballantrae ,bæl.ən'treɪ
Ballarat ,bæl.ə'ræt, '---
Ballard 'bæl.əd, -ɑːd (US) -ɚd, -ɑːrd
ballast 'bæl.əst **-s** -s
Ballater 'bæl.ə.təʳ (US) -t̬ɚ
ballcarrier 'bɔːl,kær.i.əʳ (US) -,ker.i.ɚ, 'bɑːl-, -,kær- **-s** -z
ballcock 'bɔːl.kɒk (US) 'bɔːl.kɑːk, 'bɑːl- **-s** -s
Balleine bæl'en
ballerina ,bæl.ᵊr'iː.nə (US) -ə'riː- **-s** -z
Ballesteros ,bæl.ɪ'stɪə.rɒs, ,baɪ.ɪ'-, -ə'-, -'steə- (US) ,baɪ.ə'ster.oʊs, ,bæl-
ballet 'bæl.eɪ (US) bæl'eɪ, '-- **-s** -z **'ballet ,dancer**
balletic bæl'et.ɪk, bə'let- (US) bə'let̬.ɪk
balletomane 'bæl.ɪ.təʊ.meɪn, -et.əʊ- (US) bə'let̬.ə- **-s** -z
ballgown 'bɔːl.gaʊn (US) 'bɔːl-, 'bɑːl- **-s** -z
Ballingry bə'lɪŋ.gri
Balliol 'beɪ.li.əl
ballistic bə'lɪs.tɪk **-s** -s
balloon bə'luːn **-s** -z **-ing** -ɪŋ **-ed** -d **-ist/s** -ɪst/s **go ,down/,over like a ,lead ba'lloon**
ball|ot 'bæl|.ət **-ots** -əts **-oting** -ə.tɪŋ (US) -ə.t̬ɪŋ **-oted** -ə.tɪd (US) -ə.t̬ɪd **'ballot ,box; 'ballot ,paper; 'ballot ,rigging**
ballpark 'bɔːl.pɑːk (US) -pɑːrk, 'bɑːl- **,ball-park 'figure**
ballplayer 'bɔːl,pleɪ.əʳ (US) -ɚ, 'bɑːl- **-s** -z
ball|point 'bɔːl|.pɔɪnt (US) 'bɔːl-, 'bɑːl- **-points** -pɔɪnts **-pointed** -,pɔɪn.tɪd (US) -,pɔɪn.t̬ɪd **,ball-point 'pen**
ballroom 'bɔːl.rʊm, -ruːm (US) 'bɔːl-, 'bɑːl- **-s** -z **,ballroom 'dancing** (US) **'ballroom ,dancing**
balls-up 'bɔːlz,ʌp (US) 'bɔːlz-, 'bɑːlz-
balls|y 'bɔːl.z|i (US) 'bɔːl-, 'bɑːl- **-ier** -i.əʳ (US) -i.ɚ **-iest** -i.əst, -i.ɪst
bally 'bæl.i
Ballycastle ,bæl.ɪ'kɑː.sl̩ (US) -'kæs.l̩
Ballyclare ,bæl.ɪ'kleəʳ (US) -'kler
ballyhoo ,bæl.ɪ'huː (US) '---

Ballymena ˌbæl.ɪˈmiː.nə
Ballymoney ˌbæl.ɪˈmʌn.i
balm bɑːm **-s** -z
Balmain ˈbæl.mæ̃n, -ˈ- (US) ˈbæl.meɪn, -ˈ-
Balm(e) bɑːm
Balmer ˈbɑː.məʳ (US) ˈbɑːl.mɚ, ˈbɑː-
Balmoral bælˈmɒr.əl (US) -ˈmɔːr-
balm|y ˈbɑː.m|i **-ier** -i.əʳ (US) -i.ɚ **-iest** -i.ɪst, -i.əst **-ily** -ɪ.li, -əl.i **-iness** -ɪ.nəs, -ɪ.nɪs
Balniel bælˈniː.ɪl
Balogh ˈbæl.ɒg (US) -ɑːg
baloney bəˈləʊ.ni (US) -ˈloʊ-
Baloo bəˈluː
balsa ˈbɔːl.sə, ˈbɒl- (US) ˈbɔːl-, ˈbɑːl- **ˈbalsa ˌwood**
balsam ˈbɔːl.səm, ˈbɒl- (US) ˈbɔːl-, ˈbɑːl- **-s** -z
balsamic bɔːlˈsæm.ɪk, bɒl- (US) bɔːl-, bɑːl- **balˌsamic ˈvinegar**
Balta ˈbæl.tə (US) ˈbæl-, ˈbɑːl-
Balthazar ˌbæl.θəˈzɑːʳ, ˈ---; bælˈθæz.əʳ (US) ˌbæl.θəˈzɑːr, ˈ---; bælˈθeɪ.zɚ
Note: In Shakespeare, normally /ˌbæl.θəˈzɑːʳ, ˈ--- (US) ˌbæl.θəˈzɑːr, ˈ---/.
balti **(B)** ˈbɔːl.ti, ˈbɒl- (US) ˈbɔːl-, ˈbɑːl-, ˈbʌl-
Baltic ˈbɔːl.tɪk, ˈbɒl- (US) ˈbɔːl-, ˈbɑːl- **ˌBaltic ˈSea**; **ˌBaltic ˈStates**
Baltimore ˈbɔːl.tɪ.mɔːʳ, ˈbɒl- (US) ˈbɔːl.tə.mɔːr, ˈbɑːl-, -mɚ **-s** -z
Baluchistan bəˌluː.tʃɪˈstɑːn, bælˌuː-, -kɪˈ-, -ˈstæn (US) -tʃəˈstæn, -ˈstɑːn
baluster ˈbæl.ə.stəʳ (US) -stɚ **-s** -z **-ed** -d
balustrade ˌbæl.əˈstreɪd (US) ˈ--- **-s** -z
Balzac ˈbæl.zæk (US) ˈbɔːl-, ˈbɑːl-, ˈbæl-
Bamako ˌbæm.əˈkəʊ (US) ˌbæm.əˈkoʊ, ˌbɑː.mə-
Bambi ˈbæm.bi
bambin|o bæmˈbiː.n|əʊ (US) bæmˈbiː.n|oʊ, bɑːm- **-os** -əʊz (US) -oʊz **-i** -i
bamboo bæmˈbuː **-s** -z
bamboozl|e bæmˈbuː.zl̩ **-es** -z **-ing** -ɪŋ, -ˈbuːz.lɪŋ **-ed** -d
Bamborough ˈbæm.bər.ə (US) -oʊ
Bamburgh ˈbæm.bər.ə (US) -bɚ.ə, -bɝːg
Bamfield ˈbæm.fiːld
Bamford ˈbæm.fəd (US) -fɚd
ban *prohibit:* bæn **-s** -z **-ning** -ɪŋ **-ned** -d
ban *Romanian money:* bæn (US) bɑːn **bani** ˈbɑː.ni
banal bəˈnɑːl, bænˈɑːl, -ˈnæl
banalit|y bəˈnæl.ə.t|i, bænˈæl-, -ɪ.t|i (US) -ə.t̬|i **-ies** -iz
banana bəˈnɑː.nə (US) -ˈnæn.ə **-s** -z **baˌnana reˈpublic**; **baˈnana ˌskin**; **baˌnana ˈsplit**
Banaras bəˈnɑː.rəs (US) -ˈnɑːr.əs
Banbridge ˈbæn.brɪdʒ, ˈbæm- (US) ˈbæn-
Banbury ˈbæn.bər.i, ˈbæm- (US) ˈbæn.ber-, -bɚ-
Banchory ˈbæŋ.kər.i
Bancroft ˈbæŋ.krɒft (US) ˈbæn.krɑːft, ˈbæŋ-
band bænd **-s** -z **-ing** -ɪŋ **-ed** -ɪd **ˈband ˌshell**
Banda ˈbæn.də (US) ˈbɑːn-, ˈbæn-
bandag|e ˈbæn.dɪdʒ **-es** -ɪz **-ing** -ɪŋ **-ed** -d
Band-Aid®, band-aid ˈbænd.eɪd **-s** -z
bandan(n)a bænˈdæn.ə **-s** -z
Bandaranaike ˌbæn.dər.əˈnaɪ.ɪ.kə, -ˈnaɪ.kə (US) ˌbɑːn-
Bandar Seri Begawan ˌbæn.də.ser.i.bəˈgɑː.wən, -beˈ-, -bɪˈ-, -ˈgaʊ.ən (US) ˌbɑːn.dɚ-
B and B ˌbiː.ənd̚ˈbiː, -əmˈ- (US) -ənd̚ˈ- **-s** -z
bandbox ˈbænd.bɒks (US) -bɑːks **-es** -ɪz
bandeau ˈbæn.dəʊ *as if French:* bæ̃nˈdəʊ (US) bænˈdoʊ **bandeaux** ˈbæn.dəʊ, -dəʊz *as if French:* bæ̃nˈdəʊ (US) bænˈdoʊ, -doʊz
banderole ˈbæn.dər.əʊl (US) -də.roʊl **-s** -z
bandicoot ˈbæn.dɪ.kuːt **-s** -s
bandit ˈbæn.dɪt **-s** -s **-ry** -ri
bandleader ˈbændˌliː.dəʳ (US) -dɚ **-s** -z
bandmaster ˈbændˌmɑː.stəʳ (US) -ˌmæs.tɚ **-s** -z
bandog ˈbæn.dɒg (US) -dɑːg, -dɔːg **-s** -z
bandoleer, bandolier ˌbæn.dəlˈɪəʳ (US) -dəˈlɪr **-s** -z
bandoline ˈbæn.dəʊ.liːn (US) -də-, -doʊ-
bands|man ˈbændz|.mən **-men** -mən, -men
bandstand ˈbænd.stænd **-s** -z
Bandung ˈbæn.dʊŋ, -ˈ- (US) ˈbɑːn-, ˈbæn-
bandwagon ˈbændˌwæg.ən **-s** -z
bandwidth ˈbæn.dwɪtθ, -dwɪdθ (US) ˈbænd.wɪtθ, -wɪdθ, -wɪθ **-s** -s
band|y ˈbæn.d|i **-ier** -i.əʳ (US) -i.ɚ **-iest** -i.ɪst, -i.əst **-ies** -iz **-ying** -i.ɪŋ **-ied** -id
bandy-legged ˌbæn.diˈlegd, -ˈleg.ɪd, -ˈleg.əd *stress shift:* ˌbandy-legged ˈchild
bane beɪn **-s** -z
baneful ˈbeɪn.fəl, -fʊl **-ly** -i **-ness** -nəs, -nɪs
Banff bænf **-shire** -ʃəʳ, -ˌʃɪəʳ (US) -ʃɚ, -ˌʃɪr
Banfield ˈbæn.fiːld
bang bæŋ **-s** -z **-ing** -ɪŋ **-ed** -d **go ˌoff with a ˈbang**
Bangalore ˌbæŋ.gəˈlɔːʳ (US) ˈbæŋ.gə.lɔːr, ˌ--ˈ-
banger ˈbæŋ.əʳ (US) -ɚ **-s** -z
Banger ˈbeɪn.dʒəʳ (US) -dʒɚ
Bangkok bæŋˈkɒk (US) ˈbæŋ.kɑːk, -ˈ- *stress shift, British only:* ˌBangkok ˈtemple
Bangladesh ˌbæŋ.gləˈdeʃ, -ˈdeɪʃ (US) ˌbæŋ.gləˈdeʃ, ˌbɑːŋ-
Bangladeshi ˌbæŋ.gləˈdeʃ.i, -ˈdeɪ.ʃi (US) ˌbæŋ.gləˈdeʃ-, ˌbɑːŋ- **-s** -z
bangle ˈbæŋ.gl̩ **-s** -z **-d** -d
bang-on ˌbæŋˈɒn (US) ˈbæŋ.ɑːn
Bangor *in Wales:* ˈbæŋ.gəʳ (US) -gɚ *in US:* ˈbæŋ.gɔːʳ, -gəʳ (US) -gɔːr, -gɚ
Bangui ˌbɑːŋˈgiː (US) ˌbɑːŋ-
bang-up ˌbæŋˈʌp (US) ˈ--
Banham ˈbæn.əm
bani *(plur. of* **ban***)* ˈbɑː.ni
banian ˈbæn.i.ən, ˈ-jæn **-s** -z
banish ˈbæn.ɪʃ **-es** -ɪz **-ing** -ɪŋ **-ed** -t **-ment/s** -mənt/s
banister **(B)** ˈbæn.ɪ.stəʳ (US) -ə.stɚ **-s** -z
Banja Luka ˌbæn.jəˈluː.kə (US) ˌbɑː.njəˈ-
banjo ˈbæn.dʒəʊ, -ˈ- (US) ˈbæn.dʒoʊ **-(e)s** -z
Banjul bænˈdʒuːl (US) ˈbɑːn.dʒuːl
bank bæŋk **-s** -s **-ing** -ɪŋ **-ed** -t **ˈbank aˌccount**; **ˈbank ˌcard**; **ˈbank ˌclerk**; **ˌbank ˈholiday**; **ˈbank ˌmanager**; **ˈbank ˌrate**; **ˈbank ˌstatement**; **ˌBank of ˈEngland**
bankability ˌbæŋ.kəˈbɪl.ə.ti, -ɪ.ti (US) -ə.t̬i
bankable ˈbæŋ.kə.bl̩
banker ˈbæŋ.kəʳ (US) -kɚ **-s** -z
Bankes bæŋks
Bankhead ˈbæŋk.hed
banknote ˈbæŋk.nəʊt (US) -noʊt **-s** -s
bankroll ˈbæŋk.rəʊl (US) -roʊl **-s** -z **-ing** -ɪŋ **-ed** -d
bankrupt ˈbæŋ.krʌpt, -krəpt **-s** -s **-ing** -ɪŋ **-ed** -ɪd
bankruptc|y ˈbæŋ.krəp*t*.s|i, -krʌp*t*- **-ies** -iz
Banks bæŋks
banksia ˈbæŋk.si.ə **-s** -z
Ban-Lon® ˈbæn.lɒn (US) -lɑːn
Bann bæn
Bannatyne ˈbæn.ə.taɪn
banner **(B)** ˈbæn.əʳ (US) -ɚ **-s** -z
Bannerman ˈbæn.ə.mən (US) ˈ-ɚ-
Banning ˈbæn.ɪŋ
bannister **(B)** ˈbæn.ɪ.stəʳ (US) -ə.stɚ **-s** -z
bannock ˈbæn.ək **-s** -s
Bannockburn ˈbæn.ək.bɜːn (US) -bɝːn, -bɚn
Bannon ˈbæn.ən
banns bænz
banque|t ˈbæŋ.kwɪ|t (US) -kwə|t, -kwɪ|t **-ts** -ts **-ting** -tɪŋ (US) -t̬ɪŋ **-ted** -tɪd (US) -t̬ɪd **ˈbanquet ˌroom**; **ˈbanqueting ˌhall**
banquette bæŋˈket **-s** -s
Banquo ˈbæŋ.kwəʊ (US) -kwoʊ
banshee ˈbæn.ʃiː, -ˈ- **-s** -z
Banstead ˈbæn*t*.stɪd, -sted
bant bænt **-s** -s **-ing** -ɪŋ (US) ˈbæn.t̬ɪŋ **-ed** -ɪd (US) ˈbæn.t̬ɪd
bantam **(B)** ˈbæn.təm (US) -t̬əm **-s** -z

bantamweight ˈbæn.təm.weɪt (US) -t̬əm-
bant|er ˈbæn.t|əʳ (US) -t̬|ɚ **-ers** -əz (US) -ɚz **-ering** -ᵊr.ɪŋ **-ered** -əd (US) -ɚd
Banting ˈbæn.tɪŋ (US) -t̬ɪŋ
bantling ˈbænt.lɪŋ **-s** -z
Bantry ˈbæn.tri
Bantu ˌbænˈtuː, ˌbɑːn-, ˈ-- (US) ˈbæn.tuː
bantustan (B) ˌbæn.tuˈstɑːn, ˌbɑːn-, -ˈstæn
banyan ˈbæn.jæn, -ni.ən, ˈ-jən (US) ˈ-jən, ˈ-jæn **-s** -z
Banyard ˈbæn.jɑːd (US) -jɑːrd
banzai bænˈzaɪ, bɑːn-, ˈ-- (US) bɑːnˈzaɪ, ˈ--
baobab ˈbeɪ.əʊ.bæb (US) ˈ-oʊ-, ˈbɑː- **-s** -z
bap bæp **-s** -s
baptism ˈbæp.tɪ.zᵊm **-s** -z ˌ**baptism of** ˈ**fire**
baptismal bæpˈtɪz.mᵊl **-ly** -i
baptist (B) ˈbæp.tɪst **-s** -s ˌ**John the** ˈ**Baptist**
baptister|y ˈbæp.tɪ.stᵊr|.i **-ies** -iz
baptistr|y ˈbæp.tɪ.str|i **-ies** -iz
baptiz|e, -is|e bæpˈtaɪz (US) ˈ-- **-es** -ɪz **-ing** -ɪŋ **-ed** -d
bar (B) bɑːʳ (US) bɑːr **-s** -z **-ring** -ɪŋ **-red** -d ˈ**bar** ˌ**code**; ˈ**bar** ˌ**graph**; ˈ**bar** ˌ**meal**; ˈ**bar** ˌ**staff**
Barabbas bəˈræb.əs
barb bɑːb (US) bɑːrb **-s** -z **-ing** -ɪŋ **-ed** -d
Barbadian bɑːˈbeɪ.di.ən, -dʒən (US) bɑːr- **-s** -z
Barbados bɑːˈbeɪ.dɒs, -dəs (US) bɑːrˈbeɪ.doʊs
Barbara ˈbɑː.bᵊr.ə, ˈ-brə (US) ˈbɑːr-
barbarian bɑːˈbeə.ri.ən (US) bɑːrˈber.i- **-s** -z
barbaric bɑːˈbær.ɪk (US) bɑːrˈber-, -ˈbær- **-ally** -ᵊl.i, -li
barbarism ˈbɑː.bᵊr.ɪ.zᵊm (US) ˈbɑːr- **-s** -z
barbarit|y bɑːˈbær.ə.t|i, -ɪ.t|i (US) bɑːrˈber.ə.t̬|i, -ˈbær- **-ies** -iz
barbariz|e, -ise ˈbɑː.bᵊr.aɪz (US) ˈbɑːr- **-es** -ɪz **-ing** -ɪŋ **-ed** -d
Barbarossa ˌbɑː.bᵊrˈɒs.ə (US) ˌbɑːr.bəˈroʊ.sə, -ˈrɑː-
barbarous ˈbɑː.bᵊr.əs (US) ˈbɑːr- **-ly** -li **-ness** -nəs, -nɪs
Barbary ˈbɑː.bᵊr.i (US) ˈbɑːr- ˌ**Barbary** ˈ**ape**; ˌ**Barbary** ˈ**Coast**
barbate ˈbɑː.beɪt, -bɪt, -bət (US) ˈbɑːr-
barbated ˈbɑː.beɪ.tɪd, -bɪ-, -bə-; bɑːˈbeɪ- (US) bɑːrˈbeɪ.t̬ɪd
Barbauld ˈbɑː.bᵊld (US) ˈbɑːr-
barbecu|e ˈbɑː.bɪ.kjuː, -bə- (US) ˈbɑːr- **-es** -z **-ing** -ɪŋ **-ed** -d
barbed bɑːbd (US) bɑːrbd ˌ**barbed** ˈ**wire**
barbell ˈbɑː.bel (US) ˈbɑːr- **-s** -z
barber (B) ˈbɑː.bəʳ (US) ˈbɑːr.bɚ **-s** -z
barberr|y ˈbɑː.bᵊr|.i (US) ˈbɑːr.ber|.i **-ies** -iz
barbershop ˈbɑː.bə.ʃɒp (US) ˈbɑːr.bɚ.ʃɑːp **-s** -s ˌ**barbershop quar**ˈ**tet**
barbette bɑːˈbet (US) bɑːr- **-s** -s
barbican (B) ˈbɑː.bɪ.kən (US) ˈbɑːr.bə- **-s** -z
barbie (B) ˈbɑː.bi (US) ˈbɑːr- ˈ**Barbie** ˌ**doll®**
Barbirolli ˌbɑː.bɪˈrɒl.i, -bəˈ- (US) ˌbɑːr.bəˈrɑː.li
barbitone ˈbɑː.bɪ.təʊn (US) ˈbɑːr.bə.toʊn **-s** -z
barbiturate bɑːˈbɪtʃ.ᵊr.ət, -ˈbɪt.jʊ.rət, -jᵊr.ət, -ɪt, -eɪt (US) bɑːrˈbɪtʃ.ᵊr.ət, -eɪt **-s** -s
barbituric ˌbɑː.bɪˈtʃʊə.rɪk; ˌbɑːˈbɪt.jʊ-, -jᵊr.ɪk (US) ˌbɑːr.bəˈtʃʊr.ɪk, -ˈtʊr- **barbi**ˌ**turic** ˈ**acid**
Barbour® ˈbɑː.bəʳ (US) ˈbɑːr.bɚ **-s** -z
Barbuda bɑːˈbjuː.də (US) bɑːrˈbuː-, -ˈbjuː-
barbule ˈbɑː.bjuːl (US) ˈbɑːr- **-s** -z
barbwire ˈbɑːb.waɪəʳ (US) ˈbɑːrb.waɪɚ
Barca ˈbɑː.kə (US) ˈbɑːr-
barcarol(l)e ˌbɑː.kəˈrəʊl, -ˈrɒl, ˈ--- (US) ˈbɑːr.kə.roʊl **-s** -z
Barcelona ˌbɑː.sᵊlˈəʊ.nə, -sɪˈləʊ- (US) ˌbɑːr.səˈloʊ-
Barchester ˈbɑː.tʃes.təʳ, -tʃɪ.stəʳ (US) ˈbɑːr.tʃə.stɚ, -tʃes.tɚ
Barclay ˈbɑː.kli, -kleɪ (US) ˈbɑːr- **-'s** -z
Barclaycard® ˈbɑː.kli.kɑːd, -kleɪ- (US) ˈbɑːr.kli.kɑːrd
bar code ˈbɑː.kəʊd (US) ˈbɑːr.koʊd **-s** -z
Barcroft ˈbɑː.krɒft (US) ˈbɑːr.krɑːft
bard (B) bɑːd (US) bɑːrd **-s** -z **-ic** -ɪk
Bardell bɑːˈdel; ˈbɑː.dᵊl, -del (US) bɑːrˈdel; ˈbɑːr.dᵊl, -del
Note: In Dickens' 'The Pickwick Papers' generally pronounced /bɑːˈdel (US) bɑːr-/.
bardolatry bɑːˈdɒl.ə.tri (US) bɑːrˈdɑː.lə-
Bardolph ˈbɑː.dɒlf (US) ˈbɑːr.dɑːlf
Bardot bɑːˈdəʊ (US) bɑːrˈdoʊ
Bardsey ˈbɑːd.si (US) ˈbɑːrd-
Bardsley ˈbɑːdz.li (US) ˈbɑːrdz-
Bardswell ˈbɑːdz.wəl, -wel (US) ˈbɑːrdz-
Bardwell ˈbɑːd.wəl, -wel (US) ˈbɑːrd-
bar|e beəʳ (US) ber **-er** -əʳ (US) -ɚ **-est** -ɪst, -əst **-es** -z **-ing** -ɪŋ **-ed** -d
bareback ˈbeə.bæk (US) ˈber- **-ed** -t
Barebones ˈbeə.bəʊnz (US) ˈber.boʊnz
barefaced beəˈfeɪst (US) ˈber.feɪst **-ly** -li, -ɪd.li **-ness** -nəs, -nɪs *stress shift, British only:* ˌbarefaced ˈliar
barefoot beəˈfʊt (US) ˈber.fʊt *stress shift, British only:* ˌbarefoot ˈchild
barefooted ˌbeəˈfʊt.ɪd (US) ˈber.fʊt̬- *stress shift, British only:* ˌbarefooted ˈchild
barehanded ˌbeəˈhæn.dɪd (US) ˈberˌhæn- *stress shift, British only:* ˌbarehanded ˈwarrior
bare-headed ˌbeəˈhed.ɪd (US) ˈberˌhed- *stress shift, British only:* ˌbare-headed ˈworshippers
Bareilly bəˈreɪ.li
bare-legged ˌbeəˈlegd, -ˈleg.ɪd (US) ˈberˌleg.ɪd, -legd *stress shift, British only:* ˌbare-legged ˈchild
bare|ly ˈbeə|.li (US) ˈber- **-ness** -nəs, -nɪs
Barenboim ˈbær.ən.bɔɪm, ˈbɑːr- (US) ˈber-, ˈbær-
Barents ˈbær.ənts (US) ˈber-, ˈbær-
barf bɑːf (US) bɑːrf **-s** -s **-ing** -ɪŋ **-ed** -t
Barfield ˈbɑː.fiːld (US) ˈbɑːr-
bar|fly ˈbɑː|.flaɪ (US) ˈbɑːr- **-flies** -flaɪz
Barfoot ˈbɑː.fʊt (US) ˈbɑːr-
bargain ˈbɑː.gɪn, -gən (US) ˈbɑːr- **-s** -z **-ing** -ɪŋ **-ed** -d **-er/s** -əʳ/z (US) -ɚ/z ˌ**bargain** ˈ**basement**; ˈ**bargain** ˌ**hunter**
barg|e bɑːdʒ (US) bɑːrdʒ **-es** -ɪz **-ing** -ɪŋ **-ed** -d
bargee bɑːˈdʒiː, ˈ-- (US) bɑːrˈdʒiː **-s** -z
barge|man ˈbɑːdʒ|.mən, -mæn (US) ˈbɑːrdʒ- **-men** -mən, -men
bargepole ˈbɑːdʒ.pəʊl (US) ˈbɑːrdʒ.poʊl **-s** -z
Barger ˈbɑː.dʒəʳ (US) ˈbɑːr.dʒɚ
Bargh bɑːdʒ, bɑːf (US) bɑːrdʒ, bɑːrf
Bargoed ˈbɑː.gɔɪd (US) ˈbɑːr-
Bargrave ˈbɑː.greɪv (US) ˈbɑːr-
Barham *surname:* ˈbær.əm, ˈbɑː.rəm (US) ˈber-, ˈbær-, ˈbɑːr.əm *in Kent:* ˈbær.əm (US) ˈber-, ˈbær-
Bari ˈbɑː.ri (US) ˈbɑːr.i
Baring ˈbeə.rɪŋ, ˈbær.ɪŋ (US) ˈber.ɪŋ, ˈbær-
Baring-Gould ˌbeə.rɪŋˈguːld (US) ˌber.ɪŋˈ-
baritone ˈbær.ɪ.təʊn (US) ˈber.ə.toʊn, ˈbær- **-s** -z
barium ˈbeə.ri.əm (US) ˈber.i-, ˈbær- ˌ**barium** ˈ**meal**
bark bɑːk (US) bɑːrk **-s** -s **-ing** -ɪŋ **-ed** -t **-er/s** -əʳ/z (US) -ɚ/z ˌ**bark up the wrong** ˈ**tree**; **their** ˌ**bark is** ˌ**worse than their** ˈ**bite**
barkeep ˈbɑː.kiːp (US) ˈbɑːr- **-s** -s **-er/s** -əʳ/z (US) -ɚ/z
Barker ˈbɑː.kəʳ (US) ˈbɑːr.kɚ
Barking ˈbɑː.kɪŋ (US) ˈbɑːr-
Barkston ˈbɑːk.stən (US) ˈbɑːrk-
barley ˈbɑː.li (US) ˈbɑːr- ˈ**barley** ˌ**sugar**; ˈ**barley** ˌ**water**; ˌ**barley** ˈ**wine**
barleycorn (B) ˈbɑː.li.kɔːn (US) ˈbɑːr.li.kɔːrn **-s** -z
Barlow(e) ˈbɑː.ləʊ (US) ˈbɑːr.loʊ
barm bɑːm (US) bɑːrm
barmaid ˈbɑː.meɪd (US) ˈbɑːr- **-s** -z
bar|man ˈbɑː|.mən, -mæn (US) ˈbɑːr- **-men** -mən, -men
Barmby ˈbɑːm.bi (US) ˈbɑːrm-

Barmecide ˈbɑː.mɪ.saɪd ⓤⓢ ˈbɑːr.mə-
bar mi(t)zvah bɑːˈmɪts.və ⓤⓢ bɑːr-
Barmouth ˈbɑː.məθ ⓤⓢ ˈbɑːr-
barm|y ˈbɑː.m|i ⓤⓢ ˈbɑːr- **-ier** -i.əʳ ⓤⓢ -i.ɚ **-iest** -i.ɪst, -i.əst **-iness** -ɪ.nəs, -ɪ.nɪs
barn bɑːn ⓤⓢ bɑːrn **-s** -z ˈ**barn** ˌ**dance**; ˌ**barn** ˈ**door**
Barnabas ˈbɑː.nə.bəs, -bæs ⓤⓢ ˈbɑːr-
Barnaby ˈbɑː.nə.bi ⓤⓢ ˈbɑːr-
barnacle ˈbɑː.nə.kl̩ ⓤⓢ ˈbɑːr- **-s** -z
Barnard ˈbɑː.nəd, -nɑːd ⓤⓢ ˈbɑːr.nɚd; bɑːrˈnɑːrd
Barnardiston ˌbɑː.nəˈdɪs.tən ⓤⓢ ˌbɑːr.nɚˈ-
Barnardo bəˈnɑː.dəʊ, bɑː- ⓤⓢ bɚˈnɑːr.doʊ
Barnby ˈbɑːn.bi, ˈbɑːm- ⓤⓢ ˈbɑːrn-
Barnes bɑːnz ⓤⓢ bɑːrnz
Barnet(t) ˈbɑː.nɪt ⓤⓢ bɑːrˈnet, ˈ--
barney (B) ˈbɑː.ni ⓤⓢ ˈbɑːr- **-s** -z
Barnfield ˈbɑːn.fiːld ⓤⓢ ˈbɑːrn-
Barnham ˈbɑː.nəm ⓤⓢ ˈbɑːr-
Barnicott ˈbɑː.nɪ.kət, -kɒt ⓤⓢ ˈbɑːr.nə.kɑːt, -nɪ-, -kət
Barnoldswick bɑːˈnəʊldz.wɪk *locally also:* ˈbɑː.lɪk ⓤⓢ bɑːrˈnoʊldz.wɪk
Barnsley ˈbɑːnz.li ⓤⓢ ˈbɑːrnz-
Barnstaple ˈbɑːn.stə.pl̩ *locally also:* -bl̩ ⓤⓢ ˈbɑːrn.stə.pl̩
barnstorm ˈbɑːn.stɔːm ⓤⓢ ˈbɑːrn.stɔːrm **-s** -z **-ing** -ɪŋ **-ed** -d **-er/s** -əʳ/z ⓤⓢ -ɚ/z
Barnum ˈbɑː.nəm ⓤⓢ ˈbɑːr-
barnyard ˈbɑːn.jɑːd ⓤⓢ ˈbɑːrn.jɑːrd **-s** -z
Baroda bəˈrəʊ.də ⓤⓢ -ˈroʊ-
barograph ˈbær.əʊ.grɑːf, -græf ⓤⓢ ˈber.ə.græf, ˈbær- **-s** -s
Barolo bəˈrəʊ.ləʊ ⓤⓢ -ˈroʊ.loʊ
Barolong ˌbɑː.rəʊˈləʊŋ, ˌbær.əʊ-, -ˈlɒŋ ⓤⓢ ˌbɑːr.əˈloʊŋ
barometer bəˈrɒm.ɪ.təʳ, -ə.təʳ ⓤⓢ -ˈrɑː.mə.t̬ɚ **-s** -z
barometric ˌbær.əʊˈmet.rɪk ⓤⓢ ˌber.əˈ-, ˌbær- **-al** -əl **-ally** -əl.i, -li
barometry bəˈrɒm.ɪ.tri, ˈ-ə- ⓤⓢ -ˈrɑː.mə-
baron (B) ˈbær.ən ⓤⓢ ˈber-, ˈbær- **-s** -z
baronag|e ˈbær.ən.ɪdʒ ⓤⓢ ˈber-, ˈbær- **-es** -ɪz
baroness (B) ˈbær.ən.es, -ɪs, -əs; ⓤⓢ ˈber.ən.əs, ˈbær- **-es** -ɪz
baronet ˈbær.ən.ət, -ɪt, ˌbær.ənˈet ⓤⓢ ˈber.ən.ət, ˈbær-, -ɪt **-s** -s
baronetag|e ˈbær.ə.nə.tɪdʒ, ˌbær.əˈnet.ɪdʒ ⓤⓢ ˈber.ə.nə.t̬ɪdʒ, ˈbær- **-es** -ɪz
baronetc|y ˈbær.ə.nət.s|i, -net- ⓤⓢ ˈber-, ˈbær- **-ies** -iz
baronial bəˈrəʊ.ni.əl ⓤⓢ -ˈroʊ-
baron|y ˈbær.ən|.i ⓤⓢ ˈber-, ˈbær- **-ies** -iz
baroque bəˈrɒk, bærˈɒk ⓤⓢ bəˈroʊk, bærˈoʊk, -ˈɑːk
baroscope ˈbær.əʊ.skəʊp ⓤⓢ ˈber.ə.skoʊp, ˈbær- **-s** -s
baroscopic ˌbær.əʊˈskɒp.ɪk ⓤⓢ ˌber.əˈskɑː.pɪk, ˌbær-
Barossa bəˈrɒs.ə ⓤⓢ -ˈrɑː.sə **Ba**ˌ**rossa** ˈ**Valley**
barouch|e bəˈruːʃ, bærˈuːʃ ⓤⓢ bəˈruːʃ **-es** -ɪz
barperson ˈbɑːˌpɜː.sən ⓤⓢ ˈbɑːrˌpɝː- **-s** -z
barque bɑːk ⓤⓢ bɑːrk **-s** -s
Barquisimeto ˌbɑː.kɪ.sɪˈmeɪ.təʊ ⓤⓢ bɑːrˌkə.səˈmeɪ.toʊ
Barr bɑːʳ ⓤⓢ bɑːr
Barra ˈbær.ə ⓤⓢ ˈber-, ˈbær-
barrack ˈbær.ək ⓤⓢ ˈber-, ˈbær- **-s** -s **-ing** -ɪŋ **-ed** -t
Barraclough ˈbær.ə.klʌf ⓤⓢ ˈber-, ˈbær-
barracouta ˌbær.əˈkuː.tə ⓤⓢ ˌber.əˈkuː.t̬ə, ˌbær-, -də **-s** -z
barracuda ˌbær.əˈkjuː.də, -ˈkuː- ⓤⓢ ˌber.əˈkuː-, ˌbær-
barrag|e ˈbær.ɑːdʒ ⓤⓢ bəˈrɑːdʒ **-es** -ɪz
barramund|a ˌbær.əˈmʌn.d|ə ⓤⓢ ˌber-, ˌbær- **-as** -əz **-i** -i **-is** -ɪs
Barranquilla ˌbær.əŋˈkiː.ə ⓤⓢ ˌbɑːr.ɑːnˈkiː.jɑː, ˌber-, ˌbær-
barratry ˈbær.ə.tri ⓤⓢ ˈber-, ˈbær-
Barrat(t) ˈbær.ət ⓤⓢ ˈber-, ˈbær-
barre bɑːʳ ⓤⓢ bɑːr **-s** -z
barrel ˈbær.əl ⓤⓢ ˈber-, ˈbær- **-s** -z **-(l)ing** **-(l)ed**
barrel-organ ˈbær.əlˌɔː.gən ⓤⓢ ˈber.əlˌɔːr-, ˈbær- **-s** -z
barren ˈbær.ən ⓤⓢ ˈber-, ˈbær- **-est** -ɪst, -əst **-ly** -li **-ness** -nəs, -nɪs
Barrett ˈbær.ət, -et, -ɪt ⓤⓢ ˈber-, ˈbær-
barrette bəˈret, bɑː- ⓤⓢ bəˈret **-s** -s
Barrhead ˈbɑː.hed ⓤⓢ ˈbɑːr-
barricad|e ˌbær.ɪˈkeɪd, -əˈ-, ˈ--- ⓤⓢ ˈber.ə.keɪd, ˈbær-, ˌ--ˈ- **-es** -z **-ing** -ɪŋ **-ed** -ɪd
Barrie ˈbær.i ⓤⓢ ˈber-, ˈbær-
barrier (B) ˈbær.i.əʳ ⓤⓢ ˈber.i.ɚ, ˈbær- **-s** -z ˌ**Great** ˌ**Barrier** ˈ**Reef**
barring ˈbɑː.rɪŋ ⓤⓢ ˈbɑːr.ɪŋ
Barrington ˈbær.ɪŋ.tən ⓤⓢ ˈber-
barrio ˈbær.i.əʊ ⓤⓢ ˈbɑːr.i.oʊ, ˈber-, ˈbær- **-s** -z
barrister ˈbær.ɪ.stəʳ ⓤⓢ ˈber.ɪ.stɚ, ˈbær- **-s** -z
barrister-at-law ˌbær.ɪ.stəʳ.ətˈlɔː ⓤⓢ ˌber.ə.stɚ.ətˈlɑː, ˌbær-, -ˈlɔː
barristers-at-law ˌbær.ɪ.stəz.ətˈlɔː ⓤⓢ ˌber.ə.stɚz.ətˈlɑː, ˌbær-, -ˈlɔː
barristerial ˌbær.ɪˈstɪə.ri.əl ⓤⓢ ˌber.əˈstɪr.i-, ˌbær-
Barron ˈbær.ən ⓤⓢ ˈber-, ˈbær-
barroom ˈbɑː.rʊm, -ruːm ⓤⓢ ˈbɑːr.ruːm, -rʊm **-s** -z
barrow (B) ˈbær.əʊ ⓤⓢ ˈber.oʊ, ˈbær- **-s** -z
Barrow-in-Furness ˌbær.əʊ.ɪnˈfɜː.nɪs, -nes, -nəs ⓤⓢ ˌber.oʊ.ɪnˈfɝː-, ˌbær-
Barry ˈbær.i ⓤⓢ ˈber-, ˈbær-
Barrymore ˈbær.ɪ.mɔːʳ ⓤⓢ ˈber.ɪ.mɔːr, ˈbær-
Barset ˈbɑː.sɪt, -set, -sət ⓤⓢ ˈbɑːr- **-shire** -ʃəʳ, -ˌʃɪəʳ ⓤⓢ -ʃɚ, -ˌʃɪr
barstool ˈbɑː.stuːl ⓤⓢ ˈbɑːr- **-s** -z
Barstow ˈbɑː.stəʊ ⓤⓢ ˈbɑːr.stoʊ
bart (B) bɑːt ⓤⓢ bɑːrt **-s** -s
bartend ˈbɑː.tend ⓤⓢ ˈbɑːr- **-s** -z **-ing** -ɪŋ **-ed** -ɪd
bartender ˈbɑːˌten.dəʳ ⓤⓢ ˈbɑːrˌten.dɚ **-s** -z
bart|er (B) ˈbɑː.t|əʳ ⓤⓢ ˈbɑːr.t̬|ɚ **-ers** -əz ⓤⓢ -ɚz **-ering** -ər.ɪŋ **-ered** -əd ⓤⓢ -ɚd
Barth bɑːθ ⓤⓢ bɑːrθ
Barthelme ˈbɑː.təl.meɪ ⓤⓢ ˈbɑːr.t̬əl-
Barthes bɑːt ⓤⓢ bɑːrt
Bartholomew bɑːˈθɒl.ə.mjuː, bəˈ- ⓤⓢ bɑːrˈθɑː.lə-, bɚ-
Bartle ˈbɑː.tl̩ ⓤⓢ ˈbɑːr.t̬l̩
Bartleby ˈbɑː.tl̩.bi ⓤⓢ ˈbɑːr.t̬l̩-
Bartlett ˈbɑːt.lət, -lɪt ⓤⓢ ˈbɑːrt-
Bartók ˈbɑː.tɒk ⓤⓢ ˈbɑːr.tɑːk
Bartoli bɑːˈtəʊ.li ⓤⓢ barˈtoʊ.li
Bartolommeo ˌbɑː.tɒl.əˈmeɪ.əʊ ⓤⓢ bɑːrˌtɑː.ləˈmeɪ.oʊ
Bartolozzi ˌbɑː.təˈlɒt.si ⓤⓢ ˌbɑːr.t̬əˈlɑːt-
Barton ˈbɑː.tən ⓤⓢ ˈbɑːr-
Bartram ˈbɑː.trəm ⓤⓢ ˈbɑːr-
Bart's bɑːts ⓤⓢ bɑːrts
bartsia ˈbɑːt.si.ə ⓤⓢ ˈbɑːrt-
Baruch *biblical name:* ˈbɑː.rʊk, ˈbeə-, -rək ⓤⓢ bəˈruːk; ˈbɑːr.uːk, ˈber- *modern surname:* bəˈruːk
Barugh bɑːf ⓤⓢ bɑːrf
Barum ˈbeə.rəm ⓤⓢ ˈber.əm
Barwick *in the UK:* ˈbær.ɪk ⓤⓢ ˈber.ɪk, ˈbær- *in the US:* ˈbɑː.wɪk; ˈbær.ɪk ⓤⓢ ˈbɑːr.wɪk
Baryshnikov bəˈrɪʃ.nɪ.kɒf, bærˈɪʃ-, -kəf ⓤⓢ bəˈrɪʃ.nɪ.kɔːf, bɑːˈ-, -kɑːf
barysphere ˈbær.ɪ.sfɪəʳ ⓤⓢ ˈber.ɪ.sfɪr, ˈbær- **-s** -z
barytone ˈbar.ɪ.təʊn ⓤⓢ ˈber.ə.toʊn, ˈbær- **-s** -z
basal ˈbeɪ.səl
basalt ˈbæs.ɔːlt; -əlt; bəˈsɔːlt, -ˈsɒlt ⓤⓢ bəˈsɔːlt, -ˈsɑːlt; ˈbeɪ.sɔːlt, -sɑːlt
basaltic bəˈsɔːl.tɪk, -ˈsɒl- ⓤⓢ bəˈsɔːl.t̬ɪk, -ˈsɑːl-
Basan ˈbeɪ.sæn
bascule ˈbæs.kjuːl **-s** -z
bas|e beɪs **-es** -ɪz **-er** -əʳ ⓤⓢ -ɚ **-est** -ɪst, -əst **-ely** -li **-eness** -nəs, -nɪs **-ing** -ɪŋ **-ed** -t ˌ**base** ˈ**metal**; ˈ**base** ˌ**rate**
baseball ˈbeɪs.bɔːl ⓤⓢ -bɔːl, -bɑːl ˈ**baseball** ˌ**bat**; ˈ**baseball** ˌ**cap**

baseboard 'beɪs.bɔːd US -bɔːrd **-s** -z
baseborn 'beɪs.bɔːn US -bɔːrn
Baseden 'beɪz.dən
Basel 'bɑː.zᵊl
baseless 'beɪs.ləs, -lɪs **-ly** -li **-ness** -nəs, -nɪs
baseline 'beɪs.laɪn **-s** -z
base|man 'beɪs|.mən, -mæn **-men** -mən, -men
basement 'beɪs.mənt **-s** -s
bases *(plur. of* **base***)* 'beɪ.sɪz *(plur. of* **basis***)* 'beɪ.siːz
Basford *in Nottinghamshire:* 'beɪs.fəd US -fɚd *in Staffordshire:* 'bæs.fəd US -fɚd
bash bæʃ **-es** -ɪz **-ing** -ɪŋ **-ed** -t
Basham 'bæʃ.əm
Bashan 'beɪ.ʃæn
Bashford 'bæʃ.fəd US -fɚd
bashful 'bæʃ.fᵊl, -fʊl **-lest** -ɪst, -əst **-ly** -i **-ness** -nəs, -nɪs
basho 'bæʃ.əʊ US bɑː'ʃoʊ **-s** US -z
basic (B) 'beɪ.sɪk **-s** -s **-ally** -ᵊl.i, -li
BASIC, Basic 'beɪ.sɪk
basicity bə'sɪs.ə.ti, -ɪ.ti US -ə.t̬i
Basie 'beɪ.si, -zi
basil (B) 'bæz.ᵊl, -ɪl US 'beɪ.zᵊl, -sᵊl; 'bæz.ᵊl
basilar 'bæz.ɪ.ləʳ, 'bæs-, -ᵊl.əʳ US -ɪ.lɚ, -ᵊl.ɚ ˌ**basilar 'membrane**
Basildon 'bæz.ᵊl.dən
basilect 'bæz.ɪ.lekt, '-ə- US 'bæz.ə-, 'beɪ.sə- **-s** -s **-al** -ᵊl
basilic|a bə'zɪl.ɪ.k|ə, -'sɪl- US -'sɪl- **-as** -əz **-an** -ən
basilisk 'bæz.ə.lɪsk, '-ɪ- US 'bæs-, 'bæz- **-s** -s
basin 'beɪ.sᵊn **-s** -z
basinet 'bæs.ɪ.net; '-ə-; -nɪt; ˌbæs.ɪ'net **-s** -s
Basinger 'beɪ.sɪŋ.gəʳ, 'bæs.ɪn.dʒəʳ US 'beɪ.sɪŋ.gɚ, 'bæs.ɪn.dʒɚ
Basingstoke 'beɪ.zɪŋ.stəʊk US -stoʊk
bas|is 'beɪ.s|ɪs **-es** -iːz
bask bɑːsk US bæsk **-s** -s **-ing** -ɪŋ **-ed** -t
Basker 'bɑː.skəʳ US 'bæs.kɚ
Baskervill(e) 'bæs.kə.vɪl US -kɚ-
basket 'bɑː.skɪt US 'bæs.kət **-s** -s **-ful/s** -fʊl/z **'basket ˌcase; put all one's ˌeggs in one 'basket**
basketball 'bɑː.skɪt.bɔːl US 'bæs.kət.bɔːl, -bɑːl
basketry 'bɑː.skɪ.tri US 'bæs.kə-
basketwork 'bɑː.skɪt.wɜːk US 'bæs.kət.wɝːk
Baskin-Robbins® ˌbæs.kɪn'rɒb.ɪnz US -'rɑː.bɪnz
Basle bɑːl
basmati bə'smɑː.ti, bæs'mɑː-, bəz-, bæz-
bas mi(t)zvah ˌbæs'mɪts.və US ˌbɑːs- **-ing** -ɪŋ **-ed** -d
Basnett 'bæz.nɪt, -nət, -net
Basotho bə'suː.tuː, -'səʊ.təʊ US -'soʊ.toʊ
basque (B) bæsk, bɑːsk US bæsk **-s** -s
Basra(h) 'bæz.rə, 'bʌz-, 'bæs- US 'bɑːz.rə, 'bæs-, 'bæz-, 'bɑːs-
bas-relief ˌbɑː.rɪ'liːf, ˌbæs-, ˌbɑːs-, -rə'liːf **-s** -s
bass (B) *fish, fibre, beer:* bæs
bass *in music:* beɪs **-es** -ɪz ˌ**bass clari'net**; ˌ**bass 'clef**; ˌ**bass 'drum**; ˌ**bass gui'tar**
Bassanio bə'sɑː.ni.əʊ, bæs'ɑː- US -oʊ
Bassenthwaite 'bæs.ᵊn.θweɪt
basset 'bæs.ɪt US -ət **-s** -s **'basset ˌhorn; 'basset ˌhound**
Basseterre bæs'teəʳ US -'ter
Basset(t) 'bæs.ɪt US -ət
Bassey 'bæs.i
bassinet(te) ˌbæs.ɪ'net, -ə'- **-s** -s
Bassingbourne 'bæs.ɪŋ.bɔːn US -bɔːrn
bassist 'beɪ.sɪst **-s** -s
bass|o 'bæs|.əʊ US -oʊ, 'bɑː.s|oʊ **-os** -z **-i** -iː
bassoon bə'suːn **-s** -z **-ist/s** -ɪst/s
basswood 'bæs.wʊd
bast (B) bæst
Bastable 'bæs.tə.bl̩
bastard 'bɑː.stəd, 'bæs.təd US 'bæs.tɚd **-s** -z **-y** -i
bastardiz|e, -is|e 'bɑː.stə.daɪz, 'bæs.tə- US 'bæs.tɚ- **-es** -ɪz **-ing** -ɪŋ **-ed** -d
bast|e beɪst **-es** -s **-ing** -ɪŋ **-ed** -ɪd
bastille (B) bæs'tiːl **-s** -z
bastinado ˌbæs.tɪ'nɑː.dəʊ, -'neɪ- US -doʊ **-es** -z **-ing** -ɪŋ **-ed** -d
bastion 'bæs.ti.ən US '-tʃən, '-ti.ən **-s** -z **-ed** -d
Basuto bə'suː.təʊ, -'zuː- US -toʊ **-s** -z
Basutoland bə'suː.təʊ.lænd, -'zuː- US -toʊ-
bat bæt **-s** -s **-ting** -ɪŋ US 'bæt̬.ɪŋ **-ted** -ɪd US 'bæt̬.ɪd
Ba'taan bə'tɑːn US -'tæn, -'tɑːn
Batavia bə'teɪ.vi.ə
batboy 'bæt.bɔɪ **-s** -z
batch bætʃ **-es** -ɪz
Batchelar, Batchelor 'bætʃ.ᵊl.əʳ, -ɪ.ləʳ US -ᵊl.ɚ
bat|e (B) beɪt **-es** -s **-ing** -ɪŋ US 'beɪ.t̬ɪŋ **-ed** -ɪd US 'beɪ.t̬ɪd
Bateman 'beɪt.mən **-s** -s
Bates beɪts
Bateson 'beɪt.sᵊn
Batey 'beɪ.ti US -t̬i
ba|th (B) *(n.)* bɑː|θ US bæ|θ **-ths** -ðz ˌ**Bath 'bun, 'Bath ˌbun**; ˌ**bath 'chair**; **'bath ˌcube**; **'bath ˌmat**; **'bath ˌsalts**; **'Bath ˌstone**; ˌ**Bath 'Oliver**
bath *(v.)* bɑːθ US bæθ **-s** -s **-ing** -ɪŋ **-ed** -t
bath|e beɪð **-es** -z **-ing** -ɪŋ **-ed** -d **'bathing ˌcostume**; **'bathing ˌbeauty**; **'bathing ˌsuit**
bather 'beɪ.ðəʳ US -ðɚ **-s** -z
bathetic bə'θet.ɪk, bæθ'et- US bə'θet̬-
Bathgate 'bɑːθ.geɪt US 'bæθ-
bathhou|se 'bɑːθ.haʊ|s US 'bæθ- **-ses** -zɪz
bathmat 'bɑːθ.mæt US 'bæθ- **-s** -s
Batho 'bæθ.əʊ, 'beɪ.θəʊ US 'bæθ.oʊ, 'beɪ.θoʊ
batholite 'bæθ.əʊ.laɪt US '-ə- **-s** -s
batholith 'bæθ.əʊ.lɪθ US '-ə- **-s** -s
bathors|e 'bæt.hɔːs US -hɔːrs **-es** -ɪz
bathos 'beɪ.θɒs US -θɑːs
bathrobe 'bɑːθ.rəʊb US 'bæθ.roʊb **-s** -z
bathroom 'bɑːθ.rʊm, -ruːm US 'bæθ.ruːm, -rʊm **-s** -z
Bathsheba 'bæθ.ʃɪ.bə; bæθ'ʃiː-
bathtub 'bɑːθ.tʌb US 'bæθ- **-s** -z
Bathurst 'bæθ.ɜːst, -əst, -hɜːst, 'bɑː.θɜːst, -θəst, 'bɑːθ.hɜːst US 'bæθ.ɝːst, -hɝːst
bathyscaphe 'bæθ.ɪ.skæf **-s** -s
bathysphere 'bæθ.ɪ.sfɪəʳ US -sfɪr **-s** -z
batik bæt'iːk; 'bæt.ɪk US bə'tiːk; 'bæt̬.ɪk
batiste bæt'iːst, bə'tiːst
Batley 'bæt.li
bat|man *military:* 'bæt|.mən **-men** -mən
batman *oriental weight:* 'bæt.mən **-s** -z
Batman® 'bæt.mæn
baton 'bæt.ɒn; -ᵊn US bə'tɑːn **-s** -z
Baton Rouge ˌbæt.ᵊn'ruːʒ
bats bæts
bats|man 'bæts|.mən **-men** -mən
battalion bə'tæl.i.ən, '-jən US '-jən **-s** -z
Battambang 'bæt.əm.bæŋ US 'bæt̬-
battels 'bæt.ᵊlz US 'bæt̬-
batten (B) 'bæt.ᵊn **-s** -z **-ing** -ɪŋ **-ed** -d
Battenberg 'bæt.ᵊn.bɜːg, -ᵊm- US -ᵊn.bɝːg **'Battenberg ˌcake**
batt|er 'bæt|.əʳ US 'bæt̬|.ɚ **-ers** -əz US -ɚz **-ering** -ᵊr.ɪŋ **-ered** -əd US -ɚd **'battering ˌram**
Battersby 'bæt.əz.bi US 'bæt̬.ɚz-
Battersea 'bæt.ə.si US 'bæt̬.ɚ-
batter|y 'bæt.ᵊr|.i US 'bæt̬- **-ies** -iz **'battery ˌacid**
batting *(n.)* 'bæt.ɪŋ US 'bæt̬.ɪŋ **'batting ˌaverage; 'batting ˌorder**
Battishill 'bæt.ɪ.ʃɪl, -ʃᵊl US 'bæt̬-
battl|e (B) 'bæt.l̩ US 'bæt̬- **-es** -z **-ing** -ɪŋ, 'bæt.lɪŋ **-ed** -d **-er/s** -əʳ/z, '-ləʳ/z US '-l̩.ɚ/z, '-lɚ/z **'battle ˌcry; ˌBattle of 'Britain; ˌbattle 'royal; 'battle ˌstations**
battleax|e, battle-ax 'bæt.l̩.æks US 'bæt̬- **-es** -ɪz
battledore, battledoor 'bæt.l̩.dɔːʳ US 'bæt̬.l̩.dɔːr **-s** -z
battledress 'bæt.l̩.dres
battlefield 'bæt.l̩.fiːld US 'bæt̬- **-s** -z

battleground 'bæt.l̩.graʊnd **-s** -z
battlement 'bæt.l̩.mənt ⓤⓢ 'bæţ- **-s** -s **-ed** -ɪd ⓤⓢ -mən.ţɪd
battleship 'bæt.l̩.ʃɪp ⓤⓢ 'bæţ- **-s** -s
battue bæt'uː, -'juː **-s** -z
batt|y 'bæt.|i ⓤⓢ 'bæţ- **-ier** -i.əʳ ⓤⓢ -i.ɚ **-iest** -i.ɪst, -i.əst
Battye 'bæt.i ⓤⓢ 'bæţ-
Batumi bɑː'tuː.mi
batwing 'bæt.wɪŋ ˌ**batwing** '**sleeve**
bauble 'bɔː.bl̩ ⓤⓢ 'bɑː-, 'bɔː- **-s** -z
Baucis 'bɔː.sɪs ⓤⓢ 'bɑː-, 'bɔː
Baudelaire 'bəʊ.də.leəʳ, ˌ--'- ⓤⓢ ˌboʊ.də'ler, ˌboʊd'ler
Baudouin 'bəʊ.dwæ̃n ⓤⓢ boʊ'dwɑːn
Bauer baʊəʳ ⓤⓢ baʊɚ
Baugh bɔː ⓤⓢ bɑː, bɔː
Baughan bɔːn ⓤⓢ bɑːn, bɔːn
Bauhaus 'baʊ.haʊs
baulk bɔːk, bɔːlk ⓤⓢ bɑːk, bɔːk **-s** -s **-ing** -ɪŋ **-ed** -t
Baum *US name:* bɔːm ⓤⓢ bɑːm, bɔːm *German name:* baʊm
bauxite 'bɔːk.saɪt ⓤⓢ 'bɑːk-, 'bɔːk-
Bavari|a bə'veə.ri|.ə ⓤⓢ -'ver.i- **-an/s** -ən/z
bawbee bɔː'biː, '-- ⓤⓢ 'bɑː.biː, 'bɔː-, -'- **-s** -z
bawd bɔːd ⓤⓢ bɑːd, bɔːd **-s** -z **-ry** -ri
Bawden 'bɔː.dᵊn ⓤⓢ 'bɑː-, 'bɔː-
bawd|y 'bɔː.d|i ⓤⓢ 'bɑː-, 'bɔː- **-ier** -i.əʳ ⓤⓢ -i.ɚ **-iest** -i.ɪst, -i.əst **-ily** -ɪ.li, -ᵊl.i **-iness** -ɪ.nəs, -ɪ.nɪs '**bawdy** ˌ**house**
bawl bɔːl ⓤⓢ bɑːl, bɔːl **-s** -z **-ing** -ɪŋ **-ed** -d **-er/s** -əʳ/z ⓤⓢ -ɚ/z
Bax bæks
Baxandall 'bæk.sᵊn.dɔːl ⓤⓢ -dɔːl, -dɑːl
Baxter 'bæk.stəʳ ⓤⓢ -stɚ
bay **(B)** beɪ **-s** -z **-ing** -ɪŋ **-ed** -d '**bay** ˌ**leaf**; ˌ**Bay of** '**Pigs**; '**bay** ˌ**tree**; ˌ**bay** '**window**
bayard **(B)** *horse:* beɪəd ⓤⓢ beɪɚd **-s** -z
Bayard *surname:* 'beɪ.ɑːd ⓤⓢ -ɑːrd
Bayard *airship:* 'beɪ.ɑːd, -'-; beɪəd ⓤⓢ beɪɚd; 'beɪ.ɑːrd **-s** -z
bayberr|y 'beɪ.bᵊr|.i ⓤⓢ -ˌber- **-ies** -iz
Bayer® 'beɪ.əʳ ⓤⓢ -ɚ, ber
Bayeux baɪ'jɜː, beɪ- ⓤⓢ 'beɪ.juː, 'baɪ- *stress shift, British only: see compound:* ˌ**Bayeux** '**Tapestry**
Bayley 'beɪ.li
Bayliss 'beɪ.lɪs
Bayly 'beɪ.li
Baynes beɪnz
Baynham 'beɪ.nəm
Baynton 'beɪn.tən ⓤⓢ -tᵊn
bayone|t 'beɪ.ə.nə|t, -nɪ|t, -ne|t; ˌbeɪ.ə'ne|t ⓤⓢ ˌbeɪ.ə'ne|t, '---- **-ts** -ts **-t(t)ing** -tɪŋ ⓤⓢ -ţɪŋ **-t(t)ed** -tɪd ⓤⓢ -ţɪd
Bayonne *in France:* baɪ'ɒn ⓤⓢ beɪ'oʊn, -'ɑːn, -'ɔːn *in New Jersey, U.S.A.:* beɪ'əʊn ⓤⓢ -'oʊn, -'joʊn
bayou 'baɪ.uː, -əʊ ⓤⓢ -*j*uː, -*j*oʊ **-s** -z
Bayreuth baɪ'rɔɪt, '--
bay-rum ˌbeɪ'rʌm
bay-salt ˌbeɪsɔːlt, -sɒlt ⓤⓢ
Bayston Hill ˌbeɪ.stᵊn'hɪl
Bayswater 'beɪzˌwɔː.təʳ ⓤⓢ -ˌwɑː.ţɚ, -ˌwɔː-
bazaar bə'zɑːʳ ⓤⓢ -'zɑːr **-s** -z
Bazalgette 'bæz.ᵊl.dʒɪt, -dʒet
bazooka bə'zuː.kə **-s** -z
BBC ˌbiː.biː'siː
BC biː'siː
BCG ˌbiː.siː'dʒiː
bdellium 'del.i.əm, bə'del-
be- bɪ-, bə-
Note: Prefix. Words containing **be-** are always stressed on the second syllable, e.g. **friend** /frend/, **befriend** /bɪ'frend/.
be *strong form:* biː *weak forms:* bi, bɪ **being** 'biː.ɪŋ **been** biːn, bɪn ⓤⓢ bɪn
Note: Weak form word. The strong form /biː/ is used contrastively, e.g. "the **be** all and **end** all" and in sentence-final position, e.g. "What'll it be?". The weak form is /bɪ/ before consonants, e.g. "We'll be going" /ˌwil.bɪ'gəʊ.ɪŋ ⓤⓢ -'goʊ-/; before vowels it is /bi/, e.g. "It'll be opening soon" /ˌɪt.l̩.bi'əʊ.pᵊn.ɪŋˌsuːn ⓤⓢ -'oʊ-/. See note at **been** for further weak form information.
Bea biː
beach **(B)** biːtʃ ⓤⓢ **-es** -ɪz **-ing** -ɪŋ **-ed** -t '**beach** ˌ**ball**; '**beach** ˌ**bum**
beachchair 'biːtʃ.tʃeəʳ ⓤⓢ -tʃer **-s** -z
beachcomber **(B)** 'biːtʃˌkəʊ.məʳ ⓤⓢ -ˌkoʊ.mɚ **-s** -z
beachfront 'biːtʃ.frʌnt **-s** -s
beachhead 'biːtʃ.hed **-s** -z
beach-la-mar, **Beach-la-Mar** ˌbiːtʃ.lə'mɑːʳ ⓤⓢ -'mɑːr
beachwear 'biːtʃ.weəʳ ⓤⓢ -wer
beachy **(B)** 'biː.tʃi ˌ**Beachy** '**Head**
beacon 'biː.kᵊn **-s** -z
Beaconsfield *place in Buckinghamshire:* 'bek.ᵊnz.fiːld *title of Benjamin Disraeli:* 'biː.kᵊnz.fiːld
bead biːd **-s** -z **-ing/s** -ɪŋ/z **-ed** -ɪd **-er/s** -əʳ/z ⓤⓢ -ɚ/z
beadle **(B)** 'biː.dl̩ **-s** -z
Beadon 'biː.dᵊn
beadwork 'biːd.wɜːk ⓤⓢ -wɝːk
bead|y 'biː.d|i **-ier** -i.əʳ ⓤⓢ -i.ɚ **-iest** -i.ɪst, -i.əst **-iness** -ɪ.nɪs, -ɪ.nəs
beagle 'biː.gl̩ **-s** -z
beak biːk **-s** -s **-ed** -t
beaker 'biː.kəʳ ⓤⓢ -kɚ **-s** -z
Beal(e) biːl
beam biːm **-s** -z **-ing** -ɪŋ **-ed** -d '**beam** ˌ**engine**
beam-ends ˌbiːm'endz, '--
Beaminster 'bem.ɪn*t*.stəʳ *locally also:* 'bem.ɪ.stəʳ ⓤⓢ -stɚ
Note: /'biː.mɪn*t*-/ is sometimes heard from people unfamiliar with the place.
Beamish 'biː.mɪʃ
beam|y 'biː.m|i **-ily** -ɪ.li, -ᵊl.i **-iness** -ɪ.nɪs, -ɪ.nəs
bean biːn **-s** -z ˌ**full of** '**beans**; ˌ**spill the** '**beans**
beanbag 'biːn.bæg, 'biːm- ⓤⓢ 'biːn- **-s** -z
beanfeast 'biːn.fiːst **-s** -s **-er/s** -əʳ/z ⓤⓢ -ɚ/z
beanie 'biː.ni **-s** -z
beano **(B)** 'biː.nəʊ ⓤⓢ -noʊ **-s** -z
beanpole 'biːn.pəʊl, 'biːm- ⓤⓢ 'biːn.poʊl **-s** -z
beanshoot 'biːn.ʃuːt **-s** -s
beansprout 'biːn.spraʊt **-s** -s
beanstalk 'biːn.stɔːk ⓤⓢ -stɔːk, -stɑːk **-s** -s
bear beəʳ ⓤⓢ ber **-s** -z **-ing/s** -ɪŋ/z **bore** bɔːʳ ⓤⓢ bɔːr **borne** bɔːn ⓤⓢ bɔːrn '**bear** ˌ**garden**
bearab|le 'beə.rə.b|l̩ ⓤⓢ 'ber.ə- **-ly** -li **-leness** -l̩.nəs, -l̩.nɪs
bear-baiting 'beəˌbeɪ.tɪŋ ⓤⓢ 'berˌbeɪ.ţɪŋ
beard **(B)** bɪəd ⓤⓢ bɪrd **-s** -z **-ing** -ɪŋ **-ed** -ɪd
Bearder 'bɪə.dəʳ ⓤⓢ 'bɪr.dɚ
beardless 'bɪəd.ləs, -lɪs ⓤⓢ 'bɪrd-
Beardsley 'bɪədz.li ⓤⓢ 'bɪrdz-
Beare bɪəʳ ⓤⓢ bɪr
bearer 'beə.rəʳ ⓤⓢ 'ber.ɚ **-s** -z
bearhug 'beə.hʌg ⓤⓢ 'ber- **-s** -z
bearing *(n.)* 'beə.rɪŋ ⓤⓢ 'ber.ɪŋ **-s** -z
bearing rein 'beə.rɪŋ.reɪn ⓤⓢ 'ber.ɪŋ- **-s** -z
bearish 'beə.rɪʃ ⓤⓢ 'ber.ɪʃ **-ly** -li **-ness** -nəs, -nɪs
béarnaise **(B)** ˌbeɪə'neɪz, -'nez ⓤⓢ ˌber'neɪz, ˌbeɪ.ɑːr'-, ˌbeɪɚ'-
Bearsden beəz'den ⓤⓢ berz-
bearskin 'beə.skɪn ⓤⓢ 'ber- **-s** -z
Bearsted 'bɜː.sted, 'beə.sted ⓤⓢ 'bɝː-, 'ber-
Beasant 'beɪ.zᵊnt
Beasley 'biːz.li
beast biːst **-s** -s ˌ**beast of** '**burden**
beastie 'biː.sti **-s** -z
beastings 'biː.stɪŋz
beastl|y 'biː*st*.l|i **-ier** -i.əʳ ⓤⓢ -i.ɚ **-iest** -i.ɪst, -i.əst **-iness** -ɪ.nəs, -i.nɪs
beat biːt **-s** -s **-ing/s** -ɪŋ/z ⓤⓢ 'biː.ţɪŋ/z **-en** -ᵊn ⓤⓢ 'biː.ţᵊn **-er/s** -əʳ/z ⓤⓢ 'biː.ţɚ/z ˌ**beat about the** '**bush**; '**Beat Gene**ˌ**ration**
beatific ˌbiː.ə'tɪf.ɪk **-al** -ᵊl **-ally** -ᵊl.i, -li
beatification biˌæt.ɪ.fɪ'keɪ.ʃᵊn, ˌ-ə- ⓤⓢ -ˌæţ.ə- **-s** -z

beatif|y biˈæt.ɪ.f|aɪ, ˈ-ə- (US) -ˈæt̬.ə- **-ies** -aɪz **-ying** -aɪ.ɪŋ **-ied** -aɪd
beatitude (B) biˈæt.ɪ.tjuːd, ˈ-ə-, -tʃuːd (US) -ˈæt̬.ə.tuːd, -tjuːd **-s** -z
Beatles ˈbiː.tl̩z (US) -t̬l̩z
beatnik ˈbiːt.nɪk **-s** -s
Beaton ˈbiː.tᵊn (US) -t̬ᵊn
Beatrice ˈbɪə.trɪs (US) ˈbiː.ə-
Beatrix ˈbɪə.trɪks (US) ˈbiː.ə-
Beattie ˈbiː.ti (US) -t̬i, ˈbeɪ-
Beattock ˈbiː.tək (US) -t̬ək
Beatty ˈbiː.ti (US) ˈbeɪ.t̬i, ˈbiː-
beat-up ˌbiːtˈʌp
beau (B) bəʊ (US) boʊ **-s** -z ˌ**Beau** ˈ**Brummell**
Beauchamp ˈbiː.tʃəm
Beauclerc(k) ˈbəʊ.kleəʳ (US) ˈboʊ.kler, -klɝːk
Beaufort *in South Carolina:* ˈbjuː.fət, -fɔːt (US) ˈbjuː.fɚt *other senses:* ˈbəʊ.fət, -fɔːt (US) ˈboʊ.fɚt
beau(x) geste(s) ˌbəʊˈʒest (US) ˌboʊ-
Beauharnais ˌbəʊ.ɑːˈneɪ (US) ˌboʊ.ɑːrˈ-
Beaujolais ˈbəʊ.ʒᵊl.eɪ, -ʒɒl.eɪ (US) ˌboʊ.ʒəˈleɪ
Beaujolais nouveau ˌbəʊ.ʒə.leɪ.nuːˈvəʊ, -ʒɒl.eɪ- (US) ˌboʊ.ʒə.leɪ.nuːˈvoʊ
Beaulieu *in Hampshire:* ˈbjuː.li *US family name:* ˈbəʊ.juː (US) ˈboʊ-, ˈboʊl- *in France:* bəʊˈljɜː (US) boʊ-
Beaumarchais ˈbəʊ.mɑːˌʃeɪ, ˌ--ˈ- (US) ˌboʊ.mɑːrˈʃeɪ
Beaumaris bəʊˈmær.ɪs, bjuː- (US) boʊˈmer-, -ˈmær-
beau(x) monde(s) bəʊˈmɒnd (US) ˌboʊˈmɑːnd
Beaumont ˈbəʊ.mənt, -mɒnt (US) ˈboʊ-, -mɑːnt
Beaune bəʊn (US) boʊn
Beauregard ˈbəʊ.rɪ.gɑːd (US) ˈboʊ.rə.gɑːrd
beaut bjuːt **-s** -s
beauteous ˈbjuː.ti.əs (US) -t̬i- **-ly** -li **-ness** -nəs, -nɪs
beautician bjuːˈtɪʃ.ᵊn **-s** -z
beautification ˌbjuː.tɪ.fɪˈkeɪ.ʃᵊn, -tə- (US) -t̬ə-
beautiful ˈbjuː.tɪ.fᵊl, -tə-, -fʊl (US) -t̬ə- **-ly** -i
beautif|y ˈbjuː.tɪ.f|aɪ, -tə- (US) -t̬ə- **-ies** -aɪz **-ying** -aɪ.ɪŋ **-ied** -aɪd **-ier/s** -aɪ.əʳ/z (US) -aɪ.ɚ/z
beaut|y ˈbjuː.t|i (US) -t̬|i **-ies** -iz ˈ**beauty** ˌ**contest**; ˈ**beauty** ˌ**mark**; ˈ**beauty** ˌ**parlo(u)r**; ˈ**beauty** ˌ**sleep**; ˈ**beauty** ˌ**spot**
Beauvoir ˈbəʊv.wɑː (US) boʊvˈwɑːr
beaux-arts bəʊˈzɑːʳ (US) boʊˈzɑːr
Beaux' Stratagem ˌbəʊzˈstræt.ə.dʒəm (US) ˌboʊzˈstræt̬-
Beavan, Beaven ˈbev.ᵊn
beaver (B) ˈbiː.vəʳ (US) -vɚ **-s** -z
Beaverbrook ˈbiː.və.brʊk (US) -vɚ-
beaver|y ˈbiː.vᵊr|.i **-ies** -iz
Beavis ˈbiː.vɪs
Beazley ˈbiːz.li
Bebb beb
Bebington ˈbeb.ɪŋ.tən
bebop ˈbiː.bɒp (US) -bɑːp **-per/s** -əʳ/z (US) -ɚ/z
becalm bɪˈkɑːm, bə- **-s** -z **-ing** -ɪŋ **-ed** -d
became *(from* **become***)* bɪˈkeɪm, bə-
because bɪˈkɒz, bə-, -ˈkəz *colloquially also:* kɒz, kəz (US) bɪˈkɑːz, bə-, -ˈkʌz, -ˈkəz, kəz
Note: The form /bɪˈkəz/ or /bə-/ is unusual in having a stressed schwa vowel. This is found only in a few phrases, most commonly in "because of the/a ..." The pronunciation /kəz/ (also /kɒz/ in British English) is often spelt **'cos**.
Beccles ˈbek.l̩z
bechamel, béchamel ˌbeɪ.ʃəˈmel, ˌbeʃ.əˈ- *stress shift:* ˌbechamel ˈsauce
Becher ˈbiː.tʃəʳ (US) -tʃɚ
Bechstein ˈbek.staɪn **-s** -z
Bechuana ˌbetʃ.uˈɑː.nə **-s** -z **-land** -lænd
beck (B) bek **-s** -s ˌ**beck and** ˈ**call**
Becke bek
Beckenbauer ˈbek.ᵊn.baʊəʳ (US) -baʊɚ
Beckenham ˈbek.ᵊn.əm
Becker ˈbek.əʳ (US) -ɚ
Becket(t) ˈbek.ɪt
Beckford ˈbek.fəd (US) -fɚd
Beckham ˈbek.əm
Beckinsale ˈbek.ɪn.seɪl
Beckles ˈbek.l̩z
Beckley ˈbek.li
beckon ˈbek.ᵊn **-s** -z **-ing** -ɪŋ **-ed** -d
Beckton ˈbek.tən
Beckwith ˈbek.wɪθ
Becky ˈbek.i
becloud bɪˈklaʊd, bə- **-s** -z **-ing** -ɪŋ **-ed** -ɪd
becom|e bɪˈkʌm, bə- **-es** -z **-ing** -ɪŋ **became** bɪˈkeɪm, bə-
becoming bɪˈkʌm.ɪŋ, bəˈ- **-ly** -li **-ness** -nəs, -nɪs
Becontree ˈbek.ən.triː
becquerel (B) ˌbek.əˈrel; ˈbek.ə.rel, -rᵊl **-s** -z
bed bed **-s** -z **-ding** -ɪŋ **-ded** -ɪd ˈ**bed** ˌ**rest**; ˌ**bed and** ˈ**breakfast**; ˌ**get out of** ˌ**bed on the** ˌ**wrong** ˈ**side**
BEd biːˈed
bedad bɪˈdæd, bə-
Bedale ˈbiː.dᵊl, -deɪl
Bedales ˈbiː.deɪlz
bedaub bɪˈdɔːb, bə- (US) -ˈdɑːb, -ˈdɔːb **-s** -z **-ing** -ɪŋ **-ed** -d
bedazzl|e bɪˈdæz.l̩, bə- **-es** -z **-ing** -ɪŋ **-ed** -d
bedbug ˈbed.bʌg **-s** -z
bedchamber ˈbedˌtʃeɪm.bəʳ (US) -bɚ **-s** -z
bedclothes ˈbed.kləʊðz, -kləʊz (US) -kloʊðz, -kloʊz
Beddau ˈbeð.aɪ
bedder ˈbed.əʳ (US) -ɚ **-s** -z
Beddgelert beðˈgel.ət, bed-, beɪð-, -ɜːt (US) -ɚt
bedding *(n.)* ˈbed.ɪŋ
Beddoes ˈbed.əʊz (US) -oʊz
beddy-bye ˈbed.i.baɪ **-s** -z
Bede biːd
bedeck bɪˈdek, bə- **-s** -s **-ing** -ɪŋ **-ed** -t
Bedel ˈbiː.dᵊl; bɪˈdel, bə-
bedel(l) bedˈel, bɪˈdel, bə- **-s** -z
Bedevere ˈbed.ɪ.vɪəʳ, ˈ-ə- (US) -ə.vɪr
bedevil bɪˈdev.ᵊl, bə- **-s** -z **-(l)ing** -ɪŋ **-(l)ed** -d
bedevilment bɪˈdev.ᵊl.mənt, bə-
bedew bɪˈdjuː, bə- (US) -ˈduː, -ˈdjuː **-s** -z **-ing** -ɪŋ **-ed** -d
bedfellow ˈbedˌfel.əʊ (US) -oʊ **-s** -z
Bedford ˈbed.fəd (US) -fɚd **-shire** -ʃəʳ, -ˌʃɪəʳ (US) -ʃɚ, -ˌʃɪr
bedim bɪˈdɪm, bə- **-s** -z **-ming** -ɪŋ **-med** -d
Bedivere ˈbed.ɪ.vɪəʳ, ˈ-ə- (US) -ə.vɪr
bedizen bɪˈdaɪ.zᵊn, bə-, -ˈdɪz.ᵊn **-s** -z **-ing** -ɪŋ **-ed** -d
bedjacket ˈbedˌdʒæk.ɪt **-s** -s
bedlam (B) ˈbed.ləm
Bedlamite ˈbed.lə.maɪt **-s** -s
bedlinen ˈbedˌlɪn.ɪn, -ən (US) -ən
bedmaker ˈbedˌmeɪ.kəʳ (US) -kɚ **-s** -z
Bedouin ˈbed.u.ɪn **-s** -z
bedpan ˈbed.pæn **-s** -z
bedpost ˈbed.pəʊst (US) -poʊst **-s** -s
bedraggl|e bɪˈdræg.l̩, bə- **-es** -z **-ing** -ɪŋ **-ed** -d
bedridden ˈbedˌrɪd.ᵊn
bedrock ˈbed.rɒk (US) -rɑːk **-s** -s
bedroll ˈbed.rəʊl (US) -roʊl **-s** -z
bedroom ˈbed.rʊm, -ruːm (US) -ruːm, -rʊm **-s** -z
Beds. *(abbrev. for* **Bedfordshire***)* bedz; ˈbed.fəd.ʃəʳ, -ˌʃɪəʳ (US) bedz; ˈbed.fɚd.ʃɚ, -ˌʃɪr
bedside ˈbed.saɪd ˌ**bedside** ˈ**manner**; ˌ**bedside** ˈ**table**
bedsit ˈbed.sɪt **-s** -s
bedsitter bedˈsɪt.əʳ, ˈ-ˌ-- (US) bedˈsɪt̬.ɚ, ˈ-ˌ-- **-s** -z
bedsore ˈbed.sɔːʳ (US) -sɔːr **-s** -z
bedspread ˈbed.spred **-s** -z
bedstead ˈbed.sted **-s** -z
bedstraw ˈbed.strɔː (US) -strɑː, -strɔː **-s** -z
bedtime ˈbed.taɪm
Bedwas ˈbed.wæs

Bedwell 'bed.wel, -wəl
Bedworth 'bed.wəθ (US) -wɚθ
bee (B) biː **-s** -z **'bee ˌsting; have a 'bee in one's ˌbonnet; the ˌbee's 'knees**
Beeb biːb
Beeby 'biː.bi
beech (B) biːtʃ **-es** -ɪz **-en** -ᵊn
Beecham 'biː.tʃəm **ˌBeecham's 'Powders®**
Beecher 'biː.tʃəʳ (US) -tʃɚ
Beeching 'biː.tʃɪŋ
beechnut 'biːtʃ.nʌt **-s** -s
beechwood 'biːtʃ.wʊd
bee eater 'biːˌiː.təʳ (US) -t̬ɚ **-s** -z
beef *(n)* biːf **-s** -s **beeves** biːvz
beef *(v)* biːf **-s** -s **-ing** -ɪŋ **-ed** -t
beefalo 'biː.fᵊl.əʊ (US) -fə.loʊ **-(e)s** -z
beefburger 'biːfˌbɜː.gəʳ (US) -ˌbɝː.gɚ **-s** -z
beefcake 'biːf.keɪk **-s** -s
beefeater (B) 'biːfˌiː.təʳ (US) -t̬ɚ **-s** -z
beefsteak 'biːf.steɪk, -'- **-s** -s
beef|y 'biː.f|i **-ier** -i.əʳ (US) -i.ɚ **-iest** -i.ɪst, -i.əst **-ily** -ɪ.li, -ᵊl.i **-iness** -ɪ.nəs, -ɪ.nɪs
beehive 'biː.haɪv **-s** -z
bee-keep|ing 'biːˌkiː.p|ɪŋ **-er/s** -əʳ/z (US) -ɚ/z
beeline 'biː.laɪn **-s** -z
Beelzebub biː'el.zɪ.bʌb, -zə-
been *(from* **be***)* biːn, bɪn (US) bɪn
Note: Weak form word, British English. The pronunciation /bɪn/ may be used optionally as a weak form corresponding to /biːn/, e.g. “Jane's been invited” /'dʒeɪnz.bɪn.ɪnˌvaɪ.tɪd (US) -t̬ɪd/. In American English, /biːn/ does not usually occur.
beep biːp **-s** -s **-ing** -ɪŋ **-ed** -t
beeper 'biː.pəʳ (US) -pɚ **-s** -z
beer (B) bɪəʳ (US) bɪr **-s** -z **'beer ˌgarden; 'beer ˌmat**
Beerbohm 'bɪə.bəʊm (US) 'bɪr.boʊm
Beersheba bɪə'ʃiː.bə, 'bɪə.ʃɪ- (US) bɪr'ʃiː-, ber-
beer|y 'bɪə.r|i (US) 'bɪr|.i **-ier** -i.əʳ (US) -i.ɚ **-iest** -i.ɪst, -i.əst **-ily** -ɪ.li, -ᵊl.i **-iness** -ɪ.nəs, -ɪ.nɪs
Beesl(e)y 'biːz.li
beestings 'biː.stɪŋz
Beeston 'biː.stᵊn
beeswax 'biːz.wæks
beeswing 'biːz.wɪŋ
beet biːt **-s** -s
Beetham 'biː.θəm
Beethoven *composer:* 'beɪt.həʊ.vᵊn, 'beɪ.təʊ- (US) 'beɪ.toʊ- *London street:* 'biːt.həʊ.vᵊn, 'biː.təʊ- (US) 'biː.toʊ-
beetl|e 'biː.tl̩ (US) -t̬l̩ **-es** -z **-ing** -ɪŋ, 'biːt.lɪŋ **-ed** -d
Beeton 'biː.tᵊn
beetroot 'biːt.ruːt **-s** -s
beeves *(plur. of* **beef***)* biːvz
befall bɪ'fɔːl, bə- (US) -'fɔːl, -'fɑːl **-s** -z **-ing** -ɪŋ **-en** -ən
befell *(from* **befall***)* bɪ'fel, bə-
befit bɪ'fɪt, bə- **-s** -s **-ting/ly** -ɪŋ/li (US) -'fɪt̬.ɪŋ/li **-ted** -ɪd (US) -'fɪt̬.ɪd
before bɪ'fɔːʳ, bə- (US) -'fɔːr
beforehand bɪ'fɔː.hænd, bə- (US) -'fɔːr-
before-mentioned bɪ'fɔːˌmen.*t*ʃᵊnd, -ˌ-'-- (US) bə'fɔːrˌmen-
beforetime bɪ'fɔː.taɪm, bə- (US) -'fɔːr-
befoul bɪ'faʊl, bə- **-s** -z **-ing** -ɪŋ **-ed** -d
befriend bɪ'frend, bə- **-s** -z **-ing** -ɪŋ **-ed** -ɪd
befuddl|e bɪ'fʌd.l̩, bə- **-es** -z **-ing** -ɪŋ, -'fʌd.lɪŋ **-ed** -d
befuddlement bɪ'fʌd.l̩.mᵊnt, bə-
beg beg **-s** -z **-ging** -ɪŋ **-ged** -d
begad bɪ'gæd, bə-
began *(from* **begin***)* bɪ'gæn, bə-
begat *(from* **beget***)* bɪ'gæt, bə-
beget bɪ'get, bə- **-s** -s **-ting** -ɪŋ (US) -'get̬.ɪŋ **begat** bɪ'gæt, bə- **begot** bɪ'gɒt, bə- (US) -'gɑːt **begotten** bɪ'gɒt.ᵊn, bə- (US) -'gɑː.tᵊn
Begg beg
beggar 'beg.əʳ (US) -ɚ **-s** -z **-ing** -ɪŋ **-ed** -d
beggarl|y 'beg.ᵊl|.i (US) -ɚ.l|i **-iness** -ɪ.nəs, -ɪ.nɪs
beggar-my-neighbour ˌbeg.ə.mɪ'neɪ.bəʳ, -maɪ'- (US) -ɚ.maɪ'neɪ.bɚ
beggarweed 'beg.ə.wiːd (US) '-ɚ- **-s** -z
beggary 'beg.ᵊr.i
Beggs begz
begin bɪ'gɪn, bə- **-s** -z **-ning/s** -ɪŋ/z
Begin 'beɪ.gɪn
beginner bɪ'gɪn.əʳ, bə- (US) -ɚ **-s** -z
Begley 'beg.li
begone bɪ'gɒn, bə- (US) -'gɑːn
begonia bɪ'gəʊ.ni.ə, bə- (US) -'goʊ.njə **-s** -z
begorra bɪ'gɒr.ə, bə- (US) -'gɔːr.ə
begot *(from* **beget***)* bɪ'gɒt, bə- (US) -'gɑːt **-ten** -ᵊn (US) -'gɑː.t̬ᵊn
begrim|e bɪ'graɪm, bə- **-es** -z **-ing** -ɪŋ **-ed** -d
begrudg|e bɪ'grʌdʒ, bə- **-es** -ɪz **-ing** -ɪŋ **-ed** -d
beguil|e bɪ'gaɪl, bə- **-es** -z **-ing/ly** -ɪŋ/li **-ed** -d
beguine bɪ'giːn
begum (B) 'beɪ.gəm **-s** -z
begun *(from* **begin***)* bɪ'gʌn, bə-
behalf bɪ'hɑːf, bə- (US) -'hæf
Behan 'biː.ən
behav|e bɪ'heɪv, bə- **-es** -z **-ing** -ɪŋ **-ed** -d
behavio(u)r bɪ'heɪ.vjəʳ, bə- (US) -vjɚ **-s** -z
behavio(u)ral bɪ'heɪ.vjər.əl- (US) -vjɚ.əl
behavio(u)r|ism bɪ'heɪ.vjᵊr|.ɪ.zᵊm, bə- **-ist/s** -ɪst/s
behead bɪ'hed, bə- **-s** -z **-ing** -ɪŋ **-ed** -ɪd
beheld *(from* **behold***)* bɪ'held, bə-
behemoth (B) bɪ'hiː.mɒθ, bə-, -məθ (US) -mɑːθ, -məθ; 'biː.ə.məθ **-s** -s
behest bɪ'hest, bə- **-s** -s
behind bɪ'haɪnd, bə-
behindhand bɪ'haɪnd.hænd, bə-
behind-the-scenes bɪˌhaɪn*d*.ðə'siːnz (US) bə- *stress shift:* ˌbehind-the-scenes 'tour
Behn ben
behold bɪ'həʊld, bə- (US) -'hoʊld **-s** -z **-ing** -ɪŋ **beheld** bɪ'held, bə- **beholder/s** bɪ'həʊl.dəʳ/z, bə- (US) -'hoʊl.dɚ/z
beholden bɪ'həʊl.dᵊn, bə- (US) -'hoʊl-
behoof bɪ'huːf, bə-
behoov|e bɪ'huːv, bə- **-es** -z **-ing** -ɪŋ **-ed** -d
behov|e bɪ'həʊv, bə- (US) -'hoʊv **-es** -z **-ing** -ɪŋ **-ed** -d
Behrens 'beə.rənz (US) 'ber.ənz
Behrman 'beə.mən (US) 'ber-
Beiderbecke 'baɪ.də.bek (US) -dɚ-
beige beɪʒ
Beighton 'beɪ.tᵊn, 'baɪ-
beignet 'beɪ.njeɪ, -'- (US) ˌbeɪ'njeɪ **-s** -z
Beijing beɪ'*d*ʒɪŋ
being 'biː.ɪŋ **-s** -z
Beira 'baɪ.rə (US) 'beɪ-
Beirut beɪ'ruːt
Beit baɪt
Beith *surname:* biːθ *place in Scotland:* biːð
Bejam® 'biː.dʒæm
bejan 'biː.dʒᵊn **-s** -z
bejesus, bejezus bɪ'dʒiː.zəz, bə-, -zəs
bejewel bɪ'dʒuː.əl **-s** -z **-(l)ing** -ɪŋ **-(l)ed** -d
bel bel **-s** -z
belabo(u)r bɪ'leɪ.bəʳ, bə- (US) -bɚ **-s** -z **-ing** -ɪŋ **-ed** -d
Belarius bɪ'leə.ri.əs, bə-, -'lɑː- (US) -'ler.i-
Belarus ˌbel.ə'ruːs, ˌbjel- **-rusian** -ruːs.jən, -rus.i.ən, -ru.ʃən
Belasco bɪ'læs.kəʊ, bə- (US) -koʊ
belated bɪ'leɪ.tɪd, bə- (US) -t̬ɪd **-ly** -li **-ness** -nəs, -nɪs
belay bɪ'leɪ, bə- **-s** -z **-ing** -ɪŋ **-ed** -d
bel canto ˌbel'kæn.təʊ (US) -toʊ
belch (B) beltʃ **-es** -ɪz **-ing** -ɪŋ **-ed** -t **-er/s** -əʳ/z (US) -ɚ/z
Belcher 'bel.*t*ʃəʳ (US) -*t*ʃɚ
beldam(e) 'bel.dəm **-s** -z
beleagu|er bɪ'liː.g|əʳ, bə- (US) -g|ɚ **-ers** -əz (US) -ɚz **-ering** -ᵊr.ɪŋ **-ered** -əd (US) -ɚd **-erer/s** -əʳ/z (US) -ɚ/z
Belém bə'lem, bel'em
belemnite 'bel.əm.naɪt **-s** -s

Belfast bel'fɑːst, '-- (US) 'bel.fæst, ˌ-'-
belfr|y 'bel.fr|i **-ies** -iz
Belgian 'bel.dʒən **-s** -z
Belgic 'bel.dʒɪk
Belgium 'bel.dʒəm
Belgrade bel'greɪd (US) '-- *stress shift, British only:* ˌBelgrade 'streets
Belgrano bel'grɑː.nəʊ (US) -noʊ
Belgrave bel'greɪv (US) '-- *stress shift, British only:* ˌBelgrave 'Square
Belgravia bel'greɪ.vi.ə
Belial 'biː.li.əl
bel|ie bɪ'l|aɪ, bə- **-ies** -aɪz **-ying** -aɪ.ɪŋ **-ied** -aɪd
belief bɪ'liːf, bə- **-s** -s
believab|le bɪ'liː.və.b|l̩, bə- **-ly** -li
believ|e bɪ'liːv, bə- **-es** -z **-ing/ly** -ɪŋ/li **-ed** -d
believer bɪ'liː.vəʳ, bə- (US) -vɚ **-s** -z
belike bɪ'laɪk, bə-
Belinda bə'lɪn.də, bɪ-
Belisha bə'liː.ʃə, bɪ- **Beˌlisha 'beacon**
belittl|e bɪ'lɪt.l̩, bə- (US) -'lɪt̬- **-es** -z **-ing** -ɪŋ, -'lɪt.lɪŋ **-ed** -d
Belize bə'liːz, bel'iːz
bell (B) bel **-s** -z **-ing** -ɪŋ **-ed** -d **'bell ˌjar; 'bell ˌpepper; 'bell ˌtent; 'bell ˌtower**
Bella 'bel.ə
belladonna ˌbel.ə'dɒn.ə (US) -'dɑː.nə
Bellamy 'bel.ə.mi
Bellatrix 'bel.ə.trɪks, bə'leɪ- (US) 'bel.ə-
bell-bottom 'belˌbɒt.əm (US) -ˌbɑː.t̬əm **-s** -z **-ed** -d
bellboy 'bel.bɔɪ **-s** -z
belle (B) bel **-s** -z **ˌSouthern 'belle; ˌbelle of the 'ball**
belle époque ˌbel.eɪ'pɒk (US) -'pɑːk
Belle Isle ˌbel'aɪl
Bellerophon bə'ler.ə.fən, bɪ- (US) -fən, -fɑːn
belles lettres ˌbel'let.rə
Bellevue bel'vjuː, '-- (US) 'bel.vjuː
Bellew 'bel.juː
bellhop 'bel.hɒp (US) -hɑːp **-s** -s
bellicose 'bel.ɪ.kəʊs, '-ə-, -kəʊz (US) -koʊs **-ly** -li
bellicosity ˌbel.ɪ'kɒs.ə.ti, -ɪ.ti (US) -ə'kɑː.sə.t̬i
belligeren|ce bə'lɪdʒ.ər.ən*t*|s, bɪ'- **-cy** -si
belligerent bə'lɪdʒ.ər.ənt, bɪ- **-s** -s **-ly** -li
Bellingham *in Northumberland:* 'bel.ɪn.dʒəm *surname:* 'bel.ɪn.*d*ʒəm, -ɪŋ.əm, -hæm *in London:* 'bel.ɪŋ.əm *in the US:* 'bel.ɪŋ.hæm
Bellini bel'iː.ni, bə'liː-
bell|man 'bel|.mən, -mæn **-men** -mən, -men
Belloc 'bel.ɒk (US) -ɑːk
Bellot 'bel.əʊ (US) bel'oʊ

bellow (B) 'bel.əʊ (US) -oʊ **-s** -z **-ing** -ɪŋ **-ed** -d
bellringer 'belˌrɪŋ.əʳ (US) -ɚ **-s** -z
Bellshill belz'hɪl
bellwether 'belˌweð.əʳ (US) -ɚ **-s** -z
bell|y 'bel|.i **-ies** -iz **-ying** -i.ɪŋ **-ied** -id **'belly ˌbutton; 'belly ˌdance; 'belly ˌflop; 'belly ˌlaugh**
bellyach|e 'bel.i.eɪk **-es** -s **-ing** -ɪŋ **-ed** -t
bellyful 'bel.ɪ.fʊl **-s** -z
belly-up ˌbel.i'ʌp
Belmont 'bel.mɒnt, -mənt (US) -mɑːnt
Belmopan ˌbel.məʊ'pæn (US) -moʊ'-
Belo Horizonte ˌbeɪ.ləʊ.hɒr.ɪ'zɒn.ti (US) -loʊ.hɔːr.ə'zɑːn-, ˌbel.oʊ-
belong bɪ'lɒŋ, bə- (US) -'lɑːŋ, -'lɔːŋ **-s** -z **-ing** -ɪŋ **-ed** -d
Belorussi|a ˌbel.əʊ'rʌʃ.ə, ˌbjel-, -'ruː.si- (US) -oʊ'-, -ə'- **-an/s** -ən/z
beloved *used predicatively:* bɪ'lʌvd, bə- *used attributively or as a noun:* bɪ'lʌv.ɪd, bə-, -'lʌvd
below bɪ'ləʊ, bə- (US) -'loʊ
Bel Paese ˌbel.pɑː'eɪ.zeɪ, -zi (US) -zi
Belper 'bel.pəʳ (US) -pɚ
Belsen 'bel.sən
Belsham 'bel.ʃəm
Belshaw 'bel.ʃɔː (US) -ʃɑː, -ʃɔː
Belshazzar bel'ʃæz.əʳ (US) -ɚ
Belsize 'bel.saɪz
Belstead 'bel.stɪd, -sted
belt (B) belt **-s** -s **-ing/s** -ɪŋ/z (US) 'bel.t̬ɪŋ **-ed** -ɪd (US) 'bel.t̬ɪd **beˌlow the 'belt**
Beltingham 'bel.tɪn.dʒəm
Belton 'bel.tən
beltway 'belt.weɪ **-s** -z
Beluchistan bə'luː.tʃɪ.stɑːn, bɪ-, -stæn, bəˌluː.tʃɪ'stɑːn, bə-, -kɪ'-, -'stæn
beluga bə'luː.gə, bɪ'-, bel'uː- **-s** -z
belvedere (B) 'bel.və.dɪəʳ, -vɪ-, ˌ--'- (US) 'bel.və.dɪr, ˌ--'- **-s** -z
Belvoir 'biː.vəʳ (US) -vɚ
bema 'biː.mə **-s** -z **-ta** -tə (US) -t̬ə
Bembridge 'bem.brɪdʒ
bemoan bɪ'məʊn, bə- (US) -'moʊn **-s** -z **-ing** -ɪŋ **-ed** -d
bemus|e bɪ'mjuːz, bə- **-es** -ɪz **-ing** -ɪŋ **-ed** -d **-ement** -mənt
Ben ben
Benares bɪ'nɑː.rɪz, bə-, ben'ɑː- (US) bə'nɑːr.iːz
Benbecula ben'bek.jʊ.lə, bem-, -jə- (US) ben-
Benbow 'ben.bəʊ, 'bem- (US) 'ben.boʊ
bench ben*t*ʃ **-es** -ɪz
bencher 'ben.*t*ʃəʳ (US) -*t*ʃɚ **-s** -z
Benchley 'ben*t*ʃ.li
benchmark 'ben*t*ʃ.mɑːk (US) -mɑːrk **-s** -s **-ing** -ɪŋ
bend bend **-s** -z **-ing** -ɪŋ **-ed** -ɪd **bent** bent **bendable** 'ben.də.bl̩ **ˌround the 'bend**

Bendall 'ben.dəl, -dɔːl (US) -dəl, -dɔːl, -dɑːl
bender (B) 'ben.dəʳ (US) -dɚ **-s** -z
Bendix® 'ben.dɪks
bend|y 'ben.d|i **-ier** -i.əʳ (US) -i.ɚ **-iest** -i.ɪst, -i.əst **-iness** -ɪ.nəs, -ɪ.nɪs
beneath bɪ'niːθ, bə-
Benedicite ˌben.ɪ'daɪ.sɪ.ti, -'diː.tʃɪ-, -tʃə-, -teɪ (US) -ə'dɪs.ə.t̬i, ˌbeɪ.neɪ'diː.tʃiː.teɪ **-s** -z
Benedick 'ben.ɪ.dɪk, '-ə- **-s** -s
Benedict 'ben.ɪ.dɪkt, '-ə-
benedictine *liqueur:* ˌben.ɪ'dɪk.tiːn, -ə'- **-s** -z
Benedictine *monk:* ˌben.ɪ'dɪk.tɪn, -ə'-, -taɪn (US) -tɪn, -tiːn **-s** -z
Note: Members of the Order pronounce /-tɪn/.
benediction ˌben.ɪ'dɪk.ʃən, -ə'- **-s** -z
Benedictus ˌben.ɪ'dɪk.təs, -ə'-, -tʊs **-es** -ɪz
benefaction ˌben.ɪ'fæk.ʃən, -ə'- (US) ˌben.ə'fæk-, 'ben.ə.fæk- **-s** -z
benefactive 'ben.ɪ.fæk.tɪv, -ə-, ˌben.ɪ'fæk-, -ə'- (US) 'ben.ə.fæk-, ˌben.ə'fæk-
benefactor 'ben.ɪ.fæk.təʳ, '-ə- (US) -tɚ **-s** -z
benefactress 'ben.ɪ.fæk.trəs, '-ə-, -trɪs, ˌben.ɪ'fæk-, -ə'- (US) 'ben.ə.fæk- **-es** -ɪz
benefic bɪ'nef.ɪk
benefic|e 'ben.ɪ.fɪs, '-ə- **-es** -ɪz **-ed** -t
beneficen|ce bɪ'nef.ɪ.sən|*t*s, bə- **-t/ly** -t/li
beneficial ˌben.ɪ'fɪʃ.əl, -ə'- **-ly** -li **-ness** -nəs, -nɪs
beneficiar|y ˌben.ɪ'fɪʃ.ər|.i, -ə'- **-ies** -iz
bene|fit 'ben.ɪ|.fɪt, '-ə- **-fits** -fɪts **-fit(t)ing** -fɪ.tɪŋ (US) -fɪ.t̬ɪŋ **-fit(t)ed** -fɪ.tɪd (US) -fɪ.t̬ɪd
Benelux 'ben.ɪ.lʌks
Benenden 'ben.ən.dən
Bene't 'ben.ɪt
Benet 'ben.ɪt
Benét *US surname:* ben'eɪ (US) bə'neɪ, ben'eɪ
Benetton® 'ben.ɪ.tən, '-ə-, -tɒn (US) -ə.t̬ən, -tɑːn
benevolence bɪ'nev.əl.ən*t*s, bə-
benevolent bɪ'nev.əl.ənt, bɪ- **-ly** -li
Benfleet 'ben.fliːt
BEng ˌbiː'en*d*ʒ
Bengal ˌbeŋ'gɔːl, ˌben- (US) -'gɔːl; 'beŋ.gəl, 'ben- *stress shift, British only:* ˌBengal 'tiger
Bengalese ˌbeŋ.gəl'iːz, ˌben-, -gɔː'- (US) -gə'liːz, -'liːs
Bengali beŋ'gɔː.li, ben- **-s** -z
Bengasi beŋ'gɑː.zi, ben-
Benge ben*d*ʒ
Benghazi beŋ'gɑː.zi, ben-

Ben-Gurion benˈgʊə.ri.ən, beŋ-, -ˈgʊr.i- (US) -ˈgʊr.i-, ˌben.gʊrˈjɑːn
Benham ˈben.əm
Ben-Hur benˈhɜːʳ (US) -ˈhɝː
Benidorm ˈben.ɪ.dɔːm, ˈ-ə- (US) -dɔːrm
benighted bɪˈnaɪ.tɪd, bə- (US) -t̬ɪd
benign bɪˈnaɪn, bə- **-est** -ɪst, -əst **-ly** -li
benignancy bɪˈnɪg.nən*t*.si, bə-
benignant bɪˈnɪg.nənt, bə- **-ly** -li
Benigni bəˈniː.ni
benignity bɪˈnɪg.nə.ti, bə-, -nɪ- (US) -nə.t̬i
Benin benˈiːn, bɪˈniːn, bə-
Bening ˈben.ɪŋ
benison ˈben.ɪ.sᵊn, ˈ-ə-, -zᵊn **-s** -z
Benis(s)on ˈben.ɪ.sᵊn, ˈ-ə-
Benito benˈiː.təʊ, bəˈniː- (US) bəˈniː.t̬oʊ
Benjamin ˈben.dʒə.mɪn, -ən
Benjamite ˈben.dʒə.maɪt **-s** -s
Benn ben
Bennet(t) ˈben.ɪt
Bennette benˈet, bəˈnet
Ben Nevis ˌbenˈnev.ɪs
Bennington ˈben.ɪŋ.tən
Benny ˈben.i
Bensham ˈben*t*.ʃəm
Bensley ˈbenz.li
Benson ˈben*t*.sᵊn
Benstead ˈben*t*.stɪd, -sted
bent **(B)** *(from* **bend***)* bent **-s** -s
Bentham ˈben.təm, ˈben*t*.θəm (US) ˈben*t*.θəm **-ism** -ɪ.zᵊm **-ite/s** -aɪt/s
benthic ˈben*t*.θɪk
Bentinck ˈben.tɪŋk
Bentine benˈtiːn, ˈ--
Bentley ˈbent.li **-s** -z
Benton ˈben.tən
bentwood ˈbent.wʊd
benumb bɪˈnʌm, bə- **-s** -z **-ing** -ɪŋ **-ed** -d
Benvolio benˈvəʊ.li.əʊ (US) -ˈvoʊ.li.oʊ
Benz benz, bents
Benzedrine® ˈben.zɪ.driːn, -zə-, -drɪn
benzene, benzine ˈben.ziːn, -ˈ-
benzoate ˈben.zəʊ.eɪt (US) -zoʊ-
benzoic benˈzəʊ.ɪk (US) -ˈzoʊ-
benzoin ˈben.zəʊ.ɪn, -ˈ-- (US) ˈben.zoʊ-, benˈzoʊ-
benzol ˈben.zɒl (US) -zɑːl
benzoline ˈben.zəʊ.liːn (US) -zə-
benzyl ˈben.zɪl (US) -ziː.əl, -zᵊl
Beowulf ˈbeɪ.əʊ.wʊlf, ˈbiː- (US) ˈbeɪə.wʊlf
bequea|th bɪˈkwiː|ð, bə-, -ˈkwiː|θ **-ths** -ðz, -θs **-thing** -ðɪŋ **-thed** -ðd, -θt
bequest bɪˈkwest, bə- **-s** -s
be|rate bɪ|ˈreɪt, bə-, bɪ- **-rates** -ˈreɪts **-rating** -ˈreɪ.tɪŋ (US) -ˈreɪ.t̬ɪŋ **-rated** -ˈreɪ.tɪd (US) -ˈreɪ.t̬ɪd
Berber ˈbɜː.bəʳ (US) ˈbɝː.bɚ **-s** -z
berceuse beəˈsɜːz (US) berˈsuz, -ˈsɜːz
Bere bɪəʳ (US) bɪr
Berea bəˈriː.ə, bɪ- (US) bə-
bereav|e bɪˈriːv, bə- (US) bɪ- **-es** -z **-ing** -ɪŋ **-ed** -d
bereavement bɪˈriːv.mənt, bə- **-s** -s
bereft bɪˈreft, bə-
Berengaria ˌber.ᵊŋˈgeə.ri.ə, -ɪŋˈ-, -eŋˈ- (US) -ˈger.i-
Berenice *in ancient Egypt, etc.:* ˌber.ɪˈnaɪ.si, -ki, -ˈniː.tʃeɪ *opera by Handel:* ˌber.ɪˈniː.tʃi *modern name:* ˌber.əˈniːs, -ɪˈ-
Berenson ˈber.ᵊn*t*.sən
Beresford ˈber.ɪs.fəd, -ɪz- (US) -fɚd
beret ˈber.eɪ, -i (US) bəˈreɪ **-s** -z
berg **(B)** bɜːg, beəg (US) bɝːg **-s** -z
bergamot ˈbɜː.gə.mɒt, -mət (US) ˈbɝː.gə.mɑːt **-s** -s
Bergen ˈbɜː.gən, ˈbeə- (US) ˈbɝː-
Berger *English surname:* ˈbɜː.dʒəʳ (US) ˈbɝː.dʒɚ *US surname:* ˈbɜː.gəʳ (US) ˈbɝː.gɚ
Bergerac ˈbɜː.ʒə.ræk (US) ˌbɝː.ʒəˈræk, -ˈrɑːk
Bergkamp ˈbɜːg.kæmp (US) ˈbɝːg-, -kɑːmp
Bergman ˈbɜːg.mən (US) ˈbɝːg-
Bergson ˈbɜːg.sən (US) ˈberg-, ˈbɝːg-
Bergsonian bɜːgˈsəʊ.ni.ən (US) bergˈsoʊ-, bɝːg-
beribboned bɪˈrɪb.ᵊnd, bə-
beriberi ˌber.ɪˈber.i
Bering ˈbeə.rɪŋ, ˈber- (US) ˈber.ɪŋ ˌ**Bering** ˈ**Strait**
Berio ˈber.i.əʊ (US) -oʊ
Berisford ˈber.ɪs.fəd (US) -fɚd
berk bɜːk (US) bɝːk **-s** -z
Berkeleian bɑːkˈliː.ən (US) ˈbɝː.kli.ən
Berkeley *in England:* ˈbɑː.kli (US) ˈbɑːr-, ˈbɝː- *in US:* ˈbɜː.kli (US) ˈbɝː-
berkelium bɜːˈkiː.li.əm (US) ˈbɝː.kli.əm, bɝːˈkliː.əm
Berkhamsted, Berkhampstead ˈbɜː.kəm*p*.stɪd, -sted (US) ˈbɝː-
Note: The usual British pronunciation is /ˈbɜː-/, but the form /ˈbɑː-/ is used by some residents.
Berkley ˈbɜː.kli (US) ˈbɝː-
Berkoff ˈbɜː.kɒf (US) ˈbɝː.kɑːf
Berks. *(abbrev. for* **Berkshire***)* bɑːks, ˈbɑːk.ʃəʳ, -ˌʃɪəʳ (US) bɝːks; ˈbɝːk.ʃɚ, -ˌʃɪr
Berkshire ˈbɑːk.ʃəʳ, -ˌʃɪəʳ (US) ˈbɝːk.ʃɚ, -ˌʃɪr
Berlin *in Germany:* bɜːˈlɪn (US) bɝː- *stress shift, British only, see compound:* ˌ**Berlin** ˈ**Wall**
Berlin *surname:* ˈbɜː.lɪn, -ˈ- (US) ˈbɝː-, -ˈ- *town in US:* ˈbɜː.lɪn (US) ˈbɝː-
Berliner bɜːˈlɪn.əʳ (US) bɚˈlɪn.ɚ **-s** -z
Berlioz ˈbeə.li.əʊz, ˈbɜː- (US) ˈber.li.oʊz
Berlitz bɜːˈlɪts, ˈ-- (US) ˈbɝː.lɪts, ˌ-ˈ-
Berlusconi ˌbɜː.lʊˈskəʊ.ni, ˌbeə- (US) ˌbɝː.lʊˈskoʊ-, ˌber-
Bermondsey ˈbɜː.mən*d*.zi (US) ˈbɝː-
Bermuda bəˈmjuː.də (US) bɚ- **-s** -z
Berˌ**muda** ˈ**shorts;** **Ber**ˌ**muda** ˈ**triangle**
Bern bɜːn, beən (US) bɝːn
Bernadette ˌbɜː.nəˈdet (US) ˌbɝː-
Bernard *first name:* ˈbɜː.nəd (US) ˈbɝː.nɚd *surname:* bɜːˈnɑːd, bəˈ-; ˈbɜː.nəd (US) bɚˈnɑːrd; ˈbɝː.nɚd
Berne bɜːn, beən (US) bɝːn
Berners ˈbɜː.nəz (US) ˈbɝː.nɚz
Bernese bɜːˈniːz (US) bɝː-, -ˈniːs *stress shift:* ˌBernese ˈOberland
Bernhardt ˈbɜːn.hɑːt (US) ˈbɝːn.hɑːrt
Bernice *biblical name:* bɜːˈnaɪ.si (US) bɚ- *modern name:* ˈbɜː.nɪs, bɜːˈniːs (US) ˈbɝː-; bɚˈniːs
Bernini bɜːˈniː.ni, bə- (US) bɚ-, ber-
Bernoulli bɜːˈnuː.ji, bəˈ-, -li (US) bɚˈnuː.li
Bernstein ˈbɜːn.staɪn, -stiːn (US) ˈbɝːn-
Berol® ˈbiː.rɒl, -rəʊl (US) -rɑːl, -roʊl
Berowne bəˈrəʊn (US) -ˈroʊn
Berra ˈber.ə
Berridge ˈber.ɪdʒ
berr|y **(B)** ˈber|.i **-ies** -iz
Berryman ˈber.ɪ.mæn, -mən
berserk bəˈzɜːk, -ˈsɜːk (US) bɚˈsɝːk, -ˈzɝːk **-s** -s
Bert bɜːt (US) bɝːt
Bertelsmann® ˈbɜː.tᵊlz.mæn, -mən (US) ˈbɝː.t̬ᵊlz-
berth *(n.)* bɜːθ (US) bɝːθ **-s** -s, bɜːðz (US) bɝːðz
berth *(v.)* bɜːθ (US) bɝːθ **-s** -s **-ing** -ɪŋ **-ed** -t
Bertha ˈbɜː.θə (US) ˈbɝː-
Bertie *first name:* ˈbɜː.ti (US) ˈbɝː.t̬i *surname:* ˈbɑː.ti, ˈbɜː- (US) ˈbɑːr.t̬i, ˈbɝː-
Bertolucci ˌbɜː.təʊˈluː.tʃi, -təˈ-, -ˈlʊtʃ.i (US) ˌbɝː.t̬əˈluː.tʃi, ˌber-
Bertram ˈbɜː.trəm (US) ˈbɝː-
Bertrand ˈbɜː.trənd (US) ˈbɝː-
Berwick ˈber.ɪk **-shire** -ʃəʳ, -ˌʃɪəʳ (US) -ʃɚ, -ˌʃɪr
Berwick-on-Tweed ˌber.ɪk.ɒnˈtwiːd (US) -ɑːnˈ-
beryl **(B)** ˈber.ᵊl, -ɪl (US) -ᵊl **-s** -z
beryllium bəˈrɪl.i.əm, berˈɪl- (US) bəˈrɪl-
Besançon bəˈzɑ̃ː*n*.sɔ̃ː*ŋ* (US) -ˈzɑ̃ːn.sõʊn
Besant ˈbes.ᵊnt, ˈbez-; bə-
beseech bɪˈsiːtʃ, bə- **-es** -ɪz **-ing/ly** -ɪŋ/li **-ed** -t **besought** bɪˈsɔːt, bə- (US) -ˈsɑːt, -ˈsɔːt
beseem bɪˈsiːm, bə- **-s** -z **-ing** -ɪŋ **-ed** -d
beset bɪˈset, bə- **-s** -s **-ting** -ɪŋ (US) -ˈset̬.ɪŋ
beshrew bɪˈʃruː, bə-
beside bɪˈsaɪd, bə- **-s** -z
besieg|e bɪˈsiːdʒ, bə- **-es** -ɪz **-ing** -ɪŋ **-ed** -d **-er/s** -əʳ/z (US) -ɚ/z

Besley ˈbez.li
besmear bɪˈsmɪəʳ, bə- (US) -ˈsmɪr **-s** -z **-ing** -ɪŋ **-ed** -d
besmirch bɪˈsmɜːtʃ, bə- (US) -ˈsmɝːtʃ **-es** -ɪz **-ing** -ɪŋ **-ed** -t
besom ˈbiː.zəm **-s** -z
besotted bɪˈsɒt.ɪd, bə- (US) -ˈsɑː.t̬ɪd **-ly** -li **-ness** -nəs, -nɪs
besought *(from* **beseech***)* bɪˈsɔːt, bə- (US) -ˈsɑːt, -ˈsɔːt
bespangl|e bɪˈspæŋ.gl̩, bəˈspæŋ- **-es** -z **-ing** -ɪŋ, ˈ-glɪŋ **-ed** -d
bespatt|er bɪˈspæt|.əʳ, bə- (US) -ˈspæt̬|.ɚ **-ers** -əz (US) -ɚz **-ering** -ər.ɪŋ **-ered** -əd (US) -ɚd
bespeak bɪˈspiːk, bə- **-s** -s **-ing** -ɪŋ
bespoke bɪˈspəʊk, bə- (US) -ˈspoʊk
bespoken bɪˈspəʊ.kən, bə- (US) -ˈspoʊ-
bespectacled bɪˈspek.tə.kl̩d, -tɪ.kl̩d
besprinkl|e bɪˈsprɪŋ.kl̩, bə- **-es** -z **-ing** -ɪŋ, ˈ-klɪŋ **-ed** -d
Bess bes
Bessacarr ˈbes.ə.kəʳ (US) -kɚ
Bessarabia ˌbes.əˈreɪ.bi.ə
Bessborough ˈbez.bər.ə (US) -oʊ
Bessemer ˈbes.ɪ.məʳ, ˈ-ə- (US) -mɚ
Besses o' th' Barn ˌbes.ɪz.əðˈbɑːn (US) -ˈbɑːrn
Bessette bəˈset
Bessie ˈbes.i
best (B) best **-s** -s **-ing** -ɪŋ **-ed** -ɪd ˌ**best ˈman; ˌmake the ˈbest of ˌsomething; the ˌbest of ˈboth ˌworlds** (US) **the ˌbest of ˌboth ˈworlds**
bestial ˈbes.ti.əl, ˈbiːs.ti- (US) ˈbes.tʃəl, ˈbiːs-, -ti.əl **-ly** -i **-ism** -ɪ.zəm
bestialit|y ˌbes.tiˈæl.ə.t|i, ˌbiː.stiˈ-, -ɪ.t|i (US) ˌbes.tʃiˈæl.ə.t̬|i, ˌbiːs- **-ies** -iz
bestiar|y ˈbes.ti.ər|.i, ˈbiː.sti- (US) -tʃi.er|.i **-ies** -iz
bestir bɪˈstɜːʳ, bə- (US) -ˈstɝː **-s** -z **-ring** -ɪŋ **-red** -d
bestow bɪˈstəʊ, bə- (US) -ˈstoʊ **-s** -z **-ing** -ɪŋ **-ed** -d
bestowal bɪˈstəʊ.əl, bə- (US) -ˈstoʊ- **-s** -z
bestrew bɪˈstruː, bə- **-s** -z **-ing** -ɪŋ **-ed** -d
bestrewn bɪˈstruːn, bə-
bestrid|e bɪˈstraɪd, bə- **-es** -z **-ing** -ɪŋ
bestrode bɪˈstrəʊd, bə- (US) -ˈstroʊd
bestridden bɪˈstrɪ.dən, bə-
bestseller ˌbestˈsel.əʳ (US) -ɚ **-s** -z *stress shift:* ˌbestseller ˈlistings
best-selling ˌbestˈsel.ɪŋ *stress shift:* ˌbest-selling ˈbook
Beswick ˈbez.ɪk
bet (B) bet **-s** -s **-ting** -ɪŋ (US) ˈbet̬.ɪŋ **-ted** -ɪd (US) ˈbet̬.ɪd ˌ**hedge one's ˈbets**
beta ˈbiː.tə (US) ˈbeɪ.t̬ə **-s** -z
beta-blocker ˈbiː.təˌblɒk.əʳ (US) ˈbeɪ.t̬əˌblɑː.kɚ **-s** -z
betak|e bɪˈteɪk, bə- **-es** -s **-ing** -ɪŋ
betook bɪˈtʊk, bə- **betaken** bɪˈteɪ.kən, bə-
betel ˈbiː.təl (US) -t̬əl **-nut/s** -nʌt/s
Betelgeuse, Betelgeux ˈbiː.təl.*dʒ*ɜːz, ˈbet.əl-, -*dʒ*uːz (US) ˈbiː.t̬əl.dʒuːz, ˈbet̬.əl-, -dʒuːs, -dʒɜːz
bête noire ˌbetˈnwɑːʳ (US) -ˈnwɑːr, ˌbeɪt- **bêtes noires** ˌbetˈnwɑːʳ, -ˈnwɑːz (US) -nwɑːr, beɪt-, -nwɑːrz
Beth beθ
Bethany ˈbeθ.ən.i
Bethel ˈbeθ.əl
Bethell ˈbeθ.əl, bəˈθel
Bethesda beθˈez.də, bɪˈθez-, bə- (US) bəˈθez-, bɪ-
bethink bɪˈθɪŋk, bə- **-s** -s **-ing** -ɪŋ
bethought bɪˈθɔːt, bə- (US) -ˈθɑːt, -ˈθɔːt
Bethlehem ˈbeθ.lɪ.hem, -lə- (US) -lə.hem, -həm
Bethnal ˈbeθ.nəl
bethought *(from* **bethink***)* bɪˈθɔːt, bə- (US) -ˈθɑːt, -ˈθɔːt
Bethsaida beθˈseɪ.də, -ˈsaɪ-
Bethune *surname:* ˈbiː.tən (US) bəˈθuːn *in names of streets, etc.:* beθˈjuːn, bɪˈθjuːn, bə- (US) bəˈθuːn, -ˈθjuːn
betid|e bɪˈtaɪd, bə-
betimes bɪˈtaɪmz, bə-
Betjeman ˈbetʃ.ə.mən
betoken bɪˈtəʊ.kən, bə- (US) -ˈtoʊ- **-s** -z **-ing** -ɪŋ **-ed** -ənd
betony ˈbet.ə.ni
betook *(from* **betake***)* bɪˈtʊk, bəˈtʊk
betray bɪˈtreɪ, bə- **-s** -z **-ing** -ɪŋ **-ed** -d **-er/s** -əʳ/z (US) -ɚ/z
betrayal bɪˈtreɪ.əl, bə- **-s** -z
betro|th bɪˈtrəʊ|ð, bə-, -ˈtrəʊ|θ (US) -ˈtroʊ|ð, -ˈtrɑː|θ **-ths** -ðz, -θs **-thing** -ðɪŋ, -θɪŋ **-thed** -ðd, -θt
Note: In British English, the voiceless version is unlikely before **-ing**.
betrothal bɪˈtrəʊ.ðəl, bə- (US) -ˈtroʊ-, -θəl **-s** -z
Betsy ˈbet.si
Bette bet; ˈbet.i (US) bet; ˈbet̬.i
Betteley ˈbet.əl.i (US) ˈbet̬-
bett|er ˈbet|.əʳ (US) ˈbet̬|.ɚ **-ers** -əz (US) -ɚz **-ering** -ər.ɪŋ **-ered** -əd (US) -ɚd **for ˌbetter or (for) ˈworse**
betterment ˈbet.ə.mənt (US) ˈbet̬.ɚ-
betting ˈbet.ɪŋ (US) ˈbet̬- **-s** -z ˈ**betting ˌshop**
bettor ˈbet.əʳ (US) ˈbet̬.ɚ **-s** -z
Bettws ˈbet.əs (US) ˈbet̬-
Bettws-y-Coed ˌbet.ə.siˈkɔɪd, -ʊ.siˈ-, -kəʊ.ɪd, -əd (US) ˌbet̬.ə.siˈkɔɪd
Betty ˈbet.i (US) ˈbet̬-
between bɪˈtwiːn, bə-
betweentimes bɪˈtwiːn.taɪmz, bə-
betwixt bɪˈtwɪkst, bə-
Beulah ˈbjuː.lə
Bevan ˈbev.ən
bevel ˈbev.əl **-s** -z **-(l)ing** -ɪŋ **-(l)ed** -d
Beven ˈbev.ən
beverag|e ˈbev.ər.ɪdʒ, ˈ-rɪdʒ **-es** -ɪz
Beveridge ˈbev.ər.ɪdʒ, ˈ-rɪdʒ
Beverley ˈbev.əl.i (US) -ɚ.li
Beverly ˈbev.əl.i (US) -ɚ.li ˌ**Beverly ˈHills**
Beves ˈbiː.vɪs
Bevin ˈbev.ɪn
Bevis ˈbiː.vɪs, ˈbev.ɪs
bevv|y ˈbev|.i **-ies** -iz **-ied** -id
bev|y ˈbev|.i **-ies** -iz
bewail bɪˈweɪl, bə- **-s** -z **-ing** -ɪŋ **-ed** -d
beware bɪˈweəʳ, bə- (US) -ˈwer
Bewdley ˈbjuːd.li
bewhiskered bɪˈ*h*wɪs.kəd, bə- (US) -kɚd
Bewick(e) ˈbjuː.ɪk
bewigged bɪˈwɪgd, bə-
bewild|er bɪˈwɪl.d|əʳ, bə- (US) -d|ɚ **-ers** -əz (US) -ɚ/z **-ering/ly** -ər.ɪŋ/li **-ered** -əd (US) -ɚd **-erment/s** -ə.mənt/s (US) -ɚ.mənt/s
bewitch bɪˈwɪtʃ, bə- **-es** -ɪz **-ing/ly** -ɪŋ/li **-ed** -t **-ment/s** -mənt/s
Bewley ˈbjuː.li
Bexhill beksˈhɪl *stress shift:* ˌBexhill ˈstation
Bexley ˈbek.sli
Bexleyheath ˌbek.slɪˈhiːθ
Bey beɪ **-s** -z
Beynon ˈbaɪ.nən, ˈbeɪ-
beyond biˈɒnd (US) -ˈ*j*ɑːnd
Beyrout(h) beɪˈruːt
bezant ˈbez.ənt **-s** -s
bezel ˈbez.əl **-s** -z
Béziers ˈbez.i.eɪ
bezique bɪˈziːk, bə-
BFPO ˌbiː.ef.piːˈəʊ (US) -ˈoʊ
Bhagavad-Gita ˌbæg.ə.vədˈgiː.tə, ˌbʌg-, -vædˈ- (US) ˌbɑː.gə.vɑːdˈ-
bhagwan (B) ˈbæg.wɑːn
bhaji ˈbɑː.dʒi **-s** -z
bhang bæŋ
bhangra ˈbæŋ.grə, ˈbɑːŋ-
bhindi ˈbɪn.di
Bhopal bəʊˈpɑːl (US) boʊ-
Bhutan buːˈtɑːn, -ˈtæn
Bhutanese ˌbuː.təˈniːz
Bhutto ˈbuː.təʊ, ˈbʊt.əʊ (US) ˈbuː.t̬oʊ
bi- baɪ-
Note: Prefix. Words containing **bi-** normally take secondary stress, but sometimes primary stress, on the first syllable, e.g. **bimetallic** /ˌbaɪ.metˈæl.ɪk/, British English **bicarb** /ˈbaɪ.kɑːb/, or primary stress on the second syllable, e.g. **biathlete** /baɪˈæθ.liːt/.
Biafr|a biˈæf.r|ə, baɪˈ- **-an/s** -ən/z
Bialystok biˈæl.ɪ.stɒk; ˈ-ə-; ˌbiː.əˈlɪs.tɒk (US) biˈɑː.lə.stɑːk, -ˈæl.ə-

Bianca bi'æŋ.kə (US) -'æŋ-, -'ɑːŋ-
biannual baɪ'æn.ju.əl **-s** -z **-ly** -li
Biarritz ˌbɪə'rɪts, '-- (US) ˌbiː.ə'rɪts, '---
bias 'baɪəs **-(s)es** -ɪz **-(s)ing** -ɪŋ **-(s)ed** -t
biathlete baɪ'æθ.liːt **-s** -s
biathlon baɪ'æθ.lən, -lɒn (US) -lɑːn **-s** -z
biaxal baɪ'æk.sᵊl
biaxial baɪ'æk.si.əl
bib bɪb **-s** -z
Bibby 'bɪb.i
bibelot 'bɪb.ləʊ, -ᵊl.əʊ (US) -ə.loʊ, 'biː.bloʊ **-s** -z
Bible 'baɪ.bl̩ **-s** -z **'Bible ˌBelt**
biblic|al 'bɪb.lɪ.k|ᵊl **-ally** -ᵊl.i, -li
biblio- bɪb.li.əʊ-; ˌbɪb.li'ɒ- (US) bɪb.li.oʊ-, -ə-; ˌbɪb.li'ɑː-
Note: Prefix. Normally takes either primary or secondary stress on the first syllable, e.g. **bibliophile** /'bɪb.li.əʊ.faɪl (US) -ə-/, **bibliomania** /ˌbɪb.li.əʊ'meɪ.ni.ə (US) -ə'-/, or secondary stress on the first syllable, with primary stress occurring on the third syllable, e.g. **bibliography** /ˌbɪb.li'ɒg.rə.fi (US) -'ɑː.grə-/.
bibliograph|y ˌbɪb.li'ɒg.rə.f|i (US) -'ɑː.grə- **-ies** -iz **-er/s** -əʳ/z (US) -ɚ/z
bibliolat|ry ˌbɪb.li'ɒl.ə.t|ri (US) -'ɑː.lə- **-er/z** -əʳ/z (US) -ɚ/z
bibliomania ˌbɪb.li.əʊ'meɪ.ni.ə (US) -ə'-, -oʊ'-
bibliomaniac ˌbɪb.li.əʊ'meɪ.ni.æk (US) -ə'-, -oʊ'- **-s** -s
bibliophile 'bɪb.li.əʊ.faɪl (US) -ə-, -oʊ- **-s** -z
bibulous 'bɪb.jə.ləs, -jʊ- (US) -jə- **-ly** -li
Bic® bɪk
bicameral ˌbaɪ'kæm.ᵊr.ᵊl **-ism** -ɪ.zᵊm
bicarb 'baɪ.kɑːb (US) baɪ'kɑːrb
bicarbonate ˌbaɪ'kɑː.bᵊn.ət, -eɪt, -ɪt (US) -'kɑːr- **-s** -s **biˌcarbonate of 'soda**
bice baɪs
Bice 'biː.tʃi; baɪs
bicentenar|y ˌbaɪ.sen'tiː.nᵊr|.i, -sᵊn'-, -'ten.ᵊr- (US) baɪ'sen.tᵊn.er|.i; ˌbaɪ.sen'ten.ᵊr- **-ies** -iz
bicentennial ˌbaɪ.sen'ten.i.əl, -sən'- **-s** -z
biceps 'baɪ.seps
Bicester 'bɪs.təʳ (US) -tɚ
bichloride ˌbaɪ'klɔː.raɪd (US) -'klɔːr.aɪd
bichromate ˌbaɪ'krəʊ.meɪt, -met, -mɪt (US) -'kroʊ-
bick|er 'bɪk|.əʳ (US) -ɚ **-ers** -əz (US) -ɚz **-ering/s** -ᵊr.ɪŋ/z **-ered** -əd (US) -ɚd **-erer/s** -ᵊr.əʳ/z (US) -ɚ.ɚ/z
Bickerstaff(e) 'bɪk.ə.stɑːf (US) -ɚ.stæf
Bickersteth 'bɪk.ə.steθ, -stɪθ (US) '-ɚ-
Bickerton 'bɪk.ə.tᵊn (US) '-ɚ-
Bickford 'bɪk.fəd (US) -fɚd
Bickleigh, Bickley 'bɪk.li
Bicknell 'bɪk.nᵊl
bicoastal baɪ'kəʊ.stᵊl (US) -'koʊ-
bicuspid baɪ'kʌs.pɪd **-s** -z
bicyc|le 'baɪ.sɪ.k|l̩, -sə- **-les** -l̩z **-ling** -lɪŋ **-led** -l̩d
bicyclist 'baɪ.sɪ.klɪst, -sə- **-s** -s
bid bɪd **-s** -z **-ding** -ɪŋ **-der/s** -əʳ/z (US) -ɚ/z **bade** bæd, beɪd **bidden** 'bɪd.ən
biddable 'bɪd.ə.bl̩
bidder (B) 'bɪd.əʳ (US) -ɚ **-s** -z
Biddle 'bɪd.l̩
Biddulph 'bɪd.ʌlf, -ᵊlf
bidd|y (B) 'bɪd|.i **-ies** -iz
bid|e (B) baɪd **-es** -z **-ing** -ɪŋ **-ed** -ɪd
Bideford 'bɪd.ɪ.fəd (US) -fɚd
Biden 'baɪ.dᵊn
bidet 'biː.deɪ (US) bɪ'deɪ, biː- **-s** -z
bidialectal ˌbaɪ.daɪə'lek.tᵊl
bidialectalism ˌbaɪ.daɪə'lek.tᵊl.ɪ.zᵊm
Bidwell 'bɪd.wel
Bielefeld 'biː.lə.felt, -feld
biennial baɪ'en.i.əl **-ly** -i
bier bɪəʳ (US) bɪr **-s** -z
Bierce bɪəs (US) bɪrs
biff bɪf **-s** -s **-ing** -ɪŋ **-ed** -t
Biffen 'bɪf.ɪn, -ən
bifocal baɪ'fəʊ.kᵊl (US) 'baɪˌfoʊ-, ˌ-'-- **-s** -z
bifur|cate 'baɪ.fə.keɪt, -fɜː- (US) -fɚ- **-cates** -keɪts **-cating** -keɪ.tɪŋ (US) -keɪ.t̬ɪŋ **-cated** -keɪ.tɪd (US) -keɪ.t̬ɪd
bifurcation ˌbaɪ.fə'keɪ.ʃᵊn, -fɜː'- (US) -fɚ'- **-s** -z
big bɪg **-ger** -əʳ (US) -ɚ **-gest** -ɪst, -əst **-ness** -nəs, -nɪs ˌ**Big 'Apple**; ˌ**Big 'Bang**; ˌ**Big 'Ben**; ˌ**big 'business**; ˌ**Big 'Dipper**; ˌ**big 'game**; ˌ**big 'screen**; ˌ**big 'wheel**; ˌ**hit the 'big ˌtime**
bigamist 'bɪg.ə.mɪst **-s** -s
bigamous 'bɪg.ə.məs **-ly** -li
bigam|y 'bɪg.ə.m|i **-ies** -iz
Bigelow 'bɪg.ᵊl.əʊ, -ɪ.ləʊ (US) -ə.loʊ
Bigfoot 'bɪg.fʊt
Bigge bɪg
biggie 'bɪg.i
Biggin 'bɪg.ɪn
biggish 'bɪg.ɪʃ
Biggles 'bɪg.l̩z
Biggleswade 'bɪg.l̩z.weɪd
Biggs bɪgz
biggl|y 'bɪg|.i **-ies** -iz
Bigham 'bɪg.em
bighead 'bɪg.hed **-s** -z
bigheaded ˌbɪg'hed.ɪd, -əd (US) '-ˌ-- **-ly** -li **-ness** -nəs, -nɪs *stress shift:* ˌbigheaded 'bully
bighorn 'bɪg.hɔːn (US) -hɔːrn **-s** -z
bight baɪt **-s** -s **-ing** -ɪŋ (US) 'baɪ.t̬ɪŋ **-ed** -ɪd (US) 'baɪ.t̬ɪd
big-league 'bɪg.liːg
Biglow 'bɪg.ləʊ (US) -loʊ
Bignell 'bɪg.nᵊl
big|ot 'bɪg|.ət **-ots** -əts **-oted** -ə.tɪd (US) -ə.t̬ɪd
bigotr|y 'bɪg.ə.tr|i **-ies** -iz
bigraph 'baɪ.grɑːf, -græf (US) -græf **-s** -s
Big Sur ˌbɪg'sɜːʳ (US) -'sɝː
big-ticket 'bɪgˌtɪk.ɪt
big-time 'bɪg.taɪm **-er/s** -əʳ/z (US) -ɚ/z
bigwig 'bɪg.wɪg **-s** -z
Bihar bɪ'hɑːʳ, biː- (US) -hɑːr
bijou 'biː.ʒuː, -'-
bik|e baɪk **-es** -s **-ing** -ɪŋ **-ed** -t
biker (B) 'baɪ.kəʳ (US) -kɚ **-s** -z
bikini (B) bɪ'kiː.ni, bə- **-s** -z
Biko 'biː.keʊ (US) -koʊ
bilabial (*n. adj.*) baɪ'leɪ.bi.əl **-s** -z **-ly** -i

Bilabial

Bilabial articulations involve both of the lips.

Examples for English

In English, /p b/ and /m/ are examples of bilabial sounds. These are all made with a complete closure of the lips, e.g.:

pan	/pæn/
ban	/bæn/
man	/mæn/

(/w/ is also sometimes referred to as bilabial, but, as it has tongue movement towards the velum in addition to lip rounding, it is more accurately described as 'labial-velar')

The plosives /p/ and /b/ are one of the pairs which are said to be distinguished by being FORTIS and LENIS respectively, rather than voiceless and voiced.

bilateral baɪˈlæt.ər.əl, ˈ-rəl US -ˈlæţ.ɚ.əl **-y** -i **-ness** -nəs, -nɪs
Bilbao bɪlˈbaʊ, -ˈbɑː.əʊ US -ˈbɑː.oʊ, -ˈbaʊ
bilberr|y ˈbɪl.bər|.i US -ber- **-ies** -iz
Bilborough ˈbɪl.bər.ə US -oʊ
Bilbrough ˈbɪl.brə US -broʊ
bilb|y ˈbɪl.bi **-ies** -iz
Bildungsroman ˈbɪl.dʊŋz.rəʊ.mɑːn US -roʊ- **-s** -z **-e** -ə
bile baɪl
bilg|e bɪldʒ **-es** -ɪz **-ing** -ɪŋ **-ed** -d ˈ**bilge** ˌ**pump**; ˈ**bilge** ˌ**water**
bilgy ˈbɪl.dʒi
bilharzia bɪlˈhɑː.zi.ə, -ˈhɑːt.si- US -ˈhɑːr.zi-
biliary ˈbɪl.i.ər.i
bilingual baɪˈlɪŋ.gwəl **-s** -z **-ly** -i **-ism** -ɪ.zəm *stress shift, see first compound:* ˌ**bilingual** ˈ**secretary** **bi**ˌ**lingual** ˈ**secretary**
bilious ˈbɪl.i.əs US ˈ-jəs, ˈ-i.əs **-ly** -li **-ness** -nəs, -nɪs
bilirubin ˌbɪl.ɪˈruː.bɪn
biliteral baɪˈlɪt.ər.əl, ˈ-rəl US -ˈlɪţ.ɚ.əl **-ly** -i
bilk bɪlk **-s** -s **-ing** -ɪŋ **-ed** -t
bill (B) bɪl **-s** -z **-ing** -ɪŋ **-ed** -d ˌ**bill of** ˈ**fare**; ˌ**fit the** ˈ**bill**
billable ˈbɪl.ə.bl̩
billabong ˈbɪl.ə.bɒŋ US -bɑːŋ, -bɔːŋ **-s** -z
billboard ˈbɪl.bɔːd US -bɔːrd **-s** -z
Billericay ˌbɪl.əˈrɪk.i
bille|t ˈbɪl|.ɪt, -ət US -ət **-ts** -ts **-ting** -tɪŋ US -ţɪŋ **-ted** -tɪd US -ţɪd
billet-doux ˌbɪl.eɪˈduː **billets-doux** ˌbɪl.eɪˈduː, -duːz
billfold ˈbɪl.fəʊld US -foʊld **-s** -z
billhook ˈbɪl.hʊk **-s** -s
billiard ˈbɪl.i.əd, ˈ-jəd US ˈ-jɚd **-s** -z ˈ**billiard** ˌ**ball**; ˈ**billiard** ˌ**cue**; ˈ**billiard** ˌ**room**; ˈ**billiard** ˌ**table**
Billie ˈbɪl.i
Billie-Jean ˌbɪl.iˈdʒiːn
Billing ˈbɪl.ɪŋ **-s** -z
Billinge ˈbɪl.ɪndʒ
Billingham ˈbɪl.ɪŋ.*h*əm
Billinghurst ˈbɪl.ɪŋ.hɜːst US -hɝːst
Billingsgate ˈbɪl.ɪŋz.geɪt
Billington ˈbɪl.ɪŋ.tən
billion ˈbɪl.i.ən, -jən US -jən **-s** -z
billionaire ˌbɪl.i.əˈneər, ˌ-jəˈ- US -jəˈner **-s** -z
billionth ˈbɪl.i.ənθ, ˈ-jənθ US ˈ-jənθ **-s** -s
billow ˈbɪl.əʊ US -oʊ **-s** -z **-ing** -ɪŋ **-ed** -d **-y** -i
billposter ˈbɪlˌpəʊ.stər US -ˌpoʊ.stɚ **-s** -z
billsticker ˈbɪlˌstɪk.ər US -kɚ **-s** -z
bill|y (B) ˈbɪl|.i **-ies** -iz ˈ**billy** ˌ**can**; ˈ**billy** ˌ**club**; ˈ**billy** ˌ**goat**
billycock ˈbɪl.i.kɒk US -kɑːk **-s** -s
billy-o ˈbɪl.i.əʊ US -oʊ
Biloxi bɪˈlʌk.si, bə-, -ˈlɒk- US -ˈlɑːk-, -ˈlʌk-
Bilston(e) ˈbɪl.stən
Bilton ˈbɪl.tən
biltong ˈbɪl.tɒŋ US -tɑːŋ, -tɔːŋ
bimbo ˈbɪm.bəʊ US -boʊ **-(e)s** -z
bimestrial baɪˈmes.tri.əl
bimetallic ˌbaɪ.metˈæl.ɪk, -mɪˈtæl-, -mə-
bimetall|ism baɪˈmet.əl|.ɪ.zəm US -ˈmeţ- **-ist/s** -ɪst/s
bimolecular ˌbaɪ.məˈlek.jə.lər, -jʊ- US -lɚ
bimonthl|y baɪˈmʌn*t*θ.l|i **-ies** -iz
bin bɪn **-s** -z **-ning** -ɪŋ **-ned** -d
binar|y ˈbaɪ.nər|.i **-ies** -iz ˌ**binary** ˈ**number**
binaural baɪˈnɔː.rəl, bɪ- US -ˈnɔːr.əl
Binchy ˈbɪn.*t*ʃi US ˈbɪn*t*.ʃi
bind baɪnd **-s** -z **-ing** -ɪŋ **bound** baʊnd
binder ˈbaɪn.dər US -dɚ **-s** -z
binder|y ˈbaɪn.dər|.i **-ies** -iz
bindweed ˈbaɪnd.wiːd
Binet ˈbiː.neɪ US bɪˈneɪ
Binet-Simon ˌbiː.neɪˈsaɪ.mən US bɪˌneɪ.siˈmoʊn
Bing bɪŋ
bing|e bɪndʒ **-es** -ɪz **-(e)ing** -ɪŋ **-ed** -d
Bingen ˈbɪŋ.ən
Bingham ˈbɪŋ.əm
Bingley ˈbɪŋ*g*.li
bingo ˈbɪŋ.gəʊ US -goʊ
Bink(e)s bɪŋks
bin Laden ˌbɪnˈlɑː.dən
bin|man ˈbɪn|.mæn, ˈbɪm-, -mən US ˈbɪn- **-men** -men, -mən
binnacle ˈbɪn.ə.kl̩ **-s** -z
Binney, Binnie ˈbɪn.i
Binns bɪnz
Binoche bɪˈnɒʃ, biː- US -noʊʃ
binocular *(adj.)* baɪˈnɒk.jə.lər, bɪ-, bə-, -jʊ- US -ˈnɑː.kjə.lɚ, -kjʊ-
binoculars *(n.)* bɪˈnɒk.jə.ləz, baɪ-, bə-, -jʊ- US -ˈnɑː.kjə.lɚz, -kjʊ-
binomial baɪˈnəʊ.mi.əl US -ˈnoʊ- **-s** -z **-ly** -i
Binste(a)d ˈbɪn.stɪd, -sted
bint bɪnt **-s** -s
Binyon ˈbɪn.jən
bio- baɪ.əʊ-; baɪˈɒ- US baɪ.oʊ-, -ə-; baɪˈɑː-
Note: Prefix. Normally carries primary or secondary stress on the first syllable, e.g. **biograph** /ˈbaɪ.əʊ.grɑːf US -ə.græf/, **biographic** /ˌbaɪ.əʊˈgræf.ɪk US -əˈ-/, or primary stress on the second syllable, e.g. **biographer** /baɪˈɒg.rə.fər US -ˈɑː.grə.fɚ/. There are exceptions; see individual entries.
biochemic|al ˌbaɪ.əʊˈkem.ɪ.k|əl US -oʊˈ- **-als** -əlz **-ally** -əl.i, -li
biochemist ˌbaɪ.əʊˈkem.ɪst US -oʊˈ- **-s** -s **-ry** -ri
biocoenosis ˌbaɪ.əʊ.sɪˈnəʊ.sɪs, -siːˈ- US -oʊ.sɪˈnoʊ-
biodegradability ˌbaɪ.əʊ.dɪ.greɪ.dəˈbɪl.ɪ.ti, -də.greɪ-, -ə.ti US -oʊ.dɪ.greɪ.dəˈbɪl.ə.ţi, -də-
biodegradab|le ˌbaɪ.əʊ.dɪˈgreɪ.də.b|l̩, -dəˈ- US -oʊ- **-ly** -li
biodegradation ˌbaɪ.əʊ.deg.rəˈdeɪ.ʃən US ˌ-oʊ-
biodegrad|e ˌbaɪ.əʊ.dɪˈgreɪd, -dəˈ- US -oʊ- **-es** -z **-ing** -ɪŋ **-ed** -ɪd
biodiversity ˌbaɪ.əʊ.daɪˈvɜː.sə.ti, -dɪˈ-, -sɪ- US -oʊ.dɪˈvɝː.sə.ţi, -daɪˈ-
bioengineer ˌbaɪ.əʊ.en.dʒɪˈnɪər, -dʒəˈ- US -oʊ.en.dʒɪˈnɪr, -dʒəˈ- **-s** -z
bioengineering ˌbaɪ.əʊ.en.dʒɪˈnɪə.rɪŋ, -dʒəˈ- US -oʊ.en.dʒɪˈnɪr.ɪŋ, -dʒəˈ-
biofeedback ˌbaɪ.əʊˈfiːd.bæk US -oʊˈ-
biogenesis ˌbaɪ.əʊˈdʒen.ə.sɪs, ˈ-ɪ- US -oʊˈ-
biogenetic ˌbaɪ.əʊ.dʒəˈnet.ɪk, -dʒɪˈ- US -oʊ.dʒəˈneţ- **-ally** -əl.i, -li
biogenic ˌbaɪ.əʊˈdʒen.ɪk US -oʊˈ-
biograph ˈbaɪ.əʊ.grɑːf, -græf US -ə.græf **-s** -s
biographer baɪˈɒg.rə.fər US -ˈɑː.grə.fɚ **-s** -z
biographic ˌbaɪ.əʊˈgræf.ɪk US -əˈ- **-al** -əl **-ally** -əl.i, -li
biograph|y baɪˈɒg.rə.f|i US -ˈɑː.grə- **-ies** -iz
biolinguistics ˌbaɪ.əʊ.lɪŋˈgwɪs.tɪks US ˌ-oʊ-
biologic ˌbaɪ.əˈlɒdʒ.ɪk US -ˈlɑː.dʒɪk
biologic|al ˌbaɪ.əˈlɒdʒ.ɪ.k|əl US -ˈlɑː.dʒɪ- **-ally** -əl.i, -li **bio**ˌ**logical** ˈ**clock**; **bio**ˌ**logical** ˈ**warfare**
biologist baɪˈɒl.ə.dʒɪst US -ˈɑː.lə- **-s** -s
biology baɪˈɒl.ə.dʒi US -ˈɑː.lə-
biome ˈbaɪ.əʊm US -oʊm
biomedical ˌbaɪ.əʊˈmed.ɪ.kəl US -oʊˈ-
biometric ˌbaɪ.əʊˈmet.rɪk US -oʊˈ- **-s** -s **-al** -əl
biometry baɪˈɒm.ə.tri, ˈ-ɪ- US -ˈɑː.mə-
bionic baɪˈɒn.ɪk US -ˈɑː.nɪk **-s** -s
biophysicist ˌbaɪ.əʊˈfɪz.ɪ.sɪst, -oʊˈ- **-s** -s
biophysic|s ˌbaɪ.əʊˈfɪz.ɪk|s US -oʊˈ- **-al** -əl
biopic ˈbaɪ.əʊ.pɪk US -oʊ- **-s** -s
biops|y ˈbaɪ.ɒp.s|i US -ɑːp- **-ies** -iz
biorhythm ˈbaɪ.əʊˌrɪð.əm US -oʊˌ- **-s** -z
bioscope ˈbaɪ.əʊ.skəʊp US -skoʊp **-s** -s
biosphere ˈbaɪ.əʊ.sfɪər US -ə.sfɪr **-s** -z
biotech ˈbaɪ.əʊ.tek US -oʊ-
biotechnology ˌbaɪ.əʊ.tekˈnɒl.ə.dʒi US -oʊ.tekˈnɑː.lə-
biotope ˈbaɪ.əʊ.təʊp US -toʊp **-s** -s

biparous ˈbɪp.ər.əs
bipartisan baɪˈpɑː.tɪ.zæn; ˌbaɪ.pɑː.tɪˈzæn, -zən US baɪˈpɑːr.t̬ə.zən
bipartite baɪˈpɑː.taɪt US baɪˈpɑːr- *stress shift:* ˌbipartite ˈtreaty
biped ˈbaɪ.ped **-s** -z
bipedal baɪˈpiː.dəl, -ˈped.əl US -ˈped.əl **-ism** -ɪ.zəm
biplane ˈbaɪ.pleɪn **-s** -z
bipod ˈbaɪ.pɒd US -pɑːd **-s** -z
bipolar baɪˈpəʊ.ləʳ US -ˈpoʊ.lɚ
bipolarity ˌbaɪ.pəʊˈlær.ɪ.ti, -ə.ti US -poʊˈler.ə.t̬i, -ˈlær-
biquadratic ˌbaɪ.kwɒdˈræt.ɪk, -kwəˈdræt- US -kwɑːˈdræt̬.ɪk **-s** -s
birch (B) bɜːtʃ US bɝːtʃ **-es** -ɪz **-ing** -ɪŋ **-ed** -t
Birchall ˈbɜː.tʃɔːl, -tʃəl US ˈbɝː.tʃɔːl, -tʃɑːl, -tʃəl
Birchenough ˈbɜː.tʃɪ.nʌf US ˈbɝː-
Bircher ˈbɜː.tʃəʳ US ˈbɝː.tʃɚ
Birchwood ˈbɜːtʃ.wʊd US ˈbɝːtʃ-
Bircotes ˈbɜː.kəʊts US ˈbɝː.koʊts
bird (B) bɜːd US bɝːd **-s** -z **ˈbird ˌcage; ˈbird ˌdog; ˈbird ˌfancier; ˌbird of ˈparadise; ˌbird of ˈprey; ˌkill two ˌbirds with ˌone ˈstone**
bird-brain ˈbɜːdˌbreɪn US ˈbɝːd-
bird-brained ˈbɜːdˌbreɪnd US ˈbɝːd-
birdhou|se ˈbɜːd.haʊ|s US ˈbɝːd- **-ses** -zɪz
birdie ˈbɜː.di US ˈbɝː- **-s** -z **-d** -d
birdlike ˈbɜːd.laɪk US ˈbɝːd-
birdlime ˈbɜːd.laɪm US ˈbɝːd-
birdseed ˈbɜːd.siːd US ˈbɝːd-
bird's-eye *(n. adj.)* ˈbɜːdz.aɪ US ˈbɝːdz- **-s** -z **ˌbird's-eye ˈview**
Birds Eye® ˈbɜːdz.aɪ US ˈbɝːdz-
bird's-nest ˈbɜːdz.nest US ˈbɝːdz- **-s** -s **-ing** -ɪŋ **-ed** -ɪd **ˌbird's nest ˈsoup**
birdwatch|ing ˈbɜːdˌwɒtʃ|.ɪŋ US ˈbɝːdˌwɑː.tʃ|ɪŋ, -ˌwɔː- **-er/s** -əʳ/z US -ɚ/z
bireme ˈbaɪ.riːm, -ˈ- US baɪˈriːm **-s** -z
biretta bɪˈret.ə US -ˈret̬- **-s** -z
Birgit ˈbɜː.gɪt, ˈbɪə- US ˈbɝː-, -giːt
biriani ˌbɪr.iˈɑː.ni **-s** -z
Birkbeck *surname:* ˈbɜː.bek, ˈbɜːk- US ˈbɝː-, ˈbɝːk- *college in London:* ˈbɜːk.bek US ˈbɝːk-
Birkenau ˈbɜː.kən.aʊ US ˈbɝː-
Birkenhead ˌbɜː.kənˈhed, ˈ--- US ˌbɝː.kənˈhed, ˈ---
Birkenstocks® ˈbɜː.kən.stɒks US ˈbɝː.kən.stɑːks
Birkett ˈbɜː.kɪt US ˈbɝː-
Birkin ˈbɜː.kɪn US ˈbɝː-
Birley ˈbɜː.li US ˈbɝː-
Birling ˈbɜː.lɪŋ US ˈbɝː-
Birmingham *place in UK:* ˈbɜː.mɪŋ.əm US ˈbɝː- *places in US:* ˈbɜː.mɪŋ.hæm US ˈbɝː-
Birnam ˈbɜː.nəm US ˈbɝː-
Birney ˈbɜː.ni US ˈbɝː-
Biro® ˈbaɪə.rəʊ US ˈbaɪ.roʊ **-s** -z
Biron ˈbaɪ.rən
Note: /bɪˈruːn/ in 'Love's Labour's Lost'.
birr bɜːʳ US bɝː **birrotch** ˈbɜː.rɒtʃ US ˈbɝː.ɑːtʃ
Birrell ˈbɪr.əl
birrotch *(plur. of* **birr***)* ˈbɜː.rɒtʃ US ˈbɝː.ɑːtʃ
Birstall ˈbɜː.stɔːl US ˈbɝː.stɔːl, -stɑːl
Birt bɜːt US bɝːt
birth bɜːθ US bɝːθ **-s** -s **ˈbirth cerˌtificate; ˈbirth conˌtrol; ˈbirthing ˌcenter**
birthday ˈbɜːθ.deɪ, -di US ˈbɝːθ.deɪ **-s** -z **ˈbirthday ˌcake; ˈbirthday ˌcard; ˈbirthday ˌparty; ˈbirthday ˌpresent; in one's ˈbirthday ˌsuit**
birthmark ˈbɜːθ.mɑːk US ˈbɝːθ.mɑːrk **-s** -s
birthplac|e ˈbɜːθ.pleɪs US ˈbɝːθ- **-es** -ɪz
birthrate ˈbɜːθ.reɪt US ˈbɝːθ- **-s** -s
birthright ˈbɜːθ.raɪt US ˈbɝːθ- **-s** -s
Birtwistle ˈbɜː.twɪ.sl̩ US ˈbɝː-
biryani ˌbɪr.iˈɑː.ni **-s** -z
bis bɪs
Biscay ˈbɪs.keɪ, -ki **ˌBay of ˈBiscay**
biscuit ˈbɪs.kɪt **-s** -s **ˈbiscuit ˌbarrel**
bisect baɪˈsekt US ˈbaɪ.sekt, -ˈ- **-s** -s **-ing** -ɪŋ **-ed** -ɪd
bisection baɪˈsek.ʃən **-s** -z
bisector baɪˈsek.təʳ US -tɚ **-s** -z
bisexual baɪˈsek.ʃʊəl, -ʃu.əl, -sjʊəl, -sjʊ.əl US -ʃu.əl
bisexuality baɪˌsek.ʃuˈæl.ɪ.ti, -sjuˈæl-, -ə.ti US -ʃuˈæl.ə.t̬i
bishop (B) ˈbɪʃ.əp **-s** -s
bishopric ˈbɪʃ.ə.prɪk **-s** -s
Bishopsgate ˈbɪʃ.əps.geɪt, -gɪt
Bishop's Stortford ˌbɪʃ.əpsˈstɔːt.fəd, -ˈstɔː- US -ˈstɔːrt.fɚd, -ˈstɔːr-
Bishopstoke ˈbɪʃ.əp.stəʊk US -stoʊk
Bishopston ˈbɪʃ.əp.stən
Bishopton ˈbɪʃ.əp.tən
Bisley ˈbɪz.li **-s** -z
Bismarck ˈbɪz.mɑːk US -mɑːrk
bismuth ˈbɪz.məθ
bison ˈbaɪ.sən **-s** -z
Bispham *surname:* ˈbɪs.fəm, ˈbɪs.pəm *place:* ˈbɪs.pəm
bisque biːsk, bɪsk US bɪsk **-s** -s
Bissau ˈbɪs.aʊ, -ˈ- US bɪˈsaʊ
Bissell ˈbɪs.əl
Bissett ˈbɪs.ɪt, ˈbɪz-
bissextile bɪˈsek.staɪl US -stəl, -staɪl **-s** -z
bister ˈbɪs.təʳ US -tɚ
Bisto® ˈbɪs.təʊ US -toʊ
bistour|y ˈbɪs.tər|.i **-ies** -iz
bistre ˈbɪs.təʳ US -tɚ
bistro, bistrot ˈbiː.strəʊ, ˈbɪs- US -stroʊ **-s** -z
bisulph|ate baɪˈsʌl.f|eɪt, -f|ɪt, -f|ət US -f|eɪt **-ite** -aɪt
bit bɪt **-s** -s **ˌbits and ˈpieces; take the ˌbit between one's ˈteeth**
bitch bɪtʃ **-es** -ɪz **-ed** -d
bitch|y ˈbɪtʃ|.i **-iness** -ɪ.nəs, -ɪ.nɪs **-iest** -i.ɪst, -i.əst **-ier** -i.əʳ US -i.ɚ
bit|e baɪt **-es** -s **-ing** -ɪŋ US ˈbaɪ.t̬ɪŋ **bit** bɪt **bitten** ˈbɪt.ən **biter/s** ˈbaɪ.təʳ/z US -t̬ɚ/z **ˌbite off ˌmore than one can ˈchew; ˌbite one's ˈtongue; ˌbite someone's ˈhead off; ˌbite the ˈbullet; ˌbite the ˈdust; ˌbite the ˌhand that ˈfeeds one**
Bithell ˈbɪθ.əl, bɪˈθel
Bithynia bɪˈθɪn.i.ə, baɪ-
Bitola ˈbiː.təʊ.lə US -toʊ-, -t̬əl.ə
Bitolj ˈbiː.təʊ.ljə US -toʊ-, -t̬əl.jə
bitten *(from* **bite***)* ˈbɪt.ən **once ˌbitten twice ˈshy**
bitt|er ˈbɪt|.əʳ US ˈbɪt̬|.ɚ **-erer** -ər.əʳ US -ɚ.ɚ **-erest** -ər.ɪst, -əst **-erly** -ə.li US -ɚ.li **-erness** -ə.nəs, -nɪs US -ɚ.nəs, -nɪs **to the ˌbitter ˈend**
bittern ˈbɪt.ən, -ɜːn US ˈbɪt̬.ɚn **-s** -z
bitters ˈbɪt.əz US ˈbɪt̬.ɚz
bittersweet ˈbɪt.ə.swiːt, ˌ--ˈ- US ˈbɪt̬.ɚ.swiːt
bitt|y ˈbɪt|.i US ˈbɪt̬- **-ier** -i.əʳ US -i.ɚ **-iest** -i.ɪst, -i.əst **-iness** -ɪ.nəs, -ɪ.nɪs
bitumen ˈbɪtʃ.ə.mən, ˈ-ʊ-, -mɪn US bɪˈtuː.mən, baɪ-, -ˈtjuː- **-s** -z
bituminous bɪˈtʃuː.mɪ.nəs, bə-, -ˈtjuː-, -mə- US -ˈtuː-, -ˈtjuː-
bivalen|ce ˌbaɪˈveɪ.lən|ts, bɪ-; US ˌbaɪˈveɪ.lən|ts, ˈbaɪ.veɪ- **-cy** -*t*.si **-t** -t
bivalve ˈbaɪ.vælv **-s** -z
bivouac ˈbɪv.u.æk US -u.æk, ˈ-wæk **-s** -s **-king** -ɪŋ **-ked** -t
bi-weekl|y baɪˈwiː.kl|i **-ies** -iz *stress shift:* ˌbi-weekly ˈjournal
bizarre bɪˈzɑːʳ, bə- US -ˈzɑːr **-ly** -li **-ness** -nəs, -nɪs
Bizerte, Bizerta bɪˈzɜː.tə US -ˈzɝː-
Bizet ˈbiː.zeɪ US -ˈ-
Bjork, Björk bjɔːk, bjɜːk, biˈɔːk US bjɔːrk
Bjorn, Björn bjɔːn, bjɜːn; biˈɔːn, -ˈɜːn US bjɔːrn, bjɝːn
BL ˌbiːˈel
blab blæb **-s** -z **-bing** -ɪŋ **-bed** -d **-ber/s** -əʳ/z US -ɚ/z
blabb|er ˈblæb|.əʳ US -ɚ **-ers** -əz US -ɚz **-ering** -ər.ɪŋ **-ered** -əd US -ɚd
blabber|mouth ˈblæb.əl.maʊθ US ˈ-ɚ- **-mouths** -maʊðz, -maʊθs
Blaby ˈbleɪ.bi

Blachford 'blæʃ.fəd (US) -fɚd
black (B) blæk **-s** -s **-er** -əʳ (US) -ɚ **-est** -ɪst, -əst **-ish** -ɪʃ **-ly** -li **-ness** -nəs, -nɪs **-ing** -ɪŋ **-ed** -t ˌ**black 'belt**; ˌ**black 'box**; ˌ**black 'eye**; ˌ**Black 'Forest**; ˌ**Black Forest 'gateau**; ˌ**black 'hole**; ˌ**black ˌhole of Cal'cutta**; ˌ**black 'ice**; ˌ**black 'magic**; ˌ**black 'market**; ˌ**black 'pepper**; ˌ**black 'pudding**; ˌ**Black 'Rod**; ˌ**black 'treacle**; ˌ**black and 'blue**; ˌ**black and 'tan**; ˌ**black and 'white**; ˌ**black ˌsheep of the 'family**
Blackadder 'blækˌæd.əʳ, ˌ-'-- (US) 'blækˌæd.ɚ
blackamoor 'blæk.ə.mɔːʳ (US) -mʊr **-s** -z
blackball (*v.*) 'blæk.bɔːl (US) -bɔːl, -bɑːl **-s** -z **-ing** -ɪŋ **-ed** -d
blackbeetle ˌblæk'biː.tl̩ (US) 'blækˌbiː.t̬l̩ **-s** -z
blackberr|y 'blæk.bᵊr|.i, -ˌber- (US) -ˌber- **-ies** -iz
blackberrying 'blæk.bᵊr.i.ɪŋ, -ˌber- (US) -ˌber-
blackbird 'blæk.bɜːd (US) -bɝːd **-s** -z
blackboard 'blæk.bɔːd (US) -bɔːrd **-s** -z
black box ˌblæk'bɒks (US) -'bɑːks **-es** -ɪz
blackboy 'blæk.bɔɪ **-s** -z
Blackburn(e) 'blæk.bɜːn (US) -bɝːn
blackcap 'blæk.kæp **-s** -s
blackcock 'blæk.kɒk (US) -kɑːk **-s** -s
blackcurrant ˌblæk'kʌr.ᵊnt (US) 'blækˌkɝː- **-s** -s *stress shift, British only:* ˌblackcurrant 'pie
Blackdown 'blæk.daʊn
blacken 'blæk.ᵊn **-s** -z **-ing** -ɪŋ **-ed** -d
Blackett 'blæk.ɪt
black-eyed ˌblæk'aɪd *stress shift:* ˌblack-eyed 'peas
black|fly 'blæk|.flaɪ **-flies** -flaɪz
Black|foot 'blæk|.fʊt **-feet** -fiːt
Blackford 'blæk.fəd (US) -fɚd
Blackfriars ˌblæk'fraɪəz (US) -'fraɪɚz *stress shift:* ˌBlackfriars 'Bobby
blackgame 'blæk.geɪm **-s** -z
blackguard 'blæg.ɑːd, '-əd (US) -ɑːrd, -ɚd **-s** -z **-ly** -li
blackhead 'blæk.hed **-s** -z
Blackheath ˌblæk'hiːθ *stress shift:* ˌBlackheath 'Harriers
Blackie 'blæk.i, 'bleɪ.ki (US) 'blæk.i
blacking (*n.*) 'blæk.ɪŋ **-s** -z
blackjack 'blæk.dʒæk **-s** -s
blacklead (*n.*) 'blæk.led
blacklead (*v.*) ˌblæk'led, '-- **-s** -z **-ing** -ɪŋ **-ed** -ɪd
blackleg 'blæk.leg **-s** -z
Blackley *Manchester:* 'bleɪ.kli *surname:* 'blæk.li
blacklist 'blæk.lɪst **-s** -s **-ing** -ɪŋ **-ed** -ɪd
blackmail 'blæk.meɪl **-s** -z **-ing** -ɪŋ **-ed** -d **-er/s** -əʳ/z (US) -ɚ/z
Blackman 'blæk.mən
Black Maria ˌblæk.mə'raɪə
Blackmoor, Blackmore 'blæk.mɔːʳ (US) -mɔːr
blackout 'blæk.aʊt **-s** -s
Blackpool 'blæk.puːl
Blackpudlian ˌblæk'pʌd.li.ən **-s** -z
Blackrock 'blæk.rɒk (US) -rɑːk
Blackshirt 'blæk.ʃɜːt (US) -ʃɝːt **-s** -s
blacksmith 'blæk.smɪθ **-s** -s
Blackston 'blæk.stᵊn
Blackstone 'blæk.stəʊn, -stᵊn (US) -stoʊn, -stᵊn
blackthorn (B) 'blæk.θɔːn (US) -θɔːrn **-s** -z
blacktop 'blæk.tɒp (US) -tɑːp **-s** -s **-ping** -ɪŋ **-ped** -t
Blackwall 'blæk.wɔːl (US) -wɔːl, -wɑːl
blackwater (B) 'blækˌwɔː.təʳ (US) -ˌwɑː.t̬ɚ, -ˌwɔː-
Blackwell 'blæk.wel, -wᵊl
Blackwood *surname:* 'blæk.wʊd *place in Gwent:* ˌblæk'wʊd
bladder 'blæd.əʳ (US) -ɚ **-s** -z
bladderwort 'blæd.ə.wɜːt (US) -ɚ.wɝːt, -wɔːrt **-s** -s
bladderwrack 'blæd.ᵊr.æk
blade bleɪd **-s** -z
Bladon 'bleɪ.dᵊn
blaeberr|y 'bleɪ.bᵊr|.i (US) -ber- **-ies** -iz
Blaenau Ffestiniog ˌblaɪ.naɪ.fes'tɪn.i.ɒg, ˌbleɪ.ni- (US) -ɑːg
Blaenau Gwent ˌblaɪ.naɪ'gwent, ˌbleɪ.ni-
Blaenavon blaɪ'næv.ᵊn
blah-blah 'blɑː.blɑː, ˌ-'-
Blaikie 'bleɪ.ki
Blaikley 'bleɪ.kli
blain bleɪn **-s** -z
Blair bleəʳ (US) bler **-ite/s** -aɪt/s **-ism** -ɪ.zᵊm
Blair Atholl ˌbleəʳ'æθ.ᵊl (US) ˌbler-
Blairgowrie ˌbleə'gaʊə.ri (US) ˌbler-
Blaise bleɪz
Blake bleɪk
Blakelock 'bleɪ.klɒk (US) -klɑːk
Blakely 'bleɪ.kli
Blakeney 'bleɪk.ni
Blakey 'bleɪ.ki
Blakiston 'blæk.ɪ.stᵊn, 'bleɪ.kɪ-
blamab|le 'bleɪ.mə.b|l̩ **-ly** -li **-leness** -l̩.nəs, -nɪs
blam|e bleɪm **-es** -z **-ing** -ɪŋ **-ed** -d
blameless 'bleɪm.ləs, -lɪs **-ly** -li **-ness** -nəs, -nɪs
blameworth|y 'bleɪmˌwɜː.ð|i (US) -ˌwɝː- **-iness** -ɪ.nəs, -ɪ.nɪs
Blamires blə'maɪəz (US) -'maɪɚz
Blanc *Mont:* blɑ̃ː*ŋ* (US) blɑ̃ː*ŋ*, blɑːŋk
blanch blɑːn*t*ʃ (US) blæn*t*ʃ **-es** -ɪz **-ing** -ɪŋ **-ed** -t
Blanchard 'blæn.*t*ʃəd, -*t*ʃɑːd (US) 'blæn*t*.ʃɚd, -ʃɑːrd
Blanche blɑːn*t*ʃ (US) blæn*t*ʃ
Blanchett 'blɑːn.tʃɪt (US) 'blæn-
Blanchflower 'blɑːn*t*ʃ.flaʊəʳ (US) 'blæn*t*ʃ.flaʊɚ
blancmang|e blə'mɒn*d*ʒ, -'mɒ̃*n*ʒ (US) -'mɑːn*d*ʒ **-es** -ɪz
blanco 'blæŋ.kəʊ (US) -koʊ
bland (B) blænd **-er** -əʳ (US) -ɚ **-est** -ɪst, -əst **-ly** -li **-ness** -nəs, -nɪs
Blandford 'blæn*d*.fəd (US) -fɚd
blandish 'blæn.dɪʃ **-es** -ɪz **-ing** -ɪŋ **-ed** -t
blandishment 'blæn.dɪʃ.mᵊnt
Blandy 'blæn.di
Blaney 'bleɪ.ni
blank (*n. adj. v.*) blæŋk **-s** -s **-er** -əʳ (US) -ɚ **-est** -ɪst, -əst **-ly** -li **-ness** -nəs, -nɪs **-ing** -ɪŋ **-ed** -t ˌ**blank 'cheque/check**; ˌ**blank 'verse**
blan|ket 'blæŋ|.kɪt **-kets** -kɪts **-keting** -kɪ.tɪŋ (US) -kɪ.t̬ɪŋ **-keted** -kɪ.tɪd (US) -kɪ.t̬ɪd
Blankley 'blæŋ.kli
blanquette ˌblɒŋ'ket, ˌblæŋ-, ˌblɑ̃ːŋ- (US) ˌblɑːŋ- **-s** -s
Blantyre blæn'taɪəʳ, '-- (US) blæn'taɪɚ
Note: In Malawi the preferred stress pattern is /'--/.
blar|e bleəʳ (US) bler **-es** -z **-ing** -ɪŋ **-ed** -d
blarney (B) 'blɑː.ni (US) 'blɑːr-
blasé 'blɑː.zeɪ, blɑː'zeɪ (US) -'-
blasphem|e ˌblæs'fiːm, ˌblɑːs- (US) 'blæs.fiːm **-es** -z **-ing/ly** -ɪŋ/li **-ed** -d **-er/s** -əʳ/z (US) -ɚ/z
blasphemous 'blæs.fə.məs, 'blɑːs-, -fɪ- (US) 'blæs- **-ly** -li
blasphem|y 'blæs.fə.m|i, 'blɑːs-, -fɪ- (US) 'blæs- **-ies** -iz
blast blɑːst (US) blæst **-s** -s **-ing** -ɪŋ **-ed** -ɪd '**blast ˌfurnace**
blastoderm 'blæs.təʊ.dɜːm (US) -tə.dɝːm **-s** -z
blast-off 'blɑːst.ɒf (US) 'blæst.ɑːf **-s** -s
blatancy 'bleɪ.tᵊn*t*.si
blatant 'bleɪ.tᵊnt **-ly** -li
Blatchford 'blætʃ.fəd (US) -fɚd
blath|er 'blæð|.əʳ (US) -ɚ **-ers** -əz (US) -ɚz **-ering** -ᵊr.ɪŋ **-ered** -əd (US) -ɚd
Blawith *in Cumbria:* 'blɑːð *road in Harrow:* 'bleɪ.wɪθ
blaxploitation ˌblæk.splɔɪ'teɪ.ʃᵊn
Blaydes bleɪdz
Blaydon 'bleɪ.dᵊn
blaz|e bleɪz **-es** -ɪz **-ing** -ɪŋ **-ed** -d
blazer 'bleɪ.zəʳ (US) -zɚ **-s** -z
Blazes 'bleɪ.zɪz
Blazey 'bleɪ.zi
blazon 'bleɪ.zᵊn *in original heraldic sense also:* 'blæz.ᵊn **-s** -z **-ing** -ɪŋ **-ed** -d
bleach bliːtʃ **-es** -ɪz **-ing** -ɪŋ **-ed** -t '**bleaching ˌpowder**
bleachers 'bliː.tʃəz (US) -tʃɚz

bleak bliːk **-er** -əʳ (US) -ɚ **-est** -ɪst, -əst **-ly** -li **-ness** -nəs, -nɪs
Bleakley 'bliː.kli
blear blɪəʳ (US) blɪr
blear|y 'blɪə.r|i (US) 'blɪr|.i **-ier** -i.əʳ (US) -i.ɚ **-iest** -i.ɪst (US) -i.əst **-ily** -əl.i, -ɪ.li **-iness** -ɪ.nəs, -ɪ.nɪs
bleary-eyed ˌblɪə.ri'aɪd (US) 'blɪr.i.aɪd- *stress shift, British only:* ˌbleary-eyed 'child
Bleasdale 'bliːz.deɪl
Bleasedale 'bliːz.deɪl
bleat bliːt **-s** -s **-ing** -ɪŋ (US) 'bliː.t̬ɪŋ **-ed** -ɪd (US) 'bliː.t̬ɪd
bleb bleb **-s** -z
bled *(from* **bleed***)* bled
Bledisloe 'bled.ɪ.sləʊ (US) -sloʊ
bleed bliːd **-s** -z **-ing** -ɪŋ **-er/s** -əʳ/z (US) -ɚ/z **bled** bled
bleep bliːp **-s** -s **-ing** -ɪŋ **-ed** -t
bleeper 'bliː.pəʳ (US) -pɚ **-s** -z
blemish 'blem.ɪʃ **-es** -ɪz **-ing** -ɪŋ **-ed** -t
blench **(B)** blen*t*ʃ **-es** -ɪz **-ing** -ɪŋ **-ed** -t
Blencowe 'bleŋ.kəʊ (US) -koʊ
blend blend **-s** -z **-ing** -ɪŋ **-ed** -ɪd
blende blend
blender 'blen.dəʳ (US) -dɚ **-s** -z
Blenheim 'blen.ɪm, -əm
Blenkinsop 'bleŋ.kɪn.sɒp (US) -sɑːp
Blennerhassett ˌblen.ə'hæs.ɪt (US) 'blen.ɚ.hæs-
Blériot 'bler.i.əʊ (US) ˌbler.i'oʊ, '--- **-s** -z
bless bles **-es** -ɪz **-ing** -ɪŋ **-ed** -t **blest** blest
blessed *(adj.)* 'bles.ɪd, -əd **-ly** -li **-ness** -nəs, -nɪs
blessing 'bles.ɪŋ **-s** -z **a ˌblessing in dis'guise**
Blessington 'bles.ɪŋ.tən
blest *(from* **bless***)* blest
Bletchley 'bletʃ.li
bleth|er 'bleð|.əʳ (US) -ɚ **-ers** -əz (US) -ɚz **-ering** -ər.ɪŋ **-ered** -əd (US) -ɚd
blew *(from* **blow***)* bluː
Blewett, Blewitt bluː.ɪt
Blickling 'blɪk.lɪŋ
Bligh blaɪ
blight blaɪt **-s** -s **-ing** -ɪŋ (US) 'blaɪ.t̬ɪŋ **-ed** -ɪd (US) 'blaɪ.t̬ɪd
blighter 'blaɪ.təʳ (US) -t̬ɚ **-s** -z
Blighty 'blaɪ.ti (US) -t̬i
blimey 'blaɪ.mi
blimp blɪmp **-s** -s **-ish** -ɪʃ
blind blaɪnd **-er** -əʳ (US) -ɚ **-est** -ɪst, -est **-ly** -li **-ness** -nəs, -nɪs **-s** -z **-ing** -ɪŋ **-ed** -ɪd **ˌblind 'date; 'blind ˌside; 'blind ˌspot; as ˌblind as a 'bat; (a ˌcase of) the ˌblind ˌleading the 'blind; ˌturn a ˌblind 'eye (to)**
blinder 'blaɪn.dəʳ (US) -dɚ **-s** -z
blindfold 'blaɪn*d*.fəʊld (US) -foʊld **-s** -z **-ing** -ɪŋ **-ed** -ɪd
blinding 'blaɪn.dɪŋ **-ly** -li
blindman's-buff ˌblaɪn*d*.mænz'bʌf
blindsid|e 'blaɪn*d*.saɪd **-s** -z **-ing** -ɪŋ **-ed** -ɪd
blindworm 'blaɪnd.wɜːm (US) -wɝːm **-s** -z
blini 'blɪn.i, 'bliː.ni **-s** -z
blink blɪŋk **-s** -s **-ing** -ɪŋ **-ed** -t
blinker 'blɪŋ.kəʳ (US) -kɚ **-s** -z **-ed** -d
blip blɪp **-s** -s **-ping** -ɪŋ **-ped** -t
bliss **(B)** blɪs
Blissett 'blɪs.ɪt
blissful 'blɪs.fəl, -fʊl **-ly** -i **-ness** -nəs, -nɪs
blist|er 'blɪs.t|əʳ (US) -t|ɚ **-ers** -əz (US) -ɚz **-ering** -ər.ɪŋ **-ered** -əd (US) -ɚd
blith|e blaɪð **-er** -əʳ (US) -ɚ **-est** -ɪst, -əst **-ely** -li **-eness** -nəs, -nɪs
Blithedale 'blaɪð.deɪl
blithering 'blɪð.ər.ɪŋ
blithesome 'blaɪð.səm **-ly** -li **-ness** -nəs, -nɪs
BLit(t) ˌbiː'lɪt
blitz blɪts **-es** -ɪz **-ing** -ɪŋ **-ed** -t
blitzkrieg 'blɪts.kriːg **-s** -z
Blixen 'blɪk.sən
blizzard 'blɪz.əd (US) -ɚd **-s** -z
bloat bləʊt (US) bloʊt **-s** -s **-ing** -ɪŋ (US) 'bloʊ.t̬ɪŋ **-ed/ness** -ɪd/nəs, -nɪs (US) 'bloʊ.t̬ɪd/nəs, -nɪs
bloater 'bləʊ.təʳ (US) 'bloʊ.t̬ɚ **-s** -z
blob blɒb (US) blɑːb **-s** -z
blobb|y 'blɒb|.i (US) 'blɑː.b|i **-ier** -i.əʳ (US) -i.ɚ **-iest** -i.ɪst, -ɪ.əst
bloc blɒk (US) blɑːk **-s** -s
Bloch blɒk *as if German:* blox (US) blɑːk
block **(B)** blɒk (US) blɑːk **-s** -s **-ing** -ɪŋ **-ed** -t **-er/s** -əʳ/z (US) -ɚ/z **ˌblock 'capitals; ˌblock 'booking**
blockad|e blɒk'eɪd, blə'keɪd (US) blɑː'keɪd **-es** -z **-ing** -ɪŋ **-ed** -ɪd **-er/s** -əʳ/z (US) -ɚ/z
blockag|e 'blɒk.ɪdʒ (US) 'blɑː.kɪdʒ **-es** -ɪz
blockbust|er 'blɒkˌbʌs.t|əʳ (US) 'blɑːkˌbʌs.t|ɚ **-ers** -əz (US) -ɚz **-ering** -ər.ɪŋ
blockhead 'blɒk.hed (US) 'blɑːk- **-s** -z
blockhou|se 'blɒk.haʊ|s (US) 'blɑːk- **-ses** -zɪz
Blodwen 'blɒd.wɪn, -wen (US) 'blɑːd-
Bloemfontein 'bluːm.fən.teɪn, -fɒn- (US) -fɑːn-
Blofeld 'bləʊ.felt, -feld (US) 'bloʊ-
Blois *town in France:* blwɑː *surname:* blɔɪs
bloke bləʊk (US) bloʊk **-s** -s **-ish/ly** -ɪʃ/li
Blom blɒm (US) blɑːm
Blomefield 'bluːm.fiːld
Blomfield 'blɒm.fiːld, 'blʊm-, 'blʌm-, 'bluːm- (US) 'blɑːm-, 'blʊm-, 'blʌm-, 'bluːm-
blond(e) blɒnd (US) blɑːnd **-s** -z
Blondel(l) 'blʌn.dəl, 'blɒn-; blɒn'del (US) blɑːn'del; 'blɑːn.dəl, 'blʌn-
Blondin 'blɒn.dɪn *as if French:* blɔ̃ːn'dæ̃ŋ (US) blɑːn'dæn
blood blʌd **-s** -z **-ing** -ɪŋ **-ed** -ɪd **'blood ˌcell; 'blood ˌdonor; 'blood ˌgroup; 'blood ˌmoney; 'blood ˌpoisoning; 'blood ˌpressure; ˌblood re'lation; 'blood ˌsport; 'blood ˌtest; 'blood transˌfusion; 'blood ˌvessel; ˌblood is thicker than 'water; get ˌblood out of a 'stone; in ˌcold 'blood**
bloodba|th 'blʌd.bɑː|θ (US) -bæ|θ **-ths** -ðz
bloodcurdling 'blʌdˌkɜː.dl̩.ɪŋ, -ˌkɜːd.lɪŋ (US) -ˌkɝː.dl̩.ɪŋ, -ˌkɝːd.lɪŋ **-ly** -li
bloodhound 'blʌd.haʊnd **-s** -z
bloodied 'blʌd.id
bloodless 'blʌd.ləs, -lɪs **-ly** -li **-ness** -nəs, -nɪs
bloodletting 'blʌdˌlet.ɪŋ (US) -ˌlet̬.ɪŋ
bloodline 'blʌd.laɪn
blood-red ˌblʌd'red *stress shift:* ˌblood-red 'lips
bloodshed 'blʌd.ʃed
bloodshot 'blʌd.ʃɒt (US) -ʃɑːt
bloodstain 'blʌd.steɪn **-s** -z **-ed** -d
bloodstock 'blʌd.stɒk (US) -stɑːk
bloodstone 'blʌd.stəʊn (US) -stoʊn **-s** -z
bloodstream 'blʌd.striːm **-s** -z
bloodsucker 'blʌdˌsʌk.əʳ (US) -ɚ **-s** -z
bloodthirst|y 'blʌdˌθɜː.st|i (US) -ˌθɝː- **-ier** -i.əʳ (US) -i.ɚ **-iest** -i.ɪst, -i.əst **-ily** -ɪ.li, -əl.i **-iness** -ɪ.nəs, -ɪ.nɪs
blood|y 'blʌd|.i **-ier** -i.əʳ (US) -i.ɚ **-iest** -i.ɪst, -i.əst **-ily** -ɪ.li, -əl.i **-iness** -ɪ.nəs, -ɪ.nɪs **ˌBloody 'Mary**
bloody-minded ˌblʌd.i'maɪn.dɪd *stress shift:* ˌbloody-minded 'person
bloom **(B)** bluːm **-s** -z **-ing** -ɪŋ **-ed** -d
bloomer **(B)** 'bluː.məʳ (US) -mɚ **-s** -z
Bloomfield 'bluːm.fiːld
Bloomingdale 'bluː.mɪŋ.deɪl **-'s** -z
Bloomington 'bluː.mɪŋ.tən
Bloomsbury 'bluːmz.bər.i (US) -ber-, -bɚ-
bloop bluːp **-s** -s **-ing** -ɪŋ **-ed** -t
blooper 'bluː.pəʳ (US) -pɚ **-s** -z
Blore blɔːʳ (US) blɔːr
blossom **(B)** 'blɒs.əm (US) 'blɑː.səm **-s** -z **-ing** -ɪŋ **-ed** -d
blot blɒt (US) blɑːt **-s** -s **-ting** -ɪŋ (US) 'blɑː.t̬ɪŋ **-ted** -ɪd (US) 'blɑː.t̬ɪd
blotch blɒtʃ (US) blɑːtʃ **-es** -ɪz **-ing** -ɪŋ **-ed** -t
blotch|y 'blɒtʃ|.i (US) 'blɑː.tʃ|i **-ier** -i.əʳ (US) -i.ɚ **-iest** -i.ɪst, -i.əst **-ily** -ɪ.li, -əl.i **-iness** -ɪ.nəs, -ɪ.nɪs
blotter 'blɒt.əʳ (US) 'blɑː.t̬ɚ **-s** -z
blotting 'blɒt.ɪŋ (US) 'blɑː.t̬.ɪŋ **'blotting ˌpaper**

blotto ˈblɒt.əʊ (US) ˈblɑː.t̬oʊ
Blount blʌnt, blaʊnt
blous|e blaʊz (US) blaʊs **-es** -ɪz
blouson ˈbluː.zɒn (US) -sɑːn, ˈblaʊ-, -zɑːn **-s** -z
blow (B) bləʊ (US) bloʊ **-s** -z **-ing** -ɪŋ **blew** bluː **blown** bləʊn (US) bloʊn **blowed** bləʊd (US) bloʊd **blower/s** ˈbləʊ.əʳ/z (US) ˈbloʊ.ɚ/s
blow-by-blow ˌbləʊ.baɪˈbləʊ (US) ˌbloʊ.baɪˈbloʊ *stress shift:* ˌblow-by-blow acˈcount
blow|dry ˈbləʊ|.draɪ (US) ˈbloʊ- **-dries** -draɪz **-drying** -ˌdraɪ.ɪŋ **-dried** -draɪd **-drier/s** -ˌdraɪ.əʳ/z (US) -ˌdraɪ.ɚ/z
blowfl|y ˈbləʊ.fl|aɪ (US) ˈbloʊ- **-ies** -aɪz
blowgun ˈbləʊ.gʌn (US) ˈbloʊ- **-s** -z
blowhard ˈbləʊ.hɑːd (US) ˈbloʊ.hɑːrd **-s** -z
blowhole ˈbləʊ.həʊl (US) ˈbloʊ.hoʊl **-s** -z
blowlamp ˈbləʊ.læmp (US) ˈbloʊ- **-s** -s
blown *(from* **blow***)* bləʊn (US) bloʊn
blowout ˈbləʊ.aʊt (US) ˈbloʊ- **-s** -s
blowpipe ˈbləʊ.paɪp (US) ˈbloʊ- **-s** -s
blows|y ˈblaʊ.z|i **-ier** -i.əʳ (US) -i.ɚ **-iest** -i.ɪst, -i.əst **-ily** -ɪ.li, -ᵊl.i **-iness** -ɪ.nəs, -ɪ.nɪs
blowtorch ˈbləʊ.tɔːtʃ (US) ˈbloʊ.tɔːrtʃ **-es** -ɪz
blow|y ˈbləʊ|.i (US) ˈbloʊ- **-ier** -i.əʳ (US) -i.ɚ **-iest** -i.ɪst, -i.əst **-ily** -ɪ.li, -ᵊl.i **-iness** -ɪ.nəs, -ɪ.nɪs
blowz|y ˈblaʊ.z|i **-ier** -i.əʳ (US) -i.ɚ **-iest** -i.ɪst, -i.əst **-ily** -ɪ.li, -ᵊl.i **-iness** -ɪ.nəs, -ɪ.nɪs
Blox(h)am ˈblɒk.səm (US) ˈblɑːk-
BLT ˌbiː.elˈtiː
blub blʌb **-s** -z **-bing** -ɪŋ **-bed** -d
blubb|er ˈblʌb|.əʳ (US) -ɚ **-ers** -əz (US) -ɚz **-ering** -ᵊr.ɪŋ **-ered** -əd (US) -ɚd **-erer/s** -ᵊr.əʳ/z
bludgeon ˈblʌdʒ.ᵊn **-s** -z **-ing** -ɪŋ **-ed** -d
blu|e bluː **-es** -z **-er** -əʳ (US) -ɚ **-est** -ɪst, -əst **-(e)ing** -ɪŋ **-ed** -d ˌ**blue** ˈ**cheese**; ˈ**blue** ˌ**law**; ˌ**blue** ˈ**movie**; ˈ**blue** ˌ**jay**; ˈ**blue** ˌ**tit**; ˌ**out of the** ˈ**blue**
Bluebeard ˈbluː.bɪəd (US) -bɪrd
bluebell ˈbluː.bel **-s** -z
blueberr|y ˈbluː.bᵊr|.i, -ˌber- (US) -ˌber- **-ies** -iz
bluebird ˈbluː.bɜːd (US) -bɝːd **-s** -z
blue-blooded ˌbluːˈblʌd.ɪd (US) ˈ-ˌ-- *stress shift, British only:* ˌblue-blooded ˈmonarch
bluebottle ˈbluːˌbɒt.l̩ (US) -ˌbɑː.t̬l̩ **-s** -z
blue-chip ˈbluː.tʃɪp
bluecoat ˈbluː.kəʊt (US) -koʊt **-s** -s
blue-collar ˌbluːˈkɒl.əʳ (US) ˈbluːˌkɑː.lɚ *stress shift, British only:* ˌblue-collar ˈworker
blue-eyed ˌbluːˈaɪd, ˈ-- *stress shift, British only: see compound:* ˌ**blue-eyed** ˈ**boy**
bluegrass ˈbluː.grɑːs (US) -græs
bluejacket ˈbluːˌdʒæk.ɪt **-s** -s
bluejay ˈbluː.dʒeɪ **-s** -z
bluejeans, blue jeans ˌbluːˈdʒiːnz (US) ˈ--
blueness ˈbluː.nəs, -nɪs
blue-pencil ˌbluːˈpent.sᵊl, -sɪl (US) ˈ-ˌ-- **-s** -z **-(l)ing** -ɪŋ **-(l)ed** -d
blueprint ˈbluː.prɪnt **-s** -s
bluestocking ˈbluːˌstɒk.ɪŋ (US) -ˌstɑː.kɪŋ **-s** -z
bluesy ˈbluː.zi
Bluett ˈbluː.ɪt
bluey ˈbluː.i
bluff blʌf **-s** -s **-er** -əʳ (US) -ɚ **-est** -ɪst, -əst **-ly** -li **-ness** -nəs, -nɪs **-ing** -ɪŋ **-ed** -t
bluish ˈbluː.ɪʃ
Blum bluːm
Blume bluːm
Blundell ˈblʌn.dᵊl; blʌnˈdel
Blunden ˈblʌn.dən
blund|er ˈblʌn.d|əʳ (US) -d|ɚ **-ers** -əz (US) -ɚz **-ering** -ᵊr.ɪŋ **-ered** -əd (US) -ɚd **-erer/s** -ᵊr.əʳ/z (US) -ɚ.ɚ/z
blunderbuss ˈblʌn.də.bʌs (US) -dɚ- **-es** -ɪz
Blunkett ˈblʌŋ.kɪt
Blunn blʌn
blunt (B) blʌnt **-er** -əʳ (US) ˈblʌn.t̬ɚ **-est** -ɪst, -əst (US) ˈblʌn.t̬ɪst, -t̬əst **-ly** -li **-ness** -nəs, -nɪs **-s** -s **-ing** -ɪŋ (US) ˈblʌn.t̬ɪŋ **-ed** -ɪd (US) ˈblʌn.t̬ɪd ˌ**blunt** ˈ**instrument**
blur (B) blɜːʳ (US) blɝː **-s** -z **-ring** -ɪŋ **-red** -d
blurb blɜːb (US) blɝːb **-s** -z
blurt blɜːt (US) blɝːt **-s** -s **-ing** -ɪŋ (US) ˈblɝː.t̬ɪŋ **-ed** -ɪd (US) ˈblɝː.t̬ɪd
blush blʌʃ **-es** -ɪz **-ing/ly** -ɪŋ/li **-ed** -t
blusher ˈblʌʃ.əʳ (US) -ɚ **-s** -z
blust|er ˈblʌs.t|əʳ (US) -t|ɚ **-ers** -əz (US) -ɚz **-ering/ly** -ᵊr.ɪŋ/li **-ered** -əd (US) -ɚd **-erer/s** -ᵊr.əʳ/z (US) -ɚ.ɚ/z
bluster|y ˈblʌs.tᵊr|.i **-iness** -ɪ.nəs, -ɪ.nɪs
Blu-Tack® ˈbluː.tæk
Bly blaɪ
Blyth blaɪð, blaɪθ, blaɪ
Blythborough ˈblaɪ.bᵊr.ə (US) -oʊ
Blythe blaɪð
Blyton ˈblaɪ.tᵊn
B-movie ˈbiːˌmuː.vi **-s** -z
BMus ˌbiːˈmʌz
BMW® ˌbiː.emˈdʌb.l̩.juː
BMX ˌbiː.emˈeks *stress shift, see compound:* ˌ**BMX** ˈ**bike**
bn *(abbrev. for* **billion***)* ˈbɪl.i.ən, ˈ-jən (US) ˈ-jən
Bo bəʊ (US) boʊ
BO ˌbiːˈəʊ (US) -ˈoʊ
boa bəʊə (US) boʊə **-s** -z
Boadicea ˌbəʊ.dɪˈsiː.ə, -dəˈ- (US) ˌboʊ.ə-
Boag bəʊg; ˈbəʊ.æg, -əg (US) boʊg
Boal bəʊl (US) boʊl
Boanas ˈbəʊ.nəs (US) ˈboʊ-
Boanerges ˌbəʊəˈnɜː.dʒiːz (US) ˌboʊəˈnɝː-
boar bɔːʳ (US) bɔːr **-s** -z
board bɔːd (US) bɔːrd **-s** -z **-ing** -ɪŋ **-ed** -ɪd ˈ**board** ˌ**game**; ˈ**boarding** ˌ**house**; ˈ**boarding** ˌ**pass**; ˈ**boarding** ˌ**school**; ˌ**go by the** ˈ**board**
boarder ˈbɔː.dəʳ (US) ˈbɔːr.dɚ **-s** -z
boardroom ˈbɔːd.rʊm, -ruːm (US) ˈbɔːrd.ruːm, -rʊm **-s** -z
boardwalk ˈbɔːd.wɔːk (US) ˈbɔːrd.wɔːk, -wɑːk **-s** -s
boarish ˈbɔː.rɪʃ (US) ˈbɔːr.ɪʃ
Boas ˈbəʊ.æz, -əz, -æs, -əs (US) ˈboʊ-
Boase bəʊz (US) boʊz
boast bəʊst (US) boʊst **-s** -s **-ing/ly** -ɪŋ/li **-ed** -ɪd **-er/s** -əʳ/z (US) -ɚ/z
boastful ˈbəʊst.fᵊl, -fʊl (US) ˈboʊst- **-ly** -li **-ness** -nəs, -nɪs
boat bəʊt (US) boʊt **-s** -s **-er/s** -əʳ/z (US) ˈboʊ.t̬ɚ/z ˈ**boat** ˌ**race**; ˈ**boat** ˌ**train**; ˌ**burn one's** ˈ**boats**
Boateng ˈbwɑː.teŋ, ˈbəʊ- (US) ˈbwɑː-, ˈboʊ-
boathook ˈbəʊt.hʊk (US) ˈboʊt- **-s** -s
boathou|se ˈbəʊt.haʊ|s (US) ˈboʊt- **-ses** -zɪz
boating ˈbəʊ.tɪŋ (US) ˈboʊ.t̬ɪŋ
boatload ˈbəʊt.ləʊd (US) ˈboʊt.loʊd **-s** -z
boat|man ˈbəʊt|.mən (US) ˈboʊt- **-men** -mən, -men
boatswain ˈbəʊ.sᵊn, ˈbəʊt.sweɪn (US) ˈboʊ.sᵊn **-s** -z
boatyard ˈbəʊt.jɑːd (US) ˈboʊt.jɑːrd **-s** -z
Boaz ˈbəʊ.æz (US) ˈboʊ-
bob (B) bɒb (US) bɑːb **-s** -z **-bing** -ɪŋ **-bed** -d
Bobbie ˈbɒb.i (US) ˈbɑː.bi
bobbin ˈbɒb.ɪn (US) ˈbɑː.bɪn **-s** -z
bobbish ˈbɒb.ɪʃ (US) ˈbɑː.bɪʃ **-ly** -li **-ness** -nəs, -nɪs
bobbl|e ˈbɒb.l̩ (US) ˈbɑː.bl̩ **-es** -z **-ing** -ɪŋ **-ed** -d
bobb|y (B) ˈbɒb|.i (US) ˈbɑː.b|i **-ies** -iz ˈ**bobby** ˌ**pin**
bobbysox ˈbɒb.i.sɒks (US) ˈbɑː.bi.sɑːks **-er/s** -əʳ/z (US) -ɚ/z
bobcat ˈbɒb.kæt (US) ˈbɑːb- **-s** -s
Bobo Dioulasso ˌbəʊ.bəʊ.djuˈlæs.əʊ (US) ˌboʊ.boʊ.djuˈlæs.oʊ
bobolink ˈbɒb.ə.lɪŋk (US) ˈbɑː.bə- **-s** -s
bobsled ˈbɒb.sled (US) ˈbɑːb- **-s** -z **-ding** -ɪŋ **-ded** -ɪd
bobsleigh ˈbɒb.sleɪ (US) ˈbɑːb- **-s** -z
bobstay ˈbɒb.steɪ (US) ˈbɑːb- **-s** -z
bobtail ˈbɒb.teɪl (US) ˈbɑːb- **-s** -z
bobwig ˈbɒb.wɪg (US) ˈbɑːb- **-s** -z

Boca Raton ˌbəʊ.kə.rəˈtəʊn Ⓤⓢ ˌboʊ.kə.rəˈtoʊn
Boccaccio bɒkˈɑː.tʃi.əʊ, bəˈkɑː- Ⓤⓢ boʊˈkɑː-
Boccherini ˌbɒk.ərˈiː.ni Ⓤⓢ ˌbɑː.kəˈriː-, ˌboʊ-
Boche(s) bɒʃ Ⓤⓢ bɑːʃ, bɔːʃ
Bochum ˈbəʊ.kəm Ⓤⓢ ˈboʊ-
bod bɒd Ⓤⓢ bɑːd **-s** -z
bodacious bəʊˈdeɪ.ʃəs Ⓤⓢ boʊ- **-ly** -li
Boddington ˈbɒd.ɪŋ.tən Ⓤⓢ ˈbɑː.dɪŋ-
Boddy ˈbɒd.i Ⓤⓢ ˈbɑː.di
bod|e (B) bəʊd Ⓤⓢ boʊd **-es** -z **-ing** -ɪŋ **-ed** -ɪd
bodega (B) bəˈdeɪ.ɡə, bɒdˈeɪ- Ⓤⓢ boʊˈdeɪ- **-s** -z
Boden ˈbəʊ.dən Ⓤⓢ ˈboʊ-
Bodey ˈbəʊ.di Ⓤⓢ ˈboʊ-
bodg|e bɒdʒ Ⓤⓢ bɑːdʒ **-es** -ɪz **-ing** -ɪŋ **-ed** -d
bodger ˈbɒdʒ.əʳ Ⓤⓢ ˈbɑː.dʒɚ **-s** -z
Bodiam ˈbəʊ.di.əm Ⓤⓢ ˈboʊ-
bodic|e ˈbɒd.ɪs Ⓤⓢ ˈbɑː.dɪs **-es** -ɪz
Bodie ˈbəʊ.di Ⓤⓢ ˈboʊ-
-bodied -ˈbɒd.id Ⓤⓢ -ˈbɑː.did
Note: Suffix. Always carries primary stress unless used attributively, e.g. **full-bodied** /ˌfʊlˈbɒd.id Ⓤⓢ -ˈbɑː.did/, ˈ**full-bodied** ˌ**wine**.
bodily ˈbɒd.ɪ.li, -əl.i Ⓤⓢ ˈbɑː.dəl.i ˌ**bodily** ˈ**function**
bodkin (B) ˈbɒd.kɪn Ⓤⓢ ˈbɑːd- **-s** -z
Bodleian ˈbɒd.li.ən, bɒdˈliː- Ⓤⓢ ˈbɑːd.li.ən, bɑːdˈliː-
Bodley ˈbɒd.li Ⓤⓢ ˈbɑːd-
Bodmin ˈbɒd.mɪn Ⓤⓢ ˈbɑːd-
Bodnant ˈbɒd.nænt Ⓤⓢ ˈbɑːd-
bod|y ˈbɒd|.i Ⓤⓢ ˈbɑː.d|i **-ies** -iz ˈ**body** ˌ**bag**; ˈ**body** ˌ**builder**; ˈ**body** ˌ**building**; ˈ**body** ˌ**language**; ˈ**body** ˌ**snatcher**; **keep** ˌ**body and** ˌ**soul to**ˈ**gether**; **over** ˌ**my** ˌ**dead** ˈ**body**
bodyguard ˈbɒd.i.ɡɑːd Ⓤⓢ ˈbɑː.di.ɡɑːrd **-s** -z
bodysuit ˈbɒd.i.suːt, -sjuːt Ⓤⓢ ˈbɑː.di.suːt **-s** -s
bodysurf ˈbɒd.i.sɜːf Ⓤⓢ ˈbɑː.di.sɝːf **-s** -s **-ing** -ɪŋ **-ed** -t **-er/s** -əʳ/z Ⓤⓢ -ɚ/z
bodywarmer ˈbɒd.iˌwɔː.məʳ Ⓤⓢ ˈbɑː.diˌwɔːr.mɚ **-s** -z
bodywork ˈbɒd.i.wɜːk Ⓤⓢ ˈbɑː.di.wɝːk
Boeing® ˈbəʊ.ɪŋ Ⓤⓢ ˈboʊ-
Boeoti|a biˈəʊ.ʃ|ə, -ʃi|.ə Ⓤⓢ -ˈoʊ.ʃ|ə **-an/s** -ən/z
Boer bəʊəʳ, bɔːʳ, bʊəʳ Ⓤⓢ bɔːr, boʊɚ, bʊr **-s** -z
Boethius bəʊˈiː.θi.əs Ⓤⓢ boʊ-
boeuf bourguignon ˌbɜːfˌbʊə.ɡiːˈnjɔ̃ːŋ, -ˌbɔː-, -ɡɪˈ- Ⓤⓢ ˌbɜːfˌbʊr.ɡiːˈnjõʊn
boff bɒf Ⓤⓢ bɑːf **-s** -s **-ing** -ɪŋ **-ed** -t
boffin (B) ˈbɒf.ɪn Ⓤⓢ ˈbɑː.fɪn **-s** -z
Bofors ˈbəʊ.fəz Ⓤⓢ ˈboʊ.fɔːrz, -fɔːrs
bog bɒɡ Ⓤⓢ bɑːɡ, bɔːɡ **-s** -z **-ging** -ɪŋ **-ged** -d
Bogan ˈbəʊ.ɡən Ⓤⓢ ˈboʊ-
Bogarde ˈbəʊ.ɡɑːd Ⓤⓢ ˈboʊ.ɡɑːrd
Bogart ˈbəʊ.ɡɑːt Ⓤⓢ ˈboʊ.ɡɑːrt
Bogdan ˈbɒɡ.dæn Ⓤⓢ ˈbɑːɡ-, ˈbɔːɡ-
Bogdanovich bɒɡˈdæn.ə.vɪtʃ Ⓤⓢ bɑːɡˈdɑːn-, bɔːɡ-
bogey ˈbəʊ.ɡi Ⓤⓢ ˈboʊ- **-s** -z
bogey|man ˈbəʊ.ɡi|.mæn Ⓤⓢ ˈboʊ- **-men** -men
boggl|e ˈbɒɡ.l̩ Ⓤⓢ ˈbɑː.ɡl̩ **-es** -z **-ing** -ɪŋ, ˈ-lɪŋ Ⓤⓢ ˈ-ɡlɪŋ **-ed** -d **-er/s** -əʳ/z, ˈ-ləʳ/z Ⓤⓢ ˈbɑː.ɡl̩.ɚ/z, ˈbɑːɡ.lɚ/z
bogg|y ˈbɒɡ|.i Ⓤⓢ ˈbɑː.ɡ|i **-ier** -i.əʳ Ⓤⓢ -i.ɚ **-iest** -i.ɪst, -i.əst **-iness** -ɪ.nəs, -ɪ.nɪs
bogie ˈbəʊ.ɡi Ⓤⓢ ˈboʊ- **-s** -z ˈ**bogie** ˌ**engine**; ˈ**bogie** ˌ**wheel**
Bognor ˈbɒɡ.nəʳ Ⓤⓢ ˈbɑːɡ.nɚ, ˈbɔːɡ- ˌ**Bognor** ˈ**Regis**
bog-oak ˌbɒɡˈəʊk Ⓤⓢ ˈbɑːɡ.oʊk, ˈbɔːɡ-
Bogota *in Columbia:* ˌbɒɡ.əʊˈtɑː, ˌbəʊ.ɡə- Ⓤⓢ ˌboʊ.ɡəˈtɑː, ˈ--- *in New Jersey:* bəˈɡəʊ.tə Ⓤⓢ -ˈɡoʊ.t̬ə
bogstandard ˌbɒɡˈstæn.dəd Ⓤⓢ ˈbɑːɡˌstæn.dɚd, ˈbɔːɡ-
bogus ˈbəʊ.ɡəs Ⓤⓢ ˈboʊ-
bog|y ˈbəʊ.ɡ|i Ⓤⓢ ˈboʊ- **-ies** -iz
bohea bəʊˈhiː Ⓤⓢ boʊ-
Bohème bəʊˈem, -ˈeɪm Ⓤⓢ boʊ-
Bohemia bəʊˈhiː.mi.ə Ⓤⓢ boʊ-
bohemian (B) bəʊˈhiː.mi.ən Ⓤⓢ boʊ- **-s** -z
Böhm bɜːm
Bohn bəʊn Ⓤⓢ boʊn
Bohr bɔːʳ Ⓤⓢ bɔːr
Bohun ˈbəʊ.ən, buːn Ⓤⓢ ˈboʊ-, buːn
Note: /buːn/ in Shaw's 'You never can tell'.
boil bɔɪl **-s** -z **-ing** -ɪŋ **-ed** -d ˈ**boiling** ˌ**point**
boiler ˈbɔɪ.ləʳ Ⓤⓢ -lɚ **-s** -z ˈ**boiler** ˌ**suit**
boilermaker ˈbɔɪ.ləˌmeɪ.kəʳ Ⓤⓢ -lɚˌmeɪ.kɚ **-s** -z
boilerplate ˈbɔɪ.lə.pleɪt Ⓤⓢ -lɚ- **-s** -s
boil-in-the-bag ˌbɔɪl.ɪn.ðəˈbæɡ *stress shift:* ˌboil-in-the-bag ˈmeal
boing bɔɪŋ
Boipatong ˌbɔɪ.pəˈtɒŋ, -pætˈɒŋ Ⓤⓢ ˈbɔɪ.pə.tɑːŋ, -tɔːŋ
Bois bɔɪs, bwɑː
Boise ˈbɔɪ.zi, ˈbɔɪ.si
boisterous ˈbɔɪ.stər.əs **-ly** -li **-ness** -nəs, -nɪs
Boker ˈbəʊ.kəʳ Ⓤⓢ ˈboʊ.kɚ
Bokhara bəʊˈkɑː.rə Ⓤⓢ boʊˈkɑːr.ə
Bolan ˈbəʊ.lən Ⓤⓢ ˈboʊ-
bolas ˈbəʊ.ləs, -læs Ⓤⓢ ˈboʊ- **-es** -ɪz
bold bəʊld Ⓤⓢ boʊld **-er** -əʳ Ⓤⓢ -ɚ **-est** -ɪst, -əst **-ly** -li **-ness** -nəs, -nɪs
bold-face ˌbəʊldˈfeɪs Ⓤⓢ ˈboʊld.feɪs, ˈboʊl- **-d** -t *stress shift, British only:* ˌbold-face ˈtype
Boldon ˈbəʊl.dən Ⓤⓢ ˈboʊl-
Boldre ˈbəʊl.dəʳ Ⓤⓢ ˈboʊl.dɚ
bole bəʊl Ⓤⓢ boʊl **-s** -z
bolero *dance:* bəˈleə.rəʊ, bɒlˈeə-, -ˈlɪə- Ⓤⓢ bəˈler.oʊ, boʊ- **-s** -z *garment:* ˈbɒl.ə.rəʊ Ⓤⓢ bəˈler.oʊ **-s** -z
bolet|us bəʊˈliː.t|əs Ⓤⓢ boʊˈliː.t̬|əs **-uses** -ə.sɪz **-i** -aɪ
Boleyn bəˈlɪn; bʊ-; bəʊ-; -ˈliːn; Ⓤⓢ ˈbʊ.lɪn, bʊˈlɪn
Bolingbroke ˈbɒl.ɪŋ.brʊk Ⓤⓢ ˈbɑː.lɪŋ-, ˈboʊ-
Bolinger ˈbɒl.ɪn.dʒəʳ, ˈbəʊ.lɪn- Ⓤⓢ ˈbɑː.lən.dʒɚ
Bolitho bəˈlaɪ.θəʊ, bɒlˈaɪ- Ⓤⓢ bəˈlaɪ.θoʊ
Bolivar *S. American general:* ˈbɒl.ɪ.vɑːʳ; bɒlˈiː- Ⓤⓢ ˈbɑː.lə.vɚ *places in US:* ˈbɒl.ɪ.vəʳ, ˈ-ə-, -vɑːʳ Ⓤⓢ ˈbɑː.lə.vɚ
bolivar *money:* bɒlˈiː.vɑːʳ; ˈbɒl.ɪ.vəʳ Ⓤⓢ boʊˈliː.vɑːr; ˈbɑː.lə.vɚ **-s** -z
bolivares *(alternative plur. of* **bolivar***)* ˌbɒl.ɪˈvɑː.reɪz Ⓤⓢ boʊˌliː.vɑːˈreɪs; ˌboʊ.lɪˈvɑːr.es
Bolivi|a bəˈlɪv.i|.ə, bɒlˈɪv- Ⓤⓢ bəˈlɪv-, boʊ- **-an/s** -ən/z
bolivia|no bəʊˌlɪv.iˈɑː|.nəʊ, bɒlˌɪv-; ˌbəʊ.lɪ.viˈ-, ˌbɒl.ɪv- Ⓤⓢ bəˌlɪv.iˈɑː.noʊ, boʊ- **-nos** -nɒs Ⓤⓢ -noʊs
boll bəʊl, bɒl Ⓤⓢ boʊl **-s** -z **-ed** -d ˌ**boll** ˈ**weevil** Ⓤⓢ ˈ**boll** ˌ**weevil**
Böll bɜːl Ⓤⓢ bɜːl, boʊl
bollard ˈbɒl.ɑːd, -əd Ⓤⓢ ˈbɑː.lɚd **-s** -z
Bolling ˈbəʊ.lɪŋ Ⓤⓢ ˈboʊ-
Bollinger ˈbɒl.ɪn.dʒəʳ Ⓤⓢ ˈbɑː.lən.dʒɚ
Bollington ˈbɒl.ɪŋ.tən Ⓤⓢ ˈbɑː.lɪŋ-
bollix ˈbɒl.ɪks Ⓤⓢ ˈbɑː.lɪks **-es** -ɪz **-ing** -ɪŋ **-ed** -t
bollocking ˈbɒl.ə.kɪŋ Ⓤⓢ ˈbɑː.lə-
bollocks ˈbɒl.əks Ⓤⓢ ˈbɑː.ləks
Bollywood ˈbɒl.i.wʊd Ⓤⓢ ˈbɑː.li-
bolo ˈbəʊ.ləʊ Ⓤⓢ ˈboʊ.loʊ **-s** -z
Bologna bəˈlɒn.jə, bɒlˈɒn-, -ˈləʊ.njə, -ni.ə Ⓤⓢ bəˈloʊ.njə, -ˈlɑː-
bologna *sausage:* bəˈləʊ.ni Ⓤⓢ -ˈloʊ-
bolognaise ˌbɒl.əˈneɪz, -ˈnjeɪz Ⓤⓢ ˌboʊ.ləˈnjeɪz
Bolognese ˌbɒl.əˈneɪz *as if Italian:* -ˈnjeɪ.zeɪ Ⓤⓢ ˌboʊ.ləˈniːz, -ˈnjiːz
bolometer bəʊˈlɒm.ɪ.təʳ, ˈ-ə- Ⓤⓢ boʊˈlɑː.mə.t̬ɚ **-s** -z
boloney bəˈləʊ.ni Ⓤⓢ -ˈloʊ-
Bolshevik ˈbɒl.ʃə.vɪk, -ʃɪ- Ⓤⓢ ˈboʊl-, ˈbɑːl- **-s** -s

Bolshev|ist 'bɒl.ʃə.v|ɪst, -ʃɪ- (US) 'boʊl-, 'bɑːl- **-ism** -ɪ.zᵊm

bolshie 'bɒl.ʃi (US) 'boʊl-, 'bɑːl- **-s** -z

Bolshoi, Bolshoy bɒl'ʃɔɪ, '-- (US) 'boʊl.ʃɔɪ, 'bɑːl-; boʊl'ʃɔɪ

bolsh|y 'bɒl.ʃi (US) 'boʊl-, 'bɑːl- **-ies** -z **-ier** -i.əʳ (US) -i.ɚ **-iest** -i.ɪst, -i.əst

Bolsover *surname, street in London:* 'bɒl.səʊ.vəʳ (US) 'boʊl.soʊ.vɚ *in Derbyshire:* 'bəʊl.zəʊ.vəʳ; 'bəʊl.səʊ- (US) 'boʊl.zoʊ.vɚ

bolst|er 'bəʊl.st|əʳ (US) 'boʊl.st|ɚ **-ers** -əz (US) -ɚz **-ering** -ᵊr.ɪŋ **-ered** -əd (US) -ɚd

bolt (B) bəʊlt (US) boʊlt **-s** -s **-ing** -ɪŋ (US) 'boʊl.t̬ɪŋ **-ed** -ɪd (US) 'boʊl.t̬ɪd ˌbolt 'upright

bolter (B) 'bəʊl.təʳ (US) 'boʊl.t̬ɚ **-s** -z

Bolton 'bəʊl.tᵊn (US) 'boʊl-

Bolton-le-Sands ˌbəʊl.tən.lə'sændz, -lɪ'- (US) ˌboʊl.tᵊn-

bolus 'bəʊ.ləs (US) 'boʊ- **-es** -ɪz

Bolzano bɒlt'zɑː.nəʊ (US) boʊlt'sɑː.noʊ, boʊl'zɑː-

bomb bɒm (US) bɑːm **-s** -z **-ing/s** -ɪŋ/z **-ed** -d ˌbomb dis'posal ˌunit, 'bomb diˌsposal ˌunit

bombard (*n.*) 'bɒm.bɑːd (US) 'bɑːm.bɑːrd **-s** -z

bombard (*v.*) bɒm'bɑːd (US) bɑːm'bɑːrd **-s** -z **-ing** -ɪŋ **-ed** -ɪd **-ment/s** -mənt/s

bombardier ˌbɒm.bə'dɪəʳ (US) ˌbɑːm.bə'dɪr **-s** -z

bombardon 'bɒm.bə.dᵊn; bɒm'bɑː- (US) 'bɑːm.bɚ-; bɑːm'bɑːr- **-s** -z

bombasine 'bɒm.bə.ziːn, -siːn, ˌ--'- (US) ˌbɑːm.bə'ziːn

bombast 'bɒm.bæst (US) 'bɑːm-

bombastic bɒm'bæs.tɪk (US) bɑːm- **-ally** -ᵊl.i, -li

Bombay ˌbɒm'beɪ (US) ˌbɑːm- *stress shift, see compound:* ˌBombay 'duck

bombe bɒm, bɒmb (US) bɑːm **-s** -z

bomber 'bɒm.əʳ (US) 'bɑː.mɚ **-s** -z

bombshell 'bɒm.ʃel (US) 'bɑːm- **-s** -z

bombsite 'bɒm.saɪt (US) 'bɑːm- **-s** -s

Bompas 'bʌm.pəs

bon bɔ̃ːŋ (US) bɔ̃ːn

bona fid|e ˌbəʊ.nə'faɪ.d|i, -d|eɪ (US) ˌboʊ.nə'- **-es** -iːz, -eɪz

bonanza bə'næn.zə **-s** -z

Bonapart|e 'bəʊ.nə.pɑːt (US) 'boʊ.nə.pɑːrt **-ist/s** -ɪst/s

Bonar 'bɒn.əʳ, 'bəʊ.nəʳ (US) 'bɑː.nɚ, 'boʊ-

bonbon 'bɒn.bɒn, 'bɒm- (US) 'bɑːn.bɑːn **-s** -z

Bonchurch 'bɒn.tʃɜːtʃ (US) 'bɑːn.tʃɝːtʃ

bond (B) bɒnd (US) bɑːnd **-s** -z **-ing** -ɪŋ **-ed** -ɪd 'bond ˌholder

bondage 'bɒn.dɪdʒ (US) 'bɑːn-

Bondi *in Australia:* 'bɒn.daɪ (US) 'bɑːn- ˌBondi 'Beach

Bondi *mathematician:* 'bɒn.di (US) 'bɑːn-

bondmaid 'bɒnd.meɪd (US) 'bɑːnd- **-s** -z

bond|man 'bɒnd|.mən (US) 'bɑːnd- **-men** -mən, -men

bonds|man 'bɒndz|.mən (US) 'bɑːndz- **-men** -mən, -men

bonds|woman 'bɒndz|ˌwʊm.ən (US) 'bɑːndz- **-women** -ˌwɪm.ɪn

bond|woman 'bɒnd|ˌwʊm.ən (US) 'bɑːnd- **-women** -ˌwɪm.ɪn

bon|e (B) bəʊn (US) boʊn **-es** -z **-ing** -ɪŋ **-ed** -d **-er/s** -əʳ/z (US) -ɚ/z **-eless** -ləs, -lɪs 'bone ˌmeal; 'bone ˌmarrow; ˌchilled to the 'bone; have a 'bone to pick with ˌsomeone; ˌmake no 'bones about something

bone-dry ˌbəʊn'draɪ (US) ˌboʊ- *stress shift:* ˌbone-dry 'desert

bonehead 'bəʊn.hed (US) 'boʊn- **-s** -z

bonesetter 'bəʊnˌset.əʳ (US) 'boʊnˌset̬.ɚ **-s** -z

bone-shaker 'bəʊnˌʃeɪ.kəʳ (US) 'boʊnˌʃeɪ.kɚ **-s** -z

Bo'ness bəʊ'nes (US) boʊ-

bonfire 'bɒn.faɪəʳ (US) 'bɑːn.faɪɚ **-s** -z 'Bonfire ˌNight

bong bɒŋ (US) bɑːŋ, bɔːŋ **-s** -z

bongo 'bɒŋ.gəʊ (US) 'bɑːŋ.goʊ **-(e)s** -z 'bongo ˌdrum

Bonham 'bɒn.əm (US) 'bɑː.nəm

Bonham-Carter ˌbɒn.əm'kɑː.təʳ (US) ˌbɑː.nəm'kɑːr.t̬ɚ

bonhomie 'bɒn.ɒm.i, -ə.mi, -miː, ˌ--'- (US) ˌbɑː.nə'miː, '---

Boniface 'bɒn.ɪ.feɪs, -fæs (US) 'bɑː.nɪ-

Bonifacio ˌbɒn.ɪ'fæʃ.i.əʊ, -'fæs- (US) ˌboʊ.ni'fɑː.ʃoʊ, '-ʃi.oʊ

Bonington 'bɒn.ɪŋ.tən (US) 'bɑː.nɪŋ.t̬ən

bonk bɒŋk (US) bɑːŋk, bɔːŋk **-s** -s **-ing** -ɪŋ **-ed** -t

bonkers 'bɒŋ.kəz (US) 'bɑːŋ.kɚz, 'bɔːŋ-

bon(s) mot(s) ˌbɔ̃ːm'məʊ (US) ˌbɔ̃ːn'moʊ

Bonn bɒn (US) bɑːn

Bonnard bɒn'ɑːʳ (US) bɑː'nɑːr, bɔː-

Bonner 'bɒn.əʳ (US) 'bɑː.nɚ

bonn|et 'bɒn|.ɪt (US) 'bɑː.n|ɪt **-ets** -ɪts **-eting** -ɪ.tɪŋ (US) -ɪ.t̬ɪŋ **-eted** -ɪ.tɪd (US) -ɪ.t̬ɪd

Bonnett 'bɒn.ɪt (US) 'bɑː.nɪt

Bonnie 'bɒn.i (US) 'bɑː.ni

bonn|y 'bɒn|.i (US) 'bɑː.n|i **-ier** -i.əʳ (US) -i.ɚ **-iest** -i.ɪst, -i.əst **-ily** -ɪ.li, -ᵊl.i **-iness** -ɪ.nəs, -ɪ.nɪs

Bono 'bəʊ.nəʊ, 'bɒn.əʊ (US) 'boʊ.noʊ, 'bɑː-

bonsai 'bɒn.saɪ (US) ˌbɑːn'saɪ, ˌboʊn- **-s** -z

Bonsor 'bɒnt.səʳ, -zəʳ (US) 'bɑːnt.sɚ, -zɚ

bonus 'bəʊ.nəs (US) 'boʊ- **-es** -ɪz

bon(s) vivant(s) ˌbɔ̃ːŋ.vi.'vɑ̃ːŋ (US) ˌbɑːn.viː'vɑːnt, ˌbɔ̃ː-

bon(s) viveur(s) ˌbɔ̃ːŋ.vi'vɜːʳ (US) ˌbɑːn.viː'vɝː

bon voyage ˌbɔ̃ːŋ.vɔɪ'ɑːʒ, -vwaɪ'- (US) ˌbɑːn.vwaɪ'-, -vɔɪ'-

bon|y 'bəʊ.n|i (US) 'boʊ- **-ier** -i.əʳ (US) -i.ɚ **-iest** -i.ɪst, -i.əst **-iness** -ɪ.nəs, -ɪ.nɪs

bonz|e bɒnz (US) bɑːnz **-es** -ɪz

bonzer 'bɒn.zəʳ (US) 'bɑːn.zɚ

boo buː **-s** -z **-ing** -ɪŋ **-ed** -d **-er/s** -əʳ/z (US) -ɚ/z ˌcouldn't say ˌboo to a 'goose

boob buːb **-s** -z **-ing** -ɪŋ **-ed** -d

boo-boo 'buː.buː **-s** -z

boob|y 'buː.b|i **-ies** -iz **-yish** -i.ɪʃ 'booby ˌprize; 'booby ˌtrap

boodle (B) 'buː.dl̩

booger 'buː.gəʳ, 'bʊg.əʳ (US) 'bʊg.ɚ, 'buː.gɚ **-s** -z

boogey|man 'bʊg.i|.mæn, 'buː.gi- **-men** -men

boog|ie 'buː.g|i (US) 'bʊg-, 'buː- **-ies** -iz **-ieing** -i.ɪŋ **-ied** -id

boogie-woogie ˌbuː.gi'wuː.gi, 'buː.giˌwuː-, ˌbʊg.i'wʊg.i

boohoo ˌbuː'huː **-s** -z **-ing** -ɪŋ **-ed** -d

book bʊk **-s** -s **-ing** -ɪŋ **-ed** -t **-er/s** -əʳ/z (US) -ɚ/z 'book ˌclub; 'book ˌtoken; ˌbring someone to 'book; in someone's 'good/bad ˌbooks, in someone's ˌgood/ˌbad 'books

bookable 'bʊk.ə.bl̩

bookbind|er 'bʊkˌbaɪn.d|əʳ (US) -d|ɚ **-ers** -əz (US) -ɚz **-ing** -ɪŋ

bookcas|e 'bʊk.keɪs **-es** -ɪz

bookend 'bʊk.end **-s** -z

Booker 'bʊk.əʳ (US) -ɚ

Bookham 'bʊk.əm

bookie 'bʊk.i **-s** -z

booking 'bʊk.ɪŋ **-s** -z 'booking ˌoffice

bookish 'bʊk.ɪʃ **-ly** -li **-ness** -nəs, -nɪs

bookkeep|er 'bʊkˌkiː.p|əʳ (US) -p|ɚ **-ers** -əz (US) -ɚz **-ing** -ɪŋ

bookland 'bʊk.lænd

book-learning 'bʊkˌlɜː.nɪŋ (US) -ˌlɝː-

booklet 'bʊk.lət, -lɪt **-s** -s

bookmak|er 'bʊkˌmeɪ.k|əʳ (US) -k|ɚ **-ers** -əz (US) -ɚz **-ing** -ɪŋ

book|man 'bʊk|.mən, -mæn **-men** -mən, -men

bookmark 'bʊk.mɑːk (US) -mɑːrk **-s** -s **-ing** -ɪŋ **-ed** -t **-er/s** -əʳ/z (US) -ɚ/z

bookmobile 'bʊk.məʊˌbiːl (US) -mə-, -moʊ- **-s** -z

bookplate 'bʊk.pleɪt **-s** -s

booksell|er 'bʊkˌsel|.əʳ (US) -ɚ **-ers** -əz (US) -ɚz **-ing** -ɪŋ

bookshel|f 'bʊk.ʃel|f **-ves** -vz

bookshop 'bʊk.ʃɒp (US) -ʃɑːp **-s** -s

bookstall 'bʊk.stɔːl (US) -stɔːl, -stɑːl **-s** -z

bookstand ˈbʊk.stænd **-s** -z
bookstore ˈbʊk.stɔːʳ (US) -stɔːr **-s** -z
bookwork ˈbʊk.wɜːk (US) -wɝːk
bookworm ˈbʊk.wɜːm (US) -wɝːm **-s** -z
Boolean ˈbuː.li.ən **-s** -z
boom buːm **-s** -z **-ing** -ɪŋ **-ed** -d **ˈboom ˌbox**
boomerang ˈbuː.mᵊr.æŋ (US) -mə.ræŋ **-s** -z **-ing** -ɪŋ **-ed** -d
boomlet ˈbuːm.lət, -lɪt **-s** -s
boon buːn **-s** -z
boondock ˈbuːn.dɒk (US) -dɑːk **-s** -s
boondoggl|e ˈbuːnˌdɒg.l̩ (US) -ˌdɑː.gl̩, -ˌdɔː- **-es** -z **-ing** -ɪŋ, ˌ-lɪŋ (US) -ˌdɑː.gl̩.ɪŋ, -ˌdɔː-, ˌ-glɪŋ **-ed** -d **-er/s** -əʳ/z, ˌ-ləʳ/z (US) -ˌdɑː.gl̩.ɚ/z, -ˌdɔː-, ˌ-glɚ/z
Boon(e) buːn
boonies ˈbuː.niz
boor bɔːʳ, bʊə (US) bʊr **-s** -z
Boord bɔːd (US) bɔːrd
boorish ˈbɔː.rɪʃ, ˈbʊə- (US) ˈbʊr.ɪʃ **-ly** -li **-ness** -nəs, -nɪs
Boosey ˈbuː.zi
boost buːst **-s** -s **-ing** -ɪŋ **-ed** -ɪd
booster ˈbuː.stəʳ (US) -stɚ **-s** -z
boot (B) buːt **-s** -s **-ing** -ɪŋ (US) ˈbuː.t̬ɪŋ **-ed** -ɪd (US) ˈbuː.t̬ɪd **ˈboot ˌsale; ˌput the ˈboot in; too ˌbig for one's ˈboots**
bootblack ˈbuːt.blæk **-s** -s
bootee ˌbuːˈtiː; ˈbuː.ti (US) ˈbuː.t̬i **-s** -z
Boötes bəʊˈəʊ.tiːz (US) boʊˈoʊ-
booth (B) buːð, buːθ **-s** -z, -s
Boothby ˈbuːð.bi
Boothe buːð
Boothroyd ˈbuːθ.rɔɪd, ˈbuːð-
bootie ˈbuː.ti (US) -t̬i **-s** -z
bootjack ˈbuːt.dʒæk **-s** -s
bootlac|e ˈbuːt.leɪs **-es** -ɪz
Bootle ˈbuː.tl̩ (US) ˈbuː.t̬l̩
bootleg ˈbuːt.leg **-s** -z **-ging** -ɪŋ **-ged** -d
bootlegger ˈbuːtˌleg.əʳ (US) -ɚ **-s** -z
bootless ˈbuːt.ləs, -lɪs **-ly** -li **-ness** -nəs, -nɪs
boots *(sing.) hotel servant:* buːts *(plur.)* buːts, ˈbuːt.sɪz
Boots® buːts
bootstrap ˈbuːt.stræp **-s** -s **-ping** -ɪŋ **-ped** -t
booty ˈbuː.ti (US) -t̬i
booz|e buːz **-es** -ɪz **-ing** -ɪŋ **-ed** -d **-er/s** -əʳ/z (US) -ɚ/z
booze-up ˈbuːz.ʌp **-s** -s
booz|y ˈbuː.z|i **-ier** -i.əʳ (US) -i.ɚ **-iest** -i.ɪst, -i.əst **-ily** -ɪ.li, -ᵊl.i
bop bɒp (US) bɑːp **-s** -s **-ping** -ɪŋ **-ped** -t **-py** -i
Bo-peep ˌbəʊˈpiːp (US) ˌboʊ-
Bophuthatswana ˌbɒp.uː.tætˈswɑː.nə, ˌbəʊ.puː-, -tət'- (US) ˌboʊ.puː.tɑːtˈswɑː-, -t̬ət'-
boracic bəˈræs.ɪk, bɒrˈæs- (US) bəˈræs-, bɔː-
borage ˈbɒr.ɪdʒ, ˈbʌr- (US) ˈbɔːr-
borate ˈbɔː.reɪt, -rɪt, -rət (US) ˈbɔːr.eɪt, -ɪt, -ət **-s** -s
borax ˈbɔː.ræks (US) ˈbɔːr.æks
borborygmus ˌbɔː.bəˈrɪg.məs (US) ˌbɔːr-
Bord bɔːd (US) bɔːrd
Bordeaux bɔːˈdəʊ (US) bɔːrˈdoʊ
bordello bɔːˈdel.əʊ (US) bɔːrˈdel.oʊ **-s** -z
bord|er ˈbɔː.d|əʳ (US) ˈbɔːr.d|ɚ **-ers** -əz (US) -ɚz **-ering** -ᵊr.ɪŋ **-ered** -əd (US) -ɚd **-erer/s** -ᵊr.əʳ/z (US) -ɚ.ɚ/z
borderland ˈbɔː.dᵊl.ænd (US) ˈbɔːr.dɚ.lænd **-s** -z
borderline ˈbɔː.dᵊl.aɪn (US) ˈbɔːr.dɚ.laɪn **-s** -z
Borders ˈbɔː.dəz (US) ˈbɔːr.dɚz
Bordon ˈbɔː.dᵊn (US) ˈbɔːr-
bordure ˈbɔː.djʊəʳ (US) ˈbɔːr.djɚ, -dʒɚ **-s** -z
bor|e bɔːʳ (US) bɔːr **-es** -z **-ing** -ɪŋ **-ed** -d
bore *(from* **bear***)* bɔːʳ (US) bɔːr
borealis ˌbɒr.iˈɑː.lɪs, ˌbɔː.riˈ-, -ˈeɪ- (US) ˌbɔːr.iˈæl.ɪs, -ˈeɪ.lɪs
Boreas ˈbɒr.i.æs, ˈbɔː.ri-, -əs (US) ˈbɔːr.i-
boredom ˈbɔː.dəm (US) ˈbɔːr-
Boreham ˈbɔː.rəm (US) ˈbɔːr.əm
Borehamwood ˌbɔː.rəmˈwʊd (US) ˌbɔːr.əm-
borehole ˈbɔː.həʊl (US) ˈbɔːr.hoʊl **-s** -z
borer ˈbɔː.rəʳ (US) ˈbɔːr.ɚ **-s** -z
Borg bɔːg (US) bɔːrg
Borges ˈbɔː.ges, -xes (US) ˈbɔːr.hes
Borgia ˈbɔː.*dʒ*i.ə, -*dʒ*ə (US) ˈbɔːr.*dʒ*ə
boric ˈbɔː.rɪk, ˈbɒr.ɪk (US) ˈbɔːr.ɪk **ˌboric ˈacid**
Boris ˈbɒr.ɪs (US) ˈbɔːr-
Borland ˈbɔː.lənd (US) ˈbɔːr-
borlotti (B) bɔːˈlɒt.i (US) bɔːrˈlɑː.t̬i
born bɔːn (US) bɔːrn
born-again ˌbɔːn.əˈgen, -ˈgeɪn (US) ˌbɔːrn.əˈgen *stress shift, see compound:* **ˌborn-again ˈChristian**
borne *(from* **bear***)* bɔːn (US) bɔːrn
Borneo ˈbɔː.ni.əʊ (US) ˈbɔːr.ni.oʊ
Borodin ˈbɒr.ə.dɪn (US) ˈbɔːr-
boron ˈbɔː.rɒn (US) ˈbɔːr.ɑːn
borough ˈbʌr.ə (US) ˈbɝː.oʊ, -ə **-s** -z
borrow (B) ˈbɒr.əʊ (US) ˈbɑːr.oʊ **-s** -z **-ing/s** -ɪŋ/z **-ed** -d **-er/s** -əʳ/z (US) -ɚ/z
Borrowash ˈbɒr.əʊ.wɒʃ (US) ˈbɑːr.oʊ.wɑːʃ, -wɔːʃ
Borrowdale ˈbɒr.ə.deɪl (US) ˈbɑːr-
Bors bɔːs (US) bɔːrs
borsch bɔːʃ (US) bɔːrʃ
borscht bɔːʃt (US) bɔːrʃt
borstal (B) ˈbɔː.stᵊl (US) ˈbɔːr- **-s** -z
borstch bɔːʃ, bɔːstʃ, bɔːʃtʃ (US) bɔːrʃt
Borthwick ˈbɔːθ.wɪk (US) ˈbɔːrθ-
Borwick ˈbɒr.ɪk (US) ˈbɔːr.wɪk
borzoi ˈbɔː.zɔɪ, -ˈ- (US) ˈbɔːr- **-s** -z
Bosanquet ˈbəʊ.zᵊn.ket, -kɪt (US) ˈboʊ-
boscag|e ˈbɒs.kɪdʒ (US) ˈbɑːs- **-es** -ɪz
Boscastle ˈbɒs.kɑː.sl̩, -kæs.l̩ (US) ˈbɑː.skæs-
Boscawen bɒsˈkəʊ.ən; -ɪn; -ˈkɔː-; ˈbɒs.kwɪn (US) bɑːˈskoʊ.ən; ˈbɑː.skwɪn
Bosch bɒʃ (US) bɑːʃ
bosh bɒʃ (US) bɑːʃ
Bosham ˈbɒz.əm, ˈbɒs- (US) ˈbɑː.zəm, -səm
Note: A new pronunciation /ˈbɒʃ.əm/ is also heard.
Bosher ˈbəʊ.ʃəʳ (US) ˈboʊ.ʃɚ
bosky ˈbɒs.ki (US) ˈbɑː.ski
bos'n, bo's'n ˈbəʊ.sᵊn (US) ˈboʊ- **-s** -z
Bosni|a ˈbɒz.ni|.ə (US) ˈbɑːz- **-an/s** -ən/z
Bosnia-Herzegovina ˌbɒz.ni.əˌhɜːt.səˈgɒv.ɪ.nə; -gəʊˈviː- (US) ˌbɑːz.ni.əˌhert.sə.goʊˈviː.nə, -gəˈ-
bosom ˈbʊz.ᵊm **-s** -z **-y** -i
Bosphorus ˈbɒs.fᵊr.əs, -pᵊr- (US) ˈbɑːs.fɚ-, ˈbɑː.spɚ-
Bosporus ˈbɒs.pᵊr.əs (US) ˈbɑː.spɚ-
boss (B) bɒs (US) bɑːs **-es** -ɪz **-ing** -ɪŋ **-ed** -t
bossa nova ˌbɒs.əˈnəʊ.və (US) ˌbɑː.səˈnoʊ-
boss-eyed ˌbɒsˈaɪd (US) ˈbɑːs.aɪd *stress shift:* ˌboss-eyed ˈcat
Bossuet ˈbɒs.u.eɪ (US) ˈbɑː.sweɪ
boss|y ˈbɒs|.i (US) ˈbɑː.s|i **-ier** -i.əʳ (US) -i.ɚ **-iest** -i.ɪst, -i.əst **-ily** -ɪ.li, -ᵊl.i **-iness** -ɪ.nəs, -ɪ.nɪs
Bostik® ˈbɒs.tɪk (US) ˈbɑː.stɪk
Bostock ˈbɒs.tɒk (US) ˈbɑː.stɑːk
Boston ˈbɒs.tᵊn (US) ˈbɑː.stᵊn, ˈbɔː-
Bostonian bɒsˈtəʊ.ni.ən (US) bɑːˈstoʊ-, bɔː- **-s** -z
Bostridge ˈbɒs.trɪdʒ (US) ˈbɑː.strɪdʒ
bosun ˈbəʊ.sᵊn (US) ˈboʊ- **-s** -z
Boswell ˈbɒz.wəl, -wel (US) ˈbɑːz-
Bosworth ˈbɒz.wəθ, -wɜːθ (US) ˈbɑːz.wɚθ, -wɝːθ
botanic bəˈtæn.ɪk, bɒtˈæn- (US) bəˈtæn- **-al** -ᵊl **-ally** -ᵊl.i, -li **boˌtanic ˈgarden**
botanist ˈbɒt.ᵊn.ɪst (US) ˈbɑː.tᵊn- **-s** -s
botaniz|e, -is|e ˈbɒt.ᵊn.aɪz (US) ˈbɑː.tᵊn- **-es** -ɪz **-ing** -ɪŋ **-ed** -d
botany ˈbɒt.ᵊn.i (US) ˈbɑː.tᵊn- **ˌBotany ˈBay**
botch bɒtʃ (US) bɑːtʃ **-es** -ɪz **-ing** -ɪŋ **-ed** -t **-er/s** -əʳ/z (US) -ɚ/z
botch-up ˈbɒtʃ.ʌp (US) ˈbɑːtʃ- **-s** -s
both bəʊθ (US) boʊθ
Botha ˈbəʊ.tə (US) ˈboʊ.t̬ə
Botham ˈbəʊ.θəm, ˈbɒð.əm (US) ˈboʊ.θəm, ˈbɑː.ðəm
both|er ˈbɒð|.əʳ (US) ˈbɑː.ð|ɚ **-ers** -əz (US) -ɚz **-ering** -ᵊr.ɪŋ **-ered** -əd (US) -ɚd
botheration ˌbɒð.ᵊrˈeɪ.ʃᵊn (US) ˌbɑː.ðəˈreɪ-

bothersome ˈbɒð.ə.səm (US) ˈbɑː.ðɚ-
Bothnia ˈbɒθ.ni.ə (US) ˈbɑːθ-
Bothwell ˈbɒθ.wᵊl, ˈbɒð-, -wel (US) ˈbɑːθ-, ˈbɑːð-
both|y ˈbɒθ|.i, bɒð- (US) ˈbɑː.θ|i, -ð|i **-ies** -iz
Botolph ˈbɒt.ɒlf, -ᵊlf (US) ˈbɑː.tɑːlf
Botox® ˈbəʊ.tɒks (US) ˈboʊ.tɑːks
botrytis bɒtˈraɪ.tɪs (US) boʊˈtraɪ.t̬əs
Botswana bɒtˈswɑː.nə (US) bɑːt-
Botticelli ˌbɒt.ɪˈtʃel.i (US) ˌbɑː.t̬əˈ- **-s** -z
bottl|e ˈbɒt.l̩ (US) ˈbɑː.t̬l̩ **-es** -z **-ing** -ɪŋ, ˈ-lɪŋ (US) ˈbɑː.t̬l̩.ɪŋ, ˈbɑːt.lɪŋ **-ed** -d **-er/s** -əʳ/z, ˈ-ləʳ/z (US) ˈbɑː.t̬l̩.ɚ/z, ˈbɑːt.lɚ/z ˈ**bottle** ˌ**bank**
bottle-green ˌbɒt.l̩ˈgriːn (US) ˌbɑː.t̬l̩ˈ- *stress shift:* ˌbottle-green ˈjacket
bottleneck ˈbɒt.l̩.nek (US) ˈbɑː.t̬l̩- **-s** -s
bottle-nos|e ˈbɒt.l̩.nəʊz (US) ˈbɑː.t̬l̩.noʊz **-es** -ɪz **-ed** -d
bottle-wash|er ˈbɒt.l̩ˌwɒʃ.əʳ (US) ˈbɑː.t̬l̩ˌwɑː.ʃɚ **-ers** -əz (US) -ɚs **-ing** -ɪŋ
bottom (B) ˈbɒt.əm (US) ˈbɑː.t̬əm **-s** -z **-ing** -ɪŋ **-ed** -d
Bottome bəˈtəʊm (US) -ˈtoʊm
bottomless ˈbɒt.əm.ləs, -lɪs, -les (US) ˈbɑː.t̬əm-
Bottomley ˈbɒt.əm.li (US) ˈbɑː.t̬əm-
bottomry ˈbɒt.əm.ri (US) ˈbɑː.t̬əm-
botulism ˈbɒtʃ.ə.lɪ.zᵊm, -ʊ-; ˈbɒt.jʊ-, ˈ-jə- (US) ˈbɑː.tʃə-
Bouaké ˈbwɑː.keɪ
Boucicault ˈbuː.si.kəʊ *as if French:* ˌ--ˈ- (US) ˈbuː.si.koʊ, -kɑːlt
bouclé ˈbuː.kleɪ (US) -ˈ-
Boudicca ˈbuː.dɪ.kə, ˈbəʊ- (US) buːˈdɪk.ə
boudoir ˈbuːd.wɑːʳ (US) ˈbuːd.wɑːr, ˈbʊd- **-s** -z
bouffant ˈbuː.fɑ̃ːŋ, -fɒnt (US) buːˈfɑːnt, ˈ--
bougainvillaea ˌbuː.gᵊnˈvɪl.i.ə (US) -i.ə, ˈ-jə **-s** -z
Bougainville ˈbuː.gᵊn.vɪl, -viːl
bougainvillea ˌbuː.gᵊnˈvɪl.i.ə (US) -i.ə, ˈ-jə **-s** -z
bough baʊ **-s** -z
Bough bɒf (US) bɑːf
Boughey ˈbəʊ.i (US) ˈboʊ-
bought *(from* **buy***)* bɔːt (US) bɑːt, bɔːt
Boughton ˈbɔː.tᵊn, ˈbaʊ- (US) ˈbɑː.tᵊn, ˈbɔː-, ˈbaʊ-
bougie ˈbuː.dʒiː, -ˈ- **-s** -z
boulllabaisse ˌbuː.jəˈbes, ˌbwiː-, -jɑːˈ-, -ˈbeɪs, ˈ---
bouillon ˈbuː.jɔ̃ːŋ, ˈbwiː-, -jɒn (US) ˈbʊl.jɑːn, ˈbuː-, -jən
Boulanger ˌbuː.lɑ̃ːnˈʒeɪ, ˈ---
Boulby ˈbəʊl.bi (US) ˈboʊl-
boulder ˈbəʊl.dəʳ (US) ˈboʊl.dɚ **-s** -z
Bouler ˈbuː.ləʳ (US) -lɚ
boules buːl
boulevard ˈbuː.lə.vɑːd, -lɪ-, ˈbuːl.vɑːʳ (US) ˈbʊl.ə.vɑːrd **-s** -z
Boulez ˈbuː.lez, -leɪ (US) buːˈlez
Boulogne bʊˈlɔɪn, bə- (US) -ˈloʊn, -ˈlɔɪn
Boult bəʊlt (US) boʊlt
Boulter ˈbəʊl.təʳ (US) ˈboʊl.tɚ
Boulton ˈbəʊl.tᵊn (US) ˈboʊl-
bounc|e baʊnts **-es** -ɪz **-ing** -ɪŋ **-ed** -t
bouncer (B) ˈbaʊnt.səʳ (US) -sɚ **-s** -z
bounc|y ˈbaʊnt.s|i **-ier** -i.əʳ (US) -i.ɚ **-iest** -i.ɪst, -i.əst
bound baʊnd **-s** -z **-ing** -ɪŋ **-ed** -ɪd
boundar|y ˈbaʊn.dᵊr|.i **-ies** -iz
bounden ˈbaʊn.dən ˌ**bounden** ˈ**duty**
bounder ˈbaʊn.dəʳ (US) -dɚ **-s** -z
Bounderby ˈbaʊn.də.bi (US) -dɚ-
boundless ˈbaʊnd.ləs, -lɪs **-ly** -li **-ness** -nəs, -nɪs
bounteous ˈbaʊn.ti.əs, -tʃəs (US) -t̬i.əs **-ly** -li **-ness** -nəs, -nɪs
bountiful ˈbaʊn.tɪ.fᵊl, -tə-, -fʊl (US) -t̬ə-, -t̬ɪ- **-ly** -i **-ness** -nəs, -nɪs
bount|y ˈbaʊn.t|i (US) -t̬|i **-ies** -iz ˈ**bounty** ˌ**hunter**
bouquet bʊˈkeɪ; bəʊ-; ˈbuː.keɪ (US) boʊˈkeɪ, buː- **-s** -z
bouquet(s) garni(s) bʊˌkeɪ.gɑːˈniː, ˌbuː.keɪ- (US) ˌboʊ.keɪ.gɑːrˈ-
Bourbon *French royal house:* ˈbʊə.bən, ˈbɔː-, -bɒn (US) ˈbʊr.bən, -bɔːn **-s** -z
bourbon *drink:* ˈbɜː.bən, ˈbʊə- (US) ˈbɝː- *biscuit:* ˈbɔː.bən, ˈbʊə-, -bɒn (US) ˈbɝː-
Bourchier ˈbaʊ.tʃəʳ (US) -tʃɚ
Bourdillon bəˈdɪl.i.ən, bɔː-, -ˈdɪl.ən (US) bɔːrˈdɪl.jən, bɚ-
bourdon ˈbɔː.dᵊn, ˈbʊə- (US) ˈbʊr-, ˈbɔːr- **-s** -z
bourgeois *middle class:* ˈbɔː.ʒwɑː, ˈbʊəʒ- (US) ˈbʊrʒ- *printing type:* bɜːˈdʒɔɪs (US) bɝː-
bourgeoisie ˌbɔː.ʒwɑːˈziː, ˌbʊəʒ-, -wəˈ- (US) ˌbʊrʒ-
Bourke bɜːk (US) bɝːk
bourn(e) bɔːn, bʊən (US) bɔːrn, bʊrn **-s** -z
Bourne bɔːn, bʊən *as surname also:* bɜːn (US) bɔːrn, bʊrn, bɝːn
Bournemouth ˈbɔːn.məθ (US) ˈbɔːrn-
Bournville ˈbɔːn.vɪl (US) ˈbɔːrn-
bourrée ˈbʊr.eɪ, ˈbʊə.reɪ (US) bʊˈreɪ **-s** -z
bours|e (B) bʊəs, bɔːs (US) bʊrs, bɔːrs **-es** -ɪz
boustrophedon ˌbuː.strəˈfiː.dᵊn, ˌbaʊ-, -dɒn (US) -ɑːn
bout baʊt **-s** -s
boutique buːˈtiːk **-s** -s
Boutros-Ghali ˌbuː.trɒsˈgɑː.li (US) -troʊsˈ-
Bouverie ˈbuː.vᵊr.i
bouzouki bʊˈzuː.ki, bə-, buː- **-s** -z
Bovary ˈbəʊ.vᵊr.i (US) ˈboʊ-
Bovey *place:* ˈbʌv.i *surname:* ˈbuː.vi, ˈbəʊ-, ˈbʌv.i (US) ˈbuː.vi, ˈboʊ-, ˈbʌv.i
Bovey Tracey ˌbʌv.iˈtreɪ.si
Bovill ˈbəʊ.vɪl (US) ˈboʊ-
bovine ˈbəʊ.vaɪn (US) ˈboʊ-, -viːn
Bovingdon ˈbʌv.ɪŋ.dən, ˈbɒv- (US) ˈbʌv-, ˈbɑː.vɪŋ-
Note: Locally /ˈbʌv-/.
Bovington ˈbɒv.ɪŋ.tən (US) ˈbɑː.vɪŋ-
Bovis ˈbəʊ.vɪs (US) ˈboʊ-
Bovril® ˈbɒv.rɪl, -rəl (US) ˈbɑːv-
bovver ˈbɒv.əʳ, ˈbɑː.vɚ ˈ**bovver** ˌ**boot**; ˈ**bovver** ˌ**boy**
bow *(n.) bending, fore end of ship:* baʊ **-s** -z
bow (B) *(n.) for shooting, etc., knot:* bəʊ (US) boʊ **-s** -z ˌ**bow** ˈ**tie**; ˌ**bow** ˈ**window**
bow *(v.) in playing the violin, etc.:* bəʊ (US) boʊ **-s** -z **-ing/s** -ɪŋ/z **-ed** -d
bow *(v.) bend body:* baʊ **-s** -z **-ing** -ɪŋ **-ed** -d
Bowater ˈbəʊˌwɔː.təʳ (US) ˈboʊˌwɑː.t̬ɚ, -ˌwɔː-
Bowden ˈbəʊ.dᵊn, ˈbaʊ- (US) ˈboʊ-, ˈbaʊ-
Bowdler ˈbaʊd.ləʳ (US) ˈboʊd.lɚ, ˈbaʊd-
bowdlerism ˈbaʊd.lᵊr.ɪ.zᵊm (US) ˈboʊd-, ˈbaʊd- **-s** -z
bowdlerization, -isa- ˌbaʊd.lᵊr.aɪˈzeɪ.ʃᵊn, -ɪˈ- (US) ˌboʊd.lɚ.ɪˈ-, ˌbaʊd-
bowdleriz|e, -is|e ˈbaʊd.lᵊr.aɪz (US) ˈboʊd.lə.raɪz, ˈbaʊd- **-es** -ɪz **-ing** -ɪŋ **-ed** -d
Bowdoin, Bowdon ˈbəʊ.dᵊn (US) ˈboʊ-
bowel baʊəl **-s** -z
Bowen ˈbəʊ.ɪn (US) ˈboʊ-
bower (B) baʊəʳ (US) baʊɚ **-s** -z
Bowering ˈbaʊə.rɪŋ (US) ˈbaʊɚ.ɪŋ
bowery (B) ˈbaʊə.ri (US) ˈbaʊɚ.i, ˈbaʊ.ri
Bowes bəʊz (US) boʊz
Bowie ˈbaʊ.i, ˈbəʊ- (US) ˈboʊ-, ˈbuː-
bowie-kni|fe ˈbəʊ.i.naɪ|f, ˈbuː- (US) ˈboʊ-, ˈbuː- **-ves** -vz
Bowker ˈbaʊ.kəʳ (US) -kɚ
bowl bəʊl (US) boʊl **-s** -z **-ing** -ɪŋ **-ed** -d ˈ**bowling** ˌ**alley**; ˈ**bowling** ˌ**green**
Bowland ˈbəʊ.lənd (US) ˈboʊ-
bow-legged bəʊˈlegd, -ˈleg.ɪd, -əd (US) boʊ- *stress shift:* ˌbow-legged ˈchild
bowler (B) ˈbəʊ.ləʳ (US) ˈboʊ.lɚ **-s** -z
Bowles bəʊlz (US) boʊlz
bowline ˈbəʊ.lɪn (US) ˈboʊ- **-s** -z
Bowling ˈbəʊ.lɪŋ (US) ˈboʊ-
Bowlker ˈbəʊ.kəʳ (US) ˈboʊ.kɚ
bow|man (B) ˈbəʊ|.mən (US) ˈboʊ- **-men** -mən, -men
Bowmer ˈbəʊ.məʳ (US) ˈboʊ.mɚ
Bown baʊn
Bowness bəʊˈnes (US) boʊ-
Bowra ˈbaʊ.rə
Bowring ˈbaʊ.rɪŋ

bowshot ˈbəʊ.ʃɒt (US) ˈboʊ.ʃɑːt **-s** -s
bowsprit ˈbəʊ.sprɪt, ˈbaʊ- (US) ˈbaʊ-, ˈboʊ- **-s** -s
bowstring ˈbəʊ.strɪŋ (US) ˈboʊ- **-s** -z
Bowtell bəʊˈtel (US) boʊ-
bow-wow *(interj.) sound made by a dog:* ˌbaʊˈwaʊ **-s** -z *(n.) dog:* ˈbaʊ.waʊ **-s** -z
bowyer (B) ˈbəʊ.jəʳ (US) ˈboʊ.jɚ
box (B) bɒks (US) bɑːks **-es** -ɪz **-ing** -ɪŋ **-ed** -t ˌ**box ˈbed**; ˈ**box ˌcloth**; ˌ**box ˈjunction**; ˈ**box ˌnumber**; ˈ**box ˌoffice**; ˈ**box ˌseat**; ˌ**boxed ˈset**; ˈ**box ˌscore**
boxcar ˈbɒks.kɑːʳ (US) ˈbɑːks.kɑːr **-s** -z
boxer (B) ˈbɒk.səʳ (US) ˈbɑːk.sɚ **-s** -z ˈ**boxer ˌshorts**
boxing ˈbɒk.sɪŋ (US) ˈbɑːk- ˈ**Boxing ˌDay**; ˈ**boxing ˌglove**; ˈ**boxing ˌmatch**
Boxmoor ˈbɒks.mɔːʳ *also locally:* -ˈ- (US) ˈbɑːks.mʊr, -mɔːr
boxroom ˈbɒks.rʊm, -ruːm (US) ˈbɑːks.ruːm, -rʊm **-s** -z
boxwood ˈbɒks.wʊd (US) ˈbɑːks-
box|y ˈbɒk.s|i (US) ˈbɑːk- **-iness** -ɪ.nəs, -ɪ.nɪs
boy bɔɪ **-s** -z ˌ**boy ˈscout** (US) ˈ**boy ˌscout**
boyar ˈbɔɪ.əʳ, -ɑːʳ; ˈbəʊ.jɑːʳ, -ˈ- (US) boʊˈjɑːr; ˈbɔɪ.ɚ **-s** -z
Boyce bɔɪs
boyco|tt (B) ˈbɔɪ.kɒ|t, -kə|t (US) -kɑː|t **-tts** -ts **-tting** -tɪŋ (US) -t̬ɪŋ **-tted** -tɪd (US) -t̬ɪd **-tter/s** -təʳ/z (US) -t̬ɚ/z
Boyd bɔɪd
Boyer ˈbwaɪ.eɪ; ˈbɔɪ.əʳ (US) bɔɪˈeɪ; ˈbɔɪ.ɚ
Boyet ˈbɔɪ.et, -ˈ- (US) bwɑːˈjeɪ
boyfriend ˈbɔɪ.frend **-s** -z
boyhood ˈbɔɪ.hʊd **-s** -z
boyish ˈbɔɪ.ɪʃ **-ly** -li **-ness** -nəs, -nɪs
Boyle bɔɪl
Boyne bɔɪn
boyo ˈbɔɪ.əʊ (US) -oʊ **-s** -z
boysenberr|y ˈbɔɪ.zᵊn.bᵊr|.i, -ˌber- (US) -ˌber- **-ies** -iz
Boyson ˈbɔɪ.sᵊn
Boyton ˈbɔɪ.tᵊn
Boyzone ˈbɔɪ.zəʊn (US) -zoʊn
Boz bɒz (US) bɑːz
Note: This pen-name of Charles Dickens was originally pronounced /bəʊz (US) boʊz/, but this pronunciation is not often heard now.
bozo ˈbəʊ.zəʊ (US) ˈboʊ.zoʊ **-s** -z
BP ˌbiːˈpiː
BPhil ˌbiːˈfɪl
BR ˌbiːˈɑːʳ (US) -ˈɑːr
bra brɑː **-s** -z
braai braɪ **-s** -z **-ing** -ɪŋ **-ed** -d
Brabant brəˈbænt; ˈbræb.ənt
Brabantio brəˈbæn.ti.əʊ, bræbˈæn-, -*t*ʃi- (US) brəˈbæn.t̬i.oʊ, -ˈbæn*t*.ʃi-
Brabazon ˈbræb.ə.zᵊn (US) -zɑːn
Brabham ˈbræb.əm
Brabourne *place:* ˈbreɪ.bɔːn (US) -bɔːrn *family name:* ˈbreɪ.bən, ˈbreɪ.bɔːn (US) -bɚn, -bɔːrn
brac|e (B) breɪs **-es** -ɪz **-ing** -ɪŋ **-ed** -t
Bracebridge ˈbreɪs.brɪdʒ
bracelet ˈbreɪs.lət, -lɪt **-s** -s
brach brætʃ (US) brætʃ, bræk **-es** -ɪz
brachial ˈbreɪ.ki.əl (US) ˈbreɪ-, ˈbræk.i-
brachy- ˈbræk.i-
brachycephalic ˌbræk.i.səˈfæl.ɪk, -sɪˈ-
brack bræk **-s** -s
bracken ˈbræk.ᵊn
Brackenbury ˈbræk.ᵊn.bᵊr.i (US) -ber-
Brackenridge ˈbræk.ᵊn.rɪdʒ
brack|et ˈbræk|.ɪt **-ets** -ɪts **-eting** -ɪ.tɪŋ (US) -ɪ.t̬ɪŋ **-eted** -ɪ.tɪd (US) -ɪ.t̬ɪd
brackish ˈbræk.ɪʃ **-ness** -nəs, -nɪs
Brackley ˈbræk.li
Bracknell ˈbræk.nəl
brad (B) bræd **-s** -z
bradawl ˈbræd.ɔːl (US) -ɑːl, -ɔːl **-s** -z
Bradbury ˈbræd.bᵊr.i, ˈbræb- (US) -ber-
Braddon ˈbræd.ᵊn
Braden ˈbreɪ.dᵊn
Bradfield ˈbræd.fiːld
Bradford ˈbræd.fəd (US) -fɚd
Bradgate ˈbræd.geɪt, -gɪt
Bradlaugh, Bradlaw ˈbræd.lɔː (US) -lɑː, -lɔː
Bradley ˈbræd.li
Bradman ˈbræd.mən
Bradshaw ˈbræd.ʃɔː (US) -ʃɑː, -ʃɔː
Bradstreet ˈbræd.striːt
Bradwardine ˈbræd.wə.diːn (US) -wɚ-
Brady ˈbreɪ.di
bradycardia ˌbræd.ɪˈkɑː.di.ə (US) -ˈkɑːr-
brae breɪ **-s** -z
Braemar breɪˈmɑːʳ (US) -ˈmɑːr *stress shift:* ˌBraemar ˈgames
brag bræg **-s** -z **-ging/ly** -ɪŋ/li **-ged** -d
Bragg bræg
braggadocio ˌbræg.əˈdəʊ.*t*ʃi.əʊ (US) -ˈdoʊ- **-s** -z
braggart ˈbræg.ət, -ɑːt (US) -ɚt **-s** -s
Braham ˈbreɪ.əm
Brahe ˈbrɑː.hə, -ə, -hi
brahma (B) *god:* ˈbrɑː.mə *breed of fowl or cattle:* ˈbreɪ.mə (US) ˈbrɑː-, ˈbreɪ-, ˈbræm.ə **-s** -z
Brahman ˈbrɑː.mən **-s** -z **-ism** -ɪ.zᵊm
Brahmaputra ˌbrɑː.məˈpuː.trə
brahmin (B) ˈbrɑː.mɪn **-s** -z **-ism** -ɪ.zᵊm
brahminical ˌbrɑːˈmɪn.ɪ.kᵊl
Brahms brɑːmz
braid (B) breɪd **-s** -z **-ing** -ɪŋ **-ed** -ɪd
brail breɪl **-s** -z
Braille breɪl
Brailsford ˈbreɪls.fəd (US) -fɚd
brain (B) breɪn **-s** -z **-ing** -ɪŋ **-ed** -d ˈ**brain ˌdamage**; ˈ**brain ˌdeath**; ˈ**brain ˌdrain**
brain|child ˈbreɪn|.tʃaɪld **-children** -ˌtʃɪl.drən
Braine breɪn
brainless ˈbreɪn.ləs, -lɪs **-ness** -nəs, -nɪs
brainsick ˈbreɪn.sɪk
brainstorm ˈbreɪn.stɔːm (US) -stɔːrm **-s** -z **-ing** -ɪŋ **-ed** -d
brainstorming ˈbreɪnˌstɔː.mɪŋ (US) -ˌstɔːr-
brainteaser ˈbreɪnˌtiː.zəʳ (US) -zɚ **-s** -z
Braintree ˈbreɪn.triː, -tri
brainwash ˈbreɪn.wɒʃ (US) -wɑːʃ, -wɔːʃ **-es** -ɪz **-ing** -ɪŋ **-ed** -t
brainwave ˈbreɪn.weɪv **-s** -z
brain|y ˈbreɪ.n|i **-ier** -i.əʳ (US) -i.ɚ **-iest** -i.ɪst, -i.əst
brais|e breɪz **-es** -ɪz **-ing** -ɪŋ **-ed** -d
Braithwaite ˈbreɪ.θweɪt
brak|e breɪk **-es** -s **-ing** -ɪŋ **-ed** -t ˈ**brake ˌfluid**; ˈ**brake ˌlight**
Brakenridge ˈbræk.ᵊn.rɪdʒ
Bram bræm
Bramah ˈbrɑː.mə, ˈbræm.ə
Bramall ˈbræm.ɔːl (US) -ɔːl, -ɑːl
bramble ˈbræm.bl̩ **-s** -z ˈ**bramble ˌbush**
Brambler ˈbræm.bləʳ (US) -blɚ
brambly ˈbræm.bli
Bramhall ˈbræm.hɔːl (US) -hɔːl, -hɑːl
Bramley ˈbræm.li **-s** -z
Brampton ˈbræm*p*.tən
Bramwell ˈbræm.wel, -wəl
bran (B) bræn ˌ**bran ˈmash**; ˌ**bran ˈpie**
Branagh ˈbræn.ə
branch (B) brɑːn*t*ʃ (US) bræn*t*ʃ **-es** -ɪz **-ing** -ɪŋ **-ed** -t
branchi|a ˈbræŋ.ki|.ə **-ae** -iː
branchial ˈbræŋ.ki.əl
branchiate ˈbræŋ.ki.eɪt, -ət
Brancusi bræŋˈkuː.zi (US) bræn-, brɑːŋ-
brand (B) brænd **-s** -z **-ing** -ɪŋ **-ed** -ɪd ˈ**brand ˌname**; ˌ**brand ˈnew**; ˈ**branding ˌiron**
Brandeis ˈbræn.daɪs
Brandenburg ˈbræn.dən.bɜːg (US) -bɝːg ˌ**Brandenburg ˈGate**
Brandi ˈbræn.di
brandish ˈbræn.dɪʃ **-es** -ɪz **-ing** -ɪŋ **-ed** -t
Brando ˈbræn.dəʊ (US) -doʊ
Brandon ˈbræn.dən
Brandram ˈbræn.drəm
Brandreth ˈbræn.drɪθ, -drəθ, -dreθ
Brandt brænt
brand|y (B) ˈbræn.d|i **-ies** -iz **-ied** -id **-ying** -i.ɪŋ ˌ**brandy ˈbutter** (US) ˈ**brandy ˌbutter**; ˈ**brandy ˌsnap**
brank bræŋk **-s** -s
Branksome ˈbræŋk.səm
Branson ˈbræn*t*.sᵊn
Branston ˈbræn*t*.stən
brant brænt **-s** -s
Brant brɑːnt (US) brænt
brant|-goose brænt|ˈguːs **-geese** -ˈgiːs

Braque brɑːk, bræk
Brasenose ˈbreɪz.nəʊz (US) -noʊz
brash bræʃ **-er** -əʳ (US) -ɚ **-est** -ɪst, -əst **-es** -ɪz **-ly** -li **-ness** -nəs, -nɪs
Brasher ˈbreɪ.ʃəʳ (US) -ʃɚ
brasier ˈbreɪ.zi.əʳ, ˈ-ʒəʳ (US) ˈ-ʒɚ **-s** -z
Brasilia brəˈzɪl.i.ə (US) -i.ə, ˈ-jə
Brasov ˈbræʃ.ɒv (US) ˈbrɑː.ʃɔv
brass brɑːs (US) bræs **-es** -ɪz ˌ**brass** ˈ**band**; ˌ**brass** ˈ**knuckles**; ˌ**brass** ˈ**monkey**; ˌ**brassed** ˈ**off**
brassard ˈbræs.ɑːd, -ˈ- (US) ˈbræs.ɑːrd; brəˈsɑːrd **-s** -z
brasserie ˈbræs.ᵊr.i (US) ˌbræs.əˈriː **-s** -z
Brassey ˈbræs.i
brassica ˈbræs.ɪ.kə **-s** -z
brassière ˈbræs.i.əʳ, ˈbræz- (US) brəˈzɪr **-s** -z
Brasso® ˈbrɑː.səʊ (US) ˈbræs.soʊ
brass|y, brass|ie *golf club:* ˈbrɑː.s|i (US) ˈbræs|.i **-ies** -iz
brass|y (*adj.*) ˈbrɑː.s|i (US) ˈbræs|.i **-ier** -i.əʳ (US) -i.ɚ **-iest** -i.ɪst, -i.əst
Brasted ˈbreɪ.stɪd, ˈbræs.tɪd
brat bræt **-s** -s ˈ**brat** ˌ**pack**
Bratislava ˌbræt.ɪˈslɑː.və (US) ˌbrɑː.t̬ɪˈ-
Bratsk brætsk, brɑːtsk (US) brɑːtsk
Brattleboro ˈbræt.l̩.bᵊr.ə (US) -oʊ
Braughing ˈbræf.ɪŋ
Braun brɔːn, braʊn (US) brɑːn, brɔːn, braʊn
Note: The trademark is pronounced /brɔːn/ in British English, /brɑːn, brɔːn/ in American English.
Braunton ˈbrɔːn.tən (US) ˈbrɑːn-, ˈbrɔːn-
Brautigan ˈbraʊ.tɪ.gən, ˈbrɔː-, ˈbræt.ɪ- (US) ˈbrɑː.t̬ɪ-, ˈbrɔː-
bravado brəˈvɑː.dəʊ (US) -doʊ **-(e)s** -z
brav|e breɪv **-er** -əʳ (US) -ɚ **-est** -ɪst, -əst **-ely** -li **-es** -z **-ing** -ɪŋ **-ed** -d
Braveheart ˈbreɪv.hɑːt (US) -hɑːrt
braver|y ˈbreɪ.vᵊr|.i **-ies** -iz
Bravington ˈbræv.ɪŋ.tən
bravo brɑːˈvəʊ, ˈ-- (US) ˈbrɑː.voʊ, -ˈ- **-(e)s** -z
Note: Always /ˈ--/ in the ICAO alphabet.
bravura brəˈvjʊə.rə, -ˈvjɔː-, -ˈvʊə- (US) -ˈvjʊr.ə, -ˈvʊr-
brawl brɔːl (US) brɑːl, brɔːl **-s** -z **-ing** -ɪŋ **-ed** -d **-er/s** -əʳ/z (US) -ɚ/z
brawn brɔːn (US) brɑːn, brɔːn
Brawne brɔːn (US) brɑːn, brɔːn
brawn|y ˈbrɔː.n|i (US) ˈbrɑː-, ˈbrɔː- **-ier** -i.əʳ (US) -i.ɚ **-iest** -i.ɪst, -i.əst **-iness** -ɪ.nəs, -ɪ.nɪs
Braxton ˈbræk.stᵊn
bray (**B**) breɪ **-s** -z **-ing** -ɪŋ **-ed** -d
Braybrooke ˈbreɪ.brʊk
Brayley ˈbreɪ.li
braz|e breɪz **-es** -ɪz **-ing** -ɪŋ **-ed** -d
brazen ˈbreɪ.zᵊn **-ly** -li **-ness** -nəs, -nɪs
brazen-faced ˌbreɪ.zᵊnˈfeɪst *stress shift:* ˌbrazen-faced ˈchild
brazier ˈbreɪ.zi.əʳ, ˈ-ʒəʳ (US) ˈ-ʒɚ **-s** -z
Brazier ˈbreɪ.ʒəʳ (US) -ʒɚ
Brazil *country:* brəˈzɪl *English surname:* ˈbræz.ɪl, -ᵊl; brəˈzɪl **Bra**ˈ**zil** ˌ**nut**
Brazilian brəˈzɪl.i.ən (US) -jən **-s** -z
Brazzaville ˈbræz.ə.vɪl, ˈbrɑː.zə-
breach briːtʃ **-es** -ɪz **-ing** -ɪŋ **-ed** -t ˌ**breach of the** ˈ**peace**
bread bred **-s** -z **-ed** -ɪd ˈ**bread** ˌ**basket**; ˌ**bread and** ˈ**butter**
Breadalbane *Earl:* brəˈdɔːl.bɪn, brɪ-, -bᵊn (US) -ˈdɔːl-, -ˈdɑːl- *place:* brəˈdæl.bɪn, -ˈdɔːl-, -bən (US) -ˈdæl-, -ˈdɔːl-, -ˈdɑːl-
breadboard ˈbred.bɔːd (US) -bɔːrd **-s** -z
breadbox ˈbred.bɒks (US) -bɑːks **-es** -ɪz
breadcrumb ˈbred.krʌm **-s** -z
breadfruit ˈbred.fruːt **-s** -s
breadline ˈbred.laɪn
breadth bretθ, bredθ **-s** -s
breadth|ways ˈbretθ|.weɪz, ˈbredθ- **-wise** -waɪz
breadwinner ˈbredˌwɪn.əʳ (US) -ɚ **-s** -z
break breɪk **-s** -s **-ing** -ɪŋ **broke** brəʊk (US) broʊk **broken** ˈbrəʊ.kᵊn (US) ˈbroʊ- ˌ**breaking and** ˈ**entering**
breakable ˈbreɪ.kə.bl̩ **-s** -z
breakag|e ˈbreɪ.kɪdʒ **-es** -ɪz
breakaway ˈbreɪ.kə.weɪ **-s** -z
breakdown ˈbreɪk.daʊn **-s** -z
breaker ˈbreɪ.kəʳ (US) -kɚ **-s** -z
break-even ˌbreɪkˈiː.vᵊn
breakfast ˈbrek.fəst **-s** -s **-ing** -ɪŋ **-ed** -ɪd
break-in ˈbreɪk.ɪn **-s** -z
breakneck ˈbreɪk.nek
breakout ˈbreɪk.aʊt **-s** -s
Breakspear ˈbreɪk.spɪəʳ (US) -spɪr
breakthrough ˈbreɪk.θruː **-s** -z
breakup ˈbreɪk.ʌp **-s** -s
breakwater ˈbreɪkˌwɔː.təʳ (US) -ˌwɑː.t̬ɚ, -ˌwɔː- **-s** -z
bream (**B**) briːm (US) briːm, brɪm **-s** -z
Breamore ˈbrem.əʳ (US) -ɚ
breast brest **-s** -s **-ing** -ɪŋ **-ed** -ɪd ˌ**make a** ˌ**clean** ˈ**breast of something**
breastbone ˈbrest.bəʊn (US) -boʊn **-s** -z
breast-feed ˈbrest.fiːd **-s** -z **-ing** -ɪŋ **breast-fed** ˈbrest.fed
Breaston ˈbriː.stᵊn
breastplate ˈbrest.pleɪt **-s** -s
breaststroke ˈbrest.strəʊk (US) -stroʊk
breastwork ˈbrest.wɜːk (US) -wɝːk **-s** -s
breath breθ **-s** -s ˈ**breath** ˌ**test**; ˌ**take someone's** ˈ**breath away**; ˌ**waste one's** ˈ**breath**
breathalyz|e, -ys|e ˈbreθ.ᵊl.aɪz (US) -ə.laɪz **-es** -ɪz **-ed** -d **-ing** -ɪŋ **-er/s** -əʳ/z (US) -ɚ/z
breath|e briːð **-es** -z **-ing** -ɪŋ **-ed** -d ˈ**breathing** ˌ**room**; ˈ**breathing** ˌ**space**; ˌ**breathe** ˌ**down someone's** ˈ**neck**
breathed *phonetic term:* breθt, briːðd
breather ˈbriː.ðəʳ (US) -ðɚ **-s** -z
breathiness ˈbreθ.ɪ.nəs, -nɪs
breathless ˈbreθ.ləs, -lɪs **-ly** -li **-ness** -nəs, -nɪs
breathtaking ˈbreθˌteɪ.kɪŋ **-ly** -li
breath|y ˈbreθ|.i **-ier** -i.əʳ (US) -i.ɚ **-iest** -i.ɪst, -i.əst **-iness** -ɪ.nəs, -ɪ.nɪs
Brebner ˈbreb.nəʳ (US) -nɚ
Brechin ˈbriː.kɪn, -xɪn (US) -kɪn
Brecht brekt *as if German:* brext **-ian** -i.ən
Breckenridge, -kin- ˈbrek.ᵊn.rɪdʒ, -ɪn-
Brecknock ˈbrek.nɒk, -nək (US) -nɑːk **-shire** -ʃəʳ, -ˌʃɪəʳ (US) -ʃɚ, -ˌʃɪr
Brecon ˈbrek.ᵊn ˌ**Brecon** ˈ**Beacons**
bred (*from* **breed**) bred
Bredbury ˈbred.bᵊr.i, ˈbreb- (US) ˈbred.ber-, -bɚ-
Bredon ˈbriː.dᵊn
bree briː
breech (*n.*) briːtʃ **-es** -ɪz **-ed** -t ˈ**breech** ˌ**birth**, ˌ**breech** ˈ**birth** (US) ˈ**breech** ˌ**birth**
breeches *trousers:* ˈbrɪtʃ.ɪz, ˈbriː.tʃɪz
breeching ˈbrɪtʃ.ɪŋ, ˈbriː.tʃɪŋ **-s** -z
breech-loader ˈbriːtʃˌləʊ.dəʳ (US) -ˌloʊ.dɚ **-s** -z
breed briːd **-s** -z **-ing** -ɪŋ **bred** bred ˈ**breeding** ˌ**ground**
breeder ˈbriː.dəʳ (US) -dɚ **-s** -z ˈ**breeder re**ˌ**actor**
breeks briːks
breez|e briːz **-es** -ɪz **-ing** -ɪŋ **-ed** -d
breez|y ˈbriː.z|i **-ier** -i.əʳ (US) -i.ɚ **-iest** -i.ɪst, -i.əst **-ily** -ɪ.li, -ᵊl.i **-iness** -ɪ.nəs, -ɪ.nɪs
Bremen *in Germany:* ˈbreɪ.mən (US) ˈbrem.ən, ˈbreɪ.mən *in US:* ˈbriː.mᵊn, ˈbrem.ən
Bremerhaven ˈbreɪ.məˌhɑː.vᵊn (US) ˈbrem.ɚ-, ˈbreɪ.mɚ-
Bremner ˈbrem.nəʳ (US) -nɚ
Bren bren
Brenda ˈbren.də
Brendan ˈbren.dən
Brendel ˈbren.dᵊl
Brendon ˈbren.dən
Brennan ˈbren.ən
Brenner ˈbren.əʳ (US) -ɚ
Brent brent
Brentford ˈbrent.fəd (US) -fɚd
brent|-goose ˌbrent|ˈguːs **-geese** -giːs
Brenton ˈbren.tən
Brentwood ˈbrent.wʊd
bre'r, br'er (**B**) brɜːʳ, breəʳ (US) brɝː, brer
Brereton ˈbrɪə.tᵊn (US) ˈbrɪr-
Brescia ˈbreʃ.ə, ˈbreɪ.ʃə (US) ˈbreʃ.ɑː, ˈbreɪ.ʃɑː
Breslau ˈbrez.laʊ, ˈbres-

Brest *in France:* brest
brethren 'breð.rən, -rɪn
Breton 'bret.ɒn *as if French:* bret'ɔ̃ːŋ US 'bret.ᵊn **-s** -z
Bret(t) bret
Bretwalda bret'wɔːl.də, -'wɒl-, '--- US -'wɑːl-, -'wɔːl-
Breughel 'brɔɪ.gᵊl, 'brɜː-, 'bruː- *as if Dutch:* -xəl US 'bruː.gᵊl, 'brɔɪ-, 'brɔː-
breve briːv US briːv, brev **-s** -z
brev|et 'brev|.ɪt **-ets** -ɪts **-eting** -ɪ.tɪŋ US -ɪ.t̬ɪŋ **-eted** -ɪ.tɪd US -ɪ.t̬ɪd
breviar|y 'brev.i.ᵊr|.i, 'briː.vi- US -er|.i, -ɚ|.i **-ies** -iz
breviate 'briː.vi.ət, -ɪt **-s** -s
brevier brə'vɪəʳ, brɪ- US -'vɪr
brevity 'brev.ə.ti, -ɪ.ti US -ə.t̬i
brew (B) bruː **-s** -z **-ing** -ɪŋ **-ed** -d
brewer (B) 'bruː.əʳ US -ɚ **-s** -z ˌ**brewer's 'yeast**
brewer|y 'bruː.ᵊr|.i US 'bruː.ɚ|.i, '-ri **-ies** -iz
brewpub 'bruː.pʌb **-s** -z
Brewster 'bruː.stəʳ US -stɚ
Brezhnev 'breʒ.nef, -njef US -nef, -nev
Brian braɪən
Note: /'briː.ən/ for the novelist Brian Moore.
Bria(n)na bri'æn.ə
Brianne bri'æn
briar braɪəʳ US braɪɚ **-s** -z
Briareus ˌbraɪ'eə.ri.əs US -'er.i-
brib|e braɪb **-es** -z **-ing** -ɪŋ **-ed** -d **-er/s** -əʳ/z US -ɚ/z
briber|y 'braɪ.bᵊr|.i **-ies** -iz
bric-à-brac 'brɪk.əˌbræk
Brice braɪs
brick brɪk **-s** -s **'brick ˌdust; 'brick ˌfield**
brickbat 'brɪk.bæt **-s** -s
brickie 'brɪk.i **-s** -z
brick-kiln 'brɪk.kɪln, -kɪl **-s** -z
Note: The pronunciation /-kɪl/ is used chiefly by those concerned with the working of kilns.
bricklay|er 'brɪkˌleɪ|.əʳ US -ɚ **-ers** -əz US -ɚz **-ing** -ɪŋ
brickmak|er 'brɪkˌmeɪ|.kəʳ US -kɚ **-ers** -əz US -ɚz **-ing** -ɪŋ
brickwork 'brɪk.wɜːk US -wɝːk
bricolage ˌbrɪk.əʊ'lɑːʒ, '--- US ˌbriː.koʊ'lɑːʒ, ˌbrɪk.oʊ'-
bridal 'braɪ.dᵊl
bride braɪd **-s** -z
bridegroom 'braɪd.grʊm, -gruːm US -gruːm, -grʊm **-s** -z
Brideshead 'braɪdz.hed
bridesmaid 'braɪdz.meɪd **-s** -z
brides|man 'braɪdz|.mən **-men** -mən, -men
bride-to-be ˌbraɪd.tə'biː US -tuː'- **brides-to-be** ˌbraɪdz.tə'biː US -tuː'-
Bridewell 'braɪd.wel, -wəl
bridg|e (B) brɪdʒ **-es** -ɪz **-ing** -ɪŋ **-ed** -d ˌ**burn one's 'bridges**
bridgeable 'brɪdʒ.ə.bl̩
bridgehead 'brɪdʒ.hed **-s** -z
Bridgeman 'brɪdʒ.mən
Bridgend ˌbrɪdʒ'end, '--
Bridgenorth 'brɪdʒ.nɔːθ, -'- US 'brɪdʒ.nɔːrθ, -'-
Bridgeport 'brɪdʒ.pɔːt US -pɔːrt
Bridger 'brɪdʒ.əʳ US -ɚ
Bridges 'brɪdʒ.ɪz
Bridget 'brɪdʒ.ɪt
Bridgetown 'brɪdʒ.taʊn
Bridgewater 'brɪdʒˌwɔː.təʳ US -ˌwɑː.t̬ɚ, -ˌwɔː-
bridgework 'brɪdʒ.wɜːk US -wɝːk
Bridgnorth 'brɪdʒ.nɔːθ, ˌ-'- US 'brɪdʒ.nɔːrθ, ˌ-'-
Bridgwater 'brɪdʒˌwɔː.təʳ US -ˌwɑː.t̬ɚ, -ˌwɔː-
bridie (B) 'braɪ.di **-s** -z
bridl|e 'braɪ.dl̩ **-es** -z **-ing** -ɪŋ, 'braɪd.lɪŋ **-ed** -d **'bridle ˌpath**
bridleway 'braɪ.dl̩.weɪ **-s** -z
Bridlington 'brɪd.lɪŋ.tən
bridoon brɪ'duːn **-s** -z
Bridport 'brɪd.pɔːt US -pɔːrt
brie (B) briː
brief briːf **-s** -s **-er** -əʳ US -ɚ **-est** -ɪst, -əst **-ly** -li **-ness** -nəs, -nɪs **-ing/s** -ɪŋ/z **-ed** -t
briefcas|e 'briːf.keɪs **-es** -ɪz, -əz
briefless 'briː.fləs, -flɪs
brier braɪəʳ US braɪɚ **-s** -z
Brierfield 'braɪə.fiːld US 'braɪɚ-
Brierley 'braɪə.li, 'brɪə- US 'braɪɚ-, 'brɪr-
Briers braɪəz US braɪɚz
brig brɪg **-s** -z
brigade brɪ'geɪd, brə- **-s** -z
brigadier ˌbrɪg.ə'dɪəʳ US -'dɪr **-s** -z *stress shift, see compound:* ˌ**brigadier 'general**
Brigadoon ˌbrɪg.ə'duːn
brigand 'brɪg.ᵊnd **-s** -z **-age** -ɪdʒ
brigantine 'brɪg.ᵊn.tiːn, -taɪn **-s** -z
Briges 'brɪdʒ.ɪz
Brigg brɪg **-s** -z
Brigham 'brɪg.əm
Brighouse 'brɪg.haʊs
bright (B) braɪt **-er** -əʳ US 'braɪ.t̬ɚ **-est** -ɪst, -əst US 'braɪ.t̬ɪst, -t̬əst **-ly** -li **-ness** -nəs, -nɪs
brighten 'braɪ.tᵊn **-s** -z **-ing** -ɪŋ **-ed** -d
Brightlingsea 'braɪt.lɪŋ.siː
Brighton 'braɪ.tᵊn
brights braɪts
Brigid 'brɪdʒ.ɪd
Brigit 'brɪdʒ.ɪt
Brignell 'brɪg.nəl
Brigstock(e) 'brɪg.stɒk US -stɑːk
brill (B) brɪl **-s** -z
brillian|ce 'brɪl.i.ənt|s US '-jənt|s **-cy** -si
brilliant 'brɪl.i.ənt US '-jənt **-s** -s **-ly** -li **-ness** -nəs, -nɪs
brilliantine 'brɪl.i.ən.tiːn US '-jən- **-d** -d
Brillo® 'brɪl.əʊ US -oʊ
Brillo pad® 'brɪl.əʊˌpæd US -oʊˌ-
brim brɪm **-s** -z **-ming** -ɪŋ **-med** -d
brimful brɪm'fʊl, '--
brimstone 'brɪm.stəʊn US -stoʊn
Brind brɪnd
Brindisi 'brɪn.dɪ.si, -də-, -zi
brindle (B) 'brɪn.dl̩ **-s** -z **-d** -d
brine braɪn
bring brɪŋ **-s** -z **-ing** -ɪŋ **brought** brɔːt US brɑːt, brɔːt **bringer/s** 'brɪŋ.əʳ/z US -ɚ/z
brinjal 'brɪn.*dʒ*ᵊl
brink (B) brɪŋk **-s** -s
brinkmanship 'brɪŋk.mən.ʃɪp
brinksmanship 'brɪŋ*k*s.mən.ʃɪp
Brinks-Mat® ˌbrɪŋks'mæt
Brinsley 'brɪnz.li
brin|y 'braɪ.n|i **-ier** -i.əʳ US -i.ɚ **-iest** -i.ɪst, -i.əst **-iness** -ɪ.nəs, -ɪ.nɪs
Bri-Nylon® ˌbraɪ'naɪ.lɒn US -lɑːn
brio 'briː.əʊ US -oʊ
brioch|e bri'ɒʃ, -'əʊʃ US -'oʊʃ, -'ɑːʃ **-es** -ɪz
Briony 'braɪə.ni
briquet(te) brɪ'ket **-s** -s
Brisbane 'brɪz.bən US -bən, -beɪn
Note: /'brɪz.bən/ is the pronunciation in Australia.
Briscoe 'brɪs.kəʊ US -koʊ
brisk brɪsk **-er** -əʳ US -ɚ **-est** -ɪst, -əst **-ly** -li **-ness** -nəs, -nɪs
brisket 'brɪs.kɪt **-s** -s
bristl|e 'brɪs.l̩ **-es** -z **-ing** -ɪŋ, 'brɪs.lɪŋ **-ed** -d
brist|ly 'brɪs|.l̩.i, 'brɪs|.li **-liness** -l̩.ɪ.nəs, 'brɪs|.li-, -nɪs
Bristol 'brɪs.tᵊl
Bristow(e) 'brɪs.təʊ US -toʊ
Brit brɪt **-s** -s
Brit. *(abbrev. for* **Britain***)* brɪt; 'brɪt.ᵊn
Brit. *(abbrev. for* **British***)* brɪt; 'brɪt.ɪʃ US brɪt; 'brɪt̬.ɪʃ
Britain 'brɪt.ᵊn
Britannia brɪ'tæn.i.ə, '-jə US '-jə
Britannic brɪ'tæn.ɪk **-a** -ə
britches 'brɪtʃ.ɪz, -əz
Briticism 'brɪt.ɪ.sɪ.zᵊm US 'brɪt̬- **-s** -z
British 'brɪt.ɪʃ US 'brɪt̬- **-er/s** -əʳ/z US -ɚ/z ˌ**British 'English;** ˌ**British 'Isles;** ˌ**British 'Summer ˌTime**
Britishism 'brɪt.ɪ.ʃɪ.zᵊm US 'brɪt̬- **-s** -z
British Leyland® ˌbrɪt.ɪʃ'leɪ.lənd US ˌbrɪt̬-
Britling 'brɪt.lɪŋ
Britney 'brɪt.ni
Britomart 'brɪt.əʊ.mɑːt US -oʊ.mɑːrt

Briton ˈbrɪt.^{ə}n **-s** -z
Britpop ˈbrɪt.pɒp (US) -pɑːp
Britt brɪt
Brittain ˈbrɪt.^{ə}n; brɪˈteɪn (US) ˈbrɪt.^{ə}n; brɪˈteɪn
Brittan ˈbrɪt.^{ə}n
Brittany ˈbrɪt.^{ə}n.i
Britten ˈbrɪt.^{ə}n
brittl|e ˈbrɪt.l̩ (US) ˈbrɪt̬- **-er** -ə^{r} (US) -ɚ **-est** -ɪst, -əst **-eness** -nəs, -nɪs
Brittney ˈbrɪt.ni
Britton ˈbrɪt.^{ə}n
Britvic® ˈbrɪt.vɪk
Brixham ˈbrɪk.s^{ə}m
Brixton ˈbrɪk.st^{ə}n
Brize Norton ˌbraɪzˈnɔː.t^{ə}n (US) -ˈnɔːr-
Brno ˈbɜː.nəʊ *as if Czech:* ˈbɚ- (US) ˈbɝː.noʊ
bro brəʊ (US) broʊ **-s** -z
broach brəʊtʃ (US) broʊtʃ **-es** -ɪz **-ing** -ɪŋ **-ed** -t
broad brɔːd (US) brɑːd, brɔːd **-er** -ə^{r} (US) -ɚ **-est** -ɪst, -əst **-ly** -li **-ness** -nəs, -nɪs ˌ**broad** ˈ**bean**
Broad brɔːd (US) brɑːd, brɔːd **-s** -z
broadband ˈbrɔːd.bænd (US) ˈbrɑːd-, ˈbrɔːd-
Broadbent ˈbrɔːd.bent (US) ˈbrɑːd-, ˈbrɔːd-
broadbrimmed ˌbrɔːdˈbrɪmd (US) ˌbrɑːd-, ˌbrɔːd- *stress shift:* ˌbroadbrimmed ˈhat
broadcast ˈbrɔːd.kɑːst (US) ˈbrɑːd.kæst, ˈbrɔːd- **-s** -s **-ing** -ɪŋ **-er/s** -ə^{r}/z (US) -ɚ/z
broadcloth ˈbrɔːd.klɒθ (US) ˈbrɑːd.klɑːθ, ˈbrɔːd-
broaden ˈbrɔː.d^{ə}n (US) ˈbrɑː-, ˈbrɔː- **-s** -z **-ing** -ɪŋ **-ed** -d
broad-gauge ˈbrɔːd.geɪdʒ (US) ˈbrɑːd-, ˈbrɔːd-
Broadhurst ˈbrɔːd.hɜːst (US) ˈbrɑːd.hɝːst, ˈbrɔːd-
Broadlands ˈbrɔːd.ləndz (US) ˈbrɑːd-, ˈbrɔːd-
broadloom ˈbrɔːd.luːm (US) ˈbrɑːd-, ˈbrɔːd-
broad-minded ˌbrɔːdˈmaɪn.dɪd (US) ˌbrɑːd-, ˌbrɔːd-, ˈ-ˌ-- **-ness** -nəs, -nɪs *stress shift, British only:* ˌbroad-minded ˈperson
Broadmoor ˈbrɔːd.mɔː^{r} (US) ˈbrɑːd.mʊr, ˈbrɔːd-, -mɔːr
broadsheet ˈbrɔːd.ʃiːt (US) ˈbrɑːd-, ˈbrɔːd- **-s** -s
broadside ˈbrɔːd.saɪd (US) ˈbrɑːd-, ˈbrɔːd- **-s** -z
Broadstairs ˈbrɔːd.steəz (US) ˈbrɑːd.sterz, ˈbrɔːd-
broadsword ˈbrɔːd.sɔːd (US) ˈbrɑːd.sɔːrd, ˈbrɔːd- **-s** -z
Broadwater ˈbrɔːdˌwɔː.tə^{r} (US) ˈbrɑːdˌwɑː.t̬ɚ, -ˌwɔː-
Broadway ˈbrɔːd.weɪ (US) ˈbrɑːd-, ˈbrɔːd-
Broadwood ˈbrɔːd.wʊd (US) ˈbrɑːd-, ˈbrɔːd- **-s** -z
Brobdingnag ˈbrɒb.dɪŋ.næg (US) ˈbrɑːb-
Brobdingnagian ˌbrɒb.dɪŋˈnæg.i.ən (US) ˌbrɑːb- **-s** -z
brocade brəʊˈkeɪd (US) broʊ- **-s** -z **-d** -ɪd
brocard ˈbrəʊ.kəd, -kɑːd (US) ˈbroʊ.kɚd, ˈbrɑː-, -kɑːrd **-s** -z
broc(c)oli ˈbrɒk.^{ə}l.i, -aɪ (US) ˈbrɑː.k^{ə}l-
Broch brɒk *as if German:* brox (US) broʊk
brochette brɒʃˈet (US) broʊˈʃet **-s** -s
brochure ˈbrəʊ.ʃə^{r}, -ʃʊə^{r}, brɒʃˈʊə^{r}, brəˈʃʊə^{r} (US) broʊˈʃʊr **-s** -z
brock (B) brɒk (US) brɑːk **-s** -s
Brocken ˈbrɒk.^{ə}n (US) ˈbrɑː.k^{ə}n
Brockenhurst ˈbrɒk.^{ə}n.hɜːst (US) ˈbrɑː.k^{ə}n.hɝːst
Brocket ˈbrɒk.ɪt (US) ˈbrɑː.kɪt
Brocklehurst ˈbrɒk.l̩.hɜːst (US) ˈbrɑː.kl̩.hɝːst
Brockley ˈbrɒk.li (US) ˈbrɑː.kli
Brockman ˈbrɒk.mən (US) ˈbrɑːk-
Brockovich ˈbrɒk.ə.vɪtʃ (US) ˈbrɑː.kə-
Brockwell ˈbrɒk.wəl, -wel (US) ˈbrɑː.kwəl, -kwel
Broderick ˈbrɒd.^{ə}r.ɪk (US) ˈbrɑː.d^{ə}r-
broderie anglaise ˌbrəʊ.d^{ə}r.iˈɑ̃ːŋ.gleɪz, ˌbrɒd.^{ə}r-, -ˈglez, -ɑ̃ːŋˈgleɪz, -ˈglez (US) ˌbroʊ.də.riː.ɑːŋˈgleɪz
Brodie ˈbrəʊ.di (US) ˈbroʊ-
Brodrick ˈbrɒd.rɪk (US) ˈbrɑː.drɪk
Brogan ˈbrəʊ.g^{ə}n (US) ˈbroʊ-
brogue brəʊg (US) broʊg **-s** -z
broil brɔɪl **-s** -z **-ing** -ɪŋ **-ed** -d
broiler ˈbrɔɪ.lə^{r} (US) -lɚ **-s** -z
brok|e (*v.*) brəʊk (US) broʊk **-es** -s **-ing** -ɪŋ **-ed** -t
broke *(from* **break***)* brəʊk (US) broʊk
Broke brʊk
broken ˈbrəʊ.k^{ə}n (US) ˈbroʊ- **-ly** -li
broken-down ˌbrəʊ.k^{ə}nˈdaʊn (US) ˌbroʊ- *stress shift:* ˌbroken-down ˈcar
broken-hearted ˌbrəʊ.k^{ə}nˈhɑː.tɪd (US) ˌbroʊ.k^{ə}nˈhɑːr.t̬ɪd *stress shift:* ˌbroken-hearted ˈsuitor
broker ˈbrəʊ.kə^{r} (US) ˈbroʊ.kɚ **-s** -z **-ing** -ɪŋ **-ed** -d
brokerag|e ˈbrəʊ.k^{ə}r.ɪdʒ (US) ˈbroʊ- **-es** -ɪz
broll|y ˈbrɒl|.i (US) ˈbrɑː.l|i **-ies** -iz
bromate ˈbrəʊ.meɪt (US) ˈbroʊ- **-s** -s
brome brəʊm, bruːm (US) broʊm **-s** -z
Brome brəʊm, bruːm (US) broʊm, bruːm
bromeliad brəʊˈmiː.li.æd (US) broʊ-
Bromfield ˈbrɒm.fiːld (US) ˈbrɑːm-
Bromham ˈbrɒm.əm (US) ˈbrɑː.məm
bromic ˈbrəʊ.mɪk (US) ˈbroʊ-
bromide ˈbrəʊ.maɪd (US) ˈbroʊ- **-s** -z
bromine ˈbrəʊ.miːn, -mɪn (US) ˈbroʊ-
Bromley ˈbrɒm.li, ˈbrʌm- (US) ˈbrɑːm-
Brompton ˈbrɒmp.tən, ˈbrʌmp- (US) ˈbrɑːmp-
Bromsgrove ˈbrɒmz.grəʊv (US) ˈbrɑːmz.groʊv
Bromwich *in place names:* ˈbrɒm.ɪtʃ, ˈbrʌm-, -ɪdʒ (US) ˈbrɑːm.wɪtʃ *surname:* ˈbrʌm.ɪdʒ (US) -wɪtʃ
Bromyard ˈbrɒm.jɑːd, -jəd (US) ˈbrɑːm.jɑːrd, -jɚd
bronchi|a ˈbrɒŋ.ki|.ə, ˈbrɒn- (US) ˈbrɑːŋ-, ˈbrɑːn- **-ae** -iː
bronchial ˈbrɒŋ.ki.əl, ˈbrɒn- (US) ˈbrɑːŋ-, ˈbrɑːn-
bronchiole ˈbrɒŋ.ki.əʊl, ˈbrɒn- (US) ˈbrɑːŋ.ki.oʊl, ˈbrɑːn- **-s** -z
bronchitic brɒŋˈkɪt.ɪk, brɒn- (US) brɑːŋˈkɪt̬-, brɑːn-
bronchitis brɒŋˈkaɪ.tɪs, brɒn- (US) brɑːŋˈkaɪ.t̬ɪs, brɑːn-
broncho-pneumonia ˌbrɒŋ.kəʊ.njuːˈməʊ.ni.ə, ˌbrɒn-, -njʊˈ- (US) ˌbrɑːŋ.koʊ.nuːˈmoʊ.njə, ˌbrɑːn-, -njuːˈ-
bronch|us ˈbrɒŋ.k|əs, ˈbrɒn- (US) ˈbrɑːŋ-, ˈbrɑːn- **-i** -iː, -aɪ
bronco ˈbrɒŋ.kəʊ (US) ˈbrɑːŋ.koʊ **-s** -z
Bronson ˈbrɒnt.sən (US) ˈbrɑːnt-
Bronstein ˈbrɒn.stiːn (US) ˈbrɑːn-
Bronte, Brontë ˈbrɒn.teɪ, -ti (US) ˈbrɑːn.teɪ, -t̬i
brontosaur ˈbrɒn.tə.sɔː^{r} (US) ˈbrɑːn.t̬ə.sɔːr **-s** -z
brontosaur|us ˌbrɒn.təˈsɔː.r|əs (US) ˌbrɑːn.t̬əˈsɔːr|.əs **-uses** -ə.sɪz **-i** -aɪ
Bronwen ˈbrɒn.wen, -wɪn (US) ˈbrɑːn-
Bronx brɒŋks (US) brɑːŋks ˌ**Bronx** ˈ**cheer**
bronz|e brɒnz (US) brɑːnz **-es** -ɪz **-ing** -ɪŋ **-ed** -d **-y** -i ˈ**Bronze** ˌ**Age**
bronzer ˈbrɒn.zə^{r} (US) ˈbrɑːn.zɚ **-s** -z
brooch brəʊtʃ (US) broʊtʃ, bruːtʃ **-es** -ɪz
brood bruːd **-s** -z **-ing** -ɪŋ **-ed** -ɪd
brood|y ˈbruː.d|i **-ily** -ɪ.li, -^{ə}l.i **-iness** -ɪ.nəs, -ɪ.nɪs
brook brʊk **-s** -s **-ing** -ɪŋ **-ed** -t
Brook(e) brʊk **-s** -s
Brooker ˈbrʊk.ə^{r} (US) -ɚ
Brookfield ˈbrʊk.fiːld
Brookland ˈbrʊk.lənd **-s** -z
brooklet ˈbrʊk.lət, -lɪt **-s** -s
Brookline ˈbrʊk.laɪn
Brooklyn ˈbrʊk.lɪn (US) -lɪn, -lən ˌ**Brooklyn** ˈ**Bridge**
Brookner ˈbrʊk.nə^{r} (US) -nɚ
Brooks brʊks
Brookside ˈbrʊk.saɪd
Brooksmith ˈbrʊk.smɪθ
Brookwood ˈbrʊk.wʊd
broom bruːm, brʊm **-s** -z

Broom(e) bruːm
Broomfield 'bruːm.fiːld, 'brʊm-
broomstick 'bruːm.stɪk, 'brʊm- **-s** -s
Brophy 'brəʊ.fi (US) 'broʊ-
Bros. 'brʌð.əz *sometimes humorously:* brɒs, brɒz (US) 'brʌð.ɚz
Broseley 'brəʊz.li (US) 'broʊz-
Brosnahan 'brɒz.nə.hən, 'brɒs- (US) 'brɑːz-, 'brɑːs-
Brosnan 'brɒz.nən (US) 'brɑːz-
broth brɒθ (US) brɑːθ **-s** -s
brothel 'brɒθ.ᵊl (US) 'brɑː.θᵊl **-s** -z
brother 'brʌð.əʳ (US) -ɚ **-s** -z
brotherhood 'brʌð.ə.hʊd (US) '-ɚ- **-s** -z
broth|er-in-law 'brʌð|.əʳ.ɪn.lɔː (US) -ɚ.ɪn.lɑː, -lɔː **-ers-in-law** -əz.ɪn.lɔː (US) -ɚz.ɪn.lɑː, -lɔː
brotherl|y 'brʌð.ᵊl|.i (US) -ɚ.l|i **-iness** -ɪ.nəs, -ɪ.nɪs
Brotton 'brɒt.ᵊn (US) 'brɑː.tᵊn
Brough brʌf
brougham 'bruː.əm, bruːm (US) broʊm, 'bruː.əm, bruːm **-s** -z
Brougham brʊm, bruːm, 'bruː.əm, 'brəʊ- (US) brʊm, bruːm, 'bruː.əm, 'broʊ-
Brougham and Vaux ˌbrʊm.ənd'vɔːks (US) -'vɑːks, -'vɔːks
brought *(from* **bring***)* brɔːt (US) brɑːt, brɔːt
Broughton *in Northamptonshire:* 'braʊ.tᵊn *all others in England:* 'brɔː.tᵊn (US) 'brɑː-, 'brɔː-
brouhaha 'bruː.hɑː.hɑː **-s** -z
brow braʊ **-s** -z
brow|beat 'braʊ|.biːt **-beats** -biːts **-beating** -biː.tɪŋ (US) -biː.t̬ɪŋ **-beaten** -biː.tᵊn (US) -biː.t̬ᵊn
brown (B) braʊn **-s** -z **-er** -əʳ (US) -ɚ **-est** -ɪst, -əst **-ness** -nəs, -nɪs **-ing** -ɪŋ **-ed** -d ˌ**brown 'ale**; ˌ**brown 'Betty**; ˌ**brown 'bread**; ˌ**brown 'owl**; ˌ**brown 'sauce**; ˌ**brown 'sugar**
brown-bag ˌbraʊn'bæg **-s** -z **-ging** -ɪŋ **-ged** -d
Browne braʊn
brownfield 'braʊn.fiːld
Brownhills 'braʊn.hɪlz
Brownian 'braʊ.ni.ən ˌ**Brownian 'motion** (US) '**Brownian** ˌ**motion**; ˌ**Brownian 'movement** (US) '**Brownian** ˌ**movement**
brownie (B) 'braʊ.ni **-s** -z '**Brownie** ˌ**Guide**; '**brownie** ˌ**point**
browning (B) 'braʊ.nɪŋ
brownish 'braʊ.nɪʃ
Brownjohn 'braʊn.dʒɒn (US) -dʒɑːn
Brownlee, Brownlie 'braʊn.li
Brownlow 'braʊn.ləʊ (US) -loʊ
brown-nos|e ˌbraʊn'nəʊz (US) -'noʊz **-es** -ɪz **-ing** -ɪŋ **-ed** -d
brownout 'braʊn.aʊt **-s** -s
Brownrigg 'braʊn.rɪg
brownshirt (B) 'braʊn.ʃɜːt (US) -ʃɝːt **-s** -s
Brownsmith 'braʊn.smɪθ
Brownson 'braʊn.sᵊn
brownstone 'braʊn.stəʊn (US) -stoʊn **-s** -z
brows|e (B) braʊz **-es** -ɪz **-ing** -ɪŋ **-ed** -d
browser 'braʊ.zəʳ (US) -zɚ **-s** -z
Broxbourne 'brɒks.bɔːn (US) 'brɑːks.bɔːrn
Broxburn 'brɒks.bɜːn (US) 'brɑːks.bɝːn
Brubeck 'bruː.bek
Bruce bruːs
brucellosis ˌbruː.sɪ'ləʊ.sɪs, -sə'- (US) -'loʊ-
Brucesmith 'bruːs.smɪθ
Bruch brʊk *as if German:* brʊx
Bruckner 'brʊk.nəʳ (US) -nɚ
Brueg(h)el 'brɔɪ.gᵊl, 'brɜː-, 'bruː- *as if Dutch:* -xəl (US) 'bruː.gᵊl, 'brɔɪ-, 'brɔː-
Bruges bruːʒ
bruin (B) 'bruː.ɪn, brʊɪn (US) 'bruː.ɪn **-s** -z
bruis|e bruːz **-es** -ɪz **-ing** -ɪŋ **-ed** -d
bruiser 'bruː.zəʳ (US) -zɚ **-s** -z
bruit bruːt **-s** -s **-ing** -ɪŋ (US) 'bruː.t̬ɪŋ **-ed** -ɪd (US) 'bruː.t̬ɪd
Brum brʌm
Brumaire bru'meəʳ (US) -'mer
brumb|y 'brʌm.b|i **-ies** -iz
brume bruːm
brummagem (B) 'brʌm.ə.dʒəm
Brummel 'brʌm.ᵊl
brunch brʌntʃ **-es** -ɪz
Brunei bruː'naɪ, '-- (US) bruː'nɑɪ
Brunel bruː'nel
brunette, brunet bruː'net **-s** -s
Brünnhilde brʊn'hɪl.də, '-ˌ--
Brunning 'brʌn.ɪŋ
Bruno 'bruː.nəʊ (US) -noʊ
Brunswick 'brʌnz.wɪk
brunt brʌnt
Brunton 'brʌn.tən
bruschetta brʊ'sket.ə (US) -'sket̬-, bruː'ʃet̬.ə
brush brʌʃ **-es** -ɪz **-ing** -ɪŋ **-ed** -t
brush-off 'brʌʃ.ɒf (US) -ɑːf **-s** -s ˌ**give someone the 'brush-off**
brushstroke 'brʌʃ.strəʊk (US) -stroʊk **-s** -s
brushwood 'brʌʃ.wʊd
brushwork 'brʌʃ.wɜːk (US) -wɝːk
brusque bruːsk, brʊsk, brʌsk (US) brʌsk **-ly** -li **-ness** -nəs, -nɪs
Brussels 'brʌs.ᵊlz ˌ**brussels 'sprout(s)** (US) '**brussels** ˌ**sprout(s)**
brut (B®) bruːt
brutal 'bruː.tᵊl (US) -t̬ᵊl **-ly** -i
brutalit|y bruː'tæl.ə.t|i, -ɪ.t|i (US) -ə.t̬|i **-ies** -iz
brutaliz|e, -is|e 'bruː.tᵊl.aɪz (US) -t̬ᵊl- **-es** -ɪz **-ing** -ɪŋ **-ed** -d
brute bruːt **-s** -s
brutish 'bruː.tɪʃ (US) -t̬ɪʃ **-ly** -li **-ness** -nəs, -nɪs
Brutnell 'bruːt.nel, -nᵊl
Bruton 'bruː.tᵊn (US) -tᵊn
Brutus 'bruː.təs (US) -t̬əs
Bryan braɪən **-s** -z
Bryant braɪənt
Bryce braɪs
Brydon 'braɪ.dᵊn
Bryers braɪəz (US) braɪɚz
Brylcreem® 'brɪl.kriːm **-ed** -d
Brymbo 'brɪm.bəʊ, 'brʌm- (US) 'brɪm.boʊ
Bryn brɪn
Brynamman brɪ'næm.ən
Bryncoch brɪn'kəʊx (US) -'koʊx
Brynhild 'brɪn.hɪld
Brynmawr *in Wales:* brɪn'maʊəʳ, brɪm- (US) -'maʊɚ
Bryn Mawr *in US:* brɪn'mɔːʳ (US) -'mɑːr
Brynmor 'brɪn.mɔːʳ, 'brɪm- (US) 'brɪn.mɔːr
bryony (B) 'braɪə.ni
Bryson 'braɪ.sᵊn
BS ˌbiː'es
BSc ˌbiː.es'siː
BSE ˌbiː.es'iː
BSkyB ˌbiː.skaɪ'biː
BST ˌbiː.es'tiː
BT ˌbiː'tiː
bub bʌb **-s** -z
bubbl|e 'bʌb.l̩ **-es** -z **-ing** -ɪŋ, 'bʌb.lɪŋ **-ed** -d ˌ**bubble-and-'squeak**; '**bubble** ˌ**bath**; '**bubble** ˌ**gum**; '**bubble** ˌ**wrap**
Bubblejet® 'bʌb.l̩.dʒet
bubbly 'bʌb.l̩.i, -li
Buber 'buː.bəʳ (US) -bɚ
bubo 'bjuː.bəʊ, 'buː- (US) -boʊ **-es** -z
bubonic bjuː'bɒn.ɪk, buː- (US) -'bɑː.nɪk **bu**ˌ**bonic 'plague**
Bucaramanga bʊˌkær.ə'mæŋ.gə (US) ˌbuː.kə.rɑː'mɑːŋ.gɑː, -kɑːr.ɑː'-
buccal 'bʌk.ᵊl
buccaneer ˌbʌk.ə'nɪəʳ (US) -'nɪr **-s** -z
Buccleuch bə'kluː
Bucephalus bjuː'sef.ᵊl.əs
Buchan 'bʌk.ᵊn, 'bʌx-
Buchanan bjuː'kæn.ən, bə-
Bucharest ˌbuː.kə'rest, ˌbjuː-, ˌbʊk.ə'-, '--- (US) 'buː.kə.rest, 'bjuː-
Buchel 'bjuː.ʃᵊl
Buchenwald 'buː.kᵊn.væld *as if German:* 'bʊx.ən.vælt (US) 'buː.kᵊn.wɑːld, -wɔːld
Büchner 'buːk.nəʳ *as if German:* 'buːx- (US) 'bʊk.nɚ, 'buːk-
buck (B) bʌk **-s** -s **-ing** -ɪŋ **-ed** -t ˌ**buck's 'fizz**; ˌ**buck 'teeth**; ˌ**pass the 'buck**
buckboard 'bʌk.bɔːd (US) -bɔːrd **-s** -z
buck|et 'bʌk|.ɪt **-ets** -ɪts **-eting** -ɪ.tɪŋ (US) -ɪ.t̬ɪŋ **-eted** -ɪ.tɪd (US) -ɪ.t̬ɪd ˌ**kick the 'bucket**

bucketful ˈbʌk.ɪt.fʊl **-s** -z
Buckhaven ˈbʌkˌheɪ.vᵊn
buckhorn ˈbʌk.hɔːn (US) -hɔːrn
Buckhurst ˈbʌk.*h*ɜːst (US) -*h*ɝːst
Buckie ˈbʌk.i
Buckingham ˈbʌk.ɪŋ.əm **-shire** -ʃəʳ, -ˌʃɪəʳ (US) -ʃɚ, -ˌʃɪr ˌ**Buckingham** ˈ**Palace**
Buckland ˈbʌk.lənd
buckl|e (B) ˈbʌk.l̩ **-es** -z **-ing** -ɪŋ, ˈbʌk.lɪŋ **-ed** -d
buckler ˈbʌk.ləʳ (US) -lɚ **-s** -z
Buckley ˈbʌk.li
Buckmaster ˈbʌkˌmɑː.stəʳ (US) -ˌmæs.tɚ
Bucknall ˈbʌk.nəl
Bucknell ˈbʌk.nᵊl; bʌkˈnel
Bucknill ˈbʌk.nɪl, -nᵊl
buck-passing ˈbʌkˌpɑː.sɪŋ (US) -ˌpæs.ɪŋ
buckram ˈbʌk.rəm **-s** -z
Bucks. *(abbrev. for* **Buckinghamshire***)* bʌks; ˈbʌk.ɪŋ.əm.ʃəʳ, -ˌʃɪəʳ (US) bʌks; ˈbʌk.ɪŋ.əm.ʃɚ, -ˌʃɪr
buckshee ˌbʌkˈʃiː, ˈ--
buckshot ˈbʌk.ʃɒt (US) -ʃɑːt
buckskin ˈbʌk.skɪn **-s** -z
Buckston ˈbʌk.stən
buckwheat ˈbʌk.*h*wiːt
bucolic bjuːˈkɒl.ɪk (US) -ˈkɑː.lɪk **-al** -ᵊl **-ally** -ᵊl.i, -li
Buczacki bʊˈtʃæt.ski, bjuː-
bud (B) bʌd **-s** -z **-ding** -ɪŋ **-ded** -ɪd ˌ**nip something in the** ˈ**bud**
Budapest ˌbjuː.dəˈpest, ˌbuː- (US) ˈbuː.də.pest; ˌbuː.dəˈpeʃt
Budd bʌd
Buddha ˈbʊd.ə (US) ˈbuː.də, ˈbʊd.ə
Buddh|ism ˈbʊd|.ɪ.zᵊm (US) ˈbuː.d|ɪ-, ˈbʊd|.ɪ- **-ist/s** -ɪst/s
Buddhistic bʊˈdɪs.tɪk (US) buː-, bʊ-
budding ˈbʌd.ɪŋ
Buddle ˈbʌd.l̩, ˈbʊd-
buddleia ˈbʌd.li.ə (US) bʌdˈliː-; ˈbʌd.li- **-s** -z
budd|y ˈbʌd|.i **-ies** -iz
Bude bjuːd
budg|e (B) bʌdʒ **-es** -ɪz **-ing** -ɪŋ **-ed** -d
Budgens® ˈbʌdʒ.ənz
budgerigar ˈbʌdʒ.ᵊr.ɪ.gɑːʳ (US) -gɑːr **-s** -z
budg|et ˈbʌdʒ|.ɪt **-ets** -ɪts **-eting** -ɪ.tɪŋ (US) -ɪ.t̬ɪŋ **-eted** -ɪ.tɪd (US) -ɪ.t̬ɪd
budgetary ˈbʌdʒ.ɪ.tᵊr.i, ˈ-ə- (US) -ter.i
budgie ˈbʌdʒ.i **-s** -z
Budleigh ˈbʌd.li
Budweiser® ˈbʌd.waɪ.zəʳ (US) -zɚ
Buenos Aires ˌbweɪ.nɒsˈaɪə.rez, -nəs-, -riːz, -rɪs (US) ˌbweɪ.nəsˈer.iːz, -noʊsˈ-, ˌboʊ.nəsˈ-, -aɪ.riːz
buff bʌf **-s** -s **-ing** -ɪŋ **-ed** -d
buffalo (B) ˈbʌf.ᵊl.əʊ (US) -ə.loʊ **-es** -z ˌ**Buffalo** ˈ**Bill**
buffer ˈbʌf.əʳ (US) -ɚ **-s** -z **-ing** -ɪŋ **-ed** -d ˈ**buffer** ˌ**zone**
buffet *(n.) blow:* ˈbʌf.ɪt **-s** -s
buffet *(n.) refreshment, sideboard:* ˈbʊf.eɪ, ˈbʌf-, -i (US) bəˈfeɪ, buː- **-s** -z
buff|et *(v.) hit against:* ˈbʌf|.ɪt **-ets** -ɪts **-eting** -ɪ.tɪŋ, -ə.tɪŋ (US) -ɪ.t̬ɪŋ, -ə.t̬ɪŋ **-eted** -ɪ.tɪd, -ə.tɪd (US) -ɪ.t̬ɪd, -ə.t̬ɪd
buffo ˈbʊf.əʊ (US) ˈbuː.foʊ **-s** -z
buffoon bəˈfuːn, bʌfˈuːn (US) bəˈfuːn **-s** -z
buffooner|y bəˈfuː.nᵊr|.i, bʌfˈuː- (US) bəˈfuː- **-ies** -iz
Buffs bʌfs
Buffy ˈbʌf.i
bug bʌg **-s** -z **-ging** -ɪŋ **-ged** -d
Bug *river:* buːg
bugaboo ˈbʌg.ə.buː **-s** -z
Buganda buːˈgæn.də
Bugatti bjʊˈgæt.i, bʊ- (US) -ˈgɑː.t̬i
bugbear ˈbʌg.beəʳ (US) -ber **-s** -z
bug-eyed ˌbʌgˈaɪd (US) ˈ-- *stress shift, British only:* ˌbug-eyed ˈmonster
bugg|er ˈbʌg|.əʳ (US) -ɚ **-ers** -əz (US) -ɚz **-ering** -ᵊr.ɪŋ **-ered** -əd (US) -ɚd
buggery ˈbʌg.ᵊr.i
Buggins ˈbʌg.ɪnz
Buggs bjuːgz, bʌgz
bugg|y ˈbʌg|.i **-ies** -iz
bugl|e (B) ˈbjuː.gl̩ **-es** -z **-ing** -ɪŋ, ˈbjuː.glɪŋ **-ed** -d
bugler ˈbjuː.gləʳ (US) -glɚ **-s** -z
bugloss ˈbjuː.glɒs (US) -glɑːs
Bugner ˈbʌg.nəʳ (US) -nɚ
Bugs Bunny ˌbʌgzˈbʌn.i
Buick® ˈbjuː.ɪk **-s** -s
build bɪld **-s** -z **-ing** -ɪŋ **built** bɪlt ˈ**building so**ˌ**ciety**
builder ˈbɪl.dəʳ (US) -dɚ **-s** -z
build-up ˈbɪld.ʌp **-s** -s
built *(from* **build***)* bɪlt
Builth bɪlθ
built-in ˌbɪltˈɪn (US) ˈbɪlt.ɪn *stress shift, British only:* ˌbuilt-in ˈmicrophone
Buist bjuːst, ˈbjuː.ɪst
Buitoni® bjuːˈtəʊ.ni, bwiː- (US) -ˈtoʊ-
Bujumbura ˌbuː.dʒəmˈbʊə.rə, -dʒʊmˈ- (US) -ˈbʊr.ə
Bukowski bjʊˈkɒf.ski, bjuː-, -ˈkaʊ- (US) bjuːˈkaʊ-
Bulawayo ˌbʊl.əˈweɪ.əʊ, ˌbuː.lə- (US) -oʊ
bulb bʌlb **-s** -z
bulbaceous bʌlˈbeɪ.ʃəs
bulbous ˈbʌl.bəs
bulbul ˈbʊl.bʊl **-s** -z
Bulford ˈbʊl.fəd (US) -fɚd
Bulgakov bʊlˈgɑː.kɒf (US) -kɔːf, -kɔːv
bulgar ˈbʌl.gəʳ, ˈbʊl- (US) -gɚ ˈ**bulgar** ˌ**wheat**
Bulgar ˈbʌl.gɑːʳ, ˈbʊl-, -gəʳ (US) -gɑːr, -gɚ **-s** -z
Bulgari|a bʌlˈgeə.ri|.ə (US) -ˈger.i- **-an/s** -ən/z
bulg|e bʌldʒ **-es** -ɪz **-ing** -ɪŋ **-ed** -d
Bulger ˈbʊl.dʒəʳ, ˈbʌl- (US) -dʒɚ
bulgur ˈbʊl.gəʳ (US) -gɚ
bulg|y ˈbʌl.dʒ|i **-iness** -ɪ.nəs, -ɪ.nɪs
bulim|ia bʊˈlɪm|.i.ə, buː-, bjuː-, -ˈliː.m|i- (US) bjuːˈliː.m|i-, buː- **-ic/s** -ɪk/s **bu**ˌ**limia ner**ˈ**vosa**
Bulins ˈbjuː.lɪnz
bulk bʌlk **-s** -s **-ing** -ɪŋ **-ed** -t
bulkhead ˈbʌlk.hed **-s** -z
Bulkington ˈbʌl.kɪŋ.tən
bulk|y ˈbʌl.k|i **-ier** -i.əʳ (US) -i.ɚ **-iest** -i.ɪst, -i.əst **-ily** -ɪ.li, -ᵊl.i **-iness** -ɪ.nəs, -ɪ.nɪs
bull (B) bʊl **-s** -z **-ing** -ɪŋ **-ed** -d ˌ**bull** ˈ**terrier;** ˈ**bull's** ˌ**eye; like a** ˌ**bull in a** ˈ**china shop; take the** ˌ**bull by the** ˈ**horns**
bullac|e ˈbʊl.ɪs **-es** -ɪz
Bullard ˈbʊl.ɑːd, -əd (US) -ɑːrd, -ɚd
bull-baiting ˈbʊlˌbeɪ.tɪŋ (US) -t̬ɪŋ
bull-cal|f ˈbʊlˌkɑː|f, ˌ-ˈ- (US) ˈbʊl.kæ|f **-ves** -vz
bulldog ˈbʊl.dɒg (US) -dɑːg, -dɔːg **-s** -z
bulldoz|e ˈbʊl.dəʊz (US) -doʊz **-es** -ɪz **-ing** -ɪŋ **-ed** -d
bulldozer ˈbʊlˌdəʊ.zəʳ (US) -ˌdoʊ.zɚ **-s** -z
Bulleid ˈbʊl.iːd
Bullen ˈbʊl.ən, -ɪn
Buller ˈbʌl.əʳ (US) -ɚ
bullet ˈbʊl.ɪt, -ət **-s** -s
bulletin ˈbʊl.ə.tɪn, ˈ-ɪ- (US) -ə.t̬ɪn **-s** -z ˈ**bulletin** ˌ**board**
bullet-proof ˈbʊl.ɪt.pruːf ˌ**bullet-proof** ˈ**vest**
bullfight ˈbʊl.faɪt **-s** -s
bullfight|er ˈbʊlˌfaɪ.t|əʳ (US) -t̬|ɚ **-ers** -əz (US) -ɚz **-ing** -ɪŋ
bullfinch ˈbʊl.fɪntʃ **-es** -ɪz
bullfrog ˈbʊl.frɒg (US) -frɑːg, -frɔːg **-s** -z
bullheaded ˌbʊlˈhed.ɪd (US) ˈ-ˌ-- **-ly** -li **-ness** -nəs, -nɪs *stress shift, British only:* ˌbullheaded ˈperson
bullhorn ˈbʊl.hɔːn (US) -hɔːrn **-s** -z
bullion ˈbʊl.i.ən, ˈ-jən (US) ˈ-jən
bullish ˈbʊl.ɪʃ **-ly** -li **-ness** -nəs, -nɪs
Bullman ˈbʊl.mən
bullock (B) ˈbʊl.ək **-s** -s
Bullokar ˈbʊl.ə.kɑːʳ, -kəʳ (US) -kɑːr
Bullough ˈbʊl.əʊ (US) -oʊ
bullpen ˈbʊl.pen **-s** -z
bullring ˈbʊl.rɪŋ **-s** -z
bullrush ˈbʊl.rʌʃ **-es** -ɪz
bull|shit ˈbʊl|.ʃɪt **-shits** -ʃɪts **-shitting** -ˌʃɪt.ɪŋ (US) -ˌʃɪt̬.ɪŋ **-shitted** -ˌʃɪt.ɪd (US) -ˌʃɪt̬.ɪd
bullshitter ˈbʊlˌʃɪt.əʳ (US) -ˌʃɪt̬.ɚ **-s** -z
bull|y ˈbʊl|.i **-ies** -iz **-ying** -i.ɪŋ **-ied** -id
Bulmer ˈbʊl.məʳ (US) -mɚ

bulrush ˈbʊl.rʌʃ **-es** -ɪz

Bulstrode ˈbʊl.strəʊd, ˈbʌl.strəʊd US -stroʊd

Bultitude ˈbʊl.tɪ.tjuːd, ˈ-tə- US -tuːd, -tjuːd

bulwark ˈbʊl.wək, ˈbʌl-, -wɜːk US -wɚk, -wɝːk **-s** -s

Bulwer ˈbʊl.wəʳ US -wɚ

Bulwer-Lytton ˌbʊl.wəˈlɪt.ᵊn US -wɚˈlɪt̬-

bum bʌm **-s** -z **-ming** -ɪŋ **-med** -d

bumbag ˈbʌm.bæg **-s** -z

bumbl|e ˈbʌm.bl̩ **-es** -z **-ing** -ɪŋ, ˈbʌm.blɪŋ **-ed** -d **-er/s** -əʳ/z, ˈ-bləʳ/z US ˈ-bl̩.ɚ/z, ˈ-blɚ/z

bumblebee ˈbʌm.bl̩.biː **-s** -z

bumboat ˈbʌm.bəʊt US -boʊt **-s** -s

bumf bʌm*p*f

Bumford ˈbʌm.fəd US -fɚd

bumkin ˈbʌm*p*.kɪn **-s** -z

bummaree ˌbʌm.əˈriː, ˈ--- US ˈbʌm.ə.riː **-s** -z

bummer ˈbʌm.əʳ US -ɚ **-s** -z

bump bʌmp **-s** -s **-ing** -ɪŋ **-ed** -t

bumper ˈbʌm.pəʳ US -pɚ **-s** -z ˈ**bumper** ˌ**car**; ˈ**bumper** ˌ**sticker**; ˌ**bumper to** ˈ**bumper**

bumph bʌm*p*f

bumpkin ˈbʌmp.kɪn **-s** -z

bumptious ˈbʌmp.ʃəs **-ly** -li **-ness** -nəs, -nɪs

Bumpus ˈbʌm.pəs

bump|y ˈbʌm.p|i **-ier** -i.əʳ US -i.ɚ **-iest** -i.ɪst, -i.əst **-ily** -ɪ.li, -ᵊl.i **-iness** -ɪ.nəs, -ɪ.nɪs

bun bʌn **-s** -z **have a** ˈ**bun in the** ˌ**oven**

Bunce bʌn*t*s

bunch (B) bʌn*t*ʃ **-es** -ɪz **-ing** -ɪŋ **-ed** -t

buncombe (B) ˈbʌŋ.kəm

Bundesbank ˈbʊn.dəz.bæŋk

Bundesrat ˈbʊn.dəz.rɑːt

Bundestag ˈbʊn.dəz.tɑːg *as if German:* -də.ztɑːk US -dəz.tɑːg

bundl|e ˈbʌn.dl̩ **-es** -z **-ing** -ɪŋ, ˈbʌnd.lɪŋ **-ed** -d

bung bʌŋ **-s** -z **-ing** -ɪŋ **-ed** -d

bungalow ˈbʌŋ.gᵊl.əʊ US -oʊ **-s** -z

Bungay ˈbʌŋ.gi

Bunge ˈbʌŋ.i

bungee ˈbʌn.dʒi ˈ**bungee** ˌ**jumping**

bungl|e ˈbʌŋ.gl̩ **-es** -z **-ing** -ɪŋ, ˈbʌŋ.glɪŋ **-ed** -d **-er/s** -əʳ/z, ˈ-gləʳ/z US ˈ-gl̩.ɚ/z, ˈ-glɚ/z

bunion ˈbʌn.jən **-s** -z

bunk bʌŋk **-s** -s **-ing** -ɪŋ **-ed** -t

bunk|er (B) ˈbʌŋ.k|əʳ US -k|ɚ **-ers** -əz US -ɚz **-ering** -ᵊr.ɪŋ **-ered** -əd US -ɚd

bunkhou|se ˈbʌŋk.haʊ|s **-ses** -zɪz

bunkum ˈbʌŋ.kəm

Bunnett ˈbʌn.ɪt

bunn|y ˈbʌn|.i **-ies** -iz

Bunsen ˈbʌn*t*.sᵊn US -sɪn ˌ**Bunsen** ˈ**burner** US ˈ**Bunsen** ˌ**burner**

bunt bʌnt **-s** -s

Bunter ˈbʌn.təʳ US -t̬ɚ

bunting (B) ˈbʌn.tɪŋ US -t̬ɪŋ **-s** -z

Bunty ˈbʌn.ti US -t̬i

Buñuel ˌbuː.njuˈel, ˈ---; ˌbuːnˈwel, ˌbʊn- US ˌbuːnˈwel, ˌbʊn-

Bunyan ˈbʌn.jən

buoy bɔɪ US bɔɪ, ˈbuː.i **-s** -z **-ing** -ɪŋ **-ed** -d

buoyancy ˈbɔɪ.ən*t*.si US ˈbɔɪ-, ˈbuː.jən*t*-

buoyant ˈbɔɪ.ənt US ˈbɔɪ-, ˈbuː.jənt **-ly** -li

BUPA ˈbuː.pə, ˈbjuː-

bur bɜːʳ US bɝː **-s** -z

Burbage ˈbɜː.bɪdʒ US ˈbɝː-

Burberr|y® ˈbɜː.bᵊr|.i US ˈbɝː.ber-, -bɚ- **-y's** -iz **-ies** -iz

burbl|e ˈbɜː.bl̩ US ˈbɝː- **-es** -z **-ing** -ɪŋ, ˈ-blɪŋ **-ed** -d

Burbridge ˈbɜː.brɪdʒ US ˈbɝː-

Burbury ˈbɜː.bᵊr.i US ˈbɝː.ber-, -bɚ-

Burch bɜːtʃ US bɝːtʃ

Burchell, Burchall ˈbɜː.tʃᵊl US ˈbɝː-

Burchill ˈbɜː.tʃᵊl, -tʃɪl US ˈbɝː-

Burco ˈbɜː.kəʊ US ˈbɝː.koʊ

burden (B) ˈbɜː.dᵊn US ˈbɝː- **-s** -z **-ing** -ɪŋ **-ed** -d

burdensome ˈbɜː.dᵊn.səm US ˈbɝː-

Burdett ˈbɜː.det, -ˈ- US bɝːˈdet, ˈ--

Burdett-Coutts ˌbɜː.detˈkuːts, -ˌ-ˈ- US bɝːˌdetˈ-

burdock ˈbɜː.dɒk US ˈbɝː.dɑːk **-s** -s

Burdon ˈbɜː.dᵊn US ˈbɝː-

Bure bjʊəʳ US bjʊr

bureau ˈbjʊə.rəʊ, ˈbjɔː-, bjʊəˈrəʊ US ˈbjʊr.oʊ **-s** -z

bureaucrac|y bjʊəˈrɒk.rə.s|i, bjəˈ-, bjɔːˈ- US bjʊˈrɑː.krə- **-ies** -iz

bureaucrat ˈbjʊə.rəʊ.kræt, ˈbjɔː- US ˈbjʊr.ə- **-s** -s

bureaucratic ˌbjʊə.rəʊˈkræt.ɪk, ˌbjɔː- US ˌbjʊr.əˈkræt̬- **-ally** -ᵊl.i, -li

bureaux *(alternative plur. of* **bureau***)* ˈbjʊə.rəʊ, ˈbjɔː-, -rəʊz; ˌbjʊəˈrəʊ, -ˈrəʊz US ˈbjʊr.oʊ, -oʊz

burette, buret bjʊəˈret US bjʊrˈet **-s** -s

Burford ˈbɜː.fəd US ˈbɝː.fɚd

burg bɜːg US bɝːg **-s** -z

Burgar ˈbɜː.gəʳ US ˈbɝː.gɚ

Burg|e bɜːdʒ US bɝːdʒ **-es** -ɪz

burgee ˈbɜː.dʒiː, -ˈ- US ˈbɝː.dʒi **-s** -z

burgeon ˈbɜː.dʒᵊn US ˈbɝː- **-s** -z **-ing** -ɪŋ **-ed** -d

burger ˈbɜː.gəʳ US ˈbɝː.gɚ **-s** -z

burgess (B) ˈbɜː.dʒəs, -dʒɪs, -dʒes US ˈbɝː- **-es** -ɪz

burgh ˈbʌr.ə US bɝːg, ˈbɜː.rə, ˈbɝː.oʊ **-s** -z

Burgh bɜːg US bɝːg *in Suffolk:* bɜːg; ˈbʌr.ə US bɝːg; ˈbɝː.oʊ *Baron, Heath in Surrey, place in Lincolnshire:* ˈbʌr.ə US ˈbɝː.oʊ *Burgh-by-Sands:* brʌf

Burghclere ˈbɜː.kleəʳ US ˈbɝː.kler

burgher ˈbɜː.gəʳ US ˈbɝː.gɚ **-s** -z

Burghersh ˈbɜː.gəʃ US ˈbɝː.gɚʃ

Burghley ˈbɜː.li US ˈbɝː-

burglar ˈbɜː.gləʳ US ˈbɝː.glɚ **-s** -z

burglariz|e ˈbɜː.glᵊr.aɪz US ˈbɝː.glə.raɪz **-es** -ɪz **-ing** -ɪŋ **-ed** -d

burglar|y ˈbɜː.glᵊr|.i US ˈbɝː- **-ies** -iz

burgl|e ˈbɜː.gl̩ US ˈbɝː- **-es** -z **-ing** -ɪŋ, ˈ-glɪŋ **-ed** -d

burgomaster ˈbɜː.gəʊˌmɑː.stəʳ US ˈbɝː.gəˌmæs.tɚ **-s** -z

Burgos ˈbʊə.gɒs US ˈbʊr.gɑːs

Burgoyne ˈbɜː.gɔɪn, -ˈ- US bɝːˈgɔɪn, ˈ--

burgund|y (B) ˈbɜː.gᵊn.d|i US ˈbɝː- **-ies** -iz

burial ˈber.i.əl **-s** -z ˈ**burial** ˌ**ground**; ˈ**burial** ˌ**place**

burin ˈbjʊə.rɪn US ˈbʊr.ɪn, ˈbɝː- **-s** -z

burk bɜːk US bɝːk **-s** -s

burk|e (B) bɜːk US bɝːk **-es** -s **-ing** -ɪŋ **-ed** -t

Burkina Faso bɜːˌkiː.nəˈfæs.əʊ US bʊrˌkiː.nəˈfɑː.soʊ

burlap ˈbɜː.læp US ˈbɝː-

Burleigh ˈbɜː.li US ˈbɝː-

burlesqu|e bɜːˈlesk US bɝː- **-es** -s **-ing** -ɪŋ **-ed** -t

Burley ˈbɜː.li US ˈbɝː-

Burling ˈbɜː.lɪŋ US ˈbɝː-

Burlington ˈbɜː.lɪŋ.tən US ˈbɝː-

burl|y (B) ˈbɜː.l|i US ˈbɝː- **-ier** -i.əʳ US -i.ɚ **-iest** -i.ɪst, -i.əst **-iness** -ɪ.nəs, -ɪ.nɪs

Burma ˈbɜː.mə US ˈbɝː-

Burmah ˈbɜː.mə US ˈbɝː-

Burman ˈbɜː.mən US ˈbɝː- **-s** -z

Burmese bɜːˈmiːz US bɝː-, -ˈmiːs

burn bɜːn US bɝːn **-s** -z **-ing** -ɪŋ **-ed** -d **burnt** bɜːnt US bɝːnt

Burnaby ˈbɜː.nə.bi US ˈbɝː-

Burnand bɜːˈnænd, bə- US bɚ-

Burne bɜːn US bɝːn

burner ˈbɜː.nəʳ US ˈbɝː.nɚ **-s** -z ˌ**put something on a/the** ˌ**back** ˈ**burner**

burnet (B) ˈbɜː.nɪt US ˈbɝː- **-s** -s

Burnett bɜːˈnet, bə-; ˈbɜː.nɪt US bɚˈnet; ˈbɝː.nɪt

Burney ˈbɜː.ni US ˈbɝː-

Burnham ˈbɜː.nəm US ˈbɝː-

Burnham-on-Crouch ˌbɜː.nəm.ɒnˈkraʊtʃ US ˌbɝː.nəm.ɑːnˈ-

Burnham-on-Sea ˌbɜː.nəm.ɒnˈsiː US ˌbɝː.nəm.ɑːnˈ-

burnish ˈbɜː.nɪʃ US ˈbɝː- **-es** -ɪz **-ing** -ɪŋ **-ed** -t **-er/s** -əʳ/z US -ɚ/z

Burnley ˈbɜːn.li (US) ˈbɝːn-
burnous, burnous|e bɜːˈnuːs (US) bɚ- **-es** -ɪz
burnout ˈbɜːn.aʊt (US) ˈbɝːn-
Burns bɜːnz (US) bɝːnz
Burnside ˈbɜːn.saɪd (US) ˈbɝːn-
burnt *(from* **burn***)* bɜːnt (US) bɝːnt ˌ**burnt** ˈ**offering**
Burntisland ˌbɜːntˈaɪ.lənd (US) ˌbɝːnt-
Burntwood ˈbɜːnt.wʊd (US) ˈbɝːnt-
burp bɜːp (US) bɝːp **-s** -s **-ing** -ɪŋ **-ed** -t
burqa ˈbɜː.kə (US) ˈbɝː- **-s** -z
burr (B) bɜːʳ (US) bɝː **-s** -z
Burrell ˈbʌr.ᵊl, ˈbɜːr-
Burridge ˈbʌr.ɪdʒ (US) ˈbɝː-
burrito bəˈriː.təʊ, bʊrˈiː- (US) bəˈriː.t̬oʊ **-s** -z
Burrough(e)s ˈbʌr.əʊz (US) ˈbɝː.oʊz
burrow ˈbʌr.əʊ (US) ˈbɝː.oʊ **-s** -z **-ing** -ɪŋ **-ed** -d
Burrows ˈbʌr.əʊz (US) ˈbɝː.oʊz
Burry Port ˌbʌr.iˈpɔːt (US) ˌbɝː.iˈpɔːrt
Bursa ˈbɜː.sə (US) bʊrˈsɑː, bɝː-
bursar ˈbɜː.səʳ (US) ˈbɝː.sɚ, -sɑːr **-s** -z
bursarship ˈbɜː.sə.ʃɪp (US) ˈbɝː.sɚ-, -sɑːr- **-s** -s
bursar|y ˈbɜː.sᵊr|.i (US) ˈbɝː- **-ies** -iz
Burscough Bridge ˌbɜː.skəʊˈbrɪdʒ (US) ˌbɝː.skoʊ-
Bursledon ˈbɜː.zᵊl.dᵊn (US) ˈbɝː-
Burslem ˈbɜːz.ləm (US) ˈbɝːz-
burst bɜːst (US) bɝːst **-s** -s **-ing** -ɪŋ
Burt bɜːt (US) bɝːt
burthen ˈbɜː.ðᵊn (US) ˈbɝː- **-s** -z
burton (B) ˈbɜː.tᵊn (US) ˈbɝː-
Burundi bʊˈrʊn.di, bə- **-an/s** -ən/z
Burwash ˈbɜː.wɒʃ *locally also:* ˈbʌr.əʃ (US) ˈbɝː.wɑːʃ, -wɔːʃ
bur|y *(v.)* ˈber|.i **-ies** -iz **-ying** -i.ɪŋ **-ied** -id
Bury *place:* ˈber.i *surname:* ˈbjʊə.ri, ˈber.i (US) ˈbʊr.i, ˈber-
bus bʌs **-(s)es** -ɪz **-(s)ing** -ɪŋ **-(s)ed** -t ˈ**bus** **con**ˌ**ductor**; ˈ**bus** ˌ**stop**
busbar ˈbʌs.bɑːʳ (US) -bɑːr **-s** -z
busboy ˈbʌs.bɔɪ **-s** -z
busb|y ˈbʌz.b|i **-ies** -iz
bush (B) bʊʃ **-es** -ɪz **-ing** -ɪŋ **-ed** -t ˈ**bush** ˌ**baby**; ˌ**beat about the** ˈ**bush**
bushel ˈbʊʃ.ᵊl **-s** -z
Bushell ˈbʊʃ.ᵊl (US) ˈbʊʃ.ᵊl, bʊˈʃel
Bushey ˈbʊʃ.i
Bushire bjuːˈʃaɪəʳ, buː-, -ˈʃɪəʳ (US) buːˈʃɪr
bush-league ˈbʊʃ.liːg **-s** -z
bush|man (B) ˈbʊʃ|.mən **-men** -mən, -men
Bushmills ˈbʊʃ.mɪlz
Bushnell ˈbʊʃ.nᵊl (US) -nᵊl, -nel
bushranger ˈbʊʃˌreɪn.dʒəʳ (US) -dʒɚ **-s** -z
bushwhack ˈbʊʃ.*h*wæk **-s** -s **-ing** -ɪŋ **-ed** -t
bushwhacker ˈbʊʃˌ*h*wæk.əʳ (US) -ɚ **-s** -z
bush|y (B) ˈbʊʃ|.i **-ier** -i.əʳ (US) -i.ɚ **-iest** -i.ɪst, -i.əst **-ily** -ɪ.li, -ᵊl.i **-iness** -ɪ.nəs, -ɪ.nɪs
business ˈbɪz.nɪs, -nəs **-es** -ɪz ˌ**mind one's** ˌ**own** ˈ**business**
businesslike ˈbɪz.nɪs.laɪk, -nəs-
business|man ˈbɪz.nɪs|.mæn, -nəs-, -mən **-men** -men, -mən
business|person ˈbɪz.nɪs|ˌpɜː.sᵊn, -nəsˌ- **-people** -ˌpiː.pl̩
business|woman ˈbɪz.nɪs|ˌwʊm.ən, -nəsˌ- **-women** -ˌwɪm.ɪn
busk (B) bʌsk **-s** -s **-ing** -ɪŋ **-ed** -t **-er/s** -əʳ/z (US) -ɚ/z
buskin ˈbʌs.kɪn **-s** -z **-ed** -d
bus|man ˈbʌs|.mən, -mæn **-men** -mən, -men ˌ**busman's** ˈ**holiday**
Busoni buːˈzəʊ.ni, bjuː-, -ˈsəʊ- (US) bʊˈzoʊ.ni, bjuː-
buss (B) bʌs **-es** -ɪz **-ing** -ɪŋ **-ed** -t
bust bʌst **-s** -s **-ing** -ɪŋ **-ed** -ɪd
bustard ˈbʌs.təd (US) -tɚd **-s** -z
buster (B) ˈbʌs.təʳ (US) -tɚ **-s** -z
bustier ˈbʌs.ti.əʳ, ˈbʊs-, ˈbuː.sti- (US) ˈbuː.sti.eɪ, ˈbʊs.tjeɪ **-s** -z
bustl|e ˈbʌs.l̩ **-es** -z **-ing** -ɪŋ, ˈbʌs.lɪŋ **-ed** -d
bust|y ˈbʌs.t|i **-ier** -i.əʳ (US) -i.ɚ **-iest** -i.ɪst, -i.əst **-iness** -ɪ.nəs, -ɪ.nɪs
bus|y ˈbɪz|.i **-ies** -iz **-ying** -i.ɪŋ **-ied** -ɪd **-ier** -i.əʳ (US) -i.ɚ **-iest** -i.ɪst, -i.əst **-ily** -ɪ.li, -ᵊl.i ˈ**busy** ˌ**signal**
busybod|y ˈbɪz.iˌbɒd|.i (US) -ˌbɑː.d|i **-ies** -iz
busyness ˈbɪz.i.nəs, -nɪs
but *strong form:* bʌt *weak form:* bət
Note: Weak form word. The strong form /bʌt/ is used contrastively (e.g. **ifs** and **buts**) and in sentence-final position (e.g. "It's anything but"). The weak form is /bət/ (e.g. "It's good but expensive" /ɪtsˌgʊd.bət.ɪkˈspen*t*.sɪv/)
butane ˈbjuː.teɪn (US) ˈbjuː.teɪn, -ˈ-
butch (B) bʊtʃ
butch|er (B) ˈbʊtʃ|.əʳ (US) -ɚ **-ers** -əz (US) -ɚz **-ering** -ᵊr.ɪŋ **-ered** -əd (US) -ɚd
butcher|y ˈbʊtʃ.ᵊr|.i **-ies** -iz
Bute bjuːt **-shire** -ʃəʳ, -ˌʃɪəʳ (US) -ʃɚ, -ˌʃɪr
Buthelezi ˌbuː.təˈleɪ.zi
butler (B) ˈbʌt.ləʳ (US) -lɚ **-s** -z
butler|age ˈbʌt.lᵊr|.ɪdʒ **-y** -i **-ies** -iz
Butlin ˈbʌt.lɪn **-s** -z
butt (B) bʌt **-s** -s **-ing** -ɪŋ (US) ˈbʌt̬.ɪŋ **-ed** -ɪd (US) ˈbʌt̬.ɪd
butt-end ˈbʌt.end **-s** -z
butt|er ˈbʌt|.əʳ (US) ˈbʌt̬|.ɚ **-ers** -əz (US) -ɚz **-ering** -ᵊr.ɪŋ **-ered** -əd (US) -ɚd ˈ**butter** ˌ**bean**; ˈ**butter** ˌ**dish**; ˈ**butter** ˌ**knife**; ˌ**butter wouldn't** ˌ**melt in his/her** ˈ**mouth**
butterball ˈbʌt.ə.bɔːl (US) ˈbʌt̬.ɚ.bɔːl, -bɑːl **-s** -z
buttercup ˈbʌt.ə.kʌp (US) ˈbʌt̬.ɚ- **-s** -s
butterfat ˈbʌt.ə.fæt (US) ˈbʌt̬.ɚ-
Butterfield ˈbʌt.ə.fiːld (US) ˈbʌt̬.ɚ-
butterfinger|s ˈbʌt.əˌfɪŋ.gə|z (US) ˈbʌt̬.ɚˌfɪŋ.gɚ|z **-ed** -d
butterfl|y ˈbʌt.ə.fl|aɪ (US) ˈbʌt̬.ɚ- **-ies** -aɪz
Butterick ˈbʌt.ᵊr.ɪk (US) ˈbʌt̬-
Butterleigh, Butterley ˈbʌt.ᵊl.i (US) ˈbʌt̬.ɚ.li
Buttermere ˈbʌt.ə.mɪəʳ (US) ˈbʌt̬.ɚ.mɪr
buttermilk ˈbʌt.ə.mɪlk (US) ˈbʌt̬.ɚ-
butternut ˈbʌt.ə.nʌt (US) ˈbʌt̬.ɚ- **-s** -s
butterscotch ˈbʌt.ə.skɒtʃ (US) ˈbʌt̬.ɚ.skɑːtʃ
Butterwick ˈbʌt.ᵊr.ɪk, -ə.wɪk (US) ˈbʌt̬.ɚ.ɪk, -wɪk
Butterworth ˈbʌt.ə.wəθ, -wɜːθ (US) ˈbʌt̬.ɚ.wɚθ, -wɝːθ
butter|y ˈbʌt.ᵊr|.i (US) ˈbʌt̬- **-ies** -iz
buttock ˈbʌt.ək (US) ˈbʌt̬- **-s** -s
button (B) ˈbʌt.ᵊn **-s** -z **-ing** -ɪŋ **-ed** -d
button-down ˌbʌt.ᵊnˈdaʊn *stress shift:* ˌbutton-down ˈcollar
buttonhol|e ˈbʌt.ᵊn.həʊl (US) -hoʊl **-es** -z **-ing** -ɪŋ **-ed** -d
buttonhook ˈbʌt.ᵊn.hʊk **-s** -s
buttress (B) ˈbʌt.rəs, -rɪs **-es** -ɪz **-ing** -ɪŋ **-ed** -d
butt|y ˈbʌt|.i (US) ˈbʌt̬- **-ies** -iz
butut buːˈtuːt
butyric bjʊˈtɪr.ɪk (US) bjuː-
buxom ˈbʌk.səm **-ness** -nəs, -nɪs
Buxtehude ˌbʊk.stəˈhuː.də
Buxton ˈbʌk.stən
buy baɪ **-s** -z **-ing** -ɪŋ **bought** bɔːt (US) bɑːt, bɔːt
buyable ˈbaɪ.ə.bl̩
buyback ˈbaɪ.bæk **-s** -s
buyer ˈbaɪ.əʳ (US) -ɚ **-s** -z
buyout ˈbaɪ.aʊt **-s** -s
Buzfuz ˈbʌz.fʌz
buzz bʌz **-es** -ɪz, -əz **-ing** -ɪŋ **-ed** -d
buzzard ˈbʌz.əd (US) -ɚd **-s** -z
buzzer ˈbʌz.əʳ (US) -ɚ **-s** -z
buzzword ˈbʌz.wɜːd (US) -wɝːd **-s** -z
bwana ˈbwɑː.nə
by *normal form:* baɪ *occasional weak forms:* bɪ, bə
Note: Weak form word. The strong form is /baɪ/. The weak forms /bɪ, bə/ are rarely used, but can be found occasionally, particularly in measurements (e.g. "two by three" /ˌtuː.bəˈθriː/).
by-and-by ˌbaɪ.ᵊndˈbaɪ, -ᵊm- (US) -ᵊndˈ-
Byard baɪəd (US) baɪɚd
Byars baɪəz (US) baɪɚz
Byas(s) baɪəs
Byatt baɪət

Bydgoszcz ˈbɪd.gɒʃt *as if Polish:* -gɒtʃtʃ ⓤⓢ -gɔːʃtʃ
bye (B) baɪ **-s** -z
bye-bye *goodbye:* ˌbaɪˈbaɪ, bə-, bʌbˈaɪ; ˈbaɪ.baɪ, ˈbʌb.aɪ
bye-bye *sleep:* ˈbaɪ.baɪ **-s** -z
byelaw ˈbaɪ.lɔː ⓤⓢ -lɑː, -lɔː **-s** -z
by-election ˈbaɪ.ɪˌlek.ʃᵊn, -əˌ- **-s** -z
Byelorussi|a ˌbjel.əʊˈrʌʃ|.ə, ˌbel-, -ˈruː.si- ⓤⓢ -oʊˈ-, -əˈ- **-an/s** -ᵊn/z
Byers baɪəz ⓤⓢ baɪɚz
Byfleet ˈbaɪ.fliːt
Byford ˈbaɪ.fəd ⓤⓢ -fɚd
bygone ˈbaɪ.gɒn ⓤⓢ -gɑːn **-s** -z
Bygraves ˈbaɪ.greɪvz
bylaw ˈbaɪ.lɔː ⓤⓢ -lɑː, -lɔː **-s** -z
Byles baɪlz
byline ˈbaɪ.laɪn **-s** -z
Byng bɪŋ
Bynoe ˈbaɪ.nəʊ ⓤⓢ -noʊ
BYO ˌbiː.waɪˈəʊ ⓤⓢ -ˈoʊ
bypass ˈbaɪ.pɑːs ⓤⓢ -pæs **-es** -ɪz **-ing** -ɪŋ **-ed** -d
bypa|th ˈbaɪ.pɑː|θ ⓤⓢ -pæ|θ **-ths** -ðz
byplay ˈbaɪ.pleɪ
by-product ˈbaɪˌprɒd.ʌkt, -əkt ⓤⓢ -ˌprɑː.dəkt **-s** -s
Byrd bɜːd ⓤⓢ bɝːd
byre baɪəʳ ⓤⓢ baɪɚ **-s** -z
Byrne bɜːn ⓤⓢ bɝːn
byroad ˈbaɪ.rəʊd ⓤⓢ -roʊd **-s** -z
Byrom ˈbaɪ.rəm
Byron ˈbaɪ.rən
Byronic baɪˈrɒn.ɪk ⓤⓢ -ˈrɑː.nɪk **-ally** -ᵊl.i, -li
Bysshe bɪʃ
bystander ˈbaɪˌstæn.dəʳ ⓤⓢ -dɚ **-s** -z
bystreet ˈbaɪ.striːt **-s** -s
byte baɪt **-s** -s
Bythesea ˈbaɪθ.siː
byway ˈbaɪ.weɪ **-s** -z
byword ˈbaɪ.wɜːd ⓤⓢ -wɝːd **-s** -z
Byzantian baɪˈzæn.ti.ən, bɪ-, bə-, ˈ-*t*ʃᵊn ⓤⓢ bɪˈzæn.ti.ən, bə-, baɪ-, -ˈzæn*t*.ʃᵊn
Byzantine bɪˈzæn.taɪn, baɪ-, bə-, -tiːn; ˈbɪz.ᵊn- ⓤⓢ ˈbɪz.ᵊn.tiːn, -taɪn
Byzantium bɪˈzæn.ti.əm, baɪ-, bə-, ˈ-*t*ʃᵊm ⓤⓢ bɪˈzæn.ti.əm, bə-, baɪ-, -ˈzæn*t*.ʃᵊm

Pronouncing the letter C

See also CC, CCH, CH, CK, CQU

The consonant letter **c** has four pronunciations: /s, k, ʃ/ and /tʃ/.

Before the vowel letters **i**, **e** or **y** (when functioning as a vowel letter), it is pronounced as /s/, e.g.:

specific	/spəˈsɪf.ɪk/	
cell	/sel/	
cycle	/ˈsaɪ.kl̩/	

In suffixes *-cial*, *-cious*, *-ciate*, *-cient* and their derivatives, **c** is realised as /ʃ/, e.g.:

social	/ˈsəʊ.ʃᵊl/	(US) /ˈsoʊ-/
vicious	/ˈvɪʃ.əs/	

In most other situations, **c** is pronounced as /k/, e.g.:

cat	/kæt/	
critic	/ˈkrɪt.ɪk/	(US) /ˈkrɪţ-/

In addition

C can be silent. There are two occasions when this can occur: the combination **ct** in some words, and in British place names such as *Leicester*, e.g.:

Leicester	/ˈles.təʳ/	(US) /-tɚ/
indict	/ɪnˈdaɪt/	

An exceptional pronunciation for **c** is /tʃ/ in some words borrowed from Italian, e.g.:

cello	/ˈtʃel.əʊ/	(US) /-oʊ/
Cinquecento	/ˌtʃɪŋ.kweɪˈtʃen.təʊ/	(US) /-toʊ/

A final exception:

Caesar	/ˈsiː.zəʳ/	(US) /-zɚ/

c **(C)** siː **-'s** -z
ca *(abbrev. for* **circa***)* ˈsɜː.kə (US) ˈsɝː-
CAA ˌsiː.eɪˈeɪ
cab kæb **-s** -z
CAB ˌsiː.eɪˈbiː
cabal kəˈbæl, kæbˈæl (US) kəˈbɑːl, -ˈbæl **-s** -z
cabala (C) kəˈbɑː.lə, kæbˈɑː-
cabalism ˈkæb.ə.lɪ.zᵊm
cabalistic ˌkæb.əˈlɪs.tɪk **-al** -ᵊl **-ally** -ᵊl.i, -li
caballero ˌkæb.əˈleə.rəʊ, -ˈljeə- (US) -ˈler.oʊ, -əlˈjer- **-s** -z
cabana kəˈbɑː.nə (US) -ˈbæn.ə, -ˈbɑː.nə, -njə **-s** -z
cabaret ˈkæb.ə.reɪ, ˌ--ˈ- (US) ˌkæb.əˈreɪ, ˈ--- **-s** -z
cabbag|e ˈkæb.ɪdʒ **-es** -ɪz ˈ**cabbage** ˌ**rose**
cabbala (C) kəˈbɑː.lə, kæbˈɑː- **-s** -z
cabbal|ism ˈkæb.ə.l|ɪ.zᵊm **-ist/s** -ɪst/s
cabbalistic ˌkæb.əˈlɪs.tɪk **-al** -ᵊl **-ally** -ᵊl.i, -li
cabb|ie, cabb|y ˈkæb|.i **-ies** -iz
cabdriver ˈkæbˌdraɪ.vəʳ (US) -vɚ **-s** -z
Cabell ˈkæb.ᵊl
caber ˈkeɪ.bəʳ (US) -bɚ **-s** -z
Cabernet Sauvignon ˌkæb.ə.neɪ.səʊ.viːˈnjɔ̃ːŋ, -jɒn (US) -ɚ.neɪˌsoʊ.viːˈnjoʊn
cabin ˈkæb.ɪn **-s** -z ˈ**cabin** ˌ**boy**; ˈ**cabin** ˌ**cruiser**; ˈ**cabin** ˌ**fever**
cabinet (C) ˈkæb.ɪ.nət, -ə-, -nɪt **-s** -s ˈ**Cabinet** ˌ**Minister**, ˌ**Cabinet** ˈ**Minister**
cabinetmak|er ˈkæb.ɪ.nətˌmeɪ.k|əʳ, -nɪt- (US) -k|ɚ **-ers** -əz (US) -ɚz **-ing** -ɪŋ
cabl|e (C) ˈkeɪ.bl̩ **-es** -z **-ing** -ɪŋ, ˈ-blɪŋ **-ed** -d ˈ**cable** ˌ**car**; ˌ**cable** ˈ**television**, ˌ**cable tele**ˈ**vision**
cablecast ˈkeɪ.bl̩.kɑːst (US) -kæst **-s** -s **-ing** -ɪŋ **-er/s** -əʳ/z (US) -ɚ/z
cablegram ˈkeɪ.bl̩.græm **-s** -z
cab|man ˈkæb|.mən **-men** -mən, -men
caboodle kəˈbuː.dl̩
caboos|e kəˈbuːs **-es** -ɪz
Caborn ˈkeɪ.bɔːn (US) -bɔːrn
Cabot ˈkæb.ət
cabotage ˈkæb.ə.tɑːʒ, -tɪdʒ
Cabrini kəˈbriː.ni
cabriole ˈkæb.ri.əʊl (US) -oʊl **-s** -z
cabriolet ˈkæb.ri.əʊ.leɪ, ˌkæb.ri.əʊˈleɪ (US) ˌkæb.ri.əˈleɪ **-s** -z
cabstand ˈkæb.stænd **-s** -z
ca-ca ˈkɑː.kɑː
cacao kæˈkaʊ, kækˈaʊ; kəˈkɑː.əʊ, kækˈɑː-, -ˈeɪ- (US) -oʊ **-s** -z
cachalot ˈkæʃ.ə.lɒt (US) -lɑːt, -loʊ **-s** -s, -z
cach|e kæʃ **-es** -ɪz
cachepot ˈkæʃ.pəʊ, ˌkæʃˈpɒt (US) ˈkæʃ.pɑːt, -poʊ **-s** -s, -z
cachet ˈkæʃ.eɪ (US) -ˈ- **-s** -z
cachinnat|e ˈkæk.ɪ.neɪt, ˈ-ə- **-es** -s **-ing** -ɪŋ **-ed** -ɪd
cachinnation ˌkæk.ɪˈneɪ.ʃᵊn
cachou kæʃˈuː, kəˈʃuː; ˈkæʃ.uː **-s** -z
cachucha kəˈtʃuː.tʃə **-s** -z
cacique kæsˈiːk, kəˈsiːk **-s** -s
cack-handed ˌkækˈhæn.dɪd, ˈ--- **-ly** -li **-ness** -nəs, -nɪs
cackl|e ˈkæk.l̩ **-es** -z **-ing** -ɪŋ, ˈ-lɪŋ **-ed** -d **-er/s** -əʳ/z, ˈ-ləʳ/z (US) ˈ-l̩.ɚ/z, ˈ-lɚ/z
cacodyl ˈkæk.əʊ.daɪl, -dɪl (US) ˈkæk.oʊ.dɪl, ˈ-ə-
cacoepy kækˈəʊ.ɪ.pi, -ep.i (US) -ˈoʊ.ə-
cacographic ˌkæk.əʊˈgræf.ɪk (US) -oʊˈ-, -əˈ- **-al** -ᵊl
cacography kækˈɒg.rə.fi, kəˈkɒg- (US) kəˈkɑː.grə-
cacology kækˈɒl.ə.dʒi, kəˈkɒl- (US) kəˈkɑː.lə-
cacophonic ˌkæk.əʊˈfɒn.ɪk (US) -oʊˈfɑː.nɪk, -əˈ- **-al** -ᵊl **-ally** -ᵊl.i, -li
cacophonous kəˈkɒf.ə.nəs, kækˈɒf- (US) kəˈkɑː.fə-
cacophon|y kəˈkɒf.ə.n|i, kækˈɒf- (US) kəˈkɑː.fə- **-ies** -iz
cactus ˈkæk.təs **-es** -ɪz **cacti** ˈkæk.taɪ
cacuminal kækˈjuː.mɪ.nᵊl, kəˈkjuː- (US) kəˈkjuː.mə- **-s** -z
cad kæd **-s** -z
CAD kæd
cadaster kəˈdæs.təʳ (US) -tɚ
cadastral kəˈdæs.trəl
cadastre kəˈdæs.təʳ (US) -tɚ
cadaver kəˈdɑː.vəʳ, -ˈdeɪ-, -ˈdæv.əʳ (US) -ˈdæv.ɚ **-s** -z
cadaveric kəˈdæv.ə.rɪk (US) -ɚ.ɪk
cadaverous kəˈdæv.ᵊr.əs **-ness** -nəs, -nɪs
Cadbury ˈkæd.bᵊr.i (US) ˈkæd.ber.i, -bɚ-
Cadby ˈkæd.bi, ˈkæb-
CAD/CAM ˈkæd.kæm
Caddell kəˈdel
Caddick ˈkæd.ɪk
caddie ˈkæd.i **-s** -z
caddis ˈkæd.ɪs ˈ**caddis** ˌ**fly**
caddish ˈkæd.ɪʃ **-ly** -li **-ness** -nəs, -nɪs
cadd|y ˈkæd|.i **-ies** -iz **-ying** -i.ɪŋ **-ied** -ɪd
cade (C) keɪd **-s** -z
Cadell ˈkæd.ᵊl, kəˈdel

cadenc|e ˈkeɪ.dᵊnts **-es** -ɪz
cadency ˈkeɪ.dᵊnt.si
Cadenus kəˈdiː.nəs
cadenza kəˈden.zə **-s** -z
Cader Idris ˌkæd.əʳˈɪd.rɪs (US) -ɚˈ-
cadet kəˈdet **-s** -s **caˈdet ˌcorps**
cadetship kəˈdet.ʃɪp **-s** -s
cadg|e kædʒ **-es** -ɪz **-ing** -ɪŋ **-ed** -d **-er/s** -əʳ/z (US) -ɚ/z
cadi ˈkɑː.di, ˈkeɪ- **-s** -z
Cadillac® ˈkæd.ɪ.læk, -ᵊl.æk (US) -ə.læk, -ᵊl.æk **-s** -s
Cadiz *in Spain:* kəˈdɪz *as if Spanish:* ˈkæd.ɪθ (US) kəˈdɪz; ˈkeɪ.dɪz *in Phillipines:* ˈkɑː.diːs (US) kəˈdɪz; ˈkeɪ.dɪz *in the US:* kædˈɪz; ˈkeɪ.dɪz (US) kəˈdɪz; ˈkeɪ.dɪz
Cadman ˈkæd.mən
Cadmean ˈkæd.mi.ən, kædˈmiː- (US) kædˈmiː-
cadmic ˈkæd.mɪk
cadmium ˈkæd.mi.əm, ˈkæb- (US) ˈkæd-
Cadmus ˈkæd.məs
Cadogan kəˈdʌg.ən
cadre ˈkɑː.dəʳ, ˈkeɪ-, -drə (US) ˈkæd.riː, ˈkɑː.dri, -dreɪ **-s** -z
caduce|us kəˈdjuː.si|.əs, -ˈdʒuː- (US) -ˈduː-, -ˈdjuː-, -ʃ|əs **-i** -aɪ
Cadwallader kædˈwɒl.ə.dəʳ (US) -ˈwɑː.lə.dɚ
CAE ˌsiː.eɪˈiː
caec|um ˈsiː.k|əm **-a** -ə
Caedmon ˈkæd.mən
Caen kɑ̃ː (US) kɑːn
Caerleon kɑːˈliː.ən, kə-, -ˈlɪən (US) kɑːr-
Caernarvon, Caernarfon kəˈnɑː.vᵊn (US) kɑːrˈnɑːr- **-shire** -ʃəʳ, -ˌʃɪəʳ (US) -ʃɚ, -ˌʃɪr
Caerphilly keəˈfɪl.i, kɑː-, kəˈfɪl- (US) kɑːr-
Caesar ˈsiː.zəʳ (US) -zɚ **-s** -z
Caesarea ˌsiː.zəˈriː.ə
caesarean, caesarian *way of having a baby:* sɪˈzeə.ri.ən, sə- (US) sɪˈzer.i- **caeˌsarean ˈsection**
Caesarean *of Caesarea:* ˌsiː.zəˈriː.ən *of Caesar:* siːˈzeə.ri.ən, sɪ- (US) sɪˈzer.i-
caesium ˈsiː.zi.əm
caesura sɪˈzjʊə.rə, siː-, -ˈzjɔː-, -ˈʒʊə- (US) səˈzʊr.ə, -ˈʒʊr- **-s** -z
café, cafe ˈkæf.eɪ (US) kæfˈeɪ, kəˈfeɪ **-s** -z
cafeteria ˌkæf.əˈtɪə.ri.ə, -ɪˈ- (US) -ˈtɪr.i- **-s** -z
cafetière, cafetiere ˌkæf.əˈtjeəʳ (US) -ˈtjer **-s** -z
caff kæf **-s** -s
caffein ˈkæf.iːn, -eɪn (US) kæfˈiːn
caffeinated ˈkæf.ɪ.neɪ.tɪd, ˈ-ə- (US) -ə.neɪ.t̬ɪd
caffeine ˈkæf.iːn, -eɪn (US) kæfˈiːn
caftan ˈkæf.tæn (US) -tæn, -tən **-s** -z
cag|e (C) keɪdʒ **-es** -ɪz **-ing** -ɪŋ **-ed** -d
cageling ˈkeɪdʒ.lɪŋ **-s** -z
cager ˈkeɪ.dʒəʳ (US) -dʒɚ **-s** -z
cag|ey ˈkeɪ.dʒ|i **-ier** -i.əʳ (US) -i.ɚ **-iest** -i.ɪst, -i.əst **-ily** -ɪ.li, -ᵊl.i **-iness** -ɪ.nəs, -ɪ.nɪs
Cagliari ˌkæl.jiˈɑː.ri, ˈkæl.jə.ri (US) ˈkɑːl.jɑːr.i, -jɚ-
Cagliostro kæl.jiˈɒs.trəʊ (US) kɑːlˈjɔː.stroʊ
Cagney ˈkæg.ni
cagoule kəˈguːl, kægˈuːl **-s** -z
cag|y ˈkeɪ.dʒ|i **-ier** -i.əʳ (US) -i.ɚ **-iest** -i.ɪst, -i.əst **-ily** -ɪ.li, -ᵊl.i **-iness** -ɪ.nəs, -ɪ.nɪs
Cahal kəˈhæl, ˈkæ.hᵊl
Cahan kɑːn
Cahill ˈkɑː.hɪl, ˈkeɪ.hɪl
Cahoon kəˈhuːn, kæ-
cahoots kəˈhuːts
CAI ˌsiː.eɪˈaɪ
Caiaphas ˈkaɪ.ə.fæs, -fəs
Caicos ˈkeɪ.kɒs, -kəs (US) -kəs
Caillard ˈkaɪ.ɑːʳ (US) -ɑːr
caiman ˈkeɪ.mən, ˈkaɪ-, -mæn (US) ˈkeɪ- **-s** -z
Cain(e) keɪn
caique, caïque kaɪˈiːk, kɑː- (US) kɑːˈiːk **-s** -s
Caird keəd (US) kerd
Cairene ˈkaɪə.riːn (US) ˈkaɪ-, -ˈ-
cairn keən (US) kern **-s** -z
cairngorm (C) ˌkeənˈgɔːm, ˌkeəŋ-, ˈ-- (US) ˈkern.gɔːrm **-s** -z
Cairns keənz (US) kernz
Cairo *in Egypt:* ˈkaɪə.rəʊ (US) ˈkaɪ.roʊ *in the US:* ˈkeə.rəʊ (US) ˈker.oʊ
caisson ˈkeɪ.sɒn, -sᵊn *sometimes in engineering:* kəˈsuːn (US) ˈkeɪ.sᵊn, -sɑːn **-s** -z
Caister ˈkeɪ.stəʳ (US) -stɚ
Caister-on-Sea ˌkeɪ.stəʳ.ɒnˈsiː (US) -stɚ.ɑːnˈ-
Caistor ˈkeɪ.stəʳ (US) -stɚ
Caithness ˈkeɪθ.nes, -nəs;
caitiff ˈkeɪ.tɪf (US) -t̬ɪf **-s** -s
Caitlin, Caitlín ˈkeɪt.lɪn, ˈkæt.lɪn
Caius *Roman name, character in Shakespeare's Merry Wives:* ˈkaɪ.əs, ˈkeɪ.əs *as if Latin:* ˈgaɪ- *Cambridge college:* kiːz
cajol|e kəˈdʒəʊl (US) -ˈdʒoʊl **-es** -z **-ing** -ɪŋ **-ed** -d **-er/s** -əʳ/z (US) -ɚ/z
cajoler|y kəˈdʒəʊ.lᵊr|.i (US) -ˈdʒoʊ- **-ies** -iz
Cajun ˈkeɪ.dʒən **-s** -z
cak|e keɪk **-es** -s **-ing** -ɪŋ **-ed** -t **(sell/go) like ˌhot ˈcakes** (US) **(sell/go) like ˈhot ˌcakes; ˌhave one's ˌcake and ˈeat it** (US) **ˌhave one's ˌcake and ˌeat it ˈtoo**
cakewalk ˈkeɪk.wɔːk (US) -wɑːk, -wɔːk **-s** -s
Cakovec tʃɑːˈkəʊ.vets (US) -ˈkoʊ-
CAL kæl, ˌsiː.eɪˈel
Calabar ˌkæl.əˈbɑːʳ, ˈ--- (US) ˈkæl.ə.bɑːr, ˌ--ˈ-
calabash ˈkæl.ə.bæʃ **-es** -ɪz, -əz
calaboos|e ˈkæl.ə.buːs, --ˈ- **-es** -ɪz
calabrese ˈkæl.ə.briːs, -briːz
Calabri|a kəˈlæb.ri|.ə, kælˈæb-, -ˈɑː.bri- (US) kəˈleɪ.bri-, -ˈlɑː- **-an/s** -ən/z
Calais ˈkæl.eɪ (US) kælˈeɪ
calamari ˌkæl.əˈmɑː.ri (US) -ˈmɑːr.i
calamine ˈkæl.ə.maɪn
calamitous kəˈlæm.ɪ.təs, -ə.təs (US) -ə.t̬əs **-ly** -li **-ness** -nəs, -nɪs
calamit|y kəˈlæm.ə.t|i, -ɪ.t|i (US) -ə.t̬|i **-ies** -iz **Caˌlamity ˈJane**
calamus ˈkæl.ə.məs
calash kəˈlæʃ **-es** -ɪz
calcareous kælˈkeə.ri.əs (US) -ˈker.i-, -ˈkær- **-ness** -nəs, -nɪs
calceolaria ˌkæl.si.əˈleə.ri.ə (US) -ˈler.i-, -ˈlær- **-s** -z
calces ˈkæl.siːz
Calchas ˈkæl.kæs
calciferol kælˈsɪf.ə.rɒl (US) -roʊl, -rɑːl
calciferous kælˈsɪf.ᵊr.əs
calcification ˌkæl.sɪ.fɪˈkeɪ.ʃᵊn, -sə-
calcifug|e ˈkæl.sɪ.fjuːdʒ **-es** -ɪz
calcifugous kælˈsɪf.jə.gəs
calcif|y ˈkæl.sɪ.f|aɪ, -sə- **-ies** -aɪz **-ying** -aɪ.ɪŋ **-ied** -aɪd
calcination ˌkæl.sɪˈneɪ.ʃᵊn, -səˈ-
calcin|e ˈkæl.saɪn, -sɪn **-es** -z **-ing** -ɪŋ **-ed** -d
calcite ˈkæl.saɪt **-s** -s
calcium ˈkæl.si.əm
Calcot(t) ˈkɔːl.kət, ˈkɒl-, ˈkæl- (US) ˈkɔːl.kɑːt, ˈkɑːl-, ˈkæl-
Note: In Calcot Row, Berkshire, the pronunciation is /ˈkæl.kət/.
calculab|le ˈkæl.kjə.lə.b|l̩, -kjʊ- (US) -kjə- **-ly** -li
calcu|late ˈkæl.kjə|.leɪt, -kjʊ- (US) -kjə- **-lates** -leɪts **-lating** -leɪ.tɪŋ (US) -leɪ.t̬ɪŋ **-lated** -leɪ.tɪd (US) -leɪ.t̬ɪd
calculation ˌkæl.kjəˈleɪ.ʃᵊn, -kjʊˈ- (US) -kjəˈ- **-s** -z
calculative ˈkæl.kjə.lə.tɪv, -kjʊ- (US) -kjə.lə.t̬ɪv
calculator ˈkæl.kjə.leɪ.təʳ, -kjʊ- (US) -kjə.leɪ.t̬ɚ **-s** -z
calcul|us ˈkæl.kjə.l|əs, -kjʊ- (US) -kjə- **-uses** -ə.sɪz **-i** -aɪ
Calcutt ˈkæl.kʌt
Calcutta kælˈkʌt.ə (US) -ˈkʌt̬-
Caldecote ˈkɔːl.dɪ.kət, ˈkɒl-, -də- (US) ˈkɑːl.də.koʊt, ˈkɔːl-, -kət
Caldecott ˈkɔːl.də.kət, ˈkɒl-, -dɪ-, -kɒt (US) ˈkɑːl.də.kɑːt, ˈkɔːl-, -kət
Calder ˈkɔːl.dəʳ, ˈkɒl- (US) ˈkɔːl.dɚ, ˈkɑːl-
caldera kælˈdeə.rə, ˈkɔːl.də.rə (US) kælˈder.ə

Calderon *English name:* ˈkɔːl.də.rən, ˈkɒl-, ˈkæl- (US) ˈkɔːl.də.rɑːn, ˈkɑːl- *Spanish name:* ˌkæl.dəˈrɒn (US) ˌkɑːl.ðəˈrɔːn
Caldicot(t) ˈkɔːl.dɪ.kɒt, ˈkɒl-, -də-, -kət (US) ˈkɑːl.də.kɑːt, ˈkɔːl-, -kət
caldron ˈkɔːl.drən, ˈkɒl- (US) ˈkɑːl-, ˈkɔːl- **-s** -z
Caldwell ˈkɔːld.wəl, ˈkɒld-, -wel (US) ˈkɔːld-, ˈkɑːld-
Caleb ˈkeɪ.leb, -lɪb, -ləb
Caledon ˈkæl.ɪ.dᵊn, ˈ-ə-
Caledoni|a ˌkæl.ɪˈdəʊ.ni|.ə, -əˈ- (US) -ˈdoʊ- **-an/s** -ən/z
calefaction ˌkæl.ɪˈfæk.ʃᵊn, -əˈ-
calefactor|y ˌkæl.ɪˈfæk.tᵊr|.i, -əˈ-, -tr|i **-ies** -iz
calendar ˈkæl.ən.dəʳ, -ɪn- (US) -dɚ **-s** -z
calend|er ˈkæl.ən.d|əʳ, -ɪn- (US) -d|ɚ **-ers** -əz (US) -ɚz **-ering** -ᵊr.ɪŋ **-ered** -əd (US) -ɚd
calends ˈkæl.ɪndz, -endz, -əndz (US) ˈkæl.ɪndz, ˈkeɪ.lɪndz, -lendz, -ləndz
calendula kəˈlen.djə.lə, kælˈen-, -djʊ- (US) -dʒə- **-s** -z
calenture ˈkæl.ən.tʃʊəʳ, -ɪn-, -tjʊəʳ, -tʃəʳ (US) -tʃɚ, -tʃʊr **-s** -z
cal|f kɑː|f (US) kæ|f **-ves** -vz ˌ**calf's-foot** ˈ**jelly**
calfskin ˈkɑːf.skɪn (US) ˈkæf-
Calgary ˈkæl.gᵊr.i
Calhoun kælˈhuːn, -ˈhəʊn, kəˈhuːn (US) kælˈhuːn, -ˈhoʊn, kəˈhuːn
Cali ˈkɑː.li
Caliban ˈkæl.ɪ.bæn, ˈ-ə-, -bən
caliber ˈkæl.ɪ.bəʳ, ˈ-ə- (US) ˈkæl.ə.bɚ **-s** -z
Calibra® kəˈliː.brə
cali|brate ˈkæl.ɪ|.breɪt, ˈ-ə- **-brates** -breɪts **-brating** -breɪ.tɪŋ (US) -breɪ.t̬ɪŋ **-brated** -breɪ.tɪd (US) -breɪ.t̬ɪd
calibration ˌkæl.ɪˈbreɪ.ʃᵊn, -əˈ-
calibrator ˈkæl.ɪ.breɪ.təʳ, ˈ-ə- (US) -t̬ɚ **-s** -z
calibre ˈkæl.ɪ.bəʳ, ˈ-ə- (US) ˈkæl.ə.bɚ **-s** -z
calicle ˈkæl.ɪ.kl̩ **-s** -z
calico ˈkæl.ɪ.kəʊ, ˈ-ə- (US) -koʊ **-(e)s** -z
Calicut ˈkæl.ɪ.kət, ˈ-ə-, -kʌt
calif ˈkeɪ.lɪf, ˈkæl.ɪf **-s** -s
Calif. *(abbrev. for* **California***)* ˌkæl.ɪˈfɔː.ni.ə, -əˈ-, ˈ-njə (US) -əˈfɔːr.njə, -ni.ə
Californi|a ˌkæl.ɪˈfɔː.ni|.ə, -əˈ-, ˈ-nj|ə (US) -əˈfɔːr.nj|ə, -ni|.ə **-an/s** -ən/z
californium ˌkæl.ɪˈfɔː.ni.əm, -əˈ- (US) -əˈfɔːr-
Caligula kəˈlɪg.jʊ.lə, -jə-
calipash ˈkæl.ɪ.pæʃ
calipee ˈkæl.ɪ.piː, ˌ--ˈ-
caliper ˈkæl.ɪ.pəʳ (US) -ə.pɚ **-s** -z
caliph ˈkeɪ.lɪf, ˈkæl.ɪf **-s** -s
caliphate ˈkæl.ɪ.feɪt, ˈkeɪ.lɪ-, -fɪt, -fət (US) ˈkeɪ.lɪ.fət, ˈkæl.ɪ.feɪt **-s** -s
calisthenic ˌkæl.ɪsˈθen.ɪk, -əsˈ- (US) -əsˈ- **-s** -s
Calisto kəˈlɪs.təʊ (US) -toʊ
cal|ix ˈkeɪ.l|ɪks, ˈkæl|.ɪks **-ices** -ɪs.iːz
calk kɔːk (US) kɔːk, kɑːk **-s** -s **-ing** -ɪŋ **-ed** -t
calkin ˈkæl.kɪn, ˈkɔː- (US) ˈkɔː-, ˈkɑː- **-s** -z
call kɔːl (US) kɔːl, kɑːl **-s** -z **-ing** -ɪŋ **-ed** -d ˈ**call** ˌ**girl**
Callaghan ˈkæl.ə.hən, -hæn, -gən (US) -hæn
Callahan ˈkæl.ə.hæn, -hən (US) -hæn
Callan ˈkæl.ən
Callander ˈkæl.ən.dəʳ (US) -dɚ
callanetics® ˌkæl.əˈnet.ɪks (US) -ˈnet̬-
Callao kəˈjaʊ (US) kəˈjɑː.oʊ
Callas ˈkæl.əs, -æs
callback ˈkɔːl.bæk (US) ˈkɔːl-, ˈkɑːl-
callboy ˈkɔːl.bɔɪ (US) ˈkɔːl-, ˈkɑːl- **-s** -z
Callcott ˈkɔːl.kət, ˈkɒl- (US) ˈkɔːl.kɑːt, ˈkɑːl-
Callender ˈkæl.ɪn.dəʳ, -ən- (US) -dɚ
caller ˈkɔː.ləʳ (US) ˈkɔː.lɚ, ˈkɑː- **-s** -z
Caller ˈkæl.əʳ (US) -ɚ
Callie *surname:* ˈkɔː.li (US) ˈkɔː-, ˈkɑː-
Callie *girl's name:* ˈkæl.i
calligraphic ˌkæl.ɪˈgræf.ɪk, -əˈ- **-al** -ᵊl **-ally** -ᵊl.i, -li
calligraph|y kəˈlɪg.rə.f|i, kælˈɪg- **-ist/s** -ɪst/s **-er/s** -əʳ/z (US) -ɚ/z
calling ˈkɔː.lɪŋ (US) ˈkɔː-, ˈkɑː- **-s** -z ˈ**calling** ˌ**card**
Calliope kəˈlaɪə.pi, kælˈaɪə-
calliper ˈkæl.ɪ.pəʳ (US) -ə.pɚ **-s** -z
callipygian ˌkæl.ɪˈpɪdʒ.i.ən, -əˈ- (US) -əˈ-
callipygous ˌkæl.ɪˈpaɪ.gəs, -əˈ- (US) -əˈ-
Callirrhoe kælˈɪr.əʊ.iː, kəˈlɪr- (US) kəˈlɪr.oʊ-
Callisthenes kælˈɪs.θə.niːz, kəˈlɪs- (US) kəˈlɪs-
callisthenic ˌkæl.ɪsˈθen.ɪk **-s** -s
Callistratus kælˈɪs.trə.təs, kəˈlɪs- (US) kəˈlɪs-
callosit|y kælˈɒs.ə.t|i, kəˈlɒs-, -ɪt|.i (US) kəˈlɑː.sə.t̬|i **-ies** -iz
callous ˈkæl.əs **-ly** -li **-ness** -nəs, -nɪs **-ed** -t
callow (C) ˈkæl.əʊ (US) -oʊ **-er** -əʳ (US) -ɚ **-est** -ɪst, -əst
Calloway ˈkæl.ə.weɪ
call-up ˈkɔːl.ʌp (US) ˈkɔːl-, ˈkɑːl-
callus ˈkæl.əs **-es** -ɪz **-ed**
calm kɑːm (US) kɑː*l*m **-s** -z **-er** -əʳ (US) -ɚ **-est** -ɪst, -əst **-ly** -li **-ness** -nəs, -nɪs **-ing** -ɪŋ **-ed** -d
calmative ˈkæl.mə.tɪv, ˈkɑː.mə- (US) ˈkɑː.mə.t̬ɪv, ˈkæl- **-s** -z
calmodulin kælˈmɒd.jə.lɪn, -jʊ- (US) -ˈmɑː.dʒə-, -dʒʊ-
Calne kɑːn
calomel ˈkæl.əʊ.mel (US) -ə.mel, -məl
calor ˈkæl.əʳ (US) -ɚ ˈ**Calor** ˌ**gas**
caloric kəˈlɒr.ɪk; ˈkæl.ᵊr- (US) kəˈlɔːr-
calorie ˈkæl.ᵊr.i **-s** -z
calorific ˌkæl.əˈrɪf.ɪk, -ɔːˈ- (US) -əˈ-
calorification kəˌlɒr.ɪ.fɪˈkeɪ.ʃᵊn; ˌkæl.ə.rɪ-, ˌkæl.ɔː-, ˌkæl.ɒr.ɪ- (US) kəˌlɔːr-, kælˌɔːr-
calorimeter ˌkæl.əˈrɪm.ɪ.təʳ, -ɔːˈ-, -ɒrˈɪm-, ˈ-ə- (US) -əˈrɪm.ə.t̬ɚ **-s** -z
calorimetry ˌkæl.əˈrɪm.ɪ.tri, -ɔːˈ-, -ɒrˈɪm-, ˈ-ə- (US) -əˈrɪm.ə-
calotte kəˈlɒt (US) -lɑːt **-s** -s
caloyer ˈkæl.ɔɪ.əʳ (US) ˈkæl.ə.jɚ; kəˈlɔɪ- **-s** -z
Calpurnia ˌkælˈpɜː.ni.ə (US) -ˈpɝː-
calque kælk **-s** -s
Calshot ˈkæl.ʃɒt (US) -ʃɑːt
Calthorpe *district in Birmingham:* ˈkæl.θɔːp (US) -θɔːrp *surname:* ˈkɔːl.θɔːp, ˈkɒl-, ˈkæl.θɔːp (US) ˈkɔːl.θɔːrp, ˈkɑːl-, ˈkæl-
Calton *in Edinburgh:* ˈkɔːl.tᵊn (US) ˈkɔːl-, ˈkɑːl- *in Glasgow:* ˈkɑːl.tᵊn
caltrop ˈkæl.trəp, -trɒp **-s** -s
calumet ˈkæl.jʊ.met (US) ˈkæl.jə.met, -mɪt; ˌkæl.jəˈmet **-s** -s
calumni|ate kəˈlʌm.ni|.eɪt **-ates** -eɪts **-ating** -eɪ.tɪŋ (US) -eɪ.t̬ɪŋ **-ated** -eɪ.tɪd (US) -eɪ.t̬ɪd **-ator/s** -eɪ.təʳ/z (US) -eɪ.t̬ɚ/z
calumniation kəˌlʌm.niˈeɪ.ʃᵊn **-s** -z
calumn|y ˈkæl.əm.n|i **-ies** -iz
calvados (C) ˈkæl.və.dɒs (US) ˌkæl.vəˈdoʊs, ˌkɑːl-
calvar|y (C) ˈkæl.vᵊr|.i **-ies** -iz
calv|e kɑːv (US) kæv **-es** -z **-ing** -ɪŋ **-ed** -d
Calverley *surname:* ˈkæl.vᵊl.i (US) -vɚ.li *place in West Yorkshire:* ˈkɑː.və.li, ˈkɔːv.li (US) ˈkɑː.vɚ-, ˈkɔːv-
Calvert ˈkæl.vɜːt, -vət, ˈkɔːl.vət (US) ˈkæl.vɝːt, -vɚt
Calverton ˈkæl.və.tᵊn, ˈkɔːl- (US) ˈkæl.vɚ.t̬ən
calves'-foot ˈkɑːvz.fʊt (US) ˈkævz-
Calvin ˈkæl.vɪn
Calvin|ism ˈkæl.vɪ.n|ɪ.zᵊm, -və- **-ist/s** -ɪst/s
Calvinistic ˌkæl.vɪˈnɪs.tɪk, -vəˈ- **-al** -ᵊl **-ally** -ᵊl.i, -li
cal|x kæl|ks **-ces** -siːz **-xes** -k.sɪz
Calydon ˈkæl.ɪ.dᵊn, ˈ-ə-
calypso (C) kəˈlɪp.səʊ (US) -soʊ **-(e)s** -z
ca|lyx ˈkeɪ|.lɪks, ˈkæl|.ɪks **-lyces** -lɪ.siːz **-lyxes** -lɪk.sɪz
calzone kæltˈsoʊ.ni, kælˈzəʊ-, -neɪ (US) kælˈzoʊ.ni, -ˈzoʊn **-s** -z
cam (C) kæm **-s** -z
CAm *(abbrev. for* **Central America***)* ˌsen.trᵊl.əˈmer.ɪ.kə
CAM kæm

Camalodunum ˌkæm.ə.ləʊˈdjuː.nəm ⓤⓢ -loʊˈduː-, -ˈdjuː-
camaraderie ˌkæm.əˈrɑː.dᵊr.i, -ˈræd.ᵊr-, -iː ⓤⓢ ˌkæm.əˈrɑː.dɚ.i, ˌkɑː.məˈ-, -ˈræd.ɚ-
Camargue kæmˈɑːg, kəˈmɑːg ⓤⓢ kəˈmɑːrg
camarilla ˌkæm.əˈrɪl.ə **-s** -z
Camay® ˈkæm.eɪ ⓤⓢ ˌkæmˈeɪ
camber (C) ˈkæm.bəʳ ⓤⓢ -bɚ **-s** -z
Camberley ˈkæm.bᵊl.i ⓤⓢ -bɚ.li
Camberwell ˈkæm.bə.wel, -wəl ⓤⓢ -bɚ-
cambial ˈkæm.bi.əl
cambium ˈkæm.bi.əm
Cambodi|a ˌkæmˈbəʊ.di|.ə ⓤⓢ -ˈboʊ- **-an/s** -ən
Camborne ˈkæm.bɔːn, -bən ⓤⓢ -bɔːrn
Cambray ˈkɑ̃ː*m*.breɪ, ˈkɒm- ⓤⓢ kɑːmˈbreɪ
Cambri|a ˈkæm.bri|.ə **-an/s** -ən/z
cambric ˈkæm.brɪk, ˈkeɪm-
Cambridge ˈkeɪm.brɪdʒ **-shire** -ʃəʳ, -ˌʃɪəʳ ⓤⓢ -ʃɚ, -ˌʃɪr
Cambs. *(abbrev. for* **Cambridgeshire***)* kæm*bz*; ˈkeɪm.brɪdʒ.ʃəʳ, -ˌʃɪəʳ ⓤⓢ kæm*bz*; ˈkeɪm.brɪdʒ.ʃɚ, -ˌʃɪr
Cambyses kæmˈbaɪ.siːz
camcorder ˈkæmˌkɔː.dəʳ ⓤⓢ -ˌkɔːr.dɚ **-s** -z
Camden ˈkæm.dən
came *(from* **come***)* keɪm
camel ˈkæm.ᵊl **-s** -z
Camelford ˈkæm.ᵊl.fəd ⓤⓢ -fɚd
camelhair ˈkæm.ᵊl.heəʳ ⓤⓢ -her
camel(l)ia (C) kəˈmiː.li.ə, -ˈmel.i- ⓤⓢ -ˈmiːl.jə, -ˈmiː.li.ə **-s** -z
Camelot ˈkæm.ə.lɒt, ˈ-ɪ- ⓤⓢ -lɑːt
Camembert ˈkæm.əm.beəʳ ⓤⓢ -ber
cameo ˈkæm.i.əʊ ⓤⓢ -oʊ **-s** -z **ˈcameo ˌrole**
camera ˈkæm.ᵊr.ə, ˈkæm.rə **-s** -z
cameral ˈkæm.ᵊr.ᵊl
camera|man ˈkæm.ᵊr.ə|.mæn, ˈkæm.rə-, -mən **-men** -men
camera obscura ˌkæm.ᵊr.ə.əbˈskjʊə.rə, ˌkæm.rə-, -ɒbˈ- ⓤⓢ -əbˈskjʊr.ə
camera|woman ˈkæm.ᵊr.ə|ˌwʊm.ən, -rəˌ- **-women** -ˌwɪm.ɪn
Camero kəˈmeə.rəʊ ⓤⓢ -ˈmer.oʊ
Cameron ˈkæm.ᵊr.ən, ˈkæm.rən
Cameronian ˌkæm.ᵊrˈəʊ.ni.ən ⓤⓢ -ˈroʊ- **-s** -z
Cameroon ˌkæm.əˈruːn, ˈ--- **-s** -z
camiknickers ˈkæm.iˌnɪk.əz, ˌkæm.iˈnɪk- ⓤⓢ ˈkæm.iˌnɪk.ɚz
Camilla kəˈmɪl.ə
Camille kəˈmiːl, -ˈmɪl
camis|e kəˈmiːz **-es** -ɪz
camisole ˈkæm.ɪ.səʊl ⓤⓢ -soʊl **-s** -z
Camlachie kæmˈlæk.i, -ˈlæx-
Cammell Laird ˌkæm.ᵊlˈleəd ⓤⓢ -ˈlerd
camomile ˈkæm.əʊ.maɪl ⓤⓢ -ə.miːl
Camorra kəˈmɒr.ə ⓤⓢ -ˈmɔːr-
camouflag|e ˈkæm.ə.flɑːʒ, ˈ-ʊ- ⓤⓢ -flɑːdʒ **-es** -ɪz **-ing** -ɪŋ **-ed** -d
Camoys kəˈmɔɪz
camp (C) kæmp **-s** -s **-ing** -ɪŋ **-ed** -t **-y** -i **ˈcamp ˌstool ˌcamp ˈbed ˈcamp ˌbed; ˌCamp ˈDavid; ˈcamp ˌfollower**
Campagna kæmˈpɑː.njə ⓤⓢ -njɑː
campaign kæmˈpeɪn **-s** -z **-ing** -ɪŋ **-ed** -d **-er/s** -əʳ/z ⓤⓢ -ɚ/z
campanile ˌkæm.pəˈniː.leɪ ⓤⓢ -leɪ, -li **-s** -z
campanolog|y ˌkæm.pəˈnɒl.ə.dʒ|i ⓤⓢ -ˈnɑː.lə- **-ist/s** -ɪst/s
campanula kəmˈpæn.jʊ.lə, kæm-, -jə- **-s** -z
Campari® kæmˈpɑː.ri ⓤⓢ -ˈpɑːr.i
Campbell ˈkæm.bᵊl **-s** -z
Campbellite ˈkæm.bᵊl.aɪt ⓤⓢ -bə.laɪt **-s** -s
Campbeltown ˈkæm.bᵊl.taʊn
Campden ˈkæm*p*.dən
Campeche kæmˈpiː.tʃi
camper ˈkæm.pəʳ ⓤⓢ -pɚ **-s** -z **ˈcamper ˌvan**
Camperdown ˈkæm.pə.daʊn ⓤⓢ -pɚ-
campfire ˈkæmp.faɪəʳ ⓤⓢ -faɪɚ **-s** -z
campground ˈkæmp.graʊnd **-s** -z
camphire ˈkæm*p*.faɪəʳ ⓤⓢ -faɪɚ
camphor ˈkæm*p*.fəʳ ⓤⓢ -fɚ **-s** -z
camphor|ate ˈkæm*p*.fə.r|eɪt **-ates** -eɪts **-ating** -eɪ.tɪŋ ⓤⓢ -eɪ.t̬ɪŋ **-ated** -eɪ.tɪd ⓤⓢ -eɪ.t̬ɪd ˌ**camphorated ˈoil**
camphoric kæmˈfɒr.ɪk ⓤⓢ -ˈfɔːr-
camping ˈkæm.pɪŋ
campion (C) ˈkæm.pi.ən **-s** -z
Camps kæmps
campsite ˈkæmp.saɪt **-s** -s
campus ˈkæm.pəs **-es** -ɪz
CAMRA ˈkæm.rə
camshaft ˈkæm.ʃɑːft ⓤⓢ -ʃæft **-s** -s
Camus kæmˈuː ⓤⓢ kæmˈuː, kɑːˈmuː, kə-
camwood ˈkæm.wʊd
can *(n.)* kæn **-s** -z **ˈcan ˌopener**; (ˌ**open a**) ˌ**can of ˈworms**; ˌ**carry the ˈcan**
can *(v.) put in cans:* kæn **-s** -z **-ning** -ɪŋ **-ned** -d
can *(auxil. v.) strong form:* kæn *weak forms:* kən, kn̩, kŋ
Note: Weak form word. The strong form /kæn/ is used for emphasis (e.g. “You **can** do it”, and for contrast (e.g. “I don’t know if he can or he can’t”). It is also used finally in a sentence (e.g. “I don’t know if I can”). The form /kŋ/ occurs only before words beginning with /k/ or /g/.
Cana ˈkeɪ.nə
Canaan ˈkeɪ.nən, -ni.ən *Jewish pronunciation:* kəˈneɪ.ən
Canaanite ˈkeɪ.nə.naɪt, -ni.ə- *Jewish pronunciation:* kəˈneɪ.ə.naɪt **-s** -s
Canada ˈkæn.ə.də
Canadian kəˈneɪ.di.ən **-s** -z
canaille kəˈneɪəl, -naɪ ⓤⓢ kəˈneɪl
canal kəˈnæl **-s** -z
Canaletto ˌkæn.ᵊlˈet.əʊ ⓤⓢ -əˈlet̬.oʊ
canalization, -isa- ˌkæn.ᵊl.aɪˈzeɪ.ʃᵊn, -ɪˈ- ⓤⓢ -ɪˈ-
canaliz|e, -is|e ˈkæn.ᵊl.aɪz ⓤⓢ -ə.laɪz **-es** -ɪz **-ing** -ɪŋ **-ed** -d
Cananite ˈkæn.ə.naɪt, ˈkeɪ.nə- **-s** -s
canapé ˈkæn.ə.peɪ **-s** -z
canard ˈkæn.ɑːd, kəˈnɑːd, kænˈɑːd ⓤⓢ kəˈnɑːrd **-s** -z
canar|y (C) kəˈneə.r|i ⓤⓢ -ˈner|.i **-ies** -iz **Caˈnary ˌIslands**
canasta kəˈnæs.tə
canaster kəˈnæs.təʳ ⓤⓢ -tɚ **-s** -z
Canaveral kəˈnæv.ᵊr.ᵊl
Canberra ˈkæn.bᵊr.ə, ˈkæm- ⓤⓢ ˈkæn.ber-, -bɚ-
cancan ˈkæn.kæn, ˈkæŋ- **-s** -z
cancel ˈkæn*t*.sᵊl **-s** -z **-(l)ing** -ɪŋ **-(l)ed** -d
cancell|ate ˈkæn*t*.sᵊl|.eɪt, -sɪ.l|eɪt ⓤⓢ -sə.l|eɪt **-ates** -eɪts **-ating** -eɪ.tɪŋ ⓤⓢ -eɪ.t̬ɪŋ **-ated** -eɪ.tɪd ⓤⓢ -eɪ.t̬ɪd
cancellation ˌkæn*t*.sᵊlˈeɪ.ʃᵊn, -sɪˈleɪ- ⓤⓢ -səˈleɪ- **-s** -z
cancellous ˈkæn*t*.sᵊl.əs
cancer (C) ˈkæn*t*.səʳ ⓤⓢ -sɚ **-s** -z
Cancerean, Cancerian kæn*t*ˈsɪə.ri.ən, -ˈseə- ⓤⓢ -ˈser.i-, -ˈsɪr- **-s** -z
cancerous ˈkæn*t*.sᵊr.əs
cancroid ˈkæŋ.krɔɪd
Candace kænˈdeɪ.si, ˈkæn.dɪs, -dəs
candela kænˈdel.ə, -ˈdeɪ.lə, -ˈdiː- **-s** -z
candelabr|a ˌkæn.dᵊlˈɑː.br|ə, -dɪˈlɑː-, -ˈlæb.r|ə ⓤⓢ -dəˈlɑː.br|ə, -ˈlæb.r|ə **-as** -əz **-um** -əm
Canderel® ˌkæn.dᵊrˈel, ˈ---
candescen|ce kænˈdes.ᵊn|*t*s **-t** -t
Candia ˈkæn.di.ə
Candice ˈkæn.dɪs, -diːs
candid ˈkæn.dɪd **-ly** -li **-ness** -nəs, -nɪs
Candida ˈkæn.dɪ.də
candida|cy ˈkæn.dɪ.də|.si **-cies** -siz
candidate ˈkæn.dɪ.dət, -deɪt, -dɪt **-s** -s
candidature ˈkæn.dɪ.də.tʃəʳ, ˈ-də-, -deɪ-, -dɪtʃ.əʳ ⓤⓢ ˈkæn.də.də.tʃʊr, -tʃɚ **-s** -z
Candide kɑ̃ː*n*ˈdiːd ⓤⓢ kɑːn-, kæn-
candidias|is ˌkæn.dɪˈdaɪə.s|ɪs, -dəˈ- **-es** -iːz
candle ˈkæn.dl̩ **-s** -z ˌ**burn the ˌcandle at ˌboth ˈends**
candlelight ˈkæn.dl̩.laɪt
candle-lit ˈkæn.dl̩.lɪt ˌ**candle-lit ˈdinner**
Candlemas ˈkæn.dl̩.məs, -mæs

candlepower ˈkæn.dl̩.paʊəʳ ⓤⓢ -paʊɚ **-s** -z
candlestick ˈkæn.dl̩.stɪk **-s** -s
candlewick ˈkæn.dl̩.wɪk
cando(u)r ˈkæn.dəʳ ⓤⓢ -dɚ
cand|y (C) ˈkæn.d|i **-ies** -iz **-ying** -i.ɪŋ **-ied** -id
candyfloss ˈkæn.di.flɒs ⓤⓢ -flɑːs
candytuft ˈkæn.di.tʌft
can|e (C) keɪn **-es** -z **-ing** -ɪŋ **-ed** -d ˌ**cane** ˈ**sugar**, ˈ**cane** ˌ**sugar**
Canford ˈkæn.fəd ⓤⓢ -fɚd
Canham ˈkæn.əm
canicular kəˈnɪk.jʊ.ləʳ, kænˈɪk-, -jə- ⓤⓢ -jə.lɚ
canine ˈkeɪ.naɪn, ˈkæn.aɪn ⓤⓢ ˈkeɪ.naɪn **-s** -z
Canis ˈkeɪ.nɪs, ˈkæn.ɪs
canister ˈkæn.ɪ.stəʳ ⓤⓢ -ə.stɚ **-s** -z
cank|er ˈkæŋ.k|əʳ ⓤⓢ -k|ɚ **-ers** -əz ⓤⓢ -ɚz **-ering** -ᵊr.ɪŋ **-ered** -əd ⓤⓢ -ɚd
cankerous ˈkæŋ.kᵊr.əs
canna ˈkæn.ə **-s** -z
cannabis ˈkæn.ə.bɪs
Cannan ˈkæn.ən
cannelloni ˌkæn.ᵊlˈəʊ.ni, -ɪˈləʊ- ⓤⓢ -əˈloʊ-
canner|y ˈkæn.ᵊr|.i **-ies** -iz
Cannes kæn, kænz ⓤⓢ kæn, kænz, kɑːn ˌ**Cannes** ˈ**Film** ˌ**Festival**
cannibal ˈkæn.ɪ.bᵊl, ˈ-ə- **-s** -z
cannibalism ˈkæn.ɪ.bᵊl.ɪ.zᵊm, ˈ-ə-
cannibalistic ˌkæn.ɪ.bᵊlˈɪs.tɪk, ˌ-ə- ⓤⓢ -bəˈlɪs-
cannibaliz|e, -is|e ˈkæn.ɪ.bᵊl.aɪz, ˈ-ə- ⓤⓢ -bə.laɪz **-es** -ɪz **-ing** -ɪŋ **-ed** -d
cannikin ˈkæn.ɪ.kɪn ⓤⓢ ˈ-ə- **-s** -z
Canning ˈkæn.ɪŋ
Cannizzaro ˌkæn.ɪˈzɑː.rəʊ, -əˈ- ⓤⓢ -roʊ
Cannock ˈkæn.ək
cannon (C) ˈkæn.ən **-s** -z **-ing** -ɪŋ **-ed** -d ˈ**cannon** ˌ**fodder**
cannonad|e ˌkæn.əˈneɪd **-es** -z **-ing** -ɪŋ **-ed** -ɪd
cannonball ˈkæn.ən.bɔːl ⓤⓢ -bɔːl, -bɑːl **-s** -z **-ing** -ɪŋ **-ed** -d
cannoneer ˌkæn.əˈnɪəʳ ⓤⓢ -ˈnɪr **-s** -z
cannonry ˈkæn.ən.ri
cannonshot ˈkæn.ən.ʃɒt ⓤⓢ -ʃɑːt **-s** -s
cannot ˈkæn.ɒt, -ət ⓤⓢ ˈkæn.ɑːt, kəˈnɑːt
Note: This word is usually contracted to /kɑːnt ⓤⓢ kænt/. See **can't**.
cannul|a ˈkæn.jə.l|ə, -jʊ- ⓤⓢ -jə- **-ae** -iː, -aɪ **-as** -əz
cann|y ˈkæn|.i **-ier** -i.əʳ ⓤⓢ -i.ɚ **-iest** -i.ɪst, -i.əst **-ily** -ɪ.li, -ᵊl.i **-iness** -ɪ.nəs, -ɪ.nɪs
canoe kəˈnuː **-s** -z **-ing** -ɪŋ **-d** -d
canoeist kəˈnuː.ɪst **-s** -s
canon ˈkæn.ən **-s** -z ˌ**canon** ˈ**law**
Canonbury ˈkæn.ən.bᵊr.i, -əm- ⓤⓢ -ən.ber-, -bɚ-
canoness ˌkæn.əˈnes, ˈkæn.ə.nɪs, -nes ⓤⓢ ˈkæn.ə.nəs **-es** -ɪz
Canongate ˈkæn.ən.geɪt, -əŋ-
canonic kəˈnɒn.ɪk, kænˈɒn- ⓤⓢ kəˈnɑː.nɪk **-al/s** -ᵊl/z **-ally** -ᵊl.i, -li
canonization, -isa- ˌkæn.ə.naɪˈzeɪ.ʃᵊn, -nɪˈ- ⓤⓢ -nɪˈ- **-s** -z
canoniz|e, -is|e ˈkæn.ə.naɪz **-es** -ɪz **-ing** -ɪŋ **-ed** -d
canonr|y ˈkæn.ən.r|i **-ies** -iz
canoodl|e kəˈnuː.dl̩ **-es** -z **-ing** -ɪŋ, -ˈnuːd.lɪŋ **-ed** -d
Canopus kəˈnəʊ.pəs ⓤⓢ -ˈnoʊ-
canop|y ˈkæn.ə.p|i **-ies** -iz
Canossa kəˈnɒs.ə, kænˈɒs- ⓤⓢ kəˈnɑː.sə
canst *(from* **can***) strong form:* kænst *weak form:* kənst
cant (C) kænt **-s** -s **-ing** -ɪŋ **-ed** -ɪd **-er/s** -əʳ/z ⓤⓢ -ɚ/z
can't kɑːnt ⓤⓢ kænt
Cantab. ˈkæn.tæb
cantabile kænˈtɑː.bɪ.leɪ, -bə-
Cantabria kænˈtæb.ri.ə ⓤⓢ -ˈteɪ.bri-
Cantabrian kænˈtæb.ri.ən ⓤⓢ -ˈteɪ.bri-
Cantabrigian ˌkæn.təˈbrɪdʒ.i.ən **-s** -z
cantaloup(e) ˈkæn.tə.luːp ⓤⓢ -t̬ə.loʊp **-s** -s
cantankerous ˌkænˈtæŋ.kᵊr.əs, kən- **-ly** -li **-ness** -nəs, -nɪs
cantata kænˈtɑː.tə, kən- ⓤⓢ kənˈtɑː.t̬ə **-s** -z
cantatrice ˈkæn.tə.triːs *as if French:* ˌkɑ̃ːn.tætˈriːs *as if Italian:* ˌkɑːn.təˈtriː.tʃeɪ ⓤⓢ ˌkɑːn.təˈtriːs **-s** -ɪz
canteen kænˈtiːn **-s** -z *stress shift:* ˌcanteen ˈfood
cant|er (C) ˈkæn.t|əʳ ⓤⓢ -t̬|ɚ **-ers** -əz ⓤⓢ -ɚz **-ering** -ᵊr.ɪŋ **-ered** -əd ⓤⓢ -ɚd
Canterbury ˈkæn.tə.bᵊr.i, -ber- ⓤⓢ -t̬ɚ.ber-, -bɚ- ˌ**Canterbury** ˈ**Tales**
cantharides kænˈθær.ɪ.diːz, kənt- ⓤⓢ -ˈθer-, -ˈθær-
canticle ˈkæn.tɪ.kl̩ ⓤⓢ -t̬ə- **-s** -z
Canticles *(Song of Solomon)* ˈkæn.tɪ.kl̩z ⓤⓢ -t̬ə-
cantilena ˌkæn.tɪˈleɪn.ə ⓤⓢ -t̬əˈ-
cantilever ˈkæn.tɪ.liː.vəʳ, -tə- ⓤⓢ -t̬ə.liː.vɚ, -lev.ɚ **-s** -z
Cantire kænˈtaɪəʳ ⓤⓢ -ˈtaɪɚ
Cantling ˈkænt.lɪŋ
canto ˈkæn.təʊ ⓤⓢ -toʊ **-s** -z
canton *Swiss state:* ˈkæn.tɒn, ˌ-ˈ- ⓤⓢ ˈkæn.tɑːn, -tᵊn **-s** -z *in heraldry:* ˈkæn.tən
Canton *in China:* ˌkænˈtɒn ⓤⓢ -ˈtɑːn *in Wales, surname, place in US:* ˈkæn.tən ⓤⓢ -tᵊn
canton *(v.) divide into portions or districts:* kænˈtɒn ⓤⓢ -ˈtɑːn **-s** -z **-ing** -ɪŋ **-ed** -d
canton *(v.) provide accommodation:* kænˈtuːn, kən- ⓤⓢ kænˈtoʊn, -ˈtɑːn **-s** -z **-ing** -ɪŋ **-ed** -d **-ment/s** -mənt/s
Cantona ˈkæn.tə.nɑː
cantonal ˈkæn.tə.nᵊl, kænˈtəʊ.nᵊl ⓤⓢ ˈkæn.tə.nᵊl, kænˈtɑː.nəl
Cantonese ˌkæn.təˈniːz, -tɒnˈiːz ⓤⓢ -tᵊnˈiːz, -ˈiːs
cantor ˈkæn.tɔːʳ ⓤⓢ -tɚ, -tɔːr **-s** -z
cantoris kænˈtɔː.rɪs ⓤⓢ -ˈtɔːr.ɪs
cantus ˈkæn.təs ⓤⓢ -t̬əs
Cantwell ˈkænt.wel
Canty ˈkæn.ti ⓤⓢ -t̬i
Canuck kəˈnʌk **-s** -s
Canute kəˈnjuːt ⓤⓢ -ˈnuːt, -ˈnjuːt
canvas ˈkæn.vəs **-es** -ɪz
canvasback ˈkæn.vəs.bæk **-s** -s
canvass ˈkæn.vəs **-es** -ɪz **-ing** -ɪŋ **-ed** -t **-er/s** -əʳ/z ⓤⓢ -ɚ/z
Canvey ˈkæn.vi
canyon ˈkæn.jən **-s** -z **-ing** -ɪŋ **-ed** -d
Canyonlands ˈkæn.jən.lændz
canzone kæntˈsəʊ.neɪ, kænˈzəʊ- ⓤⓢ kænˈzoʊ.ni, kɑːntˈsoʊ.neɪ **-s** -z
canzonet kæntˈsəʊ.net, kænˈzəʊ- ⓤⓢ ˌkæn.zəˈnet **-s** -s
caoutchouc ˈkaʊ.tʃʊk, -tʃuːk, -tʃuː, -ˈ-
cap kæp **-s** -s **-ping** -ɪŋ **-ped** -t
CAP ˌsiː.eɪˈpiː
capabilit|y ˌkeɪ.pəˈbɪl.ə.t|i, -ɪ.t|i ⓤⓢ -ə.t̬|i **-ies** -iz
capab|le ˈkeɪ.pə.b|l̩ **-ly** -li **-leness** -l̩.nəs, -nɪs
capacious kəˈpeɪ.ʃəs **-ly** -li **-ness** -nəs, -nɪs
capacitance kəˈpæs.ɪ.tᵊnts ⓤⓢ ˈ-ə-
capaci|tate kəˈpæs.ɪ|.teɪt ⓤⓢ ˈ-ə- **-tates** -teɪts **-tating** -teɪ.tɪŋ ⓤⓢ -teɪ.t̬ɪŋ **-tated** -teɪ.tɪd ⓤⓢ -teɪ.t̬ɪd
capacitor kəˈpæs.ɪ.təʳ, ˈ-ə- ⓤⓢ -ə.t̬ɚ **-s** -z
capacit|y kəˈpæs.ə.t|i, -ɪ.t|i ⓤⓢ -ə.t̬|i **-ies** -iz
cap-à-pie ˌkæp.əˈpiː
caparison kəˈpær.ɪ.sᵊn ⓤⓢ -ˈper.ə-, -ˈpær- **-s** -z **-ing** -ɪŋ **-ed** -d
cape (C) keɪp **-s** -s **-d** -t ˌ**Cape** **Caˈnaveral**; ˌ**Cape** ˈ**Cod**; ˌ**Cape** ˈ**Horn**; ˌ**Cape of Good** ˈ**Hope**; ˈ**Cape** ˌ**Province**; ˌ**caped cruˈsader**
Capel *surname, places in Kent and Surrey:* ˈkeɪ.pᵊl *in Wales:* ˈkæp.ᵊl
Capel Curig ˌkæp.ᵊlˈkɪr.ɪg
Capell ˈkeɪ.pᵊl
capel(l)et ˈkæp.ə.let, -lɪt **-s** -s
cap|er ˈkeɪ.p|əʳ ⓤⓢ -p|ɚ **-ers** -əz ⓤⓢ -ɚz **-ering** -ᵊr.ɪŋ **-ered** -əd ⓤⓢ -ɚd **-erer/s** -ᵊr.əʳ/z ⓤⓢ -ɚ.ɚ/z
caper *bird:* ˈkæp.əʳ ⓤⓢ -ɚ **-s** -z

capercailzie, capercaillie ˌkæp.əˈkeɪ.li, -ˈkeɪ.lji, -ˈkeɪl.zi ⓤⓢ -ɚˈkeɪ.li, -ˈkeɪl.ji, -zi **-s** -z
Capernaum kəˈpɜː.ni.əm ⓤⓢ -ˈpɝː-
Cape Town, Capetown ˈkeɪp.taʊn
Cape Verde ˌkeɪpˈvɜːd, -ˈveəd ⓤⓢ -vɝːd
Capgrave ˈkæp.greɪv
capias ˈkeɪ.pi.æs, -pjæs, -pjəs ⓤⓢ ˈkeɪ.pi.əs **-es** -ɪz
capillarity ˌkæp.ɪˈlær.ə.ti, -əˈ-, -ɪ.ti ⓤⓢ -ˈler.ə.t̬i, -ˈlær-
capillary kəˈpɪl.ər.i ⓤⓢ ˈkæp.ə.ler-
capital ˈkæp.ɪ.təl ⓤⓢ -ə.t̬əl **-s** -z **-ly** -i ˌ**capital ˈletter**; ˌ**capital ˈpunishment**
capitalism ˈkæp.ɪ.təl.ɪ.zəm, kəˈpɪt.əl-, kæpˈɪt- ⓤⓢ ˈkæp.ə.t̬əl-
capitalist ˈkæp.ɪ.təl.ɪst, kəˈpɪt.əl-, kæpˈɪt- ⓤⓢ ˈkæp.ə.t̬əl- **-s** -s
capitalistic ˌkæp.ɪ.təlˈɪs.tɪk ⓤⓢ -ə.t̬əˈlɪs- **-ally** -əl.i, -li
capitalization, -isa- ˌkæp.ɪ.təl.aɪˈzeɪ.ʃən, kæpˌɪt.əl-, kəˌpɪt- ⓤⓢ ˌkæp.ə.t̬əl.ɪˈ- **-s** -z
capitaliz|e, -is|e ˈkæp.ɪ.təl.aɪz, kæpˈɪt.əl-, kəˈpɪt- ⓤⓢ ˈkæp.ə.t̬ə.laɪz **-es** -ɪz **-ing** -ɪŋ **-ed** -d
capitation ˌkæp.ɪˈteɪ.ʃən ⓤⓢ -əˈ- **-s** -z
capitol (C) ˈkæp.ɪ.təl ⓤⓢ -ə.t̬əl **-s** -z ˌ**Capitol ˈHill**
capitolian ˌkæp.ɪˈtəʊ.li.ən ⓤⓢ -əˈtoʊ-
capitoline (C) kəˈpɪt.əʊ.laɪn ⓤⓢ ˈkæp.ə.t̬ə.laɪn, -liːn
capitular kəˈpɪt.jʊ.ləʳ, -jə-, -ˈpɪtʃ.ʊ-, ˈ-ə- ⓤⓢ -ˈpɪtʃ.əl.ɚ **-s** -z
capitular|y kəˈpɪt.jʊ.lə.r|i, -jə-, -ˈpɪtʃ.ʊ-, ˈ-ə- ⓤⓢ -ˈpɪtʃ.ə.ler|.i **-ies** -iz
capitu|late kəˈpɪt.jʊl.leɪt, -jə-, -ˈpɪtj.ʊ-, ˈ-ə- ⓤⓢ -ˈpɪtʃ.əl.leɪt, ˈ-ʊ- **-lates** -leɪts **-lating** -leɪ.tɪŋ ⓤⓢ -leɪ.t̬ɪŋ **-lated** -leɪ.tɪd ⓤⓢ -leɪ.t̬ɪd
capitulation kəˌpɪt.jʊˈleɪ.ʃən, -jəˈ-, -ˌpɪtʃ.ʊˈ-, -əˈ- ⓤⓢ -ˌpɪtʃ.əˈ-, -jʊˈ- **-s** -z
capitul|um kəˈpɪt.jʊ.l|əm, -jə-, -ˈpɪtʃ.ʊ-, ˈ-ə- ⓤⓢ -ˈpɪtʃ.ə- **-a** -ə
capo *for guitar:* ˈkæp.əʊ, ˈkeɪ.pəʊ ⓤⓢ ˈkeɪ.poʊ **-s** -z *criminal chieftain:* ˈkɑː.pəʊ, ˈkæp.əʊ ⓤⓢ ˈkɑː.poʊ, ˈkæp.oʊ
capon ˈkeɪ.pən, -pɒn ⓤⓢ -pɑːn, -pən **-s** -z
Capone kəˈpəʊn, keɪ- ⓤⓢ kəˈpoʊn
capot kəˈpɒt ⓤⓢ -ˈpɑːt **-s** -s **-ting** -ɪŋ ⓤⓢ -ˈpɑː.t̬ɪŋ **-ted** -ɪd ⓤⓢ -ˈpɑː.t̬ɪd
capote kəˈpəʊt ⓤⓢ -ˈpoʊt **-s** -s
Capote kəˈpəʊ.ti ⓤⓢ -ˈpoʊ.t̬i
Cappadoci|a ˌkæp.əˈdəʊ.si|.ə, -ʃi|.ə, -ʃ|ə ⓤⓢ -ˈdoʊ.ʃ|ə **-an/s** -ən/z
Capper ˈkæp.əʳ ⓤⓢ -ɚ
cappuccino ˌkæp.ʊˈtʃiː.nəʊ, -əˈ- ⓤⓢ ˌkæp.əˈtʃiː.noʊ, ˌkɑː.pəˈ- **-s** -z
Capra ˈkæp.rə
Capri kæpˈriː, kəˈpriː
Capriati ˌkæp.riˈɑː.ti ⓤⓢ -ˈɑː.t̬i, ˌkɑːp-
capric ˈkæp.rɪk
capriccio kəˈprɪtʃ.i.əʊ, -ˈpriː.tʃi- ⓤⓢ -ˈpriː.tʃoʊ **-s** -z
capriccioso kəˌprɪtʃ.iˈəʊ.zəʊ, -ˌpriː.tʃiˈ-, -səʊ ⓤⓢ ˌkɑː.priːˈtʃoʊ.soʊ, -tʃiˈoʊ-; kəˌpriː-
capric|e kəˈpriːs **-es** -ɪz
capricious kəˈprɪʃ.əs **-ly** -li **-ness** -nəs, -nɪs
Capricorn ˈkæp.rɪ.kɔːn ⓤⓢ -rə.kɔːrn
Capricornus ˌkæp.rɪˈkɔː.nəs ⓤⓢ -rəˈkɔːr-
capriol|e ˈkæp.ri.əʊl ⓤⓢ -oʊl **-es** -z **-ing** -ɪŋ **-ed** -d
capsicum ˈkæp.sɪ.kəm
capsiz|e kæpˈsaɪz ⓤⓢ ˈ--, -ˈ- **-es** -ɪz **-ing** -ɪŋ **-ed** -d
capstan ˈkæp.stən **-s** -z
capsular ˈkæp.sjʊ.ləʳ, -sjə- ⓤⓢ -sə.lɚ, -sjʊ-
capsule ˈkæp.sjuːl ⓤⓢ -səl, -sjʊl **-s** -z
captain ˈkæp.tɪn ⓤⓢ -tən **-s** -z **-ing** -ɪŋ **-ed** -d
captainc|y ˈkæp.tɪn.s|i, -tən- **-ies** -iz
caption ˈkæp.ʃən **-s** -z **-ing** -ɪŋ **-ed** -d
captious ˈkæp.ʃəs **-ly** -li **-ness** -nəs, -nɪs
capti|vate ˈkæp.tɪ|.veɪt ⓤⓢ -tə- **-vates** -veɪts **-vating** -veɪ.tɪŋ ⓤⓢ -veɪ.t̬ɪŋ **-vated** -veɪ.tɪd ⓤⓢ -veɪ.t̬ɪd
captivation ˌkæp.tɪˈveɪ.ʃən ⓤⓢ -təˈ-
captive ˈkæp.tɪv **-s** -z
captivit|y kæpˈtɪv.ə.t|i, -ɪ.t|i ⓤⓢ -ə.t̬|i **-ies** -iz
captor ˈkæp.təʳ, -tɔːʳ ⓤⓢ -tɚ, -tɔːr **-s** -z
capt|ure ˈkæp.tʃ|əʳ ⓤⓢ -tʃ|ɚ **-ures** -əz ⓤⓢ -ɚz **-uring** -ər.ɪŋ **-ured** -əd ⓤⓢ -ɚd
Capua ˈkæp.ju.ə
capuch|e kəˈpuːʃ, -ˈpuːtʃ **-es** -ɪz
capuchin (C) ˈkæp.jʊ.tʃɪn, -ʃɪn; ⓤⓢ ˈkæp.jʊ.tʃɪn, -jə-, -ʃɪn; kəˈpjuː- **-s** -z
Capulet ˈkæp.jʊ.let, -jə-, -lət, -lɪt
capybara ˌkæp.ɪˈbɑː.rə ⓤⓢ -ˈbɑːr.ə **-s** -z
car kɑːʳ ⓤⓢ kɑːr **-s** -z ˈ**car aˌlarm**; ˈ**car ˌferry**; ˈ**car ˌpark**; ˈ**car ˌpool**; ˈ**car ˌport**; ˈ**car ˌwash**
Cara ˈkɑː.rə ⓤⓢ ˈker.ə, ˈkær-, ˈkɑːr-
carabineer ˌkær.ə.bɪˈnɪəʳ ⓤⓢ ˌker.ə.bɪˈnɪr, ˌkær- **-s** -z
carabiner ˌkær.əˈbiː.nəʳ ⓤⓢ ˌker.əˈbiː.nɚ, ˌkær- **-s** -z
carabinieri ˌkær.ə.bɪ.niˈeə.ri ⓤⓢ ˌker.ə.bənˈjer.i, ˌkær-
caracal ˈkær.ə.kæl ⓤⓢ ˈker-, ˈkær- **-s** -z
Caracas kəˈræk.əs, -ˈrɑː.kəs ⓤⓢ -ˈrɑː-
caracole ˈkær.ə.kəʊl ⓤⓢ ˈker.ə.koʊl, ˈkær- **-s** -z
Caractacus kəˈræk.tə.kəs
Caradoc kəˈræd.ək; ˈkær.ə.dɒk ⓤⓢ ˈker.ə.dɑːk, ˈkær-; kəˈræd.ək
carafe kəˈræf, -ˈrɑːf **-s** -s
carambola ˌkær.əmˈbəʊ.lə ⓤⓢ ˌker.əmˈboʊ-, ˌkær- **-s** -z
caramel ˈkær.ə.məl, -mel ⓤⓢ ˈkɑːr.məl; ˈker.ə-, ˈkær- **-s** -z
carameliz|e, -is|e ˈkær.ə.məl.aɪz, -mel- ⓤⓢ ˈkɑːr.mə.laɪz, ˈker.ə-, ˈkær- **-es** -ɪz **-ing** -ɪŋ **-ed** -d
Caran d'Ache® ˌkær.ənˈdæʃ ⓤⓢ ˌkɑːr.ɑːnˈdɑːʃ
carapac|e ˈkær.ə.peɪs ⓤⓢ ˈker-, ˈkær- **-es** -ɪz
carat ˈkær.ət ⓤⓢ ˈker-, ˈkær- **-s** -s
Caratacus kəˈræt.ə.kəs ⓤⓢ -ˈræt̬-
Caravaggio ˌkær.əˈvædʒ.i.əʊ, ˌkɑː.rəˈ-, -ˈvɑː.dʒi- ⓤⓢ ˌker.əˈvɑː.dʒi.oʊ, ˌkær-
caravan ˈkær.ə.væn, ˌ--ˈ- ⓤⓢ ˈker.ə.væn, ˈkær- **-s** -z **-ning** -ɪŋ
caravansar|y ˌkær.əˈvæn.sər|.i ⓤⓢ ˌker-, ˌkær- **-ies** -iz
caravanserai ˌkær.əˈvæn.sər.aɪ, -eɪ, -i ⓤⓢ ˌker-, ˌkær- **-s** -z
caravel ˈkær.ə.vel, ˌ--ˈ- ⓤⓢ ˈker.ə.vel, ˈkær- **-s** -z
caraway ˈkær.ə.weɪ ⓤⓢ ˈker-, ˈkær- **-s** -z ˈ**caraway ˌseed**
Carbery ˈkɑː.bər.i ⓤⓢ ˈkɑːr.ber-, -bɚ-
carbide ˈkɑː.baɪd ⓤⓢ ˈkɑːr- **-s** -z
carbine ˈkɑː.baɪn ⓤⓢ ˈkɑːr.biːn, -baɪn **-s** -z
carbineer ˌkɑː.bɪˈnɪəʳ, -bəˈ- ⓤⓢ ˌkɑːr.bəˈnɪr **-s** -z
carbohydrate ˌkɑː.bəʊˈhaɪ.dreɪt, -drɪt ⓤⓢ ˌkɑːr.boʊˈhaɪ.dreɪt, -bəˈ- **-s** -s
carbolic kɑːˈbɒl.ɪk ⓤⓢ kɑːrˈbɑː.lɪk carˌbolic ˈ**acid**
carbon ˈkɑː.bən ⓤⓢ ˈkɑːr- **-s** -z ˌ**carbon ˈcopy** ⓤⓢ ˈ**carbon ˌcopy**; ˌ**carbon diˈoxide**
carbonaceous ˌkɑː.bəʊˈneɪ.ʃəs ⓤⓢ ˌkɑːr.bəˈ-
carbonade ˌkɑː.bəˈneɪd, ˈ--- ⓤⓢ ˌkɑːr.bəˈneɪd **-s** -z
carbonara ˌkɑː.bəˈnɑː.rə ⓤⓢ ˌkɑːr.bəˈnɑːr.ə
carbonate *(n.)* ˈkɑː.bən.eɪt, -ɪt, -ət ⓤⓢ ˈkɑːr- **-s** -s
carbon|ate *(v.)* ˈkɑː.bən|.eɪt ⓤⓢ ˈkɑːr- **-ates** -eɪts **-ating** -eɪ.tɪŋ ⓤⓢ -eɪ.t̬ɪŋ **-ated** -eɪ.tɪd ⓤⓢ -eɪ.t̬ɪd
carbon|-date ˌkɑː.bən|ˈdeɪt ⓤⓢ ˌkɑːr- **-dates** -ˈdeɪts **-dating** -ˈdeɪ.tɪŋ ⓤⓢ -ˈdeɪ.t̬ɪŋ **-dated** -ˈdeɪ.tɪd ⓤⓢ -ˈdeɪ.t̬ɪd
carbonic kɑːˈbɒn.ɪk ⓤⓢ kɑːrˈbɑː.nɪk
carboniferous ˌkɑː.bəˈnɪf.ər.əs ⓤⓢ ˌkɑːr-
carbonization, -isa- ˌkɑː.bən.aɪˈzeɪ.ʃən, -ɪˈ- ⓤⓢ ˌkɑːr.bən.ɪˈ-

Cardinal Vowel

One of the vowels of the standard classification system used in phonetics.

Description

Phoneticians have always needed some way of classifying vowels which is independent of the vowel system of a particular language. With most consonants it is quite easy to observe how their articulation is organised, and to specify the place and manner of the constriction formed; vowels, however, are much less easy to observe.

Early in the 20th century, the English phonetician Daniel Jones worked out a set of "Cardinal Vowels" that students learning phonetics could be taught to make and which would serve as reference points that other vowels could be related to.

The vowels are located on the four-sided figure shown below:

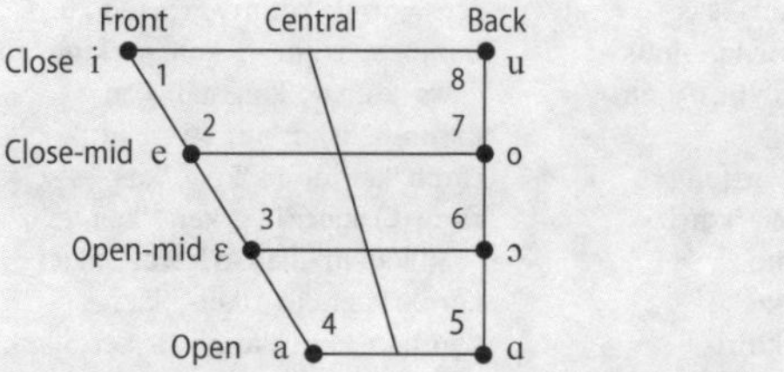

The primary cardinal vowels

The cardinal vowel figure is used to specify the qualities of the English vowels and diphthongs on pp xx and xx in the Introduction to this dictionary.

The Cardinal Vowel diagram is used both for rounded and unrounded vowels, and Jones proposed that there should be a **primary** set of Cardinal Vowels and a **secondary** set. The primary includes the unrounded front vowels [i e ɛ a], the back unrounded vowel [ɑ] and the back rounded vowels [ɔ o u], while the secondary set comprises the front rounded vowels [y ø œ ɶ], the back rounded vowel [ɒ] and the back unrounded vowels [ʌ ɤ ɯ].

Phonetic "ear-training" makes much use of the Cardinal Vowel system, and students can learn to identify and discriminate a very large number of different vowels in relation to the Cardinal vowels.

carboniz|e, -is|e ˈkɑː.bᵊn.aɪz ⓤⓢ ˈkɑːr- **-es** -ɪz **-ing** -ɪŋ **-ed** -d

carbonnade ˌkɑː.bᵊnˈeɪd, -ˈɑːd, ˈ--- ⓤⓢ ˌkɑːr.bᵊnˈeɪd **-s** -z

carbonyl ˈkɑː.bə.nɪl, -naɪl ⓤⓢ ˈkɑːr-, -niːl **-s** -z

Carborundum® ˌkɑː.bᵊrˈʌn.dəm ⓤⓢ ˌkɑːr.bɚ-

carboxyl kɑːˈbɒk.sɪl, -saɪl ⓤⓢ kɑːrˈbɑːk.sᵊl

carboy ˈkɑː.bɔɪ ⓤⓢ ˈkɑːr- **-s** -z

carbuncle ˈkɑː.bʌŋ.kl̩ ⓤⓢ ˈkɑːr- **-s** -z

carburation ˌkɑː.bjəˈreɪ.ʃᵊn, -bjʊˈ- ⓤⓢ ˌkɑːr.bə-, -bjə-

carburetter, carbure(t)tor ˌkɑː.bjəˈret.əʳ, -bjʊˈ-, ˈkɑː.bjə.ret.ə ⓤⓢ ˈkɑːr.bə.reɪ.t̬ɚ, -bjə- **-s** -z

carburization, -isa- ˌkɑː.bjə.raɪˈzeɪ.ʃᵊn, -bjʊ-, -rɪˈ- ⓤⓢ ˌkɑːr.bɚ.ɪˈ-, -bjɚ-

carburiz|e, -is|e ˈkɑː.bjə.raɪz, -bjʊ- ⓤⓢ ˈkɑːr.bə-, -bjə- **-es** -ɪz **-ing** -ɪŋ **-ed** -d

carcanet ˈkɑː.kə.net, -nɪt ⓤⓢ ˈkɑːr- **-s** -s

carcas|e ˈkɑː.kəs ⓤⓢ ˈkɑːr- **-es** -ɪz

carcass ˈkɑː.kəs ⓤⓢ ˈkɑːr- **-es** -ɪz

Carcassonne ˌkɑː.kəˈsɒn ⓤⓢ ˌkɑːr.kəˈsoʊn, -ˈsɔːn

Carchemish ˈkɑː.kə.mɪʃ, -kɪ-; kɑːˈkiː- ⓤⓢ ˈkɑːr.kə-; kɑːrˈkiː-

carcinogen kɑːˈsɪn.ə.dʒᵊn, -dʒen; ˈkɑː.sɪ.nə-, -sᵊn.ə- ⓤⓢ kɑːrˈsɪn.ə-; ˈkɑːr.sᵊn.ə- **-s** -z

carcinogenic ˌkɑː.sɪ.nəʊˈdʒen.ɪk, -sᵊn.əʊˈ- ⓤⓢ ˌkɑːr.sᵊn.oʊˈ-; kɑːrˌsɪn-

carcinom|a ˌkɑː.sɪˈnəʊ.m|ə ⓤⓢ ˌkɑːr.sᵊnˈoʊ- **-as** -əz **-ata** -ə.tə ⓤⓢ -ə.t̬ə

Carcroft ˈkɑː.krɒft ⓤⓢ ˈkɑːr.krɑːft

card kɑːd ⓤⓢ kɑːrd **-s** -z **-ing** -ɪŋ **-ed** -ɪd ˈ**card** ˌ**index**; ˈ**card** ˌ**key**; **put one's** ˌ**cards on the** ˈ**table**

cardamom, cardamum ˈkɑː.də.məm ⓤⓢ ˈkɑːr-, -mɑːm **-s** -z

cardboard ˈkɑːd.bɔːd ⓤⓢ ˈkɑːrd.bɔːrd

card-carrying ˈkɑːdˌkær.i.ɪŋ ⓤⓢ ˈkɑːrdˌker-, -ˌkær-

Cardenden ˌkɑː.dənˈdən ⓤⓢ ˌkɑːr-

Cardew ˈkɑː.djuː ⓤⓢ ˈkɑːr.duː

cardholder ˈkɑːdˌhəʊl.dəʳ ⓤⓢ ˈkɑːrdˌhoʊl.dɚ **-s** -z

cardiac ˈkɑː.di.æk ⓤⓢ ˈkɑːr- ˌ**cardiac a**ˈ**rrest**

cardiacal kɑːˈdaɪə.kᵊl ⓤⓢ kɑːr-

Cardiff ˈkɑː.dɪf ⓤⓢ ˈkɑːr-

cardigan ˈkɑː.dɪ.gən ⓤⓢ ˈkɑːr- **-s** -z

Cardigan ˈkɑː.dɪ.gən ⓤⓢ ˈkɑːr- **-shire** -ʃəʳ, -ˌʃɪəʳ ⓤⓢ -ʃɚ, -ʃɪr

Cardin ˈkɑː.dæ̃n, -dæn ⓤⓢ kɑːrˈdæn

cardinal ˈkɑː.dɪ.nᵊl, -dᵊn.ᵊl ⓤⓢ ˈkɑːr- **-s** -z ˌ**cardinal** ˈ**number**; ˌ**cardinal** ˈ**point**; ˌ**cardinal** ˈ**rule**; ˌ**cardinal** ˈ**vowel**

cardio- ˈkɑː.di.əʊ-, ˌkɑː.diˈɒ- ⓤⓢ ˈkɑːr.di.oʊ-, ˌkɑːr.diˈɑː-

Note: Prefix. Normally takes either primary or secondary stress on the first syllable, e.g. **cardiogram** /ˈkɑː.di.əʊ.græm ⓤⓢ ˈkɑːr.di.oʊ-/, **cardiological** /ˌkɑː.di.əʊˈlɒdʒ.ɪ.kᵊl ⓤⓢ ˌkɑːr.di.əˈlɑː.dʒɪ-/, or primary stress on the third syllable, e.g. **cardiology** /ˌkɑː.diˈɒl.ə.dʒi ⓤⓢ ˌkɑːr.diˈɑː.lə-/.

cardiogram ˈkɑː.di.əʊ.græm ⓤⓢ ˈkɑːr.di.oʊ- **-s** -z

cardiograph ˈkɑː.di.əʊ.grɑːf, -græf ⓤⓢ ˈkɑːr.di.oʊ.græf **-s** -s

cardiography ˌkɑː.diˈɒg.rə.fi ⓤⓢ ˌkɑːr.diˈɑː.grə-

cardioid ˈkɑː.di.ɔɪd ⓤⓢ ˈkɑːr- **-s** -z

cardiological ˌkɑː.di.əʊˈlɒdʒ.ɪ.kᵊl ⓤⓢ ˌkɑːr.di.əˈlɑː.dʒɪ-

cardiolog|y ˌkɑː.diˈɒl.ə.dʒ|i ⓤⓢ ˌkɑːr.diˈɑː.lə- **-ist/s** -ɪst/s

cardiometer ˌkɑː.di'ɒm.ɪ.təʳ, -mə- ⓤⓢ ˌkɑːr.di'ɑː.mə.t̬ɚ **-s** -z
cardiopulmonary ˌkɑː.di.əʊ'pʌl.mən.ər.i, -'pʊl- ⓤⓢ ˌkɑːr.di.oʊ'pʊl.mə.ner-, -'pʌl-
cardiovascular ˌkɑː.di.əʊ'væs.kjʊ.ləʳ, -kjə- ⓤⓢ ˌkɑːr.di.oʊ'væs.kjə.lɚ
cardoon kɑː'duːn ⓤⓢ kɑːr- **-s** -z
cardphone 'kɑːd.fəʊn ⓤⓢ 'kɑːrd.foʊn **-s** -z
cardpunch 'kɑːd.pʌntʃ ⓤⓢ 'kɑːrd- **-es** -ɪz
cardsharp 'kɑːd.ʃɑːp ⓤⓢ 'kɑːrd.ʃɑːrp **-s** -z **-er/s** -əʳ/z ⓤⓢ -ɚ/z
Cardwell 'kɑːd.wəl, -wel ⓤⓢ 'kɑːrd-
Cardy 'kɑː.di ⓤⓢ 'kɑːr-
card|y, card|ie 'kɑː.d|i ⓤⓢ 'kɑːr- **-ies** -iz
car|e keəʳ ⓤⓢ ker **-es** -z **-ing** -ɪŋ **-ed** -d **-er/s** -əʳ/z ⓤⓢ -ɚ/z
careen kə'riːn **-s** -z **-ing** -ɪŋ **-ed** -d
career kə'rɪəʳ ⓤⓢ -'rɪr **-s** -z **-ing** -ɪŋ **-ed** -d **ca'reers adˌvisor; ca'reers ˌoffice**
careerist kə'rɪə.rɪst ⓤⓢ -'rɪr.ɪst **-s** -s
carefree 'keə.friː ⓤⓢ 'ker-
careful 'keə.fəl, -fʊl ⓤⓢ 'ker- **-lest** -ɪst **-ly** -i **-ness** -nəs, -nɪs
caregiver 'keəˌgɪv.əʳ ⓤⓢ 'kerˌgɪv.ɚ **-s** -z
careless 'keə.ləs, -lɪs ⓤⓢ 'ker- **-ly** -li **-ness** -nəs, -nɪs
caress kə'res **-es** -ɪz **-ing/ly** -ɪŋ/li **-ed** -t
caret 'kær.ət, -ɪt, -et ⓤⓢ 'ker-, 'kær- **-s** -s
caretaker 'keəˌteɪ.kəʳ ⓤⓢ 'kerˌteɪ.kɚ **-s** -z **ˌcaretaker 'government** ⓤⓢ **'caretaker ˌgovernment**
Carew kə'ruː; 'keə.ri ⓤⓢ kə'ruː; 'ker.u, -i
careworn 'keə.wɔːn ⓤⓢ 'ker.wɔːrn
Carey 'keə.ri ⓤⓢ 'ker.i, 'kær-
carfare 'kɑː.feəʳ ⓤⓢ 'kɑːr.fer **-s** -z
Carfax 'kɑː.fæks ⓤⓢ 'kɑːr-
Cargill 'kɑː.gɪl, -'- ⓤⓢ 'kɑːr.gɪl, -'-
cargo 'kɑː.gəʊ ⓤⓢ 'kɑːr.goʊ **-(e)s** -z
carhop 'kɑː.hɒp ⓤⓢ 'kɑːr.hɑːp **-s** -s
Caria 'keə.ri.ə ⓤⓢ 'ker.i-
Carib 'kær.ɪb ⓤⓢ 'ker-, 'kær- **-s** -z
Caribbean ˌkær.ɪ'biː.ən, -ə-; kə'rɪb.i.ən ⓤⓢ ˌker.ɪ'biː-, ˌkær-; kə'rɪb.i-
Caribbees 'kær.ɪ.biːz ⓤⓢ 'ker-, 'kær-
caribou (C) 'kær.ɪ.buː ⓤⓢ 'ker-, 'kær- **-s** -z
caricatur|e 'kær.ɪ.kə.tʃʊəʳ, -tʃɔːʳ, -tjʊəʳ, ˌkær.ɪ.kə'tʃʊəʳ, -'tʃɔːʳ, -'tjʊəʳ ⓤⓢ 'ker.ə.kə.tʃʊr, 'kær-, -tʊr, -tʃɚ **-es** -z **-ing** -ɪŋ **-ed** -d
caricaturist 'kær.ɪ.kə.tʃʊə.rɪst, -tʃɔː-, -tjʊə-, ˌkær.ɪ.kə'tʃʊə.rɪst, -'tʃɔː-, -'tjʊə- ⓤⓢ 'ker.ə.kə.tʃʊr.ɪst, 'kær-, -tʊr-, -tʃɚ- **-s** -s
caries 'keə.riːz, -ri.iːz ⓤⓢ 'ker.iːz, -i.ɪz
carillon kær'ɪl.jən, kə'rɪl-, -ɒn; 'kær.ɪ.ljən, -əl.jən, -ɒn ⓤⓢ 'ker.ə.lɑːn, 'kær- **-s** -z
Carinthia kə'rɪnt.θi.ə, kær'ɪnt- ⓤⓢ kə'rɪnt-
carious 'keə.ri.əs ⓤⓢ 'ker.i-
Carisbrooke 'kær.ɪs.brʊk, -ɪz- ⓤⓢ 'ker-, 'kær-
carjack 'kɑː.dʒæk ⓤⓢ 'kɑːr- **-s** -z **-ing/s** -ɪŋ/z **-ed** -t **-er/s** -əz ⓤⓢ -ɚz
Carl kɑːl ⓤⓢ kɑːrl
Carla 'kɑː.lə ⓤⓢ 'kɑːr-
Carle kɑːl ⓤⓢ kɑːrl **-s** -z
Carless 'kɑː.ləs ⓤⓢ 'kɑːr-
Carleton 'kɑːl.tən ⓤⓢ 'kɑːrl-
Carlile kɑː'laɪl ⓤⓢ kɑːr-
Carlin 'kɑː.lɪn ⓤⓢ 'kɑːr-
Carling 'kɑː.lɪŋ ⓤⓢ 'kɑːr-
Carlingford 'kɑː.lɪŋ.fəd ⓤⓢ 'kɑːr.lɪŋ.fɚd
Carlisle kɑː'laɪl *locally:* '-- ⓤⓢ kɑːr'laɪl, kɚ'-; 'kɑːr.laɪl
Carlist 'kɑː.lɪst ⓤⓢ 'kɑːr- **-s** -s
Carlos 'kɑː.lɒs ⓤⓢ 'kɑːr.ləs, -loʊs
Carlovingian ˌkɑː.ləʊ'vɪn.dʒi.ən, -dʒən ⓤⓢ ˌkɑːr.lə'-
Carlow 'kɑː.ləʊ ⓤⓢ 'kɑːr.loʊ
Carlsbad 'kɑːlz.bæd ⓤⓢ 'kɑːrlz-
Carlsberg® 'kɑːlz.bɜːg ⓤⓢ 'kɑːrlz.bɝːg **-s** -z
Carlson 'kɑːl.sən ⓤⓢ 'kɑːrl-
Carlsruhe 'kɑːlzˌruː.ə ⓤⓢ 'kɑːrlz-
Carlton 'kɑːl.tən ⓤⓢ 'kɑːrl-
Carluccio kɑː'luː.tʃi.əʊ ⓤⓢ kɑːr'luː.tʃi.oʊ
Carluke kɑː'luːk ⓤⓢ kɑːr-
Carly 'kɑː.li ⓤⓢ 'kɑːr-
Carlyle kɑː'laɪl, '-- ⓤⓢ kɑːr'laɪl, '--
carmaker 'kɑːˌmeɪ.kəʳ ⓤⓢ 'kɑːrˌmeɪ.kɚ **-s** -z
car|man 'kɑː|.mən ⓤⓢ 'kɑːr- **-men** -mən, -men
Carmarthen kə'mɑː.ðən ⓤⓢ kɑːr'mɑːr- **-shire** -ʃəʳ, -ˌʃɪəʳ ⓤⓢ -ʃɚ, -ʃɪr
Carmel 'kɑː.mel, -məl, kɑː'mel ⓤⓢ 'kɑːr.mel, -məl; kɑːr'mel
Note: The form /kɑː'mel ⓤⓢ kɑːr-/ is preferred for the city in California.
Carmelite 'kɑː.məl.aɪt, -mɪ.laɪt, -mel.aɪt ⓤⓢ 'kɑːr.mə.laɪt, -mɪ-, -mel.aɪt **-s** -s
Carmen 'kɑː.men ⓤⓢ 'kɑːr-
Carmichael kɑː'maɪ.kəl, '--- ⓤⓢ 'kɑːr.maɪ-
Carmina Burana ˌkɑː.mɪ.nə.bə'rɑː.nə, kɑːˌmiː-, -bjʊ'-, -bʊ'- ⓤⓢ kɑːrˌmiː.nə.bə'-
carminative 'kɑː.mɪ.nə.tɪv, -mə- ⓤⓢ 'kɑːr.mə.nə.t̬ɪv **-s** -z
carmine 'kɑː.maɪn, -mɪn ⓤⓢ 'kɑːr-
Carnaby 'kɑː.nə.bi ⓤⓢ 'kɑːr- **'Carnaby ˌStreet**
Carnac 'kɑː.næk ⓤⓢ kɑːr'næk
carnage 'kɑː.nɪdʒ ⓤⓢ 'kɑːr-
Carnaghan 'kɑː.nə.gən, -hən ⓤⓢ 'kɑːr.nə.hæn
carnal 'kɑː.nəl ⓤⓢ 'kɑːr- **-ly** -i
carnality kɑː'næl.ə.ti, -ɪ.ti ⓤⓢ kɑːr'næl.ə.t̬i
Carnarvon kə'nɑː.vən ⓤⓢ kɑːr'nɑːr-
Carnatic kɑː'næt.ɪk ⓤⓢ kɑːr'næt̬-
carnation (C) kɑː'neɪ.ʃən ⓤⓢ kɑːr- **-s** -z
Carné kɑː'neɪ ⓤⓢ kɑːr-
Carnegie kɑː'neg.i, -'neɪ.gi, -'niː-; 'kɑː.nə.gi ⓤⓢ 'kɑːr.nə.gi; kɑːr'neɪ-, -'neg.i, -'niː.gi **Carˌnegie 'Hall**
carnelian kɑː'niː.li.ən, kə- ⓤⓢ kɑːr-, -'niːl.jən **-s** -z
carnet 'kɑː.neɪ ⓤⓢ kɑːr'neɪ **-s** -z
Carnforth 'kɑːn.fɔːθ, -fəθ ⓤⓢ 'kɑːrn.fɔːrθ, -fɚθ
carnival 'kɑː.nɪ.vəl ⓤⓢ 'kɑːr.nə- **-s** -z
carnivore 'kɑː.nɪ.vɔːʳ, -nə- ⓤⓢ 'kɑːr.nə.vɔːr **-s** -z
carnivorous kɑː'nɪv.ər.əs ⓤⓢ kɑːr-
Carnochan 'kɑː.nə.kən, -nɒk.ən, -nɒx- ⓤⓢ 'kɑːr.nə.kən, -nɑː.kən
Carnoustie kɑː'nuː.sti ⓤⓢ kɑːr-
carob 'kær.əb ⓤⓢ 'ker-, 'kær- **-s** -z
carol (C) 'kær.əl ⓤⓢ 'ker-, 'kær- **-s** -z **-(l)ing** -ɪŋ **-(l)ed** -d **'carol ˌsinger**
Carole 'kær.əl ⓤⓢ 'ker-, 'kær-
Carolina ˌkær.əl'aɪ.nə ⓤⓢ ˌker.ə'laɪ-, ˌkær-
Caroline 'kær.əl.aɪn, -ɪn ⓤⓢ 'ker.ə.laɪn, 'kær-, -əl.ɪn
carolus (C) 'kær.əl.əs ⓤⓢ 'ker-, 'kær- **-es** -ɪz
Carolyn 'kær.əl.ɪn ⓤⓢ 'ker-, 'kær-
carotene 'kær.ə.tiːn ⓤⓢ 'ker-, 'kær-
carotid kə'rɒt.ɪd ⓤⓢ -'rɑː.t̬ɪd **-s** -z
carotin 'kær.ə.tɪn ⓤⓢ 'ker-, 'kær-
carousal kə'raʊ.zəl **-s** -z
carous|e kə'raʊz **-es** -ɪz **-ing** -ɪŋ **-ed** -d **-er/s** -əʳ/z ⓤⓢ -ɚ/z
carousel ˌkær.ə'sel, -ʊ'- ⓤⓢ 'ker.ə.sel, 'kær-, ˌ--'- **-s** -z
carp kɑːp ⓤⓢ kɑːrp **-s** -s **-ing** -ɪŋ **-ed** -t **-er/s** -əʳ/z ⓤⓢ -ɚ/z
carpaccio kɑː'pætʃ.i.əʊ, -'pætʃ.əʊ ⓤⓢ kɑːr'pɑːtʃ.oʊ
carpal 'kɑː.pəl ⓤⓢ 'kɑːr- **-s** -z
Carpathian kɑː'peɪ.θi.ən ⓤⓢ kɑːr- **-s** -z
carpe diem ˌkɑː.peɪ'diː.em, -pi'- ⓤⓢ ˌkɑːr.pə'-, -peɪ'-
carpel 'kɑː.pel, -pəl ⓤⓢ 'kɑːr- **-s** -z
Carpentaria ˌkɑː.pən'teə.ri.ə, -pen'-, -pəm'- ⓤⓢ ˌkɑːr.pən'ter.i-
carpent|er (C) 'kɑː.pən.t|əʳ, -pɪn- ⓤⓢ 'kɑːr.pən.t̬|ɚ **-ers** -əz ⓤⓢ -ɚz **-ering** -ər.ɪŋ **-ered** -əd ⓤⓢ -ɚd
carpentry 'kɑː.pən.tri, -pɪn- ⓤⓢ 'kɑːr.pən-
carp|et 'kɑː.p|ɪt ⓤⓢ 'kɑːr.p|ət **-ets** -ɪts

US -əts **-eting** -ɪ.tɪŋ US -ə.t̬ɪŋ **-eted** -ɪ.tɪd US -ə.t̬ɪd **'carpet ˌbroom; 'carpet ˌslipper; 'carpet ˌsweeper**
carpetbag 'kɑː.pɪt.bæg US 'kɑːr.pət- **-s** -z **-ging** -ɪŋ
carpetbagger 'kɑː.pɪtˌbæg.əʳ US 'kɑːr.pətˌbæg.ɚ **-s** -z
carpet-bomb 'kɑː.pɪt.bɒm US 'kɑːr.pət.bɑːm **-s** -z **-ing** -ɪŋ **-ed** -d
carport 'kɑː.pɔːt US 'kɑːr.pɔːrt **-s** -s
carp|us 'kɑː.p|əs US 'kɑːr- **-i** -aɪ, -iː
Carr kɑːʳ US kɑːr
carrag(h)een 'kær.ə.giːn, --'- US 'ker.ə.giːn, 'kær-
Carrara kə'rɑː.rə US kə'rɑːr.ə
Carrauntoohill ˌkær.ən'tuː.hᵊl US ˌker-, ˌkær-
carraway 'kær.ə.weɪ US 'ker-, 'kær- **-s** -z
Carrhae 'kær.iː US 'ker-, 'kær-
carriag|e 'kær.ɪdʒ US 'ker-, 'kær- **-es** -ɪz **'carriage ˌclock**
carriageway 'kær.ɪdʒ.weɪ US 'ker-, 'kær- **-s** -z
carrick (C) 'kær.ɪk US 'ker-, 'kær-
Carrickfergus ˌkær.ɪk'fɜː.gəs US ˌker.ɪk'fɝː-, ˌkær-
Carrie 'kær.i US 'ker-, 'kær-
carrier 'kær.i.əʳ US 'ker.i.ɚ, 'kær- **-s** -z **'carrier ˌbag; 'carrier ˌpigeon**
Carrington 'kær.ɪŋ.tən US 'ker-, 'kær-
carrion 'kær.i.ən US 'ker-, 'kær- **ˌcarrion 'crow** US **'carrion ˌcrow**
Carrodus 'kær.ə.dəs US 'ker-, 'kær-
Carroll 'kær.ᵊl US 'ker-, 'kær-
Carron 'kær.ᵊn US 'ker-, 'kær-
carrot 'kær.ət US 'ker-, 'kær- **-s** -s
carroty 'kær.ə.ti US 'ker.ə.t̬i, 'kær-
carrousel ˌkær.ə'sel, -ʊ'- US ˌker.ə'sel, ˌkær-, '--- **-s** -z
Carruthers kə'rʌð.əz US -ɚz
carr|y 'kær|.i US 'ker-, 'kær- **-ies** -iz **-ying** -i.ɪŋ **-ied** -id **-ier/s** -i.əʳ/z US -i.ɚ/z
carryall 'kær.i.ɔːl US 'ker.i.ɔːl, 'kær-, -ɑːl **-s** -z
carrycot 'kær.i.kɒt US 'ker.i.kɑːt, 'kær- **-s** -s
carryings-on ˌkær.i.ɪŋz'ɒn US ˌker.i.ɪŋz'ɑːn, ˌkær-
carry-on 'kær.i.ɒn US 'ker.i.ɑːn, 'kær- **-s** -z
carryout 'kær.i.aʊt US 'ker-, 'kær- **-s** -z
Carse kɑːs US kɑːrs
Carshalton kɑː'ʃɔːl.tᵊn, kə'- *old-fashioned local pronunciation:* keɪs'hɔː.tᵊn US kɑːr'ʃɔːl-, kɚ-, -'ʃɑːl-
carsick 'kɑː.sɪk US 'kɑːr- **-ness** -nəs, -nɪs
Carson 'kɑː.sᵊn US 'kɑːr-
Carstairs 'kɑː.steəz, ˌ-'- US 'kɑːr.sterz
cart (C) kɑːt US kɑːrt **-s** -s **-ing** -ɪŋ US 'kɑːr.t̬ɪŋ **-ed** -ɪd US 'kɑːr.t̬ɪd **-er/s** -əʳ/z US 'kɑːr.t̬ɚ/z **put the ˌcart before the 'horse**
Carta 'kɑː.tə US 'kɑːr.t̬ə
cartage 'kɑː.tɪdʒ US 'kɑːr.t̬ɪdʒ
Cartagena ˌkɑː.tə'geɪ.nə US ˌkɑːr.t̬ə'dʒiː.nə, -'heɪ-, -'geɪ-
carte (C) kɑːt US kɑːrt
carte blanche ˌkɑːt'blɑ̃ːntʃ US ˌkɑːrt'blɑːnʃ, -'blæntʃ
cartel kɑː'tel US kɑːr- **-s** -z
Carter 'kɑː.təʳ US 'kɑːr.t̬ɚ
Carteret *surname:* 'kɑː.tə.ret, -rɪt US 'kɑːr.t̬ɚ.ɪt *US place name:* ˌkɑː.tə'ret US ˌkɑːr.t̬ə'-
Cartesian kɑː'tiː.zi.ən, -ʒᵊn US kɑːr'tiː.ʒᵊn **-ism** -ɪ.zᵊm
Carteton 'kɑː.tə.tᵊn US 'kɑːr.t̬ə.tən
Carthage 'kɑː.θɪdʒ US 'kɑːr-
Carthaginian ˌkɑː.θə'dʒɪn.i.ən US ˌkɑːr- **-s** -z
cart-hors|e 'kɑːt.hɔːs US 'kɑːrt.hɔːrs **-es** -ɪz
Carthusian kɑː'θjuː.zi.ən, -'θuː- US kɑːr'θuː.ʒᵊn, -'θjuː- **-s** -z
Cartier 'kɑː.ti.eɪ US ˌkɑːr.ti'eɪ; kɑːr'tjeɪ
Cartier-Bresson ˌkɑː.ti.eɪ'bres.ɔ̃ːn US ˌkɑːr.tjeɪ.breɪ'sõʊn, -bres'õʊn
cartilag|e 'kɑː.tɪ.lɪdʒ, -tᵊl.ɪdʒ US 'kɑːr.t̬ᵊl.ɪdʒ **-es** -ɪz
cartilaginous ˌkɑː.tɪ'lædʒ.ɪ.nəs, -tᵊl'ædʒ-, -ᵊn.əs US ˌkɑːr.tə'lædʒ.ᵊn.əs
carting 'kɑː.tɪŋ US 'kɑːr.t̬ɪŋ
Cartland 'kɑːt.lənd US 'kɑːrt-
cartload 'kɑːt.ləʊd US 'kɑːrt.loʊd **-s** -z
Cartmel(e) 'kɑːt.mel, -mᵊl US 'kɑːrt-
cartographic ˌkɑː.təʊ'græf.ɪk, ˌkɑːr.t̬ə'- **-ally** -ᵊl.i, -li
cartograph|y kɑː'tɒg.rə.f|i US kɑːr'tɑː.grə- **-er/s** -əʳ/z US -ɚ/z
cartomancy 'kɑː.təʊ.mænt.si US 'kɑːr.t̬ə-
carton 'kɑː.tᵊn US 'kɑːr- **-s** -z
cartoon kɑː'tuːn US kɑːr- **-s** -z **-ist/s** -ɪst/s
cartouch|e, cartouch kɑː'tuːʃ US kɑːr- **-es** -ɪz
cartridg|e 'kɑː.trɪdʒ US 'kɑːr- **-es** -ɪz **'cartridge ˌpaper**
cartwheel 'kɑːt.hwiːl US 'kɑːrt- **-s** -z **-ing** -ɪŋ **-ed** -d
cartwright (C) 'kɑːt.raɪt US 'kɑːrt- **-s** -s
caruncle 'kær.əŋ.kl̩; kə'rʌŋ- US kə'rʌŋ-, ker'ʌŋ-, kær- **-s** -z
Carus 'keə.rəs US 'ker.əs, 'kɑːr-
Caruso kə'ruː.zəʊ, -səʊ US -soʊ, -zoʊ
Caruthers kə'rʌð.əz US -ɚz
carv|e kɑːv US kɑːrv **-es** -z **-ing/s** -ɪŋ/z **-ed** -d **'carving ˌknife**
carver (C) 'kɑː.vəʳ US 'kɑːr.vɚ **-s** -z
carver|y 'kɑː.vᵊr|.i US 'kɑːr- **-ies** -iz
Carville 'kɑː.vɪl US 'kɑːr-
Carwardine 'kɑː.wə.diːn US 'kɑːr.wɚ-
carwash 'kɑː.wɒʃ US 'kɑːr.wɑːʃ, -wɔːʃ **-es** -ɪz
Cary *surname:* 'keə.ri US 'ker.i *first name:* 'kær.i US 'ker.i, 'kær-
caryatid ˌkær.i'æt.ɪd, 'kær.i.ə.tɪd US ˌker.i'æt̬.ɪd, ˌkær-; kə'raɪ.ə.t̬ɪd **-s** -z **-es** -iːz
Caryll 'kær.ɪl, -ᵊl US 'ker-, 'kær-
Carysfort 'kær.ɪs.fɔːt, -əs- US 'ker.ɪs.fɔːrt, 'kær-
Casablanca ˌkæs.ə'blæŋ.kə US ˌkæs.ə'blæŋ.kə, ˌkɑː.sə'blɑːŋ.kə
Casals kə'sæls US -'sɑːlz, -'sælz
Casamassima ˌkæs.ə'mæs.ɪ.mə
Casanova ˌkæs.ə'nəʊ.və, ˌkæz- US ˌkæs.ə'noʊ-, ˌkæz-
Casaubon kə'sɔː.bᵊn; 'kæz.ə.bɒn, -ɔː- US kə'sɑː.bᵊn, -'sɔː-; 'kæz.ə.bɑːn
casbah (C) 'kæz.bɑː US 'kæz.bɑː, 'kɑːz- **-s** -z
cascad|e kæs'keɪd **-es** -z **-ing** -ɪŋ **-ed** -ɪd
cascara kæs'kɑː.rə, kə'skɑː- US kæs'ker.ə, -'kær- **-s** -z
cascarilla ˌkæs.kə'rɪl.ə
cas|e (C) keɪs **-es** -ɪz **-ing** -ɪŋ **-ed** -t **'case ˌending; ˌcase 'history; 'case ˌknife; 'case ˌlaw; 'case ˌshot; 'case ˌstudy**
casebook 'keɪs.bʊk **-s** -s
casein 'keɪ.siːn, -siː.ɪn US -siː.ɪn, -siːn
caseload 'keɪs.ləʊd US -loʊd **-s** -z
casemate 'keɪs.meɪt **-s** -s
casement 'keɪs.mənt **-s** -s
Casement 'keɪs.mənt
casern kə'zɜːn US -'zɝːn **-s** -z
casework 'keɪs.wɜːk US -wɝːk **-er/s** -əʳ/z US -ɚ/z
Casey 'keɪ.si
cash (C) kæʃ **-es** -ɪz **-ing** -ɪŋ **-ed** -t **-less** -ləs, -lɪs **'cash ˌcrop; 'cash ˌdesk; 'cash disˌpenser; 'cash ˌflow; 'cash maˌchine; 'cash ˌregister**
cash-and-carry ˌkæʃ.ᵊnd'kær.i, -ᵊŋ'- US -ᵊnd'ker-, -'kær-
cashback 'kæʃ.bæk
cashbook 'kæʃ.bʊk **-s** -s
cashbox 'kæʃ.bɒks US -bɑːks **-es** -ɪz
cashew 'kæʃ.uː; -'-, kə'ʃuː US 'kæʃ.uː; kə'ʃuː **-s** -z **'cashew ˌnut, ca'shew ˌnut** US **ca'shew ˌnut**
cashier (*n.*) kæʃ'ɪəʳ, kə'ʃɪəʳ US kæʃ'ɪr **-s** -z
cashier (*v.*) kə'ʃɪəʳ, kæʃ'ɪəʳ US kə'ʃɪr, kæʃ'ɪr **-s** -z **-ing** -ɪŋ **-ed** -d
cash-in-hand ˌkæʃ.ɪn'hænd *stress shift:* ˌcash-in-hand 'payment
cashless 'kæʃ.ləs, -lɪs
Cashmere *place:* 'kæʃ.mɪəʳ, ˌ-'- US 'kæʃ.mɪr **-s** -z

cashmere *fabric:* ˈkæʃ.mɪəʳ, ˌ-ˈ- (US) ˈkæʒ.mɪr, ˈkæʃ-
Cashmore ˈkæʃ.mɔːʳ (US) -mɔːr
cashpoint ˈkæʃ.pɔɪnt **-s** -s
Casimir ˈkæs.ɪ.mɪəʳ (US) -ə.mɪr
casing ˈkeɪ.sɪŋ **-s** -z
casino kəˈsiː.nəʊ (US) -noʊ **-s** -z
Casio® ˈkæs.i.əʊ (US) -oʊ
cask kɑːsk (US) kæsk **-s** -s **-ing** -ɪŋ **-ed** -t
casket ˈkɑː.skɪt (US) ˈkæs.kɪt **-s** -s
Caslon ˈkæz.lᵊn, -lɒn (US) -lᵊn, -lɑːn
Caspar ˈkæs.pəʳ, -pɑːʳ (US) -pɚ
Caspian ˈkæs.pi.ən
casque kæsk, kɑːsk (US) kæsk **-s** -s
Cass kæs
Cassandra kəˈsæn.drə, -ˈsɑːn-
Cassani kəˈsɑː.ni
cassareep ˈkæs.ə.riːp
cassata kəˈsɑː.tə, kæsˈɑː- (US) kəˈsɑː.t̬ə
cassation kæsˈeɪ.ʃᵊn, kəˈseɪ- (US) kəˈseɪ- **-s** -z
Cassatt kəˈsæt
cassava kəˈsɑː.və
Cassavetes ˌkæs.əˈviː.tiːz (US) -t̬iːz
Cassel(l) ˈkæs.ᵊl
casserol|e ˈkæs.ᵊr.əʊl (US) -ə.roʊl **-es** -z **-ing** -ɪŋ **-ed** -d
cassette kəˈset, kæsˈet (US) kəˈset **-s** -s **caˈssette reˌcorder**
cassia ˈkæs.i.ə
Cassidy ˈkæs.ə.di, -ɪ.di (US) -ə.di
Cassie ˈkæs.i
Cassil(l)is ˈkæs.ᵊlz, ˈkɑː.sᵊlz
Cassio ˈkæs.i.əʊ (US) -oʊ
Cassiopeia ˌkæs.i.əʊˈpiː.ə *as name of constellation also:* ˌkæs.iˈəʊ.pi- (US) ˌkæs.i.əˈpiː-
cassis kæsˈiːs, ˈ-- (US) kæsˈiːs
Cassius ˈkæs.i.əs (US) ˈkæʃ.əs, ˈkæs.i-
Cassivelaunus ˌkæs.ɪ.vɪˈlɔː.nəs, ˌ-ə-, -vəˈ- (US) -ɪ.vəˈlɑː-, -ˈlɔː-
cassock ˈkæs.ək **-s** -s **-ed** -t
cassoulet ˌkæs.ʊˈleɪ, ˈ--- (US) ˌkæs.ʊˈleɪ **-s** -z
cassowar|y ˈkæs.ə.weə.r|i, -wə- (US) -wer|.i **-ies** -iz
Cass Timberlane ˌkæsˈtɪm.bə.leɪn (US) -bɚ-
cast kɑːst (US) kæst **-s** -s **-ing** -ɪŋ **ˌcast-ˈiron**
Castali|a kæsˈteɪ.li|.ə (US) -li|.ə, -ˈteɪl.j|ə **-an/s** -ən/z
castanet ˌkæs.təˈnet **-s** -s
castaway ˈkɑː.stə.weɪ (US) ˈkæs.tə- **-s** -z
caste kɑːst (US) kæst **-s** -s
Castel Gandolfo ˌkæs.tel.gænˈdɒl.fəʊ (US) -ˈdɑːl.foʊ, -ˈdɔːl-
castellated ˈkæs.tə.leɪ.tɪd, -tɪ-, -tel.eɪ- (US) -tə.leɪ.t̬ɪd
Castelnau ˈkɑː.sᵊl.nɔː, -nəʊ (US) ˈkæs.ᵊl.nɔː, -noʊ
caster ˈkɑː.stəʳ (US) ˈkæs.tɚ **-s** -z **ˈcaster ˌsugar**
Casterbridge ˈkɑː.stə.brɪdʒ (US) ˈkæs.tɚ-
casti|gate ˈkæs.tɪ|.geɪt, -tə|.geɪt (US) -tə- **-gates** -geɪts **-gating** -geɪ.tɪŋ (US) -geɪ.t̬ɪŋ **-gated** -geɪ.tɪd (US) -geɪ.t̬ɪd **-gator/s** -geɪ.təʳ/z (US) -geɪ.t̬ɚ/z
castigation ˌkæs.tɪˈgeɪ.ʃᵊn, -təˈ- (US) -əˈ- **-s** -z
Castile kæsˈtiːl
Castilian kæsˈtɪl.i.ən, kəˈstɪl- (US) -i.ən, -jən **-s** -z
casting ˈkɑː.stɪŋ (US) ˈkæs.tɪŋ **-s** -z **ˈcasting ˌcouch; ˈcasting ˌnet; ˌcasting ˈvote**
castl|e (C) ˈkɑː.sl̩ (US) ˈkæs.l̩ **-es** -z **-ing** -ɪŋ **-ed** -d
Castlebar ˌkɑː.sl̩ˈbɑːʳ (US) ˌkæs.l̩ˈbɑːr
Castleford ˈkɑː.sl̩.fəd (US) ˈkæs.l̩.fɚd
Castlemaine ˈkɑː.sl̩.meɪn (US) ˈkæs.l̩-
Castlenau ˈkɑː.sl̩.nɔː (US) ˈkæs.l̩.nɑː, -nɔː
Castlerea(gh) ˈkɑː.sl̩.reɪ, ˌ--ˈ- (US) ˈkæs.l̩-
Castleton ˈkɑː.sl̩.tən (US) ˈkæs.l̩.t̬ən
Castlewellan ˌkɑː.sl̩ˈwel.ən (US) ˌkæs.l̩ˈ-
cast-off ˈkɑːst.ɒf, ˌ-ˈ- (US) ˈkæst.ɑːf **-s** -s
castor (C) ˈkɑː.stəʳ (US) ˈkæs.tɚ **-s** -z **ˌcastor ˈoil; ˈcastor ˌsugar**
cas|trate kæs|ˈtreɪt (US) ˈ-- **-trates** -ˈtreɪts (US) -treɪts **-trating** -ˈtreɪ.tɪŋ (US) -treɪ.t̬ɪŋ **-trated** -ˈtreɪ.tɪd (US) -treɪ.t̬ɪd
castration kæsˈtreɪ.ʃᵊn **-s** -z
castrat|o kæsˈtrɑː.t|əʊ (US) -t|oʊ **-i** -iː
Castries kæsˈtriːz, -ˈtriːs
Castro ˈkæs.trəʊ (US) -troʊ
Castrol® ˈkæs.trɒl (US) -trɑːl, -troʊl
casual ˈkæʒ.ju.əl, -zju- (US) ˈ-uː- **-ly** -i **ˌcasual ˈsex**
casualt|y ˈkæʒ.ju.əl.t|i, ˈkæz- (US) ˈkæʒ.uː- **-ies** -iz
casuarina ˌkæz.jʊəˈriː.nə, ˌkæʒ-, ˈkæʒ.jʊə.riː- (US) ˌkæʒ.uː.əˈriː- **-s** -z
casuist ˈkæz.ju.ɪst, ˈkæʒ- (US) ˈkæʒ.u- **-s** -s
casuistic ˌkæz.juˈɪs.tɪk, ˌkæʒ- (US) ˌkæʒ.uˈ- **-al** -ᵊl
casuistry ˈkæz.ju.ɪ.stri, ˈkæʒ- (US) ˈkæʒ.u-
casus belli ˌkɑː.sʊsˈbel.iː, ˌkeɪ.səsˈbel.aɪ (US) ˌkeɪ.səsˈbel.i, ˌkɑː-
Caswell ˈkæz.wəl, -wel (US) ˈkæz-, ˈkæs-
cat kæt **-s** -s **ˈcat ˌburglar; ˌcat's ˈwhiskers; let the ˌcat out of the ˈbag; play ˌcat and ˈmouse with; set the ˌcat among the ˈpigeons**
CAT kæt **ˈCAT ˌscan**
cata- ˈkæt.ə- (US) ˈkæt̬.ə-, kəˈtæ-

Note: Prefix. This usually takes primary or secondary stress on the first syllable, e.g. **catalogue** /ˈkæt.ə.lɒg (US) ˈkæt̬.ə.lɑːg/, or on the second syllable, e.g. **catastrophe** /kəˈtæs.trə.fi/.

catabolic ˌkæt.əˈbɒl.ɪk (US) ˌkæt̬.əˈbɑː.lɪk **-ally** -ᵊl.i, -li
catabolism kəˈtæb.ᵊl.ɪ.zᵊm
catachresis ˌkæt.əˈkriː.sɪs (US) ˌkæt̬.əˈ-
cataclysm ˈkæt.ə.klɪ.zᵊm (US) ˈkæt̬- **-s** -z
cataclysmal ˌkæt.əˈklɪz.məl (US) ˌkæt̬.əˈ- **-ly** -li
cataclysmic ˌkæt.əˈklɪz.mɪk (US) ˌkæt̬.əˈ- **-ally** -ᵊl.i, -li
catacomb ˈkæt.ə.kuːm, -kəʊm (US) ˈkæt̬.ə.koʊm **-s** -z
catafalque ˈkæt.ə.fælk (US) ˈkæt̬.ə.fælk, -fɔːlk, -fɑːlk **-s** -s
Catalan ˌkæt.əˈlæn, ˈ---, -lən (US) ˈkæt̬.ə.læn, -ᵊl.ən **-s** -z
catalectic ˌkæt.əˈlek.tɪk (US) ˌkæt̬.əˈlet̬.ɪk
cataleps|y ˈkæt.ə.lep.s|i (US) ˈkæt̬.ə- **-ies** -iz
cataleptic ˌkæt.əˈlep.tɪk (US) ˌkæt̬.əˈ-
catalexis ˈkæt.ə.lek.sɪs (US) ˈkæt̬.ə-
catalog ˈkæt.ᵊl.ɒg (US) ˈkæt̬.ə.lɑːg, -lɔːg **-s** -z **-ing** -ɪŋ **-ed** -d **-er/s** -əʳ/z (US) -ɚ/z **-ist/s** -ɪst/s
catalogu|e ˈkæt.ᵊl.ɒg (US) ˈkæt̬.ə.lɑːg, -lɔːg **-es** -z **-ing** -ɪŋ **-ed** -d **-er/s** -əʳ/z (US) -ɚ/z **-ist/s** -ɪst/s
Cataloni|a ˌkæt.əˈləʊ.ni|.ə, -nj|ə (US) -ˈloʊ-, -nj|ə **-an/s** -ən/z
catalpa kəˈtæl.pə **-s** -z
catalysis kəˈtæl.ə.sɪs, ˈ-ɪ-
catalyst ˈkæt.ᵊl.ɪst (US) ˈkæt̬- **-s** -s
catalytic ˌkæt.əˈlɪt.ɪk (US) ˌkæt̬ˈə- *stress shift, see compound:* **ˌcatalytic conˈverter**
catamaran ˌkæt.ə.məˈræn, ˈkæt.ə.mə.ræn (US) ˌkæt̬.ə.məˈræn **-s** -z
Catania kəˈteɪ.ni.ə, -ˈtɑː-, -njə (US) -njə, -ni.ə
cataphora kəˈtæf.ᵊr.ə
cataphoric ˌkæt.əˈfɒr.ɪk (US) ˌkæt̬.əˈfɔːr-
cataplasm ˈkæt.ə.plæz.ᵊm (US) ˈkæt̬- **-s** -z
cata|pult ˈkæt.ə|.pʌlt (US) ˈkæt̬- **-pults** -pʌlts **-pulting** -pʌl.tɪŋ (US) -pʌl.t̬ɪŋ **-pulted** -pʌl.tɪd (US) -pʌl.t̬ɪd
cataract ˈkæt.ᵊr.ækt (US) ˈkæt̬.ər.ækt **-s** -s
catarrh kəˈtɑːʳ, kætˈɑːʳ (US) kəˈtɑːr **-s** -z **-al** -ᵊl
catastas|is kəˈtæs.tə.s|ɪs **-es** -iːz
catastrophe kəˈtæs.trə.fi **-s** -z
catastrophic ˌkæt.əˈstrɒf.ɪk (US) ˌkæt̬.əˈstrɑː.fɪk **-ally** -ᵊl.i, -li

catatonia ˌkæt.əˈtəʊ.ni.ə Ⓤⓢ ˌkæt̬.əˈtoʊ-
catatonic ˌkæt.əˈtɒn.ɪk Ⓤⓢ ˌkæt̬.əˈtɑː.nɪk
catawba (C) kəˈtɔː.bə Ⓤⓢ -ˈtɔː-, -ˈtɑː-
catbird ˈkæt.bɜːd Ⓤⓢ -bɝːd **-s** -z
catboat ˈkæt.bəʊt Ⓤⓢ -boʊt **-s** -s
catcall ˈkæt.kɔːl Ⓤⓢ -kɔːl, -kɑːl **-s** -z **-ing** -ɪŋ **-ed** -d
catch kætʃ **-es** -ɪz **-ing** -ɪŋ **caught** kɔːt Ⓤⓢ kɑːt, kɔːt
catch-22 (C) ˌkætʃˌtwen.tiˈtuː Ⓤⓢ -t̬iˈ-
catchall ˈkætʃ.ɔːl Ⓤⓢ -ɔːl, -ɑːl **-s** -z
catcher ˈkætʃ.əʳ Ⓤⓢ -ɚ **-s** -z
catching ˈkætʃ.ɪŋ
catchment ˈkætʃ.mənt **-s** -s ˈ**catchment** ˌ**area**
catchpenn|y ˈkætʃ.pen|.i **-ies** -iz
catchphras|e ˈkætʃ.freɪz **-es** -ɪz
catchpole (C) ˈkætʃ.pəʊl Ⓤⓢ -poʊl **-s** -z
catchpoll ˈkætʃ.pəʊl Ⓤⓢ -poʊl **-s** -z
catchword ˈkætʃ.wɜːd Ⓤⓢ -wɝːd **-s** -z
catch|y ˈkætʃ|.i **-ier** -i.əʳ Ⓤⓢ -i.ɚ **-iest** -i.ɪst, -i.əst **-iness** -ɪ.nəs, -ɪ.nɪs
catechism ˈkæt.ə.kɪ.zᵊm, ˈ-ɪ- Ⓤⓢ ˈkæt̬.ə- **-s** -z
catechist ˈkæt.ə.kɪst, ˈ-ɪ- Ⓤⓢ ˈkæt̬.ə- **-s** -s
catechiz|e, -is|e ˈkæt.ə.kaɪz, ˈ-ɪ- Ⓤⓢ ˈkæt̬.ə- **-es** -ɪz **-ing** -ɪŋ **-ed** -d **-er/s** -əʳ/z Ⓤⓢ -ɚ/z
catechu ˈkæt.ə.tʃuː, ˈ-ɪ- Ⓤⓢ ˈkæt̬.ə.tʃuː, -kjuː
catechumen ˌkæt.ɪˈkjuː.men, -əˈ-, -mɪn Ⓤⓢ ˌkæt̬.əˈkjuː.mən **-s** -z
categoric|al ˌkæt.əˈgɒr.ɪ.k|ᵊl, -ɪˈ- Ⓤⓢ ˌkæt̬.əˈgɔːr- **-ally** -ᵊl.i, -li
categorization, -isa- ˌkæt.ə.gᵊr.aɪˈzeɪ.ʃᵊn, ˌ-ɪ-, -ɪˈ- Ⓤⓢ ˌkæt̬.ə.gɚ.ɪˈ- **-s** -z
categoriz|e, -is|e ˈkæt.ə.gᵊr.aɪz, ˈ-ɪ- Ⓤⓢ ˈkæt̬.ə.gə.raɪz **-es** -ɪz **-ing** -ɪŋ **-ed** -d
categor|y ˈkæt.ə.gᵊr|.i, ˈ-ɪ- Ⓤⓢ ˈkæt̬.ə.gɔːr- **-ies** -iz
catenar|y kəˈtiː.nᵊr|.i **-ies** -iz
caten|ate ˈkæt.ɪ.n|eɪt, ˈ-ə- Ⓤⓢ ˈkæt.ᵊn|.eɪt **-ates** -eɪts **-ating** -eɪ.tɪŋ Ⓤⓢ -eɪ.t̬ɪŋ **-ated** -eɪ.tɪd Ⓤⓢ -eɪ.t̬ɪd
catenation ˌkæt.ɪˈneɪ.ʃᵊn, -əˈ- Ⓤⓢ ˌkæt.ənˈeɪ- **-s** -z
catenative kəˈtiː.nə.tɪv
cateniz|e, -is|e ˈkæt.ɪ.naɪz, ˈ-ə- Ⓤⓢ ˈkæt.ᵊn.aɪz **-es** -ɪz **-ing** -ɪŋ **-ed** -d
cat|er (C) ˈkeɪ.t|əʳ Ⓤⓢ -t̬|ɚ **-ers** -əz Ⓤⓢ -ɚz **-ering** -ᵊr.ɪŋ **-ered** -əd Ⓤⓢ -ɚd **-erer/s** -ᵊr.əʳ/z Ⓤⓢ -ɚ.ɚ/z
Caterham ˈkeɪ.tᵊr.əm Ⓤⓢ -t̬ɚ-
Caterina ˌkæt.ᵊrˈiː.nə Ⓤⓢ ˌkæt̬-
caterpillar ˈkæt.ə.pɪl.əʳ Ⓤⓢ ˈkæt̬.ɚ.pɪl.ɚ, ˈ-ə- **-s** -z
caterwaul ˈkæt.ə.wɔːl Ⓤⓢ ˈkæt̬.ɚ-, -wɑːl **-s** -z **-ing** -ɪŋ **-ed** -d
Catesby ˈkeɪts.bi
catfish ˈkæt.fɪʃ **-es** -ɪz
Catford ˈkæt.fəd Ⓤⓢ -fɚd
catgut ˈkæt.gʌt
Cathar ˈkæθ.əʳ, -ɑːʳ Ⓤⓢ -ɑːr **-ism** -ɪ.zᵊm **-ist/s** -ɪst/s
Catharine ˈkæθ.ᵊr.ɪn, ˈkæθ.rɪn
cathars|is kəˈθɑː.s|ɪs, kæθˈɑː- Ⓤⓢ kəˈθɑːr- **-es** -iːz
cathartic kəˈθɑː.tɪk, kæθˈɑː- Ⓤⓢ kəˈθɑːr.t̬ɪk **-s** -s
Cathay kæθˈeɪ, kəˈθeɪ
Cathcart ˈkæθ.kət, -kɑːt; kæθˈkɑːt, kəθ- Ⓤⓢ ˈkæθ.kɑːrt, -kɚt; kæθˈkɑːrt, kəθ-
cathead ˈkæt.hed **-s** -z
cathedra kəˈθiː.drə, -ˈθed.rə Ⓤⓢ kəˈθiː.drə, ˈkæθ.ə- **-s** -z
cathedra *(in phrase* **ex cathedra***)* kəˈθiː.drə, kæθˈed.rɑː, kəˈθed-
cathedral kəˈθiː.drᵊl **-s** -z
Cather ˈkæð.əʳ Ⓤⓢ -ɚ
Catherine ˈkæθ.ᵊr.ɪn, ˈkæθ.rɪn ˈ**catherine** ˌ**wheel**
catheter ˈkæθ.ɪ.təʳ, ˈ-ə- Ⓤⓢ -ət̬.ɚ **-s** -z
catheterization, -isa- ˌkæθ.ɪ.tᵊr.aɪˈzeɪ.ʃᵊn, ˌ-ə-, -ɪˈ- Ⓤⓢ -ə.t̬ɚ.ɪˈ-
catheteriz|e, -is|e ˈkæθ.ɪ.tᵊr.aɪz, ˈ-ə- Ⓤⓢ ˈ-ə.t̬ɚ- **-es** -ɪz **-ing** -ɪŋ **-ed** -d
cathetometer ˌkæθ.ɪˈtɒm.ɪ.təʳ, -əˈ-, ˈ-ə- Ⓤⓢ -əˈtɑː.mə.t̬ɚ **-s** -z
cathex|is kəˈθek.s|ɪs, kæθˈek- **-es** -iːz
Cathleen ˈkæθ.liːn, -ˈ- Ⓤⓢ -ˈ-, ˈ--
cathode ˈkæθ.əʊd Ⓤⓢ -oʊd **-s** -z ˌ**cathode** ˈ**ray**; ˌ**cathode-**ˈ**ray** ˌ**tube**
catho|lic (C) ˈkæθ.ᵊl.ɪk **-s** -s
catholicism (C) kəˈθɒl.ɪ.sɪ.zᵊm, ˈ-ə- Ⓤⓢ -ˈθɑː.lə-
catholicity (C) ˌkæθ.əʊˈlɪs.ə.ti, -ɪ.ti Ⓤⓢ ˌkæθ.əˈlɪs.ə.t̬i
catholiciz|e, -is|e kəˈθɒl.ɪ.saɪz, ˈ-ə- Ⓤⓢ -ˈθɑː.lə- **-es** -ɪz **-ing** -ɪŋ **-ed** -d
Cathy ˈkæθ.i
Catiline ˈkæt.ɪ.laɪn, -ᵊl.aɪn Ⓤⓢ -ɪ.laɪn, ˈ-ə-
cation ˈkæt.aɪən **-s** -z
catkin ˈkæt.kɪn **-s** -z
catlike ˈkæt.laɪk
catmint ˈkæt.mɪnt
catnap ˈkæt.næp **-s** -s **-ping** -ɪŋ **-ped** -t
catnip ˈkæt.nɪp
Cato ˈkeɪ.təʊ Ⓤⓢ -t̬oʊ
cat-o'-nine-tails ˌkæt.əˈnaɪn.teɪlz Ⓤⓢ ˌkæt̬-
Cator ˈkeɪ.təʳ Ⓤⓢ -t̬ɚ
Catriona kəˈtriː.ə.nə, kæˈtriː-, -triː.nə, ˌkæt.riˈəʊ.nə Ⓤⓢ -ˈoʊ-
cat's-cradle ˌkætsˈkreɪ.dl̩ Ⓤⓢ ˌ-ˈ--, ˈ-ˌ--
cat's-eye ˈkæts.aɪ **-s** -z
Catshill kætsˈhɪl *stress shift:* ˌCatshill ˈstores
Catskill ˈkæt.skɪl
catsuit ˈkæt.suːt, -sjuːt Ⓤⓢ -suːt **-s** -s
catsup ˈkæt.səp, ˈkætʃ.əp, ˈketʃ.əp **-s** -s
Cattegat ˈkæt.ɪ.gæt Ⓤⓢ ˈkæt̬-
Cattell kætˈel, kəˈtel
Catterick ˈkæt.ᵊr.ɪk Ⓤⓢ ˈkæt̬-
Cattermole ˈkæt.ə.məʊl Ⓤⓢ ˈkæt̬.ɚ.moʊl
catter|y ˈkæt.ᵊr|.i Ⓤⓢ ˈkæt̬- **-ies** -iz
cattish ˈkæt.ɪʃ Ⓤⓢ ˈkæt̬-
cattle ˈkæt.l̩ Ⓤⓢ ˈkæt̬- ˈ**cattle** ˌ**grid**; ˈ**cattle** ˌ**market**; ˈ**cattle** ˌ**pen**; ˈ**cattle** ˌ**truck**
cattle-show ˈkæt.l̩.ʃəʊ Ⓤⓢ ˈkæt̬.l̩.ʃoʊ **-s** -z
catt|y ˈkæt|.i Ⓤⓢ ˈkæt̬- **-ier** -i.əʳ Ⓤⓢ -i.ɚ **-iest** -i.ɪst, -i.əst **-ily** -ɪ.li, -ᵊl.i **-iness** -ɪ.nəs, -ɪ.nɪs
Catullus kəˈtʌl.əs
catwalk ˈkæt.wɔːk Ⓤⓢ -wɑːk, -wɔːk **-s** -s
Caucasi|a kɔːˈkeɪ.ʒ|ə, -ʒi|.ə, -zi- Ⓤⓢ kɑːˈkeɪ.ʒ|ə, kɔː-, -ʃ|ə **-an/s** -ən/z
Caucasus ˈkɔː.kə.səs, -zəs Ⓤⓢ ˈkɑː-, ˈkɔː-
caucus ˈkɔː.kəs Ⓤⓢ ˈkɑː-, ˈkɔː- **-es** -ɪz
caudal ˈkɔː.dᵊl Ⓤⓢ ˈkɑː-, ˈkɔː-
caudate ˈkɔː.deɪt Ⓤⓢ ˈkɑː-, ˈkɔː-
caudillo kaʊˈdiː.əʊ, kɔːˈdɪl-, -jəʊ Ⓤⓢ kaʊˈdiː.joʊ, -ˈdɪl- **-s** -z
Caudine ˈkɔː.daɪn Ⓤⓢ ˈkɑː-, ˈkɔː-
caudle (C) ˈkɔː.dl̩ Ⓤⓢ ˈkɑː-, ˈkɔː-
caught *(from* **catch***)* kɔːt Ⓤⓢ kɑːt, kɔːt
caul kɔːl Ⓤⓢ kɑːl, kɔːl **-s** -z
cauldron ˈkɔːl.drᵊn, ˈkɒl- Ⓤⓢ ˈkɑːl-, ˈkɔːl- **-s** -z
Caulfield ˈkɔː.fiːld, ˈkɔːl- Ⓤⓢ ˈkɑː-, ˈkɔː-, ˈkɑːl-, ˈkɔːl-
cauliflower ˈkɒl.ɪˌflaʊəʳ Ⓤⓢ ˈkɑː.lɪˌflaʊɚ, ˈkɔː- **-s** -z ˌ**cauliflower** ˈ**ear**
caulk kɔːk Ⓤⓢ kɑːk, kɔːk **-s** -s **-ing** -ɪŋ **-ed** -t
caulker ˈkɔː.kəʳ Ⓤⓢ ˈkɑː.kɚ, ˈkɔː- **-s** -z
causa ˈkaʊ.sɑː, -zɑː
causal ˈkɔː.zᵊl Ⓤⓢ ˈkɑː-, ˈkɔː- **-ly** -i
causality kɔːˈzæl.ə.ti, -ɪ.ti Ⓤⓢ kɑːˈzæl.ə.t̬i, kɔː-
causa mortis ˌkaʊ.sɑːˈmɔː.tɪs, -zɑːˈ- Ⓤⓢ -mɔːr.t̬ɪs
causation kɔːˈzeɪ.ʃᵊn Ⓤⓢ kɑː-, kɔː-
causative ˈkɔː.zə.tɪv Ⓤⓢ ˈkɑː.zə.t̬ɪv, ˈkɔː- **-ly** -li
caus|e kɔːz Ⓤⓢ kɑːz, kɔːz **-es** -ɪz **-ing** -ɪŋ **-ed** -d
cause(s) célèbre(s) ˌkɔːz.selˈeb.rə, ˌkəʊz-, -səˈleb-, -ˈleɪ.brə Ⓤⓢ ˌkɑːz.səˈleb.rə, ˌkɔːz-, ˌkoʊz-
causeless ˈkɔːz.ləs, -lɪs Ⓤⓢ ˈkɑːz-, ˈkɔːz- **-ly** -li

Pronouncing the letters CC

The consonant digraph **cc** has two pronuncations: /ks/ and /k/.

Before the vowel letters **i** or **e**, it is pronounced as /ks/, e.g.:

accident /ˈæk.sɪ.dᵊnt/

In most other situations, **cc** is pronounced as /k/, e.g.:

acclaim /əkˈleɪm/

In addition

The word *flaccid* has two possible pronunciations.

/ˈflæk.sɪd, ˈflæs.ɪd/

Words borrowed from Italian may have /tʃ/, e.g.:

cappuccino /ˌkæp.ʊˈtʃiː.nəʊ/ US /-əˈtʃiː.noʊ/

causerie ˈkəʊ.zᵊr.i, -iː US ˌkoʊ.zəˈriː **-s** -z

causeway ˈkɔːz.weɪ US ˈkɑːz-, ˈkɔːz- **-s** -z

caustic ˈkɔː.stɪk, ˈkɒs.tɪk US ˈkɑː.stɪk, ˈkɔː- **-al** -ᵊl **-ally** -ᵊl.i, -li **ˌcaustic ˈsoda**

causticity kɔːˈstɪs.ə.ti, kɒsˈtɪs-, -ɪ.ti US kɑːˈstɪs.ə.t̬i, kɔː-

cauterization, -isa- ˌkɔː.tᵊr.aɪˈzeɪ.ʃᵊn, -ɪˈ- US ˌkɑː.t̬ɚ.ɪˈ-, ˌkɔː- **-s** -z

cauteriz|e, -is|e ˈkɔː.tᵊr.aɪz US ˈkɑː.t̬ə.raɪz, ˈkɔː- **-es** -ɪz **-ing** -ɪŋ **-ed** -d

cauter|y ˈkɔː.tᵊr|.i US ˈkɑː.t̬ɚ-, ˈkɔː- **-ies** -iz

Cauthen ˈkɔː.θᵊn US ˈkɑː-, ˈkɔː-

caution ˈkɔː.ʃᵊn US ˈkɑː-, ˈkɔː- **-s** -z **-ing** -ɪŋ **-ed** -d **-er/s** -əʳ/z US -ɚ/z **ˈcaution ˌmoney; throw ˌcaution to the ˈwind**

cautionary ˈkɔː.ʃᵊn.ᵊr.i, -ʃᵊn.ri US ˈkɑː.ʃᵊn.er-, ˈkɔː- **ˌcautionary ˈtale**

cautious ˈkɔː.ʃəs US ˈkɑː-, ˈkɔː- **-ly** -li **-ness** -nəs, -nɪs

cavalcade ˌkæv.ᵊlˈkeɪd, ˈ--- **-s** -z

cavalier ˌkæv.ᵊlˈɪəʳ US -əˈlɪr **-s** -z

Cavalleria Rusticana kə.væl.əˌriː.ə.rʊs.tɪˈkɑː.nə, ˌkæv.ᵊl-, -ˌrɪə-

cavalr|y ˈkæv.ᵊl.r|i **-ies** -iz

cavalry|man ˈkæv.ᵊl.ri|.mən, -mæn **-men** -mən, -men

Cavan ˈkæv.ᵊn

Cavanagh ˈkæv.ə.nə

Cavanaugh ˈkæv.ə.nɔː US -nɑː, -nɔː

cavatina ˌkæv.əˈtiː.nə **-s** -z

cav|e (C) *(n. v.)* keɪv **-es** -z **-ing** -ɪŋ **-ed** -d **-er/s** -əʳ/z US -ɚ/z **ˈcave ˌdweller**

cave *beware:* ˈkeɪ.vi

caveat ˈkæv.i.æt, ˈkeɪ.vi- US ˈkæv.i-, ˈkeɪ.vi-, ˈkɑː- **-s** -s

caveat emptor ˌkæv.i.ætˈemp.tɔːʳ, ˌkeɪ.vi-, -təʳ US -tɔːr, ˌkɑː-, -ɑːtˈ-, -tɚ

Cavell ˈkæv.ᵊl, kəˈvel

Note: The family of Nurse Edith Cavell pronounces /ˈkæv.ᵊl/.

Pronouncing the letters CCH

The consonant letter combination **cch** only has one possible realisation: /k/, e.g.:

saccharine /ˈsæk.ᵊr.ɪn/

cave|man ˈkeɪv|.mæn **-men** -men

Cavendish ˈkæv.ᵊn.dɪʃ

cavern ˈkæv.ᵊn, -ɜːn US -ɚn **-s** -z

cavernous ˈkæv.ᵊn.əs US -ɚn- **-ly** -li

Caversham ˈkæv.ə.ʃəm US ˈ-ɚ-

cave|woman ˈkeɪv|ˌwʊm.ən **-women** -ˌwɪm.ɪn

caviar(e) ˈkæv.i.ɑːʳ, ˌ--ˈ- US ˈkæv.i.ɑːr

cavil ˈkæv.ᵊl, -ɪl **-s** -z **-(l)ing** -ɪŋ **-(l)ed** -d **-(l)er/s** -əʳ/z US -ɚ/z

cavit|y ˈkæv.ə.t|i, -ɪ.t|i US -ə.t̬|i **-ies** -iz

ca|vort kə|ˈvɔːt US -ˈvɔːrt **-vorts** -ˈvɔːts US -ˈvɔːrts **-vorting** -ˈvɔː.tɪŋ US -ˈvɔːr.t̬ɪŋ **-vorted** -ˈvɔː.tɪd US -ˈvɔːr.t̬ɪd

cav|y ˈkeɪ.v|i **-ies** -iz

caw kɔː US kɑː, kɔː **-s** -z **-ing** -ɪŋ **-ed** -d

Cawdor ˈkɔː.dəʳ, -dɔːʳ US ˈkɑː.dɚ, ˈkɔː-, -dɔːr

Cawdrey ˈkɔː.dri US ˈkɑː-, ˈkɔː-

Cawley ˈkɔː.li US ˈkɑː-, ˈkɔː-

Cawse kɔːz US kɑːz, kɔːz

Caxton ˈkæk.stᵊn

cay kiː, keɪ **-s** -z

cayenne (C) keɪˈen US kaɪ-, keɪ- *stress shift:* **ˌcayenne ˈpepper**

Cayley ˈkeɪ.li

cayman (C) ˈkeɪ.mən **-s** -z **ˈCayman ˌIslands**

Cazenove ˈkæz.ᵊn.əʊv US -oʊv

CB ˌsiːˈbiː

CBC ˌsiː.biːˈsiː

CBE ˌsiː.biːˈiː

CBI ˌsiː.biːˈaɪ

CBS ˌsiː.biːˈes *stress shift:* ˌCBS ˈrecords

cc ˌsiːˈsiː

CD ˌsiːˈdiː **-s** -z **ˌCˈD ˌplayer**

CDI ˌsiː.diːˈaɪ

Cdr. *(abbrev. for* **commander***)* kəˈmɑːn.dəʳ US -ˈmæn.dɚ

CD-ROM ˌsiː.diːˈrɒm US -ˈrɑːm **-s** -z

CDT ˌsiː.diːˈtiː

ceas|e siːs **-es** -ɪz **-ing** -ɪŋ **-ed** -t

cease-fire ˈsiːs.faɪəʳ US -faɪɚ

ceaseless ˈsiː.sləs, -slɪs **-ly** -li **-ness** -nəs, -nɪs

Ceausescu ˌtʃaʊˈʃes.kuː

Cebu siˈbuː

Cecil ˈses.ᵊl, -ɪl, ˈsɪs.ᵊl, -ɪl US ˈsiː.sᵊl, ˈses.ᵊl

Note: The family name of the Marquess of Exeter and that of the Marquess of Salisbury is /ˈsɪs.ᵊl, -ɪl/.

Cecile sesˈiːl, ˈ--, ˈses.ɪl, -ᵊl; US sɪˈsiːl

Cecilia sɪˈsiː.li.ə, sə-, -ˈsɪl.i- US -ˈsiːl.jə, -ˈsɪl-

Cecily ˈses.ɪ.li, ˈsɪs-, -ᵊl.i US ˈses-

cec|um ˈsiː.k|əm **-a** -ə

cedar ˈsiː.dəʳ US -dɚ **-s** -z

ced|e siːd **-es** -z **-ing** -ɪŋ **-ed** -ɪd

cedi ˈsiː.di **-s** -z

cedilla səˈdɪl.ə, sɪ- **-s** -z

Cedric ˈsed.rɪk, ˈsiː.drɪk

Ceefax® ˈsiː.fæks

Cefn-Mawr ˌkev.ᵊnˈmaʊəʳ US -ˈmaʊɚ

CEGB ˌsiː.iː.dʒiːˈbiː

ceilidh ˈkeɪ.li **-s** -z

ceiling ˈsiː.lɪŋ **-s** -z

celadon ˈsel.ə.dɒn, -dən US -dɑːn

celandine ˈsel.ən.daɪn, -diːn **-s** -z

Celanese® ˌsel.əˈniːz US -ˈniːz, -ˈniːs

celeb səˈleb, sɪ- **-s** -z

Celebes selˈiː.biz, səˈliː-, sɪ- US ˈsel.ə.biːz, səˈliː.biz

celebrant ˈsel.ə.brᵊnt, ˈ-ɪ- **-s** -s

cele|brate ˈsel.ə|.breɪt, ˈ-ɪ- **-brates** -breɪts **-brating** -breɪ.tɪŋ

(US) -breɪ.t̬ɪŋ **-brated** -breɪ.tɪd (US) -breɪ.t̬ɪd **-brator/s** -breɪ.təʳ/z (US) -breɪ.t̬ɚ/z
celebration ˌsel.əˈbreɪ.ʃᵊn, -ɪˈ- **-s** -z
celebratory ˌsel.əˈbreɪ.tᵊr.i, -ɪˈ-; -tri; ˈsel.ɪ.brə-, ˈ-ə- (US) ˈsel.ə.brə.tɔːr.i; səˈleb.rə-
celebrit|y səˈleb.rə.t|i, sɪ-, -rɪ- (US) səˈleb.rə.t̬|i **-ies** -iz
celeriac səˈler.i.æk, sɪ-;
celerity səˈler.ə.ti, sɪ-, -ɪ.ti (US) -ə.t̬i
Celeron® ˈsel.ᵊr.ɒn (US) -ɑːn
celery ˈsel.ᵊr.i
celeste (C) səˈlest, sɪ- **-s** -s
celestial (C) səˈles.ti.əl, sɪ- (US) ˈ-tʃᵊl **-ly** -i
celestine ˈsel.ə.staɪn, ˈ-ɪ-, -stɪn
Celestine ˈsel.ə.staɪn, ˈ-ɪ-; sɪˈles.taɪn, sə-, -tɪn, -tiːn **-s** -z
Celia ˈsiː.li.ə
celiac ˈsiː.li.æk
celibacy ˈsel.ə.bə.si, ˈ-ɪ-
celibatarian ˌsel.ə.bəˈteə.ri.ən, ˌ-ɪ- (US) -ˈter.i- **-s** -z
celibate ˈsel.ə.bət, ˈ-ɪ-, -bɪt **-s** -s
Céline selˈiːn, seɪˈliːn
cell sel **-s** -z
cellar ˈsel.əʳ (US) -ɚ **-s** -z
cellarage ˈsel.ᵊr.ɪdʒ
cellarer ˈsel.ᵊr.əʳ (US) -ɚ **-s** -z
cellaret ˌsel.ᵊrˈet, ˈsel.ᵊr.et (US) ˌsel.ɚˈet **-s** -s
cellarist ˈsel.ᵊr.ɪst **-s** -s
cellar|man ˈsel.ə|.mən, -mæn (US) -ɚ- **-men** -mən, -men
Cellini tʃelˈiː.ni, tʃɪˈliː-, tʃə-
cellist ˈtʃel.ɪst **-s** -s
cellmate ˈsel.meɪt **-s** -s
Cellnet® ˈsel.net
cello ˈtʃel.əʊ (US) -oʊ **-s** -z
Cellophane® ˈsel.ə.feɪn
cellphone ˈsel.fəʊn (US) -foʊn **-s** -z
cellular ˈsel.jə.ləʳ, -jʊ- (US) -lɚ ˌ**cellular** ˈ**phone**; ˌ**cellular** ˈ**radio**
cellule ˈsel.juːl **-s** -z
cellulite ˈsel.jə.laɪt, -jʊ-
celluloid (C) ˈsel.jə.lɔɪd, -jʊ-
cellulose ˈsel.jə.ləʊs, -jʊ- (US) -loʊs
Celsius ˈsel.si.əs (US) ˈsel.si.əs, -ʃəs
celt *axe:* selt **-s** -s
Celt *people, tribe:* kelt, selt **-s** -s *member of football or baseball team:* selt **-s** -s
Celtic *(of the people or tribe)* ˈkel.tɪk, ˈsel.tɪk
Note: In names of football and baseball teams /ˈsel.tɪk/; for **Sea** /ˈkel.tɪk/.
cembal|o ˈtʃem.bə.l|əʊ, ˈsem- (US) -loʊ **-os** -əʊz (US) -oʊz **-i** -iː
cement sɪˈment, sə- **-s** -s **-ing** -ɪŋ **-ed** -ɪd **ceˈment-**ˌ**mixer**
cementation ˌsiː.menˈteɪ.ʃᵊn **-s** -z
cementium sɪˈmen.ʃi.əm, sə-, ˈ-ti- (US) -t̬i-
cemeter|y ˈsem.ə.tr|i, ˈ-ɪ- (US) -ə.ter|.i **-ies** -iz
Cenci ˈtʃen.*t*ʃi
CENELEC ˈsen.ɪ.lek, ˈ-ə-
cenematics ˌsen.ɪˈmæt.ɪks, -əˈ- (US) -ˈmæt̬-
cenetics səˈnet.ɪks, sɪ- (US) -ˈnet̬-
CEng *(abbrev. for* **Chartered Engineer***)* ˌsiːˈendʒ, ˌtʃɑː.tədˌen.dʒɪˈnɪəʳ, -dʒəˈ- (US) ˌsiːˈendʒ, ˌtʃɑːr.t̬ɚdˌen.dʒɪˈnɪr, -dʒəˈ-
Cenis səˈniː, senˈiː
cenobite ˈsiː.nə.baɪt, ˈsen.ə- (US) ˈsen.ə- **-s** -s
cenotaph ˈsen.əʊ.tæf, -tɑːf (US) -ə.tæf **-s** -s
cens|e sen*t*s **-es** -ɪz **-ing** -ɪŋ **-ed** -t
censer ˈsen*t*.səʳ (US) -sɚ **-s** -z
cens|or ˈsen*t*.s|əʳ (US) -s|ɚ **-ors** -əz (US) -ɚz **-oring** -ᵊr.ɪŋ **-ored** -əd (US) -ɚd
censorial sen*t*ˈsɔː.ri.əl (US) -ˈsɔːr.i- **-ly** -i
censorian sen*t*ˈsɔː.ri.ən (US) -ˈsɔːr.i-
censorious sen*t*ˈsɔː.ri.əs (US) -ˈsɔːr.i- **-ly** -li **-ness** -nəs, -nɪs
censorship ˈsen*t*.sə.ʃɪp (US) -sɚ- **-s** -s
censurable ˈsen*t*.sjᵊr.ə.bl̩, -ʃᵊr- (US) -ʃɚ-
cens|ure ˈsen*t*.ʃ|əʳ, -sj|əʳ (US) ˈsen*t*.ʃ|ɚ **-ures** -əz (US) -ɚz **-uring** -ᵊr.ɪŋ **-ured** -əd (US) -ɚd
census ˈsen*t*.səs **-es** -ɪz ˈ**census** ˌ**paper**
cent sent **-s** -s
centage ˈsen.tɪdʒ
cental ˈsen.tᵊl **-s** -z
centaur ˈsen.tɔːʳ (US) -tɔːr **-s** -z
Centaur|us senˈtɔː.r|əs (US) -ˈtɔːr|.əs **-i** -aɪ, -iː
centaur|y ˈsen.tɔː.r|i (US) -tɔːr|.i **-ies** -iz
centavo senˈtɑː.vəʊ (US) -voʊ **-s** -z
centenarian ˌsen.tɪˈneə.ri.ən, -təˈ- (US) -tᵊnˈer.i- **-s** -z
centenar|y senˈtiː.nᵊr|.i, sᵊn-, -ˈten.ᵊr- (US) ˈsen.tᵊn.er-; senˈten.ᵊr- **-ies** -iz
centennial senˈten.i.əl, sᵊn- **-s** -z **-ly** -i
cent|er ˈsen.t|əʳ (US) -t̬|ɚ **-ers** -əz (US) -ɚz **-ering** -ᵊr.ɪŋ **-ered** -əd (US) -ɚd ˌ**center of** ˈ**gravity**; ˌ**center** ˈ**stage**
centerboard ˈsen.tə.bɔːd (US) -t̬ɚ.bɔːrd **-s** -z
center-field ˌsen.təˈfiːld (US) -t̬ɚˈ- **-s** -z **-er/s** -əʳ/z (US) -ɚ/z
centerfold ˈsen.tə.fəʊld (US) -t̬ɚ.foʊld **-s** -z
center-forward ˌsen.təˈfɔː.wəd (US) -t̬ɚˈfɔːr.wɚd **-s** -z
center-|half ˌsen.tə|ˈhɑːf (US) -t̬ɚ|ˈhæf **-halves** -ˈhɑːvz (US) -ˈhævz
centerpiec|e ˈsen.tə.piːs (US) -t̬ɚ- **-es** -ɪz
centesimal senˈtes.ɪ.mᵊl, ˈ-ə- **-ly** -i
centesim|o senˈtes.ɪ.m|əʊ, ˈ-ə- (US) -m|oʊ **-i** -aɪ, -iː **-os** -əʊz (US) -oʊz
centigrade ˈsen.tɪ.greɪd (US) -t̬ə-
centigram, centigramme ˈsen.tɪ.græm (US) -t̬ə- **-s** -z
centigram(me) ˈsen.tɪ.græm (US) -t̬ə- **-s** -z
centilitre, centiliter ˈsen.tɪˌliː.təʳ (US) -t̬əˌliː.t̬ɚ **-s** -z
centime ˈsɑ̃ː*n*.tiːm, ˈsɔ̃ː*n*-, ˈsɑːn-; -ˈ- (US) ˈsɑːn-, ˈsen- **-s** -z
centimetre, centimeter ˈsen.tɪˌmiː.təʳ (US) -t̬əˌmiː.t̬ɚ **-s** -z
centimo ˈsen.tɪ.məʊ (US) -moʊ **-s** -z
centipede ˈsen.tɪ.piːd (US) -t̬ə- **-s** -z
centipois|e ˈsen.tɪ.pɔɪz (US) -t̬ə- **-es** -ɪz
centner ˈsent.nəʳ (US) -nɚ **-s** -z
cento ˈsen.təʊ (US) -toʊ **-s** -z
CENTO ˈsen.təʊ (US) -toʊ
central (C) ˈsen.trᵊl **-ly** -i ˌ**Central** ˌ**African Re**ˈ**public**; ˌ**Central A**ˈ**merica**; ˌ**Central** ˈ**Daylight** ˌ**Time**; ˌ**central** ˈ**heating**; ˌ**central reser**ˈ**vation**; ˌ**Central** ˈ**Standard** ˌ**Time**
centralism ˈsen.trᵊl.ɪ.zᵊm
centralist ˈsen.trᵊl.ɪst **-s** -s
centrality senˈtræl.ə.ti, -ɪ.ti (US) -ə.t̬i
centralization, -isa- ˌsen.trᵊl.aɪˈzeɪ.ʃᵊn, -lɪˈ- (US) -lɪˈ-
centraliz|e, -is|e ˈsen.trᵊl.aɪz **-es** -ɪz **-ing** -ɪŋ **-ed** -d
cent|re ˈsen.t|əʳ (US) -t̬|ɚ **-res** -əz (US) -ɚz **-ring** -ᵊr.ɪŋ **-red** -əd (US) -ɚd ˌ**centre of** ˈ**gravity**; ˌ**centre** ˈ**stage**
centreboard ˈsen.tə.bɔːd (US) -t̬ɚ.bɔːrd **-s** -z
centre-field ˌsen.təˈfiːld (US) -t̬ɚ- **-s** -z **-er/s** -əʳ/z (US) -ɚ/z
centrefold ˈsen.tə.fəʊld (US) -t̬ɚ.foʊld **-s** -z
centre-forward ˌsen.təˈfɔː.wəd (US) -t̬ɚˈfɔːr.wɚd **-s** -z
centre-|half ˌsen.tə|ˈhɑːf (US) -t̬ɚ|ˈhæf **-halves** -ˈhɑːvz (US) -ˈhævz
centrepiec|e ˈsen.tə.piːs (US) -t̬ɚ- **-es** -ɪz
Centrepoint ˈsen.tə.pɔɪnt (US) -t̬ɚ-
centric ˈsen.trɪk **-al** -ᵊl **-ally** -ᵊl.i, -li
centrifugal ˌsen.trɪˈfjuː.gᵊl, -trəˈ-, senˈtrɪf.jʊ-, -jə- (US) senˈtrɪf.jə.gᵊl, ˈ-ə-, -juː-
centrifug|e ˈsen.trɪ.fjuːdʒ, -trə- (US) -trə- **-es** -ɪz **-ing** -ɪŋ **-ed** -d
centriole ˈsen.tri.əʊl (US) -oʊl **-s** -z
centripetal ˌsen.trɪˈp.iː.tᵊl, ˈ-ə-, senˈtrɪ.pɪ- (US) senˈtrɪ.pə.t̬ᵊl
centr|ism ˈsen.tr|ɪ.zᵊm **-ist/s** -ɪst/s
centro- ˈsen.trəʊ- (US) ˈsen.trə-
centr|um ˈsen.tr|əm **-a** -ə
centumvirate senˈtʌm.vɪ.rət, -və-, -rɪt (US) senˈtʌm.vɚ.ət, ken-, -vɪ.rət **-s** -s
Centumviri ˌsen.tʌmˈvɪ.riː (US) ˈsen.təm.vɪ-, ˈken.tʊm-, -raɪ
centuple ˈsen.tjʊ.pl̩; senˈtjuː- (US) ˈsen.t̬ə-; senˈtuː-, -ˈtjuː-

centurion sen'tjʊə.ri.ən, -'tʃʊə-, -'tjɔː-, -'tʃɔː- (US) -'tʊr.i-, -'tjʊr- **-s** -z

centur|y 'sen.*tʃ*ᵊr|.i **-ies** -iz

CEO ˌsiː.iː'əʊ (US) -'oʊ

cep sep **-s** -s

cèpe sep **-s** -s

cephalic sef'æl.ɪk, sɪf-, sə'fæl-, kef'æl-, kɪf- (US) sə'fæl.ɪk

Cephalonia ˌsef.ə'ləʊ.ni.ə (US) -'loʊ-

cephalopod 'sef.ᵊl.əʊ.pɒd (US) -ə.pɑːd **-s** -z

cephalopoda ˌsef.ə'lɒp.ə.də (US) -'lɑː.pə-

cephalous 'sef.ᵊl.əs

Cephas 'siː.fæs

Cepheid 'siː.fi.ɪd, 'sef.i- **-s** -z

Cepheus 'siː.fi.əs, -fjəs

ceramic sə'ræm.ɪk, sɪ-, kɪ-, kə- (US) sə'ræm- **-s** -s

Note: In the UK, experts tend to use the forms with /kɪ-, kə-/.

ceramicist sə'ræm.ɪ.sɪst, sɪ-, '-ə- (US) sə'ræm.ə- **-s** -s

ceramist 'ser.ə.mɪst, sə'ræm.ɪst **-s** -s

cerastes sə'ræs.tiːz, sɪ- (US) sə-

cerate 'sɪə.reɪt, -rɪt, -rət (US) 'sɪr.eɪt, -ɪt **-s** -s

Cerberus 'sɜː.bᵊr.əs (US) 'sɝː-

cercari|a sɜː'keə.ri|.ə (US) sɚ'ker.i- **-ae** -iː

cer|e sɪəʳ (US) sɪr **-es** -z **-ing** -ɪŋ **-ed** -d

cereal 'sɪə.ri.əl (US) 'sɪr.i- **-s** -z

cerebell|um ˌser.ɪ'bel|.əm, -ə'- (US) -ə'- **-ums** -əmz **-a** -ə

Cerebos® 'ser.ə.bɒs, '-ɪ- (US) -bɑːs

cerebral 'ser.ə.brᵊl, '-ɪ-; sə'riː-, sɪ- (US) 'ser.ə-; sə'riː- **-s** -z **ˌcerebral 'palsy**

cere|brate 'ser.ə|.breɪt, '-ɪ- (US) '-ə- **-brates** -breɪts **-brating** -breɪ.tɪŋ (US) -breɪ.t̬ɪŋ **-brated** -breɪ.tɪd (US) -breɪ.t̬ɪd

cerebration ˌser.ɪ'breɪ.ʃᵊn, -ə'- (US) -ə'- **-s** -z

cerebr|um sə'riː.br|əm, sɪ-; ser.ɪ-, '-ə- (US) 'ser.ə-; sə'riː- **-a** -ə **-ums** -əmz

Ceredigion ˌker.ə'dɪg.i.ɒn, -ɪ'- (US) -ɑːn

cerement 'sɪə.mənt, 'ser.ə.mənt (US) 'sɪr.mənt **-s** -s

ceremonial ˌser.ɪ'məʊ.ni.əl, -ə'- (US) -ə'moʊ- **-s** -z **-ly** -i **-ism** -ɪ.zᵊm

ceremonious ˌser.ɪ'məʊ.ni.əs, -ə'- (US) -ə'moʊ- **-ly** -li **-ness** -nəs, -nɪs

ceremon|y 'ser.ɪ.mə.n|i, '-ə- (US) '-ə.moʊ.n|i **-ies** -iz

Ceres 'sɪə.riːz (US) 'sɪr.iːz

cerif 'ser.ɪf **-s** -s

cerise sə'riːz, sɪ-, -'riːs (US) sə-

cerium 'sɪə.ri.əm (US) 'sɪr.i-

ceroplastic ˌsɪə.rəʊ'plæs.tɪk, -'plɑː.stɪk (US) 'sɪr.oʊ.plæs-, 'ser-

cert sɜːt (US) sɝːt **-s** -s

certain 'sɜː.tᵊn, -tɪn (US) 'sɝː- **-ly** -li

certaint|y 'sɜː.tᵊn.t|i, -tɪn- (US) 'sɝː- **-ies** -iz

certes 'sɜː.tiːz, -tɪz, sɜːts (US) 'sɝː.tiːz

certifiab|le ˌsɜː.tɪ'faɪ.ə.b|l̩, -tə'-, 'sɜː.tɪ.faɪ-, -tə- (US) 'sɝː.t̬ə.faɪ- **-ly** -li

certificate *(n.)* sə'tɪf.ɪ.kət, sɜː-, '-ə-, -kɪt (US) sɚ- **-s** -s

certifi|cate *(v.)* sə'tɪf.ɪ|.keɪt, sɜː-, '-ə- (US) sɚ- **-cates** -keɪts **-cating** -keɪ.tɪŋ (US) -keɪ.t̬ɪŋ **-cated** -keɪ.tɪd, -kə.tɪd, -kɪ- (US) -keɪ.t̬ɪd

certification *act of certifying:* ˌsɜː.tɪ.fɪ'keɪ.ʃᵊn, -fə'- (US) ˌsɝː.t̬ə- **-s** -z *providing with a certificate:* ˌsɜː.tɪ.fɪ'keɪ.ʃᵊn, səˌtɪ- (US) ˌsɝː.t̬ə- **-s** -z

certificatory sə'tɪf.ɪ.kə.tᵊr.i, sɜː-, -keɪ-, -tri (US) sɚ'tɪf.ɪ.kə.tɔːr.i

certif|y 'sɜː.tɪ.f|aɪ, -tə- (US) -t̬ə- **-ies** -aɪz **-ying** -aɪ.ɪŋ **-ied** -aɪd **-ier/s** -aɪ.əʳ/z (US) -aɪ.ɚ/z **ˌcertified 'mail**

certiorari ˌsɜː.ʃi.ɔː'reə.raɪ, -ti.ə'-, -'rɑː.ri (US) ˌsɝː.ʃi.ə'rer.i, -'rɑːr- **-s** -z

certitude 'sɜː.tɪ.tjuːd (US) 'sɝː.t̬ə.tuːd, -tjuːd

cerulean sə'ruː.li.ən, sɪ- (US) sə'ruː-

cerumen sə'ruː.men, sɪ-, -mən (US) sə'ruː-

Cervantes sɜː'væn.tiːz, -tɪz (US) sɚ-

cervical sə'vaɪ.kᵊl, sɜː-; 'sɜː.vɪ- (US) 'sɝː.vɪ- **cerˌvical 'smear, ˌcervical 'smear** (US) **ˌcervical 'smear**

cervine 'sɜː.vaɪn (US) 'sɝː-

cer|vix 'sɜː|.vɪks (US) 'sɝː- **-vices** -vɪ.siːz **-vixes** -vɪk.sɪz

Cerynean sə'rɪn.i.ən (US) ˌser.ə'niː.ən

César 'seɪ.zɑːʳ, -zəʳ (US) seɪ'zɑːr

cesarean, cesarian sɪ'zeə.ri.ən, sə- (US) sə'zer.i- **-s** -z **ceˌsarean 'section**

Cesarewitch *Russian prince:* sɪ'zɑː.rə.vɪtʃ, sə- (US) -'zɑːr.ə- *race:* sɪ'zær.ə.wɪtʃ, -'zɑː.rə-, -rɪ- (US) -'zɑːr.ə-

Cesario siː'zɑː.ri.əʊ, -'zær.i- (US) -'zɑːr.i.oʊ

cesium 'siː.zi.əm

cess ses **-es** -ɪz

cessation ses'eɪ.ʃᵊn, sɪ'seɪ-, sə- **-s** -z

cession 'seʃ.ᵊn **-s** -z

cessionar|y 'seʃ.ᵊn.ᵊr|.i, -ᵊn.r|i (US) -er- **-ies** -iz

Cessna® 'ses.nə

cesspit 'ses.pɪt **-s** -s

cesspool 'ses.puːl **-s** -z

c'est la vie ˌseɪ.læ'viː, -lɑː'-, -lə'-

cestui que trust ˌset.ɪ.kɪ'trʌst (US) ˌset̬-, ˌses.twɪ- **-s** -s

cestui que vie ˌset.ɪ.kɪ'viː (US) ˌset̬-, ˌses.twɪ- **-s** -z

cestuis que trust ˌset.ɪz.kɪ'trʌst (US) ˌset̬-, ˌses.twɪz-

cestuis que vie ˌset.ɪz.kɪ'viː (US) ˌset̬-, ˌses.twɪz-

cestus 'ses.təs **-es** -ɪz

cesura sɪ'zjʊə.rə, siː-, -'zjɔː-, -'ʒʊə- (US) sə'zʊr.ə, -'ʒʊr- **-s** -z

Cetacea sɪ'teɪ.ʃə, sə-, -ʃi.ə, -si.ə (US) -ʃə

cetacean sɪ'teɪ.ʃᵊn, sə-, -ʃi.ən, -si.ən (US) -ʃᵊn **-s** -z

cetaceous sɪ'teɪ.ʃəs, sə-, -ʃi.əs, -si.əs (US) -ʃəs

cetane 'siː.teɪn

Cetewayo ketʃ'waɪ.əʊ, ˌket.i'waɪ-, -wɑː.jəʊ (US) -'waɪ.oʊ

Ceuta 'sjuː.tə (US) 'seɪ.uː.t̬ə

Cévennes sev'en, sə'ven, sɪ-, -venz (US) seɪ'ven

ceviche sə'viː.tʃeɪ, -tʃiː

Ceylon sɪ'lɒn, sə- (US) sɪ'lɑːn, seɪ-

Ceylonese ˌsel.ə'niːz, ˌsiː.lə- (US) ˌsiː.lə'niːz, ˌseɪ-, -'niːs

Cézanne seɪ'zæn, sɪ-, sez'æn (US) seɪ'zɑːn

cf. *(abbrev. for* **compare***)* kəm'peəʳ, kən'fɜːʳ; ˌsiː'ef (US) kəm'per, kən'fɝː; ˌsiː'ef

CFC ˌsiː.ef'siː **-s** -z

cg *(abbrev. for* **centigramme, centigram***)* 'sen.tɪ.græm (US) -t̬ə-

Chablis 'ʃæb.liː, -bli, -'- (US) ʃæb'li, ʃɑː'bli

Chabrier 'ʃæb.ri.eɪ, 'ʃɑː.bri-, --'- (US) ˌʃɑː.bri'eɪ

cha-cha 'tʃɑː.tʃɑː **-s** -z **-ing** -ɪŋ **-ed** -d

cha-cha-cha ˌtʃɑː.tʃɑː'tʃɑː **-s** -z

chaconne ʃæk'ɒn, ʃə'kɒn (US) ʃɑː'kɑːn, ʃæk'ɑːn, -'ɔːn **-s** -z

chacun à son goût ˌʃæk.ɜːn.ɑː.sɔ̃ː*ŋ*'guː, -æ.sɒŋ'- (US) ʃɑːˌkuːn.ɑː.sɑːn'-, ʃækˌuːn-, -sɔːn'-

chad (C) tʃæd **-s** -z **-ian/s** -i.ən/z

Chadband 'tʃæd.bænd

Chadderton 'tʃæd.ə.tᵊn (US) -ɚ.t̬ən

Chadwick 'tʃæd.wɪk

chaf|e tʃeɪf **-es** -s **-ing** -ɪŋ **-ed** -t

chafer 'tʃeɪ.fəʳ (US) -fɚ **-s** -z

chaff tʃæf, tʃɑːf (US) tʃæf **-s** -s **-ing/ly** -ɪŋ/li **-ed** -t

chaff|er 'tʃæf|.əʳ (US) -ɚ **-ers** -əz (US) -ɚz **-ering** -ᵊr.ɪŋ **-ered** -əd (US) -ɚd

Chaffey 'tʃeɪ.fi

chaffinch 'tʃæf.ɪn*tʃ* **-es** -ɪz

chaff|y 'tʃæf|.i, 'tʃɑː.f|i (US) 'tʃæf|.i **-iness** -ɪ.nəs, -ɪ.nɪs

chafing-dish 'tʃeɪ.fɪŋ.dɪʃ **-es** -ɪz

Chagall ʃæg'æl, ʃə'gæl, -gɑːl (US) ʃə'gɑːl

chagrin *(n.)* 'ʃæg.rɪn, -rᵊn (US) ʃə'grɪn

chagrin *(v.)* 'ʃæg.rɪn, ʃə'griːn (US) ʃə'grɪn **-s** -z **-ing** -ɪŋ **-ed** -d

Chaim haɪm, xaɪm

chain tʃeɪn **-s** -z **-ing** -ɪŋ **-ed** -d **'chain ˌgang; ˌchain 'letter; 'chain ˌmail; ˌchain re'action; 'chain ˌstore**

Pronouncing the letters CH

The consonant digraph **ch** has three main pronunciations: /tʃ, k/ and /ʃ/. Before the letter **r**, **ch** is always realised as /k/, e.g.:

Christmas	/ˈkrɪs*t*.məs/
anachronism	/əˈnæk.rə.nɪ.zᵊm/

However, there is no reliable way of predicting whether **ch** will be pronounced as /tʃ k/ or /ʃ/ in most other situations by looking at the spelling alone, e.g.:

chap	/tʃæp/
stomach	/ˈstʌm.ək/
champagne	/ʃæmˈpeɪn/

In general, /k/ words are those originating from Greek (e.g. *chaos, chorus*). Words containing /ʃ/ are usually late borrowings from French (e.g. *champagne, chauffeur*).

The remainder, pronounced /tʃ/, are more long-established, often being common everyday words (e.g. *lunch, chew*).

In addition

Occasionally, **ch** is pronounced /dʒ/, as in the British place name *Greenwich*.

/ˈgren.ɪdʒ/

Words from Scots ending **ch** may be pronounced /x/, but can also have the realisation /k/, e.g.:

loch	/lɒk, lɒx/	US /lɑːk, lɑːx/

In the case of *yacht* **ch** is silent:

yacht	/jɒt/	US /jɑːt/

chainless ˈtʃeɪn.ləs, -lɪs
chain-link ˈtʃeɪn.lɪŋk ˌ**chain-link** ˈ**fence**
chainsaw ˈtʃeɪn.sɔː US -sɑː, -sɔː **-s** -z **-ing** -ɪŋ **-ed** -d
chain-smok|e ˈtʃeɪn.sməʊk US -smoʊk **-es** -s **-ing** -ɪŋ **-ed** -t **-er/s** -əʳ/z US -ɚ/z
chainstitch ˈtʃeɪn.stɪtʃ
chainwork ˈtʃeɪn.wɜːk US -wɝːk
chair tʃeəʳ US tʃer **-s** -z **-ing** -ɪŋ **-ed** -d
chairlift ˈtʃeə.lɪft US ˈtʃer- **-s** -s
chair|man ˈtʃeə|.mən US ˈtʃer- **-men** -mən
chairmanship ˈtʃeə.mən.ʃɪp US ˈtʃer- **-s** -s
chairperson ˈtʃeəˌpɜː.sᵊn US ˈtʃerˌpɝː- **-s** -z
chair|woman ˈtʃeə|ˌwʊm.ən US ˈtʃer- **-women** -ˌwɪm.ɪn
chais|e ʃeɪz US ʃeɪz, tʃeɪs **-es** -ɪz
chaise(s) longue(s) ˌʃeɪzˈlɒŋ, ˌʃez-, -ˈlɒŋg, -ˈlɔ̃ːŋg US ˌʃeɪzˈlɔːŋ, ˌtʃeɪs-, -ˈlɑːŋ
Chalcedon ˈkæl.sɪ.dᵊn, -dɒn US -sə.dɑːn
chalcedony kælˈsed.ᵊn.i US kælˈsed.ᵊn.i, ˈkæl.sə.doʊ.ni
chalcedonyx ˌkæl.sɪˈdɒn.ɪks US -ˈdɑː.nɪks; kælˈsed.ᵊn.ɪks; **-es** -ɪz
Chalcis ˈkæl.sɪs
chalcography kælˈkɒg.rə.fi US -ˈkɑː.grə-
Chalde|a kælˈdiː|.ə, kɔːl- US kæl- **-an/s** -ən/z
Chaldee kælˈdiː, kɔːl- US kæl- **-s** -z
chaldron ˈtʃɔːl.drᵊn US ˈtʃɔːl-, ˈtʃɑːl- **-s** -z
chalet ˈʃæl.eɪ, ˈʃæl.i US ʃælˈeɪ **-s** -z
Chalfont *in Buckinghamshire:* ˈtʃæl.fənt, -fɒnt *old-fashioned:* ˈtʃɑː- US -fɑːnt
chalic|e ˈtʃæl.ɪs **-es** -ɪz **-ed** -t
chalk (C) tʃɔːk US tʃɔːk, tʃɑːk **-s** -s **-ing** -ɪŋ **-ed** -t ˈ**chalk** ˌ**pit**; **as** ˌ**different as** ˌ**chalk and** ˈ**cheese**
chalkboard ˈtʃɔːk.bɔːd US -bɔːrd, ˈtʃɑːk- **-s** -z
Chalker ˈtʃɔː.kəʳ US ˈtʃɔː.kɚ, ˈtʃɑː-
chalkface ˈtʃɔːk.feɪs US ˈtʃɔːk-, ˈtʃɑːk-
Chalkley ˈtʃɔːk.li US ˈtʃɔːk-, ˈtʃɑːk-
chalkstone ˈtʃɔːk.stəʊn US ˈtʃɔːk.stoʊn, ˈtʃɑːk- **-s** -z
chalk|y ˈtʃɔː.k|i US ˈtʃɔː-, ˈtʃɑː- **-ier** -i.əʳ US -i.ɚ **-iest** -i.ɪst, -i.əst **-ily** -ɪ.li, -ᵊl.i **-iness** -ɪ.nəs, -ɪ.nɪs
challeng|e ˈtʃæl.ɪndʒ, -əndʒ **-es** -ɪz **-ing** -ɪŋ **-ed** -d **-er/s** -əʳ/z US -ɚ/z
Challenor ˈtʃæl.ə.nəʳ, ˈ-ɪ- US -ə.nɚ
challis (C) ˈʃæl.ɪs, ˈʃæl.i
Challoner ˈtʃæl.ə.nəʳ US -nɚ
Chalmers ˈtʃɑː.məz, ˈtʃæl- US -mɚz
Chaloner ˈtʃæl.ə.nəʳ US -nɚ
chalybeate kəˈlɪb.i.ət, -ɪt, -eɪt
chamber ˈtʃeɪm.bəʳ US -bɚ **-s** -z **-ed** -d ˈ**chamber** ˌ**music**; ˈ**chamber** ˌ**pot**
chamberlain ˈtʃeɪm.bᵊl.ɪn, -ən US -bɚ- **-s** -z
Chamberlain ˈtʃeɪm.bᵊl.ɪn, -ən, -eɪn US -bɚ-
chamberlainship ˈtʃeɪm.bᵊl.ɪn.ʃɪp, -ən- US -bɚ- **-s** -s
chambermaid ˈtʃeɪm.bə.meɪd US -bɚ- **-s** -z
Chambers ˈtʃeɪm.bəz US -bɚz
Chambourcy® ʃæmˈbʊə.si, -ˈbɔː- US ˌʃɑːm.bʊrˈsiː
chambray ˈʃæm.breɪ
chambré ˈʃɑ̃ː*m*.breɪ US ʃɑːmˈbreɪ
chameleon kəˈmiː.li.ən US -li.ən, -ˈmiːl.jən **-s** -s
chamfer ˈʃæm*p*.fəʳ, ˈtʃæm*p*- US -fɚ **-s** -z
chamois (*sing.*) *goat-antelope:* ˈʃæm.wɑː US ˈʃæm.i, ʃæmˈwɑː (*plur.*) ˈʃæm.wɑːz US ˈʃæm.iz, ʃæmˈwɑːz
chamois *leather:* ˈʃæm.i ˈ**chamois** ˌ**leather** ˌ**chamois** ˈ**leather**
chamomile ˈkæm.ə.maɪl US -miːl, -maɪl
Chamonix ˈʃæm.ə.niː, -ɒn.iː US ˌʃæm.əˈniː
champ tʃæmp **-s** -s **-ing** -ɪŋ **-ed** -t
champagne (C) ʃæmˈpeɪn **-s** -z *stress shift:* ˌchampagne ˈsocialist
champaign ˈtʃæm.peɪn **-s** -z
champers ˈʃæm.pəz US -pɚz
champerty ˈtʃæm.pɜː.ti, -pə- US -pɝː.t̬i
champignon ˈʃæm.piː.njɔ̃ː, ˈʃɑ̃ː*m*-, ˌ--ˈ-; ʃæmˈpɪn.jən, ˈ--- US ʃæmˈpɪn.jən, tʃæm- **-s** -z
champion (C) ˈtʃæm.pi.ən US -pi.ən, -pjən **-s** -z **-ing** -ɪŋ **-ed** -d
championship ˈtʃæm.pi.ən.ʃɪp US ˈtʃæm.pi.ən.ʃɪp, -pjən- **-s** -s
Champlain *French explorer:* ʃæmˈpleɪn; ʃɔ̃ː*ŋ*ˈplɑ̃ː*ŋ* US ʃæmˈpleɪn; ʃɑ̃ːˈplɑ̃ː*ŋ* *lake in US:* ʃæmˈpleɪn
Champneys ˈtʃæmp.niz
Champs Elysées ˌʃɑ̃ː*nz*.elˈiː.zeɪ, ˌʃɔ̃ː*nz*- US ˌʃɑːnz.eɪ.liːˈzeɪ
chanc|e tʃɑːn*t*s US tʃæn*t*s **-es** -ɪz **-ing** -ɪŋ **-ed** -t **-er/s** -əʳ/z US -ɚ/z
chancel ˈtʃɑːn*t*.sᵊl US ˈtʃæn*t*- **-s** -z
chanceller|y ˈtʃɑːn*t*.sᵊl.ᵊr|.i US ˈtʃæn*t*- **-ies** -iz
chancellor (C) ˈtʃɑːn*t*.sᵊl.əʳ, -sɪ.ləʳ US ˈtʃæn*t*- **-s** -z **-ship/s** -ʃɪp/s ˌ**chancellor of the ex**ˈ**chequer**
Chancellorsville ˈtʃɑːn*t*.sᵊl.əz.vɪl US ˈtʃæn*t*.sᵊl.ɚz-
chancer|y (C) ˈtʃɑːn*t*.sᵊr|.i US ˈtʃæn*t*- **-ies** -iz

chancre 'ʃæŋ.kəʳ ⓤⓢ -kɚ
chancroid 'ʃæŋ.krɔɪd **-s** -z
chanc|y 'tʃɑːnt.s|i ⓤⓢ 'tʃænt- **-ier** -i.əʳ ⓤⓢ -i.ɚ **-iest** -i.ɪst, -i.əst
chandelier ˌʃæn.də'lɪəʳ, -dɪ'- ⓤⓢ -'lɪr **-s** -z
Chandigarh ˌtʃæn.dɪ'gɜːʳ, ˌtʃʌn-, -'gɑːʳ, '--- ⓤⓢ -'gɝː, -'gɑːr
chandler (C) 'tʃɑːnd.ləʳ ⓤⓢ 'tʃænd.lɚ **-s** -z
Chandos 'ʃæn.dɒs, 'tʃæn.dɒs ⓤⓢ -dɑːs
Note: Lord Chandos pronounces /'ʃæn-/. **Chandos Street** in London is generally pronounced with /'tʃæn-/.
Chanel ʃə'nel, ʃæn'el
Chaney 'tʃeɪ.ni
Chang tʃæŋ
chang|e tʃeɪndʒ **-es** -ɪz **-ing** -ɪŋ **-ed** -d **-er/s** -əʳ/z ⓤⓢ -ɚ/z
changeability ˌtʃeɪn.dʒə'bɪl.ə.ti, -ɪ.ti ⓤⓢ -ə.t̬i
changeab|le 'tʃeɪn.dʒə.b|l̩ **-ly** -li **-leness** -l̩.nəs, -l̩.nɪs
changeful 'tʃeɪndʒ.fəl, -fʊl **-ly** -i **-ness** -nəs, -nɪs
changeless 'tʃeɪndʒ.ləs, -lɪs
changeling 'tʃeɪndʒ.lɪŋ **-s** -z
changeover 'tʃeɪndʒˌəʊ.vəʳ ⓤⓢ -ˌoʊ.vɚ **-s** -z
Chang Jiang ˌtʃæŋ.dʒi'æŋ ⓤⓢ ˌtʃɑːŋ.dʒi'ɑːŋ, ˌtʃæŋ-, -'æŋ
channel 'tʃæn.əl **-s** -z **-(l)ing** -ɪŋ **-(l)ed** -d 'Channel ˌIslands; ˌChannel 'Tunnel
channelization, -isa- ˌtʃæn.əl.aɪ'zeɪ.ʃən, -ɪ'- ⓤⓢ -ɪ'-
channeliz|e, -is|e 'tʃæn.əl.aɪz ⓤⓢ -ə.laɪz **-es** -ɪz **-ing** -ɪŋ **-ed** -d
Channell 'tʃæn.əl
Channing 'tʃæn.ɪŋ
Channon 'tʃæn.ən, 'ʃæn.ən
chanson 'ʃɑ̃ːn.sɔ̃ːŋ, -sɒn, -'- ⓤⓢ ʃɑːn'soʊn, -'sɑːn, -'sɔːn **-s** -z
chant (C) tʃɑːnt ⓤⓢ tʃænt **-s** -s **-ing** -ɪŋ ⓤⓢ 'tʃæn.t̬ɪŋ **-ed** -ɪd ⓤⓢ 'tʃæn.t̬ɪd **-er/s** -əʳ/z ⓤⓢ 'tʃæn.t̬ɚ/z
Chantal ʃɑ̃ːn'tɑːl, ʃæn-, -tæl ⓤⓢ ʃɑːn'tɑːl
Chantelle ʃɑ̃ːn'tel, ʃæn- ⓤⓢ ʃɑːn'tel, ʃæn-
Chanter 'tʃɑːn.təʳ ⓤⓢ 'tʃæn.t̬ɚ
chanterelle ˌʃɑ̃ːn.tə'rel, ˌʃæn-, ˌtʃæn- ⓤⓢ ˌʃæn.t̬ə'-, ˌʃɑːn- **-s** -z
chanteus|e ʃɑ̃ːn'tɜːz, ʃɑːn- ⓤⓢ ʃɑːn'tuːz, ʃæn-, -'tuːs **-es** -ɪz
chantey 'ʃæn.ti, 'tʃæn-, 'tʃɑːn- ⓤⓢ 'ʃæn.t̬i **-s** -z
chanticleer (C) 'tʃɑːn.tɪ.klɪəʳ, 'tʃænt-, 'ʃɑːn-, -tə-, ˌ--'- ⓤⓢ 'tʃæn.t̬ə.klɪr, 'ʃæn- **-s** -z
Chantilly *in France:* ʃæn'tɪl.i, ʃɑ̃ːn- ⓤⓢ ʃæn'tɪl.i; ˌʃɑːn.ti'ji
Note: In the song "Chantilly Lace", it is pronounced /ʃæn'tɪl.i/.
Chantilly *in US:* ʃæn'tɪli
Chantrey 'tʃɑːn.tri ⓤⓢ 'tʃæn-
chantr|y 'tʃɑːn.tr|i ⓤⓢ 'tʃæn- **-ies** -iz
chant|y 'tʃɑːn.t|i ⓤⓢ 'tʃæn.t̬|i **-ies** -iz
Chanukah 'hʌn.ʊ.kə, 'xʌn- ⓤⓢ 'hɑː.nə.kə, 'xɑː-, -nʊ.kɑː
chaos 'keɪ.ɒs ⓤⓢ -ɑːs
chaotic keɪ'ɒt.ɪk ⓤⓢ -'ɑː.t̬ɪk **-ally** -əl.i, -li
chap tʃæp **-s** -s **-ping** -ɪŋ **-ped** -t
chapat(t)i tʃə'pɑː.ti, -'pæt.i **-(e)s** -z
chapbook 'tʃæp.bʊk **-s** -s
chape tʃeɪp **-s** -s
chapeau 'ʃæp.əʊ, -'- ⓤⓢ ʃæp'oʊ **-s** -z
chapeaux *(alternative plur. of* **chapeau***)* 'ʃæp.əʊ, -əʊz ⓤⓢ ʃæp'oʊ, -'oʊz
chapel 'tʃæp.əl **-s** -z
Chapel-en-le-Frith ˌtʃæp.əl.ən.lə'frɪθ, -en.lə'-
chapelr|y 'tʃæp.əl.r|i **-ies** -iz
Chapeltown 'tʃæp.əl.taʊn
chaperon|e, chaperon 'ʃæp.ər.əʊn ⓤⓢ -ə.roʊn **-es** -z **-ing** -ɪŋ **-ed** -d **-age** -ɪdʒ
chapfallen 'tʃæpˌfɔː.lən ⓤⓢ -ˌfɔː-, -ˌfɑː-
chaplain 'tʃæp.lɪn **-s** -z
chaplainc|y 'tʃæp.lɪnt.s|i, -lənt- **-ies** -iz
chaplet 'tʃæp.lət, -lɪt, -let **-s** -s
Chaplin 'tʃæp.lɪn
Chapman 'tʃæp.mən
Chapone ʃə'pəʊn ⓤⓢ -poʊn
Chappaquiddick ˌtʃæp.ə'kwɪd.ɪk
Chappell 'tʃæp.əl
chappie, chappy 'tʃæp.i **-s** -z
Chapple 'tʃæp.l̩
chapstick 'tʃæp.stɪk **-s** -s
chapter 'tʃæp.təʳ ⓤⓢ -tɚ **-s** -z **'chapter ˌhouse; ˌchapter and 'verse**
Chapultepec tʃə'puːl.təˌpek, -'pʊl-
char tʃɑːʳ ⓤⓢ tʃɑːr **-s** -z **-ring** -ɪŋ **-red** -d
charabanc 'ʃær.ə.bæŋ, -bɑ̃ːŋ ⓤⓢ -bæŋ **-s** -s
character 'kær.ək.təʳ, -ɪk- ⓤⓢ 'ker.ək.tɚ, 'kær- **-s** -z
characteristic ˌkær.ək.tə'rɪs.tɪk, -ɪk- ⓤⓢ ˌker.ək-, ˌkær- **-s** -s **-al** -əl **-ally** -əl.i, -li
characterization, -isa- ˌkær.ək.tər.aɪ'zeɪ.ʃən, -ɪk-, -ɪ'- ⓤⓢ ˌker.ək.tɚ.ɪ'-, ˌkær- **-s** -z
characteriz|e, -is|e 'kær.ək.tər.aɪz, -ɪk- ⓤⓢ 'ker.ək.tə.raɪz, 'kær- **-es** -ɪz **-ing** -ɪŋ **-ed** -d
characterless 'kær.ək.tə.ləs, -ɪk-, -lɪs ⓤⓢ 'ker.ək.tɚ-, 'kær- **-ness** -nəs, -nɪs
charade ʃə'rɑːd ⓤⓢ -'reɪd **-s** -z
charbroil 'tʃɑː.brɔɪl ⓤⓢ 'tʃɑːr- **-s** -z **-ing** -ɪŋ **-ed** -d
charcoal 'tʃɑː.kəʊl ⓤⓢ 'tʃɑːr.koʊl
chard (C) tʃɑːd ⓤⓢ tʃɑːrd
Chardin 'ʃɑː.dæ̃ŋ, -'- ⓤⓢ ʃɑːr'dæ̃n
chardonnay (C) 'ʃɑː.dən.eɪ ⓤⓢ 'ʃɑːr-, ˌ--'- **-s** -z
char|e tʃeəʳ ⓤⓢ tʃer **-es** -z **-ing** -ɪŋ **-ed** -d
charg|e tʃɑːdʒ ⓤⓢ tʃɑːrdʒ **-es** -ɪz **-ing** -ɪŋ **-ed** -d **'charge ˌcard**
chargeab|le 'tʃɑː.dʒə.b|l̩ ⓤⓢ 'tʃɑːr- **-ly** -li **-leness** -l̩.nəs, -nɪs
chargé(s) d'affaires *sing:* ˌʃɑː.ʒeɪ.dæf'eəʳ, -də'feəʳ ⓤⓢ ˌʃɑːr.ʒeɪ.də'fer, -dæf'er *plur:* -z
charger 'tʃɑː.dʒəʳ ⓤⓢ 'tʃɑːr.dʒɚ **-s** -z
Charing Cross ˌtʃær.ɪŋ'krɒs, ˌtʃeər- ⓤⓢ ˌtʃer.ɪŋ'krɑːs, ˌtʃær-
chariot 'tʃær.i.ət ⓤⓢ 'tʃer-, 'tʃær- **-s** -s
charioteer ˌtʃær.i.ə'tɪəʳ ⓤⓢ ˌtʃer.i.ə'tɪr, ˌtʃær- **-s** -z
charisma kə'rɪz.mə
charismatic ˌkær.ɪz'mæt.ɪk ⓤⓢ ˌker.ɪz'mæt̬-, ˌkær-
charitab|le 'tʃær.ɪ.tə.b|l̩, '-ə- ⓤⓢ 'tʃer-, 'tʃær- **-ly** -li **-leness** -l̩.nəs, -nɪs
charit|y (C) 'tʃær.ɪ.t|i, -ə.t|i ⓤⓢ 'tʃer.ə.t̬|i, 'tʃær- **-ies** -iz
charivari ˌʃɑː.rɪ'vɑː.ri ⓤⓢ ʃəˌrɪv.ə'riː; ˌʃɑː.rɪ'vɑː.ri, ˌʃɪv.ə'riː **-s** -z
charivaria ˌʃɑː.rɪv'ɑː.ri.ə ⓤⓢ ˌʃɑːr.ɪ'vɑːr.i-
charlad|y 'tʃɑːˌleɪ.d|i ⓤⓢ 'tʃɑːr- **-ies** -iz
charlatan 'ʃɑː.lə.tən, -tæn ⓤⓢ 'ʃɑːr.lə.tən **-s** -z
charlatanism 'ʃɑː.lə.tən.ɪ.zəm ⓤⓢ 'ʃɑːr.lə.tən-, -t̬ə.nɪ- **-s** -z
charlatanry 'ʃɑː.lə.tən.ri ⓤⓢ 'ʃɑːr.lə.tən-, -t̬ən-
Charlbury 'tʃɑːl.bər.i ⓤⓢ 'tʃɑːrl.ber.i, -bɚ-
Charlecote 'tʃɑːl.kəʊt ⓤⓢ 'tʃɑːrl.koʊt
Charlemagne 'ʃɑː.lə.meɪn, -maɪn, ˌ--'- ⓤⓢ 'ʃɑːr.lə.meɪn
Charlemont 'tʃɑː.lɪ.mənt, 'tʃɑːl.mənt ⓤⓢ 'tʃɑːr.lɪ.mənt, 'tʃɑːrl.mənt
Charlene 'tʃɑː.liːn, 'ʃɑː-, ʃɑː'liːn ⓤⓢ ʃɑːr'liːn, '--
Charleroi 'ʃɑː.lə.rɔɪ *as if French:* ˌʃɑː.lə'rwɑː ⓤⓢ 'ʃɑːr-
Charles tʃɑːlz ⓤⓢ tʃɑːrlz
Charleston 'tʃɑːl.stən ⓤⓢ 'tʃɑːrl-
Charlestown 'tʃɑːlz.taʊn ⓤⓢ 'tʃɑːrlz-
Charlesworth 'tʃɑːlz.wəθ, -wɜːθ ⓤⓢ 'tʃɑːrlz.wɚθ, -wɝːθ
Charleville 'ʃɑː.lə.vɪl ⓤⓢ 'ʃɑːr-
Charley 'tʃɑː.li ⓤⓢ 'tʃɑːr- **'charley ˌhorse**
charlie (C) 'tʃɑː.li ⓤⓢ 'tʃɑːr- **-s** -z
charlock 'tʃɑː.lɒk ⓤⓢ 'tʃɑːr.lɑːk
charlotte (C) 'ʃɑː.lət ⓤⓢ 'ʃɑːr- **-s** -s
Charlottenburg ʃɑː'lɒt.ən.bɜːg ⓤⓢ ʃɑːr'lɑː.tən.bɝːg

Charlottesville ˈʃɑː.ləts.vɪl US ˈʃɑːr-
Charlton ˈtʃɑːl.tᵊn US ˈtʃɑːrl-
charm tʃɑːm US tʃɑːrm **-s** -z **-ed** -d **-ing** -ɪŋ **-er/s** -əʳ/z US -ɚ/z **-less/ly** -ləs/li, -lɪs/li
Charmaine ʃɑːˈmeɪn US ʃɑːr-
Charmian ˈtʃɑː.mi.ən, ˈʃɑː-, ˈkɑː- US ˈtʃɑːr-, ˈʃɑːr-, ˈkɑːr-
Charmin® ˈtʃɑː.mɪn US ˈʃɑːr-
charming ˈtʃɑː.mɪŋ US ˈtʃɑːr- **-ly** -li
charnel ˈtʃɑː.nᵊl US ˈtʃɑːr- ˈ**charnel** ˌ**house**
Charnock ˈtʃɑː.nɒk, -nək US ˈtʃɑːr.nɑːk
Charnwood ˈtʃɑːn.wʊd, -wəd US ˈtʃɑːrn-
Charolais *sing:* ˈʃær.ə.leɪ US ˌʃɑːr.əˈleɪ *plur:* ˈʃær.ə.leɪ, -leɪz US ˌʃɑːr.əˈleɪ, -ˈleɪz
Charon ˈkeə.rᵊn, -rɒn US ˈker.ᵊn
Charpentier ʃɑːˈpɑ̃ːn.ti.eɪ US ˌʃɑːr.pɑ̃ːn.tiˈeɪ, -ˈtjeɪ
Charrington ˈtʃær.ɪŋ.tən US ˈtʃer-, ˈtʃær-
chart tʃɑːt US tʃɑːrt **-s** -s **-ing** -ɪŋ US ˈtʃɑːr.t̬ɪŋ **-ed** -ɪd US ˈtʃɑːr.t̬ɪd
chart|er (C) ˈtʃɑː.t|əʳ US ˈtʃɑːr.t̬|ɚ **-ers** -əz US -ɚz **-ering** -ᵊr.ɪŋ **-ered** -əd US -ɚd **-erer/s** -ᵊr.əʳ/z US -ɚ.ɚ/z ˈ**charter** ˌ**flight**; ˌ**chartered** **aˈccountant**
Charterhouse ˈtʃɑː.tə.haʊs US ˈtʃɑːr.t̬ɚ-
Charteris ˈtʃɑː.təz, -tᵊr.ɪs US ˈtʃɑːr.t̬ɚ.ɪs
charterpart|y ˈtʃɑː.təˌpɑː.t|i US ˈtʃɑːr.t̬ɚˌpɑːr.t̬|i **-ies** -iz
chart|ism (C) ˈtʃɑː.t|ɪ.zᵊm US ˈtʃɑːr.t̬|ɪ- **-ist/s** -ɪst/s
Chartres ˈʃɑː.trə; ʃɑːt US ˈʃɑːr.trə; ʃɑːrt
Chartreuse® ʃɑːˈtrɜːz US ʃɑːrˈtruːz
Chartwell ˈtʃɑːt.wel, -wəl US ˈtʃɑːrt-
char|woman ˈtʃɑː|ˌwʊm.ən US ˈtʃɑːr- **-women** -ˌwɪm.ɪn
char|y ˈtʃeə.r|i US ˈtʃer|.i **-ier** -i.əʳ US -i.ɚ **-iest** -i.ɪst, -i.əst **-ily** -ɪ.li, -ᵊl.i **-iness** -ɪ.nəs, -ɪ.nɪs
Charybdis kəˈrɪb.dɪs
Chas tʃæz, tʃɑːlz US tʃæz, tʃɑːrlz
chas|e (C) tʃeɪs **-es** -ɪz **-ing** -ɪŋ **-ed** -t **-er/s** -əʳ/z US -ɚ/z
chasm ˈkæz.ᵊm **-s** -z
chassé ˈʃæs.eɪ US -ˈ- **-s** -z
chasseur ʃæsˈɜːʳ US -ˈɝː **-s** -z
chassis *sing:* ˈʃæs.i, -iː US ˈtʃæs-, ˈʃæs- *plur:* ˈʃæs.iz, -iːz US ˈtʃæs-, ˈʃæs-
chaste tʃeɪst **-ly** -li **-ness** -nəs, -nɪs
chasten ˈtʃeɪ.sᵊn **-s** -z **-ing** -ɪŋ **-ed** -d
chastis|e tʃæsˈtaɪz US ˈ-- **-es** -ɪz **-ing** -ɪŋ **-ed** -d
chastisement tʃæsˈtaɪz.mənt, ˈtʃæs.tɪz- US ˈtʃæs.taɪz-, -ˈ-- **-s** -s
chastiser tʃæsˈtaɪ.zəʳ US -zɚ **-s** -z
chastity (C) ˈtʃæs.tə.ti, -tɪ- US -tə.t̬i ˈ**chastity** ˌ**belt**
chasuble ˈtʃæz.jʊ.bl̩, -jə- US -jə-, ˈ-ə- **-s** -z
chat tʃæt **-s** -s **-ting** -ɪŋ US ˈtʃæt̬.ɪŋ **-ted** -ɪd US ˈtʃæt̬.ɪd ˈ**chat** ˌ**show**
Chataway ˈtʃæt.ə.weɪ US ˈtʃæt̬-
château ˈʃæt.əʊ, -ˈ- US ʃætˈoʊ **-s** -z
chateaubriand (C) ˌʃæt.əʊ.briˈɑ̃ː*nd*, ˌʃæt.əʊˈbriː-, ʃætˈəʊ- US ˌʃæt.oʊ.briˈɑ̃ː*nd*, ˌʃɑː.toʊ- **-s** -z
Châteauneuf-du-Pape ˌʃæt.əʊ.nɜːf.djuˈpæp US -oʊˌnɜːf.du-, -dju-, -ˈpɑːp
châteaux *(alternative plur. of* **chateau***)* ˈʃæt.əʊ, -əʊz, -ˈ- US ʃætˈoʊ, -ˈoʊz
chatelain ˈʃæt.ᵊl.eɪn, -æ̃*ŋ* US ˈʃæt̬.ə.leɪn **-s** -z
chatelaine ˈʃæt.ᵊl.eɪn US ˈʃæt̬.ə.leɪn **-s** -z
Chater ˈtʃeɪ.təʳ US -tɚ
Chatham ˈtʃæt.əm US ˈtʃæt̬-
chatline ˈtʃæt.laɪn **-s** -z
chatroom ˈtʃæt.ruːm, -rʊm **-s** -z
Chatsworth ˈtʃæts.wəθ, -wɜːθ US -wɚθ, -wɝːθ
Chattanooga ˌtʃæt.ᵊnˈuː.gə US ˌtʃæt̬.əˈnuː-, ˌtʃæt.ᵊnˈuː-
chattel ˈtʃæt.ᵊl US ˈtʃæt̬- **-s** -z
chatt|er ˈtʃæt|.əʳ US ˈtʃæt̬|.ɚ **-ers** -əz US -ɚz **-ering** -ᵊr.ɪŋ **-ered** -əd US -ɚd **-erer/s** -ᵊr.əʳ/z US -ɚ.ɚ/z ˈ**chattering** ˌ**classes**
chatterbox ˈtʃæt.ə.bɒks US ˈtʃæt̬.ɚ.bɑːks **-es** -ɪz
Chatteris ˈtʃæt.ᵊr.ɪs
Chatterley ˈtʃæt.ᵊl.i US ˈtʃæt̬.ɚ.li
Chatterton ˈtʃæt.ə.tᵊn US ˈtʃæt̬.ɚ-
Chatto ˈtʃæt.əʊ US -oʊ, ˈtʃæt̬-
chatt|y ˈtʃæt|.i US ˈtʃæt̬|.i **-ier** -i.əʳ US -i.ɚ **-iest** -i.ɪst, -i.əst **-ily** -ɪ.li, -ᵊl.i **-iness** -ɪ.nəs, -ɪ.nɪs
Chatwin ˈtʃæt.wɪn
Chaucer ˈtʃɔː.səʳ US ˈtʃɑː.sɚ, ˈtʃɔː-
Chaucerian tʃɔːˈsɪə.ri.ən US tʃɑːˈsɪr.i-, tʃɔː-, -ˈser-
chaudfroid ˈʃəʊ.fwɑː, -frwɑː US ˈʃoʊ-
Chaudhuri ˈtʃaʊ.dᵊr.i
chauffer ˈtʃɔː.fəʳ US ˈtʃɑː.fɚ, ˈtʃɔː- **-s** -z
chauffeur ˈʃəʊ.fəʳ, ʃəʊˈfɜːʳ US ʃoʊˈfɝː **-s** -z **-ing** -ɪŋ **-ed** -d
Chauncey ˈtʃɔːn*t*.si US ˈtʃɑːn*t*-, ˈtʃɔːn*t*-
chauvin|ism ˈʃəʊ.vɪ.n|ɪ.zᵊm, -və- US ˈʃoʊ- **-ist/s** -ɪst/s
chauvinistic ˌʃəʊ.vɪˈnɪs.tɪk, -vəˈ- US ˌʃoʊ- **-ally** -ᵊl.i, -li
Chavez ˈtʃæv.es US ˈʃɑː.vez, ˈtʃɑː-, -ves
Chaworth ˈtʃɑː.wəθ, -wɜːθ US -wɚθ, -wɝːθ
Chayefsky tʃaɪˈef.ski
Che tʃeɪ
Cheadle ˈtʃiː.dl̩
Cheam tʃiːm
cheap tʃiːp **-er** -əʳ US -ɚ **-est** -ɪst, -əst **-ly** -li **-ness** -nəs, -nɪs ˌ**cheap** ˈ**shot**
cheapen ˈtʃiː.pᵊn **-s** -z **-ing** -ɪŋ **-ed** -d
cheapie ˈtʃiː.pi **-s** -z
cheap-jack ˈtʃiːp.dʒæk **-s** -s
cheapo ˈtʃiː.pəʊ US -poʊ **-s** -z
Cheapside ˈtʃiːp.saɪd, tʃiːpˈsaɪd
cheapskate ˈtʃiːp.skeɪt **-s** -s
cheat tʃiːt **-s** -s **-ing** -ɪŋ US ˈtʃiː.t̬ɪŋ **-ed** -ɪd US ˈtʃiː.t̬ɪd
Cheatham ˈtʃiː.təm US -t̬əm
Chechen ˌtʃetʃˈen **-s** -z *stress shift:* ˌChechen ˈfighters
Chechenia ˈtʃetʃ.ni.ɑː, -ni.ə; tʃetʃ.ɪˈnjɑː US -ni.ə
Chechnya ˈtʃetʃ.ni.ə, -ni.ɑː; tʃetʃ.ɪˈnjɑː US -ni.ə
check tʃek **-s** -s **-ing** -ɪŋ **-ed** -t ˈ**checking** **acˌcount**
checkbook ˈtʃek.bʊk **-s** -s
check|er (C) ˈtʃek|.əʳ US -ɚ **-ers** -əz US -ɚz **-ering** -ᵊr.ɪŋ **-ered** -əd US -ɚd
checkerboard ˈtʃek.ə.bɔːd US -ɚ.bɔːrd **-s** -z
checkers ˈtʃek.əz US -ɚz
check-in ˈtʃek.ɪn **-s** -z ˈ**check-in** ˌ**desk**
Checkland ˈtʃek.lənd
checklist ˈtʃek.lɪst **-s** -s
checkma|te ˈtʃek.meɪ|t, ˌ-ˈ- **-tes** -ts **-ting** -tɪŋ US -t̬ɪŋ **-ted** -tɪd US -t̬ɪd
checkout ˈtʃek.aʊt **-s** -s
checkpoint ˈtʃek.pɔɪnt **-s** -s ˌ**Checkpoint** ˈ**Charlie**
checkrein ˈtʃek.reɪn **-s** -z
checkroom ˈtʃek.rʊm, -ruːm US -ruːm **-s** -z
checkup ˈtʃek.ʌp **-s** -s
cheddar (C) ˈtʃed.əʳ US -ɚ **-s** -z **-ing** -ɪŋ **-ed** -d
cheek tʃiːk **-s** -s **-ing** -ɪŋ **-ed** -t ˌ**turn the other** ˈ**cheek**
cheekbone ˈtʃiːk.bəʊn US -boʊn **-s** -z
Cheeke tʃiːk
cheek|y ˈtʃiː.k|i **-ier** -i.əʳ US -i.ɚ **-iest** -i.ɪst, -i.əst **-ily** -ɪ.li, -ᵊl.i **-iness** -ɪ.nəs, -ɪ.nɪs
cheep tʃiːp **-s** -s **-ing** -ɪŋ **-ed** -t
cheer tʃɪəʳ US tʃɪr **-s** -z **-ing** -ɪŋ **-ed** -d
cheerful ˈtʃɪə.fᵊl, -fʊl US ˈtʃɪr- **-ly** -i **-ness** -nəs, -nɪs
cheerio ˌtʃɪə.riˈəʊ US ˌtʃɪr.iˈoʊ **-s** -z
Cheerios® ˈtʃɪə.ri.əʊz, ˈtʃɪr.i.oʊz
cheerleader ˈtʃɪəˌliː.dəʳ US ˈtʃɪrˌliː.dɚ **-s** -z
cheerless ˈtʃɪə.ləs, -lɪs US ˈtʃɪr- **-ly** -li **-ness** -nəs, -nɪs
cheer|y ˈtʃɪə.r|i US ˈtʃɪr|.i **-ier** -i.əʳ US -i.ɚ **-iest** -i.ɪst, -i.əst **-ily** -ɪ.li, -ᵊl.i **-iness** -ɪ.nəs, -ɪ.nɪs

chees|e tʃiːz **-es** -ɪz **-ed** -d ˌcheesed ˈoff
cheeseboard ˈtʃiːz.bɔːd ⓤⓢ -bɔːrd **-s** -z
cheeseburger ˈtʃiːzˌbɜː.gəʳ ⓤⓢ -ˌbɝː.gɚ **-s** -z
cheesecake ˈtʃiːz.keɪk **-s** -s
cheesecloth ˈtʃiːz.klɒθ ⓤⓢ -klɑːθ
Cheeseman ˈtʃiːz.mən
cheesemonger ˈtʃiːzˌmʌŋ.gəʳ ⓤⓢ -gɚ, -ˌmɑːŋ- **-s** -z
cheeseparing ˈtʃiːzˌpeə.rɪŋ ⓤⓢ -ˌper.ɪŋ
Cheesewright ˈtʃiːz.raɪt, ˈtʃez-
chees|y ˈtʃiː.z|i **-ier** -i.əʳ ⓤⓢ -i.ɚ **-iest** -i.ɪst, -i.əst **-iness** -ɪ.nəs, -ɪ.nɪs
cheetah ˈtʃiː.tə ⓤⓢ -t̬ə **-s** -z
Cheetham ˈtʃiː.təm ⓤⓢ -t̬əm
Cheever ˈtʃiː.vəʳ ⓤⓢ -vɚ
chef ʃef **-s** -s
chef d'équipe ˌʃef.dekˈiːp
chef(s) d'oeuvre, chef(s)-d'oeuvre ˌʃeɪˈdɜːv.rə, -əʳ ⓤⓢ ˌʃeɪˈdɜːv.rə, -ˈdɝːv
Cheke tʃiːk
Chekhov ˈtʃek.ɒf, -ɒv ⓤⓢ -ɑːf, -ɔːf, -ɑːv
chela ˈtʃeɪ.lə, ˈtʃiː.lə **-s** -z
chela|te kiːˈleɪ|t, kə-, tʃiː-, kɪ-; ˈkiː.leɪ|t, ˈtʃiː- ⓤⓢ ˈkiː.leɪ|t **-tes** -ts **-ting** -tɪŋ ⓤⓢ -t̬ɪŋ **-ted** -tɪd ⓤⓢ -t̬ɪd
chelation kiːˈleɪ.ʃən, kə-, tʃiː-, kɪ-
Chelmer ˈtʃel.məʳ ⓤⓢ -mɚ
Chelmsford ˈtʃelmz.fəd, ˈtʃelmps- *old-fashioned local pronunciations:* ˈtʃemz-, ˈtʃɒmz- ⓤⓢ -fɚd
Chelsea ˈtʃel.si ˌChelsea ˈbun, ˈChelsea ˌbun; ˌChelsea ˈpensioner
Chelsey ˈtʃel.si
Cheltenham ˈtʃel.tən.əm
Chelyabinsk tʃelˈjɑː.bɪnsk
chemic ˈkem.ɪk
chemical ˈkem.ɪ.kəl **-ly** -i **-s** -z ˌchemical engiˈneering; ˌchemical ˈwarfare
chemis|e ʃəˈmiːz **-es** -ɪz
chemist ˈkem.ɪst **-s** -s
chemistry ˈkem.ɪ.stri, -ə-
Chemnitz ˈkem.nɪts
chemo- ˈkiː.məʊ-, ˈkem.əʊ- ⓤⓢ ˈkiː.moʊ-, ˈkem.oʊ-
chemotherapy ˌkiː.məʊˈθer.ə.pi, ˌkem.əʊ- ⓤⓢ ˌkiː.moʊˈ-, ˌkem.oʊˈ-
Chenevix ˈtʃen.ə.vɪks, ˈʃen.ə.vɪks
Cheney ˈtʃiː.ni, ˈtʃeɪ- ⓤⓢ ˈtʃeɪ-
Chengdu ˌtʃʌŋˈduː
Chenies *in Buckinghamshire:* ˈtʃeɪ.niz *street in London:* ˈtʃiː.niz
chenille ʃəˈniːl
cheongsam ˌtʃɒŋˈsæm, tʃiˌɒŋ- ⓤⓢ ˌtʃɔːŋ-, ˌtʃɑːŋ- **-s** -z
Cheops ˈkiː.ɒps ⓤⓢ -ɑːps
Chepstow ˈtʃep.stəʊ ⓤⓢ -stoʊ
cheque tʃek **-s** -s ˈcheque ˌcard
chequebook ˈtʃek.bʊk **-s** -s
chequecard ˈtʃek.kɑːd ⓤⓢ -kɑːrd **-s** -z
chequ|er ˈtʃek|.əʳ ⓤⓢ -ɚ **-ers** -əz ⓤⓢ -ɚz **-ering** -ər.ɪŋ **-ered** -əd ⓤⓢ -ɚd
Chequers ˈtʃek.əz ⓤⓢ -ɚz
Cher ʃeəʳ ⓤⓢ ʃer
Cherbourg ˈʃeə.bʊəg, ʃɜː-, -bɔːg, -bɜːg ⓤⓢ ˈʃer.bʊrg, -bʊr, -ˈ-
Cherie ʃəˈriː, ˈʃer.i
cherish ˈtʃer.ɪʃ **-es** -ɪz **-ing** -ɪŋ **-ed** -t
Cheriton ˈtʃer.ɪ.tən
Chernobyl tʃɜːˈnəʊ.bəl, tʃə-, -ˈnɒb.əl, -ɪl ⓤⓢ tʃɚˈnoʊ.bəl
Chernomyrdin ˌtʃɜː.nəˈmɪə.dɪn, ˌtʃeə-, -ˈmɜː-, -dən ⓤⓢ ˌtʃɝː.nəˈmɪr-, -noʊˈ-, ˌtʃer-, -ˈmɝː-
Cherokee ˈtʃer.ə.kiː, ˌ--ˈ- **-s** -z
cheroot ʃəˈruːt **-s** -s
cherr|y (C) ˈtʃer|.i **-ies** -iz ˌcherry ˈbrandy; ˌcherry ˈpie; ˌcherry toˈmato
cherrystone ˈtʃer.i.stəʊn ⓤⓢ -stoʊn **-s** -z
chersonese ˈkɜː.sə.niːs, -niːz, ˌ--ˈ- ⓤⓢ ˌkɝː.sə.niːz, -niːs
Chertsey ˈtʃɜːt.si ⓤⓢ ˈtʃɝːt-
cherub ˈtʃer.əb **-s** -z
cherubic tʃəˈruː.bɪk, tʃerˈuː- ⓤⓢ tʃəˈruː- **-ally** -əl.i, -li
cherubim ˈtʃer.ə.bɪm, ˈ-ʊ-
Cherubini ˌker.ʊˈbiː.niː, -əˈ-, -ni
chervil ˈtʃɜː.vɪl, -vəl ⓤⓢ ˈtʃɝː-
Cherwell ˈtʃɑː.wəl, -wel ⓤⓢ ˈtʃɑːr-
Cheryl ˈtʃer.əl, ˈʃer-, -ɪl ⓤⓢ ˈʃer.əl
Chesapeake ˈtʃes.ə.piːk
Chesebro, Chesebrough ˈtʃiːz.brə
Chesham ˈtʃeʃ.əm *old-fashioned local pronunciation:* ˈtʃes-
Cheshire ˈtʃeʃ.əʳ, -ɪəʳ ⓤⓢ -ɚ, -ɪr ˌCheshire ˈcat; ˌCheshire ˈcheese
Cheshunt ˈtʃes.ənt, ˈtʃeʃ-
Chesil ˈtʃez.əl ˌChesil ˈBank; ˌChesil ˈBeach
Chesney ˈtʃes.ni, ˈtʃez.ni
Chesnutt ˈtʃes.nʌt
chess tʃes
chessboard ˈtʃes.bɔːd ⓤⓢ -bɔːrd **-s** -z
chess|man ˈtʃes|.mæn, -mən **-men** -men, -mən
chest tʃest **-s** -s **-ed** -ɪd ˌchest of ˈdrawers
Chester ˈtʃes.təʳ ⓤⓢ -tɚ
chesterfield (C) ˈtʃes.tə.fiːld ⓤⓢ -tɚ- **-s** -z
Chester-le-Street ˌtʃes.tə.lɪˈstriːt, ˈ---ˌ- ⓤⓢ -tɚ-
Chesterton ˈtʃes.tə.tən ⓤⓢ -tɚ.t̬ən
chestnut ˈtʃes.nʌt, ˈtʃest- **-s** -s
Chestre ˈtʃes.təʳ ⓤⓢ -tɚ
chest|y ˈtʃes.t|i **-ier** -i.əʳ ⓤⓢ -i.ɚ **-iest** -i.ɪst, -i.əst **-ily** -ɪ.li, -əl.i **-iness** -ɪ.nəs, -ɪ.nɪs
Chetham ˈtʃet.əm
chetrum ˈtʃet.rʊm, -rəm
Chettle ˈtʃet.l̩ ⓤⓢ ˈtʃet̬-
Chetwode ˈtʃet.wʊd
Chetwynd ˈtʃet.wɪnd
cheval-glass ʃəˈvæl.glɑːs ⓤⓢ -glæs **-es** -ɪz
chevalier ˌʃev.əˈlɪəʳ ⓤⓢ -ˈlɪr **-s** -z
Chevalier *surname:* ʃəˈvæl.i.eɪ, ʃɪ- ⓤⓢ -i.eɪ, -jeɪ
Chevening ˈtʃiːv.nɪŋ
Cheves tʃiːvz
Chevette® ʃəˈvet, ʃevˈet **-s** -s
Cheviot *hills, sheep:* ˈtʃiː.vi.ət, ˈtʃev.i-, ˈtʃɪv.i- ⓤⓢ ˈʃev.i- *cloth:* ˈtʃev.i.ət ⓤⓢ ˈʃev-
Chevis ˈtʃev.ɪs
Chevrolet® ˈʃev.rə.leɪ, ˌ--ˈ- ⓤⓢ ˌʃev.rəˈleɪ **-s** -z
chevron ˈʃev.rən, -rɒn ⓤⓢ -rən **-s** -z
chev|y (C) ˈtʃev|.i **-ies** -iz **-ying** -i.ɪŋ **-ied** -id
Chevy ˈʃev.i
chew tʃuː **-s** -z **-ing** -ɪŋ **-ed** -d ˈchewing ˌgum
chew|y ˈtʃuː|.i **-ier** -i.əʳ ⓤⓢ -i.ɚ **-iest** -i.ɪst, -i.əst **-iness** -ɪ.nəs, -ɪ.nɪs
Cheyenne ˌʃaɪˈæn, -ˈen ⓤⓢ -ˈen, -ˈæn
Cheyne ˈtʃeɪ.ni, tʃeɪn
Cheyney ˈtʃeɪ.ni
chez ʃeɪ
Chiang Kai-Shek ˌtʃæŋ.kaɪˈʃek ⓤⓢ ˌtʃæŋ-, ˌdʒæŋ-
Chiang Mai tʃiˌæŋˈmaɪ ⓤⓢ ˌdʒɑːŋˈmaɪ, tʃiˌɑːŋ-
chianti (C) kiˈæn.ti ⓤⓢ -ˈɑːn.t̬i, -ˈæn-
Chiantishire kiˈæn.ti.ʃəʳ, -ˌʃɪəʳ ⓤⓢ -ˈɑːn.t̬i.ʃɚ, -ˈæn-, -ˌʃɪr
Chiapas tʃiˈæp.əs ⓤⓢ -ˈɑː.pəs
chiaroscuro kiˌɑː.rəˈskʊə.rəʊ, -rɒsˈkʊə-, -ˈkjʊə- ⓤⓢ -ˌɑːr.əˈskjʊr.oʊ
chias|ma kaɪˈæz|.mə **-mata** -mə.tə ⓤⓢ -mə.t̬ə **-mas** -məz
chiasmus kaɪˈæz.məs
chic ʃiːk, ʃɪk
Chicago ʃɪˈkɑː.gəʊ, ʃə- ⓤⓢ -goʊ, -ˈkɔː-
chican|e ʃɪˈkeɪn, ʃə- **-es** -z **-ing** -ɪŋ **-ed** -d **-er/s** -əʳ/z ⓤⓢ -ɚ/z
chicaner|y ʃɪˈkeɪ.nər|.i, ʃə- **-ies** -iz
chicano tʃɪˈkɑː.nəʊ ⓤⓢ -noʊ **-s** -z
Chichele ˈtʃɪtʃ.əl.i, -ɪ.li
Chichén Itzá tʃiˌtʃen.ɪtˈsɑː ⓤⓢ -iːtˈ-
Chichester ˈtʃɪtʃ.ɪ.stəʳ, ˈ-ə- ⓤⓢ -stɚ
chi-chi ˈʃiː.ʃiː
chick (C) tʃɪk **-s** -s
chickabidd|y ˈtʃɪk.əˌbɪd|.i **-ies** -iz
chickadee ˈtʃɪk.əˌdiː, ˌ--ˈ- **-s** -z
Chickasaw ˈtʃɪk.ə.sɔː ⓤⓢ -sɔː, -sɑː **-s** -z
chicken ˈtʃɪk.ɪn, -ən **-s** -z **-ing** -ɪŋ **-ed** -d ˈchicken ˌfeed; ˌchicken ˈKiev; ˈchicken ˌpox; ˌdon't count your ˌchickens before they ˈhatch
chickenhearted ˌtʃɪk.ɪnˈhɑː.tɪd, -ənˈ-, -təd, ˈtʃɪk.ɪnˌhɑː-, -ənˌ- ⓤⓢ ˌtʃɪk.ɪnˈhɑːr.t̬ɪd, -ənˈ-, -t̬əd

chickenshit ˈtʃɪk.ɪn.ʃɪt, -ən- **-s** -s
Chicklets® ˈtʃɪk.ləts, -lɪts
chickpea ˈtʃɪk.piː **-s** -z
chickweed ˈtʃɪk.wiːd
Chiclayo tʃiˈklaɪ.jəʊ (US) -joʊ
chicory ˈtʃɪk.ər.i
Chiddingly ˌtʃɪd.ɪŋˈlaɪ, ˈ---
chid|e tʃaɪd **-es** -z **-ing** -ɪŋ **-ed** -ɪd **chid** tʃɪd **chidden** ˈtʃɪd.ən
chief tʃiːf **-s** -s **-ly** -li **ˌchief inˈspector; ˌchief of ˈstaff**
chieftain ˈtʃiːf.tən, -tɪn **-s** -z
chieftanc|y ˈtʃiːf.tənt.s|i, -tɪnt- **-ies** -iz
chiff-chaff ˈtʃɪf.tʃæf **-s** -s
chiffon ˈʃɪf.ɒn, ʃɪˈfɒn (US) ʃɪˈfɑːn **-s** -z
chiffon(n)ier ˌʃɪf.əˈnɪər, -ni.eɪ *as if French:* ʃiː.fɔ̃ːˈnje (US) -ˈnɪr **-s** -z
chifforobe ˈʃɪf.ə.rəʊb (US) ˈʃɪf.roʊb **-s** -z
chignon ˈʃiː.njɒn, -njɒŋ, -njɔ̃ː *old-fashioned:* ʃɪˈnɒn (US) ˈʃiː.njɑːn **-s** -z
Chigwell ˈtʃɪg.wel, -wəl
chihuahua (C) tʃɪˈwɑː.wə, tʃə-, ʃɪ-, ʃə-, -wɑː **-s** -z
chilblain ˈtʃɪl.bleɪn **-s** -z
child (C) tʃaɪld **children** ˈtʃɪl.drən **ˈchild aˌbuse; ˌchild ˈbenefit; ˈchild's ˌplay; ˌchild ˈprodigy; ˌchild supˈport**
childbearing ˈtʃaɪldˌbeə.rɪŋ (US) -ˌber.ɪŋ
childbed ˈtʃaɪld.bed
childbirth ˈtʃaɪld.bɜːθ (US) -bɝːθ
childcare ˈtʃaɪld.keər (US) -ker
Childe tʃaɪld
Childermas ˈtʃɪl.də.mæs, -məs (US) -dɚ.mæs
Childers ˈtʃɪl.dəz (US) -dɚz
childhood ˈtʃaɪld.hʊd **ˌchildhood ˈsweetheart**
childish ˈtʃaɪl.dɪʃ **-ly** -li **-ness** -nəs, -nɪs
childless ˈtʃaɪld.ləs, -lɪs **-ness** -nəs, -nɪs
childlike ˈtʃaɪld.laɪk
childmind|er ˈtʃaɪldˌmaɪn.d|ər (US) -d|ɚ **-ers** -əz (US) -ɚz **-ing** -ɪŋ
childproof ˈtʃaɪld.pruːf
children *(from* **child***)* ˈtʃɪl.drən **ˈchildren's ˌhome**
Childs tʃaɪldz
Chile ˈtʃɪl.i, ˈtʃiː.leɪ
Chilean ˈtʃɪl.i.ən, tʃɪˈliː.ən (US) tʃɪˈliː-, ˈtʃɪl.i- **-s** -z
chili ˈtʃɪl.i **-s** -z
chiliad ˈkɪl.i.æd, ˈkaɪ.li-, -əd **-s** -z
chili|asm ˈkɪl.i|.æz.əm **-ast/s** -æst/s
chilidog ˈtʃɪl.i.dɒg (US) -dɑːg, -dɔːg **-s** -z
chill tʃɪl **-s** -z **-ing/ly** -ɪŋ/li **-ed** -d **-ness** -nəs, -nɪs **-er** -ər (US) -ɚ
chiller ˈtʃɪl.ər (US) -ɚ **-s** -z
chilli ˈtʃɪl.i **-es** -z **ˈchilli ˌpepper; ˈchilli ˌpowder**
chilli con carne ˌtʃɪl.i.kɒnˈkɑː.ni, -kɒŋˈ-, -kənˈ-, -kəŋˈ-, -neɪ (US) -kɑːnˈkɑːr.ni, -kənˈ-
Chillingham ˈtʃɪl.ɪŋ.əm
Chillingly ˈtʃɪl.ɪŋ.li
Chillingworth ˈtʃɪl.ɪŋ.wəθ, -wɜːθ (US) -wɚθ, -wɝːθ
Chillon ʃɪˈlɒn, ʃə-; ˈʃɪl.ən, -ɒn (US) ʃəˈlɑːn, ʃɪ-; ˈʃɪl.ən; ʃiˈjoʊn
Note: In Byron's 'Castle of Chillon' it is usual to pronounce /ˈʃɪl.ən/ or /ˈʃɪl.ɒn (US) -ɑːn/.
chill|y ˈtʃɪl|.i **-ier** -i.ər (US) -i.ɚ **-iest** -i.ɪst, -i.əst **-iness** -ɪ.nəs, -ɪ.nɪs
Chiltern ˈtʃɪl.tən (US) -tɚn **ˌChiltern ˈHills; ˌChiltern ˈHundreds**
Chilton ˈtʃɪl.tən
chimaera kaɪˈmɪə.rə, kɪ-, kə-, ʃɪ-, ʃə-, -ˈmeə-; (US) kaɪˈmɪr.ə, kɪ- **-s** -z
Chimborazo ˌtʃɪm.bəˈrɑː.zəʊ, ˌʃɪm-, -bɒrˈɑː- (US) -bəˈrɑː.zoʊ
chim|e tʃaɪm **-es** -z **-ing** -ɪŋ **-ed** -d **-er/s** -ər/z (US) -ɚ/z
chimera kaɪˈmɪə.rə, kɪ-, kə-, ʃɪ-, ʃə-, -ˈmeə-; ˈkɪm.ər.ə (US) kaɪˈmɪr.ə, kɪ- **-s** -z
chimere tʃɪˈmɪər, ʃɪ-, kɪ-, kaɪ- (US) -ˈmɪr **-s** -z
chimeric kaɪˈmer.ɪk, kɪ-, kə- **-al** -əl **-ally** -əl.i, -li
Chimkent tʃɪmˈkent
chimney ˈtʃɪm.ni **-s** -z **ˈchimney ˌbreast; ˈchimney ˌpot; ˈchimney ˌstack; ˈchimney ˌsweep; ˈchimney ˌsweeper**
chimneypiec|e ˈtʃɪm.ni.piːs **-es** -ɪz
chimp tʃɪmp **-s** -s
chimpanzee ˌtʃɪm.pənˈziː, -pænˈ- (US) tʃɪmˈpæn.ziː, ˌtʃɪm.pənˈzi **-s** -z
chin tʃɪn **-s** -z **ˌchin-ˈdeep**
china (C) ˈtʃaɪ.nə **ˈchina ˌclay ˌchina ˈclay; like a ˌbull in a ˈchina shop**
China|man ˈtʃaɪ.nə|.mən **-men** -mən
Chinatown ˈtʃaɪ.nə.taʊn
chinchilla tʃɪnˈtʃɪl.ə **-s** -z
Chindit ˈtʃɪn.dɪt **-s** -s
chin|e tʃaɪn **-es** -z **-ing** -ɪŋ **-ed** -d
Chinese tʃaɪˈniːz (US) -ˈniːz, -ˈniːs *stress shift, see compounds:* **ˌChinese ˈgooseberry; ˌChinese ˈlantern; ˌChinese ˈrestaurant**
Chingford ˈtʃɪŋ.fəd (US) -fɚd
chink (C) tʃɪŋk **-s** -s **-ing** **-ed**
Chinkie, Chinky ˈtʃɪŋ.ki
chinless ˈtʃɪn.ləs, -lɪs **ˌchinless ˈwonder**
Chinnock ˈtʃɪn.ək
Chinnor ˈtʃɪn.ər (US) -ɚ
chino ˈtʃiː.nəʊ (US) -noʊ **-s** -z
Chinook tʃɪˈnʊk, -ˈnuːk (US) ʃəˈnʊk, tʃə-
chinstrap ˈtʃɪn.stræp **-s** -s
chintz tʃɪnts **-es** -ɪz **-y** -i
chinwag ˈtʃɪn.wæg **-s** -s **-ging** -ɪŋ
Chios ˈkaɪ.ɒs, ˈkiː- (US) -ɑːs
chip tʃɪp **-s** -s **-ping** -ɪŋ **-ped** -t **ˈchip ˌshop; have a ˈchip on one's ˌshoulder**
chipboard ˈtʃɪp.bɔːd (US) -bɔːrd
chipmunk ˈtʃɪp.mʌŋk **-s** -s
chipolata ˌtʃɪp.əlˈɑː.tə (US) -əˈlɑː.t̬ə **-s** -z
Chipp tʃɪp
Chippendale ˈtʃɪp.ən.deɪl **-s** -z
Chippenham ˈtʃɪp.ən.əm
chipper ˈtʃɪp.ər (US) -ɚ
Chipperfield ˈtʃɪp.ə.fiːld (US) -ɚ-
Chippewa ˈtʃɪp.ɪ.wɑː, -wə **-s** -z
chippie ˈtʃɪp.i **-s** -z
Chipping ˈtʃɪp.ɪŋ
Chipping Sodbury ˌtʃɪp.ɪŋˈsɒd.bər.i (US) -ˈsɑːd.ber-, -bɚ-
chipp|y ˈtʃɪp|.i **-ier** -i.ər (US) -i.ɚ **-iest** -i.ɪst, -i.əst **-iness** -ɪ.nəs, -ɪ.nɪs
Chips tʃɪps
Chirac ˈʃɪə.ræk, ʃiˈræk (US) ʃəˈrɑːk, ʃɪˈræk
Chirk tʃɜːk (US) tʃɝːk
chirograph ˈkaɪə.rəʊ.grɑːf, -græf (US) ˈkaɪ.rə.græf **-s** -s
chirographer kaɪəˈrɒg.rə.fər (US) kaɪˈrɑː.grə.fɚ **-s** -z
chirographic ˌkaɪə.rəʊˈgræf.ɪk (US) ˌkaɪ.roʊˈ-
chirographist kaɪəˈrɒg.rə.fɪst (US) kaɪˈrɑː.grə- **-s** -s
chirography kaɪəˈrɒg.rə.fi (US) kaɪˈrɑː.grə-
Chirol ˈtʃɪr.əl
chiromancer ˈkaɪə.rəʊ.mænt.sər (US) ˈkaɪ.roʊ.mænt.sɚ **-s** -z
chiromancy ˈkaɪə.rəʊ.mænt.si (US) ˈkaɪ.roʊ-
Chiron ˈkaɪə.rən (US) ˈkaɪ-
chiropodist kɪˈrɒp.ə.dɪst, ʃɪ-, tʃɪ- (US) kɪˈrɑː.pə-, kaɪ-, ʃɪ- **-s** -s
chiropody kɪˈrɒp.ə.di, ʃɪ-, tʃɪ- (US) kɪˈrɑː.pə-, kaɪ-, ʃɪ-
chiropractic ˌkaɪə.rəʊˈpræk.tɪk (US) ˌkaɪ.roʊˈ-, ˈkaɪ.roʊ.præk-
chiropractor ˈkaɪə.rəʊ.præk.tər (US) ˈkaɪ.roʊ.præk.tɚ **-s** -z
chirp tʃɜːp (US) tʃɝːp **-s** -s **-ing** -ɪŋ **-ed** -t
chirp|y ˈtʃɜː.p|i (US) ˈtʃɝː- **-ier** -i.ər (US) -i.ɚ **-iest** -i.ɪst, -i.əst **-ily** -ɪ.li, -əl.i **-iness** -ɪ.nəs, -ɪ.nɪs
chirr tʃɜːr (US) tʃɝː **-s** -z **-ing** -ɪŋ **-ed** -d
chirrup ˈtʃɪr.əp (US) ˈtʃɪr-, ˈtʃɝː- **-s** -s **-ing** -ɪŋ **-ed** -t
chisel ˈtʃɪz.əl **-s** -z **-(l)ing** -ɪŋ **-(l)ed** -d **-(l)er/s** -ər/z (US) -ɚ/z
Chisholm ˈtʃɪz.əm
Chislehurst ˈtʃɪz.l̩.hɜːst (US) -hɝːst
Chiswick ˈtʃɪz.ɪk
chit tʃɪt **-s** -s
chit-chat, chitchat ˈtʃɪt.tʃæt
chitin ˈkaɪ.tɪn, -tən (US) -tən
Chittagong ˈtʃɪt.ə.gɒŋ (US) ˈtʃɪt̬.ə.gɑːŋ, -gɔːŋ
Chittenden ˈtʃɪt.ən.dən
chitterling ˈtʃɪt.əl.ɪŋ (US) ˈtʃɪt̬.ɚ.lɪŋ **-s** -z

Chitty 'tʃɪt.i ⓤⓢ 'tʃɪt̬-
chivalric 'ʃɪv.ᵊl.rɪk ⓤⓢ ʃɪ'væl-; 'ʃɪv.ᵊl-
chivalrous 'ʃɪv.ᵊl.rəs **-ly** -li **-ness** -nəs, -nɪs
chivalry 'ʃɪv.ᵊl.ri
chive tʃaɪv **-s** -z
Chivers 'tʃɪv.əz ⓤⓢ -ɚz
chivv|y 'tʃɪv|.i **-ies** -iz **-ying** -i.ɪŋ **-ied** -id
chiv|y 'tʃɪv|.i **-ies** -iz **-ying** -i.ɪŋ **-ied** -id
chlamid|ia, chlamyd|ia klə'mɪd|.i.ə **-iae** -i.i **-ial** -i.əl
chlamy|s 'klæm.ɪ|s, 'kleɪ.mɪ|s **-des** -diːz
Chloe, Chloë 'kləʊ.i ⓤⓢ 'kloʊ-
chloral 'klɔː.rᵊl ⓤⓢ 'klɔːr.ᵊl
chloramine 'klɔː.rə.miːn; -mɪn ⓤⓢ 'klɔːr.ə.miːn, ˌ--'-; klɔː'ræm.iːn, -ɪn
chlorate 'klɔː.reɪt, -rɪt ⓤⓢ 'klɔːr.eɪt, -ɪt **-s** -s
chloric 'klɔː.rɪk, 'klɒr.ɪk ⓤⓢ 'klɔːr.ɪk
chloride 'klɔː.raɪd ⓤⓢ 'klɔːr.aɪd **-s** -z
chlori|nate 'klɔː.rɪ|.neɪt, 'klɒr.ɪ- ⓤⓢ 'klɔːr.ɪ- **-nates** -neɪts **-nating** -neɪ.tɪŋ ⓤⓢ -neɪ.t̬ɪŋ **-nated** -neɪ.tɪd ⓤⓢ -neɪ.t̬ɪd
chlorine 'klɔː.riːn ⓤⓢ 'klɔːr.iːn, -ɪn
Chloris 'klɔː.rɪs, 'klɒr.ɪs ⓤⓢ 'klɔːr.ɪs
chlorite 'klɔː.raɪt ⓤⓢ 'klɔːr.aɪt **-s** -s
chloro- 'klɔː.rəʊ-, 'klɒr.əʊ- ⓤⓢ 'klɔːr.ə-, '-oʊ-
chlorodyne 'klɔː.rə.daɪn, 'klɒr.ə- ⓤⓢ 'klɔːr.ə-
chlorofluorocarbon ˌklɔː.rəʊˌflɔː.rəʊ'kɑː.bᵊn, ˌklɒr.əʊ-, -ˌflʊə- ⓤⓢ ˌklɔːr.oʊˌflɔːr.oʊ'kɑːr-, -ˌflʊr- **-s** -z
chloroform 'klɔː.rə.fɔːm, 'klɒr.ə- ⓤⓢ 'klɔːr.ə.fɔːrm **-s** -z **-ing** -ɪŋ **-ed** -d
Chloromycetin® ˌklɔː.rəʊ.maɪ'siː.tɪn, ˌklɒr.əʊ- ⓤⓢ ˌklɔːr.oʊ.maɪ'siː.tᵊn
chlorophyl(l) 'klɔː.rə.fɪl, 'klɒr.ə- ⓤⓢ 'klɔːr.ə-
chlorophyllose ˌklɔː.rə'fɪl.əʊs, ˌklɒr.ə'- ⓤⓢ ˌklɔːr.ə'fɪl.oʊs
chloroplast 'klɒr.ə.plɑːst, -plæst ⓤⓢ 'klɔːr.ə.plæst
chlorous 'klɔː.rəs ⓤⓢ 'klɔːr.əs
Choate tʃəʊt ⓤⓢ tʃoʊt
choc tʃɒk ⓤⓢ tʃɑːk **-s** -s
choc-ic|e 'tʃɒk.aɪs ⓤⓢ 'tʃɑːk- **-es** -ɪz
chock tʃɒk ⓤⓢ tʃɑːk **-s** -s ˌ**chock-'full**
chock-a-block ˌtʃɒk.ə'blɒk, '--- ⓤⓢ 'tʃɑːk.ə.blɑːk
chocker, chocka 'tʃɒk.əʳ ⓤⓢ 'tʃɑː.kɚ
chocoholic, chocaholic ˌtʃɒk.ə'hɒl.ɪk ⓤⓢ ˌtʃɑː.kə'hɑː.lɪk **-s** -s
chocolate 'tʃɒk.ᵊl.ət, -ɪt, '-lət, -lɪt ⓤⓢ 'tʃɑːk.lət, 'tʃɔːk-, 'tʃɑː.kᵊl.ət, 'tʃɔː-, -ɪt **-s** -s ˌ**chocolate 'cake,** '**chocolate** ˌ**cake;** ˌ**chocolate chip 'cookie;** '**drinking** ˌ**chocolate**
Choctaw 'tʃɒk.tɔː ⓤⓢ 'tʃɑːk.tɔː, -tɑː
choic|e tʃɔɪs **-es** -ɪz **-er** -əʳ ⓤⓢ -ɚ **-est** -ɪst, -əst **-ely** -li **-eness** -nəs, -nɪs
choir kwaɪəʳ ⓤⓢ kwaɪɚ **-s** -z '**choir** ˌ**screen**
choirboy 'kwaɪə.bɔɪ ⓤⓢ 'kwaɪɚ- **-s** -z
choirmaster 'kwaɪəˌmɑː.stəʳ ⓤⓢ 'kwaɪɚˌmæs.tɚ **-s** -z
chok|e tʃəʊk ⓤⓢ tʃoʊk **-es** -s **-ing** -ɪŋ **-ed** -t
choker 'tʃəʊ.kəʳ ⓤⓢ 'tʃoʊ.kɚ **-s** -z
chok|y 'tʃəʊ.k|i ⓤⓢ 'tʃoʊ- **-ier** -i.əʳ ⓤⓢ -i.ɚ **-iest** -i.ɪst, -i.əst **-iness** -ɪ.nəs, -ɪ.nɪs
Cholderton 'tʃəʊl.də.tᵊn ⓤⓢ 'tʃoʊl.dɚ.t̬ən
choler 'kɒl.əʳ ⓤⓢ 'kɑː.lɚ
cholera 'kɒl.ᵊr.ə ⓤⓢ 'kɑː.lɚ-
choleraic ˌkɒl.ə'reɪ.ɪk ⓤⓢ ˌkɑː.lə'-
choleric 'kɒl.ᵊr.ɪk; kɒl'er- ⓤⓢ 'kɑː.lɚ-; kə'ler-
cholesterol kə'les.tᵊr.ɒl, kɒl'es-, -ᵊl ⓤⓢ kə'les.tə.rɑːl, -rɔːl, -roʊl
choliamb 'kəʊ.li.æmb ⓤⓢ 'koʊ- **-s** -z
choliambic ˌkəʊ.li'æm.bɪk ⓤⓢ ˌkoʊ-
choline 'kəʊ.liːn ⓤⓢ 'koʊ-, -lɪn
Cholmeley 'tʃʌm.li
Cholmondeley 'tʃʌm.li
Cholsey 'tʃəʊl.zi, 'tʃɒl.si ⓤⓢ 'tʃoʊl-
Chomley 'tʃʌm.li
chomp tʃɒmp ⓤⓢ tʃɑːmp **-s** -s **-ing** -ɪŋ **-ed** -t
Chomsky 'tʃɒmp.ski ⓤⓢ 'tʃɑːmp- **-an** -ən
chon tʃəʊn ⓤⓢ tʃoʊn
Chongquing ˌtʃʊŋ'tʃɪŋ
choo-choo 'tʃuː.tʃuː **-s** -z
chook tʃʊk **-s** -s
choos|e tʃuːz **-es** -ɪz **-ing** -ɪŋ **chose** tʃəʊz ⓤⓢ tʃoʊz **chosen** 'tʃəʊ.zᵊn ⓤⓢ 'tʃoʊ- **chooser/s** 'tʃuː.zəʳ/z ⓤⓢ -zɚ/z
choos|y, choos|ey 'tʃuː.z|i **-ier** -i.əʳ ⓤⓢ -i.ɚ **-iest** -i.ɪst, -i.əst **-iness** -ɪ.nəs, -ɪ.nɪs
chop tʃɒp ⓤⓢ tʃɑːp **-s** -s **-ping** -ɪŋ **-ped** -t '**chopping** ˌ**board;** ˌ**chop 'suey**
chop-chop ˌtʃɒp'tʃɒp ⓤⓢ ˌtʃɑːp'tʃɑːp
chophou|se 'tʃɒp.haʊ|s ⓤⓢ 'tʃɑːp- **-ses** -zɪz
Chopin 'ʃɒp.æ̃ŋ, 'ʃəʊ.pæ̃ŋ, -pæŋ ⓤⓢ 'ʃoʊ.pæn; ʃoʊ'pæ̃n
chopper 'tʃɒp.əʳ ⓤⓢ 'tʃɑː.pɚ **-s** -z
chopp|y 'tʃɒp|.i ⓤⓢ 'tʃɑː.p|i **-ier** -i.əʳ ⓤⓢ -i.ɚ **-iest** -i.ɪst, -i.əst **-ily** -ɪ.li, -ᵊl.i **-iness** -ɪ.nəs, -ɪ.nɪs
chopstick 'tʃɒp.stɪk ⓤⓢ 'tʃɑːp- **-s** -s
chop-suey ˌtʃɒp'suː.i ⓤⓢ ˌtʃɑːp-
choral 'kɔː.rᵊl ⓤⓢ 'kɔːr.ᵊl **-ly** -i
chorale kɒr'ɑːl, kə'rɑːl, kɔː- ⓤⓢ kə'ræl, -'rɑːl **-s** -z
chord kɔːd ⓤⓢ kɔːrd **-s** -z
chordate 'kɔː.deɪt, -dɪt, -dət ⓤⓢ 'kɔːr-
chore tʃɔːʳ ⓤⓢ tʃɔːr **-s** -z
chorea kɒr'ɪə, kɔː'rɪə, kə- ⓤⓢ kə'riː.ə, kɔːr'iː-
choreograph 'kɒr.i.ə.grɑːf, 'kɔː.ri-, -græf ⓤⓢ 'kɔːr.i.ə.græf **-s** -s **-ing** -ɪŋ **-ed** -t
choreographer ˌkɒr.i'ɒg.rə.fəʳ, ˌkɔː.ri- ⓤⓢ ˌkɔːr.i'ɑː.grə.fɚ **-s** -z
choreographic ˌkɒr.i.əʊ'græf.ɪk, ˌkɔː.ri- ⓤⓢ ˌkɔːr.i.ə'-
choreography ˌkɒr.i'ɒg.rə.fi, ˌkɔː.ri- ⓤⓢ ˌkɔːr.i'ɑː.grə-
choriamb 'kɒr.i.æmb, 'kɔː.ri- ⓤⓢ 'kɔːr.i- **-s** -z
choriambic ˌkɒr.i'æm.bɪk, ˌkɔː.ri- ⓤⓢ ˌkɔːr.i'-
choric 'kɒr.ɪk ⓤⓢ 'kɔːr-
chorion 'kɔː.ri.ən, -ɒn ⓤⓢ 'kɔːr.i.ɑːn **-s** -z
chorionic ˌkɔː.ri'ɒn.ɪk ⓤⓢ ˌkɔːr.i'ɑː.nɪk
chorister 'kɒr.ɪ.stəʳ ⓤⓢ 'kɔːr.ɪ.stɚ **-s** -z
chorizo tʃə'riː.zəʊ, tʃɒr'iː- ⓤⓢ tʃə'riː.zoʊ, tʃoʊ-, -soʊ **-s** -z
Chorley 'tʃɔː.li ⓤⓢ 'tʃɔːr-
Chorleywood ˌtʃɔː.li'wʊd ⓤⓢ ˌtʃɔːr-
choroid 'kɔː.rɔɪd ⓤⓢ 'kɔːr.ɔɪd
chortl|e 'tʃɔː.tl̩ ⓤⓢ 'tʃɔːr.t̬l̩ **-es** -z **-ing** -ɪŋ, 'tʃɔːt.lɪŋ ⓤⓢ 'tʃɔːr.t̬l̩.ɪŋ, 'tʃɔːrt.lɪŋ **-ed** -d
chorus 'kɔː.rəs ⓤⓢ 'kɔːr.əs **-es** -ɪz **-ing** -ɪŋ **-ed** -t
chose *legal term:* ʃəʊz ⓤⓢ ʃoʊz
chose *(from* **choose***)* tʃəʊz ⓤⓢ tʃoʊz
Chosen *Japanese name for Korea:* ˌtʃəʊ'sen ⓤⓢ ˌtʃoʊ-
chosen *(from* **choose***)* 'tʃəʊ.zᵊn ⓤⓢ 'tʃoʊ-
Chou En-lai ˌtʃəʊ.en'laɪ, ˌdʒəʊ- ⓤⓢ ˌdʒoʊ-
chough tʃʌf **-s** -s
choux ʃuː ˌ**choux 'pastry**
chow tʃaʊ **-s** -z
chow-chow ˌtʃaʊ'tʃaʊ, '-- **-s** -z
chowder 'tʃaʊ.dəʳ ⓤⓢ -dɚ **-s** -z
Chowles tʃəʊlz ⓤⓢ tʃoʊlz
chow mein ˌtʃaʊ'meɪn
chrestomath|y kres'tɒm.ə.θ|i ⓤⓢ -'tɑː.mə- **-ies** -iz
Chrétien de Troyes kreɪˌtjæ̃n.də'trwɑː
Chris krɪs **-'s** -ɪz
chrism 'krɪz.ᵊm
chrisom 'krɪz.ᵊm **-s** -z
Chrissie 'krɪs.i
Christ kraɪst **-s** -s
Christa 'krɪs.tə
Christabel 'krɪs.tə.bel, -bᵊl
Christadelphian ˌkrɪs.tə'del.fi.ən **-s** -z
Christchurch 'kraɪst.tʃɜːtʃ ⓤⓢ -tʃɝːtʃ
Christdom 'kraɪst.dəm
christen 'krɪs.ᵊn **-s** -z **-ing** -ɪŋ **-ed** -d
Christendom 'krɪs.ᵊn.dəm

christening ˈkrɪs.ᵊn.ɪŋ **-s** -z

Christensen ˈkrɪs.tᵊn.sᵊn

Christi *(in* **Corpus Christi***)* ˈkrɪs.ti

Christian ˈkrɪs.tʃən, ˈkrɪʃ-; ˈkrɪs.ti.ən US ˈkrɪs.tʃən, -ti.ən **-s** -z **ˈChristian ˌname; ˌChristian ˈScience; ˌChristian ˈScientist**

Christiana ˌkrɪs.tiˈɑː.nə US -tiˈæn.ə, -tʃiˈ-, -ˈɑː.nə

Christiania ˌkrɪs.tiˈɑː.ni.ə US -tiˈæn.i-, -tʃiˈ-, -ˈɑː.ni-

Christianism ˈkrɪs.tʃᵊn.ɪ.zᵊm, ˈkrɪʃ-; ˈkrɪs.ti.ə.nɪ- US ˈkrɪs.tʃᵊn.ɪ-, -ti.ə.nɪ-

Christianity ˌkrɪs.tiˈæn.ə.ti, -ˈtʃæn-, -ɪ.ti US -tʃiˈæn.ə.t̬i, -tiˈ-

christianiz|e, -is|e (C) ˈkrɪs.tʃə.naɪz, ˈkrɪʃ-; ˈkrɪs.ti.ə- US ˈkrɪs.tʃə- **-es** -ɪz **-ing** -ɪŋ **-ed** -d

christianly (C) ˈkrɪs.tʃən.li, ˈkrɪʃ-; ˈkrɪs.ti.ən- US ˈkrɪs.tʃən-

Christie ˈkrɪs.ti **-ˈs** -z

Christina krɪˈstiː.nə

Christine ˈkrɪs.tiːn, krɪˈstiːn

Christlike ˈkraɪs*t*.laɪk **-ness** -nəs, -nɪs

Christmas ˈkrɪs*t*.məs US ˈkrɪs- **-es** -ɪz **ˈChristmas ˌbox; ˈChristmas ˌcake; ˈChristmas ˌcard; ˌChristmas ˈDay; ˌChristmas ˈEve; ˈChristmas ˌpresent; ˌChristmas ˈpudding; ˈChristmas ˌtree**

Christmassy ˈkrɪs*t*.mə.si US ˈkrɪs-

Christmastide ˈkrɪs*t*.məs.taɪd US ˈkrɪs-

Christminster ˈkraɪs*t*ˌmɪn*t*.stəʳ, ˈkrɪs*t*- US -stɚ

Christobel ˈkrɪs.tə.bel

Christophe krɪˈstɒf; ˈkrɪs.tɒf US kriːˈstɑːf, krɪ-, -ˈstɔːf

christophene ˈkrɪs.tə.fiːn **-s** -z

Christopher ˈkrɪs.tə.fəʳ US -fɚ

Christopherson krɪˈstɒf.ə.sᵊn US -ˈstɑː.fɚ-

Christy ˈkrɪs.ti

chroma ˈkrəʊ.mə US ˈkroʊ-

chromate ˈkrəʊ.meɪt, -mɪt US ˈkroʊ- **-s** -s

chromatic krə*ʊ*ˈmæt.ɪk US kroʊˈmæt̬-, krə- **-ally** -ᵊl.i, -li

chromaticity ˌkrəʊ.məˈtɪs.ə.ti, -ɪ.ti US ˌkroʊ.məˈtɪs.ə.t̬i

chromatin ˈkrəʊ.mə.tɪn US ˈkroʊ-

chromatogram ˈkrəʊ.mə.tə.græm, krə*ʊ*ˈmæt.ə- US kroʊˈmæt̬- **-s** -z

chromatographic ˌkrəʊ.mə.təˈgræf.ɪk, krə*ʊ*ˌmæt.əˈ- US kroʊˌmæt̬-

chromatography ˌkrəʊ.məˈtɒg.rə.fi US ˌkroʊ.məˈtɑː.grə-

chrome krəʊm US kroʊm

chrom|ic ˈkrəʊ.m|ɪk US ˈkroʊ- **-ous** -əs

chromite ˈkrəʊ.maɪt US ˈkroʊ- **-s** -s

chromium ˈkrəʊ.mi.əm US ˈkroʊ-

chromolithograph ˌkrəʊ.mə*ʊ*ˈlɪθ.ə*ʊ*.grɑːf, -græf US ˌkroʊ.moʊˈlɪθ.ə.græf **-s** -s

chromolithography ˌkrəʊ.mə*ʊ*.lɪˈθɒg.rə.fi US ˌkroʊ.moʊ.lɪˈθɑː.grə-

chromosomal ˌkrəʊ.məˈsəʊ.mᵊl US ˌkroʊ.məˈsoʊ-

chromosome ˈkrəʊ.mə.səʊm US ˈkroʊ.mə.soʊm **-s** -z

chromosphere ˈkrəʊ.mə.sfɪəʳ US ˈkroʊ.mə.sfɪr **-s** -z

chromotype ˈkrəʊ.mə*ʊ*.taɪp US ˈkroʊ.moʊ-

chronic ˈkrɒn.ɪk US ˈkrɑː.nɪk **-al** -ᵊl **-ally** -ᵊl.i, -li

chronicl|e ˈkrɒn.ɪ.k|l̩ US ˈkrɑː.nɪ- **-es** -z **-ing** -ɪŋ, -klɪŋ **-ed** -d **-er/s** -kləʳ/z US -klɚ/z

Chronicles ˈkrɒn.ɪ.kl̩z US ˈkrɑː.nɪ-

chrono- ˈkrɒn.əʊ-, ˈkrəʊ.nə*ʊ*-, krəˈnɒ- US ˈkrɑː.noʊ-, ˈkroʊ.noʊ-, ˈ-nə-, krəˈnɑː-

Note: Prefix. This may take primary or secondary stress on the first syllable (e.g. **chronograph** /ˈkrɒn.ə*ʊ*.grɑːf US ˈkrɑː.nə.græf/) or primary stress on the second syllable (e.g. **chronometer** /krəˈnɒm.ɪ.təʳ US krəˈnɑː.mə.t̬ɚ/).

chronogram ˈkrɒn.ə.græm, ˈkrəʊ.nə- US ˈkrɑː.nə-, ˈkroʊ- **-s** -z

chronograph ˈkrɒn.ə.grɑːf, ˈkrəʊ.nə-, -græf US ˈkrɑː.nə.græf, ˈkroʊ- **-s** -s

chronologic ˌkrɒn.əˈlɒdʒ.ɪk US ˌkrɑː.nəˈlɑː.dʒɪk **-al** -ᵊl **-ally** -ᵊl.i, -li

chronolog|y krɒnˈɒl.ə.dʒ|i, krəˈnɒl- US krəˈnɑː.lə-, krɑː- **-ies** -iz **-ist/s** -ɪst/s

chronometer krɒnˈɒm.ɪ.təʳ, krəˈnɒm-, -ə.təʳ US krəˈnɑː.mə.t̬ɚ, krɑː- **-s** -z

chronometric ˌkrɒn.əˈmet.rɪk US ˌkrɑː.nəˈ- **-al** -ᵊl **-ally** -ᵊl.i

chronometry krɒnˈɒm.ɪ.tri, krəˈnɒm-, -ə.tri US krəˈnɑː.mə-, krɑː-

chrysalid ˈkrɪs.ᵊl.ɪd **-s** -z

chrysalides krɪˈsæl.ɪ.diːz, krə-, ˈ-ə-

chrysalis ˈkrɪs.ᵊl.ɪs **-es** -ɪz

chrysanth krɪˈsæn*t*θ, krə-, -ˈzæn*t*θ **-s** -s

chrysanthemum krɪˈsæn*t*θ.ə.məm, krə-, -ˈzæn*t*θ-, ˈ-ɪ- **-s** -z

chryselephantine ˌkrɪs.el.ɪˈfæn.taɪn, -əˈ- US -taɪn, -tiːn, -tɪn

Chrysler® ˈkraɪz.ləʳ US ˈkraɪs.lɚ **-s** -z

chrysolite ˈkrɪs.ə*ʊ*.laɪt US ˈ-ə- **-s** -s

chrysopras|e ˈkrɪs.ə*ʊ*.preɪz US ˈ-ə- **-es** -ɪz

Chrysostom ˈkrɪs.ə.stəm US ˈkrɪs.ə.stəm, krɪˈsɑː-

Chryston ˈkraɪ.stən

chthonian ˈθəʊ.ni.ən, ˈkθəʊ- US ˈθoʊ-

chthonic ˈθɒn.ɪk, ˈkθɒn- US ˈθɑː.nɪk

chub tʃʌb **-s** -z

Chubb tʃʌb

chubb|y ˈtʃʌb|.i **-ier** -i.əʳ US -i.ɚ **-iest** -i.ɪst, -i.əst **-ily** -ɪ.li, -ᵊl.i **-iness** -ɪ.nəs, -ɪ.nɪs

Chuchulain(n) kuːˈkʌl.ɪn

chuck (C) tʃʌk **-s** -s **-ing** -ɪŋ **-ed** -t **ˈchuck ˌwagon**

chuckl|e ˈtʃʌk.l̩ **-es** -z **-ing** -ɪŋ, ˈ-lɪŋ **-ed** -d

Chudleigh ˈtʃʌd.li

chuff tʃʌf **-s** -s **-ing** -ɪŋ **-ed** -t

Chuffey ˈtʃʌf.i

chug tʃʌg **-s** -z **-ging** -ɪŋ **-ged** -d

chugalug ˈtʃʌg.ə.lʌg **-s** -z **-ging** -ɪŋ **-ged** -d

chukka ˈtʃʌk.ə **-s** -z

chukker ˈtʃʌk.əʳ US -ɚ **-s** -z

chum tʃʌm **-s** -z **-ming** -ɪŋ **-med** -d

Chumbi ˈtʃʊm.bi

chumm|y ˈtʃʌm|.i **-ier** -i.əʳ US -i.ɚ **-iest** -i.ɪst, -i.əst **-ily** -ɪ.li, -ᵊl.i **-iness** -ɪ.nəs, -ɪ.nɪs

chump tʃʌmp **-s** -s

chund|er ˈtʃʌn.d|əʳ US -d|ɚ **-ers** -əz US -ɚz **-ering** -ᵊr.ɪŋ **-ered** -əd US -ɚd

Chungking ˌtʃʊŋˈkɪŋ, ˌtʃʌŋ- US ˌtʃʊŋˈkɪŋ, ˌtʃʌŋ-, ˌdʒʊŋ-, ˌdʒʌŋ-, -ˈgɪŋ *stress shift:* ˌChungking ˈMansions

chunk tʃʌŋk **-s** -s

chunk|y ˈtʃʌŋ.k|i **-ier** -i.əʳ US -i.ɚ **-iest** -i.ɪst, -i.əst **-ily** -ɪ.li, -ᵊl.i **-iness** -ɪ.nəs, -ɪ.nɪs

Chunnel ˈtʃʌn.ᵊl

chunt|er ˈtʃʌn.t|əʳ US -t̬|ɚ **-ers** -əz US -ɚz **-ering** -ᵊr.ɪŋ **-ered** -əd US -ɚd

church (C) tʃɜːtʃ US tʃɝːtʃ **-es** -ɪz **ˌChurch of ˈEngland**

Churchdown ˈtʃɜːtʃ.daʊn US ˈtʃɝːtʃ-

Note: There was until recently a local pronunciation /ˈtʃəʊ.zᵊn/, which is preserved as the name of a hill near by, which is now written **Chosen**.

churchgo|er ˈtʃɜːtʃˌgəʊ|.əʳ US ˈtʃɝːtʃˌgoʊ|.ɚ **-ers** -əz US -ɚz **-ing** -ɪŋ

Churchill ˈtʃɜː.tʃɪl US ˈtʃɝː-

Churchillian tʃɜːˈtʃɪl.i.ən US tʃɝː-

church|man (C) ˈtʃɜːtʃ|.mən US ˈtʃɝːtʃ- **-men** -mən

churchwarden ˌtʃɜːtʃˈwɔː.dᵊn US ˌtʃɝːtʃˈwɔːr- **-s** -z *stress shift:* ˌchurchwarden ˈpipe

church|woman ˈtʃɜːtʃ|ˌwʊm.ən US ˈtʃɝːtʃ- **-women** -ˌwɪm.ɪn

church|y ˈtʃɜː.tʃ|i US ˈtʃɝː- **-ier** -i.əʳ US -i.ɚ **-iest** -i.ɪst, -i.əst **-ily** -ɪ.li, -ᵊl.i **-iness** -ɪ.nəs, -ɪ.nɪs

churchyard *outside church:* ˈtʃɜːtʃ.jɑːd US ˈtʃɝːtʃ.jɑːrd **-s** -z

Churchyard *surname:* 'tʃɜː.tʃəd (US) 'tʃɝː.tʃɚd
churl tʃɜːl (US) tʃɝːl **-s** -z
churlish 'tʃɜː.lɪʃ (US) 'tʃɝː- **-ly** -li **-ness** -nəs, -nɪs
churn tʃɜːn (US) tʃɝːn **-s** -z **-ing** -ɪŋ **-ed** -d
chute ʃuːt **-s** -s
Chute tʃuːt
Chuter 'tʃuː.təʳ (US) -t̬ɚ
chutney 'tʃʌt.ni **-s** -z
chutzpa(h) 'hʊt.spɑː, 'xʊt-, -spə
Chuzzlewit 'tʃʌz.l̩.wɪt
chyle kaɪl
chyme kaɪm
CIA ˌsiː.aɪ'eɪ
ciabatta tʃə'bæt.ə, -'bɑː.tə
Cian 'kiː.ən
ciao tʃaʊ
Ciara 'kɪə.rə (US) 'kɪr.ə
Ciaran 'kɪə.rᵊn (US) 'kɪr.ᵊn
Ciba-Geigy® ˌsiː.bə'gaɪ.gi
Cibber 'sɪb.əʳ (US) -ɚ
cibori|um sɪ'bɔː.ri|.əm, sə- (US) -'bɔːr.i- **-ums** -əmz **-a** -ə
cicada sɪ'kɑː.də, -'keɪ- (US) -'keɪ-, -'kɑː- **-s** -z
cicala sɪ'kɑː.lə **-s** -z
cicatric|e 'sɪk.ə.trɪs **-es** -ɪz
cicatrix 'sɪk.ə.trɪks; sə'keɪ-, sɪ- **cicatrices** ˌsɪk.ə'traɪ.siːz; sə'keɪ.trɪ-, sɪ-
cicatriz|e, -is|e 'sɪk.ə.traɪz **-es** -ɪz **-ing** -ɪŋ **-ed** -d
cicel|y (C) 'sɪs.ᵊl|.i, -ɪ.l|i **-ies** -iz
Cicero 'sɪs.ᵊr.əʊ (US) -ə.roʊ
cicerone ˌtʃɪtʃ.ə'rəʊ.ni, ˌsɪs.ə'-, ˌtʃiː.tʃə'- (US) ˌsɪs.ə'roʊ- **-s** -z
Ciceronian ˌsɪs.ᵊr'əʊ.ni.ən (US) -ə'roʊ- **-s** -z
cicisbe|o ˌtʃɪtʃ.ɪz'beɪ|.əʊ (US) sɪ'sɪs.biː|.oʊ **-i** -iː
Cid sɪd
CID ˌsiː.aɪ'diː
-cidal -'saɪ.dᵊl
-cide -saɪd
cider 'saɪ.dəʳ (US) -dɚ **-s** -z **'cider-ˌcup**
cig sɪg **-s** -z
cigar sɪ'gɑːʳ, sə- (US) -gɑːr **-s** -z **ci'gar-ˌshaped**
cigarette ˌsɪg.ᵊr'et, '--- (US) ˌsɪg.ə'ret **-s** -s **ciga'rette ˌholder** (US) **'cigarette ˌholder; ciga'rette ˌlighter** (US) **'cigarette ˌlighter**
cigarillo ˌsɪg.ə'rɪl.əʊ (US) -oʊ **-s** -z
cigg|y, cigg|ie 'sɪg|.i **-ies** -iz
cilantro sɪ'læn.trəʊ, sə- (US) -'lɑːn.troʊ, -'læn-
cilia 'sɪl.i.ə
ciliary 'sɪl.i.ᵊr.i (US) -er-
cilic|e 'sɪl.ɪs **-es** -ɪz
Cilicia saɪ'lɪʃ.i.ə, sɪ-, -'lɪs- (US) sə'lɪʃ.ə
cilium 'sɪl.i.əm
Cilla 'sɪl.ə
Ciller 'sɪl.əʳ (US) -ɚ
Cimabue ˌtʃɪm.ə'buː.eɪ, ˌtʃiː.mə'-, -i
Cimmeri|an sɪ'mɪə.ri|.ən (US) -'mɪr.i- **-i** -aɪ
C-in-C ˌsiː.ɪn'siː **-s** -z
cinch sɪntʃ **-es** -ɪz **-ing** -ɪŋ **-ed** -d
cinchona sɪŋ'kəʊ.nə (US) -'koʊ-, sɪn- **-s** -z
cinchonic sɪŋ'kɒn.ɪk (US) -'kɑː.nɪk, sɪn-
Cincinnati ˌsɪn*t*.sɪ'næt.i, -sə'- (US) -'næt̬-
Cincinnatus ˌsɪn*t*.sɪ'nɑː.təs, -'neɪ- (US) -'næt̬.əs-, -'nɑː.t̬əs, -'neɪ-
cincture 'sɪŋ*k*.tʃəʳ (US) -tʃɚ **-s** -z
cinder 'sɪn.dəʳ (US) -dɚ **-s** -z **'cinder ˌblock; 'cinder ˌpath; 'cinder ˌtrack**
Cinderella ˌsɪn.dᵊr'el.ə
Cinderford 'sɪn.də.fəd (US) -dɚ.fɚd
Cindy 'sɪn.di
cine- 'sɪn.i-
cinecamera 'sɪn.iˌkæm.ᵊr.ə, -ˌkæm.rə, ˌsɪn.i'kæm- **-s** -z
cinefilm 'sɪn.i.fɪlm **-s** -z
cinema 'sɪn.ə.mə, '-ɪ-, -mɑː (US) -mə **-s** -z
cinemago|er 'sɪn.ə.məˌgəʊ|.əʳ, '-ɪ- (US) -goʊ|.ɚ **-ers** -əz (US) -ɚz **-ing** -ɪŋ
CinemaScope® 'sɪn.ə.mə.skəʊp, '-ɪ- (US) -skoʊp **-s** -s
cinematic ˌsɪn.ɪ'mæt.ɪk, -ə'- (US) -ə'mæt̬- **-ally** -ᵊl.i, -li
cinematograph ˌsɪn.ɪ'mæt.ə.grɑːf, -ə'-, -græf (US) -ə'mæt̬.ə.græf **-s** -s
cinematographic ˌsɪn.ɪ.mæt.ə'græf.ɪk, ˌ-ə-; sɪ.nɪˌmæt- (US) ˌsɪn.əˌmæt̬- **-al** -ᵊl **-ally** -ᵊl.i, -li
cinematograph|y ˌsɪn.ɪ.mə'tɒg.rə.f|i, ˌ-ə- (US) -ə.mə'tɑː.grə- **-er/s** -əʳ/z (US) -ɚ/z
cinema verité ˌsɪn.ɪ.mɑː'ver.ɪ.teɪ, ˌ-ə-, -ə.mə'- (US) ˌsɪn.ɪ.mɑː.ver.ə'teɪ, -mə'ver.ə.teɪ
cine-projector 'sɪn.i.prəˌdʒek.təʳ (US) -tɚ **-s** -z
Cinerama® ˌsɪn.ə'rɑː.mə, -ɪ'- (US) -ə'rɑː-, -'ræm.ə
cineraria ˌsɪn.ə'reə.ri.ə (US) -'rer.i- **-s** -z
cinerari|um ˌsɪn.ə'reə.ri|.əm (US) -'rer.i- **-a** -ə
cinerary 'sɪn.ə.rᵊr.i (US) -rer-
cineration ˌsɪn.ə'reɪ.ʃᵊn
cinnabar 'sɪn.ə.bɑːʳ (US) -bɑːr
cinnamon 'sɪn.ə.mən
cinque (C) sɪŋk **'Cinque ˌPorts**
Cinquecento® ˌtʃɪŋ.kweɪ'tʃen.təʊ, -kwɪ'- (US) -toʊ
cinquefoil 'sɪŋk.fɔɪl
Cinzano® tʃɪn'zɑː.nəʊ, sɪn-, tʃɪnt'sɑː-, sɪnt'sɑː- (US) -noʊ
ciph|er 'saɪ.f|əʳ (US) -f|ɚ **-ers** -əz (US) -ɚz **-ering** -ᵊr.ɪŋ **-ered** -əd (US) -ɚd **'cipher ˌkey**
Cipriani ˌsɪp.ri'ɑː.ni
circa 'sɜː.kə (US) 'sɝː-
circadian sɜː'keɪ.di.ən, sə- (US) sɚ-; ˌsɝː.kə'diː.ən
Circassi|a sɜː'kæs.i|.ə, sə-, -'kæʃ|.ə, -i|.ə (US) sɚ- **-an/s** -ən/z
Circe 'sɜː.si (US) 'sɝː-
circl|e 'sɜː.kl̩ (US) 'sɝː- **-es** -z **-ing** -ɪŋ, '-klɪŋ (US) '-kl̩.ɪŋ, '-klɪŋ **-ed** -d
circlet 'sɜː.klət, -klɪt (US) 'sɝː- **-s** -s
circuit 'sɜː.kɪt (US) 'sɝː- **-s** -s **-ry** -ri **'circuit ˌbreaker; 'circuit ˌtraining**
circuitous sə'kjuː.ɪ.təs, sɜː-, '-ə- (US) sɚ'kjuː.ə.t̬əs **-ly** -li **-ness** -nəs, -nɪs
circular 'sɜː.kjə.ləʳ, -kjʊ- (US) 'sɝː.kjə.lɚ **-s** -z **'circular ˌsaw, ˌcircular 'saw**
circularity ˌsɜː.kjə'lær.ə.ti, -kjʊ'-, -ɪ.ti (US) -kjə'ler.ə.t̬i, -'lær-
circulariz|e, -is|e 'sɜː.kjə.lᵊr.aɪz, -kjʊ- (US) 'sɝː.kjə.lə.raɪz **-es** -ɪz **-ing** -ɪŋ **-ed** -d
circu|late 'sɜː.kjə|.leɪt, -kjʊ- (US) 'sɝː.kjə- **-lates** -leɪts **-lating** -leɪ.tɪŋ (US) -leɪ.t̬ɪŋ **-lated** -leɪ.tɪd (US) -leɪ.t̬ɪd **-lator/s** -leɪ.təʳ/z (US) -leɪ.t̬ɚ/z
circulation ˌsɜː.kjə'leɪ.ʃᵊn, -kjʊ'- (US) ˌsɝː- **-s** -z
circulatory ˌsɜː.kjə'leɪ.tᵊr.i, -kjʊ'-, -tri; 'sɜː.kjə.lə-, -kjʊ- (US) 'sɝː.kjə.lə.tɔːr.i
circum- 'sɜː.kəm-, sə'kʌm- (US) 'sɝː.kəm-, sɚ'kʌm-
Note: Prefix. This may have primary or secondary stress on the first syllable, e.g. **circumstance** /'sɜː.kəm.stɑːn*t*s (US) 'sɜːr.kəm.stæns/ or on the second syllable, e.g. **circumference** /sə'kʌm*p*.fᵊr.ᵊn*t*s (US) sɚ- /.
circumambient ˌsɜː.kəm'æm.bi.ənt (US) ˌsɝː-
circumambu|late ˌsɜː.kəm'æm.bjə|.leɪt, -bjʊ- (US) ˌsɝː.kəm'æm.bjə- **-lates** -leɪts **-lating** -leɪ.tɪŋ (US) -leɪ.t̬ɪŋ **-lated** -leɪ.tɪd (US) -leɪ.t̬ɪd
circumcis|e 'sɜː.kəm.saɪz (US) 'sɝː- **-es** -ɪz **-ing** -ɪŋ **-ed** -d
circumcision ˌsɜː.kəm'sɪʒ.ᵊn (US) ˌsɝː- **-s** -z
circumferenc|e sə'kʌm*p*.fᵊr.ᵊn*t*s (US) sɚ- **-es** -ɪz
circumferential səˌkʌm*p*.fᵊ'ren.*t*ʃᵊl (US) sɚˌkʌm*p*.fɚ'ren*t*.ʃᵊl
circumflex 'sɜː.kəm.fleks (US) 'sɝː- **-es** -ɪz
circumlocution ˌsɜː.kəm.lə'kjuː.ʃᵊn (US) ˌsɝː- **-s** -z
circumlocutory ˌsɜː.kəm.lə'kjuː.tᵊr.i,

-tri; -ˈlɒk.jʊ-
US ˌsɝː.kəmˈlɑː.kjuː.tɔːr.i
circumnavi|gate ˌsɜː.kəmˈnæv.ɪ|.ɡeɪt US ˌsɝː- **-gates** -ɡeɪts **-gating** -ɡeɪ.tɪŋ US -ɡeɪ.t̬ɪŋ **-gated** -ɡeɪ.tɪd US -ɡeɪ.t̬ɪd **-gator/s** -ɡeɪ.təʳ/z US -ɡeɪ.t̬ɚ/z
circumnavigation ˌsɜː.kəmˌnæv.ɪˈɡeɪ.ʃən US ˌsɝː- **-s** -z
circumpolar ˌsɜː.kəmˈpəʊ.ləʳ US ˌsɝː.kəmˈpoʊ.lɚ
circumscrib|e ˈsɜː.kəm.skraɪb, ˌ--ˈ- US ˈsɝː-, ˌ--ˈ- **-es** -z **-ing** -ɪŋ **-ed** -d
circumscription ˌsɜː.kəmˈskrɪp.ʃən US ˌsɝː- **-s** -z
circumspect ˈsɜː.kəm.spekt US ˈsɝː- **-ly** -li **-ness** -nəs, -nɪs
circumspection ˌsɜː.kəmˈspek.ʃən US ˌsɝː-
circumstanc|e ˈsɜː.kəm.stænts, -stənts, -stɑːnts US ˈsɝː.kəm.stænts, -stənts **-es** -ɪz **-ed** -t
circumstantial ˌsɜː.kəmˈstæn.tʃəl US ˌsɝː.kəmˈstænt.ʃəl- **-ly** -i ˌcircumstantial ˈevidence
circumstantiality ˌsɜː.kəmˌstæn.tʃiˈæl.ə.ti, -ɪ.ti US ˌsɝː.kəmˌstænt.ʃiˈæl.ə.t̬i
circumstanti|ate ˌsɜː.kəmˈstæn.tʃi|.eɪt US ˌsɝː.kəmˈstænt.ʃi-- **-ates** -eɪts **-ating** -eɪ.tɪŋ US -eɪ.t̬ɪŋ **-ated** -eɪ.tɪd US -eɪ.t̬ɪd
circumvallation ˌsɜː.kəm.vəˈleɪ.ʃən, -vælˈeɪ- US ˌsɝː- **-s** -z
circum|vent ˌsɜː.kəm|ˈvent, ˈ--|- US ˌsɝː- **-vents** -ˈvents **-venting** -ˈven.tɪŋ US -ˈven.t̬ɪŋ **-vented** -ˈven.tɪd US -ˈven.t̬ɪd
circumvention ˌsɜː.kəmˈven.tʃən US ˌsɝː.kəmˈvent.ʃən **-s** -z
circus (C) ˈsɜː.kəs US ˈsɝː- **-es** -ɪz
Cirencester ˈsaɪə.rən.ses.təʳ, ˈsɪs.ɪ.təʳ, -stəʳ US ˈsaɪ.rən.ses.tɚ
Note: The pronunciation most usually heard in the town is /ˈsaɪə.rən.ses.təʳ/ (or /-tər/ with the dialectal retroflex /r/).
cirque sɜːk, sɪək US sɝːk **-s** -s
cirrhosis sɪˈrəʊ.sɪs, sə- US səˈroʊ-
cirrocumulus ˌsɪr.əʊˈkjuː.mjə.ləs, -mjʊ- US -oʊˈkjuː.mjə-
cirrostratus ˌsɪr.əʊˈstrɑː.təs, -ˈstreɪ- US -oʊˈstreɪ.t̬əs, -ˈstræt̬.əs
cirrus ˈsɪr.əs
CIS ˌsiː.aɪˈes
Cisalpine sɪˈsæl.paɪn
Cisco® ˈsɪs.kəʊ US -koʊ
Ciskei sɪˈskaɪ, ˈsɪs.kaɪ US ˈsɪs.kaɪ
Cissie ˈsɪs.i
cissoid ˈsɪs.ɔɪd **-s** -z
cissy (C) ˈsɪs.i
cist sɪst **-s** -s
Cistercian sɪˈstɜː.ʃən, sə- US -ˈstɝː- **-s** -z
cistern ˈsɪs.tən US -tɚn **-s** -z
cistus ˈsɪs.təs **-es** -ɪz
citadel ˈsɪt.ə.del, -dəl US ˈsɪt̬- **-s** -z
citation saɪˈteɪ.ʃən **-s** -z
citatory ˈsaɪ.tə.tər.i, ˈsɪ-, -tri; saɪˈteɪ- US ˈsaɪ.t̬ə.tɔːr.i
cit|e saɪt **-es** -s **-ing** -ɪŋ US ˈsaɪ.t̬ɪŋ **-ed** -ɪd US ˈsaɪ.t̬ɪd
cithar|a ˈsɪθ.ər|.ə **-ae** -iː
cither ˈsɪθ.əʳ US -ɚ, ˈsɪð- **-s** -z
Citibank® ˈsɪt.i.bæŋk US ˈsɪt̬-
citizen ˈsɪt.ɪ.zən, ˈ-ə- US ˈsɪt̬- **-s** -z ˌcitizen's arˈrest
citizenry ˈsɪt.ɪ.zən.ri, ˈ-ə- US ˈsɪt̬-
citizenship ˈsɪt.ɪ.zən.ʃɪp, ˈ-ə- US ˈsɪt̬-
citole ˈsɪt.əʊl, sɪˈtəʊl US ˈsɪt.oʊl, sɪˈtoʊl **-s** -z
citrate ˈsɪt.reɪt, ˈsaɪ.treɪt, -trɪt **-s** -s
citric ˈsɪt.rɪk ˌcitric ˈacid
citrine sɪˈtriːn, sə-
Citroën® ˈsɪt.rəʊən, ˈsɪt.rən US ˌsɪt.roʊˈen, ˌsiː.troʊˈ- **-s** -z
citron ˈsɪt.rən **-s** -z
citronella ˌsɪt.rənˈel.ə US -rəˈnel-
citrous ˈsɪt.rəs
citrus ˈsɪt.rəs **-es** -ɪz ˈcitrus ˌfruit
cittern ˈsɪt.ɜːn, -ən US ˈsɪt̬.ɚn **-s** -z
cit|y (C) ˈsɪt|.i US ˈsɪt̬|.i **-ies** -iz ˌcity ˈfather; ˌcity ˈgent; ˌcity ˈhall; ˌcity ˈslicker US ˈcity ˌslicker
city-dweller ˈsɪt.iˌdwel.əʳ US ˈsɪt̬.iˌdwel.ɚ **-s** -z
citywide ˌsɪt.iˈwaɪd US ˈsɪt̬- *stress shift, British only:* ˌcitywide ˈmeetings
Ciudad Bolívar θjʊˌdɑːd.bɒlˈiː.vɑːʳ, θiː.ʊˌdɑːd- US sjuːˌdɑːd.boʊˈliː.vɑːr, ˌsiː.uː-
Ciudad Guayana θjʊˌdɑːd.ɡwaɪˈjɑː.nə, θiː.ʊˌdɑːd- US sjuːˌdɑːd.ɡəˈ-, ˌsiː.uː-, -ɡwəˈ-, -ɡwɑːˈ-
Ciudad Juárez θjʊˌdɑːdˈhwɑː.rez, θiː.ʊ-, -ˈwɑː- US sjuːˌdɑːdˈhwɑːr.es, ˌsiː.uː-, -ˈwɑːr.eʒ
civet ˈsɪv.ɪt **-s** -s
civic ˈsɪv.ɪk **-s** -s ˌcivic ˈcentre US ˈcivic ˌcenter
civil ˈsɪv.əl, -ɪl **-ly** -i ˌcivil deˈfence; ˌcivil disoˈbedience; ˌcivil engiˈneer; ˌcivil engiˈneering; ˌcivil ˈliberty; ˌcivil ˈrights ˌmovement; ˌcivil ˈservant; ˌcivil ˈservice; ˌcivil ˈwar
civilian sɪˈvɪl.i.ən, sə- US ˈ-jən **-s** -z
civilit|y sɪˈvɪl.ə.t|i, sə-, -ɪ.t|i US -ə.t̬|i **-ies** -iz
civilizable, -isa- ˈsɪv.ɪ.laɪ.zə.bl̩, ˈ-ə-
civilization, -isa- ˌsɪv.əl.aɪˈzeɪ.ʃən, -ɪ.laɪˈ-, -lɪˈ- US -əl.ɪˈ- **-s** -z
civiliz|e, -is|e ˈsɪv.əl.aɪz, -ɪ.laɪz US -ə.laɪz, ˈ-ɪ- **-es** -ɪz **-ing** -ɪŋ **-ed** -d
civitas ˈsɪv.ɪ.tæs, ˈkɪv-
civv|y ˈsɪv|.i **-ies** -iz ˈcivvy ˌstreet
CJD ˌsiː.dʒeɪˈdiː
cl *(abbrev. for* **centilitre/s***) singular:* ˈsen.tɪˌliː.təʳ US -t̬əˌliː.t̬ɚ *plural:* -z
clack klæk **-s** -s **-ing** -ɪŋ **-ed** -t
Clackmannan klækˈmæn.ən **-shire** -ʃəʳ, -ˌʃɪəʳ US -ʃɚ, -ˌʃɪr
Clacton ˈklæk.tən
clad klæd
cladding ˈklæd.ɪŋ
cladistics kləˈdɪs.tɪks, klædˈɪs-
Claggart ˈklæɡ.ət US -ɚt
Claiborne ˈkleɪ.bɔːn US -bɔːrn
claim kleɪm **-s** -z **-ing** -ɪŋ **-ed** -d
claimant ˈkleɪ.mənt **-s** -s
claimer ˈkleɪ.məʳ US -mɚ **-s** -z
clairaudien|ce ˌkleəˈrɔː.di.ən|ts US ˌklerˈɑː-, -ˈɔː- **-t** -t
Claire kleəʳ US kler
Clairol® ˈkleə.rɒl US ˈkler.ɑːl
clairvoyan|ce ˌkleəˈvɔɪ.ən|ts US ˌkler- **-cy** -si
clairvoyant ˌkleəˈvɔɪ.ənt US ˌkler- **-s** -s
clam klæm **-s** -z **-ming** -ɪŋ **-med** -d
clamant ˈkleɪ.mənt, ˈklæm.ənt **-ly** -li
clambake ˈklæm.beɪk **-s** -s
clamb|er ˈklæm.b|əʳ US -b|ɚ **-ers** -əz US -ɚz **-ering** -ər.ɪŋ **-ered** -əd US -ɚd
clamm|y ˈklæm|.i **-ier** -i.əʳ US -i.ɚ **-iest** -i.ɪst, -i.əst **-ily** -ɪ.li, -əl.i **-iness** -ɪ.nəs, -ɪ.nɪs
clam|or ˈklæm|.əʳ US -ɚ **-ors** -əz US -ɚz **-oring** -ər.ɪŋ **-ored** -əd US -ɚd **-orer/s** -ər.əʳ/z US -ɚ.ɚ/z
clamorous ˈklæm.ər.əs **-ly** -li **-ness** -nəs, -nɪs
clam|our ˈklæm|.əʳ US -ɚ **-ours** -əz US -ɚz **-ouring** -ər.ɪŋ **-oured** -əd US -ɚd **-ourer/s** -ər.əʳ/z US -ɚ.ɚ/z
clamp klæmp **-s** -s **-ing** -ɪŋ **-ed** -t
clampdown ˈklæmp.daʊn **-s** -z

Pronouncing the letters CK

The consonant digraph **ck** only has one possible realisation in English words: /k/, e.g.:

sock /sɒk/ US /sɑːk/

clan klæn **-s** -z
clandestine klænˈdes.tɪn, -taɪn, ˈklæn.dɪs- US klænˈdes.tɪn **-ly** -li
clang klæŋ **-s** -z **-ing** -ɪŋ **-ed** -d
clanger ˈklæŋ.əʳ US -ɚ **-s** -z
clangor ˈklæŋ.gəʳ, -əʳ US -ɚ, -gɚ
clangorous ˈklæŋ.gᵊr.əs, -ᵊr- US ˈ-ɚ-, -gɚ- **-ly** -li
clangour ˈklæŋ.gəʳ, -əʳ US -ɚ, -gɚ
clank klæŋk **-s** -s **-ing** -ɪŋ **-ed** -t
Clanmaurice klænˈmɒr.ɪs, klæm- US -ˈmɔːr-, -ˈmɑːr-
Clanmorris klænˈmɒr.ɪs, klæm- US klænˈmɔːr-
clannish ˈklæn.ɪʃ **-ly** -li **-ness** -nəs, -nɪs
Clanricarde klænˈrɪk.əd US -ɚd
clanship ˈklæn.ʃɪp
clans|man ˈklænz|.mən **-men** -mən
clap klæp **-s** -s **-ping** -ɪŋ **-ped** -t ˌ**clapped** ˈ**out** *stress shift:* ˌclapped-out ˈcar
clapboard ˈklæp.bɔːd US -bɔːrd; ˈklæb.ɚd **-s** -z
Clapham ˈklæp.ᵊm ˌ**Clapham** ˈ**omnibus**
clapometer klæpˈɒm.ɪ.təʳ US -ˈɑː.mə.t̬ɚ **-s** -z
clapper ˈklæp.əʳ US -ɚ **-s** -z
clapperboard ˈklæp.ə.bɔːd US -ɚ.bɔːrd **-s** -z
Clapton ˈklæp.tən
claptrap ˈklæp.træp
claque klæk **-s** -s
Clara ˈklɑː.rə, ˈkleə- US ˈkler.ə, ˈklær-
clarabella (C) ˌklær.əˈbel.ə US ˌkler-, ˌklær- **-s** -z
Clare kleəʳ US kler
Clarel ˈkleə.rᵊl US ˈkler.ᵊl, ˈklær.ᵊl; kləˈrel
Claremont ˈkleə.mɒnt, -mənt US ˈkler.mɑːnt
Clarence ˈklær.ᵊnts US ˈkler-, ˈklær-
Clarenc(i)eux ˈklær.ᵊn.suː, -sjuː US ˈkler-, ˈklær-
clarendon (C) ˈklær.ᵊn.dən US ˈkler-, ˈklær-
claret ˈklær.ət, -ɪt US ˈkler-, ˈklær- **-s** -s
Clarges ˈklɑː.dʒɪz, -dʒəz US ˈklɑːr-
Clarice ˈklær.ɪs US ˈkler-, ˈklær-; klerˈiːs, klær-
Claridge ˈklær.ɪdʒ US ˈkler-, ˈklær- **-'s** -ɪz
clarification ˌklær.ɪ.fɪˈkeɪ.ʃᵊn, ˌ-ə- US ˌkler-, ˌklær- **-s** -z
clari|fy ˈklær.ɪ|.faɪ, ˈ-ə- US ˈkler-, ˈklær- **-fies** -faɪz **-fying** -faɪ.ɪŋ **-fied** -faɪd **-fier/s** -faɪ.əʳ/z US -faɪ.ɚ/z
Clarina kləˈraɪ.nə
clarinet ˌklær.ɪˈnet, -əˈ- US ˌkler-, ˌklær- **-s** -s
clarinet(t)ist ˌklær.ɪˈnet.ɪst, -əˈ- US ˌkler.əˈnet̬-, ˌklær- **-s** -s
clarion ˈklær.i.ən US ˈkler-, ˈklær- **-s** -z ˈ**clarion** ˌ**call**
Clarissa kləˈrɪs.ə, klærˈɪs- US kləˈrɪs-
clarity ˈklær.ə.ti, -ɪ.ti US ˈkler.ə.t̬i, ˈklær-
Clark(e) klɑːk US klɑːrk
clarkia ˈklɑː.ki.ə US ˈklɑːr- **-s** -z
Clarkson ˈklɑːk.sᵊn US ˈklɑːrk-
Clarrie ˈklær.i US ˈkler-, ˈklær-
Clary ˈkleə.ri US ˈkler.i, ˈklær-
clash klæʃ **-es** -ɪz **-ing** -ɪŋ **-ed** -t
clasp klɑːsp US klæsp **-s** -s **-ing** -ɪŋ **-ed** -t ˈ**clasp** ˌ**knife**
class klɑːs US klæs **-es** -ɪz **-ing** -ɪŋ **-ed** -t ˈ**class** ˌ**system**; ˈ**class** ˌ**war**; ˌ**class** ˈ**war**
class-conscious ˈklɑːsˌkɒn.*t*ʃəs, ˌ-ˈ-- US ˈklæsˌkɑːn*t*.ʃəs **-ness** -nəs, -nɪs
classic ˈklæs.ɪk **-s** -s
classic|al ˈklæs.ɪ.k|ᵊl, ˈ-ə- **-ally** -ᵊl.i, -li **-alness** -ᵊl.nəs, -nɪs ˌ**classical** ˈ**music**
classicism ˈklæs.ɪ.sɪ.zᵊm, ˈ-ə- **-s** -z
classicist ˈklæs.ɪ.sɪst, ˈ-ə- **-s** -s
classifiable ˈklæs.ɪ.faɪ.ə.bl̩, ˌklæs.ɪˈfaɪ- US ˈklæs.ə.faɪ-
classification ˌklæs.ɪ.fɪˈkeɪ.ʃᵊn, ˌ-ə- US ˌ-ə- **-s** -z
classificatory ˌklæs.ɪ.fɪˈkeɪ.tᵊr.i, ˌ-ə-, -tri; ˈklæs.ɪ.fɪ.kə-, ˈ-ə- US ˈklæs.ə.fɪ.kə.tɔːr.i; kləˈsɪf.ə-
classi|fy ˈklæs.ɪ|.faɪ, ˈ-ə- **-fies** -faɪz **-fying** -faɪ.ɪŋ **-fied** -faɪd **-fier/s** -faɪ.əʳ/z US -faɪ.ɚ/z ˌ**classified** ˈ**ad** US ˈ**classified** ˌ**ad**; ˌ**classified** **inforˈmation**
class|ism ˈklɑː.s|ɪ.zᵊm US ˈklæs|.ɪ- **-ist/s** -ɪst/s
classless ˈklɑːs.ləs, -lɪs US ˈklæs- **-ness** -nəs, -nɪs
class|man ˈklɑːs|.mæn, -mən US ˈklæs- **-men** -men, -mən
classmate ˈklɑːs.meɪt US ˈklæs- **-s** -s
classroom ˈklɑːs.rʊm, -ruːm US ˈklæs.ruːm, -rʊm **-s** -z
classwork ˈklɑːs.wɜːk US ˈklæs.wɝːk
class|y ˈklɑː.s|i US ˈklæs|.i **-ier** -i.əʳ US -i.ɚ **-iest** -i.ɪst, -i.əst **-ily** -ɪ.li, -ᵊl.i **-iness** -ɪ.nəs, -ɪ.nɪs
clatt|er ˈklæt|.əʳ US ˈklæt̬|.ɚ **-ers** -əz US -ɚz **-ering** -ᵊr.ɪŋ **-ered** -əd US -ɚd
Claud(e) klɔːd US klɑːd, klɔːd
Claudette klɔːˈdet US klɑː-, klɔː-
Claudi|a ˈklɔː.di|.ə, ˈklaʊ- US ˈklɑː-, ˈklɔː-, ˈklaʊ- **-an** -ən
Claudine klɔːˈdiːn US klɑː-, klɔː-
Claudio ˈklaʊ.di.əʊ, ˈklɔː- US ˈklɑː.di.oʊ, ˈklɔː-, ˈklaʊ-
Claudius ˈklɔː.di.əs US ˈklɑː-, ˈklɔː-
claus|e klɔːz US klɑːz, klɔːz **-es** -ɪz **-al** -ᵊl
Clausewitz ˈklaʊ.sə.vɪts, -zə-
claustral ˈklɔː.strᵊl US ˈklɑː-, ˈklɔː-
claustrophob|ia ˌklɔː.strəˈfəʊ.b|i.ə, ˌklɒs.trə- US ˌklɑː.strəˈfoʊ-, ˌklɔː- **-ic** -ɪk
clave *(archaic past of* **cleave***)* kleɪv
clavecin ˈklæv.sɪn, -ə.sɪn, ˈ-ɪ- **-s** -z
Claverhouse ˈkleɪ.və.haʊs US -vɚ-
Clavering ˈkleɪ.vᵊr.ɪŋ, ˈklæv.ᵊr-
clavichord ˈklæv.ɪ.kɔːd US -kɔːrd **-s** -z
clavicle ˈklæv.ɪ.kl̩ **-s** -z
clavicular kləˈvɪk.jʊ.ləʳ, klævˈɪk-, -jə- US -jə.lɚ
clavier *keyboard:* ˈklæv.i.əʳ; klævˈɪəʳ, kləˈvɪəʳ US ˈklæv.i.ɚ; kləˈvɪr **-s** -z *instrument:* kləˈvɪəʳ, klævˈɪəʳ US ˈklæv.i.ɚ; kləˈvɪr **-s** -z
claw klɔː US klɑː, klɔː **-s** -z **-ing** -ɪŋ **-ed** -d
clawback ˈklɔː.bæk US ˈklɑː-, ˈklɔː- **-s** -s
Claxton ˈklæk.stᵊn
clay (C) kleɪ **-s** -z ˌ**clay** ˈ**pigeon**
Clayden, Claydon ˈkleɪ.dᵊn
clayey ˈkleɪ.i
Clayhanger ˈkleɪ.hæŋ.əʳ US -ɚ
claymore ˈkleɪ.mɔːʳ US -mɔːr **-s** -z
Clayton ˈkleɪ.tᵊn
Clayton-le-Moors ˌkleɪ.tᵊn.liˈmɔːʳ US -ˈmɔːr
clean kliːn **-s** -z **-ing** -ɪŋ **-ed** -d **-est** -ɪst, -əst **-ly** -li **-ness** -nəs, -nɪs
clean-cut ˌkliːnˈkʌt, ˌkliːŋ- US ˌkliːn- *stress shift:* ˌclean-cut ˈimage
cleaner ˈkliː.nəʳ US -nɚ **-s** -z
cleanliness ˈklen.lɪ.nəs, -nɪs
cleanl|y ˈkliːn.l|i **-ier** -i.əʳ US -i.ɚ **-iest** -i.ɪst, -i.əst
cleans|e klenz **-es** -ɪz **-ing** -ɪŋ **-ed** -d **-er/s** -əʳ/z US -ɚ/z **-able** -ə.bl̩
cleanshaven ˌkliːnˈʃeɪ.vᵊn *stress shift:* ˌcleanshaven ˈchin
clean-up ˈkliːn.ʌp **-s** -s
clear klɪəʳ US klɪr **-er** -əʳ US -ɚ **-est** -ɪst, -əst **-ly** -li **-ness** -nəs, -nɪs **-s** -z **-ing** -ɪŋ **-ed** -d ˌ**clear-ˈheaded** US ˈ**clear-**ˌ**headed** *stress shift, British only:* ˌclear-headed ˈthinking ˌ**clear-ˈsighted** US ˈ**clear-**ˌ**sighted** *stress shift, British only:* ˌclear-sighted ˈplanning
clearage ˈklɪə.rɪdʒ US ˈklɪr.ɪdʒ
clearanc|e ˈklɪə.rᵊnts US ˈklɪr.ᵊnts **-es** -ɪz ˈ**clearance** ˌ**sale**
clear-cut ˌklɪəˈkʌt US ˌklɪr- *stress shift:* ˌclear-cut ˈdifference
clearing-hou|se ˈklɪə.rɪŋ.haʊ|s US ˈklɪr.ɪŋ- **-ses** -zɪz
clearout ˈklɪə.raʊt US ˈklɪr- **-s** -s
clearway ˈklɪə.weɪ US ˈklɪr- **-s** -z
Cleary ˈklɪə.ri US ˈklɪr.i
cleat kliːt **-s** -s
Cleator Moor ˌkliː.təˈmɔːʳ US -t̬ɚˈmɔːr
cleavag|e ˈkliː.vɪdʒ **-es** -ɪz
cleav|e kliːv **-es** -z **-ing** -ɪŋ **-ed** -d **clove** kləʊv US kloʊv **cleft** kleft **cloven** ˈkləʊ.vᵊn US ˈkloʊ- **clave** kleɪv

Clear l

A type of LATERAL sound in which the air escapes past the sides of the tongue, found normally only before vowels. Usually contrasted with DARK L.

Examples for English

In the case of an alveolar lateral (e.g. English /l/) the blade of the tongue (the part further back than the tip) is in contact with the alveolar ridge, but the rest of the tongue is free to take up different shapes. One possibility is for the front of the tongue (the part behind the blade) to be raised in the same shape as that for a close front vowel [i]. This gives the /l/ an [i]-like sound, and the result is a "clear l". It is found in BBC English only before vowels, but in some other accents, notably Irish and Welsh ones, it is found is all positions. However, the variant most often found in all positions is "DARK L", e.g.:

pill /pɪl/ [pʰɪɫ]

cleaver (C) ˈkliː.vəʳ US -vɚ **-s** -z
Cleckheaton klekˈhiː.tᵊn US -t̬ᵊn
Clee kliː
cleek kliːk **-s** -s **-ing** -ɪŋ **-ed** -t
Cleese kliːz
Cleethorpes ˈkliː.θɔːps US -θɔːrps
clef klef **-s** -s
cleft kleft **-s** -s ˌ**cleft** ˈ**palate**
cleg kleg **-s** -z
Clegg kleg
Cleland ˈklel.ənd, ˈkliː.lənd
Clem klem
clematis ˈklem.ə.tɪs; klɪˈmeɪ.tɪs, klə-, klemˈeɪ- US ˈklem.ə.t̬əs; kləˈmæt̬.əs, -ˈmɑː.t̬əs
Clemence ˈklem.ənts
Clemenceau ˈklem.ən.səʊ, -ɑ̃ːn- US -soʊ
clemency ˈklem.ənt.si
Clemens ˈklem.ənz
clement (C) ˈklem.ənt **-ly** -li
Clementi klɪˈmen.ti, klə-, klemˈen- US -t̬i
Clementina ˌklem.ənˈtiː.nə
clementine (C) ˈklem.ən.tiːn, -taɪn US -taɪn, -tiːn **-s** -z
Clements ˈklem.ᵊnts
Clemo ˈklem.əʊ US -oʊ
clench klentʃ **-es** -ɪz **-ing** -ɪŋ **-ed** -t
Cleo ˈkliː.əʊ US -oʊ
Cleobury *places in Shropshire:* ˈklɪb.ᵊr.i, ˈkleb-, ˈklɪə.bᵊr- US -er-, ˈ-ɚ-
Cleobury *surname:* ˈkləʊ.bᵊr.i, ˈkliː- US ˈkloʊ.ber-, ˈkliː-, -bɚ-
Cleopatra ˌkli.əˈpæt.rə, -ˈpɑː.trə US ˌkli.oʊˈpæt.rə, -əˈ-, -ˈpeɪ.trə, -ˈpɑː-
clepsydr|a ˈklep.sɪ.dr|ə, klepˈsɪd.r|ə US ˈklep.sɪ.dr|ə **-ae** -iː
clerestor|y ˈklɪə.stɔː.r|i, -stə- US ˈklɪr.stɔːr|.i **-ies** -iz
clergy ˈklɜː.dʒi US ˈklɝː-
clergy|man ˈklɜː.dʒɪ|.mən US ˈklɝː- **-men** -mən
clergy|woman ˈklɜː.dʒɪ|ˌwʊm.ən US ˈklɝː- **-women** -ˌwɪm.ɪn
cleric ˈkler.ɪk **-s** -s
clerical ˈkler.ɪ.kᵊl **-s** -z **-ly** -i
Clerides klerˈiː.diːz, kləˈriː- US klerˈiː.ðiːz, -diːz
clerihew (C) ˈkler.ɪ.hjuː, ˈ-ə- US ˈ-ə- **-s** -z
clerisy ˈkler.ɪ.si, ˈ-ə- US ˈ-ə-
clerk (C) klɑːk US klɝːk **-s** -s
Clerke klɑːk US klɝːk, klɑːrk
Clerkenwell ˈklɑː.kᵊn.wel, -wəl US ˈklɝː-, ˈklɑːr-
clerkship ˈklɑːk.ʃɪp US ˈklɝːk- **-s** -s
Clermont *towns in Ireland, village in Norfolk:* ˈkleə.mɒnt, -mənt US ˈkler.mɑːnt *in US:* ˈkleə.mɒnt, ˈklɜː- US ˈkler.mɑːnt, ˈklɝː-
Clermont-Ferrand ˌkleə.mɔ̃ːn.ferˈɑ̃ːŋ US ˌkler.mɑːn.ferˈɑ̃ːn
Clery ˈklɪə.ri US ˈklɪr.i
Clevedon ˈkliːv.dən
Cleveland ˈkliːv.lənd
Cleveleys ˈkliːv.liz
clev|er ˈklev|.əʳ US -ɚ **-erer** -ᵊr.əʳ US -ɚ.ɚ **-erest** -ᵊr.ɪst, -əst **-erly** -ᵊl.i US -ɚ.li **-erness** -ə.nəs, -nɪs US -ɚ.nəs, -nɪs **-erish** -ᵊr.ɪʃ ˈ**clever** ˌ**clogs; too** ˌ**clever by** ˈ**half**
clever-dick ˈklev.ə.dɪk US ˈ-ɚ- **-s** -s
Cleverdon ˈklev.ə.dᵊn US ˈ-ɚ-
Cleves kliːvz
clew kluː **-s** -z **-ing** -ɪŋ **-ed** -d
Clews kluːz
Cley klaɪ, kleɪ
cliché ˈkliː.ʃeɪ, -ˈ- US -ˈ- **-s** -z **-d** -d
click klɪk **-s** -s **-ing** -ɪŋ **-ed** -t
client klaɪənt **-s** -s
clientage ˈklaɪən.tɪdʒ
clientele ˌkliː.ɑ̃ːnˈtel, -ɑːnˈ-, -ənˈ- US ˌklaɪ.ənˈtel, ˌkliː-, -ɑːnˈ- **-s** -z
cliff klɪf **-s** -s
Cliff(e) klɪf
cliffhanger ˈklɪfˌhæŋ.əʳ US -ɚ **-s** -z
Clifford ˈklɪf.əd US -ɚd
clifftop ˈklɪf.tɒp US -tɑːp **-s** -s
clift (C) klɪft **-s** -s
Clifton ˈklɪf.tᵊn
climacteric klaɪˈmæk.tᵊr.ɪk; ˌklaɪ.mækˈter- US klaɪˈmæk.tɚ.ɪk; ˌklaɪ.mækˈter-, -ˈtɪr- **-s** -s
climacterical ˌklaɪ.mækˈter.ɪ.kᵊl
climactic klaɪˈmæk.tɪk **-al** -ᵊl **-ally** -ᵊl.i, -li
climate ˈklaɪ.mət, -mɪt **-s** -s
climatic klaɪˈmæt.ɪk US -ˈmæt̬- **-al** -ᵊl **-ally** -ᵊl.i, -li
climatolog|y ˌklaɪ.məˈtɒl.ə.dʒ|i US -ˈtɑː.lə- **-ist/s** -ɪst/s
climax ˈklaɪ.mæks **-es** -ɪz **-ing** -ɪŋ **-ed** -t
climb klaɪm **-s** -z **-ing** -ɪŋ **-ed** -d **-able** -ə.bl̩ ˈ**climbing** ˌ**frame**
climb-down ˈklaɪm.daʊn **-s** -z
climber ˈklaɪ.məʳ US -mɚ **-s** -z
clime klaɪm **-s** -z
clinch (C) klɪntʃ **-es** -ɪz **-ing** -ɪŋ **-ed** -t **-er/s** -əʳ/z US -ɚ/z
cline (C) klaɪn **-s** -z
cling klɪŋ **-s** -z **-ing** -ɪŋ **clung** klʌŋ
clingfilm (C®) ˈklɪŋ.fɪlm
clingstone ˈklɪŋ.stəʊn US -stoʊn **-s** -z
cling|y ˈklɪŋ|.i **-ier** -i.əʳ US -i.ɚ **-iest** -i.ɪst, -i.əst **-iness** -ɪ.nəs, -ɪ.nɪs
clinic ˈklɪn.ɪk **-s** -s **-al** -ᵊl **-ally** -ᵊl.i, -li
clinician klɪˈnɪʃ.ᵊn US klɪ-, klə- **-s** -z
Clinique® klɪˈniːk
clink klɪŋk **-s** -s **-ing** -ɪŋ **-ed** -t
clinker (C) ˈklɪŋ.kəʳ US -kɚ **-s** -z
clinometer klaɪˈnɒm.ɪ.təʳ, klɪ-, ˈ-ə- US -ˈnɑː.mə.t̬ɚ **-s** -s
clinometric ˌklaɪ.nəʊˈmet.rɪk, ˌklɪn.əʊˈ- US -noʊˈ-
clinometry klaɪˈnɒm.ɪ.tri, klɪ-, ˈ-ə- US klaɪˈnɑː.mə-
Clint klɪnt
Clinton ˈklɪn.tən US ˈklɪn.tən, -tᵊn
Clio ˈkliː.əʊ, ˈklaɪ- US -oʊ
Note: The pronunciation /ˈkliː.əʊ US -oʊ/ is suitable for the motor car.
clip klɪp **-s** -s **-ping** -ɪŋ **-ped** -t ˈ**clip** ˌ**joint**
clipboard ˈklɪp.bɔːd US -bɔːrd **-s** -z
clip-clop ˈklɪp.klɒp US -klɑːp **-s** -s **-ping** -ɪŋ **-ped** -t
clipper ˈklɪp.əʳ US -ɚ **-s** -z
clippie ˈklɪp.i **-s** -z
clipping ˈklɪp.ɪŋ **-s** -z

clique kliːk US kliːk, klɪk **-s** -s **-y** -i

cliquish ˈkliː.kɪʃ US ˈkliː.kɪʃ, ˈklɪk.ɪʃ **-ly** -li **-ness** -nəs, -nɪs

cliqu|y ˈkliː.k|i US ˈkliː.k|i, ˈklɪk|.i **-ier** -i.əʳ US -i.ɚ **-iest** -i.ɪst, -i.əst **-iness** -ɪ.nəs, -ɪ.nɪs

Clissold ˈklɪs.ᵊld, -əʊld US -oʊld

Clitheroe ˈklɪð.ə.rəʊ US -roʊ

clitic ˈklɪt.ɪk US ˈklɪt̬- **-s** -s

clitoral ˈklɪt.ᵊr.ᵊl US ˈklɪt̬.ɚ-, ˈklaɪ.t̬ɚ-

clitoridectom|y ˌklɪt.ᵊr.ɪˈdek.tə.m|i US ˌklɪt- **-ies** -iz

clitor|is ˈklɪt.ᵊr|.ɪs US ˈklɪt̬.ɚ|.əs, ˈklaɪ.t̬ɚ-; klɪˈtɔːr- **-ic** -ɪk

Clive klaɪv

Cliveden ˈklɪv.dᵊn, ˈkliːv-

cloa|ca kləʊˈeɪ|.kə US kloʊ- **-cae** -kiː, -siː US -siː, -kiː **-cal** -kᵊl

cloak (C) kləʊk US kloʊk **-s** -s **-ing** -ɪŋ **-ed** -t

cloak-and-dagger ˌkləʊk.ᵊnˈdæg.əʳ US ˌkloʊk.ᵊnˈdæg.ɚ

cloakroom ˈkləʊk.rʊm, -ruːm US ˈkloʊk.ruːm, -rʊm **-s** -z

clobb|er ˈklɒb|.əʳ US ˈklɑː.b|ɚ **-ers** -əz US -ɚz **-ering** -ᵊr.ɪŋ **-ered** -əd US -ɚd

cloch|e klɒʃ, kləʊʃ US kloʊʃ **-es** -ɪz

clock klɒk US klɑːk **-s** -s **-ing** -ɪŋ **-ed** -t **ˈclock ˌface; put the ˈclock ˌback**

clockwise ˈklɒk.waɪz US ˈklɑːk-

clockwork ˈklɒk.wɜːk US ˈklɑːk.wɝːk

clod klɒd US klɑːd **-s** -z **-dy** -i

clodhopp|ing ˈklɒdˌhɒp|.ɪŋ US ˈklɑːdˌhɑː.p|ɪŋ **-er/s** -əʳ/z US -ɚ/z

Cloete kləʊˈiː.ti; ˈkluː.ti US ˈkluː.t̬i; kloʊˈiː.t̬i

clog klɒg US klɑːg, klɔːg **-s** -z **-ging** -ɪŋ **-ged** -d

clogg|y ˈklɒg|.i US ˈklɑː.g|i **-ier** -i.əʳ US -i.ɚ **-iest** -i.ɪst, -i.əst **-ily** -ɪ.li, -ᵊl.i **-iness** -ɪ.nəs, -ɪ.nɪs

Clogher ˈklɒ.həʳ, ˈklɒx.əʳ, ˈklɔː-, klɔːʳ US ˈklɑː.hɚ, -xɚ

cloisonné klwɑːˈzɒn.eɪ, klwʌzˈɒn-; US ˌklɔɪ.zəˈneɪ

cloist|er ˈklɔɪ.st|əʳ US -st|ɚ **-ers** -əz US -ɚz **-ering** -ᵊr.ɪŋ **-ered** -əd US -ɚd

cloistral ˈklɔɪ.strᵊl

clonal ˈkləʊ.nᵊl US ˈkloʊ- **-ly** -i

clon|e kləʊn US kloʊn **-es** -z **-ing** -ɪŋ **-ed** -d

Clonmel ˈklɒn.mel, -ˈ- US ˈklɑːn.mel, -ˈ-

clos|e *(v.)* kləʊz US kloʊz **-es** -ɪz **-ing** -ɪŋ **-ed** -d **-er/s** -əʳ/z US -ɚ/z **ˌclosed ˈbook; ˌclosed ˈcircuit** *stress shift:* ˌclosed circuit ˈtelevision; **ˌclosed ˈshop**

clos|e *(n.) end:* kləʊz US kloʊz **-es** -ɪz

clos|e *(adj.) near:* kləʊs US kloʊs **-er** -əʳ US -ɚ **-est** -ɪst, -əst **-ely** -li **-eness** -nəs, -nɪs **ˌclose ˈquarters; ˌclose ˈseason**

close-cut ˌkləʊsˈkʌt US ˌkloʊs-

closefisted ˌkləʊsˈfɪs.tɪd US ˌkloʊs- *stress shift:* ˌclosefisted ˈmiser

close-grained ˌkləʊsˈgreɪnd US ˌkloʊs- *stress shift:* ˌclose-grained ˈwood

close-hauled ˌkləʊsˈhɔːld US ˌkloʊsˈhɔːld, -ˈhɑːld *stress shift:* ˌclose-hauled ˈsailing

close-knit ˌkləʊsˈnɪt US ˌkloʊs- *stress shift:* ˌclose-knit ˈfamily

closely ˈkləʊ.sli US ˈkloʊ-

closely-guarded ˌkləʊ.sliˈgɑː.dɪd US ˌkloʊ.sliˈgɑːr- *stress shift:* ˌclosely-guarded ˈsecret

clos|et ˈklɒz|.ɪt US ˈklɑː.z|ɪt **-ets** -ɪts **-eting** -ɪ.tɪŋ US -ɪ.t̬ɪŋ, ˈ-ə- **-eted** -ɪ.tɪd US -ɪ.t̬ɪd, ˈ-ə- **come ˌout of the ˈcloset**

close-up ˈkləʊs.ʌp US ˈkloʊs- **-s** -s

closure ˈkləʊ.ʒəʳ US ˈkloʊ.ʒɚ **-s** -z

clot klɒt US klɑːt **-s** -s **-ting** -ɪŋ US ˈklɑː.t̬ɪŋ **-ted** -ɪd US ˈklɑː.t̬ɪd **ˌclotted ˈcream**

cloth klɒθ US klɑːθ **-s** klɒθs, klɒðz US klɑːθs, klɑːðz **ˈcloth ˌyard; cut one's ˌcoat according to one's ˈcloth**

cloth|e kləʊð US kloʊð **-es** -z **-ing** -ɪŋ **-ed** -d **clad** klæd

cloth-eared ˌklɒθˈɪəd US ˌklɑːθˈɪrd *stress shift:* ˌcloth-eared ˈlistener

clothes kləʊðz US kloʊðz **ˈclothes ˌbrush; ˈclothes ˌhanger**

clotheshors|e ˈkləʊðz.hɔːs US ˈkloʊðz.hɔːrs **-es** -ɪz

clothesline ˈkləʊðz.laɪn US ˈkloʊðz- **-s** -z

clothespeg ˈkləʊðz.peg US ˈkloʊðz- **-s** -z

clothespin ˈkləʊðz.pɪn US ˈkloʊðz- **-s** -z

clothier ˈkləʊ.ði.əʳ US ˈkloʊ.ði.ɚ **-s** -z

Clothilde ˈklɒt.ɪld, -ˈ- US kloʊˈtɪl.də

clothing ˈkləʊ.ðɪŋ US ˈkloʊ-

Clotho ˈkləʊ.θəʊ US ˈkloʊ.θoʊ

cloud klaʊd **-s** -z **-ing** -ɪŋ **-ed** -ɪd **ˈcloud-ˌcapped**

cloudberr|y ˈklaʊd.bᵊr|.i, ˈklaʊb-, -ber- US ˈklaʊd.ber- **-ies** -iz

cloudburst ˈklaʊd.bɜːst US -bɝːst **-s** -s

cloud-cuckoo-land ˌklaʊdˈkʊk.uː.lænd US -ˈkuː.kuː-, -ˈkʊk.ʊ-

Cloudesley ˈklaʊdz.li

cloudless ˈklaʊd.ləs, -lɪs **-ly** -li **-ness** -nəs, -nɪs

cloud|y ˈklaʊ.d|i **-ier** -i.əʳ US -i.ɚ **-iest** -i.ɪst, -i.əst **-ily** -ɪ.li, -ᵊl.i **-iness** -ɪ.nəs, -ɪ.nɪs

clough klʌf **-s** -s

Clough *surname:* klʌf, kluː *in Ireland:* klɒx US klʌf

Clouseau kluːˈsəʊ, ˈ-- US kluːˈzoʊ, ˈ--

clout klaʊt **-s** -s **-ing** -ɪŋ US ˈklaʊ.t̬ɪŋ **-ed** -ɪd US ˈklaʊ.t̬ɪd

clove *(n.)* kləʊv US kloʊv **-s** -z

clov|e *(from* **cleave***)* kləʊv US kloʊv **-en** -ᵊn

Clovelly kləˈvel.i

cloven ˈkləʊ.vᵊn US ˈkloʊ- **ˌcloven-ˈfooted** *stress shift:* ˌcloven-footed ˈbeast

clover (C) ˈkləʊ.vəʳ US ˈkloʊ.vɚ **-s** -z

clover|leaf ˈkləʊ.və|.liːf US ˈkloʊ.vɚ- **-leafs** -liːfs **-leaves** -liːvz

Clovis ˈkləʊ.vɪs US ˈkloʊ-

Clow kləʊ US kloʊ, klaʊ

Clowes *in Norfolk:* kluːz *surname:* klaʊz, kluːz

clown klaʊn **-s** -z **-ing** -ɪŋ **-ed** -d

Clowne klaʊn

clownish ˈklaʊ.nɪʃ **-ly** -li **-ness** -nəs, -nɪs

cloy klɔɪ **-s** -z **-ing/ly** -ɪŋ/li **-ed** -d

cloze kləʊz US kloʊz

club klʌb **-s** -z **-bing** -ɪŋ **-bed** -d **ˌclub ˈsandwich; ˌclub ˈsoda; ˌclub ˈmoss** US **ˈclub ˌmoss**

clubbable ˈklʌb.ə.bl̩

clubber ˈklʌb.əʳ US -ɚ **-s** -z

club|foot ˌklʌb|ˈfʊt, ˈ-- US ˈ-- **-feet** -ˈfiːt US -fiːt

clubfooted ˌklʌbˈfʊt.ɪd, ˈ--- US ˈklʌbˌfʊt̬.ɪd

clubhou|se ˈklʌb.haʊ|s **-ses** -zɪz

clubland ˈklʌb.lænd, -lənd

club|man ˈklʌb|.mən, -mæn **-men** -mən, -men

Club Med ˌklʌbˈmed

Club Méditerranée® ˌklʌbˌmed.ɪˌter.əˈneɪ

club-room ˈklʌb.rʊm, -ruːm US -ruːm, -rʊm **-s** -z

cluck klʌk **-s** -s **-ing** -ɪŋ **-ed** -t

clu|e kluː **-es** -z **-(e)ing** -ɪŋ **-ed** -d **ˌclued ˈup**

clueless ˈkluː.ləs, -lɪs **-ness** -nəs, -nɪs

Cluj kluːʒ

clumber (C) ˈklʌm.bəʳ US -bɚ **-s** -z

clump klʌmp **-s** -s **-ing** -ɪŋ **-ed** -t

clumpy ˈklʌm.pi

clums|y ˈklʌm.z|i **-ier** -i.əʳ US -i.ɚ **-iest** -i.ɪst, -i.əst **-ily** -ɪ.li, -ᵊl.i **-iness** -ɪ.nəs, -ɪ.nɪs

Clun klʌn

clunch klʌntʃ

clung *(from* **cling***)* klʌŋ

clunk klʌŋk **-s** -s **-ing** -ɪŋ **-ed** -t

clunk|y ˈklʌŋ.k|i **-ier** -i.əʳ US -i.ɚ **-iest** -i.ɪst, -i.əst

clust|er ˈklʌs.t|əʳ US -tɚ **-ers** -əz US -ɚz **-ering** -ᵊr.ɪŋ **-ered** -əd US -ɚd

clutch klʌtʃ **-es** -ɪz **-ing** -ɪŋ **-ed** -t **ˈclutch ˌbag**

clutt|er ˈklʌt|.əʳ US ˈklʌt̬|.ɚ **-ers** -əz US -ɚz **-ering** -ᵊr.ɪŋ **-ered** -əd US -ɚd

Clutterbuck ˈklʌt.ə.bʌk US ˈklʌt̬.ɚ-

Clutton ˈklʌt.ᵊn US ˈklʌt̬-

Cluster

Two or more CONSONANT PHONEMES in sequence, with no vowel sound between them.

Examples for English

English can allow up to three consonants in a cluster syllable initially in the ONSET, and four syllable finally in the CODA. For example, the word *stray* /streɪ/ begins with three consonants, and *sixths* /sɪksθs/ ends with four.

Some types of grammatical information are shown by adding certain consonants at the ends of words in English, giving rise to consonant clusters, e.g.:

likes	/laɪks/	
lives	/lɪvz/	
liked	/laɪkt/	
lived	/lɪvd/	
Mark's	/mɑːks/	US /mɑːrks/
John's	/dʒɒnz/	US /dʒɑːnz/
cats	/kæts/	
dogs	/dɒgz/	US /dɑːgz/

Coalescence

A kind of ASSIMILATION in which a fusion of neighbouring sounds takes place during rapid or CONNECTED SPEECH.

Examples for English

The most frequently observed situation in which coalescence occurs in English is when ALVEOLAR consonants /t d s z/ are followed by /j/, e.g.:

won't you	/wəʊnt ju/	→	/ˈwəʊntʃu/
	US /woʊnt-/		US /woʊnt-/
would you	/wʊd ju/	→	/ˈwʊdʒu/
miss you	/mɪs ju/	→	/ˈmɪʃu/
lose you	/luːz ju/	→	/ˈluːʒu/

In the case of coalescence with /s z/, there will usually be extra length to the resulting fricative sounds, e.g.:

miss you	/mɪs ju/	→	/ˈmɪʃʃu/
lose you	/luːz ju/	→	/ˈluːʒʒu/

A common very much reduced example of coalescence is *do you* being pronounced as /dʒə/.

Clwyd ˈkluː.ɪd
Clwydian kluˈɪd.i.ən
Clydach ˈklɪd.ək, ˈklʌd-, -əx US -ək
Clyde klaɪd
Clydebank ˈklaɪd.bæŋk, -ˈ-
Clydesdale ˈklaɪdz.deɪl **-s** -z
Clydeside ˈklaɪd.saɪd
Clym klɪm
clyster ˈklɪs.təʳ US -tɚ **-s** -z
Clytemnestra ˌklaɪ.təmˈnes.trə, ˌklɪt.əmˈ-, -ɪmˈ-, -emˈ-, -ˈniː.strə US ˌklaɪ.t̬əmˈnes.trə
Clytie *in Greek mythology:* ˈklɪt.i.iː, ˈklaɪ.tiː US ˈklaɪ.t̬i.iː, ˈklɪt̬.i.iː *modern first name, chignon:* ˈklaɪ.ti, -tiː US ˈklaɪ.t̬i, klɪˈʃiː.ə
cm *(abbrev. for* **centimetre/s***)* *singular:* ˈsen.tɪˌmiː.təʳ US -t̬əˌmiː.t̬ɚ *plural:* -z
CND ˌsiː.enˈdiː
Cnidus ˈnaɪ.dəs, ˈknaɪ-
CNN ˌsiː.enˈen
Cnut kəˈnjuːt, knuːt
c/o *(abbrev. for* **care of***)* ˈkeəʳ.ɒv US ˈker.ɑːv, -əv
c/o *(abbrev. for* **carried over***)* ˌkær.idˈəʊ.vəʳ US ˌker.idˈoʊ.vɚ, ˌkær-
co- kəʊ- US koʊ-
Co. *(abbrev. for* **company***)* kəʊ, ˈkʌm.pᵊn.i US koʊ, ˈkʌm.pᵊn.i
CO ˌsiːˈəʊ US -ˈoʊ
coach kəʊtʃ US koʊtʃ **-es** -ɪz **-ing** -ɪŋ **-ed** -t **ˈcoach ˌhorse; ˈcoach ˌhouse; ˈcoach ˌparty; ˈcoach ˌstation**
coach|man ˈkəʊtʃ|.mən US ˈkoʊtʃ- **-men** -mən
coac|tion kəʊˈæk|.ʃᵊn US koʊ- **-tive** -tɪv
coadjacent ˌkəʊ.əˈdʒeɪ.sᵊnt US ˌkoʊ-
coadjutant kəʊˈædʒ.ʊ.tᵊnt, ˈ-ə- US koʊˈædʒ.ə.t̬ᵊnt **-s** -s
coadjutor kəʊˈædʒ.ʊ.təʳ, ˈ-ə- US koʊˈædʒ.ə.t̬ɚ **-s** -z
co-administrator ˌkəʊ.ədˈmɪn.ɪ.streɪ.təʳ US ˌkoʊ.ædˈmɪn.ɪ.streɪ.t̬ɚ, -ədˈ- **-s** -z
coagulant kəʊˈæg.jʊ.lənt, -jə- US koʊˈæg.jə- **-s** -s
coagu|late kəʊˈæg.jə|.leɪt, -jʊ- US koʊˈæg.jə- **-lates** -leɪts **-lating** -leɪ.tɪŋ US -leɪ.t̬ɪŋ **-lated** -leɪ.tɪd US -leɪ.t̬ɪd
coagulation kəʊˌæg.jəˈleɪ.ʃᵊn, -jʊˈ- US koʊˌæg.jəˈ-
coal kəʊl US koʊl **-s** -z **-ing** -ɪŋ **-ed** -d **ˈcoal ˌbed; ˈcoal ˌblack; ˈcoal ˌbunker; ˈcoal ˌscuttle; ˈcoal ˌtar; ˌhaul someone over the ˈcoals**
coalesc|e kəʊəˈles US koʊə- **-es** -ɪz **-ing** -ɪŋ **-ed** -t
coalescen|ce kəʊəˈles.ᵊn|ts US koʊə- **-t** -t
coalfac|e ˈkəʊl.feɪs US ˈkoʊl- **-es** -ɪz
coalfield ˈkəʊl.fiːld US ˈkoʊl- **-s** -z
coalhole ˈkəʊl.həʊl US ˈkoʊl.hoʊl **-s** -z
coalhou|se ˈkəʊl.haʊ|s US ˈkoʊl- **-ses** -zɪz
Coalite® ˈkəʊ.laɪt US ˈkoʊ-
coalition kəʊəˈlɪʃ.ᵊn US koʊə- **-s** -z
coal|man ˈkəʊl|.mən, -mæn US ˈkoʊl- **-men** -men, -mən
coalmine ˈkəʊl.maɪn US ˈkoʊl- **-s** -z
coalminer ˈkəʊlˌmaɪ.nəʳ US ˈkoʊlˌmaɪ.nɚ **-s** -z
coalpit ˈkəʊl.pɪt US ˈkoʊl- **-s** -s
Coalville ˈkəʊl.vɪl US ˈkoʊl-
coanchor ˈkəʊˌæŋ.kəʳ US ˈkoʊˌæŋ.kɚ **-s** -z
coars|e kɔːs US kɔːrs **-er** -əʳ US -ɚ **-est** -ɪst, -əst **-ely** -li **-eness** -nəs, -nɪs **ˈcoarse ˌfishing, ˌcoarse ˈfishing**
coarse-grained ˌkɔːsˈgreɪnd US ˈkɔːrs.greɪnd *stress shift:* ˌcoarse-grained ˈpicture

Coarticulation

The influence of phonetic context on the articulation of speech sounds.

Examples for English

Phonetics studies coarticulation as a way of finding out how the brain controls the production of speech. When we speak, many muscles are active at the same time and sometimes the brain tries to make them do things that they are not capable of. For example, in the word *mum* the vowel phoneme is one that is normally pronounced with the soft palate raised to prevent the escape of air through the nose, while the two /m/ phonemes must have the soft palate lowered. The soft palate cannot be raised very quickly, so the vowel is likely to be pronounced with the soft palate still lowered, giving a nasalized quality to the vowel, e.g.:

mum /mʌm/ [mʌ̃m]

Another example is the lip-rounding of a consonant in the environment of rounded vowels: in the phrase 'you too', the /t/ occurs between two rounded vowels, and there is not enough time in normal speech for the lips to move from rounded to unrounded and back again in a few hundredths of a second; consequently the /t/ is pronounced with lip-rounding, e.g.:

you too /juː tuː/ [jʉːtʷʉː]

Coarticulation is a phenomenon closely related to ASSIMILATION. The major difference is that assimilation is used as a name for the process whereby one sound becomes like another neighbouring sound, while coarticulation, though it refers to a similar process, is concerned with articulatory explanations for why the assimilation occurs, and considers cases where the changes may occur over a number of segments.

coarsen ˈkɔː.sᵊn ⓤⓢ ˈkɔːr- **-s** -z **-ing** -ɪŋ **-ed** -d
coarticulation ˌkəʊ.ɑː.tɪ.kjəˈleɪ.ʃᵊn, -jʊˈ- ⓤⓢ ˌkoʊ.ɑːr.tɪ.kjəˈ-
coast kəʊst ⓤⓢ koʊst **-s** -s **-ing** -ɪŋ **-ed** -ɪd
coastal ˈkəʊs.tᵊl ⓤⓢ ˈkoʊ-
coaster ˈkəʊ.stəʳ ⓤⓢ ˈkoʊ.stɚ **-s** -z
coastguard ˈkəʊst.gɑːd ⓤⓢ ˈkoʊst.gɑːrd **-s** -z
coastline ˈkəʊst.laɪn ⓤⓢ ˈkoʊst- **-s** -z
coastwise ˈkəʊst.waɪz ⓤⓢ ˈkoʊst-
coat kəʊt ⓤⓢ koʊt **-s** -s **-ing** -ɪŋ **-ed** -ɪd **ˈcoat ˌcheck; ˈcoat ˌhanger; ˌcoat of ˈarms; ˈcoat ˌroom; ˈcoat ˌtail(s); ˌcut one's ˌcoat according to one's ˈcloth**
Coatbridge ˈkəʊt.brɪdʒ ⓤⓢ ˈkoʊt-
Coat(e)s kəʊts ⓤⓢ koʊts
coati kəʊˈɑː.ti ⓤⓢ koʊˈɑː.t̬i **-s** -z
coating ˈkəʊ.tɪŋ ⓤⓢ ˈkoʊ.t̬ɪŋ **-s** -z
coauthor kəʊˈɔː.θəʳ, ˈ--- ⓤⓢ koʊˈɑː.θɚ, -ˈɔː- **-s** -z **-ing** -ɪŋ **-ed** -d
coax kəʊks ⓤⓢ koʊks **-es** -ɪz **-ing/ly** -ɪŋ/li **-ed** -t **-er/s** -əʳ/z ⓤⓢ -ɚ/z
co-axial ˌkəʊˈæk.si.əl ⓤⓢ ˌkoʊ- **-ly** -i
cob kɒb ⓤⓢ kɑːb **-s** -z
Cobain kəʊˈbeɪn ⓤⓢ ˈkoʊ-, ˌkoʊˈbeɪn
cobalt ˈkəʊ.bɔːlt, -bɒlt ⓤⓢ ˈkoʊ.bɔːlt, -bɑːlt
Cobb(e) kɒb ⓤⓢ kɑːb
cobber ˈkɒb.əʳ ⓤⓢ ˈkɑː.bɚ **-s** -z
Cobbett ˈkɒb.ɪt ⓤⓢ ˈkɑː.bɪt
cobbl|e ˈkɒb.l̩ ⓤⓢ ˈkɑː.bl̩ **-es** -z **-ing** -ɪŋ, ˈ-lɪŋ ⓤⓢ ˈkɑː.bl̩.ɪŋ, ˈ-blɪŋ **-ed** -d
Cobbleigh ˈkɒb.li ⓤⓢ ˈkɑː.bli
cobbler ˈkɒb.ləʳ, ˈkɒb.l̩.əʳ ⓤⓢ ˈkɑː.blɚ **-s** -z
cobblestone ˈkɒb.l̩.stəʊn ⓤⓢ ˈkɑː.bl̩.stoʊn **-s** -z
Cobbold ˈkɒb.əʊld, -ᵊld ⓤⓢ ˈkɑː.boʊld
Cobden ˈkɒb.dᵊn ⓤⓢ ˈkɑːb-
Cobh kəʊv ⓤⓢ koʊv
Cobham ˈkɒb.ᵊm ⓤⓢ ˈkɑː.bᵊm
Coblenz kəʊˈblents, ˈkəʊ.blents ⓤⓢ ˈkoʊ-
cobnut ˈkɒb.nʌt ⓤⓢ ˈkɑːb- **-s** -s
COBOL, Cobol ˈkəʊ.bɒl ⓤⓢ ˈkoʊ.bɔːl, -bɑːl
cobra ˈkəʊ.brə, ˈkɒb.rə ⓤⓢ ˈkoʊ.brə **-s** -z
Coburg ˈkəʊ.bɜːg ⓤⓢ ˈkoʊ.bɝːg **-s** -z
cobweb ˈkɒb.web ⓤⓢ ˈkɑːb- **-s** -z
coca ˈkəʊ.kə ⓤⓢ ˈkoʊ.kə **-s** -z
Coca-Cola® ˌkəʊ.kəˈkəʊ.lə ⓤⓢ ˌkoʊ.kəˈkoʊ-
cocaine kəʊˈkeɪn ⓤⓢ koʊ-, ˈ--
coccal ˈkɒk.ᵊl ⓤⓢ ˈkɑː.kᵊl
coccid ˈkɒk.sɪd ⓤⓢ ˈkɑːk-
cocciferous kɒkˈsɪf.ᵊr.əs ⓤⓢ kɑːk-
coccoid ˈkɒk.ɔɪd ⓤⓢ ˈkɑː.kɔɪd
coccus ˈkɒk.əs ⓤⓢ ˈkɑː.kəs **cocci** ˈkɒk.aɪ, ˈkɒk.saɪ ⓤⓢ ˈkɑːk.saɪ
coccyx ˈkɒk.sɪks ⓤⓢ ˈkɑːk- **-es** -ɪz **coccyges** -saɪ.dʒiːz
Cochabamba ˌkəʊ.tʃəˈbæm.bə ⓤⓢ ˌkoʊ.tʃəˈbɑːm-
Cochin ˈkəʊ.tʃɪn, ˈkɒtʃ.ɪn ⓤⓢ ˈkoʊ.tʃɪn
Cochin-China ˌkɒtʃ.ɪnˈtʃaɪ.nə ⓤⓢ ˌkoʊ.tʃɪnˈ-, ˌkɑː-
cochineal ˌkɒtʃ.ɪˈniːl, -əˈ-, ˈ--- ⓤⓢ ˈkɑː.tʃə.niːl, ˌ--ˈ-
Cochise kəʊˈtʃiːs ⓤⓢ koʊ-, -ˈtʃiːz
cochle|a ˈkɒk.li.ə ⓤⓢ ˈkɑːk-, ˈkoʊk- **-as** -əz **-ae** -iː **-ar** -əʳ ⓤⓢ -ɚ
Cochran(e) ˈkɒk.rən, ˈkɒx- ⓤⓢ ˈkɑːk-
cock kɒk ⓤⓢ kɑːk **-s** -s **-ing** -ɪŋ **-ed** -t
cockade kɒkˈeɪd ⓤⓢ kɑːˈkeɪd **-s** -z
cock-a-doodle-doo ˌkɒk.ə.duː.dl̩ˈduː ⓤⓢ ˌkɑːk-
cock-a-hoop ˌkɒk.əˈhuːp ⓤⓢ ˌkɑːk-
Cockaigne kɒkˈeɪn, kəˈkeɪn ⓤⓢ kɑːˈkeɪn
cock-a-leekie ˌkɒk.əˈliː.ki ⓤⓢ ˌkɑːk-
cockalorum ˌkɒk.əˈlɔː.rᵊm ⓤⓢ ˌkɑː.kəˈlɔːr.ᵊm **-s** -z
cockamamie ˌkɒk.əˈmeɪ.mi ⓤⓢ ˈkɑː.kə.meɪ-
cock-and-bull ˌkɒk.ᵊndˈbʊl, -ᵊmˈ- ⓤⓢ ˌkɑːk.ᵊnd- *stress shift, British only, see compound:* **ˌcock-and-bull ˈstory** ⓤⓢ **ˌcock-and-ˈbull ˌstory**
cockateel, cockatiel ˌkɒk.əˈtiːl ⓤⓢ ˌkɑː.kəˈ- **-s** -z
cockatoo ˌkɒk.əˈtuː ⓤⓢ ˈkɑː.kə.tuː **-s** -z
cockatric|e ˈkɒk.ə.traɪs, -trɪs, -trəs ⓤⓢ ˈkɑː.kə- **-es** -ɪz
Cockaygne kɒkˈeɪn, kəˈkeɪn ⓤⓢ kɑːˈkeɪn
Cockburn ˈkəʊ.bɜːn, -bən ⓤⓢ ˈkoʊ.bɝːn
cockchafer ˈkɒkˌtʃeɪ.fəʳ ⓤⓢ ˈkɑːkˌtʃeɪ.fɚ **-s** -z
Cockcroft ˈkəʊk.krɒft, ˈkɒk.krɒft ⓤⓢ ˈkɑːk.krɑːft, ˈkoʊ.krɑːft
cockcrow ˈkɒk.krəʊ ⓤⓢ ˈkɑːk.kroʊ
Cocke *place:* kɒk ⓤⓢ kɑːk *surname:* kəʊk, kɒk ⓤⓢ koʊk, kɑːk
Cockell ˈkɒk.ᵊl ⓤⓢ ˈkɑː.kᵊl
cocker (C) ˈkɒk.əʳ ⓤⓢ ˈkɑː.kɚ **-s** -z **ˌcocker ˈspaniel**
cockerel ˈkɒk.ᵊr.ᵊl ⓤⓢ ˈkɑː.kɚ- **-s** -z
Cockerell ˈkɒk.ᵊr.ᵊl ⓤⓢ ˈkɑː.kɚ-
Cockermouth ˈkɒk.ə.məθ, -maʊθ *locally:* -məθ ⓤⓢ ˈkɑː.kɚ
cockeye ˈkɒk.aɪ ⓤⓢ ˈkɑːk.aɪ **-d** kɒkˈaɪd ⓤⓢ ˈkɑːk.aɪd *stress shift, British only:* ˌcockeyed ˈoptimist

Coda

The end of a syllable, which is said to be made up of an ONSET, a peak and a coda. The peak and the coda constitute the RHYME (or RIME) of the syllable.

Examples for English

English allows up to four consonants to occur in the coda, so the total number of possible codas in English is very large – several hundred in fact, e.g.

sick	/sɪk/	sixth	/sɪksθ/
six	/sɪks/	sixths	/sɪksθs/

The central part of a syllable is almost always a vowel, and if the syllable contains nothing after the vowel it is said to have no coda ('zero coda'), e.g.:

bough	baʊ
buy	baɪ

In other languages

Some languages (e.g. Japanese) have no codas in any syllables.

cock|fight ˈkɒk|.faɪt (US) ˈkɑːk- **-fights** -faɪts **-fighting** -ˌfaɪ.tɪŋ (US) -ˌfaɪ.t̬ɪŋ
Cockfosters ˌkɒkˈfɒs.təz, ˈ-ˌ-- (US) ˈkɑːkˌfɑː.stɚz, ˌ-ˈ--
cockhors|e ˌkɒkˈhɔːs (US) ˈkɑːk.hɔːrs **-es** -ɪz
cockl|e (C) ˈkɒk.l̩ (US) ˈkɑː.kl̩ **-es** -z **-ing** -ɪŋ, ˈ-lɪŋ (US) ˈkɑː.kl̩.ɪŋ, ˈ-klɪŋ **-ed** -d
cockleshell ˈkɒk.l̩.ʃel (US) ˈkɑː.kl̩- **-s** -z
cockney (C) ˈkɒk.ni (US) ˈkɑːk- **-s** -z
cockneyism ˈkɒk.ni.ɪ.zᵊm (US) ˈkɑːk- **-s** -z
cockpit ˈkɒk.pɪt (US) ˈkɑːk- **-s** -s
cockroach ˈkɒk.rəʊtʃ (US) ˈkɑːk.roʊtʃ **-es** -ɪz
Cockroft ˈkɒk.rɒft, ˈkəʊ.krɒft (US) ˈkɑː.krɑːft, ˈkoʊ-
cockscomb ˈkɒk.skəʊm (US) ˈkɑːk.skoʊm **-s** -z
Cocksedge ˈkɒk.sɪdʒ, ˈkɒs.ɪdʒ, -edʒ, ˈkəʊ.sɪdʒ (US) ˈkɑːk.sɪdʒ, ˈkɑː-, ˈkoʊ-, -sedʒ
Cockshott ˈkɒk.ʃɒt (US) ˈkɑːk.ʃɑːt
cocksh|y ˈkɒk.ʃ|aɪ (US) ˈkɑːk- **-ies** -aɪz
cockspur (C) ˈkɒk.spɜːʳ, -spəʳ (US) ˈkɑːk.spɝː **-s** -z
cocksure ˌkɒkˈʃʊəʳ, -ˈʃɔːʳ (US) ˌkɑːkˈʃʊr, -ˈʃɝː
cocktail ˈkɒk.teɪl (US) ˈkɑːk- **-s** -z ˈ**cocktail** ˌ**dress**; ˈ**cocktail** ˌ**lounge**; ˈ**cocktail** ˌ**party**; ˈ**cocktail** ˌ**stick**
cock-up ˈkɒk.ʌp (US) ˈkɑːk- **-s** -s
Cockwood ˈkɒk.wʊd (US) ˈkɑːk-
Note: There exists also a local pronunciation /ˈkɒk.ʊd (US) ˈkɑː.kʊd/.
cock|y ˈkɒk|.i (US) ˈkɑː.k|i **-ier** -i.əʳ (US) -i.ɚ **-iest** -i.ɪst, -i.əst **-ily** -ɪ.li, -ᵊl.i **-iness** -ɪ.nəs, -ɪ.nɪs
cocky-leeky ˌkɒk.iˈliː.ki (US) ˌkɑː.ki-
coco ˈkəʊ.kəʊ (US) ˈkoʊ.koʊ **-s** -z
cocoa ˈkəʊ.kəʊ (US) ˈkoʊ.koʊ **-s** -z ˈ**cocoa** ˌ**butter**
cocoanut ˈkəʊ.kə.nʌt (US) ˈkoʊ- **-s** -s
co-conspirator ˌkəʊ.kənˈspɪr.ə.təʳ, ˈ-ɪ- (US) ˌkoʊ.kənˈspɪr.ə.t̬ɚ **-s** -z
coconut ˈkəʊ.kə.nʌt (US) ˈkoʊ- **-s** -s ˌ**coconut** ˈ**ice**; ˈ**coconut** ˌ**shy**
cocoon kəˈkuːn **-s** -z **-ing** -ɪŋ **-ed** -d
Cocos ˈkəʊ.kəs, -kɒs (US) ˈkoʊ.koʊs, -kəs
cocotte kəˈkɒt, kəʊ-, kɒkˈɒt (US) koʊˈkɑːt **-s** -s
Cocteau ˈkɒk.təʊ (US) kɑːkˈtoʊ
Cocytus kəʊˈsaɪ.təs (US) koʊˈsaɪ.t̬əs
cod (C) kɒd (US) kɑːd **-s** -z **-ding** -ɪŋ **-ded** -ɪd ˌ**cod-liver** ˈ**oil**
COD ˌsiː.əʊˈdiː (US) -oʊˈ-
coda ˈkəʊ.də (US) ˈkoʊ- **-s** -z
Coddington ˈkɒd.ɪŋ.tən (US) ˈkɑː.dɪŋ-
coddl|e ˈkɒd.l̩ (US) ˈkɑː.dl̩ **-es** -z **-ing** -ɪŋ, ˈ-lɪŋ (US) ˈkɑː.dl̩.ɪŋ, ˈkɑːd.lɪŋ **-ed** -d
cod|e kəʊd (US) koʊd **-es** -z **-ing** -ɪŋ **-ed** -ɪd **-er/s** -əʳ/z (US) -ɚ/s
co-defendant ˌkəʊ.dɪˈfen.dənt, -dəˈ- (US) ˌkoʊ-
codeine ˈkəʊ.diːn (US) ˈkoʊ-
co-determination ˌkəʊ.dɪ.tɜː.mɪˈneɪ.ʃən, -də- (US) ˌkoʊ.dɪ.tɝː-, -də-
cod|ex ˈkəʊ.d|eks (US) ˈkoʊ- **-exes** -ek.sɪz, -səz **-ices** -ɪ.siːz, ˈkɒd.ɪ.siːz (US) ˈkoʊ.də.siːz, ˈkɑː-
codger ˈkɒdʒ.əʳ (US) ˈkɑː.dʒɚ **-s** -z
codicil ˈkəʊ.dɪ.sɪl, ˈkɒd.ɪ-, ˈ-ə- (US) ˈkɑː.də.sᵊl, -sɪl **-s** -z
codicillary ˌkəʊ.dɪˈsɪl.ᵊr.i, ˌkɒd.ɪˈ- (US) ˌkɑː.dəˈ-
Codicote ˈkəʊ.dɪ.kəʊt, ˈkɒd.ɪ.kət (US) ˈkoʊ.dɪ.koʊt, ˈkɑː.dɪ.kət
codification ˌkəʊ.dɪ.fɪˈkeɪ.ʃən, -də- (US) ˌkɑː-, ˌkoʊ- **-s** -z
codi|fy ˈkəʊ.dɪ|.faɪ, -də- (US) ˈkɑː-, ˈkoʊ- **-fies** -faɪz **-fying** -faɪ.ɪŋ **-fied** -faɪd
codling ˈkɒd.lɪŋ (US) ˈkɑːd- **-s** -z
codpiec|e ˈkɒd.piːs (US) ˈkɑːd- **-es** -ɪz
Codrington ˈkɒd.rɪŋ.tən (US) ˈkɑːd-
Codsall ˈkɒd.sᵊl (US) ˈkɑːd-
codswallop ˈkɒdzˌwɒl.əp (US) ˈkɑːdzˌwɑː.ləp, -ˌwɔː-
Cody ˈkəʊ.di (US) ˈkoʊ-
Coe kəʊ (US) koʊ
coed ˌkəʊˈed (US) ˈkoʊ.ed **-s** -z *stress shift, British only:* ˌcoed ˈschool
Coed kɔɪd
coeducation ˌkəʊ.edʒ.ʊˈkeɪ.ʃᵊn, -ed.jʊˈ- (US) ˌkoʊ.edʒ.ʊˈ-, -əˈ-
coeducational ˌkəʊ.edʒ.ʊˈkeɪ.ʃᵊn.ᵊl, -ed.jʊˈ-, -ˈkeɪʃ.nᵊl (US) ˌkoʊ.edʒ.əˈ- **-ly** -li
coefficient ˌkəʊ.ɪˈfɪʃ.ᵊnt, -əˈfɪʃ- (US) ˌkoʊ- **-s** -s
coelacanth ˈsiː.lə.kæn*t*θ **-s** -s
coeliac ˈsiː.li.æk
coenobite ˈsiː.nəʊ.baɪt (US) ˈsen.ə- **-s** -s
coequal ˌkəʊˈiː.kwᵊl (US) ˌkoʊ- **-ly** -i
coequality ˌkəʊ.ɪˈkwɒl.ə.ti, -ɪ.ti (US) ˌkoʊ.iːˈkwɑː.lə.t̬i
coerc|e kəʊˈɜːs (US) koʊˈɝːs **-es** -ɪz **-ing** -ɪŋ **-ed** -t
coercib|le kəʊˈɜː.sɪ.b|l̩, -sə- (US) koʊˈɝː- **-ly** -li
coercion kəʊˈɜː.ʃᵊn (US) koʊˈɝː.ʒᵊn, -ʃᵊn
coercionist kəʊˈɜː.ʃᵊn.ɪst (US) koʊˈɝː.ʒᵊn-, -ʃᵊn- **-s** -s
coercive kəʊˈɜː.sɪv (US) koʊˈɝː- **-ly** -li
co-eternal ˌkəʊ.ɪˈtɜː.nᵊl (US) ˌkoʊ.ɪˈtɝː-
Coetzee kuːtˈsɪə, -siː
Coeur de Lion ˌkɜː.dəˈliː.ɔ̃ː*ŋ*, -dᵊlˈiː-, -ɒn (US) ˌkɝː.dəˈliː.ən, -ˈlaɪən
coeval kəʊˈiː.vᵊl (US) koʊ- **-s** -z
co-executor ˌkəʊ.ɪɡˈzek.jʊ.təʳ, -eɡˈ-, -jə-; -ɪkˈsek-, -ekˈ- (US) ˌkoʊ.ɪɡˈzek.juː.t̬ɚ, -eɡˈ- **-s** -z
co-exist ˌkəʊ.ɪɡˈzɪst, -eɡˈ-, -əɡˈ-; -ɪkˈsɪst, -ekˈ-, -əkˈ- (US) ˌkoʊ.ɪɡˈzɪst, -eɡˈ- **-s** -s **-ing** -ɪŋ **-ed** -ɪd
co-existen|ce ˌkəʊ.ɪɡˈzɪs.tᵊn|ts, -eɡˈ-, -əɡˈ-; -ɪkˈsɪs-, -ekˈ-, -əkˈ- (US) ˌkoʊ.ɪɡˈ-, -eɡˈ- **-t** -t
co-extend ˌkəʊ.ɪkˈstend, -ekˈ-, -əkˈ- (US) ˌkoʊ.ɪkˈ-, -ekˈ- **-s** -z **-ing** -ɪŋ **-ed** -ɪd
co-extension ˌkəʊ.ɪkˈsten.*t*ʃᵊn, -ekˈ-, -əkˈ- (US) ˌkoʊ.ɪkˈ-, -ekˈ- **-s** -z
co-extensive ˌkəʊ.ɪkˈsten*t*.sɪv, -ekˈ-, -əkˈ- (US) ˌkoʊ.ɪkˈ-, -ekˈ-

Coey ˈkəʊ.i (US) ˈkoʊ-
C of E *(abbrev. for* **Church of England***)* ˌsiː.əvˈiː
coffee ˈkɒf.i (US) ˈkɑː.fi, ˈkɔː- **-s** -z
ˈ**coffee** ˌ**bar**; ˈ**coffee** ˌ**bean**; ˈ**coffee** ˌ**break**; ˈ**coffee** ˌ**cup**; ˈ**coffee** ˌ**mill**; ˈ**coffee** ˌ**table**
coffeehou|se ˈkɒf.i.haʊ|s (US) ˈkɑː.fi-, ˈkɔː- **-ses** -zɪz
coffee klatch, coffee klatsch ˈkɒf.iˌklætʃ (US) ˈkɑː.fi-, ˈkɔː-
coffeemaker ˈkɒf.iˌmeɪ.kəʳ (US) ˈkɑː.fiˌmeɪ.kɚ, ˈkɔː- **-s** -z
coffeepot ˈkɒf.i.pɒt (US) ˈkɑː.fi.pɑːt, ˈkɔː- **-s** -s
coffer ˈkɒf.əʳ (US) ˈkɑː.fɚ, ˈkɔː- **-s** -z
cofferdam ˈkɒf.ə.dæm (US) ˈkɑː.fɚ-, -dᵊm **-s** -z
Coffey ˈkɒf.i (US) ˈkɑː.fi, ˈkɔː-
coffin (C) ˈkɒf.ɪn (US) ˈkɔː.fɪn, ˈkɑː- **-s** -z **-ing** -ɪŋ **-ed** -d
cog kɒg (US) kɑːg, kɔːg **-s** -z **-ging** -ɪŋ **-ged** -d
cogen|ce ˈkəʊ.dʒᵊnt|s (US) ˈkoʊ- **-cy** -si
Cogenhoe ˈkʊk.nəʊ (US) -noʊ
cogent ˈkəʊ.dʒᵊnt (US) ˈkoʊ- **-ly** -li
Coggeshall *in Essex:* ˈkɒg.ɪ.ʃᵊl; ˈkɒk.sᵊl (US) ˈkɑː.gɪ.ʃᵊl, ˈkɔː-; ˈkɑːk.sᵊl *surname:* ˈkɒg.zɔːl (US) ˈkɑːg.zɔːl, ˈkɔːg-, -zɑːl
Coggin ˈkɒg.ɪn (US) ˈkɑː.gɪn, ˈkɔː-
Coghill ˈkɒg.ɪl, -hɪl (US) ˈkɑː.gɪl, ˈkɔː-, ˈkɑːg.hɪl, ˈkɔːg-
cogi|tate ˈkɒdʒ.ɪ|.teɪt, ˈ-ə- (US) ˈkɑː.dʒə- **-tates** -teɪts **-tating** -teɪ.tɪŋ (US) -teɪ.t̬ɪŋ **-tated** -teɪ.tɪd (US) -teɪ.t̬ɪd **-tator/s** -teɪ.təʳ/z (US) -teɪ.t̬ɚ/z
cogitation ˌkɒdʒ.ɪˈteɪ.ʃᵊn, -əˈ- (US) ˌkɑː.dʒəˈ- **-s** -z
cogitative ˈkɒdʒ.ɪ.tə.tɪv, ˈ-ə-, -teɪ- (US) ˈkɑː.dʒə.teɪ.t̬ɪv
cogito ergo sum ˌkɒg.ɪ.təʊˌɜː.gəʊˈsʊm (US) ˌkɑː.giː.toʊˌer.goʊˈsʌm, ˌkoʊ.gə-, -dʒiː-, -ˌɜː-, -ˈsʊm
cognac ˈkɒn.jæk (US) ˈkoʊ.njæk **-s** -s
cognate ˈkɒg.neɪt, -ˈ- (US) ˈkɑːg.neɪt, ˈkɔːg- **-s** -s
cognation kɒgˈneɪ.ʃᵊn (US) kɑːg-, kɔːg-
cognition kɒgˈnɪʃ.ᵊn (US) kɑːg-, kɔːg- **-s** -z
cognitive ˈkɒg.nə.tɪv, -nɪ- (US) ˈkɑːg.nə.t̬ɪv, ˈkɔːg-
cognizable, -isa- ˈkɒg.nɪ.zə.bl̩, ˈkɒn.ɪ-; kɒgˈnaɪ- (US) ˈkɑːg.nɪ-, ˈkɔːg-, ˈkɑː-, kɑːgˈnaɪ-, kɔːg-
cognizanc|e, -isa- ˈkɒg.nɪ.zᵊnts, ˈkɒn.ɪ-; kɒgˈnaɪ- (US) ˈkɑːg.nə-, ˈkɔːg-, ˈkɑː- **-es** -ɪz
cognizant, -isa- ˈkɒg.nɪ.zᵊnt, ˈkɒn.ɪ-; kɒgˈnaɪ- (US) ˈkɑːg.nə-, ˈkɔːg-, ˈkɑː-
cognomen kɒgˈnəʊ.men, -mən (US) kɑːgˈnoʊ-, kɔːg- **-s** -z
cognominal kɒgˈnəʊ.mɪ.nᵊl, -ˈnɒm.ɪ- (US) kɑːgˈnɑː.mə-, kɔːg-
cognoscent|e ˌkɒn.jəʊˈʃen.t|i, ˌkɒg.nəʊˈ-, -ˈsen- (US) ˌkɑːg.nəˈʃen.t̬|i, ˌkɔːg-, ˌkɑː.njəˈ- **-i** -iː, -i
cognovit kɒgˈnəʊ.vɪt (US) kɑːgˈnoʊ-, kɔːg- **-s** -s
cogwheel ˈkɒg.wiːl, -hwiːl (US) ˈkɑːg-, ˈkɔːg- **-s** -z
cohab|it kəʊˈhæb|.ɪt (US) koʊ- **-its** -ɪts **-iting** -ɪ.tɪŋ (US) -ɪ.t̬ɪŋ **-ited** -ɪ.tɪd (US) -ɪ.t̬ɪd
cohabitant kəʊˈhæb.ɪ.tᵊnt (US) koʊˈhæb.ɪ.t̬ᵊnt **-s** -s
cohabitation kəʊˌhæb.ɪˈteɪ.ʃᵊn, ˌkəʊ.hæb- (US) koʊˌhæb-
cohabitee ˌkəʊ.hæb.ɪˈtiː, kəʊˌhæb.ɪˈtiː (US) ˌkoʊ- **-s** -z
co-heir ˌkəʊˈeəʳ, ˈ-- (US) ˈkoʊ.er, -ˈ- **-s** -z
co-heiress ˌkəʊˈeə.res, -rɪs, -rəs, ˌ--ˈ- (US) ˈkoʊ.er.əs, ˌ-ˈ-- **-es** -ɪz
Cohen ˈkəʊ.ɪn, -ən (US) ˈkoʊ.ən
coher|e kəʊˈhɪəʳ (US) koʊˈhɪr **-es** -z **-ing** -ɪŋ **-ed** -d
coheren|ce kəʊˈhɪə.rᵊnt|s (US) koʊˈhɪr.ᵊnt|s **-cy** -si
coherent kəʊˈhɪə.rᵊnt (US) koʊˈhɪr.ᵊnt **-ly** -li
cohesion kəʊˈhiː.ʒᵊn (US) koʊ-
cohesive kəʊˈhiː.sɪv, -zɪv (US) koʊ- **-ly** -li **-ness** -nəs, -nɪs
Cohn kəʊn (US) koʊn
Cohn-Bendit ˌkəʊnˈben.dɪt, ˌkəʊm- (US) ˌkoʊn-
cohort ˈkəʊ.hɔːt (US) ˈkoʊ.hɔːrt **-s** -s
COHSE ˈkəʊ.zi (US) ˈkoʊ-
coif *(n.)* kɔɪf **-s** -s
coif *(v.)* kwɑːf **-s** -s **-fing** -ɪŋ **-fed** -t
coiffé ˈkwɑː.feɪ, ˈkwɒf.eɪ, ˈkwæf-, -ˈ- (US) kwɑːˈfeɪ **-s** -z **-ing** -ɪŋ **-d** -d
coiffeur kwɑːˈfɜːʳ, kwɒfˈɜːʳ, kwæf- (US) kwɑːˈfɝː **-s** -z
coiffeus|e kwɑːˈfɜːz, kwɒfˈɜːz, kwæf- (US) kwɑːˈfɜːz **-es** -ɪz
coiffure kwɒˈfjʊəʳ, kwɒfˈjʊəʳ, kwæf- (US) kwɑːˈfjʊr **-s** -z
coign kɔɪn **-s** -z
coil kɔɪl **-s** -z **-ing** -ɪŋ **-ed** -d
Coimbra ˈkwɪm.brə, ˈkwiːm-
coin kɔɪn **-s** -z **-ing** -ɪŋ **-ed** -d **-er/s** -əʳ/z (US) -ɚ/z
coinag|e ˈkɔɪ.nɪdʒ **-es** -ɪz
coin-box ˈkɔɪn.bɒks, ˈkɔɪm- (US) ˈkɔɪn.bɑːks **-es** -ɪz
coincid|e ˌkəʊ.ɪnˈsaɪd, -ənˈ- (US) ˌkoʊ- **-es** -z **-ing** -ɪŋ **-ed** -ɪd
coincidenc|e kəʊˈɪnt.sɪ.dᵊnts (US) koʊ- **-es** -ɪz
coincidental kəʊˌɪnt.sɪˈden.tᵊl, ˌkəʊ.ɪn- (US) koʊˌɪnt.sɪˈden.t̬ᵊl **-ly** -i
co-inheritor ˌkəʊ.ɪnˈher.ɪ.təʳ, ˈ-ə- (US) ˌkoʊ.ɪnˈher.ə.t̬ɚ **-s** -z
coinsurance ˌkəʊ.ɪnˈʃʊə.rᵊnts, -ˈʃɔː- (US) ˌkoʊ.ɪnˈʃʊr.ᵊnts, -ˈʃɝː-
coinsur|e ˌkəʊ.ɪnˈʃʊəʳ, -ˈʃɔːʳ (US) ˌkoʊ.ɪnˈʃʊr, -ˈʃɝː **-es** -z **-ing** -ɪŋ **-ed** -d **-er/s** -əʳ/z (US) -ɚ/z
Cointreau® ˈkwɒn.trəʊ, ˈkwɑːn-, ˈkwæn- (US) ˈkwɑːn.troʊ
coir kɔɪəʳ (US) kɔɪr
coition kəʊˈɪʃ.ᵊn (US) koʊ-
coit|us ˈkəʊ.ɪ.t|əs, ˈkɔɪ.t|əs (US) ˈkoʊ.ə.t̬|əs **-al** -ᵊl **-ally** -ᵊl.i
coitus interruptus ˌkəʊ.ɪ.təs.ɪn.təˈrʌp.təs, ˌkɔɪ- (US) ˌkoʊ.ə.t̬əs.ɪn.t̬əˈ-
coke kəʊk (US) koʊk
Coke *surname:* kəʊk, kʊk (US) koʊk
Note: Members of the Essex family pronounce /kʊk/. So also the family name of the Earl of Leicester.
Coke® kəʊk (US) koʊk
Coker ˈkəʊ.kəʳ (US) ˈkoʊ.kɚ
col kɒl (US) kɑːl **-s** -z
Col. *(abbrev. for* **Colonel***)* ˈkɜː.nᵊl (US) ˈkɝː-
cola ˈkəʊ.lə (US) ˈkoʊ-
colander ˈkʌl.ən.dəʳ, ˈkɒl- (US) ˈkʌl.ən.dɚ, ˈkɑː.lən- **-s** -z
Colbert kɒlˈbeəʳ (US) kɔːlˈber, koʊl-
Colby ˈkəʊl.bi, ˈkɒl- (US) ˈkoʊl-
colcannon kəlˈkæn.ən, ˈkɒl.kæn- (US) kəlˈkæn.ən, ˈkɑːl.kæn-
Colchester ˈkəʊl.tʃɪ.stəʳ, -tʃə- (US) ˈkoʊl.tʃes.tɚ
colchicum ˈkɒl.tʃɪ.kəm, -kɪ- (US) ˈkɑːl-
Colchis ˈkɒl.kɪs (US) ˈkɑːl-
Colclough ˈkɒl.klʌf, ˈkəʊl-, ˈkəʊ.kli (US) ˈkɑːl.klʌf, ˈkoʊl-, ˈkoʊ.kli
cold kəʊld (US) koʊld **-s** -z **-er** -əʳ (US) -ɚ **-est** -ɪst, -əst **-ly** -li **-ness** -nəs, -nɪs
ˌ**cold** ˈ**comfort**; ˈ**cold** ˌ**cream**; ˌ**cold** ˈ**feet**; ˈ**cold** ˌ**frame**; ˈ**cold** ˌ**sore**; ˌ**cold** ˈ**storage**; ˌ**cold** ˈ**turkey**; ˌ**cold** ˈ**war**; ˌ**cold** ˈ**water**; **blow** ˌ**hot and** ˈ**cold**
cold-blooded ˌkəʊldˈblʌd.ɪd (US) ˌkoʊld- **-ly** -li **-ness** -nəs, -nɪs
stress shift: ˌcold-blooded ˈkiller
cold-call *(v.)* ˈkəʊld.kɔːl (US) ˈkoʊld-, -kɑːl **-s** -z **-ing** -ɪŋ **-ed** -d
cold-hearted ˌkəʊldˈhɑː.tɪd (US) ˌkoʊldˈhɑːr.t̬ɪd **-ness** -nəs, -nɪs
coldish (C) ˈkəʊl.dɪʃ (US) ˈkoʊl-
Colditz ˈkəʊl.dɪts (US) ˈkoʊl-, ˈkɑːl-
cold-should|er ˌkəʊldˈʃəʊl.d|əʳ (US) ˌkoʊldˈʃoʊl.d|ɚ **-ers** -əz (US) -ɚz **-ering** -ᵊr.ɪŋ **-ered** -əd (US) -ɚd
Coldstream ˈkəʊld.striːm (US) ˈkoʊld-
cole (C) kəʊl (US) koʊl **-s** -z
Colebrook(e) ˈkəʊl.brʊk (US) ˈkoʊl-

Coleby ˈkəʊl.bi (US) ˈkoʊl-
Coleclough ˈkəʊl.klaʊ, -klʌf (US) ˈkoʊl-
Coleen kɒlˈiːn, ˈ-- (US) kɑːˈliːn, koʊˈliːn
Coleford ˈkəʊl.fəd (US) ˈkoʊl.fɚd
Coleman ˈkəʊl.mən (US) ˈkoʊl-
Colenso kəˈlen.zəʊ (US) -zoʊ
coleopter|a ˌkɒl.iˈɒp.tᵊr|.ə (US) ˌkɑː.liˈɑːp- **-al** -ᵊl
Coleraine kəʊlˈreɪn (US) koʊl-
Coleridge ˈkəʊ.lᵊr.ɪdʒ (US) ˈkoʊ-
Coles kəʊlz (US) koʊlz
Coleshill ˈkəʊlz.hɪl (US) ˈkoʊlz-
coleslaw ˈkəʊl.slɔː (US) ˈkoʊl.slɑː, -slɔː
Colet ˈkɒl.ɪt (US) ˈkɑː.lɪt
cole-tit ˈkəʊl.tɪt (US) ˈkoʊl- **-s** -s
Colette kɒlˈet, kəˈlet (US) koʊˈlet, kɑː-
coley (C) ˈkəʊ.li (US) ˈkoʊ- **-s** -z
Colgan ˈkɒl.gən (US) ˈkɑːl-
Colgate® ˈkəʊl.geɪt, ˈkɒl-, -gət, -gɪt (US) ˈkoʊl.geɪt
colic ˈkɒl.ɪk (US) ˈkɑː.lɪk **-ky** -i
Colin ˈkɒl.ɪn (US) ˈkɑː.lɪn
Colindale ˈkɒl.ɪn.deɪl, -ən- (US) ˈkɑː.lɪn-, -lən-
Coling ˈkəʊ.lɪŋ (US) ˈkoʊ-
coliseum (C) ˌkɒl.ɪˈsiː.əm, -əˈ- (US) ˌkɑː.ləˈ-
colitis kɒlˈaɪ.tɪs, kəʊˈlaɪ- (US) koʊˈlaɪ.t̬ɪs, kə-
collabor|ate kəˈlæb.ᵊr|.eɪt, kɒlˈæb- (US) kəˈlæb.ə.r|eɪt **-ates** -eɪts **-ating** -eɪ.tɪŋ (US) -eɪ.t̬ɪŋ **-ated** -eɪ.tɪd (US) -eɪ.t̬ɪd
collaboration kəˌlæb.ᵊˈreɪ.ʃᵊn, kɒlˌæb- (US) kəˌlæb- **-s** -z
collaborative kəˈlæb.ᵊr.ə.tɪv, kɒlˈæb- (US) kəˈlæb.ɚ.ə.t̬ɪv, -rə.t̬ɪv **-ly** -li
collaborator kəˈlæb.ᵊr.eɪ.təʳ, kɒlˈæb- (US) kəˈlæb.ə.reɪ.t̬ɚ **-s** -z
collag|e kɒlˈɑːʒ, kəˈlɑːʒ; ˈkɒl.ɑːʒ (US) kəˈlɑːʒ, kɑː-, koʊ- **-es** -ɪz
collagen ˈkɒl.ə.dʒən, -dʒɪn (US) ˈkɑː.lə-
collagenic ˌkɒl.əˈdʒen.ɪk (US) ˌkɑː.ləˈ-
collagenous kəˈlædʒ.ɪ.nəs, ˈ-ə-
collaps|e kəˈlæps **-es** -ɪz **-ing** -ɪŋ **-ed** -t
collapsible kəˈlæp.sə.bl̩, -sɪ-
coll|ar ˈkɒl|.əʳ (US) ˈkɑː.l|ɚ **-ars** -əz (US) -ɚz **-aring** -ər.ɪŋ **-ared** -əd (US) -ɚd ˌhot under the ˈcollar
collarbone ˈkɒl.ə.bəʊn (US) ˈkɑː.lɚ.boʊn **-s** -z
Collard ˈkɒl.əd (US) ˈkɑː.lɚd
coll|ate kəˈl|eɪt, kɒlˈ|eɪt (US) kəˈl|eɪt, koʊ-, kɑː- **-ates** -eɪts **-ating** -eɪ.tɪŋ (US) -eɪ.t̬ɪŋ **-ated** -eɪ.tɪd (US) -eɪ.t̬ɪd **-ator/s** -eɪ.təʳ/z (US) -eɪ.t̬ɚ/z
collateral kəˈlæt.ᵊr.ᵊl, kɒlˈæt- (US) kəˈlæt̬- **-s** -z **-ly** -i
collation kəˈleɪ.ʃᵊn, kɒlˈeɪ- (US) kɑːˈleɪ-, kə-, koʊ- **-s** -z
colleague ˈkɒl.iːg (US) ˈkɑː.liːg **-s** -z
collect (*n.*) ˈkɒl.ekt, -ɪkt (US) ˈkɑː.lekt, -ɪkt **-s** -s
collect (*v.*) kəˈlekt **-s** -s **-ing** -ɪŋ **-ed** -ɪd
collectable kəˈlek.tə.bl̩ **-s** -z
collectanea ˌkɒl.ekˈteɪ.ni.ə, -ˈtɑː- (US) ˌkɑː.lekˈ-
collected kəˈlek.tɪd, -təd **-ly** -li **-ness** -nəs, -nɪs
collectible kəˈlek.tə.bl̩, -tɪ- **-s** -z
collection kəˈlek.ʃᵊn **-s** -z
collective kəˈlek.tɪv **-ly** -li coˌllective ˈbargaining
collectiv|ism kəˈlek.tɪ.v|ɪ.zᵊm (US) -tə- **-ist/s** -ɪst/s
collectivity ˌkɒl.ekˈtɪv.ɪ.ti, kəˌlek-, -ə.ti (US) ˌkɑː.lekˈtɪv.ə.t̬i, kəˌlekˈ-
collectivization, -isa- kəˌlek.tɪ.vaɪˈzeɪ.ʃᵊn, -tə-, -vɪˈ- (US) -tɪ.vɪˈzeɪ-
collectiviz|e, -is|e kəˈlek.tɪ.vaɪz, -tə- **-es** -ɪz **-ing** -ɪŋ **-ed** -d
collector kəˈlek.təʳ (US) -tɚ **-s** -z coˈllector's ˌitem, coˌllector's ˈitem
colleen (C) ˈkɒl.iːn *in Ireland:* -ˈ- (US) kɑːˈliːn, ˈ-- **-s** -z
colleg|e (C) ˈkɒl.ɪdʒ (US) ˈkɑː.lɪdʒ **-es** -ɪz ˈCollege ˌBoard; ˌcollege ˈtry
collegian kəˈliː.dʒi.ən, kɒlˈiː-, ˈ-dʒᵊn (US) kəˈliː.dʒən, ˈ-dʒi.ən **-s** -z
collegiate kəˈliː.dʒi.ət, kɒlˈiː-, -dʒət (US) kəˈliː.dʒɪt, -dʒi.ɪt
Colles ˈkɒl.ɪs, -əs (US) ˈkɑː.lɪs
collet (C) ˈkɒl.ɪt, -ət (US) ˈkɑː.lɪt **-s** -s
Collett ˈkɒl.ɪt, -et, -ət (US) ˈkɑː.lɪt
Colley ˈkɒl.i (US) ˈkɑː.li
collid|e kəˈlaɪd **-es** -z **-ing** -ɪŋ **-ed** -ɪd
collie (C) ˈkɒl.i (US) ˈkɑː.li **-s** -z
collier (C) ˈkɒl.i.əʳ, ˈ-jəʳ (US) ˈkɑːl.jɚ **-s** -z
collier|y ˈkɒl.jə.r|i, -i.ᵊr|.i (US) ˈkɑːl.jɚ|.i **-ies** -iz
colli|gate ˈkɒl.ɪ|.geɪt, ˈ-ə- (US) ˈkɑː.lə- **-gates** -geɪts **-gating** -geɪ.tɪŋ (US) -geɪ.t̬ɪŋ **-gated** -geɪ.tɪd (US) -geɪ.t̬ɪd
colligation ˌkɒl.ɪˈgeɪ.ʃᵊn, -əˈ- (US) ˌkɑː.ləˈ-
colli|mate ˈkɒl.ɪ|.meɪt, ˈ-ə- (US) ˈkɑː.lə- **-mates** -meɪts **-mating** -meɪ.tɪŋ (US) -meɪ.t̬ɪŋ **-mated** -meɪ.tɪd (US) -meɪ.t̬ɪd
collimation ˌkɒl.ɪˈmeɪ.ʃᵊn, -əˈ- (US) ˌkɑː.ləˈ-
collimator ˈkɒl.ɪ.meɪ.təʳ, ˈ-ə- (US) ˈkɑː.lə.meɪ.t̬ɚ **-s** -z
collinear kɒlˈɪn.i.əʳ, kəʊˈlɪn- (US) kəˈlɪn.i.ɚ, kɑː-
Collingham ˈkɒl.ɪŋ.əm (US) ˈkɑː.lɪŋ-
Collings ˈkɒl.ɪŋz (US) ˈkɑː.lɪŋz
Collingwood ˈkɒl.ɪŋ.wʊd (US) ˈkɑː.lɪŋ-
Collins ˈkɒl.ɪnz (US) ˈkɑː.lɪnz
Collinson ˈkɒl.ɪn.sᵊn, -ən- (US) ˈkɑː.lɪn-
Collis ˈkɒl.ɪs (US) ˈkɑː.lɪs
collision kəˈlɪʒ.ᵊn **-s** -z coˈllision ˌcourse
collo|cate ˈkɒl.əʊ|.keɪt (US) ˈkɑː.lə- **-cates** -keɪts **-cating** -keɪ.tɪŋ (US) -keɪ.t̬ɪŋ **-cated** -keɪ.tɪd (US) -keɪ.t̬ɪd
collocation ˌkɒl.əʊˈkeɪ.ʃᵊn (US) ˌkɑː.ləˈ- **-s** -z
collodi|on kəˈləʊ.di|.ən (US) -ˈloʊ- **-um** -əm
colloid ˈkɒl.ɔɪd (US) ˈkɑː.lɔɪd **-s** -z
colloidal kəˈlɔɪ.dᵊl, kɒlˈɔɪ- (US) kəˈlɔɪ-
collop ˈkɒl.əp (US) ˈkɑː.ləp **-s** -s
colloquial kəˈləʊ.kwi.əl (US) -ˈloʊ- **-ly** -i **-ism/s** -ɪ.zᵊm/z
colloquium kəˈləʊ.kwi.əm (US) -ˈloʊ-
colloqu|y ˈkɒl.ə.kw|i (US) ˈkɑː.lə- **-ies** -iz
collotype ˈkɒl.əʊ.taɪp (US) ˈkɑː.lə- **-s** -s
Colls kɒlz (US) kɑːlz
collud|e kəˈluːd, -ljuːd (US) -ˈluːd **-es** -z **-ing** -ɪŋ **-ed** -ɪd **-er/s** -əʳ/z (US) -ɚ/z
collusion kəˈluː.ʒᵊn, -ˈljuː- (US) -ˈluː- **-s** -z
collusive kəˈluː.sɪv, -ˈljuː- (US) -ˈluː- **-ly** -li
Collyns ˈkɒl.ɪnz (US) ˈkɑː.lɪnz
collywobbles ˈkɒl.iˌwɒb.l̩z (US) ˈkɑː.liˌwɑː-
Colman ˈkəʊl.mən, ˈkɒl- (US) ˈkoʊl-, ˈkɑːl-
Colnaghi kɒlˈnɑː.gi (US) kɑːl-
Colnbrook ˈkəʊln.brʊk, ˈkəʊn- (US) ˈkoʊln-, ˈkoʊn-
Colne kəʊn, kəʊln (US) koʊn, koʊln
Colney ˈkəʊ.ni (US) ˈkoʊ-
Colo. *(abbrev. for* **Colorado***)* ˌkɒl.ᵊrˈɑː.dəʊ (US) ˌkɑː.ləˈræd.oʊ, -ˈrɑː.doʊ
cologne (C) kəˈləʊn (US) -ˈloʊn **-s** -z
Colombi|a kəˈlɒm.bi|.ə, -ˈlʌm- (US) -ˈlʌm- **-an/s** -ən/z
Colombo kəˈlʌm.bəʊ, -ˈlɒm- (US) -ˈlʌm.boʊ
colon *punctuation, part of intestine:* ˈkəʊ.lɒn, -lən (US) ˈkoʊ.lən **-s** -z **cola** ˈkəʊ.lə (US) ˈkoʊ-
colon, colón *currency:* kɒlˈɒn, kəˈlɒn (US) kəˈloʊn **-s** -z **-es** -es, -əs
colonel (C) ˈkɜː.nᵊl (US) ˈkɝː- **-s** -z ˌColonel ˈBlimp
colonelc|y ˈkɜː.nᵊl.s|i (US) ˈkɝː- **-ies** -iz
colonelship ˈkɜː.nᵊl.ʃɪp (US) ˈkɝː- **-s** -s
colonial kəˈləʊ.ni.əl (US) -ˈloʊ- **-s** -z
colonial|ism kəˈləʊ.ni.ə.l|ɪ.zᵊm (US) -ˈloʊ- **-ist/s** -ɪst/s
colonist ˈkɒl.ə.nɪst (US) ˈkɑː.lə- **-s** -s
colonization, -isa- ˌkɒl.ə.naɪˈzeɪ.ʃᵊn, -nɪˈ- (US) ˌkɑː.lə.nɪˈ-
coloniz|e, -is|e ˈkɒl.ə.naɪz (US) ˈkɑː.lə- **-es** -ɪz **-ing** -ɪŋ **-ed** -d **-er/s** -əʳ/z (US) -ɚ/z
colonnade ˌkɒl.əˈneɪd (US) ˌkɑː.ləˈ- **-s** -z

Colonus kəˈləʊ.nəs US -ˈloʊ-
colon|y ˈkɒl.ə.n|i US ˈkɑː.lə- **-ies** -iz
colophon ˈkɒl.ə.fən, -fɒn US ˈkɑː.lə.fən, -fɑːn **-s** -z
col|or ˈkʌl|.əʳ US -ɚ **-ors** -əz US -ɚz **-oring** -ᵊr.ɪŋ **-ored/s** -əd/z US -ɚd/s **-orer/s** -ᵊr.əʳ/z US -ɚ.ɚ/z **-orist/s** -ᵊr.ɪst/s
colorab|le ˈkʌl.ᵊr.ə.b|l̩ **-ly** -li
Colorado ˌkɒl.ᵊrˈɑː.dəʊ US ˌkɑː.ləˈræd.oʊ, -ˈrɑː.doʊ *stress shift, see compounds:* **ˌColorado ˈbeetle; ˌColorado ˈSprings**
colorant ˈkʌl.ᵊr.ənt **-s** -s
coloration ˌkʌl.əˈreɪ.ʃᵊn
coloratura ˌkɒl.ᵊr.əˈtjʊə.rə, -ˈtʊə- US ˌkʌl.ɚ.əˈtʊr.ə, ˌkɑː.lɚ-, -ˈtjʊr-
color|-blind ˈkʌl.ə|.blaɪnd US ˈ-ɚ- **-blindness** -ˌblaɪnd.nəs, -nɪs
colorcast ˈkʌl.ə.kɑːst US -ɚ.kæst **-s** -s **-ing** -ɪŋ **-ed** -ɪd
color-coded ˈkʌl.əˌkəʊ.dɪd US -ɚ.koʊ-
colorfast ˈkʌl.ə.fɑːst US -ɚ.fæst **-ness** -nəs, -nɪs
colorful ˈkʌl.ə.fᵊl, -fʊl US ˈ-ɚ- **-ly** -i
colorific ˌkɒl.əˈrɪf.ɪk, ˌkʌl- US ˌkʌl-
coloring ˈkʌl.ᵊr.ɪŋ **-s** -z
Colorization® ˌkɒl.ə.raɪˈzeɪ.ʃᵊn, ˌkʌl-, -rɪˈ- US ˌkʌl.ɚ.ɪˈ-
colorless ˈkʌl.ə.ləs, -lɪs US ˈ-ɚ- **-ly** -li **-ness** -nəs, -nɪs
colossal kəˈlɒs.ᵊl US -ˈlɑː.sᵊl **-ly** -i
colosseum (C) ˌkɒl.əˈsiː.əm US ˌkɑː.ləˈ-
Colossian kəˈlɒs.i.ən, -ˈlɒʃ.i.ən, -ˈlɒʃ.ᵊn US -ˈlɑː.ʃᵊn **-s** -z
coloss|us kəˈlɒs|.əs US -ˈlɑː.s|əs **-i** -aɪ **-uses** -ə.sɪz
colostom|y kəˈlɒs.tə.m|i, kɒlˈɒs- US kəˈlɑː.stə- **-ies** -iz
colostrum kəˈlɒs.trəm, kɒlˈɒs- US kəˈlɑː.strəm
col|our ˈkʌl|.əʳ US -ɚ **-ours** -əz US -ɚz **-ouring** -ᵊr.ɪŋ **-oured/s** -əd/z US -ɚd/s **-ourer/s** -ᵊr.əʳ/z US -ɚ.ɚ/z **-ourist/s** -ᵊr.ɪst/s
colourab|le ˈkʌl.ᵊr.ə.b|l̩ **-ly** -li
colourant ˈkʌl.ᵊr.ənt **-s** -s
colouration ˌkʌl.əˈreɪ.ʃᵊn
colour|-blind ˈkʌl.ə|.blaɪnd US ˈ-ɚ- **-blindness** -ˌblaɪnd.nəs, -nɪs
colourcast ˈkʌl.ə.kɑːst US -ɚ.kæst **-s** -s
colour-coded ˈkʌl.əˌkəʊ.dɪd US -ɚˌkoʊ-
colourfast ˈkʌl.ə.fɑːst US -ɚ.fæst **-ness** -nəs, -nɪs
colourful ˈkʌl.ə.fᵊl, -fʊl US ˈ-ɚ- **-ly** -i
colouring ˈkʌl.ᵊr.ɪŋ **-s** -z
colourless ˈkʌl.ə.ləs, -lɪs US ˈ-ɚ- **-ly** -li **-ness** -nəs, -nɪs
colourway ˈkʌl.ə.weɪ US -ɚ- **-s** -z
colpo- ˈkɒl.pəʊ-; kɒlˈpɒ- US ˈkɑːl.pə-, ˈkɑːl.poʊ-; kɑːlˈpɑː-
Note: Prefix. This may carry primary or secondary stress on the first syllable, e.g. **colposcope** /ˈkɒl.pə.skəʊp US ˈkɑːl.pə.skoʊp/, or on the second syllable, e.g. **colposcopy** /kɒlˈpɒs.kə.pi US kɑːlˈpɑː-/.
colporteur ˈkɒl.pɔː.təʳ, ˌkɒl.pɔːˈtɜːʳ US ˈkɑːl.pɔːr.t̬ɚ, ˌkɑːl.pɔːrˈtɝː **-s** -z
colposcope ˈkɒl.pə.skəʊp US ˈkɑːl.pə.skoʊp **-s** -s
colposcopic ˌkɒl.pəˈskɒp.ɪk US ˌkɑːl.pəˈskɑː.pɪk
colposcopy kɒlˈpɒs.kə.pi US kɑːlˈpɑː.skə-
Colquhoun kəˈhuːn
Cols. *(abbrev. for* **Colonels***)* ˈkɜː.nᵊlz US ˈkɝː-
Colson ˈkəʊl.sᵊn US ˈkoʊl-
Colston ˈkəʊl.stᵊn US ˈkoʊl-
colt kəʊlt US koʊlt **-s** -s
coltish ˈkəʊl.tɪʃ US ˈkoʊl.t̬ɪʃ **-ly** -li **-ness** -nəs, -nɪs
Coltrane kɒlˈtreɪn, kəʊl- US ˈkoʊl.treɪn
coltsfoot ˈkəʊlts.fʊt US ˈkoʊlts- **-s** -s
colubrine ˈkɒl.jʊ.braɪn, -brɪn US ˈkɑː.lə-, ˈkɑːl.jə-
Columba kəˈlʌm.bə
columbari|um ˌkɒl.əmˈbeə.ri|.əm US ˌkɑː.ləmˈber.i- **-ums** -əmz **-a** -ə
Columbi|a kəˈlʌm.bi|.ə **-an/s** -ən/z
Columbiad kəˈlʌm.bi.æd
columbine (C) ˈkɒl.əm.baɪn US ˈkɑː.ləm- **-s** -z
Columbo kəˈlʌm.bəʊ US -boʊ
Columbus kəˈlʌm.bəs
column ˈkɒl.əm US ˈkɑː.ləm **-s** -z **-ed** -d
column|al kəˈlʌm.n|ᵊl **-ar** -əʳ US -ɚ
columnist ˈkɒl.əm.nɪst, -ə.mɪst US ˈkɑː.ləm.nɪst, -lə.mɪst **-s** -s
colure kəˈljʊəʳ, -ˈlʊəʳ; ˈkəʊ.ljʊəʳ, -lʊəʳ US koʊˈlʊr, kə-; ˈkoʊ.lʊr **-s** -z
Colwyn ˈkɒl.wɪn US ˈkɑːl- **ˌColwyn ˈBay**
Colyton ˈkɒl.ɪ.tᵊn US ˈkɑː.lɪ.t̬ᵊn
colza ˈkɒl.zə US ˈkɑːl-
com- kɒm-, kəm- US kɑːm-, kəm-
Note: Prefix. This may carry primary or secondary stress, e.g. **combat** /ˈkɒm.bæt US ˈkɑːm.bæt/ or be unstressed, e.g. **complete** /kəmˈpliːt/.
coma *deep sleep:* ˈkəʊ.mə US ˈkoʊ- **-s** -z
com|a *tuft:* ˈkəʊ.m|ə US ˈkoʊ- **-as** -əz **-ae** -iː
Coma Berenices ˌkəʊ.məˌber.ɪˈnaɪ.siːz US ˌkoʊ.məˌber.əˈ-
Comanche kəˈmæn.tʃi, kəʊ- US kə- **-s** -z
Comaneci ˌkɒm.əˈnetʃ.i, -ˈnetʃ US ˌkoʊ.məˈniː.tʃi, -ˈnetʃ.i
comatose ˈkəʊ.mə.təʊs, -təʊz US ˈkoʊ.mə.toʊs, ˈkɑː-
comb kəʊm US koʊm **-s** -z **-ing/s** -ɪŋ/z **-ed** -d
combat *(n.)* ˈkɒm.bæt, ˈkʌm-, -bət US ˈkɑːm.bæt **-s** -s
comba|t *(v.)* ˈkɒm.bæ|t, ˈkʌm-, -bə|t; kəmˈbæ|t US kəmˈbæ|t, kɑːm-; ˈkɑːm.bæ|t **-ts** -ts **-(t)ting** -tɪŋ US -t̬ɪŋ **-(t)ted** -tɪd US -t̬ɪd
combatant ˈkɒm.bə.tᵊnt, ˈkʌm-; kəmˈbæt.ᵊnt US kəmˈbæt.ᵊnt; ˈkɑːm.bə.tᵊnt **-s** -s
combative ˈkɒm.bə.tɪv, ˈkʌm-; kəmˈbæt.ɪv US kəmˈbæt̬.ɪv; ˈkɑːm.bə.t̬ɪv **-ly** -li **-ness** -nəs, -nɪs
combe (C) kuːm, kəʊm US kuːm, koʊm **-s** -z
comber *combing machine:* ˈkəʊ.məʳ US ˈkoʊ.mɚ **-s** -z
comber (C) *fish:* ˈkɒm.bəʳ US ˈkɑːm.bɚ **-s** -z
combination ˌkɒm.bɪˈneɪ.ʃᵊn, -bəˈ- US ˌkɑːm.bəˈ-, -bɪˈ- **-s** -z **ˌcombiˈnation ˌlock; ˌcombiˈnation ˌroom**
combinative ˈkɒm.bɪ.nə.tɪv, -bə-, -neɪ- US ˈkɑːm.bə.neɪ.t̬ɪv, -nə-; -bɪ-, kəmˈbaɪ.nə.t̬ɪv
combinatorial ˌkɒm.bɪ.nəˈtɔː.ri.əl, -bᵊn.əˈ- US ˌkɑːm.bə.nəˈtɔːr.i-; -bɪn.əˈ-; kəmˌbaɪ-
combinatory ˈkɒm.bɪ.nə.tᵊr.i, -tri; ˌkɒm.bɪˈneɪ- US ˈkɑːm.bə.nə.tɔːr.i, -bɪ-; kəmˈbaɪ-
combine *(n.)* ˈkɒm.baɪn; kəmˈbaɪn US ˈkɑːm.baɪn **-s** -z
combin|e *(v.) join:* kəmˈbaɪn **-es** -z **-ing** -ɪŋ **-ed** -d *harvest:* ˈkɒm.baɪn US ˈkɑːm- **-es** -z **-ing** -ɪŋ **-ed** -d **ˌcombine ˈharvester**
combo ˈkɒm.bəʊ US ˈkɑːm.boʊ **-s** -z
Combs kəʊmz, kuːmz US koʊmz
combust kəmˈbʌst **-s** -s **-ing** -ɪŋ **-ed** -ɪd **-er/s** -əʳ/z US -ɚ/z
combustibility kəmˌbʌs.təˈbɪl.ə.ti, -tɪˈ-, -ɪ.ti US -ə.t̬i
combustible kəmˈbʌs.tə.bl̩, -tɪ- **-ness** -nəs, -nɪs
combustion kəmˈbʌs.tʃᵊn **-s** -z **comˈbustion ˌengine**
com|e kʌm **-es** -z **-ing/s** -ɪŋ/z **came** keɪm
come-at-able ˌkʌmˈæt.ə.bl̩ US -ˈæt̬-
comeback ˈkʌm.bæk **-s** -s
Comecon ˈkɒm.ɪ.kɒn US ˈkɑː.mɪ.kɑːn
comedian kəˈmiː.di.ən **-s** -z
comedic kəˈmiː.dɪk **-ally** -ᵊl.i, -li
comedienne kəˌmiː.diˈen, ˌkɒm.iː- US kəˌmiː- **-s** -z
comedown ˈkʌm.daʊn, ˌ-ˈ- US ˈ-- **-s** -z
comed|y ˈkɒm.ə.d|i, ˈ-ɪ- US ˈkɑː.mə- **-ies** -iz

come-hither ˌkʌmˈhɪð.əʳ US ˌkʌmˈhɪð.ɚ *stress shift:* ˌcome-hither ˈlook

comel|y ˈkʌm.l|i **-ier** -i.əʳ US -i.ɚ **-iest** -i.ɪst, -i.əst **-iness** -ɪ.nəs, -ɪ.nɪs

Comenius kəˈmeɪ.ni.əs, kɒmˈeɪ-, -ˈiː- US kəˈmiː-

come-on ˈkʌm.ɒn US -ɑːn **-s** -z

-comer -ˌkʌm.əʳ US -ɚ

comer ˈkʌm.əʳ US -ɚ **-s** -z

comestible kəˈmes.tɪ.bl̩, -tə- **-s** -z

comet ˈkɒm.ɪt US ˈkɑː.mɪt **-s** -s **-ary** -ᵊr.i US -er.i

come-uppanc|e kʌmˈʌp.ən*t*s **-es** -ɪz

comfit ˈkʌm.fɪt, ˈkɒm- US ˈkʌm-, ˈkɑːm- **-s** -s

com|fort ˈkʌmp|.fət US -fɚt **-forts** -fəts US -fɚts **-forting/ly** -fə.tɪŋ/li US -fɚ.t̬ɪŋ/li **-forted** -fə.tɪd US -fɚ.t̬ɪd **-forter/s** -fə.təʳ/z US -fɚ.t̬ɚ/z ˈcomfort ˌstation

comfortab|le ˈkʌmpf.tə.b|l̩, ˈkʌm*p*.fə.tə- US ˈkʌm*p*.fɚ.t̬ə-, ˈkʌm*p*f.tə- **-ly** -li

comforter ˈkʌm*p*.fə.təʳ US -fɚ.t̬ɚ **-s** -z

comfortless ˈkʌm*p*.fət.ləs, -lɪs US -fɚt-

comfrey ˈkʌm*p*.fri

comf|y ˈkʌm*p*.f|i **-ier** -i.əʳ US -i.ɚ **-iest** -i.ɪst, -i.əst **-ily** -ɪ.li, -ᵊl.i **-iness** -ɪ.nəs, -ɪ.nɪs

comic ˈkɒm.ɪk US ˈkɑː.mɪk **-s** -s **ˈcomic ˌbook; ˈcomic ˌstrip, ˌcomic ˈstrip**

comic|al ˈkɒm.ɪ.k|ᵊl US ˈkɑː.mɪ- **-ally** -ᵊl.i, -li **-alness** -ᵊl.nəs, -nɪs

Cominform ˈkɒm.ɪn.fɔːm, -ən-, ˌ--ˈ- US ˈkɑː.mən.fɔːrm

Comintern ˈkɒm.ɪn.tɜːn, -ən-, ˌ--ˈ- US ˈkɑː.mən.tɝːn

comity ˈkɒm.ɪ.ti, -ə.ti US ˈkɑː.mə.t̬i, ˈkoʊ-

comma ˈkɒm.ə US ˈkɑː.mə **-s** -z

command kəˈmɑːnd US -ˈmænd **-s** -z **-ing** -ɪŋ **-ed** -ɪd

commandant ˈkɒm.ən.dænt, -dɑːnt, ˌ--ˈ- US ˈkɑː.mən.dænt, -dɑːnt **-s** -s

commandantship ˌkɒm.ənˈdænt.ʃɪp, -ˈdɑːnt-, ˈkɒm.ən.dænt.ʃɪp, -dɑːnt- US ˈkɑː.mən.dænt-, -dɑːnt- **-s** -s

commandeer ˌkɒm.ənˈdɪəʳ US ˌkɑː.mənˈdɪr **-s** -z **-ing** -ɪŋ **-ed** -d

commander kəˈmɑːn.dəʳ US -ˈmæn.dɚ **-s** -z

commander-in-chief kəˌmɑːn.də.rɪnˈtʃiːf US -ˌmæn.dɚ- **commanders-in-chief** kəˌmɑːn.dəz.ɪnˈtʃiːf US -ˌmænd.ɚz-

commandership kəˈmɑːn.də.ʃɪp US -ˈmæn.dɚ- **-s** -s

commanding kəˈmɑːn.dɪŋ US -ˈmæn- **-ly** -li

commandment kəˈmɑːn*d*.mənt, -ˈmɑːm- US -ˈmæn*d*- **-s** -s

commando kəˈmɑːn.dəʊ US -ˈmæn.doʊ **-(e)s** -z

Comme des Garçons ˌkɒm.deɪ.gɑːˈsɔ̃ː*ŋ*, ˌkɒm.deɪˈgɑː.sɔ*ŋ* US ˌkɑːm.deɪ.gɑːrˈsoʊ̃n

commedia dell'arte kɒmˌeɪ.di.ə.delˈɑː.teɪ, kəˌmeɪ-, -ˌmed.i- US kəˌmeɪ.di.ə.delˈɑːr.t̬i

comme il faut ˌkɒm.iːlˈfəʊ US ˌkʌm.iːlˈfoʊ, ˌkɑːm-

commemo|rate kəˈmem.ə|.reɪt **-rates** -reɪts **-rating** -reɪ.tɪŋ US -reɪ.t̬ɪŋ **-rated** -reɪ.tɪd US -reɪ.t̬ɪd **-rator/s** -reɪ.təʳ/z US -reɪ.t̬ɚ/z

commemoration kəˌmem.əˈreɪ.ʃᵊn **-s** -z

commemorative kəˈmem.ᵊr.ə.tɪv, -eɪ- US -ə.t̬ɪv, -eɪ- **-ly** -li

commenc|e kəˈmen*t*s **-es** -ɪz **-ing** -ɪŋ **-ed** -t

commencement kəˈmen*t*s.mənt **-s** -s

commend kəˈmend **-s** -z **-ing** -ɪŋ **-ed** -ɪd

commendab|le kəˈmen.də.b|l̩ **-ly** -li **-leness** -l̩.nəs, -nɪs

commendation ˌkɒm.enˈdeɪ.ʃᵊn, -ənˈ- US ˌkɑː.mənˈ- **-s** -z

commendatory kəˈmen.də.tᵊr.i, -tri; ˌkɒm.enˈdeɪ-, -ənˈ- US kəˈmen.də.tɔːr.i

commensal kəˈmen*t*.sᵊl

commensalism kəˈmen*t*.sᵊl.ɪ.zᵊm

commensurability kəˌmen*t*.ʃᵊr.əˈbɪl.ə.ti, -ʃʊ.rə-, -sjᵊr.ə-, -ɪ.ti US -sɚ.əˈbɪl.ə.t̬i, -ʃɚ-

commensurab|le kəˈmen*t*.ʃᵊr.ə.b|l̩, -ʃʊ.rə-, -sjᵊr.ə- US -sɚ.ə-, -ʃɚ- **-ly** -li **-leness** -l̩.nəs, -nɪs

commensurate kəˈmen*t*.ʃᵊr.ət, -ʃʊ.rət, -sjᵊr.ət, -ɪt US -sɚ.ət, -ʃɚ- **-ly** -li **-ness** -nəs, -nɪs

comment (*n.*) ˈkɒm.ent US ˈkɑː.ment **-s** -s

commen|t (*v.*) ˈkɒm.en|t, -ən|t; kɒmˈent, kəˈmen|t; US ˈkɑː.men|t **-ts** -ts **-ting** -tɪŋ US -t̬ɪŋ **-ted** -tɪd US -t̬ɪd

commentar|y ˈkɒm.ən.tᵊr|.i, -tr|i US ˈkɑː.mən.ter|.i **-ies** -iz

commen|tate ˈkɒm.ən|.teɪt, -en- US ˈkɑː.mən- **-tates** -teɪts **-tating** -teɪ.tɪŋ US -teɪ.t̬ɪŋ **-tated** -teɪ.tɪd US -teɪ.t̬ɪd

commentator ˈkɒm.ən.teɪ.təʳ, -en- US ˈkɑː.mən.teɪ.t̬ɚ **-s** -z

commerce ˈkɒm.ɜːs US ˈkɑː.mɝːs

commercial kəˈmɜː.ʃᵊl US -ˈmɝː- **-s** -z **-ly** -i

commercialese kəˌmɜː.ʃᵊlˈiːz US -ˌmɝː.ʃəˈliːz

commercial|ism kəˈmɜː.ʃᵊl|.ɪ.zᵊm US -ˈmɝː- **-ist/s** -ɪst/s

commerciality kəˌmɜː.ʃiˈæl.ə.ti, -ɪ.ti US -ˌmɝː.ʃiˈæl.ə.t̬i

commercialization, -isa- kəˌmɜː.ʃə.laɪˈzeɪ.ʃᵊn, -lɪˈ- US -mɝː.ʃə.lɪˈ-

commercializ|e, -is|e kəˈmɜː.ʃᵊl.aɪz US -ˈmɝː.ʃə.laɪz **-es** -ɪz **-ing** -ɪŋ **-ed** -d

commie ˈkɒm.i US ˈkɑː.mi **-s** -z

commi|nate ˈkɒm.ɪ|.neɪt US ˈkɑː.mə- **-nates** -neɪts **-nating** -neɪ.tɪŋ US -neɪ.t̬ɪŋ **-nated** -neɪ.tɪd US -neɪ.t̬ɪd

commination ˌkɒm.ɪˈneɪ.ʃᵊn US ˌkɑː.məˈ- **-s** -z

comminatory ˈkɒm.ɪ.nə.tᵊr.i, -neɪ-, -tri US ˈkɑː.mɪ.nə.tɔːr.i; kəˈmɪn.ə-

comming|le kɒmˈɪŋ.gl̩, kəˈmɪŋ- US kəˈmɪŋ-, kɑː- **-es** -z **-ing** -ɪŋ, ˈ-glɪŋ **-ed** -d

commi|nute ˈkɒm.ɪ.njuːt US ˈkɑː.mə.nuːt, -njuːt **-nutes** -njuːts US -nuːts, -njuːts **-nuting** -njuː.tɪŋ US -nuː.t̬ɪŋ, -njuː- **-nuted** -njuː.tɪd US -nuː.t̬ɪd, -njuː-

comminution ˌkɒm.ɪˈnjuː.ʃᵊn US ˌkɑː.məˈnuː-, -ˈnjuː-

commis ˈkɒm.i, -ɪs US ˌkɑːˈmi *stress shift, American only, see compound:* **ˈcommis ˌchef, ˌcommis ˈchef**

commiser|ate kəˈmɪz.ᵊr|.eɪt, kɒmˈɪz- US kəˈmɪz- **-ates** -eɪts **-ating** -eɪ.tɪŋ US -eɪ.t̬ɪŋ **-ated** -eɪ.tɪd US -eɪ.t̬ɪd

commiseration kəˌmɪz.ᵊrˈeɪ.ʃᵊn, kɒmˌɪz- US kəˌmɪz-

commissar ˌkɒm.ɪˈsɑːʳ, -əˈ-, ˈ--- US ˈkɑː.mə.sɑːr **-s** -z

commissarial ˌkɒm.ɪˈseə.ri.əl, -əˈ-, -ˈsɑː-, -ˈsær.i- US ˌkɑː.məˈser-

commissariat ˌkɒm.ɪˈseə.ri.ət, -əˈ-, -ˈsɑː-, -ˈsær.i-, -æt US ˌkɑː.məˈser-

commissar|y ˈkɒm.ɪ.sᵊr|.i, kəˈmɪs.ᵊr- US ˈkɑː.mə.ser- **-ies** -iz

commission kəˈmɪʃ.ᵊn **-s** -z **-ing** -ɪŋ **-ed** -d **-er/s** -əʳ/z, ˈ-nəʳ/z US ˈ-ᵊn.ɚ/z, ˈ-nɚ/z **comˈmission ˌagent; comˌmissioned ˈofficer**

commissionaire kəˌmɪʃ.ᵊnˈeəʳ US -ˈer **-s** -z

commissive kəˈmɪs.ɪv, ˈkɒm.ɪ.sɪv US kəˈmɪs-

commissure ˈkɒm.ɪ.sjʊəʳ, ˈ-ə-, -ʃʊəʳ US ˈkɑː.mə.ʃʊr **-s** -z

com|mit kə|ˈmɪt **-mits** -s **-mitting** -ˈmɪt.ɪŋ US -ˈmɪt̬.ɪŋ **-mitted** -ˈmɪt.ɪd US -ˈmɪt̬.ɪd **-mitter/s** -ˈmɪt.əʳ/z US -ˈmɪt̬.ɚ/z

commitment kəˈmɪt.mənt **-s** -s

committal kəˈmɪt.ᵊl US -ˈmɪt̬- **-s** -z

committee *council:* kəˈmɪt.i US -ˈmɪt̬- **-s** -z **comˈmittee ˌmeeting**

committee *one committed:* ˌkɒm.ɪˈtiː US ˌkɑː.mɪˈtiː **-s** -z

committor ˌkɒm.ɪˈtɔːʳ, kəˈmɪt.əʳ US ˌkɑː.mɪˈt̬ɔːr; kəˈmɪt̬.ɚ **-s** -z

commixture kəˈmɪks.tʃəʳ US -tʃɚ **-s** -z

commode kəˈməʊd US -ˈmoʊd **-s** -z

commodious kəˈməʊ.di.əs US -ˈmoʊ- **-ly** -li **-ness** -nəs, -nɪs

commodit|y kəˈmɒd.ə.t|i, -ɪ.t|i US -ˈmɑː.də.t̬|i **-ies** -iz

commodore ˈkɒm.ə.dɔːʳ US ˈkɑː.mə.dɔːr **-s** -z

Commodus ˈkɒm.ə.dəs US ˈkɑː.mə-

common ˈkɒm.ən US ˈkɑː.mən **-s** -z **-er** -əʳ US -ɚ **-est** -ɪst, -əst **-ly** -li **-ness** -nəs, -nɪs **ˌcommon deˈnominator; ˌCommon ˈMarket; ˈcommon ˌroom; ˌcommon ˈsense; ˈcommon ˌtouch**

commonage ˈkɒm.ə.nɪdʒ US ˈkɑː.mə-

commonality ˌkɒm.əˈnæl.ə.ti, -ɪ.ti US ˌkɑː.məˈnæl.ə.t̬i

commonalt|y ˈkɒm.ə.nᵊl.t|i US ˈkɑː.mə- **-ies** -iz

Commondale ˈkɒm.ən.deɪl US ˈkɑː.mən-

commoner ˈkɒm.ə.nəʳ US ˈkɑː.mə.nɚ **-s** -z

common-law ˌkɒm.ənˈlɔː US ˈkɑː.mən.lɑː, -lɔː *stress shift, British only:* ˌcommon-law ˈwife

common-or-garden ˌkɒm.ən.ɔːˈgɑː.dᵊn, -əˈgɑː- US ˌkɑː.mən.ɔːrˈgɑːr-

commonplac|e ˈkɒm.ən.pleɪs, -əm- US ˈkɑː.mən- **-es** -ɪz

commons (C) ˈkɒm.ənz US ˈkɑː.mənz

commonsense ˌkɒm.ənˈsen*t*s US ˌkɑː.mənˈ-

commonsensical ˌkɒm.ənˈsen*t*.sɪ.kᵊl US ˌkɑː.mənˈ-

commonwealth (C) ˈkɒm.ən.welθ US ˈkɑː.mən- **-s** -s

commotion kəˈməʊ.ʃᵊn US -ˈmoʊ- **-s** -z

communal ˈkɒm.jʊ.nᵊl, -jə-; kəˈmjuː- US kəˈmjuː-; ˈkɑː.mjə- **-ly** -i

communard (C) ˈkɒm.jʊ.nɑːd, ˌkɒm.jʊˈnɑː US ˈkɑː.mjʊ.nɑːrd, -nɑːr **-s** -z

commune (*n.*) ˈkɒm.juːn US ˈkɑː.mjuːn **-s** -z

commun|e (*v.*) kəˈmjuːn **-es** -z **-ing** -ɪŋ **-ed** -d

communicab|le kəˈmjuː.nɪ.kə.b|l̩ **-ly** -li **-leness** -l̩.nəs, -nɪs

communicant kəˈmjuː.nɪ.kənt **-s** -s

communi|cate kəˈmjuː.nɪ|.keɪt, -nə- **-cates** -keɪts **-cating** -keɪ.tɪŋ US -keɪ.t̬ɪŋ **-cated** -keɪ.tɪd US -keɪ.t̬ɪd **-cator/s** -keɪ.təʳ/z US -keɪ.t̬ɚ/z

communication kəˌmjuː.nɪˈkeɪ.ʃᵊn, -nəˈ- **-s** -z

communicative kəˈmjuː.nɪ.kə.tɪv, -nə-, -keɪ- US -nə.keɪ.t̬ɪv, -kə- **-ly** -li **-ness** -nəs, -nɪs

communion kəˈmjuː.ni.ən US -njən **-s** -z

communiqué kəˈmjuː.nɪ.keɪ, kɒmˈjuː-, -nə- US kəˌmjuː.nɪˈkeɪ, kəˈmjuː.nɪ.keɪ **-s** -z

commun|ism ˈkɒm.jə.n|ɪ.zᵊm, -jʊ- US ˈkɑː.mjə- **-ist/s** -ɪst/s

communit|y kəˈmjuː.nə.t|i, -nɪ- US -nə.t̬|i **-ies** -iz **comˈmunity ˌcentre; comˈmunity ˌchest** US **community ˈchest; comˈmunity ˌcollege**

commutability kəˌmjuː.təˈbɪl.ə.ti, -ɪ.ti US -t̬əˈbɪl.ə.t̬i

commutable kəˈmjuː.tə.bl̩ US -t̬ə-

commu|tate ˈkɒm.jʊ|.teɪt US ˈkɑː.mjə- **-tates** -teɪts **-tating** -teɪ.tɪŋ US -teɪ.t̬ɪŋ **-tated** -teɪ.tɪd US -teɪ.t̬ɪd **-tator/s** -teɪ.təʳ/z US -teɪ.t̬ɚ/z

commutation ˌkɒm.jʊˈteɪ.ʃᵊn US ˌkɑː.mjəˈ- **-s** -z

commutative kəˈmjuː.tə.tɪv, ˈkɒm.jʊ.teɪ- US ˈkɑː.mjə.teɪ.t̬ɪv, kəˈmjuː.t̬ə- **-ly** -li

com|mute kə|ˈmjuːt **-mutes** -ˈmjuːts **-muting** -ˈmjuː.tɪŋ US -ˈmjuː.t̬ɪŋ **-muted** -ˈmjuː.tɪd US -ˈmjuː.t̬ɪd

commuter kəˈmjuː.təʳ US -t̬ɚ **-s** -z

Como ˈkəʊ.məʊ US ˈkoʊ.moʊ

Comorin ˈkɒm.ə.rɪn US ˈkɑː.mɚ.ɪn

Comoros ˈkɒm.ə.rəʊz US ˈkɑː.mə.roʊz

comose ˈkəʊ.məʊs, -məʊz, -ˈ- US ˈkoʊ.moʊs

compact (*n.*) ˈkɒm.pækt US ˈkɑːm- **-s** -s

compact (*adj. v.*) kəmˈpækt US kəm-, kɑːm- **-er** -əʳ US -ɚ **-est** -ɪst, -əst **-ly** -li **-ness** -nəs, -nɪs **-s** -s **-ing** -ɪŋ **-ed** -ɪd *stress shift, see compound:* **ˌcompact ˈdisc/ˌcompact ˈdisk**

compactor kəmˈpæk.təʳ; ˈkɒm.pæk- US kəmˈpæk.tɚ; ˈkɑːm.pæk- **-s** -z

companion kəmˈpæn.jən **-s** -z **-ship** -ʃɪp

companionab|le kəmˈpæn.jə.nə.b|l̩ **-ly** -li **-leness** -l̩.nəs, -nɪs

companionate kəmˈpæn.jə.nət, -nɪt

companionway kəmˈpæn.jən.weɪ **-s** -z

compan|y ˈkʌm.pə.n|i **-ies** -iz

Compaq® ˈkɒm.pæk US ˈkɑːm-

comparability ˌkɒm.pᵊr.əˈbɪl.ə.ti; kəmˌpær-, -ɪ.ti US ˌkɑːm.pɚ.əˈbɪl.ə.t̬i

comparab|le ˈkɒm.pᵊr.ə.b|l̩ US ˈkɑːm-; kəmˈper.ə-, -ˈpær- **-ly** -li **-leness** -l̩.nəs, -nɪs

comparative kəmˈpær.ə.tɪv US -ˈper.ə.t̬ɪv, -ˈpær- **-s** -z **-ly** -li

compar|e kəmˈpeəʳ US -per **-es** -z **-ing** -ɪŋ **-ed** -d

comparison kəmˈpær.ɪ.sᵊn US -ˈper-, -ˈpær- **-s** -z

compartment kəmˈpɑːt.mənt US -ˈpɑːrt- **-s** -s

compartmentalization, -isa- ˌkɒm.pɑːt.men.tᵊl.aɪˈzeɪ.ʃᵊn, kɒm.pɑːtˌmen-, -ɪˈ- US kəm.pɑːrtˌmen.t̬ᵊl.ɪˈ-, ˌkɑːm-

compartmentaliz|e, -is|e ˌkɒm.pɑːtˈmen.tᵊl.aɪz US kəm.pɑːrtˈmen.t̬ə.laɪz, ˌkɑːm- **-es** -ɪz **-ing** -ɪŋ **-ed** -d

compass ˈkʌm.pəs US ˈkʌm-, ˈkɑːm- **-es** -ɪz **-ing** -ɪŋ **-ed** -t

compassion kəmˈpæʃ.ᵊn

compassionate kəmˈpæʃ.ᵊn.ət, -ɪt **-ly** -li **-ness** -nəs, -nɪs

compatibility kəmˌpæt.əˈbɪl.ə.ti, -ɪˈ-, -ɪ.ti US -ˌpæt̬.əˈbɪl.ə.t̬i

compatib|le kəmˈpæt.ɪ.b|l̩, ˈ-ə- US -ˈpæt̬- **-ly** -li **-leness** -l̩.nəs, -nɪs

compatriot kəmˈpæt.ri.ət, kɒm- US kəmˈpeɪ.tri-, kɑːm- **-s** -s

compeer ˈkɒm.pɪəʳ, -ˈ- US ˈkɑːm.pɪr; -ˈ-, kəm- **-s** -z

compel kəmˈpel **-s** -z **-ling/ly** -ɪŋ/li **-led** -d **-lable** -ə.bl̩

compendious kəmˈpen.di.əs **-ly** -li **-ness** -nəs, -nɪs

compendi|um kəmˈpen.di|.əm **-ums** -əmz **-a** -ə

compen|sate ˈkɒm.pən|.seɪt, -pen- US ˈkɑːm- **-sates** -seɪts **-sating** -seɪ.tɪŋ US -seɪ.t̬ɪŋ **-sated** -seɪ.tɪd US -seɪ.t̬ɪd

compensation ˌkɒm.pənˈseɪ.ʃᵊn, -pen- US ˌkɑːm- **-s** -z

compensative kəmˈpen*t*.sə.tɪv, ˌkɒm.pənˈseɪ- US kəmˈpen*t*.sə.t̬ɪv, ˈkɑːm.pən.seɪ-

compensatory ˌkɒm.pənˈseɪ.tᵊr.i, -tri; kəmˈpen*t*.sə-; ˈkɒm.pen.seɪ-, -pən- US kəmˈpen*t*.sə.tɔːr.i

comper|e, compèr|e ˈkɒm.peəʳ US ˈkɑːm.per **-es** -z **-ing** -ɪŋ **-ed** -d

com|pete kəmˈpiːt **-petes** -ˈpiːts **-peting** -ˈpiː.tɪŋ US -ˈpiː.t̬ɪŋ **-peted** -ˈpiː.tɪd US -ˈpiː.t̬ɪd

competen|ce ˈkɒm.pɪ.tᵊn*t*|s, -pə- US ˈkɑːm- **-cies** -siz **-cy** -si

competent ˈkɒm.pɪ.tᵊnt, -pə- US ˈkɑːm.pɪ.t̬ᵊnt, -pə- **-ly** -li

competition ˌkɒm.pəˈtɪʃ.ᵊn, -pɪˈ- US ˌkɑːm- **-s** -z

competitive kəmˈpet.ɪ.tɪv, ˈ-ə- US -ˈpet̬.ə.t̬ɪv **-ly** -li **-ness** -nəs, -nɪs

competitor kəmˈpet.ɪ.təʳ, ˈ-ə- US -ˈpet̬.ə.t̬ɚ **-s** -z

compilation ˌkɒm.pɪˈleɪ.ʃᵊn, -pəˈ-, -paɪˈ- US ˌkɑːm.pəˈ- **-s** -z

compil|e kəmˈpaɪl **-es** -z **-ing** -ɪŋ **-ed** -d **-er/s** -əʳ/z US -ɚ/z

complacen|ce kəmˈpleɪ.sᵊn*t*|s **-cy** -si

complacent kəmˈpleɪ.sᵊnt **-ly** -li

Compounds

This panel looks at word stress in compounds. Compounds are words made up of two other words which can exist independently in English. They are written in a variety of ways: closed, e.g. *armchair, sunflower*; hyphenated, e.g., *front-runner, she-devil*; open, e.g. *side salad, bank manager*. Sometimes it is possible for the same compounds to be written in different ways, e.g. *shoulder blade* or *shoulderblade*.

There are some rules for compound word stress in English but they are not completely reliable. In addition, British and US English differ. The rules which follow are therefore guidelines, but exceptions exist.

Examples

Words that combine two nouns usually have primary stress on the first element, e.g.:

coffee pot	/ˈkɒf.i.pɒt/	Ⓤⓢ /ˈkɑː.fi.pɑːt/
suitcase	/ˈsuːt.keɪs/	

In US English, it is more frequently the case that compound nouns have first element stress, and this tendency is appearing among some British English speakers. For example, *ice cream* can have first or second-element stress in British English, but tends to be stressed on the first element in US English.

Other types of compound are usually stressed on the second element. These include words ending in *-ed* which are used as adjectives, words with a number as a first element, and words functioning as adverbs or verbs, e.g.:

kind-hearted	/ˌkaɪndˈhɑː.tɪd/	Ⓤⓢ /-ˈhɑːr.t̬ɪd/
three-piece	/ˌθriːˈpiːs/	
southeast	/ˌsaʊθˈiːst/	

These words are subject to stress-shift when a stressed syllable follows closely (e.g., *a ˌkindhearted ˈman*).

complain kəmˈpleɪn **-s** -z **-ing** -ɪŋ **-ed** -d **-er/s** -əʳ/z Ⓤⓢ -ɚ/z

complainant kəmˈpleɪ.nənt **-s** -s

complaint kəmˈpleɪnt **-s** -s

complaisance kəmˈpleɪ.zᵊn*t*s Ⓤⓢ -sᵊn*t*s

complaisant kəmˈpleɪ.zᵊnt Ⓤⓢ -sᵊnt **-ly** -li

compleat kəmˈpliːt

complement (*n.*) ˈkɒm.plɪ.mənt, -plə- Ⓤⓢ ˈkɑːm- **-s** -s

comple|ment (*v.*) ˈkɒm.plɪ|.ment, ˌkɒm.plɪ|ˈment Ⓤⓢ ˈkɑːm.plɪ- **-ments** -ments, -ˈments Ⓤⓢ -ments **-menting** -men.tɪŋ, -ˈmen.tɪŋ Ⓤⓢ -men.t̬ɪŋ **-mented** -men.tɪd, -ˈmen.tɪd Ⓤⓢ -men.t̬ɪd

complemental ˌkɒm.plɪˈmen.tᵊl Ⓤⓢ ˌkɑːm.plɪˈmen.t̬ᵊl

complementary ˌkɒm.plɪˈmen.tᵊr.i, -pləˈ-, ˈ-tri Ⓤⓢ ˌkɑːm.pləˈmen.t̬ɚ.i, ˈ-tri

complementation ˌkɒm.plɪ.menˈteɪ.ʃᵊn, -plə-, -mənˈ- Ⓤⓢ ˌkɑːm-

complementiser, -izer ˈkɒm.plɪ.men.taɪ.zəʳ, -plə-, -mən- Ⓤⓢ ˈkɑːm.plə.mən.taɪ.zɚ, -men- **-s** -z

com|plete kəm|ˈpliːt **-pletest** -ˈpliː.tɪst, -təst Ⓤⓢ -ˈpliː.t̬ɪst, -t̬əst **-pletely** -ˈpliːt.li **-pleteness** -ˈpliːt.nəs, -nɪs **-pletes** -ˈpliːts **-pleting** -ˈpliː.tɪŋ Ⓤⓢ -ˈpliː.t̬ɪŋ **-pleted** -ˈpliː.tɪd Ⓤⓢ -ˈpliː.t̬ɪd

completion kəmˈpliː.ʃᵊn

complex (*adj.*) ˈkɒm.pleks, kəmˈpleks Ⓤⓢ kɑːmˈpleks, kəm-; ˈkɑːm.pleks

complex (*n.*) ˈkɒm.pleks Ⓤⓢ ˈkɑːm- **-es** -ɪz

complexion kəmˈplek.ʃᵊn **-s** -z **-ed** -d

complexit|y kəmˈplek.sə.t|i, -sɪ- Ⓤⓢ -sə.t̬|i **-ies** -iz

complianc|e kəmˈplaɪ.ən*t*s **-es** -ɪz

compliant kəmˈplaɪ.ənt **-ly** -li

compli|cate ˈkɒm.plɪ|.keɪt Ⓤⓢ ˈkɑːm.plə- **-cates** -keɪts **-cating** -keɪ.tɪŋ Ⓤⓢ -keɪ.t̬ɪŋ **-cated** -keɪ.tɪd Ⓤⓢ -keɪ.t̬ɪd

complication ˌkɒm.plɪˈkeɪ.ʃᵊn Ⓤⓢ ˌkɑːm.pləˈ- **-s** -z

complicit kəmˈplɪs.ɪt

complicity kəmˈplɪs.ə.ti, -ɪ.ti Ⓤⓢ -ə.t̬i

compliment (*n.*) ˈkɒm.plɪ.mənt, -plə- Ⓤⓢ ˈkɑːm.plə- **-s** -s

compli|ment (*v.*) ˈkɒm.plɪ|.ment, -plə-, ˌkɒm.plɪ|ˈment Ⓤⓢ ˈkɑːm.plə- **-ments** -ments, -ˈments Ⓤⓢ -ments **-menting** -men.tɪŋ, -ˈmen.tɪŋ Ⓤⓢ -men.t̬ɪŋ **-mented** -men.tɪd, -ˈmen.tɪd Ⓤⓢ -men.t̬ɪd

complimentarily ˌkɒm.plɪˈmen.tᵊr.ᵊl.i, -plə- Ⓤⓢ ˌkɑːm.plə.menˈter-; -ˈmen.t̬ɚ-

complimentar|y ˌkɒm.plɪˈmen.tᵊr|.i, -pləˈ-, ˈ-tr|i Ⓤⓢ ˌkɑːm.pləˈmen.t̬ɚ|.i, ˈ-tr|i **-ies** -iz

complin ˈkɒm.plɪn Ⓤⓢ ˈkɑːm- **-s** -z

compline ˈkɒm.plɪn, -plaɪn Ⓤⓢ ˈkɑːm- **-s** -z

compl|y kəmˈpl|aɪ **-ies** -aɪz **-ying** -aɪ.ɪŋ **-ied** -aɪd **-ier/s** -aɪ.əʳ/z Ⓤⓢ -aɪ.ɚ/z

compo ˈkɒm.pəʊ Ⓤⓢ ˈkɑːm.poʊ

component kəmˈpəʊ.nənt Ⓤⓢ -ˈpoʊ- **-s** -s

componential ˌkɒm.pəʊˈnen.*t*ʃᵊl Ⓤⓢ ˌkɑːm.pəˈ- ˌcompoˌnential aˈnalysis

com|port kəm|ˈpɔːt Ⓤⓢ -ˈpɔːrt **-ports** -ˈpɔːts Ⓤⓢ -ˈpɔːrts **-porting** -ˈpɔː.tɪŋ Ⓤⓢ -ˈpɔːr.t̬ɪŋ **-ported** -ˈpɔː.tɪd Ⓤⓢ -ˈpɔːr.t̬ɪd

comportment kəmˈpɔːt.mənt Ⓤⓢ -ˈpɔːrt-

compos|e kəmˈpəʊz Ⓤⓢ -ˈpoʊz **-es** -ɪz **-ing** -ɪŋ **-ed** -d

compos|ed kəmˈpəʊz|d Ⓤⓢ -ˈpoʊz|d **-edly** -ɪd.li, -əd.li **-edness** -ɪd.nəs, -d.nəs, -nɪs

composer kəmˈpəʊ.zəʳ Ⓤⓢ -ˈpoʊ.zɚ **-s** -z

composite ˈkɒm.pə.zɪt, -sɪt, -zaɪt, -saɪt Ⓤⓢ kəmˈpɑː.zɪt **-ly** -li **-ness** -nəs, -nɪs

composition ˌkɒm.pəˈzɪʃ.ᵊn Ⓤⓢ ˌkɑːm- **-s** -z

compositor kəmˈpɒz.ɪ.təʳ Ⓤⓢ -ˈpɑː.zɪ.t̬ɚ **-s** -z

compos mentis ˌkɒm.pəsˈmen.tɪs, -pɒs- Ⓤⓢ ˌkɑːm.pəsˈmen.t̬əs

compost ˈkɒm.pɒst Ⓤⓢ ˈkɑːm.poʊst **-s** -s **-ing** -ɪŋ **-ed** -ɪd ˈcompost ˌheap

composure kəmˈpəʊ.ʒəʳ Ⓤⓢ -ˈpoʊ.ʒɚ

compote ˈkɒm.pɒt, -pəʊt Ⓤⓢ ˈkɑːm.poʊt **-s** -s

compound (*n. adj.*) ˈkɒm.paʊnd Ⓤⓢ ˈkɑːm- **-s** -z ˌcompound ˈfracture

compound (*v.*) kəmˈpaʊnd, kɒm-; ˈkɒm.paʊnd Ⓤⓢ kɑːmˈpaʊnd, kəm-; ˈkɑːm.paʊnd **-s** -z **-ing** -ɪŋ **-ed** -ɪd **-able** -ə.bl̩

comprehend ˌkɒm.prɪˈhend, -prəˈ- Ⓤⓢ ˌkɑːm- **-s** -z **-ing** -ɪŋ **-ed** -ɪd

comprehensibility ˌkɒm.prɪ.hent.səˈbɪl.ə.ti, -prə-, -sɪˈ-, -ɪ.ti (US) ˌkɑːm.prə.hent.səˈbɪl.ə.t̬i, -prɪ-
comprehensib|le ˌkɒm.prɪˈhent.sə.b|l̩, -prəˈ-, -sɪ- (US) ˌkɑːm- **-ly** -li **-leness** -l̩.nəs, -nɪs
comprehension ˌkɒm.prɪˈhen.*t*ʃᵊn, -prəˈ- (US) ˌkɑːm.prɪˈhent.ʃᵊn-, -prəˈ-
comprehensive ˌkɒm.prɪˈhent.sɪv, -prəˈ- (US) ˌkɑːm.prə-, -prɪ- **-s** -z **-ly** -li **-ness** -nəs, -nɪs **compreˈhensive ˌschool**
compress (*n.*) ˈkɒm.pres (US) ˈkɑːm- **-es** -ɪz
compress (*v.*) kəmˈpres **-es** -ɪz **-ing** -ɪŋ **-ed** -t **-or/s** -əʳ/z (US) -ɚ/z
compressibility kəmˌpres.əˈbɪl.ə.ti, -ɪˈ-, -ɪ.ti (US) -ə.t̬i
compressible kəmˈpres.ə.bl̩, ˈ-ɪ- **-ness** -nəs, -nɪs
compression kəmˈpreʃ.ᵊn **-s** -z **-al** -ᵊl
compressive kəmˈpres.ɪv
compris|e kəmˈpraɪz **-es** -ɪz **-ing** -ɪŋ **-ed** -d **-able** -ə.bl̩
compromis|e ˈkɒm.prə.maɪz (US) ˈkɑːm- **-es** -ɪz **-ing/ly** -ɪŋ/li **-ed** -d **-er/s** -əʳ/z (US) -ɚ/z
Comptometer® ˌkɒmpˈtɒm.ɪ.təʳ, ˈ-ə- (US) ˌkɑːmpˈtɑː.mə.t̬ɚ **-s** -z
Compton ˈkɒm*p*.tən, ˈkʌm*p*- (US) ˈkɑːm*p*-
Note: For British English, as surname more often /ˈkʌm*p*-/, as place name more often /ˈkɒm*p*-/. The London street is generally /ˈkɒm*p*-/.
Compton-Burnett ˌkɒmp.tən.bɜːˈnet, -ˈbɜː.nɪt (US) ˌkɑːmp.tən.bɝːˈnet
comptroller kənˈtrəʊ.ləʳ, kəmp-, kɒmp- (US) kənˈtroʊ.lɚ, kəmp-, kɑːmp-; ˈkɑːmp.troʊ- **-s** -z
compulsion kəmˈpʌl.ʃᵊn
compulsive kəmˈpʌl.sɪv **-ly** -li
compulsor|y kəmˈpʌl.sᵊr|.i **-ily** -ᵊl.i, -ɪ.li
compunction kəmˈpʌŋ*k*.ʃᵊn
compunctious kəmˈpʌŋ*k*.ʃəs
compurgation ˌkɒm.pɜːˈgeɪ.ʃᵊn (US) ˌkɑːm.pɚˈ-
computability kəmˌpjuː.təˈbɪl.ə.ti, ˌkɒm.pjʊ-, -ɪ.ti (US) kəmˌpjuː.t̬əˈbɪl.ə.t̬i
computable kəmˈpjuː.tə.bl̩; ˈkɒm.pjʊ- (US) kəmˈpjuː.t̬ə-
computation ˌkɒm.pjəˈteɪ.ʃᵊn, -pjʊˈ- (US) ˌkɑːm.pjəˈ- **-s** -z
computational ˌkɒm.pjəˈteɪ.ʃᵊn.ᵊl, -pjʊˈ-, -ˈteɪʃ.nᵊl (US) ˌkɑːm- **-ly** -i **compuˌtational linˈguistics**
computator ˈkɒm.pjə.teɪ.təʳ, -pjʊ- (US) ˈkɑːm.pjə.teɪ.t̬ɚ **-s** -z
com|pute kəm|ˈpjuːt **-putes** -ˈpjuːts **-puting** -ˈpjuː.tɪŋ (US) -ˈpjuː.t̬ɪŋ **-puted** -ˈpjuː.tɪd (US) -ˈpjuː.t̬ɪd
computer kəmˈpjuː.təʳ (US) -t̬ɚ **-s** -z **comˈputer ˌgame; comˌputer ˈprogrammer; comˌputer aided deˈsign**
computerate kəmˈpjuː.tᵊr.ət (US) -t̬ɚ-
computerization, -isa- kəmˌpjuː.tᵊr.aɪˈzeɪ.ʃᵊn, -ɪˈ- (US) -t̬ɚ.ɪˈ-
computeriz|e, -is|e kəmˈpjuː.tᵊr.aɪz (US) -t̬ə.raɪz **-es** -ɪz **-ing** -ɪŋ **-ed** -d
computist kəmˈpjuː.tɪst (US) -t̬ɪst **-s** -s
comrade ˈkɒm.reɪd, ˈkʌm-, -rɪd (US) ˈkɑːm.ræd, -rəd **-s** -z **-ship** -ʃɪp
Comsat® ˈkɒm.sæt (US) ˈkɑːm- **-s** -s
Comte kɔ̃ː*n*t, kɔːnt, kɒnt (US) kɔ̃ːnt, koʊnt
Comus ˈkəʊ.məs (US) ˈkoʊ-
Comyn ˈkʌm.ɪn
con- kɒn-, kən- (US) kɑːn-, kən-
Note: Prefix. This may carry primary or secondary stress, e.g. **concept** /ˈkɒn.sept (US) ˈkɑːn-/, or may be unstressed, e.g. **consume** /kənˈsjuːm (US) kənˈsuːm/.
con kɒn (US) kɑːn **-s** -z **-ning** -ɪŋ **-ned** -d **ˈcon ˌman; ˈcon ˌtrick**
Conakry ˌkɒn.əˈkriː, ˈkɒn.ə.kri (US) ˈkɑː.nə.kri
Conall ˈkɒn.ᵊl (US) ˈkɑː.nᵊl
Conan *personal name:* ˈkəʊ.nən, ˈkɒn.ən (US) ˈkoʊ.nən, ˈkɑː- *place in Scotland:* ˈkɒn.ən, ˈkəʊ.nən (US) ˈkɑː-, ˈkoʊ-
Conant ˈkɒn.ənt (US) ˈkoʊ.nənt
conation kəʊˈneɪ.ʃᵊn (US) koʊ-
conative ˈkəʊ.nə.tɪv (US) ˈkoʊ.nə.t̬ɪv
Concannon kɒnˈkæn.ən, kɒŋ- (US) kɑːn-
concaten|ate kənˈkæt.ᵊn|.eɪt, kəŋ-, kɒn-, kɒŋ-, ˈ-ɪ- (US) kənˈkæt̬-, kɑːn- **-ates** -eɪts **-ating** -eɪ.tɪŋ (US) -eɪ.t̬ɪŋ **-ated** -eɪ.tɪd (US) -eɪ.t̬ɪd
concatenation kənˌkæt.əˈneɪ.ʃᵊn, kəŋ-, kɒn-, kɒŋ-, -ɪˈ-; ˈkɒn.kæt-, ˈkɒŋ- (US) kənˌkæt̬.əˈ-; ˌkɑːn.kæt̬- **-s** -z
concave kɒŋˈkeɪv, kəŋ-, kɒn-, kən-; ˈkɒŋ.keɪv (US) kɑːnˈkeɪv, ˈkɑːn- *stress shift:* ˌconcave ˈlens
concavit|y kɒnˈkæv.ə.t|i, kən-, kɒŋ-, kəŋ-, -ɪ.t|i (US) kɑːnˈkæv.ə.t̬|i **-ies** -iz
conceal kənˈsiːl **-s** -z **-ing** -ɪŋ **-ed** -d **-able** -ə.bl̩ **-er/s** -əʳ/z (US) -ɚ/z
concealment kənˈsiːl.mənt **-s** -s
conced|e kənˈsiːd **-es** -z **-ing** -ɪŋ **-ed** -ɪd
conceit kənˈsiːt **-s** -s
conceited kənˈsiː.tɪd (US) -t̬ɪd **-ly** -li **-ness** -nəs, -nɪs
conceivab|le kənˈsiː.və.b|l̩ **-ly** -li **-leness** -l̩.nəs, -nɪs
conceiv|e kənˈsiːv **-es** -z **-ing** -ɪŋ **-ed** -d
concele|brate kɒnˈsel.ə|.breɪt, kən-, ˈ-ɪ- (US) kən-, kɑːn- **-brates** -breɪts **-brating** -breɪ.tɪŋ (US) -breɪ.t̬ɪŋ **-brated** -breɪ.tɪd (US) -breɪ.t̬ɪd
concelebration ˌkɒn.sel.əˈbreɪ.ʃᵊn, -ɪˈ-; kənˌsel- (US) kənˌsel-; ˌkɑːn.sel- **-s** -z
concent kənˈsent, ˌkɒn- (US) kən-
concent|er kɒnˈsen.t|əʳ (US) kənˈsen.t̬|ɚ, kɑːn- **-ers** -əz (US) -ɚz **-ering** -ᵊr.ɪŋ **-ered** -əd (US) -ɚd
concen|trate ˈkɒnt.sᵊn|.treɪt, -sɪn-, -sen- (US) ˈkɑːnt.sᵊn- **-trates** -treɪts **-trating** -treɪ.tɪŋ (US) -treɪ.t̬ɪŋ **-trated** -treɪ.tɪd (US) -treɪ.t̬ɪd
concentration ˌkɒn*t*.sᵊnˈtreɪ.ʃᵊn, -sɪnˈ-, -senˈ- (US) ˌkɑːn*t*.sᵊnˈ- **-s** -z **concenˈtration ˌcamp**
concentrative ˈkɒn*t*.sᵊn.treɪ.tɪv, -sɪn-, -sen- (US) ˈkɑːn*t*.sən.treɪ.t̬ɪv; kənˈsen.trə-
concent|re kɒnˈsen.t|əʳ (US) kənˈsen.t̬|ɚ, kɑːn- **-res** -əz (US) -ɚz **-ring** -rɪŋ **-ering** -ᵊr.ɪŋ **-red** -əd (US) -ɚd
concentric kənˈsen.trɪk, kɒn- (US) kən- **-ally** -ᵊl.i, -li
Concepción kənˌsep.siˈəʊn, ˌkɒn.sep- (US) kən-, kɑːn-, -ˈoʊn
concept ˈkɒn.sept (US) ˈkɑːn- **-s** -s
conception kənˈsep.ʃᵊn **-s** -z
conceptual kənˈsep.tʃu.əl, -ʃu-, -tju- (US) -tʃu- **-ly** -i
conceptualization, -isa- kənˌsep.tʃu.ə.laɪˈzeɪ.ʃᵊn, -ʃu-, -tju-, -ɪˈ- (US) -tʃu.ᵊl.ɪˈ-
conceptualiz|e, -is|e kənˈsep.tʃu.ə.laɪz, -ʃu-, -tju-, -tʃʊ.laɪz, -tʃə- (US) -tʃu.ə- **-es** -ɪz **-ing** -ɪŋ **-ed** -d
conceptually kənˈsep.tʃu.ə.li, -ʃu-, -tju- (US) -tʃu-
conceptus kənˈsep.təs **-es** -ɪz
concern kənˈsɜːn (US) -ˈsɝːn **-s** -z **-ing** -ɪŋ **-ed** -d **-ment/s** -mənt/s
concern|ed kənˈsɜːn|d (US) -ˈsɝːn|d **-edly** -ɪd.li **-edness** -ɪd.nəs, -d.nəs, -nɪs
concert (*n.*) *musical entertainment:* ˈkɒn.sət (US) ˈkɑːn.sɚt **-s** -s
concert (C) (*n.*) *union:* ˈkɒn.sɜːt, -sət (US) ˈkɑːn.sɚt **-s** -s
con|cert (*v.*) kən|ˈsɜːt (US) -ˈsɝːt **-certs** -ˈsɜːts (US) -ˈsɝːts **-certing** -ˈsɜː.tɪŋ (US) -ˈsɝː.t̬ɪŋ **-certed** -ˈsɜː.tɪd (US) -ˈsɝː.t̬ɪd
concerti (*plur. of* **concerto**) kənˈtʃeə.ti, -ˈtʃɜː- (US) -ˈtʃer.t̬i
concertina ˌkɒn*t*.səˈtiː.nə (US) ˌkɑːn*t*.sɚˈ- **-s** -z **-ing** -ɪŋ **-ed** -d
concertino ˌkɒn.*t*ʃəˈtiː.nəʊ (US) ˌkɑːn.tʃɚˈtiː.noʊ **-s** -z
concerto kənˈtʃeə.təʊ, -ˈtʃɜː-

US -ˈtʃer.t̬oʊ **-s** -z **concerti** kənˈtʃeə.ti, -ˈtʃɜː- US -ˈtʃer.t̬i
concerto grosso kənˌtʃeə.təʊˈgrɒs.əʊ, kɒn-, -ˌtʃɜː- US kənˌtʃer.t̬oʊˈgroʊ.soʊ, kɑːn- **concerti grossi** kənˌtʃeə.tiˈgrɒs.i US -ˌtʃer.t̬iˈgroʊ.si
concession kənˈseʃ.ᵊn **-s** -z
concessionaire kənˌseʃ.ᵊnˈeəʳ US -ˈer **-s** -z
concessional kənˈseʃ.ᵊn.ᵊl, ˈ-nᵊl US -ən.ᵊl **-ly** -i
concessionary kənˈseʃ.ᵊn.ᵊr.i, -ᵊn.ri US -ʃᵊn.er.i
concessive kənˈses.ɪv **-ly** -li
conch kɒntʃ, kɒŋk US kɑːŋk, kɑːntʃ **conches** ˈkɒn.tʃɪz US ˈkɑːn.tʃɪz **conchs** kɒŋks US kɑːŋks
concha ˈkɒŋ.kə US ˈkɑːŋ-, ˈkɔːŋ- **-s** -z
conchie ˈkɒn.tʃi US ˈkɑːn- **-s** -z
Conchobar ˈkɒŋ.kəʊ.əʳ, ˈkɒn.u.əʳ US ˈkɑː.nu.ɚ, ˈkɑːŋ.koʊ.ɚ, ˈkɔːŋ-
conchoid ˈkɒŋ.kɔɪd US ˈkɑːn- **-s** -z
conchologist kɒŋˈkɒl.ə.dʒɪst US kɑːŋˈkɑː.lə-, kɔːŋ- **-s** -s
conchology kɒŋˈkɒl.ə.dʒi US kɑːŋˈkɑː.lə-, kɔːŋ-
concierge ˌkɒn.siˈeəʒ, ˌkɔːn-, ˌkɔ̃ːn-, ˈ--- US koʊnˈsjerʒ, kɑːn-, -siˈerʒ **-s** -ɪz
concili|ate kənˈsɪl.i|.eɪt **-ates** -eɪts **-ating** -eɪ.tɪŋ US -eɪ.t̬ɪŋ **-ated** -eɪ.tɪd US -eɪ.t̬ɪd
conciliation kənˌsɪl.iˈeɪ.ʃᵊn
conciliative kənˈsɪl.i.ə.tɪv, -eɪ- US -eɪ.t̬ɪv
conciliator kənˈsɪl.i.eɪ.təʳ US -t̬ɚ **-s** -z
conciliatory kənˈsɪl.i.ə.tᵊr.i, -eɪ-, -tri; kənˌsɪl.iˈeɪ- US kənˈsɪl.i.ə.tɔːr.i
concis|e kənˈsaɪs **-er** -əʳ US -ɚ **-est** -ɪst, -əst **-ely** -li **-eness** -nəs, -nɪs
concision kənˈsɪʒ.ᵊn **-s** -z
conclave ˈkɒŋ.kleɪv, ˈkɒn- US ˈkɑːn- **-s** -z
conclud|e kənˈkluːd, kəŋ- US kən- **-es** -z **-ing** -ɪŋ **-ed** -ɪd
conclusion kənˈkluː.ʒᵊn, kəŋ- US kən- **-s** -z
conclusive kənˈkluː.sɪv, kəŋ- US kən- **-ly** -li **-ness** -nəs, -nɪs
concoct kənˈkɒkt, kəŋ- US kənˈkɑːkt **-s** -s **-ing** -ɪŋ **-ed** -ɪd **-er/s** -əʳ/z US -ɚ/z
concoction kənˈkɒk.ʃᵊn, kəŋ- US kənˈkɑːk- **-s** -z
concomitan|ce kənˈkɒm.ɪ.tᵊnt|s, kəŋ-, ˈ-ə- US kənˈkɑː.mə.t̬ᵊnt|s **-cy** -si
concomitant kənˈkɒm.ɪ.tᵊnt, kəŋ-, ˈ-ə- US kənˈkɑː.mə.t̬ᵊnt **-ly** -li
concord (*n.*) ˈkɒŋ.kɔːd, ˈkɒn- US ˈkɑːn.kɔːrd, ˈkɑːŋ-, ˈkɔːŋ- **-s** -z
concord (*v.*) kənˈkɔːd, kəŋ- US kənˈkɔːrd **-s** -z **-ing** -ɪŋ **-ed** -ɪd
Concord *place in the US, type of grape:* ˈkɒŋ.kəd US ˈkɑːŋ.kɚd
concordanc|e kənˈkɔː.dᵊnts, kəŋ- US kənˈkɔːr- **-es** -ɪz **-ing** -ɪŋ **-ed** -d
concordant kənˈkɔː.dᵊnt, kəŋ- US kənˈkɔːr- **-ly** -li
concordat kɒnˈkɔː.dæt, kɒŋ-, kən-, kəŋ- US kənˈkɔːr- **-s** -s
Concorde ˈkɒŋ.kɔːd, ˈkɒn- US ˈkɑːn.kɔːrd, ˈkɑːŋ- **-s** -z
concours|e ˈkɒŋ.kɔːs, ˈkɒn-, -kʊəs US ˈkɑːn.kɔːrs **-es** -ɪz
concrete (*n. adj.*) ˈkɒŋ.kriːt, ˈkɒn- US ˈkɑːn- **ˌconcrete ˈjungle**
con|crete (*v.*) *cover with concrete:* ˈkɒŋ|.kriːt, ˈkɒn- US ˈkɑːn- **-cretes** -kriːts **-creting** -kriː.tɪŋ US -t̬ɪŋ **-creted** -kriː.tɪd US -kriː.t̬ɪd
con|crete (*v.*) *solidify:* kən|ˈkriːt, kəŋ- US kən- **-cretes** -ˈkriːts **-creting** -ˈkriː.tɪŋ US -ˈkriː.t̬ɪŋ **-creted** -ˈkriː.tɪd US -ˈkriː.t̬ɪd
concrete|ly kɒŋˈkriːt|.li, kɒn- US kɑːn- **-ness** -nəs, -nɪs
concretion kənˈkriː.ʃᵊn, kəŋ-, kɒn- US kən-, kɑːn- **-s** -z
concretiz|e, -is|e ˈkɒŋ.kriː.taɪz, ˈkɒn-, -krɪ- US ˈkɑːn.kriː-, kɑːnˈkriː.taɪz, kɑːŋ- **-es** -ɪz **-ing** -ɪŋ **-ed** -d
concubinage kɒnˈkjuː.bɪ.nɪdʒ, kɒŋ-, kən-, kəŋ- US kənˈkjuː.bə-, kɑːn-
concubine ˈkɒŋ.kjʊ.baɪn, ˈkɒn-, -kjə- US ˈkɑːŋ-, ˈkɑːn- **-s** -z
concupiscen|ce kənˈkjuː.pɪ.sᵊn|ts, kəŋ-, ˌkɒn-, ˌkɒŋ- US kɑːn-, kənˈkjuː.pə- **-t** -t
concur kənˈkɜːʳ, kəŋ- US -ˈkɝː **-s** -z **-ring** -ɪŋ **-red** -d
concurren|ce kənˈkʌr.ᵊnt|s, kəŋ- US kən- **-cy** -si
concurrent kənˈkʌr.ᵊnt, kəŋ- US kən- **-ly** -li
concuss kənˈkʌs, kəŋ- US kən- **-es** -ɪz **-ing** -ɪŋ **-ed** -t
concussion kənˈkʌʃ.ᵊn, kəŋ- US kən- **-s** -z
condemn kənˈdem **-s** -z **-ing** -ɪŋ **-ed** -d **-able** -nə.bl̩
condemnation ˌkɒn.demˈneɪ.ʃᵊn, -dəmˈ- US ˌkɑːn- **-s** -z
condemnatory kənˈdem.nə.tᵊr.i, -tri; ˌkɒn.demˈneɪ-, -dəmˈ- US kənˈdem.nə.tɔːr.i
condensation ˌkɒn.denˈseɪ.ʃᵊn, -dənˈ- US ˌkɑːn- **-s** -z
condens|e kənˈdents **-es** -ɪz **-ing** -ɪŋ **-ed** -t **-able** -ə.bl̩ **conˌdensed ˈmilk**
condenser kənˈden.səʳ US -sɚ **-s** -z
condescend ˌkɒn.dɪˈsend, -dəˈ- US ˌkɑːn- **-s** -z **-ing** -ɪŋ **-ed** -ɪd
condescending ˌkɒn.dɪˈsen.dɪŋ, -dəˈ- US ˌkɑːn- **-ly** -li
condescension ˌkɒn.dɪˈsen.ʃᵊn, -dəˈ- US ˌkɑːn-
condign kənˈdaɪn, kɒn- US kənˈdaɪn, ˈkɑːn.daɪn **-ly** -li **-ness** -nəs, -nɪs
condiment ˈkɒn.dɪ.mənt US ˈkɑːn.də- **-s** -s
condition kənˈdɪʃ.ᵊn **-s** -z **-ing** -ɪŋ **-ed** -d
conditional kənˈdɪʃ.ᵊn.ᵊl, ˈ-nᵊl **-ly** -i
conditioner kənˈdɪʃ.ᵊn.əʳ, ˈ-nəʳ US ˈ-ᵊn.ɚ, ˈ-nɚ **-s** -z
condo ˈkɒn.dəʊ US ˈkɑːn.doʊ **-s** -z
condol|e kənˈdəʊl US -ˈdoʊl **-es** -z **-ing** -ɪŋ **-ed** -d **-ement/s** -mənt/s
condolenc|e kənˈdəʊ.lənts US -ˈdoʊ- **-es** -ɪz
condolent kənˈdəʊ.lənt US -ˈdoʊ-
condom ˈkɒn.dɒm, -dəm US ˈkɑːn.dəm, ˈkʌn- **-s** -z
condominium ˌkɒn.dəˈmɪn.i.əm US ˌkɑːn.dəˈ- **-s** -z
Condon ˈkɒn.dən US ˈkɑːn-
condonation ˌkɒn.dəʊˈneɪ.ʃᵊn US ˌkɑːn.doʊˈ- **-s** -z
condon|e kənˈdəʊn US -ˈdoʊn **-es** -z **-ing** -ɪŋ **-ed** -d
condor **(C)** ˈkɒn.dɔːʳ, -dəʳ US ˈkɑːn.dɚ, -dɔːr **-s** -z
conduc|e kənˈdjuːs US -ˈduːs, -ˈdjuːs **-es** -ɪz **-ing** -ɪŋ **-ed** -t **-ement/s** -mənt/s
conducive kənˈdjuː.sɪv US -ˈduː-, -ˈdjuː- **-ly** -li **-ness** -nəs, -nɪs
conduct (*n.*) ˈkɒn.dʌkt, -dəkt US ˈkɑːn- **-s** -s
conduct (*v.*) kənˈdʌkt **-s** -s **-ing** -ɪŋ **-ed** -ɪd
conductance kənˈdʌk.tᵊnts
conductibility kənˌdʌk.təˈbɪl.ə.ti, -tɪˈ-, -ɪ.ti US -ə.t̬i
conductible kənˈdʌk.tə.bl̩, -tɪ-
conduction kənˈdʌk.ʃᵊn
conductive kənˈdʌk.tɪv
conductivity ˌkɒn.dʌkˈtɪv.ə.ti, -dəkˈ-, -ɪ.ti US ˌkɑːn.dʌkˈtɪv.ə.t̬i
conductor kənˈdʌk.təʳ US -t̬ɚ **-s** -z
conductress kənˈdʌk.trəs, -trɪs **-es** -ɪz
conduit ˈkɒn.dju.ɪt, ˈkʌn-, -du-, -dʒu-, -dɪt US ˈkɑːn.du.ɪt, -dɪt **-s** -s
Conduit *street:* ˈkɒn.dɪt, ˈkʌn- US ˈkɑːn-
Condy ˈkɒn.di US ˈkɑːn-
condyle ˈkɒn.dɪl, -daɪl US ˈkɑːn- **-s** -z
cone kəʊn US koʊn **-s** -z
Conestoga ˌkɒn.əˈstəʊ.gə US ˌkɑː.nəˈstoʊ- **Conesˈtoga ˌwagon**
coney **(C)** ˈkəʊ.ni US ˈkoʊ- **-s** -z **ˌConey ˈIsland** *stress shift:* ˌConey Island ˈresident
confab ˈkɒn.fæb; kɒnˈfæb, kən- US ˈkɑːn.fæb **-s** -z
confabu|late kənˈfæb.jʊ|.leɪt, kɒn- US kənˈfæb.jə- **-lates** -leɪts **-lating** -leɪ.tɪŋ US -leɪ.t̬ɪŋ **-lated** -leɪ.tɪd US -leɪ.t̬ɪd

confabulation kənˌfæb.jʊˈleɪ.ʃən, kɒn- (US) kənˌfæb.jəˈ- **-s** -z

confect (*n.*) ˈkɒn.fekt (US) ˈkɑːn- **-s** -s

confect (*v.*) kənˈfekt **-s** -s **-ing** -ɪŋ **-ed** -ɪd

confection kənˈfek.ʃən **-s** -z **-ing** -ɪŋ **-ed** -d **-er/s** -əʳ/z (US) -ɚ/z

confectionery kənˈfek.ʃən.ər.i, -ʃən.ri (US) -er-

confederac|y (C) kənˈfed.ər.ə.s|i **-ies** -iz

confederate (C) (*n. adj.*) kənˈfed.ər.ət, -ɪt **-s** -s

confede|rate (*v.*) kənˈfed.ər|.reɪt **-rates** -reɪts **-rating** -reɪ.tɪŋ (US) -reɪ.t̬ɪŋ **-rated** -reɪ.tɪd (US) -reɪ.t̬ɪd

confederation kənˌfed.əˈreɪ.ʃən **-s** -z

confer kənˈfɜːʳ (US) -ˈfɝː **-s** -z **-ring** -ɪŋ **-red** -d **-rable** -ə.bl̩ **-ment** -mənt

conferenc|e ˈkɒn.fər.əntˢ (US) ˈkɑːn.fɚ- **-es** -ɪz **-ing** -ɪŋ

conferral kənˈfɜː.rəl (US) -ˈfɝː.əl **-s** -z

confess kənˈfes **-es** -ɪz **-ing** -ɪŋ **-ed** -t **-edly** -ɪd.li

Confessio Amantis kɒnˌfes.i.əʊ.əˈmæn.tɪs, kən- (US) kɑːnˌfes.i.oʊ.əˈmɑːn-

confession kənˈfeʃ.ən **-s** -z

confessional kənˈfeʃ.ən.əl, ˈ-nəl **-s** -z

confessor kənˈfes.əʳ, kɒn- (US) kənˈfes.ɚ **-s** -z

Note: In British English, may also be pronounced /kɒnˈfes.ɔːʳ/ in the sense of "Father Confessor".

confetti kənˈfet.i, kɒn- (US) kənˈfet̬-

confidant(e) ˈkɒn.fɪ.dænt, -fə-, -dənt; ˌkɒn.fɪˈdænt, -ˈdɑːnt (US) ˈkɑːn.fə.dænt, -dɑːnt, ˌ--ˈ- **-s** -s

confid|e kənˈfaɪd **-es** -z **-ing/ly** -ɪŋ/li **-ed** -ɪd **-er/s** -əʳ/z (US) -ɚ/z

confidenc|e ˈkɒn.fɪ.dəntˢ, -fə- (US) ˈkɑːn.fə- **-es** -ɪz

confident ˈkɒn.fɪ.dənt, -fə- (US) ˈkɑːn.fə- **-ly** -li

confidential ˌkɒn.fɪˈden.*t*ʃəl (US) ˌkɑːn.fəˈden*t*.ʃəl **-ly** -i

confidentiality ˌkɒn.fɪ.den.*t*ʃiˈæl.ə.ti, -fə-, -ɪ.ti (US) ˌkɑːn.fə.den*t*.ʃiˈæl.ə.t̬i

configuration kənˌfɪɡ.əˈreɪ.ʃən, ˌkɒn.fɪɡ-, -jəˈ- (US) kənˌfɪɡ.jəˈ- **-s** -z

config|ure kənˈfɪɡ|.əʳ, -j|əʳ (US) -j|ɚ **-ures** -əz (US) -ɚz **-uring** -ər.ɪŋ **-ured** -əd (US) -ɚd

confine (*n.*) ˈkɒn.faɪn (US) ˈkɑːn- **-s** -z

confin|e (*v.*) kənˈfaɪn **-es** -z **-ing** -ɪŋ **-ed** -d

confinement kənˈfaɪn.mənt **-s** -s

confirm kənˈfɜːm (US) -ˈfɝːm **-s** -z **-ing** -ɪŋ **-ed** -d **-er/s** -əʳ/z (US) -ɚ/z

confirmation ˌkɒn.fəˈmeɪ.ʃən (US) ˌkɑːn.fɚˈ- **-s** -z

confirma|tive kənˈfɜː.mə|.tɪv (US) -ˈfɝː.mə|.t̬ɪv **-tory** -tər.i, -tri (US) -tɔːr.i

confi|scate ˈkɒn.fɪ|.skeɪt, -fə- (US) ˈkɑːn.fə-, -fɪ- **-scates** -skeɪts **-scating** -skeɪ.tɪŋ (US) -skeɪ.t̬ɪŋ **-scated** -skeɪ.tɪd (US) -skeɪ.t̬ɪd **-scator/s** -skeɪ.təʳ/z (US) -skeɪ.t̬ɚ/z

confiscation ˌkɒn.fɪˈskeɪ.ʃən, -fəˈ- (US) ˌkɑːn.fəˈ-, -fɪ- **-s** -z

confiscatory kənˈfɪs.kə.tər.i, kɒn-, -tri; ˌkɒn.fɪˈskeɪ-, -fəˈ-, ˈkɒn.fɪ.skeɪ-, -fə- (US) kənˈfɪs.kə.tɔːr.i

confit kɒnˈfiː (US) koʊn-, kɔ̃ːn- **-s** -z

confiteor (C) kɒnˈfɪt.i.ɔːʳ, kən-, ˈ-eɪ- (US) kənˈfɪt̬.i.ɔːr, -ˈfiː.t̬i- **-s** -z

confiture ˈkɒn.fɪ.tjʊəʳ, -tjɔːʳ (US) ˈkɑːn.fə.tʃʊr **-s** -z

conflagration ˌkɒn.fləˈɡreɪ.ʃən (US) ˌkɑːn- **-s** -z

con|flate kən|ˈfleɪt, kɒn- (US) kən- **-flates** -ˈfleɪts **-flating** -ˈfleɪ.tɪŋ (US) -ˈfleɪ.t̬ɪŋ **-flated** -ˈfleɪ.tɪd (US) -ˈfleɪ.t̬ɪd

conflation kənˈfleɪ.ʃən, kɒn- (US) kən-

conflict (*n.*) ˈkɒn.flɪkt (US) ˈkɑːn- **-s** -s

conflict (*v.*) kənˈflɪkt **-s** -s **-ing** -ɪŋ **-ed** -ɪd

confluenc|e ˈkɒn.flu.əntˢ (US) ˈkɑːn- **-es** -ɪz

confluent ˈkɒn.flu.ənt (US) ˈkɑːn- **-s** -s **-ly** -li

conform kənˈfɔːm (US) -ˈfɔːrm **-s** -z **-ing** -ɪŋ **-ed** -d **-er/s** -əʳ/z (US) -ɚ/z

conformability kənˌfɔː.məˈbɪl.ə.ti, -ɪ.ti (US) -ˌfɔːr.məˈbɪl.ə.t̬i

conformab|le kənˈfɔː.mə.bl|̩ (US) -ˈfɔːr- **-ly** -li

conformation ˌkɒn.fɔːˈmeɪ.ʃən, -fəˈ- (US) ˌkɑːn.fɚˈ-, -fɔːrˈ- **-s** -z

conformist kənˈfɔː.mɪst (US) -ˈfɔːr- **-s** -s

conformit|y kənˈfɔː.mə.t|i, -ɪ.t|i (US) -ˈfɔːr.mə.t̬|i **-ies** -iz

confound kənˈfaʊnd, ˌkɒn- (US) kən-, ˌkɑːn- **-s** -z **-ing** -ɪŋ **-ed/ly** -ɪd/li

confraternit|y ˌkɒn.frəˈtɜː.nə.t|i, -nɪ- (US) ˌkɑːn.frəˈtɝː.nə.t̬|i **-ies** -iz

confrère ˈkɒn.freəʳ (US) kɑːnˈfrer **-s** -z

con|front kən|ˈfrʌnt **-fronts** -ˈfrʌnts **-fronting** -ˈfrʌn.tɪŋ (US) -ˈfrʌn.t̬ɪŋ **-fronted** -ˈfrʌn.tɪd (US) -ˈfrʌn.t̬ɪd

confrontation ˌkɒn.frʌnˈteɪ.ʃən, -frənˈ- (US) ˌkɑːn.frənˈ- **-s** -z

confrontational ˌkɒn.frʌnˈteɪ.ʃən.əl, -frənˈ-, -ˈteɪʃ.nəl (US) ˌkɑːn.frənˈ- **-ly** -i

Confucian kənˈfjuː.ʃən **-s** -z

Confucian|ism kənˈfjuː.ʃən|ɪ.zəm **-ist/s** -ɪst/s

confus|e kənˈfjuːz **-es** -ɪz **-ing/ly** -ɪŋ/li **-ed** -d **-edly** -ɪd.li, -d.li **-edness** -ɪd.nəs, -d.nəs, -nɪs

confusing kənˈfjuː.zɪŋ **-ly** -li

confusion kənˈfjuː.ʒən **-s** -z

confutable kənˈfjuː.tə.bl̩ (US) -t̬ə-

confutation ˌkɒn.fjʊˈteɪ.ʃən (US) ˌkɑːn.fjuːˈ- **-s** -z

con|fute kən|ˈfjuːt **-futes** -ˈfjuːts **-futing** -ˈfjuː.tɪŋ (US) -ˈfjuː.t̬ɪŋ **-futed** -ˈfjuː.tɪd (US) -ˈfjuː.t̬ɪd

conga ˈkɒŋ.ɡə (US) ˈkɑːŋ-, ˈkɔːŋ- **-s** -z

congé ˈkɔ̃ː*n*.ʒeɪ, ˈkɔːn-, ˈkɒn- (US) koʊnˈʒeɪ, kɑːn-, ˈ-- **-s** -z

congeal kənˈdʒiːl **-s** -z **-ing** -ɪŋ **-ed** -d **-able** -ə.bl̩

congee ˈkɒn.dʒiː (US) ˈkɑːn- **-s** -z

congelation ˌkɒn.dʒɪˈleɪ.ʃən, -dʒəˈ- (US) ˌkɑːn.dʒəˈ-

congener kənˈdʒiː.nəʳ; ˈkɒn.dʒɪ-, -dʒə- (US) ˈkɑːn.dʒən.ɚ; kənˈdʒiː.nɚ **-s** -z

congenial kənˈdʒiː.ni.əl (US) ˈ-njəl, ˈ-ni.əl **-ly** -i

congeniality kənˌdʒiː.niˈæl.ə.ti, -ɪ.ti (US) -ə.t̬i

congenital kənˈdʒen.ɪ.təl (US) -ə.t̬əl **-ly** -i

conger ˈkɒŋ.ɡəʳ (US) ˈkɑːŋ.ɡɚ, ˈkɔːŋ- **-s** -z ˌconger ˈeel, ˈconger ˌeel

congeries ˈkɒn.dʒər.iːz, -ɪz; kənˈdʒɪə.riːz, -rɪz (US) ˈkɑːn.dʒə.riːz

congest kənˈdʒest **-s** -s **-ing** -ɪŋ **-ed** -ɪd **-ive** -ɪv

congestion kənˈdʒes.tʃən, -ˈdʒeʃ- **-s** -z

Congleton ˈkɒŋ.ɡl̩.tən (US) ˈkɑːŋ-, ˈkɔːŋ-

conglo|bate ˈkɒŋ.ɡləʊ|.beɪt, ˈkɒn- (US) kənˈɡloʊ|.beɪt; ˈkɑːŋ.ɡloʊ-, ˈkɔːŋ- **-bates** -beɪts **-bating** -beɪ.tɪŋ (US) -beɪ.t̬ɪŋ **-bated** -beɪ.tɪd (US) -beɪ.t̬ɪd

conglobation ˌkɒn.ɡləʊˈbeɪ.ʃən, ˌkɒŋ- (US) ˌkɑːn.ɡloʊˈ-, kɑːŋ-, ˌkɔːŋ-

conglomerate (*n. adj.*) kənˈɡlɒm.ər.ət, kəŋ-, kɒn-, -eɪt, -ɪt (US) kənˈɡlɑː.mɚ- **-s** -s

conglomer|ate (*v.*) kənˈɡlɒm.ər|.eɪt, kəŋ-, kɒn- (US) kənˈɡlɑː.mə.r|eɪt **-ates** -eɪts **-ating** -eɪ.tɪŋ (US) -eɪ.t̬ɪŋ **-ated** -eɪ.tɪd (US) -eɪ.t̬ɪd

conglomeration kənˌɡlɒm.əˈreɪ.ʃən, kəŋ-, kɒn-, ˌkɒn.ɡlɒm-, ˌkɒŋ.ɡlɒm- (US) kənˌɡlɑː.məˈ- **-s** -z

Congo ˈkɒŋ.ɡəʊ (US) ˈkɑːŋ.ɡoʊ, ˈkɔːŋ-

Congolese ˌkɒŋ.ɡəʊˈliːz (US) ˌkɑːŋ.ɡəˈ-, ˌkɔːŋ-, -ˈliːs

congratu|late kənˈɡrætʃ.ʊ|.leɪt, kəŋ-, -ˈɡræt.jʊ-, -jə- (US) -ˈɡrætʃ.ə-, -ˈɡrædʒ-, ˈ-ʊ- **-lates** -leɪts **-lating** -leɪ.tɪŋ (US) -leɪ.t̬ɪŋ **-lated** -leɪ.tɪd (US) -leɪ.t̬ɪd **-lator/s** -leɪ.təʳ/z (US) -leɪ.t̬ɚ/z

congratulation kənˌɡrætʃ.ʊˈleɪ.ʃən, kəŋ-, -ˌɡræt.jʊˈ-, -jəˈ- (US) -ˌɡrætʃ.əˈ-, -ˌɡrædʒ-, -ʊˈ- **-s** -z

congratulatory kənˌɡrætʃ.ʊˈleɪ.tər.i, kəŋ-, -ˌɡræt.jʊˈ-, -jəˈ-, -tri; kənˈɡrætʃ.əl.ə- (US) kənˈɡrætʃ.əl.ə.tɔːr.i, -ˈɡrædʒ-

Connected speech phenomena

The processes which result in words being pronounced differently from their dictionary form when they occur in close contact with other words.

Examples for English

In natural speech we rarely leave gaps between words, and we can observe many processes that result in differences between isolated words and the same words occurring in connected speech: examples are ASSIMILATION and ELISION, e.g.:

(assimilation) one boy /wʌn bɔɪ/ → /wʌm bɔɪ/

(elision) last time /lɑːst taɪm/ → /lɑːs taɪm/
(US) /læst taɪm/ (US) /læs taɪm/

The study of connected speech also involves looking at the process of VOWEL REDUCTION in weak syllables (see also WEAK FORM), at RHYTHM and at prosodic phenomena such as INTONATION and STRESS.

congre|gate ˈkɒŋ.grɪ|.geɪt, -grə- (US) ˈkɑːŋ-, ˈkɔːŋ- **-gates** -geɪts **-gating** -geɪ.tɪŋ (US) -geɪ.t̬ɪŋ **-gated** -geɪ.tɪd (US) -geɪ.t̬ɪd
congregation ˌkɒŋ.grɪˈgeɪ.ʃᵊn, -grəˈ- (US) ˌkɑːŋ-, ˌkɔːŋ- **-s** -z
congregational (C) ˌkɒŋ.grɪˈgeɪ.ʃᵊn.ᵊl, -grəˈ-, -ˈgeɪʃ.nᵊl (US) ˌkɑːŋ-, ˌkɔːŋ- **-ism** -ɪ.zᵊm **-ist/s** -ɪst/s
Congresbury ˈkɒŋz.bri, ˈkuːmz.bᵊr.i (US) ˈkɑːŋz.ber-, ˈkɔːŋz-, ˈkuːmz-, -bɚ-
congress (C) ˈkɒŋ.gres (US) ˈkɑːŋ-, ˈkɔːŋ-, -grəs **-es** -ɪz
congressional (C) kənˈgreʃ.ᵊn.ᵊl, kəŋ-, kɒŋ-, ˈ-nᵊl (US) kəŋ-
congress|man ˈkɒŋ.gres|.mən (US) ˈkɑːŋ-, ˈkɔːŋ-, -grəs- **-men** -mən, -men
congress|woman ˈkɒŋ.gres|ˌwʊm.ən (US) ˈkɑːŋ-, ˈkɔːŋ-, -grəs- **-women** -ˌwɪm.ɪn
Congreve ˈkɒŋ.griːv (US) ˈkɑːn-, ˈkɑːŋ-
congruenc|e ˈkɒŋ.gru.ənts (US) ˈkɑːŋ-, ˈkɔːŋ-, kənˈgruː- **-es** -ɪz **-y** -i **-ies** -iz
congruent ˈkɒŋ.gru.ənt (US) ˈkɑːŋ-; kənˈgruː- **-ly** -li
congruit|y kɒŋˈgruː.ə.t|i, kən-, kəŋ-, -ɪ.t|i (US) kɑːnˈgruː.ə.t̬|i, kən- **-ies** -iz
congruous ˈkɒŋ.gru.əs (US) ˈkɑːŋ-, ˈkɔːŋ- **-ly** -li **-ness** -nəs, -nɪs
conic ˈkɒn.ɪk (US) ˈkɑː.nɪk **-s** -s
conical ˈkɒn.ɪ.kᵊl (US) ˈkɑː.nɪ- **-ly** -i **-ness** -nəs, -nɪs
conifer ˈkɒn.ɪ.fəʳ, ˈkəʊ.nɪ-, -nə- (US) ˈkɑː.nə.fɚ, ˈkoʊ- **-s** -z
coniferous kəʊˈnɪf.ᵊr.əs, kɒnˈɪf- (US) koʊˈnɪf-, kə-
coniform ˈkəʊ.nɪ.fɔːm (US) ˈkoʊ.nɪ.fɔːrm
Coningham ˈkʌn.ɪŋ.əm (US) -hæm
Coningsby ˈkɒn.ɪŋz.bi, ˈkʌn- (US) ˈkʌn-
Conisbrough ˈkɒn.ɪs.brə, ˈkʌn- (US) ˈkɑː.nɪs.bɚ.oʊ
Coniston ˈkɒn.ɪ.stᵊn (US) ˈkɑː.nɪ-
conjecturable kənˈdʒek.tʃᵊr.ə.bl̩
conjectural kənˈdʒek.tʃᵊr.ᵊl **-ly** -i
conject|ure kənˈdʒek.tʃ|əʳ (US) -tʃ|ɚ **-ures** -əz (US) -ɚz **-uring** -ᵊr.ɪŋ **-ured** -əd (US) -ɚd
conjoin kənˈdʒɔɪn, kɒn- (US) kən- **-s** -z **-ing** -ɪŋ **-ed** -d
conjoint kənˈdʒɔɪnt, kɒn- (US) kən- **-ly** -li
conjugal ˈkɒn.dʒʊ.gᵊl, -dʒə- (US) ˈkɑːn.dʒə- **-ly** -i ˌ**conjugal** ˈ**rights**
conjugality ˌkɒn.dʒʊˈgæl.ə.ti, -ɪ.ti (US) ˌkɑːn.dʒəˈgæl.ə.t̬i
conjugate (*n. adj*) ˈkɒn.dʒʊ.gət, -dʒə-, -gɪt, -geɪt (US) ˈkɑːn.dʒə- **-s** -s
conju|gate (*v.*) ˈkɒn.dʒʊ|.geɪt, -dʒə- (US) ˈkɑːn.dʒə- **-gates** -geɪts **-gating** -geɪ.tɪŋ (US) -geɪ.t̬ɪŋ **-gated** -geɪ.tɪd (US) -geɪ.t̬ɪd
conjugation ˌkɒn.dʒʊˈgeɪ.ʃᵊn, -dʒəˈ- (US) ˌkɑːn.dʒəˈ- **-s** -z
conjunct (*n.*) ˈkɒn.dʒʌŋ*k*t (US) ˈkɑːn- **-s** -s
conjunct (*adj.*) kənˈdʒʌŋ*k*t, kɒn- (US) kən-; ˈkɑːn.dʒʌŋ*k*t **-ly** -li
conjunction kənˈdʒʌŋk.ʃᵊn **-s** -z
conjunctiva ˌkɒn.dʒʌŋ*k*ˈtaɪ.və (US) ˌkɑːn.dʒəŋˈ-
conjunctive kənˈdʒʌŋ*k*.tɪv **-ly** -li
conjunctivitis kənˌdʒʌŋ*k*.tɪˈvaɪ.tɪs, -təˈ- (US) -təˈvaɪ.t̬ɪs
conjuncture kənˈdʒʌŋ*k*.tʃəʳ (US) -tʃɚ **-s** -z
conjuration ˌkɒn.dʒʊəˈreɪ.ʃᵊn (US) ˌkɑːn.dʒʊˈreɪ- **-s** -z
conjur|e *charge solemnly:* kənˈdʒʊəʳ (US) -ˈdʒʊr **-es** -z **-ing** -ɪŋ **-ed** -d
conj|ure *summon by magic:* ˈkʌn.dʒ|əʳ (US) -dʒ|ɚ **-ures** -əz (US) -ɚz **-uring** -ᵊr.ɪŋ **-ured** -əd (US) -ɚd **-urer/s** -ᵊr.əʳ/z (US) -ɚ.ɚ/z **-uror/s** -ᵊr.əʳ/z (US) -ɚ.ɚ/z ˈ**conjuring** ˌ**trick**
conk kɒŋk (US) kɑːŋk, kɔːŋk **-s** -s **-ing** -ɪŋ **-ed** -t
conker ˈkɒŋ.kəʳ (US) ˈkɑːŋ.kɚ, ˈkɔːŋ- **-s** -z
Conleth ˈkɒn.ləθ (US) ˈkɑːn-
Conley ˈkɒn.li (US) ˈkɑːn-
Conlon ˈkɒn.lən (US) ˈkɑːn-
con|man ˈkɒn|.mæn (US) ˈkɑːn- **-men** -men
Conn. (*abbrev. for* **Connaught**) ˈkɒn.ɔːt (US) ˈkɑː.nɑːt, -nɔːt
Conn. (*abbrev. for* **Connecticut**) kəˈnet.ɪ.kət (US) -ˈnet̬-, -kɪt
Connah's Quay ˌkɒn.əzˈkiː (US) ˌkɑː.nəzˈkiː, -ˈkeɪ, -ˈkweɪ
Connally ˈkɒn.ᵊl.i (US) ˈkɑː.nᵊl-
connate ˈkɒn.eɪt, -ˈ- (US) ˈkɑː.neɪt, -ˈ-
Connaught ˈkɒn.ɔːt (US) ˈkɑː.nɑːt, -nɔːt
connect kəˈnekt **-s** -s **-ing** -ɪŋ **-ed/ly** -ɪd/li **-able** -ə.bl̩ **-or/s** -əʳ/z (US) -ɚ/z
connectible kəˈnek.tə.bᵊl, -tɪ-
Connecticut kəˈnet.ɪ.kət (US) -ˈnet̬-, -kɪt
connection kəˈnek.ʃᵊn **-s** -z
connective kəˈnek.tɪv **-s** -z **-ly** -li
connectivity ˌkɒn.ekˈtɪv.ɪ.ti; kəˌnekˈ-, ˈ-ə- (US) ˌkɑː.nekˈtɪv.ə.t̬i
Connelly ˈkɒn.ᵊl.i (US) ˈkɑː.nᵊl-
Connemara ˌkɒn.ɪˈmɑː.rə, -əˈ- (US) ˌkɑː.nəˈ-
Conner ˈkɒn.əʳ (US) ˈkɑː.nɚ
Connery ˈkɒn.ᵊr.i (US) ˈkɑː.nɚ-
Connex® ˈkɒn.eks (US) ˈkɑː.neks
connexion kəˈnek.ʃᵊn **-s** -z
Connie ˈkɒn.i (US) ˈkɑː.ni
conning tower ˈkɒn.ɪŋˌtaʊəʳ (US) ˈkɑː.nɪŋˌtaʊɚ **-s** -z
conniption kəˈnɪp.ʃᵊn
connivance kəˈnaɪ.vᵊn*t*s
conniv|e kəˈnaɪv **-es** -z **-ing** -ɪŋ **-ed** -d **-er/s** -əʳ/z (US) -ɚ/z
connoisseur ˌkɒn.əˈsɜːʳ, -ɪˈ- (US) ˌkɑː.nəˈsɝː **-s** -z
Connolly ˈkɒn.ᵊl.i (US) ˈkɑː.nᵊl-
Connor ˈkɒn.əʳ (US) ˈkɑː.nɚ
conno|tate ˈkɒn.əʊ|.teɪt (US) ˈkɑː.nə- **-tates** -teɪts **-tating** -teɪ.tɪŋ (US) -teɪ.t̬ɪŋ **-tated** -teɪ.tɪd (US) -teɪ.t̬ɪd
connotation ˌkɒn.əʊˈteɪ.ʃᵊn (US) ˌkɑː.nəˈ- **-s** -z

connotative 'kɒn.əʊ.teɪ.tɪv; kə'nəʊ.tə- ⓤⓢ kə'noʊ.t̬ə.t̬ɪv, 'kɑː.nə.teɪ-
connot|e kə'nəʊt, kɒn'əʊt ⓤⓢ kə'noʊt **-es** -s **-ing** -ɪŋ ⓤⓢ kə'noʊ.t̬ɪŋ **-ed** -ɪd ⓤⓢ kə'noʊ.t̬ɪd
connubial kə'njuː.bi.əl, kɒn'juː- ⓤⓢ kə'nuː-, -'njuː- **-ly** -i
connubiality kəˌnjuː.bi'æl.ə.ti, kɒnˌjuː-, -ɪ.ti ⓤⓢ kəˌnuː.bi'æl.ə.t̬i, -ˌnjuː-
conoid 'kəʊ.nɔɪd ⓤⓢ 'koʊ- **-s** -z
conoidal kəʊ'nɔɪ.dᵊl ⓤⓢ koʊ-
Conolly 'kɒn.ᵊl.i ⓤⓢ 'kɑː.nᵊl-
Conor 'kɒn.əʳ ⓤⓢ 'kɑː.nɚ
conqu|er 'kɒŋ.k|əʳ ⓤⓢ 'kɑːŋ.k|ɚ, 'kɔːŋ- **-ers** -əz ⓤⓢ -ɚz **-ering** -ᵊr.ɪŋ **-ered** -əd ⓤⓢ -ɚd **-erable** -ᵊr.ə.bl̩
conqueror 'kɒŋ.kᵊr.əʳ ⓤⓢ 'kɑːŋ.kɚ.ɚ, 'kɔːŋ- **-s** -z
conquest (C) 'kɒŋ.kwest ⓤⓢ 'kɑːn-, 'kɑːŋ- **-s** -s
conquistador kɒn'kɪs.tə.dɔːʳ, kɒŋ-, -'kwɪs-; ˌkɒn.kɪ.stə'dɔːʳ, kɒŋ-, -kwɪ- ⓤⓢ kɑːŋ'kiː.stə.dɔːr, kɔːŋ-, kɑːn-, -'kwɪs.tə- **-s** -z
Conrad 'kɒn.ræd ⓤⓢ 'kɑːn-
Conran 'kɒn.rən, -ræn ⓤⓢ 'kɑːn-
Conroy 'kɒn.rɔɪ ⓤⓢ 'kɑːn-
consanguine kɒn'sæŋ.gwɪn ⓤⓢ kɑːn-
consanguineous ˌkɒn.sæŋ'gwɪn.i.əs ⓤⓢ ˌkɑːn.sæŋ'-
consanguinity ˌkɒn.sæŋ'gwɪn.ə.ti, -ɪ.ti ⓤⓢ ˌkɑːn.sæŋ'gwɪn.ə.t̬i
conscienc|e 'kɒn.tʃᵊnts ⓤⓢ 'kɑːn- **-es** -ɪz **'conscience-ˌstricken**
conscientious ˌkɒn.tʃi'en.tʃəs ⓤⓢ ˌkɑːn.tʃi'ent.ʃəs **-ly** -li **-ness** -nəs, -nɪs **consciˌentious ob'jector**
conscionab|le 'kɒn.tʃᵊn.ə.b|l̩ ⓤⓢ 'kɑːn- **-ly** -li **-leness** -l̩.nəs, -nɪs
conscious 'kɒn.tʃəs ⓤⓢ 'kɑːnt.ʃəs **-ly** -li **-ness** -nəs, -nɪs **'consciousness ˌraising**
conscrib|e kən'skraɪb **-es** -z **-ing** -ɪŋ **-ed** -d
conscript (*n.*) 'kɒn.skrɪpt ⓤⓢ 'kɑːn- **-s** -s
conscript (*v.*) kən'skrɪpt **-s** -s **-ing** -ɪŋ **-ed** -ɪd
conscription kən'skrɪp.ʃᵊn **-s** -z
conse|crate 'kɒnt.sɪ|.kreɪt, -sə- ⓤⓢ 'kɑːnt.sə- **-crates** -kreɪts **-crating** -kreɪ.tɪŋ ⓤⓢ -kreɪ.t̬ɪŋ **-crated** -kreɪ.tɪd ⓤⓢ -kreɪ.t̬ɪd **-crator/s** -kreɪ.təʳ/z ⓤⓢ -kreɪ.t̬ɚ/z
consecration ˌkɒnt.sɪ'kreɪ.ʃᵊn, -sə'- ⓤⓢ ˌkɑːnt.sə'- **-s** -z
consecutive kən'sek.jʊ.tɪv, -jə- ⓤⓢ -jə.t̬ɪv **-ly** -li **-ness** -nəs, -nɪs
consensual kən'sent.sju.ᵊl, kɒn-, -'sen.tʃu- ⓤⓢ kən'sent.ʃu-, '-ʃᵊl **-ly** -li
consensus kən'sent.səs, kɒn- ⓤⓢ kən-
con|sent kən|'sent **-sents** -'sents **-senting** -'sen.tɪŋ ⓤⓢ -'sen.t̬ɪŋ **-sented** -'sen.tɪd ⓤⓢ -'sen.t̬ɪd
consequenc|e 'kɒnt.sɪ.kwənts, -sə- ⓤⓢ 'kɑːnt- **-es** -ɪz
consequent 'kɒnt.sɪ.kwənt, -sə- ⓤⓢ 'kɑːnt- **-ly** -li
consequential ˌkɒnt.sɪ'kwen.tʃᵊl, -sə'- ⓤⓢ ˌkɑːnt- **-ly** -i
conservable kən'sɜː.və.bl̩ ⓤⓢ -'sɝː-
conservanc|y kən'sɜː.vᵊnt.s|i ⓤⓢ -'sɝː- **-ies** -iz
conservation ˌkɒnt.sə'veɪ.ʃᵊn ⓤⓢ ˌkɑːnt.sɚ'-
conservationist ˌkɒnt.sə'veɪ.ʃᵊn.ɪst ⓤⓢ ˌkɑːnt.sɚ'- **-s** -s
conservatism kən'sɜː.və.tɪ.zᵊm ⓤⓢ -'sɝː-
conservative (C) kən'sɜː.və.tɪv ⓤⓢ -'sɝː.və.t̬ɪv **-s** -z **-ly** -li **-ness** -nəs, -nɪs
conservatoire kən'sɜː.və.twɑːʳ, kɒn- ⓤⓢ kən'sɝː.və.twɑːr, -ˌsɝː.və'twɑːr **-s** -z
conservator *preserver:* 'kɒnt.sə.veɪ.təʳ ⓤⓢ 'kɑːnt.sɚ.veɪ.t̬ɚ **-s** -z
conservator *official guardian:* kən'sɜː.və.təʳ ⓤⓢ -'sɝː.və.t̬ɚ **-s** -z
conservator|y kən'sɜː.və.tr|i ⓤⓢ -'sɝː.və.tɔːr|.i **-ies** -iz
conserve (*n.*) kən'sɜːv; 'kɒn.sɜːv ⓤⓢ 'kɑːn.sɝːv **-s** -z
conserv|e (*v.*) kən'sɜːv ⓤⓢ -'sɝːv **-es** -z **-ing** -ɪŋ **-ed** -d
Consett 'kɒn.sɪt, -set, -sət ⓤⓢ 'kɑːn-
consid|er kən'sɪd|.əʳ ⓤⓢ -ɚ **-ers** -əz ⓤⓢ -ɚz **-ering** -ᵊr.ɪŋ **-ered** -əd ⓤⓢ -ɚd
considerab|le kən'sɪd.ᵊr.ə.b|l̩ **-ly** -li **-leness** -l̩.nəs, -nɪs
considerate kən'sɪd.ᵊr.ət, -ɪt **-ly** -li **-ness** -nəs, -nɪs
consideration kənˌsɪd.ᵊr'eɪ.ʃᵊn **-s** -z
consign kən'saɪn **-s** -z **-ing** -ɪŋ **-ed** -d **-er/s** -əʳ/z ⓤⓢ -ɚ/z **-able** -ə.bl̩
consignation ˌkɒn.saɪ'neɪ.ʃᵊn ⓤⓢ ˌkɑːn.sɪg'-, -sɪ'-
consignee ˌkɒn.saɪ'niː, -sɪ'- ⓤⓢ ˌkɑːn- **-s** -z
Consignia® kən'sɪg.ni.ə
consignment kən'saɪn.mənt, -'saɪm- ⓤⓢ -'saɪn- **-s** -s
consist kən'sɪst **-s** -s **-ing** -ɪŋ **-ed** -ɪd
consisten|ce kən'sɪs.tᵊnt|s **-cy** -si **-cies** -siz
consistent kən'sɪs.tᵊnt **-ly** -li
consistorial ˌkɒn.sɪ'stɔː.ri.əl ⓤⓢ ˌkɑːn.sɪ'stɔːr.i-
consistor|y kən'sɪs.tᵊr|.i, -tr|i ⓤⓢ -tɚ|.i **-ies** -iz
consolable kən'səʊ.lə.bl̩ ⓤⓢ -'soʊ-
consolation ˌkɒn.sə'leɪ.ʃᵊn ⓤⓢ ˌkɑːn- **-s** -z ˌ**conso'lation ˌprize**
consolatory kən'sɒl.ə.tᵊr.i, -'səʊ.lə-, -tri ⓤⓢ -'sɑː.lə.tɔːr.i, -'soʊ-
console (*n.*) 'kɒn.səʊl ⓤⓢ 'kɑːn.soʊl **-s** -z
consol|e (*v.*) kən'səʊl ⓤⓢ -'soʊl **-es** -z **-ing** -ɪŋ **-ed** -d **-er/s** -əʳ/z ⓤⓢ -ɚ/z
consoli|date kən'sɒl.ɪ|.deɪt, '-ə- ⓤⓢ -'sɑː.lə- **-dates** -deɪts **-dating** -deɪ.tɪŋ ⓤⓢ -deɪ.t̬ɪŋ **-dated** -deɪ.tɪd ⓤⓢ -deɪ.t̬ɪd **-dator/s** -deɪ.təʳ/z ⓤⓢ -deɪ.t̬ɚ/z **-dative** -deɪ.tɪv ⓤⓢ -deɪ.t̬ɪv
consolidation kənˌsɒl.ɪ'deɪ.ʃᵊn, -ə'- ⓤⓢ -ˌsɑː.lə'- **-s** -z
consols kən'sɒlz; 'kɒnt.sᵊlz ⓤⓢ 'kɑːn.sɑːlz; kən'sɑːlz
consommé kən'sɒm.eɪ, kɒn-; 'kɒnt.sə.meɪ ⓤⓢ ˌkɑːnt.sə'meɪ, '---
consonanc|e 'kɒnt.sᵊn.ənts ⓤⓢ 'kɑːnt- **-es** -ɪz
consonant 'kɒnt.sᵊn.ənt ⓤⓢ 'kɑːnt- **-s** -s **-ly** -li
consonantal ˌkɒnt.sᵊn'æn.tᵊl ⓤⓢ ˌkɑːnt.sə'næn.t̬ᵊl **-ly** -i
consort (*n.*) 'kɒn.sɔːt ⓤⓢ 'kɑːn.sɔːrt **-s** -s
con|sort (*v.*) kən|'sɔːt, kɒn- ⓤⓢ kən|'sɔːrt **-sorts** -'sɔːts ⓤⓢ -'sɔːrts **-sorting** -'sɔː.tɪŋ ⓤⓢ -'sɔːr.t̬ɪŋ **-sorted** -'sɔː.tɪd ⓤⓢ -'sɔːr.t̬ɪd
consorti|um kən'sɔː.ti|.əm, -ʃi-, '-ʃləm ⓤⓢ -'sɔːr.t̬i|.əm, -ʃi-, '-ʃləm **-ums** -əmz **-a** -ə
conspectus kən'spek.təs **-es** -ɪz
conspicuous kən'spɪk.ju.əs **-ly** -li **-ness** -nəs, -nɪs
conspirac|y kən'spɪr.ə.s|i **-ies** -iz **con'spiracy ˌtheory**
conspirator kən'spɪr.ə.təʳ, -ɪ.təʳ ⓤⓢ -ə.t̬ɚ **-s** -z
conspiratorial kənˌspɪr.ə'tɔː.ri.əl, kɒn- ⓤⓢ kənˌspɪr.ə'tɔːr.i-
conspir|e kən'spaɪəʳ ⓤⓢ -'spaɪɚ **-es** -z **-ing** -ɪŋ **-ed** -d **-er/s** -əʳ/z ⓤⓢ -ɚ/z
constable (C) 'kʌnt.stə.bl̩, 'kɒnt- ⓤⓢ 'kɑːnt-, 'kʌnt- **-s** -z
constabular|y kən'stæb.jʊ.lᵊr|.i, -jə- ⓤⓢ -jə.ler|.i **-ies** -iz
Constance 'kɒnt.stənts ⓤⓢ 'kɑːnt-
constancy 'kɒnt.stənt.si ⓤⓢ 'kɑːnt-
constant 'kɒnt.stənt ⓤⓢ 'kɑːnt- **-s** -s **-ly** -li **-ness** -nəs, -nɪs
Constanta kən'stæn.tə ⓤⓢ -t̬ə
Constantine *Kings and Emperors:* 'kɒnt.stᵊn.taɪn, -tiːn ⓤⓢ 'kɑːnt.stᵊn.tiːn, -taɪn *city:* 'kɒnt.stᵊn.taɪn, -tiːn ⓤⓢ 'kɑːnt-
Constantinople ˌkɒn.stæn.tɪ'nəʊ.pl̩ ⓤⓢ ˌkɑːn.stæn.tᵊn'oʊ-
constative kən'stæt.ɪv ⓤⓢ -'stæt̬-

Consonant

A speech sound which obstructs the flow of air though the vocal tract or a letter of the alphabet representing such a vowel.

Examples for English

There are many types of consonant, but what all have in common is that they obstruct the flow of air through the vocal tract. Some do this a lot, some not very much: those which make the maximum obstruction (i.e. PLOSIVES, which form a complete stoppage of the airstream) are the most consonantal, e.g.:

bat	/bæt/
keep	/kiːp/

NASAL consonants result in complete stoppage of the oral cavity but are less obstructive than plosives since air is allowed to escape through the nose, e.g.:

man	/mæn/
name	/neɪm/

FRICATIVES make a considerable obstruction to the flow of air, but not a total closure, e.g.:

sheaf	/ʃiːf/
south	/saʊθ/

The class of sounds called APPROXIMANTS comprises sounds which make very little obstruction of the flow of air.

The post-alveolar approximant that is the usual pronunciation of /r/ in BBC English involves no contact between the tongue and the palate, e.g.:

red	/red/	[ɹed]
arrive	/ə'raɪv/	[ə'ɹaɪv]

LATERAL approximants obstruct the flow of air only in the centre of the mouth, not at the sides, so obstruction is slight, e.g.:

lull	/lʌl/

Other sounds classed as approximants make so little obstruction to the flow of air that they could almost be thought to be vowels if they were in a different context. These are sometimes referred to as 'semi-vowels', e.g.:

you	/juː/
woo	/wuː/

Finally, AFFRICATES begin as plosives and are released as fricatives, with no intervening gap, e.g.:

church	/tʃɜːtʃ/	(US) /tʃɝːtʃ/
judge	/dʒʌdʒ/	

The above explanation is based on phonetic criteria. An alternative approach is to look at the *phonological* characteristics of consonants: for example, consonants are typically found at the beginning and end of syllables while vowels are typically found in the middle.

constellation ˌkɒn*t*.stə'leɪ.ʃᵊn, -stɪ'- (US) ˌkɑːn*t*- **-s** -z

conster|nate 'kɒn*t*.stə|.neɪt (US) 'kɑːn*t*.stɚ- **-nates** -neɪts **-nating** -neɪ.tɪŋ (US) -neɪ.t̬ɪŋ **-nated** -neɪ.tɪd (US) -neɪ.t̬ɪd

consternation ˌkɒn*t*.stə'neɪ.ʃᵊn (US) ˌkɑːn*t*.stɚ'-

consti|pate 'kɒn*t*.stɪ|.peɪt, -stə- (US) 'kɑːn*t*.stə- **-pates** -peɪts **-pating** -peɪ.tɪŋ (US) -peɪ.t̬ɪŋ **-pated** -peɪ.tɪd (US) -peɪ.t̬ɪd

constipation ˌkɒn*t*.stɪ'peɪ.ʃᵊn, -stə'- (US) ˌkɑːn*t*.stə'-

constituen|cy kən'stɪt.ju.ən*t*|.si, kɒn-, -'stɪtʃ.u- (US) kən'stɪtʃ.u- **-cies** -siz

constituent kən'stɪt.ju.ənt, kɒn-, -'stɪtʃ.u- (US) kən'stɪtʃ.u- **-s** -s

consti|tute 'kɒn*t*.stɪ|.tjuːt, -stə-, -tʃuːt (US) 'kɑːn*t*.stə|.tuːt, -tjuːt **-tutes** -tjuːts, -tʃuːts (US) -tuːts, -tjuːts **-tuting** -tjuː.tɪŋ, -tʃuː.tɪŋ (US) -tuː.t̬ɪŋ, -tjuː- **-tuted** -tjuː.tɪd, -tʃuː.tɪd (US) -tuː.t̬ɪd, -tjuː-

constitution ˌkɒn*t*.stɪ'tjuː.ʃᵊn, -stə'-, -'tʃuː- (US) ˌkɑːn*t*.stə'tuː-, -'tjuː- **-s** -z

constitutional ˌkɒn*t*.stɪ'tjuː.ʃᵊn.ᵊl, -stə'-, -'tʃuː-, -'tjuːʃ.nᵊl, -'tʃuːʃ- (US) ˌkɑːn*t*.stə'tuː-, -'tjuː-, -'tuːʃ.nᵊl, -'tjuːʃ- **-ly** -i

constitutional|ism ˌkɒn*t*.stɪ'tjuː.ʃᵊn.ᵊl|.ɪ.zᵊm, -stə'-, -'tʃuː- (US) ˌkɑːn*t*.stə'tuː-, -'tjuː- **-ist/s** -ɪst/s

constitutionaliz|e, -is|e ˌkɒn*t*.stɪ'tjuː.ʃᵊn.ᵊl.aɪz, -stə'-, -'tʃuː- (US) ˌkɑːn*t*.stə'tuː.ʃᵊn.ə.laɪz, -'tjuː- **-es** -ɪz **-ing** -ɪŋ **-ed** -d

constitutive kən'stɪt.jʊ.tɪv, kɒn-, -'stɪtʃ.ə-; 'kɒn*t*.stɪ.tjuː-, -stə-, -tʃuː- (US) 'kɑːn*t*.stə.tuː.t̬ɪv, -tjuː-; kən'stɪtʃ.ə-

constrain kən'streɪn **-s** -z **-ing** -ɪŋ **-ed** -d **-edly** -ɪd.li, -d.li **-able** -ə.bl̩

constraint kən'streɪnt **-s** -s

constrict kən'strɪkt **-s** -s **-ing** -ɪŋ **-ed** -ɪd **-or/s** -əʳ/z (US) -ɚ/z **-ive** -ɪv

constriction kən'strɪk.ʃᵊn **-s** -z

construct (*n.*) 'kɒn.strʌkt (US) 'kɑːn- **-s** -s

construct (*v.*) kən'strʌkt **-s** -s **-ing** -ɪŋ **-ed** -ɪd

construction kən'strʌk.ʃᵊn **-s** -z

constructional kən'strʌk.ʃᵊn.ᵊl **-ly** -i

constructionist kən'strʌk.ʃᵊn.ɪst **-s** -s

constructive kən'strʌk.tɪv **-ly** -li **-ness** -nəs, -nɪs

constructor kən'strʌk.təʳ (US) -tɚ **-s** -z

constru|e kən'struː, kɒn- (US) kən- **-es** -z **-ing** -ɪŋ **-ed** -d

consubstantial ˌkɒn.səb'stæn.*t*ʃᵊl, -'stɑːn- (US) ˌkɑːn.səb'stæn*t*.ʃᵊl **-ly** -i

consubstanti|ate ˌkɒn.səb'stæn.*t*ʃi|.eɪt, -'stɑːn-, -'stæn*t*.si-, -'stɑːn*t*.si- (US) ˌkɑːn.səb'stæn*t*.ʃi- **-ates** -eɪts **-ating** -eɪ.tɪŋ (US) -eɪ.t̬ɪŋ **-ated** -eɪ.tɪd (US) -eɪ.t̬ɪd

consubstantiation ˌkɒn.səbˌstæn.*t*ʃi'eɪ.ʃᵊn, -ˌstɑːn-, -ˌstæn*t*.si'-, -ˌstɑːn*t*.si'- (US) ˌkɑːn.səbˌstæn*t*.ʃi'-

consuetude 'kɒn*t*.swɪ.tjuːd, -tʃuːd (US) 'kɑːn*t*.swɪ.tuːd, -tjuːd

consuetudinary ˌkɒn*t*.swɪ'tjuː.dɪ.nᵊr.i (US) ˌkɑːn*t*.swɪ'tuː.dɪ.ner-, -'tjuː-

consul 'kɒn*t*.sᵊl (US) 'kɑːn*t*- **-s** -z **-ship/s** -ʃɪp/s

consular 'kɒn*t*.sjʊ.ləʳ, -sjə- (US) 'kɑːn*t*-

consulate 'kɒn*t*.sjʊ.lət, -sjə-, -lɪt (US) 'kɑːn*t*- **-s** -s

con|sult kən|'sʌlt **-sults** -'sʌlts **-sulting** -'sʌl.tɪŋ (US) -'sʌl.t̬ɪŋ **-sulted** -'sʌl.tɪd (US) -'sʌl.t̬ɪd

consultanc|y kən'sʌl.tᵊn*t*.s|i **-ies** -iz

consultant kənˈsʌl.tᵊnt **-s** -s
consultation ˌkɒn.sᵊlˈteɪ.ʃᵊn, -sʌlˈ- US ˌkɑːn- **-s** -z
consultative kənˈsʌl.tə.tɪv US -t̬ə.t̬ɪv; ˈkɑːnt.səl.teɪ-
consultatory kənˈsʌl.tə.tᵊr.i, -tri; ˌkɒnt.sᵊlˈteɪ- US kənˈsʌl.t̬ə.tɔːr.i
consumable kənˈsjuː.mə.bl̩, -ˈsuː- US -ˈsuː- **-s** -z
consum|e kənˈsjuːm, -ˈsuːm US -ˈsuːm **-es** -z **-ing** -ɪŋ **-ed** -d
consumer kənˈsjuː.məʳ, -ˈsuː- US -ˈsuː.mɚ **-s** -z **conˈsumer ˌgoods; conˈsumer soˌciety**
consumer|ism kənˈsjuː.mə.r|ɪ.zᵊm, -ˈsuː- US -ˈsuː.mɚ.ɪ- **-ist** -ɪst
consummate (*adj.*) kənˈsʌm.ət, -ɪt; ˈkɒnt.sə.mət, -sjʊ-, -mɪt US ˈkɑːnt.sə.mɪt; kənˈsʌm.ɪt **-ly** -li
consum|mate (*v.*) ˈkɒnt.səl.meɪt, -sjʊ- US ˈkɑːnt.sə- **-mates** -meɪts **-mating** -meɪ.tɪŋ US -meɪ.t̬ɪŋ **-mated** -meɪ.tɪd US -meɪ.t̬ɪd **-mator/s** -meɪ.təʳ/z US -meɪ.t̬ɚ/z
consummation ˌkɒnt.səˈmeɪ.ʃᵊn, -sjʊˈ- US ˌkɑːnt.səˈ- **-s** -z
consummative ˈkɒnt.sə.meɪ.tɪv, -sʌm.eɪ-, -sjʊ.meɪ-; kənˈsʌm.ə- US ˈkɑːnt.sə.meɪ.t̬ɪv; kənˈsʌm.ə-
consumption kənˈsʌmp.ʃᵊn
consumptive kənˈsʌmp.tɪv **-s** -z **-ly** -li **-ness** -nəs, -nɪs
contact (*n. adj.*) ˈkɒn.tækt US ˈkɑːn- **-s** -s ˈ**contact ˌlens**
contact (*v.*) ˈkɒn.tækt; -ˈ-, kən- US ˈkɑːn.tækt **-s** -s **-ing** -ɪŋ **-ed** -ɪd
contagion kənˈteɪ.dʒᵊn **-s** -z
contagious kənˈteɪ.dʒəs **-ly** -li **-ness** -nəs, -nɪs
contain kənˈteɪn **-s** -z **-ing** -ɪŋ **-ed** -d **-able** -ə.bl̩
container kənˈteɪ.nəʳ US -nɚ **-s** -z **conˈtainer ˌship**
containerization, -isa- kənˌteɪ.nᵊr.aɪˈzeɪ.ʃᵊn, -ɪˈ- US -ɪˈ-
containeriz|e, is|e kənˈteɪ.nᵊr.aɪz US -nə.raɪz **-es** -ɪz **-ing** -ɪŋ **-ed** -d
containment kənˈteɪn.mənt, -ˈteɪm- US -ˈteɪn-
contaminant kənˈtæm.ɪ.nənt, ˈ-ə- **-s** -s
contami|nate kənˈtæm.ɪl.neɪt, ˈ-ə- **-nates** -neɪts **-nating** -neɪ.tɪŋ US -neɪ.t̬ɪŋ **-nated** -neɪ.tɪd US -neɪ.t̬ɪd **-nater/s** -neɪ.təʳ/z US -neɪ.t̬ɚ/z
contamination kənˌtæm.ɪˈneɪ.ʃᵊn, -əˈ- **-s** -z
contaminative kənˈtæm.ɪ.nə.tɪv, ˈ-ə-, -neɪ- US -t̬ɪv
contango kənˈtæŋ.gəʊ, kɒn- US kənˈtæŋ.goʊ **-s** -z
contd (*abbrev. for* **continued**) kənˈtɪn.juːd, -jud
contemn kənˈtem **-s** -z **-ing** -ɪŋ **-ed** -d **-er/s** -əʳ/z, -nəʳ/z US -ɚ/z, -nɚ/z
contem|plate ˈkɒn.təml.pleɪt, -tem- US ˈkɑːn.t̬əm-, -tem- **-plates** -pleɪts **-plating** -pleɪ.tɪŋ US -pleɪ.t̬ɪŋ **-plated** -pleɪ.tɪd US -pleɪ.t̬ɪd **-plator/s** -pleɪ.təʳ/z US -pleɪ.t̬ɚ/z
contemplation ˌkɒn.təmˈpleɪ.ʃᵊn, -temˈ- US ˌkɑːn.t̬əmˈ-, -temˈ- **-s** -z
contemplative *pensive:* kənˈtem.plə.tɪv, ˈkɒn.tem.pleɪ.tɪv, -təm- US kənˈtem.plə.t̬ɪv; ˈkɑːn.t̬əm.pleɪ- **-ly** -li **-ness** -nəs, -nɪs
contemplative *of religious orders:* kənˈtem.plə.tɪv US -t̬ɪv
contemporaneity kənˌtem.pᵊr.əˈniː.ə.ti, kɒn-, -ˈneɪ-, -ɪ.ti; ˌkɒn.tem- US kənˌtem.pɚ.əˈniː.ə.t̬i, -ˈneɪ-
contemporaneous kənˌtem.pᵊrˈeɪ.ni.əs, kɒn-; ˌkɒn.tem- US kən- **-ly** -li **-ness** -nəs, -nɪs
contemporar|y kənˈtem.pᵊr.ᵊr|.i US -pə.rer- **-ies** -iz **-ily** -ᵊl.i, -ɪ.li
contempt kənˈtempt
contemptibility kənˌtemp.təˈbɪl.ə.ti, -tɪˈ-, -ɪ.ti US -təˈbɪl.ə.t̬i
contemptib|le kənˈtemp.tə.bl|̩, -tɪ- **-ly** -li **-leness** -l̩.nəs, -nɪs
contemptuous kənˈtemp.tʃu.əs, -tju- US -tʃu- **-ly** -li **-ness** -nəs, -nɪs
contend kənˈtend **-s** -z **-ing** -ɪŋ **-ed** -ɪd **-er/s** -əʳ/z US -ɚ/z
content (*n.*) *what is contained:* ˈkɒn.tent US ˈkɑːn- *contentment:* kənˈtent
con|tent (*adj. v.*) kənlˈtent **-tents** -ˈtents **-tenting** -ˈten.tɪŋ US -ˈten.t̬ɪŋ **-tented/ly** -ˈten.tɪd/li US -ˈten.t̬ɪd/li **-tentedness** -ˈten.tɪd.nəs, -nɪs US -ˈten.t̬ɪd-
contention kənˈten.tʃᵊn **-s** -z
contentious kənˈten.tʃəs **-ly** -li **-ness** -nəs, -nɪs
contentment kənˈtent.mənt
contents (*n.*) *what is contained:* ˈkɒn.tents, kənˈtents US ˈkɑːn.tents
contermin|al kɒnˈtɜː.mɪ.nl|ᵊl, kən-, -mə- US kənˈtɝː- **-ous** -əs
contest (*n.*) ˈkɒn.test US ˈkɑːn- **-s** -s
contest (*v.*) kənˈtest **-s** -s **-ing** -ɪŋ **-ed** -ɪd **-able** -ə.bl̩
contestant kənˈtes.tᵊnt **-s** -s
contestation ˌkɒn.tesˈteɪ.ʃᵊn US ˌkɑːn- **-s** -z
context ˈkɒn.tekst US ˈkɑːn- **-s** -s
contextual kənˈtek.stju.əl, kɒn-, -ˈteks.tʃu- US kənˈteks.tʃu-, kɑːn-, -tʃᵊl **-ly** -i
contextualization, -isa- kənˌtek.stju.ə.laɪˈzeɪ.ʃᵊn, -ˌteks.tʃu-, -lɪˈ- US kənˌteks.tʃu.ə.lɪˈ-, kɑːn-, -tʃᵊl.ɪˈ-
contextualiz|e, is|e kənˈtek.stju.ə.laɪz, -ˈteks.tʃu- US kənˈteks.tʃu-, -tʃə.laɪz **-es** -ɪz **-ing** -ɪŋ **-ed** -d
Conti ˈkɒn.ti US ˈkɑːn.t̬i
contiguity ˌkɒn.tɪˈgjuː.ə.ti, -təˈ-, -ɪ.ti US ˌkɑːn.t̬əˈgjuː.ə.t̬i
contiguous kənˈtɪg.ju.əs **-ly** -li **-ness** -nəs, -nɪs
continen|ce ˈkɒn.tɪ.nənt|s US ˈkɑːn.tᵊn.ənt|s **-cy** -si
continent (C) ˈkɒn.tɪ.nənt US ˈkɑːn.tᵊn.ənt **-s** -s **-ly** -li
continental ˌkɒn.tɪˈnen.tᵊl, -təˈ- US ˌkɑːn.t̬ᵊnˈen.t̬ᵊl ˌ**continental ˈbreakfast;** ˌ**continental ˈquilt**
contingen|ce kənˈtɪn.dʒᵊnt|s **-cy** -si **-cies** -siz
contingent kənˈtɪn.dʒᵊnt **-s** -s **-ly** -li
continual kənˈtɪn.ju.əl **-ly** -i
continuan|ce kənˈtɪn.ju.ənt|s **-t/s** -t/s
continuation kənˌtɪn.juˈeɪ.ʃᵊn **-s** -z
continuative kənˈtɪn.ju.ə.tɪv, -eɪ.tɪv US kənˈtɪn.ju.eɪ.t̬ɪv, -ə-
continuator kənˈtɪn.ju.eɪ.təʳ US -t̬ɚ **-s** -z
contin|ue kənˈtɪnl.juː, -ju **-ues** -juːz, -juz **-uing** -ju.ɪŋ **-ued** -juːd, -jud **-uer/s** -ju.əʳ/z US -ju.ɚ/z
continuity ˌkɒn.tɪˈnjuː.ə.ti, -təˈ-, -ɪ.ti US ˌkɑːn.tᵊnˈuː.ə.t̬i, -ˈjuː-
continuo kənˈtɪn.ju.əʊ, kɒn-, -u.əʊ US kənˈtɪn.ju.oʊ
continuous kənˈtɪn.ju.əs **-ly** -li **-ness** -nəs, -nɪs **conˌtinuous asˈsessment**
continu|um kənˈtɪn.jul.əm **-ums** -əmz **-a** -ə
contoid ˈkɒn.tɔɪd US ˈkɑːn- **-s** -z
con|tort kənlˈtɔːt US -ˈtɔːrt **-torts** -ˈtɔːts US -ˈtɔːrts **-torting** -ˈtɔː.tɪŋ US -ˈtɔːr.t̬ɪŋ **-torted** -ˈtɔː.tɪd US -ˈtɔːr.t̬ɪd
contortion kənˈtɔː.ʃᵊn US -ˈtɔːr- **-s** -z
contortionist kənˈtɔː.ʃᵊn.ɪst, kɒn- US kənˈtɔːr- **-s** -s
contour ˈkɒn.tʊəʳ, -tɔːʳ US ˈkɑːn.tʊr **-s** -z **-ing** -ɪŋ **-ed** -d
contra- ˈkɒn.trə- US ˈkɑːn.trə-
Note: Prefix. In the sense of "against", this always carries primary or secondary stress on the first syllable.
contra (C) ˈkɒn.trə, -trɑː US ˈkɑːn.trə **-s** -z
contraband ˈkɒn.trə.bænd US ˈkɑːn- **-ist/s** -ɪst/s
contrabass ˌkɒn.trəˈbeɪs, ˈ--- US ˈkɑːn.trə.beɪs **-es** -ɪz

contra bonos mores ˌkɒn.trɑːˌbəʊ.nəʊs'mɔː.reɪs, -ˌbɒn.əʊs- US ˌkɑːn.trɑːˌboʊ.noʊs'mɔːr.iːz
contraception ˌkɒn.trə'sep.ʃᵊn US ˌkɑːn-
contraceptive ˌkɒn.trə'sep.tɪv US ˌkɑːn- **-s** -z
contract *(n.)* 'kɒn.trækt US 'kɑːn- **-s** -s
contract *(v.)* kən'trækt **-s** -s **-ing** -ɪŋ **-ed** -ɪd **-ive** -ɪv
contractibility kənˌtræk.tə'bɪl.ə.ti, -tɪ'-, -ɪ.ti US kənˌtræk.tə'bɪl.ə.ṱi; ˌkɑːn.træk-
contractib|le kən'træk.tə.bl̩, -tɪ- **-ly** -li **-leness** -l̩.nəs, -nɪs
contractile kən'træk.taɪl US -tᵊl, -taɪl
contraction kən'træk.ʃᵊn **-s** -z
contractionary kən'træk.ʃᵊn.ᵊr.i, -ʃᵊn.ri US -ʃᵊn.er.i
contractor *builder:* kən'træk.təʳ; 'kɒn.træk- US 'kɑːn.træk.tɚ **-s** -z *other senses:* kən'træk.təʳ US -tɚ **-s** -z
contractual kən'træk.tʃu.ᵊl, -tju- US kən'træk.tʃu-, kɑːn-, -tʃᵊl **-ly** -i
contracture kən'træk.tʃəʳ, -tjʊəʳ, -ʃəʳ US -tʃɚ **-s** -z
contradict ˌkɒn.trə'dɪkt US ˌkɑːn- **-s** -s **-ing** -ɪŋ **-ed** -ɪd
contradiction ˌkɒn.trə'dɪk.ʃᵊn US ˌkɑːn- **-s** -z
contradictor|y ˌkɒn.trə'dɪk.tᵊr|.i, -tr|i US ˌkɑːn- **-ily** -ᵊl.i, -ɪ.li **-iness** -ɪ.nəs, -ɪ.nɪs
contradistinc|tion ˌkɒn.trə.dɪ'stɪŋ*k*|.ʃᵊn, -də'- US ˌkɑːn.trə.dɪ'-, -də'- **-tive** -tɪv
contradistinguish ˌkɒn.trə.dɪ'stɪŋ.gwɪʃ, -də'- US ˌkɑːn.trə.dɪ'-, -də'- **-es** -ɪz **-ing** -ɪŋ **-ed** -t
contrafactive ˌkɒn.trə'fæk.tɪv US ˌkɑːn-
contraflow 'kɒn.trə.fləʊ US 'kɑːn.trə.floʊ **-s** -z
contraindi|cate ˌkɒn.trə'ɪn.dɪ|.keɪt US ˌkɑːn.trə- **-cates** -keɪts **-cating** -keɪ.tɪŋ US -keɪ.ṱɪŋ **-cated** -keɪ.tɪd US -keɪ.ṱɪd
contraindication ˌkɒn.trə.ɪn.dɪ'keɪ.ʃᵊn US ˌkɑːn.trə- **-s** -z
contraindicative ˌkɒn.trə.ɪn'dɪk.ə.tɪv US ˌkɑːn.trə.ɪn'dɪk.ə.ṱɪv
contralti *(plur. of* **contralto***)* kən'træl.ti, -'trɑːl- US -'træl.ṱi
contralto kən'træl.təʊ, -'trɑːl- US -'træl.ṱoʊ **-s** -z
contra pacem ˌkɒn.trɑː'pɑː.kem, -'pɑː.tʃem US ˌkɑːn.trɑː'pɑː.kem, -'peɪ.sem
contraposition ˌkɒn.trə.pə'zɪʃ.ᵊn US ˌkɑːn-
contraption kən'træp.ʃᵊn **-s** -z
contrapuntal ˌkɒn.trə'pʌn.tᵊl US ˌkɑːn.trə'pʌn.ṱᵊl **-ly** -i
contrapuntist ˌkɒn.trə'pʌn.tɪst US ˌkɑːn.trə'pʌn.ṱɪst **-s** -s
contrariety ˌkɒn.trə'raɪ.ə.ti, -ɪ.ti US ˌkɑːn.trə'raɪ.ə.ṱi
contrariwise kən'treə.ri.waɪz; 'kɒn.trə- US kən'trer.i-; 'kɑːn.trɚ-
contrar|y *opposed:* 'kɒn.trᵊr|.i US 'kɑːn.trɚ|.i **-ies** -iz **-ily** -ᵊl.i, -ɪ.li
contrar|y *perverse, obstinate:* kən'treə.r|i US -'trer|.i **-ies** -iz **-ily** -ɪ.li, -ᵊl.i **-iness** -ɪ.nəs, -ɪ.nɪs
contrast *(n.)* 'kɒn.trɑːst US 'kɑːn.træst **-s** -s
contrast *(v.)* kən'trɑːst US -'træst **-s** -s **-ing/ly** -ɪŋ/li **-ed** -ɪd
contrastive kən'trɑː.stɪv US -'træs.tɪv
contraven|e ˌkɒn.trə'viːn US ˌkɑːn- **-es** -z **-ing** -ɪŋ **-ed** -d
contravention ˌkɒn.trə'ven.*t*ʃᵊn US ˌkɑːn- **-s** -z
contretemps *(sing.)* 'kɒn.trə.tɑ̃ːŋ, 'kɔːn-, 'kɔ̃ːn- US 'kɑːn.trə.tɑ̃ː *(plur.)* 'kɒn.trə.tɑ̃ː, -z US 'kɑːn.trə.tɑ̃ː, -z
contrib|ute kən'trɪb|.juːt, 'kɒn.trɪ.b|juːt, -jət US kən'trɪb|.juːt, -jət **-utes** -juːts US -juːts, -jəts **-uting** -jʊ.tɪŋ US -juː.ṱɪŋ, -jə- **-uted** -jʊ.tɪd US -juː.ṱɪd, -jə-
contribution ˌkɒn.trɪ'bjuː.ʃᵊn US ˌkɑːn- **-s** -z
contributive kən'trɪb.jʊ.tɪv, -jə- US -jə.ṱɪv
contributor kən'trɪb.jə.təʳ, -jʊ-; 'kɒn.trɪ.bjuː- US kən'trɪb.jə.ṱɚ, -juː.ṱɚ **-s** -z
contributory kən'trɪb.jʊ.tᵊr.i, -jə-, -tri; ˌkɒn.trɪ'bjuː- US kən'trɪb.jə.tɔːr.i
contrite kən'traɪt, kɒn- US kən-, kɑːn- **-ly** -li **-ness** -nəs, -nɪs
contrition kən'trɪʃ.ᵊn
contrivanc|e kən'traɪ.vᵊn*t*s **-es** -ɪz
contriv|e kən'traɪv **-es** -z **-ing** -ɪŋ **-ed** -d **-er/s** -əʳ/z US -ɚ/z
control *(n.)* kən'trəʊl *in machinery also:* 'kɒn.trəʊl US kən'troʊl **-s** -z
control *(v.)* kən'trəʊl US -'troʊl **-s** -z **-ling** -ɪŋ **-led** -d **-lable** -ə.bl̩
controller kən'trəʊ.ləʳ US -'troʊ.lɚ **-s** -z
controversial ˌkɒn.trə'vɜː.ʃᵊl, '-si.əl US ˌkɑːn.trə'vɝː.ʃᵊl **-ly** -i
controversialist ˌkɒn.trə'vɜː.ʃᵊl.ɪst, '-si.ᵊl- US ˌkɑːn.trə'vɝː.ʃᵊl- **-s** -s
controvers|y 'kɒn.trə.vɜː.s|i, -və.s|i; kən'trɒv.ə.s|i US 'kɑːn.trə.vɝː- **-ies** -iz
controver|t ˌkɒn.trə'vɜː|t, '--- US 'kɑːn.trə.vɝː|t, ˌ--'- **-ts** -ts **-ting** -tɪŋ US -ṱɪŋ **-ted** -tɪd US -ṱɪd
controvertib|le ˌkɒn.trə'vɜː.tə.bl̩, -tɪ- US ˌkɑːn.trə'vɝː.ṱə- **-ly** -li
contumacious ˌkɒn.tjʊ'meɪ.ʃəs US ˌkɑːn.tʊ'-, -tjuː'-, -ṱə'-, -tjə'- **-ly** -li **-ness** -nəs, -nəs
contumacy 'kɒn.tjʊ.mə.si US 'kɑːn.tuː-; -tjʊ-; kən'tuː-
contumelious ˌkɒn.tjʊ'miː.li.əs US ˌkɑːn.tʊ'-, -tjuː'-, -tə'-, -tjə'- **-ly** -li **-ness** -nəs, -nɪs
contumel|y 'kɒn.tjuː.mᵊl|.i, -tjʊ-, -mɪ.l|i; kən'tjʊm.ɪ.l|i, -ᵊl|.i, -'tjuː.mɪ.l|i, -mᵊl|.i US 'kɑːn.tuː.mᵊl|.i, -tjuː-, '-ṱəm.l|i; kən'tuː.mə.l|i, -'tjuː-, -'tʊm.ə- **-ies** -iz
contus|e kən'tjuːz US -'tuːz, -'tjuːz **-es** -ɪz **-ing** -ɪŋ **-ed** -d
contusion kən'tjuː.ʒᵊn US -'tuː-, -'tjuː- **-s** -z
conundrum kə'nʌn.drəm **-s** -z
conurbation ˌkɒn.ɜː'beɪ.ʃᵊn, -ə'- US ˌkɑː.nɝː'-, -nɚ'- **-s** -z
convalesc|e ˌkɒn.və'les US ˌkɑːn- **-es** -ɪz **-ing** -ɪŋ **-ed** -t
convalescence ˌkɒn.və'les.ᵊn*t*s US ˌkɑːn-
convalescent ˌkɒn.və'les.ᵊnt US ˌkɑːn- **-s** -s
convection kən'vek.ʃᵊn
convector kən'vek.təʳ US -tɚ **-s** -z
convenanc|e 'kɔ̃ː*n*.və.nɑ̃ː*n*s, 'kɒn-, -nɑːn*t*s US 'kɑːn.və.nən*t*s, -næn*t*s **-es** -ɪz
conven|e kən'viːn **-es** -z **-ing** -ɪŋ **-ed** -d **-er/s** -əʳ/z US -ɚ/z **-or/s** -əʳ/z US -ɚ/z
convenienc|e kən'viː.ni.ən*t*s US -'viːn.jən*t*s **-es** -ɪz **con'venience ˌfood; con'venience ˌstore**
convenient kən'viː.ni.ənt US -'viːn.jənt **-ly** -li
convent 'kɒn.vənt, -vent US 'kɑːn- **-s** -s
conventicle kən'ven.tɪ.kᵊl US -ṱə- **-s** -z
convention kən'ven.*t*ʃᵊn US -'ven*t*.ʃᵊn **-s** -z
conventional kən'ven.*t*ʃᵊn.ᵊl US -'ven*t*.ʃᵊn- **-ly** -i
conventional|ism kən'ven.*t*ʃᵊn.ᵊl|.ɪ.zᵊm US -'ven*t*.ʃᵊn- **-ist/s** -ɪst/s
conventionalit|y kənˌven.*t*ʃə'næl.ə.t|i, -ɪ.t|i US -ˌven*t*.ʃə'næl.ə.ṱ|i **-ies** -iz
conventionaliz|e, -is|e kən'ven.*t*ʃᵊn.ᵊl.aɪz US -'ven*t*.ʃᵊn.ə.laɪz **-es** -ɪz **-ing** -ɪŋ **-ed** -d
conventual kən'ven.tju.əl, -tʃu-, -tʃᵊl US -tʃu.əl **-s** -z

converg|e kənˈvɜːdʒ, kɒn- (US) kənˈvɝːdʒ **-es** -ɪz **-ing** -ɪŋ **-ed** -d

convergen|ce kənˈvɜː.dʒənt|s, kɒn- (US) kənˈvɝː- **-ces** -sɪz **-cy** -si

convergent kənˈvɜː.dʒənt, kɒn- (US) kənˈvɝː- **-ly** -li

conversable kənˈvɜː.sə.bl̩ (US) -ˈvɝː-

conversan|ce kənˈvɜː.sənt|s; ˈkɒn.və- (US) kənˈvɝː-; ˈkɑːn.vɚ- **-cy** -si

conversant kənˈvɜː.sənt; ˈkɒn.və- (US) kənˈvɝː-; ˈkɑːn.vɚ- **-ly** -li

conversation ˌkɒn.vəˈseɪ.ʃən (US) ˌkɑːn.vɚˈ- **-s** -z **converˈsation ˌpiece**

conversational ˌkɒn.vəˈseɪ.ʃən.əl, -ˈseɪʃ.nəl (US) ˌkɑːn.vɚˈ- **-ly** -i

conversationalist ˌkɒn.vəˈseɪ.ʃən.əl.ɪst, -ˈseɪʃ.nəl- (US) ˌkɑːn.vɚˈ- **-s** -s

conversazione ˌkɒn.və.sæt.siˈəʊ.neɪ, -ni (US) ˌkɑːn.vɚ.sɑːt.siˈoʊ.ni, ˌkoʊn- **-s** -z

convers|e (*n. adj.*) ˈkɒn.vɜːs; kənˈvɜːs (US) ˈkɑːn.vɝːs; kənˈvɝːs **-es** -ɪz **-ely** -li

convers|e (*v.*) kənˈvɜːs (US) -ˈvɝːs **-es** -ɪz **-ing** -ɪŋ **-ed** -t

conversion kənˈvɜː.ʃən, -ʒən (US) -ˈvɝː.ʒən, -ʃən **-s** -z **conˈversion ˌcourse**

convert (*n.*) ˈkɒn.vɜːt (US) ˈkɑːn.vɝːt **-s** -s

con|vert (*v.*) kən|ˈvɜːt (US) -ˈvɝːt **-verts** -ˈvɜːts (US) -ˈvɝːts **-verting** -ˈvɜː.tɪŋ (US) -ˈvɝː.t̬ɪŋ **-verted** -ˈvɜː.tɪd (US) -ˈvɝː.t̬ɪd **-verter/s** -ˈvɜː.təʳ/z (US) -ˈvɝː.t̬ɚ/z **-vertor/s** -ˈvɜː.təʳ/z (US) -ˈvɝː.t̬ɚ/z

convertibility kənˌvɜː.təˈbɪl.ə.ti, -tɪˈ-, -ɪ.ti (US) -ˌvɝː.t̬əˈbɪl.ə.t̬i

convertib|le kənˈvɜː.tə.bl̩|, -tɪ- (US) -ˈvɝː.t̬ə- **-les** -l̩z **-ly** -li

convex kɒnˈveks, ˈ-- (US) ˈkɑːn.veks; kənˈveks **-ly** -li

convexit|y kɒnˈvek.sə.t|i, kən-, -ɪt|.i (US) kənˈvek.sə.t̬|i **-ies** -iz

convey kənˈveɪ **-s** -z **-ing** -ɪŋ **-ed** -d **-er/s** -əʳ/z (US) -ɚ/z **-or/s** -əʳ/z (US) -ɚ/z **-able** -ə.bl̩ **conˈveyor ˌbelt**

conveyanc|e kənˈveɪ.ənts **-es** -ɪz

conveyanc|er kənˈveɪ.ənt.s|əʳ (US) -s|ɚ **-ers** -əz (US) -ɚz **-ing** -ɪŋ

convict (*n.*) ˈkɒn.vɪkt (US) ˈkɑːn- **-s** -s

convict (*v.*) kənˈvɪkt **-s** -s **-ing** -ɪŋ **-ed** -ɪd

conviction kənˈvɪk.ʃən **-s** -z

convinc|e kənˈvɪnts **-es** -ɪz **-ing** -ɪŋ **-ed** -t

convincible kənˈvɪnt.sə.bl̩

convincing kənˈvɪnt.sɪŋ **-ly** -li

convivial kənˈvɪv.i.əl **-ly** -i

conviviality kənˌvɪv.iˈæl.ə.ti, -ɪ.ti (US) -ɚ.t̬i

convocation ˌkɒn.vəʊˈkeɪ.ʃən (US) ˌkɑːn.vəˈ- **-s** -z

convok|e kənˈvəʊk (US) -ˈvoʊk **-es** -s **-ing** -ɪŋ **-ed** -t

convolu|te ˈkɒn.və.luː|t, -ljuː|t, ˌ--ˈ- (US) ˈkɑːn.və.luː|t **-ted/ly** -tɪd/li (US) -t̬ɪd/li

convolution ˌkɒn.vəˈluː.ʃən, -ˈljuː- (US) ˌkɑːn.vəˈluː- **-s** -z

convolv|e kənˈvɒlv (US) -ˈvɑːlv, -ˈvɔːlv **-es** -z **-ing** -ɪŋ **-ed** -d

convolvul|us kənˈvɒl.vjʊ.l|əs, -vjə- (US) -ˈvɑːl.vjuː-, -vjə- **-i** -aɪ **-uses** -ə.sɪz

convoy ˈkɒn.vɔɪ (US) ˈkɑːn- **-s** -z **-ing** -ɪŋ **-ed** -d

convulsant kənˈvʌl.sənt **-s** -s

convuls|e kənˈvʌls **-es** -ɪz **-ing** -ɪŋ **-ed** -t

convulsion kənˈvʌl.ʃən **-s** -z

convulsive kənˈvʌl.sɪv **-ly** -li **-ness** -nəs, -nɪs

Conway ˈkɒn.weɪ (US) ˈkɑːn-

Conwy ˈkɒn.wi (US) ˈkɑːn-

con|y ˈkəʊ.n|i (US) ˈkoʊ- **-ies** -iz

Conybeare ˈkɒn.ɪ.bɪəʳ, ˈkʌn- (US) ˈkɑː.nɪ.bɪr, ˈkʌn.ɪ-

coo kuː **-(e)s** -z **-ing** -ɪŋ **-ed** -d

Coober Pedy ˌkuː.bəˈpiː.di (US) -bɚˈ-

Cooch kuːtʃ

cooee ˈkuː.i, -iː, ˌ-ˈ- **-s** -z **-ing** -ɪŋ **-d** -d

cook kʊk **-s** -s **-ing** -ɪŋ **-ed** -t

cookbook ˈkʊk.bʊk **-s** -s

cook-chill ˌkʊkˈtʃɪl **-s** -z **-ing** -ɪŋ **-ed** -d

Cook(e) kʊk

cooker ˈkʊk.əʳ (US) -ɚ **-s** -z

cookery ˈkʊk.ər.i **ˈcookery ˌbook**

Cookham ˈkʊk.əm (US) -əm, -hæm

cookhou|se ˈkʊk.hau|s **-ses** -zɪz

cookie ˈkʊk.i **-s** -z

cookout ˈkʊk.aʊt **-s** -s

Cookson ˈkʊk.sən

Cookstown ˈkʊks.taʊn

cookware ˈkʊk.weəʳ (US) -wer

cook|y ˈkʊk|.i **-ies** -iz

cool kuːl **-er** -əʳ (US) -ɚ **-est** -ɪst, -əst **-ly** -li, -i **-ness** -nəs, -nɪs **-s** -z **-ing** -ɪŋ **-ed** -d

coolant ˈkuː.lənt **-s** -s

coolbox ˈkuːl.bɒks (US) -bɑːks **-es** -ɪz

cooler ˈkuː.ləʳ (US) -lɚ **-s** -z

coolheaded ˌkuːlˈhed.ɪd **-ness** -nəs, -nɪs *stress shift:* ˌcoolheaded ˈthinking

coolibah ˈkuː.lɪ.bɑː, -lə- **-s** -z

Coolidge ˈkuː.lɪdʒ

coolie ˈkuː.li **-s** -z

Cooling ˈkuː.lɪŋ

cooling-off period ˌkuː.lɪŋˈɒf.pɪə.ri.əd (US) -ˈɑːf.pɪr.i- **-s** -z

coom kuːm **-s** -z

coomb kuːm **-s** -z

Coomb(e) kuːm

Coomber ˈkuːm.bəʳ (US) -bɚ

Coombes kuːmz

coon kuːn **-s** -z

coop kuːp **-s** -s **-ing** -ɪŋ **-ed** -t

co-op ˈkəʊ.ɒp, -ˈ- (US) ˈkoʊ.ɑːp **-s** -s

coop|er (C) ˈkuː.p|əʳ (US) -p|ɚ **-ers** -əz (US) -ɚz **-ering** -ər.ɪŋ **-ered** -əd (US) -ɚd

cooperag|e ˈkuː.pər.ɪdʒ **-es** -ɪz

cooper|ate kəʊˈɒp.ər|.eɪt (US) koʊˈɑː.pə.r|eɪt **-ates** -eɪts **-ating** -eɪ.tɪŋ (US) -eɪ.t̬ɪŋ **-ated** -eɪ.tɪd (US) -eɪ.t̬ɪd **-ator/s** -eɪ.təʳ/z (US) -eɪ.t̬ɚ/z

cooperation kəʊˌɒp.əˈreɪ.ʃən, ˌkəʊ.ɒp- (US) koʊˌɑː.pəˈ- **-s** -z

cooperative kəʊˈɒp.ər.ə.tɪv (US) koʊˈɑː.pɚ.ə.t̬ɪv **-s** -z **-ly** -li

Cooperstown ˈkuː.pəz.taʊn (US) -pɚz-

coopery ˈkuː.pər.i

Coopman ˈkuːp.mən

co-opt kəʊˈɒpt (US) koʊˈɑːpt, ˈ-- **-s** -s **-ing** -ɪŋ **-ed** -ɪd

co-optation ˌkəʊ.ɒpˈteɪ.ʃən (US) ˌkoʊ.ɑːpˈ-

co-option kəʊˈɒp.ʃən (US) koʊˈɑːp- **-s** -z

coordinate (*n. adj.*) kəʊˈɔː.dɪ.nət, -dən.ət (US) koʊˈɔːr.dən-, -eɪt **-s** -s **-ly** -li **-ness** -nəs, -nɪs

coordin|ate (*v.*) kəʊˈɔː.dɪ.n|eɪt, -dən|.eɪt (US) koʊˈɔːr.dən- **-ates** -eɪts **-ating** -eɪ.tɪŋ (US) -eɪ.t̬ɪŋ **-ated** -eɪ.tɪd (US) -eɪ.t̬ɪd **-ator/s** -eɪ.təʳ/z (US) -eɪ.t̬ɚ/z

coordination kəʊˌɔː.dɪˈneɪ.ʃən, -dənˈeɪ- (US) koʊˌɔːr.dənˈeɪ-

coordinative kəʊˈɔː.dɪ.nə.tɪv, -dən.ə-, -eɪ- (US) koʊˈɔːr.dən.ə.t̬ɪv

Coors® kɔːz, kʊəz (US) kʊrz

coot kuːt **-s** -s

Coote kuːt

co-ownership ˌkəʊˈəʊ.nə.ʃɪp (US) ˌkoʊˈoʊ.nɚ-

cop kɒp (US) kɑːp **-s** -s **-ping** -ɪŋ **-ped** -t

Copacabana ˌkəʊ.pə.kəˈbæn.ə (US) ˌkoʊ-, -ˈbɑː.nə

copaiba kəʊˈpaɪ.bə, kɒpˈaɪ- (US) koʊˈpaɪ-

copal ˈkəʊ.pəl; kəʊˈpæl (US) ˈkoʊ.pəl, -pæl

coparcener ˌkəʊˈpɑː.sən.əʳ, -sɪ.nəʳ (US) ˌkoʊˈpɑːr.sən.ɚ **-s** -z

copartner ˌkəʊˈpɑːt.nəʳ (US) ˈkoʊˌpɑːrt.nɚ, ˌ-ˈ-- **-s** -z **-ship/s** -ʃɪp/s

cop|e (C) kəʊp (US) koʊp **-es** -s **-ing** -ɪŋ **-ed** -t

copeck ˈkəʊ.pek, ˈkɒp.ek (US) ˈkoʊ.pek **-s** -s

Copeland ˈkəʊp.lənd (US) ˈkoʊp-

Copenhagen ˌkəʊ.pənˈheɪ.gən, -ˈhɑː-, ˈkəʊ.pənˌheɪ-, -ˌhɑː-

(US) ˈkoʊ.pᵊnˌheɪ.gᵊn, -ˌhɑː-, ˌkoʊpᵊnˈheɪ-, -ˈhɑː-
coper ˈkəʊ.pəʳ (US) ˈkoʊ.pɚ **-s** -z
Copernican kəʊˈpɜː.nɪ.kᵊn (US) koʊˈpɝː-, kə-
Copernicus kəʊˈpɜː.nɪ.kəs (US) koʊˈpɝː-, kə-
copestone ˈkəʊp.stəʊn (US) ˈkoʊp.stoʊn **-s** -z
Cophetua kəʊˈfet.ju.ə (US) koʊ-
copier ˈkɒp.i.əʳ (US) ˈkɑː.pi.ɚ **-s** -z
co-pilot ˈkəʊˌpaɪ.lət, ˌ-ˈ-- (US) ˈkoʊˌpaɪ- **-s** -s
coping ˈkəʊ.pɪŋ (US) ˈkoʊ- **-s** -z
copingstone ˈkəʊ.pɪŋ.stəʊn (US) ˈkoʊ.pɪŋ.stoʊn **-s** -z
copious ˈkəʊ.pi.əs (US) ˈkoʊ- **-ly** -li **-ness** -nəs, -nɪs
Copland ˈkɒp.lənd, ˈkəʊp- (US) ˈkɑːp-, ˈkoʊp-
Note: The name of the composer Aaron Copland is pronounced /ˈkəʊp.lənd (US) ˈkoʊp-/.
Copleston ˈkɒp.l̩.stən (US) ˈkɑː.pl̩-
Copley ˈkɒp.li (US) ˈkɑː.pli
cop-out ˈkɒp.aʊt (US) ˈkɑːp- **-s** -s
Copp kɒp (US) kɑːp
copp|er ˈkɒp|.əʳ (US) ˈkɑː.p|ɚ **-ers** -əz (US) -ɚz **-ering** -ᵊr.ɪŋ **-ered** -əd (US) -ɚd ˌ**copper** ˈ**beech**; ˌ**copper** ˈ**sulphate**
copperas ˈkɒp.ᵊr.əs (US) ˈkɑː.pɚ-
copper-bottomed ˌkɒp.əˈbɒt.əmd (US) ˌkɑː.pɚˈbɑː.t̬əmd *stress shift:* ˌcopper-bottomed ˈprospect
Copperfield ˈkɒp.ə.fiːld (US) ˈkɑː.pɚ-
copperhead ˈkɒp.ə.hed (US) ˈkɑː.pɚ- **-s** -z
copperplate ˈkɒp.ə.pleɪt, ˌ--ˈ- (US) ˈkɑː.pɚ-
coppersmith (C) ˈkɒp.ə.smɪθ (US) ˈkɑː.pɚ- **-s** -s
coppery ˈkɒp.ᵊr.i (US) ˈkɑː.pɚ-
coppic|e ˈkɒp.ɪs (US) ˈkɑː.pɪs **-es** -ɪz **-ing** -ɪŋ **-ed** -t
Copping ˈkɒp.ɪŋ (US) ˈkɑː.pɪŋ
Coppola ˈkɒp.ᵊl.ə, ˈkɑː.pᵊl.ə (US) ˈkɑː.pᵊl.ə, ˈkoʊ.pᵊl.ə
Coppull ˈkɒp.ᵊl (US) ˈkɑː.pᵊl
copra ˈkɒp.rə (US) ˈkɑː.prə
copro- ˈkɒp.rəʊ- (US) ˈkɑː.proʊ-, -prə-
coproduc|e ˌkəʊ.prəˈdjuːs, -ˈdʒuːs (US) ˌkoʊ.prəˈduːs, -ˈdjuːs **-es** -ɪz **-ing** -ɪŋ **-ed** -t **-er/s** -əʳ/z (US) -ɚ/z
coproduction ˌkəʊ.prəˈdʌk.ʃᵊn (US) ˌkoʊ- **-s** -z
cops|e kɒps (US) kɑːps **-es** -ɪz
Copt kɒpt (US) kɑːpt **-s** -s
copter ˈkɒp.təʳ (US) ˈkɑːp- **-s** -z
Copthall ˈkɒp.tɔːl, ˈkɒpt.hɔːl (US) ˈkɑːp.tɔːl, -tɑːl, ˈkɑːpt.hɔːl, -hɑːl
Coptic ˈkɒp.tɪk (US) ˈkɑːp-
copul|a ˈkɒp.jə.l|ə, -jʊ- (US) ˈkɑː.pjə- **-ae** -iː **-as** -əz
copu|late ˈkɒp.jə|.leɪt, -jʊ- (US) ˈkɑː.pjə- **-lates** -leɪts **-lating** -leɪ.tɪŋ (US) -leɪ.t̬ɪŋ **-lated** -leɪ.tɪd (US) -leɪ.t̬ɪd
copulation ˌkɒp.jəˈleɪ.ʃᵊn, -jʊˈ- (US) ˌkɑː.pjəˈ- **-s** -z
copula|tive ˈkɒp.jə.lə|.tɪv, -jʊ-, -leɪ- (US) ˈkɑː.pjə.lə|.t̬ɪv **-tory** -tᵊr.i, -tri (US) -tɔːr.i
cop|y ˈkɒp|.i (US) ˈkɑː.p|i **-ies** -iz **-ying** -i.ɪŋ **-ied** -id
copybook ˈkɒp.i.bʊk (US) ˈkɑː.pi- **-s** -s ˌ**blot one's** ˈ**copybook**
copycat ˈkɒp.i.kæt (US) ˈkɑː.pi- **-s** -s
Copydex® ˈkɒp.i.deks (US) ˈkɑː.pi-
copy-ed|it ˈkɒp.iˌed|.ɪt (US) ˈkɑː.pi- **-its** -ɪts **-iting** -ɪ.tɪŋ (US) -ɪ.t̬ɪŋ **-ited** -ɪ.tɪd (US) -ɪ.t̬ɪd **-itor/s** -ɪ.təʳ/z (US) -ɪ.t̬ɚ/z
copyhold ˈkɒp.i.həʊld (US) ˈkɑː.pi.hoʊld **-s** -z **-er/s** -əʳ/z (US) -ɚ/z
copyist ˈkɒp.i.ɪst (US) ˈkɑː.pi- **-s** -s
copy|right ˈkɒp.i|.raɪt (US) ˈkɑː.pi- **-rights** -raɪts **-righting** -ˌraɪ.tɪŋ (US) -ˌraɪ.t̬ɪŋ **-righted** -ˌraɪ.tɪd (US) -ˌraɪ.t̬ɪd
copywrit|er ˈkɒp.iˌraɪ.t|əʳ (US) ˈkɑː.piˌraɪ.t̬|ɚ **-ers** -əz (US) -ɚz **-ing** -ɪŋ
coq au vin ˌkɒk.əʊˈvæn, -ˈvæ̃ŋ (US) ˌkoʊk.oʊˈ-, ˌkɑːk-
Coquelles kɒkˈel, kəʊˈkel (US) koʊˈkel
coqu|et kɒk|ˈet, kəʊˈk|et (US) koʊˈk|et **-ets** -ets **-etting** -et.ɪŋ (US) -et̬.ɪŋ **-etted** -et.ɪd (US) -et̬.ɪd
Coquet ˈkəʊ.kɪt (US) ˈkoʊ-
coquetr|y ˈkɒk.ɪ.tr|i, ˈkəʊ.kɪ-, -kə- (US) ˈkoʊ.kə.tr|i, koʊˈket.r|i **-ies** -iz
coquette kɒkˈet, kəʊˈket (US) koʊˈket **-s** -s
coquettish kɒkˈet.ɪʃ, kəʊˈket- (US) koʊˈket̬- **-ly** -li **-ness** -nəs, -nɪs
cor kɔːʳ (US) kɔːr **-s** -z
Cora ˈkɔː.rə (US) ˈkɔːr.ə
coracle ˈkɒr.ə.kl̩ (US) ˈkɔːr- **-s** -z
coral ˈkɒr.əl (US) ˈkɔːr- **-s** -z ˌ**coral** ˈ**reef**
corallaceous ˌkɒr.əˈleɪ.ʃəs (US) ˌkɔːr-
corall|ine ˈkɒr.ᵊl|.aɪn (US) ˈkɔːr.ə.l|aɪn **-ite** -aɪt
Coram ˈkɔː.rəm (US) ˈkɔːr.əm
coram nobis ˌkɔː.rəmˈnəʊ.bɪs, -ræm- (US) ˌkɔːr.æmˈnoʊ.bɪs
cor(s) anglais ˌkɔːˈrɒŋ.gleɪ, -ˈrɑːŋ- (US) ˌkɔːr.ɑːŋˈgleɪ
corban ˈkɔː.bæn, -bᵊn (US) ˈkɔːr-
corbel ˈkɔː.bᵊl (US) ˈkɔːr- **-s** -z
Corbett ˈkɔː.bɪt, -bet, -bət (US) ˈkɔːr-
Corbishley ˈkɔː.bɪʃ.li (US) ˈkɔːr-
Corbridge ˈkɔː.brɪdʒ (US) ˈkɔːr-
Corbusier kɔːˈbjuː.zi.eɪ, -ˈbuː- (US) ˌkɔːr.buːˈzjeɪ
Corby ˈkɔː.bi (US) ˈkɔːr-
Corbyn ˈkɔː.bɪn (US) ˈkɔːr-
Corcoran ˈkɔː.kᵊr.ᵊn (US) ˈkɔːr-
Corcyra ˌkɔːˈsaɪə.rə (US) ˌkɔːrˈsaɪ-
cord kɔːd (US) kɔːrd **-s** -z **-ing** -ɪŋ **-ed** -ɪd **-age** -ɪdʒ
Cordelia kɔːˈdiː.li.ə (US) kɔːrˈdiːl.jə
cordelier (C) ˌkɔː.dɪˈlɪəʳ (US) ˌkɔːr.dɪˈlɪr **-s** -z
Cordero kɔːˈdeə.rəʊ (US) kɔːrˈder.oʊ
cordial ˈkɔː.di.əl (US) ˈkɔːr.dʒəl, -djəl **-s** -z **-ly** -i
cordialit|y ˌkɔː.diˈæl.ə.t|i, -ɪ.t|i (US) ˌkɔːr.dʒiˈæl.ə.t̬|i, -ˈdjæl.ə- **-ies** -iz
cordillera (C) ˌkɔː.dɪˈljeə.rə, -dᵊlˈjeə-, -ˈeə- (US) ˌkɔːr.dᵊlˈjer.ə; kɔːrˈdɪl.ɚ-
cordite ˈkɔː.daɪt (US) ˈkɔːr-
cordless ˈkɔːd.ləs, -lɪs (US) ˈkɔːrd-
Cordoba, Córdoba ˈkɔː.də.bə (US) ˈkɔːr-
cordon ˈkɔː.dᵊn (US) ˈkɔːr- **-s** -z **-ing** -ɪŋ **-ed** -d
cordon bleu ˌkɔː.dɔ̃ːmˈblɜː, -dɒnˈ- (US) ˌkɔːr.dɔ̃ːˈbluː
cordon(s) sanitaire(s) ˌkɔː.dɔ̃ːn.sæn.ɪˈteəʳ, -dɒn-, -əˈ- (US) kɔːrˌdɔ̃ː.sɑː.niˈter
Cordov|a ˈkɔː.də.v|ə (US) ˈkɔːr- **-an/s** -ən/z
corduroy ˈkɔː.djə.rɔɪ, -djʊ-, -dʒə-, -dʒʊ-, ˌ--ˈ- (US) ˈkɔːr.də- **-s** -z
cordwainer ˈkɔːdˌweɪ.nəʳ (US) ˈkɔːrdˌweɪ.nɚ **-s** -z
cor|e kɔːʳ (US) kɔːr **-es** -z **-ing** -ɪŋ **-ed** -d **-er/s** -əʳ/z (US) -ɚ/z
CORE kɔːʳ (US) kɔːr
co-referential ˌkəʊ.ref.əˈren.tʃᵊl (US) ˌkoʊ.ref.əˈrent.ʃᵊl
co-regent ˌkəʊˈriː.dʒᵊnt (US) ˌkoʊ- **-s** -s
coreligionist ˌkəʊ.rɪˈlɪdʒ.ᵊn.ɪst, -rəˈ- (US) ˌkoʊ.rəˈ-, -rɪˈ- **-s** -s
Corelli kəˈrel.i, kɒrˈel- (US) koʊˈrel-, kəˈ-
co-representational ˌkəʊ.rep.rɪ.zenˈteɪ.ʃᵊn.ᵊl, -rə-, -ˈteɪʃ.nᵊl (US) koʊ-
co-respondent ˌkəʊ.rɪˈspɒn.dənt, -rəˈ- (US) ˌkoʊ.rɪˈspɑːn-, -rəˈ- **-s** -s
Corey ˈkɔː.ri (US) ˈkɔːr.i
corf kɔːf (US) kɔːrf **-s** -s
Corfe kɔːf (US) kɔːrf
Corfu kɔːˈfuː, -ˈfjuː (US) ˈkɔːr.fuː, -fjuː, -ˈ-
corgi (C) ˈkɔː.gi (US) ˈkɔːr- **-s** -z
coriander ˌkɒr.iˈæn.dəʳ, ˈkɒr.i.æn- (US) ˈkɔːr.i.æn.dɚ, ˌkɔːr.iˈæn-
Corin ˈkɒr.ɪn, -ᵊn (US) ˈkɔːr-
Corinne kəˈrɪn
Corinth ˈkɒr.ɪntθ (US) ˈkɔːr-
Corinthian kəˈrɪnt.θi.ən **-s** -z
Coriolanus ˌkɒr.i.əʊˈleɪ.nəs, -ˈlɑː- (US) ˌkɔːr.i.əˈ-

Corioles kəˈraɪə.liːz, kɒrˈaɪə- ⓤⓢ kəˈraɪə-
Coriolis kəˈraɪə.lɪs, kɒrˈaɪə- ⓤⓢ kəˈraɪə-
cork (C) kɔːk ⓤⓢ kɔːrk **-s** -s **-ing** -ɪŋ **-ed** -t
corkage ˈkɔː.kɪdʒ ⓤⓢ ˈkɔːr-
corker (C) ˈkɔː.kəʳ ⓤⓢ ˈkɔːr.kɚ **-s** -z
Corkery ˈkɔː.kᵊr.i ⓤⓢ ˈkɔːr-
corkscrew ˈkɔːk.skruː ⓤⓢ ˈkɔːrk- **-s** -z **-ing** -ɪŋ **-ed** -d
corky ˈkɔː.ki ⓤⓢ ˈkɔːr-
Corleone ˌkɔː.liˈəʊ.ni ⓤⓢ ˌkɔːr.liˈoʊ-
corm kɔːm ⓤⓢ kɔːrm **-s** -z
Cormac ˈkɜː.mæk, ˈkɔː- ⓤⓢ ˈkɔːr-
Cormack ˈkɔː.mæk ⓤⓢ ˈkɔːr-
cormorant ˈkɔː.mᵊr.ənt ⓤⓢ ˈkɔːr- **-s** -s
corn kɔːn ⓤⓢ kɔːrn **-s** -z **-ing** -ɪŋ **-ed** -d **ˈCorn ˌBelt; ˈcorn ˌdolly; ˌcorned ˈbeef; ˈcorn ˌexchange**
cornball ˈkɔːn.bɔːl, ˈkɔːm- ⓤⓢ ˈkɔːrn-, -bɑːl **-s** -z
cornbread ˈkɔːn.bred, ˈkɔːm- ⓤⓢ ˈkɔːrn-
Cornbury ˈkɔːn.bᵊr.i, ˈkɔːm- ⓤⓢ ˈkɔːrn.ber-, -bɚ-
corncob ˈkɔːn.kɒb ⓤⓢ ˈkɔːrn.kɑːb **-s** -z
corncrake ˈkɔːn.kreɪk, ˈkɔːŋ- ⓤⓢ ˈkɔːrn- **-s** -s
corndog ˈkɔːn.dɒg ⓤⓢ ˈkɔːrn.dɑːg, -dɔːg **-s** -z
corne|a ˈkɔː.ni|.ə; kɔːˈniː- ⓤⓢ ˈkɔːr.ni- **-as** -əz **-al** -ᵊl
Corneille kɔːˈneɪ, -ˈneɪl ⓤⓢ kɔːrˈneɪ
Cornelia kɔːˈniː.li.ə ⓤⓢ kɔːrˈniːl.jə
cornelian kɔːˈniː.li.ən ⓤⓢ kɔːrˈniːl.jən **-s** -z
Cornelius kɔːˈniː.li.əs ⓤⓢ kɔːrˈniːl.jəs
Cornell kɔːˈnel ⓤⓢ kɔːr-
corn|er ˈkɔː.n|əʳ ⓤⓢ ˈkɔːr.n|ɚ **-ers** -əz ⓤⓢ -ɚz **-ering** -ᵊr.ɪŋ **-ered** -əd ⓤⓢ -ɚd **ˌcorner ˈshop**
cornerback ˈkɔː.nə.bæk ⓤⓢ ˈkɔːr.nɚ- **-s** -s
-cornered -ˈkɔː.nəd ⓤⓢ -ˈkɔr.nɚd
cornerstone ˈkɔː.nə.stəʊn ⓤⓢ ˈkɔːr.nɚ.stoʊn **-s** -z
cornet ˈkɔː.nɪt ⓤⓢ kɔːrˈnet **-s** -s
Cornetto® kɔːˈnet.əʊ ⓤⓢ kɔːrˈnet̬.oʊ
cornfield ˈkɔːn.fiːld ⓤⓢ ˈkɔːrn- **-s** -z
cornflakes ˈkɔːn.fleɪks ⓤⓢ ˈkɔːrn-
cornflour ˈkɔːn.flaʊəʳ ⓤⓢ ˈkɔːrn.flaʊɚ
cornflower ˈkɔːn.flaʊəʳ ⓤⓢ ˈkɔːrn.flaʊɚ **-s** -z
Cornhill ˌkɔːnˈhɪl ⓤⓢ ˈkɔːrn.hɪl, ˌ-ˈ-
cornic|e ˈkɔː.nɪs ⓤⓢ ˈkɔːr- **-es** -ɪz
corniche|e (C) kɔːˈniːʃ; ˈ--, -nɪʃ ⓤⓢ kɔːrˈniːʃ **-es** -ɪz
Cornish ˈkɔː.nɪʃ ⓤⓢ ˈkɔːr- **-man** -mən **-men** -mən, -men **-woman** -ˌwʊm.ən **-women** -ˌwɪm.ɪn **ˌCornish ˈpasty**
cornmeal ˈkɔːn.miːl, ˈkɔːm- ⓤⓢ ˈkɔːrn-
cornrow ˈkɔːn.rəʊ ⓤⓢ ˈkɔːrn.roʊ **-s** -z **-ing** -ɪŋ **-ed** -d
cornstarch ˈkɔːn.stɑːtʃ ⓤⓢ ˈkɔːrn.stɑːrtʃ
cornsyrup ˈkɔːnˌsɪr.əp ⓤⓢ ˈkɔːrnˌsɪr-, -ˌsɝː-
cornucopi|a ˌkɔː.njʊˈkəʊ.pi|.ə ⓤⓢ ˌkɔːr.nəˈkoʊ-, -njəˈ- **-as** -əz **-an** -ən
Cornwall ˈkɔːn.wɔːl, -wəl ⓤⓢ ˈkɔːrn.wɔːl, -wɑːl
Cornwallis kɔːnˈwɒl.ɪs ⓤⓢ kɔːrnˈwɑː.lɪs
Cornwell ˈkɔːn.wel, -wəl ⓤⓢ ˈkɔːrn-
corn|y ˈkɔː.n|i ⓤⓢ ˈkɔːr- **-ier** -i.əʳ ⓤⓢ -i.ɚ **-iest** -i.ɪst, -i.əst
corolla (C) kəˈrɒl.ə, -ˈrəʊ.lə ⓤⓢ -ˈroʊ-, -ˈrɑː- **-s** -z
Note: The suitable pronunciation for the car in Amercian English is /kəˈroʊ-/.
corollar|y kəˈrɒl.ᵊr|.i ⓤⓢ ˈkɔːr.ə.ler- **-ies** -iz
Coromandel ˌkɒr.əʊˈmæn.dᵊl ⓤⓢ ˌkɔːr.oʊˈ-
coron|a kəˈrəʊ.n|ə ⓤⓢ -ˈroʊ- **-ae** -iː **-as** -əz
Corona *female name:* ˈkɒr.ə.nə ⓤⓢ ˈkɔːr-
coronach (C) ˈkɒr.ə.nək, -nəx, -næk ⓤⓢ ˈkɔːr.ə.nək **-s** -s
coronal *(n.)* ˈkɒr.ə.nᵊl ⓤⓢ ˈkɔːr- **-s** -z
coronal *(adj.) pertaining to the sun's corona:* kəˈrəʊ.nᵊl ⓤⓢ -ˈroʊ- *medical, botanical and phonetic senses:* ˈkɒr.ə.nᵊl; kəˈrəʊ- ⓤⓢ ˈkɔːr.ə-; kəˈroʊ-
coronar|y ˈkɒr.ə.nᵊr|.i ⓤⓢ ˈkɔːr.ə.ner- **-ies** -iz
coronation ˌkɒr.əˈneɪ.ʃᵊn ⓤⓢ ˌkɔːr- **-s** -z
Coronel ˈkɒr.ə.nel ⓤⓢ ˈkɔːr-
coroner ˈkɒr.ə.nəʳ ⓤⓢ ˈkɔːr.ᵊn.ɚ **-s** -z
coronet ˈkɒr.ə.nɪt, -net, -nət; ˌkɒr.əˈnet ⓤⓢ ˌkɔːr.əˈnet **-s** -s
corpora *(plur. of* **corpus)** ˈkɔː.pᵊr.ə, -pə.rɑː ⓤⓢ ˈkɔːr.pɚ.ə
corporal ˈkɔː.pᵊr.ᵊl, ˈ-prᵊl ⓤⓢ ˈkɔːr- **-s** -z **-ly** -i **ˌcorporal ˈpunishment**
corporality ˌkɔː.pəˈræl.ə.ti, -ɪ.ti ⓤⓢ ˌkɔːr.pəˈræl.ə.t̬i
corporate ˈkɔː.pᵊr.ət, -ɪt, ˈ-prət, ˈ-prɪt ⓤⓢ ˈkɔːr- **-ly** -li **-ness** -nəs, -nɪs
corporation ˌkɔː.pᵊrˈeɪ.ʃᵊn ⓤⓢ ˌkɔːr.pəˈreɪ- **-s** -z
corporative ˈkɔː.pᵊr.ə.tɪv ⓤⓢ ˈkɔːr.pɚ.ə.t̬ɪv
corporator ˈkɔː.pᵊr.eɪ.təʳ ⓤⓢ ˈkɔːr.pə.reɪ.t̬ɚ **-s** -z
corporeal kɔːˈpɔː.ri.əl ⓤⓢ kɔːrˈpɔːr- **-ly** -i
corps *(sing.)* kɔːʳ ⓤⓢ kɔːr *(plur.)* kɔːz ⓤⓢ kɔːrz
corps de ballet ˌkɔː.dəˈbæl.eɪ, -li ⓤⓢ ˌkɔːr.də.bælˈeɪ
corps|e kɔːps ⓤⓢ kɔːrps **-es** -ɪz **-ing** -ɪŋ **-ed** -t
corpulen|ce ˈkɔː.pjʊ.lənt|s, -pjə- ⓤⓢ ˈkɔːr.pjə- **-cy** -si
corpulent ˈkɔː.pjʊ.lənt, -pjə- ⓤⓢ ˈkɔːr.pjə-
corp|us ˈkɔː.p|əs ⓤⓢ ˈkɔːr- **-ora** -ə.rə ⓤⓢ -ɚ.ə **-uses** -ə.sɪz
Corpus Christi ˌkɔː.pəsˈkrɪs.ti ⓤⓢ ˌkɔːr-
corpuscle ˈkɔː.pʌs.l̩, -pə.sl̩; kɔːˈpʌs- ⓤⓢ ˈkɔːr.pʌs.l̩, -pə.sl̩ **-s** -z
corpuscular kɔːˈpʌs.kjə.ləʳ, -kjʊ- ⓤⓢ kɔːrˈpʌs.kjə.lɚ
corpuscule kɔːˈpʌs.kjuːl, -kjʊl ⓤⓢ kɔːrˈpʌs.kjuːl **-s** -z
corpus delicti ˌkɔː.pʌs.dɪˈlɪk.taɪ, -pəs- ⓤⓢ ˌkɔːr-
corpus juris ˌkɔː.pʌsˈdʒʊə.rɪs, -pəs- ⓤⓢ ˌkɔːr.pʌsˈdʒʊr.ɪs
Corr kɔːʳ ⓤⓢ kɔːr **-s** -z
corral kəˈrɑːl, kɒrˈɑːl ⓤⓢ kəˈræl **-s** -z **-ling** -ɪŋ **-led** -d
correct kəˈrekt **-ly** -li **-ness** -nəs, -nɪs **-s** -s **-ing** -ɪŋ **-ed** -ɪd **-or/s** -əʳ/z ⓤⓢ -ɚ/z
correction kəˈrek.ʃᵊn **-s** -z
correctional kəˈrek.ʃᵊn.ᵊl
correctitude kəˈrek.tɪ.tjuːd, -tʃuːd ⓤⓢ -tə.tuːd, -tjuːd
corrective kəˈrek.tɪv **-s** -z
Correggio kəˈredʒ.i.əʊ ⓤⓢ ˈ-oʊ
correlate *(n.)* ˈkɒr.ᵊl.ət, -ɪ.lət, -leɪt ⓤⓢ ˈkɔːr.ə.leɪt **-s** -s
corre|late *(v.)* ˈkɒr.ə|.leɪt, ˈ-ɪ- ⓤⓢ ˈkɔːr.ə- **-lates** -leɪts **-lating** -leɪ.tɪŋ ⓤⓢ -leɪ.t̬ɪŋ **-lated** -leɪ.tɪd ⓤⓢ -leɪ.t̬ɪd **-latable** -leɪ.tə.bl̩ ⓤⓢ -leɪ.t̬ə.bl̩
correlation ˌkɒr.əˈleɪ.ʃᵊn, -ɪˈ- ⓤⓢ ˌkɔːr.əˈ- **-s** -z
correlative kɒrˈel.ə.tɪv, kəˈrel- ⓤⓢ kəˈrel.ə.t̬ɪv **-ly** -li **-ness** -nəs, -nɪs
correspond ˌkɒr.ɪˈspɒnd, -əˈ- ⓤⓢ ˌkɔːr.əˈ- **-s** -z **-ing** -ɪŋ **-ed** -ɪd
correspondenc|e ˌkɒr.ɪˈspɒn.dənt|s, -əˈ- ⓤⓢ ˌkɔːr.əˈspɑːn- **-es** -ɪz **correˈspondence ˌcourse**
correspondent ˌkɒr.ɪˈspɒn.dᵊnt, -əˈ- ⓤⓢ ˌkɔːr.əˈspɑːn- **-s** -s
corresponding ˌkɒr.ɪˈspɒn.dɪŋ, -əˈ- ⓤⓢ ˌkɔːr.əˈspɑːn- **-ly** -li
corridor ˈkɒr.ɪ.dɔːʳ, ˈ-ə-, -dəʳ ⓤⓢ ˈkɔːr.ə.dɚ, ˈ-ɪ-, -dɔːr **-s** -z
corrie (C) ˈkɒr.i ⓤⓢ ˈkɔːr-
Corrientes ˌkɒr.iˈen.tes ⓤⓢ ˌkɔːr-
Corrigan ˈkɒr.ɪ.gᵊn, ˈ-ə- ⓤⓢ ˈkɔːr.ə-, ˈ-ɪ-
corrigend|um ˌkɒr.ɪˈdʒen.d|əm, -əˈ-, -ˈgen- ⓤⓢ ˌkɔːr- **-a** -ə
corrigible ˈkɒr.ɪ.dʒə.bl̩, -dʒɪ- ⓤⓢ ˈkɔːr-
Corringham ˈkɒr.ɪŋ.əm ⓤⓢ ˈkɔːr-, -hæm
corroborant kəˈrɒb.ᵊr.ᵊnt ⓤⓢ -ˈrɑː.bɚ- **-s** -s

corrobor|ate kəˈrɒb.ərˈl.eɪt ⓊⓈ -ˈrɑː.bə.r|eɪt **-ates** -eɪts **-ating** -eɪ.tɪŋ ⓊⓈ -eɪ.t̬ɪŋ **-ated** -eɪ.tɪd ⓊⓈ -eɪ.t̬ɪd **-ator/s** -eɪ.təʳ/z ⓊⓈ -eɪ.t̬ɚ/z
corroboration kəˌrɒb.əˈreɪ.ʃən ⓊⓈ -ˌrɑː.bəˈ- **-s** -z
corroborative kəˈrɒb.ər.ə.tɪv, -eɪ- ⓊⓈ -ˈrɑː.bɚ.ə.t̬ɪv
corroboratory kəˈrɒb.ər.ə.tər.i, -tri; kəˌrɒb.əˈreɪ- ⓊⓈ -ˈrɑː.bɚ.ə.tɔːr.i
corroboree kəˈrɒb.ər.i, kəˌrɒb.əˈriː ⓊⓈ -ˌrɑː.bəˈriː **-s** -z
corrod|e kəˈrəʊd ⓊⓈ -ˈroʊd **-es** -z **-ing** -ɪŋ **-ed** -ɪd
corrodible kəˈrəʊ.də.bl̩, -dɪ- ⓊⓈ -ˈroʊ.də-
corrosion kəˈrəʊ.ʒən ⓊⓈ -ˈroʊ- **-s** -z
corrosive kəˈrəʊ.sɪv, -zɪv ⓊⓈ -ˈroʊ- **-s** -z **-ly** -li **-ness** -nəs, -nɪs
corru|gate ˈkɒr.əl.geɪt, ˈ-ʊ- ⓊⓈ ˈkɔːr.ə- **-gates** -geɪts **-gating** -geɪ.tɪŋ ⓊⓈ -geɪ.t̬ɪŋ **-gated** -geɪ.tɪd ⓊⓈ -geɪ.t̬ɪd ˌ**corrugated** ˈ**iron**
corrugation ˌkɒr.əˈgeɪ.ʃən, -ʊˈ- ⓊⓈ ˌkɔːr.əˈ- **-s** -z
corrupt kəˈrʌpt **-est** -ɪst, -əst **-ly** -li **-ness** -nəs, -nɪs **-s** -s **-ing** -ɪŋ **-ed** -ɪd **-er/s** -əʳ/z ⓊⓈ -ɚ/z
corruptibility kəˌrʌp.təˈbɪl.ə.ti, -tɪˈ-, -ɪ.ti ⓊⓈ -təˈbɪl.ə.t̬i
corruptib|le kəˈrʌp.tə.bl|̩, -tɪ- ⓊⓈ -tə- **-ly** -li **-leness** -l̩.nəs, -nɪs
corruption kəˈrʌp.ʃən **-s** -z
corruptive kəˈrʌp.tɪv
Corry ˈkɒr.i ⓊⓈ ˈkɔːr-
Corsa® ˈkɔː.sə ⓊⓈ ˈkɔːr-
corsag|e kɔːˈsɑːʒ, ˈ-- ⓊⓈ kɔːrˈsɑːʒ, -sɑːdʒ **-es** -ɪz
corsair ˈkɔː.seəʳ, -ˈ- ⓊⓈ ˈkɔːr.ser, -ˈ- **-s** -z
cors|e kɔːs ⓊⓈ kɔːrs **-es** -ɪz
corselet ˈkɔː.slət, -slɪt ⓊⓈ ˈkɔːr- **-s** -s
corset ˈkɔː.sɪt, -sət ⓊⓈ ˈkɔːr- **-s** -s
corsetry ˈkɔː.sɪ.tri, -sə- ⓊⓈ ˈkɔːr-
Corsham ˈkɔː.ʃəm ⓊⓈ ˈkɔːr-
Corsic|a ˈkɔː.sɪ.k|ə ⓊⓈ ˈkɔːr- **-an/s** -ən/z
corslet ˈkɔː.slət, -slɪt ⓊⓈ ˈkɔːr- **-s** -s
cortèg|e kɔːˈteɪʒ, -ˈteʒ, ˈ-- ⓊⓈ kɔːrˈteʒ **-es** -ɪz
Cortes, Cortés ˈkɔː.tes, -tez, -ˈ- ⓊⓈ kɔːrˈtez
cort|ex ˈkɔː.t|eks ⓊⓈ ˈkɔːr- **-exes** -ek.sɪz **-ices** -ɪ.siːz
Corti ˈkɔː.ti ⓊⓈ ˈkɔːr.ti
cortical ˈkɔː.tɪ.kəl ⓊⓈ ˈkɔːr.t̬ɪ-
corticosteroid ˌkɔː.tɪ.kəʊˈstɪə.rɔɪd, -ˈster.ɔɪd ⓊⓈ ˌkɔːr.t̬ɪ.koʊˈster.ɔɪd, -ˈstɪr- **-s** -z
Cortina® kɔːˈtiː.nə ⓊⓈ kɔːr- **-s** -z
cortisone ˈkɔː.tɪ.zəʊn, -tə-, -səʊn ⓊⓈ ˈkɔːr.t̬ə.zoʊn, -soʊn
Cortney ˈkɔːt.ni ⓊⓈ ˈkɔːrt-
corundum kəˈrʌn.dəm
Corunna kɒrˈʌn.ə, kəˈrʌn- ⓊⓈ kəˈrʌn-
Corus® ˈkɔː.rəs ⓊⓈ ˈkɔːr.əs
corus|cate ˈkɒr.ə.s|keɪt, -ʌs|.keɪt ⓊⓈ ˈkɔːr.ə.s|keɪt **-cates** -keɪts **-cating** -keɪ.tɪŋ ⓊⓈ -keɪ.t̬ɪŋ **-cated** -keɪ.tɪd ⓊⓈ -keɪ.t̬ɪd
coruscation ˌkɒr.əˈskeɪ.ʃən, -ʌsˈkeɪ- ⓊⓈ ˌkɔːr.əˈskeɪ- **-s** -z
corvée ˈkɔː.veɪ ⓊⓈ kɔːrˈveɪ **-s** -z
corvette kɔːˈvet ⓊⓈ kɔːr- **-s** -s
Corwen ˈkɔː.wen, -wɪn ⓊⓈ ˈkɔːr-
Cory ˈkɔː.ri ⓊⓈ ˈkɔːr.i
Corybant ˈkɒr.ɪ.bænt ⓊⓈ ˈkɔːr- **-s** -s
Corybantes ˌkɒr.ɪˈbæn.tiːz ⓊⓈ ˌkɔːr-
Corydon ˈkɒr.ɪ.dən, ˈ-ə-, -dɒn ⓊⓈ ˈkɔːr.ə.dən, -dɑːn
corymb ˈkɒr.ɪmb, -ɪm ⓊⓈ ˈkɔːr-
coryphae|us ˌkɒr.ɪˈfiː|.əs ⓊⓈ ˌkɔːr.əˈ- **-i** -aɪ
coryphée ˌkɒr.ɪˈfeɪ ⓊⓈ ˌkɔːr-
Coryton *in Devon:* ˈkɒr.ɪ.tən, ˈ-ə- ⓊⓈ ˈkɔːr- *in Essex:* ˈkɔː.rɪ.tən, ˈ-rə- ⓊⓈ ˈkɔːr-
cos *because:* kəz, kəs, kɒz, kɒs ⓊⓈ kəz, kəs, kɑːz, kɑːs
Note: Weak form word.
cos (C) *lettuce:* kɒs, kɒz ⓊⓈ kɑːs, koʊs
Cosa Nostra ˌkəʊ.zəˈnɒs.trə ⓊⓈ ˌkoʊ.səˈnoʊ.strə, -zəˈ-
Cosby ˈkɒz.bi ⓊⓈ ˈkɑːz-
cosec ˈkəʊ.sek ⓊⓈ ˈkoʊ-
cosecant ˌkəʊˈsiː.kənt ⓊⓈ ˌkoʊ- **-s** -s
co-set ˈkəʊ.set ⓊⓈ ˈkoʊ- **-s** -s
Cosgrave ˈkɒz.greɪv ⓊⓈ ˈkɑːz-
cosh kɒʃ ⓊⓈ kɑːʃ **-es** -ɪz **-ing** -ɪŋ **-ed** -t
Cosham ˈkɒs.əm ⓊⓈ ˈkɑː.səm
cosh|er *feast, pamper:* ˈkɒʃ|.əʳ ⓊⓈ ˈkɑː.ʃ|ɚ **-ers** -əz ⓊⓈ -ɚz **-ering** -ər.ɪŋ **-ered** -əd ⓊⓈ -ɚd
cosher *according to Jewish law:* ˈkəʊ.ʃəʳ, ˈkɒʃ.əʳ ⓊⓈ ˈkoʊ.ʃɚ
Cosi Fan Tutte ˌkəʊ.si.fænˈtʊt.eɪ, -zi-, kəʊˌsiː-, -i ⓊⓈ koʊˌsiː.fɑːnˈtuː.teɪ
cosignator|y ˌkəʊˈsɪg.nə.tər|.i, -tr|i ⓊⓈ ˌkoʊˈsɪg.nə.tɔːr|.i **-ies** -iz
Cosima ˈkəʊ.sɪ.mə ⓊⓈ ˈkoʊ.zi-, -mɑː
cosine ˈkəʊ.saɪn ⓊⓈ ˈkoʊ- **-s** -z
CoSIRA kəʊˈsaɪə.rə ⓊⓈ koʊˈsaɪə-
cosmetic kɒzˈmet.ɪk ⓊⓈ kɑːzˈmet̬- **-s** -s **-al** -əl **-ally** -əl.i, -li
cosmic ˈkɒz.mɪk ⓊⓈ ˈkɑːz- **-al** -əl **-ally** -əl.i, -li
cosm|ism ˈkɒz.m|ɪ.zəm ⓊⓈ ˈkɑːz- **-ist/s** -ɪst/s
cosmo- ˈkɒz.məʊ-, kɒzˈmɒ- ⓊⓈ ˈkɑːz.moʊ-, -mə-, kɑːzˈmɑː-
Note: Prefix. This may be stressed on the initial syllable (as in **cosmonaut** /ˈkɒz.mə.nɔːt ⓊⓈ ˈkɑːz.mə.nɑːt/) or on the second syllable (e.g. **cosmology** /kɒzˈmɒl.ə.dʒi ⓊⓈ kɑːzˈmɑː.lə.dʒi/).
Cosmo ˈkɒz.məʊ ⓊⓈ ˈkɑːz.moʊ
cosmogonic ˌkɒz.məʊˈgɒn.ɪk ⓊⓈ ˌkɑːz.məˈgɑː.nɪk **-al** -əl **-ally** -əl.i, -li
cosmogon|y kɒzˈmɒg.ən|.i ⓊⓈ kɑːzˈmɑː.gən- **-ist/s** -ɪst/s
cosmographic ˌkɒz.məʊˈgræf.ɪk ⓊⓈ ˌkɑːz.məˈ- **-al** -əl **-ally** -əl.i, -li
cosmograph|y kɒzˈmɒg.rə.f|i ⓊⓈ kɑːzˈmɑː.grə- **-er/s** -əʳ/z ⓊⓈ -ɚ/z
cosmological ˌkɒz.məˈlɒdʒ.ɪ.kəl ⓊⓈ ˌkɑːz.məˈlɑː.dʒɪ-
cosmolog|y kɒzˈmɒl.ə.dʒ|i ⓊⓈ kɑːzˈmɑː.lə- **-ist/s** -ɪst/s
cosmonaut ˈkɒz.mə.nɔːt ⓊⓈ ˈkɑːz.mə.nɑːt, -nɔːt **-s** -s
cosmopolitan (C®) ˌkɒz.məˈpɒl.ɪ.tən, ˈ-ə- ⓊⓈ ˌkɑːz.məˈpɑː.lɪ- **-s** -z
cosmopolitanism ˌkɒz.məˈpɒl.ɪ.tən.ɪ.zəm, ˈ-ə-, -tɪ.nɪ- ⓊⓈ ˌkɑːz.məˈpɑː.lɪ.tən.ɪ-
cosmos (C®) ˈkɒz.mɒs ⓊⓈ ˈkɑːz.moʊs, -məs, -mɑːs
Cossack ˈkɒs.æk ⓊⓈ ˈkɑː.sæk **-s** -s
coss|et ˈkɒs|.ɪt ⓊⓈ ˈkɑː.s|ɪt **-ets** -ɪts **-e(t)ting** -ɪ.tɪŋ ⓊⓈ -ɪ.t̬ɪŋ **-e(t)ted** -ɪ.tɪd ⓊⓈ -ɪ.t̬ɪd
cost kɒst ⓊⓈ kɑːst **-s** -s **-ing** -ɪŋ **-ed** ˌ**cost-ef**ˈ**fective**; ˌ**cost of** ˈ**living**
Costa ˈkɒs.tə ⓊⓈ ˈkɑː.stə
Costa Blanca ˌkɒs.təˈblæŋ.kə ⓊⓈ ˌkɑː.stəˈblɑːŋ-, ˌkoʊ-
Costa Brava ˌkɒs.təˈbrɑː.və ⓊⓈ ˌkɑː.stə-, ˌkoʊ-
Costa del Sol ˌkɒs.tə.delˈsɒl ⓊⓈ ˌkɑː.stə.delˈsoʊl, ˌkoʊ-
Costain kɒsˈteɪn, ˈ-- ⓊⓈ ˈkɑː.steɪn, -ˈ-
costal ˈkɒs.təl ⓊⓈ ˈkɑː.stəl
co-star *(n.)* ˈkəʊ.stɑːʳ ⓊⓈ ˈkoʊ.stɑːr **-s** -z
co-star *(v.)* kəʊˈstɑːʳ ⓊⓈ ˈkoʊ.stɑːr **-s** -z **-ring** -ɪŋ **-red** -d
costard ˈkʌs.təd, ˈkɒs- ⓊⓈ ˈkɑː.stɚd **-s** -z
Costard ˈkɒs.təd, -tɑːd ⓊⓈ ˈkɑː.stɚd, -stɑːrd
Costa Ric|a ˌkɒs.təˈriː.k|ə ⓊⓈ ˌkoʊ.stəˈ-, ˌkɑː- **-an/s** -ən/z
cost-effective ˌkɒst.ɪˈfek.tɪv, -əˈ-, ˈkɒst.ɪ.fek-, ˈ-ə- ⓊⓈ ˈkɑːst.ɪˌfek-, -əˌ-, ˌkɑːst.ɪˈfekt-, -əˈ- **-ly** -li **-ness** -nəs, -nɪs
Costello kɒsˈtel.əʊ, kəˈstel-, ˈkɒs.təl.əʊ ⓊⓈ kɑːˈstel.oʊ, kə-; ˈkɑː.stə.loʊ
coster ˈkɒs.təʳ ⓊⓈ ˈkɑː.stɚ **-s** -z
costermonger ˈkɒs.təˌmʌŋ.gəʳ ⓊⓈ ˈkɑː.stɚˌmʌŋ.gɚ, -ˌmɑːŋ- **-s** -z
costive ˈkɒs.tɪv ⓊⓈ ˈkɑː.stɪv **-ly** -li **-ness** -nəs, -nɪs

costl|y 'kɒst.l|i US 'kɑːst- **-ier** -i.əʳ US -i.ɚ **-iest** -i.ɪst, -i.əst **-iness** -ɪ.nəs, -ɪ.nɪs

costmary 'kɒst.meə.ri US 'kɑːst.mer.i

Costner 'kɒs*t*.nəʳ US 'kɑːs*t*.nɚ

cost-plus ˌkɒs*t*'plʌs US ˌkɑːs*t*-

costum|e 'kɒs.tjuːm US 'kɑː.stuːm, -stjuːm **-es** -z **-ing** -ɪŋ **-ed** -d ˌ**costume 'jewellery**

costumier kɒs'tjuː.mi.əʳ, -eɪ US kɑː'stuː.mi.eɪ, -'stjuː-, -ɚ **-s** -z

Cosway 'kɒz.weɪ US 'kɑːz- **-s** -z

cos|y 'kəʊ.z|i US 'koʊ- **-ies** -iz **-ier** -i.əʳ US -i.ɚ **-iest** -i.ɪst, -i.əst **-ily** -ɪ.li, -əl.i **-iness** -ɪ.nəs, -ɪ.nɪs

cot kɒt US kɑːt **-s** -s '**cot** ˌ**death**

cotangent ˌkəʊ'tæn.dʒənt, '-ˌ-- US ˌkoʊ'tæn-, '-ˌ-- **-s** -s

cot|e kəʊt US koʊt **-es** -s **-ing** -ɪŋ US 'koʊ.t̬ɪŋ **-ed** -ɪd US 'koʊ.t̬ɪd

Côte d'Azur ˌkəʊt.dæ'ʒʊəʳ, -də'- US ˌkoʊt.də'zʊr, -dɑː'-

Côte d'Ivoire ˌkəʊt.diː'vwɑːʳ US ˌkoʊt.diː'vwɑːr

Côte d'Or ˌkəʊt'dɔːʳ US ˌkoʊt'dɔːr

cotenancy ˌkəʊ'ten.ən*t*.si US ˌkoʊ-

coterie 'kəʊ.tᵊr.i US 'koʊ.t̬ɚ- **-s** -z

coterminous ˌkəʊ'tɜː.mɪ.nəs US ˌkoʊ'tɝː- **-ly** -li

Cotgrave 'kɒt.greɪv US 'kɑːt-

cotill(i)on kə'tɪl.i.ən, kəʊ-, kɒt'ɪl- US koʊ'tɪl.jən, kə- **-s** -z

Coton 'kəʊ.tᵊn US 'koʊ-

cotoneaster kəˌtəʊ.ni'æs.təʳ US -ˌtoʊ.ni'æs.tɚ **-s** -z

Cotonou ˌkəʊ.tə'nuː, ˌkɒt.ɒn'uː US ˌkoʊ.toʊ'nuː, -tᵊn'uː

Cotopaxi ˌkɒt.əʊ'pæk.si, ˌkəʊ.təʊ'- US ˌkoʊ.t̬ə'-

Cotswold 'kɒt.swəʊld, -swəld US 'kɑːt.swoʊld **-s** -z

Cotsworth 'kɒt.swəθ, -wɜːθ US 'kɑːt.swɝːθ, -swɚθ

cottag|e 'kɒt.ɪdʒ US 'kɑː.t̬ɪdʒ **-es** -ɪz **-ing** -ɪŋ **-ey** -i ˌ**cottage 'cheese**; ˌ**cottage 'industry**; ˌ**cottage 'pie**

cottager 'kɒt.ɪ.dʒəʳ US 'kɑː.t̬ɪ.dʒɚ **-s** -z

Cottam 'kɒt.əm US 'kɑː.t̬əm

Cottbus 'kɒt.bəs, -bʊs US 'kɑːt.bəs, -bʊs

Cottenham 'kɒt.ᵊn.əm US 'kɑː.tᵊn-, -hæm

cotter (C) 'kɒt.əʳ US 'kɑː.t̬ɚ **-s** -z

Cotterell 'kɒt.ᵊr.ᵊl US 'kɑː.t̬ɚ-

Cotterill 'kɒt.ᵊr.ᵊl, -ɪl US 'kɑː.t̬ɚ-

Cottesloe 'kɒt.sləʊ, -əz.ləʊ US 'kɑːt.sloʊ, -əz.loʊ

Cottian 'kɒt.i.ən US 'kɑː.t̬i-

Cottingham 'kɒt.ɪŋ.əm US 'kɑː.t̬ɪŋ-, -hæm

cotton (C) 'kɒt.ᵊn US 'kɑː.tᵊn **-s** -z **-ing** -ɪŋ **-ed** -d '**Cotton** ˌ**Belt**; ˌ**cotton 'candy**; ˌ**cotton 'wool**

cotton grass 'kɒt.ᵊn.grɑːs US 'kɑː.tᵊn.græs

cottonseed 'kɒt.ᵊn.siːd US 'kɑː.tᵊn-

cottontail 'kɒt.ᵊn.teɪl US 'kɑː.tᵊn- **-s** -z

cottonwood 'kɒt.n̩.wʊd US 'kɑː.tn̩- **-s** -z

cottony 'kɒt.ᵊn.i US 'kɑː.tᵊn-

Cottrell 'kɒt.rᵊl; kə'trel US 'kɑː.trᵊl; kə'trel

cotyledon ˌkɒt.ɪ'liː.dᵊn, -ᵊl'iː- US ˌkɑː.t̬ə'liː- **-s** -z

cotyledonous ˌkɒt.ɪ'liː.dᵊn.əs, -ᵊl'iː- US ˌkɑː.t̬ə'liː-

couch *all verb senses, item of furniture:* kaʊtʃ **-es** -ɪz **-ing** -ɪŋ **-ed** -t '**couch poˌtato**, ˌ**couch po'tato**

couch *grass:* kuːtʃ, kaʊtʃ

Couch kuːtʃ

couchant 'kaʊ.tʃᵊnt, 'kuː-

couchée 'kuː.ʃeɪ, -'- US kuː'ʃeɪ **-s** -z

couchette kuː'ʃet **-s** -s

Coué 'kuː.eɪ **-ism** -ɪ.zᵊm

cougar 'kuː.gəʳ US -gɚ **-s** -z

cough kɒf US kɑːf, kɔːf **-s** -s **-ing** -ɪŋ **-ed** -t **-er/s** -əʳ/z US -ɚ/z '**cough** ˌ**drop**; '**cough** ˌ**mixture**; '**cough** ˌ**syrup**

Coughlan 'kɒg.lən, 'kɒf-, 'kɒk-, 'kɒx-, 'kəʊ- US 'kɑː.glən, 'koʊ.lən

Coughlin 'kɒg.lɪn, 'kɒf-, 'kɒk-, 'kɒx- US 'kɑː.glɪn, 'kɑːf-

could *(from* **can***) strong form:* kʊd *weak form:* kəd

Note: Weak form word. The strong form is used for emphasis, e.g. "You **could** be right", for contrast, e.g. "whether she could or not", and in sentence-final position, e.g. "as well as he could.".

couldn't 'kʊd.ᵊnt

couldst kʊdst

coulee 'kuː.li **-s** -z

coulisse kuː'liːs, kʊ- **-s** -ɪz

couloir 'kuːl.wɑːʳ, -wɔːʳ US kuːl'wɑːr **-s** -z

coulomb (C) 'kuː.lɒm US -lɑːm, -loʊm **-s** -z

Coulsdon 'kəʊlz.dᵊn, 'kuːlz- US 'koʊlz-, 'kuːlz-

Note: /'kəʊlz- US 'koʊlz-/ is the traditional local pronunciation. People unfamiliar with the place generally pronounce /'kuːlz-/, as also do new residents in the district.

Coulson 'kəʊl.sᵊn, 'kuːl- US 'koʊl-, 'kuːl-

coulter 'kəʊl.təʳ, 'kuː- US 'koʊl.t̬ɚ **-s** -z

Coulthard 'kuːl.tɑːd, 'kəʊl- US -tɑːrd

Coulton 'kəʊl.tᵊn US 'koʊl-

council 'kaʊn*t*.sᵊl, -sɪl **-s** -z '**council** ˌ**house**; '**council** ˌ**tax**

counci(l)lor 'kaʊn*t*.sᵊl.əʳ, -sɪ.ləʳ US -sᵊl.ɚ **-s** -z

council|man 'kaʊn*t*.sᵊl|.mən, -sɪl-, -mæn **-men** -mən, -men **-woman** -ˌwʊm.ən **-women** -ˌwɪm.ɪn

counsel 'kaʊn*t*.sᵊl **-s** -z **-(l)ing** -ɪŋ **-(l)ed** -d

counsel(l)or 'kaʊn*t*.sᵊl.əʳ US -ɚ **-s** -z

count (C) kaʊnt **-s** -s **-ing** -ɪŋ US 'kaʊn.t̬ɪŋ **-ed** -ɪd US 'kaʊn.t̬ɪd

countab|le 'kaʊn.tə.b|l US -t̬ə- **-ly** -li

countdown 'kaʊnt.daʊn

countenanc|e 'kaʊn.tᵊn.ən*t*s, -tɪ.nən*t*s US -tᵊn.ən*t*s **-es** -ɪz **-ing** -ɪŋ **-ed** -t

counter- 'kaʊn.təʳ- US 'kaʊn.t̬ɚ-

count|er 'kaʊn.t|əʳ US 'kaʊn.t̬|ɚ **-ers** -əz US -ɚz **-ering** -ᵊr.ɪŋ **-ered** -əd US -ɚd ˌ**Counter-Refor'mation**

counteract ˌkaʊn.tᵊr'ækt, '--- US ˌkaʊn.t̬ɚ'ækt **-s** -s **-ing** -ɪŋ **-ed** -ɪd

counteraction *counteracting:* ˌkaʊn.tᵊr'æk.ʃᵊn US -t̬ɚ'- **-s** -z

counter-action *action by way of reply:* 'kaʊn.təʳˌæk.ʃᵊn US -t̬ɚˌ- **-s** -z

counteractive ˌkaʊn.tᵊr'æk.tɪv US -t̬ɚ'- **-ly** -li

counterargument 'kaʊn.təʳˌɑːg.jə.mənt, -jʊ- US -t̬ɚˌɑːrg.jə- **-s** -s

counterattack 'kaʊn.təʳ.əˌtæk, ˌkaʊn.təʳ.ə'tæk US 'kaʊn.t̬ɚ.əˌtæk, ˌkaʊn.t̬ɚ.ə'tæk **-s** -s **-ing** -ɪŋ **-ed** -t

counterattraction ˌkaʊn.təʳ.ə'træk.ʃᵊn, 'kaʊn.təʳ.ə.træk- US ˌkaʊn.t̬ɚ.ə'træk-, 'kaʊn.t̬ɚ.əˌtræk- **-s** -z

counterbalanc|e *(n.)* 'kaʊn.təˌbæl.ən*t*s US -t̬ɚ- **-es** -ɪz

counterbalanc|e *(v.)* ˌkaʊn.tə'bæl.ən*t*s US -t̬ɚ'- **-es** -ɪz **-ing** -ɪŋ **-ed** -t

counterbid 'kaʊn.tə.bɪd US -t̬ɚ- **-s** -z **-ding** -ɪŋ

counterblast 'kaʊn.tə.blɑːst US -t̬ɚ.blæst **-s** -s

counterblow 'kaʊn.tə.bləʊ US -t̬ɚ.bloʊ **-s** -z

countercharg|e 'kaʊn.tə.tʃɑːdʒ US -t̬ɚ.tʃɑːrdʒ **-es** -ɪz **-ing** -ɪŋ **-ed** -d

counterclaim 'kaʊn.tə.kleɪm US -t̬ɚ- **-s** -z **-ing** -ɪŋ **-ed** -d

counterclockwise ˌkaʊn.tə'klɒk.waɪz US -t̬ɚ'klɑː.kwaɪz

counterespionage ˌkaʊn.tᵊr'es.pi.ə.nɑːʒ, -nɑːdʒ US -t̬ɚ'-

counter|feit 'kaʊn.tə|.fɪt, -fiːt US -t̬ɚ|.fɪt **-feits** -fɪts, -fiːts US -fɪts **-feiting** -fɪ.tɪŋ, -fiː- US -fɪ.t̬ɪŋ **-feited** -fɪ.tɪd, -fiː- US -fɪ.t̬ɪd **-feiter/s** -fɪ.təʳ/z, -fiː- US -fɪ.t̬ɚ/z

counterfoil 'kaʊn.tə.fɔɪl US -t̬ɚ- **-s** -z

counterinsurgen|cy ˌkaʊn.təʳ.ɪnˈsɜː.dʒᵊn|*t*.si US -t̬ɚ.ɪnˈsɝː- **-t** -t

counterintelligence ˌkaʊn.təʳ.ɪnˈtel.ɪ.dʒən*t*s, ˈkaʊn.təʳ.ɪn.tel- US ˌkaʊn.t̬ɚ.ɪnˈtel-, ˈkaʊn.t̬ɚ.ɪnˌtel-

counterintuitive ˌkaʊn.təʳ.ɪnˈtjuː.ə.tɪv, -ɪ.tɪv US -t̬ɚ.ɪnˈtuː.ə.t̬ɪv, -ˈtjuː- **-ly** -li

countermand ˌkaʊn.təˈmɑːnd, ˈ--- US ˌkaʊn.tɚˈmænd, ˈ--- **-s** -z **-ing** -ɪŋ **-ed** -ɪd

countermeasure ˈkaʊn.təˌmeʒ.əʳ US -t̬ɚˌmeʒ.ɚ **-s** -z

countermove ˈkaʊn.tə.muːv US -t̬ɚ- **-s** -z

counteroffensive ˌkaʊn.təʳ.əˈfen*t*.sɪv, ˈkaʊn.təʳ.əˌfen*t*- US ˈkaʊn.t̬ɚ.əˌfen*t*- **-s** -z

counterpane ˈkaʊn.tə.peɪn, -pɪn US -t̬ɚ- **-s** -z

counterpart ˈkaʊn.tə.pɑːt US -tɚ.pɑːrt **-s** -s

counterplot ˈkaʊn.tə.plɒt US -tɚ.plɑːt **-s** -s

counterpoint ˈkaʊn.tə.pɔɪnt US -tɚ-

counterpois|e ˈkaʊn.tə.pɔɪz US -tɚ- **-es** -ɪz **-ing** -ɪŋ **-ed** -d

counterproductive ˌkaʊn.tə.prəˈdʌk.tɪv US -tɚ- **-ly** -li **-ness** -nəs, -nɪs

counterrevolution ˌkaʊn.tə.rev.əˈluː.ʃᵊn, -ˈljuː-, ˈkaʊn.tə.rev.əˌluː-, -ˌljuː- US ˌkaʊn.t̬ɚ.rev.əˈluː-, ˈkaʊn.t̬ɚ.rev.əˌluː- **-s** -z

counterrevolutionar|y ˌkaʊn.tə.rev.əˈluː.ʃᵊn.ᵊr|.i, -ˈljuː-, ˈkaʊn.tə.rev.əˌluː-, -ˌljuː- US ˌkaʊn.t̬ɚ.rev.əˈluː.ʃᵊn.er-, ˈkaʊn.t̬ɚ.rev.əˌluː- **-ies** -iz

counterscarp ˈkaʊn.tə.skɑːp US -t̬ɚ.skɑːrp **-s** -s

countersign (*n.*) ˈkaʊn.tə.saɪn US -t̬ɚ- **-s** -z **-ed** -d

countersign (*v.*) ˈkaʊn.tə.saɪn, ˌ--ˈ- US -tɚ- **-s** -z **-ing** -ɪŋ **-ed** -d

counter|sink ˈkaʊn.tə|.sɪŋk US -tɚ- **-sinks** -sɪŋks **-sinking** -sɪŋ.kɪŋ **-sunk** -sʌŋk

countertenor ˌkaʊn.təˈten.əʳ, ˈkaʊn.təˌten- US ˈkaʊn.t̬ɚˌten.ɚ **-s** -z

counterterror|ism ˌkaʊn.təˈter.ə.r|ɪ.zᵊm US -t̬ɚˈter.ɚ|.ɪ- **-ist/s** -ɪst/s

countervail ˌkaʊn.təˈveɪl, ˈ--- US ˈkaʊn.tɚ.veɪl, ˌ--ˈ- **-s** -z **-ing** -ɪŋ **-ed** -d

counterweight ˈkaʊn.tə.weɪt US -tɚ- **-s** -s

countess (C) ˈkaʊn.tɪs, -tes, -təs; ˌkaʊnˈtes US ˈkaʊn.t̬ɪs, -təs **-es** -ɪz

Countesthorpe ˈkaʊn.tɪs.θɔːp US -θɔːrp

countinghou|se ˈkaʊn.tɪŋ.haʊ|s **-ses** -zɪz

countless ˈkaʊnt.ləs, -lɪs

countrified ˈkʌn.trɪ.faɪd

countr|y ˈkʌn.tr|i **-ies** -iz ˌ**country and ˈwestern**; ˌ**country ˈbumpkin**; ˌ**country ˈdancing** US ˈ**country** ˌ**dancing**; ˌ**country ˈhouse**; ˌ**country ˈseat**

country-danc|e ˌkʌn.triˈdɑːn*t*s US -ˈdæn*t*s **-es** -ɪz **-ing** -ɪŋ

country|man ˈkʌn.trɪ|.mən **-men** -mən

countryside ˈkʌn.trɪ.saɪd

countrywide ˌkʌn.triˈwaɪd US ˈ--- *stress shift, British only:* ˌcountrywide ˈvoting

country|woman ˈkʌn.trɪ|ˌwʊm.ən **-women** -ˌwɪm.ɪn

count|y ˈkaʊn.t|i US -t̬|i **-ies** -iz ˌ**county ˈcourt**; ˌ**county ˈfair**; ˌ**county ˈhall**; ˌ**county ˈtown**

coup kuː **-s** -z

coup(s) de foudre ˌkuː.dəˈfuː.drə

coup(s) de grâce ˌkuː.dəˈɡrɑːs

coup(s) de main ˌkuː.dəˈmæ̃ŋ, -ˈmæn

coup(s) d'état ˌkuː.deɪˈtɑː, -detˈɑː

coup(s) de théâtre ˌkuː.də.teɪˈɑː.trə

coupé, coupe ˈkuː.peɪ, -ˈ- US kuːˈpeɪ, koʊp **-s** -z

Couper ˈkuː.pəʳ US -pɚ

Couperin ˈkuː.pə.ræ̃ŋ, -ræn

Coupland ˈkuːp.lənd, ˈkəʊp- US ˈkuːp-, ˈkoʊp-

coupl|e ˈkʌp.l̩ **-es** -z **-ing** -ɪŋ, ˈ-lɪŋ **-ed** -d

coupler ˈkʌp.ləʳ US -lɚ **-s** -z

couplet ˈkʌp.lət, -lɪt **-s** -s

coupling ˈkʌp.lɪŋ **-s** -z

coupon ˈkuː.pɒn US ˈkuː.pɑːn, ˈkjuː- **-s** -z

courage (C) ˈkʌr.ɪdʒ

courageous kəˈreɪ.dʒəs **-ly** -li **-ness** -nəs, -nɪs

courante kʊˈrɑ̃ː*n*t, -ˈrɑːnt, -ˈrænt US -ˈrɑːnt **-s** -s

courgette kɔːˈʒet, kʊə- US kʊr- **-s** -s

courier (C) ˈkʊr.i.əʳ, ˈkʌr- US ˈkʊr.i.ɚ, ˈkɝː- **-s** -z

Courland ˈkʊə.lənd, -lænd US ˈkʊr-

cours|e (C) kɔːs US kɔːrs **-es** -ɪz **-ing** -ɪŋ **-ed** -t

coursebook ˈkɔːs.bʊk US ˈkɔːrs- **-s** -s

courser ˈkɔː.səʳ US ˈkɔːr.sɚ **-s** -s

coursework ˈkɔːs.wɜːk US ˈkɔːrs.wɝːk

court (C) kɔːt US kɔːrt **-s** -s **-ing** -ɪŋ US ˈkɔːr.t̬ɪŋ **-ed** -ɪd US ˈkɔːr.t̬ɪd ˈ**court** ˌ**card**; ˌ**court of apˈpeal**; ˈ**court** ˌ**order**, ˌ**court ˈorder**; ˈ**court** ˌ**shoe**

Courtauld ˈkɔː.təʊld, ˈkɔː.təʊ US ˈkɔːr.toʊld, -toʊ **-s** -z

court-bouillon ˌkɔːtˈbuː.jɒn, ˈkʊət-, ˈkʊə-, ˌ--ˈ- US ˌkɔːr.buːˈjɑːn

Courtelle® kɔːˈtel, kʊə- US kɔːr-

Courtenay ˈkɔːt.ni US ˈkɔːrt-

courteous ˈkɜː.ti.əs US ˈkɝː.t̬i- **-ly** -li **-ness** -nəs, -nɪs

courtesan ˈkɔː.tɪ.zæn, ˈkʊə-, -tə-, --ˈ- US ˈkɔːr.t̬ə.zᵊn, -zæn **-s** -z

courtes|y ˈkɜː.tə.s|i, -tɪ- US ˈkɝː.t̬ə- **-ies** -iz

Courthope ˈkɔː.təp, ˈkɔːt.həʊp US ˈkɔːr.təp, ˈkɔːrt.hoʊp

courthou|se ˈkɔːt.haʊ|s US ˈkɔːrt- **-ses** -zɪz

courtier ˈkɔː.ti.əʳ US ˈkɔːr.t̬i.ɚ **-s** -z

courtl|y ˈkɔːt.l|i US ˈkɔːrt- **-ier** -i.əʳ US -i.ɚ **-iest** -i.ɪst, -i.əst **-iness** -ɪ.nəs, -ɪ.nɪs

court-martial ˌkɔːtˈmɑː.ʃᵊl US ˈkɔːrtˌmɑːr- **-s** -z **-(l)ing** -ɪŋ **-(l)ed** -d **courts-martial** ˌkɔːts- US ˈkɔːrts-

Courtneidge ˈkɔːt.nɪdʒ US ˈkɔːrt-

Courtney ˈkɔːt.ni US ˈkɔːrt-

courtroom ˈkɔːt.rʊm, -ruːm US ˈkɔːrt.ruːm, -rʊm **-s** -z

courtship ˈkɔːt.ʃɪp US ˈkɔːrt- **-s** -s

courtyard ˈkɔːt.jɑːd US ˈkɔːrt.jɑːrd **-s** -z

Courvoisier® kʊəˈvwæz.i.eɪ, kɔːˈ-, -ˈvwɑː.zi- US ˌkɔːr.vwɑː.ziˈeɪ

couscous ˈkuːs.kuːs

cousin ˈkʌz.ᵊn **-s** -z

Cousins ˈkʌz.ᵊnz

Cousteau kuːˈstəʊ, ˈ-- US kuːˈstoʊ

couth kuːθ **-ly** -li **-ness** -nəs, -nɪs

Coutts kuːts

couture kuːˈtjʊəʳ, -tʊəʳ US kuːˈtʊr

couturier kuːˈtjʊə.ri.eɪ, -ˈtʊə-, -əʳ US -ˈtʊr.i.eɪ, -ɚ **-s** -z

Couzens ˈkʌz.ᵊnz

covalenc|y ˌkəʊˈveɪ.lən*t*.s|i, ˈkəʊ.veɪ- US ˌkoʊˈveɪ.lən*t*- **-ies** -iz

covalent ˌkəʊˈveɪ.lənt, ˈ--- US ˌkoʊˈveɪ-

covariance ˌkəʊˈveə.ri.ən*t*s, ˈkəʊ.veə- US ˌkoʊˈver.i-, -ˈvær-

cove (C) kəʊv US koʊv **-s** -z

coven ˈkʌv.ᵊn **-s** -z

coven|ant ˈkʌv.ᵊn|.ənt US -ænt **-ants** -ənts US -ænts **-anting** -ən.tɪŋ US -ən.t̬ɪŋ, -æn- **-anted** -ən.tɪd US -ən.t̬ɪd, -æn- **-anter/s** -ən.təʳ/z US -ən.t̬ɚ/z, -æn-

covenantee ˌkʌv.ᵊn.ənˈtiː US -ænˈtiː, -ənˈ- **-s** -z

covenantor ˈkʌv.ᵊn.ən.təʳ US ˈkʌv.ən.æn.t̬ɚ; ˌkʌv.ən.ænˈtɔːr **-s** -z

Covent ˈkɒv.ᵊnt, ˈkʌv- US ˈkʌv-, ˈkɑː.vᵊnt ˌ**Covent ˈGarden**

Coventry ˈkɒv.ᵊn.tri, ˈkʌv- US ˈkʌv-, ˈkɑː.vᵊn-

Pronouncing the letters CQU

The letter combination **cqu** has two possible pronunciations: /kw/ and /k/. Generally speaking, /kw/ is used where the combination begins a stressed syllable, e.g.:

acquire /əˈkwaɪəʳ/ ⓊⓈ /-ˈkwaɪɚ/
acquiesce /ˌæk.wiˈes/

The realisation /k/ tends to appear before unstressed syllables, e.g.:

racquet /ˈræk.ɪt/

cov|er ˈkʌv|.əʳ ⓊⓈ -ɚ **-ers** -əz ⓊⓈ -ɚz **-ering/s** -ᵊr.ɪŋ/z **-ered** -əd ⓊⓈ -ɚd **ˈcover ˌcharge; ˈcover ˌgirl; ˌcovered ˈwagon**
Coverack ˈkɒv.ᵊr.æk, ˈkʌv-, -ək ⓊⓈ ˈkʌv.ə.ræk, ˈkɑː.və-
coverage ˈkʌv.ᵊr.ɪdʒ
coverall ˈkʌv.ᵊr.ɔːl ⓊⓈ -ɔːl, -ɑːl **-s** -z
Coverdale ˈkʌv.ə.deɪl ⓊⓈ ˈ-ɚ-
coverlet ˈkʌv.ə.lət, -lɪt ⓊⓈ ˈ-ɚ- **-s** -s
Coverley ˈkʌv.ə.li ⓊⓈ ˈ-ɚ-
cover-point ˌkʌv.əˈpɔɪnt ⓊⓈ -ɚˈ- **-s** -s
covert (*n.*) *shelter, cloth:* ˈkʌv.ət, -ə ⓊⓈ ˈkʌv.ɚt, ˈkoʊ.vɚt **-s** -z
covert (*adj.*) ˈkəʊ.vɜːt, ˈkʌv.ət, kəʊˈvɜːt ⓊⓈ ˈkoʊ.vɝːt, ˈkʌv.ɚt; koʊˈvɝːt **-ly** -li
coverture ˈkʌv.ə.tʃəʳ, -tʃʊəʳ, -tjʊəʳ ⓊⓈ -ɚ.tʃɚ
cover-up ˈkʌv.əʳ.ʌp ⓊⓈ ˈ-ɚ- **-s** -s
cov|et ˈkʌv|.ɪt, -ət **-ets** -ɪts, -əts **-eting/ly** -ɪ.tɪŋ/li, -ə.tɪŋ/li ⓊⓈ -ə.t̬ɪŋ/li **-eted** -ɪ.tɪd, -ə.tɪd ⓊⓈ -ə.t̬ɪd **-etable** -ɪ.tə.bl̩, -ə.tə.bl̩ ⓊⓈ -ə.t̬ə.bl̩
covetous ˈkʌv.ɪ.təs, -ə.təs ⓊⓈ -ə.t̬əs **-ly** -li **-ness** -nəs, -nɪs
covey ˈkʌv.i **-s** -z
Covington ˈkʌv.ɪŋ.tən
cow kaʊ **-s** -z **-ing** -ɪŋ **-ed** -d **ˈcow ˌparsley, ˌcow ˈparsley; till the ˈcows come ˌhome**
Cowan kaʊən
coward (C) kaʊəd ⓊⓈ kaʊɚd **-s** -z
cowardice ˈkaʊə.dɪs ⓊⓈ ˈkaʊɚ-
cowardl|y ˈkaʊəd.l|i ⓊⓈ ˈkaʊɚd- **-iness** -ɪ.nəs, -ɪ.nɪs
cowbane ˈkaʊ.beɪn
cowbell ˈkaʊ.bel **-s** -z
cowboy ˈkaʊ.bɔɪ **-s** -z **ˈcowboy ˌboots; ˈcowboy ˌhat**
cowcatcher ˈkaʊˌkætʃ.əʳ ⓊⓈ -ɚ **-s** -z
Cowden ˈkaʊ.den, -dᵊn; kaʊˈden
Cowdenbeath ˌkaʊ.dᵊnˈbiːθ
Cowdray ˈkaʊ.dreɪ, -dri
Cowdrey ˈkaʊ.dri
Cowell kaʊəl, kaʊl, kəʊəl ⓊⓈ kaʊəl, kaʊl, koʊəl
Cowen kaʊən, kaʊɪn, kəʊən, kəʊɪn ⓊⓈ kaʊən, kaʊɪn, koʊən, koʊɪn
cower kaʊəʳ ⓊⓈ kaʊɚ **-s** -z **-ing** -ɪŋ **-ed** -d
Cowes kaʊz
cowgirl ˈkaʊ.gɜːl ⓊⓈ -gɝːl **-s** -z
cowhand ˈkaʊ.hænd **-s** -z
cowherd ˈkaʊ.hɜːd ⓊⓈ -hɝːd **-s** -z
cowhide ˈkaʊ.haɪd
Cowie ˈkaʊ.i
cowl kaʊl **-s** -z **-ing** -ɪŋ **-ed** -d
Cowley ˈkaʊ.li
cowlick ˈkaʊ.lɪk **-s** -s
cowlike ˈkaʊ.laɪk
Cowling ˈkaʊ.lɪŋ
cow|-man ˈkaʊ|.mæn **-men** -mən
co-worker ˈkəʊˌwɜː.kəʳ ⓊⓈ ˈkoʊˌwɝː.kɚ, ˌ-ˈ-- **-s** -z
cowpat ˈkaʊ.pæt **-s** -s
Cowper ˈkaʊ.pəʳ, ˈkuː- ⓊⓈ ˈkaʊ.pɚ, ˈkuː-
Note: The poet called himself /ˈkuː.pəʳ ⓊⓈ -pɚ/. /ˈkuː.pəʳ ⓊⓈ -pɚ/ is also the pronunciation in **Cowper Powys** /ˌkuː.pəˈpəʊ.ɪs ⓊⓈ -pɚˈpoʊ-/ and **Cowper-Black** /ˌkuː.pəˈblæk ⓊⓈ -pɚˈ-/.
cowpoke ˈkaʊ.pəʊk ⓊⓈ -poʊk **-s** -s
cowpox ˈkaʊ.pɒks ⓊⓈ -pɑːks
cowpuncher ˈkaʊˌpʌn.*t*ʃəʳ ⓊⓈ -ˌpʌn*t*.ʃɚ **-s** -z
cowr|ie, cowr|y ˈkaʊ.r|i **-ies** -iz
co-writer ˈkəʊˌraɪ.təʳ ⓊⓈ ˈkoʊˌraɪ.t̬ɚ, ˌ-ˈ-- **-s** -z
cowshed ˈkaʊ.ʃed **-s** -z
cowslip ˈkaʊ.slɪp **-s** -s
cox (C) kɒks ⓊⓈ kɑːks **-es** -ɪz **-ing** -ɪŋ **-ed** -t **-less** -ləs, -lɪs
Coxall ˈkɒk.sᵊl, -sɔːl ⓊⓈ ˈkɑːk-
coxcomb ˈkɒk.skəʊm ⓊⓈ ˈkɑːk.skoʊm **-s** -z
coxswain ˈkɒk.sᵊn, -sweɪn ⓊⓈ ˈkɑːk- **-s** -z
coy kɔɪ **-er** -əʳ ⓊⓈ -ɚ **-est** -ɪst, -əst **-ly** -li **-ness** -nəs, -nɪs
coyish ˈkɔɪ.ɪʃ **-ly** -li **-ness** -nəs, -nɪs
Coyle kɔɪl
coyote kɔɪˈəʊ.ti, kaɪ-; ˈkɔɪ.əʊt, ˈkaɪ- ⓊⓈ kaɪˈoʊ.t̬i; ˈkaɪ.oʊt **-s** -z
coypu ˈkɔɪ.puː, -pjuː, -ˈ- **-s** -z
coz kʌz
cozen ˈkʌz.ᵊn **-s** -z **-ing** -ɪŋ **-ed** -d **-er/s** -əʳ/z ⓊⓈ -ɚ/z
Cozens, Cozzens ˈkʌz.ᵊnz
coz|y ˈkəʊ.z|i ⓊⓈ koʊ- **-ier** -i.əʳ ⓊⓈ -i.ɚ **-iest** -i.ɪst, -i.əst
CPU ˌsiː.piːˈjuː
crab kræb **-s** -z **-bing** -ɪŋ **-bed** -d **ˈcrab ˌapple**
Crabbe kræb
crabbed kræbd, ˈkræb.ɪd **-ly** -li **-ness** -nəs, -nɪs
crabb|y ˈkræb|.i **-ier** -i.əʳ ⓊⓈ -i.ɚ **-iest** -i.ɪst, -i.əst **-ily** -ɪ.li, -ᵊl.i **-iness** -ɪ.nəs, -ɪ.nɪs
crabtree (C) ˈkræb.triː **-s** -z
crabwise ˈkræb.waɪz
Crace kreɪs
crack kræk **-s** -s **-ing** -ɪŋ **-ed** -t **ˌcrack of ˈdawn**
crackdown ˈkræk.daʊn **-s** -z
Crackenthorpe ˈkræk.ᵊn.θɔːp ⓊⓈ -θɔːrp
cracker ˈkræk.əʳ ⓊⓈ -ɚ **-s** -z
cracker-barrel ˈkræk.əˌbær.ᵊl ⓊⓈ -ɚˌber.ᵊl, -ˌbær-
crackerjack (*adj.*) ˈkræk.ə.dʒæk ⓊⓈ ˈ-ɚ-
Cracker Jack® ˈkræk.ə.dʒæk ⓊⓈ ˈ-ɚ-
crackhead ˈkræk.hed **-s** -z
crackhou|se ˈkræk.haʊ|s **-ses** -zɪz
crackl|e ˈkræk.l̩ **-es** -z **-ing** -ɪŋ, ˈ-lɪŋ **-ed** -d
crackling ˈkræk.lɪŋ
crackly ˈkræk.l̩.i, ˈkræk.li
cracknel ˈkræk.nᵊl **-s** -z
Cracknell ˈkræk.nᵊl
crackpot ˈkræk.pɒt ⓊⓈ -pɑːt **-s** -s
cracks|man ˈkræks|.mən **-men** -mən
Cracow ˈkræk.ɒf, -ɒv, -aʊ, -əʊ ⓊⓈ ˈkrɑː.kaʊ, ˈkræk.aʊ; ˈkrɑː.kʊf
-cracy -krə.si
Craddock ˈkræd.ək
cradl|e ˈkreɪ.dl̩ **-es** -z **-ing** -ɪŋ, ˈkreɪd.lɪŋ **-ed** -d
cradlesnatch ˈkreɪ.dl̩.snætʃ **-ing** -ɪŋ **-er/s** -əʳ/z ⓊⓈ -ɚ/z
Cradley ˈkreɪd.li, ˈkræd-
craft krɑːft ⓊⓈ kræft **-s** -s **-ing** **-ed**
-craft -krɑːft ⓊⓈ -kræft
crafts|man ˈkrɑːfts|.mən ⓊⓈ ˈkræfts- **-men** -mən **-manship** -mən.ʃɪp
crafts|woman ˈkrɑːfts|ˌwʊm.ən ⓊⓈ ˈkræfts- **-women** -ˌwɪm.ɪn

craft|y 'krɑːf.t|i (US) 'kræf- **-ier** -i.ə^r (US) -i.ɚ **-iest** -i.ɪst, -i.əst **-ily** -ɪ.li, -^{ə}l.i **-iness** -ɪ.nəs, -ɪ.nɪs
crag kræg **-s** -z
Cragg kræg
cragg|y 'kræg|.i **-ier** -i.ə^r (US) -i.ɚ **-iest** -i.ɪst, -i.əst **-ily** -ɪ.li, -^{ə}l.i **-iness** -ɪ.nəs, -ɪ.nɪs
crags|man 'krægz|.mən **-men** -mən, -men
craic kræk
Craig kreɪg
Craigavon ˌkreɪ'gæv.^{ə}n
Craigie 'kreɪ.gi
Craik kreɪk
Craiova krə'jəʊ.və, krɑː- (US) krɑː'joʊ-
crak|e kreɪk **-es** -s **-ing** -ɪŋ **-ed** -t
cram (C) kræm **-s** -z **-ming** -ɪŋ **-med** -d
crambo 'kræm.bəʊ (US) -boʊ
Cramer 'krɑː.mə^r, 'kreɪ- (US) 'kreɪ.mɚ
cram-full ˌkræm'fʊl
Cramlington 'kræm.lɪŋ.tən
crammer 'kræm.ə^r (US) -ɚ **-s** -z
cramp (C) kræmp **-s** -s **-ing** -ɪŋ **-ed** -t
cramp-iron 'kræmp.aɪən (US) -aɪɚn **-s** -z
crampon 'kræm.pɒn, -pən (US) -pɑːn **-s** -z
Crampton 'kræm*p*.tən
cran kræn **-s** -z
cranage 'kreɪ.nɪdʒ
Cranage 'kræn.ɪdʒ
cranberr|y 'kræn.b^{ə}r|.i, 'kræm- (US) -ˌber- **-ies** -iz
Cranborne 'kræn.bɔːn, 'kræm- (US) 'kræn.bɔːrn
Cranbourn(e) 'kræn.bɔːn, 'kræm- (US) 'kræn.bɔːrn
Cranbrook 'kræn.brʊk, 'kræm- (US) 'kræn-
cran|e (C) kreɪn **-es** -z **-ing** -ɪŋ **-ed** -d **'crane ˌfly**
cranesbill 'kreɪnz.bɪl **-s** -z
Cranfield 'kræn.fiːld
Cranford 'kræn.fəd (US) -fɚd
cranial 'kreɪ.ni.əl
cranio- 'kreɪ.ni.əʊ- (US) 'kreɪ.ni.oʊ-, -ə-
craniolog|y ˌkreɪ.ni'ɒl.ə.dʒ|i (US) -'ɑː.lə- **-ist/s** -ɪst/s
crani|um 'kreɪ.ni|.əm **-ums** -əmz **-a** -ə
crank kræŋk **-s** -s **-ing** -ɪŋ **-ed** -t
crankshaft 'kræŋk.ʃɑːft (US) -ʃæft **-s** -s
Crankshaw 'kræŋk.ʃɔː (US) -ʃɑː, -ʃɔː
crank|y 'kræŋ.k|i **-ier** -i.ə^r (US) -i.ɚ **-iest** -i.ɪst, -i.əst **-ily** -ɪ.li, -^{ə}l.i **-iness** -ɪ.nəs, -ɪ.nɪs
Cranleigh, Cranley 'kræn.li
Cranmer 'kræn.mə^r, 'kræm- (US) 'kræn.mɚ
crann|y 'kræn|.i **-ies** -iz **-ied** -id
Cranston 'kræn.stən
Cranwell 'kræn.wəl, -wel
Cranworth 'kræn.wəθ, -wɜːθ (US) -wɚθ, -wɝːθ
crap kræp **-s** -s **-ping** -ɪŋ **-ped** -t
crape kreɪp **-s** -s
crapper 'kræp.ə^r (US) -ɚ **-s** -z
crapp|y 'kræp|.i **-ier** -i.ə^r (US) -i.ɚ **-iest** -i.ɪst, -i.əst
craps kræps
crapshooter 'kræpˌʃuː.tə^r (US) -t̬ɚ **-s** -z
crapulen|ce 'kræp.jə.lən|*t*s, -jʊ- **-t/ly** -t/li
crapulous 'kræp.jə.ləs, -jʊ- **-ly** -li
crash kræʃ **-es** -ɪz **-ing** -ɪŋ **-ed** -t **'crash ˌbarrier; 'crash ˌhelmet, ˌcrash 'helmet**
Crashaw 'kræʃ.ɔː (US) -ɑː, -ɔː
crash-div|e 'kræʃ.daɪv, ˌ-'- **-es** -z **-ing** -ɪŋ **-ed** -d **crash-dove** 'kræʃ.dəʊv (US) -doʊv
crash-land ˌkræʃ'lænd (US) 'kræʃ.lænd, ˌ-'- **-s** -z **-ing/s** -ɪŋ/z **-ed** -ɪd *stress shift, British only:* ˌcrash-land 'heavily
cra|sis 'kreɪ|.sɪs **-ses** -siːz
crass kræs **-er** -ə^r (US) -ɚ **-est** -ɪst, -əst **-ly** -li **-ness** -nəs, -nɪs
-crat -kræt
cratch krætʃ **-es** -ɪz
Cratchit 'krætʃ.ɪt
crat|e kreɪt **-es** -s **-ing** -ɪŋ **-ed** -ɪd
crater 'kreɪ.tə^r (US) -t̬ɚ **-s** -z
Crathie 'kræθ.i
-cratic -'kræt.ɪk (US) -'kræt̬.ɪk
cra|vat krə|'væt **-vats** -væts **-vatted** -væt.ɪd (US) -væt̬.ɪd
crav|e kreɪv **-es** -z **-ing** -ɪŋ **-ed** -d **-er/s** -ə^r/z (US) -ɚ/z
craven (C) 'kreɪ.v^{ə}n **-s** -z **-ly** -li
craving 'kreɪ.vɪŋ **-s** -z
craw krɔː (US) krɑː, krɔː **-s** -z
crawfish 'krɔː.fɪʃ (US) 'krɑː-, 'krɔː- **-es** -ɪz
Crawford 'krɔː.fəd (US) 'krɑː.fɚd, 'krɔː-
crawl krɔːl (US) krɑːl, krɔːl **-s** -z **-ing** -ɪŋ **-ed** -d **-er/s** -ə^r/z (US) -ɚ/z
Crawley 'krɔː.li (US) 'krɑː-, 'krɔː-
crawl|y 'krɔː.l|i (US) 'krɑː-, 'krɔː- **-ier** -i.ə^r (US) -i.ɚ **-iest** -i.ɪst, -i.əst **-iness** -ɪ.nəs, -ɪ.nɪs
Craxi 'kræk.si
Cray kreɪ
crayfish 'kreɪ.fɪʃ **-es** -ɪz
Crayford 'kreɪ.fəd (US) -fɚd
Crayola® kreɪ'əʊ.lə (US) -'oʊ-
crayon 'kreɪ.ɒn, -ən (US) -ɑːn, -ən **-s** -z **-ing** -ɪŋ **-ed** -d
craz|e kreɪz **-es** -ɪz **-ed** -d
craz|y 'kreɪ.z|i **-ier** -i.ə^r (US) -i.ɚ **-iest** -i.ɪst, -i.əst **-ily** -ɪ.li, -^{ə}l.i **-iness** -ɪ.nəs, -ɪ.nɪs **'Crazy ˌHorse; ˌcrazy 'paving**
CRE ˌsiː.ɑː^r'iː (US) -ɑːr'-
Creagh kreɪ
creak kriːk **-s** -s **-ing** -ɪŋ **-ed** -t
creak|y 'kriː.k|i **-ier** -i.ə^r (US) -i.ɚ **-iest** -i.ɪst, -i.əst **-ily** -ɪ.li, -^{ə}l.i **-iness** -ɪ.nəs, -ɪ.nɪs
cream kriːm **-s** -z **-ing** -ɪŋ **-ed** -d **-er/s** -ə^r/z (US) -ɚ/z **ˌcream 'cheese; ˌcream 'cracker; ˌcream 'soda; ˌcream 'tea**
creamer|y 'kriː.m^{ə}r|.i **-ies** -iz
cream|y 'kriː.m|i **-ier** -i.ə^r (US) -i.ɚ **-iest** -i.ɪst, -i.əst **-ily** -ɪ.li, -^{ə}l.i **-iness** -ɪ.nəs, -ɪ.nɪs
creas|e kriːs **-es** -ɪz **-ing** -ɪŋ **-ed** -t
Creas(e)y 'kriː.si
creasy 'kriː.si
cre|ate kri|'eɪt **-ates** -eɪts **-ating** -eɪ.tɪŋ (US) -eɪ.t̬ɪŋ **-ated** -eɪ.tɪd (US) -eɪ.t̬ɪd
creation (C) kri'eɪ.ʃ^{ə}n **-s** -z
creation|ism kri'eɪ.ʃ^{ə}n|.ɪ.z^{ə}m **-ist/s** -ɪst/s
creative kri'eɪ.tɪv (US) -t̬ɪv **-ly** -li **-ness** -nəs, -nɪs
creativity ˌkriː.eɪ'tɪv.ə.ti, -ɪ.ti (US) -ə.t̬i
creator (C) kri'eɪ.tə^r (US) -t̬ɚ **-s** -z
creature 'kriː.tʃə^r (US) -tʃɚ **-s** -z **ˌcreature 'comfort** (US) **'creature ˌcomfort**
crèch|e kreʃ, kreɪʃ **-es** -ɪz
Crécy 'kres.i (US) kreɪ'siː
cred kred
Creda® 'kriː.də
credence 'kriː.d^{ə}n*t*s
credential krɪ'den.*t*ʃ^{ə}l, krə- (US) -'den*t*.ʃ^{ə}l **-s** -z
credibility ˌkred.ə'bɪl.ə.ti, -ɪ'-, -ɪ.ti (US) -ə'bɪl.ə.t̬i
credib|le 'kred.ə.b|l̩, '-ɪ- **-ly** -li **-leness** -l̩.nəs, -nɪs
cred|it 'kred|.ɪt **-its** -ɪts **-iting** -ɪ.tɪŋ (US) -ɪ.t̬ɪŋ **-ited** -ɪ.tɪd (US) -ɪ.t̬ɪd **'credit ˌcard**
creditab|le 'kred.ɪ.tə.b|l̩ (US) -t̬ə- **-ly** -li **-leness** -l̩.nəs, -nɪs
Crediton 'kred.ɪ.t^{ə}n
creditor 'kred.ɪ.tə^r (US) -t̬ɚ **-s** -z
creditworth|y 'kred.ɪtˌwɜː.ð|i (US) -ˌwɝː- **-iness** -ɪ.nəs, -ɪ.nɪs
credo 'kreɪ.dəʊ, 'kriː- (US) 'kriː.doʊ, 'kreɪ- **-s** -z
credulity krə'djuː.lə.ti, krɪ-, kred'juː-, -lɪ- (US) krə'duː.lə-, -'djuː-
credulous 'kred.jʊ.ləs, -jə- (US) 'kredʒ.ə-, 'kred.jə- **-ly** -li **-ness** -nəs, -nɪs
Cree kriː
creed (C) kriːd **-s** -z
creek (C) kriːk **-s** -s
creel kriːl **-s** -z
creep kriːp **-s** -s **-ing** -ɪŋ **crept** krept
creeper 'kriː.pə^r (US) -pɚ **-s** -z
creep|y 'kriː.p|i **-ier** -i.ə^r (US) -i.ɚ **-iest** -i.ɪst, -i.əst **-ily** -ɪ.li, -^{ə}l.i **-iness** -ɪ.nəs, -ɪ.nɪs

creepy-crawl|y ˌkriː.piˈkrɔː.l|i, ˈkriː.piˌkrɔː- ⓤⓢ ˌkriː.piˈkrɑː-, -ˈkrɔː-, ˈkriː.piˌkrɑː-, -ˌkrɔː- **-ies** -iz
Crees kriːs, kriːz
Creevey ˈkriː.vi
Creighton ˈkraɪ.tᵊn, ˈkreɪ- ⓤⓢ ˈkreɪ-, ˈkraɪ-
crema|te krɪˈmeɪ|t, krə- ⓤⓢ ˈkriː.meɪ|t; krɪˈmeɪ|t **-tes** -ts **-ting** -tɪŋ ⓤⓢ -t̬ɪŋ **-ted** -tɪd ⓤⓢ -t̬ɪd **-tor/s** -təʳ/z ⓤⓢ -t̬ɚ/z
cremation krɪˈmeɪ.ʃᵊn, krə- ⓤⓢ krɪ-, kriː- **-s** -z
crematori|um ˌkrem.əˈtɔː.ri|.əm ⓤⓢ ˌkriː.məˈtɔːr.i-, ˌkrem.əˈ- **-ums** -əmz **-a** -ə
cremator|y ˈkrem.ə.tᵊr|.i, -tr|i ⓤⓢ ˈkriː.mə.tɔːr|.i, ˈkrem.ə- **-ies** -iz
creme krem, kriːm
crème brulée ˌkrem.bruːˈleɪ, ˌkreɪm-, ˌ-ˈ--
crème caramel ˌkrem.kær.əˈmel, ˌkreɪm-, -ˈkær.ə.mel ⓤⓢ -ker.əˈmel, -kær-, -ˈker.ə.mel, -ˈkær-
crème de la crème ˌkrem.də.lɑːˈkrem, ˌkreɪm-, -ˈkreɪm
crème de menthe ˌkrem.dəˈmɑ̃ːnθ, ˌkreɪm-, -ˈmɑːntθ, -ˈmɒntθ, -ˈmɒnt ⓤⓢ -ˈmɑːnt, -ˈmentθ
crème fraîche ˌkremˈfreɪʃ, ˌkreɪm- ⓤⓢ -ˈfreɪʃ, -ˈfreʃ
Cremona krɪˈməʊ.nə, krə- ⓤⓢ -ˈmoʊ-
Cremora® krɪˈmɔː.rə, krə-
crenate ˈkriː.neɪt
crenel(l)|ate ˈkren.ᵊl|.eɪt, -ɪ.l|eɪt ⓤⓢ -ə.l|eɪt **-ates** -eɪts **-ating** -eɪ.tɪŋ ⓤⓢ -eɪ.t̬ɪŋ **-ated** -eɪ.tɪd ⓤⓢ -eɪ.t̬ɪd
crenel(l)ation ˌkren.ᵊlˈeɪ.ʃᵊn, -ɪˈleɪ- ⓤⓢ -əˈleɪ- **-s** -z
creole (C) ˈkriː.əʊl, ˈkreɪ-, -ˈ- ⓤⓢ ˈkriː.oʊl, -ˈ- **-s** -z
Creolian kriːˈəʊ.li.ən, kreɪ- ⓤⓢ -ˈoʊ-
Creon ˈkriː.ən, -ɒn ⓤⓢ -ɑːn
creo|sote ˈkriː.ə|.səʊt ⓤⓢ -soʊt **-sotes** -səʊts ⓤⓢ -soʊts **-soting** -səʊ.tɪŋ ⓤⓢ -soʊ.t̬ɪŋ **-soted** -səʊ.tɪd ⓤⓢ -soʊ.t̬ɪd
crepe kreɪp **-s** -s ˌ**crepe ˈpaper** ⓤⓢ ˈ**crepe** ˌ**paper**
crêpe de chine ˌkreɪp.dəˈʃiːn, ˌkrep-
crêpe(s) suzette ˌkrep.suːˈzet, ˌkreɪp-
crepi|tate ˈkrep.ɪ|.teɪt **-tates** -teɪts **-tating** -teɪ.tɪŋ ⓤⓢ -teɪ.t̬ɪŋ **-tated** -teɪ.tɪd ⓤⓢ -teɪ.t̬ɪd
crepitation ˌkrep.ɪˈteɪ.ʃᵊn **-s** -z
crépon ˈkrep.ɔ̃ːŋ, ˈkreɪ.pɔ̃ːŋ, -pɒn ⓤⓢ ˈkreɪ.pɑːn
crept *(from* **creep***)* krept
crepuscular krɪˈpʌs.kjə.ləʳ, krə-, krepˈʌs-, -kjʊ- ⓤⓢ -kjə.lɚ
crepuscule ˈkrep.ə.skjuːl ⓤⓢ krɪˈpʌs.kjuːl
crescendo krɪˈʃen.dəʊ, krə- ⓤⓢ -doʊ **-s** -z
crescent *moon, shape:* ˈkres.ᵊnt, ˈkrez- ⓤⓢ ˈkres- **-s** -s
crescent *growing, when applied to objects other than the moon:* ˈkres.ᵊnt
Crespigny *surname:* ˈkrep.ɪ.ni, ˈkrep.ni, ˈkres.pɪ.ni *in London streets:* kresˈpɪn.i
cress kres **-es** -ɪz
Cressida ˈkres.ɪ.də
Cresson ˈkres.ɔ̃ːŋ, -ɒn ⓤⓢ -ɑːn, -oʊn, -ɔ̃
Cresswell ˈkrez.wəl, -wel, ˈkres- ⓤⓢ ˈkres.wel, ˈkrez-, -wəl
Cressy ˈkres.i
crest krest **-s** -s **-ing** -ɪŋ **-ed** -ɪd
Cresta ˈkres.tə ˌ**Cresta ˈRun**
crestfallen ˈkrestˌfɔː.lᵊn ⓤⓢ -ˌfɔː-, -ˌfɑː- **-ness** -nəs, -nɪs
Creswell ˈkres.wəl, -wel, ˈkrez-
Creswick ˈkrez.ɪk ⓤⓢ ˈkres.wɪk; ˈkrez.ɪk
cretaceous (C) krɪˈteɪ.ʃəs, krə-, kretˈeɪ-, -ʃi.əs
Cretan ˈkriː.tᵊn **-s** -z
Crete kriːt
Cretic ˈkriː.tɪk ⓤⓢ -t̬ɪk **-s** -s
cretin ˈkret.ɪn ⓤⓢ ˈkriː.tᵊn **-s** -z
cretinism ˈkret.ɪ.nɪ.zᵊm, -ᵊn.ɪ- ⓤⓢ ˈkriː.tᵊn-
cretinous ˈkret.ɪ.nəs, -ᵊn.əs ⓤⓢ ˈkriː.tᵊn- **-ly** -li
cretonne kretˈɒn, krɪˈtɒn, krə-; ˈkret.ɒn ⓤⓢ ˈkriː.tɑːn, krɪˈtɑːn **-s** -z
Creusa kriˈuː.zə ⓤⓢ -sə
Creuse krɜːz ⓤⓢ krɝːz
Creutzfeldt-Jacob ˌkrɔɪts.feltˈjæk.ɒb ⓤⓢ -ˈjɑː.koʊb, -kɑːb ˌ**Creutzfeldt-ˈJacob diˌsease**
crevass|e krɪˈvæs, krə- ⓤⓢ krə- **-es** -ɪz **-ed** -t
Crèvecoeur krevˈkɜːʳ ⓤⓢ -ˈkʊr
crevic|e ˈkrev.ɪs **-es** -ɪz
crew kruː **-s** -z **-ing** -ɪŋ **-ed** -d ˈ**crew** ˌ**cut**; ˌ**crew ˈneck**, ˈ**crew** ˌ**neck**
Crewe kruː
crewel ˈkruː.əl, -ɪl **-s** -z
Crewkerne ˈkruː.kɜːn, ˈkrʊk.ən, kruːˈkɜːn ⓤⓢ ˈkruː.kɜːn
Crianlarich ˌkriː.ənˈlær.ɪk, -ɪx ⓤⓢ -ˈler.ɪk, -ˈlær-
crib krɪb **-s** -z **-bing** -ɪŋ **-bed** -d **-ber/s** -əʳ/z ⓤⓢ -ɚ/z ˈ**crib** ˌ**death**
cribbage ˈkrɪb.ɪdʒ
Cribbins ˈkrɪb.ɪnz
Criccieth ˈkrɪk.i.eθ, -əθ
Crich kraɪtʃ
Crichel ˈkrɪtʃ.ᵊl
Crichton ˈkraɪ.tᵊn
crick (C) krɪk **-s** -s **-ing** -ɪŋ **-ed** -t
crick|et ˈkrɪk|.ɪt **-ets** -ɪts **-eter/s** -ɪ.təʳ/z ⓤⓢ -ɪ.t̬ɚ/z **-eting** -ɪ.tɪŋ ⓤⓢ -ɪ.t̬ɪŋ
Crickhowell krɪkˈhaʊəl, -ˈhaʊl
cricoid ˈkraɪ.kɔɪd
cri(s) de coeur ˌkriː.deˈkɜːʳ ⓤⓢ -ˈkɝː
cried *(from* **cry***)* kraɪd
Crieff kriːf
crier ˈkraɪ.əʳ ⓤⓢ -ɚ **-s** -z
cries *(from* **cry***)* kraɪz
crikey ˈkraɪ.ki
crime kraɪm **-s** -z ˌ**crime of ˈpassion**
Crime|a kraɪˈmiː|.ə **-an** -ən
crimen falsi ˌkrɪm.enˈfæl.si
crime(s) passionel(s) ˌkriːm.pæs.i.əˈnel, -pæʃ.əˈ-
Crimewatch ˈkraɪm.wɒtʃ ⓤⓢ -wɑːtʃ, -wɔːtʃ
criminal ˈkrɪm.ɪ.nᵊl, ˈ-ə- **-s** -z **-ly** -li ˌ**criminal ˈdamage**; ˌ**criminal ˈlaw**, ⓤⓢ ˈ**criminal** ˌ**law**
criminality ˌkrɪm.ɪˈnæl.ə.ti, -əˈ-, -ɪ.ti ⓤⓢ -əˈnæl.ə.t̬i
criminalization, -isa- ˌkrɪm.ɪ.nᵊl.aɪˈzeɪ.ʃᵊn, -ɪˈ- ⓤⓢ -ɪˈ-
criminaliz|e, -is|e ˈkrɪm.ɪ.nᵊl.aɪz ⓤⓢ -nə.laɪz **-es** -ɪz **-ing** -ɪŋ **-ed** -d
crimi|nate ˈkrɪm.ɪ|.neɪt, ˈ-ə- **-nates** -neɪts **-nating** -neɪ.tɪŋ ⓤⓢ -neɪ.t̬ɪŋ **-nated** -neɪ.tɪd ⓤⓢ -neɪ.t̬ɪd
crimination ˌkrɪm.ɪˈneɪ.ʃᵊn, -əˈ- **-s** -z
criminolog|y ˌkrɪm.ɪˈnɒl.ə.dʒ|i, -əˈ- ⓤⓢ -ˈnɑː.lə- **-ist/s** -ɪst/s
crimp krɪmp **-s** -s **-ing** -ɪŋ **-ed** -t
Crimplene® ˈkrɪm.pliːn
crimson ˈkrɪm.zᵊn **-s** -z **-ing** -ɪŋ **-ed** -d
cring|e krɪndʒ **-es** -ɪz **-ing** -ɪŋ **-ed** -d **-er/s** -əʳ/z ⓤⓢ -ɚ/z
crinkl|e ˈkrɪŋ.kl̩ **-es** -z **-ing** -ɪŋ, ˈ-klɪŋ **-ed** -d
crinkly ˈkrɪŋ.kli
crinoid ˈkraɪ.nɔɪd, ˈkrɪn.ɔɪd **-s** -z
crinoline ˈkrɪn.ᵊl.ɪn **-s** -z
cripes kraɪps
Crippen ˈkrɪp.ɪn, -ᵊn
crippl|e ˈkrɪp.l̩ **-es** -z **-ing** -ɪŋ, ˈ-lɪŋ **-ed** -d
Cripplegate ˈkrɪp.l̩.geɪt
Cripps krɪps
Crisco® ˈkrɪs.kəʊ ⓤⓢ -koʊ
Criseyde krɪˈseɪ.də
cris|is ˈkraɪ.s|ɪs **-es** -iːz ˈ**crisis** ˌ**management**
crisp (C) krɪsp **-er** -əʳ ⓤⓢ -ɚ **-est** -ɪst, -əst **-s** -s **-ly** -li **-ness** -nəs, -nɪs
crispbread ˈkrɪsp.bred **-s** -z
Crispian ˈkrɪs.pi.ən
Crispin ˈkrɪs.pɪn
crisp|y ˈkrɪs.p|i **-ier** -i.əʳ ⓤⓢ -i.ɚ **-iest** -i.ɪst, -i.əst **-ily** -ɪ.li, -ᵊl.i **-iness** -ɪ.nəs, -ɪ.nɪs
crisscross ˈkrɪs.krɒs ⓤⓢ -krɑːs **-es** -ɪz **-ing** -ɪŋ **-ed** -t
Cristina krɪˈstiː.nə
crit krɪt **-s** -s
Critchley ˈkrɪtʃ.li

criteri|on (C) kraɪˈtɪə.ri|.ən (US) -ˈtɪr.i- **-ons** -ənz **-a** -ə
critic ˈkrɪt.ɪk (US) ˈkrɪt̬- **-s** -s
critic|al ˈkrɪt.ɪ.k|ᵊl (US) ˈkrɪt̬- **-ally** -ᵊl.i, -li **-alness** -ᵊl.nəs, -nɪs
criticism ˈkrɪt.ɪ.sɪ.zᵊm, ˈ-ə- (US) ˈkrɪt̬- **-s** -z
criticizable, -isa- ˈkrɪt.ɪ.saɪ.zə.bl̩, ˈ-ə-, ˌkrɪt.ɪˈsaɪ-, -əˈ- (US) ˈkrɪt̬.ɪ.saɪ-
criticiz|e, -is|e ˈkrɪt.ɪ.saɪz, ˈ-ə- (US) ˈkrɪt̬- **-es** -ɪz **-ing** -ɪŋ **-ed** -d
critique krɪˈtiːk, krə- **-s** -s
Crittenden ˈkrɪt.ᵊn.dən
critter ˈkrɪt.əʳ (US) ˈkrɪt̬.ɚ **-s** -z
crittur ˈkrɪt.əʳ (US) ˈkrɪt̬.ɚ **-s** -z
croak krəʊk (US) kroʊk **-s** -s **-ing/s** -ɪŋ/z **-ed** -t **-er/s** -əʳ/z (US) -ɚ/z
croak|y ˈkrəʊ.k|i (US) ˈkroʊ- **-ier** -i.əʳ (US) -i.ɚ **-iest** -i.ɪst, -i.əst **-ily** -ɪ.li, -ᵊl.i **-iness** -ɪ.nəs, -ɪ.nɪs
Croat ˈkrəʊ.æt, -ət (US) ˈkroʊ- **-s** -s
Croatia krəʊˈeɪ.ʃə (US) kroʊ-
Croatian krəʊˈeɪ.ʃᵊn (US) kroʊ- **-s** -z
croc krɒk (US) krɑːk **-s** -s
crochet ˈkrəʊ.ʃeɪ, -ʃi (US) kroʊˈʃeɪ **-s** -z **-ing** -ɪŋ **-ed** -d **ˈcrochet ˌhook** (US) **croˈchet ˌhook**
crock krɒk (US) krɑːk **-s** -s
Crocker ˈkrɒk.əʳ (US) ˈkrɑː.kɚ
crockery ˈkrɒk.ᵊr.i (US) ˈkrɑː.kɚ-
crocket ˈkrɒk.ɪt (US) ˈkrɑː.kɪt **-s** -s
Crockett ˈkrɒk.ɪt (US) ˈkrɑː.kɪt
Crockford ˈkrɒk.fəd (US) ˈkrɑːk.fɚd
Crockpot® ˈkrɒk.pɒt (US) ˈkrɑːk.pɑːt
crocodile ˈkrɒk.ə.daɪl (US) ˈkrɑː.kə- **-s** -z **ˌcrocodile ˈtears** (US) **ˈcrocodile ˌtears**
crocodilian ˌkrɒk.əˈdɪl.i.ən (US) ˌkrɑː.kəˈdɪl.jən **-s** -z
crocus ˈkrəʊ.kəs (US) ˈkroʊ- **-es** -ɪz
Croesus ˈkriː.səs
croft (C) krɒft (US) krɑːft **-s** -s
crofter ˈkrɒf.təʳ (US) ˈkrɑːf.tɚ **-s** -z
Crofton ˈkrɒf.tᵊn (US) ˈkrɑːf-
Crohn krəʊn (US) kroʊn **ˈCrohn's diˌsease**
croissant ˈkwæs.ɑ̃ːŋ, ˈkrwæs-, -ɒnt (US) kwɑːˈsɑ̃ː, krə-, krwɑː-, -ˈsɑːnt **-s** -z
Croker ˈkrəʊ.kəʳ (US) ˈkroʊ.kɚ
Cro-Magnon ˌkrəʊˈmæn.jɔ̃ːŋ, -jən, -ˈmæg.nən, -nɒn (US) kroʊˈmæg.nən, -nɑːn, -ˈmæn.jən, -jɑːn
Cromarty ˈkrɒm.ə.ti (US) ˈkrɑː.mɚ.t̬i
Crombie ˈkrɒm.bi, ˈkrʌm- (US) ˈkrɑːm-, ˈkrʌm-
Crome krəʊm (US) kroʊm
Cromer ˈkrəʊ.məʳ (US) ˈkroʊ.mɚ
cromlech ˈkrɒm.lek (US) ˈkrɑːm- **-s** -s
Crommelin ˈkrʌm.lɪn, ˈkrɒm- (US) ˈkrɑːm-, ˈkrʌm-
Crompton ˈkrʌmp.tən, ˈkrɒmp- (US) ˈkrɑːmp-
Cromwell ˈkrɒm.wəl, ˈkrʌm-, -wel (US) ˈkrɑːm-
Cromwellian krɒmˈwel.i.ən, krʌm- (US) krɑːm-
crone krəʊn (US) kroʊn **-s** -z
Cronin ˈkrəʊ.nɪn (US) ˈkroʊ-
Cronkite ˈkrɒŋ.kaɪt (US) ˈkrɑːn.kaɪt, ˈkrɑːŋ-
Cronos ˈkrəʊ.nɒs (US) ˈkroʊ.nɑːs
cron|y ˈkrəʊ.n|i (US) ˈkroʊ- **-ies** -iz
cronyism ˈkrəʊ.ni.ɪ.zᵊm (US) ˈkroʊ-
crook (C) krʊk **-s** -s **-ing** -ɪŋ **-ed** -t **by ˌhook or by ˈcrook**
Crookback ˈkrʊk.bæk
crookbacked ˈkrʊk.bækt
Crooke krʊk **-s** -s
crooked *not straight:* ˈkrʊk.ɪd **-er** -əʳ (US) -ɚ **-est** -ɪst, -əst **-ly** -li **-ness** -nəs, -nɪs
crooked *having a crook:* krʊkt
Croome kruːm
croon kruːn **-s** -z **-ing** -ɪŋ **-ed** -d **-er/s** -əʳ/z (US) -ɚ/z
crop krɒp (US) krɑːp **-s** -s **-ping** -ɪŋ **-ped** -t
cropper ˈkrɒp.əʳ (US) ˈkrɑː.pɚ **-s** -z
croquet ˈkrəʊ.keɪ, -ki (US) kroʊˈkeɪ **-s** -z **-ing** -ɪŋ **-ed** -d
croquette krɒkˈet, krəʊˈket (US) kroʊˈket **-s** -s
crore krɔːʳ (US) krɔːr **-s** -z
Crosby ˈkrɒz.bi, ˈkrɒs- (US) ˈkrɑːz-
Crosfield ˈkrɒs.fiːld (US) ˈkrɑːs-
Croshaw ˈkrəʊ.ʃɔː (US) ˈkroʊ.ʃɑː, -ʃɔː
crosier (C) ˈkrəʊ.zi.əʳ, -ʒəʳ (US) ˈkroʊ.ʒɚ **-s** -z
cross- krɒs- (US) krɑːs-
cross (C) krɒs (US) krɑːs **-es** -ɪz **-er** -əʳ (US) -ɚ **-est** -ɪst, -əst **-ly** -li **-ness** -nəs, -nɪs **-ing** -ɪŋ **-ed** -t **ˈcross ˌaction; ˈcross ˌbench**
crossbar ˈkrɒs.bɑːʳ (US) ˈkrɑːs.bɑːr **-s** -z
crossbeam ˈkrɒs.biːm (US) ˈkrɑːs- **-s** -z
crossbencher ˈkrɒsˌben.*t*ʃəʳ, ˌ-ˈ-- (US) ˈkrɑːsˌben*t*.ʃɚ **-s** -z
crossbill ˈkrɒs.bɪl (US) ˈkrɑːs- **-s** -z
crossbones ˈkrɒs.bəʊnz (US) ˈkrɑːs.boʊnz
cross-border ˌkrɒsˈbɔː.dəʳ (US) ˌkrɑːsˈbɔːr.dɚ *stress shift:* ˌcross-boarder ˈtalks
crossbow ˈkrɒs.bəʊ (US) ˈkrɑːs.boʊ **-s** -z
crossbred ˈkrɒs.bred (US) ˈkrɑːs-
crossbreed ˈkrɒs.briːd (US) ˈkrɑːs- **-s** -z **-ing** -ɪŋ
cross-Channel ˌkrɒsˈtʃæn.ᵊl (US) ˌkrɑːs- *stress shift:* ˌcross-Channel ˈferry
crosscheck *(n.)* ˈkrɒs.tʃek (US) ˈkrɑːs-
crosscheck *(v.)* ˌkrɒsˈtʃek, ˈ-- (US) ˈkrɑːs.tʃek **-s** -s **-ing** -ɪŋ **-ed** -t
cross-claim ˈkrɒs.kleɪm (US) ˈkrɑːs- **-s** -z
cross-country ˌkrɒsˈkʌn.tri (US) ˌkrɑːs- *stress shift:* ˌcross-country ˈrunner
crosscourt ˈkrɒs.kɔːt (US) ˈkrɑːs.kɔːrt
cross-cultural ˌkrɒsˈkʌl.tʃə.rᵊl (US) ˌkrɑːsˈkʌl.tʃɚ.ᵊl **-ly** -li
crosscut ˈkrɒs.kʌt, ˌ-ˈ- (US) ˈkrɑːs.kʌt **-s** -s
cross-dress|ing ˌkrɒsˈdres|.ɪŋ (US) ˌkrɑːs- **-er/s** -əʳ/z (US) -ɚ/z
Crosse krɒs (US) krɑːs
cross-examination ˌkrɒs.ɪgˌzæm.ɪˈneɪ.ʃᵊn, -egˌ-, -ɪkˌsæm-, -ekˌ-, -əˈ- (US) ˌkrɑːs.ɪgˌzæm-, -egˌ- **-s** -z
cross-examin|e ˌkrɒs.ɪgˈzæm.ɪn, -egˈ-, -ɪkˈsæm-, -ekˈ- (US) ˌkrɑːs.ɪgˈzæm-, -egˈ- **-es** -z **-ing** -ɪŋ **-ed** -d **-er/s** -əʳ/z (US) -ɚ/z
cross-eyed ˌkrɒsˈaɪd, ˈ-- (US) ˈkrɑːsˌaɪd *stress shift, British only:* ˌcross-eyed ˈstare
cross-fertilization, -isa- ˌkrɒsˌfɜː.tɪ.laɪˈzeɪ.ʃᵊn, -tə-, -lɪˈ-, -ləˈ- (US) ˌkrɑːsˌfɝː.t̬ᵊl.ɪˈ-
cross-fertiliz|e, -is|e ˌkrɒsˈfɜː.tɪ.laɪz, -tə- (US) ˌkrɑːsˈfɝː.t̬ə- **-es** -ɪz **-ing** -ɪŋ **-ed** -d
cross-fire ˈkrɒs.faɪəʳ (US) ˈkrɑːs.faɪɚ
cross-grained ˌkrɒsˈgreɪnd (US) ˌkrɑːs-, ˈ-ˌ- *stress shift:* ˌcross-grained ˈcutting
crosshatch ˈkrɒs.hætʃ (US) ˈkrɑːs- **-es** -ɪz **-ing** -ɪŋ **-ed** -t
crossing ˈkrɒs.ɪŋ (US) ˈkrɑː.sɪŋ **-s** -z
cross-legged ˌkrɒsˈlegd, ˈ--; -əd (US) ˌkrɑːsˈleg.əd, -ˈlegd
Crossley ˈkrɒs.li (US) ˈkrɑː.sli
Crossman ˈkrɒs.mən (US) ˈkrɑːs-
crossover ˈkrɒsˌəʊ.vəʳ (US) ˈkrɑːsˌoʊ.vɚ **-s** -z
cross-party ˌkrɒsˈpɑː.ti (US) ˌkrɑːsˈpɑːr.t̬i *stress shift:* ˌcross-party ˈquestions
crosspatch ˈkrɒs.pætʃ (US) ˈkrɑːs- **-es** -ɪz
cross-purpos|e ˌkrɒsˈpɜː.pəs (US) ˌkrɑːsˈpɝː-, ˈ-ˌ-- **-es** -ɪz
cross-question ˌkrɒsˈkwes.tʃᵊn, -ˈkweʃ- (US) ˌkrɑːs-, ˈ-ˌ-- **-s** -z **-ing** -ɪŋ **-ed** -d
cross-refer ˌkrɒs.rɪˈfɜːʳ, -rəˈ- (US) ˌkrɑːs.rəˈfɝː **-s** -z **-ring** -ɪŋ **-red** -d
cross-referenc|e ˌkrɒsˈref.ᵊr.ən*t*s, ˈ-rᵊn*t*s (US) ˌkrɑːs-, ˈkrɑːsˌref.ɚ.ᵊn*t*s, ˌ-rᵊn*t*s **-es** -ɪz
crossroad ˈkrɒs.rəʊd (US) ˈkrɑːs.roʊd **-s** -z
cross-section ˈkrɒs.sek.ʃᵊn, ˌ-ˈ-- (US) ˈkrɑːs.sek- **-s** -z
cross-stitch ˈkrɒs.stɪtʃ (US) ˈkrɑːs-
crosswalk ˈkrɒs.wɔːk (US) ˈkrɑːs.wɑːk, -wɔːk **-s** -s
crossway ˈkrɒs.weɪ (US) ˈkrɑːs- **-s** -z
crosswind ˈkrɒs.wɪnd (US) ˈkrɑːs- **-s** -z
crosswise ˈkrɒs.waɪz (US) ˈkrɑːs-

crossword ˈkrɒs.wɜːd ⓤⓢ ˈkrɑːs.wɝːd -s -z ˈcrossword ˌpuzzle
Crosthwaite ˈkrɒs.θweɪt ⓤⓢ ˈkrɑːs-
crotch (C) krɒtʃ ⓤⓢ krɑːtʃ -es -ɪz
crotch|et (C) ˈkrɒtʃ|.ɪt, -ət ⓤⓢ ˈkrɑː.tʃ|ət -ets -ɪts, -əts ⓤⓢ -əts
crotchet|y ˈkrɒtʃ.ɪ.t|i, -ə.t|i ⓤⓢ ˈkrɑː.tʃə.t̬|i -iness -ɪ.nəs, -ɪ.nɪs
Crothers ˈkrʌð.əz ⓤⓢ -ɚz
croton (C) ˈkrəʊ.tᵊn ⓤⓢ ˈkroʊ-
crouch (C) (*v.*) kraʊtʃ -es -ɪz -ing -ɪŋ -ed -t
Crouch *village in Kent:* kruːtʃ
Crouchback ˈkraʊtʃ.bæk
croup kruːp -s -s
croupier ˈkruː.pi.əʳ, -eɪ ⓤⓢ -eɪ, -ɚ -s -z
croustade kruːˈstɑːd -s -z
crouton ˈkruː.tɒn, -tɔ̃ːŋ ⓤⓢ ˈkruː.tɑːn, -ˈ- -s -z
crow (C) krəʊ ⓤⓢ kroʊ -s -z -ing -ɪŋ -ed -d crew kruː ˈcrow's ˌnest, ˌcrow's ˈnest; as the ˌcrow ˈflies
crowbar ˈkrəʊ.bɑːʳ ⓤⓢ ˈkroʊ.bɑːr -s -z
Crowborough ˈkrəʊ.bᵊr.ə ⓤⓢ ˈkroʊ.bɚ.oʊ
crowd kraʊd -s -z -ing -ɪŋ -ed -ɪd
Crowe krəʊ ⓤⓢ kroʊ
crow|foot ˈkrəʊ|.fʊt ⓤⓢ ˈkroʊ- -foots -fʊts -feet -fiːt
Crowhurst ˈkrəʊ.hɜːst ⓤⓢ ˈkroʊ.hɝːst
Crowland ˈkrəʊ.lənd ⓤⓢ ˈkroʊ-
Crowley ˈkrəʊ.li, ˈkraʊ- ⓤⓢ ˈkroʊ-, ˈkraʊ-
crown kraʊn -s -z -ing -ɪŋ -ed -d ˌCrown ˈCourt; ˌcrown ˈglass; ˌcrown ˈjewels; ˌcrown ˈland; ˌcrown ˈprince
Crowndale ˈkraʊn.deɪl
crow's|-foot ˈkrəʊz|.fʊt ⓤⓢ ˈkroʊz- -feet -fiːt
Crowther ˈkraʊ.ðəʳ ⓤⓢ -ðɚ
Crowthorne ˈkrəʊ.θɔːn ⓤⓢ ˈkroʊ.θɔːrn
Croxteth ˈkrɒk.stəθ ⓤⓢ ˈkrɑːk-
Croyden, Croydon ˈkrɔɪ.dᵊn
crozier (C) ˈkrəʊ.zi.əʳ, -ʒəʳ ⓤⓢ ˈkroʊ.ʒɚ -s -z
CRT ˌsiː.ɑːˈtiː ⓤⓢ -ɑːr-
cru kruː
crucial ˈkruː.ʃᵊl -ly -i
crucible ˈkruː.sɪ.bl̩, -sə- -s -z
crucifer ˈkruː.sɪ.fəʳ, -sə- ⓤⓢ -fɚ -s -z
cruciferous kruːˈsɪ.fᵊr.əs
crucifix ˈkruː.sɪ.fɪks, -sə- -es -ɪz
crucifixion (C) ˌkruː.səˈfɪk.ʃᵊn, -sɪˈ- -s -z
cruciform ˈkruː.sɪ.fɔːm, -sə- ⓤⓢ -fɔːrm
cruci|fy ˈkruː.sɪ|.faɪ, -sə- -fies -faɪz -fying -faɪ.ɪŋ -fied -faɪd -fier/s -faɪ.əʳ/z ⓤⓢ -faɪ.ɚ/z
crud krʌd -s -z -ding -ɪŋ -ded -ɪd
crudd|y ˈkrʌd|.i -ier -i.əʳ ⓤⓢ -i.ɚ -iest -i.ɪst, -i.əst
crud|e kruːd -er -əʳ ⓤⓢ -ɚ -est -ɪst, -əst -ely -li -eness -nəs, -nɪs
Cruden ˈkruː.dᵊn
crudité(s) ˈkruː.dɪ.teɪ, -də- ⓤⓢ ˌkruː.dɪˈteɪ
crudit|y ˈkruː.də.t|i, -dɪ.t|i ⓤⓢ -də.t̬|i -ies -iz
cruel ˈkruː.əl, krʊəl ⓤⓢ ˈkruː.əl -(l)er -əʳ ⓤⓢ -ɚ -(l)est -ɪst, -əst -(l)y -li -ness -nəs, -nɪs
cruelt|y ˈkruː.əl.t|i, ˈkrʊəl- ⓤⓢ ˈkruː.əl.t̬|i -ies -iz
cruet ˈkruː.ɪt -s -s
Cruft krʌft -s -s
Crui(c)kshank ˈkrʊk.ʃæŋk
cruis|e (C) kruːz -es -ɪz -ing -ɪŋ -ed -d -er/s -əʳ/z ⓤⓢ -ɚ/z ˈcruise conˌtrol; ˌcruise ˈmissile ⓤⓢ ˈcruise ˌmissile
cruiserweight ˈkruː.zə.weɪt ⓤⓢ -zɚ- -s -s
cruller ˈkrʌl.əʳ ⓤⓢ -ɚ -s -z
crumb krʌm -s -z -ing -ɪŋ -ed -d
crumbl|e ˈkrʌm.bl̩ -es -z -ing -ɪŋ, ˈ-blɪŋ -ed -d
crumbl|y ˈkrʌm.bl|i, -bl̩|.i -ier -i.əʳ ⓤⓢ -i.ɚ -iest -i.ɪst, -i.əst
crumby ˈkrʌm.i
crumhorn ˈkrʌm.hɔːn ⓤⓢ -hɔːrn -s -z
Crumlin ˈkrʌm.lɪn
Crummock ˈkrʌm.ək
crumm|y ˈkrʌm|.i -ier -i.əʳ ⓤⓢ -i.ɚ -iest -i.ɪst
crump (C) krʌmp -s -s -ing -ɪŋ -ed -t
crumpet ˈkrʌm.pɪt -s -s
crumpl|e ˈkrʌm.pl̩ -es -z -ing -ɪŋ, ˈ-plɪŋ -ed -d
crunch krʌn*t*ʃ -es -ɪz -ing -ɪŋ -ed -t
Crunchie® ˈkrʌn.*t*ʃi
crunch|y ˈkrʌn.tʃ|i -ier -i.əʳ ⓤⓢ -i.ɚ -iest -i.ɪst, -i.əst -iness -ɪ.nəs, -ɪ.nɪs
Crundale ˈkrʌn.dᵊl ⓤⓢ -deɪl
crupper ˈkrʌp.əʳ ⓤⓢ -ɚ -s -z
crusad|e (C) kruːˈseɪd -es -z -ing -ɪŋ -ed -ɪd
crusader kruːˈseɪ.dəʳ ⓤⓢ -dɚ -s -z
crus|e kruːz -es -ɪz
crush krʌʃ -es -ɪz -ing -ɪŋ -ed -t -er/s -əʳ/z ⓤⓢ -ɚ/z -able -ə.bl̩
Crusoe ˈkruː.səʊ ⓤⓢ -soʊ
crust krʌst -s -s
crustace|an krʌsˈteɪ.ʃ|ᵊn, -ʃi|.ən -a -ə -ans -ənz
crustaceous krʌsˈteɪ.ʃəs, -ʃi.əs
crustate ˈkrʌs.teɪt
crustated krʌsˈteɪ.tɪd ⓤⓢ -t̬ɪd
crustation krʌsˈteɪ.ʃᵊn -s -z
crusted ˈkrʌs.tɪd
crust|y ˈkrʌs.t|i -ier -i.əʳ ⓤⓢ -i.ɚ -iest -i.ɪst, -i.əst -ily -ɪ.li, -ᵊl.i -iness -ɪ.nəs, -ɪ.nɪs
crutch krʌtʃ -es -ɪz -ed -t
Crutched Friars ˌkrʌtʃtˈfraɪəz, ˌkrʌtʃ.ɪdˈ- ⓤⓢ -ˈfraɪɚz
Cruttwell ˈkrʌt.wəl, -wel
crux krʌks -es -ɪz
Cruyff kraɪf, krɔɪf ⓤⓢ krɔɪf
Cruz kruːz
cruzado kruːˈzɑː.dəʊ ⓤⓢ -doʊ, -ˈzeɪ- -(e)s -z
cruzeiro kruːˈzeə.rəʊ ⓤⓢ -ˈzer.oʊ -s -z
cr|y kr|aɪ -ies -aɪz -ying -aɪ.ɪŋ -ied -aɪd
cry-bab|y ˈkraɪˌbeɪ.b|i -ies -iz
cryo- ˌkraɪ.əʊ- ⓤⓢ ˌkraɪ.oʊ-, -ə-
cryogenic ˌkraɪ.əʊˈdʒen.ɪk ⓤⓢ -əˈ- -s -s
cryonic kraɪˈɒn.ɪk ⓤⓢ -ˈɑː.nɪk -s -s
crypt- krɪpt-
crypt krɪpt -s -s
cryptic ˈkrɪp.tɪk -al -ᵊl -ally -ᵊl.i, -li
crypto ˈkrɪp.təʊ ⓤⓢ -toʊ -s -z
cryptogam ˈkrɪp.təʊ.gæm ⓤⓢ -tə- -s -z
cryptogram ˈkrɪp.təʊ.græm ⓤⓢ -tə- -s -z -ic -ɪk
cryptograph ˈkrɪp.təʊ.grɑːf, -græf ⓤⓢ -tə.græf -s -s
cryptographer krɪpˈtɒg.rə.fəʳ ⓤⓢ -ˈtɑː.grə.fɚ -s -z
cryptography krɪpˈtɒg.rə.fi ⓤⓢ -ˈtɑː.grə-
cryptolog|y krɪpˈtɒl.ə.dʒ|i ⓤⓢ -ˈtɑː.lə- -ist/s -ɪst/s
crystal (C) ˈkrɪs.tᵊl -s -z ˌcrystal ˈball; ˈcrystal ˌgazing
crystalizable, -isa- ˈkrɪs.tᵊl.aɪ.zə.bl̩ ⓤⓢ -tə.laɪ-
crystalline ˈkrɪs.tᵊl.aɪn ⓤⓢ -tə.laɪn
crystallization, -isa- ˌkrɪs.tᵊl.aɪˈzeɪ.ʃᵊn, -ɪˈ- ⓤⓢ -ɪˈ- -s -z
crystalliz|e, -is|e ˈkrɪs.tᵊl.aɪz ⓤⓢ -tə.laɪz -es -ɪz -ing -ɪŋ -ed -d
crystallographer ˌkrɪs.tᵊlˈɒg.rə.fəʳ ⓤⓢ -təˈlɑː.grə.fɚ -s -z
crystallography krɪs.tᵊlˈɒg.rə.fi ⓤⓢ -təˈlɑː.grə-
crystalloid ˈkrɪs.tᵊl.ɔɪd ⓤⓢ -tə.lɔɪd -s -z
CSE ˌsiː.esˈiː
C-section ˈsiːˌsek.ʃᵊn -s -z
ct *(abbrev. for* **carat***)* ˈkær.ət ⓤⓢ ˈker-, ˈkær-
cub kʌb -s -z -bing -ɪŋ -bed -d
Cub|a ˈkjuː.b|ə -an/s -ən/z ˌCuban ˈheel
cubage ˈkjuː.bɪdʒ
cubb|y ˈkʌb|.i -ies -iz
cubbyhole ˈkʌb.i.həʊl ⓤⓢ -hoʊl -s -z
cub|e kjuːb -es -z -ing -ɪŋ -ed -d
cubic ˈkjuː.bɪk -al -ᵊl -ally -ᵊl.i, -li
cubicle ˈkjuː.bɪ.kl̩ -s -z
cub|ism ˈkjuː.b|ɪ.zᵊm -ist/s -ɪst/s
cubistic kjuːˈbɪs.tɪk
cu|bit ˈkjuː|.bɪt -bits -bɪts -bital -bɪ.tᵊl, -bɪ.t̬ᵊl
Cubitt ˈkjuː.bɪt
cuboid ˈkjuː.bɔɪd -s -z
cuchul(l)inn, cuchulain (C) kuːˈkʊl.ɪn, -ˈxʊl- ⓤⓢ -ˈkʊl-
Cuckfield ˈkʊk.fiːld
Cuckmere ˈkʊk.mɪəʳ ⓤⓢ -mɪr

cuckold ˈkʌk.əʊld, -ᵊld (US) -oʊld, -ᵊld **-s** -z **-ing** -ɪŋ **-ed** -ɪd **-er/s** -əʳ/z (US) -ɚ/z **-ry** -ri

cuckoo ˈkʊk.uː (US) ˈkuː.kuː, ˈkʊk.uː **-s** -z **-ing** -ɪŋ **-ed** -d ˈ**cuckoo** ˌ**clock**; ˈ**cuckoo** ˌ**spit**

cuckooflower ˈkʊk.uː.flaʊəʳ (US) ˈkuː.kuː.flaʊɚ, ˈkʊk.uːˌ- **-s** -z

cuckoopint ˈkʊk.uː.paɪnt (US) ˈkuː.kuː-, ˈkʊk.uː **-s** -s

cucumber ˈkjuː.kʌm.bəʳ (US) -bɚ **-s** -z

cud kʌd **-s** -z

cuddl|e ˈkʌd.l̩ **-es** -z **-ing** -ɪŋ, ˈ-lɪŋ **-ed** -d **-y** -i

cudd|y ˈkʌd|.i **-ies** -iz

cudgel ˈkʌdʒ.ᵊl **-s** -z **-(l)ing** -ɪŋ **-(l)ed** -d

Cudworth ˈkʌd.wəθ, -wɜːθ (US) -wɚθ, -wɝːθ

cu|e kjuː **-es** -z **-ing** -ɪŋ **-ed** -d

Cuenca ˈkweŋ.kɑː, -kə

Cuernavaca ˌkweə.nəˈvæk.ə (US) ˌkwer.nəˈvɑː.kə, -nɑːˈvɑː.kɑː

cuff kʌf **-s** -s **-ing** -ɪŋ **-ed** -t

Cuffley ˈkʌf.li

cufflink ˈkʌf.lɪŋk **-s** -s

cui bono ˌkuː.iˈbəʊn.əʊ, ˌkwiː-, -ˈbɒn.əʊ (US) ˌkwiːˈboʊ.noʊ

cuirass kwɪˈræs, kjuᵊ- (US) kwɪˈræs **-es** -ɪz

cuirassier ˌkwɪ.rəˈsi.əʳ, ˌkjuᵊ.rəˈ- (US) ˌkwiː.rəˈsɪr, ˈkwɪr.ə.sɪr **-s** -z

cuisenaire ˌkwiː.zᵊnˈeəʳ (US) -er

Cuisinart® ˈkwiː.zᵊn.ɑːt (US) -ɑːrt

cuisine kwɪzˈiːn, kwəˈziːn

cuisine minceur kwɪˌziːn.mæ̃nˈsɜːʳ, kwə- (US) -ˈsɝː

cuiss|e kwɪs **-es** -ɪz

cuke kjuːk **-s** -s

Culcheth ˈkʌl.tʃəθ, -tʃɪθ

cul-de-sac ˈkʌl.də.sæk, ˈkʊl-, ˌ--ˈ- **-s** -s

Culham ˈkʌl.əm

culinary ˈkʌl.ɪ.nᵊr.i, ˈ-ə-, ˈkjuː.lɪ- (US) ˈkʌl.ə.ner-

Culkin ˈkʌl.kɪn

cull kʌl **-s** -z **-ing** -ɪŋ **-ed** -d

Cullen ˈkʌl.ən, -ɪn

cullender ˈkʌl.ən.dəʳ, -ɪn- (US) -dɚ **-s** -z

Culley ˈkʌl.i

Cullinan ˈkʌl.ɪ.nən, ˈ-ə-, -næn

Culloden kəˈlɒd.ᵊn, kʌlˈɒd-; kəˈləʊ.dᵊn (US) kəˈloʊ.dᵊn, -ˈlɑː-

Cullompton kəˈlʌm*p*.tᵊn, ˈkʌl.əm*p*-

Cullum ˈkʌl.əm

culm (C) kʌlm **-s** -z

Culme kʌlm

culmi|nate ˈkʌl.mɪ|.neɪt **-nates** -neɪts **-nating** -neɪ.tɪŋ (US) -neɪ.t̬ɪŋ **-nated** -neɪ.tɪd (US) -neɪ.t̬ɪd

culmination ˌkʌl.mɪˈneɪ.ʃᵊn, -məˈ- **-s** -z

culottes kjuːˈlɒts, kuː- (US) ˈkuː.lɑːts, ˈkjuː-, -ˈ-

culpability ˌkʌl.pəˈbɪl.ə.ti, -ɪ.ti (US) -ə.t̬i

culpab|le ˈkʌl.pə.b|l̩ **-ly** -li **-leness** -l̩.nəs, -nɪs

culprit ˈkʌl.prɪt **-s** -s

Culross *Scottish surname & place:* ˈkuː.rɒs, -rəs (US) -rɑːs

Culross *English surname and London street:* ˈkʌl.rɒs, -ˈ- (US) ˈkʌl.rɑːs, -ˈ-

cult kʌlt **-s** -s

Culter ˈkuː.təʳ (US) -t̬ɚ

cultivable ˈkʌl.tɪ.və.bl̩, -tə- (US) -t̬ə-

culti|vate ˈkʌl.tɪ|.veɪt, -tə- (US) -t̬ə- **-vates** -veɪts **-vating** -veɪ.tɪŋ (US) -veɪ.t̬ɪŋ **-vated** -veɪ.tɪd (US) -veɪ.t̬ɪd **-vatable** -veɪ.tə.bl̩ (US) -veɪ.t̬ə-

cultivation ˌkʌl.tɪˈveɪ.ʃᵊn, -təˈ- (US) -t̬əˈ-

cultivator ˈkʌl.tɪ.veɪ.təʳ, -tə- (US) -t̬ə.veɪ.t̬ɚ **-s** -z

Cults kʌlts

cultural ˈkʌl.tʃᵊr.ᵊl **-ly** -i

culturality ˌkʌl.tʃᵊrˈæl.ɪ.ti, -ə.ti (US) -tʃəˈræl.ə.t̬i

culture ˈkʌl.tʃəʳ (US) -tʃɚ **-s** -z **-d** -d ˈ**culture** ˌ**shock**

culver (C) ˈkʌl.vəʳ (US) -vɚ **-s** -z

culverin ˈkʌl.vᵊr.ɪn **-s** -z

culvert ˈkʌl.vət (US) -vɚt **-s** -s **-age** -ɪdʒ (US) ˈkʌl.vɚ.t̬ɪdʒ

Culzean kəˈleɪn

cum kʌm, kʊm

Cumaean kjuːˈmiː.ən

cumbent ˈkʌm.bᵊnt

cumb|er ˈkʌm.b|əʳ (US) -b|ɚ **-ers** -əz (US) -ɚz **-ering** -ᵊr.ɪŋ **-ered** -əd (US) -ɚd **-erer/s** -ᵊr.əʳ/z (US) -ɚ.ɚ/z

Cumberland ˈkʌm.bᵊl.ənd (US) -bɚ.lənd

Cumbernauld ˌkʌm.bəˈnɔːld, ˈ--- (US) ˌkʌm.bɚˈnɑːld, -ˈnɔːld

cumbersome ˈkʌm.bə.səm (US) -bɚ- **-ly** -li **-ness** -nəs, -nɪs

Cumbri|a ˈkʌm.bri|.ə **-an/s** -ən/z

cumbrous ˈkʌmb.rəs **-ly** -li **-ness** -nəs, -nɪs

cumin ˈkjuː.mɪn, ˈkʌm.ɪn (US) ˈkuː-, ˈkjuː-

cum laude ˌkʌmˈlaʊ.deɪ, ˌkʊm-, -ˈlɔː.di (US) ˌkʊmˈlaʊ.deɪ, -ˈlɑː-, -ˈlɔː-, -di, -də

cummerbund ˈkʌm.ə.bʌnd (US) ˈ-ɚ- **-s** -z

cummin ˈkʌm.ɪn

Cumming ˈkʌm.ɪŋ **-s** -z

cummings (C) ˈkʌm.ɪŋz

Cumnock ˈkʌm.nək

Cumnor ˈkʌm.nəʳ (US) -nɚ

cumquat ˈkʌm.kwɒt (US) -kwɑːt **-s** -s

cumulate (*adj.*) ˈkjuː.mjə.lət, -mjʊ-, -lɪt, -leɪt (US) -mjə-

cumu|late (*v.*) ˈkjuː.mjə|.leɪt, -mjʊ- (US) -mjə- **-lates** -leɪts **-lating** -leɪ.tɪŋ (US) -leɪ.t̬ɪŋ **-lated** -leɪ.tɪd (US) -leɪ.t̬ɪd

cumulation ˌkjuː.mjəˈleɪ.ʃᵊn, -mjʊˈ- (US) -mjəˈ- **-s** -z

cumulative ˈkjuː.mjə.lə.tɪv, -mjʊ-, -leɪ- (US) -mjə.lə.t̬ɪv **-ly** -li **-ness** -nəs, -nɪs

cumulonimbus ˌkjuː.mjə.ləʊˈnɪm.bəs, -mjʊ- (US) -mjə.loʊˈ- **-es** -ɪz

cumul|us ˈkjuː.mjə.l|əs, -mjʊ- (US) -mjə- **-i** -aɪ, -iː (US) -aɪ

Cunard ˌkjuːˈnɑːd (US) ˌkuːˈnɑːrd, ˌkjuː- **-er/s** -əʳ/z (US) -ɚ/z

cunctation kʌŋkˈteɪ.ʃᵊn **-s** -z

cunctator kʌŋkˈteɪ.təʳ (US) -t̬ɚ **-s** -z

cuneiform ˈkjuː.nɪ.fɔːm, -ni.ɪ-, -ə.fɔːm (US) ˈkjuː.nə.fɔːrm, -ni.ə-

Cunliffe ˈkʌn.lɪf

cunnilingus ˌkʌn.ɪˈlɪŋ.gəs (US) -əˈ-

cunning ˈkʌn.ɪŋ **-est** -ɪst **-ly** -li **-ness** -nəs, -nɪs

Cunningham ˈkʌn.ɪŋ.əm (US) -hæm

cunt kʌnt **-s** -s

cup kʌp **-s** -s **-ping** -ɪŋ **-ped** -t ˈ**Cup** ˌ**Final**, ˌ**Cup** ˈ**Final**

Cupar ˈkuː.pəʳ (US) -pɚ

cupbearer ˈkʌpˌbeə.rəʳ (US) -ˌber.ɚ **-s** -z

cupboard ˈkʌb.əd (US) -ɚd **-s** -z ˈ**cupboard** ˌ**love**

cupcake ˈkʌp.keɪk **-s** -s

cupful ˈkʌp.fʊl **-s** -z

cupid (C) ˈkjuː.pɪd **-s** -z

cupidity kjuˈpɪd.ə.ti, -ɪ.ti (US) -ə.t̬i

cupola ˈkjuː.pᵊl.ə **-s** -z

cuppa ˈkʌp.ə **-s** -z

cupreous ˈkjuː.pri.əs

cupric ˈkjuː.prɪk

Cuprinol® ˈkjuː.prɪ.nɒl, -prə- (US) -nɑːl

cuprous kjuː.prəs

cur kɜːʳ (US) kɝː **-s** -z

curability ˌkjʊə.rəˈbɪl.ə.ti, ˌkjɔː-, -ɪ.ti (US) ˌkjʊr.əˈbɪl.ə.t̬i

curable ˈkjʊə.rə.bl̩, ˈkjɔː- (US) ˈkjʊr-

curaç|ao (C) ˈkjʊə.rə.s|aʊ, ˈkjɔː-, -s|əʊ, ˌ--ˈ- (US) ˈkjʊr.ə.s|oʊ, ˈkʊr-, -s|aʊ, ˌ--ˈ- **-oa** -əʊə (US) -oʊə

curac|y ˈkjʊə.rə.s|i, ˈkjɔː- (US) ˈkjʊr.ə- **-ies** -iz

Curan ˈkʌr.ən

curare kjʊəˈrɑː.ri (US) kjʊˈrɑːr.i

curate (*n.*) ˈkjʊə.rət, ˈkjɔː-, -rɪt (US) ˈkjʊr.ət, -eɪt **-s** -s ˌ**curate's** ˈ**egg**

cura|te (*v.*) ˈkjʊə.r|eɪt, ˈkjɔː-; -ˈ-, kjə- (US) ˈkjʊr.|eit; -ˈ-, kjɚ- **-tes** -ts **-ting** -tɪŋ (US) -t̬ɪŋ **-ted** -tɪd (US) -t̬ɪd

curative ˈkjʊə.rə.tɪv, ˈkjɔː- (US) ˈkjʊr.ə.t̬ɪv **-ly** li

curator kjʊəˈreɪ.təʳ, kjɔː- (US) ˈkjʊr.eɪ.t̬ɚ, ˈkjɝː- **-s** -z **-ship/s** -ʃɪp/s

curb kɜːb (US) kɝːb **-s** -z **-ing** -ɪŋ **-ed** -d

curbstone ˈkɜːb.stəʊn (US) ˈkɝːb.stoʊn **-s** -z

curd kɜːd (US) kɝːd **-s** -z

curdl|e ˈkɜː.dl̩ (US) ˈkɝː- **-es** -z **-ing** -ɪŋ, ˈkɜːd.lɪŋ (US) ˈkɝː.dl̩.ɪŋ, ˈkɝːd.lɪŋ **-ed** -d

curd|y ˈkɜː.d|i US ˈkɝː- **-ier** -i.əʳ US -i.ɚ **-iest** -i.ɪst, -i.əst **-iness** -ɪ.nəs, -ɪ.nɪs

cur|e kjʊəʳ, kjɔːʳ US kjʊr **-es** -z **-ing** -ɪŋ **-ed** -d **-er/s** -əʳ/z US -ɚ/z

cure-all ˈkjʊəʳ.ɔːl, ˈkjɔːʳ- US ˈkjʊr.ɑːl, ˈkjɝː-, -ɔːl **-s** -z

cu|ret kjʊə|ˈret US kjʊ|ˈret **-rets** -ˈrets **-retting** -ˈret.ɪŋ US -ˈreţ.ɪŋ **-retted** -ˈret.ɪd US -ˈreţ.ɪd

curettage ˌkjʊə.rɪˈtɑːʒ, kjʊəˈret.ɪdʒ US kjʊˈreţ.ɪdʒ, ˌkjʊr.əˈtɑːʒ

cu|rette kjʊə|ˈret US kjʊ- **-rettes** -ˈrets **-retting** -ˈret.ɪŋ US -ˈreţ.ɪŋ **-retted** -ˈret.ɪd US -ˈreţ.ɪd

curettment kjʊəˈret.mənt US kjʊ-

curfew ˈkɜː.fjuː US ˈkɝː- **-s** -z

cur|ia ˈkjʊə.r|i.ə, ˈkjɔː-, ˈkʊə- US ˈkjʊr|.i- **-iae** -i.iː, -i.aɪ

curie (C) ˈkjʊə.ri, -iː US ˈkjʊr.i, -iː **-s** -z

curio ˈkjʊə.ri.əʊ, ˈkjɔː- US ˈkjʊr.i.oʊ **-s** -z

curiosit|y ˌkjʊə.riˈɒs.ə.t|i, ˌkjɔː-, -ɪ.t|i US ˌkjʊr.iˈɑː.sə.ţ|i **-ies** -iz

curious ˈkjʊə.ri.əs, ˈkjɔː- US ˈkjʊr.i- **-ly** -li **-ness** -nəs, -nɪs

curium ˈkjʊə.ri.əm, ˈkjɔː- US ˈkjʊr.i-

curl kɜːl US kɝːl **-s** -z **-ing** -ɪŋ **-ed** -d ˈ**curling** ˌ**tongs**

curler ˈkɜː.ləʳ US ˈkɝː.lɚ **-s** -z

curlew ˈkɜː.ljuː US ˈkɝː.luː, ˈkɝːl.juː **-s** -z

curlicue ˈkɜː.lɪ.kjuː US ˈkɝː- **-s** -z

curling ˈkɜː.lɪŋ US ˈkɝː-

curl|y ˈkɜː.l|i US ˈkɝː- **-ier** -i.əʳ US -i.ɚ **-iest** -i.ɪst, -i.əst **-iness** -ɪ.nəs, -ɪ.nɪs

curmudgeon kɜːˈmʌdʒ.ᵊn, kə- US kɚ- **-s** -z **-ly** -li

curragh, currach (C) ˈkʌr.ə US ˈkɝː- **-s** -z

Curran ˈkʌr.ᵊn US ˈkɝː-

currant ˈkʌr.ᵊnt US ˈkɝː- **-s** -s

currawong ˈkʌr.ə.wɒŋ US -wɑːŋ, -wɔːŋ **-s** -z

currenc|y ˈkʌr.ᵊnt.s|i US ˈkɝː- **-ies** -iz

current ˈkʌr.ᵊnt US ˈkɝː- **-s** -s **-ly** -li **-ness** -nəs, -nɪs ˌ**current acˈcount**; ˌ**current afˈfairs**

Currer ˈkʌr.əʳ US ˈkɝː.ɚ

curricle ˈkʌr.ɪ.kl̩ US ˈkɝː- **-s** -z

curricul|um kəˈrɪk.jə.l|əm, -jʊ- US -jə- **-a** -ə **-ums** -əmz **-ar** -əʳ US -ɚ

curriculum vitae kəˌrɪk.jə.ləmˈviː.taɪ, -jʊ-, -teɪ US -jə.ləmˈviː.taɪ, -tiː, -ˈvaɪ.ţi **-s** -s **curricula vitae** kəˌrɪk.jə.ləˈviː.taɪ, -jʊ-, -teɪ US -jə.ləˈviː.taɪ, -tiː, -ˈvaɪ.ţi

Currie ˈkʌr.i US ˈkɝː.i

Currier ˈkʌr.i.əʳ US ˈkɝː.i.ɚ

currish ˈkɜː.rɪʃ US ˈkɝː.ɪʃ **-ly** -li **-ness** -nəs, -nɪs

curr|y (C) ˈkʌr|.i US ˈkɝː- **-ies** -iz **-ying** -i.ɪŋ **-ied** -id **-ier/s** -i.əʳ/z US -i.ɚ/z ˈ**curry** ˌ**powder**

curs|e kɜːs US kɝːs **-es** -ɪz **-ing** -ɪŋ **-ed** -t

cursed *(adj.)* ˈkɜː.sɪd US ˈkɝː- **-ly** -li **-ness** -nəs, -nɪs

cursive ˈkɜː.sɪv US ˈkɝː- **-ly** -li **-ness** -nəs, -nɪs

cursor ˈkɜː.səʳ US ˈkɝː.sɚ **-s** -z

Cursor Mundi ˌkɜː.sɔːˈmʊn.diː, -ˈmʌn.daɪ US ˌkɝː.sɔːrˈmʊn.di, -sɚˈ-

cursor|y ˈkɜː.sᵊr|.i US ˈkɝː- **-ily** -ᵊl.i, -ɪ.li **-iness** -ɪ.nəs, -ɪ.nɪs

curst kɜːst US kɝːst

cursus ˈkɜː.səs US ˈkɝː-

curt kɜːt US kɝːt **-er** -əʳ US ˈkɝː.ţɚ **-est** -ɪst, -əst US ˈkɝː.ţɪst, -ţəst **-ly** -li **-ness** -nəs, -nɪs

curtail kɜːˈteɪl US kɚ- **-s** -z **-ing** -ɪŋ **-ed** -d **-ment/s** -mənt/s

curtain ˈkɜː.tᵊn, -tɪn US ˈkɝː.tᵊn **-s** -z **-ed** -d ˈ**curtain** ˌ**call**; ˈ**curtain** ˌ**raiser**

curtes|y ˈkɜː.tə.s|i, -tɪ.s|i US ˈkɝː.ţə- **-ies** -ɪz

Curtice ˈkɜː.tɪs US ˈkɝː.ţɪs

curtilage ˈkɜː.tᵊl.ɪdʒ, -tɪ.lɪdʒ US ˈkɝː.ţᵊl-

Curtis(s) ˈkɜː.tɪs US ˈkɝː.ţɪs

curtsey ˈkɜːt.si US ˈkɝːt- **-s** -z **-ing** -ɪŋ **-ed** -d

curts|y ˈkɜːt.s|i US ˈkɝːt- **-ies** -iz **-ying** -i.ɪŋ **-ied** -id

curvaceous kɜːˈveɪ.ʃəs US kɝː- **-ly** -li **-ness** -nəs, -nɪs

curvation kɜːˈveɪ.ʃᵊn US kɝː- **-s** -z

curvature ˈkɜː.və.tʃəʳ, -tjʊəʳ US ˈkɝː.və.tʃɚ **-s** -z

curv|e kɜːv US kɝːv **-es** -z **-ing** -ɪŋ **-ed** -d ˈ**curve** ˌ**ball**

curveball ˈkɜːv.bɔːl US ˈkɝːv-, -bɑːl **-s** -z

cur|vet kɜː|ˈvet US kɝː- **-vets** -ˈvets **-vet(t)ing** -ˈvet.ɪŋ US -ˈveţ.ɪŋ **-vet(t)ed** -ˈvet.ɪd US -ˈveţ.ɪd

curviline|al ˌkɜː.vɪˈlɪn.i|.əl, -vəˈ- US ˌkɝː.vəˈ- **-ar** -əʳ US -ɚ

curv|y ˈkɜː.v|i US ˈkɝː- **-ier** -i.əʳ US -i.ɚ **-iest** -i.ɪst, -i.əst

Curwen ˈkɜː.wɪn, -wən US ˈkɝː-

Curzon ˈkɜː.zᵊn US ˈkɝː-

Cusack ˈkjuː.sæk, -zæk, -zək US ˈkuː-, ˈkjuː-

Cush kʊʃ, kʌʃ **-ite/s** -aɪt/s

Cushing ˈkʊʃ.ɪŋ

cushion ˈkʊʃ.ᵊn **-s** -z **-ing** -ɪŋ **-ed** -d

cush|y ˈkʊʃ|.i **-ier** -i.əʳ US -i.ɚ **-iest** -i.əst, -i.ɪst **-ily** -ɪ.li, -ᵊl.i **-iness** -ɪ.nəs, -ɪ.nɪs

cusp kʌsp **-s** -s

cuspid ˈkʌs.pɪd

cuspidor ˈkʌs.pɪ.dɔːʳ US -ə.dɔːr **-s** -z

cuss kʌs **-es** -ɪz **-ing** -ɪŋ **-ed** -t

cussed *(adj.)* ˈkʌs.ɪd, -əd **-ly** -li **-ness** -nəs, -nɪs

custard ˈkʌs.təd US -tɚd **-s** -z ˈ**custard** ˌ**apple**; ˌ**custard** ˈ**pie**

Custer ˈkʌs.təʳ US -tɚ kʌsˈtəʊ.diːz US -ˈtoʊ-

custodial kʌsˈtəʊ.di.əl US -ˈtoʊ-

custodian kʌsˈtəʊ.di.ən US -ˈtoʊ- **-s** -z

custody ˈkʌs.tə.di

custom ˈkʌs.təm **-s** -z

customarily ˈkʌs.tə.mᵊr.ᵊl.i, -ɪ.li; ˌkʌs.təˈmer- US ˌkʌs.təˈmer-

customar|y ˈkʌs.tə.mᵊr|.i US -mer- **-iness** -ɪ.nəs, -ɪ.nɪs

customer ˈkʌs.tə.məʳ US -mɚ **-s** -z

customhou|se ˈkʌs.təm.haʊ|s **-ses** -zɪz

customiz|e, -is|e ˈkʌs.tə.maɪz **-es** -ɪz **-ing** -ɪŋ **-ed** -d **-er/s** -əʳ/z US -ɚ/z

custom-made ˌkʌs.təmˈmeɪd *stress shift, British only:* ˌcustom-made ˈsuit

custos *(sing.)* ˈkʌs.tɒs, -təʊs US -tɑːs; ˈkʊs.toʊs *(plur.)* **custodes** kʌsˈtəʊ.diːz US -ˈtoʊ-

cut kʌt **-s** -s **-ting** -ɪŋ US ˈkʌţ.ɪŋ **-ter/s** -əʳ/z US ˈkʌţ.ɚ/z

cut-and-|dried ˌkʌt.ᵊn|ˈdraɪd **-dry** -ˈdraɪ

cut-and-paste ˌkʌt.ᵊndˈpeɪst, -ᵊmˈ- US -ᵊndˈ-

cutaneous kjuːˈteɪ.ni.əs **-ly** -li

cutaway ˈkʌt.ə.weɪ US ˈkʌţ-

cutback ˈkʌt.bæk **-s** -s

Cutch kʌtʃ

cut|e kjuːt **-er** -əʳ US ˈkjuː.ţɚ **-est** -ɪst, -əst US ˈkjuː.ţɪst, -ţəst **-ely** -li **-eness** -nəs, -nɪs

cutesy ˈkjuːt.si

cutey ˈkjuː.ti US -ţi **-s** -z

Cutforth ˈkʌt.fɔːθ US -fɔːrθ

Cuthbert ˈkʌθ.bət US -bɚt

Cuthbertson ˈkʌθ.bət.sᵊn US -bɚt-

cuticle ˈkjuː.tɪ.kl̩ US -ţə- **-s** -z

cuticular kjuːˈtɪk.jə.ləʳ, -jʊ- US -lɚ

Cuticura® ˌkjuː.tɪˈkjʊə.rə, -ˈkjɔː- US -ţəˈkjʊr.ə

cutie ˈkjuː.ti US -ţi **-s** -z

cutie-pie ˈkjuː.ti.paɪ US -ţi-

cutis ˈkjuː.tɪs US -ţɪs

cutlass ˈkʌt.ləs **-es** -ɪz

cutler (C) ˈkʌt.ləʳ US -lɚ **-s** -z

cutlery ˈkʌt.lᵊr.i

cutlet ˈkʌt.lət, -lɪt **-s** -s

cutoff ˈkʌt.ɒf US ˈkʌţ.ɑːf, -ɔːf **-s** -s

cutout ˈkʌt.aʊt US ˈkʌţ- **-s** -s

cut-price ˌkʌtˈpraɪs *stress shift:* ˌcut-price ˈgoods

Cuttell kəˈtel

cutter ˈkʌt.əʳ US ˈkʌţ.ɚ **-s** -z

cutthroat ˈkʌt.θrəʊt US -θroʊt **-s** -s

cutting ˈkʌt.ɪŋ US ˈkʌţ- **-s** -z ˌ**cutting** ˈ**edge**

cuttle (C) ˈkʌt.l̩ US ˈkʌţ- **-s** -z **-bone** -bəʊn US -boʊn

cuttlefish ˈkʌt.l̩.fɪʃ US ˈkʌţ- **-es** -ɪz

cutt|y ˈkʌt|.i US ˈkʌţ- **-ies** -iz ˌ**Cutty** ˈ**Sark**

cutwater ˈkʌtˌwɔː.təʳ (US) -ˌwɑː.t̬ɚ, -ˌwɔː- **-s** -z
cutworm ˈkʌt.wɜːm (US) -wɝːm **-s** -z
cuvette kjuːˈvet (US) kjuː-, kuː- **-s** -s
Cuvier ˈkjuː.vi.eɪ, ˈkuː- (US) ˈkjuː.vi.eɪ; ˌkuːˈvjeɪ
Cuxhaven ˈkʊksˌhɑː.vᵊn
Cuyahoga ˌkaɪ.əˈhəʊ.gə (US) -ˈhoʊ-, -ˈhɑː-, -ˈhɔː-
Cuyp kaɪp, kɔɪp (US) kɔɪp **-s** -s
Cuzco ˈkʊs.kəʊ, ˈkuː.skəʊ (US) ˈkuː.skoʊ
CV ˌsiːˈviː **-s** -z
cwm kʊm, kuːm **-s** -z
Cwm Avon kʊmˈæv.ᵊn, kuːm-
Cwmbach kʊmˈbɑːx, kuːm- (US) -ˈbɑːk
Cwmbran kʊmˈbrɑːn, kuːm-
cwt *(abbrev. for* **hundredweight***)* ˈhʌn.drəd.weɪt, -drɪd- **-s** -s
cyan ˈsaɪ.æn, -ən
cyanate ˈsaɪə.neɪt
cyanic saɪˈæn.ɪk
cyanide ˈsaɪə.naɪd **-s** -z
cyanogen saɪˈæn.ə.dʒᵊn, -dʒɪn, -dʒen
cyanosis ˌsaɪəˈnəʊ.sɪs (US) -ˈnoʊ-
cybercafe ˈsaɪ.bəˌkæf.eɪ (US) ˌsaɪ.bɚ-.kæfˈeɪ, -kəˈfeɪ **-s** -z
cybernetic ˌsaɪ.bəˈnet.ɪk (US) -bɚˈnet̬- **-s** -s
cyberpet ˈsaɪ.bə.pet (US) -bɚ- **-s** -s
cyberpunk ˈsaɪ.bə.pʌŋk (US) -bɚ- **-s** -s
cyberspace ˈsaɪ.bə.speɪs (US) -bɚ-
cybrarian saɪˈbreə.ri.ən (US) -ˈbrer.i- **-s** -z
cybrar|y ˈsaɪ.brᵊr|.i, -br|i (US) -brer|.i, -bræɹ.i **-ies** -iz
cycad ˈsaɪ.kæd, -kəd **-s** -z
Cyclades ˈsaɪ.klə.diːz, ˈsɪk.lə-
cyclamate ˈsaɪ.klə.meɪt, ˈsɪk.lə- (US) ˈsaɪ.klə- **-s** -s
cyclamen ˈsɪk.lə.mən, ˈsaɪ.klə-, -men (US) ˈsaɪ.klə- **-s** -z
cycl|e ˈsaɪ.kl̩ **-es** -z **-ing** -ɪŋ, ˈ-klɪŋ **-ed** -d
cyclic ˈsaɪ.klɪk, ˈsɪk.lɪk **-al** -ᵊl **-ally** -ᵊl.i, -li
cyclist ˈsaɪ.klɪst **-s** -s
cyclo- ˈsaɪ.kləʊ-, saɪˈklɒ-, ˈsɪk.ləʊ- (US) ˈsaɪ.kloʊ-, saɪˈklɑː-
Note: Prefix. This may be stressed on the initial syllable, e.g. **cyclostyle** /ˈsaɪ.kləʊ.staɪl (US) ˈsaɪ.kloʊ-/ or on the second syllable, e.g. **cyclometer** /saɪˈklɒm.ɪ.tə (US) saɪˈklɑː.mə.tɚ/.
cyclograph ˈsaɪ.klə*ʊ*.grɑːf, -græf (US) -klə.græf **-s** -s
cycloid ˈsaɪ.klɔɪd **-s** -z
cycloidal saɪˈklɔɪ.dᵊl
cyclometer saɪˈklɒm.ɪ.təʳ, ˈ-ə- (US) -ˈklɑː.mə.t̬ɚ **-s** -z
cyclone ˈsaɪ.kləʊn (US) -kloʊn **-s** -z
cyclonic saɪˈklɒn.ɪk (US) -ˈklɑː.nɪk
cyclopaed|ia ˌsaɪ.klə*ʊ*ˈpiː.d|i.ə (US) -kloʊˈ-, -kləˈ- **-ias** -i.əz **-ic** -ɪk
cyclopean ˌsaɪ.klə*ʊ*ˈpiː.ən; saɪˈkləʊ.pi- (US) ˌsaɪ.kloʊˈpiː-, -kləˈ-; saɪˈkloʊ.pi-
cycloped|ia ˌsaɪ.klə*ʊ*ˈpiː.d|i.ə (US) -kloʊˈ-, -kləˈ- **-ias** -i.əz **-ic** -ɪk
saɪˈkləʊ.piːz (US) -ˈkloʊ-
cyclops *(sing.)* ˈsaɪ.klɒps (US) -klɑːps *(plur.)* **cyclopes** saɪˈkləʊ.piːz (US) -ˈkloʊ-
cyclorama ˌsaɪ.kləˈrɑː.mə (US) -kloʊˈræm.ə, -kləˈ-, -ˈrɑː.mə **-s** -z
cyclostyl|e ˈsaɪ.klə*ʊ*.staɪl (US) -klə- **-es** -z **-ing** -ɪŋ **-ed** -d
cyclothymia ˌsaɪ.klə*ʊ*ˈθaɪ.mi.ə, ˌsɪk.lə*ʊ*ˈ- (US) ˌsaɪ.kloʊˈ-, -kləˈ-
cyclotron ˈsaɪ.klə*ʊ*.trɒn (US) -klə.trɑːn **-s** -z
cyder ˈsaɪ.dəʳ (US) -dɚ **-s** -z
cygnet ˈsɪg.nət, -nɪt **-s** -s
Cygnus ˈsɪg.nəs
cylinder ˈsɪl.ɪn.dəʳ, -ən- (US) -dɚ **-s** -z
cylindric səˈlɪn.drɪk, sɪ- **-al** -ᵊl **-ally** -ᵊl.i, -li
cylindriform səˈlɪn.drɪ.fɔːm, sɪ- (US) -drɪ.fɔːrm, -drə-
cylindroid ˈsɪl.ɪn.drɔɪd, səˈlɪn-, sɪ- **-s** -z
cyli|x ˈsaɪ.lɪ|ks, ˈsɪl.ɪ|ks **-ces** -siːz
cy|ma ˈsaɪ|.mə **-mae** -miː
cymbal ˈsɪm.bᵊl **-s** -z
cymbal|o ˈsɪm.bə.l|əʊ (US) -l|oʊ **-o(e)s** -əʊz (US) -oʊz
Cymbeline ˈsɪm.bə.liːn, -bɪ-
cyme saɪm **-s** -z
Cymric ˈkɪm.rɪk, ˈkʌm- (US) ˈkɪm-
Cymru ˈkɪm.ri, ˈkʌm- (US) ˈkʌm-
Cymry ˈkɪm.ri, ˈkʌm- (US) ˈkɪm-
Cynewulf ˈkɪn.ɪ.wʊlf, ˈ-ə-
cynic ˈsɪn.ɪk **-s** -s
cynical ˈsɪn.ɪ.kᵊl **-ly** -i
cynicism ˈsɪn.ɪ.sɪ.zᵊm, ˈ-ə- **-s** -z
cynocephalic ˌsaɪ.nə*ʊ*.sefˈæl.ɪk, -kefˈ- (US) -noʊ-
cynocephalous ˌsaɪ.nə*ʊ*ˈsef.ə.ləs, -ˈkef- (US) -noʊˈ-
Cynon ˈkɪn.ən, ˈkʌn-
cynosure ˈsaɪ.nə.sjʊəʳ, ˈsɪn.ə-, -ˌʃʊəʳ (US) -ʃʊr **-s** -z
Cynthi|a ˈsɪn*t*.θi|.ə **-us** -əs
cyph|er ˈsaɪ.f|əʳ (US) -f|ɚ **-ers** -əz (US) -ɚz **-ering** -ᵊr.ɪŋ **-ered** -əd (US) -ɚd
cy près ˌsiːˈpreɪ, ˌsaɪ-
cypress ˈsaɪ.prəs, -prɪs **-es** -ɪz
Cyprian ˈsɪp.ri.ən **-s** -z
Cypriot ˈsɪp.ri.ət **-s** -s
Cypriote ˈsɪp.ri.əʊt (US) -oʊt **-s** -s
Cyprus ˈsaɪ.prəs
Cyrano ˈsɪr.ə.nəʊ; sɪˈrɑː-, sə- (US) ˈsɪr.ə.noʊ **ˌCyrano de ˈBergerac**
Cyrenaica ˌsɪr.əˈneɪ.ɪ.kə, ˌsaɪə.rəˈ-, -ɪˈ-, -ˈnaɪ- (US) ˌsaɪ.rəˈ-
Cyrene saɪəˈriː.ni (US) saɪ-
Cyrenian saɪəˈriː.ni.ən (US) saɪ-
Cyrenius saɪəˈriː.ni.əs (US) saɪ-
Cyril ˈsɪr.ᵊl, -ɪl
Cyrillic səˈrɪl.ɪk, sɪ- (US) sə-
Cyrus ˈsaɪə.rəs (US) ˈsaɪ-
cyst sɪst **-s** -s
cystic ˈsɪs.tɪk **ˌcystic fibˈrosis**
cystitis sɪˈstaɪ.tɪs (US) -t̬ɪs
cystoid ˈsɪs.tɔɪd
Cythera sɪˈθɪə.rə, sə- (US) -ˈθɪr.ə
cyto- ˈsaɪ.tə*ʊ*-, saɪˈtɒ- (US) ˈsaɪ.t̬oʊ-, -t̬ə-, saɪˈtɑː-
Note: Prefix. This may carry primary or secondary stress on the initial syllable, e.g. **cytoplasm** /ˈsaɪ.tə.plæz.ᵊm (US) ˈsaɪ.t̬ə- / or on the second syllable, e.g. **cytology** /saɪˈtɒl.ədʒi (US) saɪˈtɑːl-/.
cytogenetics ˌsaɪ.tə*ʊ*.dʒəˈnet.ɪks, -dʒenˈet-, -dʒɪˈnet- (US) ˌsaɪ.t̬oʊ.dʒəˈnet̬-
cytology saɪˈtɒl.ə.dʒi (US) -ˈtɑː.lə-
cytoplasm ˈsaɪ.tə*ʊ*.plæz.ᵊm (US) -t̬ə- **-s** -z
cytoplasmic ˌsaɪ.tə*ʊ*ˈplæz.mɪk (US) -t̬əˈ-
czar (C) zɑːʳ, tsɑːʳ (US) zɑːr, tsɑːr **-s** -z
czardas ˈtʃɑː.dæʃ, ˈzɑː.dæs, -dəs (US) ˈtʃɑːr.dɑːʃ, -dæʃ **-es** -ɪz
czarevitch (C) ˈzɑː.rə.vɪtʃ, -rɪ- (US) ˈzɑːr.ə-, ˈtsɑːr- **-es** -ɪz
czarevna (C) zɑːˈrev.nə, tsɑː- **-s** -z
czarina zɑːˈriː.nə, tsɑː- **-s** -z
czarist ˈzɑː.rɪst, ˈtsɑː- (US) ˈzɑːr.ɪst, ˈtsɑːr- **-s** -s
Czech tʃek **-s** -s
Czechoslovak ˌtʃek.əʊˈsləʊ.væk (US) -oʊˈsloʊ.vɑːk, -væk **-s** -s
Czechoslovaki|a ˌtʃek.əʊ.slə*ʊ*ˈvæk.i|.ə, -ˈvɑː.ki- (US) -oʊ.sloʊˈvɑː.ki-, -ˈvæk.i- **-an** -ən
Czerny ˈtʃɜː.ni, ˈzɜː-, tʃeə- (US) ˈtʃer-

Pronouncing the letter D

When not used in the grammatical inflection *-ed*, the consonant letter **d** is most often realised as /d/, e.g.:

duck /dʌk/

However, in consonant clusters /d/ may be elided, e.g.:

grandson /ˈgrænd.sʌn/
Wednesday /ˈwenz.deɪ/

In addition

d is sometimes realised as /dʒ/, e.g.:

procedure /prəʊˈsiː.dʒəʳ/ ⓤⓢ /prəˈsiː.dʒɚ/
soldier /ˈsəʊl.dʒəʳ/ ⓤⓢ /ˈsoʊl.dʒɚ/

Due to COALESCENCE between /d/ and /j/ in British English and omission of /j/ in American English, syllables beginning with **du** may have different pronunciations, e.g.:

due /dʒuː/ ⓤⓢ /duː/

The grammatical inflection -ed

There are three possible ways of pronouncing the grammatical inflection *-ed*.

Following /t/ and /d/ the inflection is realised as /ɪd/, e.g.:

started /ˈstɑː.tɪd/ ⓤⓢ /ˈstɑːr.t̬ɪd/

Following all other voiceless consonant sounds the inflection is realised as /t/, e.g.:

shaped /ʃeɪpt/

Following all other voiced consonant sounds and after vowel sounds, the inflection is realised as /d/, e.g.:

played /pleɪd/

d (D) diː **-'s** -z
d' *(from* **do***)* də, d
Note: See also **d'you**.
'd *(from* **had, would***)* d
DA ˌdiːˈeɪ **-s** -z
dab dæb **-s** -z **-bing** -ɪŋ **-bed** -d **-ber/s** -əʳ/z ⓤⓢ -ɚ/z ˌ**dab** ˈ**hand**
dabbl|e ˈdæb.l̩ **-es** -z **-ing** -ɪŋ, ˈdæb.lɪŋ **-ed** -d **-er/s** -əʳ/z, ˈdæb.ləʳ/z ⓤⓢ -ɚ/z
dabchick ˈdæb.tʃɪk **-s** -s
da capo dɑːˈkɑː.pəʊ, də- ⓤⓢ -poʊ
Dacca ˈdæk.ə ⓤⓢ ˈdæk.ə, ˈdɑː.kə
dace deɪs
dacha ˈdætʃ.ə ⓤⓢ ˈdɑː.tʃə **-s** -z
Dachau *as if German:* ˈdæx.aʊ, ˈdæk- ⓤⓢ ˈdɑː.kaʊ
dachshund ˈdæk.sᵊnd, ˈdæʃ.ᵊnd, -hʊnd, -hʊnt ⓤⓢ ˈdɑːks.hʊnd, ˈdɑːk.sənd **-s** -z
Daci|a ˈdeɪ.si|.ə, -ʃi|-, ˈ-ʃ|ə ⓤⓢ ˈ-ʃ|ə **-an/s** -ən/z
dacoit dəˈkɔɪt **-s** -s
Dacre ˈdeɪ.kəʳ ⓤⓢ -kɚ **-s** -z
Dacron® ˈdæk.rɒn, ˈdeɪ.krɒn ⓤⓢ ˈdeɪ.krɑːn, ˈdæk.rɑːn
dactyl ˈdæk.tɪl, -tᵊl **-s** -z
dactylic dækˈtɪl.ɪk
dactylogram dækˈtɪl.əʊ.græm; ˈdæk.tɪ.ləʊ-, -tᵊl.əʊ- ⓤⓢ dækˈtɪl.ə- **-s** -z
dactylography ˌdæk.tɪˈlɒg.rə.fi ⓤⓢ -təˈlɑː.grə-
dad (D) dæd **-s** -z
Dada ˈdɑː.dɑː, -də **-ism** -ɪ.zᵊm **-ist/s** -ɪst/s
dadaistic (D) ˌdɑː.dɑːˈɪs.tɪk
Daddies® ˈdæd.iz
dadd|y ˈdæd|.i **-ies** -iz
daddy longlegs ˌdæd.iˈlɒŋ.legz ⓤⓢ -ˈlɑːŋ-, -ˈlɔːŋ-
dado ˈdeɪ.dəʊ ⓤⓢ -doʊ **-s** -z
Daedalus ˈdiː.dᵊl.əs ⓤⓢ ˈded.ᵊl-
daemon ˈdiː.mən, ˈdaɪ-, ˈdeɪ- **-s** -z
daemonic diːˈmɒn.ɪk, dɪ-, də- ⓤⓢ -ˈmɑː.nɪk
D'Aeth deɪθ, deθ, diːθ
Daewoo® ˈdeɪ.uː ⓤⓢ ˌdeɪˈwuː
DAF® dæf
daffodil ˈdæf.ə.dɪl **-s** -z
daff|y ˈdæf|.i **-ier** -i.əʳ ⓤⓢ -i.ɚ **-iest** -i.ɪst, -i.əst **-iness** -ɪ.nəs, -ɪ.nɪs
Daffyd ap Gwilym ˌdæv.ɪð.ɑːpˈgwɪl.ɪm, -ɪd- ⓤⓢ ˌdɑː.vɪð-
daft dɑːft ⓤⓢ dæft **-er** -əʳ ⓤⓢ -ɚ **-est** -ɪst, -əst **-ly** -li **-ness** -nəs, -nɪs
Dafydd ˈdæv.ɪð, ˈdæf-
dag dæg **-s** -z **-ging** -ɪŋ **-ged** -d
da Gama dəˈgɑː.mə ⓤⓢ -ˈgɑː-, -ˈgæm.ə
Dagenham ˈdæg.ᵊn.əm
Dagestan ˌdɑː.gɪˈstɑːn, -gəˈ-
dagga ˈdæx.ə, ˈdʌx-, ˈdɑː.xə ⓤⓢ ˈdæg.ə, ˈdɑː.gə
dagger ˈdæg.əʳ ⓤⓢ -ɚ **-s** -z **at** ˌ**daggers** ˈ**drawn**; **look** ˈ**daggers at someone**
Daggett ˈdæg.ɪt
dagg|y ˈdæg|.i **-ier** -i.əʳ ⓤⓢ -i.ɚ **-iest** -i.ɪst, -i.əst
Dagmar ˈdæg.mɑːʳ ⓤⓢ -mɑːr
dago ˈdeɪ.gəʊ ⓤⓢ -goʊ **-(e)s** -z
Dagobert ˈdæg.əʊ.bɜːt ⓤⓢ -ə.bɝːt
Dagon ˈdeɪ.gɒn, -gən ⓤⓢ -gɑːn
Dagonet ˈdæg.ə.nət, -nɪt
daguerreotype dəˈger.əʊ.taɪp ⓤⓢ ˈ-ə- **-s** -s
Dagwood ˈdæg.wʊd
dahl (D) dɑːl
dahlia (D) ˈdeɪ.li.ə, ˈ-ljə ⓤⓢ ˈdæl.jə, ˈdɑːl-, ˈdeɪl- **-s** -z
Dahomey dəˈhəʊ.mi ⓤⓢ -ˈhoʊ-
Dahrendorf ˈdɑː.rᵊn.dɔːf, ˈdær.ᵊn- ⓤⓢ -dɔːrf
Dai daɪ
Daiches ˈdeɪ.*t*ʃɪz, -*t*ʃəz, -*t*ʃɪs, -*t*ʃəs
Daihatsu® ˌdaɪˈhæt.suː ⓤⓢ -ˈhɑːt-
daikon ˈdaɪ.kɒn, -kən ⓤⓢ -kən, -kɑːn **-s** -z
Dail, Dáil dɔɪl
Dáil Eireann ˌdɔɪlˈeə.rən ⓤⓢ -ˈer.ən, -ˈeɪ.rən
daily ˈdeɪ.l|i **-ies** -iz
Daimler® ˈdeɪm.ləʳ ⓤⓢ -lɚ, ˈdaɪm- **-s** -z
Daintree ˈdeɪn.triː, -tri
daint|y ˈdeɪn.t|i ⓤⓢ -t̬|i **-ies** -iz **-ier** -i.əʳ ⓤⓢ -i.ɚ **-iest** -i.ɪst, -i.əst **-ily** -ɪ.li, -ᵊl.i **-iness** -ɪ.nəs, -ɪ.nɪs
daiquiri (D) ˈdaɪ.kɪ.ri, ˈdæk.ɪ-, -ᵊr.i; daɪˈkɪə.ri, də- ⓤⓢ ˈdæk.ɚ.i, ˈdaɪ.kɚ-
dair|y ˈdeə.r|i ⓤⓢ ˈder|.i **-ies** -iz **-ying** -i.ɪŋ ˈ**dairy** ˌ**farm**; ˈ**dairy** ˌ**products**
Dairylea® ˌdeə.riˈliː, ˈ--- ⓤⓢ ˌder.iˈliː, ˈ---
dairymaid ˈdeə.ri.meɪd ⓤⓢ ˈder.i- **-s** -z
dairy|man ˈdeə.ri|.mən, -mæn ⓤⓢ ˈder.i- **-men** -mən, -men
dais ˈdeɪ.ɪs, deɪs ⓤⓢ ˈdeɪ.ɪs, ˈdaɪ- **-es** -ɪz
dais|y (D) ˈdeɪ.z|i **-ies** -iz ˈ**daisy** ˌ**chain**; ˈ**daisy** ˌ**wheel**
daisywheel ˈdeɪ.zi.*h*wiːl **-s** -z

Dakar 'dæk.ɑːʳ, -əʳ (US) də'kɑːr; 'dæk.ɑːr

Dakota də'kəʊ.tə (US) -'koʊ.t̬ə **-s** -z

dal *food:* dɑːl

dal *in Italian phrases:* dæl, dɑːl (US) dɑːl

Dalai Lama ˌdæl.aɪ'lɑː.mə, ˌdɑː.laɪ'- (US) ˌdɑː.laɪ'- **-s** -z

dalasi də'lɑː.si **-s** -z

Dalbeattie dæl'biː.ti, dəl- (US) -t̬i

Dalby 'dɔːl.bi, 'dɒl-, 'dæl- (US) 'dɑːl-, 'dɔːl-, 'dæl-

Daldy 'dæl.di (US) 'dɑːl.di

dale (D) deɪl **-s** -z

Dalek 'dɑː.lek, -lɪk **-s** -s

dales|man 'deɪlz|.mən, -mæn **-men** -mən, -men **-woman** -ˌwʊm.ən **-women** -ˌwɪm.ɪn

Daley 'deɪ.li

Dalgety dæl'get.i, dəl- (US) -'get̬- *stress shift, see compound:* ˌ**Dalgety** '**Bay**

Dalgleish, Dalglish dæl'gliːʃ, dəl-

Dalhousie dæl'haʊ.zi, -'huː-

Dali 'dɑː.li

Dalkeith dæl'kiːθ

Dalkey 'dɔː.ki, 'dɔːl-

Dallas 'dæl.əs

dallianc|e 'dæl.i.ənts **-es** -ɪz

Dalloway 'dæl.ə.weɪ

dall|y 'dæl|.i **-ies** -iz **-ying** -i.ɪŋ **-ied** -id **-ier/s** -i.əʳ/z (US) -i.ɚ/z

Dalmatia dæl'meɪ.ʃə, -ʃi.ə

dalmatian (D) dæl'meɪ.ʃᵊn, -ʃi.ən **-s** -z

Dalmeny dæl'men.i, dəl-

Dalny 'dæl.ni

Dalry dæl'raɪ, dəl-

Dalrymple dæl'rɪm.pl̩, dəl-; 'dæl.rɪm- (US) 'dæl.rɪm-

Note: The family name of the Earl of Stair is /dæl'rɪm-, dəl-/.

dal segno dæl'sen.jəʊ, dɑːl- (US) dɑːl'seɪ.njoʊ, -'sen.joʊ

Dalston 'dɔːl.stᵊn, 'dɒl- (US) 'dɔːl-, 'dɑːl-

Dalton 'dɔːl.tᵊn, 'dɒl- (US) 'dɔːl-, 'dɑːl-

Dalton-in-Furness ˌdɔːl.tᵊn.ɪn'fɜː.nɪs, ˌdɒl- (US) ˌdɔːl.tᵊn.ɪn'fɝː-, ˌdɑːl-

Daltonism 'dɔːl.tᵊn.ɪ.zᵊm, 'dɒl- (US) 'dɔːl-, 'dɑːl-

Daltr(e)y 'dɔːl.tri, 'dɒl- (US) 'dɔːl-, 'dɑːl-

Dalwhinnie dæl'*h*wɪn.i, dəl-

Daly 'deɪ.li

Dalyell diː'el

Dalzell diː'el; 'dæl.zel

Dalziel diː'el; 'dæl.ziːl, -zi.əl

Note: The form /diː'el/ is chiefly used in Scotland.

dam dæm (US) **-s** -z (US) **-ming** -ɪŋ (US) **-med** -d (US)

damag|e 'dæm.ɪdʒ **-es** -ɪz **-ing/ly** -ɪŋ/li **-ed** -d

damaging 'dæm.ɪ.dʒɪŋ **-ly** -li

Damaraland də'mɑː.rə.lænd; 'dæm.ə.rə- (US) də'mɑːr.ə-

Damart® 'dæm.ɑːt, 'deɪ.mɑːt (US) 'dæm.ɑːrt, 'deɪ.mɑːrt

damascene 'dæm.ə.siːn **-s** -z

Damascus də'mæs.kəs, -'mɑː.skəs (US) -'mæs.kəs

damask 'dæm.əsk **-s** -s

dame (D) deɪm **-s** -z

Damian, Damien 'deɪ.mi.ən

Damman 'dæm.æn (US) dæm'æn

dammit 'dæm.ɪt

damn dæm **-s** -z **-ing** -ɪŋ **-ed** -d

damnab|le 'dæm.nə.b|l̩ **-ly** -li **-leness** -l̩.nəs, -l̩.nɪs

damnation dæm'neɪ.ʃᵊn **-s** -z

damnatory 'dæm.nə.tᵊr.i, -tri (US) -tɔːr.i

damnedest 'dæm.dɪst, -dəst

damni|fy 'dæm.nɪ|.faɪ **-fies** -faɪz **-fying** -faɪ.ɪŋ **-fied** -faɪd

damnum sine injuria ˌdæm.nəmˌsiː.neɪ.ɪn'dʒʊə.ri.ə (US) -'dʒʊr.i.ə

Damoclean ˌdæm.ə'kliː.ən

Damocles 'dæm.ə.kliːz

Damon 'deɪ.mən

damosel, damozel ˌdæm.əʊ'zel (US) -ə'-, -oʊ'- **-s** -z

damp dæmp **-er** -əʳ (US) -ɚ **-est** -ɪst, -əst **-ly** -li **-ness** -nəs, -nɪs **-ish** -ɪʃ **-s** -s **-ing** -ɪŋ **-ed** -t '**damp** ˌ**course**; ˌ**damp** '**squib**

dampen 'dæm.pən **-s** -z **-ing** -ɪŋ, 'dæmp.nɪŋ **-ed** -d

damper 'dæm.pəʳ (US) -pɚ **-s** -z

Dampier 'dæm.pi.əʳ, -pɪəʳ (US) -pi.ɚ

damp-proof 'dæmp.pruːf **-s** -s **-ing** -ɪŋ **-ed** -d

damsel 'dæm.zᵊl **-s** -z

damson 'dæm.zᵊn **-s** -z

dan (D) dæn **-s** -z

Dana *first name in UK:* 'dɑː.nə *in US:* 'deɪ.nə *in Canada:* 'dæn.ə

Danaan 'dæn.i.ən **-s** -z

Danaë 'dæn.eɪ.iː, '-i-

Danaides, Danäides də'neɪ.ɪ.diːz, dæn'eɪ-, '-ə-

Dan-Air® ˌdæn'eəʳ (US) -'er

Danakil ˌdæn.ə'kiːl, -'kɪl (US) 'dæn.ə.kɪl; də'nɑː.kiːl

Da Nang ˌdɑː'næŋ (US) də'næŋ, dɑː'nɑːŋ

Danbury 'dæn.bᵊr.i, 'dæm- (US) 'dæn.ber-, -bɚ-

Danby 'dæn.bi, 'dæm- (US) 'dæn-

danc|e dɑːn*t*s (US) dæn*t*s **-es** -ɪz **-ing** -ɪŋ **-ed** -t **-er/s** -əʳ/z (US) -ɚ/z

Dance dɑːn*t*s, dæn*t*s (US) dæn*t*s

Dancer 'dɑːn*t*.səʳ (US) 'dæn*t*.sɚ

dandelion 'dæn.dɪ.laɪən (US) -də-, -dɪ- **-s** -z

dandi|fy 'dæn.dɪ|.faɪ (US) -də- **-fies** -faɪz **-fying** -faɪ.ɪŋ **-fied** -faɪd

dandl|e 'dæn.dl̩ **-es** -z **-ing** -ɪŋ, 'dænd.lɪŋ **-ed** -d

Dando 'dæn.dəʊ (US) -doʊ

dandruff 'dæn.drʌf (US) -drəf

dand|y 'dæn.d|i **-ies** -iz **-yish** -i.ɪʃ **-yism** -i.ɪ.zᵊm

Dane deɪn **-s** -z

Danebury 'deɪn.bᵊr.i, 'deɪm- (US) 'deɪn.ber-, -bɚ-

danegeld 'deɪn.geld, 'deɪŋ- (US) 'deɪn-

Danelaw 'deɪn.lɔː (US) -lɑː, -lɔː

danger 'deɪn.dʒəʳ (US) -dʒɚ **-s** -z

Dangerfield 'deɪn.dʒə.fiːld (US) -dʒɚ-

dangerous 'deɪn.dʒᵊr.əs **-ly** -li **-ness** -nəs, -nɪs

dangerously 'deɪn.dʒᵊr.ə.sli

dangl|e (D) 'dæŋ.gl̩ **-es** -z **-ing** -ɪŋ, 'dæŋ.glɪŋ **-ed** -d **-er/s** -əʳ/z, '-gləʳ/z (US) '-gl̩.ɚ/z, '-glɚ/z

dangly 'dæŋ.gl̩.i, '-gli

Daniel 'dæn.jəl **-s** -z

Danielle ˌdæn.i'el, dæn'jel

Danish 'deɪ.nɪʃ ˌ**Danish** '**blue**; ˌ**Danish** '**pastry**

dank dæŋk **-er** -əʳ (US) -ɚ **-est** -ɪst, -əst **-ly** -li **-ness** -nəs, -nɪs

Danks dæŋks

Dankworth 'dæŋk.wəθ, -wɜːθ (US) -wɚθ, -wɝːθ

Dann dæn

d'Annunzio dæn'ʊnt.si.əʊ (US) dɑː'nʊnt.si.oʊ

Danny 'dæn.i

Danone dæn'əʊn, dæn'ɒn (US) -oʊn, -ɑːn

danse(s) macabre(s) ˌdɑ̃ːns.mə'kɑː.brə, -mæk'ɑː- (US) ˌdɑːn*t*s.mə'kɑː.brə

danseuse(s) ˌdɑ̃ː*n*'sɜːz (US) ˌdɑːn*t*'suːz, -'sʊz

Dansville 'dænz.vɪl

Dante 'dæn.ti, 'dɑːn-, -teɪ (US) 'dɑːn.teɪ

Dantesque dæn'tesk (US) dɑːn-

Danton 'dæn.tɒn, -tən; *as if French:* dɑ̃ː*n*'tɔ̃ː*ŋ* (US) dɑːn'tɑːn, -toʊn; '--, -tən

Danube 'dæn.juːb

Danubian dæn'juː.bi.ən, də'njuː-

Danuta də'nuː.tə, dæn'uː- (US) də'nuː.t̬ə

Danvers 'dæn.vəz (US) -vɚz

Danville 'dæn.vɪl

Danzig 'dæn*t*.sɪg, -sɪk

daphne (D) 'dæf.ni

Daphnis 'dæf.nɪs

dapp|er (D) 'dæp|.əʳ (US) -ɚ **-erest** -ᵊr.ɪst, -ᵊr.əst

dappl|e 'dæp.l̩ **-es** -z **-ing** -ɪŋ, '-lɪŋ **-ed** -d

dapple-grey ˌdæp.l̩'greɪ

DAR ˌdiː.eɪ'ɑːʳ (US) -'ɑːr

Darbishire 'dɑː.bi.ʃəʳ, -ˌʃɪəʳ (US) 'dɑːr.bi.ʃɚ, -ˌʃɪr

Darby 'dɑː.bi (US) 'dɑːr- ˌ**Darby and** '**Joan**

d'Arc dɑːk (US) dɑːrk

Dark l

A type of LATERAL sound, recognizably different from CLEAR L.

Examples for English

If, when pronouncing the sound /l/, the back of the tongue is raised as for an [u] vowel, the quality is [u]-like and 'dark'; this effect is even more noticeable if the lips are rounded at the same time. This sound is typically found when /l/ occurs before a consonant or before a pause, e.g.:

help /help/ [heɫp]
hill /hɪl/ [hɪɫ]

In several accents of English, particularly those close to London, the dark l has given way to a [w] sound, so that *help* and *hill* might be transcribed /hewp/ and /hɪw/; this process is known as 'l vocalisation'.

In other languages

The process of l vocalisation took place in Polish some time ago, and the sound represented in Polish writing with the letter ł is almost always pronounced as [w], though foreigners usually try to pronounce it as [l].

D'Arcy, Darcy ˈdɑː.si ⓤⓢ ˈdɑːr-
Dardanelles ˌdɑː.dᵊnˈelz ⓤⓢ ˌdɑːr-
Dardanus ˈdɑː.dᵊn.əs ⓤⓢ ˈdɑːr-
dar|e (D) deəʳ ⓤⓢ der **-es** -z **-ing** -ɪŋ **-ed** -d **durst** dɜːst ⓤⓢ dɝːst
daredevil ˈdeəˌdev.ᵊl ⓤⓢ ˈder- **-s** -z
daren't deənt ⓤⓢ dernt
Darent ˈdær.ᵊnt ⓤⓢ ˈder-, ˈdær-
Darenth ˈdær.ənθ ⓤⓢ ˈder-, ˈdær-
Dares ˈdeə.riːz ⓤⓢ ˈder.iːz
daresay, dare say ˌdeəˈseɪ ⓤⓢ ˌder-
Daresbury ˈdɑːz.bᵊr.i ⓤⓢ ˈdɑːrz.ber-, -bɚ-
Dar es Salaam ˌdɑː.res.səˈlɑːm, -rɪs-, -rez-, -rɪz- ⓤⓢ ˌdɑːr.es-
Darfield ˈdɑː.fiːld ⓤⓢ ˈdɑːr-
Darien ˈdeə.ri.ən, ˈdær.i.ən ⓤⓢ ˈder.i-, ˈdær-; ˌder.iˈen, ˌdær-
Darin ˈdær.ɪn ⓤⓢ ˈder-, ˈdær-
daring ˈdeə.rɪŋ ⓤⓢ ˈder.ɪŋ **-ly** -li
Dario ˈdær.i.əʊ ⓤⓢ dɑːˈriː.oʊ
dariole ˈdær.i.əʊl ⓤⓢ ˈder.i.oʊl, ˈdær- **-s** -z
Darius dəˈraɪ.əs, ˈdeə.ri-, ˈdær.i-, ˈdɑː.ri- ⓤⓢ dəˈraɪ-; ˈder.i-, ˈdær-
Darjeeling dɑːˈdʒiː.lɪŋ ⓤⓢ dɑːr-
dark dɑːk ⓤⓢ dɑːrk **-er** -əʳ ⓤⓢ -ɚ **-est** -ɪst, -əst **-ly** -li **-ness** -nəs, -nɪs ˈ**Dark** ˌ**Ages**; ˌ**dark** ˈ**glasses**; ˌ**dark** ˈ**horse**
darken ˈdɑː.kᵊn ⓤⓢ ˈdɑːr- **-s** -z **-ing** -ɪŋ, ˈdɑːk.nɪŋ ⓤⓢ ˈdɑːr.kᵊn.ɪŋ, ˈdɑːrk.nɪŋ **-ed** -d
dark|ie ˈdɑːk|.i ⓤⓢ ˈdɑːr- **-ies** -iz
darkish ˈdɑː.kɪʃ ⓤⓢ ˈdɑːr-
darkling ˈdɑː.klɪŋ ⓤⓢ ˈdɑːr-
darkroom ˈdɑːk.rʊm, -ruːm ⓤⓢ ˈdɑːrk.ruːm, -rʊm **-s** -z
darksome ˈdɑːk.səm ⓤⓢ ˈdɑːrk-
dark|y ˈdɑː.k|i ⓤⓢ ˈdɑːr- **-ies** -iz
Darlaston ˈdɑː.lə.stən ⓤⓢ ˈdɑːr-
Darleen, Darlene ˈdɑː.liːn ⓤⓢ dɑːrˈliːn
Darley ˈdɑː.li ⓤⓢ ˈdɑːr-
darling (D) ˈdɑː.lɪŋ ⓤⓢ ˈdɑːr- **-s** -z
Darlington ˈdɑː.lɪŋ.tən ⓤⓢ ˈdɑːr-
Darlow ˈdɑː.ləʊ ⓤⓢ ˈdɑːr.loʊ
Darmstadt ˈdɑːm.stæt *as if German:* -ʃtæt ⓤⓢ ˈdɑːrm-
darn dɑːn ⓤⓢ dɑːrn **-s** -z **-ing** -ɪŋ **-ed** -d **-er/s** -əʳ/z ⓤⓢ -ɚ/z ˈ**darning** ˌ**needle**
darnation dɑːˈneɪ.ʃᵊn ⓤⓢ dɑːr-
darnel ˈdɑː.nᵊl ⓤⓢ ˈdɑːr-
Darnell dɑːˈnel ⓤⓢ dɑːr-, ˈ--
Darney ˈdɑː.ni ⓤⓢ ˈdɑːr-
Darnley ˈdɑːn.li ⓤⓢ ˈdɑːrn-
Darracq ˈdær.ək, dærˈæk ⓤⓢ ˈder-, ˈdær-
Darragh ˈdær.ə, -əx ⓤⓢ ˈder.ə, ˈdær-
Darrell ˈdær.ᵊl ⓤⓢ ˈder-, ˈdær-
Darren, Darron ˈdær.ᵊn ⓤⓢ ˈder-, ˈdær-
Darrow ˈdær.əʊ ⓤⓢ ˈder.oʊ, ˈdær-
Darryl ˈdær.ᵊl, -ɪl ⓤⓢ ˈder-, ˈdær-
dart (D) dɑːt ⓤⓢ dɑːrt **-s** -s **-ing** -ɪŋ ⓤⓢ ˈdɑːr.t̬ɪŋ **-ed** -ɪd ⓤⓢ ˈdɑːr.t̬ɪd
D'Artagnan dɑːˈtæn.jən, -jɑ̃ːŋ ⓤⓢ dɑːrˈtæn.jən; ˌdɑːr.tᵊnˈjɑːn
dartboard ˈdɑːt.bɔːd ⓤⓢ ˈdɑːrt.bɔːrd **-s** -z
darter ˈdɑː.təʳ ⓤⓢ ˈdɑːr.t̬ɚ **-s** -z
Dartford ˈdɑːt.fəd ⓤⓢ ˈdɑːrt.fɚd
Darth Vader ˌdɑːθˈveɪ.dəʳ ⓤⓢ ˌdɑːrθˈveɪ.dɚ
Dartie ˈdɑː.ti ⓤⓢ ˈdɑːr.t̬i
Dartington ˈdɑː.tɪŋ.tən ⓤⓢ ˈdɑːr.t̬ɪŋ-
Dartle ˈdɑː.tl̩ ⓤⓢ ˈdɑːr.t̬l̩
Dartmoor ˈdɑːt.mɔːʳ, -mʊəʳ ⓤⓢ ˈdɑːrt.mʊr, -mɔːr
Dartmouth ˈdɑːt.məθ ⓤⓢ ˈdɑːrt-
Darton ˈdɑː.tᵊn ⓤⓢ ˈdɑːr-
darts dɑːts ⓤⓢ dɑːrts
Darwen ˈdɑː.wɪn ⓤⓢ ˈdɑːr-
Darwin ˈdɑː.wɪn ⓤⓢ ˈdɑːr- **-ism** -ɪ.zᵊm
Darwinian dɑːˈwɪn.i.ən ⓤⓢ dɑːr-
Daryl(l) ˈdær.ᵊl, -ɪl ⓤⓢ ˈder-, ˈdær-
Daschle ˈdæʃ.l̩
Dasent ˈdeɪ.sᵊnt
dash (D) dæʃ **-es** -ɪz **-ing** -ɪŋ **-ed** -t **-er/s** -əʳ/z ⓤⓢ -ɚ/z
dashboard ˈdæʃ.bɔːd ⓤⓢ -bɔːrd **-s** -z
dashing ˈdæʃ.ɪŋ **-ly** -li
Dashwood ˈdæʃ.wʊd
dastard ˈdæs.təd, ˈdɑː.stəd ⓤⓢ ˈdæs.tɚd **-s** -z **-ly** -li **-liness** -lɪ.nəs, -nɪs
DAT dæt; ˌdiː.eɪˈtiː
data ˈdeɪ.tə, ˈdɑː- ⓤⓢ ˈdeɪ.t̬ə, ˈdæt̬.ə, ˈdɑː.t̬ə
databank ˈdeɪ.tə.bæŋk, ˈdɑː- ⓤⓢ ˈdeɪ.t̬ə-, ˈdæt̬.ə-, ˈdɑː.t̬ə- **-s** -s
databas|e ˈdeɪ.tə.beɪs, ˈdɑː- ⓤⓢ ˈdeɪ.t̬ə-, ˈdæt̬.ə-, ˈdɑː.t̬ə- **-es** -ɪz
databus ˈdeɪ.tə.bʌs, ˈdɑː- ⓤⓢ ˈdeɪ.t̬ə-, ˈdæt̬.ə-, ˈdɑː.t̬ə- **-es** -ɪz
datafile ˈdeɪ.tə.faɪl, ˈdɑː- ⓤⓢ ˈdeɪ.t̬ə-, ˈdæt̬.ə-, ˈdɑː.t̬ə- **-s** -z
dataflow ˈdeɪ.tə.fləʊ, ˈdɑː- ⓤⓢ ˈdeɪ.t̬ə.floʊ, ˈdæt̬.ə-, ˈdɑː.t̬ə-
dataglove ˈdeɪ.tə.glʌv, ˈdɑː- ⓤⓢ ˈdeɪ.t̬ə-, ˈdæt̬.ə- ⓤⓢ ˈdɑː.t̬ə- **-s** -z
Datapost® ˈdeɪ.tə.pəʊst, ˈdɑː- ⓤⓢ -t̬ə.poʊst
Datchery ˈdætʃ.ᵊr.i
Datchet ˈdætʃ.ɪt
dat|e deɪt **-es** -s **-ing** -ɪŋ ⓤⓢ ˈdeɪ.t̬ɪŋ **-ed** -ɪd ⓤⓢ ˈdeɪ.t̬ɪd ˈ**dating** ˌ**agency**
dated ˈdeɪ.tɪd ⓤⓢ -t̬ɪd
Datel® ˈdeɪ.tel
Dateline® ˈdeɪt.laɪn **-s** -z
date-stamp ˈdeɪt.stæmp **-s** -s **-ing** -ɪŋ **-ed** -t
datival dəˈtaɪ.vᵊl, deɪ-
dative ˈdeɪ.tɪv ⓤⓢ -t̬ɪv **-s** -z
Datsun® ˈdæt.sᵊn ⓤⓢ ˈdɑːt-, ˈdæt-
dat|um ˈdeɪ.t|əm, ˈdɑː- ⓤⓢ ˈdeɪ.t̬|əm, ˈdæt̬|.əm, ˈdɑː.t̬|əm **-a** -ə
daub dɔːb ⓤⓢ dɑːb, dɔːb **-s** -z **-ing** -ɪŋ **-ed** -d **-er/s** -əʳ/z ⓤⓢ -ɚ/z
daube dəʊb ⓤⓢ doʊb **-s** -z
Daubeney ˈdɔː.bᵊn.i ⓤⓢ ˈdɑː-, ˈdɔː-
Daudet ˈdəʊ.deɪ ⓤⓢ doʊˈdeɪ
Daugavpils ˈdaʊ.gæf.pɪls ⓤⓢ ˈdoʊ.gʌv-, ˈdaʊ-, -gʌf-, -gɑːf-, -pɪlz, -piːlz
daughter ˈdɔː.təʳ ⓤⓢ ˈdɑː.t̬ɚ, ˈdɔː- **-s** -z
daughter-in-law ˈdɔː.təʳ.ɪn.lɔː ⓤⓢ ˈdɑː.t̬ɚ.ɪn.lɑː, ˈdɔː-, -lɔː

daughters-in-law ˈdɔː.təz.ɪn.lɔː US ˈdɑː.t̬ɚz.ɪn.lɑː, ˈdɔː-, -lɔː

daughterl|y ˈdɔː.tə.l|i US ˈdɑː.t̬ɚ-, ˈdɔː- **-iness** -ɪ.nəs, -ɪ.nɪs

Daun dɔːn US dɑːn, dɔːn

daunt (D) dɔːnt US dɑːnt, dɔːnt **-s** -s **-ing** -ɪŋ US ˈdɑːn.t̬ɪŋ, ˈdɔːn- **-ed** -ɪd US ˈdɑːn.t̬ɪd, ˈdɔːn-

dauntless ˈdɔːnt.ləs, -lɪs US ˈdɑːnt-, ˈdɔːnt **-ly** -li **-ness** -nəs, -nɪs

dauphin (D) ˈdɔː.fɪn, ˈdəʊ-, -fæ̃ŋ US ˈdɑː.fɪn, ˈdɔː-; doʊˈfæn **-s** -z

Dauphiné ˈdɔː.fɪ.neɪ, ˈdəʊ-, --ˈ- US ˌdoʊ.fiːˈneɪ

dauphine (D) ˈdɔː.fiːn, ˈdəʊ-, -fɪn US dɑːˈfiːn, dɔː-, doʊ- **-s** -z

Davao dævˈɑː.əʊ, dəˈvɑː- US dɑːˈvaʊ

Dave deɪv

Davenant, D'Avenant ˈdæv.ən.ənt, -ɪ.nənt

davenport (D) ˈdæv.ən.pɔːt, -əm- US -ən.pɔːrt **-s** -s

Daventry ˈdæv.ən.tri *old-fashioned local pronunciation:* ˈdeɪn.tri

Davey ˈdeɪ.vi

David ˈdeɪ.vɪd **-s** -z

Davidge ˈdæv.ɪdʒ

Davidson ˈdeɪ.vɪd.sən

Davie ˈdeɪ.vi

Davies ˈdeɪ.vɪs US -viːz

Davina dəˈviː.nə

da Vinci dəˈvɪn.tʃi

Davis ˈdeɪ.vɪs

Davison ˈdeɪ.vɪ.sən

davit ˈdæv.ɪt, ˈdeɪ.vɪt **-s** -s

Davos dævˈəʊs, dɑːˈvəʊs, -ˈvɒs; ˈdɑː.vɒs, -vəʊs US dɑːˈvoʊs

dav|y (D) ˈdeɪ.v|i **-ies** -iz **ˈdavy ˌlamp; ˌDavy ˌJones's ˈlocker**

daw (D) dɔː US dɑː, dɔː **-s** -z

dawdl|e ˈdɔː.dl̩ US ˈdɑː-, ˈdɔː- **-es** -z **-ing** -ɪŋ, ˈdɔːd.lɪŋ US ˈdɑːd-, ˈdɔːd- **-ed** -d **-er/s** -əʳ/z, ˈdɔːd.ləʳ/z US ˈdɑː.dl̩.ɚ/z, ˈdɔː- US ˈdɑːd.lɚ/z, ˈdɔːd-

Dawe dɔː US dɑː, dɔː **-s** -z

Dawkes dɔːks US dɑːks, dɔːks

Dawkins ˈdɔː.kɪnz US ˈdɑː-, ˈdɔː-

Dawley ˈdɔː.li US ˈdɑː-, ˈdɔː-

Dawlish ˈdɔː.lɪʃ US ˈdɑː-, ˈdɔː-

dawn (D) dɔːn US dɑːn, dɔːn **-s** -z **-ing** -ɪŋ **-ed** -d

Dawson ˈdɔː.sən US ˈdɑː-, ˈdɔː-

day (D) deɪ **-s** -z **ˈday ˌboy; ˈday ˌcamp; ˈday ˌgirl; ˈday ˌjob; ˈday ˌlily; ˈday ˌnursery; ˌday ˈout; ˈday ˌroom; ˈday ˌschool; at the ˌend of the ˈday; ˌcall it a ˈday**

daybreak ˈdeɪ.breɪk **-s** -s

daycare ˈdeɪ.keəʳ US -ker

day|dream ˈdeɪ|.driːm **-dreams** -driːmz **-dreaming** -ˌdriː.mɪŋ **-dreamed** -drempt, -driːmd **-dreamt** -drempt **-dreamer/s** -ˌdriː.məʳ/z US -ˌdriː.mɚ/z

Day-Glo®, dayglo ˈdeɪ.gləʊ US -gloʊ

Daylesford ˈdeɪlz.fəd, ˈdeɪls- US -fɚd

Day-Lewis ˌdeɪˈluː.ɪs

daylight ˈdeɪ.laɪt **-s** -s **ˌdaylight ˈrobbery; ˌdaylight ˈsaving; ˈdaylight ˌtime; ˌbeat the living ˈdaylights out of sb**

dayspring ˈdeɪ.sprɪŋ

daystar ˈdeɪ.stɑːʳ US -stɑːr **-s** -z

daytime ˈdeɪ.taɪm

day-to-day ˌdeɪ.təˈdeɪ US -t̬əˈ-

Dayton ˈdeɪ.tən

Daytona deɪˈtəʊ.nə US -ˈtoʊ- **Dayˌtona ˈBeach**

daywork ˈdeɪ.wɜːk US -wɝːk

Daz® dæz

daz|e deɪz **-es** -ɪz **-ing** -ɪŋ **-ed** -d **-edly** -əd.li, -ɪd.li

dazzl|e ˈdæz.l̩ **-es** -z **-ing/ly** -ɪŋ/li, ˈdæz.lɪŋ/li **-ed** -d **-er/s** -əʳ/z, ˈ-ləʳ/z US ˈ-l̩.ɚ/z, ˈ-lɚ/z

DBMS ˌdiː.biː.emˈes

DC ˌdiːˈsiː

D-Day ˈdiː.deɪ

DDT ˌdiː.diːˈtiː

de- diː-, dɪ-, də-

Note: Prefix. In verbs containing **de-** where the stem is free, usually a noun, it is normally pronounced /ˌdiː-/, e.g. **debag** /ˌdiːˈbæg/, **declutch** /ˌdiːˈklʌtʃ/. Attached to bound stems the pronunciation is normally /dɪ-/ or /də-/, e.g. **debilitate** /dɪˈbɪl.ɪ.teɪt/, **demand** /dɪˈmɑːnd US -mænd/. There are exceptions; see individual entries.

de *in French names:* də, dɪ, di

deacon (D) ˈdiː.kən **-s** -z

deaconess ˌdiː.kəˈnes; ˈ---, -nɪs US ˈdiː.kən.əs **-es** -ɪz

deacon|hood ˈdiː.kən|.hʊd **-ship/s** -ʃɪp/s

deaconr|y ˈdiː.kən.r|i **-ies** -iz

deacti|vate ˌdiˈæk.tɪ|.veɪt, -tə- **-vates** -veɪts **-vating** -veɪ.tɪŋ US -veɪ.t̬ɪŋ **-vated** -veɪ.tɪd US -veɪ.t̬ɪd

deactivation diˌæk.tɪˈveɪ.ʃən, ˌdiː.æk-, -təˈ- US diˌæk-

dead ded **-ness** -nəs, -nɪs **ˌdead ˈend; ˌdead ˈheat; ˌdead ˈletter; ˌdead or ˈalive; ˌdead ˈreckoning; ˌdead ˈringer; ˌDead ˈSea; ˌdead ˈset; as ˌdead as a ˈdoor-nail**

dead-and-alive ˌded.ənd.əˈlaɪv

deadbeat (*n.*) ˈded.biːt, ˈdeb- US ˈded- **-s** -s

dead beat (*adj.*) ˌdedˈbiːt, ˌdeb- US ˌded- *stress shift:* ˌdead beat ˈworker

deadbolt ˈded.bəʊlt, ˈdeb- US ˈded.boʊlt **-s** -s

deaden ˈded.ən **-s** -z **-ing** -ɪŋ **-ed** -d

dead-end ˌdedˈend *stress shift:* ˌdead-end ˈstreet

deadeye (D) ˈded.aɪ **-s** -z

deadhead ˈded.hed, -ˈ- **-s** -z

deadline ˈded.laɪn **-s** -z

deadlock ˈded.lɒk US -lɑːk **-s** -s **-ed** -t

deadl|y ˈded.l|i **-ier** -i.əʳ US -i.ɚ **-iest** -i.ɪst, -i.əst **-iness** -ɪ.nəs, -ɪ.nɪs **ˌdeadly ˈnightshade**

deadnettle ˈded.net.l̩, ˌ-ˈ-- US ˌdedˈnet̬-, ˈ-ˌ-- **-s** -z

deadpan ˈded.pæn, ˈdeb-, ˌ-ˈ- US ˈded.pæn

deadweight ˌdedˈweɪt, ˈ-- **-s** -s

deadwood ˈded.wʊd, ˌ-ˈ-

deaf def **-er** -əʳ US -ɚ **-est** -ɪst, -əst **-ly** -li **-ness** -nəs, -nɪs **ˌfall on ˌdeaf ˈears**

deaf-aid ˈdef.eɪd **-s** -z

deaf-and-dumb ˌdef.əndˈdʌm

deafen ˈdef.ən **-s** -z **-ing/ly** -ɪŋ/li, ˈ-nɪŋ/li **-ed** -d

deaf-mute ˌdefˈmjuːt, ˈ-- **-s** -s

Deakin ˈdiː.kɪn

deal (D) diːl **-s** -z **-ing** -ɪŋ **dealt** delt

dealer ˈdiː.ləʳ US -lɚ **-s** -z

dealership ˈdiː.lə.ʃɪp US -lɚ- **-s** -s

dealing ˈdiː.lɪŋ **-s** -z

dealt *(from* **deal***)* delt

Dealtry *surname:* ˈdɔːl.tri, ˈdɪəl- US ˈdɑːl-, ˈdɔːl-, ˈdiːl- *road in London:* ˈdel.tri

deami|nate diˈæm.ɪ.neɪt, ˌdiː-, ˈ-ə- US ˈ-ə- **-nates** -neɪts **-nating** -neɪ.tɪŋ US -neɪ.t̬ɪŋ **-nated** -neɪ.tɪd US -neɪ.t̬ɪd

deamination diˌæm.ɪˈneɪ.ʃən, ˌdiː-, -əˈ- US -əˈ-

dean diːn **-s** -z **-ship/s** -ʃɪp/s

Dean(e) diːn

deaner|y ˈdiː.nər|.i **-ies** -iz

Deanna diˈæn.ə; ˈdiː.nə US diˈæn.ə

Deans diːnz

dear (D) dɪəʳ US dɪr **-s** -z **-er** -əʳ US -ɚ **-est** -ɪst, -əst **-ly** -li **-ness** -nəs, -nɪs

dear|ie ˈdɪə.r|i US ˈdɪr|.i **-ies** -iz

Dearing ˈdɪə.rɪŋ US ˈdɪr.ɪŋ

Dearne dɜːn US dɝːn

dearth (D) dɜːθ US dɝːθ **-s** -s

dear|y ˈdɪə.r|i US ˈdɪr|.i **-ies** -iz

death deθ **-s** -s **ˈdeath ˌduty; ˈdeath ˌmask; ˈdeath ˌpenalty; ˈdeath ˌrate; ˈdeath ˌrattle; ˌdeath ˈrow; ˈdeath ˌtoll; ˈdeath ˌtrap; ˈdeath ˌwarrant; ˌDeath ˈValley; ˈdeath ˌwish; like ˌdeath warmed ˈup; like ˌgrim ˈdeath**

Death *surname:* deɪθ, deθ, diːθ; diːˈæθ, deɪ-, -ˈɑːθ

deathbed ˈdeθ.bed **-s** -z

deathblow ˈdeθ.bləʊ US -bloʊ **-s** -z

deathless ˈdeθ.ləs, -lɪs

deathlike ˈdeθ.laɪk

deathl|y ˈdeθ.l|i **-ier** -i.əʳ US -i.ɚ **-iest** -i.ɪst, -i.əst **-iness** -ɪ.nəs, -ɪ.nɪs
death's-head ˈdeθs.hed **-s** -z
deathwatch ˈdeθ.wɒtʃ US -wɑːtʃ, -wɔːtʃ ˌ**deathwatch** ˈ**beetle**
Deauville ˈdəʊ.vɪl, -viːl US ˈdoʊ-
Deayton ˈdiː.tᵊn
deb deb **-s** -z
débâcle deɪˈbɑː.kl̩, də-, debˈɑː-, dɪˈbɑː-; ˈdeɪ.bɑː- US dɪˈbɑː-, də-, deɪ-, -ˈbæk.l̩ **-s** -z
debag ˌdiːˈbæg **-s** -z **-ging** -ɪŋ **-ged** -d
debar ˌdiːˈbɑːʳ, dɪ- US -ˈbɑːr **-s** -z **-ring** -ɪŋ **-red** -d
debark ˌdiːˈbɑːk, dɪ- US -ˈbɑːrk **-s** -s **-ing** -ɪŋ **-ed** -t
debarkation ˌdiː.bɑːˈkeɪ.ʃᵊn US -bɑːrˈ- **-s** -z
debas|e dɪˈbeɪs **-es** -ɪz **-ing/ly** -ɪŋ/li **-ed** -t **-ement** -mənt
debatab|le dɪˈbeɪ.tə.b|l̩, də- US dɪˈbeɪ.t̬ə- **-ly** -li
de|bate dɪ|ˈbeɪt, də- US dɪ- **-bates** -ˈbeɪts **-bating** -ˈbeɪ.tɪŋ US -ˈbeɪ.t̬ɪŋ **-bated** -ˈbeɪ.tɪd US -ˈbeɪ.t̬ɪd **-bater/s** -ˈbeɪ.təʳ/z US -ˈbeɪ.t̬ɚ/z
debauch dɪˈbɔːtʃ US -ˈbɑːtʃ, -ˈbɔːtʃ **-es** -ɪz **-ing** -ɪŋ **-ed** -t **-er/s** -əʳ/z US -ɚ/z
debauchee ˌdeb.ɔːˈtʃiː, -ˈʃiː, ˌdɪb-; dɪˌbɔː-, də- US ˌdeb.ɑːˈʃiː, -ɔːˈ-; dɪˌbɑːˈtʃiː, -ˌbɔːˈ- **-s** -z
debaucher|y dɪˈbɔː.tʃᵊr|.i, dəˈ- US dɪˈbɑː-, -ˈbɔː- **-ies** -iz
Debbie ˈdeb.i
de Beauvoir dəˈbəʊ.vwɑːʳ US -ˌboʊˈvwɑːr
Deben ˈdiː.bᵊn
de bene esse ˌdeɪˌben.iˈes.i, dəˌbiː.niːˈes.iː
Debenham ˈdeb.ᵊn.əm US -hæm **-'s** -z
debenture dɪˈben.*tʃ*əʳ, də- US dɪˈben*t*.ʃɚ **-s** -z
debili|tate dɪˈbɪl.ɪ|.teɪt, də-, ˈ-ə- US dɪ- **-tates** -teɪts **-tating** -teɪ.tɪŋ US -teɪ.t̬ɪŋ **-tated** -teɪ.tɪd US -teɪ.t̬ɪd
debilitation dɪˌbɪl.ɪˈteɪ.ʃᵊn, də-, -əˈ- US dɪ-
debility dɪˈbɪl.ə.ti, də-, -ɪ.ti US dɪˈbɪl.ə.t̬i
deb|it ˈdeb|.ɪt **-its** -ɪts **-iting** -ɪ.tɪŋ US -ɪ.t̬ɪŋ **-ited** -ɪ.tɪd US -ɪ.t̬ɪd
Debnam ˈdeb.nəm
debonair ˌdeb.əˈneəʳ US -ˈner **-ly** -li **-ness** -nəs, -nɪs
de Bono dəˈbəʊ.nəʊ US -ˈboʊ.noʊ
Deborah ˈdeb.ᵊr.ə, ˈ-rə
debouch dɪˈbaʊtʃ, ˌdiː-, -buːʃ **-es** -ɪz **-ing** -ɪŋ **-ed** -t **-ment** -mənt
Debra ˈdeb.rə
Debrecen ˈdeb.rət.sᵊn US ˌdeb.rətˈsen, ˈ---
Debrett dəˈbret, dɪ- **-'s** -s
debridement, débridement dɪˈbriːd.mənt, ˌdiː-, deɪ-; *as if French:* -ˌbriːdˈmɑ̃ːŋ US dɪˈbriːd.mənt, deɪ-, -ˈbriːd.mɑ̃ːŋ
debrief ˌdiːˈbriːf **-s** -s **-ing** -ɪŋ **-ed** -t
debris ˈdeɪ.briː, ˈdeb.riː US dəˈbriː; ˈdeɪ.briː
debt det **-s** -s
debtor ˈdet.əʳ US ˈdet̬.ɚ **-s** -z
debug ˌdiːˈbʌg **-s** -z **-ging** -ɪŋ **-ged** -d
debunk ˌdiːˈbʌŋk **-s** -s **-ing** -ɪŋ **-ed** -t
De Burgh dəˈbɜːg US -ˈbɝːg
Debussy dəˈbuː.siː, -ˈbjuː-; US ˈdeɪ.bjuː.si; ˌdeɪ.bjuːˈsiː; dəˈbjuː.si
Note: US street names are always /də-/.
début ˈdeɪ.bjuː, -buː; ˈdeb.juː US deɪˈbjuː, ˈ-- **-s** -z **-ing** -ɪŋ **-ed** -d
débutant ˈdeb.jʊ.tɑ̃ːŋ, ˈdeɪ.bjʊ- US ˈdeb.juː.tɑːnt, ˌ--ˈ- **-s** -z
débutante ˈdeb.juː.tɑ̃ːŋt, ˈdeɪ.bjuː- US ˈdeb.juː.tɑːnt, ˌ--ˈ- **-s** -s
Dec. *(abbrev. for* **December***)* dɪˈsem.bəʳ, də- US dɪˈsem.bɚ
deca- dek.ə-
Note: Prefix. Normally carries primary or secondary stress on the first syllable, e.g. **decagon** /ˈdek.ə.gən US -gɑːn/, **decahedron** /ˌdek.əˈhiː.drən/.
decachord ˈdek.ə.kɔːd US -kɔːrd **-s** -z
decade *ten years:* ˈdek.eɪd; dekˈeɪd, dɪˈkeɪd **-s** -z *division of the rosary:* ˈdek.əd
decaden|ce ˈdek.ə.dᵊn*t*|s US ˈdek.ə-; dɪˈkeɪ- **-cy** -si
decadent ˈdek.ə.dᵊnt US ˈdek.ə-; dɪˈkeɪ- **-ly** -li
decaf, decaff ˈdiː.kæf
decaffei|nate dɪˈkæf.ɪ|.neɪt, ˌdiː-, ˈ-ə- **-nates** -neɪts **-nating** -neɪ.tɪŋ US -neɪ.t̬ɪŋ **-nated** -neɪ.tɪd US -neɪ.t̬ɪd
decagon ˈdek.ə.gən US -gɑːn **-s** -z
decagram, decagramme ˈdek.ə.græm **-s** -z
decahedr|on ˌdek.əˈhiː.dr|ən, -ˈhed.r|ən US -ˈhiː.dr|ən **-ons** -ənz **-a** -ə **-al** -ᵊl
decal ˈdiː.kæl; dɪˈkæl; **-s** -z
decalcification ˌdiːˌkæl.sɪ.fɪˈkeɪ.ʃᵊn, -sə-
decalci|fy ˌdiːˈkæl.sɪ|.faɪ, -sə- **-fies** -faɪz **-fying** -faɪ.ɪŋ **-fied** -faɪd
decalitre, decaliter ˈdek.əˌliː.təʳ US -t̬ɚ **-s** -z
Decalogue ˈdek.ə.lɒg US -lɑːg, -lɔːg **-s** -z
Decameron dɪˈkæm.ᵊr.ᵊn, dekˈæm-, dəˈkæm-
decametre, decameter ˈdek.əˌmiː.təʳ US -t̬ɚ **-s** -z
decamp ˌdiːˈkæmp, dɪ- **-s** -s **-ing** -ɪŋ **-ed** -t
decanal dɪˈkeɪ.nᵊl, dekˈeɪ-, dəˈkeɪ-; ˈdek.ᵊn.ᵊl
decani dɪˈkeɪ.naɪ, dekˈeɪ-
de|cant dɪ|ˈkænt, ˌdiː- **-cants** -ˈkænts **-canting** -ˈkæn.tɪŋ US -ˈkæn.t̬ɪŋ **-canted** -ˈkæn.tɪd US -ˈkæn.t̬ɪd
decantation ˌdiː.kænˈteɪ.ʃᵊn **-s** -z
decanter dɪˈkæn.təʳ, də- US dɪˈkæn.t̬ɚ **-s** -z
decapi|tate dɪˈkæp.ɪ|.teɪt, ˌdiː-, ˈ-ə- **-tates** -teɪts **-tating** -teɪ.tɪŋ US -teɪ.t̬ɪŋ **-tated** -teɪ.tɪd US -teɪ.t̬ɪd
decapitation dɪˌkæp.ɪˈteɪ.ʃᵊn, ˌdiː-, -əˈ- **-s** -z
decapod ˈdek.ə.pɒd US -pɑːd **-s** -z
Decapolis dekˈæp.ə.lɪs, dɪˈkæp-
decarbo|nate ˌdiːˈkɑː.bə|.neɪt US -ˈkɑːr- **-nates** -neɪts **-nating** -neɪ.tɪŋ US -neɪ.t̬ɪŋ **-nated** -neɪ.tɪd US -neɪ.t̬ɪd
decarbonization, -isa- diːˌkɑː.bᵊn.aɪˈzeɪ.ʃᵊn, ˌdɪ.kɑː-, -ɪˈ- US ˌdiː.kɑːr.bə.nɪˈ-
decarboniz|e, -is|e ˌdiːˈkɑː.bə.naɪz US -ˈkɑːr- **-es** -ɪz **-ing** -ɪŋ **-ed** -d
decarburiz|e, -is|e ˌdiːˈkɑː.bjʊ.raɪz, -bjᵊr.aɪz US -ˈkɑːr.bə.raɪz, -bjə-, -bjʊ- **-es** -ɪz **-ing** -ɪŋ **-ed** -d
decasyllabic ˌdek.ə.sɪˈlæb.ɪk, -səˈ-
decasyllable ˈdek.əˌsɪl.ə.bl̩, ˌdek.əˈsɪl.ə- **-s** -z
decathlete dɪˈkæθ.liːt, dekˈæθ-, dəˈkæθ- **-s** -s
decathlon dɪˈkæθ.lɒn, dekˈæθ-, dəˈkæθ-, -lən US dɪˈkæθ.lɑːn, -lən, də- **-s** -z
decay dɪˈkeɪ, də- **-s** -z **-ing** -ɪŋ **-ed** -d
Decca ˈdek.ə
Deccan ˈdek.ən, -æn
deceas|e dɪˈsiːs, də- US dɪ- **-es** -ɪz **-ing** -ɪŋ **-ed** -t
decedent dɪˈsiː.dᵊnt, də- US dɪ- **-s** -s
deceit dɪˈsiːt, də- US dɪ- **-s** -s
deceitful dɪˈsiːt.fᵊl, də-, -fʊl US dɪ- **-ly** -i **-ness** -nəs, -nɪs
deceivable dɪˈsiː.və.bl̩, də- US dɪ-
deceiv|e dɪˈsiːv, də- US dɪ- **-es** -z **-ing** -ɪŋ **-ed** -d **-er/s** -əʳ/z US -ɚ/z
deceler|ate dɪˈsel.ᵊr|.eɪt, ˌdiː- US -ə.r|eɪt **-ates** -eɪts **-ating** -eɪ.tɪŋ US -eɪ.t̬ɪŋ **-ated** -eɪ.tɪd US -eɪ.t̬ɪd
deceleration ˌdɪˌsel.əˈreɪ.ʃᵊn, ˌdiː.sel- **-s** -z
December dɪˈsem.bəʳ, də- US dɪˈsem.bɚ **-s** -z
decemvir dɪˈsem.vəʳ, də-, -vɜːʳ US diːˈsem.vɪr **-s** -z
decemvirate dɪˈsem.vɪ.rət, də-, -vᵊr.ət, -ɪt, -eɪt US diːˈsem.vɚ.ɪt, -və.reɪt **-s** -s

decenc|y ˈdiː.sᵊnt.s|i **-ies** -iz

decennial dɪˈsen.i.əl, desˈen-, dəˈsen-, diː- (US) dɪˈsen-, diː-

decent ˈdiː.sᵊnt **-ly** -li

decentralization, -isa- diːˌsen.trᵊl.aɪˈzeɪ.ʃᵊn, ˌdɪ.sen-, -ɪˈ- (US) -ɪˈ-

decentraliz|e, -is|e diːˈsen.trə.laɪz, ˌdɪ- **-es** -ɪz **-ing** -ɪŋ **-ed** -d

deception dɪˈsep.ʃᵊn, də- (US) dɪ- **-s** -z

deceptive dɪˈsep.tɪv, də- (US) dɪ- **-ly** -li **-ness** -nəs, -nɪs

de Chastelain dəˈtʃæs.tə.leɪn (US) -t̬ə.lən

deci- des.i-

Note: Prefix. Normally carries primary or secondary stress on the first syllable, e.g. **decimal** /ˈdes.ɪ.mᵊl/, **decimalization** /ˌdes.ɪ.mᵊl.aɪˈzeɪ.ʃᵊn (US) -ɪˈ-/. There are exceptions; see individual entries.

decibel ˈdes.ɪ.bel, -bəl, -bᵊl **-s** -z

decid|e dɪˈsaɪd, də- (US) dɪ- **-es** -z **-ing** -ɪŋ **-ed/ly** -ɪd/li **-er/s** -əʳ/z (US) -ɚ/z

deciduous dɪˈsɪd.ju.əs, də- (US) dɪˈsɪdʒ.u- **-ly** -li **-ness** -nəs, -nɪs

decigram, decigramme ˈdes.ɪ.ɡræm **-s** -z

decilitre, deciliter ˈdes.ɪˌliː.təʳ (US) -t̬ɚ **-s** -z

decillion dɪˈsɪl.i.ən, ˈ-jən (US) ˈ-jən **-s** -z

decimal ˈdes.ɪ.mᵊl, ˈ-ə- **-s** -z **-ly** -i **ˌdecimal ˈpoint** (US) **ˈdecimal ˌpoint**

decimalization, -isa- ˌdes.ɪ.mᵊl.aɪˈzeɪ.ʃᵊn, ˌ-ə-, -ɪˈ- (US) -ɪˈ-

decimaliz|e, -is|e ˈdes.ɪ.mᵊl.aɪz, -ə- (US) -mə.laɪz **-es** -ɪz **-ing** -ɪŋ **-ed** -d

deci|mate ˈdes.ɪ|.meɪt, ˈ-ə- **-mates** -meɪts **-mating** -meɪ.tɪŋ (US) -meɪ.t̬ɪŋ **-mated** -meɪ.tɪd (US) -meɪ.t̬ɪd **-mator/s** -meɪ.təʳ/z (US) -meɪ.t̬ɚ/z

decimation ˌdes.ɪˈmeɪ.ʃᵊn, -əˈ-

decimetre, decimeter ˈdes.ɪˌmiː.təʳ (US) -t̬ɚ **-s** -z

deciph|er dɪˈsaɪ.f|əʳ, ˌdiː- (US) -f|ɚ **-ers** -əz (US) -ɚz **-ering** -ᵊr.ɪŋ **-ered** -əd (US) -ɚd

decipherable dɪˈsaɪ.fᵊr.ə.bl̩, ˌdiː-

decision dɪˈsɪʒ.ᵊn, də- (US) dɪ- **-s** -z

decision-mak|er dɪˈsɪʒ.ᵊnˌmeɪ.k|əʳ, də-, -ᵊm- (US) dɪˈsɪʒ.ᵊnˌmeɪ.k|ɚ **-ers** -əz (US) -ɚz **-ing** -ɪŋ

decisive dɪˈsaɪ.sɪv, də-, -zɪv (US) dɪˈsaɪ.sɪv **-ly** -li **-ness** -nəs, -nɪs

Decius ˈdiː.ʃi.əs, ˈ-ʃəs, ˈ-si.əs; ˈdek.i.əs, ˈdes- (US) ˈdiː.ʃi.əs, ˈ-ʃəs, ˈ-si.əs; ˈdes.i.əs

deck dek **-s** -s **-ing** -ɪŋ **-ed** -t **-er/s** -əʳ/z (US) -ɚ/z **ˌclear the ˈdecks; ˌhit the ˈdeck**

deckchair ˈdek.tʃeəʳ (US) -tʃer **-s** -z

Decker ˈdek.əʳ (US) -ɚ

deckhand ˈdek.hænd **-s** -z

deckhou|se ˈdek.haʊ|s **-ses** -zɪz

deckle ˈdek.l̩ **-s** -z **ˌdeckle ˈedged**

declaim dɪˈkleɪm, də- (US) dɪ- **-s** -z **-ing** -ɪŋ **-ed** -d **-er/s** -əʳ/z (US) -ɚ/z **-ant/s** -ənt/s

declamation ˌdek.ləˈmeɪ.ʃᵊn **-s** -z

declamatory dɪˈklæm.ə.tᵊr.i, də-, -tri (US) dɪˈklæm.ə.tɔːr.i

Declan ˈdek.lən

declarable dɪˈkleə.rə.bl̩, də- (US) dɪˈkler.ə-, -ˈklær-

declaration ˌdek.ləˈreɪ.ʃᵊn **-s** -z

declarative dɪˈklær.ə.tɪv, də-, -kleə.rə- (US) dɪˈkler.ə.t̬ɪv, -ˈklær- **-ly** -li

declaratory dɪˈklær.ə.tᵊr.i, də-, -ˈkleə.rə-, -tri (US) dɪˈkler.ə.tɔːr.i, -ˈklær-

declar|e dɪˈkleəʳ, də- (US) dɪˈkler **-es** -z **-ing** -ɪŋ **-ed** -d **-er/s** -əʳ/z (US) -ɚ/z

declaredly dɪˈkleə.rɪd.li, də-, -rəd- (US) dɪˈkler-

declass ˌdiːˈklɑːs (US) -ˈklæs **-es** -ɪz **-ing** -ɪŋ **-ed** -t

declassification ˌdiːˌklæs.ɪ.fɪˈkeɪ.ʃᵊn, ˌ-ə-

declassi|fy ˌdiːˈklæs.ɪ|.faɪ, ˈ-ə- **-fies** -faɪz **-fying** -faɪ.ɪŋ **-fied** -faɪd

declension dɪˈklen.tʃᵊn, də- (US) dɪˈklent.ʃᵊn **-s** -z

declination ˌdek.lɪˈneɪ.ʃᵊn, -ləˈ- **-s** -z

declin|e dɪˈklaɪn, də- (US) dɪ- **-es** -z **-ing** -ɪŋ **-ed** -d **-able** -ə.bl̩

declivit|y dɪˈklɪv.ə.t|i, də-, -ɪ.t|i (US) dɪˈklɪv.ə.t̬|i **-ies** -iz

declutch ˌdiːˈklʌtʃ **-es** -ɪz **-ing** -ɪŋ **-ed** -t

decoct dɪˈkɒkt, ˌdiː- (US) -ˈkɑːkt **-s** -s **-ing** -ɪŋ **-ed** -ɪd

decod|e ˌdiːˈkəʊd (US) -ˈkoʊd **-es** -z **-ing** -ɪŋ **-ed** -ɪd

decoder ˌdiːˈkəʊ.dəʳ, dɪ- (US) -ˈkoʊ.dɚ **-s** -z

decok|e ˌdiːˈkəʊk (US) -ˈkoʊk **-es** -s **-ing** -ɪŋ **-ed** -t

décolletage ˌdeɪ.kɒlˈtɑːʒ; -kɒl.ɪˈ-, -əˈ- (US) -kɑː.ləˈ-, -kɑːlˈ-

décolleté(e) ˌdeɪ.kɒlˈteɪ; -kɒl.ɪˈ-, -əˈ- (US) -kɑː.ləˈ-, -kɑːlˈ-

decolonization ˌdiːˌkɒl.ə.naɪˈzeɪ.ʃᵊn, -nɪˈ- (US) -ˌkɑː.lə.nɪˈ-

decoloniz|e, -is|e ˌdiːˈkɒl.ə.naɪz (US) -ˈkɑː.lə- **-es** -ɪz **-ing** -ɪŋ **-ed** -d

decolo(u)rization, -isa- ˌdiː.kʌl.ə.raɪˈzeɪ.ʃᵊn, dɪˌkʌl-, -ᵊr.ɪˈ- (US) dɪˌkʌl.ɚ.ɪˈ-

decolo(u)riz|e, -is|e ˌdiːˈkʌl.ᵊr.aɪz (US) -ə.raɪz **-es** -ɪz **-ing** -ɪŋ **-ed** -d

decommission ˌdiː.kəˈmɪʃ.ᵊn **-s** -z **-ing** -ɪŋ **-ed** -d

decompos|e ˌdiː.kəmˈpəʊz (US) -ˈpoʊz **-es** -ɪz **-ing** -ɪŋ **-ed** -d **-able** -ə.bl̩

decomposition ˌdiː.kɒm.pəˈzɪʃ.ᵊn, dɪˌkɒm- (US) ˌdiː.kɑːm- **-s** -z

decompound ˌdiː.kəmˈpaʊnd **-s** -z **-ing** -ɪŋ **-ed** -ɪd

decompress ˌdiː.kəmˈpres **-es** -ɪz **-ing** -ɪŋ **-ed** -t **-er/s** -əʳ/z (US) -ɚ/z

decompression ˌdiː.kəmˈpreʃ.ᵊn

decongestant ˌdiː.kənˈdʒest.ᵊnt **-s** -s

deconsecrat|e ˌdiːˈkɒnt.sɪ.kreɪt, -sə- (US) -ˈkɑːnt- **-es** -s **-ing** -ɪŋ **-ed** -ɪd

deconsecration ˌdiː.kɒnt.sɪˈkreɪ.ʃᵊn, dɪˌkɒnt-, -səˈ- (US) ˌdiː.kɑːnt- **-s** -z

deconstruct ˌdiː.kənˈstrʌkt **-s** -s **-ing** -ɪŋ **-ed** -ɪd **-ive** -ɪv

deconstruction ˌdiː.kənˈstrʌk.ʃᵊn **-ism** -ɪ.zᵊm **-ist/s** -ɪst/s

decontami|nate ˌdiː.kənˈtæm.ɪ|.neɪt, ˈ-ə- **-nates** -neɪts **-nating** -neɪ.tɪŋ (US) -neɪ.t̬ɪŋ **-nated** -neɪ.tɪd (US) -neɪ.t̬ɪd

decontamination ˌdiː.kənˌtæm.ɪˈneɪ.ʃᵊn, -əˈ-

decontrol ˌdiː.kənˈtrəʊl (US) -ˈtroʊl **-s** -z **-ling** -ɪŋ **-led** -d

decor, décor ˈdeɪ.kɔːʳ, ˈdek.ɔːʳ, ˈdɪk- (US) deɪˈkɔːr, ˈ-- **-s** -z

decor|ate ˈdek.ᵊr|.eɪt (US) -ə.r|eɪt **-ates** -eɪts **-ating** -eɪ.tɪŋ (US) -eɪ.t̬ɪŋ **-ated** -eɪ.tɪd (US) -eɪ.t̬ɪd

decoration ˌdek.ᵊˈreɪ.ʃᵊn (US) -əˈreɪ- **-s** -z

decorative ˈdek.ᵊr.ə.tɪv (US) -t̬ɪv **-ly** -li **-ness** -nəs, -nɪs

decorator ˈdek.ᵊr.eɪ.təʳ (US) -ə.reɪ.t̬ɚ **-s** -z

decorous ˈdek.ᵊ.rəs; dɪˈkɔː- (US) ˈdek.ɚ.əs **-ly** -li **-ness** -nəs, -nɪs

decorum dɪˈkɔː.rəm, də- (US) dɪˈkɔːr-

De Courcy dəˈkʊə.si, -ˈkɔː-, -ˈkɜː- (US) -ˈkʊr-, -ˈkɔːr-, -ˈkɝː-

decoy (*n.*) ˈdiː.kɔɪ; dɪˈkɔɪ, də- (US) ˈdiː.kɔɪ; dɪˈkɔɪ **-s** -z

decoy (*v.*) dɪˈkɔɪ, də- (US) dɪ- **-s** -z **-ing** -ɪŋ **-ed** -d

decreas|e (*n.*) ˈdiː.kriːs; dɪˈ-, diː-, də- (US) ˈdiː.kriːs **-es** -ɪz

decreas|e (*v.*) dɪˈkriːs, diː-, də-; ˈdiː.kriːs (US) dɪˈkriːs; ˈdiː.kriːs **-es** -ɪz **-ing/ly** -ɪŋ/li **-ed** -t

decree dɪˈkriː, də- (US) dɪ- **-s** -z **-ing** -ɪŋ **-d** -d

decree nisi dɪˌkriːˈnaɪ.saɪ, -si

decrement ˈdek.rɪ.mənt, -rə- **-s** -s

decrepit dɪˈkrep.ɪt, də- (US) dɪ- **-est** -ɪst, -əst

decrepitation dɪˌkrep.ɪˈteɪ.ʃᵊn, də-, -əˈ- (US) dɪ- **-s** -z

decrepitude dɪˈkrep.ɪ.tjuːd, də-, ˈ-ə-, -tʃuːd (US) dɪˈkrep.ɪ.tuːd, ˈ-ə-, -tjuːd

decrescendo ˌdiː.krɪˈʃen.dəʊ, ˌdeɪ-, -krəˈ- (US) -doʊ **-s** -z

De Crespigny dəˈkrep.ɪ.ni, -ˈkres.pɪ-

decrial dɪ'kraɪ.əl **-s** -z
decriminalization, -isa- diː,krɪm.ɪ.nᵊl.aɪ'zeɪ.ʃᵊn, ,dɪ.krɪ.mɪ-, -mᵊn.ᵊl-, -ɪ'- (US) ,diː.krɪ.mɪ.nᵊl.ɪ'-
decriminaliz|e, -is|e ,diː'krɪm.ɪ.nᵊl.aɪz, dɪ-, -ᵊn.ᵊl- (US) -ɪ.nᵊl- **-es** -ɪz **-ing** -ɪŋ **-ed** -d
decr|y dɪ'kr|aɪ, də- (US) dɪ- **-ies** -aɪz **-ying** -aɪ.ɪŋ **-ied** -aɪd **-ier/s** -aɪ.əʳ/z (US) -aɪ.ɚ/z
decumben|ce dɪ'kʌm.bənt|s, ,diː- **-cy** -si
decumbent dɪ'kʌm.bənt, ,diː- **-ly** -li
decuple 'dek.jʊ.pl̩ (US) -jʊ-, -jə- **-es** -z **-ing** -ɪŋ, 'dek.jʊ.plɪŋ, -juː- **-ed** -d
Dedalus 'diː.dᵊl.əs (US) 'ded.ᵊl.əs, 'diː.dᵊl-
Deddington 'ded.ɪŋ.tᵊn
Dedham 'ded.əm
dedi|cate 'ded.ɪ|.keɪt **-cates** -keɪts **-cating** -keɪ.tɪŋ (US) -keɪ.t̬ɪŋ **-cated/ly** -keɪ.tɪd/li (US) -keɪ.t̬ɪd/li **-cator/s** -keɪ.təʳ/z (US) -keɪ.t̬ɚ/z
dedicatee ,ded.ɪ.kə'tiː **-s** -z
dedication ,ded.ɪ'keɪ.ʃᵊn **-s** -z
dedicatory 'ded.ɪ.kə.tᵊr.i, -keɪ-, -tri; ,ded.ɪ'keɪ- (US) 'ded.ɪ.kə.tɔːr-
de Dion də'diː.ən, -ɒn *as if French:* -ɔ̃ːŋ (US) də'diː.ɑːn *as if French:* -ɔ̃ːŋ **-s** -z
Dedlock 'ded.lɒk (US) -lɑːk
Dedman 'ded.mən, 'deb-, -mæn (US) 'ded-
deduc|e dɪ'djuːs, də- (US) dɪ'duːs, -'djuːs **-es** -ɪz **-ing** -ɪŋ **-ed** -t
deducibility dɪ,djuː.sə'bɪl.ə.ti, də-, -sɪ'-, -ɪ.ti (US) dɪ,duː.sə'bɪl.ə.t̬i, -,djuː-
deducible dɪ'djuː.sə.bl̩, də-, -sɪ- (US) dɪ'duː-, -'djuː-
deduct dɪ'dʌkt, də- (US) dɪ- **-s** -s **-ing** -ɪŋ **-ed** -ɪd **-ible** -ə.bl̩
deduction dɪ'dʌk.ʃᵊn, də- (US) dɪ- **-s** -z
deductive dɪ'dʌk.tɪv, də- (US) dɪ- **-ly** -li
Dee diː
deed diːd **-s** -z **'deed ,poll**
Deedes diːdz
deejay 'diː.dʒeɪ **-s** -z
Deek(e)s diːks
Deeley 'diː.li
deem diːm **-s** -z **-ing** -ɪŋ **-ed** -d
Deems diːmz
deemster 'diːm.stəʳ (US) -stɚ **-s** -z
deep diːp **-s** -s **-er** -əʳ (US) -ɚ **-est** -ɪst, -əst **-ly** -li **-ness** -nəs, -nɪs **,deep 'freeze** (US) **'deep ,freeze; ,Deep 'South; go off the 'deep ,end; ,throw (someone) in at the 'deep ,end**
deepen 'diː.pᵊn **-s** -z **-ing** -ɪŋ **-ed** -d
deep-fr|y ,diːp'fr|aɪ, '-- **-ies** -aɪz **-ying** -aɪ.ɪŋ **-ied** -aɪd *stress shift:* ,deep-fried 'chicken
deep-laid ,diːp'leɪd *stress shift:* ,deep-laid 'plans
deep-rooted ,diːp'ruː.tɪd (US) -t̬ɪd *stress shift:* ,deep-rooted 'fears
deep-sea ,diːp'siː *stress shift:* ,deep-sea 'diving
deep-seated ,diːp'siː.tɪd (US) -t̬ɪd *stress shift:* ,deep-seated 'sorrow
deep-six ,diːp'sɪks **-es** -ɪz **-ing** -ɪŋ **-ed** -t
deer dɪəʳ (US) dɪr **'deer ,forest; 'deer ,park; 'Deer ,Park**
Deerfield 'dɪə.fiːld (US) 'dɪr-
deerhound 'dɪə.haʊnd (US) 'dɪr- **-s** -z
deerskin 'dɪə.skɪn (US) 'dɪr-
Deerslayer 'dɪə,sleɪ.əʳ (US) 'dɪr,sleɪ.ɚ
deerstalk|ing 'dɪə,stɔː.k|ɪŋ (US) 'dɪr-, -,stɑː-, -,stɔː- **-er/s** -əʳ/z (US) -ɚ/z
Deery 'dɪə.ri (US) 'dɪr.i
de-escal|ate ,diː'es.kᵊl|.eɪt (US) -kə.l|eɪt **-ates** -eɪts **-ating** -eɪ.tɪŋ (US) -eɪ.t̬ɪŋ **-ated** -eɪ.tɪd (US) -eɪ.t̬ɪd
de-escalation ,diː.es.kə'leɪ.ʃᵊn, diː,es- (US) diː,es-
Deeside 'diː.saɪd
defac|e dɪ'feɪs **-es** -ɪz **-ing** -ɪŋ **-ed** -t **-er/s** -əʳ/z (US) -ɚ/z **-ement/s** -mənt/s
de facto ,deɪ'fæk.təʊ, ,diː- (US) -toʊ
defae|cate 'def.ə|.keɪt, 'diː.fə-, -fɪ- (US) 'def.ə-, '-ɪ- **-cates** -keɪts **-cating** -keɪ.tɪŋ (US) -keɪ.t̬ɪŋ **-cated** -keɪ.tɪd (US) -keɪ.t̬ɪd
defaecation ,def.ə'keɪ.ʃᵊn, ,diː.fə'-, -fɪ'- (US) ,def.ə'-, -ɪ'-
defal|cate 'diː.fæl|.keɪt, diː'fæl-; 'diː.fɔːl- (US) diː'fæl-, -'fɔːl- **-cates** -keɪts **-cating** -keɪ.tɪŋ (US) -keɪ.t̬ɪŋ **-cated** -keɪ.tɪd (US) -keɪ.t̬ɪd
defalcation ,diː.fæl'keɪ.ʃᵊn, -fɔːl'- **-s** -z
defamation ,def.ə'meɪ.ʃᵊn, ,diː.fə'- (US) ,def.ə'- **-s** -z
defamatory dɪ'fæm.ə.tᵊr.i, də-, -tri (US) dɪ'fæm.ə.tɔːr.i
defam|e dɪ'feɪm, də- (US) dɪ- **-es** -z **-ing** -ɪŋ **-ed** -d **-er/s** -əʳ/z (US) -ɚ/z
Defarge də'fɑːʒ (US) -'fɑːrʒ
default (*n.*) dɪ'fɔːlt, də-, -'fɒlt; 'diː.fɔːlt, -fɒlt (US) dɪ'fɑːlt, -'fɔːlt
defaul|t (*v.*) dɪ'fɔːl|t, də-, -'fɒl|t (US) dɪ'fɑːl|t, -'fɔːl|t **-ts** -ts **-ting** -tɪŋ (US) -t̬ɪŋ **-ted** -tɪd (US) -t̬ɪd **-ter/s** -təʳ/z (US) -t̬ɚ/z
defeasance dɪ'fiː.zᵊnts, də- (US) dɪ-
defeasib|le dɪ'fiː.zə.b|l̩, də-, -zɪ- (US) dɪ- **-ly** -li **-leness** -l̩.nəs, -nɪs
de|feat dɪ|'fiːt, də- (US) dɪ- **-feats** -'fiːts **-feating** -'fiː.tɪŋ (US) -'fiː.t̬ɪŋ **-feated** -'fiː.tɪd (US) -'fiː.t̬ɪd
defeat|ism dɪ'fiː.t|ɪ.zᵊm, də- (US) dɪ'fiː.t̬|ɪ- **-ist/s** -ɪst/s
defe|cate 'def.ə|.keɪt, 'diː.fə-, -fɪ- (US) 'def.ə-, '-ɪ- **-cates** -keɪts **-cating** -keɪ.tɪŋ (US) -keɪ.t̬ɪŋ **-cated** -keɪ.tɪd (US) -keɪ.t̬ɪd
defecation ,def.ə'keɪ.ʃᵊn, ,diː.fə'-, -fɪ'- (US) ,def.ə'-, -ɪ'- **-s** -z
defect (*n.*) 'diː.fekt; dɪ'fekt, də- (US) 'diː.fekt; dɪ'fekt **-s** -s
defect (*v.*) dɪ'fekt, də- (US) dɪ- **-s** -s **-ing** -ɪŋ **-ed** -ɪd
defection dɪ'fek.ʃᵊn, də- (US) dɪ- **-s** -z
defective dɪ'fek.tɪv, də- (US) dɪ- **-ly** -li **-ness** -nəs, -nɪs
defector dɪ'fek.təʳ, də- (US) dɪ'fek.tɚ **-s** -z
defenc|e dɪ'fen*t*s, də- (US) dɪ- **-es** -ɪz
defenceless dɪ'fen*t*.sləs, də-, -slɪs (US) dɪ- **-ly** -li **-ness** -nəs, -nɪs
defend dɪ'fend, də- (US) dɪ- **-s** -z **-ing** -ɪŋ **-ed** -ɪd **-able** -ə.bl̩
defendant dɪ'fen.dənt, də- (US) dɪ- **-s** -s
defender dɪ'fen.dəʳ, də- (US) dɪ'fen.dɚ **-s** -z
defens|e dɪ'fen*t*s, də- (US) dɪ-; *esp. in sports:* 'diː.fen*t*s **-es** -ɪz
defenseless dɪ'fen*t*.sləs, də-, -slɪs (US) dɪ- **-ly** -li **-ness** -nəs, -nɪs
defense|man dɪ'fen*t*s|.mən, də- (US) dɪ-, -mæn **-men** -mən
defensibility dɪ,fen*t*.sə'bɪl.ə.ti, də-, -sɪ'-, -ɪ.ti (US) dɪ,fen*t*.sə'bɪl.ə.t̬i
defensib|le dɪ'fen*t*.sə.b|l̩, də-, -sɪ- (US) dɪ- **-ly** -li
defensive dɪ'fen*t*.sɪv, də- (US) dɪ- **-ly** -li **-ness** -nəs, -nɪs
defer dɪ'fɜːʳ, də- (US) dɪ'fɝː **-s** -z **-ring** -ɪŋ **-red** -d **-rer/s** -əʳ/z (US) -ɚ/z
deferen|ce 'def.ᵊr.ᵊn|*t*s **-t** -t
deferential ,def.ᵊ'ren.*t*ʃᵊl (US) -'ren*t*.ʃᵊl **-ly** -i
deferment dɪ'fɜː.mənt, də- (US) dɪ'fɝː- **-s** -s
deferral dɪ'fɜː.rᵊl, də- (US) dɪ'fɝː.ᵊl **-s** -z
defiance dɪ'faɪ.ən*t*s, də- (US) dɪ-
defiant dɪ'faɪ.ənt, də- (US) dɪ- **-ly** -li **-ness** -nəs, -nɪs
defibrill|ate ,diː'fɪb.rɪ.l|eɪt, -'faɪ.brɪ-, -brᵊl|.eɪt (US) -rɪ.l|eɪt, -rə- **-ates** -eɪts **-ating** -eɪ.tɪŋ (US) -eɪ.t̬ɪŋ **-ated** -eɪ.tɪd (US) -eɪ.t̬ɪd
defibrillation diː,fɪb.rɪ'leɪ.ʃᵊn, -,faɪ.brɪ'-, -brə'-; ,diː.fɪ.brɪ'-
defibrillator ,diː'fɪb.rɪ.leɪ.təʳ, -'faɪ.brɪ-, -brə- (US) -t̬ɚ **-s** -z
deficienc|y dɪ'fɪʃ.ᵊn*t*.s|i, də- (US) dɪ- **-ies** -iz
deficient dɪ'fɪʃ.ᵊnt, də- (US) dɪ- **-ly** -li
deficit 'def.ɪ.sɪt, '-ə-; də'fɪs-, dɪ- (US) 'def.ɪ.sɪt, '-ə- **-s** -s
defilad|e ,def.ɪ'leɪd, -ə'-, '--- **-es** -z **-ing** -ɪŋ **-ed** -ɪd
defile (*n.*) dɪ'faɪl, ,diː-; 'diː.faɪl **-s** -z
defil|e (*v.*) dɪ'faɪl, də- (US) dɪ- **-es** -z **-ing**

-ɪŋ **-ed** -d **-er/s** -əʳ/z ⓤⓢ -ɚ/z **-ement** -mənt
definable dɪˈfaɪ.nə.bl̩, də- ⓤⓢ dɪ-
defin|e dɪˈfaɪn, də- ⓤⓢ dɪ- **-es** -z **-ing** -ɪŋ **-ed** -d **-er/s** -əʳ/z ⓤⓢ -ɚ/z
definite ˈdef.ɪ.nət, -ən.ət, -ɪt **-ly** -li **-ness** -nəs, -nɪs
definition ˌdef.ɪˈnɪʃ.ən, -əˈ- **-s** -z
definitive dɪˈfɪn.ə.tɪv, də-, ˈ-ɪ- ⓤⓢ dɪˈfɪn.ə.t̬ɪv **-ly** -li **-ness** -nəs, -nɪs
defla|grate ˈdiː.flə|.greɪt, ˈdef.lə- ⓤⓢ ˈdef.lə- **-grates** -greɪts **-grating** -greɪ.tɪŋ ⓤⓢ -greɪ.t̬ɪŋ **-grated** -greɪ.tɪd ⓤⓢ -greɪ.t̬ɪd **-grator/s** -greɪ.təʳ/z ⓤⓢ -greɪ.t̬ɚ/z
deflagration ˌdiː.fləˈgreɪ.ʃən, ˌdef.ləˈ- ⓤⓢ ˌdef.ləˈ- **-s** -z
de|flate dɪ|ˈfleɪt, ˌdiː- **-flates** -ˈfleɪts **-flating** -ˈfleɪ.tɪŋ ⓤⓢ -ˈfleɪ.t̬ɪŋ **-flated** -ˈfleɪ.tɪd ⓤⓢ -ˈfleɪ.t̬ɪd
deflation dɪˈfleɪ.ʃən, ˌdiː- **-ary** -ər.i ⓤⓢ -er.i
deflect dɪˈflekt, də- ⓤⓢ dɪ- **-s** -s **-ing** -ɪŋ **-ed** -ɪd **-or/s** -əʳ/z ⓤⓢ -ɚ/z
deflection, deflexion dɪˈflek.ʃən, də- ⓤⓢ dɪ- **-s** -z
defloration ˌdiː.flɔːˈreɪ.ʃən, ˌdef.lɔːˈ- ⓤⓢ ˌdef.ləˈ-, ˌdiː.fləˈ-, -flɔːˈ- **-s** -z
deflower dɪˈflaʊəʳ, ˌdiː- ⓤⓢ -ˈflaʊɚ **-s** -z **-ing** -ɪŋ **-ed** -d
Defoe dɪˈfəʊ, də- ⓤⓢ -ˈfoʊ
defog ˌdiːˈfɒg ⓤⓢ -ˈfɑːg, -ˈfɔːg **-s** -z **-ging** -ɪŋ **-ged** -d **-ger/s** -əʳ/z ⓤⓢ -ɚ/z
defoliant ˌdiːˈfəʊ.li.ənt, dɪ- ⓤⓢ -ˈfoʊ- **-s** -s
defoli|ate ˌdiːˈfəʊ.li|.eɪt, dɪ- ⓤⓢ -ˈfoʊ- **-ates** -eɪts **-ating** -eɪ.tɪŋ ⓤⓢ -eɪ.t̬ɪŋ **-ated** -eɪ.tɪd ⓤⓢ -eɪ.t̬ɪd
defoliation ˌdiː.fəʊ.liˈeɪ.ʃən; diːˌfəʊ-, dɪ- ⓤⓢ diːˌfoʊ-, dɪ-
deforest ˌdiːˈfɒr.ɪst, dɪ-, -əst ⓤⓢ -ˈfɔːr- **-s** -s **-ing** -ɪŋ **-ed** -ɪd
deforestation diːˌfɒr.ɪˈsteɪ.ʃən, dɪ-; ˌdiː.fɔːr-, -əˈ- ⓤⓢ diːˌfɔːr-, dɪ-
deform dɪˈfɔːm, də-, ˌdiː- ⓤⓢ dɪˈfɔːrm, ˌdiː- **-s** -z **-ing** -ɪŋ **-ed** -d **-er/s** -əʳ/z ⓤⓢ -ɚ/z
deformation ˌdiː.fɔːˈmeɪ.ʃən, ˌdef.əˈ- ⓤⓢ ˌdiː.fɔːrˈ-, ˌdef.ɚˈ- **-s** -z
deformit|y dɪˈfɔː.mə.t|i, də-, -mɪ- ⓤⓢ dɪˈfɔːr.mə.t̬|i **-ies** -iz
defraud dɪˈfrɔːd, ˌdiː-, də- ⓤⓢ dɪˈfrɑːd, ˌdiː-, -ˈfrɔːd **-s** -z **-ing** -ɪŋ **-ed** -ɪd **-er/s** -əʳ/z ⓤⓢ -ɚ/z
defray dɪˈfreɪ, də- ⓤⓢ dɪ- **-s** -z **-ing** -ɪŋ **-ed** -d **-er/s** -əʳ/z ⓤⓢ -ɚ/z **-ment** -mənt
defrayal dɪˈfreɪ.əl, də- ⓤⓢ dɪ- **-s** -z
De Freitas dəˈfreɪ.təs ⓤⓢ -t̬əs
defrock ˌdiːˈfrɒk ⓤⓢ -ˈfrɑːk **-s** -s **-ing** -ɪŋ **-ed** -t
defrost ˌdiːˈfrɒst, dɪ- ⓤⓢ -ˈfrɑːst **-s** -s **-ing** -ɪŋ **-ed** -ɪd **-er/s** -əʳ/z ⓤⓢ -ɚ/z
deft deft **-er** -əʳ ⓤⓢ -ɚ **-est** -ɪst, -əst **-ly** -li **-ness** -nəs, -nɪs
defunct dɪˈfʌŋkt, də-; ˈdiː.fʌnkt ⓤⓢ dɪˈfʌnkt, ˌdiː- **-s** -s
defus|e ˌdiːˈfjuːz, dɪ-, də- ⓤⓢ ˌdiː-, dɪ- **-es** -ɪz **-ing** -ɪŋ **-ed** -d
def|y dɪˈf|laɪ, də- ⓤⓢ dɪ- **-ies** -aɪz **-ying** -aɪ.ɪŋ **-ied** -aɪd **-ier/s** -aɪ.əʳ/z ⓤⓢ -aɪ.ɚ/z
Deganwy dɪˈgæn.wi, də-
Degas dəˈgɑː, ˈdeɪ.gɑː
De Gaulle dəˈgəʊl, dɪ-, -ˈgɔːl ⓤⓢ -ˈgoʊl, -ˈgɔːl, -ˈgɑːl
degauss ˌdiːˈgaʊs, -ˈgɔːs ⓤⓢ -ˈgaʊs **-es** -ɪz **-ing** -ɪŋ **-ed** -t
degeneracy dɪˈdʒen.ər.ə.si, də- ⓤⓢ dɪ-
degenerate (*adj.*) dɪˈdʒen.ər.ət, də-, -ɪt ⓤⓢ dɪ- **-ly** -li **-ness** -nəs, -nɪs
degener|ate (*v.*) dɪˈdʒen.ər|.eɪt, də- ⓤⓢ dɪˈdʒen.ə.r|eɪt **-ates** -eɪts **-ating** -eɪ.tɪŋ ⓤⓢ -eɪ.t̬ɪŋ **-ated** -eɪ.tɪd ⓤⓢ -eɪ.t̬ɪd
degeneration dɪˌdʒen.əˈreɪ.ʃən, də- ⓤⓢ dɪ-
degenerative dɪˈdʒen.ər.ə.tɪv, də-, -ə.reɪ- ⓤⓢ dɪˈdʒen.ɚ.ə.t̬ɪv, -ə.reɪ-
deglutin|ate ˌdiːˈgluː.tɪ.n|eɪt, dɪ- ⓤⓢ -tən|.eɪt **-ates** -eɪts **-ating** -eɪ.tɪŋ ⓤⓢ -eɪ.t̬ɪŋ **-ated** -eɪ.tɪd ⓤⓢ -eɪ.t̬ɪd
deglutition ˌdiː.gluːˈtɪʃ.ən
degradation ˌdeg.rəˈdeɪ.ʃən **-s** -z
degrad|e dɪˈgreɪd, də- ⓤⓢ dɪ- **-es** -z **-ed** -ɪd **-able** -ə.bl̩
degrading dɪˈgreɪ.dɪŋ, də- ⓤⓢ dɪ- **-ly** -li
degree dɪˈgriː, də- ⓤⓢ dɪ- **-s** -z
dehisc|e dɪˈhɪs, ˌdiː- ⓤⓢ ˌdiː-, dɪ- **-es** -ɪz **-ing** -ɪŋ **-ed** -t
dehiscen|ce dɪˈhɪs.ən|ts, ˌdiː- ⓤⓢ ˌdiː-, dɪ- **-t** -t
Dehra Dun ˌdeə.rəˈduːn, ˌdeɪə- ⓤⓢ ˌder.əˈ-
dehumaniz|e, -is|e ˌdiːˈhjuː.mə.naɪz **-es** -ɪz **-ing** -ɪŋ **-ed** -d
dehumidifier ˌdiː.hjuːˈmɪd.ɪ.faɪ.əʳ ⓤⓢ -ə.faɪ.ɚ **-s** -z
dehy|drate ˌdiː.haɪ|ˈdreɪt, ˈ--- **-drates** -ˈdreɪts **-drating** -ˈdre.tɪŋ ⓤⓢ -ˈdreɪ.t̬ɪŋ **-drated** -ˈdreɪ.tɪd ⓤⓢ -ˈdreɪ.t̬ɪd
dehydration ˌdiː.haɪˈdreɪ.ʃən
dehypnotiz|e, -is|e ˌdiːˈhɪp.nə.taɪz **-es** -ɪz **-ing** -ɪŋ **-ed** -d
de-ic|e ˌdiːˈaɪs **-es** -ɪz **-ing** -ɪŋ **-ed** -t **-er/s** -əʳ/z ⓤⓢ -ɚ/z
deicide ˈdeɪ.ɪ.saɪd, ˈdiː-, ˈ-ə- ⓤⓢ ˈdiː.ə- **-s** -z
dei|ctic ˈdaɪ|k.tɪk, ˈdeɪ- **-xis** -k.sɪs
deification ˌdeɪ.ɪ.fɪˈkeɪ.ʃən, ˌdiː-, ˌ-ə- ⓤⓢ ˌdiː.ə- **-s** -z
dei|fy ˈdeɪ.ɪ|.faɪ, ˈdiː-, ˈ-ə- ⓤⓢ ˈdiː- **-fies** -faɪz **-fying** -faɪ.ɪŋ **-fied** -faɪd
Deighton *surname:* ˈdeɪ.tən, ˈdaɪ- *place in North Yorkshire:* ˈdiː.tən
deign deɪn **-s** -z **-ing** -ɪŋ **-ed** -d
deindustrialization, -isa- ˌdiː.ɪnˌdʌs.tri.əl.aɪˈzeɪ.ʃən, -ɪˈ- ⓤⓢ -ɪˈ-
Deirdre ˈdɪə.dri, -dreɪ ⓤⓢ ˈdɪr.drə, -dri
de|ism ˈdeɪ|.ɪ.zəm, ˈdiː- ⓤⓢ ˈdiː- **-ist/s** -ɪst/s
deistic deɪˈɪs.tɪk, diː- ⓤⓢ diː- **-al** -əl
deit|y (D) ˈdeɪ.ɪ.t|i, ˈdiː-, ˈ-ə- ⓤⓢ ˈdiː.ə.t̬|i **-ies** -iz
déjà vu ˌdeʒ.ɑːˈvuː, -ˈvjuː ⓤⓢ ˌdeɪ.ʒɑːˈvuː, -vjuː
deject dɪˈdʒekt, də- ⓤⓢ dɪ- **-s** -s **-ing** -ɪŋ **-ed/ly** -ɪd/li **-edness** -ɪd.nəs, -nɪs
dejection dɪˈdʒek.ʃən, də- ⓤⓢ dɪ-
déjeuner ˈdeɪ.ʒə.neɪ, -ʒɜː- ⓤⓢ -ʒə- **-s** -z
de jure ˌdeɪˈdʒʊə.reɪ, di-, ˌdiː-, -ri ⓤⓢ diːˈdʒʊr.i, deɪ-
Dekker ˈdek.əʳ ⓤⓢ -ɚ
dekko ˈdek.əʊ ⓤⓢ -oʊ **-s** -z
de Klerk dəˈklɜːk, dəˈkleək ⓤⓢ -ˈklerk, -ˈklɝːk
de Kooning dəˈkəʊ.nɪŋ, -ˈkuː- ⓤⓢ -ˈkuː-
Del. (*abbrev. for* **Delaware**) ˈdel.ə.weəʳ ⓤⓢ -wer
de la Bère də.ləˈbɪəʳ ⓤⓢ də.ləˈbɪr
Delacroix ˈdel.ə.krwɑː, ˌ--ˈ-
Delafield ˈdel.ə.fiːld
Delagoa ˌdel.əˈgəʊə ⓤⓢ -ˈgoʊə
Delamain ˈdel.ə.meɪn
de la Mare də.lɑːˈmeəʳ, ˌdel.əˈ- ⓤⓢ də.ləˈmer, ˌdel.əˈ-
Delamere ˈdel.ə.mɪəʳ ⓤⓢ -mɪr
De Lancey dəˈlɑːnt.si ⓤⓢ -ˈlænt-
Delane dəˈleɪn, dɪ-
Delaney dəˈleɪ.ni, dɪ-
Delany dəˈleɪ.ni, dɪ-
De la Pole ˌdel.əˈpəʊl, də.lɑːˈ- ⓤⓢ də.ləˈpoʊl
de la Roche ˌdel.əˈrɒʃ, -ˈrəʊʃ; də.ləˈ- ⓤⓢ də.lɑːˈroʊʃ, -lə-, -ˈrɑːʃ
De la Rue ˌdel.əˈruː; də.lɑːˈ-; ˈdel.ə.ruː
de la Torre ˌdel.əˈtɔːʳ, də.lɑːˈ- ⓤⓢ -ˈtɔːr
Delaunay dəˈlɔː.neɪ ⓤⓢ -lɔːˈneɪ
Delaware ˈdel.ə.weəʳ ⓤⓢ -wer
De la Warr ˌdel.əˈweəʳ, də.lɑːˈ- ⓤⓢ -ˈwer
delay dɪˈleɪ, də- ⓤⓢ dɪ- **-s** -z **-ing** -ɪŋ **-ed** -d **-er/s** -əʳ/z ⓤⓢ -ɚ/z
Delbert ˈdel.bət ⓤⓢ -bɚt
del credere ˌdelˈkred.ər.eɪ, -ˈkreɪ.dər-, -i ⓤⓢ -ˈkreɪ.dɚ-
dele ˈdiː.liː, -li
delectab|le dɪˈlek.tə.b|l̩, də- ⓤⓢ dɪ- **-ly** -li **-leness** -l̩.nəs, -nɪs
delectation ˌdiː.lekˈteɪ.ʃən
delegac|y ˈdel.ɪ.gə.s|i, ˈ-ə- **-ies** -iz
delegate (*n.*) ˈdel.ɪ.gət, ˈ-ə-, -geɪt, -gɪt ⓤⓢ -gət, -gɪt, -geɪt **-s** -s

dele|gate *(v.)* ˈdel.ɪ|.geɪt, ˈ-ə- **-gates** -geɪts **-gating** -geɪ.tɪŋ ⓤⓢ -geɪ.t̬ɪŋ **-gated** -geɪ.tɪd ⓤⓢ -geɪ.t̬ɪd
delegation ˌdel.ɪˈgeɪ.ʃᵊn, -əˈ- **-s** -z
delend|um dɪˈlen.d|əm, diː- **-a** -ə
de|lete dɪ|ˈliːt, də- ⓤⓢ dɪ- **-letes** -ˈliːts **-leting** -ˈliː.tɪŋ ⓤⓢ -ˈliː.t̬ɪŋ **-leted** -ˈliː.tɪd ⓤⓢ -ˈliː.t̬ɪd
deleterious ˌdel.ɪˈtɪə.ri.əs, ˌdɪl-, ˌdiː.lɪˈ-, -ləˈtɪə- ⓤⓢ ˌdel.əˈtɪr.i- **-ly** -li **-ness** -nəs, -nɪs
deletion dɪˈliː.ʃᵊn, də- ⓤⓢ dɪ- **-s** -z
delf delf
Delft delft **-ware** -weəʳ ⓤⓢ -wer
Delham ˈdel.əm
Delhi ˈdel.i
deli ˈdel.i **-s** -z
Deli|a ˈdiː.li|.ə ⓤⓢ ˈdiːl.j|ə, -li|.ə, -li **-an/s** -ən/z
deliberate *(adj.)* dɪˈlɪb.ᵊr.ət, də-, -ɪt ⓤⓢ dɪ- **-ly** -li **-ness** -nəs, -nɪs
deliber|ate *(v.)* dɪˈlɪb.ᵊr|.eɪt, də- ⓤⓢ dɪˈlɪb.ə.r|eɪt **-ates** -eɪts **-ating** -eɪ.tɪŋ ⓤⓢ -eɪ.t̬ɪŋ **-ated** -eɪ.tɪd ⓤⓢ -eɪ.t̬ɪd **-ator/s** -eɪ.təʳ/z ⓤⓢ -eɪ.t̬ɚ/z
deliberation dɪˌlɪb.əˈreɪ.ʃᵊn, də- ⓤⓢ dɪ- **-s** -z
deliberative dɪˈlɪb.ᵊr.ə.tɪv, də- ⓤⓢ dɪˈlɪb.ɚ.ə.t̬ɪv, -rə.t̬ɪv **-ly** -li
Delibes dəˈliːb, dɪ-
delicac|y ˈdel.ɪ.kə.s|i, ˈ-ə- **-ies** -iz
delicate ˈdel.ɪ.kət, ˈ-ə-, -kɪt **-ly** -li **-ness** -nəs, -nɪs
delicatessen ˌdel.ɪ.kəˈtes.ᵊn, ˌ-ə- **-s** -z
delicious dɪˈlɪʃ.əs, də- ⓤⓢ dɪ- **-ly** -li **-ness** -nəs, -nɪs
delict dɪˈlɪkt; ˈdiː.lɪkt ⓤⓢ dɪˈlɪkt **-s** -s
de|light dɪ|ˈlaɪt, də- ⓤⓢ dɪ- **-lights** -ˈlaɪts **-lighting** -ˈlaɪ.tɪŋ ⓤⓢ -ˈlaɪ.t̬ɪŋ **-lighted/ly** -ˈlaɪ.tɪd/li ⓤⓢ -ˈlaɪ.t̬ɪd/li
delightful dɪˈlaɪt.fᵊl, də-, -fʊl ⓤⓢ dɪ- **-ly** -i **-ness** -nəs, -nɪs
delightsome dɪˈlaɪt.səm, də- ⓤⓢ dɪ-
Delilah dɪˈlaɪ.lə, də- ⓤⓢ dɪ-
delim|it dɪˈlɪm|.ɪt, ˌdiː-, də- ⓤⓢ dɪ- **-its** -ɪts **-iting** -ɪ.tɪŋ ⓤⓢ -ɪ.t̬ɪŋ **-ited** -ɪ.tɪd ⓤⓢ -ɪ.t̬ɪd
delimitation dɪˌlɪm.ɪˈteɪ.ʃᵊn, ˌdiː-, də- ⓤⓢ dɪ- **-s** -z
deline|ate dɪˈlɪn.i|.eɪt, də- ⓤⓢ dɪ- **-ates** -eɪts **-ating** -eɪ.tɪŋ ⓤⓢ -eɪ.t̬ɪŋ **-ated** -eɪ.tɪd ⓤⓢ -eɪ.t̬ɪd **-ator/s** -eɪ.təʳ/z ⓤⓢ -eɪ.t̬ɚ/z
delineation dɪˌlɪn.iˈeɪ.ʃᵊn, də- ⓤⓢ dɪ- **-s** -z
delinquenc|y dɪˈlɪŋ.kwənt.s|i, də- ⓤⓢ dɪ- **-ies** -iz
delinquent dɪˈlɪŋ.kwənt, də- ⓤⓢ dɪ- **-s** -s
deliquesc|e ˌdel.ɪˈkwes, -əˈ- **-es** -ɪz **-ing** -ɪŋ **-ed** -t
deliquescen|ce ˌdel.ɪˈkwes.ᵊn|*t*s **-t** -t
delirious dɪˈlɪr.i.əs, də-, -ˈlɪə.ri- ⓤⓢ dɪˈlɪr.i- **-ly** -li **-ness** -nəs, -nɪs
delirium dɪˈlɪr.i.əm, də-, -ˈlɪə.ri- ⓤⓢ dɪˈlɪr.i-
delirium tremens dɪˌlɪr.i.əmˈtriː.menz, -ˈtrem.enz, -ənz
De l'Isle *English name:* dəˈlaɪl
Delisle *French name:* dəˈliːl
Delius ˈdiː.li.əs
deliv|er dɪˈlɪv|.əʳ, də- ⓤⓢ dɪˈlɪv|.ɚ **-ers** -əz ⓤⓢ -ɚz **-ering** -ᵊr.ɪŋ **-ered** -əd ⓤⓢ -ɚd **-erer/s** -ᵊr.əʳ/z ⓤⓢ -ɚ.ɚ/z
deliverable dɪˈlɪv.ᵊr.ə.bl̩, də- ⓤⓢ dɪ- **-s** -z
deliveranc|e dɪˈlɪv.ᵊr.ᵊn*t*s, də- ⓤⓢ dɪ- **-es** -ɪz
deliver|y dɪˈlɪv.ᵊr|.i, də- ⓤⓢ dɪ- **-ies** -iz
delivery|man dɪˈlɪv.ᵊr.ɪ.mən, də-, -mæn ⓤⓢ dəˈlɪv.ri.mæn **-men** -mən, -men
dell (D) del **-s** -z
Della ˈdel.ə
Dellar ˈdel.əʳ ⓤⓢ -ɚ
della Robbia ˌdel.əˈrɒb.i.ə ⓤⓢ ˌdel.əˈroʊ.biə, -ɑːˈ-, -ˈrɑː-, -bjə
Delma ˈdel.mə
Delmar delˈmɑːʳ, ˈ-- ⓤⓢ ˈdel.mɑːr, -ˈ-
Delmarva delˈmɑː.və ⓤⓢ -ˈmɑːr- **Delˌmarva Peˌninsula**
Del Monte® delˈmɒn.teɪ, -ti ⓤⓢ -ˈmɑːn.t̬i
Deloitte dəˈlɔɪt, dɪ-
Delores dəˈlɔː.rɪz, dɪ- ⓤⓢ dɪˈlɔːr.ɪs, də-
Deloria dəˈlɔː.ri.ə ⓤⓢ -ˈlɔːr.i-
Delors dəˈlɔːʳ ⓤⓢ -ˈlɔːr
Delos ˈdiː.lɒs ⓤⓢ -lɑːs, ˈdel.oʊs
delous|e ˌdiːˈlaʊs ⓤⓢ -ˈlaʊs, -ˈlaʊz **-es** -ɪz **-ing** -ɪŋ **-ed** -t ⓤⓢ -t, -d
Delph delf
Delphi *in Greece:* ˈdel.faɪ, -fi *city in US:* ˈdel.faɪ
Delph|ian ˈdel.f|i.ən **-ic** -ɪk ˌ**Delphic ˈoracle**
Delphine delˈfiːn
delphinium delˈfɪn.i.əm **-s** -z
Delroy ˈdel.rɔɪ
delta ˈdel.tə ⓤⓢ -t̬ə **-s** -z
deltoid ˈdel.tɔɪd
delud|e dɪˈluːd, də-, -ˈljuːd ⓤⓢ dɪˈluːd **-es** -z **-ing** -ɪŋ **-ed** -ɪd **-er/s** -əʳ/z ⓤⓢ -ɚ/z
delug|e ˈdel.juːdʒ **-es** -ɪz **-ing** -ɪŋ **-ed** -d
delusion dɪˈluː.ʒᵊn, də-, -ˈljuː- ⓤⓢ dɪˈluː- **-s** -z
delusive dɪˈluː.sɪv, də-, -ˈljuː- ⓤⓢ dɪˈluː- **-ly** -li **-ness** -nəs, -nɪs
delusory dɪˈluː.sᵊr.i, də-, -ˈljuː-, -zᵊr- ⓤⓢ dɪˈluː-
de luxe, deluxe dɪˈlʌks, də-, -ˈlʊks, -ˈluːks ⓤⓢ dɪˈlʌks, də-, -ˈlʊks
delv|e delv **-es** -z **-ing** -ɪŋ **-ed** -d **-er/s** -əʳ/z ⓤⓢ -ɚ/z
Delyn ˈdel.ɪn
Dem *(abbrev. for* **Democrat***)* ˈdem.ə.kræt ˌdem.əˈkræt.ɪk
demagnetization, -isa- diːˌmæg.nə.taɪˈzeɪ.ʃᵊn, ˌdiː.mæg-, -nɪ-, -ɪˈ- ⓤⓢ diːˌmæg.nə.t̬ɪˈ- **-s** -z
demagnetiz|e, -is|e ˌdiːˈmæg.nə.taɪz, -nɪ- **-es** -ɪz **-ing** -ɪŋ **-ed** -d
demagog ˈdem.ə.gɒg ⓤⓢ -gɑːg, -gɔːg **-s** -z
demagogic ˌdem.əˈgɒg.ɪk, -ˈgɒdʒ- ⓤⓢ -ˈgɑː.dʒɪk, -gɪk; -goʊ.dʒɪk **-al** -ᵊl **-ally** -ᵊl.i, -li
demagogue ˈdem.ə.gɒg ⓤⓢ -gɑːg, -gɔːg **-s** -z
demagoguery ˈdem.ə.gɒg.ᵊr.i ⓤⓢ -gɑː.gɚ-
demagogy ˈdem.ə.gɒg.i, -gɒdʒ- ⓤⓢ -gɑː.dʒi, -gi; -goʊ.dʒi
demand dɪˈmɑːnd, də- ⓤⓢ dɪˈmænd **-s** -z **-ing/ly** -ɪŋ/li **-ed** -ɪd
demanding dɪˈmɑːn.dɪŋ, də- ⓤⓢ dɪˈmæn- **-ly** -li
demar|cate ˈdiː.mɑː|.keɪt ⓤⓢ diːˈmɑːr|.keɪt, ˈdiː.mɑːr- **-cates** -keɪts **-cating** -keɪ.tɪŋ ⓤⓢ -keɪ.t̬ɪŋ **-cated** -keɪ.tɪd ⓤⓢ -keɪ.t̬ɪd
demarcation ˌdiː.mɑːˈkeɪ.ʃᵊn ⓤⓢ -mɑːrˈ-
demarcative ˌdiːˈmɑː.kə.tɪv ⓤⓢ -ˈmɑːr.kə.t̬ɪv
démarch|e ˈdeɪ.mɑːʃ, -ˈ- ⓤⓢ deɪˈmɑːrʃ, dɪ- **-es** -ɪz
demark dɪˈmɑːk, ˌdiː- ⓤⓢ -ˈmɑːrk **-s** -s **-ing** -ɪŋ **-ed** -t
demarkation ˌdiː.mɑːˈkeɪ.ʃᵊn ⓤⓢ -mɑːrˈ-
Demas ˈdiː.mæs
dematerializ|e, -is|e ˌdiː.məˈtɪə.ri.ə.laɪz ⓤⓢ -ˈtɪr.i- **-es** -ɪz **-ing** -ɪŋ **-ed** -d
demean dɪˈmiːn, də- ⓤⓢ dɪ- **-s** -z **-ing** -ɪŋ **-ed** -d
demeano(u)r dɪˈmiː.nəʳ, də- ⓤⓢ dɪˈmiː.nɚ **-s** -z
Demelza dɪˈmel.zə, də-, demˈel-
de|ment dɪ|ˈment, də- ⓤⓢ dɪ- **-ments** -ˈments **-menting** -ˈmen.tɪŋ ⓤⓢ -ˈmen.t̬ɪŋ **-mented/ly** -ˈmen.tɪd/li ⓤⓢ -ˈmen.t̬ɪd/li
dementia dɪˈmen.*t*ʃə, də-, -*t*ʃi.ə ⓤⓢ dɪˈment.ʃə
dementia praecox dɪˌmen.*t*ʃəˈpriː.kɒks, -ˈpraɪ- ⓤⓢ -ment.ʃəˈpriː.kɑːks
demerara *sugar:* ˌdem.ᵊˈreə.rə, -ˈrɑː- ⓤⓢ -ˈrɑːr.ə
Demerara *district in Guyana:* ˌdem.əˈrɑː.rə ⓤⓢ -ˈrɑːr.ə

demerg|e ˌdiːˈmɜːdʒ (US) -ˈmɝːrdʒ, də- **-es** -ɪz **-ing** -ɪŋ **-ed** -d
demerger ˌdiːˈmɜː.dʒəʳ (US) -ˈmɝː.dʒɚ **-s** -z
demerit ˌdiːˈmer.ɪt, ˈdiː.mer- (US) dɪˈmer-, diː- **-s** -s
Demerol® ˈdem.ə.rɒl (US) -rɑːl
demesne dɪˈmeɪn, də-, -ˈmiːn (US) dɪ- **-s** -z
Demeter dɪˈmiː.təʳ, də- (US) -t̬ɚ
Demetrius dɪˈmiː.tri.əs, də-
demi- dem.i-
Note: Prefix. Normally carries primary or secondary stress on the first syllable, e.g. **demigod** /ˈdem.i.gɒd (US) -gɑːd/, **demisemiquaver** /ˌdem.iˈsem.iˌkweɪ.vəʳ (US) -vɚ/.
demigod ˈdem.i.gɒd (US) -gɑːd **-s** -z
demigoddess ˈdem.iˌgɒd.es (US) -ˌgɑː.des **-es** -ɪz
demijohn ˈdem.i.dʒɒn (US) -dʒɑːn **-s** -z
demilitarization, -isa- diːˌmɪl.ɪ.tᵊr.aɪˈzeɪ.ʃᵊn, ˌdiː.mɪ.lɪ-, -lə-, -ɪˈ- (US) diːˌmɪl.ɪ.t̬ɚ.ɪˈ-
demilitariz|e, -is|e ˌdiːˈmɪl.ɪ.tᵊr.aɪz, ˈ-ə- (US) -t̬ə.raɪz **-es** -ɪz **-ing** -ɪŋ **-ed** -d
de Mille dəˈmɪl, dɪ-
demimondaine ˌdem.i.mɒnˈdeɪn (US) -mɑːnˈ- **-s** -z
demimonde ˌdem.iˈmɔ̃ːnd, -ˈmɔːnd, -ˈmɒnd, ˈ--- (US) ˈdem.i.mɑːnd
de minimis ˌdeɪˈmɪn.ɪ.miːs, ˈ-ə-
demis|e dɪˈmaɪz, də- (US) dɪ- **-es** -ɪz **-ing** -ɪŋ **-ed** -d
demisemiquaver ˈdem.i.sem.iˌkweɪ.vəʳ, ˌdem.iˈsem.i- (US) ˌdem.iˈsem.iˌkweɪ.vɚ **-s** -z
demission dɪˈmɪʃ.ᵊn **-s** -z
demist ˌdiːˈmɪst **-s** -s **-ing** -ɪŋ **-ed** -ɪd **-er/s** -əʳ/z (US) -ɚ/z
demitass|e ˈdem.i.tæs, -tɑːs **-es** -ɪz
demiurg|e ˈdem.i.ɜːdʒ, ˈdiː.mi- (US) -ɝːdʒ **-es** -ɪz
demo ˈdem.əʊ (US) -oʊ **-s** -z
demob ˌdiːˈmɒb (US) -ˈmɑːb **-s** -z **-bing** -ɪŋ **-bed** -d
demobilization, -isa- diːˌməʊ.bᵊl.aɪˈzeɪ.ʃᵊn, dɪ-, -bɪ.laɪˈ-, -lɪˈ- (US) -ˌmoʊ.bᵊl.ɪˈ-, -bɪ.lɪˈ- **-s** -z
demobiliz|e, -is|e ˌdiːˈməʊ.bᵊl.aɪz, dɪ-, -bɪ.laɪz (US) -ˈmoʊ.bə.laɪz, -bɪ- **-es** -ɪz **-ing** -ɪŋ **-ed** -d
democrac|y dɪˈmɒk.rə.s|i, də- (US) dɪˈmɑː- **-ies** -iz
democrat (D) ˈdem.ə.kræt **-s** -s
democratic (D) ˌdem.əˈkræt.ɪk (US) -ˈkræt̬- **-al** -ᵊl **-ally** -ᵊl.i, -li
democratization, -isa- dɪˌmɒk.rə.taɪˈzeɪ.ʃᵊn, də-, -tɪˈ- (US) dɪˌmɑː.krə.t̬ɪˈ-
democratiz|e, -is|e dɪˈmɒk.rə.taɪz, də- (US) dɪˈmɑː.krə- **-es** -ɪz **-ing** -ɪŋ **-ed** -d
Democritus dɪˈmɒk.rɪ.təs, də-, -rə- (US) dɪˈmɑːk.rə.t̬əs
démodé ˌdeɪˈməʊ.deɪ (US) -moʊˈdeɪ
demodu|late ˌdiːˈmɒd.jə|.leɪt, dɪ-, -jʊ-; -ˈmɒdʒ.ə-, ˈ-ʊ- (US) -ˈmɑː.dʒə-, -dʒʊ- **-lates** -leɪts **-lating** -leɪ.tɪŋ (US) -leɪ.t̬ɪŋ **-lated** -leɪ.tɪd (US) -leɪ.t̬ɪd
demodulation ˌdiːˌmɒd.jəˈleɪ.ʃᵊn, dɪ-, -jʊˈ-; -mɒdʒ.əˈ-, -ʊˈ- (US) -ˌmɑː.dʒəˈ-, -dʒʊ-
demodulator ˌdiːˈmɒd.jə.leɪ.təʳ, dɪ-, -jʊ-; -ˈmɒdʒ.ə-, ˈ-ʊ- (US) -ˈmɑː.dʒə.leɪ.t̬ɚ, -dʒʊ- **-s** -z
demographer dɪˈmɒg.rə.fəʳ, də-, ˌdiː- (US) dɪˈmɑː.grə.fɚ, ˌdiː- **-s** -z
demographic ˌdem.əʊˈgræf.ɪk, ˌdiː.məʊˈ- (US) ˌdem.əˈ-, ˌdiː.məˈ- **-s** -s
demography dɪˈmɒg.rə.fi, də-, ˌdiː- (US) dɪˈmɑː.grə-, ˌdiː-
demoiselle ˌdem.wɑːˈzel, -wəˈ- **-s** -z
De Moivre dəˈmɔɪ.vəʳ, dɪ- (US) -vɚ
demolish dɪˈmɒl.ɪʃ, də- (US) dɪˈmɑː.lɪʃ **-es** -ɪz **-ing** -ɪŋ **-ed** -t **-er/s** -əʳ/z (US) -ɚ/z
demolition ˌdem.əˈlɪʃ.ᵊn, ˌdiː.məˈ- **-s** -z
demon ˈdiː.mən **-s** -z
demoniz|e, -is|e ˈdiː.mᵊn.aɪz **-es** -ɪz **-ing** -ɪŋ **-ed** -d
demonetization, -isa- ˌdiːˌmʌn.ɪ.taɪˈzeɪ.ʃᵊn, -ˌmɒn-, -ə-, -tɪˈ- (US) -ˌmɑː.nə.tɪˈ-
demonetiz|e, -is|e ˌdiːˈmʌn.ɪ.taɪz, -ˈmɒn-, ˈ-ə- (US) -ˈmɑː.nə- **-es** -ɪz **-ing** -ɪŋ **-ed** -d
demoniac dɪˈməʊ.ni.æk, də-, diː- (US) dɪˈmoʊ-, diː- **-s** -s
demoniac|al ˌdiː.məʊˈnaɪə.k|ᵊl (US) -məˈ- **-ally** -ᵊl.i, -li
demonic dɪˈmɒn.ɪk, də-, diː- (US) dɪˈmɑː.nɪk, diː- **-al** -ᵊl **-ally** -ᵊl.i, -li
demon|ism ˈdiː.mə.n|ɪ.zᵊm **-ist/s** -ɪst/s
demoniz|e, -is|e ˈdiː.mᵊn.aɪz **-es** -ɪz **-ing** -ɪŋ **-ed** -d
demonology ˌdiː.məˈnɒl.ə.dʒi (US) -ˈnɑː.lə-
demonstrability dɪˌmɒnt.strəˈbɪl.ə.ti, də-, -ɪ.ti; ˌdem.ən- (US) dɪˌmɑːnt.strəˈbɪl.ə.t̬i; ˌdem.ən-
demonstrab|le dɪˈmɒnt.strə.b|l̩, də-; ˈdem.ən- (US) dɪˈmɑːnt-, də-; ˈdem.ən- **-ly** -li
demon|strate ˈdem.ən|.streɪt **-strates** -streɪts **-strating** -streɪ.tɪŋ (US) -streɪ.t̬ɪŋ **-strated** -streɪ.tɪd (US) -streɪ.t̬ɪd
demonstration ˌdem.ənˈstreɪ.ʃᵊn **-s** -z
demonstrative dɪˈmɒnt.strə.tɪv, də- (US) dɪˈmɑːnt.strə.t̬ɪv **-s** -z **-ly** -li **-ness** -nəs, -nɪs
demonstrator ˈdem.ən.streɪ.təʳ (US) -t̬ɚ **-s** -z
de Montfort dəˈmɒnt.fət, -fɔːt (US) -ˈmɑːnt.fɚt, -fɔːrt
demoralization, -isa- dɪˌmɒr.ᵊl.aɪˈzeɪ.ʃᵊn, ˌdiː.mɒr-, -ɪˈ- (US) dɪˌmɔːr.ᵊl.ɪˈ-
demoraliz|e, -is|e dɪˈmɒr.ə.laɪz, ˌdiː- (US) -ˈmɔːr- **-es** -ɪz **-ing** -ɪŋ **-ed** -d
De Morgan dəˈmɔː.gən (US) -ˈmɔːr-
Demos ˈdiː.mɒs (US) -mɑːs
Demosthenes dɪˈmɒs.θə.niːz, də-, -θɪ- (US) -ˈmɑːs-
de|mote dɪ|ˈməʊt, ˌdiː- (US) -ˈmoʊt **-motes** -ˈməʊts (US) -ˈmoʊts **-moting** -ˈməʊ.tɪŋ (US) -ˈmoʊ.t̬ɪŋ **-moted** -ˈməʊ.tɪd (US) -ˈmoʊ.t̬ɪd
demotic dɪˈmɒt.ɪk, də-, diː- (US) dɪˈmɑː.t̬ɪk, diː-
demotion dɪˈməʊ.ʃᵊn, ˌdiː- (US) -ˈmoʊ-
demoti|vate ˌdiːˈməʊ.tɪ|.veɪt, -tə- (US) -ˈmoʊ.t̬ə- **-vates** -veɪts **-vating** -veɪ.tɪŋ (US) -veɪ.t̬ɪŋ **-vated** -veɪ.tɪd (US) -veɪ.t̬ɪd
Dempsey ˈdem*p*.si
Dempster ˈdem*p*.stəʳ (US) -stɚ
demulcent dɪˈmʌl.sᵊnt, də-, ˌdiː- (US) dɪ-, ˌdiː- **-s** -s
demur dɪˈmɜːʳ, də- (US) dɪˈmɝː **-s** -z **-ring** -ɪŋ **-red** -d
demur|e dɪˈmjʊəʳ, də-, -mjɔːʳ (US) dɪˈmjʊr **-er** -əʳ (US) -ɚ **-est** -ɪst, -əst **-ely** -li **-eness** -nəs, -nɪs
demurrage dɪˈmʌr.ɪdʒ, də- (US) dɪˈmɝː-
demurrer *person who demurs:* dɪˈmɜː.rəʳ, də- (US) -ˈmɝː.ɚ **-s** -z
demurrer *objection on grounds of irrelevance:* dɪˈmʌr.əʳ, də- (US) dɪˈmɝː.ɚ **-s** -z
demutualization, -isa- ˌdiː.mjuː.tʃu.ə.laɪˈzeɪ.ʃᵊn, dɪˌmjuː-, -tju-, -ɪˈ- (US) -tʃu.ə.lɪˈ-, -tʃə.laɪ-
demutualiz|e, -is|e ˌdiːˈmjuː.tʃu.ə.laɪz, dɪˈmjuː-, -tju- (US) -tʃu-, -tʃə.laɪz **-es** -ɪz **-ing** -ɪŋ **-ed** -d
dem|y dɪˈm|aɪ, də- (US) dɪ- **-ies** -aɪz
demystification ˌdiː.mɪ.stɪ.fɪˈkeɪ.ʃᵊn, -stə-; diːˌmɪs.tɪ-, -tə- (US) diːˌmɪs-
demysti|fy ˌdiːˈmɪs.tɪ|.faɪ, -tə- **-fies** -faɪz **-fying** -faɪ.ɪŋ **-fied** -faɪd
demythologiz|e, -is|e ˌdiː.mɪˈθɒl.ə.dʒaɪz, -maɪˈ-, -məˈ- (US) -mɪˈθɑː.lə- **-es** -ɪz **-ing** -ɪŋ **-ed** -d
den den **-s** -z
Denali dəˈnɑː.li
denari|us dɪˈneə.ri|.əs, də-, denˈeə-, -ˈɑː- (US) dɪˈner.i-, -ˈnær- **-i** -aɪ, -iː
denary ˈdiː.nᵊr.i, ˈden.ᵊr-
denationalization, -isa- diːˌnæʃ.ᵊn.ᵊl.aɪˈzeɪ.ʃᵊn, ˌdiː.næʃ-, -nᵊl.aɪ-, -ɪˈ- (US) diːˌnæʃ.ᵊn.ᵊl.ɪˈ-, -nᵊl.ɪ-

Dental

A sound in which there is contact between the tongue and the front teeth.

Examples for English

In English, the dentals usually referred to are the FRICATIVES /θ/ and /ð/, of which /θ/ is voiceless and /ð/ is voiced. In a careful production of these sounds, the tongue tip may be protruded between the upper and lower teeth; the sounds are sometimes referred to as 'interdental' for this reason, e.g.:

thigh	/θaɪ/	
ether	/ˈiː.θər/	(US) /-θɚ/
breath	/breθ/	
thy	/ðaɪ/	
either	/ˈaɪ.ðər/	(US) /ˈiː.ðɚ/
breathe	/briːð/	

denationaliz|e, -is|e ˌdiːˈnæʃ.ᵊn.ᵊl.aɪz, ˈ-nᵊl- **-es** -ɪz **-ing** -ɪŋ **-ed** -d
denaturalization, -isa- diːˌnætʃ.ᵊr.ᵊl.aɪˈzeɪ.ʃᵊn, ˌdiː.nætʃ-, -ɪˈ- (US) diːˌnætʃ.ɚ.ᵊl.ɪˈ-
denaturaliz|e, -is|e ˌdiːˈnætʃ.ᵊr.ᵊl.aɪz **-es** -ɪz **-ing** -ɪŋ **-ed** -d
denatur|e ˌdiːˈneɪ.tʃər (US) -tʃɚ **-es** -z **-ing** -ɪŋ **-ed** -d
Denbigh ˈden.bi, ˈdem- (US) ˈden- **-shire** -ʃər, -ˌʃɪər (US) -ʃɚ, -ˌʃɪr
Denby ˈden.bi, ˈdem- (US) ˈden-
Dench dentʃ
dendrite ˈden.draɪt **-s** -s
dendritic denˈdrɪt.ɪk (US) -ˈdrɪţ- **-al** -ᵊl
dendroid ˈden.drɔɪd
dendrology denˈdrɒl.ə.dʒi (US) -ˈdrɑː.lə-
dendron ˈden.drən (US) -drən, -drɑːn **-s** -z
dene (D) diːn **-s** -z
Deneb ˈden.eb
Denebola dɪˈneb.ə.lə, denˈeb-, dəˈneb-
Deneuve dəˈnɜːv
dengue ˈdeŋ.gi, -geɪ
Deng Xiaoping ˌdeŋ.ʃaʊˈpɪŋ (US) ˌdʌŋ-, ˌdeŋ-
Denham ˈden.əm
Denholm *place in West Yorkshire:* ˈden.hɒlm (US) -hoʊlm
Denholm(e) *name:* ˈden.əm
Denia ˈdiː.ni.ə **-s** -z
deniable dɪˈnaɪ.ə.bl̩, də- (US) dɪ-
denial dɪˈnaɪ.əl, də- (US) dɪ- **-s** -z
denier *coin:* ˈden.i.ər, -eɪ; dəˈnɪər (US) dəˈnɪr **-s** -z
denier *thickness of yarn:* ˈden.i.ər, -eɪ (US) ˈden.jɚ
denier *person who denies:* dɪˈnaɪ.ər, də- (US) dɪˈnaɪ.ɚ **-s** -z
deni|grate ˈden.ɪ|.greɪt, ˈ-ə- **-grates** -greɪts **-grating** -greɪ.tɪŋ (US) -greɪ.ţɪŋ **-grated** -greɪ.tɪd (US) -greɪ.ţɪd
denigration ˌden.ɪˈgreɪ.ʃᵊn, -əˈ-
denim ˈden.ɪm, -əm **-s** -z
De Niro dəˈnɪə.rəʊ (US) -ˈnɪr.oʊ
Denis ˈden.ɪs
Denise dəˈniːz, denˈiːz, dɪˈniːz, -ˈniːs (US) dəˈniːs, denˈiːs, dɪˈniːs, -ˈniːz
Denison ˈden.ɪ.sᵊn
denizen ˈden.ɪ.zᵊn, ˈ-ə- **-s** -z
Denktash ˈdeŋk.tæʃ (US) -tɑːʃ
Denman ˈden.mən, ˈdem- (US) ˈden-
Denmark ˈden.mɑːk, ˈdem- (US) ˈden.mɑːrk
Denning ˈden.ɪŋ
Dennis ˈden.ɪs
Dennison ˈden.ɪ.sᵊn
Denny ˈden.i **-s** -z
denomi|nate dɪˈnɒm.ɪ|.neɪt, də-, ˈ-ə- (US) dɪˈnɑː.mə- **-nates** -neɪts **-nating** -neɪ.tɪŋ (US) -neɪ.ţɪŋ **-nated** -neɪ.tɪd (US) -neɪ.ţɪd
denomination dɪˌnɒm.ɪˈneɪ.ʃᵊn, də-, -əˈ- (US) dɪˌnɑː.məˈ- **-s** -z
denominational dɪˌnɒm.ɪˈneɪ.ʃᵊn.ᵊl, də-, -əˈ- (US) dɪˌnɑː.məˈ-
denominationalism dɪˌnɒm.ɪˈneɪ.ʃᵊn.ᵊl.ɪ.zᵊm, də-, -əˈ- (US) dɪˌnɑː.məˈ-
denominative dɪˈnɒm.ɪ.nə.tɪv, də-, ˈ-ə- (US) dɪˈnɑː.mə.nə.ţɪv
denominator dɪˈnɒm.ɪ.neɪ.tər, də-, ˈ-ə- (US) dɪˈnɑː.mə.neɪ.ţɚ **-s** -z
denotation ˌdiː.nəʊˈteɪ.ʃᵊn (US) -noʊˈ-, -nəˈ- **-s** -z
denotative dɪˈnəʊ.tə.tɪv, də-; ˈdiː.nəʊ.teɪ- (US) ˈdiː.noʊ.teɪ.ţɪv; dɪˈnoʊ.ţə-
de|note dɪ|ˈnəʊt, də- (US) dɪ|ˈnoʊt **-notes** -ˈnəʊts (US) -ˈnoʊts **-noting** -ˈnəʊ.tɪŋ (US) -ˈnoʊ.ţɪŋ **-noted** -ˈnəʊ.tɪd (US) -ˈnoʊ.ţɪd
dénouement deɪˈnuː.mɑ̃ːŋ, dɪ-, də- (US) ˌdeɪ.nuːˈmɑ̃ːŋ
dénouements deɪˈnuː.mɑ̃ːŋ, dɪ-, də-, -mɑ̃ːŋz (US) ˌdeɪ.nuːˈmɑ̃ːŋ, -ˈmɑ̃ːŋz
denounc|e dɪˈnaʊnts, də- (US) dɪ- **-es** -ɪz **-ing** -ɪŋ **-ed** -t **-er/s** -ər/z (US) -ɚ/z **-ement/s** -mənt/s
de novo deɪˈnəʊ.vəʊ, diː-, də- (US) -ˈnoʊ.voʊ
dens|e dents **-er** -ər (US) -ɚ **-est** -ɪst, -əst **-ely** -li **-eness** -nəs, -nɪs
densit|y ˈdent.sɪ.t|i, -sə- (US) -sə.ţ|i **-ies** -iz
dent (D) dent **-s** -s **-ing** -ɪŋ **-ed** -ɪd
dental ˈden.tᵊl **-s** -z **ˈdental ˌfloss; ˈdental ˌsurgeon**
dentaliz|e, -is|e ˈden.tᵊl.aɪz (US) -ţə.laɪz **-es** -ɪz **-ing** -ɪŋ **-ed** -d
dentate ˈden.teɪt
dentated denˈteɪ.tɪd, ˈden.teɪ- (US) -ţɪd
denticle ˈden.tɪ.kl̩ (US) -ţɪ- **-s** -z
dentifric|e ˈden.tɪ.friːs, -tə-, -frɪs (US) -ţə.frɪs **-es** -ɪz
dentil ˈden.tɪl, -tᵊl (US) -tᵊl **-s** -z
dentilingual ˌden.tiˈlɪŋ.gwəl (US) -ţiˈ- **-s** -z
dentine ˈden.tiːn
dentist ˈden.tɪst (US) -ţɪst **-s** -s
dentistry ˈden.tɪ.stri, -tə- (US) -ţɪ-
dentition denˈtɪʃ.ᵊn
Denton ˈden.tən (US) -tᵊn
denture ˈden.tʃər (US) ˈdent.ʃɚ **-s** -z
denudation ˌdiː.njuːˈdeɪ.ʃᵊn, ˌden.juːˈ- (US) ˌdiː.nuːˈ-, -njuːˈ-; ˌden.juːˈ- **-s** -z
denud|e dɪˈnjuːd, də-, ˌdiː- (US) dɪˈnuːd, ˌdiː-, -ˈnjuːd **-es** -z **-ing** -ɪŋ **-ed** -ɪd
denunci|ate dɪˈnʌnt.si|.eɪt, də-, -ʃi- (US) dɪˈnʌnt.si- **-ates** -eɪts **-ating** -eɪ.tɪŋ (US) -eɪ.ţɪŋ **-ated** -eɪ.tɪd (US) -eɪ.ţɪd **-ator/s** -eɪ.tər/z (US) -eɪ.ţɚ/z
denunciation dɪˌnʌnt.siˈeɪ.ʃᵊn, də-, -ʃiˈ- (US) dɪˌnʌnt.siˈ- **-s** -z
denunciatory dɪˈnʌnt.si.ə.tᵊr.i, də-, -ʃi-, -tri (US) dɪˈnʌnt.si.ə.tɔːr.i
Denver ˈden.vər (US) -vɚ
den|y dɪˈn|aɪ, də- (US) dɪ- **-ies** -aɪz **-ying** -aɪ.ɪŋ **-ied** -aɪd **-ier/s** -aɪ.ər/z (US) -aɪ.ɚ/z
Denys ˈden.ɪs
Denzel ˈden.zᵊl, -zel, -zɪl, ˌdenˈzel
Denzil ˈden.zɪl, -zᵊl (US) -zᵊl
deodand ˈdiː.əʊ.dænd (US) ˈ-ə- **-s** -z
deodar ˈdiː.əʊ.dɑːr (US) -ə.dɑːr **-s** -z
deodorant diˈəʊ.dᵊr.ᵊnt (US) -ˈoʊ- **-s** -s
deodorization, -isa- diˌəʊ.dᵊr.aɪˈzeɪ.ʃᵊn, -ɪˈ- (US) -oʊ.dɚ.ɪˈ- **-s** -z

deodoriz|e, -is|e di'əʊ.dᵊr.aɪz US -'oʊ.də.raɪz **-es** -ɪz **-ing** -ɪŋ **-ed** -d **-er/s** -əʳ/z US -ɚ/z

deontic di'ɒn.tɪk, diː-, deɪ- US -'ɑːn.t̬ɪk

deoxidization, -isa- di,ɒk.sɪ.daɪ'zeɪ.ʃᵊn, ,diː-, -sə-, -dɪ'- US -,ɑːk.sə.dɪ'- **-s** -z

deoxidiz|e, -is|e di'ɒk.sɪ.daɪz, ,diː-, -sə- US -'ɑːk.sə- **-es** -ɪz **-ing** -ɪŋ **-ed** -d **-er/s** -əʳ/z US -ɚ/z

Depardieu ,dep.ɑː'djɜː, də.pɑː'-; 'dep.ɑː.djɜː US ,dep.ɑːr'djɜː, '---

de|part dɪ|'pɑːt, də- US dɪ|'pɑːrt **-parts** -'pɑːts US -'pɑːrts **-parting** -'pɑː.tɪŋ US -'pɑːr.t̬ɪŋ **-parted** -'pɑː.tɪd US -'pɑːr.t̬ɪd

department dɪ'pɑːt.mənt, də- US dɪ'pɑːrt- **-s** -s **de'partment ,store**

departmental ,diː.pɑːt'men.tᵊl US -pɑːrt'men.t̬ᵊl **-ism** -ɪ.zᵊm

departure dɪ'pɑː.tʃəʳ, də- US dɪ'pɑːr.tʃɚ **-s** -z **de'parture ,lounge**

depast|ure ,diː'pɑːs.tʃ|əʳ US -'pæs.tʃ|ɚ **-ures** -əz US -ɚz **-uring** -ᵊr.ɪŋ **-ured** -əd US -ɚd

depend dɪ'pend, də- US dɪ- **-s** -z **-ing** -ɪŋ **-ed** -ɪd

dependability dɪ,pen.də'bɪl.ə.ti, də-, -ɪ.ti US dɪ,pen.də'bɪl.ə.t̬i

dependab|le dɪ'pen.də.b|l̩, də-, dɪ- **-ly** -li **-leness** -l̩.nəs, -nɪs

dependant dɪ'pen.dənt, də- US dɪ- **-s** -s

dependenc|e dɪ'pen.dənts, də- US dɪ- **-y** -i **-ies** -iz

dependent dɪ'pen.dənt, də- US dɪ- **-s** -s **-ly** -li

De Pere dɪ'pɪəʳ, də- US -'pɪr

depersonaliz|e, is|e ,diː'pɜː.sᵊn.ᵊl.aɪz US -'pɝː- **-es** -ɪz **-ing** -ɪŋ **-ed** -d

Depew dɪ'pjuː, də-

depict dɪ'pɪkt, də- US dɪ- **-s** -s **-ing** -ɪŋ **-ed** -ɪd

depiction dɪ'pɪk.ʃᵊn, də- US dɪ- **-s** -z

depi|late 'dep.ɪ|.leɪt, '-ə- **-lates** -leɪts **-lating** -leɪ.tɪŋ US -leɪ.t̬ɪŋ **-lated** -leɪ.tɪd US -leɪ.t̬ɪd

depilation ,dep.ɪ'leɪ.ʃᵊn, -ə'-

depilator 'dep.ɪ.leɪ.təʳ, '-ə- US -t̬ɚ **-s** -z

depilator|y dɪ'pɪl.ə.tᵊr|.i, də-, -tr|i US dɪ'pɪl.ə.tɔːr|.i **-ies** -iz

deplan|e ,diː'pleɪn **-es** -z **-ing** -ɪŋ **-ed** -d

de|plete dɪ|'pliːt, də- US dɪ- **-pletes** -'pliːts **-pleting** -'pliː.tɪŋ US -'pliː.t̬ɪŋ **-pleted** -'pliː.tɪd US -'pliː.t̬ɪd

depletion dɪ'pliː.ʃᵊn, də- US dɪ- **-s** -z

deplet|ive dɪ'pliː.t|ɪv, də- US dɪ'pliː.t̬|ɪv **-ory** -ᵊr.i

deplorab|le dɪ'plɔː.rə.b|l̩, də- US dɪ'plɔːr.ə- **-ly** -li **-leness** -l̩.nəs, -nɪs

deplor|e dɪ'plɔːʳ, də- US dɪ'plɔːr **-es** -z **-ing** -ɪŋ **-ed** -d

deploy dɪ'plɔɪ, də- US dɪ- **-s** -z **-ing** -ɪŋ **-ed** -d

deployment dɪ'plɔɪ.mənt, də-, dɪ- **-s** -s

depolarization, -isa- diː,pəʊ.lᵊr.aɪ'zeɪ.ʃᵊn, ,diː.pəʊ-, -ɪ'- US diː,poʊ.lɚ.ɪ'-

depolariz|e, -is|e ,diː'pəʊ.lᵊr.aɪz US -'poʊ.lə.raɪz **-es** -ɪz **-ing** -ɪŋ **-ed** -d

depoliticization ,diː.pə,lɪt.ɪ.saɪ'zeɪ.ʃᵊn, ,-ə-, -sɪ'- US ,-lɪt̬.ɪ.sɪ'-, ,-ə-

depoliticiz|e, -is|e ,diː.pə'lɪt.ɪ.saɪz, '-ə- US -'lɪt̬- **-es** -ɪz **-ing** -ɪŋ **-ed** -d

de Pompadour də'pɒm.pə.dɔːʳ, -dʊəʳ US -'pɑːm.pə.dɔːr

deponent dɪ'pəʊ.nənt, də- US dɪ'poʊ- **-s** -s

Depo-Provera® ,dep.əʊ.prəʊ'vɪə.rə US -oʊ.proʊ'ver.ə

depopu|late ,diː'pɒp.jə|.leɪt, -jʊ- US -'pɑː.pjə- **-lates** -leɪts **-lating** -leɪ.tɪŋ US -leɪ.t̬ɪŋ **-lated** -leɪ.tɪd US -leɪ.t̬ɪd **-lator/s** -leɪ.təʳ/z US -leɪ.t̬ɚ/z

depopulation diː,pɒp.jə'leɪ.ʃᵊn, ,diː.pɒp-, -jʊ'- US diː,pɑː.pjə'-

de|port dɪ|'pɔːt, də- US dɪ|'pɔːrt **-ports** -'pɔːts US -'pɔːrts **-porting** -'pɔː.tɪŋ US -'pɔːr.t̬ɪŋ **-ported** -'pɔː.tɪd US -'pɔːr.t̬ɪd

deportation ,diː.pɔː'teɪ.ʃᵊn US -pɔːr'- **-s** -z

deportee ,diː.pɔː'tiː US -pɔːr'- **-s** -z

deportment dɪ'pɔːt.mənt, də- US dɪ'pɔːrt-

deposal dɪ'pəʊ.zᵊl, də- US dɪ'poʊ- **-s** -z

depos|e dɪ'pəʊz, də- US dɪ'poʊz **-es** -ɪz **-ing** -ɪŋ **-ed** -d

depos|it dɪ'pɒz|.ɪt, də- US dɪ'pɑː.z|ɪt **-its** -ɪts **-iting** -ɪ.tɪŋ US -ɪ.t̬ɪŋ **-ited** -ɪ.tɪd US -ɪ.t̬ɪd **de'posit ac,count**

depositar|y dɪ'pɒz.ɪ.tᵊr|.i, də-, '-ə- US dɪ'pɑː.zə.ter- **-ies** -iz

deposition ,dep.ə'zɪʃ.ᵊn, ,diː.pə'- **-s** -z

depositor dɪ'pɒz.ɪ.təʳ, də-, '-ə- US dɪ'pɑː.zə.t̬ɚ **-s** -z

depositor|y dɪ'pɒz.ɪ.tᵊr|.i, də-, '-ə-, -tr|i US dɪ'pɑː.zə.tɔːr|.i **-ies** -iz

depot 'dep.əʊ US 'diː.poʊ, 'dep.oʊ **-s** -z

Depp dep

depravation ,dep.rə'veɪ.ʃᵊn

deprav|e dɪ'preɪv, də- US dɪ- **-es** -z **-ing** -ɪŋ **-ed** -d **-edly** -d.li, -ɪd.li **-edness** -d.nəs, -ɪd.nəs, -nɪs

depravity dɪ'præv.ə.ti, də-, -ɪ.ti US dɪ'præv.ə.t̬i

depre|cate 'dep.rə|.keɪt, -rɪ- **-cates** -keɪts **-cating/ly** -keɪ.tɪŋ/li US -keɪ.t̬ɪŋ/li **-cated** -keɪ.tɪd US -keɪ.t̬ɪd **-cator/s** -keɪ.təʳ/z US -keɪ.t̬ɚ/z

deprecation ,dep.rə'keɪ.ʃᵊn, -prɪ'- **-s** -z

deprecatory 'dep.rə.kə.tᵊr.i, -rɪ-, -tri; ,dep.rə'keɪ- US 'dep.rə.kə.tɔːr.i

depreciable dɪ'priː.ʃi.ə.bl̩, də-, -si- US dɪ'priː.ʃi.ə.bl̩, '-ʃə.bl̩

depreci|ate dɪ'priː.ʃi|.eɪt, də-, -si- US dɪ'priː.ʃi- **-ates** -eɪts **-ating/ly** -eɪ.tɪŋ/li US -eɪ.t̬ɪŋ/li **-ated** -eɪ.tɪd US -eɪ.t̬ɪd **-ator/s** -eɪ.təʳ/z US -eɪ.t̬ɚ/z

depreciation dɪ,priː.ʃi'eɪ.ʃᵊn, də-, -si'- US dɪ,priː.ʃi'-

depreciatory dɪ'priː.ʃi.ə.tᵊr.i, də-, -si-, '-ʃə.tᵊr-, -tri US dɪ'priː.ʃi.ə.tɔːr.i, '-ʃə.tɔːr-

depre|date 'dep.rə|.deɪt, -rɪ- **-dates** -deɪts **-dating** -deɪ.tɪŋ US -deɪ.t̬ɪŋ **-dated** -deɪ.tɪd US -deɪ.t̬ɪd **-dator/s** -deɪ.təʳ/z US -deɪ.t̬ɚ/z

depredation ,dep.rə'deɪ.ʃᵊn, -rɪ'- **-s** -z

depredatory dɪ'pred.ə.tᵊr.i, də-, -tri; ,dep.rə'deɪ- US 'dep.rə.də.tɔːr.i, -deɪ.t̬ɚ-; dɪ'pred.ə.tɔːr-

depress dɪ'pres, də- US dɪ- **-es** -ɪz **-ing** -ɪŋ **-ed** -t **-or/s** -əʳ/z US -ɚ/z **-ant/s** -ᵊnt/s

depressing dɪ'pres.ɪŋ, də- US dɪ- **-ly** -li

depression dɪ'preʃ.ᵊn, də- US dɪ- **-s** -z

depressive dɪ'pres.ɪv, də- US dɪ- **-s** -z

depressor dɪ'pres.əʳ, də- US dɪ'pres.ɚ **-s** -z

depressurization, -isation diː,preʃ.ᵊr.aɪ'zeɪ.ʃᵊn, ,diː.preʃ-, -ɪ'- US diː,preʃ.ɚ.ɪ'-

depressuriz|e, -is|e ,diː'preʃ.ᵊr.aɪz US -ə.raɪz **-es** -ɪz **-ing** -ɪŋ **-ed** -d

deprivation ,dep.rɪ'veɪ.ʃᵊn, -rə'-; ,diː.praɪ'- **-s** -z

depriv|e dɪ'praɪv, də- US dɪ- **-es** -z **-ing** -ɪŋ **-ed** -d

de profundis ,deɪ.prɒf'ʊn.diːs, -prə'fʊn- US -proʊ'fʊn.dɪs

deprogram ,diː'prəʊ.græm US -'proʊ- **-s** -z **-(m)ing** -ɪŋ **-(m)ed** -d

deprogramm|e ,diː'prəʊ.græm US -'proʊ- **-s** -z **-ing** -ɪŋ **-er** -d

dept *(abbrev. for* **department***)* dɪ'pɑːt.mənt, də- US dɪ'pɑːrt-

Deptford 'det.fəd, 'dep.fəd US -fɚd

depth depθ **-s** -s **'depth ,charge**

deputation ,dep.jə'teɪ.ʃᵊn, -jʊ'- US -jə'- **-s** -z

de|pute dɪ|'pjuːt, də- US dɪ- **-putes** -'pjuːts **-puting** -'pjuː.tɪŋ US -'pjuː.t̬ɪŋ **-puted** -'pjuː.tɪd US -'pjuː.t̬ɪd

deputiz|e, -is|e 'dep.jə.taɪz, -jʊ- **-es** -ɪz **-ing** -ɪŋ **-ed** -d

deput|y 'dep.jə.t|i, -jʊ- US -t̬|i **-ies** -iz

De Quincey də'kwɪnt.si, dɪ-

deraci|nate dɪ'ræs.ɪ|.neɪt, ,diː-, '-ə- **-nates** -neɪts **-nating** -neɪ.tɪŋ US -neɪ.t̬ɪŋ **-nated** -neɪ.tɪd, -neɪ.t̬ɪd

deracination diːˌræs.ɪˈneɪ.ʃᵊn, ˌdiː.ræs-, -əˈ- US diːˌræs-
derail dɪˈreɪl, ˌdiː- **-s** -z **-ing** -ɪŋ **-ed** -d
derailleur dɪˈreɪ.ljəʳ, də-, -ləʳ US dɪˈreɪ.lɚ
derailment dɪˈreɪl.mənt, ˌdiː- **-s** -s
derang|e dɪˈreɪndʒ, də- US dɪ- **-es** -ɪz **-ing** -ɪŋ **-ed** -d **-ement/s** -mənt/s
de|rate ˌdiːˈreɪt **-rates** -ˈreɪts **-rating** -ˈreɪ.tɪŋ US -ˈreɪ.t̬ɪŋ **-rated** -ˈreɪ.tɪd US -ˈreɪ.t̬ɪd
deration ˌdiːˈræʃ.ᵊn **-s** -z **-ing** -ɪŋ **-ed** -d
derb|y ˈdɑː.b|i US ˈdɝː- **-ies** -iz
Der|by ˈdɑː|.bi US ˈdɑːr-, ˈdɝː- **-byshire** -bɪ.ʃəʳ, -ˌʃɪəʳ US -ʃɚ, -ˌʃɪr
Note: American pronunciation uses /ˈdɑːr-/ for British references.
Derbys. *(abbrev. for* **Derbyshire***)* ˈdɑː.bɪ.ʃəʳ, -ˌʃɪəʳ US ˈdɑːr.bɪ.ʃɚ, ˈdɝː-, -ˌʃɪr
Note: American pronunciation uses /ˈdɑːr-/ for British references.
deregu|late ˌdiːˈreg.jə|.leɪt, -jʊ- US -jə- **-lates** -leɪts **-lating** -leɪ.tɪŋ US -leɪ.t̬ɪŋ **-lated** -leɪ.tɪd US -leɪ.t̬ɪd
deregulation ˌdiː.reg.jəˈleɪ.ʃᵊn, -jʊˈ- US -jəˈ-
Dereham ˈdɪə.rəm US ˈdɪr.əm
Derek ˈder.ɪk
derelict ˈder.ə.lɪkt, ˈ-ɪ- **-s** -s
dereliction ˌder.əˈlɪk.ʃᵊn, -ɪˈ-
derequisition diːˌrek.wɪˈzɪʃ.ᵊn, ˌdiː.rek-, -wəˈ- US diːˌrek- **-s** -z **-ing** -ɪŋ **-ed** -d
De Reszke dəˈres.ki
Derg(h) dɜːg US dɝːg
Derham ˈder.əm
derid|e dɪˈraɪd, də- US dɪ- **-es** -z **-ing/ly** -ɪŋ/li **-ed** -ɪd **-er/s** -əʳ/z US -ɚ/z
de rigueur də.rɪˈgɜːʳ, ˌdeɪ-, ˌdiː-, -riːˈ- US -ˈgɝː
Dering ˈdɪə.rɪŋ US ˈdɪr.ɪŋ
derision dɪˈrɪʒ.ᵊn, də- US dɪ-
derisive dɪˈraɪ.sɪv, dəˈraɪ-, -zɪv, -ˈrɪz.ɪv US dɪˈraɪ.sɪv, -zɪv **-ly** -li **-ness** -nəs, -nɪs
derisory dɪˈraɪ.sᵊr.i, də-, -zᵊr- US dɪˈraɪ-
derivation ˌder.ɪˈveɪ.ʃᵊn, -əˈ- **-s** -z **-al** -ᵊl
derivative dɪˈrɪv.ə.tɪv, də- US dɪˈrɪv.ə.t̬ɪv **-s** -z **-ly** -li
deriv|e dɪˈraɪv, də- US dɪ- **-es** -z **-ing** -ɪŋ **-ed** -d **-able** -ə.bl̩
d'Erlanger ˌdeə.lɑ̃ːnˈʒeɪ US ˌder.lɑːnˈ-
derm dɜːm US dɝːm **-al** -ᵊl
-derm -dɜːm US -dɝːm
Note: Suffix. Does not normally carry stress, e.g. **pachyderm** /ˈpæk.ɪ.dɜːm US -ə.dɝːm/.
dermabrasion ˌdɜː.məˈbreɪ.ʒᵊn US ˌdɝː-
-dermal -dɜː.mᵊl US -dɝː-
Note: Suffix. May or may not carry stress, e.g. **epidermal** /ˌep.ɪˈdɜː.mᵊl US -ˈdɝː-/; see individual entries.
dermatitis ˌdɜː.məˈtaɪ.tɪs US ˌdɝː.məˈtaɪ.t̬ɪs
dermatolog|y ˌdɜː.məˈtɒl.ə.dʒ|i US ˌdɝː.məˈtɑː.lə- **-ist/s** -ɪst/s
dermatos|is ˌdɜː.məˈtəʊ.s|ɪs US ˌdɝː.məˈtoʊ- **-es** -iːz
dermis ˈdɜː.mɪs US ˈdɝː-
Dermot(t) ˈdɜː.mət US ˈdɝː-
dernier cri ˌdɜː.ni.eɪˈkriː, ˌdeə- US ˌder.njeɪˈ-, ˌdɝː-
dero|gate ˈder.əʊ|.geɪt, ˈdiː.rəʊ- US ˈder.ə- **-gates** -geɪts **-gating** -geɪ.tɪŋ US -geɪ.t̬ɪŋ **-gated** -geɪ.tɪd US -geɪ.t̬ɪd
derogation ˌder.əʊˈgeɪ.ʃᵊn, ˌdiː.rəʊˈ- US ˌder.əˈ-
derogator|y dɪˈrɒg.ə.tᵊr|.i, də-, -tr|i US dɪˈrɑː.gə.tɔːr|.i **-ily** -ᵊl.i, -ɪ.li **-iness** -ɪ.nəs, -ɪ.nɪs
Deronda dəˈrɒn.də, dɪ- US dəˈrɑːn-
derrick (D) ˈder.ɪk **-s** -s
Derrida dəˈriː.də, derˈiː-; ˈder.ɪ- US ˈder.iː.dɑː
derrière ˈder.i.eəʳ, ˌ--ˈ- US ˌder.iˈer, ˈ--- **-s** -z
derring-do ˌder.ɪŋˈduː, ˌdeə.rɪŋˈ- US ˌder.ɪŋˈ-
derringer (D) ˈder.ɪn.dʒəʳ, -ᵊn- US -dʒɚ **-s** -z
Derry ˈder.i
derv dɜːv US dɝːv
dervish (D) ˈdɜː.vɪʃ US ˈdɝː- **-es** -ɪz
Dervla ˈdɜːv.lə US ˈdɝːv-
Derwent ˈdɜː.wənt, ˈdɑː-, -went, -wɪnt US ˈdɝː-, ˈdɑːr- **ˈDerwent ˌWater**
Note: /ˈdɑː- US ˈdɑːr-/ is the normal pronunciation for the Baron.
Des dez US des
DES ˌdiː.iːˈes
Desai desˈaɪ; ˈdeɪ.saɪ
desali|nate ˌdiːˈsæl.ɪ|.neɪt, ˈ-ə- **-nates** -neɪts **-nating** -neɪ.tɪŋ US -neɪ.t̬ɪŋ **-nated** -neɪ.tɪd US -neɪ.t̬ɪd
desalination diːˌsæl.ɪˈneɪ.ʃᵊn, ˌdiː.sæl-, -əˈ- US diːˌsæl- **-s** -z
desalinization, -isa- diːˌsæl.ɪ.naɪˈzeɪ.ʃᵊn, ˌdiː.sæl-, ˌ-ə-, -nɪˈ- US diːˌsæl.ə.nɪˈ-
desaliniz|e, -is|e ˌdiːˈsæl.ɪ.naɪz, ˈ-ə- **-es** -ɪz **-ing** -ɪŋ **-ed** -d
Desart ˈdez.ət US -ɚt
Desborough ˈdez.brə US -bɚ.oʊ, ˈ-brə
descal|e ˌdiːˈskeɪl **-es** -z **-ing** -ɪŋ **-ed** -d
descant *(n.)* ˈdes.kænt **-s** -s
descan|t *(v.)* dɪˈskæn|t, desˈkæn|t US ˈdes.kæn|t, -ˈ- **-ts** -ts **-ting** -tɪŋ US -t̬ɪŋ **-ted** -tɪd US -t̬ɪd
Descartes ˈdeɪ.kɑːt, deɪˈkɑːt US deɪˈkɑːrt
descend dɪˈsend, də- US dɪ- **-s** -z **-ing** -ɪŋ **-ed** -ɪd
descendant, descendent dɪˈsen.dənt, də- US dɪ- **-s** -s
descender dɪˈsen.dəʳ, də- US dɪˈsen.dɚ **-s** -z
descent dɪˈsent, də- US dɪ- **-s** -s
describ|e dɪˈskraɪb, də- US dɪ- **-es** -z **-ing** -ɪŋ **-ed** -d **-er/s** -əʳ/z US -ɚ/z **-able** -ə.bl̩
description dɪˈskrɪp.ʃᵊn, də- US dɪ- **-s** -z
descriptive dɪˈskrɪp.tɪv, də- US dɪ- **-ly** -li **-ness** -nəs, -nɪs
descriptiv|ism dɪˈskrɪp.tɪ.v|ɪ.zᵊm, də- US dɪ- **-ist** -ɪst
descr|y dɪˈskr|aɪ, də- US dɪ- **-ies** -aɪz **-ying** -aɪ.ɪŋ **-ied** -aɪd
Desdemona ˌdez.dɪˈməʊ.nə, -dəˈ- US -dəˈmoʊ-
dese|crate ˈdes.ɪ|.kreɪt, ˈ-ə- **-crates** -kreɪts **-crating** -kreɪ.tɪŋ US -kreɪ.t̬ɪŋ **-crated** -kreɪ.tɪd US -kreɪ.t̬ɪd **-crator/s** -kreɪ.təʳ/z US -kreɪ.t̬ɚ/z
desecration ˌdes.ɪˈkreɪ.ʃᵊn, -əˈ- **-s** -z
deseed ˌdiːˈsiːd **-s** -z **-ing** -ɪŋ **-ed** -ɪd
desegre|gate ˌdiːˈseg.rɪ|.geɪt, -rə- **-gates** -geɪts **-gating** -geɪ.tɪŋ US -geɪ.t̬ɪŋ **-gated** -geɪ.tɪd US -geɪ.t̬ɪd
desegregation diːˌseg.rɪˈgeɪ.ʃᵊn, ˌdiː.seg-, -rəˈ- US diːˌseg-
deselect ˌdiː.səˈlekt, -sɪˈ- **-s** -s **-ing** -ɪŋ **-ed** -ɪd
deselection ˌdiː.səˈlek.ʃᵊn, -sɪˈ-
de Selincourt dəˈsel.ɪŋ.kɔːt, -ɪn- US -kɔːrt
desensitization diːˌsen*t*.sɪ.taɪˈzeɪ.ʃᵊn, ˌdiː.sen*t*-, -sə-, -tɪˈ- US diːˌsen*t*.sɪ.tɪˈ-, ˌ-sə-
desensitiz|e, -is|e ˌdiːˈsen*t*.sɪ.taɪz, -sə- **-es** -ɪz **-ing** -ɪŋ **-ed** -d
desert *(n. adj.) dry place:* ˈdez.ət US -ɚt **-s** -s ˌ**desert** ˈ**island**; ˌ**desert** ˈ**rat**
desert *(n.) what is deserved:* dɪˈzɜːt, də- US dɪˈzɝːt **-s** -s **get one's** ˌ**just de**ˈ**serts**
de|sert *(v.)* dɪ|ˈzɜːt, də- US dɪ|ˈzɝːt **-serts** -ˈzɜːts US -ˈzɝːts **-serting** -ˈzɜː.tɪŋ US -ˈzɝː.t̬ɪŋ **-serted** -ˈzɜː.tɪd US -ˈzɝː.t̬ɪd **-serter/s** -ˈzɜː.təʳ/z US -ˈzɝː.t̬ɚ/z
desertification dɪˌzɜː.tɪ.fɪˈkeɪ.ʃᵊn, də-, -tə- US dɪˌzɝː.t̬ə-
desertion dɪˈzɜː.ʃᵊn, də- US dɪˈzɝː- **-s** -z
deserv|e dɪˈzɜːv, də- US dɪˈzɝːv **-es** -z **-ing/ly** -ɪŋ/li **-ed** -d **-edly** -ɪd.li
desex ˌdiːˈseks **-es** -ɪz **-ing** -ɪŋ **-ed** -t

desexualiz|e, -is|e diːˈsek.ʃuə.laɪz, -ʃu.əl.aɪz, -sjuə.laɪz, -sju.əl.aɪz (US) -ʃu.ə.laɪz **-es** -ɪz **-ing** -ɪŋ **-ed** -d
deshabille ˌdez.æbˈiːl, ˌdeɪ.zæbˈ-, ˌdes.æbˈ-, -əˈbiːl, ˈ--- (US) ˌdes.æbˈ-, ˌdez-; ˈdɪs.ə.biːl
déshabillé ˌdeɪ.zæbˈiː.eɪ, ˌdez.æb-, ˌdes-, -əˈbiː-, -ˈbiːl
desiccant ˈdes.ɪ.kənt, ˈ-ə- **-s** -s
desic|cate ˈdes.ɪ|.keɪt, ˈ-ə- **-cates** -keɪts **-cating** -keɪ.tɪŋ (US) -keɪ.t̬ɪŋ **-cated** -keɪ.tɪd (US) -keɪ.t̬ɪd
desiccation ˌdes.ɪˈkeɪ.ʃən, -əˈ-
desiccative ˈdes.ɪ.kə.tɪv; desˈɪk.ə-, dɪˈsɪk- (US) ˈdes.ɪ.keɪ.t̬ɪv; dəˈsɪk.ə-
desiccator ˈdes.ɪ.keɪ.təʳ, ˈ-ə- (US) -t̬ɚ **-s** -z
desider|ate dɪˈzɪd.ər|.eɪt, də-, -ˈsɪd- (US) dɪˈsɪd.ə.r|eɪt, -ˈzɪd- **-ates** -eɪts **-ating** -eɪ.tɪŋ (US) -eɪ.t̬ɪŋ **-ated** -eɪ.tɪd (US) -eɪ.t̬ɪd
desideration dɪˌzɪd.əˈreɪ.ʃən, də-, -ˌsɪd- (US) dɪˌsɪd-, -ˌzɪd- **-s** -z
desiderative dɪˈzɪd.ər.ə.tɪv, də-, -ˈsɪd- (US) dɪˈsɪd.ɚ.ə.t̬ɪv, -ˈzɪd-
desiderat|um dɪˌzɪd.əˈrɑː.t|əm, də-, -ˌsɪd-, -ˈreɪ- (US) dɪˌsɪd.əˈrɑː.t̬|əm, -ˌzɪd-, -ˈreɪ- **-a** -ə
design dɪˈzaɪn, də- (US) dɪ- **-s** -z **-ing** -ɪŋ **-ed** -d **-edly** -ɪd.li **-able** -ə.bl̩
designate (*adj.*) ˈdez.ɪg.neɪt, -nɪt, -nət
desig|nate (*v.*) ˈdez.ɪg|.neɪt **-nates** -neɪts **-nating** -neɪ.tɪŋ (US) -neɪ.t̬ɪŋ **-nated** -neɪ.tɪd (US) -neɪ.t̬ɪd **-nator/s** -neɪ.təʳ/z (US) -neɪ.t̬ɚ/z
designation ˌdez.ɪgˈneɪ.ʃən **-s** -z
designer dɪˈzaɪ.nəʳ, də- (US) dɪˈzaɪ.nɚ **-s** -z
desinenc|e ˈdes.ɪ.nənts, ˈdez-, -ən.ənts **-es** -ɪz
desirability dɪˌzaɪə.rəˈbɪl.ə.ti, də-, -ɪ.ti (US) dɪˌzaɪ.rəˈbɪl.ə.t̬i
desirab|le dɪˈzaɪə.rə.b|l̩, də- (US) dɪˈzaɪ- **-ly** -li **-leness** -l̩.nəs, -nɪs
desir|e dɪˈzaɪəʳ, də (US) dɪˈzaɪɚ **-es** -z **-ing** -ɪŋ **-ed** -d **-er/s** -əʳ/z (US) -ɚ/z
Désirée deɪˈzɪə.reɪ, dezˈɪə- (US) ˌdez.əˈreɪ
desirous dɪˈzaɪə.rəs, də- (US) dɪˈzaɪ.rəs **-ly** -li
desist dɪˈsɪst, də-, dɪˈzɪst **-s** -s **-ing** -ɪŋ **-ed** -ɪd
desistance dɪˈsɪs.tənts, dəˈ-, dɪˈzɪs-
desk desk **-s** -s ˈ**desk** ˌ**job**
de-skill ˌdiːˈskɪl **-s** -z **-ing** -ɪŋ **-ed** -d
desktop ˈdesk.tɒp (US) -tɑːp ˌ**desktop** ˈ**publishing**
Des Moines dəˈmɔɪn, dɪ-, -ˈmɔɪnz (US) -ˈmɔɪn
Desmond ˈdez.mənd
desolate (*adj.*) ˈdes.əl.ət, ˈdez-, -ɪt **-ly** -li **-ness** -nəs, -nɪs
desol|ate (*v.*) ˈdes.əl|.eɪt, ˈdez.ə.l|eɪt **-ates** -eɪts **-ating** -eɪ.tɪŋ (US) -eɪ.t̬ɪŋ **-ated** -eɪ.tɪd (US) -eɪ.t̬ɪd **-ator/s** -eɪ.təʳ/z (US) -eɪ.t̬ɚ/z
desolation ˌdes.əlˈeɪ.ʃən, ˌdez- **-s** -z
de Soto dəˈsəu.təu (US) -ˈsou.tou
despair dɪˈspeəʳ, də- (US) dɪˈsper **-s** -z **-ing/ly** -ɪŋ/li **-ed** -d
Despard ˈdes.pəd, -pɑːd (US) -pɚd, -pɑːrd
despatch dɪˈspætʃ, də- (US) dɪ- **-es** -ɪz **-ing** -ɪŋ **-ed** -t **-er/s** -əʳ/z (US) -ɚ/z **des**ˈ**patch** ˌ**box; des**ˈ**patch** ˌ**rider**
desperado ˌdes.pəˈrɑː.dəu, -ˈreɪ- (US) -dou **-(e)s** -z
desperate ˈdes.pər.ət, -ɪt **-ly** -li **-ness** -nəs, -nɪs
desperation ˌdes.pəˈreɪ.ʃən
despicability dɪˌspɪk.əˈbɪl.ə.ti, də-, -ɪ.ti; ˌdes.pɪ.kəˈ- (US) dɪˌspɪk.əˈbɪl.ə.t̬i; ˌdes.pɪ.kəˈ-
despicab|le dɪˈspɪk.ə.b|l̩, də-; ˈdes.pɪ.kə- (US) dɪˈspɪk.ə-; ˈdes.pɪ.kə- **-ly** -li **-leness** -l̩.nəs, -nɪs
despis|e dɪˈspaɪz, də- (US) dɪ- **-es** -ɪz **-ing** -ɪŋ **-ed** -d **-er/s** -əʳ/z (US) -ɚ/z
despite dɪˈspaɪt, də- (US) dɪ-
despiteful dɪˈspaɪt.fəl, də-, -fʊl (US) dɪ- **-ly** -li
despoil dɪˈspɔɪl, də- (US) dɪ- **-s** -z **-ing** -ɪŋ **-ed** -d **-er/s** -əʳ/z (US) -ɚ/z
despoliation dɪˌspəu.liˈeɪ.ʃən, də-, -ˌspɒl.iˈ- (US) dɪˌspou.liˈ-
despond (D) dɪˈspɒnd, də- (US) dɪˈspɑːnd **-s** -z **-ing/ly** -ɪŋ/li **-ed** -ɪd
desponden|ce dɪˈspɒn.dən*t*|s, də- (US) dɪˈspɑːn- **-cy** -si
despondent dɪˈspɒn.dənt, də- (US) dɪˈspɑːn- **-ly** -li
despot ˈdes.pɒt, -pət (US) -pət **-s** -s
despotic dɪˈspɒt.ɪk, desˈpɒt-, dəˈspɒt- (US) desˈpɑː.t̬ɪk **-al** -əl **-ally** -əl.i, -li **-alness** -əl.nəs, -nɪs
despotism ˈdes.pə.tɪ.zəm **-s** -z
desqua|mate ˈdes.kwə|.meɪt **-mates** -meɪts **-mating** -meɪ.tɪŋ (US) -meɪ.t̬ɪŋ **-mated** -meɪ.tɪd (US) -meɪ.t̬ɪd
des res ˌdezˈrez
dessert dɪˈzɜːt, də- (US) dɪˈzɝːt **-s** -s **des**ˈ**sert** ˌ**wine, des**ˌ**sert** ˈ**wine**
dessertspoon dɪˈzɜːt.spuːn, də- (US) dɪˈzɝːt- **-s** -z
dessert|spoonful dɪˈzɜːt|ˌspuːn.fʊl, də- (US) dɪˈzɝːt- **-spoonsful** -ˌspuːnz.fʊl **-spoonfuls** -ˌspuːn.fʊlz
destabilization, -isa- ˌdiːˌsteɪ.bəl.aɪˈzeɪ.ʃən, dɪ-, -bɪ.laɪˈ- (US) -bəl.ɪˈ-, -bɪ.lɪˈ-
destabiliz|e, -is|e ˌdiːˈsteɪ.bəl.aɪz, dɪ-, -bɪ.laɪz **-es** -ɪz **-ing** -ɪŋ **-ed** -d
destination ˌdes.tɪˈneɪ.ʃən, -təˈ- **-s** -z
destin|e ˈdes.tɪn, -tən **-es** -z **-ing** -ɪŋ **-ed** -d
destin|y ˈdes.tɪ.n|i, -tən|.i **-ies** -iz
destitute ˈdes.tɪ.tjuːt, -tə- (US) -tuːt, -tjuːt **-ly** -li **-ness** -nəs, -nɪs
destitution ˌdes.tɪˈtjuː.ʃən, -təˈ- (US) -ˈtuː-, -ˈtjuː-
destroy dɪˈstrɔɪ, də- (US) dɪ- **-s** -z **-ing** -ɪŋ **-ed** -d
destroyer dɪˈstrɔɪ.əʳ, də- (US) dɪˈstrɔɪ.ɚ **-s** -z
destruct dɪˈstrʌkt, də- (US) dɪ- **-s** -s **-ing** -ɪŋ **-ed** -ɪd
destructibility dɪˌstrʌk.təˈbɪl.ə.ti, də-, -tɪˈ-, -ɪ.ti (US) dɪˌstrʌk.təˈbɪl.ə.t̬i, -tɪˈ-
destructible dɪˈstrʌk.tə.bl̩, də-, -tɪ- (US) dɪ-
destruction dɪˈstrʌk.ʃən, də- (US) dɪ- **-s** -z
destructive dɪˈstrʌk.tɪv, də- (US) dɪ- **-ly** -li **-ness** -nəs, -nɪs
destructor dɪˈstrʌk.təʳ, də- (US) dɪˈstrʌk.tɚ **-s** -z
desuetude dɪˈsjuː.ɪ.tjuːd, -tʃuːd; ˈdes.wɪ-, ˈdiː.swɪ- (US) ˈdes.wɪ.tuːd, -tjuːd; dɪˈsuː.ə-
desultor|y ˈdes.əl.tər|.i, ˈdez-, -tr|i (US) -tɔːr|.i **-ily** -əl.i, -ɪ.li **-iness** -ɪ.nəs, -ɪ.nɪs
Des Voeux deɪˈvɜː
detach dɪˈtætʃ, də- (US) dɪ- **-es** -ɪz **-ing** -ɪŋ **-ed** -t **-edly** -t.li, -ɪd.li **-able** -ə.bl̩
detachment dɪˈtætʃ.mənt, də- (US) dɪ- **-s** -s
detail ˈdiː.teɪl; dɪˈteɪl, də- (US) dɪˈteɪl; ˈdiː.teɪl **-s** -z **-ing** -ɪŋ **-ed** -d
detain dɪˈteɪn, də- (US) dɪ- **-s** -z **-ing** -ɪŋ **-ed** -d **-er/s** -əʳ/z (US) -ɚ/z
detainee ˌdiː.teɪˈniː; dɪˌteɪˈ-, də- (US) ˌdiː.teɪˈ- **-s** -z
detect dɪˈtekt, də- (US) dɪ- **-s** -s **-ing** -ɪŋ **-ed** -ɪd
detectab|le dɪˈtek.tə.b|l̩, də- (US) dɪ- **-ly** -li
detection dɪˈtek.ʃən, də- (US) dɪ- **-s** -z
detective dɪˈtek.tɪv, də- (US) dɪ- **-s** -z
detector dɪˈtek.təʳ, də- (US) dɪˈtek.tɚ **-s** -z
detent dɪˈtent, də- (US) dɪ- **-s** -s
détente ˈdeɪ.tɑ̃ːnt (US) deɪˈtɑːnt, ˈ--
detention dɪˈten.*t*ʃən, də- (US) dɪ- **-s** -z **de**ˈ**tention** ˌ**centre**
deter dɪˈtɜːʳ, də- (US) dɪˈtɝː **-s** -z **-ring** -ɪŋ **-red** -d
Deterding ˈdet.ə.dɪŋ (US) ˈdet̬.ɚ-
detergent dɪˈtɜː.dʒənt, də- (US) dɪˈtɝː- **-s** -s
deterior|ate dɪˈtɪə.ri.ər|.eɪt, də- (US) dɪˈtɪr.i.ə.r|eɪt **-ates** -eɪts **-ating** -eɪ.tɪŋ (US) -eɪ.t̬ɪŋ **-ated** -eɪ.tɪd (US) -eɪ.t̬ɪd
deterioration dɪˌtɪə.ri.əˈreɪ.ʃən, də- (US) dɪˌtɪr.i-
determinable dɪˈtɜː.mɪ.nə.bl̩, də-, -mən.ə- (US) dɪˈtɝː-

determinant dɪˈtɜː.mɪ.nənt, də- US dɪˈtɝː- **-s** -s
determinate dɪˈtɜː.mɪ.nət, də-, -nɪt US dɪˈtɝː- **-ly** -li **-ness** -nəs, -nɪs
determination dɪˌtɜː.mɪˈneɪ.ʃᵊn, də-, -məˈ- US dɪˌtɝː- **-s** -z
determinative dɪˈtɜː.mɪ.nə.tɪv, də-, -mᵊn.ə- US dɪˈtɝː.mɪ.neɪ.t̬ɪv, -nə-
determin|e dɪˈtɜː.mɪn, də-, -mən US dɪˈtɝː- **-es** -z **-ing** -ɪŋ **-ed/ly** -d/li
determined dɪˈtɜː.mɪnd, də- US dɪˈtɝː- **-ly** -li
determiner dɪˈtɜː.mɪ.nəʳ, də-, -mə- US dɪˈtɝː.mɪ.nɚ **-s** -z
determin|ism dɪˈtɜː.mɪ.nɪ.zᵊm, də-, -mə- US dɪˈtɝː- **-ist/s** -ɪst/s
deterrence dɪˈter.ᵊnts, də- US dɪ-
deterrent dɪˈter.ᵊnt, də- US dɪ- **-s** -s
detest dɪˈtest, də- US dɪ- **-s** -s **-ing** -ɪŋ **-ed** -ɪd
detestab|le dɪˈtes.tə.bl̩, də- US dɪ- **-ly** -li **-leness** -l̩.nəs, -nɪs
detestation ˌdiː.tesˈteɪ.ʃᵊn, dɪˌtes- US ˌdiː.tes-
dethron|e diːˈθrəʊn, ˌdiː-, də- US dɪˈθroʊn, ˌdiː- **-es** -z **-ing** -ɪŋ **-ed** -d **-ement** -mənt
detinue ˈdet.ɪ.njuː US -ᵊn.juː, -uː
Detlev ˈdet.lef US -ləf, -lef
Detmold ˈdet.məʊld US -moʊld
de Tocqueville dəˈtəʊk.vɪl, -ˈtɒk-, -viːl US -ˈtoʊk.vɪl, -ˈtɑːk-
deton|ate ˈdet.ᵊn|.eɪt **-ates** -eɪts **-ating** -eɪ.tɪŋ US -eɪ.t̬ɪŋ **-ated** -eɪ.tɪd US -eɪ.t̬ɪd
detonation ˌdet.ᵊnˈeɪ.ʃᵊn **-s** -z
detonator ˈdet.ᵊn.eɪ.təʳ US -t̬ɚ **-s** -z
detour ˈdiː.tʊəʳ, ˈdeɪ-, -tɔːʳ US ˈdiː.tʊr; -ˈ-, dɪ- **-s** -z
detox ˈdiː.tɒks, ˌdiːˈtɒks US diːˈtɑːks, ˈ-- **-es** -ɪz **-ing** -ɪŋ **-ed** -t
detoxi|cate ˌdiːˈtɒk.sɪ|.keɪt, dɪ-, -sə- US -ˈtɑːk- **-cates** -keɪts **-cating** -keɪ.tɪŋ US -keɪ.t̬ɪŋ **-cated** -keɪ.tɪd US -keɪ.t̬ɪd
detoxification diːˌtɒk.sɪ.fɪˈkeɪ.ʃᵊn, dɪ-, -sə-; ˌdiː.tɒk- US diːˌtɑːk-
detoxi|fy ˌdiːˈtɒk.sɪ|.faɪ, dɪ-, -sə- US ˌdiːˈtɑːk- **-fies** -faɪz **-fying** -faɪ.ɪŋ **-fied** -faɪd
detract dɪˈtrækt, də- US dɪ- **-s** -s **-ing/ly** -ɪŋ/li **-ed** -ɪd
detraction dɪˈtræk.ʃᵊn, də- US dɪ- **-s** -z
detract|ive dɪˈtræk.t|ɪv, də- US dɪ- **-ory** -ᵊr.i
detractor dɪˈtræk.təʳ, də- US dɪˈtræk.tɚ **-s** -z
detrain ˌdiːˈtreɪn **-s** -z **-ing** -ɪŋ **-ed** -d
detriment ˈdet.rɪ.mənt, -rə- **-s** -s
detrimental ˌdet.rɪˈmen.tᵊl, -rəˈ- US -t̬ᵊl
detrition dɪˈtrɪʃ.ᵊn, də- US dɪ-
detritus dɪˈtraɪ.təs, də- US dɪˈtraɪ.t̬əs
Detroit dəˈtrɔɪt, dɪ-
de trop dəˈtrəʊ US -ˈtroʊ
detrun|cate ˌdiːˈtrʌŋ|.keɪt, ˈ--- US ˌdiːˈtrʌŋ- **-cates** -keɪts **-cating** -keɪ.tɪŋ US -keɪ.t̬ɪŋ **-cated** -keɪ.tɪd US -keɪ.t̬ɪd
detruncation ˌdiː.trʌŋˈkeɪ.ʃᵊn **-s** -z
Dettol® ˈdet.ɒl, -ᵊl US -tɑːl, -t̬ᵊl
Dettori detˈɔː.ri US -ɔːr.i
detumescen|ce ˌdiː.tjuːˈmes.ᵊn|ts, -tjʊˈ- US -tuːˈ-, -tjuːˈ- **-t** -t
Deucalion djuːˈkeɪ.li.ən US duː-, djuː-
deuc|e djuːs, dʒuːs US duːs, djuːs **-es** -ɪz
deuc|ed djuːs|t, dʒuːs|t; ˈdjuː.s|ɪd, ˈdʒuː- US ˈduː.s|ɪd, ˈdjuː-; duːs|t, djuːs|t **-edly** -ɪd.li
deus ex machina ˌdeɪ.əs.eksˈmɑː.k.ɪ.nə, -ˈmæk-, ˌdiː-, -ʊs-;
deuterium djuːˈtɪə.ri.əm US duːˈtɪr.i-, djuː-
deuteronomic ˌdjuː.tᵊr.əˈnɒm.ɪk US ˌduː.t̬ɚ.əˈnɑː.mɪk, ˌdjuː-
Deuteronomy ˌdjuː.təˈrɒn.ə.mi US ˌduː.t̬əˈrɑː.nə-, ˌdjuː-
Deutsche Mark ˌdɔɪ.tʃəˈmɑːk US -ˈmɑːrk **-s** -s
deutschmark (D) ˈdɔɪtʃ.mɑːk US -mɑːrk **-s** -s
deutzia ˈdjuːt.si.ə, ˈdɔɪt- US ˈduːt-, ˈdjuːt- **-s** -z
deux chevaux ˌdɜː.ʃəˈvəʊ, -ʃɪˈ- US -ˈvoʊ
deva ˈdeɪ.və, ˈdiː.və **-s** -z
de Valera də.vəˈleə.rə, -ˈlɪə-; ˌdev.əˈ- US -ler.ə, -ˈlɪr-
de Valois dəˈvæl.wɑː
devaluation ˌdiː.væl.juˈeɪ.ʃᵊn; dɪˌvæl- US ˌdiː.væl- **-s** -z
devalu|e ˌdiːˈvæl.juː, dɪ- **-es** -z **-ing** -ɪŋ **-ed** -d
Devanagari ˌdeɪ.vəˈnɑː.gᵊr.i, ˌdev.əˈ-
Devant dəˈvænt, dɪ-
deva|state ˈdev.ə|.steɪt **-states** -steɪts **-stating/ly** -steɪ.tɪŋ/li US -steɪ.t̬ɪŋ/li **-stated** -steɪ.tɪd US -steɪ.t̬ɪd
devastation ˌdev.əˈsteɪ.ʃᵊn **-s** -z
develop dɪˈvel.əp, də- US dɪ- **-s** -s **-ing** -ɪŋ **-ed** -t **deˌveloping ˈcountry**
developer dɪˈvel.ə.pəʳ, də- US -pɚ **-s** -z
development dɪˈvel.əp.mənt, də- **-s** -s
developmental dɪˌvel.əpˈmen.tᵊl, də- US -t̬ᵊl **-ly** -li
Devenish ˈdev.ᵊn.ɪʃ
Deventer ˈdev.ᵊn.təʳ US -tɚ
De Vere dəˈvɪəʳ, dɪ- US -ˈvɪr
Devereux ˈdev.ə.ruː, -ruːks, -rɜː, -rəʊ, -reks, ˈ-ᵊr.ə US -ə.ruː, -rɝː, -rə, -uːks
Deveron ˈdev.ə.rᵊn US -ɚ.ᵊn
Devers ˈdiː.vəz, ˈdev.əz US ˈdiː.vɚz, ˈdev.ɚz
Devi ˈdeɪ.vi
devian|ce ˈdiː.vi.ən|ts **-cy** -si
deviant ˈdiː.vi.ənt **-s** -s
devi|ate ˈdiː.vi|.eɪt **-ates** -eɪts **-ating** -eɪ.tɪŋ US -eɪ.t̬ɪŋ **-ated** -eɪ.tɪd US -eɪ.t̬ɪd **-ator/s** -eɪ.təʳ/z US -eɪ.t̬ɚ/z
deviation ˌdiː.viˈeɪ.ʃᵊn **-s** -z
deviation|ism ˌdiː.viˈeɪ.ʃᵊn|.ɪ.zᵊm **-ist/s** -ɪst/s
devic|e dɪˈvaɪs, də- US dɪ- **-es** -ɪz **ˌleave someone to their ˌown deˈvices**
devil ˈdev.ᵊl **-s** -z **-(l)ing** -ɪŋ **-(l)ed** -d **ˌdevil's ˈadvocate; ˌdevil's ˈfood ˌcake, ˈdevil's food ˌcake** US **ˈdevil's food ˌcake; between the ˌdevil and the ˌdeep blue ˈsea; give the ˌdevil his ˈdue; ˌtalk of the ˈdevil**
devilfish ˈdev.ᵊl.fɪʃ **-es** -ɪz
devilish ˈdev.ᵊl.ɪʃ **-ly** -li **-ness** -nəs, -nɪs
devil-may-care ˌdev.ᵊl.meɪˈkeəʳ US -ˈker *stress shift:* ˌdevil-may-care ˈattitude
devilment ˈdev.ᵊl.mənt **-s** -s
devilr|y ˈdev.ᵊl.r|i **-ies** -iz
Devine dəˈvaɪn, dɪ-
devious ˈdiː.vi.əs **-ly** -li **-ness** -nəs, -nɪs
devis|e dɪˈvaɪz, də- US dɪ- **-es** -ɪz **-ing** -ɪŋ **-ed** -d **-er/s** -əʳ/z US -ɚ/z **-able** -ə.bl̩
devisee dɪˌvaɪˈziː, də-; ˌdev.ɪˈ- US dɪˌvaɪˈ-; ˌdev.əˈ- **-s** -z
devisor dɪˈvaɪ.zəʳ, də-; dəˌvaɪˈzɔːʳ, dɪ-; ˌdev.aɪˈ- US dɪˈvaɪ.zɚ; ˌdev.əˈzɔːr **-s** -z
devitalization, -isa- diːˌvaɪ.tᵊl.aɪˈzeɪ.ʃᵊn, ˌdiː.vaɪ-, -ɪˈ- US diːˌvaɪ.t̬ᵊl.ɪˈ-
devitaliz|e, -is|e ˌdiːˈvaɪ.tᵊl.aɪz US -t̬ᵊl- **-es** -ɪz **-ing** -ɪŋ **-ed** -d
Devizes dɪˈvaɪ.zɪz, də-, -zəz
Devlin ˈdev.lɪn, -lən
devocalization, -isa- diːˌvəʊ.kᵊl.aɪˈzeɪ.ʃᵊn, ˌdiː.vəʊ-, -ɪˈ- US diːˌvoʊ- **-s** -z
devocaliz|e, -is|e ˌdiːˈvəʊ.kᵊl.aɪz US -ˈvoʊ- **-es** -ɪz **-ing** -ɪŋ **-ed** -d
devoic|e ˌdiːˈvɔɪs **-es** -ɪz **-ing** -ɪŋ **-ed** -t
devoid dɪˈvɔɪd, də- US dɪ-
devolution ˌdiː.vəˈluː.ʃᵊn, ˌdev.əˈ-, -ˈljuː- US ˌdev.əˈluː-, ˌdiː.vəˈ- **-s** -z
devolv|e dɪˈvɒlv, də- US dɪˈvɑːlv **-es** -z **-ing** -ɪŋ **-ed** -d
Devon ˈdev.ᵊn **-shire** -ʃəʳ, -ˌʃɪəʳ US -ʃɚ, -ˌʃɪr
Devonian devˈəʊ.ni.ən, dɪˈvəʊ-, də- US dɪˈvoʊ- **-s** -z
Devonport ˈdev.ᵊn.pɔːt, -ᵊm- US -ᵊn.pɔːrt
de|vote dɪ|ˈvəʊt, də- US dɪ|ˈvoʊt **-votes** -vəʊts US -voʊts **-voting** -vəʊ.tɪŋ US -voʊ.t̬ɪŋ **-voted** -vəʊ.tɪd US -voʊ.t̬ɪd

Devoicing

A process affecting a sound which we would normally expect to be voiced but which is pronounced without VOICING in a particular context.

Examples for English

In English, the /l/ in *blade* /bleɪd/ [bleɪd̥] is usually voiced, but in *played* /pleɪd/ [pl̥eɪd̥] the /l/ is usually voiceless because of the preceding voiceless plosive. Note also that the /d/ at the end of the word in each case is devoiced if it is followed by a voiceless consonant or a pause.

The notion of devoicing leads to a rather confusing use of phonetic symbols in cases where there are separate symbols for voiced and voiceless pairs of sounds: a devoiced /d/ can be symbolised by adding a diacritic that indicates lack of voice – [d̥], but one is then left in doubt as to what the difference is between this sound and [t]. The usual reason for doing this is to leave the symbol looking like the phoneme it represents.

devoted dɪˈvəʊ.tɪd, də- ⓤⓢ dɪˈvoʊ.t̬ɪd **-ly** -li **-ness** -nəs, -nɪs
devotee ˌdev.əʊˈtiː ⓤⓢ -əˈtiː, -ˈteɪ, -oʊ- **-s** -z
devotion dɪˈvəʊ.ʃən, də- ⓤⓢ dɪˈvoʊ- **-s** -z
devotional dɪˈvəʊ.ʃən.əl, də- ⓤⓢ dɪˈvoʊ- **-ly** -i
devour dɪˈvaʊəʳ, də- ⓤⓢ dɪˈvaʊɚ **-s** -z **-ing** -ɪŋ **-ed** -d **-er/s** -əʳ/z ⓤⓢ -ɚ/z
de|vout dɪ|ˈvaʊt, də- ⓤⓢ dɪ- **-vouter** -ˈvaʊ.təʳ ⓤⓢ -ˈvaʊ.t̬ɚ **-voutest** -ˈvaʊ.tɪst, -təst ⓤⓢ -ˈvaʊ.t̬ɪst, -t̬əst **-voutly** -ˈvaʊt.li **-voutness** -ˈvaʊt.nəs, -nɪs
dew djuː, dʒuː ⓤⓢ duː, djuː **-s** -z ˈ**dew** ˌ**pond**; ˈ**dew** ˌ**point**
Dewali dɪˈwɑː.li ⓤⓢ də-, dɪ-
Dewar ˈdjuː.əʳ, ˈdʒuː-; djʊəʳ, dʒʊəʳ ⓤⓢ ˈduː.ɚ, ˈdjuː-
dewberr|y ˈdjuː.bər|.i, ˈdʒuː-, -ber- ⓤⓢ ˈduː.ber-, ˈdjuː- **-ies** -iz
dewclaw ˈdjuː.klɔː, ˈdʒuː- ⓤⓢ ˈduː.klɑː, ˈdjuː-, -klɔː **-s** -z
dewdrop ˈdjuː.drɒp, ˈdʒuː- ⓤⓢ ˈduː.drɑːp, ˈdjuː- **-s** -s
D'Ewes djuːz, dʒuːz ⓤⓢ duːz, djuːz
De Wet dəˈvet, -ˈwet
Dewey ˈdjuː.i, ˈdʒuː- ⓤⓢ ˈduː-, ˈdjuː-
Dewhurst ˈdjuː.hɜːst, ˈdʒuː- ⓤⓢ ˈduː.hɝːst, ˈdjuː-
Dewi ˈde.wi
Note: This is a Welsh place name. The anglicized pronunciation /ˈdjuː.i/ should be considered incorrect.
dewlap ˈdjuː.læp, ˈdʒuː- ⓤⓢ ˈduː-, ˈdjuː- **-s** -s
Dewsbury ˈdjuːz.bər.i, ˈdʒuːz- ⓤⓢ ˈduːz.ber-, ˈdjuːz-, -bɚ-
dew|y ˈdjuː|.i, ˈdʒuː- ⓤⓢ ˈduː-, ˈdjuː- **-iness** -ɪ.nəs, -ɪ.nɪs
Dexedrine® ˈdek.sɪ.driːn, -sə-
dexter (D) ˈdek.stəʳ ⓤⓢ -stɚ
dexterity dekˈster.ə.ti, -ɪ.ti ⓤⓢ -ə.t̬i
dexterous ˈdek.stər.əs **-ly** -li **-ness** -nəs, -nɪs
dextrose ˈdek.strəʊs, -strəʊz ⓤⓢ -stroʊs
dextrous ˈdek.strəs **-ly** -li **-ness** -nəs, -nɪs
De Zoete dəˈzuːt
de Zoete Wedd dəˌzuːtˈwed
dg *(abbrev. for* **decigram***)* ˈdes.ɪ.græm
Dhaka ˈdæk.ə ⓤⓢ ˈdæk.ə, ˈdɑː.kɑː
dhal dɑːl
dharma ˈdɑː.mə ⓤⓢ ˈdɑːr-
dhobi ˈdəʊ.bi ⓤⓢ ˈdoʊ- **-es** -z
dhoti ˈdəʊ.ti ⓤⓢ ˈdoʊ.t̬i **-es** -z
dhow daʊ **-s** -z
DHSS ˌdiː.eɪtʃ.esˈes
dhurrie ˈdʌr.i ⓤⓢ ˈdɝː- **-s** -z
di- daɪ-, dɪ-
Note: Prefix. Where the meaning is **two**, it may carry either primary or secondary stress and is pronounced /daɪ-/, e.g. **digraph** /ˈdaɪ.grɑːf ⓤⓢ -græf/, **diglossia** /ˌdaɪˈglɒs.i.ə ⓤⓢ -ˈglɑː.si-/. In other instances, it may be pronounced /daɪ-/, /dɪ-/ or occasionally /də-/, and is not normally stressed in verbs and adjectives, e.g. **digest** /daɪˈdʒest/, **diverse** /daɪˈvɜːs ⓤⓢ dɪˈvɜːrs/. In nouns, however, it may carry stress, e.g. **digest** /ˈdaɪ.dʒest/. There are exceptions; see individual entries.
Di daɪ
dia- daɪə-; daɪˈæ-
Note: Prefix. Normally carries primary or secondary stress on the first syllable, e.g. **diadem** /ˈdaɪə.dem/, **diabolic** /ˌdaɪəˈbɒl.ɪk ⓤⓢ -ˈbɑː.lɪk/, or primary stress on the second syllable, e.g. **diagonal** /daɪˈæg.ən.əl/.
diabetes ˌdaɪəˈbiː.tiːz, -tɪz, -tɪs ⓤⓢ -t̬əs, -t̬iːz
diabetic ˌdaɪəˈbet.ɪk ⓤⓢ -ˈbet̬- **-s** -s
diabolic ˌdaɪəˈbɒl.ɪk ⓤⓢ -ˈbɑː.lɪk **-al** -əl **-ally** -əl.i, -li
diabolism daɪˈæb.əl.ɪ.zəm
diaboliz|e, -is|e daɪˈæb.əl.aɪz ⓤⓢ -ə.laɪz **-es** -ɪz **-ing** -ɪŋ **-ed** -d
diabolo diˈæb.əl.əʊ, daɪ-, -ɑː.bəl- ⓤⓢ daɪˈæb.ə.loʊ
diachronic ˌdaɪ.əˈkrɒn.ɪk ⓤⓢ -ˈkrɑː.nɪk **-ally** -əl.i, -li
diacid daɪˈæs.ɪd **-s** -z
diaconal daɪˈæk.ə.nəl, di-
diaconate daɪˈæk.ə.neɪt, di-, -nɪt, -nət **-s** -s
diacritic ˌdaɪəˈkrɪt.ɪk ⓤⓢ -ˈkrɪt̬- **-s** -s **-al** -əl
diadem ˈdaɪə.dem, -dəm **-s** -z
diaeres|is daɪˈer.ə.s|ɪs, -ˈɪr.ə-, -ˈɪə.rə-, -rɪ- ⓤⓢ -ˈer.ə-, -ˈɪr- **-es** -iːz
Diaghilev diˈæg.ɪ.lef, -ˈə- ⓤⓢ -ˈɑː.gə.lef, -gɪ-
diagnos|e ˈdaɪəg.nəʊz, ˌ--ˈ- ⓤⓢ ˌdaɪəgˈnoʊs, -ˈnoʊz, ˈ--- **-es** -ɪz **-ing** -ɪŋ **-ed** -d
diagnos|is ˌdaɪəgˈnəʊ.s|ɪs ⓤⓢ -ˈnoʊ- **-es** -iːz
diagnostic ˌdaɪəgˈnɒs.tɪk ⓤⓢ -ˈnɑː.stɪk **-s** -s
diagnostician ˌdaɪəg.nɒsˈtɪʃ.ən ⓤⓢ -nɑːˈstɪʃ- **-s** -z
diagonal daɪˈæg.ən.əl **-s** -z **-ly** -i
diagram ˈdaɪə.græm **-s** -z
diagrammatic ˌdaɪə.grəˈmæt.ɪk ⓤⓢ -ˈmæt̬- **-al** -əl **-ally** -əl.i, -li
dial daɪəl ⓤⓢ daɪəl **-s** -z **-(l)ing** -ɪŋ **-(l)ed** -d ˈ**dialling** ˌ**code**; ˈ**dialling** ˌ**tone**; ˈ**dial** ˌ**tone**
dialect ˈdaɪə.lekt **-s** -s
dialectal ˌdaɪəˈlek.təl
dialectic ˌdaɪəˈlek.tɪk **-s** -s **-al** -əl **-ally** -əl.i, -li
dialectician ˌdaɪə.lekˈtɪʃ.ən **-s** -z
dialectolog|y ˌdaɪə.lekˈtɒl.ə.dʒ|i ⓤⓢ -ˈtɑː.lə- **-ist/s** -ɪst/s
diallage *figure of speech:* daɪˈæl.ə.gi, -dʒi
diallage *mineral:* ˈdaɪə.lɪdʒ
dialog|ism daɪˈæl.ə.dʒ|ɪ.zəm **-ist/s** -ɪst/s

dialogue, dialog ˈdaɪə.lɒɡ (US) -lɑːɡ **-s** -z
dial-up ˈdaɪəl.ʌp
dialys|is daɪˈæl.ə.s|ɪs, ˈ-ɪ- **-es** -iːz
diamagnetic ˌdaɪə.mæɡˈnet.ɪk, -məɡˈ- (US) -mæɡˈneţ- **-s** -s **-ally** -ᵊl.i, -li
diamagnetism ˌdaɪəˈmæɡ.nə.tɪ.zᵊm, -nɪ-
diamanté ˌdiː.əˈmɑ̃ŋ.teɪ, ˌdaɪəˈ-, -ˈmæn-, -ti (US) ˌdiː.ə.mɑːnˈteɪ, -ˈmɑːn.teɪ
diameter daɪˈæm.ɪ.təʳ, ˈ-ə- (US) -ə.ţɚ **-s** -z
diametral daɪˈæm.ɪ.trəl, ˈ-ə- **-ly** -i
diametric ˌdaɪəˈmet.rɪk **-al** -ᵊl **-ally** -ᵊl.i, -li
diamond (D) ˈdaɪə.mənd (US) ˈdaɪə-, ˈdaɪ- **-s** -z
diamondback ˈdaɪə.mənd.bæk (US) ˈdaɪə-, ˈdaɪ- **-s** -s
diamorphine ˌdaɪ.əˈmɔː.fiːn (US) -ˈmɔːr-
Diana daɪˈæn.ə
Diane daɪˈæn, di-
dianthus daɪˈæn*t*.θəs **-es** -ɪz
diapason ˌdaɪəˈpeɪ.zᵊn, -sᵊn **-s** -z
diap|er ˈdaɪə.pl|əʳ (US) -pl|ɚ **-ers** -əz (US) -ɚz **-ering** -ᵊr.ɪŋ **-ered** -əd (US) -ɚd
diaphanous daɪˈæf.ᵊn.əs
diaphone ˈdaɪə.fəʊn (US) -foʊn **-s** -z
diaphragm ˈdaɪə.fræm, -frəm (US) -fræm **-s** -z
diaphragmatic ˌdaɪə.fræɡˈmæt.ɪk, -frəɡˈ- (US) -ˈmæţ-
diapositive ˌdaɪəˈpɒz.ɪ.tɪv, ˈ-ə- (US) -ˈpɑː.zə.ţɪv **-s** -z
diarch|y ˈdaɪ.ɑː.k|i (US) -ɑːr- **-ies** -iz
diarist ˈdaɪə.rɪst **-s** -s
diarrh(o)ea ˌdaɪəˈrɪə (US) -ˈriː.ə
diar|y ˈdaɪə.r|i **-ies** -iz
diaspora (D) daɪˈæs.pᵊr.ə
diastase ˈdaɪə.steɪs, -steɪz
diastas|is daɪˈæs.tə.s|ɪs, ˌdaɪəˈsteɪ.s|ɪs **-es** -iːz
diastole daɪˈæs.tᵊl.i **-s** -z
diastolic ˌdaɪəˈstɒl.ɪk (US) -ˈstɑː.lɪk
diasystem ˈdaɪəˌsɪs.təm
diatherm|ic ˌdaɪəˈθɜː.m|ɪk (US) -ˈθɝː- **-ous** -əs
diatom ˈdaɪə.təm, -tɒm (US) -tɑːm **-s** -z
diatomaceous ˌdaɪə.təˈmeɪ.ʃəs
diatomic ˌdaɪəˈtɒm.ɪk (US) -ˈtɑː.mɪk
diatomite daɪˈæt.ə.maɪt (US) -ˈæţ-
diatonic ˌdaɪəˈtɒn.ɪk (US) -ˈtɑː.nɪk **-ally** -ᵊl.i, -li
diatribe ˈdaɪə.traɪb **-s** -z
diatype ˈdaɪə.taɪp
Diaz ˈdiː.əs, -æs, -æθ (US) -ɑːs, -ɑːz, -əs, -æz
diazepam daɪˈæz.ə.pæm, -ˈeɪ.zə-, -zɪ- (US) -ˈæz.ə-
dib dɪb **-s** -z **-bing** -ɪŋ **-bed** -d **-ber/s** -əʳ/z (US) -ɚ/z
dibasic daɪˈbeɪ.sɪk
dibasicity ˌdaɪ.beɪˈsɪs.ə.ti, -ɪ.ti (US) -ə.ţi
Dibb dɪb
dibbl|e ˈdɪb.l̩ **-es** -z **-ing** -ɪŋ, ˈdɪb.lɪŋ **-ed** -d **-er/s** -əʳ/z, ˈ-ləʳ/z (US) ˈ-l̩.ɚ/z, ˈ-lɚ/z
Dibdin ˈdɪb.dɪn
dibs dɪbz
DiCaprio dɪˈkæp.ri.əʊ, diː- (US) -oʊ
dicast ˈdɪk.æst (US) ˈdɪk.æst, ˈdaɪ.kæst **-s** -s
dice *(plur. of* **die***)* daɪs
dic|e *(v.)* daɪs **-es** -ɪz **-ing** -ɪŋ **-ed** -t
dicey (D) ˈdaɪ.si
dichloride ˌdaɪˈklɔː.raɪd (US) -ˈklɔːr.aɪd **-s** -z
dichotomous daɪˈkɒt.ə.məs, dɪ- (US) -ˈkɑː.ţə-
dichotom|y daɪˈkɒt.ə.m|i, dɪ- (US) -ˈkɑː.ţə- **-ies** -iz
dichromate ˌdaɪˈkrəʊ.meɪt (US) -ˈkroʊ- **-s** -s
dick (D) dɪk
dickens (D) ˈdɪk.ɪnz
Dickensian dɪˈken.zi.ən, də-, -si-
dick|er (D) ˈdɪk|.əʳ (US) -ɚ **-ers** -əz (US) -ɚz **-ering** -ᵊr.ɪŋ **-ered** -əd (US) -ɚd
Dickerson ˈdɪk.ə.sᵊn (US) ˈ-ɚ-
dickey (D) ˈdɪk.i **-s** -z **ˈdickey ˌbow**
dickhead ˈdɪk.hed **-s** -z
Dickie ˈdɪk.i
Dickins ˈdɪk.ɪnz
Dickinson ˈdɪk.ɪn.sᵊn
Dickson ˈdɪk.sᵊn
dick|y (D) ˈdɪk|.i **-ies** -iz
dickybird ˈdɪk.i.bɜːd (US) -bɝːd **-s** -z
dicotyledon ˌdaɪ.kɒt.ɪˈliː.dᵊn, -ᵊlˈiː- (US) -kɑː.ţᵊlˈ- **-s** -z
Dictaphone® ˈdɪk.tə.fəʊn (US) -foʊn **-s** -z
dictate *(n.)* ˈdɪk.teɪt **-s** -s
dic|tate *(v.)* dɪk|ˈteɪt (US) ˈdɪk|.teɪt, -|ˈ- **-tates** -ˈteɪts (US) -teɪts, -ˈteɪts **-tating** -ˈteɪ.tɪŋ (US) -teɪ.ţɪŋ, -ˈteɪ- **-tated** -ˈteɪ.tɪd (US) -teɪ.ţɪd, -ˈteɪ-
dictation dɪkˈteɪ.ʃᵊn **-s** -z
dictator dɪkˈteɪ.təʳ (US) ˈdɪk.teɪ.ţɚ, -ˈ-- **-s** -z
dictatorial ˌdɪk.təˈtɔː.ri.əl (US) -ˈtɔːr.i- **-ly** -i
dictatorship dɪkˈteɪ.tə.ʃɪp (US) -ţɚ- **-s** -s
diction ˈdɪk.ʃᵊn
dictionar|y ˈdɪk.ʃᵊn.ᵊr|.i, -ʃᵊn.r|i (US) -er|.i **-ies** -iz
dict|um ˈdɪk.t|əm **-a** -ə **-ums** -əmz
did *(from* **do***)* dɪd
Didache ˈdɪd.ə.ki
didact ˈdaɪ.dækt **-s** -s
didactic dɪˈdæk.tɪk, daɪ-, də- (US) daɪ-, dɪ- **-al** -ᵊl **-ally** -ᵊl.i, -li
didacticism dɪˈdæk.tɪ.sɪ.zᵊm, daɪ-, də- (US) daɪ-, dɪ-, -tə-
Didcot ˈdɪd.kət, -kɒt (US) -kɑːt
diddl|e ˈdɪd.l̩ **-es** -z **-ing** -ɪŋ, ˈ-lɪŋ **-ed** -d **-er/s** -əʳ/z, ˈ-ləʳ/z (US) ˈ-l̩.ɚ/z, ˈ-lɚ/z
diddly ˈdɪd.l̩.i, ˈ-li
diddlysquat ˌdɪd.l̩.iˈskwɒt, -liˈ- (US) -ˈskwɑːt
diddums ˈdɪd.əmz
Diderot ˈdiː.də.rəʊ (US) ˌdiː.dəˈroʊ
didgeridoo ˌdɪdʒ.ᵊr.iˈduː **-s** -z
Didier ˈdɪd.i.eɪ, ˈdiː.di-
didn't ˈdɪd.ᵊnt
Dido ˈdaɪ.dəʊ (US) -doʊ
didst dɪdst
Didymus ˈdɪd.ɪ.məs, ˈ-ə-
die *(n.) stamp:* daɪ **-s** -z
die *(n.) cube:* daɪ **dice** daɪs
die *(v.)* daɪ **-s** -z **dying** ˈdaɪ.ɪŋ **died** daɪd
die-casting ˈdaɪˌkɑː.stɪŋ (US) -ˌkæs.tɪŋ
Diego diˈeɪ.ɡəʊ (US) -ɡoʊ
diehard ˈdaɪ.hɑːd (US) -hɑːrd **-s** -z
dielectric ˌdaɪ.ɪˈlek.trɪk, -əˈ- **-s** -s
Dieppe diːˈep, di-
dieres|is daɪˈer.ə.s|ɪs, -ˈɪr-, -ˈɪə.rə-, -rɪ- (US) -ˈer.ə- **-es** -iːz
dieretic ˌdaɪəˈret.ɪk (US) -ˈreţ-
diesel ˈdiː.zᵊl (US) -sᵊl, -zᵊl **-s** -z **ˈdiesel ˌengine**
diesink ˈdaɪ.sɪŋk **-er/s** -əʳ/z (US) -ɚ/z **-ing** -ɪŋ
dies irae ˌdiː.eɪzˈɪə.raɪ, -ezˈ-, -esˈ-, -reɪ (US) -eɪzˈɪr.eɪ, -esˈ-
dies|is ˈdaɪ.ə.s|ɪs, ˈ-ɪ- **-es** -iːz
dies non ˌdaɪ.iːzˈnɒn, ˌdiː.eɪz- (US) ˈdiː.eɪs.nɑːn, -es-; ˌdiː.eɪzˈnɑːn, ˌdaɪ.iːzˈ- **-s** -z
diet daɪət **-s** -s **-ing** -ɪŋ (US) ˈdaɪə.ţɪŋ **-ed** -ɪd (US) ˈdaɪə.ţɪd **-er/s** -əʳ/z (US) -ɚ/z
dietar|y ˈdaɪə.tᵊr|.i, ˈdaɪ.ɪ-, -tr|i (US) ˈdaɪə.ter- **-ies** -iz **ˌdietary ˈfibre**
dietetic ˌdaɪəˈtet.ɪk, ˌdaɪ.ɪˈ- (US) -ˈteţ- **-s** -s **-al** -ᵊl **-ally** -ᵊl.i, -li
dietician, dietitian ˌdaɪəˈtɪʃ.ᵊn, ˌdaɪ.ɪˈ- (US) ˌdaɪəˈ- **-s** -z
Dietrich ˈdiː.trɪk, -trɪx, -trɪʃ
Dieu et mon droit ˌdjɜː.eɪ.mɔ̃ː*n*ˈdrwɑː
diff|er ˈdɪf|.əʳ (US) -ɚ **-ers** -əz (US) -ɚz **-ering** -ᵊr.ɪŋ **-ered** -əd (US) -ɚd
differenc|e ˈdɪf.ᵊr.ᵊn*t*s, ˈ-rᵊn*t*s **-es** -ɪz
different ˈdɪf.ᵊr.ᵊnt, ˈ-rᵊnt **-ly** -li
differenti|a ˌdɪf.ᵊˈren.*t*ʃi|.ə, ˈ-*t*ʃ|ə (US) -ˈren*t*.ʃi|.ə, ˈ-ʃə **-ae** -iː
differentiable ˌdɪf.ᵊˈren.*t*ʃi.ə.bl̩, ˈ-*t*ʃə- (US) -ˈren*t*.ʃi.ə-, ˈ-ʃə-
differential ˌdɪf.ᵊˈren.*t*ʃᵊl (US) -ˈren*t*.ʃᵊl **-s** -z **-ly** -i
differenti|ate ˌdɪf.ᵊˈren.*t*ʃi|.eɪt (US) -ˈren*t*.ʃi- **-ates** -eɪts **-ating** -eɪ.tɪŋ (US) -eɪ.ţɪŋ **-ated** -eɪ.tɪd (US) -eɪ.ţɪd
differentiation ˌdɪf.ᵊr.en.*t*ʃiˈeɪ.ʃᵊn, -en*t*.siˈ- (US) -ə.ren*t*.ʃiˈ-, -siˈ- **-s** -z
difficult ˈdɪf.ɪ.kᵊlt, ˈ-ə-
difficult|y ˈdɪf.ɪ.kᵊl.t|i, ˈ-ə- (US) -ţ|i **-ies** -iz
diffidence ˈdɪf.ɪ.dᵊn*t*s
diffident ˈdɪf.ɪ.dᵊnt **-ly** -li

diffract dɪˈfrækt **-s** -s **-ing** -ɪŋ **-ed** -ɪd
diffraction dɪˈfræk.ʃᵊn
diffuse *(adj.)* dɪˈfjuːs **-ly** -li **-ness** -nəs, -nɪs
diffus|e *(v.)* dɪˈfjuːz **-es** -ɪz **-ing** -ɪŋ **-ed** -d **-edly** -ɪd.li, -d.li **-edness** -ɪd.nəs, -d.nəs, -nɪs **-er/s** -əʳ/z US -ɚ/z
diffusibility dɪˌfjuː.zəˈbɪl.ə.ti, -zɪˈ-, -ɪ.ti US -zəˈbɪl.ə.t̬i
diffusible dɪˈfjuː.zə.bl̩, -zɪ-
diffusion dɪˈfjuː.ʒᵊn
diffusive dɪˈfjuː.sɪv **-ly** -li **-ness** -nəs, -nɪs
dig *(n. v.)* dɪg **-s** -z **-ging** -ɪŋ **-ged** -d **dug** dʌg
dig. *(in phrase* **infra dig.***)* dɪg
digamma daɪˈgæm.ə, ˈ--- **-s** -z
Digby ˈdɪg.bi
digest *(n.)* ˈdaɪ.dʒest **-s** -s
digest *(v.)* daɪˈdʒest, dɪ-, də- **-s** -s **-ing** -ɪŋ **-ed** -ɪd
digestibility daɪˌdʒes.təˈbɪl.ə.ti, dɪ-, də-, -tɪˈ-, -ɪ.ti US -ə.t̬i
digestible daɪˈdʒes.tə.bl̩, dɪ-, də-, -tɪ-
digestif ˌdiː.ʒesˈtɪf **-s** -s
digestion daɪˈdʒes.tʃᵊn, dɪ-, də-, -ˈdʒeʃ- **-s** -z
digestive daɪˈdʒes.tɪv, dɪ-, də- **-s** -z **-ly** -li **-ness** -nəs, -nɪs **diˌgestive ˈbiscuit, diˈgestive ˌbiscuit**
digger ˈdɪg.əʳ US -ɚ **-s** -z
Digges dɪgz
diggings ˈdɪg.ɪŋz
Diggle ˈdɪg.l̩ **-s** -z
Diggory ˈdɪg.ᵊr.i
dight daɪt
Dighton ˈdaɪ.tᵊn
digit ˈdɪdʒ.ɪt **-s** -s
digital ˈdɪdʒ.ɪ.tᵊl, ˈ-ə- US -t̬ᵊl **-s** -z **-ly** -li
digitalin ˌdɪdʒ.ɪˈteɪ.lɪn, -əˈ-, -ˈtɑː- US -ˈtæl.ɪn, -ˈteɪ.lɪn
digitalis ˌdɪdʒ.ɪˈteɪ.lɪs, -əˈ-, -ˈtɑː- US -ˈtæl.ɪs, -ˈteɪ.lɪs
digitalization, -isa- ˌdɪdʒ.ɪ.tᵊl.aɪˈzeɪ.ʃᵊn, ˌ-ə-, -ɪˈ- US -t̬ᵊl.ɪˈ-
digitaliz|e, -is|e ˈdɪdʒ.ɪ.tᵊl.aɪz, ˈ-ə- US -t̬ə.laɪz **-es** -ɪz **-ing** -ɪŋ **-ed** -d
digitization, -isa- ˌdɪdʒ.ɪ.taɪˈzeɪ.ʃᵊn, ˌ-ə-, -tɪˈ- US -t̬ɪˈ-
digitiz|e, -is|e ˈdɪdʒ.ɪ.taɪz, ˈ-ə- **-es** -ɪz **-ing** -ɪŋ **-ed** -d
digloss|ia ˌdaɪˈglɒs|.i.ə US -ˈglɑː.s|i- **-ic** -ɪk
digni|fy ˈdɪg.nɪ|.faɪ, -nə- **-fies** -faɪz **-fying** -faɪ.ɪŋ **-fied** -faɪd
dignitar|y ˈdɪg.nɪ.tᵊr|.i, -nə- US -nə.ter- **-ies** -iz
dignit|y ˈdɪg.nə.t|i, -nɪ- US -t̬|i **-ies** -iz
digraph ˈdaɪ.grɑːf US -græf **-s** -s
digress daɪˈgres, dɪ- **-es** -ɪz **-ing** -ɪŋ **-ed** -t
digression daɪˈgreʃ.ᵊn, dɪ- **-s** -z
digressive daɪˈgres.ɪv, dɪ- **-ly** -li **-ness** -nəs, -nɪs
digs dɪgz
Dijon ˈdiː.ʒɔ̃ːŋ US diːˈʒoʊn, -ˈʒɔːn
dik|e daɪk **-es** -s **-ing** -ɪŋ **-ed** -t
diktat ˈdɪk.tæt, -tɑːt US dɪkˈtɑːt, ˈ-- **-s** -s
dilapi|date dɪˈlæp.ɪ|.deɪt, də-, ˈ-ə- **-dates** -deɪts **-dating** -deɪ.tɪŋ US -deɪ.t̬ɪŋ **-dated** -deɪ.tɪd US -deɪ.t̬ɪd
dilapidation dɪˌlæp.ɪˈdeɪ.ʃᵊn, də-, -əˈ- **-s** -z
dilatability daɪˌleɪ.təˈbɪl.ə.ti, dɪ-, də-, -ɪ.ti US -t̬əˈbɪl.ə.t̬i
dilatation ˌdɪl.əˈteɪ.ʃᵊn, ˌdaɪ-, -leɪˈ- US ˌdɪl.əˈteɪ.ʃᵊn; ˈdaɪ.lə.teɪ- **-s** -z
dila|te daɪˈleɪ|t, dɪ-, də- US ˈdaɪ.leɪ|t; -ˈ-, də- **-tes** -ts **-ting** -tɪŋ US -t̬ɪŋ **-ted** -tɪd US -t̬ɪd **-ter/s** -təʳ/z US -t̬ɚ/z **-table** -tə.bl̩ US -t̬ə.bl̩
dilation daɪˈleɪ.ʃᵊn, dɪ-, də- **-s** -z
dilator daɪˈleɪ.təʳ, dɪ-, də- US -t̬ɚ **-s** -z
dilator|y ˈdɪl.ə.tᵊr|.i, -tr|i US -tɔːr|.i **-ily** -ᵊl.i, -ɪ.li **-iness** -ɪ.nəs, -ɪ.nɪs
Dilbert ˈdɪl.bət US -bɚt
dildo ˈdɪl.dəʊ US -doʊ **-(e)s** -z
dilemma dɪˈlem.ə, daɪ-, də- **-s** -z
dilettante ˌdɪl.ɪˈtæn.ti, -əˈ-, -teɪ US ˌdɪl.əˈtɑːnt, -ˈtænt, ˈ---; ˌdɪl.əˈtæn.ti, -ˈtɑːn- **-s** -z
dilettanti *(alternative plur. of* **dilettante***)* ˌdɪl.ɪˈtæn.ti, -əˈ-, -teɪ US ˌdɪl.əˈtɑːn.taɪ, -ˈtæn-, -ti
dilettantism ˌdɪl.ɪˈtæn.tɪ.zᵊm, -əˈ- US -ˈtɑːn-, -ˈtæn-
Dili ˈdɪl.i
diligenc|e ˈdɪl.ɪ.dʒᵊnts, ˈ-ə-
diligent ˈdɪl.ɪ.dʒᵊnt, ˈ-ə- **-ly** -li
Dilke dɪlk **-s** -s
dill (D) dɪl **-s** -z
Diller ˈdɪl.əʳ US -ɚ
Dilley ˈdɪl.i
Dillinger ˈdɪl.ɪn.dʒəʳ US -dʒɚ
Dillon ˈdɪl.ən
Dillwyn ˈdɪl.ɪn, ˈdɪl.wɪn
dill|y ˈdɪl|.i **-ies** -iz
dillydall|y ˈdɪl.iˌdæl|.i, ˌ--ˈ-- **-ies** -iz **-ying** -i.ɪŋ **-ied** -id
diluent ˈdɪl.ju.ənt **-s** -s
dilu|te daɪˈluː|t, dɪ-, -ˈljuː|t US -ˈluː|t **-tes** -ts **-ting** -tɪŋ US -t̬ɪŋ **-ted** -tɪd US -t̬ɪd **-teness** -t.nəs, -t.nɪs
dilution daɪˈluː.ʃᵊn, dɪ-, -ˈljuː- US -ˈluː- **-s** -z
diluvi|al daɪˈluː.vi|.əl, dɪ-, -ˈljuː- US dɪˈluː-, daɪ- **-an** -ən
diluvi|um daɪˈluː.vi|.əm, dɪ-, -ˈljuː- US dɪˈluː-, daɪ- **-a** -ə
Dilwyn, Dilwen ˈdɪl.wɪn
Dilys ˈdɪl.ɪs
dim dɪm **-mer/s** -əʳ/z US -ɚ/z **-mest** -ɪst, -əst **-ly** -li **-ness** -nəs, -nɪs **-s** -z **-ming** -ɪŋ **-med** -d
Di Maggio dɪˈmædʒ.i.əʊ US -oʊ, dəˈmɑːʒ.i.oʊ
Dimbleby ˈdɪm.bl̩.bi
dime daɪm **-s** -z
dimension ˌdaɪˈmen.tʃᵊn, dɪ-, də- US dɪˈment.ʃᵊn, də-, ˌdaɪ- **-s** -z
dimensional ˌdaɪˈmen.tʃᵊ.nᵊl, dɪ-, də- US dɪˈment.ʃᵊn-, də-, ˌdaɪ-
dimeter ˈdɪm.ɪ.təʳ, ˈ-ə- US -ə.t̬ɚ **-s** -z
diminish dɪˈmɪn.ɪʃ, də- **-es** -ɪz **-ing** -ɪŋ **-ed** -t **-able** -ə.bl̩
diminuendo dɪˌmɪn.juˈen.dəʊ, də- US -doʊ **-s** -z
diminution ˌdɪm.ɪˈnjuː.ʃᵊn US -əˈnuː-, -ˈnjuː- **-s** -z
diminutive dɪˈmɪn.jə.tɪv, də-, -jʊ- US -jə.t̬ɪv **-ly** -li **-ness** -nəs, -nɪs
dimity ˈdɪm.ɪ.ti, -ə.ti US -ə.t̬i, -ɪ.t̬i
dimmer ˈdɪm.əʳ US -ɚ **-s** -z
Dimmesdale ˈdɪmz.deɪl
dimmish ˈdɪm.ɪʃ
Dimmock ˈdɪm.ək
dimorphism daɪˈmɔː.fɪ.zᵊm US -ˈmɔːr-
dimorphous daɪˈmɔː.fəs US -ˈmɔːr-
dimout ˈdɪm.aʊt **-s** -s
dimpl|e ˈdɪm.pl̩ **-es** -z **-ing** -ɪŋ, ˈdɪm.plɪŋ **-ed** -d
Dimplex® ˈdɪm.pleks
dimply ˈdɪm.pli
dim sum ˌdɪmˈsʊm, -ˈsʌm
dimwit ˈdɪm.wɪt **-s** -s
dim-witted ˌdɪmˈwɪt.ɪd US ˈdɪmˌwɪt̬-, ˌ-ˈ-- **-ly** -li **-ness** -nəs, -nɪs *stress shift, British only:* ˌdimwitted ˈidiot
din dɪn **-s** -z **-ning** -ɪŋ **-ned** -d
Dina ˈdiː.nə, ˈdaɪ.nə
Dinah ˈdaɪ.nə
dinar ˈdiː.nɑːʳ, -ˈ- US diːˈnɑːr, ˈ-- **-s** -z
Dinaric dɪˈnær.ɪk, də-, daɪ- US -ˈner-, -ˈnær-
Dinas Powis ˌdiː.næsˈpaʊ.ɪs
din|e (D) daɪn **-es** -z **-ing** -ɪŋ **-ed** -d **ˈdining ˌcar; ˈdining ˌroom; ˈdining ˌtable**
Dinefwr dɪˈnev.ʊəʳ US -ʊr
diner ˈdaɪ.nəʳ US -nɚ **-s** -z
Dinesen ˈdɪn.ɪ.sᵊn, ˈ-ə- US ˈdiː.nə-, ˈdɪn.ə-, ˈ-ɪ-, -sɪn
dinette daɪˈnet, dɪ- US daɪ- **-s** -s
ding dɪŋ **-s** -z **-ing** -ɪŋ **-ed** -d
ding-a-ling ˈdɪŋ.ə.lɪŋ **-s** -z
dingbat ˈdɪŋ.bæt **-s** -s
ding-dong ˈdɪŋ.dɒŋ US -dɑːŋ, -dɔːŋ
dingh|y ˈdɪŋ.g|i, -i US ˈdɪŋ|.i, -g|i **-ies** -iz
dingle (D) ˈdɪŋ.gl̩ **-s** -z
Dingley ˈdɪŋ.li
dingo ˈdɪŋ.gəʊ US -goʊ **-es** -z
Dingwall ˈdɪŋ.wɔːl, -wəl US -wɑːl, -wɔːl, -wəl

Diphthong

A sound in which there is a glide from one vowel quality to another.

Examples for English

BBC English and US English contain a large number of diphthongs: in both accents, there are three ending in [ɪ] (/eɪ aɪ ɔɪ/), sometimes referred to as 'front closing', and two ending in [ʊ] (/aʊ əʊ/), sometimes referred to as 'back closing'. In US English, the preferred transcription of the BBC vowel /əʊ/ is /oʊ/, which indicates a rounded initial vowel.

BBC English also has three diphthongs ending in [ə] (/ɪə eə ʊə/), which are sometimes known as 'centring'. The /ʊə/ diphthong is now less commonly used than /ɔː/. These diphthongs usually appear in US English with an /r/ final (/ɪr er ʊr/), as words containing them generally end with an *r* in the spelling, e.g.:

bay	/beɪ/	
buy	/baɪ/	
boy	/bɔɪ/	
go	/gəʊ/	US /goʊ/
cow	/kaʊ/	
pier	/pɪə/	US /pɪr/
pear	/peə/	US /per/
poor	/pʊə/ (more often) /pɔː/	US /pʊr/

Opinions differ as to whether diphthongs should be treated as phonemes in their own right, or as combinations of two phonemes.

ding|y 'dɪn.dʒ|i **-ier** -i.əʳ US -i.ɚ **-iest** -i.ɪst, -i.əst **-ily** -ɪ.li, -ᵊl.i **-iness** -ɪ.nəs, -ɪ.nɪs
dink dɪŋk **-s** -s
Dinkins 'dɪŋ.kɪnz US 'dɪŋ-, 'dɪn-
dinkum 'dɪŋ.kəm
dink|y 'dɪŋ.k|i **-ier** -i.əʳ US -i.ɚ **-iest** -i.ɪst, -i.əst **-iness** -ɪ.nəs, -ɪ.nɪs
Dinmont 'dɪn.mɒnt, 'dɪm-, -mənt US 'dɪn.mɑːnt, -mənt
Dinneford 'dɪn.ɪ.fəd US -fɚd
dinner 'dɪn.əʳ US -ɚ **-s** -z **'dinner ˌhour; 'dinner ˌjacket; 'dinner ˌlady; 'dinner ˌparty; 'dinner ˌplate; 'dinner ˌservice; 'dinner ˌset; 'dinner ˌtable; 'dinner ˌtime**
Dinnington 'dɪn.ɪŋ.tᵊn
Dinocrates daɪ'nɒk.rə.tiːz, dɪ- US -'nɑː.krə-
Dinorah dɪ'nɔː.rə US -'nɔːr.ə
dinosaur 'daɪ.nə.sɔːʳ US -sɔːr **-s** -z
dinosaur|us ˌdaɪ.nə'sɔː.r|əs US -'sɔːr|.əs **-i** -aɪ
dinotheri|um ˌdaɪ.nəʊ'θɪə.ri|.əm US -oʊ'-, -ə'- US -'θɪr.i- **-a** -ə
dint dɪnt
Dinwiddie dɪn'wɪd.i, '---
diocesan daɪ'ɒs.ɪ.sᵊn, '-ə-, -zᵊn US -'ɑː.sə-
dioces|e 'daɪə.sɪs, -siːs, -siːz **-es** -ɪz
Diocles 'daɪə.kliːz
Diocletian ˌdaɪə'kliː.ʃᵊn, -ʃi.ən
diode 'daɪ.əʊd US -oʊd **-s** -z
Diodorus ˌdaɪə'dɔː.rəs US -'dɔːr.əs
Diogenes daɪ'ɒdʒ.ɪ.niːz, '-ə- US -'ɑː.dʒə-
Diomede 'daɪə.miːd
Diomedes ˌdaɪə'miː.diːz; daɪ'ɒm.ɪ- US ˌdaɪə'miː-
Dion *Greek:* 'daɪ.ən US -ɑːn *French:* 'diː.ən, -ɔ̃ːŋ, -ɒŋ, -ɒn US di'oʊn
Dionne diː'ɒn, di-; 'diː.ɒn US -'ɑːn
Dionysi|a ˌdaɪə'nɪs.i|.ə, -'nɪz- US -'nɪʃ.i|.ə, -'nɪs-, -'nɪz-, -'nɪʃ|.ə **-an** -ən
Dionysiac ˌdaɪə'nɪs.i.æk, -'nɪz-
Dionysius ˌdaɪə'nɪs.i.əs, -'nɪz- US -'nɪʃ.əs, '-i.əs, -'nɪs.i-, -'naɪ.si-
Dionysus ˌdaɪə'naɪ.səs US -'naɪ.səs, -'niː-
dioptre, diopter daɪ'ɒp.təʳ US -'ɑːp.tɚ **-s** -z
dioptric daɪ'ɒp.trɪk US -'ɑːp-
Dior 'diː.ɔːʳ, di'ɔːʳ US di'ɔːr
diorama ˌdaɪə'rɑː.mə US -'ræm.ə, -'rɑː.mə **-s** -z
dioramic ˌdaɪə'ræm.ɪk
Dioscuri ˌdaɪə'skjʊə.ri; ˌdaɪ.ɒs'kjʊə-; daɪ'ɒs.kjʊ.ri, -raɪ US ˌdaɪ.ɑː'skjʊr.aɪ
Diosy di'əʊ.si US -'oʊ-
dioxide daɪ'ɒk.saɪd US -'ɑːk- **-s** -z
dioxin daɪ'ɒk.sɪn US -'ɑːk- **-s** -z
dip dɪp **-s** -s **-ping** -ɪŋ **-ped** -t **-per/s** -əʳ/z US -ɚ/z
diphenyl daɪ'fiː.naɪl, -'fen.aɪl, -ᵊl, -ɪl, -'fen.ɪl US -'fen.ᵊl, -'fiː.nᵊl
diphtheria dɪf'θɪə.ri.ə, dɪp- US -'θɪr.i-
diphthong 'dɪf.θɒŋ, 'dɪp- US -θɑːŋ, -θɔːŋ **-s** -z
diphthongal 'dɪf.θɒŋ.ᵊl, 'dɪp-, -gᵊl, -'-- US dɪf'θɑːŋ.ᵊl, dɪp-, -'θɔːŋ-, -gᵊl **-ly** -i
diphthongization, -isa- ˌdɪf.θɒŋ.aɪ'zeɪ.ʃᵊn, ˌdɪp-, -gaɪ'-, -gɪ'- US -θɑːŋ.ɪ'-, -θɔːŋ-, -gɪ'- **-s** -z
diphthongiz|e, -is|e 'dɪf.θɒŋ.aɪz, 'dɪp-, -gaɪz US -θɑːŋ.aɪz, -θɔːŋ-, -gaɪz **-es** -ɪz **-ing** -ɪŋ **-ed** -d
Diplock 'dɪp.lɒk US -lɑːk
diplodoc|us dɪ'plɒd.ə.kləs, ˌdɪp.ləʊ'dəʊ- US dɪ'plɑː.də-, -'ploʊ- **-uses** -ə.sɪz **-i** -aɪ
diploid 'dɪp.lɔɪd **-s** -z
diploma dɪ'pləʊ.mə US -'ploʊ-, də- **-s** -z
diplomacy dɪ'pləʊ.mə.si US -'ploʊ-, də-
diplomat 'dɪp.lə.mæt **-s** -s
diplomatic ˌdɪp.lə'mæt.ɪk US -'mæţ- **-s** -s **-al** -ᵊl **-ally** -ᵊl.i, -li
diplomatist dɪ'pləʊ.mə.tɪst US -'ploʊ-, də- **-s** -s
diplomatiz|e, -is|e dɪ'pləʊ.mə.taɪz US -'ploʊ-, də- **-es** -ɪz **-ing** -ɪŋ **-ed** -d
diplosis dɪ'pləʊ.sɪs US -'ploʊ-
dipole 'daɪ.pəʊl US -poʊl **-s** -z
dipper 'dɪp.əʳ US -ɚ **-s** -z
dipp|y 'dɪp|.i **-ier** -i.əʳ US -i.ɚ **-iest** -i.ɪst, -i.əst
dipsomania ˌdɪp.səʊ'meɪ.ni.ə US -sə'-, -soʊ'-
dipsomaniac ˌdɪp.səʊ'meɪ.ni.æk US -sə'-, -soʊ'- **-s** -s
dipstick 'dɪp.stɪk **-s** -s
dipswitch 'dɪp.swɪtʃ **-es** -ɪz
dipteran 'dɪp.tə.rən US -tɚ.ən **-s** -z
dipter|on 'dɪp.tə.r|ən US -r|ɑːn **-ons** -ənz US -ɑːnz **-a** -ə **-ous** -əs
diptych 'dɪp.tɪk **-s** -s
dir|e daɪəʳ US daɪɚ **-er** -əʳ US -ɚ **-est** -ɪst, -əst **-ely** -li **-eness** -nəs, -nɪs
direct dɪ'rekt, daɪ-, də- US dɪ'rekt, daɪ- **-s** -s **-ing** -ɪŋ **-ed** -ɪd **-est** -ɪst, -əst **-ness** -nəs, -nɪs **ˌdirect 'mail; ˌdirect 'object**
direction dɪ'rek.ʃᵊn, daɪ-, də- US dɪ'rek-, daɪ- **-s** -z **-less** -ləs, -lɪs
directional dɪ'rek.ʃᵊn.ᵊl, daɪ-, də- US dɪ'rek-, daɪ-
directive dɪ'rek.tɪv, daɪ-, də- US dɪ'rek-, daɪ- **-s** -z

directly dɪˈrekt.li, daɪ-, də- (US) dɪ-, daɪ-
director dɪˈrek.təʳ, daɪ-, də- (US) dɪˈrek.tɚ, daɪ- **-s** -z
directorate dɪˈrek.tᵊr.ət, daɪ-, də-, -ɪt (US) dɪˈrek-, daɪ- **-s** -s
directorial dɪˌrekˈtɔː.ri.əl, daɪ-, də- (US) dɪˌrekˈtɔːr.i-, daɪ-
directorship dɪˈrek.tə.ʃɪp, daɪ-, də- (US) dɪˈrek.tɚ-, daɪ- **-s** -s
director|y dɪˈrek.tᵊr|.i, daɪ-, də- (US) dɪˈrek-, daɪ- **-ies** -iz
direful ˈdaɪə.fᵊl, -fʊl (US) ˈdaɪɚ- **-ly** -i **-ness** -nəs, -nɪs
dirg|e dɜːdʒ (US) dɝːdʒ **-es** -ɪz
dirham ˈdɪ.ræm, ˈdɪər.æm, -əm (US) dɪrˈhæm; dəˈræm **-s** -z
dirigible ˈdɪr.ɪ.dʒə.bl̩, -dʒɪ-; dɪˈrɪdʒ.ə-, də- (US) ˈdɪr.ə.dʒə-; dɪˈrɪdʒ.ə-, də- **-s** -z
dirigisme ˌdɪr.ɪˈʒiː.zᵊm; ˈdɪr.ɪ.ʒɪ- (US) ˌdɪr.ɪˈʒiː-
dirigiste ˌdɪr.ɪˈʒiːst; ˈdɪr.ɪ.ʒɪst (US) ˈdɪr.ɪ.ʒɪst; ˌdɪr.ɪˈʒiːst **-s** -s
dirk (D) dɜːk (US) dɝːk **-s** -s
dirndl ˈdɜːn.dl̩ (US) ˈdɝːn- **-s** -z
dirt dɜːt (US) dɝːt **ˌdirt ˈcheap; ˌdirt ˈpoor; ˈdirt ˌtrack**
dirt|y ˈdɜː.t|i (US) ˈdɝː.t̬|i **-ies** -iz **-ying** -i.ɪŋ **-ied** -id **-ier** -i.əʳ (US) -i.ɚ **-iest** -i.ɪst, -i.əst **-ily** -ɪ.li, -ᵊl.i **-iness** -ɪ.nəs, -ɪ.nɪs **ˌdirty ˈtrick; do someone's ˈdirty ˌwork**
dis- dɪs-, dɪz-
Note: Prefix. In words containing **dis-**, the prefix will normally either not be stressed, e.g. **disable** /dɪˈseɪ.bl̩/, or will take secondary stress if the stem is stressed on its second syllable, e.g. **ability** /əˈbɪl.ə.ti (US) -t̬i/, **disability** /ˌdɪs.əˈbɪl.ə.ti (US) -t̬i/. There is sometimes a difference in stress between nouns and verbs, e.g. **discharge**, noun /ˈdɪs.tʃɑːdʒ (US) -tʃɑːrdʒ/, verb /dɪsˈtʃɑːdʒ (US) -ˈtʃɑːrdʒ/. There are exceptions; see individual entries.
Dis dɪs
disabilit|y ˌdɪs.əˈbɪl.ə.t|i, -ɪ.t|i (US) -ə.t̬|i **-ies** -iz
disabl|e dɪˈseɪ.bl̩ **-es** -z **-ing** -ɪŋ, -ˈeɪ.blɪŋ **-ed** -d **-ement** -mənt
disabus|e ˌdɪs.əˈbjuːz **-es** -ɪz **-ing** -ɪŋ **-ed** -d
disaccharide daɪˈsæk.ᵊr.aɪd, -ɪd (US) -ə.raɪd **-s** -z
disaccustom ˌdɪs.əˈkʌs.təm **-s** -z **-ing** -ɪŋ **-ed** -d
disadvantag|e ˌdɪs.ədˈvɑːn.tɪdʒ (US) -ˈvæn.t̬ɪdʒ **-es** -ɪz **-ing** **-ed** -d
disadvantageous ˌdɪsˌæd.vənˈteɪ.dʒəs, -əd-, -vɑːnˈ-, -vænˈ-; dɪˌsæd- (US) ˌdɪsˌæd.vænˈ-, -vənˈ- **-ly** -li **-ness** -nəs, -nɪs
disaffect ˌdɪs.əˈfekt **-s** -s **-ing** -ɪŋ **-ed/ly** -ɪd/li **-edness** -ɪd.nəs, -nɪs
disaffection ˌdɪs.əˈfek.ʃᵊn
disafforest ˌdɪs.əˈfɒr.ɪst, -əst (US) -ˈfɔːr- **-s** -s **-ing** -ɪŋ **-ed** -ɪd
disafforestation ˌdɪs.əˌfɒr.ɪˈsteɪ.ʃᵊn, -əˈ- (US) -ˌfɔːr-
disagree ˌdɪs.əˈɡriː **-s** -z **-ing** -ɪŋ **-d** -d
disagreeab|le ˌdɪs.əˈɡriː.ə.bl|̩ **-ly** -li **-leness** -l̩.nəs, -nɪs
disagreement ˌdɪs.əˈɡriː.mᵊnt **-s** -s
disallow ˌdɪs.əˈlaʊ **-s** -z **-ing** -ɪŋ **-ed** -d
disallowable ˌdɪs.əˈlaʊ.ə.bl̩ *stress shift:* ˌdisallowable ˈgoals
disallowance ˌdɪs.əˈlaʊ.ənts
disambigu|ate ˌdɪs.æmˈbɪɡ.ju|.eɪt **-ates** -eɪts **-ating** -eɪ.tɪŋ (US) -eɪ.t̬ɪŋ **-ated** -eɪ.tɪd (US) -eɪ.t̬ɪd
disambiguation ˌdɪs.æmˌbɪɡ.juˈeɪ.ʃᵊn
disappear ˌdɪs.əˈpɪəʳ (US) -ˈpɪr **-s** -z **-ing** -ɪŋ **-ed** -d
disappearanc|e ˌdɪs.əˈpɪə.rᵊnts (US) -ˈpɪr.ᵊnts **-es** -ɪz
disap|point ˌdɪs.ə|ˈpɔɪnt **-points** -ˈpɔɪnts **-pointing/ly** -ˈpɔɪn.tɪŋ/li (US) -ˈpɔɪn.t̬ɪŋ/li **-pointed** -ˈpɔɪn.tɪd (US) -ˈpɔɪn.t̬ɪd
disappointment ˌdɪs.əˈpɔɪnt.mənt **-s** -s
disapprobation ˌdɪs.æp.rəʊˈbeɪ.ʃᵊn, -rʊˈ-; dɪˌsæp- (US) ˌdɪsˌæp.rəˈ-, -roʊˈ-
disapproval ˌdɪs.əˈpruː.vᵊl
disapprov|e ˌdɪs.əˈpruːv **-es** -z **-ing/ly** -ɪŋ/li **-ed** -d
disarm dɪˈsɑːm, -ˈzɑːm (US) -ˈsɑːrm **-s** -z **-ing/ly** -ɪŋ/li **-ed** -d **-er/s** -əʳ/z (US) -ɚ/z
disarmament dɪˈsɑː.mə.mənt, -ˈzɑː- (US) -ˈsɑːr-
disarrang|e ˌdɪs.ᵊˈreɪndʒ **-es** -ɪz **-ing** -ɪŋ **-ed** -d
disarrangement ˌdɪs.ᵊˈreɪndʒ.mənt **-s** -s
disarray ˌdɪs.ᵊrˈeɪ **-s** -z **-ing** -ɪŋ **-ed** -d
disarticu|late ˌdɪs.ɑːˈtɪk.jə|.leɪt, -jʊ- (US) -ɑːrˈ- **-lates** -leɪts **-lating** -leɪ.tɪŋ (US) -leɪ.t̬ɪŋ **-lated** -leɪ.tɪd (US) -leɪ.t̬ɪd
disarticulation ˌdɪs.ɑːˌtɪk.jəˈleɪ.ʃᵊn, -jʊˈ- (US) -ɑːr-
disassoci|ate ˌdɪs.əˈsəʊ.si|.eɪt, -ʃi- (US) -ˈsoʊ.ʃi-, -si- **-ates** -eɪts **-ating** -eɪ.tɪŋ (US) -eɪ.t̬ɪŋ **-ated** -eɪ.tɪd (US) -eɪ.t̬ɪd
disassociation ˌdɪs.ə.səʊ.siˈeɪ.ʃᵊn, -ʃiˈ- (US) -soʊ.ʃiˈ-, -siˈ-
disaster dɪˈzɑː.stəʳ, də- (US) dɪˈzæs.tɚ **-s** -z
disastrous dɪˈzɑː.strəs, də- (US) dɪˈzæs.trəs **-ly** -li **-ness** -nəs, -nɪs
disavow ˌdɪs.əˈvaʊ **-s** -z **-ing** -ɪŋ **-ed** -d **-al** -ᵊl
disband dɪsˈbænd **-s** -z **-ing** -ɪŋ **-ed** -ɪd **-ment** -mənt
disbar dɪsˈbɑːʳ (US) -ˈbɑːr **-s** -z **-ring** -ɪŋ **-red** -d
disbark dɪsˈbɑːk (US) -ˈbɑːrk **-s** -s **-ing** -ɪŋ **-ed** -t
disbelief ˌdɪs.bɪˈliːf, -bəˈ-
disbeliev|e ˌdɪs.bɪˈliːv, -bəˈ- **-es** -z **-ing** -ɪŋ **-ed** -d **-er/s** -əʳ/z (US) -ɚ/z
disburden dɪsˈbɜː.dᵊn (US) -ˈbɝː- **-s** -z **-ing** -ɪŋ **-ed** -d
disburdenment dɪsˈbɜː.dᵊn.mənt (US) -ˈbɝː-
disburs|e dɪsˈbɜːs (US) -ˈbɝːs **-es** -ɪz **-ing** -ɪŋ **-ed** -t
disbursement dɪsˈbɜːs.mənt (US) -ˈbɝːs- **-s** -s
disc dɪsk **-s** -s **ˈdisc ˌjockey**
discard (*n.*) ˈdɪs.kɑːd (US) -kɑːrd **-s** -z
discard (*v.*) dɪˈskɑːd (US) -ˈskɑːrd **-s** -z **-ing** -ɪŋ **-ed** -ɪd
discern dɪˈsɜːn, də- (US) dɪˈsɝːn, -ˈzɝːn **-s** -z **-ing** -ɪŋ **-ed** -d **-er/s** -əʳ/z (US) -ɚ/z
discernib|le dɪˈsɜː.nə.bl|̩, də-, -nɪ- (US) dɪˈsɝː-, -ˈzɝː- **-ly** -li **-leness** -l̩.nəs, -nɪs
discerning dɪˈsɜː.nɪŋ, də- (US) dɪˈsɝː-, -ˈzɝː- **-ly** -li
discernment dɪˈsɜːn.mənt, də- (US) dɪˈsɝːn-, -ˈzɝːn-
discharg|e (*n.*) ˈdɪs.tʃɑːdʒ, -ˈ- (US) ˈdɪs.tʃɑːrdʒ, -ˈ- **-es** -ɪz
discharg|e (*v.*) dɪsˈtʃɑːdʒ (US) -ˈtʃɑːrdʒ **-es** -ɪz **-ing** -ɪŋ **-ed** -d **-er/s** -əʳ/z (US) -ɚ/z
disciple dɪˈsaɪ.pl̩, də- (US) dɪ- **-s** -z **-ship** -ʃɪp
disciplinarian ˌdɪs.ə.plɪˈneə.ri.ən, ˌ-ɪ-, -pləˈ- (US) -ˈner.i- **-s** -z
disciplinary ˌdɪs.əˈplɪ.nᵊr.i, -ɪˈ-, ˈdɪs.ə.plɪ-, ˈ-ɪ- (US) ˈdɪs.ə.plɪ.ner- **ˌdisciplinary ˈaction, disciˌplinary ˈaction** (US) **ˈdisciplinary ˌaction**
disciplin|e ˈdɪs.ə.plɪn, ˈ-ɪ- **-es** -z **-ing** -ɪŋ **-ed** -d
disclaim dɪsˈkleɪm **-s** -z **-ing** -ɪŋ **-ed** -d
disclaimer dɪsˈkleɪm.əʳ (US) -mɚ **-s** -z
disclos|e dɪsˈkləʊz (US) -ˈkloʊz **-es** -ɪz **-ing** -ɪŋ **-ed** -d
disclosure dɪsˈkləʊ.ʒəʳ (US) -ˈkloʊ.ʒɚ **-s** -z
disco ˈdɪs.kəʊ (US) -koʊ **-s** -z **-ing** -ɪŋ
discobol|us dɪˈskɒb.ᵊl|.əs (US) -ˈskɑː.bᵊl- **-i** -aɪ
discol|o(u)r dɪˈskʌl|.əʳ (US) -ˈskʌl|.ɚ **-o(u)rs** -əz (US) -ɚz **-o(u)ring** -ᵊr.ɪŋ **-o(u)red** -əd (US) -ɚd
discolo(u)ration dɪˌskʌl.əˈreɪ.ʃᵊn; ˌdɪs.kʌl- (US) dɪˌskʌl- **-s** -z
discombobu|late ˌdɪs.kəmˈbɒb.jə|.leɪt, -jʊ- (US) -ˈbɑː.bjə-, -bjʊ- **-lates** -leɪts **-lating** -leɪ.tɪŋ (US) -leɪ.t̬ɪŋ **-lated** -leɪ.tɪd (US) -leɪ.t̬ɪd

discom|fit dɪˈskʌmp|.fɪt **-fits** -fɪts **-fiting** -fɪ.tɪŋ (US) -fɪ.t̬ɪŋ **-fited** -fɪ.tɪd (US) -fɪ.t̬ɪd

discomfiture dɪˈskʌmp.fɪ.tʃəʳ, -fə- (US) -tʃɚ

discom|fort dɪˈskʌmp|.fət (US) -fɚt **-forts** -fəts (US) -fɚts **-forting** -fə.tɪŋ (US) -fɚ.t̬ɪŋ **-forted** -fə.tɪd (US) -fɚ.t̬ɪd

discommod|e ˌdɪs.kəˈməʊd (US) -ˈmoʊd **-es** -z **-ing** -ɪŋ **-ed** -ɪd

discompos|e ˌdɪs.kəmˈpəʊz (US) -ˈpoʊz **-es** -ɪz **-ing** -ɪŋ **-ed** -d

discomposure ˌdɪs.kəmˈpəʊ.ʒəʳ (US) -ˈpoʊ.ʒɚ

discon|cert ˌdɪs.kən|ˈsɜːt (US) -ˈsɝːt **-certs** -ˈsɜːts (US) -ˈsɝːts **-certing/ly** -ˈsɜː.tɪŋ/li (US) -ˈsɝː.t̬ɪŋ/li **-certed** -ˈsɜː.tɪd (US) -ˈsɝː.t̬ɪd

disconnect ˌdɪs.kəˈnekt **-s** -s **-ing** -ɪŋ **-ed** -ɪd

disconnection ˌdɪs.kəˈnek.ʃᵊn

disconsolate dɪˈskɒnt.sᵊl.ət, -ɪt (US) -ˈskɑːnt- **-ly** -li **-ness** -nəs, -nɪs

discon|tent ˌdɪs.kən|ˈtent **-tented** -ˈten.tɪd (US) -ˈten.t̬ɪd **-tentedly** -ˈten.tɪd.li (US) -ˈten.t̬ɪd.li **-tentedness** -ˈten.tɪd.nəs, -nɪs (US) -ˈten.t̬ɪd.nəs, -nɪs **-tentment** -ˈtent.mənt

discontinuance ˌdɪs.kənˈtɪn.ju.ənts

discontinuation ˌdɪs.kənˌtɪn.juˈeɪ.ʃᵊn

discontinu|e ˌdɪs.kənˈtɪn.juː **-es** -z **-ing** -ɪŋ **-ed** -d

discontinuit|y ˌdɪsˌkɒn.tɪˈnjuː.ə.t|i, -kɒn-, -ɪ.t|i; dɪˌskɒn- (US) ˌdɪs.kɑːn.tᵊnˈuː.ə.t̬|i, -ˈjuː- **-ies** -iz

discontinuous ˌdɪs.kənˈtɪn.ju.əs **-ly** -li

discord (*n.*) ˈdɪs.kɔːd (US) -kɔːrd **-s** -z

discord (*v.*) dɪˈskɔːd (US) -ˈskɔːrd **-s** -z **-ing** -ɪŋ **-ed** -ɪd

discordan|ce dɪˈskɔː.dᵊnt|s (US) -ˈskɔːr- **-cy** -si

discordant dɪˈskɔː.dᵊnt (US) -ˈskɔːr- **-ly** -li

discotheque, discothèque ˈdɪs.kə.tek **-s** -s

discount (*n.*) ˈdɪs.kaʊnt **-s** -s

dis|count (*v.*) dɪˈs|kaʊnt **-counts** -kaʊnts **-counting** -kaʊn.tɪŋ (US) -kaʊn.t̬ɪŋ **-counted** -kaʊn.tɪd (US) -kaʊn.t̬ɪd **-counter/s** -kaʊn.təʳ/z (US) -kaʊn.t̬ɚ/z

discountenanc|e dɪˈskaʊn.tɪ.nənts, -tə- (US) -tᵊn.ənts **-es** -ɪz **-ing** -ɪŋ **-ed** -t

discourag|e dɪˈskʌr.ɪdʒ (US) -ˈskɝː- **-es** -ɪz **-ing/ly** -ɪŋ/li **-ed** -d

discouragement dɪˈskʌr.ɪdʒ.mənt (US) -ˈskɝː- **-s** -s

discours|e (*n.*) ˈdɪs.kɔːs (US) -kɔːrs **-es** -ɪz

discours|e (*v.*) dɪˈskɔːs (US) -ˈskɔːrs **-es** -ɪz **-ing** -ɪŋ **-ed** -t **-er/s** -əʳ/z (US) -ɚ/z

discourteous dɪˈskɜː.ti.əs (US) -ˈskɝː.t̬i- **-ly** -li **-ness** -nəs, -nɪs

discourtesy dɪˈskɜː.tə.si, -tɪ- (US) -ˈskɝː.t̬ə-

discov|er dɪˈskʌv|.əʳ (US) -ɚ **-ers** -əz (US) -ɚz **-ering** -ᵊr.ɪŋ **-ered** -əd (US) -ɚd **-erer/s** -ᵊr.əʳ/z (US) -ɚ.ɚ/z

discoverable dɪˈskʌv.ᵊr.ə.bl̩

discovert dɪˈskʌv.ət (US) -ɚt

discover|y dɪˈskʌv.ᵊr|.i **-ies** -iz

discred|it dɪˈskred|.ɪt **-its** -ɪts **-iting** -ɪ.tɪŋ (US) -ɪ.t̬ɪŋ **-ited** -ɪ.tɪd (US) -ɪ.t̬ɪd

discreditab|le dɪˈskred.ɪ.tə.b|l̩ (US) -t̬ə- **-ly** -li **-leness** -l̩.nəs, -nɪs

dis|creet dɪˈs|kriːt **-creetest** -ˈkriː.tɪst, -təst (US) -ˈkriː.t̬ɪst, -t̬əst **-creetly** -ˈkriːt.li **-creetness** -ˈkriːt.nəs, -nɪs

discrepan|cy dɪˈskrep.ᵊn|*t*.si **-cies** -*t*.siz **-t** -t

discrete dɪˈskriːt **-ly** -li **-ness** -nəs, -nɪs

discretion dɪˈskreʃ.ᵊn **-s** -z

discretional dɪˈskreʃ.ᵊn.ᵊl **-ly** -i

discretionar|y dɪˈskreʃ.ᵊn.ᵊr|.i, -r|i (US) -er|.i **-ily** -ᵊl.i, -ɪ.li

discriminate (*adj.*) dɪˈskrɪm.ɪ.nət, ˈ-ə-, -nɪt **-ly** -li

discrimi|nate (*v.*) dɪˈskrɪm.ɪ|.neɪt, ˈ-ə- **-nates** -neɪts **-nating/ly** -neɪ.tɪŋ/li (US) -neɪ.t̬ɪŋ/li **-nated** -neɪ.tɪd (US) -neɪ.t̬ɪd

discrimination dɪˌskrɪm.ɪˈneɪ.ʃᵊn, -əˈ- **-s** -z

discriminative dɪˈskrɪm.ɪ.nə.tɪv, ˈ-ə-, -neɪ- (US) -neɪ.t̬ɪv, -nə- **-ly** -li

discriminatory dɪˈskrɪm.ɪ.nə.tᵊr.i, ˈ-ə-, -tri; dɪˌskrɪm.ɪˈneɪ-, -əˈ- (US) dɪˈskrɪm.ɪ.nə.tɔːr.i

discursion dɪˈskɜː.ʃᵊn, -ʒᵊn (US) -ˈskɝː.ʒᵊn, -ʃᵊn **-s** -z

discursive dɪˈskɜː.sɪv (US) -skɝː- **-ly** -li **-ness** -nəs, -nɪs

discursory dɪˈskɜː.sᵊr.i (US) -ˈskɝː-

disc|us ˈdɪs.k|əs **-i** -aɪ **-uses** -ə.sɪz

discuss dɪˈskʌs **-es** -ɪz **-ing** -ɪŋ **-ed** -t **-able** -ə.bl̩

discussant dɪˈskʌs.ᵊnt **-s** -s

discussion dɪˈskʌʃ.ᵊn **-s** -z

disdain dɪsˈdeɪn, dɪz- **-s** -z **-ing** -ɪŋ **-ed** -d

disdainful dɪsˈdeɪn.fᵊl, dɪz-, -fʊl **-ly** -i **-ness** -nəs, -nɪs

diseas|e dɪˈziːz, də- (US) dɪ- **-es** -ɪz **-ed** -d

disembark ˌdɪs.ɪmˈbɑːk, -em'- (US) -ˈbɑːrk, ˈ--- **-s** -s **-ing** -ɪŋ **-ed** -t

disembarkation ˌdɪs.ɪm.bɑːˈkeɪ.ʃᵊn, -em- (US) -bɑːr'- **-s** -z

disembarkment ˌdɪs.ɪmˈbɑːk.mənt, -em'- (US) -ˈbɑːrk- **-s** -s

disembarrass ˌdɪs.ɪmˈbær.əs, -em'- (US) -ˈber-, -ˈbær- **-es** -ɪz **-ing** -ɪŋ **-ed** -t

disembarrassment ˌdɪs.ɪmˈbær.əs.mənt, -em'- (US) -ˈber-, -ˈbær- **-s** -s

disembod|y ˌdɪs.ɪmˈbɒd|.i, -em'- (US) -ˈbɑː.d|i **-ies** -iz **-ying** -i.ɪŋ **-ied** -id

disembowel ˌdɪs.ɪmˈbaʊəl, -em'- **-s** -z **-(l)ing** -ɪŋ **-(l)ed** -d

disen|chant ˌdɪs.ɪn|ˈtʃɑːnt, -en'-, -ᵊn'- (US) -ˈtʃænt **-chants** -ˈtʃɑːnts (US) -ˈtʃænts **-chanting** -ˈtʃɑːn.tɪŋ (US) -ˈtʃæn.t̬ɪŋ **-chanted** -ˈtʃɑːn.tɪd (US) -ˈtʃæn.t̬ɪd

disenchantment ˌdɪs.ɪnˈtʃɑːnt.mənt, -en'-, -ᵊn'- (US) -ˈtʃænt- **-s** -s

disencumb|er ˌdɪs.ɪnˈkʌm.b|əʳ, -ɪŋ'-, -en'-, -eŋ'- (US) -b|ɚ **-ers** -əz (US) -ɚz **-ering** -ᵊr.ɪŋ **-ered** -əd (US) -ɚd

disendow ˌdɪs.ɪnˈdaʊ, -en'- **-s** -z **-ing** -ɪŋ **-ed** -d

disendowment ˌdɪs.ɪnˈdaʊ.mənt, -en'-

disenfranchis|e ˌdɪs.ɪnˈfræn.*t*ʃaɪz, -en'- **-es** -ɪz **-ing** -ɪŋ **-ed** -d

disenfranchisement ˌdɪs.ɪnˈfræn.*t*ʃɪz.mənt, -en'-, -*t*ʃaɪz- (US) -*t*ʃaɪz-, -*t*ʃɪz-

disengag|e ˌdɪs.ɪnˈgeɪdʒ, -ɪŋ'-, -en'-, -eŋ'- (US) -ɪn'-, -en'- **-es** -ɪz **-ing** -ɪŋ **-ed** -d

disengagement ˌdɪs.ɪnˈgeɪdʒ.mənt, -ɪŋ'-, -en'-, -eŋ'- (US) -ɪn'-, -en'-

disentail ˌdɪs.ɪnˈteɪl, -en'-, -ᵊn'- **-s** -z **-ing** -ɪŋ **-ed** -d

disentangl|e ˌdɪs.ɪnˈtæŋ.gl̩, -en'- **-es** -z **-ing** -ɪŋ, -ˈtæŋ.glɪŋ **-ed** -d

disentanglement ˌdɪs.ɪnˈtæŋ.gl̩.mənt, -en'-

disequilibrium ˌdɪs.ek.wɪˈlɪb.ri.əm, -iː.kwɪ'-, -kwə'- (US) ˌdɪs.iː.kwɪ'-; dɪˌsek.wɪ'-

disestablish ˌdɪs.ɪˈstæb.lɪʃ, -esˈtæb-, -əˈstæb- (US) -ɪˈstæb-, -esˈtæb-, ˈdɪs.ɪ.stæb-, -es.tæb- **-es** -ɪz **-ing** -ɪŋ **-ed** -t

disestablishment ˌdɪs.ɪˈstæb.lɪʃ.mənt, -esˈtæb-, -əˈstæb- (US) -ɪˈstæb-, -esˈtæb-

disestablishmentarian ˌdɪs.ɪˌstæb.lɪʃ.mənˈteə.ri.ən, -esˌtæb-, -əˌstæb- (US) -ɪˌstæb.lɪʃ.mənˈter.i-, -esˌtæb-

disfavo(u)r dɪsˈfeɪ.vəʳ (US) -vɚ

disfiguration dɪsˌfɪg.əˈreɪ.ʃᵊn, ˌdɪs.fɪg-, -jʊ'- (US) dɪsˌfɪg.jə'- **-s** -z

disfig|ure dɪsˈfɪg|.əʳ (US) -j|ɚ **-ures** -əz (US) -ɚz **-uring** -ᵊr.ɪŋ **-ured** -əd (US) -ɚd **-urement/s** -ə.mənt/s (US) -ɚ.mənt/s

disforest dɪsˈfɒr.ɪst, -əst (US) -ˈfɔːr- **-s** -s **-ing** -ɪŋ **-ed** -ɪd

disfranchis|e dɪsˈfræn.*t*ʃaɪz **-es** -ɪz **-ing** -ɪŋ **-ed** -d

disfranchisement dɪsˈfræn.*t*ʃɪz.mənt, -*t*ʃəz-, -*t*ʃaɪz- (US) -tʃaɪz-, -tʃɪz-

disgorg|e dɪsˈgɔːdʒ (US) -ˈgɔːrdʒ **-es** -ɪz **-ing** -ɪŋ **-ed** -d

disgrac|e dɪsˈɡreɪs, dɪz- Ⓤⓢ dɪs- **-es** -ɪz **-ing** -ɪŋ **-ed** -t
disgraceful dɪsˈɡreɪs.fəl, dɪz-, -fʊl Ⓤⓢ dɪs- **-ly** -i **-ness** -nəs, -nɪs
disgruntled dɪsˈɡrʌn.tl̩d Ⓤⓢ -t̬l̩d
disgruntlement dɪsˈɡrʌn.tl̩.mənt Ⓤⓢ -t̬l̩-
disguis|e dɪsˈɡaɪz, dɪz- Ⓤⓢ dɪs- **-es** -ɪz **-ing** -ɪŋ **-ed** -d **-er/s** -əʳ/z Ⓤⓢ -ɚ/z
disgust dɪsˈɡʌst, dɪz- Ⓤⓢ dɪs- **-s** -s **-ing** -ɪŋ **-ed/ly** -ɪd/li
disgusting dɪsˈɡʌs.tɪŋ, dɪz- Ⓤⓢ dɪs- **-ly** -li
dish dɪʃ **-es** -ɪz **-ing** -ɪŋ **-ed** -t
dishabille ˌdɪs.æbˈiːl, -əˈbiːl Ⓤⓢ -əˈ-
disharmony dɪsˈhɑː.mən.i Ⓤⓢ -ˈhɑːr-
dish|cloth ˈdɪʃ|.klɒθ Ⓤⓢ -klɑːθ **-cloths** -klɒθs, -klɒðz Ⓤⓢ -klɑːθs, -klɑːðz
dishearten dɪsˈhɑː.tən Ⓤⓢ -ˈhɑːr- **-s** -z **-ing/ly** -ɪŋ/li **-ed** -d
dishevel dɪˈʃev.əl **-s** -z **-(l)ing** -ɪŋ **-(l)ed** -d
dishful ˈdɪʃ.fʊl **-s** -z
dishonest dɪˈsɒn.ɪst, -ˈzɒn-, -əst Ⓤⓢ -ˈsɑː.nɪst, -nəst **-ly** -li
dishonest|y dɪˈsɒn.ɪ.st|i, -ˈzɒn-, ˈ-ə- Ⓤⓢ -ˈsɑː.nə- **-ies** -iz
dishono(u)r dɪˈsɒn.əʳ, -ˈzɒn- Ⓤⓢ -ˈsɑː.nɚ **-s** -z **-ing** -ɪŋ **-ed** -d **-er/s** -əʳ/z Ⓤⓢ -ɚ/z
dishono(u)rab|le dɪˈsɒn.ər.ə.b|l̩, -ˈzɒn- Ⓤⓢ -ˈsɑː.nɚ- **-ly** -li **-leness** -l̩.nəs, -nɪs
dishrag ˈdɪʃ.ræɡ **-s** -z
dishtowel ˈdɪʃ.taʊəl **-s** -z
dishwash|er ˈdɪʃˌwɒʃ|.əʳ Ⓤⓢ -ˌwɑː.ʃ|ɚ, -ˌwɔː- **-ers** -əz Ⓤⓢ -ɚz **-ing** -ɪŋ
dishwater ˈdɪʃˌwɔː.təʳ Ⓤⓢ -ˌwɑː.t̬ɚ, -ˌwɔː-
dish|y ˈdɪʃ|.i **-ier** -i.əʳ Ⓤⓢ -i.ɚ **-iest** -i.ɪst, -i.əst
disillusion ˌdɪs.ɪˈluː.ʒən, -əˈ-, -ˈljuː- Ⓤⓢ -ˈluː- **-s** -z **-ing** -ɪŋ **-ed** -d **-ment/s** -mənt/s
disincentive ˌdɪs.ɪnˈsen.tɪv Ⓤⓢ -t̬ɪv **-s** -z
disinclination ˌdɪs.ɪn.klɪˈneɪ.ʃən, -ɪŋ-, -kləˈ- Ⓤⓢ -ɪn-
disinclin|e ˌdɪs.ɪnˈklaɪn, -ɪŋˈ- Ⓤⓢ -ɪn- **-es** -z **-ing** -ɪŋ **-ed** -d
disinfect ˌdɪs.ɪnˈfekt **-s** -s **-ing** -ɪŋ **-ed** -ɪd
disinfectant ˌdɪs.ɪnˈfek.tənt **-s** -s
disinfection ˌdɪs.ɪnˈfek.ʃən **-s** -z
disinfestation ˌdɪs.ɪn.fesˈteɪ.ʃən
disinflation ˌdɪs.ɪnˈfleɪ.ʃən
disinformation ˌdɪs.ɪn.fəˈmeɪ.ʃən, -fɔːˈ- Ⓤⓢ -fɚˈ-
disingenuous ˌdɪs.ɪnˈdʒen.ju.əs **-ly** -li **-ness** -nəs, -nɪs
disinher|it ˌdɪs.ɪnˈher|.ɪt **-its** -ɪts **-iting** -ɪ.tɪŋ Ⓤⓢ -ɪ.t̬ɪŋ **-ited** -ɪ.tɪd Ⓤⓢ -ɪ.t̬ɪd
disinheritance ˌdɪs.ɪnˈher.ɪ.tənts Ⓤⓢ -t̬ənts
disintegrable dɪˈsɪn.tɪ.ɡrə.bl̩, -tə- Ⓤⓢ -t̬ə-
disinte|grate dɪˈsɪn.tɪ|.ɡreɪt, -tə- Ⓤⓢ -t̬ə- **-grates** -ɡreɪts **-grating** -ɡreɪ.tɪŋ Ⓤⓢ -ɡreɪ.t̬ɪŋ **-grated** -ɡreɪ.tɪd Ⓤⓢ -ɡreɪ.t̬ɪd **-grator/s** -ɡreɪ.təʳ/z Ⓤⓢ -ɡreɪ.t̬ɚ/z
disintegration dɪˌsɪn.tɪˈɡreɪ.ʃən, -təˈ-; ˌdɪs.ɪn- Ⓤⓢ ˌdɪs.ɪn.t̬əˈ- **-s** -z
disinter ˌdɪs.ɪnˈtɜːʳ Ⓤⓢ -ˈtɝː **-s** -z **-ring** -ɪŋ **-red** -d
disinterest dɪˈsɪn.trəst, -trest, -trɪst; ˈ-tər.əst, -est, -ɪst Ⓤⓢ -ˈsɪn.trɪst, -trəst, -trest; ˈ-t̬ɚ.ɪst, -əst, -est
disinterested dɪˈsɪn.trə.stɪd, -tres.tɪd, -trɪ.stɪd; ˈ-tər.ə.stɪd, -es.tɪd, -ɪ.stɪd Ⓤⓢ -ˈsɪn.trɪ.stɪd, -trə-, -tres.tɪd; ˈ-t̬ɚ.ɪ.stɪd, -ə-, -es.tɪd **-ly** -li **-ness** -nəs, -nɪs
disinterment ˌdɪs.ɪnˈtɜː.mənt Ⓤⓢ -ˈtɝː- **-s** -s
disinvest ˌdɪs.ɪnˈvest **-s** -s **-ing** -ɪŋ **-ed** -ɪd **-ment** -mənt
disjoin dɪsˈdʒɔɪn, dɪz- Ⓤⓢ dɪs- **-s** -z **-ing** -ɪŋ **-ed** -d
disjoint dɪsˈdʒɔɪnt, dɪz- Ⓤⓢ dɪs- **-s** -s **-ing** -ɪŋ **-ed** -ɪd
disjointed dɪsˈdʒɔɪn.tɪd, dɪz- Ⓤⓢ dɪsˈdʒɔɪn.t̬ɪd **-ly** -li **-ness** -nəs, -nɪs
disjunct dɪsˈdʒʌŋ*k*t, ˈ--
disjunction dɪsˈdʒʌŋ*k*.ʃən **-s** -z
disjunctive dɪsˈdʒʌŋ*k*.tɪv **-ly** -li
disk dɪsk **-s** -s ˈ**disk** ˌ**drive**
diskette dɪˈsket **-s** -s
dislik|e dɪˈslaɪk, dɪzˈlaɪk Ⓤⓢ dɪˈslaɪk **-es** -s **-ing** -ɪŋ **-ed** -t **-able** -ə.bl̩
Note: The stress /ˈ--/ is, however, used in the expression **likes and dislikes.**
dislo|cate ˈdɪs.ləʊ|.keɪt Ⓤⓢ dɪˈsloʊ-; ˈdɪs.loʊ- **-cates** -keɪts **-cating** -keɪ.tɪŋ Ⓤⓢ -keɪ.t̬ɪŋ **-cated** -keɪ.tɪd Ⓤⓢ -keɪ.t̬ɪd
dislocation ˌdɪs.ləʊˈkeɪ.ʃən Ⓤⓢ -loʊˈ- **-s** -z
dislodg|e dɪˈslɒdʒ Ⓤⓢ -ˈslɑːdʒ **-es** -ɪz **-ing** -ɪŋ **-ed** -d **-(e)ment** -mənt
disloyal dɪˈslɔɪəl; ˌdɪsˈlɔɪəl **-ly** -i
disloyalt|y dɪˈslɔɪəl.t|i; ˌdɪsˈlɔɪəl- Ⓤⓢ -t̬|i **-ies** -iz
dismal ˈdɪz.məl **-ly** -i **-ness** -nəs, -nɪs
dismantl|e dɪˈsmæn.tl̩, dɪzˈmæn- Ⓤⓢ dɪˈsmæn.t̬l̩ **-es** -z **-ing** -ɪŋ, dɪˈsmænt.lɪŋ, dɪzˈmænt- Ⓤⓢ dɪˈsmæn.tl̩.ɪŋ, -ˈsmænt.lɪŋ **-ed** -d
dismast ˌdɪsˈmɑːst Ⓤⓢ -ˈmæst **-s** -s **-ing** -ɪŋ **-ed** -ɪd
dismay dɪˈsmeɪ, dɪzˈmeɪ **-s** -z **-ing** -ɪŋ **-ed** -d
dismemb|er dɪˈsmem.b|əʳ Ⓤⓢ -b|ɚ **-ers** -əz Ⓤⓢ -ɚz **-ering** -ər.ɪŋ **-ered** -əd Ⓤⓢ -ɚd **-erment** -ə.mənt Ⓤⓢ -ɚ.mənt
dismiss dɪˈsmɪs **-es** -ɪz **-ing** -ɪŋ **-ed** -t
dismissal dɪˈsmɪs.əl **-s** -z
dismissive dɪˈsmɪs.ɪv **-ly** -li **-ness** -nəs, -nɪs
dis|mount dɪˈs|maʊnt **-mounts** -maʊnts **-mounting** -maʊn.tɪŋ Ⓤⓢ -maʊn.t̬ɪŋ **-mounted** -maʊn.tɪd Ⓤⓢ -maʊn.t̬ɪd
Disney ˈdɪz.ni ˈ**Disney** ˌ**World®**
Disneyland® ˈdɪz.ni.lænd
disobedience ˌdɪs.əʊˈbiː.di.ən*t*s Ⓤⓢ -əˈ-, -oʊˈ-
disobedient ˌdɪs.əʊˈbiː.di.ənt Ⓤⓢ -əˈ-, -oʊˈ- **-ly** -li
disobey ˌdɪs.əʊˈbeɪ Ⓤⓢ -əˈ-, -oʊˈ- **-s** -z **-ing** -ɪŋ **-ed** -d
disoblig|e ˌdɪs.əˈblaɪdʒ **-es** -ɪz **-ing/ly** -ɪŋ/li **-ingness** -ɪŋ.nəs, -nɪs **-ed** -d
disord|er dɪˈsɔː.d|əʳ, -ˈzɔː- Ⓤⓢ -ˈsɔːr.d|ɚ, -ˈzɔːr- **-ers** -əz Ⓤⓢ -ɚz **-ering** -ər.ɪŋ **-ered** -əd Ⓤⓢ -ɚd
disorderl|y dɪˈsɔː.dəl|.i, -ˈzɔː- Ⓤⓢ -ˈsɔːr.dɚ.l|i, -ˈzɔːr- **-iness** -ɪ.nəs, -ɪ.nɪs
disorganization, -isa- dɪˌsɔː.ɡə.naɪˈzeɪ.ʃən, -ˌzɔː-, -nɪˈ-; ˌdɪs.ɔː-, ˌdɪz- Ⓤⓢ dɪˌsɔːr.ɡə.nɪˈ-, -ˌzɔːr-
disorganiz|e, -is|e dɪˈsɔː.ɡə.naɪz, -ˈzɔː-; ˌdɪsˈɔː-, ˌdɪzˈɔː- Ⓤⓢ dɪˈsɔːr-, -ˈzɔːr- **-es** -ɪz **-ing** -ɪŋ **-ed** -d
disorien|t dɪˈsɔː.ri.ən|t, -en|t Ⓤⓢ -ˈsɔːr.i.en|t **-ts** -ts **-ting** -tɪŋ Ⓤⓢ -t̬ɪŋ **-ted** -tɪd Ⓤⓢ -t̬ɪd
disorien|tate dɪˈsɔː.ri.ən|.teɪt, -en-; ˌdɪsˈɔːr- Ⓤⓢ dɪˈsɔːr.i- **-tates** -teɪts **-tating** -teɪ.tɪŋ Ⓤⓢ -teɪ.t̬ɪŋ **-tated** -teɪ.tɪd Ⓤⓢ -teɪ.t̬ɪd
disorientation dɪˌsɔː.ri.ənˈteɪ.ʃən, -enˈ-; ˌdɪsˌɔː- Ⓤⓢ dɪˌsɔːr.i-
disown dɪˈsəʊn; ˌdɪsˈəʊn Ⓤⓢ dɪˈsoʊn **-s** -z **-ing** -ɪŋ **-ed** -d
disparag|e dɪˈspær.ɪdʒ Ⓤⓢ -ˈsper-, -ˈspær- **-es** -ɪz **-ing/ly** -ɪŋ/li **-ed** -d **-er/s** -əʳ/z Ⓤⓢ -ɚ/z **-ement** -mənt
disparate ˈdɪs.pər.ət, -ɪt, -eɪt Ⓤⓢ -ət, -ɪt; dɪˈsper-, -ˈspær- **-s** -s
disparit|y dɪˈspær.ə.t|i, -ɪ.t|i Ⓤⓢ -ˈper.ə.t̬|i, -ˈpær- **-ies** -iz
dispassionate dɪˈspæʃ.ən.ət, -ɪt **-ly** -li **-ness** -nəs, -nɪs
dispatch (*n.*) dɪˈspætʃ, də-; ˈdɪs.pætʃ Ⓤⓢ dɪˈspætʃ; ˈdɪs.pætʃ **-es** -ɪz disˈ**patch** ˌ**box**; disˈ**patch** ˌ**rider**
dispatch (*v.*) dɪˈspætʃ, də- Ⓤⓢ dɪ- **-es** -ɪz **-ing** -ɪŋ **-ed** -t **-er/s** -əʳ/z Ⓤⓢ -ɚ/z
dispel dɪˈspel **-s** -z **-(l)ing** -ɪŋ **-(l)ed** -d
dispensable dɪˈspen*t*.sə.bl̩
dispensar|y dɪˈspen*t*.sər|.i **-ies** -iz
dispensation ˌdɪs.penˈseɪ.ʃən, -pənˈ- **-s** -z
dispensator|y dɪˈspen.sə.tər|.i, -tr|i Ⓤⓢ -tɔːr|.i **-ies** -iz

dispens|e dɪˈspent*s* **-es** -ɪz **-ing** -ɪŋ **-ed** -t **-er/s** -əʳ/z (US) -ɚ/z

dispersal dɪˈspɜː.sᵊl (US) -ˈspɝː- **-s** -z

dispers|e dɪˈspɜːs (US) -spɝːs **-es** -ɪz **-ing** -ɪŋ **-ed** -t **-er/s** -əʳ/z (US) -ɚ/z **-ant/s** -ᵊnt/s

dispersion (D) dɪˈspɜː.ʃᵊn (US) -ˈspɝː.ʒᵊn, -ʃᵊn **-s** -z

dispersive dɪˈspɜː.sɪv (US) -ˈspɝː.zɪv, -sɪv

dispir|it dɪˈspɪr|.ɪt **-its** -ɪts **-iting** -ɪ.tɪŋ (US) -ɪ.t̬ɪŋ **-ited/ly** -ɪ.tɪd/li (US) -ɪ.t̬ɪd/li **-itedness** -ɪ.tɪd.nəs, -nɪs (US) -ɪ.t̬ɪd.nəs, -nɪs

displac|e dɪˈspleɪs **-es** -ɪz **-ing** -ɪŋ **-ed** -t

displacement dɪˈspleɪs.mənt

display dɪˈspleɪ **-s** -z **-ing** -ɪŋ **-ed** -d **-er/s** -əʳ/z (US) -ɚ/z

displeas|e dɪˈspliːz **-es** -ɪz **-ing/ly** -ɪŋ/li **-ed** -d

displeasure dɪˈspleʒ.əʳ (US) -ɚ

di|sport dɪ|ˈspɔːt (US) -|ˈspɔːrt **-sports** -ˈspɔːts (US) -ˈspɔːrts **-sporting** -ˈspɔː.tɪŋ (US) -ˈspɔːr.t̬ɪŋ **-sported** -ˈspɔː.tɪd (US) -ˈspɔːr.t̬ɪd

disposable dɪˈspəʊ.zə.bl̩, də- (US) dɪˈspoʊ-

disposal dɪˈspəʊ.zᵊl, də- (US) dɪˈspoʊ- **-s** -z

Disposall® dɪˈspəʊ.zɔːl, də- (US) dɪˈspoʊ.zɑːl, -zɔːl

dispos|e dɪˈspəʊz, də- (US) -ˈspoʊz **-es** -ɪz **-ing** -ɪŋ **-ed** -d **-er/s** -əʳ/z (US) -ɚ/z

disposition ˌdɪs.pəˈzɪʃ.ᵊn **-s** -z

dispossess ˌdɪs.pəˈzes **-es** -ɪz **-ing** -ɪŋ **-ed** -t

dispossession ˌdɪs.pəˈzeʃ.ᵊn

Disprin® ˈdɪs.prɪn **-s** -z

disproof dɪˈspruːf

disproportion ˌdɪs.prəˈpɔː.ʃᵊn (US) -ˈpɔːr- **-ed** -d

disproportional ˌdɪs.prəˈpɔː.ʃᵊn.ᵊl, -ˈpɔːʃ.nᵊl (US) -ˈpɔːr.ʃᵊn.ᵊl, -ˈpɔːrʃ.nᵊl **-ly** -i

disproportionate ˌdɪs.prəˈpɔː.ʃᵊn.ət, -ɪt (US) -ˈpɔːr- **-ly** -li **-ness** -nəs, -nɪs

disproval dɪˈspruː.vᵊl; dɪsˈpruː-

disprov|e dɪˈspruːv; ˌdɪsˈpruːv **-es** -z **-ing** -ɪŋ **-ed** -d

disputable dɪˈspjuː.tə.bl̩, də-; ˈdɪs.pjʊ- (US) dɪˈspjuː.t̬ə-; ˈdɪs.pjʊ-, -pjə-

disputableness dɪˈspjuː.tə.bl̩.nəs, də-, -nɪs (US) dɪˈspjuː.t̬ə-

disputant dɪˈspjuː.tᵊnt; ˈdɪs.pjʊ- (US) ˈdɪs.pjʊ.tᵊnt, -pjə-; dɪˈspjuː- **-s** -s

disputation ˌdɪs.pjʊˈteɪ.ʃᵊn (US) -pjuːˈ- **-s** -z

disputatious ˌdɪs.pjʊˈteɪ.ʃəs (US) -pjuːˈ- **-ly** -li **-ness** -nəs, -nɪs

disputative dɪˈspjuː.tə.tɪv (US) -t̬ə.t̬ɪv

dispute (*n.*) dɪˈspjuːt; ˈdɪs.pjuːt (US) dɪˈspjuːt **-s** -s

di|spute (*v.*) dɪ|ˈspjuːt **-sputes** -ˈspjuːts **-sputing** -ˈspjuː.tɪŋ (US) -ˈspjuː.t̬ɪŋ **-sputed** -ˈspjuː.tɪd (US) -ˈspjuː.t̬ɪd **-sputer/s** -ˈspjuː.təʳ/z (US) -ˈspjuː.t̬ɚ/z

disqualification dɪˌskwɒl.ɪ.fɪˈkeɪ.ʃᵊn, ˌ-ə-; ˌdɪsˌkwɒl- (US) dɪˌskwɑː.lə- **-s** -z

disquali|fy dɪˈskwɒl.ɪ|.faɪ, ˈ-ə-; ˌdɪsˈkwɒl- (US) dɪˈskwɑː.lə- **-fies** -faɪz **-fying** -faɪ.ɪŋ **-fied** -faɪd

di|squiet (*n. v.*) dɪ|ˈskwaɪət **-squiets** -ˈskwaɪəts **-squieting** -ˈskwaɪə.tɪŋ (US) -ˈskwaɪə.t̬ɪŋ **-squieted** -ˈskwaɪə.tɪd (US) -ˈskwaɪə.t̬ɪd

disquietude dɪˈskwaɪə.tjuːd, -ˈskwaɪ.ɪ- (US) -ˈskwaɪə.tuːd, -tjuːd

disquisition ˌdɪs.kwɪˈzɪʃ.ᵊn, -kwəˈ- **-s** -z

disquisitional ˌdɪs.kwɪˈzɪʃ.ᵊn.ᵊl, -kwəˈ-, ˈ-nᵊl

disquisitive dɪˈskwɪz.ə.tɪv, -ɪ.tɪv (US) -ə.t̬ɪv

Disraeli dɪzˈreɪ.li, dɪs-

d'Israeli dɪzˈreɪ.li, dɪs-

disregard ˌdɪs.rɪˈgɑːd, -rəˈ- (US) -rɪˈgɑːrd **-s** -z **-ing** -ɪŋ **-ed** -ɪd

disregardful ˌdɪs.rɪˈgɑːd.fᵊl, -rəˈ-, -fʊl (US) -rɪˈgɑːrd- **-ly** -i

disrepair ˌdɪs.rɪˈpeəʳ, -rəˈ- (US) -rɪˈper

disreputability dɪsˌrep.jə.təˈbɪl.ə.ti, -jʊ-, -ɪ.ti (US) -jə.t̬əˈ-

disreputab|le dɪsˈrep.jə.tə.bl|, -jʊ- (US) -jə.t̬ə- **-ly** -li **-leness** -l̩.nəs, -nɪs

disrepute ˌdɪs.rɪˈpjuːt, -rəˈ- (US) -rɪˈ-

disrespect ˌdɪs.rɪˈspekt, -rəˈ- (US) -rɪˈ-

disrespectful ˌdɪs.rɪˈspekt.fᵊl, -rəˈ-, -fʊl (US) -rɪˈ- **-ly** -i **-ness** -nəs, -nɪs

disrob|e dɪsˈrəʊb (US) -ˈroʊb **-es** -z **-ing** -ɪŋ **-ed** -d

disrupt dɪsˈrʌpt **-s** -s **-ing** -ɪŋ **-ed** -ɪd

disruption dɪsˈrʌp.ʃᵊn **-s** -z

disruptive dɪsˈrʌp.tɪv **-ly** -li **-ness** -nəs, -nɪs

Diss dɪs

dis(s) dɪs **-es** -ɪz **-ing** -ɪŋ **-ed** -t

dissatisfaction dɪsˌsæt.ɪsˈfæk.ʃᵊn, ˌdɪs.sæt-, -əsˈ- (US) ˌdɪs.sæt̬.əsˈ-

dissatisfactor|y dɪsˌsæt.ɪsˈfæk.tᵊr|.i, ˌdɪs.sæt-, -əsˈ- (US) ˌdɪs.sæt̬.əsˈ- **-ily** -ᵊl.i, -ɪ.li **-iness** -i.nəs, -i.nɪs

dissatis|fy dɪsˈsæt.ɪs|.faɪ, ˌdɪs-, -əs- (US) -ˈsæt̬.əs- **-fies** -faɪz **-fying** -faɪ.ɪŋ **-fied** -faɪd

dissect dɪˈsekt, də-, daɪ- (US) dɪˈsekt, daɪ-; ˈdaɪ.sekt **-s** -s **-ing** -ɪŋ **-ed** -ɪd **-or/s** -əʳ/z (US) -ɚ/z **-ible** -ə.bl̩, -ɪ.bl̩

dissection dɪˈsek.ʃᵊn, də-, daɪ- (US) dɪˈsek-, daɪ-; ˈdaɪ.sek- **-s** -z

dissemblanc|e dɪˈsem.blən*t*s **-es** -ɪz

dissembl|e dɪˈsem.bl̩ **-es** -z **-ing** -ɪŋ, ˈ-blɪŋ **-ed** -d **-er/s** -əʳ/z, ˈ-bləʳ/z (US) -ə/z

dissemi|nate dɪˈsem.ɪ|.neɪt, ˈ-ə- **-nates** -neɪts **-nating** -neɪ.tɪŋ (US) -neɪ.t̬ɪŋ **-nated** -neɪ.tɪd (US) -neɪ.t̬ɪd **-nator/s** -neɪ.təʳ/z (US) -neɪ.t̬ɚ/z

dissemination dɪˌsem.ɪˈneɪ.ʃᵊn, -əˈ-

dissension, dissention dɪˈsen.*t*ʃᵊn **-s** -z

dis|sent dɪ|ˈsent **-sents** -ˈsents **-senting** -ˈsen.tɪŋ (US) -ˈsen.t̬ɪŋ **-sented** -ˈsen.tɪd (US) -ˈsen.t̬ɪd **-senter/s** -ˈsen.təʳ/z (US) -ˈsen.t̬ɚ/z

dissentient dɪˈsen.*t*ʃi.ənt, -*t*ʃᵊnt (US) -ˈsen*t*.ʃᵊnt **-s** -s

dissertation ˌdɪs.əˈteɪ.ʃᵊn, -ɜːˈ- (US) -ɚˈ- **-s** -z

disservic|e ˌdɪsˈsɜː.vɪs, dɪ- (US) -ˈsɝː- **-es** -ɪz

dissev|er dɪsˈsev|.əʳ (US) -ɚ **-ers** -əz (US) -ɚz **-ering** -ᵊr.ɪŋ **-ered** -əd (US) -ɚd **-erment** -ə.mənt (US) -ɚ.mənt **-erance** -ᵊr.ᵊn*t*s

dissidence ˈdɪs.ɪ.dᵊn*t*s, ˈ-ə-

dissident ˈdɪs.ɪ.dᵊnt, ˈ-ə- **-s** -s

dissimilar ˌdɪsˈsɪm.ɪ.ləʳ, dɪ-, ˈ-ə- (US) -lɚ **-ly** -li

dissimilarit|y ˌdɪsˌsɪm.ɪˈlær.ə.t|i, dɪ-, -əˈ-, -ɪ.t|i (US) -ˈler.ə.t̬|i, -ˈlær- **-ies** -iz

dissimi|late dɪˈsɪm.ɪ|.leɪt, ˌdɪs-, ˈ-ə- **-lates** -leɪts **-lating** -leɪ.tɪŋ (US) -leɪ.t̬ɪŋ **-lated** -leɪ.tɪd (US) -leɪ.t̬ɪd

dissimilation ˌdɪsˌsɪm.ɪˈleɪ.ʃᵊn, dɪ-, -əˈ- **-s** -z

dissimilitude ˌdɪs.sɪˈmɪl.ɪ.tjuːd, -ɪˈ-, ˈ-ə- (US) -tuːd, -tjuːd

dissimu|late dɪˈsɪm.jə|.leɪt, ˌdɪs-, -jʊ- **-lates** -leɪts **-lating** -leɪ.tɪŋ (US) -leɪ.t̬ɪŋ **-lated** -leɪ.tɪd (US) -leɪ.t̬ɪd **-lator/s** -leɪ.təʳ/z (US) -leɪ.t̬ɚ/z

dissimulation ˌdɪsˌsɪm.jəˈleɪ.ʃᵊn, dɪ-, -jʊˈ- **-s** -z

dissi|pate ˈdɪs.ɪ|.peɪt, ˈ-ə- **-pates** -peɪts **-pating** -peɪ.tɪŋ (US) -peɪ.t̬ɪŋ **-pated** -peɪ.tɪd (US) -peɪ.t̬ɪd **-pative** -peɪ.tɪv (US) -peɪ.t̬ɪv

dissipation ˌdɪs.ɪˈpeɪ.ʃᵊn, -əˈ- **-s** -z

dissociable *separable:* dɪˈsəʊ.ʃi.ə.bl̩, ˌdɪs- (US) -ˈsoʊ-, -ʃə.bl̩ *unsociable:* ˌdɪsˈsəʊ.ʃə.bl̩, dɪ- (US) -ˈsoʊ-

dissoci|ate dɪˈsəʊ.ʃi|.eɪt, -si- (US) -ˈsoʊ- **-ates** -eɪts **-ating** -eɪ.tɪŋ (US) -eɪ.t̬ɪŋ **-ated** -eɪ.tɪd (US) -eɪ.t̬ɪd

dissociation dɪˌsəʊ.ʃiˈeɪ.ʃᵊn, ˌdɪs-, -siˈ- (US) -ˌsoʊ-

dissolubility dɪˌsɒl.jəˈbɪl.ə.ti, -jʊˈ-, -ɪ.ti (US) -ˌsɑːl.jəˈbɪl.ə.t̬i, -jʊˈ-

dissolub|le dɪˈsɒl.jə.bl|, -jʊ- (US) -ˈsɑːl- **-ly** -li **-leness** -l̩.nəs, -nɪs

dissolute ˈdɪs.ə.luːt, -ljuːt (US) -luːt **-s** -s **-ly** -li **-ness** -nəs, -nɪs

dissolution ˌdɪs.əˈluː.ʃᵊn, -ˈljuː- (US) -ˈluː- **-s** -z

dissolvability dɪˌzɒl.vəˈbɪl.ə.ti,

də,zɒl-, -ˌsɒl-, -ɪ.ti (US) dɪˌzɑːl.və'bɪl.ə.ţi, -ˌzɔːl-

dissolv|e dɪ'zɒlv, -'sɒlv (US) -'zɑːlv, -'zɔːlv **-es** -z **-ing** -ɪŋ **-ed** -d **-able** -ə.bḷ

dissolvent dɪ'zɒl.vənt, -'sɒl- (US) -'zɑːl-, -'zɔːl- **-s** -s

dissonanc|e 'dɪs.ᵊn.ən*t*s **-es** -ɪz

dissonant 'dɪs.ᵊn.ənt **-ly** -li

dissuad|e dɪ'sweɪd **-es** -z **-ing** -ɪŋ **-ed** -ɪd

dissuasion dɪ'sweɪ.ʒᵊn

dissuasive dɪ'sweɪ.sɪv, -zɪv (US) -sɪv **-ly** -li **-ness** -nəs, -nɪs

dissymmetric ˌdɪs.ɪ'met.rɪk, -sɪm'-

dissymmetry dɪ'sɪm.ɪ.tri, ˌdɪs-, '-ə-

distaff 'dɪs.tɑːf (US) -tæf **-s** -s

distanc|e 'dɪs.tᵊn*t*s **-es** -ɪz **-ing** -ɪŋ **-ed** -t

distant 'dɪs.tᵊnt **-ly** -li

distaste dɪ'steɪst **-s** -s

distasteful dɪ'steɪst.fᵊl, -fʊl **-ly** -i **-ness** -nəs, -nɪs

distemp|er dɪ'stem.pləʳ (US) -plɚ **-ers** -əz (US) -ɚz **-ering** -ᵊr.ɪŋ **-ered** -əd (US) -ɚd

distend dɪ'stend **-s** -z **-ing** -ɪŋ **-ed** -ɪd

distensible dɪ'sten*t*.sə.bḷ, -sɪ-

distension dɪ'sten.*t*ʃᵊn (US) -'sten*t*.ʃᵊn

distich 'dɪs.tɪk **-s** -s **-ous** -əs

distil(l) dɪ'stɪl, də- (US) dɪ- **-s** -z **-ing** -ɪŋ **-ed** -d

distillate 'dɪs.tɪ.lət, -tᵊl.ət, -eɪt, -ɪt (US) -tə.leɪt, -tᵊl.ɪt; dɪ'stɪl.ɪt **-s** -s

distillation ˌdɪs.tɪ'leɪ.ʃᵊn, -tə'- **-s** -z

distillatory dɪ'stɪl.ə.tᵊr.i, də-, -tri (US) dɪ'stɪl.ə.tɔːr.i

distiller dɪ'stɪl.əʳ, də- (US) dɪ'stɪl.ɚ **-s** -z

distiller|y dɪ'stɪl.ᵊr|.i, də- (US) dɪ- **-ies** -iz

distinct dɪ'stɪŋ*k*t, də- (US) dɪ- **-est** -ɪst, -əst **-ly** -li **-ness** -nəs, -nɪs

distinction dɪ'stɪŋ*k*.ʃᵊn, də- (US) dɪ- **-s** -z

distinctive dɪ'stɪŋ*k*.tɪv, də- (US) dɪ- **-ly** -li **-ness** -nəs, -nɪs

distinguish dɪ'stɪŋ.gwɪʃ, də- (US) dɪ- **-es** -ɪz **-ing** -ɪŋ **-ed** -t

distinguishab|le dɪ'stɪŋ.gwɪ.ʃə.b|ḷ, də- (US) dɪ- **-ly** -li

di|stort dɪ|'stɔːt (US) -'stɔːrt **-storts** -'stɔːts (US) -'stɔːrts **-storting** -'stɔː.tɪŋ (US) -'stɔːr.ţɪŋ **-storted** -'stɔː.tɪd (US) -'stɔːr.ţɪd

distortion dɪ'stɔː.ʃᵊn (US) -'stɔːr- **-s** -z

distract dɪ'strækt, də'strækt (US) dɪ- **-s** -s **-ing** -ɪŋ **-ed/ly** -ɪd/li **-edness** -ɪd.nəs, -nɪs

distraction dɪ'stræk.ʃᵊn, də- **-s** -z

distrain dɪ'streɪn, də- (US) dɪ- **-s** -z **-ing** -ɪŋ **-ed** -d **-er/s** -əʳ/z (US) -ɚ/z **-able** -ə.bḷ

distrainee ˌdɪs.treɪ'niː **-s** -z

distrainor ˌdɪs.treɪ'nɔːʳ (US) -'nɔːr, dɪ'streɪ.nɚ **-s** -z

distraint dɪ'streɪnt **-s** -s

distrait dɪ'streɪ; 'dɪs.treɪ (US) dɪ'streɪ

distraught dɪ'strɔːt (US) -'strɑːt, -'strɔːt

distress dɪ'stres **-es** -ɪz **-ing/ly** -ɪŋ/li **-ed** -t

distressful dɪ'stres.fᵊl, -fʊl **-ly** -i

distributable dɪ'strɪb.jə.tə.bḷ, -jʊ- (US) -ţə-

distribu|te dɪ'strɪb.juː|t; 'dɪs.trɪ.bjuː|t, -trə- (US) dɪ'strɪb.juː|t, -jʊ|t, -jə|t **-tes** -ts **-ting** -tɪŋ (US) -ţɪŋ **-ted** -tɪd (US) -ţɪd

distribution ˌdɪs.trɪ'bjuː.ʃᵊn, -trə'- **-s** -z

distributive dɪ'strɪb.jə.tɪv, -jʊ- (US) -jə.ţɪv **-ly** -li

distributor dɪ'strɪb.jə.təʳ, -jʊ- (US) -ţɚ **-s** -z

district 'dɪs.trɪkt **-s** -s ˌ**district at'torney**; ˌ**District of Co'lumbia**

distrust dɪ'strʌst; ˌdɪs'trʌst **-s** -s **-ing** -ɪŋ **-ed** -ɪd

distrustful dɪ'strʌst.fᵊl, -fʊl; ˌdɪs'trʌst- **-ly** -i **-ness** -nəs, -nɪs

disturb dɪ'stɜːb (US) -'stɝːb **-s** -z **-ing/ly** -ɪŋ/li **-ed** -d **-er/s** -əʳ/z (US) -ɚ/z

disturbanc|e dɪ'stɜː.bᵊn*t*s (US) -'stɝː- **-es** -ɪz

distyle 'dɪs.taɪl; 'daɪ.staɪl **-s** -z

disulphate daɪ'sʌl.feɪt, -fɪt **-s** -s

disulphide daɪ'sʌl.faɪd **-s** -z

disunion dɪ'sjuː.njən, -ni.ən (US) '-njən **-s** -z

disu|nite ˌdɪs.juː|'naɪt **-nites** -'naɪts **-niting** -'naɪ.tɪŋ (US) -'naɪ.ţɪŋ **-nited** -'naɪ.tɪd (US) -'naɪ.ţɪd

disunity dɪ'sjuː.nɪ.ti, -nə- (US) -ţi

disuse (*n.*) dɪ'sjuːs

disus|e (*v.*) dɪ'sjuːz **-es** -ɪz **-ing** -ɪŋ **-ed** -d

disyllabic ˌdaɪ.sɪ'læb.ɪk, ˌdɪs.ɪ'-, -ə'-

disyllable daɪ'sɪl.ə.bḷ, dɪ- **-s** -z

ditch dɪtʃ **-es** -ɪz **-ing** -ɪŋ **-ed** -t **-er/s** -əʳ/z (US) -ɚ/z

Ditchling 'dɪtʃ.lɪŋ

ditchwater 'dɪtʃˌwɔː.təʳ (US) -ˌwɑː.ţɚ, -ˌwɔː- **as** ˌ**dull as 'ditch-water**

dith|er 'dɪð|.əʳ (US) -ɚ **-ers** -əz (US) -ɚz **-ering** -ᵊr.ɪŋ **-ered** -əd (US) -ɚd **-erer/s** -ᵊr.əʳ/z (US) -ɚ.ɚ/z **-ery** -ᵊr.i

dithyramb 'dɪθ.ɪ.ræm*b*, '-ə- **-s** -z

Note: The /b/ is rarely pronounced.

dithyramb|us ˌdɪθ.ɪ'ræm.b|əs, -ə'- **-i** -aɪ **-ic/s** -ɪk/s

ditransitive ˌdaɪ'træn.sɪ.tɪv, -'trɑːn-, -sə- (US) -'træn.sə.ţɪv **-s** -z **-ly** -li

dits|y 'dɪt.s|i **-ier** -i.əʳ (US) -i.ɚ **-iest** -i.ɪst, -i.əst

ditto 'dɪt.əʊ (US) 'dɪţ.oʊ **-s** -z

Ditton 'dɪt.ᵊn

ditt|y 'dɪt|.i (US) 'dɪţ- **-ies** -iz

diures|is ˌdaɪ.jʊə'riː.s|ɪs, -jə'- (US) -jə'-, -ə'-, -jʊr'- **-es** -iːz

diuretic ˌdaɪ.jʊə'ret.ɪk, -jə'- (US) -jə'reţ-, -ə'- **-s** -s

diurnal ˌdaɪ'ɜː.nᵊl (US) -'ɝː- **-s** -z **-ly** -i

diva 'diː.və **-s** -z

diva|gate 'daɪ.vəl.geɪt; -veɪ-; 'dɪv.ə- (US) 'daɪ.və-, 'dɪv.ə- **-gates** -geɪts **-gating** -geɪ.tɪŋ (US) -geɪ.ţɪŋ **-gated** -geɪ.tɪd (US) -geɪ.ţɪd

divagation ˌdaɪ.və'geɪ.ʃᵊn, -veɪ'- (US) ˌdaɪ.və'-, ˌdɪv.ə'- **-s** -z

divalent ˌdaɪ'veɪ.lənt, 'daɪ.veɪ-

Divali dɪ'vɑː.li

divan dɪ'væn, də-, daɪ-; 'daɪ.væn (US) dɪ'væn, daɪ-; 'daɪ.væn **-s** -z

div|e daɪv **-es** -z **-ing** -ɪŋ **-ed** -d **dove** dəʊv (US) doʊv **'diving** ˌ**bell**; **'diving** ˌ**board**; **'diving** ˌ**suit**

dive-bomb 'daɪv.bɒm (US) -bɑːm **-s** -z **-ing** -ɪŋ **-ed** -d **-er/s** -əʳ/z (US) -ɚ/z

diver (D) 'daɪ.vəʳ (US) -vɚ **-s** -z

diverg|e daɪ'vɜːdʒ, dɪ- (US) dɪ'vɝːdʒ, daɪ- **-es** -ɪz **-ing** -ɪŋ **-ed** -d

divergenc|e daɪ'vɜː.dʒən*t*s, dɪ- (US) dɪ'vɝː-, daɪ- **-es** -ɪz **-y** -i **-ies** -iz

divergent daɪ'vɜː.dʒənt, dɪ- (US) dɪ'vɝː-, daɪ- **-ly** -li

divers 'daɪ.vəz, -vɜːz, -vɜːs; daɪ'vɜːs (US) 'daɪ.vɚz

diverse daɪ'vɜːs, '-- (US) dɪ'vɝːs, daɪ-; 'daɪ.vɝːs **-ly** -li

diversification daɪˌvɜː.sɪ.fɪ'keɪ.ʃᵊn, dɪ-, də-, -sə- (US) dɪˌvɝː-, daɪ- **-s** -z

diversi|fy daɪ'vɜː.sɪ|.faɪ, dɪ- (US) dɪ'vɝː-, daɪ- **-fies** -faɪz **-fying** -faɪ.ɪŋ **-fied** -faɪd

diversion daɪ'vɜː.ʃᵊn, dɪ-, -ʒən (US) dɪ'vɝː-, daɪ- **-s** -z

diversionary daɪ'vɜː.ʃᵊn.ᵊr.i, dɪ-, -ʒᵊn- (US) dɪ'vɝː.ʒᵊn.er.i, daɪ-, -ʃᵊn-

diversionist daɪ'vɜː.ʃᵊn.ɪst, dɪ-, -ʒᵊn- (US) dɪ'vɝː-, daɪ- **-s** -s

diversit|y daɪ'vɜː.sə.t|i, dɪ-, -ɪ.t|i (US) dɪ'vɝː.sə.ţ|i, daɪ- **-ies** -iz

di|vert daɪ|'vɜːt, dɪ- (US) dɪ|'vɝːt, daɪ- **-verts** -'vɜːts (US) -'vɝːts **-verting/ly** -'vɜː.tɪŋ/li (US) -'vɝː.ţɪŋ/li **-verted** -'vɜː.tɪd (US) -'vɝː.ţɪd

diverticulitis ˌdaɪ.vəˌtɪk.jʊ'laɪ.tɪs, -vɜːˌ-, -jə'- (US) -vɚˌtɪk.jə'laɪ.ţɪs, -jʊ'-

diverticulosis ˌdaɪ.vəˌtɪk.jʊ'ləʊ.sɪs, -vɜːˌ-, -jə'- (US) -vɚˌtɪk.jə'loʊ-, -jʊ'-

diverticulum ˌdaɪ.və'tɪk.jʊ.ləm, -vɜː'-, -jə- (US) -vɚ'tɪk.jə-, -jʊ-

divertimento dɪˌvɜː.tɪ'men.təʊ, -ˌveə-, -tə'- (US) -ˌvɝː.ţə'men.toʊ

divertissement ˌdiː.veə'tiːs.mɑ̃ːŋ, -və'-, -vɜː'-, dɪ'vɜː.tɪs.mənt (US) ˌdɪv.er'tiːs.mɑ̃

Dives *in Bible:* 'daɪ.viːz *surname:* daɪvz

divest daɪ'vest, dɪ- (US) dɪ-, daɪ- **-s** -s **-ing** -ɪŋ **-ed** -ɪd

divestiture daɪ'ves.tɪ.tʃəʳ, dɪ- (US) dɪ'ves.tɪ.tʃɚ, daɪ-

divestment daɪˈvest.mənt, dɪ- US dɪ-, daɪ- **-s** -s
divid|e dɪˈvaɪd, də- **-es** -z **-ing** -ɪŋ **-ed/ly** -ɪd/li **-able** -ə.bl̩
dividend ˈdɪv.ɪ.dend, ˈ-ə-, -dənd **-s** -z
divider dɪˈvaɪ.də^r, də- US -dɚ **-s** -z
divination ˌdɪv.ɪˈneɪ.ʃ^{ə}n, -əˈ- **-s** -z
divin|e (*n. adj.*) dɪˈvaɪn, də- **-es** -z **-er** -ə^r US -ɚ **-est** -ɪst, -əst **-ely** -li **-eness** -nəs, -nɪs **diˌvine ˈright**
divin|e (*v.*) dɪˈvaɪn, də- **-es** -z **-ing** -ɪŋ **-ed** -d **-er/s** -ə^r/z US -ɚ/z **diˈvining ˌrod**
divinit|y dɪˈvɪn.ə.t|i, də-, -ɪ.t|i US -ə.t̬|i **-ies** -iz
divisibility dɪˌvɪz.ɪˈbɪl.ə.ti, də-, -əˈ-, -ɪ.ti US -əˈbɪl.ə.t̬i
divisib|le dɪˈvɪz.ə.bl|̩, də-, ˈ-ɪ- **-ly** -li
division dɪˈvɪʒ.^{ə}n, də- **-s** -z
divisional dɪˈvɪʒ.^{ə}n.^{ə}l, də-, ˈ-n^{ə}l
divisive dɪˈvaɪ.sɪv, də- **-ly** -li **-ness** -nəs, -nɪs
divisor dɪˈvaɪ.zə^r, də- US -zɚ **-s** -z
divorc|e dɪˈvɔːs, də- US -ˈvɔːrs **-es** -ɪz **-ing** -ɪŋ **-ed** -t **-er/s** -ə^r/z US -ɚ/z
divorcé(e), divorcee dɪˌvɔːˈsiː, də-, -ˈseɪ; ˌdɪv.ɔːˈ- US dɪˌvɔːrˈseɪ, də-, -ˈsiː; -ˈvɔːr.seɪ, -siː **-s** -z
divot ˈdɪv.ət **-s** -s
divulg|e daɪˈvʌldʒ, dɪ- US dɪ-, daɪ- **-es** -ɪz **-ing** -ɪŋ **-ed** -d
divulsion daɪˈvʌl.ʃ^{ə}n, dɪ- US dɪ-, daɪ- **-s** -z
divv|y ˈdɪv|.i **-ies** -iz **-ying** -i.ɪŋ **-ied** -id
divvy-up ˌdɪv.iˈʌp
Diwali dɪˈwɑː.li
Dix dɪks
Dixey, Dixie ˈdɪk.si
dixieland (D) ˈdɪk.si.lænd
Dixon ˈdɪk.s^{ə}n
Dixwell ˈdɪk.swəl, -swel
DIY ˌdiː.aɪˈwaɪ
dizz|y ˈdɪz|.i **-ier** -i.ə^r US -i.ɚ **-iest** -i.ɪst, -i.əst **-ily** -ɪ.li, -^{ə}l.i **-iness** -ɪ.nəs, -ɪ.nɪs **-ies** -iz **-ying/ly** -i.ɪŋ **-ied** -id
DJ ˌdiːˈdʒeɪ US ˈ-- **-s** -z *stress shift, British only:* ˌDJ ˈculture
Djakarta dʒəˈkɑː.tə US -ˈkɑːr.t̬ə
Django ˈdʒæŋ.gəʊ US -goʊ
djellaba(h) dʒəˈlɑː.bə **-s** -z
Djibouti dʒɪˈbuː.ti, dʒə- US -t̬i
djinn dʒɪn **-s** -z
djinni dʒɪˈni, ˈdʒɪn.i
Djukanovic dʒʊˈkæn.ə.vɪtʃ US -ˈkɑːn-, dʒuː-, -oʊ-
dl (*abbrev. for* **decilitres/s, deciliter/s**) *singular:* ˈdes.ɪˌliː.tə^r US -t̬ɚ *plural:* -z
DLit(t) ˌdiːˈlɪt
dm (*abbrev. for* **decimetre/s, decimeter/s**) *singular:* ˈdes.ɪˌmiː.tə^r US -t̬ɚ *plural:* -z
D-mark ˈdɔɪtʃ.mɑːk US -mɑːrk **-s** -s
DNA ˌdiː.enˈeɪ
Dnepropetrovsk ˌ*d*njep.rɒp.jetˈrɒfsk US ˌnep.roʊ.pəˈtrɔːfsk, ˌdjnep-, -pjə-
Dnieper ˈ*d*niː.pə^r US -pɚ
D-notic|e ˈdiːˌnəʊ.tɪs US -ˌnoʊ.t̬ɪs **-es** -ɪz
do (*v.*) *strong form:* duː *weak forms:* də, du *strong form:* **dost** dʌst *weak form:* dəst *strong form:* **doth** dʌθ *weak form:* dəθ **doeth** ˈduː.ɪθ *strong form:* **does** dʌz *weak form:* dəz **doing** ˈduː.ɪŋ **did** dɪd **done** dʌn **doer/s** ˈduː.ə^r/z US -ɚ/z

Note: Weak form word. The strong form /duː/ is normally used in final position (e.g. “Yes, I do”), when it is used as a full verb rather than as an auxilliary (e.g. “Do it yourself”), for emphasis (e.g. “Why **do** you like him?”) or for contrast (e.g. “I do and I don’t”). There are two weak forms: /də/ before consonants (e.g. “How do they do it” /ˌhaʊ.də.ðeɪˈduː.ɪt/) and /du/ before vowels (e.g. “Why do all the books disappear?” /ˌwaɪ.du.ɔːl.ðəˈbʊks.dɪs.ə.pɪə^r US -pɪɚ/).

do (*n.*) *entertainment:* duː **-s** -z
do (*n.*) *musical note:* dəʊ US doʊ **-s** -z
do. (*abbrev. for* **ditto**) ˈdɪt.əʊ US ˈdɪt̬.oʊ
DOA ˌdiː.əʊˈeɪ US -oʊˈ-
doable ˈduː.ə.bl̩
Doane dəʊn US doʊn
dob dɒb US dɑːb **-s** -z **-bing** -ɪŋ **-bed** -d **-ber/s** -ə^r/z US -ɚ/z
Dobb dɒb US dɑːb **-s** -z
dobbin (D) ˈdɒb.ɪn US ˈdɑː.bɪn **-s** -z
Dobell dəʊˈbel, ˈdəʊ.b^{ə}l US ˈdoʊ.b^{ə}l, -bel
doberman (D) ˈdəʊ.bə.mən US ˈdoʊ.bɚ- **-s** -z
Doberman pinscher ˌdəʊ.bə.mənˈpɪn.*t*ʃə^r US ˌdoʊ.bɚ.mənˈpɪn*t*.ʃɚ
Dobie ˈdəʊ.bi US ˈdoʊ-
dobra ˈdəʊ.brə US ˈdoʊ- **-s** -z
Dobrée ˈdəʊ.breɪ US ˈdoʊ-
Dobson ˈdɒb.s^{ə}n US ˈdɑːb-
doc dɒk US dɑːk **-s** -s
docent ˈdəʊ.s^{ə}nt, dəʊˈsent US ˈdoʊ.sənt, -sent; doʊˈsent **-s** -s
Docet|ism dəʊˈsiː.t|ɪ.z^{ə}m; ˈdəʊ.sɪ- US doʊˈsiː.t|ɪ-; ˈdoʊ.sə.t̬|ɪ- **-ist/s** -ɪst/s
Docherty ˈdɒk.ə.ti, ˈdɒx- US ˈdɑː.kɚ.t̬i
docile ˈdəʊ.saɪl, ˈdɒs.aɪl US ˈdɑː.s^{ə}l, -saɪl **-ly** -li
docility dəʊˈsɪl.ə.ti, -ɪ.ti US dɑːˈsɪl.ə.t̬i, doʊ-
dock dɒk US dɑːk **-s** -s **-ing** -ɪŋ **-ed** -t
dockage ˈdɒk.ɪdʒ US ˈdɑː.kɪdʒ
docker (D) ˈdɒk.ə^r US ˈdɑː.kɚ **-s** -z
Dockerill ˈdɒk.^{ə}r.^{ə}l US ˈdɑː.kɚ-
dock|et ˈdɒk|.ɪt US ˈdɑː.k|ɪt **-ets** -ɪts **-eting** -ɪ.tɪŋ US -ɪ.t̬ɪŋ **-eted** -ɪ.tɪd US -ɪ.t̬ɪd
dockland (D) ˈdɒk.lænd, -lənd US ˈdɑːk- **-s** -z
dockside ˈdɒk.saɪd US ˈdɑːk-
dockworker ˈdɒkˌwɜː.kə^r US ˈdɑːkˌwɝː.kɚ **-s** -z
dockyard ˈdɒk.jɑːd US ˈdɑːk.jɑːrd **-s** -z
Doc Martens® ˌdɒkˈmɑː.tɪnz US ˌdɑːkˈmɑːr.t^{ə}nz
doct|or ˈdɒk.t|ə^r US ˈdɑːk.t|ɚ **-ors** -əz US -ɚz **-oring** -^{ə}r.ɪŋ **-ored** -əd US -ɚd
doctoral ˈdɒk.t^{ə}r.^{ə}l US ˈdɑːk-
doctorate ˈdɒk.t^{ə}r.ət, -ɪt US ˈdɑːk- **-s** -s
Doctorow ˈdɒk.t^{ə}r.əʊ US ˈdɑːk.tə.roʊ
doctrinaire ˌdɒk.trɪˈneə^r, -trəˈ- US ˌdɑːk.trəˈner **-s** -z
doctrinal dɒkˈtraɪ.n^{ə}l; ˈdɒk.trɪ- US ˈdɑːk.trɪ- **-ly** -i
doctrinarian ˌdɒk.trɪˈneə.ri.ən, -trəˈ- US ˌdɑːk.trɪˈner.i- **-s** -z
doctrine ˈdɒk.trɪn US ˈdɑːk- **-s** -z
docudrama ˈdɒk.juˌdrɑː.mə US ˈdɑː.kjʊˌdrɑː.mə, -ˌdræm.ə **-s** -z
document (*n.*) ˈdɒk.jə.mənt, -jʊ- US ˈdɑː.kjə-, -jʊ- **-s** -s
docu|ment (*v.*) ˈdɒk.jə|.ment, -jʊ- US ˈdɑː.kjə-, -jʊ- **-ments** -ments **-menting** -men.tɪŋ US -men.t̬ɪŋ **-mented** -men.tɪd US -men.t̬ɪd
documental ˌdɒk.jəˈmen.t^{ə}l, -jʊˈ- US ˌdɑː.kjəˈmenˈt̬^{ə}l, -jʊ-
documentar|y (*n. adj.*) ˌdɒk.jəˈmen.t^{ə}r|.i, -jʊˈ-, ˈ-tr|i US ˌdɑː.kjəˈmen.t̬ɚ|.i, -kjʊˈ- **-ies** -iz
documentation ˌdɒk.jə.menˈteɪ.ʃ^{ə}n, -jʊ-, -mənˈ- US ˌdɑː.kjə-, -jʊ-
docusoap ˈdɒk.ju.səʊp, -jʊ- US ˈdɑː.kjə.soʊp, -kjʊ- **-s** -s
Docwra ˈdɒk.rə US ˈdɑːk-
Dod(d) dɒd US dɑːd **-s** -z
dodd|er ˈdɒd|.ə^r US ˈdɑː.d|ɚ **-ers** -əz US -ɚz **-ering** -^{ə}r.ɪŋ **-ered** -əd US -ɚd **-erer/s** -^{ə}r.ə^r/z US -ɚ.ɚ/z
doddery ˈdɒd.^{ə}r.i US ˈdɑː.dɚ-
Doddington ˈdɒd.ɪŋ.tən US ˈdɑː.dɪŋ-
doddle ˈdɒd.l̩ US ˈdɑː.dl̩ **-s** -z
Doddridge ˈdɒd.rɪdʒ US ˈdɑː.drɪdʒ
dodecagon ˌdəʊˈdek.ə.gən US ˌdoʊ- **-s** -z
dodecahedr|on ˌdəʊ.dek.əˈhiː.dr|^{ə}n, -dɪk-, -ˈhed.r|^{ə}n US ˌdoʊ.dek.əˈhiː.dr|^{ə}n **-ons** -^{ə}nz **-a** -ə **-al** -^{ə}l
Dodecanese ˌdəʊ.dɪ.kəˈniːz, -dek.əˈ- US ˌdoʊ.dek-, -ˈniːs
dodg|e (D) dɒdʒ US dɑːdʒ **-es** -ɪz **-ing** -ɪŋ **-ed** -d **-er/s** -ə^r/z US -ɚ/z ˌ**Dodge ˈCity**

dodgem 'dɒdʒ.əm ⓤⓢ 'dɑː.dʒəm **-s** -z
Dodgson 'dɒdʒ.sᵊn ⓤⓢ 'dɑːdʒ-
dodg|y 'dɒdʒ|.i ⓤⓢ 'dɑː.dʒ|i **-ier** -i.əʳ ⓤⓢ -i.ɚ **-iest** -i.ɪst, -i.əst **-ily** -ɪ.li, -ᵊl.i **-iness** -ɪ.nəs, -ɪ.nɪs
Dodington 'dɒd.ɪŋ.tən ⓤⓢ 'dɑː.dɪŋ-
dodo (D) 'dəʊ.dəʊ ⓤⓢ 'doʊ.doʊ **-(e)s** -z
Dodoma 'dəʊ.də.mə, -mɑː ⓤⓢ 'doʊ.də.mɑː, -doʊ-, doʊ'-
Dodona dəʊ'dəʊ.nə ⓤⓢ də'doʊ-
Dodsley 'dɒdz.li ⓤⓢ 'dɑːdz-
Dodson 'dɒd.sᵊn ⓤⓢ 'dɑːd-
Dodsworth 'dɒdz.wəθ, -wɜːθ ⓤⓢ 'dɑːdz.wɚθ, -wɝːθ
Dodwell 'dɒd.wəl, -wel ⓤⓢ 'dɑːd-
doe (D) dəʊ ⓤⓢ doʊ **-s** -z
doer 'duː.əʳ ⓤⓢ -ɚ **-s** -z
-doer -ˌduː.əʳ ⓤⓢ -ɚ
Note: Suffix. Normally carries secondary stress, e.g. **wrongdoer** /'rɒŋˌduː.əʳ ⓤⓢ 'rɑːŋˌduː.ɚ/.
does *(from* **do***) strong form:* dʌz *weak form:* dəz
Note: Weak form word. The strong form is used when **does** is used as a full verb (e.g. "That's what he does for a living"), for emphasis (e.g. "That **does** look nice") and for contrast (e.g. "It **does** cost a lot, but it **doesn't** need repairing"). The strong form also occurs in final position (e.g. "I don't like it as much as she does"). When **does** occurs in other positions as an auxiliary, the weak form is normally used (e.g. "Why does it stop?" /ˌwaɪ.dəz.ɪt'stɒp ⓤⓢ -stɑːp/).
doeskin 'dəʊ.skɪn ⓤⓢ 'doʊ- **-s** -z
doesn't 'dʌz.ᵊnt
doeth *(from* **do***)* 'duː.ɪθ
Note: Archaic.
doff (D) dɒf ⓤⓢ dɑːf, dɔːf **-s** -s **-ing** -ɪŋ **-ed** -t **-er/s** -əʳ/z ⓤⓢ -ɚ/z
dog dɒg ⓤⓢ dɑːg, dɔːg **-s** -z **-ging** -ɪŋ **-ged** -d **'dog ˌbiscuit; 'dog ˌcollar; 'dog ˌdays; 'dog ˌpaddle; 'dog ˌrose; ˌdog's 'breakfast; 'Dog ˌStar; dressed up like a ˌdog's 'dinner; it's a 'dog's ˌlife; let ˌsleeping dogs 'lie; ˌgo to the 'dogs**
dogbane 'dɒg.beɪn ⓤⓢ 'dɑːg-, 'dɔːg-
Dogberry 'dɒg.ber.i, -bᵊr- ⓤⓢ 'dɑːg.ber-, 'dɔːg-
dogcart 'dɒg.kɑːt ⓤⓢ 'dɑːg.kɑːrt, 'dɔːg- **-s** -s
dogcatcher 'dɒgˌkætʃ.əʳ ⓤⓢ 'dɑːgˌkætʃ.ɚ, 'dɔːg- **-s** -z
dog|e dəʊdʒ, dəʊʒ ⓤⓢ doʊdʒ **-es** -ɪz
dog-ear 'dɒg.ɪəʳ ⓤⓢ 'dɑːg.ɪr, 'dɔːg- **-s** -z **-ing** -ɪŋ **-ed** -d
dog-eat-dog ˌdɒg.iːt'dɒg ⓤⓢ ˌdɑːg.iːt'dɑːg; ˌdɔːg.iːt'dɔːg
dog-end 'dɒg.end ⓤⓢ 'dɑːg-, 'dɔːg- **-s** -z
dogfight 'dɒg.faɪt ⓤⓢ 'dɑːg-, 'dɔːg- **-s** -s
dogfish 'dɒg.fɪʃ ⓤⓢ 'dɑːg-, 'dɔːg- **-es** -ɪz
Doggart 'dɒg.ət ⓤⓢ 'dɑː.gɚt, 'dɔː-
dogged 'dɒg.ɪd ⓤⓢ 'dɑː.gɪd, 'dɔː- **-ly** -li **-ness** -nəs, -nɪs
dogger (D) 'dɒg.əʳ ⓤⓢ 'dɑː.gɚ, 'dɔː- **-s** -z **ˌDogger 'Bank** ⓤⓢ **'Dogger ˌBank**
doggerel 'dɒg.ᵊr.ᵊl, -ɪl ⓤⓢ 'dɑː.gɚ.ᵊl, 'dɔː-, '-grᵊl
Doggert 'dɒg.ət ⓤⓢ 'dɑː.gɚt, 'dɔː-
Doggett 'dɒg.ɪt ⓤⓢ 'dɑː.gɪt, 'dɔː-
doggo 'dɒg.əʊ ⓤⓢ 'dɑː.goʊ, 'dɔː-
doggone 'dɒg.ɒn ⓤⓢ 'dɑː.gɑːn; 'dɔː.gɔːn **-d** -d
dogg|y, dogg|ie 'dɒg|.i ⓤⓢ 'dɑː.g|i, 'dɔː- **-ies** -iz **'doggie ˌbag**
doghou|se 'dɒg.haʊ|s ⓤⓢ 'dɑːg-, 'dɔːg- **-ses** -zɪz
dogie 'dəʊ.gi ⓤⓢ 'doʊ- **-s** -z
dogleg 'dɒg.leg ⓤⓢ 'dɑːg-, 'dɔːg- **-s** -z **-ging** -ɪŋ **-ged** -ɪd, -legd
dogma 'dɒg.mə ⓤⓢ 'dɑːg-, 'dɔːg- **-s** -z
dogmatic dɒg'mæt.ɪk ⓤⓢ dɑːg'mæṭ-, dɔːg- **-s** -s **-al** -ᵊl **-ally** -ᵊl.i, -li
dogmat|ism 'dɒg.mə.t|ɪ.zᵊm ⓤⓢ 'dɑːg.mə.t|ɪ-, 'dɔːg- **-ist/s** -ɪst/s
dogmatiz|e, -is|e 'dɒg.mə.taɪz ⓤⓢ 'dɑːg-, 'dɔːg- **-es** -ɪz **-ing** -ɪŋ **-ed** -d **-er/s** -əʳ/z ⓤⓢ -ɚ/z
do-good|er ˌduː'gʊd|.əʳ ⓤⓢ 'duːˌgʊd|.ɚ **-ers** -əz ⓤⓢ -ɚz **-ing** -ɪŋ
dogsbod|y 'dɒgz.bɒd|.i ⓤⓢ 'dɑːgz.bɑː.d|i, 'dɔːgz- **-ies** -iz
dogsled 'dɒg.sled ⓤⓢ 'dɑːg-, 'dɔːg- **-s** -z
dog-tired ˌdɒg'taɪəd ⓤⓢ ˌdɑːg'taɪɚd, ˌdɔːg- *stress shift:* ˌdog-tired 'worker
dog|tooth 'dɒg|.tuːθ ⓤⓢ 'dɑːg-, 'dɔːg- **-teeth** -tiːθ
dogwatch 'dɒg.wɒtʃ ⓤⓢ 'dɑːg.wɑːtʃ, 'dɔːg- **-es** -ɪz
dogwood 'dɒg.wʊd ⓤⓢ 'dɑːg-, 'dɔːg-
doh dəʊ ⓤⓢ doʊ **-s** -z
Doha 'dəʊ.hɑː, -ə ⓤⓢ 'doʊ-
Doherty 'dəʊ.ə.ti; 'dɒ.hə-; 'dɒx.ə-; dəʊ'hɜː- ⓤⓢ 'dɔːr.ə.ṭi; 'doʊ.ɚ-
Dohnanyi dɒk'nɑːn.jiː, dɒx-, -ji ⓤⓢ 'doʊ.ɑː.nji; dɑːk'nɑːn.ji, dɑːx-
Doig dɔɪg, 'dəʊ.ɪg ⓤⓢ dɔɪg, 'doʊ.ɪg
doil|y 'dɔɪ.l|i **-ies** -iz
doing *(from* **do***)* 'duː.ɪŋ **-s** -z
Doister 'dɔɪ.stəʳ ⓤⓢ -stɚ
doit dɔɪt **-s** -s
do-it-yourself ˌduː.ɪ.tʃə'self, -ɪt.jɔː'-, -jə'- ⓤⓢ ˌduː.ɪt.jɚ'self, -ɪ.tʃɚ'-
Dokic 'dɒk.ɪtʃ ⓤⓢ 'dɑː.kɪtʃ
Dolan 'dəʊ.lən ⓤⓢ 'doʊl-
Dolby 'dɒl.bi ⓤⓢ 'dɑːl-, 'doʊl-
dolce 'dɒl.tʃi, 'dəʊl-, -tʃeɪ ⓤⓢ 'doʊl.tʃeɪ
dolce vita ˌdɒl.tʃi'viː.tə, ˌdəʊ-, -tʃeɪ'- ⓤⓢ ˌdoʊl.tʃeɪ'viː.tə
Dolcis® 'dɒl.sɪs, -tʃɪs ⓤⓢ 'dɑːl-
doldrum 'dɒl.drəm ⓤⓢ 'doʊl-, 'dɑːl- **-s** -z
dol|e (D) dəʊl ⓤⓢ doʊl **-es** -z **-ing** -ɪŋ **-ed** -d
doleful 'dəʊl.fᵊl, -fʊl ⓤⓢ 'doʊl- **-ly** -i **-ness** -nəs, -nɪs
dolerite 'dɒl.ə.raɪt ⓤⓢ 'dɑː.lə-
Dolgellau, Dolgelley dɒl'geθ.laɪ, -li ⓤⓢ dɑːl-
dolichocephalic ˌdɒl.ɪ.kəʊ.sef'æl.ɪk, -sɪ'fæl-, -sə'-, -kef'æl-, -kɪ'fæl- ⓤⓢ ˌdɑː.lɪ.koʊ-
Dolittle 'duː.lɪ.tl̩ ⓤⓢ -ṭl̩
doll dɒl ⓤⓢ dɑːl **-s** -z **'doll's ˌhouse**
dollar (D) 'dɒl.əʳ ⓤⓢ 'dɑː.lɚ **-s** -z **ˌbet one's ˌbottom 'dollar**
Dollond 'dɒl.ənd ⓤⓢ 'dɑː.lənd
dollop 'dɒl.əp ⓤⓢ 'dɑː.ləp **-s** -s
doll|y (D) 'dɒl|.i ⓤⓢ 'dɑː.l|i **-ies** -iz **'dolly ˌmixture**
dolman 'dɒl.mən ⓤⓢ 'doʊl- **-s** -z
dolmen 'dɒl.men ⓤⓢ 'doʊl- **-s** -z
dolomite (D) 'dɒl.ə.maɪt ⓤⓢ 'doʊ.lə-, 'dɑː- **-s** -s
dolor 'dɒl.əʳ, 'dəʊ.ləʳ ⓤⓢ 'doʊ.lɚ, 'dɑː-
Dolores də'lɔː.res, dɒl'ɔː-, -rɪs, -rəs, -rez, -rɪz, -rəz ⓤⓢ də'lɔːr.əs, -ɪs
dolorous 'dɒl.ᵊr.əs ⓤⓢ 'doʊ.lɚ-, 'dɑː- **-ly** -li **-ness** -nəs, -nɪs
dolour 'dɒl.əʳ, 'dəʊ.ləʳ ⓤⓢ 'doʊ.lɚ, 'dɑː-
dolphin 'dɒl.fɪn ⓤⓢ 'dɑːl- **-s** -z
dolt dəʊlt ⓤⓢ doʊlt **-s** -s
doltish 'dəʊl.tɪʃ ⓤⓢ 'doʊl- **-ly** -li **-ness** -nəs, -nɪs
-dom -dəm
Note: Suffix. Normally unstressed, e.g. **kingdom** /'kɪŋ.dəm/.
domain dəʊ'meɪn ⓤⓢ doʊ-, də- **-s** -z
Dombey 'dɒm.bi ⓤⓢ 'dɑːm-
dome dəʊm ⓤⓢ doʊm **-s** -z **-d** -d
Domecq dəʊ'mek, dɒm'ek ⓤⓢ doʊ-
Domesday 'duːmz.deɪ **'Domesday ˌbook**
domestic də'mes.tɪk **-s** -s **-ally** -ᵊl.i, -li **doˌmestic 'animal; doˌmestic 'violence**
domesti|cate də'mes.tɪ|.keɪt **-cates** -keɪts **-cating** -keɪ.tɪŋ ⓤⓢ -keɪ.ṭɪŋ **-cated** -keɪ.tɪd ⓤⓢ -keɪ.ṭɪd
domestication dəˌmes.tɪ'keɪ.ʃᵊn
domesticity ˌdɒm.es'tɪs.ə.ti, ˌdəʊ.mes-, -ɪ.ti ⓤⓢ ˌdoʊ.mes'-, dəˌmes'-
Domestos® də'mes.tɒs, dəʊ- ⓤⓢ də'mes.toʊs
domett dəʊ'met ⓤⓢ də-, doʊ-; 'dɑː.mət
Domett 'dɒm.ɪt ⓤⓢ 'dɑː.mɪt
domicil|e 'dɒm.ɪ.saɪl, 'dəʊ.mɪ-, -sɪl ⓤⓢ 'dɑː.mə-, 'doʊ.mə- **-es** -z **-ing** -ɪŋ **-ed** -d

domiciliary ˌdɒm.ɪˈsɪl.i.ᵊr.i, -əˈ- (US) ˌdɑː.məˈsɪl.i.er-, ˌdoʊ-

dominance ˈdɒm.ɪ.nən*t*s, ˈ-ə- (US) ˈdɑː.mə-

dominant ˈdɒm.ɪ.nənt, ˈ-ə- (US) ˈdɑː.mə- **-s** -s **-ly** -li

domi|nate ˈdɒm.ɪ|.neɪt, ˈ-ə- (US) ˈdɑː.mə- **-nates** -neɪts **-nating** -neɪ.tɪŋ (US) -neɪ.t̬ɪŋ **-nated** -neɪ.tɪd (US) -neɪ.t̬ɪd **-nator/s** -neɪ.təʳ/z (US) -neɪ.t̬ɚ/z

domination ˌdɒm.ɪˈneɪ.ʃᵊn, -əˈ- (US) ˌdɑː.məˈ- **-s** -z

dominatr|ix ˌdɒm.ɪˈneɪ.tr|ɪks, -əˈ- (US) ˌdɑː.məˈ- **-ixes** -ɪk.sɪz **-ices** -ɪ.siːz

domineer ˌdɒm.ɪˈnɪəʳ, -əˈ- (US) ˌdɑː.məˈnɪr **-s** -z **-ing/ly** -ɪŋ/li **-ed** -d

Domingo dəˈmɪŋ.gəʊ, dɒmˈɪŋ- (US) dəˈmɪŋ.goʊ

Dominic ˈdɒm.ɪ.nɪk, ˈ-ə- (US) ˈdɑː.mə-

Dominica dəˈmɪn.ɪ.kə; dɒm.ɪn.ˈiː- (US) ˌdɑː.mɪˈniː-, dəˈmɪn.ɪ-

dominical dəˈmɪn.ɪ.kᵊl, dɒmˈɪn-, dəʊˈmɪn- (US) doʊˈmɪn-, də-

Dominican *republic, religious order:* dəˈmɪn.ɪ.kən, dɒmˈɪn- (US) doʊˈmɪn-, də- **-s** -z *of Dominica:* ˌdɒm.ɪˈniː.kən (US) ˌdɑː.mɪˈniː- **-s** -z

dominie ˈdɒm.ɪ.ni, ˈ-ə- (US) ˈdɑː.mɪ- **-s** -z

dominion **(D)** dəˈmɪn.jən, -i.ən (US) ˈ-jən **-s** -z

Dominique ˌdɒm.ɪˈniːk, -əˈ-, ˈ--- (US) ˌdɑː.məˈ-, ˈ---

domino **(D)** ˈdɒm.ɪ.nəʊ, ˈ-ə- (US) ˈdɑː.mə.noʊ **-(e)s** -z **ˈdomino efˌfect**

Domitian dəʊˈmɪʃ.i.ən, dɒmˈɪʃ-, -ˈɪʃ.ən (US) dəˈmɪʃ.ən, -i.ən

don **(D)** dɒn (US) dɑːn **-s** -z **-ning** -ɪŋ **-ned** -d

doña, dona ˈdɒn.jə (US) ˈdoʊ.njə, -nə

dona(h) ˈdəʊ.nə (US) ˈdoʊ- **-s** -z

Donal ˈdəʊ.nᵊl (US) ˈdoʊ-

Donalbain ˈdɒn.ᵊl.beɪn (US) ˈdɑː.nᵊl-

Donald ˈdɒn.ᵊld (US) ˈdɑː.nᵊld

Donaldson ˈdɒn.ᵊld.sᵊn (US) ˈdɑː.nᵊld-

Donat ˈdəʊ.næt (US) ˈdoʊ-

do|nate dəʊ|ˈneɪt (US) ˈdoʊ|.neɪt, -|ˈ- **-nates** -ˈneɪts (US) -neɪts, -ˈneɪts **-nating** -ˈneɪ.tɪŋ (US) -neɪ.t̬ɪŋ, -ˈneɪ- **-nated** -ˈneɪ.tɪd (US) -neɪ.t̬ɪd, -ˈneɪ-

Donatello ˌdɒn.əˈtel.əʊ (US) ˌdɑː.nəˈtel.oʊ

donatio dəʊˈnɑː.ti.əʊ (US) doʊˈnɑː.ti.oʊ, -ˈneɪ-, -ʃi-

donation dəʊˈneɪ.ʃᵊn (US) doʊˈneɪ- **-s** -z

Donatist ˈdəʊ.nə.tɪst, ˈdɒn.ə- (US) ˈdoʊ.nə-, ˈdɑː- **-s** -s

donative ˈdəʊ.nə.tɪv, ˈdɒn.ə- (US) ˈdoʊ.nə.t̬ɪv, ˈdɑː- **-s** -z

donator dəʊˈneɪ.təʳ (US) ˈdoʊ.neɪ.t̬ɚ, ˌdoʊˈneɪ- **-s** -z

donatory ˈdəʊ.nə.tᵊr.i, ˈdɒn.ə-; -tri, dəʊˈneɪ- (US) ˈdoʊ.nə.tɔːr.i

Donatus dəʊˈneɪ.təs, -ˈnɑː- (US) doʊˈneɪ.t̬əs, -ˈnɑː-

Don Carlos ˌdɒnˈkɑː.lɒs, ˌdɒŋ- (US) ˌdɑːnˈkɑːr.loʊs

Doncaster ˈdɒŋ.kə.stəʳ, -ˌkɑː-, -ˌkæs.təʳ (US) ˈdɑːŋˌkæs.tɚ, -kə.stɚ, ˈdɑːn-

done *(from* **do)** dʌn

Done dəʊn (US) doʊn

donee dəʊˈniː (US) doʊ- **-s** -z

Donegal ˌdɒn.ɪˈgɔːl, ˌdʌn-, ˈ--- (US) ˌdɑː.nɪˈgɔːl, -ˈgɑːl, ˈ---

Note: /ˌdʌn.ɪˈgɔːl/ appears to be the most usual pronunciation in Ireland.

Donegall ˈdɒn.ɪ.gɔːl (US) ˈdɑː.nɪ.gɔːl, -gɑːl

Donelson ˈdɒn.ᵊl.sᵊn (US) ˈdɑː.nᵊl-

doner ˈdɒn.əʳ (US) ˈdoʊ.nɚ **ˌdoner keˈbab**

Donetsk dɒnˈ*j*etsk (US) dəˈnjetsk, doʊ-

Donetz dɒnˈ*j*ets (US) dəˈnets, dɑːˈnjets

dong *(v.)* dɒŋ (US) dɑːŋ, dɔːŋ **-s** -z **-ing** -ɪŋ **-ed** -d

dông *Vietnam currency:* dɒŋ (US) dɑːŋ, dɔːŋ

donga ˈdɒŋ.gə (US) ˈdɑːŋ.gə, ˈdɔːŋ- **-s** -z

Dönges ˈdɜːn.jes

Don Giovanni ˌdɒn.dʒəʊˈvɑː.ni, -dʒi.əʊˈ-, -ˈvæn.i (US) ˌdɑːn.dʒi.əˈvɑː.ni, -dʒoʊˈ-

Dongola ˈdɒŋ.gə.lə (US) ˈdɑːŋ-

Donington ˈdɒn.ɪŋ.tᵊn, ˈdʌn- (US) ˈdɑː.nɪŋ-

Donizetti ˌdɒn.ɪˈzet.i, -ɪdˈze-, -ɪtˈset- (US) ˌdɑː.nəˈzet̬.i, -nətˈset̬-

donjon ˈdɒn.*d*ʒᵊn, ˈdʌn- (US) ˈdɑːn- **-s** -z

Don Juan ˌdɒnˈdʒuː.ən, -ˈ*h*wɑːn (US) ˌdɑːn-

donkey ˈdɒŋ.ki (US) ˈdɑːŋ-, ˈdɔːŋ-, ˈdʌŋ- **-s** -z **ˈdonkey ˌengine; ˈdonkey ˌjacket; ˈdonkey's ˌyears**

donkeywork ˈdɒŋ.ki.wɜːk (US) ˈdɑːŋ.ki.wɝːk, ˈdɔːŋ-, ˈdʌŋ-

Donleavy, Donlevy dɒnˈliː.vi, -ˈlev.i (US) ˈdɑːn.liː.vi, ˈdʌn-, -lev.i, -ˈ--

Donmar ˈdɒn.mɑːʳ (US) ˈdɑːn-

donna **(D)** ˈdɒn.ə (US) ˈdɑː.nə

Donnan ˈdɒn.ən (US) ˈdɑː.nən

Donne dʌn, dɒn (US) dʌn, dɑːn

Donnell ˈdɒn.ᵊl (US) ˈdɑː.nᵊl

Donnelly ˈdɒn.ᵊl.i (US) ˈdɑː.nᵊl-

Donnington ˈdɒn.ɪŋ.tən (US) ˈdɑː.nɪŋ-

donnish ˈdɒn.ɪʃ (US) ˈdɑː.nɪʃ **-ly** -li **-ness** -nəs, -nɪs

Donny ˈdɒn.i (US) ˈdɑː.ni

Donnybrook ˈdɒn.i.brʊk (US) ˈdɑː.ni-

Donoghue ˈdʌn.ə.hjuː, ˈdɒn-, -hjuː (US) ˈdɑː.nə.huː, ˈdʌn.ə-, -huː

Donohoe ˈdʌn.ə.həʊ, ˈdɒn-, -huː (US) ˈdɑː.nə.hoʊ, ˈdʌn.ə-, -huː

Donohue ˈdʌn.ə.hjuː, ˈdɒn-, -huː (US) ˈdɑː.nə.hjuː, ˈdʌn.ə-, -huː

donor ˈdəʊ.nəʳ, -nɔːʳ (US) ˈdoʊ.nɚ **-s** -z

Donovan ˈdɒn.ə.vən (US) ˈdɑː.nə-, ˈdʌn.ə-

Don Pasquale ˌdɒn.pæsˈkwɑː.leɪ, ˈdɒm-, -li (US) ˌdɑːn.pəˈ-

Don Quixote ˌdɒnˈkwɪk.sət, ˌdɒŋ-, -səʊt, -sɒt; *as if Spanish:* ˌdɒn.kiˈhəʊ.teɪ, ˌdɒŋ-, -ti (US) ˌdɑːn.kiːˈhoʊ.teɪ, -t̬i; -ˈkwɪk.sət

donship ˈdɒn.ʃɪp (US) ˈdɑːn- **-s** -s

don't dəʊnt (US) doʊnt

Note: Weak forms /dən, dn̩/ may sometimes be heard in the expression "I don't know", and a weak form /dəm/ in the expression "I don't mind".

do|nut ˈdəʊ|.nʌt (US) ˈdoʊ- **-nuts** -nʌts **-nutting** -nʌt.ɪŋ (US) -nʌt̬.ɪŋ

Doo duː

Doobie ˈduː.bi

doodad ˈduː.dæd **-s** -z

doodah ˈduː.dɑː **-s** -z

doodl|e ˈduː.dl̩ **-es** -z **-ing** -ɪŋ, ˈduːd.lɪŋ **-ed** -d **-er/s** -əʳ/z, ˈduːd.ləʳ/z (US) ˈduː.dl̩.ɚ/z, ˈduːd.lɚ/z

doodlebug ˈduː.dl̩.bʌg **-s** -z

doohickey ˈduːˌhɪk.i **-s** -z

Doolittle ˈduː.lɪ.tl̩ (US) -t̬l̩

doom duːm **-s** -z **-ing** -ɪŋ **-ed** -d

doomsayer ˈduːmˌseɪ.əʳ (US) -ɚ **-s** -z

doomsday **(D)** ˈduːmz.deɪ

Doona® ˈduː.nə **-s** -z

Doon(e) duːn

door dɔːʳ (US) dɔːr **-s** -z **ˌshut the ˌdoor in someone's ˈface; ˌshow someone the ˈdoor**

doorbell ˈdɔː.bel (US) ˈdɔːr- **-s** -z

doorframe ˈdɔː.freɪm (US) ˈdɔːr- **-s** -z

doorjamb ˈdɔː.dʒæm (US) ˈdɔːr- **-s** -z

doorkeeper ˈdɔːˌkiː.pəʳ (US) ˈdɔːrˌkiː.pɚ **-s** -z

doorknob ˈdɔː.nɒb (US) ˈdɔːr.nɑːb **-s** -z

doorknocker ˈdɔːˌnɒk.əʳ (US) ˈdɔːrˌnɑː.kɚ **-s** -z

door|man ˈdɔː|.mən, -mæn (US) ˈdɔːr- **-men** -mən, -men

doormat ˈdɔː.mæt (US) ˈdɔːr- **-s** -s

doornail ˈdɔː.neɪl (US) ˈdɔːr- **-s** -z **as ˌdead as a ˈdoornail**

doorplate ˈdɔː.pleɪt (US) ˈdɔːr- **-s** -s

doorpost ˈdɔː.pəʊst (US) ˈdɔːr.poʊst **-s** -s

doorstep ˈdɔː.step (US) ˈdɔːr- **-s** -s **-ping** -ɪŋ **-ped** -t **-per/s** -əʳ/z (US) -ɚ/z

doorstop ˈdɔː.stɒp (US) ˈdɔːr.stɑːp **-s** -s

door-to-door ˌdɔː.təˈdɔːʳ (US) ˌdɔːr.t̬əˈdɔːr

doorway ˈdɔː.weɪ (US) ˈdɔːr- **-s** -z

doo-wop ˈduː.wɒp (US) -wɑːp

dopa ˈdəʊ.pə (US) ˈdoʊ-, -pɑː

dopamine ˈdəʊ.pə.miːn, -mɪn (US) ˈdoʊ-

dop|e dəʊp US doʊp **-es** -s **-ing** -ɪŋ **-ed** -t **-er/s** -əʳ/z US -ɚ/z
dop|ey 'dəʊ.p|i US 'doʊ- **-ier** -i.əʳ US -i.ɚ **-iest** -i.ɪst, -i.əst **-ily** -ɪ.li, -ᵊl.i **-iness** -ɪ.nəs, -ɪ.nɪs
doppelganger 'dɒp.ᵊl,gæŋ.əʳ US 'dɑː.pᵊl,gæŋ.ɚ **-s** -z
doppelgänger 'dɒp.ᵊl,geŋ.əʳ US 'dɑː.pᵊl,geŋ.ɚ **-s** -z
Doppler 'dɒp.ləʳ US 'dɑː.plɚ **'Doppler ef,fect**
dop|y 'dəʊ.p|i US 'doʊ- **-ier** -i.əʳ US -i.ɚ **-iest** -i.ɪst, -i.əst **-ily** -ɪ.li, -ᵊl.i **-iness** -ɪ.nəs, -ɪ.nɪs
Dora 'dɔː.rə US 'dɔːr.ə
dorado (D) də'rɑː.dəʊ, dɒr'ɑː- US doʊ'rɑː.doʊ, də'- **-s** -z
Doran 'dɔː.rən US 'dɔːr.ən
Dorando də'ræn.dəʊ, dɒr'æn- US dɔːr'æn.doʊ
Dorcas 'dɔː.kəs, -kæs US 'dɔːr-
Dorchester 'dɔː.tʃɪ.stəʳ US 'dɔːr.tʃes.tɚ
Dordogne dɔː'dɔɪn US dɔːr'doʊn
Dordon 'dɔː.dᵊn US 'dɔːr-
Dordrecht 'dɔː.drext, -drekt US 'dɔːr.drekt, -drext
Dore dɔːʳ US dɔːr
Doreen 'dɔː.riːn; -'-, də-, dɒr'iːn US dɔːr'iːn
Dorian 'dɔː.ri.ən US 'dɔːr.i- **-s** -z
Doric 'dɒr.ɪk US 'dɔːr-
Doricism 'dɒr.ɪ.sɪ.zᵊm, '-ə- US 'dɔːr- **-s** -z
Dorigen 'dɒr.ɪ.gᵊn US 'dɔːr-
Doris *modern first name:* 'dɒr.ɪs US 'dɔːr-, 'dɑːr- *district and female name in Greek history:* 'dɔː.rɪs, 'dɒr.ɪs US 'dɔːr.ɪs, 'dɑːr-
dork dɔːk US dɔːrk **-s** -s
Dorking 'dɔː.kɪŋ US 'dɔːr-
Dorling 'dɔː.lɪŋ US 'dɔːr-
dorm dɔːm US dɔːrm **-s** -z
dormancy 'dɔː.mənt.si US 'dɔːr-
dormant 'dɔː.mənt US 'dɔːr-
dormer (D) 'dɔː.məʳ US 'dɔːr.mɚ **-s** -z **,dormer 'window**
dormie 'dɔː.mi US 'dɔːr-
dormitor|y 'dɔː.mɪ.tᵊr|.i, -mə-, -tr|i US 'dɔːr.mə.tɔːr|.i **-ies** -iz
Dormobile® 'dɔː.mə.biːl US 'dɔːr- **-s** -z
dor|mouse 'dɔː|.maʊs US 'dɔːr- **-mice** -maɪs
dormy 'dɔː.mi US 'dɔːr-
Dornoch 'dɔː.nɒk, -nək, -nɒx, -nəx US 'dɔːr.nɑːk, -nək
Dornton 'dɔːn.tᵊn US 'dɔːrn-
Dorothea ,dɒr.ə'θi.ə US ,dɔːr-, ,dɑːr-
Dorothy 'dɒr.ə.θi US 'dɔːr-, 'dɑːr-
Dorr dɔːʳ US dɔːr
Dorriforth 'dɒr.ɪ.fɔːθ US 'dɔːr.ɪ.fɔːrθ, 'dɑːr-
Dorrit 'dɒr.ɪt US 'dɔːr-
Dors dɔːz US dɔːrz
dorsal 'dɔː.sᵊl US 'dɔːr- **-ly** -i
Dorset 'dɔː.sɪt, -sət US 'dɔːr- **-shire** -ʃəʳ, -,ʃɪəʳ US -ʃɚ, -,ʃɪr
Dorsey 'dɔː.si US 'dɔːr-
dorsum 'dɔː.səm US 'dɔːr-
Dortmund 'dɔːt.mənd, -mʊnd US 'dɔːrt-
dor|y (D) 'dɔː.r|i US 'dɔːr|.i **-ies** -iz
DOS dɒs US dɑːs
dosag|e 'dəʊ.sɪdʒ US 'doʊ- **-es** -ɪz
dos|e dəʊs US doʊs **-es** -ɪz **-ing** -ɪŋ **-ed** -t **like a ,dose of 'salts**
dosh dɒʃ US dɑːʃ
do-si-do ,dəʊ.si'dəʊ, -saɪ'- US ,doʊ.si'doʊ **-s** -z
Dos Passos ,dɒs'pæs.ɒs US ,doʊs'pæs.oʊs, dəs-, ,dɑːs-
doss dɒs US dɑːs **-es** -ɪz **-ing** -ɪŋ **-ed** -t **-er/s** -əʳ/z US -ɚ/z
dossal 'dɒs.ᵊl US 'dɑː.sᵊl **-s** -z
dosshou|se 'dɒs.haʊ|s US 'dɑːs- **-ses** -zɪz
dossier 'dɒs.i.eɪ, -əʳ US 'dɑː.si.eɪ, -ɚ **-s** -z
dost *(from* **do***) strong form:* dʌst *weak form:* dəst
Dostoievski, Dostoevsky ,dɒs.tɔɪ'ef.ski US ,dɔː.stə'jef-, ,dɑː-, 'dʌs.tə'-, -tɔɪ'-
dot (D) dɒt US dɑːt **-s** -s **-ting** -ɪŋ US 'dɑː.t̬ɪŋ **-ted** -ɪd US 'dɑː.t̬ɪd **,dotted 'line**
dotage 'dəʊ.tɪdʒ US 'doʊ.t̬ɪdʒ
dotard 'dəʊ.təd, -tɑːd US 'doʊ.t̬ɚd **-s** -z
dot.com ,dɒt'kɒm US 'dɑːt.kɑːm, ,-'- **-s** -z *stress shift:* ,dot.com 'company
dot|e dəʊt US doʊt **-es** -s **-ing/ly** -ɪŋ/li US 'doʊ.t̬ɪŋ/li **-ed** -ɪd US 'doʊ.t̬ɪd **-er/s** -əʳ/z US 'doʊ.t̬ɚ/z
doth *(from* **do***) strong form:* dʌθ *weak form:* dəθ
Dotheboys Hall ,duː.ðə.bɔɪz'hɔːl US -'hɔːl, -'hɑːl
dot-matrix ,dɒt'meɪ.trɪks, '-,-- US ,dɑːt'meɪ- **,dot-matrix 'printer, dot-,matrix 'printer** US **,dot-'matrix printer**
dotterel 'dɒt.rᵊl US 'dɑː.trᵊl **-s** -z
dottle 'dɒt.l̩ US 'dɑː.t̬l̩ **-s** -z
dott|y 'dɒt|.i US 'dɑː.t̬|i **-ier** -i.əʳ US -i.ɚ **-iest** -i.ɪst, -i.əst **-ily** -ɪ.li, -ᵊl.i **-iness** -ɪ.nəs, -ɪ.nɪs
Douai *French town:* 'duː.eɪ US -'- *school near Reading:* 'daʊ.eɪ, 'duː-, -i US duː'eɪ *version of Bible:* 'daʊ.eɪ, 'duː-, -i US duː'eɪ, '--
Douala du'ɑː.lə
doubl|e 'dʌb.l̩ **-y** -i, '-li **-eness** -nəs, -nɪs **-es** -z **-ing** -ɪŋ, '-lɪŋ **-ed** -d **,double 'agent; ,double 'bass; ,double 'chin; ,double 'dutch; ,double 'entry; ,double 'first; ,Double 'Gloucester; ,double in'demnity; ,double 'jeopardy; ,double 'take;** US **'double ,take;**
double-barrel(l)ed ,dʌb.l̩'bær.l̩d US -'ber-, -'bær- *stress shift:* ,double-barrel(l)ed 'name
double-breasted ,dʌb.l̩'bres.tɪd *stress shift:* ,double-breasted 'jacket
double-check ,dʌb.l̩'tʃek US 'dʌb.l̩,tʃek, ,--'- **-s** -s **-ing** -ɪŋ **-ed** -t
double-cross ,dʌb.l̩'krɒs US -'krɑːs **-es** -ɪz **-ing** -ɪŋ **-ed** -t
Doubleday 'dʌb.l̩.deɪ
double-deal|er ,dʌb.l̩'diː.l|əʳ US -l|ɚ **-ers** -əʳ/z US -ɚ/z **-ing** -ɪŋ
double-decker ,dʌb.l̩'dek.əʳ US 'dʌb.l̩,dek.ɚ, ,dʌb.l̩'dek- **-s** -z *stress shift, British only:* ,double-decker 'bus
double-dip ,dʌb.l̩'dɪp **-s** -s **-ping** -ɪŋ **-ped** -t
double-edged ,dʌb.l̩'edʒd *stress shift:* ,double-edged 'sword
double entendre ,duː.bl̩.ɑ̃ːn'tɑ̃ːn.drə, -ɑːn'tɑːn- US ,dʌb.l̩.ɑːn'tɑːn.drə, ,duː.blɑːn'trɑːn
double-glaz|e ,dʌb.l̩'gleɪz **-es** -ɪz **-ing** -ɪŋ **-ed** -d *stress shift:* ,double-glazed 'windows
double-glazing ,dʌb.l̩'gleɪ.zɪŋ
double-header ,dʌb.l̩'hed.əʳ US -ɚ **-s** -z
double-jointed ,dʌb.l̩'dʒɔɪn.tɪd US -t̬ɪd *stress shift:* ,double-jointed 'gymnast
double-park ,dʌb.l̩'pɑːk US -'pɑːrk **-s** -s **-ing** -ɪŋ **-ed** -t
double-quick ,dʌb.l̩'kwɪk *stress shift:* ,double-quick 'time
doublespeak 'dʌb.l̩.spiːk
double-stop ,dʌb.l̩'stɒp US -'stɑːp **-s** -s **-ping** -ɪŋ **-ped** -t
doublet 'dʌb.lɪt, -lət **-s** -s
doubletalk 'dʌb.l̩.tɔːk US -tɔːk, -tɑːk
doublethink 'dʌb.l̩.θɪŋk
double-tongued ,dʌb.l̩'tʌŋd
doubloon dʌb'luːn **-s** -z
doubt daʊt **-s** -s **-ing/ly** -ɪŋ/li US 'daʊ.t̬ɪŋ/li **-ed** -ɪd US 'daʊ.t̬ɪd **-er/s** -əʳ/z US 'daʊ.t̬ɚ/z **,doubting 'Thomas**
doubtful 'daʊt.fᵊl, -fʊl **-lest** -ɪst, -əst **-ly** -i **-ness** -nəs, -nɪs
doubtless 'daʊt.ləs, -lɪs **-ly** -li
douch|e duːʃ **-es** -ɪz **-ing** -ɪŋ **-ed** -t
Doug dʌg
Dougal(l) 'duː.gᵊl
Dougan 'duː.gən
dough dəʊ US doʊ
Dougherty 'dɒx.ə.ti, 'dəʊ-, 'daʊ- US 'dɔːr.ə.t̬i, 'dɔːr.t̬i, 'doʊ.ɚ-, 'daʊ-, 'dɑː.kɚ-

doughfaced 'dəʊ.feɪst US 'doʊ-

dough|nut 'dəʊ|.nʌt US 'doʊ- **-nuts** -nʌts **-nutting** -nʌt.ɪŋ US -nʌt̬.ɪŋ

dought|y (D) 'daʊ.t|i US -t̬|i **-ier** -i.əʳ US -i.ɚ **-iest** -i.ɪst, -i.əst **-ily** -ɪ.li, -ᵊl.i **-iness** -ɪ.nəs, -ɪ.nɪs

dough|y 'dəʊ|.i US 'doʊ- **-ily** -ɪ.li, -ᵊl.i **-iness** -ɪ.nəs, -ɪ.nɪs

Douglas-Home ˌdʌg.ləs'hjuːm

Douglas(s) 'dʌg.ləs

douloureux ˌduː.lə'rɜː, -luː'-, -lʊ'-

Doulton 'dəʊl.tᵊn US 'doʊl-

Dounreay 'duːn.reɪ, -'-

dour dʊəʳ, daʊəʳ US dʊr, daʊɚ **-ly** -li **-ness** -nəs, -nɪs

Douro 'dʊə.rəʊ US 'dɔːr.oʊ

dous|e daʊs **-es** -ɪz **-ing** -ɪŋ **-ed** -t

dove (D) dʌv **-s** -z

dove *(from* **dive***)* dəʊv US doʊv

dovecot(e) 'dʌv.kɒt US -kɑːt **-s** -s

Dovedale 'dʌv.deɪl

Dover 'dəʊ.vəʳ US 'doʊ.vɚ **ˌDover 'sole**

dovetail 'dʌv.teɪl **-s** -z **-ing** -ɪŋ **-ed** -d

Dovey 'dʌv.i

Dow daʊ **ˌDow 'Jones; ˌDow Jones 'index**

dowager 'daʊə.dʒəʳ, 'daʊɪ- US -dʒɚ **-s** -z

Dowden 'daʊ.dᵊn

Dowds daʊdz

dowd|y 'daʊ.d|i **-ies** -iz **-ier** -i.əʳ US -i.ɚ **-iest** -i.ɪst, -i.əst **-ily** -ɪ.li, -ᵊl.i **-iness** -ɪ.nəs, -ɪ.nɪs

dowel daʊəl **-s** -z **-(l)ing** -ɪŋ **-(l)ed** -d

Dowell daʊəl; 'daʊ.ɪl, -el

dower daʊəʳ US daʊɚ **-s** -z **-less** -ləs, -lɪs

Dowgate 'daʊ.gɪt, -geɪt

Dowie 'daʊ.i

Dowland 'daʊ.lənd

dowlas (D) 'daʊ.ləs

Dowler 'daʊ.ləʳ US -lɚ

Dowling 'daʊ.lɪŋ

down (D) daʊn **-s** -z **-ing** -ɪŋ **-ed** -d **ˌdown 'payment; 'Down's ˌsyndrome; ˌdown 'under**

Down *county:* daʊn **-shire** -ʃəʳ, -ˌʃɪəʳ US -ʃɚ, -ˌʃɪr

down-and-out ˌdaʊn.ənd'aʊt **-s** -s *stress shift:* ˌdown-and-out 'person

down-at-heel ˌdaʊn.ət'hiːl *stress shift:* ˌdown-at-heel 'person

downbeat 'daʊn.biːt, 'daʊm- US 'daʊn- **-s** -s

downcast 'daʊn.kɑːst, 'daʊŋ-, ˌ-'- US 'daʊn.kæst

downdraught 'daʊn.drɑːft US -dræft **-s** -s

downdrift 'daʊn.drɪft

Downe daʊn **-s** -z

downer 'daʊ.nəʳ US -nɚ **-s** -z

Downey 'daʊ.ni

downfall 'daʊn.fɔːl US -fɔːl, -fɑːl **-s** -z

downgrad|e ˌdaʊn'greɪd, ˌdaʊŋ- US 'daʊn.greɪd **-es** -z **-ing** -ɪŋ **-ed** -ɪd *stress shift, British only:* ˌdowngraded 'worker

Downham 'daʊ.nəm

downhearted ˌdaʊn'hɑː.tɪd US -'hɑːr.t̬ɪd **-ly** -li **-ness** -nəs, -nɪs *stress shift:* ˌdownhearted 'person

downhill ˌdaʊn'hɪl *stress shift:* ˌdownhill 'slide

down-home ˌdaʊn'həʊm US -'hoʊm

Downie 'daʊ.ni

Downing 'daʊ.nɪŋ **'Downing ˌStreet**

downland (D) 'daʊn.lænd, -lənd

download ˌdaʊn'ləʊd, '-- US 'daʊn.loʊd **-s** -z **-ing** -ɪŋ **-ed** -ɪd **-able**

downmarket ˌdaʊn'mɑː.kɪt, ˌdaʊm- US 'daʊnˌmɑːr- *stress shift, British only:* ˌdownmarket 'area

Downpatrick ˌdaʊn'pæt.rɪk, ˌdaʊm- US ˌdaʊn-

downpipe 'daʊn.paɪp, 'daʊm- US 'daʊn- **-s** -s

downplay ˌdaʊn'pleɪ, ˌdaʊm- US 'daʊn.pleɪ **-s** -z **-ing** -ɪŋ **-ed** -d *stress shift, British only:* ˌdownplayed 'incident

downpour 'daʊn.pɔːʳ, 'daʊm- US 'daʊn.pɔːr **-s** -z

downright 'daʊn.raɪt **-ness** -nəs, -nɪs

downriver ˌdaʊn'rɪv.əʳ, -ɚ *stress shift:* ˌdownriver 'settlement

downrush 'daʊn.rʌʃ **-es** -ɪz

Downs daʊnz

downside (D) 'daʊn.saɪd

downsiz|e ˌdaʊn'saɪz US '-- **-es** -ɪz **-ing** -ɪŋ **-ed** -d *stress shift, British only:* ˌdownsized 'payments

downspout 'daʊn.spaʊt **-s** -s

downstage ˌdaʊn'steɪdʒ US '-- *stress shift, British only:* ˌdownstage 'action

downstairs ˌdaʊn'steəz US -'sterz *stress shift:* ˌdownstairs 'bathroom

downstream ˌdaʊn'striːm *stress shift:* ˌdownstream 'settlement

downswing 'daʊn.swɪŋ **-s** -z

downtime 'daʊn.taɪm

down-to-earth ˌdaʊn.tu'ɜːθ US -'ɝːθ *stress shift:* ˌdown-to-earth 'person

Downton 'daʊn.tən US -tᵊn

downtown ˌdaʊn'taʊn US ˌdaʊn'taʊn, '-- *stress shift, British only:* ˌdowntown 'area

downtrodden 'daʊnˌtrɒd.ᵊn, ˌ-'-- US 'daʊnˌtrɑː.dᵊn

downturn 'daʊn.tɜːn US -tɝːn **-s** -z

downward 'daʊn.wəd US -wɚd **-s** -z

downwind ˌdaʊn'wɪnd US ˌdaʊn'wɪnd, '--

down|y 'daʊ.n|i **-ier** -i.əʳ US -i.ɚ **-iest** -i.ɪst, -i.əst

dowr|y 'daʊ.r|i **-ies** -iz

dows|e daʊz, daʊs **-es** -ɪz **-ing** -ɪŋ **-ed** -d **-er/s** -əʳ/z US -ɚ/z **'dowsing ˌrod**

Dowse daʊs

Dowson 'daʊ.sᵊn

Dowton 'daʊ.tᵊn

doxolog|y dɒk'sɒl.ə.dʒ|i US dɑːk'sɑː.lə- **-ies** -iz

dox|y 'dɒk.s|i US 'dɑːk- **-ies** -iz

doyen 'dɔɪ.en, -ən; 'dwaɪ.æ̃ŋ; dɔɪ'en US 'dɔɪ.ən, -ən, dwɑː'jen **-s** -z

doyenne dɔɪ'en; dwaɪ'æ̃ŋ US dɔɪ'en, -'jen, dwɑː'jen **-s** -z

Doyle dɔɪl

doyl|(e)y 'dɔɪ.li **-(e)ys** -z **-lies** -z

D'Oyl(e)y 'dɔɪ.li

d'Oyly Carte ˌdɔɪ.li'kɑːt US -'kɑːrt

doz|e dəʊz US doʊz **-es** -ɪz **-ing** -ɪŋ **-ed** -d **-er/s** -əʳ/z US -ɚ/z

dozen 'dʌz.ᵊn **-s** -z **-th** -θ

doz|y 'dəʊ.z|i US 'doʊ- **-ier** -i.əʳ US -i.ɚ **-iest** -i.ɪst, -i.əst **-ily** -ɪ.li, -ᵊl.i **-iness** -ɪ.nəs, -ɪ.nɪs

DPhil ˌdiː'fɪl

dr *(abbrev. for* **dram***)* dræm

Dr. *(abbrev. for* **Doctor***)* 'dɒk.təʳ US 'dɑːk.tɚ

drab dræb **-s** -z **-ber** -əʳ US -ɚ **-best** -ɪst, -əst **-ness** -nəs, -nɪs

drabbl|e (D) 'dræb.l̩ **-es** -z **-ing** -ɪŋ, '-lɪŋ **-ed** -d

dracaena drə'siː.nə **-s** -z

drachm dræm **-s** -z

drachm|a 'dræk.m|ə **-as** -əz **-ae** -iː, -eɪ

Draco *Greek legislator:* 'dreɪ.kəʊ US -koʊ *English surname:* 'drɑː.kəʊ US -koʊ

draconian (D) drə'kəʊ.ni.ən, dræk'əʊ- US drə'koʊ-, dreɪ-

Dracula 'dræk.jə.lə, -jʊ-

draff dræf, drɑːf US dræf

draft drɑːft US dræft **-s** -s **-ing** -ɪŋ **-ed** -ɪd **-er/s** -əʳ/z US -ɚ/z **'draft ˌdodger**

draftee ˌdrɑːf'tiː US ˌdræf- **-s** -z

drafts|man 'drɑːfts|.mən US 'dræfts- **-men** -mən, -men **-manship** -mən.ʃɪp

drafts|woman 'drɑːfts|ˌwʊm.ən US 'dræfts- **-women** -ˌwɪm.ɪn

draft|y 'drɑːf.t|i US 'dræf- **-ier** -i.əʳ US -i.ɚ **-iest** -i.ɪst, -i.əst **-iness** -ɪ.nəs, -ɪ.nɪs

drag dræg **-s** -z **-ging** -ɪŋ **-ged** -d **'drag ˌrace; 'drag ˌqueen**

Drage dreɪdʒ

dragee, dragée dræʒ'eɪ US dræʒ'eɪ, drɑː'ʒeɪ **-s** -z

draggl|e 'dræg.l̩ **-es** -z **-ing** -ɪŋ, '-lɪŋ **-ed** -d

dragg|y 'dræg|.i **-ier** -i.əʳ US -i.ɚ **-iest** -i.ɪst, -i.əst

dragnet 'dræg.net **-s** -s

drago|man 'dræg.əʊ|.mən, -mæn

US -ə-, -oʊ- **-mans** -mənz, -mænz **-men** -mən, -men
dragon ˈdræg.ən **-s** -z ˈ**dragon's** ˌ**blood**, ˌ**dragon's** ˈ**blood**
dragonet ˈdræg.ə.nɪt, -net **-s** -s
dragonfl|y ˈdræg.ən.fl|aɪ **-ies** -aɪz
dragonnade ˌdræg.əˈneɪd **-s** -z
dragoon drəˈguːn **-s** -z
dragster ˈdræg.stəʳ US -stɚ **-s** -z
drain dreɪn **-s** -z **-ing** -ɪŋ **-ed** -d **-er/s** -əʳ/z US -ɚ/z ˈ**draining** ˌ**board**
drainage ˈdreɪ.nɪdʒ
drainpipe ˈdreɪn.paɪp, ˈdreɪm- US ˈdreɪn- **-s** -s
drake (D) dreɪk **-s** -s
Drakensberg ˈdræk.ənz.bɜːg US ˈdrɑː.kənz.bɝːg
Dralon® ˈdreɪ.lɒn US -lɑːn
dram dræm **-s** -z **-ming** -ɪŋ **-med** -d
drama ˈdrɑː.mə US ˈdrɑːm.ə, ˈdræm.ə **-s** -z
Dramamine® ˈdræm.ə.miːn
dramatic drəˈmæt.ɪk US -ˈmæţ- **-al** -əl **-ally** -əl.i, -li **-s** -s
dramatis personae ˌdrɑː.mə.tɪs.pɜːˈsəʊ.naɪ, ˌdræm.ə-, -pəˈ- US ˌdrɑː.mə.ţɪs.pɚˈsoʊ-, ˌdræm.ə-, -ni
dramatist ˈdræm.ə.tɪst, ˈdrɑː.mə- US ˈdrɑː.mə.ţɪst, ˈdræm.ə- **-s** -s
dramatization, -isa- ˌdræm.ə.taɪˈzeɪ.ʃən, ˌdrɑː.mə-, -tɪˈ- US ˌdrɑː.mə.ţɪˈ-, ˌdræm.ə- **-s** -z
dramatiz|e, -is|e ˈdræm.ə.taɪz, ˈdrɑː.mə- US ˈdrɑː.mə-, ˈdræm.ə- **-es** -ɪz **-ing** -ɪŋ **-ed** -d **-able** -ə.bl̩
dramaturg|e ˈdræm.ə.tɜːdʒ, ˈdrɑː.mə- US ˈdrɑː.mə-, ˈdræm.ə.tɝːdʒ **-es** -ɪz
dramaturgic ˌdræm.əˈtɜː.dʒɪk, ˌdrɑː.mə- US ˈdrɑː.mə.tɝː-; ˌdræm.əˈtɝː- **-al** -əl **-ally** -əl.i, -li
dramaturgy ˈdræm.ə.tɜː.dʒi, ˈdrɑː.mə- US ˈdrɑː.mə.tɝː-, ˈdræm.ə-
Drambuie® dræmˈbjuː.i, -ˈbuː-
Drane dreɪn
drank *(from* **drink**) dræŋk
drap|e dreɪp **-es** -s **-ing** -ɪŋ **-ed** -t
draper (D) ˈdreɪ.pəʳ US -pɚ **-s** -z
draper|y ˈdreɪ.pər|.i **-ies** -iz
Drapier ˈdreɪ.pi.əʳ US -ɚ
Draskovic ˈdræs.kə.vɪtʃ US drɑːs-
drastic ˈdræs.tɪk, ˈdrɑː.stɪk US ˈdræs.tɪk **-ally** -əl.i, -li
drat dræt
draught drɑːft US dræft **-s** -s
draughtboard ˈdrɑːft.bɔːd US ˈdræft.bɔːrd **-s** -z
draught-proof ˈdrɑːft.pruːf US ˈdræft- **-s** -s **-ing** -ɪŋ **-d** -t
draughts|man ˈdrɑːfts|.mən US ˈdræfts- **-men** -mən
draughts|woman ˈdrɑːfts|ˌwʊm.ən US ˈdræfts- **-women** -ˌwɪm.ɪn
draught|y ˈdrɑːf.t|i US ˈdræf- **-ier** -i.əʳ US -i.ɚ **-iest** -i.ɪst, -i.əst **-ily** -ɪ.li, -əl.i **-iness** -ɪ.nəs, -ɪ.nɪs
Drava ˈdrɑː.və
Dravidian drəˈvɪd.i.ən **-s** -z
draw drɔː US drɑː, drɔː **-s** -z **-ing** -ɪŋ **drew** druː **drawn** drɔːn US drɑːn, drɔːn **drawable** ˈdrɔː.ə.bl̩ US ˈdrɑː-, ˈdrɔː- ˈ**drawing** ˌ**board**; ˈ**drawing** ˌ**pin**; ˈ**drawing** ˌ**room**; ˈ**drawing** ˌ**table**; **go** ˌ**back to the** ˈ**drawing** ˌ**board**
drawback ˈdrɔː.bæk US ˈdrɑː-, ˈdrɔː- **-s** -s
drawbridg|e ˈdrɔː.brɪdʒ US ˈdrɑː-, ˈdrɔː- **-es** -ɪz
drawdown ˈdrɔː.daʊn US ˈdrɑː-, ˈdrɔː-
drawee ˌdrɔːˈiː US ˌdrɑː-, ˌdrɔː- **-s** -z
drawer *sliding box:* drɔːʳ US drɔːr **-s** -z
drawer *person who draws:* ˈdrɔː.əʳ US ˈdrɑː.ɚ, ˈdrɔː- **-s** -z
drawers *garment:* drɔːz US drɔːrz
drawl drɔːl US drɑːl, drɔːl **-s** -z **-ing** -ɪŋ **-ed** -d **-er/s** -əʳ/z US -ɚ/z
drawn *(from* **draw**) drɔːn US drɑːn, drɔːn
drawstring ˈdrɔː.strɪŋ US ˈdrɑː-, ˈdrɔː- **-s** -z
Drax dræks
dray dreɪ **-s** -z
dray|man ˈdreɪ|.mən, -mæn **-men** -mən, -men
Drayton ˈdreɪ.tən
dread dred **-s** -z **-ing** -ɪŋ **-ed** -ɪd
dreadful ˈdred.fəl, -fʊl **-ly** -i **-ness** -nəs, -nɪs
dreadlocks ˈdred.lɒks US -lɑːks
dreadnought, dreadnaught (D) ˈdred.nɔːt US -nɑːt, -nɔːt **-s** -s
dream driːm **-s** -z **-ing/ly** -ɪŋ/li **-ed** drempt, driːmd US driːmd, drempt **-t** drempt **-er/s** ˈdriː.məʳ/z US -mɚ/z **-like** -laɪk ˈ**dream** ˌ**world**
dreamboat ˈdriːm.bəʊt US -boʊt **-s** -s
Dreamcast® ˈdriːm.kɑːst US -kæst
dreamland ˈdriːm.lænd
dreamless ˈdriːm.ləs, -lɪs **-ly** -li
dreamtime ˈdriːm.taɪm
dream|y ˈdriː.m|i **-ier** -i.əʳ US -i.ɚ **-iest** -i.ɪst, -i.əst **-ily** -ɪ.li, -əl.i **-iness** -ɪ.nəs, -ɪ.nɪs
drear drɪəʳ US drɪr
drear|y ˈdrɪə.r|i US ˈdrɪr|.i **-ier** -i.əʳ US -i.ɚ **-iest** -i.ɪst, -i.əst **-ily** -ɪ.li, -əl.i **-iness** -ɪ.nəs, -ɪ.nɪs
dredg|e dredʒ **-es** -ɪz **-ing** -ɪŋ **-ed** -d
dredger ˈdredʒ.əʳ US -ɚ **-s** -z
Dre-fach Felindre drevˌɑːx.velˈɪn.drə
dregg|y ˈdreg|.i **-ily** -ɪ.li, -əl.i **-iness** -ɪ.nəs, -ɪ.nɪs
dregs dregz
Dreiser ˈdraɪ.zəʳ, -səʳ US -zɚ, -sɚ
drench drentʃ **-es** -ɪz **-ing** -ɪŋ **-ed** -t **-er/s** -əʳ/z US -ɚ/z
Dresden ˈdrez.dən
dress dres **-es** -ɪz **-ing** -ɪŋ **-ed** -t ˌ**dress** ˈ**circle** US ˈ**dress** ˌ**circle**; ˌ**dress** ˈ**coat** US ˈ**dress** ˌ**coat**; ˈ**dress** ˌ**code**; ˌ**dress** **re**ˈ**hearsal** US ˈ**dress** **re**ˌ**hearsal**; ˈ**dress** ˌ**sense**; ˌ**dress** ˈ**suit**; US ˈ**dress** ˌ**suit**
dressage ˈdres.ɑːʒ; -ɑːdʒ; -ɪdʒ; drəˈsɑːʒ US drəˈsɑːʒ, dresˈɑːʒ
dresser ˈdres.əʳ US -ɚ **-s** -z
dressing ˈdres.ɪŋ **-s** -z ˈ**dressing** ˌ**gown**; ˈ**dressing** ˌ**room**; ˈ**dressing** ˌ**table**;
dressing-down ˌdres.ɪŋˈdaʊn **-s** -z
dressmak|er ˈdresˌmeɪ.k|əʳ US -k|ɚ **-ers** -əz US -ɚz **-ing** -ɪŋ
dress|y ˈdres|.i **-ier** -i.əʳ US -i.ɚ **-iest** -i.ɪst, -i.əst **-ily** -ɪ.li, -əl.i **-iness** -ɪ.nəs, -ɪ.nɪs
drew *(from* **draw**) druː
Drew druː **-s** -z
Dreyfus(s) ˈdreɪ.fəs, ˈdraɪ-, -fʊs
dribbl|e ˈdrɪb.l̩ **-es** -z **-ing** -ɪŋ **-ed** -d, ˈ-lɪŋ **-er/s** -əʳ/z, ˈ-ləʳ/z US ˈ-l̩.ɚ/z, ˈ-lɚ/z
driblet ˈdrɪb.lət, -lɪt **-s** -s
dribs and drabs ˌdrɪbz.ənˈdræbz
dried *(from* **dry**) draɪd
drier ˈdraɪ.əʳ US -ɚ **-s** -z
dries *(from* **dry**) draɪz
driest ˈdraɪ.ɪst, -əst
Driffield ˈdrɪf.iːld
drift drɪft **-s** -s **-ing** -ɪŋ **-ed** -ɪd
drifter ˈdrɪf.təʳ US -tɚ **-s** -z
driftless ˈdrɪft.ləs, -lɪs
driftnet ˈdrɪft.net **-s** -s
driftwood ˈdrɪft.wʊd
drifty ˈdrɪf.ti
drill drɪl **-s** -z **-ing** -ɪŋ **-ed** -d ˈ**drill** ˌ**sergeant**
drily ˈdraɪ.li
drink drɪŋk **-s** -s **-ing** -ɪŋ **drank** dræŋk **drunk** drʌŋk **drinker/s** ˈdrɪŋ.kəʳ/z US -kɚ/z ˈ**drinking** ˌ**fountain**; ˈ**drinking** ˌ**horn**; ˈ**drinking** ˌ**water**
drinkable ˈdrɪŋ.kə.bl̩
drink-driv|ing ˌdrɪŋkˈdraɪ.v|ɪŋ **-er/s** -əʳ/z US -ɚ/z
Drinkwater ˈdrɪŋkˌwɔː.təʳ US -ˌwɑː.ţɚ, -ˌwɔː-
drip drɪp **-s** -s **-ping** -ɪŋ **-ped** -t
drip|-dry ˈdrɪp|.draɪ, ˌ-|ˈ- **-dries** -draɪz **-drying** -ˌdraɪ.ɪŋ **-dried** -draɪd
drip|-feed ˈdrɪp|.fiːd **-feeds** -fiːdz **-feeding** -ˌfiː.dɪŋ **-fed** -fed
dripping ˈdrɪp.ɪŋ **-s** -z
dripp|y ˈdrɪp|.i **-ier** -i.əʳ US -i.ɚ **-iest** -i.ɪst, -i.əst
dripstone ˈdrɪp.stəʊn US -stoʊn **-s** -z
Driscoll ˈdrɪs.kəl

driv|e draɪv **-es** -z **-ing** -ɪŋ **drove** drəʊv (US) droʊv **driven** ˈdrɪv.ən **ˈdriving ˌiron; ˈdriving ˌlicence/license; ˈdriving ˌseat; ˈdriving ˌtest**
driveaway ˈdraɪv.əˌweɪ
drive-by ˈdraɪv.baɪ
drive-in ˈdraɪv.ɪn **-s** -z
drivel ˈdrɪv.əl **-s** -z **-(l)ing** -ɪŋ **-(l)ed** -d **-(l)er/s** -əʳ/z (US) -ɚ/z
driven *(from* **drive***)* ˈdrɪv.ən
driver (D) ˈdraɪ.vəʳ (US) -vɚ **-s** -z **ˈdriver's ˌlicense; in the ˈdriver's ˌseat**
driveway ˈdraɪv.weɪ **-s** -z
Driza-bone® ˈdraɪ.zə.bəʊn (US) -boʊn
drizzl|e ˈdrɪz.l̩ **-es** -z **-ing** -ɪŋ, ˈ-lɪŋ **-ed** -d
drizzly ˈdrɪz.l̩.i, ˈ-li
Drogheda *place:* ˈdrɔɪ.ɪ.də, ˈdrɔː-, ˈ-ə-, ˈdrɒ.hə- (US) ˈdrɔː.ɪ-, ˈdrɑː-, ˈ-ə- *Earl:* ˈdrɔɪ.ɪ.də
droid drɔɪd **-s** -z
droit drɔɪt, drwɑː **-s** -s
droit de seigneur ˌdrwɑː.də.seɪˈnjɜːʳ, -senˈjɜːʳ, -siːˈnjɜːʳ (US) -seɪˈnjʊr, -senˈjʊr, -ˈjɝː
Droitwich ˈdrɔɪ.twɪtʃ
droll drəʊl (US) droʊl **-ness** -nəs, -nɪs **-er** -əʳ (US) -ɚ **-est** -ɪst, -əst **-y** -li, ˈdrəʊ.li (US) ˈdroʊ.li
droller|y ˈdrəʊ.ləʳl.i (US) ˈdroʊ- **-ies** -iz
-drome -drəʊm (US) -droʊm
Note: Suffix. Normally unstressed, e.g. **aerodrome** /ˈeə.rə.drəʊm (US) ˈer.ə.droʊm/.
dromedar|y ˈdrɒm.ə.dərl.i, ˈdrʌm-, ˈ-ɪ- (US) ˈdrɑː.mə.der-, ˈdrʌm.ə- **-ies** -iz
Dromio ˈdrəʊ.mi.əʊ (US) ˈdroʊ.mi.oʊ
Dromore ˈdrəʊ.mɔːʳ; drəˈmɔːʳ (US) ˈdroʊ.mɔːr; drəˈmɔːr
dron|e drəʊn (US) droʊn **-es** -z **-ing** -ɪŋ **-ed** -d
Dronfield ˈdrɒn.fiːld (US) ˈdrɑːn-
drongo ˈdrɒŋ.gəʊ (US) ˈdrɑːŋ.goʊ **-(e)s** -z
Drood druːd
drool druːl **-s** -z **-ing** -ɪŋ **-ed** -d
droop druːp **-s** -s **-ing/ly** -ɪŋ/li **-ed** -t
droop|y ˈdruː.pli **-ier** -i.əʳ (US) -i.ɚ **-iest** -i.ɪst, -i.əst **-ily** -ɪ.li, -əl.i **-iness** -ɪ.nəs, -ɪ.nɪs
drop drɒp (US) drɑːp **-s** -s **-ping** -ɪŋ **-ped** -t **ˈdrop ˌscone; ˈdrop ˌshot; a ˌdrop in the ˈocean; at the ˌdrop of a ˈhat**
drop-in ˈdrɒp.ɪn (US) ˈdrɑːp-
dropkick ˈdrɒp.kɪk (US) ˈdrɑːp- **-s** -s
droplet ˈdrɒp.lət, -lɪt (US) ˈdrɑːp- **-s** -s
dropout ˈdrɒp.aʊt (US) ˈdrɑːp- **-s** -s
dropper ˈdrɒp.əʳ (US) ˈdrɑː.pɚ **-s** -z
dropping ˈdrɒp.ɪŋ (US) ˈdrɑː.pɪŋ **-s** -z
dropsic|al ˈdrɒp.sɪ.kləl (US) ˈdrɑːp- **-ally** -əl.i, -li **-alness** -əl.nəs, -nɪs
dropsy ˈdrɒp.si (US) ˈdrɑːp-
droshk|y ˈdrɒʃ.kli (US) ˈdrɑːʃ- **-ies** -iz
drosophila drəˈsɒf.ɪ.lə, drɒsˈɒf-, -əl.ə (US) droʊˈsɑː.fəl.ə, drə- **-s** -z
dross drɒs (US) drɑːs **-y** -i
drought draʊt **-s** -s **-y** -i
drove drəʊv (US) droʊv **-s** -z
drover ˈdrəʊ.vəʳ (US) ˈdroʊ.vɚ **-s** -z
Drower draʊəʳ (US) draʊɚ
drown draʊn **-s** -z **-ing** -ɪŋ **-ed** -d
drows|e draʊz **-es** -ɪz **-ing** -ɪŋ **-ed** -d
drows|y ˈdraʊ.zli **-ier** -i.əʳ (US) -i.ɚ **-iest** -i.ɪst, -i.əst **-ily** -ɪ.li, -əl.i **-iness** -ɪ.nəs, -ɪ.nɪs
Droylsden ˈdrɔɪlz.dən
Drs. *(abbrev. for* **Doctors***)* ˈdɒk.təz (US) ˈdɑːk.tɚz
drub drʌb **-s** -z **-bing** -ɪŋ **-bed** -d
Druce druːs
Drucker ˈdrʊk.əʳ (US) ˈdrʌk.ɚ, ˈdrʊk-
drudg|e drʌdʒ **-es** -ɪz **-ing/ly** -ɪŋ/li **-ed** -d
drudgery ˈdrʌdʒ.ər.i
drug drʌg **-s** -z **-ging** -ɪŋ **-ged** -d
drugget ˈdrʌg.ɪt **-s** -s
druggie ˈdrʌg.i **-s** -z
druggist ˈdrʌg.ɪst **-s** -s
drugg|y ˈdrʌgl.i **-ies** -iz
drugstore ˈdrʌg.stɔːʳ (US) -stɔːr **-s** -z
druid ˈdruː.ɪd **-s** -z **-ess/es** -ɪs/ɪz, -es/ɪz **-ism** -ɪ.zəm
druidic druˈɪd.ɪk **-al** -əl
drum drʌm **-s** -z **-ming** -ɪŋ **-med** -d **ˌdrum ˈmajor** (US) **ˈdrum ˌmajor; ˌdrum majorˈette**
drumbeat ˈdrʌm.biːt **-s** -s
Drumcree drʌmˈkriː *stress shift:* ˌDrumcree ˈresidents
drumfire ˈdrʌm.faɪəʳ (US) -faɪɚ
drumhead ˈdrʌm.hed **-s** -z
drummer ˈdrʌm.əʳ (US) -ɚ **-s** -z
Drummond ˈdrʌm.ənd
drumroll ˈdrʌm.rəʊl (US) -roʊl **-s** -z
drumstick ˈdrʌm.stɪk **-s** -s
drunk *(n. adj.) (also from* **drink***)* drʌŋk **-s** -s **-er** -əʳ (US) -ɚ
drunkard ˈdrʌŋ.kəd (US) -kɚd **-s** -z
drunk-driv|ing ˌdrʌŋkˈdraɪ.vlɪŋ **-er/s** -əʳ/z (US) -ɚ/z
drunken ˈdrʌŋ.kən **-ly** -li **-ness** -nəs, -nɪs
drupe druːp **-s** -s
Drury ˈdrʊə.ri (US) ˈdrʊr.i
drus|e *geological term:* druːz **-es** -ɪz
Druse *surname:* druːz, druːs
Drus|e, Druz|e *member of sect in Syria and Lebanon:* druːz **-es** -ɪz
Drusilla druːˈsɪl.ə, drʊ-
druthers ˈdrʌð.əz (US) -ɚz
dr|y drlaɪ **-ier** -aɪ.əʳ (US) -aɪ.ɚ **-iest** -aɪ.ɪst, -əst **-yly** -aɪ.li **-yness** -aɪ.nəs, -nɪs **-ies** -aɪz **-ying** -aɪ.ɪŋ **-ied** -aɪd **ˌdry ˈgoods** (US) **ˈdry ˌgoods; ˌdry ˈice; ˌdry ˈland; ˌdry ˈrot**
dryad ˈdraɪ.æd, -əd **-s** -z
Dryburgh ˈdraɪ.bər.ə (US) -bɝːg, -bɚ.ə
dry-clean ˌdraɪˈkliːn (US) ˈ-- **-s** -z **-ing** -ɪŋ **-ed** -d **-er/s** -əʳ/z (US) -ɚ/z
Dryden ˈdraɪ.dən
dry-dock ˌdraɪˈdɒk, ˈ-- (US) ˈdraɪ.dɑːk **-s** -s **-ing** -ɪŋ **-ed** -t
dryer ˈdraɪ.əʳ (US) -ɚ **-s** -z
Dryfesdale ˈdraɪfs.deɪl
Dryhurst ˈdraɪ.hɜːst (US) -hɝːst
drying *(from* **dry***)* ˈdraɪ.ɪŋ
dryly ˈdraɪ.li
dryness ˈdraɪ.nəs, -nɪs
dry-nurs|e ˈdraɪ.nɜːs (US) -nɝːs **-es** -ɪz **-ing** -ɪŋ **-ed** -t
drypoint ˈdraɪ.pɔɪnt
Drysdale ˈdraɪz.deɪl
dryshod ˈdraɪ.ʃɒd (US) ʃɑːd
drywall ˈdraɪ.wɔːl (US) -wɔːl, -wɑːl **-s** -z **-ing** -ɪŋ **-ed** -d
DTI ˌdiː.tiːˈaɪ
DTP ˌdiː.tiːˈpiː
DTs ˌdiːˈtiːz
dual ˈdjuː.əl, ˈdʒuː-; djʊəl, dʒʊəl (US) ˈduː.əl, ˈdjuː- **ˌdual ˈcarriageway**
dual|ism ˈdjuː.ə.llɪ.zəm, ˈdʒuː-; ˈdjʊə.llɪ-, ˈdʒʊə- (US) ˈduː.əll.ɪ-, ˈdjuː- **-ist/s** -ɪst/s
dualistic ˌdjuː.əˈlɪs.tɪk, ˌdʒuː-; ˌdjʊəˈlɪs-, ˌdʒʊə- (US) ˌduː.əlˈɪs-, ˌdjuː-
dualit|y djuˈæl.ə.tli, dʒu-, -ɪ.tli (US) duˈæl.ə.t̬li, dju- **-ies** -iz
dual-purpose ˌdjuː.əlˈpɜː.pəs, ˌdʒuː-; ˌdjʊəl-, ˌdʒʊəl- (US) ˌduː.əlˈpɝː-, ˌdjuː- *stress shift:* ˌdual-purpose ˈimplement
Duane dweɪn; duˈeɪn
dub dʌb **-s** -z **-bing** -ɪŋ **-bed** -d
Dubai duːˈbaɪ, dʊ-, djʊ- (US) duː-, də-
Du Barry djuːˈbær.i, duː- (US) duːˈber-, djuː-, -ˈbær-
dubbin ˈdʌb.ɪn
Dubcek ˈdʊb.tʃek (US) ˈduːb-
dubiety djuːˈbaɪ.ə.ti, djʊ-, dʒuː-, dʒʊ-, -ɪ.ti (US) duːˈbaɪ.ə.t̬i, djuː-
dubious ˈdjuː.bi.əs, ˈdʒuː- (US) ˈduː-, ˈdjuː- **-ly** -li **-ness** -nəs, -nɪs
dubi|tate ˈdjuː.bɪl.teɪt, ˈdʒuː- (US) ˈduː.bə-, ˈdjuː- **-tates** -teɪts **-tating** -teɪ.tɪŋ (US) -teɪ.t̬ɪŋ **-tated** -teɪ.tɪd (US) -teɪ.t̬ɪd
dubitation ˌdjuː.bɪˈteɪ.ʃən, ˌdʒuː- (US) ˌduː.bəˈ-, ˌdjuː- **-s** -z
dubitative ˈdjuː.bɪ.tə.tɪv, ˈdʒuː-, -teɪ- (US) ˈduː.bə-, ˈdjuː- **-ly** -li
Dublin ˈdʌb.lɪn
Dubliner ˈdʌb.lɪ.nəʳ (US) -nɚ **-s** -z
DuBois, Du Bois duːˈbwɑː, djuː-
Dubonnet® djuːˈbɒn.eɪ, duː-, ˈ--- (US) ˌduː.bəˈneɪ, ˌdjuː-
Dubrovnik dʊˈbrɒv.nɪk, dʊ- (US) duːˈbrɑːv-
Dubya ˈdʌb.jə

ducal ˈdjuː.kᵊl, ˈdʒuː- ⓤⓢ ˈduː-, ˈdjuː- **-ly** -i
Du Cane djuːˈkeɪn, duː- ⓤⓢ du-, djuː-
ducat ˈdʌk.ət **-s** -s
duce **(D)** ˈduː.tʃeɪ, -tʃi ⓤⓢ ˈduː.tʃeɪ
duces tecum ˌduː.kesˈteɪ.kʊm ⓤⓢ -siːzˈ-
Duchamp ˈdjuː.ʃɑ̃ŋ, ˈduː-, ˌ-ˈ- ⓤⓢ ˌ-ˈ-, ˌduˈʃɑːmp
Duchesne djuːˈʃeɪn, duː-
duchess **(D)** ˈdʌtʃ.ɪs, -es; dʌtʃˈes ⓤⓢ ˈdʌtʃ.ɪs **-es** -ɪz
duchesse duːˈʃes; ˈdʌtʃ.ɪs, -es ⓤⓢ ˈdʌtʃ.ɪs
Duchovny dʊˈkɒv.ni, duː- ⓤⓢ -ˈkɑːv-
duch|y ˈdʌtʃ|.i **-ies** -iz
Ducie ˈdjuː.si, ˈdʒuː- ⓤⓢ ˈduː-, ˈdjuː-
duck dʌk **-s** -s **-ing** -ɪŋ **-ed** -t **ˈduck ˌpond; ˌducks and ˈdrakes; ˌtake to something like a ˌduck to ˈwater**
duckbill ˈdʌk.bɪl **-s** -z **-ed** -d **ˌduckbilled ˈplatypus**
duckboard ˈdʌk.bɔːd ⓤⓢ -bɔːrd **-s** -z
duck-egg ˈdʌk.eg **-s** -z
duckling ˈdʌk.lɪŋ **-s** -z
duckweed ˈdʌk.wiːd
Duckworth ˈdʌk.wəθ, -wɜːθ ⓤⓢ -wɚθ, -wɝːθ
duck|y ˈdʌk|.i **-ies** -iz
duct dʌkt **-s** -s
ductile ˈdʌk.taɪl ⓤⓢ -tɪl, -taɪl
ductility dʌkˈtɪl.ə.ti, -ɪ.ti ⓤⓢ -ə.t̬i
ductless ˈdʌkt.ləs, -lɪs **ˌductless ˈgland**
dud dʌd **-s** -z
Duddeston ˈdʌd.ɪ.stᵊn
Duddington ˈdʌd.ɪŋ.tᵊn
Duddon ˈdʌd.ᵊn
dude duːd, djuːd **-s** -z **ˈdude ˌranch**
Dudeney ˈduːd.ni, ˈdjuːd-
dudgeon ˈdʌdʒ.ᵊn **-s** -z
Dudley ˈdʌd.li
due djuː, dʒuː ⓤⓢ duː, djuː **-s** -z
duel ˈdjuː.əl, ˈdʒuː- ⓤⓢ ˈduː.əl, ˈdjuː- **-s** -z **-(l)ing** -ɪŋ **-(l)ed** -d **-(l)er/s** -əʳ/z ⓤⓢ -ɚ/z
duel(l)ist ˈdjuː.ᵊl.ɪst, ˈdʒuː- ⓤⓢ ˈduː-, ˈdjuː- **-s** -s
duenna djuˈen.ə, du- ⓤⓢ du-, dju- **-s** -z
Duer ˈdjuː.əʳ, ˈdʒuː- ⓤⓢ ˈduː.ɚ, ˈdjuː-
Duessa djuˈes.ə, dʒu- ⓤⓢ du-, dju-
duet djuˈet, dʒu- ⓤⓢ du-, dju- **-s** -s
duettino ˌdjuː.etˈiː.nəʊ, ˌdʒuː- ⓤⓢ ˌduː.etˈiː.noʊ, ˌdjuː- **-s** -z
duettist djuˈet.ɪst, dʒu- ⓤⓢ duˈet̬-, dju- **-s** -s
duetto djuˈet.əʊ, dʒu- ⓤⓢ duˈet̬.oʊ, dju- **-s** -z
duff **(D)** dʌf **-s** -s **-ing** -ɪŋ **-ed** -t
duffel ˈdʌf.ᵊl **ˈduffel ˌbag; ˈduffel ˌcoat**
duffer ˈdʌf.əʳ ⓤⓢ -ɚ **-s** -z
Dufferin ˈdʌf.ᵊr.ɪn
Duffield ˈdʌf.iːld
Duffin ˈdʌf.ɪn
Duffy ˈdʌf.i
Dufy ˈduː.fi ⓤⓢ duːˈfiː
dug *(n.) (also from* **dig***)* dʌg **-s** -z
Dugald ˈduː.gᵊld
Dugan ˈduː.gᵊn
Dugdale ˈdʌg.deɪl
Duggan ˈdʌg.ᵊn
Dugmore ˈdʌg.mɔːʳ ⓤⓢ -mɔːr
dugong ˈdjuː.gɒŋ, ˈduː- ⓤⓢ ˈduː.gɑːŋ, -gɔːŋ **-s** -z
dugout ˈdʌg.aʊt **-s** -s
Duguid ˈdjuː.gɪd, ˈduː.gɪd ⓤⓢ ˈduː-, ˈdjuː-
DUI ˌdiː.juːˈaɪ
duiker ˈdaɪ.kəʳ ⓤⓢ -kɚ **-s** -z
Duisburg ˈdjuːz.bɜːg, ˈdjuːs- ⓤⓢ ˈduːs.bɝːg, ˈduːz-
Duisenberg ˈdaɪ.zᵊn.bɜːg, ˈdɔɪ-, -zᵊm- ⓤⓢ ˈduː.zᵊn.bɝg, daɪ-
Dukakis dʊˈkɑː.kɪs, djʊ-, dʒʊ-, də- ⓤⓢ dʊˈkɑː.kəs, də-
Dukas ˈdjuː.kɑː, ˈduː-, -ˈ- ⓤⓢ duːˈkɑː, djuː-
duke **(D)** djuːk, dʒuːk ⓤⓢ duːk, djuːk **-s** -s
dukedom ˈdjuːk.dəm, ˈdʒuːk- ⓤⓢ ˈduːk-, ˈdjuːk- **-s** -z
duker|y ˈdjuː.kᵊr|.i, ˈdʒuː- ⓤⓢ ˈduː-, ˈdjuː- **-ies** -iz
Dukinfield ˈdʌk.ɪn.fiːld
Dulce ˈdʌl.si
dulcet ˈdʌl.sɪt, -sət
Dulcie ˈdʌl.si
dulci|fy ˈdʌl.sɪ|.faɪ, -sə- **-fies** -faɪz **-fying** -faɪ.ɪŋ **-fied** -faɪd
dulcimer ˈdʌl.sɪ.məʳ, -sə- ⓤⓢ -mɚ **-s** -z
Dulcinea ˌdʌl.sɪˈniː.ə, -ˈneɪ-; dʌlˈsɪn.i- ⓤⓢ ˌdʌl.səˈniː-; dʌlˈsɪn.i-
dulia djʊˈlaɪə, dʊ- ⓤⓢ duːˈlaɪə, djuː-; ˈduː.li.ə
dull dʌl **-er** -əʳ ⓤⓢ -ɚ **-est** -ɪst, -əst **-y** -li, -i **-ness** -nəs, -nɪs **-s** -z **-ing** -ɪŋ **-ed** -d **as ˌdull as ˈditch-water**
dullard ˈdʌl.əd, -ɑːd ⓤⓢ -ɚd **-s** -z
Dulles ˈdʌl.ɪs, -əs
dullish ˈdʌl.ɪʃ
dullsville ˈdʌlz.vɪl
dulness ˈdʌl.nəs, -nɪs
Duluth dəˈluːθ, djʊ-, dʊ-, də- ⓤⓢ də-
Dulux® ˈdjuː.lʌks
Dulwich ˈdʌl.ɪdʒ, -ɪtʃ
duly ˈdjuː.li, ˈdʒuː- ⓤⓢ ˈduː-, ˈdjuː-
Duma ˈduː.mə, ˈdjuː- ⓤⓢ ˈduː-
Dumain djʊˈmeɪn, dʒʊ- ⓤⓢ duː-, djuː-
Dumas ˈdjuː.mɑː, ˈduː-; dʊˈmɑː ⓤⓢ duːˈmɑː, djuː-
Du Maurier djuːˈmɔː.ri.eɪ, duː-, -ˈmɒr.i- ⓤⓢ duːˈmɔːr.i-, djuː-
dumb dʌm **-er -est -ly** -li **-ness** -nəs, -nɪs **-s** -z **-ing** -ɪŋ **-ed** -d **ˈdumb ˌshow; ˌdumb ˈwaiter** ⓤⓢ **ˈdumb ˌwaiter**
Dumbarton dʌmˈbɑː.tᵊn, dəm- ⓤⓢ -ˈbɑːr-
Note: In **Dumbarton Oaks** (Washington DC), however, the pronunciation is /ˌdʌm.bɑːr.tᵊnˈəʊks ⓤⓢ -bɑːr.tᵊnˈoʊks/.
dumbbell ˈdʌm.bel **-s** -z
dumbfound ˌdʌmˈfaʊnd, ˈ-- ⓤⓢ ˈdʌm.faʊnd, ˌ-ˈ- **-s** -z **-ing** -ɪŋ **-ed** -ɪd
dumbo **(D)** ˈdʌm.bəʊ ⓤⓢ -boʊ
dumbstricken ˈdʌmˌstrɪk.ᵊn
dumbstruck ˈdʌm.strʌk
dum-dum ˈdʌm.dʌm **-s** -z
dumfound ˌdʌmˈfaʊnd, ˈ-- ⓤⓢ ˈdʌm.faʊnd, ˌ-ˈ- **-s** -z **-ing** -ɪŋ **-ed** -ɪd
Dumfries dʌmˈfriːs, dəm- **-shire** -ʃəʳ, -ˌʃɪəʳ, dʌmˈfriːʃ.ʃəʳ ⓤⓢ dʌmˈfriːs.ʃɚ, -ˌʃɪr
dumm|y ˈdʌm|.i **-ies** -iz
dump dʌmp **-s** -s **-ing** -ɪŋ **-ed** -t **ˈdump ˌtruck**
dumper ˈdʌm.pəʳ ⓤⓢ -pɚ **-s** -z
Dumphreys ˈdʌm*p*.frɪz, -friz
dumpish ˈdʌm.pɪʃ **-ly** -li **-ness** -nəs, -nɪs
dumpling ˈdʌm.plɪŋ **-s** -z
dumps dʌmps
Dumpster® ˈdʌmp.stəʳ ⓤⓢ -stɚ
dump|y ˈdʌm.p|i **-ier** -i.əʳ ⓤⓢ -i.ɚ **-iest** -i.ɪst, -i.əst **-iness** -ɪ.nəs, -ɪ.nɪs
dun dʌn **-s** -z **-ning** -ɪŋ **-ned** -d
Dunalley dʌnˈæl.i
Dunaway ˈdʌn.ə.weɪ
Dunbar dʌnˈbɑːʳ, dʌm-, ˈ-- ⓤⓢ ˈdʌn.bɑːr, -ˈ-
Note: In Scotland always -ˈ-.
Dunbarton dʌnˈbɑː.tᵊn, dʌm- ⓤⓢ dʌnˈbɑːr- **-shire** -ʃəʳ, -ˌʃɪəʳ ⓤⓢ -ʃɚ, -ˌʃɪr
Dunblane dʌnˈbleɪn, dʌm- ⓤⓢ dʌn-
Duncan ˈdʌŋ.kən, ˈdʌn-
Duncannon dʌnˈkæn.ən, dʌŋ- ⓤⓢ dʌn-
Duncansby ˈdʌŋ.kənz.bi, ˈdʌn-
dunc|e dʌn*t*s **-es** -ɪz
Dunciad ˈdʌn*t*.si.æd
Duncombe ˈdʌn.kəm, ˈdʌŋ-
Dundalk dʌnˈdɔːk, -ˈdɔːlk ⓤⓢ -ˈdɔːk, -ˈdɑːk
Dundas dʌnˈdæs, ˈdʌn.dæs, ˈdʌn.dəs ⓤⓢ dʌnˈdæs, ˈdʌn.dəs
Dundee dʌnˈdiː, ˌdʌn- *stress shift:* ˌDundee ˈstation
dunderhead ˈdʌn.də.hed ⓤⓢ -dɚ- **-s** -z
Dundonald dʌnˈdɒn.ᵊld ⓤⓢ -ˈdɑː.nᵊld
dundrear|y **(D)** dʌnˈdrɪə.r|i ⓤⓢ -ˈdrɪr|.i **-ies** -iz
Dundrum dʌnˈdrʌm, ˈdʌn.drəm
dune djuːn, dʒuːn ⓤⓢ duːn, djuːn **-s** -z
Dunedin dʌnˈiː.dɪn, -dᵊn

Dunell djʊˈnel, ˌdjuː-, dʒʊ-, ˌdʒuː- ⓤⓢ duː-, djuː-
Dunfermline dʌnˈfɜːm.lɪn, -lən ⓤⓢ -ˈfɝːm-
dung dʌŋ
Dungannon dʌnˈgæn.ən, dʌŋ-
dungaree ˌdʌŋ.gəˈriː, ˈ--- **-s** -z
Dungarvan dʌnˈgɑː.vən, dʌŋ- ⓤⓢ dʌnˈgɑːr-
Dungeness ˌdʌn.*dʒ*əˈnes, -*dʒ*ɪˈ-
dungeon ˈdʌn.dʒən **-s** -z
dunghill ˈdʌŋ.hɪl **-s** -z
Dunglison ˈdʌŋ.glɪ.sən
dungy ˈdʌŋ.i
Dunham ˈdʌn.əm
Dunhill ˈdʌn.hɪl
Dunholme ˈdʌn.əm
dunk (D) dʌŋk **-s** -s **-ing** -ɪŋ **-ed** -t
Dunkeld dʌnˈkeld, dʌŋ- ⓤⓢ dʌn-
Dunker ˈdʌŋ.kər ⓤⓢ -kɚ **-s** -z
Dunkirk dʌnˈkɜːk, ˌdʌn-, dʌŋ-, ˌdʌŋ- ⓤⓢ ˈdʌn.kɝːk, dʌnˈkɝːk, ˌdʌn-
Dunkley ˈdʌŋ.kli
Dun Laoghaire dʌnˈlɪə.ri, duːn-, -ˈleə-, -rə ⓤⓢ -ˈler.ə, -i
Dunlap ˈdʌn.ləp, -læp ⓤⓢ -læp, -ləp
dunlin ˈdʌn.lɪn, -lən **-s** -z
Dunlop *surname:* ˈdʌn.lɒp, -ˈ- ⓤⓢ ˈdʌn.lɑːp, -ˈ-
Dunlop® ˈdʌn.lɒp ⓤⓢ -lɑːp **-s** -s
Dunmail dʌnˈmeɪl, dʌm- ⓤⓢ dʌn-
Dunmore dʌnˈmɔːr, dʌm- ⓤⓢ dʌnˈmɔːr
Dunmow ˈdʌn.məʊ, ˈdʌm- ⓤⓢ ˈdʌn.moʊ
dunnage ˈdʌn.ɪdʒ
Dunn(e) dʌn
Dunnet(t) ˈdʌn.ɪt
Dunning ˈdʌn.ɪŋ
dunno dəˈnəʊ ⓤⓢ -ˈnoʊ
dunnock ˈdʌn.ək **-s** -s
Dunnottar dʌnˈɒt.ər, dəˈnɒt- ⓤⓢ dʌnˈɑː.t̬ɚ, dəˈnɑː-
dunn|y ˈdʌn|.i **-ies** -ɪz
Dunoon dʌnˈuːn, dəˈnuːn
Dunraven dʌnˈreɪ.vən
Dunrobin dʌnˈrɒb.ɪn ⓤⓢ -ˈrɑː.bɪn
Dunsany dʌnˈseɪ.ni, -ˈsæn.i
Dunse dʌn*t*s
Dunsinane dʌnˈsɪn.ən
Note: This name has to be pronounced /ˌdʌn*t*.sɪˈneɪn/ in Shakespeare's 'Macbeth'.
Duns Scotus ˌdʌnzˈskɒt.əs, -ˈskəʊ.təs ⓤⓢ -ˈskoʊ.t̬əs
Dunstable ˈdʌn*t*.stə.bl̩
Dunstaffnage dʌnˈstæf.nɪdʒ, -ˈstɑːf- ⓤⓢ -ˈstæf-
Dunstan ˈdʌn*t*.stən
Dunster ˈdʌn*t*.stər ⓤⓢ -stɚ
Dunston ˈdʌn*t*.stən
Dunton ˈdʌn.tən ⓤⓢ -tən
Dunwich ˈdʌn.ɪtʃ

Dunwoody dʌnˈwʊd.i
duo- djuː.əʊ-, dʒuː.əʊ-; djuˈɒ-, dʒuˈɒ- ⓤⓢ duː.oʊ-, djuː-, -ə-; duˈɑː-, djuˈɑː-
Note: Prefix. Either carries primary or secondary stress on the first syllable, e.g. **duologue** /ˈdjuː.ə.lɒg ⓤⓢ ˈduː.ə.lɑːg/, **duodecimal** /ˌdjuː.əʊˈdes.ɪ.məl ⓤⓢ ˌduː.oʊˈ-/, or primary stress on the second syllable, e.g. **duopoly** /djuˈɒp.əl.i ⓤⓢ duˈɑː.pəl-/.
duo ˈdjuː.əʊ, ˈdʒuː- ⓤⓢ ˈduː.oʊ, ˈdjuː- **-s** -z
duodecennial ˌdjuː.əʊ.dɪˈsen.i.əl, ˌdʒuː-, -dəˈ- ⓤⓢ ˌduː.oʊ.dəˈ-, ˌdjuː-
duodecimal ˌdjuː.əʊˈdes.ɪ.məl, ˌdʒuː-, ˈ-ə- ⓤⓢ ˌduː.oʊˈ-, ˌdjuː- **-s** -z
duodecimo ˌdjuː.əʊˈdes.ɪ.məʊ, ˌdʒuː- ⓤⓢ ˌduː.oʊˈdes.ə.moʊ, ˌdjuː- **-s** -z
duodenal ˌdjuː.əʊˈdiː.nəl, ˌdʒuː- ⓤⓢ ˌduː.əˈ-, ˌdjuː-; duːˈɑː.dən.əl, djuː-
duodenary ˌdjuː.əʊˈdiː.nər.i, ˌdʒuː- ⓤⓢ ˌduː.əˈ-, ˌdjuː-, -ˈden.ɚ.i
duoden|um ˌdjuː.əʊˈdiː.n|əm, ˌdʒuː- ⓤⓢ ˌduː.əˈ-, ˌdjuː-; duːˈɑː.dən|.əm, djuː- **-ums** -əmz **-a** -ə
duologue ˈdjuː.ə.lɒg, ˈdʒuː- ⓤⓢ ˈduː.ə.lɑːg, ˈdjuː- **-s** -z
duopol|y djuˈɒp.əl|.i, dʒu- ⓤⓢ duˈɑː.pəl-, dju- **-ies** -iz
dup|e djuːp, dʒuːp ⓤⓢ duːp, djuːp **-es** -s **-ing** -ɪŋ **-ed** -t
dupery ˈdjuː.pər.i, ˈdʒuː- ⓤⓢ ˈduː-, ˈdjuː-
duple ˈdjuː.pl̩, ˈdʒuː- ⓤⓢ ˈduː-, ˈdjuː-
Dupleix *governor in India:* djuːˈpleɪks ⓤⓢ duːˈpleɪks, djuː- *historian:* djuːˈpleɪ ⓤⓢ duːˈpleɪ, djuː-
duplex ˈdjuː.pleks, ˈdʒuː- ⓤⓢ ˈduː-, ˈdjuː- **-es** -ɪz
duplicate (*n. adj.*) ˈdjuː.plɪ.kət, ˈdʒuː-, -plə-, -kɪt ⓤⓢ ˈduː-, ˈdjuː- **-s** -s
dupli|cate (*v.*) ˈdjuː.plɪ|.keɪt, ˈdʒuː-, -plə- ⓤⓢ ˈduː-, ˈdjuː- **-cates** -keɪts **-cating** -keɪ.tɪŋ ⓤⓢ -keɪ.t̬ɪŋ **-cated** -keɪ.tɪd ⓤⓢ -keɪ.t̬ɪd **-cator/s** -keɪ.tər/z ⓤⓢ -keɪ.t̬ɚ/z
duplication ˌdjuː.plɪˈkeɪ.ʃən, ˌdʒuː-, -pləˈ- ⓤⓢ ˌduː-, ˌdjuː- **-s** -z
duplicature ˈdjuː.plɪ.keɪ.tʃər, ˈdʒuː-, -kə- ⓤⓢ ˈduː.plə.kə.tʃʊr, ˈdjuː-, -keɪ-, -tʃɚ **-s** -z
duplicitous djʊˈplɪs.ɪ.təs, dʒʊ-, ˈ-ə- ⓤⓢ duːˈplɪs.ə.t̬əs, djuː- **-ly** -li **-ness** -nəs, -nɪs
duplicity djʊˈplɪs.ə.ti, dʒʊ-, -ɪ.ti ⓤⓢ duːˈplɪs.ə.t̬i, djuː-
dupl|y djʊˈpl|aɪ, dʒʊ- ⓤⓢ duː-, djuː- **-ies** -aɪz
Dupont djʊˈpɒnt; ˈdjuː.pɒnt ⓤⓢ duːˈpɑːnt, djuː-, ˈ--

du Pré dʊˈpreɪ, djʊ- ⓤⓢ duː-, djuː-
Dupré(e) dʊˈpreɪ, djʊ-, -ˈpriː ⓤⓢ duː-, djuː-
Dupuytren dʊˈpwiː.trən, djʊ-; ˈdjuː.pɪ.træ̃ŋ, ˌ--ˈ- ⓤⓢ ˈduː.pwiː.træn, ˈdjuː-
Duquesne *French naval commander:* djʊˈkeɪn, dʊ- ⓤⓢ duː-, djuː- *place in US:* djuːˈkeɪn, duː- ⓤⓢ duː-, dju-
durability ˌdjʊə.rəˈbɪl.ə.ti, ˌdjɔː-, ˌdʒʊə-, ˌdʒɔː-, -ɪ.ti ⓤⓢ ˌdʊr.əˈbɪl.ə.t̬i, ˌdjʊr-, ˌdɝː-
durab|le ˈdjʊə.rə.bl̩|, ˈdjɔː-, ˈdʒʊə-, ˈdʒɔː- ⓤⓢ ˈdʊr.ə-, ˈdjʊr-, ˈdɝː- **-ly** -li **-leness** -l̩.nəs, -nɪs
Duracell® ˈdjʊə.rə.sel, ˈdʒʊə-, ˈdjɔː-, ˈdʒɔː- ⓤⓢ ˈdʊr.ə-, ˈdjʊr-, ˈdɝː-
Duraglit® ˈdjʊə.rə.glɪt, ˈdʒʊə- ⓤⓢ ˈdʊr.ə-, ˈdjʊr-
dural ˈdjʊə.rəl, ˈdjɔː-, ˈdʒʊə-, ˈdʒɔː- ⓤⓢ ˈdʊr.əl, ˈdjʊr-
Duralumin® djʊəˈræl.jʊ.mɪn, djɔː-, dʒʊə-, dʒɔː-, -jə- ⓤⓢ duːˈræl.jə-, djuː-
duramen djʊəˈreɪ.men, dʒʊə- ⓤⓢ dʊ-, djʊ-, -mən
Duran djʊəˈræn, dʊə-, dʒʊə- ⓤⓢ dʊˈræn, də- **Duˌran Duˈran**
durance ˈdjʊə.rən*t*s, ˈdʒʊə- ⓤⓢ ˈdʊr.ən*t*s, ˈdjʊr-
Durand djʊəˈrænd, dʒʊə- ⓤⓢ dʊˈrænd, də-
Durango dəˈræŋ.gəʊ, dʊ- ⓤⓢ -goʊ
Durant djʊˈrɑːnt, dʒʊ-, -ˈrænt ⓤⓢ ˈduː.rænt; dəˈrænt
Durante djʊˈræn.ti, dʒʊ-, -teɪ ⓤⓢ dəˈræn.t̬i, dʊ-
duration djʊəˈreɪ.ʃən, djɔː-, dʒʊə-, dʒɔː- ⓤⓢ dʊ-, djʊ-, də- **-s** -z
durative ˈdjʊə.rə.tɪv, ˈdjɔː-, ˈdʒʊə-, ˈdʒɔː- ⓤⓢ ˈdʊr.ə.t̬ɪv, ˈdjʊr-
Durban ˈdɜː.bən ⓤⓢ ˈdɝː-
durbar ˈdɜː.bɑːr, ˌ-ˈ- ⓤⓢ ˈdɝː.bɑːr **-s** -z
d'Urberville ˈdɜː.bə.vɪl ⓤⓢ ˈdɝː.bɚ- **-s** -z
Durbin ˈdɜː.bɪn ⓤⓢ ˈdɝː-
Durden ˈdɜː.dən ⓤⓢ ˈdɝː-
durdle ˈdɜː.dl̩ ⓤⓢ ˈdɝː- **-s** -z
Durell djʊəˈrel, dʒʊə- ⓤⓢ duː-, djuː-
Dürer ˈdjʊə.rər ⓤⓢ ˈdjuː.rɚ **-s** -z
duress djʊˈres, dʒʊ- ⓤⓢ dʊ-, djʊ-
durex® (D) ˈdjʊə.reks, ˈdjɔː-, ˈdʒʊə-, ˈdʒɔː- ⓤⓢ ˈdʊr.eks, ˈdjʊr- **-es** -ɪz
Durham ˈdʌr.əm ⓤⓢ ˈdɝː-
durian, durion ˈdjʊə.ri.ən, ˈdʊr.i-, -æn ⓤⓢ ˈdʊr.i- **-s** -z
during ˈdjʊə.rɪŋ, ˈdjɔː-, ˈdʒʊə-, ˈdʒɔː- ⓤⓢ ˈdʊr.ɪŋ, ˈdjʊr-, ˈdɝː-
Durnford ˈdɜːn.fəd ⓤⓢ ˈdɝːn.fɚd
Durocher dəˈrəʊ.ʃər, -tʃər ⓤⓢ -ˈroʊ.ʃɚ, -tʃɚ

Durran dʌr'æn, də'ræn (US) də'ræn
Durrant 'dʌr.ᵊnt (US) 'dɝː-; də'rænt
Durrell 'dʌr.ᵊl (US) 'dɝː-
Dürrenmat 'djʊə.rᵊn.mæt, 'dʊə- (US) 'dʊr.ən.mɑːt
durrie 'dʌr.i (US) 'dɝː- **-s** -z
Durrington 'dʌr.ɪŋ.tᵊn (US) 'dɝː-
Dursley 'dɜːz.li (US) 'dɝːz-
durst *(from* **dare***)* dɜːst (US) dɝːst **-n't** 'dɜː.sᵊnt (US) 'dɝː-
durum 'djʊə.rəm, 'dʒʊə-, 'djɔː-, 'dʒɔː- (US) 'dʊr.əm, 'dɝː-
Durward 'dɜː.wəd (US) 'dɝː.wɚd
Dury 'djʊə.ri, 'dʒʊə- (US) 'dʊr.i, 'djʊr-
Duse 'duː.zi
Dushanbe duː'ʃæn.bə, -'ʃæm-, -'ʃɑːn-, -'ʃɑːm-, -bi (US) duː'ʃɑːn.bi
dusk dʌsk **-s** -s **-ing** -ɪŋ **-ed** -t
dusk|y 'dʌs.k|i **-ier** -i.əʳ (US) -i.ɚ **-iest** -i.ɪst, -i.əst **-ily** -ɪ.li, -ᵊl.i **-iness** -ɪ.nəs, -ɪ.nɪs
Düsseldorf 'dʊs.ᵊl.dɔːf (US) 'duː.sᵊl.dɔːrf, 'dʊs.ᵊl-
dust dʌst **-s** -s **-ing** -ɪŋ **-ed** -ɪd **'Dust ˌBowl; 'dust ˌcover; 'dust ˌjacket; ˌbite the 'dust**
dustbin 'dʌs*t*.bɪn **-s** -z
dustcart 'dʌs*t*.kɑːt (US) -kɑːrt **-s** -s
dustcoat 'dʌs*t*.kəʊt (US) -koʊt **-s** -s
duster 'dʌs.təʳ (US) -tɚ **-s** -z
Dustin 'dʌs.tɪn
dust|man 'dʌs*t*|.mən **-men** -mən
dustpan 'dʌs*t*.pæn **-s** -z
dustproof 'dʌs*t*.pruːf
dustsheet 'dʌs*t*.ʃiːt **-s** -s
dust-up 'dʌst.ʌp **-s** -s
dust|y (D) 'dʌs.t|i **-ier** -i.əʳ (US) -i.ɚ **-iest** -i.ɪst, -i.əst **-ily** -ɪ.li, -ᵊl.i **-iness** -ɪ.nəs, -ɪ.nɪs
Dutch dʌtʃ **-man** -mən **-men** -mən **ˌDutch 'cap; ˌDutch 'courage; ˌDutch 'elm diˌsease; ˌDutch 'oven; ˌDutch 'treat**
Dutch|woman 'dʌtʃ|ˌwʊm.ən **-women** -ˌwɪm.ɪn
duteous 'djuː.ti.əs, 'dʒuː- (US) 'duː.t̬i-, 'djuː- **-ly** -li **-ness** -nəs, -nɪs
Duthie 'dʌθ.i
dutiable 'djuː.ti.ə.bl̩, 'dʒuː- (US) 'duː.t̬i-, 'djuː-
dutiful 'djuː.tɪ.fᵊl, 'dʒuː-, -fʊl (US) 'duː.t̬ɪ-, 'djuː- **-ly** -i **-ness** -nəs, -nɪs
Dutton 'dʌt.ᵊn
dut|y 'djuː.t|i, 'dʒuː- (US) 'duː.t̬|i, 'djuː- **-ies** -iz
duty-free ˌdjuː.ti'friː, ˌdʒuː- (US) ˌduː.t̬i-, ˌdjuː- **ˌduty-'free shop**
duumvir dju'ʌm.vəʳ, du-, -'ʊm-; 'djuː.əm.vəʳ, 'duː- (US) du'ʌm.vɚ, dju- **-s** -z **-i** -aɪ, -iː
duumvirate dju'ʌm.vɪ.rət, du-, -vᵊr.ət, -ɪt, -eɪt (US) du'ʌm.vɪ.rət, dju-, -vɚ.ət, -ɪt **-s** -s
Duvalier djʊ'væl.i.eɪ, dʊ- (US) duː'vɑːl.jeɪ, djuː-
Duveen djʊ'viːn (US) duː-, djuː-, də-
duvet 'djuː.veɪ, 'duː- (US) duː'veɪ, djuː- **-s** -z
dux dʌks **-es** -ɪz
Duxbury 'dʌks.bᵊr.i (US) -ber-, -bɚ-
Duxford 'dʌks.fəd (US) -fɚd
DV ˌdiː'viː
DVD ˌdiː.viː'diː **-s** -z
Dvořák *Czech composer:* 'dvɔː.ʒɑːk, 'vɔː-, -ʒæk (US) 'dvɔːr.ʒɑːk
Dvorak *US family name:* 'dvɔː.ræk (US) 'dvɔːr.æk
dwale dweɪl
dwar|f *(n.)* dwɔː|f (US) dwɔːr|f **-s** -s **-ves** -vz
dwarf *(v.)* dwɔːf (US) dwɔːrf **-s** -s **-ing** -ɪŋ **-ed** -t
dwarfish 'dwɔː.fɪʃ (US) 'dwɔːr- **-ly** -li **-ness** -nəs, -nɪs
Dwayne dweɪn
dweeb dwiːb **-s** -z
dwell dwel **-s** -z **-ing** -ɪŋ **-ed** -t, -d **dwelt** dwelt **dweller/s** 'dwel.əʳ/z (US) -ɚ/z
dwelling 'dwel.ɪŋ **-s** -z
dwelt *(from* **dwell***)* dwelt
DWI ˌdiː.dʌb.l̩.juː'aɪ (US) -juː'-, -jə'-
Dwight dwaɪt
dwindl|e 'dwɪn.dl̩ **-es** -z **-ing** -ɪŋ **-ed** -d
Dworkin 'dwɔː.kɪn (US) 'dwɔːr-
Dwyer dwaɪəʳ (US) dwaɪɚ
dyad 'daɪ.æd, -əd **-s** -z
Dyak 'daɪ.æk, -ək **-s** -s
dyarch|y 'daɪ.ɑː.k|i (US) -ɑːr- **-ies** -iz
Dyce daɪs
dy|e (D) daɪ **-es** -z **-eing** -ɪŋ **-ed** -d **-er/s** -əʳ/z (US) -ɚ/z
dyed-in-the-wool ˌdaɪd.ɪn.ðə'wʊl
Dyer daɪəʳ (US) daɪɚ
dyestuff 'daɪ.stʌf **-s** -s
dyewood 'daɪ.wʊd
dyeworks 'daɪ.wɜːks (US) -wɝːks
Dyfed 'dʌv.ɪd, -ed, -əd
Dyffryn 'dʌf.rɪn, -rᵊn
dying *(from* **die***)* 'daɪ.ɪŋ
dyk|e (D) daɪk **-es** -s **-ing** -ɪŋ **-ed** -t
Dylan 'dɪl.ən, 'dʌl- (US) 'dɪl-
Dymchurch 'dɪm.tʃɜːtʃ (US) -tʃɝːtʃ
Dymock, Dymoke 'dɪm.ək
Dymond 'daɪ.mənd
Dymphna 'dɪmp.nə
dynameter daɪ'næm.ɪ.təʳ, dɪ-, '-ə- (US) -ə.t̬ɚ **-s** -z
dynamic daɪ'næm.ɪk, dɪ- **-al** -ᵊl **-ally** -ᵊl.i, -li **-s** -s
dynamism 'daɪ.nə.mɪ.zᵊm
dyna|mite 'daɪ.nə|.maɪt **-mites** -maɪts **-miting** -maɪ.tɪŋ (US) -maɪ.t̬ɪŋ **-mited** -maɪ.tɪd (US) -maɪ.t̬ɪd **-miter/s** -maɪ.təʳ/z (US) -maɪ.t̬ɚ/z
dynamo 'daɪ.nə.məʊ (US) -moʊ **-s** -z
dynamometer ˌdaɪ.nə'mɒm.ɪ.təʳ, '-ə- (US) -'mɑː.mə.t̬ɚ **-s** -z
dynamometric ˌdaɪ.nə.məʊ'met.rɪk (US) -moʊ'- **-al** -ᵊl
dynast 'dɪn.əst, 'daɪ.nəst, -næst (US) 'daɪ.næst, -nəst **-s** -s
dynastic dɪ'næs.tɪk, daɪ-, də- (US) daɪ-
dynast|y 'dɪn.ə.st|i, 'daɪ.nə- (US) 'daɪ.nə- **-ies** -iz
dynatron 'daɪ.nə.trɒn (US) -trɑːn **-s** -z
dyne daɪn **-s** -s
Dynevor 'dɪn.ɪ.vəʳ, '-ə- (US) -vɚ
d'you *strong forms:* dʒuː, djuː *weak forms:* dʒə, djə, dʒu, dju
Note: Abbreviated form of "do you": the spelling represents a pronunciation that is usually unstressed, and the pronunciation therefore parallels that of unstressed **you**, which has weak forms /jə/ before a consonant and /ju/ before vowels. When used contrastively, the strong form /djuː/ or /dʒuː/ may be used (e.g. "I don't like it. **D'you** like it?").
Dysart 'daɪ.sət, -zət, -sɑːt, -zɑːt (US) -sɑːrt, -zɑːrt, -sɚt
dysarthria dɪ'sɑː.θri.ə (US) -'sɑːr-
dysenteric ˌdɪs.ᵊn'ter.ɪk, -en'- (US) -en'-
dysentery 'dɪs.ᵊn.tᵊr.i, -tri (US) -ter.i
dysfunction dɪs'fʌŋ*k*.ʃᵊn **-s** -z **-ing** -ɪŋ **-ed** -d **-al** -ᵊl
dysfunctional dɪs'fʌŋ*k*.ʃᵊn.ᵊl
dysgraphia dɪs'græf.i.ə
dysgraphic dɪs'græf.ɪk
dyslalia dɪ'sleɪ.li.ə, -'slæl.i-
dyslexia dɪ'slek.si.ə
dyslexic dɪ'slek.sɪk
dysmenorrh(o)ea ˌdɪs.men.ə'rɪə (US) -'riː.ə
Dyson 'daɪ.sᵊn
dyspepsia dɪ'spep.si.ə
dyspeptic dɪ'spep.tɪk **-s** -s
dysphagia dɪs'feɪ.dʒi.ə (US) -dʒə, -dʒi.ə
dysphasia dɪs'feɪ.zi.ə, -ʒi-, '-ʒə (US) '-ʒə, '-ʒi.ə
dysphasic dɪs'feɪ.zɪk **-s** -s
dysphonia dɪs'fəʊ.ni.ə (US) -'foʊ-
dysphonic dɪs'fɒn.ɪk (US) -'fɑː.nɪk
dyspn(o)ea dɪs*p*'niː.ə
dysprosium dɪ'sprəʊ.zi.əm, -si- (US) -'sproʊ-
dystrophic dɪ'strɒf.ɪk (US) -'strɑː.fɪk, -'stroʊ-
dystrophy 'dɪs.trə.fi
dysuria dɪ'sjʊə.ri.ə (US) -'sjʊr.i-
dziggetai 'dzɪg.ɪ.taɪ, '-ə-, --'- (US) 'dʒɪg.ɪ.taɪ, **-s** -z

Pronouncing the letter E

See also EA, EE, EI, EO, EOU, EU/EW, EY

The vowel letter **e** has two main strong pronunciations linked to spelling: a 'short' pronunciation /e/ and a 'long' pronunciation /iː/. However, the situation is not clear cut and other pronunciations are available.

The 'short' pronunciation always occurs when the **e** is followed by a consonant which closes the syllable, or a double consonant before another vowel, e.g.:

bed	/bed/	
bedding	/ˈbed.ɪŋ/	

The 'long' pronunciation is usually found when the **e** is followed by a single consonant and then a vowel, e.g.:

Eve	/iːv/	
credence	/ˈkriː.dᵊnts/	

However, the 'short' pronunciation occurs in many cases where the **e** is followed by a single consonant and then a vowel, e.g.:

ever	/ˈev.əʳ/	US /-ɚ/
prejudice	/ˈpredʒ.ə.dɪs/	

The 'long' pronunciation may also occur where the **e** is followed by two consonants, e.g.:

negro	/ˈniː.grəʊ/	US /-roʊ/
secret	/ˈsiː.krət/	

When there is an **r** in the spelling, the strong pronunciation is one of four possibilities: /ɪə US ɪr/, /eə US er/, /ɜː US ɝː/ or /e/, e.g.:

here	/hɪəʳ/	US /hɪr/
there	/ðeəʳ/	US /ðer/
were	/wɜːʳ/	US /wɝː/
very	/ˈver.i/	

It frequently happens that the letter **e** has no pronunciation at all, but is used as a spelling convention to show that a preceding vowel is realised with its 'long' pronunciation, e.g.:

brave	/breɪv/	
mice	/maɪs/	
hope	/həʊp/	US /hoʊp/
use (v.)	/juːz/	

In addition

There are other vowel sounds associated with the letter **e**, e.g.:

eɪ	ballet	/ˈbæl.eɪ/	US /bælˈeɪ/

And, in rare cases:

/ɑː/ US /ɝː/	clerk	/klɑːk/	US /klɝːk/
/ɪ/	women	/ˈwɪm.ɪn/	

In weak syllables

The vowel letter **e** is realised with the vowels /ɪ/, /i/ and /ə/ in weak syllables, or may also not be pronounced at all due to syllabic consonant formation or compression, e.g.:

begin	/bɪˈgɪn/	
react	/riˈækt/	
arithmetic	/əˈrɪθ.mə.tɪk/	
castle	/ˈkɑː.sl̩/	US /ˈkæs.l̩/

e (E) iː **-'s** -z **'E ˌnumber**
E *(abbrev. for east)* iːst
E111 ˌiːˌwʌn.ɪˈlev.ən, -əˈ-
each iːtʃ **ˌeach 'other**
EACSO iːˈæk.səʊ, -ˈɑːk- US -soʊ
Eadie, Eady ˈiː.di
eager ˈiː.gəʳ US -gɚ **-ly** -li **-ness** -nəs, -nɪs **ˌeager 'beaver**
eagle (E) ˈiː.gl̩ **-s** -z **'eagle ˌowl; ˌEagle 'Scout** US **'Eagle ˌScout**
eagle-eyed ˌiː.gl̩ˈaɪd, ˈiː.gl̩.aɪd
Eaglefield ˈiː.gl̩.fiːld
Eaglehawk ˈiː.gl̩.hɔːk US -hɑːk, -hɔːk
Eaglescliffe ˈiː.gl̩z.klɪf
eaglet ˈiː.glɪt, -lət **-s** -s
eagre ˈeɪ.gəʳ, ˈiː- US ˈiː.gɚ, ˈeɪ- **-s** -z
Eakin ˈeɪ.kɪn, ˈiː- **-s** -z
Ealing ˈiː.lɪŋ
Eames iːmz, eɪmz
Eamon(n) ˈeɪ.mən
-ean -iː.ən, -i.ən
Note: Suffix. **-ean** may take primary stress or alternatively words containing it may be stressed on the syllable before the prefix. An example where both possibilities occur is **Caribbean**, which is either /ˌkær.ɪˈbiː.ən US ˌker-/, or /kəˈrɪb.i.ən/.
ear ɪəʳ US ɪr **-s** -z **'ear ˌtrumpet; ˌturn a ˌdeaf 'ear to; ˌkeep one's ˌear to the 'ground; ˌprick up one's 'ears; ˌgive someone a ˌthick 'ear**
earache ˈɪə.reɪk US ˈɪr-
Eardley ˈɜːd.li US ˈɝːd-
eardrop ˈɪə.drɒp US ˈɪr.drɑːp **-s** -s
eardrum ˈɪə.drʌm US ˈɪr- **-s** -z
eared ɪəd US ɪrd
earful ˈɪə.fʊl US ˈɪr-
Earhart ˈeə.hɑːt US ˈer.hɑːrt
earl (E) ɜːl US ɝːl **-s** -z **-dom/s** -dəm/z **ˌEarl's 'Court; ˌEarl 'Grey; ˌearl 'marshal**
Earl(e) ɜːl US ɝːl
earlobe ˈɪə.ləʊb US ˈɪr.loʊb **-s** -z
earl|y ˈɜː.l|i US ˈɝː- **-ier** -i.əʳ US -i.ɚ **-iest** -i.ɪst, -i.əst **-iness** -ɪ.nəs, -ɪ.nɪs **'early ˌbird; ˌearly 'warning ˌsystem**
earmark ˈɪə.mɑːk US ˈɪr.mɑːrk **-s** -s **-ing** -ɪŋ **-ed** -t
earmuffs ˈɪə.mʌfs US ˈɪr-
earn (E) ɜːn US ɝːn **-s** -z **-ing** -ɪŋ **-ed** -d, ɜːnt US ɝːnt **-er/s** -əʳ/z US -ɚ/z
earnest ˈɜː.nɪst, -nəst US ˈɝː- **-s** -s **-ly** -li **-ness** -nəs, -nɪs
earnings ˈɜː.nɪŋz US ˈɝː-
Earnshaw ˈɜːn.ʃɔː US ˈɝːn.ʃɑː, -ʃɔː
Earp ɜːp US ɝːp
earphone ˈɪə.fəʊn US ˈɪr.foʊn **-s** -z
earpiec|e ˈɪə.piːs US ˈɪr- **-es** -ɪz

Pronouncing the letters EA

The vowel digraph **ea** has two main strong pronunciations linked to spelling: a 'short' pronunciation /e/ and a 'long' pronunciation /iː/. However, it is not normally predictable which one will occur, e.g.:

bread	/bred/
bead	/biːd/
cleanse	/klenz/
clean	/kliːn/

When the digraph is followed by an **r** in the spelling, the strong pronunciation is one of four possibilities: /ɪə US ɪr/, /eə US er/, /ɜː US ɝː/ or /ɑː US ɑːr/, e.g:

fear (n.)	/fɪəʳ/	US /fɪr/
tear (v.)	/teəʳ/	US /ter/
pearl	/pɜːl/	US /pɝːl/
heart	/hɑːt/	US /hɑːrt/

In addition

There are other vowel sounds associated with the digraph **ea**, e.g.:

/ɪə/	idea	/aɪˈdɪə/	
/i.ə/	area	/ˈeə.ri.ə/	US /ˈer.i-/
/eɪ/	great	/greɪt/	
/i.æ/	theatrical	/θiˈæt.rɪ.kᵊl/	
/i.eɪ/	create	/kriˈeɪt/	

In addition, there are instances when the two letters **e** and **a** come together in closed compounds, e.g.:

whereas	/*h*weəˈræz/	US /*h*werˈæz/
hereafter	/hɪərˈɑːf.təʳ/	US /hɪrˈæf.tɚ/

In weak syllables

The vowel digraph **ea** is realised with the vowels /i/ and /ə/ in weak syllables and may result in a syllabic consonant, e.g.:

guinea	/ˈgɪn.i/	
ocean	/ˈəʊ.ʃᵊn/	US /ˈoʊ-/

earplug ˈɪə.plʌg US ˈɪr- **-s** -z
earring ˈɪə.rɪŋ US ˈɪr.ɪŋ, -rɪŋ **-s** -z
earshot ˈɪə.ʃɒt US ˈɪr.ʃɑːt
earsplitting ˈɪəˌsplɪt.ɪŋ US ˈɪrˌsplɪt̬.ɪŋ **-ly** -li
earth (E) *(n.)* ɜːθ US ɝːθ **-s** -s, ɜːðz US ɝːðz ˈ**earth** ˌ**mother**
earth *(v.)* ɜːθ US ɝːθ **-s** -s **-ing** -ɪŋ **-ed** -t
earthborn ˈɜːθ.bɔːn US ˈɝːθ.bɔːrn
earthbound ˈɜːθ.baʊnd US ˈɝːθ-
earthen ˈɜː.θᵊn, -ðᵊn US ˈɝː-
earthenware ˈɜː.θᵊn.weəʳ, -ðᵊn- US ˈɝː.θᵊn.wer, -ðᵊn-
earthiness ˈɜː.θɪ.nəs, -nɪs US ˈɝː-
earthling ˈɜːθ.lɪŋ US ˈɝːθ- **-s** -z
earthl|y ˈɜːθ.l|i US ˈɝːθ- **-ier** -i.əʳ US -i.ɚ **-iest** -i.ɪst, -i.əst **-iness** -ɪ.nəs, -ɪ.nɪs
earthmover ˈɜːθˌmuː.vəʳ US ˈɝːθˌmuː.vɚ **-s** -z
earthquake ˈɜːθ.kweɪk US ˈɝːθ- **-s** -s
Earthsea ˈɜːθ.siː US ˈɝːθ-
earthshaking ˈɜːθˌʃeɪ.kɪŋ US ˈɝːθ-
earth-shattering ˈɜːθˌʃæt.ᵊr.ɪŋ US ˈɝːθˌʃæt̬- **-ly** -li
earthward ˈɜːθ.wəd US ˈɝːθ.wɚd **-s** -z
earthwork ˈɜːθ.wɜːk US ˈɝːθ.wɝːk **-s** -s
earthworm ˈɜːθ.wɜːm US ˈɝːθ.wɝːm **-s** -z
earth|y ˈɜː.θ|i US ˈɝː- **-ier** -i.əʳ US -i.ɚ **-iest** -i.əst, -i.ɪst **-ily** -ɪ.li, -ᵊl.i **-iness** -ɪ.nəs, -ɪ.nɪs
earwax ˈɪə.wæks US ˈɪr-
earwig ˈɪə.wɪg US ˈɪr- **-s** -z **-ging** -ɪŋ **-ged** -d
Easdale ˈiːz.deɪl
Easdaq iˈæz.dæk
eas|e iːz **-es** -ɪz **-ing** -ɪŋ **-ed** -d
Easebourne ˈiːz.bɔːn US -bɔːrn
easeful ˈiːz.fᵊl, -fʊl **-ly** -li **-ness** -nəs, -nɪs
easel ˈiː.zᵊl **-s** -z
easement ˈiːz.mənt **-s** -s
Easey ˈiː.zi
easiness *(from* **easy***)* ˈiː.zɪ.nəs, -nɪs
Easington ˈiː.zɪŋ.tən
east (E) iːst ˌ**East** ˈ**Anglia;** ˌ**East** ˈ**End** *stress shift:* ˌEast End ˈpub; ˌEast ˈCoast *stress shift:* ˌEast Coast ˈaccent
East Bergholt ˌiːstˈbɜːg.həʊlt US -ˈbɝːg.hoʊlt
eastbound ˈiːs*t*.baʊnd
Eastbourne ˈiːs*t*.bɔːn US -bɔːrn
Eastcheap ˈiːs*t*.tʃiːp
Eastender ˌiːstˈen.dəʳ US -dɚ **-s** -z
Easter ˈiː.stəʳ US -stɚ **-s** -z ˌ**Easter** ˈ**bonnet** US ˈ**Easter** ˌ**bonnet;** ˌ**Easter** ˈ**Bunny** US ˈ**Easter** ˌ**Bunny;** ˌ**Easter** ˈ**Day;** ˈ**Easter** ˌ**egg;** ˈ**Easter** ˌ**Island;** ˌ**Easter** ˈ**Sunday**
Easterby ˈiː.stə.bi US -stɚ-
easterl|y ˈiː.stᵊl.l|i US -stɚ.l|i **-ies** -iz
eastern (E) ˈiː.stᵊn US -stɚn **-most** -məʊst, -məst US -moʊst, -məst ˌ**Eastern** ˈ**Shore;** ˌ**Eastern** ˈ**Standard** ˌ**Time**
easterner (E) ˈiːs.tᵊn.əʳ US -tɚ.nɚ **-s** -z
Eastertide ˈiː.stə.taɪd US -stɚ-
Eastfield ˈiːst.fiːld
Eastham ˈiːst.*h*əm
Easthampton ˌiːstˈhæm*p*.tən
easting ˈiː.stɪŋ **-s** -z
East Kilbride ˌiːst.kɪlˈbraɪd
Eastlake ˈiːst.leɪk
Eastleigh ˈiːst.liː, ˌiːstˈliː
Eastman ˈiːs*t*.mən
east-northeast ˌiːst.nɔːθˈiːst US -nɔːrθˈ- *in nautical usage also:* -nɔːˈriːst US -nɔːrˈiːst
Easton ˈiː.stən
Easton-in-Gordano ˌiː.stᵊn.ɪn.gɔːˈdɑː.nəʊ, -ɪŋ- US -gɔːrˈdɑː.noʊ
Eastport ˈiːs*t*.pɔːt US -pɔːrt
east-southeast ˌiːst.saʊθˈiːst *in nautical usage also:* -saʊˈ-
eastward ˈiːst.wəd US -wɚd **-ly** -li **-s** -z
East-West ˌiːstˈwest *stress shift, see compound:* ˌ**East-West** **re**ˈ**lations**
Eastwood ˈiːst.wʊd
eas|y (E) ˈiː.z|i **-ier** -i.əʳ US -i.ɚ **-iest** -i.ɪst, -i.əst **-ily** -ɪ.li, -ᵊl.i **-iness** -ɪ.nəs, -ɪ.nɪs ˈ**easy** ˌ**chair;** **as** ˌ**easy as** ˈ**pie;** ˌ**take it** ˈ**easy;** **on** ˈ**easy** ˌ**street**
easygoing ˌiː.ziˈgəʊ.ɪŋ US -ˈgoʊ- *stress shift:* ˌeasygoing ˈperson
EasyJet® ˈiː.zi.dʒet
eat iːt **-s** -s **-ing** -ɪŋ US ˈiː.t̬ɪŋ **ate** et, eɪt US eɪt **eaten** ˈiː.tᵊn US -t̬ən **eater/s** ˈiː.təʳ/z US -t̬ɚ/z ˈ**eating di**ˌ**sorder;** ˌ**eat one's** ˈ**heart out;** ˌ**eat one's** ˈ**words;** ˌ**eat someone out of** ˌ**house and** ˈ**home**
eatable ˈiː.tə.bl̩ US -t̬ə- **-s** -z
eaterie ˈiː.tᵊr.i US -t̬ɚ- **-s** -z

eater|y 'iː.tᵊr|.i (US) -t̬ɚ- **-ies** -iz
Eaton 'iː.tᵊn
Eaton Socon ˌiː.tᵊn'səʊ.kᵊn (US) -'soʊ-
eau de cologne ˌəʊ.də.kə'ləʊn, -dɪ- (US) ˌoʊ.də.kə'loʊn *stress shift:* ˌeau de cologne 'spray
eau de nil ˌəʊ.də'niːl (US) ˌoʊ- *stress shift:* ˌeau de nil 'paint
eau de parfum ˌəʊ.də.pɑː'fʌm (US) ˌoʊ.də.pɑːr'-
eau de toilette ˌəʊ.də.twɑː'let, -twə'- (US) ˌoʊ-
eau-de-vie ˌəʊ.də'viː (US) ˌoʊ-
eave (E) iːv **-s** -z
eavesdrop 'iːvz.drɒp (US) -drɑːp **-s** -s **-ping** -ɪŋ **-ped** -t **-per/s** -əʳ/z (US) -ɚ/z
ebb eb **-s** -z **-ing** -ɪŋ **-ed** -d ˌ**ebb** '**tide**
Ebbsfleet 'ebz.fliːt
Ebbw 'eb.uː, -ə
Ebel eb'el, 'iː.bᵊl
Ebenezer ˌeb.ə'niː.zəʳ, -ɪ'- (US) -zɚ *stress shift:* ˌEbenezer 'Scrooge
Eberhart 'eɪ.bə.hɑːt (US) 'eb.ɚ.hɑːrt, 'eɪ.bɚ-
Ebionite 'iː.bjə.naɪt, -bɪə- **-s** -s
Eblis 'eb.lɪs
ebola (E) ɪ'bəʊ.lə, 'eb.əʊ.lə (US) -'boʊ-
ebon 'eb.ən
ebonite 'eb.ə.naɪt
eboniz|e, -is|e 'eb.ə.naɪz **-es** -ɪz **-ing** -ɪŋ **-ed** -d
ebony (E) 'eb.ᵊn.i
Eboracum iː'bɒr.ə.kəm, ɪ- (US) ɪ'bɔːr-
Ebrington 'eb.rɪŋ.tən
Ebro 'iː.brəʊ, 'eb.rəʊ (US) 'eɪ.broʊ, 'iː-, 'eb.roʊ
ebullien|ce ɪ'bʌl.i.ən|ts, -'bʊl- (US) -'bʊl.jən|ts, -'bʌl- **-cy** -*t*si
ebullient ɪ'bʌl.i.ənt, -'bʊl- (US) -'bʊl.jənt, -'bʌl- **-ly** -li
ebullition ˌeb.ə'lɪʃ.ᵊn, -ʊ'- (US) -ə'-, -juː'- **-s** -z
Ebury 'iː.bᵊr.i (US) -ˌber-, -bɚ-
e-business 'iːˌbɪz.nɪs, -nəs **-es** -ɪz
EC ˌiː'siː
écarté eɪ'kɑː.teɪ (US) ˌeɪ.kɑːr'teɪ
Ecbatana ek'bæt.ᵊn.ə, ˌek.bə'tɑː.nə (US) ek'bæt.ᵊn.ə
ecce homo ˌek.eɪ'həʊ.məʊ, ˌetʃ-, -'hɒm.əʊ (US) -'hoʊ.moʊ
eccentric ɪk'sen.trɪk, ek- **-s** -s **-al** -ᵊl **-ally** -ᵊl.i, -li
eccentricit|y ˌek.sen'trɪs.ə.t|i, -sᵊn'-, -ɪ.t|i (US) -ə.t̬|i **-ies** -iz
Ecclefechan ˌek.l̩'fek.ᵊn, -'fex-
Eccles 'ek.l̩z '**Eccles** ˌ**cake**
Ecclesfield 'ek.l̩z.fiːld
ecclesi|a ɪ'kliː.zi|.ə (US) ɪ'kliː-, ek'liː-, -'leɪ- **-ast/s** -æst/s
Ecclesiastes ɪˌkliː.zi'æs.tiːz (US) ɪˌkliː-, ekˌliː-
ecclesiastic ɪˌkliː.zi'æs.tɪk (US) ɪˌkliː-, ekˌliː- **-s** -s **-al** -ᵊl **-ally** -ᵊl.i, -li
ecclesiasticism ɪˌkliː.zi'æs.tɪ.sɪ.zᵊm (US) ɪˌkliː-, ekˌliː-
Ecclesiasticus ɪˌkliː.zi'æs.tɪ.kəs (US) ɪˌkliː-, ekˌliː-
Eccleston 'ek.l̩.stən
Ecclestone 'ek.l̩.stən
eccrine 'ek.rɪn, -riːn, -rən, -raɪn
ECG ˌiː.siː'dʒiː
echelon 'eʃ.ə.lɒn, 'eɪ.ʃə- (US) 'eʃ.ə.lɑːn **-s** -z **-ned** -d
echidn|a ek'ɪd.n|ə, ɪ'kɪd- (US) iː'kɪd- **-ae** -iː **-as** -əz
echinacea ˌek.ɪ'neɪ.ʃə, -ə'-, -si.ə
echin|us ek'aɪ.n|əs; ɪ'kaɪ-; ə-; 'ek.ɪn|.əs (US) ɪ'kaɪ.n|əs **-i** -aɪ
echo 'ek.əʊ (US) -oʊ **-es** -z **-ing** -ɪŋ **-ed** -d
echocardio|gram ˌek.əʊ'kɑː.di.əʊ|.græm (US) -oʊ'kɑːr.di.ə-, -oʊ- **-s** -z **-graph/s** -grɑːf/s, -græf/s (US) -græf/s
echoic ek'əʊ.ɪk, ɪ'kəʊ-, ə- (US) ek'oʊ-
echolalia ˌek.əʊ'leɪ.li.ə (US) -oʊ'-
echolo|cate ˌek.əʊ.ləʊ|'keɪt (US) -oʊ.loʊ'- **-cates** -'keɪts **-cating** -'keɪ.tɪŋ (US) -'keɪ.t̬ɪŋ **-cated** -'keɪ.tɪd (US) -'keɪ.t̬ɪd
echolocation ˌek.əʊ.ləʊ'keɪ.ʃᵊn (US) -oʊ.loʊ'-
echt ext, ekt
Eckersl(e)y 'ek.əz.li (US) -ɚz-
Eckert 'ek.ət (US) -ɚt
Eckertford 'ek.ət.fəd (US) -ɚt.fɚd
Eckington 'ek.ɪŋ.tən
éclair eɪ'kleəʳ, ɪ-; 'eɪ.kleəʳ (US) eɪ'kler, ɪ- **-s** -z
eclampsia ɪ'klæm*p*.si.ə, ek'læm*p*-, ə'klæm*p*-
éclat eɪ'klɑː, '-- **-s** -z
eclectic ek'lek.tɪk, ɪ'klek-, iː- (US) ek'lek- **-s** -s **-al** -ᵊl **-ally** -ᵊl.i, -li
eclecticism ek'lek.tɪ.sɪ.zᵊm, ɪ'klek-, iː-, -tə- (US) ek'lek.tə-
eclips|e ɪ'klɪps, ə-, iː- **-es** -ɪz **-ing** -ɪŋ **-ed** -t
ecliptic ɪ'klɪp.tɪk, ə-, iː- **-s** -s
eclogue 'ek.lɒg (US) -lɑːg, -lɔːg **-s** -z
eco- iː.kəʊ-, ek.əʊ-; ɪ.kɒ- (US) ek.oʊ-, -ə-, iː.koʊ-, -kə-; ɪ.kɑː-
Note: Prefix. Either takes primary or secondary stress on the first syllable, e.g. **ecosphere** /'iː.kəʊ.sfɪəʳ (US) 'ek.oʊ.sfɪr/, **economic** /ˌiː.kə'nɒm.ɪk (US) ˌiː.kə'nɑː.mɪk/, or primary or secondary stress on the second syllable, e.g. **ecology** /iː'kɒl.ə.dʒi (US) -'kɑː.lə-/, **econometric** /ɪˌkɒn.ə'met.rɪk (US) -kɑː.nə'-/.
eco-friendly 'iː.kəʊˌfrend.li (US) 'ek.oʊˌ-, 'iː.koʊˌ-
E coli ˌiː'kəʊ.laɪ (US) -'koʊ-
ecologic|al ˌiː.kə'lɒdʒ.ɪ.k|ᵊl, ˌek.ə'- (US) -'lɑː.dʒɪ- **-ally** -ᵊl.i, -li ˌ**eco**ˌ**logically** '**sound**
ecolog|y iː'kɒl.ə.dʒ|i, ɪ-, ek'ɒl- (US) iː'kɑː.lə-, ɪ'kɑː-, ek'ɑː- **-ist/s** -ɪst/s
e-commerce 'iːˌkɒm.ɜːs (US) -ˌkɑː.mɝːs
econometric ɪˌkɒn.ə'met.rɪk, iː- (US) -ˌkɑː.nə'- **-s** -s
econometrician ɪˌkɒn.ə.met'rɪʃ.ᵊn, iː-, -mə'trɪʃ- (US) -ˌkɑː.nə.mə'- **-s** -z
econometrics ɪˌkɒn.ə'met.rɪks, iː- (US) -ˌkɑː.nə'-
economic ˌiː.kə'nɒm.ɪk, ˌek.ə'- (US) -'nɑː.mɪk **-s** -s **-al** -ᵊl **-ally** -ᵊl.i, -li ˌ**economic** '**growth**
economist ɪ'kɒn.ə.mɪst, iː- (US) -'kɑː.nə- **-s** -s
economiz|e, -is|e ɪ'kɒn.ə.maɪz, ə'kɒn- (US) ɪ'kɑː.nə-, iː- **-es** -ɪz **-ing** -ɪŋ **-ed** -d **-er/s** -əʳ/z (US) -ɚ/z
econom|y ɪ'kɒn.ə.m|i, ə'kɒn- (US) ɪ'kɑː.nə-, iː- **-ies** -iz **e'conomy** ˌ**class**
ecosphere 'iː.kəʊ.sfɪəʳ, 'ek.əʊ- (US) 'ek.oʊ.sfɪr, 'iː.koʊ-
ecosystem 'iː.kəʊˌsɪs.təm, 'ek.əʊ-, -tɪm (US) 'ek.oʊˌsɪs.təm, 'iː.koʊ- **-s** -z
eco-tour|ism 'iː.kəʊˌtʊə.r|ɪ.zᵊm, 'ek.əʊ-, -ˌtɔː- (US) 'iː.koʊˌtʊr-, 'ek.oʊ- **-ist/s** -ɪst/s
ecru 'eɪ.kruː, 'ek.ruː
ecstas|y 'ek.stə.s|i **-ies** -iz
ecstatic ɪk'stæt.ɪk, ek-, ək- (US) ek'stæt̬-, ɪk- **-al** -ᵊl **-ally** -ᵊl.i, -li
ECT ˌiː.siː'tiː
ecto- ek.təʊ- (US) ek.toʊ-, -tə-
Note: Prefix. Normally takes primary or secondary stress on the first syllable, e.g. **ectomorph** /'ek.təʊ.mɔːf (US) 'ek.toʊ.mɔːrf/, **ectomorphic** /ˌek.təʊ'mɔː.fɪk (US) ˌek.toʊ'mɔːr-/.
ectoderm 'ek.təʊ.dɜːm (US) -toʊ.dɝːm, -tə-
ectoderm|al ˌek.təʊ'dɜː.m|ᵊl (US) -toʊ'dɝː-, -tə'- **-ic** -ɪk
ectomorph 'ek.təʊ.mɔːf (US) -toʊ.mɔːrf, -tə- **-s** -s
ectomorph|ic ˌek.təʊ'mɔː.f|ɪk (US) -toʊ'mɔːr-, -tə'- **-ism** -ɪ.zᵊm **-y** -i
-ectomy -'ek.tə.mi
Note: Suffix. Always carries primary stress, e.g. **appendix** /ə'pen.dɪks/, **appendectomy** /ˌæp.en'dek.tə.mi/.
ectopic ek'tɒp.ɪk, ˌek-, ɪk- (US) ek'tɑː.pɪk **ec**ˌ**topic** '**pregnancy**
ectoplasm 'ek.təʊ.plæz.ᵊm (US) -toʊ-, -tə-
ecu *(abbrev. for* **European Currency Unit), ECU** 'ek.juː, 'eɪ.kjuː, 'iː-; ˌiː.siː'juː (US) 'eɪ.kuː; ˌiː.siː'juː **-s** -z

Ecuador ˈek.wə.dɔːʳ US -dɔːr
ecumenic ˌiː.kjʊˈmen.ɪk, ˌek.jʊˈ-, -jəˈ- US ˌek.jʊˈ-, -jəˈ- **-al** -ᵊl
ecumenicism ˌiː.kjʊˈmen.ɪ.sɪ.zᵊm, ˌek.jʊˈ-, -jəˈ- US ˌek.jʊˈ-, -jəˈ-
ecumen|ism iːˈkjuː.mə.n|ɪ.zᵊm; ɪ-; ˈek.jʊ-, -jə- US ˈek.juː-, -jə-; ekˈjuː-, ɪˈkjuː- **-ist/s** -ɪst/s
eczema ˈek.sɪ.mə, -sᵊm.ə US ˈek.sə.mə; ˈeg.zə-; ɪgˈziː.mə
eczematous ekˈsem.ə.təs, ɪk-; ɪgˈzem- US ɪgˈzem.ə.ţəs, eg-; ɪkˈsem-
Ed ed
-ed -t, -d, -ɪd
Note: Suffix. Unstressed. When preceded by /t/ or /d/, the pronunciation is /-ɪd/, e.g. **batted** /ˈbæt.ɪd US ˈbæţ.ɪd/. When preceded by a voiceless consonant other than /t/, the pronunciation is /t/, e.g. **picked** /pɪkt/. When preceded by a voiced sound, including vowels and consonants, the pronunciation is /d/, e.g. **rigged** /rɪgd/. There are, however, exceptions, particularly in adjectival forms, including **dogged** /ˈdɒg.ɪd US ˈdɑː.gɪd/, and **learned** /ˈlɜː.nɪd US ˈlɜːr-/; see individual entries.
edacious ɪˈdeɪ.ʃəs, iː-, edˈeɪ- US ɪˈdeɪ-, iː-
Edam ˈiː.dæm US ˈiː.dəm, -dæm
edaphic ɪˈdæf.ɪk, iː-
Edda ˈed.ə **-s** -z
Eddery ˈed.ᵊr.i
Eddie ˈed.i
Eddington ˈed.ɪŋ.tən
edd|y (E) ˈed|.i **-ies** -iz **-ying** -i.ɪŋ **-ied** -id
Eddystone ˈed.ɪ.stᵊn, -stəʊn US -stoʊn, -stən
Ede iːd
edelweiss ˈeɪ.dᵊl.vaɪs
edem|a ɪˈdiː.m|ə, iː- **-as** -əz **-ata** -ə.tə US -ə.ţə
edematous ɪˈdiː.mə.təs, iː- US -ţəs
Eden ˈiː.dᵊn ˌ**Garden of** ˈ**Eden**
Edenbridge ˈiː.dᵊn.brɪdʒ
Edenfield ˈiː.dᵊn.fiːld
edentate iːˈden.teɪt, ɪ- **-s** -s
Edessa ɪˈdes.ə, iː-
Edgar ˈed.gəʳ US -gɚ
Edgbaston ˈedʒ.bə.stᵊn, -bæs.tᵊn
edg|e (E) edʒ **-es** -ɪz **-ing** -ɪŋ **-ed** -d
Edgecomb(e) ˈedʒ.kəm
Edgecote ˈedʒ.kəʊt, -kət US -koʊt
Edgecumbe ˈedʒ.kəm, -kuːm
Edgehill *name of a hill:* ˌedʒˈhɪl *surname:* ˈedʒ.hɪl
edgeless ˈedʒ.ləs, -lɪs
Edgerton ˈedʒ.ə.tᵊn US -ɚ.ţən
edge|ways ˈedʒ|.weɪz **-wise** -waɪz
edgewise ˈedʒ.waɪz
Edgeworth ˈedʒ.wəθ, -wɜːθ US -wɚθ, -wɝːθ
edging ˈedʒ.ɪŋ **-s** -z
Edgington ˈedʒ.ɪŋ.tən
Edgley ˈedʒ.li
Edgware ˈedʒ.weəʳ US -wer
edg|y ˈedʒ|.i **-ier** -i.əʳ US -i.ɚ **-iest** -i.ɪst, -i.əst **-ily** ɪ.li, ᵊl.i
edibility ˌed.ɪˈbɪl.ə.ti, -əˈ-, -ɪ.ti US -ə.ţi
edible ˈed.ɪ.bl̩, ˈ-ə- **-s** -z **-ness** -nəs, -nɪs
edict ˈiː.dɪkt **-s** -s
Edie ˈiː.di
edification ˌed.ɪ.fɪˈkeɪ.ʃᵊn, ˌ-ə-
edific|e ˈed.ɪ.fɪs, ˈ-ə- **-es** -ɪz
edi|fy ˈed.ɪ|.faɪ, ˈ-ə- **-fies** -faɪz **-fying** -faɪ.ɪŋ **-fied** -faɪd
Edina ɪˈdaɪ.nə, iː-, edˈaɪ-, -ˈiː-
Edinburgh ˈed.ɪn.bᵊr.ə, -ɪm-, -ᵊn-, -bʌr- US -bʌr.ə, -oʊ
Edington ˈed.ɪŋ.tən
Edison ˈed.ɪ.sᵊn, ˈ-ə-
ed|it ˈed|.ɪt **-its** -ɪts **-iting** -ɪ.tɪŋ US -ɪ.ţɪŋ **-ited** -ɪ.tɪd US -ɪ.ţɪd
Edith ˈiː.dɪθ
edition ɪˈdɪʃ.ᵊn, ə- US ɪ- **-s** -z
editor ˈed.ɪ.təʳ US -ţɚ **-s** -z
editorial ˌed.ɪˈtɔː.ri.əl, -əˈ- US -əˈtɔːr.i- **-s** -z **-ly** -i
editorializ|e, -is|e ˌed.ɪˈtɔː.ri.ᵊl.aɪz, -əˈ- US -əˈtɔːr.i.ə.laɪz **-es** -ɪz **-ing** -ɪŋ **-ed** -d
editor-in-chief ˌed.ɪ.təʳ.ɪnˈtʃiːf US -ţɚ-
editorship ˈed.ɪ.tə.ʃɪp US -ţɚ- **-s** -s
Edmond ˈed.mənd **-s** -z
Edmonton ˈed.mən.tən
Edmund ˈed.mənd **-s** -z
Edna ˈed.nə
Edom ˈiː.dəm **-ite/s** -aɪt/s
Edridge ˈed.rɪdʒ
Edsall ˈed.sᵊl
educability ˌedʒ.ʊ.kəˈbɪl.ə.ti, ˌed.jʊ-, -ɪ.ti US ˌedʒ.ʊ.kəˈbɪl.ə.ţi, ˌ-ə-
educable ˈedʒ.ʊ.kə.bl̩, ˈed.jʊ- US ˈedʒ.ʊ-, ˈ-ə-
edu|cate ˈedʒ.ʊ|.keɪt, ˈed.jʊ- US ˈedʒ.ʊ|.keɪt, ˈ-ə- **-cates** -keɪts **-cating** -keɪ.tɪŋ US -keɪ.ţɪŋ **-cated** -keɪ.tɪd US -keɪ.ţɪd **-cator/s** -keɪ.təʳ/z US -keɪ.ţɚ/z
education ˌedʒ.ʊˈkeɪ.ʃᵊn, ˌed.jʊˈ- US ˌedʒ.ʊˈkeɪ.ʃᵊn, -əˈ-
educational ˌedʒ.ʊˈkeɪ.ʃᵊn.ᵊl, ˌed.jʊˈ- US ˌedʒ.ʊˈkeɪ.ʃᵊn.ᵊl, -əˈ- **-ly** -i
educationalist ˌedʒ.ʊˈkeɪ.ʃᵊn.ᵊl.ɪst, ˌed.jʊˈ- US ˌedʒ.ʊˈkeɪ.ʃᵊn.ᵊl.ɪst, -əˈ- **-s** -s
educationist ˌedʒ.ʊˈkeɪ.ʃᵊn.ɪst, ˌed.jʊˈ- US ˌedʒ.ʊˈkeɪ.ʃᵊn.ɪst, -əˈ- **-s** -s
educative ˈedʒ.ʊ.kə.tɪv, ˈed.jʊ-, -keɪ- US ˈedʒ.ʊ.keɪ.ţɪv, ˈ-ə-
educ|e ɪˈdjuːs, iː-, -ˈdʒuːs US -ˈduːs, -ˈdjuːs **-es** -ɪz **-ing** -ɪŋ **-ed** -t
eduction ɪˈdʌk.ʃᵊn, iː- **-s** -z
Edward ˈed.wəd US -wɚd **-(e)s** -z
Edwardian edˈwɔː.di.ən US -ˈwɔːr-, -ˈwɑːr- **-s** -z
Edwin ˈed.wɪn
Edwina edˈwiː.nə
Edwinstowe ˈed.wɪn.stəʊ US -stoʊ
-ee -iː, -i
Note: Suffix. May be stressed or unstressed, e.g. **employee** /ˌem.plɔɪˈiː, ɪmˈplɔɪ.iː/, **committee** /kəˈmɪt.i US -ˈmɪţ-/.
-ée, -ee -eɪ
Note: Suffix. May be stressed or unstressed in British English, e.g. **soirée** /ˈswɑː.reɪ, -ˈ-/, but normally stressed in American English, e.g. /swɑːˈreɪ/.
EEC ˌiː.iːˈsiː
EEG ˌiː.iːˈdʒiː
eejit ˈiː.dʒɪt **-s** -s
eel iːl **-s** -z
eelgrass ˈiːl.grɑːs US -græs
eelworm ˈiːl.wɜːm US -wɝːm **-s** -z
e'en iːn
eeny, meeny, miney, mo ˌiː.niˌmiː.niˌmaɪ.niˈməʊ US -ˈmoʊ
e'er eəʳ US er
-eer -ˈɪəʳ US -ˈɪr
Note: Suffix. Normally carries stress, e.g., **musket** /ˈmʌskɪt/, **musketeer** /ˌmʌs.kɪˈtɪəʳ US -kəˈtɪr/.
eer|ie ˈɪə.r|i US ˈɪr|.i **-y** -i **-ily** -ɪ.li, -ᵊl.i **-iness** -ɪ.nəs, -ɪ.nɪs
Eeyore ˈiː.ɔːʳ US -ɔːr
eff ef **-ing** -ɪŋ ˌ**eff** ˈ**off**; ˌ**effing and** ˈ**blinding**
effac|e ɪˈfeɪs, efˈeɪs US ɪˈfeɪs, ə- **-es** -ɪz **-ing** -ɪŋ **-ed** -t **-ement** -mənt **-eable** -ə.bl̩
effect ɪˈfekt US ɪˈfekt, ə-, iː- **-s** -s **-ing** -ɪŋ **-ed** -ɪd
effective ɪˈfek.tɪv US ɪˈfek-, ə-, iː- **-s** -z **-ly** -li **-ness** -nəs, -nɪs
effectual ɪˈfek.tʃu.əl, -tju-, -tʃʊl, -tjʊl US ɪˈfek.tʃuː.əl, ə-, iː- **-ly** -i
effectuality ɪˌfek.tʃuˈæl.ə.ti, -tjuˈ-, -ɪ.ti US ɪˌfek.tʃuːˈæl.ə.ţi, ə-, iː-
effectu|ate ɪˈfek.tʃu|.eɪt, -tju- US ɪˈfek.tʃuː-, ə-, iː- **-ates** -eɪts **-ating** -eɪ.tɪŋ US -eɪ.ţɪŋ **-ated** -eɪ.tɪd US -eɪ.ţɪd
effeminacy ɪˈfem.ɪ.nə.si, efˈem-, əˈfem-, ˈ-ə-
effeminate (*adj.*) ɪˈfem.ɪ.nət, efˈem-, əˈfem-, ˈ-ə-, -nɪt **-ly** -li **-ness** -nəs, -nɪs
effemi|nate (*v.*) ɪˈfem.ɪ|.neɪt, efˈem-, ˈ-ə- **-nates** -neɪts **-nating** -neɪ.tɪŋ US -neɪ.ţɪŋ **-nated** -neɪ.tɪd US -neɪ.ţɪd

Pronouncing the letters EE

The most common pronunciation for the vowel digraph **ee** is /iː/, e.g.:

bee /biː/

When followed by an **r** in the spelling, **ee** is pronounced as either /ɪə (US) ɪr/ or /iː.ə (US) iː.ɚ/, e.g.:

steer /stɪəʳ/ (US) /stɪr/
freer (comparative adj.) /ˈfriː.əʳ/ (US) /-ɚ/

In addition

There are other vowel sounds associated with the digraph **ee**, e.g.:

eɪ fiancée /fiˈɑ̃ːn.seɪ/ (US) /fiˈɑːn.seɪ/
iː.ɪst freest (superlative adj.) /ˈfriː.ɪst/

In weak syllables

The vowel digraph **ee** is realised with the vowel sound /i/ in weak syllables, e.g.:

coffee /ˈkɒf.i/ (US) /ˈkɑː.fi/

effendi efˈen.di, ɪˈfen-
efferent ˈef.ər.ənt, ˈiː.fər- (US) ˈef.ər-
effervesc|e ˌef.əˈves (US) -ɚˈ- **-es** -ɪz **-ing** -ɪŋ **-ed** -t
effervescen|t ˌef.əˈves.ən|t (US) -ɚˈ- **-ce** -*t*s *stress shift:* ˌeffervescent ˈpowder
effete ɪˈfiːt, efˈiːt
efficacious ˌef.ɪˈkeɪ.ʃəs, -əˈ- **-ly** -li **-ness** -nəs, -nɪs
efficacity ˌef.ɪˈkæs.ə.ti, -əˈ-, -ɪ.ti (US) -ə.t̬i
efficacy ˈef.ɪ.kə.si, ˈ-ə-
efficienc|y ɪˈfɪʃ.ə*n*t.s|i, ə- (US) ɪˈfɪʃ-, ə-, iː- **-ies** -iz
efficient ɪˈfɪʃ.ənt, ə- (US) ɪˈfɪʃ-, ə-, iː- **-ly** -li
Effie ˈef.i
effig|y ˈef.ɪ.dʒ|i, ˈ-ə- **-ies** -iz
Effingham *in the UK:* ˈef.ɪŋ.əm (US) ˈef.ɪŋ.əm, -hæm *in the US:* ˈef.ɪŋ.hæm
effloresc|e ˌef.lɔːˈres, -lɒrˈes, -ləˈres (US) -ləˈres, -lɔːrˈ- **-es** -ɪz **-ing** -ɪŋ **-ed** -t
efflorescen|t ˌef.lɔːˈres.ən|t (US) -ləˈ-, -lɔːrˈ- **-ce** -*t*s
effluence ˈef.lu.ən*t*s
effluent ˈef.lu.ənt **-s** -s
effluvi|um ɪˈfluː.vi|.əm, efˈluː- **-a** -ə **-al** -əl
efflux ˈef.lʌks **-es** -ɪz
effluxion efˈluk.ʃən, ɪˈflʌk- **-s** -z
effort ˈef.ət (US) -ɚt **-s** -s
effortless ˈef.ət.ləs, -lɪs (US) -ɚt- **-ly** -li **-ness** -nəs, -nɪs
effronter|y ɪˈfrʌn.tər|.i, efˈrʌn- (US) efˈrʌn-, ɪˈfrʌn- **-ies** -iz
effulg|e ɪˈfʌldʒ, efˈʌldʒ **-es** -ɪz **-ing** -ɪŋ **-ed** -d
effulgen|ce ɪˈfʌl.dʒən|*t*s, efˈʌl- **-t/ly** -t/li
effuse (*adj.*) ɪˈfjuːs, efˈjuːs
effus|e (*v.*) ɪˈfjuːz, efˈjuːz **-es** -ɪz **-ing** -ɪŋ **-ed** -d
effusion ɪˈfjuː.ʒən, efˈjuː- **-s** -z
effusive ɪˈfjuː.sɪv, efˈjuː- **-ly** -li **-ness** -nəs, -nɪs
Efik ˈef.ɪk
EFL ˌiː.efˈel
eft eft **-s** -s
EFTA ˈef.tə
e.g. ˌiːˈdʒiː; fər.ɪgˈzɑːm.pl̩ (US) ˌiːˈdʒiː; fɚ.ɪgˈzæm.pl̩
egad iːˈgæd, ɪ-
egalitarian ɪˌgæl.ɪˈteə.ri.ən, iː-, -əˈ-; ˌiː.gæl- (US) -ˈter.i- **-ism** -ɪ.zəm
Egan ˈiː.gən
Egbert ˈeg.bət, -bɜːt (US) -bɚt, -bɝːt
Egdon ˈeg.dən
Egeria ɪˈdʒɪə.ri.ə, iː- (US) -ˈdʒɪr.i-
Egerton ˈedʒ.ə.tən (US) ˈ-ɚ-
Egeus *in Greek mythology:* ˈiː.dʒuːs; ɪˈdʒiː.əs, iː- (US) iːˈdʒiː.əs *Shakespearean character:* iːˈdʒiː.əs, ɪ-
egg eg **-s** -z **-ing** -ɪŋ **-ed** -d **ˈegg ˌtimer; have ˈegg on one's ˌface; put ˌall one's ˌeggs in one ˈbasket**
eggcup ˈeg.kʌp **-s** -s
egghead ˈeg.hed **-s** -z
Eggleston ˈeg.l̩z.tən (US) -l̩.stən
Eggleton ˈeg.l̩.tən
eggnog ˌegˈnɒg, ˈ-- (US) ˈeg.nɑːg **-s** -z
eggplant ˈeg.plɑːnt (US) -plænt **-s** -s
egg-shaped ˈeg.ʃeɪpt
eggshell ˈeg.ʃel **-s** -z
Egham ˈeg.əm
Eglamore, Eglamour ˈeg.lə.mɔːʳ (US) -mɔːr
eglantine (E) ˈeg.lən.taɪn, -tiːn
Eglingham ˈeg.lɪn.dʒəm
Eglinton ˈeg.lɪn.tən
Eglon ˈeg.lɒn (US) -lɑːn
Egmont ˈeg.mɒnt, -mənt (US) -mɑːnt
ego ˈiː.gəʊ, ˈeg.əʊ (US) ˈiː.goʊ, ˈeg.oʊ **-s** -z **ˈego ˌtrip**
egocentric ˌiː.gəʊˈsen.trɪk, ˌeg.əʊˈ- (US) ˌiː.goʊˈ-, ˌeg.oʊˈ- **-ally** -əl.i, -li
egocentricity ˌiː.gəʊ.senˈtrɪs.ɪ.ti, ˌeg.əʊ-, -ə.ti (US) ˌiː.goʊ.senˈtrɪs.ə.t̬i, ˌeg.oʊ-
egocentrism ˌiː.gəʊˈsen.trɪ.zəm, ˌeg.əʊˈ- (US) ˌiː.goʊˈ-, ˌeg.oʊˈ-
ego|ism ˈiː.gəʊ|.ɪ.zəm, ˈeg.əʊ- (US) ˈiː.goʊ-, ˈeg.oʊ- **-ist/s** -ɪst/s
egoistic ˌiː.gəʊˈɪs.tɪk, ˌeg.əʊˈ- (US) ˌiː.goʊˈ-, ˌeg.oʊˈ- **-al** -əl **-ally** -əl.i, -li
egomania ˌiː.gəʊˈmeɪ.ni.ə, ˌeg.əʊˈ- (US) ˌiː.goʊˈ-, ˌeg.oʊˈ-
egomaniac ˌiː.gəʊˈmeɪ.ni.æk, ˌeg.əʊˈ- (US) ˌiː.goʊˈ-, ˌeg.oʊˈ- **-s** -s
Egon ˈeg.ən, ˈiː.gən, -gɒn (US) ˈeɪ.gɑːn, -gən
Note: The restaurant critic Egon Ronay is popularly pronunced as /ˈiː.gɒn/ in the UK.
egot|ism ˈiː.gəʊ.t|ɪ.zəm, ˈeg.əʊ- (US) ˈiː.goʊ-, ˈeg.oʊ- **-ist/s** -ɪst/s
egotistic ˌiː.gəʊˈtɪs.tɪk, ˌeg.əʊˈ- (US) ˌiː.goʊˈ-, ˌeg.oʊˈ- **-al** -əl **-ally** -əl.i, -li
egregious ɪˈgriː.dʒəs, əˈgriː-, -dʒi.əs (US) iː-, ɪ- **-ly** -li **-ness** -nəs, -nɪs
Egremont ˈeg.rə.mənt, -rɪ-, -mɒnt (US) -mɑːnt
egress ˈiː.gres **-es** -ɪz
egression ɪˈgreʃ.ən, iː- **-s** -z
egressive ɪˈgres.ɪv, iː-
egret ˈiː.grət, -grɪt, -gret (US) ˈiː.gret, ˈeg.ret, -rɪt **-s** -s
Egton ˈeg.tən
Egypt ˈiː.dʒɪpt
Egyptian ɪˈdʒɪp.ʃən, ə-, iː- **-s** -z
Egyptolog|y ˌiː.dʒɪpˈtɒl.ə.dʒ|i (US) -ˈtɑː.lə- **-ist/s** -ɪst/s
eh eɪ
Ehrlich *European family name:* ˈeə.lɪk, -lɪx (US) ˈer- *US family name:* ˈɜː.lɪk (US) ˈɝː-, ˈer-

Pronouncing the letters EI

There are several pronunciation possibilities for the vowel digraph **ei**. One is /iː/ when following a **c**; this is immortalised in the spelling rhyme "I before **E** except after **C**, but only if the sound is /iː/", e.g.:

receive	/rɪˈsiːv/	

When followed by a silent **gh** in the spelling, it is usually pronounced as /eɪ/ but may be pronounced /aɪ/, e.g.:

eight	/eɪt/	
height	/haɪt/	

The pronunciation /aɪ/ also occurs in two words which do not include **gh**, but only in British English, e.g.:

either	/ˈaɪ.ðəʳ/	US /ˈiː.ðɚ/
neither	/ˈnaɪ.ðəʳ/	US /ˈniː.ðɚ/

When followed by an **r** in the spelling, **ei** is pronounced as /eə US er/ and /ɪə US ɪr/, e.g.:

their	/ðeəʳ/	US /ðer/
weir	/wɪəʳ/	US /wɪr/

In addition

Other vowel sounds are associated with the digraph **ei**, e.g.:

e	Leicester	/ˈles.təʳ/ US /-tɚ/
eɪ	rein	/reɪn/

In weak syllables

The vowel digraph **ei** is realised with the vowel /ɪ/ in weak syllables, e.g.:

foreign	/ˈfɒr.ɪn/	US /ˈfɔːr-/

eider ˈaɪ.dəʳ US -dɚ **-s** -z ˈ**eider** ˌ**duck**
eiderdown ˈaɪ.də.daʊn US -dɚ- **-s** -z
Eidos® ˈaɪ.dɒs, ˈeɪ- US -dɑːs, -doʊs
Eifel ˈaɪ.fəl
Eiffel Tower ˌaɪ.fəlˈtaʊəʳ US -ˈtaʊɚ **-s** -z
Eiger ˈaɪ.gəʳ US -gɚ
Eigg eg
eight eɪt **-s** -s
eighteen ˌeɪˈtiːn **-s** -z **-th/s** -θ/s *stress shift:* ˌeighteen ˈmonths
eightfold ˈeɪt.fəʊld US -foʊld
eighth eɪtθ **-s** -s
eightieth ˈeɪ.ti.əθ, -ti.ɪθ US -t̬i.əθ **-s** -s
eightsome ˈeɪt.səm
eight|y ˈeɪ.t|i US -t̬|i **-ies** -iz
eightyfold ˈeɪ.ti.fəʊld US -t̬i.foʊld
eighty-six ˌeɪ.tiˈsɪks US -t̬iˈ- **-es** -ɪz **-ing** -ɪŋ **-ed** -t
Eilat eɪˈlɑːt, -ˈlæt US -ˈlɑːt
Eilean ˈel.ən, ˈiː.lən
Eileen ˈaɪ.liːn US aɪˈliːn
Eiloart ˈaɪ.ləʊ.ɑːt US -loʊ.ɑːrt
Eindhoven ˈaɪnd.həʊ.vən US -hoʊ-
Einstein ˈaɪn.staɪn
einsteinium ˌaɪnˈstaɪ.ni.əm
Eire ˈeə.rə US ˈer.ə, -iː; ˈaɪ.rə, -riː
eirenicon aɪəˈriː.nɪ.kɒn, -ˈren.ɪ- US aɪˈriː.nɪ.kɑːn **-s** -z
Eisenhower ˈaɪ.zən.haʊəʳ US -haʊɚ
eisteddfod (E) aɪˈsteð.vɒd, ɪ-, -ˈsted.fəd US -ˈsteð.vɑːd, eɪ- **-s** -z
either ˈaɪ.ðəʳ, ˈiː- US ˈiː.ðɚ, ˈaɪ-
ejacu|late (*v.*) ɪˈdʒæk.jə|.leɪt, iː-, -jʊ- **-lates** -leɪts **-lating** -leɪ.tɪŋ US -leɪ.t̬ɪŋ **-lated** -leɪ.tɪd US -leɪ.t̬ɪd
ejaculate (*n.*) ɪˈdʒæk.jə.lət, iː-, -jʊ-, -lɪt, -leɪt US -lət, -lɪt
ejaculation ɪˌdʒæk.jəˈleɪ.ʃən, iː-, -jʊˈ- **-s** -z
ejaculative ɪˈdʒæk.jə.lə.tɪv, -jʊ-, -leɪ.tɪv US -jə.lə.t̬ɪv
ejaculatory ɪˈdʒæk.jə.lə.tər.i, iː-, -jʊ-, -leɪ-, -tri; ɪˌdʒæk.jəˈleɪ-, iː-, -jʊˈ- US ɪˈdʒæk.jə.lə.tɔːr.i, iː-, -jʊ-
eject ɪˈdʒekt, iː- **-s** -s **-ing** -ɪŋ **-ed** -ɪd
ejection ɪˈdʒek.ʃən, iː- **-s** -z
ejective ɪˈdʒek.tɪv, iː- **-s** -z
ejectment ɪˈdʒekt.mənt, iː- **-s** -s
ejector ɪˈdʒek.təʳ, iː- US -tɚ **-s** -z
ejusdem generis eɪˌʊs.demˈgen.ər.ɪs US edʒˌuːs.demˈgen.ɚ.əs; iː.dʒəs.demˈdʒen-
Ekaterinburg ɪˌkæt.ərˈiːn.bɜːg US -bɝːg
ek|e iːk **-es** -s **-ing** -ɪŋ **-ed** -t
EKG ˌiː.keɪˈdʒiː
Ekron ˈek.rɒn US -rɑːn
Ektachrome® ˈek.tə.krəʊm US -kroʊm
el el
elaborate (*adj.*) ɪˈlæb.ər.ət, -ɪt **-ly** -li **-ness** -nəs, -nɪs
elabor|ate (*v.*) ɪˈlæb.ə.r|eɪt **-ates** -eɪts **-ating** -eɪ.tɪŋ US -eɪ.t̬ɪŋ **-ated** -eɪ.tɪd US -eɪ.t̬ɪd **-ator/s** -eɪ.təʳ/z US -eɪ.t̬ɚ/z
elaboration ɪˌlæb.əˈreɪ.ʃən **-s** -z
elaborative ɪˈlæb.ər.ə.tɪv, -eɪ- US -ə.t̬ɪv
Elaine ɪˈleɪn, ə-, elˈeɪn
El Al® ˌelˈæl
El Alamein ˌelˈæl.ə.meɪn; elˌæl.əˈmeɪn US ˌelˈæl.ə.mein, -ˈɑː.lə-; elˌæl.əˈmeɪn, -ˌɑː.ləˈ-
Elam ˈiː.ləm **-ite/s** -aɪt/s
élan eɪˈlɑ̃ːn, ɪ-, -ˈlæn US -ˈlɑːn, -ˈlɑ̃ːŋ, -ˈlæn *stress shift, see compound:* ˌ**élan viˈtal**
eland (E) ˈiː.lənd **-s** -z
elaps|e ɪˈlæps **-es** -ɪz **-ing** -ɪŋ **-ed** -t
elastic ɪˈlæs.tɪk, -ˈlɑː.stɪk US -ˈlæs.tɪk **-s** -s **-ally** -əl.i, -li **e**ˌ**lastic** ˈ**band**
elasti|cate ɪˈlæs.tɪ|.keɪt, -ˈlɑː.stɪ-, -stə- US -ˈlæs.tɪ- **-cates** -keɪts **-cating** -keɪ.tɪŋ US -keɪ.t̬ɪŋ **-cated** -keɪ.tɪd US -keɪ.t̬ɪd
elasticity ˌɪl.æsˈtɪs.ə.ti, ˌel-, ˌiː.læs-, -ləˈstɪs-, -lɑːˈ-, -ɪ.ti; ɪˌlæsˈtɪs-, -ˌlɑːˈstɪs- US ɪˌlæsˈtɪs.ə.t̬i; ˌiː.læsˈ-
elasticiz|e, -ise ɪˈlæs.tɪ.saɪz, -ˈlɑː.stɪ-, -stə-, -ˈlæs.tɪ- **-es** -ɪz **-ing** -ɪŋ **-ed** -d
elastin ɪˈlæs.tɪn, ə-, -ˈlɑː.stɪn US ɪˈlæs.tɪn
Elastoplast® ɪˈlæs.təʊ.plɑːst, el-, iːˈlæs-, -plæst; -ˈlɑː.stəʊ.plɑːst US ɪˈlæs.toʊ.plæst, iː-, -tə-
e|late ɪ|ˈleɪt, iː- **-lates** -leɪts **-lating** -leɪ.tɪŋ US -leɪ.t̬ɪŋ **-lated/ly** -leɪ.tɪd/li US -leɪ.t̬ɪd/li
elation ɪˈleɪ.ʃən, iː-
Elba ˈel.bə
Elbe ˈel.bə, elb
elbow ˈel.bəʊ US -boʊ **-s** -z **-ing** -ɪŋ **-ed** -d ˈ**elbow** ˌ**grease**; ˈ**elbow** ˌ**room**
El Cid ˌelˈsɪd
elder (E) ˈel.dəʳ US -dɚ **-s** -z ˌ**elder** ˈ**statesman**
elderberr|y ˈel.dəˌber|.i, -bər- US -dɚˌber- **-ies** -ɪz
elderflower ˈel.dəˌflaʊəʳ US -dɚˌflaʊɚ **-s** -z
elderl|y ˈel.dəl|.i US -dɚ.l|i **-iness** -ɪ.nəs, -ɪ.nɪs
eldest ˈel.dɪst, -dəst
Eldon ˈel.dən
El Dorado, Eldorado ˌel.dəˈrɑː.dəʊ, -dɒrˈɑː- US -dəˈrɑː.doʊ, -ˈreɪ-
Eldred ˈel.drɪd, -dred, -drəd

Eldridge 'el.drɪdʒ
Eleanor 'el.ɪ.nəʳ, '-ə- ⓊⓈ -nɚ, -nɔːr
Eleanora ˌel.i.ə'nɔː.rə ⓊⓈ -'nɔːr.ə-
Eleazar ˌel.i'eɪ.zəʳ ⓊⓈ -zɚ
elecampane ˌel.ɪ.kæm'peɪn, ˌ-ə- **-s** -z
elect ɪ'lekt **-s** -s **-ing** -ɪŋ **-ed** -ɪd **-able** -ə.bl̩
election ɪ'lek.ʃᵊn **-s** -z
electioneer ɪˌlek.ʃə'nɪəʳ ⓊⓈ -'nɪr **-s** -z **-ing** -ɪŋ **-ed** -d **-er/s** -əʳ/z ⓊⓈ -ɚ/z
elective ɪ'lek.tɪv **-ly** -li
elector ɪ'lek.təʳ ⓊⓈ -tɚ **-s** -z
electoral ɪ'lek.tᵊr.ᵊl, '-trᵊl
electorate ɪ'lek.tᵊr.ət, -ɪt, '-trət, '-trɪt **-s** -s
Electra ɪ'lek.trə **E'lectra ˌcomplex**
electric ɪ'lek.trɪk **-al** -ᵊl **-ally** -ᵊl.i, -li **-s** -s **eˌlectric 'blanket; eˌlectric 'chair; eˌlectric gui'tar; eˌlectric 'shock; eˌlectric 'shock ˌtherapy**
electrician ˌel.ɪk'trɪʃ.ᵊn, ˌiː.lek'-; ɪˌlek'- ⓊⓈ ɪˌlek'-; ˌiː.lek'- **-s** -z
electricity ˌel.ɪk'trɪs.ə.ti, ˌiː.lek-, -ɪ.ti; ɪˌlek'- ⓊⓈ ɪˌlek'-; ˌiː.lek'-
electrification ɪˌlek.trɪ.fɪ'keɪ.ʃᵊn, -trə- **-s** -z
electri|fy ɪ'lek.trɪ|.faɪ, -trə- **-fies** -faɪz **-fying** -faɪ.ɪŋ **-fied** -faɪd **-fiable** -faɪ.ə.bl̩
electro- ɪ.lek.trəʊ-; ˌel.ɪk'trɒ-, ˌiː.lek'-; ɪˌlek'- ⓊⓈ ɪ.lek.troʊ-; ɪˌlek'trɑː-; ˌiː.lek'-
Note: Prefix. Either takes primary or secondary stress on the second syllable, e.g. **electrocute** /ɪ'lek.trə.kjuːt/, **electrocution** /ɪˌlek.trə'kjuː.ʃᵊn/, or primary stress on the third syllable, with secondary stress on either the first or second syllable,e.g. **electrolysis** /ˌel.ɪk'trɒl.ɪ.sɪs, ɪˌlek'- ⓊⓈ ɪˌlek'trɑː.lə-, ˌiː.lek'-/.
electrobiology ɪˌlek.trəʊ.baɪ'ɒl.ə.dʒi ⓊⓈ -troʊ.baɪ'ɑː.lə-
electrocardiogram ɪˌlek.trəʊ'kɑː.di.əʊ.græm ⓊⓈ -troʊ'kɑːr.di.ə- **-s** -z
electrocardiograph ɪˌlek.trəʊ'kɑː.di.əʊ.grɑːf, -græf ⓊⓈ -troʊ'kɑːr.di.ə.græf **-s** -s
electrochemistry ɪˌlek.trəʊ'kem.ɪ.stri, -ə.stri ⓊⓈ -troʊ'kem.ə-
electroconvulsive ɪˌlek.trəʊ.kən'vʌl.sɪv ⓊⓈ -troʊ- **eˌlectroconˌvulsive 'therapy**
electro|cute ɪ'lek.trə|.kjuːt **-cutes** -kjuːts **-cuting** -kjuː.tɪŋ ⓊⓈ -kjuː.t̬ɪŋ **-cuted** -kjuː.tɪd ⓊⓈ -kjuː.t̬ɪd
electrocution ɪˌlek.trə'kjuː.ʃᵊn **-s** -z
electrode ɪ'lek.trəʊd ⓊⓈ -troʊd **-s** -z
electrodynamic ɪˌlek.trəʊ.daɪ'næm.ɪk, -dɪ'- ⓊⓈ -troʊ.daɪ'- **-s** -s
electroencephalo|gram ɪˌlek.trəʊ.en'sef.ᵊl.əʊ|.græm, -ɪn'-, -'kef-, -eŋ'kef-, -ɪŋ'kef- ⓊⓈ -troʊ.en'sef.ə.loʊ-, -lə- **-s** -z **-graph/s** -grɑːf/s, -græf/s ⓊⓈ -græf/s
electrokinetic ɪˌlek.trəʊ.kɪ'net.ɪk, -kaɪ'- ⓊⓈ -troʊ.kɪ'net̬-, -trə- **-s** -s
electrolier ɪˌlek.trəʊ'lɪəʳ ⓊⓈ -trə'lɪr **-s** -z
Electrolux® ɪ'lek.trəʊ.lʌks ⓊⓈ -trə-
electrolys|is ˌel.ɪk'trɒl.ə.s|ɪs, ˌiː.lek-, -ɪ.s|ɪs; ɪˌlek'-, ə- ⓊⓈ ɪˌlek'trɑː.lə-; ˌiː.lek- **-es** -iːz
electrolyte ɪ'lek.trə.laɪt **-s** -s
electrolytic ɪˌlek.trə'lɪt.ɪk ⓊⓈ -'lɪt̬-
electrolyz|e, -ys|e ɪ'lek.trᵊl.aɪz ⓊⓈ -trə.laɪz **-es** -ɪz **-ing** -ɪŋ **-ed** -d
electromagnet ɪˌlek.trəʊ'mæg.nɪt, -nət ⓊⓈ -troʊ'-, -trə'- **-s** -s **-ism** -ɪ.zᵊm
electromagnetic ɪˌlek.trəʊ.mæg'net.ɪk, -məg'- ⓊⓈ -troʊ.mæg'net̬-, -trə-
electrometer ˌel.ɪk'trɒm.ɪ.təʳ, ˌiː.lek-, -mə.təʳ; ɪˌlek'- ⓊⓈ ɪ.lek'trɑː.mə.t̬ɚ; ˌiː.lek'- **-s** -z
electromotive ɪˌlek.trəʊ'məʊ.tɪv ⓊⓈ -troʊ'moʊ.t̬ɪv, -trə'-
electromotor ɪˌlek.trəʊ'məʊ.təʳ ⓊⓈ -troʊ'moʊ.t̬ɚ, -trə'- **-s** -z
electron ɪ'lek.trɒn ⓊⓈ -trɑːn **-s** -z
electronic ˌel.ek'trɒn.ɪk, -ɪk'-, ˌiː.lek'-; ɪˌlek'- ⓊⓈ ɪˌlek'trɑː.nɪk; ˌiː.lek'- **-s** -s **-ally** -ᵊl.i, -li *stress shift, see compound:* **ˌelectronic 'mail**
electropalatogram ɪˌlek.trəʊ'pæl.ə.təʊ.græm ⓊⓈ -troʊ'pæl.ə.t̬ə- **-s** -z
electropalatography ɪˌlek.trəʊˌpæl.ə'tɒg.rə.fi ⓊⓈ -troʊˌpæl.ə'tɑː.grə-
electrophone ɪ'lek.trə.fəʊn ⓊⓈ -foʊn **-s** -z
electrophorus ˌel.ɪk'trɒf.ᵊr.əs, ˌiː.lek'- ⓊⓈ ɪˌlek'trɑː.fɚ-; ˌiː.lek'- **-es** -ɪz
electropla|te ɪ'lek.trəʊ.pleɪ|t, ɪˌlek.trəʊ'pleɪ|t ⓊⓈ ɪ'lek.troʊ.pleɪ|t, iː-, -trə- **-tes** -ts **-ting** -tɪŋ ⓊⓈ -t̬ɪŋ **-ted** -tɪd ⓊⓈ -t̬ɪd **-ter/s** -təʳ/z ⓊⓈ -t̬ɚ/z
electropolar ɪˌlek.trəʊ'pəʊ.ləʳ ⓊⓈ -troʊ'poʊ.lɚ
electropositive ɪˌlek.trəʊ'pɒz.ə.tɪv, -ɪ.tɪv ⓊⓈ -troʊ'pɑː.zə.t̬ɪv
electroscope ɪ'lek.trəʊ.skəʊp ⓊⓈ -troʊ.skoʊp, -trə- **-s** -s
electrostatic ɪˌlek.trəʊ'stæt.ɪk ⓊⓈ -troʊ'stæt̬- **-s** -s
electrotherapeutic ɪˌlek.trəʊˌθer.ə'pjuː.tɪk ⓊⓈ -troʊˌθer.ə'pjuː.t̬ɪk **-s** -s
electrotherapy ɪˌlek.trəʊ'θer.ə.pi ⓊⓈ -troʊ'-
electrothermal ɪˌlek.trəʊ'θɜː.mᵊl ⓊⓈ -troʊ'θɝː-
electrotype ɪ'lek.trəʊ.taɪp ⓊⓈ -troʊ- **-s** -s
electrovalency ɪˌlek.trəʊ'veɪ.lənt.si ⓊⓈ -troʊ'-
electrum ɪ'lek.trəm
electuar|y ɪ'lek.tjʊə.r|i ⓊⓈ -tʃuː.er|.i **-ies** -iz
eleemosynary ˌel.i.iː'mɒs.ɪ.nᵊr.i, ˌel.iː'-, ˌel.ɪ'-, -'mɒz-, -'məʊ.zɪ-, -zᵊn.ᵊr- ⓊⓈ ˌel.ɪ'mɑː.sə.ner.i, -iː.ə'-
elegance 'el.ɪ.gᵊnts ⓊⓈ '-ə-
elegant 'el.ɪ.gᵊnt ⓊⓈ '-ə- **-ly** -li
elegiac ˌel.ɪ'dʒaɪ.ək, -ə'-, -æk ⓊⓈ ˌel.ɪ'dʒaɪ.ək, -ə'-, -æk; ɪ'liː.dʒiː.æk **-s** -s **-al** -ᵊl
elegist 'el.ɪ.dʒɪst, '-ə- **-s** -s
elegit ɪ'liː.dʒɪt, el'iː-
elegiz|e, -is|e 'el.ɪ.dʒaɪz, '-ə- **-es** -ɪz **-ing** -ɪŋ **-ed** -d
eleg|y 'el.ɪ.dʒ|i, '-ə- **-ies** -iz
Elektra ɪ'lek.trə
element 'el.ɪ.mənt, '-ə- ⓊⓈ '-ə- **-s** -s
elemental ˌel.ɪ'men.tᵊl, -ə'- ⓊⓈ -ə'men.t̬ᵊl **-s** -z **-ly** -i
elementar|y ˌel.ɪ'men.tᵊr|.i, -ə'-, '-tr|i ⓊⓈ -ə'men.t̬ɚ|.i, '-tr|i **-ily** -ɪ.li, -ᵊl.i **-iness** -ɪ.nəs, -ɪ.nɪs **ele'mentary ˌschool**
elemi 'el.ɪ.mi
elenchus ɪ'leŋ.kəs, ə-
Eleonora ˌel.i.ə'nɔː.rə ⓊⓈ -'nɔːr.ə
Eleonore 'el.i.ə.nɔːʳ ⓊⓈ -nɔːr
elephant 'el.ɪ.fənt, '-ə- **-s** -s
elephantiasis ˌel.ɪ.fən'taɪə.sɪs, ˌ-ə-, -fæn'-
elephantine ˌel.ɪ'fæn.taɪn, -ə'- ⓊⓈ -taɪn, -tiːn, 'el.ə.fən-
Eleusinian ˌel.juː'sɪn.i.ən, -uː'-
Eleusis el'juː.sɪs, ɪ'ljuː-, ə-, -'luː- ⓊⓈ ɪ'luː.sɪs
Eleuthera ɪ'luː.θᵊr.ə, el'uː-, -'juː- ⓊⓈ ɪ'luː-
ele|vate 'el.ɪ|.veɪt, '-ə- **-vates** -veɪts **-vating** -veɪ.tɪŋ ⓊⓈ -veɪ.t̬ɪŋ **-vated** -veɪ.tɪd ⓊⓈ -veɪ.t̬ɪd
elevation ˌel.ɪ'veɪ.ʃᵊn, -ə'- **-s** -z
elevator 'el.ɪ.veɪ.təʳ, '-ə- ⓊⓈ -t̬ɚ **-s** -z
elevatory ˌel.ɪ'veɪ.tᵊr.i, -ə'-, '-tri ⓊⓈ -t̬ɚ.i
eleven ɪ'lev.ᵊn, ə- **-s** -z **-th/s** -θ/s
eleven-plus ɪˌlev.ᵊn'plʌs, ə-, -əm'- ⓊⓈ -ən'- **-es** -ɪz
elevenses ɪ'lev.ᵊn.zɪz, ə-
el|f el|f **-ves** -vz
elfin 'el.fɪn **-s** -z
elfish 'el.fɪʃ **-ly** -li
Elfrida el'friː.də
Elgar *composer:* 'el.gɑːʳ ⓊⓈ -gɑːr *surname:* 'el.gɑːʳ, -gəʳ ⓊⓈ -gɑːr, -gɚ

Elision

The omission of sounds which are normally present if words are pronounced slowly and clearly but appear not to be pronounced when the same words are produced in a rapid, colloquial style, or when the words occur in a different context. These missing sounds are said to have been 'elided'. See also CONNECTED SPEECH PHENOMENA.

Examples for English

It is easy to find examples of elision, but very difficult to state rules that govern which sounds may be elided and which may not. Elision of vowels in English usually happens when a short, unstressed vowel occurs between voiceless consonants, e.g. in the first syllable of *perhaps*, *potato*, the second syllable of *bicycle*, or the third syllable of *philosophy*.

Elision also occurs when a weak vowel occurs between a PLOSIVE or FRICATIVE consonant and a consonant such as a NASAL or a LATERAL: this process leads to SYLLABIC CONSONANTS, e.g.:

sudden	/ˈsʌd.ən/	→	/ˈsʌd.n̩/
awful	/ˈɔː.fʊl/	→	/ˈɔː.fl̩/
	(US) /ˈɑː-/		(US) /ˈɑː-/

Elision of consonants in English happens most commonly when a speaker 'simplifies' a complex consonant cluster, e.g.

acts	/ækts/	→	/æks/
twelfth night	/ˌtwelfθˈnaɪt/	→	/ˌtwelθˈnaɪt/ or ˌtwelfˈnaɪt/

In *twelfth night* above, it seems much less likely that any of the other consonants could be left out: the /l/ and the /n/ seem to be unelidable.

It is very important to note that sounds do not simply 'disappear' like a light being switched off. A transcription such as /æks/ for *acts* implies that the /t/ phoneme has dropped out altogether, but detailed examination of speech shows that such effects are more gradual: in slow speech the /t/ may be fully pronounced, with an audible transition from the preceding /k/ and to the following /s/, while in a more rapid style it may be articulated but not given any audible realisation, and in very rapid speech it may be observable, if at all, only as a rather early movement of the tongue blade towards the /s/ position. Much more research in this area is needed (not only on English) for us to understand what processes are involved when speech is 'reduced' in rapid articulation.

Elgin ˈel.gɪn (US) -gɪn, -dʒɪn ˌ**Elgin ˈMarbles**
El Greco ˌelˈgrek.əʊ (US) -oʊ
Elham ˈiː.ləm
Eli ˈiː.laɪ
Elia ˈiː.li.ə
Elias ɪˈlaɪəs, elˈaɪ-, əˈlaɪ-, -ˈlaɪ.æs
Elibank ˈel.ɪ.bæŋk
elic|it ɪˈlɪs|.ɪt, ə-, iː- **-its** -ɪts **-iting** -ɪ.tɪŋ (US) -ɪ.t̬ɪŋ **-ited** -ɪ.tɪd (US) -ɪ.t̬ɪd
elicitation ɪˌlɪs.ɪˈteɪ.ʃən, ə-, iː-, -əˈ-
elid|e ɪˈlaɪd, iː- **-es** -z **-ing** -ɪŋ **-ed** -ɪd **-able** -ə.bl̩
Elie ˈiː.li
eligibility ˌel.ɪ.dʒəˈbɪl.ə.ti, ˌ-ə-, -dʒɪˈ-, -ɪ.ti (US) -dʒəˈbɪl.ə.t̬i
eligib|le ˈel.ɪ.dʒə.b|l̩, ˈ-ə-, -dʒɪ- (US) -dʒə- **-ly** -li **-leness** -l̩.nəs, -nɪs
Elihu ɪˈlaɪ.hjuː, elˈaɪ- (US) ˈel.ɪ-; iːˈlaɪ-, ɪ-
Elijah ɪˈlaɪ.dʒə
Eliman ˈel.ɪ.mən
elimi|nate ɪˈlɪm.ɪ|.neɪt, ə-, ˈ-ə- **-nates** -neɪts **-nating** -neɪ.tɪŋ (US) -neɪ.t̬ɪŋ **-nated** -neɪ.tɪd (US) -neɪ.t̬ɪd **-nator/s** -neɪ.təʳ/z (US) -neɪ.t̬ɚ/z
elimination ɪˌlɪm.ɪˈneɪ.ʃən, ə-, -əˈ- **-s** -z
Elinor ˈel.ɪ.nəʳ, ˈ-ə- (US) -nɚ, -nɔːr
Eliot ˈel.i.ət
Eliotson ˈel.i.ət.sən
Eliott ˈel.i.ət
Eliphaz ˈel.ɪ.fæz
Elis ˈiː.lɪs
Elisabeth ɪˈlɪz.ə.bəθ, ə-
Elise ɪˈliːz (US) ɪˈliːz, -ˈliːs
Elisha *prophet:* ɪˈlaɪ.ʃə *place in Northumberland:* elˈɪʃ.ə
elision ɪˈlɪʒ.ən **-s** -z
elite, élite ɪˈliːt, eɪ- **-s** -s
elitism, élitism ɪˈliː.tɪ.zəm, eɪˈliː-
elitist, élitist ɪˈliː.tɪst, eɪˈliː- **-s** -s
elixir ɪˈlɪk.səʳ, elˈɪk-, əˈlɪk-, iː-, -sɪəʳ (US) -sɚ **-s** -z
Eliza ɪˈlaɪ.zə
Elizabeth ɪˈlɪz.ə.bəθ, ə-
Elizabethan ɪˌlɪz.əˈbiː.θən, ə- **-s** -z *stress shift:* EˌlizabethanˈPoet
Elizabethian ɪˌlɪz.əˈbiː.θi.ən, ə- **-s** -z *stress shift:* Eˌlizabethian ˈpoet
elk elk **-s** -s
Elkhart ˈelk.hɑːt (US) -hɑːrt
Elkin ˈel.kɪn
Elkington ˈel.kɪŋ.tən
Elkins ˈel.kɪnz
ell el **-s** -z
Ella ˈel.ə
Elland ˈel.ənd
Ellangowan ˌel.ənˈgaʊən, -əŋˈ-
Elle el
Ellen ˈel.ən, -ɪn
Ellenborough ˈel.ən.bər.ə, -ɪn- (US) -oʊ
Ellery ˈel.ər.i
Ellesmere ˈelz.mɪəʳ (US) -mɪr
Ellice ˈel.ɪs
Ellicott ˈel.ɪ.kət, -kɒt (US) -kət, -kɑːt
Elliman ˈel.ɪ.mən
Ellingham *in Northumberland:* ˈel.ɪn.dʒəm *surname:* ˈel.ɪŋ.əm
Ellington ˈel.ɪŋ.tən
Elliot ˈel.i.ət
Elliotson ˈel.i.ət.sən
Elliott ˈel.i.ət
ellipse ɪˈlɪps **-s** -ɪz
ellips|is ɪˈlɪp.s|ɪs **-es** -iːz
ellipsoid ɪˈlɪp.sɔɪd **-s** -z
ellipsoidal ˌel.ɪpˈsɔɪ.dəl; ɪˌlɪpˈ-; elˌɪp- (US) ɪˌlɪpˈ-; ˌel.ɪpˈ-
elliptic ɪˈlɪp.tɪk **-al** -əl **-ally** -əl.i, -li
ellipticity ˌel.ɪpˈtɪs.ə.ti, ˌɪl-, -ɪ.ti (US) ɪˌlɪpˈtɪs.ə.t̬i; ˌel.ɪpˈ-
Ellis ˈel.ɪs
Ellison ˈel.ɪ.sən
Elliston ˈel.ɪ.stən
Ellon ˈel.ən
Ellsworth ˈelz.wəθ, -wɜːθ (US) -wɚθ, -wɝːθ
Ellwood ˈel.wʊd
elm (E) elm **-s** -z
Elmer ˈel.məʳ (US) -mɚ
Elmer Gantry ˌel.məˈgæn.tri (US) -mɚˈ-
Elmes elmz
Elmhurst ˈelm.hɜːst (US) -hɝːst
Elmina elˈmiː.nə
Elmo ˈel.məʊ (US) -moʊ
Elmore ˈel.mɔːʳ (US) -mɔːr
Elmsley ˈelmz.li
Elmwood ˈelm.wʊd

elocution ˌel.əˈkjuː.ʃᵊn
elocutionary ˌel.əˈkjuː.ʃᵊn.ᵊr.i, -ri (US) -er.i
elocutionist ˌel.əˈkjuː.ʃᵊn.ɪst **-s** -s
Elohim elˈəʊ.hɪm, ɪˈləʊ-, ə-, -hiːm; ˌel.əʊˈhiːm (US) elˈoʊ.hɪm, ɪˈloʊ-, ə-, -hiːm, ˌel.oʊˈhɪm, -ˈoʊ-
Eloi ɪˈləʊ.aɪ; ˈiː.ləʊ.aɪ, -lɔɪ (US) ˈiː.lɔɪ, ˈeɪ-
Eloisa ˌel.əʊˈiː.zə, -sə (US) -oʊˈ-
Éloise, Eloise ˌel.əʊˈiːz (US) -oʊˈ-
elon|gate ˈiː.lɒŋ|.geɪt (US) ɪˈlɑːŋ-, -ˈlɔːŋ- **-gates** -geɪts **-gating** -geɪ.tɪŋ (US) -geɪ.t̬ɪŋ **-gated** -geɪ.tɪd (US) -geɪ.t̬ɪd
elongation ˌiː.lɒŋˈgeɪ.ʃᵊn (US) ˌiː.lɑːŋˈ-, -lɔːŋˈ-; ɪˌlɑːŋˈ-, -ˌlɔːŋˈ- **-s** -z
elop|e ɪˈləʊp (US) -ˈloʊp **-es** -s **-ing** -ɪŋ **-ed** -t **-ement/s** -mənt/s
eloquence ˈel.ə.kwənts
eloquent ˈel.ə.kwənt **-ly** -li
El Paso ˌelˈpæs.əʊ (US) -oʊ
Elphick ˈel.fɪk
Elphin ˈel.fɪn
Elphinstone ˈel.fɪn.stən
Els els
Elsa *English name:* ˈel.sə *German name:* ˈel.zə
El Salvador ˌelˈsæl.və.dɔːʳ (US) -dɔːr
Elsan® ˈel.sæn
else els **-'s** -ɪz
elsewhere ˌelsˈ*h*weəʳ, ˈ-- (US) ˈels.*h*wer
Elsie ˈel.si
Elsinore ˈel.sɪ.nɔːʳ, ˌ--ˈ- (US) ˈel.sə.nɔːr, ˌ--ˈ-
Note: The stressing /ˌ--ˈ-/ has to be used in Shakespeare's 'Hamlet'.
Elsmere ˈelz.mɪəʳ (US) -mɪr
Elson ˈel.sᵊn
Elspeth ˈel.spəθ, -speθ
Elstree ˈel.striː, ˈelz.triː, -tri
Elswick ˈel.sɪk, ˈel.zɪk, ˈelz.wɪk
Note: **Elswick** in Tyne and Wear is locally /ˈel.sɪk/ or /ˈel.zɪk/.
Elsworthy ˈelz.wɜː.ði (US) -wɝː-
ELT ˌiː.elˈtiː
Eltham ˈel.təm
Elton ˈel.tᵊn
eluci|date ɪˈluː.sɪ|.deɪt, əˈluː-, -ˈljuː-, -sə- (US) ɪˈluː.sɪ-, -sə- **-dates** -deɪts **-dating** -deɪ.tɪŋ (US) -deɪ.t̬ɪŋ **-dated** -deɪ.tɪd (US) -deɪ.t̬ɪd **-dator/s** -deɪ.təʳ/z (US) -deɪ.t̬ɚ/z
elucidation ɪˌluː.sɪˈdeɪ.ʃᵊn, əˌluː-, -ˌljuː-, -səˈ- (US) ɪˌluː.sɪˈdeɪ-, -səˈ- **-s** -z
elucidative ɪˈluː.sɪ.deɪ.tɪv, əˈluː-, -ˈljuː-, -sə-, -də- (US) ɪˈluː.sɪ.deɪ.t̬ɪv, -sə-
elucidatory ɪˈluː.sɪ.deɪ.tᵊr.i, əˈluː-, -ˈljuː-, -sə-, -tri; ɪˌluː.sɪˈdeɪ-, ə-, -ˌljuː-, -səˈ- (US) ɪˈluː.sɪ.deɪ.tɔːr.i, -sə-; ɪˌluː.sɪˈdeɪ.t̬ɚ-, -səˈ-
elud|e ɪˈluːd, əˈluːd, -ˈljuːd (US) ɪˈluːd **-es** -z **-ing** -ɪŋ **-ed** -ɪd
elusion ɪˈluː.ʒᵊn, əˈluː, -ˈljuː- (US) ɪˈluː- **-s** -z
elusive ɪˈluː.sɪv, əˈluː-, -ˈljuː- (US) ɪˈluː- **-ly** -li **-ness** -nəs, -nɪs
elusory ɪˈluː.sᵊr.i, əˈluː-, -ˈljuː- (US) ɪˈluː-
elvan ˈel.vən
Elvedon ˈelv.dən, ˈel.dən
elver ˈel.vəʳ (US) -vɚ **-s** -z
elves *(plur. of* **elf***)* elvz
Elvey ˈel.vi
Elvin ˈel.vɪn
Elvira elˈvɪə.rə, -ˈvaɪə- (US) -ˈvaɪ.rə, -ˈvɪr.ə
Elvis ˈel.vɪs
Elwell ˈel.wel, -wəl
Elwes ˈel.wɪz, -wɪs, -wez
Ely *cities:* ˈiː.li *first name in US:* ˈiː.laɪ
Elyot ˈel.i.ət
Elyse elˈiːz (US) ɪˈliːs
Elysée eɪˈliː.zeɪ, ɪ-, ə- (US) ˌeɪ.liːˈzeɪ
Elysi|an ɪˈlɪz.i|.ən, iː- (US) ɪˈlɪʒ|.ən **-um** -əm **Eˌlysian ˈfields**
elzevir (E) ˈel.zɪ.vɪəʳ, -sɪ-, -zə-, -sə- (US) -vɪr
em- em-, ɪm-
Note: Prefix. Either takes primary or secondary stress and is pronounced /em-/, e.g. **emblem** /ˈem.bləm/, **emblematic** /ˌem.bləˈmæt.ɪk (US) -ˈmæt̬-/, or is unstressed and may be pronounced either /ɪm-/ or /em-/, e.g. **embed** /ɪmˈbed, em- (US) em-, ɪm-/.
em em **-s** -z
'em *(weak form of* **them***)* əm, m
emaci|ate ɪˈmeɪ.ʃi|.eɪt, iː-, -si- **-ates** -eɪts **-ating** -eɪ.tɪŋ (US) -eɪ.t̬ɪŋ **-ated** -eɪ.tɪd (US) -eɪ.t̬ɪd
emaciation ɪˌmeɪ.ʃiˈeɪ.ʃᵊn, iː-, -siˈ-
e-mail, E-mail ˈiː.meɪl **-s** -z **-ing** -ɪŋ **-ed** -d
emalangeni *(plur. of* **lilangeni***)* ˈem.ə.lɑːŋˌgen.i (US) ˌem.ə.lənˈgen-
ema|nate ˈem.ə|.neɪt **-nates** -neɪts **-nating** -neɪ.tɪŋ (US) -neɪ.t̬ɪŋ **-nated** -neɪ.tɪd (US) -neɪ.t̬ɪd **-native** -neɪ.tɪv (US) -neɪ.t̬ɪv
emanation ˌem.əˈneɪ.ʃᵊn **-s** -z
emanci|pate ɪˈmænt.sɪ|.peɪt, -sə- **-pates** -peɪts **-pating** -peɪ.tɪŋ (US) -peɪ.t̬ɪŋ **-pated** -peɪ.tɪd (US) -peɪ.t̬ɪd **-pator/s** -peɪ.təʳ/z (US) -peɪ.t̬ɚ/z
emancipation ɪˌmænt.sɪˈpeɪ.ʃᵊn, -səˈ- **-s** -z
Emanuel ɪˈmæn.ju.əl, -el
emasculate *(adj.)* ɪˈmæs.kjʊ.lɪt, iː-, -kjə-, -lət
emascu|late *(v.)* ɪˈmæs.kjʊ|.leɪt, iː-, -kjə- **-lates** -leɪts **-lating** -leɪ.tɪŋ (US) -leɪ.t̬ɪŋ **-lated** -leɪ.tɪd (US) -leɪ.t̬ɪd **-lator/s** -leɪ.təʳ/z (US) -leɪ.t̬ɚ/z
emasculation ɪˌmæs.kjʊˈleɪ.ʃᵊn, iː-, -kjəˈ- **-s** -z
embalm ɪmˈbɑːm, em- (US) em-, ɪm- **-s** -z **-ing** -ɪŋ **-ed** -d **-er/s** -əʳ/z (US) -ɚ/z **-ment/s** -mənt/s
embank ɪmˈbæŋk, em- (US) em-, ɪm- **-s** -s **-ing** -ɪŋ **-ed** -t
embankment (E) ɪmˈbæŋk.mənt, em- (US) em-, ɪm- **-s** -s
embarcation ˌem.bɑːˈkeɪ.ʃᵊn (US) -bɑːrˈ- **-s** -z
embargo ɪmˈbɑː.gəʊ, em- (US) emˈbɑːr.goʊ, ɪm- **-es** -z **-ing** -ɪŋ **-ed** -d
embark ɪmˈbɑːk, em- (US) emˈbɑːrk, ɪm- **-s** -s **-ing** -ɪŋ **-ed** -t
embarkation ˌem.bɑːˈkeɪ.ʃᵊn (US) -bɑːrˈ- **-s** -z
embarras de richesses ˌɑː*m*.bærˌɑː.də.riːˈʃes, ɑ̃ː*m*- (US) ˌɑːm.bɑː.rɑː-
embarrass ɪmˈbær.əs, em- (US) emˈber-, ɪm-, -ˈbær- **-es** -ɪz **-ing/ly** -ɪŋ/li **-ed** -t
embarrassment ɪmˈbær.əs.mənt, em- (US) emˈber-, ɪm-, -ˈbær- **-s** -s
embass|y ˈem.bə.s|i **-ies** -iz
embattl|e ɪmˈbæt.l̩, em- (US) emˈbæt̬-, ɪm- **-es** -z **-ing** -ɪŋ, -ˈbæt.lɪŋ **-ed** -d
embay ɪmˈbeɪ, em- (US) em-, ɪm- **-s** -z **-ing** -ɪŋ **-ed** -d
embed ɪmˈbed, em- (US) em-, ɪm- **-s** -z **-ding** -ɪŋ **-ded** -ɪd **-ment** -mənt
embellish ɪmˈbel.ɪʃ, em- (US) em-, ɪm- **-es** -ɪz **-ing** -ɪŋ **-ed** -t **-er/s** -əʳ/z (US) -ɚ/z
embellishment ɪmˈbel.ɪʃ.mənt, em- (US) em-, ɪm- **-s** -s
ember (E) ˈem.bəʳ (US) -bɚ **-s** -z **ˈEmber ˌday**
embezzl|e ɪmˈbez.l̩, em- (US) em-, ɪm- **-es** -z **-ing** -ɪŋ, -ˈ-lɪŋ **-ed** -d **-er/s** -əʳ/z, ˈ-ləʳ/z (US) -ɚ/z, ˈ-lɚ/z
embezzlement ɪmˈbez.l̩.mənt, em- (US) em-, ɪm-
embitt|er ɪmˈbɪt|.əʳ, em- (US) emˈbɪt̬|.ɚ, ɪm- **-ers** -əz (US) -ɚz **-ering** -ᵊr.ɪŋ **-ered** -əd (US) -ɚd **-erment** -ə.mənt (US) -ɚ.mənt
emblazon ɪmˈbleɪ.zᵊn, em- (US) em-, ɪm- **-s** -z **-ing** -ɪŋ **-ed** -d **-ment/s** -mənt/s **-ry** -ri
emblem ˈem.bləm, -blem, -blɪm (US) -bləm **-s** -z
emblematic ˌem.bləˈmæt.ɪk, -blɪˈ- (US) -bləˈmæt̬- **-al** -ᵊl **-ally** -ᵊl.i, -li
emblematiz|e, -is|e emˈblem.ə.taɪz, ˈ-ɪ-; ˈem.blem.ə- (US) emˈblem.ə- **-es** -ɪz **-ing** -ɪŋ **-ed** -d
emblements ˈem.blə.mənts, -bl̩- (US) -blə-

embodiment ɪmˈbɒd.ɪ.mənt, em- ⓤⓢ emˈbɑː.di-, ɪm- **-s** -s
embod|y ɪmˈbɒd|.i, em- ⓤⓢ emˈbɑː.d|i, ɪm- **-ies** -iz **-ying** -i.ɪŋ **-ied** -id
embolden ɪmˈbəʊl.dᵊn, em- ⓤⓢ emˈboʊl-, ɪm- **-s** -z **-ing** -ɪŋ **-ed** -d
embolism ˈem.bə.lɪ.zᵊm **-s** -z
embonpoint ˌɑ̃ːm.bɔ̃ːmˈpwɑ̃ːŋ ⓤⓢ ˌɑ̃ːm.bɔ̃ʊnˈpwæ̃n, -ˈpwɑ̃ːn
embosom ɪmˈbʊz.ᵊm, em- ⓤⓢ em-, ɪm- **-s** -z **-ing** -ɪŋ **-ed** -d
emboss ɪmˈbɒs, em- ⓤⓢ emˈbɑːs, ɪm- **-es** -ɪz **-ing** -ɪŋ **-ed** -t **-er/s** -əʳ/z ⓤⓢ -ɚ/z **-ment/s** -mənt/s
embouchure ˌɑ̃ːm.buːˈʃʊəʳ, ˈ--- ⓤⓢ ˌɑːm.buːˈʃʊr, ˈ--- **-s** -z
embowel ɪmˈbaʊəl, em- ⓤⓢ emˈbaʊᵊl, ɪm- **-s** -z **-(l)ing** -ɪŋ **-(l)ed** -d
embower ɪmˈbaʊəʳ, em- ⓤⓢ emˈbaʊɚ, ɪm- **-s** -z **-ing** -ɪŋ **-ed** -d
embrac|e ɪmˈbreɪs, em- ⓤⓢ em-, ɪm- **-es** -ɪz **-ing** -ɪŋ **-ed** -t
embracery ɪmˈbreɪ.sᵊr.i, em- ⓤⓢ em-, ɪm-
embranchment ɪmˈbrɑːntʃ.mənt, em- ⓤⓢ emˈbræntʃ-, ɪm- **-s** -s
embrasure ɪmˈbreɪ.ʒəʳ, em-, -ʒʊəʳ ⓤⓢ emˈbreɪ.ʒɚ, ɪm- **-s** -z
embro|cate ˈem.brəʊ|.keɪt ⓤⓢ -broʊ-, -brə- **-cates** -keɪts **-cating** -keɪ.tɪŋ ⓤⓢ -keɪ.t̬ɪŋ **-cated** -keɪ.tɪd ⓤⓢ -keɪ.t̬ɪd
embrocation ˌem.brəʊˈkeɪ.ʃᵊn ⓤⓢ -broʊˈ-, -brəˈ- **-s** -z
embroglio ɪmˈbrəʊ.li.əʊ, em- ⓤⓢ emˈbroʊ.ljoʊ, ɪm- **-s** -z
embroid|er ɪmˈbrɔɪ.d|əʳ, em- ⓤⓢ emˈbrɔɪ.d|ɚ, ɪm- **-ers** -əz ⓤⓢ -ɚz **-ering** -ᵊr.ɪŋ **-ered** -əd ⓤⓢ -ɚd **-erer/s** -ᵊr.əʳ/z ⓤⓢ -ɚ.ɚ/z
embroider|y ɪmˈbrɔɪ.dᵊr|.i, em- ⓤⓢ em-, ɪm- **-ies** -iz
embroil ɪmˈbrɔɪl, em- ⓤⓢ em-, ɪm- **-s** -z **-ing** -ɪŋ **-ed** -d **-ment/s** -mənt/s
embryo ˈem.bri.əʊ ⓤⓢ -oʊ **-s** -z
embryolog|y ˌem.briˈɒl.ə.dʒ|i ⓤⓢ -ˈɑː.lə- **-ist/s** -ɪst/s
embryonic ˌem.briˈɒn.ɪk ⓤⓢ -ˈɑː.nɪk
Embury, Emburey ˈem.bᵊr.i, -bjʊ.ri, -bjə.ri ⓤⓢ -bɚ.i
emcee ˌemˈsiː **-s** -z **-ing** -ɪŋ **-d** -d
-eme -iːm
Note: Suffix. Unstressed, e.g. **lexeme** /ˈlek.siːm/.
Emeline ˈem.ɪ.liːn, ˈ-ə- ⓤⓢ -ə.laɪn, -liːn
emend ɪˈmend, iː- **-s** -z **-ing** -ɪŋ **-ed** -ɪd **-able** -ə.bl̩
emen|date ˈiː.men|.deɪt, ˈem.en- ⓤⓢ ˈiː.men-, -mən-; ɪˈmen- **-dates** -deɪts **-dating** -deɪ.tɪŋ ⓤⓢ -deɪ.t̬ɪŋ **-dated** -deɪ.tɪd ⓤⓢ -deɪ.t̬ɪd **-dator/s** -deɪ.təʳ/z ⓤⓢ -deɪ.t̬ɚ/z
emendation ˌiː.menˈdeɪ.ʃᵊn, ˌem.enˈ-, -ənˈ- **-s** -z
emendatory ɪˈmen.də.tᵊr.i, iː-, -tri ⓤⓢ -tɔːr.i
emerald ˈem.ᵊr.ᵊld, ˈ-rᵊld **-s** -z ˈ**Emerald** ˌ**Isle**
emerg|e ɪˈmɜːdʒ, iː- ⓤⓢ -ˈmɝːdʒ **-es** -ɪz **-ing** -ɪŋ **-ed** -d
emergen|ce ɪˈmɜː.dʒᵊn|ts, iː- ⓤⓢ -ˈmɝː- **-t** -t
emergenc|y ɪˈmɜː.dʒᵊnt.s|i, iː- ⓤⓢ -ˈmɝː- **-ies** -iz **eˈmergency** ˌ**room**
emeritus ɪˈmer.ɪ.təs, iː-, -ə.təs ⓤⓢ -ə.t̬əs
emersion ɪˈmɜː.ʃᵊn, iː-, -ʒᵊn ⓤⓢ -ˈmɝː.ʒᵊn, -ʃᵊn **-s** -z
Emerson ˈem.ə.sᵊn ⓤⓢ ˈ-ɚ-
emery (E) ˈem.ᵊr.i ˈ**emery** ˌ**board**; ˈ**emery** ˌ**paper**
emetic ɪˈmet.ɪk, iː- ⓤⓢ -ˈmet̬- **-s** -s **-al** -ᵊl **-ally** -ᵊl.i, -li
émeute eɪˈmɜːt **-s** -s
EMF ˌiː.emˈef
EMI® ˌiː.emˈaɪ
emigrant ˈem.ɪ.grənt ⓤⓢ ˈ-ɪ-, ˈ-ə- **-s** -s
emi|grate ˈem.ɪ|.greɪt ⓤⓢ ˈ-ɪ-, ˈ-ə- **-grates** -greɪts **-grating** -greɪ.tɪŋ ⓤⓢ -greɪ.t̬ɪŋ **-grated** -greɪ.tɪd ⓤⓢ -greɪ.t̬ɪd **-grator/s** -greɪ.təʳ/z ⓤⓢ -greɪ.t̬ɚ/z
emigration ˌem.ɪˈgreɪ.ʃᵊn ⓤⓢ -ɪˈ-, -əˈ- **-s** -z
emigratory ˈem.ɪ.grə.tᵊr.i, -greɪ-, -tri; ˌem.ɪˈgreɪ- ⓤⓢ ˈem.ɪ.grə.tɔːr.i, ˈ-ə-
émigré ˈem.ɪ.greɪ **-s** -z
Emil emˈiːl, eɪˈmiːl ⓤⓢ ˈiː.məl, ˈeɪ-
Emile, Émile emˈiːl, eɪˈmiːl ⓤⓢ ˈiː.məl; eɪˈmiːl
Emilia ɪˈmɪl.i.ə, -ˈjə, emˈiː.li.ə ⓤⓢ ɪˈmɪl.jə, emˈiː.ljə
Emily ˈem.ɪ.li, ˈ-ə-
Emin ˈem.ɪn
Eminem ˌem.ɪˈnem
eminen|ce ˈem.ɪ.nənt|s, ˈ-ə- **-ces** -sɪz **-cy** -si
éminence grise ˌem.ɪ.nənt*s*ˈgriːz *as if French:* ˌeɪ.mɪˌnɑ̃ːntsˈgriːz ⓤⓢ ˌeɪ.miː.nɑːntsˈ-
eminent ˈem.ɪ.nənt, ˈ-ə- **-ly** -li
emir (E) emˈɪəʳ, ɪˈmɪr, ə-, eɪ-; ˈem.ɪəʳ ⓤⓢ emˈɪr, əˈmɪr; ˌeɪˈmɪr **-s** -z
emirate ˈem.ɪ.rət, -ᵊr.ət, -ɪt, -eɪt; emˈɪə.rət, ɪˈmɪə-, ə-, eɪ-, -rɪt, -reɪt ⓤⓢ emˈɪr.eɪt, əˈmɪr-, -ət **-s** -s
emissar|y ˈem.ɪ.sᵊr|.i ⓤⓢ -ser- **-ies** -iz
emission ɪˈmɪʃ.ᵊn, iː- **-s** -z
emissive ɪˈmɪs.ɪv, iː-
e|mit ɪ|ˈmɪt, iː- **-mits** -ˈmɪts **-mitting** -ˈmɪt.ɪŋ ⓤⓢ -ˈmɪt̬- **-mitted** -ˈmɪt.ɪd ⓤⓢ -ˈmɪt̬- **-mitter/s** -ˈmɪt.əʳ/z ⓤⓢ -ˈmɪt̬.ɚ/z
Emley ˈem.li
Emlyn ˈem.lɪn
Emma ˈem.ə
Emmanuel ɪˈmæn.ju.əl, -el
Emmanuelle ɪˌmæn.juˈel, emˌæn-
Emmaus emˈeɪ.əs, ɪˈmeɪ-
Emmeline ˈem.ɪ.liːn, ˈ-ə- ⓤⓢ -ə.laɪn, -liːn
Emmental, Emmenthal ˈem.ən.tɑːl
Emmerdale ˈem.ə.deɪl ⓤⓢ ˈ-ɚ-
emmet (E) ˈem.ɪt **-s** -s
Emmie ˈem.i
Emmy ˈem.i **-s** -z ˈ**Emmy A**ˌ**ward**
emollient ɪˈmɒl.i.ənt, iː- ⓤⓢ -ˈmɑːl.jənt **-s** -s
emolument ɪˈmɒl.jʊ.mənt, -jə- ⓤⓢ -ˈmɑːl- **-s** -s
Emory ˈem.ᵊr.i
e|mote ɪ|ˈməʊt, iː- ⓤⓢ -ˈmoʊt **-motes** -ˈməʊts ⓤⓢ -ˈmoʊts **-moting** -ˈməʊ.tɪŋ ⓤⓢ -ˈmoʊ.t̬ɪŋ **-moted** -ˈməʊ.tɪd ⓤⓢ -ˈmoʊ.t̬ɪd
emoticon ɪˈməʊ.tɪ.kɒn ⓤⓢ -ˈmoʊ.t̬ɪ.kɑːn **-s** -z
emotion ɪˈməʊ.ʃᵊn ⓤⓢ -ˈmoʊ- **-s** -z **-less** -ləs, -lɪs
emotional ɪˈməʊ.ʃᵊn.ᵊl ⓤⓢ -ˈmoʊ- **-ly** -i
emotionalism ɪˈməʊ.ʃᵊn.ᵊl.ɪ.zᵊm ⓤⓢ -ˈmoʊ-
emotionaliz|e, -is|e ɪˈməʊ.ʃᵊn.ᵊl.aɪz ⓤⓢ -ˈmoʊ.ʃᵊn.ə.laɪz **-es** -ɪz **-ing** -ɪŋ **-ed** -d
emotive ɪˈməʊ.tɪv ⓤⓢ -ˈmoʊ.t̬ɪv **-ly** -li
empanel ɪmˈpæn.ᵊl, em- ⓤⓢ em-, ɪm- **-s** -z **-(l)ing** -ɪŋ **-(l)ed** -d **-ment/s** -mənt/s
empathetic ˌem.pəˈθet.ɪk ⓤⓢ -ˈθet̬-
empathic emˈpæθ.ɪk, ɪm-
empathiz|e, -is|e ˈem.pə.θaɪz **-es** -ɪz **-ing** -ɪŋ **-ed** -d
empathy ˈem.pə.θi
Empedocles emˈped.ə.kliːz, ɪm-
emperor (E) ˈem.pᵊr.əʳ ⓤⓢ -ɚ.ɚ **-s** -z
emphas|is ˈem*p*.fə.s|ɪs **-es** -iːz
emphasiz|e, -is|e ˈem*p*.fə.saɪz **-es** -ɪz **-ing** -ɪŋ **-ed** -d
emphatic ɪmˈfæt.ɪk, em- ⓤⓢ emˈfæt̬-, ɪm- **-al** -ᵊl **-ally** -ᵊl.i, -li
emphysema ˌem*p*.fɪˈsiː.mə ⓤⓢ -fəˈsiː-, -ˈziː- **-s** -z
empire (E) ˈem.paɪəʳ ⓤⓢ -paɪɚ **-s** -z ˌ**Empire** ˈ**State** ˌ**Building**
empiric ɪmˈpɪr.ɪk, em- ⓤⓢ em-, ɪm- **-s** -s **-al** -ᵊl **-ally** -ᵊl.i, -li
empiric|ism ɪmˈpɪr.ɪ.s|ɪ.zᵊm, em-, ˈ-ə- ⓤⓢ em-, ɪm- **-ist/s** -ɪst/s
emplacement ɪmˈpleɪs.mənt, em- ⓤⓢ em-, ɪm- **-s** -s
employ ɪmˈplɔɪ, em- ⓤⓢ em-, ɪm- **-s** -z **-ing** -ɪŋ **-ed** -d **-able** -ə.bl̩
employé ɑ̃ːmˈplɔɪ.eɪ, ɔ̃ːm- **-s** -z
employee ɪmˈplɔɪ.iː, em-, əm-; ˌem.plɔɪˈiː ⓤⓢ emˈplɔɪ.iː, ɪm-; ˌem.plɔɪˈiː **-s** -z

employer ɪmˈplɔɪ.əʳ, em- US emˈplɔɪ.ɚ, ɪm- **-s** -z

employment ɪmˈplɔɪ.mənt, em- US em-, ɪm- **-s** -s **emˈployment ˌagency**

empori|um emˈpɔː.ri|.əm, ɪm- US -ˈpɔːr.i- **-ums** -əmz **-a** -ə

empower ɪmˈpaʊəʳ, em- US emˈpaʊɚ, ɪm- **-s** -z **-ing** -ɪŋ **-ed** -d

empowerment ɪmˈpaʊə.mənt, em- US emˈpaʊɚ-, ɪm-

empress (E) ˈem.prəs, -prɪs, -pres **-es** -ɪz

Empson ˈemp.sᵊn

emption ˈemp.ʃᵊn

empt|y ˈemp.t|i **-ier** -i.əʳ US -i.ɚ **-iest** -i.ɪst, -i.əst **-ily** -ɪ.li, -ᵊl.i **-iness** -ɪ.nəs, -ɪ.nɪs **-ies** -iz **-ying** -i.ɪŋ **-ied** -id

empty-handed ˌemp.tiˈhæn.dɪd *stress shift:* ˌempty-handed ˈbeggar

empty-headed ˌemp.tiˈhed.ɪd **-ness** -nəs, -nɪs *stress shift:* ˌempty-headed ˈnonsense

empyema ˌem.paɪˈiː.mə US -paɪˈ-, -piˈ-

empyre|al ˌem.paɪəˈriː|.əl, -pɪˈ- US emˈpɪr.i-, -ˈpaɪ.ri-; ˌem.paɪˈriː-, -pəˈ- **-an** -ən

EMS ˌiː.emˈes

Emsworth ˈemz.wəθ, -wɜːθ US -wɚθ, -wɝːθ

emu ˈiː.mjuː US -mjuː, -muː **-s** -z

EMU ˌiː.emˈjuː, ˈiː.mjuː

emu|late ˈem.jə|.leɪt, -jʊ- **-lates** -leɪts **-lating** -leɪ.tɪŋ US -leɪ.t̬ɪŋ **-lated** -leɪ.tɪd US -leɪ.t̬ɪd **-lator/s** -leɪ.təʳ/z US -leɪ.t̬ɚ/z

emulation ˌem.jəˈleɪ.ʃᵊn, -jʊˈ-

emulative ˈem.jə.lə.tɪv, -jʊ-, -leɪ- US -leɪ.t̬ɪv

emulous ˈem.jə.ləs, -jʊ- **-ly** -li

emulsifier ɪˈmʌl.sɪ.faɪ.əʳ, -sə- US -ɚ **-s** -z

emulsi|fy ɪˈmʌl.sɪ|.faɪ, -sə- **-fies** -faɪz **-fying** -faɪ.ɪŋ **-fied** -faɪd

emulsion ɪˈmʌl.ʃᵊn **-s** -z

emunctor|y ɪˈmʌŋ*k*.tᵊr|.i **-ies** -iz

en *in French phrases:* ɑ̃ːŋ, ɒn, ɑːn

en- ɪn-, en-, ən-

Note: Prefix. Either takes primary or secondary stress and is pronounced /en-/, e.g. **energy** /ˈen.ə.dʒi US ˈ-ɚ-/, **energetic** /ˌen.əˈdʒet.ɪk US -ɚˈdʒet̬.ɪk/, or is unstressed and may be pronounced either /ɪn-/ or /en-/, e.g. **endear** /ɪnˈdɪəʳ, en- US -ˈdɪr/. NB When followed by a /k/ or /g/, assimilation may take place, e.g. **encage** may also be /ɪŋˈkeɪdʒ, eŋ-/.

enabl|e ɪˈneɪ.bl̩, enˈeɪ- **-es** -z **-ing** -ɪŋ, ˈ-blɪŋ **-ed** -d

enabler ɪˈneɪ.bləʳ, enˈeɪ-, -bl̩.əʳ US ˈ-blɚ, ˈ-bl̩.ɚ **-s** -z

enact ɪˈnækt, enˈækt **-s** -s **-ing** -ɪŋ **-ed** -ɪd **-or/s** -əʳ/z US -ɚ/z **-ment/s** -mənt/s **-ive** -ɪv

enaction ɪˈnæk.ʃᵊn, enˈæk- **-s** -z

enamel ɪˈnæm.ᵊl **-s** -z **-(l)ing** -ɪŋ **-(l)ed** -d **-(l)er/s** -əʳ/z US -ɚ/z **-(l)ist/s** -ɪst/s

enamelware ɪˈnæm.ᵊl.weəʳ US -wer

enamo(u)r ɪˈnæm.əʳ, enˈæm- US -ɚ **-s** -z **-ing** -ɪŋ **-ed** -d

en banc ɑ̃ːmˈbɑ̃ːŋk US ɑ̃ːnˈbɑ̃ːŋ

en bloc ˌɑ̃ːmˈblɒk US ɑ̃ːnˈblɑːk, en-

Encaenia enˈsiː.ni.ə

encag|e ɪnˈkeɪdʒ, ɪŋ-, en-, eŋ- US en-, ɪn- **-es** -ɪz **-ing** -ɪŋ **-ed** -d

encamp ɪnˈkæmp, ɪŋ-, en-, eŋ- US en-, ɪn- **-s** -s **-ing** -ɪŋ **-ed** -t, -kæmt **-ment/s** -mənt/s

encapsu|late ɪnˈkæp.sjə|.leɪt, ɪŋ-, en-, eŋ-, -sjʊ- US en-, ɪn- **-lates** -leɪts **-lating** -leɪ.tɪŋ US -leɪ.t̬ɪŋ **-lated** -leɪ.tɪd US -leɪ.t̬ɪd

encapsulation ɪnˌkæp.sjəˈleɪ.ʃᵊn, ɪŋ-, en-, eŋ-, -sjʊˈ- US en-, ɪn-

Encarta® enˈkɑː.tə, eŋ-, ɪn-, ɪŋ- US -ˈkɑːr.t̬ə

encas|e ɪnˈkeɪs, ɪŋ-, en-, eŋ- US en-, ɪn- **-es** -ɪz **-ing** -ɪŋ **-ed** -t **-ement/s** -mənt/s

encaustic ɪnˈkɔː.stɪk, ɪŋ-, en-, eŋ-, enˈkɒs.tɪk US enˈkɑː.stɪk, -ˈkɔː-, ɪn- **-s** -s **-ally** -ᵊl.i, -li

-ence -ᵊn*t*s

Note: Suffix. Normally, **-ence** does not affect the stress pattern of the word it is attached to, e.g. **depend** /dɪˈpend/, **dependence** /dɪˈpen.dən*t*s/. In other cases, the stress may be on the penultimate or antepenultimate syllable, e.g. **excellence**/ˈek.sᵊl.ᵊn*t*s/. See individual entries.

enceinte ˌɑ̃ːnˈsæ̃nt US ˌɑ̃ːn-; enˈseɪnt **-s** -s

Enceladus enˈsel.ə.dəs

encephalic ˌen.kəˈfæl.ɪk, ˌeŋ-, ˌɪn-, ˌɪŋ-, -kɪˈ-; ˌen.səˈ-, ˌɪn-, -sefˈæl-, -sɪˈfæl- US ˌen.səˈfæl.ɪk, -sɪˈ-

encephalitis ˌen.kef.əˈlaɪ.tɪs, ˌeŋ-, ˌɪn-, ˌɪŋ-, -kɪ.fəˈ-; ˌen.sə-, ˌɪn-, -sef.əˈ-; enˌkef-, eŋ-, ɪn-, ɪŋ-; enˌsef-, ɪn- US enˌsef.əˈlaɪ.t̬ɪs

encephalogram enˈkef.ə.lə.græm, eŋ-, ɪn-, ɪŋ-; enˈsef-, ɪn- US enˈsef.ə.loʊ- **-s** -z

encephalograph enˈkef.ə.lə.grɑːf, eŋ-, ɪn-, ɪŋ; enˈsef-, ɪn-, -græf US enˈsef.ə.loʊ.græf **-s** -s

encephalomyelitis enˌkef.ə.ləʊ.maɪəˈlaɪ.tɪs, eŋ-, ɪn-, ɪŋ-; enˌsef-, ɪnˌsef-; ˌen.kef-, ˌeŋ-, ˌɪn-, ˌɪŋ-; ˌen.sef-, ˌɪn.sef- US enˌsef.ə.loʊ.maɪəˈlaɪ.t̬ɪs

encephalopathic enˌkef.ə.ləʊˈpæθ.ɪk, eŋ-, ɪn-, ɪŋ-, enˌsef-, ɪnˌsef- US enˌsef.ə.loʊˈ-

encephalopathy enˌkef.əˈlɒp.ə.θi, eŋ-, ɪn-, ɪŋ-; enˌsef-, ɪnˌsef-; ˌen.kef-, ˌeŋ-, ˌɪn-, ˌɪŋ-; ˌen.sef-, ˌɪn.sef- US enˌsef.əˈlɑː.pə-

enchain ɪnˈtʃeɪn, en- US en-, ɪn- **-s** -z **-ing** -ɪŋ **-ed** -d **-ment** -mənt

enchan|t ɪnˈtʃɑːn|t, en- US enˈtʃæn|t, ɪn- **-ts** -ts **-ting/ly** -tɪŋ/li US -t̬ɪŋ/li **-ted** -tɪd US -t̬ɪd **-ter/s** -təʳ/z US -t̬ɚ/z **-tress/es** -trɪs/ɪz **-tment/s** -t.mənt/s

enchilada ˌen.tʃɪˈlɑː.də **-s** -z

enchiridion ˌen.kaɪˈrɪd.i.ən, ˌeŋ-, -kɪˈ-, -ɒn US ˌen.kaɪˈrɪd.i.ən, -kɪˈ- **-s** -z

enciph|er ɪnˈsaɪ.f|əʳ, en- US enˈsaɪ.f|ɚ, ɪn- **-ers** -əz US -ɚz **-ering** -ᵊr.ɪŋ **-ered** -əd US -ɚd

encircl|e ɪnˈsɜː.kl̩, en- US enˈsɝː-, ɪn- **-es** -z **-ing** -ɪŋ, ˈ-klɪŋ **-ed** -d **-ement/s** -mənt/s

Encke ˈeŋ.kə

enclasp ɪnˈklɑːsp, ɪŋ-, en-, eŋ- US enˈklæsp, ɪn- **-s** -s **-ing** -ɪŋ **-ed** -t

enclave ˈen.kleɪv, ˈeŋ- US ˈen-, ˈɑːn- **-s** -z

enclitic ɪnˈklɪt.ɪk, ɪŋ-, en-, eŋ- US enˈklɪt̬-, ɪn- **-s** -s **-ally** -ᵊl.i, -li

enclos|e ɪnˈkləʊz, ɪŋ-, en-, eŋ- US enˈkloʊz, ɪn- **-es** -ɪz **-ing** -ɪŋ **-ed** -d

enclosure ɪnˈkləʊ.ʒəʳ, ɪŋ-, en-, eŋ- US enˈkloʊ.ʒɚ, ɪn- **-s** -z

encod|e ɪnˈkəʊd, en-, eŋ-, ɪŋ- US enˈkoʊd, ɪn- **-es** -z **-ing** -ɪŋ **-ed** -ɪd **-er/s** -əʳ/z US -ɚ/z

encomi|ast ɪnˈkəʊ.mi|.æst, ɪŋ-, en-, eŋ- US enˈkoʊ-, ɪn- **-asts** -æsts **-um/s** -əm/z **-a** -ə

encompass ɪnˈkʌm.pəs, ɪŋ-, en-, eŋ- US en-, ɪn- **-es** -ɪz **-ing** -ɪŋ **-ed** -t

encore ˈɒŋ.kɔːʳ, ˈɑ̃ːŋ-, -ˈ- US ˈɑːn.kɔːr, -ˈ- **-es** -z **-ing** -ɪŋ **-ed** -d

encoun|ter ɪnˈkaʊn|.təʳ, ɪŋ-, en-, eŋ- US enˈkaʊn|.t̬ɚ, ɪn- **-ters** -təz US -t̬ɚz **-tering** -tᵊr.ɪŋ US -t̬ɚ.ɪŋ **-tered** -təd US -t̬ɚd

encourag|e ɪnˈkʌr.ɪdʒ, ɪŋ-, en-, eŋ- US en.kɝː-, ɪn- **-es** -ɪz **-ing/ly** -ɪŋ/li **-ed** -d

encouragement ɪnˈkʌr.ɪdʒ.mənt, ɪŋ-, en-, eŋ- US en.kɝː-, ɪn- **-s** -s

encroach ɪnˈkrəʊtʃ, ɪŋ-, en-, eŋ- US enˈkroʊtʃ, ɪn- **-es** -ɪz **-ing** -ɪŋ **-ed** -t **-ment/s** -mənt/s

en croûte ˌɑ̃ːŋˈkruːt US ˌɑːnˈkruːt

encrust ɪnˈkrʌst, ɪŋ-, en-, eŋ- US en-, ɪn- **-s** -s **-ing** -ɪŋ **-ed** -ɪd

encrustation ˌen.krʌsˈteɪ.ʃᵊn, ˌeŋ- US ˌen- **-s** -z

encrypt ɪnˈkrɪpt, ɪŋ-, en-, eŋ- (US) en-, ɪn- **-s** -s **-ing** -ɪŋ **-ed** -ɪd
encryption ɪnˈkrɪp.ʃᵊn, ɪŋ-, en-, eŋ- (US) en-, ɪn-
encumb|er ɪnˈkʌm.b|əʳ, ɪŋ-, en-, eŋ- (US) enˈkʌm.b|ɚ, ɪn- **-ers** -əz (US) -ɚz **-ering** -ᵊr.ɪŋ **-ered** -əd (US) -ɚd
encumbranc|e ɪnˈkʌm.brənts, ɪŋ-, en-, eŋ- (US) en-, ɪn- **-es** -ɪz
-ency -ᵊnt.si
Note: Suffix. Words containing **-ency** are stressed in a similar way to those containing **-ence**; see above.
encyclic ɪnˈsɪk.lɪk, en-, -ˈsaɪ.klɪk (US) en-, ɪn- **-s** -s **-al/s** -ᵊl/z
encyclop(a)edia ɪnˌsaɪ.kləˈpiː.di.ə, enˌsaɪ-, ˌɪn.saɪ-, ˌen- (US) enˌsaɪ-, ɪn-, ˌen.saɪ-, ˌɪn- **-s** -z
encyclop(a)edic ɪnˌsaɪ.kləˈpiː.dɪk, enˌsaɪ-, ˌɪn.saɪ-, ˌen- (US) enˌsaɪ-, ɪn-, ˌen.saɪ-, ˌɪn- **-ally** -ᵊl.i, -li
encyclop(a)ed|ism ɪnˌsaɪ.kləˈpiː.d|ɪ.zᵊm, enˌsaɪ-, ˌɪn.saɪ-, ˌen- (US) enˌsaɪ-, ɪn-, ˌen.saɪ-, ˌɪn- **-ist/s** -ɪst/s
end end **-s** -z **-ing** -ɪŋ **-ed** -ɪd **ˌend ˈproduct; ˈend ˌuser; be at a ˌloose ˈend; be at ˌloose ˈends; ˌmake ends ˈmeet** (US) **ˌmake ˈends ˌmeet; go off the ˈdeep ˌend; ˌthrown in at the ˈdeep ˌend; at the ˌend of the ˈday**
endang|er ɪnˈdeɪn.dʒ|əʳ, en- (US) enˈdeɪn.dʒ|ɚ, ɪn- **-ers** -əz (US) -ɚz **-ering** -ᵊr.ɪŋ **-ered** -əd (US) -ɚd **-erment** -ə.mənt (US) -ɚ.mənt
endear ɪnˈdɪəʳ, en- (US) enˈdɪr, ɪn- **-s** -z **-ing/ly** -ɪŋ/li **-ed** -d **-ment** -mənt
endeav|o(u)r ɪnˈdev|.əʳ, en- (US) enˈdev|.ɚ, ɪn- **-o(u)rs** -əz (US) -ɚz **-o(u)ring** -ᵊr.ɪŋ **-o(u)red** -əd (US) -ɚd
Endell ˈen.dᵊl
endemic enˈdem.ɪk **-s** -s **-al** -ᵊl **-ally** -ᵊl.i, -li
Enderby ˈen.də.bi (US) -dɚ-
endermic enˈdɜː.mɪk (US) -ˈdɝː- **-al** -ᵊl **-ally** -ᵊl.i, -li
endgame ˈend.geɪm, ˈeŋ- (US) ˈend- **-s** -z
Endicott ˈen.dɪ.kət, -də-, -kɒt (US) -kɑːt, -kət
ending ˈen.dɪŋ **-s** -z
endive ˈen.daɪv, -dɪv (US) ˈen.daɪv, ˈɑːn.diːv **-s** -z
endless ˈend.ləs, -lɪs **-ly** -li **-ness** -nəs, -nɪs
endlong ˈend.lɒŋ (US) -lɑːŋ, -lɔːŋ
endmost ˈend.məʊst (US) -moʊst
endnote ˈend.nəʊt (US) -noʊt **-s** -s
endo- en.dəʊ-; enˈdɒ-, ɪn- (US) en.doʊ-, -də-; enˈdɑː-, ɪn-
Note: Prefix. Either carries primary or secondary stress on the first syllable, e.g. **endomorph** /ˈen.dəʊ.mɔːf (US) -doʊ.mɔːrf/, **endomorphic** /ˌen.dəʊˈmɔː.fɪk (US) -doʊˈmɔːr-/, or primary stress on the second syllable, e.g. **endogenous** /ɪnˈdɒdʒ.ɪ.nəs (US) enˈdɑː.dʒə-/.
endocentric ˌen.dəʊˈsen.trɪk (US) -doʊˈ-
endocrine ˈen.dəʊ.kraɪn, -krɪn, -kriːn (US) -də.krɪn, -kriːn, -kraɪn **ˈendocrine ˌgland**
endocrinolog|y ˌen.dəʊ.kraɪˈnɒl.ə.dʒ|i, -krɪˈ- (US) -doʊ.krɪˈnɑː.lə- **-ist/s** -ɪst/s
endoderm ˈen.dəʊ.dɜːm (US) -doʊ.dɝːm
endoderm|al ˌen.dəʊˈdɜː.m|ᵊl (US) -doʊˈdɝː- **-ic** -ɪk
endogamy ɪnˈdɒg.ə.mi, en- (US) enˈdɑː.gə-, ɪn-
endogenous ɪnˈdɒdʒ.ə.nəs, en-, ˈ-ɪ- (US) enˈdɑː.dʒə-, ɪn-
endometrial ˌen.dəʊˈmiː.tri.əl (US) -doʊˈ-
endometriosis ˌen.dəʊˌmiː.triˈəʊ.sɪs (US) -doʊˌmiː.triˈoʊ-
endometri|um ˌen.dəʊˈmiː.tri|.əm (US) -doʊˈ- **-a** -ə
endomorph ˈen.dəʊ.mɔːf (US) -doʊ.mɔːrf **-s** -s **-y** -i
endomorph|ic ˌen.dəʊˈmɔː.f|ɪk (US) -doʊˈmɔːr- **-ism** -ɪ.zᵊm
endophoric ˌen.dəʊˈfɒr.ɪk (US) -doʊˈfɔːr-
endoplasm ˈen.dəʊ.plæz.ᵊm (US) -doʊ-
endoplasmic ˌen.dəʊˈplæz.mɪk (US) -doʊˈ-
Endor ˈen.dɔːʳ (US) -dɔːr
endorphin enˈdɔː.fɪn (US) -ˈdɔːr-, ɪn- **-s** -z
endors|e ɪnˈdɔːs, en- (US) enˈdɔːrs, ɪn- **-es** -ɪz **-ing** -ɪŋ **-ed** -t **-er/s** -əʳ/z (US) -ɚ/z **-ement/s** -mənt/s **-able** -ə.bl̩
endorsee ˌen.dɔːˈsiː (US) -dɔːrˈ- **-s** -z
endoscope ˈen.dəʊ.skəʊp (US) -doʊ.skoʊp, -də- **-s** -s
endoscop|y enˈdɒs.kə.p|i (US) -ˈdɑː.skə- **-ies** -iz
endoskeleton ˌen.dəʊˈskel.ɪ.tᵊn, ˈ-ə- (US) -doʊˈ- **-s** -z
endosperm ˈen.dəʊ.spɜːm (US) -doʊ.spɝːm **-s** -z
endow ɪnˈdaʊ, en- (US) en-, ɪn- **-s** -z **-ing** -ɪŋ **-ed** -d **-ment/s** -mənt/s
endpaper ˈendˌpeɪ.pəʳ (US) -pɚ **-s** -z
endpoint ˈend.pɔɪnt **-s** -s
end-stopped ˈend.stɒpt (US) -stɑːpt
endu|e ɪnˈdjuː, en- (US) enˈduː, ɪn-, -ˈdjuː **-es** -z **-ing** -ɪŋ **-ed** -d
endurab|le ɪnˈdjʊə.rə.b|l̩, en-, -ˈdjɔː- (US) enˈdʊr.ə-, ɪn-, -ˈdjʊr- **-ly** -li
endurance ɪnˈdjʊə.rᵊnts, en-, -ˈdjɔː- (US) enˈdʊr.ᵊnts, ɪn-, -ˈdjʊr-
endur|e ɪnˈdjʊəʳ, en-, -ˈdjɔːʳ (US) enˈdʊr, ɪn, -ˈdjʊr **-es** -z **-ing/ly** -ɪŋ/li **-ed** -d
end|ways ˈend|.weɪz **-wise** -waɪz
Endymion enˈdɪm.i.ən, ɪn-
-ene -iːn
Note: Suffix. **-ene** is not stressed, e.g. **ethylene** /ˈeθ.ɪ.liːn/.
ENE ˌiːst.nɔːθˈiːst (US) -nɔːrθ- *in nautical usage also:* -nɔːˈriːst (US) -nɔːrˈiːst
Eneas iːˈniː.əs, ɪ-, -æs
Eneid ˈiː.ni.ɪd, ɪˈniː-
enema ˈen.ə.mə, ˈ-ɪ- (US) ˈ-ə- **-s** -z
enem|y ˈen.ə.m|i, ˈ-ɪ- **-ies** -iz
energetic ˌen.əˈdʒet.ɪk (US) -ɚˈdʒet̬- **-s** -s **-ally** -ᵊl.i, -li
energiz|e, -is|e ˈen.ə.dʒaɪz (US) ˈ-ɚ- **-es** -ɪz **-ing** -ɪŋ **-ed** -d **-er/s** -əʳ/z (US) -ɚ/z
energumen ˌen.əˈgjuː.men (US) -ɚˈ- **-s** -z
energ|y ˈen.ə.dʒ|i (US) ˈ-ɚ- **-ies** -iz
ener|vate ˈen.ə|.veɪt, -ɜː- (US) ˈ-ɚ- **-vates** -veɪts **-vating** -veɪ.tɪŋ (US) -veɪ.t̬ɪŋ **-vated** -veɪ.tɪd (US) -veɪ.t̬ɪd
enervation ˌen.əˈveɪ.ʃᵊn, -ɜːˈ- (US) -ɚˈ-
en famille ˌɑ̃ːn.fæmˈiː (US) ˌɑ̃ːn.fɑːˈmiː.jə
enfant(s) terrible(s) ˌɑ̃ːn.fɑ̃ːn.terˈiː.blə, ˌɒn.fɒn-, -təˈriː- (US) ˌɑːn.fɑːn.terˈiː-, ˌɑ̃n.fɑ̃n-
enfeebl|e ɪnˈfiː.bl̩, en- (US) en-, ɪn- **-es** -z **-ing** -ɪŋ, ˈ-blɪŋ **-ed** -d **-ement** -mənt
enfeoff ɪnˈfiːf, en-, -ˈfef (US) en-, ɪn- **-s** -s **-ing** -ɪŋ **-ed** -t **-ment/s** -mənt/s
Enfield ˈen.fiːld
enfilad|e ˌen.fɪˈleɪd, ˈ--- (US) ˈen.fə.leɪd **-es** -z **-ing** -ɪŋ **-ed** -ɪd
enfold ɪnˈfəʊld, en- (US) enˈfoʊld, ɪn- **-s** -z **-ing** -ɪŋ **-ed** -ɪd **-ment** -mənt
enforc|e ɪnˈfɔːs, en- (US) enˈfɔːrs, ɪn- **-es** -ɪz **-ing** -ɪŋ **-ed** -t **-edly** -ɪd.li **-eable** -ə.bl̩
enforcement ɪnˈfɔːs.mənt, en- (US) enˈfɔːrs-, ɪn-
enforcer ɪnˈfɔː.səʳ (US) -ˈfɔːr.sɚ **-s** -z
enfranchis|e ɪnˈfræn.tʃaɪz, en- (US) en-, ɪn- **-es** -ɪz **-ing** -ɪŋ **-ed** -d
enfranchisement ɪnˈfræn.tʃɪz.mənt, en-, -tʃəz- (US) enˈfræn.tʃaɪz-, ɪn-, -tʃəz- **-s** -s
Engadine ˈeŋ.gə.diːn, ˌ--ˈ-
engag|e ɪnˈgeɪdʒ, ɪŋ-, en-, eŋ- (US) en-, ɪn- **-es** -ɪz **-ing/ly** -ɪŋ/li **-ed** -d
engagement ɪnˈgeɪdʒ.mənt, ɪŋ-, en-, eŋ- (US) en-, ɪn- **-s** -s **enˈgagement ˌring**
en garde ɑ̃ːŋˈgɑːd (US) ˌɑːnˈgɑːrd, ˌɑ̃ːn-
Engels ˈeŋ.gᵊlz
engend|er ɪnˈdʒen.d|əʳ, en- (US) enˈdʒen.d|ɚ, ɪn- **-ers** -əz (US) -ɚz **-ering** -ᵊr.ɪŋ **-ered** -əd (US) -ɚd
engine ˈen.dʒɪn **-s** -z **ˈengine ˌdriver**

engineer ˌen.dʒɪˈnɪəʳ, -dʒəˈ- (US) -ˈnɪr **-s** -z **-ing** -ɪŋ **-ed** -d

engird ɪnˈɡɜːd, ɪŋ-, en-, eŋ- (US) enˈɡɝːd, ɪn- **-s** -z **-ing** -ɪŋ **-ed** -ɪd

England ˈɪŋ.ɡlənd **-er/s** -əʳ/z (US) -ɚ/z

Englefield ˈeŋ.ɡl̩.fiːld

Englewood ˈeŋ.ɡl̩.wʊd

English ˈɪŋ.ɡlɪʃ ˌ**English** ˈ**Channel**; ˌ**English** ˈ**horn** (US) ˈ**English** ˌ**horn**

English|man ˈɪŋ.ɡlɪʃ|.mən **-men** -mən, -men

English|woman ˈɪŋ.ɡlɪʃ|ˌwʊm.ən **-women** -ˌwɪm.ɪn

engorg|e ɪnˈɡɔːdʒ, ɪŋ-, en-, eŋ- (US) -ˈɡɔːrdʒ **-es** -ɪz **-ing** -ɪŋ **-ed** -d

engraft ɪnˈɡrɑːft, ɪŋ-, en-, eŋ- (US) enˈɡræft, ɪn- **-s** -s **-ing** -ɪŋ **-ed** -ɪd **-ment** -mənt

engrailed ɪnˈɡreɪld, ɪŋ-, en-, eŋ- (US) en-, ɪn-

engrain ɪnˈɡreɪn, ɪŋ-, en-, eŋ- (US) en-, ɪn- **-s** -z **-ing** -ɪŋ **-ed** -d

engrav|e ɪnˈɡreɪv, ɪŋ-, en-, eŋ- (US) en-, ɪn- **-es** -z **-ing/s** -ɪŋ/z **-ed** -d **-er/s** -əʳ/z (US) -ɚ/z **-ery** -əʳr.i

en gros ˌɑ̃ːŋˈɡrəʊ, ˌɑːnˈɡroʊ

engross ɪnˈɡrəʊs, ɪŋ-, en-, eŋ- (US) enˈɡroʊs, ɪn- **-es** -ɪz **-ing** -ɪŋ **-ed** -t **-ment** -mənt

engulf ɪnˈɡʌlf, ɪŋ-, en-, eŋ- (US) en-, ɪn- **-s** -s **-ing** -ɪŋ **-ed** -t **-ment** -mənt

enhanc|e ɪnˈhɑːnts, en- (US) -ˈhænts **-es** -ɪz **-ing** -ɪŋ **-ed** -t **-ement/s** -mənt/s **-er/s** -əʳ/z (US) -ɚ/z

enharmonic ˌen.hɑːˈmɒn.ɪk (US) -hɑːrˈmɑː.nɪk **-al** -əl **-ally** -əl.i, -li

Enid ˈiː.nɪd

enigma ɪˈnɪɡ.mə, enˈɪɡ-, əˈnɪɡ- (US) ɪˈnɪɡ.mə, ə-, enˈɪɡ- **-s** -z

enigmatic ˌen.ɪɡˈmæt.ɪk (US) -ˈmæţ- **-al** -əl **-ally** -əl.i, -li *stress shift:* ˌenigmatic ˈsmile

enigmatist ɪˈnɪɡ.mə.tɪst, enˈɪɡ-, əˈnɪɡ- (US) ɪˈnɪɡ-, ə-, enˈɪɡ- **-s** -s

enigmatiz|e, -is|e ɪˈnɪɡ.mə.taɪz, enˈɪɡ-, əˈnɪɡ- (US) ɪˈnɪɡ-, ə-, enˈɪɡ- **-es** -ɪz **-ing** -ɪŋ **-ed** -d

enjamb(e)ment ɪnˈdʒæm*b*.mənt, en- (US) en-, ɪn- **-s** -s

enjoin ɪnˈdʒɔɪn, en- (US) en-, ɪn- **-s** -z **-ing** -ɪŋ **-ed** -d

enjoy ɪnˈdʒɔɪ, en- (US) en-, ɪn- **-s** -z **-ing** -ɪŋ **-ed** -d

enjoyab|le ɪnˈdʒɔɪ.ə.b|l̩, en- (US) en-, ɪn- **-ly** -li **-leness** -l̩.nəs, -nɪs

enjoyment ɪnˈdʒɔɪ.mənt, en- (US) en-, ɪn- **-s** -s

enkindl|e ɪnˈkɪn.dl̩, en-, ɪŋ-, eŋ- (US) en-, ɪn- **-es** -z **-ing** -ɪŋ, ˈ-lɪŋ **-ed** -d

enlac|e ɪnˈleɪs, en- (US) en-, ɪn- **-es** -ɪz **-ing** -ɪŋ **-ed** -t **-ement/s** -mənt/s

Enlai ˌenˈlaɪ

enlarg|e ɪnˈlɑːdʒ, en- (US) enˈlɑːrdʒ, ɪn- **-es** -ɪz **-ing** -ɪŋ **-ed** -d **-er/s** -əʳ/z (US) -ɚ/z **-ement/s** -mənt/s

enlighten ɪnˈlaɪ.tən, en- (US) en-, ɪn- **-s** -z **-ing** -ɪŋ **-ed** -d

enlightenment (E) ɪnˈlaɪ.tən.mənt, en- (US) en-, ɪn-

enlist ɪnˈlɪst, en- (US) en-, ɪn- **-s** -s **-ing** -ɪŋ **-ed** -ɪd **-ment/s** -mənt/s

enliven ɪnˈlaɪ.vən, en- (US) en-, ɪn- **-s** -z **-ing** -ɪŋ **-ed** -d

en masse ɑ̃ːmˈmæs, ɒn- (US) ɑːn-, ɑ̃n-

enmesh ɪnˈmeʃ, en- (US) en-, ɪn- **-es** -ɪz **-ing** -ɪŋ **-ed** -t

enmit|y ˈen.mə.t|i, -mɪ- **-ies** -iz

Ennis ˈen.ɪs

Enniscorthy ˌen.ɪˈskɔː.θi (US) -ˈskɔːr-

Enniskillen ˌen.ɪˈskɪl.ən, -əˈ-, -ɪn

Ennius ˈen.i.əs

ennobl|e ɪˈnəʊ.bl̩, enˈəʊ- (US) enˈoʊ-, ɪˈnoʊ- **-es** -z **-ing** -ɪŋ, ˈ-blɪŋ **-ed** -d **-ement** -mənt

ennui ˈɑ̃n.wiː, ˈɒn-, -ˈ- (US) ˌɑːnˈwiː, ˈ--

Eno® ˈiː.nəʊ (US) -noʊ **-'s** -z

Enoch ˈiː.nɒk (US) -nɑːk, -nək

enormit|y ɪˈnɔː.mə.t|i, ə-, -mɪ- (US) -ˈnɔːr.mə.ţ|i **-ies** -iz

enormous ɪˈnɔː.məs, ə- (US) -ˈnɔːr- **-ly** -li **-ness** -nəs, -nɪs

Enos ˈiː.nɒs (US) -nɑːs, -nəs

enough ɪˈnʌf, ə-

enounc|e ɪˈnaʊnts **-es** -ɪz **-ing** -ɪŋ **-ed** -t

enow ɪˈnaʊ

en passant ˌɑ̃ːmˈpæs.ɑ̃ːŋ, ˌ--ˈ- (US) ˌɑ̃ːn.pɑːˈsɑ̃ːn, -pəˈ-

enquir|e ɪnˈkwaɪəʳ, ɪŋ-, en-, eŋ- (US) enˈkwaɪɚ, ɪn- **-es** -z **-ing/ly** -ɪŋ/li **-ed** -d **-er/s** -əʳ/z (US) -ɚ/z

enquir|y ɪnˈkwaɪə.r|i, ɪŋ-, en-, eŋ- (US) enˈkwaɪ-, ɪn-; ˈɪn.kwɚ.i **-ies** -iz

enrag|e ɪnˈreɪdʒ, en- (US) en-, ɪn- **-es** -ɪz **-ing** -ɪŋ **-ed** -d

enrapt ɪnˈræpt, en- (US) en-, ɪn-

enrapt|ure ɪnˈræp.tʃ|əʳ, en- (US) enˈræp.tʃ|ɚ, ɪn- **-ures** -əz (US) -ɚz **-uring** -əʳr.ɪŋ **-ured** -əd (US) -ɚd

enregist|er ɪnˈredʒ.ɪ.st|əʳ, en-, ˈ-ə- (US) enˈredʒ.ɪ.st|ɚ, ɪn-, ˈ-ə- **-ers** -əz (US) -ɚz **-ering** -əʳr.ɪŋ **-ered** -əd (US) -ɚd

enrich ɪnˈrɪtʃ, en- (US) en-, ɪn- **-es** -ɪz **-ing** -ɪŋ **-ed** -t **-ment** -mənt

Enright ˈen.raɪt

enrob|e ɪnˈrəʊb, en- (US) enˈroʊb, ɪn- **-es** -z **-ing** -ɪŋ **-ed** -d

enrol ɪnˈrəʊl, en- (US) enˈroʊl, ɪn- **-s** -z **-ling** -ɪŋ **-led** -d

enroll ɪnˈrəʊl, en- (US) enˈroʊl, ɪn- **-s** -z **-ing** -ɪŋ **-ed** -d

enrol(l)ment ɪnˈrəʊl.mənt, en- (US) enˈroʊl-, ɪn- **-s** -s

Enron® ˈen.rɒn (US) -rɑːn

en route ˌɑ̃ːnˈruːt, ˌɒn- (US) ˌɑːn-

en|s en|z **-tia** -ʃi.ə, -ʃə, -ti.ə

ENSA ˈen*t*.sə

ensample enˈsɑːm.pl̩, ɪn- (US) -ˈsæm- **-s** -z

ensanguined ɪnˈsæŋ.ɡwɪnd, en- (US) en-, ɪn-

ensconc|e ɪnˈskɒn*t*s, en- (US) enˈskɑːn*t*s, ɪn- **-es** -ɪz **-ing** -ɪŋ **-ed** -t

ensemble ɑ̃ːnˈsɑ̃ːm.bəl, ɒnˈsɒm- (US) ˌɑːnˈsɑːm- **-s** -z

enshrin|e ɪnˈʃraɪn, en- (US) en-, ɪn- **-es** -z **-ing** -ɪŋ **-ed** -d **-ement** -mənt

enshroud ɪnˈʃraʊd, en- (US) en-, ɪn- **-s** -z **-ing** -ɪŋ **-ed** -ɪd

ensign *flag:* ˈen.saɪn *in the navy:* ˈen*t*.sən **-s** -z

ensign *officer:* ˈen.saɪn (US) ˈen.sɪn **-s** -z

ensign (*v.*) enˈsaɪn, ɪn- **-s** -z **-ing** -ɪŋ **-ed** -d

ensilag|e ˈen*t*.sɪ.lɪdʒ, -sə; ɪnˈsaɪ-, en- (US) ˈen*t*.sə- **-es** -ɪz

ensil|e enˈsaɪl, ˈen*t*.saɪl **-es** -z **-ing** -ɪŋ **-ed** -d

enslav|e ɪnˈsleɪv, en- (US) en-, ɪn- **-es** -z **-ing** -ɪŋ **-ed** -d **-er/s** -əʳ/z (US) -ɚ/z **-ement** -mənt

ensnar|e ɪnˈsneəʳ, en- (US) enˈsner, ɪn- **-es** -z **-ing** -ɪŋ **-ed** -d **-er/s** -əʳ/z (US) -ɚ/z

ensoul ɪnˈsəʊl, en- (US) enˈsoʊl, ɪn- **-s** -z **-ing** -ɪŋ **-ed** -d

ensu|e ɪnˈsjuː, en-, -ˈsuː (US) enˈsuː, ɪn-, -ˈsjuː **-es** -z **-ing** -ɪŋ **-ed** -d

en suite ˌɑ̃ːnˈswiːt, ˌɒn- (US) ˌɑːn- *stress shift:* ˌen suite ˈbathroom

ensur|e ɪnˈʃɔːʳ, en-, -ˈʃʊəʳ, -ˈsjʊəʳ (US) enˈʃʊr, ɪn- **-es** -z **-ing** -ɪŋ **-ed** -d

-ent -ənt

Note: Suffix. Words containing **-ent** are stressed in a similar way to those containing **-ence**; see above.

entablature enˈtæb.lə.tʃəʳ, ɪn-, -lɪ-, -tʃʊəʳ, -tjʊəʳ (US) -lə.tʃɚ **-s** -z

entail ɪnˈteɪl, en- (US) en-, ɪn- **-s** -z **-ing** -ɪŋ **-ed** -d **-er/s** -əʳ/z (US) -ɚ/z **-ment** -mənt

entangl|e ɪnˈtæŋ.ɡl̩, en- (US) en-, ɪn- **-es** -z **-ing** -ɪŋ, ˈ-ɡlɪŋ **-ed** -d **-ement/s** -mənt/s

Entebbe enˈteb.i, ɪn- (US) -ə

entendre ɑ̃ːnˈtɑ̃ːn.drə (US) ɑːnˈtɑːn.drə

entente ɑ̃ːnˈtɑ̃ːnt (US) ɑːnˈtɑːnt **-s** -s

entente cordiale ˌɑ̃ːn.tɑ̃ːnt.kɔː.diˈɑːl (US) ˌɑːn.tɑːnt.kɔːr-

ent|er ˈen.t|əʳ (US) -ţ|ɚ **-ers** -əz (US) -ɚz **-ering** -əʳr.ɪŋ **-ered** -əd (US) -ɚd

enteric enˈter.ɪk

enteritis ˌen.təˈraɪ.tɪs (US) -ţɪs

enterokinas|e ˌen.təʳr.əʊˈkaɪ.neɪz (US) -ţə.roʊˈkaɪ.neɪs, -ˈkɪn.eɪs, -eɪz **-es** -ɪz

enterology ˌen.təˈrɒl.ə.dʒi (US) -ţəˈrɑː.lə-

enterotomy ˌen.təˈrɒt.ə.mi
 Ⓤⓢ -t̬əˈrɑː.t̬ə-
enterovirus ˌen.tᵊr.əʊˈvaɪə.rəs
 Ⓤⓢ -t̬ə.roʊˈvaɪ.rəs **-es** -ɪz
enterpris|e ˈen.tə.praɪz Ⓤⓢ -t̬ɚ- **-es** -ɪz **-ing/ly** -ɪŋ/li
entertain ˌen.təˈteɪn Ⓤⓢ -t̬ɚˈ- **-s** -z **-ing/ly** -ɪŋ/li **-ed** -d **-er/s** -əʳ/z Ⓤⓢ -ɚ/z
entertainment ˌen.təˈteɪn.mənt
 Ⓤⓢ -t̬ɚˈ- **-s** -s
enthral ɪnˈθrɔːl, en- Ⓤⓢ enˈθrɔːl, ɪn-, -ˈθrɑːl **-s** -z **-ling** -ɪŋ **-led** -d **-ment** -mənt
enthrall ɪnˈθrɔːl, en- Ⓤⓢ enˈθrɔːl, ɪn-, -ˈθrɑːl **-s** -z **-ing** -ɪŋ **-ed** -d **-ment** -mənt
enthron|e ɪnˈθrəʊn, en- Ⓤⓢ enˈθroʊn, ɪn- **-es** -z **-ing** -ɪŋ **-ed** -d **-ement/s** -mənt/s
enthus|e ɪnˈθjuːz, en- Ⓤⓢ enˈθuːz, ɪn-, -ˈθjuːz **-es** -ɪz **-ing** -ɪŋ **-ed** -d
enthusi|asm ɪnˈθjuː.zi|.æz.ᵊm, en-, -ˈθuː- Ⓤⓢ enˈθuː-, ɪn-, -ˈθjuː- **-asms** -æzmz **-ast/s** -æst/s
enthusiastic ɪnˌθjuː.ziˈæs.tɪk, en-, -ˌθuː- Ⓤⓢ enˌθuː-, ɪn-, -ˌθjuː- **-ally** -ᵊl.i, -li
entia *(plur. of* **ens***)* ˈen.ʃi.ə, -ʃə, -ti.ə
entic|e ɪnˈtaɪs, en- Ⓤⓢ en-, ɪn- **-es** -ɪz **-ing/ly** -ɪŋ/li **-ed** -t **-ement/s** -mənt/s
entire ɪnˈtaɪəʳ, en- Ⓤⓢ enˈtaɪɚ, ɪn- **-ly** -li **-ness** -nəs, -nɪs
entiret|y ɪnˈtaɪə.rə.t|i, en-
 Ⓤⓢ enˈtaɪ.rə.t̬|i, -ˈtaɪr.t̬|i, ɪn- **-ies** -iz
entitl|e ɪnˈtaɪ.tḷ, en- Ⓤⓢ enˈtaɪ.t̬ḷ, ɪn- **-es** -z **-ing** -ɪŋ, -ˈtaɪt.lɪŋ **-ed** -d
entitlement ɪnˈtaɪ.tḷ.mənt, en-
 Ⓤⓢ enˈtaɪ.t̬ḷ-, ɪn- **-s** -s
entit|y ˈen.tɪ.t|i, -tə- Ⓤⓢ -t̬ə.t̬|i **-ies** -iz
entomb ɪnˈtuːm, en- Ⓤⓢ en-, ɪn- **-s** -z **-ing** -ɪŋ **-ed** -d **-ment/s** -mənt/s
entomological ˌen.tə.məˈlɒdʒ.ɪ.kḷ
 Ⓤⓢ -t̬ə.məˈlɑː.dʒɪ- **-ly** -i
entomologiz|e, -is|e ˌen.təˈmɒl.ə.dʒaɪz
 Ⓤⓢ -t̬əˈmɑː.lə- **-es** -ɪz **-ing** -ɪŋ **-ed** -d
entomolog|y ˌen.təˈmɒl.ə.dʒ|i
 Ⓤⓢ -t̬əˈmɑː.lə- **-ist/s** -ɪst/s
entourag|e ˈɒn.tʊ.rɑːʒ, ˈɑ̃ː*n*-, -tʊə-, ˌ--ˈ- Ⓤⓢ ˌɑːn.tʊˈrɑːʒ **-es** -ɪz
entr'acte ˈɒn.trækt, ˈɑ̃ː*n*-, ˌ-ˈ-
 Ⓤⓢ ˈɑːnˌtrækt, ɑ̃ːn-, ˌ-ˈ- **-s** -s
entrails ˈen.treɪlz
entrain ɪnˈtreɪn, en- Ⓤⓢ en-, ɪn- **-s** -z **-ing** -ɪŋ **-ed** -d
entrammel ɪnˈtræm.ᵊl, en- Ⓤⓢ en-, ɪn- **-s** -z **-(l)ing** -ɪŋ **-(l)ed** -d
entranc|e *(n.) entry, place of entry, etc.:* ˈen.trən*t*s **-es** -ɪz
entranc|e *(v.) put in state of trance, delight:* ɪnˈtrɑːn*t*s, en- Ⓤⓢ enˈtræn*t*s, ɪn- **-es** -ɪz **-ing** -ɪŋ **-ed** -t **-ement/s** -mənt/s
entrant ˈen.trənt **-s** -s
entrap ɪnˈtræp, en- Ⓤⓢ en-, ɪn- **-s** -s **-ping** -ɪŋ **-ped** -t **-ment** -mənt
en|treat ɪn|ˈtriːt, en- Ⓤⓢ en-, ɪn- **-treats** -ˈtriːts **-treating/ly** -ˈtriː.tɪŋ/li
 Ⓤⓢ -ˈtriː.t̬ɪŋ/li **-treated** -ˈtriː.tɪd
 Ⓤⓢ -ˈtriː.t̬ɪd **-treatment** -ˈtriːt.mənt
entreat|y ɪnˈtriː.t|i, en- Ⓤⓢ enˈtriː.t̬|i, ɪn- **-ies** -iz
entrechat ˈɑ̃ː*n*.trə.ʃɑː, ˈɒn-
 Ⓤⓢ ˌɑːn.trəˈʃɑː, ˈ--- **-s** -z
entrecôte ˈɑ̃ː*n*.trə.kəʊt, ˈɒn-
 Ⓤⓢ ˈɑːn.trə.koʊt, ˈɑ̃ːn-, ˌ--ˈ- **-s** -s
entrée ˈɑ̃ː*n*.treɪ, ˈɒn- Ⓤⓢ ˈɑːn-, ˌ-ˈ- **-s** -z
entremets *(sing.)* ˈɑ̃ː*n*.trə.meɪ, ˈɒnt-
 Ⓤⓢ ˈɑːn.trə-, ˌ--ˈ- *(plur.)* -z
entrench ɪnˈtrenʃ, en- Ⓤⓢ en-, ɪn- **-es** -ɪz **-ing** -ɪŋ **-ed** -t **-ment/s** -mənt/s
entre nous ˌɑ̃ː*n*.trəˈnuː, ˌɒn- Ⓤⓢ ˌɑːn-
entrepôt ˈɑ̃ː*n*.trə.pəʊ, ˈɒn-
 Ⓤⓢ ˈɑːn.trə.poʊ; ˌ--ˈ- **-s** -z
entrepreneur ˌɒn.trə.prəˈnɜːʳ, ˌɑ̃ː*n*-, -prenˈɜːʳ Ⓤⓢ ˌɑːn.trə.prəˈnɝː, -ˈnʊr, -ˈnjʊr **-s** -z **-ship** -ʃɪp
entrepreneurial ˌɒn.trə.prəˈnɜː.ri.əl, ˌɑ̃ː*n*- Ⓤⓢ ˌɑːn.trə.prəˈnɝː.i-, -ˈnʊr-, -ˈnjʊr-
entresol ˈɑ̃ː*n*.trə.sɒl, ˈɒn-
 Ⓤⓢ ˈɑːn.trə.sɑːl, ˌ--ˈ- **-s** -z
entropy ˈen.trə.pi
entrust ɪnˈtrʌst, en- Ⓤⓢ en-, ɪn- **-s** -s **-ing** -ɪŋ **-ed** -ɪd
entr|y ˈen.tr|i **-ies** -iz
entry|ism ˈen.tri|.ɪ.zᵊm **-ist/s** -ɪst/s
entryphone ˈen.tri.fəʊn Ⓤⓢ -foʊn **-s** -z
entryway ˈen.tri.weɪ **-s** -z
entwin|e ɪnˈtwaɪn, en- Ⓤⓢ en-, ɪn- **-es** -z **-ing** -ɪŋ **-ed** -d
entwist ɪnˈtwɪst, en- Ⓤⓢ en-, ɪn- **-s** -s **-ing** -ɪŋ **-ed** -ɪd
enumerable ɪˈnjuː.mᵊr.ə.bḷ Ⓤⓢ -ˈnuː-, -ˈnjuː-
enumer|ate ɪˈnjuː.mᵊr|.eɪt
 Ⓤⓢ -ˈnuː.mə.r|eɪt, -ˈnjuː- **-ates** -eɪts **-ating** -eɪ.tɪŋ Ⓤⓢ -eɪ.t̬ɪŋ **-ated** -eɪ.tɪd
 Ⓤⓢ -eɪ.t̬ɪd **-ator/s** -eɪ.təʳ/z
 Ⓤⓢ -eɪ.t̬ɚ/z
enumeration ɪˌnjuː.mᵊrˈeɪ.ʃᵊn
 Ⓤⓢ -ˌnuː.məˈreɪ-, -ˌnjuː- **-s** -z
enumerative ɪˈnjuː.mᵊr.ə.tɪv, -eɪ.tɪv
 Ⓤⓢ -ˈnuː.mɚ.ə.t̬ɪv, -ˈnjuː-
enunciable ɪˈnʌn*t*.si.ə.bḷ, -ʃi.ə-
enunci|ate ɪˈnʌn*t*.si|.eɪt, -ʃi- **-ates** -eɪts **-ating** -eɪ.tɪŋ Ⓤⓢ -eɪ.t̬ɪŋ **-ated** -eɪ.tɪd
 Ⓤⓢ -eɪ.t̬ɪd **-ator/s** -eɪ.təʳ/z
 Ⓤⓢ -eɪ.t̬ɚ/z
enunciation ɪˌnʌn*t*.siˈeɪ.ʃᵊn **-s** -z
enunciative ɪˈnʌn*t*.si.ə.tɪv, -ʃi.ə-, -eɪ.tɪv Ⓤⓢ -ə.t̬ɪv
enur|e ɪˈnjʊəʳ Ⓤⓢ -ˈnjʊr **-es** -z **-ing** -ɪŋ **-ed** -d
enuresis ˌen.jʊəˈriː.sɪs Ⓤⓢ -juːˈ-
envelop ɪnˈvel.əp, en- Ⓤⓢ en-, ɪn- **-s** -s **-ing** -ɪŋ **-ed** -t **-ment/s** -mənt/s
envelope ˈen.və.ləʊp, ˈɒn-
 Ⓤⓢ ˈen.və.loʊp, ˈɑːn- **-s** -s
envenom ɪnˈven.əm, en- Ⓤⓢ en-, ɪn- **-s** -z **-ing** -ɪŋ **-ed** -d
enviab|le ˈen.vi.ə.b|ḷ **-ly** -li **-leness** -ḷ.nəs, -nɪs
envious ˈen.vi.əs **-ly** -li **-ness** -nəs, -nɪs
environ *(v.)* ɪnˈvaɪə.rᵊn, en- Ⓤⓢ enˈvaɪ-, ɪn-, -ɚn **-s** -z **-ing** -ɪŋ **-ed** -d
environment ɪnˈvaɪə.rᵊn.mənt, en-
 Ⓤⓢ enˈvaɪ-, ɪn-, -ɚn- **-s** -s
environmental ɪnˌvaɪə.rᵊnˈmen.tᵊl, en-, -rᵊmˈ- Ⓤⓢ enˌvaɪ.rənˈmen.t̬ᵊl, ɪn-, -ɚnˈ- **-ly** -i
environmental|ism
 ɪnˌvaɪə.rᵊnˈmen.tᵊl|.ɪ.zᵊm, en-, -rᵊmˈ- Ⓤⓢ enˌvaɪ.rᵊnˈmen.t̬ᵊl-, ɪn-, -ɚnˈ- **-ist/s** -ɪst/s
environmentally-friendly
 ɪnˌvaɪᵊ.rᵊnˌmen.tᵊl.iˈfrend.li, en-, -rᵊmˌ- Ⓤⓢ enˌvaɪ.rᵊn.men.t̬ᵊl-, ɪn-, ˌ-ɚn-
environs *(n.)* ɪnˈvaɪə.rᵊnz, en-; ˈen.vɪ-, -vᵊr.ᵊnz Ⓤⓢ enˈvaɪ.rᵊnz, ɪn-, -ɚnz
envisag|e ɪnˈvɪz.ɪdʒ, en- Ⓤⓢ en-, ɪn- **-es** -ɪz **-ing** -ɪŋ **-ed** -d
envision ɪnˈvɪʒ.ᵊn, en- Ⓤⓢ en-, ɪn- **-s** -z **-ing** -ɪŋ **-ed** -d
envoy ˈen.vɔɪ Ⓤⓢ ˈɑːn-, ˈen- **-s** -z
env|y ˈen.v|i **-ies** -iz **-ying** -i.ɪŋ **-ied** -id
enwrap ɪnˈræp, en- Ⓤⓢ en-, ɪn- **-s** -s **-ping** -ɪŋ **-ped** -t
enwreath|e ɪnˈriːð, en- Ⓤⓢ en-, ɪn- **-es** -z **-ing** -ɪŋ **-ed** -d
enzyme ˈen.zaɪm **-s** -z
enzymolog|y ˌen.zaɪˈmɒl.ə.dʒ|i
 Ⓤⓢ -zɪˈ-, -ˈmɑː.lə- **-ist/s** -ɪst/s
Eocene ˈiː.əʊ.siːn Ⓤⓢ -oʊ-, -ə-
eolian (E) iˈəʊ.li.ən Ⓤⓢ -ˈoʊ-
eolith ˈiː.əʊ.lɪθ Ⓤⓢ -oʊ-, -ə- **-s** -s
eolithic ˌiː.əʊˈlɪθ.ɪk Ⓤⓢ -oʊˈ-, -əˈ-
eon ˈiː.ɒn Ⓤⓢ -ɑːn **-s** -z
-eous -i.əs, -əs
Note: Suffix. Words containing **-eous** are normally stressed on the syllable preceding the suffix, e.g. **advantage** /ədˈvɑːn.tɪdʒ Ⓤⓢ -ˈvæn.t̬ɪdʒ/, **advantageous** /ˌæd.vənˈteɪ.dʒəs Ⓤⓢ -vænˈ-/.
EP ˌiːˈpiː
EPA ˌiː.piːˈeɪ
epact ˈiː.pækt, ˈep.ækt **-s** -s
Epaminondas epˌæm.ɪˈnɒn.dæs, ɪˌpæm-, -əˈ- Ⓤⓢ ɪˌpæm.əˈnɑːn-
eparch ˈep.ɑːk Ⓤⓢ -ɑːrk **-s** -s **-y** -i **-ies** -iz
epaulette, epaulet ˌep.əˈlet, -ɔːˈ-, ˈ--- Ⓤⓢ ˌep.əˈlet, ˈ--- **-s** -s
Epcot® ˈep.kɒt Ⓤⓢ -kɑːt ˈEpcot ˌCenter
epee, épée ˈep.eɪ, ˈeɪ.peɪ, -ˈ- Ⓤⓢ eɪˈpeɪ; ˈep.eɪ **-s** -z **-ist/s** -ɪst/s

Pronouncing the letters EO

There are several pronunciation possibilities for the vowel digraph **eo**, e.g.:

iː	people	/ˈpiː.pl̩/	
e	leopard	/ˈlep.əd/	(US) /-ɚd/
i.ə	chameleon	/kəˈmiː.li.ən/	

When followed by an **r** in the spelling, **eo** is pronounced as /ɔː (US) ɔːr/ and /ɪə (US) ɪr/, e.g.:

George	/dʒɔːdʒ/	(US) /dʒɔːrdʒ/
theory	/ˈθɪə.ri/	(US) /ˈθɪr.i/

Where *geo-* is a prefix, there are several possible realisations, e.g.:

/i.ɒ (US) i.ɑː/	geography	/dʒiˈɒg.rə.fi/ (US) /-ˈɑː.grə-/
/iː.əʊ (US) iː.oʊ/	geothermal	/ˌdʒiː.əʊˈθɜː.məl/ (US) /-oʊˈθɝː-/

(In *geography*, the prefix may also be pronounced as /ˈdʒɒg-/ in British English.)

In addition

There are instances when the two letters **e** and **o** come together in closed compounds, e.g.:

thereof	/ðeəˈrɒv/	(US) /ðerˈɑːv/
whereon	/*h*weəˈrɒn/	(US) /*h*werˈɑːn/

In weak syllables

The vowel digraph **eo** is realised with the vowel /ə/ in weak syllables, e.g.:

pigeon	/ˈpɪdʒ.ən/
luncheon	/ˈlʌntʃ.ən/

Pronouncing the letters EOU

The vowel letter combination **eou** has two possible pronunciations. After **c** or **g** the pronunciation is /ə/, e.g.:

cretaceous	/krɪˈteɪ.ʃəs/	
gorgeous	/ˈgɔː.dʒəs/	(US) /ˈgɔːr-/

After other letters, the pronunciation is /i.ə/, e.g.:

spontaneous	/spɒnˈteɪ.ni.əs/	(US) /spɑːn-/

epenthes|is epˈent.θə.s|ɪs, ɪˈpen*t*-, -θɪ- (US) ɪˈpen*t*.θə- **-es** -iːz
epenthetic ˌep.enˈθet.ɪk, -ənˈ- (US) -enˈθet̬-
epergne ɪˈpɜːn, epˈɜːn, -ˈeən (US) iːˈpɝːn, eɪ- **-s** -z
epexegesis epˌek.sɪˈdʒiː.sɪs, ɪˌpek-, -səˈ- (US) -səˈ-
epexegetic epˌek.sɪˈdʒet.ɪk, ɪˌpek-, -səˈ- (US) -səˈdʒet̬- **-al** -əl **-ally** -əl.i, -li
ephah ˈiː.fə **-s** -z
ephedrine ˈef.ə.drɪn, ˈ-ɪ-, -driːn, ɪˈfed.rɪn, -riːn (US) ɪˈfed.rin; ˈef.ə.driːn, -drɪn
ephemer|a ɪˈfem.ər|.ə, efˈem-, əˈfem-, -ˈfiː.mər- (US) ɪˈfem.ɚ-, efˈem-, ˈ-r|ə **-as** -əz **-al** -əl
ephemeralit|y ɪˌfem.əˈræl.ə.t|i, efˌem-, əˌfem-, -ˌfiː.məˈ-, -ɪ.t|i (US) ɪˌfem.əˈræl.ə.t̬|i, efˌem- **-ies** -iz
ephemeris ɪˈfem.ər.ɪs, efˈem-, əˈfem-, -ˈfiː.mər- (US) ɪˈfem-, efˈem-
ephemerides ˌef.ɪˈmer.ɪ.diːz (US) -əˈmer.ə-
ephemeron ɪˈfem.ər.ɒn, efˈem-, əˈfem-, -ˈfiː.mər-, -ən (US) ɪˈfem.ə.rɑːn, efˈem-, -rən **-s** -z
ephemerous ɪˈfem.ər.əs, efˈem-, əˈfem-, -ˈfiː.mər- (US) ɪˈfem.ɚ-, efˈem-
Ephesian ɪˈfiː.ʒən, efˈiː-, -ʒi.ən, -zi- **-s** -z
Ephesus ˈef.ə.səs, ˈ-ɪ-
ephod ˈiː.fɒd, ˈef.ɒd (US) -ɑːd **-s** -z
Ephraim ˈiː.freɪ.ɪm, -fri-, -əm, -frəm (US) ˈiː.fri.əm, -frəm
Ephron ˈef.rɒn, ˈiː.frɒn (US) -frɑːn
epi- ep.i-, ep.ə-; epˈɪ-
Note: Prefix. Normally takes either primary or secondary stress on the first syllable, e.g. **epicycle** /ˈep.ɪ.saɪ.kl̩/, **epicyclic** /ˌep.ɪˈsɪk.lɪk/, but may also be stressed on the second syllable, e.g. **epigraphy** /eˈpɪg.rə.fi/.
epiblast ˈep.ɪ.blæst **-s** -s
epic ˈep.ɪk **-s** -s
epicanth|ic ˌep.ɪˈkæn*t*.θ|ɪk **-us/es** -əs/ɪz **-i** -aɪ
epicene ˈep.ɪ.siːn **-s** -z
epicenter ˈep.ɪ.sen.təʳ (US) -t̬ɚ **-s** -z
epicentral ˌep.ɪˈsen.trəl
epicentre ˈep.ɪ.sen.təʳ (US) -t̬ɚ **-s** -z
epicentr|um ˌep.ɪˈsen.tr|əm **-ums** -əmz **-a** -ə
Epicharmus ˌep.ɪˈkɑː.məs (US) -ˈkɑːr-
epic|ism ˈep.ɪ.s|ɪ.zəm **-ist/s** -ɪst/s
Epicoene ˈep.ɪ.siː.ni (US) ˈep.ɪ.siːn
epicotyl ˈep.ɪ.kɒt.ɪl (US) -kɑː.t̬əl **-s** -z
Epictetus ˌep.ɪkˈtiː.təs (US) -t̬əs
epicure ˈep.ɪ.kjʊəʳ, -kjɔːʳ (US) -kjʊr **-s** -z
epicurean (E) ˌep.ɪ.kjʊəˈriː.ən, -kjɔːˈ- (US) -kjʊrˈiː- **-s** -z
epicurism ˈep.ɪ.kjʊə.rɪ.zəm, -kjɔː- (US) -kjʊr.ɪ-
Epicurus ˌep.ɪˈkjʊə.rəs, -ˈkjɔː- (US) -əˈkjʊr.əs
epicycle ˈep.ɪ.saɪ.kl̩ (US) ˈ-ə- **-s** -z
epicyclic ˌep.ɪˈsaɪ.klɪk, -ˈsɪk.lɪk (US) -əˈ-
epicycloid ˌep.ɪˈsaɪ.klɔɪd (US) -əˈ- **-s** -z
Epidaurus ˌep.ɪˈdɔː.rəs (US) -əˈdɔːr.əs
epideictic ˌep.ɪˈdaɪk.tɪk (US) -əˈ-
epidemic ˌep.ɪˈdem.ɪk (US) -əˈ- **-s** -s **-al** -əl **-ally** -əl.i, -li
epidemiological ˌep.ɪ.diː.mi.əˈlɒdʒ.ɪ.kəl (US) -əˌdiː.mi.əˈlɑː.dʒɪ-, -ˌdem.i- **-ly** -i
epidemiolog|y ˌep.ɪˌdiː.miˈɒl.ə.dʒ|i (US) -əˌdiː.miˈɑː.lə-, -ˌdem.iˈ- **-ist/s** -ɪst/s
epiderm|al ˌep.ɪˈdɜː.m|əl (US) -əˈdɝː- **-ic** -ɪk **-oid** -ɔɪd

epidermis ˌep.ɪˈdɜː.mɪs (US) -əˈdɝː-
epidiascope ˌep.ɪˈdaɪə.skəʊp (US) -əˈdaɪə.skoʊp **-s** -s
epididymis ˌep.ɪˈdɪd.ə.mɪs, ˈ-ɪ- (US) -əˈ- **epididymides** ˌep.ɪ.dɪˈdɪm.ɪ.diːz (US) -ə-
epidural ˌep.ɪˈdjʊə.rəl, -ˈdjɔː- (US) -əˈdʊr.əl, -ˈdjʊr- **-s** -z
epige|al ˌep.ɪˈdʒiː|.əl (US) -əˈ- **-an** -ən
epigene ˈep.ɪ.dʒiːn (US) ˈ-ə-
epigenesis ˌep.ɪˈdʒen.ə.sɪs, ˈ-ɪ- (US) -əˈ-
epiglott|al ˌep.ɪˈglɒt|.əl, ˈep.ɪ.glɒt- (US) ˌep.əˈglɑː.t̬|əl **-ic** -ɪk
epiglottis ˌep.ɪˈglɒt.ɪs, ˈep.ɪ.glɒt- (US) -əˈglɑː.t̬ɪs **-es** -ɪz
epigone ˈep.ɪ.gəʊn (US) -ə.goʊn **-s** -z
Epigoni epˈɪ.gə.naɪ, ɪˈpɪg-, -niː
epigram ˈep.ɪ.græm (US) ˈ-ə- **-s** -z
epigrammatic ˌep.ɪ.grəˈmæt.ɪk (US) -ə.grəˈmæt̬- **-al** -əl **-ally** -əl.i, -li
epigrammatist ˌep.ɪˈgræm.ə.tɪst (US) -əˈgræm.ə.t̬ɪst **-s** -s
epigrammatiz|e, -is|e ˌep.ɪˈgræm.ə.taɪz (US) -əˈ- **-es** -ɪz **-ing** -ɪŋ **-ed** -d
epigraph ˈep.ɪ.grɑːf, -græf (US) -ə.græf **-s** -s
epigrapher epˈɪg.rə.fəʳ, ɪˈpɪg- (US) -fɚ **-s** -z
epigraphic ˌep.ɪˈgræf.ɪk (US) -əˈ-
epigraph|y epˈɪg.rə.f|i, ɪˈpɪg- **-ist/s** -ɪst/s
epilepsy ˈep.ɪ.lep.si, ˈ-ə-
epileptic ˌep.ɪˈlep.tɪk, -əˈ- **-s** -s **-al** -əl
epilog ˈep.ɪ.lɒg (US) -ə.lɑːg, -lɔːg **-s** -z
epilogic ˌep.ɪˈlɒdʒ.ɪk, -əˈ- (US) -əˈlɑː.dʒɪk
epilogiz|e, -is|e epˈɪl.ə.dʒaɪz, ɪˈpɪl- **-es** -ɪz **-ing** -ɪŋ **-ed** -d
epilogue ˈep.ɪ.lɒg (US) -ə.lɑːg, -lɔːg **-s** -z
Epimenides ˌep.ɪˈmen.ɪ.diːz, -ə.diːz (US) -əˈ-
Epinal ˈep.ɪ.nəl (US) ˌeɪ.piːˈnɑːl
epiphan|y (E) ɪˈpɪf.ən|.i, epˈɪf-, əˈpɪf- (US) ɪˈpɪf.ə.n|i **-ies** -iz
epiphyte ˈep.ɪ.faɪt (US) ˈ-ə- **-s** -s
Epirus epˈaɪə.rəs, ɪˈpaɪə- (US) ɪˈpaɪ-
episcopac|y ɪˈpɪs.kə.pə.s|i, epˈɪs- **-ies** -iz
episcopal ɪˈpɪs.kə.pəl, epˈɪs- **-ly** -i
episcopalian (E) ɪˌpɪs.kəˈpeɪ.li.ən, epˌɪs- (US) -ˈpeɪ.li.ən, -ˈpeɪl.jən **-s** -z **-ism** -ɪ.zəm
episcopate ɪˈpɪs.kə.pət, epˈɪs-, -pɪt, -peɪt **-s** -s
episcope ˈep.ɪ.skəʊp (US) -ə.skoʊp **-s** -s
episcopiz|e, -is|e ɪˈpɪs.kə.paɪz, epˈɪs- **-es** -ɪz **-ing** -ɪŋ **-ed** -d
episiotom|y ɪˌpɪz.iˈɒt.ə.m|i, epˌɪz-, -ˌiː.ziˈ-; ˌep.ɪ.ziˈ- (US) ɪˌpiː.ziːˈɑː.t̬ə-; ˌep.ɪ.saɪˈ- **-ies** -iz
episode ˈep.ɪ.səʊd (US) -ə.soʊd **-s** -z
episodic ˌep.ɪˈsɒd.ɪk (US) -əˈsɑː.dɪk **-al** -əl **-ally** -əl.i, -li
epistemic ˌep.ɪˈstiː.mɪk, -ˈstem.ɪk
epistemological ɪˌpɪs.tɪ.məˈlɒdʒ.ɪ.kəl, epˌɪs-, -tə-, -tiː- (US) -ˈlɑː.dʒɪ- **-ly** -li
epistemology ɪˌpɪs.təˈmɒl.ə.dʒi, epˌɪs-, -tɪˈ- (US) -təˈmɑː.lə-
epistle (E) ɪˈpɪs.l̩, epˈɪs- (US) ɪˈpɪs- **-s** -z
epistler ɪˈpɪst.ləʳ, epˈɪs- (US) ɪˈpɪst.lɚ **-s** -z
epistolary ɪˈpɪs.təl.ər.i, epˈɪs- (US) ɪˈpɪs.təl.er-
epistoler ɪˈpɪs.təl.əʳ, epˈɪs- (US) ɪˈpɪs.təl.ɚ **-s** -z
epistoliz|e, -is|e ɪˈpɪs.təl.aɪz, epˈɪs- (US) ɪˈpɪs.tə.laɪz **-es** -ɪz **-ing** -ɪŋ **-ed** -d
epistyle ˈep.ɪ.staɪl **-s** -z
epitaph ˈep.ɪ.tɑːf, -tæf (US) -ə.tæf **-s** -s
Epithalamion ˌep.ɪ.θəˈleɪ.mi.ən
epithalami|um ˌep.ɪ.θəˈleɪ.mi|.əm **-a** -ə **-ums** -əmz
epitheli|um ˌep.ɪˈθiː.li|.əm **-ums** -əmz **-a** -ə
epithet ˈep.ɪ.θet (US) -θet, -θət **-s** -s
epithetic ˌep.ɪˈθet.ɪk (US) -əˈθet̬-
epitome ɪˈpɪt.ə.mi, epˈɪt-, əˈpɪt- (US) ɪˈpɪt̬- **-s** -z
epitomic ˌep.ɪˈtɒm.ɪk (US) -ˈtɑː.mɪk **-al** -əl
epitomist ɪˈpɪt.ə.mɪst, epˈɪt- (US) ɪˈpɪt̬- **-s** -s
epitomiz|e, -is|e ɪˈpɪt.ə.maɪz, epˈɪt- (US) ɪˈpɪt̬- **-es** -ɪz **-ing** -ɪŋ **-ed** -d
epoch ˈiː.pɒk, ˈep.ək (US) ˈep.ək, -ɑːk, ˌiːˈpɑːk **-s** -s
epochal ˈiː.pɒk.əl, ˈep.ɒk-, -ə.kəl; iːˈpɒk.əl (US) ˈep.ə.kəl; -ɑː.kəl
epoch-making ˈiː.pɒkˌmeɪ.kɪŋ (US) ˈep.əkˌ-, -ɑːkˌ-
epode ˈep.əʊd (US) -oʊd **-s** -z
eponym ˈep.ə.nɪm **-s** -z
eponymous ɪˈpɒn.ɪ.məs, epˈɒn-, ˈ-ə- (US) ɪˈpɑː.nə-
eponymy ɪˈpɒn.ɪ.mi, epˈɒn-, ˈ-ə- (US) ɪˈpɑː.nə-
epos ˈep.ɒs, ˈiː.pɒs (US) ˈep.ɑːs **-es** -ɪz
Epos, EPOS ˈiː.pɒs (US) -pɑːs
epox|y ɪˈpɒk.si, epˈɒk- (US) ɪˈpɑːk- **-ies** -ɪz **-ing** -ɪŋ **ied** -ɪd eˌpoxy ˈresin
Epping ˈep.ɪŋ
Epps eps
EPROM ˈiː.prɒm (US) -prɑːm **-s** -z
epsilon epˈsaɪ.lən, -lɒn; ˈep.sɪ.lən, -sə-, -lɒn (US) ˈep.sə.lɑːn, -lən **-s** -z
Epsom ˈep.səm ˈ**Epsom ˌsalts, ˌEpsom ˈsalts**
Epstein ˈep.staɪn
Epstein-Barr ˌep.staɪnˈbɑːʳ, -staɪmˈ- (US) -staɪn.ˈbɑːr
Epworth ˈep.wəθ, -wɜːθ (US) -wɚθ, -wɝːθ
epylli|on epˈɪl.i|.ɒn, ɪˈpɪl-, -ən (US) -ɑːn, -ən **-a** -ə
equability ˌek.wəˈbɪl.ə.ti, ˌiː.kwəˈ-, -ɪ.ti (US) -ə.t̬i
equab|le ˈek.wə.b|l̩, ˈiː.kwə- **-ly** -li **-leness** -l̩.nəs, -nɪs
equal ˈiː.kwəl **-ly** -i **-ness** -nəs, -nɪs **-s** -z **-(l)ing** -ɪŋ **-(l)ed** -d ˌ**Equal Opporˈtunities Comˌmission; ˌEqual ˈRights Aˌmendment; ˌequal ˈrights; ˈequals ˌsign**
equalit|y ɪˈkwɒl.ə.t|i, iː-, -ɪ.t|i (US) -ˈkwɑː.lə.t̬|i, -ˈkwɔː- **-ies** -iz
equalization, -isa- ˌiː.kwəl.aɪˈzeɪ.ʃən, -ɪˈ- (US) -ɪˈ- **-s** -z
equaliz|e, -is|e ˈiː.kwəl.aɪz (US) -kwə.laɪz **-es** -ɪz **-ing** -ɪŋ **-ed** -d
equalizer, -iser ˈiː.kwə.laɪ.zəʳ (US) -zɚ **-s** -z
equanimity ˌek.wəˈnɪm.ə.ti, ˌiː.kwəˈ-, -ɪ.ti (US) -ə.t̬i
equanimous ɪˈkwæn.ɪ.məs, iː-, ekˈwæn-, -ˈwɒn-, -ə.məs (US) ɪˈkwæn-, iː-, ekˈwæn- **-ly** -li **-ness** -nəs, -nɪs
e|quate ɪˈkweɪt, iː- **-quates** -kweɪts **-quating** -kweɪ.tɪŋ (US) -kweɪ.t̬ɪŋ **-quated** -kweɪ.tɪd (US) -kweɪ.t̬ɪd **-quatable** -kweɪ.tə.bl̩ (US) -kweɪ.t̬ə.bl̩
equation ɪˈkweɪ.ʒən (US) ɪˈ-, iːˈ- **-s** -z
equational ɪˈkweɪ.ʒən.əl, iː-
equative ɪˈkweɪ.tɪv (US) -t̬ɪv
equator ɪˈkweɪ.təʳ (US) -t̬ɚ **-s** -z
equatorial ˌek.wəˈtɔː.ri.əl, ˌiː.kwəˈ- (US) -ˈtɔːr.i- **-ly** -i
equerr|y ˈek.wə.r|i; ɪˈkwer|.i (US) ˈek.wɚ|.i; ɪˈkwer- **-ies** -iz
Note: The pronunciation at court is /ɪˈkwer.i/.
equestrian ɪˈkwes.tri.ən, ekˈwes- (US) ɪˈkwes- **-s** -z **-ism** -ɪ.zəm
equestrienne ɪˌkwes.triˈen, ekˌwes- (US) ɪˌkwes- **-s** -z
equi- iː.kwɪ-, ek.wɪ-, -wi-, -wə-; ɪˈkwɪ-
Note: Prefix. Either takes primary or secondary stress on the first syllable, e.g. **equinox** /ˈiː.kwɪ.nɒks (US) -nɑːks/, **equinoctial** /ˌiː.kwɪnˈɒk.ʃəl (US) -ˈnɑːk-/, or primary or secondary stress on the second syllable, e.g. **equivocate** /ɪˈkwɪv.ə.keɪt/, **equivocation** /ɪˌkwɪv.əˈkeɪ.ʃən/.
equiangular ˌiː.kwiˈæŋ.gjʊ.ləʳ, -gjə- (US) -lɚ
equidistant ˌiː.kwɪˈdɪs.tənt, ˌek.wɪˈ-, -wəˈ- **-ly** -li
equilateral ˌiː.kwɪˈlæt.ər.əl, -kwəˈ- (US) -ˈlæt̬-, ˌek.wəˈ-
equilib|rate ˌiː.kwɪˈlaɪ.b|reɪt, ˌek.wɪˈ-, -wəˈ-, -ˈlɪb|.reɪt; iːˈkwɪl.ɪ.b|reɪt, ɪ- (US) ɪˈkwɪl-, iː- **-rates** -reɪts **-rating**

-reɪ.tɪŋ ⓤⓢ -reɪ.t̬ɪŋ **-rated** -reɪ.tɪd ⓤⓢ -reɪ.t̬ɪd
equilibration ˌiː.kwɪ.laɪˈbreɪ.ʃᵊn, ˌek.wɪ-, -wə-, -lɪˈbreɪ-; iːˌkwɪl.ɪˈ-, ɪ- ⓤⓢ ɪˌkwɪl.ɪˈ-, iːˌ-
equilibrist iːˈkwɪl.ɪ.brɪst, ɪ-; ˌiː.kwɪˈlɪb.rɪst, ˌek.wɪˈ-, -wəˈ- ⓤⓢ ɪˈkwɪl.ə.brɪst, iː-; ˌiː.kwəˈlɪb.rɪst **-s** -s
equilibrium ˌiː.kwɪˈlɪb.ri.əm, ˌek.wɪˈ-, -wəˈ-
equimultiple ˌiː.kwɪˈmʌl.tɪ.pl̩, ˌek.wɪˈ-, -wəˈ-, -tə- ⓤⓢ -t̬ə- **-s** -z
equine ˈek.waɪn, ˈiː.kwaɪn ⓤⓢ ˈiː.kwaɪn, ˈek.waɪn
equinoctial ˌiː.kwɪˈnɒk.ʃᵊl, ˌek.wɪˈ-, -wəˈ- ⓤⓢ -ˈnɑːk- **-s** -z
equinox ˈiː.kwɪ.nɒks, ˈek.wɪ-, -wə- ⓤⓢ -nɑːks **-es** -ɪz
equip ɪˈkwɪp **-s** -s **-ping** -ɪŋ **-ped** -t
equipag|e ˈek.wɪ.pɪdʒ, -wə- **-es** -ɪz
equipment ɪˈkwɪp.mənt
equipois|e ˈek.wɪ.pɔɪz, ˈiː.kwɪ-, -kwə- **-es** -ɪz **-ing** -ɪŋ **-ed** -d
equipollent ˌiː.kwɪˈpɒl.ənt, ˌek.wɪˈ-, -wəˈ- ⓤⓢ -ˈpɑː.lənt
equitab|le ˈek.wɪ.tə.bl̩, -wə- ⓤⓢ -t̬ə- **-ly** -li **-leness** -l̩.nəs, -nɪs
equitation ˌek.wɪˈteɪ.ʃᵊn, -wəˈ-
equit|y (E) ˈek.wɪ.t|i, -wə- ⓤⓢ -t̬|i **-ies** -iz
equivalen|ce ɪˈkwɪv.ᵊl.ənt|s **-cy** -si
equivalent ɪˈkwɪv.ᵊl.ənt **-s** -s **-ly** -li
equivocal ɪˈkwɪv.ə.kᵊl, ˈ-ɪ- **-ly** -i **-ness** -nəs, -nɪs
equivo|cate ɪˈkwɪv.ə|.keɪt **-cates** -keɪts **-cating** -keɪ.tɪŋ ⓤⓢ -keɪ.t̬ɪŋ **-cated** -keɪ.tɪd ⓤⓢ -keɪ.t̬ɪd **-cator/s** -keɪ.təʳ/z ⓤⓢ -keɪ.t̬ɚ/z
equivocation ɪˌkwɪv.əˈkeɪ.ʃᵊn **-s** -z
equivoque, equivoke ˈek.wɪ.vəʊk, -wə- ⓤⓢ -voʊk **-s** -s
Equuleus ekˈwʊl.i.əs
er ɜːʳ ⓤⓢ ɝː
-er -əʳ ⓤⓢ -ɚ
Note: Suffix. Normally unstressed, e.g. **paint** /peɪnt/, **painter** /ˈpeɪn.təʳ ⓤⓢ -t̬ɚ/, **soon** /suːn/, **sooner** /ˈsuː.nəʳ ⓤⓢ -nɚ/.
ER ˌiːˈɑːʳ ⓤⓢ -ˈɑːr
era ˈɪə.rə ⓤⓢ ˈɪr.ə, ˈer- **-s** -z
ERA ˌiː.ɑːʳˈeɪ ⓤⓢ -ɑːrˈ-
eradi|ate ɪˈreɪ.di|.eɪt, iː- **-ates** -eɪts **-ating** -eɪ.tɪŋ ⓤⓢ -eɪ.t̬ɪŋ **-ated** -eɪ.tɪd ⓤⓢ -eɪ.t̬ɪd
eradiation ɪˌreɪ.diˈeɪ.ʃᵊn, iː-
eradicable ɪˈræd.ɪ.kə.bl̩
eradi|cate ɪˈræd.ɪ|.keɪt **-cates** -keɪts **-cating** -keɪ.tɪŋ ⓤⓢ -keɪ.t̬ɪŋ **-cated** -keɪ.tɪd ⓤⓢ -keɪ.t̬ɪd
eradication ɪˌræd.ɪˈkeɪ.ʃᵊn
eradicative ɪˈræd.ɪ.kə.tɪv, -keɪ- ⓤⓢ -kə.t̬ɪv
Érard ˈer.ɑːd ⓤⓢ eɪˈrɑːrd, ˈer.ɑːrd **-s** -z
eras|e ɪˈreɪz ⓤⓢ -ˈreɪs **-es** -ɪz **-ing** -ɪŋ **-ed** -d **-er/s** -əʳ/z ⓤⓢ -ɚ/z **-able** -ə.bl̩
erasion ɪˈreɪ.ʒᵊn **-s** -z
Erasmian ɪˈræz.mi.ən, erˈæz- **-s** -z **-ism** -ɪ.zᵊm
Erasmus ɪˈræz.məs, erˈæz-
Erastian ɪˈræs.ti.ən, erˈæs- **-s** -z **-ism** -ɪ.zᵊm
Erastus ɪˈræs.təs, erˈæs-
erasure ɪˈreɪ.ʒəʳ ⓤⓢ -ʃɚ **-s** -z
erbium ˈɜː.bi.əm ⓤⓢ ˈɝː-
Erdington ˈɜː.dɪŋ.tən ⓤⓢ ˈɝː-
ere eəʳ ⓤⓢ er
Erebus ˈer.ɪ.bəs, ˈ-ə-
Erec ˈɪə.rek ⓤⓢ ˈiː.rek, ˈer.ek
Erechtheum ˌer.ekˈθiː.əm, -ɪkˈ-, -əkˈ-
Erechtheus ɪˈrek.θjuːs, erˈek-, -θi.əs
erect ɪˈrekt **-ly** -li **-ness** -nəs, -nɪs **-s** -s **-ing** -ɪŋ **-ed** -ɪd
erectile ɪˈrek.taɪl ⓤⓢ -təl, -taɪl
erection ɪˈrek.ʃᵊn **-s** -z
erector ɪˈrek.təʳ ⓤⓢ -tɚ **-s** -z
eremite ˈer.ɪ.maɪt, ˈ-ə- **-s** -s
eremitic ˌer.ɪˈmɪt.ɪk, -əˈ- ⓤⓢ -əˈmɪt̬- **-al** -ᵊl
erepsin ɪˈrep.sɪn
Eretri|a ɪˈret.ri|.ə, erˈet- **-an/s** -ən/z
erewhile eəˈhwaɪl ⓤⓢ erˈ-
Erewhon ˈer.ɪ.hwɒn ⓤⓢ -hwɑːn, -hwʌn
Erfurt ˈeə.fɜːt *as if German:* -fʊət ⓤⓢ ˈer.fʊrt, -fɝːt
erg ɜːg ⓤⓢ ɝːg **-s** -z
ergative ˈɜː.gə.tɪv ⓤⓢ ˈɝː.gə.t̬ɪv
ergativity ˌɜː.gəˈtɪv.ə.ti, -ɪ.ti ⓤⓢ ˌɝː.gəˈtɪv.ə.t̬i
ergo ˈɜː.gəʊ, ˈeə- ⓤⓢ ˈer.goʊ, ˈɝː-
ergon ˈɜː.gɒn ⓤⓢ ˈɝː.gɑːn **-s** -z
ergonic ɜːˈgɒn.ɪk ⓤⓢ ɝːˈgɑː.nɪk **-s** -s **-ally** -ᵊl.i, -li
ergonomic ˌɜː.gəˈnɒm.ɪk ⓤⓢ ˌɝː.gəˈnɑː.mɪk **-s** -s
ergonomical ˌɜː.gəˈnɒm.ɪ.kᵊl ⓤⓢ ˌɝː.gəˈnɑː.mɪ- **-ly** -i
ergonomist ɜːˈgɒn.ə.mɪst ⓤⓢ ɝːˈgɑː.nə- **-s** -s
ergosterol ɜːˈgɒs.tə.rɒl, -tɪᵊ- ⓤⓢ ɝːˈgɑː.stə.rɑːl, -rɔːl, -roʊl
ergot ˈɜː.gət, -gɒt ⓤⓢ ˈɝː.gət, -gɑːt **-ism** -ɪ.zᵊm
Eric ˈer.ɪk
Erica, erica ˈer.ɪ.kə
ericaceous ˌer.ɪˈkeɪ.ʃəs
Ericht ˈer.ɪxt
Eric(k)son ˈer.ɪk.sᵊn
Ericsson® ˈer.ɪk.sᵊn
Erie ˈɪə.ri ⓤⓢ ˈɪr.i
Erik ˈer.ɪk
Erika ˈer.ɪ.kə
Erin ˈɪə.rɪn, ˈer.ɪn, ˈeə.rɪn ⓤⓢ ˈer.ɪn, ˈɪr-
Eris ˈer.ɪs ⓤⓢ ˈɪr-, ˈer-
eristic erˈɪs.tɪk ⓤⓢ ɪˈrɪs-, erˈɪs- **-s** -s
Erith ˈɪə.rɪθ ⓤⓢ ˈɪr.ɪθ
Eritre|a ˌer.ɪˈtreɪ|.ə, -əˈtreɪ-, -ˈtriː- ⓤⓢ -ˈtriː- **-an/s** -ən/z
Erle ɜːl ⓤⓢ ɝːl
erl-king ˈɜːl.kɪŋ, ˌ-ˈ- ⓤⓢ ˈɝːl.kɪŋ, ˈerl- **-s** -z
ERM ˌiː.ɑːʳˈem ⓤⓢ -ɑːrˈ-
ermine ˈɜː.mɪn ⓤⓢ ˈɝː- **-s** -z **-d** -d
erne (E) ɜːn ⓤⓢ ɝːn **-s** -z
Ernest ˈɜː.nɪst, -nəst ⓤⓢ ˈɝː-
Ernie ˈɜː.ni ⓤⓢ ˈɝː-
Ernle ˈɜːn.li ⓤⓢ ˈɝːn-
Ernst ɜːntst *as if German:* eəntst ⓤⓢ ɝːntst *as if German:* ernst
erod|e ɪˈrəʊd ⓤⓢ -ˈroʊd **-es** -z **-ing** -ɪŋ **-ed** -ɪd
erogenous ɪˈrɒdʒ.ɪ.nəs, erˈɒdʒ-, əˈrɒdʒ-, ˈ-ə- ⓤⓢ ɪˈrɑː.dʒɪ-, -dʒə-
Eroica erˈəʊ.ɪ.kə, ɪˈrəʊ-, əˈrəʊ- ⓤⓢ ɪˈroʊ-, erˈoʊ-
Eros ˈɪə.rɒs, ˈer.ɒs ⓤⓢ ˈer.ɑːs, ˈɪr-, ˈer.oʊs
erosion ɪˈrəʊ.ʒᵊn ⓤⓢ -ˈroʊ- **-s** -z
erosive ɪˈrəʊ.sɪv, -zɪv ⓤⓢ -ˈroʊ-
erotic ɪˈrɒt.ɪk ⓤⓢ -ˈrɑː.t̬ɪk **-s** -s **-a** -ə **-ally** -ᵊl.i, -li
eroticism ɪˈrɒt.ɪ.sɪ.zᵊm, ˈ-ə- ⓤⓢ -ˈrɑː.t̬ə-
eroticization, -isa- ɪˌrɒt.ɪ.saɪˈzeɪ.ʃᵊn, ˌ-ə-, -sɪˈ- ⓤⓢ -ˌrɑː.t̬ə.sɪˈ-
eroticiz|e, -is|e ɪˈrɒt.ɪ.saɪz, ˈ-ə- ⓤⓢ -ˈrɑː.t̬ə- **-es** -ɪz **-ing** -ɪŋ **-ed** -d
erotogenic ɪˌrɒt.əˈdʒen.ɪk, -ˌrəʊ.təˈ- ⓤⓢ ɪˌrɑː.t̬əˈdʒen-, -ˌroʊ- **-ally** -ᵊl.i, -li
erotomani|a ɪˌrɒt.əʊˈmeɪ.ni|.ə, -ˌrəʊ.təʊˈ- ⓤⓢ ɪˌrɑː.t̬əˈmeɪ.ni|.ə, -ˌroʊ- **-ac/s** -æk/s
err ɜːʳ ⓤⓢ ɝː, er **-s** -z **-ing** -ɪŋ **-ed** -d
errand ˈer.ənd **-s** -z
errant ˈer.ənt **-ly** -li **-ry** -ri
errata *(plur. of* **erratum***)* erˈɑː.tə, ɪˈrɑː-, -ˈreɪ- ⓤⓢ -t̬ə
erratic ɪˈræt.ɪk, erˈæt- ⓤⓢ ɪˈræt̬- **-ally** -ᵊl.i, -li
errat|um erˈɑː.t|əm, ɪˈrɑː-, -ˈreɪ- ⓤⓢ -t̬|əm **-a** -ə
Errol(l) ˈer.əl
erroneous ɪˈrəʊ.ni.əs, erˈəʊ- ⓤⓢ əˈroʊ-, erˈoʊ-, ɪˈroʊ- **-ly** -li **-ness** -nəs, -nɪs
error ˈer.əʳ ⓤⓢ -ɚ **-s** -z
ersatz ˈeə.sæts *as if German:* ˈeə.zɑːts ⓤⓢ ˈer.zɑːts, -ˈ-
Erse ɜːs ⓤⓢ ɝːs
Erskine ˈɜː.skɪn ⓤⓢ ˈɝː-
erst ɜːst ⓤⓢ ɝːst
erstwhile ˈɜːst.hwaɪl ⓤⓢ ˈɝːst-
erubescen|ce ˌer.ʊˈbes.ᵊn|ts, -uːˈ- **-cy** -tsi **-t** -t
eruct ɪˈrʌkt, iː- **-s** -s **-ing** -ɪŋ **-ed** -ɪd
eruc|tate ɪˈrʌk|.teɪt, iː- **-tates** -teɪts **-tating** -teɪ.tɪŋ ⓤⓢ -teɪ.t̬ɪŋ **-tated** -teɪ.tɪd ⓤⓢ -teɪ.t̬ɪd

eructation ˌiː.rʌkˈteɪ.ʃᵊn, ˌer.ʌk-, -əkˈ-; ɪˌrʌkˈ- US ˌiː.rʌkˈ-, ɪˌrʌkˈ- **-s** -z
erudite ˈer.ʊ.daɪt, -jʊ- US -jə-, -ə-, -juː-, -uː- **-ly** -li **-ness** -nəs, -nɪs
erudition ˌer.ʊˈdɪʃ.ᵊn, -jʊˈ- US -juːˈ-, -uːˈ-, -jəˈ-, -əˈ-
erupt ɪˈrʌpt **-s** -s **-ing** -ɪŋ **-ed** -ɪd
eruption ɪˈrʌp.ʃᵊn **-s** -z
eruptive ɪˈrʌp.tɪv **-ly** -li **-ness** -nəs, -nɪs
Ervine ˈɜː.vɪn US ˈɝː-
Erving ˈɜː.vɪŋ US ˈɝː-
erysipelas ˌer.ɪˈsɪp.ᵊl.əs, -əˈ-, -ɪ.ləs, -lɪs
erythema ˌer.ɪˈθiː.mə, -əˈ-
erythrocyte ɪˈrɪθ.rəʊ.saɪt US erˈɪθ.roʊ- **-s** -s
erythrocytic ɪˌrɪθ.rəʊˈsɪt.ɪk US erˌɪθ.roʊˈsɪţ-
erythromycin ɪˌrɪθ.rəʊˈmaɪ.sɪn, əˌrɪθ- US ɪ.rɪθ.roʊˈ-, -rəˈ-
Erzerum ˈeə.zə.ruːm US ˈer-
Esau ˈiː.sɔː US -sɑː, -sɔː
Esbjerg ˈes.bjɜːg US -bjerg
escalad|e ˌes.kəˈleɪd, ˈ--- **-es** -z **-ing** -ɪŋ **-ed** -ɪd
esca|late ˈes.kə|.leɪt **-lates** -leɪts **-lating** -leɪ.tɪŋ US -leɪ.ţɪŋ **-lated** -leɪ.tɪd US -leɪ.ţɪd
escalation ˌes.kəˈleɪ.ʃᵊn
escalator ˈes.kə.leɪ.təʳ US -ţɚ **-s** -z
escal(l)op ɪˈskɒl.əp, esˈkɒl-, -ˈkæl-, -ɒp; ˈes.kə.lɒp US esˈkɑː.ləp, ɪˈskɑː-, -ˈskæl- **-ed** -t
escalope ˈes.kə.lɒp, ˈɪs-, -ləp; esˈkæl.əp, -ɒp US ˌes.kəˈloʊp **-s** -s
escapade ˌes.kəˈpeɪd, ˈ--- **-s** -z
escap|e ɪˈskeɪp, esˈkeɪp, əˈskeɪp **-es** -s **-ing** -ɪŋ **-ed** -t **-ement/s** -mənt/s
escapee ɪˌskeɪˈpiː, ˌes.keɪˈ- **-s** -z
escap|ism ɪˈskeɪ.p|ɪ.zᵊm, esˈkeɪ- **-ist/s** -ɪst/s
escapolog|y ˌes.kəˈpɒl.ə.dʒ|i, -keɪˈ- US -keɪˈpɑː.lə- **-ist/s** -ɪst/s
escargot ɪˈskɑː.gəʊ, esˈkɑː- *as if French:* ˌes.kɑːˈgəʊ US ˌes.kɑːrˈgoʊ **-s** -z
escarole ˈes.kə.rəʊl US -kə.roʊl
escarp ɪˈskɑːp, esˈkɑːp US esˈkɑːrp **-s** -s **-ing** -ɪŋ **-ed** -t
escarpment ɪˈskɑːp.mənt, esˈkɑːp- US esˈkɑːrp- **-s** -s
-esce -ˈes
Note: Suffix. Always carries primary stress, e.g. **convalesce** /ˌkɒn.vəˈles US ˌkɑːn-/.
-escen|ce -ˈes.ᵊn|ts **-t** -t
Note: Suffix. Always carries primary stress, e.g. **convalescence** /ˌkɒn.vəˈles.ᵊnts US ˌkɑːn-/.
eschar ˈes.kɑːʳ US -kɑːr, -kɚ **-s** -z
eschatological ˌes.kə.təˈlɒdʒ.ɪ.kᵊl, -kæt.əˈ- US -kə.ţəˈlɑː.dʒɪ-; esˌkæţ.ᵊlˈɑː-
eschatolog|y ˌes.kəˈtɒl.ə.dʒ|i US -ˈtɑː.lə- **-ist/s** -ɪst/s
es|cheat ɪs|ˈtʃiːt, es- **-cheats** -ˈtʃiːts **-cheating** -ˈtʃiː.tɪŋ US -ˈtʃiː.ţɪŋ **-cheated** -ˈtʃiː.tɪd US -ˈtʃiː.ţɪd
Escher ˈeʃ.əʳ US -ɚ
eschew ɪsˈtʃuː, es- US es-, ɪs- **-s** -z **-ing** -ɪŋ **-ed** -d
eschscholtzia ɪˈskɒl.ʃə, esˈkɒl-, -tʃə; ɪʃˈɒlt.si.ə, eʃ-, əˈʃɒlt-, -ˈskɒlt- US eʃˈoʊlt.si.ə **-s** -z
Escoffier ɪˈskɒf.i.eɪ, esˈkɒf- US ˌes.kɑːˈfjeɪ
Escom ˈes.kɒm, -kɑːm US -kɑːm
Escombe ˈes.kəm
Escondido ˌes.kənˈdiː.dəʊ US -doʊ
Escorial ˌes.kɒr.iˈɑːl, -ˈæl; esˈkɔː.ri.æl, -ɑːl US esˈkɔːr.i.əl; esˌkɔːr.iˈæl
escort® **(E)** *(n.)* ˈes.kɔːt US -kɔːrt **-s** -s
escor|t *(v.)* ɪˈskɔː|t, esˈkɔː|t; ˈes.kɔː|t US esˈkɔːr|t, ɪˈskɔːr|t; ˈes.kɔːr|t **-ts** -ts **-ting** -tɪŋ US -ţɪŋ **-ted** -tɪd US -ţɪd
Escott ˈes.kɒt US -kɑːt
Escow ˈes.kəʊ US -koʊ
escritoire ˌes.kriːˈtwɑːʳ, ˈ--- US ˌes.kriːˈtwɑːr **-s** -z
escrow ˈes.krəʊ, -ˈ- US ˈes.kroʊ, -ˈ-
escudo esˈkuː.dəʊ, ɪˈskuː-, -ˈskjuː-; ɪʃˈkuː-, eʃ- US esˈkuː.doʊ, ɪˈskuː- **-s** -z
esculent ˈes.kjə.lənt, -kjʊ- **-s** -s
Escurial esˈkjʊə.ri.əl US -ˈkjʊr.i-
escutcheon ɪˈskʌtʃ.ᵊn, esˈkʌtʃ- **-s** -z
Esda ˈes.də, ˈez- ˈ**Esda** ˌ**test**
Esdaile ˈez.deɪl
Esdras ˈez.dræs, -drəs
-ese -ˈiːz US -ˈiːz, -ˈiːs
Note: Suffix. Always carries primary stress, e.g. **Japan** /dʒəˈpæn/, **Japanese** /ˌdʒæp.əˈniːz/.
ESE ˌiːst.saʊθˈiːst *in nautical usage also:* -saʊˈ-
Esfahan ˈeʃ.fə.hɑːn, ˈes- US ˌes.fəˈhɑːn
Esher ˈiː.ʃəʳ US -ʃɚ
Esias ɪˈzaɪ.əs, ezˈaɪ-, -æs
Esk esk
Eskimo ˈes.kɪ.məʊ US -kə.moʊ **-s** -z
ESL ˌiː.esˈel
Esmé ˈez.mi, -meɪ
Esmeralda ˌez.məˈræl.də, -mɪˈ-
Esmond(e) ˈez.mənd
ESN ˌiː.esˈen
ESOL ˈiː.sɒl US -sɑːl
ESOP ˈiː.sɒp US -sɑːp
esophageal ɪˌsɒf.əˈdʒiː.əl, iː-, ə-; ˌiː.sɒf- US ɪˌsɑː.fəˈ-; ˌiː.sɑː-
esopha|gus iːˈsɒf.ə|.gəs, ɪ-, ə- US ɪˈsɑː.fə-, iː- **-gi** -gaɪ, -dʒaɪ **-guses** -gə.sɪz
esoteric ˌes.əʊˈter.ɪk, ˌiː.səʊˈ- US ˌes.əˈ- **-al** -ᵊl **-ally** -ᵊl.i, -li
ESP ˌiː.esˈpiː
Espace® esˈpæs
espadrille ˌes.pəˈdrɪl, ˈ--- US ˈes.pə.drɪl **-s** -z
espalier ɪˈspæl.i.eɪ, esˈpæl-, -i.əʳ US -ˈspæl.jɚ, -jeɪ **-s** -z **-ing** -ɪŋ **-ed** -d
esparto esˈpɑː.təʊ, ɪˈspɑː- US esˈpɑːr.ţoʊ **-s** -z
especial ɪˈspeʃ.ᵊl, esˈpeʃ-, əˈspeʃ- **-ly** -i
Esperant|o ˌes.pᵊrˈæn.t|əʊ US -pəˈræn.t|oʊ, -ˈrɑːn- **-ist/s** -ɪst/s
espial ɪˈspaɪ.əl, esˈpaɪ-
espionage ˈes.pi.ə.nɑːʒ, -nɑːdʒ, -nɪdʒ; ˌes.pi.əˈnɑːʒ, -ˈnɑːdʒ
esplanade ˌes.pləˈneɪd, -ˈnɑːd, ˈ--- US ˈes.plə.nɑːd, -neɪd **-s** -z
Esplanade *in Western Australia:* ˈes.plə.nɑːd
ESPN ˌiː.esˌpiːˈen
Espoo ˈes.pəʊ US -poʊ
espous|e ɪˈspaʊz, esˈpaʊz **-es** -ɪz **-ing** -ɪŋ **-ed** -d **-er/s** -əʳ/z US -ɚ/z **-al/s** -ᵊl/z
espressivo ˌes.presˈiː.vəʊ US -voʊ
espresso esˈpres.əʊ, ɪˈspres- US -oʊ **-s** -z
esprit esˈpriː, ɪˈspriː, əˈspriː; ˈes.priː US esˈpriː, ɪˈspriː
esprit de corps esˌpriː.dəˈkɔːʳ, ɪˌspriː-, əˌspriː-; ˌes.priː- US esˌpriː.dəˈkɔːr, ɪˌspriː-
esp|y ɪˈsp|aɪ, esˈp|aɪ **-ies** -aɪz **-ying** -aɪ.ɪŋ **-ied** -aɪd
Espy ˈes.pi
Esq. *(abbrev. for* **Esquire***)* ɪˈskwaɪəʳ, esˈkwaɪəʳ US ˈes.kwaɪɚ; ɪˈskwaɪɚ, esˈkwaɪɚ
-esque -ˈesk
Note: Suffix. Always carries primary stress, e.g. **picturesque** /ˌpɪk.tʃᵊrˈesk/.
Esquiline ˈes.kwɪ.laɪn, -kwᵊl.aɪn US -kwə.laɪn
Esquimalt esˈkwaɪ.mɔːlt, ɪˈskwaɪ-, -mɒlt US -mɑːlt, -mɔːlt
esquire ɪˈskwaɪəʳ, esˈkwaɪəʳ US ˈes.kwaɪɚ; ɪˈskwaɪɚ, esˈkwaɪɚ **-s** -z
ess es **-es** -ɪz
essay *(n.) piece of writing:* ˈes.eɪ **-s** -z **-ist/s** -ɪst/s
essay *(n. v.) attempt:* esˈeɪ, ˈ-- **-s** -z **-ing** -ɪŋ **-ed** -d **-er/s** -əʳ/z US -ɚ/z
esse ˈes.i
Essen ˈes.ᵊn
essenc|e ˈes.ᵊnts **-es** -ɪz
Essene ˈes.iːn, -ˈ- **-s** -z
essential ɪˈsen.*t*ʃᵊl US ɪˈsent.ʃᵊl, esˈent- **-s** -z **-ly** -i **-ness** -nəs, -nɪs **es**ˌ**sential** ˈ**oil**
essentiality ɪˌsen.*t*ʃiˈæl.ə.ti, esˌen-, -ɪ.ti US -ə.ţi
Essex ˈes.ɪks
essive ˈes.ɪv **-s** -z

Esso® 'es.əʊ (US) -oʊ
-est -ɪst, -əst
Note: Suffix. Does not affect the stress pattern of the word, e.g. **happy** /'hæp.i/, **happiest** /'hæp.i.ɪst/.
EST ˌiː.es'tiː
establish ɪ'stæb.lɪʃ, es'tæb- **-es** -ɪz **-ing** -ɪŋ **-ed** -t **-er/s** -əʳ/z (US) -ɚ/z **-ment/s** -mənt/s
estate ɪ'steɪt, es'teɪt **-s** -s **es'tate ˌagent; es'tate ˌcar**
Estcourt 'est.kɔːt (US) -kɔːrt
Este 'es.ti (US) -teɪ
Estée 'es.teɪ, -tiː (US) -teɪ
esteem ɪ'stiːm, es'tiːm **-s** -z **-ing** -ɪŋ **-ed** -d
Estelle ɪ'stel, es'tel
ester 'es.təʳ (US) -tɚ **-s** -z
Esterhazy 'es.tə.hɑː.zi (US) -tɚ.hɑː.zi
Esther 'es.təʳ, -θəʳ (US) -tɚ
esthete 'iːs.θiːt (US) 'es- **-s** -s
esthetic es'θet.ɪk, ɪs- (US) es'θet̬- **-al** -ᵊl **-ally** -ᵊl.i, -li **-s** -s
esthetic|ism es'θet.ɪ.s|ɪ.zᵊm, ɪs- (US) es'θet̬- **-ist/s** -ɪst/s
estimab|le 'es.tɪ.mə.b|l̩, -tə- **-ly** -li **-leness** -l̩.nəs, -nɪs
estimate *(n.)* 'es.tɪ.mət, -tə-, -mɪt, -meɪt (US) -mɪt, -mət **-s** -s
esti|mate *(v.)* 'es.tɪ|.meɪt, -tə-, -mət (US) -meɪt **-mates** -meɪts, -məts (US) -meɪts **-mating** -meɪ.tɪŋ, -mə- (US) -meɪ.t̬ɪŋ **-mated** -meɪ.tɪd, -mə- (US) -meɪ.t̬ɪd **-mator/s** -meɪ.təʳ/z, -mə- (US) -meɪ.t̬ɚ/z
estimation ˌes.tɪ'meɪ.ʃᵊn, -tə'-
estival iː'staɪ.vᵊl, es'taɪ- (US) 'es.tə-, es'taɪ-
Eston 'es.tən
Estoni|a es'təʊ.ni|.ə, ɪ'stəʊ- (US) es'toʊ- **-an/s** -ən/z
estop ɪ'stɒp, es'tɒp (US) es'tɑːp **-s** -s **-ping** -ɪŋ **-ped** -t **-page** -ɪdʒ **-pel/s** -ᵊl/z
Estoril ˌes.tᵊr'ɪl (US) ˌiː.stə'rɪl
estovers ɪ'stəʊ.vəz, es'təʊ- (US) es'toʊ.vɚz
estrade es'trɑːd, ɪ'strɑːd (US) es'trɑːd **-s** -z
Estragon 'es.trə.gɒn (US) -gɑːn
estrang|e ɪ'streɪndʒ, es'treɪndʒ **-es** -ɪz **-ing** -ɪŋ **-ed** -d
estrangement ɪ'streɪndʒ.mənt, es'treɪndʒ- **-s** -s
estrea|t ɪ'striː|t, es'triː|t (US) es'triː|t **-ts** -ts **-ting** -tɪŋ (US) -t̬ɪŋ **-ted** -tɪd (US) -t̬ɪd
Estremadura ˌes.trə.mə'dʊə.rə, -'dɔː- (US) -'dʊr.ə
estrogen 'iː.strə.dʒᵊn, 'es.trə- (US) 'es.trə.dʒᵊn, -dʒen
estr(o)us 'iː.strəs, 'es.trəs (US) 'es.trəs **-es** -ɪz
estuarine 'es.tju.ə.raɪn, -riːn, -rɪn (US) 'es.tʃuː.ə.raɪn, -ɚ.ɪn
estuar|y 'es.tjʊə.r|i, -tju.ə-, -tʃʊə-, -tʃu.ə-, -tjʊr|.i, -tʃʊr|.i (US) 'es.tʃuː.er|.i **-ies** -iz
esurien|ce ɪ'sjʊə.ri.ən|*t*s (US) iː'sʊr.i-, -'sjʊr- **-cy** -*t*.si **-t** -t
eta *Greek alphabet:* 'iː.tə (US) 'eɪ.t̬ə, 'iː-
ETA *estimated time of arrival:* ˌiː.tiː'eɪ
ETA *Basque separatist group:* 'et.ə (US) 'et̬-
étagère, etagere ˌeɪ.tə'ʒeəʳ, ˌet.ə-, -tæʒ'eəʳ, -tɑː'ʒeəʳ (US) -tɑː'ʒer **-s** -z
Etah 'iː.tə (US) -t̬ə
e-tail 'iː.teɪl **-er/s** -əʳ/z (US) -ɚz
Etain 'et.eɪn
et al et'æl (US) et'ɑːl, -'æl, -'ɔːl
Etam® 'iː.tæm
etc. ɪt'set.ᵊr.ə, et-, ət- (US) -'set̬.ɚ-
etcetera ɪt'set.ᵊr.ə, et-, ət- (US) -'set̬.ɚ- **-s** -z
etch etʃ **-es** -ɪz **-ing/s** -ɪŋ/z **-ed** -t **-er/s** -əʳ/z (US) -ɚ/z
eternal ɪ'tɜː.nᵊl (US) -'tɝː- **-ly** -i
eternaliz|e, -is|e ɪ'tɜː.nᵊl.aɪz (US) -'tɝː.nə.laɪz **-es** -ɪz **-ing** -ɪŋ **-ed** -d
eternit|y ɪ'tɜː.nə.t|i, -nɪ.t|i (US) -'tɝː.nə.t̬|i **-ies** -iz
eterniz|e, -is|e ɪ'tɜː.naɪz (US) -'tɝː- **-es** -ɪz **-ing** -ɪŋ **-ed** -d
Etesian ɪ'tiː.ʒi.ən, -zi-, -ʒᵊn
Ethan 'iː.θᵊn
ethane 'iː.θeɪn, 'eθ.eɪn (US) 'eθ.eɪn
ethanoic ˌeθ.ə'nəʊ.ɪk, 'iː.θə'- (US) ˌeθ.ə'noʊ-
ethanol 'eθ.ə.nɒl, 'iː.θə- (US) 'eθ.ə.nɑːl, -noʊl
Ethel 'eθ.ᵊl
Ethelbald 'eθ.ᵊl.bɔːld (US) -bɔːld, -bɑːld
Ethelbert 'eθ.ᵊl.bɜːt, -bət (US) -bɝːt, -bɚt
Ethelberta ˌeθ.ᵊl'bɜː.tə, 'eθ.ᵊlˌbɜː- (US) ˌeθ.ᵊl'bɝː.t̬ə
Ethelburga ˌeθ.ᵊl'bɜː.gə, 'eθ.ᵊlˌbɜː- (US) ˌeθ.ᵊl'bɝː-
Ethelred 'eθ.ᵊl.red
Ethelwulf 'eθ.ᵊl.wʊlf
ethene 'eθ.iːn
ether 'iː.θəʳ (US) -θɚ **-s** -z
ethereal ɪ'θɪə.ri.əl, iː-, ə- (US) -'θɪr.i- **-ly** -i
etherealiz|e, -is|e ɪ'θɪə.ri.ᵊl.aɪz, iː-, ə- (US) -'θɪr.i.ə.laɪz **-es** -ɪz **-ing** -ɪŋ **-ed** -d
Etherege 'eθ.ᵊr.ɪdʒ
etheric iː'θer.ɪk, ɪ- **-s** -s **-ally** -ᵊl.i, -li
Etherington 'eð.ᵊr.ɪŋ.tən
etheriz|e, -is|e 'iː.θᵊr.aɪz (US) -θə.raɪz **-es** -ɪz **-ing** -ɪŋ **-ed** -d
ethic 'eθ.ɪk **-s** -s **-al** -ᵊl **-ally** -ᵊl.i, -li
Ethiop 'iː.θi.ɒp (US) -ɑːp **-s** -s
Ethiopi|a ˌiː.θi'əʊ.pi|.ə (US) -'oʊ- **-an/s** -ən/z
Ethiopic ˌiː.θi'ɒp.ɪk, -'əʊ.pɪk (US) -'ɑː-, -'oʊ-
ethnic 'eθ.nɪk **-al** -ᵊl **-ally** -ᵊl.i, -li
ethnicity eθ'nɪs.ə.ti, -ɪ.ti (US) -ə.t̬i
ethno- eθ.nəʊ-; eθ'nɒ- (US) eθ.noʊ-; eθ'nɑː-
Note: Prefix. Either takes primary or secondary stress on the first syllable, e.g. **ethnographic** /ˌeθ.nəʊ'græf.ɪk (US) -noʊ'-/, or primary stress on the second syllable, e.g. **ethnographer** /eθ'nɒg.rə.fəʳ (US) -'nɑː.grə.fɚ/.
ethnocentr|ic ˌeθ.nəʊ'sen.tr|ɪk (US) -noʊ'-, -nə'- **-ism** -ɪ.zᵊm **-ically** -ɪ.kᵊl.i, -ɪ.kli
ethnocentricity ˌeθ.nəʊ.sen'trɪs.ə.ti, -ɪ.ti (US) -noʊ.sen'trɪs.ə.t̬i
ethnographer eθ'nɒg.rə.fəʳ (US) -'nɑː.grə.fɚ **-s** -z
ethnographic ˌeθ.nəʊ'græf.ɪk (US) -noʊ'-, -nə'- **-al** -ᵊl
ethnography eθ'nɒg.rə.fi (US) -'nɑː.grə-
ethnologic ˌeθ.nəʊ'lɒdʒ.ɪk (US) -noʊ'lɑː.dʒɪk, -nə'- **-al** -ᵊl **-ally** -ᵊl.i, -li
ethnolog|y eθ'nɒl.ə.dʒ|i (US) -'nɑː.lə- **-ist/s** -ɪst/s
ethologic ˌiː.θə'lɒdʒ.ɪk (US) -'lɑː.dʒɪk **-al** -ᵊl
etholog|y iː'θɒl.ə.dʒ|i, ɪ- (US) iː'θɑː.lə-, ɪ'- **-ist/s** -ɪst/s
ethos 'iː.θɒs (US) -θɑːs, 'eθ.ɑːs, -oʊs
ethyl *commercial and general pronunciation:* 'eθ.ɪl, -ᵊl (US) -ᵊl *chemists' pronunciation:* 'iː.θaɪl
ethylene 'eθ.ɪ.liːn, -ᵊl.iːn (US) -ə.liːn
etio|late 'iː.ti.əʊ|.leɪt (US) -ə- **-lates** -leɪts **-lating** -leɪ.tɪŋ (US) -leɪ.t̬ɪŋ **-lated** -leɪ.tɪd (US) -leɪ.t̬ɪd
etiolog|y ˌiː.ti'ɒl.ə.dʒ|i (US) -'ɑː.lə- **-ist/s** -ɪst/s
etiquette 'et.ɪ.ket, -kət; (US) 'et̬.ɪ.kɪt, -ket
Etna 'et.nə
Eton 'iː.tᵊn
Etonian iː'təʊ.ni.ən, ɪ- (US) -'toʊ- **-s** -z
Etruri|a ɪ'trʊə.ri|.ə (US) -'trʊr.i- **-an/s** -ən/z
Etruscan ɪ'trʌs.kᵊn **-s** -z
-ette -et
Note: Suffix. Normally takes primary stress, e.g. **majorette** /ˌmeɪ.dʒᵊr'et/; there are exceptions, however, e.g. **etiquette** /'et.ɪ.ket (US) 'et̬.ɪ.kɪt/. See individual entries.
Ettrick 'et.rɪk
Etty 'et.i (US) 'et̬-
étude 'eɪ.tjuːd, -'- (US) 'eɪ.tuːd, -tjuːd **-s** -z
etui et'wiː (US) eɪ'twiː **-s** -z

etymologic ˌet.ɪ.məˈlɒdʒ.ɪk, ˌ-ə- (US) ˌet̬.ɪ.məˈlɑː.dʒɪk **-al** -əl **-ally** -əl.i, -li
etymologist ˌet.ɪˈmɒl.ə.dʒɪst, -əˈ- (US) ˌet̬.ɪˈmɑː.lə- **-s** -s
etymologiz|e, -is|e ˌet.ɪˈmɒl.ə.dʒaɪz, -əˈ- (US) ˌet̬.ɪˈmɑː.lə- **-es** -ɪz **-ing** -ɪŋ **-ed** -d
etymolog|y ˌet.ɪˈmɒl.ə.dʒ|i, -əˈ- (US) ˌet̬.ɪˈmɑː.lə- **-ies** -iz
etymon ˈet.ɪ.mɒn, ˈ-ə- (US) ˈet̬.ə.mɑːn **-s** -z
EU ˌiːˈjuː
Euan ˈjuː.ən
Eubank ˈjuː.bæŋk
Euboea juːˈbiː.ə
eucalyptus ˌjuː.kəlˈɪp.təs **-es** -ɪz
Eucharist ˈjuː.kər.ɪst **-s** -s
eucharistic ˌjuː.kərˈɪs.tɪk **-al** -əl **-ally** -əl.i, -li
euchre ˈjuː.kər (US) -kɚ **-s** -z **-ing** -ɪŋ **-d** -d
Euclid ˈjuː.klɪd **-s** -z
Euclidean juːˈklɪd.i.ən
eud(a)emon|ism juːˈdiː.mə.n|ɪ.zəm **-ist/s** -ɪst/s
eudiometer ˌjuː.diˈɒm.ɪ.tər, ˈ-ə- (US) -ˈɑː.mə.t̬ɚ **-s** -z
Eudocia juːˈdəʊ.ʃi.ə, -ʃə, -si.ə (US) -ˈdoʊ-
Eudora juːˈdɔː.rə (US) -ˈdɔːr.ə
Eudoxia juːˈdɒk.si.ə (US) -ˈdɑːk-
Eudoxus juːˈdɒk.səs (US) -ˈdɑːk-
Eugen *English name:* ˈjuː.dʒen, -dʒɪn, -dʒən *German name:* ˈɔɪ.gən
Eugene juːˈdʒiːn, -ˈdʒeɪn; ˈjuː.dʒiːn (US) juːˈdʒiːn, ˈ--
Eugene Onegin ˌjuː.dʒiːn.ɒnˈjeɪ.gɪn (US) -ɑːnˈ-, -oʊnˈ-
Eugénia juːˈdʒiː.ni.ə, -ˈʒiː-, -ˈdʒeɪ-, -ˈʒeɪ-
eugenic juːˈdʒen.ɪk **-s** -s
eugenicist juːˈdʒen.ɪ.sɪst, ˈ-ə- **-s** -s
Eugénie juːˈʒeɪ.ni, -ˈʒiː-, -ˈdʒiː-
Eugenius juːˈdʒiː.ni.əs, -ˈʒiː-, -ˈdʒeɪ- (US) -ˈʒeɪ-
Eulalia juːˈleɪ.li.ə
Eulenspiegel ˈɔɪ.lənˌʃpiː.gəl
Euler *English name:* ˈjuː.lər (US) -lɚ *German name:* ˈɔɪ.lər (US) -lɚ
eulogist ˈjuː.lə.dʒɪst **-s** -s
eulogistic ˌjuː.ləˈdʒɪs.tɪk **-al** -əl **-ally** -əl.i, -li
eulogi|um juːˈləʊ.dʒi|.əm (US) -ˈloʊ- **-ums** -z **-a** -ə
eulogiz|e, -is|e ˈjuː.lə.dʒaɪz **-es** -ɪz **-ing** -ɪŋ **-ed** -d
eulog|y ˈjuː.lə.dʒ|i **-ies** -iz
Eumenides juːˈmen.ɪ.diːz, ˈ-ə-
Eunice *modern Christian name:* ˈjuː.nɪs *biblical name:* juːˈnaɪ.si
eunuch ˈjuː.nək **-s** -s **-ism** -ɪ.zəm
euonymus juːˈɒn.ɪ.məs, ˈ-ə- (US) -ˈɑː.nə- **-es** -ɪz
eupepsia juːˈpep.si.ə
eupeptic juːˈpep.tɪk
Euphemia juːˈfiː.mi.ə
euphemism ˈjuː.fə.mɪ.zəm, -fɪ- **-s** -z
euphemistic ˌjuː.fəˈmɪs.tɪk, -fɪˈ- **-al** -əl **-ally** -əl.i, -li
euphemiz|e, -is|e ˈjuː.fə.maɪz, -fɪ- **-es** -ɪz **-ing** -ɪŋ **-ed** -d
euphonic juːˈfɒn.ɪk (US) -ˈfɑː.nɪk **-al** -əl **-ally** -əl.i, -li
euphonious juːˈfəʊ.ni.əs (US) -ˈfoʊ- **-ly** -li
euphonium juːˈfəʊ.ni.əm (US) -ˈfoʊ- **-s** -z
euphoniz|e, -is|e ˈjuː.fə.naɪz **-es** -ɪz **-ing** -ɪŋ **-ed** -d
euphony ˈjuː.fən.i
euphorbia juːˈfɔː.bi.ə (US) -ˈfɔːr-
euphoria juːˈfɔː.ri.ə (US) -ˈfɔːr.i-
euphoric juːˈfɒr.ɪk (US) -ˈfɔːr.ɪk **-ally** -əl.i, -li
euphrasy ˈjuː.frə.si
Euphrates juːˈfreɪ.tiːz (US) -t̬iːz
Euphronius juːˈfrəʊ.ni.əs (US) -ˈfroʊ-
Euphrosyne juːˈfrɒz.ɪ.niː, ˈ-ə- (US) -ˈfrɑː.zə-
Euphues ˈjuː.fju.iːz
euphu|ism ˈjuː.fju.|ɪ.zəm **-isms** -ɪ.zəmz **-ist/s** -ɪst/s
euphuistic ˌjuː.fjuˈɪs.tɪk
eupnoea ˈjuːp.niː.ə (US) ˈ--
Eurasi|a jʊəˈreɪ.ʒ|ə, jɔːˈ-, ˈ-ʒi|.ə, ˈ-ʃ|ə (US) jʊˈreɪ.ʒ|ə **-a** -ən
Euratom jʊəˈræt.əm, jɔːˈ- (US) jʊˈræt̬-
eureka (E) jʊəˈriː.kə, jɔːˈ- (US) jʊ-
eurhythm|ic jʊəˈrɪð.m|ɪk, jɔːˈ-, -ˈrɪθ- (US) jʊˈrɪð- **-ics** -ɪks **-y** -i
Euripides jʊəˈrɪp.ɪ.diːz, jɔːˈ-, ˈ-ə- (US) jʊ-
Euripus jʊəˈraɪ.pəs, jɔːˈ- (US) jʊ-
Euro- ˈjʊə.rəʊ-, jɔː-; jʊəˈrɒ- (US) ˈjʊr.oʊ-, -ə-; jʊˈroʊ-
Note: Prefix. Usually takes primary stress on the first syllable, e.g. **Eurocrat** /ˈjʊə.rəʊ.kræt (US) ˈjʊr.ə-/.
euro ˈjʊə.rəʊ, ˈjɔː- (US) ˈjʊr.oʊ **-s** -z

Pronouncing the letters EU, EW

The vowel digraphs **eu** and **ew** are similar in that their most common pronunciation is one of /juː/ or /uː/, e.g.:

feud	/fjuːd/
flew	/fluː/

Many words in British English which have /juː/ are pronounced without the /j/ in American English, e.g.:

news	/njuːz/	(US) /nuːz/

When the digraph **eu** is followed by an **r** in the spelling, the strong pronunciation is usually /jʊə (US) jʊr/, although words borrowed from French may have /ɜː (US) ɝː/ in stressed syllables, and /ər (US) ɚ/ in unstressed syllables, e.g.:

European	/ˌjʊə.rəˈpiː.ən/	(US) /ˌjʊr.ə-/
connoisseur	/ˌkɒn.əˈsɜːr/	(US) /ˌkɑː.nəˈsɝː/
amateur	/ˈæm.ə.tər/	(US) /-tʃɚ/

In addition

Other sounds associated with the digraphs **eu** and **ew** are as follows:

/əʊ (US) oʊ/	sew	/səʊ/ (US) /soʊ/
/i.ə/	museum	/mjuːˈzi.əm/
/ɔɪ/	schadenfreude	/ˈʃɑː.dənˌfrɔɪ.də/
/ɜː (US) ɜː,uː/	masseuse	/mæsˈɜːz/ (US) /məˈsɜːz, -suːz/

In words borrowed from German, **eu** is pronounced /ɔɪ/, e.g.:

/ɔɪ/	schadenfreude	/ˈʃɑː.dənˌfrɔɪ.də/

Eurobond ˈjʊə.rəʊ.bɒnd, ˈjɔː- US ˈjʊr.oʊ.bɑːnd **-s** -z

eurocentric ˌjʊə.rəʊˈsen.trɪk, ˌjɔː- US ˌjʊr.oʊˈ-

Eurocheque® ˈjʊə.rəʊ.tʃek, ˈjɔː- US ˈjʊr.oʊ- **-s** -s

Eurocommun|ism ˌjʊə.rəʊˈkɒm.jə.n|ɪ.zᵊm, ˌjɔː-, -jʊ-, ˈjʊə.rəʊˌkɒm-, ˈjɔː- US ˌjʊr.oʊˈkɑːm.jə-, -əˈ- **-ist/s** -ɪst/s

Eurocrat ˈjʊə.rəʊ.kræt, ˈjɔː- US ˈjʊr.ə- **-s** -s

Eurodisney® ˈjʊə.rəʊˌdɪz.ni, ˈjɔː- US ˈjʊr.oʊ-

Eurodollar® ˈjʊə.rəʊˌdɒl.əʳ, ˈjɔː- US ˈjʊr.oʊˌdɑː.lɚ **-s** -z

Europa jʊəˈrəʊ.pə, jɔːˈ- US jʊˈroʊ-

Europe ˈjʊə.rəp, ˈjɔː- US ˈjʊr.əp

European ˌjʊə.rəˈpiː.ən, ˌjɔː- US ˌjʊr.əˈ- **-s** -z *stress shift:* ˌEuropean Comˈmunity; ˌEuropean Ecoˈnomic Comˈmunity; ˌEuropean ˈMonetary System

europeaniz|e, -is|e ˌjʊə.rəˈpiː.ə.naɪz, ˌjɔː- US ˌjʊr.əˈ- **-es** -ɪz **-ing** -ɪŋ **-ed** -d

europium jʊəˈrəʊ.pi.əm, jɔːˈ- US jʊˈroʊ-

Eurosceptic ˈjʊə.rəʊˌskep.tɪk, ˈjɔː- US ˈjʊr.oʊ-, ˈ-ə- **-s** -s

Eurostar® ˈjʊə.rəʊ.stɑːʳ, ˈjɔː- US ˈjʊr.oʊ.stɑːr, -ə-

Eurotunnel® ˈjʊə.rəʊˌtʌn.ᵊl, ˈjɔː- US ˈjʊr.oʊ-, ˈ-ə-

Eurovision® ˈjʊə.rəʊ.vɪ.ʒᵊn, ˈjɔː- US ˈjʊr.ə-, -oʊ- ˌ**Eurovision ˈSong ˌContest**

eurozone ˈjʊə.rəʊ.zəʊn, ˈjɔː- US ˈjʊr.oʊ.zoʊn, -ə- **-s** -z

Eurus ˈjʊə.rəs, ˈjɔː- US ˈjʊr.əs

Eurydice jʊəˈrɪd.ɪ.si, jɔːˈ-, ˈ-ə- US jʊ-

eurythm|ic jʊəˈrɪð.m|ɪk, jɔːˈ-, -ˈrɪθ- US jʊˈrɪð- **-ics** -ɪks **-y** -i

Eusden ˈjuːz.dən

Eusebius juːˈsiː.bi.əs

Eustace ˈjuː.stəs, -stɪs

eustachian juːˈsteɪ.ʃᵊn, -ʃi.ən, -ki.ən **euˌstachian ˈtube** US **euˈstachian ˌtube**

Eustachius juːˈsteɪ.ki.əs

Eustacia juːˈsteɪ.si.ə, -ʃə

Euston ˈjuː.stᵊn

Euterpe juːˈtɜː.pi US -ˈtɝː-

euthanasia ˌjuː.θəˈneɪ.zi.ə, ˈ-ʒə US ˈ-ʒə, ˈ-zi.ə

Eutropius juːˈtrəʊ.pi.əs US -ˈtroʊ-

Euxine ˈjuːk.saɪn

Euxton ˈek.stən

Eva ˈiː.və US ˈiː.və, ˈeɪ-

evacu|ate ɪˈvæk.ju|.eɪt **-ates** -eɪts **-ating** -eɪ.tɪŋ US -eɪ.t̬ɪŋ **-ated** -eɪ.tɪd US -eɪ.t̬ɪd **-ator/s** -eɪ.təʳ/z US -eɪ.t̬ɚ/z

evacuation ɪˌvæk.juˈeɪ.ʃᵊn **-s** -z

evacuee ɪˌvæk.juˈiː **-s** -z

evad|e ɪˈveɪd **-es** -z **-ing** -ɪŋ **-ed** -ɪd **-er/s** -əʳ/z US -ɚ/z

Evadne ɪˈvæd.ni

evalu|ate ɪˈvæl.ju|.eɪt **-ates** -eɪts **-ating** -eɪ.tɪŋ US -eɪ.t̬ɪŋ **-ated** -eɪ.tɪd US -eɪ.t̬ɪd

evaluation ɪˌvæl.juˈeɪ.ʃᵊn **-s** -z

evaluative ɪˈvæl.ju.ə.tɪv US -eɪ.t̬ɪv **-ly** -li

Evan ˈev.ᵊn

Evander ɪˈvæn.dəʳ US -dɚ

evanesc|e ˌiː.vəˈnes, ˌev.əˈ- US ˌev.əˈ- **-es** -ɪz **-ing** -ɪŋ **-ed** -t

evanescen|ce ˌiː.vəˈnes.ᵊn|ts, ˌev.əˈ- US ˌev.əˈ- **-t/ly** -t/li

evangel ɪˈvæn.dʒəl, -dʒel **-s** -z

evangelic ˌiː.vænˈdʒel.ɪk, ˌev.ænˈ-, -ənˈ- **-s** -s

evangelic|al ˌiː.vænˈdʒel.ɪ.k|ᵊl, ˌev.ænˈ-, -ənˈ- **-als** -ᵊlz **-ally** -li **-alism** -ᵊl.ɪ.zᵊm

Evangeline ɪˈvæn.dʒɪ.liːn, -dʒᵊl.iːn, -aɪn US -dʒə.lɪn, -dʒɪ-, -liːn, -laɪn

evangel|ism ɪˈvæn.dʒə.l|ɪ.zᵊm, -dʒɪ- **-ist/s** -ɪst/s

evangelistic ɪˌvæn.dʒəˈlɪs.tɪk, -dʒɪˈ-

evangelization, -isa- ɪˌvæn.dʒᵊl.aɪˈzeɪ.ʃᵊn, -dʒɪ.laɪˈ-, -lɪˈ- US -dʒᵊl.ɪˈ-

evangeliz|e, -is|e ɪˈvæn.dʒᵊl.aɪz, -dʒɪ- US -dʒə.laɪz, -dʒɪ- **-es** -ɪz **-ing** -ɪŋ **-ed** -d

Evans ˈev.ᵊnz

Evanson ˈev.ᵊn.sᵊn

Evanston ˈev.ᵊn.stən

Evansville ˈev.ᵊnz.vɪl

evaporable ɪˈvæp.ᵊr.ə.bl̩

evapor|ate ɪˈvæp.ᵊr|.eɪt US -ə.r|eɪt **-ates** -eɪts **-ating** -eɪ.tɪŋ US -eɪ.t̬ɪŋ **-ated** -eɪ.tɪd US -eɪ.t̬ɪd **-ator/s** -eɪ.təʳ/z US -eɪ.t̬ɚ/z **eˌvaporated ˈmilk**

evaporation ɪˌvæp.əˈreɪ.ʃᵊn **-s** -z

evasion ɪˈveɪ.ʒᵊn **-s** -z

evasive ɪˈveɪ.sɪv **-ly** -li **-ness** -nəs, -nɪs

eve (E) iːv **-s** -z

Evele(i)gh ˈiːv.li

Evelina ˌev.ɪˈliː.nə, -əˈ-

Eveline ˈiːv.lɪn, ˈev.lɪn, ˈev.ɪ.liːn

Evelyn ˈiːv.lɪn, ˈev.lɪn, ˈev.ə- US ˈev.ə-, ˈev.lɪn, ˈiːv-

Note: The pronunciation /ˈiːv.lɪn/ is used in the US only for British people of that name.

even ˈiː.vᵊn **-ly** -li **-ness** -nəs, -nɪs **-s** -z **-ing** -ɪŋ **-ed** -d

Evenden ˈev.ᵊn.dən

evenhanded ˌiː.vᵊnˈhæn.dɪd **-ly** -li **-ness** -nəs, -nɪs *stress shift:* ˌevenhanded adˈministrator

evening *(n.)* ˈiːv.nɪŋ **-s** -z ˈ**evening ˌdress**, ˌ**evening ˈdress**; ˈ**evening ˌgown**; ˌ**evening ˈprimrose**; ˌ**evening ˈprimrose ˌoil**

Evens ˈev.ᵊnz

evensong ˈiː.vᵊn.sɒŋ US -sɑːŋ, -sɔːŋ **-s** -z

even-steven ˌiː.vᵊnˈstiː.vᵊn **-s** -z

e|vent ɪ|ˈvent **-vents** -ˈvents **-venting** -ˈven.tɪŋ US -ˈven.t̬ɪŋ **-vented** -ˈven.tɪd US -ˈven.t̬ɪd **-venter/s** -ˈven.təʳ/z US -ˈven.t̬ɚ/z

eventful ɪˈvent.fᵊl, -fʊl **-ly** -i

eventide ˈiː.vᵊn.taɪd **-s** -z

eventive ɪˈven.tɪv US -t̬ɪv

eventual ɪˈven.tʃu.əl, -tju-, -tʃʊl, -tjʊl US -tʃu.əl **-ly** -i

eventualit|y ɪˌven.tʃuˈæl.ə.t|i, -tjuˈ-, -ɪ.t|i US -tʃuˈæl.ə.t̬|i **-ies** -iz

eventu|ate ɪˈven.tʃu|.eɪt, -tju- US -tʃu- **-ates** -eɪts **-ating** -eɪ.tɪŋ US -eɪ.t̬ɪŋ **-ated** -eɪ.tɪd US -eɪ.t̬ɪd

ever ˈev.əʳ US -ɚ

Everard ˈev.ᵊr.ɑːd US -ə.rɑːrd

Everest ˈev.ᵊr.est US -ə.rest, -ɚ.ɪst, ˈ-rɪst

Everett ˈev.ᵊr.et US -ə.ret, ˈev.rɪt

Everglades ˈev.ə.gleɪdz US ˈ-ɚ-

evergreen ˈev.ə.griːn US ˈ-ɚ- **-s** -z

Everitt ˈev.ᵊr.ɪt

everlasting ˌev.əˈlɑː.stɪŋ US -ɚˈlæs.tɪŋ **-ly** -li **-ness** -nəs, -nɪs

Everl(e)y ˈev.ə.li US ˈ-ɚ-

evermore ˌev.əˈmɔːʳ US -ɚˈmɔːr

EverReady® ˈev.əˌred.i US -ɚˌ-

Evers ˈev.əz US -ɚz

Evershed ˈev.ə.ʃed US ˈ-ɚ-

eversion ɪˈvɜː.ʃᵊn, iː- US -ˈvɝː.ʒᵊn, -ʃᵊn

Eversley ˈev.əz.li US -ɚz-

e|vert ɪ|ˈvɜːt, iː- US -ˈvɝːt **-verts** -ˈvɜːts US -ˈvɝːts **-verting** -ˈvɜː.tɪŋ US -ˈvɝː.t̬ɪŋ **-verted** -ˈvɜː.tɪd US -ˈvɝː.t̬ɪd

Evert ˈev.ət US -ɚt

Everton ˈev.ə.tᵊn US ˈ-ɚ-

every ˈev.ri ˌ**every ˌwhich ˈway** US ˌ**every ˈwhich ˌway** US ˈ**every ˌwhich ˌway**

Note: The meaning is slightly different in American English depending on the stress pattern. ˌ**Every which way** means "akimbo". ˈ**Every which ˌway** means "in all possible ways.".

everybody ˈev.riˌbɒd.i US -ˌbɑː.di

everyday ˈev.ri.deɪ, ˌ--ˈ-

Everyman ˈev.ri.mæn

everyone ˈev.ri.wʌn

everyplace ˈev.ri.pleɪs

everything ˈev.ri.θɪŋ

everywhere 'ev.ri.*h*weəʳ ⓤⓢ -*h*wer
Evesham 'iːv.ʃᵊm *locally also:* 'iː.vɪ-
Evett 'ev.ɪt
Evian® 'ev.i.ɒ̃ŋ ⓤⓢ ˌev.i'ɑːn, 'ev.i.ən
evict ɪ'vɪkt **-s** -s **-ing** -ɪŋ **-ed** -ɪd
eviction ɪ'vɪk.ʃᵊn **-s** -z
evidenc|e 'ev.ɪ.dᵊnts, '-ə- **-es** -ɪz **-ing** -ɪŋ **-ed** -t
evident 'ev.ɪ.dᵊnt, '-ə- **-ly** -li
evidential ˌev.ɪ'den.*t*ʃᵊl, -ə'- ⓤⓢ -ʃᵊl **-ly** -i
evidentiary ˌev.ɪ'den.*t*ʃᵊr.i, -ə'- ⓤⓢ -'den*t*.ʃɚ.i
evil 'iː.vᵊl, -vɪl ⓤⓢ -vᵊl **-s** -z **-ly** -i ˌ**evil** '**eye** ⓤⓢ '**evil** ˌ**eye**
evildoer 'iː.vᵊlˌduː.əʳ, -vɪlˌ-, ˌiː.vᵊl'duː-, -vɪl'- ⓤⓢ 'iː.vᵊlˌduː.ɚ, ˌiː.vᵊl'duː- **-s** -z
evil-minded ˌiː.vᵊl'maɪn.dɪd, -vɪl'-, 'iː.vᵊlˌmaɪn-, -vɪlˌ- ⓤⓢ ˌiː.vᵊl'maɪn-, 'iː.vᵊlˌmaɪn- **-ness** -nəs, -nɪs
evinc|e ɪ'vɪnts **-es** -ɪz **-ing** -ɪŋ **-ed** -t **-ive** -ɪv
evincib|le ɪ'vɪnt.sə.b|l̩, -sɪ- **-ly** -li
evi|rate 'iː.vɪ|.reɪt, 'ev.ɪ- **-rates** -reɪts **-rating** -reɪ.tɪŋ ⓤⓢ -reɪ.t̬ɪŋ **-rated** -reɪ.tɪd ⓤⓢ -reɪ.t̬ɪd
evisce|rate ɪ'vɪs.ə|.reɪt, iː- **-rates** -reɪts **-rating** -reɪ.tɪŋ ⓤⓢ -reɪ.t̬ɪŋ **-rated** -reɪ.tɪd ⓤⓢ -reɪ.t̬ɪd
evisceration ɪˌvɪs.ə'reɪ.ʃᵊn, iːˌvɪs-
Evita ev'iː.tə, ɪ'viː- ⓤⓢ -tə, -t̬ə
evo|cate 'ev.əʊ|.keɪt, 'iː.vəʊ- ⓤⓢ 'ev.ə-, 'iː.voʊ- **-cates** -keɪts **-cating** -keɪ.tɪŋ ⓤⓢ -keɪ.t̬ɪŋ **-cated** -keɪ.tɪd ⓤⓢ -keɪ.t̬ɪd
evocation ˌev.əʊ'keɪ.ʃᵊn, ˌiː.vəʊ'- ⓤⓢ ˌev.ə'-, ˌiː.voʊ'- **-s** -z
evocative ɪ'vɒk.ə.tɪv ⓤⓢ -'vɑː.kə.t̬ɪv **-ly** -li
evok|e ɪ'vəʊk ⓤⓢ -'voʊk **-es** -s **-ing** -ɪŋ **-ed** -t
evolute ˌiː.və'luːt, ˌev.ə'-, -'ljuːt ⓤⓢ ˌev.ə'luːt, ˌiː.və'- **-s** -s
evolution ˌiː.və'luː.ʃᵊn, ˌev.ə'-, -'ljuː- ⓤⓢ ˌev.ə'luː.ʃᵊn, ˌiː.və'- **-s** -z
evolutional ˌiː.və'luː.ʃᵊn.ᵊl, ˌev.ə'-, -'ljuː- ⓤⓢ ˌev.ə'luː-, ˌiː.və'-
evolutionary ˌiː.və'luː.ʃᵊn.ᵊr.i, ˌev.ə'-, -'ljuː-, -ri ⓤⓢ ˌev.ə'luː.ʃᵊn.er-, ˌiː.və'-
evolution|ism ˌiː.və'luː.ʃᵊn|.ɪ.zᵊm, ˌev.ə'-, -'ljuː- ⓤⓢ ˌev.ə'luː-, ˌiː.və'- **-ist/s** -ɪst/s
evolutive ɪ'vɒl.jə.tɪv, iː-, -jʊ- ⓤⓢ ˌev.ə'luː.t̬ɪv, ˌiː.və'-; iː'vɑːl.jə-
evolv|e ɪ'vɒlv ⓤⓢ -'vɑːlv **-es** -z **-ing** -ɪŋ **-ed** -d **-able** -ə.bl̩
Évora 'ev.ə.rə ⓤⓢ ev'ʊr.ə
Evo-stik® 'iː.vəʊ.stɪk ⓤⓢ -voʊ-
evulsion ɪ'vʌl.ʃᵊn, iː- **-s** -z
Ewan 'juː.ən

Ewart 'juː.ət, jʊət ⓤⓢ 'juː.ɚt
Ewbank 'juː.bæŋk
ewe juː **-s** -z
Ewell 'juː.əl, jʊəl ⓤⓢ 'juː.əl
Ewen 'juː.ən, -ɪn; jʊən ⓤⓢ 'juː.ən
ewer 'juː.əʳ, jʊəʳ ⓤⓢ 'juː.ɚ **-s** -z
Ewing 'juː.ɪŋ
ex- eks-, ɪks-, egz-, ɪgz-
Note: Prefix. Takes either primary or secondary stress, e.g. **excellent** /'ek.sᵊl.ᵊnt/, **excitation** /ˌek.sɪ'teɪ.ʃᵊn ⓤⓢ -saɪ'-/ or may be unstressed, e.g. **excel** /ɪk'sel/.
ex eks
exacer|bate ɪg'zæs.ə|.beɪt, eg-; ɪk'sæs-, ek- ⓤⓢ ɪg'zæs.ɚ-, eg'- **-bates** -beɪts **-bating** -beɪ.tɪŋ ⓤⓢ -beɪ.t̬ɪŋ **-bated** -beɪ.tɪd ⓤⓢ -beɪ.t̬ɪd
exacerbation ɪgˌzæs.ə'beɪ.ʃᵊn, egˌ-; ɪkˌsæs-, ekˌ- ⓤⓢ ɪgˌzæs.ɚ'-, eg'- **-s** -z
exact ɪg'zækt, eg'-; ɪk'sækt, ek'- ⓤⓢ ɪg'zækt, eg'- **-ly** -li, -'zæk.li, -'sæk- ⓤⓢ -'zæk- **-ness** -nəs, -nɪs **-s** -s **-ing/ly** -ɪŋ/li **-ed** -ɪd **-er/s** -əʳ/z ⓤⓢ -ɚ/z **-or/s** -əʳ/z ⓤⓢ -ɚ/z
exaction ɪg'zæk.ʃᵊn, eg'-; ɪk'sæk-, ek'- ⓤⓢ ɪg'zæk-, eg'- **-s** -z
exactitude ɪg'zæk.tɪ.tjuːd, eg'-, -tə-; ɪk'sæk-, ek'- ⓤⓢ ɪg'zæk.tə.tuːd, eg'-, -tjuːd
exactly ɪg'zækt.li, eg'-; ɪk'sækt-, ek'- ⓤⓢ ɪg'zækt-, eg'-
exagger|ate ɪg'zædʒ.ᵊr|.eɪt, eg'-; ɪk'sædʒ-, ek'- ⓤⓢ ɪg'zædʒ.ə.r|eɪt, eg'- **-ates** -eɪts **-ating** -eɪ.tɪŋ ⓤⓢ -eɪ.t̬ɪŋ **-ated/ly** -eɪ.tɪd/li ⓤⓢ -eɪ.t̬ɪd/li **-ator/s** -eɪ.təʳ/z ⓤⓢ -eɪ.t̬ɚ/z
exaggeration ɪgˌzædʒ.ə'reɪ.ʃᵊn, egˌ-; ɪkˌsædʒ-, ekˌ- ⓤⓢ ɪgˌzædʒ-, egˌ- **-s** ⓤⓢ -z
exaggerative ɪg'zædʒ.ᵊr.ə.tɪv, eg'-; ɪk'sædʒ-, ek'- ⓤⓢ ɪg'zædʒ.ɚ.ə.t̬ɪv, eg'-
exal|t ɪg'zɔːl|t, eg'-, -'zɒl|t; ɪk'sɔːl|t, ek'-, -'sɒl|t ⓤⓢ ɪg'zɔːl|t, eg-, -'zɑːl|t **-ts** -ts **-ting** -tɪŋ ⓤⓢ -t̬ɪŋ **-ted/ly** -tɪd/li ⓤⓢ -t̬ɪd/li **-tedness** -tɪd.nəs ⓤⓢ -t̬ɪd.nəs, -nɪs
exaltation ˌeg.zɔːl'teɪ.ʃᵊn, ˌek.sɔːl'-, -sɒl'- ⓤⓢ ˌeg.zɔːl'-, -zɑːl'-; ˌek.sɔːl'-, -sɑːl'- **-s** -z
exam ɪg'zæm, eg'-; ɪk'sæm, ek'- ⓤⓢ ɪg'zæm, eg'- **-s** -z
examen eg'zeɪ.men, ɪg'- **-s** -z
examination ɪgˌzæm.ɪ'neɪ.ʃᵊn, egˌ-; ɪkˌsæm-, ekˌ-, -ə'- ⓤⓢ ɪgˌzæm-, egˌ- **-s** -z **exˌami'nation** ˌ**paper**
examin|e ɪg'zæm.ɪn, eg'-; ɪk'sæm-, ek'- ⓤⓢ ɪg'zæm-, eg'- **-es** -z **-ing** -ɪŋ **-ed** -d **-er/s** -əʳ/z ⓤⓢ -ɚ/z

examinee ɪgˌzæm.ɪ'niː, egˌ-; ɪkˌsæm-, ekˌ-, -ə'- ⓤⓢ ɪgˌzæm-, egˌ- **-s** -z
exampl|e ɪg'zɑːm.pl̩, eg'-; ɪk'sɑːm-, ek'- ⓤⓢ ɪg'zæm-, eg'- **-es** -z **-ing** -ɪŋ, '-plɪŋ **-ed** -d
exarch 'ek.sɑːk ⓤⓢ -sɑːrk **-s** -s **-ate/s** -eɪt/s
exasper|ate ɪg'zæs.pᵊr|.eɪt, eg'-; ɪk'sæs-, ek'-, -'zɑː.spᵊr- ⓤⓢ ɪg'zæs.pə.r|eɪt, eg'- **-ates** -eɪts **-ating/ly** -eɪ.tɪŋ/li ⓤⓢ -eɪ.t̬ɪŋ/li **-ated/ly** -eɪ.tɪd/li ⓤⓢ -eɪ.t̬ɪd/li
exasperation ɪgˌzæs.pə'reɪ.ʃᵊn, egˌ-; ɪkˌsæs-, ekˌ-, -ˌzɑː.spə'- ⓤⓢ ɪg'zæs.pə'-, eg-
Excalibur ek'skæl.ɪ.bəʳ, ɪk'-, '-ə- ⓤⓢ -bɚ
ex cathedra ˌeks.kə'θiː.drə, -'θed.rə, -rɑː ⓤⓢ -kə'θiː.drə; -'kæθ.ɪ-
exca|vate 'ek.skə|.veɪt **-vates** -veɪts **-vating** -veɪ.tɪŋ ⓤⓢ -veɪ.t̬ɪŋ **-vated** -veɪ.tɪd ⓤⓢ -veɪ.t̬ɪd **-vator/s** -veɪ.təʳ/z ⓤⓢ -veɪ.t̬ɚ/z
excavation ˌeks.kə'veɪ.ʃᵊn **-s** -z
exceed ɪk'siːd, ek- **-s** -z **-ing/ly** -ɪŋ/li **-ed** -ɪd
exceeding ɪk'siː.dɪŋ, ek- **-ly** -li
excel ɪk'sel, ek- **-s** -z **-ling** -ɪŋ **-led** -d
excellenc|e 'ek.sᵊl.ᵊn*t*s **-es** -ɪz
excellenc|y (E) 'ek.sᵊl.ᵊn*t*.s|i **-ies** -iz
excellent 'ek.sᵊl.ᵊnt **-ly** -li
excelsior ek'sel.si.ɔːʳ, ɪk-, -əʳ ⓤⓢ -ɔːr, -ɚ
except ɪk'sept, ek- **-s** -s **-ing** -ɪŋ **-ed** -ɪd
exception ɪk'sep.ʃᵊn, ek- **-s** -z
exceptionab|le ɪk'sep.ʃᵊn.ə.b|l̩, ek- **-ly** -li **-leness** -l̩.nəs, -nɪs
exceptional ɪk'sep.ʃᵊn.ᵊl, ek- **-ly** -i
excerpt (*n.*) 'ek.sɜːpt, 'eg.zɜːpt ⓤⓢ 'ek.sɝːpt, 'eg.zɝːpt **-s** -s
excerpt (*v.*) ek'sɜːpt, ɪk'- ⓤⓢ ek'sɝːpt, eg'zɝːpt **-s** -s **-ing** -ɪŋ **-ed** -ɪd
excerption ek'sɜːp.ʃᵊn, ɪk- ⓤⓢ ek'sɝːp-, eg'zɝːp- **-s** -z
excess ɪk'ses, ek'- **-es** -ɪz **-ing** -ɪŋ **-ed** -t *stress shift:* ˌexcess 'baggage
excessive ɪk'ses.ɪv, ek'- **-ly** -li **-ness** -nəs, -nɪs
exchang|e ɪks'tʃeɪndʒ, eks'- **-es** -ɪz **-ing** -ɪŋ **-ed** -d **-er/s** -əʳ/z ⓤⓢ -ɚ/z **-eable** -ə.bl̩ **ex'change** ˌ**rate**; **Ex'change** ˌ**Rate** ˌ**Mechanism**
exchangeability ɪksˌtʃeɪn.dʒə'bɪl.ə.ti, eksˌ-, -ɪ.ti ⓤⓢ -ə.t̬i
exchangee ˌeks.tʃeɪn'dʒiː; ɪksˌtʃeɪn'- **-s** -z
exchequer (E) ɪks'tʃek.əʳ, eks'- ⓤⓢ -ɚ **-s** -z ˌ**Chancellor of the Ex'chequer**
excisable ek'saɪ.zə.bl̩, ɪk'- ⓤⓢ ek'saɪ-, 'ek.saɪ-

excise (*n.*) *tax:* ˈek.saɪz; ekˈsaɪz, ɪk- ⓤⓢ ˈek.saɪz, -saɪs **-man** -mæn **-men** -men

excis|e (*v.*) *cut out:* ekˈsaɪz, ɪk- **-es** -ɪz **-ing** -ɪŋ **-ed** -d

excision ekˈsɪʒ.ən, ɪk- **-s** -z

excitability ɪkˌsaɪ.təˈbɪl.ə.ti, ekˌ-, -ɪ.ti ⓤⓢ -ə.t̬i

excitab|le ɪkˈsaɪ.tə.bl̩, ek- ⓤⓢ -t̬ə- **-ly** -li **-leness** -l̩.nəs, -nɪs

excitant ˈek.sɪ.tənt; ɪkˈsaɪ-, ek- ⓤⓢ ɪkˈsaɪ.tənt **-s** -s

excitation ˌek.sɪˈteɪ.ʃən, -səˈ-, -saɪˈ- ⓤⓢ ˌek.saɪˈ- **-s** -z

excita|tive ekˈsaɪ.tə|.tɪv, ɪk- ⓤⓢ -t̬ə|.t̬ɪv **-tory** -tər.i, -tri ⓤⓢ -tɔːr.i

ex|cite ɪk|ˈsaɪt, ek|- **-cites** -ˈsaɪts **-citing/ly** -ˈsaɪ.tɪŋ/li ⓤⓢ -ˈsaɪ.t̬ɪŋ/li **-cited** -ˈsaɪ.tɪd ⓤⓢ -ˈsaɪ.t̬ɪd **-citer/s** -ˈsaɪ.təʳ/z ⓤⓢ -ˈsaɪ.t̬ɚ/z

excitement ɪkˈsaɪt.mənt, ek- **-s** -s

exclaim ɪksˈkleɪm, eks- **-s** -z **-ing** -ɪŋ **-ed** -d

exclamation ˌeks.kləˈmeɪ.ʃən **-s** -z **exclaˈmation ˌmark; exclaˈmation ˌpoint**

exclamatory eksˈklæm.ə.tər.i, ɪks-, -tri ⓤⓢ -tɔːr.i

exclave ˈeks.kleɪv **-s** -z

exclud|e ɪksˈkluːd, eks- **-es** -z **-ing** -ɪŋ **-ed** -ɪd

exclusion ɪksˈkluː.ʒən, eks- **-s** -z

exclusionary ɪksˈkluː.ʒən.ər.i, eks- ⓤⓢ -er-

exclusionist ɪksˈkluː.ʒən.ɪst, eks- **-s** -s

exclusive ɪksˈkluː.sɪv, eks- **-ly** -li **-ness** -nəs, -nɪs

exclusiv|ism ɪksˈkluː.sɪ.v|ɪ.zəm, eks-, -sə- **-ist/s** -ɪst/s

exclusivistic ɪksˌkluː.sɪˈvɪs.tɪk, eks-, -sə-

exclusivity ˌeks.kluːˈsɪv.ə.ti, -ɪ.ti ⓤⓢ -ə.t̬i

excogi|tate ekˈskɒdʒ.ɪ|.teɪt, ɪk- ⓤⓢ -ˈskɑː.dʒɪ- **-tates** -teɪts **-tating** -teɪ.tɪŋ ⓤⓢ -teɪ.t̬ɪŋ **-tated** -teɪ.tɪd ⓤⓢ -teɪ.t̬ɪd

excogitation ˌek.skɒdʒ.ɪˈteɪ.ʃən; ɪkˌskɒdʒ.ɪˈ-, ekˌ- ⓤⓢ ɪkˌskɑː.dʒɪˈ-, ekˌ- **-s** -z

excommuni|cate ˌek.skəˈmjuː.nɪ|.keɪt, -nə- **-cates** -keɪts **-cating** -keɪ.tɪŋ ⓤⓢ -keɪ.t̬ɪŋ **-cated** -keɪ.tɪd ⓤⓢ -keɪ.t̬ɪd

excommunication ˌek.skəˌmjuː.nɪˈkeɪ.ʃən, -nəˈ- **-s** -z

excori|ate ekˈskɔː.ri|.eɪt, ɪk-, -ˈskɒr.i- ⓤⓢ -ˈskɔːr.i- **-ates** -eɪts **-ating** -eɪ.tɪŋ ⓤⓢ -eɪ.t̬ɪŋ **-ated** -eɪ.tɪd ⓤⓢ -eɪ.t̬ɪd

excoriation ekˌskɔː.riˈeɪ.ʃən, ɪkˌ-, -ˌskɒr.iˈ- ⓤⓢ -ˌskɔːr.iˈ- **-s** -z

excrement ˈek.skrə.mənt, -skrɪ- **-s** -s

excremental ˌek.skrəˈmen.təl, -skrɪˈ- ⓤⓢ -t̬əl

excrescen|ce ɪkˈskres.ən|*t*s, ek- **-ces** -*t*.sɪz **-t** -t

excreta ɪkˈskriː.tə, ek- ⓤⓢ -t̬ə

ex|crete ɪkˈs|kriːt, ek- **-cretes** -kriːts **-creting** -kriː.tɪŋ ⓤⓢ -kriː.t̬ɪŋ **-creted** -kriː.tɪd ⓤⓢ -kriː.t̬ɪd **-cretive** -kriː.tɪv ⓤⓢ -kriː.t̬ɪv **-cretory** -kriː.tər.i ⓤⓢ -kriː.t̬ɚ.i

excretion ɪkˈskriː.ʃən, ek- **-s** -z

excret|um ɪkˈskriː.t|əm, ek- ⓤⓢ -t̬|əm **-a** -ə

excruci|ate ɪkˈskruː.ʃi|.eɪt, ek-, -si- ⓤⓢ -ʃi- **-ates** -eɪts **-ating/ly** -eɪ.tɪŋ/li ⓤⓢ -eɪ.t̬ɪŋ/li **-ated** -eɪ.tɪd ⓤⓢ -eɪ.t̬ɪd

excruciation ɪkˌskruː.ʃiˈeɪ.ʃən, ekˌ-, -siˈ- ⓤⓢ -ʃiˈ-

excul|pate ˈek.skʌl|.peɪt; ɪkˈskʌl-, ekˈ- **-pates** -peɪts **-pating** -peɪ.tɪŋ ⓤⓢ -peɪ.t̬ɪŋ **-pated** -peɪ.tɪd ⓤⓢ -peɪ.t̬ɪd

exculpation ˌek.skʌlˈpeɪ.ʃən

exculpatory ekˈskʌl.pə.tər.i, -tri ⓤⓢ -tɔːr.i

excurs|e ɪkˈskɜːs, ek- ⓤⓢ -ˈskɝːs **-es** -ɪz **-ing** -ɪŋ **-ed** -t

excursion ɪkˈskɜː.ʃən, ek-, -ʒən ⓤⓢ -ˈskɝː.ʒən **-s** -z

excursionist ɪkˈskɜː.ʃən.ɪst, ek-, -ʒən- ⓤⓢ -ˈskɝː.ʒən- **-s** -s

excursioniz|e, -is|e ɪkˈskɜː.ʃən.aɪz, ek-, -ʒən- ⓤⓢ -ˈskɝː.ʒən- **-es** -ɪz **-ing** -ɪŋ **-ed** -d

excursive ɪkˈskɜː.sɪv, ek- ⓤⓢ -ˈskɝː- **-ly** -li **-ness** -nəs, -nɪs

excursus ekˈskɜː.səs, ɪk- ⓤⓢ -ˈskɝː- **-es** -ɪz

excusab|le ɪkˈskjuː.zə.bl̩, ek- **-ly** -li **-leness** -l̩.nəs, -nɪs

excusatory ɪkˈskjuː.zə.tər.i, ek-, -tri ⓤⓢ -tɔːr.i

excus|e (*n.*) ɪkˈskjuːs, ek- **-es** -ɪz

excus|e (*v.*) ɪkˈskjuːz, ek- **-es** -ɪz **-ing** -ɪŋ **-ed** -d

ex delicto ˌeks.delˈɪk.təʊ ⓤⓢ -diːˈlɪk.toʊ, -dɪˈ-

ex-directory ˌeks.dəˈrek.tər.i, -dɪˈ-, -daɪˈ-, ˈ-tri

Exe eks

exeat ˈek.si.æt, -seɪ- **-s** -s

exec ɪgˈzek, eg-, ɪkˈsek, ek- ⓤⓢ ɪgˈzek, əg- **-s** -s

execrab|le ˈek.sɪ.krə.bl̩, -sə- **-ly** -li **-leness** -l̩.nəs, -nɪs

exe|crate ˈek.sɪ|.kreɪt, -sə- **-crates** -kreɪts **-crating** -kreɪ.tɪŋ ⓤⓢ -kreɪ.t̬ɪŋ **-crated** -kreɪ.tɪd ⓤⓢ -kreɪ.t̬ɪd

execration ˌek.sɪˈkreɪ.ʃən, -səˈ- **-s** -z

execra|tive ˈek.sɪ.kreɪ|.tɪv, -sə- ⓤⓢ -t̬ɪv **-tively** -tɪv.li ⓤⓢ -t̬ɪv.li **-tory** -tər.i, -tri ⓤⓢ -tɔːr.i

executant ɪgˈzek.jə.tənt, eg-, -jʊ-; ɪkˈsek-, ek- ⓤⓢ ɪgˈzek.jə-, eg- **-s** -s

exe|cute ˈek.sɪ|.kjuːt, -sə- **-cutes** -kjuːts **-cuting** -kjuː.tɪŋ ⓤⓢ -kjuː.t̬ɪŋ **-cuted** -kjuː.tɪd ⓤⓢ -kjuː.t̬ɪd **-cuter/s** -kjuː.təʳ/z ⓤⓢ -kjuː.t̬ɚ/z **-cutable** -kjuː.tə.bl̩ ⓤⓢ -kjuː.t̬ə.bl̩

execution ˌek.sɪˈkjuː.ʃən, -səˈ- **-s** -z

executioner ˌek.sɪˈkjuː.ʃən.əʳ, -səˈ- ⓤⓢ -ɚ **-s** -z

executive ɪgˈzek.jə.tɪv, eg-, -jʊ-; ɪkˈsek-, ek- ⓤⓢ ɪgˈzek.jə.t̬ɪv, eg- **-s** ⓤⓢ -z **-ly** ⓤⓢ -li **exˌecutive ˈprivilege**

executor ɪgˈzek.jə.təʳ, eg-, -jʊ-; ɪkˈsek-, ek- ⓤⓢ ɪgˈzek.jə.t̬ɚ, eg- **-s** -z **-ship/s** -ʃɪp/s

executory ɪgˈzek.jə.tər.i, eg-, -jʊ-, -tri, ɪkˈsek-, ek- ⓤⓢ ɪgˈzek.jə.tɔːr.i, eg-

executr|ix ɪgˈzek.jə.tr|ɪks, eg-, -jʊ-; ɪkˈsek-, ek- ⓤⓢ ɪgˈzek.jə-, eg- **-ixes** -ɪk.sɪz **executrices** ɪgˌzek.jəˈtraɪ.siːz, eg-, -jʊ-; ɪkˌsek-, ek- ⓤⓢ ɪgˌzek.jəˈ-, eg-

exeges|is ˌek.sɪˈdʒiː.s|ɪs, -səˈ- **-es** -iːz

exegetic ˌek.sɪˈdʒet.ɪk, -səˈ-, ˈdʒiː.tɪk ⓤⓢ -ˈdʒet̬- **-al** -əl **-ally** -əl.i, -li **-s** -s

exemplar ɪgˈzem.pləʳ, eg-; ɪkˈsem-, ek-, -plɑːʳ ⓤⓢ ɪgˈzem.plɚ, eg-, -plɑːr **-s** -z

exemplarity ˌeg.zemˈplær.ə.ti, -ɪ.ti ⓤⓢ -ˈpler-, -ˈplær-, -ə.t̬i

exemplar|y ɪgˈzem.plər|.i, eg-; ɪkˈsem-, ek- ⓤⓢ ɪgˈzem-, eg- **-ily** -əl.i, -ɪ.li **-iness** -ɪ.nəs, -ɪ.nɪs

exemplification ɪgˌzem.plɪ.fɪˈkeɪ.ʃən, eg-, -plə-; ɪkˌsem-, ek- ⓤⓢ ɪgˌzem.plə-, eg- **-s** -z

exempli|fy ɪgˈzem.plɪ|.faɪ, eg-, -plə-; ɪkˈsem-, ek- ⓤⓢ ɪgˈzem-, eg- **-fies** -faɪz **-fying** -faɪ.ɪŋ **-fied** -faɪd

exemplum ɪgˈzem.pləm, egˈ-; ɪkˈsem-, ekˈ-

exempt ɪgˈzempt, egˈ-; ɪkˈsempt, ekˈ- ⓤⓢ ɪgˈzempt, egˈ- **-s** -s **-ing** -ɪŋ **-ed** -ɪd

exemption ɪgˈzemp.ʃən, egˈ-; ɪkˈsemp-, ekˈ- ⓤⓢ ɪgˈzemp-, egˈ **-s** -z

exequatur ˌek.sɪˈkweɪ.təʳ, -səˈ- ⓤⓢ -t̬ɚ **-s** -z

exequies ˈek.sɪ.kwɪz, -sə- ⓤⓢ -kwiːz

exercis|e ˈek.sə.saɪz ⓤⓢ -sɚ- **-es** -ɪz **-ing** -ɪŋ **-ed** -d **-er/s** -əʳ/z ⓤⓢ -ɚ/z **ˈexercise ˌbook**

exercitation egˌzɜː.sɪˈteɪ.ʃən, ɪgˌ- ⓤⓢ -ˌzɝː-

exergue ekˈsɜːg, ˈ-- ⓤⓢ ˈek.sɝːg, ˈeg.zɝːg **-s** -z

exer|t ɪgˈzɜː|t, eg-; ɪkˈsɜː|t, ek- ⓤⓢ ɪgˈzɝː|t, eg- **-ts** -ts **-ting** -tɪŋ

Ⓤ -t̬ɪŋ **-ted** -tɪd Ⓤ -t̬ɪd **-tive** -tɪv Ⓤ -t̬ɪv

exertion ɪɡˈzɜː.ʃᵊn, eɡ-; ɪkˈsɜː-, ek- Ⓤ ɪɡˈzɝː-, eɡ- **-s** -z

Exeter ˈek.sɪ.təʳ, -sə- Ⓤ -t̬ɚ

exeunt ˈek.si.ʌnt, -seɪ-, -ʊnt, -si.ənt Ⓤ -si.ʌnt, -ənt

exfoli|ate eksˈfəʊ.li|.eɪt Ⓤ -ˈfoʊ- **-ates** -eɪts **-ating** -eɪ.tɪŋ Ⓤ -eɪ.t̬ɪŋ **-ated** -eɪ.tɪd Ⓤ -eɪ.t̬ɪd **-ator** -eɪ.təʳ Ⓤ -eɪ.t̬ɚ/z

exfoliation eksˌfəʊ.liˈeɪ.ʃᵊn, ˌeks.fəʊ- Ⓤ eksˌfoʊ- **-s** -z

ex gratia eksˈɡreɪ.ʃə, -ʃi.ə

exhalant, exhalent eksˈheɪ.lənt, ɪks-; eɡˈzeɪ- Ⓤ eksˈheɪ-

exhalation ˌeks.*h*əˈleɪ.ʃᵊn **-s** -z

exhal|e eksˈheɪl, ɪks-; eɡˈzeɪl Ⓤ eksˈheɪl, ˈ-- **-es** -z **-ing** -ɪŋ **-ed** -d

exhaust ɪɡˈzɔːst, eɡˈ-; ɪkˈsɔːst, ekˈ- Ⓤ ɪɡˈzɑːst, eɡˈ-, -ˈzɔːst **-s** -s **-ing** -ɪŋ **-ed** -ɪd **-er/s** -əʳ/z Ⓤ -ɚ/z **-ible** -ə.bl̩, -ɪ.bl̩ **-less** -ləs, -lɪs **exˈhaust ˌpipe**

exhaustion ɪɡˈzɔːs.tʃᵊn, eɡ-; ɪkˈsɔː-, ek- Ⓤ ɪɡˈzɑː-, eɡ-, -ˈzɔː-

exhaustive ɪɡˈzɔː.stɪv, eɡ-; ɪkˈsɔː-, ek- Ⓤ ɪɡˈzɑː-, eɡ-, -ˈzɔː- **-ly** -li **-ness** -nəs, -nɪs

exhibit (*n.*) ɪɡˈzɪb.ɪt, eɡ-; ɪkˈsɪb-, ek-; ˈeɡ.zɪb-, ˈek.sɪb- Ⓤ ɪɡˈzɪb-, eɡ- **-s** -s

exhib|it (*v.*) ɪɡˈzɪb|.ɪt, eɡ-; ɪkˈsɪb-, ek- Ⓤ ɪɡˈzɪb-, eɡ- **-its** -ɪts **-iting** -ɪ.tɪŋ Ⓤ -ɪ.t̬ɪŋ **-ited** -ɪ.tɪd Ⓤ -ɪ.t̬ɪd **-itor/s** -ɪ.təʳ/z Ⓤ -ɪ.t̬ɚ/z **-itive** -ɪ.tɪv Ⓤ -ɪ.t̬ɪv **-itory** -ɪ.tᵊr.i, -ɪ.tri Ⓤ -ɪ.tɔːr.i

exhibition ˌek.sɪˈbɪʃ.ᵊn, -səˈ- **-s** -z

exhibitioner ˌek.sɪˈbɪʃ.ᵊn.əʳ, -səˈ- Ⓤ -ɚ **-s** -z

exhibitionism ˌek.sɪˈbɪʃ.ᵊn.ɪ.zᵊm, -səˈ-

exhibitionist ˌek.sɪˈbɪʃ.ᵊn.ɪst, -səˈ- **-s** -s

exhibitionistic ˌek.sɪ.bɪ.ʃᵊnˈɪs.tɪk, -sə- **-ally** -ᵊl.i, -li

exhilarant ɪɡˈzɪl.ᵊr.ᵊnt, eɡ-; ɪkˈsɪl-, ek- Ⓤ ɪɡˈzɪl-, eɡ- **-s** -s

exhilar|ate ɪɡˈzɪl.ᵊr|.eɪt, eɡ-; ɪkˈsɪl-, ek- Ⓤ ɪɡˈzɪl-, eɡ- **-ates** -eɪts **-ating** -eɪ.tɪŋ Ⓤ -eɪ.t̬ɪŋ **-ated** -eɪ.tɪd Ⓤ -eɪ.t̬ɪd

exhilaration ɪɡˌzɪl.ᵊrˈeɪ.ʃᵊn, eɡ-; ɪkˌsɪl-, ek- Ⓤ ɪɡˌzɪl-, eɡ-

exhilarative ɪɡˈzɪl.ᵊr.ə.tɪv, eɡ-, -eɪ-; ɪkˈsɪl-, ek- Ⓤ ɪɡˈzɪl.ə.reɪ.t̬ɪv, eɡ-

exhor|t ɪɡˈzɔː|t, eɡ-; ɪkˈsɔː|t, ek- Ⓤ ɪɡˈzɔːr|t, eɡ- **-ts** -ts **-ting** -tɪŋ Ⓤ -t̬ɪŋ **-ted** -tɪd Ⓤ -t̬ɪd

exhortation ˌeɡ.zɔːˈteɪ.ʃᵊn, ˌek.sɔːˈ- Ⓤ ˌeɡ.zɔːrˈ-, -zɚˈ-; ˌek.sɔːrˈ-, -sɚˈ- **-s** -z

exhorta|tive ɪɡˈzɔː.tə|.tɪv, eɡ-; ɪkˈsɔː-, ek- Ⓤ ɪɡˈzɔːr.t̬ə|.t̬ɪv, eɡ- **-tory** -tᵊr.i, -tri Ⓤ -tɔːr.i

exhumation ˌeks.*h*juːˈmeɪ.ʃᵊn Ⓤ ˌeks.*h*juːˈ-, ˌeɡ.zjuːˈ- **-s** -z

exhum|e eksˈ*h*juːm, ɪksˈ-; ɪɡˈzjuːm, eɡˈ- Ⓤ eɡˈzuːm, ɪɡˈ-, -ˈzjuːm **-es** -z **-ing** -ɪŋ **-ed** -d **-er/s** -əʳ/z Ⓤ -ɚ/z

exigen|ce ˈek.sɪ.dʒən*t*|s, -sə-; ˈeɡ.zɪ-, -zə- **-ces** -sɪz

exigenc|y ˈek.sɪ.dʒən*t*.s|i, -sə-; ˈeɡ.zɪ-, -zə-; ɪɡˈzɪdʒ.ən*t*-, eɡ-; ɪkˈsɪdʒ-, ek- **-ies** -iz

exigent ˈek.sɪ.dʒənt, -sə-; ˈeɡ.zɪ-, -zə- **-ly** -li

exiguity ˌek.sɪˈɡjuː.ə.ti, -ɪ.ti Ⓤ ˌek.sɪˈɡjuː.ə.t̬i, ˌeɡ.zɪˈ-

exiguous eɡˈzɪɡ.ju.əs, ɪɡ-; ekˈsɪɡ-, ɪk- Ⓤ eɡˈzɪɡ-, ɪɡ- **-ness** -nəs, -nɪs

exil|e ˈek.saɪl, ˈeɡ.zaɪl **-es** -z **-ing** -ɪŋ **-ed** -d

exility eɡˈzɪl.ə.ti, ekˈsɪl-, -ɪ.ti Ⓤ -ə.t̬i

exist ɪɡˈzɪst, eɡ-; ɪkˈsɪst, ek- Ⓤ ɪɡˈzɪst, eɡ- **-s** -s **-ing** -ɪŋ **-ed** -ɪd

existen|ce ɪɡˈzɪs.tᵊn|*t*s, eɡ-; ɪkˈsɪs-, ek- Ⓤ ɪɡˈzɪs-, eɡ- **-ces** -*t*.sɪz

existent ɪɡˈzɪs.tᵊnt, eɡ-; ɪkˈsɪs-, ek- Ⓤ ɪɡˈzɪs-, eɡ-

existential ˌeɡ.zɪˈsten.*t*ʃᵊl, -zəˈ-; ˌek.sɪˈ-, -səˈ-

existential|ism ˌeɡ.zɪˈsten.*t*ʃᵊl|.ɪ.zᵊm, -zəˈ-; ˌek.sɪˈ-, -səˈ- **-ist/s** -ɪst/s

exit ˈek.sɪt, ˈeɡ.zɪt **-s** -s **ˈexit ˌpoll** **-ing** -ɪŋ **-ed** -ɪd

ex libris ˌeksˈlɪb.riːs, -rɪs, -ˈlaɪ.brɪs Ⓤ -ˈliː.brɪs

Exmoor ˈek.smɔːʳ, -smʊəʳ Ⓤ -smʊr

Exmouth *in Devon:* ˈek.smaʊθ, -sməθ *in Australia:* ˈek.smaʊθ

exo- ek.səʊ-; ɪkˈsɒ-, ek- Ⓤ ek.soʊ-; ɪkˈsɑː-, ek-

Note: Prefix. Either carries primary or secondary stress on the first syllable, e.g. **exocrine** /ˈek.səʊ.kraɪn Ⓤ -sə.krən/, **exocentric** /ˌek.səʊˈsen.trɪk Ⓤ -soʊˈ-/, or primary stress on the second syllable, e.g. **exogamy** /ekˈsɒɡ.ə.mi Ⓤ -ˈsɑː.ɡə-/.

exocentric ˌek.səʊˈsen.trɪk Ⓤ -soʊˈ- **-ally** -ᵊ.li, -li

Exocet® ˈek.səʊ.set Ⓤ -soʊ- **-s** -s

exocrine ˈek.səʊ.kraɪn, -krɪn Ⓤ ˈek.sə.krən, -soʊ-, -kraɪn, -kriːn

exode ˈek.səʊd Ⓤ -soʊd **-s** -z

exodus (E) ˈek.sə.dəs **-es** -ɪz

ex officio ˌeks.əˈfɪʃ.i.əʊ, -ɒfˈɪʃ-, -ˈɪs- Ⓤ -əˈfɪʃ.i.oʊ, -ˈfɪs-

exogam|y ekˈsɒɡ.ə.m|i Ⓤ -ˈsɑː.ɡə- **-ous** -əs

exogenous ɪkˈsɒdʒ.ə.nəs, ek-, -ɪ.nəs Ⓤ -ˈsɑː.dʒə-

exon ˈek.sɒn Ⓤ -sɑːn **-s** -z

exoner|ate ɪɡˈzɒn.ᵊr|.eɪt, eɡ-; ɪkˈsɒn-, ek- Ⓤ ɪɡˈzɑː.nə.r|eɪt, eɡ- **-ates** -eɪts **-ating** -eɪ.tɪŋ Ⓤ -eɪ.t̬ɪŋ **-ated** -eɪ.tɪd Ⓤ -eɪ.t̬ɪd

exoneration ɪɡˌzɒn.əˈreɪ.ʃᵊn, eɡ-; ɪkˌsɒn-, ek- Ⓤ ɪɡˌzɑː.nəˈ-, eɡ-

exonerative ɪɡˈzɒn.ᵊr.ə.tɪv, eɡ-, -eɪ-; ɪkˈsɒn-, ek-, -eɪ.tɪv Ⓤ ɪɡˈzɑː.nə.reɪ.t̬ɪv, eɡ-

exophora ekˈsɒf.ᵊr.ə Ⓤ -ˈsɑː.fɚ-

exophoric ˌek.səʊˈfɒr.ɪk Ⓤ -səˈfɔːr-

exorbitan|ce ɪɡˈzɔː.bɪ.tᵊn*t*|s, eɡ-, -bə-; ɪkˈsɔː-, ek- Ⓤ ɪɡˈzɔːr.bə.t̬ᵊn*t*|s, eɡ- **-cy** -si

exorbitant ɪɡˈzɔː.bɪ.tᵊnt, eɡ-, -bə-; ɪkˈsɔː-, ek- Ⓤ ɪɡˈzɔːr.bə.t̬ᵊnt, eɡ- **-ly** -li

exorc|ism ˈek.sɔː.s|ɪ.zᵊm, -sə-; ˈeɡ.zɔː-, -zə- Ⓤ ˈek.sɔːr-, -sɚ- **-ist/s** -ɪst/s

exorciz|e, -is|e ˈek.sɔː.saɪz, -sə-; ˈeɡ.zɔː-, -zə- Ⓤ ˈek.sɔːr-, -sɚ- **-es** -ɪz **-ing** -ɪŋ **-ed** -d

exordi|um ekˈsɔː.di|.əm; eɡˈzɔː- Ⓤ eɡˈzɔːr.di-, ɪɡ-; ekˈsɔːr-, ɪk- **-ums** -əmz **-a** -ə

exoskelet|on ˌek.səʊˈskel.ɪ.t|ᵊn, ˈ-ə-, ˈek.səʊˌskel- Ⓤ ˌek.soʊˈskel.ə- **-ons** -ənz **-al** -ᵊl

exoteric ˌek.səʊˈter.ɪk Ⓤ -səˈ-, -soʊˈ- **-s** -s **-al** -ᵊl **-ally** -ᵊl.i, -li

exotic ɪɡˈzɒt.ɪk, eɡ-; ɪkˈsɒt-, ek- Ⓤ ɪɡˈzɑː.t̬ɪk, eɡ- **-s** -s **-a** -ə **-ally** -ᵊl.i, -li

exoticism ɪɡˈzɒt.ɪ.sɪ.zᵊm, eɡ-, ˈ-ə-; ɪkˈsɒt-, ek-, ək- Ⓤ ɪɡˈzɑː.t̬ə-, eɡ-

expand ɪkˈspænd, ek- **-s** -z **-ing** -ɪŋ **-ed** -ɪd **-er/s** -əʳ/z Ⓤ -ɚ/z **-able** -ə.bl̩

expans|e ɪkˈspæn*t*s, ek- **-es** -ɪz

expansibility ɪkˌspæn*t*.səˈbɪl.ə.ti, ek-, -sɪˈ-, -ɪ.ti Ⓤ -ə.t̬i

expansib|le ɪkˈspæn*t*.sə.b|l̩, ek-, -sɪ- **-ly** -li **-leness** -l̩.nəs, -nɪs

expansile ɪkˈspæn*t*.saɪl, ek- Ⓤ -sɪl

expansion ɪkˈspæn.*t*ʃᵊn, ek- **-s** -z

expansion|ism ɪkˈspæn.*t*ʃᵊn|.ɪ.zᵊm, ek-, ək- **-ist/s** -ɪst/s

expansive ɪkˈspæn*t*.sɪv, ek- **-ly** -li **-ness** -nəs, -nɪs

ex parte ˌeksˈpɑː.teɪ, -ti Ⓤ -ˈpɑːr.t̬i

expat ˌekˈspæt **-s** -s *stress shift:* ˌexpat comˈmunity

expati|ate ekˈspeɪ.ʃi|.eɪt, ɪk- **-ates** -eɪts **-ating** -eɪ.tɪŋ Ⓤ -eɪ.t̬ɪŋ **-ated** -eɪ.tɪd Ⓤ -eɪ.t̬ɪd

expatiation ekˌspeɪ.ʃiˈeɪ.ʃᵊn, ɪk- **-s** -z

expatia|tive ekˈspeɪ.ʃi.ə|.tɪv, ɪk-, -tɪv Ⓤ -eɪ|.t̬ɪv **-tory** -tᵊr.i, -tri Ⓤ -tɔːr.i

expatriate (*n. adj.*) ɪk'spæt.ri.ət, ek'-, -'speɪ.tri-, -ɪt, -eɪt (US) ek'speɪ-, ɪk'- **-s** -s

expatri|ate (*v.*) ɪk'spæt.ri|.eɪt, ek'-, -'speɪ.tri- (US) ek'speɪ-, ɪk'- **-ates** -eɪts **-ating** -eɪ.tɪŋ (US) -eɪ.t̬ɪŋ **-ated** -eɪ.tɪd (US) -eɪ.t̬ɪd

expatriation ekˌspæt.ri'eɪ.ʃᵊn, ɪk-, -ˌspeɪ.tri'-, ˌek.speɪ-, ˌek.spæt.ri'- (US) ekˌspeɪ.tri'eɪ-, ɪk-

expect ɪk'spekt, ek- **-s** -s **-ing** -ɪŋ **-ed** -ɪd

expectan|cy ɪk'spek.tᵊnt|si, ek- **-ce** -s **-cies** -siz

expectant ɪk'spek.tᵊnt, ek- **-ly** -li

expectation ˌek.spek'teɪ.ʃᵊn **-s** -z

expectorant ɪk'spek.tᵊr.ᵊnt, ek- **-s** -s

expector|ate ɪk'spek.tᵊr|.eɪt, ek- **-ates** -eɪts **-ating** -eɪ.tɪŋ (US) -eɪ.t̬ɪŋ **-ated** -eɪ.tɪd (US) -eɪ.t̬ɪd

expectoration ɪkˌspek.tᵊr'eɪ.ʃᵊn, ek-

Expedia ɪk'spiː.di.ə, ek-

expedien|cy ɪk'spiː.di.ənt|si, ek- **-ce** -s

expedient ɪk'spiː.di.ənt, ek- **-s** -s **-ly** -li

expe|dite 'ek.spɪ|.daɪt, -spə- **-dites** -daɪts **-diting** -daɪ.tɪŋ (US) -daɪ.t̬ɪŋ **-dited** -daɪ.tɪd (US) -daɪ.t̬ɪd

expediter 'ek.spɪ.daɪ.təʳ, -spə- (US) -t̬ɚ **-s** -z

expedition ˌek.spɪ'dɪʃ.ᵊn, -spə'- **-s** -z

expeditionary ˌek.spɪ'dɪʃ.ᵊn.ᵊr.i, -spɪ'-, -ri (US) -er-

expeditious ˌek.spɪ'dɪʃ.əs, -spə'- **-ly** -li **-ness** -nəs, -nɪs

expeditor 'ek.spɪ.daɪ.təʳ, -spə- (US) -t̬ɚ **-s** -z

expel ɪk'spel, ek- **-s** -z **-ling** -ɪŋ **-led** -d **-lable** -ə.bl̩

expend ɪk'spend, ek- **-s** -z **-ing** -ɪŋ **-ed** -ɪd

expendable ɪk'spen.də.bl̩, ek- **-s** -z

expenditure ɪk'spen.dɪ.tʃəʳ, ek-, -də- (US) -tʃɚ **-s** -z

expens|e ɪk'spen*t*s, ek- **-es** -ɪz **ex'pense acˌcount**

expensive ɪk'spen*t*.sɪv, ek- **-ly** -li **-ness** -nəs, -nɪs

experienc|e ɪk'spɪə.ri.ən*t*s, ek- (US) -'spɪr.i- **-es** -ɪz **-ing** -ɪŋ **-ed** -t

experiential ɪkˌspɪə.ri'en.*t*ʃᵊl, ek- (US) -ˌspɪr.i'- **-ly** -li

experiment (*n.*) ɪk'sper.ɪ.mənt, ek-, '-ə- **-s** -s

experiment (*v.*) ɪk'sper.ɪ.ment, ek-, '-ə- **-s** -s **-ing** -ɪŋ **-ed** -ɪd **-er/s** -əʳ/z (US) -ɚ/z

experimental ɪkˌsper.ɪ'men.tᵊl, ek-, -ə'-; ˌek.sper- (US) ekˌsper-, ɪk- **-ly** -i

experimental|ism ɪkˌsper.ɪ'ment.ᵊl|.ɪ.zᵊm, ek-, -ə'-; ˌek.sper-, -ə'men- (US) ekˌsper-, ɪk- **-ist/s** -ɪst/s

experimentaliz|e, -is|e ɪkˌsper.ɪ'men.tᵊl.aɪz, ek-, -ə'-; ˌek.sper- (US) ekˌsper.ɪ'men.t̬ᵊ.laɪz, ɪk- **-es** -ɪz **-ing** -ɪŋ **-ed** -d

experimentation ɪkˌsper.ɪ.men'teɪ.ʃᵊn, ek-, ˌ-ə- **-s** -z

expert 'ek.spɜːt (US) -spɝːt **-s** -s **-ly** -li **-ness** -nəs, -nɪs

expertise ˌek.spɜː'tiːz, -spə'tiːz (US) -spɝː'-, -spɚ'-

expiable 'ek.spi.ə.bl̩

expi|ate 'ek.spi|.eɪt **-ates** -eɪts **-ating** -eɪ.tɪŋ (US) -eɪ.t̬ɪŋ **-ated** -eɪ.tɪd (US) -eɪ.t̬ɪd **-ator/s** -eɪ.təʳ/z (US) -eɪ.t̬ɚ/z

expiation ˌek.spi'eɪ.ʃᵊn **-s** -z

expiatory 'ek.spi.ə.tᵊr.i, -eɪ-, -tri; ˌek.spi'eɪ- (US) 'ek.spi.ə.tɔːr.i

expiration ˌek.spɪ'reɪ.ʃᵊn, -spə'-, -spaɪə'- (US) -spə'- **-s** -z

expiratory ɪk'spɪr.ə.tᵊr.i, ek-, -'spaɪə.rə-, -tri (US) -'spaɪ.rə.tɔːr.i

expir|e ɪk'spaɪəʳ, ek'- (US) -'spaɪɚ **-es** -z **-ing** -ɪŋ **-ed** -d

expiry ɪk'spaɪə.ri, ek- (US) -'spaɪ-; 'ek.spɚ.i **ex'piry ˌdate**

explain ɪk'spleɪn, ek'- **-s** -z **-ing** -ɪŋ **-ed** -d **-er/s** -əʳ/z (US) -ɚ/z **-able** -ə.bl̩

explanation ˌek.splə'neɪ.ʃᵊn **-s** -z

explanator|y ɪk'splæn.ə.tᵊr|.i, ek'-, '-ɪ-, -tr|i (US) -ə.tɔːr|.i **-ily** -ᵊl.i, -ɪ.li **-iness** -ɪ.nəs, -ɪ.nɪs

expletive ɪk'spliː.tɪv, ek'- (US) 'ek.splə.t̬ɪv **-s** -z

expletory ɪk'spliː.tᵊr.i, ek'-, '-tri (US) -t̬ɚ.i

explicab|le ɪk'splɪk.ə.bl|l̩, ek-; 'ek.splɪ.kə- **-ly** -li

expli|cate 'ek.splɪ|.keɪt **-cates** -keɪts **-cating** -keɪ.tɪŋ (US) -keɪ.t̬ɪŋ **-cated** -keɪ.tɪd (US) -keɪ.t̬ɪd

explication ˌek.splɪ'keɪ.ʃᵊn **-s** -z

explicative ek'splɪk.ə.tɪv, ɪk-; 'ek.splɪ.keɪ.tɪv (US) -t̬ɪv

explicatory ek'splɪk.ə.tᵊr.i, ɪk-, -tri; 'ek.splɪ.keɪ-, ˌek.splɪ'keɪ- (US) 'ek.splɪ.kə.tɔːr.i; ɪk'splɪk.ə-, ek-

explicit ɪk'splɪs.ɪt, ek- **-ly** -li **-ness** -nəs, -nɪs

explod|e ɪk'spləʊd, ek- (US) -'sploʊd **-es** -z **-ing** -ɪŋ **-ed** -ɪd **-er/s** -əʳ/z (US) -ɚ/z

exploit (*n.*) 'ek.splɔɪt **-s** -s

exploi|t (*v.*) ɪk'splɔɪ|t, ek- **-ts** -ts **-ting** -tɪŋ (US) -t̬ɪŋ **-ted** -tɪd (US) -t̬ɪd **-ter/s** -təʳ/z (US) -t̬ɚ/z

exploitation ˌek.splɔɪ'teɪ.ʃᵊn

exploitative ɪk'splɔɪ.tə.tɪv, ek- (US) -t̬ə.t̬ɪv **-ly** -li

exploitive ɪk'splɔɪ.tɪv, ek- (US) -t̬ɪv **-ly** -li

exploration ˌek.splə'reɪ.ʃᵊn, -splɔː'- (US) -splɔːr- **-s** -z

explorative ɪk'splɒr.ə.tɪv, ek-, -'splɔː.rə- (US) -'splɔːr.ə.t̬ɪv

exploratory ɪk'splɒr.ə.tᵊr.i, ek-, -'splɔː.rə-, -tri (US) -'splɔːr.ə.tɔːr.i

explor|e ɪk'splɔːʳ, ek- (US) -'splɔːr **-es** -z **-ing** -ɪŋ **-ed** -d **-er/s** -əʳ/z (US) -ɚ/z

explosion ɪk'spləʊ.ʒᵊn, ek- (US) -'sploʊ- **-s** -z

explosive ɪk'spləʊ.sɪv, ek-, -zɪv (US) -'sploʊ.sɪv **-s** -z **-ly** -li **-ness** -nəs, -nɪs

expo 'ek.spəʊ (US) -spoʊ **-s** -z

exponent ɪk'spəʊ.nənt, ek- (US) -'spoʊ- **-s** -s

exponential ˌek.spəʊ'nen.*t*ʃᵊl (US) -spoʊ'nen*t*.ʃᵊl **-ly** -li

export (*n.*) 'ek.spɔːt (US) -spɔːrt **-s** -s

expor|t (*v.*) ɪk'spɔː|t, ek-; 'ek.spɔː|t (US) ɪk'spɔːr|t, ek-; 'ek.spɔːr|t **-ts** -ts **-ting** -tɪŋ (US) -t̬ɪŋ **-ted** -tɪd (US) -t̬ɪd **-ter/s** -təʳ/z (US) -t̬ɚ/z

exportable ɪk'spɔː.tə.bᵊl, ek- (US) -'spɔːr.t̬ə-

exportation ˌek.spɔː'teɪ.ʃᵊn (US) -spɔːr'-

expos|e ɪk'spəʊz, ek- (US) -'spoʊz **-es** -ɪz **-ing** -ɪŋ **-ed** -d **-edness** -d.nəs, -nɪs **-er/s** -əʳ/z (US) -ɚ/z

exposé ek'spəʊ.zeɪ, ɪk- (US) ˌek.spoʊ'zeɪ, '--- **-s** -z

exposition ˌek.spəʊ'zɪʃ.ᵊn (US) -pə'- **-s** -z

expositive ɪk'spɒz.ɪ.tɪv, ek-, -ə.tɪv (US) -'spɑː.zə.t̬ɪv

exposi|tor ɪk'spɒz.ɪ|.təʳ, ek-, -ə|.təʳ (US) -'spɑː.zə|.t̬ɚ **-tors** -təz (US) -t̬ɚz **-tory** -tᵊr.i, -tri (US) -tɔːr.i

ex post facto ˌeks.pəʊs*t*'fæk.təʊ (US) -poʊst'fæk.toʊ

expostu|late ɪk'spɒs.tʃə|.leɪt, ek-, -tʃʊ-, -tjə-, -tjʊ- (US) -'spɑːs.tʃə- **-lates** -leɪts **-lating** -leɪ.tɪŋ (US) -leɪ.t̬ɪŋ **-lated** -leɪ.tɪd (US) -leɪ.t̬ɪd **-lator/s** -leɪ.təʳ/z (US) -leɪ.t̬ɚ/z

expostulation ɪkˌspɒs.tʃə'leɪ.ʃᵊn, ek-, -tʃʊ'-, -tjə'-, -tjʊ'- (US) -ˌpɑːs.tʃə'- **-s** -z

expostulative ɪk'spɒs.tʃə.lə.tɪv, ek-, -tʃʊ-, -tjə-, -tjʊ-, -leɪ- (US) -'pɑːs.tʃə.leɪ.t̬ɪv

expostulatory ɪk'spɒs.tʃə.lə.tᵊr.i, ek-, -tʃʊ-, -tjə-, -tjʊ-, -leɪ-, -tri (US) -'spɑːs.tʃə.lə.tɔːr.i

exposure ɪk'spəʊ.ʒəʳ, ek- (US) -'spoʊ.ʒɚ **-s** -z

expound ɪk'spaʊnd, ek- **-s** -z **-ing** -ɪŋ **-ed** -ɪd **-er/s** -əʳ/z (US) -ɚ/z

express ɪk'spres, ek- **-es** -ɪz **-ly** -li **-ness** -nəs, -nɪs **-ing** -ɪŋ **-ed** -t **ˌexpress de'livery, exˌpress de'livery** (US) **ˌexpress de'livery**

expressible ɪk'spres.ə.bl̩, ek-, -sɪ-

expression ɪk'spreʃ.ᵊn, ek- **-s** -z

expressional ɪk'spreʃ.ᵊn.ᵊl, ek-

expression|ism ɪkˈspreʃ.ən|.ɪ.zəm, ek- **-ist/s** -ɪst/s
expressionistic ɪkˌspreʃ.əˈnɪs.tɪk, ek- **-ally** -əl.i, -li
expressionless ɪkˈspreʃ.ən.ləs, ek-, -lɪs **-ly** -li **-ness** -nəs, -nɪs
expressive ɪkˈspres.ɪv, ek- **-ly** -li **-ness** -nəs, -nɪs
expresso ɪkˈspres.əʊ, ek- ⓤⓢ -oʊ **-s** -z
expressway ɪkˈspres.weɪ, ek- **-s** -z
expropri|ate ɪkˈsprəʊ.pri|.eɪt, ek- ⓤⓢ -ˈsproʊ- **-ates** -eɪts **-ating** -eɪ.tɪŋ ⓤⓢ -eɪ.t̬ɪŋ **-ated** -eɪ.tɪd ⓤⓢ -eɪ.t̬ɪd **-ator/s** -eɪ.təʳ/z ⓤⓢ -eɪ.t̬ɚ/z
expropriation ɪkˌsprəʊ.priˈeɪ.ʃən, ek-; ˌek.sprəʊ- ⓤⓢ ɪkˌsproʊ-, ek- **-s** -z
expulsion ɪkˈspʌl.ʃən, ek- **-s** -z
expulsive ɪkˈspʌl.sɪv, ek-
expung|e ɪkˈspʌndʒ, ek- **-es** -ɪz **-ing** -ɪŋ **-ed** -d
expur|gate ˈek.spə|.geɪt, -spɜː- ⓤⓢ -spɚ- **-gates** -geɪts **-gating** -geɪ.tɪŋ ⓤⓢ -geɪ.t̬ɪŋ **-gated** -geɪ.tɪd ⓤⓢ -geɪ.t̬ɪd **-gator/s** -geɪ.təʳ/z ⓤⓢ -geɪ.t̬ɚ/z
expurgation ˌek.spəˈgeɪ.ʃən, -spɜːˈ- ⓤⓢ -spɚˈ- **-s** -z
expurgatory ekˈspɜː.gə.tər.i, ɪkˈ-, -tri ⓤⓢ -ˈspɝː.gə.tɔːr.i
exquisite ɪkˈskwɪz.ɪt, ek-; ˈek.skwɪ.zɪt, -zət **-s** -s **-ly** -li **-ness** -nəs, -nɪs
exscind ekˈsɪnd, ɪk- **-s** -z **-ing** -ɪŋ **-ed** -ɪd
exsect ekˈsekt, ɪk- **-s** -s **-ing** -ɪŋ **-ed** -ɪd
exsection ekˈsek.ʃən, ɪk- **-s** -z
ex-service ˌeksˈsɜː.vɪs ⓤⓢ ˌeksˈsɝː-
exsic|cate ˈek.sɪ|.keɪt, ˈeks- **-cates** -keɪts **-cating** -keɪ.tɪŋ ⓤⓢ -keɪ.t̬ɪŋ **-cated** -keɪ.tɪd ⓤⓢ -keɪ.t̬ɪd **-cator/s** -keɪ.təʳ/z ⓤⓢ -keɪ.t̬ɚ/z
extant ekˈstænt, ɪk-; ˈek.stənt ⓤⓢ ˈek.stənt; ˌekˈstænt
extemporaneous ɪkˌstem.pəˈreɪ.ni.əs, ek-; ˌek.stem- ⓤⓢ ɪkˌstem.pəˈ-, ek- **-ly** -li **-ness** -nəs, -nɪs
extemporary ɪkˈstem.pər.ə.ri, ek- ⓤⓢ -er.i
extempore ɪkˈstem.pər.i, ek-
extemporization, -isa- ɪkˌstem.pər.aɪˈzeɪ.ʃən, ek-, -ɪˈ- ⓤⓢ -ɪˈ- **-s** -z
extemporiz|e, -is|e ɪkˈstem.pər.aɪz, ek- ⓤⓢ -pə.raɪz **-es** -ɪz **-ing** -ɪŋ **-ed** -d **-er/s** -əʳ/z ⓤⓢ -ɚ/z
extend ɪkˈstend, ek- **-s** -z **-ing** -ɪŋ **-ed** -ɪd **-able** -ə.bl̩ **exˌtended ˈfamily**
extensibility ɪkˌstent.səˈbɪl.ə.ti, ek-, -sɪˈ-, -ɪ.ti ⓤⓢ -ə.t̬i
extensible ɪkˈstent.sə.bl̩, ek-, -sɪ-
extensile ɪkˈstent.saɪl, ek- ⓤⓢ -sɪl
extension ɪkˈsten.tʃən, ek- **-s** -z **exˈtension ˌlead**
extensive ɪkˈstent.sɪv, ek- **-ly** -li **-ness** -nəs, -nɪs
extensor ɪkˈstent.səʳ, ek- ⓤⓢ -sɚ **-s** -z
extent ɪkˈstent, ek- **-s** -s
extenu|ate ɪkˈsten.ju|.eɪt, ek- **-ates** -eɪts **-ating/ly** -eɪ.tɪŋ/li ⓤⓢ -eɪ.t̬ɪŋ/li **-ated** -eɪ.tɪd ⓤⓢ -eɪ.t̬ɪd **exˌtenuating ˈcircumstances**
extenuation ɪkˌsten.juˈeɪ.ʃən, ek- **-s** -z
extenuative ɪkˈsten.ju.ə.tɪv, ek-, -eɪ- ⓤⓢ -eɪ.t̬ɪv
extenuatory ɪkˈsten.ju.ə.tər.i, ek-, -eɪ-, -tri ⓤⓢ -ə.tɔːr.i
exterior ɪkˈstɪə.ri.əʳ, ek- ⓤⓢ -ˈstɪr.i.ɚ **-s** -z **-ly** -li
exteriority ɪkˌstɪə.riˈɒr.ə.ti, ek-, -ɪ.ti; ˌek.stɪə- ⓤⓢ ɪkˌstɪr.iˈɔːr.ə.t̬i, ek-
exterioriz|e, -is|e ɪkˈstɪə.ri.ər.aɪz, ek- ⓤⓢ -ˈstɪr.i.ə.raɪz **-es** -ɪz **-ing** -ɪŋ **-ed** -d
exterminable ɪkˈstɜː.mɪ.nə.bl̩, ek-, -mə- ⓤⓢ -ˈstɝː-
extermi|nate ɪkˈstɜː.mɪ|.neɪt, ek-, -mə- ⓤⓢ -ˈstɝː- **-nates** -neɪts **-nating** -neɪ.tɪŋ ⓤⓢ -neɪ.t̬ɪŋ **-nated** -neɪ.tɪd ⓤⓢ -neɪ.t̬ɪd **-nator/s** -neɪ.təʳ/z ⓤⓢ -neɪ.t̬ɚ/z
extermination ɪkˌstɜː.mɪˈneɪ.ʃən, ek-, -məˈ- ⓤⓢ -ˌstɝː- **-s** -z
exterminative ɪkˈstɜː.mɪ.nə.tɪv, ek-, -mə-, -neɪ- ⓤⓢ -ˈstɝː.mə.neɪ.t̬ɪv, -nə-
exterminatory ɪkˈstɜː.mɪ.nə.tər.i, ek-, -mə-, -neɪ-, -tri ⓤⓢ -ˈstɝː.mə.nə.tɔːr.i
extern ˈek.stɜːn; ɪkˈstɜːn, ek- ⓤⓢ ˈek.stɝːn **-s** -z
external ɪkˈstɜː.nəl, ek-; ˈek.stɜː- ⓤⓢ ɪkˈstɝː-, ek-; ˈek.stɝː- **-s** -z **-ly** -i
external|ism ɪkˈstɜː.nəl|.ɪ.zəm, ek- ⓤⓢ -ˈstɝː- **-ist/s** -ɪst/s
externality ˌek.stɜːˈnæl.ə.ti, -ɪ.ti ⓤⓢ -stɝːˈnæl.ə.t̬i
externalization, -isa- ɪkˌstɜː.nəl.aɪˈzeɪ.ʃən, ek-, -ɪˈ- ⓤⓢ -ˌstɝː.nəl.ɪˈ-
externaliz|e, -is|e ɪkˈstɜː.nəl.aɪz, ek- ⓤⓢ -ˈstɝː.nə.laɪz **-es** -ɪz **-ing** -ɪŋ **-ed** -d
exterritorial ˌek.ster.ɪˈtɔː.ri.əl ⓤⓢ -ˈtɔːr.i-
extinct ɪkˈstɪŋkt, ek-
extinction ɪkˈstɪŋk.ʃən, ek- **-s** -z
extinctive ɪkˈstɪŋk.tɪv, ek-
extinguish ɪkˈstɪŋ.gwɪʃ, ek- **-es** -ɪz **-ing** -ɪŋ **-ed** -t **-er/s** -əʳ/z ⓤⓢ -ɚ/z **-ment** -mənt **-able** -ə.bl̩
extir|pate ˈek.stɜː|.peɪt, -stə- ⓤⓢ -stɚ-; ɪkˈstɝː-, ek- **-pates** -peɪts **-pating** -peɪ.tɪŋ ⓤⓢ -peɪ.t̬ɪŋ **-pated** -peɪ.tɪd ⓤⓢ -peɪ.t̬ɪd **-pator/s** -peɪ.təʳ/z ⓤⓢ -peɪ.t̬ɚ/z
extirpation ˌek.stɜːˈpeɪ.ʃən, -stəˈ- ⓤⓢ -stɚˈ- **-s** -z
extol ɪkˈstəʊl, ek-, -ˈstɒl ⓤⓢ -ˈstoʊl, -ˈstɑːl **-s** -z **-ling** -ɪŋ **-led** -d
extoll ɪkˈstəʊl, ek-, -stɒl ⓤⓢ -ˈstoʊl, -ˈstɑːl **-s** -z **-ing** -ɪŋ **-ed** -d
Exton ˈek.stən
extor|t ɪkˈstɔː|t, ek- ⓤⓢ -ˈstɔːr|t **-ts** -ts **-ting** -tɪŋ ⓤⓢ -t̬ɪŋ **-ted** -tɪd ⓤⓢ -t̬ɪd **-ter/s** -təʳ/z ⓤⓢ -t̬ɚ/z
extortion ɪkˈstɔː.ʃən, ek- ⓤⓢ -ˈstɔːr- **-s** -z
extortionate ɪkˈstɔː.ʃən.ət, ek-, -ɪt ⓤⓢ -ˈstɔːr- **-ly** -li
extortioner ɪkˈstɔː.ʃən.əʳ, ek- ⓤⓢ -ˈstɔːr.ʃən.ɚ **-s** -z
extortionist ɪkˈstɔː.ʃən.ɪst, ek- ⓤⓢ -ˈstɔːr- **-s** -s
extra- ˈek.strə-; ɪkˈstræ-, ek-
Note: Prefix. Normally takes either primary or secondary stress on the first syllable, e.g. **extradite** /ˈek.strə.daɪt/, **extramural** /ˌeks.trəˈmjʊə.rəl ⓤⓢ -ˈmjʊr.əl/, but may also take primary stress on the second syllable, e.g. **extrapolate** /ɪkˈstræp.ə.leɪt/. In some cases, the second syllable seems to disappear altogether, e.g. **extraordinary** /ekˈstrɔː.dən.ər.i ⓤⓢ -ˈstrɔːr.dən.er-/.
extra ˈek.strə **-s** -z **ˌextra ˈtime**
extract (*n.*) ˈek.strækt **-s** -s
extract (*v.*) ɪkˈstrækt, ek- **-s** -s **-ing** -ɪŋ **-ed** -ɪd **-able** -ə.bl̩ **exˈtractor ˌfan**
extraction ɪkˈstræk.ʃən, ek- **-s** -z
extractive ɪkˈstræk.tɪv, ek- **-ly** -li
extractor ɪkˈstræk.təʳ, ek- ⓤⓢ -tɚ **-s** -z **exˈtractor ˌfan**
extracurricular ˌek.strə.kəˈrɪk.jə.ləʳ, -jʊ- ⓤⓢ -kəˈrɪk.jə.lɚ **ˌextracurˌricular acˈtivities**
extra|dite ˈek.strə|.daɪt **-dites** -daɪts **-diting** -daɪ.tɪŋ ⓤⓢ -daɪ.t̬ɪŋ **-dited** -daɪ.tɪd ⓤⓢ -daɪ.t̬ɪd **-ditable** -daɪ.tə.bl̩ ⓤⓢ -daɪ.t̬ə.bl̩
extradition ˌek.strəˈdɪʃ.ən **-s** -z
extrados ekˈstreɪ.dɒs ⓤⓢ -dɑːs, -doʊs **-es** -ɪz
extragalactic ˌek.strə.gəˈlæk.tɪk
extrajudicial ˌek.strə.dʒuːˈdɪʃ.əl **-ly** -i
extramarital ˌek.strəˈmær.ɪ.təl ⓤⓢ -ˈmer.ə.t̬əl, -ˈmær- **ˌextramarital ˈsex**
extramural ˌek.strəˈmjʊə.rəl, -ˈmjɔː- ⓤⓢ -ˈmjʊr.əl
extraneous ɪkˈstreɪ.ni.əs, ek- **-ly** -li
extranet ˈek.strə.net **-s** -s
extraordinaire ɪkˌstrɔː.dɪˈneəʳ, ek-, -dənˈeəʳ ⓤⓢ -ˌstrɔːr.dəˈner

extraordinar|y ɪkˈstrɔː.dᵊn.ᵊr|.i, ek-, -dɪ.nᵊr-; ˌek.strəˈɔː- (US) ɪkˈstrɔːr.dᵊn.er-, ek-; ˌek.strəˈɔːr- **-ily** -ᵊl.i, -ɪ.li **-iness** -ɪ.nəs, -ɪ.nɪs

extrapo|late ɪkˈstræp.ə|.leɪt, ek- **-lates** -leɪts **-lating** -leɪ.tɪŋ (US) -leɪ.t̬ɪŋ **-lated** -leɪ.tɪd (US) -leɪ.t̬ɪd

extrapolation ɪkˌstræp.əˈleɪ.ʃᵊn, ek- **-s** -z

extrasensory ˌek.strəˈsent.sᵊr.i **ˌextraˌsensory perˈception**

extraterrestrial ˌeks.trə.təˈres.tri.əl, -terˈes-, -tɪˈres- (US) -təˈ- **-s** -z

extraterritorial ˌeks.trəˌter.ɪˈtɔː.ri.əl, -əˈ- (US) -ˈtɔːr.i-

extravagan|ce ɪkˈstræv.ə.gənt|s, ek-, ˈ-ɪ- **-ces** -sɪz

extravagant ɪkˈstræv.ə.gənt, ˈ-ɪ- **-ly** -li

extravaganza ɪkˌstræv.əˈgæn.zə, ek-; ˌek.stræv- (US) ɪkˌstræv-, ek- **-s** -z

extrava|sate ekˈstræv.ə|.seɪt, ɪk- **-sates** -seɪts **-sating** -seɪ.tɪŋ (US) -seɪ.t̬ɪŋ **-sated** -seɪ.tɪd (US) -seɪ.t̬ɪd

extravasation ekˌstræv.əˈseɪ.ʃᵊn, ɪk-; -ˈzeɪ-, ˌek.stræv- (US) ɪkˌstræv-, ek- **-s** -z

extra|vert ˈek.strə|.vɜːt (US) -vɝːt **-verts** -vɜːts (US) -vɝːts **-verted** -vɜː.tɪd (US) -vɝː.t̬ɪd

Extremadura ˌek.strə.məˈdjʊə.rə (US) -ˈdʊr.ə, -ˈdjʊr.ə

extrem|e ɪkˈstriːm, ek- **-es** -z **-est** -ɪst, -əst **-ly** -li **-eness** -nəs, -nɪs

extrem|ism ɪkˈstriː.m|ɪ.zᵊm, ek- **-ist/s** -ɪst/s

extremit|y ɪkˈstrem.ə.t|i, ek-, -ɪ.t|i (US) -ə.t̬|i **-ies** -iz

extricable ɪkˈstrɪk.ə.bl̩, ek-; ˈek.strɪ.kə-

extri|cate ˈek.strɪ|.keɪt **-cates** -keɪts **-cating** -keɪ.tɪŋ (US) -keɪ.t̬ɪŋ **-cated** -keɪ.tɪd (US) -keɪ.t̬ɪd

extrication ˌek.strɪˈkeɪ.ʃᵊn

extrinsic ekˈstrɪnt.sɪk, ɪk-, -ˈstrɪn.zɪk **-al** -ᵊl **-ally** -ᵊl.i, -li

extroversion ˌek.strəˈvɜː.ʃᵊn, -ʒᵊn (US) ˈek.strə.vɝː.ʒən, -stroʊ-

extro|vert ˈek.strə|.vɜːt (US) -strə|.vɝːt, -stroʊ- **-verts** -vɜːts (US) -vɝːts **-verted** -vɜː.tɪd (US) -vɝː.t̬ɪd

extrud|e ɪkˈstruːd, ek- **-es** -z **-ing** -ɪŋ **-ed** -ɪd

extrusion ɪkˈstruː.ʒᵊn, ek- **-s** -z

extrus|ive ɪkˈstruː.s|ɪv, ek- **-ory** -ᵊr.i (US) -ɔːr.i

exuberan|ce ɪgˈzjuː.bᵊr.ᵊnt|s, eg-, -ˈzuː-; ɪkˈsjuː-, ek-, -ˈsuː- (US) ɪgˈzuː-, eg- **-cy** -si

exuberant ɪgˈzjuː.bᵊr.ᵊnt, eg-, -ˈzuː-; ɪkˈsjuː-, ek-, -ˈsuː- (US) ɪgˈzuː-, eg- **-ly** -li

exuber|ate ɪgˈzjuː.bᵊr|.eɪt, eg-, -ˈzuː-; ɪkˈsjuː-, ek-, -ˈsuː- (US) ɪgˈzuː.bə.r|eɪt, eg- **-ates** -eɪts **-ating** -eɪ.tɪŋ (US) -eɪ.t̬ɪŋ **-ated** -eɪ.tɪd (US) -eɪ.t̬ɪd

exudation ˌek.sjuːˈdeɪ.ʃᵊn, ˌeg.zjuːˈ- (US) ˌek.sjuːˈ-, -suːˈ-, -səˈ-, ˌeg.zjuːˈ-, -zuːˈ- **-s** -z

exud|e ɪgˈzjuːd, eg-, -ˈzuːd; ɪkˈsjuːd, ek-, -ˈsuːd (US) ɪgˈzuːd, ɪkˈsuːd, ek- **-es** -z **-ing** -ɪŋ **-ed** -ɪd

exul|t ɪgˈzʌl|t, eg-; ɪkˈsʌl|t, ek- (US) ɪgˈzʌl|t, eg- **-ts** -ts **-ting/ly** -tɪŋ/li (US) -t̬ɪŋ/li **-ted** -tɪd (US) -t̬ɪd

exultan|ce ɪgˈzʌl.tᵊnt|s, eg-; ɪkˈsʌl-, ek- (US) ɪgˈzʌl-, eg- **-cy** -si

exultant ɪgˈzʌl.tᵊnt, eg-; ɪkˈsʌl-, ek- (US) ɪgˈzʌl-, eg- **-ly** -li

exultation ˌeg.zʌlˈteɪ.ʃᵊn, -zᵊlˈ-; ˌek.sʌlˈ-, -sᵊlˈ- (US) ˌek.sʌlˈ-, -sᵊlˈ-; ˌeg.zʌlˈ-, -zᵊlˈ- **-s** -z

exurb ˈek.sɜːb; ˈeg.zɜːb (US) ˈek.sɝːb; ˈeg.zɝːb

exur|ban ekˈsɜː|.bᵊn; egˈzɜː- (US) ekˈsɝː-; egˈzɝː- **-banite** -bᵊn.aɪt **-bia** -bi.ə

exuviae ɪgˈzjuː.vi.iː, eg-; -ˈzuː-; ɪkˈsjuː-, ek-, -ˈsuː-, -aɪ (US) ɪgˈzuː.vi.iː, ekˈsuː-, egˈzuː-, -aɪ

exuvial ɪgˈzjuː.vi.əl, eg-, -ˈzuː-; ɪkˈsjuː-, ek-, -ˈsuː- (US) ɪgˈzuː-, ekˈsuː-, egˈzuː-

exuvi|ate ɪgˈzjuː.vi|.eɪt, eg-, -ˈzuː-; ɪkˈsjuː-, ek-, -ˈsuː- (US) ɪgˈzuː-, ekˈsuː-, egˈzuː- **-ates** -eɪts **-ating** -eɪ.tɪŋ (US) -eɪ.t̬ɪŋ **-ated** -eɪ.tɪd (US) -eɪ.t̬ɪd

exuviation ɪgˌzjuː.viˈeɪ.ʃᵊn, eg-, -ˌzuː-; ɪkˌsjuː-, ek-, -ˌsuː- (US) ɪgˈzuː-, ekˈsuː-, egˈzuː-

ex voto ˌeksˈvəʊ.təʊ (US) -ˈvoʊ.t̬oʊ

Exxon® ˈek.sɒn (US) -sɑːn

Eyam ˈiː.əm, iːm

eyas aɪəs **-es** -ɪz

Eyck aɪk

eye (*n. v.*) aɪ **-s** -z **-ing** -ɪŋ **-d** -d **have ˌeyes in the ˌback of one's ˈhead; in a ˌpig's ˈeye; ˌone in the ˈeye; ˌup to one's ˈeyes; ˌgive one's ˌeye ˈteeth;** see **ˌeye to ˈeye**

Eye *place:* aɪ

eyeball ˈaɪ.bɔːl (US) -bɔːl, -bɑːl **-s** -z **-ing** -ɪŋ **-ed** -d

eyebath ˈaɪ.bɑːθ (US) -bæθ **-s** -s

eyebright ˈaɪ.braɪt

eyebrow ˈaɪ.braʊ **-s** -z **ˈeyebrow ˌpencil**

eye-catching ˈaɪˌkætʃ.ɪŋ **-ly** -li

eyeful ˈaɪ.fʊl **-s** -z

eyeglass ˈaɪ.glɑːs (US) -glæs **-es** -ɪz

eyelash ˈaɪ.læʃ **-es** -ɪz

eyelet ˈaɪ.lət, -lɪt **-s** -s

eyelid ˈaɪ.lɪd **-s** -z

eyeliner ˈaɪˌlaɪ.nəʳ (US) -nɚ **-s** -z

Eyemouth ˈaɪ.maʊθ

eye-open|er ˈaɪˌəʊ.pᵊn|.əʳ, -ˌəʊp.n|əʳ (US) -ˌoʊ.pᵊn|.ɚ **-ers** -əz, -ɚz **-ing** -ɪŋ

eyepatch ˈaɪ.pætʃ **-es** -ɪz

eyepiec|e ˈaɪ.piːs **-es** -ɪz

eyeshade ˈaɪ.ʃeɪd **-s** -z

eyeshot ˈaɪ.ʃɒt (US) -ʃɑːt

eyesight ˈaɪ.saɪt

eyesore ˈaɪ.sɔːʳ (US) -sɔːr **-s** -z

eyestrain ˈaɪ.streɪn

Eyetie ˈaɪ.taɪ **-s** -z

eye|tooth ˈaɪ|.tuːθ **-teeth** -tiːθ

eyewash ˈaɪ.wɒʃ (US) -wɑːʃ, -wɔːʃ

Pronouncing the letters EY

The most common position for the vowel digraph **ey** is in word final position in an unstressed syllable.

In weak syllables the vowel digraph **ey** is realised with the vowel /i/, e.g.:

donkey	/ˈdɒŋ.ki/	(US) /ˈdɑːŋ-/
Surrey	/ˈsʌr.i/	(US) /ˈsɝː-/

However, there are several pronunciation possibilities for the digraph in stressed syllables, e.g.:

/eɪ/	they	/ðeɪ/	
/iː/	key	/kiː/	
/aɪ/	geyser	/ˈgiː.zəʳ, ˈgaɪ-/	(US) /-zɚ/

eyewitness ˈaɪ.wɪt.nɪs, -nəs, -ˈ--
 -es -ɪz
Eynon ˈaɪ.nən (US) -nɑːn
Eynsford ˈeɪnz.fəd, ˈeɪnts- (US) -fɚd
Eynsham *in Oxfordshire:* ˈeɪn.ʃᵊm *locally:* ˈen.ʃᵊm

eyot eɪt, eɪət, aɪt **-s** -s
Note: The local pronunciation in the Thames valley is /eɪt/.
Eyre, eyre eəʳ (US) er
eyr|ie, eyr|y ˈaɪə.r|i, ˈɪə-, ˈeə- (US) ˈer.i, ˈɪr- **-ies** -iz

Eysenck ˈaɪ.zeŋk
Eyton *in Shropshire:* ˈaɪ.tᵊn *in Hereford and Worcester:* ˈeɪ.tᵊn *surname:* ˈaɪ.tᵊn, ˈiː-
Ezekiel ɪˈziː.ki.əl, ezˈiː-
Ezra ˈez.rə

Pronouncing the letter F

The consonant letter **f** is most often realised as /f/, and is given as a double consonant **ff** at the ends of many words, e.g.:

fit /fɪt/
cuff /kʌf/

However, in one of the most common words containing **f** it is pronounced /v/:

of /ɒv, əv/ (US) /ɑːv, əv/

f (F) ef **-'s** -s
fa fɑː *stress shift:* ˌFA 'cup;
FA ˌef'eɪ ˌ**sweet** ˌ**F'A**
fab fæb
Faber *English name:* 'feɪ.bəʳ (US) -bɚ *German name:* 'fɑː.bəʳ (US) -bɚ
Fabergé 'fæb.ə.ʒeɪ, -dʒeɪ (US) ˌfæb.ɚ'ʒeɪ
Fabian 'feɪ.bi.ən **-s** -z **-ism** -ɪ.zᵊm '**Fabian So**ˌ**ciety**
Fabius 'feɪ.bi.əs
fable 'feɪ.bl̩ **-s** -z **-d** -d
fabliau 'fæb.li.əʊ (US) -oʊ **-x** -z
Fablon® 'fæb.lɒn (US) -lɑːn
fabric 'fæb.rɪk **-s** -s '**fabric** ˌ**softener**
fabri|cate 'fæb.rɪ|.keɪt **-cates** -keɪts **-cating** -keɪ.tɪŋ (US) -keɪ.t̬ɪŋ **-cated** -keɪ.tɪd (US) -keɪ.t̬ɪd **-cator/s** -keɪ.təʳ/z (US) -keɪ.t̬ɚ/z
fabrication ˌfæb.rɪ'keɪ.ʃᵊn, -rə'- **-s** -z
Fabricius fə'brɪʃ.i.əs, -ʃəs
fabulist 'fæb.jə.lɪst, -jʊ- (US) -jə- **-s** -s
fabulous 'fæb.jə.ləs, -jʊ- (US) -jə- **-ly** -li **-ness** -nəs, -nɪs
Fabyan 'feɪ.bi.ən
facade, façade fə'sɑːd, fæs'ɑːd (US) fə'sɑːd **-s** -z
fac|e (*n. v.*) feɪs **-es** -ɪz **-ing** -ɪŋ **-ed** -t '**face** ˌ**pack**; ˌ**face** '**value**; ˌ**cut off one's** ˌ**nose to** ˌ**spite one's** '**face**; **put a** ˌ**brave** '**face on**; ˌ**fly in the** '**face of**; ˌ**laugh on the other** ˌ**side of one's** '**face**
face|cloth 'feɪs|.klɒθ (US) -klɑːθ **-cloths** -klɒθs, -klɒðz (US) -klɑːθs, -klɑːðz
faceless 'feɪs.ləs, -lɪs **-ness** -nəs, -nɪs
face-lift 'feɪs.lɪft **-s** -s
facemask 'feɪs.mɑːsk (US) -mæsk **-s** -s
face-off 'feɪs.ɒf (US) -ɑːf **-s** -s
faceplate 'feɪs.pleɪt **-s** -s
facer 'feɪ.səʳ (US) -sɚ **-s** -z
face-sav|er 'feɪsˌseɪ.vəʳ (US) -vɚ **-ers** -z **-ing** -ɪŋ
fac|et 'fæs|.ɪt, -ət, -et (US) -ɪt **-ets** -ɪts **-et(t)ed** -ɪ.tɪd (US) -ɪ.t̬ɪd
facetiae fə'siː.ʃi.iː, -ʃiː (US) -ʃi.iː
facetious fə'siː.ʃəs **-ly** -li **-ness** -nəs, -nɪs
face-to-face ˌfeɪs.tə'feɪs (US) -t̬ə- *stress shift:* ˌface-to-face 'talk
facia 'feɪ.ʃə (US) -ʃi.ə, -ʃə **-s** -z
facial 'feɪ.ʃᵊl **-ly** -i **-s** -z
facies 'feɪ.ʃi.iːz, -ʃiːz
facile 'fæs.aɪl (US) -ɪl, -əl **-ly** -li **-ness** -nəs, -nɪs
facili|tate fə'sɪl.ɪ|.teɪt, '-ə- **-tates** -teɪts **-tating** -teɪ.tɪŋ (US) -teɪ.t̬ɪŋ **-tated** -teɪ.tɪd (US) -teɪ.t̬ɪd **-tator/s** -teɪ.təʳ/z (US) -teɪ.t̬ɚ/z
facilitation fəˌsɪl.ɪ'teɪ.ʃᵊn, -ə'-
facilit|y fə'sɪl.ə.t|i, -ɪ.t|i (US) -ə.t̬|i **-ies** -iz
facing 'feɪ.sɪŋ **-s** -z
facsimile fæk'sɪm.ᵊl.i, -ɪ.li **-s** -z
fact fækt **-s** -s ˌ**fact of** '**life**
fact-find|ing 'fæktˌfaɪn.d|ɪŋ **-er/s** -əʳ/z (US) -ɚ/z
faction 'fæk.ʃᵊn **-s** -z
factional 'fæk.ʃᵊn.ᵊl
factional|ism 'fæk.ʃᵊn.ᵊl|.ɪ.zᵊm **-ist/s** -ɪst/s
factionalization, -isa- ˌfæk.ʃᵊn.ᵊl.aɪ'zeɪ.ʃᵊn, -ɪ'- (US) -ɪ'-
factionaliz|e, -is|e 'fæk.ʃᵊn.ᵊl.aɪz (US) -ə.laɪz **-es** -ɪz **-ing** -ɪŋ **-ed** -d
factious 'fæk.ʃəs **-ly** -li **-ness** -nəs, -nɪs
factitious fæk'tɪʃ.əs **-ly** -li **-ness** -nəs, -nɪs
factitive 'fæk.tɪ.tɪv, -tə.tɪv (US) -tə.t̬ɪv
factive 'fæk.tɪv
factivity fæk'tɪv.ə.ti, -ɪ.ti (US) -ə.t̬i
fact|or 'fæk.t|əʳ (US) -t|ɚ **-ors** -əz (US) -ɚz **-oring** -ᵊr.ɪŋ **-ored** -ᵊrd **-orage** -ᵊr.ɪdʒ ˌ**Factor** '**5**
factorial fæk'tɔː.ri.əl (US) -'tɔːr.i-
factorization, -isa- ˌfæk.tᵊr.aɪ'zeɪ.ʃᵊn, -ɪ'- (US) -ɪ'-
factoriz|e, -is|e 'fæk.tᵊr.aɪz (US) -tə.raɪz **-es** -ɪz **-ing** -ɪŋ **-ed** -d
factor|y 'fæk.tᵊr|.i, '-tr|i **-ies** -iz '**factory** ˌ**farming**, ˌ**factory** '**farming**; ˌ**factory** '**floor**
factotum fæk'təʊ.təm (US) -'toʊ.t̬əm **-s** -z
factsheet 'fækt.ʃiːt **-s** -s
factual 'fæk.tʃʊəl, -tjʊəl (US) -tʃuː.əl **-ly** -li **-ness** -nəs, -nɪs
factum 'fæk.təm
factum probandum ˌfæk.təm.prəʊ'bæn.dəm (US) -proʊ'bɑːn-
facul|a 'fæk.jə.l|ə, -jʊ- (US) -jə-, -juː- **-ae** -iː
facultative 'fæk.ᵊl.tə.tɪv, -teɪ- (US) -teɪ.t̬ɪv **-ly** -li
facult|y 'fæk.ᵊl.t|i (US) -t̬|i **-ies** -iz
fad fæd **-s** -z
faddish 'fæd.ɪʃ **-ly** -li **-ness** -nəs, -nɪs
fadd|ism 'fæd|.ɪ.zᵊm **-ist/s** -ɪst/s
fadd|y 'fæd|.i **-ier** -i.əʳ (US) -i.ɚ **-iest** -i.ɪst, -i.əst **-ily** -ɪ.li, -ᵊl.i **-iness** -ɪ.nəs, -ɪ.nɪs
fad|e feɪd **-es** -z **-ing** -ɪŋ **-ed** -ɪd
fadeout 'feɪd.aʊt **-s** -s
fado 'fɑː.du (US) 'fɑː.ðuː, -ðoʊ, -doʊ **-s** -z
faecal 'fiː.kᵊl
faeces 'fiː.siːz
Faed feɪd
faerie, faery (F) 'feə.ri, 'feɪ.ᵊr.i (US) 'fer.i
Faeroe 'feə.rəʊ (US) 'fer.oʊ **-s** -z
Faeroese ˌfeə.rəʊ'iːz (US) ˌfer.oʊ'-
faff fæf **-s** -s **-ing** -ɪŋ **-ed** -t
Fafner 'fɑːf.nəʳ, 'fæf- (US) -nɚ
Fafnir 'fæf.nɪəʳ, 'fæv- (US) -nɪr
fag fæg **-s** -z **-ging** -ɪŋ **-ged** -d '**fag** ˌ**end**, ˌ**fag** '**end**; '**fag** ˌ**hag**
Fagan 'feɪ.gən
Fagg(e) fæg
faggot 'fæg.ət **-s** -s
Fagin 'feɪ.gɪn
fagot 'fæg.ət **-s** -s
fah fɑː
Fahd fɑːd
Fahey, Fahie 'feɪ.i; feɪ
Fahrenheit 'fær.ᵊn.haɪt, 'fɑː.rᵊn- (US) 'fer.ᵊn-, 'fær-
Fahy 'fɑː.i, -hi; feɪ (US) 'feɪ.i; feɪ
faience, faïence faɪ'ɑ̃ːns, feɪ-, -ɑːnts (US) faɪ'ɑːnts, feɪ'-; 'faɪ.ənts
fail feɪl **-s** -z **-ing/s** -ɪŋ/z **-ed** -d
faille feɪəl (US) faɪl, feɪl
failsafe 'feɪl.seɪf, -'- (US) '--
Failsworth 'feɪlz.wəθ, -wɜːθ (US) -wɚθ, -wɝːθ
failure 'feɪ.ljəʳ (US) 'feɪl.jɚ **-s** -z
fain feɪn
Fainall 'feɪ.nɔːl (US) -nɔːl, -nɑːl
faint feɪnt **-er** -əʳ (US) 'feɪn.t̬ɚ **-est** -ɪst, -əst (US) 'feɪn.t̬ɪst, 'feɪn.t̬əst **-ly** -li **-ness** -nəs, -nɪs **-s** -s **-ing** -ɪŋ (US) 'feɪn.t̬ɪŋ **-ed** -ɪd (US) 'feɪn.t̬ɪd
fainthearted ˌfeɪnt'hɑː.tɪd (US) -'hɑːr.t̬ɪd **-ly** -li **-ness** -nəs, -nɪs *stress shift:* ˌfainthearted 'hero

Fainwell ˈfeɪn.wel, -wəl
fair (F) feəʳ ⓊⓈ fer **-s** -z **-er** -əʳ ⓊⓈ -ɚ **-est** -ɪst, -əst **-ness** -nəs, -nɪs ˌ**fair** ˈ**do's**; ˌ**fair** ˈ**dinkum**; ˌ**fair** ˈ**game**; ˈ**Fair** ˌ**Isle**; ˌ**fair** ˈ**play**; ˌ**fair's** ˈ**fair**; ˌ**fair and** ˈ**square**
Fairbairn ˈfeə.beən ⓊⓈ ˈfer.bern **-s** -z
Fairbank ˈfeə.bæŋk ⓊⓈ ˈfer- **-s** -s
Fairbeard ˈfeə.bɪəd ⓊⓈ ˈfer.bɪrd
Fairbrother ˈfeəˌbrʌð.əʳ ⓊⓈ ˈferˌbrʌð.ɚ
Fairburn ˈfeə.bɜːn ⓊⓈ ˈfer.bɝːn
Fairbury ˈfeə.bᵊr.i ⓊⓈ ˈferˌber-, -bɚ-
Fairchild ˈfeə.tʃaɪld ⓊⓈ ˈfer-
Fairclough ˈfeə.klʌf, -kləʊ ⓊⓈ ˈfer.klʌf
fairfaced ˌfeəˈfeɪst ⓊⓈ ˌfer- *stress shift:* ˌfairfaced ˈchild
Fairfax ˈfeə.fæks ⓊⓈ ˈfer-
Fairfield ˈfeə.fiːld ⓊⓈ ˈfer-
Fairford ˈfeə.fəd ⓊⓈ ˈfer.fɚd
Fairgrieve ˈfeə.griːv ⓊⓈ ˈfer-
fairground ˈfeə.graʊnd ⓊⓈ ˈfer- **-s** -z
fair-haired ˌfeəˈheəd ⓊⓈ ˌferˈherd *stress shift:* ˌfair-haired ˈchild
Fairhaven ˈfeəˌheɪ.vᵊn ⓊⓈ ˈfer-
Fairholme ˈfeə.həʊm ⓊⓈ ˈfer.hoʊm, -hoʊlm
Fairholt ˈfeə.həʊlt ⓊⓈ ˈfer.hoʊlt
fairish ˈfeə.rɪʃ ⓊⓈ ˈfer.ɪʃ
Fairleigh ˈfeə.li, -liː ⓊⓈ ˈfer-
Fairlight ˈfeə.laɪt ⓊⓈ ˈfer-
fairly ˈfeə.li ⓊⓈ ˈfer-
Fairman ˈfeə.mən ⓊⓈ ˈfer-
fair-minded ˌfeəˈmaɪn.dɪd ⓊⓈ ˌfer- **-ly** -li **-ness** -nəs, -nɪs *stress shift:* ˌfair-minded ˈjudge
Fairmont ˈfeə.mɒnt, -mənt ⓊⓈ ˈfer.mɑːnt
Fairmount ˈfeə.maʊnt ⓊⓈ ˈfer-
Fairport ˈfeə.pɔːt ⓊⓈ ˈfer.pɔːrt
Fairscribe ˈfeə.skraɪb ⓊⓈ ˈfer-
Fairview ˈfeə.vjuː ⓊⓈ ˈfer-
fairway ˈfeə.weɪ ⓊⓈ ˈfer- **-s** -z
Fairweather ˈfeəˌweð.əʳ ⓊⓈ ˈferˌweð.ɚ
fair-weather ˈfeəˌweð.əʳ ⓊⓈ ˈferˌweð.ɚ
fair|y ˈfeə.r|i ⓊⓈ ˈfer|.i **-ies** -iz ˌ**fairy** ˈ**godmother**; ˈ**fairy** ˌ**light**; ˌ**fairy** ˈ**ring** ⓊⓈ ˈ**fairy** ˌ**ring**; ˈ**fairy** ˌ**story**; ˈ**fairy** ˌ**tale**
fairyland ˈfeə.ri.lænd ⓊⓈ ˈfer.i-
fairylike ˈfeə.ri.laɪk ⓊⓈ ˈfer.i-
Faisal ˈfaɪ.sᵊl
Faisalabad ˈfaɪ.sᵊl.ə.bæd, -zᵊl- ⓊⓈ ˌfaɪ.sɑː.ləˈbɑːd, -sæl.əˈbæd
fait accompli ˌfeɪt.əˈkɒm.pliː, ˌfet-, -ˈkʌm- *as if French:* -kɔ̃ːmˈpliː ⓊⓈ ˌfeɪt.ə.kɑːmˈpliː, ˌfet- **faits accomplis** ˌfeɪz-, ˌfeɪts-, ˌfeɪt-, ˌfez-, -pliːz ⓊⓈ ˌfeɪt.ə.kɑːmˈpliː, ˌfet-, -ˈpliːz
faith (F) feɪθ **-s** -s ˈ**faith** ˌ**healer**
faithful (F) ˈfeɪθ.fᵊl, -fʊl **-ly** -i **-ness** -nəs, -nɪs
Faithfull ˈfeɪθ.fᵊl, -fʊl
faithless ˈfeɪθ.ləs, -lɪs **-ly** -li **-ness** -nəs, -nɪs
Faithorne ˈfeɪ.θɔːn ⓊⓈ -θɔːrn
fajita fæˈhiː.tə ⓊⓈ fæ-, fə-, -t̬ə
fak|e feɪk **-es** -s **-ing** -ɪŋ **-ed** -t **-er/s** -əʳ/z ⓊⓈ -ɚ/z
Fakenham ˈfeɪ.kᵊn.əm
fakir ˈfeɪ.kɪəʳ, ˈfɑː-, ˈfæk.ɪəʳ, fəˈkɪəʳ, fækˈɪəʳ ⓊⓈ fɑːˈkɪr, fækˈɪr; ˈfeɪ.kɚ **-s** -z **-ism** -ɪ.zᵊm
Fal fæl
falafel fəˈlɑː.fᵊl, -ˈlæf.ᵊl ⓊⓈ -ˈlɑː.fᵊl
Falange fəˈlændʒ; ˈfæl.ændʒ ⓊⓈ fəˈlændʒ, -ˈlɑːndʒ
Falangist fəˈlæn.dʒɪst **-s** -s
Falasha fəˈlæʃ.ə ⓊⓈ -ˈlɑː.ʃə, fɑːˈ- **-s** -z
fal|cate ˈfæl|.keɪt **-cated** -keɪ.tɪd ⓊⓈ -keɪ.t̬ɪd
falchion ˈfɔːl.*t*ʃᵊn ⓊⓈ ˈfɔːl-, ˈfɑːl- **-s** -z
falcon (F) ˈfɔːl.kᵊn, ˈfɔː-, ˈfɒl-, ˈfæl- ⓊⓈ ˈfæl-, ˈfɔːl-, ˈfɑːl-, ˈfɔː- **-s** -z **-er/s** -əʳ/z ⓊⓈ -ɚ/z
Note: /ˈfɔː-/ is the usual British pronunciation among people who practise the sport of falconry, with /ˈfɔː-/ and /ˈfɔːl-/ most usual among them in the US.
Falconbridge ˈfɔːl.kᵊn.brɪdʒ, ˈfɔː-, ˈfɒl-, ˈfæl-, -kᵊm- ⓊⓈ ˈfɔː.kᵊn-, ˈfɔːl-, ˈfæl-, ˈfɑːl-
Falconer ˈfɔːl.kᵊn.əʳ, ˈfɔː-, ˈfɒl-, ˈfæl- ⓊⓈ ˈfɔː.kᵊn.ɚ, ˈfɔːl-, ˈfæl-, ˈfɑːl-
falconry ˈfɔːl.kᵊn.ri, ˈfɔː-, ˈfɒl-, ˈfæl- ⓊⓈ ˈfæl-, ˈfɔːl-, ˈfɑːl-, ˈfɔː-
Note: See note at **falcon**.
Falder ˈfɔːl.dəʳ, ˈfɒl- ⓊⓈ ˈfɑːl.dɚ, ˈfɔːl-
falderal ˈfæl.də.ræl, -dɪ-, ˌ--ˈ- ⓊⓈ ˈfɑːl.də.rɑːl, ˈfæl.də.ræl **-s** -z
Faldo ˈfæl.dəʊ ⓊⓈ -doʊ
faldstool ˈfɔːl*d*.stuːl **-s** -z
Falerii fəˈlɪə.ri.aɪ, fælˈɪə-, -iː ⓊⓈ fəˈlɪr.i-
Falernian fəˈlɜː.ni.ən ⓊⓈ -ˈlɝː-
Falk fɔːk, fɔːlk ⓊⓈ fɔːk, fɔːlk, fɑːlk
Falkenbridge ˈfɔː.kᵊn.brɪdʒ, ˈfɔːl-, ˈfɒl-, ˈfæl-, -kᵊm- ⓊⓈ ˈfɔː.kᵊn-, ˈfɔːl-, ˈfæl-, ˈfɑːl-
Falkender ˈfɔːl.kən.dəʳ ⓊⓈ -dɚ
Falkirk ˈfɔːl.kɜːk, ˈfɒl-, -kək ⓊⓈ ˈfɔːl.kɝːk, -kɚk
Falkland *Viscount:* ˈfɔː.klənd, ˈfɒl- ⓊⓈ ˈfɔː- *place in Scotland:* ˈfɔːl.klənd, ˈfɒl- ⓊⓈ ˈfɔːl-
Falkland Islands ˈfɔː.kləndˌaɪ.ləndz, ˈfɔːl-, ˈfɒl- ⓊⓈ ˈfɔː-, ˈfɔːl-
Falkner ˈfɔːk.nəʳ, ˈfɔːlk-, ˈfɒlk-, ˈfælk- ⓊⓈ ˈfɔːk.nɚ, ˈfɔːlk-, ˈfɑːlk-, ˈfælk-
fall fɔːl ⓊⓈ fɔːl, fɑːl **-s** -z **-ing** -ɪŋ **fell** fel **fallen** ˈfɔː.lən ⓊⓈ ˈfɔː-, ˈfɑː- ˈ**fall** ˌ**guy**; ˌ**falling** ˈ**star**
Falla ˈfaɪ.jə; ˈfɑː.ljə, ˈfæl.jə, -ə ⓊⓈ ˈfaɪ.jə; ˈfɑːl.jɑː
fallacious fəˈleɪ.ʃəs **-ly** -li **-ness** -nəs, -nɪs
fallac|y ˈfæl.ə.s|i **-ies** -iz
fallal fælˈæl, -ˈlæl ⓊⓈ fælˈæl, fɑːˈlɑːl **-s** -z
fallback ˈfɔːl.bæk ⓊⓈ ˈfɔːl-, ˈfɑːl- **-s** -s
Faller ˈfæl.əʳ ⓊⓈ -ɚ
fallibility ˌfæl.əˈbɪl.ə.ti, -ɪˈ-, -ɪ.ti ⓊⓈ -ə.t̬i
fallib|le ˈfæl.ə.b|l̩, ˈ-ɪ- **-ly** -li **-leness** -l̩.nəs, -nɪs
falling-out ˌfɔː.lɪŋˈaʊt ⓊⓈ ˌfɔː-, ˌfɑː- **fallings-out** ˌfɔː.lɪŋzˈaʊt ⓊⓈ ˌfɔː-, ˌfɑː- **falling-outs** ˌfɔː.lɪŋˈaʊts ⓊⓈ ˌfɔː-, ˌfɑː-
fall-off ˈfɔːl.ɒf ⓊⓈ -ɑːf, ˈfɑːl- **-s** -s
Fallon ˈfæl.ən
fallopian (F) fəˈləʊ.pi.ən, fælˈəʊ- ⓊⓈ fəˈloʊ- **fa**ˌ**llopian** ˈ**tube**
fallout ˈfɔːl.aʊt ⓊⓈ ˈfɔːl-, ˈfɑːl-
fallow (F) ˈfæl.əʊ ⓊⓈ -oʊ **-s** -z **-ness** -nəs, -nɪs **-ing** -ɪŋ **-ed** -d ˈ**fallow** ˌ**deer**, ˌ**fallow** ˈ**deer**
Fallowfield ˈfæl.əʊ.fiːld ⓊⓈ -oʊ-
Fallows ˈfæl.əʊz ⓊⓈ -oʊz
Falls fɔːlz ⓊⓈ fɔːlz, fɑːlz ˌ**Falls** ˈ**Road**
Falmer ˈfæl.məʳ, ˈfɔːl- ⓊⓈ ˈfɑːl.mɚ, ˈfɔːl-
Falmouth ˈfæl.məθ
fals|e fɔːls, fɒls ⓊⓈ fɔːls, fɑːls **-er** -əʳ ⓊⓈ -ɚ **-est** -ɪst, -əst **-eness** -nəs, -nɪs ˌ**false a**ˈ**larm**; ˌ**false pre**ˈ**tences**; ˌ**false** ˈ**start**; ˌ**false** ˈ**teeth**
falsehood ˈfɔːls.*h*ʊd, ˈfɒls- ⓊⓈ ˈfɔːls.hʊd, ˈfɑːls- **-s** -z
falsely ˈfɔːl.sli, ˈfɒl- ⓊⓈ ˈfɔːl-, ˈfɑːl-
falsetto fɒlˈset.əʊ, fɔːl- ⓊⓈ fɔːlˈset̬.oʊ, fɑːl- **-s** -z
Falshaw ˈfɔːl.ʃɔː, ˈfɒl- ⓊⓈ ˈfɔːl.ʃɑː, ˈfɑːl-, -ʃɔː
falsification ˌfɔːl.sɪ.fɪˈkeɪ.ʃᵊn, ˌfɒl-, -sə- ⓊⓈ ˌfɔːl-, ˌfɑːl- **-s** -z
falsi|fy ˈfɔːl.sɪ|.faɪ, ˈfɒl-, -sə- ⓊⓈ ˈfɔːl-, ˈfɑːl- **-fies** -faɪz **-fying** -faɪ.ɪŋ **-fied** -faɪd **-fier/s** -faɪ.əʳ/z ⓊⓈ -faɪ.ɚ/z
falsit|y ˈfɔːl.sə.t|i, ˈfɒl-, -ɪ.t|i ⓊⓈ ˈfɔːl.sə.t̬|i, ˈfɑːl- **-ies** -iz
Falstaff ˈfɔːl.stɑːf, ˈfɒl- ⓊⓈ ˈfɔːl.stæf, ˈfɑːl-
Falstaffian fɔːlˈstɑː.fi.ən, fɒl- ⓊⓈ fɔːlˈstæf.i-, fɑːl-
falt|er ˈfɔːl.t|əʳ, ˈfɒl- ⓊⓈ ˈfɔːl.t̬|ɚ, ˈfɑːl- **-ers** -əz ⓊⓈ -ɚz **-ering/ly** -ᵊr.ɪŋ/li **-ered** -əd ⓊⓈ -ɚd **-erer/s** -ᵊr.əʳ/z ⓊⓈ -ɚ.ɚ/z
Faludi fəˈluː.di, fælˈuː.di
Famagusta ˌfæm.əˈgʊs.tə, ˌfɑː.məˈ- ⓊⓈ ˌfɑː.məˈguː.stə
fame feɪm **-d** -d
familial fəˈmɪl.i.əl
familiar fəˈmɪl.i.əʳ ⓊⓈ ˈ-jɚ, -i.ɚ **-s** -z **-ly** -li
familiarit|y fəˌmɪl.iˈær.ə.t|i, -ɪ.t|i ⓊⓈ -ˈer.ə.t̬|i, -ˈær- **-ies** -iz

familiariz|e, -is|e fəˈmɪl.i.ᵊr.aɪz (US) ˈ-jə.raɪz, ˈ-i.ə- **-es** -ɪz **-ing** -ɪŋ **-ed** -d
famil|y ˈfæm.ᵊl|.i, -ɪ.l|i **-ies** -iz ˌ**family alˈlowance**; ˌ**family ˈcredit**; ˈ**family ˌman**; ˌ**family ˈplanning**; ˈ**family ˌroom**; ˈ**family ˌstyle**; ˌ**family ˈtree**
famine ˈfæm.ɪn **-s** -z
famish ˈfæm.ɪʃ **-es** -ɪz **-ing** -ɪŋ **-ed** -t
famosus libellus fæmˌəʊ.səs.lɪˈbel.əs (US) -ˌoʊ-
famous ˈfeɪ.məs **-ly** -li **-ness** -nəs, -nɪs
fan fæn **-s** -z **-ning** -ɪŋ **-ned** -d
Fan *Welsh mountains:* væn
fan-assisted ˌfæn.əˈsɪs.tɪd *stress shift:* ˌfan-assisted ˈoven
fanatic fəˈnæt.ɪk (US) -ˈnæt̬- **-s** -s **-al** -ᵊl **-ally** -ᵊl.i, -li
fanaticism fəˈnæt.ɪ.sɪ.zᵊm, ˈ-ə- (US) -ˈnæt̬-
fanaticiz|e, -is|e fəˈnæt.ɪ.saɪz (US) -ˈnæt̬- **-es** -ɪz **-ing** -ɪŋ **-ed** -d
fanbelt ˈfæn.belt **-s** -s
fanciful ˈfænt.sɪ.fᵊl, -fʊl **-ly** -i **-ness** -nəs, -nɪs
Fancourt ˈfæn.kɔːt, ˈfæŋ- (US) -kɔːrt
fanc|y ˈfænt.s|i **-ies** -iz **-ying** -i.ɪŋ **-ied** -id **-ier/s** -i.əʳ/z (US) -i.ɚ/z ˌ**fancy ˈdress**
fancy-free ˌfænt.siˈfriː ˌ**footloose and ˌfancy-ˈfree** (US) ˈ**footloose and ˌfancy ˌfree**
fancywork ˈfænt.si.wɜːk (US) -wɝːk
fandango fænˈdæŋ.gəʊ (US) -goʊ **-s** -z
fane **(F)** feɪn **-s** -z
Faneuil ˈfæn.ᵊl, -jəl, -jʊəl (US) -jə.wəl
fanfare ˈfæn.feəʳ (US) -fer **-s** -z
fanfaronade ˌfæn.fær.əˈnɑːd, -fᵊr-, -ˈneɪd (US) -fər.əˈneɪd, -ˈnɑːd **-s** -z
fang **(F)** fæŋ **-s** -z **-ed** -d
fanjet ˈfæn.dʒet **-s** -s
fanlight ˈfæn.laɪt **-s** -s
fanner ˈfæn.əʳ (US) -ɚ **-s** -z
Fanning ˈfæn.ɪŋ
fann|y **(F)** ˈfæn|.i **-ies** -iz ˈ**fanny ˌpack**
Fanshawe ˈfæn.ʃɔː (US) -ʃɑː, -ʃɔː
Fanta® ˈfæn.tə (US) -t̬ə
fantabulous fænˈtæb.jə.ləs, -jʊ-
fantail ˈfæn.teɪl **-s** -z
fantasia fænˈteɪ.zi.ə, -ˈtɑː-, ˈ-ʒə; ˌfæn.təˈziː.ə, -ˈsiː- (US) fænˈteɪ.ʒə, -ʒi.ə; ˌfæn.t̬əˈziː.ə **-s** -z
fantasist ˈfæn.tə.sɪst (US) -t̬ə- **-s** -s
fantasiz|e, -is|e ˈfæn.tə.saɪz (US) -t̬ə- **-es** -ɪz **-ing** -ɪŋ **-ed** -d
fantasm ˈfæn.tæz.ᵊm **-s** -z
fantastic fænˈtæs.tɪk, fən- (US) fæn- **-al** -ᵊl **-ally** -ᵊl.i, -li **-alness** -ᵊl.nəs, -nɪs
fantas|y ˈfæn.tə.s|i, -z|i (US) -t̬ə- **-ies** -iz
Fanti, Fante ˈfæn.ti (US) ˈfæn.ti, ˈfɑːn- **-s** -z
fanzine ˈfæn.ziːn **-s** -z
far fɑːʳ (US) fɑːr ˌ**Far ˈEast**
farad ˈfær.əd, -æd (US) ˈfer-, ˈfær- **-s** -z
faraday **(F)** ˈfær.ə.deɪ (US) ˈfer-, ˈfær- **-s** -z
faradic fəˈræd.ɪk
faraway ˌfɑː.rəˈweɪ (US) ˌfɑːr.əˈ- *stress shift:* ˌfaraway ˈlook
farc|e fɑːs (US) fɑːrs **-es** -ɪz
farceur ˌfɑːˈsɜːʳ (US) ˌfɑːrˈsɝː **-s** -z
farcical ˈfɑː.sɪ.kᵊl, -sə- (US) ˈfɑːr- **-ly** -i
farci(e) ˌfɑːˈsiː (US) ˌfɑːr-
farcy ˈfɑː.si (US) ˈfɑːr-
far|e (*n. v.*) feəʳ (US) fer **-es** -z **-ing** -ɪŋ **-ed** -d
Far East ˌfɑːʳˈiːst (US) ˌfɑːr-
Farebrother ˈfeəˌbrʌð.əʳ (US) ˈferˌbrʌð.ɚ
Fareham ˈfeə.rəm (US) ˈfer.əm
farewell ˌfeəˈwel (US) ˌfer- **-s** -z *stress shift:* ˌfarewell ˈkiss
Farewell ˈfeə.wel, -wᵊl (US) ˈfer-
farfalle fɑːˈfæl.eɪ (US) fɑːr-
far-fetched ˌfɑːˈfetʃt (US) ˌfɑːr- *stress shift:* ˌfar-fetched ˈtale
far-flung ˌfɑːˈflʌŋ (US) ˌfɑːr- *stress shift:* ˌfar-flung ˈplaces
Fargo ˈfɑː.gəʊ (US) ˈfɑːr.goʊ
Farhi ˈfɑː.hi (US) ˈfɑːr-
Faribault ˈfær.ɪ.bəʊ (US) ˈfer.ɪ.boʊ, ˈfær-
farina fəˈriː.nə, -ˈraɪ- (US) -ˈriː-
Farina fəˈriː.nə
farinaceous ˌfær.ɪˈneɪ.ʃəs, -əˈ- (US) ˌfer-, ˌfær-
Faringdon ˈfær.ɪŋ.dən (US) ˈfer-, ˈfær-
Faringford ˈfær.ɪŋ.fəd (US) ˈfer.ɪŋ.fɚd, ˈfær-
Farington ˈfær.ɪŋ.tən (US) ˈfer-, ˈfær-
farinose ˈfær.ɪ.nəʊs, -nəʊz (US) ˈfer.ə.noʊs, ˈfær-
Farjeon ˈfɑː.dʒᵊn (US) ˈfɑːr-
Farleigh, Farley ˈfɑː.li (US) ˈfɑːr-
farm fɑːm (US) fɑːrm **-s** -z **-ing** -ɪŋ **-ed** -d
Farman ˈfɑː.mən (US) ˈfɑːr-
Farmaner ˈfɑː.mə.nəʳ (US) ˈfɑːr.mə.nɚ
farmer **(F)** ˈfɑː.məʳ (US) ˈfɑːr.mɚ **-s** -z
farmhand ˈfɑːm.hænd (US) ˈfɑːrm- **-s** -z
farmhou|se ˈfɑːm.haʊ|s (US) ˈfɑːrm- **-ses** -zɪz
Farmington ˈfɑː.mɪŋ.tən (US) ˈfɑːr-
farmland ˈfɑːm.lænd, -lənd (US) ˈfɑːrm.lænd
farmstead ˈfɑːm.sted (US) ˈfɑːrm- **-s** -z
farmyard ˈfɑːm.jɑːd (US) ˈfɑːrm.jɑːrd **-s** -z
Farnaby ˈfɑː.nə.bi (US) ˈfɑːr-
Farnborough ˈfɑːn.bᵊr.ə, ˈfɑːm- (US) ˈfɑːrn-, -oʊ
Farn(e) fɑːn (US) fɑːrn
Farnham ˈfɑː.nəm (US) ˈfɑːr-
Farnhamworth ˈfɑː.nəm.wəθ, -wɜːθ (US) ˈfɑːr.nəm.wɚθ, -wɝːθ
faro *gambling game:* ˈfeə.rəʊ (US) ˈfer.oʊ, ˈfær-
Faro *in Portugal:* ˈfɑː.rəʊ, ˈfeə- (US) ˈfɑːr.oʊ, ˈfer-
Faroe ˈfeə.rəʊ (US) ˈfer.oʊ
Faroese ˌfeə.rəʊˈiːz (US) ˌfer.oʊˈ-
far-off ˌfɑːʳˈɒf (US) ˌfɑːrˈɑːf *stress shift:* ˌfar-off ˈtown
farouche fəˈruːʃ, fɑː-
Farouk fəˈruːk, færˈuːk (US) fəˈruːk
far-out ˌfɑːʳˈaʊt (US) ˌfɑːr- *stress shift:* ˌfar-out ˈmusic
Farquhar ˈfɑː.kwəʳ, -kəʳ (US) ˈfɑːr.kwɚ, -kwɑːr, -kɚ
Farquharson ˈfɑː.kwə.sᵊn, -kə- (US) ˈfɑːr.kwɚ-, -kɚ-
Farr fɑːʳ (US) fɑːr
farraginous fəˈreɪ.dʒɪ.nəs, -ˈrædʒ.ɪ-, -ᵊn.əs (US) fəˈrædʒ.ɪ.nəs, ˈ-ə-
farrago fəˈrɑː.gəʊ, -ˈreɪ- (US) fəˈrɑː.goʊ, -ˈreɪ- **-(e)s** -z
Farragut ˈfær.ə.gət (US) ˈfer-, ˈfær-
Farrah ˈfær.ə (US) ˈfer-, ˈfær-
Farrakhan ˈfær.ə.kæn (US) ˈfer-, ˈfær-, -kɑːn, ˈfer.kɑːn
Farrant ˈfær.ᵊnt (US) ˈfer-, ˈfær-
far-reaching ˌfɑːˈriː.tʃɪŋ (US) ˌfɑːr- *stress shift:* ˌfar-reaching ˈconsequences
Farrell ˈfær.ᵊl (US) ˈfer-, ˈfær-
Farren ˈfær.ᵊn (US) ˈfer-, ˈfær-
Farrener ˈfær.ə.nəʳ (US) ˈfer.ə.nɚ, ˈfær-
farrier ˈfær.i.əʳ (US) ˈfer.i.ɚ, ˈfær- **-s** -z **-y** -i **-ies** -iz
Farringdon ˈfær.ɪŋ.dən (US) ˈfer-, ˈfær-
Farringford ˈfær.ɪŋ.fəd (US) ˈfer.ɪŋ.fɚd, ˈfær-
Farrington ˈfær.ɪŋ.tən (US) ˈfer-, ˈfær-
farrow **(F)** ˈfær.əʊ (US) ˈfer.oʊ, ˈfær- **-s** -z **-ing** -ɪŋ **-ed** -d
farseeing ˌfɑːˈsiː.ɪŋ (US) ˌfɑːr- *stress shift:* ˌfarseeing ˈleader
Farsi ˈfɑː.siː, ˌ-ˈ- (US) ˈfɑːr- **-s** -z
farsighted fɑːˈsaɪ.tɪd (US) fɑːrˈsaɪ.t̬ɪd **-ly** -li **-ness** -nəs, -nɪs
Farsley ˈfɑːz.li (US) ˈfɑːrz-
fart fɑːt (US) fɑːrt **-s** -s **-ing** -ɪŋ (US) ˈfɑːr.t̬ɪŋ **-ed** -ɪd (US) ˈfɑːr.t̬ɪd
farth|er ˈfɑː.ð|əʳ (US) ˈfɑːr.ð|ɚ **-est** -ɪst, -əst
farthing ˈfɑː.ðɪŋ (US) ˈfɑːr- **-s** -z
farthingale ˈfɑː.ðɪŋ.geɪl (US) ˈfɑːr- **-s** -z
fartlek ˈfɑːt.lek (US) ˈfɑːrt- **-s** -s
Faruk fəˈruːk, færˈuːk (US) fəˈruːk
Farwell ˈfɑː.wel, -wəl (US) ˈfɑːr-
fasces ˈfæs.iːz
fasci|a *medical term:* ˈfæʃ.i|.ə, -ʃ|ə (US) -ʃi|.ə **-as** -əs **-ae** -iː *other senses:* ˈfeɪ.ʃ|ə, -ʃi|.ə (US) ˈfæʃ.i|.ə, ˈfæʃ|.ə *also when referring to classical architecture:* ˈfeɪ.si|.ə (US) -ʃi- **-as** -əz **-ae** -iː
fasciated ˈfæʃ.i.eɪ.tɪd (US) -t̬ɪd

fascicle ˈfæs.ɪ.kl̩, ˈ-ə- **-s** -z
fascicule ˈfæs.ɪ.kjuːl, ˈ-ə- **-s** -z
fascin|ate ˈfæs.ɪ.n|eɪt, -ᵊn|.eɪt (US) -ᵊn|.eɪt **-ates** -eɪts **-ated** -eɪ.tɪd (US) -eɪ.t̬ɪd **-ator/s** -eɪ.təʳ/z (US) -eɪ.t̬ɚ/z
fascinating ˈfæs.ɪ.neɪ.tɪŋ, -ᵊn.eɪ- (US) -ᵊn.eɪ.t̬ɪŋ **-ly** -li
fascination ˌfæs.ɪˈneɪ.ʃᵊn, -ᵊnˈeɪ- (US) -ᵊnˈeɪ- **-s** -z
fascine fæsˈiːn, fəˈsiːn **-s** -z
fascism (F) ˈfæʃ.ɪ.zᵊm
fascist (F) ˈfæʃ.ɪst **-s** -s
Fascisti fæʃˈɪs.tiː, fəˈʃɪs-
fascistic (F) fæʃˈɪs.tɪk, fəˈʃɪs- **-ally** -ᵊl.i, -li
fash fæʃ **-es** -ɪz **-ing** -ɪŋ **-ed** -t
fashion ˈfæʃ.ᵊn **-s** -z **-ing** -ɪŋ **-ed** -d **-er/s** -əʳ/z (US) -ɚ/z **ˈfashion ˌplate**
fashionab|le ˈfæʃ.ᵊn.ə.b|l̩, ˈfæʃ.nə- **-ly** -li **-leness** -l̩.nəs, -nɪs
Faslane fæzˈleɪn, fəˈsleɪn
Fassbinder ˈfæs.bɪn.dəʳ (US) ˈfɑːs.bɪn.dɚ
fast (F) fɑːst (US) fæst **-s** -s **-est** -ɪst, -əst **-ness** -nəs, -nɪs **-ing** -ɪŋ **-ed** -ɪd **-er/s** -əʳ/z (US) -ɚ/z **ˌfast and ˈloose; ˈfast ˌday; ˌfast ˈfood; ˈfast ˌlane; ˌfast reˈactor; ˈfast ˌtrack; ˌlife in the ˈfast ˌlane ˌpull a ˈfast ˌone**
fastball ˈfɑːs*t*.bɔːl (US) ˈfæs*t*-, -bɑːl **-s** -z
fasten ˈfɑː.sᵊn (US) ˈfæs.ᵊn **-s** -z **-ing** -ɪŋ, ˈfɑːs.nɪŋ (US) ˈfæs- **-ed** -d
fastener ˈfɑːs.ᵊn.əʳ (US) ˈfæs.ᵊn.ɚ **-s** -z
fastening ˈfɑː.sᵊn.ɪŋ; ˈfɑːs.nɪŋ (US) ˈfæs.ᵊn.ɪŋ; ˈfæs.nɪŋ **-s** -z
fast-forward ˌfɑːs*t*ˈfɔː.wəd (US) ˌfæs*t*ˈfɔːr.wɚd **-s** -z **-ing** -ɪŋ **-ed** -ɪd
fasti (F) ˈfæs.tiː, -taɪ
fastidious fæsˈtɪd.i.əs, fəˈstɪd- **-ly** -li **-ness** -nəs, -nɪs
fastness ˈfɑːs*t*.nəs, -nɪs (US) ˈfæs*t*- **-es** -ɪz
Fastnet ˈfɑːs*t*.net, -nɪt (US) ˈfæs*t*-
fast-talk ˌfɑːs*t*ˈtɔːk (US) ˌfæs*t*-, -ˈtɑːk **-s** -s **-ing** -ɪŋ **-ed** -t **-er/s** -əʳ/z (US) -ɚ/z
fast-track ˈfɑːs*t*.træk (US) ˈfæs*t*- **-s** -s **-ing** -ɪŋ **-ed** -t
fat fæt **-ter** -əʳ (US) ˈfæt̬.ɚ **-test** -ɪst, -əst (US) ˈfæt̬.ɪst, -əst **-ness** -nəs, -nɪs **ˈfat ˌcat; ˌfat ˈcity**
fatal ˈfeɪ.tᵊl (US) -t̬ᵊl **-ly** -i
fatal|ism ˈfeɪ.tᵊl|.ɪ.zᵊm (US) -t̬ᵊl- **-ist/s** -ɪst/s
fatalistic ˌfeɪ.tᵊlˈɪs.tɪk (US) -t̬ᵊlˈ- **-ally** -ᵊl.i, -li
fatalit|y fəˈtæl.ə.t|i, feɪ-, -ɪ.t|i (US) -ə.t̬|i **-ies** -iz
fat|e (F) feɪt **-es** -s **-ed** -ɪd (US) ˈfeɪ.t̬ɪd
fateful ˈfeɪt.fᵊl, -fʊl **-ly** -i
fathead ˈfæt.hed **-s** -z
fath|er (F) ˈfɑː.ð|əʳ (US) -ð|ɚ **-ers** -əz (US) -ɚz **-ering** -ᵊr.ɪŋ **-ered** -əd (US) -ɚd **ˌFather ˈChristmas; ˈfather ˌfigure**
fatherhood ˈfɑː.ðə.hʊd (US) -ðɚ-
father-in-law ˈfɑː.ðəʳ.ɪn.lɔː (US) -ðɚ.ɪn.lɑː, -lɔː **fathers-in-law** ˈfɑː.ðəz- (US) -ðɚz-
fatherland ˈfɑː.ðə.lænd (US) -ðɚ- **-s** -z
fatherless ˈfɑː.ðə.ləs, -lɪs (US) -ðɚ-
fatherl|y ˈfɑː.ðᵊl|.i (US) -ðɚ.l|i **-iness** -ɪ.nəs, -ɪ.nɪs
fathom ˈfæð.əm **-s** -z **-ing** -ɪŋ **-ed** -d **-able** -ə.bl̩ **-less** -ləs, -lɪs
fatigu|e fəˈtiːg **-es** -z **-ing/ly** -ɪŋ/li **-ed** -d **ˌchronic faˈtigue ˌsyndrome**
Fatima ˈfæt.ɪ.mə (US) ˈfæt̬-, ˈfɑː.t̬ɪ-; fəˈtiː-
fatling ˈfæt.lɪŋ **-s** -z
fatsia ˈfæt.si.ə **-s** -z
fatso ˈfæt.səʊ (US) -soʊ **-es** -z
fatted ˈfæt.ɪd (US) ˈfæt̬- **ˌfatted ˈcalf**
fatten ˈfæt.ᵊn **-s** -z **-ing** -ɪŋ **-ed** -d **-er/s** -əʳ/z (US) -ɚ/z
fattish ˈfæt.ɪʃ (US) ˈfæt̬-
fatt|y ˈfæt|.i (US) ˈfæt̬- **-ies** -iz **-ier** -i.əʳ (US) -i.ɚ **-iest** -i.ɪst, -i.əst **-iness** -ɪ.nəs, -ɪ.nɪs **ˌfatty ˈacid**
fatuity fəˈtjuː.ə.ti, fætˈjuː-, -ɪ.ti (US) fəˈtuː.ə.t̬i, -ˈtjuː-
fatuous ˈfæt.ju.əs (US) ˈfætʃ.u- **-ly** -li **-ness** -nəs, -nɪs
fatwa ˈfæt.wɑː, -wə (US) ˈfæt.wɑː, ˈfʌt- **-s** -z
fatwood ˈfæt.wʊd
faubourg ˈfəʊ.bʊəg, -bɜːg (US) ˈfoʊ.bʊr, -bʊrg **-s** -z
faucal ˈfɔː.kᵊl (US) ˈfɑː-, ˈfɔː-
fauces ˈfɔː.siːz (US) ˈfɑː-, ˈfɔː-
faucet ˈfɔː.sɪt, -sət (US) ˈfɑː-, ˈfɔː- **-s** -s
Faucett, Faucit ˈfɔː.sɪt, -ət (US) ˈfɑː-, ˈfɔː-
Faulconbridge ˈfɔː.kᵊn.brɪdʒ, ˈfɔːl-, -kᵊm- (US) ˈfɑː.kᵊn-, ˈfɑːl-, ˈfɔː-, ˈfɔːl-
Fauldhouse ˈfɔːld.haʊs (US) ˈfɑːld-, ˈfɔːld-
Faulds fəʊldz, fɔːldz (US) foʊldz, fɑːldz, fɔːldz
Faulhorn ˈfaʊl.hɔːn (US) -hɔːrn
Faulk fɔːk (US) fɑːk, fɔːk, fɑːlk
Faulkes fɔːks, fɔːlks (US) fɑːks, fɑːlks, fɔːks, fɔːlks
Faulkland ˈfɔː.klənd, ˈfɔːl- (US) ˈfɑː-, ˈfɑːl-, ˈfɔː-, ˈfɔːl-
Faulkner ˈfɔːk.nəʳ (US) ˈfɑːk.nɚ, ˈfɔːk-, ˈfɑːlk-
Faulks fəʊks (US) foʊks
faul|t fɔːl|t, fɒl|t (US) fɔːl|t, fɑːl|t **-ts** -ts **-ting** -tɪŋ (US) -t̬ɪŋ **-ted** -tɪd (US) -t̬ɪd
faultfind|er ˈfɔːltˌfaɪn.d|əʳ, ˈfɒlt- (US) ˈfɔːltˌfaɪn.d|ɚ, ˈfɑːlt- **-ers** -əz (US) -ɚz **-ing** -ɪŋ
faultless ˈfɔːlt.ləs, ˈfɒlt-, -lɪs (US) ˈfɔːlt-, ˈfɑːlt- **-ly** -li **-ness** -nəs, -nɪs
fault|y ˈfɔːl.t|i, ˈfɒl- (US) ˈfɔːl.t̬|i, ˈfɑːl- **-ier** -i.əʳ (US) -i.ɚ **-iest** -i.ɪst, -i.əst **-ily** -ɪ.li, -ᵊl.i **-iness** -ɪ.nəs, -ɪ.nɪs
faun fɔːn (US) fɑːn, fɔːn **-s** -z
fauna ˈfɔː.nə (US) ˈfɑː-, ˈfɔː-
Faunch fɔːn*t*ʃ (US) fɑːn*t*ʃ, fɔːn*t*ʃ
Fauntleroy ˈfɔːnt.lə.rɔɪ, ˈfɒnt- (US) ˈfɑːnt-, ˈfɔːnt-
Fauré ˈfɔː.reɪ, ˈfɒr.eɪ (US) foʊˈreɪ, fɔː-
Faust faʊst
Faustian ˈfaʊ.sti.ən
Faustina fɔːˈstiː.nə, faʊ- (US) faʊ-, fɔː-
Faustus ˈfɔː.stəs, ˈfaʊ- (US) ˈfaʊ-, ˈfɔː-
fauteuil ˈfəʊ.tɜː.i, fəʊˈtɜː.i, -ˈtɜːl (US) ˈfoʊ.tɪl; foʊˈtɜː.jə **-s** -z
fauve fəʊv (US) foʊv
fauv|ism (F) ˈfəʊ.v|ɪ.zᵊm (US) ˈfoʊ- **-ist/s** -ɪst/s
Faux fəʊ, fɔːks (US) foʊ
faux ami ˌfəʊz.æmˈi (US) ˌfoʊz- **-s** -z
faux-naïf ˌfəʊ.naɪˈiːf (US) ˌfoʊ.nɑːˈ- **-s** -s
faux pas *singular:* ˌfəʊˈpɑː (US) ˌfoʊ-
faux pas *plural:* ˌfəʊˈpɑː, -ˈpɑːz (US) ˌfoʊ-
fave feɪv **-s** -z
Favel ˈfeɪ.vᵊl
Faversham ˈfæv.ə.ʃəm (US) ˈ-ɚ-
Favoni|an fəˈvəʊ.ni|.ən, feɪ- (US) -ˈvoʊ- **-us** -əs
Favorit® ˈfæv.ᵊr.ɪt
fav|o(u)r ˈfeɪ.v|əʳ (US) -v|ɚ **-o(u)rs** -əz (US) -ɚz **-o(u)ring** -ᵊr.ɪŋ **-o(u)red** -əd (US) -ɚd **-o(u)rer/s** -ᵊr.əʳ/z (US) -ɚ.ɚ/z
favo(u)rab|le ˈfeɪ.vᵊr.ə.b|l̩ **-ly** -li **-leness** -l̩.nəs, -nɪs
favo(u)rit|e ˈfeɪ.vᵊr.ɪt, -ət, ˈfeɪv.rɪt **-es** -s **-ism** -ɪ.zᵊm **ˌfavo(u)rite ˈson**
favo(u)rless ˈfeɪ.və.ləs, -lɪs (US) -vɚ-
Fawcett ˈfɔː.sɪt, -sət, ˈfɒs.ɪt, -ət (US) ˈfɑː.sɪt, ˈfɔː-, -sət
Fawkes fɔːks (US) fɑːks, fɔːks
Fawkner ˈfɔːk.nəʳ (US) ˈfɑːk.nɚ, ˈfɔːk-
Fawley ˈfɔː.li (US) ˈfɑː-, ˈfɔː-
Fawlty ˈfɔːl.ti (US) ˈfɑːl-, ˈfɔːl-
fawn fɔːn (US) fɑːn, fɔːn **-s** -z **-ing/ly** -ɪŋ/li **-ed** -d **-er/s** -əʳ/z (US) -ɚ/z
Fawssett ˈfɔː.sɪt, -sət (US) ˈfɑː.sɪt, ˈfɔː-, -sət
fax fæks **-es** -ɪz **-ing** -ɪŋ **-ed** -t **ˈfax maˌchine**
fay (F) feɪ **-s** -z
Faye feɪ
Fayette feɪˈet *stress shift, see compound:* **ˌFayette ˈCity**
Fayetteville ˈfeɪ.et.vɪl, -ɪt-, -ət- *locally also:* (US) ˈfeɪt.vəl
Faygate ˈfeɪ.geɪt
Faza(c)kerley fəˈzæk.ᵊl.i (US) -ɚ.li
faz|e feɪz **-es** -ɪz **-ing** -ɪŋ **-ed** -d
FBI ˌef.biːˈaɪ
FC ˌefˈsiː
FCO ˌef.siːˈəʊ (US) -ˈoʊ

FDA ˌef.diːˈeɪ
fe *name of note in Tonic Sol-fa:* fiː
fe *syllable used in Tonic Sol-fa for counting a short note off the beat:* fi
FE *(abbrev. for* **Further Education***)* ˌefˈiː
fealty ˈfiːl.ti
fear fɪəʳ US fɪr **-s** -z **-ing** -ɪŋ **-ed** -d
fearful ˈfɪə.fəl, -fʊl US ˈfɪr- **-ly** -i **-ness** -nəs, -nɪs
Fearghal ˈfɜː.gəl US ˈfɝː-
Feargus ˈfɜː.gəs US ˈfɝː-
Fearing ˈfɪə.rɪŋ US ˈfɪr.ɪŋ
fearless ˈfɪə.ləs, -lɪs US ˈfɪr- **-ly** -li **-ness** -nəs, -nɪs
Fearn(e) fɜːn US fɝːn
Fearnside ˈfɜːn.saɪd US ˈfɝːn-
Fearon ˈfɪə.rən US ˈfɪr.ən
fearsome ˈfɪə.səm US ˈfɪr- **-ly** -li **-ness** -nəs, -nɪs
feasibility ˌfiː.zəˈbɪl.ə.ti, -zɪˈ-, -ɪ.ti US -ə.t̬i
feasib|le ˈfiː.zə.b|l̩, -zɪ- **-ly** -li **-leness** -l̩.nəs, -nɪs
feast (F) fiːst **-s** -s **-ing** -ɪŋ **-ed** -ɪd **-er/s** -əʳ/z US -ɚ/z
feat fiːt **-s** -s
feath|er ˈfeð|.əʳ US -ɚ **-ers** -əz US -ɚz **-ering** -ər.ɪŋ **-ered** -əd US -ɚd ˌ**feather ˈbed**
featherbed ˈfeð.ə.bed, ˌ--ˈ- US -ɚ- **-s** -z **-ding** -ɪŋ **-ded** -ɪd
featherbrain ˈfeð.ə.breɪn US ˈ-ɚ- **-s** -z **-ed** -d
featheredg|e ˈfeð.əʳ.edʒ, ˌ--ˈ- US -ɚ- **-es** -ɪz
featherhead ˈfeð.ə.hed US ˈ-ɚ- **-s** -z **-ed** -ɪd
featherstitch ˈfeð.ə.stɪtʃ US ˈ-ɚ- **-es** -ɪz **-ing** -ɪŋ **-ed** -t
Featherston ˈfeð.ə.stən US ˈ-ɚ-
Featherstone ˈfeð.ə.stən, -stəʊn US -ɚ.stən, -stoʊn
Featherstonehaugh ˈfeð.ə.stən.hɔː; ˈfæn.ʃɔː; ˈfes.tən.hɔː, ˈfɪə.stən-; ˈfiː.sən.heɪ US ˈfeð.ɚ.stən.θɑː, -hɔː; ˈfæn.ʃɑː, -ʃɔː; ˈfes.tən.hɑː, ˈfɪr.stən-, -hɔː; ˈfiː.sən.heɪ
featherweight ˈfeð.ə.weɪt US ˈ-ɚ- **-s** -s
feather|y ˈfeð.ər|.i **-iness** -ɪ.nəs, -ɪ.nɪs
Featley ˈfiːt.li
featly ˈfiːt.li
feat|ure ˈfiː.tʃ|əʳ US -tʃ|ɚ **-ures** -əz US -ɚz **-uring** -ər.ɪŋ **-ured** -əd US -ɚd **-ureless** -ə.ləs, -lɪs US -ɚ.ləs, -lɪs
Feaver ˈfiː.vəʳ US -vɚ
Feb. *(abbrev. for* **February***)* feb, ˈfeb.ru.ər.i, ˈ-jʊ.ər.i, ˈ-jʊ.ri, ˈ-jər.i US ˈfeb.ruː.er.i, ˈ-juː-, ˈ-jə.wer-
febrifug|e ˈfeb.rɪ.fjuːdʒ, -rə- **-es** -ɪz
febrile ˈfiː.braɪl US -brɪl, ˈfeb.rɪl
February ˈfeb.ru.ər.i, ˈ-ju.ər.i, ˈ-jʊ.ri, ˈ-jər.i US ˈfeb.ruː.er.i, ˈ-juː-, ˈ-jə.wer-
fecal ˈfiː.kəl
feces ˈfiː.siːz
fecit ˈfiː.sɪt, ˈfeɪ.kɪt
Feckenham ˈfek.ən.əm
feckless ˈfek.ləs, -lɪs **-ly** -li **-ness** -nəs, -nɪs
feculen|t ˈfek.jə.lən|t, -jʊ- US -jə-, -juː- **-ce** -*ts*
fecund ˈfek.ənd, ˈfiː.kənd, -kʌnd
fecun|date ˈfek.ən|.deɪt, ˈfiː.kən-, -kʌn- **-dates** -deɪts **-dating** -deɪ.tɪŋ US -deɪ.t̬ɪŋ **-dated** -deɪ.tɪd US -deɪ.t̬ɪd
fecundation ˌfek.ənˈdeɪ.ʃən, ˌfiː.kənˈ-, -kʌnˈ-
fecundity fɪˈkʌn.də.ti, fiːˈkʌn-, fekˈʌn-, -dɪ.ti US -də.t̬i
fed *(from* **feed***)* fed ˌ**fed ˈup**
Fed fed
federal (F) ˈfed.ər.əl, ˈ-rəl **-ly** -i ˌ**Federal ReˈServe**
federal|ism ˈfed.ər.əl|.ɪ.zəm, ˈ-rəl- **-ist/s** -ɪst/s
federalization, -isa- ˌfed.ər.əl.aɪˈzeɪ.ʃən, ˌ-rəl-, -ɪˈ- US -ɪˈ-
federaliz|e, -is|e ˈfed.ər.əl.aɪz, ˈ-rəl- US ˈ-ɚ.ə.laɪz, ˈ-rə- **-es** -ɪz **-ing** -ɪŋ **-ed** -d
federate *(n. adj.)* ˈfed.ər.ət, -ɪt, -eɪt **-s** -s
feder|ate *(v.)* ˈfed.ər|.eɪt **-ates** -eɪts **-ating** -eɪ.tɪŋ US -eɪ.t̬ɪŋ **-ated** -eɪ.tɪd US -eɪ.t̬ɪd
federation ˌfed.ərˈeɪ.ʃən US -əˈreɪ- **-s** -z
federative ˈfed.ər.ə.tɪv, -eɪ- US -ɚ.ə.t̬ɪv, -ə.reɪ- **-ly** -li
fedora (F) fɪˈdɔː.rə, fə-, fedˈɔː- US fəˈdɔːr.ə **-s** -z
fed up ˌfedˈʌp
fee fiː **-s** -z **-ing** -ɪŋ **-d** -d ˌ**fee ˈsimple**; ˌ**fee ˈtail**
feeb|le ˈfiː.b|l̩ **-ler** -ləʳ US -lɚ **-lest** -l̩.ɪst, -əst, -lɪst, -ləst **-ly** -li **-leness** -l̩.nəs, -nɪs
feebleminded ˌfiː.bl̩ˈmaɪn.dɪd US ˌfiː.bl̩ˈmaɪn.dɪd, ˈfiː.bl̩ˌmaɪn.dɪd **-ness** -nəs, -nɪs *stress shift, British only:* ˌfeebleminded ˈsimpleton
feed fiːd **-s** -z **-ing** -ɪŋ **fed** fed **feeder/s** ˈfiː.dəʳ/z US -dɚ/z ˈ**feeding** ˌ**bottle**; ˈ**feed** ˌ**pipe**; ˈ**feed** ˌ**tank**
feedback ˈfiːd.bæk
feedbag ˈfiːd.bæg **-s** -z
feel fiːl **-s** -z **-ing** -ɪŋ **felt** felt
feeler ˈfiː.ləʳ US -lɚ **-s** -z
feelgood ˈfiːl.gʊd ˈ**feelgood** ˌ**factor**
feeling ˈfiː.lɪŋ **-s** -z **-ly** -li
Feeney ˈfiː.ni
feet *(plur. of* **foot***)* fiːt ˌ**drag one's ˈfeet**; ˌ**fall on one's ˈfeet**; ˌ**find one's ˈfeet**; **have/keep** ˌ**both feet on the ˈground**; **be** ˌ**rushed off one's ˈfeet**; ˌ**sweep someone off their ˈfeet**
Fegan ˈfiː.gən
Feiffer ˈfaɪ.fəʳ US -fɚ
feign feɪn **-s** -z **-ing** -ɪŋ **-ed** -d **-edly** -ɪd.li **-edness** -ɪd.nəs, -nɪs
Feilden ˈfiːl.dən
Feilding ˈfiːl.dɪŋ
Feinstein ˈfaɪn.staɪn
feint feɪnt **-s** -s **-ing** -ɪŋ US ˈfeɪn.t̬ɪŋ **-ed** -ɪd US ˈfeɪn.t̬ɪd
Feisal ˈfaɪ.səl, ˈfeɪ-
Feist fiːst
feist|y ˈfaɪ.st|i **-ier** -i.əʳ US -i.ɚ **-iest** -i.ɪst, -i.əst **-ily** -ɪ.li, -əl.i
felafel fəˈlɑː.fəl, -ˈlæf.əl US -ˈlɑː.fəl **-s** -z
Feldman ˈfeld.mən
feldspar ˈfeld.spɑːʳ, ˈfel- US ˈfeld.spɑːr
Felicia fəˈlɪs.i.ə, felˈɪs-, fɪˈlɪs-, -ˈlɪʃ- US fəˈlɪʃ.ə, -i.ə, -ˈliː.ʃə, -ˈlɪs.i.ə
felicitat|e fɪˈlɪs.ɪ|.teɪt, fə-, felˈɪs-, ˈ-ə- US fəˈlɪs- **-es** -teɪts **-ing** -teɪ.tɪŋ US -teɪ.t̬ɪŋ **-ed** -teɪ.tɪd US -teɪ.t̬ɪd
felicitation fɪˌlɪs.ɪˈteɪ.ʃən, fə-, felˌɪs-, -əˈ- US fəˌlɪs- **-s** -z
felicitous fɪˈlɪs.ɪ.təs, fə-, felˈɪs-, ˈ-ə- US fəˈlɪs.ɪ.t̬əs, ˈ-ə- **-ly** -li **-ness** -nəs, -nɪs
felicity (F) fɪˈlɪs.ə.ti, fə-, felˈɪs-, -ɪ.ti US fəˈlɪs.ə.t̬i
feline ˈfiː.laɪn **-s** -z
felinity fɪˈlɪn.ə.ti, fiː-, fə-, -ɪ.ti US -ə.t̬i, -ɪ.t̬i
Felix ˈfiː.lɪks
Felixstowe ˈfiː.lɪk.stəʊ US -stoʊ
Felkin ˈfel.kɪn
fell (F) fel **-s** -z **-ing** -ɪŋ **-ed** -d
fella ˈfel.ə **-s** -z
fellah ˈfel.ə US ˈfel.ə; fəˈlɑː **-in** -hiːn, ˌfel.əˈhiːn US -hiːn **-een** -hiːn, ˌfel.əˈhiːn US -hiːn
fella|te felˈeɪ|t, fəˈleɪ|t, fɪ- US ˈfel.eɪ|t, -ˈ- **-tes** -ts **-ting** -tɪŋ US -t̬ɪŋ **-ted** -tɪd US -t̬ɪd **-tor/s** -təʳ/z US -t̬ɚ/z **-trix/es** -trɪks/ɪz **-trice/s** -trɪs/ɪz
fellatio fəˈleɪ.ʃi.əʊ, felˈeɪ-, fɪˈleɪ- US fəˈleɪ.ʃi.oʊ, -ʃoʊ; -ˈlɑː.ti.oʊ
fellation fəˈleɪ.ʃən, felˈeɪ-, fɪˈleɪ- US fə-
feller ˈfel.əʳ US -ɚ **-z** -z
Felling ˈfel.ɪŋ
Fellini felˈiː.ni, fəˈliː-, fɪ- US fə-
felloe ˈfel.əʊ US -oʊ **-s** -z
fellow ˈfel.əʊ US -oʊ **-s** -z ˌ**fellow ˈcitizen**; ˌ**fellow ˈfeeling**; ˌ**fellow ˈtraveller**
Fellow(e)s ˈfel.əʊz US -oʊz
fellowship ˈfel.əʊ.ʃɪp US -oʊ- **-s** -s
Felltham ˈfel.θəm
felo-de-se ˌfiː.ləʊ.diːˈsiː, ˌfel.əʊ-, -dɪˈ-, -ˈseɪ US ˌfiː.loʊ.dɪˈsiː, ˌfel.oʊ-

felos-de-se ˌfiː.ləʊz-, ˌfel.əʊz- (US) ˌfiː.loʊz-, ˌfel.oʊz- **felones-de-se** ˌfiː.ləʊ.niːz-, ˌfel.əʊ.niːz- (US) ˌfel.oʊ.niː.dɪˈsiː, ˌfiː.loʊ-

felon ˈfel.ən **-s** -z

felonious fəˈləʊ.ni.əs, felˈəʊ-, fɪˈləʊ- (US) fəˈloʊ- **-ly** -li **-ness** -nəs, -nɪs

felon|y ˈfel.ə.n|i **-ies** -iz

Felpham ˈfel.pəm

felspar ˈfel.spɑːʳ (US) -spɑːr

Felste(a)d ˈfel.stɪd, -sted

felt felt **-s** -s

Feltham *place:* ˈfel.təm *personal name:* ˈfel.θəm

felting ˈfel.tɪŋ **-s** -z

Felton ˈfel.tᵊn

felt-tip ˌfeltˈtɪp **-s** -s *stress shift, see compound:* **ˌfelt-tip ˈpen**

felucca felˈʌk.ə, fəˈlʌk-, fɪ- (US) fəˈlʌk-, -ˈluː.kə **-s** -z

female ˈfiː.meɪl **-s** -z **-ness** -nəs, -nɪs

feme fiːm, fem (US) fem **-s** -z

Femidom® ˈfem.ɪ.dɒm (US) -dɑːm

feminine ˈfem.ɪ.nɪn, ˈ-ə- **-ly** -li **-ness** -nəs, -nɪs

femininit|y ˌfem.ɪˈnɪn.ə.t|i, -əˈ-, -ɪ.t|i (US) -ə.t̬|i **-ies** -iz

femin|ism ˈfem.ɪ.n|ɪ.zᵊm, ˈ-ə- **-ist/s** -ɪst/s

feminiz|e, -is|e ˈfem.ɪ.naɪz, ˈ-ə- **-es** -ɪz **-ing** -ɪŋ **-ed** -d

femme(s) fatale(s) ˌfæm.fəˈtɑːl (US) ˌfem.fəˈtæl

femora *(alternative plur. of* **femur***)* ˈfem.ᵊr.ə, ˈfiː.mᵊr- (US) ˈfem.ᵊr-

femoral ˈfem.ᵊr.ᵊl, ˈfiː.mᵊr- (US) ˈfem.ᵊr-

femur ˈfiː.məʳ (US) -mɚ **-s** -z **femora** ˈfem.ᵊr.ə, ˈfiː.mᵊr- (US) ˈfem.ᵊr-

fen (F) fen **-s** -z

fenc|e fen*t*s **-es** -ɪz **-ing** -ɪŋ **-ed** -t **-er/s** -əʳ/z (US) -ɚ/z **-eless** -ləs, -lɪs **ˌsit on the ˈfence**

fencesitt|er ˈfen*t*sˌsɪt|.əʳ (US) -ˌsɪt̬- **-ers** -əʳ/z (US) -ɚ/z **-ing** -ɪŋ

Fenchurch ˈfen.tʃɜːtʃ (US) -tʃɝːtʃ

fend fend **-s** -z **-ing** -ɪŋ **-ed** -ɪd

fender ˈfen.dəʳ (US) -dɚ **-s** -z

fender-bender ˈfen.dəˌben.dəʳ (US) -dɚˌben.dɚ **-s** -z

Fendi ˈfen.di

Fenella fɪˈnel.ə, fə-

fenestr|a fɪˈnes.tr|ə, fə- **-ae** -iː **-al** -ᵊl

fenes|trate fɪˈnes|.treɪt, fəˈnes-; ˈfen.ɪ.s|treɪt, ˈ-ə- (US) ˈfen.ɪ.s|treɪt; fəˈnes|.treɪt **-trates** -treɪts **-trating** -treɪ.tɪŋ (US) -treɪ.t̬ɪŋ **-trated** -treɪ.tɪd (US) -treɪ.t̬ɪd

fenestration ˌfen.ɪˈstreɪ.ʃᵊn, -əˈ- **-s** -z

feng shui ˌfeŋˈʃuː.i (US) ˌfʌŋˈʃweɪ

Fenham ˈfen.əm

Fenian ˈfiː.ni.ən **-s** -z **-ism** -ɪ.zᵊm

Fenimore ˈfen.ɪ.mɔːʳ (US) -mɔːr

fenland (F) ˈfen.lənd, -lænd

Fenn fen

fennec ˈfen.ek, -ɪk **-s** -s

fennel ˈfen.ᵊl

Fennell ˈfen.ᵊl

Fennessy ˈfen.ɪ.si, ˈ-ə-

Fennimore ˈfen.ɪ.mɔːʳ (US) -mɔːr

fenny (F) ˈfen.i

Fenrir ˈfen.rɪəʳ (US) -rɪr

Fenton ˈfen.tən (US) -tᵊn

fenugreek ˈfen.jʊ.griːk, -ʊ- (US) -juː-, -jə-

Fenwick *English surname:* ˈfen.ɪk, -wɪk *American surname:* ˈfen.wɪk *places in UK:* ˈfen.ɪk

Feodor ˈfiː.əʊ.dɔːʳ (US) -ə.dɔːr

Feodora ˌfiː.əʊˈdɔː.rə (US) -əˈdɔːr.ə

feoff fiːf, fef **-s** -s **-ing** -ɪŋ **-ed** -t **-er/s** -əʳ/z (US) -ɚ/z **-ment/s** -mənt/s

feoffee fiːˈfiː, fefˈiː **-s** -z

feoffor fiːˈfɔːʳ, fefˈɔːʳ (US) fiːˈfɔːr, fefˈɔːr **-s** -z

ferae naturae ˌfer.aɪˌnɑːˈtjʊə.raɪ, -ˈtjɔː- (US) ˌfiː.riː.nəˈtuː.riː, -ˈtʊr.iː

feral ˈfer.ᵊl, ˈfɪə.rᵊl (US) ˈfer.ᵊl, ˈfɪr-

Ferdinand ˈfɜː.dɪ.nænd, -də-, -dᵊn.ænd, -ənd (US) ˈfɝː.dᵊn.ænd

feretor|y ˈfer.ɪ.tᵊr|.i, -tr|i (US) -tɔːr|.i **-ies** -iz

Fergal ˈfɜː.gᵊl (US) ˈfɝː-

Fergie ˈfɜː.gi (US) ˈfɝː-

Fergus ˈfɜː.gəs (US) ˈfɝː-

Fergus(s)on ˈfɜː.gə.sᵊn (US) ˈfɝː-

feri|a ˈfer.i.ə, ˈfɪə.ri- (US) ˈfɪr-, ˈfer- **-al** -əl

Feringhee fəˈrɪŋ.gi **-s** -z

Fermanagh fəˈmæn.ə, fɜː- (US) fɚ-, fɝː-

ferment *(n.)* ˈfɜː.ment (US) ˈfɝː- **-s** -s

fer|ment *(v.)* fə|ˈment, fɜː- (US) fɚ- **-ments** -ˈments **-menting** -ˈmen.tɪŋ (US) -ˈmen.t̬ɪŋ **-mented** -ˈmen.tɪd (US) -ˈmen.t̬ɪd **-mentable** -ˈmen.tə.bl̩ (US) -ˈmen.t̬ə.bl̩

fermentation ˌfɜː.menˈteɪ.ʃᵊn, -mənˈ- (US) ˌfɝː- **-s** -z

fermentative fəˈmen.tə.tɪv (US) -t̬ə.t̬ɪv **-ly** -li **-ness** -nəs, -nɪs

Fermi ˈfeə.mi (US) ˈfer-

fermium ˈfɜː.mi.əm (US) ˈfɝː-

Fermor ˈfɜː.mɔːʳ (US) ˈfɝː.mɔːr

Fermoy *near Cork:* fəˈmɔɪ, fɜː- (US) fɚ-, fɝː- *street in London:* ˈfɜː.mɔɪ (US) ˈfɝː-

fern (F) fɜːn (US) fɝːn **-s** -z

Fernandez fɜːˈnæn.dez, fə- (US) fɚ-

Fernando fəˈnæn.dəʊ (US) fɚˈnæn.doʊ

Ferndale ˈfɜːn.deɪl (US) ˈfɝːn-

Ferndown ˈfɜːn.daʊn (US) ˈfɝːn-

ferner|y ˈfɜː.nᵊr|.i (US) ˈfɝː- **-ies** -iz

Fernhough ˈfɜːn.həʊ (US) ˈfɝːn.hoʊ

Fernihough, Fernyhough ˈfɜː.ni.hʌf, -həʊ (US) ˈfɝː.ni.hʌf, -hoʊ

ferny ˈfɜː.ni (US) ˈfɝː-

ferocious fəˈrəʊ.ʃəs, fɪ- (US) fəˈroʊ- **-ly** -li **-ness** -nəs, -nɪs

ferocity fəˈrɒs.ə.ti, fɪ-, -ɪ.ti (US) fəˈrɑː.sə.t̬i

-ferous -fᵊr.əs

Note: Suffix. Words containing **-ferous** are normally stressed on the preceding syllable, e.g. **conifer** /ˈkɒn.ɪ.fəʳ (US) ˈkɑː.nə.fɚ/, **coniferous** /kəʊˈnɪf.ᵊr.əs (US) koʊˈnɪf-/.

Ferrand ˈfer.ᵊnd

Ferranti fəˈræn.ti, fɪ-, ferˈæn- (US) fəˈrɑːn.t̬i

Ferrar ˈfer.əʳ; fəˈrɑːʳ (US) ˈfer.ɚ; fəˈrɑːr

Ferrara fəˈrɑː.rə, fɪˈ-, ferˈɑː- (US) -ˈrɑːr.ə

Ferrari® fəˈrɑː.ri, fɪˈ-, ferˈɑː- (US) fəˈrɑːr.i

Ferraro fəˈrɑː.rəʊ, fɪˈ-, ferˈɑː- (US) fəˈrɑːr.oʊ

Ferraud fəˈrəʊ, ferˈəʊ (US) fəˈroʊ

ferrel (F) ˈfer.ᵊl **-s** -z

ferreous ˈfer.i.əs

Ferrer ˈfer.əʳ; fəˈreəʳ (US) ˈfer.ɚ; fəˈrer **-s** -z

ferre|t (F) ˈfer.ɪ|t, -ə|t **-ts** -ts **-ting** -tɪŋ (US) -t̬ɪŋ **-ted** -tɪd (US) -t̬ɪd

ferri- ˈfer.i-

ferric ˈfer.ɪk

Ferrier ˈfer.i.əʳ (US) -ɚ

ferris (F) ˈfer.ɪs **ˈferris ˌwheel**

Ferrisburg ˈfer.ɪs.bɜːg (US) -bɝːg

ferrite ˈfer.aɪt

ferritic ferˈɪt.ɪk, fəˈrɪt- (US) fəˈrɪt̬-, ferˈɪt̬-

ferro- fer.əʊ- (US) fer.oʊ-

Note: Prefix. Normally carries either primary or secondary stress on the first syllable, e.g. **ferrotype** /ˈfer.əʊ.taɪp (US) -oʊ-/, **ferromagnetic** /ˌfer.əʊ.mægˈnet.ɪk (US) -oʊ.mægˈnet̬-/.

ferroconcrete ˌfer.əʊˈkɒŋ.kriːt (US) -oʊˈkɑːn.kriːt

ferromagnetic ˌfer.əʊ.mægˈnet.ɪk (US) -oʊ.mægˈnet̬-

ferromagnetism ˌfer.əʊˈmæg.nə.tɪ.zᵊm (US) -oʊˈ-

ferrotype ˈfer.əʊ.taɪp (US) -oʊ- **-s** -s

ferrous ˈfer.əs

ferruginous ferˈuː.dʒɪ.nəs, fəˈruː-, fɪ-, -dʒᵊn- (US) fəˈruː.dʒɪ.nəs, ferˈuː-

ferrule ˈfer.uːl, -ᵊl, -juːl (US) -ᵊl, -uːl **-s** -z

Note: /ˈfer.ᵊl/ is the pronunciation used by those connected with the umbrella trade.

ferr|y (F) ˈfer|.i **-ies** -iz **-ying** -i.ɪŋ **-ied** -id

ferryboat ˈfer.i.bəʊt (US) -boʊt **-s** -s

Ferryhill ˈfer.i.hɪl

ferry|man ˈfer.i|.mən, -mæn **-men** -mən, -men

fertile 'fɜː.taɪl (US) 'fɝː.t̬ᵊl **-ly** -li

fertility fə'tɪl.ə.ti, fɜː-, -ɪ.ti (US) fɚ'tɪl.ə.t̬i

fertilization, -isa- ˌfɜː.tɪ.laɪ'zeɪ.ʃᵊn, -tᵊl.aɪ'-, -ɪ'- (US) ˌfɝː.t̬ᵊl.ɪ'-

fertiliz|e, -is|e 'fɜː.tɪ.laɪz, -tᵊl.aɪz (US) 'fɝː.t̬ə.laɪz **-es** -ɪz **-ing** -ɪŋ **-ed** -d

fertilizer, -ise- 'fɜː.tɪ.laɪ.zəʳ, -tᵊl.aɪ- (US) 'fɝː.t̬ᵊl- **-s** -z

ferule 'fer.uːl, -ᵊl, -juːl (US) -ᵊl, -uːl **-s** -z

fervency 'fɜː.vᵊn*t*.si (US) 'fɝː-

fervent 'fɜː.vᵊnt (US) 'fɝː- **-ly** -li **-ness** -nəs, -nɪs

fervid 'fɜː.vɪd (US) 'fɝː- **-ly** -li **-ness** -nəs, -nɪs

fervo(u)r 'fɜː.vəʳ (US) 'fɝː.vɚ

fescue 'fes.kjuː **-s** -z

fess fes **-es** -ɪs **-ing** -ɪŋ **-ed** -t

fess|e fes **-es** -ɪz

Fessenden 'fes.ᵊn.dən

fest fest **-s** -s

festal 'fes.tᵊl **-ly** -i

Feste 'fes.ti (US) -teɪ

fest|er 'fes.t|əʳ (US) -t|ɚ **-ers** -əz (US) -ɚz **-ering** -ᵊr.ɪŋ **-ered** -əd (US) -ɚd

Festiniog fes'tɪn.i.ɒg (US) -ɑːg, -ɔːg

festival 'fes.tɪ.vᵊl, -tə- **-s** -z

festive 'fes.tɪv **-ly** -li **-ness** -nəs, -nɪs

festivit|y fes'tɪv.ə.t|i, -ɪ.t|i (US) -ə.t̬|i **-ies** -iz

festoon fes'tuːn (US) fes'tuːn, fə'stuːn **-s** -z **-ing** -ɪŋ **-ed** -d

festschrift 'fes*t*.ʃrɪft, 'feʃ- **-en** -ən **-s** -s

Festus 'fes.təs

feta 'fet.ə (US) 'fet̬- ˌ**feta 'cheese**

fetal 'fiː.tᵊl (US) -t̬ᵊl '**fetal poˌsition**

fetch fetʃ **-es** -ɪz **-ing** -ɪŋ **-ed** -t **-er/s** -əʳ/z (US) -ɚ/z

fetching 'fetʃ.ɪŋ **-ly** -li

fet|e, fêt|e feɪt (US) feɪt, fet **-es** -s **-ing** -ɪŋ (US) 'feɪ.t̬ɪŋ, 'fet̬.ɪŋ **-ed** -ɪd (US) 'feɪ.t̬ɪd, 'fet̬.ɪd ˌ**garden 'fete** (US) '**garden ˌfete**

fête(s) champêtre(s) ˌfet.ʃɑ̃ː*m*'pet.rə (US) -ʃɑːm'-

fetich 'fet.ɪʃ (US) 'fet̬- **-es** -ɪz

fetich|ism 'fet.ɪ.ʃ|ɪ.zᵊm (US) 'fet̬- **-ist/s** -ɪst/s

fetichistic ˌfet.ɪ'ʃɪs.tɪk (US) ˌfet̬- **-ally** -ᵊl.i, -li

fetid 'fet.ɪd, 'fiː.tɪd (US) 'fet̬.ɪd, 'fiː.t̬ɪd **-ly** -li **-ness** -nəs, -nɪs

fetish 'fet.ɪʃ (US) 'fet̬- **-es** -ɪz

fetish|ism 'fet.ɪ.ʃ|ɪ.zᵊm (US) 'fet̬- **-ist/s** -ɪst/s

fetishistic ˌfet.ɪ'ʃɪs.tɪk (US) ˌfet̬- **-ally** -ᵊl.i, -li

fetlock 'fet.lɒk (US) -lɑːk **-s** -s **-ed** -t

fetolog|y fiː'tɒl.ə.dʒ|i (US) -'tɑː.lə- **-ist/s** -ɪst/s

fetta 'fet.ə (US) 'fet̬- ˌ**fetta 'cheese**

fett|er (F) 'fet|.əʳ (US) 'fet̬|.ɚ **-ers** -əz (US) -ɚz **-ering** -ᵊr.ɪŋ **-ered** -əd (US) -ɚd

Fettes *place:* 'fet.ɪs (US) 'fet̬- *surname:* 'fet.ɪs, -ɪz (US) 'fet̬-

Fettesian fet'iː.zi.ən, -ʒᵊn **-s** -z

fettl|e 'fet.l̩ (US) 'fet̬- **-es** -z **-ing** -ɪŋ, '-lɪŋ (US) 'fet̬.l̩.ɪŋ, 'fet.lɪŋ **-ed** -d

fettuccine ˌfet.ʊ'tʃiː.ni (US) ˌfet̬.ə'-

fetus 'fiː.təs (US) -t̬əs **-es** -ɪz

feu fjuː **-s** -z **-ing** -ɪŋ **-ed** -d

feud fjuːd **-s** -z **-ing** -ɪŋ

feudal 'fjuː.dᵊl **-ly** -i

feudal|ism 'fjuː.dᵊl|.ɪ.zᵊm **-ist/s** -ɪst/s

feudality fjuː'dæl.ə.ti, -ɪ.ti (US) -ə.t̬i

feudalization, -isa- ˌfjuː.dᵊl.aɪ'zeɪ.ʃᵊn, -ɪ'- (US) -ɪ'-

feudaliz|e, -is|e 'fjuː.dᵊl.aɪz (US) -də.laɪz **-es** -ɪz **-ing** -ɪŋ **-ed** -d

feudatory 'fjuː.də.tᵊr.i, -tri (US) -tɔːr.i

feuilleton 'fɜː.ɪ.tɔ̃ː*ŋ*, 'fɜːl.tɔ̃ː*ŋ* (US) 'fɜː.jə.tɑːn, 'fɝː-, -tɔ̃ː*n* **-s** -z

fever 'fiː.vəʳ (US) -vɚ **-s** -z **-ed** -d '**fever ˌblister**; '**fever ˌpitch**

feverfew 'fiː.və.fjuː (US) -vɚ-

feverish 'fiː.vᵊr.ɪʃ **-ly** -li **-ness** -nəs, -nɪs

Feversham 'fev.ə.ʃᵊm (US) '-ɚ-

few (F) fjuː **-er** -əʳ (US) -ɚ **-est** -ɪst, -əst **-ness** -nəs, -nɪs

fey feɪ **-ness** -nəs, -nɪs

Feydeau 'feɪ.dəʊ (US) feɪ'doʊ

Feynman 'faɪn.mən

fez (F) fez **-(z)es** -ɪz

Fezzan fez'ɑːn, -'æn (US) -'æn

Ffestiniog fes'tɪn.i.ɒg (US) -ɑːg, -ɔːg

Ffion 'fiː.ɒn (US) -ɑːn

Ffitch fɪtʃ

Ffoulkes fəʊks, fəʊlks, faʊks, fuːks (US) foʊks, foʊlks, faʊks, fuːks

Ffrangcon 'fræŋ.kᵊn

-fiable -faɪ.ə.bl̩

Note: Suffix. Normally unstressed, e.g. **rectifiable** /'rek.tɪ.faɪ.ə.bl̩ (US) -tə-/, although some words containing **-fiable** may also be stressed on the antepenultimate syllable, especially in British English (e.g. **justifiable** /ˌdʒʌs.tɪ'faɪ.ə.bl̩/); see alsoentry for **-fy**.

fiacre fi'ɑː.krə (US) -kɚ **-s** -z

fiancé(e) fi'ɑ̃ː*n*.seɪ, -'ɒn*t*- (US) ˌfiː.ɑːn'seɪ, -'-- **-s** -z

Fianna Fail, Fianna Fáil ˌfiː.ə.nə'fɔɪl, ˌfiː.nə'-, -'fɔːl (US) -'fɔɪl, -'fiːl

fiasco fi'æs.kəʊ (US) -koʊ **-(e)s** -z

fiat *decree:* 'faɪ.æt (US) 'fiː.ət, -æt, -ɑːt **-s** -s

Fiat® fɪət, 'fiː.æt (US) 'fiː.ɑːt **-s** -s

fiat justicia ˌfiː.æt.jʊs'tɪs.i.ə (US) ˌfiː.ɑːt'jʊs.tɪ.ʃə

fib fɪb **-s** -z **-bing** -ɪŋ **-bed** -d **-ber/s** -əʳ/z (US) -ɚ/z

fiber 'faɪ.bəʳ (US) -bɚ **-s** -z

fiberglass 'faɪ.bə.glɑːs (US) -bɚ.glæs

fiberlike 'faɪ.bə.laɪk (US) -bɚ-

Fibonacci ˌfɪb.ə'nɑː.tʃi, ˌfiː.bə'-

fibre 'faɪ.bəʳ (US) -bɚ **-s** -z **-d** -d **-less** -ləs, -lɪs

fibreglass 'faɪ.bə.glɑːs (US) -bɚ.glæs

fibreoptic ˌfaɪ.bəʳ'ɒp.tɪk (US) -bɚ'ɑːp- **-s** -s

fibre optics ˌfaɪ.bəʳ'ɒp.tɪks (US) -bɚ'ɑːp-

fibriform 'faɪ.brɪ.fɔːm, 'fɪb.rɪ- (US) -fɔːrm

fibril 'faɪ.brɪl, -brəl (US) 'faɪ.brɪl, 'fɪb.rɪl **-s** -s **-lar** -əʳ (US) -ɚ **-lose** -əʊs (US) -oʊs

fibril|late 'faɪ.brɪ|.leɪt, 'fɪb.rɪ-, -rə- (US) 'fɪb.rɪ-, 'faɪ.brɪ- **-lates** -leɪts **-lating** -leɪ.tɪŋ (US) -leɪ.t̬ɪŋ **-lated** -leɪ.tɪd (US) -leɪ.t̬ɪd

fibrillation ˌfaɪ.brɪ'leɪ.ʃᵊn, ˌfɪb.rɪ'-, -rə'- (US) ˌfɪb.rɪ'-, ˌfaɪ.brɪ'- **-s** -z

fibrilliform faɪ'brɪl.ɪ.fɔːm, fɪ- (US) fɪ'-, faɪ'-, -fɔːrm

fibrin 'fɪb.rɪn, 'faɪ.brɪn (US) 'faɪ- **-ous** -əs

fibrinogen fɪ'brɪn.əʊ.dʒᵊn, faɪ-, -dʒen (US) faɪ'brɪn.ə-

fibro- faɪ.brəʊ-; faɪ'brəʊ- (US) faɪ.broʊ-, -brə-; faɪ'broʊ-

Note: Prefix. Normally carries primary or secondary stress on the first syllable, e.g. **fibrositis** /ˌfaɪ.brəʊ'saɪ.tɪs (US) -broʊ'saɪ.t̬ɪs/, or primary stress on the second syllable, e.g. **fibrosis** /faɪ'brəʊ.sɪs (US) -'broʊ-/.

fibroid 'faɪ.brɔɪd **-s** -z

fibroma faɪ'brəʊ.mə (US) -'broʊ- **-s** -z **-ta** -tə (US) -t̬ə

fibrosis faɪ'brəʊ.sɪs (US) -'broʊ-

fibrositis ˌfaɪ.brəʊ'saɪ.tɪs (US) -broʊ'saɪ.t̬ɪs

fibrous 'faɪ.brəs **-ly** -li **-ness** -nəs, -nɪs

fibul|a 'fɪb.jə.l|ə, -jʊ- (US) -jə- **-as** -əz **-ae** -iː

FICA 'fiː.kə (US) 'faɪ-, 'fiː-

fich|e fiːʃ **-es** -ɪz

fichu 'fiː.ʃuː, 'fɪʃ.uː (US) 'fɪʃ.uː; fiː'ʃuː **-s** -z

fickl|e 'fɪk.l̩ **-er** -əʳ, '-ləʳ (US) '-lɚ, -l̩.ɚ **-est** -ɪst, -əst **-eness** -nəs, -nɪs

fiction 'fɪk.ʃᵊn **-s** z

fictional 'fɪk.ʃᵊn.ᵊl **-ly** -i

fictionalization ˌfɪk.ʃᵊn.ᵊl.aɪ'zeɪ.ʃᵊn, -ɪ'- (US) -ɪ'-

fictionaliz|e, -is|e 'fɪk.ʃᵊn.ᵊl.aɪz (US) -ə.laɪz **-es** -ɪz **-ing** -ɪŋ **-ed** -d

fictionist 'fɪk.ʃᵊn.ɪst **-s** -s

fictitious fɪk'tɪʃ.əs **-ly** -li **-ness** -nəs, -nɪs

fictive 'fɪk.tɪv

fid fɪd **-s** -z

fiddl|e 'fɪd.l̩ **-es** -z **-ing** -ɪŋ, '-lɪŋ **-ed** -d **-er/s** -əʳ/z, '-ləʳ/z, '-l̩.ɚ/z (US) '-lɚ/z **as ˌfit as a 'fiddle**

fiddledededee ˌfɪd.l̩.dɪˈdiː US -diːˈdiː

fiddle-faddl|e ˈfɪd.l̩ˌfæd.l̩ **-es** -z **-ing** -ɪŋ, ˌ-lɪŋ **-ed** -d

fiddlesticks ˈfɪd.l̩.stɪks

fiddl|y ˈfɪd.l̩|.i, ˈfɪd.l|i **-ier** -i.əʳ US -i.ɚ **-iest** -i.ɪst, -i.əst **-iness** -ɪ.nəs, -ɪ.nɪs

Fidel fɪˈdel, fiː-, ˈfɪd.el

Fidelia fɪˈdiː.li.ə, fə-, -ˈdeɪ- US -ˈdiː.li.ə, -ˈdiːl.jə

Fidelio fɪˈdeɪ.li.əʊ US -oʊ

fidelity fɪˈdel.ə.ti, fə-, -ɪ.ti US -ə.t̬i

fidg|et ˈfɪdʒ|.ɪt **-ets** -ɪts **-eting** -ɪ.tɪŋ US -ɪ.t̬ɪŋ **-eted** -ɪ.tɪd US -ɪ.t̬ɪd

fidget|y ˈfɪdʒ.ɪ.t|i, ˈ-ə- **-ier** -i.əʳ US -i.ɚ **-iest** -i.ɪst, -i.əst **-iness** -ɪ.nəs, -ɪ.nɪs

Fido ˈfaɪ.dəʊ US -doʊ

fiducial fɪˈdjuː.ʃi.əl, fə-, faɪ-, -si- US -ˈduː.ʃəl, -ˈdjuː- **-ly** -i

fiduciar|y fɪˈdjuː.ʃi.ə.r|i, fə-, faɪ-, -si-, -ʃər|.i US fɪˈduː.ʃi.er-, -ʃər-, -ˈdjuː- **-ies** -iz

fie faɪ

Fiedler ˈfiːd.ləʳ US -lɚ

fief fiːf **-s** -s

fiefdom ˈfiːf.dəm **-s** -z

field (F) ˈfiːld **-s** -z **-ing** -ɪŋ **-ed** -ɪd **-er/s** -əʳ/z US -ɚ/z ˈ**field** ˌ**glass**; ˈ**field** ˌ**goal**; ˈ**field** ˌ**gun**; ˌ**field** ˈ**hospital** US ˈ**field** ˌ**hospital**; ˌ**field** ˈ**marshal** US ˈ**field** ˌ**marshal**; ˈ**field** ˌ**mouse**; ˈ**field** ˌ**officer**; ˌ**field of** ˈ**vision**; ˈ**field** ˌ**trip**; **have a** ˈ**field** ˌ**day**

Fielden ˈfiːl.dən

Fieldener ˈfiːl.dən.əʳ US -ɚ

fielder (F) ˈfiːl.dəʳ US -dɚ **-s** -z

fieldfare ˈfiːld.feəʳ US -fer **-s** -z

Fielding ˈfiːl.dɪŋ

Fields fiːldz

fields|man ˈfiːldz|.mən **-men** -mən, -men

field-test ˈfiːld.test **-s** -s **-ing** -ɪŋ **-ed** -ɪd

fieldwork ˈfiːld.wɜːk US -wɝːk **-s** -s **-er/s** -əʳ/z US -ɚ/z

fiend (F) fiːnd **-s** -z

fiendish ˈfiːn.dɪʃ **-ly** -li **-ness** -nəs, -nɪs

Fiennes faɪnz

fierc|e fɪəs US fɪrs **-er** -əʳ US -ɚ **-est** -ɪst, -əst **-ely** -li **-eness** -nəs, -nɪs

fier|y ˈfaɪə.r|i US ˈfaɪ-, ˈfaɪɚ|.i **-ier** -i.əʳ US -i.ɚ **-iest** -i.ɪst, -i.əst **-ily** -ɪ.li, -əl.i **-iness** -ɪ.nəs, -ɪ.nɪs

fiesta® (F) fiˈes.tə **-s** -z

FIFA, Fifa ˈfiː.fə

fif|e (F) faɪf **-es** -s **-ing** -ɪŋ **-ed** -t **-er/s** -əʳ/z US -ɚ/z

Fife faɪf **-shire** -ʃəʳ, -ˌʃɪəʳ US -ʃɚ, -ʃɪr

Fifi ˈfiː.fiː

Fifield ˈfaɪ.fiːld

fifteen ˌfɪfˈtiːn **-s** -z **-th/s** -θ/s *stress shift:* ˌfifteen ˈyears

fifth fɪfθ **-s** -s **-ly** -li ˌ**Fifth A**ˈ**mendment**; ˌ**Fifth** ˈ**Avenue**

fifth-column ˌfɪfθˈkɒl.əm US -ˈkɑː.ləm **-ist/s** -ɪst/s, -nɪst/s **-ism** -ɪ.zəm, -nɪ.zəm

fiftieth ˈfɪf.ti.əθ **-s** -s

fift|y ˈfɪf.t|i **-ies** -iz

fifty-fifty ˌfɪf.tiˈfɪf.ti

fiftyfold ˈfɪf.ti.fəʊld US -foʊld

fig fɪg **-s** -z ˈ**fig** ˌ**leaf**; ˈ**fig** ˌ**tree**

Figaro ˈfɪg.ə.rəʊ US -roʊ

Figes ˈfɪg.ɪs

Figg fɪg

Figgis ˈfɪg.ɪs

fight faɪt **-s** -s **-ing** -ɪŋ US ˈfaɪ.t̬ɪŋ **fought** fɔːt US fɑːt, fɔːt ˈ**fighting** ˌ**cock**

fightback ˈfaɪt.bæk **-s** -s

fighter ˈfaɪ.təʳ US -t̬ɚ **-s** -z

figment ˈfɪg.mənt **-s** -s

Figo ˈfiː.gəʊ US -goʊ

Figueroa ˌfɪg.əˈrəʊ.ə US -ˈroʊ-

figurability ˌfɪg.jər.əˈbɪl.ə.ti, -ər-, -jʊ.rəˈ-, -ɪ.ti US -jɚ.əˈbɪl.ə.t̬i, -jʊ.rəˈ-

figurable ˈfɪg.jər.ə.bl̩, -ər-, -jʊ.rə- US -jɚ.ə-, -jʊ.rə-

figurative ˈfɪg.jər.ə.tɪv, -ər-, -jʊ.rə- US -jɚ.ə.t̬ɪv, -jʊ.rə- **-ly** -li **-ness** -nəs, -nɪs

figur|e ˈfɪg.əʳ US -jɚ, -jʊr **-es** -z **-ing** -ɪŋ **-ed** -d ˌ**figure** ˈ**eight**; ˌ**figure of** ˈ**eight**; ˌ**figure of** ˈ**speech**; ˈ**figure** ˌ**skating**

figurehead ˈfɪg.ə.hed US -jɚ- **-s** -z

figurine ˈfɪg.jə.riːn, ˈ-ə-, -jʊ-, ˌ--ˈ- US ˌfɪg.juːˈriːn, -jəˈ- **-s** -z

Fiji ˈfiː.dʒiː, -ˈ- US ˈ--

Fijian fɪˈdʒiː.ən, fiː- US ˈfiː.dʒiː-, -ˈ-- **-s** -z

filament ˈfɪl.ə.mənt **-s** -s

filamentous ˌfɪl.əˈmen.təs

filari|a fɪˈleə.ri|.ə US -ˈler.i- **-ae** -iː **-al** -əl

filarias|is ˌfɪl.əˈraɪə.s|ɪs; fɪˌleə.riˈeɪ-, fə- US ˌfɪl.əˈraɪ.ə.s|ɪs **-es** -iːz

filature ˈfɪl.ə.tʃəʳ, -tjəʳ US -tʃɚ **-s** -z

filbert ˈfɪl.bət US -bɚt **-s** -s

filch fɪltʃ **-es** -ɪz **-ing** -ɪŋ **-ed** -t

Fildes faɪldz

fil|e faɪl **-es** -z **-ing/s** -ɪŋ/z **-ed** -d ˈ**filing** ˌ**clerk**

filemot ˈfɪl.ɪ.mɒt US -mɑːt

filet ˈfɪl.eɪ, ˈfiː.leɪ US fɪˈleɪ, ˈfɪl.eɪ **-s** -z **-(t)ing** -ɪŋ **-(t)ed** -d

filet(s) mignon(s) ˌfɪl.eɪˈmiː.njɔ̃ːŋ, ˌfiː.leɪ-, -ˈmɪn.jɒn US ˌfɪl.eɪ.miːˈnjɑːn, -ˈnjoʊn; fɪˌleɪ-

Filey ˈfaɪ.li

filial ˈfɪl.i.əl **-ly** -i **-ness** -nəs, -nɪs

filiation ˌfɪl.iˈeɪ.ʃən

filibeg ˈfɪl.ɪ.beg, ˈ-ə- **-s** -z

filibust|er ˈfɪl.ɪ.bʌs.t|əʳ, ˈ-ə- US -t|ɚ **-ers** -əz US -ɚz **-ering** -ər.ɪŋ **-ered** -əd US -ɚd

filigree ˈfɪl.ɪ.griː, ˈ-ə- **-s** -z **-ing** -ɪŋ **-d** -d

filing ˈfaɪ.lɪŋ **-s** -z ˈ**filing** ˌ**cabinet**

Filioque ˌfiː.liˈəʊ.kwi, ˌfaɪ-, ˌfɪl.iˈ- US -ˈoʊ-

Filipino ˌfɪl.ɪˈpiː.nəʊ, -əˈ- US -noʊ **-s** -z

Filkin ˈfɪl.kɪn **-s** -z

fill fɪl **-s** -z **-ing/s** -ɪŋ/z **-ed** -d ˈ**filling** ˌ**station**; ˌ**fill the** ˈ**bill**

filler *thing or person that fills:* ˈfɪl.əʳ US -ɚ **-s** -z

filler, fillér *Hungarian currency:* ˈfiː.leəʳ US ˈfɪl.er, ˈfiː.ler **-s** -z

fill|et ˈfɪl|.ɪt **-ets** -ɪts **-eting** -ɪ.tɪŋ US -ɪ.t̬ɪŋ **-eted** -ɪ.tɪd US -ɪ.t̬ɪd

fillibeg ˈfɪl.ɪ.beg, ˈ-ə- **-s** -z

fillip ˈfɪl.ɪp **-s** -s **-ing** -ɪŋ **-ed** -t

Fillmore ˈfɪl.mɔːʳ US -mɔːr

fill|y ˈfɪl|.i **-ies** -iz

film fɪlm **-s** -z **-ing** -ɪŋ **-ed** -d ˈ**film** ˌ**star**

filmgoer ˈfɪlmˌgəʊ.əʳ US -ˌgoʊ.ɚ **-s** -z

filmgoing ˈfɪlmˌgəʊ.ɪŋ US -ˌgoʊ-

filmic ˈfɪl.mɪk

filmmaker ˈfɪlmˌmeɪ.kəʳ US -kɚ **-s** -z

film(s) noir(s) ˌfɪlmˈnwɑː, -ˈnwɑːr

film|set ˈfɪlm|.set **-sets** -sets **-setting** -ˌset.ɪŋ US -ˌset̬.ɪŋ

filmstrip ˈfɪlm.strɪp **-s** -s

film|y ˈfɪl.m|i **-ier** -i.əʳ US -i.ɚ **-iest** -i.ɪst, -i.əst **-ily** -ɪ.li, -əl.i **-iness** -ɪ.nəs, -ɪ.nɪs

filo ˈfaɪ.ləʊ, ˈfiː-, ˈfɪl.əʊ US ˈfiː.loʊ, ˈfaɪ- ˌ**filo** ˈ**pastry** US ˈ**filo** ˌ**pastry**

Filofax® ˈfaɪ.ləʊ.fæks US -loʊ-, -lə- **-es** -ɪz

Filon ˈfaɪ.lən, -lɒn US ˌfiːˈlɑːn

fils *son:* fiːs

fils *monetary unit:* fɪls

filt|er *(n. v.)* ˈfɪl.t|əʳ US -t̬|ɚ **-ers** -əz US -ɚz **-ering** -ər.ɪŋ **-ered** -əd US -ɚd ˈ**filter** ˌ**coffee**; ˈ**filter** ˌ**paper**; ˈ**filter** ˌ**tip**

filth fɪlθ

filth|y ˈfɪl.θ|i **-ier** -i.əʳ US -i.ɚ **-iest** -i.ɪst, -i.əst **-ily** -ɪ.li, -əl.i **-iness** -ɪ.nəs, -ɪ.nəs

filtrate *(n.)* ˈfɪl.treɪt **-s** -s

fil|trate *(v.)* fɪl|ˈtreɪt US ˈ-- **-trates** -ˈtreɪts US -treɪts **-trating** -ˈtreɪ.tɪŋ US -treɪ.t̬ɪŋ **-trated** -ˈtreɪ.tɪd US -treɪ.t̬ɪd

filtration fɪlˈtreɪ.ʃən **-s** -z

FIMBRA ˈfɪm.brə

fin fɪn **-s** -z

Fina® ˈfiː.nə, ˈfaɪ

finable ˈfaɪ.nə.bl̩

finagl|e fɪˈneɪ.gl̩ **-es** -z **-ing** -ɪŋ, ˈ-glɪŋ **-ed** -d **-er/s** -əʳ/z, ˈ-gləʳ/z US ˈ-ɚ/z, ˈ-glɚ/z

final ˈfaɪ.nəl **-s** -z **-ly** -i

finale fɪˈnɑː.li, fə-, -leɪ US -ˈnæl.i, -ˈnɑː.leɪ, -li **-s** -z

finalist ˈfaɪ.nəl.ɪst **-s** -s

finality faɪˈnæl.ə.ti, -ɪ.ti US faɪˈnæl.ə.t̬i, fə-

finaliz|e, -is|e ˈfaɪ.nᵊl.aɪz US -nə.laɪz **-es** -ɪz **-ing** -ɪŋ **-ed** -d
financ|e ˈfaɪ.nænts; faɪˈnænts, fɪ-, fə- **-es** -ɪz **-ing** -ɪŋ **-ed** -t
financial faɪˈnæn.tʃᵊl, fɪ-, fə- US -ˈnænt.ʃᵊl **-ly** -i **Fiˌnancial ˈTimes**
financier faɪˈnænt.si.əʳ, fɪ-, fə- US fɪˈnænt.si.ɚ, fə-; ˌfɪn.ənˈsɪr, ˌfaɪ.nænˈ-, -nənˈ- **-s** -z
Finbar ˈfɪn.bɑːʳ, ˈfɪm- US ˈfɪn.bɑːr
finch (F) fɪntʃ **-es** -ɪz
Finchale ˈfɪŋ.kᵊl
Fincham ˈfɪn.tʃəm
Finchampsted ˈfɪn.tʃəm.sted, -tʃəmp-, -stɪd
Finchley ˈfɪntʃ.li
find faɪnd **-s** -z **-ing/s** -ɪŋ/z **found** faʊnd **finder/s** ˈfaɪn.dəʳ/z US -dɚ/z
fin de siècle ˌfæ̃n.dəˈsjek.l̩, ˌfæn-, -siˈek-, -lə US ˌfæ̃n.də.siˈek.lə, -ˈsjek-, -l̩
Findlater ˈfɪnd.lə.təʳ, -leɪ.təʳ US -t̬ɚ
Findlay ˈfɪnd.leɪ, -li
Findley ˈfɪnd.li
Findus ˈfɪn.dəs
fin|e faɪn **-es** -z **-er** -əʳ US -ɚ **-est** -ɪst, -əst **-eness** -nəs, -nɪs **-ing** -ɪŋ **-ed** -d **ˌfine ˈart; ˈfine ˌprint, ˌfine ˈprint**
finely ˈfaɪn.li
finery ˈfaɪ.nᵊr.i
fines herbes ˌfiːnˈeəb, -ˈɜːb US ˌfiːnˈzerb
finespun ˌfaɪnˈspʌn US ˈ-- *stress shift, British only:* ˌfinespun ˈyarn
finess|e (*n. v.*) fɪˈnes, fə- **-es** -ɪz **-ing** -ɪŋ **-ed** -t
fine-tooth ˌfaɪnˈtuːθ **-ed** -t **ˌfine-toothed ˈcomb**
fine-tun|e ˌfaɪnˈtjuːn, -ˈtʃuːn US -ˈtuːn, -ˈtjuːn **-es** -z **-ing** -ɪŋ **-ed** -d *stress shift:* ˌfine-tuned ˈinstrument
Fingal ˈfɪŋ.gᵊl **ˌFingal's ˈCave**
Fingall ˈfɪŋ.gɔːl US -gɔːl, -gɑːl
fing|er ˈfɪŋ.g|əʳ US -g|ɚ **-ers** -əz US -ɚz **-ering/s** -ᵊr.ɪŋ/z **-ered** -əd US -ɚd **ˈfinger ˌbowl; ˈFinger ˌLakes; ˌburn one's ˈfingers; ˌall ˌfingers and ˈthumbs; have a ˌfinger in every ˈpie; keep one's ˈfingers ˌcrossed; ˌtwist someone round one's ˌlittle ˈfinger; ˌwork one's ˌfingers to the ˈbone**
fingerboard ˈfɪŋ.gə.bɔːd US -gɚ.bɔːrd **-s** -z
fingermark ˈfɪŋ.gə.mɑːk US -gɚ.mɑːrk **-s** -s
fingernail ˈfɪŋ.gə.neɪl US -gɚ- **-s** -z
fingerplate ˈfɪŋ.gə.pleɪt US -gɚ- **-s** -s
fingerpost ˈfɪŋ.gə.pəʊst US -gɚ.poʊst **-s** -s
fingerprint ˈfɪŋ.gə.prɪnt US -gɚ- **-s** -s **-ing** -ɪŋ
fingerstall ˈfɪŋ.gə.stɔːl US -gɚ.stɔːl, -stɑːl **-s** -z
fingertip ˈfɪŋ.gə.tɪp US -gɚ- **-s** -s
Fingest ˈfɪn.dʒɪst
finial ˈfɪn.i.əl, ˈfaɪ.ni- US ˈfɪn.i- **-s** -z
finical ˈfɪn.ɪ.kᵊl **-ly** -i **-ness** -nəs, -nɪs
finicking ˈfɪn.ɪ.kɪŋ
finick|y ˈfɪn.ɪ.k|i **-ier** -i.əʳ US -i.ɚ **-iest** -i.ɪst, -i.əst **-ily** -ɪ.li, -ᵊl.i **-iness** -ɪ.nəs, -ɪ.nɪs
finis ˈfɪn.ɪs, ˈfiː.nɪs US ˈfɪn.ɪs; fiːˈniː; ˈfaɪ.nɪs
finish ˈfɪn.ɪʃ **-es** -ɪz **-ing** -ɪŋ **-ed** -t **-er/s** -əʳ/z US -ɚ/z **ˈfinishing ˌschool**
Finisterre ˌfɪn.ɪˈsteəʳ, -əˈ-, ˈ--- US ˌfɪn.ɪˈster
finite ˈfaɪ.naɪt **-ly** -li **-ness** -nəs, -nɪs
finito fɪˈniː.təʊ, fə- US -toʊ
finitude ˈfaɪ.nɪ.tjuːd, ˈfɪn.ɪ-, -tʃuːd US ˈfɪn.ɪ.tuːd, -tjuːd
fink fɪŋk **-s** -s **-ing** -ɪŋ **-ed** -t
Finlaison ˈfɪn.lɪ.sᵊn
Finland ˈfɪn.lənd **-er/s** -əʳ/z US -ɚ/z
Finlandization, -isa- ˌfɪn.lən.daɪˈzeɪ.ʃᵊn, -dɪˈ- US -dɪˈ-
Finlandiz|e, -is|e ˈfɪn.lən.daɪz **-es** -ɪz **-ing** -ɪŋ **-ed** -d
Finlay ˈfɪn.leɪ, -li
Finlayson ˈfɪn.lɪ.sᵊn
Finley ˈfɪn.li
Finn fɪn **-s** -z
Finnan ˈfɪn.ən
Finnegan ˈfɪn.ɪ.gən, ˈ-ə-
Finney ˈfɪn.i
Finnic ˈfɪn.ɪk
Finnie ˈfɪn.i
Finnish ˈfɪn.ɪʃ
Finnon ˈfɪn.ən
Finno-Ugrian ˌfɪn.əʊˈjuː.gri.ən US -oʊˈuː-, -ˈjuː-
Finno-Ugric ˌfɪn.əʊˈjuː.grɪk US -oʊˈuː-, -ˈjuː-
fino ˈfiː.nəʊ US -noʊ **-s** -z
Finsberg ˈfɪnz.bɜːg US -bɝːg
Finsbury ˈfɪnz.bᵊr.i US -ˌber-, -bɚ- **ˌFinsbury ˈPark**
Finucane fɪˈnuː.kᵊn, fə-, fɪn.əˈkeɪn
Finzi ˈfɪn.zi
Fiona fiˈəʊ.nə US -ˈoʊ-
fiord fjɔːd; fiˈɔːd; ˈfiː.ɔːd US fjɔːrd; fiˈɔːrd **-s** -z
fiorin ˈfaɪə.rɪn US ˈfaɪɚ.ɪn
Fiorino® ˌfiː.ɔːˈriː.nəʊ US -noʊ
fioritur|a ˌfjɔː.riˈtjʊə.r|ə, ˌfiː.ə.riˈ- US ˌfjɔː.riːˈtuː.r|ɑː **-e** -eɪ
fir fɜːʳ US fɝː **-s** -z **ˈfir ˌtree**
Firbank ˈfɜː.bæŋk US ˈfɝː-
fir|e faɪəʳ US faɪɚ **-es** -z **-ing** -ɪŋ **-ed** -d **-er/s** -əʳ/z US -ɚ/z **ˈfire aˌlarm; ˈfire briˌgade; ˈfire conˌtrol; ˈfire deˌpartment; ˈfire ˌdrill; ˈfire ˌengine; ˈfire esˌcape; ˈfire exˌtinguisher; ˈfire ˌfighter; ˈfire ˌhydrant; ˈfire ˌiron; ˈfire ˌscreen; ˌout of the ˌfrying pan ˌinto the ˈfire**
firearm ˈfaɪəʳ.ɑːm US ˈfaɪɚ.ɑːrm **-s** -z
fireball ˈfaɪə.bɔːl US ˈfaɪɚ.bɔːl, -bɑːl **-s** -z
firebomb ˈfaɪə.bɒm US ˈfaɪɚ.bɑːm **-s** -z **-ing** -ɪŋ **-ed** -d
firebox ˈfaɪə.bɒks US ˈfaɪɚ.bɑːks **-es** -ɪz
firebrand ˈfaɪə.brænd US ˈfaɪɚ- **-s** -z
firebreak ˈfaɪə.breɪk US ˈfaɪɚ- **-s** -s
firebrick ˈfaɪə.brɪk US ˈfaɪɚ- **-s** -s
firebug ˈfaɪə.bʌg US ˈfaɪɚ- **-s** -z
fireclay ˈfaɪə.kleɪ US ˈfaɪɚ-
firecracker ˈfaɪəˌkræk.əʳ US ˈfaɪɚˌkræk.ɚ **-s** -z
firecrest ˈfaɪə.krest US ˈfaɪɚ- **-s** -s
firedamp ˈfaɪə.dæmp US ˈfaɪɚ-
firedog ˈfaɪə.dɒg US ˈfaɪɚ.dɑːg, -dɔːg **-s** -z
fire-eat|er ˈfaɪəʳˌiː.t|əʳ US ˈfaɪɚˌiː.t̬|ɚ **-ers** -əz US -ɚz **-ing** -ɪŋ
firefighter ˈfaɪəˌfaɪ.təʳ US ˈfaɪɚˌfaɪ.t̬ɚ **-s** -z
firefl|y ˈfaɪə.fl|aɪ US ˈfaɪɚ- **-ies** -aɪz
fireguard ˈfaɪə.gɑːd US ˈfaɪɚ.gɑːrd **-s** -z
firehou|se ˈfaɪə.haʊ|s US ˈfaɪɚ- **-ses** -zɪz
fire|light ˈfaɪə|.laɪt US ˈfaɪɚ- **-lighter/s** -ˌlaɪ.təʳ/z US -ˌlaɪ.t̬ɚ/z
firelock ˈfaɪə.lɒk US ˈfaɪɚ.lɑːk **-s** -s
fire|man ˈfaɪə|.mən US ˈfaɪɚ- **-men** -mən, -men
fireplac|e ˈfaɪə.pleɪs US ˈfaɪɚ- **-es** -ɪz
fireplug ˈfaɪə.plʌg US ˈfaɪɚ- **-s** -z
firepower ˈfaɪəˌpaʊəʳ US ˈfaɪɚˌpaʊɚ
fireproof ˈfaɪə.pruːf US ˈfaɪɚ-
fireship ˈfaɪə.ʃɪp US ˈfaɪɚ- **-s** -s
fireside ˈfaɪə.saɪd US ˈfaɪɚ- **-s** -z
firestone ˈfaɪə.stəʊn US ˈfaɪɚ.stoʊn
firestorm ˈfaɪə.stɔːm US ˈfaɪɚ.stɔːrm **-s** -z
firetrail ˈfaɪə.treɪl US ˈfaɪɚ- **-s** -z
firetrap ˈfaɪə.træp US ˈfaɪɚ- **-s** -s
firewall ˈfaɪə.wɔːl US ˈfaɪɚ-, -wɑːl **-s** -z
firewarden ˈfaɪəˌwɔː.dᵊn US ˈfaɪɚˌwɔːr- **-s** -z
firewater ˈfaɪəˌwɔː.təʳ US ˈfaɪɚˌwɑː.t̬ɚ, -ˌwɔː-
firewood ˈfaɪə.wʊd US ˈfaɪɚ-
firework ˈfaɪə.wɜːk US ˈfaɪɚ.wɝːk **-s** -s
firing ˈfaɪə.rɪŋ US ˈfaɪɚ.ɪŋ **ˈfiring ˌline; ˈfiring ˌparty; ˈfiring ˌsquad**
firkin ˈfɜː.kɪn US ˈfɝː- **-s** -z
firm fɜːm US fɝːm **-s** -z **-er** -əʳ US -ɚ **-est** -ɪst, -əst **-ing** -ɪŋ **-ed** -d **-ly** -li **-ness** -nəs, -nɪs
firmament ˈfɜː.mə.mənt US ˈfɝː- **-s** -s
firmware ˈfɜːm.weəʳ US ˈfɝːm.wer

Firsby ˈfɜːz.bi (US) ˈfɝːz-

first ˈfɜːst (US) ˈfɝːst **-s** -s **-ly** -li ˌ**first ˈaid;** ˌ**first ˈbase;** ˌ**first ˈclass;** ˌ**first ˈfloor;** ˌ**first ˈlady;** ˌ**First** ˌ**World ˈWar**

first base ˌfɜːstˈbeɪs (US) ˌfɝːst-

firstborn ˈfɜːst.bɔːn (US) ˈfɝːst.bɔːrn

first-degree ˌfɜːst.dɪˈgriː, -dəˈ- (US) ˌfɝːst.dɪˈ- *stress shift, see compound:* ˌ**first-degree ˈmurder**

firstfruits ˈfɜːst.fruːts (US) ˈfɝːst-

firsthand ˌfɜːstˈhænd (US) ˌfɝːst- *stress shift:* ˌfirsthand acˈcount

firstling ˈfɜːst.lɪŋ (US) ˈfɝːst- **-s** -z

firstly ˈfɜːst.li (US) ˈfɝːst-

first-past-the-post ˌfɜːstˌpɑːst.ðəˈpəʊst (US) ˌfɝːstˌpæst.ðəˈpoʊst *stress shift:* ˌfirst-past-the-post ˈsystem

first-rate ˌfɜːstˈreɪt (US) ˌfɝːst- *stress shift:* ˌfirst-rate ˈgame

first-time ˌfɜːstˈtaɪm (US) ˌfɝːst- *stress shift, see compound:* ˌ**first-time ˈbuyer**

firth (F) fɜːθ (US) fɝːθ **-s** -s

fisc fɪsk

fiscal ˈfɪs.kəl **-s** -z

Fischer ˈfɪʃ.əʳ (US) -ɚ

Fischler ˈfɪʃ.ləʳ (US) -lɚ

fish (F) fɪʃ **-es** -ɪz **-ing** -ɪŋ **-ed** -t ˌ**fish and ˈchips;** ˌ**fish ˈfinger;** ˈ**fishing** ˌ**rod;** ˈ**fishing** ˌ**tackle;** ˈ**fish** ˌ**knife;** ˈ**fish** ˌ**slice;** ˈ**fish** ˌ**stick; have** ˌ**other ˈfish to** ˌ**fry; like a** ˌ**fish out of ˈwater; a ˈpretty** ˌ**kettle of** ˌ**fish**

fishbone ˈfɪʃ.bəʊn (US) -boʊn **-s** -z

fishbowl ˈfɪʃ.bəʊl (US) -boʊl **-s** -z

fishcake ˈfɪʃ.keɪk **-s** -s

fisher (F) ˈfɪʃ.əʳ (US) -ɚ **-s** -z

fisher|man ˈfɪʃ.ə|.mən (US) ˈ-ɚ- **-men** -mən, -men

fisher|y ˈfɪʃ.ər|.i **-ies** -iz

fisheye ˈfɪʃ.aɪ ˌ**fisheye ˈlens**

Fishguard ˈfɪʃ.gɑːd (US) -gɑːrd

fishhook ˈfɪʃ.hʊk (US) -hʊk **-s** -s

Fishkill ˈfɪʃ.kɪl

fishmonger ˈfɪʃˌmʌŋ.gəʳ (US) -ˌmʌŋ.gɚ, -ˌmɑːŋ- **-s** -z

fish 'n' chips ˌfɪʃ.ənˈtʃɪps

fishnet ˈfɪʃ.net **-s** -s ˌ**fishnet ˈstockings**

fishplate ˈfɪʃ.pleɪt **-s** -s

fishpond ˈfɪʃ.pɒnd (US) -pɑːnd **-s** -z

fishtail ˈfɪʃ.teɪl **-s** -z **-ing** -ɪŋ **-ed** -d

fishtank ˈfɪʃ.tæŋk **-s** -s

Fishwick ˈfɪʃ.wɪk

fish|wife ˈfɪʃ|.waɪf **-wives** -waɪvz

fish|y ˈfɪʃ|.i **-ier** -i.əʳ (US) -i.ɚ **-iest** -i.ɪst, -i.əst **-ily** -ɪ.li, -əl.i **-iness** -ɪ.nəs, -ɪ.nɪs

Fisk(e) fɪsk

Fison ˈfaɪ.sən

fissile ˈfɪs.aɪl (US) -ɪl

fission ˈfɪʃ.ən (US) ˈfɪʃ-, ˈfɪʒ- **-s** -z **-al** -əl

fissionable ˈfɪʃ.ən.ə.bl̩ (US) ˈfɪʃ-, ˈfɪʒ-

fissiparous fɪˈsɪp.ər.əs, fə-

fiss|ure ˈfɪʃ|.əʳ, -ʊəʳ (US) -ɚ **-ures** -əz (US) -ɚz **-uring** -ər.ɪŋ **-ured** -əd (US) -ɚd

fist fɪst **-s** -s **-ing** -ɪŋ **-ed** -ɪd **-ic** -ɪk

fistfight ˈfɪst.faɪt **-s** -s

fistful ˈfɪst.fʊl **-s** -z

fisticuffs ˈfɪs.tɪ.kʌfs

fistul|a ˈfɪs.tjə.l|ə, -tjʊ-, -tʃə-, -tʃʊ- (US) -tjə-, -tʃuː- **-as** -əz **-ae** -iː **-ous** -əs

fit fɪt **-s** -s **-ting/ly** -ɪŋ/li (US) ˈfɪt̬.ɪŋ/li **-ted** -ɪd (US) ˈfɪt̬.ɪd **-ter/s** -əʳ/z (US) ˈfɪt̬.ɚ/z **-test** -ɪst (US) ˈfɪt̬.ɪst, -əst **-ly** -li ˌ**fitted ˈkitchen;** ˈ**fitting** ˌ**room; as** ˌ**fit as a ˈfiddle**

fitch (F) fɪtʃ **-es** -ɪz

Fitchburg ˈfɪtʃ.bɜːg (US) -bɝːg

fitchew ˈfɪtʃ.uː **-s** -z

fitful ˈfɪt.fəl, -fʊl **-ly** -i **-ness** -nəs, -nɪs

fitment ˈfɪt.mənt **-s** -s

fitness ˈfɪt.nəs, -nɪs

fitt fɪt **-s** -s

Fitzalan fɪtsˈæl.ən

Fitzcharles fɪtsˈtʃɑːlz (US) -ˈtʃɑːrlz

Fitzclarence fɪtsˈklær.ənts (US) -ˈkler-, -ˈklær-

Fitzgeorge fɪtsˈdʒɔːdʒ (US) -ˈdʒɔːrdʒ

Fitzgerald, FitzGerald fɪtsˈdʒer.əld

Fitzgibbon fɪtsˈgɪb.ən

Fitzhardinge fɪtsˈhɑː.dɪŋ (US) -ˈhɑːr-

Fitzharris fɪtsˈhær.ɪs (US) -ˈher-, -ˈhær-

Fitzherbert fɪtsˈhɜː.bət (US) -ˈhɝː.bɚt

Fitzhugh fɪtsˈhjuː

Fitzjames fɪtsˈdʒeɪmz

Note: In **James Fitzjames** often /ˈfɪts.dʒeɪmz/.

Fitzjohn fɪtsˈdʒɒn (US) -ˈdʒɑːn

Fitzmaurice fɪtsˈmɒr.ɪs (US) -ˈmɑːr-, -ˈmɔːr-

Fitzpatrick fɪtsˈpæt.rɪk

Fitzroy *surname:* fɪtsˈrɔɪ, ˈ-- *square and street in London:* ˈfɪts.rɔɪ

Fitzsimmons fɪtsˈsɪm.ənz

Fitzstephen fɪtsˈstiː.vən

Fitzwalter fɪtsˈwɔːl.təʳ, -ˈwɒl- (US) -ˈwɔːl.t̬ɚ, -ˈwɑːl-

Fitzwilliam fɪtsˈwɪl.jəm, ˈ-i.əm (US) ˈ-jəm

five faɪv **-s** -z **-fold** -fəʊld (US) -foʊld

five-and-dime ˌfaɪv.əndˈdaɪm **-s** -z

fivepen|ce ˈfaɪf.pənt|s, ˈfaɪv- **-ces** -sɪz

fivepenny ˈfaɪv.pən.i

fiver ˈfaɪ.vəʳ (US) -vɚ **-s** -z

fix fɪks **-es** -ɪz **-ing** -ɪŋ **-ed** -t **-edness** -ɪd.nəs, -nɪs **-er/s** -əʳ/z (US) -ɚ/z

fixable ˈfɪk.sə.bl̩

fixa|te fɪkˈseɪ|t (US) ˈ-- **-tes** -ts **-ting** -tɪŋ (US) -t̬ɪŋ **-ted** -tɪd (US) -t̬ɪd

fixation fɪkˈseɪ.ʃən **-s** -z

fixative ˈfɪk.sə.tɪv (US) -t̬ɪv **-s** -z

fixedly ˈfɪk.sɪd.li, -səd-

fixit|y ˈfɪk.sə.t|i, -ɪ.t|i (US) -ə.t̬|i **-ies** -iz

fixture ˈfɪks.tʃəʳ (US) -tʃɚ **-s** -z

fizz fɪz **-es** -ɪz **-ing** -ɪŋ **-ed** -d **-er/s** -əʳ/z (US) -ɚ/z

fizzl|e ˈfɪz.l̩ **-es** -z **-ing** -ɪŋ, ˈ-lɪŋ **-ed** -d

fizz|y ˈfɪz|.i **-ier** -i.əʳ (US) -i.ɚ **-iest** -i.ɪst, -i.əst **-iness** -ɪ.nəs, -ɪ.nɪs

fjord fjɔːd; fiˈɔːd; ˈfiː.ɔːd (US) fjɔːrd **-s** -z

Fla. *(abbrev. for* **Florida***)* ˈflɒr.ɪ.də (US) ˈflɔːr-, ˈflɑːr-

flab flæb

flabbergast ˈflæb.ə.gɑːst (US) -ɚ.gæst **-s** -s **-ing** -ɪŋ **-ed** -ɪd

flabb|y ˈflæb|.i **-ier** -i.əʳ (US) -i.ɚ **-iest** -i.ɪst, -i.əst **-ily** -ɪ.li, -əl.i **-iness** -ɪ.nəs, -ɪ.nɪs

flaccid ˈflæk.sɪd, ˈflæs.ɪd **-ly** -li **-ness** -nəs, -nɪs

flaccidity flækˈsɪd.ə.ti, flæsˈɪd-, -ɪ.ti (US) -ə.t̬i

flack (F) flæk **-s** -s

Flackwell ˈflæk.wel, -wəl

flag flæg **-s** -z **-ging** -ɪŋ **-ged** -d ˈ**flag** ˌ**day;** ˈ**flag** ˌ**officer**

flagellant ˈflædʒ.əl.ənt, -ɪ.lənt; fləˈdʒel.ənt, flædʒˈel- (US) ˈflædʒ.əl.ənt, -ɪ.lənt; fləˈdʒel.ənt **-s** -s

flagellate *(n, adj.)* ˈflædʒ.əl.ət, -ɪ.lət, -ɪt, -eɪt (US) ˈflædʒ.əl.eɪt, -ɪt; fləˈdʒel.ɪt **-s** -s

flagell|ate *(v.)* ˈflædʒ.əl|.eɪt, ˈ-ɪ- (US) -ə.l|eɪt **-ates** -eɪts **-ating** -eɪ.tɪŋ (US) -eɪ.t̬ɪŋ **-ated** -eɪ.tɪd (US) -eɪ.t̬ɪd **-ator/s** -eɪ.təʳ/z (US) -eɪ.t̬ɚ/z

flagellation ˌflædʒ.əˈleɪ.ʃən, -ɪˈ- **-s** -z

flagell|um fləˈdʒel|.əm, flædʒˈel- (US) fləˈdʒel- **-ums** -əmz **-a** -ə

flageolet ˌflæd.ʒəʊˈlet, -ˈleɪ, ˈ--- (US) ˌflædʒ.əˈlet, -ˈleɪ **-s** -s

Flagg flæg

flag|man ˈflæg|.mən, -mæn **-men** -mən, -men

flagon ˈflæg.ən **-s** -z

flagpole ˈflæg.pəʊl (US) -poʊl **-s** -z

flagrancy ˈfleɪ.grənt.si

flagrant ˈfleɪ.grənt **-ly** -li

flagrante delicto fləˌgræn.teɪ.dɪˈlɪk.təʊ, flægˌræn-, -ti-, -dəˈ-, -deɪˈ- (US) fləˌgræn.ti.diːˈlɪk.toʊ

flagship ˈflæg.ʃɪp **-s** -s

flagstaff ˈflæg.stɑːf (US) -stæf **-s** -s

flagstone ˈflæg.stəʊn (US) -stoʊn **-s** -z

flag-waving ˈflægˌweɪ.vɪŋ

Flaherty ˈfleə.ti, ˈflɑː.hə.ti, ˈflæ.hə.ti (US) ˈflæ.ɚ.t̬i, ˈflɑː-; ˈfler.ə-

flail fleɪl **-s** -z **-ing** -ɪŋ **-ed** -d

flair fleəʳ (US) fler **-s** -z

flak flæk

flak|e fleɪk **-es** -s **-ing** -ɪŋ **-ed** -t ˌ**flake ˈwhite**

Flap

A type of consonant sound that is closely similar to the TAP. It is usually voiced, and is produced by slightly curling back the tip of the tongue, then throwing it forward and allowing it to strike the alveolar ridge as it descends. The phonetic symbol for the sound is [ɽ]

Examples in English

This sound, although occurring in some accents of English, is not a PHONEME, and is uncommon in British English. It appears, however, in US English, where it is sometimes heard in words like *party* and *birdie*, where the /r/ consonant causes retroflexion of the tongue and the stress pattern favours a flap-like articulation, e.g.:

party	/ˈpɑː.ti/	(US) /ˈpɑːr.t̬i/ [ˈpʰɑːɻ.ɽti]
birdie	/ˈbɜː.di/	(US) /ˈbɝː.di/ [ˈb̥ɝː.ɽi]

In other languages

A flap is most commonly heard in languages which have other RETROFLEX consonants, such as languages of the Indian sub-continent; it is also heard in the English of native speakers of such languages, often as a realisation of /r/.

flak|y ˈfleɪ.k|i **-ily** -ɪ.li, -əl.i **-iness** -ɪ.nəs, -ɪ.nɪs ˌ**flaky** ˈ**pastry**
flam flæm **-s** -z
Flambard ˈflæm.bɑːd, -bəd (US) -bɑːrd, -bɚd
flambé, flambe ˈflɑ̃ːm.beɪ (US) flɑːmˈbeɪ **-s** -z **-ing** -ɪŋ **-ed** -d
flambeau (F) ˈflæm.bəʊ (US) -boʊ **-s** -z
flambée, flambee ˈflɑ̃ːm.beɪ (US) flɑːmˈbeɪ **-d** -d
Flamborough ˈflæm.bər.ə (US) -oʊ
flamboyance flæmˈbɔɪ.ənts
flamboyant flæmˈbɔɪ.ənt **-ly** -li
flam|e fleɪm **-es** -z **-ing** -ɪŋ **-ed** -d
flamen ˈfleɪ.men **-s** -z
flamenco fləˈmeŋ.kəʊ (US) -koʊ **-s** -z
flameproof ˈfleɪm.pruːf **-s** -s **-ing** -ɪŋ **-ed** -t
flamethrower ˈfleɪmˌθrəʊ.əʳ (US) -ˌθroʊ.ɚ **-s** -z
flamingo fləˈmɪŋ.gəʊ, flæmˈɪŋ- (US) fləˈmɪŋ.goʊ **-(e)s** -z
Flaminius fləˈmɪn.i.əs, flæmˈɪn- (US) fləˈmɪn-
flammability ˌflæm.əˈbɪl.ə.ti, -ɪ.ti (US) -ə.t̬i
flammable ˈflæm.ə.bl̩
Flamstead ˈflæm.stiːd, -stɪd
Flamsteed ˈflæm.stiːd
flan flæn **-s** -z
Flanagan ˈflæn.ə.gən
Flanders ˈflɑːn.dəz (US) ˈflæn.dɚz
flang|e flændʒ **-es** -ɪz **-ing** -ɪŋ **-ed** -d
flank flæŋk **-s** -s **-ing** -ɪŋ **-ed** -t **-er/s** -əʳ/z (US) -ɚ/z
Flann flæn
flannel ˈflæn.əl **-s** -z **-(l)ing** -ɪŋ **-(l)ed** -d
flannelette, flannelet ˌflæn.əlˈet (US) ˌflæn.əlˈet, -əˈlet
flannelly ˈflæn.əl.i
flap flæp **-s** -s **-ping** -ɪŋ **-ped** -t
flapdoodle ˈflæpˌduː.dl̩
flapjack ˈflæp.dʒæk **-s** -s
flapper ˈflæp.əʳ (US) -ɚ **-s** -z
flar|e fleəʳ (US) fler **-es** -z **-ing/ly** -ɪŋ/li **-ed** -d
flarepa|th ˈfleə.pɑː|θ (US) ˈfler.pæ|θ **-ths** -ðz
flare-up ˈfleəʳ.ʌp (US) ˈfler- **-s** -s
flash (F) flæʃ **-es** -ɪz **-ing** -ɪŋ **-ed** -t ˈ**flash** ˌ**card**; ˈ**flash** ˌ**point**; ˌ**flash in the** ˈ**pan**; ˌ**quick as a** ˈ**flash**
flashback ˈflæʃ.bæk **-s** -s
flashbulb ˈflæʃ.bʌlb **-s** -z
flasher ˈflæʃ.əʳ (US) -ɚ **-s** -z
flashgun ˈflæʃ.gʌn **-s** -z
flashlight ˈflæʃ.laɪt **-s** -s
Flashman ˈflæʃ.mən
flash|y ˈflæʃ|.i **-ier** -i.əʳ (US) -i.ɚ **-iest** -i.ɪst, -i.əst **-ily** -ɪ.li, -əl.i **-iness** -ɪ.nəs, -ɪ.nɪs
flask flɑːsk (US) flæsk **-s** -s
flat flæt **-s** -s **-ter** -əʳ (US) ˈflæt̬.ɚ **-test** -ɪst, -əst (US) ˈflæt̬.ɪst, -əst **-ly** -li **-ness** -nəs, -nɪs
Flatbush ˈflæt.bʊʃ
flat-chested ˌflætˈtʃes.tɪd **-ness** -nəs, -nɪs *stress shift:* ˌflat-chested ˈwaif
flatfish ˈflæt.fɪʃ **-es** -ɪz
flatfoot ˈflæt.fʊt
flat-footed ˌflætˈfʊt.ɪd (US) -ˈfʊt̬-, ˈ--- **-ly** -li **-ness** -nəs, -nɪs *stress shift, British only:* ˌflat-footed ˈperson
flathead (F) ˈflæt.hed **-s** -z
flatiron ˈflætˌaɪən (US) ˈflætˌaɪɚn **-s** -z
Flatland ˈflæt.lænd
flatlet ˈflæt.lət, -lɪt **-s** -s
flatmate ˈflæt.meɪt **-s** -s
flat-out ˌflætˈaʊt *stress shift:* ˌflat-out ˈdash
flatten ˈflæt.ən **-s** -z **-ing** -ɪŋ **-ed** -d
flatt|er ˈflæt|.əʳ (US) ˈflæt̬|.ɚ **-ers** -əz, -ɚz **-ering/ly** -ər.ɪŋ/li **-ered** -əd, -ɚd **-erer/s** -ər.əʳ/z (US) -ɚ.ɚ/z
flatter|y ˈflæt.ər|.i (US) ˈflæt̬- **-ies** -iz
flatties ˈflæt.iz (US) ˈflæt̬-
flattish ˈflæt.ɪʃ (US) ˈflæt̬-
flattop ˈflæt.tɒp (US) -tɑːp **-s** -s
flatulen|ce ˈflæt.jə.lənt|s, -jʊ-, ˈflætʃ.ə- (US) ˈflætʃ.ə- **-cy** -si
flatulent ˈflæt.jə.lənt, -jʊ-, ˈflætʃ.ə-, ˈ-ʊ- (US) ˈflætʃ.ə- **-ly** -li
flatus ˈfleɪ.təs (US) -t̬əs **-es** -ɪz
flatware ˈflæt.weəʳ (US) -wer
flat|ways ˈflæt|.weɪz **-wise** -waɪz
flatworm ˈflæt.wɜːm (US) -wɝːm **-s** -z
Flaubert ˈfləʊ.beəʳ (US) ˈfloʊ.ber, -ˈ-
flaun|t flɔːn|t (US) flɑːn|t, flɔːn|t **-ts** -ts **-ting/ly** -tɪŋ/li (US) -t̬ɪŋ/li **-ted** -tɪd (US) -t̬ɪd
flautist ˈflɔː.tɪst (US) ˈflɑː.t̬ɪst, ˈflɔː-, ˈflaʊ- **-s** -s
Flavel ˈflæv.əl, ˈfleɪ.vəl
Flavell fləˈvel, ˈfleɪ.vəl
Flavi|a ˈfleɪ.vi|.ə **-an** -ən
flavin ˈfleɪ.vɪn, ˈflæv.ɪn (US) ˈfleɪ.vɪn **-s** -z
flavin(e) ˈfleɪ.viːn, ˈflæv.iːn, -ɪn (US) ˈfleɪ.viːn
Flavius ˈfleɪ.vi.əs
flav|or ˈfleɪ.v|əʳ (US) -v|ɚ **-ors** -əz (US) -ɚz **-oring/s** -ər.ɪŋ/z **-ored** -əd (US) -ɚd ˌ**flavor of the** ˈ**month**
flavorful ˈfleɪ.və.fəl, -fʊl (US) -vɚ-
flavoring ˈfleɪ.vər.ɪŋ
flavorless ˈfleɪ.və.ləs, -lɪs (US) -vɚ- **-ness** -nəs, -nɪs
flavorous ˈfleɪ.vər.əs
flavorsome ˈfleɪ.və.səm (US) -vɚ-
flav|our (*n. v.*) ˈfleɪ.v|əʳ (US) -v|ɚ **-ours** -əz (US) -ɚz **-ouring/s** -ər.ɪŋ/z **-oured** -əd (US) -ɚd ˌ**flavour of the** ˈ**month**
flavourful ˈfleɪ.və.fəl, -fʊl (US) -vɚ-
flavouring ˈfleɪ.vər.ɪŋ **-s** -z
flavourless ˈfleɪ.və.ləs, -lɪs (US) -vɚ- **-ness** -nəs, -nɪs
flavoursome ˈfleɪ.və.səm (US) -vɚ-
flaw flɔː (US) flɑː, flɔː **-s** -z **-ing** -ɪŋ **-ed** -d
flawless ˈflɔː.ləs, -lɪs (US) ˈflɑː-, ˈflɔː- **-ly** -li **-ness** -nəs, -nɪs
flax flæks **-en** -ən
Flaxman ˈflæks.mən

flay fleɪ -s -z -ing -ɪŋ -ed -d -er/s -ər/z US -ɚ/z

flea fliː -s -z 'flea ˌmarket

fleabag 'fliː.bæg -s -z

fleabane 'fliː.beɪn

flea|bite 'fliː|.baɪt -bites -baɪts -bitten -bɪt.ən US -bɪt̬-

fleadh flɑː

fleam fliːm -s -z

fleapit 'fliː.pɪt -s -s

flèch|e, flech|e fleɪʃ, fleʃ -es -ɪz

fleck flek -s -s -ing -ɪŋ -ed -t

Flecker 'flek.ər US -ɚ

Flecknoe 'flek.nəʊ US -noʊ

flection 'flek.ʃən -s -z

flectional 'flek.ʃən.əl

fled *(from* **flee***)* fled

fledg|e fledʒ -es -ɪz -ing -ɪŋ -ed -d

fledg(e)ling 'fledʒ.lɪŋ -s -z

flee fliː -s -z -ing -ɪŋ **fled** fled

fleec|e fliːs -es -ɪz -ing -ɪŋ -ed -t

fleec|y 'fliː.s|i -ier -i.ər US -i.ɚ -iest -i.ɪst, -i.əst -iness -ɪ.nəs, -ɪ.nɪs

fleer flɪər US flɪr -s -z -ing -ɪŋ -ed -d

fleet (F) fliːt -s -s -er -ər US 'fliː.t̬ɚ -est -ɪst, -əst US 'fliː.t̬ɪst, -t̬əst -ly -li -ness -nəs, -nɪs -ing -ɪŋ US 'fliː.t̬ɪŋ -ed -ɪd US 'fliː.t̬ɪd 'Fleet ˌStreet

fleeting 'fliː.tɪŋ US -t̬ɪŋ -ly -li

Fleetwood 'fliːt.wʊd

Fleming 'flem.ɪŋ -s -z

Flemings 'flem.ɪŋz

Flemington 'flem.ɪŋ.tən

Flemish 'flem.ɪʃ

Flemming 'flem.ɪŋ

flens|e flenz, flen*t*s US flen*t*s -es -ɪz -ing -ɪŋ -ed -d

flesh fleʃ -es -ɪz -ing/s -ɪŋ/z -ed -t ˌflesh and 'blood; 'flesh ˌwound; ˌmake someone's 'flesh ˌcreep

fleshless 'fleʃ.ləs, -lɪs

fleshl|y 'fleʃ.l|i -iness -ɪ.nəs, -ɪ.nɪs

fleshpot 'fleʃ.pɒt US -pɑːt -s -s

flesh|y 'fleʃ|.i -iness -ɪ.nəs, -ɪ.nɪs

fletcher (F) 'fletʃ.ər US -ɚ -s -z

Flete fliːt

fletton (F) 'flet.ən US 'flet̬-

Fleur flɜːr US flɝː

fleur-de-lis ˌflɜː.də'liː, -liːs US ˌflɝː-, ˌflʊr-

fleuron 'flʊə.rɒn, 'flɜː-, -rən US 'flɝː.ɑːn, 'flʊr- -s -z

flew *(from* **fly***)* fluː

flex fleks -es -ɪz -ing -ɪŋ -ed -t

flexibility ˌflek.sɪ'bɪl.ə.ti, -sə'-, -ɪ.ti US -ə.t̬i

flexib|le 'flek.sɪ.b|l̩, -sə- -ly -li -leness -l̩.nəs, -nɪs

flexion 'flek.ʃən -s -z

flexitime 'flek.si.taɪm

flexor 'flek.sər US -sɚ, -sɔːr -s -z

flextime 'fleks.taɪm

flexure 'flek.ʃər US -ʃɚ -s -z

flibbertigibbet ˌflɪb.ə.ti'dʒɪb.ɪt, -ət US 'flɪb.ɚ.t̬iˌdʒɪb- -s -s

flick flɪk -s -s -ing -ɪŋ -ed -t

flick|er 'flɪk|.ər US -ɚ -ers -əz US -ɚz -ering -ər.ɪŋ -ered -əd US -ɚd

flick-kni|fe 'flɪk.naɪ|f -ves -vz

flier 'flaɪ.ər US -ɚ -s -z

flight (F) flaɪt -s -s -less -ləs, -lɪs 'flight atˌtendant; 'flight ˌdeck; 'flight ˌpath

flight|y 'flaɪ.t|i US -t̬|i -ier -i.ər US -i.ɚ -iest -i.ɪst, -i.əst -ily -ɪ.li, -əl.i -iness -ɪ.nəs, -ɪ.nɪs

flimflam 'flɪm.flæm -s -z -ming -ɪŋ -med -d

flims|y 'flɪm.z|i -ier -i.ər US -i.ɚ -iest -i.ɪst, -i.əst -ily -ɪ.li, -əl.i -iness -ɪ.nəs, -ɪ.nɪs

flinch flɪntʃ -es -ɪz -ing/ly -ɪŋ/li -ed -t -er/s -ər/z US -ɚ/z

flinders (F) 'flɪn.dəz US -dɚz

fling flɪŋ -s -z -ing -ɪŋ **flung** flʌŋ

flint flɪnt -s -s 'flint ˌglass

Flint flɪnt -shire -ʃər, -ˌʃɪər US -ʃɚ, -ˌʃɪr

flintlock 'flɪnt.lɒk US -lɑːk -s -s

Flintoff 'flɪn.tɒf US -tɑːf

Flintshire 'flɪnt.ʃər, -ˌʃɪər US -ʃɚ, -ˌʃɪr

flintstone (F) 'flɪnt.stəʊn US -stoʊn -s -z

flint|y 'flɪn.t|i US -t̬|i -ier -i.ər US -i.ɚ -iest -i.ɪst, -i.əst -ily -ɪ.li, -əl.i -iness -ɪ.nəs, -ɪ.nɪs

flip flɪp -s -s -ping -ɪŋ -ped -t 'flip ˌside

flip-flap 'flɪp.flæp -s -s -ping -ɪŋ -ped -t

flip-flop 'flɪp.flɒp US -flɑːp -s -s -ping -ɪŋ -ped -t

flippancy 'flɪp.ən*t*.si

flippant 'flɪp.ənt -ly -li -ness -nəs, -nɪs

flipper 'flɪp.ər US -ɚ -s -z

flipside 'flɪp.saɪd -s -z

flirt flɜːt US flɝːt -s -s -ing/ly -ɪŋ/li US 'flɝː.t̬ɪŋ/li -ed -ɪd US 'flɝː.t̬ɪd

flirtation flɜː'teɪ.ʃən US flɝː- -s -z

flirtatious flɜː'teɪ.ʃəs US flɝː- -ly -li -ness -nəs, -nɪs

flirty 'flɜː.ti US 'flɝː.t̬i

flit flɪt -s -s -ting -ɪŋ US 'flɪt̬.ɪŋ -ted -ɪd US 'flɪt̬.ɪd

flitch (F) flɪtʃ -es -ɪz

flitt|er 'flɪt|.ər US 'flɪt̬|.ɚ -ers -əz US -ɚz -ering -ər.ɪŋ -ered -əd US -ɚd

Flitwick 'flɪt.ɪk US 'flɪt̬-

flivver 'flɪv.ər US -ɚ -s -z

Flixton 'flɪk.stən

float fləʊt US floʊt -s -s -ing -ɪŋ US 'floʊ.t̬ɪŋ -ed -ɪd US 'floʊ.t̬ɪd -er/s -ər/z US 'floʊ.t̬ɚ/z -age -ɪdʒ US 'floʊ.t̬ɪdʒ ˌfloating 'bridge; ˌfloating 'dock

floatation fləʊ'teɪ.ʃən US floʊ-

floatplane 'fləʊt.pleɪn US 'floʊt- -s -z

floccu|late 'flɒk.jə|.leɪt, -jʊ- US 'flɑː.kjuː-, -kjə- -lates -leɪts -lating -leɪ.tɪŋ US -leɪ.t̬ɪŋ -lated -leɪ.tɪd US -leɪ.t̬ɪd

flocculent 'flɒk.jə.lənt, -jʊ- US 'flɑː.kjuː-, -kjə-

flock flɒk US flɑːk -s -s -ing -ɪŋ -ed -t

Flockhart 'flɒk.hɑːt US 'flɑːk.hɑːrt

Flockton 'flɒk.tən US 'flɑːk-

Flodden 'flɒd.ən US 'flɑː.dən

floe fləʊ US floʊ -s -z

Floella fləʊ'el.ə US floʊ-

flog flɒg US flɑːg, flɔːg -s -z -ging/s -ɪŋ/z -ged -d

Flo-Jo 'fləʊ.dʒəʊ US 'floʊ.dʒoʊ

flood (F) flʌd -s -z -ing -ɪŋ -ed -ɪd ˌflood 'tide

floodgate 'flʌd.geɪt -s -s

flood|light 'flʌd|.laɪt -lights -laɪts -lighting -laɪ.tɪŋ US -laɪ.t̬ɪŋ -lit -lɪt

floodwater 'flʌdˌwɔː.tər US -ˌwɑː.t̬ɚ, -ˌwɔː- -s -z

Flook flʊk, fluːk

floor flɔːr US flɔːr -s -z -ing -ɪŋ -ed -d -er/s -ər/z US -ɚ/z 'floor ˌcloth; 'floor ˌplan; 'floor ˌshow

floorboard 'flɔː.bɔːd US 'flɔːr.bɔːrd -s -z

floorwalker 'flɔːˌwɔː.kər US 'flɔːrˌwɔː.kɚ, -ˌwɑː- -s -z

floosie 'fluː.zi -s -z

flooz|y, flooz|ie 'fluː.z|i -ys -iz -ies -iz

flop flɒp US flɑːp -s -s -ping -ɪŋ -ped -t

flophou|se 'flɒp.haʊ|s US 'flɑːp- -ses -zɪz

flopp|y 'flɒp|.i US 'flɑː.p|i -ier -i.ər US -i.ɚ -iest -i.ɪst, -i.əst -ily -ɪ.li, -əl.i -iness -ɪ.nəs, -ɪ.nɪs ˌfloppy 'disk

Flopsy 'flɒp.si US 'flɑːp-

floptical 'flɒp.tɪ.kəl US 'flɑːp- ˌfloptical 'disk

flor|a (F) 'flɔː.r|ə US 'flɔːr|.ə, 'floʊ.r|ə -as -əz -ae -iː

floral 'flɔː.rəl, 'flɒr.əl US 'flɔːr-, 'floʊ.rəl

Florence 'flɒr.ən*t*s US 'flɔːr-

florentine (F) 'flɒr.ən.taɪn, -tiːn US 'flɔːr- -s -z

Flores 'flɔː.rɪz US 'flɔːr.es, -ɪz

florescen|ce flɔː'res.ən|*t*s, flɒr'es-, flə'res- US flɔː'res-, flə-, floʊ- -t -t

floret 'flɒr.ɪt, 'flɔː.rɪt, -ret US 'flɔːr.ɪt-, 'floʊ.rɪt -s -s

Florian 'flɔː.ri.ən US 'flɔːr.i-

flori|ate 'flɔː.ri|.eɪt US 'flɔːr.i-, 'floʊ.ri- -ates -eɪts -ating -eɪ.tɪŋ US -eɪ.t̬ɪŋ -ated -eɪ.tɪd US -eɪ.t̬ɪd

floribunda ˌflɒr.ɪ'bʌn.də, ˌflɔː.rɪ'- US ˌflɔːr.ɪ'-, ˌfloʊ.rɪ'-

floricultur|al ˌflɔː.rɪ'kʌl.tʃər|.əl, ˌflɒr.ɪ'-, -tʃʊ.r|əl US ˌflɔːr.ɪ'kʌl.tʃɚ|.əl, ˌfloʊ.rɪ'- -ist/s -ɪst/s

floriculture ˈflɔː.rɪ.kʌl.tʃəʳ, ˈflɒr.ɪ- ⓤⓢ ˈflɔːr.ɪ.kʌl.tʃɚ, ˈfloʊ.rɪ-
florid ˈflɒr.ɪd ⓤⓢ ˈflɔːr- **-est** -ɪst, -əst **-ly** -li **-ness** -nəs, -nɪs
Florida ˈflɒr.ɪ.də ⓤⓢ ˈflɔːr-, ˈflɑːr- ˌ**Florida** ˈ**Keys**
Floridian flɒrˈɪd.i.ən, fləˈrɪd- ⓤⓢ flɔːˈrɪd-, flɑːˈ- **-s** -z
floridity flɒrˈɪd.ə.ti, fləˈrɪd-, flɔː-, -ɪ.ti ⓤⓢ flɔːˈrɪd.ə.t̬i
floriferous flɔːˈrɪf.ᵊr.əs, flɒrˈɪf-, fləˈrɪf- ⓤⓢ flɔːˈrɪf-, floʊˈ-
florin ˈflɒr.ɪn ⓤⓢ ˈflɔːr- **-s** -z
Florinda flɔːˈrɪn.də, flɒrˈɪn-, fləˈrɪn- ⓤⓢ flɔːˈrɪn-, floʊ-
Florio ˈflɔː.ri.əʊ ⓤⓢ ˈflɔːr.i.oʊ
florist ˈflɒr.ɪst, ˈflɔː.rɪst ⓤⓢ ˈflɔːr.ɪst, ˈfloʊ.rɪst **-s** -s
floristry ˈflɒr.ɪ.stri, ˈflɔː.rɪ- ⓤⓢ ˈflɔːr.ɪ-, ˈfloʊ.rɪ-
Florrie ˈflɒr.i ⓤⓢ ˈflɔːr-
floruit ˈflɔː.ru.ɪt, ˈflɒr.u- ⓤⓢ ˈflɔːr.ju-, ˈfloʊr-
floss (F) flɒs ⓤⓢ flɑːs **-y** -i **-es** -ɪz **-ing** -ɪŋ **-ed** -t
Flossie ˈflɒs.i ⓤⓢ ˈflɑː.si
flotage ˈfləʊ.tɪdʒ ⓤⓢ ˈfloʊ.t̬ɪdʒ
flotation fləʊˈteɪ.ʃᵊn ⓤⓢ floʊ- **-s** -z
flotilla flə(ʊ)ˈtɪl.ə ⓤⓢ floʊ- **-s** -z
flotsam ˈflɒt.səm ⓤⓢ ˈflɑːt- ˌ**flotsam and** ˈ**jetsam**
Flotta ˈflɒt.ə ⓤⓢ ˈflɑː.t̬ə
flounc|e flaʊnts **-es** -ɪz **-ing** -ɪŋ **-ed** -t
flouncy ˈflaʊnt.si
flound|er ˈflaʊn.d|əʳ ⓤⓢ -d|ɚ **-ers** -əz ⓤⓢ -ɚz **-ering** -ᵊr.ɪŋ **-ered** -əd ⓤⓢ -ɚd
flour flaʊəʳ ⓤⓢ flaʊɚ **-s** -z **-ing** -ɪŋ **-ed** -d
flourish ˈflʌr.ɪʃ ⓤⓢ ˈflɝː.ɪʃ **-es** -ɪz **-ing/ly** -ɪŋ/li **-ed** -t
floury ˈflaʊə.ri ⓤⓢ ˈflaʊə.ri
flout flaʊt **-s** -s **-ing** -ɪŋ ⓤⓢ ˈflaʊ.t̬ɪŋ **-ed** -ɪd ⓤⓢ ˈflaʊ.t̬ɪd
flow fləʊ ⓤⓢ floʊ **-s** -z **-ing/ly** -ɪŋ/li **-ingness** -ɪŋ.nəs, -nɪs **-ed** -d ˈ**flow** ˌ**chart**; ˈ**flow** ˌ**diagram**
flower (F) flaʊəʳ ⓤⓢ flaʊɚ **-s** -z **-ing** -ɪŋ **-ed** -d **-er/s** -əʳ/z ⓤⓢ -ɚ/z ˈ**flower** ˌ**child**; ˈ**flower** ˌ**garden**; ˈ**flower** ˌ**girl**; ˈ**flower** ˌ**power**
flowerbed ˈflaʊə.bed ⓤⓢ ˈflaʊɚ- **-s** -z
floweret ˈflaʊə.rɪt, -ret ⓤⓢ ˈflaʊɚ.ɪt, -et **-s** -s
flowerless ˈflaʊə.ləs, -lɪs ⓤⓢ ˈflaʊɚ-
flowerpot ˈflaʊə.pɒt ⓤⓢ ˈflaʊɚ.pɑːt **-s** -s
flowery ˈflaʊə.ri
flown *(from* **fly***)* fləʊn ⓤⓢ floʊn
Floyd flɔɪd
Floyder ˈflɔɪ.dəʳ ⓤⓢ -dɚ
fl oz *(abbrev. for* **fluid ounce***) singular:* ˌfluː.ɪdˈaʊnts *plural:* -ˈaʊnt.sɪz
flu, ˈ**flu** fluː
flub flʌb **-s** -z **-bing** -ɪŋ **-bed** -d
fluctuant ˈflʌk.tʃu.ənt, -tju- ⓤⓢ -tʃu-, -tʃə.wənt
fluctu|ate ˈflʌk.tʃu|.eɪt, -tju- ⓤⓢ -tʃu-, -tʃə.w|eɪt **-ates** -eɪts **-ating** -eɪ.tɪŋ ⓤⓢ -eɪ.t̬ɪŋ **-ated** -eɪ.tɪd ⓤⓢ -eɪ.t̬ɪd
fluctuation ˌflʌk.tʃuˈeɪ.ʃᵊn, -tjuˈ- ⓤⓢ -tʃu-, -tʃəˈweɪ- **-s** -z
Flud(d) flʌd
Fludyer ˈflʌd.jəʳ, -i.əʳ ⓤⓢ ˈflʌd.jɚ
flue fluː **-s** -z ˈ**flue** ˌ**pipe**
Fluellen fluˈel.ɪn, -ən
fluency ˈfluː.ənt.si
fluent ˈfluː.ənt **-ly** -li **-ness** -nəs, -nɪs
fluff flʌf **-s** -s **-ing** -ɪŋ **-ed** -t
fluff|y ˈflʌf|.i **-ier** -i.əʳ ⓤⓢ -i.ɚ **-iest** -i.ɪst, -i.əst **-iness** -ɪ.nəs, -ɪ.nɪs
flugelhorn, flügelhorn ˈfluː.gᵊl.hɔːn ⓤⓢ -hɔːrn **-s** -z
fluid ˈfluː.ɪd **-s** -z ˌ**fluid** ˈ**ounce**
fluidity fluˈɪd.ə.ti, -ɪ.ti ⓤⓢ -ə.t̬i
fluidization, -isa- ˌfluː.ɪ.daɪˈzeɪ.ʃᵊn, -dɪˈ- ⓤⓢ -dɪˈ-
fluidiz|e, -is|e ˈfluː.ɪ.daɪz **-es** -ɪz **-ing** -ɪŋ **-ed** -d **-er/s** -əʳ/z ⓤⓢ -ɚ/z
fluk|e fluːk **-es** -s **-ing** -ɪŋ **-ed** -t **-er/s** -əʳ/z ⓤⓢ -ɚ/z **-ish** -ɪʃ
fluk|y, fluk|ey ˈfluː.k|i **-ier** -i.əʳ ⓤⓢ -i.ɚ **-iest** -i.ɪst, -i.əst **-iness** -ɪ.nəs, -ɪ.nɪs
flume fluːm **-s** -z
flummery ˈflʌm.ᵊr.i
flummox ˈflʌm.əks **-es** -ɪz **-ing** -ɪŋ **-ed** -t
flung *(from* **fling***)* flʌŋ
flunk flʌŋk **-s** -s **-ing** -ɪŋ **-ed** -t
flunkey ˈflʌŋ.ki **-s** -z **-ism** -ɪ.zᵊm
flunk|y ˈflʌŋ.k|i **-ys** -iz **-ies** -iz **-yism** -i.ɪ.zᵊm
fluor ˈfluː.ɔːʳ, -əʳ ⓤⓢ -ɔːr, -ɚ
fluorescence flɔːˈres.ᵊnts, flʊə-, flə-; ⓤⓢ flɔː-, flʊ-, fluː-, floʊ-
fluorescent flɔːˈres.ᵊnt, flʊə-, flə- ⓤⓢ flɔː-, flʊ-, fluː-, floʊ-
fluoric fluˈɒr.ɪk ⓤⓢ -ˈɔːr-
fluori|date ˈflɔː.rɪ|.deɪt, ˈflʊə-, -rə- ⓤⓢ ˈflɔːr.ə-, ˈflʊr- **-dates** -deɪts **-dating** -deɪ.tɪŋ ⓤⓢ -deɪ.t̬ɪŋ **-dated** -deɪ.tɪd ⓤⓢ -deɪ.t̬ɪd
fluoridation ˌflɔː.rɪˈdeɪ.ʃᵊn, ˌflʊə-, -raɪˈ-, -rəˈ- ⓤⓢ ˌflɔːr.əˈ-, ˌflʊr.əˈ-
fluoride ˈflɔː.raɪd, ˈflʊə- ⓤⓢ ˈflɔːr.aɪd, ˈflʊr- **-s** -z
fluoridization, -isa- ˌflɔː.rɪ.daɪˈzeɪ.ʃᵊn, ˌflʊə-, -raɪ-, -dɪˈ- ⓤⓢ ˌflɔːr.ə.dɪˈ-, ˌflʊr-
fluoridiz|e, -is|e- ˈflɔː.rɪ.daɪz, ˈflʊə- ⓤⓢ ˈflɔːr.ə-, ˈflʊr- **-es** -ɪz **-ing** -ɪŋ **-ed** -d
fluori|nate ˈflɔː.rɪ|.neɪt, ˈflʊə-, ˈflɒr.ɪ-, ˈ-ə- ⓤⓢ ˈflɔːr.ə-, ˈflʊr- **-nates** -neɪts **-nating** -neɪ.tɪŋ ⓤⓢ -neɪ.t̬ɪŋ **-nated** -neɪ.tɪd ⓤⓢ -neɪ.t̬ɪd
fluorination ˌflɔː.rɪˈneɪ.ʃᵊn, ˌflʊə-, ˌflɒr.ɪˈ-, -əˈ- ⓤⓢ ˌflɔːr.əˈ-, ˌflʊr-
fluorine ˈflɔː.riːn, ˈflʊə- ⓤⓢ ˈflɔːr.iːn, ˈflʊr-, -ɪn
fluorisis flɔːˈraɪ.sɪs, flʊə-, flə- ⓤⓢ flɔː-, flʊ-
fluorite ˈflɔː.raɪt, ˈflʊə- ⓤⓢ ˈflɔːr.aɪt, ˈflʊr-
fluoro- flɔː.rəʊ-, flʊə-; flɔːˈrɒ-, flʊə-, flə-, -ˈrəʊ- ⓤⓢ flɔːr.ə-, flʊr-, ˈ-oʊ-; flɔːˈrɑː-, flʊ-, -ˈroʊ-
Note: Prefix. Either takes primary or secondary stress on the first syllable, e.g. **fluoroscope** /ˈflɔː.rəʊ.skəʊp ⓤⓢ ˈflɔːr.ə.skoʊp/, **fluoroscopic** /ˌflɔː.rəʊˈskɒp.ɪk ⓤⓢ ˌflɔːr.əˈskɑː.pɪk/, or primary stress on the second syllable, e.g. **fluoroscopy** /flɔːˈrɒs.kə.pi ⓤⓢ -ˈrɑː.skə-/.
fluorocarbon ˌflɔː.rəʊˈkɑː.bᵊn, ˌflʊə- ⓤⓢ ˌflɔːr.əˈkɑːr-, ˌflʊr-, -oʊˈ- **-s** -z *stress shift:* ˌfluorocarbon ˈdating techˌnique
fluoroscop|e ˈflɔː.rəʊ.skəʊp, ˈflʊə- ⓤⓢ ˈflɔːr.ə-, ˈflʊr-, -oʊ- **-es** -s **-ing** -ɪŋ **-ed** -t
fluoroscopic ˌflɔː.rəʊˈskɒp.ɪk, ˌflʊə- ⓤⓢ ˌflɔːr.əˈ-, ˌflʊr-, -oʊˈ- **-ally** -ᵊl.i, -li
fluoroscop|y flɔːˈrɒs.kə.p|i, flʊə-, flə- ⓤⓢ flɔːˈrɑː.skə-, flʊ- **-ies** -iz **-ist/s** -ɪst/s
fluorosis flɔːˈrəʊ.sɪs, flʊə-, flə- ⓤⓢ flɔːˈroʊ-, flʊ-
fluorspar ˈflɔː.spɑːʳ, ˈflʊə- ⓤⓢ ˈflɔːr.spɑːr, ˈfluː.ɔːr-
flurr|y ˈflʌr|.i ⓤⓢ ˈflɝː- **-ies** -iz **-ying** -i.ɪŋ **-ied** -id
flush flʌʃ **-es** -ɪz **-ing** -ɪŋ **-ed** -t
flushing (F) ˈflʌʃ.ɪŋ **-s** -z
flust|er ˈflʌs.t|əʳ ⓤⓢ -t|ɚ **-ers** -əz ⓤⓢ -ɚz **-ering** -ᵊr.ɪŋ **-ered** -əd ⓤⓢ -ɚd
flut|e (F) fluːt **-es** -s **-ing** -ɪŋ ⓤⓢ ˈfluː.t̬ɪŋ **-ed** -ɪd ⓤⓢ ˈfluː.t̬ɪd **-y** -i ⓤⓢ ˈfluː.t̬i **-ier** -i.əʳ ⓤⓢ ˈfluː.t̬i.ɚ **-iest** -i.ɪst, -i.əst ⓤⓢ ˈfluː.t̬i.ɪst, -əst **-iness** -ɪ.nəs, -ɪ.nɪs ⓤⓢ ˈfluː.t̬ɪ.nəs, -nɪs
flutist ˈfluː.tɪst ⓤⓢ -t̬ɪst **-s** -s
flutt|er (F) ˈflʌt|.əʳ ⓤⓢ ˈflʌt̬|.ɚ **-ers** -əz ⓤⓢ -ɚz **-ering** -ᵊr.ɪŋ **-ered** -əd ⓤⓢ -ɚd **-erer/s** -ᵊr.əʳ/z ⓤⓢ -ɚ.ɚ/z
fluvial ˈfluː.vi.əl
flux flʌks **-es** -ɪz
fluxion ˈflʌk.ʃᵊn **-s** -z
fluxional ˈflʌk.ʃᵊn.ᵊl
fl|y (F) fl|aɪ **-ies** -aɪz **-ying** -aɪ.ɪŋ **flew** fluː **flown** fləʊn ⓤⓢ floʊn **flier/s** ˈflaɪ.əʳ/z ⓤⓢ -ɚ/z ˈ**fly** ˌ**ball**; ˌ**flying** ˈ**buttress**; ˈ**flying** ˌ**fish**; ˈ**flying** ˌ**officer**; ˌ**flying** ˈ**saucer**; ˈ**flying** ˌ**squad**; ˌ**flying** ˈ**start**; ˈ**fly** ˌ**sheet**; **he/she** ˌ**wouldn't harm a** ˈ**fly**

flyable 'flaɪ.ə.bl̩
flyaway 'flaɪ.ə.weɪ
flyb|y 'flaɪ.b|aɪ **-ies** -aɪz
fly-by-night 'flaɪ.baɪ.naɪt **-s** -s **-er/s** -ə^r/z US ɚ/z
fly-by-wire 'flaɪ.baɪ.waɪə^r, ˌ--'- US -waɪɚ
flycatcher 'flaɪˌkætʃ.ə^r US -ɚ **-s** -z
fly-drive 'flaɪ.draɪv, ˌ-'- **-s** -z
flyer 'flaɪ.ə^r US -ɚ **-s** -z
fly-fishing 'flaɪˌfɪʃ.ɪŋ
flyingsaucer ˌflaɪ.ɪŋ'sɔː.sə^r US -'sɑː.sɚ, -'sɔː- **-s** -z
flying squad 'flaɪ.ɪŋ.skwɒd US -skwɑːd **-s** -z
flylea|f 'flaɪ.liː|f **-ves** -vz
Flymo® 'flaɪ.məʊ US -moʊ
Flyn(n) flɪn
Flynt flɪnt
flyover 'flaɪˌəʊ.və^r US -ˌoʊ.vɚ **-s** -z
flypaper 'flaɪˌpeɪ.pə^r US -pɚ **-s** -z
flypast 'flaɪ.pɑːst US -pæst **-s** -s
flyposter 'flaɪˌpəʊ.stə^r US -ˌpoʊ.stɚ **-s** -z
flyswatter 'flaɪˌswɒt.ə^r US -ˌswɑː.t̬ɚ **-s** -z
Flyte flaɪt
flyway 'flaɪ.weɪ **-s** -z
flyweight 'flaɪ.weɪt **-s** -s
flywheel 'flaɪ.*h*wiːl **-s** -z
FM ˌef'em
Fo fəʊ US foʊ
foal fəʊl US foʊl **-s** -z **-ing** -ɪŋ **-ed** -d
foam fəʊm US foʊm **-s** -z **-ing** -ɪŋ **-ed** -d **-y** -i **-iness** -ɪ.nəs, -ɪ.nɪs
Foard fɔːd US fɔːrd
fob fɒb US fɑːb **-s** -z **-bing** -ɪŋ **-bed** -d
focal 'fəʊ.k^{ə}l US 'foʊ- **'focal ˌpoint, ˌfocal 'point**
Foch fɒʃ US fɑːʃ, fɔːʃ
Fochabers 'fɒk.ə.bəz, 'fɒx- US 'fɑːk.ə.bɚz
Focke fɒk US fɑːk
fo'c'sle 'fəʊk.s^{ə}l US 'foʊk- **-s** -z
fo|cus (*n.*) 'fəʊ|.kəs US 'foʊ- **-cuses** -kə.sɪz **-ci** -saɪ, -kiː
focus (*v.*) 'fəʊ.kəs US 'foʊ- **-(s)es** -ɪz **-(s)ing** -ɪŋ **-(s)ed** -t
fodder 'fɒd.ə^r US 'fɑː.dɚ
foe fəʊ US foʊ **-s** -z
FoE *(abbrev. for* **Friends of the Earth***)* ˌef.əʊ'iː US -oʊ'-
foehn fɜːn US feɪn, fɜːn
foe|man 'fəʊ|.mən, -mæn US 'foʊ- **-men** -mən, -men
foetal 'fiː.t^{ə}l US -t̬^{ə}l **'foetal poˌsition**
foetid 'fiː.tɪd, 'fet.ɪd US 'fet̬.ɪd, 'fiː.t̬ɪd **-ly** -li **-ness** -nəs, -nɪs
foetus 'fiː.təs US -t̬əs **-es** -ɪz
fog fɒg US fɑːg, fɔːg **-s** -z **-ging** -ɪŋ **-ged** -d **'fog ˌlamp**
fogbound 'fɒg.baʊnd US 'fɑːg-, 'fɔːg-
Fogerty 'fəʊ.gə.ti, 'fɒg.ə.ti US 'foʊ.gɚ.t̬i
fogey 'fəʊ.gi US 'foʊ- **-s** -z **-ish** -ɪʃ **-ism** -ɪ.z^{ə}m
Fogg fɒg US fɑːg, fɔːg
fogg|y 'fɒg|.i US 'fɑː.g|i, 'fɔː- **-ier** -i.ə^r US -i.ɚ **-iest** -i.ɪst, -i.əst **-ily** -ɪ.li, -^{ə}l.i **-iness** -ɪ.nəs, -ɪ.nɪs **ˌFoggy 'Bottom**
foghorn 'fɒg.hɔːn US 'fɑːg.hɔːrn, 'fɔːg- **-s** -z
fog|y 'fəʊ.g|i US 'foʊ- **-ies** -iz **-yish** -i.ɪʃ **-yism** -i.ɪ.z^{ə}m
fohn, föhn fɜːn US feɪn, fɜːn
foible 'fɔɪ.bl̩ **-s** -z
foie gras ˌfwɑː'grɑː
foil fɔɪl **-s** -z **-ing** -ɪŋ **-ed** -d
foist fɔɪst **-s** -s **-ing** -ɪŋ **-ed** -ɪd
Fokker® 'fɒk.ə^r US 'fɑː.kɚ
fold fəʊld US foʊld **-s** -z **-ing** -ɪŋ **-ed** -ɪd
foldaway 'fəʊld.ə.weɪ US 'foʊld-
folder 'fəʊl.də^r US 'foʊl.dɚ **-s** -z
folderol 'fɒl.dɪ.rɒl, -də- US 'fɑːl.də.rɑːl **-s** -z
foldout 'fəʊld.aʊt US 'foʊld- **-s** -s
Foley 'fəʊ.li US 'foʊ-
Folgate 'fɒl.gɪt, -geɪt US 'fɑːl.geɪt
Folger 'fəʊl.dʒə^r, 'fɒl- US 'foʊl.dʒɚ
foliage 'fəʊ.li.ɪdʒ US 'foʊ- **-d** -d
foliar 'fəʊ.li.ə US 'foʊ.li.ɚ
foliate (*adj.*) 'fəʊ.li.ət, -ɪt, -eɪt US 'foʊ-
foli|ate (*v.*) 'fəʊ.li|.eɪt US 'foʊ- **-ates** -eɪts **-ating** -eɪ.tɪŋ US -eɪ.t̬ɪŋ **-ated** -eɪ.tɪd US -eɪ.t̬ɪd
foliation ˌfəʊ.li'eɪ.ʃ^{ə}n US ˌfoʊ- **-s** -z
folic 'fɒl.ɪk, 'fəʊ.lɪk US 'foʊ- **ˌfolic 'acid**
Folies Bergère ˌfɒl.i.bɜː'ʒeə^r, -bə'-, -beə'- US ˌfoʊ.li.ber'ʒer
folio 'fəʊ.li.əʊ US 'foʊ.li.oʊ **-s** -z
Foliot 'fɒl.i.ət US 'fɑː.li-
folk fəʊk US foʊk **-s** -s **'folk ˌdance; 'folk ˌsong**
Folkes fəʊlks, fuːks US foʊlks
Folkestone 'fəʊk.stən US 'foʊk-
folklore 'fəʊk.lɔː^r US 'foʊk.lɔːr
folklorist 'fəʊkˌlɔː.rɪst US 'foʊkˌlɔːr.ɪst **-s** -s
folksinger 'fəʊkˌsɪŋ.ə^r US 'foʊkˌsɪŋ.ɚ **-s** -z
folks|y 'fəʊk.s|i US 'foʊk- **-ier** -i.ə^r US -i.ɚ **-iest** -i.ɪst, -i.əst **-ily** -ɪ.li, -^{ə}l.i **-iness** -ɪ.nəs, -ɪ.nɪs
folktale 'fəʊk.teɪl US 'foʊk- **-s** -z
Follen 'fɒl.ɪn, -ən US 'fɑː.lɪn, -lən
Follett 'fɒl.ɪt, -ət US 'fɑː.lɪt, -lət
Follick 'fɒl.ɪk US 'fɑː.lɪk
follicle 'fɒl.ɪ.kl̩ US 'fɑː.lɪ- **-s** -z
follow 'fɒl.əʊ US 'fɑː.loʊ **-s** -z **-ing/s** -ɪŋ/z **-ed** -d **-er/s** -ə^r/z US -ɚ/z
follow-my-leader ˌfɒl.əʊ.mə'liː.də^r, -mɪ'-, -maɪ'- US ˌfɑː.loʊ.maɪ'liː.dɚ
follow-on 'fɒl.əʊ.ɒn US 'fɑː.loʊ.ɑːn **-s** -z
follow-the-leader ˌfɒl.əʊ.ðə'liː.də^r US ˌfɑː.loʊ.ðə'liː.dɚ
follow-through ˌfɒl.əʊ'θruː US '---, 'fɑː.loʊ.θruː **-s** -z
follow-up 'fɒl.əʊ.ʌp US 'fɑː.loʊ- **-s** -s
foll|y (F) 'fɒl|.i US 'fɑː.l|i **-ies** -iz
Fomalhaut 'fəʊ.mə.ləʊt, 'fɒm-, -^{ə}l.hɔːt US 'foʊ.m^{ə}l.hɑːt, -hɔːt, -mə.loʊ
fo|ment fəʊ|'ment US foʊ- **-ments** -'ments **-menting** -'men.tɪŋ US -'men.t̬ɪŋ **-mented** -'men.tɪd US -'men.t̬ɪd **-menter/s** -'men.tə^r/z US -'men.t̬ɚ/z
fomentation ˌfəʊ.men'teɪ.ʃ^{ə}n, -mən'- US ˌfoʊ- **-s** -z
fond fɒnd US fɑːnd **-er** -ə^r US -ɚ **-est** -ɪst, -əst **-ly** -li **-ness** -nəs, -nɪs
Fonda 'fɒn.də US 'fɑːn-
fondant 'fɒn.dənt US 'fɑːn- **-s** -s
fondl|e 'fɒn.dl̩ US 'fɑːn- **-es** -z **-ing** -ɪŋ, 'fɒnd.lɪŋ US 'fɑːnd- **-ed** -d
fondly 'fɒnd.li US 'fɑːnd-
fondu(e) 'fɒn.djuː, -duː, -'- US fɑːn'duː, -'djuː, '-- **-s** -z
font fɒnt US fɑːnt **-s** -s **-al** -^{ə}l US 'fɑːn.t̬^{ə}l
Fontainebleau 'fɒn.tɪn.bləʊ, -tɪm-, -təm- US 'fɑːn.t^{ə}n.bloʊ
Fontane 'fɒn.teɪn *as if German:* fɒn'tɑː.nə US 'fɑːn-
fontanelle, fontanel ˌfɒn.tə'nel US ˌfɑːn.t^{ə}n'el **-s** -z
Fontenoy 'fɒn.tə.nɔɪ, -tɪ.nɔɪ US 'fɑːn.t^{ə}n.ɔɪ
Fonteyn fɒn'teɪn, '-- US fɑːn'teɪn, '--
Fonthill 'fɒnt.hɪl US 'fɑːnt-
Foochow ˌfuː'tʃaʊ
food fuːd **-s** -z **-less** -ləs, -lɪs **'food ˌpoisoning; 'food ˌprocessor**
foodie 'fuː.di **-s** -z
foodstuff 'fuːd.stʌf **-s** -s
fool fuːl **-s** -z **-ing** -ɪŋ **-ed** -d **ˌfool's 'gold, 'fool's ˌgold; ˌmake a 'fool of oneˌself**
fooler|y 'fuː.l^{ə}r|.i **-ies** -iz
foolhard|y 'fuːlˌhɑː.d|i US -ˌhɑːr- **-iest** -i.ɪst, -i.əst **-ily** -ɪ.li, -^{ə}l.i **-iness** -ɪ.nəs, -ɪ.nɪs
foolish 'fuː.lɪʃ **-ly** -li **-ness** -nəs, -nɪs
foolproof 'fuːl.pruːf
foolscap, fool's cap *hat:* 'fuːlz.kæp **s** -s
foolscap *paper size:* 'fuːl.skæp, 'fuːlz.kæp
foot (F) (*n.*) fʊt **feet** fiːt **'foot ˌfault; 'foot ˌpassenger; 'foot ˌsoldier; ˌone foot in the 'grave; put one's ˌbest foot 'forward; ˌput one's 'foot down; ˌput one's 'foot in it**
foot (*v.*) fʊt **-s** -s **-ing** -ɪŋ US 'fʊt̬.ɪŋ **-ed** -ɪd US 'fʊt̬.ɪd
footage 'fʊt.ɪdʒ US 'fʊt̬-

foot-and-mouth ˌfʊt.ᵊnd'maʊθ, -ᵊm'- (US) -ᵊnd'- ˌ**foot-and-'mouth diˌsease**

football 'fʊt.bɔːl (US) -bɔːl, -bɑːl **-s** -z **-ing** -ɪŋ **-er/s** -əʳ/z (US) -ɚ/z **'football ˌmatch**; **'football ˌpools**

footba|th 'fʊt.bɑː|θ (US) -bæ|θ **-ths** -ðz

footboard 'fʊt.bɔːd (US) -bɔːrd **-s** -z

footbridg|e 'fʊt.brɪdʒ **-es** -ɪz

Foote fʊt

footer 'fʊt.əʳ (US) 'fʊt̬.ɚ

footfall 'fʊt.fɔːl (US) -fɔːl, -fɑːl **-s** -z

foothill 'fʊt.hɪl **-s** -z

foothold 'fʊt.həʊld (US) -hoʊld **-s** -z

footie 'fʊt.i (US) 'fʊt̬-

footing 'fʊt.ɪŋ (US) 'fʊt̬- **-s** -z

footl|e 'fuː.tl̩ (US) -t̬l̩ **-es** -z **-ing** -ɪŋ, 'fuːt.lɪŋ **-ed** -d

footlight 'fʊt.laɪt **-s** -s

footlocker 'fʊtˌlɒk.əʳ (US) -ˌlɑː.kɚ **-s** -z

footloose 'fʊt.luːs ˌ**footloose and ˌfancy-'free**

foot|man 'fʊt|.mən **-men** -mən

footmark 'fʊt.mɑːk (US) -mɑːrk **-s** -s

footnote 'fʊt.nəʊt (US) -noʊt **-s** -s

footpad 'fʊt.pæd **-s** -z

footpa|th 'fʊt.pɑː|θ (US) -pæ|θ **-ths** -ðz

footplate 'fʊt.pleɪt **-s** -s

foot-pound 'fʊt.paʊnd **-s** -z

footprint 'fʊt.prɪnt **-s** -s

footrac|e 'fʊt.reɪs **-es** -ɪz

footrest 'fʊt.rest **-s** -s

footrule 'fʊt.ruːl **-s** -z

footsie (F) 'fʊt.si

footslog 'fʊt.slɒg (US) -slɑːg, -slɔːg **-s** -z **-ging** -ɪŋ **-ged** -d

footsore 'fʊt.sɔːʳ (US) -sɔːr

footstep 'fʊt.step **-s** -s

footstool 'fʊt.stuːl **-s** -z

footsure 'fʊt.ʃʊəʳ, -ʃɔːʳ (US) -ʃʊr, -ʃɝː **-ness** -nəs, -nɪs

footwear 'fʊt.weəʳ (US) -wer

footwork 'fʊt.wɜːk (US) -wɝːk

footy 'fʊt.i (US) 'fʊt̬-

foozl|e (F) 'fuː.zl̩ **-es** -z **-ing** -ɪŋ, 'fuːz.lɪŋ **-ed** -d **-er/s** -əʳ/z, 'fuːz.ləʳ/z (US) 'fuː.zl̩.ɚ/z, 'fuːz.lɚ/z

fop fɒp (US) fɑːp **-s** -s

fopper|y 'fɒp.ᵊr|.i (US) 'fɑː.pɚ- **-ies** -iz

foppish 'fɒp.ɪʃ (US) 'fɑː.pɪʃ **-ly** -li **-ness** -nəs, -nɪs

for *(prep. conj.) strong form:* fɔːʳ (US) fɔːr *weak form:* fəʳ (US) fɚ *alternative weak form before vowels:* frɯ

Note: Weak form word. The strong form /fɔːʳ (US) fɔːr/ is used contrastively (e.g. "**for** and **against**") and in sentence-final position (e.g. "That's what it's for"). The weak form is /fə (US) fɚ/ before consonants (e.g. "Thanks for coming" /ˌθæŋks.fə'kʌm.ɪŋ (US) -fɚ'-/); before vowels it is /fər (US) fɚ/ (e.g. "One for all" /ˌwʌn.fər'ɔːl (US) -fɚ'ɑːl/) or, in rapid speech, /frɯ/ (e.g. "Time for another" /ˌtaɪm.frɯ.ə'nʌð.əʳ (US) -ɚ/).

forag|e 'fɒr.ɪdʒ (US) 'fɔːr- **-es** -ɪz **-ing** -ɪŋ **-ed** -d **-er/s** -əʳ/z (US) -ɚ/z

foramen fə'reɪ.men, fɒr'eɪ-, -mən (US) fə'reɪ.mən, fɔː-, foʊ- **foramina** fə'ræm.ɪ.nə, fɒr'eɪ- (US) fə'ræm.ə-, fɔː-, foʊ-

forasmuch fᵊr.əz'mʌtʃ, ˌfɔː.rəz-, ˌfɒr.əz- (US) ˌfɔːr.æz'-, ˌfɚ-, -əz'-

foray 'fɒr.eɪ (US) 'fɔːr- **-s** -z **-ing** -ɪŋ **-ed** -d

forbad *(from* **forbid***)* fə'bæd, fɔː- (US) fɚ-, fɔːr-

forbade *(from* **forbid***)* fə'bæd, fɔː-, -beɪd (US) fɚ'bæd, fɔːr-

forbear *(n.)* 'fɔː.beəʳ (US) 'fɔːr.ber **-s** -z

for|bear *(v.)* fɔː|'beəʳ, fə- (US) fɔːr|'ber **-bears** -'beəz (US) -'berz **-bearing/ly** -'beə.rɪŋ/li (US) -'ber.ɪŋ/li **-bore** -'bɔːʳ (US) -'bɔːr **-borne** -'bɔːn (US) -'bɔːrn

forbearance fɔː'beə.rənts, fə- (US) fɔːr'ber.ənts

Forbes fɔːbz, 'fɔː.bɪs (US) fɔːrbz

for|bid fə|'bɪd, fɔː- (US) fɚ-, fɔːr- **-bids** -'bɪdz **-bidding/ly** -'bɪd.ɪŋ/li **-bad** -'bæd **-bade** -'bæd, -'beɪd (US) -'bæd **-bidden** -'bɪd.ᵊn

forbore *(from* **forbear***)* fɔː'bɔːʳ (US) fɔːr'bɔːr

forc|e (F) fɔːs (US) fɔːrs **-es** -ɪz **-ing** -ɪŋ **-ed** -t **-edly** -ɪd.li **-edness** -ɪd.nəs, -nɪs **'force ˌpump**; ˌ**forced 'march**

forcefeed ˌfɔːs'fiːd, '-- (US) 'fɔːrs.fiːd, ˌ-'- **-s** -z **-ing** -ɪŋ **forcefed** ˌfɔːs'fed, '-- (US) 'fɔːrs.fed, ˌ-'-

forceful 'fɔːs.fᵊl, -fʊl (US) 'fɔːrs- **-ly** -i **-ness** -nəs, -nɪs

force majeure ˌfɔːs.mæʒ'ɜːʳ, -mædʒ'ʊəʳ (US) ˌfɔːrs.mɑː'ʒɝː

forcemeat 'fɔːs.miːt (US) 'fɔːrs-

forceps 'fɔː.seps, -sɪps, -səps (US) 'fɔːr-

forcer 'fɔː.səʳ (US) 'fɔːr.sɚ **-s** -z

forcib|le 'fɔː.sə.b|l̩, -sɪ- (US) 'fɔːr- **-ly** -li **-leness** -l̩.nəs, -nɪs

ford (F) fɔːd (US) fɔːrd **-s** -z **-ing** -ɪŋ **-ed** -ɪd **-able** -ə.bl̩

Fordcombe 'fɔːd.kəm (US) 'fɔːrd-

Forde fɔːd (US) fɔːrd

Forder 'fɔː.dəʳ (US) 'fɔːr.dɚ

Fordham 'fɔː.dəm (US) 'fɔːr-

Fordingbridge 'fɔː.dɪŋ.brɪdʒ (US) 'fɔːr-

Fordoun 'fɔː.dᵊn (US) 'fɔːr-

Fordyce 'fɔː.daɪs (US) 'fɔːr-

fore fɔːʳ (US) fɔːr

forearm *(n.)* 'fɔːʳ.ɑːm (US) 'fɔːr.ɑːrm **-s** -z

forearm *(v.)* fɔːʳ'ɑːm (US) fɔːr'ɑːrm **-s** -z **-ing** -ɪŋ **-ed** -d

forebear 'fɔː.beəʳ (US) 'fɔːr.ber **-s** -s

forebod|e fɔː'bəʊd, fə- (US) fɔːr'boʊd, fɚ- **-es** -z **-ing/ly** -ɪŋ/li **-ed** -ɪd **-er/s** -əʳ/z (US) -ɚ/z

foreboding fɔː'bəʊ.dɪŋ, fə- (US) fɔːr'boʊ-, fɚ- **-s** -z

forecast *(n.)* 'fɔː.kɑːst (US) 'fɔːr.kæst **-s** -s

forecast *(v.)* 'fɔː.kɑːst (US) 'fɔːr.kæst **-s** -s **-ing** -ɪŋ **-ed** -ɪd **-er/s** -əʳ/z (US) -ɚ/z

forecastle 'fəʊk.sᵊl (US) 'foʊk- **-s** -z

foreclos|e fɔː'kləʊz (US) fɔːr'kloʊz **-es** -ɪz **-ing** -ɪŋ **-ed** -d

foreclosure fɔː'kləʊ.ʒəʳ (US) fɔːr'kloʊ.ʒɚ **-s** -z

forecourt 'fɔː.kɔːt (US) 'fɔːr.kɔːrt **-s** -s

forefather 'fɔːˌfɑː.ðəʳ (US) 'fɔːrˌfɑː.ðɚ **-s** -z

forefinger 'fɔːˌfɪŋ.gəʳ (US) 'fɔːrˌfɪŋ.gɚ **-s** -z

fore|foot 'fɔː|.fʊt (US) 'fɔːr- **-feet** -fiːt

forefront 'fɔː.frʌnt (US) 'fɔːr-

fore|go fɔː|'gəʊ (US) fɔːr|'goʊ **-goes** -'gəʊz (US) -'goʊz **-going** -'gəʊ.ɪŋ (US) -'goʊ.ɪŋ **-went** -'went **-gone** -'gɒn (US) -'gɑːn **-goer/s** -'gəʊ.əʳ/z (US) -'goʊ.ɚ/z

foregone *(from* **forego***)* fɔː'gɒn (US) fɔːr'gɑːn

foregone *(adj.)* 'fɔː.gɒn (US) 'fɔːr.gɑːn ˌ**foregone con'clusion**

foreground 'fɔː.graʊnd (US) 'fɔːr- **-s** -z

foregrounding 'fɔːˌgraʊn.dɪŋ (US) 'fɔːr-

forehand 'fɔː.hænd (US) 'fɔːr- **-s** -z

forehanded fɔː'hæn.dɪd (US) 'fɔːrˌ-, ˌ-'-- **-ly** -li **-ness** -nəs, -nɪs *stress shift, British only:* ˌforehanded 'volley

forehead 'fɔː.hed, 'fɒr.ɪd, -ed; (US) 'fɔːr.ed, -hed **-s** -z

foreign 'fɒr.ɪn, -ən (US) 'fɔːr- ˌ**foreign af'fairs**; ˌ**foreign corre'spondent**; ˌ**foreign ex'change**; ˌ**foreign 'legion**; **'Foreign ˌOffice**; ˌ**foreign 'policy**; ˌ**foreign 'secretary**; ˌ**Foreign 'Service**

foreigner 'fɒr.ɪ.nəʳ, '-ə- (US) 'fɔːr- **-s** -z

forejudg|e fɔː'dʒʌdʒ (US) fɔːr- **-es** -ɪz **-ing** -ɪŋ **-ed** -d

fore|know fɔː|'nəʊ (US) fɔːr|'noʊ **-knows** -'nəʊz (US) -'noʊz **-knowing** -'nəʊ.ɪŋ (US) -'noʊ.ɪŋ **-knew** -'njuː (US) -'nuː, -'njuː **-known** -'nəʊn (US) -'noʊn

foreknowledge fɔː'nɒl.ɪdʒ (US) fɔːr'nɑː.lɪdʒ

foreland (F) 'fɔː.lənd (US) 'fɔːr- **-s** -z

foreleg 'fɔː.leg (US) 'fɔːr- **-s** -z

forelock 'fɔː.lɒk (US) 'fɔːr.lɑːk **-s** -s

fore|man (F) 'fɔː|.mən (US) 'fɔːr- **-men** -mən

foremast 'fɔː.mɑːst (US) 'fɔːr.mæst *nautical pronunciation:* -məst **-s** -s

foremost 'fɔː.məʊst, -məst (US) 'fɔːr.moʊst

forename ˈfɔː.neɪm (US) ˈfɔːr- **-s** -z
forenoon ˈfɔː.nuːn (US) ˈfɔːr-, ˌ-ˈ- **-s** -z
forensic fəˈrent.sɪk, fɒrˈent-, -ˈen.zɪk (US) fəˈrent.sɪk, -ˈren.zɪk **-s** -s
foreordain ˌfɔːʳ.ɔːˈdeɪn (US) ˌfɔːr.ɔːrˈ- **-s** -z **-ing** -ɪŋ **-ed** -d
forepart ˈfɔː.pɑːt (US) ˈfɔːr.pɑːrt **-s** -s
foreplay ˈfɔː.pleɪ (US) ˈfɔːr-
fore|run fɔː|ˈrʌn (US) fɔːr- **-runs** -ˈrʌnz **-running** -ˈrʌn.ɪŋ **-ran** -ˈræn
forerunner ˈfɔːˌrʌn.əʳ, ˌ-ˈ-- (US) ˈfɔːrˌrʌn.ɚ, ˌ-ˈ-- **-s** -z
foresail ˈfɔː.seɪl (US) ˈfɔːr- *nautical pronunciation:* -sᵊl **-s** -z
fore|see fɔː|ˈsiː, fə- (US) fɔːr-, fɚ- **-sees** -ˈsiːz **-seeing** -ˈsiː.ɪŋ **-saw** -ˈsɔː (US) -ˈsɑː, -ˈsɔː **-seen** -ˈsiːn **-seeable** -ˈsiː.ə.bl̩
foreseeability fɔːˌsiː.əˈbɪl.ə.ti, ˌfɔː.siː-; fəˌsiː- (US) fɔːrˌsiː.əˈbɪl.ə.t̬i, fɚ-
foreshadow fɔːˈʃæd.əʊ (US) fɔːrˈʃæd.oʊ **-s** -z **-ing** -ɪŋ **-ed** -d **-er/s** -əʳ/z (US) -ɚ/z
foreshore ˈfɔː.ʃɔːʳ (US) ˈfɔːr.ʃɔːr **-s** -z
foreshorten fɔːˈʃɔː.tᵊn (US) fɔːrˈʃɔːr- **-s** -z **-ing** -ɪŋ **-ed** -d
foreshow fɔːˈʃəʊ (US) fɔːrˈʃoʊ **-s** -z **-ing** -ɪŋ **-ed** -d **-n** -n
foresight ˈfɔː.saɪt (US) ˈfɔːr- **-s** -s
foreskin ˈfɔː.skɪn (US) ˈfɔːr- **-s** -z
forest (F) ˈfɒr.ɪst (US) ˈfɔːr- **-s** -s ˌ**Forest ˈHills; ˌforest ˈranger** (US) **ˈforest ˌranger; not see the ˌforest for the ˈtrees**
forestall fɔːˈstɔːl (US) fɔːrˈstɔːl, -ˈstɑːl **-s** -z **-ing** -ɪŋ **-ed** -d **-er/s** -əʳ/z (US) -ɚ/z
forester (F) ˈfɒr.ɪ.stəʳ, ˈ-ə- (US) ˈfɔːr- **-s** -z
forestry ˈfɒr.ɪ.stri, ˈ-ə- (US) ˈfɔːr-
foretaste *(n.)* ˈfɔː.teɪst (US) ˈfɔːr- **-s** -s
foretast|e *(v.)* fɔːˈteɪst (US) fɔːr- **-es** -s **-ing** -ɪŋ **-ed** -ɪd
fore|tell fɔː|ˈtel (US) fɔːr- **-tells** -ˈtelz **-telling** -ˈtel.ɪŋ **-told** -ˈtəʊld (US) -ˈtoʊld **-teller/s** -ˈtel.əʳ/z (US) -ˈtel.ɚ/z
forethought ˈfɔː.θɔːt (US) ˈfɔːr.θɑːt, -θɔːt
foretop, fore-top ˈfɔː.tɒp (US) ˈfɔːr.tɑːp *nautical pronunciation:* -təp **-s** -s
fore-topmast fɔːˈtɒp.mɑːst (US) fɔːrˈtɑːp.mæst *nautical pronunciation:* -məst **-s** -s
fore-topsail fɔːˈtɒp.seɪl (US) fɔːrˈtɑːp- *nautical pronunciation:* -sᵊl **-s** -z
forever fəˈre.vəʳ (US) fɔːrˈev.ɚ, fɚ-
forewarn fɔːˈwɔːn (US) fɔːrˈwɔːrn **-s** -z **-ing** -ɪŋ **-ed** -d
forewent *(from **forego**)* fɔːˈwent (US) fɔːr-
fore|woman ˈfɔː|ˌwʊm.ən (US) ˈfɔːr- **-women** -ˌwɪm.ɪn
foreword ˈfɔː.wɜːd (US) ˈfɔːr.wɝːd **-s** -z

Forfar ˈfɔː.fəʳ, -fɑːʳ (US) ˈfɔːr.fɚ, -fɑːr
forfei|t ˈfɔː.fɪ|t (US) ˈfɔːr-, -fə|t **-ts** -ts **-ting** -tɪŋ (US) -t̬ɪŋ **-ted** -tɪd (US) -t̬ɪd **-ter/s** -təʳ/z (US) -t̬ɚ/z **-table** -tə.bl̩ (US) -t̬ə.bl̩
forfeiture ˈfɔː.fɪ.tʃəʳ (US) ˈfɔːr.fə- **-s** -z
forfend fɔːˈfend (US) fɔːr- **-s** -z **-ing** -ɪŋ **-ed** -ɪd
forgath|er fɔːˈgæð|.əʳ (US) fɔːrˈgæð|.ɚ **-ers** -əz (US) -ɚz **-ering** -ᵊr.ɪŋ **-ered** -əd (US) -ɚd
forgave *(from **forgive**)* fəˈgeɪv (US) fɚ-, fɔːr-
forg|e fɔːdʒ (US) fɔːrdʒ **-es** -ɪz **-ing** -ɪŋ **-ed** -d **-er/s** -əʳ/z (US) -ɚ/z
forger|y ˈfɔː.dʒᵊr|.i (US) ˈfɔːr- **-ies** -iz
for|get fə|ˈget (US) fɚ-, fɔːr- **-gets** -ˈgets **-getting** -ˈget.ɪŋ (US) -ˈget̬.ɪŋ **-got** -ˈgɒt (US) -ˈgɑːt **-gotten** -ˈgɒt.ᵊn (US) -ˈgɑː.tᵊn
forgetful fəˈget.fᵊl, -fʊl (US) fɚ-, fɔːr- **-ly** -i **-ness** -nəs, -nɪs
forget-me-not fəˈget.mi.nɒt (US) fɚˈget.mi.nɑːt, fɔːr- **-s** -s
forgettab|le fəˈget.ə.b|l̩ (US) fɚˈget̬-, fɔːr- **-ly** -li
for|give fə|ˈgɪv (US) fɚ-, fɔːr- **-gives** -ˈgɪvz **-giving** -ˈgɪv.ɪŋ **-gave** -ˈgeɪv **-given** -ˈgɪv.ᵊn **-givable** -ˈgɪv.ə.bl̩ **-giveness** -ˈgɪv.nəs, -nɪs
for|go fɔː|ˈgəʊ (US) fɔːr|ˈgoʊ **-goes** -ˈgəʊz (US) -ˈgoʊz **-going** -ˈgəʊ.ɪŋ (US) -ˈgoʊ.ɪŋ **-went** -ˈwent **-gone** -ˈgɒn (US) -ˈgɑːn
forgot *(from **forget**)* fəˈgɒt (US) fɚˈgɑːt, fɔːr-
forgotten *(from **forget**)* fəˈgɒt.ᵊn (US) fɚˈgɑː.tᵊn, fɔːr-
Forington ˈfɒr.ɪŋ.tən (US) ˈfɔːr-
forint ˈfɒr.ɪnt (US) ˈfɔːr- **-s** -s
fork fɔːk (US) fɔːrk **-s** -s **-ing** -ɪŋ **-ed** -t **-ful/s**
forklift ˈfɔːk.lɪft, ˌ-ˈ- (US) ˈfɔːrk.lɪft **-s** -s **-ing** -ɪŋ **-ed** -ɪd ˌ**forklift ˈtruck**
forlorn fəˈlɔːn, fɔː- (US) fɔːrˈlɔːrn, fɚ- **-ly** -li **-ness** -nəs, -nɪs
form fɔːm (US) fɔːrm **-s** -z **-ing** -ɪŋ **-ed** -d
formal ˈfɔː.mᵊl (US) ˈfɔːr- **-ly** -i
formaldehyde fɔːˈmæl.dɪ.haɪd, -də- (US) fɔːr-, fɚ-
formalin ˈfɔː.mᵊl.ɪn (US) ˈfɔːr.mə.lɪn
formal|ism ˈfɔː.mᵊl|.ɪ.zᵊm (US) ˈfɔːr- **-ist/s** -ɪst/s
formalit|y fɔːˈmæl.ə.t|i, -ɪ.t|i (US) -ə.t̬|i **-ies** -iz
formalization, -isa- ˌfɔː.mᵊl.aɪˈzeɪ.ʃᵊn, -ɪˈ- (US) ˌfɔːr.mᵊl.ɪˈ- **-s** -z
formaliz|e, -is|e ˈfɔː.mᵊl.aɪz (US) ˈfɔːr.mə.laɪz **-es** -ɪz **-ing** -ɪŋ **-ed** -d
Forman ˈfɔː.mən (US) ˈfɔːr-
formant ˈfɔː.mənt (US) ˈfɔːr- **-s** -s
for|mat ˈfɔː|.mæt (US) ˈfɔːr- **-mats** -mæts **-matting** -mæt.ɪŋ (US) -mæt̬.ɪŋ **-matted** -mæt.ɪd (US) -mæt̬.ɪd **-matter/s** -mæt.əʳ/z (US) -mæt̬.ɚ/z

formation fɔːˈmeɪ.ʃᵊn (US) fɔːr- **-s** -z
formative ˈfɔː.mə.tɪv (US) ˈfɔːr.mə.t̬ɪv **-ly** -li **-ness** -nəs, -nɪs
Formby ˈfɔːm.bi (US) ˈfɔːrm-
forme fɔːm (US) fɔːrm **-s** -z
former ˈfɔː.məʳ (US) ˈfɔːr.mɚ **-ly** -li
formic ˈfɔː.mɪk (US) ˈfɔːr- ˌ**formic ˈacid**
Formica® fɔːˈmaɪ.kə, fəˈmaɪ- (US) fɔːr-, fɚ-
formidab|le ˈfɔː.mɪ.də.b|l̩; fɔːˈmɪd.ə-, fə- (US) ˈfɔːr.mə.də.b|l̩; fɔːrˈmɪd.ə-, fɚ- **-ly** -li **-leness** -l̩.nəs, -nɪs
Formidable *name of ship:* fɔːˈmɪd.ə.bl̩; ˈfɔː.mɪ.də- (US) ˈfɔːr.mə.də-; fɔːrˈmɪd.ə-
formless ˈfɔːm.ləs (US) ˈfɔːrm-, -lɪs **-ness** -nəs, -nɪs
Formos|a fɔːˈməʊ.s|ə, -z|ə (US) fɔːrˈmoʊ- **-an/s** -ən/z
formul|a ˈfɔː.mjə.l|ə, -mjʊ- (US) ˈfɔːr.mjʊ-, -mjə- **-ae** -iː **-as** -əz
formulaic ˌfɔː.mjəˈleɪ.ɪk, -mjʊˈ- (US) ˌfɔːr.mjʊˈ-, -mjəˈ-
formular|y ˈfɔː.mjə.lə.r|i, -mjʊ- (US) ˈfɔːr.mjʊ.ler|.i, -mjə- **-ies** -iz
formu|late ˈfɔː.mjə|.leɪt, -mjʊ- (US) ˈfɔːr.mjʊ-, -mjə- **-lates** -leɪts **-lating** -leɪ.tɪŋ (US) -leɪ.t̬ɪŋ **-lated** -leɪ.tɪd (US) -leɪ.t̬ɪd
formulation ˌfɔː.mjəˈleɪ.ʃᵊn, -mjʊˈ- (US) ˌfɔːr.mjʊˈ-, -mjəˈ- **-s** -z
Fornax ˈfɔː.næks (US) ˈfɔːr-
Forney ˈfɔː.ni (US) ˈfɔːr-
forni|cate ˈfɔː.nɪ|.keɪt, -nə- (US) ˈfɔːr- **-cates** -keɪts **-cating** -keɪ.tɪŋ (US) -keɪ.t̬ɪŋ **-cated** -keɪ.tɪd (US) -keɪ.t̬ɪd **-cator/s** -keɪ.təʳ/z (US) -keɪ.t̬ɚ/z
fornication ˌfɔː.nɪˈkeɪ.ʃᵊn, -nəˈ- (US) ˌfɔːr-
Forres ˈfɒr.ɪs (US) ˈfɔːr-
Forrest ˈfɒr.ɪst (US) ˈfɔːr-
Forrester ˈfɒr.ɪ.stəʳ (US) ˈfɔːr.ɪ.stɚ
for|sake fə|ˈseɪk, fɔː- (US) fɔːr-, fɚ- **-sakes** -ˈseɪks **-saking** -ˈseɪ.kɪŋ **-sook** -ˈsʊk **-saken** -ˈseɪ.kᵊn
Forshaw ˈfɔː.ʃɔː (US) ˈfɔːr.ʃɑː, -ʃɔː
forsooth fəˈsuːθ, fɔː- (US) fɔːr-, fɚ-
Forster ˈfɔː.stəʳ (US) ˈfɔːr.stɚ
for|swear fɔː|ˈsweəʳ (US) fɔːr|ˈswer **-swears** -ˈsweəz (US) -ˈswerz **-swearing** -ˈsweə.rɪŋ (US) -ˈswer.ɪŋ **-swore** -ˈswɔːʳ (US) -ˈswɔːr **-sworn** -ˈswɔːn (US) -ˈswɔːrn
Forsyte ˈfɔː.saɪt (US) ˈfɔːr-
Forsyth ˈfɔː.saɪθ, -ˈ- (US) ˈfɔːr-, -ˈ-
forsythia fɔːˈsaɪ.θi.ə, fə-, -ˈsɪθ.i- (US) fɔːrˈsɪθ-, -ˈsaɪ.θi- **-s** -z
fort fɔːt (US) fɔːrt **-s** -s ˌ**Fort ˈKnox;** ˌ**Fort**

Fortis

Fortis sounds are said to be made with a relatively high degree of effort.

Examples for English

It is claimed that in some languages (including English) there are pairs of consonants whose members can be distinguished from each other in terms of whether they are 'strong' (fortis) or 'weak' (LENIS). These terms refer to the amount of energy used in their production, and are similar to the terms TENSE and LAX more usually used in relation to vowels. It is argued that English /b d g v ð z ʒ/ often have little or no voicing in normal speech, and it is therefore a misnomer to call them voiced. Since they seem to be more weakly articulated than /p t k f θ s ʃ/ it would be appropriate to use the term lenis instead, e.g.:

pin	/pɪn/	[pʰɪ̃n]
bin	/bɪn/	[b̥ɪ̃n]
fine	/faɪn/	[faɪ̃n]
vine	/vaɪn/	[v̥aɪ̃n]

ˈLauderdale; ˌFort ˈWorth; ˌhold the ˈfort
Fortaleza ˌfɔː.təˈleɪ.zə (US) ˌfɔːr.t̬əˈ-
forte *strong point:* ˈfɔː.teɪ, -ti (US) fɔːrt, ˈfɔːr.teɪ **-s** -z (US) fɔːrts; ˈfɔːr.teɪz
forte *in music:* ˈfɔː.teɪ, -ti (US) ˈfɔːr- **-s** -z
Fortescue ˈfɔː.tɪ.skjuː, -tə- (US) ˈfɔːr.t̬ə-
Forteviot fɔːˈtiː.vi.ət (US) fɔːr-
forth (F) fɔːθ (US) fɔːrθ
forthcoming ˌfɔːθˈkʌm.ɪŋ (US) ˌfɔːrθˈ-, ˈ-ˌ-- *stress shift, British only:* ˌforthcoming ˈbook
forthright ˈfɔːθ.raɪt, ˌ-ˈ- (US) ˈfɔːrθ-, ˌ-ˈ- **-ness** -nəs, -nɪs
forthwith ˌfɔːθˈwɪθ, -ˈwɪð (US) ˌfɔːrθˈ-
Forties *area in the North Sea:* ˈfɔː.tiz, -tɪz (US) ˈfɔːr.t̬iz
fortieth ˈfɔː.ti.əθ, -ɪθ (US) ˈfɔːr.t̬i- **-s** -s
fortification ˌfɔː.tɪ.fɪˈkeɪ.ʃᵊn, -tə- (US) ˌfɔːr.t̬ə- **-s** -z
forti|fy ˈfɔː.tɪ|.faɪ, -tə- (US) ˈfɔːr.t̬ə- **-fies** -faɪz **-fying** -faɪ.ɪŋ **-fied** -faɪd **-fier/s** -faɪ.əʳ/z (US) -faɪ.ɚ/z **-fiable** -faɪ.ə.bl̩
Fortinbras ˈfɔː.tɪn.bræs, -tɪm- (US) ˈfɔːr.tᵊn-, -t̬ɪn-
fort|is ˈfɔː.t|ɪs (US) ˈfɔːr.t̬|ɪs **-es** -iːz, -eɪz
fortissimo fɔːˈtɪs.ɪ.məʊ, -ə- (US) fɔːrˈtɪs.ə.moʊ **-s** -z
fortition fɔːˈtɪʃ.ᵊn (US) fɔːr-
fortitude ˈfɔː.tɪ.tjuːd, -tʃuːd (US) ˈfɔːr.t̬ə.tuːd, -tjuːd
fortnight ˈfɔːt.naɪt (US) ˈfɔːrt- **-s** -s
fortnightl|y (F) ˈfɔːt.naɪt.l|i (US) ˈfɔːrt- **-ies** -iz
Fortnum ˈfɔːt.nəm (US) ˈfɔːrt-
Fortran, FORTRAN ˈfɔː.træn (US) ˈfɔːr-
fortress ˈfɔː.trəs, -trɪs (US) ˈfɔːr- **-es** -ɪz
fortuitous fɔːˈtjuː.ɪ.təs, -ˈtʃuː-, ˈ-ə- (US) fɔːrˈtuː.ə.t̬əs, -ˈtjuː- **-ly** -li **-ness** -nəs, -nɪs
fortuit|y fɔːˈtjuː.ɪ.t|i, -ˈtʃuː-, ˈ-ə- (US) fɔːrˈtuː.ə.t̬|i, -ˈtjuː- **-ies** -iz
Fortuna fɔːˈtjuː.nə (US) fɔːrˈtuː-, -ˈtjuː-
fortunate ˈfɔː.tʃᵊn.ət, -ɪt (US) ˈfɔːr- **-ly** -li **-ness** -nəs, -nɪs
Fortunatus ˌfɔː.tjuːˈneɪ.təs, -ˈnɑː- (US) ˌfɔːr.tuːˈnɑː.t̬əs, -ˈneɪ-
fortune (F) ˈfɔː.tʃuːn, -tjuːn, -tʃən (US) ˈfɔːr.tʃən **-s** -z **-less** -ləs, -lɪs **ˈfortune ˌcookie**
fortune-teller ˈfɔː.tʃuːnˌtel.əʳ, -tjuːnˌ-, -tʃənˌ- (US) ˈfɔːr.tʃənˌtel.ɚ **-s** -z
fort|y ˈfɔː.t|i (US) ˈfɔːr.t̬|i **-ies** -iz **ˌforty ˈwinks**
forty-five ˌfɔː.tiˈfaɪv (US) ˌfɔːr.t̬iˈ- **-s** -z
fortyfold ˈfɔː.ti.fəʊld (US) ˈfɔːr.t̬i-
forty-niner ˌfɔː.tiˈnaɪ.nəʳ (US) ˌfɔːr.t̬iˈnaɪ.nɚ **-s** -z
forum ˈfɔː.rəm (US) ˈfɔːr.əm **-s** -z
forward ˈfɔː.wəd (US) ˈfɔːr.wɚd *nautical pronunciation:* ˈfɒr.əd (US) ˈfɔːr- **-ly** -li **-ness** -nəs, -nɪs **-er** -əʳ (US) -ɚ **-est** -ɪst, -əst **-s** -z **-ing** -ɪŋ **-ed** -ɪd **ˌbackwards and ˈforwards**
forwards ˈfɔː.wədz (US) ˈfɔːr.wɚdz
forwent *(from* **forgo***)* fɔːˈwent (US) fɔːr-
Fosbery ˈfɒz.bᵊr.i (US) ˈfɑːzˌber-, -bɚ-
Fosbroke ˈfɒz.brʊk (US) ˈfɑːz-
Fosbury ˈfɒz.bᵊr.i (US) ˈfɑːzˌber-, -bɚ-
Fosco ˈfɒs.kəʊ (US) ˈfɑː.skoʊ
Foss fɒs (US) fɑːs
foss|e fɒs (US) fɑːs **-es** -ɪz
fossick ˈfɒs.ɪk (US) ˈfɑː.sɪk **-s** -s **-ing** -ɪŋ **-ed** -t
fossil ˈfɒs.ᵊl, -ɪl (US) ˈfɑː.sᵊl **-s** -z
fossilization, -isa- ˌfɒs.ᵊl.aɪˈzeɪ.ʃᵊn, -ɪ.laɪˈ-, -lɪˈ- (US) ˌfɑː.sᵊl.ɪˈ-
fossiliz|e, -is|e ˈfɒs.ᵊl.aɪz, -ɪ.laɪz (US) ˈfɑː.sə.laɪz **-es** -ɪz **-ing** -ɪŋ **-ed** -d
fost|er (F) ˈfɒs.t|əʳ (US) ˈfɑː.st|ɚ **-ers** -əz (US) -ɚz **-ering** -ᵊr.ɪŋ **-ered** -əd (US) -ɚd **-erer/s** -ᵊr.əʳ/z (US) -ɚ.ɚ/z **-erage** -ᵊr.ɪdʒ **ˈfoster ˌbrother; ˈfoster ˌchild; ˈfoster ˌchildren; ˈfoster ˌfather; ˈfoster ˌhome; ˈfoster ˌmother; ˈfoster ˌparent; ˈfoster ˌsister**
Fothergill ˈfɒð.ə.gɪl (US) ˈfɑː.ðɚ-
Fotheringay ˈfɒð.ᵊr.ɪŋ.heɪ, -geɪ (US) ˈfɑː.ðɚ-
Fotheringham ˈfɒð.ᵊr.ɪŋ.əm (US) ˈfɑː.ðɚ-
Foucault ˈfuː.kəʊ, -ˈ- (US) ˌfuːˈkoʊ
fouetté ˈfuː.ə.teɪ (US) fwetˈeɪ **-s** -z
fought *(from* **fight***)* fɔːt (US) fɑːt, fɔːt
foul faʊl **-er** -əʳ (US) -ɚ **-est** -ɪst, -əst **-ly** -li, ˈfaʊ.li **-ness** -nəs, -nɪs **-s** -z **-ing** -ɪŋ **-ed** -d **ˌfoul ˈplay**
foulard ˈfuː.lɑːʳ, -lɑːd, -ˈ- (US) fuːˈlɑːrd
Foulden ˈfəʊl.dən (US) ˈfoʊl-
Foulds fəʊldz (US) foʊldz
Foulerton ˈfʊl.ə.tᵊn (US) ˈ-ɚ-
Foulger ˈfuːl.dʒəʳ, -gəʳ (US) ˈfuːl.dʒɚ, ˈfoʊl-, -gɚ
Foulis faʊlz
Foulkes fəʊks, faʊks (US) foʊks, faʊks
foulmouthed ˌfaʊlˈmaʊðd, -ˈmaʊθt (US) ˌ-ˈ-, ˈ-ˌ- *stress shift, British only:* ˌfoulmouthed ˈlanguage
foulness ˈfaʊl.nəs
Foulness ˌfaʊlˈnes, -nɪs *stress shift:* ˌFoulness ˈbeach
Foulsham ˈfəʊl.ʃᵊm (US) ˈfoʊl-
foul-up ˈfaʊl.ʌp **-s** -s
found faʊnd **-s** -z **-ing** -ɪŋ **-ed** -ɪd
found *(from* ***find****)* faʊnd
foundation faʊnˈdeɪ.ʃᵊn **-s** -z **founˈdation ˌcourse; founˈdation ˌstone**
foundationer faʊnˈdeɪ.ʃᵊn.əʳ (US) -ɚ **-s** -z
found|er ˈfaʊn.d|əʳ (US) -d|ɚ **-ers** -əz (US) -ɚz **-ering** -ᵊr.ɪŋ **-ered** -əd (US) -ɚd **ˌfounder ˈmember**
foundling (F) ˈfaʊnd.lɪŋ **-s** -z
foundr|y ˈfaʊn.dr|i **-ies** -iz
fount *fountain, source:* faʊnt **-s** -s
fount *in printing:* faʊnt, fɒnt (US) faʊnt, fɑːnt **-s** -s
Note: Those connected with the printing trade generally pronounce /fɒnt, (US) fɑːnt/.

fountain (F) ˈfaʊn.tɪn, -tən (US) -tᵊn **-s** -z
ˈ**fountain** ˌ**pen**
fountainhead ˈfaʊn.tɪn.hed, -tən-, ˌ--ˈ- (US) ˈfaʊn.tᵊn.hed **-s** -z
four fɔːʳ (US) fɔːr **-s** -z **-th/s** -θ/s **-thly** -θ.li ˌ**Four** ˈ**Corners**
four-cornered ˌfɔːˈkɔː.nəd (US) ˌfɔːrˈkɔːr.nɚd *stress shift:* ˌfour-cornered ˈhat
four-dimensional ˌfɔː.dɪˈmen.*t*ʃᵊn.ᵊl, -daɪˈ- (US) ˌfɔːr.dəˈmen*t*.ʃᵊn- *stress shift:* ˌfour-dimensional ˈmodel
fourfold ˈfɔː.fəʊld (US) ˈfɔːr.foʊld
four-footed ˌfɔːˈfʊt.ɪd (US) ˌfɔːrˈfʊt̬- *stress shift:* ˌfour-footed ˈbeast
Fourier ˈfʊə.ri.əʳ, ˈfʊr.i-, -eɪ (US) ˈfʊr.i.eɪ
four-in-hand ˌfɔːʳ.ɪnˈhænd (US) ˈfɔːr.ɪnˌhænd **-s** -z
four-legged ˌfɔːˈlegd, -ˈleg.ɪd (US) ˌfɔːr-, ˈfɔːrˌ- *stress shift:* ˌfour-legged ˈfriend
four-letter ˌfɔːˈlet.əʳ (US) ˌfɔːrˈlet̬.ɚ *stress shift, see compound:* ˌ**four-letter** ˈ**word**
fourpence ˈfɔː.pᵊn*t*s (US) ˈfɔːr-
fourpenny ˈfɔː.pᵊn.i (US) ˈfɔːr-
four-ply ˈfɔː.plaɪ, ˌ-ˈ- (US) ˈfɔːr.plaɪ, ˌ-ˈ-
four-poster ˌfɔːˈpəʊ.stəʳ (US) ˌfɔːrˈpoʊ.stɚ **-s** -z *stress shift, see compound:* ˌ**four-poster** ˈ**bed**
fourscore ˌfɔːˈskɔːʳ (US) ˌfɔːrˈskɔːr *stress shift:* ˌfourscore ˈyears
foursome ˈfɔː.səm (US) ˈfɔːr- **-s** -z
foursquare ˌfɔːˈskweəʳ, ˈ-- (US) ˌfɔːrˈskwer, ˈ--
fourteen ˌfɔːˈtiːn (US) ˌfɔːr- **-s** -z **-th/s** -θ/s *stress shift:* ˌfourteen ˈyears
fourteener fɔːˈtiː.nəʳ (US) fɔːrˈtiː.nɚ **-s** -z
fourth fɔːθ (US) fɔːrθ **-s** -s **-ly** -li ˌ**Fourth of Ju**ˈ**ly**
four-wheel drive ˌfɔː.*h*wiːlˈdraɪv (US) ˌfɔːr- *stress shift, British only:* ˌfour-wheel drive ˈcar
four-wheeler ˌfɔːˈ*h*wiː.ləʳ (US) ˌfɔːrˈ*h*wiː.lɚ **-s** -z
fov|ea ˈfɒv|.i.ə, ˈfəʊ.v|i- (US) ˈfoʊ- **-eae** -i.iː
Fowey fɔɪ, ˈfəʊ.i (US) fɔɪ, ˈfoʊ.i
Fowke faʊk, fəʊk (US) faʊk, foʊk
Fowkes fəʊks, faʊks (US) foʊks, faʊks
fowl faʊl **-s** -z **-ing** -ɪŋ **-ed** -d **-er/s** -əʳ/z (US) -ɚ/z ˈ**fowling** ˌ**piece**
Fowler ˈfaʊ.ləʳ (US) -lɚ
Fowles faʊlz
fox (F) fɒks (US) fɑːks **-es** -ɪz **-ing** -ɪŋ **-ed** -t ˌ**fox** ˈ**terrier**
Foxboro' ˈfɒks.bᵊr.ə (US) ˈfɑːks.bɚ.oʊ
Foxcroft ˈfɒks.krɒft (US) ˈfɑːks.krɑːft
Foxe fɒks (US) fɑːks
Foxfield ˈfɒks.fiːld (US) ˈfɑːks-
foxglove ˈfɒks.glʌv (US) ˈfɑːks- **-s** -z
foxhole ˈfɒks.həʊl (US) ˈfɑːks.hoʊl **-s** -z
foxhound ˈfɒks.haʊnd (US) ˈfɑːks- **-s** -z
fox|hunt ˈfɒks|.hʌnt (US) ˈfɑːks- **-hunts** -hʌnts **-hunting** -ˌhʌn.tɪŋ (US) -ˌhʌn.t̬ɪŋ
foxtrot ˈfɒks.trɒt (US) ˈfɑːks.trɑːt **-s** -s
Foxwell ˈfɒks.wəl, -wel (US) ˈfɑːks-
fox|y ˈfɒk.s|i (US) ˈfɑːk- **-ier** -i.əʳ (US) -i.ɚ **-iest** -i.ɪst, -i.əst **-ily** -ɪ.li, -ə.li **-iness** -ɪ.nəs, -ɪ.nɪs
Foy fɔɪ
foyer ˈfɔɪ.eɪ, -əʳ; ˈfwaɪ.eɪ (US) ˈfɔɪ.ɚ, -eɪ; fɔɪˈeɪ, fwɑːˈ- **-s** -z
Foyers ˈfɔɪ.əz (US) -ɚz
Foyle fɔɪl
Fr. *(abbrev. for* **Father***)* ˈfɑː.ðəʳ (US) -ðɚ
frabjous ˈfræb.dʒəs
fracas *singular:* ˈfræk.ɑː (US) ˈfreɪ.kəs, ˈfræk.əs *American usage only:* **-es** (US) -ɪz *plural:* ˈfræk.ɑːz (US) ˈfreɪ.kəs, ˈfræk.əs
fractal ˈfræk.tᵊl **-s** -z
fraction ˈfræk.ʃᵊn **-s** -z
fractional ˈfræk.ʃᵊn.ᵊl **-ly** -i
fraction|ate ˈfræk.ʃᵊn|.eɪt **-ates** -eɪts **-ating** -eɪ.tɪŋ (US) -eɪ.t̬ɪŋ **-ated** -eɪ.tɪd (US) -eɪ.t̬ɪd
fractious ˈfræk.ʃəs **-ly** -li **-ness** -nəs, -nɪs
fract|ure ˈfræk.*t*ʃ|əʳ (US) -tʃ|ɚ **-ures** -əz (US) -ɚz **-uring** -ᵊr.ɪŋ **-ured** -əd (US) -ɚd
fragile ˈfrædʒ.aɪl (US) ˈfrædʒ.ᵊl **-ly** -li
fragility frəˈdʒɪl.ə.ti, frædʒˈɪl-, -ɪ.ti (US) frəˈdʒɪl.ə.t̬i
fragment (*n.*) ˈfræg.mənt **-s** -s
fragmen|t (*v.*) frægˈmen|t (US) ˈfræg.men|t, -ˈ- **-ts** -ts **-ting** -tɪŋ (US) -t̬ɪŋ **-ted** -tɪd (US) -t̬ɪd
fragmental frægˈmen.tᵊl (US) -t̬ᵊl
fragmentar|y ˈfræg.mən.tᵊr|.i, -tr|i; frægˈmen- (US) ˈfræg.mən.ter|.i **-ily** -ᵊl.i, -ɪ.li **-iness** -ɪ.nəs, -ɪ.nɪs
fragmentation ˌfræg.mənˈteɪ.ʃᵊn, -menˈ-
Fragonard ˈfræg.ɒn.ɑːʳ, -ən- (US) ˌfræg.əˈnɑːr, ˌfrɑː.goʊˈ-
fragranc|e ˈfreɪ.grən*t*s **-es** -ɪz **-ed** -t
fragrant ˈfreɪ.grənt **-ly** -li **-ness** -nəs, -nɪs
frail freɪl **-er** -əʳ (US) -ɚ **-est** -ɪst, -əst **-ly** -li **-ness** -nəs, -nɪs
frailt|y ˈfreɪl.t|i (US) -t̬|i **-ies** -iz
frambesia, framboesia fræmˈbiː.zi.ə, -ʒə, ʒi.ə (US) -ʒə, -ʒi.ə
fram|e (F) freɪm **-es** -z **-ing** -ɪŋ **-ed** -d **-er/s** -əʳ/z (US) -ɚ/z
frame-up ˈfreɪm.ʌp **-s** -s
framework ˈfreɪm.wɜːk (US) -wɝːk **-s** -s
Framingham *in UK:* ˈfreɪ.mɪŋ.əm *in US:* ˈfræm.ɪŋ.hæm
Framley ˈfræm.li
Framlingham ˈfræm.lɪŋ.əm
Framlington ˈfræm.lɪŋ.tən
Frampton ˈfræm*p*.tən
Fran fræn
franc fræŋk **-s** -s
France frɑːn*t*s (US) fræn*t*s
Frances ˈfrɑːn*t*.sɪs (US) ˈfræn*t*-
Francesca frænˈtʃes.kə (US) fræn-, frɑːn-
Franche-Comté ˌfrɑ̃ːn*ʃ*.kɔ̃ː*n*ˈteɪ (US) -koʊ̃nˈ-
franchis|e ˈfræn.*t*ʃaɪz **-es** -ɪz **-ing** -ɪŋ **-ed** -d **-er/s** -əʳ/z (US) -ɚ/z
franchisee ˌfræn.*t*ʃaɪˈziː **-s** -z
Francie ˈfrɑːn*t*.si (US) ˈfræn*t*-
Francine fræn*t*ˈsiːn, ˈ--
Francis ˈfrɑːn*t*.sɪs (US) ˈfræn*t*-
Franciscan frænˈsɪs.kən **-s** -z
Francisco frænˈsɪs.kəʊ (US) -koʊ *in* ***San Francisco:*** frənˈsɪs.kəʊ, fræn- (US) -koʊ
francium ˈfræn*t*.si.əm
Franck frɑ̃ːŋk, frɑːŋk, fræŋk (US) frɑ̃ːŋk
Franco-, franco- fræŋ.kəʊ- (US) fræŋ.koʊ-, -kə-
Note: Prefix. Normally either takes primary or secondary stress on the first syllable, e.g. **francophile** /ˈfræŋ.kəʊ.faɪl (US) -koʊ-/, **Franco-German** /ˌfræŋ.kəʊˈdʒɜː.mən (US) -koʊˈdʒɜːr-/.
Franco ˈfræŋ.kəʊ (US) -koʊ
Franco-German ˌfræŋ.kəʊˈdʒɜː.mən (US) -koʊˈdʒɝː-
Francois, François ˈfrɑ̃ː*n*.swɑː, -ˈ- (US) frɑ̃ːn*t*ˈswɑː, fræn*t*ˈ-, ˈ-ˌ-
Francoise, Françoise ˈfrɑːn*t*.swɑːz, ˈfrɒn*t*-, ˈfræn*t*-, ˌ-ˈ- (US) ˌfrɑːn*t*ˈswɑːz
francolin ˈfræŋ.kəʊ.lɪn (US) -koʊ- **-s** -z
Franconi|a fræŋˈkəʊ.ni|.ə (US) fræŋˈkoʊ-, fræn- **-an** -ən
francophile ˈfræŋ.kəʊ.faɪl (US) -koʊ-, -kə- **-s** -z
francophobe ˈfræŋ.kəʊ.fəʊb (US) -koʊ.foʊb, -kə- **-s** -z
francophone (F) ˈfræŋ.kəʊ.fəʊn (US) -koʊ.foʊn, -kə- **-s** -z
francophonic (F) ˌfræŋ.kəʊˈfɒn.ɪk (US) -koʊˈfɑː.nɪk, -kəˈ-
frangibility ˌfræn.dʒɪˈbɪl.ə.ti, -dʒəˈ-, -ɪ.ti (US) -ə.t̬i
frangible ˈfræn.dʒɪ.bl̩, -dʒə- **-ness** -nəs, -nɪs
frangipani ˌfræn.dʒɪˈpɑː.ni, -ˈpæn.i **-s** -z
franglais ˈfrɑ̃ː*ŋ*.gleɪ, ˈfrɒŋ- (US) frɑ̃ːnˈgleɪ
frank (F) fræŋk **-er** -əʳ (US) -ɚ **-est** -ɪst, -əst **-ly** -li **-ness** -nəs, -nɪs **-s** -s **-ing** -ɪŋ **-ed** -t
Frankau ˈfræŋ.kəʊ, -kaʊ (US) -kaʊ
Frankenstein ˈfræŋ.kᵊn.staɪn, -kɪn-
Frankfort *places in US:* ˈfræŋk.fət (US) -fɚt

Frankfurt *in Germany:* 'fræŋk.fɜːt, -fət (US) -fɝːt, -fɚt
frankfurter (F) 'fræŋk.fɜː.təʳ (US) -fɝː.t̬ɚ **-s** -z
Frankie 'fræŋ.ki
frankincense 'fræŋ.kɪn.sen*t*s, -kᵊn-
Frankish 'fræŋ.kɪʃ
Frankland 'fræŋk.lənd
franklin (F) 'fræŋk.lɪn **-s** -z
Franklyn 'fræŋk.lɪn
Franks fræŋks
frantic 'fræn.tɪk (US) -t̬ɪk **-ally** -ᵊl.i, -li **-ness** -nəs, -nɪs
Franz *German name:* fræn*t*s, frɑːn*t*s *US name:* frænz
frap fræp **-s** -s **-ping** -ɪŋ **-ped** -t
frappé 'fræp.eɪ (US) -'-
Frascati fræs'kɑː.ti
Fraser 'freɪ.zəʳ (US) -zɚ
Fraserburgh 'freɪ.zə.bᵊr.ə, -bʌr- (US) -zɚ.bɚ-
Frasier 'freɪ.ʒəʳ, 'freɪ.zi.ə (US) -ʒɚ
frat fræt **-s** -s
fraternal frə'tɜː.nᵊl (US) -'tɝː- **-ly** -i
fraternit|y frə'tɜː.nə.t|i, -ɪ.t|i (US) -'tɝː.nə.t̬|i **-ies** -iz
fraternization, -isa- ˌfræt.ᵊn.aɪ'zeɪ.ʃᵊn, -ɪ'- (US) -ɚ.nɪ'-
fraterniz|e, -is|e 'fræt.ə.naɪz (US) '-ɚ- **-es** -ɪz **-ing** -ɪŋ **-ed** -d **-er/s** -əʳ/z (US) -ɚ/z
fratricidal ˌfræt.rɪ'saɪ.dᵊl, ˌfreɪ.trɪ'-, -trə'- (US) ˌfræt.rə'saɪ-
fratricide 'fræt.rɪ.saɪd, 'freɪ.trɪ-, -trə- (US) 'fræt.rə- **-s** -z
Fratton 'fræt.ᵊn
Frau fraʊ
fraud frɔːd (US) frɑːd, frɔːd **-s** -z
fraudster 'frɔːd.stəʳ (US) 'frɑːd.stɚ, 'frɔːd- **-s** -z
fraudulence 'frɔː.djə.lən*t*s, -djʊ-, -dʒə-, -dʒʊ- (US) 'frɑː.dʒə-, 'frɔː-, -djuː-, -djə-
fraudulent 'frɔː.djə.lənt, -djʊ-, -dʒə-, -dʒʊ- (US) 'frɑː.dʒə-, 'frɔː-, -djuː-, -djə- **-ly** -li
fraught frɔːt (US) frɑːt, frɔːt
fraülein 'frɔɪ.laɪn, 'fraʊ- **-s** -z
fray freɪ **-s** -z **-ing** -ɪŋ **-ed** -d
Fray Bentos® ˌfreɪ'ben.tɒs (US) -toʊs
Frayn freɪn
Frazer 'freɪ.zəʳ (US) -zɚ
Frazier 'freɪ.zi.əʳ (US) -ʒɚ, -ʒi.ɚ
frazil 'freɪ.zɪl, 'fræz.ɪl, -ᵊl (US) 'freɪ.zɪl; 'fræz.ᵊl; frə'zɪl, -'ziːl
frazzl|e 'fræz.l̩ **-es** -z **-ing** -ɪŋ, '-lɪŋ **-ed** -d
freak friːk **-s** -s **-ing** -ɪŋ **-ed** -t
Freake friːk
freakish 'friː.kɪʃ **-ly** -li **-ness** -nəs, -nɪs
freak|y 'friː.k|i **-ier** -i.əʳ (US) -i.ɚ **-iest** -i.ɪst, -i.əst **-ily** -ɪ.li, -ᵊl.i **-iness** -ɪ.nəs, -ɪ.nɪs
Frean friːn
Frears frɪəz, freəz (US) frɪrz, frerz
freckl|e 'frek.l̩ **-es** -z **-ing** -ɪŋ, '-lɪŋ **-ed** -d
Freckleton 'frek.l̩.tən
freckly 'frek.l̩.i, 'frek.li
Fred fred
Freda 'friː.də
Freddie, Freddy 'fred.i
Frederica ˌfred.ᵊr'iː.kə (US) -ə'riː-
Frederic(k) 'fred.ᵊr.ɪk
Fredericksburg 'fred.ᵊr.ɪks.bɜːg (US) -bɝːg
free (F) friː **-r** -əʳ (US) -ɚ **-st** -ɪst, -əst **-ly** -li **-s** -z **-ing** -ɪŋ **-d** -d **-r/s** -əʳ/z (US) -ɚ/z ˌ**free 'enterprise;** '**free** ˌ**house;** ˌ**free 'kick;** ˌ**free 'market;** ˌ**free 'ride;** ˌ**free 'trade;** ˌ**free 'will; give someone a** ˌ**free 'hand**
freebas|e 'friː.beɪs **-es** -ɪz **-ing** -ɪŋ **-ed** -t
freebie, freebee 'friː.bi **-s** -z
freeboard 'friː.bɔːd (US) -bɔːrd
freebooter 'friːˌbuː.təʳ (US) -t̬ɚ **-s** -z
freeborn ˌfriː'bɔːn (US) -'bɔːrn *stress shift:* ˌfreeborn 'citizen
Freeborn 'friː.bɔːn (US) -bɔːrn
Freeburn 'friː.bɜːn (US) -bɝːn
freed|man 'friːd|.mæn, -mən **-men** -men, -mən
freedom 'friː.dəm **-s** -z '**freedom** ˌ**fighter**
free-fall (*v.*) 'friː.fɔːl, ˌ-'- (US) 'friː.fɔːl, -fɑːl **-ing** -ɪŋ **-er/s** -əʳ/z (US) -ɚ/z
Freefone® 'friː.fəʊn (US) -foʊn
free-for-all 'friː.fəʳˌɔːl, ˌ--'- (US) 'friː.fɚ.ɔːl, -ɑːl
freehand 'friː.hænd
freehearted ˌfriː'hɑː.tɪd (US) -'hɑːr.t̬ɪd, '-ˌ-- **-ly** -li **-ness** -nəs, -nɪs *stress shift, British only:* ˌfreehearted 'friend
freehold 'friː.həʊld (US) -hoʊld **-s** -z **-er/s** -əʳ/z (US) -ɚ/z
freelanc|e 'friː.lɑːn*t*s, ˌ-'- (US) 'friː.læn*t*s **-es** -ɪz **-ing** -ɪŋ **-ed** -t **-er/s** -əʳ/z (US) -ɚ/z
Freeling 'friː.lɪŋ
freeload 'friː.ləʊd (US) -loʊd **-s** -z **-ing** -ɪŋ **-ed** -ɪd **-er/s** -əʳ/z (US) -ɚ/z
free|man 'friː|.mən, -mæn **-men** -mən, -men
Freeman *surname:* 'friː.mən
free-market (*adj.*) 'friːˌmɑː.kɪt (US) -ˌmɑːr-
free market (*n.*) ˌfriː'mɑː.kɪt (US) -'mɑːr-
freemason 'friːˌmeɪ.sᵊn **-s** -z
freemasonry 'friːˌmeɪ.sᵊn.ri, ˌfriː'meɪ-
freephone 'friː.fəʊn (US) -foʊn
Freeport 'friː.pɔːt (US) -pɔːrt
Freepost® 'friː.pəʊst (US) -poʊst
free-range ˌfriː'reɪndʒ *stress shift, see compounds:* ˌ**free-range 'eggs;** ˌ**free-range 'chickens**
Freeserve® 'friː.sɜːv (US) -sɝːv
freesheet 'friː.ʃiːt **-s** -s
freesia 'friː.zi.ə, -ʒə, -ʒi.ə (US) -ʒi.ə, -ʒə **-s** -z
free-spoken ˌfriː'spəʊ.kᵊn (US) ˌfriː'spoʊ-, '-ˌ-- *stress shift, British only:* ˌfree-spoken 'person
free-standing ˌfriː'stæn.dɪŋ (US) ˌfriː'stæn.dɪŋ, '-ˌ-- *stress shift, British only:* ˌfree-standing 'column
freestone (F) 'friː.stəʊn (US) -stoʊn
freestyle 'friː.staɪl
Freeth friːθ
freethinker ˌfriː'θɪŋ.kəʳ (US) -kɚ, '-ˌ-- **-s** -z
Freetown 'friː.taʊn
freeway 'friː.weɪ **-s** -z
freewheel ˌfriː'*h*wiːl (US) 'friː.*h*wiːl **-s** -z **-ing** -ɪŋ **-ed** -d *stress shift, British only:* ˌfreewheel 'mechanism
freewill ˌfriː'wɪl, '--
freez|e friːz **-es** -ɪz **-ing** -ɪŋ **froze** frəʊz (US) froʊz **frozen** 'frəʊ.zᵊn (US) 'froʊ- **freezer/s** 'friː.zəʳ/z (US) -zɚ/z '**freeze** ˌ**frame** ˌ**freeze 'frame**
freeze|-dry 'friːz|.draɪ **-dries** -draɪz **-drying** -ˌdraɪ.ɪŋ **-dried** -draɪd
Freiburg 'fraɪ.bɜːg (US) -bɝːg
freight freɪt **-s** -s **-ing** -ɪŋ (US) 'freɪ.t̬ɪŋ **-ed** -ɪd (US) 'freɪ.t̬ɪd **-age** -ɪdʒ (US) 'freɪ.t̬ɪdʒ '**freight** ˌ**car**
freighter 'freɪ.təʳ (US) -t̬ɚ **-s** -z
freightliner 'freɪtˌlaɪ.nəʳ (US) -nɚ **-s** -z
Fremantle 'friː.mæn.tl̩ (US) -t̬l̩
fremitus 'frem.ɪ.təs (US) -t̬əs
Fremont 'friː.mɒnt, frɪ'mɒnt (US) 'friː.mɑːnt
French, french fren*t*ʃ ˌ**French 'bean;** ˌ**French 'bread;** ˌ**French 'dressing;** ˌ**french 'fry;** (US) '**french** ˌ**fry;** ˌ**French 'loaf;** ˌ**French Revo'lution;** ˌ**French 'stick;** ˌ**French 'windows**
frenchi|fy 'fren.*t*ʃɪ|.faɪ (US) 'fren*t*.ʃɪ- **-fies** -faɪz **-fying** -faɪ.ɪŋ **-fied** -faɪd
French|man 'fren*t*ʃ|.mən **-men** -mən
french-polish ˌfren*t*ʃ'pɒl.ɪʃ (US) -'pɑː.lɪʃ **-es** -ɪz **-ing** -ɪŋ **-ed** -t **-er/s** -əʳ/z (US) -ɚ/z
French|woman 'fren*t*ʃ|ˌwʊm.ən **-women** -ˌwɪm.ɪn
frenetic frə'net.ɪk, frɪ-, fren'et- (US) frə'net̬- **-ally** -ᵊl.i, -li
frenz|y 'fren.z|i **-ies** -iz **-ied/ly** -ɪd/li
frequen|ce 'friː.kwən*t*|s **-cy** -si **-cies** -siz
frequent (*adj.*) 'friː.kwənt **-ly** -li **-ness** -nəs, -nɪs
frequen|t (*v.*) frɪ'kwen|t, friː-, frə- (US) friː-; 'friː.kwen|t, -kwən|t **-ts** -ts **-ting** -tɪŋ (US) -t̬ɪŋ **-ted** -tɪd (US) -t̬ɪd **-ter/s** -təʳ/z (US) -t̬ɚ/z
frequentative frɪ'kwen.tə.tɪv, friː-, frə- (US) friː'kwen.t̬ə.t̬ɪv **-s** -z

French words and phrases

French has provided a substantial proportion of English vocabulary since the Norman Conquest in 1066, with new words being incorporated all the time. The longest-established and the most commonly-used words are usually the most completely anglicised, and the most noticeable changes from the French original are found where English phonology does not easily accommodate them. Often there are many possible anglicised pronunciations: see for example the many listed for *restaurant*.

Examples

Word-final /r/: this is not usually pronounced in British English unless followed by a vowel in a following word. However, it is pronounced in US English, e.g.:

savoir faire /ˌsæv.wɑːˈfeəʳ/
(US) /-wɑːrˈfer, -wɑːˈ-/

Nasalized vowels: although some English speakers who have a good command of French may attempt to produce the French nasalized vowels /ɛ̃ ɑ̃ ɔ̃/ and even occasionally /œ̃/, these are pronounced by many people with a following /ŋ/. *Croissant* is given the pronunciation /ˈkwæs.ɑ̃ːŋ/ for British English, indicating that the vowel in the last syllable will be pronounced with a nasalised vowel but possibly also a velar nasal consonant. In US English, however, a velar nasal is not usually produced following a nasalised vowel, and *croissant* is pronounced /kwɑːˈsɑ̃ː/. (It should be noted that in both cases other pronunciations exist.) This example also shows the simplification of the initial consonant cluster /krw/, which occurs in French but not in English.

Word-final stress: many French words and names with final stress are modified by British English speakers to have the stress at the beginning of the word. In US English, this occurs in some words, but not in others, e.g.:

ballet	/ˈbæl.eɪ/	(US) /bælˈeɪ, ˈ--/
Paris	/ˈpær.ɪs/	(US) /ˈper-, ˈpær-/
restaurant	/ˈres.tᵊr.ɔ̃ːŋ/	(US) /-tə.rɑːnt/

The phoneme /ʒ/: while this phoneme occurs frequently in the middle of words, it is rare at the beginning and end. Many such cases are in words of French origin. English speakers sometimes substitute /dʒ/ for this sound, e.g.:

gigolo /ˈdʒɪg.ə.ləʊ, ˈʒɪg-/
(US) /-loʊ/
garage /ˈgær.ɑːʒ, -ɪdʒ, -ɑːdʒ/
(US) /gəˈrɑːʒ, -ˈrɑːdʒ/

Frere frɪəʳ (US) frer
fresco ˈfres.kəʊ (US) -koʊ **-(e)s** -z
fresh freʃ **-er** -əʳ (US) -ɚ **-est** -ɪst, -əst **-ly** -li **-ness** -nəs, -nɪs
freshen ˈfreʃ.ᵊn **-s** -z **-ing** -ɪŋ **-ed** -d
fresher ˈfreʃ.əʳ (US) -ɚ **-s** -z
freshet ˈfreʃ.ɪt, -ət **-s** -s
fresh|man ˈfreʃ|.mən **-men** -mən
freshwater (F) ˈfreʃˌwɔː.təʳ, ˌ-ˈ-- (US) ˈfreʃˌwɑː.t̬ɚ, -ˌwɔː-
Fresno ˈfrez.nəʊ (US) -noʊ
fret fret **-s** -s **-ting** -ɪŋ (US) ˈfret̬.ɪŋ **-ted** -ɪd (US) ˈfret̬.ɪd
fretboard ˈfret.bɔːd, ˈfrep- (US) ˈfret.bɔːrd **-s** -z
fretful ˈfret.fᵊl, -fʊl **-ly** -i **-ness** -nəs, -nɪs
fretsaw ˈfret.sɔː (US) -sɑː, -sɔː **-s** -z
Fretwell ˈfret.wel, -wəl
fretwork ˈfret.wɜːk (US) -wɝːk
Freud frɔɪd **-ian** -i.ən ˌ**Freudian** ˈ**slip**
Frew fruː
Frey freɪ
Freya freɪə
Freyberg ˈfraɪ.bɜːg (US) -bɝːg
Freyer frɪəʳ; ˈfraɪ.əʳ (US) ˈfraɪ.ɚ, -ɚ; frɪr
Freyja freɪə
Fri. *(abbrev. for* **Friday**) ˈfraɪ.deɪ, -di
friability ˌfraɪ.əˈbɪl.ə.ti, -ɪ.ti (US) -ə.t̬i
friable ˈfraɪ.ə.bl̩ **-ness** -nəs, -nɪs
friar fraɪəʳ (US) fraɪɚ **-s** -z
friar|y ˈfraɪə.r|i **-ies** -iz
fribbl|e ˈfrɪb.l̩ **-es** -z **-ing** -ɪŋ, ˈ-lɪŋ **-ed** -d
fricandeau ˈfrɪk.ən.dəʊ, -ɑ̃ːn- (US) ˌfrɪk.ənˈdoʊ, ˈ--- **-s** -z
fricandeaux *(alternative plur. of* **fricandeau**) ˈfrɪk.ən.dəʊ, -ɑ̃ːn-, -dəʊz (US) ˌfrɪk.ənˈdoʊ, -ˈdoʊz, ˈ---
fricassee ˌfrɪk.əˈsiː, -ˈseɪ, ˈ--- (US) ˌfrɪk.əˈsiː, ˈ--- **-s** -z **-ing** -ɪŋ **-d** -d
fricative ˈfrɪk.ə.tɪv (US) -t̬ɪv **-s** -z
friction ˈfrɪk.ʃᵊn **-s** -z **-less** -ləs, -les, -lɪs
frictional ˈfrɪk.ʃᵊn.ᵊl
Friday ˈfraɪ.deɪ, -di **-s** -z
fridg|e frɪdʒ **-es** -ɪz ˌ**fridge**-ˈ**freezer**
fried *(from* **fry**) fraɪd
Frieda ˈfriː.də
Friedan friːˈdæn, frɪ-
Friedland ˈfriːd.lənd, -lænd
Friedman ˈfriːd.mən
Friel friːl
friend (F) frend **-s** -z
friendless ˈfrend.ləs, -lɪs **-ness** -nəs, -nɪs
friendl|y (F) ˈfrend.l|i **-ies** -iz **-ier** -i.əʳ (US) -i.ɚ **-iest** -i.ɪst, -i.əst **-iness** -ɪ.nəs, -ɪ.nɪs
Friendl|y ˈfrend.l|i **-ies** -iz
friendship ˈfrend.ʃɪp **-s** -s
Friern ˈfraɪ.ən, ˈfriː- (US) -ɚn
fries *(from* **fry**) fraɪz
Fries friːs, friːz
Friesian ˈfriː.ʒən, ˈ-zi.ən (US) ˈfriː.ʒᵊn
Friesland ˈfriːz.lənd, -lænd **-er/s** -əʳ/z (US) -ɚ/z
friez|e (F) friːz **-es** -ɪz
frig frɪg **-s** -z **-ging** -ɪŋ **-ged** -d
frigate ˈfrɪg.ət, -ɪt **-s** -s
fright fraɪt **-s** -s **-ing** -ɪŋ (US) ˈfraɪ.t̬ɪŋ **-ed** -ɪd (US) ˈfraɪ.t̬ɪd
frighten ˈfraɪ.tᵊn **-s** -z **-ing/ly** -ɪŋ/li **-ed** -d **-er/s** -əʳ/z (US) -ɚ/z
frightful ˈfraɪt.fᵊl, -fʊl **-ly** -i **-ness** -nəs, -nɪs
frigid ˈfrɪdʒ.ɪd **-ly** -li **-ness** -nəs, -nɪs
Frigidaire® ˌfrɪdʒ.ɪˈdeəʳ, -əˈ- (US) -ˈder, ˈ--ˌ-
frigidity frɪˈdʒɪd.ə.ti, -ɪ.ti (US) -ə.t̬i
Friis friːs
frijole frɪˈhəʊ.li, -eɪ (US) friːˈhoʊ.liː, -ˈhoʊ, -ˈhoʊl **-s** -z
frill frɪl **-s** -z **-ing** -ɪŋ **-ed** -d
frill|y ˈfrɪl|.i **-ier** -i.əʳ (US) -i.ɚ **-iest** -i.ɪst, -i.əst **-iness** -ɪ.nəs, -ɪ.nɪs
Frimley ˈfrɪm.li
fring|e frɪndʒ **-es** -ɪz **-ing** -ɪŋ **-ed** -d **-eless** -ləs, -lɪs ˈ**fringe** ˌ**benefit**, ˌ**fringe** ˈ**benefit**; ˌ**fringe** ˈ**theatre**/ˈ**theater**
Frink frɪŋk
Frinton ˈfrɪn.tən
fripper|y ˈfrɪp.ᵊr|.i **-ies** -iz
Frisbee® ˈfrɪz.bi **-s** -z

Fricative

A type of consonant made by forcing air through a narrow gap so that a hissing noise is generated. This may be accompanied by VOICING, in which case the sound is a voiced fricative, such as [z], or it may be voiceless, such as [s].

Examples for English

British and US English have nine fricative phonemes: /f θ s ʃ h/ (voiceless) and /v ð z ʒ/ (voiced).

All except /h/ are permitted to occur in all positions in English, but /ʒ/ as in 'measure' /ˈmeʒə/ is of rather low frequency compared to the other eight sounds. /h/ may not end a syllable.

The quality and intensity of fricative sounds varies greatly, but all are acoustically composed of energy at relatively high frequency – an indication of this is that much of the fricative sound is too high to be transmitted over a phone (which usually cuts out the highest and lowest frequencies in order to reduce the cost), giving rise to the confusions that often arise over sets of words like English *fin*, *thin*, *sin* and *shin*. In order for the sound quality to be produced accurately, the size and direction of the jet of air has to be very precisely controlled.

A distinction is sometimes made between 'sibilant' or 'strident' fricatives (such as [s] and [ʃ]) which are strong and clearly audible and others which are weak and less audible (such as [θ] and [f]).

frisé(e) ˈfriː.zeɪ ⓤⓢ friːˈzeɪ, frɪ- **-s** -z
frisette frɪˈzet, friː- **-s** -s
Frisian ˈfrɪz.i.ən, ˈfriː.zi-, -ʒi-, -ʒᵊn ⓤⓢ ˈfrɪʒ.ᵊn, ˈfriː.ʒᵊn **-s** -z
frisk frɪsk **-s** -s **-ing** -ɪŋ **-ed** -t **-er/s** -əʳ/z ⓤⓢ -ɚ/z
frisket ˈfrɪs.kɪt **-s** -s
frisk|y ˈfrɪs.k|i **-ier** -i.əʳ ⓤⓢ -i.ɚ **-iest** -i.ɪst, -i.əst **-ily** -ɪ.li, -ᵊl.i **-iness** -ɪ.nəs, -ɪ.nɪs
frisson ˈfriː.sɔ̃ːŋ, -ˈ- ⓤⓢ friːˈsõʊn **-s** -z
Friston ˈfrɪs.tᵊn
Friswell ˈfrɪz.wəl, -wel
frit frɪt **-s** -s **-ting** -ɪŋ ⓤⓢ ˈfrɪt̬.ɪŋ **-ted** -ɪd ⓤⓢ ˈfrɪt̬.ɪd
frith (F) frɪθ **-s** -s
Frithsden ˈfriːz.dən, ˈfrɪz-, ˈfrɪθs.dən
fritillar|y frɪˈtɪl.ᵊr|.i, frə- ⓤⓢ ˈfrɪt̬.ᵊl.er|.i **-ies** -iz
Fritos® ˈfriː.təʊz ⓤⓢ -t̬oʊz, -toʊz
fritt|er ˈfrɪt|.əʳ ⓤⓢ ˈfrɪt̬|.ɚ **-ers** -əz ⓤⓢ -ɚz **-ering** -ᵊr.ɪŋ **-ered** -əd ⓤⓢ -ɚd
fritz (F) frɪts
Friuli friˈuː.li
frivol ˈfrɪv.ᵊl **-s** -z **-(l)ing** -ɪŋ **-(l)ed** -d
frivolit|y frɪˈvɒl.ə.t|i, frə-, -ɪ.t|i ⓤⓢ -ˈvɑː.lə.t̬|i **-ies** -iz
frivolous ˈfrɪv.ᵊl.əs **-ly** -li **-ness** -nəs, -nɪs
Frizelle frɪˈzel
friz(z) frɪz **-es** -ɪz **-ing** -ɪŋ **-ed** -d
frizzl|e ˈfrɪz.l̩ **-es** -z **-ing** -ɪŋ, ˈ-lɪŋ **-ed** -d
frizzl|y ˈfrɪz.l̩|.i, ˈfrɪz.l|i **-iness** -ɪ.nəs, -ɪ.nɪs
frizz|y ˈfrɪz|.i **-ier** -i.əʳ ⓤⓢ -i.ɚ **-iest** -i.ɪst, -i.əst **-iness** -ɪ.nəs, -ɪ.nɪs
fro frəʊ ⓤⓢ froʊ
Frobisher ˈfrəʊ.bɪ.ʃəʳ ⓤⓢ ˈfroʊ.bɪ.ʃɚ
frock frɒk ⓤⓢ frɑːk **-s** -s ˌ**frock ˈcoat**
Frodo ˈfrəʊ.dəʊ ⓤⓢ ˈfroʊ.doʊ
Frodsham ˈfrɒd.ʃᵊm ⓤⓢ ˈfrɑːd-
Froebel ˈfrəʊ.bᵊl, ˈfrɜː- ⓤⓢ ˈfrɜː-, ˈfroʊ-
frog frɒg ⓤⓢ frɑːg, frɔːg **-s** -z **have a ˈfrog in one's ˌthroat**
Froggatt ˈfrɒg.ɪt, -ət ⓤⓢ ˈfrɑː.gɪt, -gət
frogg|y ˈfrɒg|.i ⓤⓢ ˈfrɑː.g|i **-ies** -iz
frog|man ˈfrɒg|.mən ⓤⓢ ˈfrɑːg-, ˈfrɔːg- **-men** -mən
frogmarch ˈfrɒg.mɑːtʃ ⓤⓢ ˈfrɑːg.mɑːrtʃ, ˈfrɔːg- **-es** -ɪz **-ing** -ɪŋ **-ed** -t
Frogmore ˈfrɒg.mɔːʳ ⓤⓢ ˈfrɑːg.mɔːr, ˈfrɔːg-
frogspawn ˈfrɒg.spɔːn ⓤⓢ ˈfrɑːg.spɑːn, ˈfrɔːg-, -spɔːn
Froissart ˈfrɔɪ.sɑːt, ˈfrwæs.ɑː ⓤⓢ -sɑːrt; *as if French:* ˌfrwɑːˈsɑːr
frolic ˈfrɒl.ɪk ⓤⓢ ˈfrɑː.lɪk **-s** -s **-king** -ɪŋ **-ked** -t
frolicsome ˈfrɒl.ɪk.səm ⓤⓢ ˈfrɑː.lɪk- **-ness** -nəs, -nɪs
from *strong form:* frɒm ⓤⓢ frɑːm *weak forms:* frəm, frm
Note: Weak form word. The strong from /frɒm ⓤⓢ frɑːm/ is used contrastively (e.g. "Travelling **to** and **from** London") and in sentence-final position (e.g. "Where is it from?"). The weak form is /frəm/ (e.g. "back from abroad" /ˌbæk.frəm.əˈbrɔːd ⓤⓢ -ˈbrɑːd/). In rapid speech this may be further weakened to /frm/ (e.g. "one from each" /ˌwʌn.frmˈiːtʃ/).
fromage frais ˌfrɒm.ɑːʒˈfreɪ ⓤⓢ frəˌmɑːʒˈ-; ˌfrɑː.mɑːʒˈ-
Frome *in Somerset:* fruːm *lake in Australia:* frəʊm ⓤⓢ froʊm
Note: /frəʊm ⓤⓢ froʊm/ is suitable in the Edith Wharton novel "Ethan Frome".
Fromm frɒm ⓤⓢ frɑːm
frond frɒnd ⓤⓢ frɑːnd **-s** -z
front frʌnt **-s** -s **-ing** -ɪŋ ⓤⓢ ˈfrʌn.t̬ɪŋ **-ed** -ɪd ⓤⓢ ˈfrʌn.t̬ɪd ˌ**front ˈline**; ˈ**front ˌmatter**; ˈ**front ˌmoney**
frontag|e ˈfrʌn.tɪdʒ ⓤⓢ -t̬ɪdʒ **-es** -ɪz
frontal ˈfrʌn.tᵊl ⓤⓢ -t̬ᵊl **-s** -z
frontbench ˌfrʌntˈbentʃ **-er/s** -əʳ/z ⓤⓢ -ɚ/z *stress shift:* ˌfrontbench ˈspokesman
Frontera® frʌnˈteə.rə, frɒn- ⓤⓢ frʌnˈter.ə, frɑːn-
frontier frʌnˈtɪəʳ; ˈ--, ˈfrɒn- ⓤⓢ frʌnˈtɪr, frɑːn- **-s** -z
frontispiec|e ˈfrʌn.tɪs.piːs, -təs- ⓤⓢ -t̬ɪs- **-es** -ɪz
frontless ˈfrʌnt.ləs, -lɪs, -les
frontlet ˈfrʌnt.lɪt, -lət **-s** -s
front-load ˌfrʌntˈləʊd ⓤⓢ -ˈloʊd, ˈ-- **-s** -z **-ing** -ɪŋ **-ed** -ɪd **-er/s** -əʳ/z ⓤⓢ -ɚ/z *stress shift, British only:* ˌfront-loading ˈdrier
front|man ˈfrʌnt|.mæn **-men** -men
front-page ˌfrʌntˈpeɪdʒ *stress shift, see compound:* ˌ**front-page ˈnews**
front-runner ˈfrʌntˌrʌn.əʳ, ˌ-ˈ-- ⓤⓢ ˈfrʌntˌrʌn.ɚ **-s** -z
frosh frɒʃ ⓤⓢ frɑːʃ **-es** -ɪz
frost (F) frɒst ⓤⓢ frɑːst **-s** -s **-ing/s** -ɪŋ/z **-ed** -ɪd
frost|bite ˈfrɒst|.baɪt ⓤⓢ ˈfrɑːst- **-bitten** -ˌbɪt.ᵊn ⓤⓢ -ˌbɪt̬-
Frosties® ˈfrɒs.tiz ⓤⓢ ˈfrɑː.stiz
frostwork ˈfrɒst.wɜːk ⓤⓢ ˈfrɑːst.wɝːk
frost|y ˈfrɒs.t|i ⓤⓢ ˈfrɑː.st|i **-ier** -i.əʳ ⓤⓢ -i.ɚ **-iest** -i.ɪst, -i.əst **-ily** -ɪ.li, -ᵊl.i **-iness** -ɪ.nəs, -ɪ.nɪs
froth (*n.*) frɒθ ⓤⓢ frɑːθ **-s** -s
fro|th (*v.*) frɒ|θ ⓤⓢ frɑː|θ, frɑː|ð **-ths** -θs ⓤⓢ -θs, -ðz **-thing** -θɪŋ ⓤⓢ -θɪŋ, -ðɪŋ **-thed** -θt ⓤⓢ -θt, -ðd
Frothingham ˈfrɒð.ɪŋ.əm ⓤⓢ ˈfrɑː.ðɪŋ-

froth|y ˈfrɒθ|.i US ˈfrɑː.θ|i, -ð|i **-ier** -i.əʳ US -i.ɚ **-iest** -i.ɪst, -i.əst **-ily** -ɪ.li, -ᵊl.i **-iness** -ɪ.nəs, -ɪ.nɪs
frottage ˈfrɒt.ɑːʒ, -ɪdʒ; frɒtˈɑːʒ US frəˈtɑːʒ, frɑː-
Froud fraʊd, fruːd
Froude fruːd
froufrou ˈfruː.fruː
froward ˈfrəʊ.əd US ˈfroʊ.ɚd **-ly** -li **-ness** -nəs, -nɪs
frown fraʊn **-s** -z **-ing/ly** -ɪŋ/li **-ed** -d
frowst fraʊst **-s** -s **-ing** -ɪŋ **-ed** -ɪd
frowst|y ˈfraʊ.st|i **-iness** -ɪ.nəs, -ɪ.nɪs
frows|y, frowz|y ˈfraʊ.z|i **-ier** -i.əʳ US -i.ɚ **-iest** -i.ɪst, -i.əst **-iness** -ɪ.nəs, -ɪ.nɪs
froz|e *(from* **freeze***)* frəʊz US froʊz **-en** -ᵊn
fructiferous frʌkˈtɪf.ᵊr.əs US frʌk-, frʊk-
fructification ˌfrʌk.tɪ.fɪˈkeɪ.ʃᵊn US ˌfrʌk.tə-, ˌfrʊk-
fructi|fy ˈfrʌk.tɪ|.faɪ US ˈfrʌk.tə-, ˈfrʊk- **-fies** -faɪz **-fying** -faɪ.ɪŋ **-fied** -faɪd
fructose ˈfrʌk.təʊs, ˈfrʊk-, -təʊz US -toʊs
frugal ˈfruː.gᵊl **-ly** -i
frugality fruːˈgæl.ə.ti, -ɪ.ti US -ə.t̬i
fruit fruːt **-s** -s **-ing** -ɪŋ US ˈfruː.t̬ɪŋ **-ed** -ɪd US ˈfruː.t̬ɪd **ˈfruit maˌchine**
fruitarian fruːˈteə.ri.ən US -ˈter.i- **-s** -z
fruitcake ˈfruːt.keɪk **-s** -s
fruiterer ˈfruː.tᵊr.əʳ US -t̬ɚ.ɚ **-s** -z
fruitful ˈfruːt.fᵊl, -fʊl **-ly** -i **-ness** -nəs, -nɪs
fruition fruˈɪʃ.ᵊn
fruitless ˈfruːt.ləs, -lɪs **-ly** -li **-ness** -nəs, -nɪs
fruit|y ˈfruː.t|i US -t̬|i **-ier** -i.əʳ US -i.ɚ **-iest** -i.ɪst, -i.əst **-iness** -ɪ.nəs, -ɪ.nɪs
frumenty ˈfruː.mən.ti US -t̬i
frump frʌmp **-s** -s **-ish** -ɪʃ
frump|y ˈfrʌm.p|i **-ier** -i.əʳ US -i.ɚ **-iest** -i.ɪst, -i.əst **-ily** -ɪ.li, -ᵊl.i **-iness** -ɪ.nəs, -ɪ.nɪs
frustra|te frʌsˈtreɪ|t, ˈ-- US ˈfrʌs.treɪ|t **-tes** -ts **-ting/ly** -tɪŋ/li US -t̬ɪŋ/li **-ted** -tɪd US -t̬ɪd
frustration frʌsˈtreɪ.ʃᵊn **-s** -z
frust|um ˈfrʌs.t|əm **-a** -ə **-ums** -əmz
fr|y (F) fr|aɪ **-ies** -aɪz **-ying** -aɪ.ɪŋ **-ied** -aɪd **-yer** -aɪ.əʳ US -aɪ.ɚ **ˈfrying ˌpan; ˌout of the ˌfrying pan ˌinto the ˈfire**
Frye fraɪ
ft *(abbrev. for* **foot** *or* **feet***) singular:* fʊt *plural:* fiːt
FT ˌefˈtiː
FTSE, FT-SE ˈfʊt.si **ˈFT-SE ˌIndex**
FT-SE 100 ˌfʊt.si.wʌnˈhʌn.drəd, -drɪd
Fuad fuːˈɑːd, -ˈæd US ˈfuː.ɑːd
fuchsia ˈfjuː.ʃə **-s** -z
fuchsine ˈfuːk.siːn, -sɪn US ˈfuːk.sɪn, ˈfjuːk-, ˈfʊk-, -siːn
fuck fʌk **-s** -s **-ing** -ɪŋ **-ed** -t **-er/s** -əʳ/z US -ɚ/z
fu|cus ˈfjuː|.kəs **-ci** -saɪ **-cuses** -kə.sɪz
fuddl|e ˈfʌd.l̩ **-es** -z **-ing** -ɪŋ, ˈ-lɪŋ **-ed** -d
fuddy-dudd|y ˈfʌd.iˌdʌd|.i **-ies** -iz
fudg|e fʌdʒ **-es** -ɪz **-ing** -ɪŋ **-ed** -d
Fudge fʌdʒ, fjuːdʒ
fuehrer ˈfjʊə.rə, ˈfjɔː- US ˈfjʊr.ɚ
fuel ˈfjuː.əl, fjʊəl US ˈfjuː.əl, fjuːl **-s** -z **-(l)ing** -ɪŋ **-(l)ed** -d **add ˌfuel to the ˈfire**
Fuentes ˈfwen.tes, -teɪz
fug fʌg **-s** -z
fugacious fjuːˈgeɪ.ʃəs **-ly** -li **-ness** -nəs, -nɪs
fugacity fjuːˈgæs.ə.ti, -ɪ.ti US -ə.t̬i
fugal ˈfjuː.gᵊl
Fugard ˈfuː.gɑːd, ˈfjuː- US -gɑːrd
fuggles ˈfʌg.l̩z
fugg|y ˈfʌg|.i **-ier** -i.əʳ US -i.ɚ **-iest** -i.ɪst, -i.əst **-iness** -ɪ.nəs, -ɪ.nɪs
fugitive ˈfjuː.dʒə.tɪv, -dʒɪ- US -t̬ɪv **-s** -z **-ly** -li **-ness** -nəs, -nɪs
fugle|man ˈfjuː.gl̩|.mæn, -mən **-men** -men, -mən
fugue fjuːg **-s** -z
führer (F) ˈfjʊə.rəʳ, ˈfjɔː- US ˈfjʊr.ɚ **-s** -z
Fujairah fuːˈdʒaɪə.rə US -ˈdʒaɪ-
Fuji ˈfuː.dʒi
Fujian fuːˈdʒɑːn
Fujimori ˌfuː.dʒiˈmɔːr.i
Fuji-san ˈfuː.dʒi.sæn US -sɑːn
Fujitsu fʊˈdʒɪt.suː, fuː- US fuː-ˈ, fʊ-
Fujiyama ˌfuː.dʒiˈjɑː.mə
Fukuoka ˌfʊk.uːˈəʊ.kə, ˌfuː.kuːˈ- US ˌfuː.kuːˈoʊ-, ˌfʊk.uːˈ-
-ful -fᵊl, -fʊl
Note: Two suffixes are covered by this entry, both of which are not stressed. The first forms an adjective, e.g. **beauty** /ˈbjuː.ti US -t̬i/, **beautiful** /ˈbjuː.tɪ.fᵊl US -t̬ɪ-/; in this the pronunciation /-fᵊl/ is preferred. The second forms a measuring noun, e.g. **bucket** /ˈbʌk.ɪt/, **bucketful** /ˈbʌk.ɪt.fʊl/, and is normally /-fʊl/.
Fulani fuːˈlɑː.ni, ˈ--- **-s** -z
Fulbright ˈfʊl.braɪt **-s** -s
Fulcher ˈfʊl.tʃəʳ US -tʃɚ
fulcr|um ˈfʊl.kr|əm, ˈfʌl- **-a** -ə **-ums** -əmz
fuler|um fʊlkr|əm, fʌl- **-a** -ə **-ums** -əmz
fulfil fʊlˈfɪl **-s** -z **-ling** -ɪŋ **-led** -d **-ment** -mənt
fulfill fʊlˈfɪl **-s** -z **-ing** -ɪŋ **-ed** -d **-ment** -mənt
Fulford ˈfʊl.fəd US -fɚd
fulgent ˈfʌl.dʒənt **-ly** -li
Fulham ˈfʊl.əm
fuliginous fjuːˈlɪdʒ.ɪ.nəs **-ly** -li
Fulke fʊlk
full fʊl **-er** -əʳ US -ɚ **-est** -ɪst, -əst **-ness** -nəs, -nɪs **ˌfull ˈboard; ˌfull ˈface; ˌfull ˈmoon; ˌfull ˈstop**
fullback ˈfʊl.bæk, ˌ-ˈ- US ˈ-- **-s** -s
full-blooded ˌfʊlˈblʌd.ɪd *stress shift:* ˌfull-blooded ˈmale
full-blown ˌfʊlˈbləʊn US -ˈbloʊn *stress shift:* ˌfull-blown ˈargument
full-bodied ˌfʊlˈbɒd.ɪd US -ˈbɑː.did *stress shift:* ˌfull-bodied ˈwine
fuller (F) ˈfʊl.əʳ US -ɚ **-s** -z
Fullerton ˈfʊl.ə.tᵊn US -ɚ-
full-face ˌfʊlˈfeɪs *stress shift:* ˌfull-face ˈphotograph
full-fledged ˌfʊlˈfledʒd *stress shift:* ˌfull-fledged ˈbird
full-grown ˌfʊlˈgrəʊn US -ˈgroʊn *stress shift:* ˌfull-grown ˈman
full-length ˌfʊlˈleŋ*k*θ *stress shift:* ˌfull-length ˈcoat
full-scale ˌfʊlˈskeɪl *stress shift:* ˌfull-scale ˈwar
full-time ˌfʊlˈtaɪm *stress shift:* ˌfull-time ˈmother
fully ˈfʊl.i
-fully -fᵊl.i, -fʊl.i
Note: Suffix. Words containing **-fully** are stressed in a similar way to adjectives containing **-ful**; see above.
fully-fledged ˌfʊl.iˈfledʒd *stress shift:* ˌfully-fledged ˈbird
fulmar ˈfʊl.məʳ, -mɑːʳ US -mɚ, -mɑːr **-s** -z
Fulmer ˈfʊl.məʳ US -mɚ
fulmi|nate ˈfʊl.mɪ|.neɪt, ˈfʌl-, -mə- **-nates** -neɪts **-nating** -neɪ.tɪŋ US -neɪ.t̬ɪŋ **-nated** -neɪ.tɪd US -neɪ.t̬ɪd
fulmination ˌfʊl.mɪˈneɪ.ʃᵊn, ˌfʌl-, -məˈ- **-s** -z
fulness ˈfʊl.nəs, -nɪs
fulsome ˈfʊl.səm **-ly** -li **-ness** -nəs, -nɪs
Fulton ˈfʊl.tᵊn
Fulvia ˈfʊl.vi.ə, ˈfʌl-
fulvous ˈfʌl.vəs, ˈfʊl-
Fulwood ˈfʊl.wʊd
Fu Manchu ˌfuː.mænˈtʃuː
fumbl|e ˈfʌm.bl̩ **-es** -z **-ing** -ɪŋ, ˈ blɪŋ **-ed** -d **-er/s** -əʳ/z, ˈ-bləʳ/z US ˈ-bl̩.ɚ/z, ˈ-blɚ/z
fum|e fjuːm **-es** -z **-ing** -ɪŋ **-ed** -d
fumi|gate ˈfjuː.mɪ|.geɪt, -mə- **-gates** -geɪts **-gating** -geɪ.tɪŋ US -geɪ.t̬ɪŋ **-gated** -geɪ.tɪd US -geɪ.t̬ɪd **-gator/s** -geɪ.təʳ/z US -geɪ.t̬ɚ/z
fumigation ˌfjuː.mɪˈgeɪ.ʃᵊn, -məˈ- **-s** -z
fun fʌn
Funafuti ˌfuː.nəˈfuː.ti

funambulist fjuːˈnæm.bjə.lɪst, fjʊ-, -bjʊ- (US) fjuːˈnæm.bjə-, -bjuː- **-s** -s
Funchal fʊnˈʃɑːl, -ˈtʃɑːl
function ˈfʌŋ*k*.ʃᵊn **-s** -z **-ing** -ɪŋ **-ed** -d
functional ˈfʌŋ*k*.ʃᵊn.ᵊl **-ly** -i
functional|ism ˈfʌŋ*k*.ʃᵊn.ᵊl|.ɪ.zᵊm **-ist/s** -ɪst/s
functionality ˌfʌŋ*k*.ʃᵊnˈæl.ɪ.ti, -ə.ti (US) -ə.t̬i
functionar|y ˈfʌŋ*k*.ʃᵊn.ᵊr.|i, -r|i (US) -er|.i **-ies** -iz
functor ˈfʌŋ*k*.təʳ, -tɔːʳ (US) -tɚ, -tɔːr **-s** -z
fund fʌnd **-s** -z **-ing** -ɪŋ **-ed** -ɪd
fundament ˈfʌn.də.mənt **-s** -s
fundamental ˌfʌn.dəˈmen.tᵊl (US) -t̬ᵊl **-s** -z **-ly** -i
fundamental|ism (F) ˌfʌn.dəˈmen.tᵊl|.ɪ.zᵊm (US) -t̬ᵊl- **-ist/s** -ɪst/s
fundamentality ˌfʌn.də.menˈtæl.ə.ti, -ɪ.ti (US) -ə.t̬i
fundless ˈfʌnd.ləs, -lɪs, -les
fundrais|er ˈfʌndˌreɪ.z|əʳ (US) -z|ɚ **-er/s** -əz (US) -ɚz **-ing** -ɪŋ
Fundy ˈfʌn.di
funeral ˈfjuː.nᵊr.əl **-s** -z ˈ**funeral** ˌ**home**; ˈ**funeral** ˌ**parlo(u)r**
funerary ˈfjuː.nᵊr.ə.ri (US) -er.i
funereal fjuːˈnɪə.ri.əl (US) -ˈnɪr.i- **-ly** -i
funfair ˈfʌn.feəʳ (US) -fer **-s** -z
fungal ˈfʌŋ.gᵊl
fungible ˈfʌn.dʒɪ.bl̩, -dʒə- **-s** -z
fungicidal ˌfʌŋ.gɪˈsaɪ.dᵊl, ˌfʌn.dʒɪˈ- (US) ˌfʌn.dʒɪˈ-, ˌfʌŋ.gəˈ- **-li** -i
fungicide ˈfʌŋ.gɪ.saɪd, ˈfʌn.dʒɪ- (US) ˈfʌn.dʒɪ-, ˈfʌŋ.gə- **-s** -z
fungo ˈfʌŋ.gəʊ (US) -goʊ **-es** -z
fun|gus ˈfʌŋ.|gəs **-gi** -gaɪ, -giː, ˈfʌn.dʒiː, -dʒaɪ **-guses** -gə.sɪz **-goid** -gɔɪd **-gous** -gəs
funicle ˈfjuː.nɪ.kl̩ **-s** -z
funicular fjuːˈnɪk.jə.ləʳ, fə-, -jʊ- (US) -juː.lɚ **-s** -z
funicul|us fjuːˈnɪk.jə.l|əs, fə-, -jʊ- (US) -juː- **-i** -aɪ
funk (F) fʌŋk **-s** -s **-ing** -ɪŋ **-ed** -t
funk|y ˈfʌŋ.k|i **-ier** -i.əʳ (US) -i.ɚ **-iest** -i.ɪst, -i.əst **-ily** -ɪ.li, -ᵊl.i **-iness** -ɪ.nəs, -ɪ.nɪs
funnel ˈfʌn.ᵊl **-s** -z **-(l)ing** -ɪŋ **-(l)ed** -d
funnies ˈfʌn.iz
funn|y ˈfʌn|.i **-ier** -i.əʳ (US) -i.ɚ **-iest** -i.ɪst, -i.əst **-ily** -ɪ.li, -ᵊl.i **-iness** -ɪ.nəs, -ɪ.nɪs ˈ**funny** ˌ**bone**; ˈ**funny** ˌ**business**
funny|man ˈfʌn.i|.mæn **-men** -men
fur fɜːʳ (US) fɝː **-s** -z **-ring** -ɪŋ **-red** -d
fur *(abbrev. for* **furlong***)* ˈfɜː.lɒŋ (US) ˈfɝː.lɑːŋ, -lɔːŋ
Furbear ˈfɜː.beəʳ (US) ˈfɝː.ber
furbelow ˈfɜː.bɪ.ləʊ, -bə- (US) ˈfɝː.bɪ.loʊ, -bə- **-s** -z
furbish ˈfɜː.bɪʃ (US) ˈfɝː- **-es** -ɪz **-ing** -ɪŋ **-ed** -t
furcate *(adj.)* ˈfɜː.keɪt, -kɪt, -kət (US) ˈfɝː-
fur|cate *(v.)* ˈfɜː|.keɪt, -|ˈ- (US) ˈfɝː|.keɪt **-cates** -keɪts, -ˈkeɪts (US) -keɪts **-cating** -keɪ.tɪŋ, -ˈkeɪ- (US) -keɪ.t̬ɪŋ **-cated** -keɪ.tɪd, -ˈkeɪ- (US) -keɪ.t̬ɪd
furcation fɜːˈkeɪ.ʃᵊn (US) fɝː- **-s** -z
furibund ˈfjʊə.rɪ.bʌnd, ˈfjɔː-, -bənd (US) ˈfjʊr.i-
furioso ˌfjʊə.riˈəʊ.zəʊ, ˌfjɔː-, -səʊ (US) ˌfjʊr.iˈoʊ.soʊ, ˌfjɝː-, -zoʊ
furious ˈfjʊə.ri.əs, ˈfjɔː- (US) ˈfjʊr.i-, ˈfjɝː- **-ly** -li
furl fɜːl (US) fɝːl **-s** -z **-ing** -ɪŋ **-ed** -d
furlong ˈfɜː.lɒŋ (US) ˈfɝː.lɑːŋ, -lɔːŋ **-s** -z
furlough ˈfɜː.ləʊ (US) ˈfɝː.loʊ **-s** -z
furnac|e ˈfɜː.nɪs, -nəs (US) ˈfɝː- **-es** -ɪz
Furneaux ˈfɜː.nəʊ (US) fɝːˈnoʊ
Furness ˈfɜː.nɪs, fɜːˈnes (US) ˈfɝː.nɪs, fɝːˈnes
Furneux ˈfɜː.nɪks, -nəʊ (US) ˈfɝː.nɪks, -nuː, -noʊ
Note: /ˈfɜː.nɪks/ is the more usual local pronunciation.
furnish ˈfɜː.nɪʃ (US) ˈfɝː- **-es** -ɪz **-ing/s** -ɪŋ/z **-ed** -t **-er/s** -əʳ/z (US) -ɚ/z
furniture ˈfɜː.nɪ.tʃəʳ (US) ˈfɝː.nɪ.tʃɚ
Furnival(l) ˈfɜː.nɪ.vᵊl (US) ˈfɝː-
furor ˈfjʊr.ɔː (US) ˈfjʊr.ɔːr, -ɚ
furore fjʊəˈrɔː.ri, -reɪ; ˈfjʊə.rɔːʳ, ˈfjɔː- (US) ˈfjʊr.ɔːr, -ɚ **-s** -z
furph|y (F) ˈfɜː.f|i (US) ˈfɝː- **-ies** -iz
furrier ˈfʌr.i.əʳ (US) ˈfɝː.i.ɚ **-s** -z
furrier|y ˈfʌr.i.ᵊr|.i (US) ˈfɝː- **-ies** -iz
furrow ˈfʌr.əʊ (US) ˈfɝː.oʊ **-s** -z **-ing** -ɪŋ **-ed** -d
furr|y ˈfɜː.r|i (US) ˈfɝː|.i **-ier** -i.əʳ (US) -i.ɚ **-iest** -i.ɪst, -i.əst **-iness** -ɪ.nəs, -ɪ.nɪs
furth|er ˈfɜː.ð|əʳ (US) ˈfɝː.ð|ɚ **-ers** -əz (US) -ɚz **-ering** -ᵊr.ɪŋ **-ered** -əd (US) -ɚd **-erer/s** -ᵊr.əʳ/z (US) -ɚ.ɚ/z ˌ**further** **eduˈcation**
furtherance ˈfɜː.ðᵊr.ᵊn*t*s (US) ˈfɝː-
furthermore ˌfɜː.ðəˈmɔːʳ, ˈ--- (US) ˈfɝː.ðɚ.mɔːr
furthermost ˈfɜː.ðə.məʊst (US) ˈfɝː.ðɚ.moʊst
furthest ˈfɜː.ðɪst, -ðəst (US) ˈfɝː-
furtive ˈfɜː.tɪv (US) ˈfɝː.t̬ɪv **-ly** -li **-ness** -nəs, -nɪs
furuncle ˈfjʊə.rʌŋ.kᵊl, ˈfjɔː- (US) ˈfjʊr.ʌŋ- **-s** -z
fur|y (F) ˈfjʊə.r|i, ˈfjɔː- (US) ˈfjʊr|.i **-ies** -iz
furze fɜːz (US) fɝːz
fus|e fjuːz **-es** -ɪz **-ing** -ɪŋ **-ed** -d ˈ**fuse** ˌ**box**
fusee fjuːˈziː (US) fjuːˈziː, ˈ-- **-s** -z
fusel ˈfjuː.zᵊl (US) ˈfjuː.zᵊl, -sᵊl ˈ**fusel** ˌ**oil**, ˌ**fusel** ˈ**oil**
fuselag|e ˈfjuː.zᵊl.ɑːʒ, -zɪ.lɑːʒ (US) -sə.lɑːʒ, -zə-, -lɑːdʒ **-es** -ɪz
fusibility ˌfjuː.zɪˈbɪl.ə.ti, -zəˈ-, -ɪ.ti (US) -ə.t̬i
fusible ˈfjuː.zɪ.bl̩, -zə-
fusil ˈfjuː.zɪl (US) -zɪl, -sɪl **-s** -z
fusile ˈfjuː.saɪl, -zaɪl (US) -zᵊl, -zaɪl, -sɪl
fusilier ˌfjuː.zᵊlˈɪəʳ, -zɪˈlɪəʳ (US) -zɪˈlɪr **-s** -z
fusillade ˌfjuː.zəˈleɪd, -zɪˈ- (US) ˌfjuː.səˈlɑːd, -zəˈ-, -ˈleɪd, ˈ--- **-s** -z
fusilli fʊˈsiː.li, fjʊˈzɪl.i (US) ˈfjuː.siː.li, -zə-
fusion ˈfjuː.ʒᵊn **-s** -z
fuss fʌs **-es** -ɪz **-ing** -ɪŋ **-ed** -t **-er/s** -əʳ/z (US) -ɚ/z
fussbudget ˈfʌsˌbʌdʒ.ɪt **-s** -s
fusspot ˈfʌs.pɒt (US) -pɑːt **-s** -s
fuss|y ˈfʌs|.i **-ier** -i.əʳ (US) -i.ɚ **-iest** -i.ɪst, -i.əst **-ily** -ɪ.li, -ᵊl.i **-iness** -ɪ.nəs, -ɪ.nɪs
fustian ˈfʌs.ti.ən (US) -tʃᵊn
fustic ˈfʌs.tɪk
fusti|gate ˈfʌs.tɪ|.geɪt, -tə- **-gates** -geɪts **-gating** -geɪ.tɪŋ (US) -geɪ.t̬ɪŋ **-gated** -geɪ.tɪd (US) -geɪ.t̬ɪd
fustigation ˌfʌs.tɪˈgeɪ.ʃᵊn, -təˈ- **-s** -z
fust|y ˈfʌs.t|i **-ier** -i.əʳ (US) -i.ɚ **-iest** -i.ɪst, -i.əst **-ily** -ɪ.li, -ᵊl.i **-iness** -ɪ.nəs, -ɪ.nɪs
futhark ˈfuː.θɑːk (US) -θɑːrk
futile ˈfjuː.taɪl (US) -t̬əl, -taɪl **-ly** -li **-ness** -nəs, -nɪs
futilit|y fjuːˈtɪl.ə.t|i, -ɪ.t|i (US) -ə.t̬|i **-ies** -iz
futon ˈfuː.tɒn, ˈfjuː-, ˈfʊt.ɒn, -ᵊn; ˌfuːˈtɒn (US) ˈfuː.tɑːn **-s** -z
futtock ˈfʌt.ək (US) ˈfʌt̬- **-s** -s
future ˈfjuː.tʃəʳ (US) -tʃɚ **-s** -z
futur|ism ˈfjuː.tʃᵊr|.ɪ.zᵊm **-ist/s** -ɪst/s
futuristic ˌfjuː.tʃəˈrɪs.tɪk **-ally** -ᵊl.i, -li
futurit|y fjuːˈtjʊə.rə.t|i, -ˈtjɔː-, -ˈtʃʊə-, -ˈtʃɔː-, -ɪ.t|i (US) fjuːˈtʊr.ə.t̬|i, -ˈtjʊr-, -ˈtʃʊr-, -ˈtʃɝː- **-ies** -iz
futurolog|ist ˌfjuː.tʃəˈrɒl.ə.dʒ|ɪst (US) -ˈrɑː.lə- **-ists** -ɪsts **-y** -i
fuz|e fjuːz **-es** -ɪz **-ing** -ɪŋ **-ed** -d
fuzee fjuːˈziː (US) fjuːˈziː, ˈ-- **-s** -z
Fuzhou ˈfuː.dʒəʊ (US) -dʒoʊ
fuzz fʌz **-es** -ɪz **-ing** -ɪŋ **-ed** -d
fuzz|y ˈfʌz|.i **-ier** -i.əʳ (US) -i.ɚ **-iest** -i.ɪst, -i.əst **-ily** -ɪ.li, -ᵊl.i **-iness** -ɪ.nəs, -ɪ.nɪs
fuzzy-wuzz|y ˈfʌz.iˌwʌz|.i, ˌ--ˈ-- **-ies** -iz
f-word ˈefˌwɜːd (US) -ˌwɝːd
Fyf(f)e faɪf
Fyfield ˈfaɪ.fiːld
Fylingdales ˈfaɪ.lɪŋ.deɪlz
Fyne faɪn

Pronouncing the letter G

See also GG, GH, GU, NG

There are two main pronunciations for the consonant letter **g**: /dʒ/ and /g/, e.g.:

gem	/dʒem/
age	/eɪdʒ/
geese	/giːs/
gig	/gɪg/

A following vowel letter **e**, **i** or **y** may lead to the pronunciation /dʒ/. However, as can be seen in the above examples, this is not reliable as an indicator of which pronunciation to use. More reliably, before vowel letters **a**, **o** or **u** the pronunciation is highly likely to be /g/, although there are exceptions, e.g.:

gaol	/dʒeɪl/

In addition

g is often silent before a consonant letter **m** or **n** at the beginning and end of words, e.g.:

gnat	/næt/
paradigm	/ˈpær.ə.daɪm/

g (**G**) dʒiː **-'s** -z
g *(abbrev. for* **gram/s***) singular:* græm *plural:* -z
Ga. *(abbrev. for* **Georgia***)* ˈdʒɔː.dʒə (US) ˈdʒɔːr-
gab gæb **-s** -z **-bing** -ɪŋ **-bed** -d
gabardine ˌgæb.əˈdiːn, ˈ--- (US) ˈgæb.ɚ.diːn, ˌ--ˈ- **-s** -z
Gabbatha ˈgæb.ə.θə
gabbl|e ˈgæb.l̩ **-es** -z **-ing** -ɪŋ, ˈ-lɪŋ **-ed** -d **-er/s** -əʳ/z, ˈ-ləʳ/z (US) ˈ-l̩.ɚ/z, ˈ-lɚ/z
gabbro ˈgæb.rəʊ (US) -roʊ **-s** -z
gabb|y ˈgæb|.i **-ier** -i.əʳ (US) -i.ɚ **-iest** -i.ɪst, -i.əst
gaberdine ˌgæb.əˈdiːn, ˈ--- (US) ˈgæb.ɚ.diːn, ˌ--ˈ- **-s** -z
gaberlunzie ˌgæb.əˈlʌn.zi, -ˈluː.nji, ˈgæb.ə.lʌn.zi, -luː.nji (US) ˌgæb.ɚˈlʌn.zi **-s** -z
gabfest ˈgæbˌfest **-s** -s
Gabii ˈgæb.i.iː, -bi.aɪ (US) ˈgæb.i.aɪ, ˈgeɪ.bi-
gabion ˈgeɪ.bi.ən **-s** -z
gable (**G**) ˈgeɪ.bl̩ **-s** -z **-d** -d
gablet ˈgeɪ.blɪt, -blət (US) -blət **-s** -s
Gabon gæbˈɒn, gəˈbɒn; ˈgæb.ɒn *as if French:* gæbˈɔ̃ːŋ (US) gæbˈoʊn, gəˈboʊn
Gabonese ˌgæb.ɒnˈiːz, -əˈniːz (US) -əˈniːz
Gaboon gəˈbuːn
Gabor gəˈbɔːʳ; ˈgɑː.bɔːʳ (US) gəˈbɔːr; ˈgɑː.bɔːr
Gaborone ˌgæb.əˈrəʊ.ni (US) ˌgɑː.bəˈroʊ.neɪ, -ni
Gabriel ˈgeɪ.bri.əl
Gabriella ˌgæb.riˈel.ə, ˌgeɪ.briˈ-
Gabrielle ˌgæb.riˈel, ˌgeɪ.briˈ-
gab|y ˈgeɪ.b|i **-ies** -iz
Gaby ˈgæb.i, ˈgɑː.bi
gad (**G**) gæd **-s** -z **-ding** -ɪŋ **-ded** -ɪd
gadabout ˈgæd.ə.baʊt **-s** -s
Gadafy, Gadaffi gəˈdæf.i, -ˈdɑː.fi (US) -ˈdɑː-
Gadara ˈgæd.ᵊr.ə
Gadarene ˌgæd.əˈriːn, ˈ--- (US) ˈ--- **-s** -z
Gaddafi gəˈdæf.i, -ˈdɑː.fi (US) -ˈdɑː-
Gaddesden ˈgædz.dᵊn
Gaddis ˈgæd.ɪs
Gade *English river:* geɪd *Danish composer:* ˈgɑː.də
Gades ˈgeɪ.diːz
gadfl|y ˈgæd.fl|aɪ **-ies** -aɪz
gadget ˈgædʒ.ɪt, -ət **-s** -s
gadgetry ˈgædʒ.ɪ.tri, ˈ-ə-
Gadhafi gəˈdæf.i, -ˈdɑː.fi (US) -ˈdɑː-
Gadhel ˈgæd.el (US) -əl **-s** -z
Gadhelic gædˈel.ɪk, gəˈdel-
gadolinium ˌgæd.əʊˈlɪn.i.əm, -ᵊlˈɪn- (US) -oʊˈlɪn-, gædˈlɪn-
gadroon gəˈdruːn **-s** -z
Gadsby ˈgædz.bi
Gadsden ˈgædz.dᵊn
Gadshill ˈgædz.hɪl
gadwall ˈgæd.wɔːl (US) -wɔːl **-s** -z
gadzooks ˌgædˈzuːks, gæd- (US) -ˈzuːks, -ˈzʊks
Gael geɪl **-s** -z
Gaelic ˈgeɪ.lɪk, ˈgæl.ɪk
Gaeltacht ˈgeɪl.tæxt, -təxt
Gaetulia *in Ireland:* giːˈtjuː.li.ə, gaɪ-, dʒi-, -ˈtuː- (US) dʒiˈtuː-, giː- *in Libya:* dʒɪˈtjuː.li.ə (US) -ˈtuː-, -ˈtjuː-
gaff gæf **-s** -s **-ing** -ɪŋ **-ed** -t
gaffe gæf **-s** -s
gaffer ˈgæf.əʳ (US) -ɚ **-s** -z
gag gæg **-s** -z **-ging** -ɪŋ **-ged** -d
gaga ˈgɑː.gɑː, ˈgæg.ɑː (US) ˈgɑː.gɑː **-s** -z
Gagarin gəˈgɑː.rɪn, gægˈɑː- (US) gəˈgɑːr.ɪn
gag|e (**G**) geɪdʒ **-es** -ɪz **-ing** -ɪŋ **-ed** -d
gaggle ˈgæg.l̩ **-s** -z
Gaia ˈgaɪ.ə, ˈgeɪ-
gaiet|y (**G**) ˈgeɪ.ə.t|i, -ɪ.t|i (US) -ə.t̬|i **-ies** -iz
Gail ˈgeɪl
gaily *(from* **gay***)* ˈgeɪ.li
gain geɪn **-s** -z **-ing/s** -ɪŋ/z **-ed** -d **-er/s** -əʳ/z (US) -ɚ/z
Gaines geɪnz
Gainesville ˈgeɪnz.vɪl (US) -vɪl, -vəl
gainful ˈgeɪn.fᵊl, -fʊl **-ly** -i **-ness** -nəs, -nɪs
gain|say ˌgeɪn|ˈseɪ **-says** -ˈseɪz, -ˈsez **-saying** -ˈseɪ.ɪŋ **-sayed** -ˈseɪd **-said** -ˈsed, -ˈseɪd **-sayer/s** -ˈseɪ.əʳ/z (US) -ˈseɪ.ɚ/z
Gainsborough ˈgeɪnz.bᵊr.ə (US) -oʊ, -ə **-s** -z
Gairdner ˈgeəd.nəʳ, ˈgɑːd- (US) ˈgerd.nɚ, ˈgɑːrd-
Gairloch ˈgeə.lɒx, -lɒk (US) ˈger.lɑːk
Gaisford ˈgeɪs.fəd (US) -fɚd
gait geɪt **-s** -s
gaiter ˈgeɪ.təʳ (US) -t̬ɚ **-s** -z
Gaitskell ˈgeɪt.skᵊl, -skɪl
Gaius ˈgaɪ.əs (US) ˈgeɪ-, ˈgaɪ-
gal *girl:* gæl **-s** -z
gal *(abbrev. for* **gallon***)* ˈgæl.ən
gala *special occasion:* ˈgɑː.lə, ˈgeɪ- (US) ˈgeɪ-, ˈgæl.ə, ˈgɑː.lə **-s** -z
Gala *river:* ˈgɑː.lə (US) ˈgɑː.lə, ˈgæl.ə
galactic gəˈlæk.tɪk **-ally** -ᵊl.i, -li
galacto- gəˈlæk.təʊ- (US) ˈ-tə-, ˈ-toʊ-
galactose gəˈlæk.təʊs, -təʊz (US) -toʊs
galah gəˈlɑː **-s** -z
Galahad ˈgæl.ə.hæd
galantine ˈgæl.ən.tiːn, ˌ--ˈ- **-s** -z
Galapagos gəˈlæp.ə.gəs, -gɒs (US) gəˈlɑː.pə.goʊs, -gəz
Galashiels ˌgæl.əˈʃiːlz *stress shift:* ˌGalashiels ˈstreets
Galata ˈgæl.ə.tə (US) -t̬ə
Galatasaray ˌgæl.əˈtæs.ə.raɪ
Galatea ˌgæl.əˈti.ə
Galatia gəˈleɪ.ʃə, -ʃi.ə, ˌgæl.əˈti.ə
Galatian gəˈleɪ.ʃᵊn, -ʃi.ən, ˌgæl.əˈti.ən **-s** -z
galax|y ˈgæl.ək.s|i **-ies** -iz
Galba ˈgæl.bə
galbanum ˈgæl.bə.nəm

Galbraith gælˈbreɪθ ⓤⓢ ˈ--
gale (G) geɪl **-s** -z
Galen ˈgeɪ.lən, -lɪn
galena (G) gəˈliː.nə
Galenic gəˈlen.ɪk, geɪ-, -ˈliː.nɪk **-al** -əl
Galerius gəˈlɪə.ri.əs ⓤⓢ -ˈlɪr.i-
Galesburg ˈgeɪlz.bɜːg ⓤⓢ -bɝːg
Galic|ia gəˈlɪs|.i.ə, gælˈɪs-, -ˈɪʃ|.ə, -ˈɪʃ|.i.ə ⓤⓢ gəˈlɪʃ|.ə **-ian/s** -i.ən/z ⓤⓢ -ən/z, -i.ən/z
Galilean ˌgæl.ɪˈliː.ən, -əˈ- ⓤⓢ -əˈ- **-s** -z
Galilee ˈgæl.ɪ.liː, ˈ-ə- ⓤⓢ ˈ-ə-
Galileo ˌgæl.ɪˈleɪ.əʊ, -əˈ-, -ˈliː.əʊ ⓤⓢ -əˈliː-, -ˈleɪ-
galingale ˈgæl.ɪŋ.geɪl
Galion ˈgæl.i.ən ⓤⓢ ˈgæl.jən
galipot ˈgæl.ɪ.pɒt ⓤⓢ -pɑːt
gall gɔːl ⓤⓢ gɔːl, gɑːl **-s** -z **-ing** -ɪŋ **-ed** -d **ˈgall ˌbladder**
Gallacher ˈgæl.ə.həʳ, -xəʳ ⓤⓢ -hɚ
Gallagher ˈgæl.ə.həʳ, -xəʳ ⓤⓢ -gɚ, -hɚ
Gallaher ˈgæl.ə.həʳ, -xəʳ ⓤⓢ -hɚ
gallant *(n.)* ˈgæl.ənt **-s** -s
gallant *(adj.) brave:* ˈgæl.ənt **-ly** -li **-ness** -nəs, -nɪs
gallant *(adj.) attentive to women:* ˈgæl.ənt; gəˈlænt ⓤⓢ ˈgæl.ənt; gəˈlænt, -ˈlɑːnt **-ly** -li **-ness** -nəs, -nɪs
Gallant gəˈlɔ̃ːŋ
gallantr|y ˈgæl.ən.tr|i **-ies** -iz
Gallatin ˈgæl.ə.tɪn
Gallaudet gæl.əˈdet *stress shift:* ˌGallaudet ˈCollege
Galle *port in Sri Lanka:* gɑːl ⓤⓢ gɑːl, gæl
Galle *German astronomer:* ˈgæl.ə
galleon ˈgæl.i.ən ⓤⓢ -i.ən, ˈ-jən **-s** -z
galler|y ˈgæl.ᵊr|.i **-ies** -iz **-ied** -id
galley ˈgæl.i **-s** -z **ˈgalley ˌproof**; **ˈgalley ˌslave**
gallfl|y ˈgɔːl.fl|aɪ ⓤⓢ ˈgɔːl-, ˈgɑːl- **-ies** -aɪz
Gallia ˈgæl.i.ə
galliambic ˌgæl.iˈæm.bɪk **-s** -s
galliard ˈgæl.i.ɑːd, -əd ⓤⓢ ˈ-jɚd **-s** -z
gallic (G) ˈgæl.ɪk
Gallican ˈgæl.ɪ.kən **-s** -z
gallice ˈgæl.ɪ.siː, -si
gallicism ˈgæl.ɪ.sɪ.zᵊm, ˈ-ə- ⓤⓢ ˈ-ə- **-s** -z
gallicizl|e, -is|e ˈgæl.ɪ.saɪz, ˈ-ə- ⓤⓢ ˈ-ə- **-es** -ɪz **-ing** -ɪŋ **-ed** -d
gallimaufr|y ˌgæl.ɪˈmɔː.fr|i, -əˈ- ⓤⓢ -əˈmɑː-, -ˈmɔː- **-ies** -iz
gallinaceous ˌgæl.ɪˈneɪ.ʃəs, -əˈ- ⓤⓢ -əˈ-
Gallio ˈgæl.i.əʊ ⓤⓢ -oʊ
galliot ˈgæl.i.ət **-s** -s
Gallipoli gəˈlɪp.ᵊl.i, gæˈlɪp-
Gallipolis *in US:* ˌgæl.ɪ.pəˈliːs ⓤⓢ ˌ-ə-, -ˈlɪs
gallipot ˈgæl.ɪ.pɒt ⓤⓢ -ə.pɑːt **-s** -s
gallium ˈgæl.i.əm
gallivant ˈgæl.ɪ.vænt, ˈ-ə-, ˌ--ˈ- ⓤⓢ ˈgæl.ə.vænt, ˌ--ˈ- **-s** -s **-ing** -ɪŋ **-ed** -ɪd
gallnut ˈgɔːl.nʌt ⓤⓢ ˈgɔːl-, ˈgɑːl- **-s** -s
gallon ˈgæl.ən **-s** -z
galloon gəˈluːn
gallop ˈgæl.əp **-s** -s **-ing** -ɪŋ **-ed** -t **-er/s** -əʳ/z ⓤⓢ -ɚ/s
gallopade ˌgæl.əˈpeɪd, -ˈpɑːd ⓤⓢ -ˈpeɪd **-s** -z
Gallovidian ˌgæl.əʊˈvɪd.i.ən ⓤⓢ -əˈ- **-s** -z
galloway (G) ˈgæl.ə.weɪ **-s** -z
gallows ˈgæl.əʊz ⓤⓢ -oʊz
gallstone ˈgɔːl.stəʊn ⓤⓢ -stoʊn, ˈgɑːl- **-s** -z
Gallup ˈgæl.əp **ˈGallup ˌpoll**
Gallus ˈgæl.əs
galoot gəˈluːt **-s** -s
galop ˈgæl.əp; gælˈɒp ⓤⓢ ˈgæl.əp **-s** -s
galore gəˈlɔːʳ ⓤⓢ -ˈlɔːr
galosh gəˈlɒʃ ⓤⓢ -ˈlɑːʃ **-es** -ɪz
Galpin ˈgæl.pɪn
Galsham ˈgɔːl.səm, ˈgɒl- ⓤⓢ ˈgɔːl-, ˈgɑːl-
Galston ˈgɔːl.stᵊn, ˈgɒl- ⓤⓢ ˈgɔːl-, ˈgɑːl-
Galsworthy ˈgɔːlz.wɜː.ði, ˈgɒlz-, ˈgælz- ⓤⓢ ˈgɔːlz.wɝː-, ˈgɑːlz-, ˈgælz-
Note: John Galsworthy, the author, is commonly called /ˈgɔːlz.wɜː.ði ⓤⓢ -wɜːr-/.
Galt gɔːlt, gɒlt ⓤⓢ gɑːlt, gɔːlt
Galton ˈgɔːl.tᵊn, ˈgɒl- ⓤⓢ ˈgɔːl-, ˈgɑːl-
Galvani gælˈvɑː.ni
galvanic gælˈvæn.ɪk
galvanism ˈgæl.və.nɪ.zᵊm
galvaniz|e, -is|e ˈgæl.və.naɪz **-es** -ɪz **-ing** -ɪŋ **-ed** -d **-er/s** -əʳ/z ⓤⓢ -ɚ/z
galvanometer ˌgæl.vəˈnɒm.ɪ.təʳ, -ə.təʳ ⓤⓢ -ˈnɑː.mə.t̬ɚ **-s** -z
Galveston, Galvestone ˈgæl.vɪ.stᵊn, -və-
Galway ˈgɔːl.weɪ ⓤⓢ ˈgɔːl-, ˈgɑːl-
gam gæm **-s** -z
Gama ˈgɑː.mə
Gamage ˈgæm.ɪdʒ **-ˈs** -ɪz
Gamaliel gəˈmeɪ.li.əl *in Jewish usage also:* -ˈmɑː-; ˌgæm.əˈliː.əl
Gamay ˈgæm.eɪ, -ˈ- ⓤⓢ gæmˈeɪ
gamba ˈgæm.bə ⓤⓢ ˈgɑːm-, ˈgæm- **-s** -z
gambado *jump:* gæmˈbeɪ.dəʊ, -ˈbɑː- ⓤⓢ -ˈbeɪ.doʊ **-(e)s** -z
gambadoes *leggings:* gæmˈbeɪ.dəʊz ⓤⓢ -doʊz
Gambetta gæmˈbet.ə ⓤⓢ -ˈbet̬-
Gambia ˈgæm.bi.ə **-n/s** -n/z
gambier *substance used in dyeing:* ˈgæm.bɪəʳ ⓤⓢ ˈgæm.bɪr
Gambier *surname:* ˈgæm.bi.əʳ, -bɪəʳ, -bi.eɪ ⓤⓢ ˈgæm.bɪr
gambit ˈgæm.bɪt **-s** -s
gambl|e (G) ˈgæm.bl̩ **-es** -z **-ing** -ɪŋ, ˈ-blɪŋ **-ed** -d **-er/s** -əʳ/z, ˈ-bləʳ/z ⓤⓢ ˈ-bl̩.ɚ/z, ˈ-blɚ/z
gamboge gæmˈbəʊʒ, -ˈbəʊdʒ, -ˈbuːʒ ⓤⓢ -ˈboʊdʒ
gambol ˈgæm.bᵊl **-s** -z **-(l)ing** -ɪŋ **-(l)ed** -d
Gambon ˈgæm.bən
gambrel ˈgæm.brəl **-s** -z
gam|e geɪm **-es** -z **-er** -əʳ ⓤⓢ -ɚ **-est** -ɪst, -əst **-ely** -li **-eness** -nəs, -nɪs **-ing** -ɪŋ **-ed** -d **ˈgame ˌshow**
gamebag ˈgeɪm.bæg **-s** -z
gamecock ˈgeɪm.kɒk ⓤⓢ -ˈkɑːk **-s** -s
gamekeeper ˈgeɪmˌkiː.pəʳ ⓤⓢ -pɚ **-s** -z
gamelan ˈgæm.ə.læn, ˈ-ɪ- **-s** -z
gameplay ˈgeɪm.pleɪ
gamesmanship ˈgeɪmz.mən.ʃɪp
games|-master ˈgeɪmz|ˌmɑː.stəʳ ⓤⓢ -ˌmæs.tɚ **-masters** -ˌmɑː.stəz ⓤⓢ -ˌmæs.tɚz **-mistress/es** -ˌmɪs.trəs/ɪz, -trɪs/ɪz
gamester ˈgeɪm.stəʳ ⓤⓢ -stɚ **-s** -z
gamete ˈgæm.iːt, gəˈmiːt **-s** -s
gametic gəˈmet.ɪk, gæmˈet- ⓤⓢ gəˈmet̬-
gamin ˈgæm.ɪn, gæˈmæ̃ŋ **-s** -z
gamine ˈgæm.iːn, -ˈ- **-s** -z
gamma ˈgæm.ə **-s** -z **ˈgamma ˌray**
Gammell ˈgæm.ᵊl
gammer ˈgæm.əʳ ⓤⓢ -ɚ **-s** -z
gammon ˈgæm.ən **-s** -z **-ing** -ɪŋ **-ed** -d
gamm|y ˈgæm|.i **-ier** -i.əʳ ⓤⓢ -i.ɚ **-iest** -i.ɪst, -i.əst
-gamous -gə.məs
Note: Suffix. Usually unstressed, e.g. **monogamous** /məˈnɒg.ə.məs ⓤⓢ -ˈnɑː.gə-/.
gamp (G) gæmp **-s** -s
gamut ˈgæm.ət, -ʌt **-s** -s
gam|y ˈgeɪ.m|i **-ier** -i.əʳ ⓤⓢ -i.ɚ **-iest** -i.ɪst, -i.əst **-iness** -ɪ.nəs, -ɪ.nɪs
-gamy -gə.mi
Note: Suffix. Normally unstressed, e.g. **monogamy** /məˈnɒg.ə.mi ⓤⓢ -ˈnɑː.gə-/.
Gandalf ˈgæn.dælf ⓤⓢ -dælf, -dɑːlf
gander (G) ˈgæn.dəʳ ⓤⓢ -dɚ **-s** -z
Gandh|i ˈgæn.d|i, ˈgɑːn- ⓤⓢ ˈgɑːn-, ˈgæn- **-ian** -i.ən
Ganes(h)a gænˈiː.sə, -ˈeɪ.sə ⓤⓢ -ʃə
gang gæŋ **-s** -z **-ing** -ɪŋ **-ed** -d
gang-bang ˈgæŋˌbæŋ **-s** -z **-ing** -ɪŋ **-ed** -d
Ganges ˈgæn.dʒiːz
gangland ˈgæŋ.lænd, -lənd
gangling ˈgæŋ.glɪŋ
gangli|on ˈgæŋ.gli|.ən, -ɒn ⓤⓢ -ən **-a** -ə **-ons** -ənz, -ɒnz ⓤⓢ -ənz
gangl|y ˈgæŋ.gl|i **-ier** -i.əʳ ⓤⓢ -i.ɚ **-iest** -i.ɪst, -i.əst
gangplank ˈgæŋ.plæŋk **-s** -s
gangren|e ˈgæŋ.griːn ⓤⓢ ˈ--, ˌ-ˈ- **-es** -z **-ing** -ɪŋ **-ed** -d

gangrenous ˈgæŋ.grɪ.nəs ⓊⓈ -grə-
gangsta ˈgæŋ*k*.stə
gangster ˈgæŋ*k*.stəʳ ⓊⓈ -stɚ **-s** -z
-ism -ɪ.zᵊm
gangway ˈgæŋ.weɪ **-s** -z
ganister ˈgæn.ɪ.stəʳ ⓊⓈ -stɚ
ganja ˈgæn.dʒə, ˈgɑːn- ⓊⓈ ˈgɑːn-
gannet ˈgæn.ɪt, -ət **-s** -s
Gannett ˈgæn.ɪt, -ət
gannister ˈgæn.ɪ.stəʳ ⓊⓈ -stɚ
Gannon ˈgæn.ən
gantr|y (G) ˈgæn.tr|i **-ies** -iz
Ganymede ˈgæn.ɪ.miːd ⓊⓈ ˈ-ə-
gaol dʒeɪl **-s** -z **-ing** -ɪŋ **-ed** -d
gaolbird ˈdʒeɪl.bɜːd ⓊⓈ -bɝːd **-s** -z
gaolbreak ˈdʒeɪl.breɪk **-s** -s
gaoler ˈdʒeɪ.ləʳ ⓊⓈ -lɚ **-s** -z
gap gæp **-s** -s
gap|e geɪp **-es** -s **-ing** -ɪŋ **-ed** -t
garag|e ˈgær.ɑːʒ, -ɪdʒ, -ɑːdʒ
occasionally: gəˈrɑːdʒ, -rɑːʒ
ⓊⓈ gəˈrɑːʒ, -ˈrɑːdʒ **-es** -ɪz **-ing** -ɪŋ
-ed -d ˈ**garage** ˌ**sale** ⓊⓈ **gaˈrage** ˌ**sale**
garam masala ˌgɑː.rəm.məˈsɑː.lə,
-mɑːˈsɑː-
Garamond ˈgær.ə.mɒnd ⓊⓈ ˈger-,
ˈgær-, -mɑːnd
garb gɑːb ⓊⓈ gɑːrb **-s** -z **-ed** -d
garbage ˈgɑː.bɪdʒ ⓊⓈ ˈgɑːr- ˈ**garbage**
ˌ**can**; ˈ**garbage disˌposal**; ˈ**garbage**
ˌ**man**
garbanzo gɑːˈbæn.zəʊ
ⓊⓈ gɑːrˈbɑːn.zoʊ **-s** -z
garbl|e ˈgɑː.bl̩ ⓊⓈ ˈgɑːr- **-es** -z **-ing** -ɪŋ,
ˈ-blɪŋ **-ed** -d
Garbo ˈgɑː.bəʊ ⓊⓈ ˈgɑːr.boʊ
Garcia *English surname:* ˈgɑː.si.ə,
ˈgɑː.ʃi.ə ⓊⓈ gɑːrˈsiː.ə, ˈgɑːr.si-
García, Garcia *Spanish surname:*
gɑːˈsiː.ə ⓊⓈ gɑːr-
García Lorca gɑːˌsiː.əˈlɔː.kə
ⓊⓈ gɑːrˌsiː.əˈlɔːr.kə
García Márquez gɑːˌsiː.əˈmɑː.kez,
-kes ⓊⓈ gɑːrˌsiː.ə.mɑːrˈkez, -ˈkes,
-ˈkeθ
garçon, garcon ˈgɑː.sɒŋ, -sɒn; gɑːˈsɔ̃*ŋ*
ⓊⓈ gɑːrˈsoʊn, -ˈsɔ̃ **-s** -z
garda *Irish police:* ˈgɑː.də ⓊⓈ ˈgɑːr-
gardai gɑːˈdiː ⓊⓈ gɑːr-
Garda *Italian lake:* ˈgɑː.də ⓊⓈ ˈgɑːr-
garden (G) ˈgɑː.dᵊn ⓊⓈ ˈgɑːr- **-s** -z **-ing**
-ɪŋ **-ed** -d ˈ**garden** ˌ**centre**; ˌ**garden**
ˈ**city**; ˈ**garden** ˌ**party**
gardener ˈgɑː.dᵊn.əʳ; ˈgɑːd.nəʳ
ⓊⓈ ˈgɑːr.dᵊn.ɚ; ˈgɑːrd.nɚ **-s** -z
gardenia gɑːˈdiː.ni.ə ⓊⓈ gɑːr-, ˈ-njə **-s** -z
Gardiner ˈgɑː.dᵊn.əʳ; ˈgɑːd.nəʳ
ⓊⓈ ˈgɑːr.dᵊn.ɚ; ˈgɑːrd.nɚ
Gardner ˈgɑːd.nəʳ ⓊⓈ ˈgɑːrd.nɚ
Gare du Nord ˌgɑː.djuːˈnɔːʳ
ⓊⓈ ˌgɑːr.duːˈnɔːr, -djuːˈ-
garefowl ˈgeə.faʊl ⓊⓈ ˈger- **-s** -z

Gareth ˈgær.əθ, -eθ, -ɪθ ⓊⓈ ˈger-, ˈgær-
Garfield ˈgɑː.fiːld ⓊⓈ ˈgɑːr-
garfish ˈgɑː.fɪʃ ⓊⓈ ˈgɑːr-
Garforth ˈgɑː.fəθ, -fɔːθ ⓊⓈ ˈgɑːr.fɚθ,
-fɔːrθ
Garfunkel ˌgɑːˈfʌŋ.kᵊl, ˈ---
ⓊⓈ ˈgɑːr.fʌŋ-
garganey ˈgɑː.gᵊn.i ⓊⓈ ˈgɑːr- **-s** -z
Gargantua gɑːˈgæn.tju.ə, -tʃu-
ⓊⓈ gɑːrˈgæn.tʃu-, -tju-
gargantuan gɑːˈgæn.tju.ən, -tʃu-
ⓊⓈ gɑːrˈgæn.tʃu-, -tʃu-
Gargery ˈgɑː.dʒᵊr.i ⓊⓈ ˈgɑːr-
gargl|e ˈgɑː.gl̩ ⓊⓈ ˈgɑːr- **-es** -z **-ing/s**
-ɪŋ/z, ˈ-glɪŋ **-ed** -d
gargoyle ˈgɑː.gɔɪl ⓊⓈ ˈgɑːr- **-s** -z
garibaldi (G) ˌgær.ɪˈbɔːl.di, -əˈ-, -ˈbæl-,
-ˈbɒl- ⓊⓈ ˌger-, ˌgær-, -ˈbɑːl- **-s** -z
Garioch ˈgær.i.ɒk, -ɒx ⓊⓈ ˈger.i.ɑːk,
ˈgær-
garish ˈgeə.rɪʃ, ˈgɑː- ⓊⓈ ˈger.ɪʃ, ˈgær-
-ly -li **-ness** -nəs, -nɪs
garland (G) ˈgɑː.lənd ⓊⓈ ˈgɑːr- **-s** -z
-ing -ɪŋ **-ed** -ɪd
garlic ˈgɑː.lɪk ⓊⓈ ˈgɑːr- **-ky** -i
Garlick ˈgɑː.lɪk ⓊⓈ ˈgɑːr-
Garman ˈgɑː.mən ⓊⓈ ˈgɑːr-
gar|ment ˈgɑː|.mənt ⓊⓈ ˈgɑːr- **-ments**
-mənts **-mented** -mən.tɪd
ⓊⓈ -mən.t̬ɪd
garner (G) ˈgɑː.nəʳ ⓊⓈ ˈgɑːr.nɚ **-s** -z
-ing -ɪŋ **-ed** -d
garnet ˈgɑː.nɪt, -nət ⓊⓈ ˈgɑːr- **-s** -s
Garnet(t) ˈgɑː.nɪt, -nət ⓊⓈ ˈgɑːr-
Garnham ˈgɑː.nəm ⓊⓈ ˈgɑːr-
garnish ˈgɑː.nɪʃ ⓊⓈ ˈgɑːr- **-es** -ɪz **-ing**
-ɪŋ **-ed** -t
garnishee ˌgɑː.nɪˈʃiː ⓊⓈ ˌgɑːr- **-s** -z **-ing**
-ɪŋ **-d** -d
garnishment ˈgɑː.nɪʃ.mənt ⓊⓈ ˈgɑːr-
-s -s
garniture ˈgɑː.nɪ.tʃəʳ ⓊⓈ ˈgɑːr.nɪ.tʃɚ
Garonne gærˈɒn ⓊⓈ -ˈɔːn, -ˈɑːn
Garrard ˈgær.əd, -ɑːd ⓊⓈ ˈger.ɚd,
ˈgær-; gəˈrɑːrd
Garratt ˈgær.ət ⓊⓈ ˈger-, ˈgær-
Garraway ˈgær.ə.weɪ ⓊⓈ ˈger-, ˈgær-
garret ˈgær.ət, -ɪt ⓊⓈ ˈger-, ˈgær- **-s** -s
Garret(t) ˈgær.ət, -ɪt ⓊⓈ ˈger-, ˈgær-
Garrick ˈgær.ɪk ⓊⓈ ˈger-, ˈgær-
Garrioch *district in Scotland:* ˈgɪə.ri
ⓊⓈ ˈger.i *surname:* ˈgær.i.ək, -əx
ⓊⓈ ˈger-, ˈgær-
garrison (G) ˈgær.ɪ.sᵊn, ˈ-ə- ⓊⓈ ˈger.ə-,
ˈgær- **-s** -z **-ing** -ɪŋ **-ed** -d
Garrod ˈgær.əd ⓊⓈ ˈger-, ˈgær-
Garrold ˈgær.ᵊld ⓊⓈ ˈger-, ˈgær-
garrot ˈgær.ət ⓊⓈ ˈger-, ˈgær- **-s** -s
garro|t(t)e gəˈrɒ|t ⓊⓈ -ˈrɑː|t, -ˈroʊ|t;
ˈger.ə|t **-t(t)es** -ts **-t(t)ing** -tɪŋ ⓊⓈ -t̬ɪŋ
-t(t)ed -tɪd ⓊⓈ -t̬ɪd **-t(t)er/s** -təʳ/z
ⓊⓈ -t̬ɚ/z

garrulity gærˈuː.lə.ti, gəˈruː-, -ˈrjuː-,
-lɪ- ⓊⓈ gerˈuː.lə.t̬i, gær-
garrulous ˈgær.ᵊl.əs, -ʊl-, -jʊl-
ⓊⓈ ˈger.ᵊl-, -jᵊl- **-ly** -li **-ness** -nəs, -nɪs
Garston ˈgɑː.stᵊn ⓊⓈ ˈgɑːr-
gart|er ˈgɑː.t|əʳ ⓊⓈ ˈgɑːr.t̬|ɚ **-ers** -əz
ⓊⓈ -ɚz **-ering** -ᵊr.ɪŋ **-ered** -əd ⓊⓈ -ɚd
garth (G) gɑːθ ⓊⓈ gɑːrθ **-s** -s
Gartmore ˈgɑːt.mɔːʳ ⓊⓈ ˈgɑːrt.mɔːr
Gartward ˈgɑːt.wəd, -wɔːd
ⓊⓈ ˈgɑːrt.wɚd
Garuda gærˈuː.də ⓊⓈ ger-, gær-
Garvagh ˈgɑː.və ⓊⓈ ˈgɑːr-
Garvaghy ˌgɑːˈvæ.hi ⓊⓈ ˈgɑːr-
Garwood ˈgɑː.wʊd ⓊⓈ ˈgɑːr-
Gary ˈgær.i ⓊⓈ ˈger-, ˈgær-
Garza ˈgɑː.zə ⓊⓈ ˈgɑːr-
gas (*n.*) gæs **-(s)es** -ɪz ˈ**gas** ˌ**chamber**;
ˈ**gas** ˌ**mask**; ˈ**gas** ˌ**station**
gas (*v.*) gæs **-ses** -ɪz **-sing** -ɪŋ **-sed** -t
gasbag ˈgæs.bæg **-s** -z
Gascoigne ˈgæs.kɔɪn ⓊⓈ gæsˈkɔɪn, ˈ--
Gascon ˈgæs.kən **-s** -z
gasconad|e ˌgæs.kəˈneɪd **-es** -z **-ing** -ɪŋ
-ed -ɪd
Gascony ˈgæs.kə.ni
Gascoyne ˈgæs.kɔɪn ⓊⓈ gæsˈkɔɪn, ˈ--
gaselier ˌgæs.əˈlɪəʳ ⓊⓈ -ˈlɪr **-s** -z
gaseous ˈgæs.i.əs, ˈgeɪ.si-, ˈ-ʃəs;
ˈgæʃ.əs ⓊⓈ ˈgæs.i.əs, ˈgæʃ-; ˈgæʃ.əs
-ness -nəs, -nɪs
gas-guzzler ˈgæsˌgʌz.ləʳ, -ˌgʌz.l̩.əʳ
ⓊⓈ ˌ-l̩.ɚ, ˌ-lɚ **-s** -z
gash gæʃ **-es** -ɪz **-ing** -ɪŋ **-ed** -t
gasholder ˈgæsˌhəʊl.dəʳ ⓊⓈ -ˌhoʊl.dɚ
-s -z
gasi|fy ˈgæs.ɪ|.faɪ, ˈ-ə- ⓊⓈ ˈ-ə- **-fies** -faɪz
-fying -faɪ.ɪŋ **-fied** -faɪd
Gaskell ˈgæs.kᵊl, -kel
gasket ˈgæs.kɪt **-s** -s
gaskin (G) ˈgæs.kɪn **-s** -z
gaslight ˈgæs.laɪt **-s** -s
gas|man ˈgæs|.mæn **-men** -men
gasohol ˈgæs.ə.hɒl ⓊⓈ -hɔːl, -hɑːl
gasoline, gasolene ˈgæs.ᵊl.iːn, ˌ--ˈ-
gasometer gæsˈɒm.ɪ.təʳ, gəˈsɒm-,
-ə.təʳ ⓊⓈ gæsˈɑː.mə.t̬ɚ **-s** -z
gasp gɑːsp ⓊⓈ gæsp **-s** -s **-ing** -ɪŋ
-ed -t
Gaspé gæsˈpeɪ
gasper ˈgɑː.spəʳ ⓊⓈ ˈgæs.pɚ **-s** -z
gass|y ˈgæs|.i **-ier** -i.əʳ ⓊⓈ -i.ɚ **-iest**
-i.ɪst, -i.əst **-iness** -ɪ.nəs, -ɪ.nɪs
gasteropod ˈgæs.tᵊr.əʊ.pɒd
ⓊⓈ -ə.pɑːd **-s** -z
Gaston ˈgæs.tɒn, gæsˈtɔ̃ː*ŋ* ⓊⓈ -tən,
gæsˈtɑːn, -ɔ̃ːn
gastric ˈgæs.trɪk
gastrin ˈgæs.trɪn
gastritis gæsˈtraɪ.tɪs ⓊⓈ -t̬ɪs
gastro- gæs.trəʊ-; gæsˈtrɒ-
ⓊⓈ gæs.troʊ-, -trə-; gæsˈtrɑː-

Note: Prefix. Normally takes either primary or secondary stress on the first syllable, e.g. **gastronome** /ˈgæs.trə.nəʊm US -noʊm/, **gastronomic** /ˌgæs.trəˈnɒm.ɪk US -ˈnɑː.mɪk/, or primary stress on the second syllable, e.g. **gastronomy** /gæsˈtrɒn.ə.mi US -ˈtrɑː.nə-/.

gastroenteritis ˌgæs.trəʊˌen.təˈraɪ.tɪs US -troʊˌen.t̬əˈraɪ.t̬ɪs

gastroenterolog|ist ˌgæs.trəʊˌen.təˈrɒl.ə.dʒ|ɪst US -troʊˌen.t̬əˈrɑː.lə.dʒ|ɪst **-ists** -ɪsts **-y** -i

gastrointestinal ˌgæs.trəʊˌɪn.tesˈtaɪ.nəl, -ɪnˈtes.tɪ.nəl, -tən.əl US -troʊ.ɪnˈtes.tən.əl

gastronome ˈgæs.trə.nəʊm US -noʊm **-s** -z

gastronomic ˌgæs.trəˈnɒm.ɪk US -ˈnɑː.mɪk **-al** -əl

gastronom|y gæsˈtrɒn.ə.m|i US -ˈtrɑː.nə- **-ist/s** -ɪst/s

gastropod ˈgæs.trəʊ.pɒd US -trə.pɑːd **-s** -z

gastropub ˈgæs.trəʊ.pʌb US -troʊ- **-s** -z

gasworks ˈgæs.wɜːks US -wɝːks

gat|e geɪt **-es** -s **-ing** -ɪŋ US ˈgeɪ.t̬ɪŋ **-ed** -ɪd US ˈgeɪ.t̬əd

gâteau, gateau ˈgæt.əʊ US gætˈoʊ **-s** -z

gâteaux, gateaux US gætˈoʊ, -z

gatecrash ˈgeɪt.kræʃ **-es** -ɪz **-ing** -ɪŋ **-ed** -t **-er/s** -ər/z US -ɚ/z

gatehou|se ˈgeɪt.haʊ|s **-ses** -zɪz

gatekeeper ˈgeɪtˌkiː.pər US -pɚ **-s** -z

gateleg ˈgeɪt.leg **-s** -z

gate-legged ˈgeɪtˌlegd

gateless ˈgeɪt.ləs, -lɪs

gatepost ˈgeɪt.pəʊst US -poʊst **-s** -s

Gates geɪts

Gateshead ˈgeɪts.hed, ˌgeɪtsˈhed

gateway (G) ˈgeɪt.weɪ **-s** -z

Gath gæθ

gath|er ˈgæð|.ər US -ɚ **-ers** -əz US -ɚz **-ering/s** -ər.ɪŋ/z **-ered** -əd US -ɚd **-erer/s** -ər.ər/z US -ɚ.ɚ/z

Gatley ˈgæt.li

Gatling ˈgæt.lɪŋ

gator ˈgeɪ.tə US -t̬ɚ **-s** -z

Gatorade® ˌgeɪ.tərˈeɪd US ˈgeɪ.t̬əˌreɪd

Gatsby ˈgæts.bi

Gatt, GATT gæt

Gatting ˈgæt.ɪŋ US ˈgæt̬-

Gatty ˈgæt.i US ˈgæt̬-

Gatwick ˈgæt.wɪk ˌ**Gatwick ˈAirport**

gauche gəʊʃ US goʊʃ **-ly** -li **-ness** -nəs, -nɪs

gaucherie ˈgəʊ.ʃər.i; ˌgəʊ.ʃərˈiː US ˌgoʊ.ʃəˈriː **-s** -z

gaucho ˈgaʊ.tʃəʊ US -tʃoʊ **-s** -z

gaud gɔːd US gɑːd, gɔːd **-s** -z

Gauden ˈgɔː.dən US ˈgɑː-, ˈgɔː-

Gaudí ˈgaʊ.di, -ˈ-

gaud|y ˈgɔː.d|i US ˈgɑː-, ˈgɔː- **-ier** -i.ər US -i.ɚ **-iest** -i.ɪst, -i.əst **-ily** -ɪ.li, -əl.i **-iness** -ɪ.nəs, -ɪ.nɪs

gaug|e geɪdʒ **-es** -ɪz **-ing** -ɪŋ **-ed** -d **-eable** -ə.bl̩

gauger ˈgeɪ.dʒər US -dʒɚ **-s** -z

Gauguin ˈgəʊ.gæ̃n, -gæn US goʊˈgæ̃, -ˈgæn

Gaul gɔːl **-s** -z **-ish** -ɪʃ

gauleiter ˈgaʊ.laɪ.tər US -t̬ɚ **-s** -z

Gaull|ism ˈgəʊ.l|ɪ.zəm US ˈgɑː-, ˈgoʊ- **-ist/s** -ɪst/s

Gauloise(s)® ˈgəʊl.wɑːz, ˌ-ˈ- US goʊlˈwɑːz, gɑːl-

Gault gɔːlt, gɒlt US gɔːlt, gɑːlt

Gaultier ˈgɔːl.ti.eɪ US ˈgɔːl-, ˈgɑːl-

Gaumont® ˈgəʊ.mɒnt, -mənt US ˈgoʊ.mɑːnt

gaun|t (G) gɔːn|t US gɑːn|t, gɔːn|t **-ter** -tər US -t̬ɚ **-test** -tɪst, -təst US -t̬ɪst, -t̬əst **-tly** -t.li **-tness** -t.nəs, -nɪs

gauntle|t (G) ˈgɔːnt.lə|t, -lɪ|t US ˈgɑːnt-, ˈgɔːnt- **-ts** -ts **-ted** -tɪd US -t̬ɪd

Gauntlett ˈgɔːnt.lət, -lɪt US ˈgɑːnt-, ˈgɔːnt

gauss (G) gaʊs **-es** -ɪz

gauz|e gɔːz US gɑːz, gɔːz **-es** -ɪz **-y** -i **-iness** -ɪ.nəs, -ɪ.nɪs

gave *(from* **give***)* geɪv

gavel ˈgæv.əl **-s** -z

gavelkind ˈgæv.əl.kaɪnd, -kɪnd

gavel-to-gavel ˌgæv.əl.təˈgæv.əl

Gaveston ˈgæv.ɪ.stən, ˈ-ə-

Gavey ˈgeɪ.vi

Gavin ˈgæv.ɪn

gavotte gəˈvɒt, gæ- US -ˈvɑːt **-s** -s

Gawain ˈgɑː.weɪn, ˈgæw.eɪn, -ɪn;

gawd gɔːd US gɔːd, gɑːd

Gawith ˈgeɪ.wɪθ, ˈgaʊ.ɪθ

gawk gɔːk US gɑːk, gɔːk **-s** -s **-ing** -ɪŋ **-ed** -t

gawk|y ˈgɔː.k|i US ˈgɑː-, ˈgɔː- **-ier** -i.ər US -i.ɚ **-iest** -i.ɪst, -i.əst **-iness** -ɪ.nəs, -ɪ.nɪs

gawp gɔːp US gɑːp, gɔːp **-s** -s **-ing** -ɪŋ **-ed** -t

Gawthrop ˈgɔː.θrɒp, -θrəp US ˈgɑː.θrɑːp, ˈgɔː-, -θrəp

gay (G) geɪ **-er** -ər US -ɚ **-est** -ɪst, -əst **-s** -z **gaily** ˈgeɪ.li **gayness** ˈgeɪ.nəs, -nɪs

Gaye geɪ

Gayle geɪl

Gaylord ˈgeɪ.lɔːd US -lɔːrd

Gay-Lussac ˌgeɪˈluː.sæk US -ləˈsæk

Gaynham ˈgeɪ.nəm

Gaynor ˈgeɪ.nər US -nɚ

Gaza *in the Middle East:* ˈgɑː.zə *in biblical use also:* ˈgeɪ.zə US ˈgɑː.zə, ˈgæz.ə, ˈgeɪ.zə ˌ**Gaza ˈStrip**

Gaza *Greek scholar:* ˈgɑː.zə

gaz|e geɪz **-es** -ɪz **-ing** -ɪŋ **-ed** -d **-er/s** -ər/z US -ɚ/z

gazebo gəˈziː.bəʊ US -ˈziː.boʊ, -ˈzeɪ- **-s** -z

gazelle gəˈzel **-s** -z

ga|zette gə|ˈzet **-zettes** -ˈzets **-zetting** -ˈzet.ɪŋ US -ˈzet̬.ɪŋ **-zetted** -ˈzet.ɪd US -ˈzet̬.əd

gazetteer ˌgæz.əˈtɪər, -ɪˈ- US -ˈtɪr **-s** -z

Gaziantep ˌgɑː.zi.ɑːnˈtep

gazogene ˈgæz.əʊ.dʒiːn US ˈ-ə-

gazpacho gæsˈpætʃ.əʊ US gəˈspɑː.tʃoʊ, gəzˈpɑː-

gazump gəˈzʌmp **-s** -s **-ing** -ɪŋ **-ed** -t, -ˈzʌmt

gazunder gəˈzʌn.dər US -dɚ **-s** -s **-ing** -ɪŋ **-ed** -d

Gazza ˈgæz.ə

GB ˌdʒiːˈbiː

GBH ˌdʒiː.biːˈeɪtʃ

GCE ˌdʒiː.siːˈiː **-s** -z

GCHQ ˌdʒiː.siː.eɪtʃˈkjuː

GCSE ˌdʒiː.siː.esˈiː **-s** -z

Gdansk gəˈdæntsk, -ˈdaɪntsk US -ˈdɑːntsk, -ˈdæntsk

g'day gəˈdeɪ

GDP ˌdʒiː.diːˈpiː

GDR ˌdʒiː.diːˈɑːr US -ˈɑːr

GE® ˌdʒiːˈiː

gear gɪər US gɪr **-s** -z **-ing** -ɪŋ **-ed** -d ˈ**gear** ˌ**lever**

gearbox ˈgɪə.bɒks US ˈgɪr.bɑːks **-es** -ɪz

Geare gɪər US gɪr

gearshift ˈgɪə.ʃɪft US ˈgɪr- **-s** -s

Geary ˈgɪə.ri US ˈgɪr.i

Geat giːt **-s** -s

gecko ˈgek.əʊ US -oʊ **-(e)s** -z

Ged ged, dʒed

GED ˌdʒiː.iːˈdiː

Geddes ˈged.ɪs US -iːz

geddit ˈged.ɪt US -ət

gee (G) dʒiː **-s** -z **-ing** -ɪŋ **-d** -d ˌ**gee** ˈ**whiz**

geegaw ˈgiː.gɔː US -gɑː, -gɔː **-s** -z

geegee ˈdʒiː.dʒiː **-s** -z

geek giːk **-s** -s

geek|y ˈgiː.k|i **-ier** -i.ər US -i.ɚ **-iest** -i.ɪst, -i.əst

Geelong dʒɪˈlɒŋ, dʒə- US -ˈlɑːŋ, -ˈlɔːŋ

Geering ˈgɪə.rɪŋ US ˈgɪr.ɪŋ

geese *(plur. of* **goose***)* giːs

Geeson ˈdʒiː.sən, ˈgiː-

gee-up ˌdʒiːˈʌp, ˈdʒiː.ʌp

geezer ˈgiː.zər US -zɚ **-s** -z

Geffen ˈgef.ən

gefilte gəˈfɪl.tə, gɪ- **geˈfilte** ˌ**fish**, **geˌfilte** ˈ**fish**

Gehazi gɪˈheɪ.zaɪ, ge-, gə-, -ˈhɑː-, -zi

Gehenna gɪˈhen.ə, gə-

Gehrig ˈger.ɪg

Gehry ˈgeə.ri US ˈger.i

Geierstein ˈgaɪə.staɪn US ˈgaɪɚ-

Geiger 'gaɪ.gəʳ (US) -gɚ **'Geiger ˌcounter**
Geikie 'giː.ki
geisha 'geɪ.ʃə (US) 'geɪ-, 'giː- **-s** -z
gel *girl:* gel **-s** -z
gel *jelly:* dʒel **-s** -s **-ling** -ɪŋ **-led** -d
gelatin 'dʒel.ə.tɪn
gelatine 'dʒel.ə.tiːn, -tɪn, ˌ--'-
gelatiniz|e, -is|e dʒə'læt.ɪ.naɪz, dʒel'æt-, dʒɪ'læt-, -ᵊn.aɪz (US) dʒə'læt.ᵊn.aɪz **-es** -ɪz **-ing** -ɪŋ **-ed** -d
gelatinous dʒə'læt.ɪ.nəs, dʒel'æt-, dʒɪ'læt-, -ᵊn.əs (US) dʒə'læt.ᵊn.əs **-ly** -li
geld geld **-s** -z **-ing** -ɪŋ **-ed** -ɪd
Gelderland 'gel.də.lænd (US) -dɚ-
gelding 'gel.dɪŋ **-s** -z
Geldof 'gel.dɒf (US) -dɑːf
gelid 'dʒel.ɪd **-ly** -li **-ness** -nəs, -nɪs
gelignite 'dʒel.ɪg.naɪt, -əg-
Gell gel, dʒel
Gellan 'gel.ən
Gellatl(e)y 'gel.ət.li, gel'æt-, gə'læt- (US) gel'æt-, gə'læt-
Geller 'gel.əʳ (US) -ɚ
Gelligaer ˌgeθ.li'geəʳ, -'gaɪ.əʳ (US) -'ger, -'gaɪɚ
gem (G) dʒem **-s** -z
Gemara gə'mɑː.rə, gem'ɑː-, gɪ'mɑː-
gemfish 'dʒem.fɪʃ **-es** -ɪz
gemi|nate *(v.)* 'dʒem.ɪ|.neɪt, '-ə- **-nates** -neɪts **-nating** -neɪ.tɪŋ (US) -neɪ.t̬ɪŋ **-nated** -neɪ.tɪd (US) -neɪ.t̬əd
geminate *(adj.)* 'dʒem.ɪ.nət
gemination ˌdʒem.ɪ'neɪ.ʃᵊn, -ə'-
Gemini *constellation:* 'dʒem.ɪ.naɪ, '-ə-, -niː *aircraft:* 'dʒem.ɪ.ni, '-ə-
Geminian ˌdʒem.ɪ'naɪ.ən, -ə'-, -'niː- **-s** -z
gem|ma (G) 'dʒem|.ə **-mae** -iː
gemmiferous dʒə'mɪf.ᵊr.əs, dʒem'ɪf-
gemmology dʒem'ɒl.ə.dʒi (US) -'ɑː.lə-
gemmule 'dʒem.juːl **-s** -z
gemology dʒem'ɒl.ə.dʒi (US) -'ɑː.lə-
gemsbok 'gemz.bɒk, -bʌk (US) -bɑːk **-s** -s
gemshorn 'gemz.hɔːn (US) -hɔːrn **-s** -z
gemstone 'dʒem.stəʊn (US) -stoʊn **-s** -z
gen dʒen **-s** -z **-ning** -ɪŋ **-ed** -d
gendarme 'ʒɑ̃ːn.dɑːm, 'ʒɔ̃ːn-, 'ʒɑːn- (US) 'ʒɑːn.dɑːrm **-s** -z
gender 'dʒen.dəʳ (US) -dɚ **-s** -z **-ing** -ɪŋ **-ed** -d
gender-bender 'dʒen.də,ben.dəʳ (US) -dɚ,ben.dɚ **-s** -z
gene (G) dʒiːn **-s** -z
genealogical ˌdʒiː.ni.ə'lɒdʒ.ɪ.kᵊl (US) ˌdʒiː.ni.ə'lɑː.dʒɪ-, ˌdʒen.i- **-ly** -i
genealogist ˌdʒiː.ni'æl.ə.dʒɪst (US) ˌdʒiː.ni'-, ˌdʒen.i'- **-s** -s
genealog|y ˌdʒiː.ni'æl.ə.dʒ|i (US) ˌdʒiː.ni'-, ˌdʒen.i'- **-ies** -iz
genera *(plur. of* **genus**) 'dʒen.ᵊr.ə
general 'dʒen.ᵊr.ᵊl **-s** -z **-ly** -i **ˌgeneral as'sembly; ˌgeneral e'lection; ˌgeneral prac'titioner; ˌgeneral 'store; ˌGeneral 'Motors®**
generalissimo ˌdʒen.ᵊr.ə'lɪs.ɪ.məʊ, '-ə- (US) -ə.moʊ **-s** -z
generalist 'dʒen.ᵊr.ᵊl.ɪst, 'dʒen.rᵊl- **-s** -s
generalit|y ˌdʒen.ᵊ'ræl.ə.t|i, -ɪ.t|i (US) -ə.t̬|i **-ies** -iz
generalization, -isa- ˌdʒen.ᵊr.ᵊl.aɪ'zeɪ.ʃᵊn, -ɪ'- (US) -ɪ'- **-s** -z
generaliz|e, -is|e 'dʒen.ᵊr.ᵊl.aɪz (US) -ə.laɪz **-es** -ɪz **-ing** -ɪŋ **-ed** -d **-able** -ə.bl̩
generalship 'dʒen.ᵊr.ᵊl.ʃɪp **-s** -s
gener|ate 'dʒen.ᵊr|.eɪt (US) -ə.r|eɪt **-ates** -eɪts **-ating** -eɪ.tɪŋ (US) -eɪ.t̬ɪŋ **-ated** -eɪ.tɪd (US) -eɪ.t̬ɪd
generation ˌdʒen.ə'reɪ.ʃᵊn **-al** -s -z **gene'ration ˌgap**
generative 'dʒen.ᵊr.ə.tɪv (US) -ə.t̬ɪv, '-ə.reɪ.t̬ɪv
generator 'dʒen.ᵊ.reɪ.təʳ (US) -t̬ɚ **-s** -z
generatri|x 'dʒen.ᵊ.reɪ.trɪ|ks (US) ˌdʒen.ə'reɪ- **-ces** -siːz
generic dʒə'ner.ɪk, dʒɪ-, dʒen'er- **-ally** -ᵊl.i, -li
generosity ˌdʒen.ᵊ'rɒs.ə.ti, -ɪ.ti (US) -'rɑː.sə.t̬i
generous 'dʒen.ᵊr.əs **-ly** -li **-ness** -nəs, -nɪs
gene|sis (G) 'dʒen.ə|.sɪs, '-ɪ- **-ses** -siːz
Genesius dʒə'niː.si.əs, dʒen'iː-, dʒɪ'niː- (US) -si-, -ʃi-, -zi-
Genesta dʒə'nes.tə, dʒen'es-, dʒɪ'nes-
genet *(D) animal:* 'dʒen.ɪt (US) 'dʒen.ɪt, dʒə'net **-s** -s
Genet *French writer:* ʒə'neɪ
genetic dʒə'net.ɪk, dʒɪ- (US) -'net̬.ɪk **-s** -s **-ally** -ᵊl.i, -li **geˌnetic engiˈneering; geˌnetic 'fingerprint**
geneticist dʒə'net.ɪ.sɪst, dʒɪ-, '-ə- (US) -'net̬.ə- **-s** -s
Geneva dʒə'niː.və, dʒɪ- **GeˌnevaCon'vention**
Geneviève *French name:* ˌʒen.ə'vjev (US) ˌʒen.ə'vjev, 'dʒen.ə.viːv
Genevieve *English name:* 'dʒen.ə.viːv, '-ɪ-, ˌ--'-
Genghis Khan ˌgeŋ.gɪs'kɑːn, ˌdʒeŋ-, -gɪz'-
genial *amiable:* 'dʒiː.ni.əl **-ly** -i **-ness** -nəs, -nɪs
genial *of the chin:* dʒɪ'niː.əl, dʒə-, -'naɪ-
geniality ˌdʒiː.ni'æl.ə.ti, -ɪ.ti (US) -ə.t̬i
-genic -'dʒen.ɪk, -'dʒiː.nɪk
Note: Suffix. Words ending **-genic** normally carry primary stress on the penultimate syllable, e.g. **photogenic** /ˌfəʊ.təʊ'dʒen.ɪk (US) ˌfoʊ.t̬oʊ'-/.
genie (G) 'dʒiː.ni **-s** -z
genii *(from* **genius**) 'dʒiː.ni.aɪ
genista dʒə'nɪs.tə, dʒɪ-, dʒen'ɪs- **-s** -z
genital 'dʒen.ɪ.tᵊl, '-ə- (US) -ət̬.ᵊl **-s** -z **-ly** -li
genitalia ˌdʒen.ɪ'teɪ.li.ə, -ə'- (US) -'teɪ.li.ə, -'teɪl.jə
genitival ˌdʒen.ɪ'taɪ.vᵊl, -ə'-
genitive 'dʒen.ɪ.tɪv, '-ə- (US) -ə.t̬ɪv **-s** -z
genito-urinary ˌdʒen.ɪ.təʊ'jʊə.rɪ.nᵊr.i, ˌ-ə-, -'jɔː-, -rᵊn.ᵊr- (US) -ə.t̬oʊ'jʊr.ə.ner.i
geni|us 'dʒiː.ni|.əs **-i** -aɪ **-uses** -ə.sɪz
genius loci ˌdʒiː.ni.əs'ləʊ.saɪ (US) -'loʊ- **genii loci** ˌdʒiː.ni.aɪ'-
Gennadi dʒə'nɑː.di, ge-
Gennesare|t gə'nez.ᵊr.ɪ|t, gɪ-, gen'ez-, -e|t, -ə|t (US) gə'nes-, dʒə- **-th** -θ
Genoa 'dʒen.əʊ.ə, dʒə'nəʊ-, dʒɪ-, dʒen'əʊ- (US) 'dʒen.ə.wə, dʒə'noʊ.ə
genocidal ˌdʒen.ə'saɪ.dᵊl *stress shift:* ˌgenocidal 'policies
genocide 'dʒen.ə.saɪd
Genoese ˌdʒen.əʊ'iːz (US) -oʊ'iːz *stress shift:* ˌGenoese 'sailor
genome 'dʒiː.nəʊm (US) -noʊm **-s** -z
genotype 'dʒen.əʊ.taɪp (US) '-oʊ-
-genous -dʒə.nəs, -dʒɪ.nəs
Note: Suffix. Words containing **-genous** are normally stressed on the antepenultimate syllable, e.g. **androgenous** /æn'drɒdʒ.ᵊn.əs (US) -'drɑː.dʒᵊn-/. Exceptions exist: see individual entries.
genre 'ʒɑ̃ːn.rə (US) 'ʒɑːn.rə **-s** -z
gen|s dʒen|z **-tes** -tiːz
Genseric 'gen.sᵊr.ɪk, 'dʒen-
Gensing 'gen.zɪŋ, 'gent.sɪŋ
gent *gentleman:* dʒent **-s** -s
Gent *surname:* gent
Gent *place in Belgium:* gent, xent
genteel dʒen'tiːl, dʒən- **-ly** -li **-ness** -nəs, -nɪs
gentes *(plur. of* **gens**) 'dʒen.tiːz
gentian 'dʒen.tʃᵊn, -tʃi.ən **-s** -z
gentile (G) 'dʒen.taɪl **-s** -z
gentility ˌdʒen'tɪl.ə.ti (US) -t̬i
gent|le (G) 'dʒen.t|l̩ **-ler** -l̩.əʳ, 'dʒent.ləʳ (US) 'dʒen.t̬l̩.ɚ, 'dʒent.lɚ **-lest** -l̩.əst, -ɪst, 'dʒent.lɪst, -ləst **-ly** -li **-leness** -l̩.nəs, -nɪs **'gentle ˌsex**
gentlefolk 'dʒen.tl̩.fəʊk (US) 'dʒen.t̬l̩-foʊk **-s** -s
gentle|man 'dʒen.tl̩|.mən (US) 'dʒen.t̬l̩- **-men** -mən, -men **ˌgentleman's 'gentleman**
gentle|man-at-arms ˌdʒen.tl̩|.mən.ət'ɑːmz (US) -t̬l̩|.mən.ət'ɑːrmz **-men-at-arms** -mən.ət'ɑːmz, -men- (US) -'ɑːrmz
gentlemanlike 'dʒen.tl̩.mən.laɪk (US) 'dʒen.t̬l̩.-

gentlemanl|y ˈdʒen.tl̩.mən.l|i (US) ˈdʒen.t̬l̩- **-iness** -ɪ.nəs, -ɪ.nɪs
gentle|woman ˈdʒen.tl̩|ˌwʊm.ən (US) ˈdʒen.t̬l̩- **-women** -ˌwɪm.ɪn
gentrification ˌdʒen.trɪ.fɪˈkeɪ.ʃᵊn, -trə- **-s** -z
gentrifier ˈdʒen.trɪ.faɪ.əʳ, -trə- (US) -ɚ **-s** -z
gentrif|y ˈdʒen.trɪ.f|aɪ, -trə- **-ies** -aɪz **-ying** -aɪ.ɪŋ **-ied** -aɪd
gentry (G) ˈdʒen.tri
genuflect ˈdʒen.jʊ.flekt, -jə- **-s** -s **-ing** -ɪŋ **-ed** -ɪd
genuflection, genuflexion ˌdʒen.jʊˈflek.ʃᵊn, -jə- **-s** -z
genuine ˈdʒen.ju.ɪn **-ly** -li **-ness** -nəs, -nɪs
genus ˈdʒiː.nəs, ˈdʒen.əs **genera** ˈdʒen.ᵊr.ə
-geny -dʒə.ni, -dʒɪ.ni
Note: Suffix. Words containing **-geny** are stressed in a similar way to those containing **-genous**; see above.
geo- dʒiː.əʊ-; dʒiˈɒ-, ˈdʒɒ- (US) dʒiː.oʊ-, -ə-; dʒiˈɑː-
Note: Prefix. Normally takes either primary or secondary stress on the first syllable, e.g. **geomancy** /ˈdʒiː.əʊ.mænt.si (US) ˈ-ə-/, **geocentric** /ˌdʒiː.əʊˈsen.trɪk (US) -oʊˈ-/, or primary stress on the second syllable, e.g. **geography** /dʒiˈɒg.rə.fi (US) -ˈɑː.grə-/.
geocentric ˌdʒiː.əʊˈsen.trɪk (US) -oʊˈ- **-al** -ᵊl **-ally** -ᵊl.i, -li
geochemical ˌdʒiː.əʊˈkem.ɪ.kᵊl (US) -oʊˈ-
geochemist ˌdʒiː.əʊˈkem.ɪst, ˈdʒiː.əʊˌkem- (US) ˌdʒiː.oʊˈkem- **-s** -s
geochemistry ˌdʒiː.əʊˈkem.ɪ.stri (US) -oʊˈ-
geode ˈdʒiː.əʊd (US) -oʊd **-s** -z
geodesic ˌdʒiː.əʊˈdes.ɪk, -ˈdiː.sɪk (US) -əˈ- **-al** -ᵊl
geodesy dʒiˈɒd.ɪ.si, ˈ-ə- (US) -ˈɑː.də-
geodic dʒiˈɒd.ɪk (US) -ˈɑː.dɪk
Geoff dʒef
Geoffr(e)y ˈdʒef.ri
Geoghegan ˈgeɪ.gᵊn, ˈgəʊ.gᵊn, gɪˈheɪ.gᵊn (US) ˈgoʊ.gᵊn
geographer dʒiˈɒg.rə.fəʳ (US) -ˈɑː.grə.fɚ **-s** -z
geographic ˌdʒiː.əʊˈgræf.ɪk (US) -əˈ- **-al** -ᵊl **-ally** -ᵊl.i, -li
geograph|y dʒiˈɒg.rə.f|i; ˈdʒɒg- (US) dʒiˈɑː.grə- **-ies** -iz
geologic ˌdʒi.əʊˈlɒdʒ.ɪk (US) -əˈlɑː.dʒɪk **-al** -ᵊl **-ally** -ᵊl.i, -li
geologist dʒiˈɒl.ə.dʒɪst (US) -ˈɑː.lə- **-s** -s
geologiz|e, -is|e dʒiˈɒl.ə.dʒaɪz (US) -ˈɑː.lə- **-es** -ɪz **-ing** -ɪŋ **-ed** -d
geology dʒiˈɒl.ə.dʒi (US) -ˈɑː.lə-
geomagnetic ˌdʒiː.əʊ.mægˈnet.ɪk, -məg- (US) -oʊ.mægˈnet̬.ɪk
geomagnetism ˌdʒiː.əʊˈmæg.nɪ.tɪ.zᵊm, -nə- (US) -oʊˈmæg.nə-
geomancy ˈdʒiː.əʊ.mænt.si (US) ˈ-ə-
geometer dʒiˈɒm.ɪ.təʳ, ˈ-ə- (US) -ˈɑː.mə.t̬ɚ **-s** -z
geometric ˌdʒiː.əʊˈmet.rɪk (US) -əˈ- **-al** -ᵊl **-ally** -ᵊl.i, -li
geometrician ˌdʒiː.əʊ.məˈtrɪʃ.ᵊn, dʒiˌɒm.əˈ-, -ɪˈ- (US) ˌdʒiː.ə.məˈ-; dʒiˌɑː- **-s** -z
geometr|y dʒiˈɒm.ɪ.tr|i, ˈ-ə-; ˈdʒɒm- (US) dʒiˈɑː.mə- **-ies** -iz
geomorphologic ˌdʒiː.əʊˌmɔː.fəˈlɒdʒ.ɪk (US) -oʊˌmɔːr.fəˈlɑː.dʒɪk **-al** -ᵊl **-ally** -ᵊl.i, -li
geomorpholog|y ˌdʒiː.əʊ.mɔːˈfɒl.ə.dʒ|i (US) -oʊ.mɔːrˈfɑː.lə- **-ist/s** -ɪst/s
geophysical ˌdʒiː.əʊˈfɪz.ɪ.kᵊl (US) -oʊˈ-
geophysicist ˌdʒi.əʊˈfɪz.ɪ.sɪst (US) -oʊˈ- **-s** -s
geophysics ˌdʒiː.əʊˈfɪz.ɪks (US) -oʊˈ-
geopolitical ˌdʒiː.əʊ.pəˈlɪt.ɪ.kᵊl (US) -oʊ.pəˈlɪt̬- **-ly** -i
geopolitics ˌdʒiː.əʊˈpɒl.ə.tɪks, ˈ-ɪ- (US) -oʊˈpɑː.lə-
Geordie ˈdʒɔː.di (US) ˈdʒɔːr- **-s** -z
George dʒɔːdʒ (US) dʒɔːrdʒ
Georgetown ˈdʒɔːdʒ.taʊn (US) ˈdʒɔːrdʒ-
georgette dʒɔːˈdʒet (US) dʒɔːr-
Georgi|a ˈdʒɔː.dʒ|ə, -dʒi|.ə (US) ˈdʒɔːr- **-an/s** -ən/z
Georgiana ˌdʒɔː.dʒiˈɑː.nə (US) ˌdʒɔːrˈdʒæn.ə, -dʒiˈæn-
georgic (G) ˈdʒɔː.dʒɪk (US) ˈdʒɔːr- **-s** -s
Georgina dʒɔːˈdʒiː.nə (US) dʒɔːrˈ-
geoscience ˌdʒiː.əʊˈsaɪ.ənts (US) -oʊˈ-
geostationary ˌdʒiː.əʊˈsteɪ.ʃᵊn.ᵊr.i, -ri (US) -oʊˈsteɪ.ʃᵊn.er-
geothermal ˌdʒiː.əʊˈθɜː.mᵊl (US) -oʊˈθɝː-
geotropic ˌdʒiː.əʊˈtrɒp.ɪk (US) -əˈtrɑː.pɪk
geotropism dʒiˈɒt.rə.pɪ.zᵊm (US) -ˈɑː.trə- **-s** -z
Geraint ˈger.aɪnt, -ˈ- (US) dʒəˈreɪnt
Gerald ˈdʒer.ᵊld
Geraldine ˈdʒer.ᵊl.diːn, -daɪn
Note: /ˈdʒer.ᵊl.daɪn/ in Coleridge's 'Christabel'.
Geraldton ˈdʒer.ᵊld.tᵊn
geranium dʒəˈreɪ.ni.əm, dʒɪ- **-s** -z
Gerard ˈdʒer.ɑːd, ˈdʒer.əd, dʒerˈɑːd, dʒəˈrɑːd (US) dʒəˈrɑːrd
Gerbeau dʒeəˈbəʊ, dʒɜː-, ˈ-- (US) dʒerˈboʊ, ˈ--
gerbil ˈdʒɜː.bᵊl, -bɪl (US) ˈdʒɝː.bᵊl **-s** -z
gerfalcon ˈdʒɜːˌfɔːl.kᵊn, -ˌfɔː.kᵊn (US) ˈdʒɝːˌfɑːl-, -ˌfæl-, -ˌfɔː- **-s** -z
Note: In British English, those who practise the sport of falconry pronounce /-ˌfɔː-/.
Gergesene ˈgɜː.gɪ.siːn, -gə-, -ges.iːn, ˌ-ˈ-- (US) ˈgɝː.gə- **-s** -z
Gerhardt ˈgeə.hɑːt (US) ˈger.hɑːrd, -hɑːrt
geriatric ˌdʒer.iˈæt.rɪk **-s** -s
geriatrician ˌdʒer.i.əˈtrɪʃ.ᵊn **-s** -z
geriatry ˈdʒer.i.ə.tri, -æt.ri
Geritol® ˈdʒer.ɪ.tɒl (US) -tɑːl
Gerizim gerˈaɪ.zɪm, gəˈraɪ-, -ˈriː-; ˈger.ɪ.zɪm
germ dʒɜːm (US) dʒɝːm **-s** -z **ˌgerm ˈwarfare**
Germain ˈdʒɜː.mən, -meɪn (US) ˈdʒɝː-
Germaine dʒəˈmeɪn, dʒɜː- (US) dʒɚ-
German ˈdʒɜː.mən (US) ˈdʒɝː- **-s** -z **ˌGerman ˈmeasles**
germander dʒəˈmæn.dəʳ, dʒɜː- (US) dʒɚˈmæn.dɚ
germane (G) dʒəˈmeɪn, dʒɜː-; ˈdʒɜː.meɪn (US) dʒɚˈmeɪn **-ly** -li **-ness** -nəs, -nɪs
Germanic dʒəˈmæn.ɪk, dʒɜː- (US) dʒɚ-
German|ism ˈdʒɜː.mə.n|ɪ.zᵊm (US) ˈdʒɝː- **-isms** -ɪ.zᵊmz **-ist/s** -ɪst/s
germanium dʒəˈmeɪ.ni.əm, dʒɜː- (US) dʒɚ-
germanization, -isa- ˌdʒɜː.mə.naɪˈzeɪ.ʃᵊn, -ɪˈ- (US) ˌdʒɝː.mə.nɪˈ-
germaniz|e, -is|e ˈdʒɜː.mə.naɪz (US) ˈdʒɝː- **-es** -ɪz **-ing** -ɪŋ **-ed** -d
German|y ˈdʒɜː.mə.n|i (US) ˈdʒɝː- **-ies** -iz
germicidal ˌdʒɜː.mɪˈsaɪ.dᵊl, -məˈ-, ˈdʒɜː.mɪ.saɪ-, -mə- (US) ˌdʒɝː.məˈsaɪ-
germicide ˈdʒɜː.mɪ.saɪd, -mə- (US) ˈdʒɝː.mə- **-s** -z
germinal ˈdʒɜː.mɪ.nᵊl, -mə- (US) ˈdʒɝː.mə-
germi|nate ˈdʒɜː.mɪ|.neɪt, -mə- (US) ˈdʒɝː.mə- **-nates** -neɪts **-nating** -neɪ.tɪŋ (US) -neɪ.t̬ɪŋ **-nated** -neɪ.tɪd (US) -neɪ.t̬ɪd
germination ˌdʒɜː.mɪˈneɪ.ʃᵊn, -məˈ- (US) ˌdʒɝː.məˈ- **-s** -z
Germiston ˈdʒɜː.mɪ.stᵊn (US) ˈdʒɝː.mɪ-, -mə-
Germolene® ˈdʒɜː.mə.liːn (US) ˈdʒɝː-
Geronimo dʒəˈrɒn.ɪ.məʊ, dʒɪ-, dʒerˈɒn-, ˈ-ə- (US) -ˈrɑː.nə.moʊ
Gerontius gəˈrɒn.ti.əs, gɪ-, dʒə-, dʒɪ-, gerˈɒn-, -ʃi.əs, -ʃəs (US) dʒəˈrɑːn-
gerontocrac|y ˌdʒer.ɒnˈtɒk.rə.s|i, -ənˈ- (US) -ᵊnˈtɑː.krə- **-cies** -iz
gerontocratic dʒəˌrɒn.təˈkræt.ɪk, ˌdʒer.ɒn-, -ən.təˈ- (US) dʒəˌrɑːn.t̬əˈkræt̬.ɪk

Pronouncing the letters GG

The main pronunciation for the consonant digraph **gg** is /g/, e.g.:

rugged /ˈrʌg.ɪd/

In addition

gg may be pronounced as /dʒ/, e.g.:

exaggerate /ɪgˈzædʒ.ər.eɪt/ (US) /-ə.reɪt/

And in rare cases for American English as /gdʒ/:

suggest /səˈdʒest/ (US) /səgˈdʒest/

Pronouncing the letters GH

The consonant digraph **gh** can be pronounced as /g/, /f/ or may be silent.

In syllable-initial position, **gh** is always pronounced as /g/, e.g.:

ghost /gəʊst/ (US) /goʊst/
aghast /əˈgɑːst/ (US) /-ˈgæst/

Following a vowel letter, the pronunciation may be silent. This is always the case after **i** and **ei**, e.g.:

high /haɪ/
height /haɪt/
plough /plaʊ/
caught /kɔːt/ (US) /kɑːt/

Alternatively, the pronunciation may be /f/, e.g.:

rough /rʌf/
laugh /lɑːf/ (US) /læf/

In addition

A unique pronunciation of the consonant digraph **gh** is /p/, e.g.:

hiccough /ˈhɪk.ʌp/

gerontolog|y ˌdʒer.ɒnˈtɒl.ə.dʒ|i, ˌger-, -ənˈ- (US) ˌdʒer.ənˈtɑː.lə- **-ist/s** -ɪst/s
Gerrard ˈdʒer.əd, -ɑːd; dʒerˈɑːd, dʒəˈrɑːd (US) ˈdʒer.ɚd ˌ**Gerrard's ˈCross**
Gerry ˈdʒer.i
gerrymand|er ˈdʒer.i.mæn.d|əʳ, ˌdʒer.iˈmæn- (US) -d|ɚ **-ers** -əz (US) -ɚz **-ering** -ər.ɪŋ **-ered** -əd (US) -ɚd
Gershwin ˈgɜːʃ.wɪn (US) ˈgɝːʃ-, -wən
Gertie ˈgɜː.ti (US) ˈgɝː.t̬i
Gertrude ˈgɜː.truːd (US) ˈgɝː-
Gerty ˈgɜː.ti (US) ˈgɝː.t̬i
gerund ˈdʒer.ənd, -ʌnd **-s** -z
gerundival ˌdʒer.ənˈdaɪ.vəl
gerundive dʒəˈrʌn.dɪv, dʒɪ-, dʒerˈʌn- **-s** -z
Gerva(i)se ˈdʒɜː.veɪz, -vɪz; dʒɜːˈveɪz, -ˈveɪs (US) ˈdʒɝː-
Geryon ˈger.i.ən (US) ˈdʒɪr-, ˈger-
gesso ˈdʒes.əʊ (US) -oʊ **-es** -z
gest dʒest **-s** -s
gestalt gəˈʃtælt, -ʃtɑːlt; ˈgeʃ.tælt (US) gəˈʃtɑːlt
Gestapo gesˈtɑː.pəʊ, geʃ- (US) gəˈstɑː.poʊ, gəʃˈtɑː-
Gesta Romanorum ˌdʒes.tə.rəʊ.məˈnɔː.rəm, -mɑː-, ˌges- (US) -roʊ.məˈnɔːr.əm, -mɑ-
ges|tate dʒes|ˈteɪt, ˈ-- (US) ˈdʒes|.teɪt **-tates** -ˈteɪts (US) -teɪts **-tating** -ˈteɪ.tɪŋ (US) -teɪ.t̬ɪŋ **-tated** -ˈteɪ.tɪd (US) -teɪ.t̬ɪd
gestation dʒesˈteɪ.ʃən **-s** -z
gestatorial ˌdʒes.təˈtɔː.ri.əl
gestatory dʒesˈteɪ.tər.i; ˈdʒes.tə- (US) ˈdʒes.tə.tɔːr-
Gestetner® gesˈtet.nəʳ, gɪˈstet-, gə- (US) -nɚ
gesticu|late dʒesˈtɪk.jə|.leɪt, -jʊ- (US) -jə- **-lates** -leɪts **-lating** -leɪ.tɪŋ (US) -leɪ.t̬ɪŋ **-lated** -leɪ.tɪd (US) -leɪ.t̬ɪd **-lator/s** -leɪ.təʳ/z (US) -leɪ.t̬ɚ/z
gesticulation dʒesˌtɪk.jəˈleɪ.ʃən, -jʊˈ- (US) -jəˈ- **-s** -z
gesticulatory dʒesˈtɪk.jʊ.leɪ.tər.i, -lə-, -je- (US) -jə.lə.tɔːr-
gestur|e ˈdʒes.tʃəʳ (US) -tʃɚ **-es** -z **-ing** -ɪŋ **-ed** -d
Gesundheit gəˈzʊnd.haɪt
get get **-s** -s **-ting** -ɪŋ (US) ˈget̬.ɪŋ **got** gɒt (US) gɑːt **gotten** ˈgɒt.ən (US) ˈgɑː.tən ˌ**give as ˌgood as one ˈgets**
Getae ˈgeɪ.taɪ, ˈdʒiː.tiː
getatable getˈæt.ə.bl̩ (US) get̬ˈæt̬-
getaway ˈget.ə.weɪ (US) ˈget̬- **-s** -z
Gethin ˈgeθ.ɪn
Gethsemane geθˈsem.ə.ni
get-rich-quick ˌget.rɪtʃˈkwɪk
get-together ˈget.tə.geð.ə (US) -geð.ɚ **-s** -z
Getty ˈget.i (US) ˈget̬.i
Gettysburg ˈget.iz.bɜːg (US) ˈget̬.iz.bɝːg ˌ**Gettysburg Adˈdress**
getup ˈget.ʌp (US) ˈget̬- **-s** -s
get-up-and-go ˌget.ʌp.ənˈgəʊ, -əŋˈ- (US) ˌget̬.ʌp.ənˈgoʊ
geum ˈdʒiː.əm **-s** -z
gewgaw ˈgjuː.gɔː (US) ˈguː.gɑː, ˈgjuː-, -gɔː **-s** -z
Gewürztraminer gəˈvʊət.strəˌmiː.nə, -ˈvɜːt- (US) -ˈvɝːt.strəˌmiː.nɚ
geyser *hot spring:* ˈgiː.zəʳ, ˈgaɪ- (US) ˈgaɪ.zɚ **-s** -z
Note: In New Zealand the pronunciation is /ˈgaɪ.zəʳ/.
apparatus for heating water: ˈgiː.zəʳ (US) -zɚ **-s** -z
Ghana ˈgɑː.nə
Ghanaian gɑːˈneɪ.ən (US) -ˈniː-, -ˈneɪ- **-s** -z
ghastl|y ˈgɑːst.l|i (US) ˈgæst.l|i **-ier** -i.əʳ (US) -i.ɚ **-iest** -i.ɪst, -i.əst **-iness** -ɪ.nəs, -ɪ.nɪs
Ghat gɑːt, gɔːt **-s** -s
ghee giː
Ghent gent

gherkin ˈgɜː.kɪn ⓤⓢ ˈgɝː- **-s** -z
ghetto ˈget.əʊ ⓤⓢ ˈget̬.oʊ **-(e)s** -z
ˈ**ghetto** ˌ**blaster**
ghettoiz|e, -i|se ˈget.əʊ.aɪz ⓤⓢ ˈget̬.oʊ- **-es** -ɪz **-ing** -ɪŋ **-ed** -d
Ghia ˈgiː.ə
Ghibelline ˈgɪb.ɪ.laɪn, ˈ-ə-, -liːn **-s** -z
ghillie ˈgɪl.i **-s** -z
ghost gəʊst ⓤⓢ goʊst **-s** -s **-ing** -ɪŋ **-ed** -ɪd **-like** -laɪk ˈ**ghost** ˌ**town**; ˌ**give up the** ˈ**ghost**
ghostl|y ˈgəʊst.l|i ⓤⓢ ˈgoʊst- **-iness** -ɪ.nəs, -ɪ.nɪs
ghost|write ˈgəʊst|.raɪt ⓤⓢ ˈgoʊst- **-writes** -raɪts **-writing** -ˌraɪ.tɪŋ ⓤⓢ -ˌraɪ.t̬ɪŋ **-wrote** -rəʊt ⓤⓢ -roʊt
ghostwriter ˈgəʊstˌraɪ.təʳ ⓤⓢ ˈgoʊstˌraɪ.t̬ɚ **-s** -z
ghoul guːl **-s** -z **-ish/ly** -ɪʃ/li
ghyll gɪl **-s** -z
GI ˌdʒiːˈaɪ *stress shift:* ˌGI ˈbride
giant dʒaɪənt **-s** -s **-like** -laɪk ˌ**Giant's** ˈ**Causeway**
giantess ˈdʒaɪən.tes, -tɪs, -təs; ⓤⓢ ˈdʒaɪən.t̬əs **-es** -ɪz
Giaour ˈdʒaʊəʳ ⓤⓢ -ɚ
Gibb gɪb
gibb|er ˈdʒɪb|.əʳ ⓤⓢ -ɚ **-ers** -əz ⓤⓢ -ɚz **-ering** -ər.ɪŋ **-ered** -əd ⓤⓢ -ɚd
gibberish ˈdʒɪb.ə.rɪʃ
gibbet ˈdʒɪb.ɪt, -ət **-s** -s **-ing** -ɪŋ ⓤⓢ ˈdʒɪb.ɪ.t̬ɪŋ **-ed** -ɪd ⓤⓢ ˈdʒɪb.ɪ.t̬ɪd
Gibbie ˈdʒɪb.i
Gibbins ˈgɪb.ɪnz
gibbon (G) ˈgɪb.ən **-s** -z
gibbosity gɪˈbɒs.ə.ti, dʒɪ-, -ɪ.ti ⓤⓢ gɪˈbɑː.sə.t̬i
gibbous ˈgɪb.əs, ˈdʒɪb- ⓤⓢ ˈgɪb- **-ly** -li **-ness** -nəs, -nɪs
Gibbs gɪbz
gib|e dʒaɪb **-es** -z **-ing/ly** -ɪŋ/li **-ed** -d **-er/s** -əʳ/z ⓤⓢ -ɚ/z
Gibeon ˈgɪb.i.ən
giblet ˈdʒɪb.lət, -lɪt **-s** -s
Gibraltar dʒɪˈbrɔːl.təʳ, dʒə-, -ˈbrɒl- ⓤⓢ -ˈbrɑːl.tɚ, -ˈbrɔːl-
Gibraltarian ˌdʒɪb.rɔːlˈteə.ri.ən, -rɒlˈ-; dʒɪˌbrɔːlˈ-, dʒə-, -ˌbrɒlˈ- ⓤⓢ ˌdʒɪb.rɑːlˌter.i-, -rɔːlˈ- **-s** -z
Gibson ˈgɪb.sən
Gidding ˈgɪd.ɪŋ **-s** -z
Giddis ˈgɪd.ɪs
gidd|y (G) ˈgɪd|.i **-ier** -i.əʳ ⓤⓢ -i.ɚ **-iest** -i.ɪst, -i.əst **-ily** -ɪ.li, -əl.i **-iness** -ɪ.nəs, -ɪ.nɪs
Gide ʒiːd
Gidea ˈgɪd.i.ə
Gideon ˈgɪd.i.ən
Gielgud ˈgiːl.gʊd
GIF gɪf, dʒɪf
Giffard ˈdʒɪf.əd, ˈgɪf- ⓤⓢ -ɚd
Giffen ˈgɪf.ɪn, ˈdʒɪf.ɪn, -ən
Giffnock ˈgɪf.nək
Gifford *place near Haddington:* ˈgɪf.əd ⓤⓢ -ɚd *surname:* ˈgɪf.əd, ˈdʒɪf.əd ⓤⓢ -ɚd
gift gɪft **-s** -s **-ed** -ɪd ˈ**gift cer**ˌ**tificate**; ˈ**gift** ˌ**token**; ˌ**gift of the** ˈ**gab**; ˌ**look a** ˌ**gift horse in the** ˈ**mouth**
gift-wrap ˈgɪft.ræp **-s** -s **-ping** -ɪŋ **-ped** -t
gig gɪg **-s** -z
giga- ˈgɪg.ə-, ˈgaɪ.gə-, ˈdʒɪg.ə-
gigabyte ˈgɪg.ə.baɪt, ˈgaɪ.gə-, ˈdʒɪg.ə- **-s** -s
gigahertz ˈgɪg.ə.hɜːts, ˈgaɪ.gə-, ˈdʒɪg.ə- ⓤⓢ -hɝːts
gigantesque ˌdʒaɪ.gænˈtesk, -gən-
gigantic dʒaɪˈgæn.tɪk, ˌdʒaɪ- ⓤⓢ -t̬ɪk **-ally** -əl.i, -li
gigantism dʒaɪˈgæn.tɪ.zəm, ˈdʒaɪ.gæn- ⓤⓢ -t̬ɪ-
giggl|e *(n. v.)* ˈgɪg.l̩ **-es** -z **-ing** -ɪŋ, ˈ-lɪŋ **-ed** -d **-er/s** -əʳ/z, ˈ-ləʳ/z ⓤⓢ ˈ-l̩.ɚ/z, ˈ-lɚ/z
giggleswick (G) ˈgɪg.l̩z.wɪk
giggly ˈgɪg.l̩.i, ˈgɪg.li
Giggs gɪgz
Gight gɪkt, gɪxt
Gigi ˈʒiː.ʒiː
Gigli ˈdʒiː.li, -lji ⓤⓢ ˈdʒiː.li, ˈdʒiːl.ji
Giglio ˈdʒiː.li.əʊ, ˈ-ljəʊ ⓤⓢ ˈ-li.oʊ
GIGO ˈgaɪ.gəʊ, ˈdʒaɪ- ⓤⓢ ˈgɪg.oʊ, ˈgaɪ.goʊ, ˈgiː-
gigolo ˈdʒɪg.ə.ləʊ, ˈʒɪg- ⓤⓢ -loʊ **-s** -z
gigot ˈdʒɪg.ət, ˈzɪg-, -əʊ, ˈdʒiː.gəʊ ⓤⓢ ziːˈgoʊ **-s** -s
gigue ʒiːg, ʒɪg **-s** -z
Gihon ˈgaɪ.hɒn *in Jewish usage sometimes:* ˈgiː.həʊn
gila (G) ˈhiː.lə, ˈgiː- ⓤⓢ ˈhiː- **-s** -z
Gilbert ˈgɪl.bət ⓤⓢ -bɚt
Gilbertian gɪlˈbɜː.ti.ən, -ʃən ⓤⓢ -ˈbɝː.t̬i.ən
Gilbey ˈgɪl.bi
Gilboa gɪlˈbəʊ.ə ⓤⓢ -ˈboʊ-
Gilchrist ˈgɪl.krɪst
gild gɪld **-s** -z **-ing** -ɪŋ **-ed** -ɪd **gilt** gɪlt
Gildas ˈgɪl.dæs
gilder (G) ˈgɪl.dəʳ ⓤⓢ -dɚ **-s** -z
Gildersleeve ˈgɪl.də.sliːv ⓤⓢ -dɚ-
Gildersome ˈgɪl.də.səm ⓤⓢ -dɚ-
Gilding ˈgɪl.dɪŋ
Gildredge ˈgɪl.drɪdʒ, -dredʒ
Gilead ˈgɪl.i.æd ⓤⓢ -əd
Giles dʒaɪlz
Gilfil ˈgɪl.fɪl
Gilfillan gɪlˈfɪl.ən
Gilford ˈgɪl.fəd ⓤⓢ -fɚd
Gilgal ˈgɪl.gæl, -gɔːl
Gilgamesh ˈgɪl.gə.meʃ
Gilham ˈgɪl.əm
Gilkes dʒɪlks
gill *respiratory organ, ravine:* gɪl **-s** -z *measure:* dʒɪl **-s** -z
Gill gɪl, dʒɪl
Gillam ˈgɪl.əm
Gillard ˈgɪl.ɑːd, -əd; gɪˈlɑːd ⓤⓢ ˈgɪl.ɚd
Gillen ˈgɪl.ən
Gilleney ˈgɪl.ən.i
Gillespie gɪˈles.pi, gə-
Gillett ˈgɪl.ɪt, ˈgɪl.et, gɪˈlet, dʒɪˈlet, dʒəˈlet
Gillette® dʒɪˈlet ⓤⓢ dʒəˈlet, dʒɪ- **-s** -s
Gilley ˈgɪl.i
Gilliam ˈgɪl.i.əm
Gillian ˈdʒɪl.i.ən, ˈgɪl-
Gilliat ˈgɪl.i.ət, -æt
Gillick ˈgɪl.ɪk
gillie (G) ˈgɪl.i **-s** -z
Gillies ˈgɪl.ɪs
Gilliland ˈgɪl.ɪ.lænd
Gilling ˈgɪl.ɪŋ **-s** -z
Gillingham *in Kent:* ˈdʒɪl.ɪŋ.əm *in Dorset & Norfolk:* ˈgɪl- *surname:* ˈgɪl-, ˈdʒɪl-
Gillison ˈgɪl.ɪ.sən
Gillmore ˈgɪl.mɔːʳ ⓤⓢ -mɔːr
Gillon ˈgɪl.ən
Gillott ˈdʒɪl.ət, ˈgɪl.ət
Gillow ˈgɪl.əʊ ⓤⓢ -oʊ
Gillray ˈgɪl.reɪ
Gills gɪlz
Gillson ˈdʒɪl.sən
gilly ˈgɪl.i **-s** -z
gillyflower ˈdʒɪl.ɪˌflaʊəʳ ⓤⓢ -ˌflaʊɚ **-s** -z
Gilman ˈgɪl.mən
Gilmer ˈgɪl.məʳ ⓤⓢ -mɚ
Gilmore ˈgɪl.mɔːʳ, -məʳ ⓤⓢ -mɔːr
Gilmour ˈgɪl.mɔːʳ, -məʳ ⓤⓢ -mɔːr
Gilpatrick gɪlˈpæt.rɪk
Gilpin ˈgɪl.pɪn
Gilroy ˈgɪl.rɔɪ
Gilson ˈdʒɪl.sən, ˈgɪl.sən
gilt gɪlt **-s** -s
gilt-edged ˌgɪltˈedʒd *stress shift:* ˌgilt-edged ˈstocks
gimbal ˈgɪm.bəl, ˈdʒɪm- **-s** -z
gimbl|e ˈgɪm.bl̩ **-es** -z **-ing** -ɪŋ, ˈ-blɪŋ **-ed** -d
Gimblett ˈgɪm.blɪt, -ət
gimcrack ˈdʒɪm.kræk **-s** -s
gimlet ˈgɪm.lət, -lɪt **-s** -s
gimme ˈgɪm.i
gimmick ˈgɪm.ɪk **-s** -s **-ry** -ri **-y** -i
gimp gɪmp
Gimson ˈgɪmp.sən, ˈdʒɪmp.sən
gin dʒɪn **-s** -z ˈ**gin** ˌ**mill**; ˌ**gin** ˈ**rummy**; ˌ**gin** ˈ**sling**
Gina ˈdʒiː.nə
Gingell ˈgɪn.dʒəl
ginger ˈdʒɪn.dʒəʳ ⓤⓢ -dʒɚ **-s** -z ˌ**ginger** ˈ**ale**; ˌ**ginger** ˈ**beer**
gingerbread (G) ˈdʒɪn.dʒə.bred ⓤⓢ -dʒɚ- **-s** -z ˈ**gingerbread** ˌ**man**
gingerly ˈdʒɪn.dʒəl.i ⓤⓢ -dʒɚ.li

ginger|y ˈdʒɪn.dʒᵊr|.i **-iness** -ɪ.nəs, -ɪ.nɪs
gingham ˈɡɪŋ.əm **-s** -z
gingival dʒɪnˈdʒaɪ.vᵊl, ˈdʒɪn.dʒɪ.vᵊl
gingivitis ˌdʒɪn.dʒɪˈvaɪ.tɪs, -dʒəˈ- US -dʒəˈvaɪ.t̬ɪs
gingko ˈɡɪŋ.kəʊ US -koʊ **-s** -z
Gingold ˈɡɪŋ.ɡəʊld US -ɡoʊld
Gingrich ˈɡɪŋ.ɡrɪtʃ
Ginkel(l) ˈɡɪŋ.kᵊl
ginkgo ˈɡɪŋ.kəʊ, ˈɡɪŋk.ɡəʊ US ˈɡɪŋ.koʊ, ˈɡɪŋk.ɡoʊ **-es** -z
Ginn ɡɪn
ginnel ˈɡɪn.ᵊl, ˈdʒɪn- **-s** -z
Ginny ˈdʒɪn.i
Ginola ˈdʒɪ.nəʊ.lə, ˈʒɪn- US -nə-, -ˌnoʊ-
ginormous dʒaɪˈnɔː.məs US -ˈnɔːr-
Ginsberg ˈɡɪnz.bɜːɡ US -bɝːɡ
ginseng ˈdʒɪn.seŋ
Gioconda ˌdʒɪəˈkɒn.də US -ˈkɑːn-
Giotto ˈdʒɒt.əʊ, dʒiˈɒt- US ˈdʒɑː.t̬oʊ
Giovanni ˌdʒiː.əʊˈvɑː.ni, dʒəʊˈ-, -ˈvæn.i US dʒoʊˈvɑː-, dʒə-
gip ɡɪp **-s** -s **-ping** -ɪŋ **-ped** -t
Gipp ɡɪp
Gippsland ˈɡɪps.lænd
gippy ˈdʒɪp.i
gips|y ˈdʒɪp.s|i **-ies** -iz
giraffe dʒɪˈrɑːf, dʒə-, -ˈræf US dʒəˈræf **-s** -s
Giralda dʒɪˈræl.də, hɪ-
girandole ˈdʒɪr.ən.dəʊl US -doʊl **-s** -z
gird ɡɜːd US ɡɝːd **-s** -z **-ing** -ɪŋ **-ed** -ɪd
girt ɡɜːt US ɡɝːt
girder ˈɡɜː.dəʳ US ˈɡɝː.dɚ **-s** -z
girdl|e ˈɡɜː.dl̩ US ˈɡɝː- **-es** -z **-ing** -ɪŋ, ˈɡɜːd.lɪŋ US ˈɡɝː.dl̩.ɪŋ, ˈɡɝːd.lɪŋ **-ed** -d
Girdlestone ˈɡɜː.dl̩.stᵊn US ˈɡɝː-
girl ɡɜːl US ɡɝːl **-s** -z **-hood** -hʊd
girlfriend ˈɡɜːl.frend US ˈɡɝːl- **-s** -z
girlie ˈɡɜː.li US ˈɡɝː-
girlish ˈɡɜː.lɪʃ US ˈɡɝː- **-ly** -li **-ness** -nəs, -nɪs
girly ˈɡɜː.li US ˈɡɝː-
giro (G) ˈdʒaɪə.rəʊ US ˈdʒaɪ.roʊ **-s** -z
Girobank® ˈdʒaɪə.rəʊ.bæŋk US ˈdʒaɪ.roʊ-
Gironde dʒɪˈrɒnd, ʒɪ-; US dʒəˈrɑːnd
Girondist dʒɪˈrɒn.dɪst, ʒɪ- US dʒəˈrɑːn- **-s** -s
girt (*n.*) ɡɜːt US ɡɝːt **-s** -s
girt (*from* **gird**) ɡɜːt US ɡɝːt
girth ɡɜːθ US ɡɝːθ **-s** -s
Girtin ˈɡɜː.tɪn US ˈɡɝː.tɪn, -tᵊn
Girton ˈɡɜː.tᵊn US ˈɡɝː-
Girtonian ɡɜːˈtəʊ.ni.ən US ɡɚˈtoʊ- **-s** -z
Girvan ˈɡɜː.vən US ˈɡɝː.vᵊn
Gisbourne ˈɡɪz.bɔːn, -bən US -bɔːrn
Giscard d'Estaing *dʒ*ɪs.kɑː.des.ˈtæŋ, *dʒ*iː-, -ˈtæ̃ŋ US ʒiːsˌkɑːr.desˈtæ̃ŋ
Giselle ʒɪˈzel, dʒɪ-
Gish ɡɪʃ
gismo ˈɡɪz.məʊ US -moʊ **-s** -z
Gissing ˈɡɪs.ɪŋ
gist dʒɪst **-s** -s
git ɡɪt **-s** -s
Gita ˈɡiː.tə US -t̬ə
Gitane® ʒɪˈtɑːn US -ˈtɑːn, -ˈtæn **-s** -z
gîte, gite ʒiːt **-s** -s
gittern ˈɡɪt.ɜːn US -ɚn **-s** -z
Gitty ˈɡɪt.i US ˈɡɪt̬.i
Giuliani ˌdʒuː.liˈɑː.ni
Giuseppe dʒuˈsep.i
giv|e ɡɪv **-es** -z **-ing** -ɪŋ **gave** ɡeɪv **giv|en** ˈɡɪv|.ᵊn **-er/s** -əʳ/z US -ɚ/z ˈ**given** ˌ**name**; ˌ**give as** ˌ**good as one** ˈ**gets**
give-and-take ˌɡɪv.ᵊnd*ˈ*teɪk
giveaway ˈɡɪv.ə.weɪ **-s** -z
giveback ˈɡɪv.bæk **-s** -s
Givenchy® ʒiːˈvɑ̃ːn.ʃi, ɡɪ- US ʒiːˈvɑ̃ːn-, -ˈʃiː
Giza, Gîza ˈɡiː.zə
Gizeh ˈɡiː.zeɪ, -zə
gizmo ˈɡɪz.məʊ US -moʊ **-s** -z
gizzard ˈɡɪz.əd US -ɚd **-s** -z
glabrous ˈɡleɪ.brəs
glacé, glace ˈɡlæs.eɪ US ɡlæsˈeɪ **-ed** -d
glacial ˈɡleɪ.si.əl, -ʃᵊl; ˈɡlæs.i.əl US ˈɡleɪ.ʃəl **-ly** -i
glaciation ˌɡleɪ.siˈeɪ.ʃᵊn, ˌɡlæs- US ˌɡleɪ.ʃiˈ-
glacier ˈɡlæs.i.əʳ, ˈɡleɪ.si- US ˈɡleɪ.ʃɚ **-s** -z
glacis ˈɡlæs.ɪs, -i US ˈɡleɪ.sɪs, ˈɡlæs.ɪs, ɡlæsˈiː ˈɡlæs.ɪz US ˈɡleɪ.siːz, ˈɡlæs.iːz, -ˈ-
glacises (*alternative plur. of* **glacis**) ˈɡlæs.ɪ.sɪz US ˈɡleɪ.sɪ.ziːz, ˈɡlæs.ɪ-
glad ɡlæd **-der** -əʳ US -ɚ **-dest** -ɪst, -əst **-ness** -nəs, -nɪs ˈ**glad** ˌ**rags**
gladden ˈɡlæd.ᵊn **-s** -z **-ing** -ɪŋ **-ed** -d
glade ɡleɪd **-s** -z
glad-hand ˈɡlædˌhænd, ˌ-ˈ- **-s** -z **-ing** -ɪŋ **-ed** -ɪd **-er/s** -əʳ/z
gladiator ˈɡlæd.i.eɪ.təʳ US -t̬ɚ **-s** -z
gladiatorial ˌɡlæd.i.əˈtɔː.ri.əl US -tɔːr.i.əl
gladiole ˈɡlæd.i.əʊl US -oʊl **-s** -z
gladiol|us ˌɡlæd.iˈəʊ.l|əs US -ˈoʊ- **-i** -aɪ **-uses** -əs.ɪz
gladly ˈɡlæd.li
gladsome ˈɡlæd.səm **-ly** -li **-ness** -nəs, -nɪs
Gladstone ˈɡlæd.stᵊn US -stoʊn, -stᵊn
Gladstonian ɡlædˈstəʊ.ni.ən US -ˈstoʊ-
Gladwin ˈɡlæd.wɪn
Gladys ˈɡlæd.ɪs
glagolitic (G) ˌɡlæɡ.əʊˈlɪt.ɪk US -əˈlɪt̬-
glair ɡleəʳ US ɡler
Glaisdale ˈɡleɪz.deɪl *locally:* -dᵊl
Glaisher ˈɡleɪ.ʃəʳ US -ʃɚ
glam ɡlæm
Glam. (*abbrev. for* **Glamorgan**) ɡləˈmɔː.ɡən US -ˈmɔːr-
Glamis ɡlɑːmz
Note: In Shakespeare /ˈɡlæm.ɪs/.
Glamorgan ɡləˈmɔː.ɡən US -ˈmɔːr- **-shire** -ʃə, -ˌʃɪəʳ US -ʃɚ, -ˌʃɪr
glamoriz|e, -is|e ˈɡlæm.ᵊr.aɪz US -ə.raɪz **-es** -ɪz **-ing** -ɪŋ **-ed** -d
glamorous ˈɡlæm.ᵊr.əs **-ly** -li **-ness** -nəs, -nɪs
glamour ˈɡlæm.əʳ US -ɚ
glamourous ˈɡlæm.ᵊr.əs **-ly** -li **-ness** -nəs, -nɪs
glamourpuss ˈɡlæm.ə.pʊs US -ɚ- **-es** -ɪz
glanc|e ɡlɑːn*t*s US ɡlæn*t*s **-es** -ɪz **-ing/ly** -ɪŋ/li **-ed** -t
gland ɡlænd **-s** -z
glander|s ˈɡlæn.də|z, ˈɡlɑːn- US ˈɡlæn.dɚ|z **-ed** -d
glandes (*plur. of* **glans**) ˈɡlæn.diːz
glandular ˈɡlæn.djʊ.ləʳ, -dʒə.ləʳ US -dʒə.lɚ ˌ**glandular** ˈ**fever**
glandule ˈɡlæn.djuːl US -dʒuːl **-s** -z
glans ɡlænz **glandes** ˈɡlæn.diːz
Glanvill(e) ˈɡlæn.vɪl
Glapthorne ˈɡlæp.θɔːn US -θɔːrn
glar|e ɡleəʳ US ɡler **-es** -z **-ing/ly** -ɪŋ/li **-ingness** -ɪŋ.nəs, -nɪs **-ed** -d
Glarus *place in US:* ˈɡlær.əs US ˈɡler-, ˈɡlær- *other senses:* ˈɡlɑː.rəs
Glasgow ˈɡlɑːz.ɡəʊ, ˈɡlɑːs-, ˈɡlɑːs.kəʊ, ˈɡlæz.ɡəʊ, ˈɡlæs-, ˈɡlæs.kəʊ US ˈɡlæs.koʊ, ˈɡlæz.ɡoʊ
glasier (G) ˈɡleɪ.zi.əʳ, -ʒəʳ US -ʒɚ **-s** -z
glasnost ˈɡlæs.nɒst, ˈɡlæz- US ˈɡlæs.nɑːst, -noʊst
glass (G) ɡlɑːs US ɡlæs **-es** -ɪz ˌ**glass** ˈ**ceiling**; ˈ**glass** ˌ**cutter**
glassblow|er ˈɡlɑːsˌbləʊ|.əʳ US ˈɡlæsˌbloʊ|.ɚ **-ers** -əz US -ɚz **-ing** -ɪŋ
Glasscock ˈɡlɑːs.kɒk, -kəʊ US ˈɡlæs.kɑːk, -koʊ
glassful ˈɡlɑːs.fʊl, -fᵊl US ˈɡlæs- **-s** -z
glasshou|se ˈɡlɑːs.haʊ|s US ˈɡlæs- **-ses** -zɪz
glasspaper, glass-paper ˈɡlɑːsˌpeɪ.pəʳ US ˈɡlæsˌpeɪ.pɚ
glassware ˈɡlɑːs.weəʳ US ˈɡlæs.wer
glasswork ˈɡlɑːs.wɜːk US ˈɡlæs.wɝːk **-s** -s
glasswort ˈɡlɑːs.wɜːt US ˈɡlæs.wɝːt, -wɔːrt
glass|y ˈɡlɑː.s|i US ˈɡlæs|.i **-ier** -i.əʳ US -i.ɚ **-iest** -i.ɪst, -i.əst **-ily** -ɪ.li, -ᵊl.i **-iness** -ɪ.nəs, -ɪ.nɪs
Glastonbury ˈɡlæs.tᵊn.bᵊr.i, ˈɡlɑː.stᵊn- US ˈɡlæs.tᵊnˌber.i, -bᵊr.i
Glaswegian ɡlæzˈwiː.dʒᵊn, ɡlɑːz-, ɡlæs-, ɡlɑːs-, -dʒi.ən US ɡlæs-, ɡlæz- **-s** -z

glaucoma glɔːˈkəʊ.mə, glaʊ- (US) glɑːˈkoʊ-, glɔː- **-tous** -təs
glaucous ˈglɔː.kəs (US) ˈglɑː-, ˈglɔː-
Glaxo® ˈglæk.səʊ (US) -soʊ
glaz|e gleɪz **-es** -ɪz **-ing** -ɪŋ **-ed** -d **-er/s** -əʳ/z (US) -ɚ/z
Glazebrook ˈgleɪz.brʊk
glazier ˈgleɪ.zi.əʳ, ˈ-ʒəʳ (US) ˈ-ʒɚ **-s** -z
Glazunov ˈglæz.u.nɒf (US) ˈglæz.ə.nɑːf, ˈglɑː.zə-, -noʊf
gleam gliːm **-s** -z **-ing** -ɪŋ **-ed** -d **-y** -i
glean gliːn **-s** -z **-ing/s** -ɪŋ/z **-ed** -d **-er/s** -əʳ/z **-er/z** (US) -ɚ/z
Gleason ˈgliː.sᵊn
glebe gliːb **-s** -z
glee gliː ˈ**glee** ˌ**club**
gleeful ˈgliː.fᵊl, -fʊl **-ly** -i **-ness** -nəs, -nɪs
glee|man ˈgliː|.mən, -mæn **-men** -mən, -men
Glegg gleg
Gleichen ˈglaɪ.kən
Glemsford ˈglems.fəd, ˈglemz- (US) -fɚd
glen (G) glen **-s** -z
Glenallan glenˈæl.ən
Glenalmond glenˈɑː.mənd
Glenavon glenˈæv.ᵊn
Glenavy glenˈeɪ.vi
Glencairn glenˈkeən, gleŋ- (US) glenˈkern
Glencoe glenˈkəʊ, gleŋ- (US) glenˈkoʊ
Glenda ˈglen.də
Glendale glenˈdeɪl, ˈglen.deɪl (US) ˈglen-
Glendenning glenˈden.ɪŋ
Glendin(n)ing glenˈdɪn.ɪŋ
Glendower glenˈdaʊ.əʳ (US) -ɚ
Gleneagles glenˈiː.gl̩z
Glenelg glenˈelg
Glenfiddich glenˈfɪd.ɪk, -ɪx
Glenfinnan glenˈfɪn.ən
glengarr|y (G) glenˈgær|.i, gleŋ- (US) glenˈger-, -ˈgær-, ˈ--- **-ies** -iz
Glenlivet glenˈlɪv.ɪt, -ət
Glenmorangie ˌglen.məˈræn.dʒi, ˌglem-, glenˈmɒr.ən.dʒi (US) ˌglen-
Glenmore glenˈmɔːʳ, glem- (US) ˈglen.mɔːr, -ˈ-
Glenn glen
Glenrothes glenˈrɒθ.ɪs (US) -ˈrɑː.θəs
Glen Trool ˌglenˈtruːl
Glenwood ˈglen.wʊd
Glenys ˈglen.ɪs
glib glɪb **-ber** -əʳ (US) -ɚ **-best** -ɪst, -əst **-ly** -li **-ness** -nəs, -nɪs
glid|e glaɪd **-es** -z **-ing/ly** -ɪŋ/li **-ed** -ɪd
glider ˈglaɪ.dəʳ (US) -dɚ **-s** -z
glimmer ˈglɪm.əʳ (US) -ɚ **-s** -z **-ing/s** -ɪŋ/z **-ingly** -ɪŋ.li **-ed** -d
glimps|e glɪmps **-es** -ɪz **-ing** -ɪŋ **-ed** -t
glinch glɪntʃ **-es** -ɪz
Glinka ˈglɪŋ.kə
glint glɪnt **-s** -s **-ing** -ɪŋ **-ed** -ɪd
gliom|a glaɪˈəʊ.m|ə (US) -ˈoʊ-, gli- **-as** -əz **-ata** -ə.tə (US) -ə.t̬ə
glissad|e *(n. v.)* glɪˈsɑːd, -ˈseɪd **-es** -z **-ing** -ɪŋ **-ed** -ɪd
glissand|o glɪˈsæn.d|əʊ (US) -ˈsɑːn.d|oʊ **-i** -iː **-os** -əʊz (US) -oʊz
Glisson ˈglɪs.ᵊn
glisten ˈglɪs.ᵊn **-s** -z **-ing** -ɪŋ **-ed** -d
glist|er ˈglɪs.t|əʳ (US) -t|ɚ **-ers** -əz (US) -ɚz **-ering** -ᵊr.ɪŋ **-ered** -əd (US) -ɚd
glitch glɪtʃ **-es** -ɪz
glitt|er ˈglɪt|.əʳ (US) ˈglɪt̬|.ɚ **-ers** -əz (US) -ɚz **-ering/ly** -ᵊr.ɪŋ/li **-ered** -əd (US) -ɚd **-ery** -ᵊr.i
glitterati ˌglɪt.əˈrɑː.tiː, -ti (US) ˌglɪt̬.əˈrɑː.t̬i
glitz glɪts
glitz|y ˈglɪt.s|i **-ier** -i.əʳ (US) -i.ɚ **-iest** -i.ɪst, -i.əst **-iness** -ɪ.nəs, -ɪ.nɪs
Gloag gləʊg (US) gloʊg
gloaming ˈgləʊ.mɪŋ (US) ˈgloʊ-
gloat gləʊt (US) gloʊt **-s** -s **-ing/ly** -ɪŋ (US) ˈgloʊ.t̬ɪŋ **-ed** -ɪd (US) ˈgloʊ.t̬əd
glob glɒb (US) glɑːb **-s** -z
global ˈgləʊ.bᵊl (US) ˈgloʊ- **-ly** -i **-ism** -ɪ.zᵊm ˌ**global** ˈ**village**; ˌ**global** ˈ**warming**
globalization, -isa- ˌgləʊ.bᵊl.aɪˈzeɪ.ʃᵊn, -ɪˈ- (US) ˌgloʊ.bᵊl.ɪˈ-
globaliz|e, -is|e ˈgləʊ.bᵊl.aɪz (US) ˈgloʊ.bə.laɪz **-es** -ɪz **-ing** -ɪŋ **-ed** -d
globe gləʊb (US) gloʊb **-s** -z
globe-trott|er ˈgləʊbˌtrɒt|.əʳ (US) ˈgloʊbˌtrɑː.t̬|ɚ **-ers** -əz (US) -ɚz **-ing** -ɪŋ
globose ˈgləʊ.bəʊs, gləʊˈbəʊs (US) ˈgloʊ.boʊs, -ˈ-
globosity gləʊˈbɒs.ə.ti, -ɪ.ti (US) gloʊˈbɑː.sə.t̬i
globous ˈgləʊ.bəs (US) ˈgloʊ-
globular ˈglɒb.jʊ.ləʳ, -jə- (US) ˈglɑː.bjə.lɚ **-ly** -li
globule ˈglɒb.juːl (US) ˈglɑː.bjuːl **-s** -z
globulin ˈglɒb.jʊ.lɪn, -jə- (US) ˈglɑː.bjə- **-s** -z
glockenspiel ˈglɒk.ᵊn.ʃpiːl, -spiːl (US) ˈglɑː.kᵊn.spiːl, -ʃpiːl **-s** -z
glom glɒm (US) glɑːm **-s** -z **-ming** -ɪŋ **-med** -d
gloom gluːm **-s** -z **-ing** -ɪŋ **-ed** -d
gloom|y ˈgluː.m|i **-ier** -i.əʳ (US) -i.ɚ **-iest** -i.ɪst, -i.əst **-ily** -ɪ.li, -ᵊl.i **-iness** -ɪ.nəs, -ɪ.nɪs
glop glɒp (US) glɑːp **-py** -i
Gloria ˈglɔː.ri.ə (US) ˈglɔːr.i- **-s** -z
Gloriana ˌglɔː.riˈɑː.nə (US) ˌglɔːr.iˈæn.ə, -ˈeɪ.nə
glorification ˌglɔː.rɪ.fɪˈkeɪ.ʃᵊn, -rə- (US) ˌglɔːr.ə.fə-
glori|fy ˈglɔː.rɪ|.faɪ, -rə- (US) ˈglɔːr.ə- **-fies** -faɪz **-fying** -faɪ.ɪŋ **-fied** -faɪd **-fier/s** -faɪ.əʳ/z (US) -faɪ.ɚ/z
glorious ˈglɔː.ri.əs (US) ˈglɔːr.i- **-ly** -li **-ness** -nəs, -nɪs
glor|y ˈglɔː.r|i (US) ˈglɔːr|.i **-ies** -iz **-ying** -i.ɪŋ **-ied** -id ˈ**glory** ˌ**hole**
Glos. *(abbrev. for* **Gloucestershire***)* ˈglɒs.tə.ʃəʳ, -ˌʃɪəʳ (US) ˈglɑː.stɚ.ʃɚ, -ˌʃɪr
gloss glɒs (US) glɑːs **-es** -ɪz **-ing** -ɪŋ **-ed** -t **-er/s** -əʳ/z (US) -ɚ/z
glossal ˈglɒs.ᵊl (US) ˈglɑː.sᵊl
glossarial glɒsˈeə.ri.əl (US) glɑːˈser.i-
glossar|y ˈglɒs.ᵊr|.i (US) ˈglɑː.sᵊr- **-ies** -iz
glossectomy glɒsˈek.tə.mi (US) glɑːˈsek-
glossematics ˌglɒs.ɪˈmæt.ɪks, -əˈ- (US) ˌglɑː.səˈmæt̬.ɪks
glosseme ˈglɒs.iːm (US) ˈglɑː.siːm **-s** -z
glossitis glɒsˈaɪ.tɪs (US) glɑːˈsaɪ.t̬ɪs
glossolalia ˌglɒs.əʊˈleɪ.li.ə (US) ˌglɑː.səˈ-
Glossop ˈglɒs.əp (US) ˈglɑː.səp
glossopharyngeal ˌglɒs.əʊˌfær.ɪnˈdʒiː.əl, -fəˈrɪn.dʒi.əl (US) ˌglɑː.soʊˌfer.ᵊnˈdʒiː.əl, -ˌfær-
gloss|y ˈglɒs|.i (US) ˈglɑː.s|i **-ies** -iz **-ier** -i.əʳ (US) -i.ɚ **-iest** -i.ɪst, -i.əst **-ily** -ɪ.li, -ᵊl.i **-iness** -ɪ.nəs, -ɪ.nɪs
Gloster ˈglɒs.təʳ (US) ˈglɑː.stɚ
glottal ˈglɒt.ᵊl (US) ˈglɑː.t̬əl ˌ**glottal** ˈ**stop**
glottalic glɒtˈæl.ɪk, gləˈtæl- (US) glɑːˈtæl-
glott|is ˈglɒt|.ɪs (US) ˈglɑː.t̬|əs **-ises** -ɪ.sɪz, -ə.sɪz **-ides** -ɪ.diːz
glottochronology ˌglɒt.əʊ.krəˈnɒl.ə.dʒi (US) ˌglɑː.t̬oʊ.krəˈnɑː.lə-
glottology glɒtˈɒl.ə.dʒi (US) glɑːˈtɑː.lə-
Gloucester *in the UK:* ˈglɒs.təʳ (US) ˈglɑː.stɚ **-shire** -ʃəʳ, -ˌʃɪəʳ (US) -ʃɚ, -ˌʃɪr *in the US:* ˈglaʊ.stəʳ (US) -stɚ
glove glʌv **-s** -z **-d** -d ˈ**glove** **com**ˌ**partment**; ˈ**glove** ˌ**puppet**
glover (G) ˈglʌv.əʳ (US) -ɚ **-s** -z
glow gləʊ (US) gloʊ **-s** -z **-ing/ly** -ɪŋ/li **-ed** -d
glower glaʊəʳ (US) glaʊɚ **-s** -z **-ing** -ɪŋ **-ed** -d
glowworm ˈgləʊ.wɜːm (US) ˈgloʊ.wɝːm **-s** -z
gloxinia glɒkˈsɪn.i.ə (US) glɑːkˈ- **-s** -z
gloz|e gləʊz (US) gloʊz **-es** -ɪz **-ing** -ɪŋ **-ed** -d
Gluck glʊk, gluːk, glʌk
glucose ˈgluː.kəʊs, -kəʊz (US) -koʊs, -koʊz
glu|e gluː **-es** -z **-(e)ing** -ɪŋ **-ed** -d **-er/s** -əʳ/z (US) -ɚ/z
gluesniff|ing ˈgluːˌsnɪf|.ɪŋ **-er/s** -əʳ/z (US) -ɚz
gluey ˈgluː.i **-ness** -nəs, -nɪs

Glottal stop

A consonant made by closure of the vocal folds. The phonetic symbol for a glottal stop is [ʔ].

Examples for English

In some British accents, a glottal stop can actually replace the voiceless alveolar plosive [t] as the realisation of the /t/ phoneme when it follows a stressed vowel, e.g.:

getting better /ˌget.ɪŋˈbet.əʳ/ → [ˌgeʔ.ĩŋˈbeʔ.ə]

This type of pronunciation is found in many urban accents, notably London (Cockney), Leeds, Glasgow, Edinburgh and others, and is increasingly accepted among educated young people.

Sometimes a glottal stop is pronounced in front of a /p t/ or /k/ if there is not a vowel immediately following (see GLOTTALISATION).

In a true glottal stop there is complete obstruction to the passage of air, and the result is a period of silence. In casual speech it often happens that a speaker aims to produce a complete glottal stop but instead makes a low-pitched creak-like sound.

Glottalisation

The addition of a glottal stop before a consonant.

Examples for English

Adding a glottal stop before certain consonants has the effect of making the preceding vowel somewhat shorter. In English this usually happens before a voiceless PLOSIVE or AFFRICATE consonant if there is not a vowel immediately following (e.g. in *captive, catkin, arctic*; a similar case is that of /tʃ/ when following a stressed vowel or when syllable-final, as in *butcher*). This addition of a glottal stop is sometimes called 'glottal reinforcement', e.g.:

back	/bæk/	[b̥a̰ʔk]	(US)	/bæk/	[b̥æʔk]
captive	/ˈkæp.tɪv/	[ˈkʰa̰ʔp˺.tɪv]	(US)	/ˈkæp.tɪv/	[ˈkʰæʔp˺.tɪv]
catkin	/ˈkæt.kɪn/	[ˈkʰa̰ʔk˺.kĩn]	(US)	/ˈkæt.kɪn/	[ˈkʰæʔk˺.kĩn]
arctic	/ˈɑːk.tɪk/	[ˈɑˑʔk˺.tɪk]	(US)	/ˈɑːrk.tɪk/	[ˈɑˑɹ̥ʔk˺.tɪk]
butcher	/ˈbʊtʃ.əʳ/	[ˈbʊʔ.t͡ʃə]	(US)	/ˈbʊtʃ.ɚ/	[ˈbʊʔ.t͡ʃɚ]

This feature of English is an important one for perception. As the difference in voicing between /p t k tʃ/ and /b d g dʒ/ in syllable-final position is negligible, it is the length of the vowel rather than the voicing of the final consonant which contributes strongly to a native speaker's decision of whether a speaker has produced e.g. *back* or *bag*.

glühwein ˈgluː.vaɪn
glum glʌm **-mer** -əʳ (US) -ɚ **-mest** -ɪst, -əst **-ly** -li **-ness** -nəs, -nɪs
Glusburn ˈglʌz.bɜːn (US) -bɝːn
glut glʌt **-s** -s **-ting** -ɪŋ (US) ˈglʌt̬.ɪŋ **-ted** -ɪd (US) ˈglʌt̬.əd
glutamate ˈgluː.tə.meɪt (US) -t̬ə- **-s** -s
gluteal ˈgluː.ti.əl (US) -t̬i-
gluten ˈgluː.tᵊn, -tɪn
glute|us ˈgluː.ti|.əs (US) -t̬i- **-i** -aɪ
gluteus maximus ˌgluː.ti.əsˈmæk.sɪm.əs (US) -t̬i-
glutinous ˈgluː.tɪ.nəs, -tᵊn.əs (US) -tᵊn- **-ly** -li **-ness** -nəs, -nɪs
glutton ˈglʌt.ᵊn **-s** -z
gluttoniz|e, -is|e ˈglʌt.ᵊn.aɪz **-es** -ɪz **-ing** -ɪŋ **-ed** -d
gluttonous ˈglʌt.ᵊn.əs **-ly** -li
gluttony ˈglʌt.ᵊn.i
glyceride ˈglɪs.ᵊ.raɪd **-s** -z
glycerin ˈglɪs.ᵊr.ɪn, -iːn; ˌglɪs.əˈriːn
glycerine ˈglɪs.ᵊr.iːn, -ɪn; ˌglɪs.əˈriːn
glycerol ˈglɪs.ᵊ.rɒl (US) -rɑːl, -roʊl
glycogen ˈglaɪ.kəʊ.dʒən, ˈglɪk.əʊ-, -dʒen (US) ˈglaɪ.koʊ-, -kə-
glycol ˈglaɪ.kɒl, ˈglɪk.ɒl (US) ˈglaɪ.kɑːl, -koʊl
Glyde glaɪd
Glyn glɪn
Glynde glaɪnd
Glyndebourne ˈglaɪnd.bɔːn, ˈglaɪm- (US) ˈglaɪnd.bɔːrn
Glyndwr glɪnˈdaʊəʳ, glen- (US) -ˈdaʊɚ
Glynis ˈglɪn.ɪs
Glynne glɪn
Glyn-Neath ˌglɪnˈniːθ
glyph glɪf **-s** -s
glyptic ˈglɪp.tɪk
gm *(abbrev. for* **gram/s***) singular:* græm *plural:* -z
GM ˌdʒiːˈem *stress shift:* ˌGM ˈfood
G|-man ˈdʒiː|ˌmæn **-men** -ˌmen
GMT ˌdʒiː.emˈtiː
gnarl nɑːl (US) nɑːrl **-s** -z **-ed** -d
gnash næʃ **-es** -ɪz **-ing** -ɪŋ **-ed** -t
gnat næt **-s** -s
gnathic ˈnæθ.ɪk
gnaw nɔː (US) nɑː, nɔː **-s** -z **-ing** -ɪŋ **-ed** -d
gneiss naɪs, gəˈnaɪs
gnocchi ˈnjɒk.i (US) ˈnjɑː.ki
gnome *goblin:* nəʊm (US) noʊm **-s** -z
gnome *maxim:* ˈnəʊ.miː (US) noʊm **-s** -z
gnomic ˈnəʊ.mɪk (US) ˈnoʊ-
gnomish ˈnəʊ.mɪʃ (US) ˈnoʊ-
gnomon ˈnəʊ.mɒn, -mən (US) ˈnoʊ.mɑːn, -mən **-s** -z
gnomonic nəʊˈmɒn.ɪk (US) noʊˈmɑː.nɪk **-al** -ᵊl **-ally** -ᵊl.i, -li
Gnosall ˈnəʊ.səl (US) ˈnoʊ-
gnostic (G) ˈnɒs.tɪk (US) ˈnɑː.stɪk **-s** -s
gnosticism (G) ˈnɒs.tɪ.sɪ.zᵊm (US) ˈnɑː.stə-
gnu nuː, -njuː **-s** -z
go gəʊ (US) goʊ **-es** -z **-ing** -ɪŋ **went** went **gone** gɒn (US) gɑːn, gɔːn **goer/s** ˈgəʊ.əʳ/z (US) ˈgoʊ.ɚ/z
Goa gəʊə (US) goʊə
goad gəʊd (US) goʊd **-s** -z **-ing** -ɪŋ **-ed** -ɪd
go-ahead *(adj.)* ˈgəʊ.ə.hed, ˌ--ˈ- (US) ˈgoʊ-
go-ahead *(n.)* ˈgəʊ.ə.hed (US) ˈgoʊ-
goal gəʊl (US) goʊl **-s** -z
goalie ˈgəʊ.li (US) ˈgoʊ.li **-s** -z
goalkeeper ˈgəʊlˌkiː.pəʳ (US) ˈgoʊlˌkiː.pɚ **-s** -z

goalless ˈgəʊl.ləs, -lɪs US ˈgoʊl-

goalmouth ˈgəʊl.maʊθ US ˈgoʊl-

goalpost ˈgəʊl.pəʊst US ˈgoʊl.poʊst **-s** -s

goalscorer ˈgəʊlˌskɔː.rəʳ US ˈgoʊlˌskɔːr.ɚ **-s** -z

goaltender ˈgəʊlˌten.dəʳ US ˈgoʊlˌten.dɚ **-s** -z

Goan gəʊ.ən US goʊ.ən

Goanese ˌgəʊ.əˈniːz US ˌgoʊ.ə-

goanna gəʊˈæn.ə US goʊ- **-s** -z

goat gəʊt US goʊt **-s** -s ˌ**get someone's ˈgoat**

goatee gəʊˈtiː US goʊ- **-s** -z *stress shift, British only, see compounds:* ˌ**goatee ˈbeard** US **goaˈtee ˌbeard**

goatherd ˈgəʊt.hɜːd US ˈgoʊt.hɝːd **-s** -z

Goathland ˈgəʊθ.lənd US ˈgoʊθ-

goatish ˈgəʊ.tɪʃ US ˈgoʊ-

goatskin ˈgəʊt.skɪn US ˈgoʊt- **-s** -z

goatsucker ˈgəʊtˌsʌk.əʳ US ˈgoʊtˌsʌk.ɚ **-s** -z

gob gɒb US gɑːb **-s** -z **-bing** -ɪŋ **-bed** -d

gobbet ˈgɒb.ɪt US ˈgɑː.bɪt **-s** -s

Gobbi ˈgɒb.i US ˈgɑː.bi

gobbl|e ˈgɒb.l̩ US ˈgɑː.bl̩ **-es** -z **-ing** -ɪŋ, ˈgɒb.lɪŋ US ˈgɑː.bl̩.ɪŋ, ˈ-blɪŋ **-ed** -d **-er/s** -əʳ/z, ˈgɒb.ləʳ/z US ˈgɑː.bl̩.ɚ/z, ˈ-blɚ/z

gobbledygook, gobbledegook ˈgɒb.l̩.diˌguːk, -ˌgʊk US ˈgɑː.bl̩-

Gobbo ˈgɒb.əʊ US ˈgɑː.boʊ

Gobelin ˈgəʊ.bᵊl.ɪn, ˈgɒb.ᵊl- US ˈgoʊ.bᵊl-

go-between ˈgəʊ.bɪˌtwiːn, -bə- US ˈgoʊ.bə- **-s** -z

Gobi ˈgəʊ.bi US ˈgoʊ-

goblet ˈgɒb.lət, -lɪt US ˈgɑː.blət **-s** -s

goblin ˈgɒb.lɪn US ˈgɑː.blɪn **-s** -z

gobsmack ˈgɒb.smæk US ˈgɑːb- **-s** -s **-ing** -ɪŋ **-ed** -t

gobstopper ˈgɒbˌstɒp.əʳ US ˈgɑːbˌstɑː.pɚ **-s** -z

gob|y ˈgəʊ.b|i US ˈgoʊ- **-ies** -iz

go-by ˈgəʊˌbaɪ US ˈgoʊ-

go-cart ˈgəʊ.kɑːt US ˈgoʊ.kɑːrt **-s** -s

god (G) gɒd US gɑːd **-s** -z

Godalming ˈgɒd.ᵊl.mɪŋ US ˈgɑː.dᵊl-

Godard ˈgɒd.ɑː US goʊˈdɑːr

god-awful ˌgɒdˈɔː.fᵊl US ˌgɑːdˈɑː-, -ˈɔː- *stress shift:* ˌgod-awful ˈnoise

god|child ˈgɒd|.tʃaɪld US ˈgɑːd- **-children** -ˌtʃɪl.drᵊn

goddam(n) ˈgɒd.æm, ˈgɒd.dæm US ˌgɑːdˈdæm, ˈgɑːd-

goddamned ˈgɒd.æmd, ˈgɒd.dæmd US ˈgɑːd.æmd

Goddard ˈgɒd.ɑːd, -əd US ˈgɑː.dɚd, -dɑːrd

goddaughter ˈgɒdˌdɔː.təʳ US ˈgɑːdˌdɑː.t̬ɚ, -ˌdɔː- **-s** -z

Godden ˈgɒd.ᵊn US ˈgɑː.dᵊn

goddess ˈgɒd.es, -ɪs, -əs US ˈgɑː.dɪs, -dəs **-es** -ɪz

Goderich ˈgəʊ.drɪtʃ US ˈgoʊ-

godetia gəʊˈdiː.ʃə, -ʃi.ə US gə- **-s** -z

godfather (G) ˈgɒd.fɑː.ðəʳ US ˈgɑːdˌfɑː.ðɚ **-s** -z

god-fearing (G) ˈgɒdˌfɪə.rɪŋ US ˈgɑːd.fɪr.ɪŋ

godforsaken ˈgɒd.fəˌseɪ.kᵊn US ˈgɑːd.fɚ-

Godfrey ˈgɒd.fri US ˈgɑːd-

god-given ˈgɒdˌgɪv.ᵊn US ˈgɑːd-

godhead (G) ˈgɒd.hed US ˈgɑːd- **-s** -z

Godiva gəˈdaɪ.və

Godkin ˈgɒd.kɪn US ˈgɑːd-

godless ˈgɒd.ləs, -lɪs US ˈgɑːd- **-ly** -li **-ness** -nəs, -nɪs

godlike ˈgɒd.laɪk US ˈgɑːd-

godl|y ˈgɒd.l|i US ˈgɑːd- **-ier** -i.əʳ US -i.ɚ **-iest** -i.ɪst, -i.əst **-iness** -ɪ.nəs, -ɪ.nɪs

Godman ˈgɒd.mən US ˈgɑːd-

Godmanchester ˈgɒd.mənˌtʃes.təʳ US ˈgɑːd.mənˌtʃes.tɚ

godmother ˈgɒdˌmʌð.əʳ US ˈgɑːdˌmʌð.ɚ **-s** -z

Godolphin gəˈdɒl.fɪn US -ˈdɑːl-

Godot ˈgɒd.əʊ US gəˈdoʊ, gɑː-

godown ˈgəʊ.daʊn US ˈgoʊ- **-s** -z

godparent ˈgɒdˌpeə.rᵊnt US ˈgɑːdˌper.ᵊnt, -ˌpær- **-s** -s

godsend ˈgɒd.send US ˈgɑːd- **-s** -z

God-slot ˈgɒdˌslɒt US ˈgɑːdˌslɑːt **-s** -s

godson ˈgɒd.sʌn US ˈgɑːd- **-s** -z

Godspeed ˌgɒdˈspiːd US ˌgɑːd-

Godunov ˈgɒd.ə.nɒf, ˈgʊd-, -u- US ˈgʊd.ə.nɑːf

Godward ˈgɒd.wəd US ˈgɑːd.wɚd

Godwin ˈgɒd.wɪn US ˈgɑːd-

godwit ˈgɒd.wɪt US ˈgɑːd- **-s** -s

Godzilla gɒdˈzɪl.ə US gɑːd-

Goebbels ˈgɜː.bᵊlz, -bᵊls

Goering ˈgɜː.rɪŋ US ˈgɝː-

Goethe ˈgɜː.tə

gofer ˈgəʊ.fəʳ US ˈgoʊ.fɚ **-s** -z

Goff(e) gɒf US gɑːf

goff|er ˈgəʊ.f|əʳ, ˈgɒf|.əʳ US ˈgɑː.f|ɚ **-ers** -əz US -ɚz **-ering** -ᵊr.ɪŋ **-ered** -əd US -ɚd

Gog gɒg US gɑːg, gɔːg

Gogarty ˈgəʊ.gə.ti US ˈgoʊ.gɚ.t̬i

go-getter ˈgəʊˌget.əʳ, ˌ-ˈ-- US ˈgoʊˌget̬.ɚ **-s** -z

goggl|e ˈgɒg.l̩ US ˈgɑː.gl̩ **-es** -z **-ing** -ɪŋ, ˈ-lɪŋ US ˈ-gl̩.ɪŋ, ˈ-glɪŋ **-ed** -d

goggle-box ˈgɒg.l̩.bɒks US ˈgɑː.gl̩.bɑːks **-es** -ɪz

goggle-eyed ˌgɒg.l̩ˈaɪd US ˈgɑː.gl̩ˌaɪd *stress shift, British only:* ˌgoggle-eyed ˈcrowd

Gogmagog ˈgɒg.mə.gɒg US ˈgɑːg.mə.gɑːg, ˈgɔːg-, -gɔːg

a go-go, à go-go əˈgəʊ.gəʊ US -ˈgoʊ.goʊ

go-go ˈgəʊ.gəʊ US ˈgoʊ.goʊ **ˈgo-go ˌdancer**

Gogo ˈgəʊ.gəʊ US ˈgoʊ.goʊ

Gogol ˈgəʊ.gɒl US ˈgoʊ.gɑːl, -gᵊl

Goiânia gɔɪˈɑː.ni.ə

Goidelic gɔɪˈdel.ɪk

goings ˈgəʊ.ɪŋz US ˈgoʊ- ˌ**comings and ˈgoings**; ˌ**goings-ˈon**

goiter ˈgɔɪ.təʳ US -t̬ɚ **-s** -z **-ed** -d

goitre ˈgɔɪ.təʳ US -t̬ɚ **-s** -z **-d** -d

goitrous ˈgɔɪ.trəs

go-kart ˈgəʊ.kɑːt US ˈgoʊ.kɑːrt **-s** -s

Golan ˈgəʊ.læn, -lɑːn; US ˈgoʊ.lɑːn ˌ**Golan ˈHeights**

Golborne ˈgəʊl.bɔːn US ˈgoʊl.bɔːrn

Golby ˈgəʊl.bi US ˈgoʊl-

Golconda gɒlˈkɒn.də US gɑːlˈkɑːn.də

gold (G) gəʊld US goʊld **-s** -z **ˈGold ˌCoast**; **ˈgold ˌdust**; ˌ**gold ˈleaf**; ˌ**gold ˈmedal**; **ˈgold ˌmine**; **ˈgold ˌrush**; **as ˌgood as ˈgold**

Golda ˈgəʊl.də US ˈgoʊl-

Goldberg ˈgəʊld.bɜːg US ˈgoʊld.bɝːg

goldbrick ˈgəʊld.brɪk US ˈgoʊld- **-s** -s **-ing** -ɪŋ **-ed** -d **-er/s** -əʳ/z US -ɚ/z

goldcrest ˈgəʊld.krest US ˈgoʊld- **-s** -s

gold-digger ˈgəʊldˌdɪg.əʳ US ˈgoʊldˌdɪg.ɚ **-s** -z

golden (G) ˈgəʊl.dᵊn US ˈgoʊl- ˌ**golden ˈage** US **ˈgolden ˌage**; ˌ**golden ˈhandshake**; ˌ**golden ˈrule**; ˌ**golden ˈsyrup**

goldeneye ˈgəʊl.dᵊn.aɪ US ˈgoʊl- **-s** -z

goldfield ˈgəʊld.fiːld US ˈgoʊld- **-s** -z

goldfinch ˈgəʊld.fɪntʃ US ˈgoʊld- **-es** -ɪz

goldfish ˈgəʊld.fɪʃ US ˈgoʊld- **-es** -ɪz **ˈgoldfish ˌbowl**

Goldilocks ˈgəʊl.dɪ.lɒks US ˈgoʊl.di.lɑːks

Golding ˈgəʊl.dɪŋ US ˈgoʊl-

Goldman ˈgəʊld.mən US ˈgoʊld-

Goldsborough ˈgəʊldz.bᵊr.ə US ˈgoʊldz.bɚ.oʊ

Goldschmidt ˈgəʊld.ʃmɪt US ˈgoʊld-

goldsmith (G) ˈgəʊld.smɪθ US ˈgoʊld- **-s** -s

Goldstein ˈgəʊld.staɪn, -stiːn US ˈgoʊld-

Goldwyn ˈgəʊl.dwɪn US ˈgoʊl-

golem ˈgəʊ.lem US ˈgoʊ- **-s** -z

golf *(n. v.)* gɒlf *old-fashioned, sometimes used by players:* gɒf US gɑːlf **-s** -s **-ing** -ɪŋ **-ed** -t **ˈgolf ˌclub**; **ˈgolf ˌcourse**; **ˈgolf ˌlinks**

golfer ˈgɒl.fəʳ, ˈgɒf.əʳ US ˈgɑːl.fɚ **-s** -z

Golgotha ˈgɒl.gə.θə US ˈgɑːl-

Goliath gəʊˈlaɪ.əθ US gə-

Golightly gəʊˈlaɪt.li US goʊ-

Gollancz gəˈlænts, -ˈlæŋks, gɒlˈænts,

-ˈæŋks, ˈgɒl.ənts, -æŋks US gəˈlænts, ˈgɑː.lənts, -lænts

golliwog ˈgɒl.ɪ.wɒg US ˈgɑː.li.wɔːg, -wɑːg **-s** -z

golly ˈgɒl.i US ˈgɑː.li

gollywog ˈgɒl.ɪ.wɒg US ˈgɑː.lɪ.wɔːg, -wɑːg **-s** -z

golosh gəˈlɒʃ US gəˈlɑːʃ **-es** -ɪz

Gomar ˈgəʊ.məʳ US ˈgoʊ.mɚ

Gomer ˈgəʊ.məʳ US ˈgoʊ.mɚ

Gomersal ˈgɒm.ə.səl US ˈgɑː.mɚ.səl

Gomes ˈgəʊ.mez US ˈgoʊ-

Gomez, Gómez ˈgəʊ.mez US ˈgoʊ-

Gomme gɒm US gɑːm

Gomorrah gəˈmɒr.ə US -ˈmɔːr.ə, -ˈmɑːr-

Gompers ˈgɒm.pəz US ˈgɑːm.pɚz

Gomshall ˈgʌm.ʃəl, ˈgɒm- US ˈgɑːm-

gonad ˈgəʊ.næd US ˈgoʊ- **-s** -z

Goncourt ˌgɒnˈkʊəʳ, ˌgɒŋ-, ˌgɔ̃ːŋ- US ˌgoʊnˈkʊr

gondola ˈgɒn.dəl.ə US ˈgɑːn- **-s** -z

gondolier ˌgɒn.dəˈlɪəʳ, -dəlˈɪəʳ US ˌgɑːn.dəˈlɪr **-s** -z

Gondwana gɒndˈwɑː.nə US gɑːnd- **-land** -lænd

gone *(from* **go***)* gɒn US gɑːn

goner ˈgɒn.əʳ US ˈgɑː.nɚ **-s** -z

Goneril ˈgɒn.ər.ɪl, -əl US ˈgɑː.nər.əl

gonfalon ˈgɒn.fəl.ən US ˈgɑːn- **-s** -z

gong gɒŋ US gɑːŋ, gɔːŋ **-s** -z

goniometer ˌgəʊ.niˈɒm.ɪ.təʳ, ˈ-ə- US ˌgoʊ.niˈɑː.mə.t̬ɚ **-s** -z

goniometric ˌgəʊ.ni.əˈmet.rɪk US ˌgoʊ-

gonk gɒŋk US gɑːŋk, gɔːŋk **-s** -s

gonna gən.ə, ˈgɒn.ə US ˈgɑː.nə, ˈgɔː-

gonorrh(o)e|a ˌgɒn.əˈriː|.ə US ˌgɑː.nəˈ- **-al** -əl

Gonville ˈgɒn.vɪl US ˈgɑːn-

Gonzales gɒnˈzɑː.lɪs, gən-, -lez US gənˈzɑː.ləs, gɑːn-, -ˈsɑː-, -leɪs

Gonzalez gɒnˈzɑː.lɪs, gən-, -lez US gənˈzɑːl.əs, gɑːn-, -ˈsɑː-, -leɪs

gonzo ˈgɒn.zəʊ US ˈgɑːn.zoʊ

goo guː

goober ˈguː.bəʳ US -bɚ **-s** -z

Gooch guːtʃ

good (G) *(n. adj. interj.)* gʊd **-s** -z **-ness** -nəs, -nɪs **ˌgood ˈday; ˌGood ˈFriday; ˌgood ˈgrief!; ˌGood ˈHeavens!; ˈgoods ˌtrain; as ˌgood as ˈgold**

Goodale ˈgʊd.eɪl

Goodall ˈgʊd.ɔːl US -ɔːl, -ɑːl

Goodbody ˈgʊd.bɒd.i US -bɑː.di

goodbye *(n.)* gʊdˈbaɪ **-s** -z

goodbye *(interj.)* gʊdˈbaɪ

Goodchild ˈgʊd.tʃaɪld

Goode gʊd

Goodell gʊˈdel

Goodenough ˈgʊd.ɪ.nʌf, ˈ-ə-, -ən.ʌf

Goodfellow ˈgʊdˌfel.əʊ US -oʊ

good-for-nothing ˈgʊd.fəˌnʌθ.ɪŋ, ˌgʊd.fəˈnʌθ- US ˈgʊd.fɚˌnʌθ-, ˌgʊd.fɚˈnʌθ- **-s** -z

Goodge guːdʒ, gʊdʒ

Goodhart ˈgʊd.hɑːt US -hɑːrt

good-hearted ˌgʊdˈhɑː.tɪd US -ˈhɑːr.t̬əd **-ness** -nəs, -nɪs *stress shift:* ˌgood-hearted ˈperson

good-humo(u)red ˌgʊdˈhjuː.məd US -ˈhjuː.mɚd, -ˈjuː- **-ly** -li **-ness** -nəs, -nɪs *stress shift:* ˌgood-humo(u)red ˈfriend

goodie ˈgʊd.i **-s** -z

goodish ˈgʊd.ɪʃ

Goodison ˈgʊd.ɪ.sən, -ə-

Goodliffe ˈgʊd.lɪf

good-looking ˌgʊdˈlʊk.ɪŋ *stress shift:* ˌgood-looking ˈguy

goodl|y ˈgʊd.l|i **-ier** -i.əʳ US -i.ɚ **-iest** -i.ɪst, -i.əst **-iness** -ɪ.nəs, -ɪ.nɪs

good|man ˈgʊd|.mæn **-men** -men

Goodman ˈgʊd.mən

good morning gʊdˈmɔː.nɪŋ US -ˈmɔːr-

good-natured ˌgʊdˈneɪ.tʃəd US -tʃɚd **-ly** -li **-ness** -nəs, -nɪs *stress shift:* ˌgood-natured ˈsmile

goodness ˈgʊd.nəs, -nɪs

good night ˌgʊdˈnaɪt

Goodrich ˈgʊd.rɪtʃ

Goodson ˈgʊd.sən

goods-train ˈgʊdz.treɪn **-s** -z

good-tempered ˌgʊdˈtem.pəd US -pɚd **-ly** -li **-ness** -nəs, -nɪs *stress shift:* ˌgood-tempered ˈhorse

goodwill gʊdˈwɪl **-s** -z

Goodwin ˈgʊd.wɪn

Goodwood ˈgʊd.wʊd

good|y (G) ˈgʊd|.i **-ies** -iz **ˌgoody-ˈtwo-shoes**

Goodyear® ˈgʊd.jɪəʳ, -jəʳ, -jɜːʳ US -jɪr, -jɚ, ˈgʊdʒ.ɪr

Goodyer ˈgʊd.jəʳ

goody-good|y ˈgʊd.iˌgʊd|.i **-ies** -iz

goo|ey ˈguː|.i **-ier** -i.əʳ US -i.ɚ **-iest** -i.ɪst, -i.əst **-iness** -ɪ.nəs, -ɪ.nɪs

goof guːf **-s** -s **-ing** -ɪŋ **-ed** -t

goofball ˈguːf.bɔːl US -bɔːl, -bɑːl **-s** -z

goof|y (G) ˈguː.f|i **-ier** -i.əʳ US -i.ɚ **-iest** -i.ɪst, -i.əst **-ily** -ɪ.li, -əl.i **-iness** -ɪ.nəs, -ɪ.nɪs

Googe guːdʒ, gʊdʒ

Googie ˈguː.gi

Google ˈguː.gl̩

googl|y ˈguː.gl|i **-ies** -iz

googol ˈguː.gɒl, -gəl US -gɑːl, -gəl **-s** -z

googolplex ˈguː.gɒl.pleks, -gəl- US -gɑːl-, -gəl-

Goole guːl

gooll|ie, gooll|y ˈguː.l|i **-ies** -iz

goon guːn **-s** -z

Goonhilly ˌguːnˈhɪl.i, ˌgʊn- *stress shift:* ˌGoonhilly ˈDown

goop guːp

goop|y ˈguː.p|i **-ier** -i.əʳ US -i.ɚ **-iest** -i.ɪst, -i.əst **-ily** -ɪ.li, -əl.i **-iness** -ɪ.nəs, -ɪ.nɪs

goosander guːˈsæn.dəʳ US -dɚ **-s** -z

goose *bird:* guːs **geese** giːs **ˈgoose ˌbumps; ˈgoose ˌgrass; ˈgoose ˌpimples; ˌcook someone's ˈgoose; (kill) the ˌgoose that ˌlays the ˌgolden ˈeggs; ˌcouldn't say ˌboo to a ˈgoose**

goos|e *(v.)* guːs **-es** -ɪz **-ing** -ɪŋ **-ed** -t

goos|e *tailor's iron:* guːs **-es** -ɪz

gooseberr|y ˈgʊz.bər|.i, ˈguːz-, ˈ-br|i US ˈguːsˌber|.i, ˈguːz-, -bɚ- **-ies** -iz **ˌgooseberry ˈfool**

gooseflesh ˈguːs.fleʃ

goose-step ˈguːsˌstep **-s** -s **-ping** -ɪŋ **-ped** -t

goosey ˈguː.si **-s** -z

GOP ˌdʒiː.əʊˈpiː US -oʊˈ-

gopher ˈgəʊ.fəʳ US ˈgoʊ.fɚ **-s** -z

Gorazde gɔːˈræʒ.deɪ, gəˈ-

Gorbachev ˈgɔː.bə.tʃɒf, ˌ--ˈ- US ˈgɔːr.bə.tʃɑːf, ˌ--ˈ-

Gorbals ˈgɔː.bəlz US ˈgɔːr-

gorblimey ˌgɔːˈblaɪ.mi US ˌgɔːr-

Gorboduc ˈgɔː.bə.dʌk US ˈgɔːr-

Gordale ˈgɔː.deɪl US ˈgɔːr-

Gordano gɔːˈdɑː.nəʊ, -ˈdeɪ- US gɔːrˈdɑː.noʊ

Gordian knot ˌgɔː.di.ənˈnɒt US ˌgɔːr.di.ənˈnɑːt

Gordimer ˈgɔː.dɪ.məʳ US ˈgɔːr-

Gordon ˈgɔː.dən US ˈgɔːr-

Gordonstoun ˈgɔː.dən.stən US ˈgɔːr-

gor|e (G) gɔːʳ US gɔːr **-es** -z **-ing** -ɪŋ **-ed** -d

Gorebridge ˈgɔː.brɪdʒ US ˈgɔːr-

Gorell ˈgɒr.əl US ˌgɔːˈrel, ˈgɑː.rəl

Gore-Tex® ˈgɔː.teks US ˈgɔːr-

gorg|e gɔːdʒ US gɔːrdʒ **-es** -ɪz **-ing** -ɪŋ **-ed** -d

gorgeous ˈgɔː.dʒəs US ˈgɔːr- **-ly** -li **-ness** -nəs, -nɪs

Gorges ˈgɔː.dʒɪz US ˈgɔːr-

gorget ˈgɔː.dʒɪt, -dʒət US ˈgɔːr.dʒət **-s** -s

Gorgie ˈgɔː.gi US ˈgɔːr-

gorgon (G) ˈgɔː.gən US ˈgɔːr- **-s** -z

Gorgonzola ˌgɔː.gənˈzəʊ.lə US ˌgɔːr.gənˈzoʊ-

Gorham ˈgɔː.rəm US ˈgɔːr.əm

gorilla gəˈrɪl.ə **-s** -z

Goring ˈgɔː.rɪŋ US ˈgɔːr.ɪŋ ˈgɜː.rɪŋ US ˈgɝː.ɪŋ, ˈgɔːr-

Gorki, Gorky ˈgɔː.ki US ˈgɔːr-

Gorleston ˈgɔːl.stən US ˈgɔːrl-

Gorman ˈgɔː.mən US ˈgɔːr-

gormandiz|e, -is|e ˈgɔː.mən.daɪz US ˈgɔːr- **-es** -ɪz **-ing** -ɪŋ **-ed** -d **-er/s** -əʳ/z US -ɚ/z

Gormenghast ˈgɔː.mən.gɑːst, -məŋ- ⓤⓢ ˈgɔːr.mən.gæst, -məŋ-
gormless ˈgɔːm.ləs, -lɪs ⓤⓢ ˈgɔːrm- **-ly** -li **-ness** -nəs, -nɪs
Gormley ˈgɔːm.li ⓤⓢ ˈgɔːrm-
Goronwy gəˈrɒn.wi ⓤⓢ -ˈrɑːn-
gorp gɔːp ⓤⓢ gɔːrp
Gorringe ˈgɒr.ɪndʒ, -əndʒ ⓤⓢ ˈgɑː.rɪndʒ, ˈgɔː-
gorse gɔːs ⓤⓢ gɔːrs
Gorseinon gɔːˈsaɪ.nən ⓤⓢ gɔːr-
Gorst gɔːst ⓤⓢ gɔːrst
Gorton ˈgɔː.tᵊn ⓤⓢ ˈgɔːr-
gor|y ˈgɔː.r|i ⓤⓢ ˈgɔːr|.i **-ier** -i.əʳ ⓤⓢ -i.ɚ **-iest** -i.ɪst, -i.əst **-ily** -ᵊl.i, -ɪ.li **-iness** -ɪ.nəs, -ɪ.nɪs
Goschen ˈgəʊ.ʃᵊn, ˈgɒʃ.ᵊn ⓤⓢ ˈgoʊ-
gosh gɒʃ ⓤⓢ gɑːʃ
goshawk ˈgɒs.hɔːk ⓤⓢ ˈgɑːs.hɑːk, -hɔːk **-s** -s
Goshen ˈgəʊ.ʃᵊn, ˈgɒʃ.ᵊn ⓤⓢ ˈgoʊ-
gosling (G) ˈgɒz.lɪŋ ⓤⓢ ˈgɑːz- **-s** -z
go-slow ˌgəʊˈsləʊ, ˈ-- ⓤⓢ ˈgoʊ.sloʊ **-s** -z
gospel (G) ˈgɒs.pᵊl, -pel ⓤⓢ ˈgɑːs- **-s** -z **ˈgospel ˌmusic**
gospel(l)er ˈgɒs.pᵊl.əʳ ⓤⓢ ˈgɑː.spᵊl.ɚ **-s** -z
Gosport ˈgɒs.pɔːt ⓤⓢ ˈgɑːs.pɔːrt
gossamer ˈgɒs.ə.məʳ ⓤⓢ ˈgɑː.sə.mɚ
Goss(e) gɒs ⓤⓢ gɑːs
gossip *(n. v.)* ˈgɒs.ɪp ⓤⓢ ˈgɑː.səp **-s** -s **-ing** -ɪŋ **-ed** -t **-y** -i
got *(from* **get***)* gɒt ⓤⓢ gɑːt
Göteborg ˈjɜː.tə.bɔː ⓤⓢ -bɔːr
goth (G) gɒθ ⓤⓢ gɑːθ **-s** -s
Gotha *in Germany:* ˈgəʊ.θə, ˈgəʊ.tə ⓤⓢ ˈgoʊ.t̬ə *old-fashioned English spelling of* ***Göta*** *in Sweden:* ˈgəʊ.tə ⓤⓢ ˈgoʊ.t̬ə
Gotham *in Nottinghamshire:* ˈgəʊ.təm ⓤⓢ ˈgoʊ.t̬əm *New York:* ˈgɒθ.əm ⓤⓢ ˈgɑː.θəm
Gothenburg ˈgɒθ.ᵊn.bɜːg, ˈgɒt-, -ᵊm- ⓤⓢ ˈgɑː.θᵊn.bɝːg, -tᵊn-
gothic (G) ˈgɒθ.ɪk ⓤⓢ ˈgɑː.θɪk
Gothicism ˈgɒθ.ɪ.sɪ.zᵊm, ˈ-ə- ⓤⓢ ˈgɑː.θə-
gothiciz|e, -is|e ˈgɒθ.ɪ.saɪz, ˈ-ə- ⓤⓢ ˈgɑː.θə- **-es** -ɪz **-ing** -ɪŋ **-ed** -d
Gothland ˈgɒθ.lənd ⓤⓢ ˈgɑːt-
Gotland ˈgɒt.lənd ⓤⓢ ˈgɑːt-
gotta ˈgɒt.ə ⓤⓢ ˈgɑː.t̬ə
gotten *(from* **get***)* ˈgɒt.ᵊn ⓤⓢ ˈgɑː.tᵊn
götterdämmerung (G) ˌgɜː.təˈdem.ə.rʊŋ, -ˈdeɪ.mə- ⓤⓢ ˌgɜː.t̬ɚˈdem-
Gotthard ˈgɒt.ɑːd ⓤⓢ ˈgɑː.tɑːrd
Gotti ˈgɒt.i ⓤⓢ ˈgɑː.t̬i
Göttingen ˈgɜː.tɪŋ.ən ⓤⓢ ˈgɝː-
gouache guˈɑːʃ, -ˈæʃ, gwɑːʃ, gwæʃ
Gouda ˈgaʊ.də ⓤⓢ ˈguː-
Goudie ˈgaʊ.di
goug|e gaʊdʒ, guːdʒ ⓤⓢ gaʊdʒ **-es** -ɪz **-ing** -ɪŋ **-ed** -d
Gough gɒf ⓤⓢ gɑːf
goujon ˈguː.dʒɒn, -ʒɒn, -ʒɔ̃ːŋ ⓤⓢ guːˈʒoʊn **-s** -z
goulash ˈguː.læʃ ⓤⓢ -lɑːʃ, -læʃ **-es** -ɪz
Goulburn *place-name:* ˈgəʊl.bɜːn ⓤⓢ ˈgoʊl.bɝːn *surname:* ˈguːl.bɜːn, ˈgəʊl.bən ⓤⓢ ˈguːl.bɝːn, ˈgoʊl.bɚn
Gould guːld
Goulden ˈguːl.dən
Goulding ˈguːl.dɪŋ
Gouler ˈguː.ləʳ ⓤⓢ -lɚ
Gounod ˈguː.nəʊ ⓤⓢ -noʊ
gourd gʊəd, gɔːd ⓤⓢ gɔːrd, gʊrd **-s** -z
gourde gʊəd, gɔːd ⓤⓢ gɔːrd, gʊrd **-s** -z
Gourl|ay ˈgʊə.l|eɪ, -l|i ⓤⓢ ˈgʊr.l|i **-ey** -i
gourmand ˈgʊə.mənd, ˈgɔː-, -mɑ̃ŋ ⓤⓢ ˈgʊr.mɑːnd, -mənd; **-s** -z
gourmet ˈgʊə.meɪ, ˈgɔː- ⓤⓢ ˈgʊr.meɪ, -ˈ- **-s** -z
Gourock ˈgʊə.rək ⓤⓢ ˈgʊr.ək
gout gaʊt **-y** -i ⓤⓢ ˈgaʊ.t̬i **-ily** -ɪ.li, -ᵊl.i ⓤⓢ ˈgaʊ.t̬ɪ.li, -t̬ᵊl.i **-iness** -ɪ.nəs, -ɪ.nɪs ⓤⓢ ˈgaʊ.t̬ɪ.nəs, -t̬ɪ-
Govan ˈgʌv.ᵊn
Gover ˈgəʊ.vəʳ ⓤⓢ ˈgoʊ.vɚ
govern ˈgʌv.ᵊn ⓤⓢ -ɚn **-s** -z **-ing** -ɪŋ **-ed** -d **-able** -ə.bl̩
governance ˈgʌv.ᵊn.ənts ⓤⓢ -ɚ.nᵊnts
governess ˈgʌv.ᵊn.əs, -ɪs, -es ⓤⓢ -ɚ.nəs **-es** -ɪz
government ˈgʌv.ᵊn.mənt, -ᵊm.mənt, -və.mənt ⓤⓢ -ɚn- **-s** -s
governmental ˌgʌv.ᵊnˈmen.tᵊl, -ᵊmˈmen-, -əˈmen- ⓤⓢ -ɚnˈmen.t̬ᵊl
governor ˈgʌv.ᵊn.əʳ ⓤⓢ -ɚ.nɚ **-s** -z
governor-general ˌgʌv.ᵊn.əˈdʒen.ᵊr.ᵊl ⓤⓢ -ɚ.nɚˈ- **-s** -z
governorship ˈgʌv.ᵊn.ə.ʃɪp ⓤⓢ -ɚ.nɚ- **-s** -s
Govey ˈgəʊ.vi ⓤⓢ ˈgoʊ-
Govier ˈgəʊ.vi.əʳ ⓤⓢ ˈgoʊ.vi.ɚ
Gow gaʊ
Gowan gaʊən
Gowdy ˈgaʊ.di
Gowen gaʊən, gaʊɪn
Gower gaʊəʳ, gɔːʳ ⓤⓢ gaʊɚ
Note: /gaʊəʳ/ is used in **Gower Street** and for the place in Wales. /gɔːʳ/ is the family name of the Duke of Sutherland; this pronunciation is also used in **Leveson-Gower** .
Gowing ˈgaʊ.ɪŋ
gowk gaʊk **-s** -s
Gowlett ˈgaʊ.lət, -lɪt
gown gaʊn **-s** -z **-ed** -d
gowns|man ˈgaʊnz|.mən **-men** -mən, -men
Gowrie ˈgaʊ.ri
Gowther ˈgaʊ.ðəʳ ⓤⓢ -ðɚ
Gowy ˈgaʊ.i
goy gɔɪ **-s** -z **-im** -ɪm **-ish** -ɪʃ
Goya ˈgɔɪ.ə
Gozo ˈgəʊ.zəʊ ⓤⓢ ˈgoʊ.zoʊ
GP ˌdʒiːˈpiː **-s** -z
GPA ˌdʒiː.piːˈeɪ
GPO ˌdʒiː.piːˈəʊ ⓤⓢ -ˈoʊ
GPS ˌdʒiː.piːˈes
grab græb **-s** -z **-bing** -ɪŋ **-bed** -d **-ber/s** -əʳ/z ⓤⓢ -ɚ/z **ˈgrab ˌbag; ˌup for ˈgrabs**
grabbl|e ˈgræb.l̩ **-es** -z **-ing** -ɪŋ, ˈ-lɪŋ **-ed** -d
grabb|y ˈgræb|.i **-ier** -i.əʳ ⓤⓢ -i.ɚ **-iest** -i.ɪst, -i.əst
Grabham ˈgræb.əm
Gracch|us ˈgræk|.əs **-i** -iː, -aɪ
grac|e (G) greɪs **-es** -ɪz **-ing** -ɪŋ **-ed** -t **ˈgrace ˌnote; ˌfall from ˈgrace**
Gracechurch ˈgreɪs.tʃɜːtʃ ⓤⓢ -tʃɝːtʃ
graceful ˈgreɪs.fᵊl, -fʊl **-ly** -i **-ness** -nəs, -nɪs
Graceland ˈgreɪs.lænd, -lənd
graceless ˈgreɪ.sləs, -slɪs **-ly** -li **-ness** -nəs, -nɪs
Gracie ˈgreɪ.si
gracious ˈgreɪ.ʃəs **-ly** -li **-ness** -nəs, -nɪs
grackle ˈgræk.l̩ **-s** -z
grad græd **-s** -z **ˈgrad ˌschool**
gradability ˌgreɪ.dəˈbɪl.ə.ti, -ɪ.ti ⓤⓢ -ə.t̬i
gradable ˈgreɪ.də.bl̩
gra|date grə|ˈdeɪt ⓤⓢ ˈgreɪ|.deɪt **-dates** -ˈdeɪts ⓤⓢ -deɪts **-dating** -ˈdeɪ.tɪŋ ⓤⓢ -deɪ.t̬ɪŋ **-dated** -ˈdeɪ.tɪd ⓤⓢ -deɪ.t̬əd
gradation grəˈdeɪ.ʃᵊn ⓤⓢ greɪ- **-s** -z
gradational grəˈdeɪ.ʃᵊn.ᵊl ⓤⓢ greɪ-
grad|e greɪd **-es** -z **-ing** -ɪŋ **-ed** -ɪd **ˌgrade point ˈaverage** ⓤⓢ **ˈgrade point ˌaverage; ˈgrade ˌschool; ˌmake the ˈgrade**
gradeable ˈgreɪ.də.bl̩
gradely ˈgreɪd.li
Gradgrind ˈgræd.graɪnd
gradient ˈgreɪ.di.ənt **-s** -s
gradin ˈgreɪ.dɪn **-s** -z
graditative ˈgreɪ.dɪ.tə.tɪv, -də- ⓤⓢ -də-
gradual ˈgrædʒ.u.əl, ˈgræd.ju.əl ⓤⓢ ˈgrædʒ.u.əl **-s** -z **-ly** -i
graduate *(n.)* ˈgrædʒ.u.ət, ˈgræd.ju-, -ɪt ⓤⓢ ˈgrædʒ.u.ət, -ɪt **-s** -s
gradu|ate *(v.)* ˈgræd.ju|.eɪt, ˈgrædʒ.u- ⓤⓢ ˈgrædʒ.u- **-ates** -eɪts **-ating** -eɪ.tɪŋ ⓤⓢ -eɪ.t̬ɪŋ **-ated** -eɪ.tɪd ⓤⓢ -eɪ.t̬ɪd
graduation ˌgrædʒ.uˈeɪ.ʃᵊn, ˌgræd.juˈ- ⓤⓢ ˌgrædʒ.uˈ- **-s** -z
graduator ˈgrædʒ.u.eɪ.təʳ, ˈgræd.ju- ⓤⓢ ˈgrædʒ.u.eɪ.t̬ɚ **-s** -z
gradus ˈgræd.əs, ˈgreɪ.dəs **-es** -ɪz
Grady ˈgreɪ.di
Graecism ˈgriː.sɪ.zᵊm

Graeco- ˈgriː.kəʊ-, ˈgrek.əʊ- ⓤⓢ ˈgrek.oʊ-, ˈgriː.koʊ-
Graeme greɪəm, greɪm
Graf grɑːf, græf ⓤⓢ græf
Graf(f)ham ˈgræf.əm
graffiti grəˈfiː.ti, græfˈiː- ⓤⓢ grəˈfiː.ţi
graft grɑːft ⓤⓢ græft **-s** -s **-ing** -ɪŋ **-ed** -ɪd **-er/s** -əʳ/z ⓤⓢ -ɚ/z
Grafton ˈgrɑːf.tᵊn ⓤⓢ ˈgræf-
graham cracker ˈgreɪəm,kræk.əʳ ⓤⓢ -ɚ, ˈgræm- **-s** -z
Graham(e) ˈgreɪəm
graham flour ˈgreɪəm,flaʊəʳ ⓤⓢ -,flaʊɚ
Grahamston ˈgreɪəm.stᵊn
Grahamstown ˈgreɪəmz.taʊn
grail (G) greɪl **-s** -z
grain greɪn **-s** -z **-ing** -ɪŋ **-ed** -d **-er/s** -əʳ/z ⓤⓢ -ɚ/z **,go a,gainst the ˈgrain**
Grainger ˈgreɪn.dʒəʳ ⓤⓢ -dʒɚ
grain|y ˈgreɪ.n|i **-ier** -i.əʳ ⓤⓢ -i.ɚ **-iest** -i.ɪst, -i.əst
gram græm **-s** -z
gramercy grəˈmɜː.si ⓤⓢ -ˈmɝː-
graminaceous ,græm.ɪˈneɪ.ʃəs, ,greɪ.mɪˈ-, -məˈ- ⓤⓢ ,græm.əˈ-
gramineous grəˈmɪn.i.əs, græmˈɪn-
graminivorous ,græm.ɪˈnɪv.ᵊr.əs, ,greɪ-
grammalogue ˈgræm.ə.lɒg ⓤⓢ -lɑːg, -lɔːg **-s** -z
grammar ˈgræm.əʳ ⓤⓢ -ɚ **-s** -z **ˈgrammar ,school**
grammarian grəˈmeə.ri.ən ⓤⓢ -ˈmer.i- **-s** -z
grammatical grəˈmæt.ɪ.kᵊl ⓤⓢ -ˈmæţ.ɪ- **-ly** -i
grammaticality grə,mæt.ɪˈkæl.ə.ti, -ɪ.ti ⓤⓢ -,mæţ.əˈkæl.ə.ţi
grammaticiz|e, -is|e grəˈmæt.ɪ.saɪz, ˈ-ə- ⓤⓢ -ˈmæţ.ə- **-es** -ɪz **-ing** -ɪŋ **-ed** -d
gramme græm **-s** -z
Grammer ˈgræm.əʳ ⓤⓢ -ɚ
Gramm|y ˈgræm|.i **-ys** -iz **-ies** -iz
gramophone ˈgræm.ə.fəʊn ⓤⓢ -foʊn **-s** -z
Grampian ˈgræm.pi.ən **-s** -z
gramps græmps
grampus ˈgræm.pəs **-es** -ɪz
gran græn **-s** -z
Granada grəˈnɑː.də
granar|y ˈgræn.ᵊr|.i **-ies** -iz **ˈgranary ,bread**
Granbury ˈgræn.bᵊr.i, ˈgræm- ⓤⓢ ˈgræn,ber-, -bɚ-
Granby ˈgræn.bi, ˈgræm- ⓤⓢ ˈgræn-
Gran Canaria ,græn.kəˈneə.ri.ə, ,græŋ- ⓤⓢ ,grɑːn.kəˈnɑː-, -ˈner-
Gran Chaco ,grænˈtʃɑː.kəʊ, -ˈtʃæk.əʊ ⓤⓢ ,grɑːnˈtʃɑː.koʊ
grand grænd **-er** -əʳ ⓤⓢ -ɚ **-est** -ɪst, -əst **-ly** -li **-ness** -nəs, -nɪs, ˈgræn.nəs, -nɪs **,Grand Caˈnary; ,Grand ˈCanyon; ,grand ˈduchess; ,grand ˈduke; ,Grand ˈForks; ,grand ˈjury; ,Grand ˈNational; ,grand piˈano**
grandad (G) ˈgræn.dæd **-s** -z
grandadd|y ˈgræn.dæd|.i **-ies** -iz
grandam ˈgræn.dæm, -dəm **-s** -z
grandaunt ˈgrænd,ɑːnt ⓤⓢ -,ænt, -,ɑːnt **-s** -s
grand|child ˈgrænd|.tʃaɪld **-children** -,tʃɪl.drᵊn
granddad (G) ˈgrænd.dæd **-s** -z
granddadd|y ˈgrænd.dæd|.i **-ies** -iz
granddaughter ˈgrænd,dɔː.təʳ ⓤⓢ -,dɑː.ţɚ, -,dɔː- **-s** -z
grande dame ,grɑːndˈdɑːm, ,grɑ̃ːn-, -ˈdæm **-s** -z
grandee grænˈdiː **-s** -z
grandeur ˈgræn.djəʳ, -dʒəʳ, -djʊəʳ ⓤⓢ -dʒɚ, -dʒʊr
grandfather ˈgrænd,fɑː.ðəʳ ⓤⓢ -ðɚ **-s** -z **ˈgrandfather ,clause; ,grandfather ˈclock** ⓤⓢ **ˈgrandfather ,clock**
Grand Guignol ,grɑ̃ːŋ.giːˈnjɒl ⓤⓢ ,grɑ̃ː.giːˈnjoʊl, ,grɑːn-, -ˈnjɑːl
grandiloquen|ce grænˈdɪl.ə.kwən|ts **-t/ly** -t/li
grandiose ˈgræn.di.əʊs, -əʊz ⓤⓢ -oʊs, -oʊz, ,--ˈ- **-ly** -li
grandiosity ,græn.diˈɒs.ə.ti, -ɪ.ti ⓤⓢ -ˈɑː.sə.ţi
Grandison ˈgræn.dɪ.sᵊn
Grandissimes ˈgrænd.ɪ.siːmz
grandma ˈgrænd.mɑː, ˈgræm- **-s** -z **,Grandma ˈMoses**
grand mal ,grɑ̃ːndˈmæl ⓤⓢ ,grɑːndˈmɑːl, ,grænd-, -ˈmæl
grandmamma ˈgrænd.mə,mɑː, ˈgræm- **-s** -z
Grand Marnier® ,grɑ̃ːndˈmɑː.ni.eɪ ⓤⓢ ,grɑːn.mɑːrˈnjeɪ **-s** -z
grandmaster ˈgrænd,mɑː.stəʳ, ˈgræm- ⓤⓢ ˈgrænd,mæs.tɚ **-s** -z
grandmother ˈgrænd,mʌð.əʳ, ˈgræm- ⓤⓢ ˈgrænd,mʌð.ɚ **-s** -z
grandnephew ˈgrænd,nev.juː, -,nef-, ,-ˈ-- ⓤⓢ ˈgrænd,nef.juː **-s** -z
grandniec|e ˈgrænd.niːs, ,-ˈ- **-es** -ɪz
grandpa ˈgrænd.pɑː, ˈgræm- **-s** -z
grandpapa ˈgrænd.pə,pɑː, ˈgræm- **-s** -z
grandparent ˈgrænd,peə.rᵊnt, ˈgræm- ⓤⓢ ˈgrænd,per.ᵊnt, -,pær- **-s** -s
grand prix ,grɑ̃ːnˈpriː, ,grɒn-, ,grɒm- ⓤⓢ ,grɑːn- **grands prix** ,grɑ̃ːˈpriː, ,grɒn-, ,grɒm- ⓤⓢ ,grɑːn-
grandsire ˈgrænd.saɪəʳ ⓤⓢ -saɪɚ **-s** -z
grandson ˈgrænd.sʌn **-s** -z
grands prix ,grɑ̃ːˈpriː, ,grɒn-, ,grɒm- ⓤⓢ ,grɑːn
grandstand ˈgrænd.stænd **-s** -z **-ing** -ɪŋ **-ed** -ɪd
granduncle ˈgrænd,ʌŋ.kḷ **-s** -z
grang|e (G) ˈgreɪndʒ **-es** -ɪz
Grangemouth ˈgreɪndʒ.məθ, -maʊθ
Granger ˈgreɪn.dʒəʳ ⓤⓢ -dʒɚ
grangeriz|e, -is|e ˈgreɪn.dʒᵊr.aɪz ⓤⓢ -dʒə.raɪz **-es** -ɪz **-ing** -ɪŋ **-ed** -d
Grangetown ˈgreɪndʒ.taʊn
Grangeville ˈgreɪndʒ.vɪl
granite (G) ˈgræn.ɪt, -ət **-s** -s
granitic grænˈɪt.ɪk, grəˈnɪt- ⓤⓢ grəˈnɪţ-
grann|y ˈgræn|.i **-ies** -iz **ˈgranny ,flat; ˈgranny ,knot; ,Granny ˈSmith**
granola grəˈnəʊ.lə, grænˈəʊ- ⓤⓢ grəˈnoʊ-
granolithic ,græn.əʊˈlɪθ.ɪk ⓤⓢ -əˈ-
grant (G) grɑːnt ⓤⓢ grænt **-s** -s **-ing** -ɪŋ ⓤⓢ ˈgræn.ţɪŋ **-ed** -ɪd ⓤⓢ ˈgræn.ţɪd
Granta ˈgræn.tə, ˈgrɑːn- ⓤⓢ ˈgræn-
Grantchester ˈgrɑːn.tʃɪ.stəʳ, ˈgræn-, -tʃə, -tʃes.təʳ ⓤⓢ ˈgræn,tʃes-
grantee ,grɑːnˈtiː ⓤⓢ ,græn- **-s** -z
Granth grʌnt
Grantham ˈgrænt.θəm
Granton ˈgrɑːn.tən, ˈgræn- ⓤⓢ ˈgræn-
grantor ,grɑːnˈtɔːʳ; ˈgrɑːn.təʳ ⓤⓢ ˈgræn.ţɚ; ,grænˈtɔːr **-s** -z
Grantown ˈgræn.taʊn
granular ˈgræn.jə.ləʳ, -jʊ- ⓤⓢ -jə.lɚ **-ly** -li
granularity ,græn.jəˈlær.ə.ti, -jʊˈ-, -ɪ.ti ⓤⓢ -jəˈler.ə.ţi, -ˈlær-
granu|late ˈgræn.jə|.leɪt, -jʊ- ⓤⓢ -jə- **-lates** -leɪts **-lating** -leɪ.tɪŋ ⓤⓢ -leɪ.ţɪŋ **-lated** -leɪ.tɪd ⓤⓢ -leɪ.ţɪd
granulation ,græn.jəˈleɪ.ʃᵊn, -jʊˈ- ⓤⓢ -jəˈ- **-s** -z
granule ˈgræn.juːl **-s** -z
granulite ˈgræn.jə.laɪt, -jʊ- ⓤⓢ -jə-
granulitic ,græn.jəˈlɪt.ɪk, -jʊˈ- ⓤⓢ -jəˈlɪţ-
Granville ˈgræn.vɪl
Granville-Barker ,græn.vɪlˈbɑː.kəʳ ⓤⓢ -ˈbɑːr.kɚ
grape (G) greɪp **-s** -s **ˈgrape ,sugar**
grapefruit ˈgreɪp.fruːt **-s** -s
grapeshot ˈgreɪp.ʃɒt ⓤⓢ -ʃɑːt
grapevine ˈgreɪp.vaɪn **-s** -z
graph grɑːf, græf ⓤⓢ græf **-s** -s **ˈgraph ,paper**
grapheme ˈgræf.iːm **-s** -z
graphemic græfˈiː.mɪk, grəˈfiː- **-ally** -ᵊl.i, -li
-grapher -grə.fəʳ ⓤⓢ -grə.fɚ
Note: Suffix. Words containing -**grapher** are normally stressed on the antepenultimate syllable, e.g. **photographer** /fəˈtɒg.rə.fəʳ ⓤⓢ -ˈtɑː.grə.fɚ/.
graphic (G) ˈgræf.ɪk **-s** -s **-al** -ᵊl **-ally** -ᵊl.i, -li **,graphic deˈsign**
-graphic -ˈgræf.ɪk
Note: Suffix. Normally carries primary stress, e.g. **photographic** /,fəʊ.təˈgræf.ɪk ⓤⓢ ,foʊ.ţəˈ-/.

graphite ˈgræf.aɪt
graphitic græfˈɪt.ɪk, grəˈfɪt- (US) grəˈfɪt̬-
graphological ˌgræf.əˈlɒdʒ.ɪ.k^əl (US) -ˈlɑː.dʒɪ- **-ly** -i
graphology|y græfˈɒl.ə.dʒ|i, grəˈfɒl- (US) grəˈfɑː.lə- **-ist/s** -ɪst/s
graphometer græfˈɒm.ɪ.tə^r, grəˈfɒm-, ˈ-ə- (US) grəˈfɑː.mə.t̬ɚ **-s** -z
-graphy -grə.fi
Note: Suffix. Words containing **-graphy** are normally stressed on the antepenultimate syllable, e.g. **photography** /fəˈtɒg.rə.fi (US) -ˈtɑː.grə-/.
grapnel ˈgræp.n^əl **-s** -z
grappa ˈgræp.ə (US) ˈgrɑː.pə **-s** -z
Grappelli græpˈel.i, grəpˈ-
grappl|e ˈgræp.l̩ **-es** -z **-ing** -ɪŋ, ˈ-lɪŋ **-ed** -d **-er/s** -ə^r/z, ˈ-lə^r/z (US) ˈ-l̩.ɚ/z, ˈ-lɚ/z **ˈgrappling ˌiron**
grapy ˈgreɪ.pi
Grasmere ˈgrɑːs.mɪə^r (US) ˈgræs.mɪr
grasp grɑːsp (US) græsp **-s** -s **-ing** -ɪŋ **-ed** -t **-er/s** -ə^r/z (US) -ɚ/z **-able** -ə.bl̩
grass (G) grɑːs (US) græs **-es** -ɪz **-ing** -ɪŋ **-ed** -t **ˌgrass ˈwidow; let the ˌgrass ˌgrow under one's ˈfeet**
grasshopper ˈgrɑːsˌhɒp.ə^r (US) ˈgræsˌhɑː.pɚ **-s** -z
grassland ˈgrɑːs.lænd, -lənd (US) ˈgræs-
grass-roots *(adj.)* ˌgrɑːsˈruːts (US) ˌgræs- *stress shift:* ˌgrass-roots ˈfeeling
grass roots *(n.)* ˌgrɑːsˈruːts (US) ˌgræs-
grasstree ˈgrɑːs.triː (US) ˈgræs.triː **-s** -z
grass|y ˈgrɑː.s|i (US) ˈgræs|.i **-ier** -i.ə^r (US) -i.ɚ **-iest** -i.ɪst, -i.əst
grat|e *(n. v.)* greɪt **-es** -s **-ing/ly** -ɪŋ/li (US) ˈgreɪ.t̬ɪŋ/li **-ed** -ɪd (US) ˈgreɪ.t̬ɪd **-er/s** -ə^r/z (US) ˈgreɪ.t̬ɚ/z
grateful ˈgreɪt.f^əl, -fʊl **-ly** -i **-ness** -nəs, -nɪs
Gratian ˈgreɪ.ʃ^ən, -ʃi.ən
graticule ˈgræt.ɪ.kjuːl, ˈ-ə- (US) ˈ-ə- **-s** -z
gratification ˌgræt.ɪ.fɪˈkeɪ.ʃ^ən, ˌ-ə- (US) ˌgræt̬.ə- **-s** -z
grati|fy ˈgræt.ɪ|.faɪ, ˈ-ə- (US) ˈgræt̬.ə- **-fies** -faɪz **-fying/ly** -faɪ.ɪŋ/li **-fied** -faɪd
gratin ˈgræ.tæ̃ŋ, -tæn (US) ˈgrɑː.t^ən
grating *(n.)* ˈgreɪ.tɪŋ (US) -t̬ɪŋ **-s** -z
Gratiot ˈgræʃ.i.ət, ˈgræʃ.ət, ˈgreɪ.ʃi.ət, -ʃət (US) ˈgræʃ.ət
gratis ˈgrɑː.tɪs, ˈgreɪ-, ˈgræt.ɪs, -əs (US) ˈgræt̬.əs, ˈgrɑː.t̬əs, ˈgreɪ-
gratitude ˈgræt.ɪ.tjuːd, -tʃuːd, ˈ-ə- (US) ˈgræt̬.ə.tuːd, -tjuːd
Grattan ˈgræt.^ən
gratuitous grəˈtjuː.ɪ.təs, -ˈtʃuː- (US) -ˈtuː.ə.t̬əs, -ˈtjuː- **-ly** -li **-ness** -nəs, -nɪs
gratuit|y grəˈtjuː.ə.t|i, -ˈtʃuː-, -ɪ.t|i (US) -ˈtuː.ə.t̬|i, -ˈtjuː- **-ies** -iz
graupel ˈgraʊ.p^əl
gravadlax ˈgræv.əd.læks (US) ˈgrɑː.vəd.lɑːks
gravamen grəˈveɪ.men, -ˈvɑː-, -mən (US) -mən **-s** -z **gravamina** grəˈveɪ.mɪn.ə, -ˈvɑː- (US) -ˈvæm.ɪn-
grave *accent above a letter:* grɑːv (US) grɑːv, greɪv
grav|e *other senses:* greɪv **-es** -z **-er** -ə^r (US) -ɚ **-est** -ɪst, -əst **-ely** -li **-eness** -nəs, -nɪs **-ing** -ɪŋ **-ed** -d **-er/s** -ə^r/z (US) -ɚ/z **ˌturn in one's ˈgrave**
graveclothes ˈgreɪv.kləʊðz (US) -kloʊðz
gravedigger ˈgreɪvˌdɪg.ə^r (US) -ɚ **-s** -z
gravel ˈgræv.^əl **-s** -z **-(l)ing** -ɪŋ **-(l)ed** -d **-ly** -i
graven ˈgreɪ.v^ən **ˌgraven ˈimage**
Graves *surname:* greɪvz *wine:* grɑːv
Gravesend ˌgreɪvzˈend
graveside ˈgreɪv.saɪd
gravestone ˈgreɪv.stəʊn (US) -stoʊn **-s** -z
graveyard ˈgreɪv.jɑːd (US) -jɑːrd **-s** -z **ˈgraveyard ˌshift, ˌgraveyard ˈshift**
gravid ˈgræv.ɪd **-ly** -li **-ness** -nəs, -nɪs
gravid|a ˈgræv.ɪ.d|ə **-as** -əz **-ae** -iː
gravidity grævˈɪd.ɪ.ti, grəˈvɪd- (US) grəˈvɪd.ə.t̬i
gravitas ˈgræv.ɪ.tæs, ˈ-ə-, -tɑːs
gravi|tate ˈgræv.ɪ|.teɪt, ˈ-ə- **-tates** -teɪts **-tating** -teɪ.tɪŋ (US) -teɪ.t̬ɪŋ **-tated** -teɪ.tɪd (US) -teɪ.t̬ɪd
gravitation ˌgræv.ɪˈteɪ.ʃ^ən, -əˈ- **-al** -^əl **-ally** -^əl.i
gravitative ˈgræv.ɪ.teɪ.tɪv, ˈ-ə-, -tə.tɪv (US) -teɪ.t̬ɪv
gravity ˈgræv.ə.ti, -ɪ.ti (US) -ə.t̬i
gravlax ˈgræv.læks (US) ˈgrɑːv.lɑːks
gravure grəˈvjʊə^r, -ˈvjɔː^r (US) -ˈvjʊr
grav|y ˈgreɪ.v|i **-ies** -iz **ˈgravy ˌtrain**
gray (G) greɪ **-s** -z **-er** -ə^r (US) -ɚ **-est** -ɪst, -əst **-ness** -nəs, -nɪs **-ing** -ɪŋ
grayish ˈgreɪ.ɪʃ
grayling ˈgreɪ.lɪŋ **-s** -z
Grayson ˈgreɪ.s^ən
graystone (G) ˈgreɪ.stəʊn (US) -stoʊn
Graz grɑːts
graz|e greɪz **-es** -ɪz **-ing** -ɪŋ **-ed** -d
grazier ˈgreɪ.zi.ə^r, -ʒə^r (US) -ʒɚ **-s** -z
GRE ˌdʒiː.ɑːrˈiː **-s** -z
Greasby ˈgriːz.bi
greas|e griːs **-es** -ɪz **-ing** -ɪŋ **-ed** -t
greasepaint ˈgriːs.peɪnt
greaseproof ˈgriːs.pruːf **ˌgreaseproof ˈpaper**
greaser ˈgriː.sə^r (US) -sɚ, -zɚ **-s** -z
Greasley ˈgriːz.li
greas|y ˈgriː.s|i **-ier** -i.ə^r (US) -i.ɚ **-iest** -i.ɪst, -i.əst **-ily** -ɪ.li, -^əl.i **-iness** -ɪ.nəs, -ɪ.nɪs
great greɪt **-er** -ə^r (US) ˈgreɪ.t̬ɚ **-est** -ɪst, -əst (US) ˈgreɪ.t̬ɪst, -t̬əst **-s** -s **-ness** -nəs, -nɪs **ˌGreat ˌBarrier ˈReef; ˌGreat ˈBritain; ˌGreat ˈFalls; ˌGreat ˈLakes; ˌGreat ˈPlains**
great-aunt ˌgreɪtˈɑːnt (US) ˌgreɪtˈænt, -ˈɑːnt **-s** -s *stress shift:* ˌgreat-aunt ˈMaud
Note: p
greatcoat ˈgreɪt.kəʊt (US) -koʊt **-s** -s
great-grand|child ˌgreɪtˈgrænd|.tʃaɪld **-children** -ˌtʃɪl.dr^ən
great-granddaughter ˌgreɪtˈgrændˌdɔː.tə^r (US) -ˌdɑː.t̬ɚ, -ˌdɔː- **-s** -z
great-grandfather ˌgreɪtˈgrændˌfɑː.ðə^r (US) -ðɚ **-s** -z
great-grandmother ˌgreɪtˈgrændˌmʌð.ə^r, -ˈgræm- (US) -ˈgrændˌmʌð.ɚ **-s** -z
great-grandparent ˌgreɪtˈgrændˌpeə.r^ənt (US) -ˌper.^ənt, -ˌpær- **-s** -s
great-grandson ˌgreɪtˈgrænd.sʌn **-s** -z
Greatham *in Durham:* ˈgriː.təm (US) ˈgriː.t̬əm *in Northamptonshire, Hampshire, and West Sussex:* ˈgret.əm (US) ˈgreɪ.t̬əm
Greathead ˈgreɪt.hed
Greatheart ˈgreɪt.hɑːt (US) -hɑːrt
greathearted ˌgreɪtˈhɑː.tɪd (US) -ˈhɑːr.t̬ɪd *stress shift:* ˌgreathearted ˈwarrior
greatly ˈgreɪt.li
Greatorex ˈgreɪ.tə.reks (US) -t̬ə-
Greats greɪts
great-uncle ˌgreɪtˈʌŋ.kl̩, ˈ-ˌ-- **-s** -z *stress shift:* ˌgreat-uncle ˈJohn
Great Yarmouth ˌgreɪtˈjɑː.məθ (US) -ˈjɑːr-
greave griːv **-s** -z
Greaves griːvz, greɪvz
grebe griːb **-s** -z
Grecian ˈgriː.ʃ^ən **-s** -z
Grecism ˈgriː.sɪ.z^əm
Greco- ˈgriː.kəʊ-, ˈgrek.əʊ- (US) ˈgrek.oʊ-, ˈgriː.koʊ-
Greece griːs
greed griːd
greed|y ˈgriː.d|i **-ier** -i.ə^r (US) -i.ɚ **-iest** -i.ɪst, -i.əst **-ily** -ɪ.li, -^əl.i **-iness** -ɪ.nəs, -ɪ.nɪs **ˈgreedy ˌguts**
Greek griːk **-s** -s **ˌGreek ˌOrthodox ˈChurch**
Greel(e)y ˈgriː.li
green (G) griːn **-s** -z **-er** -ə^r (US) -ɚ **-est** -ɪst, -əst **-ly** -li **-ness** -nəs, -nɪs **-ing** -ɪŋ **-ed** -d **ˌgreen ˈbean** (US) **ˈgreen ˌbean; ˌGreen Beˈret; ˈgreen ˌcard; ˌgreen cross ˈcode; ˈGreen ˌParty**
Greenall ˈgriː.nɔːl **-s** -z
Greenaway ˈgriː.nə.weɪ
greenback ˈgriːn.bæk, ˈgriːm- (US) ˈgriːn- **-s** -s

greenbelt (G) ˈgriːn.belt, ˈgriːm- (US) ˈgriːn- **-s** -s
Green(e) griːn
greenery ˈgriː.nᵊr.i
green-eyed ˌgriːnˈaɪd (US) ˈgriːn.aɪd *stress shift, British only:* ˌgreen-eyed ˈmonster
greenfield (G) ˈgriːn.fiːld
greenfinch ˈgriːn.fɪn*t*ʃ **-es** -ɪz
green|fly ˈgriːn|.flaɪ **-flies** -flaɪz
Greenford ˈgriːn.fəd (US) -fɚd
greengag|e ˈgriːn.geɪdʒ, ˈgriːŋ- (US) ˈgriːn- **-es** -ɪz
greengrocer ˈgriːnˌgrəʊ.səʳ, ˈgriːŋ- (US) ˈgriːnˌgroʊ.sɚ **-s** -z
Greenhalgh ˈgriːn.hælʃ, -hældʒ, -hɔː
Greenham ˈgriː.nəm **ˌGreenham ˈCommon**
Greenhaulgh ˈgriːn.hɔː
Greenhill ˈgriːn.hɪl
Greenhithe ˈgriːn.haɪð
greenhorn ˈgriːn.hɔːn (US) -hɔːrn **-s** -z
greenhou|se ˈgriːn.haʊ|s **-ses** -zɪz **ˈgreenhouse efˌfect; ˌgreenhouse ˈgas**
greenish (G) ˈgriː.nɪʃ
Greenland ˈgriːn.lənd, -lænd **-er/s** -əʳ/z
Greenleaf ˈgriːn.liːf
greenmarket ˈgriːnˌmɑː.kɪt, ˈgriːm- (US) ˈgriːnˌmɑːr.kɪt **-s** -s
Greenock ˈgriː.nək, ˈgrɪn.ək, ˈgren-
Greenore ˈgriː.nɔːʳ (US) -nɔːr
Greenough ˈgriː.nəʊ (US) -noʊ
Greenpeace ˈgriːn.piːs, ˈgriːm- (US) ˈgriːn-
Greenpoint ˈgriːn.pɔɪnt, ˈgriːm- (US) ˈgriːn-
Greenport ˈgriːn.pɔːt, ˈgriːm- (US) ˈgriːn.pɔːrt
greenroom ˈgriːn.rʊm, -ruːm (US) -ruːm, -rʊm **-s** -z
greensand ˈgriːn.sænd
greenshank ˈgriːn.ʃæŋk **-s** -s
Greenslade ˈgriːn.sleɪd
Greensleeves ˈgriːn.sliːvz
Greenspan ˈgriːn.spæn
greenstick ˈgriːn.stɪk **-s** -z **ˌgreenstick ˈfracture**
greenstone ˈgriːn.stəʊn (US) -stoʊn
greensward ˈgriːn.swɔːd (US) -swɔːrd
Greenville ˈgriːn.vɪl
Greenway ˈgriːn.weɪ
Greenwell ˈgriːn.wᵊl, -wel
Greenwich ˈgren.ɪdʒ, ˈgrɪn-, -ɪtʃ (US) ˈgren.ɪdʒ, ˈgrɪn-, -nɪtʃ, -wɪtʃ **ˌGreenwich ˈMean Time, ˌGreenwich ˌMean ˈTime**
greenwood (G) ˈgriːn.wʊd **-s** -z
Greer grɪəʳ (US) grɪr
greet (G) griːt **-s** -s **-ing/s** -ɪŋ/z (US) ˈgriː.t̬ɪŋ/z **-ed** -ɪd (US) ˈgriː.t̬ɪd **ˈgreetings ˌcard** (US) **ˈgreeting ˌcard**

Greetland ˈgriːt.lənd
gregarious grɪˈgeə.ri.əs, grə- (US) -ˈger.i- **-ly** -li **-ness** -nəs, -nɪs
Greg(g) greg
Gregor ˈgreg.əʳ (US) -ɚ
Gregorian grɪˈgɔː.ri.ən, grə-, gregˈɔː- **-s** -z **Greˌgorian ˈchant**
Gregory ˈgreg.ᵊr.i
Greig greg
greige greɪʒ
greisen ˈgraɪ.zᵊn
gremlin ˈgrem.lɪn **-s** -z
grenache grenˈæʃ
Grenada grəˈneɪ.də, grɪ-, grenˈeɪ-
grenade grəˈneɪd, grɪ-, grenˈeɪd **-s** -z
grenadier (G) ˌgren.əˈdɪəʳ (US) -ˈdɪr **-s** -z
grenadine ˈgren.ə.diːn, ˌgren.əˈdiːn
Grenadines ˌgren.əˈdiːnz
Grendel ˈgren.dᵊl
Grenfell ˈgren.fel, -fᵊl
Grenoble grəˈnəʊ.bl̩, grɪˈnəʊ- (US) grəˈnoʊ-
Grenville ˈgren.vɪl, -vᵊl
Gresham ˈgreʃ.əm
Gresley ˈgrez.li
Greswell ˈgrez.wᵊl, -wel
Greta ˈgriː.tə, ˈgret.ə, ˈgreɪ.tə (US) ˈgret̬.ə, ˈgriː.t̬ə, ˈgreɪ.t̬ə
Gretchen ˈgretʃ.ᵊn
Gretel ˈgret.ᵊl
Gretna ˈgret.nə **ˌGretna ˈGreen**
Greuz|e grɜːz (US) grɜːz **-es** -ɪz
Greville ˈgrev.ɪl, -ᵊl
grew *(from* **grow***)* (G) gruː
grey (G) greɪ **-s** -z **-er** -əʳ (US) -ɚ **-est** -ɪst, -əst **-ness** -nəs, -nɪs **-ing** -ɪŋ
greybeard ˈgreɪ.bɪəd (US) -bɪrd **-s** -z
greycoat (G) ˈgreɪ.kəʊt (US) -koʊt **-s** -s
grey-haired ˌgreɪˈheəd (US) -ˈherd *stress-shift:* **ˌgrey-haired ˈperson**
greyhound ˈgreɪ.haʊnd **-s** -z **ˌGreyhound ˈbus®**
greyish ˈgreɪ.ɪʃ
greylag ˈgreɪ.læg **-s** -z
Greylock ˈgreɪ.lɒk (US) -lɑːk
Greyson ˈgreɪ.sᵊn
Greystoke ˈgreɪ.stəʊk (US) -stoʊk
Gribbin ˈgrɪb.ɪn
gribble (G) ˈgrɪb.l̩ **-s** -z
Grice graɪs
grid grɪd **-s** -z
griddl|e ˈgrɪd.l̩ **-es** -z **-ing** -ɪŋ **-ed** -d
gridiron ˈgrɪd.aɪən (US) -aɪɚn **-s** -z
Gridley ˈgrɪd.li
gridlock ˈgrɪd.lɒk (US) -lɑːk **-s** -s **-ed** -t
grief griːf **-s** -z **ˈgrief-ˌstricken**
Grieg griːg
Grierson ˈgrɪə.sᵊn (US) ˈgrɪr-
grievanc|e ˈgriː.vᵊn*t*s **-es** -ɪz
griev|e (G) griːv **-es** -z **-ing** -ɪŋ **-ed** -d **-er/s** -əʳ/z (US) -ɚ/z

grievous ˈgriː.vəs **-ly** -li **-ness** -nəs, -nɪs **ˌgrievous ˌbodily ˈharm**
griffin (G) ˈgrɪf.ɪn **-s** -z
Griffith ˈgrɪf.ɪθ **-s** -s
griffon ˈgrɪf.ᵊn **-s** -z
grift grɪft **-s** -s **-ing** -ɪŋ **-ed** -ɪd
grifter ˈgrɪf.təʳ (US) -tɚ **-s** -z
grig grɪg **-s** -z
Grigg grɪg **-s** -z
Grigson ˈgrɪg.sᵊn
grill grɪl **-s** -z **-ing** -ɪŋ **-ed** -d **-er/s** -əʳ/z (US) -ɚ/z
grillag|e ˈgrɪl.ɪdʒ **-es** -ɪz
grille grɪl **-s** -z
grillroom ˈgrɪl.rʊm, -ruːm (US) -ruːm, -rʊm **-s** -z
grilse grɪls
grim grɪm **-mer** -əʳ (US) -ɚ **-mest** -ɪst, -əst **-ly** -li **-ness** -nəs, -nɪs **ˌGrim ˈReaper**
grimac|e ˈgrɪm.əs, grɪˈmeɪs (US) ˈgrɪm.əs; grɪˈmeɪs **-es** -ɪz **-ing** -ɪŋ **-ed** -t
Grimald ˈgrɪm.ᵊld
Grimaldi grɪˈmɔːl.di, grə-, -ˈmɒl-, -ˈmæl- (US) -ˈmɑːl-, -ˈmɔːl-
grimalkin grɪˈmæl.kɪn, -ˈmɔːl- **-s** -z
grim|e graɪm **-es** -z **-ing** -ɪŋ **-ed** -d
Grimes graɪmz
Grimethorpe ˈgraɪm.θɔːp (US) -θɔːrp
Grimké ˈgrɪm.ki
Grimm grɪm
Grimond ˈgrɪm.ənd
Grimsby ˈgrɪmz.bi
Grimshaw ˈgrɪm.ʃɔː (US) -ʃɑː, -ʃɔː
Grimwood ˈgrɪm.wʊd
grim|y ˈgraɪ.m|i **-ier** -i.əʳ (US) -i.ɚ **-iest** -i.ɪst, -i.əst **-ily** -ɪ.li, -ᵊl.i **-iness** -ɪ.nəs, -ɪ.nɪs
grin grɪn **-s** -z **-ning** -ɪŋ **-ned** -d
Grinch grɪntʃ
grind graɪnd **-s** -z **-ing** -ɪŋ **ground** graʊnd **grinder/s** ˈgraɪn.dəʳ/z (US) -dɚ/z
Grindal ˈgrɪnd.ᵊl
Grindelwald ˈgrɪn.dᵊl.vɑːld, -væld (US) -vɑːld, -væld, -wɔːld
Grindon ˈgrɪn.dən
grindstone ˈgraɪn*d*.stəʊn (US) -stoʊn **-s** -z **ˌkeep one's ˌnose to the ˈgrindstone**
gringo ˈgrɪŋ.gəʊ (US) -goʊ **-s** -z
Grinnell grɪˈnel
Grinstead ˈgrɪn.stɪd, -sted (US) -sted
grip grɪp **-s** -s **-ping** -ɪŋ **-ped** -t
grip|e graɪp **-es** -s **-ing** -ɪŋ **-ed** -t **ˈgripe ˌwater**
gripes graɪps
grippe griːp, grɪp (US) grɪp
grisaille grɪˈzeɪl, grə-, griː-, -ˈzaɪ, -ˈzaɪl (US) -ˈzaɪ, -ˈzeɪl
Griselda grɪˈzel.də, grə-
grisette grɪˈzet **-s** -s

Grisewood ˈgraɪz.wʊd

Grisham ˈgrɪʃ.ᵊm

griskin ˈgrɪs.kɪn

grisl|y ˈgrɪz.l|i **-ier** -i.əʳ (US) -i.ɚ **-iest** -i.ɪst, -i.əst **-iness** -ɪ.nəs, -ɪ.nɪs

Grisons griːˈzɔ̃ːŋ, -ˈzɔːŋ (US) griːˈzɔ̃ːŋ, -ˈzɔːŋ

Grissel ˈgrɪs.ᵊl

grist grɪst

gristle ˈgrɪs.l̩

gristly ˈgrɪs.l̩.i, ˈgrɪs.li

Griswold ˈgrɪz.wəʊld, -wᵊld (US) -wɔːld, -wᵊld

grit grɪt **-s** -s **-ting** -ɪŋ (US) ˈgrɪt̬.ɪŋ **-ted** -ɪd (US) ˈgrɪt̬.ɪd

gritter ˈgrɪt.əʳ (US) ˈgrɪt̬.ɚ **-s** -z

Gritton ˈgrɪt.ᵊn

gritt|y ˈgrɪt|.i (US) ˈgrɪt̬|.i **-ier** -i.əʳ (US) -i.ɚ **-iest** -i.ɪst, -i.əst **-ily** -ɪ.li, -ᵊl.i **-iness** -ɪ.nəs, -ɪ.nɪs

Grizedale ˈgraɪz.deɪl

Grizel grɪˈzel

grizzl|e ˈgrɪz.l̩ **-es** -z **-ing** -ɪŋ, ˈ-lɪŋ **-ed** -d

grizzl|y ˈgrɪz.l|i **-ies** -iz **-ier** -i.əʳ (US) -i.ɚ **-iest** -i.ɪst, -i.əst **ˈgrizzly ˌbear**

Gro grəʊ, gruː, grɔː (US) groʊ, grɔː

groan grəʊn (US) groʊn **-s** -z **-ing/s** -ɪŋ/z **-ed** -d

groat grəʊt (US) groʊt **-s** -s

grocer ˈgrəʊ.səʳ (US) ˈgroʊ.sɚ **-s** -z

grocer|y ˈgrəʊ.sᵊr|.i (US) ˈgroʊ- **-ies** -iz

grockle ˈgrɒk.l̩ (US) ˈgrɑː.kl̩ **-s** -z

Grocott ˈgrɒk.ət, ˈgrəʊ.kɒt (US) ˈgrɑː.kət, ˈgroʊ-

Grocyn ˈgrəʊ.sɪn (US) ˈgroʊ-

grog grɒg (US) grɑːg, grɔːg

grogg|y ˈgrɒg|.i (US) ˈgrɑː.g|i, ˈgrɔː- **-ier** -i.əʳ (US) -i.ɚ **-iest** -i.ɪst, -i.əst **-ily** -ɪ.li, -ᵊl.i **-iness** -ɪ.nəs, -ɪ.nɪs

grogram ˈgrɒg.rəm (US) ˈgrɑː.grəm

groin grɔɪn **-s** -z

grommet ˈgrɒm.ɪt, ˈgrʌm- (US) ˈgrɑː.mɪt **-s** -s

gromwell ˈgrɒm.wᵊl, -wel (US) ˈgrɑːm-

Gromyko grəˈmiː.kəʊ (US) -koʊ

Grongar ˈgrɒŋ.gəʳ (US) ˈgrɑːŋ.gɚ, ˈgrɔːŋ

Groningen ˈgrəʊ.nɪŋ.ən, ˈgrɒn.ɪŋ- (US) ˈgroʊ-

groom (G) gruːm, grʊm **-s** -z **-ing** -ɪŋ **-ed** -d

grooms|man ˈgruːmz|.mən, ˈgrʊmz- **-men** -mən, -men

groov|e gruːv **-es** -z **-ing** -ɪŋ **-ed** -d

groov|y ˈgruː.v|i **-ier** -i.əʳ (US) -i.ɚ **-iest** -i.ɪst, -i.əst **-iness** -ɪ.nəs, -ɪ.nɪs

grop|e grəʊp (US) groʊp **-es** -s **-ing/ly** -ɪŋ/li **-ed** -t **-er/s** -əʳ/z (US) -ɚ/z

Gropius ˈgrəʊ.pi.əs (US) ˈgroʊ-

Grosart ˈgrəʊ.zɑːt (US) ˈgroʊ.zɑːrt

grosbeak ˈgrəʊs.biːk, ˈgrɒs-, ˈgrɒz- (US) ˈgroʊs- **-s** -s

groschen ˈgrɒʃ.ᵊn, ˈgrəʊʃ.ᵊn (US) ˈgroʊ.ʃᵊn

Grose grəʊs, grəʊz (US) groʊs, groʊz

grosgrain ˈgrəʊ.greɪn (US) ˈgroʊ-

Grosmont *in North Yorkshire:* ˈgrəʊ.mənt, -mɒnt *locally also:* ˈgrəʊs.mənt (US) ˈgroʊ.mɑːnt, ˈgroʊs- *in Gwent:* ˈgrɒs.mənt (US) ˈgrɑːs-

gros point ˌgrəʊˈpɔɪnt (US) ˈgroʊ.pɔɪnt

gross grəʊs (US) groʊs **-er** -əʳ (US) -ɚ **-est** -ɪst, -əst **-ly** -li **-ness** -nəs, -nɪs **-es** -ɪz **-ing** -ɪŋ **-ed** -t **ˌgross doˌmestic ˈproduct; ˌgross ˌnational ˈproduct**

Gross *surname:* grɒs, grəʊs (US) grɑːs, groʊs

Grosseteste ˈgrəʊs.test (US) ˈgroʊs-

Grossmith ˈgrəʊ.smɪθ (US) ˈgroʊ-

grosso modo ˌgrɒs.əʊˈmɒd.əʊ, -ˈməʊ.dəʊ (US) ˌgroʊ.soʊˈmoʊ.doʊ

Grosvenor ˈgrəʊv.nəʳ (US) ˈgroʊv.nɚ

grosz grɔːʃ (US) grɑːʃ, grɔːʃ **groszy** ˈgrɔː.ʃi (US) ˈgrɑː-, ˈgrɔː-

Grote grəʊt (US) groʊt

grotesque grəʊˈtesk (US) groʊ- **-ly** -li **-ness** -nəs, -nɪs

Grotius ˈgrəʊ.ti.əs (US) ˈgroʊ.ʃəs, -ʃi.əs

grotto ˈgrɒt.əʊ (US) ˈgrɑː.t̬oʊ **-(e)s** -z

grott|y ˈgrɒt|.i (US) ˈgrɑː.t̬|i **-ier** -i.əʳ (US) -i.ɚ **-iest** -i.ɪst, -i.əst **-ily** -ɪ.li, -ᵊl.i **-iness** -ɪ.nəs, -ɪ.nɪs

grouch graʊtʃ **-es** -ɪz **-ing** -ɪŋ **-ed** -t

Groucho ˈgraʊ.tʃəʊ (US) -tʃoʊ

grouch|y ˈgraʊ.tʃ|i **-ier** -i.əʳ (US) -i.ɚ **-iest** -i.ɪst, -i.əst **-ily** -ɪ.li, -ᵊl.i **-iness** -ɪ.nəs, -ɪ.nɪs

ground graʊnd **-s** -z **-ing** -ɪŋ **-ed** -ɪd **-er/s** -əʳ/z (US) -ɚ/z **ˈground ˌplan; ˈground ˌrule; ˈground ˌstroke; ˈground ˌswell; ˌsuit someone ˌdown to the ˈground**

groundbreaking ˈgraʊndˌbreɪ.kɪŋ

ground|cloth ˈgraʊnd|.klɒθ, ˈgraʊŋ- (US) ˈgraʊnd|.klɑːθ **-cloths** -klɒθs, -klɒðz (US) -klɑːθs, -klɑːðz

groundcover ˈgraʊndˌkʌv.əʳ, ˈgraʊŋ- (US) ˈgraʊndˌkʌv.ɚ

groundhog ˈgraʊnd.hɒg (US) -hɑːg, -hɔːg **-s** -z **ˈGroundhog ˌDay**

groundless ˈgraʊnd.ləs, -lɪs **-ly** -li **-ness** -nəs, -nɪs

groundling ˈgraʊnd.lɪŋ **-s** -z

groundnut ˈgraʊnd.nʌt **-s** -s

groundout ˈgraʊnd.aʊt **-s** -s

groundsel ˈgraʊnd.sᵊl

groundsheet ˈgraʊnd.ʃiːt **-s** -s

grounds|man ˈgraʊndz|.mən **-men** -mən, -men

groundspeed ˈgraʊnd.spiːd **-s** -z

groundstroke ˈgraʊnd.strəʊk (US) -stroʊk **-s** -s

groundwater ˈgraʊndˌwɔː.təʳ (US) -ˌwɑː.t̬ɚ, -ˌwɔː-

groundwork ˈgraʊnd.wɜːk (US) -wɝːk

group gruːp **-s** -s **-ing/s** -ɪŋ/z **-ed** -t

grouper ˈgruː.pəʳ (US) -pɚ **-s** -z

groupie ˈgruː.pi **-s** -z

grous|e (G) graʊs **-es** -ɪz **-ing** -ɪŋ **-ed** -t **-er/s** -əʳ/z (US) -ɚ/z

grout graʊt **-s** -s **-ing** -ɪŋ (US) ˈgraʊ.t̬ɪŋ **-ed** -ɪd (US) ˈgraʊ.t̬ɪd **-er/s** -əʳ/z (US) ˈgraʊ.t̬ɚ/z

grove (G) grəʊv (US) groʊv **-s** -z

grovel ˈgrɒv.ᵊl (US) ˈgrɑː.vᵊl, ˈgrʌv.ᵊl **-s** -z **-(l)ing** -ɪŋ **-(l)ed** -d **-(l)er/s** -əʳ/z (US) -ɚ/z

Grover ˈgrəʊ.vəʳ (US) ˈgroʊ.vɚ

grow grəʊ (US) groʊ **-s** -z **-ing** -ɪŋ **grew** gruː **grown** grəʊn (US) groʊn **ˈgrow ˌbag; ˈgrowing ˌpains**

grow-bag ˈgrəʊ.bæg (US) ˈgroʊ- **-s** -z

grower ˈgrəʊ.əʳ (US) ˈgroʊ- **-s** -z

growl graʊl **-s** -z **-ing** -ɪŋ **-ed** -d **-er/s** -əʳ/z (US) -ɚ/z

grown *(from* **grow***)* grəʊn (US) groʊn

grown-up *(n.)* ˈgrəʊn.ʌp (US) ˈgroʊn- **-s** -s *stress shift:* ˌgrown-up ˈlanguage

grown-up *(adj.)* ˌgrəʊnˈʌp (US) ˌgroʊnˈ-

growth grəʊθ (US) groʊθ **-s** -s

groyne grɔɪn **-s** -z

Grozny ˈgrɒz.ni (US) ˈgrɑːz-

grub grʌb **-s** -z **-bing** -ɪŋ **-bed** -d **-ber/s** -əʳ/z (US) -ɚ/z

grubb|y ˈgrʌb|.i **-ier** -i.əʳ (US) -i.ɚ **-iest** -i.ɪst, -i.əst **-iness** -ɪ.nəs, -ɪ.nɪs

grubstak|e ˈgrʌb.steɪk **-es** -s **-ing** -ɪŋ **-ed** -t

grudg|e grʌdʒ **-es** -ɪz **-ing/ly** -ɪŋ/li **-ed** -d

gruel grʊəl, ˈgruː.əl (US) ˈgruː.əl

gruel(l)ing ˈgrʊə.lɪŋ, ˈgruː.ᵊl.ɪŋ (US) ˈgruː.lɪŋ, -ᵊl.ɪŋ

Gruenther ˈgrʌn.θəʳ (US) -θɚ

gruesome ˈgruː.səm **-ly** -li **-ness** -nəs, -nɪs

gruff grʌf **-er** -əʳ (US) -ɚ **-est** -ɪst, -əst **-ly** -li **-ness** -nəs, -nɪs

grumbl|e ˈgrʌm.bl̩ **-es** -z **-ing** -ɪŋ, ˈ-blɪŋ **-ed** -d **-er/s** -əʳ/z, ˈ-bləʳ/z (US) ˈ-bl̩.ɚ/z, ˈ-blɚ/z

grummet ˈgrʌm.ɪt, -ət **-s** -s

grump grʌmp **-s** -s

grump|y ˈgrʌm.p|i **-ier** -i.əʳ (US) -i.ɚ **-iest** -i.ɪst, -i.əst **-ily** -ɪ.li, -ᵊl.i **-iness** -ɪ.nəs, -ɪ.nɪs

Grundig® ˈgrʌn.dɪg, ˈgrʊn-

Grundtvig ˈgrʊnt.vɪg

Grundy ˈgrʌn.di

grunge grʌndʒ

grung|y ˈgrʌn.dʒ|i **-ier** -i.əʳ (US) -i.ɚ **-iest** -i.ɪst, -i.əst

grunt grʌnt **-s** -s **-ing** -ɪŋ (US) ˈgrʌn.t̬ɪŋ **-ed** -ɪd (US) ˈgrʌn.t̬ɪd **-er/s** -əʳ/z (US) ˈgrʌn.t̬ɚz

Gruyère ˈgruː.jeəʳ, -jəʳ; gruˈjeəʳ (US) gruˈjer

Pronouncing the letters G U

At the beginning of words, the consonant digraph **gu** is usually realised as /g/, e.g.:

guest /gest/

Word-finally, **gu** is usually followed by **e** in nouns and is pronounced /g/, e.g.:

fatigue /fə'tiːg/

gu may also be pronounced as /gw/, e.g.:

language /'læŋ.gwɪdʒ/

Gryll grɪl
gryphon 'grɪf.ᵊn **-s** -z
G-seven ˌdʒiː'sev.ᵊn
g-spot 'dʒiː.spɒt (US) -spɑːt
Gstaad kʃtɑːd; gə'ʃtɑːd (US) gə'ʃtɑːt, -'ʃtɑːd
G-string 'dʒiː.strɪŋ **-s** -z
GTech® 'dʒiː.tek
GTI ˌdʒiː.tiː'aɪ **-s** -z
guacamole ˌgwɑː.kə'məʊ.li, ˌgwæk-, -leɪ (US) ˌgwɑːk.ə'moʊ.li
Guadalajara ˌgwɑː.dᵊl.ə'hɑː.rə, ˌgwæd.ᵊl- (US) ˌgwɑː.dᵊl.ə'hɑːr.ə
Guadalquivir ˌgwɑː.dᵊl.kwɪ'vɪəʳ, ˌgwæd.ᵊl-, -kɪ'- (US) ˌgwɑː.dᵊl'kwɪ.vɚ, -kɪ'vɪr
Guadeloupe ˌgwɑː.də'luːp, -dᵊl'uːp, '---
Guam gwɑːm
Guangdong ˌgwæŋ'dɒŋ, ˌgwɒŋ-, -'dʊŋ (US) ˌgwɑːŋ'dɑːŋ, -'dʊŋ
Guangzhou ˌgwæŋ'ʒəʊ, ˌgwɒŋ- (US) ˌgwɑːŋ'dʒoʊ
guano 'gwɑː.nəʊ (US) -noʊ **-s** -z
Guantánamo gwæn'tæn.ə.məʊ, gwɑːn- (US) gwɑːn'tɑː.nə.moʊ
Guarani, Guaraní ˌgwɑː.rə'niː, 'gwɑː.rᵊn.i **-s** -z
guarantee ˌgær.ᵊn'tiː (US) ˌger-, ˌgær-, '--- **-s** -z **-ing** -ɪŋ **-d** -d
guarantor ˌgær.ᵊn'tɔːʳ (US) 'ger.ᵊn.tɔːr, 'gær-, ˌ--'- **-s** -z
guarant|y 'gær.ᵊn.t|i (US) 'ger.ᵊn.t̬|i, 'gær- **-ies** -iz
guard (G) gɑːd (US) gɑːrd **-s** -z **-ing** -ɪŋ **-ed/ly** -ɪd/li **-edness** -ɪd.nəs, -nɪs **'guard's ˌvan**
guardian (G) 'gɑː.di.ən (US) 'gɑːr- **-s** -z **-ship** -ʃɪp
guardrail 'gɑːd.reɪl (US) 'gɑːrd- **-s** -z
guardroom 'gɑːd.rʊm, -ruːm (US) 'gɑːrd.ruːm, -rʊm **-s** -z
guards|man 'gɑːdz|.mən, -mæn (US) 'gɑːrdz- **-men** -mən, -men
Guarneri gwɑː'neə.ri (US) gwɑːr'ner.i
Guatemal|a ˌgwæ.tə'mɑː.l|ə, ˌgwɑːt.ə'-, -ɪm'ɑː- (US) ˌgwɑː.t̬ə'- **-an/s** -ən/z
guava 'gwɑː.və **-s** -z
Guayaquil ˌgwaɪ.ə'kiːl, -'kɪl
Guayra 'gwaɪ.rə
gubbins (G) 'gʌb.ɪnz
gubernatorial ˌguː.bᵊn.ə'tɔː.ri.əl, ˌgjuː- (US) ˌguː.bɚ.nə'tɔːr.i-
Gucci® 'guː.tʃi
gudgeon 'gʌdʒ.ᵊn **-s** -z
Gudrun 'gʊd.ruːn, gʊ'druːn
Gue gjuː
guelder-ros|e 'gel.də.rəʊz, ˌ--'- (US) 'gel.dɚ.roʊz, ˌ--'- **-es** -ɪz
Guelph, Guelf gwelf **-s** -s
Guenevere 'gwɪn.ɪ.vɪəʳ, 'gwen-, '-ə- (US) -vɪr
guerdon 'gɜː.dᵊn (US) 'gɝː- **-s** -z
guerilla gə'rɪl.ə, gjə-, gɜː- (US) gə- **-s** -z
Guernica 'gɜː.nɪk.ə, 'gwɜː-; (US) 'gwer.nɪk-
guernsey (G) 'gɜːn.zi (US) 'gɝːn- **-s** -z
guerrilla gə'rɪl.ə, gjə-, gɜː- (US) gə- **-s** -z
guess ges **-es** -ɪz **-ing** -ɪŋ **-ed** -t **-er/s** -əʳ/z (US) -ɚ/z **-able** -ə.bl̩ **'guessing ˌgame**
guesstimate (*n.*) 'ges.tɪ.mət, -tə-, -mɪt, -meɪt **-s** -s
guessti|mate (*v.*) 'ges.tɪ|.meɪt, -tə- (US) -tə- **-mates** -meɪts **-mating** -meɪ.tɪŋ (US) -meɪ.t̬ɪŋ **-mated** -meɪ.tɪd (US) -meɪ.t̬ɪd
guesswork 'ges.wɜːk (US) -wɝːk
guest (G) gest **-s** -s **-ing** -ɪŋ **-ed** -ɪd **'guest ˌnight; 'guest ˌroom**
guesthou|se 'gest.haʊ|s **-ses** -zɪz
Guevara gə'vɑː.rə, gɪ-, gev'ɑː-
guff gʌf
guffaw gʌf'ɔː, gə'fɔː (US) gʌf'ɑː, -'ɔː, gə'fɑː, -'fɔː **-s** -z **-ing** -ɪŋ **-ed** -d
Guggenheim 'gʊg.ᵊn.haɪm, 'guː.gᵊn-
Guggisberg 'gʌg.ɪs.bɜːg (US) -bɝːg
Guiana gaɪ'æn.ə, gi'ɑː.nə (US) gi'æn.ə, gaɪ-, -'ɑː.nə **-s** -z
Guianese ˌgaɪ.ə'niːz (US) ˌgiː.ə'niːz, ˌgaɪ-, -'niːs *stress shift:* ˌGuianese 'people
guidance 'gaɪ.dᵊnts
guid|e gaɪd **-es** -z **-ing** -ɪŋ **-ed** -ɪd **'guide ˌdog**
guidebook 'gaɪd.bʊk **-s** -s
guideline 'gaɪd.laɪn **-s** -z
guidepost 'gaɪd.pəʊst (US) -poʊst **-s** -s
Guido 'gwiː.dəʊ, 'giː- (US) -doʊ
guidon 'gaɪ.dᵊn **-s** -z
guild gɪld **-s** -z
Guildenstern 'gɪl.dᵊn.stɜːn (US) -stɝːn
guilder 'gɪl.dəʳ (US) -dɚ **-s** -z
Guildford 'gɪl.fəd (US) -fɚd
guildhall (G) 'gɪldˌhɔːl, ˌ-'- (US) -hɔːl, -hɑːl **-s** -z
Guilding 'gɪl.dɪŋ
guile gaɪl
guileful 'gaɪl.fᵊl, -fʊl **-ly** -i **-ness** -nəs, -nɪs
guileless 'gaɪl.ləs, -lɪs **-ly** -li **-ness** -nəs, -nɪs
Guilford 'gɪl.fəd (US) -fɚd
guillemot 'gɪl.ɪ.mɒt, '-ə- (US) -ə.mɑːt **-s** -s
Guillim 'gwɪl.ɪm
guillotin|e 'gɪl.ə.tiːn, ˌ--'- **-es** -z **-ing** -ɪŋ **-ed** -d
Note: Some people use /'gɪl.ə.tiːn/ for the noun and /ˌgɪl.ə'tiːn/ for the verb.
guilt gɪlt
guiltless 'gɪlt.ləs, -lɪs **-ly** -li **-ness** -nəs, -nɪs
guilt|y 'gɪl.t|i (US) -t̬|i **-ier** -i.əʳ (US) -i.ɚ **-iest** -i.ɪst, -i.əst **-ily** -ɪ.li, -ᵊl.i **-iness** -ɪ.nəs, -ɪ.nɪs
guimpe gɪmp, gæmp **-s** -s
guinea (G) 'gɪn.i **-s** -z **'guinea ˌfowl; 'guinea ˌpig**
Guinea-Bissau ˌgɪn.i.bɪ'saʊ
Guiness 'gɪn.ɪs
Guinevere 'gwɪn.ɪ.vɪəʳ, 'gɪn-, '-ə- (US) 'gwɪn.ɪ.vɪr, '-ə-
Guinness 'gɪn.ɪs, -əs; gɪ'nes
Note: The beer is called /'gɪn.ɪs/.
guipure gɪ'pjʊəʳ (US) -'pjʊr, -'pʊr
Guisborough 'gɪz.bᵊr.ə (US) -bɚ.oʊ, -bɚ.ə
guis|e gaɪz **-es** -ɪz
Guise giːz, gwiːz
Guiseley 'gaɪz.li
guitar gɪ'tɑːʳ (US) -'tɑːr **-s** -z
guitarist gɪ'tɑː.rɪst, gə- (US) -'tɑːr.ɪst **-s** -s

Gujarat ˌgʊdʒ.əˈrɑːt, ˌguː.dʒəˈ-
Gujarati ˌgʊdʒ.əˈrɑː.ti, ˌguː.dʒəˈ- ⓊⓈ -t̬i
Gujranwala guːdʒˈrɑːn.wʌl.ə ⓊⓈ -rənˈwɑː.lə
gulag (G) ˈguː.læg, -lɑːg ⓊⓈ -lɑːg **-s** -z
Gulbenkian gʊlˈbeŋ.ki.ən
gulch gʌltʃ **-es** -ɪz
gulden ˈgʊl.dən, ˈguːl- **-s** -z
gules gjuːlz, dʒuːlz
gulf gʌlf **-s** -s **-y** -i ˌ**Gulf** ˈ**States**; ˈ**Gulf** ˌ**Stream**; ˈ**Gulf** ˌ**War** ˌ**Gulf** ˈ**War**
gull (G) gʌl **-s** -z **-ing** -ɪŋ **-ed** -d
gullet ˈgʌl.ɪt, -ət **-s** -s
gulley ˈgʌl.i **-s** -z
gullibility ˌgʌl.ɪˈbɪl.ə.ti, -əˈ-, -ɪ.ti ⓊⓈ -əˈbɪl.ə.t̬i
gullible ˈgʌl.ɪ.bl̩, ˈ-ə- ⓊⓈ ˈ-ə-
Gullit ˈhʊl.ɪt *as if Dutch* ˈxʊl.ɪt
Gulliver ˈgʌl.ɪ.vəʳ, ˈ-ə- ⓊⓈ -ə.vɚ
gull|y (G) ˈgʌl|.i **-ies** -iz
gulp gʌlp **-s** -s **-ing** -ɪŋ **-ed** -t
gum gʌm **-s** -z **-ming** -ɪŋ **-med** -d **-mer/s** -əʳ/z ⓊⓈ -ɚ/z
gumball ˈgʌm.bɔːl ⓊⓈ -bɔːl, -bɑːl **-s** -z
Gumbley ˈgʌm.bli
gumbo (G) ˈgʌm.bəʊ ⓊⓈ -boʊ **-s** -z
gumboil ˈgʌm.bɔɪl **-s** -z
gumboot ˈgʌm.buːt **-s** -s
gumdrop ˈgʌm.drɒp ⓊⓈ -drɑːp **-s** -s
Gummidge ˈgʌm.ɪdʒ
gumm|y ˈgʌm|.i **-ier** -i.əʳ ⓊⓈ -i.ɚ **-iest** -i.ɪst, -i.əst **-iness** -ɪ.nəs, -ɪ.nɪs
gumption ˈgʌmp.ʃən
gumshield ˈgʌm.ʃiːld **-s** -z
gumshoe ˈgʌm.ʃuː **-s** -z **-ing** -ɪŋ **-d** -d
gumtree ˈgʌm.triː **-s** -z
gun gʌn **-s** -z **-ning** -ɪŋ **-ned** -d **-ner/s** -əʳ/z ⓊⓈ -ɚ/z ˈ**gun** ˌ**carriage**; ˈ**gun** ˌ**dog**; ˈ**gun** ˌ**room**; ˌ**jump the** ˈ**gun**
gunboat ˈgʌn.bəʊt, ˈgʌm- ⓊⓈ ˈgʌn.boʊt **-s** -s
Gunby Hadath ˌgʌn.biˈhæd.əθ, ˌgʌm- ⓊⓈ ˌgʌn-
guncatcher ˈgʌnˌkætʃ.əʳ, ˈgʌŋ- ⓊⓈ ˈgʌnˌkætʃ.ɚ
guncotton ˈgʌn.kɒt.ən, ˈgʌŋ- ⓊⓈ ˈgʌn.kɑː.tən
gunfight ˈgʌn.faɪt **-s** -s **-er/s** -əʳ/z ⓊⓈ ɚ/z
gunfire ˈgʌn.faɪəʳ ⓊⓈ -faɪɚ
Gunga Din ˌgʌŋ.gəˈdɪn
gung|e gʌndʒ **-y** -i
gung ho ˌgʌŋˈhəʊ ⓊⓈ -ˈhoʊ
gunk gʌŋk **-y** -i
gun|man ˈgʌn|.mən, ˈgʌm-, -mæn ⓊⓈ ˈgʌn- **-men** -mən, -men
gunmetal ˈgʌnˌmet.əl, ˈgʌm- ⓊⓈ ˈgʌnˌmet̬.əl
Gunn gʌn
Gunnar ˈgʊn.ɑːʳ ⓊⓈ -ɑːr
gunnel (G) ˈgʌn.əl **-s** -z
Gunnell ˈgʌn.əl
Gunner ˈgʌn.əʳ ⓊⓈ -ɚ
Gunnersbury ˈgʌn.əz.bər.i ⓊⓈ -ɚzˌber-, -bər-
gunnery ˈgʌn.ər.i
Gunning ˈgʌn.ɪŋ
Gunnison ˈgʌn.ɪ.sən
gunny ˈgʌn.i
gunnysack ˈgʌn.i.sæk **-s** -s
gunpoint ˈgʌn.pɔɪnt, ˈgʌm- ⓊⓈ ˈgʌn-
gunpowder ˈgʌnˌpaʊ.dəʳ, ˈgʌm- ⓊⓈ ˈgʌnˌpaʊ.dɚ ˌ**Gunpowder** ˈ**Plot** ⓊⓈ ˈ**Gunpowder** ˌ**Plot**
gunrunn|er ˈgʌnˌrʌn|.əʳ ⓊⓈ -ɚ **-ers** -əz ⓊⓈ -ɚz **-ing** -ɪŋ
gunship ˈgʌn.ʃɪp **-s** -s
gunshot ˈgʌn.ʃɒt ⓊⓈ -ʃɑːt **-s** -s
gunslinger ˈgʌn.slɪŋ.əʳ **-s** -z
gunsmith ˈgʌn.smɪθ **-s** -s
Gunter ˈgʌn.təʳ ⓊⓈ -tɚ
Guntram ˈgʌn.trəm
gunwale ˈgʌn.əl **-s** -z
gupp|y (G) ˈgʌp|.i **-ies** -iz
Gupta ˈgʊp.tə, ˈgʌp.tə
gurgl|e ˈgɜː.gl̩ ⓊⓈ ˈgɝː- **-es** -z **-ing** -ɪŋ, ˈ-glɪŋ **-ed** -d
Gurkha ˈgɜː.kə ⓊⓈ ˈgɝː- **-s** -z
Gurkhali ˌgɜːˈkɑː.li, ˌgʊə- ⓊⓈ ˌgɝː-
Gurley ˈgɜː.li ⓊⓈ ˈgɝː-
Gurnall ˈgɜː.nəl ⓊⓈ ˈgɝː-
gurnard (G) ˈgɜː.nəd ⓊⓈ ˈgɝː.nɚd **-s** -z
gurnet ˈgɜː.nɪt, -nət ⓊⓈ ˈgɝː- **-s** -s
gurney (G) ˈgɜː.ni ⓊⓈ ˈgɝː-
Gurton ˈgɜː.tən ⓊⓈ ˈgɝː-
guru ˈgʊr.uː, ˈguː.ruː, ˈgʊə- ⓊⓈ ˈguː.ruː **-s** -z
Gus gʌs
gush gʌʃ **-es** -ɪz **-ing/ly** -ɪŋ/li **-ed** -t **-er/s** -əʳ/z ⓊⓈ -ɚ/z
Gushington ˈgʌʃ.ɪŋ.tən
gusset ˈgʌs.ɪt **-s** -s **-ing** -ɪŋ **-ed** -ɪd
Gussie, Gussy ˈgʌs.i
gust gʌst **-s** -s **-ing** -ɪŋ **-ed** -ɪd
Gustafson ˈgʊs.tæf.sən ⓊⓈ ˈgʌs.təf-, -tɑːf-
gustation gʌsˈteɪ.ʃən
gustatory ˈgʌs.tə.tər.i; gʌsˈteɪ- ⓊⓈ ˈgʌs.tə.tɔːr-
Gustav, Gustave ˈgʊs.tɑːv, ˈgʌs- ⓊⓈ ˈgʌs-
Gustavus gʊsˈtɑː.vəs, gʌs-, gəˈstɑː- ⓊⓈ gʌsˈteɪ.vəs, -ˈtɑː-
gusto ˈgʌs.təʊ ⓊⓈ -toʊ
gust|y ˈgʌs.t|i **-ier** -i.əʳ ⓊⓈ -i.ɚ **-iest** -i.ɪst, -i.əst **-ily** -ɪ.li, -əl.i **-iness** -ɪ.nəs, -ɪ.nɪs
gut gʌt **-s** -s **-ting** -ɪŋ ⓊⓈ ˈgʌt̬.ɪŋ **-ted** -ɪd ⓊⓈ ˈgʌt̬.ɪd
Gutenberg ˈguː.tən.bɜːg ⓊⓈ -bɝːg
Guthrie ˈgʌθ.ri
Gutierrez guːˈtjer.ez
gutless ˈgʌt.ləs, -lɪs **-ly** -li **-ness** -nəs, -nɪs
guts|y ˈgʌt.s|i **-ier** -i.əʳ ⓊⓈ -i.ɚ **-iest** -i.ɪst, -i.əst **-ily** -ɪ.li, -əl.i **-iness** -ɪ.nəs, -ɪ.nɪs
gutt|a ˈgʌt|.ə ⓊⓈ ˈgʌt̬|.ə **-ae** -iː
gutta-percha ˌgʌt.əˈpɜː.tʃə ⓊⓈ ˌgʌt̬.əˈpɝː-
gutt|er ˈgʌt|.əʳ ⓊⓈ ˈgʌt̬|.ɚ **-ers** -əz ⓊⓈ -ɚz **-ering** -ər.ɪŋ **-ered** -əd ⓊⓈ -ɚd ˌ**gutter** ˈ**press** ⓊⓈ ˈ**gutter** ˌ**press**
guttersnipe ˈgʌt.ə.snaɪp ⓊⓈ ˈgʌt̬.ɚ- **-s** -s
guttural ˈgʌt.ər.əl ⓊⓈ ˈgʌt̬- **-s** -z **-ly** -i
guv gʌv
guvnor ˈgʌv.nəʳ ⓊⓈ -nɚ **-s** -z
guy (G) gaɪ **-s** -z
Guyana gaɪˈɑː.nə, giˈɑː.nə ⓊⓈ giˈæn.ə, gaɪ-, -ˈɑː.nə
Guyanese ˌgaɪ.əˈniːz ⓊⓈ ˌgiː.əˈniːz, ˌgaɪ-, -ˈniːs *stress shift:* ˌGuyanese ˈpeople
Guy Fawkes ˌgaɪˈfɔːks, ˈ-- ⓊⓈ -ˈfɔːks, -ˈfɑːks *stress shift, see compound:* ˈ**Guy Fawkes** ˌ**night**
Guylian ˈgiː.li.ən
Guysborough ˈgaɪz.bər.ə ⓊⓈ -bɚ.oʊ
guzzl|e ˈgʌz.l̩ **-es** -z **-ing** -ɪŋ, ˈ-lɪŋ **-ed** -d **-er/s** -əʳ/z, ˈ-ləʳ/z ⓊⓈ ˈ-l̩.ɚ/z, ˈ-lɚ/z
Gwalia ˈgwɑː.li.ə
Gwalior ˈgwɑː.li.ɔːʳ ⓊⓈ -ɔːr
Gwatkin ˈgwɒt.kɪn ⓊⓈ ˈgwɑːt-
Gwaun-Cae-Gurwen ˌgwaɪn.kəˈgɜː.wən, ˌgwaɪŋ- ⓊⓈ -ˈgɝː-
Gwen gwen
Gwenda ˈgwen.də
Gwendol|en ˈgwen.də.l|ɪn, -dəl.|ɪn **-ine** -ɪn, -iːn **-yn** -ɪn
Gwent gwent
Gwersyllt ˌgweəˈsɪlt ⓊⓈ ˌgwer-
Gwinnett gwɪˈnet
Gwladys ˈglæd.ɪs
Gwrych gʊˈriːk, -ˈriːx
Gwydion ˈgwɪd.i.ən
Gwydyr ˈgwɪd.ɪəʳ, -əʳ; ⓊⓈ ˈgwɪd.ɪr
Gwynedd ˈgwɪn.əð, -ɪð, -eð
Gwyneth ˈgwɪn.əθ, -ɪθ, -eθ
gwyniad ˈgwɪn.i.æd **-s** -z
Gwyn(ne) gwɪn
gyb|e dʒaɪb **-es** -z **-ing** -ɪŋ **-ed** -d
Gye dʒaɪ, gaɪ
Gyges ˈgaɪ.dʒiːz
Gyle gaɪl
Gyles gaɪlz
gym dʒɪm **-s** -z
gymkhana dʒɪmˈkɑː.nə **-s** -z
gymnas|ium dʒɪmˈneɪ.z|i.əm **-iums** -z **-ia** -i.ə
gymnast ˈdʒɪm.næst ⓊⓈ -næst, -nəst **-s** -s
gymnastic dʒɪmˈnæs.tɪk **-s** -s **-al** -əl **-ally** -əl.i, -li

gymnosophist dʒɪmˈnɒs.ə.fɪst (US) -ˈnɑː.sə- **-s** -s
gymnosperm ˈdʒɪm.nəʊ.spɜːm, ˈgɪm- (US) -nə.spɝːm **-s** -z
gymnospermous ˌdʒɪm.nəʊˈspɜː.məs, ˌgɪm- (US) -nəˈspɝː-
Gympie ˈgɪm.pi
gymslip ˈdʒɪm.slɪp **-s** -s
gyn(a)ecological ˌgaɪ.nə.kəˈlɒdʒ.ɪ.kəl, -nɪ- (US) -ˈlɑː.dʒɪ- **-li** -i
gyn(a)ecolog|y ˌgaɪ.nəˈkɒl.ə.dʒ|i, -ɪˈ- (US) -ˈkɑː.lə- **-ist/s** -ɪst/s
gyneci|um ˌdʒaɪˈniː.si|əm, ˌgaɪ- **-a** -ə
Gyngell ˈgɪn.dʒəl
gynoeci|um ˌdʒaɪˈniː.si|.əm, ˌgaɪ- **-a** -ə
Györ djɜːʳ (US) djɝː, djɔːr
gyp dʒɪp **-s** -s **-ping** -ɪŋ **-ped** -t
Gyp *nickname:* dʒɪp *French novelist:* ʒiːp
gypsophila dʒɪpˈsɒf.ɪ.lə, -əl.ə (US) -ˈsɑː.fɪ- **-s** -z
gypsum ˈdʒɪp.səm
gyps|y ˈdʒɪp.s|i **-ies** -iz
gyrate (*adj.*) ˈdʒaɪə.rət, -reɪt, -rɪt (US) ˈdʒaɪ.reɪt
gy|rate (*v.*) dʒaɪə|ˈreɪt (US) ˈdʒaɪ|.reɪt **-rates** -ˈreɪts (US) -reɪts **-rating** -ˈreɪ.tɪŋ (US) -reɪ.t̬ɪŋ **-rated** -ˈreɪ.tɪd (US) -reɪ.t̬ɪd
gyration dʒaɪəˈreɪ.ʃən (US) dʒaɪ- **-s** -z
gyratory ˈdʒaɪə.rə.tər.i; dʒaɪəˈreɪ- (US) ˈdʒaɪ.rə.tɔːr-
gyr|e dʒaɪəʳ (US) dʒaɪɚ **-es** -z **-ing** -ɪŋ **-ed** -d
gyrfalcon ˈdʒɜːˌfɔːl.kən, ˈdʒɪə-, -ˌfɔː- (US) ˈdʒɝː.fæl-, -fɔːl- **-s** -z
gyro- dʒaɪə.rəʊ- (US) dʒaɪ.roʊ-, -rə-
Note: Prefix. Normally takes either primary or secondary stress on the first syllable, e.g. **gyroscope** /ˈdʒaɪə.rə.skəʊp (US) ˈdʒaɪ.rə.skoʊp/, **gyroscopic** /ˌdʒaɪə.rəˈskɒp.ɪk (US) ˌdʒaɪ.rəˈskɑː.pɪk/.
gyro ˈdʒaɪə.rəʊ (US) ˈdʒaɪ.roʊ, ˈgɪr.oʊ **-s** -z
gyrocompass ˈdʒaɪə.rəʊˌkʌm.pəs (US) ˈdʒaɪ.roʊ- **-es** -ɪz
gyromagnetic ˌdʒaɪə.rəʊ.mægˈnet.ɪk, -məgˈ- (US) ˌdʒaɪ.roʊ.mægˈnet̬.ɪk
gyron ˈdʒaɪə.rən, -rɒn (US) ˈdʒaɪ.rən, -rɑːn **-s** -z
gyroscope ˈdʒaɪə.rə.skəʊp (US) ˈdʒaɪ.rə.skoʊp **-s** -s
gyroscopic ˌdʒaɪə.rəˈskɒp.ɪk (US) ˌdʒaɪ.rəˈskɑː.pɪk **-ally** -əl.i, -li
gyrostat ˈdʒaɪə.rəʊ.stæt (US) ˈdʒaɪ.rə-, -roʊ- **-s** -s
gyrostatic ˌdʒaɪə.rəʊˈstæt.ɪk (US) ˌdʒaɪ.rəˈstæt̬- **-s** -s
gyv|e dʒaɪv **es**-z **-ing** -ɪŋ **-ed** -d

Pronouncing the letter H

There are two main pronunciations for the consonant letter **h**: /h/ and silent.

The usual pronunciation is /h/, e.g.:

head	/hed/

h has a silent realisation at the end of a word, e.g.:

oh	/əʊ/	(US) /oʊ/
loofah	/ˈluː.fə/	

There is a group of words in which it is also silent initially: *heir, honest, honour* and *hour*, and their derivatives, and *herb* for American English.

Following an initial **r**, **h** is silent, e.g.:

rhythm	/ˈrɪð.ᵊm/

In weak forms, **h** is often not pronounced, e.g.:

him	/ɪm/
have	/əv/

h (H) eɪtʃ **-'s** -ɪz
H_2O ˌeɪtʃ.tuːˈəʊ (US) -ˈoʊ
ha *exclamation:* hɑː
ha *(abbrev. for* **hectare***)* ˈhek.teəʳ, -tɑːʳ, -təʳ (US) -ter
Haagen Dazs® ˌhɑː.gənˈdɑːz (US) ˈhɑː.gənˌdæs
Haakon ˈhɔː.kɒn, ˈhɑː-, -kᵊn (US) ˈhɔː.kʊn, ˈhɑː-, -kɑːn, -kən
Haarlem ˈhɑː.ləm, -lem (US) ˈhɑːr-
Habacuc, Habakkuk ˈhæb.ə.kək, -kʌk; həˈbæk.ək
Habberton ˈhæb.ə.tən (US) -ɚ.t̬ən
habeas corpus ˌheɪ.bi.əsˈkɔː.pəs, -æsˈ- (US) -ˈkɔːr-
haberdasher ˈhæb.ə.dæʃ.əʳ (US) -ɚ.dæʃ.ɚ **-s** -z
haberdasher|y ˌhæb.əˈdæʃ.ᵊr|.i, ˈhæb.ə.dæʃ- (US) ˈhæb.ɚ.dæʃ- **-ies** -iz
Habgood ˈhæb.gʊd
Habibie həˈbiː.bi, hæbˈiː-
habiliment həˈbɪl.ɪ.mənt, hæbˈɪl-, ˈ-ə- (US) həˈbɪl.ə- **-s** -s
habili|tate həˈbɪl.ɪ|teɪt, hæbˈɪl-, ˈ-ə- (US) həˈbɪl.ə- **-tates** -teɪts **-tating** -teɪ.tɪŋ (US) -teɪ.t̬ɪŋ **-tated** -teɪ.tɪd (US) -teɪ.t̬ɪd
habilitation həˌbɪl.ɪˈteɪ.ʃᵊn, hæbˌɪl-, -əˈ- (US) həˌbɪl.əˈ-
Habington ˈhæb.ɪŋ.tən
habit ˈhæb.ɪt **-s** -s
habitab|le ˈhæb.ɪ.tə.b|l̩ (US) -t̬ə- **-ly** -li **-leness** -l̩.nəs, -nɪs
habitant *inhabitant:* ˈhæb.ɪ.tᵊnt (US) -t̬ᵊnt **-s** -s
habitant *in Canada and Louisiana:* ˈhæb.ɪ.tɔ̃ːŋ, ˈæb-, -tɒŋ (US) ˈhæb.ɪ.tɑːnt, -tɑ̃nt; ˌæb.iˈtɑːn **-s** -z
habitat (H®) ˈhæb.ɪ.tæt, ˈ-ə- **-s** -s
habitation ˌhæb.ɪˈteɪ.ʃᵊn, -əˈ- **-s** -z
habit-forming ˈhæb.ɪtˌfɔː.mɪŋ (US) -ˌfɔːr-
habit|ual həˈbɪtʃ|.u.əl, hæbˈɪtʃ-, -ˈbɪt.j|u- (US) həˈbɪtʃ|.u.əl **-ually** -ʊ.li, -ə.li
habitu|ate həˈbɪtʃ.u|.eɪt, hæbˈɪtʃ-, -ˈbɪt.ju- (US) həˈbɪtʃ.u- **-ates** -eɪts **-ating** -eɪ.tɪŋ (US) -eɪ.t̬ɪŋ **-ated** -eɪ.tɪd (US) -eɪ.t̬ɪd
habitude ˈhæb.ɪ.tjuːd, -tʃuːd (US) -tuːd, -tjuːd **-s** -z
habitué həˈbɪt.ju.eɪ, hæbˈɪt-, -ˈbɪtʃ.u.eɪ (US) həˌbɪtʃ.uˈeɪ, həˈbɪtʃ.u.eɪ **-s** -z
Note: Also occasionally /əˈbɪt.ju.eɪ/ in British English, when not initial.
Habsburg ˈhæps.bɜːg (US) -bɝːg
hacek ˈhɑː.tʃek, ˈhætʃ.ek
hachure hæʃˈjʊəʳ, -ˈʊəʳ (US) hæʃˈʊr, -ˈjʊr, ˈhæʃ.ʊr **-s** -z
hacienda ˌhæs.iˈen.də (US) ˌhɑː.siˈ- **-s** -z
hack (H) hæk **-s** -s **-ing** -ɪŋ **-ed** -t
hackamore ˈhæk.ə.mɔːʳ (US) -mɔːr **-s** -z
hackberr|y ˈhækˌberǀ.i, -bᵊr|.i (US) -ˌber- **-ies** -iz
hacker (H) ˈhæk.əʳ (US) -ɚ **-s** -z
Hackett ˈhæk.ɪt
hackl|e ˈhæk.l̩ **-es** -z **-ing** -ɪŋ, ˈhæk.lɪŋ **-ed** -d
hackney (H) ˈhæk.ni **-s** -z **-ed** -d
hacksaw ˈhæk.sɔː (US) -sɑː, -sɔː **-s** -z
hackwork ˈhæk.wɜːk (US) -wɝːk
had *(from* **have***) strong form:* hæd *weak forms:* həd, əd, d
Note: The strong form is used when **had** is used as a full verb rather than an auxiliary, e.g. 'We had some tea.' The auxiliary verb is a weak form word: the strong form /hæd/ is used contrastively, e.g. 'I don't know if she had or she hadn't', in final position, e.g. 'I'd read as much as he had' and quite frequently in initial position, e.g. 'Had anyone seen it before?'. It is also used for emphasis, e.g. 'It had to break down when it was raining'. Elsewhere, the weak form is usually /həd/ or /əd/. The form /d/ is usually used only after vowels.
Hadar ˈheɪ.dɑːʳ (US) -dɑːr
hadarim *(plur. of* **heder***)* ˌhæd.ɑːˈriːm (US) ˌhɑː- *as if Hebrew:* ˌxæd- (US) ˌxɑː-
Hadden ˈhæd.ᵊn
Haddington ˈhæd.ɪŋ.tən
haddock (H) ˈhæd.ək **-s** -s
Haddon ˈhæd.ᵊn
had|e heɪd **-es** -z **-ing** -ɪŋ **-ed** -ɪd
Haden ˈheɪ.dᵊn
Hades ˈheɪ.diːz
Hadfield ˈhæd.fiːld
hadj hædʒ, hɑːdʒ (US) hædʒ **-es** -ɪz
hadji ˈhædʒ.i, ˈhɑː.dʒi, -dʒiː (US) ˈhædʒ.iː **-s** -z
Hadleigh, Hadley ˈhæd.li
Hadlow ˈhæd.ləʊ (US) -loʊ
hadn't ˈhæd.ᵊnt
Hadrian ˈheɪ.dri.ən ˌ**Hadrian's** ˈ**Wall**
hadst *strong form:* hædst *weak form:* hədst
Note: Weak form word, rarely used. See the note for **had**.
haecceity hekˈsiː.ə.ti, hiːk-, haɪk-, -ɪ.ti (US) hekˈsiː.ə.t̬i, hiːk-
haem hiːm
haematite ˈhiː.mə.taɪt, ˈhem.ə- (US) ˈhiː.mə-
haematologic ˌhiː.mə.təˈlɒdʒ.ɪk (US) -t̬əˈlɑːdʒ- **-al** -ᵊl
haematolog|y ˌhiː.məˈtɒl.ə.dʒ|i (US) -ˈtɑː.lə- **-ist/s** -ɪst/s
haematoma ˌhiː.məˈtəʊ.mə, ˌhem.əˈ- (US) ˌhiː.məˈtoʊ- **-s** -əz **-ta** -tə
haemoglobin ˌhiː.məʊˈgləʊ.bɪn, ˌhem.əʊˈ- (US) ˈhiː.mə.gloʊ-, -mə-
haemophili|a ˌhiː.məˈfɪl.i|.ə, ˌhem.əˈ- (US) ˌhiː.moʊˈ-, -məˈ-, -ˈfiːl.j|ə **-ac/s** -æk/s
haemorrhag|e ˈhem.ᵊr.ɪdʒ (US) -ɚ.ɪdʒ, ˈ-rɪdʒ **-es** -ɪz **-ing** -ɪŋ **-ed** -d
haemorrhoid ˈhem.ᵊr.ɔɪd (US) -ə.rɔɪd, ˈ-rɔɪd **-s** -z
haemosta|sis ˌhiː.məˈsteɪ|.sɪs, ˌhem.əˈ- (US) ˌhiː.məˈ- **-ses** -siːz
hafnium ˈhæf.ni.əm
haft hɑːft (US) hæft **-s** -s
hag hæg **-s** -s

Hag® hɑːg
Hagan ˈheɪ.gᵊn ⓤⓢ ˈheɪ-, ˈhɑː-
Hagar *biblical name:* ˈheɪ.gɑːʳ, -gəʳ ⓤⓢ -gɑːr *modern personal name:* ˈheɪ.gəʳ ⓤⓢ -gɑːr, -gɚ
Hagarene ˈhæg.ᵊr.iːn, ˈheɪ.gᵊr-, ˌ--ˈ- ⓤⓢ ˈhæg.ə.riːn, ˈheɪ.gə- **-s** -z
Hagerstown ˈheɪ.gəz.taʊn ⓤⓢ -gɚz-
Haggada(h) hægˈʌd.ə, -ˈɒd- ⓤⓢ həˈgɑː.dɑː, -də; ˌhɑː.gɑːˈdɑː
Haggai ˈhæg.eɪ.aɪ, -i.aɪ, ˈhæg.aɪ; hægˈeɪ.aɪ ⓤⓢ ˈhæg.i.aɪ, ˈhæg.aɪ
Haggar ˈhæg.ɑːʳ, -əʳ ⓤⓢ -ɑːr, -ɚ
haggard (H) ˈhæg.əd ⓤⓢ -ɚd **-ly** -li **-ness** -nəs, -nɪs
Hagger ˈhæg.əʳ ⓤⓢ -ɚ
Haggerston ˈhæg.ə.stᵊn ⓤⓢ ˈ-ɚ-
haggis ˈhæg.ɪs **-es** -ɪz
haggl|e ˈhæg.l̩ **-es** -z **-ing** -ɪŋ, ˈhæg.lɪŋ **-ed** -d **-er/s** -əʳ/z ⓤⓢ -ɚ/z, ˈhæg.ləʳ/z ⓤⓢ -lɚ/z
hagiograph|y ˌhæg.iˈɒg.rə.f|i, ˌheɪ.dʒiˈ- ⓤⓢ -ˈɑː.grə- **-er/s** -əʳ/z ⓤⓢ -ɚ/z
hagiolatry ˌhæg.iˈɒl.ə.tri, ˌheɪ.dʒiˈ- ⓤⓢ -ˈɑː.lə-
hagiolog|y ˌhæg.iˈɒl.ə.dʒ|i, ˌheɪ.dʒiˈ- ⓤⓢ -ˈɑː.lə- **-ist/s** -ɪst/s
hagioscope ˈhæg.i.ə.skəʊp, ˈheɪ.dʒi- ⓤⓢ -skoʊp **-s** -s
Hagley ˈhæg.li
Hagman ˈhæg.mən
hagridden ˈhægˌrɪd.ᵊn
Hague heɪg
ha-ha (*interj.*) hɑːˈhɑː, ˈ--
ha-ha *sunken fence:* ˈhɑː.hɑː **-s** -z
Hahn hɑːn
hahnium ˈhɑː.ni.əm
Haider ˈhaɪ.dəʳ ⓤⓢ -dɚ
Haifa ˈhaɪ.fə
Haig heɪg
Haigh heɪg, heɪ
Haight-Ashbury ˌheɪtˈæʃ.bᵊr.i ⓤⓢ -ˌber-
haiku ˈhaɪ.kuː
hail heɪl **-s** -z **-ing** -ɪŋ **-ed** -d ˌ**Hail ˈMary**
Hailes heɪlz
Haile Selassie ˌhaɪ.li.səˈlæs.i, -sɪˈ- ⓤⓢ -ˈlæs.i, -ˈlɑː.si
Hailey ˈheɪ.li
Haileybury ˈheɪ.lɪ.bᵊr.i ⓤⓢ -ˌber-
hail-fellow-well-met ˌheɪl,fel.əʊ,welˈmet ⓤⓢ ˌ-oʊˌ-
Hailsham ˈheɪl.ʃəm
hailstone ˈheɪl.stəʊn ⓤⓢ -stoʊn **-s** -z
hailstorm ˈheɪl.stɔːm ⓤⓢ -stɔːrm **-s** -z
Hain heɪn
Hainan ˌhaɪˈnæn
Hainault ˈheɪ.nɔːt, -nɔːlt, -nɒlt ⓤⓢ -nɑːlt, -nɔːlt
Haines heɪnz
Haiphong ˌhaɪˈfɒŋ ⓤⓢ -ˈfɑːŋ
hair heəʳ ⓤⓢ her **-s** -z ˈ**hair** ˌ**gel**; ˈ**hair's** ˌ**breadth**; ˈ**hair** ˌ**piece**; ˌ**hair** ˈ**shirt**; ˈ**hair** ˌ**slide**; ˌ**hair** ˈ**trigger**; **let one's** ˈ**hair** ˌ**down**; ˌ**make someone's** ˈ**hair stand on** ˌ**end**
hairball ˈheə.bɔːl ⓤⓢ ˈher-, -bɑːl **-s** -z
hairband ˈheə.bænd ⓤⓢ ˈher- **-s** -z
hairbreadth ˈheə.bretθ, -bredθ ⓤⓢ ˈher- **-s** -s
hairbrush ˈheə.brʌʃ ⓤⓢ ˈher- **-es** -ɪz
haircloth ˈheə.klɒθ ⓤⓢ ˈher.klɑːθ
haircut ˈheə.kʌt ⓤⓢ ˈher- **-s** -s
haircutt|er ˈheəˌkʌt|.əʳ ⓤⓢ ˈherˌkʌt̬|.ɚ **-ers** -əz ⓤⓢ -ɚz **-ing** -ɪŋ
hairdo ˈheə.duː ⓤⓢ ˈher- **-s** -z
hairdress|er ˈheəˌdres|.əʳ ⓤⓢ ˈherˌdres|.ɚ **-ers** -ez ⓤⓢ -ɚz **-ing** -ɪŋ
hairdryer, hairdrier ˈheəˌdraɪ.əʳ ⓤⓢ ˈherˌdraɪ.ɚ **-s** -z
-haired -ˈheəd ⓤⓢ -herd
Note: Suffix. Compounds ending **-haired** normally carry primary stress on the suffix in British English, but there is a stress shift when such words are used attributively, e.g. ˌ**goldenhaired** ˈ**child**. In American English, compounds ending **-haired** are normally stressed on the first element, e.g. **goldenhaired** /ⓤⓢ ˈgoʊl.dᵊn.herd/.
hairgrass ˈheə.grɑːs ⓤⓢ ˈher.græs
hairgrip ˈheə.grɪp ⓤⓢ ˈher- **-s** -s
hairless ˈheə.ləs, -lɪs ⓤⓢ ˈher- **-ness** -nəs, -nɪs
hairline ˈheə.laɪn ⓤⓢ ˈher- **-s** -z
hairnet ˈheə.net ⓤⓢ ˈher- **-s** -s
hairpiec|e ˈheə.piːs ⓤⓢ ˈher- **-es** -ɪz
hairpin ˈheə.pɪn ⓤⓢ ˈher- **-s** -z ˌ**hairpin** ˈ**bend**; ˌ**hairpin** ˈ**turn**
hair-raising ˈheəˌreɪ.zɪŋ ⓤⓢ ˈher-
hairsplitting ˈheəˌsplɪt.ɪŋ ⓤⓢ ˈherˌsplɪt̬-
hairspray ˈheə.spreɪ ⓤⓢ ˈher- **-s** -z
hairspring ˈheə.sprɪŋ ⓤⓢ ˈher- **-s** -z
hairstyle ˈheə.staɪl ⓤⓢ ˈher- **-s** -z
hairstylist ˈheəˌstaɪ.lɪst ⓤⓢ ˈher- **-s** -s
hair|y ˈheə.r|i ⓤⓢ ˈher|.i **-ier** -i.əʳ ⓤⓢ -i.ɚ **-iest** -i.ɪst, -i.əst **-iness** -ɪ.nəs, -ɪ.nɪs
Haiti ˈheɪ.ti, ˈhaɪ-; haɪˈiː.ti, hɑː- ⓤⓢ ˈheɪ.t̬i, -ti
Haitian ˈheɪ.ʃᵊn, -ʃi.ən, -ti-; haɪˈiː.ʃᵊn, hɑː-, -ʃi.ən ⓤⓢ ˈheɪ.ʃᵊn, -ti.ən **-s** -z
Haitink ˈhaɪ.tɪŋk
hajj hædʒ, hɑːdʒ ⓤⓢ hædʒ
hajji ˈhædʒ.i, ˈhɑː.dʒi, -dʒiː ⓤⓢ ˈhædʒ.iː **-s** -z
haka ˈhɑː.kə **-s** -z
hake heɪk **-s** -s
hakim *doctor:* hɑːˈkiːm, hə-, hækˈiːm ⓤⓢ hɑːˈkiːm **-s** -z *ruler:* ˈhɑː.kiːm, -ˈ- ⓤⓢ ˈhɑː.kiːm, -kɪm
Hakkinen ˈhæk.ɪ.nən
Hakluyt ˈhæk.luːt
Hakodate ˌhæk.əʊˈdɑː.ti ⓤⓢ ˌhɑː.koʊˈdɑː.teɪ
Hal hæl
Halakah hælˈʌk.ə ⓤⓢ ˌhɑː.lɑːˈkɑː, -ˈxɑː; həˈlɑː.kə, -xə
halal hælˈæl; həˈlɑːl
halala, halalah həˈlæl.ə, hælˈæl.ə ⓤⓢ həˈlɑː.lə **-s** -z
halation həˈleɪ.ʃᵊn, hælˈeɪ- ⓤⓢ həˈleɪ- **-s** -z
halberd ˈhæl.bəd, ˈhɔːl-, -bɜːd ⓤⓢ ˈhæl.bɚd, ˈhɑːl- **-s** -z
halberdier ˌhæl.bəˈdɪəʳ ⓤⓢ -bɚˈdɪr **-s** -z
halcyon ˈhæl.si.ən **-s** -z
Halcyone hælˈsaɪə.ni
Haldane ˈhɔːl.deɪn, ˈhɒl- ⓤⓢ ˈhɔːl-, ˈhɑːl-
Haldon ˈhɔːl.dᵊn
hal|e (H) (*adj. v.*) heɪl **-er** -əʳ ⓤⓢ -ɚ **-est** -ɪst, -əst **-es** -z **-ing** -ɪŋ **-ed** -d
haler ˈhɑː.ləʳ ⓤⓢ -lɚ, -ler **-s** -z **-u** -uː
Hales heɪlz
Halesowen ˌheɪlzˈəʊ.ɪn, -ən ⓤⓢ -ˈoʊ-
Halesworth ˈheɪlz.wəθ, -wɜːθ ⓤⓢ -wɝːθ, -wɚθ
Halex® ˈheɪ.leks
Haley ˈheɪ.li
hal|f hɑː|f ⓤⓢ hæ|f **-ves** -vz ˌ**half a** ˈ**dozen**; ˌ**half an** ˈ**hour**; ˌ**half** ˈ**cock**; ˌ**half** ˈ**measures**; ˌ**half** ˈ**nelson**; ˌ**half** ˈ**pay**; ˌ**half** ˈ**term**
Note: Compound words beginning with **half-** usually have secondary stress on this syllable and primary stress later in the compound word (e.g. **half-baked** has the stress pattern ˈ-ˌ-); however, the word is liable to undergo stress shift when a strongly stressed syllable follows (e.g. **half-baked plan** often has the pattern ˈ--ˌ-). Since there are many such words, notes about this stress shift for individual words are not given.
half-a-crown ˌhɑːf.əˈkraʊn ⓤⓢ ˌhæf-
halfback ˈhɑːf.bæk ⓤⓢ ˈhæf- **-s** -s
half-baked ˌhɑːfˈbeɪkt ⓤⓢ ˌhæf-
half-blood ˈhɑːf.blʌd ⓤⓢ ˈhæf-
half-board ˌhɑːfˈbɔːd ⓤⓢ ˌhæfˈbɔːrd
half-bred ˈhɑːf.bred ⓤⓢ ˈhæf-
half-breed ˈhɑːf.briːd ⓤⓢ ˈhæf- **-s** -z
half-brother ˈhɑːfˌbrʌð.əʳ ⓤⓢ ˈhæfˌbrʌð.ɚ **-s** -z
half-caste ˈhɑːf.kɑːst ⓤⓢ ˈhæf.kæst **-s** -s
half-crown ˌhɑːfˈkraʊn ⓤⓢ ˌhæf- **-s** -z
half-dozen ˌhɑːfˈdʌz.ᵊn ⓤⓢ ˌhæf- **-s** -z
half-hardy ˌhɑːfˈhɑː.di ⓤⓢ ˌhæfˈhɑːr-
half-hearted ˌhɑːfˈhɑː.tɪd ⓤⓢ ˌhæfˈhɑːr.t̬ɪd
half-hearted|ly ˌhɑːfˈhɑː.tɪd|.li ⓤⓢ ˌhæfˈhɑːr.t̬ɪd- **-ness** -nəs, -nɪs

half-holiday ˌhɑːfˈhɒl.ə.deɪ, ˈ-ɪ-, -di ⓤⓢ ˌhæfˈhɑː.lə.deɪ **-s** -z

half-hour ˌhɑːfˈaʊəʳ ⓤⓢ ˌhæfˈaʊr, -ˈaʊɚ **-s** -z

half-hourly ˌhɑːfˈaʊə.li ⓤⓢ ˌhæfˈaʊr-, -ˈaʊɚ-

half-length ˌhɑːfˈleŋθ, -ˈleŋkθ ⓤⓢ ˌhæf- **-s** -s

half-li|fe ˈhɑːf.laɪ|f ⓤⓢ ˈhæf- **-ves** -vz

half-mast ˌhɑːfˈmɑːst ⓤⓢ ˌhæfˈmæst

half-moon ˌhɑːfˈmuːn ⓤⓢ ˌhæf- **-s** -z

Halford ˈhæl.fəd, ˈhɔːl-, ˈhɒl- ⓤⓢ ˈhæl.fɚd, ˈhɔːl-, ˈhɑːl-

halfpence ˈheɪ.pᵊnts

halfpenn|y ˈheɪp.n|i, ˈheɪ.pᵊn|.i **-ies** -iz

Halfpenny ˈhɑːf.pen.i, -pə.ni ⓤⓢ ˈhæf-

halfpennyworth ˈheɪp.ni.wəθ, ˈheɪ.pᵊn.i-, -wɜːθ; ˌhɑːfˈpen.əθ ⓤⓢ ˈheɪ.pᵊn.i.wɝːθ **-s** -s

half-pint ˌhɑːfˈpaɪnt ⓤⓢ ˌhæf- **-s** -s

half-price ˌhɑːfˈpraɪs ⓤⓢ ˌhæf-

half-sister ˈhɑːfˌsɪs.təʳ ⓤⓢ ˈhæfˌsɪs.tɚ **-s** -z

half-size ˌhɑːfˈsaɪz ⓤⓢ ˈhæf.saɪz

half-time ˌhɑːfˈtaɪm ⓤⓢ ˈhæf.taɪm

halftone ˌhɑːfˈtəʊn ⓤⓢ ˈhæf.toʊn **-s** -z

half-tru|th ˌhɑːfˈtruː|θ ⓤⓢ ˈhæf.truː|θ **-ths** -ðz

half-volley ˌhɑːfˈvɒl.i ⓤⓢ ˈhæfˌvɑː.li **-s** -z

halfway ˌhɑːfˈweɪ ⓤⓢ ˌhæf- ˌ**halfway** ˈ**house** ⓤⓢ ˈ**halfway** ˌ**house**

half-wit ˈhɑːf.wɪt ⓤⓢ ˈhæf- **-s** -s

half-witted ˌhɑːfˈwɪt.ɪd ⓤⓢ ˌhæfˈwɪt̬-

half-year ˌhɑːfˈjɪəʳ ⓤⓢ ˌhæfˈjɪr **-s** -z **-ly** -li

Haliburton ˌhæl.ɪˈbɜː.tᵊn ⓤⓢ ˈhæl.ɪ.bɝː-

halibut ˈhæl.ɪ.bət, -bʌt **-s** -s

Halicarnassus ˌhæl.ɪ.kɑːˈnæs.əs ⓤⓢ -kɑːrˈ-

halidom ˈhæl.ɪ.dəm

Halidon ˈhæl.ɪ.dᵊn

Halifax ˈhæl.ɪ.fæks

halitosis ˌhæl.ɪˈtəʊ.sɪs ⓤⓢ -ˈtoʊ-

Halkett ˈhɔːl.kɪt, ˈhæl.kɪt, ˈhæk.ɪt

hall (H) hɔːl ⓤⓢ hɔːl, hɑːl **-s** -z ˌ**Hall of** ˈ**Fame**; ˌ**hall of** ˈ**residence**; ˈ**residence** ˌ**hall**

hallal hælˈæl, həˈlɑːl

Hallam ˈhæl.əm

Hallé ˈhæl.eɪ, -i ⓤⓢ ˈhæl.eɪ

Halle ˈhæl.ə ⓤⓢ ˈhɑː.lə

hallelujah (H) ˌhæl.ɪˈluː.jə, -əˈ- **-s** -z

Haller ˈhæl.əʳ ⓤⓢ -ɚ

Hallett ˈhæl.ɪt

Halley ˈhæl.i, ˈhɔː.li ⓤⓢ ˈhæl.i, ˈheɪ.li ˌ**Halley's** ˈ**Comet**

Note: Halley's Comet is usually referred to as /ˈhæl.iz/, with the popular variant /ˈheɪ.liz/ in the US.

halliard ˈhæl.jəd, -i.əd ⓤⓢ -jɚd **-s** -z

Halliday ˈhæl.ɪ.deɪ, ˈ-ə-

Halliwell ˈhæl.ɪ.wel

hallmark ˈhɔːl.mɑːk ⓤⓢ -mɑːrk, ˈhɑːl- **-s** -s **-ing** -ɪŋ **-ed** -t

hallo(a) həˈləʊ, hælˈəʊ, helˈ-, ˈhʌl.əʊ ⓤⓢ həˈloʊ

halloo həˈluː, hælˈuː ⓤⓢ həˈluː **-s** -z **-ing** -ɪŋ **-ed** -d

hallow ˈhæl.əʊ ⓤⓢ -oʊ **-s** -z **-ing** -ɪŋ **-ed** -d

Halloween, Hallowe'en ˌhæl.əʊˈiːn ⓤⓢ ˌhæl.oʊˈ-, ˌhɑː.loʊˈ-, -ləˈwiːn

Hallowmas ˈhæl.əʊ.mæs, -məs ⓤⓢ -oʊ- **-es** -ɪz

Hallows ˈhæl.əʊz ⓤⓢ -oʊz

hallstand ˈhɔːl.stænd ⓤⓢ ˈhɔːl-, ˈhɑːl- **-s** -z

halluci|nate həˈluː.sɪ|.neɪt, -ˈljuː-, -sə- ⓤⓢ -ˈluː- **-nates** -neɪts **-nating** -neɪ.tɪŋ ⓤⓢ -neɪ.t̬ɪŋ **-nated** -neɪ.tɪd ⓤⓢ -neɪ.t̬ɪd

hallucination həˌluː.sɪˈneɪ.ʃᵊn, -ˌljuː-, -səˈ- ⓤⓢ -ˌluː- **-s** -z

hallucinatory həˈluː.sɪ.nə.tᵊr.i, -ˈljuː-, -sᵊn.ə-, -tri; həˌluː.sɪˈneɪ-, -ˌljuː-, -sᵊnˈeɪ- ⓤⓢ həˈluː.sɪ.nə.tɔːr.i

hallucinogen həˈluː.sɪ.nə.dʒen, -dʒᵊn; ˌhæl.uːˈsɪn- ⓤⓢ həˈluː.sɪ.nə.dʒen; ˌhæl.juːˈsɪn.ə-, -jəˈ- **-s** -z

hallucinogenic həˌluː.sɪ.nəʊˈdʒen.ɪk, -ˌljuː-, -sᵊn.əˈ- ⓤⓢ -ˌluː.sɪ.noʊˈ-

hallway ˈhɔːl.weɪ ⓤⓢ ˈhɔːl-, ˈhɑːl- **-s** -z

halma ˈhæl.mə

halo ˈheɪ.ləʊ ⓤⓢ -loʊ **-(e)s** -z **-ing** -ɪŋ **-ed** -d

halogen ˈhæl.ə.dʒen, ˈheɪ.lə-, -dʒən ⓤⓢ ˈhæl.oʊ-, ˈ-ə- **-s** -z

halogenous həˈlɒdʒ.ɪ.nəs, -ᵊn.əs ⓤⓢ -ˈlɑː.dʒə.nəs

Halper ˈhæl.pəʳ ⓤⓢ -pɚ

Halpern ˈhæl.pən ⓤⓢ -pɚn

Hals hæls, hælz ⓤⓢ hɑːls, hɑːlz

Halsbury ˈhɔːlz.bᵊr.i, ˈhɒlz- ⓤⓢ ˈhɔːlzˌber-, ˈhɑːlz-

Halsey ˈhɔːl.si, ˈhæl-, -zi ⓤⓢ ˈhɔːl.zi, ˈhɑːl-

Halstead ˈhɔːl.sted, ˈhɒl-, ˈhæl-, -stɪd ⓤⓢ ˈhɔːl-, ˈhɑːl-, ˈhæl-

halt hɒlt, hɔːlt ⓤⓢ hɔːlt, hɑːlt **-s** -s **-ing/ly** -ɪŋ/li ⓤⓢ ˈhɔːl.t̬ɪŋ/li, ˈhɑːl- **-ed** -ɪd ⓤⓢ ˈhɔːl.t̬ɪd, ˈhɑːl-

halter ˈhɔːl.təʳ, ˈhɒl- ⓤⓢ ˈhɔːl.t̬ɚ, ˈhɑːl- **-s** -z

halterneck ˈhɒl.tə.nek, ˈhɔːl- ⓤⓢ ˈhɔːl.t̬ɚ-, ˈhɑːl- **-s** -s

halva(h) ˈhæl.və, -vɑː ⓤⓢ hɑːlˈvɑː; ˈ--, -və

halv|e hɑːv ⓤⓢ hæv **-es** -z **-ing** -ɪŋ **-ed** -d

Halvergate ˈhæl.və.geɪt ⓤⓢ -vɚ-

halves *(plur. of* **half***)* hɑːvz ⓤⓢ hævz

halyard ˈhæl.jəd ⓤⓢ -jɚd **-s** -z

ham (H) hæm **-s** -z **-ming** -ɪŋ **-med** -d

hamadryad ˌhæm.əˈdraɪəd, -ˈdraɪ.æd **-s** -z

Hamah ˈhæm.ə ⓤⓢ ˈhɑː.mɑː

Haman *biblical name:* ˈheɪ.mæn, -mən ⓤⓢ -mən *modern surname:* ˈheɪ.mən

Hamar ˈheɪ.mɑːʳ ⓤⓢ -mɑːr

hamartia ˌhɑː.mɑːˈtiː.ə ⓤⓢ -mɑːrˈ-

Hamas hæmˈæs, ˈ--

Hamble ˈhæm.bl̩

Hambleden ˈhæm.bl̩.dən

Hambledon ˈhæm.bl̩.dən

Hambleton ˈhæm.bl̩.tən

Hamblin ˈhæmb.lɪn

Hambro ˈhæm.brəʊ, -brə ⓤⓢ ˈhæm.brə, -broʊ

Hamburg ˈhæm.bɜːg ⓤⓢ -bɝːg, ˈhɑːm.bʊrg

hamburger ˈhæmˌbɜː.gəʳ ⓤⓢ -ˌbɝː.gɚ **-s** -z

Hamed ˈhæm.ed ⓤⓢ ˈhɑːməd

Hamelin ˈhæm.lɪn, -ᵊl.ɪn, -ɪ.lɪn

Hamer ˈheɪ.məʳ ⓤⓢ -mɚ

Hamerton ˈhæm.ə.tᵊn ⓤⓢ ˈ-ɚ-

ham-fisted ˌhæmˈfɪs.tɪd ⓤⓢ ˈ--- **-ly** -li **-ness** -nəs, -nɪs *stress shift, British only:* ˌham-fisted ˈeffort

ham-handed ˌhæmˈhæn.dɪd ⓤⓢ ˈhæmˌhæn- **-ly** -li **-ness** -nəs, -nɪs *stress shift, British only:* ˌham-handed ˈgesture

Hamhung ˌhɑːmˈhʊŋ

Hamilcar hæmˈɪl.kɑːʳ, həˈmɪl-; ˈhæm.ɪl-, -ᵊl- ⓤⓢ -kɑːr

Hamill ˈhæm.ᵊl

Hamilton ˈhæm.ᵊl.tən, -ɪl-

Hamiltonian ˌhæm.ᵊlˈtəʊ.ni.ən, -ɪlˈ- ⓤⓢ -ˈtoʊ-

Hamish ˈheɪ.mɪʃ

Hamite ˈhæm.aɪt **-s** -s

Hamitic hæmˈɪt.ɪk, həˈmɪt- ⓤⓢ hæmˈɪt̬-, həˈmɪt̬-

hamlet (H) ˈhæm.lət, -lɪt **-s** -s

Hamley ˈhæm.li

Hamlin, Hamlyn ˈhæm.lɪn

hammam ˈhæm.æm, -əm, ˈhʌm.ʌm; həˈmɑːm ⓤⓢ ˈhæm.əm **-s** -z

Hammarskjöld ˈhæm.ə.ʃəʊld ⓤⓢ -ɚ.ʃoʊld, ˈhɑː.mɚ-

hamm|er (H) ˈhæm|.əʳ ⓤⓢ -ɚ **-ers** -əz ⓤⓢ -ɚz **-ering** -ᵊr.ɪŋ **-ered** -əd ⓤⓢ -ɚd ˌ**go at it** ˌ**hammer and** ˈ**tongs**

Hammerfest ˈhæm.ə.fest ⓤⓢ ˈ-ɚ-

hammerhead ˈhæm.ə.hed ⓤⓢ ˈ-ɚ- **-s** -z

hammerlock ˈhæm.ə.lɒk ⓤⓢ -ɚ.lɑːk **-s** -s

Hammersmith ˈhæm.ə.smɪθ ⓤⓢ ˈ-ɚ-

Hammerstein ˈhæm.ə.staɪn, -stiːn ⓤⓢ ˈ-ɚ-

Hammett ˈhæm.ɪt

hammock ˈhæm.ək **-s** -s

Ham(m)ond ˈhæm.ənd

Hammurabi ˌhæm.ʊˈrɑː.bi (US) ˌhɑː.mʊˈ-, ˌhæm.əˈ-
hamm|y ˈhæm|.i **-ier** -i.əʳ (US) -i.ɚ **-iest** -i.ɪst, -i.əst **-ily** -ɪ.li, -ᵊl.i **-iness** -ɪ.nəs, -ɪ.nɪs
Hampden ˈhæm*p*.dən
hamp|er ˈhæm.p|əʳ (US) -p|ɚ **-ers** -əz (US) -ɚz **-ering** -ᵊr.ɪŋ **-ered** -əd (US) -ɚd
Hampshire ˈhæmp.ʃəʳ, -ˌʃɪəʳ (US) -ʃɚ, -ˌʃɪr
Hampstead ˈhæm*p*.sted, -stɪd **ˌHampstead ˈHeath**
Hampton ˈhæm*p*.tən **ˌHampton ˈCourt**
Hamshaw ˈhæm.ʃɔː (US) -ʃɑː, -ʃɔː
hamster ˈhæm*p*.stəʳ (US) -stɚ **-s** -z
ham|string ˈhæm|.strɪŋ **-strings** -strɪŋz **-stringing** -strɪŋ.ɪŋ **-strung** -strʌŋ
hamza ˈhæm.zə **-s** -z
Han hæn (US) hɑːn
Hanan ˈhæn.ən
Hananiah ˌhæn.əˈnaɪ.ə
Hanbury ˈhæn.bᵊr.i, ˈhæm- (US) ˈhænˌber-
Hancock ˈhæn.kɒk, ˈhæŋ- (US) ˈhæn.kɑːk
Hancox ˈhæn.kɒks, ˈhæŋ- (US) ˈhæn.kɑːks
hand **(H)** hænd **-s** -z **-ing** -ɪŋ **-ed** -ɪd **-er/s** -əʳ/z (US) -ɚ/z **-edness** -ɪd.nəs, -nɪs **ˈhand ˌcream; ˈhand greˌnade; ˌknow somewhere like the ˌback of one's ˈhand; ˌbite the ˌhand that ˈfeeds ˌone; ˌforce someone's ˈhand; ˌhand in ˈglove (with); ˌwait on someone ˌhand and ˈfoot**
handbag ˈhæn*d*.bæg, ˈhæm- (US) ˈhæn*d*- **-s** -z **-ging** -ɪŋ **-ged** -d
handball ˈhæn*d*.bɔːl, ˈhæm- (US) ˈhæn*d*.bɔːl, -bɑːl **-s** -z
handbarrow ˈhæn*d*ˌbær.əʊ, ˈhæm- (US) ˈhæn*d*ˌber.oʊ, -ˌbær- **-s** -z
handbasin ˈhæn*d*ˌbeɪ.sᵊn, ˈhæm-, -sɪn (US) ˈhæn*d*- **-s** -z
handbell ˈhæn*d*.bel, ˈhæm- (US) ˈhæn*d*- **-s** -z
handbill ˈhæn*d*.bɪl, ˈhæm- (US) ˈhæn*d*- **-s** -z
handbook ˈhæn*d*.bʊk, ˈhæm- (US) ˈhæn*d*- **-s** -s
handbrake ˈhæn*d*.breɪk, ˈhæm- (US) ˈhæn*d*- **-s** -s
handcart ˈhæn*d*.kɑːt, ˈhæŋ- (US) ˈhæn*d*.kɑːrt **-s** -s
handclap ˈhæn*d*.klæp, ˈhæŋ- (US) ˈhæn*d*- **-s** -s
Handcock ˈhæn*d*.kɒk (US) -kɑːk
handcraft ˈhæn*d*.krɑːft, ˈhæŋ- (US) ˈhæn*d*.kræft **-s** -s
handcuff ˈhæn*d*.kʌf **-s** -s **-ing** -ɪŋ **-ed** -t
Handel ˈhæn.dᵊl
Handelian hænˈdiː.li.ən (US) -ˈdel.i-, -ˈdiː.li-
handful ˈhæn*d*.fʊl **-s** -z
handgrip ˈhæn*d*.grɪp, ˈhæŋ- (US) ˈhæn*d*- **-s** -s
handgun ˈhæn*d*.gʌn, ˈhæŋ- (US) ˈhæn*d*- **-s** -z
hand-held ˌhændˈheld (US) ˌ-ˈ-, ˈ-- *stress shift, British only:* ˌhand-held ˈcamera
handhold ˈhænd.həʊld (US) -hoʊld **-s** -z
hand-holding ˈhændˌhəʊl.dɪŋ (US) -ˌhoʊl-
handicap ˈhæn.dɪ.kæp (US) ˈ-dɪ-, ˈ-di- **-s** -s **-ping** -ɪŋ **-ped** -t **-per/s** -əʳ/z (US) -ɚ/z
handicraft ˈhæn.dɪ.krɑːft (US) ˈ-dɪ.kræft, ˈ-di- **-s** -s
handiwork ˈhæn.dɪ.wɜːk (US) ˈ-dɪ.wɝːk, ˈ-di-
handkerchie|f ˈhæŋ.kə.tʃiː|f, -tʃɪ|f (US) -kɚ.tʃɪ|f, -tʃiː|f **-fs** -fs **-ves** -vz
handknit ˌhæn*d*ˈnɪt **-s** -ˈnɪts **-ting** -ˈnɪt.ɪŋ (US) -ˈnɪt̬.ɪŋ **-ted** -ˈnɪt.ɪd (US) -ˈnɪt̬.ɪd *stress shift:* ˌhandknit ˈsweater
handl|e ˈhæn.dl̩ **-es** -z **-ing** -ɪŋ, -ˈhænd.lɪŋ **-ed** -d **-er/s** -əʳ/z (US) -ɚ/z, ˈhænd.ləʳ/z (US) -lɚ/z
handlebar ˈhæn.dl̩.bɑːʳ (US) -bɑːr **-s** -z
Handley ˈhæn*d*.li
handmade ˌhæn*d*ˈmeɪd, ˌhæm- (US) ˌhæn*d*- *stress shift:* ˌhandmade ˈsweets
handmaid ˈhæn*d*.meɪd, ˈhæm- (US) ˈhæn*d*- **-s** -z
handmaiden ˈhæn*d*ˌmeɪ.dᵊn, ˈhæm- (US) ˈhæn*d*- **-s** -z
hand-me-down ˈhæn*d*.mi.daʊn, ˈhæm- (US) ˈhæn*d*- **-s** -z
handout ˈhænd.aʊt **-s** -s
handover ˈhænˌdəʊ.vəʳ (US) -ˌdoʊ.vɚ **-s** -z
hand-pick ˌhæn*d*ˈpɪk, ˌhæm- (US) ˌhæn*d*- **-s** -s **-ing** -ɪŋ **-ed** -t
handrail ˈhænd.reɪl **-s** -z
Hands hændz
handsaw ˈhæn*d*.sɔː (US) -sɑː, -sɔː **-s** -z
handsel ˈhæn*d*.sᵊl **-s** -z **-ling** -ɪŋ **-led** -d
handset ˈhæn*d*.set **-s** -s
handsful *(plur. of* **handful***)* ˈhæn*d*z.fʊl
handshak|e ˈhæn*d*.ʃeɪk **-es** -s **-ing** -ɪŋ
hands-off ˌhæn*d*zˈɒf (US) -ˈɑːf, -ˈɔːf *stress shift:* ˌhands-off ˈmanner
handsom|e ˈhæn*d*.səm **-er** -əʳ (US) -ɚ **-est** -ɪst, -əst **-ely** -li **-eness** -nəs, -nɪs
hands-on ˌhæn*d*zˈɒn (US) -ˈɑːn *stress shift:* ˌhands-on ˈpractice
handspring ˈhæn*d*.sprɪŋ **-s** -z
handstand ˈhæn*d*.stænd **-s** -z
hand-to-hand ˌhæn*d*.təˈhænd *stress shift:* ˌhand-to-hand ˈfighting
hand-to-mouth ˌhæn*d*.təˈmaʊθ *stress shift:* ˌhand-to-mouth ˈliving
handwork ˈhænd.wɜːk (US) -wɝːk
handwriting ˈhændˌraɪ.tɪŋ (US) -t̬ɪŋ **-s** -z
handwritten ˌhændˈrɪt.ᵊn *stress shift:* ˌhandwritten ˈnote
hand|y **(H)** ˈhæn.d|i **-ier** -i.əʳ (US) -i.ɚ **-iest** -i.ɪst, -i.əst **-ily** -ɪ.li, -ᵊl.i **-iness** -ɪ.nəs, -ɪ.nɪs
handy|man ˈhæn.di|.mæn, -mən **-men** -men
hang hæŋ **-s** -z **-ing/s** -ɪŋ/z **-ed** -d **hung** hʌŋ
hangar ˈhæŋ.gəʳ, -əʳ (US) -ɚ **-s** -z
hangdog ˈhæŋ.dɒg (US) -dɑːg, -dɔːg **-s** -z
hanger **(H)** ˈhæŋ.əʳ (US) -ɚ **-s** -z
hanger-on ˌhæŋ.əʳˈɒn (US) -ɚˈɑːn **hangers-on** ˌhæŋ.əzˈɒn (US) -ɚzˈ-
hang-glid|er ˈhæŋˌglaɪ.d|əʳ (US) -ɚ **-ers** -əz (US) -ɚz **-ing** -ɪŋ
hang|man ˈhæŋ|.mən, -mæn **-men** -mən
hangnail ˈhæŋ.neɪl **-s** -z
hangout ˈhæŋ.aʊt **-s** -s
hangover ˈhæŋ.əʊ.vəʳ (US) -oʊ.vɚ **-s** -z
hang-up ˈhæŋ.ʌp **-s** -s
hank **(H)** hæŋk **-s** -s
hank|er ˈhæŋ.k|əʳ (US) -k|ɚ **-ers** -əz (US) -ɚz **-ering** -ᵊr.ɪŋ **-ered** -əd (US) -ɚd
hankie ˈhæŋ.ki **-s** -z
Hankow ˌhænˈkaʊ, ˌhæŋ- (US) ˌhæn-, ˌhɑːn-, -ˈkoʊ
Hanks hæŋks
hank|y ˈhæŋ.k|i **-ies** -iz
hanky-panky ˌhæŋ.kiˈpæŋ.ki (US) ˌhæŋ.kiˈpæŋ-, ˈhæŋ.kiˌpæŋ-
Hanley ˈhæn.li
Hanna(h) ˈhæn.ə
Hannay ˈhæn.eɪ
Hannen ˈhæn.ən
Hannibal ˈhæn.ɪ.bᵊl, ˈ-ə-
Hannington ˈhæn.ɪŋ.tən
Hanoi hænˈɔɪ, həˈnɔɪ (US) hænˈɔɪ, hɑːˈnɔɪ, hə- *stress shift:* ˌHanoi ˈRocks
Hanover ˈhæn.əʊ.vəʳ (US) -oʊ.vɚ
Hanoverian ˌhæn.əʊˈvɪə.ri.ən, -ˈveə- (US) -əˈvɪr.i-, -ˈver **-s** -z
Hansa ˈhæn*t*.sə, ˈhæn.zə
Hansard ˈhæn*t*.sɑːd, -səd (US) -sɚd
Hansberry ˈhænz.bᵊr.i (US) -ˌber-
Hans|e hæn*t*s **-es** -ɪz
Hanseatic ˌhæn*t*.siˈæt.ɪk, ˌhæn.ziˈ- (US) -ˈæt̬-
hansel **(H)** ˈhæn*t*.sᵊl **-s** -z **-(l)ing** -ɪŋ **-(l)ed** -d
Hänsel ˈhæn*t*.sᵊl, ˈhen*t*-
Hansell ˈhæn*t*.sᵊl
Hansen ˈhæn*t*.sen
hansom **(H)** ˈhæn*t*.səm **-s** -z **ˈhansom ˌcab**
Hanson ˈhæn*t*.sᵊn
Hants. *(abbrev. for* **Hampshire***)* hænts
Hanuk(k)ah ˈhʌn.ʊ.kə, ˈhæn- (US) ˈhɑː.nə.kə, ˈxɑː-, -nuː-, -kɑː

Hanuman ˌhʌn.ʊˈmɑːn (US) ˌhɑː.nʊˈmɑːn, ˈ---
Hanway ˈhæn.weɪ
Hanwell ˈhæn.wəl, -wel
hào haʊ
hap hæp **-s** -s **-ping** -ɪŋ **-ped** -t
haphazard ˌhæpˈhæz.əd (US) -ɚd **-ly** -li **-ness** -nəs, -nɪs
hapless ˈhæp.ləs, -lɪs **-ly** -li **-ness** -nəs, -nɪs
haploid ˈhæp.lɔɪd **-s** -z
haplology hæpˈlɒl.ə.dʒi (US) -ˈlɑː.lə-
haply ˈhæp.li
hap'orth ˈheɪ.pəθ (US) -pɚθ **-s** -s
happ|en ˈhæp|.ən **-ens** -ənz **-ening/s** -ən.ɪŋ/z, ˈhæp.nɪŋ/z **-ened** -ənd
happenstance ˈhæp.ən.stænts, -əm-, -stɑːnts (US) -ən.stænts
Happisburgh ˈheɪz.bər.ə
happ|y ˈhæp|.i **-ier** -i.əʳ (US) -i.ɚ **-iest** -i.ɪst, -i.əst **-ily** -ɪ.li, -əl.i **-iness** -ɪ.nəs, -ɪ.nɪs **ˈhappy ˌhour; ˌhappy ˈmedium**
happy-go-lucky ˌhæp.i.gəʊˈlʌk.i (US) -goʊˈ- *stress shift:* ˌhappy-go-lucky ˈfellow
Hapsburg ˈhæps.bɜːg (US) -bɝːg
hara-kiri ˌhær.əˈkɪr.i, -ˈkɪə.ri (US) ˌhɑːr.əˈkɪr.i, ˌhær-
harangu|e həˈræŋ **-es** -z **-ing** -ɪŋ **-ed** -d **-er/s** -əʳ/z (US) -ɚ/z
Harare həˈrɑː.ri, -reɪ (US) hɑːˈrɑːr.i, hə-, -eɪ
harass ˈhær.əs; həˈræs (US) həˈræs; ˈher.əs, ˈhær- **-es** -ɪz **-ing** -ɪŋ **-ed** -t **-er/s** -əʳ/z (US) -ɚ/z **-ment** -mənt
Harben ˈhɑː.bən (US) ˈhɑːr-
Harberton ˈhɑː.bə.tən (US) ˈhɑːr.bɚ.t̬ən
Harbin hɑːˈbiːn, -ˈbɪn (US) ˈhɑːr.bɪn
harbinger ˈhɑː.bɪn.dʒəʳ (US) ˈhɑːr.bɪn.dʒɚ **-s** -z
harb|or ˈhɑː.b|əʳ (US) ˈhɑːr.b|ɚ **-ors** -əz (US) -ɚz **-oring** -ər.ɪŋ **-ored** -əd (US) -ɚd **-orage** -ər.ɪdʒ **-orless** -ə.ləs, -lɪs (US) -ɚ.ləs, -lɪs **ˈharbor ˌmaster**
Harborough ˈhɑː.bər.ə (US) ˈhɑːr.bə.roʊ
harb|our ˈhɑː.b|əʳ (US) ˈhɑːr.b|ɚ **-ours** -əz (US) -ɚz **-ouring** -ər.ɪŋ **-oured** -əd (US) -ɚd **-ourage** -ər.ɪdʒ **-ourless** -ə.ləs, -lɪs (US) -ɚ.ləs, -lɪs **ˈharbour ˌmaster**
Harcourt ˈhɑː.kət, -kɔːt (US) ˈhɑːr.kɔːrt, -kɚt
hard (H) hɑːd (US) hɑːrd **-er** -əʳ (US) -ɚ **-est** -ɪst, -əst **-ness** -nəs, -nɪs **ˌhard ˈcopy ˈhard ˌcopy; ˌhard ˈcurrency; ˌhard ˈdisk; ˌno ˌhard ˈfeelings; ˌhard ˈlabour; ˌhard ˈluck; ˌhard ˈluck ˌstory; ˌhard of ˈhearing; ˌhard ˈsell; ˌhard ˈshoulder**
hardback ˈhɑːd.bæk (US) ˈhɑːrd- **-s** -s
hardbake ˈhɑːd.beɪk (US) ˈhɑːrd-
hard-baked ˌhɑːdˈbeɪkt (US) ˌhɑːrd- *stress shift:* ˌhard-baked ˈcharacter
hard-bitten ˌhɑːdˈbɪt.ən (US) ˌhɑːrd- *stress shift:* ˌhard-bitten ˈcynic
hardboard ˈhɑːd.bɔːd (US) ˈhɑːrd.bɔːrd
hard-boiled ˌhɑːdˈbɔɪld (US) ˌhɑːrd- *stress shift:* ˌhard-boiled ˈegg
Hardcastle ˈhɑːdˌkɑː.sl̩ (US) ˈhɑːrdˌkæs-
hard-core *(adj.)* ˌhɑːdˈkɔːʳ, ˈ-- (US) ˌhɑːrdˈkɔːr *stress shift:* ˌhard-core ˈporn
hard core *(n.) (nucleus:)* ˌhɑːdˈkɔː (US) ˌhɑːrdˈkɔːr
hardcore *(n.) rubble:* ˈhɑːd.kɔːʳ (US) ˈhɑːrd.kɔːr
hardcover ˈhɑːdˌkʌv.əʳ (US) ˈhɑːrdˌkʌv.ɚ **-s** -z
hard-earned ˌhɑːdˈɜːnd (US) ˌhɑːrdˈɝːnd *stress shift:* ˌhard-earned ˈcash
harden (H) ˈhɑː.dən (US) ˈhɑːr- **-s** -z **-ing** -ɪŋ, ˈhɑːd.nɪŋ (US) ˈhɑːrd- **-ed** -d
Hardern ˈhɑː.dən (US) ˈhɑːr.dɚn
hard-fought ˌhɑːdˈfɔːt (US) ˌhɑːrdˈfɑːt, -ˈfɔːt *stress shift:* ˌhard-fought ˈbattle
hardheaded ˌhɑːdˈhed.ɪd (US) ˌhɑːrd- **-ness** -nəs, -nɪs *stress shift:* ˌhardheaded ˈbargaining
hardhearted ˌhɑːdˈhɑː.tɪd (US) ˌhɑːrdˈhɑːr.t̬ɪd **-ly** -li **-ness** -nəs, -nɪs *stress shift:* ˌhardhearted ˈvillain
hard-hit ˌhɑːdˈhɪt (US) ˌhɑːrd- **-ting** -ɪŋ *stress shift:* ˌhard-hit ˈregion
Hardicanute ˈhɑː.dɪ.kəˌnjuːt, -də-; ˌhɑː.dɪ.kəˈnjuːt (US) ˌhɑːr.dɪ.kəˈnuːt, -ˈnjuːt
Hardie ˈhɑː.di (US) ˈhɑːr-
hardihood ˈhɑː.di.hʊd (US) ˈhɑːr-
Harding ˈhɑː.dɪŋ (US) ˈhɑːr-
Hardinge ˈhɑː.dɪŋ, -dɪndʒ (US) ˈhɑːr-
hardline ˌhɑːdˈlaɪn (US) ˌhɑːrd- *stress shift:* ˌhardline ˈleader
hardliner ˌhɑːdˈlaɪ.nəʳ, ˈ-ˌ-- (US) ˌhɑːrdˈlaɪ.nɚ, ˈ-ˌ-- **-s** -z
hardly ˈhɑːd.li (US) ˈhɑːrd-
hard-nosed ˌhɑːdˈnəʊzd (US) ˌhɑːrdˈnoʊzd *stress shift:* ˌhard-nosed ˈpolicy
hard-on ˈhɑːd.ɒn (US) ˈhɑːrd.ɑːn
hard-pressed ˌhɑːdˈprest (US) ˌhɑːrd- *stress shift:* ˌhard-pressed ˈleader
hardship ˈhɑːd.ʃɪp (US) ˈhɑːrd- **-s** -s
hardtop ˈhɑːd.tɒp (US) ˈhɑːrd.tɑːp **-s** -s
hard-up ˌhɑːdˈʌp (US) ˌhɑːrd- *stress shift:* ˌhard-up ˈpensioner
hardware ˈhɑːd.weəʳ (US) ˈhɑːrd.wer
hard-wearing ˌhɑːdˈweə.rɪŋ (US) ˌhɑːrdˈwer.ɪŋ *stress shift:* ˌhard-wearing ˈcarpet
Hardwick(e) ˈhɑːd.wɪk (US) ˈhɑːrd-
hardwood ˈhɑːd.wʊd (US) ˈhɑːrd- **-s** -z
hard-working ˌhɑːdˈwɜː.kɪŋ (US) ˌhɑːrdˈwɝː- *stress shift:* ˌhard-working ˈsecretary
hard|y (H) ˈhɑː.d|i (US) ˈhɑːr- **-ier** -i.əʳ (US) -i.ɚ **-iest** -i.ɪst, -i.əst **-ily** -ɪ.li, -əl.i **-iness** -ɪ.nəs, -ɪ.nɪs
har|e (H) heəʳ (US) her **-es** -z **-ing** -ɪŋ **-ed** -d
harebell ˈheə.bel (US) ˈher- **-s** -z
harebrained ˈheə.breɪnd (US) ˈher-
Harefield ˈheə.fiːld (US) ˈher-
Hare Krishna ˌhær.iˈkrɪʃ.nə, ˌhɑː.riˈ- (US) ˌhɑː.riˈ- **-s** -z
harelip ˌheəˈlɪp (US) ˌher- **-s** -s **-ped** -t
harem ˈhɑː.riːm, ˈheə-, -rəm; həˈriːm, hɑː- (US) ˈher.əm, ˈhær- **-s** -z
Harewood ˈhɑː.wʊd, ˈheə.wʊd (US) ˈhɑːr-, ˈher-
Note: The Earl of Harewood pronounces /ˈhɑː.wʊd (US) ˈhɑːr-/, and his house is called /ˌhɑː.wʊdˈhaʊs (US) ˌhɑːr-/. The village in West Yorkshire is now generally pronounced /ˈheə.wʊd (US) ˈher-/, though /ˈhɑː.wʊd (US) ˈhɑːr-/ may sometimes be heard from old people there. Other people with the surname **Harewood** pronounce /ˈheə.wʊd (US) ˈher-/.
Harford ˈhɑː.fəd (US) ˈhɑːr.fɚd
Hargraves ˈhɑː.greɪvz (US) ˈhɑːr-
Hargreaves ˈhɑː.griːvz, -greɪvz (US) ˈhɑːr-
haricot ˈhær.ɪ.kəʊ (US) ˈher.ɪ.koʊ, ˈhær- **-s** -z **ˌharicot ˈbean, ˈharicot ˌbean**
Haringey ˈhær.ɪŋ.geɪ (US) ˈher-, ˈhær-
Harington ˈhær.ɪŋ.tən (US) ˈher-, ˈhær-
Hariot ˈhær.i.ət (US) ˈher-, ˈhær-, -ɑːt
hark hɑːk (US) hɑːrk **-s** -s **-ing** -ɪŋ **-ed** -t
Harker ˈhɑː.kəʳ (US) ˈhɑːr.kɚ
Harkin ˈhɑː.kɪn (US) ˈhɑːr-
Harkinson ˈhɑː.kɪnt.sən (US) ˈhɑːr-
Harkness ˈhɑːk.nəs, -nɪs (US) ˈhɑːrk-
Harland ˈhɑː.lənd (US) ˈhɑːr-
Harlech ˈhɑː.lek, -lex, -lək, -ləx (US) ˈhɑːr.lek
Harleian hɑːˈliː.ən; ˈhɑː.li- (US) ˈhɑːr.li-; hɑːrˈliː-
Harlem ˈhɑː.ləm, -lem (US) ˈhɑːr- **ˌHarlem ˈGlobetrotters**
harlequin ˈhɑː.lɪ.kwɪn, -lə-, -kɪn (US) ˈhɑːr.lɪ- **-s** -z
harlequinade ˌhɑː.lɪ.kwɪˈneɪd, -lə-, -kɪˈ- (US) ˌhɑːr.lɪ- **-s** -z
Harlesden ˈhɑːlz.dən (US) ˈhɑːrlz-
Harley ˈhɑː.li (US) ˈhɑːr- **ˈHarley ˌStreet**
Harley Davidson® ˌhɑː.liˈdeɪ.vɪd.sən (US) ˌhɑːr-
Harlock ˈhɑː.lɒk (US) ˈhɑːr.lɑːk
harlot ˈhɑː.lət (US) ˈhɑːr- **-s** -s **-ry** -ri
Harlow(e) ˈhɑː.ləʊ (US) ˈhɑːr.loʊ
harm hɑːm (US) hɑːrm **-s** -z **-ing** -ɪŋ **-ed** -d **ˌout of ˌharm's ˈway**

Harman ˈhɑː.mən (US) ˈhɑːr-
Harmer ˈhɑː.məʳ (US) ˈhɑːr.mɚ
harmful ˈhɑːm.fᵊl, -fʊl (US) ˈhɑːrm- **-ly** -i **-ness** -nəs, -nɪs
harmless ˈhɑːm.ləs, -lɪs (US) ˈhɑːrm- **-ly** -li **-ness** -nəs, -nɪs
Harmon ˈhɑː.mən (US) ˈhɑːr-
Harmondsworth ˈhɑː.məndz.wəθ, -wɜːθ (US) ˈhɑːr.məndz.wɝːθ
Harmonia hɑːˈməʊ.ni.ə (US) hɑːrˈmoʊ-
harmonic hɑːˈmɒn.ɪk (US) hɑːrˈmɑː.nɪk **-s** -s **-al** -ᵊl **-ally** -ᵊl.i, -li
harmonica hɑːˈmɒn.ɪ.kə (US) hɑːrˈmɑː.nɪ- **-s** -z
harmonious hɑːˈməʊ.ni.əs (US) hɑːrˈmoʊ- **-ly** -li **-ness** -nəs, -nɪs
harmonist ˈhɑː.mə.nɪst (US) ˈhɑːr- **-s** -s
harmonium hɑːˈməʊ.ni.əm (US) hɑːrˈmoʊ- **-s** -z
harmonization, -isa- ˌhɑː.mə.naɪˈzeɪ.ʃᵊn, -nɪˈ- (US) ˌhɑːr.mə.nɪˈ- **-s** -z
harmoniz|e, -is|e ˈhɑː.mə.naɪz (US) ˈhɑːr- **-es** -ɪz **-ing** -ɪŋ **-ed** -d **-er/s** -əʳ/z (US) -ɚ/z
harmon|y ˈhɑː.mə.n|i (US) ˈhɑːr- **-ies** -iz
Harmsworth ˈhɑːmz.wəθ, -wɜːθ (US) ˈhɑːrmz.wɝːθ
Harnack ˈhɑː.næk (US) ˈhɑːr-
harness (H) ˈhɑː.nɪs, -nəs (US) ˈhɑːr- **-es** -ɪz **-ing** -ɪŋ **-ed** -t **-er/s** -əʳ/z (US) -ɚ/z
Harold ˈhær.əld (US) ˈher-, ˈhær-
harp hɑːp (US) hɑːrp **-s** -s **-ing** -ɪŋ **-ed** -t
Harpenden ˈhɑː.pᵊn.dən (US) ˈhɑːr-
Harper ˈhɑː.pəʳ (US) ˈhɑːr.pɚ
Harpham ˈhɑː.pəm (US) ˈhɑːr-
Harpic® ˈhɑː.pɪk (US) ˈhɑːr-
harpist ˈhɑː.pɪst (US) ˈhɑːr- **-s** -s
harpoon ˌhɑːˈpuːn (US) ˌhɑːr- **-s** -z **-ing** -ɪŋ **-ed** -d **-er/s** -əʳ/z (US) -ɚ/z
harpsichord ˈhɑːp.sɪ.kɔːd (US) ˈhɑːrp.sɪ.kɔːrd **-s** -z
harp|y (H) ˈhɑː.p|i (US) ˈhɑːr- **-ies** -iz
harquebus ˈhɑː.kwɪ.bəs, -kwə- (US) ˈhɑːr.kwə- **-es** -ɪz
Harraden ˈhær.ə.dᵊn, -den (US) ˈher-, ˈhær-
Harrap ˈhær.əp (US) ˈher-, ˈhær-
Harrell ˈhær.ᵊl (US) ˈher-, ˈhær-
harridan ˈhær.ɪ.dᵊn, ˈ-ə- (US) ˈher-, ˈhær- **-s** -z
Harrie ˈhær.i (US) ˈher-, ˈhær-
harrier ˈhær.i.əʳ (US) ˈher.i.ɚ, ˈhær- **-s** -z
Harries ˈhær.ɪs, -iz (US) ˈher-, ˈhær-
Harriet ˈhær.i.ət (US) ˈher-, ˈhær-
Harriman ˈhær.ɪ.mən (US) ˈher-, ˈhær-
Harrington ˈhær.ɪŋ.tən (US) ˈher-, ˈhær-
Harriot ˈhær.i.ət (US) ˈher-, ˈhær-
Harris ˈhær.ɪs (US) ˈher-, ˈhær- **ˌHarris ˈTweed**
Harrisburg ˈhær.ɪs.bɜːg (US) ˈher.ɪs.bɝːg, ˈhær-
Harris(s)on ˈhær.ɪ.sᵊn (US) ˈher-, ˈhær-
Harrod ˈhær.əd (US) ˈher-, ˈhær- **-s** -z
Harrogate ˈhær.ə.gət, -geɪt, -gɪt (US) ˈher-, ˈhær-
Harrop ˈhær.əp (US) ˈher-, ˈhær-
Harrovian hærˈəʊ.vi.ən, həˈrəʊ- (US) həˈroʊ- **-s** -z
harrow (H) ˈhær.əʊ (US) ˈher.oʊ, ˈhær- **-s** -z **-ing/ly** -ɪŋ/li **-ed** -d
Harrowby ˈhær.əʊ.bi (US) ˈher.oʊ-, ˈhær-
harrumph həˈrʌmpf **-s** -s **-ing** -ɪŋ **-ed** -t
harr|y (H) ˈhær|.i (US) ˈher-, ˈhær- **-ies** -iz **-ying** -i.ɪŋ **-ied** -id
harsh hɑːʃ (US) hɑːrʃ **-er** -əʳ (US) -ɚ **-est** -ɪst, -əst **-ly** -li **-ness** -nəs, -nɪs
hart (H) hɑːt (US) hɑːrt **-s** -s
Harte hɑːt (US) hɑːrt
hartebeest ˈhɑː.tɪ.biːst, -tə- (US) ˈhɑːr.t̬ə-, -tə- **-s** -s
Hartford ˈhɑːt.fəd (US) ˈhɑːrt.fɚd
Harthan ˈhɑː.ðᵊn, ˈhɑː.θᵊn (US) ˈhɑːr-
Hartington ˈhɑː.tɪŋ.tən (US) ˈhɑːr.t̬ɪŋ-
Hartland ˈhɑːt.lənd (US) ˈhɑːrt-
Hartlepool ˈhɑːt.lɪ.puːl, -lə- (US) ˈhɑːrt-
Hartley ˈhɑːt.li (US) ˈhɑːrt-
Hartman ˈhɑːt.mən (US) ˈhɑːrt-
Hartnell ˈhɑːt.nᵊl (US) ˈhɑːrt-
Hartshill ˈhɑːts.hɪl (US) ˈhɑːrts-
hartshorn (H) ˈhɑːts.hɔːn (US) ˈhɑːrts.hɔːrn
hart's-tongue ˈhɑːts.tʌŋ (US) ˈhɑːrts- **-s** -z
Hartz hɑːts (US) hɑːrts
harum-scarum ˌheə.rəmˈskeə.rəm (US) ˌher.əmˈsker.əm, ˌhær-, -ˈskær-
Harun-al-Rashid hærˌuːn.æl.ræʃˈiːd, hɑːˌruːn-; ˌhær.uːn.ælˈræʃ.iːd, ˌhɑː.ruːn-, -ɪd (US) hɑːˌruːn.ɑːl.rɑːˈʃiːd
haruspex həˈrʌs.peks, hærˈʌs-; ˈhær.ə.speks **haruspices** həˈrʌs.pɪ.siːz, hærˈʌs-
Harvard ˈhɑː.vəd (US) ˈhɑːr.vɚd
Harverson ˈhɑː.və.sᵊn (US) ˈhɑːr.vɚ-
harvest ˈhɑː.vɪst, -əst (US) ˈhɑːr- **-s** -s **-ing** -ɪŋ **-ed** -ɪd **-er/s** -əʳ/z (US) -ɚ/z **ˌharvest ˈfestival; ˈharvest ˌmite; ˌharvest ˈmoon; ˈharvest ˌmouse**
Harvey ˈhɑː.vi (US) ˈhɑːr-
Harwich ˈhær.ɪtʃ, -ɪdʒ (US) ˈhær-, ˈher-
Harwood ˈhɑː.wʊd (US) ˈhɑːr-
Harworth ˈhɑː.wəθ (US) ˈhɑːr.wɚθ
Haryana ˌhær.iˈɑː.nə (US) ˌhɑːrˈjɑː-
Harz hɑːts (US) hɑːrts
has *(from* **have***) strong form:* hæz *weak forms:* həz, əz, z, s
Note: The strong form is used when **has** is used as a full verb rather than as an auxiliary, e.g. ‘He has some money’. The auxiliary verb is a weak form word: the strong form /hæz/ is used contrastively, e.g. ‘I don’t know if she has or she hasn’t’, in final position, e.g. ‘I’ve read as much as he has’ and quite frequently in initial position, e.g. ‘Has anyone seen my glasses?’. It is also used for emphasis, e.g. ‘She **has** to have one’. Elsewhere, the weak form is usually /həz/ or /əz/. The shortest weak forms are /s/ and /z/: the form /s/ is used only after voiceless consonants other than /s, ʃ, tʃ/, while the form /z/ is used only after a vowel or a voiced consonant other than /z, ʒ, dʒ/. After /s, z, ʃ, ʒ, tʃ, dʒ/, the weak form is usually /əz/.
has-been ˈhæz.biːn, -bɪn (US) -bɪn **-s** -z
Hasdrubal ˈhæz.drʊ.bᵊl, -druː-, -bæl
Haselden ˈhæz.ᵊl.dən, ˈheɪz-
hash hæʃ **-es** -ɪz **-ing** -ɪŋ **-ed** -t **ˌhash ˈbrown**
Hashemite ˈhæʃ.ɪ.maɪt, -ə-
Hashimoto ˌhæʃ.ɪˈməʊ.təʊ (US) -ˈmoʊ.t̬oʊ, ˌhɑːʃ-, -toʊ
hashish ˈhæʃ.ɪʃ, -iːʃ; hæsˈiːʃ
Hasid hæsˈiːd, hɑːˈsiːd **-im** -ɪm
Hasidic hæsˈɪd.ɪk, hɑːˈsɪd- (US) hæsˈɪd-, həˈsɪd-, hɑː-
Hasidism hæsˈɪd.ɪ.zᵊm, ˈhæs- (US) ˈhæs.ɪ.dɪ-, ˈhɑː.sɪ-; hæsˈɪd.ɪ-, həˈsɪd-, hɑː-
Haslam ˈhæz.ləm
Haslemere ˈheɪ.zl̩.mɪəʳ (US) -mɪr
haslet ˈhæz.lət, ˈheɪz-, -lɪt (US) ˈhæs-, ˈheɪz-
Haslett ˈhæz.lət, ˈheɪz.lət, -lɪt
Haslingden ˈhæz.lɪŋ.dən
Hasluck ˈhæz.lʌk, -lək
hasn't ˈhæz.ᵊnt
hasp hɑːsp, hæsp (US) hæsp **-s** -s **-ing** -ɪŋ **-ed** -t
Hassall ˈhæs.ᵊl
Hassan *district in India:* ˈhʌs.ᵊn, ˈhæs- *Arabic name:* həˈsɑːn, hæsˈɑːn; ˈhæs.ᵊn, ˈhʌs- (US) ˈhɑː.sɑːn; həˈsɑːn
Hasselhoff ˈhæs.ᵊl.hɒf (US) -hɑːf
hassl|e ˈhæs.l̩ **-es** -z **-ing** -ɪŋ, ˈhæs.lɪŋ **-ed** -d
hassock (H) ˈhæs.ək **-s** -s
hast (H) *(from* **have***) strong form:* hæst *weak forms:* həst, əst, st
Note: This weak form word is little used. See the note for **have** for guidance on when to use the strong form.
hast|e heɪst **-es** -s **-ing** -ɪŋ **-ed** -ɪd
hasten ˈheɪ.sᵊn **-s** -z **-ing** -ɪŋ, ˈheɪs.nɪŋ **-ed** -d
Hastie ˈheɪ.sti
Hastings ˈheɪ.stɪŋz
hast|y ˈheɪ.st|i **-ier** -i.əʳ (US) -i.ɚ **-iest** -i.ɪst, -i.əst **-ily** -ɪ.li, -ᵊl.i **-iness** -ɪ.nəs, -ɪ.nɪs

hat hæt **-s** -s ˈ**hat** ˌ**rack** ˈ**hat** ˌ**stand**; ˈ**hat** ˌ**trick**; **at the** ˌ**drop of a** ˈ**hat**; ˌ**keep something** ˌ**under one's** ˈ**hat**; **I'll** ˌ**eat my** ˈ**hat**
hatband ˈhæt.bænd **-s** -z
hatbox ˈhæt.bɒks (US) -bɑːks **-es** -ɪz
hatch (H) *(n. v.)* hætʃ **-es** -ɪz **-ing** -ɪŋ **-ed** -t
hatchback ˈhætʃ.bæk **-s** -s
hatcher|y ˈhætʃ.ᵊr|.i **-ies** -iz
hatchet ˈhætʃ.ɪt **-s** -s ˈ**hatchet** ˌ**job**; ˌ**bury the** ˈ**hatchet**
hatchling ˈhætʃ.lɪŋ **-s** -z
hatchment ˈhætʃ.mənt **-s** -s
hatchway (H) ˈhætʃ.weɪ **-s** -z
hat|e heɪt **-es** -s **-ing** -ɪŋ (US) ˈheɪ.t̬ɪŋ **-ed** -ɪd (US) ˈheɪ.t̬ɪd **-er/s** -əʳ/z (US) ˈheɪ.t̬ɚ/z
hateful ˈheɪt.fᵊl, -fʊl **-ly** -i **-ness** -nəs, -nɪs
Hatfield ˈhæt.fiːld
hath *(from* **have***) strong form:* hæθ *weak forms:* həθ, əθ
Note: This weak form word is little used. See the note for **has** for guidance on when to use the strong form.
hatha ˈhæθ.ə, ˈhʌθ-
Hathaway ˈhæθ.ə.weɪ
Hatherell ˈhæð.ᵊr.ᵊl
Hatherleigh ˈhæð.ə.li (US) ˈ-ɚ-
Hatherley ˈhæð.ə.li (US) ˈ-ɚ-
Hathersage ˈhæð.ə.seɪdʒ, -sɪdʒ, -sedʒ (US) ˈ-ɚ-
Hatherton ˈhæð.ə.tᵊn (US) -ɚ.t̬ᵊn
Hathorn(e) ˈhɔː.θɔːn (US) ˈhɑː.θɔːrn, ˈhɔː-
Hathway ˈhæθ.weɪ
hatless ˈhæt.ləs, -lɪs, -les
hatpin ˈhæt.pɪn **-s** -z
hatred ˈheɪ.trɪd, -trəd
hatter ˈhæt.əʳ (US) ˈhæt̬.ɚ **-s** -z **as** ˌ**mad as a** ˈ**hatter**
Hatteras ˈhæt.ᵊr.əs (US) ˈhæt̬.ɚ-
Hattersley ˈhæt.əz.li (US) ˈhæt̬.ɚz-
Hattie ˈhæt.i (US) ˈhæt̬-
Hatton ˈhæt.ᵊn
hauberk ˈhɔː.bɜːk (US) ˈhɑː.bɝːk, ˈhɔː- **-s** -s
haugh hɔː (US) hɑː, hɔː **-s** -z
Haughey ˈhɔː.hi, ˈhɒ- (US) ˈhɑː-, ˈhɔː-
Haughton ˈhɔː.tᵊn (US) ˈhɑː-, ˈhɔː-
haught|y ˈhɔː.t|i (US) ˈhɑː.t̬|i, ˈhɔː- **-ier** -i.əʳ (US) -i.ɚ **-iest** -i.ɪst, -i.əst **-ily** -ɪ.li, -ᵊl.i **-iness** -ɪ.nəs, -ɪ.nɪs
haul hɔːl (US) hɑːl, hɔːl **-s** -z **-ing** -ɪŋ **-ed** -d **-er/s** -əʳ/z (US) -ɚ/z
haulage ˈhɔː.lɪdʒ (US) ˈhɑː-, ˈhɔː-
haulier ˈhɔː.li.əʳ (US) ˈhɑːl.jɚ, ˈhɔː- **-s** -z
haulm hɔːm (US) hɔːm, hɑːm **-s** -z
haunch hɔːntʃ (US) hɑːntʃ, hɔːntʃ **-es** -ɪz
haunt hɔːnt (US) hɑːnt, hɔːnt **-s** -s **-ing/ly** -ɪŋ/li (US) ˈhɑːn.t̬ɪŋ/li, ˈhɔːn- **-ed** -ɪd (US) ˈhɑːn.t̬ɪd, ˈhɔːn-
Hausa ˈhaʊ.sə, -zə **-s** -z
hausfrau ˈhaʊs.fraʊ **-s** -z **-en** -ᵊn
Haussmann ˈhaʊs.mæn (US) -mæn, -mən
hautbois *(sing.)* ˈəʊ.bɔɪ, ˈhəʊ-, ˈhɔːt- (US) ˈhoʊ-, ˈoʊ- ˈəʊ.bɔɪz, ˈhəʊ-, ˈhɔːt- (US) ˈhoʊ-, ˈoʊ-
hautboy ˈəʊ.bɔɪ, ˈhəʊ-, ˈhɔːt- (US) ˈhoʊ-, ˈoʊ- **-s** -z
haute couture ˌəʊt.kʊˈtjʊəʳ, -kuːˈ-, -ˈtʊəʳ (US) ˌoʊt.kuːˈtʊr
haute cuisine ˌəʊt.kwɪˈziːn, -kwəˈ- (US) ˌoʊt-
hauteur əʊˈtɜːʳ, ˈ-- (US) hoʊˈtɝː, oʊˈ-
Havana həˈvæn.ə, hævˈæn-, -ˈvɑː.nə (US) -ˈvæn.ə **-s** -z
Havant ˈhæv.ᵊnt
Havard ˈhæv.ɑːd, -əd (US) -ɑːrd, -ɚd
Havarti həˈvɑː.ti (US) -ˈvɑːr-
have *one who has:* hæv **-s** -z
Note: This word usually occurs only in conjunction with **have-not**, in expressions such as 'There's a conflict between the haves and have-nots'.
have *(v.) strong form:* hæv *weak forms:* həv, əv, v **hast** *strong form:* hæst *weak forms:* həst, əst, st *strong form:* **has** hæz *weak forms:* həz, əz, z, s **having** ˈhæv.ɪŋ **had** *strong form:* hæd *weak forms:* həd, əd, d
Note: When **have** occurs as a full verb, e.g. 'to have and to hold', the strong form is used. As an auxiliary verb, it is a weak form word: the strong form is used contrastively, e.g. 'I don't know if you have or haven't', for emphasis, e.g. 'You **have** to see it', and also in final position, e.g. 'I've got as much as you have'. It is also quite often used in initial position, e.g. 'Have you seen my book?'. Elsewhere the weak form is commonly used; the form /v/ is only found after vowels. For **hast**, **has**, **had** and **hadst**, see notes provided for those word entries.
Havel ˈhɑː.vᵊl (US) -fᵊl
Havell ˈhæv.ᵊl
Havelo(c)k ˈhæv.lɒk, -lək (US) -lɑːk, -lək
haven ˈheɪ.vᵊn **-s** -z
have-not ˈhæv.nɒt, ˌ-ˈ- (US) ˈhæv.nɑːt, ˌ-ˈ- **-s** -s
haven't ˈhæv.ᵊnt
hav|er ˈheɪ.v|əʳ (US) -v|ɚ **-ers** -əz (US) -ɚz **-ering** -ᵊr.ɪŋ **-ered** -əd (US) -ɚd
Haverford ˈhæv.ə.fəd (US) -ɚ.fɚd
Haverfordwest ˌhæv.ə.fədˈwest, ˌhɑː.fədˈwest (US) ˌhæv.ɚ.fɚdˈ-, ˌhɑː.fɚdˈ-
Havergal ˈhæv.ə.gᵊl (US) ˈ-ɚ-
Haverhill ˈheɪ.vᵊr.ɪl, -ᵊl; ˈheɪ.və.hɪl (US) -vɚ-
Havering ˈheɪ.vᵊr.ɪŋ
Havers ˈheɪ.vəz (US) -vɚz
haversack ˈhæv.ə.sæk (US) ˈ-ɚ- **-s** -s
haversian canal (H) həˌvɜː.ʃᵊn.kəˈnæl, hævˌɜː-, -ʒᵊn- (US) həˌvɝː.ʒᵊn
Haverstock ˈhæv.ə.stɒk (US) -ɚ.stɑːk
Havilah ˈhæv.ɪ.lə (US) -lə, -lɑː
Haviland ˈhæv.ɪ.lænd, ˈ-ə-, -lənd
Havisham ˈhæv.ɪ.ʃᵊm
havoc ˈhæv.ək
Havre *place in France:* ˈhɑː.vrə, -vəʳ (US) -vrə, -vɚ *place in Maryland:* ˈhɑː.vəʳ (US) -vɚ, ˈhæv.ɚ *place in Montana:* ˈhæv.əʳ (US) -ɚ
Havre de Grace ˌhɑː.və.dəˈgrɑːs, ˌhæv.ə-, -ˈgræs, -ˈgreɪs (US) ˌhɑː.vɚ-, ˌhæv.ɚ-
haw hɔː (US) hɑː, hɔː **-s** -z **-ing** -ɪŋ **-ed** -d
Hawaii həˈwaɪ.iː, hɑː-, -i (US) həˈwɑː-, -ˈwaɪ-
Hawaiian həˈwaɪ.ən, hɑː-, ˈ-i.ən (US) həˈwɑː.jən **-s** -z
Haward ˈheɪ.wəd, ˈhɔː.əd, hɑːd, hɔːd (US) ˈheɪ.wɚd, ˈhɔː.ɚd, hɑːrd, hɔːrd
Hawarden *in Clwyd:* ˈhɑː.dᵊn, ˈhɔː- (US) ˈhɑːr-, ˈhɔːr *Viscount:* ˈheɪˌwɔː.dᵊn (US) -ˌwɔːr- *town in US:* ˈheɪˌwɑː.dᵊn (US) -ˌwɑːr-
Haweis ˈhɔː.ɪs (US) ˈhɔː.ɪs, hɔɪs
Hawes hɔːz (US) hɑːz, hɔːz
hawfinch ˈhɔː.fɪntʃ (US) ˈhɑː-, ˈhɔː- **-es** -ɪz
haw-haw ˈhɔːˌhɔː, ˌ-ˈ- (US) ˈhɑː.hɑː, ˈhɔː.hɔː, ˌ-ˈ- **-s** -z
Hawick ˈhɔː.ɪk, hɔɪk (US) ˈhɑː.ɪk, ˈhɔː-, hɔɪk
hawk hɔːk (US) hɑːk, hɔːk **-s** -s **-ing** -ɪŋ **-ed** -t **-er/s** -əʳ/z (US) -ɚ/z
Hawke hɔːk (US) hɑːk, hɔːk **-s** -s
Hawker-Siddeley® ˌhɔː.kəˈsɪd.ᵊl.i, ˈ-li (US) ˌhɑː.kɚˈ-, ˌhɔː-
Hawkeye ˈhɔːk.aɪ (US) ˈhɑːk-, ˈhɔːk-
hawk-eyed ˈhɔːk.aɪd (US) ˈhɑːk-, ˈhɔːk-
Hawking ˈhɔː.kɪŋ (US) ˈhɑː-, ˈhɔː-
Hawkins ˈhɔː.kɪnz (US) ˈhɑː-, ˈhɔː-
hawkish ˈhɔː.kɪʃ (US) ˈhɑː-, ˈhɔː- **-ly** -li **-ness** -nes, -nɪs
hawkmoth ˈhɔːk.mɒθ (US) ˈhɑːk.mɑːθ, ˈhɔːk- **-s** -s
Hawks hɔːks (US) hɑːks, hɔːks
hawksbill ˈhɔːks.bɪl (US) ˈhɑːks-, ˈhɔːks- **-s** -z
Hawkshaw ˈhɔːk.ʃɔː (US) ˈhɑːk.ʃɑː, ˈhɔːk-, -ʃɔː
Hawksley ˈhɔːk.sli (US) ˈhɑːks-, ˈhɔːks-
Hawksmoor ˈhɔːks.mɔːʳ (US) ˈhɑːks.mɔːr, ˈhɔːks-, -mʊr
hawkweed ˈhɔːk.wiːd (US) ˈhɑːk-, ˈhɔːk-
Hawkwood ˈhɔːk.wʊd (US) ˈhɑːk-, ˈhɔːk-
Hawley ˈhɔː.li (US) ˈhɑː-, ˈhɔː-

Hawn hɔːn ⓤⓢ hɑːn, hɔːn
Haworth *place in Yorkshire:* ˈhaʊ.əθ, ˈhɔː.əθ ⓤⓢ ˈhɔː.wɚθ *surname:* ˈhaʊ.əθ ⓤⓢ ˈheɪ.wɚθ, ˈhaʊ.ɚθ, ˈhoʊ-; hɑːrθ *place in New Jersey:* ˈhɔː.wəθ ⓤⓢ -wɚθ
haws|e hɔːz ⓤⓢ hɑːz, hɔːz **-es** -ɪz
hawser ˈhɔː.zəʳ ⓤⓢ ˈhɑː.zɚ, ˈhɔː- **-s** -z
hawthorn ˈhɔː.θɔːn ⓤⓢ ˈhɑː.θɔːrn, ˈhɔː- **-s** -z
Hawthornden ˈhɔː.θɔːn.dən ⓤⓢ ˈhɑː.θɔːrn-, ˈhɔː-
Hawthorne ˈhɔː.θɔːn ⓤⓢ ˈhɑː.θɔːrn, ˈhɔː-
Haxby ˈhæks.bi
hay (H) heɪ **ˈhay ˌfever**
haybox ˈheɪ.bɒks ⓤⓢ -bɑːks **-es** -ɪz
haycart ˈheɪ.kɑːt ⓤⓢ -kɑːrt **-s** -s
haycock (H) ˈheɪ.kɒk ⓤⓢ -kɑːk **-s** -s
Hayden ˈheɪ.dᵊn
Haydn *English surname:* ˈheɪ.dᵊn *Austrian composer:* ˈhaɪ.dᵊn
Haydock ˈheɪ.dɒk ⓤⓢ -dɑːk
Haydon ˈheɪ.dᵊn
Hayes heɪz
Hayesford ˈheɪz.fəd ⓤⓢ -fɚd
Hayhurst ˈhaɪ.əst, ˈheɪ.hɜːst ⓤⓢ ˈhaɪ.ɚst, ˈheɪ.hɝːst
Hayle heɪl
Hayles heɪlz
Hayley ˈheɪ.li
Hayling Island ˌheɪ.lɪŋˈaɪ.lənd, ˈheɪ.lɪŋˌaɪ-
hayloft ˈheɪ.lɒft ⓤⓢ -lɑːft **-s** -s
haymak|er ˈheɪˌmeɪ.k|əʳ ⓤⓢ -k|ɚ **-ers** -əz ⓤⓢ -ɚz **-ing** -ɪŋ
Haymarket ˈheɪˌmɑː.kɪt ⓤⓢ -ˌmɑːr-
Haynes heɪnz
hayrick ˈheɪ.rɪk **-s** -s
Hays heɪz
hayseed ˈheɪ.siːd **-s** -z
haystack ˈheɪ.stæk **-s** -s
Hayter, Haytor ˈheɪ.təʳ ⓤⓢ -t̬ɚ
hayward (H) ˈheɪ.wəd ⓤⓢ -wɚd **-s** -z
haywire ˈheɪ.waɪəʳ ⓤⓢ -waɪr
Haywood ˈheɪ.wʊd
Hazara həˈzɑː.rə ⓤⓢ -ˈzɑːr.ə
hazard (H) ˈhæz.əd ⓤⓢ -ɚd **-s** -z **-ing** -ɪŋ **-ed** -ɪd
hazardous ˈhæz.ə.dəs ⓤⓢ ˈ-ɚ- **-ly** -li **-ness** -nəs, -nɪs
haz|e heɪz **-es** -ɪz **-ing** -ɪŋ **-ed** -d
hazel ˈheɪ.zᵊl **-s** -z
Hazelhurst ˈheɪ.zᵊl.hɜːst ⓤⓢ -hɝːst
hazelnut ˈheɪ.zᵊl.nʌt **-s** -s
Hazen ˈheɪ.zᵊn
Hazledean ˈheɪ.zl̩.diːn
Hazlemere ˈheɪ.zl̩.mɪəʳ ⓤⓢ -mɪr
Hazlett ˈheɪz.lɪt, ˈhæz-, -lət
Hazlitt ˈheɪz.lɪt, ˈhæz-
Note: William Hazlitt, the essayist, called himself /ˈheɪz.lɪt/, and the present members of his family pronounce the name thus. He is, however, commonly referred to as /ˈhæz.lɪt/. In the **Hazlitt Gallery** in London the pronunciation is /ˈhæz.lɪt/.
Hazor ˈheɪ.zɔːʳ ⓤⓢ -zɔːr
haz|y ˈheɪ.z|i **-ier** -i.əʳ ⓤⓢ -i.ɚ **-iest** -i.ɪst, -i.əst **-ily** -ɪ.li, -ᵊl.i **-iness** -ɪ.nəs, -ɪ.nɪs
Hazzard ˈhæz.əd ⓤⓢ -ɚd
H-Block ˈeɪtʃ.blɒk ⓤⓢ -blɑːk
H-bomb ˈeɪtʃ.bɒm ⓤⓢ -bɑːm **-s** -z
HDTV ˌeɪtʃ.diː.tiːˈviː
he *strong form:* hiː *weak forms:* hi, i
Note: Weak form word. The strong form /hiː/ is usually used contrastively, e.g. 'I'm not interested in what **he** says, it's **her** I'm listening to' or for emphasis, e.g. '**he**'s the one'. The weak form is /hi/ in careful speech, e.g. 'Does he live here?' /ˌdʌz.hiˌlɪvˈhɪə ⓤⓢ -ˈhɪr/; in rapid speech it may be pronounced /i/ when following a consonant, e.g. 'What does he want?' /ˌwɒt.dəz.iˈwɒnt/ ⓤⓢ ˌwɑːt.dəz.iˈwɑːnt/.
head (H) hed **-s** -z **-ing** -ɪŋ **-ed** -ɪd **ˌhead of ˈstate; ˌhead ˈstart; ˌhead ˈteacher; ˌbite someone's ˈhead off; have ˌeyes in the ˌback of one's ˈhead; ˌbang one's ˌhead against a ˌbrick ˈwall; ˌbury one's ˌhead in the ˈsand; ˌhave one's ˈhead screwed on; ˌhead over ˈheels; keep one's ˌhead above ˈwater; make ˌhead or ˈtail of; ˌhold one's ˌhead ˈhigh**
head|ache ˈhed|.eɪk **-aches** -eɪks **-achy** -ˌeɪ.ki
headband ˈhed.bænd **-s** -z
headbang ˈhed.bæŋ **-s** -z **-ing** -ɪŋ **-ed** -d **-er/s** -əʳ/z ⓤⓢ -ɚ/z
headboard ˈhed.bɔːd ⓤⓢ -bɔːrd **-s** -z
headcas|e ˈhed.keɪs, ˈheg- ⓤⓢ ˈhed- **-es** -ɪz
headcheese ˈhed.tʃiːz
headdress ˈhed.dres **-es** -ɪz
header ˈhed.əʳ ⓤⓢ -ɚ **-s** -z
headfirst ˌhedˈfɜːst ⓤⓢ -ˈfɝːst *stress shift:* ˌheadfirst ˈleap
headgear ˈhed.gɪəʳ ⓤⓢ -gɪr **-s** -z
headhun|t ˈhed.hʌn|t **-ts** -ts **-ting** -tɪŋ ⓤⓢ -t̬ɪŋ **-ted** -tɪd ⓤⓢ -t̬ɪd
headhunt|er ˈhedˌhʌn.t|əʳ ⓤⓢ -t̬|ɚ **-ers** -əz ⓤⓢ -ɚz **-ing** -ɪŋ
heading (H) ˈhed.ɪŋ **-s** -z
Headingl(e)y ˈhed.ɪŋ.li
Headlam ˈhed.ləm
headlamp ˈhed.læmp **-s** -s
headland ˈhed.lənd, -lænd **-s** -z
headless ˈhed.ləs, -lɪs **-ness** -nəs, -nɪs
headlight ˈhed.laɪt **-s** -s
headlin|e ˈhed.laɪn **-es** -z **-ing** -ɪŋ **-ed** -d
headlock ˈhed.lɒk ⓤⓢ -lɑːk
headlong ˈhed.lɒŋ ⓤⓢ -lɑːŋ, -lɔːŋ
headman *of group of workers:* ˌhedˈmæn, ˈ-- **headmen** ˌhedˈmen, ˈ-- *of tribe:* ˈhed|.mæn, -mən **-men** -men, -mən
headmaster ˌhedˈmɑː.stəʳ, ˈ-ˌ-- ⓤⓢ ˈhedˌmæs.tɚ **-s** -z
headmistress ˌhedˈmɪs.trəs, -trɪs, ˈ-ˌ-- ⓤⓢ ˈhedˌ-- **-es** -ɪz
headnote ˈhed.nəʊt ⓤⓢ -noʊt **-s** -s
head-on ˌhedˈɒn ⓤⓢ -ˈɑːn *stress shift:* ˌhead-on ˈimpact
headphones ˈhed.fəʊnz ⓤⓢ -foʊnz
headpiec|e ˈhed.piːs **-es** -ɪz
headquarters ˌhedˈkwɔː.təz, ˈ--- ⓤⓢ ˈhedˌkwɔːr.t̬ɚz
headrest ˈhed.rest **-s** -s
headroom ˈhed.rʊm, -ruːm ⓤⓢ -ruːm, -rʊm
headscar|f ˈhed.skɑː|f ⓤⓢ -skɑːr|f **-ves** -vz
headset ˈhed.set **-s** -s
headship ˈhed.ʃɪp **-s** -s
heads|man ˈhedz|.mən **-men** -mən
headstand ˈhed.stænd **-s** -z
headstone (H) ˈhed.stəʊn ⓤⓢ -stoʊn **-s** -z
headstrong ˈhed.strɒŋ ⓤⓢ -strɑːŋ
headteacher ˌhedˈtiː.tʃəʳ ⓤⓢ -tʃɚ **-s** -z
headwater ˈhedˌwɔː.təʳ ⓤⓢ -ˌwɑː.t̬ɚ, -ˌwɔː- **-s** -z
headway ˈhed.weɪ
headwind ˈhed.wɪnd **-s** -z
headword ˈhed.wɜːd ⓤⓢ -wɝːd **-s** -z
headwork ˈhed.wɜːk ⓤⓢ -wɝːk
head|y ˈhed|.i **-ier** -i.əʳ ⓤⓢ -i.ɚ **-iest** -i.ɪst, -i.əst **-ily** -ɪ.li, -ᵊl.i **-iness** -ɪ.nəs, -ɪ.nɪs
Heagerty ˈheg.ə.ti ⓤⓢ -ɚ.t̬i
heal (H) hiːl **-s** -z **-ing** -ɪŋ **-ed** -d **-er/s** -əʳ/z ⓤⓢ -ɚ/z
Healey ˈhiː.li
health helθ **ˌhealth and ˈsafety; ˈhealth ˌfarm; ˈhealth ˌfood; ˈhealth ˌservice; ˈhealth ˌvisitor**
healthcare ˈhelθ.keəʳ ⓤⓢ -ker
healthful ˈhelθ.fᵊl, -fʊl **-ly** -i **-ness** -nəs, -nɪs
health-giving ˈhelθˌgɪv.ɪŋ
health|y ˈhel.θ|i **-ier** -i.əʳ ⓤⓢ -i.ɚ **-iest** -i.ɪst, -i.əst **-ily** -ɪ.li, -ᵊl.i **-iness** -ɪ.nəs, -ɪ.nɪs
Healy ˈhiː.li
Heaney ˈhiː.ni
Heanor ˈhiː.nəʳ ⓤⓢ -nɚ
heap hiːp **-s** -s **-ing** -ɪŋ **-ed** -t
hear hɪəʳ ⓤⓢ hɪr **-s** -z **-ing/s** -ɪŋ/z **heard** hɜːd ⓤⓢ hɝːd **hearer/s** ˈhɪə.rəʳ/z ⓤⓢ ˈhɪr.ɚ/z **ˈhearing ˌaid; ˌhard of ˈhearing**

heard (H) *(from* **hear***)* hɜːd US hɝːd
hearing-impaired ˈhɪə.rɪŋ.ɪmˌpeəd US ˈhɪr.ɪŋ.ɪmˌperd
hearken ˈhɑː.kᵊn US ˈhɑːr- **-s** -z **-ing** -ɪŋ, ˈhɑːk.nɪŋ US ˈhɑːr.kᵊn.ɪŋ, ˈhɑːrk.nɪŋ **-ed** -d
Hearn(e) hɜːn US hɝːn
hearsay ˈhɪə.seɪ US ˈhɪr-
hears|e hɜːs US hɝːs **-es** -ɪz
Hearsey ˈhɜː.si US ˈhɝː-
Hearst hɜːst US hɝːst
heart hɑːt US hɑːrt **-s** -s **ˈheart atˌtack; ˈheart ˌfailure; ˌeat one's ˈheart out; have one's ˌheart in the ˌright ˈplace; in one's ˌheart of ˈhearts; ˌset one's ˈheart on something; ˌwear one's ˌheart on one's ˈsleeve**
heartache ˈhɑːt.eɪk US ˈhɑːrt-
heartbeat ˈhɑːt.biːt US ˈhɑːrt- **-s** -s
heartbreak ˈhɑːt.breɪk US ˈhɑːrt-
heartbreaking ˈhɑːtˌbreɪ.kɪŋ US ˈhɑːrt- **-ly** -li
heartbroken ˈhɑːtˌbrəʊ.kᵊn US ˈhɑːrtˌbroʊ-
heartburn ˈhɑːt.bɜːn US ˈhɑːrt.bɝːn **-ing** -ɪŋ
-hearted -ˈhɑː.tɪd US -ˈhɑːr.t̬ɪd
Note: Suffix. Compounds containing **-hearted** are normally stressed on the suffix as shown, but a stress shift occurs when the word is used attributively, e.g. **ˈbrokenhearted ˌlover**.
hearten ˈhɑː.tᵊn US ˈhɑːr- **-s** -z **-ing/ly** -ɪŋ/li, ˈhɑːt.nɪŋ/li US ˈhɑːrt- **-ed** -d
heartfelt ˈhɑːt.felt US ˈhɑːrt-
hear|th hɑː|θ US hɑːr|θ **-ths** -θs, -ðz **ˈhearth ˌrug**
hearthstone ˈhɑːθ.stəʊn US ˈhɑːrθ.stoʊn **-s** -z
heartland ˈhɑːt.lænd US ˈhɑːrt- **-s** -z
heartless ˈhɑːt.ləs, -lɪs US ˈhɑːrt- **-ly** -li **-ness** -nəs, -nɪs
heart-rending ˈhɑːtˌren.dɪŋ US ˈhɑːrt- **-ly** -li
heart-searching ˈhɑːtˌsɜː.tʃɪŋ US ˈhɑːrtˌsɝː- **-s** -z
heart's-ease ˈhɑːts.iːz US ˈhɑːrts-
heart-shaped ˈhɑːt.ʃeɪpt US ˈhɑːrt-
heartsick ˈhɑːt.sɪk US ˈhɑːrt- **-ness** -nəs, -nɪs
heartsore ˈhɑːt.sɔːʳ US ˈhɑːrt.sɔːr
heartstrings ˈhɑːt.strɪŋz US ˈhɑːrt-
heart-throb ˈhɑːt.θrɒb US ˈhɑːrt.θrɑːb **-s** -z
heart-to-heart ˌhɑːt.təˈhɑːt US ˌhɑːrt.tuːˈhɑːrt, -təˈ- **-s** -s *stress shift:* ˌheart-to-heart ˈtalk
heart-warming ˈhɑːtˌwɔː.mɪŋ US ˈhɑːrtˌwɔːr- **-ly** -li
heartwood ˈhɑːt.wʊd US ˈhɑːrt-
heart|y ˈhɑː.t|i US ˈhɑːr.t̬|i **-ier** -i.əʳ US -i.ɚ **-iest** -i.ɪst, -i.əst **-ily** -ɪ.li, -ᵊl.i **-iness** -ɪ.nəs, -ɪ.nɪs
heat hiːt **-s** -s **-ing** -ɪŋ US ˈhiː.t̬ɪŋ **-ed/ly** -ɪd/li US ˈhiː.t̬ɪd/li **ˈheat ˌrash; ˈheat ˌspot; ˈheat ˌwave**
heater ˈhiː.təʳ US -t̬ɚ **-s** -z
heath (H) hiːθ **-s** -s **ˌHeath ˈRobinson**
Heathcliff(e) ˈhiːθ.klɪf
Heathcoat ˈhiːθ.kəʊt US -koʊt
Heathcote ˈheθ.kət, ˈhiːθ.kət US ˈhiːθ.koʊt, -kət
heathen ˈhiː.ðᵊn **-s** -z **-ish** -ɪʃ **-dom** -dəm
heathenism ˈhiː.ðᵊn.ɪ.zᵊm
heatheniz|e, -is|e ˈhiː.ðᵊn.aɪz **-es** -ɪz **-ing** -ɪŋ **-ed** -d
heath|er (H) *shrub, girl's name:* ˈheð|.əʳ US -ɚ **-ers** -əz US -ɚz **-ery** -ᵊr.i
Heather *place in Leicestershire:* ˈhiː.ðəʳ US -ðɚ
Heathfield ˈhiːθ.fiːld
heathland ˈhiːθ.lənd, -lænd
Heathrow ˌhiːθˈrəʊ, ˈ-- US -roʊ **ˌHeathrow ˈAirport**
Heath-Stubbs ˌhiːθˈstʌbz
heath|y ˈhiː.θ|i **-ier** -i.əʳ US -i.ɚ **-iest** -i.ɪst, -i.əst
Heaton ˈhiː.tᵊn
heat-seeking ˈhiːtˌsiː.kɪŋ
heatstroke ˈhiːt.strəʊk US -stroʊk
heav|e hiːv **-es** -z **-ing** -ɪŋ **-ed** -d **hove** həʊv US hoʊv **heaver/s** ˈhiː.vəʳ/z US -vɚ/z
heave-ho ˌhiːvˈhəʊ US -hoʊ
heaven (H) ˈhev.ᵊn **-s** -z **move ˌheaven and ˈearth**
heavenl|y ˈhev.ᵊn.l|i **-iness** -ɪ.nəs, -ɪ.nɪs
heaven-sent ˌhev.ᵊnˈsent US ˈ--- *stress shift, British only:* ˌheaven-sent ˈchance
heavenward ˈhev.ᵊn.wəd US -wɚd **-s** -z
Heaviside ˈhev.ɪ.saɪd
heav|y ˈhev|.i **-ier** -i.əʳ US -i.ɚ **-iest** -i.ɪst, -i.əst **-ily** -ɪ.li, -ᵊl.i **-iness** -ɪ.nəs, -ɪ.nɪs **ˌheavy ˈbreather; ˌheavy ˈcream; ˌheavy ˈmetal**
heavy-duty ˌhev.iˈdjuː.ti US -ˈduː.t̬i, -ˈdjuː- *stress shift:* ˌheavy-duty ˈbattery
heavy-handed ˌhev.iˈhæn.dɪd **-ly** -li **-ness** -nəs, -nɪs *stress shift:* ˌheavy-handed ˈcriticism
heavy-hearted ˌhev.iˈhɑː.tɪd US -ˈhɑːr.t̬ɪd **-ly** -li **-ness** -nəs, -nɪs *stress shift:* ˌheavy-hearted ˈlover
heavyweight ˈhev.i.weɪt **-s** -s
Heazell ˈhiː.zᵊl
Hebburn ˈheb.ɜːn, -ən US -ɝːn, -ɚn
Hebden ˈheb.dən
hebdomadal hebˈdɒm.ə.dᵊl US -ˈdɑː.mə- **-ly** -li
Hebe ˈhiː.bi
Heber ˈhiː.bəʳ US -bɚ
Heberden ˈheb.ə.dᵊn US ˈ-ɚ-
Hebraic hiːˈbreɪ.ɪk, hɪˈbreɪ-, hebˈreɪ- US hiːˈbreɪ-, hɪ- **-al** -ᵊl **-ally** -ᵊl.i, -li
Hebra|ism ˈhiː.breɪ|.ɪ.zᵊm, -brɪ- **-isms** -ɪ.zᵊmz **-ist/s** -ɪst/s
Hebraistic ˌhiː.breɪˈɪst.ɪk, -brɪˈ-
hebraiz|e, -is|e ˈhiː.breɪ.aɪz, -brɪ- **-es** -ɪz **-ing** -ɪŋ **-ed** -d
Hebrew ˈhiː.bruː **-s** -z
Hebridean ˌheb.rɪˈdiː.ən, -rəˈ- **-s** -z *stress shift:* ˌHebridean ˈcattle
Hebrides ˈheb.rɪ.diːz, -rə-
Hebron *biblical place-name:* ˈheb.rɒn, ˈhiː.brɒn, -brən US ˈhiː.brən, ˈheb- *modern surname:* ˈheb.rən, -rɒn US -rən, -rɑːn
Hecate ˈhek.ə.ti *in Shakespeare sometimes:* ˈhek.ət
hecatomb ˈhek.ə.tuːm, -təʊm, -təm US -toʊm, -tʊm **-s** -z
Hecht hekt
heck hek
heckl|e ˈhek.l̩ **-es** -z **-ing** -ɪŋ, ˈhek.lɪŋ **-ed** -d **-er/s** -əʳ/z US -ɚ/z, ˈhek.ləʳ/z US -lɚ/z
Heckmondwike ˈhek.mənd.waɪk
Hecla ˈhek.lə
hectare ˈhek.teəʳ, -tɑːʳ, -təʳ US -ter **-s** -z
hectic ˈhek.tɪk **-ally** -ᵊl.i, -li
hectogram, hectogramme ˈhek.təʊ.græm US -toʊ-, -tə- **-s** -z
hectograph ˈhek.təʊ.grɑːf, -græf US -toʊ.græf, -tə- **-s** -s **-ing** -ɪŋ **-ed** -t
hectographic ˌhek.təʊˈgræf.ɪk US -toʊˈ-, -təˈ-
hectolitre, hectoliter ˈhek.təʊˌliː.təʳ US -toʊˌliː.t̬ɚ, -təˌ- **-s** -z
hectometre, hectometer ˈhek.təʊˌmiː.təʳ US -toʊˌmiː.t̬ɚ, -təˌ- **-s** -z
hector (H) ˈhek.təʳ US -tɚ **-s** -z **-ing** -ɪŋ **-ed** -d
Hecuba ˈhek.jə.bə, -jʊ-
heder ˈheɪ.dəʳ US ˈheɪ.dɚ *as if Hebrew:* ˈxeɪ- **-s** -z **hadarim** ˌhæd.ɑːˈriːm US ˌhɑː- *as if Hebrew:* ˌxæd- US ˌxɑː-
Hedgcock ˈhedʒ.kɒk US -kɑːk
hedg|e hedʒ **-es** -ɪz **-ing** -ɪŋ **-ed** -d **-er/s** -əʳ/z US -ɚ/z **ˈhedge ˌsparrow; ˌhedge one's ˈbets**
hedgehog ˈhedʒ.hɒg US -hɑːg, -hɔːg **-s** -z
hedgehop ˈhedʒ.hɒp US -hɑːp **-s** -s **-ping** -ɪŋ **-ped** -t
Hedgeley ˈhedʒ.li
Hedger ˈhedʒ.əʳ US -ɚ
Hedgerley ˈhedʒ.ə.li US ˈ-ɚ-

hedgerow 'hedʒ.rəʊ ⓊⓈ -roʊ **-s** -z
Hedges 'hedʒ.ɪz
Hedley 'hed.li
hedon|ism 'hiː.dᵊn|.ɪ.zᵊm, 'hed.ᵊn- ⓊⓈ 'hiː.dᵊn- **-ist/s** -ɪst/s
hedonistic ˌhiː.dᵊn'ɪs.tɪk, ˌhed.ᵊn'- ⓊⓈ ˌhiː.dᵊn'- **-ally** -ᵊl.i, -li
heebie-jeebies ˌhiː.bi'dʒiː.biz
heed hiːd **-s** -z **-ing** -ɪŋ **-ed** -ɪd
heedful 'hiːd.fᵊl, -fʊl **-ly** -i **-ness** -nəs, -nɪs
heedless 'hiːd.ləs, -lɪs **-ly** -li **-ness** -nəs, -nɪs
heehaw 'hiːˌhɔː, ˌ-'- ⓊⓈ 'hiː.hɑː, -hɔː, ˌ-'- **-s** -z **-ing** -ɪŋ **-ed** -d
heel hiːl **-s** -z **-ing** -ɪŋ **-ed** -d **ˌcool one's 'heels; ˌdig one's 'heels in; ˌdrag one's 'heels; ˌhard on the 'heels of; ˌkick one's 'heels**
heeler 'hiː.ləʳ ⓊⓈ -lɚ **-s** -z
Heeley 'hiː.li
Heenan 'hiː.nən
Heep hiːp
Heffer 'hef.əʳ ⓊⓈ -ɚ
Hefner 'hef.nəʳ ⓊⓈ -nɚ
heft heft **-s** -s **-ing** -ɪŋ **-ed** -tɪd
heft|y 'hef.t|i **-ier** -i.əʳ ⓊⓈ -i.ɚ **-iest** -i.ɪst, -i.əst **-ily** -ɪ.li, -ᵊl.i **-iness** -ɪ.nəs, -ɪ.nɪs
Hegarty 'heg.ə.ti ⓊⓈ -ɚ.t̬i
Hegel 'heɪ.gᵊl
Hegelian hɪ'geɪ.li.ən, heg'eɪ-; heɪ'giː-, heg'iː- **-ism** -ɪ.zᵊm
hegemonic ˌheg.ɪ'mɒn.ɪk, ˌhiː.gɪ'-, ˌhedʒ.ɪ'-, -ə'- ⓊⓈ ˌhedʒ.ɪ'mɑː.nɪk
hegemony hɪ'gem.ə.ni, hiː'gem-, -'dʒem-; 'heg.ɪ.mə-, 'hedʒ- ⓊⓈ hɪ'dʒem.ə-; 'hedʒ.ə.moʊ-
hegira (H) 'hedʒ.ɪ.rə, -ᵊr.ə, hɪ'dʒaɪᵊ.rə, hedʒ'aɪᵊ- ⓊⓈ 'hedʒ.ɪ.rə, -ɚ.ə, hɪ'dʒaɪ-, hedʒ'aɪ- **-s** -z
Hegley 'heg.li
Heidegger 'haɪ.deg.əʳ, -dɪ.gəʳ ⓊⓈ -dɪ.gɚ
Heidelberg 'haɪ.dᵊl.bɜːg ⓊⓈ -bɝːg
Heidi 'haɪ.di
heifer 'hef.əʳ ⓊⓈ -ɚ **-s** -z
heigh heɪ
heigh-ho ˌheɪ'həʊ ⓊⓈ -'hoʊ
Heighington 'heɪ.ɪŋ.tən, 'hiː-
height haɪt **-s** -s
heighten 'haɪ.tᵊn **-s** -z **-ing** -ɪŋ, 'haɪt.nɪŋ **-ed** -d
Heighton 'heɪ.tᵊn
Heighway 'haɪ.weɪ, 'heɪ-
Heimlich manoeuvre, Heimlich maneuver 'haɪm.lɪk.məˌnuː.vəʳ, -lɪx- ⓊⓈ -vɚ
Heineken® 'haɪ.nɪ.kᵊn, -nə-
Heinekey 'haɪ.nɪ.ki
Heinemann 'haɪ.nə.mən, -mæn
Heinlein 'haɪn.laɪn
heinous 'heɪ.nəs, 'hiː- ⓊⓈ 'heɪ- **-ly** -li **-ness** -nəs, -nɪs
Heinz haɪnts, haɪnz
Note: The trademark is always pronounced /haɪnz/.
heir eəʳ ⓊⓈ er **-s** -z **-dom** -dəm **-less** -ləs, -lɪs, -les **ˌheir ap'parent; ˌheir pre'sumptive**
heiress 'eə.res, -rɪs, -res; eə'res ⓊⓈ 'er.ɪs **-es** -ɪz
heirloom 'eə.luːm ⓊⓈ 'er- **-s** -z
heirship 'eə.ʃɪp ⓊⓈ 'er-
heist haɪst **-s** -s **-ing** -ɪŋ **-ed** -ɪd
heister 'haɪ.stəʳ ⓊⓈ -stɚ **-s** -z
hejira (H) 'hedʒ.ɪ.rə, -ᵊr.ə; hɪ'dʒaɪᵊ.rə, hə- **-s** -z
Hekla 'hek.lə
Hel hel
held *(from* **hold***)* held
Helen 'hel.ən, -ɪn
Helena 'hel.ɪ.nə, '-ə-; hel'iː.nə, hɪ'liː-, hə-
Note: /'hel.ɪ.nə, 'hel.ə.nə/ are the more usual pronunciations, except in the name of the island **St. Helena**; the city in Montana is normally /'hel-/.
Helene hel'eɪn, hɪ'leɪn, hə-, -'liːn
Helensburgh 'hel.ənzˌbᵊr.ə, -ɪnzˌ-, -ˌbʌr- ⓊⓈ -bɝːg
Helenus 'hel.ɪ.nəs, '-ə-
Helga 'hel.gə
heliacal hɪ'laɪə.kᵊl, hiː-, hel'aɪə- **-ly** -i
Heliades hel'aɪə.diːz, hɪ'laɪə-
helianth|us ˌhiː.li'æn*t*.θ|əs, ˌhel.i'- **-i** -aɪ **-uses** -ə.sɪz
helical 'hel.ɪ.kᵊl, 'hiː.lɪ- **-ly** -i
helices *(plur. of* **helix***)* 'hiː.lɪ.siːz, 'hel.ɪ-, -lə-
Helicon 'hel.ɪ.kᵊn, '-ə-, -ɪ.kɒn ⓊⓈ -kɑːn, -kᵊn
helicopter 'hel.ɪ.kɒp.təʳ, '-əˌ- ⓊⓈ -kɑːp.tɚ **-s** -z
Heligoland 'hel.ɪ.gəʊ.lænd, '-ə- ⓊⓈ -goʊ-
heliocentric ˌhiː.li.əʊ'sen.trɪk ⓊⓈ -oʊ'-, -ə'- **-al** -ᵊl **-ally** -ᵊl.i, -li *stress shift:* ˌheliocentric 'force
Heliogabalus ˌhiː.li.əʊ'gæb.ᵊl.əs ⓊⓈ -oʊ'-, -ə'-
heliogram 'hiː.li.əʊ.græm ⓊⓈ -oʊ-, -ə- **-s** -z
heliograph 'hiː.li.əʊ.grɑːf, -græf ⓊⓈ -oʊ.græf, -ə- **-s** -s
heliograph|er ˌhiː.li'ɒg.rə.f|əʳ ⓊⓈ -'ɑː.grə.f|ɚ **-ers** -əz ⓊⓈ -ɚz **-y** -i
heliographic ˌhiː.li.əʊ'græf.ɪk ⓊⓈ -oʊ-', -ə'- **-al** -ᵊl
heliometer ˌhiː.li'ɒm.ɪ.təʳ, '-ə- ⓊⓈ -'ɑː.mə.t̬ɚ **-s** -z
heliometric ˌhiː.li.əʊ'met.rɪk ⓊⓈ -oʊ'- **-ally** -ᵊl.i, -li
Heliopolis ˌhiː.li'ɒp.ᵊl.ɪs ⓊⓈ -'ɑː.pᵊl-
Helios 'hiː.li.ɒs ⓊⓈ -ɑːs
helioscope 'hiː.li.əʊ.skəʊp ⓊⓈ -oʊ.skoʊp, -ə- **-s** -s
heliostat 'hiː.li.əʊ.stæt ⓊⓈ -oʊ-, -ə- **-s** -s
heliotrope 'hiː.li.ə.trəʊp, 'hel.i- ⓊⓈ 'hiː.li.ə.troʊp **-s** -s
heliotropic ˌhiː.li.ə'trɒp.ɪk ⓊⓈ -'trɑː.pɪk **-ally** -ᵊl.i, -li
heliotropism ˌhiː.li'ɒt.rə.pɪ.zᵊm; 'hiː.li.əˌtrəʊ-, ˌhiː.li.ə'trəʊ- ⓊⓈ ˌhiː.li'ɑː.trə-
helipad 'hel.ɪ.pæd **-s** -z
heliport 'hel.ɪ.pɔːt ⓊⓈ -pɔːrt **-s** -s
helium 'hiː.li.əm
helix 'hiː.lɪks **-es** -ɪz **helices** 'hiː.lɪ.siːz, 'hel.ɪ-, -lə-
hell (H) hel **-s** -z **ˌHell's 'Angel; come ˌhell or ˌhigh 'water**
he'll *(=* **he will***)* hiːl
hellacious hel'eɪ.ʃəs
Hellas 'hel.æs ⓊⓈ -æs, -əs
hellbent ˌhel'bent ⓊⓈ '-,-
hellebore 'hel.ɪ.bɔːʳ, '-ə- ⓊⓈ -bɔːr
helleborine 'hel.ɪ.bə.raɪn, '-ə-, -riːn; ˌhel.ɪ'bɔː.riːn, -ə'- ⓊⓈ ˌhel.ə'bɔːr.ɪn, -iːn
Hellene 'hel.iːn **-s** -z
Hellenic hel'iː.nɪk, hɪ'liː-, hə-, -'len- ⓊⓈ hə'len-
Hellen|ism 'hel.ɪ.n|ɪ.zᵊm, '-ə- **-isms** -ɪ.zᵊmz **-ist/s** -ɪst/s
Hellenistic ˌhel.ɪ'nɪs.tɪk, -ə'- **-al** -ᵊl **-ally** -ᵊl.i, -li
helleniz|e, -is|e 'hel.ɪ.naɪz, '-ə- **-es** -ɪz **-ing** -ɪŋ **-ed** -d
Heller 'hel.əʳ ⓊⓈ -ɚ
Hellespont 'hel.ɪ.spɒnt, '-ə- ⓊⓈ -spɑːnt
hellfire ˌhel'faɪəʳ, '-- ⓊⓈ 'hel.faɪr
hellhole 'hel.həʊl ⓊⓈ -hoʊl **-s** -z
hellhound 'hel.haʊnd **-s** -z
Hellingly ˌhel.ɪŋ'laɪ
hellish 'hel.ɪʃ **-ly** -li **-ness** -nəs, -nɪs
Hellman 'hel.mən
hello hel'əʊ, hə'ləʊ ⓊⓈ hel'oʊ, hə'loʊ, 'hel.oʊ **-(e)s** -z **-ing** -ɪŋ **-ed** -d
helluva 'hel.ə.və
hellward 'hel.wəd ⓊⓈ -wɚd
helm helm **-s** -z
helme|t 'hel.mə|t, -mɪ|t **-ts** -ts **-ted** -tɪd ⓊⓈ -t̬ɪd
Helmholtz 'helm.həʊlts ⓊⓈ -hoʊlts
helminth 'hel.mɪn*t*θ **-s** -s
helminthiasis ˌhel.mɪn*t*'θaɪə.sɪs
Helmsley 'helmz.li *locally:* 'hemz-
helms|man 'helmz|.mən **-men** -mən, -men
Helmut 'hel.mʊt
Héloïse ˌel.əʊ'iːz ⓊⓈ -oʊ'-; 'el.ə.wiːz
hel|ot 'hel|.ət **-ots** -əts **-otage** -ə.tɪdʒ ⓊⓈ -ə.t̬ɪdʒ **-otism** -ə.tɪ.zᵊm ⓊⓈ -ə.t̬ɪ.zᵊm **-otry** -ət.ri

help help **-s** -s **-ing/s** -ɪŋ/s **-ed** -t **-er/s** -əʳ/z (US) -ɚ/z

helpful ˈhelp.fᵊl, -fʊl **-ly** -i **-ness** -nəs, -nɪs

helpless ˈhelp.ləs, -lɪs **-ly** -li **-ness** -nəs, -nɪs

helpline ˈhelp.laɪn **-s** -z

helpmate ˈhelp.meɪt **-s** -s

helpmeet ˈhelp.miːt **-s** -s

Helsingborg ˈhel.sɪŋ.bɔːg (US) -bɔːrg

Helsinki helˈsɪŋ.ki, ˈ--- (US) ˈhel.siŋ.ki, -ˈ--

Helston(e) ˈhel.stən

helter-skelter ˌhel.təˈskel.təʳ (US) -t̬ɚˈskel.t̬ɚ **-s** -z

helve helv **-s** -z

Helvellyn helˈvel.ɪn

Helveti|a helˈviː.ʃ|ə, -ʃi|.ə **-an/s** -ən/z

Helvetic helˈvet.ɪk (US) -ˈvet̬-

Helvétius helˈviː.ʃəs, -ʃi.əs (US) -ˈviː-, -ˈveɪ-

Hely ˈhiː.li

hem (*n. v.*) hem **-s** -z **-ming** -ɪŋ **-med** -d

hemal ˈhiː.mᵊl

he|-man ˈhiː|.mæn **-men** -men

Hemans ˈhem.ənz

hematite ˈhiː.mə.taɪt, ˈhem.ə- (US) ˈhiː.mə-

hematologic ˌhiː.mə.təˈlɒdʒ.ɪk (US) -ˈlɑː.dʒɪk **-al** -ᵊl

hematolog|y ˌhiː.məˈtɒl.ə.dʒ|i (US) -ˈtɑː.lə- **-ist/s** -ɪst/s

hematoma ˌhiː.məˈtəʊ.mə, ˌhem.əˈ- (US) ˌhiː.məˈtoʊ- **-s** -z **-ta** -tə

heme hiːm

Hemel Hempstead ˌhem.ᵊlˈhem*p*.stɪd, -stəd, -sted

hemicycle ˈhem.iˌsaɪ.kl̩ **-s** -z

hemidemisemiquaver ˌhem.iˌdem.iˈsem.iˌkweɪ.vəʳ (US) -vɚ **-s** -z

Heming ˈhem.ɪŋ

Hemingway ˈhem.ɪŋ.weɪ

hemipleg|ia ˌhem.iˈpliː.dʒ|i.ə, -dʒ|ə **-ic** -ɪk

hemisphere ˈhem.ɪ.sfɪəʳ, ˈ-ə- (US) -sfɪr **-s** -z

hemispheric ˌhem.ɪˈsfer.ɪk, -əˈ- (US) -ˈsfɪr-, -ˈsfer- **-al** -ᵊl **-ally** -ᵊl.i, -li

hemistich ˈhem.i.stɪk **-s** -s

hemline ˈhem.laɪn **-s** -z

hemlock ˈhem.lɒk (US) -lɑːk **-s** -s

Hemming ˈhem.ɪŋ

Hemmings ˈhem.ɪŋz

hemoglobin ˌhiː.məʊˈgləʊ.bɪn, ˌhem.əʊˈ- (US) ˈhiː.moʊ.gloʊ-, ˈ-ə-

hemophili|a ˌhiː.məˈfɪl.i|.ə, ˌhem.əˈ- (US) ˌhiː.moʊˈ-, -məˈ- **-ac/s** -æk/s

hemorrhag|e ˈhem.ᵊr.ɪdʒ (US) -ɚ.ɪdʒ, ˈ-rɪdʒ **-es** -ɪz **-ing** -ɪŋ **-ed** -d

hemorrhoid ˈhem.ᵊr.ɔɪd (US) -ə.rɔɪd, ˈ-rɔɪd **-s** -z

hemosta|sis ˌhiː.məˈsteɪ|.sɪs, ˌhem.əˈ- (US) ˌhiː.məˈ- **-ses** -siːz

hemp hemp **-en** -ən

Hemp(e)l ˈhem.pᵊl

hemstitch ˈhem.stɪtʃ **-es** -ɪz **-ing** -ɪŋ **-ed** -t

Hemy ˈhem.i

hen hen **-s** -z ˈ**hen** ˌ**party**

henbane ˈhen.beɪn, ˈhem- (US) ˈhen-

hence hen*t*s

henceforth ˌhen*t*sˈfɔːθ (US) ˈhen*t*s.fɔːrθ

henceforward ˌhen*t*sˈfɔː.wəd (US) -ˈfɔːr.wɚd

Henchard ˈhen.tʃɑːd, -tʃəd (US) -tʃɚd, -tʃɑːrd

hench|man ˈhen*t*ʃ|.mən **-men** -mən

hencoop ˈhen.kuːp **-s** -s

hendecagon henˈdek.ə.gən (US) -gɑːn **-s** -z

hendecagonal ˌhen.dɪˈkæg.ᵊn.ᵊl, -dekˈæg-

hendecasyllabic henˌdek.ə.sɪˈlæb.ɪk, -səˈ- **-s** -s

hendecasyllable ˌhen.dek.əˈsɪl.ə.bᵊl **-s** -z

Henderson ˈhen.də.sᵊn (US) -dɚ-

hendiadys henˈdaɪə.dɪs

Hendon ˈhen.dən

Hendricks ˈhen.drɪks

Hendrickson ˈhen.drɪk.sᵊn

Hendrix ˈhen.drɪks

Hendry ˈhen.dri

Heneage ˈhen.ɪdʒ

heng|e hendʒ **-es** -ɪz

Hengist ˈheŋ.gɪst

Henley ˈhen.li

Henlow ˈhen.ləʊ (US) -loʊ

Henman ˈhen.mən

henna ˈhen.ə **-s** -z **-ing** -ɪŋ **-ed** -d

henner|y ˈhen.ᵊr|.i **-ies** -iz

Henness(e)y ˈhen.ə.si, ˈ-ɪ-

Henniker ˈhen.ɪ.kəʳ (US) -kɚ

Henning ˈhen.ɪŋ

henpeck ˈhen.pek, ˈhem- (US) ˈhen- **-s** -s **-ing** -ɪŋ **-ed** -t

Henri *French name:* ˈɑ̃ːn.riː, -ˈ- (US) ɑ̃ːnˈriː *US surname:* ˈhen.ri

Henrietta ˌhen.riˈet.ə (US) -ˈet̬-

Henriques henˈriː.kɪz

henr|y (H) ˈhen.r|i **-ys** -iz **-ies** -iz

Henryson ˈhen.rɪ.sᵊn

Hensen ˈhen*t*.sᵊn

Hensley ˈhenz.li

Henslow(e) ˈhenz.ləʊ (US) -loʊ

Henson ˈhen*t*.sᵊn

Henty ˈhen.ti (US) -t̬i

Hentzau ˈhent.zaʊ

hepatic hɪˈpæt.ɪk, hepˈæt- (US) hɪˈpæt̬-

hepatica hɪˈpæt.ɪ.kə, hepˈæt- (US) hɪˈpæt̬- **-s** -z

hepatite ˈhep.ə.taɪt

hepati|tis ˌhep.əˈtaɪ|.tɪs, -təs (US) -t̬ɪs **-tides** -tɪ.diːz

Hepburn ˈheb.ɜːn, -bən; ˈhep.bɜːn (US) ˈhep.bɝːn, -bɚn

Note: The names of Katharine and Audrey Hepburn are usually pronounced /ˈhep.bɜːn (US) -bɜːrn/.

Hephaestus hɪˈfiː.stəs, hefˈiː-, həˈfiː- (US) hɪˈfes.təs

Hephzibah ˈhef.sɪ.bɑː, ˈhep-, -sə-

Hepplewhite ˈhep.l̩.*h*waɪt

hepta- ˈhep.tə-; hepˈtæ-

Note: Prefix. Normally takes either primary or secondary stress on the first syllable, e.g. **heptagon** /ˈhep.tə.gᵊn (US) -gɑːn/, **heptahedron** /ˌhep.təˈhiː.drᵊn/, or primary stress on the second syllable, e.g. **heptathlete** /hepˈtæθ.liːt/.

heptagon ˈhep.tə.gᵊn, -gɒn (US) -gɑːn **-s** -z

heptagonal hepˈtæg.ᵊn.ᵊl

heptahedr|on ˌhep.təˈhiː.dr|ən, -ˈhed.r|ən, -r|ɒn; ˈhep.təˌhiː.dr|ən, -ˌhed.r|ən, -r|ɒn (US) ˌhep.təˈhiː.dr|ən **-ons** -ənz **-a** -ə **-al** -ᵊl

heptameter hepˈtæm.ɪ.təʳ, ˈ-ə- (US) -ə.t̬ɚ **-s** -z

heptarch ˈhep.tɑːk (US) -tɑːrk **-s** -s **-y** -i **-ies** -iz

Heptateuch ˈhep.tə.tjuːk (US) -tuːk, -tjuːk

heptathlete hepˈtæθ.liːt **-s** -s

heptathlon hepˈtæθ.lɒn, -lən (US) -lɑːn **-s** -z

Hepworth ˈhep.wəθ, -wɜːθ (US) -wɝːθ, -wɚθ

her *strong form:* hɜːʳ (US) hɝː *weak forms:* həʳ, əʳ (US) hɚ, ɚ **-s** -z

Note: Weak form word. The strong form /hɜːʳ (US) hɜːr/ is used for emphasis, e.g. 'it was **her** fault' or contrast, e.g. 'his or her bank'. There is a weak form /həʳ (US) hɚ/ which is used at the beginning of sentences, e.g. 'Her train was late' /həˈtreɪn.wəzˌleɪt (US) hɚ-/ and elsewhere in slow, careful speech, e.g. 'I admired her skill', /aɪ.ədˌmaɪəd.həˈskɪl (US) -ˌmaɪrd.hɚˈ-/. In rapid speech the weak form is likely to be /əʳ (US) ɚ/, e.g. 'Let her through', /ˌlet.əˈθruː (US) ˌlet̬.ɚˈ-/.

Hera ˈhɪə.rə (US) ˈhɪr.ə, ˈhiː.rə

Heraclean ˌher.əˈkliː.ən

Heracles ˈher.ə.kliːz, ˈhɪə.rə- (US) ˈher.ə-

Heraclitus ˌher.əˈklaɪ.təs (US) -t̬əs

Heraklion herˈæk.li.ən

herald ˈher.əld **-s** -z **-ing** -ɪŋ **-ed** -ɪd

heraldic hɪˈræl.dɪk, həˈræl-, herˈæl- (US) həˈræl-, herˈæl- **-ally** -ᵊl.i, -li

heraldr|y ˈher.ᵊl.dr|i **-ies** -iz

Herat herˈæt, hɪˈræt, həˈræt, -ˈrɑːt (US) herˈɑːt

herb (H) hɜːb (US) ɝːb, hɝːb **-s** -z **-age** -ɪdʒ **-y** -i

Note: The US pronunciation for the name **Herb** is always /hɜːrb/.

herbaceous hɜːˈbeɪ.ʃəs, hə- (US) hɝˈ-, ɝˈ- **her,baceous ˈborder**

herbal ˈhɜː.bᵊl (US) ˈhɝː-, ˈɝː-

herbal|ism ˈhɜː.bᵊl|.ɪ.zᵊm (US) ˈhɝː-, ˈɝː- **-ist/s** -ɪst/s

herbarium hɜːˈbeə.ri.əm (US) hɝːˈber.i-, ɝː- **-s** -z

Herbert ˈhɜː.bət (US) ˈhɝː.bɚt

herbicidal ˌhɜː.bɪˈsaɪ.dᵊl (US) ˌhɝː-, ˌɝː-

herbicide ˈhɜː.bɪ.saɪd (US) ˈhɝː-, ˈɝː- **-s** -z

Herbie ˈhɜː.bi (US) ˈhɝː-

herbivore ˈhɜː.bɪ.vɔːʳ (US) ˈhɝː.bə.vɔːr, ˈɝː- **-s** -z

herbivorous hɜːˈbɪv.ᵊr.əs, hə- (US) hɝː-, hɚ-, ɝː-, ɚ-

herboriz|e, -is|e ˈhɜː.bᵊr.aɪz (US) ˈhɝː-, ˈɝː- **-es** -ɪz **-ing** -ɪŋ **-ed** -d

Herbst hɜːbst (US) hɝːpst

Herculaneum ˌhɜː.kjəˈleɪ.ni.əm, -kjʊˈ- (US) ˌhɝː.kjəˈ-

Hercule ˈeə.kjuːl, ˈɜː-, ˌ-ˈ- (US) erˈkjuːl, ɝː- ˌ**Hercule ˈPoirot, ˌHercule Poiˈrot**

herculean (H) ˌhɜː.kjəˈliː.ən, -kjʊˈ-; hɜːˈkjuː.li- (US) ˌhɝː.kjuːˈliː-; hɚˈkjuː.li-

Hercules ˈhɜː.kjə.liːz, -kjʊ- (US) ˈhɝː.kjə-

herd (H) hɜːd (US) hɝːd **-s** -z **-ing** -ɪŋ **-ed** -ɪd ˌ**herd ˈinstinct**

herds|man ˈhɜːdz|.mən (US) ˈhɝːdz- **-men** -mən

here hɪəʳ (US) hɪr ˌ**here, ˌthere, and ˈeverywhere; ˌneither ˌhere nor ˈthere**

hereabouts ˌhɪər.əˈbaʊts, ˈ--- (US) ˌhɪr.əˈbaʊts, ˈ---

hereafter ˌhɪərˈɑːf.təʳ (US) ˌhɪrˈæf.tɚ

hereby ˌhɪəˈbaɪ, ˈ-- (US) ˌhɪrˈbaɪ, ˈ--

hereditable hɪˈred.ɪ.tə.bl̩, hə-, herˈed-, ˈ-ə- (US) həˈred.ɪ.t̬ə-

hereditament ˌher.ɪˈdɪt.ə.mənt, -əˈ-, ˈ-ɪ- (US) -əˈdɪt̬.ə- **-s** -s

hereditar|y hɪˈred.ɪ.tᵊr|.i, hə-, herˈed-, ˈ-ə- (US) həˈred.ɪ.ter- **-ily** -ᵊl.i, -ɪ.li **-iness** -ɪ.nəs, -ɪ.nɪs

heredity hɪˈred.ə.ti, hə-, herˈed-, -ɪ.ti (US) həˈred.ɪ-

Hereford *place in UK:* ˈher.ɪ.fəd, -ə.fəd (US) -ə.fɚd **-shire** -ʃəʳ, -ˌʃɪəʳ (US) -ʃɚ, -ˌʃɪr *in US:* ˈhɜː.fəd (US) ˈhɝː.fɚd

herein ˌhɪəʳˈɪn (US) ˌhɪr-

hereinabove ˌhɪəʳ.ɪn.əˈbʌv (US) ˌhɪr-

hereinafter ˌhɪəʳ.ɪnˈɑːf.təʳ (US) ˌhɪr.ɪnˈæf.tɚ

hereinbefore ˌhɪəʳ.ɪn.bɪˈfɔːʳ, -bəˈfɔːʳ (US) ˌhɪr.ɪn.bɪˈfɔːr, -bəˈ-

hereinbelow ˌhɪəʳ.ɪn.bɪˈləʊ, -bəˈ- (US) ˌhɪr.ɪn.bɪˈloʊ, -bəˈ-

hereof ˌhɪəʳˈɒv (US) ˌhɪrˈɑːv

hereon ˌhɪəʳˈɒn (US) ˌhɪrˈɑːn

Herero həˈreə.rəʊ, herˈeə-, -ˈɪə-; ˈhɪə.rə.rəʊ, ˈher.ə- (US) həˈrer.oʊ; ˈher.ə.roʊ **-s** -z

heresiarch həˈriː.zi.ɑːk, hɪ-, herˈiː-; -si-, ˈher.ə.si- (US) həˈriː.zi.ɑːrk; ˈher.ə.si- **-s** -s

heres|y ˈher.ə.s|i, ˈ-ɪ- **-ies** -iz

heretic ˈher.ə.tɪk, -ɪ.tɪk (US) ˈ-ə- **-s** -s

heretic|al həˈret.ɪ.k|ᵊl, hɪˈ-, herˈet- (US) həˈret̬- **-ally** -ᵊl.i, -li

hereto ˌhɪəˈtuː (US) ˌhɪr-

heretofore ˌhɪə.tuːˈfɔːʳ (US) ˌhɪr.tuːˈfɔːr, ˈ---

hereunder ˌhɪəʳˈʌn.dəʳ (US) ˌhɪrˈʌn.dɚ, ˈ---

hereunto ˌhɪəʳ.ʌnˈtuː, -ˈʌn.tuː (US) ˌhɪr-, ˈ---

hereupon ˌhɪəʳ.əˈpɒn (US) ˌhɪr.əˈpɑːn, ˈ---

Hereward ˈher.ɪ.wəd, -ə- (US) -wɚd

herewith ˌhɪəˈwɪð, -ˈwɪθ (US) ˌhɪrˈwɪð, ˈ--

Herford ˈhɜː.fəd, ˈhɑː- (US) ˈhɝː.fɚd

Hergé eəˈʒeɪ (US) er-

heriot (H) ˈher.i.ət, -ɒt (US) -ət **-s** -s

Heriot-Watt ˌher.i.ətˈwɒt (US) -ˈwɑːt

heritable ˈher.ɪ.tə.bl̩, ˈ-ə- (US) -ɪ.t̬ə-

heritag|e ˈher.ɪ.tɪdʒ, ˈ-ə- (US) -ɪ.t̬ɪdʒ **-es** -ɪz

heritor ˈher.ɪ.təʳ, ˈ-ə- (US) -ɪ.t̬ɚ **-s** -z

Herkomer ˈhɜː.kə.məʳ (US) ˈhɝː.kə.mɚ **-s** -z

Herman ˈhɜː.mən (US) ˈhɝː-

hermaphrodite hɜːˈmæf.rə.daɪt, hə- (US) hɚˈmæf.roʊ-, -rə- **-s** -s

hermaphroditic hɜːˌmæf.rəˈdɪt.ɪk, hə- (US) hɚˌmæf.roʊˈdɪt̬-, -rəˈ- **-ally** -ᵊl.i, -li

hermeneutic ˌhɜː.mɪˈnjuː.tɪk, -məˈ- (US) ˌhɝː.məˈnuː.t̬ɪk, -ˈnjuː- **-s** -s **-al** -ᵊl **-ally** -ᵊl.i, -li

Hermes ˈhɜː.miːz (US) ˈhɝː-

Hermès® eəˈmes (US) er-

Hermesetas® ˌhɜː.mɪˈsiː.təz, -məˈ-, -təs (US) ˌhɝː.məˈsiː.t̬əz, -təs

hermetic hɜːˈmet.ɪk, hə- (US) hɚˈmet̬- **-al** -ᵊl **-ally** -ᵊl.i, -li

Hermia ˈhɜː.mi.ə (US) ˈhɝː-

Hermione hɜːˈmaɪə.ni, hə- (US) hɚ-

Hermiston ˈhɜː.mɪ.stᵊn (US) ˈhɝː-

hermit ˈhɜː.mɪt (US) ˈhɝː- **-s** -s ˈ**hermit ˌcrab**

hermitag|e (H) ˈhɜː.mɪ.tɪdʒ, -mə- *as if French:* ˌeə.mɪˈtɑːʒ (US) ˈhɝː.mɪ.t̬ɪdʒ **-es** -ɪz

hermitic hɜːˈmɪt.ɪk, hə- (US) hɚˈmɪt̬-

Hermocrates hɜːˈmɒk.rə.tiːz, hə- (US) hɚˈmɑː.krə-

Hermogenes hɜːˈmɒdʒ.ɪ.niːz, hə-, -ən.iːz (US) hɚˈmɑː.dʒə.niːz

Hermon ˈhɜː.mən (US) ˈhɝː-

hern hɜːn (US) hɝːn **-s** -z

Hernandez hɜːˈnæn.dez (US) hɚ-; erˈnɑːn.des

Herne hɜːn (US) hɝːn

herni|a ˈhɜː.ni|.ə (US) ˈhɝː- **-as** -əz **-ae** -iː **-al** -əl

herni|ate ˈhɜː.ni|.eɪt (US) ˈhɝː- **-ates** -eɪts **-ating** -eɪ.tɪŋ (US) -t̬ɪŋ **-ated** -eɪ.tɪd (US) -t̬ɪd

herniation ˌhɜː.niˈeɪ.ʃᵊn (US) ˌhɝː- **-s** -z

hero (H) ˈhɪə.rəʊ (US) ˈhɪr.oʊ, ˈhiː.roʊ **-es** -z ˈ**hero ˌworship**

Herod ˈher.əd ˌ**Herod ˈAntipas**

Herodian herˈəʊ.di.ən, həˈrəʊ-, hɪ- (US) həˈroʊ- **-s** -z

Herodias herˈəʊ.di.æs, həˈrəʊ-, hɪ-, -əs (US) həˈroʊ-

Herodotus herˈɒd.ə.təs, həˈrɒd-, hɪ- (US) həˈrɑː.də.t̬əs

heroic hɪˈrəʊ.ɪk, hə-, herˈəʊ- (US) hɪˈroʊ-, hiː- **-s** -s **-al** -ᵊl **-ally** -ᵊl.i, -li **heˌroic ˈverse**

heroin ˈher.əʊ.ɪn (US) -oʊ-

heroine ˈher.əʊ.ɪn (US) -oʊ- **-s** -z

heroism ˈher.əʊ.ɪ.zᵊm (US) -oʊ-

heron (H) ˈher.ᵊn **-s** -z **-ry** -ri **-ries** -riz

herpes ˈhɜː.piːz (US) ˈhɝː-

herpetologic ˌhɜː.pɪ.təˈlɒdʒ.ɪk, -pə- (US) ˌhɝː.pə.t̬əˈlɑː.dʒɪk **-al** -ᵊl **-ally** -ᵊl.i, -li

herpetolog|y ˌhɜː.pɪˈtɒl.ə.dʒ|i, -pəˈ- (US) -pəˈtɑː.lə- **-ist/s** -ɪst/s

Herr heəʳ (US) her

Herrick ˈher.ɪk

Herries ˈher.ɪs, -ɪz

herring (H) ˈher.ɪŋ **-s** -z

herringbone ˈher.ɪŋ.bəʊn (US) -boʊn **-s** -z

Herriot ˈher.i.ət

Herron ˈher.ən

hers hɜːz (US) hɝːz

Herschel(l) ˈhɜː.ʃᵊl (US) ˈhɝː-

herself həˈself (US) hɚ- *when not initial:* ə- (US) ɚ-

Hershey ˈhɜː.ʃi (US) ˈhɝː-

Herstmonceux ˌhɜːst.mənˈzuː, -mɒn-, -ˈsjuː, -ˈsuː (US) ˌhɝːst.mənˈ-, -mɑːnˈ-

Hertford *in England:* ˈhɑːt.fəd, ˈhɑː- (US) ˈhɑːrt.fɚd, ˈhɑːr- **-shire** -ʃəʳ, -ˌʃɪəʳ (US) -ʃɚ, -ʃɪr

Hertford *in US:* ˈhɜːt.fəd (US) ˈhɝːt.fɚd

Herts. *(abbrev. for* **Hertfordshire***)* hɑːts; ˈhɑːt.fəd.ʃəʳ, ˈhɑː-, -ˌʃɪəʳ (US) hɑːrts; ˈhɑːrt.fɚd.ʃɚ, ˈhɑːr-, -ˌʃɪr

Hertslet ˈhɜːt.slɪt (US) ˈhɝːt-
hertz hɜːts (US) hɝːts
Hertz hɜːts, heəts (US) hɝːts, herts **-ian** -i.ən
Note: The trademark is pronounced /hɜːts (US) hɜːrts/.
Hertzog ˈhɜːt.sɒɡ (US) ˈhɝːt.sɑːɡ, -sɔːɡ
Hervey ˈhɑː.vi, ˈhɜː.vi (US) ˈhɝː-
Herzegovina ˌhɜːt.sə.ɡəʊˈviː.nə, ˌheət-, -sɪ.ɡəʊˈ-; -sɪˈɡɒv.ɪ.nə (US) ˌhɝːt.sə.ɡoʊˈviː.nə
Herzog ˈhɜːt.sɒɡ (US) ˈhɝːt.sɑːɡ, -sɔːɡ
he's (**he is** *or* **he has**) *strong form:* hiːz *occasional weak forms:* hiz, iz
Note: See note for **he**.
Hesba ˈhez.bə
Heseltine ˈhes.əl.taɪn, ˈhez-
Heshbon ˈheʃ.bɒn (US) -bɑːn
Hesiod ˈhiː.si.əd, ˈhes.i-, -ɒd (US) -əd
hesitan|ce ˈhez.ɪ.tᵊnt|s, ˈ-ə- **-cy** -si
hesitant ˈhez.ɪ.tᵊnt, ˈ-ə- **-ly** -li
hesi|tate ˈhez.ɪ|.teɪt, ˈ-ə- **-tates** -teɪts **-tating/ly** -teɪ.tɪŋ/li (US) -teɪ.t̬ɪŋ/li **-tated** -teɪ.tɪd (US) -teɪ.t̬ɪd
hesitation ˌhez.ɪˈteɪ.ʃᵊn, -əˈ- **-s** -z
Hesketh ˈhes.kəθ, -kɪθ
Heskey ˈhes.ki
Hesperian hesˈpɪə.ri.ən (US) -ˈpɪr.i-
Hesperides hesˈper.ɪ.diːz, hɪˈsper-, hə-, ˈ-ə- (US) hesˈper.ɪ-
Hesperus ˈhes.pᵊr.əs
Hess hes
Hessayon ˈhes.i.ən
Hesse ˈhes.ə, hes
hessian (**H**) ˈhes.i.ən (US) ˈheʃ.ᵊn **-s** -z
Hester ˈhes.təʳ (US) -tɚ
Heston ˈhes.tᵊn
Heswall ˈhez.wəl (US) ˈhes.wɔːl
Hesychius hesˈɪk.i.əs
hetero ˈhet.ᵊr.əʊ (US) ˈhet̬.ə.roʊ **-s** -z
heteroclite ˈhet.ᵊr.əʊ.klaɪt (US) ˈhet.ɚ.ə- **-s** -s
heterodox ˈhet.ᵊr.əʊ.dɒks (US) ˈhet̬.ɚ.ə.dɑːks **-y** -i
heterodyne ˈhet.ᵊr.əʊ.daɪn (US) ˈhet̬.ɚ.ə-
heterogeneity ˌhet.ᵊr.əʊ.dʒəˈniː.ə.ti, -dʒɪˈ-, -ɪ.ti (US) ˌhet̬.ə.roʊ.dʒəˈniː.ə.t̬i, ˈ-ɚ.ə-
heterogeneous ˌhet.ᵊr.əʊˈdʒiː.ni.əs (US) ˌhet̬.ə.roʊˈ-, -ɚ.əˈ- **-ly** -li **-ness** -nəs, -nɪs
heterogenesis ˌhet.ᵊr.əʊˈdʒen.ə.sɪs, ˈ-ɪ- (US) ˌhet̬.ə.roʊˈdʒen.ə.sɪs, -ɚ.əˈ-
heteronym ˈhet.ᵊr.əʊ.nɪm (US) ˈhet̬.ə.roʊ-, -ɚ.ə- **-s** -z
heteronym|ous ˌhet.əˈrɒn.ɪ.m|əs, ˈ-ə- (US) ˌhet̬.əˈrɑː.nɪ- **-y** -i
heterosex|ism ˌhet.ᵊr.əʊˈsek.s|ɪ.zᵊm (US) ˌhet̬.ə.roʊˈ-, -ɚ.əˈ- **-ist/s** -ɪst/s
heterosexual ˌhet.ᵊr.əʊˈsek.ʃu.əl, ˈ-sju-, -ʃᵊl (US) ˌhet̬.ə.roʊˈsek.ʃu.əl, -ɚ.əˈ- **-s** -z **-ly** -i
heterosexuality ˌhet.ᵊr.əʊˌsek.ʃuˈæl.ə.ti, -sjuˈ- (US) ˌhet̬.ə.roʊˌsek.ʃuˈæl.ə.t̬i, -ɚ.əˌ-
heterozygous ˌhet.ᵊr.əʊˈzaɪ.ɡəs (US) ˌhet̬.ə.roʊˈ-, -ɚ.əˈ-
Hetherington ˈheð.ᵊr.ɪŋ.tən
Hetton-le-Hole ˌhet.ᵊn.ləˈhəʊl, -lɪˈ- (US) ˌhet̬.ᵊn.ləˈhoʊl
Hetty ˈhet.i (US) ˈhet̬-
het up ˌhetˈʌp (US) ˌhet̬- *stress shift:* ˌhet up ˈteenager
Heugh *place:* hjuːf *surname:* hjuː
heuristic hjʊəˈrɪs.tɪk (US) hjuːˈ- **-s** -s **-ally** -ᵊl.i, -li
Hever ˈhiː.vəʳ (US) -vɚ
hew hjuː **-s** -z **-ing** -ɪŋ **-ed** -d **-n** -n **-er/s** -əʳ/z (US) -ɚ/z
Heward ˈhjuː.əd (US) -ɚd
Hewart ˈhjuː.ət (US) -ɚt
Hewetson ˈhjuː.ɪt.sᵊn
Hewett, Hewitt ˈhjuː.ɪt
Hewke hjuːk
Hewlett ˈhjuː.lɪt, -lət
Hewlettson ˈhjuː.lɪt.sᵊn, -lət-
hewn (*from* **hew**) hjuːn
hex heks **-es** -ɪz **-ing** -ɪŋ **-ed** -t
hexa- ˈhek.sə-; hekˈsæ-
Note: Prefix. Normally either takes primary or secondary stress on the first syllable, e.g. **hexagon** /ˈhek.sə.ɡᵊn (US) -ɡɑːn/, **hexahedron** /ˌhek.səˈhiː.drᵊn/, or primary stress on the second syllable, e.g. **hexagonal** /hekˈsæɡ.ᵊn.ᵊl/.
hexachord ˈhek.sə.kɔːd (US) -kɔːrd **-s** -z
hexagon ˈhek.sə.ɡən (US) -ɡɑːn **-s** -z
hexagonal hekˈsæɡ.ᵊn.ᵊl **-ly** -i
hexagram ˈhek.sə.ɡræm **-s** -z
hexahedr|on ˌhek.səˈhiː.dr|ən, -ˈhed.r|ən (US) -ˈhiː.dr|ən **-ons** -ənz **-a** -ə **-al** -əl
Hexam ˈhek.səm
hexameter hekˈsæm.ɪ.təʳ, hɪkˈ-, ˈ-ə- (US) -ə.t̬ɚ **-s** -z
Hexateuch ˈhek.sə.tjuːk (US) -tuːk, -tjuːk
Hexham ˈhek.səm
Hextable ˈhek.stə.bl̩
hey heɪ
Heycock ˈheɪ.kɒk (US) -kɑːk
heyday ˈheɪ.deɪ
Heyer heɪəʳ (US) heɪɚ
Heyerdahl ˈheɪə.dɑːl (US) ˈheɪɚ-, ˈhaɪɚ-
hey presto ˌheɪˈpres.təʊ (US) -toʊ
Heysham ˈhiː.ʃᵊm
Heyward ˈheɪ.wəd (US) -wɚd
Heywood ˈheɪ.wʊd
Hezbollah ˌhɪz.bɒlˈɑː, ˈhez- (US) ˌhez.bəˈlɑː
Hezekiah ˌhez.ɪˈkaɪə, -əˈ-
Hezlewood ˈhez.l̩.wʊd
HGV ˌeɪtʃ.dʒiːˈviː
hi haɪ
hiatus haɪˈeɪ.təs, hi- (US) haɪˈeɪ.t̬əs **-es** -ɪz
Hiawatha ˌhaɪ.əˈwɒθ.ə (US) -ˈwɑː.θə
hibachi hɪˈbɑː.tʃi, hiː- **-s** -z
Hibbert ˈhɪb.ət, -ɜːt (US) -ɚt, -ɝːt
hibernal haɪˈbɜː.nᵊl (US) -ˈbɝː-
hiber|nate ˈhaɪ.bə|.neɪt (US) -bɚ- **-nates** -neɪts **-nating** -neɪ.tɪŋ (US) -neɪ.t̬ɪŋ **-nated** -neɪ.tɪd (US) -neɪ.t̬ɪd
hibernation ˌhaɪ.bəˈneɪ.ʃᵊn (US) -bɚˈ- **-s** -z
Hibernia haɪˈbɜː.ni.ə, hɪ- (US) -ˈbɝː-
Hibernian (*n. adj.*) haɪˈbɜː.ni.ən (US) -ˈbɝː- **-s** -z *in name of football club:* hɪˈbɜː.ni.ən (US) -ˈbɝː- **-s** -z
Hibernicism haɪˈbɜː.nɪ.sɪ.zᵊm, -nə- (US) -ˈbɝː- **-s** -z
hibiscus hɪˈbɪs.kəs, haɪ- (US) haɪ-, hɪ-
hiccough ˈhɪk.ʌp, -əp **-s** -s **-ing** -ɪŋ **-ed** -t
hiccup ˈhɪk.ʌp, -əp **-s** -s **-(p)ing** -ɪŋ **-(p)ed** -t
hick hɪk **-s** -s
hickey ˈhɪk.i **-s** -z
Hickman ˈhɪk.mən
Hickok ˈhɪk.ɒk (US) -ɑːk
hickory (**H**) ˈhɪk.ᵊr.i (US) -ɚ.i, ˈ-ri
Hicks hɪks
Hickson ˈhɪk.sᵊn
hid (*from* **hide**) hɪd
hidalgo (**H**) hɪˈdæl.ɡəʊ (US) -ɡoʊ **-s** -z
hid|e haɪd **-es** -z **-ing/s** -ɪŋ/z **hid** hɪd **hidden** ˈhɪd.ᵊn **ˌhide-and-ˈseek**; **ˈhiding ˌplace**
hideaway ˈhaɪd.ə.weɪ **-s** -z
hidebound ˈhaɪd.baʊnd
hideous ˈhɪd.i.əs **-ly** -li **-ness** -nəs, -nɪs
hideout ˈhaɪd.aʊt **-s** -s
hid(e)y-hole ˈhaɪ.di.həʊl (US) -hoʊl **-s** -z
hie haɪ **-s** -z **-ing** -ɪŋ **-d** -d
Hierapolis ˌhaɪəˈræp.ᵊl.ɪs (US) ˌhaɪˈræp.ə.lɪs
hierarch ˈhaɪə.rɑːk (US) ˈhaɪ.rɑːrk **-s** -s
hierarchal ˌhaɪəˈrɑː.kᵊl (US) ˌhaɪˈrɑːr-
hierarchic ˌhaɪəˈrɑː.kɪk (US) ˌhaɪˈrɑːr- **-al** -ᵊl **-ally** -ᵊl.i, -li
hierarch|y ˈhaɪə.rɑː.k|i (US) ˈhaɪ.rɑːr- **-ies** -iz
hieratic ˌhaɪəˈræt.ɪk (US) ˌhaɪˈræt̬-
hieroglyph ˈhaɪə.rəʊ.ɡlɪf (US) ˈhaɪ.roʊ- **-s** -s
hieroglyphic ˌhaɪə.rəʊˈɡlɪf.ɪk (US) ˌhaɪ.roʊˈ- **-s** -s **-al** -ᵊl **-ally** -ᵊl.i, -li
Hieronimo hɪəˈrɒn.ɪ.məʊ (US) hɪˈrɑː.nɪ.moʊ
Hieronymus hɪəˈrɒn.ɪ.məs, haɪəˈ- (US) haɪˈrɑː.nɪ-
hierophant ˈhɪə.rəʊ.fænt, ˈhaɪə- (US) ˈhaɪ.roʊ- **-s** -s

hifalutin ˌhaɪ.fəˈluː.tɪn, -tᵊn *stress shift:* ˌhifalutin ˈattitude
hi-fi ˈhaɪ.faɪ, ˌ-ˈ- **-s** -z
Higginbotham ˈhɪg.ɪnˌbɒt.əm, -ᵊnˌ-, -ᵊmˌ-, -ˌbɒθ.əm ⓤⓢ -ˌbɑː.t̬əm, -θəm
Higginbottom ˈhɪg.ɪnˌbɒt.əm, -ᵊnˌ-, -ᵊmˌ- ⓤⓢ -ˌbɑː.t̬əm
Higgins ˈhɪg.ɪnz
Higginson ˈhɪg.ɪn.sᵊn
higgl|e ˈhɪg.l̩ **-es** -z **-ing** -ɪŋ, ˈhɪg.lɪŋ **-ed** -d **-er/s** -əʳ/z ⓤⓢ -ɚ/z, ˈhɪg.ləʳ/z ⓤⓢ -lɚ/z
higgledy-piggledy ˌhɪg.l̩.diˈpɪg.l̩.di
Higgs hɪgz
high haɪ **-er** -əʳ ⓤⓢ -ɚ **-est** -ɪst, -əst **-s** -z **-ly** -li **-ness** -nəs, -nɪs ˌ**High ˈCourt** *stress shift, British only:* ˌHigh Court ˌjudge; ˈ**high ˌchair**; ˌ**high ˈchurch**; ˌ**high ˈchurchman**; ˈ**high ˌday**; ˌ**high ˈfrequency**; ˌ**high ˈheels**; ˌ**high ˈhorse**; ˈ**high ˌjump**; ˌ**high ˈroller**; ˈ**high ˌschool**; ˈ**high ˌstreet**; ˌ**high ˈtide**; ˌ**high ˈwater**; ˌ**high ˈwater mark**; ˌ**high and ˈdry**; ˌ**high and ˈlow**; ˌ**higher eduˈcation**
Higham ˈhaɪ.əm **-s** -z
high-and-mighty ˌhaɪ.ənˈmaɪ.ti, -əmˈ- ⓤⓢ -ənˈmaɪ.t̬i *stress shift:* ˌhigh-and-mighty ˈmanners
highball ˈhaɪ.bɔːl ⓤⓢ -bɔːl, -bɑːl **-s** -z **-ing** -ɪŋ **-ed** -d
highborn ˌhaɪˈbɔːn ⓤⓢ ˈhaɪ.bɔːrn *stress shift, British only:* ˌhighborn ˈlady
highboy ˈhaɪ.bɔɪ **-s** -z
Highbridge ˈhaɪ.brɪdʒ
highbrow ˈhaɪ.braʊ **-s** -z
Highbury ˈhaɪ.bᵊr.i ⓤⓢ -ber.i, -bɚ-
highchair ˈhaɪ.tʃeəʳ, ˌ-ˈ- ⓤⓢ -tʃer **-s** -z
High Church ˌhaɪˈtʃɜːtʃ ⓤⓢ -ˈtʃɝːtʃ **-man** -mən **-men** -mən, -men *stress shift:* ˌHigh Church ˈmannerism
high-class ˌhaɪˈklɑːs ⓤⓢ -ˈklæs *stress shift:* ˌhigh-class ˈbutcher
Highclere ˈhaɪ.klɪəʳ ⓤⓢ -klɪr
highfalut|in ˌhaɪ.fəˈluː.t|ɪn, -t|ᵊn **-ing** -ɪŋ *stress shift:* ˌhighfalutin ˈattitude
Highfield ˈhaɪ.fiːld
highflier, highflyer ˌhaɪˈflaɪ.əʳ ⓤⓢ -ɚ **-s** -z
highflown ˌhaɪˈfləʊn ⓤⓢ -ˈfloʊn *stress shift:* ˌhigh-flown ˈrhetoric
Highgate ˈhaɪ.geɪt, -gɪt, -gət
Highgrove ˈhaɪ.grəʊv ⓤⓢ -groʊv
high-handed ˌhaɪˈhæn.dɪd **-ly** -li **-ness** -nəs, -nɪs *stress shift:* ˌhigh-handed ˈruler
high-heeled ˌhaɪˈhiːld *stress shift:* ˌhigh-heeled ˈshoes
highjack ˈhaɪ.dʒæk **-s** -s **-ing** -ɪŋ **-ed** -t **-er/s** -əʳ/z ⓤⓢ -ɚ/z
highjinks ˈhaɪ.dʒɪŋks
highland (H) ˈhaɪ.lənd **-s** -z **-er/s** -əʳ/z ⓤⓢ -ɚ/z ˌ**Highland ˈfling**
high-level ˌhaɪˈlev.ᵊl *stress shift:* ˌhigh-level ˈlanguage
high|light ˈhaɪ|.laɪt **-lights** -laɪts **-lighting** -ˌlaɪ.tɪŋ ⓤⓢ -ˌlaɪ.t̬ɪŋ **-lighted** -ˌlaɪ.tɪd ⓤⓢ -ˌlaɪ.t̬ɪd
highlighter ˈhaɪˌlaɪ.təʳ ⓤⓢ -t̬ɚ **-s** -z
highly ˈhaɪ.li
high-minded ˌhaɪˈmaɪn.dɪd **-ness** -nəs, -nɪs *stress shift:* ˌhigh-minded ˈthinker
Highness ˈhaɪ.nəs, -nɪs **-es** -ɪz
high-octane ˌhaɪˈɒk.teɪn ⓤⓢ -ˈɑːk- *stress shift:* ˌhigh-octane ˈfuel
high-pitched ˌhaɪˈpɪtʃt *stress shift:* ˌhigh-pitched ˈvoice
high-powered ˌhaɪˈpaʊəd ⓤⓢ -ˈpaʊ.ɚd *stress shift:* ˌhigh-powered ˈengine
high-pressure ˌhaɪˈpreʃ.əʳ ⓤⓢ -ɚ *stress shift:* ˌhigh-pressure ˈsalesman
high-priced ˌhaɪˈpraɪst *stress shift:* ˌhigh-priced ˈgoods
high-priest ˌhaɪˈpriːst **-s** -s **-hood/s** -hʊd/z
high-priestess ˌhaɪ.priːˈstes, ˌ-ˈ-- ⓤⓢ ˌhaɪˈpriː- **-es** -ɪz
high-profile ˌhaɪˈprəʊ.faɪl ⓤⓢ -ˈproʊ- *stress shift:* ˌhigh-profile ˈmission
high-ranking ˌhaɪˈræŋ.kɪŋ, ˈ--- *stress shift:* ˌhigh-ranking ˈofficer
high-ris|e ˌhaɪˈraɪz, ˈ-- ⓤⓢ ˈ-- **-s** -ɪz *stress shift:* ˌhigh-rise ˈflats
high-risk ˌhaɪˈrɪsk *stress shift:* ˌhigh-risk ˈstrategy
highroad ˈhaɪ.rəʊd ⓤⓢ -roʊd **-s** -z
high-speed ˌhaɪˈspiːd *stress shift:* ˌhigh-speed ˈchase
high-spirited ˌhaɪˈspɪr.ɪ.tɪd ⓤⓢ -t̬ɪd **-ly** -li **-ness** -nəs, -nɪs
highspot ˈhaɪ.spɒt ⓤⓢ -spɑːt **-s** -s
high-strung ˌhaɪˈstrʌŋ *stress shift:* ˌhigh-strung ˈhorse
hightail ˈhaɪ.teɪl **-s** -z **-ing** -ɪŋ **-ed** -d
high-tech ˌhaɪˈtek *stress shift:* ˌhigh-tech ˈoffice
Highton ˈhaɪ.tᵊn
high-up ˌhaɪˈʌp **-s** -s *stress shift:* ˌhigh-up ˈsource
highway ˈhaɪ.weɪ **-s** -z ˌ**Highway ˈCode**, ˈ**Highway ˌCode**; ˌ**highway ˈrobbery**
highway|man ˈhaɪ.weɪ|.mən **-men** -mən
Highworth ˈhaɪ.wəθ, -wɜːθ ⓤⓢ -wɚθ
High Wycombe ˌhaɪˈwɪk.əm
hijack ˈhaɪ.dʒæk **-s** -s **-ing** -ɪŋ **-ed** -t **-er/s** -əʳ/z ⓤⓢ -ɚ/z
hijinks ˈhaɪ.dʒɪŋks
hik|e haɪk **-es** -s **-ing** -ɪŋ **-ed** -t **-er/s** -əʳ/z ⓤⓢ -ɚ/z
Hilaire hɪˈleəʳ; ˈhɪl.eəʳ ⓤⓢ hɪˈler; ˈhɪl.er
hilarious hɪˈleə.ri.əs, hə- ⓤⓢ hɪˈler.i-, -ˈlær- **-ly** -li **-ness** -nəs, -nɪs
hilarity hɪˈlær.ə.ti, hə-, -ɪ.ti ⓤⓢ hɪˈler.ə.t̬i, -ˈlær-
Hilary ˈhɪl.ᵊr.i
Hilda ˈhɪl.də
Hildebrand ˈhɪl.də.brænd, -dɪ-
Hildegard(e) ˈhɪl.də.gɑːd, -dɪ- ⓤⓢ -gɑːrd
hill (H) hɪl **-s** -z ˌ**over the ˈhill**; **as** ˌ**old as the ˈhills**
Hillary ˈhɪl.ᵊr.i
hillbill|y ˈhɪlˌbɪl|.i **-ies** -iz
Hillborn ˈhɪl.bɔːn ⓤⓢ -bɔːrn
Hillel ˈhɪl.el, -əl; hɪˈlel
Hillhead hɪlˈhed, ˈ--
Note: The pronunciation in Scotland is /-ˈ-/.
Hilliard ˈhɪl.i.əd, -ɑːd ⓤⓢ ˈ-jɚd
Hillingdon ˈhɪl.ɪŋ.dən
hill|man ˈhɪl|.mæn, -mən **-men** -men
Hillman ˈhɪl.mən **-s** -z
hillock ˈhɪl.ək **-s** -s
Hillsboro ˈhɪlz.bᵊr.ə ⓤⓢ -oʊ
Hillsborough ˈhɪlz.bᵊr.ə ⓤⓢ -oʊ
hillside (H) ˈhɪl.saɪd, ˌ-ˈ- **-s** -z
hilltop ˈhɪl.tɒp ⓤⓢ -tɑːp **-s** -s
hill|y ˈhɪl|.i **-ier** -i.əʳ ⓤⓢ -i.ɚ **-iest** -i.ɪst, -i.əst **-iness** -ɪ.nəs, -ɪ.nɪs
Hillyard ˈhɪl.jəd, -jɑːd ⓤⓢ -jɚd
Hillyer ˈhɪl.i.əʳ ⓤⓢ ˈ-jɚ
hilt hɪlt **-s** -s **-ed** -ɪd ⓤⓢ ˈhɪl.t̬ɪd
Hilton ˈhɪl.tᵊn
hil|um ˈhaɪ.l|əm **-ums** -əmz **-a** -ə **-i** -aɪ **-us** -əs
Hilversum ˈhɪl.və.sʊm, -sᵊm ⓤⓢ -vɚ-
him *strong form:* hɪm *weak form:* ɪm
Note: Weak form word. The strong form is mainly used for contrastive purposes, e.g. 'The gift is for **him**, not **her**'.
Himachal Pradesh hɪˌmɑː.tʃᵊl.prɑːˈdeʃ ⓤⓢ -prəˈ-
Himalaya ˌhɪm.əˈleɪə, hɪˈmɑː.li.ə, -lə.jə **-as** -əz **-an** -ən
Himes haɪmz
Himmler ˈhɪm.ləʳ ⓤⓢ -lɚ
himself hɪmˈself *when not initial:* ɪm-
Himyaritic ˌhɪm.jəˈrɪt.ɪk ⓤⓢ -ˈrɪt̬-
Hinayana ˌhiː.nəˈjɑː.nə, ˌhɪn.əˈ- ⓤⓢ ˌhiː.nəˈ-
Hinchcliffe ˈhɪnt*ʃ*.klɪf
Hinchingbrooke ˈhɪn.t*ʃ*ɪŋ.brʊk
Hinchliffe ˈhɪnt*ʃ*.lɪf
Hinckley ˈhɪŋ.kli
hind (H) haɪnd **-s** -z
Hinde haɪnd
Hindemith ˈhɪnd.ə.mɪt, -mɪθ
Hindenburg ˈhɪn.dən.bɜːg, -dəm- ⓤⓢ -bɝːg
hinder *(adj.)* ˈhaɪn.dəʳ ⓤⓢ -dɚ **-most** -məʊst ⓤⓢ -moʊst

hind|er (*v.*) ˈhɪn.d|əʳ US -d|ɚ **-ers** -əz US -ɚz **-ering** -ᵊr.ɪŋ **-ered** -əd US -ɚd **-erer/s** -ᵊr.əʳ/z US -ɚ.ɚ/z
Hinderwell ˈhɪn.də.wel, -wəl US -dɚ-
Hindhead ˈhaɪnd.hed
Hindi ˈhɪn.diː, -di
Hindle ˈhɪn.dl̩
Hindley *surname:* ˈhɪnd.li, ˈhaɪnd- *town in Greater Manchester:* ˈhɪnd.li
Hindlip ˈhɪnd.lɪp
hindmost ˈhaɪn*d*.məʊst US -moʊst
hindquarters ˌhaɪn*d*ˈkwɔː.təz, ˌhaɪŋ-, ˈ--- US ˈhaɪndˌkwɔːr.t̬ɚz
hindranc|e ˈhɪn.drən*t*s **-es** -ɪz
hindsight ˈhaɪnd.saɪt
Hindu ˈhɪn.duː US ˈhɪn.duː **-s** -z
Hinduism ˈhɪn.duː.ɪ.zᵊm, ˌhɪnˈduː- US ˈhɪn.duː-
Hinduja hɪnˈduː.dʒə
Hindu Kush ˌhɪn.duːˈkuːʃ, -ˈkʊʃ
Hindustan ˌhɪn.dʊˈstɑːn, -ˈstæn **-i** -i
Hines haɪnz
hing|e ˈhɪndʒ **-es** -ɪz **-ing** -ɪŋ **-ed** -d
Hingis ˈhɪŋ.gɪs
Hingston ˈhɪŋ*k*.stən
Hinkley ˈhɪŋ.kli
Hinkson ˈhɪŋk.sən
hinn|y ˈhɪn|.i **-ies** -iz **-ying** -i.ɪŋ **-ied** -id
hint hɪnt **-s** -s **-ing** -ɪŋ US ˈhɪn.t̬ɪŋ **-ed** -ɪd US ˈhɪn.t̬ɪd
hinterland ˈhɪn.tə.lænd, -lənd US -t̬ɚ-
Hinton ˈhɪn.tən
hip hɪp **-s** -s **-ped** -t **-per** -əʳ US -ɚ **-pest** -ɪst, -əst ˈ**hip** ˌ**bath**; ˈ**hip** ˌ**joint**
hipbone ˈhɪp.bəʊn US -boʊn **-s** -z
hip-hop ˈhɪp.hɒp US -hɑːp
Hipomenes haɪˈpɒm.ɪ.niːz US -ˈpɑː.mɪ-
Hipparchus hɪˈpɑː.kəs US -ˈpɑːr-
Hippias ˈhɪp.i.æs US -æs, -əs
hippie ˈhɪp.i **-s** -z
hippo ˈhɪp.əʊ US -oʊ **-s** -z
hippocamp|us ˌhɪp.əʊˈkæm.p|əs US -oʊˈ- **-i** -aɪ
Hippocrates hɪˈpɒk.rə.tiːz US -ˈpɑː.krə-
Hippocratic ˌhɪp.əʊˈkræt.ɪk US -əˈkræt̬- ˌ**Hippocratic** ˈ**oath**
Hippocrene ˌhɪp.əʊˈkriː.niː, -ni *also in poetry:* ˈhɪp.əʊ.kriːn US ˈhɪp.oʊ.kriːn, ˌhɪp.oʊˈkriː.ni
hippodrome (H) ˈhɪp.ə.drəʊm US -droʊm **-s** -z
Hippolyta hɪˈpɒl.ɪ.tə, ˈ-ə- US -ˈpɑː.lɪ.tə
Hippolyte hɪˈpɒl.ɪ.tiː, ˈ-ə- US -ˈpɑː.lɪ.tiː
Hippolytus hɪˈpɒl.ɪ.təs, ˈ-ə- US -ˈpɑː.lɪ.təs
hippopotam|us ˌhɪp.əˈpɒt.ə.m|əs US -ˈpɑː.t̬ə- **-uses** -ə.sɪz **-i** -aɪ
hipp|y ˈhɪp|.i **-ies** -iz
hipster ˈhɪp.stəʳ US -stɚ **-s** -z
Hiram *biblical name:* ˈhaɪə.rəm, -ræm US ˈhaɪ.rəm *modern names:* ˈhaɪə.rəm US ˈhaɪ-
hircine ˈhɜː.saɪn US ˈhɝː-, -sɪn
Hird hɜːd US hɝːd
hir|e haɪəʳ US haɪr **-es** -z **-ing** -ɪŋ **-ed** -d **-er/s** -əʳ/z US -ɚ/z **-eling/s** -lɪŋ/z ˌ**hire** ˈ**purchase**; ˌ**hired** ˈ**hand**
hireling ˈhaɪə.lɪŋ US ˈhaɪr- **-s** -z
Hirohito ˌhɪr.əʊˈhiː.təʊ US -oʊˈhiː.toʊ
Hiroshima hɪˈrɒʃ.ɪ.mə, hə-, ˈ-ə-; ˌhɪr.ɒʃˈiː-, -əˈʃiː- US ˌhɪr.əˈʃiː-, hɪˈroʊ.ʃɪ-
Hirst hɜːst US hɝːst
hirsute ˈhɜː.sjuːt, -suːt, -ˈ- US ˈhɝː.suːt, ˈhɪr-; hɚˈsuːt **-ness** -nəs, -nɪs
hirsutism ˈhɜː.sjuː.tɪ.zᵊm, -suː-; hɜːˈsjuː-, -ˈsuː- US ˈhɝː.suː.t̬ɪ-, ˈhɪr-; hɚˈsuː-
his *strong form:* hɪz *weak form:* ɪz
Note: Weak form word. The strong form /hɪz/ is always used when the word occurs contrastively, e.g. 'It's **his**, not **hers**' and when it is in final position, e.g. 'He said it was **his**'. When the word is unstressed the weak pronuciation is usually /ɪz/, e.g. 'on his back', /ɒn.ɪzˈbæk US ɑːn-/, though /hɪz/ occurs when it is the first word in a sentence, e.g. 'His shoes were wet', /hɪzˈʃuːz.wəˌwet US -wɚ-/, and when the style of speech is slow and careful.
Hislop ˈhɪz.lɒp, -ləp US -lɑːp
his'n'hers ˌhɪz.ᵊnˈhɜːz US -ˈhɝːz
Hispanic hɪˈspæn.ɪk **-s** -s
Hispanic|ism hɪˈspæn.ɪ.s|ɪ.zᵊm, ˈ-ə- **-ist/s** -ɪst/s
Hispaniola ˌhɪs.pæn.iˈəʊ.lə; -pænˈjəʊ-; hɪˌspæn- US ˌhɪs.pənˈjoʊ-
hiss (H) hɪs **-es** -ɪz **-ing** -ɪŋ **-ed** -t **-er/s** -əʳ/z US -ɚ/z
hist sːt, hɪst
Note: This spelling is used to represent the hissing sound made to attract someone's attention; it has a connotation of secrecy.
histamine ˈhɪs.tə.miːn, -mɪn **-s** -z
histogram ˈhɪs.tə.græm US -toʊ-, -tə- **-s** -z
histological ˌhɪs.təˈlɒdʒ.ɪ.kᵊl US -toʊˈlɑː.dʒɪ-, -təˈ- **-ly** -li
histolog|y hɪˈstɒl.ə.dʒ|i US ˈtɑː.lə- **-ist/s** -ɪst/s
Histon ˈhɪs.tᵊn
historian hɪˈstɔː.ri.ən US -ˈstɔːr.i- **-s** -z
historic hɪˈstɒr.ɪk US hɪˈstɔːr.ɪk **-al** -ᵊl **-ally** -ᵊl.i, -li
Note: In British English, the pronunciation /ɪsˈtɒr.ɪk/ is sometimes used, though only after 'an' /ən/.
historicism hɪˈstɒr.ɪ.sɪ.zᵊm, ˈ-ə- US -ˈstɔːr.ə-
historicity ˌhɪs.tɒrˈɪs.ə.ti, -təˈrɪs-, -ɪ.ti US -təˈrɪs.ə.t̬i
historiograph|y hɪˌstɒr.iˈɒg.rə.f|i US -ˌstɔːr.iˈɑː.grə- **-er/s** -əʳ/z US -ɚ/z
histor|y ˈhɪs.tᵊr|.i **-ies** -iz
histrionic ˌhɪs.triˈɒn.ɪk US -ˈɑː.nɪk **-s** -s **-al** -ᵊl **-ally** -ᵊl.i, -li
histrionism ˈhɪs.tri.ə.nɪ.zᵊm
hit hɪt **-s** -s **-ting** -ɪŋ US ˈhɪt̬.ɪŋ **-ter/s** -əʳ/z US ˈhɪt̬.ɚ/z ˈ**hit** ˌ**list**; ˈ**hit** **pa**ˌ**rade**
Hitachi® hɪˈtɑː.tʃi, -ˈtætʃ.i US -ˈtɑː.tʃi
hit-and-miss ˌhɪt.ᵊnˈmɪs, -ᵊmˈ- US -ᵊnˈ-
hit-and-run ˌhɪt.ᵊnˈrʌn, -ᵊmˈ- US -ᵊnˈ- *stress shift, see compound:* ˌ**hit-and-run** ˈ**driver**
hitch hɪtʃ **-es** -ɪz **-ing** -ɪŋ **-ed** -t
Hitchcock ˈhɪtʃ.kɒk US -kɑːk
Hitchens ˈhɪtʃ.ɪnz
hitchhik|e ˈhɪtʃ.haɪk **-es** -s **-ing** -ɪŋ **-ed** -t **-er/s** -əʳ/z US -ɚ/z
Hitchin ˈhɪtʃ.ɪn **-s** -z
Hite haɪt
hi-tech ˌhaɪˈtek *stress shift:* ˌhi-tech ˈproduct
hither (H) ˈhɪð.əʳ US -ɚ
hithermost ˈhɪð.ə.məʊst US -ɚ.moʊst
hitherto ˌhɪð.əˈtuː US -ɚˈ- *stress shift:* ˌhitherto ˈnamed
hitherwards ˈhɪð.ə.wədz US -ɚ.wɚdz
Hitler ˈhɪt.ləʳ US -lɚ
Hitlerian hɪtˈlɪə.ri.ən US -ˈlɪr.i-
Hitlerism ˈhɪt.ləʳ.ɪ.zᵊm US -lɚ-
Hitlerite ˈhɪt.ləʳ.aɪt US -lɚ.aɪt **-s** -s
hit|man ˈhɪt|.mæn **-men** -men
Hittite ˈhɪt.aɪt US ˈhɪt̬- **-s** -s
HIV ˌeɪtʃ.aɪˈviː *stress shift, see compound:* ˌ**HIV** ˈ**positive**
hiv|e (*n. v.*) haɪv **-es** -z **-ing** -ɪŋ **-ed** -d
Hivite ˈhaɪ.vaɪt **-s** -s
Hizbollah ˌhɪz.bɒlˈɑː US ˌhez.bəˈlɑː
Hizbullah ˌhɪz.bʊˈlɑː, -bəˈ-
HMO ˌeɪtʃ.emˈəʊ US -ˈoʊ
HMS ˌeɪtʃ.emˈes
HNC ˌeɪtʃ.enˈsiː
HND ˌeɪtʃ.enˈdiː
ho həʊ US hoʊ
Hoadl(e)y ˈhəʊd.li US ˈhoʊd-
hoag|ie, hoag|y ˈhəʊ.g|i US ˈhoʊ- **-ies** -iz
hoar (H) hɔːʳ US hɔːr
hoard hɔːd US hɔːrd **-s** -z **-ing** -ɪŋ **-ed** -ɪd **-er/s** -əʳ/z US -ɚ/z
hoarding ˈhɔː.dɪŋ US ˈhɔːr- **-s** -z
Hoare hɔːʳ US hɔːr
hoarfrost ˈhɔː.frɒst, ˌ-ˈ- US ˈhɔːr.frɑːst **-s** -s
hoars|e hɔːs US hɔːrs **-er** -əʳ US -ɚ **-est** -ɪst, -əst **-ely** -li **-eness** -nəs, -nɪs
hoar|y ˈhɔː.r|i US ˈhɔːr|.i **-ier** -i.əʳ US -i.ɚ **-iest** -i.ɪst, -i.əst **-ily** -ᵊl.i, -ɪ.li **-iness** -ɪ.nəs, -ɪ.nɪs

hoax həʊks (US) hoʊks **-es** -ɪz **-ing** -ɪŋ **-ed** -t **-er/s** -əʳ/z (US) -ɚ/z
hob hɒb (US) hɑːb **-s** -z
Hoban ˈhəʊ.bən (US) ˈhoʊ-
Hobart ˈhəʊ.bɑːt, -bət; ˈhʌb.ət (US) ˈhoʊ.bɑːrt, -bɚt; ˈhʌb.ɚt
Hobbema ˈhɒb.ɪ.mə (US) ˈhɑː.bə.mɑː, -mə **-s** -z
Hobbes hɒbz (US) hɑːbz
hobbit (H) ˈhɒb.ɪt (US) ˈhɑː.bɪt **-s** -s
hobbl|e ˈhɒb.l̩ (US) ˈhɑː.bl̩ **-es** -z **-ing** -ɪŋ, ˈhɒb.lɪŋ (US) ˈhɑː.blɪŋ **-ed** -d **-er/s** -əʳ/z (US) -ɚ/z, ˈhɒb.ləʳ/z (US) ˈhɑː.blɚ/z
hobbledehoy ˌhɒb.l̩.diˈhɔɪ, ˈhɒb.l̩.di.hɔɪ (US) ˈhɑː.bl̩.di.hɔɪ **-s** -z
Hobbs hɒbz (US) hɑːbz
hobb|y ˈhɒb|.i (US) ˈhɑː.b|i **-ies** -iz
hobbyhors|e ˈhɒb.i.hɔːs (US) ˈhɑː.bi.hɔːrs **-es** -ɪz
Hobday ˈhɒb.deɪ (US) ˈhɑːb-
hobgoblin ˌhɒbˈgɒb.lɪn, ˈ-ˌ-- (US) ˈhɑːbˌgɑːb- **-s** -z
Hobhouse ˈhɒb.haʊs (US) ˈhɑːb-
hobnail ˈhɒb.neɪl (US) ˈhɑːb- **-s** -z **-ed** -d **ˌhobnail ˈboots**
hobnob ˈhɒb.nɒb, ˌ-ˈ- (US) ˈhɑːb.nɑːb **-s** -z **-bing** -ɪŋ **-bed** -d
hobo ˈhəʊ.bəʊ (US) ˈhoʊ.boʊ **-(e)s** -z
Hoboken ˈhəʊ.bəʊ.kən (US) ˈhoʊ.boʊ-
Hobsbaum ˈhɒbz.baʊm (US) ˈhɑːbz-
Hobsbawm ˈhɒbz.bɔːm (US) ˈhɑːbz.bɑːm, -bɔːm
Hobson ˈhɒb.sən (US) ˈhɑːb- **ˌHobson's ˈchoice**
Hobson-Jobson ˌhɒb.sənˈdʒɒb.sən (US) ˌhɑːb.sənˈdʒɑːb-
Hoby ˈhəʊ.bi (US) ˈhoʊ-
Hoccleve ˈhɒk.liːv (US) ˈhɑːk-
Ho Chi Minh ˌhəʊ.tʃiːˈmɪn (US) ˌhoʊ-
Ho Chi Minh City ˌhəʊ.tʃiː.mɪnˈsɪt.i (US) ˌhoʊ.tʃiː.mɪnˈsɪt̬-
hock hɒk (US) hɑːk **-s** -s **-ing** -ɪŋ **-ed** -t
hockey ˈhɒk.i (US) ˈhɑː.ki **ˈhockey ˌstick**
Hockin ˈhɒk.ɪn (US) ˈhɑː.kɪn
Hocking ˈhɒk.ɪŋ (US) ˈhɑː.kɪŋ
Hockley ˈhɒk.li (US) ˈhɑːk-
Hockney ˈhɒk.ni (US) ˈhɑːk-
hockshop ˈhɒk.ʃɒp (US) ˈhɑːk.ʃɑːp **-s** -s
hocus ˈhəʊ.kəs (US) ˈhoʊ- **-es** -ɪz **-(s)ing** -ɪŋ **-(s)ed** -t
hocus-pocus ˌhəʊ.kəsˈpəʊ.kəs (US) ˌhoʊ.kəsˈpoʊ-
hod hɒd (US) hɑːd **-s** -z
Hodder ˈhɒd.əʳ (US) ˈhɑː.dɚ
Hoddesdon ˈhɒdz.dən (US) ˈhɑːdz-
Hoddinott ˈhɒd.ɪ.nɒt, -ən.ɒt (US) ˈhɑː.dən.ɑːt
Hoddle ˈhɒd.l̩ (US) ˈhɑː.dl̩
Hodge hɒdʒ (US) hɑːdʒ
hodgepodge ˈhɒdʒ.pɒdʒ (US) ˈhɑːdʒ.pɑːdʒ
Hodges ˈhɒdʒ.ɪz (US) ˈhɑː.dʒɪz
Hodgetts ˈhɒdʒ.ɪts (US) ˈhɑː.dʒɪts
Hodgins ˈhɒdʒ.ɪnz (US) ˈhɑː.dʒɪnz
Hodgkin ˈhɒdʒ.kɪn (US) ˈhɑːdʒ- **ˈHodgkin's diˌsease**
Hodgkins ˈhɒdʒ.kɪnz (US) ˈhɑːdʒ-
Hodgkinson ˈhɒdʒ.kɪn.sən (US) ˈhɑːdʒ-
Hodgkiss ˈhɒdʒ.kɪs (US) ˈhɑːdʒ-
Hodgson ˈhɒdʒ.sən *in the North of England also:* ˈhɒdʒ.ən (US) ˈhɑːdʒ.sən
hodometer hɒdˈɒm.ɪ.təʳ, -ə.təʳ (US) hɑːˈdɑː.mə.t̬ɚ **-s** -z
Hodson ˈhɒd.sən (US) ˈhɑːd-
hoe (H) həʊ (US) hoʊ **-s** -z **-ing** -ɪŋ **-d** -d
hoedown ˈhəʊ.daʊn (US) ˈhoʊ- **-s** -z
Hoey hɔɪ, ˈhəʊ.i (US) ˈhoʊ.i
Hoffa ˈhɒf.ə (US) ˈhɑː.fə
Hoffman(n) ˈhɒf.mən (US) ˈhɑːf-
Hofmannsthal ˈhɒf.mən.stɑːl (US) ˈhɑːf.mɑːn-, ˈhɔːf-
Hofmeister ˈhɒfˌmaɪ.stəʳ (US) ˈhɑːfˌmaɪ.stɚ
hog hɒg (US) hɑːg, hɔːg **-s** -z **-ging** -ɪŋ **-ged** -d
Hogan ˈhəʊ.gən (US) ˈhoʊ-
Hogarth ˈhəʊ.gɑːθ, ˈhɒg.ət (US) ˈhoʊ.gɑːrθ
Hogarthian həʊˈgɑː.θi.ən (US) hoʊˈgɑːr-
Hogben ˈhɒg.bən, -ben (US) ˈhɑːg-, ˈhɔːg
Hogg hɒg (US) hɑːg, hɔːg
Hoggart ˈhɒg.ət (US) ˈhɑː.gɚt, ˈhɔː-
hogget (H) ˈhɒg.ɪt (US) ˈhɑː.gɪt, ˈhɔː- **-s** -s
hoggish ˈhɒg.ɪʃ (US) ˈhɑː.gɪʃ, ˈhɔː- **-ly** -li **-ness** -nəs, -nɪs
hogmanay (H) ˈhɒg.mə.neɪ, ˌ--ˈ- (US) ˈhɑːg.mə.neɪ, ˈhɔːg-
hogshead ˈhɒgz.hed (US) ˈhɑːgz-, ˈhɔːgz- **-s** -z
Hogwarts ˈhɒg.wɔːts
hogwash ˈhɒg.wɒʃ (US) ˈhɑːg.wɑːʃ, ˈhɔːg-, -wɔːʃ
hogweed ˈhɒg.wiːd (US) ˈhɑːg-, ˈhɔːg- **-s** -z
Hohenlinden ˌhəʊ.ənˈlɪn.dən (US) ˌhoʊ.ənˈ-, ˈhoʊ.ənˌlɪn-
Hohenzollern ˌhəʊ.ənˈzɒl.ən (US) ˈhoʊ.ənˌzɑː.lɚn **-s** -z
hoi(c)k hɔɪk **-s** -s **-ing** -ɪŋ **-ed** -t
hoi polloi ˌhɔɪ.pəˈlɔɪ, -pɒlˈɔɪ; -ˈpɒl.ɔɪ (US) ˌhɔɪ.pəˈlɔɪ
hoisin ˈhɔɪ.sɪn, -ˈ- **ˌhoisin ˈsauce**
hoist hɔɪst **-s** -s **-ing** -ɪŋ **-ed** -ɪd
hoity-toity ˌhɔɪ.tiˈtɔɪ.ti (US) ˌhɔɪ.t̬iˈtɔɪ.t̬i
hokey ˈhəʊ.ki (US) ˈhoʊ- **ˌhokey ˈcokey**
hokey-pokey ˌhəʊ.kiˈpəʊ.ki (US) ˌhoʊ.kiˈpoʊ-
Hokkaido hɒkˈaɪ.dəʊ (US) hɑːˈkaɪ.doʊ
hokum ˈhəʊ.kəm (US) ˈhoʊ-
Holbeach ˈhɒl.biːtʃ, ˈhəʊl- (US) ˈhɑːl-, ˈhoʊl-
Holbech ˈhəʊl.biːtʃ, ˈhɒl- (US) ˈhoʊl-
Holbeck ˈhɒl.bek, ˈhəʊl- (US) ˈhoʊl-
Holbein ˈhɒl.baɪn (US) ˈhoʊl- **-s** -z
Holborn ˈhəʊ.bən, ˈhəʊl-, ˈhɒl- (US) ˈhoʊl.bɚn, ˈhoʊ-
Holbrook(e) ˈhəʊl.brʊk, ˈhɒl- (US) ˈhoʊl-
Holburn ˈhɒl.bɜːn, ˈhəʊl- (US) ˈhoʊl.bɝːn
Holcroft ˈhəʊl.krɒft (US) ˈhoʊl.krɑːft
hold həʊld (US) hoʊld **-s** -z **-ing/s** -ɪŋ/z **held** held **ˌno ˌholds ˈbarred**; **ˈholding ˌcompany**; **ˌhold one's ˈown**
holdall ˈhəʊld.ɔːl (US) ˈhoʊld-, -ɑːl **-s** -z
Holden ˈhəʊl.dən (US) ˈhoʊl-
holder (H) ˈhəʊl.dəʳ (US) ˈhoʊl.dɚ **-s** -z
Holderness ˈhəʊl.də.nəs, -nɪs, -nes (US) ˈhoʊl.dɚ-
holdover ˈhəʊldˌəʊ.vəʳ (US) ˈhoʊldˌoʊ.vɚ **-s** -z
Holdsworth ˈhəʊldz.wəθ, -wɜːθ (US) ˈhoʊldz.wɚθ, -wɝːθ
holdup ˈhəʊld.ʌp (US) ˈhoʊld- **-s** -s
hol|e (H) həʊl (US) hoʊl **-es** -z **-ing** -ɪŋ **-ed** -d **ˌhole in ˈone** (US) **ˈhole in ˌone**; **ˌneed something like a ˌhole in the ˈhead** (US) **ˌneed something like a ˈhole in the ˌhead**
hole-and-corner ˌhəʊl.əndˈkɔː.nəʳ, -əŋˈ- (US) ˌhoʊl.əndˈkɔːr.nɚ
hole-in-the-wall ˌhəʊl.ɪn.ðəˈwɔːl (US) ˌhoʊl.ɪn.ðəˈwɔːl, -wɑːl
Holford ˈhəʊl.fəd, ˈhɒl- (US) ˈhoʊl.fɚd
holiday (H) ˈhɒl.ə.deɪ, ˈ-ɪ-, -di (US) ˈhɑː.lə.deɪ **-s** -z **-ing** -ɪŋ **-ed** -d **ˈholiday ˌcamp**
holidaymaker ˈhɒl.ə.diˌmeɪ.kəʳ, ˈ-ɪ-, -deɪˌ- (US) ˈhɑː.lə.deɪˌmeɪ.kɚ **-s** -z
holier-than-thou ˌhəʊ.li.ə.ðənˈðaʊ (US) ˌhoʊ.li.ɚ- *stress shift:* ˌholier-than-thou ˈattitude
Holies ˈhəʊ.lɪz (US) ˈhoʊ-
Holifield ˈhɒl.ɪ.fiːld (US) ˈhoʊ.lɪ-, ˈhɑː-
Holinshed ˈhɒl.ɪn.ʃed (US) ˈhɑː.lɪn-
holism ˈhəʊ.lɪ.zəm, ˈhɒl.ɪ- (US) ˈhoʊ.lɪ-
holistic həʊˈlɪs.tɪk, hɒlˈɪs- (US) hoʊlˈɪs- **-ally** -əl.i, -li
Holland, holland ˈhɒl.ənd (US) ˈhɑː.lənd **-s** -z
hollandaise ˌhɒl.ənˈdeɪz (US) ˌhɑː.lənˈ- *stress shift, see compound:* **ˌhollandaise ˈsauce** (US) **ˈhollandaise ˌsauce**
Hollander ˈhɒl.ən.dəʳ (US) ˈhɑː.lən.dɚ **-s** -z
holl|er ˈhɒl|.əʳ (US) ˈhɑː.l|ɚ **-ers** -əz (US) -ɚz **-ering** -ər.ɪŋ **-ered** -əd (US) -ɚd
Holles ˈhɒl.ɪs (US) ˈhɑː.lɪs
Hollick ˈhɒl.ɪk (US) ˈhɑː.lɪk
Holliday ˈhɒl.ɪ.deɪ, ˈ-ə-, -di (US) ˈhɑː.lə-
Hollings ˈhɒl.ɪŋz (US) ˈhɑː.lɪŋz
Hollingsworth ˈhɒl.ɪŋz.wəθ, -wɜːθ (US) ˈhɑː.lɪŋz.wɚθ, -wɝːθ

Hollingworth ˈhɒl.ɪŋ.wəθ, -wɜːθ (US) ˈhɑː.lɪŋ.wɚθ, -wɝːθ
Hollins ˈhɒl.ɪnz (US) ˈhɑː.lɪnz
Hollis ˈhɒl.ɪs (US) ˈhɑː.lɪs
hollo ˈhɒl.əʊ (US) ˈhɑː.loʊ; həˈloʊ **-es** -z **-ing** -ɪŋ **-ed** -d
hollo(a) ˈhɒl.əʊ (US) ˈhɑː.loʊ; həˈloʊ **-s** -z **-ing** -ɪŋ **-ed** -d
Hollom ˈhɒl.əm (US) ˈhɑː.ləm
hollow ˈhɒl.əʊ (US) ˈhɑː.loʊ **-s** -z **-er** -əʳ (US) -ɚ **-est** -ɪst, -əst **-ly** -li **-ness** -nəs, -nɪs **-ing** -ɪŋ **-ed** -d
Holloway ˈhɒl.ə.weɪ (US) ˈhɑː.lə-
holl|y (H) ˈhɒl|.i (US) ˈhɑː.l|i **-ies** -iz
hollyhock ˈhɒl.i.hɒk (US) ˈhɑː.li.hɑːk **-s** -s
Hollywood ˈhɒl.i.wʊd (US) ˈhɑː.li-
holm (H) həʊm (US) hoʊ*l*m **-s** -z ˈ**holm** ˌ**oak**
Holman ˈhəʊl.mən, ˈhɒl- (US) ˈhoʊl-
Holmby ˈhəʊm.bi (US) ˈhoʊ*l*m-
Holmer ˈhəʊl.məʳ, ˈhəʊ- (US) ˈhoʊ*l*.mɚ
Holmes həʊmz (US) hoʊ*l*mz
Holmesdale ˈhəʊmz.deɪl (US) ˈhoʊ*l*mz-
Holmfirth ˈhəʊm.fəθ, -fɜːθ (US) ˈhoʊ*l*m.fɚθ, -fɝːθ
holmium ˈhəʊl.mi.əm, ˈhɒl- (US) ˈhoʊl-
holo- hɒl.əʊ-; hɒlˈɒ- (US) hɑː.loʊ-, hoʊ-, -lə-; hoʊˈlɑː-
Note: Prefix. Normally either takes primary or secondary stress on the first syllable, e.g. **holograph** /ˈhɒl.ə.grɑːf (US) ˈhɑː.lə.græf/, **holographic** /ˌhɒl.əˈgræf.ɪk (US) ˌhɑː.ləˈ-/, or primary stress on the second syllable, e.g. **holography** /hɒlˈɒg.rə.fi (US) hoʊˈlɑː.grə-/.
holocaust (H) ˈhɒl.ə.kɔːst, -kɒst (US) ˈhɑː.lə.kɑːst, ˈhoʊ-, -kɔːst **-s** -s
Holofernes ˌhɒl.əʊˈfɜː.niːz, həˈlɒf.ə- (US) ˌhɑː.ləˈfɝː-
hologram ˈhɒl.ə.græm (US) ˈhɑː.lə-, ˈhoʊ- **-s** -z
holograph ˈhɒl.ə.grɑːf, -græf (US) ˈhɑː.lə.græf, ˈhoʊ- **-s** -s
holographic ˌhɒl.əˈgræf.ɪk (US) ˌhɑː.lə-, ˌhoʊ- **-ally** -əl.i, -li
holography hɒlˈɒg.rə.fi (US) hoʊˈlɑː.grə-
Holon ˈhɒl.ən (US) ˈhɑː.lən; ˈhoʊ.lɑːn
holophras|e ˈhɒl.ə.freɪz (US) ˈhɑː.lə-, ˈhoʊ- **-es** -ɪz
holophrastic ˌhɒl.əˈfræs.tɪk (US) ˌhɑː.ləˈ-, ˌhoʊ-
Holroyd ˈhɒl.rɔɪd, ˈhəʊl- (US) ˈhɑːl-
Holst həʊlst (US) hoʊlst
holstein (H) ˈhɒl.staɪn, ˈhəʊl- (US) ˈhoʊl.staɪn, -stiːn
holster ˈhəʊl.stəʳ (US) ˈhoʊl.stɚ **-s** -z **-ed** -d
holt (H) həʊlt (US) hoʊlt **-s** -s
Holtby ˈhəʊlt.bi (US) ˈhoʊlt-
Holtham ˈhəʊl.θəm, ˈhɒl-, ˈhəʊ- (US) ˈhoʊl-
holus-bolus ˌhəʊ.ləsˈbəʊ.ləs (US) ˌhoʊ.ləsˈboʊ-
hol|y (H) ˈhəʊ.l|i (US) ˈhoʊ- **-ier** -i.əʳ (US) -i.ɚ **-iest** -i.ɪst, -i.əst **-iness** -ɪ.nəs, -ɪ.nɪs ˌ**Holy** ˈ**Bible**; ˌ**Holy Com**ˈ**munion**; ˌ**Holy** ˈ**Ghost**; ˌ**Holy** ˈ**Grail**; ˈ**Holy** ˌ**Land**; ˌ**Holy** ˌ**Roman** ˈ**Empire**; ˌ**Holy** ˈ**Spirit**; ˈ**Holy** ˌ**Week**
Holycross ˈhəʊ.li.krɒs (US) ˈhoʊl.i.krɑːs
Holyfield ˈhəʊl.ɪ.fiːld (US) ˈhɑː.lɪ-
Holyhead ˌhɒl.iˈhed, ˈ--- (US) ˈhɑː.li-
Holyoake *place in Massachusetts:* ˈhəʊl.jəʊk (US) ˈhoʊl.joʊk *all other senses:* ˈhəʊ.li.əʊk (US) ˈhoʊ.li.oʊk
Holyrood ˈhɒl.i.ruːd (US) ˈhɑː.li-
holyston|e ˈhəʊl.i.stəʊn (US) ˈhoʊl.i.stoʊn **-es** -z **-ing** -ɪŋ **-ed** -d
Holywell ˈhɒl.i.wəl, -wel (US) ˈhɑː.li-
homage ˈhɒm.ɪdʒ (US) ˈhɑː.mɪdʒ, ˈɑː-
hombre ˈɒm.breɪ, -bri (US) ˈɑːm- **-s** -z
homburg (H) ˈhɒm.bɜːg (US) ˈhɑːm.bɝːg **-s** -z
home həʊm (US) hoʊm **-s** -z ˌ**home** ˈ**brew**; ˌ**Home** ˈ**Counties**; ˌ**home eco**ˈ**nomics**; ˌ**home** ˈ**free**; ˌ**home** ˈ**front** (US) ˈ**home** ˌ**front**; ˌ**home** ˈ**help**; ˈ**Home** ˌ**Office**; ˈ**home** ˌ**page**; ˌ**home** ˈ**rule**; ˌ**Home** ˈ**Secretary**; ˌ**home** ˈ**truth**; ˌ**close to** ˈ**home**; ˌ**home from** ˈ**home**
Home həʊm, hjuːm (US) hoʊm, hjuːm
Note: /hjuːm/ in **Milne-Home, Douglas-Home,** and **Baron Home of the Hirsel.**
Homebase® ˈhəʊm.beɪs (US) ˈhoʊm-
homeboy ˈhəʊm.bɔɪ (US) ˈhoʊm- **-s** -z
homebred ˌhəʊmˈbred (US) ˌhoʊm- *stress shift:* ˌhomebred ˈlivestock
homecoming ˈhəʊmˌkʌm.ɪŋ (US) ˈhoʊm- **-s** -z
homegrown ˌhəʊmˈgrəʊn (US) ˌhoʊmˈgroʊn *stress shift:* ˌhomegrown ˈfood
homeland (H) ˈhəʊm.lænd, -lənd (US) ˈhoʊm- **-s** -z
homeless ˈhəʊm.ləs, -lɪs (US) ˈhoʊm- **-ness** -nəs, -nɪs
homelike ˈhəʊm.laɪk (US) ˈhoʊm-
homel|y ˈhəʊm.l|i (US) ˈhoʊm- **-ier** -i.əʳ (US) -i.ɚ **-iest** -i.ɪst, -i.əst **-iness** -ɪ.nəs, -ɪ.nɪs
homemade ˌhəʊmˈmeɪd (US) ˌhoʊm- *stress shift:* ˌhomemade ˈjam
homemaker ˈhəʊmˌmeɪ.kəʳ (US) ˈhoʊmˌmeɪ.kɚ **-s** -z
homeo- ˈhəʊ.mi.əʊ-, ˈhɒm.i.əʊ-; ˌhəʊ.miˈɒ-, ˌhɒm.iˈɒ- (US) ˈhoʊ.mi.oʊ-, -ə-; ˌhoʊ.miˈɑː-
Note: Prefix. Normally ether takes primary or secondary stress on the first syllable, e.g. **homeopath** /ˈhəʊ.mi.əʊ.pæθ (US) ˈhoʊ.mi.oʊ-/, **homeopathic** /ˌhəʊ.mi.əʊˈpæθ.ɪk (US) ˌhoʊ.mi.oʊˈ-/, or primary stress on the third syllable with secondary stress on the first, e.g. **homeopathy** /ˌhəʊ.miˈɒp.ə.θi (US) ˌhoʊ.miˈɑː.pə-/.
homeopath ˈhəʊ.mi.əʊ.pæθ, ˈhɒm.i- (US) ˈhoʊ.mi.oʊ-, -ə- **-s** -s
homeopathic ˌhəʊ.mi.əʊˈpæθ.ɪk, ˌhɒm.i- (US) ˌhoʊ.mi.oʊˈ-, -ə- **-al** -əl **-ally** -əl.i, -li
homeopathy ˌhəʊ.miˈɒp.ə.θi, ˌhɒm.iˈ- (US) ˌhoʊ.miˈɑː.pə-
homeostasis ˌhəʊ.mi.əʊˈsteɪ.sɪs, ˌhɒm.i-, ˌ--ˈɒs.tə- (US) ˌhoʊ.mi.oʊˈ-, -ˈstæs.ɪs
homeostatic ˌhəʊ.mi.əʊˈstæt.ɪk, ˌhɒm.i- (US) ˌhoʊ.mi.oʊˈstæt̬- **-ally** -əl.i, -li
homeowner ˈhəʊmˌəʊ.nəʳ (US) ˈhoʊmˌoʊ.nɚ **-s** -z
homepag|e ˈhəʊm.peɪdʒ (US) ˈhoʊm- **-es** -ɪz
Homer ˈhəʊ.məʳ (US) ˈhoʊ.mɚ
homer ˈhəʊ.məʳ (US) ˈhoʊ.mɚ **-s** -z
Homeric *relating to Homer:* həʊˈmer.ɪk (US) hoʊ- *name of ship:* ˈhəʊ.mər.ɪk (US) ˈhoʊ-
Homerton ˈhɒm.ə.tən (US) ˈhɑː.mɚ-
homesick ˈhəʊm.sɪk (US) ˈhoʊm- **-ness** -nəs, -nɪs
homespun ˈhəʊm.spʌn (US) ˈhoʊm- **-s** -z
homestead ˈhəʊm.sted, -stɪd (US) ˈhoʊm- **-s** -z
homesteader ˈhəʊmˌsted.əʳ (US) ˈhoʊmˌsted.ɚ **-s** -z
homestretch ˌhəʊmˈstretʃ, ˈ-- (US) ˌhoʊmˈstretʃ, ˈ-- **-es** -ɪz
homeward ˈhəʊm.wəd (US) ˈhoʊm.wɚd **-s** -z
homework ˈhəʊm.wɜːk (US) ˈhoʊm.wɝːk
homey ˈhəʊ.mi (US) ˈhoʊ-
homicidal ˌhɒm.ɪˈsaɪ.dəl, -əˈ- (US) ˌhɑː.məˈ-, ˌhoʊ- *stress shift:* ˌhomicidal ˈmaniac
homicide ˈhɒm.ɪ.saɪd, ˈ-ə- (US) ˈhɑː.mə-, ˈhoʊ- **-s** -z
homil|y ˈhɒm.ɪ.l|i, ˈ-ə- (US) ˈhɑː.mə- **-ies** -iz
homing ˈhəʊ.mɪŋ (US) ˈhoʊ- ˈ**homing de**ˌ**vice**; ˈ**homing** ˌ**pigeon**
hominid ˈhɒm.ɪ.nɪd, ˈ-ə- (US) ˈhɑː.mɪ-, -mə- **-s** -z
hominoid ˈhɒm.ɪ.nɔɪd, -ə- (US) ˈhɑː.mɪ-, -mə- **-s** -z
hominy ˈhɒm.ɪ.ni, ˈ-ə- (US) ˈhɑː.mɪ-, -mə-
homo ˈhəʊ.məʊ, ˈhɒm.oʊ (US) ˈhoʊ.moʊ **-s** -z

Homographs

When two lexical items have the same form in spelling, these are known as homographs. Homographs can be pronounced the same as or different to each other.

Examples

Here are some examples of homographs with the same pronunciation:

- bank /bæŋk/ (*e.g. financial institution; area of ground by a river*)
- well /wel/ (*e.g. source of water; healthy; adv.*)

Other homographs differ in their pronunciation, but usually only in the vowel sound used, e.g.:

- bow
  — (*e.g. a slip knot with a double loop; a device for shooting arrows*) /bəʊ/ US /boʊ/
  — (*e.g. incline the head or trunk; submit*) /baʊ/
- dove
  — (*pigeon*) /dʌv/
  — (*past tense of* dive) /dəʊv/ US /doʊv/

Homographs also appear in noun/verb, noun/adjective and verb/adjective pairs. The difference in pronunciation indicates which part of speech is being used, e.g.:

insert	(*n.*)	/ˈɪn.sɜːt/	US /-sɝːt/
	(*v.*)	/ɪnˈsɜːt/	US /-ˈsɝːt/
deliberate	(*adj.*)	/dɪˈlɪb.ᵊr.ət/	
	(*v.*)	/dɪˈlɪb.ᵊr.eɪt/	US /ˈ-ə.reɪt/
arithmetic	(*n.*)	/əˈrɪθ.mə.tɪk/	
	(*adj.*)	/ˌær.ɪθˈmet.ɪk/	US /ˌer.ɪθˈmet̬-/

Pronunciation tip

In most cases it is necessary to check the pronunciation of a word individually, as the correct realisation is not obvious from the form of the word. However, some rules are available. For example, the pronunciation of word pairs ending with *–ate* is predictable depending on the part of speech. In two-syllable words where the stress moves to show the difference between a noun and a verb (e.g. *insert*, *export*), the noun is almost always stressed on the first syllable and the verb on the second.

homo- həʊ.məʊ-, hɒm.əʊ-; həˈmɒ-, hɒmˈɒ- US hoʊ.moʊ-, hɑː-, -mə-; həˈmɑː-, hoʊ-
Note: Prefix. Normally either takes primary or secondary stress on the first syllable, e.g. **homonym** /ˈhɒm.ə.nɪm US ˈhɑː.mə-/, **homophobia** /ˌhɒm.əˈfəʊ.bi.ə US ˌhoʊ.məˈfoʊ-/, or primary stress on the second syllable, e.g. **homonymy** /həˈmɒn.ɪ.mi US hoʊˈmɑː.nə-/.

homoeopath ˈhəʊ.mi.əʊ.pæθ, ˈhɒm.i- US ˈhoʊ.mi.oʊ- **-s** -s

homoeopathic ˌhəʊ.mi.əʊˈpæθ.ɪk, ˌhɒm.i- US ˌhoʊ.mi.oʊˈ- **-al** -ᵊl **-ally** -əl.i, -li

homoeopathy ˌhəʊ.miˈɒp.ə.θi, ˌhɒm.iˈ- US ˌhoʊ.miˈɑː.pə-

homoeostasis ˌhəʊ.mi.əʊˈsteɪ.sɪs, ˌ--ˈɒs.tə- US ˌhoʊ.mi.oʊˈ-, -ˈstæs.ɪs

homoeostatic ˌhəʊ.mi.əʊˈstæt.ɪk US ˌhoʊ.mi.oʊˈstæt̬- **-ally** -ᵊl.i, -li

homoerotic ˌhəʊ.məʊ.ɪˈrɒt.ɪk, ˌhɒm.əʊ-, -əˈ- US ˌhoʊ.moʊ.ɪˈrɑː.t̬ɪk, -əˈ-

homoeroticism ˌhəʊ.məʊ.ɪˈrɒt.ɪ.sɪ.z.ᵊm, ˌhɒm.əʊ-, -əˈ-, ˈ-ə- US ˌhoʊ.moʊ.ɪˈrɑː.t̬ə-, -əˈ-

homogeneity ˌhəʊ.məʊ.dʒəˈneɪ.ə.ti, ˌhɒm.əʊ-, -dʒenˈeɪ-, -dʒɪˈneɪ-, -ɪ.ti US ˌhoʊ.moʊ.dʒəˈniː.ə.t̬i, ˌhɑː-, -mə-, -ˈneɪ-

homogeneous ˌhɒm.əˈdʒiː.ni.əs, ˌhəʊ.mə- US ˌhoʊ.moʊˈdʒiː-, ˌhɑː-, -məˈ- **-ly** -li **-ness** -nəs, -nɪs

homogeniz|e, -is|e həˈmɒdʒ.ə.naɪz, hɒmˈɒdʒ-, ˈ-ɪ- US həˈmɑː.dʒə- **-es** -ɪz **-ing** -ɪŋ **-ed** -d

homograph ˈhɒm.ə.grɑːf, ˈhəʊ.mə-, -græf US ˈhɑː.mə.græf, ˈhoʊ- **-s** -s

homographic ˌhɒm.əˈgræf.ɪk, ˌhəʊ.məˈ- US ˌhɑː.məˈ-, ˌhoʊ-

homoiotherm həˈmɔɪ.ə.θɜːm, hɒmˈɔɪ- US hoʊˈmɔɪ.oʊ.θɝːm, -ə.θɝːm **-s** -z

homoiothermic həˌmɔɪ.əˈθɜː.mɪk, hɒmˌɔɪ- US hoʊˌmɔɪ.oʊˈθɝː-, -əˈθɝː-

homolog ˈhɒm.ə.lɒg US ˈhɑː.mə.lɑːg, ˈhoʊ-, -lɔːg **-s** -z

homologous həˈmɒl.ə.gəs, hɒmˈɒl- US hoʊˈmɑː.lə-, hə-

homologue ˈhɒm.ə.lɒg US ˈhɑː.mə.lɑːg, ˈhoʊ-, -lɔːg **-s** -z

homolog|y həˈmɒl.ə.dʒ|i, hɒmˈɒl- US hoʊˈmɑː.lə-, hə- **-ies** -iz

homonym ˈhɒm.ə.nɪm US ˈhɑː.mə- **-s** -z

homonymous həˈmɒn.ɪ.məs, hɒmˈɒn-, -ə.məs US hoʊˈmɑː.nə-, hə- **-ly** -li

homonymy həˈmɒn.ɪ.mi, hɒmˈɒn-, -ə.mi US hoʊˈmɑː.nə-, hə-

homophobe ˈhəʊ.mə.fəʊb US ˈhoʊ.mə.foʊb **-s** -z

homophobia ˌhəʊ.məˈfəʊ.bi.ə US ˌhoʊ.məˈfoʊ-

homophobic ˌhəʊ.məˈfəʊ.bɪk US ˌhoʊ.məˈfoʊ-

homophone ˈhɒm.ə.fəʊn, ˈhəʊ.mə- US ˈhɑː.mə.foʊn, ˈhoʊ- **-s** -z

homophonic ˌhɒm.əˈfɒn.ɪk, ˌhəʊ.məˈ- US ˌhɑː.məˈfɑː.nɪk, ˌhoʊ- **-ally** -ᵊl.i, -li

homophon|ous həˈmɒf.ᵊn|.əs, hɒmˈɒf- US hoʊˈmɑː.fᵊn-, hə- **-y** -i

homorganic ˌhɒm.ɔːˈgæn.ɪk US ˌhoʊ.mɔːrˈ-, ˌhɑː-

homo sapiens ˌhəʊ.məʊˈsæp.i.enz, -ənz US ˌhoʊ.moʊˈ-

homosexual ˌhəʊ.məʊˈsek.ʃu.ᵊl, ˌhɒm.əʊˈ-, ˈ-sju-, -ʃᵊl US ˌhoʊ.moʊˈsek.ʃu.ᵊl, -məˈ- **-s** -z **-ist/s** -ɪst/s

homosexuality ˌhəʊ.məʊˌsek.ʃuˈæl.ə.ti, ˌhɒm.əʊ-, -sjuˈ-, -ɪ.ti US ˌhoʊ.moʊ.sek.ʃuˈæl.ə.t̬i, -mə-

homozygous ˌhɒm.əˈzaɪ.gəs US ˌhoʊ.məˈ-, ˌhɑː-

Homs hɒmz US hɔːmz

homuncul|us hɒmˈʌŋ.kjə.l|əs, həˈmʌŋ-, -kjʊ- US hoʊˈmʌŋ.kjə-, hə- **-i** -aɪ

hon. (**H**) *(abbrev. for* **honourable***)* ˈɒn.ᵊr.ə.bl̩ US ˈɑː.nɚ- *(abbrev. for* **honorary***)* ˈɒn.ᵊr.ə.ri, ˈ-ᵊr.i US ˈɑː.nɚ.er.i

honcho ˈhɒn.tʃəʊ US ˈhɑːn.tʃoʊ **-s** -z **-ing** -ɪŋ **-ed** -d

Honda® ˈhɒn.də US ˈhɑːn.də

Hondur|as hɒnˈdjʊə.r|əs, -ˈdʊə-, -ˈdjɔː-, -r|æs US hɑːnˈdʊr|.əs, -ˈdjʊr- **-an/s** -ən/z

hon|e (H) həʊn US hoʊn **-es** -z **-ing** -ɪŋ **-ed** -d

Honecker ˈhɒn.ɪ.kəʳ, -ek.əʳ US ˈhɑː.nɪ.kɚ

Honegger ˈhɒn.ɪ.gəʳ, -eg.əʳ US ˈhɑː.nɪ.gɚ, ˈhoʊ-

honest ˈɒn.ɪst, -əst US ˈɑː.nɪst **-ly** -li

honest-to-goodness ˌɒn.ɪs*t*.təˈgʊd.nəs, -əs*t*-, -nɪs US ˌɑː.nɪst.təˈ-

honesty ˈɒn.ɪ.sti, ˈ-ə- US ˈɑː.nɪ-

hon|ey ˈhʌn|.i **-eyed** -id **-ied** -id

honeybee ˈhʌn.i.biː **-s** -z

Honeybourne ˈhʌn.i.bɔːn US -bɔːrn

honeybun ˈhʌn.i.bʌn **-s** -z

honeybunch ˈhʌn.i.bʌn*t*ʃ **-es** -ɪz

Honeychurch ˈhʌn.i.tʃɜːtʃ US -tʃɝːtʃ

honeycomb (H) ˈhʌn.i.kəʊm US -koʊm **-s** -z **-ed** -d

honeydew ˈhʌn.i.djuː US -duː, -djuː ˌ**honeydew** ˈ**melon**

honeyeater ˈhʌn.iˌiː.təʳ US -t̬ɚ **-s** -z

honeymoon ˈhʌn.i.muːn **-s** -z **-ing** -ɪŋ **-ed** -d **-er/s** -əʳ/z US -ɚ/z

honeysucker ˈhʌn.iˌsʌk.əʳ US -ɚ **-s** -z

honeysuckle ˈhʌn.iˌsʌk.l̩ **-s** -z

hong hɒŋ US hɑːŋ **-s** -z

Hong Kong ˌhɒŋˈkɒŋ US ˈhɑːŋˌkɑːŋ, ˈhɔːŋ-, -ˌkɔːŋ, ˌ-ˈ-

Honiara ˌhəʊ.niˈɑː.rə US ˌhoʊ.niˈɑːr.ə

Honi soit qui mal y pense ˌɒn.iˌswɑː.kiːˌmæl.iˈpɑ̃ː*nt*s US ˌɔː.ni-

Honiton ˈhɒn.ɪ.tᵊn *locally:* ˈhʌn- US ˈhɑː.nə.t̬ən

honk hɒŋk US hɑːŋk, hɔːŋk **-s** -s **-ing** -ɪŋ **-ed** -t

honk|ie, honk|y ˈhɒŋ.k|i US ˈhɑːŋ-, ˈhɔːŋ- **-ies** -iz

honky-tonk ˈhɒŋ.ki.tɒŋk, ˌ--ˈ- US ˈhɑːŋ.ki.tɑːŋk, ˈhɔːŋ-, -tɔːŋk

Honolulu ˌhɒn.ᵊlˈuː.luː US ˌhɑː.nəˈluː-

hon|or (H) ˈɒn|.əʳ US ˈɑː.n|ɚ **-ors** -əz US -ɚz **-oring** -ᵊr.ɪŋ **-ored** -əd US -ɚd

honorab|le ˈhɒn.ᵊr.ə.b|l̩ US ˈɑː.nɚ- **-ly** -li **-leness** -l̩.nəs, -nɪs

honorarium ˌɒn.əˈreə.ri.əm, -ˈrɑː- US ˌɑː.nəˈrer.i- **-s** -z

honorary ˈɒn.ᵊr.ə.ri, ˈ-ᵊr.i US ˈɑː.nə.rer.i

honorific ˌɒn.ᵊrˈɪf.ɪk US ˌɑː.nəˈrɪf- **-s** -s

Honorius həˈnɔː.ri.əs, hɒnˈɔː- US hoʊˈnɔːr.i-, hə-

hon|our ˈɒn|.əʳ US ˈɑː.n|ɚ **-ours** -əz US -ɚz **-ouring** -ᵊr.ɪŋ **-oured** -əd US -ɚd ˈ**honours** ˌ**list**

honourab|le (H) ˈɒn.ᵊr.ə.b|l̩ US ˈɑː.nɚ- **-ly** -li **-leness** -l̩.nəs, -nɪs

Honshu ˈhɒn.ʃuː US ˈhɑːn-

Honyman ˈhʌn.i.mən

Hoo huː

hooch huːtʃ

hood (H) hʊd **-s** -z **-ing** -ɪŋ **-ed** -ɪd **-less** -ləs, -lɪs

-hood -hʊd

Note: Suffix. Normally unstressed, e.g. **womanhood** /ˈwʊm.ən.hʊd/.

hoodlum ˈhuːd.ləm, ˈhʊd- **-s** -z

hoodwink ˈhʊd.wɪŋk **-s** -s **-ing** -ɪŋ **-ed** -t

hooey ˈhuː.i

hoo|f huː|f US hʊ|f, huː|f **-fs** -fs **-ves** -vz **-fing** -fɪŋ **-fed** -ft **-fer/s** -fəʳ/z US -fɚ/z

Hoog(h)ly ˈhuː.gli

hook (H) hʊk **-s** -s **-ing** -ɪŋ **-ed** -t ˌ**hook and** ˈ**eye**; ˌ**Hook of** ˈ**Holland**; **by** ˌ**hook or by** ˈ**crook**; ˌ**hook,** ˌ**line, and** ˈ**sinker**

hookah ˈhʊk.ə, -ɑː US ˈhʊk.ə, ˈhuː.kə, -kɑː **-s** -z

Hooke hʊk

hooker (H) ˈhʊk.əʳ US -ɚ **-s** -z

hookey ˈhʊk.i

hookup ˈhʊk.ʌp **-s** -s

hookworm ˈhʊk.wɜːm US -wɝːm **-s** -z

hooky ˈhʊk.i

Hooley ˈhuː.li

hooligan (H) ˈhuː.lɪ.gᵊn, -lə- US -lɪ- **-s** -z **-ism** -ɪ.zᵊm

Hoon huːn

hoop huːp US huːp, hʊp **-s** -s **-ing** -ɪŋ **-ed** -t

hooper (H) ˈhuː.pəʳ US -pɚ **-s** -z

hoopla ˈhuːp.lɑː, ˈhʊp-

hoopoe ˈhuː.puː **-s** -z

hoorah hʊˈrɑː, hə-, ˌhuː- **-s** -z

hooray hʊˈreɪ, hə-, ˌhuː-

hooray Henr|y ˌhuː.reɪˈhen.r|i **-ies** -iz

hoot huːt **-s** -s **-ing** -ɪŋ US ˈhuː.t̬ɪŋ **-ed** -ɪd US ˈhuː.t̬ɪd

hootch huːtʃ

hootenan|ny ˈhuː.tᵊn.æn|.i **-nies** -iz

hooter ˈhuː.təʳ US -t̬ɚ **-s** -z

hoov|er (H®) ˈhuː.v|əʳ US -v|ɚ **-ers** -əz US -ɚz **-ering** -ᵊr.ɪŋ **-ered** -əd US -ɚd

hooves *(from* **hoof***)* huːvz US hʊvz, huːvz

hop hɒp US hɑːp **-s** -s **-ping** -ɪŋ **-ped** -t ˌ**hopping** ˈ**mad**

Hopcraft ˈhɒp.krɑːft US ˈhɑːp.kræft

hop|e (H) həʊp US hoʊp **-es** -s **-ing** -ɪŋ **-ed** -t ˈ**hope** ˌ**chest**

hopeful (H) ˈhəʊp.fᵊl, -fʊl US ˈhoʊp- **-s** -z **-ly** -i **-ness** -nəs, -nɪs

hopeless ˈhəʊp.ləs, -lɪs US ˈhoʊp- **-ly** -li **-ness** -nəs, -nɪs

Hopi ˈhəʊ.pi US ˈhoʊ-

Hopkins ˈhɒp.kɪnz US ˈhɑːp-

Hopkinson ˈhɒp.kɪn.sən US ˈhɑːp-

hoplite ˈhɒp.laɪt US ˈhɑː.plaɪt **-s** -s

hopper (H) ˈhɒp.əʳ US ˈhɑː.pɚ **-s** -z

hop-pick|er ˈhɒpˌpɪk|.əʳ US ˈhɑːpˌpɪk|.ɚ **-ers** -əz US -ɚz **-ing** -ɪŋ

Hoppner ˈhɒp.nəʳ US ˈhɑːp.nɚ **-s** -z

hopscotch ˈhɒp.skɒtʃ US ˈhɑːp.skɑːtʃ

Hopton ˈhɒp.tən US ˈhɑːp-

Hor hɔːʳ US hɔːr

Horace ˈhɒr.ɪs, -əs US ˈhɔːr.ɪs

Horae ˈhɔː.riː US ˈhoʊ.riː, ˈhɔːr.iː

Horatian həˈreɪ.ʃᵊn, hɒrˈeɪ-, -ʃi.ən US hɔːˈreɪ-, hə-

Horatio həˈreɪ.ʃi.əʊ, hɒrˈeɪ- US hɔːˈreɪ-, hə-

Horati|us həˈreɪ.ʃ|əs, hɒrˈeɪ-, -ʃi|.əs US hɔːˈreɪ-, hə-

Horbury ˈhɔː.bᵊr.i US ˈhɔːrˌber-

horde hɔːd US hɔːrd **-s** -z

Horeb ˈhɔː.reb US ˈhɔːr.eb

horehound ˈhɔː.haʊnd US ˈhɔːr- **-s** -z

horizon həˈraɪ.zᵊn **-s** -z

horizontal ˌhɒr.ɪˈzɒn.tᵊl, -əˈ- US ˌhɔːr.ɪˈzɑːn- **-ly** -i

Horley ˈhɔː.li US ˈhɔːr-

Horlick ˈhɔː.lɪk US ˈhɔːr-

Horlicks® ˈhɔː.lɪks US ˈhɔːr-

hormonal hɔːˈməʊ.nᵊl US hɔːrˈmoʊ-

hormone ˈhɔː.məʊn US ˈhɔːr.moʊn **-s** -z ˌ**hormone re**ˈ**placement** ˌ**therapy**

Hormuz ˌhɔːˈmuːz, ˈhɔː.məz US ˈhɔːr.mʌz, -muːz

horn (H) hɔːn US hɔːrn **-s** -z ˌ**Horn of** ˈ**Africa**; ˌ**horn of** ˈ**plenty**; **take the** ˌ**bull by the** ˈ**horns**

hornbeam ˈhɔːn.biːm, ˈhɔːm- US ˈhɔːrn- **-s** -z

hornbill ˈhɔːn.bɪl, ˈhɔːm- US ˈhɔːrn- **-s** -z

hornblende ˈhɔːn.blend, ˈhɔːm- US ˈhɔːrn-

Hornblower ˈhɔːnˌbləʊ.əʳ, ˈhɔːm- US ˈhɔːrnˌbloʊ.ɚ

hornbook ˈhɔːn.bʊk, ˈhɔːm- US ˈhɔːrn- **-s** -s

Hornby ˈhɔːn.bi, ˈhɔːm- US ˈhɔːrn-

Horncastle ˈhɔːnˌkɑː.sᵊl, ˈhɔːŋ- US ˈhɔːrnˌkæs.ᵊl

Hornchurch ˈhɔːn.tʃɜːtʃ US ˈhɔːrn.tʃɝːtʃ

Horne hɔːn US hɔːrn

horned *of cattle, birds, etc.:* hɔːnd US hɔːrnd *poetic:* ˈhɔː.nɪd US ˈhɔːr-

Hornell hɔːˈnel US hɔːr-

Horner ˈhɔː.nəʳ US ˈhɔːr.nɚ

hornet ˈhɔː.nɪt, -nət US ˈhɔːr- **-s** -s ˈ**hornet's** ˌ**nest,** ˌ**hornet's** ˈ**nest**

Horniman ˈhɔː.nɪ.mən US ˈhɔːr-

hornpipe ˈhɔːn.paɪp, ˈhɔːm- US ˈhɔːrn- **-s** -s

horn-rimmed ˌhɔːnˈrɪmd US ˈhɔːrn.rɪmd *stress shift, British only:* ˌhorn-rimmed ˈspectacles

Hornsea ˈhɔːn.siː US ˈhɔːrn-

Hornsey ˈhɔːn.zi US ˈhɔːrn-

hornswoggl|e ˈhɔːnˌswɒg.l̩ US ˈhɔːrnˌswɑː.gl̩ **-es** -z **-ing** -ɪŋ **-ed** -d

Hornung ˈhɔː.nəŋ US ˈhɔːr-

hornwork ˈhɔːn.wɜːk US ˈhɔːrn.wɝːk **-s** -s

horn|y ˈhɔː.n|i US ˈhɔːr- **-ier** -i.əʳ US -i.ɚ **-iest** -i.ɪst, -i.əst **-iness** -ɪ.nəs, -ɪ.nɪs

horography hɒrˈɒg.rə.fi, hɔːˈrɒg-, hə- US hɔːˈrɑːg-

horolog|e ˈhɒr.ə.lɒdʒ, ˈhɔː.rə-, -ləʊdʒ US ˈhɔːr.ə.loʊdʒ **-es** -ɪz

horologic ˌhɒr.əˈlɒdʒ.ɪk, ˌhɔː.rəˈ- US ˌhɔːr.əˈlɑː.dʒɪk **-al** -ᵊl

horological ˌhɒr.əˈlɒdʒ.ɪ.kᵊl, ˌhɔː.rəˈ- US ˌhɔːr.əˈlɑː.dʒɪ-

horolog|y hɒrˈɒl.ə.dʒ|i, hɔːˈrɒl-, hə- US hɔːrˈɑː.lə- **-er/s** -əʳ/z US -ɚ/z **-ist/s** -ɪst/s

horoscope ˈhɒr.ə.skəʊp US ˈhɔːr.ə.skoʊp **-s** -s

horoscopic ˌhɒr.əˈskɒp.ɪk US ˌhɔːr.əˈskɑː.pɪk

Horovitz ˈhɒr.ə.vɪts US ˈhɔːr-

Horowitz ˈhɒr.ə.vɪts, -wɪts US ˈhɔːr.ə.wɪts

horrendous hɒrˈen.dəs, həˈren- US hɔːˈren-, hə- **-ly** -li **-ness** -nəs, -nɪs

horrib|le ˈhɒr.ə.b|l̩, ˈ-ɪ- US ˈhɔːr- **-ly** -li **-leness** -l̩.nəs, -nɪs

horrid ˈhɒr.ɪd US ˈhɔːr- **-er** -əʳ US -ɚ **-est** -ɪst, -əst **-ly** -li **-ness** -nəs, -nɪs

horrific hɒrˈɪf.ɪk, həˈrɪf- US hɔːˈrɪf-, hə- **-ally** -ᵊl.i, -li

horri|fy ˈhɒr.ɪ|.faɪ, ˈ-ə- US ˈhɔːr- **-fies** -faɪz **-fying/ly** -faɪ.ɪŋ/li **-fied** -faɪd

horripilation hɒrˌɪp.ɪˈleɪ.ʃᵊn, -əˈ-; ˌhɒr.ɪ.pɪˈ-, ˌ-ə- US ˌhɔːr.ɪ.pəˈleɪ-

Horrocks ˈhɒr.əks US ˈhɔːr-

horror ˈhɒr.əʳ US ˈhɔːr.ɚ **-s** -z

horror|-stricken ˈhɒr.ə|ˌstrɪk.ᵊn US ˈhɔːr.ɚ|ˌ- **-struck** -strʌk

Horsa ˈhɔː.sə US ˈhɔːr-

hors de combat ˌhɔː.dəˈkɔ̃ːm.bɑː, -ˈkɔːm-, -ˈkɒm-, -bæt US ˌɔːr.də.kɔ̃ːmˈbɑː

hors d'oeuvre ˌɔːˈdɜːv, -ˈdɜːv.rə US ˌɔːrˈdɝːv, -ˈdɝːv.rə **-s** -z

hors|e hɔːs US hɔːrs **-es** -ɪz **-ing** -ɪŋ **-ed** -t ˌhorse ˈchestnut; ˈhorse ˌopera; ˈhorse ˌsense; ˈhorse ˌshow; ˈhorse ˌtrials; ˌflog a ˌdead ˈhorse; ˌhold your ˈhorses; (ˌstraight) from the ˌhorse's ˈmouth

horse-and-buggy ˌhɔː.sᵊndˈbʌg.i, -ᵊmˈ- US ˌhɔːrs-

horseback ˈhɔːs.bæk US ˈhɔːrs- ˈhorseback ˌriding

horsebox ˈhɔːs.bɒks US ˈhɔːrs.bɑːks **-es** -ɪz

horseflesh ˈhɔːs.fleʃ US ˈhɔːrs-

horsefl|y ˈhɔːs.fl|aɪ US ˈhɔːrs- **-ies** -aɪz

Horseguard ˈhɔːs.gɑːd US ˈhɔːrs.gɑːrd **-s** -z

horsehair ˈhɔːs.heəʳ US ˈhɔːrs.her **-s** -z

horselaugh ˈhɔːs.lɑːf US ˈhɔːrs.læf **-s** -s

horse|man (H) ˈhɔːs|.mən US ˈhɔːrs- **-men** -mən, -men **-manship** -mən.ʃɪp

horseplay ˈhɔːs.pleɪ US ˈhɔːrs-

horsepower ˈhɔːsˌpaʊəʳ US ˈhɔːrsˌpaʊr

horseradish ˈhɔːsˌræd.ɪʃ US ˈhɔːrs- **-es** -ɪz

horseshoe ˈhɔːs.ʃuː, ˈhɔːʃ- US ˈhɔːrs-, ˈhɔːrʃ- **-s** -z

horsetail ˈhɔːs.teɪl US ˈhɔːrs- **-s** -z

horsetrad|e ˈhɔːs.treɪd US ˈhɔːrs- **-es** -z **-ing** -ɪŋ **-ed** -ɪd **-er/s** -əʳ/z US -ɚ/z

horse-trading ˈhɔːsˌtreɪ.dɪŋ US ˈhɔːrs-

horsewhip ˈhɔːs.*h*wɪp US ˈhɔːrs- **-s** -s **-ping** -ɪŋ **-ped** -t

horse|woman ˈhɔːs|ˌwʊm.ən US ˈhɔːrs- **-women** -ˌwɪm.ɪn

hors|ey ˈhɔː.s|i US ˈhɔːr- **-ier** -i.əʳ US -i.ɚ **-iest** -i.ɪst, -i.əst **-ily** -ɪ.li, -ᵊl.i **-iness** -ɪ.nəs, -ɪ.nɪs

Horsfall ˈhɔːs.fɔːl US ˈhɔːrs.fɔːl, -fɑːl

Horsforth ˈhɔːs.fəθ US ˈhɔːrs.fɚθ

Horsham ˈhɔː.ʃᵊm US ˈhɔːr-

Horsley ˈhɔːz.li, ˈhɔːs- US ˈhɔːrz-, ˈhɔːrs-

Horsmonden *in Kent:* ˌhɔːz.mənˈden *old-fashioned local pronunciation:* ˌhɔː.sᵊn- US ˌhɔːrz.mᵊnˈ-

hors|y ˈhɔː.s|i US ˈhɔːr- **-ier** -i.əʳ US -i.ɚ **-iest** -i.ɪst, -i.əst **-ily** -ɪ.li, -ᵊl.i **-iness** -ɪ.nəs, -ɪ.nɪs

horta|tive ˈhɔː.tə|.tɪv US ˈhɔːr.t̬ə|.t̬ɪv **-tory** -tᵊr.i US -tɔːr.i

Hortensi|a hɔːˈten*t*.si|.ə, -ˈten.*t*ʃi|.ə, -*t*ʃ|ə US hɔːrˈten.*t*ʃi- **-us** -əs

horticultural ˌhɔː.tɪˈkʌl.tʃᵊr.ᵊl, -təˈ-, -tʃʊ.rᵊl US ˌhɔːr.t̬əˈkʌl.tʃɚ.ᵊl **-ist/s** -ɪst/s

horticulture ˈhɔː.tɪ.kʌl.tʃəʳ, -tə- US ˈhɔːr.t̬ə.kʌl.tʃɚ

Horton ˈhɔː.tᵊn US ˈhɔːr-

Horus ˈhɔː.rəs US ˈhɔːr.əs

Horwich ˈhɒr.ɪtʃ US ˈhɔːr.ɪtʃ

Hosack ˈhɒs.ək US ˈhɑː.sək

hosanna həʊˈzæn.ə US hoʊ- **-s** -z

hos|e həʊz US hoʊz **-es** -ɪz **-ing** -ɪŋ **-ed** -d

Hosea həʊˈzɪə US hoʊˈzeɪ.ə, -ˈziː-

hosepipe ˈhəʊz.paɪp US ˈhoʊz- **-s** -s

hoser ˈhəʊ.zəʳ US ˈhoʊ.zɚ **-s** -z

hosier (H) ˈhəʊ.zi.əʳ, -ʒəʳ US ˈhoʊ.ʒɚ **-s** -z

hosiery ˈhəʊ.zi.ə.ri, -ʒᵊr.i US ˈhoʊ.ʒɚ.i

Hoskins ˈhɒs.kɪnz US ˈhɑː.skɪnz

Hosmer ˈhɒz.məʳ US ˈhɑːz.mɚ

hospic|e ˈhɒs.pɪs US ˈhɑː.spɪs **-es** -ɪz

hospitab|le hɒsˈpɪt.ə.b|l̩, həˈspɪt-; ˈhɒs.pɪ.tə- US ˈhɑː.spɪ.t̬ə-; hɑːˈspɪt̬.ə- **-ly** -li **-leness** -l̩.nəs, -nɪs

hospital ˈhɒs.pɪ.tᵊl US ˈhɑː.spɪ.t̬ᵊl **-s** -z

Hospitaler ˈhɒs.pɪ.tᵊl.əʳ US ˈhɑː.spɪ.t̬ᵊl.ɚ **-s** -z

hospitalit|y ˌhɒs.pɪˈtæl.ə.t|i, -pəˈ-, -ɪ.t|i US ˌhɑː.spɪˈtæl.ə.t̬|i **-ies** -iz

hospitalization, -isa- ˌhɒs.pɪ.tᵊl.aɪˈzeɪ.ʃᵊn, -pə-, -ɪˈ- US ˌhɑː.spɪ.t̬ᵊl.ɪˈ-

hospitaliz|e, -is|e ˈhɒs.pɪ.tᵊl.aɪz, -pə- US ˈhɑː.spɪ.t̬ᵊl- **-es** -ɪz **-ing** -ɪŋ **-ed** -d

Hospitaller ˈhɒs.pɪ.tᵊl.əʳ US ˈhɑː.spɪ.t̬ᵊl.ɚ **-s** -z

host (H) həʊst US hoʊst **-s** -s **-ing** -ɪŋ **-ed** -ɪd

hosta ˈhɒs.tə, ˈhəʊ.stə US ˈhɑː-, ˈhoʊ- **-s** -z

hostag|e ˈhɒs.tɪdʒ US ˈhɑː.stɪdʒ **-es** -ɪz

hostel ˈhɒs.tᵊl US ˈhɑː.stᵊl **-s** -z

hostel|ler ˈhɒs.tᵊl|.əʳ US ˈhɑː.stᵊl|.ɚ **-ers** -əz US -ɚz **-ing** -ɪŋ

hostelr|y ˈhɒs.tᵊl.r|i US ˈhɑː.stᵊl- **-ies** -iz

hostess ˈhəʊ.stɪs, -stes, -stəs; ˌhəʊˈstes US ˈhoʊ.stɪs, -stəs **-es** -ɪz

hostile ˈhɒs.taɪl US ˈhɑː.stᵊl, -staɪl **-ly** -li

hostilit|y hɒsˈtɪl.ə.t|i, -ɪ.t|i US hɑːˈstɪl.ə.t̬|i **-ies** -iz

hostler ˈɒs.ləʳ, ˈhɒs- US ˈhɑː.slɚ, ˈɑː- **-s** -z

hot hɒt US hɑːt **-ter** -əʳ US ˈhɑː.t̬ɚ **-test** -ɪst, -əst US ˈhɑː.t̬ɪst, -t̬əst **-ly** -li **-ness** -nəs, -nɪs **-s** -s **-ting** -ɪŋ US ˈhɑː.t̬ɪŋ **-ted** -ɪd US ˈhɑː.t̬ɪd ˌhot ˈair; ˌhot cross ˈbun; ˈhot ˌdog; ˌhot ˈdog ˈhot ˌpants; ˌhot poˈtato; ˈhot ˌseat, ˌhot ˈseat; ˌhot ˈstuff; ˌhot ˈticket; ˌhot ˈwater; ˌblow ˌhot and ˈcold; ˌsell like ˌhot ˈcakes; US ˌsell like ˈhot ˌcakes

hotbed ˈhɒt.bed US ˈhɑːt- **-s** -z

hot-blooded ˌhɒtˈblʌd.ɪd US ˌhɑːt- *stress shift:* ˌhot-blooded ˈyouth

Hotchkiss ˈhɒtʃ.kɪs US ˈhɑːtʃ-

hotchpot ˈhɒtʃ.pɒt US ˈhɑːtʃ.pɑːt **-s** -s

hotchpotch ˈhɒtʃ.pɒtʃ US ˈhɑːtʃ.pɑːtʃ **-es** -ɪz

hotdog ˈhɒt.dɒg US ˈhɑːt.dɑːg, -dɔːg **-s** -z **-ging** -ɪŋ **-ged** -d

hotel həʊˈtel, əʊ- US hoʊ- **-s** -z

Note: Some British speakers use the form /əʊˈtel/ always; others use it occasionally when the word is not initial, with ‘an’ as preceding indefinite article.

hotelier həʊˈtel.i.eɪ, əʊ-, -əʳ US ˌhoʊ.tᵊlˈjeɪ, ˌoʊ-; hoʊˈtel.jɚ **-s** -z

hotfoo|t ˌhɒtˈfʊ|t, ˈ-- US ˈhɑːt.fʊ|t **-ts** -ts **-ting** -tɪŋ US -t̬ɪŋ **-ted** -tɪd US -t̬ɪd

Hotham ˈhʌð.əm

hothead ˈhɒt.hed US ˈhɑːt- **-s** -z

hotheaded ˌhɒtˈhed.ɪd, ˈ-ˌ-- US ˈhɑːtˌhed.ɪd, ˌ-ˈ-- **-ly** -li **-ness** -nəs, -nɪs

hothou|se ˈhɒt.haʊ|s US ˈhɑːt- **-ses** -zɪz

hotline ˈhɒt.laɪn US ˈhɑːt- **-s** -z

Hotol ˈhɒt.ɒl, ˈhəʊ.tɒl US ˈhɑː.tɑːl, ˈhoʊ-

hotplate ˈhɒt.pleɪt US ˈhɑːt- **-s** -s

Hotpoint® ˈhɒt.pɔɪnt (US) ˈhɑːt-

hotpot ˈhɒt.pɒt (US) ˈhɑːt.pɑːt **-s** -s

hotrod ˈhɒt.rɒd (US) ˈhɑːt.rɑːd **-s** -z **-ding** -ɪŋ **-ded** -ɪd **-der/s** -əʳ/z (US) -ɚ/z

hotshot ˈhɒt.ʃɒt (US) ˈhɑːt.ʃɑːt **-s** -s

hotspot ˈhɒt.spɒt (US) ˈhɑːt.spɑːt **-s** -s

hotspur (H) ˈhɒt.spɜːʳ, -spəʳ (US) ˈhɑːt.spɝː, -spɚ **-s** -z

hot-tempered ˌhɒtˈtem.pəd (US) ˌhɑːtˈtem.pɚd *stress shift:* ˌhot-tempered ˈfighter

Hottentot ˈhɒt.ᵊn.tɒt (US) ˈhɑː.tᵊn.tɑːt **-s** -s

hot-water bottle ˌhɒtˈwɔː.təˌbɒt.l̩ (US) ˌhɑːtˈwɑː.t̬ɚˌbɑː.t̬l̩, -ˈwɔː- **-s** -z

Houdini huːˈdiː.ni

hough hɒk (US) hɑːk **-s** -s **-ing** -ɪŋ **-ed** -t

Hough hʌf, hɒf, haʊ (US) hʌf, hɔːf, hɑːf

Houghall ˈhɒf.ᵊl (US) ˈhɑː.fᵊl

Hougham ˈhʌf.əm

Houghton ˈhɔː.tᵊn, ˈhaʊ-, ˈhəʊ- (US) ˈhoʊ-, ˈhɔː-, ˈhɑː-, ˈhaʊ-

Note: /ˈhɔː.tᵊn, ˈhaʊ.tᵊn/ are more usual in British English when the word is a surname. The city in Michigan is /ˈhəʊ- (US) ˈhoʊ-/.

Houghton-le-Spring ˌhəʊ.tᵊn.ləˈsprɪŋ, ˌhaʊ-, -liˈ- (US) ˌhoʊ-, ˌhaʊ-

Houllier ˈ*h*uː.li.eɪ

Houltby ˈhəʊlt.bi (US) ˈhoʊlt-

houm(o)us ˈhuː.mʊs, ˈhʊm.ʊs, -əs (US) ˈhʌm.əs, ˈhʊm-

hound haʊnd **-s** -z **-ing** -ɪŋ **-ed** -ɪd

Houndsditch ˈhaʊn*d*z.dɪtʃ

houndstooth ˈhaʊn*d*z.tuːθ, ˌ-ˈ- (US) ˈ--

Hounslow ˈhaʊnz.ləʊ (US) -loʊ

hour aʊəʳ (US) aʊr, aʊɚ **-s** -z **-ly** -li

hourglass ˈaʊə.glɑːs (US) ˈaʊr.glæs, ˈaʊɚ- **-es** -ɪz

houri ˈhʊə.ri (US) ˈhʊr.i, ˈhuːr- **-s** -z

Housden ˈhaʊz.dən

hou|se (H) *(n.)* haʊ|s **-ses** -zɪz ˌ**house arˈrest; ˈhouse ˌhusband; ˈhouse ˌmartin; ˈhouse ˌmusic; ˌHouse of ˈCommons; ˌHouse of ˈLords; ˌHouse of Repreˈsentatives; ˌHouses of ˈParliament; ˈhouse ˌparty; ˈhouse ˌsparrow; ˌeat one out of ˌhouse and ˈhome; ˌbring the ˈhouse ˌdown; get ˌon like a ˈhouse on ˌfire; ˌset one's ˈhouse in ˌorder**

hous|e *(v.)* haʊz **-es** -ɪz **-ing** -ɪŋ **-ed** -d

houseboat ˈhaʊs.bəʊt (US) -boʊt **-s** -s

housebound ˈhaʊs.baʊnd

housebreak|er ˈhaʊsˌbreɪ.k|əʳ (US) -k|ɚ **-ers** -əz (US) -ɚz **-ing** -ɪŋ

house-broken ˈhaʊsˌbrəʊ.kᵊn (US) -ˌbroʊ-

housebuy|er ˈhaʊsˌbaɪ|.əʳ (US) -ɚ **-ers** -z **-ing** -ɪŋ

housecoat ˈhaʊs.kəʊt (US) -koʊt **-s** -s

housefather ˈhaʊsˌfɑː.ðəʳ (US) -ðɚ **-s** -z

housefl|y ˈhaʊs.fl|aɪ **-ies** -aɪz

houseful ˈhaʊs.fʊl **-s** -z

houseguest ˈhaʊs.gest **-s** -s

household (H) ˈhaʊs.*h*əʊld (US) -*h*oʊld **-s** -z **-er/s** -əʳ/z (US) -ɚ/z

housekeeper ˈhaʊsˌkiː.pəʳ (US) -pɚ **-s** -z (US) -z

housekeeping ˈhaʊsˌkiː.pɪŋ

Housel ˈhaʊ.zᵊl

houseleek ˈhaʊs.liːk **-s** -s

housemaid ˈhaʊs.meɪd **-s** -z

house|man ˈhaʊs|.mən, -mæn **-men** -mən, -men

housemaster ˈhaʊsˌmɑː.stəʳ (US) -ˌmæs.tɚ **-s** -z

housemate ˈhaʊs.meɪt **-s** -s

housemother ˈhaʊsˌmʌð.əʳ (US) -ɚ **-s** -z

houseplant ˈhaʊs.plɑːnt (US) -plænt **-s** -s

houseproud ˈhaʊs.praʊd

houseroom ˈhaʊs.rʊm, -ruːm (US) -ruːm, -rʊm

house|sit ˈhaʊs|.sɪt **-sits** -sɪts **-sitting** -ˌsɪt.ɪŋ (US) -ˌsɪt̬.ɪŋ **-sat** -sæt **-sitter/s** -ˌsɪt.əʳ/z (US) -ˌsɪt̬.ɚ/z

Housestead's Fort ˌhaʊs.stedzˈfɔːt (US) -ˈfɔːrt

house-to-house ˌhaʊs.təˈhaʊs *stress shift:* ˌhouse-to-house ˈsearch

housetop ˈhaʊs.tɒp (US) -tɑːp **-s** -s

housewares ˈhaʊs.weəz (US) -werz

housewarming ˈhaʊsˌwɔː.mɪŋ (US) -ˌwɔːr- **-s** -z

housewife *woman:* ˈhaʊs.waɪf; *old-fashioned:* ˈhʌz.ɪf **housewives** ˈhaʊs.waɪvz; *old-fashioned:* -ɪvz **housewifes** *old-fashioned:* ˈhʌz.ɪfs

housewi|fe *needle-case:* ˈhʌz.ɪ|f **-fes** -fs **-ves** -vz

housewifel|y ˈhaʊsˌwaɪf.l|i **-iness** -ɪ.nəs, -ɪ.nɪs

housewifery ˈhaʊsˌwɪf.ᵊr.i; *old-fashioned:* ˈhʌz.ɪ.fri (US) ˈhaʊsˌwaɪ.fɚ.i, ˌ-fri

housework ˈhaʊs.wɜːk (US) -wɝːk

housey-housey, housie-housie ˌhaʊ.siˈhaʊ.si, -ziˈhaʊ.zi

housing ˈhaʊ.zɪŋ **ˈhousing asˌsociation; ˈhousing deˌvelopment; ˈhousing eˌstate; ˈhousing ˌlist**

Housman ˈhaʊs.mən

Houston *English surname:* ˈhuː.stᵊn, ˈhaʊ- *Scottish surname:* ˈhuː.stᵊn *in US:* ˈhjuː.stᵊn

Houyhnhnm ˈhuː.ɪ.nᵊm (US) ˈhwɪn.ᵊm, huˈɪn- **-s** -z

hove (H) *(from* **heave***)* həʊv (US) hoʊv

hovel ˈhɒv.ᵊl, ˈhʌv- (US) ˈhʌv-, ˈhɑː.vᵊl **-s** -z

Hovell ˈhəʊ.vᵊl, ˈhɒv.ᵊl, həʊˈvel (US) ˈhoʊ.vᵊl, ˈhɑː-, hoʊˈvel

Hovenden ˈhɒv.ᵊn.dən (US) ˈhoʊ.vᵊn-

hov|er ˈhɒv|.əʳ (US) ˈhʌv|.ɚ, ˈhɑː.v|ɚ **-ers** -əz (US) -ɚz **-ering** -ᵊr.ɪŋ **-ered** -əd (US) -ɚd

hovercraft ˈhɒv.ə.krɑːft (US) ˈhʌv.ɚ.kræft, ˈhɑː.vɚ- **-s** -s

hoverfl|y ˈhɒv.ə.fl|aɪ (US) ˈhʌv.ɚ-, ˈhɑː.vɚ- **-ies** -aɪz

hoverport ˈhɒv.ə.pɔːt (US) ˈhʌv.ɚ.pɔːrt, ˈhɑː.vɚ- **-s** -s

Hovis® ˈhəʊ.vɪs (US) ˈhoʊ-

how (H) haʊ

Howard haʊəd (US) haʊɚd

Howarth haʊəθ (US) haʊɚθ

howdah ˈhaʊ.də **-s** -z

Howden ˈhaʊ.dᵊn

how-do-you-do ˌhaʊ.djʊˈduː, -djəˈ-, -dʒʊˈ-, -dʒəˈ-, ˈ--- (US) ˈhaʊ.də.juː.duː, ˈ-djə.duː

howdy ˈhaʊ.di

howdy-do ˌhaʊ.diˈduː **-s** -z

Howe haʊ

Howell haʊəl **-s** -z

Howerd haʊəd (US) haʊɚd

Howers haʊəz (US) haʊɚz

Howes haʊz

however haʊˈev.əʳ (US) -ɚ

Howick ˈhaʊ.ɪk

Howie ˈhaʊ.i

Howitt ˈhaʊ.ɪt

howitzer ˈhaʊ.ɪt.səʳ (US) -sɚ **-s** -z

howl haʊl **-s** -z **-ing** -ɪŋ **-ed** -d

howler ˈhaʊ.ləʳ (US) -lɚ **-s** -z

Howlett ˈhaʊ.lɪt

Howley ˈhaʊ.li

Howorth haʊəθ (US) haʊɚθ

Howse haʊz

howsoever ˌhaʊ.səʊˈev.əʳ (US) -soʊˈev.ɚ

Howson ˈhaʊ.sᵊn

Howth həʊθ (US) hoʊθ

how-to ˈhaʊ.tuː **-s** -z

Hoxha ˈhɒdʒ.ə (US) ˈhɔː.ʒdɑː

Hoxton ˈhɒk.stᵊn (US) ˈhɑːk-

hoy (H) hɔɪ **-s** -z

hoyden (H) ˈhɔɪ.dᵊn **-s** -z

Hoylake ˈhɔɪ.leɪk

Hoyland Nether ˌhɔɪ.lən*d*ˈneð.əʳ (US) -ɚ

HP ˌeɪtʃˈpiː

HQ ˌeɪtʃˈkjuː

HRH ˌeɪtʃ.ɑːʳˈeɪtʃ (US) -ɑːrˈ-

HRT ˌeitʃ.ɑːˈtiː (US) -ɑːrˈ-

HSBC ˌeɪtʃ.es.biːˈsiː

Huang Ho ˌhwæŋˈhəʊ (US) ˌhwɑːŋˈhoʊ, ˌhwæŋ-

hub hʌb **-s** -z

Hubbard ˈhʌb.əd (US) -ɚd

Hubble ˈhʌb.l̩

hubble-bubble ˈhʌb.l̩ˌbʌb.l̩ **-s** -z

hubbub ˈhʌb.ʌb, -əb (US) -ʌb **-s** -z

hubb|y ˈhʌb|.i **-ies** -iz

hubcap ˈhʌb.kæp **-s** -s

Hubert ˈhjuː.bət (US) -bɚt

hubris ˈhjuː.brɪs, ˈhuː- (US) ˈhjuː-

hubristic hjuːˈbrɪs.tɪk, huː- (US) hjuː-
huckaback ˈhʌk.ə.bæk **-s** -s
Huckle ˈhʌk.l̩
huckleberr|y (H) ˈhʌk.l̩.bᵊr|.i, -ˌber|.i (US) -ˈber- **-ies** -iz
Hucknall, Hucknell ˈhʌk.nᵊl
huckster ˈhʌk.stəʳ (US) -stɚ **-s** -z
Huddersfield ˈhʌd.əz.fiːld (US) -ɚz-
huddl|e ˈhʌd.l̩ **-es** -z **-ing** -ɪŋ, ˈhʌd.lɪŋ **-ed** -d
Hud(d)leston(e) ˈhʌd.l̩.stᵊn
Hudibras ˈhjuː.dɪ.bræs, -də-
Hudnott ˈhʌd.nɒt, -nət (US) -nɑːt
Hudson ˈhʌd.sᵊn
hue hjuː **-s** -z ˌ**hue and** ˈ**cry**
Hueffer ˈhef.əʳ (US) -ɚ
Huelva ˈwel.və (US) -və, -vɑː
huevos rancheros ˌweɪ.vɒs.rænˈtʃeə.rɒs (US) -voʊs.rænˈtʃer.oʊs
huff (H) hʌf **-s** -s **-ing** -ɪŋ **-ed** -t
huffish ˈhʌf.ɪʃ **-ly** -li **-ness** -nəs, -nɪs
Huffman ˈhʌf.mən
huff|y ˈhʌf|.i **-ier** -i.əʳ (US) -i.ɚ **-iest** -i.ɪst, -i.əst **-ily** -ɪ.li, -ᵊl.i **-iness** -ɪ.nəs, -ɪ.nɪs
hug hʌg **-s** -z **-ging** -ɪŋ **-ged** -d
Hugall ˈhjuː.gᵊl
hug|e hjuːdʒ **-er** -əʳ (US) -ɚ **-est** -ɪst, -əst **-ely** -li **-eness** -nəs, -nɪs
hugger-mugger ˈhʌg.əˌmʌg.əʳ, ˌhʌg.əˈmʌg- (US) ˈhʌg.ɚˌmʌg.ɚ
Huggin ˈhʌg.ɪn **-s** -z
Hugh hjuː
Hughenden ˈhjuː.ᵊn.dᵊn
Hughes hjuːz
Hugo ˈhjuː.gəʊ (US) -goʊ
Hugon ˈhjuː.gᵊn, -gɒn (US) -gɑːn
Huguenot ˈhjuː.gə.nəʊ, ˈhuː-, -nɒt (US) ˈhjuː.gə.nɑːt **-s** -z
Huish ˈhjuː.ɪʃ
hula ˈhuː.lə **-s** -z
Hula-Hoop® ˈhuː.lə.huːp **-s** -s
Hulbert ˈhʌl.bət (US) -bɚt
hulk hʌlk **-s** -s **-ing** -ɪŋ
hull (H) hʌl **-s** -z **-ing** -ɪŋ **-ed** -d
hullabaloo ˌhʌl.ə.bəˈluː **-s** -z
Hullah ˈhʌl.ə
Hullbridge ˈhʌl.brɪdʒ
hullo həˈləʊ, hʌlˈəʊ (US) həˈloʊ, hʌlˈoʊ **-s** -z
Hulme hjuːm, huːm
Hulse hʌls
Hulsean hʌlˈsiː.ən
hum (*n. v.*) hʌm **-s** -z **-ming** -ɪŋ **-med** -d ˈ**humming** ˌ**top**
human (H) ˈhjuː.mən **-s** -z **-ly** -li ˌ**human** ˈ**being**; ˌ**human** ˈ**nature**; ˌ**human** ˈ**race**; ˌ**human** ˈ**rights**
human|e hjuːˈmeɪn **-er** -əʳ (US) -ɚ **-est** -ɪst, -əst **-ely** -li **-eness** -nəs, -nɪs
human|ism ˈhjuː.mə.n|ɪ.zᵊm **-ist/s** -ɪst/s
humanistic ˌhjuː.məˈnɪs.tɪk
humanitarian hjuːˌmæn.ɪˈteə.ri.ən, -əˈ-; ˌhjuː.mæn- (US) hjuːˌmæn.əˈter.i- **-s** -z **-ism** -ɪ.zᵊm
humanit|y hjuːˈmæn.ə.t|i, -ɪ.t|i (US) -ə.t̬|i **-ies** -iz
humanization, -isa- ˌhjuː.mə.naɪˈzeɪ.ʃᵊn, -nɪˈ- (US) -nɪˈ-
humaniz|e, -is|e ˈhjuː.mə.naɪz **-es** -ɪz **-ing** -ɪŋ **-ed** -d
humankind ˌhjuː.mənˈkaɪnd, -məŋˈ- (US) -mənˈ-
humanoid ˈhjuː.mə.nɔɪd **-s** -z
Humber ˈhʌm.bəʳ (US) -bɚ **-s** -z **-side** -saɪd
Humberston ˈhʌm.bə.stᵊn (US) -bɚ-
Humbert ˈhʌm.bət (US) -bɚt
humb|le ˈhʌm.b|l̩ **-ler** -ləʳ (US) -lɚ **-lest** -lɪst, -ləst **-ly** -li **-leness** -l̩.nəs, -nɪs **-les** -l̩z **-ling** -l̩.ɪŋ (US) -lɪŋ **-led** -l̩d **eat** ˌ**humble** ˈ**pie**
Humblethwaite ˈhʌm.bl̩.θweɪt
Humboldt ˈhʌm.bəʊlt, ˈhʊm- (US) -boʊlt
Humbrol® ˈhʌm.brɒl (US) -brɑːl
humbug ˈhʌm.bʌg **-s** -z **-ging** -ɪŋ **-ged** -d
humdinger ˌhʌmˈdɪŋ.əʳ (US) -ɚ **-s** -z
humdrum ˈhʌm.drʌm
Hume hjuːm
humectant hjuːˈmek.tᵊnt **-s** -s
humer|us ˈhjuː.mᵊr|.əs **-i** -aɪ **-al** -ᵊl
Humian ˈhjuː.mi.ən
humid ˈhjuː.mɪd **-ness** -nəs, -nɪs
humidification hjuːˌmɪd.ɪ.fɪˈkeɪ.ʃᵊn, ˌ-ə-
humidifier hjuːˈmɪd.ɪ.faɪ.əʳ, ˈ-ə- **-s** -z
humidif|y hjuːˈmɪd.ɪ.f|aɪ, ˈ-ə- **-ies** -aɪz **-ying** -aɪ.ɪŋ **-ied** -aɪd **-ier/s** -aɪ.əʳ/z (US) -aɪ.ɚ/z
humidity hjuːˈmɪd.ə.ti, -ɪ.ti (US) -ə.t̬i
humili|ate hjuːˈmɪl.i|.eɪt **-ates** -eɪts **-ating/ly** -eɪ.tɪŋ/li (US) -eɪ.t̬ɪŋ/li **-ated** -eɪ.tɪd (US) -eɪ.t̬ɪd
humiliation hjuːˌmɪl.iˈeɪ.ʃᵊn, ˌhjuː.mɪ.liˈ- (US) hjuːˌmɪl.iˈ- **-s** -z
humility hjuːˈmɪl.ə.ti, -ɪt.i (US) -ə.t̬i
hummingbird ˈhʌm.ɪŋ.bɜːd (US) -bɝːd **-s** -z
hummock ˈhʌm.ək **-s** -s **-y** -i
hummus ˈhʊm.ʊs, ˈhʌm-, -əs, ˈhuː.məs (US) ˈhʌm.əs, ˈhʊm-
humongous hjuːˈmʌŋ.gəs
hum|or ˈhjuː.m|əʳ (US) -m|ɚ **-ors** -əz (US) -ɚz **-oring** -ᵊr.ɪŋ **-ored** -əd (US) -ɚd **-orless/ly** -ə.ləs/li, -ɚ.lɪs/li
humoral ˈhjuː.mᵊr.ᵊl
humoresque ˌhjuː.mᵊrˈesk (US) -məˈresk **-s** -s
humorist ˈhjuː.mᵊr.ɪst **-s** -s
humoristic ˌhjuː.mᵊrˈɪs.tɪk
humorous ˈhjuː.mᵊr.əs **-ly** -li **-ness** -nəs, -nɪs
hum|our ˈhjuː.m|əʳ (US) -m|ɚ **-ours** -əz (US) -ɚz **-ouring** -ᵊr.ɪŋ **-oured** -əd (US) -ɚd **-ourless/ly** -ə.ləs/li, -ɚ.lɪs/li
humoursome ˈhjuː.mə.sᵊm (US) -mɚ- **-ly** -li **-ness** -nəs, -nɪs
hump hʌmp **-s** -s **-ing** -ɪŋ **-ed** -t
humpback ˈhʌmp.bæk **-s** -s **-ed** -t ˌ**humpbacked** ˈ**bridge**
Humperdinck ˈhʌm.pə.dɪŋk (US) -pɚ-
humph (*interj.*) ˌm̥m, hə̃h, hʌmf
Note: Interjection indicating annoyance or disapproval, with rapid fall in pitch. The transcriptions reflect a wide range of possible pronunciations. The small circle uncer the /m/ symbol indicates a voiceless consonant.
Humphr(e)y ˈhʌm*p*.fri **-s** -z
Humphries ˈhʌm*p*.friz
Humpty Dumpty ˌhʌm*p*.tiˈdʌm*p*.ti
hump|y ˈhʌm.p|i **-ier** -i.əʳ (US) -i.ɚ **-iest** -i.ɪst, -i.əst **-iness** -ɪ.nəs, -ɪ.nɪs
humus ˈhjuː.məs
Hun hʌn **-s** -z
hunch hʌn*t*ʃ **-es** -ɪz **-ing** -ɪŋ **-ed** -t
hunchback ˈhʌn*t*ʃ.bæk **-s** -s **-ed** -t
hundred ˈhʌn.drəd, -drɪd **-s** -z
hundredfold ˈhʌn.drəd.fəʊld, -drɪd- (US) -foʊld
hundredth ˈhʌn.drədθ, -drɪdθ, -drətθ, -drɪtθ **-s** -s
hundredweight ˈhʌn.drəd.weɪt, -drɪd- **-s** -s
hung (*from* **hang**) hʌŋ ˌ**hung** ˈ**jury**; ˌ**hung** ˈ**parliament**
Hungarian hʌŋˈgeə.ri.ən (US) -ˈger.i- **-s** -z
Hungary ˈhʌŋ.gᵊr.i
hung|er ˈhʌŋ.g|əʳ (US) -g|ɚ **-ers** -əz (US) -ɚz **-ering** -ᵊr.ɪŋ **-ered** -əd (US) -ɚd ˈ**hunger** ˌ**strike**; ˈ**hunger** ˌ**striker**
Hungerford ˈhʌŋ.gə.fəd (US) -gɚ.fɚd
hungerstrik|e ˈhʌŋ.gə.straɪk (US) -gɚ- **-es** -s **-ing** -ɪŋ **hungerstruck** ˈhʌŋ.gə.strʌk (US) -gɚ-
hungover ˌhʌŋˈəʊ.vəʳ (US) -ˈoʊ.vɚ
hungr|y ˈhʌŋ.gr|i **-ier** -i.əʳ (US) -i.ɚ **-iest** -i.ɪst, -i.əst **-ily** -ᵊl.i, -ɪ.li **-iness** -ɪ.nəs, -ɪ.nɪs
hunk hʌŋk **-s** -s
hunk|y ˈhʌŋ.k|i **-ier** -i.əʳ (US) -i.ɚ **-iest** -i.ɪst, -i.əst
hunky-dory ˌhʌŋ.kiˈdɔː.ri (US) -ˈdɔːr.i
hunnish (H) ˈhʌn.ɪʃ
Hunslet ˈhʌnz.lət, -lɪt, ˈhʌn.slɪt, -slət
Hunstanton hʌnˈstæn.tən *locally:* ˈhʌn.stən-
Hunsworth ˈhʌnz.wəθ (US) -wɚθ
hunt (H) hʌnt **-s** -s **-er/s** -əʳ/z (US) -ɚ/z **-ing** -ɪŋ (US) ˈhʌn.t̬ɪŋ **-ed** -ɪd (US) ˈhʌn.t̬ɪd ˈ**hunting** ˌ**ground**; ˈ**hunting** ˌ**horn**; ˈ**hunting** ˌ**knife**

hunter-gatherer ˌhʌn.təˈgæð.ər.əʳ (US) -t̬ɚˈgæð.ɚ.ɚ **-s** -z

Hunterian hʌnˈtɪə.ri.ən (US) -ˈtɪr.i-

Huntingdon ˈhʌn.tɪŋ.dən **-shire** -ʃəʳ, -ˌʃɪəʳ (US) -ʃɚ, -ˌʃɪr

Huntingdonian ˌhʌn.tɪŋˈdəʊ.ni.ən (US) -ˈdoʊ- **-s** -z

Huntingford ˈhʌn.tɪŋ.fəd (US) -fɚd

Huntington ˈhʌn.tɪŋ.tən ˌ**Huntington's choˈrea**

Huntl(e)y ˈhʌnt.li

Hunton ˈhʌn.tən (US) -tən

huntress ˈhʌn.trəs, -trɪs **-es** -ɪz

Hunts. *(abbrev. for* **Huntingdonshire***)* hʌnts; ˈhʌn.tɪŋ.dən.ʃəʳ, -ˌʃɪəʳ (US) hʌnts; ˈhʌn.tɪŋ.dən.ʃɚ, -ˌʃɪr

hunts|man ˈhʌnts|.mən **-men** -mən, -men **-manship** -mən.ʃɪp

Huntsville ˈhʌnts.vɪl

Hunyadi ˈhʊn.jɑː.di, ˈhʌn-, -ˈ-- (US) ˈhʊn.jɑː.di

Hurd hɜːd (US) hɝːd

hurdl|e ˈhɜː.dl̩ **-es** -z **-ing** -ɪŋ, ˈhɜːd.lɪŋ (US) ˈhɝːd- **-ed** -d **-er/s** -əʳ/z (US) -ɚ/z

hurdy-gurd|y ˈhɜː.diˌgɜː.d|i, ˌhɜː.diˈgɜː- (US) ˌhɝː.diˈgɝːr.d|i, ˈhɝː.diˌgɝːr- **-ies** -iz

Hurford ˈhɜː.fəd (US) ˈhɝː.fɚd

hurl hɜːl (US) hɝːl **-s** -z **-ing** -ɪŋ **-ed** -d **-er/s** -əʳ/z (US) -ɚ/z

hurley (H) ˈhɜː.li (US) ˈhɝː- **-s** -z

hurling ˈhɜː.lɪŋ (US) ˈhɝː-

Hurlingham ˈhɜː.lɪŋ.əm (US) ˈhɝː-

Hurlstone ˈhɜːl.stən (US) ˈhɝːl-

hurly-burly ˈhɜː.liˌbɜː.li, ˌhɜː.liˈbɜː- (US) ˈhɝː.liˌbɝːr-, ˌhɝː.liˈbɝːr-

Huron ˈhjʊə.rən, -rɒn (US) ˈhjʊr.ɑːn, -ən

hurrah həˈrɑː, hʊ- (US) -ˈrɑː, -ˈrɔː **-s** -z **-ing** -ɪŋ **-ed** -d

hurray həˈreɪ, hʊ- **-s** -z

Hurrell ˈhʌr.əl, ˈhʊə.rəl (US) ˈhɝː.əl

hurricane ˈhʌr.ɪ.kən, ˈ-ə-, -keɪn (US) ˈhɝː.ɪ.keɪn, -kən **-s** -z **ˈhurricane ˌlamp**

hurried ˈhʌr.id (US) ˈhɝː- **-ly** -li

hurr|y (H) ˈhʌr|.i (US) ˈhɝː- **-ies** -i.z **-ying** -i.ɪŋ

hurry-scurry ˌhʌr.iˈskʌr.i (US) ˌhɝː.iˈskɝːr-

hurst (H) hɜːst (US) hɝːst **-s** -s

Hurstmonceux ˌhɜːs*t*.mənˈzuː, -mɒnˈ-, -ˈsjuː, -ˈsuː (US) ˈhɝːs*t*.mən.suː, ˌ--ˈ-

Hurston ˈhɜː.stən (US) ˈhɝː-

Hurstpierpoint ˌhɜːs*t*.pɪəˈpɔɪnt (US) ˌhɝːs*t*.pɪrˈ-

hurt (H) hɜːt (US) hɝːt **-s** -s **-ing** -ɪŋ (US) ˈhɝː.t̬ɪŋ

hurtful ˈhɜːt.fəl, -fʊl (US) ˈhɝːt- **-ly** -i **-ness** -nəs, -nɪs

hurtl|e ˈhɜː.tl̩ (US) -t̬l̩ **-es** -z **-ing** -ɪŋ, ˈhɜːt.lɪŋ (US) ˈhɝːt- **-ed** -d

husband ˈhʌz.bənd **-s** -z **-ing** -ɪŋ **-ed** -ɪd **-ly** -li

husband|man ˈhʌz.bənd|.mən **-men** -mən, -men

husbandry ˈhʌz.bən.dri

hush hʌʃ **-es** -ɪz **-ing** -ɪŋ **-ed** -t **ˈhush ˌmoney**

hushaby ˈhʌʃ.ə.baɪ

hush-hush ˌhʌʃˈhʌʃ *stress shift:* ˌhush-hush ˈservice

Hush Puppies® ˈhʌʃˌpʌp.iz

husk (H) hʌsk **-s** -s

Huskisson ˈhʌs.kɪ.sən, -kə-

husk|y ˈhʌs.k|i **-ier** -i.əʳ (US) -i.ɚ **-iest** -i.ɪst, -i.əst **-ily** -ɪ.li, -əl.i **-iness** -ɪ.nəs, -ɪ.nɪs

Hussain hʊˈseɪn (US) huː-

hussar hʊˈzɑːʳ, hə- (US) -ˈzɑːr **-s** -z

Hussein hʊˈseɪn (US) huː-

Hussey ˈhʌs.i

Hussite ˈhʌs.aɪt, ˈhʊs- (US) ˈhʌs- **-s** -s

huss|y (H) ˈhʌs|.i, ˈhʌz- **-ies** -iz

hustings ˈhʌs.tɪŋz

hustl|e ˈhʌs.l̩ **-es** -z **-ing** -ɪŋ, ˈhʌs.lɪŋ **-ed** -d **-er/s** -əʳ/z (US) -ɚ/z, ˈhʌs.ləʳ/z (US) -lɚ/z

Huston ˈhjuː.stən

hut hʌt **-s** -s

hutch hʌtʃ **-es** -ɪz

Hutchence ˈhʌtʃ.ən*t*s, -en*t*s

Hutcheson ˈhʌtʃ.ɪ.sən, ˈ-ə-

Hutchings ˈhʌtʃ.ɪŋz

Hutchinson ˈhʌtʃ.ɪn.sən

Hutchinsonian ˌhʌtʃ.ɪnˈsəʊ.ni.ən (US) -ˈsoʊ- **-s** -z

Hutchison ˈhʌtʃ.ɪ.sən

Huth huːθ

Huthwaite ˈhuːθ.weɪt

hutment ˈhʌt.mənt **-s** -s

Hutton ˈhʌt.ən

Hutu ˈhuː.tuː **-s** -z

hutzpah ˈhʊt.spɑː, ˈxʊt-, -spə

Huw hjuː

Huxley ˈhʌk.sli

Huxtable ˈhʌk.stə.bl̩

Huygens ˈhaɪ.gənz

Huyton ˈhaɪ.tən

huzza(h) hʊˈzɑː, hʌzˈɑː-, həˈzɑː (US) həˈzɑː, -ˈzɔː **-s** -z

Hwang-ho ˌhwæŋˈhəʊ (US) ˌhwɑːŋˈhoʊ

hwyl ˈhuː.ɪl, -əl

hyacinth (H) ˈhaɪə.sɪn*t*θ **-s** -s

hyacinthine ˌhaɪəˈsɪn*t*.θaɪn (US) -θaɪn, -θɪn

Hyades ˈhaɪ.ə.diːz

hyaena haɪˈiː.nə **-s** -z

hyalin ˈhaɪ.ə.lɪn

hyaline ˈhaɪə.lɪn, -liːn, -laɪn

hyalite ˈhaɪə.laɪt

hyaloid ˈhaɪə.lɔɪd

Hyam haɪəm

Hyamson ˈhaɪəm.sən

Hyannis haɪˈæn.ɪs

hybrid ˈhaɪ.brɪd **-s** -z **-ism** -ɪ.zəm

hybridity haɪˈbrɪd.ə.ti, -ɪ.ti (US) -ə.t̬i

hybridization, -isa- ˌhaɪ.brɪ.daɪˈzeɪ.ʃən, ˌ-brə-, -dɪˈ- (US) -dɪˈ-

hybridiz|e, -is|e ˈhaɪ.brɪ.daɪz, -brə- **-es** -ɪz **-ing** -ɪŋ **-ed** -d **-er/s** -əʳ/z (US) -ɚ/z

Hyde haɪd ˌ**Hyde ˈPark**; ˌ**Hyde ˌPark ˈCorner**

Hyder® ˈhaɪ.dəʳ (US) -dɚ

Hyderabad ˈhaɪ.dər.ə.bæd, -bɑːd, ˌhaɪ.dər.əˈbæd, -ˈbɑːd (US) ˈhaɪ.dɚ.ə.bæd, -bɑːd, ˈ-drə.bæd, -bɑːd

hydra (H) ˈhaɪ.drə **-s** -z

hydrangea haɪˈdreɪn.dʒə, -dʒi.ə (US) -ˈdreɪn-, -ˈdræn- **-s** -z

hydrant ˈhaɪ.drənt **-s** -s

hydrate *(n.)* ˈhaɪ.dreɪt, -drɪt **-s** -s

hydra|te *(v.)* haɪˈdreɪ|t, ˈ-- (US) ˈ-- **-tes** -ts **-ting** -tɪŋ (US) -t̬ɪŋ **-ted** -tɪd (US) -t̬ɪd

hydration haɪˈdreɪ.ʃən

hydraulic haɪˈdrɔː.lɪk, -ˈdrɒl.ɪk (US) -ˈdrɑː-, -ˈdrɔː- **-s** -s

hydrazine ˈhaɪ.drə.ziːn, -zɪn

hydro- haɪ.drəʊ-; haɪˈdrɒ- (US) haɪ.droʊ-, -drə-; haɪˈdrɑː-

Note: Prefix. Normally either takes primary or secondary stress on the first syllable, e.g. **hydrofoil** /ˈhaɪ.drəʊ.fɔɪl (US) -droʊ-/, **hydrochloric** /ˌhaɪ.drəʊˈklɒr.ɪk (US) -droʊˈklɔːr-/, or primary stress on the second syllable, e.g. **hydrogenate** /haɪˈdrɒdʒ.ɪ.neɪt (US) -ˈdrɑː.dʒə-/.

hydro ˈhaɪ.drəʊ (US) -droʊ **-s** -z

hydrocarbon ˌhaɪ.drəʊˈkɑː.bən (US) -droʊˈkɑːr-, -drəˈ- **-s** -z

hydrocephalus ˌhaɪ.drəʊˈsef.əl.əs, -ˈkef- (US) -droʊˈsef-

hydrochloric ˌhaɪ.drəʊˈklɒr.ɪk, -ˈklɔː.rɪk (US) -droʊˈklɔːr.ɪk, -drəˈ- *stress shift, see compound:* ˌ**hydrochloric ˈacid**

hydrodynamic ˌhaɪ.drəʊ.daɪˈnæm.ɪk, -dɪˈ- (US) -droʊ.daɪˈ-, -drə- **-al** -əl **-ally** -əl.i, -li **-s** -s

hydroelectric ˌhaɪ.drəʊ.ɪˈlek.trɪk, -əˈ- (US) -droʊ- **-s** -s *stress shift:* ˌhydroelectric ˈpower

hydroelectricity ˌhaɪ.drəʊ.ɪ.lekˈtrɪs.ɪ.ti, -ə- (US) -droʊ.ɪ.lekˈtrɪs.ɪ.t̬i, -ə.t̬i

hydrofoil ˈhaɪ.drəʊ.fɔɪl (US) -droʊ-, -drə- **-s** -z

hydrogen ˈhaɪ.drə.dʒən, -drɪ-, -dʒɪn (US) -drə.dʒən **ˈhydrogen ˌbomb**; ˌ**hydrogen ˈchloride**; ˌ**hydrogen ˈfluoride**; ˌ**hydrogen peˈroxide**

hydroge|nate haɪˈdrɒdʒ.ɪ|.neɪt, ˈ-ə-; ˈhaɪ.drə.dʒɪ-, -dʒə- US haɪˈdrɑː.dʒə-; ˈhaɪ.drə- **-nates** -neɪts **-nating** -neɪ.tɪŋ US -neɪ.t̬ɪŋ **-nated** -neɪ.tɪd US -neɪ.t̬ɪd

hydrogenation ˌhaɪ.drə.dʒəˈneɪ.ʃᵊn, -dʒɪˈ- US haɪˌdrɑː.dʒəˈ-

hydrogenous haɪˈdrɒdʒ.ɪ.nəs, ˈ-ə- US -ˈdrɑː.dʒɪ-, -dʒə-

hydrographic ˌhaɪ.drəʊˈgræf.ɪk US -droʊˈgræf- **-al** -ᵊl **-ally** -ᵊl.i, -li

hydrograph|y haɪˈdrɒg.rə.f|i US -ˈdrɑː.grə- **-er/s** -əʳ/z US -ɚ/z

hydrology haɪˈdrɒl.ə.dʒi US -ˈdrɑː.lə-

hydrolysis haɪˈdrɒl.ə.sɪs, ˈ-ɪ- US -ˈdrɑː.lɪ-

hydrolytic ˌhaɪ.drəˈlɪt.ɪk US -ˈlɪt̬- **-ally** -ᵊl.i, -li

hydrolyz|e, -ys|e ˈhaɪ.drə.laɪz **-es** -ɪz **-ing** -ɪŋ **-ed** -d

hydromechanics ˌhaɪ.drəʊ.mɪˈkæn.ɪks, -məˈ- US -droʊ.məˈ-

hydrometer haɪˈdrɒm.ɪ.təʳ, ˈ-ə- US -ˈdrɑː.mə.t̬ɚ **-s** -z

hydrometric ˌhaɪ.drəʊˈmet.rɪk US -droʊˈ-, -drəˈ- **-al** -ᵊl **-ally** -ᵊl.i, -li

hydrometry haɪˈdrɒm.ə.tri, ˈ-ɪ- US -ˈdrɑː.mə-

hydropathic ˌhaɪ.drəʊˈpæθ.ɪk US -droʊˈ-, -drəˈ- **-s** -s **-al** -ᵊl **-ally** -ᵊl.i, -li

hydropath|y haɪˈdrɒp.ə.θ|i US -ˈdrɑː.pə- **-ist/s** -ɪst/s

hydrophilic ˌhaɪ.drəʊˈfɪl.ɪk US -droʊˈ-, -drəˈ-

hydrophobia ˌhaɪ.drəʊˈfəʊ.bi.ə US -droʊˈfoʊ-, -drəˈ-

hydrophobic ˌhaɪ.drəʊˈfəʊ.bɪk US -droʊˈfoʊ-, -drəˈ-

hydrophyte ˈhaɪ.drəʊ.faɪt US -droʊ-, -drə- **-s** -s

hydroplan|e ˈhaɪ.drəʊ.pleɪn US -droʊ-, -drə- **-es** -z **-ing** -ɪŋ **-ed** -d

hydroponic ˌhaɪ.drəʊˈpɒn.ɪk US -droʊˈpɑː.nɪk, -drəˈ- **-s** -s **-ally** -ᵊl.i, -li

hydroscope ˈhaɪ.drəʊ.skəʊp US -droʊ.skoʊp, -drə- **-s** -s

hydrostat ˈhaɪ.drəʊ.stæt US -droʊ-, -drə- **-s** -s

hydrostatic ˌhaɪ.drəʊˈstæt.ɪk US -droʊˈstæt̬-, -drəˈ- **-al** -ᵊl **-ally** -ᵊl.i, -li **-s** -s

hydrotherapy ˌhaɪ.drəʊˈθer.ə.pi US -droʊˈ-, -drəˈ-

hydrotropism haɪˈdrɒt.rə.pɪ.zᵊm US -ˈdrɑː.trə-

hydrous ˈhaɪ.drəs

hydroxide haɪˈdrɒk.saɪd US -ˈdrɑːk- **-s** -z

hydroxyl haɪˈdrɒk.sɪl US -ˈdrɑːk-

hyena haɪˈiː.nə **-s** -z

Hygeia haɪˈdʒiː.ə

hygiene ˈhaɪ.dʒiːn

hygienic haɪˈdʒiː.nɪk US ˌhaɪ.dʒiˈen.ɪk; haɪˈdʒen-, -ˈdʒiː.nɪk **-ally** -ᵊl.i, -li

hygienist ˈhaɪ.dʒiː.nɪst US ˈhaɪ.dʒiː.nɪst; -ˈ--, -ˈdʒen.ɪst **-s** -s

hygrometric ˌhaɪ.grəʊˈmet.rɪk US -groʊˈ-, -grəˈ- **-al** -ᵊl **-ally** -ᵊl.i, -li

hygromet|ry haɪˈgrɒm.ə.t|ri US -ˈgrɑː.mə- **-er/s** -əʳ/z US -ɚ/z

hygroscope ˈhaɪ.grəʊ.skəʊp US -groʊ.skoʊp, -grə- **-s** -s

hygroscopic ˌhaɪ.grəʊˈskɒp.ɪk US -groʊˈskɑː.pɪk, -grəˈ- **-ally** -ᵊl.i, -li

Hyksos ˈhɪk.sɒs US -sɑːs

Hylas ˈhaɪ.læs, -ləs

Hylton ˈhɪl.tən

Hyman ˈhaɪ.mən

hymen (H) ˈhaɪ.men, -mən US -mən **-s** -z

hymene|al ˌhaɪ.menˈiː|.əl, -məˈniː-, -mɪˈ- US -məˈ- **-an** -ən

Hymettus haɪˈmet.əs US -ˈmet̬-

hymn hɪm **-s** -z **-ing** -ɪŋ **-ed** -d ˈ**hymn** ˌ**book**

hymnal ˈhɪm.nᵊl **-s** -z

hymnar|y ˈhɪm.nᵊr|.i **-ies** -iz

hymnic ˈhɪm.nɪk

hymnody ˈhɪm.nə.di

hymnolog|y hɪmˈnɒl.ə.dʒi US -nɑː.lə- **-ist/s** -ɪst/s

Hyndley ˈhaɪnd.li

Hyndman ˈhaɪnd.mən

Hynes haɪnz

hyoid ˈhaɪ.ɔɪd

hyoscine ˈhaɪ.əʊ.siːn US -ə.siːn, -sɪn

hypallage haɪˈpæl.ə.gi, -dʒi US haɪ-, hə-; ˌhaɪ.pəˈlædʒ.i, ˌhɪp.əˈ-

Hypatia haɪˈpeɪ.ʃə, -ʃi.ə

hyp|e haɪp **-es** -s **-ing** -ɪŋ **-ed** -t ˌ**hyped** ˈ**up**

hyper- haɪ.pəʳ-; haɪˈpɜː- US haɪ.pɚ-; haɪˈpɝː-

Note: Prefix. Normally either takes primary or secondary stress on the first syllable, e.g. **hypermarket** /ˈhaɪ.pəˌmɑː.kɪt US -pɚˌmɑːr-/, **hyperactive** /ˌhaɪ.pəʳˈæk.tɪv US -pɚˈ-/, or primary stress on the second syllable, e.g. **hyperbole** /haɪˈpɜː.bᵊl.i US -ˈpɝːr-/. Note also that, although /r/ is normally assigned to a following strong syllable in US transcriptions, in **hyper-** it is perceived to be morphemically linked to that morpheme and is retained in the prefix as /ɚ/.

hyper ˈhaɪ.pəʳ US -pɚ

hyperactive ˌhaɪ.pəʳˈæk.tɪv US -pɚˈ- *stress shift* ˌhyperactive ˈchild

hyperactivity ˌhaɪ.pᵊr.ækˈtɪv.ə.ti, -ɪ.ti US -pɚ.ækˈtɪv.ə.t̬i

hyperacute ˌhaɪ.pəʳ.əˈkjuːt US -pɚ- **-ness** -nəs, -nɪs

hyperbol|a haɪˈpɜː.bᵊl|.ə US -ˈpɝː- **-ae** -iː **-as** -əz

hyperbole haɪˈpɜː.bᵊl.i US -ˈpɝː- **-s** -z

hyperbolic ˌhaɪ.pəˈbɒl.ɪk US -pɚˈbɑː.lɪk **-al** -ᵊl **-ally** -ᵊl.i, -li

hyperbol|ism haɪˈpɜː.bᵊl|.ɪ.zᵊm US -ˈpɝː- **-ist/s** -ɪst/s

hyperboliz|e, -is|e haɪˈpɜː.bᵊl.aɪz US -ˈpɝː- **-es** -ɪz **-ing** -ɪŋ **-ed** -d

hyperboloid haɪˈpɜː.bᵊl.ɔɪd US -ˈpɝː- **-s** -z

hyperborean ˌhaɪ.pəˈbɔː.ri.ən; -bɔːˈriː.ən, -bɒrˈiː.ən US -pɚ.bɔːˈriː-, -bəˈ- **-s** -z

hypercorrect ˌhaɪ.pə.kəˈrekt US -pɚ.kəˈrekt **-ly** -li **-ness** -nəs, -nɪs

hypercorrection ˌhaɪ.pə.kəˈrek.ʃᵊn US -pɚ.kəˈrek- **-s** -z

hypercritic|al ˌhaɪ.pəˈkrɪt.ɪ.k|ᵊl US -pɚˈkrɪt̬- **-ally** -ᵊl.i US -li

hypercriticism ˌhaɪ.pəˈkrɪt.ɪ.sɪ.zᵊm US -pɚˈkrɪt̬.ɪ-

hypercriticiz|e, -is|e ˌhaɪ.pəˈkrɪt.ɪ.saɪz US -pɚˈkrɪt̬- **-es** -ɪz **-ing** -ɪŋ **-ed** -d

hyperglycaem|ia ˌhaɪ.pə.glaɪˈsiː.m|i.ə US -pɚ- **-ic** -ɪk

hypericum haɪˈper.ɪ.kəm **-s** -z

Hyperides haɪˈper.ɪ.diːz; ˌhaɪ.pəˈraɪ- US haɪˈper.ɪ-, hɪ-

hyperinflation ˌhaɪ.pᵊr.ɪnˈfleɪ.ʃᵊn US -pɚ-

Hyperion haɪˈpɪə.ri.ən, -ˈper.i- US -ˈpɪr-

hyperlink ˈhaɪ.pə.lɪŋk US -pɚ- **-s** -s

hypermarket ˈhaɪ.pəˌmɑː.kɪt US -pɚˌmɑːr- **-s** -s

hypernym ˈhaɪ.pə.nɪm US -pɚ- **-s** -z

hypersensitive ˌhaɪ.pəˈsent.sə.tɪv, -sɪ- US -pɚˈsent.sə.t̬ɪv

hypersensitivity ˌhaɪ.pəˌsent.səˈtɪv.ə.ti, -sɪˈ-, -ɪ.ti US -pɚˌsent.səˈtɪv.ə.t̬i

hyperspace ˈhaɪ.pə.speɪs US -pɚ-

hypertension ˌhaɪ.pəˈten.tʃᵊn, ˈhaɪ.pəˌten- US ˌhaɪ.pɚˈtent.ʃᵊn

hypertext ˈhaɪ.pə.tekst US -pɚ-

hyperthyroid ˌhaɪ.pəˈθaɪ.rɔɪd US -pɚˈ- **-ism** -ɪ.zᵊm

hypertroph|y haɪˈpɜː.trə.f|i US -ˈpɝː- **-ied** -id

hyperventi|late ˌhaɪ.pəˈven.tɪ|.leɪt, -tə- US -pɚˈven.t̬ə- **-lates** -leɪts **-lating** -leɪ.tɪŋ US -leɪ.t̬ɪŋ **-lated** -leɪ.tɪd US -leɪ.t̬ɪd

hyperventilation ˌhaɪ.pəˌven.tɪˈleɪ.ʃᵊn, -təˈ- US -pɚˌven.t̬əˈ-

hyph|a ˈhaɪ.f|ə **-ae** -iː

hyphal ˈhaɪ.fᵊl

hyphen 'haɪ.f^{ə}n **-s** -z **-ing** -ɪŋ **-ed** -d

hyphen|ate 'haɪ.f^{ə}n|.eɪt, -fɪ.n|eɪt (US) -fə- **-ates** -eɪts **-ating** -eɪ.tɪŋ (US) -eɪ.t̬ɪŋ **-ated** -eɪ.tɪd (US) -eɪ.t̬ɪd

hyphenation ˌhaɪ.f^{ə}n'eɪ.ʃ^{ə}n

hypno- 'hɪp.nəʊ-; hɪp'nɒ-, -'nəʊ- (US) 'hɪp.noʊ-, -nə-; hɪp'nɑː-, -'noʊ-

Note: Prefix. Normally either takes primary or secondary stress on the first syllable, e.g. **hypnotism** /'hɪp.nə.tɪ.z^{ə}m/, **hypnotherapy** /ˌhɪp.nəʊ'θer.ə.pi (US) -noʊ'-/, or primary stress on the second syllable, e.g. **hypnotic** /hɪp'nɒt.ɪk (US) -'nɑː.t̬ɪk/.

hypnosis hɪp'nəʊ.sɪs (US) -'noʊ-

hypnotherapist ˌhɪp.nəʊ'θer.ə.pɪst (US) -noʊ'- **-s** -s

hypnotherapy ˌhɪp.nəʊ'θer.ə.pi (US) -noʊ'-

hypnotic hɪp'nɒt.ɪk (US) -'nɑː.t̬ɪk

hypnot|ism 'hɪp.nə.t|ɪ.z^{ə}m **-ist/s** -ɪst/s

hypnotization, -isa- ˌhɪp.nə.taɪ'zeɪ.ʃ^{ə}n, -tɪ'- (US) -tɪ'-

hypnotiz|e, -is|e 'hɪp.nə.taɪz **-es** -ɪz **-ing** -ɪŋ **-ed** -d **-er/s** -ə^{r}/z (US) -ɚ/z

hypo- 'haɪ.pəʊ-; haɪ'pɒ- (US) 'haɪ.poʊ-, -pə-; haɪ'pɑː-, hɪ-

Note: Prefix. Normally either takes primary or secondary stress on the first syllable, e.g. **hypocaust** /'haɪ.pəʊ.kɔːst (US) -poʊ-/, **hypothetic** /ˌhaɪ.pəʊ'θet.ɪk (US) -poʊ'θet̬-/, or primary stress on the second syllable, e.g. **hypotenuse** /haɪ'pɒt.^{ə}n.juːz (US) -'pɑː.t^{ə}n.uːs/.

hypo 'haɪ.pəʊ (US) -poʊ **-s** -z

hypoallergenic ˌhaɪ.pəʊˌæl.ə'dʒen.ɪk, -ɜː'- (US) -poʊˌæl.ɚ'-

hypocaust 'haɪ.pəʊ.kɔːst, -kɒst (US) -poʊ.kɔːst, -pə-, -kɑːst **-s** -s

hypochondri|a ˌhaɪ.pəʊ'kɒn.dri|.ə (US) -poʊ'kɑːn-, -pə'- **-ac/s** -æk/s

hypochondriacal ˌhaɪ.pəʊ.kɒn'draɪ.ə.k^{ə}l, -kən'- (US) -poʊ.kɑːn'-, -pə-

hypochondriasis ˌhaɪ.pəʊ.kɒn'draɪ.ə.sɪs, -kən'- (US) -poʊ.kɑːn'-, -pə-

hypocotyl ˌhaɪ.pə'kɒt.ɪl (US) -poʊ'kɑː.t̬^{ə}l

hypocris|y hɪ'pɒk.rə.s|i, -rɪ- (US) -'pɑː.krə- **-ies** -iz

hypocrite 'hɪp.ə.krɪt **-s** -s

hypocritic|al ˌhɪp.əʊ'krɪt.ɪ.k|^{ə}l (US) -ə'krɪt̬- **-ally** -^{ə}l.i, -li

hypocycloid ˌhaɪ.pəʊ'saɪ.klɔɪd (US) -poʊ'-, -pə'- **-s** -z

hypodermic ˌhaɪ.pəʊ'dɜː.mɪk (US) -poʊ'dɝː-, -pə'- *stress shift, see compounds:* ˌ**hypodermic** '**needle**; *stress shift, see compounds:* ˌ**hypodermic sy'ringe**

hypodermis ˌhaɪ.pəʊ'dɜː.mɪs (US) -poʊ'dɝː-, -pə'-

hypogeal ˌhaɪ.pəʊ'dʒiː.əl (US) -poʊ'-

hypoglyc(a)em|ia ˌhaɪ.pəʊ.glaɪ'siː.m|i.ə (US) -poʊ- **-ic** -ɪk

hypophosphate ˌhaɪ.pəʊ'fɒs.feɪt, -fɪt (US) -poʊ'fɑːs-, -pə'- **-s** -s

hyposta|sis haɪ'pɒs.tə|.sɪs (US) -'pɑː.stə-, hɪ- **-ses** -siːz

hypostatiz|e, -is|e haɪ'pɒs.tə.taɪz (US) -'pɑː.stə-, hɪ- **-es** -ɪz **-ing** -ɪŋ **-ed** -d

hypostyle 'haɪ.pəʊ.staɪl (US) -poʊ-

hyposulphite ˌhaɪ.pəʊ'sʌl.faɪt (US) -poʊ'-, -pə'- **-s** -s

hypotactic ˌhaɪ.pəʊ'tæk.tɪk (US) -poʊ'-, -pə'-

hypotax|is ˌhaɪ.pəʊ'tæk.s|ɪs, 'haɪ.pəʊ.tæk- (US) ˌhaɪ.poʊ'tæk-, -pə'- **-es** -iːz

hypotension ˌhaɪ.pəʊ'ten.tʃ^{ə}n (US) 'haɪ.poʊˌten-, -pəˌ-

hypotenus|e haɪ'pɒt.^{ə}n.juːz, -ɪ.njuːz, -juːs (US) -'pɑː.t^{ə}n.uːs, -tɪ.nuːs, -njuːs **-es** -ɪz

hypothalamus ˌhaɪ.pəʊ'θæl.ə.məs (US) -poʊ'-, -pə'-

hypothe|cate haɪ'pɒθ.ə|.keɪt, '-ɪ- (US) -'pɑː.θə-, hɪ- **-cates** -keɪts **-cating** -keɪ.tɪŋ (US) -keɪ.t̬ɪŋ **-cated** -keɪ.tɪd (US) -keɪ.t̬ɪd

hypothecation haɪˌpɒθ.ə'keɪ.ʃ^{ə}n, -ɪ'- (US) -pɑː.θə'-, hɪ- **-s** -z

hypothermal ˌhaɪ.pəʊ'θɜː.m^{ə}l (US) -poʊ'θɝː-, -pə'-

hypothermia ˌhaɪ.pəʊ'θɜː.mi.ə (US) -poʊ'θɝː-, -pə'-

hypothes|is haɪ'pɒθ.ə.s|ɪs, '-ɪ- (US) -'pɑː.θə-, hɪ- **-es** -iːz

hypothesiz|e, -is|e haɪ'pɒθ.ə.saɪz (US) -'pɑː.θə-, hɪ- **-es** -ɪz **-ing** -ɪŋ **-ed** -d

hypothetic ˌhaɪ.pəʊ'θet.ɪk (US) -poʊ'θet̬-, -pə'- **-al** -^{ə}l **-ally** -^{ə}l.i, -li

hypothyroid ˌhaɪ.pəʊ'θaɪ.rɔɪd (US) -poʊ'- **-ism** -ɪ.z^{ə}m

hypoxia haɪ'pɒk.si.ə (US) -'pɑːk-, hɪ-

hypoxic haɪ'pɒk.sɪk (US) -'pɑːk-, hɪ-

hypsome|try hɪp'sɒm.ə|.tri (US) -'sɑː.mə- **-ter/s** -tə^{r}/z (US) -t̬ɚ/z

hyrax 'haɪ.ræks **-es** -ɪz

Hyslop 'hɪz.ləp, -lɒp (US) -lɑːp, -ləp

hyson (H) 'haɪ.s^{ə}n

hyssop 'hɪs.əp

hysterectom|y ˌhɪs.t^{ə}r'ek.tə.m|i (US) -tə'rek- **-ies** -iz

hysteria hɪ'stɪə.ri.ə (US) -'ster.i-, -'stɪr-

hysteric hɪ'ster.ɪk **-s** -s **-al** -^{ə}l **-ally** -^{ə}l.i, -li

hysteron proteron ˌhɪs.tə.rɒn'prɒt.ə.rɒn, -rɒm'-, -'prəʊ.tə- (US) -rɑːn'prɑː.t̬ə.rɑːn

hythe (H) haɪð **-s** -z

Hytner 'haɪt.nə^{r} (US) -nɚ

Hyundai® 'haɪ.ʌn.daɪ, -ən-, 'hjʊn-, 'hjʊn.deɪ (US) 'hjʌn.deɪ, 'hʌn-

Hywel haʊəl

Hz *(abbrev. for* **Hertz***)* hɜːts, heəts (US) hɝːts, herts

Pronouncing the letter I

See also IE, IEU, IO

The vowel letter **i** has two main strong pronunciations linked to spelling: a 'short' pronunciation /ɪ/ and a 'long' pronunciation /aɪ/. In the 'short' pronunciation, the **i** is generally followed by a consonant which closes the syllable, or a double consonant before another vowel, e.g.:

ship /ʃɪp/
shipping /ˈʃɪp.ɪŋ/

The 'long' pronunciation is usually found when the **i** is followed by a single consonant and then a vowel, although it should be noted that this spelling does not regularly predict a 'long' pronunciation, e.g.:

pipe /paɪp/
piping /ˈpaɪ.pɪŋ/

In many cases, the 'short' pronunciation results from the above kind of spelling, e.g.:

give /gɪv/
living /ˈlɪv.ɪŋ/

Also, the 'long' pronunciation appears in some words where the vowel is followed by two consonants, e.g.:

mind /maɪnd/
wild /waɪld/

Preceding the letters **gh**, **i** is pronounced /aɪ/, except in some names such as *Brigham* and *Brighouse* e.g.:

high /haɪ/
light /laɪt/
Brigham /ˈbrɪg.əm/

When **i** is followed by **r**, the strong pronunciation is one of two possibilities: /aɪə US aɪɚ/ or /ɜː US ɝː/. E.g., in:

fire /faɪəʳ/ US /faɪɚ/
fir /fɜːʳ/ US /fɝː/

Another vowel sound associated with the letter **i** is /iː/, e.g.:

/iː/ machine /məˈʃiːn/

In weak syllables

The vowel letter **i** is realised with the vowels /ɪ/ and /ə/ in weak syllables, and may also be elided in British English, e.g.:

divide /dɪˈvaɪd, də-/
medicine /ˈmed.sᵊn/ US /ˈ-ɪ.sən/

i (I) aɪ **-'s** -z
Ia. *(abbrev. for* **Iowa***)* ˈaɪ.əʊə; ˈaɪə.wə US ˈaɪə.wə; ˈaɪ.oʊ-
-iac i.æk, iː-, -ək
Note: Suffix. Does not normally affect stress patterning, e.g. **mania** /ˈmeɪ.ni.ə/, **maniac** /ˈmeɪ.ni.æk/.
Iachimo iˈæk.ɪ.məʊ, aɪ- US -moʊ
Iago iˈɑː.gəʊ US -goʊ
Iain ˈiː.ən
-ial -i.əl, -əl
Note: Suffix. Normally stressed on the syllable before the prefix, e.g. **facial** /ˈfeɪ.ʃᵊl/.
iamb ˈaɪ.æmb **-s** -z
iamb|ic aɪˈæm.b|ɪk **-us/es** -əs/ɪz
Ian ˈiː.ən
-ian -i.ən
Note: Suffix. Words ending **-ian** are stressed in a similar way to those ending **-ial**; see above.
I'Anson aɪˈænt.sən
Ianthe aɪˈænt.θi
IATA aɪˈɑː.tə, iː- US ˌaɪˌeɪˌtiːˈeɪ, aɪˈɑː.t̬ə
iatrogenic aɪˌæt.rəʊˈdʒen.ɪk, ˌaɪ.æt- US aɪˌæt.roʊˈ-, iː-, -rəˈ- **-ally** -ᵊl.i, -li
Ibadan ɪˈbæd.ᵊn US iːˈbɑː.dɑːn, -dᵊn
Ibbertson ˈɪb.ət.sᵊn US -ɚt-
Ibbetson ˈɪb.ɪt.sᵊn, -ət-
I-beam ˈaɪ.biːm **-s** -z
Iberi|a aɪˈbɪə.ri|.ə US -ˈbɪr.i- **-an/s** -ən/z
iberis aɪˈbɪə.rɪs US -ˈbɪr.ɪs
Iberus aɪˈbɪə.rəs US -ˈbɪr.əs
ibex ˈaɪ.beks **-es** -ɪz
ibid ɪˈbɪd, ˈɪb.ɪd
ibidem ˈɪb.ɪ.dem, ˈ-ə-; ɪˈbaɪ.dem US ˈɪb.ɪ.dem, ˈ-ə-; ɪˈbiː.dem, -ˈbaɪ-
-ibility -ɪˈbɪl.ɪ.ti, -əˈ-, -ə.ti US -ə.t̬i
Note: Suffix. Words containing **-ibility** always exhibit primary stress as shown above, e.g. **eligibility** /ˌel.ɪ.dʒəˈbɪl.ə.ti US -t̬i/.
ibis ˈaɪ.bɪs **-es** -ɪz
Ibiza ɪˈbiː.θə, iː- US ɪˈbiː.zə, -sə; -ˈviː.θə, -θɑː
-ible -ə.bl̩, -ɪ-
Note: Suffix. Words containing **-ible** are normally stressed either on the antepenultimate syllable, e.g. **susceptible** /səˈsep.tə.bl̩/, or two syllables preceding the suffix, e.g. **eligible** /ˈel.ɪ.dʒə.bl̩/.
IBM® ˌaɪ.biːˈem
Ibo ˈiː.bəʊ US -boʊ **-s** -z
iBook® ˈaɪ.bʊk
Ibrahim ˈɪb.rə.hiːm, -hɪm, ˌ--ˈ-
Ibrox ˈaɪ.brɒks US -brɑːks
Ibsen ˈɪb.sᵊn
Ibstock ˈɪb.stɒk US -stɑːk
ibuprofen ˌaɪ.bjuːˈprəʊ.fen, -fᵊn; aɪˈbjuː.prəʊ- US ˌaɪ.bjuːˈproʊ.fᵊn
IC ˌaɪˈsiː **-s** -z
-ic -ɪk
Note: Suffix. Words containing **-ic** are normally stressed on the penultimate syllable, e.g. **music** /ˈmjuː.zɪk/.
-ic|al -ɪ.k|ᵊl **-ally** -ᵊl.i, -li
Note: Suffix. Words containing **-ical** are normally stressed on the antepenultimate syllable, e.g. **musical** /ˈmjuː.zɪ.kᵊl/.
Icari|a ɪˈkeə.ri|.ə, aɪ- US -ˈker.i- **-an** -ən
Icarus ˈɪk.ᵊr.əs, ˈaɪ.kᵊr- US ˈɪk.ɚ-
ICBM ˌaɪ.siː.biːˈem
ic|e aɪs **-es** -ɪz **-ing** -ɪŋ **-ed** -t ˈ**ice** ˌ**age**; ˈ**ice** ˌ**axe**; ˈ**ice** ˌ**bucket**; ˈ**ice** ˌ**cap**; ˈ**ice** ˌ**field**; ˈ**ice** ˌ**floe**; ˈ**ice** ˌ**hockey**, ˌ**ice** ˈ**hockey**; ˈ**ice** ˌ**lolly** ˌ**ice** ˈ**lolly**; ˈ**ice** ˌ**pack**; ˈ**ice** ˌ**rink**; ˌ**break the** ˈ**ice**; ˌ**skate on** ˌ**thin** ˈ**ice**
iceberg ˈaɪs.bɜːg US -bɝːg **-s** -z ˌ**iceberg** ˈ**lettuce**
icebound ˈaɪs.baʊnd
icebox ˈaɪs.bɒks US -bɑːks **-es** -ɪz
icebreaker ˈaɪsˌbreɪ.kəʳ US -kɚ **-s** -z
ice cream ˌaɪsˈkriːm, ˈ-- US ˈ-- **-s** -z ˌ**ice** ˈ**cream** ˌ**parlo(u)r**; ˌ**ice cream** ˈ**soda**
icefall ˈaɪs.fɔːl US -fɔːl, -fɑːl **-s** -z

icehou|se 'aɪs.haʊ|s **-ses** -zɪz
Iceland 'aɪs.lənd
Icelander 'aɪs.lən.dəʳ, -læn- (US) -dɚ **-s** -z
Icelandic aɪs'læn.dɪk
icemaker 'aɪs,meɪ.kəʳ (US) -kɚ **-s** -z
ice|man 'aɪs|.mæn, -mən **-men** -men, -mən
Iceni aɪ'siː.naɪ, -ni
icepick 'aɪs.pɪk **-s** -s
ice|skate 'aɪs|.skeɪt **-skates** -skeɪts **-skating** -,skeɪ.tɪŋ (US) -,skeɪ.t̬ɪŋ **-skated** -,skeɪ.tɪd (US) -,skeɪ.t̬ɪd **-skater/s** -,skeɪ.təʳ/z (US) -,skeɪ.t̬ɚ/z
Ichabod 'ɪk.ə.bɒd, 'ɪx- (US) ɪk-, -bɑːd
ich dien ,ɪx'diːn
I Ching ,iː'tʃɪŋ, ,aɪ-, -'dʒɪŋ (US) ,iː-
ich-laut 'ɪx.laut, 'ɪk-
ichneumon ɪk'njuː.mən (US) -'nuː-, -'njuː- **-s** -z
ichnographic ,ɪk.nəʊ'græf.ɪk (US) -noʊ'- **-al** -ᵊl **-ally** -ᵊl.i, -li
ichnography ɪk'nɒg.rə.fi (US) -'nɑː.grə-
ichnological ,ɪk.nəʊ'lɒdʒ.ɪ.kᵊl (US) -noʊ'lɑː.dʒɪ-
ichnology ɪk'nɒl.ə.dʒi (US) -'nɑː.lə-
ichor 'aɪ.kɔːʳ (US) -kɔːr, -kɚ
ichthyologic|al ,ɪk.θi.ə'lɒdʒ.ɪ.k|ᵊl (US) -'lɑː.dʒɪ- **-ally** -ᵊl.i, -li
ichthyolog|y ,ɪk.θi'ɒl.ə.dʒ|i (US) -'ɑː.lə- **-ist/s** -ɪst/s
ichthyosaur 'ɪk.θi.ə.sɔːʳ (US) -sɔːr **-s** -z
ichthyosaur|us ,ɪk.θi.əʊ'sɔː.r|əs (US) -oʊ'sɔːr|.əs, -ə'- **-i** -aɪ **-uses** -ə.sɪz
ICI® ,aɪ.siː'aɪ
-ician -'ɪʃ.ᵊn
Note: Suffix. Normally carries primary stress as shown above, e.g. **musician** /mjuː'zɪʃ.ᵊn/, **technician** /tek'nɪʃ.ᵊn/.
icicle 'aɪ.sɪ.kl̩, -sə- **-s** -z
icing 'aɪ.sɪŋ **'icing ,sugar**
Icke aɪk, ɪk
Icknield 'ɪk.niːld
ick|y 'ɪk|.i **-ier** -i.əʳ (US) -i.ɚ **-iest** -i.ɪst, -i.əst
icon 'aɪ.kɒn, -kən (US) -kɑːn, -kən **-s** -z
iconic aɪ'kɒn.ɪk (US) -'kɑː.nɪk
Iconium aɪ'kəʊ.ni.əm, ɪ- (US) aɪ'koʊ-
iconoclasm aɪ'kɒn.əʊ,klæz.ᵊm (US) -'kɑː.nə-
iconoclast aɪ'kɒn.əʊ.klæst, -klɑːst (US) -'kɑː.nə.klæst **-s** -s
iconoclastic aɪ,kɒn.əʊ'klæs.tɪk, ,aɪ.kɒn- (US) aɪ,kɑː.nə'- **-ally** -ᵊl.i, -li
iconographic ,aɪ.kə.nəʊ'græf.ɪk (US) -noʊ-
iconograph|y ,aɪ.kə'nɒg.rə.f|i, -kɒn'ɒg- (US) -kə'nɑː.grə- **-er/s** -əʳ/z (US) -ɚ/z
iconoscope aɪ'kɒn.ə.skəʊp (US) -'kɑː.nə.skoʊp **-s** -s

icosahedr|on ,aɪ.kɒs.ə'hiː.dr|ən, -kə.sə'-; aɪ,kɒs- (US) ,aɪ.koʊ.sə'-; aɪ,kɑː- **-ons** -ənz **-a** -ə **-al** -əl
ictus 'ɪk.təs **-es** -ɪz
ICU ,aɪ.siː'juː
ic|y 'aɪ.s|i **-ier** -i.əʳ (US) -i.ɚ **-iest** -i.ɪst, -i.əst **-ily** -ɪ.li, -ᵊl.i **-iness** -ɪ.nəs, -ɪ.nɪs
id ɪd
'Id iːd
ID ,aɪ'diː ,**I'D ,card**
I'd (= **I would, I should** *or* **I had**) aɪd
Ida 'aɪ.də
Ida. (*abbrev. for* **Idaho**) 'aɪ.də.həʊ (US) -hoʊ
Idaho 'aɪ.də.həʊ (US) -hoʊ
Iddesleigh 'ɪdz.li
Ide iːd
-ide -aɪd
Note: Suffix. Words containing **-ide** are normally stressed on the penultimate or antepenultimate syllable, e.g. **hydroxide** /haɪ'drɒk.saɪd (US) -'drɑːk-/.
idea aɪ'dɪə (US) -'diː.ə **-s** -z
Note: In British English, the pronunciation /'aɪ.dɪə/ is also sometimes heard, especially when a stress immediately follows, e.g. "I thought of the 'idea ,first".
ideal (*n.*) aɪ'dɪəl, -'diː.əl (US) -'diː- **-s** -z *stress shift:* ,ideal 'home
ideal (*adj.*) aɪ'dɪəl, -'diː.əl, '-- (US) -'diː-
ideal|ism aɪ'dɪə.l|ɪ.zᵊm; 'aɪ.dɪə- (US) aɪ'diː.ə.l|ɪ- **-ist/s** -ɪst/s
idealistic aɪ,dɪə'lɪs.tɪk; ,aɪ.dɪə- (US) ,aɪ.di.ə'- **-ally** -ᵊl.i, -li
ideality ,aɪ.di'æl.ə.ti, -ɪ.ti (US) -ə.t̬i
idealization, -isa- aɪ,dɪə.laɪ'zeɪ.ʃᵊn, -lɪ'-; ,aɪ.dɪə- (US) aɪ,diː.ə.lə'- **-s** -z
idealiz|e, -is|e aɪ'dɪə.laɪz (US) -'diː.ə- **-es** -ɪz **-ing** -ɪŋ **-ed** -d **-er/s** -əʳ/z (US) -ɚ/z
ideally aɪ'dɪə.li, -'dɪəl.li (US) -'diː.li, -ə.li
ide|ate 'aɪ.di|.eɪt **-ates** -eɪts **-ating** -eɪ.tɪŋ (US) -t̬ɪŋ **-ated** -eɪ.tɪd (US) -t̬ɪd
ideational ,aɪ.di'eɪ.ʃᵊn.ᵊl, -'eɪʃ.nᵊl
idée fixe ,iː.deɪ'fiːks **idées fixes** ,iː.deɪ'fiːks, -deɪz'-
idée reçue ,iː.deɪ.rə'suː **idées reçues** ,iː.deɪ.rə'suː, -deɪz-
idem 'ɪd.em, 'iː.dem, 'aɪ- (US) 'aɪ-, 'iː-, 'ɪd.em
idempotent ,ɪd.əm'pəʊ.tənt, ,iː.dəm-, ,aɪ-, -dem'- (US) ,aɪ.dem'poʊ-, ,iː-, ,ɪd.em'-
identic|al aɪ'den.tɪ.k|ᵊl, ɪ- (US) -t̬ə- **-ally** -ᵊl.i, -li **-alness** -ᵊl.nəs, -ᵊl.nɪs
identifiable aɪ'den.tɪ.faɪ.ə.bl̩, -tə'-, aɪ,den.tɪ'faɪ-, -tə- (US) aɪ,den.t̬ə'-
identification aɪ,den.tɪ.fɪ'keɪ.ʃᵊn, -tə- (US) -t̬ə- **-s** -z

identi|fy aɪ'den.tɪ|.faɪ, -tə- (US) -t̬ə- **-fies** -faɪz **-fying** -faɪ.ɪŋ **-fied** -faɪd **-fier/s** -faɪ.əʳ/z (US) -faɪ.ɚ/z
identikit (I) aɪ'den.tɪ.kɪt (US) -t̬ə- **-s** -s
identit|y aɪ'den.tə.t|i, -ɪ.t|i (US) -t̬ə.t̬|i **-ies** -iz **i'dentity ,card; i'dentity ,crisis; i'dentity pa,rade; i'dentity ,lineup**
ideogram 'ɪd.i.əʊ.græm, 'aɪ.di- (US) -oʊ-, -ə- **-s** -z
ideograph 'ɪd.i.əʊ.grɑːf, 'aɪ.di-, -græf (US) -oʊ.græf, -ə- **-s** -s
ideographic ,ɪd.i.əʊ'græf.ɪk, ,aɪ.di- (US) -oʊ'-, -ə'- **-al** -ᵊl **-ally** -ᵊl.i, -li
ideography ,ɪd.i'ɒg.rə.fi, ,aɪ.di'- (US) -'ɑː.grə-
ideologic|al ,aɪ.di.ə'lɒdʒ.ɪ.k|ᵊl, ,ɪd.i- (US) -'lɑː.dʒɪ- **-ally** -ᵊl.i, -li
ideologue 'aɪ.di.əʊ.lɒg, 'ɪd.i- (US) -ə.lɑːg **-s** -z
ideolog|y ,aɪ.di'ɒl.ə.dʒ|i, ,ɪd.i'- (US) -'ɑː.lə- **-ies** -iz **-ist/s** -ɪst/s
ides (I) aɪdz ,**Ides of 'March**
Idi Amin ,iː.di,ɑː'miːn
idio- ɪd.i.əʊ-; ,ɪd.i'ɒ- (US) ɪd.i.oʊ-, -ə-; ,ɪd.i'ɑː-
Note: Prefix. Normally takes either primary or secondary stress on the first syllable, e.g. **idiolect** /'ɪd.i.əʊ.lekt (US) -oʊ-/, **idiomatic** /,ɪd.i.əʊ'mæt.ɪk (US) -ə'mæt̬-/, or secondary stress on the first syllable and primary stress on the third, e.g. **idiotic** /,ɪd.i'ɒt.ɪk (US) -'ɑː.t̬ɪk/.
idioc|y 'ɪd.i.ə.s|i **-ies** -iz
idiolect 'ɪd.i.əʊ.lekt (US) -oʊ-, -ə- **-s** -s **-al** -ᵊl
idiom 'ɪd.i.əm **-s** -z
idiomatic ,ɪd.i.əʊ'mæt.ɪk (US) -ə'mæt̬- **-al** -ᵊl **-ally** -ᵊl.i, -li
idiophone 'ɪd.i.əʊ.fəʊn (US) -oʊ.foʊn, -ə- **-s** -z
idiosyncras|y ,ɪd.i.əʊ'sɪŋ.krə.s|i (US) -oʊ'sɪn-, -ə'-, -'sɪŋ- **-ies** -iz
idiosyncratic ,ɪd.i.əʊ.sɪŋ'kræt.ɪk (US) -oʊ.sɪn'kræt̬-, -ə-, -sɪŋ'- **-ally** -ᵊl.i, -li
idiot 'ɪd.i.ət **-s** -s **'idiot ,box**
idiotic ,ɪd.i'ɒt.ɪk (US) -'ɑː.t̬ɪk **-al** -ᵊl **-ally** -ᵊl.i, -li
idiotism 'ɪd.i.ə.tɪ.zᵊm (US) -t̬ɪ- **-s** -z
idiot-proof 'ɪd.i.ət,pruːf
idiot(s) savant(s) ,iː.di.əʊ.sæv'ɑ̃ːŋ, ,ɪd.i.ət'sæv.ᵊnt (US) ,iː.diː.oʊ.sæv'ɑːnt, -'ænt
Idist 'iː.dɪst **-s** -s
id|le (I) 'aɪ.d|l̩ **-ly** -li **-lest** -lɪst, -ləst **-leness** -l̩.nəs, -nɪs **-les** -l̩z **-ling** -lɪŋ **-led** -l̩d **-ler/s** -ləʳ/z (US) -lɚ/z
Ido 'iː.dəʊ (US) -doʊ
idol 'aɪ.dᵊl **-s** -z
idolater aɪ'dɒl.ə.təʳ (US) -'dɑː.lə.t̬ɚ **-s** -z

Pronouncing the letters IE

There are several pronunciation possibilities for the vowel digraph **ie**. One of the most common is /iː/:

achieve /ə'tʃiːv/
piece /piːs/

Another common pronunciation is /aɪ/, e.g.:

pie /paɪ/
magnifies /'mæg.nɪ.faɪz/

When followed by an **r** in the spelling, **ie** is pronounced as /ɪə/, (US) ɪr/, e.g.:

pier /pɪəʳ/ (US) /pɪr/
fierce /fɪəs/ (US) /fɪrs/

In addition

Other vowel sounds are associated with the digraph **ie**, e.g.:

/ɪ/ handkerchief /'hæŋ.kə.tʃɪf/ (US) /-kɚ-/
/aɪə/ diet /daɪət/
/e/ friend /frend/
/i.e/ conscientious /ˌkɒn.tʃi'en.tʃəs/ (US) /ˌkɑːn.tʃi'ent.ʃəs/
/i.iː/ medieval /ˌmed.i'iː.vᵊl/ (US) /ˌmiː.di'-/

In weak syllables

The vowel digraph **ie** is realised with the vowel /ə/ in weak syllables, or can cause the following consonant to be realised as syllabic, e.g.:

patient /'peɪ.ʃᵊnt/

Pronouncing the letters IEU

The vowel letter combination **ieu** has a number of possible pronunciations, but most are associated with particular words, e.g.:

lieutenant /lef'ten.ənt/ (US) /luː-/
lieu /ljuː, luː/ (US) /luː/

idolatrous aɪ'dɒl.ə.trəs (US) -'dɑː.lə- **-ly** -li **-ness** -nəs, -nɪs
idolatr|y aɪ'dɒl.ə.tr|i (US) -'dɑː.lə- **-ies** -iz
idolization, -isa- ˌaɪ.dᵊl.aɪ'zeɪ.ʃᵊn, -ɪ'- (US) -ɪ'-
idoliz|e, -is|e 'aɪ.dᵊl.aɪz **-es** -ɪz **-ing** -ɪŋ **-ed** -d **-er/s** -əʳ/z (US) -ɚ/z
Idomeneus aɪ'dɒm.ɪ.njuːs, ɪ'-, '-ə-; ɪˌdɒm.ɪ'niː.əs, aɪˌ-, -ə'- (US) -'dɑː.mə.nuːs, -njuːs
Idris 'ɪd.rɪs, 'aɪ.drɪs
Idumea ˌaɪ.djʊ'miː.ə, ˌɪd.jʊ'- (US) ˌɪd.juː'miː.ə, ˌiː.djuː'-, ˌiː.dʒuː'-
idyll 'ɪd.ᵊl, 'aɪ.dᵊl, -dɪl (US) 'aɪ.dᵊl **-s** -z
idyllic ɪ'dɪl.ɪk, aɪ- (US) aɪ- **-ally** -ᵊl.i, -li
idyllist 'ɪd.ᵊl.ɪst, 'aɪ.dᵊl-, -dɪl- (US) 'aɪ.dᵊl- **-s** -s
i.e. ˌaɪ'iː
if ɪf
Ife *surname:* aɪf *town in Nigeria:* 'iː.feɪ
Iffley 'ɪf.li
iffy 'ɪf.i
Ifor 'aɪ.vəʳ, -fəʳ, 'iː.vɔːʳ (US) 'aɪ.vɚ, 'iː-
-ify -ɪ.faɪ, -ə-
Note: Suffix. Words containing **-ify** normally carry stress on the antepenultimate syllable, e.g. **person** /'pɜː.sᵊn (US) 'pɜːr-/, **personify** /pə'sɒn.ɪ.faɪ (US) pɚ'sɑː.nɪ-/. Exceptions exist; see individual entries.
Igbo 'iː.bəʊ (US) -boʊ **-s** -z
Ightham 'aɪ.təm (US) -t̬əm
Iglesias ɪ'gleɪ.si.æs, -əs, -zi- (US) -əs
igloo 'ɪg.luː **-s** -z
Ignatieff ɪg'næt.i.ef (US) -'næt̬-
Ignatius ɪg'neɪ.ʃəs
igneous 'ɪg.ni.əs
ignis fatu|us ˌɪg.nɪs'fæt.ju|.əs (US) -'fætʃ.uː- **-i** -iː
ig|nite ɪg|'naɪt **-nites** -'naɪts **-niting** -'naɪ.tɪŋ (US) -'naɪ.t̬ɪŋ **-nited** -'naɪ.tɪd (US) -'naɪ.t̬ɪd **-nitable** -'naɪ.tə.bl̩ (US) -'naɪ.t̬ə.bl̩
ignition ɪg'nɪʃ.ᵊn **-s** -z
ignobility ˌɪg.nəʊ'bɪl.ə.ti, -ɪ.ti (US) -noʊ'bɪl.ə.t̬i, -nə'-
ignob|le ɪg'nəʊ.b|l̩ (US) -'noʊ- **-ly** -li **-leness** -l̩.nəs, -nɪs
ignominious ˌɪg.nəʊ'mɪn.i.əs (US) -nə'- **-ly** -li **-ness** -nəs, -nɪs
ignominy 'ɪg.nə.mɪ.ni, -mə.ni (US) -nə.mɪ-
ignoramus ˌɪg.nə'reɪ.məs **-es** -ɪz
ignorance 'ɪg.nᵊr.ᵊnts
ignorant 'ɪg.nᵊr.ᵊnt **-ly** -li
ignor|e ɪg'nɔːʳ (US) -'nɔːr **-es** -z **-ing** -ɪŋ **-ed** -d **-able** -ə.bl̩
Igoe 'aɪ.gəʊ (US) -goʊ
Igor 'iː.gɔːʳ (US) -gɔːr
Igorot ˌiː.gə'rəʊt, ˌɪg.ə'- (US) ˌiː.goʊ'roʊt, ˌɪg.oʊ'- **-s** -s
Igraine ɪ'greɪn, iː-
Iguaçú ˌiː.gwɑː'suː
iguana ɪ'gwɑː.nə, ˌɪg.ju'ɑː- (US) ɪ'gwɑː-, iː- **-s** -z
iguanodon ɪ'gwɑː.nə.dɒn, ˌɪg.ju'ɑː-, -'æn.ə-, -dən (US) ɪ'gwɑː.nə.dɑːn, iː- **-s** -z
Iguazú ˌiː.gwɑː'suː
ikat 'iː.kɑːt
IKBS ˌaɪ.keɪ.biː'es
Ike aɪk
Ikea® aɪ'kiː.ə *as if Swedish:* ɪ'keɪ.ə
ikon 'aɪ.kɒn, -kən (US) -kɑːn, -kən **-s** -z
Ilchester 'ɪl.tʃɪs.təʳ (US) -tɚ
ILEA 'ɪl.ɪ.ə, ˌaɪ.el.iː'eɪ
ilea *(plur. of* **ileum***)* 'ɪl.i.ə
ileostom|y ˌɪl.i'ɒs.tə.m|i (US) -'ɑː.stə- **-ies** -iz
ile|um 'ɪl.i|.əm **-a** -ə **-al** -əl
ilex 'aɪ.leks **-es** -ɪz
Ilford 'ɪl.fəd (US) -fɚd
Ilfracombe 'ɪl.frə.kuːm
ilia *(plur. of* **ilium***)* 'ɪl.i.ə
iliac 'ɪl.i.æk
Iliad 'ɪl.i.æd, -əd (US) -əd, -æd

Iliffe 'aɪ.lɪf
ili|um 'ɪl.i|.əm **-a** -ə
Ilium 'ɪl.i.əm, 'aɪ.li-
ilk ɪlk
Ilkeston(e) 'ɪl.kɪ.stᵊn, -kə-
Ilkley 'ɪl.kli
ill ɪl **-s** -z ˌ**ill at 'ease**; ˌ**ill 'will**
I'll *(=* **I will** *or* **I shall***)* aɪl
Ill. *(abbrev. for* **Illinois***)* ˌɪl.ɪ'nɔɪ, -ə'-
ill-advised ˌɪl.əd'vaɪzd *stress shift:* ˌill-advised 'plan
ill-advisedly ˌɪl.əd'vaɪ.zɪd.li
ill-assorted ˌɪl.ə'sɔː.tɪd ⓤⓢ -'sɔːr.t̬ɪd *stress shift:* ˌill-assorted 'candidates
illative ɪ'leɪ.tɪv, 'ɪl.ə.tɪv ⓤⓢ -t̬ɪv **-ly** -li
ill-bred ˌɪl'bred *stress shift:* ˌill-bred 'lout
ill-breeding ˌɪl'briː.dɪŋ
ill-conceived ˌɪl.kən'siːvd *stress shift:* ˌill-conceived 'plan
ill-conditioned ˌɪl.kən'dɪʃ.ᵊnd *stress shift:* ˌill-conditioned 'crew
ill-considered ˌɪl.kən'sɪd.əd ⓤⓢ -ɚd *stress shift:* ˌill-considered 'action
ill-disposed ˌɪl.dɪ'spəʊzd ⓤⓢ -'spoʊzd *stress shift:* ˌill-disposed 'patient
illegal ɪ'liː.gᵊl ⓤⓢ ɪ'liː-, ˌɪl- **-ly** -i **il**ˌ**legal 'alien**; **il**ˌ**legal 'immigrant**
illegalit|y ˌɪl.iː'gæl.ə.t|i, -ɪ'-, -ɪ.t|i ⓤⓢ -ə.t̬|i **-ies** -iz
illegibility ɪˌledʒ.ə'bɪl.ə.ti, ˌɪl.ledʒ-, -ɪ'-, -ɪ.ti ⓤⓢ -ə.t̬i
illegib|le ɪ'ledʒ.ə.b|l̩, ˌɪl'ledʒ-, '-ɪ- **-ly** -li **-leness** -l̩.nəs, -nɪs
illegitimacy ˌɪl.ɪ'dʒɪt.ə.mə.si, -ə'-, '-ɪ- ⓤⓢ -'dʒɪt̬.ə-
illegitimate ˌɪl.ɪ'dʒɪt.ə.mət, -ə'-, '-ɪ-, -mɪt ⓤⓢ -'dʒɪt̬.ə- **-ly** -li
ill-equipped ˌɪl.ɪ'kwɪpt *stress shift:* ˌill-equipped 'project
ill-fated ˌɪl'feɪ.tɪd ⓤⓢ -t̬ɪd *stress shift:* ˌill-fated 'lovers
ill-favoured ˌɪl'feɪ.vəd ⓤⓢ -vɚd **-ly** -li **-ness** -nəs, -nɪs *stress shift:* ˌill-favoured 'couple
ill-feeling ˌɪl'fiː.lɪŋ
ill-founded ˌɪl'faʊn.dɪd *stress shift:* ˌill-founded 'rumo(u)r
ill-gotten ˌɪl'gɒt.ᵊn ⓤⓢ -'gɑː.tᵊn *stress shift, see compound:* ˌ**ill-gotten 'gains**
illiberal ɪ'lɪb.ᵊr.ᵊl, ˌɪl- **-ly** -i **-ness** -nəs, -nɪs
illiberalism ɪ'lɪb.ᵊr.ᵊl.ɪ.zᵊm, ˌɪl-
illiberality ɪˌlɪb.ə'ræl.ə.ti, ˌɪl-, -ɪ.ti ⓤⓢ -ə.t̬i
illicit ɪ'lɪs.ɪt, ˌɪl- **-ly** -li **-ness** -nəs, -nɪs
illimitab|le ɪ'lɪm.ɪ.tə.b|l̩, ˌɪl- ⓤⓢ -t̬ə- **-ly** -li **-leness** -l̩.nəs, -nɪs
Illingworth 'ɪl.ɪŋ.wəθ, -wɜːθ ⓤⓢ -wɚθ, -wɝːθ
Illinois ˌɪl.ɪ'nɔɪ, -ə'-
illiteracy ɪ'lɪt.ᵊr.ə.si, ˌɪl- ⓤⓢ -'lɪt̬-
illiterate ɪ'lɪt.ᵊr.ət, ˌɪl-, -ɪt ⓤⓢ -'lɪt̬- **-s** -s **-ly** -li **-ness** -nəs, -nɪs
ill-judged ˌɪl'dʒʌdʒd *stress shift:* ˌill-judged 'move
ill-mannered ˌɪl'mæn.əd ⓤⓢ -ɚd *stress shift:* ˌill-mannered 'man
ill-natured ˌɪl'neɪ.tʃəd ⓤⓢ -tʃɚd **-ly** -li *stress shift:* ˌill-natured 'dog
illness 'ɪl.nəs, -nɪs **-es** -ɪz
illocution ˌɪl.ə'kjuː.ʃᵊn **-s** -z **-ary** -ᵊr.i ⓤⓢ -er-
Illogan ɪ'lʌg.ən
illogic|al ɪ'lɒdʒ.ɪ.k|ᵊl, ˌɪl- ⓤⓢ -'lɑː.dʒɪ- **-ally** -ᵊl.i, -li **-alness** -ᵊl.nəs, -nɪs
illogicalit|y ɪˌlɒdʒ.ɪ'kæl.ə.t|i, ˌɪl-, -ɪ.t|i ⓤⓢ -ˌlɑː.dʒɪ'kæl.ə.t̬|i **-ies** -iz
ill-omened ˌɪl'əʊ.mend, -mənd, -mɪnd ⓤⓢ -'oʊ- *stress shift:* ˌill-omened 'voyage
ill-starred ˌɪl'stɑːd ⓤⓢ -'stɑːrd *stress shift:* ˌill-starred 'love
ill-tempered ˌɪl'tem.pəd ⓤⓢ -pɚd *stress shift:* ˌill-tempered 'customer
ill-timed ˌɪl'taɪmd *stress shift:* ˌill-timed 'entrance
ill|-treat ˌɪl'triːt, ɪl- **-treats** -'triːts **-treating** -'triː.tɪŋ ⓤⓢ -'triː.t̬ɪŋ **-treated** -'triː.tɪd ⓤⓢ -'triː.t̬ɪd **-treatment** -'triːt.mənt
illum|e ɪ'ljuːm, -'luːm ⓤⓢ -'luːm **-es** -z **-ing** -ɪŋ **-ed** -d
illuminant ɪ'luː.mɪ.nənt, -'ljuː-, -mə- ⓤⓢ -'luː.mə- **-s** -s
illumi|nate ɪ'luː.mɪ|.neɪt, -'ljuː-, -mə- ⓤⓢ -'luː.mə- **-nates** -neɪts **-nating** -neɪ.tɪŋ ⓤⓢ -neɪ.t̬ɪŋ **-nated** -neɪ.tɪd ⓤⓢ -neɪ.t̬ɪd **-nator/s** -neɪ.təʳ/z ⓤⓢ -neɪ.t̬ɚ/z
illuminati (I) ɪˌluː.mɪ'nɑː.tiː, -mə'- ⓤⓢ -'nɑː.t̬i
illumination ɪˌluː.mɪ'neɪ.ʃᵊn, -ˌljuː-, -mə'- ⓤⓢ -ˌluː- **-s** -z
illuminative ɪ'luː.mɪ.nə.təv, -'ljuː-, -mə-, -neɪ- ⓤⓢ -'luː.mɪ.neɪ.t̬ɪv, -mə-
illumin|e ɪ'ljuː.mɪn, -'luː- ⓤⓢ -'luː- **-es** -z **-ing** -ɪŋ **-ed** -d
ill-usage ˌɪl'juː.zɪdʒ, -sɪdʒ ⓤⓢ -sɪdʒ, -zɪdʒ **-s** -ɪz
ill-used ˌɪl'juːzd *stress shift:* ˌill-used 'servant
illusion ɪ'luː.ʒᵊn, -'ljuː- ⓤⓢ -'luː- **-s** -z
illusion|ism ɪ'luː.ʒᵊn|.ɪ.zᵊm, -'ljuː- ⓤⓢ -'luː- **-ist/s** -ɪst/s
illusive ɪ'luː.sɪv, -'ljuː- ⓤⓢ -'luː- **-ly** -li **-ness** -nəs, -nɪs
illusor|y ɪ'luː.sᵊr|.i, -'ljuː-, -zᵊr- ⓤⓢ -'luː- **-ily** -ᵊl.i, -ɪ.li **-iness** -ɪ.nəs, -ɪ.nɪs
illu|strate 'ɪl.ə|.streɪt **-strates** -streɪts **-strating** -streɪ.tɪŋ ⓤⓢ -streɪ.t̬ɪŋ **-strated** -streɪ.tɪd ⓤⓢ -streɪ.t̬ɪd **-strator/s** -streɪ.təʳ/z ⓤⓢ -streɪ.t̬ɚ/z
illustration ˌɪl.ə'streɪ.ʃᵊn **-s** -z
illustrative 'ɪl.ə.strə.tɪv, -streɪ-; ɪ'lʌs.trə.tɪv ⓤⓢ ɪ'lʌs.trə.t̬ɪv; 'ɪl.ə.streɪ- **-ly** -li
illustrious ɪ'lʌs.tri.əs **-ly** -li **-ness** -nəs, -nɪs
illuvi|um ɪ'luː.vi|.əm **-ums** -əmz **-a** -ə **-al** -əl
Illyri|a ɪ'lɪr.i|.ə **-an/s** -ən/z
Illyricum ɪ'lɪr.ɪ.kəm
Ilminster 'ɪl.mɪn.stəʳ ⓤⓢ -stɚ
Ilorin ɪ'lɒr.ɪn ⓤⓢ -'lɔːr-
Ilyushin ɪ'ljuː.ʃɪn, -ʃᵊn ⓤⓢ ɪl'juː-, ɪ'luː-
im- ɪm-
Note: Prefix. The form of **in-** where the stem begins with /p/, /b/, or /m/. When a negative prefix, **im-** does not affect the stress pattern of the stem, e.g. **balance** /'bæl.ənts/, **imbalance** /ɪm'bæl.ənts/. In other cases, the prefix is normally stressed in nouns but not in verbs, e.g. **imprint**, noun /'ɪm.prɪnt/, verb /ɪm'prɪnt/.
I'm *(=* **I am***)* aɪm
imag|e 'ɪm.ɪdʒ **-es** -ɪz **-ing** -ɪŋ **-ed** -d
imager|y 'ɪm.ɪ.dʒᵊr|.i, '-ə- **-ies** -iz
imaginab|le ɪ'mædʒ.ɪ.nə.b|l̩, -ᵊn.ə- **-ly** -li **-leness** -l̩.nəs, -nɪs
imaginar|y ɪ'mædʒ.ɪ.nᵊr|.i, -ᵊn.ᵊr-, -'-nᵊr|.i ⓤⓢ -ə.ner- **-ily** -ᵊl.i, -ɪ.li **-iness** -ɪ.nəs, -ɪ.nɪs
imagination ɪˌmædʒ.ɪ'neɪ.ʃᵊn, -ə'- **-s** -z
imaginative ɪ'mædʒ.ɪ.nə.tɪv, '-ə- ⓤⓢ -nə.t̬ɪv, -neɪ- **-ly** -li **-ness** -nəs, -nɪs
imagin|e ɪ'mædʒ.ɪn, -ᵊn **-es** -z **-ing/s** -ɪŋ/z **-ed** -d
imagines *(plur. of* **imago***)* ɪ'meɪ.dʒɪ.niːz, ɪ'mɑː-, -neɪz ⓤⓢ -niːz
imagism 'ɪm.ɪ.dʒɪ.zᵊm
ima|go ɪ'meɪ|.gəʊ, ɪ'mɑː- ⓤⓢ -goʊ **-goes** -gəʊz ⓤⓢ -goʊz **-gines** -dʒɪ.niːz, -neɪz ⓤⓢ -niːz
imam ɪ'mɑːm, 'iː.mɑːm ⓤⓢ ɪ'mɑːm **-s** -z
imbalanc|e ˌɪm'bæl.ənts **-es** -ɪz
imbecile 'ɪm.bə.siːl, -bɪ-, -saɪl ⓤⓢ -sɪl, -səl **-s** -z
imbecilic ˌɪm.bə'sɪl.ɪk, -bɪ'-
imbecilit|y ˌɪm.bə'sɪl.ə.t|i, -bɪ'-, -ɪ.t|i ⓤⓢ -ə.t̬|i **-ies** -iz
imbed ɪm'bed **-s** -z **-ding** -ɪŋ **-ded** -ɪd
Imbert 'ɪm.bət ⓤⓢ -bɚt
imbib|e ɪm'baɪb **-es** -z **-ing** -ɪŋ **-ed** -d **-er/s** -əʳ/z ⓤⓢ -ɚ/z
imbroglio ɪm'brəʊ.li.əʊ ⓤⓢ -'broʊ.li.oʊ **-s** -z
imbru|e ɪm'bruː **-es** -z **-ing** -ɪŋ **-ed** -d
imbu|e ɪm'bjuː **-es** -z **-ing** -ɪŋ **-ed** -d
Imelda ɪ'mel.də
Imeson 'aɪ.mɪ.sᵊn
IMF ˌaɪ.em'ef
imitability ˌɪm.ɪ.tə'bɪl.ə.ti, ˌ-ə-, -ɪ.ti ⓤⓢ -ə.t̬i

imitable ˈɪm.ɪ.tə.bl̩, ˈ-ə- US -ə.t̬ə-
imi|tate ˈɪm.ɪ|.teɪt, ˈ-ə- **-tates** -teɪts **-tating** -teɪ.tɪŋ US -teɪ.t̬ɪŋ **-tated** -teɪ.tɪd US -teɪ.t̬ɪd **-tator/s** -teɪ.təʳ/z US -teɪ.t̬ɚ/z
imitation ˌɪm.ɪˈteɪ.ʃᵊn, -əˈ- **-s** -z **-al** -ᵊl
imitative ˈɪm.ɪ.tə.tɪv, ˈ-ə-, -teɪ- US -teɪ.t̬ɪv **-ly** -li **-ness** -nəs, -nɪs
Imlay ˈɪm.leɪ
immaculate ɪˈmæk.jə.lət, -jʊ-, -lɪt **-ly** -li **-ness** -nəs, -nɪs **Imˌmaculate Conˈception**
immanen|ce ˈɪm.ə.nən|*t*s **-t** -t
Immanuel ɪˈmæn.ju.əl US -el, -ᵊl
immaterial ˌɪm.əˈtɪə.ri.əl US -ˈtɪr.i- **-ly** -i **-ness** -nəs, -nɪs
immaterial|ism ˌɪm.əˈtɪə.ri.ᵊl|.ɪ.zᵊm US -ˈtɪr.i- **-ist/s** -ɪst/s
immateriality ˌɪm.əˌtɪə.riˈæl.ə.ti, -ɪ.ti US -ˌtɪr.iˈæl.ə.t̬i
immaterializ|e, -is|e ˌɪm.əˈtɪə.ri.ᵊl.aɪz US -ˈtɪr.i- **-es** -ɪz **-ing** -ɪŋ **-ed** -d
immature ˌɪm.əˈtjʊəʳ, -ˈtʃʊəʳ, -ˈtjɔːʳ, -ˈtʃɔːʳ US -ˈtʊr, -ˈtjʊr, -ˈtʃʊr **-ly** -li **-ness** -nəs, -nɪs
immaturit|y ˌɪm.əˈtjʊə.rə.t|i, -ˈtʃʊə-, -ˈtjɔː-, -ˈtʃɔː-, -rɪ- US -ˈtʊr.ə.t̬|i, -ˈtjʊr-, -ˈtʃʊr- **-ies** -iz
immeasurab|le ɪˈmeʒ.ᵊr.ə.b|l̩, ˌɪm- **-ly** -li **-leness** -l̩.nəs, -nɪs
immediacy ɪˈmiː.di.ə.si
immediate ɪˈmiː.di.ət, -ɪt, -dʒət US -di.ɪt **-ly** -li
immemorial ˌɪm.ɪˈmɔː.ri.əl, -əˈ- US -ˈmɔːr.i- **-ly** -li
immense ɪˈmen*t*s **-ly** -li **-ness** -nəs, -nɪs
immensit|y ɪˈmen*t*.sə.t|i, -sɪ- US -sə.t̬|i **-ies** -iz
immers|e ɪˈmɜːs US -ˈmɝːs **-es** -ɪz **-ing** -ɪŋ **-ed** -t
immersion ɪˈmɜː.ʃᵊn, -ʒᵊn US -ˈmɝː- **-s** -z **imˈmersion ˌheater**
immigrant ˈɪm.ɪ.grənt, ˈ-ə- **-s** -s
immi|grate ˈɪm.ɪ|.greɪt, ˈ-ə- **-grates** -greɪts **-grating** -greɪ.tɪŋ US -greɪ.t̬ɪŋ **-grated** -greɪ.tɪd US -greɪ.t̬ɪd
immigration ˌɪm.ɪˈgreɪ.ʃᵊn, -əˈ- **-s** -z
imminence ˈɪm.ɪ.nən*t*s, ˈ-ə-
imminent ˈɪm.ɪ.nənt, ˈ-ə- **-ly** -li
Immingham ˈɪm.ɪŋ.əm US -hæm, -həm, -əm
immiscibility ɪˌmɪs.ɪˈbɪl.ə.ti, ˌɪm-, -əˈ-, -ɪ.ti US -ə.t̬i
immiscib|le ɪˈmɪs.ə.b|l̩, ˌɪm-, ˈ-ɪ- **-ly** -li
immobile ɪˈməʊ.baɪl, ɪm- US -ˈmoʊ.bᵊl, -bɪl, -baɪl
immobility ˌɪm.əʊˈbɪl.ə.ti, -ɪ.ti US -moʊˈbɪl.ə.t̬i
immobilization, -isa- ɪˌməʊ.bᵊl.aɪˈzeɪ.ʃᵊn, ˌɪm-, -bɪ.laɪˈ-, -lɪˈ- US -ˌmoʊ.bə.lɪˈ-
immobiliz|e, -is|e ɪˈməʊ.bᵊl.aɪz, ˌɪm-, -bɪ.laɪz US -ˈmoʊ- **-es** -ɪz **-ing** -ɪŋ **-ed** -d
immobilizer, -ise- ɪˈməʊ.bᵊl.aɪ.zəʳ US -zɚ **-s** -z
immoderate ɪˈmɒd.ᵊr.ət, ˌɪm-, -ɪt US -ˈmɑː.dɚ- **-ly** -li **-ness** -nəs, -nɪs
immoderation ɪˌmɒd.əˈreɪ.ʃᵊn, ˌɪm- US -ˌmɑː.dəˈ-
immodest ɪˈmɒd.ɪst, ˌɪm- US -ˈmɑː.dɪst **-ly** -li
immodesty ɪˈmɒd.ə.sti, ˌɪm-, ˈ-ɪ- US -ˈmɑː.də-
immo|late ˈɪm.əʊ|.leɪt US ˈ-ə- **-lates** -leɪts **-lating** -leɪ.tɪŋ US -leɪ.t̬ɪŋ **-lated** -leɪ.tɪd US -leɪ.t̬ɪd **-lator/s** -leɪ.təʳ/z US -leɪ.t̬ɚ/z
immolation ˌɪm.əʊˈleɪ.ʃᵊn US -əˈ- **-s** -z
immoral ɪˈmɒr.ᵊl, ˌɪm- US -ˈmɔːr- **-ly** -i
immoralit|y ˌɪm.əˈræl.ə.t|i, -ɒrˈæl-, -ɪ.t|i US -mɔːˈræl.ə.t̬|i, -məˈ- **-ies** -iz
immortal ɪˈmɔː.tᵊl, ˌɪm- US -ˈmɔːr.t̬ᵊl **-s** -z **-ly** -i
immortality ˌɪm.ɔːˈtæl.ə.ti, -ɪ.ti US -ɔːrˈtæl.ə.t̬i
immortaliz|e, -is|e ɪˈmɔː.tᵊl.aɪz, ˌɪm- US -ˈmɔːr.t̬ᵊl- **-es** -ɪz **-ing** -ɪŋ **-ed** -d
immortelle ˌɪm.ɔːˈtel US -ɔːrˈ- **-s** -z
immovability ɪˌmuː.vəˈbɪl.ə.ti, ˌɪm-, -ɪ.ti US -ə.t̬i
immovab|le ɪˈmuː.və.b|l̩, ˌɪm- **-ly** -li **-leness** -l̩.nəs, -nɪs
immune ɪˈmjuːn **imˈmune ˌsystem**
immunit|y ɪˈmjuː.nə.t|i, -nɪ- US -nə.t̬|i **-ies** -iz
immunization, -isa- ˌɪm.jə.naɪˈzeɪ.ʃᵊn, -jʊ-, -nɪˈ- US -nɪˈ- **-s** -z
immuniz|e, -is|e ˈɪm.jə.naɪz, -jʊ- **-es** -ɪz **-ing** -ɪŋ **-ed** -d
immuno- ˌɪm.jə.nəʊ-, -jʊ-; ɪˌmjuː.nəʊ- US -noʊ-
immunodeficiency ˌɪm.jə.nəʊ.dɪˈfɪʃ.ᵊn*t*.si, -jʊ-; ɪˌmjuː- US -noʊ-
immunologic|al ˌɪm.jə.nəʊˈlɒdʒ.ɪ.k|ᵊl, -jʊ-; ɪˌmjuː.nəʊˈ- US ˌɪm.jə.noʊˈlɑː.dʒɪ-, -jʊ- **-ally** -ᵊl.i, -li
immunolog|y ˌɪm.jəˈnɒl.ə.dʒ|i, -jʊˈ- US -ˈnɑː.lə- **-ist/s** -ɪst/s
immunosuppress|ant ˌɪm.jə.nəʊ.səˈpres|.ᵊnt, -jʊ-; ɪˌmjuː- US -noʊ- **-ive** -ɪv
immunosuppression ˌɪm.jə.nəʊ.səˈpreʃ.ᵊn, -jʊ-; ɪˌmjuː- US -noʊ-
immur|e ɪˈmjʊəʳ, -ˈmjɔːʳ US -ˈmjʊr **-es** -z **-ing** -ɪŋ **-ed** -d **-ement** -mənt
immutability ɪˌmjuː.təˈbɪl.ə.ti, -ɪ.ti; ˌɪm.jə-, -jʊ- US ɪˌmjuː.t̬əˈbɪl.ə.t̬i
immutab|le ɪˈmjuː.tə.b|l̩ US -t̬ə- **-ly** -li **-leness** -l̩.nəs, -nɪs
Imogen ˈɪm.ə.dʒᵊn, -dʒen, -dʒɪn US -dʒen, -dʒᵊn
Imogene ˈɪm.ə.dʒiːn
Imola ˈɪm.əʊ.lə US -ə-, -ˌoʊ-
imp ɪmp **-s** -s **-ing** -ɪŋ **-ed** -t
impact (*n.*) ˈɪm.pækt **-s** -s
impact (*v.*) ɪmˈpækt, ˈ-- **-s** -s **-ing** -ɪŋ **-ed** -ɪd
impair ɪmˈpeəʳ US -ˈper **-s** -z **-ing** -ɪŋ **-ed** -d
impairment ɪmˈpeə.mənt US -ˈper- **-s** -s
impala ɪmˈpɑː.lə US -ˈpɑː.lə, -ˈpæl.ə **-s** -z
impal|e ɪmˈpeɪl **-es** -z **-ing** -ɪŋ **-ed** -d **-ement** -mənt
impalpab|le ɪmˈpæl.pə.b|l̩, ˌɪm- **-ly** -li
impanel ɪmˈpæn.ᵊl **-s** -z **-(l)ing** -ɪŋ **-(l)ed** -d
imparisyllabic ɪmˌpær.ɪ.sɪˈlæb.ɪk, ˌɪm.pær-, ˌ-ə- US ɪmˌper-, -ˌpær-
im|part ɪm|ˈpɑːt US -ˈpɑːrt **-parts** -ˈpɑːts US -ˈpɑːrts **-parting** -ˈpɑː.tɪŋ US -ˈpɑːr.t̬ɪŋ **-parted** -ˈpɑː.tɪd US -ˈpɑːr.t̬ɪd
impartation ˌɪm.pɑːˈteɪ.ʃᵊn US -pɑːrˈ-
impartial ɪmˈpɑː.ʃᵊl, ˌɪm- US -ˈpɑːr- **-ly** -i **-ness** -nəs, -nɪs
impartiality ɪmˌpɑː.ʃiˈæl.ə.ti, ˌɪm.pɑː-, ˌɪmˌpɑː-, -ɪ.ti US ɪmˌpɑːr-, ˌɪm-
impassability ɪmˌpɑː.səˈbɪl.ə.ti, ˌɪm.pɑː-, ˌɪmˌpɑː-, -ɪ.ti US ɪmˌpæs.əˈbɪl.ə.t̬i, ˌɪm-
impassable ɪmˈpɑː.sə.bl̩, ˌɪm- US -ˈpæs.ə- **-ness** -nəs, -nɪs
impasse ˈæ̃m.pɑːs, ˈæm-, ˈɪm-, -pæs, -ˈ- US ˈɪm.pæs, -ˈ- **-es** -ɪz
impassibility ɪmˌpæs.əˈbɪl.ə.ti, ˌɪm.pæs-, -sɪˈ-, -ɪ.ti US ɪmˌpæs-
impassible ɪmˈpæs.ə.bl̩, ˈ-ɪ-
impassioned ɪmˈpæʃ.ᵊnd
impassive ɪmˈpæs.ɪv **-ly** -li **-ness** -nəs, -nɪs
impassivity ˌɪm.pæsˈɪv.ə.ti, -ɪ.ti US -ə.t̬i
impasto ɪmˈpæs.təʊ US -toʊ, -ˈpɑː.stoʊ **-ed** -d
impatience ɪmˈpeɪ.ʃᵊn*t*s
impatiens ɪmˈpeɪ.ʃi.enz, -ˈpæt.i-
impatient ɪmˈpeɪ.ʃᵊnt **-ly** -li
impeach ɪmˈpiːtʃ **-es** -ɪz **-ing** -ɪŋ **-ed** -t **-er/s** -əʳ/z US -ɚ/z **-ment/s** -mənt/s **-able** -ə.bl̩
impeccability ɪmˌpek.əˈbɪl.ə.ti, ˌɪm.pek-, -ɪ.ti US ɪmˌpek.əˈbɪl.ə.t̬i
impeccab|le ɪmˈpek.ə.b|l̩ **-ly** -li
impecunious ˌɪm.pɪˈkjuː.ni.əs, -pəˈ- **-ly** -li **-ness** -nəs, -nɪs
impedanc|e ɪmˈpiː.dᵊn*t*s **-es** -ɪz
imped|e ɪmˈpiːd **-es** -z **-ing** -ɪŋ **-ed** -ɪd
impediment ɪmˈped.ɪ.mənt, ˈ-ə- **-s** -s
impedimenta ɪmˌped.ɪˈmen.tə, ˌɪm.ped-

impel ɪmˈpel **-s** -z **-ling** -ɪŋ **-led** -d **-ler/s** -əʳ/z (US) -ɚ/z **-lent** -ənt

impend ɪmˈpend **-s** -z **-ing** -ɪŋ **-ed** -ɪd

impenetrability ɪmˌpen.ɪ.trəˈbɪl.ə.ti, ˌɪm.pen-, ˌ-ə-, -ɪ.ti (US) ɪmˌpen.ɪ.trəˈbɪl.ə.t̬i, ˌ-ə-

impenetrab|le ɪmˈpen.ɪ.trə.b|l̩, ˌɪm-, ˈ-ə- **-ly** -li **-leness** -l̩.nəs, -nɪs

impenitence ɪmˈpen.ɪ.tᵊnts, ˌɪm- (US) ˈ-ə-

impenitent ɪmˈpen.ɪ.tᵊnt, ˌɪm- (US) ˈ-ə- **-ly** -li

imperative ɪmˈper.ə.tɪv (US) -t̬ɪv **-s** -z **-ly** -li **-ness** -nəs, -nɪs

imperator ˌɪm.pəˈrɑː.tɔːʳ, -ˈreɪ-, -təʳ (US) -ˈreɪ.tɔːr, -ˈrɑː-, -t̬ɚ **-s** -z

imperatorial ɪmˌper.əˈtɔː.ri.əl; ˌɪm.per-, -pᵊr- (US) ˌɪm.pɚ.əˈtɔːr.i.əl

imperceptibility ˌɪm.pəˌsep.təˈbɪl.ə.ti, -tɪˈ-, -ɪ.ti (US) -pɚˌsep.təˈbɪl.ə.t̬i

imperceptib|le ˌɪm.pəˈsep.tə.b|l̩, -tɪ- (US) -pɚˈsep.tə- **-ly** -li **-leness** -l̩.nəs, -nɪs

imperceptive ˌɪm.pəˈsep.tɪv (US) -pɚˈ- **-ness** -nəs, -nɪs

imperfect ɪmˈpɜː.fɪkt, ˌɪm-, -fekt (US) -ˈpɝː- **-s** -s **-ly** -li **-ness** -nəs, -nɪs

imperfection ˌɪm.pəˈfek.ʃᵊn (US) -pɚˈ- **-s** -z

imperfective ˌɪm.pəˈfek.tɪv (US) -pɚˈ-

imperforat|e ɪmˈpɜː.fᵊr.ət, ˌɪm-, -ɪt (US) -ˈpɝː- **-ed** -ɪd **-s** -s

imperial ɪmˈpɪə.ri.əl (US) -ˈpɪr- **-s** -z **-ly** -i

imperial|ism ɪmˈpɪə.ri.ə.l|ɪ.zᵊm (US) -ˈpɪr.i- **-ist/s** -ɪst/s

imperialist ɪmˈpɪə.ri.ə.lɪst (US) -ˈpɪr.i-

imperialistic ɪmˌpɪə.ri.əˈlɪs.tɪk (US) -ˈpɪr.i-

imperil ɪmˈper.ᵊl, -ɪl (US) -ᵊl **-s** -z **-(l)ing** -ɪŋ **-(l)ed** -d

imperious ɪmˈpɪə.ri.əs (US) -ˈpɪr.i- **-ly** -li **-ness** -nəs, -nɪs

imperishab|le ɪmˈper.ɪ.ʃə.b|l̩, ˌɪm- **-ly** -li **-leness** -l̩.nəs, -nɪs

impermanence ɪmˈpɜː.mə.nənts, ˌɪm- (US) -ˈpɝː-

impermanent ɪmˈpɜː.mə.nənt, ˌɪm- (US) -ˈpɝː- **-ly** -li

impermeability ɪmˌpɜː.mi.əˈbɪl.ə.ti, ˌɪm-, -ɪ.ti (US) -ˌpɝː.mi.əˈbɪl.ə.t̬i

impermeable ɪmˈpɜː.mi.ə.b|l̩, ˌɪm- (US) -ˈpɝː- **-ly** -li **-leness** -l̩.nəs, -nɪs

impermissibility ˌɪm.pəˌmɪs.əˈbɪl.ə.ti, -ɪˈ-, -ɪ.ti (US) -pɚˌmɪs.əˈbɪl.ə.t̬i, -ɪˈ-

impermissib|le ˌɪm.pəˈmɪs.ə.b|l̩, ˈ-ɪ- (US) -pɚˈ- **-ly** -li

impers|onal ɪmˈpɜː.s|ᵊn.ᵊl, ˌɪm- (US) -ˈpɝː- **-onally** -nə.li, -ᵊn.ᵊl.i

impersonality ɪmˌpɜː.sᵊnˈæl.ə.ti, ˌɪm-, -ɪ.ti (US) -ˌpɝː.sᵊnˈæl.ə.t̬i

imperson|ate ɪmˈpɜː.sᵊn|.eɪt (US) -ˈpɝː- **-ates** -eɪts **-ating** -eɪ.tɪŋ (US) -eɪ.t̬ɪŋ **-ated** -eɪ.tɪd (US) -eɪ.t̬ɪd **-ator/s** -eɪ.təʳ/z (US) -eɪ.t̬ɚ/z

impersonation ɪmˌpɜː.sᵊnˈeɪ.ʃᵊn (US) -ˌpɝː- **-s** -z

impertinence ɪmˈpɜː.tɪ.nənts, ˌɪm-, -tᵊn.ənts (US) -ˈpɝː.t̬ᵊn-

impertinent ɪmˈpɜː.tɪ.nənt, ˌɪm-, -tᵊn.ənt (US) -ˈpɝː.t̬ᵊn- **-ly** -li

imperturbability ˌɪm.pəˌtɜː.bəˈbɪl.ə.ti, -ɪ.ti (US) -pɚˌtɝː.bəˈbɪl.ə.t̬i

imperturbab|le ˌɪm.pəˈtɜː.bə.b|l̩ (US) -pɚˈtɝː- **-ly** -li **-leness** -l̩.nəs, -nɪs

impervious ɪmˈpɜː.vi.əs, ˌɪm- (US) -ˈpɝː- **-ly** -li **-ness** -nəs, -nɪs

impetigo ˌɪm.pɪˈtaɪ.gəʊ, -pəˈ-, -petˈaɪ- (US) -pəˈtaɪ.goʊ

impetuosity ɪmˌpet.juˈɒs.ə.ti (US) ˌɪm-, -ˌpetʃ.uˈ-, -ɪ.ti (US) ɪmˌpetʃ.uˈɑː.sə.t̬i

impetuous ɪmˈpetʃ.u.əs, ˌɪm-, -ˈpet.ju- (US) -ˈpetʃ.u- **-ly** -li **-ness** -nəs, -nɪs

impetus ˈɪm.pɪ.təs, -pə- (US) -t̬əs

Impey ˈɪm.pi

impiet|y ɪmˈpaɪ.ə.t|i, ˌɪm-, -ɪ.t|i (US) -ə.t̬|i **-ies** -iz

imping|e ɪmˈpɪndʒ **-es** -ɪz **-ing** -ɪŋ **-ed** -d **-ement/s** -mənt/s

impious ˈɪm.pi.əs; ɪmˈpaɪ-, ˌɪm- (US) ˈɪm.pi-; ɪmˈpaɪ- **-ly** -li **-ness** -nəs, -nɪs

impish ˈɪm.pɪʃ **-ly** -li **-ness** -nəs, -nɪs

implacability ɪmˌplæk.əˈbɪl.ə.ti, ˌɪm-, -ɪ.ti (US) -ə.t̬i

implacab|le ɪmˈplæk.ə.b|l̩ **-ly** -li **-leness** -l̩.nəs, -nɪs

implant (*n.*) ˈɪm.plɑːnt (US) -plænt **-s** -s

implan|t (*v.*) ɪmˈplɑːn|t (US) -ˈplæn|t **-ts** -ts **-ting** -tɪŋ (US) -t̬ɪŋ **-ted** -tɪd (US) -t̬ɪd **-ter/s** -təʳ/z (US) -t̬ɚ/z

implantation ˌɪm.plɑːnˈteɪ.ʃᵊn, -plænˈ- (US) -plænˈ-

implausibilit|y ɪmˌplɔː.zəˈbɪl.ə.t|i, ˌɪm.plɔː-, ˌɪmˌplɔː-, -zɪˈ-, -ɪ.t|i (US) ɪmˌplɑː.zəˈbɪl.ə.t̬|i, ˌɪm-, -ˌplɔː- **-ies** -iz

implausib|le ɪmˈplɔː.zə.b|l̩, ˌɪm-, -zɪ- (US) -ˈplɑː-, -ˈplɔː- **-ly** -li **-leness** -l̩.nəs, -nɪs

impleader ɪmˈpliː.dəʳ (US) -dɚ **-s** -z

implement (*n.*) ˈɪm.plɪ.mənt, -plə- **-s** -s

implemen|t (*v.*) ˈɪm.plɪ.men|t, -plə-, -mən|t (US) -men|t **-ts** -ts **-ting** -tɪŋ (US) -t̬ɪŋ **-ted** -tɪd (US) -t̬ɪd

implementation ˌɪm.plɪ.menˈteɪ.ʃᵊn, -plə-, -mənˈ- **-s** -z

impli|cate ˈɪm.plɪ|.keɪt, -plə- **-cates** -keɪts **-cating** -keɪ.tɪŋ (US) -keɪ.t̬ɪŋ **-cated** -keɪ.tɪd (US) -keɪ.t̬ɪd

implication ˌɪm.plɪˈkeɪ.ʃᵊn, -pləˈ- **-s** -z

implicative ɪmˈplɪk.ə.tɪv; ˈɪm.plɪ.keɪ.tɪv, -plə- (US) ˈɪm.plɪ.keɪ.t̬ɪv; ɪmˈplɪk.ə- **-ly** -li

implicature ɪmˈplɪk.ə.tʃəʳ, -tjʊəʳ (US) -tʃɚ **-s** -z

implicit ɪmˈplɪs.ɪt **-ly** -li **-ness** -nəs, -nɪs

implod|e ɪmˈpləʊd (US) -ˈploʊd **-es** -z **-ing** -ɪŋ **-ed** -ɪd

implor|e ɪmˈplɔːʳ (US) -ˈplɔːr **-es** -z **-ing/ly** -ɪŋ/li **-ed** -d **-er/s** -əʳ/z (US) -ɚ/z

implosion ɪmˈpləʊ.ʒᵊn (US) -ˈploʊ- **-s** -z

implosive ɪmˈpləʊ.sɪv, ˌɪm-, -zɪv (US) -ˈploʊ.sɪv **-s** -z

impl|y ɪmˈpl|aɪ **-ies** -aɪz **-ying** -aɪ.ɪŋ **-ied** -aɪd

impolic|y ɪmˈpɒl.ə.s|i, ˌɪm-, ˈ-ɪ- (US) -ˈpɑː.lə- **-ies** -iz

impolite ˌɪm.pᵊlˈaɪt (US) -pəˈlaɪt **-ly** -li **-ness** -nəs, -nɪs

impolitic ɪmˈpɒl.ə.tɪk, ˌɪm-, ˈ-ɪ- (US) -ˈpɑː.lə-

imponderab|le ɪmˈpɒn.dᵊr.ə.b|l̩, ˌɪm- (US) -ˈpɑːn- **-les** -l̩z **-ly** -li **-leness** -l̩.nəs, -nɪs

import (*n.*) ˈɪm.pɔːt (US) -pɔːrt **-s** -s

impor|t (*v.*) ɪmˈpɔː|t, ˌɪm-, ˈ-- (US) ɪmˈpɔːr|t, ˈ-- **-ts** -ts **-ting** -tɪŋ (US) -t̬ɪŋ **-ted** -tɪd (US) -t̬ɪd **-ter/s** -təʳ/z (US) -t̬ɚ/z

importable ɪmˈpɔː.tə.bl̩, ˌɪm- (US) -ˈpɔːr.t̬ə-

importance ɪmˈpɔː.tᵊnts (US) -ˈpɔːr-

important ɪmˈpɔː.tᵊnt (US) -ˈpɔːr- **-ly** -li

importation ˌɪm.pɔːˈteɪ.ʃᵊn (US) -pɔːrˈ- **-s** -z

importunate ɪmˈpɔː.tjʊ.nət, -tʃʊ-, -tʃə-, -ɪt (US) -ˈpɔːr.tʃə.nɪt **-ly** -li **-ness** -nəs, -nɪs

importun|e ˌɪm.pəˈtjuːn, -ˈtʃuːn; ɪmˈpɔː.tjuːn, -tʃuːn (US) ˌɪm.pɔːrˈtuːn, -ˈtjuːn, ɪmˈpɔːr.tʃən **-es** -z **-ing** -ɪŋ **-ed** -d

importunit|y ˌɪm.pɔːˈtjuː.nə.t|i, -nɪ- (US) -pɔːrˈtuː.nə.t̬|i, -ˈtjuː- **-ies** -iz

impos|e ɪmˈpəʊz (US) -ˈpoʊz **-es** -ɪz **-ing** -ɪŋ **-ed** -d **-er/s** -əʳ/z (US) -ɚ/z **-able** -ə.bl̩

imposing ɪmˈpəʊ.zɪŋ (US) -ˈpoʊ- **-ly** -li **-ness** -nəs, -nɪs

imposition ˌɪm.pəˈzɪʃ.ᵊn **-s** -z

impossibilit|y ɪmˌpɒs.əˈbɪl.ə.t|i, ˌɪm.pɒs-, ˌɪmˌpɒs-, -ɪˈ-, -ɪ.t|i (US) ɪmˌpɑː.səˈbɪl.ə.t̬|i, ˌɪm- **-ies** -iz

impossib|le ɪmˈpɒs.ə.b|l̩, ˌɪm-, ˈ-ɪ- (US) -ˈpɑː.sə- **-ly** -li

impost ˈɪm.pəʊst, -pɒst (US) -poʊst **-s** -s

impostor, imposter ɪmˈpɒs.təʳ (US) -ˈpɑː.stɚ **-s** -z

imposture ɪmˈpɒs.tjəʳ, -tʃəʳ (US) -ˈpɑːs.tʃɚ **-s** -z

impoten|ce ˈɪm.pə.tᵊnt|s (US) -t̬ᵊnt|s **-cy** -si

impotent ˈɪm.pə.tᵊnt (US) -t̬ᵊnt **-ly** -li

impound ɪmˈpaʊnd **-s** -z **-ing** -ɪŋ **-ed** -ɪd

impoverish ɪm'pɒv.ᵊr.ɪʃ US -'pɑː.vɚ-, -'pɑːv.rɪʃ **-es** -ɪz **-ing** -ɪŋ **-ed** -t **-ment** -mənt

impracticabilit|y ɪmˌpræk.tɪ.kə'bɪl.ə.t|i, ˌɪm-, -ɪ.t|i US -ə.t̬|i **-ies** -iz

impracticab|le ɪm'præk.tɪ.kə.b|l̩, ˌɪm- **-ly** -li **-leness** -l̩.nəs, -nɪs

impractic|al ɪm'præk.tɪ.k|ᵊl, ˌɪm- **-ally** -ᵊl.i US -li **-alness** -ᵊl.nəs, -nɪs

impracticalit|y ɪmˌpræk.tɪ'kæl.ə.t|i, ˌɪm.præk-, ˌɪmˌpræk-, -ɪ.t|i US ɪmˌpræk.tɪ'kæl.ə.t̬|i, ˌɪm- **-ies** -iz

impre|cate 'ɪm.prɪ|.keɪt, -prə- **-cates** -keɪts **-cating** -keɪ.tɪŋ US -keɪ.t̬ɪŋ **-cated** -keɪ.tɪd US -keɪ.t̬ɪd **-cator/s** -keɪ.təʳ/z US -keɪ.t̬ɚ/z

imprecation ˌɪm.prɪ'keɪ.ʃᵊn, -prə'-, -prek'eɪ- US -prɪ'keɪ- **-s** -z

imprecatory 'ɪm.prɪ.keɪ.tᵊr.i, ˌɪm.prɪ'keɪ-; ɪm'prek.ə- US 'ɪm.prɪ.kə.tɔːr.i

imprecise ˌɪm.prɪ'saɪs, -prə'- **-ly** -li **-ness** -nəs, -nɪs

imprecision ˌɪm.prɪ'sɪʒ.ᵊn, -prə'-

impregnability ɪmˌpreg.nə'bɪl.ə.ti, ˌɪm-, -ɪ.ti US -ə.t̬i

impregnab|le ɪm'preg.nə.b|l̩ **-ly** -li

impregnate (*adj.*) ɪm'preg.nɪt, -nət, -neɪt

impregna|te (*v.*) 'ɪm.preg.neɪ|t, -'-- US ɪm'preg.neɪ|t **-tes** -ts **-ting** -tɪŋ US -t̬ɪŋ **-ted** -tɪd US -t̬ɪd

impregnation ˌɪm.preg'neɪ.ʃᵊn, -prɪg'- US -preg'- **-s** -z

impresario ˌɪm.prɪ'sɑː.ri.əʊ, -prə'-, -pres'ɑː-, -'ɑː- US ˌɪm.prə'sɑːr.i.oʊ, -'ser- **-s** -z

imprescriptible ˌɪm.prɪ'skrɪp.tə.bl̩

impress (*n.*) 'ɪm.pres **-es** -ɪz

impress (*v.*) ɪm'pres **-es** -ɪz **-ing** -ɪŋ **-ed** -t

impressibility ɪmˌpres.ɪ'bɪl.ə.ti, -ə'-, -ɪ.ti US -ə.t̬i

impressib|le ɪm'pres.ə.b|l̩, '-ɪ- **-ly** -li **-leness** -l̩.nəs, -nɪs

impression ɪm'preʃ.ᵊn **-s** -z

impressionability ɪmˌpreʃ.ᵊn.ə'bɪl.ə.ti, -ˌpreʃ.nə'-, -ɪ.ti US -ə.t̬i

impressionab|le ɪm'preʃ.ᵊn.ə.b|l̩, -'preʃ.nə- **-ly** -li

impression|ism (I) ɪm'preʃ.ᵊn|.ɪ.zᵊm **-ist/s** -ɪst/s

impressionistic ɪmˌpreʃ.ᵊn'ɪs.tɪk **-ally** -ᵊl.i, -li

impressive ɪm'pres.ɪv **-ly** -li **-ness** -nəs, -nɪs

impressment ɪm'pres.mənt **-s** -s

imprest 'ɪm.prest, -'- **-s** -s

imprimatur ˌɪm.prɪ'meɪ.təʳ, -praɪ'-, -'mɑː-, -tʊəʳ, -tɜːʳ US -prɪ'mɑː.tɚ, -'meɪ-, -tʊr **-s** -z

imprint (*n.*) 'ɪm.prɪnt **-s** -s

im|print (*v.*) ɪm|'prɪnt, ˌɪm- **-prints** -'prɪnts **-printing** -'prɪn.tɪŋ US -'prɪn.t̬ɪŋ **-printed** -'prɪn.tɪd US -'prɪn.t̬ɪd

imprison ɪm'prɪz.ᵊn, ˌɪm- **-s** -z **-ing** -ɪŋ, -'prɪz.nɪŋ **-ed** -d

imprisonment ɪm'prɪz.ᵊn.mənt, -ᵊm- US -ᵊn-

improbabilit|y ɪmˌprɒb.ə'bɪl.ə.t|i, ˌɪm.prɒb-, ˌɪmˌprɒb-, -ɪ.ti US ˌɪm.prɑː.bə'bɪl.ə.t̬|i **-ies** -iz

improbab|le ɪm'prɒb.ə.b|l̩, ˌɪm- US -'prɑː.bə- **-ly** -li

improbity ɪm'prəʊ.bə.ti, ˌɪm-, -bɪ- US -'proʊ.bə.t̬i

impromptu ɪm'prɒmp.tjuː, -tʃuː US -'prɑːmp.tuː, -tjuː **-s** -z

improper ɪm'prɒp.əʳ, ˌɪm- US -'prɑː.pɚ **-ly** -li ˌ**improper 'fraction, imˌproper 'fraction**

impropri|ate ɪm'prəʊ.pri|.eɪt US -'proʊ- **-ates** -eɪts **-ating** -eɪ.tɪŋ US -eɪ.t̬ɪŋ **-ated** -eɪ.tɪd US -eɪ.t̬ɪd **-ator/s** -eɪ.təʳ/z US -eɪ.t̬ɚ/z

impropriation ɪmˌprəʊ.pri'eɪ.ʃᵊn, ˌɪm.prəʊ-, ˌɪmˌprəʊ- US ɪmˌproʊ-, ˌɪm- **-s** -z

impropriet|y ˌɪm.prə'praɪ.ə.t|i US -t̬|i **-ies** -iz

improvability ɪmˌpruː.və'bɪl.ə.ti, -ɪ.ti US -ə.t̬i

improvab|le ɪm'pruː.və.b|l̩ **-ly** -li **-leness** -l̩.nəs, -nɪs

improv|e ɪm'pruːv **-es** -z **-ing** -ɪŋ **-ed** -d **-er/s** -əʳ/z US -ɚ/z

improvement ɪm'pruːv.mənt **-s** -s

improvidence ɪm'prɒv.ɪ.dᵊnts, ˌɪm-, '-ə- US -'prɑː.və-

improvident ɪm'prɒv.ɪ.dᵊnt, ˌɪm- US -'prɑː.və- **-ly** -li

improvisation ˌɪm.prə.vaɪ'zeɪ.ʃᵊn US ɪmˌprɑː.vɪ'-; ˌɪm.prə- **-s** -z

improvisatory ˌɪm.prə.vaɪ'zeɪ.tᵊr.i; -'vaɪ.zə- US ɪm'prɑː.və.zə.tɔːr-; ˌɪm.prə'vaɪ-

improvis|e 'ɪm.prə.vaɪz **-es** -ɪz **-ing** -ɪŋ **-ed** -d **-er/s** -əʳ/z US -ɚ/z **-or/s** -əʳ/z US -ɚ/z

imprudence ɪm'pruː.dᵊnts, ˌɪm-

imprudent ɪm'pruː.dᵊnt, ˌɪm- **-ly** -li

impudence 'ɪm.pjə.dᵊnts, -pjʊ-

impudent 'ɪm.pjə.dᵊnt, -pjʊ- **-ly** -li

impugn ɪm'pjuːn **-s** -z **-ing** -ɪŋ **-ed** -d **-er/s** -əʳ/z US -ɚ/z **-able** -ə.bl̩ **-ment** -mənt

impuissan|ce ɪm'pjuː.ɪ.sᵊn|ts US -'pjuː.ɪ-, -'pwɪ.sᵊnts; ˌɪm.pjuː'ɪs.ᵊnts **-t** -t

impuls|e 'ɪm.pʌls **-es** -ɪz '**impulse ˌbuying**

impulsion ɪm'pʌl.ʃᵊn **-s** -z

impulsive ɪm'pʌl.sɪv **-ly** -li **-ness** -nəs, -nɪs

impunit|y ɪm'pjuː.nə.t|i, -nɪ- US -t̬|i **-ies** -iz

impure ɪm'pjʊəʳ, ˌɪm-, -'pjɔːʳ US -'pjʊr **-ly** -li **-ness** -nəs, -nɪs

impurit|y ɪm'pjʊə.rə.t|i, ˌɪm-, -'pjɔː-, -rɪ- US -'pjʊr.ə.t̬|i **-ies** -iz

imputability ɪmˌpjuː.tə'bɪl.ə.ti, ˌɪm.pjuː-, ˌɪmˌpjuː-, -ɪ.ti US ɪmˌpjuː.t̬ə'bɪl.ə.t̬i, ˌɪm-

imputation ˌɪm.pjʊ'teɪ.ʃᵊn **-s** -z

im|pute ɪm|'pjuːt **-putes** -'pjuːts **-puting** -'pjuː.tɪŋ US -'pjuː.t̬ɪŋ **-puted** -'pjuː.tɪd US -'pjuː.t̬ɪd **-putable** -'pjuː.tə.bl̩ US -'pjuː.t̬ə.bl̩

Imray 'ɪm.reɪ

Imrie 'ɪm.ri

IMRO 'ɪm.rəʊ US -roʊ

in- ɪn-

Note: Prefix. When the meaning of the prefix is "in", it often carries secondary stress, e.g. **inbuilt** /ˌɪn'bɪlt/. The resulting compounds may undergo stress-shift (see entry for **inbuilt**). As a negative prefix, **in-** does not normally affect the stress pattern of the stem to which it is added, e.g. **active** /'æk.tɪv/, **inactive** /ɪn'æk.tɪv/. In other cases, the prefix is normally stressed in nouns but not in verbs, e.g. **increase** noun /'ɪn.kriːs /, verb /ɪn'kriːs/.

in ɪn ˌ**ins and 'outs**

in. (*abbrev. for* **inch/es**) *singular:* ɪntʃ *plural:* -ɪz

Ina 'iː.nə, 'aɪ- US 'aɪ-

inabilit|y ˌɪn.ə'bɪl.ə.t|i, -ɪ.t|i US -ə.t̬|i **-ies** -iz

in absentia ˌɪn.æb'sen.ti.ə, -tʃi-, -ɑː US -'sen.tʃə, -tʃi.ə

inaccessibility ˌɪn.əkˌses.ə'bɪl.ə.ti, -ækˌ-, -ɪ'-, -ɪ.ti US -ə.t̬i

inaccessib|le ˌɪn.ək'ses.ə.b|l̩, -æk'-, '-ɪ- **-ly** -li **-leness** -l̩.nəs, -nɪs

inaccurac|y ɪn'æk.jə.rə.s|i, ˌɪn-, -jʊ-, -rɪ.s|i US -jɚ.ə- **-ies** -iz

inaccurate ɪn'æk.jə.rət, ˌɪn-, -jʊ-, -rɪt US -jɚ.ət **-ly** -li

inaction ɪn'æk.ʃᵊn, ˌɪn-

inacti|vate ɪn'æk.tɪ|.veɪt, ˌɪn-, -tə- **-vates** -veɪts **-vating** -veɪ.tɪŋ US -veɪ.t̬ɪŋ **-vated** -veɪ.tɪd US -veɪ.t̬ɪd

inactive ɪn'æk.tɪv, ˌɪn- **-ly** -li

inactivity ˌɪn.æk'tɪv.ə.ti, -ɪ.ti US -ə.t̬i

inadequac|y ɪ'næd.ɪ.kwə.s|i, ˌɪn'æd-, '-ə- **-ies** -iz

inadequate ɪ'næd.ɪ.kwət, ˌɪn'æd-, -kwɪt **-ly** -li **-ness** -nəs, -nɪs

inadmissibility ˌɪn.ədˌmɪs.ə'bɪl.ə.ti, -ɪ'-, -ɪ.ti US -ə.t̬i

inadmissib|le ˌɪn.ədˈmɪs.ə.bl̩, ˈ-ɪ- **-ly** -li
inadverten|ce ˌɪn.ədˈvɜː.tənt|s ⓤⓢ -ˈvɝː- **-cy** -si
inadvertent ˌɪn.ədˈvɜː.tənt ⓤⓢ -ˈvɝː- **-ly** -li
inadvisability ˌɪn.ədˌvaɪ.zəˈbɪl.ə.ti, -ɪ.ti ⓤⓢ -ə.t̬i
inadvisable ˌɪn.ədˈvaɪ.zə.bl̩
inalienability ɪˌneɪ.li.ə.nəˈbɪl.ə.ti, ˌɪnˌeɪ-, -ɪ.ti ⓤⓢ -ə.t̬i
inalienab|le ɪˈneɪ.li.ə.nə.bl̩|, ˌɪnˈeɪ- **-ly** -li **-leness** -l̩.nəs, -nɪs
inamora|ta ɪˌnæm.əˈrɑː|.tə, ˌɪn.æm- ⓤⓢ -ˈrɑː|.t̬ə, -ˌnæm- **-as** -təz ⓤⓢ -t̬əz **-o/s** -təʊ/z ⓤⓢ -toʊ/z
inane ɪˈneɪn **-ly** -li **-ness** -nəs, -nɪs
inanimate ɪˈnæn.ɪ.mət, ˌɪnˈæn-, -mɪt **-ly** -li **-ness** -nəs, -nɪs
inanition ˌɪn.əˈnɪʃ.ən, -ænˈɪʃ-
inanit|y ɪˈnæn.ə.t|i, -ɪ.t|i ⓤⓢ -ə.t̬|i **-ies** -iz
inappeasable ˌɪn.əˈpiː.zə.bl̩
inapplicability ɪˌnæp.lɪ.kəˈbɪl.ə.ti, ˌɪnˌæp-, -ɪ.ti; ˌɪn.əˌplɪk.əˈ- ⓤⓢ ɪˌnæp.lɪ.kəˈbɪl.ə.t̬i, ˌɪnˌæp-; ˌɪn.ə.plɪ.kəˈbɪl.ə.ti
inapplicable ˌɪn.əˈplɪk.ə.bl̩; ɪˈnæp.lɪ.kə-, ˌɪnˈæp- ⓤⓢ ɪˈnæp-, ˌɪnˈæp-; ˌɪn.əˈplɪk.ə- **-ness** -nəs, -nɪs
inapposite ɪˈnæp.ə.zɪt, ˌɪnˈæp- **-ly** -li **-ness** -nəs, -nɪs
inappreciab|le ˌɪn.əˈpriː.ʃi.ə.bl̩|, -ʃə- **-ly** -li
inapprehensible ɪnˌæp.rɪˈhent.sə.bl̩, ˈ-sɪ-
inapproachab|le ˌɪn.əˈprəʊ.tʃə.bl̩| ⓤⓢ -ˈproʊ- **-ly** -li
inappropriate ˌɪn.əˈprəʊ.pri.ət, -ɪt ⓤⓢ -ˈproʊ- **-ly** -li **-ness** -nəs, -nɪs
inapt ɪˈnæpt, ˌɪnˈæpt **-ly** -li **-ness** -nəs, -nɪs
inaptitude ɪˈnæp.tɪ.tjuːd, ˌɪnˈæp- ⓤⓢ -tə.tuːd, -tjuːd
inarguab|le ɪˈnɑː.gju.ə.bl̩|, ˌɪnˈɑː- ⓤⓢ ˌɪnˈɑːr- **-ly** -li
inarticulate ˌɪn.ɑːˈtɪk.jə.lət, -jʊ-, -lɪt ⓤⓢ -ɑːrˈ- **-ly** -li **-ness** -nəs, -nɪs
inartistic ˌɪn.ɑːˈtɪs.tɪk ⓤⓢ -ɑːrˈ- **-al** -əl **-ally** -əl.i, -li
inasmuch ˌɪn.əzˈmʌtʃ
inattention ˌɪn.əˈten.*t*ʃən
inattentive ˌɪn.əˈten.tɪv ⓤⓢ -t̬ɪv **-ly** -li **-ness** -nəs, -nɪs
inaudibility ɪˌnɔː.dəˈbɪl.ə.ti, ˌɪn.ɔː-, -dɪˈ-, -ɪ.ti ⓤⓢ ɪˌnɑː.dɪˈbɪl.ə.t̬i, ˌɪnˌɑː-, ɪˌnɔː-, ˌɪnˌɔː-
inaudib|le ɪˈnɔː.də.bl̩|, ˌɪn.ɔː-, -dɪ- ⓤⓢ ɪˈnɑː-, ˌɪnˈɑː-, ɪˈnɔː-, ˌɪnˈɔː- **-ly** -li **-leness** -l̩.nəs, -nɪs
inaugural ɪˈnɔː.gjə.rəl, -jʊ- ⓤⓢ ɪˈnɑː.gjʊr.əl, -ˈnɔː.g-, -jɚ-, ˈ-ɚ-
inaugu|rate ɪˈnɔː.gjə|.reɪt, -jʊ- ⓤⓢ ɪˈnɑː.gjʊ|.reɪt, ɪˈnɔː.g-, -jə-, ˈ-ə- **-rates** -reɪts **-rating** -reɪ.tɪŋ ⓤⓢ -reɪ.t̬ɪŋ **-rated** -reɪ.tɪd ⓤⓢ -reɪ.t̬ɪd **-rator/s** -reɪ.təʳ/z ⓤⓢ -reɪ.t̬ɚ/z
inauguration ɪˌnɔː.gjəˈreɪ.ʃən, -jʊˈ- ⓤⓢ ɪˌnɑː.gjʊˈ-, -ˌnɔː.g-, -jəˈ-, -əˈ- **-s** -z
inauspicious ˌɪn.ɔːˈspɪʃ.əs, -ɒsˈpɪʃ- ⓤⓢ -ɑːˈspɪʃ-, -ɔːˈ- **-ly** -li **-ness** -nəs, -nɪs
inboard ˌɪnˈbɔːd, ˌɪm- ⓤⓢ ˈɪn.bɔːrd *stress shift, British only:* ˌinboard ˈmotor
inborn ˌɪnˈbɔːn, ˌɪm- ⓤⓢ ˈɪn.bɔːrn *stress shift, British only:* ˌinborn ˈtalent
inbox ˈɪn.bɒks, ˈɪm- ⓤⓢ ˈɪn.bɑːks **-es** -ɪz
inbreath|e ˌɪnˈbriːð, ˌɪm- ⓤⓢ ˌɪn- **-es** -z **-ing** -ɪŋ **-ed** -d
inbreed ˌɪnˈbriːd, ˌɪm- ⓤⓢ ˈɪn.briːd **-s** -z **-ing** -ɪŋ **inbred** ˌɪnˈbred, ˌɪm- ⓤⓢ ˈɪn.bred *stress shift, British only:* ˌinbred ˈtrait
inbuilt ˌɪnˈbɪlt, ˌɪm-, ˈ-- ⓤⓢ ˈɪn.bɪlt *stress shift, British only:* ˌinbuilt ˈhazard
inc. *(abbrev. for* **incorporated***)* ɪŋˈkɔː.pər.eɪ.tɪd, ɪŋk ⓤⓢ ɪnˈkɔːr.pə.reɪ.t̬ɪd, ɪŋk
Inca ˈɪŋ.kə **-s** -z
incalculability ɪnˌkæl.kjə.ləˈbɪl.ə.ti, ˌɪn-, ɪŋ-, ˌɪŋ-, -kjʊ-, -ɪ.ti ⓤⓢ ɪnˌkæl.kjə.ləˈbɪl.ə.t̬i, ˌɪn-, -kjʊ-
incalculab|le ɪnˈkæl.kjə.lə.bl̩|, ˌɪn-, ɪŋ-, ˌɪŋ-, -kjʊ- ⓤⓢ ɪnˈkæl-, ˌɪn- **-ly** -li **-leness** -l̩.nəs, -nɪs
in camera ˌɪnˈkæm.ər.ə, ˌɪŋ-, ˈ-rə ⓤⓢ ˌɪn-
incandescence ˌɪn.kænˈdes.ənts, ˌɪŋ-, -kənˈ- ⓤⓢ ˌɪn.kənˈ-
incandescent ˌɪn.kænˈdes.ənt, ˌɪŋ-, -kənˈ- ⓤⓢ ˌɪn.kənˈ- **-ly** -li
incantation ˌɪn.kænˈteɪ.ʃən, ˌɪŋ- ⓤⓢ ˌɪn- **-s** -z
incapabilit|y ɪnˌkeɪ.pəˈbɪl.ə.t|i, ˌɪn-, ɪŋ-, ˌɪŋ-, -ɪ.t|i ⓤⓢ ɪnˌkeɪ.pəˈbɪl.ə.t̬|i, ˌɪn- **-ies** -iz
incapab|le ɪnˈkeɪ.pə.bl̩|, ˌɪn-, ɪŋ-, ˌɪŋ- ⓤⓢ ɪnˈkeɪ-, ˌɪn- **-ly** -li **-leness** -l̩.nəs, -nɪs
incapaci|tate ˌɪn.kəˈpæs.ɪ|.teɪt, ˌɪŋ-, ˈ-ə- ⓤⓢ ˌɪn- **-tates** -teɪts **-tating** -teɪ.tɪŋ ⓤⓢ -teɪ.t̬ɪŋ **-tated** -teɪ.tɪd ⓤⓢ -teɪ.t̬ɪd
incapacitation ˌɪn.kəˌpæs.ɪˈteɪ.ʃən, ˌɪŋ-, -əˈ- ⓤⓢ ˌɪn- **-s** -z
incapacit|y ˌɪn.kəˈpæs.ə.t|i, ˌɪŋ-, -ɪ.t|i ⓤⓢ ˌɪn.kəˈpæs.ə.t̬|i **-ies** -iz
in capite ˌɪnˈkæp.ɪ.teɪ ⓤⓢ -teɪ, -ti
incarcer|ate ɪnˈkɑː.sər|.eɪt, ɪŋ- ⓤⓢ ɪnˈkɑːr.sə.r|eɪt **-ates** -eɪts **-ating** -eɪ.tɪŋ ⓤⓢ -eɪ.t̬ɪŋ **-ated** -eɪ.tɪd ⓤⓢ -eɪ.t̬ɪd
incarceration ɪnˌkɑː.sərˈeɪ.ʃən, ˌɪn.kɑː-, ˌɪnˌkɑː-, ɪŋˌkɑː-, ˌɪŋ.kɑː- ⓤⓢ ɪnˌkɑːr.səˈreɪ-, ˌɪn- **-s** -z
incarnadine ɪnˈkɑː.nə.daɪn, ɪŋ- ⓤⓢ ɪnˈkɑːr-, -diːn, -dɪn
incarnate *(adj.)* ɪnˈkɑː.nət, ɪŋ-, -neɪt, -nɪt ⓤⓢ ɪnˈkɑːr-
incar|nate *(v.)* ˈɪn.kɑː|.neɪt, ˈɪŋ-, -ˈ-- ⓤⓢ ɪnˈkɑːr- **-nates** -neɪts **-nating** -neɪ.tɪŋ ⓤⓢ -neɪ.t̬ɪŋ **-nated** -neɪ.tɪd ⓤⓢ -neɪ.t̬ɪd
incarnation (I) ˌɪn.kɑːˈneɪ.ʃən, ˌɪŋ- ⓤⓢ ˌɪn.kɑːrˈ- **-s** -z
incautious ɪnˈkɔː.ʃəs, ˌɪn-, ɪŋ-, ˌɪŋ- ⓤⓢ ɪnˈkɑː-, ˌɪn-, -ˈkɔː- **-ly** -li **-ness** -nəs, -nɪs
Ince ɪn*t*s
Ince-in-Makerfield ˌɪn*t*s.ɪnˈmeɪ.kə.fiːld ⓤⓢ -kɚ-
incendiar|y ɪnˈsen.di.ər|.i, -djər- ⓤⓢ -di.er|.i, -ɚ|.i **-ies** -iz **-ism** -ɪ.zəm
incense *(n.)* ˈɪn.sen*t*s
incens|e *(v.) enrage:* ɪnˈsen*t*s **-es** -ɪz **-ing** -ɪŋ **-ed** -t
incens|e *(v.) burn incense:* ˈɪn.sen*t*s **-es** -ɪz **-ing** -ɪŋ **-ed** -t
incentive ɪnˈsen.tɪv ⓤⓢ -t̬ɪv **-s** -z
incept ɪnˈsept **-s** -s **-ing** -ɪŋ **-ed** -ɪd **-or/s** -əʳ/z ⓤⓢ -ɚ/z **-ive** -ɪv
inception ɪnˈsep.ʃən **-s** -z
incertitude ɪnˈsɜː.tɪ.tjuːd, ˌɪn- ⓤⓢ -ˈsɝː.t̬ɪ.tuːd, -tjuːd **-s** -z
incessant ɪnˈses.ənt **-ly** -li
incest ˈɪn.sest
incestuous ɪnˈses.tju.əs, -tʃu- ⓤⓢ -tʃu- **-ly** -li **-ness** -nəs, -nɪs
inch (I) ɪn*t*ʃ **-es** -ɪz **-ing** -ɪŋ **-ed** -t **ˌgive him an ˌinch and he'll ˌtake a ˈmile; not ˌbudge an ˈinch**
Inchcape ˈɪn*t*ʃ.keɪp, ˌ-ˈ-
Inchinnan ɪnˈʃɪn.ən
inchoate *(adj.)* ɪnˈkəʊ.eɪt, ɪŋ-, -ɪt, ˈ--- ⓤⓢ ɪnˈkoʊ- **-ly** -li
incho|ate *(v.)* ˈɪn.kəʊ|.eɪt, ˈɪŋ- ⓤⓢ ˈɪn.koʊ- **-ates** -eɪts **-ating** -eɪ.tɪŋ ⓤⓢ -eɪ.t̬ɪŋ **-ated** -eɪ.tɪd ⓤⓢ -eɪ.t̬ɪd
inchoation ˌɪn.kəʊˈeɪ.ʃən, ˌɪŋ- ⓤⓢ ˌɪn.koʊˈ-
inchoative ˈɪn.kəʊ.eɪ.tɪv, ˈɪŋ-; ɪnˈkəʊ.ə.tɪv, ɪŋ- ⓤⓢ ɪnˈkoʊ.ə.t̬ɪv
Inchon ˌɪnˈtʃɒn ⓤⓢ ˈɪn.tʃɑːn
inchworm ˈɪn*t*ʃ.wɜːm ⓤⓢ -wɝːm **-s** -z
incidence ˈɪn*t*.sɪ.dən*t*s
incident ˈɪn*t*.sɪ.dənt **-s** -s
incident|al ˌɪn*t*.sɪˈden.t|əl ⓤⓢ -t̬|əl **-ly** -əl.i, -li **-ness** -nəs, -nɪs **-s** -z *stress shift:* ˌincidental ˈmusic
inciner|ate ɪnˈsɪn.ər|.eɪt ⓤⓢ -ə.r|eɪt **-ates** -eɪts **-ating** -eɪ.tɪŋ ⓤⓢ -eɪ.t̬ɪŋ **-ated** -eɪ.tɪd ⓤⓢ -eɪ.t̬ɪd
incineration ɪnˌsɪn.ərˈeɪ.ʃən ⓤⓢ -əˈreɪ-
incinerator ɪnˈsɪn.ər.eɪ.təʳ ⓤⓢ -ə.reɪ.t̬ɚ **-s** -z
incipien|ce ɪnˈsɪp.i.ənt|s **-cy** -si
incipient ɪnˈsɪp.i.ənt **-ly** -li

incis|e ɪn'saɪz **-es** -ɪz **-ing** -ɪŋ **-ed** -d

incision ɪn'sɪʒ.ᵊn **-s** -z

incisive ɪn'saɪ.sɪv **-ly** -li **-ness** -nəs, -nɪs

incisor ɪn'saɪ.zəʳ US -zɚ **-s** -z

incitation ˌɪnt.saɪ'teɪ.ʃᵊn, -sɪ'- US -sə'- **-s** -z

in|cite ɪn|'saɪt **-cites** -'saɪts **-citing** -'saɪ.tɪŋ US -'saɪ.t̬ɪŋ **-cited** -'saɪ.tɪd US -'saɪ.t̬ɪd

incitement ɪn'saɪt.mənt **-s** -s

incivilit|y ˌɪn.sɪ'vɪl.ə.t|i, -sə'-, -ɪ.t|i US -ə.t̬|i **-ies** -iz

incl. *(abbrev. for* **including***)* ɪn'kluː.dɪŋ, ɪŋ- US ɪn- *(abbrev. for* **inclusive***)* ɪn'kluː.sɪv, ɪŋ- US ɪn-

Incledon 'ɪŋ.kl̩.dən

inclemency ɪn'klem.ənt.si, ˌɪn-, ɪŋ-, ˌɪŋ- US ɪn'klem-, ˌɪn-

inclement ɪn'klem.ənt, ˌɪn-, ɪŋ-, ˌɪŋ- US ɪn'klem-, ˌɪn- **-ly** -li

inclination ˌɪn.klɪ'neɪ.ʃᵊn, ˌɪŋ-, -klə'- US ˌɪn- **-s** -z

incline (*n.*) 'ɪn.klaɪn, 'ɪŋ-, ˌ-'- US 'ɪn.klaɪn, ˌ-'- **-s** -z

inclin|e (*v.*) ɪn'klaɪn, ɪŋ- US ɪn- **-es** -z **-ing** -ɪŋ **-ed** -d **-able** -ə.bl̩

inclos|e ɪn'kləʊz, ɪŋ- US ɪn'kloʊz **-es** -ɪz **-ing** -ɪŋ **-ed** -d

inclosure ɪn'kləʊ.ʒəʳ, ɪŋ- US ɪn'kloʊ.ʒɚ **-s** -z

includ|e ɪn'kluːd, ɪŋ- US ɪn- **-es** -z **-ing** -ɪŋ **-ed** -ɪd

inclusion ɪn'kluː.ʒᵊn, ɪŋ- US ɪn- **-s** -z

inclusive ɪn'kluː.sɪv, ɪŋ- US ɪn- **-ly** -li **-ness** -nəs, -nɪs

incognito ˌɪn.kɒg'niː.təʊ, ˌɪŋ-; ɪn'kɒg.nɪ.təʊ, ɪŋ-, -nə- US ˌɪn.kɑːg'niː.toʊ; ɪn'kɑːg.nɪ-, -t̬oʊ **-s** -z

incognizan|ce ɪn'kɒg.nɪ.zᵊn|ts, ɪŋ- US ɪn'kɑːg- **-t** -t

incoherence ˌɪn.kəʊ'hɪə.rᵊnts, ˌɪŋ- US ˌɪn.koʊ'hɪr.ᵊnts, -'her-

incoherent ˌɪn.kəʊ'hɪə.rᵊnt, ˌɪŋ- US ˌɪn.koʊ'hɪr.ᵊnt, -'her- **-ly** -li

incombustibility ˌɪn.kəmˌbʌs.tə'bɪl.ə.ti, ˌɪŋ-, -tɪ'-, -ɪ.ti US ˌɪn.kəmˌbʌs.tə'bɪl.ə.t̬i, -tɪ'-

incombustible ˌɪn.kəm'bʌs.tə.bl̩, ˌɪŋ-, -tɪ- US ˌɪn- **-ness** -nəs, -nɪs

income 'ɪŋ.kʌm, 'ɪn-, -kəm US 'ɪn- **-s** -z ˌincome sup'port, 'income supˌport; 'income ˌtax

incomer 'ɪnˌkʌm.əʳ, 'ɪŋ- US 'ɪnˌkʌm.ɚ **-s** -z

incoming 'ɪnˌkʌm.ɪŋ, 'ɪŋ- US 'ɪnˌkʌm- **-s** -z

incommensurability ˌɪn.kəˌmen.tʃᵊr.ə'bɪl.ə.ti, ˌɪŋ-, -tʃʊr-, -ɪ.ti US ˌɪn.kəˌment.sɚ.ə'bɪl.ə.t̬i, -ʃɚ-

incommensurab|le ˌɪn.kə'men.tʃᵊr.ə.b|l̩, ˌɪŋ-, -tʃʊr- US ˌɪn.kə'ment.sɚ-, -ʃɚ- **-les** -l̩z **-ly** -li **-leness** -l̩.nəs, -nɪs

incommensurate ˌɪn.kə'men.tʃᵊr.ət, ˌɪŋ-, -tʃʊr-, -ɪt US ˌɪn.kə'ment.sɚ-, -ʃɚ- **-ly** -li **-ness** -nəs, -nɪs

incommod|e ˌɪn.kə'məʊd, ˌɪŋ- US ˌɪn.kə'moʊd **-es** -z **-ing** -ɪŋ **-ed** -ɪd

incommodious ˌɪn.kə'məʊ.di.əs, ˌɪŋ- US ˌɪn.kə'moʊ- **-ly** -li **-ness** -nəs, -nɪs

incommunicab|le ˌɪn.kə'mjuː.nɪ.kə.b|l̩, ˌɪŋ- US ˌɪn- **-ly** -li **-leness** -l̩.nəs, -nɪs

incommunicado ˌɪn.kəˌmjuː.nɪ'kɑː.dəʊ, ˌɪŋ-, -nə'- US ˌɪn.kəˌmjuː.nɪ'kɑː.doʊ, -nə'-

incommutab|le ˌɪn.kə'mjuː.tə.b|l̩, ˌɪŋ- US ˌɪn.kə'mjuː.t̬ə.b|l̩ **-ly** -li **-leness** -l̩.nəs, -nɪs

incomparability ɪnˌkɒm.pᵊr.ə'bɪl.ə.ti, ɪŋ-, -ɪ.ti US ɪnˌkɑːm.pɚ.ə'bɪl.ə.t̬i

incomparab|le ɪn'kɒm.pᵊr.ə.b|l̩, ɪŋ- US ɪn'kɑːm- **-ly** -li **-leness** -l̩.nəs, -nɪs

incompatibilit|y ˌɪn.kəmˌpæt.ə'bɪl.ə.t|i, ˌɪŋ-, -ɪ'-, -ɪ.t|i US ˌɪn.kəmˌpæt̬.ə'bɪl.ə.t̬|i **-ies** -iz

incompatib|le ˌɪn.kəm'pæt.ə.b|l̩, ˌɪŋ-, '-ɪ- US ˌɪn.kəm'pæt̬- **-ly** -li **-leness** -l̩.nəs, -nɪs

incompeten|ce ɪn'kɒm.pɪ.tᵊnt|s, ˌɪn-, ɪŋ-, ˌɪŋ-, -pə- US ɪn'kɑːm.pə.t̬ənt|s, ˌɪn- **-cy** -si

incompetent ɪn'kɒm.pɪ.tᵊnt, ˌɪn-, ɪŋ-, ˌɪŋ-, -pə- US ɪn'kɑːm.pə.t̬ənt, ˌɪn- **-ly** -li

incomplete ˌɪn.kəm'pliːt, ˌɪŋ- US ˌɪn- **-ly** -li **-ness** -nəs, -nɪs

incompletion ˌɪn.kəm'pliː.ʃᵊn, ˌɪŋ- US ˌɪn-

incomprehensibility ɪnˌkɒm.prɪˌhent.sə'bɪl.ə.ti, ˌɪn-, ɪŋ-, ˌɪŋ-, -prəˌ-, -sɪ'-, -ɪ.ti US ˌɪn.kɑːm.prɪ.hent.sə'bɪl.ə.t̬i

incomprehensib|le ɪnˌkɒm.prɪ'hent.sə.b|l̩, ˌɪn-, ɪŋ-, ˌɪŋ-, -sɪ- US ˌɪn.kɑːm- **-ly** -li **-leness** -l̩.nəs, -nɪs

incomprehension ɪnˌkɒm.prɪ'hen.tʃᵊn, ˌɪn-, ɪŋ-, ˌɪŋ-, -prə'- US ˌɪn.kɑːm-

incompressibility ˌɪn.kəmˌpres.ə'bɪl.ə.ti, ˌɪŋ-, -ɪ'-, -ɪ.ti US ˌɪn.kəmˌpres.ə'bɪl.ə.t̬i

incompressible ˌɪn.kəm'pres.ə.bl̩, ˌɪŋ-, '-ɪ- US ˌɪn- **-ness** -nəs, -nɪs

incomputab|le ˌɪn.kəm'pjuː.tə.b|l̩, ˌɪŋ-; ɪn'kɒm.pjə.tə.b|l̩, ˌɪn-, ɪŋ-, ˌɪŋ-, -pjʊ- US ˌɪn.kəm'pjuː.t̬ə- **-ly** -li

inconceivability ˌɪn.kənˌsiː.və'bɪl.ə.ti, ˌɪŋ-, -ɪ.ti US ˌɪn.kənˌsiː.və'bɪl.ə.t̬i

inconceivab|le ˌɪn.kən'siː.və.b|l̩, ˌɪŋ- US ˌɪn- **-ly** -li **-leness** -l̩.nəs, -nɪs

inconclusive ˌɪn.kən'kluː.sɪv, ˌɪŋ-, -kəŋ'- US ˌɪn.kən'- **-ly** -li **-ness** -nəs, -nɪs

incondite ɪn'kɒn.dɪt, ɪŋ-, -daɪt US ɪn'kɑːn-

incongruent ɪn'kɒŋ.gru.ənt, ɪŋ- US ɪn'kɑːŋ-; ˌɪn.kən'gruː- **-ly** -li

incongruit|y ˌɪn.kɒŋ'gruː.ə.t|i, ˌɪŋ-, -ɪ.t|i US ˌɪn.kən'gruː.ə.t̬|i **-ies** -iz

incongruous ɪn'kɒŋ.gru.əs, ɪŋ- US ɪn'kɑːŋ- **-ly** -li **-ness** -nəs, -nɪs

inconsequenc|e ɪn'kɒnt.sɪ.kwənts, ɪŋ-, -sə- US ɪn'kɑːnt- **-es** -ɪz

inconsequent ɪn'kɒnt.sɪ.kwənt, ɪŋ-, -sə- US ɪn'kɑːnt- **-ly** -li

inconsequential ɪnˌkɒnt.sɪ'kwen.tʃᵊl, ˌɪn-, ɪŋ-, ˌɪŋ-, -sə'- US ɪnˌkɑːnt- **-ly** -i

inconsiderab|le ˌɪn.kən'sɪd.ᵊr.ə.b|l̩, ˌɪŋ- US ˌɪn- **-ly** -li **-leness** -l̩.nəs, -nɪs

inconsiderate ˌɪn.kən'sɪd.ᵊr.ət, ˌɪŋ-, -ɪt US ˌɪn- **-ly** -li **-ness** -nəs, -nɪs

inconsideration ˌɪn.kənˌsɪd.ə'reɪ.ʃᵊn, ˌɪŋ- US ˌɪn-

inconsistenc|y ˌɪn.kən'sɪs.tᵊnt.s|i, ˌɪŋ- US ˌɪn- **-ies** -iz

inconsistent ˌɪn.kən'sɪs.tənt, ˌɪŋ- US ˌɪn- **-ly** -li

inconsolab|le ˌɪn.kən'səʊ.lə.b|l̩, ˌɪŋ- US ˌɪn.kən'soʊ- **-ly** -li **-leness** -l̩.nəs, -nɪs

inconsonant ɪn'kɒnt.sə.nənt, ɪŋ- US ɪn'kɑːnt-

inconspicuous ˌɪn.kən'spɪk.ju.əs, ˌɪŋ- US ˌɪn- **-ly** -li **-ness** -nəs, -nɪs

inconstanc|y ɪn'kɒnt.stᵊnt.s|i, ˌɪn-, ɪŋ-, ˌɪŋ- US ɪn'kɑːnt-, ˌɪn- **-ies** -iz

inconstant ɪn'kɒnt.stənt, ˌɪn-, ɪŋ-, ˌɪŋ- US ɪn'kɑːnt-, ˌɪn- **-ly** -li

incontestability ˌɪn.kənˌtes.tə'bɪl.ə.ti, ˌɪŋ-, -ɪ.ti US ˌɪn.kənˌtes.tə'bɪl.ə.t̬i

incontestab|le ˌɪn.kən'tes.tə.b|l̩, ˌɪŋ- US ˌɪn- **-ly** -li

incontinence ɪn'kɒn.tɪ.nənts, ˌɪn-, ɪŋ-, ˌɪŋ-, -tə- US ɪn'kɑːn.tᵊn.ᵊnts, ˌɪn-

incontinent ɪn'kɒn.tɪ.nənt, ˌɪn-, ɪŋ-, ˌɪŋ-, -tə- US ɪn'kɑːn.tᵊn.ᵊnt, ˌɪn- **-ly** -li

incontrollab|le ˌɪn.kən'trəʊ.lə.b|l̩, ˌɪŋ- US ˌɪn.kən'troʊ- **-ly** -li

incontrovertibility ˌɪnˌkɒn.trəˌvɜː.tə'bɪl.ə.ti, ˌɪŋ-, -tɪ'-, -ɪ.ti US ˌɪn.kɑːn.trəˌvɝː.t̬ə'bɪl.ə.t̬i

incontrovertib|le ˌɪnˌkɒn.trə'vɜː.tə.b|l̩, ˌɪŋ-, -tɪ- US ˌɪnˌkɑːn.trə'vɝː.t̬ə- **-ly** -li

inconvenienc|e ˌɪn.kən'viː.ni.ənts, ˌɪŋ- US ˌɪn-, '-njənts **-es** -ɪz **-ing** -ɪŋ **-ed** -t

inconvenient ˌɪn.kən'viː.ni.ənt, ˌɪŋ- US ˌɪn-, '-njənt **-ly** -li

inconvertibility ˌɪn.kənˌvɜː.təˈbɪl.ə.ti, ˌɪŋ-, -tɪˈ-, -ɪ.ti (US) ˌɪn.kənˌvɝː.t̬əˈbɪl.ə.t̬i

inconvertib|le ˌɪn.kənˈvɜː.tə.bl̩, ˌɪŋ-, -tɪ- (US) ˌɪn.kənˈvɝː.t̬ə- **-ly** -li

incorporate *(adj.)* ɪnˈkɔː.pᵊr.ət, ˌɪn-, ɪŋ-, ˌɪŋ-, -ɪt (US) ɪnˈkɔːr-, ˌɪn-

incorpor|ate *(v.)* ɪnˈkɔː.pᵊr|.eɪt, ɪŋ- (US) ɪnˈkɔːr.pə.r|eɪt **-ates** -eɪts **-ating** -eɪ.tɪŋ (US) -eɪ.t̬ɪŋ **-ated** -eɪ.tɪd (US) -eɪ.t̬ɪd

incorporation ɪnˌkɔː.pᵊrˈeɪ.ʃᵊn, ɪŋ- (US) ɪnˌkɔːr.pəˈreɪ- **-s** -z

incorporeal ˌɪn.kɔːˈpɔː.ri.əl, ˌɪŋ- (US) ˌɪn.kɔːrˈpɔːr.i- **-ly** -i

incorrect ˌɪn.kᵊrˈekt, ˌɪŋ- (US) ˌɪn.kəˈrekt **-ly** -li **-ness** -nəs, -nɪs

incorrigibility ɪnˌkɒr.ɪ.dʒəˈbɪl.ə.ti, ɪŋ-, -dʒɪˈ-, -ɪ.ti (US) ɪnˌkɔːr.ə.dʒəˈbɪl.ə.t̬i

incorrigib|le ɪnˈkɒr.ɪ.dʒə.bl̩, ɪŋ-, -dʒɪ- (US) ɪnˈkɔːr.ə.dʒə- **-ly** -li **-leness** -l̩.nəs, -nɪs

incorruptibility ˌɪn.kəˌrʌp.təˈbɪl.ə.ti, ˌɪŋ-, -tɪˈ-, -ɪ.ti (US) ˌɪn.kəˌrʌp.təˈbɪl.ə.t̬i

incorruptib|le ˌɪn.kəˈrʌp.tə.bl̩, ˌɪŋ-, -tɪ- (US) ˌɪn- **-ly** -li **-leness** -l̩.nəs, -nɪs

incorruption ˌɪn.kəˈrʌp.ʃᵊn, ˌɪŋ- (US) ˌɪn-

increas|e *(n.)* ˈɪn.kriːs, ˈɪŋ-, -ˈ- (US) ˈɪn.kriːs, -ˈ- **-es** -ɪz

increas|e *(v.)* ɪnˈkriːs, ɪŋ-, ˈ-- (US) ɪnˈkriːs, ˈ-- **-es** -ɪz **-ing/ly** -ɪŋ/li **-ed** -t

incredibility ɪnˌkred.ɪˈbɪl.ə.ti, ɪŋ-, -əˈ-, -ɪ.ti (US) ɪnˌkred.ɪˈbɪl.ə.t̬i, -əˈ-

incredib|le ɪnˈkred.ɪ.bl̩, ɪŋ-, ˈ-ə- (US) ˌɪn- **-ly** -li **-leness** -l̩.nəs, -nɪs

incredulity ˌɪn.krəˈdjuː.lə.ti, ˌɪŋ-, -krɪˈ-, -kredˈjuː-, -ɪ.ti (US) ˌɪn.krəˈduː.lə.t̬i, -ˈdjuː-

incredulous ɪnˈkred.jə.ləs, ɪŋ-, -jʊ-, -ˈkredʒ.ə-, ˈ-ʊ- (US) ɪnˈkredʒ.ʊ- **-ly** -li **-ness** -nəs, -nɪs

increment ˈɪn.krə.mənt, ˈɪŋ-, -krɪ- (US) ˈɪn- **-s** -s

incremental ˌɪn.krəˈmen.tᵊl, ˌɪŋ-, -krɪˈ- (US) ˌɪn.krəˈmen.t̬ᵊl **-ly** -i

incrimi|nate ɪnˈkrɪm.ɪ|.neɪt, ɪŋ-, ˈ-ə- (US) ɪn- **-nates** -neɪts **-nating** -neɪ.tɪŋ (US) -neɪ.t̬ɪŋ **-nated** -neɪ.tɪd (US) -neɪ.t̬ɪd

incrimination ɪnˌkrɪm.ɪˈneɪ.ʃᵊn, ɪŋ-, -əˈ- (US) ɪn-

incriminatory ɪnˈkrɪm.ɪ.nə.tᵊr.i, ɪŋ-, -ᵊn.ə-, -neɪ.tᵊr-; ɪnˌkrɪm.ɪˈneɪ-, ˌɪn-, ɪŋ-, ˌɪŋ- (US) ɪnˈkrɪm.ɪ.nə.tɔːr.i

incrust ɪnˈkrʌst, ɪŋ- (US) ɪn- **-s** -s **-ing** -ɪŋ **-ed** -ɪd

incrustation ˌɪn.krʌsˈteɪ.ʃᵊn, ˌɪŋ- (US) ˌɪn- **-s** -z

incu|bate ˈɪŋ.kjʊ|.beɪt, ˈɪn-, -kjə- **-bates** -beɪts **-bating** -beɪ.tɪŋ (US) -beɪ.t̬ɪŋ **-bated** -beɪ.tɪd (US) -beɪ.t̬ɪd **-bative** -beɪ.tɪv (US) -beɪ.t̬ɪv

incubation ˌɪŋ.kjʊˈbeɪ.ʃᵊn, ˌɪn-, -kjəˈ- **-s** -z

incubator ˈɪŋ.kjʊ.beɪ.təʳ, ˈɪn-, -kjə- (US) -t̬ɚ **-s** -z

incubatory ˈɪŋ.kjʊ.beɪ.tᵊr.i, ˈɪn-, -kjə- (US) -bə.tɔːr-, ˌɪŋ.kjʊˈbeɪ.tɚ-, ˌɪn-, -kjəˈ-

incub|us ˈɪŋ.kjʊ.b|əs, ˈɪn-, -kjə- **-uses** -ə.sɪz **-i** -aɪ

incul|cate ˈɪn.kʌl|.keɪt, ˈɪŋ-, -kəl-; ɪnˈkʌl-, ɪŋ- (US) ˈɪn.kʌl-, -kəl-; ɪnˈkʌl- **-cates** -keɪts **-cating** -keɪ.tɪŋ (US) -keɪ.t̬ɪŋ **-cated** -keɪ.tɪd (US) -keɪ.t̬ɪd **-cator/s** -keɪ.təʳ/z (US) -keɪ.t̬ɚ/z

inculcation ˌɪn.kʌlˈkeɪ.ʃᵊn, ˌɪŋ-, -kəlˈ- (US) ˌɪn-

incul|pate ˈɪn.kʌl|.peɪt, ˈɪŋ-, -kəl-; ɪnˈkʌl-, ɪŋ- (US) ˈɪn.kʌl-, -kəl-; ɪnˈkʌl- **-pates** -peɪts **-pating** -peɪ.tɪŋ (US) -peɪ.t̬ɪŋ **-pated** -peɪ.tɪd (US) -peɪ.t̬ɪd

inculpation ˌɪn.kʌlˈpeɪ.ʃᵊn, ˌɪŋ-, -kəlˈ- (US) ˌɪn-

inculpatory ɪnˈkʌl.pə.tᵊr.i, ɪŋ-; ˈɪn.kʌl.peɪ-, ˈɪŋ-, -kəl-, ˌɪn.kʌlˈpeɪ-, ˌɪŋ-, -kəlˈ- (US) ɪnˈkʌl.pə.tɔːr.i

incumbenc|y ɪnˈkʌm.bən*t*.s|i, ɪŋ- (US) ɪn- **-ies** -iz

incumbent ɪnˈkʌm.bənt, ɪŋ- (US) ɪn- **-s** -s **-ly** -li

incumbranc|e ɪnˈkʌm.brən*t*s, ɪŋ- (US) ɪn- **-es** -ɪz

incunabul|um ˌɪn.kjuːˈnæb.jə.l|əm, ˌɪŋ-, -jʊ- (US) -kjəˈ-, -kjʊˈ- **-a** -ə

incur ɪnˈkɜːʳ, ɪŋ- (US) ɪnˈkɝː **-s** -z **-ring** -ɪŋ **-red** -d **-rable** -ə.bl̩

incurability ɪnˌkjʊə.rəˈbɪl.ə.ti, ˌɪn-, ɪŋ-, ˌɪŋ-, -ˌkjɔː-, -ɪ.ti (US) ɪnˌkjʊr.əˈbɪl.ə.t̬i

incurab|le ɪnˈkjʊə.rə.bl̩, ˌɪn-, ɪŋ-, ˌɪŋ-, -ˈkjɔː- (US) ɪnˈkjʊr.ə- **-ly** -li **-leness** -l̩.nəs, -nɪs

incurious ɪnˈkjʊə.ri.əs, ˌɪn-, ɪŋ-, ˌɪŋ-, -ˈkjɔː- (US) ɪnˈkjʊr.i- **-ly** -li **-ness** -nəs, -nɪs

incursion ɪnˈkɜː.ʃᵊn, ɪŋ-, -ʒᵊn (US) ɪnˈkɝː- **-s** -z

incursive ɪnˈkɜː.sɪv, ɪŋ- (US) ɪnˈkɝː-

incurvate *(adj.)* ɪnˈkɜː.veɪt, ɪŋ-, -vət, -vɪt (US) ɪnˈkɝː-

incur|vate *(v.)* ˈɪn.kɜː|.veɪt, ˈɪŋ- (US) ɪnˈkɝː-, ˈɪn.kɝː- **-vates** -veɪts **-vating** -veɪ.tɪŋ (US) -veɪ.t̬ɪŋ **-vated** -veɪ.tɪd (US) -veɪ.t̬ɪd

incurvation ˌɪn.kɜːˈveɪ.ʃᵊn, ˌɪŋ- (US) ˌɪn.kɝːˈ-

incurv|e ˌɪnˈkɜːv, ˌɪŋ- (US) ˌɪnˈkɝːv **-es** -z **-ing** -ɪŋ **-ed** -d *stress shift:* ˌincurved ˈsurface

incus|e ɪnˈkjuːz, ɪŋ- (US) ɪnˈkjuːz, -ˈkjuːs **-es** -ɪz **-ing** -ɪŋ **-ed** -d

Ind *surname:* ɪnd *India:* ɪnd, aɪnd

Ind. *(abbrev. for* **Indiana***)* ˌɪn.diˈæn.ə, -ˈɑː.nə (US) -ˈæn.ə

ind. *(abbrev. for* **independent***)* ˌɪn.dɪˈpen.dənt, -dəˈ- *(abbrev. for* **indicative***)* ɪnˈdɪk.ə.tɪv (US) -t̬ɪv *(abbrev. for* **industrial***)* ɪnˈdʌs.tri.əl

Indaur ɪnˈdɔːʳ (US) -ˈdɔːr

Ind Coope® ˌɪndˈkuːp

indebted ɪnˈdet.ɪd (US) -ˈdet̬- **-ness** -nəs, -nɪs

indecenc|y ɪnˈdiː.sᵊn*t*.s|i, ˌɪn- **-ies** -iz

indecent ɪnˈdiː.sᵊnt, ˌɪn- **-ly** -li **inˌdecent asˈsault; inˌdecent exˈposure**

indecipherable ˌɪn.dɪˈsaɪ.fᵊr.ə.bl̩, -dəˈ-

indecision ˌɪn.dɪˈsɪʒ.ᵊn, -dəˈ-

indecisive ˌɪn.dɪˈsaɪ.sɪv, -dəˈ- **-ly** -li **-ness** -nəs, -nɪs

indeclinable ˌɪn.dɪˈklaɪ.nə.bl̩, -dəˈ- **-s** -z

indecomposable ɪnˌdiː.kəmˈpəʊ.zə.bl̩, ˌɪn- (US) -ˈpoʊ-

indecorous ɪnˈdek.ᵊr.əs, ˌɪn- **-ly** -li **-ness** -nəs, -nəs

indecorum ˌɪn.dɪˈkɔː.rəm, -dəˈ- (US) -ˈkɔːr.əm

indeed *(adv.)* ɪnˈdiːd *(interj.)* ɪnˈdiːd, ˌɪn.diːd

indefatigab|le ˌɪn.dɪˈfæt.ɪ.gə.bl̩, -dəˈ- (US) -ˈfæt̬- **-ly** -li **-leness** -l̩.nəs, -nɪs

indefeasibility ˌɪn.dɪˌfiː.zəˈbɪl.ə.ti, -dəˌ-, -zɪˈ-, -ɪ.ti (US) -ə.t̬i

indefeasib|le ˌɪn.dɪˈfiː.zə.bl̩, -dəˈ-, -zɪ- **-ly** -li

indefensibility ˌɪn.dɪˌfen*t*.səˈbɪl.ə.ti, -dəˌ-, -sɪˈ-, -ɪ.ti (US) -ə.t̬i

indefensib|le ˌɪn.dɪˈfen*t*.sə.bl̩, -dəˈ-, -sɪ- **-ly** -li

indefinab|le ˌɪn.dɪˈfaɪ.nə.bl̩, -dəˈ- **-ly** -li

indefinite ɪnˈdef.ɪ.nət, ˌɪn-, -ᵊn.ət, ˈ-nət, -nɪt (US) -ə.nət, ˈ-nət **-ly** -li **-ness** -nəs, -nɪs **inˌdefinite ˈarticle**

indelibility ɪnˌdel.ɪˈbɪl.ə.ti, ˌɪn-, -əˈ-, -ɪ.ti (US) -ə.t̬i

indelib|le ɪnˈdel.ə.bl̩, ˌɪn-, ˈ-ɪ- **-ly** -li

indelicac|y ɪnˈdel.ɪ.kə.s|i, ˌɪn-, ˈ-ə- **-ies** -iz

indelicate ɪnˈdel.ɪ.kət, ˌɪn-, ˈ-ə-, -kɪt **-ly** -li

in delicto ˌɪn.delˈɪk.təʊ, -dɪˈlɪk- (US) -dəˈlɪk.toʊ

indemnification ɪnˌdem.nɪ.fɪˈkeɪ.ʃᵊn, -nə- **-s** -z

indemni|fy ɪnˈdem.nɪ|.faɪ, -nə- **-fies** -faɪz **-fying** -faɪ.ɪŋ **-fied** -faɪd

indemnit|y ɪnˈdem.nə.t|i, -nɪ- (US) -t̬|i **-ies** -iz

indemonstrab|le ɪnˈdem.ən*t*.strə.bl̩, ˌɪn-; ˌɪn.dɪˈmɒn*t*.strə-, -dəˈ- (US) ˌɪn.dɪˈmɑːn*t*.strə-; ɪnˈdem.ən*t*-, ˌɪn- **-ly** -li

indent (*n.*) 'ɪn.dent, -'- **-s** -s

in|dent (*v.*) ɪn|'dent, ˌɪn- **-dents** -'dents **-denting** -'den.tɪŋ (US) -'den.t̬ɪŋ **-dented** -'den.tɪd (US) -'den.t̬ɪd

indentation ˌɪn.den'teɪ.ʃᵊn **-s** -z

indenture ɪn'den.tʃəʳ (US) -tʃɚ **-s** -z **-d** -d

independen|ce ˌɪn.dɪ'pen.dənt|s, -də'- **-cy** -si **Inde'pendence ˌDay**

independent (I) ˌɪn.dɪ'pen.dənt, -də'- **-s** -s **-ly** -li

in-depth ˌɪn'depθ *stress shift:* ˌin-depth 'treatment

indescribab|le ˌɪn.dɪ'skraɪ.bə.b|l̩, -də'- **-ly** -li

indestructibility ˌɪn.dɪˌstrʌk.tə'bɪl.ə.ti, -tɪ'-, -ɪ.ti (US) -ə.t̬i

indestructib|le ˌɪn.dɪ'strʌk.tə.b|l̩, -tɪ- **-ly** -li **-leness** -l̩.nəs, -l̩.nɪs

indetectab|le, -ib|le ˌɪn.dɪ'tek.tə.b|l̩, -də'- **-ly** -li

indeterminab|le ˌɪn.dɪ'tɜː.mɪ.nə.b|l̩, -də'- (US) -'tɝː- **-ly** -li **-leness** -l̩.nəs, -l̩.nɪs

indeterminacy ˌɪn.dɪ'tɜː.mɪ.nə.si, -də'-, -mᵊn.ə- (US) -'tɝː-

indeterminate ˌɪn.dɪ'tɜː.mɪ.nət, -də'-, -nɪt (US) -'tɝː- **-ly** -li **-ness** -nəs, -nɪs

indetermination ˌɪn.dɪˌtɜː.mɪ'neɪ.ʃᵊn, -dəˌ-, -mə'- (US) -ˌtɝː-

ind|ex 'ɪn.d|eks **-exes** -ek.sɪz **-exing** -eks.ɪŋ **-exed** -ekst **-ices** -ɪ.siːz, -ə- **'index ˌcard; ˌindex 'finger, 'index ˌfinger; 'index ˌnumber**

indexer 'ɪn.dek.səʳ (US) -sɚ **-s** -z

index-linked ˌɪn.deks'lɪŋ*k*t

Indi|a 'ɪn.di|.ə **-an/s** -ən/z **ˌIndian 'Ocean; ˌIndia 'rubber; ˌIndian 'summer**

Indiana ˌɪn.di'æn.ə, -'ɑː.nə (US) -'æn.ə

Indianapolis ˌɪn.di.ə'næp.ᵊl.ɪs (US) -ə.lɪs

Indic 'ɪn.dɪk

indi|cate 'ɪn.dɪ|.keɪt, -də- **-cates** -keɪts **-cating** -keɪ.tɪŋ (US) -keɪ.t̬ɪŋ **-cated** -keɪ.tɪd (US) -keɪ.t̬ɪd

indication ˌɪn.dɪ'keɪ.ʃᵊn, -də'- **-s** -z

indicative (*n. adj.*) *in grammar:* ɪn'dɪk.ə.tɪv (US) -t̬ɪv **-s** -z **-ly** -li

indicative (*adj.*) *indicating:* ɪn'dɪk.ə.tɪv; 'ɪn.dɪ.keɪ- (US) ɪn'dɪk.ə.t̬ɪv **-ly** -li

indicator 'ɪn.dɪ.keɪ.təʳ, -də- (US) -t̬ɚ **-s** -z

indicatory ɪn'dɪk.ə.tᵊr.i; 'ɪn.dɪ.keɪ-, ˌɪn.dɪ'keɪ- (US) 'ɪn.dɪ.kə.tɔːr-; ɪn'dɪk.ə-

indices (*plur. of* **index**) 'ɪn.dɪ.siːz, -də-

indicia ɪn'dɪʃ.i.ə (US) -'dɪʃ.ə, -i.ə

in|dict ɪn|'daɪt **-dicts** -'daɪts **-dicting** -'daɪ.tɪŋ (US) -'daɪ.t̬ɪŋ **-dicted** -'daɪ.tɪd (US) -'daɪ.t̬ɪd **-dicter/s** -'daɪ.təʳ/z (US) -'daɪ.t̬ɚ/z **-dictable** -'daɪ.tə.bl̩ (US) -'daɪ.t̬ə.bl̩

indiction ɪn'dɪk.ʃᵊn **-s** -z

indictment ɪn'daɪt.mənt **-s** -s

indie 'ɪn.di **-s** -z

Indies 'ɪn.diz

indifference ɪn'dɪf.ᵊr.ᵊn*t*s, '-rᵊn*t*s

indifferent ɪn'dɪf.ᵊr.ᵊnt, '-rᵊnt **-ly** -li

indigen 'ɪn.dɪ.dʒən, -də- **-s** -z

indigence 'ɪn.dɪ.dʒən*t*s

indigene 'ɪn.dɪ.dʒiːn **-s** -z

indigenous ɪn'dɪdʒ.ɪ.nəs, -ᵊn.əs **-ly** -li **-ness** -nəs, -nɪs

indigent 'ɪn.dɪ.dʒənt **-s** -s **-ly** -li

indigestibility ˌɪn.dɪˌdʒes.tə'bɪl.ə.ti, -tɪ'-, -ɪ.ti (US) -dɪˌdʒes.tə'bɪl.ə.t̬i, -daɪˌ-

indigestib|le ˌɪn.dɪ'dʒes.tə.b|l̩, -də'-, -tɪ- (US) -dɪ'-, -daɪ'- **-leness** -l̩.nəs, -nɪs **-ly** -li

indigestion ˌɪn.dɪ'dʒes.tʃᵊn, -də'-, -'dʒeʃ- (US) -dɪ'dʒes-, -daɪ'-

indignant ɪn'dɪg.nənt **-ly** -li

indignation ˌɪn.dɪg'neɪ.ʃᵊn

indignit|y ɪn'dɪg.nə.t|i, -nɪ- (US) -nə.t̬|i **-ies** -iz

indigo 'ɪn.dɪ.gəʊ (US) -goʊ **-(e)s** -z

Indira 'ɪn.dɪ.rə, -dᵊr.ə; ɪn'dɪə.rə (US) ɪn'dɪr.ə

indirect ˌɪn.dɪ'rekt, -daɪ'-, -də'- **-ly** -li **-ness** -nəs, -nɪs **ˌindirect 'object; ˌindirect 'speech**

indiscernib|le ˌɪn.dɪ'sɜː.nə.b|l̩, -'zɜː-, -nɪ- (US) -'sɝː-, -'zɝː- **-ly** -li

indisciplin|e ɪn'dɪs.ə.plɪn, ˌɪn-, '-ɪ- **-ed** -d **-able** -ə.bl̩

indiscreet ˌɪn.dɪ'skriːt, -də'- **-ly** -li **-ness** -nəs, -nɪs

indiscrete ˌɪn.dɪ'skriːt, -də'-

indiscretion ˌɪn.dɪ'skreʃ.ᵊn, -də'- **-s** -z

indiscriminate ˌɪn.dɪ'skrɪm.ɪ.nət, -də'-, '-ə-, -nɪt **-ly** -li **-ness** -nəs, -nɪs

indiscrimination ˌɪn.dɪˌskrɪm.ɪ'neɪ.ʃᵊn, -dəˌ-, -ə'-

indispensability ˌɪn.dɪˌspen*t*.sə'bɪl.ə.ti, -dəˌ-, -ɪ.ti (US) -ə.t̬i

indispensab|le, -ib|le ˌɪn.dɪ'spen*t*.sə.b|l̩, -də'- **-ly** -li **-leness** -nəs, -nɪs

indispos|e ˌɪn.dɪ'spəʊz, -də'- (US) -'spoʊz **-es** -ɪz **-ing** -ɪŋ **-ed** -d

indisposition ˌɪn.dɪ.spə'zɪʃ.ᵊn; ɪnˌdɪs.pə'- (US) ˌɪn.dɪ.spə'- **-s** -z

indisputability ˌɪn.dɪˌspjuː.tə'bɪl.ə.ti; ɪnˌdɪs.pjuː-, -ɪ.ti (US) ˌɪn.dɪˌspjuː.tə'bɪl.ə.t̬i

indisputab|le ˌɪn.dɪ'spjuː.tə.b|l̩; ɪn'dɪs.pjuː- (US) ˌɪn.dɪ'spjuː.t̬ə-; ɪn'dɪs.pjuː-, -pjə- **-ly** -li **-leness** -l̩.nəs, -nɪs

indissociable ˌɪn.dɪ'səʊ.ʃi.ə.bl̩, -ʃə.bl̩ (US) -'soʊ-

indissolubility ˌɪn.dɪˌsɒl.jə'bɪl.ə.ti, -dəˌ-, -jʊ'-, -ɪ.ti (US) -ˌsɑːl.jə'bɪl.ə.t̬i

indissolub|le ˌɪn.dɪ'sɒl.jə.b|l̩, -də'-, -jʊ- (US) -'sɑːl- **-ly** -li **-leness** -l̩.nəs, -nɪs

indistinct ˌɪn.dɪ'stɪŋ*k*t, -də'- **-ly** -li **-ness** -nəs, -nɪs

indistinctive ˌɪn.dɪ'stɪŋ*k*.tɪv, -də'- **-ly** -li **-ness** -nəs, -nɪs

indistinguishab|le ˌɪn.dɪ'stɪŋ.gwɪ.ʃə.b|l̩, -də'- **-ly** -li **-leness** -l̩.nəs, -nɪs

in|dite ɪn|'daɪt **-dites** -'daɪts **-diting** -'daɪ.tɪŋ (US) -'daɪ.t̬ɪŋ **-dited** -'daɪ.tɪd (US) -'daɪ.t̬ɪd **-diter/s** -'daɪ.təʳ/z (US) -'daɪ.t̬ɚ/z

indium 'ɪn.di.əm

individual ˌɪn.dɪ'vɪdʒ.u.əl, -də'-, -'vɪd.ju- (US) -'vɪdʒ.u-, -'vɪdʒ.ᵊl **-s** -z **-ly** -i

individual|ism ˌɪn.dɪ'vɪdʒ.u.ə.l|ɪ.zᵊm, -də'-, -'vɪd.ju.ə.l|ɪz- (US) -'vɪdʒ.u-, -'vɪdʒ.ᵊl|.ɪ- **-ist/s** -ɪst/s

individualistic ˌɪn.dɪˌvɪdʒ.u.ə'lɪs.tɪk, -dəˌ-, -ˌvɪd.ju- (US) -ˌvɪdʒ.u-, -ˌvɪdʒ.ᵊl'ɪs- **-ally** -ᵊl.i, -li

individualit|y ˌɪn.dɪˌvɪdʒ.u'æl.ə.t|i, -dəˌ-, -ˌvɪd.ju'-, -ɪ.t|i (US) -ˌvɪdʒ.u'æl.ə.t̬|i **-ies** -iz

individualization, -isa- ˌɪn.dɪˌvɪdʒ.u.ᵊl.aɪ'zeɪ.ʃᵊn, -dəˌ-, -ˌvɪd.ju-, -ɪ'- (US) -ˌvɪdʒ.u.ᵊl.ɪ'-, -ˌvɪdʒ.ᵊl-

individualiz|e, -is|e ˌɪn.dɪ'vɪdʒ.u.ə.laɪz, -də'-, -'vɪd.ju- (US) -'vɪdʒ.u-, -'vɪdʒ.ᵊl.aɪz **-es** -ɪz **-ing** -ɪŋ **-ed** -d

individu|ate ˌɪn.dɪ'vɪdʒ.u|.eɪt, -də'-, -'vɪd.ju- (US) -'vɪdʒ.u- **-ates** -eɪts **-ating** -eɪ.tɪŋ (US) -eɪ.t̬ɪŋ **-ated** -eɪ.tɪd (US) -eɪ.t̬ɪd

individuation ˌɪn.dɪˌvɪdʒ.u'eɪ.ʃᵊn, -dəˌ-, -ˌvɪd.ju'- (US) -ˌvɪdʒ.u'- **-s** -s

indivisibility ˌɪn.dɪˌvɪz.ɪ'bɪl.ə.ti, -ə'-, -ɪ.ti (US) -ə.t̬i

indivisib|le ˌɪn.dɪ'vɪz.ə.b|l̩, '-ɪ- **-ly** -li **-leness** -l̩.nəs, -nɪs

Indo-China ˌɪn.dəʊ'tʃaɪ.nə (US) -doʊ'-

Indo-Chinese ˌɪn.dəʊ.tʃaɪ'niːz (US) -doʊ-

indocile ɪn'dəʊ.saɪl, ˌɪn- (US) -'dɑː.səl

indocility ˌɪn.dəʊ'sɪl.ə.ti, -ɪ.ti (US) -dɑː'sɪl.ə.t̬i, -doʊ'-

indoctri|nate ɪn'dɒk.trɪ|.neɪt, -trə- (US) -'dɑːk- **-nates** -neɪts **-nating** -neɪ.tɪŋ (US) -neɪ.t̬ɪŋ **-nated** -neɪ.tɪd (US) -neɪ.t̬ɪd **-nator/s** -neɪ.təʳ/z (US) -neɪ.t̬ɚ/z

indoctrination ɪnˌdɒk.trɪ'neɪ.ʃᵊn, ˌɪn-, -trə'- (US) -ˌdɑːk- **-s** -z

Indo-European ˌɪn.dəʊˌjʊə.rə'piː.ən, -ˌjɔː- (US) -doʊ.jʊr.ə'- **-s** -z

Indo-Germanic ˌɪn.dəʊ.dʒɜː'mæn.ɪk, -dʒə'- (US) -doʊ.dʒɝː'-

indolence ˈɪn.dᵊl.ənts
indolent ˈɪn.dᵊl.ənt **-ly** -li
indomitab|le ɪnˈdɒm.ɪ.tə.b|l̩, ˈ-ə- (US) -ˈdɑː.mə.t̬ə- **-ly** -li **-leness** -l̩.nəs, -nɪs
Indonesi|a ˌɪn.dəʊˈniː.ʒ|ə, -zi|.ə, -si|.ə, -ˈniː.ʃ|ə (US) -dəˈniː.ʒ|ə, -ʃ|ə **-an/s** -ən/z
indoor ˌɪnˈdɔːʳ (US) -ˈdɔːr *stress shift:* ˌindoor ˈgames
indoors ˌɪnˈdɔːz (US) -ˈdɔːrz
Indore ˌɪnˈdɔːʳ (US) -ˈdɔːr
indors|e ɪnˈdɔːs (US) -ˈdɔːrs **-es** -ɪz **-ing** -ɪŋ **-ed** -t
indorsement ɪnˈdɔːs.mənt (US) -ˈdɔːrs- **-s** -s
Indra ˈɪn.drə
indrawn ˌɪnˈdrɔːn (US) ˈɪn.drɑːn, -drɔːn *stress shift, British only:* ˌindrawn ˈbreath
indubitab|le ɪnˈdjuː.bɪ.tə.b|l̩, ˌɪn- (US) -ˈduː.bɪ.t̬ə-, -ˈdjuː- **-ly** -li **-leness** -l̩.nəs, -nɪs
induc|e ɪnˈdjuːs (US) -ˈduːs, -ˈdjuːs **-es** -ɪz **-ing** -ɪŋ **-ed** -t **-er/s** -əʳ/z (US) -ɚ/z
inducement ɪnˈdjuːs.mənt (US) -ˈduːs-, -ˈdjuːs- **-s** -s
induct ɪnˈdʌkt **-s** -s **-ing** -ɪŋ **-ed** -ɪd **-or/s** -əʳ/z (US) -ɚ/z
inductanc|e ɪnˈdʌk.tᵊnts **-es** -ɪz
inductee ˌɪn.dʌkˈtiː **-s** -z
inductile ɪnˈdʌk.taɪl, ˌɪn- (US) -tɪl
inductility ˌɪn.dʌkˈtɪl.ə.ti, -ɪ.ti (US) -ə.t̬i
induction ɪnˈdʌk.ʃᵊn **-s** -z **inˈduction ˌcoil**
inductive ɪnˈdʌk.tɪv **-ly** -li
indulg|e ɪnˈdʌldʒ **-es** -ɪz **-ing** -ɪŋ **-ed** -d **-er/s** -əʳ/z (US) -ɚ/z
indulgenc|e ɪnˈdʌl.dʒənts **-es** -ɪz
indulgent ɪnˈdʌl.dʒənt **-ly** -li
indur|ate ˈɪn.djʊə.r|eɪt, -djʊr|.eɪt (US) -dʊ.r|eɪt, -djʊ-, -də-, -djə- **-ates** -eɪts **-ating** -eɪ.tɪŋ (US) -eɪ.t̬ɪŋ **-ated** -eɪ.tɪd (US) -eɪ.t̬ɪd **-ative** -ə.tɪv (US) -t̬ɪv
induration ɪn.djʊəˈreɪ.ʃᵊn, -djʊˈ- (US) -dʊˈ-, -djʊˈ-, -dəˈ-, -djəˈ-
Indus ˈɪn.dəs
industrial ɪnˈdʌs.tri.əl **-ly** -i **inˌdustrial ˈaction; inˌdustrial disˈpute, inˌdustrial ˈdispute; inˌdustrial ˈespionage; inˌdustrial esˈtate; inˈdustrial ˌpark; inˌdustrial reˈlations; Inˌdustrial Revoˈlution; inˌdustrial triˈbunal**
industrial|ism ɪnˈdʌs.tri.əl|.ɪ.zᵊm **-ist/s** -ɪst/z
industrialization, -isa- ɪnˌdʌs.tri.ə.laɪˈzeɪ.ʃᵊn, -lɪˈ- (US) -lɪˈ-
industrializ|e, -is|e ɪnˈdʌs.tri.ə.laɪz **-es** -ɪz **-ing** -ɪŋ **-ed** -d
industrious ɪnˈdʌs.tri.əs **-ly** -li **-ness** -nəs, -nɪs
industr|y ˈɪn.də.str|i **-ies** -iz
industrywide ˌɪn.də.striˈwaɪd *stress shift:* ˌindustrywide ˈslump
indwel|l ˌɪnˈdwel, ˈ-- **-ls** -z **-ling** -ɪŋ **-t** -t
indweller ˈɪnˌdwel.əʳ (US) -ɚ **-s** -z
-ine -aɪn, -iːn, -ɪn
inebriate (*n. adj.*) ɪˈniː.bri.ət, -ɪt, -eɪt **-s** -s
inebri|ate (*v.*) ɪˈniː.bri|.eɪt **-ates** -eɪts **-ating** -eɪ.tɪŋ (US) -eɪ.t̬ɪŋ **-ated** -eɪ.tɪd (US) -eɪ.t̬ɪd
inebriation ɪˌniː.briˈeɪ.ʃᵊn
inebriety ˌɪn.iːˈbraɪ.ə.ti, -ɪˈ-, -ɪ.ti (US) -ə.t̬i
inedible ɪˈned.ɪ.bl̩, ˌɪnˈed-, ˈ-ə- (US) ˌɪnˈed-, ɪˈned-
inedited ɪˈned.ɪ.tɪd, ˌɪnˈed-, ˈ-ə- (US) ˌɪnˈed.ɪ.t̬ɪd, ɪˈned-, ˈ-ə-
ineducable ɪˈned.jə.kə.bl̩, ˌɪnˈed-, -ˈedʒ.ə-, ˈ-ʊ- (US) ˌɪnˈedʒ.ʊ-, ɪˈnedʒ-, ˈ-ə-
ineffab|le ɪˈnef.ə.b|l̩, ˌɪnˈef- (US) ˌɪnˈef-, ɪˈnef- **-ly** -li **-leness** -l̩.nəs, -nɪs
ineffaceab|le ˌɪn.ɪˈfeɪ.sə.b|l̩, -efˈeɪ-, -əˈfeɪ- **-ly** -li
ineffective ˌɪn.ɪˈfek.tɪv, -əˈ- **-ly** -li **-ness** -nəs, -nɪs
ineffectual ˌɪn.ɪˈfek.tʃu.ᵊl, -əˈ-, -tju- (US) -tʃu- **-ly** -i **-ness** -nəs, -nɪs
inefficacious ˌɪn.ef.ɪˈkeɪ.ʃəs, ɪˌnef- **-ly** -li
inefficacy ɪˈnef.ɪ.kə.si, ˌɪnˈef- (US) ˌɪnˈef-, ɪˈnef-
inefficiency ˌɪn.ɪˈfɪʃ.ᵊnt.si, -əˈ-
inefficient ˌɪn.ɪˈfɪʃ.ᵊnt, -əˈ- **-ly** -li
inelastic ˌɪn.ɪˈlæs.tɪk, -əˈ-, -ˈlɑː.stɪk (US) -iːˈlæs-, -ɪˈ-
inelasticity ˌɪn.ɪ.læsˈtɪs.ə.ti, ˌ-ə-, -ˌiː.læsˈ-, -lɑːˈstɪs-, -ɪ.ti (US) -iː.læsˈtɪs.ə.t̬i, ˌ-ɪ-
inelegance ɪˈnel.ɪ.gənts, ˌɪnˈel-, ˈ-ə- (US) ˌɪnˈel-, ɪˈnel-
inelegant ɪˈnel.ɪ.gənt, ˌɪnˈel-, ˈ-ə- (US) ˌɪnˈel-, ɪˈnel- **-ly** -li
ineligibility ɪˌnel.ɪ.dʒəˈbɪl.ə.ti, ˌɪn.el-, -dʒɪˈ-, -ɪ.ti (US) ˌɪn.el.ɪ.dʒəˈbɪl.ə.t̬i, ɪˌnel-, -dʒɪˈ-
ineligib|le ɪˈnel.ɪ.dʒə.b|l̩, ˌɪnˈel-, -dʒɪ- (US) ˌɪnˈel-, ɪˈnel- **-ly** -li
ineluctab|le ˌɪn.ɪˈlʌk.tə.b|l̩, -əˈ- **-ly** -li
inept ɪˈnept, ˌɪnˈept (US) ˌɪnˈept, ɪˈnept **-ly** -li **-ness** -nəs, -nɪs
ineptitude ɪˈnep.tɪ.tjuːd, ˌɪnˈep-, -tə- (US) ˌɪnˈep.tɪ.tuːd, ɪˈnep-, -tə-, -tjuːd
inequab|le ɪˈnek.wə.b|l̩, ˌɪnˈek- (US) ˌɪnˈek-, ɪˈnek- **-ly** -li
inequalit|y ˌɪn.ɪˈkwɒl.ə.t|i, -iːˈ-, -əˈ-, -ɪ.t|i (US) -ˈkwɑː.lə.t̬|i **-ies** -iz
inequitab|le ɪˈnek.wɪ.tə.b|l̩, ˌɪnˈek- (US) ˌɪnˈek.wə.t̬ə-, ɪˈnek- **-ly** -li
inequit|y ɪˈnek.wə.t|i, ˌɪnˈek-, -wɪ- (US) ˌɪnˈek.wə.t̬|i, ɪˈnek- **-ies** -iz
ineradicab|le ˌɪn.ɪˈræd.ɪ.kə.b|l̩, -əˈ- **-ly** -li
inert ɪˈnɜːt (US) ˌɪnˈɝːt, ɪˈnɝːt **-ly** -li **-ness** -nəs, -nɪs
inertia ɪˈnɜː.ʃə, -ʃi.ə (US) ˌɪnˈɝː-, ɪˈnɝː-
inescapab|le ˌɪn.ɪˈskeɪ.pə.b|l̩, -əˈ- **-ly** -li
inessential ˌɪn.ɪˈsen.tʃᵊl, -əˈ-
inessive ɪˈnes.ɪv, ˌɪnˈes- (US) ˌɪnˈes-, ɪˈnes-
inestimab|le ɪˈnes.tɪ.mə.b|l̩, ˌɪnˈes-, -tə- (US) ˌɪnˈes-, ɪˈnes- **-ly** -li
inevitability ɪˌnev.ɪ.təˈbɪl.ə.ti, ˌɪnˌev-, ˌ-ə-, -ɪ.ti (US) ˌɪnˌev.ɪ.t̬əˈbɪl.ə.t̬i, ɪˌnev-, ˌ-ə-
inevitab|le ɪˈnev.ɪ.tə.b|l̩, ˌɪnˈev-, ˈ-ə- (US) ˌɪnˈev.ɪ.t̬ə-, ɪˈnev-, ˈ-ə- **-ly** -li **-leness** -l̩.nəs, -nɪs
inexact ˌɪn.ɪgˈzækt, -egˈ-; -ɪkˈsækt, -ekˈ- (US) -ɪgˈzækt, -egˈ- **-ly** -li **-ness** -nəs, -nɪs
inexactitude ˌɪn.ɪgˈzæk.tɪ.tjuːd, -egˈ-, -tə-; -ɪkˈsæk-, -ekˈ- (US) -ɪgˈzæk.tə.tuːd, -egˈ- **-s** -z
inexcusab|le ˌɪn.ɪkˈskjuː.zə.b|l̩, -ekˈ- **-ly** -li **-leness** -l̩.nəs, -nɪs
inexhaustibility ˌɪn.ɪgˌzɔː.stəˈbɪl.ə.ti, -egˌ-, -stɪˈ-, -ɪ.ti; -ɪkˌsɔː-, -ekˌ- (US) -ɪgˌzɑː.stəˈbɪl.ə.t̬i, -egˌ-, -ˌzɔː-
inexhaustib|le ˌɪn.ɪgˈzɔː.stə.b|l̩, -egˈ-, -stɪ-; -ɪkˈsɔː-, -ekˈ- (US) -ɪgˈzɑː.stə-, -egˈ-, -ˈzɔː- **-ly** -li **-leness** -l̩.nəs, -nɪs
inexisten|t ˌɪn.ɪgˈzɪs.tᵊn|t, -ekˈ-; -ɪkˈsɪs-, -ekˈ- (US) -ɪgˈzɪs-, -egˈ- **-ce** -ts
inexorability ɪˌnek.sᵊr.əˈbɪl.ə.ti, ˌɪnˌek-, -ɪ.ti (US) ˌɪnˌek.sɚ.əˈbɪl.ə.t̬i, ɪˌnek-
inexorab|le ɪˈnek.sᵊr.ə.b|l̩, ˌɪnˈek- (US) ˌɪnˈek-, ɪˈnek- **-ly** -li **-leness** -l̩.nəs, -nɪs
inexpedien|ce ˌɪn.ɪkˈspiː.di.ən|ts, -ekˈ- **-cy** -si
inexpedient ˌɪn.ɪkˈspiː.di.ənt, -ekˈ- **-ly** -li
inexpensive ˌɪn.ɪkˈspent.sɪv, -ekˈ- **-ly** -li **-ness** -nəs, -nɪs
inexperience ˌɪn.ɪkˈspɪə.ri.ənts, -ekˈ- (US) -ˈspɪr.i- **-d** -t
inexpert ɪˈnek.spɜːt, ˌɪnˈek- (US) ˌɪnˈek.spɝːt, ɪˈnek-; ˌɪn.ɪkˈspɝːt, -ekˈ- **-ly** -li **-ness** -nəs, -nɪs
inexpiab|le ɪˈnek.spi.ə.b|l̩, ˌɪnˈek- (US) ˌɪnˈek-, ɪˈnek- **-ly** -li **-leness** -l̩.nəs, -nɪs
inexplicability ˌɪn.ɪkˌsplɪk.əˈbɪl.ə.ti, -ekˌ-, -ɪ.ti; ɪnˌek.splɪk.əˈ-, ˌɪn- (US) ɪˌnek.splɪ.kəˈbɪl.ə.t̬i, ˌɪn.ek-
inexplicab|le ˌɪn.ɪkˈsplɪk.ə.b|l̩, -ekˈ-; ɪˈnek.splɪ.kə-, ˌɪnˈek-, -splə- (US) ˌɪnˈek.splɪ.kə-, ɪˈnek-, -splə-; ˌɪn.ɪkˈsplɪk.ə- **-ly** -li **-leness** -l̩.nəs, -nɪs

inexplicit ˌɪn.ɪkˈsplɪs.ɪt, -ekˈ- **-ly** -li **-ness** -nəs, -nɪs

inexplorable ˌɪn.ɪkˈsplɔː.rə.bl̩, -ekˈ- (US) -ˈsplɔːr.ə-

inexpressib|le ˌɪn.ɪkˈspres.ə.b|l̩, -ekˈ-, ˈ-ɪ- **-ly** -li

inexpressive ˌɪn.ɪkˈspres.ɪv, -ekˈ- **-ly** -li **-ness** -nəs, -nɪs

inexpugnab|le ˌɪn.ɪkˈspʌg.nə.b|l̩, -ekˈ- (US) -ˈspʌg-, -ˈspjuː- **-ly** -li **-leness** -l̩.nəs, -nɪs

inextensible ˌɪn.ɪkˈstent.sə.bl̩, -ekˈ-, -sɪ-

inextinguishab|le ˌɪn.ɪkˈstɪŋ.gwɪ.ʃə.b|l̩, -ekˈ-, -wɪ- **-ly** -li

in extremis ˌɪn.ɪkˈstriː.mɪs (US) -ɪkˈ-, -ekˈ-

inextricab|le ˌɪn.ɪkˈstrɪk.ə.b|l̩, -ekˈ-; ɪˈnek.strɪ.kə-, ˌɪnˈek- **-ly** -li **-leness** -l̩.nəs, -nɪs

Inez ˈiː.nez, ˈaɪ- (US) iːˈnez, ɪ-, aɪ-, ˈiː.nez, ˈaɪ-, -nes

infallibility ɪnˌfæl.əˈbɪl.ə.ti, ˌɪn-, -ɪˈ-, -ɪ.ti (US) -ə.t̬i

infallib|le ɪnˈfæl.ə.b|l̩, ˈ-ɪ- **-ly** -li

infamous ˈɪn.fə.məs **-ly** -li **-ness** -nəs, -nɪs

infam|y ˈɪn.fə.m|i **-ies** -iz

infanc|y ˈɪn.fənt.s|i **-ies** -iz

infant ˈɪn.fənt **-s** -s **ˈinfant ˌschool; ˌinfant morˈtality ˌrate**

infanta ɪnˈfæn.tə (US) -t̬ə, -ˈfɑːn- **-s** -z

infante ɪnˈfæn.ti (US) -teɪ, -ˈfɑːn- **-s** -z

infanticide ɪnˈfæn.tɪ.saɪd, -tə- (US) -t̬ə- **-s** -z

infant|ile ˈɪn.fən.t|aɪl (US) -t|aɪl, -t|ɪl **-ine** -aɪn **ˌinfantile paˈralysis**

infantilism ɪnˈfæn.tɪ.lɪ.zᵊm, -tə- (US) ˈɪn.fən.t̬ə-, -taɪ-; ɪnˈfæn.t̬ə-

infantry ˈɪn.fən.tri **-man** -mən, -mæn **-men** -mən, -men

infarct ˈɪn.fɑːkt, ˌ-ˈ- (US) ˈɪn.fɑːrkt, ˌ-ˈ- **-s** -s

infarction ɪnˈfɑːk.ʃᵊn (US) -ˈfɑːrk- **-s** -z

infatu|ate ɪnˈfæt.ju|.eɪt, -ˈfætʃ.u- (US) -ˈfætʃ.u- **-ates** -eɪts **-ating** -eɪ.tɪŋ (US) -eɪ.t̬ɪŋ **-ated** -eɪ.tɪd (US) -eɪ.t̬ɪd

infatuation ɪnˌfæt.juˈeɪ.ʃᵊn, -ˌfætʃ.uˈ- (US) -ˌfætʃ.uˈ- **-s** -z

infect ɪnˈfekt **-s** -s **-ing** -ɪŋ **-ed** -ɪd

infection ɪnˈfek.ʃᵊn **-s** -z

infectious ɪnˈfek.ʃəs **-ly** -li **-ness** -nəs, -nɪs

infecundity ˌɪn.fɪˈkʌn.də.ti, -fiːˈ-, -fekˈʌn-, -dɪ- (US) -fiːˈkʌn.də.t̬i, -fɪˈ-

infelicitous ˌɪn.fəˈlɪs.ɪ.təs, -fɪˈ-, -felˈɪs-, ˈ-ə- (US) -fəˈlɪs.ə.t̬əs **-ly** -li

infelicit|y ˌɪn.fəˈlɪs.ə.t|i, -fɪˈ-, -felˈɪs-, -ɪ- (US) -ə.t̬|i **-ies** -iz

infer ɪnˈfɜːʳ (US) -ˈfɝː **-s** -z **-ring** -ɪŋ **-red** -d **-able** -ə.bl̩

inferenc|e ˈɪn.fᵊr.ᵊnts, ˈ-frᵊnts **-es** -ɪz

inferential ˌɪn.fᵊrˈen.tʃᵊl (US) -fəˈren- **-ly** -i

inferior ɪnˈfɪə.ri.əʳ, ˌɪn- (US) -ˈfɪr.i.ɚ **-s** -z

inferiority ɪnˌfɪə.riˈɒr.ə.ti, ˌɪn-, -ɪ.ti (US) -ˌfɪr.iˈɔːr.ə.t̬i **inferiˈority ˌcomplex**

infernal ɪnˈfɜː.nᵊl (US) -ˈfɝː- **-ly** -i

inferno (I) ɪnˈfɜː.nəʊ (US) -ˈfɝː.noʊ **-s** -z

infertile ɪnˈfɜː.taɪl, ˌɪn- (US) -ˈfɝː.t̬ᵊl

infertility ˌɪn.fəˈtɪl.ə.ti, -fɜːˈ-, -ɪ.ti (US) -fɚˈtɪl.ə.t̬i

infest ɪnˈfest **-s** -s **-ing** -ɪŋ **-ed** -ɪd

infestation ˌɪn.fesˈteɪ.ʃᵊn **-s** -z

infibu|late ɪnˈfɪb.jə|.leɪt, -jʊ- **-lates** -leɪts **-lating** -leɪ.tɪŋ (US) -leɪ.t̬ɪŋ **-lated** -leɪ.tɪd (US) -leɪ.t̬ɪd

infibulation ɪnˌfɪb.jəˈleɪ.ʃᵊn, -jʊˈ-

infidel ˈɪn.fɪ.dᵊl, -fə-, -del (US) -fə.del, -dᵊl **-s** -z

infidelit|y ˌɪn.fɪˈdel.ə.t|i, -fəˈ-, -ɪ.t|i (US) -fəˈdel.ə.t̬|i **-ies** -iz

infield ˈɪn.fiːld **-s** -z

infielder ˈɪnˌfiːl.dəʳ (US) -dɚ **-s** -z

infighting ˈɪnˌfaɪ.tɪŋ

infill ˈɪn.fɪl **-s** -z **-ing** -ɪŋ **-ed** -d

infilling ˈɪnˌfɪl.ɪŋ

infil|trate ˈɪn.fɪl|.treɪt, -fᵊl- (US) ɪnˈfɪl|.treɪt, ˈɪn.fɪl- **-trates** -treɪts **-trating** -treɪ.tɪŋ (US) -treɪ.t̬ɪŋ **-trated** -treɪ.tɪd (US) -treɪ.t̬ɪd **-trator/s** -treɪ.təʳ/z (US) -treɪ.t̬ɚ/z

infiltration ˌɪn.fɪlˈtreɪ.ʃᵊn, -fᵊlˈ- **-s** -z

in fine ˌɪnˈfaɪ.ni, -ˈfiː-, -neɪ

infinite *in non-technical sense:* ˈɪn.fɪ.nət, -fᵊn.ət, -ɪt *in church music:* ˈɪn.fɪ.naɪt, -faɪ- (US) ˈɪn.fə.nɪt **-ly** -li **-ness** -nəs, -nɪs *in grammar:* ˌɪnˈfaɪ.naɪt *in mathematics:* ˈɪn.fɪ.nət, -fᵊn.ət, -ɪt, -ˌfaɪ.naɪt

infinitesimal ˌɪn.fɪ.nɪˈtes.ɪ.mᵊl, -fᵊn.ɪˈ-, -əˈ-, -ᵊm.ᵊl (US) -ˈtes-, -ˈtez- **-ly** -i

infinitival ɪnˌfɪn.ɪˈtaɪ.vᵊl, -əˈ-; ˌɪn.fɪ.nɪˈ-, -nəˈ- (US) ɪnˌfɪn.ɪˈtaɪ-

infinitive ɪnˈfɪn.ə.tɪv, ˈ-ɪ- (US) -t̬ɪv **-s** -z **-ly** -li

infinitude ɪnˈfɪn.ɪ.tjuːd, ˈ-ə- (US) -tuːd, -tjuːd **-s** -z

infinit|y ɪnˈfɪn.ə.t|i, -ɪ.t|i (US) -ə.t̬|i **-ies** -iz

infirm ɪnˈfɜːm, ˌɪn- (US) -ˈfɝːm **-ly** -li

infirmar|y ɪnˈfɜː.mᵊr|.i (US) -ˈfɝː- **-ies** -iz

infirmit|y ɪnˈfɜː.mə.t|i, -mɪ- (US) -ˈfɝː.mə.t̬|i **-ies** -iz

infix *(n.)* ˈɪn.fɪks **-es** -ɪz

infix *(v.)* ˈɪn.fɪks, ˌ-ˈ- **-es** -ɪz **-ing** -ɪŋ **-ed** -t

in flagrante delicto ɪn.fləˌgræn.teɪ.dɪˈlɪk.təʊ, -ti-, -dəˈ-, -diːˈ-, -deɪˈ- (US) -ˌgrɑːn.teɪ.dɪˈlɪk.toʊ, -ˌgræn-, -ti-, -dəˈ-, -diːˈ-, -deɪˈ-

inflam|e ɪnˈfleɪm **-es** -z **-ing** -ɪŋ **-ed** -d

inflammability ɪnˌflæm.əˈbɪl.ə.ti, -ɪ.ti (US) -ə.t̬i

inflammable ɪnˈflæm.ə.bl̩ **-ness** -nəs, -nɪs

inflammation ˌɪn.fləˈmeɪ.ʃᵊn **-s** -z

inflammatory ɪnˈflæm.ə.tᵊr.i (US) -tɔːr-

inflatable ɪnˈfleɪ.tə.bl̩ (US) -t̬ə- **-s** -z

in|flate ɪn|ˈfleɪt **-flates** -ˈfleɪts **-flating** -ˈfleɪ.tɪŋ (US) -ˈfleɪ.t̬ɪŋ **-flated** -ˈfleɪ.tɪd (US) -ˈfleɪ.t̬ɪd **-flator/s** -ˈfleɪ.təʳ/z (US) -ˈfleɪ.t̬ɚ/z

inflation ɪnˈfleɪ.ʃᵊn **-s** -z **-ary** -ᵊr.i

inflationism ɪnˈfleɪ.ʃᵊn.ɪ.zᵊm

inflect ɪnˈflekt **-s** -s **-ing** -ɪŋ **-ed** -ɪd

inflection ɪnˈflek.ʃᵊn **-s** -z

inflectional ɪnˈflek.ʃᵊn.ᵊl

inflective ɪnˈflek.tɪv

inflexibility ɪnˌflek.səˈbɪl.ə.ti, ˌɪn-, -sɪˈ-, -ɪ.ti (US) -ə.t̬i

inflexib|le ɪnˈflek.sə.b|l̩, -sɪ- **-ly** -li **-leness** -l̩.nəs, -nɪs

inflexion ɪnˈflek.ʃᵊn **-s** -z

inflexional ɪnˈflek.ʃᵊn.ᵊl

inflict ɪnˈflɪkt **-s** -s **-ing** -ɪŋ **-ed** -ɪd

infliction ɪnˈflɪk.ʃᵊn **-s** -z

in-flight ˌɪnˈflaɪt (US) ˈ--, ˌ-ˈ- *stress shift, British only:* ˌin-flight ˈservice

inflorescence ˌɪn.flɔːˈres.ᵊnts, -flɒrˈes-, -fləˈres- (US) -fləˈres-, -flɔː-, -floʊ-

inflow ˈɪn.fləʊ (US) -floʊ **-s** -z

influenc|e ˈɪn.flu.ənts, -flʊənts (US) -flu.ənts **-es** -ɪz **-ing** -ɪŋ **-ed** -t

influent ˈɪn.flu.ənt, -flʊənt (US) -flu.ənt **-s** -s

influential ˌɪn.fluˈen.tʃᵊl **-ly** -i

influenza ˌɪn.fluˈen.zə

influx ˈɪn.flʌks **-es** -ɪz

influxion ɪnˈflʌk.ʃᵊn

info ˈɪn.fəʊ (US) -foʊ

infomercial ˌɪn.fəʊˈmɜː.ʃᵊl (US) ˈɪn.foʊ.mɝː- **-s** -z

inform ɪnˈfɔːm (US) -ˈfɔːrm **-s** -z **-ing** -ɪŋ **-ed** -d **inˌformed oˈpinion**

informal ɪnˈfɔː.mᵊl, ˌɪn- (US) -ˈfɔːr- **-ly** -i

informalit|y ˌɪn.fɔːˈmæl.ə.t|i, -ɪ.t|i (US) -fɔːrˈmæl.ə.t̬|i **-ies** -iz

informant ɪnˈfɔː.mənt (US) -ˈfɔːr- **-s** -s

in forma pauperis ɪnˌfɔː.məˈpaʊ.pᵊr.ɪs (US) ɪnˌfɔːr.məˈpɑː.pɚ-, -ˈpɔː-

informatics ˌɪn.fəˈmæt.ɪks, -fɔːˈ- (US) -fɚˈmæt̬-

information ˌɪn.fəˈmeɪ.ʃᵊn, -fɔːˈ- (US) -fɚˈ- **-s** -z **inforˌmation techˈnology** (US) **inforˌmation techˈnology, inforˈmation techˌnology**

informa|tive ɪnˈfɔː.mə|.tɪv (US) -ˈfɔːr.mə|.t̬ɪv **-tory** -tᵊr.i (US) -tɔːr.i
informer ɪnˈfɔː.məʳ (US) -ˈfɔːr.mɚ **-s** -z
infotainment ˌɪn.fəʊˈteɪn.mənt (US) ˈɪn.foʊ.teɪn-, ˌɪn.foʊˈteɪn-
infra ˈɪn.frə ˌ**infra** ˈ**dig**
infract ɪnˈfrækt **-s** -s **-ing** -ɪŋ **-ed** -ɪd
infraction ɪnˈfræk.ʃᵊn **-s** -z
infralapsarian ˌɪn.frə.læpˈseə.ri.ən (US) -ˈser.i- **-s** -z
infrangibility ɪnˌfræn.dʒɪˈbɪl.ə.ti, ˌɪn-, -dʒəˈ-, -ɪ.ti (US) -ə.t̬i
infrangib|le ɪnˈfræn.dʒɪ.b|l̩, ˌɪn-, -dʒə- **-ly** -li **-leness** -l̩.nəs, -nɪs
infrared ˌɪn.frəˈred *stress shift:* ˌinfrared ˈcamera
infrastructure ˈɪn.frəˌstrʌk.tʃəʳ (US) -tʃɚ **-s** -z
infrequency ɪnˈfriː.kwənt.si, ˌɪn-
infrequent ɪnˈfriː.kwənt, ˌɪn- **-ly** -li
infring|e ɪnˈfrɪndʒ **-es** -ɪz **-ing** -ɪŋ **-ed** -d **-er/s** -əʳ/z (US) -ɚ/z
infringement ɪnˈfrɪndʒ.mənt **-s** -s
infuri|ate ɪnˈfjʊə.ri|.eɪt, -ˈfjɔː- (US) -ˈfjʊr.i- **-ates** -eɪts **-ating/ly** -eɪ.tɪŋ/li (US) -eɪ.t̬ɪŋ/li **-ated** -eɪ.tɪd (US) -eɪ.t̬ɪd
infus|e ɪnˈfjuːz **-es** -ɪz **-ing** -ɪŋ **-ed** -d **-er/s** -əʳ/z (US) -ɚ/z
infusible *capable of being infused:* ɪnˈfjuː.zə.bl̩, -zɪ- *not fusible:* ɪnˈfjuː.zə.bl̩, ˌɪn-, -zɪ-
infusion ɪnˈfjuː.ʒᵊn **-s** -z
infusori|an ˌɪn.fjʊˈzɔː.ri|.ən, -ˈsɔː- (US) -ˈsɔːr.i- **-al** -əl
infusory ɪnˈfjuː.zᵊr.i, -sᵊr- (US) -sɚ-, -zɚ-
in futuro ˌɪn.fjuːˈtjʊə.rəʊ (US) -ˈtʊr.oʊ, -ˈtjʊr-
-ing -ɪŋ
Note: Suffix. Normally unstressed, e.g. **shopping** /ˈʃɒp.ɪŋ (US) ˈʃɑː.pɪŋ/.
Inga ˈɪŋ.ə, -gə (US) -gə
Ingall ˈɪŋ.gɔːl (US) -gəl
Ingalls ˈɪŋ.gɔːlz (US) -gəlz
Ingatestone ˈɪŋ.gət.stəʊn, ˈɪŋ- (US) -stoʊn
ingathering ˈɪnˌgæð.ᵊr.ɪŋ **-s** -z
Inge *surname:* ɪŋ, ɪndʒ
Note: The American playwright is pronounced /ɪndʒ/. *girl's name:* ˈɪŋ.ə, -gə (US) -gə
Ingelow ˈɪn.dʒɪ.ləʊ (US) -loʊ
in genere ˌɪnˈdʒen.ᵊr.eɪ (US) -ɚ.i
ingenious ɪnˈdʒiː.ni.əs, ˌɪn- (US) ˈ-njəs, -ni.əs **-ly** -li **-ness** -nəs, -nɪs
ingénue, ingenue ˈæ̃n.ʒeɪ.njuː, ˈæn-, -ʒə-, -ʒen.juː, ˌ--ˈ- (US) ˈæn.ʒə.nuː, ˈɑːn-, -dʒə-, -njuː **-s** -z
ingenuit|y ˌɪn.dʒɪˈnjuː.ə.t|i, -dʒəˈ-, -ɪ.t|i (US) -ə.t̬|i **-ies** -iz
ingenuous ɪnˈdʒen.ju.əs **-ly** -li **-ness** -nəs, -nɪs

Ingersoll® ˈɪŋ.gə.sɒl (US) -gɚ.sɑːl, -sɔːl **-s** -z
ingest ɪnˈdʒest **-s** -s **-ing** -ɪŋ **-ed** -ɪd **-ible** -ə.bl̩, -ɪ-
inges|tion ɪnˈdʒes|.tʃᵊn **-tive** -tɪv
Ingham ˈɪŋ.əm
ingle (I) ˈɪŋ.gl̩ **-s** -z
Ingleborough ˈɪŋ.gl̩.bᵊr.ə (US) -oʊ
Ingleby ˈɪŋ.gl̩.bi
inglenook ˈɪŋ.gl̩.nʊk **-s** -s
Inglewood ˈɪŋ.gl̩.wʊd
Inglis ˈɪŋ.gᵊlz, -glɪs
inglorious ɪnˈglɔː.ri.əs, ˌɪn-, ɪŋ-, ˌɪŋ- (US) -ˈglɔːr.i- **-ly** -li **-ness** -nəs, -nɪs
Ingmar ˈɪŋ.mɑːʳ (US) -mɑːr
ingoing ˈɪnˌgəʊ.ɪŋ, ˈɪŋ- (US) ˈɪnˌgoʊ-
Ingold ˈɪŋ.gəʊld (US) -goʊld
Ingoldsby ˈɪn.gᵊl*d*z.bi
ingot ˈɪŋ.gət, -gɒt (US) -gət **-s** -s
Ingraham ˈɪŋ.grə.həm, -grɪəm (US) ˈɪŋ.grəm
ingrain ɪnˈgreɪn, ˌɪn-, ɪŋ-, ˌɪŋ- (US) ɪn-, ˌɪn- **-s** -z **-ing** -ɪŋ **-ed** -d *stress shift:* ˌingrained ˈhabits
Ingram ˈɪŋ.grəm
Ingrams ˈɪŋ.grəmz
ingrate ˈɪn.greɪt, ˈɪŋ-, -ˈ- (US) ˈɪn.greɪt, -ˈ- **-s** -s **-ly** -li
ingrati|ate ɪnˈgreɪ.ʃi|.eɪt, ɪŋ- (US) ɪn- **-ates** -eɪts **-ating** -eɪ.tɪŋ (US) -eɪ.t̬ɪŋ **-ated** -eɪ.tɪd (US) -eɪ.t̬ɪd
ingratitude ɪnˈgræt.ɪ.tjuːd, ˌɪn-, ɪŋ-, ˌɪŋ-, ˈ-ə- (US) ɪnˈgræt̬.ə.tuːd, ˌɪn-, -tjuːd
Ingrebourne ˈɪŋ.grɪ.bɔːn (US) -bɔːrn
ingredient ɪnˈgriː.di.ənt, ɪŋ- (US) ɪn- **-s** -s
Ingres ˈæŋ.grə, ˈæ̃*ŋ*- (US) ˈæŋ-, ˈæ̃*ŋ*, ˈæn-
ingress ˈɪn.gres, ˈɪŋ- (US) ˈɪn-
ingressive ɪnˈgres.ɪv, ɪŋ- (US) ɪn-
Ingrey ˈɪŋ.gri
Ingrid ˈɪŋ.grɪd
in-group ˈɪn.gruːp, ˈɪŋ- (US) ˈɪn- **-s** -s
ingrow|ing ɪnˈgrəʊ|.ɪŋ, ˌɪn-, ɪŋ-, ˌɪŋ-, ˈ-ˌ-- (US) ˈɪn.groʊ- ˌ**ingrowing** ˈ**toenail**
ingrown ɪnˈgrəʊn, ˌɪn-, ɪŋ-, ˌɪŋ (US) ˈɪn.groʊn *stress shift, British only:* ˌingrown ˈtoenail
ingrowth ˈɪn.grəʊθ, -ˈɪŋ- (US) -groʊθ **-s** -s
inguinal ˈɪŋ.gwɪ.nᵊl, -gwə-
Ingushetia ˌɪŋ.gʊˈʃet.i.ə
inhab|it ɪnˈhæb|.ɪt **-its** -ɪts **-iting** -ɪ.tɪŋ (US) -ɪ.t̬ɪŋ **-ited** -ɪ.tɪd (US) -ɪ.t̬ɪd **-iter/s** -ɪ.təʳ/z (US) -ɪ.t̬ɚ/z **-itable** -ɪ.tə.bl̩ (US) -ɪ.t̬ə.bl̩
inhabitant ɪnˈhæb.ɪ.tᵊnt **-s** -s
inhabitation ɪnˌhæb.ɪˈteɪ.ʃᵊn
inhalation ˌɪn.*h*əˈleɪ.ʃᵊn **-s** -z
inhal|e ɪnˈheɪl **-es** -z **-ing** -ɪŋ **-ed** -d **-ant/s** -ənt/s **-er/s** -əʳ/z (US) -ɚ/z
inharmonious ˌɪn.hɑːˈməʊ.ni.əs (US) -hɑːrˈmoʊ- **-ly** -li **-ness** -nəs, -nɪs

inher|e ɪnˈhɪəʳ (US) -ˈhɪr **-es** -z **-ing** -ɪŋ **-ed** -d
inheren|ce ɪnˈher.ᵊnt|s, -ˈhɪə.rᵊnt|s (US) -ˈhɪr.ᵊnt|s, -ˈher- **-cy** -si
inherent ɪnˈher.ᵊnt, -ˈhɪə.rᵊnt (US) -ˈhɪr.ᵊnt, -ˈher- **-ly** -li
inher|it ɪnˈher|.ɪt **-its** -ɪts **-iting** -ɪ.tɪŋ (US) -ɪ.t̬ɪŋ **-ited** -ɪ.tɪd (US) -ɪ.t̬ɪd **-itor/s** -ɪ.təʳ/z (US) -ɪ.t̬ɚ/z **-itable** -ɪ.tə.bl̩ (US) -ɪ.t̬ə.bl̩
inheritanc|e ɪnˈher.ɪ.tᵊnts **-es** -ɪz
inheritrix ɪnˈher.ɪ.trɪks **-es** -ɪz
inhib|it ɪnˈhɪb|.ɪt **-its** -ɪts **-iting** -ɪ.tɪŋ (US) -ɪ.t̬ɪŋ **-ited** -ɪ.tɪd (US) -ɪ.t̬ɪd **-itor/s** -ɪ.təʳ/z (US) -ɪ.t̬ɚ/z **-itory** -ɪ.tᵊr.i (US) -ɪ.tɔːr.i
inhibition ˌɪn.*h*ɪˈbɪʃ.ᵊn **-s** -z
inhospitab|le ˌɪn.hɒsˈpɪt.ə.b|l̩; ɪnˈhɒs.pɪ.tə-, ˌɪn-, -pə- (US) ɪnˈhɑː.spɪ.t̬ə-, ˌɪn-; ˌɪn.hɑːˈspɪt̬.ə- **-ly** -li **-leness** -l̩.nəs, -nɪs
inhospitality ɪnˌhɒs.pɪˈtæl.ə.ti, ˌɪn-, -ɪ.ti (US) -ˌhɑː.spəˈtæl.ə.t̬i
in-house ˌɪnˈhaʊs *stress shift:* ˌin-house proˈduction
inhuman ɪnˈhjuː.mən, ˌɪn- **-ly** -li
inhumane ˌɪn.hjuːˈmeɪn, -hjʊˈ- **-ly** -li
inhumanit|y ˌɪn.hjuːˈmæn.ə.t|i, -hjʊˈ-, -ɪ.t|i (US) -ə.t̬|i **-ies** -iz
inhumation ˌɪn.hjuːˈmeɪ.ʃᵊn, -hjʊˈ- **-s** -z
inhum|e ɪnˈhjuːm **-es** -z **-ing** -ɪŋ **-ed** -d
Inigo ˈɪn.ɪ.gəʊ (US) -goʊ
inimic|al ɪˈnɪm.ɪ.k|ᵊl **-ally** -ᵊl.i, -li
inimitability ɪˌnɪm.ɪ.təˈbɪl.ə.ti, ˌ-ə-, -ɪ.ti (US) -t̬əˈbɪl.ə.t̬i
inimitab|le ɪˈnɪm.ɪ.tə.b|l̩, ˈ-ə- (US) -t̬ə- **-ly** -li **-leness** -l̩.nəs, -nɪs
iniquitous ɪˈnɪk.wɪ.təs, -wə- (US) -t̬əs **-ly** -li
iniquit|y ɪˈnɪk.wə.t|i, -wɪ- (US) -t̬|i **-ies** -iz
initial ɪˈnɪʃ|.ᵊl **-s** -ᵊlz **-ly** -ᵊl.i, -li **-(l)ing** -ᵊl.ɪŋ, -lɪŋ **-(l)ed** -ᵊld
initialization, -isa- ɪˌnɪʃ.ᵊl.aɪˈzeɪ.ʃᵊn, -ɪˈ- (US) -ɪˈ-
initializ|e, -is|e ɪˈnɪʃ.ᵊl.aɪz **-es** -ɪz **-ing** -ɪŋ **-ed** -d
initiate *(n.)* ɪˈnɪʃ.i.ət, -eɪt, -ɪt **-s** -s
initi|ate *(v.)* ɪˈnɪʃ.i|.eɪt **-ates** -eɪts **-ating** -eɪ.tɪŋ (US) -eɪ.t̬ɪŋ **-ated** -eɪ.tɪd (US) -eɪ.t̬ɪd **-ator/s** -eɪ.təʳ/z (US) -eɪ.t̬ɚ/z
initiation ɪˌnɪʃ.iˈeɪ.ʃᵊn **-s** -z
initiative ɪˈnɪʃ.ə.tɪv, -i.ə- (US) -t̬ɪv **-s** -z
initiatory ɪˈnɪʃ.ə.tᵊr.i, -i.ə-, -eɪ- (US) -ə.tɔːr.i
initio ɪˈnɪʃ.i.əʊ, -ˈnɪt-, -ˈnɪs- (US) -oʊ
inject ɪnˈdʒekt **-s** -s **-ing** -ɪŋ **-ed** -ɪd **-or/s** -əʳ/z (US) -ɚ/z **-able** -ə.bl̩
injection ɪnˈdʒek.ʃᵊn **-s** -z

injudicious ˌɪn.dʒuːˈdɪʃ.əs **-ly** -li **-ness** -nəs, -nɪs

Injun ˈɪn.dʒən **-s** -z

injunction ɪnˈdʒʌŋk.ʃᵊn **-s** -z

injurant ˈɪn.dʒʊ.rənt, -dʒə.rənt **-s** -s

inj|ure ˈɪn.dʒ|əʳ (US) -dʒ|ɚ **-ures** -əz (US) -ɚz **-uring** -ᵊr.ɪŋ **-ured** -əd (US) -ɚd **-urer/s** -ᵊr.əʳ/z (US) -ɚ.ɚ/z

injuria absque damno ɪnˌdʒʊə.ri.əˌæb.skweɪˈdæm.nəʊ (US) -ˌdʒʊr.i.əˌæb.skweɪˈdæm.noʊ

injurious ɪnˈdʒʊə.ri.əs, -ˈdʒɔː- (US) -ˈdʒʊr.i- **-ly** -li **-ness** -nəs, -nɪs

injur|y ˈɪn.dʒᵊr|.i **-ies** -iz ˈ**injury** ˌ**time**

injustic|e ɪnˈdʒʌs.tɪs, ˌɪn- **-es** -ɪz

ink ɪŋk **-s** -s **-ing** -ɪŋ **-ed** -t **-er/s** -əʳ/z (US) -ɚ/z

Inkatha ɪnˈkɑː.tə, ɪŋˈ-

inkblot ˈɪŋk.blɒt (US) -blɑːt **-s** -s

Inkerman ˈɪŋ.kə.mən (US) -kɚ-

inkhorn ˈɪŋk.hɔːn (US) -hɔːrn **-s** -z

inkjet ˈɪŋk.dʒet **-s** -s

inkling ˈɪŋk.lɪŋ **-s** -z

Inkpen ˈɪŋk.pen

inkpot ˈɪŋk.pɒt (US) -pɑːt **-s** -s

ink-stain ˈɪŋk.steɪn **-s** -z

inkstand ˈɪŋk.stænd **-s** -z

inkwell ˈɪŋk.wel **-s** -z

ink|y ˈɪŋ.k|i **-ier** -i.əʳ (US) -i.ɚ **-iest** -i.ɪst, -i.əst **-iness** -ɪ.nəs, -ɪ.nɪs

INLA ˌaɪ.en.elˈeɪ

inlaid *(from* **inlay***)* ɪnˈleɪd (US) ˈ-- *stress shift, British only:* ˌinlaid ˈgold

inland *(n. adj.)* ˈɪn.lənd, -lænd **-s** -z ˌ**Inland** ˈ**Revenue**

inland *(adv.)* ˈɪn.lænd, -ˈ-

inlander ˈɪn.lən.dəʳ (US) -dɚ, -læn- **-s** -z

in-law ˈɪn.lɔː (US) -lɑː, -lɔː **-s** -z

inlay *(n.)* ˈɪn.leɪ

in|lay *(v.)* ɪn|ˈleɪ, ˌɪn- (US) ɪn|ˈleɪ, ˌɪn-, ˈɪn|.leɪ **-lays** -ˈleɪz (US) -ˈleɪz, -leɪz **-laying** -ˈleɪ.ɪŋ (US) -ˈleɪ-, -ˌleɪ-

inlet ˈɪn.let, -lət, -lɪt **-s** -s

in loco parentis ɪnˌləʊ.kəʊ.pəˈren.tɪs, -ˌlɒk.əʊ- (US) -ˌloʊ.koʊ.pəˈren.t̬ɪs

inly ˈɪn.li

Inman ˈɪn.mən, ˈɪm- (US) ˈɪn-

inmate ˈɪn.meɪt, ˈɪm- (US) ˈɪn- **-s** -s

in medias res ɪnˌmiː.di.æsˈreɪs, ɪm-, -ˌmeɪ-, -ˌmed.i-, -ɑːsˈ-, -əsˈ-, -ˈreɪz (US) ɪnˌmiː.di.əsˈreɪs, -ˌmed.i-, -ˈreɪz

in memoriam ˌɪn.mɪˈmɔː.ri.əm, ˌɪm-, -məˈ-, -æm (US) ˌɪn.mɪˈmɔːr.i-, -məˈ-

inmost ˈɪn.məʊst, ˈɪm- (US) ˈɪn.moʊst

inn ɪn **-s** -z

innards ˈɪn.ədz (US) -ɚdz

innate ɪˈneɪt, ˌɪnˈeɪt **-ly** -li **-ness** -nəs, -nɪs

innavigable ɪ*n*ˈnæv.ɪ.gə.bl̩, ˌɪnˈ*n*æv-, ˈ-ə-

inner ˈɪn.əʳ (US) -ɚ ˌ**inner** ˈ**city**; ˈ**inner** ˌ**tube**

inner-city ˈɪn.əˌsɪt.i (US) -ɚˌsɪt̬-

innermost ˈɪn.ə.məʊst (US) -ɚ.moʊst

inner|vate ˈɪn.ə|.veɪt; ɪˈnɜː-, ˌɪnˈɜː- (US) ɪˈnɝː-, ˌɪnˈɝː-; ˈɪn.ɚ- **-vates** -veɪts **-vating** -veɪ.tɪŋ (US) -veɪ.t̬ɪŋ **-vated** -veɪ.tɪd (US) -veɪ.t̬ɪd

innervation ˌɪn.əˈveɪ.ʃᵊn (US) -ɚˈ-

Innes(s) ˈɪn.ɪs

inning ˈɪn.ɪŋ **-s** -z **-ses** -zɪz

innings ˈɪn.ɪŋz **-es** -ɪz

Innisfail ˌɪn.ɪsˈfeɪl, -əsˈ-

Innisfree ˌɪn.ɪsˈfriː, -əsˈ-

innit ˈɪn.ɪt

innkeeper ˈɪnˌkiː.pəʳ, ˈɪŋ- (US) -pɚ **-s** -z

innocen|ce ˈɪn.ə.sᵊn*t*|s **-cy** -si

innocent (I) ˈɪn.ə.sᵊnt **-s** -s **-ly** -li

innocuous ɪˈnɒk.ju.əs (US) -ˈnɑːk- **-ly** -li **-ness** -nəs, -nɪs

innominate ɪˈnɒm.ɪ.nət, ˈ-ə-, -nɪt, -neɪt (US) -ˈnɑːm.ə-

inno|vate ˈɪn.əʊ|.veɪt (US) ˈ-ə- **-vates** -veɪts **-vating** -veɪ.tɪŋ (US) -veɪ.t̬ɪŋ **-vated** -veɪ.tɪd (US) -veɪ.t̬ɪd **-vator/s** -veɪ.təʳ/z (US) -veɪ.t̬ɚ/z

innovation ˌɪn.əʊˈveɪ.ʃᵊn (US) -əˈ- **-s** -z

innovative ˈɪn.ə.və.tɪv, -veɪ-; ɪˈnəʊ.və.tɪv (US) ˈɪn.ə.veɪ.t̬ɪv

innovatory ˈɪn.əʊ.veɪ.tᵊr.i, -və- (US) ˈɪn.ə.və.tɔːr.i

innoxious ɪˈnɒk.ʃəs (US) -ˈnɑːk- **-ly** -li **-ness** -nəs, -nɪs

Innsbruck ˈɪnz.brʊk

Innsworth ˈɪnz.wəθ, -wɜːθ (US) -wɚθ, -wɝːθ

innuendo ˌɪn.juˈen.dəʊ (US) -doʊ **-(e)s** -z

Innuit ˈɪn.u.ɪt, -ju- (US) ˈ-u- **-s** -s

innumerability ɪˌnjuː.mᵊr.əˈbɪl.ə.ti, ˌɪnˌjuː-, -ɪ.ti (US) ɪˌnuː.mɚ.əˈbɪl.ə.t̬i, ˌɪnˌuː-, -ˌjuː-

innumerab|le ɪˈnjuː.mᵊr.ə.b|l̩, ˌɪnˈjuː- (US) ɪˈnuː-, ˌɪnˈuː-, -ˈjuː- **-ly** -li **-leness** -l̩.nəs, -nɪs

innumeracy ɪˈnjuː.mᵊr.ə.si, ˌɪnˈjuː- (US) ɪˈnuː-, ˌɪnˈuː-, -ˈjuː-

innumerate ɪˈnjuː.mᵊr.ət, ˌɪnˈjuː- (US) ɪˈnuː.mɚ-, ˌɪnˈuː-, -ˈjuː- **-s** -s

innutriti|on ˌɪn.*n*juːˈtrɪʃ|.ᵊn (US) -*n*uːˈ-, -*n*juːˈ- **-ous** -əs

inobservan|ce ˌɪn.əbˈzɜː.vᵊn|*t*s (US) -ˈzɝː- **-t** -t

inoccupation ɪˌnɒk.jʊˈpeɪ.ʃᵊn, ˌɪnˌɒk- (US) ɪˌnɑː.kjəˈ-, ˌɪnˌɑː-

inocu|late ɪˈnɒk.jə|.leɪt, -jʊ- (US) -ˈnɑː.kjə- **-lates** -leɪts **-lating** -leɪ.tɪŋ (US) -leɪ.t̬ɪŋ **-lated** -leɪ.tɪd (US) -leɪ.t̬ɪd **-lator/s** -leɪ.təʳ/z (US) -leɪ.t̬ɚ/z

inoculation ɪˌnɒk.jəˈleɪ.ʃᵊn, -jʊˈ- (US) -ˌnɑː.kjəˈ- **-s** -z

inodorous ɪˈnəʊ.dᵊr.əs, ˌɪnˈəʊ- (US) ˌɪnˈnoʊ-, ɪˈnoʊ-

inoffensive ˌɪn.əˈfen*t*.sɪv **-ly** -li **-ness** -nəs, -nɪs

inofficious ˌɪn.əˈfɪʃ.əs

in omnibus ˌɪnˈɒm.nɪ.bəs, -bʊs (US) -ˈɑːm.nɪ-, -niː-

inoperable ɪˈnɒp.ᵊr.ə.bl̩, ˌɪnˈɒp- (US) ˌɪnˈɑː.pɚ-, ɪˈnɑː-

inoperative ɪˈnɒp.ᵊr.ə.tɪv, ˌɪnˈɒp- (US) ˌɪnˈɑː.pɚ.ə.t̬ɪv, ɪˈnɑː-

inopportune ɪˈnɒp.ə.tjuːn, ˌɪnˈɒp-, -tʃuːn; ˌɪn.ɒp.əˈtjuːn, -ˈtʃuːn (US) ˌɪnˌɑː.pɚˈtuːn, ɪˌnɑː-, -ˈtjuːn **-ly** -li **-ness** -nəs, -nɪs

inordinate ɪˈnɔː.dɪ.nət, ˌɪnˈɔː-, -dᵊn.ət, -ɪt (US) ˌɪnˈɔːr.dᵊn.ɪt, ɪˈnɔːr- **-ly** -li **-ness** -nəs, -nɪs

inorganic ˌɪn.ɔːˈgæn.ɪk (US) -ɔːrˈ- **-ally** -ᵊl.i, -li

inoscu|late ɪˈnɒs.kjə|.leɪt, -kjʊ- (US) -ˈnɑː.skjuː-, ˌɪnˈɑː- **-lates** -leɪts **-lating** -leɪ.tɪŋ (US) -leɪ.t̬ɪŋ **-lated** -leɪ.tɪd (US) -leɪ.t̬ɪd

inosculation ɪˌnɒs.kjəˈleɪ.ʃᵊn (US) -ˌnɑː.skjuːˈ-, ˌɪnˌɑː-

in pais ˌɪnˈpeɪs (US) ˌɪnˈpeɪ

in pari delicto ɪnˌpær.i.dɪˈlɪk.təʊ (US) -dəˈlɪk.toʊ, -ˌpɑːr-

in pari materia ɪnˌpær.i.məˈtɪə.ri.ə (US) -ˈtɪr.i.ə, -ˌpɑːr-

inpatient ˈɪnˌpeɪ.ʃᵊnt **-s** -s

in personam ˌɪn.pɜːˈsəʊ.næm, ˌɪm-, -pəˈ-, -nəm (US) ˌɪn.pɚˈsoʊ.næm

in praesenti ˌɪn.praɪˈsen.tiː (US) -prɪˈzen.tiː

in|put ˈɪn|.pʊt, ˈɪm- **-puts** -pʊts **-putting** -ˌpʊt.ɪŋ (US) -ˌpʊt̬.ɪŋ **-putted** -ˌpʊt.ɪd (US) -ˌpʊt̬.ɪd **-putter/s** -ˌpʊt.əʳ/z (US) -ˌpʊt̬.ɚ/z

input-output ˌɪn.pʊtˈaʊt.pʊt, ˌɪm-

inquest ˈɪŋ.kwest, ˈɪn- (US) ˈɪn- **-s** -s

inquietude ɪnˈkwaɪə.tjuːd, ɪŋ-, -ˈkwaɪ.ɪ- (US) ɪnˈkwaɪə.tuːd, -ˈkwaɪ.ɪ-, -tjuːd

inquiline ˈɪŋ.kwɪ.laɪn, ˈɪn- (US) ˈɪn.kwɪ.laɪn, -lɪn **-s** -z

inquir|e ɪnˈkwaɪəʳ, ɪŋ- (US) ɪnˈkwaɪr **-es** -z **-ing/ly** -ɪŋ/li **-ed** -d **-er/s** -əʳ/z (US) -ɚ/z

inquir|y ɪnˈkwaɪə.r|i, ɪŋ- (US) ɪnˈkwaɪ-; ˈɪn.kwɚ|.i **-ies** -iz

inquisition (I) ˌɪŋ.kwɪˈzɪʃ.ᵊn, ˌɪn- (US) ˌɪn- **-s** -z

inquisitional ˌɪŋ.kwɪˈzɪʃ.ᵊn.ᵊl, ˌɪn- (US) ˌɪn-

inquisitive ɪnˈkwɪz.ə.tɪv, ɪŋ-, ˈ-ɪ- (US) ɪnˈkwɪz.ə.t̬ɪv, ˈ-ɪ- **-ly** -li **-ness** -nəs, -nɪs

inquisitor ɪnˈkwɪz.ɪ.təʳ, ɪŋ- (US) ɪnˈkwɪz.ɪ.t̬ɚ **-s** -z

inquisitorial ɪnˌkwɪz.ɪˈtɔː.ri.əl, ɪŋ-; ˌɪn.kwɪ.zɪˈ-, ˌɪŋ- (US) ɪnˌkwɪz.ɪˈtɔːr.i- **-ly** -i

inquorate ˌɪnˈkwɔː.reɪt, ˌɪŋ-, -rət, -rɪt (US) ɪnˈkwɔːr.eɪt, -ət, -ɪt

in re ˌɪn'reɪ

in rem ˌɪn'rem

inroad 'ɪn.rəʊd (US) -roʊd **-s** -z

inrush 'ɪn.rʌʃ **-es** -ɪz

INS ˌaɪ.en'es

insalubr|ious ˌɪn.sə'luː.br|i.əs, -'ljuː- (US) -'luː- **-ity** -ə.ti, -ɪ.ti (US) -ə.t̬i

insane ɪn'seɪn, ˌɪn- **-ly** -li **-ness** -nəs, -nɪs

insanitar|y ɪn'sæn.ɪ.tᵊr|.i, ˌɪn-, '-ə-, -tr|i (US) -ter|.i **-iness** -ɪ.nəs, -nɪs

insanity ɪn'sæn.ə.ti, ˌɪn-, -ɪ.ti (US) -ə.t̬i

insatiability ɪnˌseɪ.ʃə'bɪl.ə.ti, -ʃi.ə'-, -ɪ.ti (US) -ə.t̬i

insatiab|le ɪn'seɪ.ʃə.b|l̩, -ʃi.ə- **-ly** -li **-leness** -l̩.nəs, -nɪs

insatiate ɪn'seɪ.ʃi.ət, -ɪt, -eɪt

inscape 'ɪn.skeɪp

inscrib|e ɪn'skraɪb **-es** -z **-ing** -ɪŋ **-ed** -d **-er/s** -əʳ/z (US) -ɚ/z

inscription ɪn'skrɪp.ʃᵊn **-s** -z

inscrutability ɪnˌskruː.tə'bɪl.ə.ti, ˌɪn-, -ɪ.ti (US) -ˌskruː.t̬ə'bɪl.ə.t̬i

inscrutab|le ɪn'skruː.tə.b|l̩, ˌɪn- (US) -t̬ə- **-ly** -li **-leness** -l̩.nəs, -nɪs

inseam 'ɪn.siːm

insect 'ɪn.sekt **-s** -s

insectari|um ˌɪn.sek'teə.ri|.əm (US) -'ter.i- **-ums** -əmz **-a** -ə

insecticidal ɪnˌsek.tɪ'saɪ.dᵊl, -tə'- **-ly** -i

insecticide ɪn'sek.tɪ.saɪd, -tə- **-s** -z

insectivore ɪn'sek.tɪ.vɔːʳ, -tə- (US) -vɔːr **-s** -z

insectivorous ˌɪn.sek'tɪv.ᵊr.əs

insecure ˌɪn.sɪ'kjʊəʳ, -sə'-, -'kjɔːʳ (US) -'kjʊr **-ly** -li

insecurit|y ˌɪn.sɪ'kjʊə.rə.t|i, -sə'-, -'kjɔː-, -rɪ- (US) -'kjʊr.ə.t̬|i **-ies** -iz

insemi|nate ɪn'sem.ɪ|.neɪt, '-ə- **-nates** -neɪts **-nating** -neɪ.tɪŋ (US) -neɪ.t̬ɪŋ **-nated** -neɪ.tɪd (US) -neɪ.t̬ɪd **-nator/s** -neɪ.təʳ/z (US) -neɪ.t̬ɚ/z

insemination ɪnˌsem.ɪ'neɪ.ʃᵊn, ˌɪn-, -ə'-

insensate ɪn'sent.seɪt, ˌɪn-, -sət, -sɪt **-ly** -li **-ness** -nəs, -nɪs

insensibility ɪnˌsent.sə'bɪl.ə.ti, ˌɪn-, -sɪ'-, -ɪ.ti (US) -ə.t̬i

insensib|le ɪn'sent.sə.b|l̩, ˌɪn-, -sɪ- **-ly** -li **-leness** -l̩.nəs, -nɪs

insensitive ɪn'sent.sə.tɪv, ˌɪn-, -sɪ- (US) -t̬ɪv **-ness** -nəs, -nɪs

insensitivity ɪnˌsent.sə'tɪv.ə.ti, ˌɪn-, -sɪ'-, -ɪ.ti (US) -ə.t̬i

insentien|t ˌɪn'sen.tʃᵊn|t, -tʃi.ən|t **-ce** -ts

inseparability ɪnˌsep.ᵊr.ə'bɪl.ə.ti, ˌɪn-, -rə'-, -ɪ.ti (US) -ə.t̬i

inseparab|le ɪn'sep.ᵊr.ə.b|l̩, ˌɪn-, '-rə- **-ly** -li **-leness** -l̩.nəs, -nɪs

insert (*n.*) 'ɪn.sɜːt (US) -sɝːt **-s** -s

in|sert (*v.*) ɪn|'sɜːt (US) -'sɝːt **-serts** -'sɜːts (US) -'sɝːts **-serting** -'sɜː.tɪŋ (US) -'sɝː.t̬ɪŋ **-serted** -'sɜː.tɪd (US) -'sɝː.t̬ɪd

insertion ɪn'sɜː.ʃᵊn (US) -'sɝː- **-s** -z

in-service ˌɪn'sɜː.vɪs (US) 'ɪnˌsɝː- *stress shift, British only:* ˌin-service 'training

inset (*n.*) 'ɪn.set **-s** -s

inse|t (*v.*) ˌɪn'se|t (US) ɪn'se|t, '-- **-ts** -ts **-tting** -tɪŋ (US) -t̬ɪŋ

inseverable ɪn'sev.ᵊr.ə.bl̩, ˌɪn-

inshore ˌɪn'ʃɔːʳ (US) -'ʃɔːr *stress shift:* ˌinshore 'rescue

inside ˌɪn'saɪd, '-- **-s** -z ˌ**inside 'job** (US) '**inside** ˌ**job**; ˌ**inside 'out**

insider ɪn'saɪ.dəʳ, ˌɪn- (US) 'ɪnˌsaɪ.dɚ, -'-- **-s** -z **in**ˌ**sider 'dealing** (US) ˌ**insider 'dealing; in**ˌ**sider 'trading** (US) ˌ**insider 'trading**

insidious ɪn'sɪd.i.əs **-ly** -li **-ness** -nəs, -nɪs

insight 'ɪn.saɪt **-s** -s

insightful 'ɪn.saɪt.fᵊl, -fʊl (US) 'ɪn.saɪt.fᵊl, -'-- **-ly** -li

insignia ɪn'sɪg.ni.ə **-s** -z

insignifican|ce ˌɪn.sɪg'nɪf.ɪ.kᵊnt|s **-cy** -si

insignificant ˌɪn.sɪg'nɪf.ɪ.kᵊnt **-ly** -li

insincere ˌɪn.sɪn'sɪəʳ, -sᵊn'- (US) -'sɪr **-ly** -li

insincerit|y ˌɪn.sɪn'ser.ə.t|i, -sᵊn'-, -ɪ.t|i (US) -ə.t̬|i **-ies** -iz

insinu|ate ɪn'sɪn.ju|.eɪt **-ates** -eɪts **-ating/ly** -eɪ.tɪŋ/li (US) -eɪ.t̬ɪŋ/li **-ated** -eɪ.tɪd (US) -eɪ.t̬ɪd **-ator/s** -eɪ.təʳ/z (US) -eɪ.t̬ɚ/z

insinuation ɪnˌsɪn.ju'eɪ.ʃᵊn, ˌɪn- **-s** -z

insipid ɪn'sɪp.ɪd **-ly** -li **-ness** -nəs, -nɪs

insipidity ˌɪn.sɪ'pɪd.ə.ti, -ɪ.ti (US) -ɪ.t̬i

insipien|ce ɪn'sɪp.i.ən|ts **-t** -t

insist ɪn'sɪst **-s** -s **-ing** -ɪŋ **-ed** -ɪd

insisten|ce ɪn'sɪs.tᵊnt|s **-cy** -si

insistent ɪn'sɪs.tᵊnt **-ly** -li

in situ ˌɪn'sɪt.juː, -'sɪtʃ.uː, -'saɪ.tjuː, -tʃuː (US) -'saɪ.tuː, -'siː-, -'sɪt.uː, -juː

Inskip 'ɪn.skɪp

insobriety ˌɪn.səʊ'braɪ.ə.ti, -'braɪ.ɪ- (US) -soʊ'braɪ.ə.t̬i

insofar ˌɪn.səʊ'fɑːʳ (US) -soʊ'fɑːr

insolation ˌɪn.səʊ'leɪ.ʃᵊn (US) -soʊ'-

insole 'ɪn.səʊl (US) -soʊl **-s** -z

insolence 'ɪnt.sᵊl.ənts

insolent 'ɪnt.sᵊl.ənt **-ly** -li

insolubility ɪnˌsɒl.jə'bɪl.ə.ti, ˌɪn-, -jʊ'-, -ɪ.ti (US) -ˌsɑːl.jə'bɪl.ə.t̬i

insolub|le ɪn'sɒl.jə.b|l̩, ˌɪn-, -jʊ- (US) -'sɑːl.jə- **-ly** -li **-leness** -l̩.nəs, -nɪs

insolvable ɪn'sɒl.və.bl̩, ˌɪn- (US) -'sɑːl-

insolven|cy ɪn'sɒl.vᵊn|t.si, ˌɪn- (US) -'sɑːl- **-t** -t

insomnia ɪn'sɒm.ni.ə (US) -'sɑːm-

insomniac ɪn'sɒm.ni.æk (US) -'sɑːm- **-s** -s

insomuch ˌɪn.səʊ'mʌtʃ (US) -soʊ'-

insouciance ɪn'suː.si.ənts (US) -si.ənts, -ʃənts

insouciant ɪn'suː.si.ənt (US) -si.ənt, -ʃənt **-ly** -li

in specie ˌɪn'spes.i.eɪ (US) ˌɪn'spiː.ʃi, -si

inspect ɪn'spekt **-s** -s **-ing** -ɪŋ **-ed** -ɪd

inspection ɪn'spek.ʃᵊn **-s** -z

inspector ɪn'spek.təʳ **-s** -z

inspectorate ɪn'spek.tᵊr.ət, -ɪt **-s** -s

inspectorship ɪn'spek.tə.ʃɪp (US) -tɚ- **-s** -s

inspiration ˌɪnt.spᵊr'eɪ.ʃᵊn, -spɪ'reɪ- (US) -spə'reɪ- **-s** -z

inspirational ˌɪnt.spᵊr'eɪ.ʃᵊn.əl, -spɪ'reɪ- (US) -spə'reɪ- **-ly** -i

inspirator 'ɪnt.spᵊr.eɪ.təʳ, -spɪ.reɪ- (US) -spə.reɪ.t̬ɚ **-s** -z

inspiratory ɪn'spaɪə.rə.tᵊr.i, -'spɪr.ə- (US) -'spaɪ.rə.tɔːr-

inspir|e ɪn'spaɪəʳ (US) -'spaɪr **-es** -z **-ing/ly** -ɪŋ/li **-ed** -d **-er/s** -əʳ/z (US) -ɚ/z

inspir|it ɪn'spɪr|.ɪt **-its** -ɪts **-iting** -ɪ.tɪŋ (US) -ɪ.t̬ɪŋ **-ited** -ɪ.tɪd (US) -ɪ.t̬ɪd

inspiss|ate ɪn'spɪs|.eɪt; 'ɪn.spɪ.s|eɪt (US) ɪn'spɪs|.eɪt **-ates** -eɪts **-ating** -eɪ.tɪŋ (US) -eɪ.t̬ɪŋ **-ated** -eɪ.tɪd (US) -eɪ.t̬ɪd

inst. *(abbrev. for* **instant***)* ɪntst, 'ɪnt.stᵊnt

inst. (I) *(abbrev. for* **institute***)* ɪntst, 'ɪnt.stɪ.tjuːt, -stə-, -tʃuːt (US) -tuːt, -tjuːt

instabilit|y ˌɪn.stə'bɪl.ə.t|i, -ɪ.t|i (US) -ə.t̬|i **-ies** -iz

instal ɪn'stɔːl (US) -'stɔːl, -'stɑːl **-s** -z **-ling** -ɪŋ **-led** -d

install ɪn'stɔːl (US) -'stɔːl, -'stɑːl **-s** -z **-ing** -ɪŋ **-ed** -d **-able** -ə.bl̩

installation ˌɪn.stə'leɪ.ʃᵊn **-s** -z

installer ɪn'stɔː.ləʳ (US) -'stɔː.lɚ, -'stɑː- **-s** -z

instal(l)ment ɪn'stɔːl.mənt (US) -'stɔːl-, -'stɑːl- **-s** -s **in'stallment** ˌ**plan**

instanc|e 'ɪnt.stənts **-es** -ɪz **-ing** -ɪŋ **-ed** -t

instant 'ɪnt.stənt **-s** -s **-ly** -li

instantaneous ˌɪnt.stən'teɪ.ni.əs **-ly** -li **-ness** -nəs, -nɪs

instanter ɪn'stæn.təʳ (US) -t̬ɚ

in statu quo ɪnˌstæt.juː'kwəʊ (US) -ˌsteɪ.tuː'kwoʊ, -ˌstɑː-

instead ɪn'sted

instep 'ɪn.step **-s** -s

insti|gate 'ɪnt.stɪ|.geɪt, -stə- **-gates** -geɪts **-gating** -geɪ.tɪŋ (US) -geɪ.t̬ɪŋ **-gated** -geɪ.tɪd (US) -geɪ.t̬ɪd **-gator/s** -geɪ.təʳ/z (US) -geɪ.t̬ɚ/z

instigation ˌɪnt.stɪ'geɪ.ʃᵊn, -stə'- **-s** -z

instil ɪn'stɪl **-s** -z **-ling** -ɪŋ **-led** -d **-ment** -mənt

instill ɪn'stɪl **-s** -z **-ing** -ɪŋ **-ed** -d **-ment** -mənt

instillation ˌɪnt.stɪˈleɪ.ʃᵊn, -stəˈ-
instinct ˈɪnt.stɪŋkt **-s** -s
instinctive ɪnˈstɪŋk.tɪv **-ly** -li
institu|te ˈɪnt.stɪ.tjuː|t, -stə-, -tʃuː|t (US) -tuː|t, -tjuː|t **-tes** -ts **-ting** -tɪŋ (US) -t̬ɪŋ **-ted** -tɪd (US) -t̬ɪd **-tor/s** -təʳ/z (US) -t̬ɚ/z
institution ˌɪnt.stɪˈtjuː.ʃᵊn, -stəˈ-, -ˈtʃuː- (US) -ˈtuː-, -ˈtjuː- **-s** -z
institutional ˌɪnt.stɪˈtjuː.ʃᵊn.ᵊl, -stəˈ-, -ˈtʃuː- (US) -ˈtuː-, -ˈtjuː- **-ly** -li
institutionalization, -isa- ˌɪnt.stɪˌtjuː.ʃᵊn.ᵊl.aɪˈzeɪ.ʃᵊn, -stəˌ-, -ˌtʃuː-, -ɪˈ- (US) -ˌtuː.ʃᵊn.ᵊl.ɪˈ-, -ˌtjuː-
institutionaliz|e, -is|e ˌɪnt.stɪˈtjuː.ʃᵊn.ə.laɪz, -stəˈ-, -ˈtʃuː- (US) -ˈtuː-, -ˈtjuː- **-es** -ɪz **-ing** -ɪŋ **-ed** -d
in-store ˌɪnˈstɔːʳ (US) -ˈstɔːr *stress shift:* ˌin-store ˈrestaurant
instress ˌɪnˈstres
instruct ɪnˈstrʌkt **-s** -s **-ing** -ɪŋ **-ed** -ɪd
instruction ɪnˈstrʌk.ʃᵊn **-s** -z
instructional ɪnˈstrʌk.ʃᵊn.ᵊl **-ly** -i
instructive ɪnˈstrʌk.tɪv **-ly** -li **-ness** -nəs, -nɪs
instructor ɪnˈstrʌk.təʳ (US) -tɚ **-s** -z
instrument ˈɪnt.strə.mənt, -strʊ- (US) -strə- **-s** -s
instrumental ˌɪnt.strəˈmen.tᵊl, -strʊˈ- (US) -strəˈmen.t̬ᵊl **-s** -z **-ly** -i **-ist/s** -ɪst/s
instrumentality ˌɪnt.strə.menˈtæl.ə.ti, -strʊ-, -mənˈ-, -ɪ.ti (US) -strə.menˈtæl.ə.t̬i, -mənˈ-
instrumentation ˌɪnt.strə.menˈteɪ.ʃᵊn, -strʊ-, -mənˈ- (US) -strə-
insubordinate ˌɪn.səˈbɔː.dᵊn.ət, -dɪ.nət, -nɪt (US) -ˈbɔːr.dᵊn.ɪt **-s** -s
insubordination ˌɪn.səˌbɔː.dɪˈneɪ.ʃᵊn, -dəˈ- (US) -ˌbɔːr-
insubstantial ˌɪn.səbˈstæn.tʃᵊl, -ˈstɑːn- (US) -ˈstæn- **-ly** -i
insufferab|le ɪnˈsʌf.ᵊr.ə.b|l̩ **-ly** -li
insufficien|ce ˌɪn.səˈfɪʃ.ᵊnt|s **-cy** -si
insufficient ˌɪn.səˈfɪʃ.ᵊnt **-ly** -li
insular ˈɪnt.sjə.ləʳ, -sjʊ- (US) -sə.lɚ, -sjə- **-ly** -li **-ism** -ɪ.zᵊm
insularity ˌɪnt.sjəˈlær.ə.ti, -sjʊˈ-, -ɪ.ti (US) -səˈler.ə.t̬i, -sjəˈ-, -ˈlær-
insu|late ˈɪnt.sjə|.leɪt, -sjʊ- (US) -sə-, -sjə- **-lates** -leɪts **-lating** -leɪ.tɪŋ (US) -leɪ.t̬ɪŋ **-lated** -leɪ.tɪd (US) -leɪ.t̬ɪd **-lator/s** -leɪ.təʳ/z (US) -leɪ.t̬ɚ/z ˈ**insulating** ˌ**tape**
insulation ˌɪnt.sjəˈleɪ.ʃᵊn, -sjʊˈ- (US) -səˈ-, -sjəˈ-
insulin ˈɪnt.sjə.lɪn, -sjʊ- (US) -sə-
insult (*n.*) ˈɪn.sʌlt **-s** -s **add** ˌ**insult to** ˈ**injury**
in|sult (*v.*) ɪn|ˈsʌlt **-sults** -ˈsʌlts **-sulting/ly** -ˈsʌl.tɪŋ/li (US) -ˈsʌl.t̬ɪŋ/li **-sulted** -ˈsʌl.tɪd (US) -ˈsʌl.t̬ɪd **-sulter/s** -ˈsʌl.təʳ/z (US) -ˈsʌl.t̬ɚ/z

insuperability ɪnˌsuː.pᵊr.əˈbɪl.ə.ti, ˌɪn-, -ˌsjuː-, -ɪ.ti (US) -ˌsuː.pɚ.əˈbɪl.ə.t̬i
insuperab|le ɪnˈsuː.pᵊr.ə.b|l̩, ˌɪn-, -ˈsjuː- (US) -ˈsuː- **-ly** -li
insupportab|le ˌɪn.səˈpɔː.tə.b|l̩ (US) -ˈpɔːr.t̬ə- **-ly** -li **-leness** -l̩.nəs, -nɪs
insuppressib|le ˌɪn.səˈpres.ə.b|l̩, ˈ-ɪ- **-ly** -li
insuranc|e ɪnˈʃʊə.rᵊnts, -ˈʃɔː- (US) -ˈʃʊr.ᵊnts **-es** -ɪz **inˈsurance** ˌ**broker; inˈsurance** ˌ**policy**
insur|e ɪnˈʃʊəʳ, -ʃɔːʳ (US) -ˈʃʊr **-es** -z **-ing** -ɪŋ **-ed** -d **-er/s** -əʳ/z (US) -ɚ/z **-able** -ə.bl̩
insurgen|ce ɪnˈsɜː.dʒᵊnt|s (US) -ˈsɝː- **-cy** -si
insurgent ɪnˈsɜː.dʒᵊnt (US) -ˈsɝː- **-s** -s
insurmountability ˌɪn.səˌmaʊn.təˈbɪl.ə.ti, -ɪ.ti (US) -sɚˌmaʊn.t̬əˈbɪl.ə.t̬i
insurmountab|le ˌɪn.səˈmaʊn.tə.b|l̩ (US) -sɚˈmaʊn.t̬ə- **-ly** -li
insurrection ˌɪn.sᵊrˈek.ʃᵊn (US) -səˈrek- **-s** -z
insurrectional ˌɪn.sᵊrˈek.ʃᵊn.ᵊl (US) -səˈrek-
insurrectionar|y ˌɪn.sᵊrˈek.ʃᵊn.ᵊr|.i (US) -səˈrek.ʃᵊn.er- **-ies** -iz
insurrection|ism ˌɪn.sᵊrˈek.ʃᵊn|.ɪ.zᵊm (US) -səˈrek- **-ist/s** -ɪst/s
insusceptibility ˌɪn.səˌsep.təˈbɪl.ə.ti, -tɪˈ-, -ɪ.ti (US) -ə.t̬i
insusceptib|le ˌɪn.səˈsep.tə.b|l̩, -tɪ- **-ly** -li
intact ɪnˈtækt, ˌɪn- **-ness** -nəs, -nɪs
intaglio ɪnˈtɑː.li.əʊ, -ˈtæl.i- (US) -ˈtæl.joʊ, -ˈtɑːl- **-s** -z
intake ˈɪn.teɪk **-s** -s
intangibility ɪnˌtæn.dʒəˈbɪl.ə.ti, ˌɪn-, -dʒɪˈ-, -ɪ.ti (US) -ə.t̬i
intangib|le ɪnˈtæn.dʒə.b|l̩, ˌɪn-, -dʒɪ- **-ly** -li **-leness** -l̩.nəs, -nɪs
integer ˈɪn.tɪ.dʒəʳ, -tə- (US) -dʒɚ, -t̬ə- **-s** -z
integral (*n.*) ˈɪn.tɪ.grəl, -tə- (US) -t̬ə- **-s** -z
integral (*adj.*) ˈɪn.tɪ.grəl, -tə-; ɪnˈteg.rəl (US) ˈɪn.t̬ə.grəl; ɪnˈteg.rəl **-ly** -i
Note: As a mathematical term always /ˈɪn.tɪ.grəl (US) -t̬ə-/.
inte|grate ˈɪn.tɪ|.greɪt, -tə- (US) -t̬ə- **-grates** -greɪts **-grating** -greɪ.tɪŋ (US) -greɪ.t̬ɪŋ **-grated** -greɪ.tɪd (US) -greɪ.t̬ɪd **-grator/s** -greɪ.təʳ/z (US) -greɪ.t̬ɚ/z ˌ**integrated** ˈ**circuit**
integration ˌɪn.tɪˈgreɪ.ʃᵊn, -təˈ- (US) -t̬əˈ- **-s** -z
integrity ɪnˈteg.rə.ti, -rɪ- (US) -t̬i
integument ɪnˈteg.jə.mənt, -jʊ- **-s** -s
Intel® ˈɪn.tel
intellect ˈɪn.tᵊl.ekt, -tɪ.lekt (US) -t̬ə.lekt **-s** -s

intellection ˌɪn.tᵊlˈek.ʃᵊn, -tɪˈlek- (US) -t̬əˈlek-
intellective ˌɪn.tᵊlˈek.tɪv, -tɪˈlek- (US) -t̬əˈlek-
intellectual ˌɪn.tᵊlˈek.tju.əl, -tɪˈlek-, -tʃu- (US) -t̬ᵊlˈek.tʃu- **-s** -z **-ly** -i
intellectual|ism ˌɪn.tᵊlˈek.tju.ə.l|ɪ.zᵊm, -tɪˈlek-, -tʃu- (US) -t̬ᵊlˈek.tʃu- **-ist/s** -ɪst/s
intellectuality ˌɪn.tᵊlˌek.tjuˈæl.ə.ti, -tɪˌlek-, -tʃuˈ-, -ɪ.ti (US) -tʃuˈæl.ə.t̬i
intellectualiz|e, -is|e ˌɪn.tᵊlˈek.tju.ə.laɪz, -tɪˈlek-, -tʃu- (US) -t̬ᵊlˈek.tʃu- **-es** -ɪz **-ing** -ɪŋ **-ed** -d
intelligence ɪnˈtel.ɪ.dʒᵊnts, ˈ-ə- **-es** -ɪz **-er/s** -əʳ/z (US) -ɚ/z **inˈtelligence** ˌ**test**
intelligent ɪnˈtel.ɪ.dʒᵊnt, ˈ-ə- **-ly** -li
intelligentsia ɪnˌtel.ɪˈdʒent.si.ə, ˌɪn- (US) -ˈdʒent-, -ˈgent-
intelligibility ɪnˌtel.ɪ.dʒəˈbɪl.ə.ti, ˌ-ə-, -dʒɪˈ-, -ɪ.ti (US) -ə.t̬i
intelligib|le ɪnˈtel.ɪ.dʒə.b|l̩, ˈ-ə-, -dʒɪ- **-ly** -li **-leness** -l̩.nəs, -nɪs
intemperance ɪnˈtem.pᵊr.ᵊnts, ˌɪn-, ˈ-prᵊnts
intemperate ɪnˈtem.pᵊr.ət, ˌɪn-, -ɪt, ˈ-prət (US) -prɪt **-ly** -li **-ness** -nəs, -nɪs
intend ɪnˈtend **-s** -z **-ing** -ɪŋ **-ed** -ɪd
intendan|ce ɪnˈten.dən|ts **-cy** -tsi **-t/s** -t/s
intens|e ɪnˈtents **-er** -əʳ **-est** -ɪst, -əst **-ely** -li **-eness** -nəs, -nɪs
intensification ɪnˌtent.sɪ.fɪˈkeɪ.ʃᵊn, -sə- **-s** -z
intensi|fy ɪnˈtent.sɪ|.faɪ, -sə- **-fies** -faɪz **-fying** -faɪ.ɪŋ **-fied** -faɪd **-fier/s** -faɪ.əʳ/z (US) -faɪ.ɚ/z
intension ɪnˈten.tʃᵊn
intensit|y ɪnˈtent.sə.t|i, -sɪ- (US) -sə.t̬|i **-ies** -iz
intensive ɪnˈtent.sɪv **-ly** -li **-ness** -nəs, -nɪs **inˌtensive** ˈ**care**
in|tent ɪn|ˈtent **-tents** -ˈtents **-tenter** -ˈten.təʳ (US) -ˈten.t̬ɚ **-tentest** -ˈten.tɪst, -ˈten.təst (US) -ˈten.t̬ɪst, -ˈten.t̬əst **-tently** -ˈtent.li **-tentness** -ˈtent.nəs, -ˈtent.nɪs
intention ɪnˈten.tʃᵊn **-s** -z **-ed** -d
intentional ɪnˈten.tʃᵊn.ᵊl **-ly** -i
inter- ɪn.təʳ- (US) ɪn.t̬ɚ-
Note: Prefix. Normally takes either primary stress or secondary stress on the first syllable, with nouns often receiving front stress, e.g. **intercom** (noun) /ˈɪn.tə.kɒm (US) -t̬ɚ.kɑːm/, **interact** (verb) /ˌɪn.təʳˈækt (US) -t̬ɚˈækt/. Exceptions exist; see individual entries. Note also that, although /r/ is normally assigned to a following strong syllable in US transcriptions, in **inter-** it is perceived to be

morphemically linked to that morpheme and is retained in the prefix as /ɚ/.

inter (*v.*) ɪnˈtɜːʳ US -ˈtɝː **-s** -z **-ring** -ɪŋ **-red** -d

inter (*Latin prep., in such phrases as* **inter alia, inter se**) ˈɪn.təʳ US -t̬ɚ

interact (*n.*) ˈɪn.təʳ.ækt US -t̬ɚˈækt **-s** -s

interact (*v.*) ˌɪn.təʳˈækt US -t̬ɚˈækt **-s** -s **-ing** -ɪŋ **-ed** -ɪd

interaction ˌɪn.təʳˈæk.ʃᵊn US -t̬ɚˈæk- **-s** -z

interactive ˌɪn.təʳˈæk.tɪv US -t̬ɚˈæk- **-ly** -li

interactivity ˌɪn.təʳ.ækˈtɪv.ə.ti, -ɪ.ti US -t̬ɚ.ækˈtɪv.ə.t̬i

Interahamwe ˌɪn.tᵊr.əˈhæm.weɪ US -t̬ɚ-

inter alia ˌɪn.təʳˈeɪ.li.ə, -ˈæl.i- US -t̬ɚˈɑː-, -ˈeɪ-, -ɑː

interblend ˌɪn.təˈblend US -t̬ɚˈ- **-s** -z **-ing** -ɪŋ **-ed** -ɪd

inter|breed ˌɪn.tə|ˈbriːd US -t̬ɚˈ- **-breeds** -ˈbriːdz **-breeding** -ˈbriː.dɪŋ **-bred** -ˈbred

intercalary ɪnˈtɜː.kᵊl.ᵊr.i; ˌɪn.təˈkæl- US ɪnˈtɝː.kə.ler-, ˌɪn.t̬ɚˈkæl.ɚ.i

interca|late ɪnˈtɜː.kə|.leɪt, ˈɪn.tə.kə- US -ˈtɝː- **-lates** -leɪts **-lating** -leɪ.tɪŋ US -leɪ.t̬ɪŋ **-lated** -leɪ.tɪd US -leɪ.t̬ɪd

intercalation ɪnˌtɜː.kəˈleɪ.ʃᵊn US -ˌtɝː- **-s** -z

interced|e ˌɪn.təˈsiːd US -t̬ɚˈ- **-es** -z **-ing** -ɪŋ **-ed** -ɪd **-er/s** -əʳ/z US -ɚ/z

intercept (*n.*) ˈɪn.tə.sept US -t̬ɚ- **-s** -s

intercept (*v.*) ˌɪn.təˈsept US -t̬ɚˈ- **-s** -s **-ing** -ɪŋ **-ed** -ɪd **-er/s** -əʳ/z US -ɚ/z **-or/s** -əʳ/z US -ɚ/z

interception ˌɪn.təˈsep.ʃᵊn US -t̬ɚˈ- **-s** -z

interceptive ˌɪn.təˈsep.tɪv US -t̬ɚˈ-

intercession ˌɪn.təˈseʃ.ᵊn US -t̬ɚˈ- **-s** -z

intercessional ˌɪn.təˈseʃ.ᵊn.ᵊl US -t̬ɚˈ-

intercessor ˌɪn.təˈses.əʳ, ˈɪn.tə.ses- US ˌɪn.t̬ɚˈses.ɚ, ˈɪn.t̬ɚ.ses- **-s** -z

intercessory ˌɪn.təˈses.ᵊr.i US -t̬ɚˈ-

interchang|e (*n.*) ˈɪn.tə.tʃeɪndʒ US -t̬ɚ- **-es** -ɪz

interchang|e (*v.*) ˌɪn.təˈtʃeɪndʒ US -t̬ɚˈ- **-es** -ɪz **-ing** -ɪŋ **-ed** -d

interchangeability ˌɪn.təˌtʃeɪn.dʒəˈbɪl.ə.ti, -ɪ.ti US -t̬ɚˌtʃeɪn.dʒəˈbɪl.ə.t̬i

interchangeab|le ˌɪn.təˈtʃeɪn.dʒə.b|l̩ US -t̬ɚˈ- **-ly** -li **-leness** -l̩.nəs, -nɪs

intercity (I) ˌɪn.təˈsɪt.i US -t̬ɚˈsɪt̬- *stress shift:* ˌintercity ˈtrain

intercollegiate ˌɪn.tə.kəˈliː.dʒət, -kɒlˈiː-, -dʒi.ət, -ɪt US -t̬ɚ.kəˈliː.dʒɪt

intercolonial ˌɪn.tə.kəˈləʊ.ni.əl US -t̬ɚ.kəˈloʊ-

intercom ˈɪn.tə.kɒm US -t̬ɚ.kɑːm **-s** -z

intercommuni|cate ˌɪn.tə.kəˈmjuː.nɪ|.keɪt, -nə- US -t̬ɚ- **-cates** -keɪts **-cating** -keɪ.tɪŋ US -keɪ.t̬ɪŋ **-cated** -keɪ.tɪd US -keɪ.t̬ɪd **-cator/s** -keɪ.təʳ/z US -keɪ.t̬ɚ/z

intercommunication ˌɪn.tə.kəˌmjuː.nɪˈkeɪ.ʃᵊn, -nəˈ- US -t̬ɚ-

intercommunion ˌɪn.tə.kəˈmjuː.ni.ən US -t̬ɚ.kəˈmjuː.njən

intercommunity ˌɪn.tə.kəˈmjuː.nə.ti, -nɪ- US -t̬ɚ.kəˈmjuː.nə.t̬i

interconnect ˌɪn.tə.kəˈnekt US -t̬ɚ- **-s** -s **-ing** -ɪŋ **-ed** -ɪd

interconnection ˌɪn.tə.kəˈnek.ʃᵊn US -t̬ɚ- **-s** -z

intercontinental ˌɪn.təˌkɒn.tɪˈnen.tᵊl, -təˈ- US -t̬ɚˌkɑːn.təˈnen.t̬ᵊl

intercostal ˌɪn.təˈkɒs.tᵊl US -t̬ɚˈkɑː.stᵊl

intercourse ˈɪn.tə.kɔːs US -t̬ɚ.kɔːrs

intercurrent ˌɪn.təˈkʌr.ᵊnt US -t̬ɚˈkɝː- **-ly** -li

interdenominational ˌɪn.tə.dɪˌnɒm.ɪˈneɪ.ʃᵊn.ᵊl, -dəˌ-, -əˈ- US -t̬ɚ.dɪˌnɑː.məˈ-, -diˌ- **-ism** -ɪ.zᵊm **-ly** -i

interdental ˌɪn.təˈden.tᵊl US -t̬ɚˈden.t̬ᵊl

interdepartmental ˌɪn.təˌdiː.pɑːtˈmen.tᵊl; ˌɪn.tə.dɪˌpɑːtˈ-, -dəˌ- US -t̬ɚˌdiː.pɑːrtˈmen.t̬ᵊl, -dɪ-

interdependence ˌɪn.tə.dɪˈpen.dənts, -dəˈ- US -t̬ɚ.diːˈ-, -dɪˈ-

interdependent ˌɪn.tə.dɪˈpen.dᵊnt, -dəˈ- US -t̬ɚ.diːˈ-, -dɪˈ- **-ly** -li

interdict (*n.*) ˈɪn.tə.dɪkt, -daɪt US -t̬ɚ.dɪkt **-s** -s

interdict (*v.*) ˌɪn.təˈdɪkt, -ˈdaɪt US -t̬ɚˈdɪkt **-s** -s **-ing** -ɪŋ **-ed** -ɪd

interdiction ˌɪn.təˈdɪk.ʃᵊn US -t̬ɚˈ- **-s** -z

interdigi|tate ˌɪn.təˈdɪdʒ.ɪ|.teɪt, ˈ-ə- US -t̬ɚˈ- **-tates** -teɪts **-tating** -teɪ.tɪŋ US -teɪ.t̬ɪŋ **-tated** -teɪ.tɪd US -teɪ.t̬ɪd

interdisciplinary ˌɪn.təˈdɪs.ɪ.plɪ.nᵊr.i, ˈ-ə-; ˌɪn.təˌdɪs.ɪˈplɪn.ᵊr-, -əˈ- US -t̬ɚˈdɪs.ə.plɪ.ner-

interest ˈɪn.trəst, -trest, -trɪst; -tᵊr.əst, -est, -ɪst US ˈɪn.trɪst, -trəst, -trest; -t̬ɚ.ɪst, -əst, -est **-s** -s **-ing** -ɪŋ **-ed/ly** -ɪd/li ˈ**interest** ˌ**rate**

interesting ˈɪn.trə.stɪŋ, -tres.tɪŋ, -trɪ.stɪŋ, -tᵊr.ə-, -es.tɪŋ, -ɪ.stɪŋ US ˈɪn.trɪ.stɪŋ, -trə-, -tres.tɪŋ, -t̬ɚ.ɪ.stɪŋ, -es.tɪŋ **-ly** -li

interfac|e (*n.*) ˈɪn.tə.feɪs US -t̬ɚ- **-es** -ɪz

interfac|e (*v.*) ˌɪn.təˈfeɪs, ˈ--- US ˈɪn.t̬ɚ.feɪs **-es** -ɪz **-ing** -ɪŋ **-ed** -t

Note: The computer world uses first-syllable stress for both noun and verb.

interfaith ˌɪn.təˈfeɪθ US ˈɪn.t̬ɚ.feɪθ *stress shift, British only:* ˌinterfaith ˈservice

interfer|e ˌɪn.təˈfɪəʳ US -t̬ɚˈfɪr **-es** -z **-ing** -ɪŋ **-ed** -d **-er/s** -əʳ/z US -ɚ/z

interferenc|e ˌɪn.təˈfɪə.rᵊnts US -t̬ɚˈfɪr.ᵊnts **-es** -ɪz

interferon ˌɪn.təˈfɪə.rɒn US -t̬ɚˈfɪr.ɑːn **-s** -z

Interflora® ˌɪn.təˈflɔː.rə US -t̬ɚˈflɔːr.ə

interfus|e ˌɪn.təˈfjuːz US -t̬ɚˈ- **-es** -ɪz **-ing** -ɪŋ **-ed** -d

interfusion ˌɪn.təˈfjuː.ʒᵊn US -t̬ɚˈ-

intergalactic ˌɪn.tə.gəˈlæk.tɪk US -t̬ɚ-

interglacial ˌɪn.təˈgleɪ.si.əl, -ʃi-, -ʃᵊl US -t̬ɚˈgleɪ.ʃᵊl

intergovernmental ˌɪn.tə.gʌv.ᵊnˈmen.tᵊl, -ᵊmˈ- US -t̬ɚˌgʌv.ɚnˈmen.t̬ᵊl

interim ˈɪn.tᵊr.ɪm US -t̬ɚ-

interior ɪnˈtɪə.ri.əʳ US -ˈtɪr.i.ɚ **-s** -z **in**ˌ**terior** ˈ**decorator; in**ˌ**terior de**ˈ**signer**

interioriz|e, -is|e ɪnˈtɪə.ri.ə.raɪz US -ˈtɪr.i- **-es** -ɪz **-ing** -ɪŋ **-ed** -d

interject ˌɪn.təˈdʒekt US -t̬ɚˈ- **-s** -s **-ing** -ɪŋ **-ed** -ɪd **-or/s** -əʳ/z US -ɚ/z

interjection ˌɪn.təˈdʒek.ʃᵊn US -t̬ɚˈ- **-s** -z **-al/ly** -əl/i

inter|knit ˌɪn.tə|ˈnɪt US -t̬ɚˈ- **-knits** -ˈnɪts **-knitting** -ˈnɪt.ɪŋ US -ˈnɪt̬.ɪŋ **-knitted** -ˈnɪt.ɪd US -ˈnɪt̬.ɪd

interlac|e ˌɪn.təˈleɪs US -t̬ɚˈ- **-es** -ɪz **-ing** -ɪŋ **-ed** -t **-ement** -mənt

Interlaken ˈɪn.tə.lɑː.kᵊn, ˌɪn.təˈlɑː- US ˈɪn.t̬ɚ.lɑː-, ˌɪn.t̬ɚˈlɑː, -t̬ɚ-

interlanguage ˈɪn.təˌlæŋ.gwɪdʒ US -t̬ɚ-

interlard ˌɪn.təˈlɑːd US -t̬ɚˈlɑːrd **-s** -z **-ing** -ɪŋ **-ed** -ɪd

interlea|f ˈɪn.tə.liː|f US -t̬ɚ- **-ves** -vz

interleav|e ˌɪn.təˈliːv US -t̬ɚˈ- **-es** -z **-ing** -ɪŋ **-ed** -d

interlin|e ˌɪn.təˈlaɪn US -t̬ɚˈ- **-es** -z **-ing** -ɪŋ **-ed** -d

interlinear ˌɪn.təˈlɪn.i.əʳ US -t̬ɚˈlɪn.i.ɚ

interlineation ˌɪn.təˌlɪn.iˈeɪ.ʃᵊn US -t̬ɚ- **-s** -z

interlink ˌɪn.təˈlɪŋk US -t̬ɚˈ- **-s** -s **-ing** -ɪŋ **-ed** -t

interlock ˌɪn.təˈlɒk US -t̬ɚˈlɑːk **-s** -s **-ing** -ɪŋ **-ed** -t

interlocution ˌɪn.tə.ləˈkjuː.ʃᵊn, -lɒkˈjuː- US -t̬ɚ.loʊˈkjuː- **-s** -z

interlocutor ˌɪn.təˈlɒk.jə.təʳ, -jʊ- US -t̬ɚˈlɑː.kjə.t̬ɚ, -kjʊ- **-s** -z **-y** -i

interlocu|tress ˌɪn.təˈlɒk.jə|.trəs, -jʊ-, -trɪs US -t̬ɚˈlɑː.kjʊ|.trɪs, -kjə- **-trice** -trɪs **-trix** -trɪks

interlop|e ˌɪn.təˈləʊp ⓤⓢ ˈɪn.t̬ɚ.loʊp **-es** -s **-ing** -ɪŋ **-ed** -t
interloper ˈɪn.təˌləʊ.pəʳ, ˌɪn.təˈləʊ.pəʳ ⓤⓢ ˈɪn.t̬ɚˌloʊ.pɚ **-s** -z
interlude ˈɪn.tə.luːd, -ljuːd ⓤⓢ -t̬ɚ.luːd **-s** -z
intermarriag|e ˌɪn.təˈmær.ɪdʒ ⓤⓢ -t̬ɚˈmer-, -ˈmær- **-es** -ɪz
intermarr|y ˌɪn.təˈmær|.i ⓤⓢ ˈɪn.t̬ɚˌmer-, -ˈmær- **-ies** -iz **-ying** -i.ɪŋ **-ied** -id
intermeddl|e ˌɪn.təˈmed.l̩ ⓤⓢ -t̬ɚˈ- **-es** -z **-ing** -ɪŋ, -ˈmed.lɪŋ **-ed** -d **-er/s** -əʳ/z, -ˈmed.ləʳ/z ⓤⓢ -lɚ/z
intermediar|y ˌɪn.təˈmiː.di.ə.r|i ⓤⓢ -t̬ɚˈmiː.di.er-, -ɚ- **-ies** -iz
intermediate ˌɪn.təˈmiː.di.ət, -ɪt ⓤⓢ -t̬ɚˈ- **-s** -s **-ly** -li
interment ɪnˈtɜː.mənt ⓤⓢ -ˈtɝː- **-s** -s
intermezz|o ˌɪn.təˈmet.s|əʊ, -ˈmed.z|əʊ ⓤⓢ -t̬ɚˈmet.s|oʊ, -ˈmed.z|oʊ **-os** -əʊz ⓤⓢ -oʊz **-i** -i, -iː
interminab|le ɪnˈtɜː.mɪ.nə.b|l̩, ˌɪn-, -mᵊn.ə- ⓤⓢ -ˈtɝː- **-ly** -li **-leness** -l̩.nəs, -nɪs
intermingl|e ˌɪn.təˈmɪŋ.gl̩ ⓤⓢ -t̬ɚˈ- **-es** -z **-ing** -ɪŋ, -ˈmɪŋ.glɪŋ **-ed** -d
intermission ˌɪn.təˈmɪʃ.ᵊn ⓤⓢ -t̬ɚˈ- **-s** -z
inter|mit ˌɪn.tə|ˈmɪt ⓤⓢ -t̬ɚˈ- **-mits** -ˈmɪts **-mitting/ly** -ˈmɪt.ɪŋ/li ⓤⓢ -ˈmɪt̬.ɪŋ/li **-mitted** -ˈmɪt.ɪd ⓤⓢ -ˈmɪt̬.ɪd
intermittent ˌɪn.təˈmɪt.ᵊnt ⓤⓢ -t̬ɚˈmɪt- **-ly** -li
intermix ˌɪn.təˈmɪks ⓤⓢ -t̬ɚˈ- **-es** -ɪz **-ing** -ɪŋ **-ed** -t
intermixture ˌɪn.təˈmɪks.tʃəʳ ⓤⓢ -t̬ɚˈmɪks.tʃɚ **-s** -z
intermodal ˌɪn.təˈməʊ.dᵊl ⓤⓢ -t̬ɚˈmoʊ-
intern (*n.*) ˈɪn.tɜːn, -ˈ- ⓤⓢ ˈɪn.tɝːn **-s** -z
intern (*v.*) ɪnˈtɜːn ⓤⓢ ɪnˈtɝːn, ˈ-- **-s** -z **-ing** -ɪŋ **-ed** -d
internal ɪnˈtɜː.nᵊl, ˌɪn- ⓤⓢ -ˈtɝː- **-ly** -i **inˌternal comˈbustion; inˌternal comˈbustion ˌengine** ⓤⓢ **inˌternal comˌbustion ˈengine; Inˌternal ˈRevenue ˌService**
internalization ɪnˌtɜː.nᵊl.aɪˈzeɪ.ʃᵊn, ˌɪn-, -ɪˈ- ⓤⓢ -ˌtɝː.nᵊl.ɪˈ-
internaliz|e, -is|e ɪnˈtɜː.nᵊl.aɪz ⓤⓢ -ˈtɝː- **-es** -ɪz **-ing** -ɪŋ **-ed** -d
international ˌɪn.təˈnæʃ.ᵊn.ᵊl, -təˈnæʃ.nᵊl ⓤⓢ -t̬ɚˈ- **-s** -z **-ly** -i
Internationale ˌɪn.təˌnæʃ.əˈnɑːl, -ˌnæʃ.i.əˈnɑːl ⓤⓢ -t̬ɚˌnæʃ.əˈnæl, -ˈnɑːl
international|ism ˌɪn.təˈnæʃ.ᵊn.ᵊl|.ɪ.zᵊm, -ˈnæʃ.nᵊl- ⓤⓢ -t̬ɚˈ- **-ist/s** -ɪst/s
internationalization, -isa- ˌɪn.təˌnæʃ.ᵊn.ᵊl.aɪˈzeɪ.ʃᵊn, ˌ-nᵊl-, -ɪˈ- ⓤⓢ -t̬ɚˌnæʃ.ᵊn.ᵊl.ɪˈ-, ˌ-nᵊl-
internationaliz|e, -is|e ˌɪn.təˈnæʃ.ᵊn.ᵊl.aɪz, -ˈnæʃ.nᵊl- ⓤⓢ -t̬ɚˈ- **-es** -ɪz **-ing** -ɪŋ **-ed** -d
interne ˈɪn.tɜːn ⓤⓢ -tɝːn **-s** -z
internecine ˌɪn.təˈniː.saɪn, -tɜːˈ- ⓤⓢ -t̬ɚˈniː.sɪn, -siːn, -ˈnes.ɪn, -iːn
internee ˌɪn.tɜːˈniː ⓤⓢ -tɝːˈ- **-s** -z
Internet ˈɪn.tə.net ⓤⓢ -t̬ɚ-
internist ˈɪn.tɜː.nɪst, -ˈ-- ⓤⓢ ˈɪn.tɝː-, -ˈ-- **-s** -s
internment ɪnˈtɜːn.mənt, -ˈtɜːm- ⓤⓢ -ˈtɝːn- **-s** -s
internodal ˌɪn.təˈnəʊ.dᵊl ⓤⓢ -t̬ɚˈnoʊ-
internode ˈɪn.tə.nəʊd ⓤⓢ -t̬ɚ.noʊd **-s** -z
internship ˈɪn.tɜːn.ʃɪp, -ˈ-- ⓤⓢ ˈɪn.tɝːn-, -ˈ-- **-s** -s
interoceanic ˌɪn.tərˌəʊ.ʃiˈæn.ɪk ⓤⓢ -t̬ɚˌoʊ-
inter pares ˌɪn.təˈpɑː.riːz, -ˈpeə-, -reɪs ⓤⓢ -tɚˈpɑː.res
inter partes ˌɪn.təˈpɑː.tiːz, -teɪs ⓤⓢ ˌɪn.tɚˈpɑːr.tes
interpellant ˌɪn.təˈpel.ənt ⓤⓢ -t̬ɚˈ- **-s** -s
interpell|ate ɪnˈtɜː.pə.l|eɪt, -pɪ-, -pel|.eɪt; ˌɪn.təˈpel|.eɪt ⓤⓢ ˌɪn.t̬ɚˈpel-; ɪnˈtɜː.pə.l|eɪt **-ates** -eɪts **-ating** -eɪ.tɪŋ ⓤⓢ -eɪ.t̬ɪŋ **-ated** -eɪ.tɪd ⓤⓢ -eɪ.t̬ɪd
interpellation ɪnˌtɜː.pəˈleɪ.ʃᵊn, -pɪˈ-, -pelˈeɪ-; ˌɪn.tə.pəˈleɪ- ⓤⓢ ˌɪn.tɚ.pəˈleɪ-; ɪnˌtɝː- **-s** -z
interpene|trate ˌɪn.təˈpen.ɪ|.treɪt, ˈ-ə- ⓤⓢ -t̬ɚˈ- **-trates** -treɪts **-trating** -treɪ.tɪŋ ⓤⓢ -treɪ.t̬ɪŋ **-trated** -treɪ.tɪd ⓤⓢ -treɪ.t̬ɪd
interpenetration ˌɪn.təˌpen.ɪˈtreɪ.ʃᵊn, -əˈ- ⓤⓢ -t̬ɚˌ-
interpersonal ˌɪn.təˈpɜː.sᵊn.ᵊl ⓤⓢ -t̬ɚˈpɝː- **-ly** -i
interplanetary ˌɪn.təˈplæn.ɪ.tᵊr.i, ˈ-ə- ⓤⓢ -t̬ɚˈplæn.ə.ter-
interplay ˈɪn.tə.pleɪ ⓤⓢ -t̬ɚ-
interpleader ˌɪn.təˈpliː.dəʳ ⓤⓢ -t̬ɚˈpliː.dɚ **-s** -z
Interpol ˈɪn.tə.pɒl ⓤⓢ -t̬ɚ.pɑːl, -poʊl
interpo|late ɪnˈtɜː.pə|.leɪt ⓤⓢ -ˈtɝː- **-lates** -leɪts **-lating** -leɪ.tɪŋ ⓤⓢ -leɪ.t̬ɪŋ **-lated** -leɪ.tɪd ⓤⓢ -leɪ.t̬ɪd **-lator/s** -leɪ.təʳ/z ⓤⓢ -leɪ.t̬ɚ/z
interpolation ɪnˌtɜː.pəˈleɪ.ʃᵊn ⓤⓢ -ˌtɝː- **-s** -z
interposal ˌɪn.təˈpəʊ.zᵊl ⓤⓢ -t̬ɚˈpoʊ- **-s** -z
interpos|e ˌɪn.təˈpəʊz ⓤⓢ -t̬ɚˈpoʊz **-es** -ɪz **-ing** -ɪŋ **-ed** -d **-er/s** -əʳ/z ⓤⓢ -ɚ/z
interposition ˌɪn.tə.pəˈzɪʃ.ᵊn; ɪnˌtɜː- ⓤⓢ ˌɪn.t̬ɚ.pəˈ- **-s** -z
interpre|t ɪnˈtɜː.prɪ|t, -prə|t ⓤⓢ -ˈtɝː.prə|t **-ts** -ts **-ting** -tɪŋ ⓤⓢ -t̬ɪŋ **-ted** -tɪd ⓤⓢ -t̬ɪd **-table** -tə.bl̩ ⓤⓢ -t̬ə.bl̩
interpretation ɪnˌtɜː.prɪˈteɪ.ʃᵊn, -prəˈ- ⓤⓢ -ˌtɝː.prəˈ- **-s** -z **-al** -ᵊl
interpretative ɪnˈtɜː.prɪ.tə.tɪv, -prə-, -teɪ- ⓤⓢ -ˈtɝː.prə.teɪ.t̬ɪv, -t̬ə- **-ly** -li
interpreter ɪnˈtɜː.prɪ.təʳ, -prə- ⓤⓢ -ˈtɝː.prə.t̬ɚ **-s** -z
interpretive ɪnˈtɜː.prɪ.tɪv, -prə- ⓤⓢ -ˈtɝː.prə.t̬ɪv **-ly** -li
interquartile ˌɪn.təˈkwɔː.taɪl ⓤⓢ -t̬ɚˈkwɔːr-, -tɪl, -t̬ᵊl
interracial ˌɪn.təˈreɪ.ʃᵊl, -ʃi.əl ⓤⓢ -t̬ɚˈreɪ.ʃᵊl
interregn|um ˌɪn.təˈreg.n|əm ⓤⓢ -t̬ɚˈ- **-ums** -əmz **-a** -ə
interre|late ˌɪn.tə.rɪ|ˈleɪt, -rəˈ- ⓤⓢ -t̬ɚ.riˈ-, -rɪˈ- **-lates** -ˈleɪts **-lating** -ˈleɪ.tɪŋ ⓤⓢ -ˈleɪ.t̬ɪŋ **-lated** -ˈleɪ.tɪd ⓤⓢ -ˈleɪ.t̬ɪd
interrelation ˌɪn.tə.rɪˈleɪ.ʃᵊn, -rəˈ- ⓤⓢ -t̬ɚ.riˈ-, -rɪˈ- **-s** -z
interrelationship ˌɪn.tə.rɪˈleɪ.ʃᵊn.ʃɪp
interro|gate ɪnˈter.ə|.geɪt **-gates** -geɪts **-gating** -geɪ.tɪŋ ⓤⓢ -geɪ.t̬ɪŋ **-gated** -geɪ.tɪd ⓤⓢ -geɪ.t̬ɪd **-gator/s** -geɪ.təʳ/z ⓤⓢ -geɪ.t̬ɚ/z
interrogation ɪnˌter.əˈgeɪ.ʃᵊn **-s** -z
interrogative ˌɪn.təˈrɒg.ə.tɪv ⓤⓢ -t̬ɚˈrɑː.gə.t̬ɪv **-s** -z **-ly** -li
interrogator|y ˌɪn.təˈrɒg.ə.tᵊr|.i ⓤⓢ -t̬ɚˈrɑː.gə.tɔːr- **-ies** -iz
interrupt (*v.*) ˌɪn.təˈrʌpt ⓤⓢ -t̬ɚˈ- **-s** -s **-ing** -ɪŋ **-ed** -ɪd **-er/s** -əʳ/z ⓤⓢ -ɚ/z
interrupt (*n.*) ˈɪn.tə.rʌpt ⓤⓢ -t̬ɚ-
interruption ˌɪn.təˈrʌp.ʃᵊn ⓤⓢ -t̬ɚˈ- **-s** -z
intersect ˌɪn.təˈsekt ⓤⓢ -t̬ɚˈ- **-s** -s **-ing** -ɪŋ **-ed** -ɪd **-or/s** -əʳ/z ⓤⓢ -ɚ/z
intersection ˌɪn.təˈsek.ʃᵊn, ˈɪn.təˌsek- ⓤⓢ ˌɪn.t̬ɚˈsek-, ˈɪn.t̬ɚˌsek- **-s** -z
Note: /ˈɪn.t̬ɚˌsek.ʃᵊn/ is the common US pronunciation for a place where streets meet.
interspac|e (*n.*) ˈɪn.tə.speɪs, ˌ--ˈ- ⓤⓢ ˈɪn.t̬ɚ.speɪs **-es** -ɪz
interspac|e (*v.*) ˌɪn.təˈspeɪs ⓤⓢ -t̬ɚˈ-, ˈ--- **-es** -ɪz **-ing** -ɪŋ **-ed** -t
interspers|e ˌɪn.təˈspɜːs ⓤⓢ -t̬ɚˈspɝːs **-es** -ɪz **-ing** -ɪŋ **-ed** -t
interspersion ˌɪn.təˈspɜː.ʃᵊn, -ʒᵊn ⓤⓢ -t̬ɚˈspɝː-
interstate (I) ˌɪn.təˈsteɪt ⓤⓢ ˈɪn.t̬ɚ.steɪt *stress shift, British only:* ˌinterstate ˈhighway
interstellar ˌɪn.təˈstel.əʳ ⓤⓢ -t̬ɚˈstel.ɚ *stress shift:* ˌinterstellar ˈtravel
interstic|e ɪnˈtɜː.stɪs ⓤⓢ -ˈtɝː- **-es** -ɪz, -iːz
interstitial ˌɪn.təˈstɪʃ.ᵊl ⓤⓢ -t̬ɚˈ-
intertribal ˌɪn.təˈtraɪ.bᵊl ⓤⓢ -t̬ɚˈ-
intertwin|e ˌɪn.təˈtwaɪn ⓤⓢ -t̬ɚˈ- **-es** -z **-ing** -ɪŋ **-ed** -d

intertwist ˌɪn.tə'twɪst US -t̬ɚ'- **-s** -s **-ing** -ɪŋ **-ed** -ɪd

interurban ˌɪn.təʳ'ɜː.bᵊn US -t̬ɚ'ɝː-

interval 'ɪn.tə.vᵊl US -t̬ɚ- **-s** -z

interven|e ˌɪn.tə'viːn US -t̬ɚ'- **-es** -z **-ing** -ɪŋ **-ed** -d **-er/s** -əʳ/z US -ɚ/z

intervention ˌɪn.tə'ven.*t*ʃᵊn US -t̬ɚ'- **-s** -z

intervention|ism ˌɪn.tə'ven.*t*ʃᵊn|.ɪ.zᵊm US -t̬ɚ'- **-ist/s** -ɪst/s

interventionist ˌɪn.tə'ven.tʃᵊn.ɪst US -t̬ɚ'-

interview 'ɪn.tə.vjuː US -t̬ɚ- **-s** -z **-ing** -ɪŋ **-ed** -d **-er/s** -əʳ/z US -ɚ/z

interviewee ˌɪn.tə.vju'iː US -t̬ɚ- **-s** -z

inter vivos ˌɪn.tə'viː.vəʊs US -tɚ'viː.voʊs, -'vaɪ-

intervocalic ˌɪn.tə.və*ʊ*'kæl.ɪk US -t̬ɚ.voʊ'-

interweav|e ˌɪn.tə'wiːv US -t̬ɚ'-, '--- **-es** -z **-ing** -ɪŋ **-ed** -d **interwove** ˌɪn.tə'wəʊv US -t̬ɚ'woʊv, '--- **interwoven** ˌɪn.tə'wəʊ.vᵊn US -t̬ɚ'woʊ.vᵊn, 'ɪn.t̬ɚˌwoʊ-

intestac|y ɪn'tes.tə.s|i **-ies** -iz

intestate ɪn'tes.teɪt, -tɪt, -tət **-s** -s

intestinal ɪn'tes.tɪ.nᵊl, -tᵊn.ᵊl, ˌɪn.tes'taɪ.nᵊl US ɪn'tes.tɪ-

intestine ɪn'tes.tɪn, -tiːn US -tɪn, -tən **-s** -z

inthral(l) ɪn'θrɔːl US -'θrɑːl, -'θrɔːl **-s** -z **-ing** -ɪŋ **-ed** -d

intifada ˌɪn.tɪ'fɑː.də **-s** -z

intimac|y 'ɪn.tɪ.mə.s|i, -tə- US -t̬ə-, -t̬ɪ- **-ies** -iz

intimate (*n. adj.*) 'ɪn.tɪ.mət, -tə-, -mɪt US -t̬ə.mət, -t̬ɪ- **-s** -s **-ly** -li

inti|mate (*v.*) 'ɪn.tɪ|.meɪt, -tə- US -t̬ə-, -t̬ɪ- **-mates** -meɪts **-mating** -meɪ.tɪŋ US -meɪ.t̬ɪŋ **-mated** -meɪ.tɪd US -meɪ.t̬ɪd **-mater/s** -meɪ.təʳ/z US -meɪ.t̬ɚ/z

intimation ˌɪn.tɪ'meɪ.ʃᵊn, -tə'- US -t̬ə'-, -t̬ɪ'- **-s** -z

intimi|date ɪn'tɪm.ɪ|.deɪt, '-ə- **-dates** -deɪts **-dating** -deɪ.tɪŋ US -deɪ.t̬ɪŋ **-dated** -deɪ.tɪd US -deɪ.t̬ɪd **-dator/s** -deɪ.təʳ/z US -deɪ.t̬ɚ/z

intimidation ɪnˌtɪm.ɪ'deɪ.ʃᵊn, -ə'-

intituled ɪn'tɪt.juːld

into 'ɪn.tə, -tu, -tuː US -tə, -tu

Note: In British English, the pronunciation /'ɪn.tuː/ is sometimes used in final position (e.g. 'That's the wall he walked into'), though the /u/ vowel is more usual. Elsewhere, the pronunciation /'ɪn.tə/ is used before consonants (e.g. 'into debt' /ˌɪn.tə'det/) and /'ɪn.tu/ before vowels (e.g. 'into each' /ɪn.tu'iːtʃ/). In American English the schwa form is usual before consonants and also vowels (e.g. 'into each' /ˌɪn.tə'iːtʃ/).

intolerab|le ɪn'tɒl.ᵊr.ə.b|l̩, ˌɪn- US -'tɑː.lɚ- **-ly** -li **-leness** -l̩.nəs, -nɪs

intolerance ɪn'tɒl.ᵊr.ᵊn*t*s, ˌɪn- US -'tɑː.lɚ-

intolerant ɪn'tɒl.ᵊr.ᵊnt, ˌɪn- US -'tɑː.lɚ- **-ly** -li

into|nate 'ɪn.tə*ʊ*|.neɪt US -toʊ-, -tə- **-nates** -neɪts **-nating** -neɪ.tɪŋ US -neɪ.t̬ɪŋ **-nated** -neɪ.tɪd US -neɪ.t̬ɪd

intonation ˌɪn.tə*ʊ*'neɪ.ʃᵊn US -toʊ'-, -tə'- **-s** -z

intonational ˌɪn.tə*ʊ*'neɪ.ʃᵊn.ᵊl US -toʊ'-, -tə'-

inton|e ɪn'təʊn US -'toʊn **-es** -z **-ing** -ɪŋ **-ed** -d **-er/s** -əʳ/z US -ɚ/z

in toto ɪn'təʊ.təʊ US -'toʊ.toʊ

Intourist® 'ɪnˌtʊə.rɪst, -ˌtɔː- US -ˌtʊr.ɪst

Intonation

The use of the pitch of the voice to convey linguistic information. The word is used with two rather different meanings. In a restricted sense, it is the variations in the pitch of a speaker's voice used to convey or alter meaning. In a broader and more popular sense, intonation is equivalent to 'prosody', where variations in such things as voice quality, tempo and loudness are included.

Examples for English

Intonation is said to convey emotions and attitudes. Other linguistic functions have also been claimed: interesting relationships exist in English between intonation and grammar, for example. In a few extreme cases a perceived difference in grammatical meaning may depend on the pitch movement, e.g.:

- she didn't go because of her ˇ <u>time</u>table
  (meaning 'she did go, but it was not because of her timetable')
- she didn't go because of her ˋ <u>time</u>table
  (meaning 'she didn't go, the reason being her timetable').

Other 'meanings' of intonation include things like the difference between statement and question, e.g.:

- it was ˋ <u>cold</u>
  (meaning "it was cold")
- it was ˊ <u>cold</u>
  (meaning "was it cold?)

the contrast between 'open' and 'closed' lists, e.g.:

- would you like ˊ <u>wine</u>, ˊ <u>sherry</u> or ˊ <u>beer</u>
  ('open', implying other things are also on offer)
- would you like ˊ <u>wine</u>, ˊ <u>sherry</u> or ˋ <u>beer</u>
  ('closed', implying no further choices are available)

and the indication of whether a relative clause is restrictive or non-restrictive, e.g.:

- the students who were ˇ <u>ner</u>vous ˋ <u>failed</u>
  (restrictive relative clause: only students who were nervous failed)
- the ˇ <u>stu</u>dents, who were ˇ <u>ner</u>vous, ˋ <u>failed</u>
  (non-restrictive relative clause: all students were nervous and all failed)

Another approach to intonation is to concentrate on its role in conversational discourse: this involves such aspects as indicating whether the particular thing being said constitutes new information or old, the regulation of turn-taking in conversation, the establishment of dominance and the elicitation of co-operative responses. As with the signalling of attitudes, it seems that though analysts concentrate on pitch movements there are many other prosodic factors being used to create these effects.

intoxicant ɪn'tɒk.sɪ.kᵊnt, -sə- US -'tɑːk.sɪ- **-s** -s

intoxi|cate ɪn'tɒk.sɪ|.keɪt, -sə- US -'tɑːk.sɪ- **-cates** -keɪts **-cating** -keɪ.tɪŋ US -keɪ.t̬ɪŋ **-cated** -keɪ.tɪd US -keɪ.t̬ɪd **-cator/s** -keɪ.təʳ/z US -keɪ.t̬ɚ/z

intoxication ɪnˌtɒk.sɪ'keɪ.ʃᵊn, -sə'- US -ˌtɑːk.sɪ'-

intra- ˌɪn.trə-
Note: Prefix. Normally takes secondary stress on the first syllable, e.g. **intravenous** /ˌɪn.trə'viː.nəs/.

intractability ɪnˌtræk.tə'bɪl.ə.ti, ˌɪn-, -ɪ.ti US -ə.t̬i

intractab|le ɪn'træk.tə.b|l̩, ˌɪn- **-ly** -li **-leness** -l̩.nəs, -nɪs

intradepartmental ˌɪn.trəˌdiː.pɑːt'men.tᵊl US -pɑːrt'men.t̬ᵊl

intrados ɪn'treɪ.dɒs US -dɑːs; 'ɪn.trə.dɑːs, -doʊs **-es** -ɪz

intramural ˌɪn.trə'mjʊə.rᵊl, -'mjɔː- US -'mjʊr.ᵊl

intramuscular ˌɪn.trə'mʌs.kjə.ləʳ, -kjʊ- US -lɚ **-ly** -li

intranet 'ɪn.trə.net **-s** -s

intransigence ɪn'trænt.sɪ.dʒᵊnts, -'trɑːnt-, -sə-; -'træn.zɪ-, -'trɑːn-, -zə- US -'trænt.sə-

intransigent ɪn'trænt.sɪ.dʒᵊnt, -'trɑːnt-, -sə-; -'træn.zɪ-, -'trɑːn-, -zə- US -'trænt.sə- **-s** -s **-ly** -li

intransitive ɪn'trænt.sə.tɪv, ˌɪn-, -'trɑːnt-, -sɪ-; -'træn.zə-, -'trɑːn-, -zɪ- US -'trænt.sə.t̬ɪv **-s** -z **-ly** -li

intransitivity ɪnˌtrænt.sə'tɪv.ə.ti, ˌɪn-, -ˌtrɑːnt-, -sɪ'-; -ˌtræn.zə'-, -ˌtrɑːn-, -zɪ'-, -ɪ.ti US -ˌtrænt.sə'tɪv.ə.t̬i

intrapersonal ˌɪn.trə'pɜː.sᵊn.ᵊl US -'pɝː-

intrauterine ˌɪn.trə'juː.tᵊr.aɪn US -t̬ɚ.ɪn, -t̬ə.raɪn ˌ**intra**ˌ**uterine de**'**vice**

intravenous ˌɪn.trə'viː.nəs **-ly** -li

in-tray 'ɪn.treɪ **-s** -z

intrench ɪn'trentʃ **-es** -ɪz **-ing** -ɪŋ **-ed** -t **-ment/s** -mənt/s

intrepid ɪn'trep.ɪd **-ly** -li

intrepidity ˌɪn.trə'pɪd.ə.ti, -trɪ'-, -trep'ɪd-, -ɪ.ti US ˌɪn.trə'pɪd.ə.t̬i, -trɪ'-

intricac|y 'ɪn.trɪ.kə.s|i, -trə- **-ies** -iz

intricate 'ɪn.trɪ.kət, -trə-, -kɪt **-ly** -li **-ness** -nəs, -nɪs

intrigue (*n.*) 'ɪn.triːg, ˌ-'-

intrigu|e (*v.*) ɪn'triːg **-es** -z **-ing/ly** -ɪŋ/li **-ed** -d **-er/s** -əʳ/z US -ɚ/z

intrinsic ɪn'trɪnt.sɪk; -'trɪn.zɪk **-ally** -ᵊl.i, -li

intro- ɪn.trəʊ- US ɪn.troʊ-, -trə-
Note: Prefix. Normally takes either primary or secondary stress on the first syllable, e.g. **introvert** (noun), /'ɪn.trəʊ.vɜːt US -troʊ.vɜːrt/, **introspect** /ˌɪn.trəʊ'spekt US -troʊ'-/.

intro 'ɪn.trəʊ US -troʊ **-s** -z

introduc|e ˌɪn.trə'djuːs, -'dʒuːs US -'duːs, -'djuːs **-es** -ɪz **-ing** -ɪŋ **-ed** -t **-er/s** -əʳ/z US -ɚ/z

introduction ˌɪn.trə'dʌk.ʃᵊn **-s** -z

introductor|y ˌɪn.trə'dʌk.tᵊr|.i **-ily** -ᵊl.i, -ɪ.li **-iness** -ɪ.nəs, -nɪs

introit 'ɪn.trɔɪt, -trəʊ.ɪt; ɪn'trəʊ.ɪt US ɪn'troʊ.ɪt; 'ɪn.trɔɪt **-s** -s

intromission ˌɪn.trəʊ'mɪʃ.ᵊn US -troʊ'-, -trə'- **-s** -z

intro|mit ˌɪn.trəʊ|'mɪt US -troʊ'-, -trə'- **-mits** -'mɪts **-mitting** -'mɪt.ɪŋ US -'mɪt̬.ɪŋ **-mitted** -'mɪt.ɪd US -'mɪt̬.ɪd

introspect ˌɪn.trəʊ'spekt US -troʊ'-, -trə'- **-s** -s **-ing** -ɪŋ **-ed** -ɪd

introspection ˌɪn.trəʊ'spek.ʃᵊn US -troʊ'-, -trə'- **-ist/s** -ɪsts/s **-al** -ᵊl

introspective ˌɪn.trəʊ'spek.tɪv US -troʊ'-, -trə'- **-ly** -li **-ness** -nəs, -nɪs

introversion ˌɪn.trəʊ'vɜː.ʃᵊn, -ʒᵊn US -troʊ'vɝː-, -trə'-

introvert (*n.*) 'ɪn.trəʊ.vɜːt US -troʊ.vɝːt, -trə- **-s** -s

introver|t (*v.*) ˌɪn.trəʊ'vɜː|t US -troʊ'vɝː|t, -trə'-, '--- **-ts** -ts **-ting** -tɪŋ US -t̬ɪŋ **-ted** -tɪd US -t̬ɪd

intrud|e ɪn'truːd **-es** -z **-ing** -ɪŋ **-ed** -ɪd **-er/s** -əʳ/z US -ɚ/z

intrusion ɪn'truː.ʒᵊn **-s** -z

intrusive ɪn'truː.sɪv **-ly** -li **-ness** -nəs, -nɪs

intu|it ɪn'tjuː|.ɪt US ɪn'tuː-, -'tjuː-, 'ɪn.tu|.ɪt **-its** -ɪts **-iting** -ɪ.tɪŋ US -ɪ.t̬ɪŋ **-ited** -ɪ.tɪd US -ɪ.t̬ɪd **-itable** -ɪ.tə.bl̩

intuition ˌɪn.tju'ɪʃ.ᵊn US -tu'-, -tju'- **-s** -z **-al** -ᵊl

intuitive ɪn'tjuː.ɪ.tɪv, '-ə- US -'tuː.ɪ.t̬ɪv, -'tjuː- **-ly** -li **-ness** -nəs, -nɪs

intumescen|ce ˌɪn.tjuː'mes.ᵊn|ts US -tuː'-, -tjuː'- **-t** -t

Inuit 'ɪn.u.ɪt, -ju- US '-u- **-s** -s

inun|date 'ɪn.ʌn|.deɪt, -ən- US -ən- **-dates** -deɪts **-dating** -deɪ.tɪŋ US -deɪ.t̬ɪŋ **-dated** -deɪ.tɪd US -deɪ.t̬ɪd

inundation ˌɪn.ʌn'deɪ.ʃᵊn, -ən'- US -ən'- **-s** -z

inur|e ɪ'njʊəʳ, -'njɔːʳ US -'njʊr, -'nʊr **-es** -z **-ing** -ɪŋ **-ed** -d **-ement** -mənt

in utero ɪn'juː.tᵊr.əʊ US -t̬ɚ.oʊ

inutility ˌɪn.juː'tɪl.ə.ti, -ɪ.ti US -ə.t̬i

invad|e ɪn'veɪd **-es** -z **-ing** -ɪŋ **-ed** -ɪd **-er/s** -əʳ/z US -ɚ/z

invalid (*n. v. adj.*) *infirm through illness, etc.:* 'ɪn.və.lɪd, -liːd US -lɪd **-s** -z **-ing** -ɪŋ **-ed** -ɪd

invalid (*adj.*) *not valid:* ɪn'væl.ɪd, ˌɪn-

invali|date ɪn'væl.ɪ|.deɪt, ˌɪn-, '-ə- **-dates** -deɪts **-dating** -deɪ.tɪŋ US -deɪ.t̬ɪŋ **-dated** -deɪ.tɪd US -deɪ.t̬ɪd

invalidation ɪnˌvæl.ɪ'deɪ.ʃᵊn, ˌɪn-, -ə'-

invalidity ˌɪn.və'lɪd.ə.ti, -ɪ.ti US -ə.t̬i **inva**'**lidity** ˌ**benefit**

invaluab|le ɪn'væl.ju.ə.b|l̩, -jə.b|l̩, -jʊ- US -ju.ə- **-ly** -li

Invar® ɪn'vɑːʳ, '--, 'ɪn.vəʳ US 'ɪn.vɑːr

invariability ɪnˌveə.ri.ə'bɪl.ə.ti, ˌɪn-, -ɪ.ti US -ˌver.i.ə'bɪl.ə.t̬i

invariab|le ɪn'veə.ri.ə.b|l̩, ˌɪn- US -'ver.i- **-ly** -li **-leness** -l̩.nəs, -nɪs

invariance ɪn'veə.ri.ənts, ˌɪn- US -'ver.i-

invasion ɪn'veɪ.ʒᵊn **-s** -z

invasive ɪn'veɪ.sɪv, -zɪv US -zɪv, -sɪv **-ly** -li **-ness** -nəs, -nɪs

invective ɪn'vek.tɪv **-s** -z

inveigh ɪn'veɪ **-s** -z **-ing** -ɪŋ **-ed** -d

inveigl|e ɪn'veɪ.gl̩, -'viː- **-es** -z **-ing** -ɪŋ, -'veɪ.glɪŋ, -'viː- **-ed** -əd **-ement/s** -mənt/s

in|vent ɪn|'vent **-vents** -'vents **-venting** -'ven.tɪŋ US -'ven.t̬ɪŋ **-vented** -'ven.tɪd US -'ven.t̬ɪd

invention ɪn'ven.tʃᵊn **-s** -z

inventive ɪn'ven.tɪv US -t̬ɪv **-ly** -li **-ness** -nəs, -nɪs

inventor ɪn'ven.təʳ US -t̬ɚ **-s** -z

inventor|y 'ɪn.vᵊn.tr|i, -tᵊr|.i, ɪn'ven.tᵊr|.i US -tɔːr- **-ies** -iz

Inverary ˌɪn.vᵊr'eə.ri, -rə US -və'rer.i

Invercargill *in Scotland:* ˌɪn.və'kɑː.gɪl, -gᵊl; -kɑː'gɪl US -vɚ'kɑːr.gɪl *in New Zealand:* ˌɪn.və'kɑː.gɪl US -vɚ'kɑːr-

Invergordon ˌɪn.və'gɔː.dᵊn US -vɚ'gɔːr-

Inverkeithing ˌɪn.və'kiː.ðɪŋ US -vɚ'-

Inverness, inverness ˌɪn.və'nes US -vɚ'- **-es** -ɪz *stress shift:* ˌInverness 'train

Inverness-shire ˌɪn.və'nes.ʃəʳ, -'neʃ-, -ˌʃɪəʳ US -vɚ'nes.ʃɚ, -ˌʃɪr

inverse ɪn'vɜːs, '-- US -'vɝːs, '-- **-s** -ɪz **-ly** -li

inversion ɪn'vɜː.ʃᵊn, -ʒᵊn US -'vɝː.ʒᵊn, -ʃᵊn **-s** -z

invert (*n. adj.*) 'ɪn.vɜːt US -vɝːt **-s** -s

in|vert (*v.*) ɪn|'vɜːt US -'vɝːt **-verts** -'vɜːts US -'vɝːts **-verting** -'vɜː.tɪŋ US -'vɝː.t̬ɪŋ **-verted** -'vɜː.tɪd US -'vɝː.t̬ɪd **in**ˌ**verted** '**comma**; **in**ˌ**verted** '**snob**; **in**ˌ**verted** '**snobbery**

invertase ɪn'vɜː.teɪz US -'vɝː.teɪs, -teɪz, '---

invertebrate ɪn'vɜː.tɪ.breɪt, ˌɪn-, '-tə-, -brət, -brɪt (US) -'vɝː.t̬ə.brɪt, -breɪt **-s** -s

Inverurie ˌɪn.vᵊr'ʊə.ri (US) -və'rʊr.i

invest ɪn'vest **-s** -s **-ing** -ɪŋ **-ed** -ɪd

investi|gate ɪn'ves.tɪ|.geɪt, -tə- **-gates** -geɪts **-gating** -geɪ.tɪŋ (US) -geɪ.t̬ɪŋ **-gated** -geɪ.tɪd (US) -geɪ.t̬ɪd **-gator/s** -geɪ.təʳ/z (US) -geɪ.t̬ɚ/z

investigation ɪnˌves.tɪ'geɪ.ʃᵊn, -tə'- **-s** -z

investigative ɪn'ves.tɪ.gə.tɪv, -tə-, -geɪ- (US) -geɪ.t̬ɪv

investigatory ɪn'ves.tɪ.gə.tᵊr.i, -tə-, -geɪ-; ɪnˌves.tɪ'geɪ-, -tə'- (US) ɪn'ves.tɪ.gə.tɔːr-, -tə-

investiture ɪn'ves.tɪ.tʃəʳ, -tə-, -tjʊəʳ (US) -tʃɚ **-s** -z

investment ɪn'ves*t*.mənt **-s** -s **in'vestment ˌbond**

investor ɪn'ves.təʳ (US) -tɚ **-s** -z

inveteracy ɪn'vet.ᵊr.ə.si (US) -'vet̬-

inveterate ɪn'vet.ᵊr.ət, -ɪt (US) -'vet̬- **-ly** -li **-ness** -nəs, -nɪs

invidious ɪn'vɪd.i.əs **-ly** -li **-ness** -nəs, -nɪs

invigi|late ɪn'vɪdʒ.ɪ|.leɪt, '-ɪ- **-lates** -leɪts **-lating** -leɪ.tɪŋ (US) -leɪ.t̬ɪŋ **-lated** -leɪ.tɪd (US) -leɪ.t̬ɪd **-lator/s** -leɪ.təʳ/z (US) -leɪ.t̬ɚ/z

invigilation ɪnˌvɪdʒ.ɪ'leɪ.ʃᵊn, -ɪ'- **-s** -z

invigor|ate ɪn'vɪg.ᵊr|.eɪt (US) -ə.r|eɪt **-ates** -eɪts **-ating** -eɪ.tɪŋ (US) -eɪ.t̬ɪŋ **-ated** -eɪ.tɪd (US) -eɪ.t̬ɪd **-ator/s** -eɪ.təʳ/z (US) -eɪ.t̬ɚ/z

invigoration ɪnˌvɪg.ᵊr'eɪ.ʃᵊn (US) -ə'reɪ-

invincibility ɪnˌvɪn*t*.sə'bɪl.ə.ti, -sɪ'-, -ɪ.ti (US) -ə.t̬i

invincib|le ɪn'vɪn*t*.sə.b|l̩, -sɪ- **-ly** -li **-leness** -l̩.nəs, -nɪs

inviolability ɪnˌvaɪə.lə'bɪl.ə.ti, ˌɪn-, -ɪ.ti (US) -ə.t̬i

inviolab|le ɪn'vaɪə.lə.b|l̩ **-ly** -li **-leness** -l̩.nəs, -nɪs

inviolate ɪn'vaɪə.lət, -lɪt, -leɪt **-ly** -li **-ness** -nəs, -nɪs

invisibility ɪnˌvɪz.ə'bɪl.ə.ti, ˌɪn-, -ɪ'-, -ɪ.ti (US) -ə.t̬i

invisib|le ɪn'vɪz.ə.b|l̩, ˌɪn-, '-ɪ- **-ly** -li **-leness** -l̩.nəs, -nɪs

invitation ˌɪn.vɪ'teɪ.ʃᵊn, -və'- **-s** -z **-al/s** -ᵊl/z

in|vite (*v.*) ɪn|'vaɪt **-vites** -'vaɪts **-viting/ly** -'vaɪ.tɪŋ/li (US) -'vaɪ.t̬ɪŋ/li **-vited** -'vaɪ.tɪd (US) -'vaɪ.t̬ɪd **-viter/s** -'vaɪ.təʳ/z (US) -'vaɪ.t̬ɚ/z

invite (*n.*) 'ɪn.vaɪt **-s** -s

invitee ˌɪn.vaɪ'tiː, -vɪ'- (US) -vaɪ'-, -və'-

in vitro ˌɪn'viː.trəʊ, -'vɪt.rəʊ (US) -'viː.troʊ, -'vɪt.roʊ **in ˌvitro fertili'zation**

in vivo ˌɪn'viː.vəʊ (US) -voʊ

invo|cate 'ɪn.vəʊ|.keɪt (US) -və- **-cates** -keɪts **-cating** -keɪ.tɪŋ (US) -keɪ.t̬ɪŋ **-cated** -keɪ.tɪd (US) -keɪ.t̬ɪd

invocation ˌɪn.vəʊ'keɪ.ʃᵊn (US) -və'- **-s** -z **-al** -ᵊl

invoic|e 'ɪn.vɔɪs **-es** -ɪz **-ing** -ɪŋ **-ed** -t

invok|e ɪn'vəʊk (US) -'voʊk **-es** -s **-ing** -ɪŋ **-ed** -t

involucre 'ɪn.və.luː.kəʳ, -ljuː-, ˌɪn.və'luː.kəʳ, -'ljuː- (US) ˌɪn.voʊ'luː.kɚ, -və'- **-s** -z

involuntar|y ɪn'vɒl.ən.tᵊr|.i, ˌɪn-, -ᵊn-, -tr|i (US) -'vɑː.lən.ter|.i **-ily** -ᵊl.i, -ɪ.li **-iness** -ɪ.nəs, -ɪ.nɪs

involu|te 'ɪn.və.luː|t, -ljuː|t, ˌ--'- (US) 'ɪn.və.luː|t **-tes** -ts **-ting** -tɪŋ (US) -t̬ɪŋ **-ted** -tɪd (US) -t̬ɪd

involution ˌɪn.və'luː.ʃᵊn, -'ljuː- (US) -'luː- **-s** -z

involv|e ɪn'vɒlv (US) -'vɑːlv, -'vɔːlv **-es** -z **-ing** -ɪŋ **-ed** -d

involvement ɪn'vɒlv.mənt (US) -'vɑːlv-, -'vɔːlv- **-s** -s

invulnerability ɪnˌvʌl.nᵊr.ə'bɪl.ə.ti, ˌɪn-, -ˌvʌn.ᵊr-, -ɪ.ti (US) -ˌvʌl.nɚ.ə'bɪl.ə.t̬i

invulnerab|le ɪn'vʌl.nᵊr.ə.b|l̩, ˌɪn-, -'vʌn.ᵊr- (US) -'vʌl.nɚ- **-ly** -li **-leness** -l̩.nəs, -nɪs

inward 'ɪn.wəd (US) -wɚd **-s** -z **-ly** -li **-ness** -nəs, -nɪs

Inwards 'ɪn.wədz (US) -wɚds

inweav|e ɪn'wiːv **-es** -z **-ing** -ɪŋ **-ed** -d **inwove** ɪn'wəʊv (US) -'woʊv **inwoven** ɪn'wəʊ.vᵊn (US) -'woʊ-

Inwood 'ɪn.wʊd

inwov|e (*from* **inweave**) ɪn'wəʊv (US) -'woʊv **-en** -ᵊn

inwrought ɪn'rɔːt (US) -'rɑːt, -'rɔːt

io (I) 'aɪ.əʊ (US) -oʊ **-s** -z

io|date 'aɪ.əʊ|.deɪt (US) '-ə- **-dates** -deɪts **-dating** -deɪ.tɪŋ (US) -deɪ.t̬ɪŋ **-dated** -deɪ.tɪd (US) -deɪ.t̬ɪd

iodic aɪ'ɒd.ɪk (US) -'ɑː.dɪk

iodide 'aɪ.əʊ.daɪd (US) '-ə- **-s** -z

iodine 'aɪ.ə.diːn, -daɪn (US) -daɪn, -dɪn, -diːn

iodiz|e, -is|e 'aɪ.ə.daɪz **-es** -ɪz **-ing** -ɪŋ **-ed** -d

iodoform aɪ'ɒd.ə.fɔːm (US) -'oʊ.də.fɔːrm, -'ɑː-

Iolanthe ˌaɪ.əʊ'læn*t*.θi (US) ˌaɪə'-, ˌaɪ.oʊ'-

iolite 'aɪ.əʊ.laɪt (US) '-oʊ-

Iolo 'jəʊ.ləʊ (US) 'joʊ.loʊ

ion 'aɪ.ən, -ɒn (US) -ən, -ɑːn **-s** -z

Iona aɪ'əʊ.nə (US) -'oʊ-

Ione aɪ'əʊ.ni (US) -'oʊ-

Ionesco jɒn'es.kəʊ, ˌiː.ɒn'-, ˌiː.ə'nes-, -kuː (US) jə'nes.koʊ, ˌiː.ə'-

Ioni|a aɪ'əʊ.ni|.ə (US) -'oʊ- **-an/s** -ən/z

ionic (I) aɪ'ɒn.ɪk (US) -'ɑː.nɪk **-s** -s

Ionica® aɪ'ɒn.ɪ.kə (US) -'ɑːnɪ-

ionization, -isa- ˌaɪə.naɪ'zeɪ.ʃᵊn, -nɪ'- (US) -nɪ'- **-s** -z

ioniz|e, -is|e 'aɪə.naɪz **-es** -ɪz **-ing** -ɪŋ **-ed** -d **-er/s** -əʳ/z (US) -ɚ/z **-able** -ə.bl̩

Pronouncing the letters IO

There are several pronunciation possibilities for the vowel digraph **io**, e.g.:

/aɪə/	lion	/laɪən/
/i.əʊ (US) i.oʊ/	radio	/'reɪ.di.əʊ/ (US) /-oʊ/
/aɪ.ɒ (US) aɪ.ɑː, aɪ.ɔː/	priority	/praɪ'ɒr.ə.ti/ (US) /-'ɔːr.ə.t̬i/
/i.ɒ (US) i.ɑː/	curiosity	/ˌkjʊə.ri'ɒs.ə.ti/ (US) /ˌkjʊr.i'ɑː.sə.t̬i/

In weak syllables

In weak syllables where it is preceded by the letters **s** and **t**, the vowel digraph **io** is realised with the vowel /ə/, and may result in a syllabic consonant, e.g.:

station	/'steɪ.ʃᵊn/
invasion	/ɪn'veɪ.ʒᵊn/

In other weak syllable contexts, **io** is realised with /i.ə/ or /jə/, e.g.:

million	/'mɪl.jən, -i.ən/	(US) /-jən/
patriot	/'pæt.ri.ət/	(US) /'peɪ.tri-/

ionosphere aɪˈɒn.ə.sfɪəʳ (US) -ˈɑː.nə.sfɪr **-s** -z

iota aɪˈəʊ.tə (US) -ˈoʊ.t̬ə **-s** -z

iotacism aɪˈəʊ.tə.sɪ.zᵊm (US) -ˈoʊ.t̬ə- **-s** -z

IOU ˌaɪ.əʊˈjuː (US) -oʊˈ- **-s** -z

Iowa ˈaɪ.əʊə, ˈaɪə.wə (US) ˈaɪə.wə ˌ**Iowa ˈCity**

IPA ˌaɪ.piːˈeɪ

ipecac ˈɪp.ɪ.kæk, ˈ-ə-

ipecacuanha ˌɪp.ɪˌkæk.juˈæn.ə, -əˌ-, -ˈɑː.nə (US) -juˈæn.ə

Iphicrates ɪˈfɪk.rə.tiːz

Iphigenia ˌɪf.ɪ.dʒɪˈnaɪə, ˌaɪ.fɪ-, -dʒəˈ-; ɪˌfɪdʒ.ɪˈ-, -əˈ- (US) ˌɪf.ə.dʒəˈ-

Ipoh ˈiː.pəʊ (US) -poʊ

ipse dixit ˌɪp.siˈdɪk.sɪt, -seɪˈ- (US) -siˈ-

ipso facto ˌɪp.səʊˈfæk.təʊ (US) -soʊˈfæk.toʊ

ipso jure ˌɪp.səʊˈjʊə.reɪ, -ri (US) -soʊˈdʒʊr.i

Ipswich ˈɪp.swɪtʃ

IQ ˌaɪˈkjuː **IˈQ ˌtest**

Iqbal ˈɪk.bæl, ˈɪg-, -bɑːl (US) ɪkˈbɑːl

Iquique ɪˈkiː.ki, -keɪ (US) iːˈkiː.keɪ

Iquitos ɪˈkiː.tɒs (US) iːˈkiː.toʊs, -tɔːs

Ira ˈaɪə.rə (US) ˈaɪ-

IRA ˌaɪ.ɑːʳˈeɪ (US) -ɑːrˈ-

Irabu ɪˈrɑː.bu, ˈɪr.ə.buː

Irak ɪˈrɑːk, -ˈræk (US) ɪ-, iː- **-i/s** -i/z

Iran ɪˈrɑːn, -ˈræn (US) -ˈræn

Iranian ɪˈreɪ.ni.ən, -ˈrɑː- (US) ɪ- **-s** -z

Iraq ɪˈrɑːk, -ˈræk (US) ɪ- **-i/s** -i/z

irascibility ɪˌræs.əˈbɪl.ə.ti, -ɪˈ-, -ɪ.ti (US) -ə.t̬i

irascib|le ɪˈræs.ə.b|l̩, ˈ-ɪ- **-ly** -li **-leness** -l̩.nəs, -nɪs

irate aɪˈreɪt, ˌaɪ- (US) aɪˈreɪt, ˈ-- **-ly** -li

Irbid ˈɪə.bɪd (US) ˈɪr-

ire aɪəʳ (US) aɪr

Iredell ˈaɪə.del (US) ˈaɪr-

ireful ˈaɪə.fᵊl, -fʊl (US) ˈaɪr **-ly** -i **-ness** -nəs, -nɪs

Ireland ˈaɪə.lənd (US) ˈaɪr-

Iremonger ˈaɪəˌmʌŋ.gəʳ (US) ˈaɪrˌmʌŋ.gɚ, -ˌmɑːŋ-

Irene ˈaɪ.riːn, -ˈ-; -ˈriː.ni (US) -ˈriːn; -ˈriː.ni

irenic aɪˈriː.nɪk, -ˈren.ɪk (US) -ˈren-, -ˈriː.nɪk **-al** -ᵊl

Ireton ˈaɪə.tᵊn (US) ˈaɪr-

Irian ˈɪr.i.ən, -ɑːn (US) -ɑːn, -ən

Irian Jaya ˌɪr.i.ɑːnˈdʒɑː.jə, -ənˈ-, -jɑː

irides *(plur. of* **iris***)* ˈaɪə.rɪ.diːz, ˈɪr.ɪ- (US) ˈaɪ.rɪ-, ˈɪr.ɪ-

iridescence ˌɪr.ɪˈdes.ᵊnts, -əˈ-

iridescent ˌɪr.ɪˈdes.ᵊnt, -əˈ- **-ly** -li

iridium ɪˈrɪd.i.əm, aɪ-

iridolog|y ˌɪr.ɪˈdɒl.ə.dʒ|i (US) -ˈdɑː.lə- **-ist/s** -ɪst/s

Irion ˈɪr.i.ən, -ɒn (US) -ɑːn, -ən

iris (I) ˈaɪə.rɪs (US) ˈaɪ- **irises** ˈaɪə.rɪ.sɪz (US) ˈaɪ- **irides** ˈaɪə.rɪ.diːz, ˈɪr.ɪ- (US) ˈaɪ.rɪ-, ˈɪr.ɪ-

Irish ˈaɪə.rɪʃ (US) ˈaɪ- **-ism/s** -ɪ.zᵊm/z ˌ**Irish ˈcoffee**; ˌ**Irish Reˈpublic**; ˌ**Irish ReˌpublicanˈArmy**; ˌ**Irish ˈSea**; ˌ**Irish ˈstew**

Irish|man ˈaɪə.rɪʃ|.mən (US) ˈaɪ- **-men** -mən, -men

Irishry ˈaɪə.rɪʃ.ri (US) ˈaɪ-

Irish|woman ˈaɪə.rɪʃ|ˌwʊm.ən (US) ˈaɪ- **-women** -ˌwɪm.ɪn

irk ɜːk (US) ɝːk **-s** -s **-ing** -ɪŋ **-ed** -t

irksome ˈɜːk.səm (US) ˈɝːk- **-ly** -li **-ness** -nəs, -nɪs

Irkutsk ɜːˈkʊtsk, ɪə- (US) ɪr-

Irlam ˈɜː.ləm (US) ˈɝː-

Irma ˈɜː.mə (US) ˈɝː-

iron (I) aɪən (US) ˈaɪ.ɚn, aɪrn **-s** -z **-ing** -ɪŋ **-ed** -d ˈ**Iron ˌAge**; ˈ**ironing ˌboard**; ˌ**Iron ˈCurtain**; ˌ**iron ˈlung**; ˈ**iron ˌmould**; ˌ**strike while the ˌiron's ˈhot**

ironbark ˈaɪən.bɑːk (US) ˈaɪ.ɚn.bɑːrk, ˈaɪrn- **-s** -s

ironbound ˈaɪən.baʊnd (US) ˈaɪ.ɚn-, ˈaɪrn-

Ironbridge ˈaɪən.brɪdʒ, -ˈ- (US) ˈaɪ.ɚn-, ˈaɪrn-

ironclad ˈaɪən.klæd (US) ˈaɪ.ɚn-, ˈaɪrn- **-s** -z

irongray, irongrey ˌaɪənˈgreɪ, ˌaɪəŋ- (US) ˌaɪ.ɚnˈ-, ˌaɪrn- *stress shift:* ˌ**irongray ˈbattleship**

ironic aɪəˈrɒn.ɪk (US) aɪˈrɑː.nɪk **-al** -ᵊl **-ally** -ᵊl.i, -li

ironmonger ˈaɪənˌmʌŋ.gəʳ, ˈaɪəm- (US) ˈaɪ.ɚnˌmʌŋ.gɚ, ˈaɪrn-, -ˌmɑːŋ- **-s** -z

ironmongery ˈaɪənˌmʌŋ.gᵊr.i, ˈaɪəm- (US) ˈaɪ.ɚnˌ-, ˈaɪrn-, -ˌmɑːŋ-

ironside (I) ˈaɪən.saɪd (US) ˈaɪ.ɚn-, ˈaɪrn- **-s** -z

ironstone ˈaɪən.stəʊn (US) ˈaɪ.ɚn.stoʊn, ˈaɪrn-

Ironton ˈaɪən.tən (US) ˈaɪ.ɚn-, ˈaɪrn-

ironware ˈaɪən.weəʳ (US) ˈaɪ.ɚn.wer, ˈaɪrn-

ironwood (I) ˈaɪən.wʊd (US) ˈaɪ.ɚn-, ˈaɪrn-

ironwork ˈaɪən.wɜːk (US) ˈaɪ.ɚn.wɝːk, ˈaɪrn- **-s** -s

iron|y *(n.) sarcasm, etc.:* ˈaɪə.rᵊn|.i (US) ˈaɪ- **-ies** -iz

irony *(adj.) like iron:* ˈaɪə.ni (US) ˈaɪ.ɚ-, ˈaɪr-

Iroquoian ˌɪr.əʊˈkwɔɪ.ən (US) -əˈ-

Iroquois *(sing.)* ˈɪr.ə.kwɔɪ, -kwɔɪ *(plur.)* ˈɪr.ə.kwɔɪz, -kwɔɪ

irradian|ce ɪˈreɪ.di.ənt|s (US) ɪrˈ- **-cy** -si

irradi|ate ɪˈreɪ.di|.eɪt (US) ɪrˈ- **-ates** -eɪts **-ating** -eɪ.tɪŋ (US) -eɪ.t̬ɪŋ **-ated** -eɪ.tɪd (US) -eɪ.t̬ɪd

irradiation ɪˌreɪ.diˈeɪ.ʃᵊn, ˌɪr.eɪ- (US) ɪrˈ-, ɪˌreɪ- **-s** -z

irradicab|le ɪˈræd.ɪ.kə.b|l̩ (US) ɪrˈ- **-ly** -li

irrational ɪˈræʃ.ᵊn.ᵊl, ˌɪrˈæʃ-, -ˈræʃ.nᵊl **-ly** -i

irrationality ɪˌræʃ.ᵊnˈæl.ə.ti, ˌɪrˌæʃ-, -ɪ.ti (US) -ə.t̬i

Irrawaddy ˌɪr.əˈwɒd.i (US) -ˈwɑː.di, -ˈwɔː-

irrebuttable ˌɪr.ɪˈbʌt.ə.bl̩ (US) -ˈbʌt̬-

irreceptive ˌɪr.ɪˈsep.tɪv

irreclaimab|le ˌɪr.ɪˈkleɪ.mə.b|l̩ **-ly** -li

irrecognizable, -isa- ɪˌrek.əgˈnaɪ.zə.bl̩, ˌɪrˌek-

irreconcilability ɪˌrek.ᵊnˌsaɪ.ləˈbɪl.ə.ti, ˌɪrˌek-, -ɪ.ti (US) -ə.t̬i

irreconcilab|le ˌɪr.ek.ᵊnˈsaɪ.lə.b|l̩, ɪˌrek- **-ly** -li **-leness** -l̩.nəs, -nɪs

irrecoverab|le ˌɪr.ɪˈkʌv.ᵊr.ə.b|l̩, -əˈ- **-ly** -li **-leness** -l̩.nəs, -nɪs

irredeemab|le ˌɪr.ɪˈdiː.mə.b|l̩, -əˈ- **-ly** -li **-leness** -l̩.nəs, -nɪs

irredent|ism ˌɪr.ɪˈden.t|ɪ.zᵊm, -əˈ- **-ist/s** -ɪst/s

irreducib|le ˌɪr.ɪˈdjuː.sə.b|l̩, -əˈ-, -sɪ- (US) -ˈduː-, -ˈdjuː- **-ly** -li **-leness** -l̩.nəs, -nɪs

irrefutability ɪˌref.jə.təˈbɪl.ə.ti, -jʊ-, -ɪ.ti; ˌɪr.ɪˌfjuː.təˈ-, -əˌ- (US) -t̬əˈbɪl.ə.t̬i

irrefutab|le ˌɪr.ɪˈfjuː.tə.b|l̩, -əˈ-; ɪˈref.jə-, -jʊ- (US) ɪˈref.jə.t̬ə-; ˌɪr.ɪˈfjuː-, -əˈ- **-ly** -li **-leness** -l̩.nəs, -nɪs

irregardless ˌɪr.ɪˈgɑːd.ləs, -əˈ-, -lɪs (US) -ɪˈgɑːrd-

irregular ɪˈreg.jə.ləʳ, -jʊ- (US) -lɚ **-ly** -li

irregularit|y ɪˌreg.jəˈlær.ə.t|i, ˌɪrˌeg-, -jʊˈ-, -ɪ.t|i (US) ɪˌreg.jəˈler.ə.t̬|i, -ˈlær- **-ies** -iz

irrelevan|ce ɪˈrel.ə.vᵊnt|s, ˈ-ɪ- (US) ɪrˈ- **-cy** -si **-cies** -siz

irrelevant ɪˈrel.ə.vᵊnt, ˈ-ɪ- (US) ɪrˈ- **-ly** -li

irreligion ˌɪr.ɪˈlɪdʒ.ᵊn, -əˈ-

irreligious ˌɪr.ɪˈlɪdʒ.əs, -əˈ- **-ly** -li **-ness** -nəs, -nɪs

irremediab|le ˌɪr.ɪˈmiː.di.ə.b|l̩ **-ly** -li

irremovability ˌɪr.ɪˌmuː.vəˈbɪl.ə.ti, -əˌ-, -ɪ.ti (US) -ə.t̬i

irremovab|le ˌɪr.ɪˈmuː.və.b|l̩, -əˈ- **-ly** -li

irreparability ɪˌrep.ᵊr.əˈbɪl.ə.ti, ˌɪrˌep-, -ɪ.ti (US) -ə.t̬i

irreparab|le ɪˈrep.ᵊr.ə.b|l̩ **-ly** -li **-leness** -l̩.nəs, -nɪs

irreplaceable ˌɪr.ɪˈpleɪ.sə.bl̩

irrepressib|le ˌɪr.ɪˈpres.ə.b|l̩, -əˈ-, ˈ-ɪ- **-ly** -li **-leness** -l̩.nəs, -nɪs

irreproachability ˌɪr.ɪˌprəʊ.tʃəˈbɪl.ə.ti, -əˌ-, -ɪ.ti (US) -ˌproʊ.tʃəˈbɪl.ə.t̬i

irreproachab|le ˌɪr.ɪˈprəʊ.tʃə.b|l̩, -əˈ- (US) -ˈproʊ- **-ly** -li **-leness** -l̩.nəs, -nɪs

irresistibility ˌɪr.ɪˌzɪs.təˈbɪl.ə.ti, -əˌ-, -tɪˈ-, -ɪ.ti ⓊⓈ -ə.t̬i
irresistib|le ˌɪr.ɪˈzɪs.tə.b|l̩, -əˈ-, -tɪ- **-ly** -li **-leness** -l̩.nəs, -nɪs
irresoluble ɪˈrez.əl.jə.bl̩, -jʊ- ⓊⓈ ˌɪr.ɪˈzɑːl.jə-
irresolute ɪˈrez.ᵊl.uːt, ˌɪrˈez-, -juːt ⓊⓈ -uːt **-ly** -li **-ness** -nəs, -nɪs
irresolution ɪˌrez.ᵊlˈuː.ʃᵊn, -ˈljuː- ⓊⓈ -ˈuː-
irresolvability ˌɪr.ɪˌzɒl.vəˈbɪl.ə.ti, -əˌ-, -ɪ.ti ⓊⓈ -ˌzɑːl.vəˈbɪl.ə.t̬i
irresolvab|le ˌɪr.ɪˈzɒl.və.b|l̩ ⓊⓈ -ˈzɑːl.və- **-ly** -li **-leness** -l̩.nəs, -nɪs
irrespective ˌɪr.ɪˈspek.tɪv, -əˈ- **-ly** -li
irresponsibility ˌɪr.ɪˌspɒnt.səˈbɪl.ə.ti, -əˌ-, -sɪˈ-, -ɪ.ti ⓊⓈ -ˌspɑːnt.səˈbɪl.ə.t̬i
irresponsib|le ˌɪr.ɪˈspɒnt.sə.b|l̩, -əˈ-, -sɪ- ⓊⓈ -ˈspɑːnt- **-ly** -li **-leness** -l̩.nəs, -nɪs
irresponsive ˌɪr.ɪˈspɒnt.sɪv, -əˈ- ⓊⓈ -ˈspɑːnt- **-ly** -li **-ness** -nəs, -nɪs
irretentive ˌɪr.ɪˈten.tɪv, -əˈ- ⓊⓈ -t̬ɪv
irretrievability ˌɪr.ɪˌtriː.vəˈbɪl.ə.ti, -əˌ-, -ɪ.ti ⓊⓈ -ə.t̬i
irretrievab|le ˌɪr.ɪˈtriː.və.b|l̩, -əˈ- **-ly** -li **-leness** -l̩.nəs, -nɪs
irreverence ɪˈrev.ᵊr.ᵊnts, ˌɪrˈev-
irreverent ɪˈrev.ᵊr.ᵊnt, ˌɪrˈev- **-ly** -li
irreversibility ˌɪr.ɪˌvɜː.səˈbɪl.ə.ti, -əˌ-, -sɪˈ-, -ɪ.ti ⓊⓈ -ˌvɝː.səˈbɪl.ə.t̬i, -sɪˈ-
irreversib|le ˌɪr.ɪˈvɜː.sə.b|l̩, -əˈ-, -sɪ- ⓊⓈ -ˈvɝː- **-ly** -li **-leness** -l̩.nəs, -nɪs
irrevocability ɪˌrev.ə.kəˈbɪl.ə.ti, -ɪ.ti ⓊⓈ -ə.t̬i
irrevocab|le ɪˈrev.ə.kə.b|l̩ **-ly** -li *when applied to letters of credit:* ˌɪr.ɪˈvəʊ.kə.bl̩, -əˈ- ⓊⓈ ɪˈrev.ə.kə-; ˌɪr.ɪˈvoʊ-
irrigable ˈɪr.ɪ.gə.bl̩, ˈ-ə-
irri|gate ˈɪr.ɪ|.geɪt, ˈ-ə- **-gates** -geɪts **-gating** -geɪ.tɪŋ ⓊⓈ -geɪ.t̬ɪŋ **-gated** -geɪ.tɪd ⓊⓈ -geɪ.t̬ɪd **-gator/s** -geɪ.təʳ/z ⓊⓈ -geɪ.t̬ɚ/z
irrigation ˌɪr.ɪˈgeɪ.ʃᵊn, -əˈ- **-s** -z
irritability ˌɪr.ɪ.təˈbɪl.ə.ti, ˈ-ə-, -ɪ.ti ⓊⓈ -t̬əˈbɪl.ə.t̬i
irritab|le ˈɪr.ɪ.tə.b|l̩, ˈ-ə- ⓊⓈ -t̬ə- **-ly** -li **-leness** -l̩.nəs, -nɪs **ˌirritable ˈbowel ˌsyndrome**
irritant ˈɪr.ɪ.tᵊnt, ˈ-ə- ⓊⓈ -t̬ənt **-s** -s
irri|tate ˈɪr.ɪ|.teɪt, ˈ-ə- **-tates** -teɪts **-tating/ly** -teɪ.tɪŋ/li ⓊⓈ -teɪ.t̬ɪŋ/li **-tated** -teɪ.tɪd ⓊⓈ -teɪ.t̬ɪd **-tative** -teɪ.tɪv ⓊⓈ -teɪ.t̬ɪv **-tator/s** -teɪ.təʳ/z ⓊⓈ -teɪ.t̬ɚ/z
irritation ˌɪr.ɪˈteɪ.ʃᵊn, -əˈ- **-s** -z
irrupt ɪˈrʌpt **-s** -s **-ing** -ɪŋ **-ed** -ɪd **-ive/ly** -ɪv/li
irruption ɪˈrʌp.ʃᵊn **-s** -z
Irvine *name:* ˈɜː.vɪn, -vaɪn ⓊⓈ ˈɝː- *US city:* ˈɜː.vaɪn ⓊⓈ ˈɝː-
Irvinestown ˈɜː.vɪnz.taʊn ⓊⓈ ˈɝː-
Irving ˈɜː.vɪŋ ⓊⓈ ˈɝː-
Irwin ˈɜː.wɪn ⓊⓈ ˈɝː-
is *(from* **be***) strong form:* ɪz *weak forms:* z, s
Note: /z/ is used only when the preceding word ends in a vowel or a voiced consonant other than /z/ or /ʒ/. /s/ is used only when the preceding word ends in a voiceless consonant other than /s/ or /ʃ/.
ISA, Isa ˈaɪ.sə **-s** -z
Isaac ˈaɪ.zək **-s** -s
Isaacson ˈaɪ.zək.sᵊn
Isabel ˈɪz.ə.bel
Isabella ˌɪz.əˈbel.ə
Isabelle ˈɪz.ə.bel
Isaiah aɪˈzaɪə ⓊⓈ aɪˈzeɪə, -ˈzaɪə
Isambard ˈɪz.ᵊm.bɑːd ⓊⓈ -bɑːrd
Isard ˈɪz.ɑːd ⓊⓈ -ɑːrd
-isation -aɪˈzeɪ.ʃᵊn, -ɪˈ- ⓊⓈ -ɪˈ-
Note: Suffix. Words containing **-isation** alway carry primary stress as shown above, e.g. **decimalisation** /ˌdes.ɪ.mᵊl.aɪˈzeɪ.ʃᵊn ⓊⓈ -ɪˈ-/.
ISBN ˌaɪ.es.biːˈen
Iscariot ɪsˈkær.i.ət ⓊⓈ -ˈker-, -ˈkær-
Ischia ˈɪs.ki.ə
-ise -aɪz, -iːz
Note: Suffix. Where **-ise** forms a verb, the pronunciation is /-aɪz/. See note for **-ize**. Where **-ise** forms a noun, it usually carries primary stress (e.g. **experˈtise**) and is pronounced /-iːz/.
Iseult iˈzuːlt, -ˈsuːlt ⓊⓈ -ˈsuːlt
-ish -ɪʃ
Note: Suffix. When forming an adjective, **-ish** does not affect the stress pattern of the word, e.g. **yellowish** /ˈjel.əʊ.ɪʃ ⓊⓈ -oʊ-/. When forming a verb, the antepenultimate syllable is stressed, e.g. **demolish** /dɪˈmɒl.ɪʃ ⓊⓈ -ˈmɑː.lɪʃ/.
Isham ˈaɪ.ʃᵊm
Isherwood ˈɪʃ.ə.wʊd ⓊⓈ ˈ-ɚ-
Ishiguro ˌɪʃ.ɪˈgʊər.əʊ ⓊⓈ -ˈgʊr.oʊ
Ishmael ˈɪʃ.meɪəl, -mi.əl
Ishmae|lite ˈɪʃ.mi.ə|.laɪt, -meɪə|.laɪt, -mə|.laɪt **-lites** -laɪts **-litish** -laɪ.tɪʃ ⓊⓈ -laɪ.t̬ɪʃ
Ishtar ˈɪʃ.tɑːʳ ⓊⓈ -tɑːr
Isidore ˈɪz.ɪ.dɔːʳ, ˈ-ə- ⓊⓈ -ə.dɔːr
Isidorian ˌɪz.ɪˈdɔː.ri.ən, -əˈ- ⓊⓈ -ˈdɔːr.i-
isinglass ˈaɪ.zɪŋ.glɑːs ⓊⓈ -zɪn.glæs, -zɪŋ-
Isis ˈaɪ.sɪs
Isla ˈaɪ.lə
Islam ˈɪz.lɑːm, ˈɪs-, -læm, -ləm; ɪzˈlɑːm, ɪs-
Islamabad ɪzˈlɑː.mə.bæd, ɪs-, -ˈlæm.ə-, -bɑːd ⓊⓈ -ˈlɑː.mə.bɑːd
Islamic ɪzˈlæm.ɪk, ɪs-, -ˈlɑː.mɪk ⓊⓈ -ˈlɑː-, -ˈlæm.ɪk **-s** -s
Islam|ism ˈɪz.lə.m|ɪ.zᵊm, ˈɪs- **-ist/s** -ɪst/s
island ˈaɪ.lənd **-s** -z **-er/s** -əʳ/z ⓊⓈ -ɚ/z
Islay ˈaɪ.leɪ *locally:* ˈaɪ.lə
isle aɪl **-s** -z
Isle of Dogs ˌaɪl.əvˈdɒgz ⓊⓈ -ˈdɑːgz, -ˈdɔːgz
Isle of Man ˌaɪl.əvˈmæn
Isle of Wight ˌaɪl.əvˈwaɪt
islet ˈaɪ.lət, -lɪt, -let ⓊⓈ -lɪt **-s** -s
Isleworth ˈaɪ.zᵊl.wəθ, -wɜːθ ⓊⓈ -wɝːθ, -wɚθ
Islington ˈɪz.lɪŋ.tən
Islip *archbishop:* ˈɪz.lɪp *in Oxfordshire:* ˈaɪ.slɪp
Islwyn ˈɪs.lu.ɪn; ɪzˈluː.ɪn, ɪs-
-ism -ɪ.zᵊm **-s** -z
Note: Suffix. When added to a free stem, **-ism** does not normally affect the stress pattern of the word, e.g. **absentee** /ˌæb.sᵊnˈtiː/, **absenteeism** /ˌæb.sᵊnˈtiː.ɪ.zᵊm/. When added to a bound stem, the word is normally stressed two syllables before the suffix, e.g. **exorcism** /ˈek.sɔː.sɪ.zᵊm ⓊⓈ -sɔːr-/. Exceptions exist; see individual entries.
Ismail ˌɪz.mɑːˈiːl, ˌɪs-; ˈɪz.maɪl, -meɪl
Ismailiya ˌɪz.maɪˈliː.ə, ˌɪs- ⓊⓈ ˌɪs.meɪ.əˈ-, ˌɪz-
Ismay ˈɪz.meɪ
isn't ˈɪz.ᵊnt
iso- aɪ.səʊ-; aɪˈsɒ- ⓊⓈ aɪ.soʊ-, -sə-; aɪˈsɑː-
Note: Prefix. Normally takes either primary or secondary stress on the first syllable, e.g. **isotope** /ˈaɪ.sə.təʊp ⓊⓈ -toʊp/, **isotopic** /ˌaɪ.səˈtɒp.ɪk ⓊⓈ -ˈtɑː.pɪk/, or primary stress on the second syllable, e.g. **isotropy** /aɪˈsɒt.rə.pi ⓊⓈ -ˈsɑː.trə-/.
ISO ˌaɪ.esˈəʊ ⓊⓈ -ˈoʊ
isobar ˈaɪ.səʊ.bɑːʳ ⓊⓈ -soʊ.bɑːr, -sə- **-s** -z
Isobel ˈɪz.ə.bel
isochromatic ˌaɪ.səʊ.krəʊˈmæt.ɪk ⓊⓈ -soʊ.kroʊˈmæt̬.ɪk, -sə-
isochronal aɪˈsɒk.rə.nᵊl ⓊⓈ -ˈsɑː.krə- **-ly** -i
isochronous aɪˈsɒk.rə.nəs ⓊⓈ -ˈsɑː.krə- **-ly** -li
Isocrates aɪˈsɒk.rə.tiːz ⓊⓈ -ˈsɑː.krə-
isogloss ˈaɪ.səʊ.glɒs ⓊⓈ -soʊ.glɑːs, -sə- **-es** -ɪz
isolate *(n.)* ˈaɪ.sᵊl.ət, -ɪt, -eɪt ⓊⓈ -sə.lɪt **-s** -s

iso|late (*v.*) 'aɪ.səl.leɪt **-lates** -leɪts **-lating** -leɪ.tɪŋ (US) -leɪ.t̬ɪŋ **-lated** -leɪ.tɪd (US) -leɪ.t̬ɪd **-lator/s** -leɪ.təʳ/z (US) -leɪ.t̬ɚ/z

isolation ˌaɪ.sᵊl'eɪ.ʃᵊn

isolation|ism ˌaɪ.sᵊl'eɪ.ʃᵊn|.ɪ.zᵊm **-ist/s** -ɪst/s

isolative 'aɪ.sᵊl.ə.tɪv, -eɪ.tɪv (US) -sə.leɪ.t̬ɪv, -soʊ- **-ly** -li

Isolda ɪ'zɒl.də (US) -'soʊl-, -'zoʊl-

Isolde ɪ'zɒl.də (US) -'soʊl-, -'zoʊl-; -'soʊld, -'zoʊld

isomer 'aɪ.sə.məʳ (US) -soʊ.mɚ, -sə- **-s** -z

isomeric ˌaɪ.səʊ'mer.ɪk (US) -soʊ'-, -sə'-

isomer|ism aɪ'sɒm.ᵊr|.ɪ.zᵊm (US) -'sɑː.mɚ- **-ous** -əs

isometric ˌaɪ.səʊ'met.rɪk (US) -soʊ'-, -sə'- **-al** -ᵊl **-ally** -ᵊl.i, -li

isomorph 'aɪ.səʊ.mɔːf (US) -soʊ.mɔːrf, -sə- **-s** -s

isomorph|ism ˌaɪ.səʊ'mɔː.f|ɪ.zᵊm (US) -soʊ'mɔːr- **-ic** -ɪk **-ous** -əs

Ison 'aɪ.sᵊn

isophone 'aɪ.səʊ.fəʊn (US) -soʊ.foʊn, -sə- **-s** -z

isosceles aɪ'sɒs.ᵊl.iːz, -ɪ.liːz (US) -'sɑː.sᵊl.iːz

isotherm 'aɪ.səʊ.θɜːm (US) -soʊ.θɝːm, -sə- **-s** -z

isothermal ˌaɪ.sə'θɜː.mᵊl (US) -'θɝː- **-ly** -i

isotonic ˌaɪ.sə'tɒn.ɪk (US) -'tɑː.nɪk

isotope 'aɪ.sə.təʊp (US) -toʊp **-s** -s

isotopic ˌaɪ.sə'tɒp.ɪk (US) -'tɑː.pɪk **-ally** -ᵊl.i, -li

isotropic ˌaɪ.sə'trɒp.ɪk (US) -'trɑː.pɪk **-ally** -ᵊl.i, -li

isotropy aɪ'sɒt.rə.pi (US) -'sɑː.trə-

ISP ˌaɪ.es'piː

I-spy ˌaɪ'spaɪ

Israel 'ɪz.reɪəl, -ri.əl, -reɪ.el (US) -ri.əl, -reɪ-, -rᵊl

Israeli ɪz'reɪ.li **-s** -z

Israelite 'ɪz.ri.ə.laɪt, -reɪ-, -rə.laɪt, -rɪ- (US) -ri.ə-, -reɪ- **-s** -s

Issachar 'ɪs.ə.kəʳ, -kɑːʳ (US) -kɑːr

iss|ue 'ɪʃ|.uː, 'ɪs.j|uː (US) 'ɪʃ|.uː **-ues** -uːz **-uing** -uː.ɪŋ **-ued** -uːd **-uer/s** -uː.əʳ/z (US) -uː.ɚ/z **-uable** -u.ə.bl̩ **-uance** -u.ᵊnts

-ist -ɪst

Note: Suffix. When attached to a free stem, **-ist** does not normally affect the stress pattern of the stem, e.g. **modern** /'mɒd.ᵊn (US) 'mɑː.dɚn/, **modernist** /'mɒd.ᵊn.ɪst (US) 'mɑː.dɚ.nɪst/. When attached to a bound stem, the word is normally stressed on the penultimate syllable, e.g. **Baptist** /'bæp.tɪst/. Exceptions exist; see individual entries.

Istanbul ˌɪs.tæn'bʊl, -tɑːn'-, -tæm'-, -tɑːm'- (US) -tɑːn'-, -tæn'-, -'buːl

isthmi *(plur. of* **isthmus***)* 'ɪs.maɪ, 'ɪsθ-, 'ɪst- (US) 'ɪs-

isthmian (**I**) 'ɪsθ.mi.ən, 'ɪst-, 'ɪs- (US) 'ɪs-

isthmus 'ɪs.məs, 'ɪsθ-, 'ɪst- (US) 'ɪs- **-es** -ɪz

-istic -'ɪs.tɪk

Note: Suffix. Normally takes primary stress as shown, e.g. **impressionistic** /ɪmˌpreʃ.ᵊn'ɪs.tɪk/.

istle 'ɪst.li

Istria 'ɪs.tri.ə

it ɪt

IT ˌaɪ'tiː

Italian ɪ'tæl.i.ən (US) '-jən **-s** -z

italianate ɪ'tæl.i.ə.neɪt, -nət, -nɪt (US) '-jə.nɪt

italianism ɪ'tæl.i.ə.nɪ.zᵊm (US) '-jə- **-s** -z

italianiz|e, -is|e ɪ'tæl.i.ə.naɪz (US) '-jə- **-es** -ɪz **-ing** -ɪŋ **-ed** -d

italic (**I**) ɪ'tæl.ɪk **-s** -s

italicization, -isa- ɪˌtæl.ɪ.saɪ'zeɪ.ʃᵊn, ˌ-ə-, -sɪ'- (US) -sɪ'-

italiciz|e, -is|e ɪ'tæl.ɪ.saɪz, '-ə- **-es** -ɪz **-ing** -ɪŋ **-ed** -d

Italy 'ɪt.ᵊl.i (US) 'ɪt̬-

itch ɪtʃ **-es** -ɪz **-ing** -ɪŋ **-ed** -t

Itchen 'ɪtʃ.ɪn, -ᵊn

itch|y 'ɪtʃ|.i **-ier** -i.əʳ (US) -i.ɚ **-iest** -i.ɪst, -i.əst **-iness** -ɪ.nəs, -ɪ.nɪs

it'd 'ɪt.əd (US) 'ɪt̬-

item 'aɪ.təm, -tɪm, -tem (US) -t̬əm **-s** -z

itemiz|e, -is|e 'aɪ.tə.maɪz, -tɪ- (US) -t̬ə- **-es** -ɪz **-ing** -ɪŋ **-ed** -d

iter|ate 'ɪt.ᵊr|.eɪt (US) 'ɪt̬.ə.r|eɪt **-ates** -eɪts **-ating** -eɪ.tɪŋ (US) -eɪ.t̬ɪŋ **-ated** -eɪ.tɪd (US) -eɪ.t̬ɪd

iteration ˌɪt.ᵊr'eɪ.ʃᵊn (US) ˌɪt̬.ə'reɪ- **-s** -z

iterative 'ɪt.ᵊr.ə.tɪv, -eɪ- (US) 'ɪt̬.ə.reɪ.t̬ɪv, -ɚ.ə- **-ly** -li **-ness** -nəs, -nɪs

Ithaca 'ɪθ.ə.kə

itinerancy aɪ'tɪn.ᵊr.ᵊnt.si, ɪ-

itinerant aɪ'tɪn.ᵊr.ᵊnt, ɪ- **-s** -s

itinerar|y aɪ'tɪn.ᵊr.ᵊr|.i, ɪ- (US) -ə.rer- **-ies** -iz

itiner|ate aɪ'tɪn.ᵊr|.eɪt, ɪ- (US) -ə.r|eɪt **-ates** -eɪts **-ating** -eɪ.tɪŋ (US) -eɪ.t̬ɪŋ **-ated** -eɪ.tɪd (US) -eɪ.t̬ɪd

-ition -'ɪʃ.ᵊn

Note: Suffix. Always stressed as shown, e.g. **edition** /ɪ'dɪʃ.ᵊn/.

-itious -'ɪʃ.əs

Note: Suffix. Always stressed as shown, e.g. **surreptitious** /ˌsʌr.əp'tɪʃ.əs (US) ˌsɜːr.əp'-/.

-itis -'aɪ.tɪs (US) -'aɪ.t̬ɪs, -t̬əs

Note: Suffix. Always stressed as shown, e.g. **tonsilitis** /ˌtɒnt.sᵊl'aɪ.tɪs (US) ˌtɑːnt.sə'laɪ.t̬ɪs/.

-itive -ɪ.tɪv, -ə- (US) -ə.t̬ɪv, -ɪ-

Note: Suffix. Words containing **-itive** are normally stressed on the antepenultimate syllable, e.g. **competitive** /kəm'pet.ɪ.tɪv (US) -ə.t̬ɪv/. Exceptions exist; see individual entries.

it'll (= **it will, it shall**) 'ɪt.ᵊl (US) 'ɪt̬-

ITN ˌaɪ.tiː'en

-itory -ə.tᵊr.i, -ɪ-, -tri (US) -ə.tɔːr.i, -ɪ-

Note: Suffix. Words containing **-itory** are normally stressed on the syllable preceding the prefix, e.g. **territory** /'ter.ɪ.tᵊr.i (US) 'ter.ɪ.tɔːr.i/. Exceptions exist; see individual entries.

its ɪts

it's (= **it is, it has**) ɪts

itself ɪt'self

itsy-bitsy ˌɪt.si'bɪt.si

itty-bitty ˌɪt.i'bɪt.i (US) ˌɪt̬.i'bɪt̬-

ITV ˌaɪ.tiː'viː

-ity -ə.ti, -ɪ.ti (US) -ə.t̬i

Note: Suffix. Words containing **-ity** are normally stressed on the antepenultimate syllable, e.g. **conformity** /kən'fɔː.mə.ti (US) -'fɔːr.mə.t̬i/.

IUD ˌaɪ.juː'diː

Ivan 'aɪ.vᵊn; (US) 'aɪ.vən *foreign name:* iː'væn, ɪ-, -'vɑːn (US) -'vɑːn

Ivanhoe 'aɪ.vᵊn.həʊ (US) -hoʊ

Ivanoff ɪ'vɑː.nəf, iː-, -nɒf (US) 'iː.və.nɑːf; iː'vɑː-

Ivanov 'aɪ.və.nɒf, ɪ'vɑː.nɒf (US) iː.və'nɑːf, aɪ-

Ivatt 'aɪ.vət, -væt **-s** -s

I've (= **I have**) aɪv

-ive -ɪv

Note: Suffix. Words containing **-ive** are either stressed on the penultimate syllable, e.g. **expensive** /ɪk'spent.sɪv/, or on the antepenultimate syllable, e.g. **executive** /ɪg'zek.jə tɪv (US) -t̬ɪv/.

Iveagh 'aɪ.və, -veɪ

Iveco® ɪ'veɪ.kəʊ, aɪ'-, -'viː- (US) -'veɪ.koʊ

Ivens 'aɪ.vᵊnz

Iver 'aɪ.vəʳ (US) -vɚ

Ives *surname, and towns* **St. Ives** *in Cornwall and Cambridgeshire:* aɪvz *in Stevenson's 'St. Ives':* iːvz

Ivey 'aɪ.vi

IVF ˌaɪ.viː'ef

Ivor 'aɪ.vəʳ (US) -vɚ, 'iː-

ivor|y (**I**) 'aɪ.vᵊr|.i **-ies** -iz ˌ**Ivory** '**Coast**; ˌ**ivory** '**tower**

ivory-black ˌaɪ.vᵊr.i'blæk

iv|y (**I**) 'aɪ.v|i **-ies** -iz **-ied** -id '**Ivy** ˌ**League**

Ivybridge 'aɪ.vi.brɪdʒ

ixia 'ɪk.si.ə **-s** -z

Ixion ɪk'saɪən (US) -'saɪən, -'saɪ.ɑːn

Iza 'aɪ.zə

Izaby ˈɪz.ə.bi
Izal® ˈaɪ.zəl
izard ˈɪz.əd ⓤⓢ -ɚd **-s** -z
Izard ˈaɪ.zɑːd, -zəd; ˈɪz.əd ⓤⓢ ˈaɪ.zɑːrd, -zɚd; ˈɪz.ɚd
-ization -aɪˈzeɪ.ʃən, -ɪˈ- ⓤⓢ -ɪˈ-
Note: Suffix. Words containing **-ization** always carry primary stress as shown above, e.g. **decimalization** /ˌdes.ɪ.məl.aɪˈzeɪ.ʃən ⓤⓢ -ɪˈ-/.
-ize, -ise -aɪz
Note: Suffix. When attached to a free stem, **-ize** does not normally affect the stress pattern of the stem, e.g. **decimal** /ˈdes.ɪ.məl/, **decimalize** /ˈdes.ɪ.məl.aɪz ⓤⓢ -mə.laɪz/. When attached to a bound stem, the word is normally stressed on the antepenultimate syllable, e.g. **recognize** /ˈrek.əg.naɪz/. Exceptions exist; see individual entries.
Izmir ˈɪz.mɪəʳ, -ˈ- ⓤⓢ ɪzˈmɪr
Izzard ˈɪz.əd, -ɑːd ⓤⓢ -ɚd, -ɑːrd

Pronouncing the letter J

In general, the consonant letter **j** is pronounced /dʒ/, e.g.:

jam /dʒæm/
raj /rɑːdʒ/

(The latter can also be pronounced /rɑːʒ/ in British English.)

In some exceptional cases, **j** is pronounced /j/, e.g.:
hallelujah /ˌhæl.ɪˈluː.jə/

j (J) dʒeɪ **-'s** -z
jab dʒæb **-s** -z **-bing** -ɪŋ **-bed** -d
jabb|er ˈdʒæb|.əʳ ⓤⓢ -ɚ **-ers** -əz ⓤⓢ -ɚz **-ering** -ər.ɪŋ **-ered** -əd ⓤⓢ -ɚd **-erer/s** -ər.əʳ/z ⓤⓢ -ɚ.ɚ/z
Jabberwock ˈdʒæb.ə.wɒk ⓤⓢ -ɚ.wɑːk **-y** -i
jabberwocky (J) ˈdʒæb.ə.wɒk.i ⓤⓢ -ɚ.wɑː.ki, -wɔːk.i
Jabez ˈdʒeɪ.bez, -bɪz
jabiru ˌdʒæb.əˈruː, -ɪˈ-, ˈ--- ⓤⓢ ˈdʒæb.ə.ruː, ˌ--ˈ- **-s** -z
jaborandi ˌdʒæb.əˈræn.di, ˌʒæb-, -ɔːˈ-; -rænˈdiː ⓤⓢ ˌdʒæb.əˈræn.di; -rænˈdiː
jabot ˈʒæb.əʊ ⓤⓢ ʒæbˈoʊ **-s** -z
jacamar ˈdʒæk.ə.mɑːʳ, ˈʒæk- ⓤⓢ ˈdʒæk.ə.mɑːr **-s** -z
jacaranda ˌdʒæk.əˈræn.də **-s** -z
Jacinta dʒəˈsɪn.tə, hə-
jacinth (J) ˈdʒæs.ɪnʈθ, ˈdʒeɪ.sɪnʈθ **-s** -s
Jacintha dʒəˈsɪnʈ.θə, dʒæsˈɪnʈ-
jack (J) dʒæk **-s** -s **-ing** -ɪŋ **-ed** -t ˌ**Jack ˈFrost**; ˌ**Jack ˈRobinson**; ˌ**Jack ˈRussell**; ˌ**jack ˈtar**; ˌ**Jack the ˈlad**
jackal ˈdʒæk.ɔːl, -əl ⓤⓢ -əl **-s** -z
jackanapes ˈdʒæk.ə.neɪps **-es** -ɪz
jackaroo ˌdʒæk.ərˈuː ⓤⓢ -əˈruː **-s** -z
jackass ˈdʒæk.æs **-es** -ɪz
jackboot ˈdʒæk.buːt **-s** -s **-ed** -ɪd
jackdaw ˈdʒæk.dɔː ⓤⓢ -dɑː, -dɔː **-s** -z
jackeroo ˌdʒæk.ərˈuː ⓤⓢ -əˈruː **-s** -z
jack|et ˈdʒæk|.ɪt **-ets** -ɪts **-eting** -ɪ.tɪŋ ⓤⓢ -ɪ.t̬ɪŋ **-eted** -ɪ.tɪd ⓤⓢ -ɪ.t̬ɪd
jackhammer ˈdʒækˌhæm.əʳ ⓤⓢ -ɚ **-s** -z
Jackie ˈdʒæk.i
jack-in-office ˈdʒæk.ɪnˌɒf.ɪs ⓤⓢ -ˌɑː.fɪs **jacks-in-office** ˈdʒæks-
jack-in-the-box ˈdʒæk.ɪn.ðə.bɒks ⓤⓢ -bɑːks **-es** -ɪz
jack-kni|fe (*n.*) ˈdʒæk.naɪ|f **-ves** -vz
jackknif|e (*v.*) ˈdʒæk.naɪf **-es** -s **-ing** -ɪŋ **-ed** -t
Jacklin ˈdʒæk.lɪn
Jacklyn ˈdʒæk.lɪn
Jackman ˈdʒæk.mən
jack-of-all-trades ˌdʒæk.əvˈɔːl.treɪdz, -ɔːlˈtreɪdz ⓤⓢ -ˈɔːl-, -ˈɑːl- **jacks-of-all-trades** ˌdʒæks-
jack-o'-lantern ˌdʒæk.əʊˈlæn.tən, ˈdʒæk.əʊˌlæn.tən ⓤⓢ ˈdʒæk.əˌlæn.tɚn **-s** -z
jackpot ˈdʒæk.pɒt ⓤⓢ -pɑːt **-s** -s ˌ**hit the ˈjackpot**
jackrabbit ˈdʒækˌræb.ɪt **-s** -s
Jackson ˈdʒæk.sən
Jacksonian ˌdʒækˈsəʊ.ni.ən ⓤⓢ -ˈsoʊ-
Jacksonville ˈdʒæk.sən.vɪl
jack-tar ˌdʒækˈtɑːʳ, ˈ-- ⓤⓢ ˌdʒækˈtɑːr, ˈ-- **-s** -z
Jacob ˈdʒeɪ.kəb ˌ**Jacob's ˈladder**
jacobean (J) ˌdʒæk.əʊˈbiː.ən ⓤⓢ -əˈ-, -oʊˈ- **-s** -z
Jacobi ˈdʒæk.ə.bi; dʒəˈkəʊ- ⓤⓢ -ˈkoʊ-
jacobian (J) dʒəˈkəʊ.bi.ən ⓤⓢ -ˈkoʊ- **-s** -z
Jacobin ˈdʒæk.əʊ.bɪn ⓤⓢ ˈ-ə- **-s** -z **-ism** -ɪ.zəm
Jacobit|e ˈdʒæk.əʊ.baɪt ⓤⓢ ˈ-ə- **-es** -s **-ism** -ɪ.zəm
Jacobs ˈdʒeɪ.kəbz
Jacobson ˈdʒæk.əb.sən, ˈjæk- ⓤⓢ ˈdʒeɪ.kəb-
jacobus (J) dʒəˈkəʊ.bəs ⓤⓢ -ˈkoʊ- **-es** -ɪz
Jacoby dʒəˈkəʊ.bi; ˈdʒæk.ə- ⓤⓢ dʒəˈkoʊ-; ˈdʒæk.ə-
Jacquard ˈdʒæk.ɑːd, dʒəˈkɑːd ⓤⓢ dʒəˈkɑːrd
Jacqueline ˈdʒæk.ə.liːn, ˈʒæk-, -lɪn; ˈdʒæk.liːn, -lɪn ⓤⓢ ˈdʒæk.ə.lɪn, -liːn; ˈ-wə.lɪn
Jacques *English surname:* dʒeɪks, dʒæks *French name:* ʒæk ⓤⓢ ʒɑːk
Jacqui ˈdʒæk.i
jactitation ˌdʒæk.tɪˈteɪ.ʃən **-s** -z
jacuzzi (J®) dʒəˈkuː.zi, dʒækˈuː- ⓤⓢ dʒəˈkuː- **-s** -z
jad|e (J) dʒeɪd **-es** -z **-ing** -ɪŋ **-ed** -ɪd
jaeger (J®) ˈjeɪ.gəʳ, ˈdʒeɪ- ⓤⓢ -gɚ **-s** -z
Jael dʒeɪəl, dʒeɪl, ˈdʒeɪ.el ⓤⓢ dʒeɪəl
Jaffa ˈdʒæf.ə ⓤⓢ ˈdʒæf-, ˈdʒɑː.fə, ˈjɑː- **-s** -z
Jaffna ˈdʒæf.nə
Jaffrey ˈdʒæf.ri
jag dʒæg **-s** -z **-ging** -ɪŋ **-ged** -d
Jaggard ˈdʒæg.əd ⓤⓢ -ɚd
jagged ˈdʒæg.ɪd **-ly** -li **-ness** -nəs, -nɪs
jagger (J) ˈdʒæg.əʳ ⓤⓢ -ɚ **-s** -z
jagg|y ˈdʒæg|.i **-ier** -i.əʳ ⓤⓢ -i.ɚ **-iest** -i.ɪst, -i.əst **-iness** -ɪ.nəs, -ɪ.nɪs
Jago ˈdʒeɪ.gəʊ ⓤⓢ -goʊ
jaguar (J) ˈdʒæg.ju.əʳ ⓤⓢ ˈdʒæg.wɑːr, ˈ-ju.ɑːr **-s** -z
Jah dʒɑː, jɑː
Jahveh ˈjɑː.veɪ, ˌjɑːˈveɪ, ˈdʒɑː.veɪ, ˈjɑː.və ⓤⓢ ˈjɑː.veɪ
jai alai ˌhaɪ.əˈlaɪ, ˈ---, ˌhaɪˈlaɪ, ˈ-- ⓤⓢ ˈhaɪˌlaɪ, -əˌlaɪ; ˌhaɪ.əˈlaɪ
jail dʒeɪl **-s** -z **-ing** -ɪŋ **-ed** -d
jailbait ˈdʒeɪl.beɪt
jailbird ˈdʒeɪl.bɜːd ⓤⓢ -bɝːd **-s** -z
jailbreak ˈdʒeɪl.breɪk **-s** -s
jailer, jailor ˈdʒeɪ.ləʳ ⓤⓢ -lɚ **-s** -z
jailhou|se ˈdʒeɪl.haʊ|s **-ses** -zɪz
Jaime *English name:* ˈdʒeɪ.mi *Spanish name:* ˈhaɪ.mi
Jain dʒaɪn, dʒeɪn ⓤⓢ dʒaɪn **-s** -z **-ism** -ɪ.zəm
Jaipur ˌdʒaɪˈpʊəʳ, -ˈpɔːʳ ⓤⓢ -ˈpʊr
Jairus ˈdʒaɪə.rəs, dʒeɪˈaɪə- ⓤⓢ ˈdʒaɪ-, dʒeɪˈaɪ-
Jaish-e-Mohamed dʒɑːˌiːʃ.ɪ.məʊˈhæm.ɪd, -ˌeɪ-, -əd, -ɪd ⓤⓢ dʒaɪ.iːʃ.ə.moʊˈhɑː.mɪd, -ˈhæm-
Jakarta dʒəˈkɑː.tə ⓤⓢ -ˈkɑːr.t̬ə
Jake dʒeɪk
Jakes dʒeɪks
Jalalabad dʒəˈlɑː.lə.bɑːd, -ˈlæl.ə-, -bæd; dʒəˌlɑː.ləˈbɑːd, -ˌlæl.əˈ-, -ˈbæd
jalap ˈdʒæl.əp
jalapeño ˌhæl.əˈpeɪ.njəʊ ⓤⓢ ˌhɑː.ləˈpeɪ.njoʊ, ˌhæl.əˈ- **-s** -z
Jalisco hɑːˈles.kəʊ ⓤⓢ -ˈliːs.koʊ
jalop|y dʒəˈlɒp|.i ⓤⓢ -ˈlɑː.p|i **-ies** -iz
jalousie ˈʒæl.u.ziː, ˌ--ˈ-, dʒəˈluː.si ⓤⓢ ˈdʒæl.ə.si **-s** -z
jam dʒæm **-s** -z **-ming** -ɪŋ **-med** -d ˈ**jam ˌjar**; ˌ**jam ˈtart**; ˈ**jam ˌsession**
Jam *Indian title:* dʒɑːm **-s** -z
Jamaic|a dʒəˈmeɪ.k|ə **-an/s** -ən/z
Jamal dʒəˈmɑːl
jamb dʒæm*b* **-s** -z
jambalaya ˌdʒæm.bəˈlaɪ.ə, ˌdʒʌm- **-s** -z
jamboree ˌdʒæm.bərˈiː, ˈ--- ⓤⓢ ˌdʒæm.bəˈriː **-s** -z
James dʒeɪmz
Jameson ˈdʒeɪm.sən, ˈdʒɪm-, ˈdʒem-, ˈdʒæm-; ˈdʒeɪ.mɪ.sən, ˈdʒɪm.ɪ-, ˈdʒem-, ˈdʒæm-, ˈ-ə- ⓤⓢ ˈdʒeɪm.sən; ˈdʒeɪ.mɪ-
James's ˈdʒeɪm.zɪz
Jamestown ˈdʒeɪmz.taʊn
Jamia ˈdʒʌm.i.ə, ˈdʒæm-

Jamie 'dʒeɪ.mi
Jamieson 'dʒeɪ.mɪ.sᵊn, 'dʒæm.ɪ-, 'dʒem-, 'dʒɪm-, '-ə- ⓤⓢ 'dʒeɪ.mɪ-
jam-jar 'dʒæm.dʒɑːʳ ⓤⓢ -dʒɑːr
Jammu 'dʒæm.uː, 'dʒʌm- ⓤⓢ 'dʒʌm-
jamm|y 'dʒæm|.i **-ier** -i.əʳ ⓤⓢ -i.ɚ **-iest** -i.ɪst, -i.əst **-iness** -ɪ.nəs, -ɪ.nɪs
jam-pot 'dʒæm.pɒt ⓤⓢ -pɑːt **-s** -s
Jamy 'dʒeɪ.mi
Jan *female first name:* dʒæn *male first name:* jæn
Jan. *(abbrev. for* **January***)* dʒæn, 'dʒæn.ju.ᵊr.i, -jʊə.ri, -jʊ- ⓤⓢ -ju.er.i
Jana 'dʒæn.ə, 'dʒeɪ.nə *as if Czech or Polish:* 'jɑː.nə ⓤⓢ 'dʒæn.ə
Janácek 'jæn.ə.tʃek, '-ɑː- ⓤⓢ 'jɑː.nə-
Jane dʒeɪn ˌ**Jane 'Doe**
Janeiro dʒə'nɪə.rəʊ, -'neə- ⓤⓢ ʒə'ner.oʊ, dʒə-, -'nɪr-
Janet 'dʒæn.ɪt, -ət
jangl|e 'dʒæŋ.gl̩ **-es** -z **-ing** -ɪŋ, 'dʒæŋ.glɪŋ **-ed** -d **-er/s** -əʳ/z ⓤⓢ -ɚ/z, 'dʒæŋ.gləʳ/z ⓤⓢ -glɚ/z
Janice 'dʒæn.ɪs
Janine dʒə'niːn
janissar|y 'dʒæn.ɪ.sᵊr|.i ⓤⓢ -ə.ser- **-ies** -iz
janitor 'dʒæn.ɪ.təʳ ⓤⓢ -ə.t̬ɚ **-s** -z
Jan(n)ette dʒə'net, dzæn'et
Jansen 'dʒænt.sᵊn
Jansen|ism 'dʒænt.sᵊn|.ɪ.zᵊm **-ist/s** -ɪst/s
Jantzen® 'jænt.sᵊn, 'dʒænt- ⓤⓢ 'dʒænt-
Januarius ˌdʒæn.ju'eə.ri.əs ⓤⓢ -'er.i-
Januar|y 'dʒæn.ju.ᵊr|.i, -jʊə.r|i, -jʊ- ⓤⓢ -ju.er|.i **-ies** -iz
Janus 'dʒeɪ.nəs
Jap dʒæp **-s** -s
Japan, japan dʒə'pæn **-s** -z **-ning** -ɪŋ **-ned** -d **-ner/s** -əʳ/z ⓤⓢ -ɚ/z
Japanese ˌdʒæp.ᵊn'iːz ⓤⓢ -'iːz, -'iːs
jap|e dʒeɪp **-es** -s **-ing** -ɪŋ **-ed** -t
Japhet 'dʒeɪ.fet, -fɪt
Japheth 'dʒeɪ.feθ, -fɪθ
japhetic dʒeɪ'fet.ɪk, dʒə- ⓤⓢ dʒə'fet̬-
japonica dʒə'pɒn.ɪ.kə ⓤⓢ -'pɑː.nɪ- **-s** -z
Jaques *name:* dʒeɪks, dʒæks *Shakespearian character:* 'dʒeɪ.kwɪz ⓤⓢ -kwɪz, -kiːz; dʒeɪks, dʒæks
jar dʒɑːʳ ⓤⓢ dʒɑːr **-s** -z **-ring/ly** -ɪŋ/li **-red** -d
Jardine 'dʒɑː.diːn, -'- ⓤⓢ 'dʒɑːr.diːn, -'-
jardinière ˌʒɑː.dɪ.ni'eəʳ, ˌdʒɑː-, -dɪ'njeəʳ ⓤⓢ ˌdʒɑːr.dᵊn'ɪr, ˌʒɑːr-, -'jer **-s** -z
Jared 'dʒær.əd ⓤⓢ 'dʒer-, 'dʒær-
jarful 'dʒɑː.fʊl ⓤⓢ 'dʒɑːr- **-s** -z
jargon 'dʒɑː.gən ⓤⓢ 'dʒɑːr- **-s** -z
jargonelle ˌdʒɑː.gə'nel ⓤⓢ ˌdʒɑːr- **-s** -z
Jarley 'dʒɑː.li ⓤⓢ 'dʒɑːr-
Jarlsberg® 'jɑːlz.bɜːg ⓤⓢ 'jɑːrlz.bɝːg
Jarlshof 'jɑːlz.hɒf ⓤⓢ 'jɑːrlz.hɑːf
Jarmaine dʒɑː'meɪn ⓤⓢ dʒɑːr-
Jarman 'dʒɑː.mən ⓤⓢ 'dʒɑːr-
Jarndyce 'dʒɑːn.daɪs ⓤⓢ 'dʒɑːrn-
Jarratt 'dʒær.ət ⓤⓢ 'dʒer-, 'dʒær-
Jarrell dʒə'rel ⓤⓢ dʒə'rel; 'dʒer.ᵊl, 'dʒær-
Jarrett 'dʒær.ət ⓤⓢ 'dʒer-, 'dʒær-
Jarrod 'dʒær.əd ⓤⓢ 'dʒer-, 'dʒær-
Jarrold 'dʒær.ᵊld ⓤⓢ 'dʒer-, 'dʒær-
Jarrow 'dʒær.əʊ ⓤⓢ 'dʒer.oʊ, 'dʒær-
Jarry 'ʒær.i ⓤⓢ ʒɑː'riː
Jaruzelski ˌjær.u'zel.ski ⓤⓢ ˌjɑː.ruː'-
jarvey 'dʒɑː.vi ⓤⓢ 'dʒɑːr- **-s** -z
Jarvie 'dʒɑː.vi ⓤⓢ 'dʒɑːr-
Jarvis 'dʒɑː.vɪs ⓤⓢ 'dʒɑːr-
Jas. *(abbrev. for* **James***)* dʒeɪmz, dʒæs ⓤⓢ dʒeɪmz
jasey 'dʒeɪ.zi **-s** -z
Jasher 'dʒæʃ.əʳ ⓤⓢ -ɚ
jasmine (J) 'dʒæz.mɪn, 'dʒæs-
Jason 'dʒeɪ.sᵊn
jasper (J) 'dʒæs.pəʳ ⓤⓢ 'dʒæs.pɚ **-s** -z
Jaspers 'jæs.pəz ⓤⓢ 'jɑː.spɚz
Jassy 'dʒæs.i
jaundice 'dʒɔːn.dɪs ⓤⓢ 'dʒɑːn-, 'dʒɔːn- **-d** -t
jaun|t dʒɔːn|t ⓤⓢ dʒɑːn|t, dʒɔːn|t **-ts** -ts **-ting/ly** -tɪŋ/li ⓤⓢ -t̬ɪŋ/li **-ted** -tɪd ⓤⓢ -t̬ɪd
jaunt|y 'dʒɔːn.t|i ⓤⓢ 'dʒɑːn.t̬|i, 'dʒɔːn- **-ier** -i.əʳ ⓤⓢ -i.ɚ **-iest** -i.ɪst, -i.əst **-ily** -ɪ.li, -ᵊl.i **-iness** -ɪ.nəs, -ɪ.nɪs
Java 'dʒɑː.və ⓤⓢ 'dʒɑː-, 'dʒæv.ə
Note: **Java coffee** is more likely to be /'dʒæv.ə/ in the US.
Javan *of Java:* 'dʒɑː.vᵊn ⓤⓢ 'dʒɑː-, 'dʒæv.ᵊn *biblical name:* 'dʒeɪ.væn
Javanese ˌdʒɑː.vᵊn'iːz ⓤⓢ -'iːz, -'iːs *stress shift:* ˌJavanese 'people
javelin (J) 'dʒæv.ᵊl.ɪn, -lɪn **-s** -z
jaw dʒɔː ⓤⓢ dʒɑː, dʒɔː **-s** -z **-ing** -ɪŋ **-ed** -d
jawbone 'dʒɔː.bəʊn ⓤⓢ 'dʒɑː.boʊn, 'dʒɔː- **-s** -z
jawboning 'dʒɔːˌbəʊ.nɪŋ ⓤⓢ 'dʒɑːˌboʊ-, 'dʒɔː-
jawbreak|er 'dʒɔːˌbreɪ.k|ə ⓤⓢ 'dʒɑːˌbreɪ.k|ɚ, 'dʒɔː- **-ers** -əz ⓤⓢ -ɚz **-ing** -ɪŋ
jay (J) dʒeɪ **-s** -z
Jayne dʒeɪn
jaywalk 'dʒeɪ.wɔːk ⓤⓢ -wɑːk, -wɔːk **-s** -s **-ing** -ɪŋ **-ed** -t **-er/s** -əʳ/z ⓤⓢ -ɚ/z
jazz dʒæz '**jazz** ˌ**band**
jazz|y 'dʒæz|.i **-ier** -i.əʳ ⓤⓢ -i.ɚ **-iest** -i.ɪst, -i.əst **-ily** -ɪ.li, -ᵊl.i **-iness** -ɪ.nəs, -ɪ.nɪs
JCB ˌdʒeɪ.siː'biː
JD ˌdʒeɪ'diː
Jeakes dʒeɪks
jealous 'dʒel.əs **-ly** -li **-ness** -nəs, -nɪs
jealous|y 'dʒel.ə.s|i **-ies** -iz
Jean *female name:* dʒiːn *French name:* ʒɑ̃ːn ⓤⓢ ʒɑ̃ːn
jean *cotton fabric:* dʒeɪn ⓤⓢ dʒiːn
Jeanette dʒə'net, dʒɪ-
Jeanne *English name:* dʒiːn *French name:* ʒæn ⓤⓢ ʒɑ̃ːn
Jeannie 'dʒiː.ni
jeans dʒiːnz
Jeavons 'dʒev.ᵊnz
Jebb dʒeb
Jebusite 'dʒeb.ju.zaɪt ⓤⓢ -jə.saɪt **-s** -s
Jed dʒed
Jedburgh 'dʒed.bᵊr.ə ⓤⓢ -bɝːg
Jeddah 'dʒed.ə
Jedediah ˌdʒed.ɪ'daɪ.ə
Jeep® dʒiːp **-s** -s
jeepers 'dʒiː.pəz ⓤⓢ -pɚz
jeer dʒɪəʳ ⓤⓢ dʒɪr **-s** -z **-ing/ly** -ɪŋ/li **-ed** -d **-er/s** -əʳ/z ⓤⓢ -ɚ/z
Jeeves dʒiːvz
jeez dʒiːz
Jeff dʒef
Jefferies 'dʒef.riz
Jeffers 'dʒef.əz ⓤⓢ -ɚz
Jefferson 'dʒef.ə.sᵊn ⓤⓢ '-ɚ-
Jeffersonian ˌdʒef.ə'səʊ.ni.ən ⓤⓢ -ɚ'soʊ-
Jeffery 'dʒef.ri **-s** -z
Jeffrey 'dʒef.ri **-s** -z
Jeffries 'dʒef.riz
Jehoiachin dʒɪ'hɔɪ.ə.kɪn, dʒə-
Jehoiakim dʒɪ'hɔɪ.ə.kɪm, dʒə-
Jehoram dʒɪ'hɔː.rəm, dʒə-, -ræm ⓤⓢ -'hɔːr.əm, -æm
Jehoshaphat dʒɪ'hɒʃ.ə.fæt, dʒə-, -'hɒs- ⓤⓢ -'hɑː.ʃə-, -sə-
Jehovah dʒɪ'həʊ.və, dʒə- ⓤⓢ -'hoʊ- **Je**ˌ**hovah's 'witness**
jehu (J) 'dʒiː.hjuː ⓤⓢ -hjuː, -huː **-s** -z
jejune dʒɪ'dʒuːn, dʒə- **-ly** -li **-ness** -nəs, -nɪs
jejunum dʒɪ'dʒuː.nəm, dʒə- **-s** -z
Jekyll 'dʒek.ᵊl, -ɪl, 'dʒiː.kɪl
jell dʒel **-s** -z **-ing** -ɪŋ **-ed** -d
jellaba(h) 'dʒel.ə.bə **-s** -z
Jellicoe 'dʒel.ɪ.kəʊ ⓤⓢ -koʊ
jello 'dʒel.əʊ ⓤⓢ -oʊ **-s** -z
Jell-O® 'dʒel.əʊ ⓤⓢ -oʊ
jell|y 'dʒel|.i **-ies** -iz **-ying** -i.ɪŋ **-ied** -id '**jelly** ˌ**bag**; '**jelly** ˌ**baby**, ˌ**jelly 'baby**; '**jelly** ˌ**bean**
jellyfish 'dʒel.i.fɪʃ **-es** -ɪz
jellygraph 'dʒel.i.grɑːf, -græf ⓤⓢ -græf **-s** -s **-ing** -ɪŋ **-ed** -t
jellyroll 'dʒel.i.rəʊl ⓤⓢ -roʊl **-s** -z
Jemima dʒɪ'maɪ.mə, dʒə-
Jemma 'dʒem.ə
jemm|y 'dʒem|.i **-ies** -iz **-ying** -i.ɪŋ **-ied** -id

Jena ˈdʒeɪ.nə (US) -nɑː
je ne sais quoi ˌʒə.nə.seɪˈkwɑː (US) -seɪˈ-, -seˈ-
Jenkin ˈdʒeŋ.kɪn **-s** -z
Jenkinson ˈdʒeŋ.kɪn.sᵊn
Jenna ˈdʒen.ə
Jenner ˈdʒen.əʳ (US) -ɚ
jennet ˈdʒen.ɪt **-s** -s
Jennifer ˈdʒen.ɪ.fəʳ, ˈ-ə- (US) -fɚ
Jennings ˈdʒen.ɪŋz
Jenny *female name:* ˈdʒen.i, ˈdʒɪn- (US) ˈdʒen-
jenn|y *in machinery:* ˈdʒen|.i *in billiards:* ˈdʒɪn|.i, ˈdʒen- **-ies** -iz
Jensen ˈdʒent.sᵊn **-s** -z
jeopardiz|e, -is|e ˈdʒep.ə.daɪz (US) ˈ-ɚ- **-es** -ɪz **-ing** -ɪŋ **-ed** -d
jeopardy ˈdʒep.ə.di (US) ˈ-ɚ-
Jephthah ˈdʒef.θə
jerboa dʒɜːˈbəʊ.ə, dʒə- (US) dʒɚˈboʊ- **-s** -z
jeremiad ˌdʒer.ɪˈmaɪ.əd, -əˈ-, -æd (US) -əˈ- **-s** -z
Jeremiah ˌdʒer.ɪˈmaɪ.ə, -əˈ- (US) -əˈ-
Jeremy ˈdʒer.ə.mi, ˈ-ɪ-
Jerez həˈrez *as if Spanish:* herˈeθ (US) -ˈres, -ˈreθ
Jericho ˈdʒer.ɪ.kəʊ (US) -koʊ
jerk dʒɜːk (US) dʒɝːk **-s** -s **-ing** -ɪŋ **-ed** -t
jerkin ˈdʒɜː.kɪn (US) ˈdʒɝː- **-s** -z
jerkwater ˈdʒɜːkˌwɔː.təʳ (US) ˈdʒɝːkˌwɑː.t̬ɚ, -ˌwɔː- **ˈjerkwater ˌtown**
jerk|y ˈdʒɜː.k|i (US) ˈdʒɝː- **-ier** -i.əʳ (US) -i.ɚ **-iest** -i.ɪst, -i.əst **-ily** -ɪ.li, -ᵊl.i **-iness** -ɪ.nəs, -ɪ.nɪs
Jermaine dʒɜːˈmeɪn, dʒə-, dʒɜːr- (US) dʒɚ-
Jermyn ˈdʒɜː.mɪn (US) ˈdʒɝː-
jeroboam (J) ˌdʒer.əˈbəʊ.əm (US) -ˈboʊ- **-s** -z
Jerome *Saint:* dʒəˈrəʊm, dʒerˈəʊm, dʒɪˈrəʊm (US) dʒəˈroʊm, dʒerˈoʊm, dʒɪˈroʊm *surname:* dʒəˈrəʊm, dʒerˈəʊm, dʒɪˈrəʊm, ˈdʒer.əm (US) dʒəˈroʊm, dʒerˈoʊm, dʒɪˈroʊm, ˈdʒer.əm
Note: Jerome K. Jerome, the author, is pronounced /dʒəˈrəʊm (US) -roʊm/.
Jerram ˈdʒer.əm
Jerrold ˈdʒer.ᵊld
jerr|y (J) ˈdʒer|.i **-ies** -iz **ˈjerry ˌcan**
jerry-build ˈdʒer.i.bɪld **-s** -z **-ing** -ɪŋ **jerry-built** ˈdʒer.i.bɪlt **jerry-builder/s** ˈdʒer.iˌbɪl.dəʳ/z (US) -dɚ/z
jersey (J) ˈdʒɜː.zi (US) ˈdʒɝː- **-s** -z
Jerusalem dʒəˈruː.sᵊl.əm, dʒɪ-, -lem **JeˌrusaIem ˈartichoke**
Jervaulx ˈdʒɜː.vəʊ, ˈdʒɑː-, -vɪs, -vəs (US) ˈdʒɝː.voʊ, -vɪs, -vəs
Jervis ˈdʒɑː.vɪs, ˈdʒɜː.vɪs (US) ˈdʒɝː-
Jervois ˈdʒɜː.vɪs (US) ˈdʒɝː-
Jespersen ˈjes.pə.sᵊn (US) -pɚ-
jess (J) dʒes **-es** -ɪz **-ing** -ɪŋ **-ed** -t
jessamine (J) ˈdʒes.ə.mɪn
Jesse ˈdʒes.i
Jessel ˈdʒes.ᵊl
Jessica ˈdʒes.ɪ.kə
Jessie ˈdʒes.i
Jessop ˈdʒes.əp
jest dʒest **-s** -s **-ing/ly** -ɪŋ/li **-ed** -ɪd
jester ˈdʒes.təʳ (US) -tɚ **-s** -z
Jesu ˈdʒiː.zjuː (US) ˈdʒiː.zjuː, ˈdʒeɪ-, ˈjeɪ-, -suː, -zuː
Jesu|it ˈdʒez.ju|.ɪt, ˈ-u-, ˈdʒeʒ.u|.ɪt **-its** -ɪts **-itism** -ɪ.tɪ.zᵊm (US) -ɪ.t̬ɪ-
jesuitic ˌdʒez.juˈɪt.ɪk, -uˈ-, ˌdʒeʒ.uˈ- (US) -ˈɪt- **-al** -ᵊl **-ally** -ᵊl.i, -li
Jesus ˈdʒiː.zəs **ˌJesus ˈChrist**
jet dʒet **-s** -s **-ting** -ɪŋ (US) ˈdʒet̬.ɪŋ **-ted** -ɪd (US) ˈdʒet̬.ɪd **ˌjet ˈengine; ˈjet ˌlag; ˈjet ˌset; ˈjet ˌsetter; ˈjet ˌstream**
jeté ʒəˈteɪ **-s** -z
jetfoil ˈdʒet.fɔɪl **-s** -z
Jethro ˈdʒeθ.rəʊ (US) -roʊ
jetliner ˈdʒetˌlaɪ.nəʳ (US) -nɚ **-s** -z
jetsam ˈdʒet.səm, -sæm (US) -səm
jettison ˈdʒet.ɪ.sᵊn, -zᵊn (US) ˈdʒet̬.ə- **-s** -z **-ing** -ɪŋ **-ed** -d
jett|y ˈdʒet|.i (US) ˈdʒet̬- **-ies** -iz
Jetway® ˈdʒet.weɪ
jeu ʒɜː **-s** -z
jeunesse dorée ˌʒɜː.nes.dɔːˈreɪ (US) ʒɜːˌnes.dɔːˈ-
Jevons ˈdʒev.ᵊnz
Jew dʒuː **-s** -z **ˌJew's ˈharp** (US) **ˈJew's ˌharp**
jewel (J) ˈdʒuː.əl, dʒʊəl (US) ˈdʒuː.əl **-s** -z **-(l)ing** -ɪŋ **-(l)ed** -d
Jewell ˈdʒuː.əl, dʒʊəl (US) ˈdʒuː.əl
jewel(l)er ˈdʒuː.ə.ləʳ, ˈdʒʊə.ləʳ (US) ˈdʒuː.ə.lɚ, ˈdʒuː.lɚ **-s** -z
jewellery, jewelry ˈdʒuː.əl.ri, ˈdʒʊəl- (US) ˈdʒuː.əl-
Jewess ˈdʒuː.es, -ɪs, -əs; dʒuːˈes (US) ˈdʒuː.ɪs **-es** -ɪz
Jewett ˈdʒuː.ɪt
Jewish ˈdʒuː.ɪʃ **-ness** -nəs, -nɪs
Jewry ˈdʒʊə.ri, ˈdʒuː- (US) ˈdʒuː.ri
Jewsbury ˈdʒuːz.bᵊr.i (US) -ˌber-
Jeyes dʒeɪz
Jezebel ˈdʒez.ə.bel, ˈ-ɪ-, -bᵊl
Jezreel ˈdʒez.ri.əl, ˌdʒezˈriːl
Jhabvala ˌdʒɑːbˈvɑː.lə
Jiang Qing ˌdʒæŋˈtʃɪŋ
jiao dʒaʊ
jib dʒɪb **-s** -z **-bing** -ɪŋ **-bed** -d
jib-boom dʒɪ*b*ˈbuːm, ˈ-- **-s** -z
jib|e dʒaɪb **-es** -z **-ing** -ɪŋ **-ed** -d **-er/s** -əʳ/z (US) -ɚ/z
Jif® dʒɪf
jiff dʒɪf
jiff|y ˈdʒɪf|.i **-ies** -iz **ˈJiffy ˌbag®**
jig dʒɪg **-s** -z **-ging** -ɪŋ **-ged** -d
jigger ˈdʒɪg.əʳ (US) -ɚ **-s** -z **-ing** -ɪŋ **-ed** -d
jiggered ˈdʒɪg.əd (US) -ɚd
jiggery-pokery ˌdʒɪg.ᵊr.iˈpəʊ.kᵊr.i (US) -ˈpoʊ-
jiggl|e ˈdʒɪg.l̩ **-es** -z **-ing** -ɪŋ, ˈdʒɪg.lɪŋ **-ed** -d
jigsaw ˈdʒɪg.sɔː (US) -sɑː, -sɔː **-s** -z **ˈjigsaw ˌpuzzle**
jihad dʒɪˈhæd, dʒə-, -ˈhɑːd (US) dʒɪˈhɑːd, dʒiː-
Jill dʒɪl
jillaroo ˌdʒɪl.əˈruː **-s** -z
Jillian ˈdʒɪl.i.ən
jilt dʒɪlt **-s** -s **-ing** -ɪŋ (US) ˈdʒɪl.t̬ɪŋ **-ed** -ɪd (US) ˈdʒɪl.t̬ɪd
Jim dʒɪm **-my** -i
jim-dandy ˌdʒɪmˈdæn.di
jimjams ˈdʒɪm.dʒæmz
jimm|y (J) ˈdʒɪm.i **-ies** -iz **-ying** -i.ɪŋ **-ied** -id
jimsonweed ˈdʒɪm*p*.sᵊn.wiːd
jingl|e (J) ˈdʒɪŋ.gl̩ **-es** -z **-ing** -ɪŋ, ˈdʒɪŋ.glɪŋ **-ed** -d **-y** -i **-er/s** -əʳ/z (US) -ɚ/z
jingo (J) ˈdʒɪŋ.gəʊ (US) -goʊ **-es** -z
jingo|ism ˈdʒɪŋ.gəʊ|.ɪ.zᵊm (US) -goʊ- **-ist/s** -ɪst/s
jingoistic ˌdʒɪŋ.gəʊˈɪs.tɪk (US) -goʊˈ- **-ally** -ᵊl.i, -li
jink dʒɪŋk **-s** -s **-ing** -ɪŋ **-ed** -t
jinks (J) dʒɪŋks
jinn dʒɪn **-s** -z
Jinnah ˈdʒɪn.ə
jinrick|sha ˌdʒɪnˈrɪk|.ʃə (US) -ʃɑː, -ʃɔː **-shas** -ʃəz (US) -ʃɑːz, -ʃɔːz **-shaw/s** -ʃɔː/z (US) -ʃɑː/z, -ʃɔː/z
jinx dʒɪŋks **-es** -ɪz **-ing** -ɪŋ **-ed** -t
jitney ˈdʒɪt.ni **-s** -z
jitter ˈdʒɪt.əʳ (US) ˈdʒɪt̬.ɚ **-s** -z **-ing** -ɪŋ **-ed** -d
jitterbug ˈdʒɪt.ə.bʌg (US) ˈdʒɪt̬.ɚ- **-s** -z **-ging** -ɪŋ **-ged** -d
jitters ˈdʒɪt.əz (US) ˈdʒɪt̬.ɚz
jitter|y ˈdʒɪt.ᵊr|.i (US) ˈdʒɪt̬- **-iness** -ɪ.nəs, -ɪ.nɪs
jiujitsu ˌdʒjuːˈdʒɪt.suː
jiv|e dʒaɪv **-es** -z **-ing** -ɪŋ **-ed** -d
jnr (J) *(abbrev. for* **junior***)* ˈdʒuː.ni.əʳ (US) ˈ-njɚ
jo (J) dʒəʊ (US) dʒoʊ **-es** -z
Joab ˈdʒəʊ.æb (US) ˈdʒoʊ-
Joachim ˈjəʊ.ə.kɪm (US) ˈjoʊ-
Joan dʒəʊn (US) dʒoʊn
Joanna dʒəʊˈæn.ə (US) dʒoʊ-
Joanne dʒəʊˈæn (US) dʒoʊ-
Joash ˈdʒəʊ.æʃ (US) ˈdʒoʊ-
job dʒɒb (US) dʒɑːb **-s** -z **-bing** -ɪŋ **-bed** -d **ˈJob ˌCentre; ˈjob desˌcription, ˌjob desˈcription; ˌjob ˈlot** (US) **ˈjob ˌlot; ˈjob ˌshare; ˌgive something ˌup as a ˌbad ˈjob;**
Job dʒəʊb (US) dʒoʊb
jobber ˈdʒɒb.əʳ (US) ˈdʒɑː.bɚ **-s** -z

jobbery ˈdʒɒb.ər.i US ˈdʒɑː.bɚ-
job-hop ˈdʒɒb.hɒp US ˈdʒɑːb.hɑːp **-s** -s **-ping** -ɪŋ **-ped** -t **-per/s** -əʳ/z US -ɚ/z
jobhunting ˈdʒɒbˌhʌn.tɪŋ US ˈdʒɑːbˌhʌn.t̬ɪŋ
jobless ˈdʒɒb.ləs, -lɪs US ˈdʒɑːb- **-ness** -nəs, -nɪs
jobmaster ˈdʒɒbˌmɑː.stəʳ US ˈdʒɑːbˌmæs.tɚ **-s** -z
jobseeker ˈdʒɒbˌsiː.kəʳ, ˈdʒɑːbˌsiː.kɚ **-s** -z
jobsharing ˈdʒɒbˌʃeə.rɪŋ US ˈdʒɑːbˌʃer.ɪŋ
Jobson ˈdʒɒb.sən, ˈdʒəʊb- US ˈdʒɑːb-, ˈdʒoʊb-
Jocasta dʒəʊˈkæs.tə US dʒoʊ-
Jocelyn ˈdʒɒs.lɪn, ˈ-əl.ɪn US ˈdʒɑː.səl.ɪn, ˈ-slɪn
jock (J) dʒɒk US dʒɑːk
jockey ˈdʒɒk.i US ˈdʒɑː.ki **-s** -z **-ing** -ɪŋ **-ed** -d **-ship** -ʃɪp **ˈJockey ˌClub**
jockstrap ˈdʒɒk.stræp US ˈdʒɑːk- **-s** -s
jocose dʒəʊˈkəʊs US dʒoʊˈkoʊs **-ly** -li **-ness** -nəs, -nɪs
jocosity dʒəʊˈkɒs.ə.ti, -ɪ.ti US dʒoʊˈkɑː.sə.t̬i
jocular ˈdʒɒk.jə.ləʳ, -jʊ- US ˈdʒɑː.kjə.lɚ **-ly** -li
jocularity ˌdʒɒk.jəˈlær.ə.ti, -jʊˈ-, -ɪ.ti US ˌdʒɑː.kjəˈler.ə.t̬i, -ˈlær-
jocund ˈdʒɒk.ənd, ˈdʒəʊ.kənd, -kʌnd US ˈdʒɑː.kənd, ˈdʒoʊ- **-ly** -li **-ness** -nəs, -nɪs
jocundity dʒəʊˈkʌn.də.ti, dʒɒkˈʌn-, -dɪ- US dʒoʊˈkʌn.də.t̬i
jod jɒd US jɑːd *as if Hebrew:* jʊd **-s** -z
jodhpurs ˈdʒɒd.pəz, -pɜːz US ˈdʒɑːd.pɚz
Jodi ˈdʒəʊ.di US ˈdʒoʊ-
Jodie ˈdʒəʊ.di US ˈdʒoʊ-
Jodrell ˈdʒɒd.rəl US ˈdʒɑː.drəl **ˌJodrell ˈBank**
Jody ˈdʒəʊ.di US ˈdʒoʊ-
Joe dʒəʊ US dʒoʊ **ˌJoe ˈBloggs; ˌJoe ˈBlow; ˌJoe ˈPublic**
Joel ˈdʒəʊ.əl, -el US ˈdʒoʊ-
Joely ˈdʒəʊ.li, ˈdʒəʊ.ə.li US ˈdʒoʊ-
joey (J) ˈdʒəʊ.i US ˈdʒoʊ- **-s** -z
Joffe ˈdʒɒf.i US ˈdʒɑː.fi
jog dʒɒg US dʒɑːg **-s** -z **-ging** -ɪŋ **-ged** -d **-ger/s** -əʳ/z US -ɚ/z **ˈjog ˌtrot**
joggl|e ˈdʒɒg.l̩ US ˈdʒɑː.gl̩ **-es** -z **-ing** -ɪŋ, ˈdʒɒg.lɪŋ US ˈdʒɑː.glɪŋ **-ed** -d **-er/s** -əʳ/z US -ɚ/z
johannes *coin:* dʒəʊˈæn.ɪs US dʒoʊˈhæn.iːz **-es** -ɪz
Johannes *personal name:* jəʊˈhæn.ɪs US joʊˈhɑː.nɪs
Johannesburg dʒəʊˈhæn.ɪs.bɜːg, -ɪz-, -əs-, -əz- US dʒoʊˈhæn.ɪs.bɝːg, joʊˈhɑː.nɪs-

Note: There exists also a local pronunciation /dʒəˈhɒn.ɪs.bɜːg/, which is used by many English-speaking South Africans.

Johannine dʒəʊˈhæn.aɪn US dʒoʊˈhæn.ɪn, -aɪn
Johannisburger jəʊˈhæn.ɪsˌbɜː.gəʳ, -ɪz-, -əs-, -əz- US dʒoʊˈhæn.ɪsˌbɝː.gɚ, joʊˈhɑː.nɪs-
john (J) dʒɒn US dʒɑːn **-s** -z **ˌJohn ˈBull; ˌJohn ˈDoe; ˌJohn ˈDory**
Johnes dʒəʊnz, dʒɒnz US dʒoʊnz, dʒɑːnz
Johnian ˈdʒəʊ.ni.ən US ˈdʒoʊ- **-s** -z
johnn|y (J) ˈdʒɒn|.i US ˈdʒɑː.n|i **-ies** -iz
Johnny-come-latel|y ˌdʒɒn.i.kʌmˈleɪt.l|i US ˌdʒɑː.ni- **-ies** -iz
John o' Groat's ˌdʒɒn.əˈgrəʊts US ˌdʒɑːn.əˈgroʊts
Johns dʒɒnz US dʒɑːnz
Johnson ˈdʒɒnt.sən US ˈdʒɑːnt-
Johnsonese ˌdʒɒnt.sənˈiːz US ˌdʒɑːnt-
Johnsonian dʒɒnˈsəʊ.ni.ən US dʒɑːnˈsoʊ-
Johnston(e) ˈdʒɒnt.stən, -sən US ˈdʒɑːnt-
Johore dʒəʊˈhɔːʳ US dʒəˈhɔːr
Johor(e) Baharu ˌdʒəʊ.hɔːˈbɑː.ruː US dʒəˌhɔːrˈbɑːr.uː
joie de vivre ˌʒwɑː.dəˈviː.vrə, -ˈviːv
join dʒɔɪn **-s** -z **-ing** -ɪŋ **-ed** -d
joinder ˈdʒɔɪn.dəʳ US -dɚ
joiner ˈdʒɔɪ.nəʳ US -nɚ **-s** -z
joinery ˈdʒɔɪ.nər.i
joint dʒɔɪnt **-s** -s **-ly** -li **-ing** -ɪŋ US ˈdʒɔɪn.t̬ɪŋ **-ed** -ɪd US ˈdʒɔɪn.t̬ɪd **-er/s** -əʳ/z US ˈdʒɔɪn.t̬ɚ/z
joint-stock ˌdʒɔɪntˈstɒk US -ˈstɑːk *stress shift:* ˌjoint-stock ˈbank
jointure ˈdʒɔɪn.tʃəʳ US -tʃɚ **-s** -z
Joinville ˈʒwæ̃ːn.viːl US -ˈ-
joist dʒɔɪst **-s** -s
jojoba həʊˈhəʊ.bə US hoʊˈhoʊ-, hə-
jok|e dʒəʊk US dʒoʊk **-es** -s **-ing/ly** -ɪŋ/li **-ed** -t **-(e)y** -i
joker ˈdʒəʊ.kəʳ US ˈdʒoʊ.kɚ **-s** -z
Jolie ˈdʒəʊ.li, dʒəʊˈliː, ʒəʊ-
Jolley ˈdʒɒl.i US ˈdʒɑː.li
Jolliffe ˈdʒɒl.ɪf US ˈdʒɑː.lɪf
jollification ˌdʒɒl.ɪ.fɪˈkeɪ.ʃən, ˌ-ə- US ˌdʒɑː.lə- **-s** -z
jolli|fy ˈdʒɒl.ɪ|.faɪ US ˈdʒɑː.lɪ- **-fies** -faɪz **-fying** -faɪ.ɪŋ **-fied** -faɪd
jollit|y ˈdʒɒl.ə.t|i, -ɪ.t|i US ˈdʒɑː.lə.t̬|i **-ies** -iz
joll|y (J) ˈdʒɒl|.i US ˈdʒɑː.l|i **-ier** -i.əʳ US -i.ɚ **-iest** -i.ɪst, -i.əst **-ily** -ɪ.li, -əl.i **-iness** -ɪ.nəs, -ɪ.nɪs **-ies** -ɪz **-ying** -i.ɪŋ **-ied** -ɪd **ˌJolly ˈRoger**
jollyboat ˈdʒɒl.i.bəʊt US ˈdʒɑː.li.boʊt **-s** -s
Jolson ˈdʒɒl.sən, ˈdʒəʊl- US ˈdʒoʊl-
jolt dʒəʊlt US dʒoʊlt **-s** -s **-ing/ly** -ɪŋ/li US ˈdʒoʊl.t̬ɪŋ/li **-ed** -ɪd US ˈdʒoʊl.t̬ɪd
jolt|y ˈdʒəʊl.t|i US ˈdʒoʊl.t̬|i **-ier** -i.əʳ US -i.ɚ **-iest** -i.ɪst, -i.əst **-ily** -ɪ.li, -əl.i **-iness** -ɪ.nəs, -ɪ.nɪs
Jolyon ˈdʒəʊ.li.ən, ˈdʒɒl.i- US ˈdʒoʊ.li-, ˈdʒɑː-
Jon dʒɒn US dʒɑːn
Jonah ˈdʒəʊ.nə US ˈdʒoʊ-
Jonas ˈdʒəʊ.nəs, -næs US ˈdʒoʊ.nəs
Jonathan, Jonathon ˈdʒɒn.ə.θən US ˈdʒɑː.nə-
Jones dʒəʊnz US dʒoʊnz
Jonesboro ˈdʒəʊnz.bər.ə US ˈdʒoʊnz.bɚ.oʊ
jongleur ʒɔ̃ːŋˈglɜːʳ, ʒɔːŋ-, ʒɒŋ- US ˈdʒɑːŋ.glɚ **-s** -z
jonquil ˈdʒɒŋ.kwɪl, -kwəl US ˈdʒɑːŋ.kwɪl, ˈdʒɑːn- **-s** -z
Jonson ˈdʒɒnt.sən US ˈdʒɑːnt-
Jonty ˈdʒɒn.ti US ˈdʒɑːn-
Joplin ˈdʒɒp.lɪn US ˈdʒɑːp-
Joppa ˈdʒɒp.ə US ˈdʒɑː.pə
Jopson ˈdʒɒp.sən US ˈdʒɑːp-
Joram ˈdʒɔː.rəm, -ræm US ˈdʒɔːr.əm
Jordan ˈdʒɔː.dən US ˈdʒɔːr- **-s** -z
Jordanian dʒɔːˈdeɪ.ni.ən US dʒɔːr- **-s** -z
Jorge dʒɔːdʒ *as if Spanish:* ˈhɔː.heɪ, ˈxɔː.xeɪ US ˈhɔːr.heɪ
jorum ˈdʒɔː.rəm US ˈdʒɔːr.əm, ˈdʒoʊ.rəm **-s** -z
Josceline ˈdʒɒs.lɪn, ˈ-əl.ɪn US ˈdʒɑː.səl.ɪn, ˈ-slɪn
José, Jose həʊˈzeɪ, -ˈseɪ US hoʊ-
joseph (J) ˈdʒəʊ.zɪf, -zəf US ˈdʒoʊ- **-s** -s
Josephine ˈdʒəʊ.zə.fiːn, -zɪ- US ˈdʒoʊ-
Josephus dʒəʊˈsiː.fəs US dʒoʊ-
josh (J) dʒɒʃ US dʒɑːʃ **-es** -ɪz **-ing/ly** -ɪŋ/li **-ed** -t **-er/s** -əʳ/z US -ɚ/z
Joshua ˈdʒɒʃ.ju.ə, ˈ-u- US ˈdʒɑːʃ-
Josiah dʒəʊˈsaɪ.ə, -ˈzaɪ- US dʒoʊ-
Josias dʒəʊˈsaɪ.əs, -ˈzaɪ- US dʒoʊ-
Josie ˈdʒəʊ.zi, -si US ˈdʒoʊ-
Jospin ˈʒɒs.pæ̃, -ˈ-, dʒɑːsˈpæ̃n
joss dʒɒs US dʒɑːs **-es** -ɪz **ˈjoss ˌhouse; ˈjoss ˌstick**
Jost jəʊst US joʊst
jostl|e ˈdʒɒs.l̩ US ˈdʒɑː.sl̩ **-es** -z **-ing** -ɪŋ, ˈdʒɒs.lɪŋ US ˈdʒɑː.slɪŋ **-ed** -d **-er/s** -əʳ/z US -ɚ/z
jot dʒɒt US dʒɑːt **-s** -s **-ting/s** -ɪŋ/z US ˈdʒɑː.t̬ɪŋ/z **-ted** -ɪd US ˈdʒɑː.t̬ɪd
jotter ˈdʒɒt.əʳ US ˈdʒɑː.t̬ɚ **-s** -z
joule *unit of energy:* dʒuːl, dʒaʊl **-s** -z
Joule *English surname:* dʒuːl, dʒəʊl, dʒaʊl US dʒuːl, dʒoʊl, dʒaʊl
jounc|e dʒaʊnts **-es** -ɪz **-ing** -ɪŋ **-ed** -t
journal ˈdʒɜː.nəl US ˈdʒɝː- **-s** -z

journalese ˌdʒɜː.nᵊlˈiːz (US) ˌdʒɝː-
journal|ism ˈdʒɜː.nᵊl|.ɪ.zᵊm (US) ˈdʒɝː- **-ist/s** -ɪst/s
journalistic ˌdʒɜː.nᵊlˈɪs.tɪk (US) ˌdʒɝː- **-ally** -ᵊl.i, -li
journaliz|e, -is|e ˈdʒɜː.nᵊl.aɪz (US) ˈdʒɝː- **-es** -ɪz **-ing** -ɪŋ **-ed** -d
journey ˈdʒɜː.ni (US) ˈdʒɝː- **-s** -z **-ing/s** -ɪŋ/z **-ed** -d
journey|man ˈdʒɜː.ni|.mən (US) ˈdʒɝː- **-men** -mən
joust dʒaʊst **-s** -s **-ing** -ɪŋ **-ed** -ɪd **-er/s** -əʳ/z (US) -ɚ/z
Jove dʒəʊv (US) dʒoʊv
jovial ˈdʒəʊ.vi.əl (US) ˈdʒoʊ- **-ly** -i **-ness** -nəs, -nɪs
joviality ˌdʒəʊ.viˈæl.ə.ti, -ɪ.ti (US) ˌdʒoʊ.viˈæl.ə.t̬i
Jowell dʒaʊəl, dʒəʊəl (US) dʒaʊəl, dʒoʊəl
Jowett, Jowitt ˈdʒaʊ.ɪt, ˈdʒəʊ- (US) ˈdʒaʊ-, ˈdʒoʊ-
jowl dʒaʊl **-s** -z
joy (J) dʒɔɪ **-s** -z **-ing** -ɪŋ **-ed** -d
Joyce dʒɔɪs
joyful ˈdʒɔɪ.fᵊl, -fʊl **-lest** -ɪst, -əst **-ly** -i **-ness** -nəs, -nɪs
joyless ˈdʒɔɪ.ləs, -lɪs **-ly** -li **-ness** -nəs, -nɪs
joyous ˈdʒɔɪ.əs **-ly** -li **-ness** -nəs, -nɪs
joy|ride ˈdʒɔɪ|.raɪd **-rides** -raɪdz **-riding** -ˌraɪ.dɪŋ **-rode** -rəʊd (US) -roʊd **-ridden** -rɪd.ᵊn **-rider/s** -ˌraɪ.dəʳ/z (US) -dɚ/z
joystick ˈdʒɔɪ.stɪk **-s** -s
JPEG ˈdʒeɪ.peg
jr (J) *(abbrev. for* **junior***)* ˈdʒuː.ni.əʳ (US) ˈ-njɚ
Juan *h*wɑːn; ˈdʒuː.ən *as if Spanish:* xwɑːn, xwæn (US) *h*wɑːn
Note: In Byron's Don Juan, the pronunciation is /ˈdʒuː.ən/ in both British and American English.
Juan Carlos ˌ*h*wɑːnˈkɑː.lɒs, ˌ*h*wɑːŋ- *as if Spanish:* ˌxwɑːn-, ˌxwæn- (US) ˌ*h*wɑːnˈkɑːr.loʊs
Juan Fernandez ˌ*h*wɑːn.fəˈnæn.dez, -des *as if Spanish:* ˌxwɑːn.fəˈnæn.dez, ˌxwæn- (US) ˌ*h*wɑːn.fɚˈnɑːn.des
Juanita ˌdʒuː.əˈniː.tə; hwɑːˈniː.tə, hwænˈiː (US) *h*wɑːˈniː.t̬ə, *h*wə-
jubilant ˈdʒuː.bɪ.lənt, -bᵊl.ənt **-ly** -li
jubi|late *(v.)* ˈdʒuː.bɪ|.leɪt, -bə- **-lates** -leɪts **-lating** -leɪ.tɪŋ (US) -leɪ.t̬ɪŋ **-lated** -leɪ.tɪd (US) -leɪ.t̬ɪd
Jubilate *(n.)* ˌdʒuː.bɪˈlɑː.teɪ, ˌjuː-, -bəˈ-, -ti (US) ˌjuː.biːˈlɑː.teɪ **-s** -z
jubilation ˌdʒuː.bɪˈleɪ.ʃᵊn, -bəˈ- **-s** -z
jubilee ˈdʒuː.bɪ.liː, -bə-, ˌ--ˈ- **-s** -z
Judae|a dʒuːˈdiː|.ə **-an/s** -ən/z
Juda(h) ˈdʒuː.də
Judaic dʒuːˈdeɪ.ɪk **-al** -ᵊl **-ally** -ᵊl.i, -li
Juda|ism ˈdʒuː.deɪ|.ɪ.zᵊm, -di- (US) -deɪ-, -di-, -də- **-ist/s** -ɪst/s
judaiz|e, -is|e ˈdʒuː.deɪ.aɪz (US) -deɪ-, -di-, -də- **-es** -ɪz **-ing** -ɪŋ **-ed** -d **-er/s** -əʳ/z (US) -ɚ/z
Judas ˈdʒuː.dəs **-es** -ɪz ˈ**Judas** ˌ**tree**
Judd dʒʌd
judder ˈdʒʌd.əʳ (US) -ɚ **-s** -z **-ing** -ɪŋ **-ed** -d
Jude dʒuːd
Jude|a dʒuːˈdiː|.ə **-an/s** -ən/z
judg|e (J) dʒʌdʒ **-es** -ɪz **-ing** -ɪŋ **-ed** -d
judg(e)ment ˈdʒʌdʒ.mənt **-s** -s ˈ**Judgement** ˌ**Day**
judgeship ˈdʒʌdʒ.ʃɪp, ˈdʒʌd- **-s** -s
judgmental dʒʌdʒˈmen.tᵊl (US) -t̬ᵊl **-ly** -i
judicator|y ˈdʒuː.dɪ.kə.tᵊr|.i (US) -tɔːr- **-ies** -iz
judicature ˈdʒuː.dɪ.kə.tʃəʳ, -tjʊəʳ (US) -tʃɚ
judicial dʒuːˈdɪʃ.ᵊl **-ly** -i **ju**ˌ**dicial re**ˈ**view**
judiciar|y dʒuːˈdɪʃ.ᵊr|.i, -i.əʳ- (US) -i.er-, -ˈdɪʃ.ɚ-, -i.ɚ- **-ies** -iz
judicious dʒuːˈdɪʃ.əs **-ly** -li **-ness** -nəs, -nɪs
Judith ˈdʒuː.dɪθ
judo ˈdʒuː.dəʊ (US) -doʊ
Judson ˈdʒʌd.sᵊn
Judy ˈdʒuː.di
jug dʒʌg **-s** -z **-ging** -ɪŋ **-ged** -d
jugful ˈdʒʌg.fʊl **-s** -z
juggernaut (J) ˈdʒʌg.ə.nɔːt (US) -ɚ.nɑːt, -nɔːt **-s** -s
juggins (J) ˈdʒʌg.ɪnz **-es** -ɪz
juggl|e ˈdʒʌg.l̩ **-es** -z **-ing** -ɪŋ, ˈdʒʌg.lɪŋ **-ed** -d **-er/s** -əʳ/z, ˈdʒʌg.ləʳ/z (US) -ɚ/z, ˈdʒʌg.lɚ/z
jugglery ˈdʒʌg.lᵊr.i
Jugoslav ˈjuː.gəʊ.slɑːv, ˌ--ˈ- (US) ˈjuː.goʊ.slɑːv **-s** -z
Jugoslavi|a ˌjuː.gəʊˈslɑː.vi|.ə (US) -goʊˈ- **-an** -ən
jugular ˈdʒʌg.jə.ləʳ, -jʊ- (US) -lɚ ˌ**jugular** ˈ**vein** ˈ**jugular** ˌ**vein** (US) ˈ**jugular** ˌ**vein**
Jugurtha dʒʊˈgɜː.θə, jʊ- (US) dʒuːˈgɝː-
juic|e dʒuːs **-es** -ɪz **-ing** -ɪŋ **-ed** -t **-er/s** -əʳ/z (US) -ɚ/z
juic|y ˈdʒuː.s|i **-ier** -i.əʳ (US) -i.ɚ **-iest** -i.ɪst, -i.əst **-ily** -ɪ.li, -ᵊl.i **-iness** -ɪ.nəs, -ɪ.nɪs
Juilliard ˈdʒuː.li.ɑːd (US) -ɑːrd
jujitsu dʒuːˈdʒɪt.suː
jujube ˈdʒuː.dʒuːb **-s** -z
jukebox ˈdʒuːk.bɒks (US) -bɑːks **-es** -ɪz
Jukes dʒuːks
Jul. *(abbrev. for* **July***)* dʒʊˈlaɪ, dʒə-, dʒuː-
julep ˈdʒuː.lɪp, -lep, -ləp (US) -ləp **-s** -s
Julia ˈdʒuː.li.ə (US) ˈdʒuːl.jə
Julian ˈdʒuː.li.ən (US) ˈdʒuːl.jən
Juliana ˌdʒuː.liˈɑː.nə (US) -ˈæn.ə, -ˈɑː.nə
Julie ˈdʒuː.li
julienne ˌdʒuː.liˈen, ˌʒuː- (US) ˌdʒuː-
Juliet ˈdʒuː.li.ət; ˌdʒuː.liˈet (US) ˈdʒuː.li.et, -ɪt; ˌdʒuː.liˈet; ˈdʒuːl.jɪt
Juliette ˌdʒuː.liˈet, ˈ---
Julius ˈdʒuː.li.əs (US) ˈdʒuːl.jəs
Julius Caesar ˌdʒuː.li.əsˈsiː.zəʳ (US) ˌdʒuːl.jəsˈsiː.zɚ
Jul|y dʒʊˈl|aɪ, dʒə-, ˌdʒuː- **-ies** -aɪz
Julyan ˈdʒuː.li.ən (US) ˈdʒuːl.jən
jumbl|e ˈdʒʌm.bl̩ **-es** -z **-ing** -ɪŋ, ˈdʒʌm.blɪŋ **-ed** -d ˈ**jumble** ˌ**sale**
Jumbl|y ˈdʒʌm.bl|i **-ies** -iz
jumbo (J) ˈdʒʌm.bəʊ (US) -boʊ **-s** -z ˌ**jumbo** ˈ**jet,** ˈ**jumbo** ˌ**jet**
Jumna ˈdʒʌm.nə
jump dʒʌmp **-s** -s **-ing** -ɪŋ **-ed** -t **-er/s** -əʳ/z (US) -ɚ/z ˈ**jumper** ˌ**cables;** ˌ**jumping** ˈ**jack** (US) ˈ**jumping** ˌ**jack;** ˈ**jump** ˌ**leads;** ˈ**jump** ˌ**rope;** ˌ**jump the** ˈ**gun**
jumped-up ˌdʒʌmptˈʌp *stress shift:* ˌjumped-up ˈtyrant
jumper ˈdʒʌm.pəʳ (US) -pɚ **-s** -z
jump-jet ˈdʒʌmp.dʒet **-s** -s
jump-off ˈdʒʌmp.ɒf (US) -ɑːf **-s** -s
jump|-start ˈdʒʌmp|.stɑːt (US) -stɑːrt **-starts** -stɑːts (US) -stɑːrts **-starting** -ˌstɑː.tɪŋ (US) -ˌstɑːr.t̬ɪŋ **-started** -ˌstɑː.tɪd (US) -ˌstɑːr.t̬ɪd
jumpsuit ˈdʒʌmp.suːt, -sjuːt (US) -suːt **-s** -s
jump|y ˈdʒʌm.p|i **-ier** -i.əʳ (US) -i.ɚ **-iest** -i.ɪst, -i.əst **-ily** -ɪ.li, -ᵊl.i **-iness** -ɪ.nəs, -ɪ.nɪs
jun. *(abbrev. for* **junior***)* ˈdʒuː.ni.əʳ (US) ˈ-njɚ
Jun. *(abbrev. for* **June***)* dʒuːn
junction ˈdʒʌŋ*k*.ʃᵊn **-s** -z ˈ**junction** ˌ**box**
juncture ˈdʒʌŋ*k*.tʃəʳ (US) -tʃɚ **-s** -z
June dʒuːn **-s** -z
Juneau ˈdʒuː.nəʊ, -ˈ- (US) ˈdʒuː.noʊ
Jung jʊŋ
Jungfrau ˈjʊŋ.fraʊ
Jungian ˈjʊŋ.i.ən **-s** -z
jungl|e ˈdʒʌŋ.gl̩ **-es** -z **-y** -i ˈ**jungle** ˌ**fowl;** ˈ**jungle** ˌ**gym** ˌ**jungle** ˈ**gym**
junior ˈdʒuː.ni.əʳ (US) ˈ-njɚ **-s** -z
juniority ˌdʒuː.niˈɒr.ə.ti, -ɪ.ti (US) -ˈɔːr.ə.t̬i
juniper ˈdʒuː.nɪ.pəʳ, -nə- (US) -pɚ **-s** -z
Junius ˈdʒuː.ni.əs (US) -njəs
junk dʒʌŋk **-s** -s **-ing** -ɪŋ **-ed** -t ˈ**junk** ˌ**bond;** ˈ**junk** ˌ**food,** ˌ**junk** ˈ**food;** ˈ**junk** ˌ**mail,** ˌ**junk** ˈ**mail;** ˈ**junk** ˌ**shop**
junker (J) ˈjʊŋ.kəʳ (US) -kɚ *old car:* ˈdʒʌŋ.kəʳ (US) -kɚ **-s** -z
jun|ket ˈdʒʌŋ|.kɪt **-kets** -kɪts **-keting** -kɪ.tɪŋ (US) -kɪ.t̬ɪŋ **-keted** -kɪ.tɪd (US) -t̬ɪd

junkie ˈdʒʌŋ.ki **-s** -z
junkyard ˈdʒʌŋk.jɑːd ⓤⓢ -jɑːrd **-s** -z
Juno ˈdʒuː.nəʊ ⓤⓢ -noʊ
Junoesque ˌdʒuː.nəʊˈesk ⓤⓢ -noʊˈ-
junta ˈdʒʌn.tə, ˈdʒʊn-, ˈhʊn- ⓤⓢ ˈhʊn-, ˈdʒʊn-, ˈdʒʌn-, ˈhʌn- **-s** -z
junto ˈdʒʌn.təʊ, ˈdʒʊn-, ˈhʊn ⓤⓢ -toʊ **-s** -z
jupe ʒuːp ⓤⓢ dʒuːp **-s** -s
Jupiter ˈdʒuː.pɪ.təʳ, -pə- ⓤⓢ -t̬ɚ
jupon ˈʒuː.pɒn, ˈdʒuː-, -pɔ̃ːŋ, -pɒŋ ⓤⓢ ˈdʒuː.pɑːn, -ˈ- **-s** -z
Jura ˈdʒʊə.rə ⓤⓢ ˈdʒʊr.ə
Jurassic dʒʊəˈræs.ɪk ⓤⓢ dʒʊ-, dʒə-
jurat ˈdʒʊə.ræt ⓤⓢ ˈdʒʊr.æt **-s** -s
Jürgen ˈjɜː.gən, ˈjʊə- ⓤⓢ ˈjɝː-
juridic|al dʒʊəˈrɪd.ɪ.k|əl ⓤⓢ dʒʊ- **-ally** -əl.i, -li
jurisdiction ˌdʒʊə.rɪsˈdɪk.ʃən, -rəsˈ-, -rɪzˈ-, -rəzˈ- ⓤⓢ ˌdʒʊr.ɪsˈ- **-s** -z **-al** -əl
jurisprudence ˌdʒʊə.rɪsˈpruː.dənts, -rəs-; ˈdʒʊə.rɪsˌpruː-, -rəs- ⓤⓢ ˌdʒʊr.ɪsˈpruː-
jurist ˈdʒʊə.rɪst ⓤⓢ ˈdʒʊr.ɪst **-s** -s
juror ˈdʒʊə.rəʳ ⓤⓢ ˈdʒʊr.ɚ, -ɔːr **-s** -z
jur|y ˈdʒʊə.r|i ⓤⓢ ˈdʒʊr.|i **-ies** -iz **ˈjury ˌbox; ˈjury ˌservice**
jury|man ˈdʒʊə.ri|.mən ⓤⓢ ˈdʒʊr.i- **-men** -mən, -men
jury-mast ˈdʒʊə.ri.mɑːst ⓤⓢ ˈdʒʊr.i.mæst *nautical pronunciation:* -məst **-s** -s
just (J) *(adj.)* dʒʌst **-er** -əʳ ⓤⓢ -ɚ **-est** -ɪst, -əst **-ly** -li **-ness** -nəs, -nɪs
just *(adv.) strong form:* dʒʌst *weak form:* dʒəst
jus tertii ˌjʊsˈtɜː.ti.iː ⓤⓢ ˌdʒʌsˈterti:, ˌjuːs-
justic|e ˈdʒʌs.tɪs **-es** -ɪz **ˌjustice of the ˈpeace**
justiciable dʒʌsˈtɪʃ.i.ə.bl̩, -ˈtɪʃ.ə- ⓤⓢ -i.ə-
justiciar dʒʌsˈtɪʃ.i.ɑːʳ, -ˈtɪs- ⓤⓢ -ˈtɪʃ.i.ɚ **-s** -z
justiciar|y dʒʌsˈtɪʃ.i.ər|.i, -ˈtɪʃ.ər-, -ˈtɪs.i- ⓤⓢ -ˈtɪʃ.i.er- **-ies** -iz
justifiab|le ˈdʒʌs.tɪ.faɪ.ə.b|l̩, -tə-; ˌdʒʌs.tɪˈfaɪ-, -təˈ- ⓤⓢ ˈdʒʌs.tə.faɪ-, -tɪ- **-ly** -li **-leness** -l̩.nəs, -nɪs
justification ˌdʒʌs.tɪ.fɪˈkeɪ.ʃən, -tə- ⓤⓢ -tə-, -tɪ- **-s** -z
justificatory ˈdʒʌs.tɪ.fɪ.keɪ.tər.i, -tə-; ˌdʒʌs.tɪ.fɪˈkeɪ-; ˌdʒʌs.tɪˈfɪk.ə- ⓤⓢ dʒəˈstɪf.ɪ.kə.tɔːr-; ˈdʒʌs.tə.fɪ.keɪ.tɚ-
justi|fy ˈdʒʌs.tɪ|.faɪ, -tə- **-fies** -faɪz **-fying** -faɪ.ɪŋ **-fied** -faɪd **-fier/s** -faɪ.əʳ/z ⓤⓢ -faɪ.ɚ/z
Justin ˈdʒʌs.tɪn
Justine dʒʌsˈtiːn, ˈ--
Justinian dʒʌsˈtɪn.i.ən
Justus ˈdʒʌs.təs
jut dʒʌt **-s** -s **-ting** -ɪŋ ⓤⓢ ˈdʒʌt̬.ɪŋ **-ted** -ɪd ⓤⓢ ˈdʒʌt̬.ɪd
Juta ˈdʒuː.tə
jute (J) dʒuːt **-s** -s
Jutland ˈdʒʌt.lənd
Juvenal ˈdʒuː.vən.əl, -vɪ.nəl
juvenescen|ce ˌdʒuː.vənˈes.ən|ts, -vɪˈnes- **-t** -t
juvenile ˈdʒuː.vən.aɪl, -vɪ.naɪl ⓤⓢ -və.nəl, -naɪl **-s** -z **ˌjuvenile deˈlinquent**
juvenilia ˌdʒuː.vəˈnɪl.i.ə, -vɪˈ-, -ˈniː.li- ⓤⓢ -vəˈnɪl.i-, ˈ-jə
juvenility ˌdʒuː.vəˈnɪl.ə.ti, -vɪˈ-, -ɪ.ti ⓤⓢ -ə.t̬i
Juventus juːˈven.təs
juxtapos|e ˌdʒʌk.stəˈpəʊz, ˈ--- ⓤⓢ ˈdʒʌk.stə.poʊz, ˌ--ˈ- **-es** -ɪz **-ing** -ɪŋ **-ed** -d
juxtaposition ˌdʒʌk.stə.pəˈzɪʃ.ən **-s** -z **-al** -əl

Pronouncing the letter K

In general, the consonant letter **k** is pronounced /k/, e.g.:

Kate /keɪt/

This is also the case in the digraph **kh**, e.g.:

khaki /ˈkɑː.ki/ (US) /ˈkæk.i/

In words beginning **kn**, **k** is usually silent, e.g.:

knack /næk/

However, where the **k** appears before an **n** at a morpheme boundary, it is pronounced, e.g.:

sickness /ˈsɪk.nəs/

k (K) keɪ **-'s** -z
K2 ˌkeɪˈtuː
Kaaba ˈkɑː.bə, ˈkɑː.ə.bɑː (US) -bə
kabaka (K) kəˈbɑː.kə **-s** -z
kabbadi kɑːˈbɑː.di
Kab(b)ala kəˈbɑː.lə, kæbˈɑː- (US) ˈkæb.ə-; kəˈbɑː-
Kabila kəˈbiː.lə, kæbˈiː- (US) kɑːˈbiːlə
kabob kəˈbɒb (US) -ˈbɑːb
kabuki kəˈbuː.ki, kæbˈuː- (US) kə-, kɑː-
Kabul ˈkɑː.bᵊl, ˈkɔː-, -bʊl; kəˈbʊl (US) ˈkɑː.bʊl; kəˈbʊl
Kabwe ˈkæb.weɪ (US) ˈkɑːb-
Kabyle kəˈbaɪl, kæbˈaɪl, -iːl **-s** -z
kachina (K) kəˈtʃiː.nə **-s** -z
Kaczynski kəˈzɪn*t*.ski
Kaddish ˈkæd.ɪʃ (US) ˈkɑː.dɪʃ **-im** -ɪm, -iːm
kaf(f)ir (K) ˈkæf.əʳ **-s** -z
Kafka ˈkæf.kə (US) ˈkɑːf-
Kafkaesque ˌkæf.kəˈesk (US) ˌkɑːf-
kaftan ˈkæf.tæn (US) -tən, -tæn **-s** -z
kagoule kəˈguːl **-s** -z
Kahn kɑːn
kailyard ˈkeɪl.jɑːd (US) -jɑːrd **-s** -z
Kaiser ˈkaɪ.zəʳ (US) -zɚ **-s** -z
Kaiserslautern ˈkaɪ.zəzˌlaʊ.tɜːn, -tən (US) ˌkaɪ.zɚzˈlaʊ.tɚn
Kaitlin, Kaitlyn ˈkeɪt.lɪn
Kakadu ˈkæk.ə.duː, --ˈ-
kakemono ˌkæk.iˈməʊ.nəʊ (US) ˌkɑː.kəˈmoʊ.noʊ **-s** -z
Kalahari ˌkæl.əˈhɑː.ri (US) ˌkɑː.lɑːˈhɑːr.i, ˌkæl-
Kalamazoo ˌkæl.ə.məˈzuː
Kalashnikov® kəˈlæʃ.nɪ.kɒf, -nə- (US) -ˈlɑːʃ.nɪ.kɑːf **-s** -s
Kalat kəˈlɑːt
kale keɪl
kaleidoscope kəˈlaɪ.də.skəʊp (US) -skoʊp **-s** -s
kaleidoscopic kəˌlaɪ.dəˈskɒp.ɪk (US) -ˈskɑː.pɪk
kalends ˈkæl.endz, -ɪndz, -əndz (US) -əndz, ˈkeɪ.ləndz
Kalevala ˌkɑː.ləˈvɑː.lə (US) -lə, -lɑː
Kalgoorlie kælˈgʊə.li (US) -ˈgʊr-
Kali ˈkɑː.li
kalif ˈkeɪ.lɪf, ˈkæl.ɪf, ˈkɑː.lɪf; kəˈlɪf (US) ˈkeɪ.lɪf, ˈkæl.ɪf **-s** -s
Kalimantan ˌkæl.ɪˈmæn.tən (US) ˌkɑː.liːˈmɑːn.tɑːn
Kam|a *Hindu god:* ˈkɑː.m|ə **-ic** -ɪk *Russian river:* ˈkɑː.mə
Kamasutra ˌkɑː.məˈsuː.trə
Kamchatka kæmˈtʃæt.kə (US) kæmˈtʃæt-, kɑːmˈtʃɑːt-
kamikaze ˌkæm.ɪˈkɑː.zi (US) ˌkɑː.məˈkɑː.zi **-s** -z
Kampala kæmˈpɑː.lə (US) kɑːm-
kampong ˈkæm.pɒŋ, -ˈ- (US) ˈkɑːm.pɔːŋ, -pɑːŋ
Kampuche|a ˌkæm.pʊˈtʃiː|.ə (US) -puːˈ- **-an/s** -ən/z
kana ˈkɑː.nə (US) -nə, -nɑː
Kananga kəˈnæŋ.gə (US) -ˈnɑːŋ-
Kanarese ˌkæn.ᵊrˈiːz (US) ˌkɑː.nəˈriːz, -ˈriːs
Kanchenjunga ˌkæn.tʃənˈdʒʊŋ.gə, -ˈdʒʌŋ- (US) ˌkɑːn.tʃənˈdʒʊŋ-
Kandahar ˌkæn.dəˈhɑːʳ (US) ˌkɑːn.dəˈhɑːr
Kandinsky kænˈdɪn*t*.ski
Kandy ˈkæn.di (US) ˈkæn-, ˈkɑːn-
Kane keɪn
Kanga ˈkæŋ.gə
kangaroo ˌkæŋ.gᵊrˈuː *sometimes in Australia:* ˈ--- (US) ˌkæŋ.gəˈruː **-s** -z *stress shift, see compound:* **ˌkangaroo ˈcourt**
Kangchenjunga ˌkæn.tʃənˈdʒʊŋ.gə, -ˈdʒʌŋ- (US) ˌkɑːn.tʃənˈdʒʊŋ-
kanji ˈkæn.dʒi, ˈkɑːn- (US) ˈkɑːn.*d*ʒi **-s** -z
Kano ˈkɑː.nəʊ, ˈkeɪ- (US) ˈkɑː.noʊ
Kanpur kɑːnˈpʊəʳ (US) ˈkɑːn.pʊr
Kans. *(abbrev. for* **Kansas***)* ˈkæn.zəs
Kansas ˈkæn.zəs ˌ**Kansas ˈCity**; ˌ**Kansas ˌCity ˈsteak**
Kant kænt (US) kænt, kɑːnt
Kantian ˈkæn.ti.ən (US) ˈkæn.ṭi-, ˈkɑːn-
Kant|ism ˈkæn.t|ɪ.zᵊm (US) ˈkæn.t|ɪ-, ˈkɑːn- **-ist/s** -ɪst/s
Kaohsiung ˌkaʊ.ʃiˈʊŋ (US) -ˈʃʊŋ
Kaolak ˈkɑː.əʊ.læk, ˈkaʊ.læk (US) ˈkɑː.oʊ-, ˈkaʊ.læk
kaolin ˈkeɪ.ə.lɪn
kapellmeister kəˈpel.maɪ.stəʳ, kæpˈel- (US) kɑːˈpel.maɪ.stɚ, kə- **-s** -z
Kaplan ˈkæp.lən
kapok ˈkeɪ.pɒk (US) -pɑːk
Kaposi kəˈpəʊ.zi, kæpˈəʊ-, -si; ˈkɑː.pə.ʃi, ˈkæp.ə- (US) kəˈpoʊ.zi, -si; ˈkæp.ə- **Kaˌposiˈs sarˈcoma**
kappa ˈkæp.ə
kaput(t) kəˈpʊt, kæpˈʊt (US) kəˈpʊt, -ˈpuːt
Kara ˈkɑː.rə (US) ˈkɑːr.ə
Karachi kəˈrɑː.tʃi
Karadzic ˈkær.ə.*d*ʒɪtʃ, -dɪtʃ (US) kəˈrɑː.dʒɪtʃ
Karaganda ˌkær.əˈgæn.də (US) ˌkɑːr.əˈgɑːn-
Karajan ˈkær.ə.jɑːn (US) ˈkɑːr-, -jən
karaoke ˌkær.iˈəʊ.ki (US) ˌker.iˈoʊ.ki, ˌkær- **-s** -z
karat ˈkær.ət (US) ˈker-, ˈkær- **-s** -z
karate kəˈrɑː.ti, kærˈɑː- (US) kəˈrɑː.ṭi
Kareli|a kəˈreɪ.li|.ə, -ˈriː- (US) -li|.ə, -lj|ə **-ans** -ənz
Karen *female name:* ˈkær.ən (US) ˈker-, ˈkær- *of Burma:* kəˈren **-s** -z
Karenina kəˈren.ɪ.nə
Karl kɑːl (US) kɑːrl
Karla ˈkɑː.lə (US) ˈkɑːr-
Karl-Marx-Stadt ˌkɑːlˈmɑːksˌʃtæt (US) ˌkɑːrˈmɑːrksˌʃtɑːt
Karloff ˈkɑː.lɒf (US) ˈkɑːr.lɑːf
Karlsbad ˈkɑːlz.bæd (US) ˈkɑːrlz-
Karlsruhe ˈkɑːlz.ruː.ə (US) ˈkɑːrlz-
karm|a ˈkɑː.m|ə, ˈkɜː- (US) ˈkɑːr-, ˈkɝː- **-ik** -ɪk
Karnak ˈkɑː.næk (US) ˈkɑːr-
Karnataka kəˈnɑː.tə.kə (US) kɑːrˈnɑː.ṭə-
Karpov ˈkɑː.pɒf (US) ˈkɑːr.pɑːf
karroo kəˈruː **-s** -z
Kars kɑːz (US) kɑːrz
Karsh kɑːʃ (US) kɑːrʃ
kart kɑːt (US) kɑːrt **-s** -s **-ing** -ɪŋ (US) ˈkɑːr.ṭɪŋ
Karzai ˈkɑː.zaɪ (US) ˈkɑːr-
Kasakhstan ˌkæz.ækˈstɑːn, ˌkɑː.zækˈ-, -zɑːkˈ-, -ˈstæn (US) ˌkɑː.zɑːkˈstɑːn
kasbah (K) ˈkæz.bɑː, -bə (US) -bɑː, ˈkɑːz- **-s** -z

Kasey ˈkeɪ.si
kasha ˈkæʃ.ə, ˈkɑː.ʃə (US) ˈkɑː.ʃə
Kashgar ˈkæʃ.gɑːʳ (US) ˈkɑːʃ.gɑːr
Kashmir ˌkæʃˈmɪəʳ (US) ˈkæʃ.mɪr, -ˈ- **-i/s** -i/z *stress shift, British only:* ˌKashmir ˈborder
Kaspar ˈkæs.pəʳ, -pɑːʳ (US) -pɚ, -pɑːr
Kasparov kæsˈpɑː.rɒf; ˈkæs.pə- (US) kæsˈpɑːr.ɔːf, kəˈspɑːr-; ˈkæs.pə.rɔːf
Kassala kəˈsɑː.lə (US) kə-, kɑː-
Kassel ˈkæs.əl (US) ˈkɑː.səl, ˈkæs.əl
Kasur kʌsˈɔːʳ (US) -ˈʊr
katakana ˌkæt.əˈkɑː.nə (US) ˌkɑː.t̬ə-
Kate keɪt
Katelyn ˈkeɪt.lɪn
Kater ˈkeɪ.təʳ (US) -t̬ɚ
Katerina ˌkæt.ᵊrˈiː.nə (US) ˌkæt̬.əˈriː-
Kath kæθ
Katharina ˌkæθ.ᵊrˈiː.nə (US) -əˈriː-
Katharine, Katherine ˈkæθ.rɪn, -ᵊr.ɪn
Kathie ˈkæθ.i
Kathleen ˈkæθ.liːn, ˌ-ˈ-
Kathmandu ˌkæt.mænˈduː, ˌkɑːt-, -mənˈ-, -mɑːnˈ- (US) ˌkɑːt.mɑːnˈ-, ˌkæt-
Kathryn ˈkæθ.rɪn
Kathy ˈkæθ.i
Katie ˈkeɪ.ti (US) -t̬i
Katin ˈkeɪ.tɪn (US) -t̬ɪn
Katmandu ˌkæt.mænˈduː, ˌkɑːt-, -mənˈ-, -mɑːnˈ- (US) ˌkɑːt.mɑːnˈ-, ˌkæt-
Katowice ˌkæt.əʊˈvɪt.seɪ, -ˈviːt- (US) -təˈviːt.sə, -tɔːˈviːt.seɪ
Katrina kəˈtriː.nə
Katrine ˈkæt.rɪn
Kattegat ˌkæt.iˈgæt, ˈ--- (US) ˈkæt̬-
Katty ˈkæt.i (US) ˈkæt̬-
Katy ˈkeɪ.ti (US) -t̬i
katydid ˈkeɪ.ti.dɪd (US) -t̬i- **-s** -z
Katz kæts, keɪts
katzenjammer ˈkæt.sᵊnˌdʒæm.əʳ (US) -ɚ
Kaufman ˈkɔːf.mən, ˈkaʊf- (US) ˈkɑːf-, ˈkɔːf-
Kaunas ˈkaʊ.nəs (US) -nɑːs
Kaunda kɑːˈʊn.də, -ˈuːn-
Kaur kaʊəʳ (US) kaʊr
Kavanagh ˈkæv.ᵊn.ə; kəˈvæn.ə (US) ˈkæv.ə.nɑː, -nɔː
Note: In Ireland always /ˈkæv.ᵊn.ə/.
Kawasaki® ˌkaʊ.əˈsɑː.ki, ˌkɑː.wəˈ-, -ˈsæk.i (US) ˌkɑː.wəˈsɑː.ki
Kay keɪ
kayak ˈkaɪ.æk **-s** -s **-ing** -ɪŋ **-ed** -t
Kaye keɪ **-s** -z
Kayla ˈkeɪ.lə
Kayleigh ˈkeɪ.li
Kayseri ˈkeɪ.sᵊr.i
Kazakh ˈkæ.zæk, -ˈzɑːk; (US) kəˈzɑːk, kɑː-, -ˈzæk **-s** -s
Kazakhstan, Kazakstan ˌkæz.ækˈstɑːn, ˌkɑː.zækˈ-, -zɑːkˈ-, -ˈstæn (US) kəˈzɑːk.stɑːn, kɑː-, -ˈzæk-, -stæn
Kazan kəˈzæn, -ˈzɑːn (US) kəˈzæn, kɑː-, -ˈzɑːn
kazi ˈkɑː.zi **-s** -z
kazoo kəˈzuː **-s** -z
kcal *(abbrev. for* **kilocalorie***)* ˈkɪl.əʊˌkæl.ᵊr.i (US) ˈ-oʊ-, ˈ-ə-
kea ˈkeɪ.ə, ˈkiː- **-s** -z
Keady ˈkiː.di (US) ˈkeɪ-
Kean(e) kiːn
Kearn(e)y ˈkɜː.ni, ˈkɑː- (US) ˈkɑːr-, ˈkɝː-
Kearsley ˈkɪəz.li *locally:* ˈkɜːz- (US) ˈkɪrz-
Kearsney ˈkɜːz.ni (US) ˈkɝːz-
Kearton ˈkɪə.tᵊn, ˈkɜː- (US) ˈkɪr-, ˈkɝː-
Keary ˈkɪə.ri (US) ˈkɪr.i
Keating(e) ˈkiː.tɪŋ (US) -t̬ɪŋ
Keaton ˈkiː.tᵊn
Keats kiːts
kebab kɪˈbæb, kə- (US) -ˈbɑːb **-s** -z
Keble ˈkiː.bl̩
kebob kəˈbɒb (US) -ˈbɑːb **-s** -z
kedg|e kedʒ **-es** -ɪz **-ing** -ɪŋ **-ed** -d
kedgeree ˌkedʒ.ᵊrˈiː; ˈkedʒ.ᵊr.i (US) ˈkedʒ.ᵊr-; ˌkedʒ.əˈriː **-s** -z
Kedleston ˈked.l̩.stᵊn
Kedron ˈked.rɒn, ˈkiː.drɒn (US) ˈkiː.drɑːn, -drən
Keeble ˈkiː.bl̩
Keegan ˈkiː.gən
keel kiːl **-s** -z **-ing** -ɪŋ **-ed** -d **on an ˌeven ˈkeel**
Keele kiːl
Keeler ˈkiː.ləʳ (US) -lɚ
keelhaul ˈkiːl.hɔːl (US) -hɑːl, -hɔːl **-s** -z **-ing** -ɪŋ **-ed** -d
Keeling ˈkiː.lɪŋ
keelson ˈkel.sᵊn, ˈkiːl- **-s** -z
keen kiːn **-er** -əʳ (US) -ɚ **-est** -ɪst, -əst **-s** **-ing** **-ed** **-ly** -li **-ness** -nəs, -nɪs **as ˌkeen as ˈmustard**
Keenan ˈkiː.nən
Keen(e) kiːn
keep kiːp **-s** -s **-ing** -ɪŋ **kept** kept **keeper/s** ˈkiː.pəʳ/z (US) -pɚ/z
keepnet ˈkiːp.net **-s** -s
keepsake ˈkiːp.seɪk **-s** -s
Kefauver ˈkiːˌfɔː.vəʳ, -ˌfəʊ- (US) -ˌfɑː.vɚ, -ˌfɔː-
Keflavik ˈkef.lə.vɪk
keg keg **-s** -z
Kegan ˈkiː.gən
Keig kiːg
Keighley *in West Yorkshire:* ˈkiːθ.li *surname:* ˈkiːθ.li, ˈkiː-, ˈkaɪ-
Keightley ˈkiːt.li, ˈkaɪt-
Keigwin ˈkeg.wɪn
Keiller, Keillor ˈkiː.ləʳ (US) -lɚ
Keir kɪəʳ (US) kɪr
Keisha ˈkiː.ʃə
Keitel ˌkaɪˈtel
Keith kiːθ
Kelland ˈkel.ənd
Kellas ˈkel.æs
Keller ˈkel.əʳ (US) -ɚ
Kelley, Kellie ˈkel.i
Kellogg ˈkel.ɒg (US) -ɑːg, -ɔːg
Kelly ˈkel.i
kelly-green ˌkel.iˈgriːn *stress shift:* ˌkelly-green ˈfabric
Kelman ˈkel.mən
kelp kelp
kelpie ˈkel.pi **-s** -z
Kelsey ˈkel.si, -zi
Kelso ˈkel.səʊ (US) -soʊ
kelson ˈkel.sᵊn **-s** -z
Kelt kelt **-s** -s **-ic** -ɪk
Kelty ˈkel.ti (US) -t̬i
kelvin (K) ˈkel.vɪn
Kelway ˈkel.wi, -weɪ
Kemal kemˈɑːl, kəˈmɑːl (US) kəˈmɑːl
Kemble ˈkem.bl̩
kemp kemp **-y** -i
Kemp(e) kemp
Kempenfelt ˈkem.pən.felt
Kempis ˈkem.pɪs
Kempson ˈkemp.sᵊn
Kempston ˈkemp.stᵊn
kempt kem*p*t
Kempton ˈkem*p*.tən
Kemsing ˈkem.zɪŋ
ken (K) ken **-s** -z **-ning** -ɪŋ **-ned** -d
Ken. *(abbrev. for* **Kentucky***)* kenˈtʌk.i, kən- (US) kən-
Kendal(l) ˈken.dᵊl
kendo ˈken.dəʊ (US) -doʊ
Kendra ˈken.drə
Kendrick ˈken.drɪk
Keneal(l)y kɪˈniː.li, kə-, kenˈiː-
Kenelm ˈken.elm
Kenilworth ˈken.ᵊl.wəθ, -ɪl-, -wɜːθ (US) -wɚθ, -wɝːθ
Kenite ˈkiː.naɪt **-s** -s
Kénitra ˈkeɪ.niː.trə; kenˈiː-
Kenmare kenˈmeəʳ (US) -ˈmer
Kenmore ˈken.mɔːʳ (US) -mɔːr
Kennaird kəˈneəd, kenˈeəd (US) kenˈerd, kəˈnerd
Kennan ˈken.ən
Kennard ˈken.ɑːd; kɪˈnɑːd (US) ˈken.ɑːrd, kɪˈnɑːrd
Kennedy ˈken.ə.di, ˈ-ɪ-
kennel (K) ˈken.ᵊl **-s** -z **-(l)ing** -ɪŋ **-(l)ed** -d
Kennerley ˈken.ᵊl.i (US) -ɚ.li
Kennet ˈken.ɪt, -ət
Kenneth ˈken.ɪθ, -əθ
Kenney ˈken.i
Kennicot ˈken.ɪ.kət (US) -kət, -kɑːt
Kennington ˈken.ɪŋ.tən
Kennish ˈken.ɪʃ
Kennoway ˈken.ə.weɪ

Kenny ˈken.i

keno ˈkiː.nəʊ (US) -noʊ

Kenosha kiːˈnəʊ.ʃə, kə- (US) kəˈnoʊ-

Kenrick ˈken.rɪk

Kensal ˈken.sᵊl

Kensington ˈken.zɪŋ.tən

Kensit ˈken.zɪt, -sɪt

Kent kent **-s** -s **-ish** -ɪʃ

Kentucky kenˈtʌk.i, kən- (US) kən- **Kenˌtucky ˈDerby; Kenˌtucky ˌFried ˈChicken**

Kenwood® ˈken.wʊd

Kenya ˈken.jə, ˈkiː.njə **-n/s** -n/z

Note: Both pronunciations are heard locally.

Kenyatta kenˈjæt.ə (US) -ˈjɑː.t̬ə

Kenyon ˈken.jən

Keogh kjəʊ; ˈkiː.əʊ (US) ˈkiː.oʊ

Keown kjəʊn; kiˈoʊn; ˈkiː.əʊn; (US) kjoʊn; kiˈoʊn; ˈkiː.oʊn;

kepi ˈkeɪ.pi (US) ˈkeɪ-, ˈkep.i **-s** -z

Kepler ˈkep.ləʳ (US) -lɚ

Keppel ˈkep.ᵊl

kept *(from* **keep***)* kept

Ker kɑːʳ, keəʳ, kɜːʳ *in Scotland* kɛr (US) kɝː

Kerala ˈker.ᵊl.ə, kəˈrɑː.lə (US) ˈker.ə.lə

Kerans ˈker.ənz

keratin ˈker.ə.tɪn (US) -t̬ɪn

keratitis ˌker.əˈtaɪ.tɪs (US) -t̬ɪs

kerb kɜːb (US) kɝːb **-s** -z

kerbside ˈkɜːb.saɪd (US) ˈkɝːb-

kerbstone ˈkɜːb.stəʊn (US) ˈkɝːb.stoʊn **-s** -z

ker|chief ˈkɜː|.tʃɪf, -tʃiːf, -tʃəf (US) ˈkɝː|.tʃɪf, -tʃiːf **-chiefs** -tʃɪfs, -tʃiːfs **-chieves** -tʃɪvz, -tʃiːvz **-chiefed** -tʃɪft **-chieft** -tʃiːft

Kerensky kəˈren*t*.ski

kerfuffl|e kəˈfʌf.l̩ (US) kɚ- **-es** -z **-ing** -ɪŋ **-ed** -d

Kerguelen ˈkɜː.gɪ.lɪn, -gᵊl.ɪn, -ən (US) ˈkɝː.gᵊl.ən

Keri ˈker.i

Kerith ˈkɪə.rɪθ, ˈker.ɪθ (US) ˈkɪr-, ˈker-

kermes ˈkɜː.mɪz, -miːz (US) ˈkɝː.miːz

Kermit ˈkɜː.mɪt (US) ˈkɝː-

Kermode ˈkɜː.məʊd, -ˈ- (US) ˈkɝː.moʊd, -ˈ-

kern (K) kɜːn (US) kɝːn **-s** -z **-ing** -ɪŋ **-ed** -d

Kernahan ˈkɜː.nə.hən, -ni.ən (US) ˈkɝː-, -nə.hæn

kernel ˈkɜː.nᵊl (US) ˈkɝː- **-s** -z

Kernohan ˈkɜː.nə.hən (US) ˈkɝː-, -hæn

kerosene ˈker.ə.siːn, ˌ--ˈ-

Kerouac ˈker.u.æk (US) ˈker.u.æk, ˈ-ə-

Kerr kɜːʳ, keəʳ, kɑːʳ (US) kɝː, kɑːr

Kerri ˈker.i

kerria ˈker.i.ə **-s** -z

Kerridge ˈker.ɪdʒ

Kerry ˈker.i

Kerse kɜːs (US) kɝːs

kersey (K) ˈkɜː.zi (US) ˈkɝː- **-s** -z

kerseymere (K) ˈkɜː.zi.mɪəʳ (US) ˈkɝː.zi.mɪr

Kershaw ˈkɜː.ʃɔː (US) ˈkɝː.ʃɑː, -ʃɔː

Kes kes, kez

Kesey ˈkes.i, ˈkiː.si, -zi (US) ˈkiː.si, -zi

Kesteven *Barony:* ˈkes.tɪ.vᵊn *Lincolnshire:* kesˈtiː.vᵊn, kəˈstiː-

Keston ˈkes.tᵊn

kestrel ˈkes.trᵊl **-s** -z

Keswick ˈkez.ɪk

ketch (K) ketʃ **-es** -ɪz

ketchup ˈketʃ.ʌp, -əp (US) -əp **-s** -s

Ketteridge ˈket.ᵊr.ɪdʒ (US) ˈket̬-

Kettering ˈket.ᵊr.ɪŋ (US) ˈket̬-

kettle (K) ˈket.l̩ (US) ˈket̬- **-s** -z **a ˈpretty ˌkettle of ˌfish**

kettledrum ˈket.l̩.drʌm (US) ˈket̬- **-s** -z

Kevin ˈkev.ɪn

Kevlar® ˈkev.lɑːʳ (US) -lɑːr

Kevorkian kəˈvɔː.ki.ən, kevˈ- (US) -ˈvɔːr-

Kew kjuː **ˌKew ˈGardens**

kewpie ˈkjuː.pi **-s** -z

key (K) kiː **-s** -z **-ing** -ɪŋ **-ed** -d **ˈkey ˌring; ˈkey ˌsignature; ˌKey ˈWest**

keyboard ˈkiː.bɔːd (US) -bɔːrd **-s** -z **-ing** -ɪŋ **-ed** -ɪd **-er/s** -əʳ/z (US) -ɚ/z **-ist/s** -ɪst/s

keycard ˈkiː.kɑːd (US) -kɑːrd **-s** -z

Keyes kiːz, kaɪz

keyhole ˈkiː.həʊl (US) -hoʊl **-s** -z **ˌkeyhole ˈsurgery**

Key Largo ˌkiːˈlɑː.gəʊ (US) -ˈlɑːr.goʊ

Keymer ˈkiː.məʳ, ˈkaɪ- (US) -mɚ

Keymour ˈkiː.məʳ (US) -mɚ

Keyne kiːn

Keynes *in Milton Keynes:* kiːnz *surname, other places:* keɪnz

Keynesian ˈkeɪn.zi.ən **-ism** -ɪ.zᵊm

keynote ˈkiː.nəʊt, ˌ-ˈ- (US) ˈkiː.noʊt **-s** -s

Keynsham ˈkeɪn.ʃᵊm

keypad ˈkiː.pæd **-s** -z

keypunch ˈkiː.pʌn*t*ʃ **-es** -ɪz

Keyser ˈkiː.zəʳ, ˈkaɪ.zəʳ (US) ˈkaɪ.zɚ

keystone (K) ˈkiː.stəʊn (US) -stoʊn **-s** -z

keystroke ˈkiː.strəʊk (US) -stroʊk **-s** -s

keyword ˈkiː.wɜːd (US) -wɝːd **-s** -z

Keyworth ˈkiː.wəθ, -wɜːθ (US) -wɚθ, -wɝːθ

kg *(abbrev. for* **kilogram/s***) singular:* ˈkɪl.ə.græm *plural:* ˈkɪl.ə.græmz

KGB ˌkeɪ.dʒiːˈbiː

Khabarovsk kɑːˈbɑː.rɒfsk (US) -rɔːfsk

Khachaturian ˌkætʃ.əˈtʊə.ri.ən, ˌkɑː.tʃəˈ-, -ˈtjʊə- (US) -ˈtʊr.i-

khaki ˈkɑː.ki (US) ˈkæk.i, ˈkɑː.ki **-s** -z

khalif ˈkeɪ.lɪf (US) ˈkɑː-, ˈkæl.ɪf, ˈkɑː.lɪf; kælˈɪf (US) ˈkeɪ.lɪf, ˈkæl.ɪf **-s** -s

Khalifa kɑːˈliː.fə, kəˈliː- **-s** -z

khalifate ˈkæl.ɪ.feɪt, ˈkeɪ.lɪ-, -lə- (US) ˈkæl.ɪ-, ˈ-ə- **-s** -s

Khan kɑːn (US) kɑːn, kæn

Khanpur ˌkɑːnˈpʊəʳ, ˌkɑːmˈ-, ˈ-- (US) ˌkɑːnˈpʊr

Kharkov ˈkɑː.kɒf (US) ˈkɑːr.kɔːf

Khartoum ˌkɑːˈtuːm, kɑː- (US) kɑːr-

Khatami kəˈtɑː.mi, kætˈ- (US) ˈkɑː.tɑː.mi, kəˈ-, hɑː.tɑːˈmiː

Khayyam kaɪˈæm, -ˈɑːm (US) -ˈjɑːm, -ˈjæm

khazi ˈkɑː.zi **-s** -z

khedival kɪˈdiː.vᵊl, kedˈiː-, kəˈdiː- (US) kəˈdiː-

khedive kɪˈdiːv, kedˈiːv, kəˈdiːv (US) kəˈdiːv **-s** -z

khedivial kɪˈdiː.vi.əl, kedˈiː-, kəˈdiː- (US) kəˈdiː-

Khmer kmeəʳ, kəˈmeəʳ (US) kəˈmer **Khˌmer ˈRouge**

Khomeini kɒmˈeɪ.ni, kəʊˈmeɪ- (US) koʊ-, kə-

khoums kuːmz

Khrus(h)chev ˈkrʊs.tʃɒf, ˈkrʊʃ-, ˌ-ˈ- (US) ˈkruː.tʃef, -tʃɔːf; kruːʃˈtʃɔːf

Khyber ˈkaɪ.bəʳ (US) -bɚ **ˌKhyber ˈPass**

kHz *(abbrev. for* **kilohertz***)* ˈkɪl.əʊ.hɜːts (US) -ə.hɝːts

Kia Ora® ˌkɪəˈɔː.rə, ˌkiː.əˈ- (US) ˌkiː.əˈɔːr.ə

kibbl|e ˈkɪb.l̩ **-es** -z **-ing** -ɪŋ, ˈkɪb.lɪŋ **-ed** -d

kibbutz kɪˈbʊts (US) -ˈbʊts, -ˈbuːts **-nik/s** -nɪk **-es** -ɪz **kibbutzim** ˌkɪb.ʊtˈsiːm; kɪˈbʊt.siːm (US) ˌkiː.buːtˈsiːm

kibe kaɪb **-s** -z

kibitz ˈkɪb.ɪts **-es** -ɪz **-ing** -ɪŋ **-ed** -t **-er/s** -əʳ/z (US) -ɚ/z

kibosh ˈkaɪ.bɒʃ (US) ˈkaɪ.bɑːʃ; kɪˈbɑːʃ **-es** -ɪz **-ing** -ɪŋ **-ed** -t

kick kɪk **-s** -s **-ing** -ɪŋ **-ed** -t **-er/s** -əʳ/z (US) -ɚ/z

kickabout ˈkɪk.ə.baʊt **-s** -s

kickback ˈkɪk.bæk **-s** -s

Kickham ˈkɪk.əm

kick-off ˈkɪk.ɒf (US) -ɑːf **-s** -s

kickshaw ˈkɪk.ʃɔː (US) -ʃɑː, -ʃɔː **-s** -z

kick|-start ˈkɪk|.stɑːt (US) -stɑːrt **-starts** -stɑːts (US) -stɑːrts **-starting** -ˌstɑː.tɪŋ (US) -ˌstɑːr.t̬ɪŋ **-started** -ˌstɑː.tɪd (US) -ˌstɑːr.t̬ɪd **-starter/s** -ˌstɑː.təʳ/z (US) -ˌstɑːr.t̬ɚ/z

kid kɪd **-s** -z **-ding** -ɪŋ **-ded** -ɪd **ˌkid ˈglove**

Kidd kɪd

Kidderminster ˈkɪd.ə.mɪn*t*.stəʳ (US) -ɚ.mɪn*t*.stɚ

kiddie ˈkɪd.i **-s** -z

kiddle (K) ˈkɪd.l̩ **-s** -z

kidd|y ˈkɪd|.i **-ies** -iz

Kidlington ˈkɪd.lɪŋ.tən

Kidman ˈkɪd.mən

kidnap ˈkɪd.næp **-s** -s **-(p)ing/s** -ɪŋ/z **-(p)ed** -t **-(p)er/s** -əʳ/z (US) -ɚ/z

kidney 'kɪd.ni **-s** -z '**kidney** ˌ**bean**; '**kidney ma**ˌ**chine**
Kidsgrove 'kɪdz.grəʊv (US) -groʊv
Kiel kiːl
kielbas(s)a kiːl'bæs.ə (US) -'bɑː.sə, kɪl-
Kielder 'kiːl.dəʳ (US) -dɚ
kier (K) kɪəʳ (US) kɪr **-s** -z
Kieran 'kɪə.rᵊn (US) 'kɪr.ᵊn
Kierkegaard 'kɪə.kə.gɑːd, -gɔːd (US) 'kɪr.kə.gɑːrd, -gɔːrd
Kiev 'kiː.ev, -ef, ˌ-'-
Kigali kɪ'gɑː.li (US) kə-
Kikuyu kɪ'kuː.juː (US) kiː-
Kilbirnie kɪl'bɜː.ni (US) -'bɝː-
Kilbride kɪl'braɪd (US) 'kɪl.braɪd, -'-
Kilburn 'kɪl.bən, -bɜːn (US) -bɚn, -bɝːn
Kilby 'kɪl.bi
Kildale 'kɪl.deɪl
Kildare kɪl'deəʳ (US) -'der
kilderkin 'kɪl.də.kɪn (US) -dɚ- **-s** -z
Kilen 'kaɪ.lən
Kiley 'kaɪ.li
Kilfoyle kɪl'fɔɪl
Kilham 'kɪl.əm
kilim (K) kɪ'liːm **-s** -z
Kilimanjaro ˌkɪl.ɪ.mən'dʒɑː.rəʊ, ˌ-ə-, -mæn'- (US) -ə.mən'dʒɑːr.oʊ
Kilkeel kɪl'kiːl
Kilkenny kɪl'ken.i
kill kɪl **-s** -z **-ing/s** -ɪŋ/z **-ed** -d ˌ**dressed to** '**kill**
Killaloe ˌkɪl.ə'luː (US) kɪ'læl.oʊ
Killamarsh 'kɪl.ə.mɑːʃ (US) -mɑːrʃ
Killarney kɪ'lɑː.ni (US) -'lɑːr-
Killearn kɪ'lɜːn (US) -'lɝːn
killer 'kɪl.əʳ (US) -ɚ **-s** -z '**killer** ˌ**instinct**; '**killer** ˌ**whale**
Killick 'kɪl.ɪk
Killiecrankie ˌkɪl.ɪ'kræŋ.ki
Killigrew 'kɪl.ɪ.gruː
Killin 'kɪl.ɪn
Killingworth 'kɪl.ɪŋ.wəθ, -wɜːθ (US) -wɚθ, -wɝːθ
killjoy 'kɪl.dʒɔɪ **-s** -z
Killwick 'kɪl.wɪk
Kilmainham kɪl'meɪ.nəm
Kilmarnock kɪl'mɑː.nək, -nɒk (US) -'mɑːr.nək, -nɑːk
kiln kɪln, kɪl **-s** -z
Note: The pronunciation /kɪl/ appears to be used only by those concerned with the working of kilns.
Kilnsey 'kɪln.zi
kilo- kɪl.əʊ-; kɪ'lɒ- (US) kɪl.oʊ-, -ə-; kɪ'lɑː-
Note: Prefix. Normally carries primary stress on the first syllable, e.g. **kilometre** /'kɪl.əʊˌmiː.təʳ (US) -əˌmiː.t̬ɚ-/.
kilo 'kiː.ləʊ (US) -loʊ **-s** -z
kilobyte 'kɪl.əʊ.baɪt (US) '-oʊ-, '-ə- **-s** -s
kilocalorie 'kɪl.əʊˌkæl.ᵊr.i (US) '-oʊ-, '-ə- **-s** -z
kilocycle 'kɪl.əʊˌsaɪ.kl̩ (US) -oʊˌ-, -əˌ- **-s** -z
kilogram, kilogramme 'kɪl.əʊ.græm (US) '-oʊ-, '-ə- **-s** -z
kilohertz 'kɪl.əʊ.hɜːts, -heəts (US) -oʊ.herts, '-ə-, -hɝːts
kilojoule 'kɪl.əʊ.dʒuːl (US) '-oʊ-, '-ə- **-s** -z
kilolitre, kiloliter 'kɪl.əʊˌliː.təʳ (US) -oʊˌliː.t̬ɚ, -əˌ- **-s** -z
kilometre, kilometer kɪ'lɒm.ɪ.təʳ, '-ə-; 'kɪl.əʊˌmiː- (US) kɪ'lɑː.mə.t̬ɚ; 'kɪl.əˌmiː- **-s** -z
kiloton 'kɪl.əʊ.tʌn (US) '-oʊ-, '-ə- **-s** -z
kilovolt 'kɪl.əʊ.vəʊlt (US) -oʊ.voʊlt, '-ə- **-s** -s
kilowatt 'kɪl.əʊ.wɒt (US) -oʊ.wɑːt, '-ə- **-s** -s
Kilpatrick kɪl'pæt.rɪk
Kilrush kɪl'rʌʃ
Kilsyth kɪl'saɪθ
kilt kɪlt **-s** -s **-ing** -ɪŋ (US) 'kɪl.t̬ɪŋ **-ed** -ɪd (US) 'kɪl.t̬ɪd
kilter 'kɪl.təʳ (US) -t̬ɚ
Kilvert 'kɪl.vət (US) -vɚt
Kilwarden kɪl'wɔː.dᵊn (US) -'wɔːr-
Kilwinning kɪl'wɪn.ɪŋ
Kim kɪm
Kimball 'kɪm.bᵊl
Kimberl(e)y 'kɪm.bəl.i (US) -bɚ.li
Kimbolton kɪm'bəʊl.tᵊn (US) -'boʊl-
Kimmeridge 'kɪm.ᵊr.ɪdʒ
Kimmins 'kɪm.ɪnz
kimono kɪ'məʊ.nəʊ (US) kə'moʊ.nə, -noʊ **-s** -z
kin kɪn
kina 'kiː.nə
kinaesthetic ˌkɪn.iːs'θet.ɪk, ˌkaɪ.niːs'-, -nɪs'- (US) ˌkɪn.es'θet̬.ɪk
Kincardine kɪn'kɑː.dɪn, kɪŋ-, -dᵊn (US) kɪn'kɑːr- **-shire** -ʃəʳ, -ˌʃɪəʳ (US) -ʃɚ, -ˌʃɪr
Kinchinjunga ˌkɪn.tʃɪn'dʒʌŋ.gə (US) -tʃɪn'dʒʊŋ-
kind kaɪnd **-s** -z **-er** -əʳ (US) -ɚ **-est** -ɪst, -əst **-ly** -li **-ness/es** -nəs/ɪz, -nɪs/ɪz
kinda 'kaɪn.də
kindergarten 'kɪn.dəˌgɑː.tᵊn (US) -dɚˌgɑːr- **-s** -z
Kinder Scout ˌkɪn.də'skaʊt (US) -dɚ-
Kindersley 'kɪn.dəz.li (US) -dɚz-
kind-hearted ˌkaɪnd'hɑː.tɪd (US) -'hɑːr.t̬ɪd **-ly** -li **-ness** -nəs, -nɪs *stress shift:* ˌkindhearted 'person
kindl|e 'kɪn.dl̩ **-es** -z **-ing** -ɪŋ, 'kɪnd.lɪŋ **-ed** -d **-er/s** -əʳ/z, 'kɪnd.ləʳ/z (US) -ɚ/z, 'kɪnd.lɚ/z
kindling 'kɪnd.lɪŋ, 'kɪn.dl̩.ɪŋ
kindl|y 'kaɪnd.l|i **-ier** -i.əʳ (US) -i.ɚ **-iest** -i.ɪst, -i.əst **-iness** -ɪ.nəs, -ɪ.nɪs
kindred 'kɪn.drəd, -drɪd ˌ**kindred** '**spirit**
kine kaɪn
kinema 'kɪn.ɪ.mə, '-ə- **-s** -z
kinematic ˌkɪn.ɪ'mæt.ɪk, ˌkaɪ.nɪ'-, -nə'- (US) ˌkɪn.ə'mæt̬- **-al** -ᵊl **-ally** -ᵊl.i, -li **-s** -s
kinematograph ˌkɪn.ɪ'mæt.ə.grɑːf, ˌkaɪ.nɪ'-, -nə'-, -græf (US) ˌkɪn.ə'mæt̬.ə.græf **-s** -s
kinesics kɪ'niː.sɪks, kaɪ- (US) -sɪks, -zɪks
kinesis kɪ'niː.sɪs, kaɪ- (US) -sɪs, -zɪs
kinesthetic ˌkɪn.iːs'θet.ɪk, ˌkaɪ.niːs'-, -nɪs'- (US) ˌkɪn.ɪs'θet̬-
kinetic kɪ'net.ɪk, kaɪ- (US) kɪ'net̬- **-ally** -ᵊl.i, -li **-s** -s
kinfolk 'kɪn.fəʊk (US) -foʊk **-s** -s
king (K) kɪŋ **-s** -z ˌ**King's** '**Bench**; ˌ**King Charles** '**spaniel**; ˌ**King's** '**Counsel**; ˌ**King's** '**English**; ˌ**king's** '**evidence**; ˌ**King's** '**Lynn**; ˌ**king** '**prawn**; '**king-**ˌ**size**
king-at-arms ˌkɪŋ.ət'ɑːmz (US) -'ɑːrms **kings-at-arms** ˌkɪŋz-
kingcraft 'kɪŋ.krɑːft (US) -kræft
kingcup 'kɪŋ.kʌp **-s** -s
kingdom (K) 'kɪŋ.dəm **-s** -z ˌ**kingdom** '**come**; ˌ**Kingdom** '**Hall**
Kingdon 'kɪŋ.dən
kingfisher 'kɪŋˌfɪʃ.əʳ (US) -ɚ **-s** -z
Kinghorn 'kɪŋ.hɔːn (US) -hɔːrn
Kinglake 'kɪŋ.leɪk
kingless 'kɪŋ.ləs, -lɪs
kinglet 'kɪŋ.lət, -lɪt **-s** -s
kinglike 'kɪŋ.laɪk
kingl|y 'kɪŋ.l|i **-ier** -i.əʳ (US) -i.ɚ **-iest** -i.ɪst, -i.əst **-iness** -ɪ.nəs, -ɪ.nɪs
kingmaker (K) 'kɪŋˌmeɪ.kəʳ (US) -kɚ **-s** -z
kingpin 'kɪŋ.pɪn, ˌ-'- (US) 'kɪŋ.pɪn **-s** -z
Kingsborough 'kɪŋz.bᵊr.ə (US) -oʊ
Kingsbury 'kɪŋz.bᵊr.i (US) -ˌber-
Kingscote -kəʊt (US) -kət, -koʊt
Kings Cross ˌkɪŋz'krɒs (US) -'krɑːs *stress shift:* ˌKings Cross 'Station
kingship 'kɪŋ.ʃɪp
king-size 'kɪŋ.saɪz **-d** -d
Kingsley 'kɪŋz.li
Kings|man 'kɪŋz|.mən, -mæn **-men** -mən, -men
Kingsteignton kɪŋ'steɪn.tən (US) -tᵊn
Kingston(e) 'kɪŋ.stən, 'kɪŋk-, 'kɪŋz.tən
Kingstown 'kɪŋz.taʊn, 'kɪŋ.stən, 'kɪŋk-
Kingsway 'kɪŋz.weɪ
Kingswinford kɪŋ'swɪn.fəd (US) -fɚd
Kingswood 'kɪŋz.wʊd
Kington 'kɪŋ.tən, 'kɪŋk-
Kingussie kɪŋ'juː.si
kink kɪŋk **-s** -s **-ing** -ɪŋ **-ed** -t
kinkajou 'kɪŋ.kə.dʒuː **-s** -z
Kinkel 'kɪŋ.kᵊl
kink|y 'kɪŋ.k|i **-ier** -i.əʳ (US) -i.ɚ **-iest** -i.ɪst, -i.əst **-iness** -ɪ.nəs, -ɪ.nɪs
kinless 'kɪn.ləs, -lɪs

Kinnaird kɪˈneəd (US) -ˈnerd
Kinnear kɪˈnɪəʳ, -ˈneəʳ (US) -ˈnɪr, -ˈner
Kinnock ˈkɪn.ək
Kinnoull kɪˈnuːl
kino ˈkiː.nəʊ (US) -noʊ
Kinros|s kɪnˈrɒs (US) -ˈrɑːs **-shire** -ʃəʳ, -ˌʃɪəʳ (US) -ʃɚ, -ˌʃɪr
Kinsale kɪnˈseɪl
Kinsella kɪnˈsel.ə, ˈkɪnt.sel.ə
Kinsey ˈkɪn.zi
kinsfolk ˈkɪnz.fəʊk (US) -foʊk
Kinshasa kɪnˈʃɑː.sə, -ˈʃæs.ə (US) -ˈʃɑː.sə, -sɑː
kinship ˈkɪn.ʃɪp
Kinski ˈkɪn*t*.ski
kins|man ˈkɪnz|.mən **-men** -mən, -men
kins|woman ˈkɪnz|ˌwʊm.ən **-women** -ˌwɪm.ɪn
Kintore kɪnˈtɔːʳ (US) -ˈtɔːr
Kintyre kɪnˈtaɪəʳ (US) -ˈtaɪr
kiosk ˈkiː.ɒsk (US) -ɑːsk, kiˈɑːsk **-s** -s
kip kɪp **-s** -s **-ping** -ɪŋ **-ped** -t
Kipling ˈkɪp.lɪŋ
Kippax ˈkɪp.æks, -əks
kipp|er ˈkɪp|.əʳ (US) -ɚ **-ers** -əz (US) -ɚz **-ering** -ᵊr.ɪŋ **-ered** -əd (US) -ɚd
Kipps kɪps
kir kɪəʳ (US) kɪr **-s** -z
Kirby ˈkɜː.bi (US) ˈkɝː-
Kircaldie kɜːˈkɔːl.di, kə- (US) kɝː-, kɚ-
Kirchner ˈkɜːk.nəʳ (US) ˈkɪrk.nɚ *US family name:* ˈkɜːtʃ.nəʳ, ˈkɜːʃ- (US) ˈkɝːtʃ.nɚ, ˈkɝːʃ-
Kirghiz ˈkɜː.gɪz, ˈkɪə- (US) kɪrˈgiːz
Kirghizia kɜːˈgɪz.i.ə, kɪə- (US) kɪrˈgiː.ʒə, -ʒi.ə
Kiribati ˌkɪr.əˈbæs, ˌkɪə.rəˈ-, -rɪˈ-; ˌkɪr.iˈbɑː.ti (US) ˌkɪr.iˈbɑː.ti; ˈkɪr.ə.bæs
Kiri Te Kanawa ˌkɪr.i.tɪˈkæn.ə.wə, ˌkɪə.ri-, -ˈkɑː.nə-, -teɪ- (US) ˌkɪr.i.təˈkɑː.nə.wɑː
Kiriyenko ˌkɪr.iˈjeŋ.kəʊ (US) -koʊ
kirk kɜːk (US) kɝːk **-s** -s
Kirkby *surname:* ˈkɜː.bi, ˈkɜːk.bi (US) ˈkɝː-, ˈkɝːk- *place:* ˈkɜː.bi (US) ˈkɝː-
Kirkcaldy *place:* kɜːˈkɔː.di, kəˈkɒd.i, -ˈkɔː.di (US) kɝː-, kɚ- *surname:* kɜːˈkɔː.di, kə- (US) kɝː-, kɚ-
Kirkcudbright kɜːˈkuː.bri, kə- (US) kɝː-, kɚ- **-shire** -ʃəʳ, -ˌʃɪəʳ (US) -ʃɚ, -ˌʃɪr
Kirkdale ˈkɜːk.deɪl (US) ˈkɝːk-
Kirk(e) kɜːk (US) kɝːk
Kirkham ˈkɜː.kəm (US) ˈkɝː-
Kirkintilloch ˌkɜː.kɪnˈtɪl.ək *as if Scots:* -əx (US) ˌkɝː.kɪnˈtɪl.ək
Kirkland ˈkɜːk.lənd (US) ˈkɝːk-
Kirklees ˌkɜːkˈliːz (US) ˌkɝːk-
Kirkman ˈkɜːk.mən (US) ˈkɝːk-
Kirkness ˌkɜːkˈnes (US) ˌkɝːk-
Kirkpatrick ˌkɜːkˈpæt.rɪk (US) ˌkɝːk-
Kirkstall ˈkɜːk.stɔːl *locally also:* -stᵊl (US) ˈkɝːk-
Kirkuk kɜːˈkʊk, ˈ-- (US) kɪrˈkuːk
Kirkwall ˈkɜːk.wɔːl (US) ˈkɝːk-
Kirkwood ˈkɜːk.wʊd (US) ˈkɝːk-
Kirov ˈkɪə.rɒf, -rɒv (US) ˈkiː.rɔːf
Kirovabad kɪəˈrɒv.ə.bæd, kɪ- (US) kiːˈroʊ.və-, kɪ-
Kirriemuir ˌkɪr.iˈmjʊəʳ, -ˈmjɔːʳ (US) -ˈmjʊɚ
kirsch kɪəʃ, kɜːʃ (US) kɪrʃ
kirschwasser ˈkɪəʃˌvæs.əʳ, -ˌvɑː.səʳ (US) ˈkɪrʃˌvɑː.sɚ
Kirsten ˈkɜː.stɪn, ˈkɪə-, -stᵊn (US) ˈkɝː-, ˈkɪr-
Kirstie, Kirsty ˈkɜː.sti (US) ˈkɝː-
kirtle ˈkɜː.tl̩ (US) ˈkɝː.t̬l̩ **-s** -z
Kisangani ˌkɪs.æŋˈgɑː.ni (US) ˌkiː.sɑːnˈgɑː-
kish kɪʃ
Kishinev ˈkɪʃ.ɪ.nɒf, -nef (US) -nev, -nef, -nɔːf
Kishon ˈkaɪ.ʃɒn *with some Jews:* ˈkiː.ʃɒn (US) ˈkaɪ.ʃɑːn, -ʃᵊn
kismet ˈkɪz.met, ˈkɪs-, -mɪt, -mət (US) -met, -mɪt
kiss kɪs **-es** -ɪz **-ing** -ɪŋ **-ed** -t **-er/s** -əʳ/z (US) -ɚ/z ˌ**kiss of ˈdeath**; ˌ**kiss of ˈlife**
kissagram, kiss-a-gram, kissogram ˈkɪs.ə.græm **-s** -z
kiss-and-tell ˌkɪs.ᵊndˈtel
Kissinger ˈkɪs.ɪn.dʒəʳ, -ɪŋ.əʳ (US) -ən.dʒɚ, -ɪn-
kiss-off ˈkɪs.ɒf (US) -ɑːf
Kisumu kɪˈsuː.muː (US) kiː-
kit (K) kɪt **-s** -s **-ting** -ɪŋ (US) ˈkɪt̬.ɪŋ **-ted** -ɪd (US) ˈkɪt̬.ɪd ˌ**kit and caˈboodle**; ˈ**kit ˌbag**; ˈ**kit ˌcar**
kitbag ˈkɪt.bæg **-s** -z
kit-cat (K) ˈkɪt.kæt **-s** -s
kitchen (K) ˈkɪtʃ.ɪn, -ᵊn **-s** -z ˌ**kitchen ˈcabinet**; ˌ**kitchen ˈgarden**; ˌ**kitchen ˈsink**; ˌ**kitchen ˈunit**
kitchener (K) ˈkɪtʃ.ɪ.nəʳ, -ᵊn.əʳ (US) -ə.nɚ **-s** -z
kitchenette ˌkɪtʃ.ɪˈnet, -əˈ- **-s** -s
kitchenmaid ˈkɪtʃ.ɪn.meɪd, -ᵊn- **-s** -z
kitchenware ˈkɪtʃ.ɪn.weəʳ, -ᵊn- (US) -wer
Kitchin ˈkɪtʃ.ɪn
Kitching ˈkɪtʃ.ɪŋ
kit|e kaɪt **-es** -s **-ing** -ɪŋ **-ed** -əd
Kit-E-Kat® ˈkɪt.iˌkæt
kitemark ˈkaɪt.mɑːk (US) -mɑːrk
kith kɪθ
Kithnos ˈkɪθ.nɒs (US) -nɑːs
Kit-Kat® ˈkɪt.kæt
kitsch kɪtʃ **-y** -i
Kitson ˈkɪt.sᵊn
kitten ˈkɪt.ᵊn **-s** -z
kittenish ˈkɪt.ᵊn.ɪʃ **-ly** -li
kittiwake ˈkɪt.ɪ.weɪk (US) ˈkɪt̬- **-s** -s
Kitto ˈkɪt.əʊ (US) ˈkɪt̬.oʊ
Kittredge ˈkɪt.rɪdʒ
Kitts kɪts
Kittson ˈkɪt.sᵊn
kitt|y (K) ˈkɪt|.i (US) ˈkɪt̬- **-ies** -iz ˈ**Kitty ˌHawk**
Kitwe ˈkɪt.weɪ
Kitzbuhel, Kitzbühel ˈkɪts.bjuː.əl, -buː-, -bjuːl, -buːl
kiwi (K®) ˈkiː.wiː, -wi **-s** -z ˈ**kiwi ˌfruit**
kJ *(abbrev. for* **kilojoule***)* ˈkɪl.əʊˌdʒuːl (US) ˈ-oʊ-, ˈ-ə-
KKK *(abbrev. for* **Ku Klux Klan***)* ˌkeɪ.keɪˈkeɪ
kl *(abbrev. for* **kilolitre/s***) singular:* ˈkɪl.əʊˌliː.təʳ (US) -oʊˌliː.t̬ɚ, ˈ-ə- *plural:* ˈkɪl.əʊˌliː.təz (US) -oʊˌliː.t̬ɚz, ˈ-ə-
Klagenfurt ˈklɑː.gᵊn.fɜːt (US) -fɝːt
Klan klæn
Klans|man ˈklænz|.mən, -mæn **-men** -mən, -men
klatch klætʃ (US) klætʃ, klɑːtʃ **-es** -ɪz
klaxon ˈklæk.sᵊn **-s** -z
Klee kleɪ
Kleenex® ˈkliː.neks
Klein klaɪn
Kleinwort ˈkleɪn.wɔːt (US) -wɔːrt
Kleist klaɪst
Klemperer ˈklem.pᵊr.əʳ (US) -ɚ
kleptomani|a ˌklep.təʊˈmeɪ.ni|.ə (US) -toʊˈ-, -təˈ- **-ac/s** -æk/s
Kline klaɪn
Klondike ˈklɒn.daɪk (US) ˈklɑːn-
Kluge *English name:* kluːdʒ *German name:* ˈkluː.gə
klutz klʌts **-es** -ɪz
klutz|y ˈklʌt.s|i **-iness** -ɪ.nəs, -ɪ.nɪs
km *(abbrev. for* **kilometre/s***) singular:* kɪˈlɒm.ɪ.təʳ, -ˈə-; ˈkɪl.əʊˌmiː- (US) kɪˈlɑː.mə.t̬ɚ; ˈkɪl.əˌmiː- *plural:* kɪˈlɒm.ɪ.təz, ˈ-ə-; ˈkɪl.əʊˌmiː.təz (US) kɪˈlɑː.mɪ.t̬ɚz; ˈkɪl.əˌmiː.t̬ɚz
K Mart® ˈkeɪˌmɑːt (US) -ˌmɑːrt
knack næk **-s** -s
knack|er ˈnæk|.əʳ (US) -ɚ **-ers** -əz (US) -ɚz **-ering** -ᵊr.ɪŋ **-ered** -əd (US) -ɚd
knacker|y ˈnæk.ᵊr|.i **-ies** -iz
knag næg **-s** -z **-gy** -i
knap næp **-s** -s **-ping** -ɪŋ **-ped** -t
Knapp næp
knapsack ˈnæp.sæk **-s** -s
knar nɑːʳ (US) nɑːr **-s** -z
Knaresborough ˈneəz.bᵊr.ə, ˈ-brə (US) ˈnerz.bɚ.oʊ, ˈ-brə
knave neɪv **-s** -z
knaver|y ˈneɪ.vᵊr|.i **-ies** -iz
knavish ˈneɪ.vɪʃ **-ly** -li **-ness** -nəs, -nɪs
knead niːd **-s** -z **-ing** -ɪŋ **-ed** -ɪd
Knebworth ˈneb.wəθ, -wɜːθ (US) -wɚθ, -wɝːθ

knee niː **-s** -z **-ing** -ɪŋ **-d** -d ˌ**knee-ˈdeep; ˌweak at the ˈknees**
knee-breeches ˈniːˌbrɪtʃ.ɪz
kneecap ˈniː.kæp **-s** -s **-ping** -ɪŋ **-ped** -t
knee-high (*adj.*) ˌniːˈhaɪ *stress shift:* ˌknee-high ˈsocks
kneehigh (*n.*) ˈniː.haɪ **-s** -z
knee-jerk ˈniː.dʒɜːk US -dʒɝːk
knee-joint ˈniː.dʒɔɪnt **-s** -s
kneel niːl **-s** -z **-ing** -ɪŋ **-ed** -d **knelt** nelt
knees-up ˈniːz.ʌp
knell nel **-s** -z **-ing** -ɪŋ **-ed** -d
Kneller ˈnel.əʳ US -ɚ **-s** -z
knelt (*from* **kneel**) nelt
Knesset ˈknes.et, kəˈnes-, -ɪt
knew (*from* **know**) njuː, nuː US nuː, njuː
knicker ˈnɪk.əʳ US -ɚ **-s** -z
knickerbocker (K) ˈnɪk.əˌbɒk.əʳ US -ɚˌbɑː.kɚ **-s** -z ˌ**knickerbocker ˈglory**
knick-knack ˈnɪk.næk **-s** -s **-ery** -ᵊr.i
kni|fe (*n.*) naɪ|f **-ves** -vz
knif|e (*v.*) naɪf **-es** -s **-ing** -ɪŋ **-ed** -t
knight (K) naɪt **-s** -s **-ing** -ɪŋ US ˈnaɪ.t̬ɪŋ **-ed** -ɪd US ˈnaɪ.t̬ɪd
knight-errant ˌnaɪtˈer.ᵊnt **knights-errant** ˌnaɪtsˈer.ᵊnt
knighthood ˈnaɪt.hʊd **-s** -z
Knightley ˈnaɪt.li
knightl|y ˈnaɪt.l|i **-ier** -i.əʳ US -i.ɚ **-iest** -i.ɪst, -i.əst **-iness** -ɪ.nəs, -ɪ.nɪs
Knighton ˈnaɪ.tᵊn
Knightsbridge ˈnaɪts.brɪdʒ
knish kəˈnɪʃ **-es** -ɪz
knit nɪt **-s** -s **-ting** -ɪŋ US ˈnɪt̬.ɪŋ **-ted** -ɪd US ˈnɪt̬.ɪd **-ter/s** -əʳ/z US ˈnɪt̬.ɚ/z **ˈknitting maˌchine; ˈknitting ˌneedle**
knitwear ˈnɪt.weəʳ US -wer
knob nɒb US nɑːb **-s** -z
knobbly ˈnɒb.l̩.i, ˈ-li US ˈnɑː.bl̩.i, ˈ-bli
knobb|y ˈnɒb|.i US ˈnɑː.b|i **-ier** -i.əʳ US -i.ɚ **-iest** -i.ɪst, -i.əst **-iness** -ɪ.nəs, -ɪ.nɪs
knock nɒk US nɑːk **-s** -s **-ing/s** -ɪŋ/z **-ed** -t **-er/s** -əʳ/z US -ɚ/z
knockabout ˈnɒk.əˌbaʊt US ˈnɑːk- **-s** -s
Knockbreda nɒkˈbreɪ.də US nɑːk-
knock-down ˈnɒk.daʊn US ˈnɑːk.daʊn
knock-down-drag-out ˌnɒk.daʊnˈdræg.aʊt US ˌnɑːk- *stress shift:* ˌknock-down-ˌdrag-out ˈfight
knock-kneed ˌnɒkˈniːd US ˈnɑːk.niːd *stress shift:* ˌknock-kneed ˈchild
knockoff ˈnɒk.ɒf US ˈnɑːk.ɑːf **-s** -s
knock-on (*adj.*) ˌnɒkˈɒn US ˌnɑːkˈɑːn *stress shift, see compound:* **ˈknock-on efˌfect**
knock-on (*n.*) (*in rugby*) ˌnɒkˈɒn, ˈ-- US ˌnɑːkˈɑːn, ˈ--
knock-out ˈnɒk.aʊt US ˈnɑːk- **-s** -s **ˈknockout ˌdrops**
knock-up ˈnɒk.ʌp US ˈnɑːk- **-s** -s
knockwurst ˈnɒk.wɜːst US ˈnɑːk.wɝːst, -wʊrst
Knole nəʊl US noʊl
knoll nəʊl US noʊl **-s** -z
Knolles, Knollys nəʊlz US noʊlz
knop nɒp US nɑːp **-s** -s
Knopfler ˈnɒp.fləʳ US ˈnɑːp.flɚ
Knossos ˈknɒs.ɒs, ˈknəʊ.sɒs, -səs US ˈnɑː.səs
knot nɒt US nɑːt **-s** -s **-ting** -ɪŋ US ˈnɑː.t̬ɪŋ **-ted** -ɪd US ˈnɑː.t̬ɪd **at a ˌrate of ˈknots**
knotgrass ˈnɒt.grɑːs US ˈnɑːt.græs
knothole ˈnɒt.həʊl US ˈnɑːt.hoʊl **-s** -z
Knott nɒt US nɑːt
Knottingley ˈnɒt.ɪŋ.li US ˈnɑː.t̬ɪŋ-
knott|y ˈnɒt|.i US ˈnɑː.t̬|i **-ier** -i.əʳ US -i.ɚ **-iest** -i.ɪst, -i.əst **-ily** -ɪ.li, -ᵊl.i **-iness** -ɪ.nəs, -ɪ.nɪs
Knotty Ash ˌnɒt.iˈæʃ US ˌnɑː.t̬i-
knout naʊt **-s** -s **-ing** -ɪŋ US ˈnaʊ.t̬ɪŋ **-ed** -ɪd US ˈnaʊ.t̬ɪd
know nəʊ US noʊ **-s** -z **-ing** -ɪŋ **knew** njuː US nuː **known** nəʊn US noʊn **knower/s** ˈnəʊ.əʳ/z US ˈnoʊ.ɚ/z **knowable** ˈnəʊ.ə.bl̩ US ˈnoʊ-
know-all ˈnəʊ.ɔːl US ˈnoʊ-, -ɑːl **-s** -z
know-how ˈnəʊ.haʊ US ˈnoʊ-
knowing ˈnəʊ.ɪŋ US ˈnoʊ- **-ly** -li **-ness** -nəs, -nɪs
know-it-all ˈnəʊ.ɪt.ɔːl US ˈnoʊ.ɪt̬-, -ɑːl **-s** -z
Knowle nəʊl US noʊl
knowledg|e ˈnɒl.ɪdʒ US ˈnɑː.lɪdʒ **-es** -ɪz
knowledgeab|le ˈnɒl.ɪ.dʒə.b|l̩ US ˈnɑː.lɪ- **-ly** -li
Knowles nəʊlz US noʊlz
known (*from* **know**) nəʊn US noʊn
know-nothing ˈnəʊˌnʌθ.ɪŋ US ˈnoʊ- **-s** -z
Knox nɒks US nɑːks
Knoxville ˈnɒks.vɪl US ˈnɑːks-, -vᵊl
knuckl|e ˈnʌk.l̩ **-es** -z **-ing** -ɪŋ, ˈ-lɪŋ **-ed** -d **-y** -i, ˈ-li ˌ**knuckle ˈsandwich**
knuckleball ˈnʌk.l̩.bɔːl US -bɔːl, -bɑːl
knucklebone ˈnʌk.l̩.bəʊn US -boʊn **-s** -z
knuckle-duster ˈnʌk.l̩ˌdʌs.təʳ US -tɚ **-s** -z
knucklehead ˈnʌk.l̩.hed **-ed** -ɪd
knurled nɜːld US nɝːld
Knutsford ˈnʌts.fəd US -fɚd
KO, k.o. ˌkeɪˈəʊ US -ˈoʊ **-'s** -z **-'ing** -ɪŋ **-'d** -d
koala kəʊˈɑː.lə US koʊ- **-s** -z
Kobe ˈkəʊ.beɪ, -bi US ˌkoʊˈbeɪ, ˈkoʊ.bi
Koblenz kəʊˈblents US ˈkoʊ.blents
kobo ˈkɒb.əʊ US ˈkɑː.boʊ, ˈkoʊ-; ˈkɔː.bɔː
kobold ˈkɒb.əʊld, ˈkəʊ.bəʊld, -bᵊld US ˈkoʊ.bɔːld, -bɑːld **-s** -z
Koch kəʊk, kɒtʃ *as if German:* kɒx US koʊk, kɑːk, kɑːtʃ *as if German:* kɔːx, koʊx
Köchel ˈkɜː.kᵊl *as if German:* -xᵊl US ˈkɝː- **ˈKöchel ˌnumber**
Kodak® ˈkəʊ.dæk US ˈkoʊ- **-s** -s
Kodály ˈkəʊ.daɪ, -dɑː.i US ˈkoʊ-; koʊˈdɑː.i
Kodiak ˈkəʊ.di.æk US ˈkoʊ-
Koestler ˈkɜːst.ləʳ US ˈkest.lɚ
Koh-i-noor ˌkəʊ.iˈnʊəʳ, -ˈnɔəʳ, -ˈnɔːʳ, ˈ--- US ˈkoʊ.ɪ.nʊr
kohl kəʊl US koʊl
Kohl kəʊl US koʊl
kohlrab|i ˌkəʊlˈrɑː.b|i US ˌkoʊl-, ˈ--- **-ies** -iz
koine (K) ˈkɔɪ.neɪ, -niː, -ni US kɔɪˈneɪ; ˈkɔɪ.neɪ, -niː
Kojak ˈkəʊ.dʒæk US ˈkoʊ-
kola (K) ˈkəʊ.lə US ˈkoʊ-
kolkhoz ˌkɒlˈkɒz, -ˈkɔːz, -ˈhɔːz US ˌkɑːlˈkɔːz **-es** -ɪz
Kolnai ˈkɒl.naɪ US ˈkɑːl-
Komodo kəˈməʊ.dəʊ US -ˈmoʊ.doʊ
Kongo ˈkɒŋ.gəʊ US ˈkɑːŋ.goʊ
Konica® ˈkɒn.ɪ.kə, ˈkəʊ.nɪ- US ˈkɑː.nɪ-
Königsberg ˈkɜː.nɪgz.bɜːg, -beəg US ˈkɝː.nɪgz.bɝːg, -berg
Konrad ˈkɒn.ræd US ˈkɑːn-
Konya ˈkɔː.njɑː
koodoo ˈkuː.duː **-s** -z
kook kuːk **-s** -s
kookaburra ˈkʊk.əˌbʌr.ə US -ˌbɝː-, -ˌbʌr- **-s** -z
kook|y ˈkuː.k|i **-ier** -i.əʳ US -i.ɚ **-iest** -i.ɪst, -i.əst **-iness** -ɪ.nəs, -ɪ.nɪs
Kool-Aide® ˈkuːl.eɪd
Koori(e) ˈkʊə.ri, ˈkɔː- US ˈkʊr.i
Kop kɒp US kɑːp
kope(c)k ˈkəʊ.pek, ˈkɒp.ek US ˈkoʊ.pek **-s** -s
kopje ˈkɒp.i US ˈkɑː.pi **-s** -z
Kops kɒps US kɑːps
Korah ˈkɔː.rə US ˈkɔːr.ə
Koran kɒrˈɑːn, kɔːˈrɑːn, kʊ-, kə- US kəˈræn, -ˈrɑːn; ˈkɔːr.æn, -ɑːn
Koranic kɒrˈæn.ɪk, kɔːˈræn-, kʊ-, kə- US kəˈræn.ɪk, -ˈrɑː.nɪk; ˈkɔːr.æn.ɪk, -ɑː.nɪk
Kore|a kəˈriː|.ə, kɒrˈiː- US kəˈriː-, kɔː- **-an/s** -ᵊn/z
korma ˈkɔː.mə US ˈkɔːr-
koruna kɒrˈuː.nə, kəˈruː- US ˈkɔːr.uː- **-s** -z
koruny (*plur. of* **koruna**) kɒrˈuː.ni, kəˈruː- US ˈkɔːr.uː-
kosher ˈkəʊ.ʃəʳ *occasionally, by non-Jews:* ˈkɒʃ.əʳ US ˈkoʊ.ʃɚ
Kosice kɒʃˈɪt.sə US ˈkɔː.ʃiːt.seɪ, -ʃɪt-
Kosov|o ˈkɒs.ə.v|əʊ US ˈkoʊ.sə.v|oʊ, ˈkɑː-, ˈkɔː- **-an** -ən **-ar/s** -ɑːʳ/z US -ɑːr/z

Kostunica kɒs'tuː.nɪt.sə (US) kaːs.tuː.'nit.sə
Kosygin kə'siː.gɪn (US) kə-, koʊ-
Kotex® 'kəʊ.teks (US) 'koʊ-
kotow ˌkəʊ'taʊ (US) ˌkoʊ- **-s** -z **-ing** -ɪŋ **-ed** -d **-er/s** -əʳ/z (US) -ɚ/z
Kough kjəʊ, kəʊ (US) kjoʊ, koʊ
koumiss 'kuː.mɪs, -məs
Kournikova ˌkɔː.nɪ'kəʊ.və, -nə'- (US) ˌkɔːr.nɪ'koʊ-, -nə'-
Kowasaki kəʊ.ə'sɑː.ki, -'sæk.i (US) koʊ-
Kowloon ˌkaʊ'luːn
kowtow ˌkaʊ'taʊ (US) ˌkaʊ'taʊ, '-- **-s** -z **-ing** -ɪŋ **-ed** -d **-er/s** -əʳ/z (US) -ɚ/z
kraal krɑːl, krɔːl **-s** -z
Note: Usually pronounced /krɑːl/ in England, but /krɔːl/ in South Africa.
Kraft® krɑːft (US) kræft
Kragujevac kræg'uː.jə.væts (US) 'krɑː.guː.jə.vɑːts
krait kraɪt **-s** -s
Krajicek 'kraɪ.tʃek, 'krɑː.jɪ.tʃek, 'kraɪ.ə.tʃek
Krakatoa ˌkræk.ə'təʊ.ə (US) -'toʊ-
kraken 'krɑː.kᵊn, 'kreɪ- (US) 'krɑː- **-s** -z
Krakow 'kræk.ɒv, -ɒf, -aʊ (US) 'krɑː.kaʊ, 'kræk.aʊ, 'kreɪ.kaʊ; 'krɑː.kʊf
Kramer 'kreɪ.məʳ (US) -mɚ
krantz (K) krænts
Krasnodar ˌkrɑːs.nəʊ'dɑːʳ (US) -noʊ'dɑːr
Krasnoyarsk ˌkrɑːs.nəʊ'jɑːsk (US) -noʊ'jɑːrsk
Kravchuk kræv'tʃʊk
Kray kreɪ
kremlin (K) 'krem.lɪn **-s** -z
Kremlinolog|y ˌkrem.lɪ'nɒl.ə.dʒ|i (US) -'nɑː.lə- **-ist/s** -ɪst/s
kreu(t)zer (K) 'krɔɪt.səʳ (US) -sɚ **-s** -z
krill krɪl
kris kriːs **-es** -ɪz
Krishna 'krɪʃ.nə
Kris Kringle, Kriss Kringle ˌkrɪs'krɪŋ.gl̩
Krista 'krɪs.tə
Kristen 'krɪs.tᵊn, -tɪn
Kristi 'krɪs.ti
Kristiansand 'krɪs.tʃᵊn.sænd
Kristie 'krɪs.ti
Kristin 'krɪs.tɪn
Kristina krɪ'stiː.nə
Kristine krɪ'stiːn
Kristopher 'krɪs.tə.fəʳ (US) -fɚ
kro|na 'krəʊ|.nə (US) 'kroʊ- **-nor** -nɔːʳ (US) -nɔːr
kró|na 'krəʊ|.nə (US) 'kroʊ- **-nur** -nʊəʳ (US) -nɚ
kro|ne 'krəʊ|.nə (US) 'kroʊ- **-nes** -nəz **-ner** -nəʳ **-nen** -nən
Kronin 'krəʊ.nɪn (US) 'kroʊ-
Krons(h)tadt 'krɒnt.ʃtæt (US) 'krɔːnt.ʃtɑːt
kroon kruːn
Krug kruːg
Kruger 'kruː.gəʳ (US) -gɚ
krugerrand (K) 'kruː.gᵊr.ænd (US) -gɚ- **-s** -z
Krupp krʊp, krʌp
Krushchev 'krʊs.tʃɒf, 'krʊʃ-, ˌ-'- (US) 'kruː.tʃef, -tʃɔːf, -tʃev, kruːʃ'tʃɔːf
krypton 'krɪp.tɒn, -tən (US) -tɑːn
kryptonite 'krɪp.tᵊn.aɪt (US) -tə.naɪt
Krystal 'krɪs.tᵊl
Krystle 'krɪs.tl̩
Kuala Lumpur ˌkwɑː.lə'lʊm.pʊəʳ, ˌkwɒl-, -'lʌm-, -pəʳ (US) ˌkwɑː.lə'lʊm.pʊr
Kubla Khan ˌkuː.blə'kɑːn, ˌkʊb.lə'- (US) ˌkuː.blə'-
Kubrick 'kjuː.brɪk, 'kuː-
kudos 'kjuː.dɒs (US) 'kuː.doʊz, 'kjuː-, -doʊs, -dɑːs
Kudrow 'kʊd.rəʊ (US) 'kuːdroʊ
kudu 'kuː.duː **-s** -z
Ku Klux Klan ˌkuː.klʌks'klæn, ˌkjuː-
kulak 'kuː.læk (US) kuː'lɑːk, '-- **-s** -s
kultur (K) kʊl'tʊəʳ (US) -'tʊr
Kumanovo ˌkuː.mə'nəʊ.vəʊ (US) 'kʊm.əˌnoʊ.voʊ
Kumar kuː'mɑːʳ (US) 'kuː.mɑːr
Kumasi kʊ'mæs.i, -'mɑː.si (US) -'mɑː.si
Kumin 'kjuː.mɪn, 'kuː- (US) 'kuː-
kümmel 'kʊm.ᵊl, 'kɪm- (US) 'kɪm-
kumquat 'kʌm.kwɒt (US) -kwɑːt **-s** -s
Kundera 'kʊn.də.rə (US) -dɚ.ə
kung fu ˌkʊŋ'fuː, ˌkʌŋ- (US) ˌkʌŋ-, ˌkʊŋ-, ˌgʊn-
Kunitz 'kjuː.nɪts, 'kuː- (US) 'kuː-
Kuomintang ˌkwəʊ.mɪn'tæŋ, ˌgwəʊ- (US) ˌkwoʊ-
Kuoni® kʊ'əʊ.ni (US) -'oʊ-
Kurath 'kjʊə.ræθ (US) 'kʊr.ɑːt, 'kjʊr- (US) -ɑːθ
Kurd kɜːd (US) kɝːd, kʊrd **-s** -z **-ish** -ɪʃ
Kurdistan ˌkɜː.dɪ'stɑːn, -də'-, -'stæn (US) ˌkɝː.dɪ'stæn, ˌkʊr-, -də'-, -'stɑːn
Kureishi kʊ'reʃ.i, -'reɪ.ʃi, -'riː-
Kuril(e) kʊ'riːl, kjuː- (US) 'kuː.rɪl; kuː'riːl **-s** -z
Kurosawa ˌkʊə.rəʊ'sɑː.wə (US) ˌkʊr.ə'-
kursaal 'kʊə.zɑːl, 'kɜː-, -sɑːl, -sᵊl (US) 'kʊr-, 'kɝː- **-s** -z
Kursk kɜːsk, kʊəsk (US) kɝːsk
Kurt kɜːt (US) kɝːt
Kurtis 'kɜː.tɪs (US) 'kɝː.t̬ɪs
Kurtz kɜːts (US) kɝːts
kurus kʊ'rʊʃ, -'ruːʃ (US) -'ruːʃ
Kutaisi kʊ'taɪ.si (US) kʊ'taɪ.si, ˌkuː.tə'ʃiː.si
Ku|wait kuː|'weɪt, kjuː-, kə- (US) kuː|'weɪt, -'waɪt **-waiti/s** -'weɪ.ti/z (US) -'weɪ.t̬i/z, -'waɪ.t̬i/z
Kuyper 'kaɪ.pəʳ (US) -pɚ
kvas(s) kvɑːs, kvæs (US) kvɑːs, kə'vɑːs
kvetch kvetʃ, kə'vetʃ **-es** -ɪz **-ing** -ɪŋ **-ed** -t
kW *(abbrev. for* **kilowatt***)* 'kɪl.əʊ.wɒt (US) -oʊ.wɑːt, '-ə-
kwacha 'kwɑː.tʃɑː
Kwangtung ˌkwæn'tʌŋ, ˌkwæŋ- (US) ˌkwɑːŋ'tʊŋ, ˌgwɑːŋ-
Kwantung ˌkwæn'tʌŋ (US) ˌkwɑːŋ'tʊŋ, ˌgwɑːŋ-
kwanza 'kwæn.zə (US) 'kwɑːn.zɑː, -zə **-s** -z
Kwanzaa 'kwɑːn.zə, 'kwæn-, -zɑː (US) 'kwɑːn- **-s** -z
kwashiorcor ˌkwæʃ.i'ɔː.kɔːʳ, -kəʳ (US) ˌkwɑː.ʃiː'ɔːr.kɔːr
KwaZulu kwɑː'zuː.luː
KwaZulu-Natal kwɑːˌzuː.luː.nə'tæl, -'tɑːl
kwela 'kweɪ.lə
KWIC kwɪk
Ky. *(abbrev. for* **Kentucky***)* ken'tʌk.i, kən- (US) kən-
kyat ki'ɑːt (US) tʃɑːt, kjɑːt
Kyd kɪd
Kyla 'kaɪ.lə
kyle (K) kaɪl **-s** -z
Kylie 'kaɪ.li
kylin 'kaɪ.lɪn **-s** -z
Kyllachy 'kaɪ.lə.ki, -xi (US) -ki
kyloe 'kaɪ.ləʊ (US) -loʊ **-s** -z
kymogram 'kaɪ.məʊ.græm (US) -moʊ-, -mə-
kymograph 'kaɪ.məʊ.grɑːf, -græf (US) -moʊ.græf, -mə- **-s** -s
kymographic ˌkaɪ.məʊ'græf.ɪk (US) -moʊ'-, -mə'-
Kynance 'kaɪ.nænts
Kynaston 'kɪn.ə.stᵊn
Kyoto 'kjəʊ.təʊ, ki'əʊ.təʊ (US) kiː'oʊ.toʊ, 'kjoʊ-
Kyrgyzstan ˌkɜː.gɪ'stɑːn (US) 'kɪr.gɪ.stɑːn, -stæn, ˌ--'-
kyrie 'kɪr.i.eɪ, 'kɪə.ri-, -iː (US) 'kɪr.i.eɪ **-s** -z
Kyrle kɜːl (US) kɝːl
Kythe 'kaɪ.θi
Kyushu 'kjuː.ʃuː, ki'uː-
Kyzyl-Kum kəˌzɪl'kuːm, -'kʊm

Pronouncing the letter L

See also LL

In general, the consonant letter l is pronounced /l/, e.g.:

like /laɪk/
wool /wʊl/

However, l is frequently silent, particularly when preceded by an a, e.g.:

calf /kɑːf/ (US) /kæf/
calm /kɑːm/ (US) /kɑːlm/

In the past tense form of modal verbs spelt **ould**, l is also silent, e.g.:

could /kʊd/
would /wʊd/

l (L) el **-'s** -z

l *(abbrev. for* **litre/s***) singular:* 'liː.təʳ (US) -t̬ɚ *plural:* 'liː.təz (US) -t̬ɚz

la lɑː **-s** -z

La. *(abbrev. for* **Louisiana***)* luˌiː.zi'æn.ə, -'ɑː.nə; ˌluː.i.zi'- (US) luˌiː.zi'æn.ə; ˌluː.zi'-

LA ˌel'eɪ *stress shift:* ˌLA 'Law

laager 'lɑː.gəʳ (US) -gɚ **-s** -z

laari 'lɑː.ri (US) 'lɑːr.i **-s** -z

lab læb **-s** -z

Laban *biblical character:* 'leɪ.bən, -bæn (US) -bən *US family name:* lə'bæn

label 'leɪ.bᵊl **-s** -z **-(l)ing** -ɪŋ, 'leɪ.blɪŋ **-(l)ed** -d

labia *(from* **labium***)* 'leɪ.bi.ə

labial 'leɪ.bi.əl **-s** -z **-ly** -i

labialization, -isa- ˌleɪ.bi.ᵊl.aɪ'zeɪ.ʃᵊn, -ɪ'- (US) -ɪ'-

labializ|e, -is|e 'leɪ.bi.ᵊl.aɪz **-es** -ɪz **-ing** -ɪŋ **-ed** -d

labia majora ˌleɪ.bi.ə.mə'dʒɔː.rə, -maɪ'ɔː- (US) -mə'dʒɔːr.ə

labia minora ˌleɪ.bi.ə.mɪ'nɔː.rə (US) -'nɔːr.ə

labiate 'leɪ.bi.eɪt, -ət, -ɪt **-s** -s

Labienus ˌlæb.i'iː.nəs, -'eɪ-

labile 'leɪ.baɪl (US) -baɪl, -bᵊl

labiodental ˌleɪ.bi.əʊ'den.tᵊl (US) -oʊ'den.t̬ᵊl **-s** -z

labiopalatal ˌleɪ.bi.əʊ'pæl.ə.tᵊl (US) -oʊ'pæl.ə.t̬ᵊl **-s** -z **-ly** -li

labiovelar ˌleɪ.bi.əʊ'viː.ləʳ (US) -oʊ'viː.lɚ **-s** -z

labiovelariz|e, -is|e ˌleɪ.bi.əʊ'viː.lᵊr.aɪz (US) -oʊ'viː.lə.raɪz **-es** -ɪz **-ing** -ɪŋ **-ed** -d

labi|um 'leɪ.bi|.əm **-a** -ə

La Bohème ˌlɑː.bəʊ'em, ˌlæ-, -'eɪm (US) ˌlɑː.boʊ'-

lab|or (L) 'leɪ.b|əʳ (US) -b|ɚ **-ors** -əz (US) -ɚz **-oring** -ᵊr.ɪŋ **-ored** -əd (US) -ɚd **-orer/s** -ᵊr.əʳ/z (US) -ɚ.ɚ/z ˌ**labor of** '**love**; '**labor** ˌ**union**

laborator|y lə'bɒr.ə.tᵊr|.i, -tr|i (US) 'læb.rə.tɔːr|.i, 'læb.ɚ.ə- **-ies** -iz

labor-intensive ˌleɪ.bəʳ.ɪn'ten*t*.sɪv (US) -bɚ- *stress shift:* ˌlabor-intensive 'work

laborious lə'bɔː.ri.əs (US) -'bɔːr.i- **-ly** -li **-ness** -nəs, -nɪs

laborite (L) 'leɪ.bᵊr.aɪt (US) -bə.raɪt **-s** -s

labor-saving 'leɪ.bəˌseɪ.vɪŋ (US) -bɚˌ- *stress shift:* ˌlabor-saving 'gadget

Labouchere ˌlæb.uː'ʃeəʳ, -ʊ'-, '--- (US) ˌlæb.uː'ʃer

lab|our (L) 'leɪ.b|əʳ (US) -b|ɚ **-ours** -əz (US) -ɚz **-ouring** -ᵊr.ɪŋ **-oured** -əd (US) -ɚd **-ourer/s** '-ᵊr.əʳ/z '**labour ex**ˌ**change**; ˌ**labour of** '**love**; '**Labour** ˌ**Party**

labour-intensive ˌleɪ.bəʳ.ɪn'ten*t*.sɪv (US) -bɚ- *stress shift:* ˌlabour-intensive 'work

labourite (L) 'leɪ.bᵊr.aɪt (US) -bə.raɪt **-s** -s

labour-saving 'leɪ.bəˌseɪ.vɪŋ (US) -bɚˌ- *stress shift:* ˌlabour-saving 'gadget

Labrador 'læb.rə.dɔːʳ (US) -dɔːr **-s** -z

Labuan lə'buː.ən (US) ˌlɑː.buː'ɑːn, lə'buː.ən

laburnum lə'bɜː.nəm (US) -'bɝː- **-s** -z

labyrinth 'læb.ᵊr.ɪntθ, -ɪ.rɪnt*θ* (US) -ɚ.ɪntθ, '-rəntθ **-s** -s

labyrinth|ian ˌlæb.ə'rɪn*t*.θ|i.ən, -ɪ'- (US) -ə'rɪn*t*- **-ine** -aɪn (US) -ɪn, -iːn, -aɪn

lac læk **-s** -s

Laccadive 'læk.ə.dɪv, 'lɑː.kə-, -diːv, -daɪv (US) 'læk.ə.daɪv; 'lɑː.kə.diːv **-s** -z

laccolith 'læk.ə.lɪθ

lac|e leɪs **-es** -ɪz **-ing** -ɪŋ **-ed** -t **-er/s** -əʳ/z (US) -ɚ/z

Lacedaemon ˌlæs.ə'diː.mən, -ɪ'- (US) -ə'-

Lacedaemonian ˌlæs.ə.dɪ'məʊ.ni.ən, -ɪ-, -də'- (US) -ə.dɪ'moʊ.ni- **-s** -z

lacer|ate 'læs.ᵊr|.eɪt (US) -ə.r|eɪt **-ates** -eɪts **-ating** -eɪ.tɪŋ (US) -eɪ.t̬ɪŋ **-ated** -eɪ.tɪd (US) -eɪ.t̬ɪd

laceration ˌlæs.ᵊr'eɪ.ʃᵊn (US) -ə'reɪ- **-s** -z

Lacert|a lə'sɜː.t|ə (US) -'sɝː.t̬|ə **-ae** -iː

Lacey 'leɪ.si

laches 'lætʃ.ɪz, 'leɪ.tʃɪz, -tʃəz (US) 'lætʃ.ɪz, 'leɪ.tʃɪz

Lachesis 'læk.ə.sɪs, -ɪ- (US) 'læk-, 'lætʃ-

Lachish 'leɪ.kɪʃ

Lachlan 'læk.lən, 'lɒk.lən (US) 'lɑːk-

lachrymal 'læk.rɪ.mᵊl

lachrymatory ˌlæk.rɪ'meɪ.tᵊr.i; 'læk.rɪ.mə-, -meɪ- (US) 'læk.rɪ.mə.tɔːr-

lachrymose 'læk.rɪ.məʊs, -rə-, -məʊz (US) -rɪ.moʊs **-ly** -li

lack læk **-s** -s **-ing** -ɪŋ **-ed** -t

lackadaisic|al ˌlæk.ə'deɪ.zɪ.k|ᵊl **-ally** -ᵊl.i, -li **-alness** -nəs, -nɪs

lackaday 'læk.ə.deɪ, ˌ--'-

lackey 'læk.i **-s** -z **-ing** -ɪŋ **-ed** -d

lacklustre, lackluster 'lækˌlʌs.təʳ, ˌ-'-- (US) 'lækˌlʌs.tɚ

Lacon 'leɪ.kən

Laconi|a lə'kəʊ.ni|.ə (US) -'koʊ- **-an/s** -ən/z

laconic (L) lə'kɒn.ɪk (US) -'kɑː.nɪk **-al** -ᵊl **-ally** -ᵊl.i, -li

lacqu|er 'læk|.əʳ (US) -ɚ **-ers** -əz (US) -ɚz **-ering** -ᵊr.ɪŋ **-ered** -əd (US) -ɚd **-erer/s** -ᵊr.əʳ/z (US) -ɚ.ɚ/z

lacquey 'læk.i **-s** -z **-ing** -ɪŋ **-ed** -d

Lacroix læk'rwɑː (US) lə'kwɑː, -'krɔɪ

lacrosse lə'krɒs (US) -'krɑːs

lactase 'læk.teɪs, -teɪz (US) -teɪs

lactate *(n.)* 'læk.teɪt

lacta|te *(v.)* læk'teɪ|t (US) '-- **-tes** -ts **-ting** -tɪŋ (US) -t̬ɪŋ **-ted** -tɪd (US) -t̬ɪd

lactation læk'teɪ.ʃᵊn

lacteal 'læk.ti.əl

lactic 'læk.tɪk ˌ**lactic** '**acid**

lactometer læk'tɒm.ɪ.təʳ, -ə.təʳ (US) -'tɑː.mə.t̬ɚ **-s** -z

lactose 'læk.təʊs, -təʊz (US) -toʊs

lacun|a lə'kjuː.n|ə, læk'juː- (US) lə'kjuː- **-ae** -iː **-as** -əz

lacy (L) 'leɪ.si

lad læd **-s** -z

Lada® 'lɑː.də **-s** -z

Ladakh lə'dɑːk, -'dɔːk (US) -'dɑːk

Ladbroke 'læd.brʊk, -brəʊk (US) -brʊk, -broʊk

Ladbrokes 'læd.brəʊks, -brʊks (US) -broʊks, -brʊks

Labiodental

A consonant articulated with contact between the lips and the teeth.

Examples for English

By far the most common type of labiodental articulation is one where the lower surface of the lower lip touches the upper front teeth, as in the fricatives [f] (voiceless) and [v] (voiced); these two occur in English, e.g.:

fine	/faɪn/	safe	/seɪf/
vine	/vaɪn/	save	/seɪv/

The fricative noise made by /f/ and /v/ is very weak. In final position, as /f/ is FORTIS and /v/ is LENIS, 'pre-fortis clipping' of the vowel occurs. This has the effect of shortening the vowel in *safe*, making it much shorter than the one in *save*.

ladd|er 'læd|.ə^{r} (US) -ɚ **-ers** -əz (US) -ɚz **-ering** -^{ə}r.ɪŋ **-ered** -əd (US) -ɚd
ladderback 'læd.ə.bæk (US) '-ɚ-
laddie 'læd.i **-s** -z
laddish 'læd.ɪʃ **-ly** -li **-ness** -nəs, -nɪs
lad|e leɪd **-es** -z **-ing** -ɪŋ **-ed** -ɪd **-en** -^{ə}n
Ladefoged 'læd.ɪ.fəʊ.gɪd, '-ə-, -gəd (US) -ə.foʊ.gəd
laden *(from* **lade)** 'leɪ.d^{ə}n
la-di-da, lah-di-dah ˌlɑː.dɪ'dɑː (US) -diː'- *stress shift:* ˌla-di-da 'voice
ladies 'leɪ.diz **'ladies' ˌman; 'ladies' ˌroom**
ladieswear 'leɪ.diz.weə^{r} (US) -wer
Ladislaus 'læd.ɪ.slɔːs (US) -slɔːs, -slɑːs
Ladislaw 'læd.ɪ.slɔː (US) -slɔː, -slɑː
ladl|e 'leɪ.dl̩ **-es** -z **-ing** -ɪŋ, 'leɪd.lɪŋ **-ed** -d
ladleful 'leɪ.dl̩.fʊl **-s** -z
Ladoga 'læd.əʊ.gə, 'lɑː.dəʊ-; lə'dəʊ- (US) 'lɑː.dɔː.gɑː, -də.gə
la dolce vita lɑːˌdɒl.tʃeɪ'viː.tə (US) -ˌdoʊl.tʃeɪ'-, -tʃə'-, -t̬ə
Ladrone lə'drəʊn (US) -'droʊn
lad|y (L) 'leɪ.d|i **-ies** -iz **ˌLady 'Bountiful; 'lady ˌchapel; 'Lady ˌDay; 'lady ˌfriend**
ladybird (L®) 'leɪ.di.bɜːd (US) -bɝːd **-s** -z
ladybug 'leɪ.di.bʌg **-s** -z
ladyfinger 'leɪ.diˌfɪŋ.gə^{r} (US) -gɚ **-s** -z
lady-in-waiting ˌleɪ.di.ɪn'weɪ.tɪŋ (US) -t̬ɪŋ **ladies-in-waiting** ˌleɪ.diz-
lady-killer 'leɪ.diˌkɪl.ə^{r} (US) -ɚ **-s** -z
ladylike 'leɪ.di.laɪk
ladylove 'leɪ.di.lʌv **-s** -z
ladyship 'leɪ.di.ʃɪp **-s** -s
Ladysmith 'leɪ.di.smɪθ
Laertes leɪ'ɜː.tiːz (US) -'ɝː-, -'er-
Laestrygones liː'straɪ.gə.niːz (US) les'trɪg.ə-
Laetitia lɪ'tɪʃ.i.ə, liː-, lə-, -'tiː.ʃi-, '-ʃə (US) lə'tɪʃ.ə, -'tiː.ʃə
Lafarge lə'fɑːʒ (US) -'ɑːrʒ
Lafayette *French name:* ˌlɑː.faɪ'et, ˌlæf-, -feɪ'- (US) ˌlæf.iː'-, ˌlɑː.fiː'-, -faɪ'- *in Louisiana:* ˌlɑː'feɪt, lə-
Lafcadio læf'kɑː.di.əʊ (US) lɑːf'kɑː.di.oʊ
Laffan 'læf.ən; lə'fæn
Laf(f)itte læf'iːt, lɑː'fiːt, lə- (US) lɑː'fiːt, lə-
Lafontaine ˌlæf.ɒn'ten, ˌlɑːfɒn-, -'teɪn (US) ˌlɑː.fɔːn-, -foʊn'-
lag læg **-s** -z **-ging** -ɪŋ **-ged** -d **-ger/s** -ə^{r}/z (US) -ɚ/z
Lagan 'læg.^{ə}n
lager *beer:* 'lɑː.gə^{r} (US) -gɚ **-s** -z **'lager ˌlout**
Lager *English surname:* 'leɪ.gə^{r} (US) -gɚ
Lagerfeld 'lɑː.gə.felt (US) -gɚ-
laggard 'læg.əd (US) -ɚd **-s** -z **-ly** -li
lagn(i)appe 'læn.jæp, ˌ-'-
lagoon lə'guːn **-s** -z
Lagos 'leɪ.gɒs (US) -gɑːs; 'lɑː.goʊs
Lagrange læg'rɑ̃ːnʒ, lə'-, -'greɪndʒ (US) lɑː'grɑ̃ːndʒ, lə-
La Guardia lə'gwɑː.di.ə (US) -'gwɑːr-
Laguna Beach ləˌguː.nə'biːtʃ
lah lɑː **-s** -z
Lahore lə'hɔː^{r}, lɑː- (US) -'hɔːr
laic 'leɪ.ɪk **-al** -^{ə}l
laid *(from* **lay)** leɪd
laid-back ˌleɪd'bæk *stress shift:* ˌlaid-back 'attitude
Laidlaw 'leɪd.lɔː (US) -lɑː, -lɔː
lain *(from* **lie)** leɪn
Laindon 'leɪn.dən
Laing læŋ, leɪŋ
lair leə^{r} (US) ler **-s** -z
laird (L) leəd (US) lerd **-s** -z **-ship** -ʃɪp
laissez-faire, laisser-faire ˌleɪ.seɪ'feə^{r}, ˌles.eɪ'- (US) ˌles.eɪ'fer, ˌleɪ.seɪ'- *stress shift:* ˌlaissez-faire 'attitude
laity 'leɪ.ə.ti, -ɪ.ti (US) -ti, -t̬i
Laius 'laɪ.əs, 'leɪ- (US) 'leɪ-, 'laɪ-
lake (L) leɪk **-s** -s
Lakeland 'leɪk.lənd, -lænd
Lakenheath 'leɪ.k^{ə}n.hiːθ
Lake Placid ˌleɪk'plæs.ɪd
Laker 'leɪ.kə^{r} (US) -kɚ
lakeside (L) 'leɪk.saɪd **-s** -z
lakh lɑːk, læk **-s** -s
Lakin 'leɪ.kɪn
Lalage 'læl.ə.gi, -dʒi
Lalique® læl'iːk, lə'liːk (US) lɑː'liːk, lə-
lam læm **-s** -z **-ming** -ɪŋ **-med** -d
lama (L) 'lɑː.mə **-s** -z
Lamarr lə'mɑː^{r} (US) -'mɑːr
lamaser|y 'lɑː.mə.s^{ə}r|.i, 'læm.ə- (US) 'lɑː.mə.ser- **-ies** -iz
Lamaze lə'mɑːz **La'maze ˌmethod**
lamb (L) læm **-s** -z **-ing** -ɪŋ **-ed** -d **ˌlamb's 'lettuce; 'lamb's ˌwool; ˌmutton dressed as 'lamb**
lambada læm'bɑː.də (US) lɑːm- **-s** -z **-ing** -ɪŋ **-ed** -d
lambast læm'bæst (US) -'beɪst, -'bæst **-s** -s **-ing** -ɪŋ **-ed** -ɪd
lambast|e læm'beɪst (US) -'beɪst, -'bæst **-es** -s **-ing** -ɪŋ **-ed** -ɪd
lambda 'læm.də **-s** -z
lambdacism 'læm.də.sɪ.z^{ə}m **-s** -z
Lambe læm
lamben|cy 'læm.bən|*t*.si **-t** -t
Lambert 'læm.bət (US) -bɚt
Lambeth 'læm.bəθ
lambkin 'læm.kɪn **-s** -z
lamblike 'læm.laɪk
Lamborghini® ˌlæm.bɔː'giː.ni, -bə'- (US) ˌlɑːm.bɔːr'-, ˌlæm-, -bɚ'-
Lambretta® læm'bret.ə (US) -'bret̬-
lambrusco (L) læm'brʊs.kəʊ (US) -'bruː.skoʊ, lɑːm-, -'brʊs.koʊ
lambskin 'læm.skɪn **-s** -z
Lambton 'læm*p*.tən
lam|e leɪm **-er** -ə^{r} (US) -ɚ **-est** -ɪst, -əst **-ely** -li **-eness** -nəs, -nɪs **-es** -z **-ing** -ɪŋ **-ed** -d **ˌlame 'duck**
lamé 'lɑː.meɪ (US) læm'eɪ, lɑː'meɪ
lamebrain 'leɪm.breɪn **-s** -z
Lamech 'leɪ.mek, 'lɑː-, -mex (US) 'leɪ.mek
lamell|a lə'mel|.ə **-ae** -iː **-as** -əz **-ar** -ə^{r} (US) -ɚ
la|ment lə|'ment **-ments** -'ments **-menting** -'men.tɪŋ (US) -'men.t̬ɪŋ **-mented** -'men.tɪd (US) -'men.t̬ɪd
lamentab|le 'læm.ən.tə.b|l̩, -ɪn-; lə'men- (US) lə'men.t̬ə-; 'læm.ən.t̬ə- **-ly** -li
lamentation (L) ˌlæm.en'teɪ.ʃ^{ə}n, -ən'-, -ɪn'- (US) -ən'- **-s** -z

Lamia *Greek town:* læm'iː.ə US lə'miː- *literary title, Keats:* 'lɑː.mi.ə, 'leɪ- US 'leɪ-

lamin|a 'læm.ɪ.n|ə, '-ə- **-al** -ᵊl **-ae** -iː **-as** -əz **-ar** -əʳ US -ɚ

lami|nate (*v.*) 'læm.ɪ|.neɪt, '-ə- **-nates** -neɪts **-nating** -neɪ.tɪŋ US -neɪ.t̬ɪŋ **-nated** -neɪ.tɪd US -neɪ.t̬ɪd

laminate (*n.*) 'læm.ɪ.nət, '-ə-, -nɪt, -neɪt US -nɪt

lamination ˌlæm.ɪ'neɪ.ʃᵊn, -ə'-

lamington (L) 'læm.ɪŋ.tən

Lammas 'læm.əs **-tide** -taɪd

lammergeier, lammergeyer 'læm.ə.gaɪəʳ US -ɚ.gaɪɚ **-s** -z

Lammermoor 'læm.ə.mʊəʳ, -mɔːʳ, ˌ--'- US 'læm.ɚ.mʊr, -mɔːr, ˌ--'-

Lammermuir 'læm.ə.mjʊəʳ, -mjɔːʳ US -ɚ.mjʊr, -mjʊɚ

Lamond 'læm.ənd

Lamont *surname:* lə'mɒnt; 'læm.ənt US lə'mɑːnt *in US:* lə'mɒnt US -'mɑːnt

lamp læmp **-s** -s

lampas *silk material:* 'læm.pəs *swelling in horse's mouth:* 'læm.pəz

lampblack 'læmp.blæk

Lampedusa ˌlæm.pɪ'djuː.zə US -pə'duː.sə, -zə

Lampet 'læm.pɪt

Lampeter 'læm.pɪ.təʳ, -pə- US -t̬ɚ

lampion 'læm.pi.ən **-s** -z

lamp|light 'læmp|.laɪt **-lighter/s** -ˌlaɪ.təʳ/z US -ˌlaɪ.t̬ɚ/s

Lamplough 'læm.pluː, -plʌf

Lamplugh 'læm.pluː, -plə

lampoon læm'puːn **-s** -z **-ing** -ɪŋ **-ed** -d **-er/s** -əʳ/z US -ɚ/z

lamp-post 'læmp.pəʊst US -poʊst **-s** -s

lamprey 'læm.pri **-s** -z

lampshade 'læmp.ʃeɪd **-s** -z

Lampson 'læmp.sᵊn

lampstand 'læmp.stænd **-s** -z

LAN læn **-s** -z

Lana 'lɑː.nə US 'læn.ə, 'lɑː.nə

Lanagan 'læn.ə.gᵊn

Lanark 'læn.ək US -ɚk **-shire** -ʃəʳ, -ˌʃɪəʳ US -ʃɚ, -ˌʃɪr

Lancashire 'læŋ.kə.ʃəʳ, -ˌʃɪəʳ US -ʃɚ, -ˌʃɪr

Lancaster 'læŋ.kə.stəʳ, -kæs.təʳ US 'læŋ.kə.stɚ, 'læn-, -kæs.tɚ

Lancasterian ˌlæŋ.kæs'tɪə.ri.ən, -kə'stɪə- US ˌlæŋ.kæs'tɪr.i-, ˌlæn-, -kə'stɪr- **-s** -z

Lancastrian læŋ'kæs.tri.ən US læŋ-, læn- **-s** -z

lanc|e (L) lɑːnts US lænts **-es** -ɪz **-ing** -ɪŋ **-ed** -t ˌ**lance** '**corporal**

Lancelot 'lɑːnt.sə.lɒt, -sᵊl.ɒt, -ət US 'lænt.sə.lɑːt, 'lɑːnt-, -lət

lancer 'lɑːnt.səʳ US 'lænt.sɚ **-s** -z

lancet (L) 'lɑːnt.sɪt US 'lænt- **-s** -s

Lancia® 'lɑːnt.si.ə, 'lænt- **-s** -z

Lancing 'lɑːnt.sɪŋ US 'lænt-

Lancôme®, Lancome 'lɑ̃ːŋ.kəʊm, -'- US 'læn.koʊm, -kəm, ˌlæn'koʊm

Lancs. *(abbrev. for* **Lancashire***)* læŋks

land (L) lænd **-s** -z **-ing** -ɪŋ **-ed** -ɪd

landau 'læn.dɔː, -daʊ **-s** -z

Lander 'læn.dəʳ US -dɚ

landfall 'lænd.fɔːl US -fɔːl, -fɑːl **-s** -z

landfill 'lænd.fɪl **-s** -z

landforc|e 'lænd.fɔːs US -fɔːrs **-es** -ɪz

landgrabb|er 'lænd,græb|.əʳ, 'læŋ- US 'lænd,græb|.ɚ **-ers** -əz US -ɚz **-ing** -ɪŋ

landgrave 'lænd.greɪv, 'læŋ- US 'lænd- **-s** -z

landholder 'lænd,həʊl.dəʳ US -ˌhoʊl.dɚ **-s** -z

landing 'læn.dɪŋ **-s** -z '**landing** ˌ**gear;** '**landing** ˌ**net;** '**landing** ˌ**stage;** '**landing** ˌ**strip**

landlad|y 'lænd,leɪ.d|i **-ies** -iz

landlocked 'lænd.lɒkt US -lɑːkt

landlord 'lænd.lɔːd US -lɔːrd **-s** -z **-ism** -ɪ.zᵊm

landlubber 'lænd,lʌb.əʳ US -ɚ **-s** -z

landmark 'lænd.mɑːk, 'læm- US 'lænd.mɑːrk **-s** -s

landmass 'lænd.mæs, 'læm- US 'lænd- **-es** -ɪz

landmine 'lænd.maɪn, 'læm- US 'lænd- **-s** -z

Landon 'læn.dən

Landor 'læn.dɔːʳ, -dəʳ US -dɚ, -dɔːr

land-own|er 'lænd,əʊ.n|əʳ US -ˌoʊ.n|ɚ **-ers** -əz US -ɚz **-ing** -ɪŋ

landrail 'lænd.reɪl **-s** -z

Land Rover® 'lænd,rəʊ.vəʳ US -ˌroʊ.vɚ **-s** -z

landscap|e 'lænd.skeɪp **-es** -s **-ing** -ɪŋ **-ed** -t **-er/s** -əʳ/z US -ɚ/z ˌ**landscape** '**gardener** US '**landscape** ˌ**gardener;** '**landscape** ˌ**mode**

Landseer 'lænd,siː.əʳ, -sɪəʳ US -ˌsiː.ɚ, -ˌsɪr

Land's End ˌlændz'end

landslide 'lænd.slaɪd **-s** -z

landslip 'lænd.slɪp **-s** -s

lands|man 'lændz|.mən **-men** -mən

landward 'lænd.wəd US -wɚd

landwehr 'lænd.veəʳ US -veɪr

landwind 'lænd.wɪnd **-s** -z

lane (L) leɪn **-s** -z **in the** '**fast** ˌ**lane**

Lanfranc 'læn.fræŋk

Lang læŋ

Langbaine 'læŋ.beɪn

Langbourne 'læŋ.bɔːn US -bɔːrn

Langdale 'læŋ.deɪl

Langer 'læŋ.əʳ US -ɚ

Langerhans 'læŋ.ə.hænz, -hænts US 'læŋ.ɚ.hænz, 'lɑːŋ.ɚ.hɑːnz

Langford 'læŋ.fəd US -fɚd

Langham, Langholm(e) 'læŋ.əm

Langhorne 'læŋ.hɔːn US -hɔːrn

Langland 'læŋ.lənd

langlauf 'lɑːŋ.laʊf **-s** -s

Langley 'læŋ.li

Langmere 'læŋ.mɪəʳ US -mɪr

langoustine ˌlɑ̃ŋ.gʊ'stiːn, ˌlæn- US ˌlæŋ.gə'- **-s** -z

Langridge 'læŋ.grɪdʒ

Langside 'læŋ.saɪd, -'-

lang syne ˌlæŋ'saɪn US -'zaɪn, -'saɪn

Langton 'læŋk.tən

Langtry 'læŋk.tri

languag|e 'læŋ.gwɪdʒ **-es** -ɪz

langue lɑ̃ːŋg US lɑ̃ːŋg, lɑːŋ

langue de chat ˌlɑ̃ːŋ.də'ʃɑː US ˌlɑ̃ːŋg-, ˌlɑːŋ-

Languedoc 'lɑ̃ːŋ.gə.dɒk, ˌ--'- US lɑ̃ːŋg'dɔːk, lɑːŋ-

languid 'læŋ.gwɪd **-ly** -li **-ness** -nəs, -nɪs

languish (L) 'læŋ.gwɪʃ **-es** -ɪz **-ing/ly** -ɪŋ/li **-ed** -t **-ment** -mənt

languor 'læŋ.gəʳ US -gɚ **-ous/ly** -əs/li

langur 'læŋ.gəʳ, 'lʌŋ-, -gʊəʳ US lɑːŋ'gʊr **-s** -z

Lanier 'læn.jəʳ; lə'nɪəʳ US lə'nɪr

Lanigan 'læn.ɪ.gᵊn, '-ə-

lank læŋk **-er** -əʳ US -ɚ **-est** -ɪst, -əst **-ly** -li **-ness** -nəs, -nɪs

Lankester 'læŋ.kɪ.stəʳ, -kə- US -stɚ

lank|y 'læŋ.k|i **-ier** -i.əʳ US -i.ɚ **-iest** -i.ɪst, -i.əst **-ily** -ɪ.li, -ᵊl.i **-iness** -ɪ.nəs, -ɪ.nɪs

lanolin(e) 'læn.ᵊl.ɪn, -ə.liːn US -ə.lɪn

Lansbury 'lænz.bᵊr.i US -ber.i

Lansdown(e) 'lænz.daʊn

Lansing 'lɑːnt.sɪŋ, 'lænt- US 'lænt-

Lansley 'lændz.li

Lantau 'læn.taʊ

lantern 'læn.tən US -t̬ɚn **-s** -z

lanthanum 'lænt.θə.nəm

lanyard 'læn.jəd, -jɑːd US -jɚd, -jɑːrd **-s** -z

Lanzarote ˌlæn.zə'rɒt.i US ˌlɑːnt.sə'roʊ.t̬i, -teɪ

Laocoön leɪ'ɒk.əʊ.ɒn, -ən US -'ɑː.koʊ.ɑːn

Laodamia ˌleɪ.əʊ.də'maɪə, -'miː.ə US leɪˌɑː.də'maɪ.ə

Laodice|a ˌleɪ.əʊ.dɪ'siː|.ə, -də'- US leɪˌɑː.dɪ'-; ˌleɪ.ə.də'- **-an/s** -ən/z

Laois liːʃ

Laomedon leɪ'ɒm.ɪ.dən, '-ə- US -'ɑː.mə.dɑːn

Laos 'leɪ.ɒs, 'lɑː-; laʊs, laʊz US laʊs; 'leɪ.ɑːs, -oʊs

Laotian leɪ'əʊ.ʃᵊn; 'laʊ.ʃi.ən, -ʃᵊn; lɑː'ɒʃ.ᵊn US leɪ'oʊ.ʃᵊn; 'laʊ.ʃᵊn

Lao-tsze ˌlɑː.əʊ'tseɪ, ˌlaʊ'tseɪ, -'tsiː US ˌlaʊ'dzuː, -'tseɪ

Larynx

The larynx is located in the throat and its main biological function is to act as a valve that can stop air entering or escaping from the lungs and also (usually) prevents food and other solids from entering the lungs. It consists of a rigid framework or box made of cartilage and, inside, the vocal folds, which are two small lumps of muscular tissue like a very small pair of lips with the division between them (the 'glottis') running from front to back of the throat. There is a complex set of muscles inside the larynx that can open and close the vocal folds as well as changing their length and tension.

In speech the larynx has many important functions including the following:

i) the distinction between voiced and voiceless sounds
ii) the control of pitch
iii) the production of the glottal fricative [h] and the glottal stop [ʔ]
iv) producing variation in voice quality.

lap læp **-s** -s **-ping** -ɪŋ **-ped** -t **-per/s** -əʳ/z (US) -ɚ/z **in the ˌlap of ˈluxury**

laparoscop|y ˌlæp.ᵊrˈɒs.kə.p/i **-ies** -iz

laparotom|y ˌlæp.ᵊrˈɒt.ə.m|i (US) -əˈrɑː.t̬ə- **-ies** -iz

La Paz lɑːˈpæz, læ- (US) ləˈpɑːz, lɑː-, -ˈpɑːs

lapdog ˈlæp.dɒg (US) -dɑːg, -dɔːg **-s** -z

lapel ləˈpel **-s** -z

lapful ˈlæp.fʊl **-s** -z

lapidar|y ˈlæp.ɪ.dᵊr|.i, ˈ-ə- (US) -ə.der- **-ies** -iz

lapis lazuli ˌlæp.ɪsˈlæz.jʊ.li, -jə-, -laɪ (US) -ˈlæz.ə.li, -ˈlæʒ-, -jʊ-

Lapithae ˈlæp.ɪ.θiː

Lapland ˈlæp.lænd **-er/s** -əʳ/z (US) -ɚ/z

La Porte ləˈpɔːt (US) -ˈpɔːrt

Lapp læp **-s** -s **-ish** -ɪʃ

lapp|et ˈlæp|.ɪt **-ets** -ɪts **-eted** -ɪ.tɪd (US) -ɪ.t̬ɪd

Lappin ˈlæp.ɪn

Lapsang ˈlæp.sæŋ

Lapsang Souchong ˌlæp.sæŋ.suːˈʃɒŋ, -ˈtʃɒŋ (US) -tʃɔːŋ, -ʃɔːŋ

laps|e læps **-es** -ɪz **-ing** -ɪŋ **-ed** -t

lapsus linguae ˌlæp.səsˈlɪŋ.gwaɪ, -sʊsˈ-, -gweɪ (US) -səsˈlɪŋ.gwiː, -gwaɪ

laptop ˈlæp.tɒp (US) -tɑːp **-s** -s

Laput|a ləˈpjuː.t|ə (US) -t̬|ə **-an/s** -ᵊn/z

lapwing ˈlæp.wɪŋ **-s** -z

lar (L) lɑːʳ (US) lɑːr **lares** ˈleə.riːz, ˈlɑː.reɪz (US) ˈler.iːz, ˈlɑːr.iːz

Lara ˈlɑː.rə (US) ˈlɑːr.ə, ˈler.ə

Laramie ˈlær.ə.mi (US) ˈler-, ˈlær-

Larbert ˈlɑː.bət, -bɜːt (US) ˈlɑːr.bɚt, -bɝːt

larboard ˈlɑː.bəd, -bɔːd (US) -bɚd, -bɔːrd

larcenous ˈlɑː.sᵊn.əs, -sɪ.nəs (US) ˈlɑːr.sə- **-ly** -li

larcen|y ˈlɑː.sᵊn|.i, -sɪ.n|i (US) ˈlɑːr.sə- **-ies** -iz

larch lɑːtʃ (US) lɑːrtʃ **-es** -ɪz

lard lɑːd (US) lɑːrd **-s** -z **-ing** -ɪŋ **-ed** -ɪd

larder ˈlɑː.dəʳ (US) ˈlɑːr.dɚ **-s** -z

Lardner ˈlɑːd.nəʳ (US) ˈlɑːrd.nɚ

lardon ˈlɑː.dᵊn (US) ˈlɑːr- **-s** -z

Laredo ləˈreɪ.dəʊ (US) -doʊ

lares *(plur. of* **lar***)* ˈleə.riːz, ˈlɑː.reɪz (US) ˈler.iːz, ˈlɑːr.iːz

Largactil® lɑːˈgæk.tɪl, -tᵊl (US) lɑːr-

larg|e lɑːdʒ (US) lɑːrdʒ **-er** -əʳ (US) -ɚ **-est** -ɪst, -əst **-ely** -li **-eness** -nəs, -nɪs **as ˌlarge as ˈlife**

largehearted ˌlɑːdʒˈhɑː.tɪd (US) ˌlɑːrʒˈhɑːr.t̬ɪd **-ness** -nəs, -nɪs *stress shift:* ˌlargehearted ˈperson

large-scale ˌlɑːdʒˈskeɪl (US) ˌlɑːrdʒ- *stress shift:* ˌlarge-scale ˈchanges

largess|(e) lɑːˈʒes, -ˈdʒes; ˈ-- (US) lɑːrˈdʒes, -ˈʒes; ˈlɑːr.dʒəs **-es** -ɪz

larghetto lɑːˈget.əʊ (US) lɑːrˈget̬.oʊ **-s** -z

largish ˈlɑː.dʒɪʃ (US) ˈlɑːr-

largo ˈlɑː.gəʊ (US) ˈlɑːr.goʊ **-s** -z

Largs lɑːgz (US) lɑːrgz

Larham ˈlɑː.rəm (US) ˈlɑːr-

lari|at ˈlær.i|.ət (US) ˈler-, ˈlær- **-ats** -əts **-ating** -ə.tɪŋ (US) -ə.t̬ɪŋ **-ated** -ə.tɪd (US) -ə.t̬ɪd

Larisa, Larissa ləˈrɪs.ə

lark lɑːk (US) lɑːrk **-s** -s **-ing** -ɪŋ **-ed** -t

Larkhall ˈlɑːk.hɔːl (US) ˈlɑːrk-, -hɑːl

Larkin ˈlɑː.kɪn (US) ˈlɑːr-

larkspur ˈlɑːk.spɜːʳ, -spəʳ (US) ˈlɑːrk.spɝː, -spɚ **-s** -z

lark|y ˈlɑː.k|i (US) ˈlɑːr- **-ier** -i.əʳ (US) -i.ɚ **-iest** -i.ɪst, -i.əst **-iness** -ɪ.nəs, -ɪ.nɪs

Larmor, Larmour ˈlɑː.məʳ (US) ˈlɑːr.mɚ, -mɔːr

Larne lɑːn (US) lɑːrn

Larousse lærˈuːs (US) lɑːˈruːs

larrikin ˈlær.ɪ.kɪn, ˈ-ə- (US) ˈler-, ˈlær- **-s** -z

larrup ˈlær.əp (US) ˈler-, ˈlær- **-s** -s **-ping** -ɪŋ **-ped** -t

Larry ˈlær.i (US) ˈler-, ˈlær-

Larsen, Larson ˈlɑː.sᵊn (US) ˈlɑːr-

Lars Porsena ˌlɑːzˈpɔː.sɪ.nə, -sə- (US) ˌlɑːrzˈpɔːr-

larum ˈlær.əm (US) ˈler-, ˈlær-; ˈlɑːr.ʊm **-s** -z

larv|a ˈlɑː.v|ə (US) ˈlɑːr- **-ae** -iː **-al** -ᵊl

laryngal ləˈrɪŋ.gᵊl, lærˈɪŋ- (US) ləˈrɪŋ-, lerˈɪŋ-, lær-

laryngeal ləˈrɪn.dʒi.əl, lærˈɪn-, -dʒᵊl; ˌlær.ɪnˈdʒiː.əl, -ənˈ- (US) ləˈrɪn.dʒi.əl, -dʒᵊl

laryngectom|y ˌlær.ɪnˈdʒek.tə.m|i, -ənˈ- (US) ˌler-, ˌlær- **-ies** -iz

larynges *(plur. of* **larynx***)* lærˈɪn.dʒiːz, ləˈrɪn- (US) lə-, lerˈɪn-, lær-

laryngitis ˌlær.ɪnˈdʒaɪ.tɪs, -ənˈ- (US) ˌler.ɪnˈdʒaɪ.t̬ɪs, ˌlær-

laryngolog|y ˌlær.ɪŋˈgɒl.ə.dʒ|i, -əŋˈ- (US) ˌler.ɪŋˈgɑː.lə-, ˌlær-, -ɪnˈdʒɑː- **-ist/s** -ɪst/s

laryngoscope ləˈrɪŋ.gə.skəʊp, lærˈɪŋ-; ˈlær.ɪŋ- (US) ləˈrɪŋ.goʊ.skoʊp, -gə-, -ˈrɪn.dʒə- **-s** -s

laryngoscopic ləˌrɪŋ.gəˈskɒp.ɪk, lærˌɪŋ-; ˌlær.ɪŋ- (US) ləˌrɪŋ.goʊˈskɑː.pɪk, -gəˈ-, -ˌrɪn.dʒəˈ-

laryngoscop|y ˌlær.ɪŋˈgɒs.kə.p|i, -əŋˈ- (US) ˌler.ɪŋˈgɑː.skə-, ˌlær-, -ɪnˈdʒɑː- **-ist/s** -ɪst/s

larynx ˈlær.ɪŋks (US) ˈler-, ˈlær- **-es** -ɪz **larynges** lærˈɪn.dʒiːz, ləˈrɪn- (US) lə-, lerˈɪn-, lær-

lasagne, lasagna ləˈzæn.jə, -ˈsæn-, -ˈzɑː.njə, -ˈsɑː- (US) -ˈzɑː.njə, -ˈsɑː-

Lascar ˈlæs.kəʳ (US) -kɚ **-s** -z

Lascaux ˈlæs.kəʊ, -ˈ- (US) læsˈkoʊ

Lascelles ˈlæs.ᵊlz, ləˈselz

lascivious ləˈsɪv.i.əs **-ly** -li **-ness** -nəs, -nɪs

laser ˈleɪ.zəʳ (US) -zɚ **-s** -z **ˈlaser ˌdisk, ˈlaser ˌprinter**

laserjet ˈleɪ.zə.dʒet (US) -zɚ- **-s** -s

lash læʃ **-es** -ɪz **-ing/s** -ɪŋ/z **-ed** -t **-er/s** -əʳ/z (US) -ɚ/z

Lasham ˈlæʃ.əm *locally also:* ˈlæs.əm

Las Palmas ˌlæsˈpæl.məs, -ˈpɑːl- (US) ˌlɑːsˈpɑːl-, -mɑːs

lass læs **-es** -ɪz

Lassa ˈlæs.ə, ˈlɑː.sə (US) ˈlɑː.sə, ˈlæs.ə **ˌLassa ˈfever**

Lassalle ləˈsæl

Lateral

A lateral consonant is one where there is obstruction to the passage of air in the centere (mid-line) of the air-passage and the air flows to the side of the obstruction.

Examples for English

In English the /l/ phoneme is lateral both in its "clear" and its "dark" allophones (see CLEAR L and DARK L): the blade of the tongue is in contact with the alveolar ridge as for /t d n/ but the sides of the tongue are lowered to allow the passage of air, e.g.:

lip /lɪp/ pill /pɪl/

When an alveolar plosive precedes a lateral consonant in English it is usual for it to have a 'lateral release'. This means that to go from /t/ or /d/ to /l/ we simply lower the sides of the tongue to release the compressed air, rather than lowering and then raising the tongue blade. A syllabic /l/ is the usual result of this in word final position (see SYLLABIC CONSONANT), e.g.:

bottle /ˈbɒt.l̩/ puddle /ˈpʌd.l̩/

Most laterals are produced with the air passage to both sides of the obstruction (they are 'bilateral'), but sometimes we find air passing to one side only ('unilateral').

In other languages

Other lateral consonants are found in other languages: the Welsh ll sound is a voiceless lateral fricative [ɬ], and Xhosa and Zulu have a voiced lateral fricative [ɮ]. Several Southern African languages have lateral clicks (where the plosive occlusion is released laterally) and at least one language (of Papua New Guinea) has a contrast between alveolar and velar lateral.

Lassell læsˈel, ləˈsel
lassie (L) ˈlæs.i **-s** -z
lassitude ˈlæs.ɪ.tjuːd, ˈ-ə- (US) -tuːd, -tjuːd
lasso *(n.)* læsˈuː; ˈlæs.əʊ (US) ˈlæs.oʊ, -uː **-(e)s** -z
lasso *(v.)* læsˈuː, ləˈsuː (US) ˈlæs.oʊ, -uː **-(e)s** -z **-ing** -ɪŋ **-ed** -d
last (L) lɑːst (US) læst **-s** -s **-ing/ly** -ɪŋ/li **-ed** -ɪd **-ly** ˈlɑːst.li (US) ˈlæst.li ˌ**Last ˈJudgment; ˌlast ˈstraw; ˌLast ˈSupper; ˌlast ˈword; at the ˌlast ˈminute**
last-ditch ˌlɑːstˈdɪtʃ (US) ˌlæst- *stress shift, see compound:* ˌ**last-ditch atˈtempt**
last-minute ˌlɑːstˈmɪn.ɪt (US) ˌlæst- *stress shift:* ˌlast-minute ˈplans
Las Vegas ˌlæsˈveɪ.gəs, ˌlɑːs- (US) ˌlɑːs-
lat læt **-s** -s
Latakia ˌlæt.əˈkiː.ə (US) ˌlɑː.t̬əˈ-, ˌlæt̬.əˈ-
latch lætʃ **-es** -ɪz **-ing** -ɪŋ **-ed** -t
latchet ˈlætʃ.ɪt, -ət **-s** -s
latchkey ˈlætʃ.kiː **-s** -z ˈ**latchkey ˌchild, ˌlatchkey ˈchild**
lat|e leɪt **-er** -əʳ (US) ˈleɪ.t̬ɚ **-est** -ɪst, -əst (US) ˈleɪ.t̬ɪst, -t̬əst **-ely** -li **-eness** -nəs, -nɪs
latecomer ˈleɪtˌkʌm.əʳ (US) -ɚ **-s** -z
lateen ləˈtiːn (US) lætˈiːn, ləˈtiːn **-s** -z
latency ˈleɪ.tᵊnt.si
late-night ˈleɪtˌnaɪt ˌ**late-ˌnight ˈshopping**
latent ˈleɪ.tᵊnt **-ly** -li
lateral ˈlæt.ᵊr.ᵊl, ˈ-rᵊl (US) ˈlæt̬.ɚ.ᵊl **-s** -z **-ly** -i ˌ**lateral ˈthinking**
Lateran ˈlæt.ᵊr.ᵊn (US) ˈlæt̬-
laterite ˈlæt.ᵊr.aɪt (US) ˈlæt̬.ə.raɪt
latex ˈleɪ.teks **-es** -ɪz **latices** ˈlæt.ɪ.siːz, ˈleɪ.tɪ- (US) ˈlæt̬.ɪ-, ˈleɪ.t̬ɪ-
lath læθ, lɑːθ (US) læθ **-s** -s, lɑːðz (US) -s, læðz
Latham ˈleɪ.θəm, -ðəm
Note: Generally /ˈleɪ.θəm/ in S. of England; always /ˈleɪ.ðəm/ in N.
Lathbury ˈlæθ.bᵊr.i (US) -ber-
lath|e leɪð **-es** -z **-ing** -ɪŋ **-ed** -d
lath|er ˈlɑː.ðl|əʳ, ˈlæðl.əʳ (US) ˈlæðl.ɚ **-ers** -əz (US) -ɚz **-ering** -ᵊr.ɪŋ **-ered** -əd (US) -ɚd
lathi ˈlɑː.ti **-s** -z
Lathom ˈleɪ.θəm, -ðəm
Lathrop ˈleɪ.θrəp
latices *(plur. of* **latex***)* ˈlæt.ɪ.siːz, ˈleɪ.tɪ- (US) ˈlæt̬.ɪ-, ˈleɪ.t̬ɪ-
Latimer ˈlæt.ɪ.məʳ, ˈ-ə- (US) ˈlæt̬.ə.mɚ
Latin ˈlæt.ɪn (US) -ᵊn **-ate** -eɪt ˌ**Latin Aˈmerica**
latin|ism ˈlæt.ɪ.nl.ɪ.zᵊm (US) -ᵊnl.ɪ- **-isms** -ɪ.zᵊmz **-ist/s** -ɪst/s
latinity ləˈtɪn.ə.ti, lætˈɪn-, -ɪ.ti (US) lætˈɪn.ə.t̬i
latiniz|e, -is|e ˈlæt.ɪ.naɪz (US) -ᵊn.aɪz **-es** -ɪz **-ing** -ɪŋ **-ed** -d
latin|o (L) ləˈtiː.nləʊ, lætˈiː- (US) -nloʊ **-os** -əʊz (US) -oʊz **-a/s** -ə/z (US) -ɑː/z
Latinus ləˈtaɪ.nəs
latish ˈleɪ.tɪʃ (US) -t̬ɪʃ
latitude ˈlæt.ɪ.tjuːd, ˈ-ə-, -tʃuːd (US) ˈlæt̬.ə.tuːd, -tjuːd **-s** -z
latitudinal ˌlæt.ɪˈtjuː.dɪ.nᵊl, -əˈ-, -ˈtʃuː-, -dᵊn.ᵊl (US) ˌlæt̬.əˈtuː-, -ˈtjuː-
latitudinarian ˌlæt.ɪˌtjuː.dɪˈneə.ri.ən, -əˌ-, -ˌtʃuː- (US) ˌlæt̬.əˌtuː.dɪˈner.i-, -ˌtjuː- **-s** -z **-ism** -ɪ.zᵊm
Latium ˈleɪ.ʃi.əm, ˈlæt.i- (US) ˈleɪ.ʃᵊm, -ʃi.əm
latke ˈlɑːt.kə **-s** -z
Latoya ləˈtɔɪ.ə
latria ləˈtraɪə
latrine ləˈtriːn **-s** -z
Lattakia ˌlæt.əˈkiː.ə (US) ˌlɑː.t̬əˈ-, ˌlæt̬.əˈ-
latte ˈlæt.eɪ (US) ˈlɑː.teɪ
latter ˈlæt.əʳ (US) ˈlæt̬.ɚ **-ly** -li
latter-day ˈlæt.ə.deɪ (US) ˈlæt̬.ɚ- ˌ**Latter-Day ˈSaint**
lattic|e ˈlæt.ɪs (US) ˈlæt̬- **-es** -ɪz **-ed** -t
latticework ˈlæt.ɪs.wɜːk (US) ˈlæt̬.ɪs.wɝːk
Latvi|a ˈlæt.vil.ə **-an/s** -ən/z
laud (L) lɔːd (US) lɑːd, lɔːd **-s** -z **-ing** -ɪŋ **-ed** -ɪd
Lauda ˈlaʊ.də
laudab|le ˈlɔː.də.bl̩ (US) ˈlɑː-, ˈlɔː- **-ly** -li **-leness** -l̩.nəs, -nɪs
laudanum ˈlɔː.dᵊn.əm (US) ˈlɑː-, ˈlɔː-
laudatory ˈlɔː.də.tᵊr.i (US) ˈlɑː.də.tɔːr-, ˈlɔː-
Lauder ˈlɔː.dəʳ (US) ˈlɑː.dɚ, ˈlɔː-
Lauderdale ˈlɔː.də.deɪl (US) ˈlɑː.dɚ-, ˈlɔː-
laugh lɑːf (US) læf **-s** -s **-ing/ly** -ɪŋ/li **-ed** -t **-er/s** -əʳ/z (US) -ɚ/z ˈ**laughing ˌgas; ˌlaughing ˈjackass; no ˌlaughing ˈmatter, no ˈlaughing ˌmatter; have the ˌlast ˈlaugh**
laughab|le ˈlɑː.fə.bl̩ (US) ˈlæf.ə- **-ly** -li **-leness** -l̩.nəs, -nɪs
Laugharne lɑːn (US) lɑːrn
laughingstock ˈlɑː.fɪŋ.stɒk (US) ˈlæf.ɪŋ.stɑːk **-s** -s
Laughland ˈlɒk.lənd (US) ˈlɑːk-
Laughlin ˈlɒk.lɪn, ˈlɒx-, ˈlɒf-, ˈlɑː.flɪn (US) ˈlɑː-, ˈlɔː-

Latin words and phrases

Words, names and phrases from Latin have entered the English language at many different times. Some words and names are in relatively common use and have been completely anglicised, while others are used in particular types of discourse which to some extent determine their pronunciation. The pronunciation used by academic scholars of Latin has tended to be based on a reconstruction of what was supposed to be the pronunciation in Roman times. Ecclesiastical Latin, previously used in the Roman Catholic church and closely similar to the pronunciation of Italian, has largely disappeared, but phrases such as *Gloria in excelsis* or *Humanae Vitae* are still heard. Legal Latin is also now much less widely used than it used to be, but some phrases survive, such as *habeas corpus, ultra vires* (usual pronunciation /ˌheɪ.bi.əsˈkɔː.pəs, US -ˈkɔːr-/ and /ˌʌl.trəˈvaɪə.riːz, ˌʊl.trɑːˈvɪə.reɪz, US ˌʌl.trəˈvaɪ.riːz/). Most of the Latin words, phrases and names in this dictionary are ones that have been fully anglicized, but there is no set of rules to determine exactly how this is done.

Examples

Words, e.g.:

accidia	/ækˈsɪd.i.ə/
flamen	/ˈfleɪ.men/
vale	/ˈvɑː.leɪ, ˈveɪ.li, ˈvæl.eɪ/
	US /ˈveɪ.li, ˈvɑː.leɪ/

Names, e.g.:

Aeneas	/ˈiː.ni.əs, iːˈniː-, -æs/
Flaminius	/fləˈmɪn.i.əs, flæmˈɪn-/
	US /fləˈmɪn-/

Phrases, e.g.:

ad hoc	/ˌædˈhɒk, -ˈhəʊk/
	US /-ˈhɑːk, -ˈhoʊk/
ex voto	/ˌeksˈvəʊ.təʊ/
	US /-ˈvoʊ.t̬oʊ/
flagrante delicto	/fləˌgræn.teɪ.dɪˈlɪk.təʊ/, /flægˌræn-, -ti-, -dəˈ-, -deɪˈ-/
	US /fləˌgræn.ti.diːˈlɪk.toʊ/

laughter ˈlɑːf.təʳ US ˈlæf.tɚ
Laughton ˈlɔː.tᵊn US ˈlɑː-, ˈlɔː-
launc|e lɑːnts US lænts, lɑːnts, lɔːnts **-es** -ɪz
Launce lɑːnts, lɔːnts US lænts, lɑːnts, lɔːnts
Launcelot ˈlɑːnt.sᵊl.ɒt, ˈlɔːnt-, -ət US ˈlænt.sə.lɑːt, ˈlɑːnt-, ˈlɔːnt-, -lət
Launceston *in Cornwall:* ˈlɔːnt.stən, -sᵊn *locally:* ˈlɑːnt- *in Tasmania:* ˈlɔːnt.səs.tᵊn *locally:* ˈlɒnt- US ˈlɑːnt-, ˈlɔːnt-
launch lɔːntʃ US lɑːntʃ, lɔːntʃ **-es** -ɪz **-ing** -ɪŋ **-ed** -t **-er/s** -əʳ/z US -ɚ/z
launchpad ˈlɔːntʃ.pæd US ˈlɑːntʃ-, ˈlɔːntʃ- **-s** -z
laund|er ˈlɔːn.d|əʳ US ˈlɑːn.d|ɚ, ˈlɔːn- **-ers** -əz US -ɚz **-ering** -ᵊr.ɪŋ **-ered** -əd US -ɚd
launderette ˌlɔːn.dᵊrˈet, ˌ-ˈdret US ˌlɑːn.dəˈret, ˌlɔːn-, ˌ-ˈdret **-s** -s
laundress ˈlɔːn.dres, -drəs, -drɪs US ˈlɑːn.drɪs, ˈlɔːn- **-es** -ɪz
laundrette ˌlɔːnˈdret US ˌlɑːn-, ˌlɔːn- **-s** -s
Laundromat® ˈlɔːn.drə.mæt US ˈlɔːn.droʊ-, ˈlɑːn-, -drə- **-s** -s
laundr|y ˈlɔːn.dr|i US ˈlɑːn-, ˈlɔːn- **-ies** -iz **ˈlaundry ˌbasket; ˈlaundry ˌlist**
laundry|man ˈlɔːn.dri|.mæn, -mən US ˈlɑːn-, ˈlɔːn- **-men** -mən, -men **-woman** -ˌwʊm.ən **-women** -ˌwɪm.ɪn
Laundy ˈlɔːn.di US ˈlɑːn-, ˈlɔːn-
Laura ˈlɔː.rə US ˈlɔːr.ə
laureate *(n. adj.)* ˈlɔː.ri.ət, ˈlɒr.i-, -ɪt US ˈlɔːr.i.ɪt, ˈlɑːr- **-s** -s **-ship/s** -ʃɪp/s
laure|ate *(v.)* ˈlɔː.ri|.eɪt, ˈlɒr.i- US ˈlɔːr.i-, ˈlɑːr- **-ates** -eɪts **-ating** -eɪ.tɪŋ US -eɪ.t̬ɪŋ **-ated** -eɪ.tɪd US -eɪ.t̬ɪd
laurel (L) ˈlɒr.ᵊl US ˈlɔːr-, ˈlɑːr- **-s** -z
Lauren ˈlɔː.rən, ˈlɒr.ən US ˈlɔːr.ən, ˈlɑːr-
Laurence ˈlɒr.ᵊnts US ˈlɔːr-, ˈlɑːr-
Laurent lɔːˈrɑ̃ːŋ, lə- US lɑːˈrɑːnt, lə-
Laurie ˈlɒr.i, ˈlɔː.ri US ˈlɔːr.i, ˈlɑːr-
Laurier *English name:* ˈlɒr.i.əʳ US ˈlɔːr.i.ɚ, ˈlɑːr- *Canadian name:* ˈlɒr.i.eɪ US ˈlɔːr.i.eɪ
Lauriston ˈlɒr.ɪ.stᵊn, ˈ-ə- US ˈlɔːr-, ˈlɑːr-
laurustinus ˌlɒr.əˈstaɪ.nəs, ˌlɔː.rəˈ- US ˌlɑːr-, ˌlɔːr- **-es** -ɪz
Lausanne ləʊˈzæn US loʊ-, -ˈzɑːn
Lauterbrunnen ˈlaʊ.tə.brʊn.ən US -t̬ɚ-
Lautrec ləʊˈtrek US loʊ-, lə-
lav læv **-s** -z
lava ˈlɑː.və US ˈlɑː-, ˈlæv.ə
lavabo *ritual:* ləˈvɑː.bəʊ, lævˈɑː-, -ˈeɪ- US ləˈvɑː.boʊ, -ˈveɪ- **-s** -z *basin:* ləˈveɪ.bəʊ; ˈlæv.ə.bəʊ US ləˈvɑː.boʊ, -ˈveɪ- **-s** -z
lavage lævˈɑːʒ, ləˈvɑːʒ, -ˈvɑːdʒ; ˈlæv.ɪdʒ, -ɑːʒ US ləˈvɑːʒ; ˈlæv.ɪdʒ
Lavater lɑːˈvɑː.təʳ, ˈ--- US -t̬ɚ
lavatorial ˌlæv.əˈtɔː.ri.əl US -ˈtɔːr.i-
lavator|y ˈlæv.ə.tᵊr|.i, -tr|i US -tɔːr.i **-ies** -iz
lav|e leɪv **-es** -z **-ing** -ɪŋ **-ed** -d
lavender (L) ˈlæv.ᵊn.dəʳ, -ɪn- US -dɚ **ˈlavender ˌwater**
Lavengro ləˈveŋ.grəʊ, lævˈeŋ- US -groʊ
Lavenham ˈlæv.ᵊn.əm
laver *seaweed:* ˈlɑː.vəʳ US ˈleɪ.vɚ, ˈlɑː- **-s** -z *all other senses:* ˈleɪ.vəʳ US -vɚ **-s** -z
Laver *name:* ˈleɪ.vəʳ US -vɚ
Laverty ˈlæv.ə.ti US -ɚ.t̬i
Lavery ˈleɪ.vᵊr.i, ˈlæv.ᵊr-
Lavin ˈlæv.ɪn
Lavington ˈlæv.ɪŋ.tən
Lavini|a ləˈvɪn.i|.ə **-an** -ən
lavish ˈlæv.ɪʃ **-ly** -li **-ness** -nəs, -nɪs **-es** -ɪz **-ing** -ɪŋ **-ed** -t
Lavoisier ləˈvwɑː.zi.eɪ, lævˈwɑː-, -ˈwæz.i- US ləˈvwɑː.zi-
law (L) lɔː US lɑː, lɔː **-s** -z **ˈlaw ˌlord; be a ˌlaw unto oneˈself; take the ˌlaw into one's ˌown ˈhands**
law-abiding ˈlɔː.əˌbaɪ.dɪŋ US ˈlɑː-, ˈlɔː-
lawbreak|er ˈlɔːˌbreɪ.k|əʳ US ˈlɑːˌbreɪ.k|ɚ, ˈlɔː- **-ers** -əz US -ɚz **-ing** -ɪŋ
Lawes lɔːz US lɑːz, lɔːz
Lawesford ˈlɔːz.fəd US ˈlɑːz.fɚd, ˈlɔːz-
lawful ˈlɔː.fᵊl, -fʊl US ˈlɑː-, ˈlɔː- **-ly** -i **-ness** -nəs, -nɪs
lawgiv|er ˈlɔːˌgɪv|.əʳ US ˈlɑːˌgɪv|.ɚ, ˈlɔː- **-ers** -əz US -ɚz **-ing** -ɪŋ
lawks lɔːks US lɑːks, lɔːks
lawless (L) ˈlɔː.ləs, -lɪs US ˈlɑː-, ˈlɔː- **-ly** -li **-ness** -nəs, -nɪs
Lawley, Lawly ˈlɔː.li US ˈlɑː-, ˈlɔː-
lawmak|er ˈlɔːˌmeɪ.k|əʳ US ˈlɑːˌmeɪ.k|ɚ, ˈlɔː- **-ers** -əz US -ɚz **-ing** -ɪŋ

Lax

A lax sound is produced with relatively little articulatory energy. Since there is no established standard for measuring articulatory energy, this concept only has meaning if it is used relative to some other sounds that are felt to be articulated with a comparatively greater amount of energy (i.e. TENSE).

Examples for English

It is mainly American phonologists who use the terms lax and tense in describing English vowels; the short vowels /ɪ e æ ʌ ɒ ʊ ə/ are classed as lax, while what are referred to in our description of BBC pronunciation as the long vowels and the diphthongs are tense. The terms can also be used of consonants as equivalent to FORTIS (tense) and LENIS (lax), though this is not commonly done in present-day descriptions.

lawn lɔːn US lɑːn, lɔːn **-s** -z ˈ**lawn** ˌ**mower**; ˌ**lawn** ˈ**tennis** US ˈ**lawn** ˌ**tennis**
Lawrence, Lawrance ˈlɒr.ənts US ˈlɔːr-, ˈlɑːr-
lawrencium ləˈrent.si.əm, lɔː-, lɒrˈent- US lɔːˈrent-, lɑː-
Lawrenson ˈlɒr.ənt.sən US ˈlɔːr.ənt-, ˈlɑːr-
Lawrentian ləˈren.ʃi.ən, lɒrˈen-, -ʃən US ləˈrent-, lɔː-, lɑː-
Lawson ˈlɔː.sən US ˈlɑː-, ˈlɔː-
lawsuit ˈlɔː.suːt, -sjuːt US ˈlɑː.suːt, ˈlɔː- **-s** -s
Lawton ˈlɔː.tən US ˈlɑː-, ˈlɔː-
lawyer ˈlɔɪ.əʳ, ˈlɔː.jəʳ US ˈlɑː.jɚ, ˈlɔː-, ˈlɔɪ- **-s** -z
lax læks **-er** -əʳ US -ɚ **-est** -ɪst, -əst **-ly** -li **-ness** -nəs, -nɪs
laxative ˈlæk.sə.tɪv US -t̬ɪv **-s** -z
laxity ˈlæk.sə.ti, -sɪ- US -sə.t̬i
lay (L) leɪ **-s** -z **-ing** -ɪŋ **laid** leɪd ˌ**lay** ˈ**reader** US ˈ**lay** ˌ**reader**; ˌ**lay of the** ˈ**land**
layabout ˈleɪ.əˌbaʊt **-s** -s
Layamon ˈlaɪ.ə.mən, -mɒn US ˈleɪ.ə.mən, ˈlaɪ-
Layard ˈleɪ.ɑːd, leəd US ˈleɪ.ɑːrd, lerd
layaway ˈleɪ.ə.weɪ
lay-by ˈleɪ.baɪ **-s** -z
Laycock ˈleɪ.kɒk US -kɑːk
layer leɪəʳ, leəʳ US ˈleɪ.ɚ **-s** -z **-ing** -ɪŋ **-ed** -d
layette leɪˈet **-s** -s
lay|man ˈleɪ|.mən **-men** -mən
layoff ˈleɪ.ɒf US -ɑːf **-s** -s
layout ˈleɪ.aʊt **-s** -s
layover ˈleɪˌəʊ.vəʳ US -ˌoʊ.vɚ
lay|person ˈleɪˌpɜː.sən US -ˌpɝː- **-people** -ˌpiː.pl̩
Layton ˈleɪ.tən
layup ˈleɪ.ʌp **-s** -s
lay|woman ˈleɪ|ˌwʊm.ən **-women** -ˌwɪm.ɪn
lazar ˈlæz.əʳ US ˈleɪ.zɚ, ˈlæz.ɚ **-s** -z
lazaretto ˌlæz.əˈret.əʊ, -ərˈet- US -ˈret̬.oʊ **-s** -z
Lazarus ˈlæz.ər.əs
laz|e leɪz **-es** -ɪz **-ing** -ɪŋ **-ed** -d
Lazenby ˈleɪ.zən.bi, -zəm- US -zən-
Lazio ˈlæt.si.əʊ US ˈlɑːt.si.oʊ
lazuli ˈlæz.jə.liː, -jʊ-, ˈlæʒ.ə-, ˈ-ʊ-, -laɪ US ˈlæʒ.juː-, ˈlæz-, ˈ-ə-
lazulite ˈlæz.jə.laɪt, -jʊ-, ˈlæʒ.ə-, -ˈʊ- US ˈlæʒ.juː-, ˈlæz-, ˈ-ə-
laz|y ˈleɪ.z|i **-ier** -i.əʳ US -i.ɚ **-iest** -i.ɪst, -i.əst **-ily** -ɪ.li, -əl.i **-iness** -ɪ.nəs, -ɪ.nɪs
lazybones ˈleɪ.ziˌbəʊnz US -ˌboʊnz
lb *(abbrev. for* **pound/s***) singular:* paʊnd *plural:* paʊndz
lbw ˌel.biːˈdʌb.l̩.juː
LCD ˌel.siːˈdiː
L-dopa ˌelˈdəʊ.pə US -ˈdoʊ-
lea (L) liː **-s** -z
LEA ˌel.iːˈeɪ
leach (L) liːtʃ **-es** -ɪz **-ing** -ɪŋ **-ed** -t
Leachman ˈliːtʃ.mən
Leacock ˈliː.kɒk, ˈleɪ- US -kɑːk
lead *metal:* led **-s** -z **-ing** -ɪŋ **-ed** -ɪd ˌ**lead** ˈ**pencil**; US ˈ**lead** ˌ**pencil**; ˌ**lead** ˈ**poisoning**
lead *cable, flex:* liːd **-s** -z
lead *guide:* liːd **-s** -z **-ing** -ɪŋ **led** led ˌ**leading** ˈ**light**; ˈ**leading** ˌ**rein**; ˈ**lead** ˌ**time**
Lead *surname:* liːd
Leadbetter ˈledˌbet.əʳ, -ˈ-- US ˈledˌbet̬.ɚ, -ˈ--
leaden ˈled.ən **-ly** -li **-ness** -nəs, -nɪs
Leadenhall ˈled.ən.hɔːl US -hɔːl, -hɑːl
leader (L) ˈliː.dəʳ US -dɚ **-s** -z ˌ**leader of the** ˌ**oppo**ˈ**sition**
leaderboard ˈliː.də.bɔːd US -dɚ.bɔːrd **-s** -z
leaderette ˌliː.dərˈet **-s** -s
leadership ˈliː.də.ʃɪp US -dɚ- **-s** -s
lead-in ˈliːd.ɪn **-s** -z
lead-off ˈliːd.ɒf US -ɑːf **-s** -s
leads *(n.) roofing:* ledz
lea|f *(n.)* liː|f **-ves** -vz ˈ**leaf** ˌ**mould**; **take a** ˌ**leaf out of** ˌ**someone's** ˈ**book**; ˌ**turn over a** ˌ**new** ˈ**leaf**
leaf *(v.)* liːf **-s** -s **-ing** -ɪŋ **-ed** -t
leafless ˈliːf.ləs, -lɪs
leafle|t ˈliː.flə|t, -flɪ|t **-ts** -ts **-(t)ting** -tɪŋ US -t̬ɪŋ **-(t)ted** -tɪd US -t̬ɪd
leaf|y ˈliː.f|i **-ier** -i.əʳ US -i.ɚ **-iest** -i.ɪst, -i.əst **-iness** -ɪ.nəs, -ɪ.nɪs
leagu|e liːg **-es** -z **-ing** -ɪŋ **-ed** -d ˈ**league** ˌ**table**
leaguer (L) ˈliː.gəʳ US -gɚ **-s** -z
Leah ˈliː.ə; lɪə US ˈliː.ə
Leahy ˈliː.hi US ˈleɪ-
leak liːk **-s** -s **-ing** -ɪŋ **-ed** -t
leakag|e ˈliː.kɪdʒ **-es** -ɪz
Leake liːk
Leakey ˈliː.ki
leak|y ˈliː.k|i **-ier** -i.əʳ US -i.ɚ **-iest** -i.ɪst, -i.əst **-iness** -ɪ.nəs, -ɪ.nɪs
Leamington ˈlem.ɪŋ.tən ˌ**Leamington** ˈ**Spa**
lean liːn **-er** -əʳ US -ɚ **-est** -ɪst, -əst **-ly** -li **-ness** -nəs, -nəs **-s** -z **-ing/s** -ɪŋ/z **leaned** -d, lent **leant** lent
Leander liˈæn.dəʳ US -dɚ
Leanne liˈæn
lean-to ˈliːn.tuː **-s** -z
leap liːp **-s** -s **-ing** -ɪŋ **-ed** lept, liːpt **-t** lept **-er/s** -əʳ/z US -ɚ/z ˈ**leap** ˌ**year**; **by** ˌ**leaps and** ˈ**bounds**
leapfrog ˈliːp.frɒg US -frɑːg, -frɔːg **-s** -z **-ging** -ɪŋ **-ged** -d
Lear lɪəʳ US lɪr
learn lɜːn US lɝːn **-s** -z **-ing** -ɪŋ **-ed** -d, -t **-t** -t **-er/s** -əʳ/z US -ɚ/z ˈ**learning** ˌ**curve**; ˈ**learning disa**ˌ**bility**
learned *scholarly:* ˈlɜː.nɪd US ˈlɝː- **-ly** -li **-ness** -nəs, -nɪs
Learney ˈleə.ni US ˈler-
leas|e liːs **-es** -ɪz **-ing** -ɪŋ **-ed** -t **a** ˌ**new** ˌ**lease of** ˈ**life**; **a** ˌ**new** ˌ**lease on** ˈ**life**
leaseback ˈliːs.bæk
leasehold ˈliːs.həʊld US -hoʊld **-s** -z **-er/s** -əʳ/z US -ɚ/z
lease-|lend ˌliːs|ˈlend **-lends** -ˈlendz **-lending** -ˈlen.dɪŋ **-lent** -ˈlent

leash liːʃ **-es** -ɪz **-ing** -ɪŋ **-ed** -t
least liːst
leastways ˈliːst.weɪz
leastwise ˈliːst.waɪz
leat liːt **-s** -s
Leatham ˈliː.θəm, -ðəm
Leathart ˈliː.θɑːt (US) -θɑːrt
leath|er ˈleð|.əʳ (US) -ɚ **-ers** -əz (US) -ɚz **-ering** -ər.ɪŋ **-ered** -əd (US) -ɚd
leatherback ˈleð.ə.bæk (US) ˈ-ɚ-
Leatherette® ˌleð.ərˈet
Leatherhead ˈleð.ə.hed (US) ˈ-ɚ-
leatherjacket ˈleð.əˌdʒæk.ɪt (US) -ɚˌ- **-s** -s
leathern ˈleð.ən (US) -ɚn
leatherneck ˈleð.ə.nek (US) ˈ-ɚ- **-s** -s
leather|y ˈleð.ər|.i **-iness** -ɪ.nəs, -ɪ.nɪs
Leathes liːðz
leave *(n.)* liːv **-s** -z
Note: Formerly, the pronunciation /liːf/ was used in the British army (plural: /liːfs/).
leav|e *(v.)* liːv **-es** -z **-ing/s** -ɪŋ/z **left** left **-er/s** -əʳ/z (US) -ɚ/z
leaved liːvd
leaven ˈlev.ən **-s** -z **-ing** -ɪŋ, ˈlev.nɪŋ **-ed** -d
Leavenworth ˈlev.ən.wəθ, -wɜːθ (US) -wɚθ, -wɝːθ
leaves *(plur. of* **leaf***)* liːvz
leave-taking ˈliːvˌteɪ.kɪŋ
Leavis ˈliː.vɪs
Leavisite ˈliː.vɪ.saɪt **-s** -s
Leavitt ˈlev.ɪt
Lebanese ˌleb.əˈniːz *stress shift:* ˌLebanese ˈcapital
Lebanon ˈleb.ə.nən, -nɒn (US) -nɑːn, -nən
Le Beau ləˈbəʊ (US) -ˈboʊ
Lebed ˈleb.jed, -ed, -ˈ- (US) -ed
lebensraum (L) ˈleɪ.bənz.raʊm, -bəmz- (US) -bənz-
Le Bon ləˈbɒn (US) -ˈbɔːn
Lebowa ləˈbəʊ.ə (US) -ˈboʊ-
Lebrun ləˈbrɜ̃ːŋ (US) -ˈbrɜ̃n
Leburn ˈliː.bɜːn (US) -bɝːn
Lec® lek
Le Carré, le Carré ləˈkær.eɪ (US) -ˈkær.eɪ; -kɑːˈreɪ
lech letʃ **-es** -ɪz **-ing** -ɪŋ **-ed** -t
Lech lek *as if Polish:* lex
lecher ˈletʃ.əʳ (US) -ɚ **-s** -z
lecherous ˈletʃ.ər.əs **-ly** -li **-ness** -nəs, -nɪs
lechery ˈletʃ.ər.i
Lechlade ˈletʃ.leɪd
Lechmere ˈleʃ.mɪəʳ, ˈletʃ- (US) -mɪr
lecithin ˈles.ɪ.θɪn, ˈ-ə-, -θən (US) -ɪ.θɪn
Leckhampton ˈlekˌhæm*p*.tən
Leckie ˈlek.i
Lecky ˈlek.i
Leclanché ləˈklɑ̃ːn.ʃeɪ
Leconfield ˈlek.ən.fiːld
Leconte ləˈkɒnt, ləˈkɔ̃ːt, -ˈkɑːnt
Le Corbusier lə.kɔːˈbuː.zi.eɪ, -ˈbjuː- (US) -kɔːr.buːˈzjeɪ, -ziˈeɪ
lect lekt **-al** -əl
lectern ˈlek.tən, -tɜːn (US) -tɚn, -tɝːn **-s** -z
lection ˈlek.ʃən **-s** -z
lectionar|y ˈlek.ʃən.ər|.i (US) -er- **-ies** -iz
lector ˈlek.tɔːʳ (US) -tɚ, -tɔːr **-s** -z
lect|ure ˈlek.tʃ|əʳ (US) -tʃ|ɚ **-ures** -əz (US) -ɚz **-uring** -ər.ɪŋ **-ured** -əd (US) -ɚd
lecturer ˈlek.tʃər.əʳ (US) -ɚ **-s** -z
lectureship ˈlek.tʃə.ʃɪp (US) -tʃɚ- **-s** -s
led *(from* **lead***)* led
LED ˌel.iːˈdiː
Leda ˈliː.də
Ledbury ˈled.bər.i (US) ˈled.ber-
lederhosen ˈleɪ.dəˌhəʊ.zən (US) -dɚˌhoʊ-
ledg|e ledʒ **-es** -ɪz
ledger ˈledʒ.əʳ (US) -ɚ **-s** -z **ˈledger ˌline**
Ledi ˈled.i
Lediard ˈled.i.əd, -ɑːd, ˈ-jəd (US) ˈled.jɚd, ˈ-i.ɚd, -ɑːrd
Ledward ˈled.wəd (US) -wɚd
Ledyard ˈled.jəd (US) -jɚd
lee (L) liː **-s** -z
leech (L) liːtʃ **-es** -ɪz
Leeds liːdz
Lee-Enfield ˌliːˈen.fiːld
leek (L) liːk **-s** -s
leer lɪəʳ (US) lɪr **-s** -z **-ing/ly** -ɪŋ/li **-ed** -d
leer|y ˈlɪə.r|i (US) ˈlɪr|.i **-ier** -i.əʳ (US) -i.ɚ **-iest** -i.ɪst, -i.əst **-ily** -ɪ.li, -əl.i **-iness** -ɪ.nəs, -ɪ.nɪs
lees (L) liːz
leeson liː.sən
leet liːt **-s** -s
leeward ˈliː.wəd (US) -wɚd *nautical pronunciation:* ˈluː.əd, ˈljuː.əd (US) ˈluː.ɚd
Leeward *islands:* ˈliː.wəd (US) -wɚd
leeway ˈliː.weɪ
Lefanu, Le Fanu ˈlef.ə.njuː, -nuː; ləˈfɑː.nuː (US) ˈlef.ə.nuː, ləˈfɑː-
Lefevre ləˈfiː.vəʳ, -ˈfeɪ-, -ˈfɛːv.rə (US) -ˈfiː.vɚ
Note: /ləˈfiː.vəʳ (US) -vɚ/ in Sterne's 'Sentimental Journey'.
Lefroy ləˈfrɔɪ
left left ˌ**Left** ˈ**Bank** *stress shift:* ˌLeft Bank ˈartist
left|ie ˈlef.t|i **-ies** -iz
left-hand ˌleftˈhænd, ˈ--
left-hand|ed ˌleftˈhæn.d|ɪd **-edness** -ɪd.nəs, -nɪs **-er/s** -əʳ/z (US) -ɚ/z *stress shift:* ˌleft-handed ˈscissors
leftist ˈlef.tɪst **-s** -s
left-luggage office ˌleftˈlʌg.ɪdʒˌɒf.ɪs (US) -ˌɑː.fɪs
leftover ˈleftˌəʊ.vəʳ (US) -ˌoʊ.vɚ **-s** -z
leftward ˈleft.wəd (US) -wɚd **-s** -z
left-wing ˌleftˈwɪŋ **-er/s** -əʳ/z (US) -ɚ/z *stress shift:* ˌleft-wing ˈtendencies
left|y ˈlef.t|i **-ies** -iz
leg leg **-s** -z **-ging** -ɪŋ **-ged** -d ˌ**leg before** ˈ**wicket**; ˌ**leg** ˈ**bye**; **on one's** ˌ**last** ˈ**legs**; **not have a** ˌ**leg to** ˈ**stand on**
legac|y ˈleg.ə.s|i **-ies** -iz
legal ˈliː.gəl **-ly** -i ˌ**legal** ˈ**aid**; ˌ**legal** ˈ**tender**
legalese ˌliː.gəlˈiːz
legal|ism ˈliː.gəl|.ɪ.zəm **-ist/s** -ɪst/s
legalistic ˌliː.gəlˈɪs.tɪk **-ally** -əl.i, -li
legalit|y liːˈgæl.ə.t|i, lɪ-, -ɪ.t|i (US) -ə.t̬|i **-ies** -iz
legalization, -isa- ˌliː.gəl.aɪˈzeɪ.ʃən, -ɪˈ- (US) -ɪˈ-
legaliz|e, -is|e ˈliː.gəl.aɪz **-es** -ɪz **-ing** -ɪŋ **-ed** -d
legal-size ˈliː.gəlˌsaɪz
legate ˈleg.ət, -ɪt, -eɪt (US) -ɪt **-s** -s
legatee ˌleg.əˈtiː **-s** -z
legation lɪˈgeɪ.ʃən, lə-, legˈeɪ- (US) lɪˈgeɪ- **-s** -z
legatissimo ˌleg.ɑːˈtɪs.ɪ.məʊ, -əˈ- (US) -ɪ.moʊ
legato lɪˈgɑː.təʊ, lə-, legˈɑː- (US) -toʊ **-s** -z
legend ˈledʒ.ənd **-s** -z
legendary ˈledʒ.ən.dər.i, -ɪn- (US) -der-
Leger ˈledʒ.əʳ (US) -ɚ
Léger leɪˈʒeɪ
legerdemain ˌledʒ.ə.dəˈmeɪn *as if French:* ˌleʒ.ə.dəˈmæ̃ŋ (US) ˌ-ɚ-
Leggatt ˈleg.ət
Legge leg
-legged -ˈleg.ɪd, -ˈlegd
Note: Suffix. Normally carries primary stress on the penultimate syllable, e.g. **three-legged** /ˌθriːˈleg.ɪd/, but when a strong stress follows closely it undergoes stress shift, e.g. ˈ**three-legged** ˌ**stool**. However, the phrase "three-legged race" is usually ˈ**three-**ˌ**legged** ˈ**race**.
Leggett ˈleg.ɪt, -ət
Leggetter ˈleg.ɪ.təʳ, ˈ-ə- (US) -t̬ɚ
legging ˈleg.ɪŋ **-s** -z
leggy ˈleg.i
Legh liː
leghorn *fowl:* legˈɔːn, lɪˈgɔːn; ˈleg.ɔːn, ˈlɪg- (US) ˈleg.hɔːrn, -ɚn **-s** -z
leghorn *straw hat:* ˈleg.hɔːn; legˈɔːn, lɪˈgɔːn, lə- (US) ˈleg.hɔːrn, -ɚn **-s** -z
Leghorn *place:* ˈleg.hɔːn, -ˈ- (US) -hɔːrn, ˌ-ˈ-
legibility ˌledʒ.əˈbɪl.ə.ti, -ɪˈ-, -ɪ.ti (US) -ə.t̬i
legib|le ˈledʒ.ə.b|l̩, ˈ-ɪ- **-ly** -li **-leness** -l̩.nəs, -nɪs

legion (L) ˈliː.dʒən **-s** -z ˌ**Legion of ˈHonour**

legionar|y ˈliː.dʒə.nᵊr|.i (US) -er- **-ies** -iz

legionnaire (L) ˌliː.dʒəˈneəʳ (US) -ˈner **-s** -z **Legionˈnaire's diˌsease**

legi|slate ˈledʒ.ɪ|.sleɪt, ˈ-ə- **-slates** -sleɪts **-slating** -sleɪ.tɪŋ (US) -sleɪ.t̬ɪŋ **-slated** -sleɪ.tɪd (US) -sleɪ.t̬ɪd

legislation ˌledʒ.ɪˈsleɪ.ʃᵊn, -əˈ-

legislative ˈledʒ.ɪ.slə.tɪv, ˈ-ə-, -sleɪ- (US) -sleɪ.t̬ɪv

legislator ˈledʒ.ɪ.sleɪ.təʳ, ˈ-ə- (US) -t̬ɚ **-s** -z

legislature ˈledʒ.ɪ.slə.tʃəʳ, -sleɪ-, -tjʊəʳ, -tʃʊəʳ (US) -sleɪ.tʃɚ **-s** -z

legit ləˈdʒɪt, lɪ-

legitimacy lɪˈdʒɪt.ə.mə.si, lə-, ˈ-ɪ- (US) ləˈdʒɪt̬.ə-

legitimate *(adj.)* lɪˈdʒɪt.ə.mət, lə-, ˈ-ɪ-, -mɪt (US) ləˈdʒɪt̬.ə- **-ly** -li **-ness** -nəs, -nɪs

legiti|mate *(v.)* lɪˈdʒɪt.ə|.meɪt, lə-, ˈ-ɪ- (US) ləˈdʒɪt̬.ə- **-mates** -meɪts **-mating** -meɪ.tɪŋ (US) -meɪ.t̬ɪŋ **-mated** -meɪ.tɪd (US) -meɪ.t̬ɪd

legitimation lɪˌdʒɪt.əˈmeɪ.ʃᵊn, lə-, -ɪˈ- (US) ləˌdʒɪt̬.əˈ-

legitimatiz|e, -is|e lɪˈdʒɪt.ə.mə.taɪz, lə-, ˈ-ɪ- (US) ləˈdʒɪt̬.ə- **-es** -ɪz **-ing** -ɪŋ **-ed** -d

legitimist lɪˈdʒɪt.ə.mɪst, lə-, ˈ-ɪ- (US) ləˈdʒɪt̬.ə- **-s** -s

legitimiz|e, -is|e lɪˈdʒɪt.ə.maɪz, lə-, ˈ-ɪ- (US) ləˈdʒɪt̬.ə- **-es** -ɪz **-ing** -ɪŋ **-ed** -d

legless ˈleg.ləs, -lɪs

Lego® ˈleg.əʊ (US) -oʊ

Legoland® ˈleg.əʊ.lænd (US) -oʊ-

leg-pull ˈleg.pʊl **-s** -z **-ing** -ɪŋ **-ed** -d

Legree lɪˈgriː, lə-

legroom ˈleg.rʊm, -ruːm (US) -ruːm, -rʊm

Legros ləˈgrəʊ (US) -ˈgroʊ

legume ˈleg.juːm; lɪˈgjuːm, lə- **-s** -z

leguminous lɪˈgjuː.mɪ.nəs, lə-, legˈjuː-, -mə- (US) ləˈgjuː-

leg-warmer ˈlegˌwɔː.məʳ (US) -ˌwɔːr.mɚ **-s** -z

legwork ˈleg.wɜːk (US) -wɝːk

Lehar, Lehàr leɪˈhɑːʳ, lɪ-, lə-; ˈleɪ.hɑːʳ (US) ˈleɪ.hɑːr

Le Havre ləˈhɑː.vrə, -vəʳ (US) -ˈhɑː.vrə, -vɚ

Lehigh ˈliː.haɪ

Lehman(n) ˈleɪ.mən, ˈliː-

lehr lɪəʳ, leəʳ (US) lɪr, ler **-s** -z

lei ˈleɪ.iː **-s** -z

lei *(plur. of* **leu***)* leɪ

Leibni(t)z ˈlaɪb.nɪts, ˈliːb-

Leica® ˈlaɪ.kə

Leicester ˈles.təʳ (US) -tɚ **-shire** -ʃəʳ, -ˌʃɪəʳ (US) -ʃɚ, -ˌʃɪr

Leics. *(abbrev. for* **Leicestershire***)* ˈles.tə.ʃəʳ, -ˌʃɪəʳ (US) -ʃɚ, -ˌʃɪr

Leiden ˈlaɪ.dᵊn, ˈleɪ- (US) ˈlaɪ-

Leigh *surname:* liː *place name:* liː, laɪ

Leighton ˈleɪ.tᵊn

Leila ˈliː.lə, ˈleɪ-

Leinster *Irish province:* ˈlent.stəʳ (US) -stɚ *Duke of:* ˈlɪnt.stəʳ (US) -stɚ *square in London:* ˈlent.stəʳ, ˈlɪnt- (US) -stɚ

Leipzig ˈlaɪp.sɪg, -sɪk

Leishman ˈliːʃ.mən, ˈlɪʃ-

leishmania ˌliːʃˈmeɪ.ni.ə

leishmaniasis ˌliː.ʃ.məˈnaɪ.ə.sɪs

leishmaniosis ˌleɪʃ.mə.niˈəʊ.sɪs, -meɪ- (US) -meɪ.niˈoʊ-

leister ˈliː.stəʳ (US) -stɚ **-s** -z

Leister ˈles.təʳ (US) -tɚ

Leiston ˈleɪ.stᵊn

leisure ˈleʒ.əʳ (US) ˈliː.ʒɚ, ˈleʒ.ɚ **-d** -d **-ly** -li **-liness** -lɪ.nəs, -nɪs

Leith liːθ

leitmotif, leitmotiv ˈlaɪt.məʊˌtiːf, -ˌməʊ.tɪv (US) -moʊˌtiːf **-s** -s, -z (US) -s

Leitrim ˈliː.trɪm

Leix liːʃ

lek lek **-s** -s **-king** -ɪŋ **-ked** -t

lekker ˈlek.əʳ (US) -ɚ

Leland ˈliː.lənd

Lelean ləˈliːn

Lely ˈliː.li, ˈlɪl.i

leman ˈlem.ən, ˈliː.mən **-s** -z

Leman *lake:* ˈlem.ən, ˈliː.mən; lɪˈmæn, ləˈmæn, ləˈmɑ̃ːŋ (US) ˈliː.mən; ləˈmæn *surname:* ˈle.mən, ˈliː.mən *street in London:* ˈlem.ən *formerly:* ˈlɪm.æn

Le Mans ləˈmɑ̃ːŋ (US) -ˈmɑːn, -ˈmɑ̃ːn

Le Marchant ləˈmɑː.tʃᵊnt (US) -ˈmɑːr-

Lemare ləˈmeəʳ (US) -ˈmer

Lemberg ˈlem.bɜːg (US) -bɝːg

Lemesurier, Le Mesurier ləˈmeʒ.ᵊr.əʳ; lə.məˈʒʊə.ri.eɪ (US) ləˈmeʒ.ɚ.ɚ; lə.məˈʒʊr.i.eɪ

lemma ˈlem.ə **-s** -z

lemmatization, -isa- ˌlem.ə.taɪˈzeɪ.ʃᵊn, -tɪˈ- (US) -t̬ɪˈ-

lemmatiz|e, -is|e ˈlem.ə.taɪz **-es** -ɪz **-ing** -ɪŋ **-ed** -d **-er/s** -əʳ/z (US) -ɚ/z

lemme ˈlem.i

lemming ˈlem.ɪŋ **-s** -z

Lemmon ˈlem.ən

lemnis|cus lemˈnɪs|.kəs **-ci** -aɪ, -kaɪ, -iː, -kiː (US) -aɪ, -kaɪ

Lemnos ˈlem.nɒs (US) -nɑːs, -noʊs

Lemoine ləˈmɔɪn

lemon (L) ˈlem.ən **-s** -z ˈ**lemon ˌgrass;** ˈ**lemon ˌjuice;** ˌ**lemon ˈsole;** ˌ**lemon ˈsquash;** ˌ**lemon meˌringue ˈpie**

lemonade ˌlem.əˈneɪd **-s** -z

Le Morte D'Arthur ləˌmɔːtˈdɑː.θəʳ (US) -ˌmɔːrtˈdɑːr.θɚ

lempira lemˈpɪə.rə (US) -ˈpɪr.ə **-s** -z

Lempriere ˈlem.pri.eəʳ (US) -er

Lemsip® ˈlem.sɪp

Lemuel ˈlem.juəl, -ju.əl (US) -ju.əl, -jʊl

lemur ˈliː.məʳ (US) -mɚ **-s** -z

Len len

Lena *first name:* ˈliː.nə *Siberian river:* ˈleɪ.nə

lend lend **-s** -z **-ing** -ɪŋ **lent** lent **lender/s** ˈlen.dəʳ/z (US) -dɚ/z ˈ**lending ˌlibrary**

lenes *(plur. of* **lenis***)* ˈliː.neɪz, ˈleɪ- (US) ˈliː.niːz, ˈleɪ-

length leŋkθ **-s** -s

lengthen ˈleŋk.θən **-s** -z **-ing** -ɪŋ, ˈleŋkθ.nɪŋ **-ed** -d

length|man ˈleŋkθ|.mən **-men** -mən

lengthways ˈleŋkθ.weɪz

lengthwise ˈleŋkθ.waɪz

length|y ˈleŋk.θ|i **-ier** -i.əʳ (US) -i.ɚ **-iest** -i.ɪst, -i.əst **-ily** -ɪ.li, -ᵊl.i **-iness** -ɪ.nəs, -ɪ.nɪs

lenien|ce ˈliː.ni.ənt|s **-cy** -si

lenient ˈliː.ni.ənt **-ly** -li

Lenin ˈlen.ɪn **-ism** -ɪ.zᵊm **-ist/s** -ɪst/s **-ite/s** -aɪt/s

Leningrad ˈlen.ɪn.græd, -ɪŋ-, -grɑːd (US) -græd

lenis ˈliː.nɪs, ˈleɪ- (US) ˈliː.nɪs, ˈleɪ- **lenes** ˈliː.niːz, ˈleɪ-, -neɪz

lenition lɪˈnɪʃ.ᵊn, lə-

lenitive ˈlen.ɪ.tɪv (US) -ə.t̬ɪv **-s** -z

lenity ˈlen.ə.ti, ˈliː.nə-, -nɪ- (US) ˈlen.ə.t̬i

Lennie ˈlen.i

Lennon ˈlen.ən

Lennox ˈlen.əks

Lenny ˈlen.i

leno ˈliː.nəʊ (US) -noʊ ˈlen.əʊ, ˈliː.nəʊ (US) ˈlen.oʊ, ˈliː.noʊ

Lenoir *surname:* ləˈnwɑːʳ (US) -ˈnwɑːr *town in US:* ləˈnɔːʳ (US) -ˈnɔːr

Lenor® lɪˈnɔːʳ, lə- (US) -ˈnɔːr

Lenore lɪˈnɔːʳ, lə- (US) -ˈnɔːr

Lenox ˈlen.əks

lens lenz **-es** -ɪz

lent *(from* **lend***)* lent

Lent lent **-en** -ən

Lenthall *surname:* ˈlen.tɔːl *place in Yorkshire:* ˈlen.θɔːl, -θᵊl

Lenthéric®, Lentheric ˈlɒnt.θᵊr.ɪk, ˈlɑ̃ːn- (US) ˈlɑːnt-

lenticel ˈlen.tɪ.sel (US) -t̬ɪ- **-s** -z

lenticular lenˈtɪk.jə.ləʳ, -jʊ- (US) -jə.lɚ

lentil ˈlen.tᵊl, -tɪl (US) -t̬ᵊl **-s** -z

lentivirus ˈlen.tɪ.vaɪə.rəs (US) -t̬ɪ.vaɪ- **-es** -ɪz

lento ˈlen.təʊ (US) -toʊ

Lenton ˈlen.tən

Lentulus ˈlen.tjə.ləs, -tjʊ- (US) -tuː-, -tə-

Lenz lents

Leo ˈliː.əʊ (US) -oʊ

Leofric ˈleɪ.əʊ.frɪk, ˈlef.rɪk (US) leɪˈɑː.frɪk, -ˈoʊ-

Leominster *place in Britain:* ˈlemp.stəʳ (US) -stɚ *place in US:* ˈlem.ɪnt.stəʳ (US) -stɚ

Length

A term used in phonetics to refer to a subjective impression of how much time a sound takes; it is distinct from physically measurable 'duration'. Usually, however, the term is used as synonymous with duration.

Examples for English

Length is important in many ways in speech: in English and most other languages, stressed syllables tend to be longer than unstressed (see RHYTHM, STRESS and WEAK FORM). Some languages have phonemic differences between long and short sounds, and BBC English is claimed by some writers to be of this type, contrasting short vowels /ɪ e æ ʌ ɒ ʊ ə/ with long vowels /iː ɜː ɑː ɔː uː/ (though other, equally valid analyses have been put forward). However, the context in which these sounds occur must be taken into account. For example, the vowel /iː/ is said to be longer than /ɪ/ as well as having a different quality, but the vowel in *beat* is unlikely to be longer than the vowel in *bid* as the phonetic environment in *beat* causes the vowel to be shorter.

In other languages

When languages have long/short consonant differences, as does Arabic, for example, it is usual to treat the long consonants as **geminate**; it is odd that this is not done equally regularly in the case of vowels. Perhaps the most interesting example of length differences comes from Estonian, which has traditionally been said to have a three-way distinction between short, long and extra-long consonants and vowels.

Lenis

A lenis sound is weakly articulated (the word comes from Latin, where it means 'smooth, gentle'). The opposite term is FORTIS.

Examples for English

In general, the term lenis is used of voiced consonants (which are supposed to be less strongly articulated than their corresponding voiceless ones), and is resorted to for languages such as German, Russian and English where voiced PHONEMES like /b d g/ are not always voiced. (See the entry at FORTIS for examples.) However, it is claimed that the language which most clearly shows a distinction between fortis and lenis consonants is Korean.

Leon 'liː.ɒn, 'leɪ-, -ən US -ɑːn

León leɪ'ɒn US -'oʊn

Leonard 'len.əd US -ɚd **-s** -z

Leonardo ˌliː.ə'nɑː.dəʊ, ˌleɪ- US ˌliː.ə'nɑːr.doʊ **-s** -z

leone (L) li'əʊ.ni US -'oʊ- **-s** -z

Leonid 'liː.əʊ.nɪd, 'leɪ- US '-ə- **-s** -z

Leonidas li'ɒn.ɪ.dæs, '-ə- US -'ɑː.nə.dəs

Leonie li'əʊ.ni US -'oʊ-

leonine 'liː.əʊ.naɪn US '-ə-

Leonora ˌliː.ə'nɔː.rə US -'nɔːr.ə

Leontes li'ɒn.tiːz, leɪ- US li'ɑːn-

leopard 'lep.əd US -ɚd **-s** -z **-ess/es** -es/ɪz, -ɪs/ɪz, -əs/ɪz

Leopardstown 'lep.ədz.taʊn US -ɚrdz-

Leopold 'liː.ə.pəʊld, 'lɪə.pəʊld US 'liː.ə.poʊld

leotard 'liː.ə.tɑːd US -tɑːrd **-s** -z

Lepanto lɪ'pæn.təʊ, lə- US lɪ'pæn.toʊ, -'pɑːn-

leper 'lep.əʳ US -ɚ **-s** -z

lepidopter|an ˌlep.ɪ'dɒp.tᵊr|.ən US -'dɑːp- **-ans** -ənz **-a** -ə

lepidopterist ˌlep.ɪ'dɒp.tᵊr.ɪst US -'dɑːp- **-s** -s

lepidopterology ˌlep.ɪˌdɒp.tᵊr'ɒl.ə.dʒi US -ˌdɑːp.tə'rɑː.lə-

lepidopter|on ˌlep.ɪ'dɒp.tᵊr|.ən US -'dɑːp- **-ons** -ənz **-a** -ə

Lepidus 'lep.ɪ.dəs

Le Play lə'pleɪ

leprechaun 'lep.rə.kɔːn, -rɪ-, -hɔːn US -rə.kɑːn, -kɔːn **-s** -z

leprosy 'lep.rə.si

leprous 'lep.rəs **-ly** -li **-ness** -nəs, -nɪs

Lepsius 'lep.si.əs

lept|on 'lep.t|ɒn, -t|ən US -t|ɑːn **-a** -ə

Lepus 'liː.pəs, 'lep.əs US 'liː.pəs

Lermontov 'leə.mɒn.tɒf, -mən-, -təf US 'ler.mɑːn.tɔːf

Lerner 'lɜː.nəʳ US 'lɝː.nɚ

Leroy 'liː.rɔɪ, lə'rɔɪ

Lerwick 'lɜː.wɪk US 'lɝː-

les *in French phrases:* leɪ, leɪz

Note: The form /leɪz/ only occurs when the following word begins with a vowel.

Les *first name:* lez US les

Lesbi|a 'lez.bi|.ə **-an** -ən

lesbian 'lez.bi.ən **-s** -z **-ism** -ɪ.zᵊm

Lesbos 'lez.bɒs US -bɑːs, -boʊs

lèse-majesté, lese-majesty ˌleɪz'mædʒ.ə.steɪ, ˌliːz-, '-ɪ-, -sti US ˌliːzˌmæʒ.es'teɪ; -'mædʒ.ɪ.sti

lesion 'liː.ʒᵊn **-s** -z

Leskovac 'les.kəʊ.vɑːts, -væts US -kɔː-

Leslie, Lesley 'lez.li US 'les-, 'lez-

Lesmahagow ˌles.mə'heɪ.gəʊ US -goʊ

Lesotho lə'suː.tuː, lɪ-, leɪ-, -'səʊ-, -təʊ US lə'soʊ.toʊ, -'suː.tuː

less les **-er** -əʳ US -ɚ

lessee les'iː **-s** -z

lessen 'les.ᵊn **-s** -z **-ing** -ɪŋ, 'les.nɪŋ **-ed** -d

Lesseps 'les.əps, -eps; les'eps US 'les.əps

Lessing 'les.ɪŋ

lesson 'les.ᵊn **-s** -z ˌ**learn one's** '**lesson**

lessor les'ɔːʳ, '-- US 'les.ɔːr, -'- **-s** -z

lest lest

Lester 'les.təʳ US -tɚ

L'Estrange lə'streɪndʒ, lɪ-

Le Sueur lə'suː.əʳ US -'sʊr

let let **-s** -s **-ting** -ɪŋ US 'leţ.ɪŋ

letch letʃ **-es** -ɪz **-ing** -ɪŋ **-ed** -t

Letchworth 'letʃ.wəθ, -wɜːθ US -wɚθ, -wɝːθ

letdown 'let.daʊn **-s** -z

lethal 'liː.θᵊl **-ly** -i

lethargic lə'θɑː.dʒɪk, lɪ-, leθ'ɑː- ⓊⓈ lɪ'θɑːr-, lə- **-ally** -əl.i, -li
lethargy 'leθ.ə.dʒi ⓊⓈ '-ɚ-
Lethe 'liː.θi, -θiː
Letheby 'leθ.ə.bi
Lethem 'leθ.əm
Letitia lɪ'tɪʃ.i.ə, liː-, lə-, -'tiː.ʃi-, '-ʃə ⓊⓈ lə'tɪʃ.ə, -'tiː.ʃə
Letraset® 'let.rə.set
Lett let **-s** -s
lett|er 'let|.əʳ ⓊⓈ 'leţ|.ɚ **-ers** -əz ⓊⓈ -ɚz **-ering** -ər.ɪŋ **-ered** -əd ⓊⓈ -ɚd **'letter ˌbomb; 'letter ˌbox; 'letter ˌcarrier; 'letter ˌopener**
letterhead 'let.ə.hed ⓊⓈ 'leţ.ɚ- **-s** -z
Letterman 'let.ə.mən ⓊⓈ 'leţ.ɚ-
letter-perfect ˌlet.ə'pɜː.fɪkt, -fekt ⓊⓈ ˌleţ.ɚ'pɝː.fɪkt
letterpress 'let.ə.pres ⓊⓈ 'leţ.ɚ-
letter-quality 'let.əˌkwɒl.ə.ti, -ɪ.ti ⓊⓈ 'leţ.ɚˌkwɑː.lə.ţi
letter-size 'let.ə.saɪz ⓊⓈ 'leţ.ɚ-
Lettice 'let.ɪs ⓊⓈ 'leţ-
Lettish 'let.ɪʃ ⓊⓈ 'leţ-
lettuc|e 'let.ɪs, -əs ⓊⓈ 'leţ- **-es** -ɪz
Letty 'let.i ⓊⓈ 'leţ-
letup 'let.ʌp ⓊⓈ 'leţ- **-s** -s
leu 'leɪ.uː **lei** leɪ
Leuchars *place in Scotland:* 'luː.kəz, 'ljuː-, -xəz ⓊⓈ 'luː.kɚz *surname:* 'luː.kəs, 'ljuː- ⓊⓈ 'luː.kɚs
leucine 'ljuː.siːn, 'luː-, -saɪn ⓊⓈ 'luː-
leucite 'ljuː.saɪt, 'luː- ⓊⓈ 'luː-
leucocyte 'ljuː.kəʊ.saɪt, 'luː- ⓊⓈ 'luː.koʊ-, -kə- **-s** -s
leucotom|y ljuː'kɒt.ə.m|i, luː- ⓊⓈ luː'kɑː.ţə- **-ies** -iz
Leuctra 'ljuːk.trə ⓊⓈ 'luːk-
leuk(a)emia ljuː'kiː.mi.ə, luː- ⓊⓈ luː-
lev lev ⓊⓈ lef **leva** 'lev.ə
le|vant (L) *(n.v.)* lə|'vænt, lɪ- ⓊⓈ lə- **-vants** -'vænts **-vanting** -'væn.tɪŋ ⓊⓈ -'væn.ţɪŋ **-vanted** -'væn.tɪd ⓊⓈ -'væn.ţɪd
levant *(adj.)* 'lev.ənt
levanter (L) lə'væn.təʳ, lɪ- ⓊⓈ lə'væn.ţɚ **-s** -z
Levantine 'lev.ən.taɪn, -tiːn ⓊⓈ 'lev.ən.tiːn, -taɪn; lɪ'væn-
levee *royal reception:* 'lev.i, -eɪ ⓊⓈ 'lev.i; lə'viː, -'veɪ **-s** -z
levee *embankment:* 'lev.i **-s** -z
level 'lev.əl **-s** -z **-(l)ing** -ɪŋ, 'lev.lɪŋ **-(l)ed** -d **-(l)er/s** -əʳ/z ⓊⓈ -ɚ/z **-ness** -nəs, -nɪs **-ly** -li ˌ**level 'crossing**
level-headed ˌlev.əl'hed.ɪd ⓊⓈ 'lev.əlˌhed.ɪd *stress shift, British only:* ˌlevel-headed 'person
Leven *loch:* 'liː.vən *surname:* 'lev.ən, 'liː.vən
Note: The Earl pronounces /'liː.vən/
lev|er *(n. v.)* *on machine:* 'liː.v|əʳ ⓊⓈ 'lev.|ɚ, 'liː.v|ɚ **-ers** -əz ⓊⓈ -ɚz **-ering** -ər.ɪŋ **-ered** -əd ⓊⓈ -ɚd
Lever *surname:* 'liː.vəʳ ⓊⓈ -vɚ
leverag|e 'liː.vər.ɪdʒ ⓊⓈ 'lev.ɚ-, 'liː.vɚ- **-ing** -ɪŋ **-ed** -d
leveret 'lev.ər.ɪt, -ət **-s** -s
Leverett 'lev.ər.ɪt
Leverhulme 'liː.və.hjuːm ⓊⓈ -vɚ-
Levertov 'lev.ə.tɒf ⓊⓈ -ɚ.tɑːf
Leveson 'lev.ɪ.sən
Leveson-Gower ˌluː.sən'gɔːʳ, ˌljuː-, -səŋ'- ⓊⓈ ˌluː.sən'gɔːr
Levett 'lev.ɪt
Levey 'liː.vi, 'lev.i
Levi 'liː.vaɪ, 'lev.i, 'liː.vi
leviable 'lev.i.ə.bl̩
leviathan (L) lɪ'vaɪə.θən, lə- **-s** -z
Levin 'lev.ɪn
Levine lə'viːn, -'vaɪn
levirate 'liː.vɪ.rət, 'lev.ɪ-, -rɪt ⓊⓈ 'lev.ə.rɪt, 'liː.və-, -reɪt
Levis *in Quebec:* 'lev.i
Levis *trademark, jeans brand:* 'liː.vaɪz
Lévi-Strauss ˌlev.i'straʊs ⓊⓈ ˌleɪ.vi-, ˌlev.i'-
levi|tate 'lev.ɪ|.teɪt, '-ə- **-tates** -teɪts **-tating** -teɪ.tɪŋ ⓊⓈ -teɪ.ţɪŋ **-tated** -teɪ.tɪd ⓊⓈ -teɪ.ţɪd
levitation ˌlev.ɪ'teɪ.ʃən, -ə'- **-s** -z
Levite 'liː.vaɪt **-s** -s
levitic lə'vɪt.ɪk, lɪ- ⓊⓈ lə'vɪţ- **-al** -əl **-ally** -əl.i, -li
Leviticus lə'vɪt.ɪ.kəs, lɪ- ⓊⓈ lə'vɪţ-
Levitt 'lev.ɪt
levit|y 'lev.ə.t|i, -ɪ.t|i ⓊⓈ -ə.ţ|i **-ies** -iz
lev|y *(n. v.)* 'lev|.i **-ies** -iz **-ying** -i.ɪŋ **-ied** -id **-ier/s** -i.əʳ/z ⓊⓈ -i.ɚ/z
Levy *surname:* 'liː.vi, 'lev.i
lewd ljuːd, luːd ⓊⓈ luːd **-er** -əʳ ⓊⓈ -ɚ **-est** -ɪst, -əst **-ly** -li **-ness** -nəs, -nɪs
Lewes 'luː.ɪs
Lewin 'luː.ɪn
Lewinsky lə'wɪnt.ski ⓊⓈ luː'wɪn.ski
lewis (L) 'luː.ɪs **-es** -ɪz
Lewisham 'luː.ɪ.ʃəm
Lewison 'luː.ɪ.sən
Lewsey 'ljuː.si ⓊⓈ 'luː-
lexeme 'lek.siːm **-s** -z
lexic|al 'lek.sɪ.k|əl **-ally** -əl.i, -li
lexicographic ˌlek.sɪ.kəʊ'græf.ɪk ⓊⓈ -koʊ'-, -kə'- **-al** -əl **-ally** -əl.i, -li
lexicograph|y ˌlek.sɪ'kɒg.rə.f|i ⓊⓈ -kɑː'grə- **-er/s** -əʳ/z ⓊⓈ -ɚ/z
lexicological ˌlek.sɪ.kə'lɒdʒ.ɪ.kəl ⓊⓈ -'lɑː.dʒɪ-
lexicolog|y ˌlek.sɪ'kɒl.ə.dʒ|i ⓊⓈ -'kɑː.lə- **-ist/s** -ɪst/s
lexicon 'lek.sɪ.kən, -kɒn ⓊⓈ -kɑːn, -kən **-s** -z
Lexington 'lek.sɪŋ.tən
lexis 'lek.sɪs
lex loci contractus ˌleksˌləʊ.saɪ.kɒn'træk.təs, -ˌləʊ.kiː- ⓊⓈ -ˌloʊ.saɪ.kɑːn'-, -kiː-, -siː-
lex loci delicti ˌleksˌləʊ.saɪ.del'ɪk.tiː, -ˌləʊ.kiː-, -taɪ ⓊⓈ -ˌloʊ.saɪ.də'lɪk-, -kiː-, -siː-
ley (L) leɪ, liː **'ley ˌline**
Leybourne 'leɪ.bɔːn ⓊⓈ -bɔːrn
Leyburn 'leɪ.bɜːn ⓊⓈ -bɝːn
Leyden jar ˌleɪ.dən'dʒɑːʳ ⓊⓈ 'laɪ.dənˌdʒɑːr **-s** -z
Leyland 'leɪ.lənd
Leys liːz
Leyton 'leɪ.tən
Lhasa 'lɑː.sə, 'læs.ə
li liː **-s** -z
liabilit|y ˌlaɪ.ə'bɪl.ə.t|i, -ɪ.t|i ⓊⓈ -ə.ţ|i **-ies** -iz
liable 'laɪ.ə.bl̩
liais|e li'eɪz **-es** -ɪz **-ing** -ɪŋ **-ed** -d
liaison li'eɪ.zən, -zɒn *as if French:* -zɔ̃ːŋ ⓊⓈ 'liː.ə.zɑːn; li'eɪ-, -zən **-s** -z
Note: In military use always /li'eɪ.zən ⓊⓈ -zɑːn, -zən/.
Liam 'liː.əm
liana li'ɑː.nə, -'æn.ə
liar 'laɪ.əʳ ⓊⓈ -ɚ **-s** -z
Lias 'laɪ.əs
Liassic laɪ'æs.ɪk, li-
lib lɪb ˌ**women's 'lib**
Libanus 'lɪb.ə.nəs
libation laɪ'beɪ.ʃən, lɪ- ⓊⓈ laɪ- **-s** -z
libber 'lɪb.əʳ ⓊⓈ -ɚ **-s** -z ˌ**women's 'libber**
Libby 'lɪb.i
Libdem ˌlɪb'dem **-s** -z *stress shift:* ˌLibdem 'vote
libel 'laɪ.bəl **-s** -z **-(l)ing** -ɪŋ **-(l)ed** -d **-(l)er/s** -əʳ/z ⓊⓈ -ɚ/z
libel(l)ous 'laɪ.bəl.əs **-ly** -li
Liber 'laɪ.bəʳ ⓊⓈ -bɚ
Liberace ˌlɪb.ər'ɑː.tʃi ⓊⓈ -ə'rɑː-
liberal (L) 'lɪb.ər.əl, '-rəl **-s** -z **-ly** -i
Liberal Democrat ˌlɪb.ər.əl'dem.ə.kræt, -rəl'- **-s** -s
liberalism (L) 'lɪb.ər.əl.ɪ.zəm, '-rəl-
liberality ˌlɪb.ər'æl.ə.ti, lɪ'bræl- ⓊⓈ ˌlɪb.ə'ræl-, -ɪ.ti ⓊⓈ -ə.ţi
liberalization, -isa- ˌlɪb.ər.əl.aɪ'zeɪ.ʃən, ˌ-rəl-, -ɪ'- ⓊⓈ -ɪ'-
liberaliz|e, -is|e 'lɪb.ər.əl.aɪz, '-rəl- **-es** -ɪz **-ing** -ɪŋ **-ed** -d
liber|ate 'lɪb.ər|.eɪt ⓊⓈ -ə.r|eɪt **-ates** -eɪts **-ating** -eɪ.tɪŋ ⓊⓈ -eɪ.ţɪŋ **-ated** -eɪ.tɪd ⓊⓈ -eɪ.ţɪd **-ator/s** -eɪ.təʳ/z ⓊⓈ -eɪ.ţɚ/z
liberation ˌlɪb.ər'eɪ.ʃən ⓊⓈ -ə'reɪ-
Liberi|a laɪ'bɪə.ri|.ə ⓊⓈ -'bɪr.i- **-an/s** -ən/z
libertarian ˌlɪb.ə'teə.ri.ən ⓊⓈ -ɚ'ter.i- **-s** -z **-ism** -ɪ.zəm
libertine 'lɪb.ə.tiːn, -taɪn ⓊⓈ -ɚ.tiːn, -tɪn **-s** -z
Liberton 'lɪb.ə.tən ⓊⓈ '-ɚ-

Liaison

The linking or joining together of sounds.

Examples for English

In English the best-known case of liaison is the 'linking r': there are many words in English (e.g. *car, here, tyre*) which in a RHOTIC accent such as US English or Scots would be pronounced with a final /r/, but which in BBC pronunciation end in a vowel when they are pronounced before a pause or before a consonant. When they are followed by a vowel, British English speakers pronounce /r/ at the end, e.g.:

the car stopped	/ðə kɑː stɒpt/
	US /ðə kɑːr stɑːpt/
the car is blue	/ðə kɑːr ɪz bluː/
	US /ðə kɑːr ɪz bluː/

In BBC English there is also 'intrusive r' – an /r/ inserted between two vowels at word boundaries where there is none in the spelling. This does not occur after close vowels (/iː uː/), or diphthongs which end with a close element (/eɪ aɪ ɔɪ aʊ əʊ/), e.g.:

China and Japan	tʃaɪnə r ən dʒə'pæn
	US tʃaɪnə ən dʒə'pæn
law and order	lɔː r ən 'ɔː.də
	US lɑː ən 'ɔːr.dɚ

It is said that liaison is done to link the words without sliding the two vowels together though many languages do run vowels together.

Another aspect of liaison in English is the movement of a single consonant at the end of an unstressed word to the beginning of the next if that is strongly stressed. A well-known example in British English is *none at all*, where the /t/ of *at* becomes initial (and therefore strongly aspirated) in the final syllable for many speakers.

libert|y (L) 'lɪb.ə.t|i US -ɚ.ţ|i **-ies** -iz ˌ**Liberty 'Island**
libidinous lɪ'bɪd.ɪ.nəs, lə-, -ən.əs US lə'bɪd.ən.əs **-ly** -li **-ness** -nəs, -nɪs
libido lɪ'biː.dəʊ, lə- US -doʊ **-s** -z
libr|a *pound:* 'liː.br|ə, 'laɪ- US 'liː- **-ae** -iː, -eɪ, -aɪ
Libr|a *constellation:* 'liː.br|ə, 'lɪb.r|ə, 'laɪ.br|ə US 'liː-, 'laɪ- **-an/s** -ən/z
librarian laɪ'breə.ri.ən US -'brer.i- **-s** -z **-ship** -ʃɪp
librar|y 'laɪ.brər|.i, -br|i US -brer|.i **-ies** -iz
libration laɪ'breɪ.ʃən **-s** -z
librettist lɪ'bret.ɪst, lə- US lɪ'breţ- **-s** -s
librett|o lɪ'bret|.əʊ, lə- US lɪ'breţ|.oʊ **-os** -əʊz US -oʊz **-i** -iː
Libreville 'liː.brə.vɪl US -viːl, -vɪl
Librium® 'lɪb.ri.əm
Liby|a 'lɪb.i|.ə **-an/s** -ən/z
lice *(plur. of* **louse***)* laɪs
licenc|e 'laɪ.sənts **-es** -ɪz **-ed** -t
licens|e 'laɪ.sənts **-es** -ɪz **-ing** -ɪŋ **-ed** -t **-er/s** -ər/z US -ɚ/z **-or/s** -ər/z US -ɚ/z **'license ˌplate**
licensee ˌlaɪ.sənt'siː **-s** -z
licentiate laɪ'sen.tʃi.ət, lɪ-, -tʃət, -tʃi.ɪt US -ʃi.ɪt, -ʃi.eɪt, -ʃət **-s** -s
licentious laɪ'sen.tʃəs **-ly** -li **-ness** -nəs, -nɪs
lichee ˌlaɪ'tʃiː; 'laɪ.tʃiː, 'liː- US 'liː.tʃiː **-s** -z
lichen 'laɪ.kən, -kɪn, 'lɪtʃ.ən, -ɪn US 'laɪ.kən **-s** -z **-ed** -d
lichenous 'laɪ.kə.nəs, -kɪ-, 'lɪtʃ.ə-, '-ɪ- US 'laɪ.kə-
Lichfield 'lɪtʃ.fiːld
lichgate 'lɪtʃ.geɪt **-s** -s
Lichtenstein 'lɪx.tən.staɪn, 'lɪk- US lɪk-
Licini|an laɪ'sɪn.i|.ən, lɪ- **-us** -əs
licit 'lɪs.ɪt **-ly** -li **-ness** -nəs, -nɪs
lick lɪk **-s** -s **-ing/s** -ɪŋ/z **-ed** -t
lickety-split ˌlɪk.ə.ti'splɪt, ˌ-ɪ- US -ə.ţi'-
licorice 'lɪk.ər.ɪs, -ɪʃ, 'lɪk.rɪs, -rɪʃ US 'lɪk.ɚ.ɪʃ, '-rɪʃ, 'lɪk.ɚ.ɪs
lictor 'lɪk.tər, -tɔːr US -tɚ **-s** -z
lid lɪd **-s** -z **-ded** -ɪd
Liddell 'lɪd.əl, lɪ'del
Liddesdale 'lɪdz.deɪl
Liddiment 'lɪd.ɪ.mənt
Liddle 'lɪd.l̩
Liddon 'lɪd.ən
Lidell lɪ'del
Lidgate 'lɪd.geɪt, -gɪt
lido (L) 'liː.dəʊ, 'laɪ- US 'liː.doʊ **-s** -z
lie *(n. v.) falsehood:* laɪ **-s** -z **lying/ly** 'laɪ.ɪŋ/li **lied** laɪd ˌ**lie through one's 'teeth**
lie *(v.) recline:* laɪ **-s** -z **lying** 'laɪ.ɪŋ **lay** leɪ **lain** leɪn
lie-abed 'laɪ.ə.bed **-s** -z
Lieberman 'liː.bə.mən US -bɚ-
liebfraumilch (L) 'liːb.fraʊ.mɪltʃ *as if German:* -mɪlx US -mɪlk, 'liːp-
Liebig 'liː.bɪg *as if German:* -bɪx US -bɪg *as if German:* bɪx
Liebknecht 'liːb.knekt *as if German:* -knext
Liechtenstein 'lɪk.tən.staɪn *as if German:* 'lɪx-
lied *German song:* liːd *as if German:* liːt **lieder** 'liː.dər US -dɚ
lief liːf **-er** -ər US -ɚ
lieg|e liːdʒ **-es** -ɪz
Liège li'eɪʒ, -'eʒ
lie-in ˌlaɪ'ɪn, '-- **-s** -z
lien 'liː.ən, liːn US liːn, 'liː.ən **-s** -z
Liepaja lɪ'pɑː.jə US li'ep.ə-, lɪ'pɑː-
lieu ljuː, luː US luː
lieutenanc|y lef'ten.ənt.s|i, ləf- US luː- **-ies** -iz
lieutenant lef'ten.ənt, ləf- US luː- **-s** -s **lieuˌtenant 'colonel; lieuˌtenant com'mander; lieuˌtenant 'general; lieuˌtenant 'governor**
li|fe laɪ|f **-ves** -vz **'life ˌcycle; 'life exˌpectancy; 'life inˌsurance; ˌlife 'savings; ˌlife 'sentence**
life-and-death ˌlaɪf.ən'deθ *stress shift:* ˌlife-and-death 'issue
lifebelt 'laɪf.belt **-s** -s
lifeblood 'laɪf.blʌd
lifeboat 'laɪf.bəʊt US -boʊt **-s** -s
life-buoy 'laɪf.bɔɪ US -bɔɪ, -ˌbuː.i **-s** -z
life-giving 'laɪfˌgɪv.ɪŋ
lifeguard 'laɪf.gɑːd US -gɑːrd **-s** -z
lifejacket 'laɪfˌdʒæk.ɪt **-s** -s
lifeless 'laɪf.ləs, -lɪs **-ly** -li **-ness** -nəs, -nɪs
lifelike 'laɪf.laɪk
lifeline 'laɪf.laɪn **-s** -z
lifelong ˌlaɪf'lɒŋ US ˌlaɪf'lɑːŋ, -'lɔːŋ *stress shift:* ˌlifelong 'dream
life of Riley ˌlaɪf.əv'raɪ.li
life-or-death ˌlaɪf.ɔː'deθ US -ɔːr'- *stress shift:* ˌlife-or-death 'issue
life-preserver 'laɪf.prɪˌzɜː.vər, -prəˌ- US -priːˌzɝː.vɚ, -prɪˌ- **-s** -z
lifer 'laɪ.fər US -fɚ **-s** -z
lifesaver 'laɪfˌseɪ.vər US -vɚ **-s** -z
life-saving 'laɪfˌseɪ.vɪŋ *stress shift:* ˌlife-saving 'medicine
life-size 'laɪf.saɪz, ˌ-'-
lifespan 'laɪf.spæn **-s** -z
lifestyle 'laɪf.staɪl **-s** -z

life-support 'laɪf.sə,pɔːt, ,--'- ⓤⓢ 'laɪf.sə,pɔːrt **,life-sup'port ,system, 'life-sup,port ,system** ⓤⓢ **'life-sup,port ,system**
life-threatening 'laɪf,θret.ᵊn.ɪŋ
lifetime 'laɪf.taɪm **-s** -z
lifework ,laɪf'wɜːk, '-- ⓤⓢ ,laɪf'wɝːk, '-- **-s** -s
Liffe laɪf
Liffey 'lɪf.i
Lifford 'lɪf.əd ⓤⓢ -ɚd
lift lɪft **-s** -s **-ing** -ɪŋ **-ed** -ɪd **-er/s** -əʳ/z ⓤⓢ -ɚ/z
lift-off 'lɪft.ɒf ⓤⓢ -ɑːf
ligament 'lɪg.ə.mənt **-s** -s
ligament|al ,lɪg.ə'men.t|ᵊl ⓤⓢ -t̬|ᵊl **-ous** -əs
ligature 'lɪg.ə.tʃəʳ, -tjʊəʳ, -tʃʊəʳ ⓤⓢ -tʃɚ **-s** -z **-d** -d
liger 'laɪ.gəʳ ⓤⓢ -gɚ **-s** -z
Ligeti 'lɪg.et.i
Liggett 'lɪg.ɪt, -ət
light laɪt **-s** -s **-er** -əʳ ⓤⓢ 'laɪ.t̬ɚ **-est** -ɪst, -əst ⓤⓢ 'laɪ.t̬ɪst, -t̬əst **-ly** -li **-ness** -nəs, -nɪs **-ing** -ɪŋ ⓤⓢ 'laɪ.t̬ɪŋ **-ed** -ɪd ⓤⓢ 'laɪ.t̬ɪd **lit** lɪt **,light 'aircraft; 'light ,bulb; 'light ,meter**
lighten 'laɪ.tᵊn **-s** -z **-ing** -ɪŋ, 'laɪt.nɪŋ **-ed** -d
lighter 'laɪ.təʳ ⓤⓢ -t̬ɚ **-s** -z
lighterage 'laɪ.tᵊr.ɪdʒ ⓤⓢ -t̬ɚ-
light-fingered ,laɪt'fɪŋ.gəd ⓤⓢ -gɚd *stress shift:* ,light-fingered 'thief
lightfoot (L) 'laɪt.fʊt
light-headed ,laɪt'hed.ɪd **-ly** -li **-ness** -nəs, -nɪs *stress shift:* ,light-headed 'daze
light-hearted ,laɪt'hɑː.tɪd ⓤⓢ -'hɑːr.t̬ɪd **-ly** -li **-ness** -nəs, -nɪs *stress shift:* ,light-hearted 'comment
lighthou|se 'laɪt.haʊ|s **-ses** -zɪz
lighthousekeeper 'laɪt.haʊs,kiː.pəʳ ⓤⓢ -pɚ **-s** -z
lighting-up time ,laɪ.tɪŋ'ʌp,taɪm ⓤⓢ -t̬ɪŋ'-
lightning 'laɪt.nɪŋ **-s** -z
lightning-conductor 'laɪt.nɪŋ.kən,dʌk.təʳ ⓤⓢ -t̬ɚ **-s** -z
lightship 'laɪt.ʃɪp **-s** -s
lightweight 'laɪt.weɪt **-s** -s
light-year 'laɪt.jɪəʳ ⓤⓢ -jɪr **-s** -z
ligneous 'lɪg.ni.əs
lignite 'lɪg.naɪt
lignum 'lɪg.nəm
Liguri|a lɪg'jʊə.ri|.ə, -'jɔː- ⓤⓢ -'jʊr.i- **-an/s** -ən/z
likable 'laɪ.kə.bl̩ **-ness** -nəs, -nɪs
lik|e laɪk **-es** -s **-ing** -ɪŋ **-ed** -t
likeable 'laɪ.kə.bl̩ **-ness** -nəs, -nɪs
likelihood 'laɪ.kli.hʊd
likel|y 'laɪ.kl|i **-ier** -i.əʳ ⓤⓢ -i.ɚ **-iest** -i.ɪst, -i.əst **-iness** -ɪ.nəs, -ɪ.nɪs
likeminded ,laɪk'maɪn.dɪd ⓤⓢ '-,--, ,-'-- *stress shift, British only:* ,likeminded 'friend
liken 'laɪ.kᵊn **-s** -z **-ing** -ɪŋ **-ed** -d
likeness 'laɪk.nəs, -nɪs **-es** -ɪz
likewise 'laɪk.waɪz
liking 'laɪ.kɪŋ **-s** -z
Likud lɪ'kʊd, -'kuːd ⓤⓢ -'kuːd
likuta liː'kuː.tɑː
lilac 'laɪ.lək ⓤⓢ -lək, -læk, -lɑːk **-s** -s
liliaceous ,lɪl.i'eɪ.ʃəs
Lilian 'lɪl.i.ən
Lilias 'lɪl.i.əs
Liliburlero ,lɪl.i.bə'leə.rəʊ ⓤⓢ -bɚ'ler.oʊ
Lilith 'lɪl.ɪθ
Lilla 'lɪl.ə
Lille liːl
Lillehammer 'lɪl.ɪ.hæm.əʳ, -ə,- ⓤⓢ -ə.hɑː.mɚ, -hæm.ɚ
Lil-lets® lɪ'lets
Lilley 'lɪl.i
Lillian 'lɪl.i.ən
Lilliput 'lɪl.ɪ.pʌt, '-ə-, -pʊt, -pət ⓤⓢ -ə.pʌt, -pət, -pʊt
lilliputian (L) ,lɪl.ɪ'pjuː.ʃᵊn, -ə'-, -ʃi.ən ⓤⓢ -ə'pjuː.ʃᵊn **-s** -z
Lilly 'lɪl.i
Lillywhite 'lɪl.i.*h*waɪt
Lilo® 'laɪ.ləʊ ⓤⓢ -loʊ **-s** -z
Lilongwe lɪ'lɒŋ.weɪ ⓤⓢ -'lɔːŋ-, -'lɑːŋ-
lilt lɪlt **-s** -s **-ing** -ɪŋ ⓤⓢ 'lɪl.t̬ɪŋ **-ed** -ɪd ⓤⓢ 'lɪl.t̬ɪd
lil|y (L) 'lɪl|.i **-ies** -iz **,lily of the 'valley**
lily-livered ,lɪl.i'lɪv.əd ⓤⓢ -ɚd *stress shift:* ,lily-livered 'scoundrel
lily-white ,lɪl.i'*h*waɪt *stress shift:* ,lily-white 'hands
Lima *in Peru:* 'liː.mə *in US:* 'laɪ.mə
lima *bean:* 'liː.mə ⓤⓢ 'laɪ-
Limavady ,lɪm.ə'væd.i
limb lɪm **-s** -z **-ed** -d **,out on a 'limb**
limber *(n. adj.)* 'lɪm.bəʳ ⓤⓢ -bɚ **-s** -z
limbo (L) 'lɪm.bəʊ ⓤⓢ -boʊ **-s** -z **-ing** -ɪŋ **-ed** -d
Limburg 'lɪm.bɜːg ⓤⓢ -bɝːg
lim|e *(n. v.)* laɪm **-es** -z **-ing** -ɪŋ **-ed** -d **,lime 'green**
limeade ,laɪ'meɪd ⓤⓢ ,-'-, 'laɪ.meɪd
Limehouse 'laɪm.haʊs
limekiln 'laɪm.kɪln, -kɪl **-s** -z
limelight 'laɪm.laɪt **-s** -s
limen 'laɪ.men, -mən ⓤⓢ -mən
limerick (L) 'lɪm.ᵊr.ɪk ⓤⓢ -ɚ.ɪk, '-rɪk **-s** -s
limescale 'laɪm.skeɪl
limestone 'laɪm.stəʊn ⓤⓢ -stoʊn
limewash 'laɪm.wɒʃ ⓤⓢ -wɑːʃ, -wɔːʃ **-es** -ɪz **-ing** -ɪŋ **-ed** -t
limewater 'laɪm,wɔː.təʳ ⓤⓢ -,wɑː.t̬ɚ, -,wɔː-
limey 'laɪ.mi **-s** -z
liminal 'lɪm.ɪ.nᵊl
lim|it *(n. v.)* 'lɪm|.ɪt **-its** -ɪts **-iting** -ɪ.tɪŋ ⓤⓢ -ɪ.t̬ɪŋ **-ited/ness** -ɪ.tɪd/nəs, -nɪs ⓤⓢ -ɪ.t̬ɪd/nəs, -nɪs **-itable** -ɪ.tə.bl̩ ⓤⓢ -ɪ.t̬ə.bl̩
limitation ,lɪm.ɪ'teɪ.ʃᵊn, -ə'- **-s** -z
limitless 'lɪm.ɪt.ləs, -lɪs
limn lɪm **-s** -z **-ing** -ɪŋ, -nɪŋ **-ed** -d **-er/s** -nəʳ/z ⓤⓢ -ɚ/z, -nɚ/z
limo 'lɪm.əʊ ⓤⓢ -oʊ **-s** -z
Limoges lɪ'məʊʒ ⓤⓢ liː'moʊʒ
Limousin ,lɪm.uː'zæn *as if French:* -'zæ̃ŋ ⓤⓢ ,liː.muː'zæn
limousine ,lɪm.ə'ziːn, -ʊ'-, '--- ⓤⓢ 'lɪm.ə.ziːn, ,--'- **-s** -z
limp lɪmp **-s** -s **-er** -əʳ ⓤⓢ -ɚ **-est** -ɪst, -əst **-ly** -li **-ness** -nəs, -nɪs **-ing/ly** -ɪŋ/li **-ed** -t
limpet 'lɪm.pɪt **-s** -s
limpid 'lɪm.pɪd **-ly** -li **-ness** -nəs, -nɪs
limpidity lɪm'pɪd.ə.ti, -ɪ.ti ⓤⓢ -ə.t̬i
Limpopo lɪm'pəʊ.pəʊ ⓤⓢ -'poʊ.poʊ
limp-wristed ,lɪmp'rɪs.tɪd ⓤⓢ ,-'--, 'lɪmp,rɪs-
limy 'laɪ.mi
Linacre 'lɪn.ə.kəʳ, '-ɪ- ⓤⓢ -kɚ
linag|e 'laɪ.nɪdʒ **-es** -ɪz
Linares lɪ'nɑː.rɪs ⓤⓢ lɪ'ner.ɪs
linchpin 'lɪn*t*ʃ.pɪn **-s** -z
Lincoln 'lɪŋ.kən **-shire** -ʃəʳ, -,ʃɪəʳ ⓤⓢ -ʃɚ, -,ʃɪr
Lincs. *(abbrev. for* **Lincolnshire***)* lɪŋks, lɪŋ.kən.ʃəʳ, -ʃɪəʳ ⓤⓢ -ʃɚ, -,ʃɪr
linctus 'lɪŋk.təs **-es** -ɪz
Lind lɪnd
Linda 'lɪn.də
Lindbergh 'lɪn*d*.bɜːg ⓤⓢ -bɝːg
linden (L) 'lɪn.dən **-s** -z
Lindisfarne 'lɪn.dɪs.fɑːn, -dəs- ⓤⓢ -fɑːrn
Lindley 'lɪn*d*.li
Lindon 'lɪn.dən
Lindsay, Lindsey 'lɪn*d*.zi
lin|e (L) laɪn **-es** -z **-ing** -ɪŋ **-ed** -d **'line ,drawing; ,read be,tween the 'lines**
lineag|e *family:* 'lɪn.i.ɪdʒ ⓤⓢ '-ɪdʒ, -i.ɪdʒ **-es** -ɪz
lineag|e *alternative spelling of* **linage**: 'laɪ.nɪdʒ **-es** -ɪz
lineal 'lɪn.i.əl **-ly** -i
lineament 'lɪn.i.ə.mənt **-s** -s
linear 'lɪn.i.əʳ ⓤⓢ -ɚ **-ly** -li
lineation ,lɪn.i'eɪ.ʃᵊn **-s** -z
linebacker 'laɪn,bæk.əʳ, 'laɪm- ⓤⓢ 'laɪn,bæk.ɚ **-s** -z
line-engraving 'laɪn.ɪn,greɪ.vɪŋ, -ɪŋ,- ⓤⓢ -ɪn,- **-s** -z
Lineker 'lɪn.ɪ.kəʳ, '-ə- ⓤⓢ -kɚ
line|man 'laɪn|.mən, 'laɪm- ⓤⓢ 'laɪn- **-men** -mən, -men
linen 'lɪn.ɪn, -ən **-s** -z
lineout 'laɪn.aʊt **-s** -s

liner 'laɪ.nəʳ ⓤⓢ -nɚ **-s** -z
lines|man 'laɪnz|.mən **-men** -mən, -men
lineup 'laɪn.ʌp **-s** -s
Linford 'lɪn.fəd ⓤⓢ -fɚd
ling (L) lɪŋ **-s** -z
lingam 'lɪŋ.gəm, -æm
Lingay 'lɪŋ.gi
Lingen 'lɪŋ.ən
ling|er 'lɪŋ.g|əʳ ⓤⓢ -g|ɚ **-ers** -əz ⓤⓢ -ɚz **-ering/ly** -ᵊr.ɪŋ/li **-ered** -əd ⓤⓢ -ɚd **-erer/s** -ᵊr.əʳ/z ⓤⓢ -ɚ.ɚ/z
lingerie 'læ̃n.ʒᵊr.i, 'lɒn-, -dʒᵊr-, -ri, -reɪ ⓤⓢ ˌlɑːn.ʒə'reɪ; ˌlæn.ʒə'riː, -dʒə'-
Lingfield 'lɪŋ.fiːld
lingo 'lɪŋ.gəʊ ⓤⓢ -goʊ **-s** -z
lingua franca ˌlɪŋ.gwə'fræŋ.kə
lingual 'lɪŋ.gwəl **-ly** -i
Linguaphone® 'lɪŋ.gwə.fəʊn ⓤⓢ -foʊn
Linguarama® ˌlɪŋ.gwə'rɑː.mə ⓤⓢ -'ræm.ə, -'rɑː.mə
linguine, linguini lɪŋ'gwiː.ni
linguist 'lɪŋ.gwɪst **-s** -s
linguistic lɪŋ'gwɪs.tɪk **-s** -s **-al** -ᵊl **-ally** -ᵊl.i, -li
linguistician ˌlɪŋ.gwɪ'stɪʃ.ᵊn **-s** -z
liniment 'lɪn.ɪ.mənt, '-ə- **-s** -s
lining 'laɪ.nɪŋ **-s** -z
link (*n. v.*) lɪŋk **-s** -s **-ing** -ɪŋ **-ed** -t
linkag|e 'lɪŋ.kɪdʒ **-es** -ɪz
Linklater 'lɪŋkˌleɪ.təʳ ⓤⓢ -t̬ɚ
links lɪŋks
linkup 'lɪŋk.ʌp
Linley 'lɪn.li
Linlithgow lɪn'lɪθ.gəʊ ⓤⓢ -goʊ **-shire** -ʃəʳ, -ˌʃɪəʳ ⓤⓢ -ʃɚ, -ˌʃɪr
Linnaean lɪ'niː.ən, -'neɪ-
Linnaeus lɪ'niː.əs, -'neɪ-
Linnean lɪ'niː.ən, -'neɪ-
linnet (L) 'lɪn.ɪt **-s** -s
lino 'laɪ.nəʊ ⓤⓢ -noʊ **-s** -z
linocut 'laɪ.nəʊ.kʌt ⓤⓢ -noʊ-, -nə- **-s** -s
linoleum lɪ'nəʊ.li.əm ⓤⓢ -'noʊ- **-s** -z
Linotype® 'laɪ.nəʊ.taɪp ⓤⓢ -nə- **-s** -s
linseed 'lɪn.siːd 'linseed ˌoil ˌlinseed 'oil
linsey (L) 'lɪn.zi
linsey-woolsey (L) ˌlɪn.zi'wʊl.zi
lint lɪnt
lintel 'lɪn.tᵊl ⓤⓢ -t̬ᵊl **-s** -z
Linthwaite 'lɪn.θweɪt
Linton 'lɪn.tən
Lintot(t) 'lɪn.tɒt ⓤⓢ -tɑːt
Linus 'laɪ.nəs
Linux 'lɪn.əks, 'laɪ.nəks, -nʌks ⓤⓢ 'lɪn.əks
Linz lɪnts
lion laɪən **-s** -z 'lion ˌtamer
Lionel 'laɪə.nᵊl
lioness 'laɪə.nes, -nɪs; ˌlaɪə'nes ⓤⓢ 'laɪə.nes, -nɪs **-es** -ɪz
Lionheart 'laɪən.hɑːt ⓤⓢ -hɑːrt
lion-hearted ˌlaɪən'hɑː.tɪd ⓤⓢ 'laɪənˌhɑːr.t̬ɪd *stress shift, British only:* ˌlion-hearted 'warrior
lionization, -isa- ˌlaɪə.naɪ'zeɪ.ʃᵊn, -nɪ'- ⓤⓢ -nɪ'-
lioniz|e, -is|e 'laɪə.naɪz **-es** -ɪz **-ing** -ɪŋ **-ed** -d
lip lɪp **-s** -s **-ping** -ɪŋ **-ped** -t 'lip ˌservice
Lipari 'lɪp.ᵊr.i, 'liː.pær-
lipas|e 'laɪ.peɪz, 'lɪp.eɪz, -eɪs ⓤⓢ 'lɪp.eɪs, 'laɪ.peɪs **-es** -ɪz
lipbrush 'lɪp.brʌʃ **-es** -ɪz
lipid(e) 'lɪp.ɪd, 'laɪ.pɪd ⓤⓢ 'lɪp.ɪd **-s** -z
Lipman 'lɪp.mən
lipoid 'lɪp.ɔɪd, 'laɪ.pɔɪd
lipoprotein ˌlɪp.əʊ'prəʊ.tiːn, ˌlaɪ.pəʊ'- ⓤⓢ ˌlɪp.oʊ'proʊ.tiːn, ˌlaɪ.poʊ'-, -pə'-, -tiː.ɪn **-s** -z
liposome 'lɪp.əʊ.səʊm ⓤⓢ -ə.soʊm, 'laɪ.pə- **-s** -z
liposuction 'lɪp.əʊˌsʌk.ʃᵊn ⓤⓢ 'lɪp.oʊˌ-, 'laɪ.poʊˌ-, -pəˌ-
Lippi 'lɪp.i
Lippincott 'lɪp.ɪŋ.kət, -kɒt ⓤⓢ -ɪn.kɑːt, -kət
Lippizaner ˌlɪp.ɪt'sɑː.nəʳ, -ət'- ⓤⓢ -nɚ **-s** -z
Lippmann 'lɪp.mən
lipp|y 'lɪp|.i **-ier** -i.əʳ ⓤⓢ -i.ɚ **-iest** -i.ɪst, -i.əst **-iness** -ɪ.nəs, -ɪ.nɪs
lip|-read 'lɪp|.riːd **-reads** -riːdz **-reading** -ˌriː.dɪŋ *past tense:* **-read** -red **-readers** -ˌriː.dəz ⓤⓢ -ˌriː.dɚz
lip-salve 'lɪp.sælv, -sɑːlv ⓤⓢ -sæv, -sɑːv **-s** -z
Lipscomb(e) 'lɪp.skəm
Lipstadt 'lɪp.stæt
lipstick 'lɪp.stɪk **-s** -s
lip-synch 'lɪp.sɪŋk **-s** -s **-ing** -ɪŋ **-ed** -t
Lipton 'lɪp.tən
liquefaction ˌlɪk.wɪ'fæk.ʃᵊn, -wə'-
lique|fy 'lɪk.wɪ|.faɪ, -wə- **-fies** -faɪz **-fying** -faɪ.ɪŋ **-fied** -faɪd **-fier/s** -faɪ.əʳ/z ⓤⓢ -faɪ.ɚ/z **-fiable** -faɪ.ə.bl̩
liqueur lɪ'kjʊəʳ, lə-, -'kjɔːʳ, -'kjɜːʳ ⓤⓢ lɪ'kɝː, -'kʊr, -'kjʊr **-s** -z
liquid 'lɪk.wɪd **-s** -z **-ly** -li **-ness** -nəs, -nɪs
liqui|date 'lɪk.wɪ|.deɪt, -wə- **-dates** -deɪts **-dating** -deɪ.tɪŋ ⓤⓢ -deɪ.t̬ɪŋ **-dated** -deɪ.tɪd ⓤⓢ -deɪ.t̬ɪd **-dator/s** -deɪ.təʳ/z ⓤⓢ -deɪ.t̬ɚ/z
liquidation ˌlɪk.wɪ'deɪ.ʃᵊn, -wə'- **-s** -z
liquidity lɪ'kwɪd.ə.ti, lə-, -ɪ.ti ⓤⓢ -ə.t̬i
liquidiz|e, -is|e 'lɪk.wɪ.daɪz, -wə- **-es** -ɪz **-ing** -ɪŋ **-ed** -d
liquidizer, -iser 'lɪk.wɪ.daɪ.zəʳ, -wə- ⓤⓢ -zɚ **-s** -z
liquif|y 'lɪk.wɪ.f|aɪ, -wə- **-ies** aɪz **-ying** aɪ.ɪŋ **-ied** -aɪd
liqu|or 'lɪk|.əʳ ⓤⓢ -ɚ **-ors** -əz ⓤⓢ -ɚz **-oring** -ᵊr.ɪŋ **-ored** -əd ⓤⓢ -ɚd
liquorice 'lɪk.ᵊr.ɪs, -ɪʃ, 'lɪk.rɪs, -rɪʃ ⓤⓢ 'lɪk.ɚ.ɪʃ, '-rɪʃ, 'lɪk.ɚ.ɪs
lir|a 'lɪə.r|ə ⓤⓢ 'lɪr|.ə **-as** -əz **-e** -i, -eɪ
Lisa 'liː.sə, -zə
Lisbet 'lɪz.bət, -bet, -bɪt
Lisbeth 'lɪz.bəθ, -beθ, -bɪθ
Lisbon 'lɪz.bən
Lisburn 'lɪz.bɜːn ⓤⓢ -bɝːn
lisente lɪ'sen.teɪ ⓤⓢ -ti
Lisette lɪ'zet, 'liː.zet
Liskeard 'lɪs.kɑːd ⓤⓢ -kɑːrd
lisle *thread:* laɪl
Lisle laɪl, liːl
Note: Baron Lisle pronounces /laɪl/.
Lismore *in Scotland and Ireland:* lɪz'mɔːʳ ⓤⓢ -'mɔːr *in Australia:* 'lɪz.mɔːʳ ⓤⓢ -mɔːr
lisp, LISP lɪsp **-s** -s **-ing/ly** -ɪŋ/li **-ed** -t **-er/s** -əʳ/z ⓤⓢ -ɚ/z
lis pendens ˌlɪs'pen.denz
Liss lɪs
lissom(e) 'lɪs.əm **-ness** -nəs, -nɪs
Lisson 'lɪs.ᵊn
list lɪst **-s** -s **-ing/s** -ɪŋ/z **-ed** -ɪd
listen 'lɪs.ᵊn **-s** -z **-ing** -ɪŋ, 'lɪs.nɪŋ **-ed** -d **-er/s** -əʳ/z, 'lɪs.nəʳ/z **-er/z** ⓤⓢ 'lɪs.ᵊn.ɚ/z **-er/s** ⓤⓢ 'lɪs.nɚ/z
Lister 'lɪs.təʳ ⓤⓢ -tɚ
listeria lɪ'stɪə.ri.ə ⓤⓢ -'stɪr.i-
listeriasis ˌlɪs.tə'riː.ə.sɪs
Listerine® 'lɪs.tᵊr.iːn ⓤⓢ ˌlɪs.tə'riːn
listeriosis lɪˌstɪə.ri'əʊ.sɪs, ˌlɪs.tɪə- ⓤⓢ lɪˌstɪr.i'oʊ-
listless 'lɪst.ləs, -lɪs **-ly** -li **-ness** -nəs, -nɪs
Liston 'lɪs.tᵊn
Listowel lɪ'stəʊəl ⓤⓢ -'stoʊəl, -'staʊl
Liszt lɪst
lit (*from* **light**) lɪt
litan|y 'lɪt.ᵊn|.i **-ies** -iz
Litchfield 'lɪtʃ.fiːld
litchi ˌlaɪ'tʃiː; 'laɪ.tʃiː, 'liː- ⓤⓢ 'liː.tʃiː **-s** -z
lite laɪt
liter 'liː.təʳ ⓤⓢ -t̬ɚ **-s** -z
literacy 'lɪt.ᵊr.ə.si, '-rə.si ⓤⓢ 'lɪt̬.ɚ.ə-
literal 'lɪt.ᵊr.ᵊl, '-rᵊl ⓤⓢ 'lɪt̬.ɚ.ᵊl **-ly** -i **-ness** -nəs, -nɪs
literal|ism 'lɪt.ᵊr.ᵊl|.ɪ.zᵊm, '-rᵊl- ⓤⓢ 'lɪt̬.ɚ.ᵊl- **-ist/s** -ɪst/s
literality ˌlɪt.ᵊr'æl.ə.ti, -ɪ.ti ⓤⓢ -ə'ræl.ə.t̬i
literar|y 'lɪt.ᵊr.ᵊr|.i, '-ᵊr|.i ⓤⓢ 'lɪt̬.ə.rer- **-ily** -ᵊl.i, -ɪ.li **-iness** -ɪ.nəs, -ɪ.nɪs
literate 'lɪt.ᵊr.ət, -ɪt, '-rət, -rɪt ⓤⓢ 'lɪt̬.ɚ.ət **-s** -s
literati ˌlɪt.ᵊr'ɑː.tiː ⓤⓢ ˌlɪt̬.ə'rɑː.t̬iː
literatim ˌlɪt.ᵊr'ɑː.tɪm ⓤⓢ ˌlɪt̬.ə'reɪ.t̬ɪm, -'rɑː-
literature 'lɪt.rə.tʃəʳ, -rɪ-, '-ᵊr.ə-, -ɪ- ⓤⓢ 'lɪt̬.ɚ.ə.tʃɚ, -tʃʊr **-s** -z
litharge 'lɪθ.ɑːdʒ ⓤⓢ -ɑːrdʒ; lɪ'θɑːrdʒ

lith|e laɪð **-er** -əʳ US -ɚ **-est** -ɪst, -əst **-ely** -li **-eness** -nəs, -nɪs
Litheby ˈlɪð.ɪ.bi, ˈ-ə-
Litherland ˈlɪð.ə.lænd US ˈ-ɚ-
lithesome ˈlaɪð.səm **-ness** -nəs, -nɪs
Lithgow ˈlɪθ.gəʊ US -goʊ
lithia ˈlɪθ.i.ə
lithic ˈlɪθ.ɪk
lithium ˈlɪθ.i.əm
litho ˈlɪθ.əʊ, ˈlaɪ.θəʊ US ˈlɪθ.oʊ **-s** -z
lithograph ˈlɪθ.əʊ.grɑːf, -græf US -ə.græf, ˈ-oʊ- **-s** -s **-ing** -ɪŋ **-ed** -t
Note: In British printers' usage /ˈlaɪ.θəʊ-/. So also with derived words (**lithographer,** etc.).
lithographer lɪˈθɒg.rə.fəʳ US -ˈθɑː.grə.fɚ **-s** -z
lithographic ˌlɪθ.əʊˈgræf.ɪk US -oʊˈ-, -əˈ- **-al** -ᵊl **-ally** -ᵊl.i, -li
lithography lɪˈθɒg.rə.fi US -ˈθɑː.grə-
lithosphere ˈlɪθ.əʊˌsfɪəʳ US -oʊˌsfɪr, -əˌ- **-s** -z
Lithuani|a ˌlɪθ.juˈeɪ.ni|.ə, -uˈ- US -uˈeɪ-, -əˈweɪ- **-an/s** -ən/z
litigant ˈlɪt.ɪ.gənt, ˈ-ə- US ˈlɪţ- **-s** -s
liti|gate ˈlɪt.ɪ|.geɪt, ˈ-ə- US ˈlɪţ- **-gates** -geɪts **-gating** -geɪ.tɪŋ US -geɪ.ţɪŋ **-gated** -geɪ.tɪd US -geɪ.ţɪd **-gator/s** -geɪ.təʳ/z US -geɪ.ţɚ/z
litigation ˌlɪt.ɪˈgeɪ.ʃᵊn, -əˈ- US ˌlɪţ- **-s** -z
litigious lɪˈtɪdʒ.əs, lə- US lɪ- **-ly** -li **-ness** -nəs, -nɪs
litmus ˈlɪt.məs ˈ**litmus** ˌ**paper**; ˈ**litmus** ˌ**test**
litotes laɪˈtəʊ.tiːz; ˈlaɪ.təʊ- US ˈlaɪ.ţə.tiːz; laɪˈtoʊ-; ˈlɪt.oʊ-
litre ˈliː.təʳ US -ţɚ **-s** -z
Littel lɪˈtel
litt|er ˈlɪt|.əʳ US ˈlɪţ|.ɚ **-ers** -əz US -ɚz **-ering** -ᵊr.ɪŋ **-ered** -əd US -ɚd
litterbug ˈlɪt.ə.bʌg US ˈlɪţ.ɚ- **-s** -z
littl|e (L) ˈlɪt.l̩ US ˈlɪţ.l̩ **-er** -əʳ US -ɚ **-est** -ɪst, -əst **-eness** -nəs, -nɪs
Littleborough ˈlɪt.l̩.bᵊr.ə, -ˌbʌr.ə US ˈlɪţ.l̩.bɚ.oʊ
Littlechild ˈlɪt.l̩.tʃaɪld
little-englander ˌlɪt.l̩ˈɪŋ.glən.dəʳ US ˌlɪţ.l̩ˈɪŋ.glən.dɚ **-s** -z
little-go ˈlɪt.l̩.gəʊ US ˈlɪţ.l̩.goʊ **-es** -z
Littlehampton ˈlɪt.l̩ˌhæmp.tən, ˌlɪt.l̩ˈhæmp- US ˌlɪţ.l̩ˈ-, ˈlɪţ.l̩ˌ-
Littlejohn ˈlɪt.l̩.dʒɒn US ˈlɪţ.l̩.dʒɑːn
littleneck ˈlɪt.l̩.nek US ˈlɪţ- **-s** -s
Littler ˈlɪt.l̩.əʳ, ˈ-ləʳ US ˈlɪt.lɚ, ˈlɪţ.l̩.ɚ
Littleton ˈlɪt.l̩.tᵊn US ˈlɪţ-
Littlewoods ˈlɪt.l̩.wʊdz
Litton ˈlɪt.ᵊn
littoral ˈlɪt.ᵊr.ᵊl US ˈlɪţ- **-s** -z
liturgic lɪˈtɜː.dʒɪk, lə- US lɪˈtɝː- **-s** -s **-al** -ᵊl **-ally** -ᵊl.i, -li
liturgist ˈlɪt.ə.dʒɪst, ˈ-ɜː- US ˈlɪţ.ɚ- **-s** -s
liturg|y ˈlɪt.ə.dʒ|i, ˈ-ɜː- US ˈlɪţ.ɚ- **-ies** -iz
livable ˈlɪv.ə.bl̩
live (*adj.*) laɪv
liv|e (*v.*) lɪv **-es** -z **-ing** -ɪŋ **-ed** -d **-er/s** -əʳ/z US -ɚ/z ˌ**living** ˈ**will**
live-circuit ˌlaɪvˈsɜː.kɪt US -ˈsɝː- **-s** -s
live-in ˌlɪvˈɪn, ˈ-- ˌ**live-in** ˈ**lover**
livelihood ˈlaɪv.li.hʊd **-s** -z
livelong ˈlɪv.lɒŋ, ˈlaɪv- US ˈlɪv.lɑːŋ, -lɔːŋ
livel|y (L) ˈlaɪv.l|i **-ier** -i.əʳ US -i.ɚ **-iest** -i.ɪst, -i.əst **-iness** -ɪ.nəs, -ɪ.nɪs
liven ˈlaɪ.vᵊn **-s** -z **-ing** -ɪŋ, ˈlaɪv.nɪŋ **-ed** -d
Livens ˈlɪv.ᵊnz
liv|er ˈlɪv|.əʳ US -ɚ **-ers** -əz US -ɚz **-erish** -ᵊr.ɪʃ
Livermore ˈlɪv.ə.mɔːʳ US -ɚ.mɔːr
Liverpool ˈlɪv.ə.puːl US ˈ-ɚ-
Liverpudlian ˌlɪv.əˈpʌd.li.ən US -ɚˈ- **-s** -z
Liversedge ˈlɪv.ə.sedʒ US ˈ-ɚ-
liverwort ˈlɪv.ə.wɜːt US -ɚ.wɝːt, -wɔːrt **-s** -s
liverwurst ˈlɪv.ə.wɜːst US -ɚ.wɝːst
liver|y ˈlɪv.ᵊr|.i, ˈ-r|i **-ies** -iz **-ied** -id
livery|man ˈlɪv.ᵊr.i|.mən US ˈ-ri-, -mæn **-men** -mən, -men
livery-stable ˈlɪv.ᵊr.iˌsteɪ.bl̩ US ˈ-riˌ- **-s** -z
lives (*plur. of* **life**) laɪvz (*from* **live** *v.*) lɪvz
Livesey ˈlɪv.si, -zi
livestock ˈlaɪv.stɒk US -stɑːk
live wire ˌlaɪvˈwaɪəʳ US -ˈwaɪr, ˈ-- **-s** -z
Livia ˈlɪv.i.ə
livid ˈlɪv.ɪd **-ly** -li **-ness** -nəs, -nɪs
lividity lɪˈvɪd.ə.ti, -ɪ.ti US -ə.ţi
living ˈlɪv.ɪŋ **-s** -z
living-room ˈlɪv.ɪŋ.rʊm, -ruːm US -ruːm, -rʊm **-s** -z
Livingston(e) ˈlɪv.ɪŋ.stᵊn
Livoni|a lɪˈvəʊ.ni|.ə US -ˈvoʊ-, ˈ-nj|ə **-an/s** -ən/z
Livorno lɪˈvɔː.nəʊ US ləˈvɔːr.noʊ
Livy ˈlɪv.i
lixivi|ate lɪkˈsɪv.i|.eɪt **-ates** -eɪts **-ating** -eɪ.tɪŋ US -eɪ.ţɪŋ **-ated** -eɪ.tɪd US -eɪ.ţɪd
Liz lɪz
Liza ˈlaɪ.zə, ˈliː- US ˈlaɪ-
lizard (L) ˈlɪz.əd US -ɚd **-s** -z
Lizzie ˈlɪz.i
Ljubljana ˌlʊb.liˈɑː.nə *as if Slovene:* ˌljuːbˈljɑː.nə US ˌluː.bliˈɑː.nə
llama (L) ˈlɑː.mə US ˈlɑː-, ˈjɑː- **-s** -z
Llanberis *h*lænˈber.ɪs, θlæn- US *h*læn-
Llandaff ˈ*h*læn.dəf, ˈθlæn-; lænˈdæf, θlæn- US *h*lænˈdɑːf
Llandeilo *h*lænˈdaɪ.ləʊ, θlæn- US *h*lænˈdaɪ.loʊ
Llandovery *h*lænˈdʌv.ᵊr.i, θlæn- US *h*læn-
Llandrindod Wells *h*lænˌdrɪn.dɒdˈwelz, θlæn- US *h*lænˌdrɪn.dɑːdˈ-
Llandudno *h*lænˈdɪd.nəʊ, θlæn-, -ˈdʌd- US *h*lænˈdɪd.noʊ, -ˈdʌd-
Llanelli *h*lænˈeθ.li, ləˈneθ-, θlænˈeθ-, θləˈneθ- US *h*lænˈel.i
Llanfair *h*lænˈfeəʳ, θlæn-, -ˈvaɪəʳ US *h*lænˈfer
Llanfairfechan ˌ*h*læn.feəˈfek.ən, ˌθlæn-, -vaɪəˈ-, -ˈvek-, -ˈvex- US ˌ*h*læn.ferˈfek-
Llanfair PG ˌ*h*læn.feəˌpiːˈdʒiː, ˌθlæn-, -vaɪəˌ- US ˌ*h*læn.fer-
Note: This is the accepted abbreviation of the following entry.

Pronouncing the letters LL

In general, the consonant digraph ll is pronounced /l/, e.g.:

fall /fɔːl/ US /fɑːl/
illustrate /ˈɪl.ə.streɪt/

Where the ll is produced by adding the suffix *–ly* or *–less* to a word ending in a single l, the pronunciation reflects this, e.g.:

coolly /ˈkuːl.li/
soulless /ˈsəʊl.ləs/ US /ˈsoʊl-/

In addition

In Welsh words, ll may be pronounced by English speakers in a variety of different ways. In this dictionary, we suggest /*h*l/, which stands both for the phonetic [ɬ] used in Welsh and for the English approximation of either a voiceless or voiced [l], and also the variant /θl/ for British English speakers, e.g.:

Llanberis /*h*lænˈber.ɪs, θlæn-/ US /*h*læn-/

Llanfairpwllgwyngyllgogerychwyrndrobwllllantysiliogogogoch ˌ*h*læn.feə.pʊlˌgwɪŋ.gɪl.gəʊˌger.əˌkwɜːnˌdrəʊ.bʊlˌ*h*læn.dəˌsɪl.i.əʊˌgəʊ.gəʊˈgɒf, ˌθlæn-, ˌ-vaɪə-, -ˌθlæn- *as if Welsh:* -xwɜːn-, -ˈgɒx ⓤⓢ ˌ*h*læn.fer.pʊlˌgwɪn.gɪl.goʊˌger.ə.kwɝːnˌdroʊ.bʊlˌ*h*læn.dəˌsɪl.i.oʊˌgoʊ.goʊˈgɑːf

Llangattock *h*lænˈgæt.ək, θlæn-, læŋ-, θlæŋ- ⓤⓢ *h*lænˈgæt̬.ək

Llangollen *h*lænˈgɒθ.lən, θlæn-, læŋ-, θlæŋ-, -len ⓤⓢ *h*lænˈgɑː.lən

Llanharan *h*lænˈhær.ən, θlæn- ⓤⓢ *h*lænˈhɑːr.ən

Llanrwst *h*lænˈruːst, θlæn- ⓤⓢ *h*læn-

Llantrisant *h*lænˈtrɪs.ənt

Llantwit Major ˌ*h*læn.twɪtˈmeɪ.dʒəʳ ⓤⓢ -dʒɚ

Llanuwchllyn *h*lænˈjuː.klɪn, θlæn-, -ˈjuːx.lɪn ⓤⓢ *h*lænˈjuː.klɪn

Llanwern *h*lænˈweən ⓤⓢ -ˈwern

Llechwedd *h*lekˈwed

Llewel(l)yn *English name:* luːˈel.ɪn, ləˈwel- *Welsh name:* *h*luːˈel.ɪn, θluː- ⓤⓢ *h*luː-

Lleyn *h*liːn, θliːn, *h*leɪn, θleɪn ⓤⓢ *h*liːn, *h*leɪn

Lliw *h*luː

Lloyd lɔɪd **ˈs** -z

Lloyd Webber ˌlɔɪdˈweb.əʳ ⓤⓢ -ɚ

Llyn Tegid ˌ*h*lɪnˈteg.ɪd, ˌθlɪn- ⓤⓢ ˌ*h*lɪn-

Llywelyn *h*ləˈwel.ɪn, θlə- ⓤⓢ *h*lə-

lo ləʊ ⓤⓢ loʊ

Loach ləʊtʃ ⓤⓢ loʊtʃ

load ləʊd ⓤⓢ loʊd **-s** -z **-ing** -ɪŋ **-ed** -ɪd **-er/s** -əʳ/z ⓤⓢ -ɚ/z

loadstone ˈləʊd.stəʊn ⓤⓢ ˈloʊd.stoʊn **-s** -z

loa|f *(n.)* ləʊ|f ⓤⓢ loʊ|f **-ves** -vz

loaf *(v.)* ləʊf ⓤⓢ loʊf **-s** -s **-ing** -ɪŋ **-ed** -t

loafer ˈləʊ.fəʳ ⓤⓢ ˈloʊ.fɚ **-s** -z

loam ləʊm ⓤⓢ loʊm

loam|y ˈləʊ.m|i ⓤⓢ ˈloʊ.m|i **-ier** -i.əʳ ⓤⓢ -i.ɚ **-iest** -i.ɪst, -i.əst **-iness** -ɪ.nəs, -ɪ.nɪs

loan ləʊn ⓤⓢ loʊn **-s** -z **-ing** -ɪŋ **-ed** -d **-er/s** -əʳ/z ⓤⓢ -ɚ/z **ˈloan ˌshark**

Loanhead ˌləʊnˈhed ⓤⓢ ˌloʊn-

loanword ˈləʊn.wɜːd ⓤⓢ ˈloʊn.wɝːd **-s** -z

loath ləʊθ, ləʊð ⓤⓢ loʊð **-ness** -nəs, -nɪs

loath|e ləʊð ⓤⓢ loʊð **-es** -z **-ing/ly** -ɪŋ/li **-ed** -d

loathsome ˈləʊð.səm, ˈləʊθ- ⓤⓢ ˈloʊð-, ˈloʊθ- **-ly** -li **-ness** -nəs, -nɪs

loaves *(plur. of* **loaf***)* ləʊvz ⓤⓢ loʊvz

lob (L) lɒb ⓤⓢ lɑːb **-s** -z **-bing** -ɪŋ **-bed** -d **-ber/s** -əʳ/z ⓤⓢ -ɚ/z

lobb|y ˈlɒb|.i ⓤⓢ ˈlɑː.b|i **-ies** -iz **-ying** -i.ɪŋ **-ied** -id

lobbyist ˈlɒb.i.ɪst ⓤⓢ ˈlɑː.bi- **-s** -s

lobe ləʊb ⓤⓢ loʊb **-s** -z **-d** -d

lobelia ləʊˈbiː.li.ə ⓤⓢ loʊˈbiːl.jə, -ˈbiː.li.ə **-s** -z

lobotomiz|e, -is|e ləʊˈbɒt.ə.maɪz ⓤⓢ loʊˈbɑː.t̬ə-, lə- **-es** -ɪz **-ing** -ɪŋ **-ed** -d

lobotom|y ləʊˈbɒt.ə.m|i ⓤⓢ loʊˈbɑː.t̬ə-, lə- **-ies** -iz

lobster ˈlɒb.stəʳ ⓤⓢ ˈlɑːb.stɚ **-s** -z

lobular ˈlɒb.jə.ləʳ, -jʊ- ⓤⓢ ˈlɑː.bjə.lɚ

lobule ˈlɒb.juːl ⓤⓢ ˈlɑː.bjuːl **-s** -z

local ˈləʊ.kᵊl ⓤⓢ ˈloʊ- **-s** -z **-ly** -i **ˌlocal ˈcolo(u)r; ˈlocal ˌtime, ˌlocal ˈtime**

locale ləʊˈkɑːl ⓤⓢ loʊˈkæl **-s** -z

localism ˈləʊ.kᵊl.ɪ.zᵊm ⓤⓢ ˈloʊ-

localit|y ləʊˈkæl.ə.t|i, -ɪ.t|i ⓤⓢ loʊˈkæl.ə.t̬|i **-ies** -iz

localization, -isa- ˌləʊ.kᵊl.aɪˈzeɪ.ʃᵊn, -ɪˈ- ⓤⓢ ˌloʊ.kᵊl.ɪˈ-

localiz|e, -is|e ˈləʊ.kᵊl.aɪz ⓤⓢ ˈloʊ- **-es** -ɪz **-ing** -ɪŋ **-ed** -d **-er/s** -əʳ/z ⓤⓢ -ɚ/z

Locarno ləʊˈkɑː.nəʊ, lɒkˈɑː- ⓤⓢ loʊˈkɑːr.noʊ

loca|te ləʊˈkeɪ|t ⓤⓢ ˈloʊ.keɪ|t, -ˈ- **-tes** -ts **-ting** -tɪŋ ⓤⓢ -t̬ɪŋ **-ted** -tɪd ⓤⓢ -t̬ɪd

location ləʊˈkeɪ.ʃᵊn ⓤⓢ loʊ- **-s** -z

locative ˈlɒk.ə.tɪv ⓤⓢ ˈlɑː.kə.t̬ɪv **-s** -z

loc. cit. ˌlɒkˈsɪt, ˌlɒk.əʊ.sɪˈtɑː.təʊ *old-fashioned:* ˌləʊ.kəʊ.sɪˈteɪ.təʊ ⓤⓢ ˌlɑːkˈsɪt

loch (L) lɒk *as if Scots:* lɒx ⓤⓢ lɑːk *as if Scots:* lɑːx **-s** -s

Lochaber lɒkˈɑː.bəʳ, -ˈæb.əʳ *as if Scots:* lɒx- ⓤⓢ lɑːˈkɑː.bɚ *as if Scots:* -ˈxɑː-

Lochgelly lɒkˈgel.i *as if Scots:* lɒx- ⓤⓢ lɑːk- *as if Scots:* lɑːx-

Lochhead ˈlɒk.hed *as if Scots:* ˈlɒx- ⓤⓢ ˈlɑːk- *as if Scots:* ˈlɑːx-

Lochiel lɒkˈiːl *as if Scots:* lɒx- ⓤⓢ lɑːˈkiːl *as if Scots:* -ˈxiːl

Lochinvar ˌlɒk.ɪnˈvɑːʳ *as if Scots:* ˌlɒx- ⓤⓢ ˌlɑː.kɪnˈvɑːr *as if Scots:* -xɪnˈ-

Lochleven lɒkˈliː.vᵊn *as if Scots:* lɒx- ⓤⓢ lɑːk- *as if Scots:* lɑːx-

Lochnagar ˌlɒk.nəˈgɑːʳ *as if Scots:* ˌlɒx- ⓤⓢ ˌlɑːk.nəˈgɑːr *as if Scots:* ˌlɑːx-

loci *(plur. of* **locus***)* ˈləʊ.saɪ, -kaɪ, -kiː; ˈlɒk.aɪ, ˈlɒs- ⓤⓢ ˈloʊ.saɪ, -kaɪ, -ki

lock (L) lɒk ⓤⓢ lɑːk **-s** -s **-ing** -ɪŋ **-ed** -t **ˌlock, ˌstock, and ˈbarrel; under ˌlock and ˈkey**

Locke lɒk ⓤⓢ lɑːk

locker (L) ˈlɒk.əʳ ⓤⓢ ˈlɑː.kɚ **-s** -z **ˈlocker ˌroom**

Lockerbie ˈlɒk.ə.bi ⓤⓢ ˈlɑː.kɚ-

locket ˈlɒk.ɪt ⓤⓢ ˈlɑː.kɪt **-s** -s

Lockhart ˈlɒk.ət, -hɑːt ⓤⓢ ˈlɑːk.hɑːrt, ˈlɑː.kɚt

Note: The Bruce-Lockhart family pronounce /ˈlɒk.ət/ (or in the Scottish manner /ˈlɒk.ərt/).

Lockheed ˈlɒk.hiːd ⓤⓢ ˈlɑːk-

Lockie ˈlɒk.i ⓤⓢ ˈlɑː.ki

lockjaw ˈlɒk.dʒɔː ⓤⓢ ˈlɑːk.dʒɑː, -dʒɔː

lock-keeper ˈlɒkˌkiː.pəʳ ⓤⓢ ˈlɑːkˌkiː.pɚ **-s** -z

locknut ˈlɒk.nʌt ⓤⓢ ˈlɑːk- **-s** -s

lockout ˈlɒk.aʊt ⓤⓢ ˈlɑːk- **-s** -s

Locksley ˈlɒk.sli ⓤⓢ ˈlɑːk-

locksmith ˈlɒk.smɪθ ⓤⓢ ˈlɑːk- **-s** -s

lockstep ˈlɒk.step ⓤⓢ ˈlɑːk-

lockstitch ˈlɒk.stɪtʃ ⓤⓢ ˈlɑːk- **-es** -ɪz

lockup ˈlɒk.ʌp ⓤⓢ ˈlɑːk- **-s** -s

Lockwood ˈlɒk.wʊd ⓤⓢ ˈlɑːk-

Lockyer ˈlɒk.jəʳ ⓤⓢ ˈlɑː.kjɚ

loco ˈləʊ.kəʊ ⓤⓢ ˈloʊ.koʊ **-s** -z

locomotion ˌləʊ.kəˈməʊ.ʃᵊn ⓤⓢ ˌloʊ.kəˈmoʊ-

locomotive ˌləʊ.kəˈməʊ.tɪv, ˈləʊ.kəˌməʊ- ⓤⓢ ˌloʊ.kəˈmoʊ.t̬ɪv **-s** -z

locomotor ˌləʊ.kəˈməʊ.təʳ, ˈləʊ.kəˌməʊ- ⓤⓢ ˌloʊ.kəˈmoʊ.t̬ɚ *stress shift, see compound:* **ˌlocoˌmotor aˈtaxia**

Locri|a ˈləʊ.kri|.ə ⓤⓢ ˈloʊ- **-an/s** -ən/z

Locrine ˈlɒk.raɪn ⓤⓢ ˈlɑː.kraɪn

Locris ˈləʊ.krɪs ⓤⓢ ˈloʊ-

Loctite® ˈlɒk.taɪt ⓤⓢ ˈlɑːk-

locum ˈləʊ.kəm ⓤⓢ ˈloʊ- **-s** -z

locum-tenens ˌləʊ.kəmˈten.enz, -ˈtiː.nenz ⓤⓢ ˌloʊ.kəmˈtiː.nenz, -ˈten.enz

locus ˈləʊ.kəs, ˈlɒk.əs ⓤⓢ ˈloʊ.kəs **-es** -ɪz **loci** ˈləʊ.saɪ, -kaɪ, -kiː; ˈlɒk.aɪ, ˈlɒs- ⓤⓢ ˈloʊ.saɪ

locus delicti ˌləʊ.kəs.delˈɪk.taɪ ⓤⓢ ˌloʊ.kəs.dəˈlɪk.ti, -taɪ

locus in quo ˌləʊ.kəsˌɪnˈkwəʊ, -ˌɪŋˈ- ⓤⓢ ˌloʊ.kəs.ɪnˈkwoʊ

locust ˈləʊ.kəst ⓤⓢ ˈloʊ- **-s** -s

locution ləʊˈkjuː.ʃᵊn, lɒkˈjuː- ⓤⓢ loʊˈkjuː- **-s** -z

locutionary ləʊˈkjuː.ʃᵊn.ᵊr.i, lɒkˈjuː- ⓤⓢ loʊˈkjuː-

locutor|y ˈlɒk.jə.tᵊr|.i, -jʊ- ⓤⓢ ˈlɑː.kjə.tɔːr- **-ies** -iz

lode ləʊd ⓤⓢ loʊd **-s** -z

loden ˈləʊ.dᵊn ⓤⓢ ˈloʊ-

lodestar ˈləʊd.stɑːʳ ⓤⓢ ˈloʊd.stɑːr **-s** -z

lodestone ˈləʊd.stəʊn ⓤⓢ ˈloʊd.stoʊn **-s** -z

lodg|e (L) lɒdʒ ⓤⓢ lɑːdʒ **-es** -ɪz **-ing/s** -ɪŋ/z **-ed** -d

lodg(e)ment ˈlɒdʒ.mənt ⓤⓢ ˈlɑːdʒ- **-s** -s

lodger ˈlɒdʒ.əʳ ⓤⓢ ˈlɑː.dʒɚ **-s** -z

lodging-hou|se ˈlɒdʒ.ɪŋ.haʊ|s ⓤⓢ ˈlɑː.dʒɪŋ- **-ses** -zɪz

Lodore ləʊˈdɔːʳ ⓤⓢ loʊˈdɔːr

Lódz wʊdʒ, wuːdʒ ⓤⓢ luːdʒ, lɑːdʒ, loʊdz, wuːdʒ

Loe luː

Loeb lɜːb, ləʊb ⓤⓢ loʊb

loess ˈləʊ.es, -ɪs, -əs; lɜːs (US) ˈloʊ.es, less, lɜːs
Loewe ˈləʊ.i (US) loʊ
Lofoten ləʊˈfəʊ.tᵊn; ˈləʊ.fəʊ- (US) ˈloʊ.fʊ-, -foʊ-
loft lɒft (US) lɑːft **-s** -s **-ing** -ɪŋ **-ed** -ɪd **-er/s** -əʳ/z (US) -ɚ/z
Lofthouse ˈlɒf.təs, ˈlɒft.haʊs (US) ˈlɑːf.təs, ˈlɑːft.haʊs
Lofting ˈlɒf.tɪŋ (US) ˈlɑːf-
Loftus ˈlɒf.təs (US) ˈlɑːf-
loft|y ˈlɒf.t|i (US) ˈlɑːf- **-ier** -i.əʳ (US) -i.ɚ **-iest** -i.ɪst, -i.əst **-ily** -ɪ.li, -ᵊl.i **-iness** -ɪ.nəs, -ɪ.nɪs
log lɒg (US) lɑːg, lɔːg **-s** -z **-ging** -ɪŋ **-ged** -d **-ger/s** -əʳ/z (US) -ɚ/z **ˌlog ˈcabin; ˌsleep like a ˈlog**
-log -lɒg (US) -lɑːg, -lɔːg
Logan ˈləʊ.gən (US) ˈloʊ-
loganberr|y ˈləʊ.gᵊn.bᵊr.|i, -gəm-, -ˌber- (US) ˈloʊ.gənˌber- **-ies** -iz
logarithm ˈlɒg.ᵊr.ɪ.ðᵊm, -θᵊm (US) ˈlɑː.gɚ.ɪ.ðᵊm, ˈlɔː- **-s** -z
logarithmic ˌlɒg.ᵊrˈɪð.mɪk, -ˈrɪθ- (US) ˌlɑː.gəˈrɪθ-, ˌlɔː- **-al** -ᵊl **-ally** -ᵊl.i, -li
logbook ˈlɒg.bʊk (US) ˈlɑːg-, ˈlɔːg- **-s** -s
logger ˈlɒg.əʳ (US) ˈlɑː.gɚ, ˈlɔː- **-s** -z
loggerhead ˈlɒg.ə.hed (US) ˈlɑː.gɚ-, ˈlɔː- **-s** -z
loggia ˈləʊ.dʒə, ˈlɒdʒ.ə, -i.ə (US) ˈlɑː.dʒə, -dʒi.ə **-s** -z
Logia ˈlɒg.i.ə (US) ˈloʊ.gi-, ˈlɑː-
logic ˈlɒdʒ.ɪk (US) ˈlɑː.dʒɪk **-al** -ᵊl **-ally** -ᵊl.i, -li
Logica® ˈlɒdʒ.ɪ.kə (US) ˈlɑː.dʒɪ-
logician lɒdʒˈɪʃ.ᵊn (US) loʊˈdʒɪ- **-s** -z
Logie ˈləʊ.gi (US) ˈloʊ-
-logist -lə.dʒɪst
Note: Suffix. Words containing **-logist** are normally stressed on the syllable preceding the suffix, e.g. **sociologist** /ˌsəʊ.ʃiˈɒl.ə.dʒɪst (US) ˌsoʊ.siˈɑː.lə-/.
logistic ləˈdʒɪs.tɪk, lɒdʒˈɪs- (US) loʊˈdʒɪs- **-s** -s **-al** -ᵊl **-ally** -ᵊl.i, -li
logjam ˈlɒg.dʒæm (US) ˈlɑːg-, ˈlɔːg- **-s** -z
logo ˈləʊ.gəʊ, ˈlɒg.əʊ (US) ˈloʊ.goʊ **-s** -z
logogram ˈlɒg.əʊ.græm (US) ˈlɑː.goʊ-, ˈlɔː-, ˈloʊ-, -gə- **-s** -z
logograph ˈlɒg.əʊ.grɑːf, -græf (US) ˈlɑː.goʊ.græf, ˈlɔː-, ˈloʊ-, -gə- **-s** -s
logographic ˌlɒg.əʊˈgræf.ɪk (US) ˌlɑː.goʊ-, ˌlɔː-, ˌloʊ-, -gə- **-al** -ᵊl **-ally** -ᵊl.i, -li
Logos ˈlɒg.ɒs, ˈləʊ.gɒs (US) ˈloʊ.goʊs, ˈlɔː-, ˈlɑː-, -gɔːs, -gɑːs
logotype ˈlɒg.əʊ.taɪp (US) ˈlɑː.gə-, ˈlɔː- **-s** -s
logroll ˈlɒg.rəʊl (US) ˈlɑːg.roʊl, ˈlɔːg- **-s** -z **-ing** -ɪŋ **-ed** -d **-er/s** -əʳ/z (US) -ɚ/z

Logue ləʊg (US) loʊg
-logue -lɒg (US) -lɑːg, -lɔːg
-logy -lə.dʒi
Note: Suffix. Words containing **-logy** are normally stressed on the syllable preceding the suffix, e.g. **biology** /baɪˈɒl.ə.dʒi (US) -ˈɑː.lə-/.
Lohengrin ˈləʊ.ən.grɪn, -ɪn-, -əŋ-, -ɪŋ- (US) ˈloʊ.ən-
loin lɔɪn **-s** -z
loin|cloth ˈlɔɪn|.klɒθ (US) -klɑːθ **-cloths** -klɒθs (US) -klɑːθs
Loire lwɑːʳ (US) lwɑːr
Lois ˈləʊ.ɪs (US) ˈloʊ-
loit|er ˈlɔɪ.t|əʳ (US) -t̬|ɚ **-ers** -əz (US) -ɚz **-ering** -ᵊr.ɪŋ **-ered** -əd (US) -ɚd **-erer/s** -ᵊr.əʳ/z (US) -ɚ.ɚ/z
Loki ˈləʊ.ki (US) ˈloʊ-
Lola ˈləʊ.lə (US) ˈloʊ-
Lolita lɒlˈiː.tə, ləʊˈliː- (US) loʊˈliː.t̬ə
loll lɒl (US) lɑːl **-s** -z **-ing** -ɪŋ **-ed** -d
Lollard ˈlɒl.əd, -ɑːd (US) ˈlɑː.lɚd **-s** -z
lollipop ˈlɒl.i.pɒp (US) ˈlɑː.li.pɑːp **-s** -s
lollop ˈlɒl.əp (US) ˈlɑː.ləp **-s** -s **-ing** -ɪŋ **-ed** -t
lollo rosso ˌlɒl.əʊˈrɒs.əʊ (US) ˌlɑː.loʊˈrɑː.soʊ, ˌloʊ-, ˈ-roʊ-
loll|y ˈlɒl|.i (US) ˈlɑː.l|i **-ies** -iz
lollypop ˈlɒl.i.pɒp (US) ˈlɑː.li.pɑːp **-s** -s
Loman ˈləʊ.mən (US) ˈloʊ-
Lomas ˈləʊ.mæs, -məs (US) ˈloʊ.mæs
Lomax ˈləʊ.mæks, -məks (US) ˈloʊ.mæks
Lombard ˈlɒm.bəd, -bɑːd (US) ˈlɑːm.bɑːrd, -bɚd, ˈlʌm- **-s** -z
Lombardy ˈlɒm.bə.di (US) ˈlɑːm.bɚ-, ˈlʌm-
Lombok ˈlɒm.bɒk (US) ˈlɑːm.bɑːk
Lomé ˈləʊ.meɪ (US) loʊˈmeɪ
Lomond ˈləʊ.mənd (US) ˈloʊ-
Londesborough ˈlɒnz.bᵊr.ə (US) ˈlɑːndz.bɚ.oʊ
London ˈlʌn.dən **-er/s** -əʳ/z (US) -ɚ/z **ˌLondon ˈBridge; ˌLondon ˈpride; ˌLondon ˈweighting**
Londonderry *place:* ˈlʌn.dən.der.i, ˌlʌn.dənˈder- (US) ˈlʌn.dən.der- *Lord:* ˈlʌn.dən.dᵊr.i (US) -der-
lone ləʊn (US) loʊn
lonel|y ˈləʊn.l|i (US) ˈloʊn- **-ier** -i.əʳ (US) -i.ɚ **-iest** -i.ɪst, -i.əst **-iness** -ɪ.nəs, -ɪ.nɪs **ˌlonely ˈhearts**
loner ˈləʊ.nəʳ (US) ˈloʊ.nɚ **-s** -z
lonesome ˈləʊn.səm (US) ˈloʊn- **-ness** -nəs, -nɪs
long (L) *(n. adj.)* lɒŋ (US) lɑːŋ, lɔːŋ **-er** -gəʳ (US) -gɚ **-est** -gɪst, -gəst **ˌLong ˈIsland; ˈlong ˌjump; ˈlong ˌshot; ˈlong ˌwave; ˌlong weekˈend;** (US) **ˌlong ˈweekend the ˌlong and the ˈshort of it; in the ˈlong ˌrun**
long *(v.)* lɒŋ (US) lɑːŋ, lɔːŋ **-s** -z **-ing/ly** -ɪŋ/li **-ed** -d **-er/s** -əʳ/z (US) -ɚ/z

Longannet lɒŋˈæn.ɪt, -ət (US) lɑːŋ-, lɔːŋ-
long-awaited ˌlɒŋ.əˈweɪ.tɪd (US) ˌlɑːŋ.əˈweɪ.t̬ɪd, ˌlɔːŋ- *stress shift:* ˌlong-awaited ˈmoment
longboat ˈlɒŋ.bəʊt (US) ˈlɑːŋ.boʊt, ˈlɔːŋ- **-s** -s
longbow (L) ˈlɒŋ.bəʊ (US) ˈlɑːŋ.boʊ, ˈlɔːŋ- **-s** -z
Longbridge ˈlɒŋ.brɪdʒ (US) ˈlɑːŋ-, ˈlɔːŋ-
Longdendale ˈlɒŋ.ən.deɪl (US) ˈlɑːŋ-, ˈlɔːŋ-
long-distance ˌlɒŋˈdɪs.tᵊn*t*s (US) ˌlɑːŋ-, ˌlɔːŋ- *stress shift:* ˌlong-distance ˈdriver
long-drawn-out ˌlɒŋ.drɔːnˈaʊt (US) ˌlɑːŋ.drɑːnˈ-, ˌlɔːŋ-, -drɔːnˈ- *stress shift:* ˌlong-drawn-out ˈsigh
longeron ˈlɒn.dʒᵊr.ᵊn (US) ˈlɑːn.dʒə.rɑːn, -dʒɚ.ən **-s** -z
longevity lɒnˈdʒev.ə.ti, ˈlɒŋ-, -ɪ.ti (US) lɑːnˈdʒev.ə.t̬i, lɑːŋ-, lɔːŋ-
Longfellow ˈlɒŋˌfel.əʊ (US) ˈlɑːŋˌfel.oʊ, ˈlɔːŋ-
Longfield ˈlɒŋ.fiːld (US) ˈlɑːŋ-, ˈlɔːŋ-
Longford ˈlɒŋ.fəd (US) ˈlɑːŋ.fɚd, ˈlɔːŋ-
longhand ˈlɒŋ.hænd (US) ˈlɑːŋ-, ˈlɔːŋ-
long-haul ˌlɒŋˈhɔːl, ˈ-- (US) ˌlɑːŋˈhɑːl, ˌlɔːŋ-, -hɔːl, ˈ-- *stress shift:* ˌlong-haul ˈjet
longheaded ˌlɒŋˈhed.ɪd (US) ˌlɑːŋ-, ˌlɔːŋ- *stress shift:* ˌlongheaded ˈelder
longhorn ˈlɒŋ.hɔːn (US) ˈlɑːŋ.hɔːrn, ˈlɔːŋ- **-s** -z
Longines® ˈlɒn.*d*ʒiːn, -ˈ- (US) ˌlɑːnˈdʒiːn
longing ˈlɒŋ.ɪŋ (US) ˈlɑːŋ-, ˈlɔːŋ- **-s** -z
Longinus lɒnˈdʒaɪ.nəs, lɒŋˈgiː- (US) lɑːnˈdʒaɪ-
longish ˈlɒŋ.ɪʃ (US) ˈlɑːŋ-, ˈlɔːŋ-
longitude ˈlɒn.dʒɪ.tjuːd, ˈlɒŋ.gɪ- (US) ˈlɑːn.dʒə.tuːd, -tjuːd **-s** -z
longitudinal ˌlɒn.dʒɪˈtjuː.dɪ.nᵊl, -dʒəˈ-, ˌlɒŋ.gɪˈ-, -gəˈ-, -də- (US) ˌlɑːn.dʒəˈtuː-, -ˈtjuː- **-ly** -i
long johns ˈlɒŋ.dʒɒnz, ˌ-ˈ- (US) ˈlɑːŋ.dʒɑːnz, ˈlɔːŋ-, ˌ-ˈ-
Longland ˈlɒŋ.lənd (US) ˈlɑːŋ-, ˈlɔːŋ-
Longleat ˈlɒŋ.liːt (US) ˈlɑːŋ-, ˈlɔːŋ-
long-lived ˌlɒŋˈlɪvd (US) ˌlɑːŋ-, ˌlɔːŋ-, -laɪvd *stress shift:* ˌlong-lived ˈperson
Longman ˈlɒŋ.mən (US) ˈlɑːŋ-, ˈlɔːŋ-
long-range ˌlɒŋˈreɪndʒ (US) ˌlɑːŋ-, ˌlɔːŋ- *stress shift:* ˌlong-range ˈmissile
Longridge ˈlɒŋ.rɪdʒ (US) ˈlɑːŋ-, ˈlɔːŋ-
long-running ˌlɒŋˈrʌn.ɪŋ (US) ˌlɑːŋ-, ˌlɔːŋ- *stress shift:* ˌlong-running ˈproblems
longshore|man ˈlɒŋ.ʃɔː|.mən (US) ˈlɑːŋ.ʃɔːr-, ˈlɔːŋ- **-men** -mən, -men
long-sighted ˌlɒŋˈsaɪ.tɪd (US) ˌlɑːŋˈsaɪ.t̬ɪd, ˌlɔːŋ-, ˈ-ˌ-- **-ness** -nəs, -nɪs *stress shift, British only:* ˌlong-sighted ˈperson

Longstaff ˈlɒŋ.stɑːf US ˈlɑːŋ.stæf, ˈlɔːŋ-
long-standing ˌlɒŋˈstæn.dɪŋ US ˌlɑːŋ-, ˌlɔːŋ- *stress shift:* ˌlong-standing ˈfeud
Longstreet ˈlɒŋ.striːt US ˈlɑːŋ-, ˈlɔːŋ-
long-suffering ˌlɒŋˈsʌf.ᵊr.ɪŋ US ˌlɑːŋ-, ˌlɔːŋ- *stress shift:* ˌlong-suffering ˈfamily
long-term ˌlɒŋˈtɜːm US ˌlɑːŋˈtɝːm, ˌlɔːŋ- *stress shift:* ˌlong-term ˈgoal
long-time ˈlɒŋˌtaɪm US ˈlɑːŋ-, ˈlɔːŋ-
Longton ˈlɒŋ*k*.tən US ˈlɑːŋ-, ˈlɔːŋ-
Longtown ˈlɒŋ.taʊn US ˈlɑːŋ-, ˈlɔːŋ-
longueur lɔ̃ːŋˈgɜːʳ, lɔːŋ-, lɒŋ- US lɔːŋˈgɝː **-s** -z
Longus ˈlɒŋ.gəs US ˈlɑːŋ-, ˈlɔːŋ-
longways ˈlɒŋ.weɪz US ˈlɑːŋ-, ˈlɔːŋ-
long-winded ˌlɒŋˈwɪn.dɪd US ˌlɑːŋ-, ˌlɔːŋ- **-ness** -nəs, -nɪs *stress shift:* ˌlong-winded ˈstory
longwise ˈlɒŋ.waɪz US ˈlɑːŋ-, ˈlɔːŋ-
lonicera lɒnˈɪs.ᵊr.ə, ləˈnɪs- US loʊ-; ˌlɑː.nɪˈsɪr.ə **-s** -z
Lonrho® ˈlɒn.rəʊ, ˈlʌn- US ˈlɑːn.roʊ
Lonsdale ˈlɒnz.deɪl US ˈlɑːnz-
loo luː **-s** -z
loob|y ˈluː.b|i **-ies** -iz
Looe luː
loofah ˈluː.fə **-s** -z
look lʊk **-s** -s **-ing** -ɪŋ **-ed** -t **-er/s** -əʳ/z US -ɚ/z
lookalike ˈlʊk.ə.laɪk **-s** -s
looker-on ˌlʊk.əʳˈɒn US -kɚˈɑːn **lookers-on** ˌlʊk.əzˈɒn US -kɚzˈɑːn
looking-glass ˈlʊk.ɪŋ.glɑːs US -glæs **-es** -ɪz
lookout ˈlʊk.aʊt **-s** -s
look-see ˈlʊk.siː
loom luːm **-s** -z **-ing** -ɪŋ **-ed** -d
loon luːn **-s** -z
loonie ˈluː.ni **-s** -z
loon|y ˈluː.n|i **-ies** -iz ˈ**loony** ˌ**bin**; ˌ**loony** ˈ**left**
loop luːp **-s** -s **-ing** -ɪŋ **-ed** -t
loophol|e ˈluːp.həʊl US -hoʊl **-es** -z **-ing** -ɪŋ **-ed** -d
loop|y ˈluː.p|i **-ier** -i.əʳ US -i.ɚ **-iest** -i.ɪst, -i.əst
Loos ləʊs, luːs US luːs
loos|e luːs **-er** -əʳ US -ɚ **-est** -ɪst, -əst **-eness** -nəs, -nɪs **-es** -ɪz **-ing** -ɪŋ **-ed** -t ˌ**let someone** ˈ**loose on**
looseleaf ˌluːsˈliːf *stress shift:* ˌlooseleaf ˈfolder
loosely ˈluː.sli
loosen ˈluː.sᵊn **-s** -z **-ing** -ɪŋ, ˈluːs.nɪŋ **-ed** -d
loosestrife ˈluːs.straɪf
loot luːt **-s** -s **-ing** -ɪŋ US ˈluː.t̬ɪŋ **-ed** -ɪd US ˈluː.t̬ɪd **-er/s** -əʳ/z US ˈluː.t̬ɚ/z
lop lɒp US lɑːp **-s** -s **-ping** -ɪŋ **-ped** -t
lop|e ləʊp US loʊp **-es** -s **-ing** -ɪŋ **-ed** -t
lop-eared ˌlɒpˈɪəd US ˈlɑːp.ɪrd *stress shift, British only:* ˌlop-eared ˈrabbit
Lopez ˈləʊ.pez US ˈloʊ-
lopping ˈlɒp.ɪŋ US ˈlɑː.pɪŋ **-s** -z
lop-sided ˌlɒpˈsaɪ.dɪd US ˌlɑːp- **-ness** -nəs, -nɪs *stress shift:* ˌlop-sided ˈsmile
loquacious ləʊˈkweɪ.ʃəs, lɒkˈweɪ- US loʊˈkweɪ- **-ly** -li **-ness** -nəs, -nɪs
loquacity ləʊˈkwæs.ə.ti, lɒkˈwæs-, -ɪ.ti US loʊˈkwæs.ə.t̬i
loquat ˈləʊ.kwɒt, ˈlɒk.wɒt, -wæt US ˈloʊ.kwɑːt, -kwæt **-s** -s
lor lɔːʳ US lɔːr
Loraine ləˈreɪn, lɒrˈeɪn US ləˈreɪn
Loral ˈlɔː.ræl, ˈlɒr.æl US ˈlɔːr.æl
Loram ˈlɔː.rəm US ˈlɔːr.əm
Lorca ˈlɔː.kə US ˈlɔːr-
lord (L) lɔːd US lɔːrd **-s** -z **-ing** -ɪŋ **-ed** -ɪd ˌ**Lord's** ˈ**Prayer**
Note: British lawyers addressing a judge in court sometimes pronounce **my lord** as /mɪˈlʌd/ instead of the normal /mɪˈlɔːd/.
lordling ˈlɔːd.lɪŋ US ˈlɔːrd- **-s** -z
lordl|y ˈlɔːd.l|i US ˈlɔːrd- **-ier** -i.əʳ US -i.ɚ **-iest** -i.ɪst, -i.əst **-iness** -ɪ.nəs, -ɪ.nɪs
lordship (L) ˈlɔːd.ʃɪp US ˈlɔːrd- **-s** -s
lore lɔːʳ US lɔːr
L'Oréal® ˈlɒr.i.æl US ˌlɔːr.iˈæl
Lorelei ˈlɔː.rə.laɪ, ˈlɒr.ə- US ˈlɔːr-
Loren ˈlɔː.ren, -rᵊn; lɔːˈren US ˈlɔːr.ən
Lorenzo ləˈren.zəʊ, lɒrˈen- US ləˈren.zoʊ, lɔː-
Loretto ləˈret.əʊ, lɔː- US ləˈret̬.oʊ, lɔː-
lorgnette lɔːˈnjet US lɔːr- **-s** -s
Lori(e) ˈlɒr.i US ˈlɔːr-
lorikeet ˈlɒr.ɪ.kiːt, ˈ-ə- US ˈlɔːr.ɪ- **-s** -s
lorimer (L) ˈlɒr.ɪ.məʳ US ˈlɔːr.ɪ.mɚ **-s** -z
loris ˈlɔː.rɪs US ˈlɔːr.ɪs **-es** -ɪz
lorn lɔːn US lɔːrn
Lorna ˈlɔː.nə US ˈlɔːr-
Lorne lɔːn US lɔːrn
Lorraine ləˈreɪn, lɒrˈeɪn US ləˈreɪn, lɔː-
lorr|y ˈlɒr|.i US ˈlɔːr- **-ies** -iz
lor|y ˈlɔː.r|i US ˈlɔːr|.i **-ies** -iz
losable ˈluː.zə.bl̩
Los Alamos ˌlɒsˈæl.ə.mɒs, -məʊs US ˌlɑːsˈæl.ə.moʊs, ˌlɔːs-
Los Angeles lɒsˈæn.*dʒ*ɪ.liːz, -*dʒ*ə-, -lɪz, -lɪs US lɑːsˈæn.dʒə.ləs, lɔːs-, -gə-, -liːz
los|e luːz **-es** -ɪz **-ing** -ɪŋ **lost** lɒst US lɑːst
loser ˈluː.zəʳ US -zɚ **-s** -z
Losey ˈləʊ.zi US ˈloʊ-
loss lɒs US lɑːs **-es** -ɪz ˈ**loss** ˌ**leader**
Lossiemouth ˌlɒs.iˈmaʊθ, ˈlɒs.i.maʊθ US ˌlɑː.si-
lost *(from* **lose**) lɒst US lɑːst ˌ**lost** ˈ**property**
Lostwithiel lɒs*t*ˈwɪθ.i.əl, -ˈwɪð- US lɑːs*t*-
lot (L) lɒt US lɑːt **-s** -s **-ting** -ɪŋ US ˈlɑː.t̬ɪŋ **-ted** -ɪd US ˈlɑː.t̬ɪd
loth ləʊθ US loʊθ, loʊð
Lothair ləʊˈθeəʳ US loʊˈθer
Lothario ləʊˈθɑː.ri.əʊ, lɒθˈɑː-, -ˈeə- US loʊˈθer.i.oʊ, -ˈθɑːr-
Lothbury ˈləʊθ.bᵊr.i, ˈlɒθ- US ˈloʊθ.ber-, ˈlɑːθ-, -bɚ-
Lothian ˈləʊ.ði.ən US ˈloʊ-
loti ˈləʊ.ti US ˈloʊ-
lotion ˈləʊ.ʃᵊn US ˈloʊ- **-s** -z
lotta ˈlɒt.ə US ˈlɑː.t̬ə
lotter|y ˈlɒt.ᵊr|.i US ˈlɑː.t̬ɚ- **-ies** -iz
Lottie ˈlɒt.i US ˈlɑː.t̬i
lotto (L) ˈlɒt.əʊ US ˈlɑː.t̬oʊ
lotus ˈləʊ.təs US ˈloʊ.t̬əs **-es** -ɪz ˈ**lotus** **po**ˌ**sition**
Lou luː
louche luːʃ **-ly** -li **-ness** -nəs, -nɪs
loud laʊd **-er** -əʳ US -ɚ **-est** -ɪst, -əst **-ly** -li **-ness** -nəs, -nɪs
loud-hailer ˌlaʊdˈheɪ.ləʳ US -lɚ **-s** -z
loud|mouth ˈlaʊd|.maʊθ **-mouths** -maʊðz **-mouthed** -maʊθt
Loudo(u)n ˈlaʊ.dᵊn
loudspeaker ˌlaʊdˈspiː.kəʳ US ˈlaʊdˌspiː.kɚ **-s** -z
Loudwater ˈlaʊdˌwɔː.təʳ US -ˌwɑː.t̬ɚ, -ˌwɔː-
lough *lake:* lɒk *as if Irish:* lɒx US lɑːk *as if Irish:* lɑːx **-s** -s
Lough *surname:* lʌf, ləʊ US lʌf, loʊ
Loughborough ˈlʌf.bᵊr.ə US -bɚ.oʊ, -ə
Loughlin ˈlɒk.lɪn, -lən *as if Irish:* ˈlɒx- US ˈlɑːks- *as if Irish:* ˈlɑːx-
Loughman ˈlʌf.mən
Loughran *as if Irish:* ˈlɒx.rən *as if Irish:* US ˈlɑːx-
Loughrea lɒkˈreɪ *as if Irish:* lɒx- US lɑːk- *as if Irish:* lɑːx-
Loughrey *as if Irish:* ˈlɒx.ri US ˈlɑːk-, ˈlɑːf- *as if Irish:* ˈlɑːx-
Loughton ˈlaʊ.tᵊn
Louie ˈluː.i
Louis *English name:* ˈluː.i, -ɪs *French name:* ˈluː.i, -iː, luˈi
Louisa luˈiː.zə
Louisburg ˈluː.ɪs.bɜːg US -bɝːg
louis-d'or ˌluː.iˈdɔːʳ US -ˈdɔːr **-s** -z
Louise luˈiːz
Louisiana luˌiː.ziˈæn.ə, -ˈɑː.nə; ˌluː.ɪ.ziˈ- US luˌiː.ziˈæn.ə; ˌluː.ziˈ-
Louis Quatorze ˌluː.i.kætˈɔːz US -ˈɔːrz
Louis Quinze ˌluː.iˈkæ̃nz
Louisville ˈluː.i.vɪl US -ɪ.vɪl *locally:* ˈluː.ə.vəl
loung|e laʊndʒ **-es** -ɪz **-ing** -ɪŋ **-ed** -d **-er/s** -əʳ/z US -ɚ/z ˈ**lounge** ˌ**bar**; ˈ**lounge** ˌ**lizard**; ˈ**lounge** ˌ**suit**
Lounsbury ˈlaʊnz.bᵊr.i US -ber-, -bɚ-

lour lauəʳ (US) laur **-s** -z **-ing** -ɪŋ **-ed** -d
Lourdes lʊəd, lʊədz, lɔːdz (US) lʊrd, lʊrdz
Lourenço Marques lə,rent.səʊ'mɑː.kez, -kes (US) -soʊ'mɑːr.kes
louse (*n.*) laʊs **lice** laɪs
lous|e (*v.*) laʊz, laʊs (US) laʊs, laʊz **-es** -ɪz **-ing** -ɪŋ **-ed** -d, laʊst
lous|y 'laʊ.z|i **-ier** -i.əʳ (US) -i.ɚ **-iest** -i.ɪst, -i.əst **-ily** -ɪ.li, -əl.i **-iness** -ɪ.nəs, -ɪ.nɪs
lout laʊt **-s** -s
Louth *in Ireland:* laʊð *in Lincolnshire:* laʊθ
loutish 'laʊ.tɪʃ (US) -t̬ɪʃ **-ly** -li **-ness** -nəs, -nɪs
Louvain 'luː.vǣŋ, -veɪn; lʊ'vǣŋ, -'væn (US) luː'væn, -'vǣn
louver, louvre 'luː.vəʳ (US) -vɚ **-s** -z
Louvre 'luː.vrə (US) -vrə, luːv
lovab|le 'lʌv.ə.b|l̩ **-ly** -li **-leness** -l̩.nəs, -nɪs
lovage 'lʌv.ɪdʒ
Lovat 'lʌv.ət
lov|e (L) lʌv **-es** -z **-ing/ly** -ɪŋ/li **-ed** -d 'love af,fair; 'love ,letter; ,make 'love; 'love song; 'love ,story; not for ,love nor 'money
loveab|le 'lʌv.ə.b|l̩ **-ly** -li **-leness** -l̩.nəs, -nɪs
lovebird 'lʌv.bɜːd (US) -bɝːd **-s** -z
lovebite 'lʌv.baɪt **-s** -s
love|-child 'lʌv|.tʃaɪld **-children** -,tʃɪl.drən
Loveday 'lʌv.deɪ
Lovejoy 'lʌv.dʒɔɪ
Lovel 'lʌv.əl
Lovelace 'lʌv.leɪs
loveless 'lʌv.ləs, -lɪs **-ly** -li **-ness** -nəs, -nɪs
Lovell 'lʌv.əl
lovelorn 'lʌv.lɔːn (US) -lɔːrn
lovel|y 'lʌv.l|i **-ies** -i.z **-ier** -i.əʳ (US) -i.ɚ **-iest** -i.ɪst, -i.əst **-iness** -ɪ.nəs, -ɪ.nɪs
lovemaking 'lʌv,meɪ.kɪŋ
love-match 'lʌv.mætʃ **-es** -ɪz
love-potion 'lʌv,pəʊ.ʃən (US) -,poʊ- **-s** -z
lover 'lʌv.əʳ (US) -ɚ **-s** -z
Loveridge 'lʌv.rɪdʒ, -ər.ɪdʒ
lovesick 'lʌv.sɪk **-ness** -nəs, -nɪs
love-stor|y 'lʌv,stɔː.r|i (US) -,stɔːr|.i **-ies** -ɪz
Lovett 'lʌv.ɪt
lovey-dovey ,lʌv.i'dʌv.i, 'lʌv.i,dʌv-
Loveys 'lʌv.ɪs
Lovibond 'lʌv.ɪ.bɒnd (US) -bɑːnd
Lovick 'lʌv.ɪk
loving-cup 'lʌv.ɪŋ.kʌp **-s** -s
low (L) ləʊ (US) loʊ **-er** -əʳ (US) -ɚ **-est** -ɪst, -əst **-ness** -nəs, -nɪs **-s** -z **-ing** -ɪŋ **-ed** -d ,Low 'Church; ,low 'profile; 'low ,season
lowborn ,ləʊ'bɔːn (US) 'loʊ.bɔːrn *stress shift, British only:* ,lowborn 'person
lowbred ,ləʊ'bred (US) 'loʊ.bred *stress shift, British only:* ,lowbred 'person
lowbrow 'ləʊ.braʊ (US) 'loʊ-
lowdown (*n.*) 'ləʊ.daʊn (US) 'loʊ- *stress shift:* ,low-down 'scoundrel
low-down (*adj.*) ,ləʊ'daʊn (US) ,loʊ-
Lowe ləʊ (US) loʊ
Lowell 'ləʊ.əl (US) 'loʊ-
low|er (*v. adj.*) *cause to descend:* 'ləʊ|.əʳ (US) 'loʊ|.ɚ **-ers** -əz, -ɚs **-ering** -ər.ɪŋ **-ered** -əd (US) -ɚd
lower (*v.*) *look threatening:* laʊəʳ (US) laʊr, laʊɚ **-s** -z **-ing/ly** -ɪŋ/li **-ed** -d
lower-case ,ləʊ.ə'keɪs (US) ,loʊ.ɚ'- *stress shift:* ,lower-case 'letter
lowermost 'ləʊ.ə.məʊst, -məst (US) 'loʊ.ɚ.moʊst
Lowery 'laʊə.ri (US) 'laʊ.ri
Lowes ləʊz (US) loʊz
Lowestoft 'ləʊ.stɒft, 'ləʊ.ɪ-, -stəft (US) 'loʊ.stɑːft, 'loʊ.ɪ- *locally:* 'ləʊ.stəf (US) 'loʊ-
Lowick 'ləʊ.ɪk (US) 'loʊ-
Lowis 'laʊ.ɪs
lowkey ,ləʊ'kiː (US) ,loʊ-
lowland (L) 'ləʊ.lənd (US) 'loʊ- **-s** -z **-er/s** -əʳ/z (US) -ɚ/z
low-life 'ləʊ.laɪf, ,-'- (US) 'loʊ-, ,-'- **-s** -s
low-loader ,ləʊ'ləʊ.dəʳ (US) 'loʊ,loʊ.dɚ **-s** -z
lowl|y 'ləʊ.l|i (US) 'loʊ- **-ier** -i.əʳ (US) -i.ɚ **-iest** -i.ɪst, -i.əst **-iness** -ɪ.nəs, -ɪ.nɪs
low-lying ,ləʊ'laɪ.ɪŋ (US) ,loʊ- *stress shift:* ,low-lying 'cloud
Lowndes laʊndz
low-necked ,ləʊ'nekt (US) ,loʊ- *stress shift:* ,low-necked 'sweater
Lowood 'ləʊ.wʊd (US) 'loʊ-
Lowries 'laʊə.rɪz, 'laʊ- (US) 'laʊ-
Lowry 'laʊə.ri, 'laʊ- (US) 'laʊ-
Lowsley 'ləʊz.li (US) 'loʊz-
Lowson 'ləʊ.sən, 'laʊ- (US) 'loʊ-, 'laʊ-
Lowth laʊθ
Lowther 'laʊ.ðəʳ (US) -ðɚ
Lowton 'ləʊ.tən (US) 'loʊ-
Lowville 'laʊ.vɪl
lox lɒks (US) lɑːks
Loxley 'lɒk.sli (US) 'lɑːk-
loyal lɔɪəl (US) 'lɔɪ.əl **-ly** -i
loyalist 'lɔɪə.lɪst (US) 'lɔɪ.ə.lɪst **-s** -s
loyalt|y 'lɔɪəl.t|i (US) 'lɔɪ.əl.t̬|i **-ies** -iz
Loyd lɔɪd
Loyola 'lɔɪ.əʊ.lə; lɔɪ'əʊ- (US) lɔɪ'oʊ-
lozeng|e 'lɒz.ɪndʒ, -əndʒ (US) 'lɑː.zəndʒ **-es** -ɪz
LP ,el'piː
L-plate 'el.pleɪt **-s** -s
LPN ,el.piː'en
LSD ,el.es'diː
LSE ,el.es'iː
Ltd. 'lɪm.ɪ.tɪd, '-ə- (US) -ə.t̬ɪd
Luanda lu'æn.də (US) -'æn-, -'ɑːn-
luau 'luː.aʊ
Lubavitcher 'luː.bə.vɪ.tʃəʳ (US) -tʃɚ **-s** -z
lubber 'lʌb.əʳ (US) -ɚ **-s** -z
Lubbock 'lʌb.ək
lube luːb **-s** -z
Lübeck 'luː.bek, 'ljuː- (US) 'luː-
Lubin 'luː.bɪn
Lublin 'luː.blɪn
lubricant 'luː.brɪ.kənt, 'ljuː-, -brə- (US) 'luː- **-s** -s
lubri|cate 'luː.brɪ|.keɪt, 'ljuː-, -brə- (US) 'luː- **-cates** -keɪts **-cating** -keɪ.tɪŋ (US) -keɪ.t̬ɪŋ **-cated** -keɪ.tɪd (US) -keɪ.t̬ɪd **-cator/s** -keɪ.təʳ/z (US) -keɪ.t̬ɚ/z
lubrication ,luː.brɪ'keɪ.ʃən, ,ljuː-, -brə'- (US) ,luː- **-s** -z
lubricious luː'brɪʃ.əs, ljuː- (US) luː- **-ly** -li **-ness** -nəs, -nɪs
lubricity luː'brɪs.ə.ti, ljuː-, -ɪ.ti (US) luː'brɪs.ə.t̬i
Lubumbashi ,luː.bʊm'bæʃ.i (US) -'bɑː.ʃi
Luca 'luː.kə
Lucan 'luː.kən, 'ljuː- (US) 'luː-
Lucania luː'keɪ.ni.ə, ljuː- (US) luː-
lucarne luː'kɑːn, ljuː- (US) luː'kɑːrn **-s** -z
Lucas 'luː.kəs
Luce luːs
lucen|t 'luː.sən|t, 'ljuː- (US) 'luː- **-cy** -*t*.si
lucern(e) luː'sɜːn, ljuː-, '-- (US) luː'sɝːn
Lucerne luː'sɜːn, ljuː- (US) luː'sɝːn
luces (*plur. of* **lux**) 'luː.siːz
Lucia 'luː.si.ə, '-ʃə; luː'tʃiː.ə
Lucian 'luː.si.ən, '-ʃən, -ʃi.ən (US) 'luː.ʃən
Luciana ,luː.si'ɑː.nə, ,ljuː- (US) ,luː-, -'æn.ə
Lucianus ,luː.si'ɑː.nəs, ,ljuː-, -'eɪ- (US) ,luː.si'ɑː-
lucid 'luː.sɪd, 'ljuː- (US) 'luː- **-ly** -li **-ness** -nəs, -nɪs
lucidity luː'sɪd.ə.ti, ljuː-, -ɪ.ti (US) luː'sɪd.ə.t̬i
Lucie 'luː.si, 'ljuː- (US) 'luː-
Lucien 'luː.si.ən, 'ljuː- (US) 'luː-
Lucie-Smith ,luː.si'smɪθ, ,ljuː- (US) ,luː-
lucifer (L) 'luː.sɪ.fəʳ, 'ljuː-, -sə- (US) 'luː.sə.fɚ **-s** -z
Lucilius luː'sɪl.i.əs, ljuː- (US) luː-
Lucille luː'siːl
Lucina luː'siː.nə, ljuː-, -'saɪ-, -'tʃiː- (US) luː'saɪ-, -'siː-
Lucinda luː'sɪn.də, ljuː- (US) luː-
Lucite® 'luː.saɪt, 'ljuː- (US) 'luː-
Lucius 'luː.si.əs, 'ljuː-, '-ʃəs, -ʃi.əs (US) 'luː.ʃəs
luck (L) lʌk to be ,down on one's 'luck

luckless 'lʌk.ləs, -lɪs **-ly** -li **-ness** -nəs, -nɪs
Lucknow 'lʌk.naʊ, ˌ-'- (US) 'lʌk.naʊ
luck|y 'lʌk|.i **-ier** -i.ə^{r} (US) -i.ɚ **-iest** -i.ɪst, -i.əst **-ily** -ɪ.li, -^{ə}l.i **-iness** -ɪ.nəs, -ɪ.nɪs
Lucock 'luː.kɒk, 'ljuː- (US) 'luː.kɑːk
Lucozade® 'luː.kə.zeɪd
lucrative 'luː.krə.tɪv, 'ljuː- (US) 'luː.krə.ţɪv **-ly** -li **-ness** -nəs, -nɪs
lucre 'luː.kə^{r}, 'ljuː- (US) 'luː.kɚ
Lucrece luː'kriːs, ljuː- (US) luː-
Lucretia luː'kriː.ʃə, ljuː-, -ʃi.ə (US) luː'kriː.ʃə
Lucretius luː'kriː.ʃəs, ljuː-, -ʃi.əs (US) luː'kriː.ʃəs
lucu|brate 'luː.kjə|.breɪt, -kjʊ-, 'ljuː- (US) 'luː- **-brates** -breɪts **-brating** -breɪ.tɪŋ (US) -breɪ.ţɪŋ **-brated** -breɪ.tɪd (US) -breɪ.ţɪd
lucubration ˌluː.kjə'breɪ.ʃ^{ə}n, -kjʊ'-, ˌljuː- (US) ˌluː- **-s** -z
Lucullus luː'kʌl.əs, ljuː-, -'sʌl- (US) luː'kʌl-
Lucy 'luː.si
Lud lʌd
Luddite 'lʌd.aɪt **-s** -s
Ludgate 'lʌd.gət, -gɪt, -geɪt
ludicrous 'luː.dɪ.krəs, 'ljuː-, -də- (US) 'luː- **-ly** -li **-ness** -nəs, -nɪs
Ludlow 'lʌd.ləʊ (US) -loʊ
Ludmilla lʊd'mɪl.ə, lʌd-
ludo 'luː.dəʊ (US) -doʊ
Ludovic 'luː.də.vɪk
Ludwig 'lʊd.vɪg, 'luːd- (US) 'lʊd-, 'luːd-, 'lʌd-, -wɪg
luff (L) lʌf **-s** -s **-ing** -ɪŋ **-ed** -t
Lufthansa® 'lʊft.hænt.sə, -ˌhæn.zə (US) lʊf'tɑːn.zə
Luftwaffe 'lʊft.wæf.ə, -ˌvæf-, -ˌwɑː.fə, -ˌvɑː- (US) -ˌvɑː-, -ˌwɑː-
lug lʌg **-s** -z **-ging** -ɪŋ **-ged** -d
Lugano luː'gɑː.nəʊ, lə- (US) luː'gɑː.noʊ
Lugard 'luː.gɑːd, -'- (US) 'luː.gɑːrd, -'-
lug|e luːʒ, luːdʒ (US) luːʒ **-es** -ɪz **-(e)ing** -ɪŋ **-ed** -d
Luger® 'luː.gə^{r} (US) -gɚ
luggable 'lʌg.ə.bl̩
luggage 'lʌg.ɪdʒ **'luggage ˌlabel**; **'luggage ˌrack**
lugger 'lʌg.ə^{r} (US) -ɚ **-s** -z
lughole 'lʌg.həʊl, -əʊl (US) -hoʊl **-s** -z
Lugosi luː'gəʊ.si (US) -'goʊ-
lugsail 'lʌg.seɪl *nautical pronunciation:* -s^{ə}l **-s** -z
lugubrious luː'guː.bri.əs, ljuː-, lə- (US) lə'guː-, luː- **-ly** -li **-ness** -nəs, -nɪs
lugworm 'lʌg.wɜːm (US) -wɝːm **-s** -z
Luis 'luː.ɪs
Luka 'luː.kə
Lukacs, Lukács 'luː.kætʃ (US) -kɑːtʃ
Luke luːk
lukewarm ˌluːk'wɔːm, '-- (US) 'luːk.wɔːrm, ˌ-'- **-ly** -li **-ness** -nəs, -nɪs
lull lʌl **-s** -z **-ing** -ɪŋ **-ed** -d
lullab|y 'lʌl.ə.b|aɪ **-ies** -aɪz
Lully 'lʊl.i; *as if French:* luː'liː (US) luː'liː
lulu (L) 'luː.luː
lumbago lʌm'beɪ.gəʊ (US) -goʊ
lumbar 'lʌm.bə^{r}, -bɑː^{r} (US) -bɑːr, -bɚ
lumb|er 'lʌm.b|ə^{r} (US) -b|ɚ **-ers** -əz (US) -ɚz **-ering** -^{ə}r.ɪŋ **-ered** -əd (US) -ɚd **-erer/s** -^{ə}r.ə^{r}/z (US) -ɚ.ɚ/z **-erman** -ə.mən (US) -ɚ.mən **-ermen** -ə.mən, -ə.men (US) -ɚ.mən, -ɚ.men
lumberjack 'lʌm.bə.dʒæk (US) -bɚ- **-s** -s
lumberyard 'lʌm.bə.jɑːd (US) -bɚ.jɑːrd **-s** -z
lumiere, lumière 'luː.mi.eə^{r}, ˌ--'- (US) ˌluː.mi'er
luminar|y 'luː.mɪ.n^{ə}r|.i, 'ljuː-, -mə- (US) 'luː.mə.ner- **-ies** -iz
luminesc|e ˌluː.mɪ'nes, ˌljuː-, -mə'- (US) ˌluː.mə'- **-es** -ɪz **-ing** -ɪŋ **-ed** -t
luminescen|ce ˌluː.mɪ'nes.^{ə}n|ts, ˌljuː-, -mə'- (US) ˌluː.mə'- **-t** -t
luminiferous ˌluː.mɪ'nɪf.^{ə}r.əs, ˌljuː-, -mə'- (US) ˌluː.mə'-
luminosity ˌluː.mɪ'nɒs.ə.ti, ˌljuː-, -mə'-, -ɪ.ti (US) ˌluː.mə'nɑː.sə.ţi
luminous 'luː.mɪ.nəs, 'ljuː-, -mə- (US) 'luː.mə- **-ly** -li **-ness** -nəs, -nɪs
Lumley 'lʌm.li
lumme 'lʌm.i
lummox 'lʌm.əks **-es** -ɪz
lump lʌmp **-s** -s **-ing** -ɪŋ **-ed** -t
lumpectom|y lʌm'pek.tə.m|i **-ies** -iz
lumpen 'lʌm.pən, 'lʊm-
lumpenproletariat ˌlʌm.pənˌprəʊ.lə'teə.ri.ət, ˌlʊm-, -pəmˌ-, -lɪ'-, -æt (US) -pənˌproʊ.lə'ter.i.ət
lumpfish 'lʌmp.fɪʃ **-es** -ɪz
lumpish 'lʌm.pɪʃ **-ly** -li **-ness** -nəs, -nɪs
Lumpkin 'lʌmp.kɪn
lump|y 'lʌm.p|i **-ier** -i.ə^{r} (US) -i.ɚ **-iest** -i.ɪst, -i.əst **-iness** -ɪ.nəs, -ɪ.nɪs
Lumsden 'lʌmz.dən
Luna 'luː.nə, 'ljuː- (US) 'luː-
lunacy 'luː.nə.si, 'ljuː- (US) 'luː-
lunar 'luː.nə^{r}, 'ljuː- (US) 'luː.nɚ
lunate 'luː.neɪt, 'ljuː-, -nət, -nɪt (US) 'luː.neɪt, -nɪt
lunatic 'luː.nə.tɪk, 'ljuː- (US) 'luː- **-s** -s **'lunatic aˌsylum**; **ˌlunatic 'fringe**
lunation luː'neɪ.ʃ^{ə}n, ljuː- (US) luː- **-s** -z
Luncarty 'lʌŋ.kə.ti (US) -kɚ.ţi
lunch lʌntʃ **-es** -ɪz **-ing** -ɪŋ **-ed** -t
lunchbox 'lʌntʃ.bɒks (US) -bɑːks **-es** -ɪz
luncheon 'lʌn.tʃən **-s** -z **'luncheon ˌmeat**; **'luncheon ˌvoucher**
luncheonette ˌlʌn.tʃə'net **-s** -s
lunchroom 'lʌntʃ.ruːm, -rʊm **-s** -z
lunchtime 'lʌntʃ.taɪm **-s** -z
Lund *place in Sweden:* lʊnd (US) lʊnd, lʌnd *family name:* lʌnd
Lundy 'lʌn.di
lune (L) luːn, ljuːn (US) luːn **-s** -z
Lüneburg 'luː.nə.bɜːg (US) -bɝːg
lunette luː'net, ljuː- (US) luː- **-s** -s
lung lʌŋ **-s** -z
lung|e lʌndʒ **-es** -ɪz **-ing** -ɪŋ **-ed** -d **-er/s** -ə^{r}/z (US) -ɚ/z
lungfish 'lʌŋ.fɪʃ **-es** -ɪz
lunkhead 'lʌŋk.hed **-s** -z
Lunn lʌn
lunul|a 'luː.njə.l|ə, 'ljuː- (US) -njʊ-, 'luː.njə- **-ae** -iː
lunule 'luː.njuːl, 'ljuː- (US) 'luː- **-s** -z
Lupercal 'luː.pə.kæl, 'ljuː-, -pɜː- (US) 'luː.pɚ.kæl
Lupercalia ˌluː.pə'keɪ.li.ə, ˌljuː-, -pɜː'- (US) ˌluː.pɚ'keɪl.jə
lupin(e) *flower:* 'luː.pɪn **-s** -z
lupine *(adj.) wolfish:* 'luː.paɪn, 'ljuː- (US) 'luː-
lupus (L) 'luː.pəs, 'ljuː- (US) 'luː-
lurch lɜːtʃ (US) lɝːtʃ **-es** -ɪz **-ing** -ɪŋ **-ed** -t **-er/s** -ə^{r}/z (US) -ɚ/z **ˌleave someone in the 'lurch**
lur|e lʊə^{r}, ljʊə^{r}, ljɔː^{r} (US) lʊr **-es** -z **-ing** -ɪŋ **-ed** -d
Lurex® 'ljʊə.reks, 'lʊə-, 'ljɔː- (US) 'lʊr.eks
Lurgan 'lɜː.g^{ə}n (US) 'lɝː-
lurg|y 'lɜː.g|i (US) 'lɝː- **-ies** -iz
lurid 'lʊə.rɪd, 'ljʊə-, 'ljɔː- (US) 'lʊr.ɪd **-ly** -li **-ness** -nəs, -nɪs
lurk lɜːk (US) lɝːk **-s** -s **-ing** -ɪŋ **-ed** -t **-er/s** -ə^{r}/z (US) -ɚ/z
Lurpak® 'lɜː.pæk (US) 'lɝː-
Lusaka luː'sɑː.kə, lʊ-, -'zɑː- (US) luː'sɑː.kɑː
Lusardi luː'sɑː.di (US) -'sɑːr-
Lusati|a luː'seɪ.ʃ|ə, -ʃi|.ə **-an/s** -ən/z
luscious 'lʌʃ.əs **-ly** -li **-ness** -nəs, -nɪs
lush (L) lʌʃ **-es** -ɪz **-er** -ə^{r} (US) -ɚ **-est** -ɪst, -əst **-ing** -ɪŋ **-ed** -t **-ness** -nəs, -nɪs
Lushington 'lʌʃ.ɪŋ.tən
Lusiad 'luː.si.æd, 'ljuː- (US) 'luː- **-s** -z
Lusitania ˌluː.sɪ'teɪ.ni.ə, ˌljuː-, -sə'- (US) ˌluː-
lust lʌst **-s** -s **-ing** -ɪŋ **-ed** -ɪd
luster 'lʌs.tə^{r} (US) -tɚ **-s** -z **-less** -ləs, -lɪs
lustful 'lʌst.f^{ə}l, -fʊl **-ly** -i **-ness** -nəs, -nɪs
lustral 'lʌs.tr^{ə}l
lustration lʌs'treɪ.ʃ^{ə}n **-s** -z
lustre 'lʌs.tə^{r} (US) -tɚ **-s** -z **-less** -ləs, -lɪs
lustrous 'lʌs.trəs **-ly** -li **-ness** -nəs, -nɪs
lustr|um 'lʌs.tr|əm **-ums** -əmz **-a** -ə
lust|y 'lʌs.t|i **-ier** -i.ə^{r} (US) -i.ɚ **-iest** -i.ɪst, -i.əst **-ily** -ɪ.li, -^{ə}l.i **-iness** -ɪ.nəs, -ɪ.nɪs

lutanist ˈluː.tᵊn.ɪst, ˈljuː- US ˈluː-
lute luːt, ljuːt US luːt **-s** -s
lutein ˈluː.ti.ɪn, ˈljuː-, -tiːn, ˈluː.ti.ɪn
luteiniz|e, -is|e ˈluː.ti.ɪ.naɪz, ˈljuː-, -ə-; -tɪ.naɪz, -tə-, -tiː-, -tᵊn.aɪz US ˈluː.ti.ə.naɪz, -ə- **-es** -ɪz **-ing** -ɪŋ **-ed** -d
lutenist ˈluː.tᵊn.ɪst, ˈljuː- US ˈluː- **-s** -s
lutetium luːˈtiː.ʃəm, ljuː-, -ʃi.əm US luːˈtiː.ʃi.əm
Luth|er ˈluː.θ|əʳ US ˈluː.θ|ɚ **-eran/s** -ᵊr.ᵊn/z **-eranism** -ᵊr.ᵊn.ɪ.zᵊm **-erism** -ᵊr.ɪ.zᵊm
Lutine luːˈtiːn, ˈ--
lutist ˈluː.tɪst, ˈljuː- US ˈluː.t̬ɪst **-s** -s
Luton ˈluː.tᵊn
Lutterworth ˈlʌt.ə.wəθ, -wɜːθ US ˈlʌt̬.ɚ.wɚθ, -wɝːθ
Lutton ˈlʌt.ᵊn
Luttrell ˈlʌt.rəl
Lutyens ˈlʌt.jənz, ˈlʌtʃ.ənz
luv lʌv **-s** -z
luvv|ie, luvv|y ˈlʌv|.i **-ies** -ɪz
lux lʌks **luxes** ˈlʌk.sɪz
Lux® lʌks
luxe lʌks, luːks, lʊks
Luxemb(o)urg ˈlʌk.sᵊm.bɜːg US -bɝːg
Luxor ˈlʌk.sɔːʳ US -sɔːr, ˈlʊk-
luxuriance lʌgˈʒʊə.ri.ənts, ləg-, -ˈʒɔː-, -ˈzjʊə-, -ˈzjɔː-; lʌkˈsjʊə-, lək-, -ˈsjɔː- US lʌgˈʒʊr.i-, -ˈzjʊr-; lʌkˈʃʊr-, -ˈsjʊr-
luxuriant lʌgˈʒʊə.ri.ənt, ləg-, -ˈʒɔː-, -ˈzjʊə-, -ˈzjɔː-; lʌkˈsjʊə-, lək-, -ˈsjɔː- US lʌgˈʒʊr.i-, -ˈzjʊr-; lʌkˈʃʊr-, -ˈsjʊr- **-ly** -li
luxuri|ate lʌgˈʒʊə.ri|.eɪt, ləg-, -ˈʒjɔː-, -ˈzjʊə-, -ˈzjɔː-; lʌkˈsjʊə-, lək-, -ˈsjɔː- US lʌgˈʒʊr.i-, -ˈʒjʊr-; lʌkˈʃʊr-, -ˈsjʊr- **-ates** -eɪts **-ating** -eɪ.tɪŋ US -eɪ.t̬ɪŋ **-ated** -eɪ.tɪd US -eɪ.t̬ɪd
luxurious lʌgˈʒʊə.ri.əs, ləg-, -ˈʒɔː-, -ˈzjʊə-, -ˈzjɔː-; lʌkˈsjʊə-, lək-, -ˈsjɔː- US lʌgˈʒʊr.i-, -ˈzjʊr-; lʌkˈʃʊr-, -ˈsjʊr- **-ly** -li **-ness** -nəs, -nɪs
luxur|y ˈlʌk.ʃᵊr|.i US ˈlʌk.ʃɚ|.i, -ʃʊr-; ˈlʌg.ʒɚ-, -ʒʊr- **-ies** -iz **in the ˌlap of ˈluxury**
Luzon luːˈzɒn US -ˈzɑːn
Lvov ləˈvɒf US -ˈvɑːf
lwei ləˈweɪ **-s** -z
-ly -li
Note: Suffix. Does not alter the stress pattern of the stem to which it is added, e.g. **rapid** /ˈræp.ɪd/, **rapidly** /ˈræp.ɪd.li/.*
Lyall ˈlaɪ.əl, laɪəl
lycanthrope ˈlaɪ.kᵊn.θrəʊp; laɪˈkænt.θrəʊp US -θroʊp **-s** -s
lycanthropic ˌlaɪ.kᵊnˈθrɒp.ɪk US -ˈθrɑː.pɪk
lycanthropy laɪˈkænt.θrə.pi
lycée ˈliː.seɪ US liːˈseɪ **-s** -z
Lycett ˈlaɪ.sɪt, -set
lyceum (L) laɪˈsiː.əm, ˈlaɪ- **-s** -z
lychee ˌlaɪˈtʃiː; ˈlaɪ.tʃiː, ˈliː- US ˈliː.tʃiː **-s** -z
lychgate ˈlɪtʃ.geɪt **-s** -s
lychnis ˈlɪk.nɪs
Lyci|a ˈlɪs.i|.ə, ˈlɪʃ-, ˈlɪʃ|.ə US ˈlɪʃ|.ə, -i|.ə **-an/s** -ən/z
Lycidas ˈlɪs.ɪ.dæs US -dæs, -dəs
Lycoming laɪˈkɒm.ɪŋ US -ˈkʌm-
lycopodium ˌlaɪ.kəʊˈpəʊ.di.əm US -koʊˈpoʊ- **-s** -z
Lycra® ˈlaɪ.krə
Lycurgus laɪˈkɜː.gəs US -ˈkɝː-
Lydall ˈlaɪ.dᵊl
Lydd lɪd
lyddite ˈlɪd.aɪt
Lydekker laɪˈdek.əʳ US -ɚ
Lydgate *fifteenth century poet, place in Greater Manchester:* ˈlɪd.geɪt, -gɪt *place in Yorkshire:* ˈlɪd.gɪt, ˈlɪ.gɪt *lane in Sheffield:* ˈlɪdʒ.ɪt
Lydi|a ˈlɪd.i|.ə **-an/s** -ən/z
Lydiate ˈlɪd.i.ət
Lydney ˈlɪd.ni
Lydon ˈlaɪ.dᵊn
lye (L) laɪ
Lyell ˈlaɪ.əl; laɪəl
Lygon ˈlɪg.ən
lying *(from* **lie***)* ˈlaɪ.ɪŋ **ˌtake something ˌlying ˈdown**
Lyle laɪl
Lyly ˈlɪl.i
Lyme laɪm **ˈLyme diˌsease**
Lyme Regis ˌlaɪmˈriː.dʒɪs
Lymeswold® ˈlaɪmz.wəʊld US -woʊld
Lymington ˈlɪm.ɪŋ.tən
Lymm lɪm
Lympany ˈlɪm.pə.ni
lymph lɪmpf **-s** -s
lymphatic lɪmˈfæt.ɪk US -ˈfæt̬- **-s** -s **-ally** -ᵊl.i, -li
lymphocyte ˈlɪmp.fəʊ.saɪt US -foʊ-, -fə- **-s** -s
lymphoid ˈlɪmp.fɔɪd
lymphoma lɪmˈfəʊ.mə US -ˈfoʊ- **-s** -z
Lympne lɪm
Lyn lɪn
Lynam ˈlaɪ.nəm
Lynas ˈlaɪ.nəs
lynch (L) lɪntʃ US lɪntʃ **-es** -ɪz **-ing** -ɪŋ **-ed** -t
Lynchburg ˈlɪntʃ.bɜːg US -bɝːg
lynchpin ˈlɪntʃ.pɪn **-s** -z
Lynda ˈlɪn.də
Lyndhurst ˈlɪnd.hɜːst US -hɝːst
Lyndon ˈlɪn.dən
Lyndsay, Lyndsey ˈlɪnd.zi
Lyness ˈlaɪ.nɪs, -nəs, -nes
Lynette lɪˈnet
Lynmouth ˈlɪn.məθ
Lynn(e) lɪn
Lynton ˈlɪn.tən
lynx lɪŋks **-es** -ɪz
Lyon laɪən
lyonnaise ˌlaɪəˈneɪz, ˌliː.əˈ-
Lyons laɪənz *French city:* ˈliː.ɔ̃ːŋ, -ɒn; laɪənz *as if French:* liˈɔ̃ŋ US liˈoʊn
Lyr|a ˈlaɪə.r|ə US ˈlaɪ- **-ae** -iː
lyrate ˈlaɪə.rɪt, -reɪt, -rət US ˈlaɪ.reɪt
lyre laɪəʳ US laɪr **-s** -z
lyrebird ˈlaɪə.bɜːd US ˈlaɪr.bɝːd **-s** -z
lyric (L) ˈlɪr.ɪk **-s** -s **-al** -ᵊl **-ally** -ᵊl.i, -li
lyricism ˈlɪr.ɪ.sɪ.zᵊm, ˈ-ə-
lyricist ˈlɪr.ɪ.sɪst, ˈ-ə- **-s** -s
lyrist *player on the lyre:* ˈlaɪə.rɪst, ˈlɪr.ɪst US ˈlaɪr.ɪst **-s** -s
lyrist *lyric poet:* ˈlɪr.ɪst **-s** -s
Lysander laɪˈsæn.dəʳ US -dɚ
lysergic laɪˈsɜː.dʒɪk, lɪ- US laɪˈsɝː-
Lysias ˈlɪs.i.æs
Lysicrates laɪˈsɪk.rə.tiːz
Lysippus laɪˈsɪp.əs
-lysis -lə.sɪs, -lɪ-
Note: Suffix. Words containing **-lysis** are normally stressed on the syllable preceding the suffix, e.g. **paralysis** /pəˈræl.ə.sɪs/.
Lysistrata laɪˈsɪs.trə.tə US ˌlɪs.ɪˈstrɑː-; laɪˈsɪs.trə-
Lysol® ˈlaɪ.sɒl US -sɑːl
Lystra ˈlɪs.trə
Lyte laɪt
Lytham ˈlɪð.əm
Lythe laɪð
Lyttelton ˈlɪt.ᵊl.tən US ˈlɪt̬-
Lyttle ˈlɪt.l̩ US ˈlɪt̬-
Lytton ˈlɪt.ᵊn

Pronouncing the letter M

See also MN

The consonant letter **m** is always realised as /m/.

m (M) em **-'s** -z
m *(abbrev. for* **metre/s***) singular:* 'miː.təʳ (US) -t̬ɚ *plural:* -z
ma *(mother)* mɑː **-s** -z
MA ˌem'eɪ
ma'am *(abbrev. for* **madam***)* mæm, mɑːm, məm, m (US) mæm
Note: /mɑːm/, or alternatively /mæm/, is used in addressing members of the royal family.
Maas mɑːs
Maastricht 'mɑː.strɪkt, -strɪxt; *as if Dutch:* mɑː'strɪxt (US) 'mɑː.strɪkt, -strɪxt
Mab mæb
Mabel 'meɪ.bᵊl
Mabinogion ˌmæb.ɪ'nɒg.i.ɒn, -ə'-, -ən (US) -'noʊ.gi.ɑːn, -'nɑː-, -ən
Mablethorpe 'meɪ.bl̩.θɔːp (US) -θɔːrp
Mabley 'mæb.li (US) 'mæb-, 'meɪb-
Mabs mæbz
Mac mæk
mac, mack mæk **-s** -s
macabre mə'kɑː.brə, mæk'ɑː-, -bəʳ (US) mə'kɑː.brə, -'kɑːb, -'kɑː.bɚ
macadam mə'kæd.əm
MacAdam mə'kæd.əm
macadamia ˌmæk.ə'deɪ.mi.ə **-s** -z **ˌmaca'damia ˌnut**
macadamization, -isa- məˌkæd.ə.maɪ'zeɪ.ʃᵊn, -mɪ'- (US) -mə'-
macadamiz|e, -is|e mə'kæd.ə.maɪz **-es** -ɪz **-ing** -ɪŋ **-ed** -d
Macalister mə'kæl.ɪ.stəʳ (US) -stɚ
Macan mə'kæn
Macao mə'kaʊ, mæk'aʊ (US) mə'kaʊ
macaque mə'kɑːk, -'kæk; 'mæk.æk (US) mə'kɑːk **-s** -s
macaroni ˌmæk.ᵊr'əʊ.ni (US) -ə'roʊ- **-(e)s** -z *stress shift, see compound:* **ˌmacaroni 'cheese**
macaroon ˌmæk.ᵊr'uːn (US) -ə'ruːn **-s** -z
MacArthur mə'kɑː.θəʳ (US) -'kɑːr.θɚ
macassar (M) mə'kæs.əʳ (US) -ɚ **ma'cassar ˌoil**
Macau mə'kaʊ, mæk'aʊ (US) mə'kaʊ
Macaulay mə'kɔː.li (US) -'kɑː.li, -'kɔː-
Macavity mə'kæv.ə.ti, -ɪ.ti (US) -ə.t̬i
MacAvoy 'mæk.ə.vɔɪ
macaw mə'kɔː (US) -'kɑː, -'kɔː **-s** -z
MacBain mək'beɪn
Macbeth mək'beθ, mæk-
Note: In Scotland always /mək-/.

Maccabaeus ˌmæk.ə'biː.əs, -'beɪ- (US) -'biː-
Maccabean ˌmæk.ə'biː.ən, -'beɪ- (US) -'biː-
Maccabees 'mæk.ə.biːz
Maccabeus ˌmæk.ə'biː.əs, -'beɪ- (US) -'biː-
MacCaig mə'keɪg
MacCall mə'kɔːl (US) -'kɔːl, -'kɑːl
MacCallum mə'kæl.əm
MacCarthy mə'kɑː.θi (US) -'kɑːr-
Macclesfield 'mæk.l̩z.fiːld, -l̩s-
MacCunn mə'kʌn
MacDaire mək'dɑː.rə (US) mək'der
MacDiarmid mək'dɜː.mɪd, -'deə- (US) -'dɝː-
Macdonald, MacDonald mək'dɒn.ᵊld, mæk- (US) -'dɑː.nᵊld
MacDonaugh mək'dɒn.ə (US) -'dɑː.nə
MacDon(n)ell mək'dɒn.ᵊl (US) -'dɑː.nᵊl
MacDougal mək'duː.gᵊl
MacDuff mək'dʌf, mæk-
Note: In Scotland always /mək-/.
mace meɪs **-s** -ɪz
macedoine, macédoine ˌmæs.ɪ'dwɑːn, -ə'-, '--- (US) ˌmæs.ɪ'dwɑːn **-s** -z
Macedon 'mæs.ɪ.dᵊn, '-ə- (US) -ə.dɑːn, -dən
Macedoni|a ˌmæs.ɪ'dəʊ.ni|.ə (US) -ə'doʊ.ni-, '-nj|ə **-an/s** -ən/z
MacElder(r)y ˌmæk.ᵊl'der.i, mə'kel.dᵊr- (US) mə'kel.dɚ-
MacElwain 'mæk.ᵊl.weɪn, mə'kel.weɪn
MacElwin 'mæk.ᵊl.wɪn
macer|ate 'mæs.ᵊr|.eɪt (US) -ə.r|eɪt **-ates** -eɪts **-ating** -eɪ.tɪŋ (US) -eɪ.t̬ɪŋ **-ated** -eɪ.tɪd (US) -eɪ.t̬ɪd
maceration ˌmæs.ᵊr'eɪ.ʃᵊn (US) -ə'reɪ- **-s** -z
macerator 'mæs.ᵊr.eɪ.təʳ (US) -ə.reɪ.t̬ɚ **-s** -z
MacFarlane mək'fɑː.lən (US) -'fɑːr-
Macfarren mək'fær.ᵊn (US) -'fer-, -'fær-
Macgillicuddy, MacGillicuddy mə'gɪl.i.kʌd.i; 'mæg.li-, 'mæk.ɪl- (US) mə'gɪl.i-
Note: **Macgillicuddy's Reeks** is pronounced /məˌgɪl.i.kʌd.iz'riːks/.
Macgregor, MacGregor mə'greg.əʳ (US) -ɚ
Mach mæk, mɑːk (US) mɑːk, mæk
Machakos mə'tʃɑː.kɒs (US) -kɑːs
Macheath mək'hiːθ (US) mæk-, mək-

Machen 'meɪ.tʃɪn, -tʃən; 'mæk.ɪn *as if Welsh:* 'mæx- (US) 'mæk.ɪn
machete mə'tʃet.i, mætʃ'et-, -'eɪ.ti (US) mə'tʃet̬.i **-s** -z
Machiavelli ˌmæk.i.ə'vel.i, ˌ-jə'-
Machiavellian ˌmæk.i.ə'vel.i.ən, ˌmæk.jə- **-s** -z **-ism** -ɪ.zᵊm
machico|late mə'tʃɪk.əʊ|.leɪt, mætʃ'ɪk- (US) mə'tʃɪk.oʊ-, '-ə- **-lates** -leɪts **-lating** -leɪ.tɪŋ (US) -leɪ.t̬ɪŋ **-lated** -leɪ.tɪd (US) -leɪ.t̬ɪd
machicolation məˌtʃɪk.əʊ'leɪ.ʃᵊn, mætʃˌɪk- (US) məˌtʃɪk.oʊ'-, -ə'- **-s** -z
Machin 'meɪ.tʃɪn
machi|nate 'mæk.ɪ|.neɪt, 'mæʃ-, '-ə- (US) -ə|.neɪt **-nates** -neɪts **-nating** -neɪ.tɪŋ (US) -neɪ.t̬ɪŋ **-nated** -neɪ.tɪd (US) -neɪ.t̬ɪd **-nator/s** -neɪ.təʳ/z (US) -neɪ.t̬ɚ/s
machination ˌmæk.ɪ'neɪ.ʃᵊn, ˌmæʃ-, -ə'- (US) -ə'- **-s** -z
machin|e mə'ʃiːn **-es** -z **-ing** -ɪŋ **-ed** -d **ma'chine ˌcode; ma'chine ˌtool**
machine-gun mə'ʃiːn.gʌn, -'ʃiːŋ.- (US) -'ʃiːn.- **-s** -z **-ning** -ɪŋ **-ned** -d **-ner/s** -əʳ/z (US) -ɚ/z
machine-made mə'ʃiːn.meɪd
machine-readable məˌʃiːn'riː.də.bl̩ *stress shift:* maˌchine-readable 'dictionary
machiner|y mə'ʃiː.nᵊr.i **-ies** -ɪz
machine-washable məˌʃiːn'wɒʃ.ə.bl̩ (US) -'wɑː.ʃə- *stress shift:* maˌchine-washable 'wool
machinist mə'ʃiː.nɪst **-s** -s
machismo mætʃ'ɪz.məʊ, mə'tʃɪz-, -'kɪz- (US) mɑː'tʃiːz.moʊ, mə'kɪz-
macho 'mætʃ.əʊ (US) 'mɑː.tʃoʊ **-s** -z
macho-|man 'mætʃ.əʊ|ˌmæn (US) 'mɑː.tʃoʊ- **-men** -men
Machu Picchu ˌmɑː.tʃuː'piːk.tʃuː
Machynlleth mə'kʌn.*h*ləθ
MacIlwain 'mæk.ᵊl.weɪn, -ɪl-
MacIlwraith 'mæk.ɪl.reɪθ
Macindoe, MacIndoe 'mæk.ɪn.dəʊ, -ᵊn- (US) -doʊ
MacInnes, MacInnis mə'kɪn.ɪs
macintosh 'mæk.ɪn.tɒʃ (US) -tɑːʃ **-es** -ɪz
MacIntyre 'mæk.ɪn.taɪəʳ, -ᵊn- (US) -taɪɚ
MacIver mə'kaɪ.vəʳ, -'kɪv.əʳ (US) -vɚ
MacIvor mə'kaɪ.vəʳ (US) -vɚ
Mack mæk
Mackay(e), MacKay(e) mə'kaɪ, mə'keɪ
Note: /mə'keɪ/ mainly in U.S.A.
Mackenzie mə'ken.zi
mackerel 'mæk.rᵊl, 'mæk.ᵊr.ᵊl **-s** -z
Mackerras mə'ker.əs
Mackeson 'mæk.ɪ.sᵊn, '-ə-
Mackie 'mæk.i
Mackin 'mæk.ɪn
mackinaw 'mæk.ɪ.nɔː (US) -nɑː, -nɔː **-s** -z

Mackinlay, Mackinley mə'kɪn.li
mackintosh (M) 'mæk.ɪn.tɒʃ ⓤⓢ -tɑːʃ -es -ɪz
Mackowie, MacKowie mə'kaʊ.i
MacLachlan mə'klɒk.lən, -'klɒx-, -'klæk-, -'klæx- ⓤⓢ -'klɑː.klən
MacLagan mə'klæg.ən ⓤⓢ mək'lɑː.ken, -'glɑː.kən
MacLaglan mə'klæg.lən ⓤⓢ -'klæg-, -'klɑːg-
Maclaren mə'klær.ən ⓤⓢ -'kler-, -'klær-
MacLaverty mə'klæv.ə.ti ⓤⓢ -ɚ.t̬i
Maclean mə'kleɪn, -'kliːn ⓤⓢ -'kliːn
Macleans® mə'kliːnz
MacLeish mə'kliːʃ
MacLeod mə'klaʊd
Maclise mə'kliːs
MacManus mək'mæn.əs, -meɪ.nəs
Macmillan mək'mɪl.ən, mæk-
Macmorran mək'mɒr.ən, mæk- ⓤⓢ -'mɔːr-
MacNab mək'næb
Macnamara ˌmæk.nə'mɑː.rə ⓤⓢ 'mæk.nə.mer.ə, -mær-
MacNaught mək'nɔːt ⓤⓢ -nɑːt, -nɔːt
MacNeice mək.niːs
Mâcon 'mɑː.kɔ̃ːŋ, 'mæk.ɔ̃ːŋ, -ɒn, -ən ⓤⓢ mɑː'koʊn
Macon 'meɪ.kən
Maconchy mə'kɒŋ.ki ⓤⓢ -'kɑːŋ-, -'kɔːŋ-
Maconochie mə'kɒn.ə.ki, -xi ⓤⓢ -'kɑː.nə-
MacPhee mək'fiː
MacPherson, Macpherson mək'fɜː.sən, mæk-, -'fɪə- ⓤⓢ -'fɝː-, -'fɪr-
Macquarie mə'kwɒr.i ⓤⓢ -'kwɑːr-, -'kwɔːr-
macrame, macramé mə'krɑː.meɪ, -mi ⓤⓢ 'mæk.rə.meɪ
Macready mə'kriː.di
macro- 'mæk.rəʊ- ⓤⓢ 'mæk.roʊ-, -rə-
macro 'mæk.rəʊ ⓤⓢ -roʊ **-s** -z
macrobiotic ˌmæk.rəʊ.baɪ'ɒt.ɪk ⓤⓢ -roʊ.baɪ'ɑː.t̬ɪk, -rə- **-s** -s
macroclimate 'mæk.rəʊˌklaɪ.mɪt, -mət ⓤⓢ -roʊˌ- **-s** -s
macroclimatic ˌmæk.rəʊ.klaɪ'mæt.ɪk ⓤⓢ -roʊ.klaɪ'mæt̬-, -rə-
macrocosm 'mæk.rəʊˌkɒz.əm ⓤⓢ -roʊˌkɑː.zəm, -rə- **-s** -z
macroeconomic ˌmæk.rəʊ.iː.kə'nɒm.ɪk, -ek.ə'- ⓤⓢ -roʊˌek.ə'nɑː.mɪk, -ˌiː.kə'- **-s** -s
macron 'mæk.rɒn ⓤⓢ 'meɪ.krɑːn, 'mæk.rɑːn, -rən **-s** -z
macrophag|e 'mæk.rəʊ.feɪdʒ ⓤⓢ -roʊ- **-es** -ɪz
macrophagic ˌmæk.rəʊ'feɪ.dʒɪk ⓤⓢ -roʊ'fædʒ.ɪk
macroscopic ˌmæk.rəʊ'skɒp.ɪk ⓤⓢ -roʊ'skɑː.pɪk **-al** -əl

Macrow mə'krəʊ ⓤⓢ -'kroʊ
MacSwiney mək'swiː.ni, -'swɪn-
MacTavish mək'tæv.ɪʃ
macul|a 'mæk.jʊ.l|ə, -jə- ⓤⓢ -jə-, -juː- **-as** -əz **-ae** -iː
Macy® 'meɪ.si 'meɪ.siz
mad mæd **-der** -əʳ ⓤⓢ -ɚ **-dest** -ɪst, -əst **-ly** -li **-ness** -nəs, -nɪs **as ˌmad as a 'hatter; ˌmad 'cow diˌsease**
Madagasc|ar ˌmæd.ə'gæs.k|əʳ ⓤⓢ -k|ɚ **-an/s** -ən/z
madam 'mæd.əm **-s** -z
madame (M) 'mæd.əm, mə'dæm, -'dɑːm; **-s** -z
Madan 'mæd.ən, 'meɪ.dən
madcap 'mæd.kæp **-s** -s
Maddalo 'mæd.əl.əʊ ⓤⓢ -oʊ
madden (M) 'mæd.ən **-s** -z **-ing** -ɪŋ **-ed** -d
madder 'mæd.əʳ ⓤⓢ -ɚ **-s** -z
Maddie 'mæd.i
madding 'mæd.ɪŋ
Maddison 'mæd.ɪ.sən, '-ə-
Maddox 'mæd.əks
made *(from* **make***)* meɪd
Madeira mə'dɪə.rə ⓤⓢ -'dɪr.ə **-s** -z **Ma'deira ˌcake**
Madeleine 'mæd.əl.ɪn, -eɪn
Madeley 'meɪd.li
Madeline 'mæd.əl.ɪn, -eɪn
mademoiselle (M) ˌmæd.ə.mwə'zel, ˌmæm.wə'-, ˌmæm'zel ⓤⓢ ˌmæd.ə.mə'-, ˌmæm'- **-s** -z
made-to-measure ˌmeɪd.tə'meʒ.əʳ ⓤⓢ -ɚ *stress shift:* ˌmade-to-measure 'suit
made-to-order ˌmeɪd.tu'ɔː.dəʳ ⓤⓢ -'ɔːr.dɚ *stress-shift:* **ˌmade-to-order 'suit**
Madge mædʒ
madhou|se 'mæd.haʊ|s **-ses** -zɪz
Madhya Pradesh ˌmʌd.jə.prɑː'deʃ, ˌmɑːd- ⓤⓢ -'prɑː.deʃ
Madingley 'mæd.ɪŋ.li
Madison 'mæd.ɪ.sən, '-ə- **ˌMadison 'Avenue**
mad|man 'mæd|.mən ⓤⓢ -mən, -mæn **-men** -mən, -men **-woman** -ˌwʊm.ən **-women** -ˌwɪm.ɪn
Madoc 'mæd.ək
madonna (M) mə'dɒn.ə ⓤⓢ -'dɑː.nə **-s** -z
Madras *in India:* mə'drɑːs, -dræs
madras *fabric:* 'mæd.rəs ⓤⓢ 'mæd.rəs, mə'dræs, -'drɑːs
madrepore ˌmæd.rɪ'pɔːʳ, -rə'-, '--- ⓤⓢ 'mæd.rə.pɔːr **-s** -z
Madrid mə'drɪd
madrigal 'mæd.rɪ.gəl, -rə- **-s** -z
madrigalist 'mæd.rɪ.gəl.ɪst, -rə- **-s** -s
Madura mə'djʊə.rə, -'dʒʊə-, -'dʊə- ⓤⓢ mɑː'dʊr.ə

madwort 'mæd.wɜːt ⓤⓢ -wɝːt, -wɔːrt
Mae meɪ
Maecenas maɪ'siː.næs, miː'-, -nəs ⓤⓢ miː'-, mɪ-
maelstrom (M) 'meɪl.strɒm, -strəʊm ⓤⓢ -strəm **-s** -z
maenad 'miː.næd **-s** -z
Maerdy 'mɑː.di, 'meə- ⓤⓢ 'mɑːr-, 'mer-
Maesteg ˌmaɪ'steɪg
maestoso ˌmɑː.es'təʊ.zəʊ, maɪ'stəʊ-, -səʊ ⓤⓢ maɪ'stoʊ.zoʊ
maestr|o (M®) 'maɪ.str|əʊ ⓤⓢ -str|oʊ **-os** -əʊz ⓤⓢ -oʊz **-i** -i
Maeterlinck 'meɪ.tə.lɪŋk ⓤⓢ 'meɪ.tɚ-, 'met.ɚ-
Maev(e) meɪv
Mae West ˌmeɪ'west **-s** -s
Mafeking 'mæf.ɪ.kɪŋ, '-ə-
MAFF, Maff mæf
maffick 'mæf.ɪk **-s** -s **-ing** -ɪŋ **-ed** -t **-er/s** -əʳ/z ⓤⓢ -ɚ/z
mafia (M) 'mæf.i.ə, 'mɑː.fi- ⓤⓢ 'mɑː-
Mafikeng 'mæf.ɪ.keŋ, '-ə-
mafios|o (M) ˌmæf.i'əʊ.s|əʊ, ˌmɑː.fi'-, -z|əʊ ⓤⓢ ˌmɑː.fi'oʊ.s|oʊ **-os** -əʊz ⓤⓢ -oʊz **-i** -iː
mag (M) mæg **-s** -z
magalog 'mæg.ə.lɒg ⓤⓢ -lɑːg **-s** -z
Magan 'meɪ.gən, mə'gæn
magazine ˌmæg.ə'ziːn, '--- ⓤⓢ 'mæg.ə.ziːn, ˌ--'- **-s** -z
Note: The stressing /'---/ is usual in the north of England, but uncommon in the south.
Magdala 'mæg.dəl.ə, ˌmæg'dɑː.lə ⓤⓢ 'mæg.dəl.ə
Magdalen *biblical name, modern first name, Canadian islands:* 'mæg.dəl.ɪn, -ən ⓤⓢ -ən, -ɪn *Oxford college and bridge:* 'mɔːd.lɪn ⓤⓢ 'mɑːd-, 'mɔːd- *Oxford street:* 'mæg.dəl.ɪn, -ən ⓤⓢ -ən, -ɪn
Magdalene *biblical name:* ˌmæg.də'liː.ni; 'mæg.dəl.iːn, -ɪn ⓤⓢ 'mæg.dəl.iːn, -ən, -ɪn; ˌmæg.də'liː.nə *modern first name:* 'mæg.dəl.iːn, -ɪn ⓤⓢ -iːn, -ən, -ɪn *Cambridge college and street:* 'mɔːd.lɪn ⓤⓢ 'mɑːd-, 'mɔːd-
Magdalenian ˌmæg.dəl'iː.ni.ən
Magdeburg 'mæg.də.bɜːg, '-dɪ- ⓤⓢ 'mæg.də.bɝːg, 'mɑːg.də.bʊrg
mag|e meɪdʒ **-es** -ɪz
Magee mə'giː
Magellan mə'gel.ən ⓤⓢ -'dʒel-
magenta (M) mə'dʒen.tə ⓤⓢ -t̬ə
Maggie 'mæg.i
Maggiore ˌmædʒ'ɔː.reɪ, -ri; ˌ-i'-, mə'dʒɔː- ⓤⓢ mə'dʒɔːr.i
magg|ot 'mæg|.ət **-ots** -əts **-oty** -ə.ti ⓤⓢ -ə.t̬i
Maghera ˌmæk.ə'rɑː, ˌmæ.hə'-

Magherafelt ˌmæk.ᵊr.əˈfelt, ˌmæ.hᵊr-
Maghreb, Maghrib ˈmɑː.greb, ˈmʌg.reb, ˈmæg.reb, -rɪb, -rəb; məˈgreb, mɑː- (US) ˈmʌg.rəb
Maghull məˈgʌl
Magi *(plur. of* **Magus***)* ˈmeɪ.dʒaɪ, -gaɪ (US) -dʒaɪ
magic ˈmædʒ.ɪk **-al** -ᵊl **-ally** -ᵊl.i, -li ˌ**magic ˈcarpet**; ˌ**magic ˈeye**; ˌ**magic ˈlantern**; ˌ**magic ˈmushroom**; ˌ**magic ˈwand**
magician məˈdʒɪʃ.ᵊn **-s** -z
Maginot ˈmæʒ.ɪ.nəʊ, ˈmædʒ-, ˈ-ə- (US) -ə.noʊ ˈ**Maginot** ˌ**Line**
magisterial ˌmædʒ.ɪˈstɪə.ri.əl, -əˈ- (US) -ɪˈstɪr.i- **-ly** -i
magistrac|y ˈmædʒ.ɪ.strə.s|i, ˈ-ə- (US) ˈ-ɪ- **-ies** -iz
magistral məˈdʒɪs.trᵊl, mædʒˈɪs-; ˈmædʒ.ɪ.strᵊl, ˈ-ə- (US) ˈmædʒ.ɪ.strᵊl
magistrate ˈmædʒ.ɪ.streɪt, ˈ-ə-, -strɪt, -strət (US) -ɪ.streɪt, -strɪt **-s** -s
magistrature ˈmædʒ.ɪ.strə.tʃəʳ, ˈ-ə-, -ˌtjʊəʳ, -ˌtʃʊəʳ (US) -ɪ.streɪ.tʃɚ, -strə.tʃʊr **-s** -z
magma ˈmæg.mə
magmatic mægˈmæt.ɪk (US) -ˈmæt̬-
Magna Carta ˌmæg.nəˈkɑː.tə (US) -ˈkɑːr.t̬ə
magna cum laude ˌmæg.nɑː.kʊmˈlaʊ.deɪ
magnanimity ˌmæg.nəˈnɪm.ə.ti, -nænˈɪm-, -ɪ.ti (US) -nəˈnɪm.ə.t̬i
magnanimous mægˈnæn.ɪ.məs, məg- (US) mægˈnæn.ə- **-ly** -li
magnate ˈmæg.neɪt, -nɪt **-s** -s
magnesia *substance:* mægˈniː.zi.ə, məg-, ˈ-si.ə, -ʒi.ə, -ʒə (US) mægˈniː.ʒə, -ʃə
Magnesia *city:* mægˈniː.zi.ə, -ʒi.ə, -ʒə (US) -zi.ə, -ʒi.ə, -ʒə, -ʃə
magnesium mægˈniː.zi.əm, məg-, -si-, -ʒi- (US) mægˈniː.zi-, -ʒi-, ˈ-ʒᵊm
magnet ˈmæg.nət, -nɪt **-s** -s
magnetic mægˈnet.ɪk, məg- (US) mægˈnet̬- **-al** -ᵊl **-ally** -ᵊl.i, -li magˌ**netic ˈfield**; magˌ**netic ˈnorth**; magˌ**netic ˈstorm**; magˌ**netic ˈtape**
magnetism ˈmæg.nə.tɪ.zᵊm, -nɪ- (US) -t̬ɪ-
magnetiz|e, -is|e ˈmæg.nə.taɪz, -nɪ- **-es** -ɪz **-ing** -ɪŋ **-ed** -d **-er/s** -əʳ/z (US) -ɚ/z
magneto mægˈniː.təʊ, məg (US) mægˈniː.t̬oʊ **-s** -z
magnetron ˈmæg.nə.trɒn, -nɪ- (US) -trɑːn **-s** -z
Magnificat mægˈnɪf.ɪ.kæt, məg-, ˈ-ə- (US) mægˈnɪf-; mɑːˈnjɪ.fɪ.kɑːt **-s** -s
magnification ˌmæg.nɪ.fɪˈkeɪ.ʃᵊn, -nə- **-s** -z
magnificence mægˈnɪf.ɪ.sᵊnts, məg-, ˈ-ə- (US) mæg-
magnificent mægˈnɪf.ɪ.sᵊnt, məg-, ˈ-ə- (US) mæg- **-ly** -li
magnifico mægˈnɪf.ɪ.kəʊ, ˈ-ə- (US) -koʊ **-(e)s** -z
magni|fy ˈmæg.nɪ|.faɪ, -nə- **-fies** -faɪz **-fying** -faɪ.ɪŋ **-fied** -faɪd **-fier/s** -faɪ.əʳ/z (US) -faɪ.ɚ/z **-fiable** -faɪ.ə.bl̩ ˈ**magnifying** ˌ**glass**
magniloquen|ce mægˈnɪl.ə.kwən|ts **-t** -t
magnitude ˈmæg.nɪ.tjuːd, -nə-, -tʃuːd (US) -tuːd, -tjuːd **-s** -z
magnolia mægˈnəʊ.li.ə, məg- (US) mægˈnoʊl.jə, -ˈnoʊ.li.ə **-s** -z
Magnox ˈmæg.nɒks (US) -nɑːks
magnum ˈmæg.nəm **-s** -z
magnum bonum ˌmæg.nəmˈbəʊ.nəm, -ˈbɒn.əm (US) -ˈboʊ.nəm **-s** -z
magnum opus ˌmæg.nəmˈəʊ.pəs, -ˈɒp.əs (US) -ˈoʊ.pəs
Magnus ˈmæg.nəs
Magnyficence mægˈnɪf.ɪ.sᵊnts, ˈ-ə-
Magog ˈmeɪ.gɒg (US) -gɑːg, -gɔːg
magpie ˈmæg.paɪ **-s** -z
Magrath məˈgrɑː, -ˈgrɑːθ, -ˈgræθ (US) -ˈgræθ
Magritte mægˈriːt, məˈgriːt (US) mɑː-
Magruder məˈgruː.dəʳ (US) -dɚ
Maguiness məˈgɪn.ɪs, -əs
Maguire məˈgwaɪəʳ (US) -ˈgwaɪɚ
ma|gus (M) ˈmeɪ|.gəs **-gi** -dʒaɪ, -gaɪ (US) -dʒaɪ
Magwitch ˈmæg.wɪtʃ
Magyar ˈmæg.jɑːʳ (US) -jɑːr **-s** -z
Mahabharata məˌhɑːˈbɑː.rə.tə, ˌmɑː.həˈ- (US) məˌhɑːˈbɑːr.ə-, ˌmɑː-, -ˈrɑː.tɑː
Mahaffy məˈhæf.i
Mahan məˈhæn; mɑːn (US) məˈhæn
Mahany ˈmɑː.ni
maharaja(h) ˌmɑː.*h*əˈrɑː.dʒə (US) -həˈ- **-s** -z
maharani, maharanee ˌmɑː.*h*əˈrɑː.ni (US) -həˈ- **-s** -z
Maharashtra ˌmɑː.*h*əˈræʃ.trə, -ˈrɑːʃ- (US) -hɑːˈrɑːʃ-
maharishi (M) ˌmɑː.*h*əˈriː.ʃi (US) -həˈ- **-s** -z
mahatma (M) məˈhɑːt.mə, -ˈhæt- **-s** -z
Mahayana məˌhɑːˈjɑː.nə, ˌmɑː.həˈ- (US) ˌmɑː.həˈ-
Mahdi ˈmɑː.diː, -di **-s** -z
Mahé ˈmɑː.*h*eɪ (US) mɑːˈheɪ
Mahican məˈ*h*iː.kᵊn, mɑː- **-s** -z
mah-jong(g) ˌmɑːˈdʒɒŋ (US) -ˈdʒɔːŋ, -ˈdʒɑːŋ, -ˈʒɔːŋ, -ˈʒɑːŋ
Mahler ˈmɑː.ləʳ (US) -lɚ
mahlstick ˈmɔːl.stɪk (US) ˈmɑːl-, ˈmɔːl- **-s** -s
Mahmud mɑːˈmuːd
mahogany məˈhɒg.ᵊn.i (US) -ˈhɑː.gᵊn-
Mahomet, Mahomed məˈhɒm.ɪt, -et (US) məˈhɑː.mɪt
Mahometan məˈhɒm.ɪ.tᵊn, ˈ-ə- (US) -ˈhɑː.mə.t̬ən **-s** -z
Mahommed məˈhɒm.ɪd, -ed (US) -ˈhɑː.mɪd
Mahommedan məˈhɒm.ɪ.dᵊn (US) -ˈhɑː.mə- **-s** -z
Mahon mɑːn; ˈmæ.hən; məˈhuːn, -ˈhəʊn (US) mæn; məˈhoʊn, -ˈhuːn
Mahon(e)y ˈmɑː.ə.ni, ˈmɑː.ni, məˈhəʊ.ni (US) məˈhoʊ-
mahonia məˈhəʊ.ni.ə, mɑː- (US) məˈhoʊ- **-s** -z
mahout məˈhaʊt, mɑː-, -ˈhuːt (US) məˈhoʊt **-s** -s
Mahratta məˈræt.ə (US) -ˈrɑː.t̬ə **-s** -z
Maia ˈmaɪ.ə, ˈmeɪ-
maid meɪd **-s** -z
Maida ˈmeɪ.də
maidan (M) maɪˈdɑːn, mædˈɑːn **-s** -z
maiden ˈmeɪ.dᵊn **-s** -z **-ly** -li ˌ**maiden ˈname**
maidenhair ˈmeɪ.dᵊn.heəʳ (US) -her **-s** -z
maidenhead (M) ˈmeɪ.dᵊn.hed
maidenhood ˈmeɪ.dᵊn.hʊd
Maidens ˈmeɪ.dᵊnz
maid-servant ˈmeɪdˌsɜː.vᵊnt (US) -ˌsɝː- **-s** -s
Maidstone ˈmeɪd.stᵊn, -stəʊn (US) -stoʊn, -stᵊn
maieutic meɪˈuː.tɪk, maɪ- (US) -ˈjuː.t̬ik
Maigret ˈmeɪ.greɪ (US) ˌ-ˈ-
mail meɪl **-s** -z **-ing** -ɪŋ **-ed** -d **-er/s** -əʳ/z (US) -ɚ/z ˈ**mail** ˌ**drop**; ˈ**mailing** ˌ**list**;
mailbag ˈmeɪl.bæg **-s** -z
mailbox ˈmeɪl.bɒks (US) -bɑːks **-es** -ɪz
Mailer ˈmeɪ.ləʳ (US) -lɚ
Mailgram® ˈmeɪl.græm
Maillard ˈmeɪ.ləd (US) -lɚd
mail|man ˈmeɪl|.mæn **-men** -men, -mən
mail-order ˌmeɪlˈɔː.dəʳ (US) ˈmeɪlˌɔːr.dɚ *stress shift, British English:* ˌmail-order ˈcatalogue
mailroom ˈmeɪl.rʊm, -ruːm (US) -ruːm, -rʊm **-s** -z
mailshot ˈmeɪl.ʃɒt (US) -ʃɑːt **-s** -s
maim meɪm **-s** -z **-ing** -ɪŋ **-ed** -d
main meɪn **-s** -z ˌ**main ˈdrag**; ˌ**main ˈline**; ˈ**Main** ˌ**Street**
Main *German river:* maɪn, meɪn
mainbrac|e ˈmeɪn.breɪs, ˈmeɪm- (US) ˈmeɪn- **-es** -ɪz
Maine meɪn
mainframe ˈmeɪn.freɪm **-s** -z
mainland ˈmeɪn.lənd, -lænd
Mainland ˈmeɪn.lænd
mainlin|e ˈmeɪn.laɪn, ˌ-ˈ- (US) ˈ-- **-es** -z **-ing** -ɪŋ **-ed** -d **-er/s** -əʳ/z (US) -ɚ/z
mainly ˈmeɪn.li

mainmast 'meɪn.mɑːst, 'meɪm- ⓤⓢ 'meɪn.mæst *nautical pronunciation:* -məst **-s** -s
mainsail 'meɪn.seɪl *nautical pronunciation:* -sᵊl **-s** -z
mainspring 'meɪn.sprɪŋ **-s** -z
mainstay 'meɪn.steɪ **-s** -z
mainstream 'meɪn.striːm, ˌ-'- ⓤⓢ '--
mainstreaming 'meɪnˌstriː.mɪŋ
maintain meɪn'teɪn, mən-, men- ⓤⓢ meɪn- **-s** -z **-ing** -ɪŋ **-ed** -d **-able** -ə.bl̩ **-er/s** -əʳ/z ⓤⓢ -ɚ/z
maintenance 'meɪn.tᵊn.ənts, -tɪ.nənts ⓤⓢ -tᵊn.ənts
Mainwaring *surname:* 'mæn.ᵊr.ɪŋ *in Wales:* 'meɪn.wə.rɪŋ, -weə-; ˌmeɪn'weə- ⓤⓢ 'meɪn.wɚ.ɪŋ, -wer-; ˌmeɪn'wer-
Mainz maɪnts
Maisie 'meɪ.zi
maisonette ˌmeɪ.zᵊn'et, -sᵊn'- **-s** -s
Maitland 'meɪt.lənd
maître d', maitre d' ˌmeɪ.trə'diː, ˌmet.rə'- ⓤⓢ ˌmeɪ.trə'-, -t̬ɚ'- **-s** -z
maître(s) d'hôtel ˌmeɪ.trə.dəʊ'tel, ˌmet.rə- ⓤⓢ ˌmeɪ.trə.doʊ'-, -t̬ɚ-
maize meɪz
majestic (M) mə'dʒes.tɪk **-al** -ᵊl **-ally** -ᵊl.i, -li
majest|y (M) 'mædʒ.ə.st|i, '-ɪ- **-ies** -iz
majolica mə'jɒl.ɪ.kə, -'dʒɒl- ⓤⓢ -'dʒɑː.lɪ-
maj|or (M) 'meɪ.dʒ|əʳ ⓤⓢ -dʒ|ɚ **-ors** -əz ⓤⓢ -ɚz **-oring** -ᵊr.ɪŋ **-ored** -əd ⓤⓢ -ɚd
Majorca mə'jɔː.kə, maɪ'ɔː-, -'dʒɔː- ⓤⓢ -'jɔːr-, -'dʒɔːr-
majordomo ˌmeɪ.dʒə'dəʊ.məʊ ⓤⓢ -dʒɚ'doʊ.moʊ **-s** -z
majorette ˌmeɪ.dʒᵊr'et **-s** -s
major-general ˌmeɪ.dʒə'dʒen.ᵊr.ᵊl, '-rᵊl ⓤⓢ -dʒɚ'- **-s** -z
majorit|y mə'dʒɒr.ə.t|i, -ɪ.t|i ⓤⓢ -'dʒɔːr.ə.t̬|i **-ies** -iz
major-league ˌmeɪ.dʒə'liːg ⓤⓢ ˌmeɪ.dzɚ'liːg *stress shift:* ˌmajor-league 'player
majuscule 'mædʒ.ə.skjuːl ⓤⓢ mə'dʒʌs.kjuːl; 'mædʒ.ə.skjuːl **-s** -z
Makarios mə'kɑː.ri.ɒs, -'kær.i- ⓤⓢ mə'kɑːr.i.oʊs, -'kær.i-, -ɑːs, -əs
mak|e meɪk **-es** -s **-ing** -ɪŋ **made** meɪd **maker/s** 'meɪ.kəʳ/z ⓤⓢ -kɚ/z
Makeba mə'keɪ.bə
make-believe 'meɪk.bɪˌliːv, -bəˌ-, ˌ--'-
Makeham 'meɪ.kəm
make-or-break ˌmeɪk.ɔː'breɪk ⓤⓢ -ɔːr'-, -ɚ'- *stress shift:* ˌmake-or-break 'deal
makeover 'meɪkˌəʊ.vəʳ ⓤⓢ -ˌoʊ.vɚ **-s** -z
Makepeace 'meɪk.piːs
Makerere mə'ker.ᵊr.i
makeshift 'meɪk.ʃɪft
make-up 'meɪk.ʌp **-s** -s
makeweight 'meɪk.weɪt **-s** -s
makings 'meɪ.kɪŋz
Makins 'meɪ.kɪnz
Makower mə'kaʊəʳ ⓤⓢ -'kaʊɚ
makuta *(plur. of* **likuta)** mɑː'kuː.tɑː
mal- mæl-
Note: Prefix. In verbs or adjectives, **mal-** usually carries secondary stress, e.g. **malfunction** /ˌmæl'fʌŋk.ʃᵊn/, **maladjusted** /ˌmæl.ə'dʒʌs.tɪd/. Nouns containing **mal-** normally carry stress on the first syllable, e.g. **malcontent** /'mæl.kən.tent/. Exceptions exist: see individual entries.
Malabar 'mæl.ə.bɑːʳ, ˌ--'- ⓤⓢ 'mæl.ə.bɑːr
Malabo mə'lɑː.bəʊ ⓤⓢ -boʊ; 'mæl.ə-
malabsorption ˌmæl.əb'zɔːp.ʃᵊn, -'sɔːp- ⓤⓢ -'sɔːrp-, -'zɔːrp-
Malacca mə'læk.ə ⓤⓢ -'læk-, -'lɑː.kə
Malachi 'mæl.ə.kaɪ
malachite 'mæl.ə.kaɪt
maladjusted ˌmæl.ə'dʒʌs.tɪd *stress shift:* ˌmaladjusted 'person
maladjustment ˌmæl.ə'dʒʌst.mənt **-s** -s
maladministration ˌmæl.əd,mɪn.ɪ'streɪ.ʃᵊn ⓤⓢ -ə'-
maladroit ˌmæl.ə'drɔɪt, '--- **-ly** -li **-ness** -nəs, -nɪs *stress shift:* ˌmaladroit 'tactics
malad|y 'mæl.ə.d|i **-ies** -iz
mala fide ˌmeɪ.lə'faɪ.di, ˌmæl.ə'fɪd.i, -eɪ ⓤⓢ ˌmeɪ.lə'fiː.di, ˌmæl.ə'fiː.deɪ
Malaga, Málaga 'mæl.ə.gə ⓤⓢ 'mɑː.lɑː.gɑː, 'mæl.ə.gə
Malagasy ˌmæl.ə'gæs.i, -'gɑː.zi ⓤⓢ -'gæs.i
Malahide 'mæl.ə.haɪd
malaise mə'leɪz, mæl'eɪz
Malamud 'mæl.ə.mʊd ⓤⓢ -məd, -mʊd
Malan *English surname:* 'mæl.ən *South African name:* mə'læn, -'lɑːn
malaprop (M) 'mæl.ə.prɒp ⓤⓢ -prɑːp **-s** -s
malapropism 'mæl.ə.prɒp.ɪ.zᵊm ⓤⓢ -prɑː.pɪ- **-s** -z
malapropos ˌmælˌæp.rə'pəʊ, ˌ-'--- ⓤⓢ ˌmæl.æp.rə'poʊ
malari|a mə'leə.ri|.ə ⓤⓢ -'ler.i- **-al** -əl **-an** -ən
malark(e)y mə'lɑː.ki ⓤⓢ -'lɑːr-
Malawi mə'lɑː.wi ⓤⓢ mɑː-, mə- **-an/s** -ən/z
Malay mə'leɪ ⓤⓢ 'meɪ.leɪ, mə'leɪ **-s** -z
Malay|a mə'leɪ|.ə **-an/s** -ən/z
Malayalam ˌmæl.i'ɑː.ləm, -eɪ'-; -ə'jɑː- ⓤⓢ ˌmæl.ə'jɑː.ləm
Malaysi|a mə'leɪ.zi|.ə, -ʒi-, '-ʒ|ə ⓤⓢ -ʒ|ə, -ʃ|ə **-an/s** -ən/z
Malchus 'mæl.kəs
Malcolm 'mæl.kəm
malcontent 'mæl.kənˌtent **-s** -s
Malden 'mɔːl.dᵊn, 'mɒl- ⓤⓢ 'mɔːl-, 'mɑːl-
Maldive 'mɔːl.diːv, 'mɒl-, -dɪv, -daɪv ⓤⓢ 'mæl.daɪv, 'mɑːl-, -diːv **-s** -z
Maldivian mɔːl'dɪv.i.ən, mɒl-, mɑːl- ⓤⓢ mæl'daɪ.vi-, mɑːl-, -'diː- **-s** -z
Maldon 'mɔːl.dᵊn, 'mɒl- ⓤⓢ 'mɔːl-, 'mɑːl-
male meɪl **-s** -z **-ness** -nəs, -nɪs ˌ**male 'chauvinist;** ˌ**male** ˌ**chauvinist 'pig**
Malé 'mɑː.liː, -leɪ ⓤⓢ -liː
malediction ˌmæl.ɪ'dɪk.ʃᵊn, -ə'- ⓤⓢ -ə'- **-s** -z
maledictory ˌmæl.ɪ'dɪk.tᵊr.i, -ə'- ⓤⓢ -ə'-
malefaction ˌmæl.ɪ'fæk.ʃᵊn, -ə'- ⓤⓢ -ə'- **-s** -z
malefactor 'mæl.ɪ.fæk.təʳ, '-ə- ⓤⓢ -ə.fæk.tɚ **-s** -z
malefic mə'lef.ɪk
maleficen|ce mə'lef.ɪ.sᵊn|ts, mæl'ef- ⓤⓢ mə'lef.ə- **-t** -t
Malet 'mæl.ɪt
malevolence mə'lev.ᵊl.ənts, mæl'ev- ⓤⓢ mə'lev-
malevolent mə'lev.ᵊl.ənt, mæl'ev- ⓤⓢ mə'lev- **-ly** -li
malfeasance mæl'fiː.zᵊnts
Malfi 'mæl.fi
malformation ˌmæl.fɔː'meɪ.ʃᵊn, -fə'- ⓤⓢ -fɔːr'- **-s** -z
malformed ˌmæl'fɔːmd ⓤⓢ -'fɔːrmd
malfunction ˌmæl'fʌŋk.ʃᵊn **-s** -z **-ing** -ɪŋ **-ed** -d
Malham 'mæl.əm
Mali 'mɑː.li
Malibu 'mæl.ɪ.buː, '-ə-
malic 'mæl.ɪk, 'meɪ-
malice 'mæl.ɪs
malicious mə'lɪʃ.əs **-ly** -li **-ness** -nəs, -nɪs
Malick 'mæl.ɪk
malign mə'laɪn **-ly** -li **-s** -z **-ing** -ɪŋ **-ed** -d **-er/s** -əʳ/z ⓤⓢ -ɚ/z
malignancy mə'lɪg.nənt.si
malignant mə'lɪg.nənt **-ly** -li
malignity mə'lɪg.nə.ti, -nɪ- ⓤⓢ -nə.t̬i
Malik 'mæl.ɪk
Malin 'mæl.ɪn, 'meɪ.lɪn
Malines mæl'iːn
maling|er mə'lɪŋ.g|əʳ ⓤⓢ -g|ɚ **-ers** -əz ⓤⓢ -ɚz **-ering** -ᵊr.ɪŋ **-ered** -əd ⓤⓢ -ɚd **-erer/s** -ᵊr.əʳ/z ⓤⓢ -ɚ.ɚ/z
Malins 'meɪ.lɪnz, 'mæl.ɪnz
malkin 'mɔː.kɪn, 'mɔːl-, 'mɒl- ⓤⓢ 'mɔː-, 'mɔːl- **-s** -z

Malkin ˈmæl.kɪn
Malkovich ˈmæl.kə.vɪtʃ
mall mɔːl, mæl US mɔːl, mɑːl **-s** -z
Mall *(in* **The Mall, Chiswick Mall, Pall Mall***)* mæl
mallard (M) ˈmæl.ɑːd, -ləd US -ɚd **-s** -z
Mallarmé ˈmæl.ɑː.meɪ US ˌmæl.ɑːrˈmeɪ
Malle mæl, mɑːl US mɑːl
malleability ˌmæl.i.əˈbɪl.ə.ti, ˌmæl.əˈbɪl-, -ɪ.ti US ˌmæl.i.əˈbɪl.ə.t̬i
malleable ˈmæl.i.ə.bl̩, ˈ-ə.bl̩ US ˈ-i.ə- **-ness** -nəs, -nɪs
mallee ˈmæl.i
malleolar məˈliː.ə.ləʳ US -lɚ
malleo|lus məˈliː.əl.ləs **-li** -laɪ
mallet (M) ˈmæl.ɪt, -ət **-s** -s
Mallett ˈmæl.ɪt, -ət
malle|us ˈmæl.i|.əs **-i** -aɪ
Malling ˈmɔː.lɪŋ US ˈmɔː-, ˈmɑː-
Mallon ˈmæl.ən
Mallorca məˈjɔː.kə, -ˈljɔː-, -ˈlɔː- US mɑːˈjɔːr.kɑː, mɑːl-, mə-, -kə
Mallory ˈmæl.ᵊr.i
mallow (M) ˈmæl.əʊ US -oʊ **-s** -z
Malmaison ˌmælˈmeɪ.zɔ̃ːŋ, -zɒn, ˌ--ˈ- US -ˈzɑːn, -ˈzɔ̃ːn **-s** -z
Malmesbury ˈmɑːmz.bᵊr.i US -ber-, -bɚ-
Malmö ˈmæl.məʊ, -mɜː US -moʊ
malmsey (M) ˈmɑːm.zi
malnourished ˌmælˈnʌr.ɪʃt US -ˈnɝː-
malnutrition ˌmæl.njuːˈtrɪ.ʃᵊn US -nuːˈ-
malodor ˌmælˈəʊ.dəʳ US -ˈoʊ.dɚ **-s** -z
malodorous ˌmælˈəʊ.dᵊr.əs US -ˈoʊ- **-ly** -li **-ness** -nəs, -nɪs
Malone məˈləʊn US -ˈloʊn
Maloney məˈləʊ.ni US -ˈloʊ-
Malory ˈmæl.ᵊr.i
Malpas *near Truro:* ˈməʊ.pəs US ˈmoʊ- *in Gwent:* ˈmæl.pəs *in Cheshire:* ˈmɔːl.pəs, ˈmɔː-, ˈmæl-
Note: Viscount Malpas pronounces /ˈmɔːl.pəs/
Malpighi mælˈpiː.gi US mɑːl-, mæl-
Malpighian mælˈpɪg.i.ən, -ˈpiː.gi- US mɑːlˈpɪg.i-, mæl- **Malˌpighian ˈlayer**
Malplaquet ˈmæl.plə.keɪ, ˌ--ˈ- US ˌmæl.plækˈeɪ, -pləˈkeɪ
malpractic|e ˌmælˈpræk.tɪs **-es** -ɪz
Malraux ˈmæl.rəʊ US ˈmæl.roʊ, mɑːlˈroʊ
mal|t mɔːl|t, mɒl|t US mɔːl|t, mɑːl|t **-ts** -ts **-ting** -tɪŋ US -t̬ɪŋ **-ted** -tɪd US -t̬ɪd **ˌmalted ˈmilk**
Malta ˈmɔːl.tə, ˈmɒl- US ˈmɔːl.t̬ə, ˈmɑːl-
maltase ˈmɔːl.teɪz, ˈmɒl- US ˈmɔːl.teɪs, ˈmɑːl-
Maltby ˈmɔːlt.bi, ˈmɒlt- US ˈmɔːlt-, ˈmɑːlt-
Maltese ˌmɔːlˈtiːz, ˌmɒl- US ˌmɔːlˈtiːz, ˌmɑːl-, -ˈtiːs *stress shift, see compounds:* **ˌMaltese ˈcross**; **ˌMaltese ˈfalcon**
Maltesers® mɔːlˈtiː.zəz, mɒl- US mɔːlˈtiː.zɚz, mɑːl-
Malthus ˈmæl.θəs
Malthusian mælˈθjuː.zi.ən, mɔːl-, mɒl-, -ˈθuː- US mælˈθuː.ʒᵊn, -zi.ən **-s** -z **-ism** -ɪ.zᵊm
maltings ˈmɔːl.tɪŋz, ˈmɒl- US ˈmɔːl.t̬ɪŋz, ˈmɑːl-
Malton ˈmɔːl.tᵊn, ˈmɒl- US ˈmɔːl-, ˈmɑːl-
maltose ˈmɔːl.təʊz, ˈmɒl- US ˈmɔːl.toʊz, ˈmɑːl-, -toʊs
Maltravers mælˈtræv.əz US -ɚz
mal|treat ˌmæl|ˈtriːt **-treats** -ˈtriːts **-treating** -ˈtriː.tɪŋ US -ˈtriː.t̬ɪŋ **-treated** -ˈtriː.tɪd US -ˈtriː.t̬ɪd **-treatment** -ˈtriːt.mənt **-treater/s** -ˈtriː.təʳ/z US -ˈtriː.t̬ɚ/z
maltster ˈmɔːlt.stəʳ, ˈmɒlt- US ˈmɔːlt.stɚ, ˈmɑːlt- **-s** -z
Maltz mɔːlts, mɒlts US mɔːlts, mɑːlts
malum in se ˌmɑː.lʊm.ɪnˈseɪ US ˌmɑː.ləm.ɪnˈseɪ
malum prohibitum ˌmɑː.lʊm.prəʊˈhɪb.ɪ.tʊm US ˌmɑː.ləm.proʊˈhɪb.ɪ.təm
Malvasia ˌmæl.vəˈsiː.ə
Malvern *in UK:* ˈmɔːl.vᵊn, ˈmɒl-, -vɜːn *locally also:* ˈmɔː.vᵊn US ˈmɔːl.vɚn *in US:* ˈmæl.vən US -vɚn
malversation ˌmæl.vɜːˈseɪ.ʃᵊn, -vəˈ- US -vɚˈ-
Malvinas mælˈviː.nəs
Malvolio mælˈvəʊ.li.əʊ US -ˈvoʊ.li.oʊ, -ˈvoʊl.joʊ
Malyon ˈmæl.jən
mam mæm **-s** -z
mama məˈmɑː; ˈmæm.ə US ˈmɑː.mə; məˈmɑː **-s** -z
mamba ˈmæm.bə US ˈmɑːm- **-s** -z
mambo ˈmæm.bəʊ US ˈmɑːm.boʊ **-es** -z **-ing** -ɪŋ **-ed** -d
Mameluke ˈmæm.ɪ.luːk, ˈ-ə-, -ljuːk US -ə.luːk **-s** -s
Mamet ˈmæm.ɪt US -ət
Mamie ˈmeɪ.mi
Mamilius məˈmɪl.i.əs, mæmˈɪl-
mamma *mother:* məˈmɑː US ˈmɑː.mə, məˈmɑː **-s** -z
mamm|a *milk-secreting organ:* ˈmæm|.ə **-ae** -iː
mammal ˈmæm.ᵊl **-s** -z
mammalian mæmˈeɪ.li.ən, məˈmeɪ-
mammary ˈmæm.ᵊr.i **ˈmammary ˌgland**
mammogram ˈmæm.ə.græm **-s** -z
mammograph ˈmæm.əʊ.grɑːf, -græf US -græf, -ə-, -oʊ- **-s** -s
mammography mæmˈɒg.rə.fi, məˈmɒg- US məˈmɑː.grə-, mæmˈɑːg-
mammon (M) ˈmæm.ən
mammoth ˈmæm.əθ **-s** -s
mamm|y ˈmæm|.i **-ies** -iz
man (M) *(n.)* mæn **men** men **ˌman ˈFriday**; **ˌman of the ˈworld**
man *(v.)* mæn **-s** -z **-ning** -ɪŋ **-ned** -d
manacl|e ˈmæn.ə.kl̩ **-es** -z **-ing** -ɪŋ, ˈmæn.ə.klɪŋ **-ed** -d
manag|e ˈmæn.ɪdʒ, -ədʒ **-es** -ɪz **-ing** -ɪŋ **-ed** -d **ˌmanaging diˈrector**
manageability ˌmæn.ɪ.dʒəˈbɪl.ə.ti, ˌ-ə-, -ɪ.ti US -ə.t̬i
manageab|le ˈmæn.ɪ.dʒə.bl|̩, ˈ-ə- **-ly** -li **-leness** -l̩.nəs, -nɪs
management ˈmæn.ɪdʒ.mənt, -ədʒ- **-s** -s
manager ˈmæn.ɪ.dʒəʳ, ˈ-ə- US -dʒɚ **-s** -z
manageress ˌmæn.ɪ.dʒᵊrˈes, ˌ-ə-; ˈmæn.ɪ.dʒᵊr.es, ˈ-ə- US ˈmæn- **-es** -ɪz
managerial ˌmæn.əˈdʒɪə.ri.əl US -ˈdʒɪr.i- **-ly** -i
Managua məˈnæg.wə, mænˈæg-, -ˈɑː.gwə US məˈnɑː.gwɑː, mɑː-, -gwə
Manama məˈnɑː.mə US -ˈnæm.ə
mañana mænˈjɑː.nə, məˈnjɑː- US məˈnjɑː-, mɑː-
Manassas məˈnæs.əs
Manasseh məˈnæs.i, -ə US -ə
Manasses məˈnæs.ɪz, -iːz
manatee (M) ˌmæn.əˈtiː US ˈmæn.ə.ti, ˌmæn.əˈtiː **-s** -z
Manáus məˈnaʊs US mə-, mɑː-
Manchester ˈmæn.tʃɪs.təʳ, -tʃes-, -tʃəs- US -tʃes.tɚ, -tʃɪ.stɚ
Manchu ˌmænˈtʃuː **-s** -z *stress shift:* ˌManchu ˈdynasty
Manchukuo ˌmænˌtʃuːˈkwəʊ US -ˈkwoʊ
Manchuri|a mænˈtʃʊə.ri|.ə, -ˈtʃɔː- US -ˈtʃʊr.i- **-an/s** -ən/z
Mancini mænˈsiː.ni
manciple ˈmænt.sɪ.pl̩, -sə- **-s** -z
Mancunian mæŋˈkjuː.ni.ən, mæn- US mæn- **-s** -z
mandala ˈmæn.dᵊl.ə, ˈmʌn-; mənˈdɑː.lə, mæn- US ˈmʌn.də- **-s** -z
Mandalay ˌmæn.dᵊlˈeɪ, ˈ---
mandamus mænˈdeɪ.məs **-es** -ɪz
mandarin (M) ˈmæn.dᵊr.ɪn, ˌ--ˈ- US ˈmæn.dɚ.ɪn **-s** -z
mandate *(n.)* ˈmæn.deɪt, -dɪt, -dət US -deɪt **-s** -s
manda|te *(v.)* mænˈdeɪ|t, ˈ-- US ˈ-- **-tes** -ts **-ting** -tɪŋ US -t̬ɪŋ **-ted** -tɪd US -t̬ɪd **-tor/s** -təʳ/z US -t̬ɚ/z
mandator|y ˈmæn.də.tᵊr|.i, -tr|i; mænˈdeɪ- US ˈmæn.də.tɔːr|.i **-ies** -iz
Mandela mænˈdel.ə, -ˈdeɪ.lə US -ˈdel.ə
Mandelson ˈmæn.dᵊl.sᵊn US -sᵊn, -soʊn

Mandelstam ˈmæn.dᵊl.stæm, -stəm
Mander ˈmɑːn.dəʳ, ˈmæn- US -dɚ
Mandeville ˈmæn.də.vɪl, -dɪ-
mandible ˈmæn.dɪ.bl̩, -də- **-s** -z
Mandingo mænˈdɪŋ.gəʊ US -goʊ **-(e)s** -z
mandolin ˌmæn.dᵊlˈɪn, ˈ--- **-s** -z
mandoline ˌmæn.dᵊlˈiːn **-s** -z
mandragora mænˈdræg.ᵊr.ə, mən- US mæn-
mandrake ˈmæn.dreɪk **-s** -s
mandrax (M®) ˈmæn.dræks **-es** -ɪz
mandrill ˈmæn.drɪl, -drᵊl US -drɪl **-s** -z
Mandy ˈmæn.di
mane meɪn **-s** -z **-d** -d
man-eater ˈmænˌiː.təʳ US -t̬ɚ **-s** -z
manège, manege mænˈeɪʒ, -ˈeʒ, ˈ-- US mænˈeʒ, məˈneʒ, -ˈneɪʒ **-s** -ɪz
manes (M) ˈmɑː.neɪz, -neɪs, ˈmeɪ.niːz US ˈmeɪ.niːz, ˈmɑː.neɪs
Manet ˈmæn.eɪ US mænˈeɪ, məˈneɪ
Manette mænˈet
maneuv|er məˈnuː.v|əʳ US -v|ɚ **-ers** -əz US -ɚz **-ering/s** -ᵊr.ɪŋ/z **-ered** -əd US -ɚd **-erer/s** -ᵊr.əʳ/z US -ɚ.ɚ/z
maneuverability məˌnuː.vᵊr.əˈbɪl.ə.ti, -ɪ.ti US -ə.t̬i
maneuverable məˈnuː.vᵊr.ə.bl̩
Manfred ˈmæn.fred, -frɪd
manful ˈmæn.fᵊl, -fʊl **-ly** -i **-ness** -nəs, -nɪs
Mangan ˈmæŋ.gən
manganate ˈmæŋ.gə.neɪt **-s** -s
manganese ˈmæŋ.gə.niːz, ˌ--ˈ- US ˈ---, -niːs
manganic mæŋˈgæn.ɪk, mæn- US mæn-
mange meɪndʒ
mangel-wurzel ˈmæŋ.gᵊlˌwɜː.zᵊl, ˌmæŋ.gᵊlˈwɜː- US ˈmæŋ.gᵊlˌwɝː-, -ˌwɝːt.sᵊl **-s** -z
manger ˈmeɪn.dʒəʳ US -dʒɚ **-s** -z
mangetout ˌmɑ̃ːnʒˈtuː US ˌmɑ̃ːndʒ- **-s** -z
mangl|e ˈmæŋ.gl̩ **-es** -z **-ing** -ɪŋ, ˈmæŋ.glɪŋ **-ed** -d **-er/s** -əʳ/z US -ɚ/z
mango ˈmæŋ.gəʊ US -goʊ **-(e)s** -z
mangold (M) ˈmæŋ.gəʊld US -goʊld **-s** -z
mangosteen ˈmæŋ.gəʊ.stiːn US -gə- **-s** -z
Mangotsfield ˈmæŋ.gəts.fiːld
mangrove ˈmæŋ.grəʊv US ˈmæn.groʊv, ˈmæŋ- **-s** -z
mang|y ˈmeɪn.dʒ|i **-ier** -i.əʳ US -i.ɚ **-iest** -i.ɪst, -i.əst **-ily** -ɪ.li, -ᵊl.i **-iness** -ɪ.nəs, -ɪ.nɪs
manhandl|e ˈmænˌhæn.dl̩, ˌ-ˈ-- US ˈ--- **-es** -z **-ing** -ɪŋ, -ˌhænd.lɪŋ **-ed** -d
manhattan (M) mænˈhæt.ᵊn US mæn-, mən-
manhole ˈmæn.həʊl US -hoʊl **-s** -z
manhood (M) ˈmæn.hʊd
manhour ˈmæn.aʊəʳ US -aʊr, -aʊɚ **-s** -z
manhunt ˈmæn.hʌnt **-s** -s
mania ˈmeɪ.ni.ə US -ni.ə, ˈ-njə **-s** -z
maniac ˈmeɪ.ni.æk **-s** -s
maniac|al məˈnaɪə.k|ᵊl **-ally** -ᵊl.i US -li
manic ˈmæn.ɪk **-s** -s ˌ**manic deˈpression**
manic-depressive ˌmæn.ɪk.dɪˈpres.ɪv, -dəˈ- **-s** -z
Manich(a)ean ˌmæn.ɪˈkiː.ən, -əˈ- **-s** -z
manicur|e ˈmæn.ɪ.kjʊəʳ, ˈ-ə-, -kjɔːʳ US -kjʊr **-es** -z **-ing** -ɪŋ **-ed** -d **-ist/s** -ɪst/s
manifest ˈmæn.ɪ.fest, ˈ-ə- **-ly** -li **-s** -s **-ing** -ɪŋ **-ed** -ɪd **-ness** -nəs, -nɪs
manifestation ˌmæn.ɪ.fesˈteɪ.ʃᵊn, ˌ-ə-, -fəˈsteɪ- **-s** -z
manifesto ˌmæn.ɪˈfes.təʊ, -əˈ- US -toʊ **-(e)s** -z
manifold ˈmæn.ɪ.fəʊld, ˈ-ə- US -foʊld **-ness** -nəs, -nɪs
manikin ˈmæn.ɪ.kɪn, ˈ-ə- **-s** -z
manila (M) məˈnɪl.ə **-s** -z
manilla məˈnɪl.ə **-s** -z
Manilow ˈmæn.ɪ.ləʊ, ˈ-ə- US -loʊ
manioc ˈmæn.i.ɒk US -ɑːk
maniple ˈmæn.ɪ.pl̩, ˈ-ə- **-s** -z
manipu|late məˈnɪp.jə|.leɪt, -jʊ- US -jə-, -juː- **-lates** -leɪts **-lating** -leɪ.tɪŋ US -leɪ.t̬ɪŋ **-lated** -leɪ.tɪd US -leɪ.t̬ɪd **-lator/s** -leɪ.təʳ/z US -leɪ.t̬ɚ/z
manipulation məˌnɪp.jəˈleɪ.ʃᵊn, -jʊˈ- US -jəˈ-, -juːˈ- **-s** -z
manipulative məˈnɪp.jə.lə.tɪv, -jʊ- US -jə.leɪ.t̬ɪv, -juː-, -lə- **-ly** -li **-ness** -nəs, -nɪs
Manitoba ˌmæn.ɪˈtəʊ.bə, -əˈ- US -əˈtoʊ-
manit(o)u ˈmæn.ɪ.tuː US ˈ-ə- **-s** -z
mankind *general use:* mænˈkaɪnd, mæŋ- US mæn-
mank|y ˈmæŋ.k|i **-ier** -i.əʳ US -i.ɚ **-iest** -i.ɪst, -i.əst
Manley ˈmæn.li
manlike ˈmæn.laɪk
Manlius ˈmæn.li.əs
manl|y (M) ˈmæn.l|i **-ier** -i.əʳ US -i.ɚ **-iest** -i.ɪst, -i.əst **-iness** -ɪ.nəs, -ɪ.nɪs
man-made ˌmænˈmeɪd, ˌmæm- US ˌmæn- *stress shift:* ˌman-made ˈfibre
Mann mæn
manna ˈmæn.ə
mannequin ˈmæn.ɪ.kɪn, ˈ-ə- **-s** -z
manner ˈmæn.əʳ US -ɚ **-s** -z **-ed** -d
mannerism (M) ˈmæn.ᵊr.ɪ.zᵊm **-s** -z
mannerist (M) ˈmæn.ᵊr.ɪst
mannerl|y ˈmæn.ᵊl|.i US -ɚ.l|i **-iness** -ɪ.nəs, -ɪ.nɪs
Manners ˈmæn.əz US -ɚz
Mannesmann ˈmæn.ə.smæn, -smən
Mannheim ˈmæn.haɪm
mannikin ˈmæn.ɪ.kɪn, ˈ-ə- **-s** -z
Manning ˈmæn.ɪŋ
mannish ˈmæn.ɪʃ **-ly** -li **-ness** -nəs, -nɪs
Manns mænz
Manny ˈmæn.i
Mannyng of Brunne ˌmæn.ɪŋ.əvˈbrʊn
manoeuvrability məˌnuː.vᵊr.əˈbɪl.ə.tɪ, -ɪ.ti US -ə.t̬i
manoeuvrable məˈnuː.vᵊr.ə.bl̩
manoeuv|re məˈnuː.v|əʳ US -v|ɚ **-res** -əz US -ɚz **-ring/s** -ᵊr.ɪŋ/z **-red** -əd US -ɚd **-rer/s** -ᵊr.əʳ/z US -ɚ.ɚ/z
man-of-war ˌmæn.əvˈwɔːʳ US -ˈwɔːr **men-of-war** ˌmen-
manometer məˈnɒm.ɪ.təʳ, mænˈɒm-, ˈ-ə- US məˈnɑː.mə.t̬ɚ **-s** -z
manometric ˌmæn.əʊˈmet.rɪk US -əˈ- **-al** -ᵊl **-ally** -ᵊl.i, -li
manor ˈmæn.əʳ US -ɚ **-s** -z
manor-hou|se ˈmæn.ə.haʊ|s US ˈ-ɚ- **-ses** -zɪz
manorial məˈnɔː.ri.əl, mænˈɔː- US məˈnɔːr.i-
manpower ˈmænˌpaʊəʳ, ˈmæm- US ˈmænˌpaʊɚ
manqué ˈmɑ̃ːŋ.keɪ US mɑ̃ːŋˈkeɪ
Manresa mænˈreɪ.sə, -zə US mɑːnˈreɪ.sə, mæn-
Mansa ˈmænt.sə
mansard ˈmænt.sɑːd US -sɑːrd **-s** -z
mans|e mænts **-es** -ɪz
Mansel(l) ˈmænt.sᵊl
Mansergh *surname:* ˈmæn.zəʳ, ˈmænt.səʳ, -sɜːdʒ US ˈmæn.zɚ, ˈmænt.sɚ, -sɝːdʒ *place in Cumbria:* ˈmæn.zəʳ US -zɚ
manservant ˈmænˌsɜː.vᵊnt US -ˌsɝː- **menservants** ˈmenˌsɜː.vᵊnts US -ˌsɝː-
Mansfield ˈmænts.fiːld US ˈmænz-
-manship -mən.ʃɪp
mansion (M) ˈmæn.tʃᵊn **-s** -z
mansion-hou|se (M) ˈmæn.tʃᵊn.haʊ|s **-ses** -zɪz
manslaughter ˈmænˌslɔː.təʳ US -ˌslɑː.t̬ɚ, -ˌslɔː-
Manson ˈmænt.sᵊn
Manston ˈmænt.stᵊn
mansuetude ˈmæn.swɪ.tjuːd US -tuːd, -tjuːd
Manta ˈmæn.tə
Mantegna mænˈten.jə US mɑːnˈten.jɑː, -jə
mantel ˈmæn.tᵊl **-s** -z
mantelpiec|e ˈmæn.tᵊl.piːs **-es** -ɪz
mantelshel|f ˈmæn.tᵊl.ʃel|f **-ves** -vz
-mantic -ˈmæn.tɪk
mantilla mænˈtɪl.ə US -ˈtɪl-, -ˈtiː.jə **-s** -z
mantis ˈmæn.tɪs US -t̬ɪs **-es** -ɪz
mantissa mænˈtɪs.ə **-s** -z
mantl|e ˈmæn.tl̩ **-es** -z **-ing** -ɪŋ, ˈmænt.lɪŋ **-ed** -d
Mantovani ˌmæn.təˈvɑː.ni US ˌmɑːn-

mantra 'mæn.trə, 'mʌn- (US) 'mæn-, 'mɑːn-, 'mʌn- **-s** -z
mantrap 'mæn.træp **-s** -s
Mantu|a (M) 'mæn.tjul.ə, -tu-, -tʃu- (US) -tʃu.w|ə, -tu- **-an/s** -ənz
manual 'mæn.ju.əl **-s** -z **-ly** -i
Manuel *surname:* 'mæn.ju.el, -əl
Manuel *first name:* mæn'wel; ˌmæn.u'el, -ju'- (US) mæn'wel, mɑːn-
manufact|ure ˌmæn.jə'fæk.tʃ|əʳ, -jʊ'-, -ə'- (US) -jə'fæk.tʃ|ɚ, -juː'- **-ures** -əz (US) -ɚz **-uring** -ᵊr.ɪŋ **-ured** -əd (US) -ɚd **-urer/s** -ᵊr.əʳ/z (US) -ɚ.ɚ/z
manumission ˌmæn.jə'mɪʃ.ᵊn, -jʊ'- (US) -jə'-, -juː- **-s** -z
manu|mit ˌmæn.jə|'mɪt, -jʊ'- (US) -jə'-, -juː'- **-mits** -'mɪts **-mitting** -'mɪt.ɪŋ (US) -'mɪţ.ɪŋ **-mitted** -'mɪt.ɪd (US) -'mɪţ.ɪd
manur|e mə'njʊəʳ, -njɔːʳ (US) -'nʊr, -'njʊr **-es** -z **-ing** -ɪŋ **-ed** -d
manuscript 'mæn.jə.skrɪpt, -jʊ- **-s** -s
Manutius mə'njuː.ʃi.əs, '-ʃəs (US) -'nuː.ʃi.əs, -'njuː-
Manwaring 'mæn.ᵊr.ɪŋ
Manx mæŋks ˌ**Manx 'cat**
Manx|man 'mæŋks|.mæn, -mən **-men** -men, -mən **-woman** -ˌwʊm.ən **-women** -ˌwɪm.ɪn
many 'men.i
manyfold 'men.i.fəʊld (US) -foʊld
many-sided ˌmen.i'saɪ.dɪd **-ness** -nəs, -nɪs *stress shift:* ˌ**many-sided 'shape**
manzanilla (M) ˌmæn.zə'nɪl.ə, -jə (US) -'niːl.jə, -'niː-, -'nɪl.ə
Manzoni mæn'zəʊ.ni (US) mɑːn'zoʊ-
Mao maʊ
Mao|ism 'maʊ|.ɪ.zᵊm **-ist/s** -ɪst/s
Maori 'maʊə.ri (US) 'maʊ.ri; 'mɑː.oʊ.ri **-s** -z
Mao Tse-tung ˌmaʊ.tseɪ'tʊŋ, ˌmaʊ.dzeɪ'dʊŋ (US) -tsə'dʊŋ
Mao Zedong ˌmaʊ.dʒeɪ'dʊŋ, ˌmaʊ.tseɪ'tʊŋ (US) -dʒə'-, -'dɑːŋ
map mæp **-s** -s **-ping** -ɪŋ **-ped** -t
maple (M) 'meɪ.pl̩ **-s** -z '**Maple** ˌ**Leaf**; ˌ**maple 'syrup**
Maplin Sands ˌmæp.lɪn'sændz, -lən'-
mapmak|er/s 'mæp.meɪ.k|əʳ/z, -k|ɚ/z **-ing** -ɪŋ
Mappin 'mæp.ɪn
Mapplethorpe 'mæp.l̩.θɔːp (US) 'meɪ.pl̩.θɔːrp
Maputo mə'puː.təʊ (US) -toʊ
maquillage ˌmæk.iː'ɑːʒ, -'jɑːʒ (US) ˌmɑː.ki'ɑːʒ
maquis mæk'iː, '-- (US) mɑː'kiː, mæk'iː
mar (M) mɑːʳ (US) mɑːr **-s** -z **-ring** -ɪŋ **-red** -d
Mar. *(abbrev. for* **March***)* mɑːtʃ (US) mɑːrtʃ
marabou 'mær.ə.buː (US) 'mer-, 'mær- **-s** -z
maraca mə'ræk.ə (US) -'rɑː.kə **-s** -z
Maracaibo ˌmær.ə'kaɪ.bəʊ (US) ˌmer.ə'kaɪ.boʊ, ˌmær-
Maradona ˌmær.ə'dɒn.ə (US) ˌmer.ə'dɑː.nə, ˌmær-
maraschino (M) ˌmær.ə'ʃiː.nəʊ, -'skiː- (US) ˌmer.ə'ʃiː.noʊ, ˌmær-, -'skiː- **-s** -z ˌ**mara**ˌ**schino 'cherry**
Marat 'mær.ɑː (US) mɑː'rɑː, mə-
Marathi mə'rɑː.ti **-s** -z
marathon (M) 'mær.ə.θᵊn (US) 'mer.ə.θɑːn, 'mær- **-s** -z
maraud mə'rɔːd (US) -'rɑːd, -'rɔːd **-s** -z **-ing** -ɪŋ **-ed** -ɪd **-er/s** -əʳ/z (US) -ɚ/z
Marazion ˌmær.ə'zaɪən (US) ˌmer-, ˌmær-
Marbella mɑː'beɪ.ə, -jə (US) mɑːr-
marbl|e 'mɑː.bl̩ (US) 'mɑːr- **-es** -z **-ing** -ɪŋ, 'mɑː.blɪŋ (US) 'mɑːr- **-ed** -d
Marburg 'mɑː.bʊəg, -bɜːg (US) 'mɑːr.bɝːg, -bʊrg
Marc mɑːk (US) mɑːrk
marcasite 'mɑː.kə.saɪt (US) 'mɑːr-
Marceau ˌmɑː'səʊ, '-- (US) mɑːr'soʊ
Marcel mɑː'sel (US) mɑːr-
Marcella mɑː'sel.ə (US) mɑːr-
Marcelle mɑː'sel (US) mɑːr-
Marcellus mɑː'sel.əs (US) mɑːr-
march (M) mɑːtʃ (US) mɑːrtʃ **-es** -ɪz **-ing** -ɪŋ **-ed** -t **-er/s** -əʳ/z (US) -ɚ/z
Marchant 'mɑː.tʃᵊnt (US) 'mɑːr-
Marchbank 'mɑːtʃ.bæŋk (US) 'mɑːrtʃ- **-s** -s
marchioness ˌmɑː.ʃᵊn'es, -'ɪs; 'mɑː.ʃᵊn.əs (US) 'mɑːr.ʃᵊn.ɪs; ˌmɑːr.ʃᵊn'es **-es** -ɪz
Marchmain 'mɑːtʃ.meɪn (US) 'mɑːrtʃ-
Marchmont 'mɑːtʃ.mənt (US) 'mɑːrtʃ-
Marcia 'mɑː.si.ə, '-ʃə (US) 'mɑːr.ʃə
Marciano ˌmɑː.si'ɑː.nəʊ, -ʃi'- (US) ˌmɑːr.si'æn.oʊ, -ʃi'-, -'ɑː.noʊ
Marco 'mɑː.kəʊ (US) 'mɑːr.koʊ
Marconi mɑː'kəʊ.ni (US) mɑːr'koʊ-
marconigram mɑː'kəʊ.ni.græm (US) mɑːr'koʊ- **-s** -z
Marcos 'mɑː.kɒs (US) 'mɑːr.koʊs
Marcus 'mɑː.kəs (US) 'mɑːr-
Marcuse mɑː'kuː.zə; mɑː'kjuːz (US) mɑːr'kuː.zə
Mar del Plata ˌmɑː.del'plɑː.tə (US) ˌmɑːr.del'plɑː.tə
Marden *in Kent:* 'mɑː.dᵊn; mɑː'den (US) 'mɑːr.dᵊn; mɑːr'den *other places:* 'mɑː.dᵊn (US) 'mɑːr-
Mardi Gras ˌmɑː.di'grɑː (US) 'mɑːr.diˌgrɑː, ˌ--'-
Marduk 'mɑː.dʊk (US) 'mɑːr-
mare *female horse:* meəʳ (US) mer **-s** -z
mare *lunar plain:* 'mɑː.reɪ (US) 'mɑːr.eɪ **maria** 'mɑː.ri.ə (US) 'mɑːr.i-
Marengo mə'reŋ.gəʊ (US) -goʊ
mare's-nest 'meəz.nest, ˌ-'- (US) 'merz.nest **-s** -s
mare's-tail 'meəz.teɪl, ˌ-'- (US) 'merz- **-s** -z
Margaret 'mɑː.gᵊr.ət, -ɪt, '-grət, -grɪt (US) 'mɑːr.grət
margarine ˌmɑː.dʒə'riːn, -gə'-, '--- (US) 'mɑːr.dʒɚ.ɪn
margarita (M) ˌmɑː.gᵊr'iː.tə (US) -gə'riː.ţə **-s** -z
Margate 'mɑː.geɪt, -gɪt (US) 'mɑːr-
marge mɑːdʒ (US) mɑːrdʒ
Margerison mɑː'dʒer.ɪ.sᵊn, '-ə-; 'mɑː.dʒᵊr- (US) mɑːr'dʒer-; 'mɑːr.dʒə.rɪ-, -rə-
Margery 'mɑː.dʒᵊr.i (US) 'mɑːr-
Margetts 'mɑː.gɪts (US) 'mɑːr-
margin 'mɑː.dʒɪn (US) 'mɑːr- **-s** -z
marginal 'mɑː.dʒɪ.nᵊl, -dʒᵊn.ᵊl (US) 'mɑːr- **-s** -z **-ly** -i
marginalia ˌmɑː.dʒɪ'neɪ.li.ə, -dʒə'- (US) ˌmɑːr-, -'neɪl.jə
marginalization, -isa- ˌmɑː.dʒɪ.nᵊl.aɪ'zeɪ.ʃᵊn, -dʒᵊn.ᵊl-, -ɪ'- (US) ˌmɑːr.dʒɪ.nᵊl.ɪ'-, -dʒᵊn.ᵊl-
marginaliz|e, -is|e 'mɑː.dʒɪ.nᵊl.aɪz, -dʒᵊn.ᵊl- (US) 'mɑːr- **-es** -ɪz **-ing** -ɪŋ **-ed** -d
Margolis mɑː'gəʊ.lɪs (US) mɑːr'goʊ-
Margot 'mɑː.gəʊ (US) 'mɑːr.goʊ
margrave (M) 'mɑː.greɪv (US) 'mɑːr- **-s** -z
margravine 'mɑː.grə.viːn (US) 'mɑːr- **-s** -z
marguerite (M) ˌmɑː.gᵊr'iːt (US) ˌmɑːr.gə'riːt **-s** -s
Margulies 'mɑː.gʊ.lɪs (US) 'mɑːr'guː.lɪz
Marham *in Norfolk:* 'mær.əm, 'mɑː.rəm (US) 'mær.əm, 'mɑːr-
Note: The pronunciation of the local residents is /'mær.əm/.
Marhamchurch 'mær.əm.tʃɜːtʃ (US) -tʃɝːtʃ
Maria *first name:* mə'riː.ə, mə'raɪ.ə
maria *(plur. of* **mare***)* 'mɑː.ri.ə (US) 'mɑːr.i-
Marian *first name:* 'mær.i.ən (US) 'mer-, 'mær-
Marian *(n. adj.) of Mary, or person devoted to Mary:* 'meə.ri.ən (US) 'mer.i-, 'mær-
Mariana *English name:* ˌmær.i'æn.ə, ˌmeə.ri'-, -'ɑː.nə (US) ˌmer.i'æn.ə, ˌmær- *Spanish historian:* ˌmɑː.ri'ɑː.nə (US) ˌmɑːr.i'ɑː-
Marianne ˌmær.i'æn (US) ˌmer.i'æn, ˌmær-
Maribor 'mær.i.bɔːʳ (US) 'mɑːr.i.bɔːr
Marie mə'riː, 'mɑː.ri, 'mær.i (US) mə'riː
Marie Antoinette ˌmær.iˌæn.twə'net, -ˌɑ̃ːn- (US) məˌriː.æn-

Marienbad 'mær.i.ən.bæd, -əm-; mə'riː- ⓤⓢ 'mer.i.ən-, 'mær-
marigold (M) 'mær.ɪ.gəʊld ⓤⓢ 'mer.ɪ.goʊld, 'mær- **-s** -z
marijuana, marihuana ˌmær.ɪ'wɑː.nə, -ə'- ⓤⓢ ˌmer.ɪ'-, ˌmær-
Marilla mə'rɪl.ə
Marilyn 'mær.ɪ.lɪn, '-ə- ⓤⓢ 'mer-, 'mær-
marimba mə'rɪm.bə **-s** -z
marina (M) mə'riː.nə **-s** -z
marinad|e ˌmær.ɪ'neɪd, '--- ⓤⓢ ˌmer.ɪ'neɪd, ˌmær-, '--- **-es** -z **-ing** -ɪŋ **-ed** -ɪd
marinara ˌmær.ɪ'nɑː.rə, -ə'- ⓤⓢ ˌmer.ɪ'ner.ə, -nær.ə, -nɑː.rə
marinat|e 'mær.ɪ.neɪt, '-ə- ⓤⓢ 'mer-, 'mær- **-es** -s **-ing** -ɪŋ **-ed** -ɪd
marination ˌmær.ɪ'neɪ.ʃən, -ə'- ⓤⓢ ˌmer-, ˌmær-
marine mə'riːn **-s** -z
mariner 'mær.ɪ.nər, '-ə- ⓤⓢ 'mer.ɪ.nɚ, 'mær-, '-ə- **-s** -z
Marino Faliero məˌriː.nəʊ.fə'lɪə.rəʊ ⓤⓢ -noʊ.fə'lɪr.oʊ
Mario 'mær.i.əʊ, 'mɑː.ri- ⓤⓢ 'mɑːr.i.oʊ, 'mer-, 'mær-
Marion 'mær.i.ən, 'meə.ri- ⓤⓢ 'mer.i-, 'mær-
marionette ˌmær.i.ə'net ⓤⓢ ˌmer-, ˌmær- **-s** -s
Marisa mə'rɪs.ə
Marischal 'mɑː.ʃəl ⓤⓢ 'mɑːr.ɪ.ʃɑːl, '-ʃɑːl, '-ʃəl
Marissa mə'rɪs.ə
marital 'mær.ɪ.təl, '-ə- ⓤⓢ 'mer.ɪ.t̬əl, 'mær- **-ly** -i
maritime (M) 'mær.ɪ.taɪm, '-ə- ⓤⓢ 'mer-, 'mær-
Marius 'mær.i.əs, 'meə.ri-, 'mɑː- ⓤⓢ 'mer.i-, 'mær-
Marivaux 'mær.i.vəʊ, --'-
marjoram 'mɑː.dʒər.əm ⓤⓢ 'mɑːr.dʒɚ.əm
Marjoribanks 'mɑːtʃ.bæŋks ⓤⓢ 'mɑːrtʃ-
Marjorie, Marjory 'mɑː.dʒər.i ⓤⓢ 'mɑːr-
mark (M) mɑːk ⓤⓢ mɑːrk **-s** -s **-ing/s** -ɪŋ/z **-ed** -t **-edly** -ɪd.li **-er/s** -ər/z ⓤⓢ -ɚ/z ˌ**Mark 'Antony**
Markby 'mɑːk.bi ⓤⓢ 'mɑːrk-
markdown 'mɑːk.daʊn ⓤⓢ 'mɑːrk-
mar|ket (M) 'mɑː|.kɪt ⓤⓢ 'mɑːr- **-kets** -kɪts **-keting** -kɪ.tɪŋ ⓤⓢ -kɪ.t̬ɪŋ **-keted** -kɪ.tɪd **-keter/s** -kɪ.tər/z ⓤⓢ -kɪ.t̬ɚ/z **-keted** ⓤⓢ -kɪ.t̬ɪd **-ketable** -kɪ.tə.bl̩ ⓤⓢ -kɪ.t̬ə.bl̩ ˌ**market e'conomy**; ˌ**market 'gardening**; ˌ**market re'search**; ⓤⓢ '**market** ˌ**research**, '**market re**ˌ**search**; '**market** ˌ**town**, ˌ**market 'town**
marketability ˌmɑː.kɪ.tə'bɪl.ə.ti, -ɪ.ti ⓤⓢ ˌmɑːr.kɪ.t̬ə'bɪl.ə.t̬i
Market Deeping ˌmɑː.kɪt'diː.pɪŋ ⓤⓢ ˌmɑːr-
marketeer ˌmɑː.kɪ'tɪər, -kə'- ⓤⓢ ˌmɑːr.kə'tɪr **-s** -z
market-plac|e 'mɑː.kɪt.pleɪs ⓤⓢ 'mɑːr- **-es** -ɪz
Market Rasen ˌmɑː.kɪt'reɪ.zən ⓤⓢ ˌmɑːr-
Markham 'mɑː.kəm ⓤⓢ 'mɑːr-
markk|a 'mɑː.k|ɑː, -k|ə ⓤⓢ 'mɑːr- **-aa** -ɑː
Markov 'mɑː.kɒf, -kɒv ⓤⓢ 'mɑːr.kɔːf
Markova mɑː'kəʊ.və ⓤⓢ mɑːr'koʊ-
Marks mɑːks ⓤⓢ mɑːrks
Marks and Spencer® ˌmɑːks.ənd'spent.sər ⓤⓢ ˌmɑːrks.ənd'spent.sɚ
marks|man 'mɑːks|.mən ⓤⓢ 'mɑːrks- **-men** -mən, -men **-woman** -ˌwʊm.ən **-women** -ˌwɪm.ɪn
marksmanship 'mɑːks.mən.ʃɪp ⓤⓢ 'mɑːrks-
markup 'mɑːk.ʌp ⓤⓢ 'mɑːrk- **-s** -s
marl mɑːl ⓤⓢ mɑːrl
Marlboro® 'mɑːl.bər.ə, 'mɔːl- ⓤⓢ 'mɑːrl-
Marlborough *town in Wiltshire, family name:* 'mɔːl.bər.ə ⓤⓢ 'mɑːrl.bə.roʊ *London streets, town in US, New Zealand district:* 'mɑːl.bər.ə ⓤⓢ 'mɑːrl.bɚ-
Marlene *English name:* 'mɑː.liːn, -'- ⓤⓢ mɑːr'- *German name:* mɑː'leɪ.nə ⓤⓢ mɑːr-
Marler 'mɑː.lər ⓤⓢ 'mɑːr.lɚ
Marley 'mɑː.li ⓤⓢ 'mɑːr-
marlin 'mɑː.lɪn ⓤⓢ 'mɑːr- **-s** -z
Marling 'mɑː.lɪŋ ⓤⓢ 'mɑːr-
Marlovian mɑː'ləʊ.vi.ən ⓤⓢ mɑːr'loʊ-
Marlow(e) 'mɑː.ləʊ ⓤⓢ 'mɑːr.loʊ
Marmaduke 'mɑː.mə.djuːk ⓤⓢ 'mɑːr.mə.duːk, -djuːk
marmalade 'mɑː.məl.eɪd ⓤⓢ 'mɑːr- **-s** -z
Marmion 'mɑː.mi.ən ⓤⓢ 'mɑːr-
marmite (M®) 'mɑː.maɪt ⓤⓢ 'mɑːr-
Marmora 'mɑː.mər.ə ⓤⓢ 'mɑːr-
marmoreal mɑː'mɔː.ri.əl ⓤⓢ mɑːr'mɔːr.i- **-ly** -i
marmoset 'mɑː.mə.set, -zet, ˌ--'- ⓤⓢ 'mɑːr.mə- **-s** -s
marmot 'mɑː.mət ⓤⓢ 'mɑːr- **-s** -s
Marne mɑːn ⓤⓢ mɑːrn
Marner 'mɑː.nər ⓤⓢ 'mɑːr.nɚ
marocain 'mær.ə.keɪn, ˌ--'- ⓤⓢ 'mer-, 'mær-
maroon mə'ruːn **-s** -z **-ing** -ɪŋ **-ed** -d
Marple 'mɑː.pl̩ ⓤⓢ 'mɑːr-
Marprelate 'mɑː.prel.ət, -ɪt ⓤⓢ 'mɑːr-
Marquand 'mɑː.kwənd ⓤⓢ 'mɑːr-
marque mɑːk ⓤⓢ mɑːrk **-s** -s
marquee mɑː'kiː ⓤⓢ mɑːr- **-s** -z
Marquesas mɑː'keɪ.səs, -zəs, -sæs, -zæs ⓤⓢ mɑːr'keɪ.zəs, -səs
marquess 'mɑː.kwɪs, -kwəs ⓤⓢ 'mɑːr- **-es** -ɪz
marquetr|y 'mɑː.kɪ.tr|i, -kə- ⓤⓢ 'mɑːr- **-ies** -iz
marquis (M) 'mɑː.kwɪs, -kwəs; mɑː'kiː ⓤⓢ 'mɑːr.kwɪs, -kwəs; mɑːr'kiː **marquises** 'mɑː.kwɪ.sɪz, -kwə- ⓤⓢ 'mɑːr.kwɪ- *(alternative plur. of* **marquis***)* mɑː'kiːz ⓤⓢ mɑːr-
marquis|e mɑː'kiːz ⓤⓢ mɑːr- **-es** -ɪz
Marr mɑːr ⓤⓢ mɑːr
Marrakesh, Marrakech ˌmær.ə'keʃ, mə'ræk.eʃ ⓤⓢ 'mer.ə.keʃ, 'mær-; ˌmə'rɑː.keʃ
marram grass 'mær.əmˌgrɑːs ⓤⓢ 'mer.əm.græs, 'mær-
marriag|e 'mær.ɪdʒ ⓤⓢ 'mer-, 'mær- **-es** -ɪz **-eable** -ə.bl̩
Marriner 'mær.ɪ.nər ⓤⓢ 'mer.ɪ.nɚ, 'mær-
Marriott 'mær.i.ət ⓤⓢ 'mer-, 'mær-, -ɑːt
marron 'mær.ən, -ɔ̃ːŋ ⓤⓢ 'mer.ən, 'mær-; mə'roʊn **-s** -z
marrons glacés ˌmær.ən'glæs.eɪ, -əŋ'-, -ɔ̃ːŋ'- ⓤⓢ məˌroʊn.glɑː'seɪ
marrow 'mær.əʊ ⓤⓢ 'mer.oʊ, 'mær- **-s** -z **-y** -i
marrowbone 'mær.əʊ.bəʊn ⓤⓢ 'mer.oʊ.boʊn, 'mær- **-s** -z
marrowfat 'mær.əʊ.fæt ⓤⓢ 'mer.oʊ-, 'mær- **-s** -s
marr|y 'mær|.i ⓤⓢ 'mer-, 'mær- **-ies** -iz **-ying** -i.ɪŋ **-ied** -id **-ier/s** -i.ər/z ⓤⓢ -i.ɚ/z
Marryat 'mær.i.ət ⓤⓢ 'mer-, 'mær-
Mars mɑːz ⓤⓢ mɑːrz '**Mars** ˌ**bar®**
Marsala mɑː'sɑː.lə ⓤⓢ mɑːr'sɑː.lɑː
Marsalis mɑː'sɑː.lɪs ⓤⓢ mɑːr.sæ-
Marsden 'mɑːz.dən ⓤⓢ 'mɑːrz-
Marseillaise ˌmɑː.seɪ'jeɪz, -'eɪz, -səl'eɪz ⓤⓢ ˌmɑːr.səl'eɪz, -seɪ'ez
Marseilles, Marseille ˌmɑː'seɪ ⓤⓢ ˌmɑːr-
marsh (M) mɑːʃ ⓤⓢ mɑːrʃ **-es** -ɪz
Marsha 'mɑː.ʃə ⓤⓢ 'mɑːr-
marshal 'mɑː.ʃəl ⓤⓢ 'mɑːr- **-s** -z **-(l)ing** -ɪŋ **-(l)ed** -d **-(l)er/s** -ər/z ⓤⓢ -ɚ/z
Marshall 'mɑː.ʃəl ⓤⓢ 'mɑːr-
marshland 'mɑːʃ.lænd, -lənd ⓤⓢ 'mɑːrʃ-
marshmallow ˌmɑːʃ'mæl.əʊ ⓤⓢ 'mɑːrʃ.mel.oʊ, -mæl- **-s** -z
marsh|y 'mɑː.ʃ|i ⓤⓢ 'mɑːr- **-ier** -i.ər ⓤⓢ -i.ɚ **-iest** -i.ɪst, -i.əst **-iness** -ɪ.nəs, -ɪ.nɪs
Marske mɑːsk ⓤⓢ mɑːrsk
Marsland 'mɑːz.lənd ⓤⓢ 'mɑːrz-
Marston 'mɑː.stən ⓤⓢ 'mɑːr-
marsupial mɑː'suː.pi.əl, -'sjuː- ⓤⓢ mɑːr'suː- **-s** -z

mart mɑːt (US) mɑːrt **-s** -s
Martel(l) mɑːˈtel (US) mɑːr-
Martello tower mɑːˌtel.əʊˈtaʊəʳ (US) mɑːrˌtel.oʊˈtaʊɚ **-s** -z
marten ˈmɑː.tɪn (US) ˈmɑːr.tᵊn **-s** -z
Martens ˈmɑː.tɪnz; mɑːˈtenz (US) ˈmɑːr.tᵊnz; mɑːrˈtenz
Martha ˈmɑː.θə (US) ˈmɑːr- ˌ**Martha's** ˈ**Vineyard**
martial (M) ˈmɑː.ʃᵊl (US) ˈmɑːr- **-ly** -i ˌ**martial** ˈ**law**
Martian ˈmɑː.ʃᵊn (US) ˈmɑːr- **-s** -z
martin (M) ˈmɑː.tɪn (US) ˈmɑːr.tᵊn **-s** -z
Martina mɑːˈtiː.nə (US) mɑːr-
Martine mɑːˈtiːn (US) mɑːr-
Martineau ˈmɑː.tɪ.nəʊ, -tə- (US) ˈmɑːr.tə.noʊ
martinet (M) ˌmɑː.tɪˈnet, -təˈ-, -ˈneɪ (US) ˌmɑːr.tᵊnˈet, -ˈeɪ, ˈ--- **-s** -s
Martinez mɑːˈtiː.nez (US) mɑːr-, -nəs
martingale ˈmɑː.tɪŋ.geɪl (US) ˈmɑːr.tᵊn- **-s** -z
martini (M®) mɑːˈtiː.ni (US) mɑːr- **-s** -z
Martinique ˌmɑː.tɪˈniːk, -təˈ- (US) ˌmɑːr.tᵊnˈiːk
Martinmas ˈmɑː.tɪn.məs, -tɪm-, -mæs (US) ˈmɑːr.tᵊn.məs
Martyn ˈmɑː.tɪn (US) ˈmɑːr.tᵊn
mart|yr (M) ˈmɑː.t|əʳ (US) ˈmɑːr.t̬|ɚ **-yrs** -əz (US) -ɚz **-yring** -ᵊr.ɪŋ **-yred** -əd (US) -ɚd
martyrdom ˈmɑː.tə.dəm (US) ˈmɑːr.t̬ɚ- **-s** -z
martyriz|e, -is|e ˈmɑː.tᵊr.aɪz, -tɪ.raɪz (US) ˈmɑːr.t̬ə.raɪz **-es** -ɪz **-ing** -ɪŋ **-ed** -d
marvel ˈmɑː.vᵊl (US) ˈmɑːr- **-s** -z **-(l)ing** -ɪŋ, ˈmɑːv.lɪŋ **-(l)ed** -d
Marvell ˈmɑː.vᵊl (US) ˈmɑːr-
marvel(l)ous ˈmɑː.vᵊl.əs; ˈmɑːv.ləs (US) ˈmɑːr.vᵊl.əs; ˈmɑːrv.ləs **-ly** -li **-ness** -nəs, -nɪs
Marvin ˈmɑː.vɪn (US) ˈmɑːr-
Marx mɑːks (US) mɑːrks ˈ**Marx** ˌ**Brothers**
Marxian ˈmɑːk.si.ən (US) ˈmɑːrk-
Marx|ism ˈmɑːk.s|ɪ.zᵊm (US) ˈmɑːrk- **-ist/s** -ɪst/s
Marxism-Leninism ˌmɑːk.sɪ.zᵊmˈlen.ɪ.nɪ.zᵊm (US) ˌmɑːrk-
Marxist-Leninist ˌmɑːk.sɪstˈlen.ɪ.nɪst (US) ˌmɑːrk- **-s** -s
Mary ˈmeə.ri (US) ˈmer.i
Maryborough ˈmeə.ri.bᵊr.ə, -ˌbʌr.ə (US) ˈmer.i.bə.roʊ
Maryland ˈmeə.ri.lænd, ˈmer.ɪ-, -lənd (US) ˈmer.ə.lənd
Marylebone *road, district:* ˈmær.ᵊl.ə.bən, -bəʊn; ˈ-ə.bən, ˈ-ɪ-; ˈmɑː.lɪ- (US) ˈmer.ᵊl.ə.bən, -boʊn; ˈ-ə.bən, ˈ-ɪ-; ˈmɑːr.lɪ-
Mary-le-Bone *preceded by 'St.':* ˈmær.ɪ.lə.bən, -ᵊl.ə- (US) ˈmer-
Maryport ˈmeə.ri.pɔːt (US) ˈmer.i.pɔːrt
marzipan ˈmɑː.zɪ.pæn, -zə-, ˌ--ˈ- (US) ˈmɑːr.zɪ.pæn, ˈmɑːrt.sɪ-, -pɑːn
Masaccio məˈzɑː.tʃəʊ, -ˈzætʃ.əʊ, -tʃi.əʊ (US) -ˈsɑː.tʃi.oʊ
Masada məˈsɑː.də, mæsˈɑː- (US) məˈsɑː.də; ˌmɑː.sɑːˈdɑː
Masai ˈmɑː.saɪ; -ˈ-, məˈ- (US) mɑːˈsaɪ, məˈ-
masala məˈsɑː.lə, mɑː-
Masaryk ˈmæs.ə.rɪk, ˈmæz- (US) ˈmæs.ɚ.ɪk
Mascagni mæsˈkɑː.nji, -ˈkæn.ji (US) mɑːs-
mascara məˈskɑː.rə, mæsˈkɑː- (US) mæsˈker.ə, -ˈkær- **-s** -z
mascarpone ˌmæs.kɑːˈpəʊ.neɪ (US) ˌmɑːs.kɑːrˈpoʊ-, ˌmæs-
mascot ˈmæs.kɒt, -kət (US) -kɑːt, -kət **-s** -s
masculine ˈmæs.kjə.lɪn, -kjʊ- (US) ˈmæs.kjə-, -kjuː- **-s** -z
masculinity ˌmæs.kjəˈlɪn.ə.ti, -kjʊˈ-, -ɪ.ti (US) ˌmæs.kjəˈlɪn.ə.t̬i, -kjuːˈ-
Masefield ˈmeɪs.fiːld
Masekela ˌmæs.əˈkeɪ.lə
maser ˈmeɪ.zəʳ (US) -zɚ **-s** -z
Maserati® ˌmæz.ᵊrˈɑː.ti (US) ˌmɑː.səˈrɑː.t̬i, ˌmæz.əˈ- **-s** -z
Maseru məˈsɪə.ruː, -ˈseə- (US) ˈmæz.ə.ruː, ˌmɑː.səˈruː
mash (M) mæʃ **-es** -ɪz **-ing** -ɪŋ **-ed** -t
MASH mæʃ
Masham *in North Yorkshire:* ˈmæs.əm *surname:* ˈmæs.əm, ˈmæʃ-
masher ˈmæʃ.əʳ (US) -ɚ **-s** -z
mashie ˈmæʃ.i **-s** -z
Mashona məˈʃɒn.ə, -ˈʃəʊ.nə (US) -ˈʃɑː-, -ˈʃoʊ- **-s** -z **-land** -lænd
mash|y ˈmæʃ|.i **-ies** -iz
Masie ˈmeɪ.zi
mask mɑːsk (US) mæsk **-s** -s **-ing** -ɪŋ **-ed** -t ˈ**masking** ˌ**tape**
Maskell ˈmæs.kᵊl
Maskelyne ˈmæs.kɪ.lɪn, -kᵊl.ɪn (US) -ɪn, -aɪn
masoch|ism ˈmæs.ə.k|ɪ.zᵊm, ˈmæz- **-ist/s** -ɪst/s
masochistic ˌmæs.əˈkɪs.tɪk, ˌmæz- **-ally** -ᵊl.i, -li
mason (M) ˈmeɪ.sᵊn **-s** -z ˈ**mason** ˌ**jar**
Mason-Dixon ˌmeɪ.sᵊnˈdɪk.sᵊn ˌ**Mason-**ˈ**Dixon** ˌ**line**
masonic (M) məˈsɒn.ɪk (US) -ˈsɑː.nɪk
Masonite® ˈmeɪ.sᵊn.aɪt
masonr|y (M) ˈmeɪ.sᵊn.r|i **-ies** -iz
masque mɑːsk, mæsk (US) mæsk **-s** -s
masquerad|e ˌmæs.kᵊrˈeɪd, ˌmɑː.skᵊrˈ- (US) ˌmæs.kəˈreɪd **-es** -z **-ing** -ɪŋ **-ed** -ɪd **-er/s** -əʳ/z (US) -ɚ/z
mass mæs **-es** -ɪz **-ing** -ɪŋ **-ed** -t ˌ**mass** ˈ**media**; ˌ**mass pro**ˈ**duction**
mass (M) *(n.) religious service:* mæs, mɑːs (US) mæs **-es** -ɪz
Mass. *(abbrev. for* **Massachusetts***)* mæs
Massachusetts ˌmæs.əˈtʃuː.sɪts, -səts (US) -sɪts
massac|re ˈmæs.ə.k|əʳ, ˈ-ɪ- (US) -k|ɚ **-res** -əz (US) -ɚz **-ring** -ᵊr.ɪŋ **-red** -əd (US) -ɚd
massag|e ˈmæs.ɑːdʒ (US) məˈsɑːdʒ **-es** -ɪz **-ing** -ɪŋ **-ed** -d **-er/s** -əʳ/z **-er/z** (US) -ɚ/z **-ist/s** -ɪst/s ˈ**massage** ˌ**parlour** (US) **mas**ˈ**sage** ˌ**parlor**
Massawa məˈsɑː.wə (US) mɑːˈsɑː.wɑː, məˈsɑː.wə
Massenet ˈmæs.ᵊn.eɪ (US) ˌ--ˈ-
masseur mæsˈɜːʳ, məˈsɜːʳ (US) -ˈsɝː, -ˈsuːr, -ˈsʊr **-s** -z
masseus|e mæsˈɜːz, məˈsɜːz (US) -ˈsɜːz, -ˈsuːz, -ˈsʊz **-es** -ɪz
Massey ˈmæs.i
massif mæsˈiːf, ˈ-- (US) mæsˈiːf **-s** -s
Massif Central ˌmæs.iːf.sɑ̃ːnˈtrɑːl
Massinger ˈmæs.ɪn.dʒəʳ (US) -dʒɚ
massive ˈmæs.ɪv **-ly** -li **-ness** -nəs, -nɪs
mass-market ˌmæsˈmɑː.kɪt (US) -ˈmɑːr- **-s** -s **-ing** -ɪŋ **-ed** -ɪd
mass-meeting ˌmæsˈmiː.tɪŋ, ˈ-ˌ-- (US) -t̬ɪŋ **-s** -z
Masson ˈmæs.ᵊn (US) ˈmæs.ɑːn, -ˈ-
Massow ˈmæs.əʊ (US) -oʊ
mass-produc|e ˌmæs.prəˈdjuːs, -ˈdʒuːs (US) ˌmæs.prəˈduːs, -proʊˈ-, -ˈdjuːs **-es** -ɪz **-ing** -ɪŋ **-ed** -t **-er/s** -əʳ/z (US) -ɚ/z *stress shift:* ˌmass-produced ˈgoods
mass-production ˌmæs.prəˈdʌk.ʃᵊn, ˈmæs.prəˌ- (US) ˌmæs.prəˈdʌk-, -proʊˈ-
mass|y ˈmæs|.i **-iness** -ɪ.nəs, -ɪ.nɪs
mast mɑːst (US) mæst **-s** -s
mastectom|y mæsˈtek.tə.m|i (US) məˈstek-, mæsˈtek- **-ies** -iz
mast|er ˈmɑː.st|əʳ (US) ˈmæs.t|ɚ **-ers** -əz (US) -ɚz **-ering** -ᵊr.ɪŋ **-ered** -əd (US) -ɚd ˌ**master** ˈ**bedroom**; ˈ**master** ˌ**class**; ˌ**master of** ˈ**ceremonies**; ˈ**master** ˌ**key**; ˈ**master** ˌ**race**
master-at-arms ˌmɑː.stəʳ.ətˈɑːmz (US) ˌmæs.tɚ.ətˈɑːrmz **masters-at-arms** ˌmɑː.stəz- (US) ˌmæs.tɚz-
Mastercard® ˈmɑː.stə.kɑːd (US) ˈmæs.tɚ.kɑːrd
masterclass ˈmɑː.stə.klɑːs (US) ˈmæs.tɚ.klæs **-es** -ɪz
masterful ˈmɑː.stə.fᵊl, -fʊl (US) ˈmæs.tɚ- **-ly** -i **-ness** -nəs, -nɪs
masterl|y ˈmɑː.stə.l|i (US) ˈmæs.tɚ- **-iness** -ɪ.nəs, -ɪ.nɪs
Masterman ˈmɑː.stə.mən (US) ˈmæs.tɚ-
mastermind ˈmɑː.stə.maɪnd (US) ˈmæs.tɚ- **-s** -z **-ing** -ɪŋ **-ed** -ɪd

masterpiec|e ˈmɑː.stə.piːs US ˈmæs.tɚ- **-es** -ɪz
Masters ˈmɑː.stəz US ˈmæs.tɚz
mastership ˈmɑː.stə.ʃɪp US ˈmæs.tɚ-
master-stroke ˈmɑː.stə.strəʊk US ˈmæs.tɚ.stroʊk **-s** -s
masterwork ˈmɑː.stə.wɜːk US ˈmæs.tɚ.wɝːk **-s** -s
master|y ˈmɑː.stᵊr|.i US ˈmæs.tɚ- **-ies** -iz
masthead ˈmɑːst.hed US ˈmæst- **-s** -z
mastic ˈmæs.tɪk
masti|cate ˈmæs.tɪ|.keɪt, -tə- **-cates** -keɪts **-cating** -keɪ.tɪŋ US -keɪ.t̬ɪŋ **-cated** -keɪ.tɪd US -keɪ.t̬ɪd **-cator/s** -keɪ.təʳ/z US -keɪ.t̬ɚ/z
mastication ˌmæs.tɪˈkeɪ.ʃᵊn, -təˈ-
masticatory ˈmæs.tɪ.kə.tᵊr.i, -keɪ-; ˌmæs.tɪˈkeɪ-, -təˈ- US ˈmæs.tɪ.kə.tɔːr-, -tə-
mastiff ˈmæs.tɪf, ˈmɑː.stɪf US ˈmæs.tɪf **-s** -s
mastitis mæsˈtaɪ.tɪs, məˈstaɪ- US mæsˈtaɪ.t̬ɪs, məˈstaɪ- **mastitides** mæsˈtɪt.ə.diːz, məˈstɪt- US mæsˈtɪt̬.ə-, məˈstɪt̬-
mastodon ˈmæs.tə.dɒn, -dən US -dɑːn **-s** -z
mastoid ˈmæs.tɔɪd **-s** -z
Mastroianni ˌmæs.trəʊˈjɑː.ni, ˌmɑːs.trəʊ-, -ˈjæn.i US -troʊˈ-
mastur|bate ˈmæs.tə|.beɪt US -tɚ- **-bates** -beɪts **-bating** -beɪ.tɪŋ US -beɪ.t̬ɪŋ **-bated** -beɪ.tɪd US -beɪ.t̬ɪd **-bator/s** -beɪ.təʳ/z US -beɪ.t̬ɚ/z
masturbation ˌmæs.təˈbeɪ.ʃᵊn US -tɚˈ- **-s** -z
masturbatory ˌmæs.təˈbeɪ.tᵊr.i, ˈmæs.tə.beɪ- US ˈmæs.tɚ.bə.tɔːr-
Masur məˈzʊəʳ US -ˈzʊr
mat mæt **-s** -s **-ting** -ɪŋ US ˈmæt̬.ɪŋ **-ted** -ɪd US ˈmæt̬.ɪd
Matabel|e ˌmæt.əˈbiː.li US ˌmæt̬- **-ies** -iz **-ie** -i
Matabeleland ˌmæt.əˈbiː.li.lænd US ˌmæt̬-
matador ˈmæt.ə.dɔːʳ US ˈmæt̬.ə.dɔːr **-s** -z
Mata Hari ˌmɑː.təˈhɑː.ri US ˌmɑː.t̬əˈhɑːr.i, ˌmæt̬.əˈher-, -ˈhær-
match mætʃ **-es** -ɪz **-ing** -ɪŋ **-ed** -t **-er/s** -əʳ/z US -ɚ/z ˌ**match ˈpoint**
matchboard ˈmætʃ.bɔːd US -bɔːrd
matchbook ˈmætʃ.bʊk **-s** -s
matchbox ˈmætʃ.bɒks US -bɑːks **-es** -ɪz
matchless ˈmætʃ.ləs, -lɪs **-ly** -li **-ness** -nəs, -nɪs
matchlock ˈmætʃ.lɒk US -lɑːk **-s** -s
matchmaker ˈmætʃˌmeɪ.kəʳ US -kɚ **-s** -z
matchmaking ˈmætʃˌmeɪ.kɪŋ
matchplay ˈmætʃ.pleɪ
matchstick ˈmætʃ.stɪk **-s** -s
matchwood ˈmætʃ.wʊd
mat|e meɪt **-es** -s **-ing** -ɪŋ US ˈmeɪ.t̬ɪŋ **-ed** -ɪd US ˈmeɪ.t̬ɪd
maté ˈmɑː.teɪ, ˈmæt.eɪ
matelot ˈmæt.ləʊ, ˈ-əl.əʊ US -ᵊl.oʊ **-s** -z
mater ˈmeɪ.təʳ, ˈmɑː- US -t̬ɚ **-s** -z
materfamilias ˌmæt.ə.fəˈmɪl.i.æs US ˌmeɪ.t̬ɚ.fəˈmɪl.i.əs, ˌmɑː-
material məˈtɪə.ri.əl US -ˈtɪr.i- **-s** -z **-ly** -i
material|ism məˈtɪə.ri.ə.l|ɪ.zᵊm US -ˈtɪr.i- **-ist/s** -ɪst/s
materialistic məˌtɪə.ri.əˈlɪs.tɪk US -ˌtɪr.i-
materialization, -isa- məˌtɪə.ri.əl.aɪˈzeɪ.ʃən, -ɪˈ- US -ˌtɪr.i.əl.ɪˈ- **-s** -z
materializ|e, -is|e məˈtɪə.ri.ə.laɪz US -ˈtɪr.i- **-es** -ɪz **-ing** -ɪŋ **-ed** -d
matériel, materiel məˌtɪə.riˈel, mæt,ɪə-; məˈtɪə.ri.əl US məˌtɪr.iˈel; məˈtɪr.i.əl
maternal məˈtɜː.nᵊl US -ˈtɝː- **-ly** -i
maternit|y məˈtɜː.nə.t|i, -ɪ.t|i US -ˈtɝː.nə.t̬|i **-ies** -iz **maˈternity ˌleave; maˈternity ˌward**
matey ˈmeɪ.ti US -t̬i **-ness** -ɪ.nəs, -ɪ.nɪs
math mæθ
mathematic ˌmæθ.ᵊmˈæt.ɪk, -ɪˈmæt-, mæθˈmæt- US ˌmæθ.əˈmæt̬-, mæθˈmæt̬-
mathematic|al ˌmæθ.ᵊmˈæt.ɪ.k|ᵊl, -ɪˈmæt, mæθˈmæt- US ˌmæθ.əˈmæt̬-, mæθˈmæt̬- **-ally** -ᵊl.i, -li
mathematician ˌmæθ.ᵊm.əˈtɪʃ.ᵊn, -ɪ.məˈ-, ˌmæθ.məˈ- US ˌmæθ.ə.məˈ-, ˌmæθ.məˈ- **-s** -z
mathematics mæθ.ᵊmˈæt.ɪks, -ɪˈmæt-, mæθˈmæt- US ˌmæθ.əˈmæt̬-, mæθˈmæt̬-
Mather ˈmeɪ.ðəʳ, -θəʳ; ˈmæð.əʳ US ˈmæð.ɚ **-s** -z
Matheson ˈmæθ.ɪ.sᵊn, ˈ-ə-
Mathew ˈmæθ.juː, ˈmeɪ.θjuː
Mathews ˈmæθ.juːz, ˈmeɪ.θjuːz
Mathias məˈθaɪəs
Mathilda məˈtɪl.də
Mathis ˈmæθ.ɪs
maths mæθs
Matilda məˈtɪl.də
matinée, matinee ˈmæt.ɪ.neɪ, -ᵊn.eɪ US ˌmæt.ᵊnˈeɪ **-s** -z **ˈmatinée ˌidol matinˈée ˌidol**
matins ˈmæt.ɪnz US -ᵊnz
Matisse məˈtiːs US mə-, mɑː-
Matlock ˈmæt.lɒk US -lɑːk
Mato Grosso ˌmæt.əʊˈgrəʊ.səʊ, ˌmɑː.təʊˈ- US ˌmæt̬.əˈgroʊ.soʊ, ˌmɑː.tuːˈgroʊ.suː, -ˈgrɔː-
Maton ˈmeɪ.tᵊn
Matravers məˈtræv.əz US -ɚz
matriarch ˈmeɪ.tri.ɑːk, ˈmæt.ri- US ˈmeɪ.tri.ɑːrk **-y** -i
matriarchal ˌmeɪ.triˈɑː.kᵊl, ˌmæt.riˈ- US ˌmeɪ.triˈɑːr-
matric məˈtrɪk
matrices *(plur. of* **matrix***)* ˈmeɪ.trɪ.siːz, -trə, ˈmæt.rɪ-, -rə- US ˈmeɪ.trɪ-
matricidal ˌmæt.rɪˈsaɪ.dᵊl, ˌmeɪ.trɪˈ-, -trəˈ-
matricide ˈmæt.rɪ.saɪd, ˈmeɪ.trɪ-, -trə- **-s** -z
matricu|late məˈtrɪk.jə|.leɪt, -jʊ- US -jə-, -juː- **-lates** -leɪts **-lating** -leɪ.tɪŋ US -leɪ.t̬ɪŋ **-lated** -leɪ.tɪd US -leɪ.t̬ɪd **-lator/s** -leɪ.təʳ/z US -leɪ.t̬ɚ/z
matriculation məˌtrɪk.jəˈleɪ.ʃᵊn, -jʊˈ- US -jəˈ-, -juːˈ- **-s** -z
matrilineal ˌmæt.rɪˈlɪn.i.əl, ˌmeɪ.trɪˈ-, -trəˈ- US -trəˈ- **-ly** -i
matrimonial ˌmæt.rɪˈməʊ.ni.əl, -rəˈ- US -rəˈmoʊ- **-ly** -i
matrimon|y ˈmæt.rɪ.mə.n|i, -rə- US -rə.moʊ- **-ies** -iz
mat|rix ˈmeɪ.t|rɪks, ˈmæt|.rɪks US ˈmeɪ.t|rɪks **-rixes** -rɪk.sɪz **-rices** -rɪ.siːz, -rə-

Note: British doctors generally pronounce /ˈmeɪ.trɪks/ when talking about the cell type. Those connected with the printing trade pronounce /ˈmæt.rɪks/.

matron ˈmeɪ.trᵊn **-s** -z **-ly** -li ˌ**matron of ˈhonour**
Matrûh mætˈruː
Matsui® mætˈsuː.i
Matsushita® ˌmæt.suˈʃiː.tə US -t̬ə
matt(e) mæt
matt|er ˈmæt|.əʳ US ˈmæt̬|.ɚ **-ers** -əz US -ɚz **-ering** -ᵊr.ɪŋ **-ered** -əd US -ɚz **as a ˌmatter of ˈfact**
Matterhorn ˈmæt.ə.hɔːn US ˈmæt̬.ɚ.hɔːrn
matter-of-fact ˌmæt.əʳ.əvˈfækt US ˌmæt̬.ɚ-
Matthau ˈmæθ.aʊ, ˈmæt-
Matthes ˈmæθ.əs
Matthew ˈmæθ.juː
Matthews ˈmæθ.juːz
Matthias məˈθaɪəs
Matthiessen ˈmæθ.ɪ.sᵊn
matting ˈmæt.ɪŋ US ˈmæt̬-
mattins ˈmæt.ɪnz US -ᵊnz
mattock ˈmæt.ək US ˈmæt̬- **-s** -s
mattress ˈmæt.rəs, -trɪs **-es** -ɪz
matur|ate ˈmæt.jᵊr|.eɪt, -jʊ.r|eɪt; ˈmætʃ.ᵊr|.eɪt US ˈmætʃ.ə.r|eɪt, -ʊ- **-ates** -eɪts **-ating** -eɪ.tɪŋ US -eɪ.t̬ɪŋ **-ated** -eɪ.tɪd US -eɪ.t̬ɪd

maturation ˌmæt.jəˈreɪ.ʃən, -jʊˈreɪ-; ˌmætʃ.əˈreɪ- ⓤⓢ ˌmætʃ.əˈreɪ-, -ʊˈ-
matur|e (M) məˈtjʊəʳ, -ˈtjɔːʳ, -ˈtʃʊəʳ, -ˈtʃɔːʳ ⓤⓢ -ˈtʊr, -ˈtjʊr, -ˈtʃʊr **-ely** -li **-eness** -nəs, -nɪs **-es** -z **-ing** -ɪŋ **-ed** -d
Maturin *surname:* ˈmæt.jʊə.rɪn, -jəˈ- ⓤⓢ ˌmɑː.tuːˈriːn, -təˈ-
Maturín *in Venezuela:* ˌmæt.jʊəˈrɪn, -jəˈ- ⓤⓢ ˌmɑː.tuːˈriːn, -t̬əˈ-
maturity məˈtjʊə.rə.ti, -ˈtjɔː-, -ˈtʃʊə-, -ˈtʃɔː-, -rɪ- ⓤⓢ -ˈtʊr.ə.t̬i, -ˈtjʊr-, -ˈtʃʊr-
matutinal ˌmæt.jʊˈtaɪ.nəl; məˈtjuː.tɪ-, -tə- ⓤⓢ məˈtuː.tən.əl, -ˈtjuː-
matzo(h) ˈmɒt.sə, ˈmæt-, ˈmɑːt-, -səʊ ⓤⓢ ˈmɑːt.sə, -soʊ **-s** -z **matzoth** ˈmɒt.səʊt, ˈmæt-, ˈmɑːt-, -səʊθ ⓤⓢ -soʊt
maud (M) mɔːd ⓤⓢ mɑːd, mɔːd **-s** -z
Maude mɔːd ⓤⓢ mɑːd, mɔːd
maudlin ˈmɔːd.lɪn ⓤⓢ ˈmɑːd-, ˈmɔːd-
Maudsley ˈmɔːdz.li ⓤⓢ ˈmɑːdz-, ˈmɔːdz-
Mauger ˈmeɪ.dʒəʳ, ˈmɔː.gəʳ ⓤⓢ ˈmɑː.gɚ, ˈmɔː-, ˈmeɪ.dʒɚ
Maugham mɔːm; ˈmɒf.əm ⓤⓢ mɑːm, mɔːm
Note: The author Somerset Maugham is pronounced /mɔːm/.
Maughan mɔːn ⓤⓢ mɑːn, mɔːn
maugre ˈmɔː.gəʳ ⓤⓢ ˈmɑː.gɚ, ˈmɔː-
Maui ˈmaʊ.i
maul mɔːl ⓤⓢ mɑːl, mɔːl **-s** -z **-ing** -ɪŋ **-ed** -d **-er/s** -əʳ/z ⓤⓢ -ɚ/z
Mauleverer mɔːˈlev.ər.əʳ, mə- ⓤⓢ mɑːˈlev.ɚ.ɚ, mɔː-, mə-
maulstick ˈmɔːl.stɪk ⓤⓢ ˈmɑːl-, ˈmɔːl- **-s** -s
Mau Mau ˈmaʊˌmaʊ, ˌ-ˈ-
Mauna Kea ˌmaʊ.nəˈkeɪ.ə ⓤⓢ ˌmaʊ-, ˌmɑː-, ˌmɔː-
Mauna Loa ˌmaʊ.nəˈləʊ.ə ⓤⓢ -ˈloʊ-, ˌmɑː-, ˌmɔː-
maunder ˈmɔːn.dəʳ ⓤⓢ ˈmɑːn.dɚ, ˈmɔːn- **-s** -z **-ing** -ɪŋ **-ed** -d
maundy (M) ˈmɔːn.di ⓤⓢ ˈmɑːn-, ˈmɔːn- ˌ**Maundy** ˈ**Thursday**
Maunsell ˈmænt.səl
Maupassant ˈməʊ.pæs.ɑ̃ːŋ ⓤⓢ ˈmoʊ.pə.sɑːnt
Maupin ˈmɔː.pɪn, -pæ̃ ⓤⓢ ˈmɑː-
Maureen ˈmɔː.riːn, -ˈ- ⓤⓢ mɔːˈriːn, mə-
Mauretani|a ˌmɒr.ɪˈteɪ.ni|.ə, ˌmɔː.rɪˈ- ⓤⓢ ˌmɔːr.ɪˈ-, ˌmɑːr-, -ˈnj|ə **-an/s** -ən/z
Mauriac ˈmɒr.i.æk, ˈmɔː.ri- ⓤⓢ ˈmɔːr-, ˈmɑːr-
Maurice ˈmɒr.ɪs, mɒrˈiːs ⓤⓢ mɔːˈriːs, mɑː-, mə-; ˈmɑːr.ɪs, ˈmɔːr-
Mauritani|a ˌmɒr.ɪˈteɪ.ni|.ə, ˌmɔː.rɪˈ- ⓤⓢ ˌmɔːr.ɪˈ-, ˌmɑːr-, -ˈnj|ə **-an/s** -ən/z
Maurit|ius məˈrɪʃ|.əs, mɔː-, mɒrˈɪʃ- ⓤⓢ mɔːˈrɪʃ.i|.əs, mɑː-, ˈ-əs **-ian/s** -ən/z
Mauser ˈmaʊ.zəʳ ⓤⓢ -zɚ **-s** -z
mausoleum ˌmɔː.səˈliː.əm, ˌmaʊ-, -zəˈ-, -ˈleɪ- ⓤⓢ ˌmɑː.səˈliː-, ˌmɔː-, -zəˈ- **-s** -z
mauve məʊv ⓤⓢ moʊv, mɑːv, mɔːv **-s** -z
maven ˈmeɪ.vən **-s** -z
maverick ˈmæv.ər.ɪk ⓤⓢ ˈmæv.ɚ-, ˈ-rɪk **-s** -s
mavis (M) ˈmeɪ.vɪs
maw (M) mɔː ⓤⓢ mɑː, mɔː **-s** -z
Mawer ˈmɔː.əʳ, mɔːʳ ⓤⓢ ˈmɔː.ɚ
Mawhinney, Mawhinny məˈhwɪn.i
mawkish ˈmɔː.kɪʃ ⓤⓢ ˈmɑː-, ˈmɔː- **-ly** -li **-ness** -nəs, -nɪs
max (M) mæks
Maxey ˈmæk.si
Max Factor® ˌmæksˈfæk.təʳ ⓤⓢ -tɚ
maxi ˈmæk.si **-s** -z
maxill|a mækˈsɪl|.ə **-ae** -iː **-as** -əz **-ary** -ər.i
maxim (M) ˈmæk.sɪm **-s** -z
maximal ˈmæk.sɪ.məl, -sə- **-ly** -i
maximalist ˈmæk.sɪ.məl.ɪst, -sə- **-s** -s
Maximilian ˌmæk.sɪˈmɪl.i.ən, -səˈ- ⓤⓢ ˈ-jən, ˈ-i.ən
maximization, -isa- ˌmæk.sɪ.maɪˈzeɪ.ʃən, -sə-, -mɪˈ- ⓤⓢ -mɪˈ- **-s** -z
maximiz|e, -is|e ˈmæk.sɪ.maɪz, -sə- **-es** -ɪz **-ing** -ɪŋ **-ed** -d **-er/s** -əʳ/z ⓤⓢ -ɚ/z
maxim|um ˈmæk.sɪ.m|əm, -sə- **-ums** -əmz **-a** -ə
Maximus ˈmæk.sɪ.məs, -sə-
Maxine mækˈsiːn, ˈ-- ⓤⓢ mækˈsiːn
Maxse ˈmæk.si
Maxwell ˈmæk.swəl, -swel
may *(auxil. v.)* meɪ
May meɪ ˈ**May** ˌ**Day**
May|a ˈmaɪ|.ə ⓤⓢ ˈmɑː.j|ə, ˈmaɪ|.ə **-as** -əz **-an/s** -ən/z
Mayall ˈmeɪ.ɔːl, -əl ⓤⓢ -ɔːl, -ɑːl, -əl
mayapple ˈmeɪˌæp.l̩ **-s** -z
maybe ˈmeɪ.bi, -biː, ˌ-ˈ-
maybug ˈmeɪ.bʌg **-s** -z
mayday (M) ˈmeɪ.deɪ **-s** -z
Mayer ˈmeɪ.əʳ ⓤⓢ -ɚ
mayest ˈmeɪ.ɪst, -əst; meɪst
Mayfair ˈmeɪ.feəʳ ⓤⓢ -fer
Mayfield ˈmeɪ.fiːld
mayflower (M) ˈmeɪ.flaʊəʳ ⓤⓢ -flaʊɚ **-s** -z
mayfl|y ˈmeɪ.fl|aɪ **-ies** -aɪz
mayhap ˈmeɪ.hæp
mayhem ˈmeɪ.hem
Mayhew ˈmeɪ.hjuː
maying ˈmeɪ.ɪŋ
Maynard ˈmeɪ.nɑːd, -nəd ⓤⓢ -nɚd
Maynooth məˈnuːθ, meɪ-
mayn't meɪnt; ˈmeɪ.ənt
Maynwaring ˈmæn.ər.ɪŋ
Mayo *in Ireland, surname:* ˈmeɪ.əʊ, -ˈ- ⓤⓢ -oʊ, -ˈ- **-s** -z *American Indian:* ˈmaɪ.əʊ ⓤⓢ -oʊ **-s** -z
mayo *(abbrev. for* **mayonnaise***)* ˈmeɪ.əʊ ⓤⓢ -oʊ
mayonnaise ˌmeɪ.əˈneɪz ⓤⓢ ˈmeɪ.ə.neɪz, ˌ--ˈ-
mayor (M) meəʳ ⓤⓢ meɪɚ, mer **-s** -z
mayoral ˈmeə.rəl ⓤⓢ ˈmeɪ.ɔːr.əl
mayoralt|y ˈmeə.rəl.t|i ⓤⓢ ˈmeɪɚ.əl.t̬|i, ˈmer- **-ies** -iz
mayoress (M) ˌmeəˈres; ˈmeə.res, -rɪs, -rəs ⓤⓢ ˈmeɪɚ.ɪs, ˈmer-, -əs **-es** -ɪz
mayorship ˈmeə.ʃɪp ⓤⓢ ˈmeɪɚ-, ˈmer- **-s** -s
Mayotte maɪˈjɒt ⓤⓢ mɑːˈjɑːt
Mayou ˈmeɪ.uː
maypole ˈmeɪ.pəʊl ⓤⓢ -poʊl **-s** -z
mayst meɪst
Mazda® ˈmæz.də ⓤⓢ ˈmɑːz- **-s** -z
maz|e meɪz **-es** -ɪz
Mazeppa məˈzep.ə
Mazo de la Roche ˌmæz.əʊ.də.lɑːˈrɒʃ, ˌmeɪ.zəʊ- ⓤⓢ ˌmɑː.zoʊ.də.lɑːˈroʊʃ
mazourka məˈzɜː.kə ⓤⓢ -ˈzɝː-, -ˈzʊr- **-s** -z
mazuma məˈzuː.mə
mazurka məˈzɜː.kə ⓤⓢ -ˈzɝː-, -ˈzʊr- **-s** -z
mazuzah məˈzuː.zə
maz|y ˈmeɪ.z|i **-ier** -i.əʳ ⓤⓢ -i.ɚ **-iest** -i.ɪst, -i.əst **-ily** -ɪ.li, -əl.i **-iness** -ɪ.nəs, -ɪ.nɪs
MBA ˌem.biːˈeɪ
Mbabane əm.bɑːˈbɑː.neɪ ⓤⓢ ˌem-
MBE ˌem.biːˈiː
Mbeki əmˈbek.i
Mbuji-Mayi əmˈbuː.dʒi.maɪ.i ⓤⓢ emˌbuː.dʒiˈmaɪ.ji, -ˈmɑː-
Mc mək, mæk
MC ˌemˈsiː
McAdam məˈkæd.əm
McAfee məˈkæf.i; ˌmæk.əˈfiː ⓤⓢ ˈmæk.ə.fiː; məˈkæf.i
McAiley məˈkeɪ.li
McAleer ˌmæk.əˈlɪəʳ ⓤⓢ -ˈlɪr
McAleese ˌmæk.əˈliːs
McAlinden ˌmæk.əˈlɪn.dən
McAlister məˈkæl.ɪ.stəʳ ⓤⓢ -stɚ
McAll məˈkɔːl ⓤⓢ -ˈkɔːl, -ˈkɑːl
McAl(l)ister məˈkæl.ɪ.stəʳ, ˈ-ə- ⓤⓢ -stɚ
McAlpine məˈkæl.pɪn, -paɪn
McAnally ˌmæk.əˈnæl.i ⓤⓢ ˈmæk.ən.æl.i
McArdle məˈkɑː.dl̩ ⓤⓢ -ˈkɑːr-
McArthur məˈkɑː.θəʳ ⓤⓢ -ˈkɑːr.θɚ
McAteer ˌmæk.əˈtɪəʳ, ˈ--- ⓤⓢ ˌmæk.əˈtɪr, ˈ---
McAulay məˈkɔː.li ⓤⓢ -ˈkɔː-, -ˈkɑː-
McAvoy ˈmæk.ə.vɔɪ
McBain məkˈbeɪn
McBeal məkˈbiːl

McBean mək'beɪn, -'biːn
McBeth mək'beθ
McBrain mək'breɪn
McBride mək'braɪd
MCC ˌem.siː'siː
McCabe mə'keɪb
McCaffrey mə'kæf.ri
McCain® mə'keɪn
McCall mə'kɔːl US -'kɔːl, -'kɑːl
McCallie mə'kɔː.li US -'kɑː.li, -'kɔː-
McCallion mə'kæl.i.ən
McCallum mə'kæl.əm
McCann mə'kæn
McCartan, McCarten mə'kɑː.tᵊn US -'kɑːr-
McCarthy mə'kɑː.θi US -'kɑːr- **-ism** -ɪ.zᵊm **-ite/s** -aɪt/s
McCartney mə'kɑːt.ni US -'kɑːrt-
McCaughey mə'kæx.i, -'kæ.hi, -'kɒf.i US -'kæ.hi, -'kɑː.fi
McCausland mə'kɔːz.lənd US -'kɑːz-, -'kɔːz-
McClain mə'kleɪn
McClean mə'kleɪn, -'kliːn
McClear mə'klɪəʳ US -'klɪr
McClellan mə'klel.ən
McClelland mə'klel.ənd
McClintock mə'klɪn.tək, -tɒk US -t̬ək, -tɑːk
McCloskey mə'klɒs.ki US -'klɑː.ski, -'klʌs.ki
McClure mə'klʊəʳ, -'klɔːʳ US -'klʊr
McColl mə'kɒl US -'kɑːl, -'kɔːl
McCollum mə'kɒl.əm US -'kɑː.ləm
McComb mə'kəʊm US -'koʊm
McConnell mə'kɒn.əl US -'kɑː.nəl
McConochie mə'kɒn.ə.ki, -xi US -'kɑː.nə-
McConville mə'kɒn.vɪl US -'kɑːn-
McCormack mə'kɔː.mək US -'kɔːr-
McCormick mə'kɔː.mɪk US -'kɔːr-
McCorquodale mə'kɔː.kə.deɪl US -'kɔːr-
McCorry mə'kɒr.i US -'kɔːr-
McCourt mə'kɔːt US -'kɔːrt
McCoy mə'kɔɪ
McCrae, McCrea mə'kreɪ
McCready mə'kriː.di
McCrory mə'krɔː.ri US -'krɔːr.i
McCullagh mə'kʌl.ə
McCullam mə'kʌl.əm
McCullers mə'kʌl.əz US -ɚz
McCulloch mə'kʌl.ək, -əx
McCusker mə'kʌs.kəʳ US -kɚ
McDade mək'deɪd
McDaniels mək'dæn.jəlz
McDermot(t) mək'dɜː.mət US -'dɝː-
McDiarmid mək'dɜː.mɪd, -'deə- US -'dɝː-
McDonald mək'dɒn.ᵊld, mæk- US -'dɑː.nᵊld
McDonaugh mək'dɒn.ə US -'dɑː.nə
McDon(n)ell mək'dɒn.ᵊl, ˌmæk.də'nel US -'dɑː.nəl
McDono(u)gh mək'dʌn.ə, -'dɒn- US -'dɑː.nə, -'dʌn-
McDougal mək'duː.gᵊl
McDougall mək'duː.gᵊl
McDougall's® mək'duː.gᵊlz, mæk-
McDowell, McDowall mək'daʊəl, -'dəʊəl US -'daʊəl, -'doʊəl
McDuff mək'dʌf, mæk-
Note: In Scotland always /mək-/.
McElder(r)y 'mæk.ᵊlˌder.i, ˌmæk.ᵊl'der-
McEldowney ˌmæk.ᵊl'daʊ.ni, 'mæk.ᵊlˌdaʊ-
McElroy 'mæk.ᵊl.rɔɪ
McElwain mə'kel.weɪn; 'mæk.ᵊl.weɪn
McElwin mə'kel.wɪn
McEnroe 'mæk.ɪn.rəʊ, -ᵊn- US -roʊ
McEwen, McEwan mə'kjuː.ən, -ɪn
McFadzean mək'fæd.i.ən
McFarland mək'fɑː.lənd US -'fɑːr-
McFarlane mək'fɑː.lɪn, -lən US -'fɑːr-
McGahey mə'gæx.i, -'gæ.hi US -'geɪ.hi
McGee mə'giː
McGillicuddy 'mæg.li.kʌd.i, 'mæk.ɪl-; mə'gɪl.i- US mə'gɪl.i-
McGillivray mə'gɪl.ɪ.vri, -'gɪl.vri, -'glɪv.ri, -reɪ
McGoldrick mə'gəʊl.drɪk US -goʊl-
McGough mə'gɒf US -'gɑːf
McGovern mə'gʌv.ən US -ɚn
McGowan mə'gaʊən
McGrath mə'grɑː, -'grɑːθ, -'græθ US -'græθ
McGraw mə'grɔː US -'grɑː, -'grɔː
McGregor mə'greg.əʳ US -ɚ
McGuane mə'gweɪn
McGuigan mə'gwɪg.ən
McGuinness mə'gɪn.ɪs, -əs
McGuire mə'gwaɪəʳ US -'gwaɪɚ
McIlrath 'mæk.ᵊl.rɑːθ, -ɪl- US -ræθ
McIlroy 'mæk.ᵊl.rɔɪ, -ɪl-, ˌ--'-
McIlvanney ˌmæk.ᵊl'væn.i, -ɪl'-
McIlwraith 'mæk.ᵊl.reɪθ, -ɪl-
McInlay, McInley mə'kɪn.li US mək'ɪn.li
McInroy 'mæk.ɪn.rɔɪ, -ᵊn-
McIntosh 'mæk.ɪn.tɒʃ, -ᵊn- US -tɑːʃ
McIntyre 'mæk.ɪn.taɪəʳ, -ᵊn- US -taɪɚ
McIver mə'kaɪ.vəʳ, -'kɪv.əʳ US -vɚ
McIvor mə'kiː.vəʳ, -'kaɪ.vəʳ US -vɚ
McKee mə'kiː
McKellen mə'kel.ᵊn
McKenna mə'ken.ə
McKenzie mə'ken.zi
McKeown mə'kjəʊn, -'kjʊən US -'kjoʊn
McKerras mə'ker.əs
McKie mə'kaɪ, -'kiː
McKinlay, McKinley mə'kɪn.li
McKinnon mə'kɪn.ən
McKinny mə'kɪn.i
McKnight mək'naɪt
McLachlan mə'klɒk.lən, -'klɒx-, -'klæk-, -'klæx- US -'klɑː.klən
McLagan mə'klæg.ᵊn
McLaine mə'kleɪn
McLaren mə'klær.ᵊn US -'kler-, -'klær-, -ən
McLaughlin mə'klɒk.lɪn, -'klɒx- US -'klɑː.klɪn, -'klɑːf-, -'klɔːf-
McLay mə'kleɪ
McLean mə'kleɪn, -'kliːn US -'kliːn
McLeish mə'kliːʃ
McLeod mə'klaʊd
McMahon mək'mɑːn US -'mæn, -'meɪən, -'mɑːn
McManaman mək'mæn.ə.mən
McManus mək'mæn.əs, -'meɪ.nəs
McMaster mək'mɑː.stəʳ US -'mæs.tɚ
McMenem(e)y mək'men.ə.mi
McMichael mək'maɪ.kᵊl
McMillan mək'mɪl.ən
McMullen mək'mʌl.ən
McMurdo mək'mɜː.dəʊ US -'mɝː.doʊ
McNab mək'næb
McNaghten, McNachton mək'nɔː.tᵊn US -'nɑː-, -'nɔː-
McNally mək'næl.i
McNamara ˌmæk.nə'mɑː.rə US 'mæk.nə.mer.ə, -mær-
McNaught mək'nɔːt US -'nɑːt, -'nɔːt **-on** -ᵊn **-en** -ᵊn
McNeice mək'niːs
McNeil mək'niːl
McPhee mək'fiː
McQuarie mə'kwɒr.i, -'kwɑːr-, -'kwɔːr- US mə'kwɑː.ri
McQueen mə'kwiːn
McRae mə'kreɪ
McReady mə'kriː.di
McShane mək'ʃeɪn
McShea mək'ʃeɪ
McSwiney mək'swiː.ni, -'swɪn-
McTaggart mək'tæg.ət US -ɚt
McTavish mək'tæv.ɪʃ
McTeague mək'tiːg
McVay mək'veɪ
McVeagh mək'veɪ
McVean mək'veɪn, -viːn
McVeigh mək'veɪ
McVey mək'veɪ
McVicar mək'vɪk.əʳ US -ɚ
McVitie's® mək'vɪt.iz US -'vɪt̬-
McVit(t)ie mək'vɪt.i US -'vɪt̬-
McWhirter mək'*h*wɜː.təʳ US -'*h*wɝː.t̬ɚ
McWilliams mək'wɪl.jəmz, -i.əmz US '-jəmz
MD ˌem'di
Md. *(abbrev. for* **Maryland***)* 'meə.rɪ.lænd, 'mer.ɪ-, -lənd US 'mer.ɪ.lənd

me *note in Tonic Sol-fa:* miː **-s** -z
me *(pron.) normal form:* miː *freq. weak form:* mi
Me. *(abbrev. for* **Maine***)* meɪn
ME ˌemˈiː
Meacher ˈmiː.tʃəʳ US -tʃɚ
mea culpa ˌmeɪ.əˈkʊl.pə, -ɑːˈ-, -ˈkʌl-, -pɑː US -ɑːˈkʊl.pɑː, miː-, -əˈkʌl.pə
mead (M) miːd **-s** -z
Meaden ˈmiː.dᵊn
meadow ˈmed.əʊ US -oʊ **-s** -z **-y** -i
meadowlark ˈmed.əʊ.lɑːk US -oʊ.lɑːrk **-s** -s
Meadows ˈmed.əʊz US -oʊz
meadowsweet ˈmed.əʊ.swiːt US -oʊ-
Meagan ˈmiː.gᵊn
meag|er ˈmiː.g|əʳ US -g|ɚ **-erer** -ᵊr.əʳ US -ɚ.ɚ **-erest** -ᵊr.ɪst, -əst **-erly** -ᵊl.i US -ɚ.li **-erness** -ə.nəs, -nɪs US -ɚ-
Meagher mɑːʳ US mɑːr
meag|re ˈmiː.g|əʳ US -gɚ **-rer** -ᵊr.əʳ US -ɚ.ɚ **-rest** -ᵊr.ɪst, -əst **-rely** -ᵊl.i US -ɚ.li **-reness** -ə.nəs, -nɪs US -ɚ-
Meaker ˈmiː.kəʳ US -kɚ
meal miːl **-s** -z ˌ**meals on ˈwheels; ˈmeal ˌticket**
mealie ˈmiː.li **-s** -z
mealtime ˈmiːl.taɪm **-s** -z
meal|y ˈmiː.l|i **-ier** -i.əʳ US -i.ɚ **-iest** -i.ɪst, -i.əst **-iness** -ɪ.nəs, -ɪ.nɪs
mealybug ˈmiː.li.bʌg
mealy-mouthed ˌmiː.liˈmaʊðd US ˈmiː.li.maʊðd, -maʊθt, ˌ--ˈ- *stress shift, British only:* ˌmealy-mouthed ˈperson
mean miːn **-s** -z **-er** -əʳ US -ɚ **-est** -ɪst, -əst **-ly** -li **-ness** -nəs, -nɪs **-ing** -ɪŋ **meant** ment ˈ**means** ˌ**test**
meand|er (M) miˈæn.d|əʳ US -d|ɚ **-ers** -əz US -ɚz **-ering/s** -ᵊr.ɪŋ **-ered** -əd US -ɚd
meanie ˈmiː.ni **-s** -z
meaning ˈmiː.nɪŋ **-s** -z **-ly** -li
meaningful ˈmiː.nɪŋ.fᵊl, -fʊl **-ly** -i **-ness** -nəs, -nɪs
meaningless ˈmiː.nɪŋ.ləs, -lɪs **-ly** -li **-ness** -nəs, -nɪs
means-test ˈmiːnz.test **-s** -s **-ing** -ɪŋ **-ed** -ɪd
meant *(from* **mean***)* ment
meantime ˌmiːnˈtaɪm, ˈ-- US ˈmiːn-
meanwhile ˌmiːnˈ*h*waɪl, ˈ-- US ˈmiːn-
mean|y ˈmiː.n|i **-ies** -iz
Meany ˈmiː.ni
Mearns mɜːnz, meənz, mɪənz US mɝːnz, mernz, mɪrnz
Mears mɪəz US mɪrz
measles ˈmiː.zl̩z
measly ˈmiːz.li
measurab|le ˈmeʒ.ᵊr.ə.b|l̩ **-ly** -li **-leness** -l̩.nəs, -nɪs
meas|ure ˈmeʒ|.əʳ US -ɚ **-ures** -əz US -ɚz **-uring** -ᵊr.ɪŋ **-ured** -əd US -ɚd **-urer/s** -ᵊr.əʳ/z US -ɚ.ɚ/z
measureless ˈmeʒ.ə.ləs, -lɪs US ˈ-ɚ- **-ly** -li **-ness** -nəs, -nɪs
measurement ˈmeʒ.ə.mənt US ˈ-ɚ- **-s** -s
meat miːt **-s** -s
meat-and-potatoes ˌmiːt.ᵊn*d*.pəˈteɪ.təʊz, -ᵊm- US -ᵊn*d*.pəˈteɪ.t̬oʊz
meatball ˈmiːt.bɔːl US -bɔːl, -bɑːl **-s** -z
Meates miːts
Meath *Irish county:* miːð
Note: Often pronounced /miːθ/ by English people.
meathead ˈmiːt.hed **-s** -z
meatless ˈmiːt.ləs, -lɪs
meatloa|f ˈmiːt.ləʊ|f US -loʊ|f **-ves** -vz
meatpacking ˈmiːtˌpæk.ɪŋ
meatus miˈeɪ.təs US -t̬əs **-es** -ɪz
meat|y ˈmiː.t|i US -t̬|i **-ier** -i.əʳ US -i.ɚ **-iest** -i.ɪst, -i.əst **-iness** -ɪ.nəs, -ɪ.nɪs
mecca (M) ˈmek.ə
Meccano® mɪˈkɑː.nəʊ, mekˈɑː-, məˈkɑː- US -noʊ
mechanic mɪˈkæn.ɪk, mə- **-s** -s **-al** -ᵊl **-ally** -ᵊl.i, -li
mechanician ˌmek.əˈnɪʃ.ᵊn **-s** -z
mechanism ˈmek.ə.nɪ.zᵊm **-s** -z
mechanistic ˌmek.əˈnɪs.tɪk **-ally** -ᵊl.i, -li
mechanization, -isa- ˌmek.ə.naɪˈzeɪ.ʃᵊn, -nɪˈ- US -nɪˈ-
mechaniz|e, -is|e ˈmek.ə.naɪz **-es** -ɪz **-ing** -ɪŋ **-ed** -d
Mecklenburg ˈmek.lɪn.bɜːg, -lən-, -lɪm-, -ləm- US -lɪn.bɝːg, -lən-
MEd ˌemˈed
Med med
medal ˈmed.ᵊl **-s** -z
medalist ˈmed.ᵊl.ɪst **-s** -s
medallion mɪˈdæl.i.ən, medˈæl-, məˈdæl- US məˈdæl.jən **-s** -z
medallist ˈmed.ᵊl.ɪst **-s** -s
Medan ˈmed.ɑːn, ˈmeɪ.dɑːn, -ˈ- US meɪˈdɑːn, ˈ--
Medawar ˈmed.ə.wəʳ US -wɚ
meddl|e ˈmed.l̩ **-es** -z **-ing** -ɪŋ, ˈ-lɪŋ **-ed** -d **-er/s** -əʳ/z US -ɚ/z, ˈ-ləʳ/z US ˈ-l̩.ɚ/z, ˈ-lɚ/z
meddlesome ˈmed.l̩.səm **-ness** -nəs, -nɪs
Mede miːd **-s** -z
Medea mɪˈdɪə, mə-, -ˈdiː.ə US mɪˈdiː-, mə-
Medellín ˌmed.ᵊlˈɪn, -ˈiːn *as if Spanish:* ˌmed.eɪˈjin US -ˈiːn
medfl|y ˈmed.fl|aɪ **-ies** -aɪz
media *(plur. of* **medium***)* ˈmiː.di.ə
mediaeval (M) ˌmed.iˈiː.vᵊl, medˈiː- US ˌmiː.diˈ-, ˌmed.iˈ-; məˈdiː- **-ism** -ɪ.zᵊm **-ist/s** -ɪst/s
medial ˈmiː.di.əl
median ˈmiː.di.ən **-s** -z ˈ**median** ˌ**strip**
mediant ˈmiː.di.ənt **-s** -s
mediastin|um ˌmiː.di.əˈstaɪ.n|əm US -æsˈtaɪ- **-a** -ə
mediate *(adj.)* ˈmiː.di.ət, -ɪt **-ly** -li **-ness** -nəs, -nɪs
medi|ate *(v.)* ˈmiː.di|.eɪt **-ates** -eɪts **-ating** -eɪ.tɪŋ US -eɪ.t̬ɪŋ **-ated** -eɪ.tɪd US -eɪ.t̬ɪd
mediation ˌmiː.diˈeɪ.ʃᵊn **-s** -z
mediative ˈmiː.di.ə.tɪv US -t̬ɪv
mediator ˈmiː.di.eɪ.təʳ US -t̬ɚ **-s** -z
mediatorial ˌmiː.di.əˈtɔː.ri.əl US -ˈtɔːr.i- **-ly** -i
mediatory ˈmiː.di.ə.tᵊr.i, -tri US -tɔːr.i
medic ˈmed.ɪk **-s** -s
Medicaid ˈmed.ɪ.keɪd
medic|al ˈmed.ɪ.k|ᵊl **-als** -ᵊlz **-ally** -ᵊl.i, -li
medicament məˈdɪk.ə.mənt, mɪ-, medˈɪk-; ˈmed.ɪ.kə- US məˈdɪk.ə-; ˈmed.ɪ.kə- **-s** -s
Medicare ˈmed.ɪ.keəʳ US -ker
medi|cate ˈmed.ɪ|.keɪt **-cates** -keɪts **-cating** -keɪ.tɪŋ US -keɪ.t̬ɪŋ **-cated** -keɪ.tɪd US -keɪ.t̬ɪd
medication ˌmed.ɪˈkeɪ.ʃᵊn **-s** -z
Medici ˈmed.ɪ.tʃiː, -tʃi; medˈiː.tʃi, məˈdiː-, mɪ- US ˈmed.ə.tʃiː
medicinal məˈdɪs.ɪ.nᵊl, mɪ-, medˈɪs-, -ᵊn.ᵊl US məˈdɪs- **-ly** -i
medicine ˈmed.sᵊn, -sɪn, ˈ-ɪ.sᵊn, ˈ-ə-, -sɪn US ˈmed.ɪ.sən **-s** -z ˈ**medicine** ˌ**ball;** ˈ**medicine** ˌ**chest;** ˌ**give someone a** ˌ**taste of their** ˌ**own** ˈ**medicine**
medico ˈmed.ɪ.kəʊ US -koʊ **-s** -z
medico- ˌmed.ɪ.kəʊ- US -koʊ-
medieval (M) ˌmed.iˈiː.vᵊl, medˈiː- US ˌmiː.diˈ-, ˌmed.iˈ-; məˈdiː- **-ism** -ɪ.zᵊm **-ist/s** -ɪst/s
Medill məˈdɪl
Medina *in Saudi Arabia:* medˈiː.nə, mɪˈdiː-, mə- US mə- *in US:* medˈaɪ.nə, mɪˈdaɪ-, mə- US mə-
mediocre ˌmiː.diˈəʊ.kəʳ, ˈmiː.di.əʊ- US ˌmiː.diˈoʊ.kɚ, ˈmiː.di.oʊ-
mediocrit|y ˌmiː.diˈɒk.rə.t|i, ˌmed.iˈ-, -ɪ.t|i US ˌmiː.diˈɑː.krə.t̬|i **-ies** -iz
medi|tate ˈmed.ɪ|.teɪt, ˈ-ə- **-tates** -teɪts **-tating** -teɪ.tɪŋ US -teɪ.t̬ɪŋ **-tated** -teɪ.tɪd US -teɪ.t̬ɪd **-tator/s** -teɪ.təʳ/z US -teɪ.t̬ɚ/z
meditation ˌmed.ɪˈteɪ.ʃᵊn, -əˈ- **-s** -z
meditative ˈmed.ɪ.tə.tɪv, ˈ-ə-, -teɪ- US -teɪ.t̬ɪv **-ly** -li **-ness** -nəs, -nɪs
Mediterranean ˌmed.ɪ.tᵊrˈeɪ.ni.ən, ˌ-ə- US -təˈreɪ-
medi|um ˈmiː.di|.əm **-a** -ə **-ums** -əmz ˈ**medium** ˌ**wave**
Medjugorje ˈmet.jʊ.gɔː.tʃə US -gɔːr-

medlar ˈmed.ləʳ (US) -lɚ **-s** -z
medley (M) ˈmed.li **-s** -z
Medlock ˈmed.lɒk (US) -lɑːk
Médoc ˈmeɪ.dɒk, ˈmed.ɒk, -ˈ- (US) ˈmeɪ.dɑːk, -ˈ- **-s** -s
medulla medˈʌl.ə, mɪˈdʌl-, mə- (US) mɪ- **-s** -z
medus|a (M) mɪˈdjuː.z|ə, mə-, medˈjuː-, -s|ə (US) məˈduː-, -ˈdjuː- **-as** -əz **-ae** -iː
Medway ˈmed.weɪ
Mee miː
meed miːd **-s** -z
meek (M) miːk **-er** -əʳ (US) -ɚ **-est** -ɪst, -əst **-ly** -li **-ness** -nəs, -nɪs
meerkat ˈmɪə.kæt (US) ˈmɪr- **-s** -s
meerschaum ˈmɪə.ʃəm, -ʃaʊm (US) ˈmɪr-, -ʃɑːm, -ʃɔːm **-s** -z
Meerut ˈmɪə.rət (US) ˈmiː-
meet miːt **-s** -s **-ness** -nəs, -nɪs **-ing** -ɪŋ, ˈmiː.t̬ɪŋ **met** met
meeting ˈmiː.tɪŋ (US) -t̬ɪŋ **-s** -z
Meg meg
mega- ˈmeg.ə-, ˌmeg.əˈ-
Note: Prefix. May carry primary or secondary stress on the first syllable, e.g. **megalith** /ˈmeg.ə.lɪθ/, **megalithic** /ˌmeg.əˈlɪθ.ɪk/.
megabit ˈmeg.ə.bɪt **-s** -s
megabucks ˈmeg.ə.bʌks
megabyte ˈmeg.ə.baɪt **-s** -s
megacycle ˈmeg.əˌsaɪ.kl̩ **-s** -z
megadeath ˈmeg.ə.deθ **-s** -s
megahertz ˈmeg.ə.hɜːts (US) -hɝːts, -herts
megalith ˈmeg.ə.lɪθ **-s** -s
megalithic ˌmeg.əˈlɪθ.ɪk
megalomania ˌmeg.ᵊl.əʊˈmeɪ.ni.ə (US) -oʊˈmeɪ-, -əˈ-, ˈ-njə
megalomaniac ˌmeg.ᵊl.əʊˈmeɪ.ni.æk (US) -oʊˈ-, -əˈ- **-s** -s
megalomaniacal ˌmeg.ᵊl.əʊ.məˈnaɪ.ə.kᵊl
megalopolis ˌmeg.ᵊlˈɒp.ə.lɪs (US) -ˈɑː.pə-
Megan ˈmeg.ən (US) ˈmeg-, ˈmiː.gən
megaphone ˈmeg.ə.fəʊn (US) -foʊn **-s** -z
megaplex ˈmeg.ə.pleks **-es** -ɪz
megastar ˈmeg.ə.stɑːʳ (US) -stɑːr **-s** -z
megastore ˈmeg.ə.stɔːʳ (US) -stɔːr **-s** -z
megatheri|um ˌmeg.əˈθɪə.ri|.əm (US) -ˈθɪr.i- **-a** -ə
megaton ˈmeg.ə.tʌn **-s** -z
megavolt ˈmeg.ə.vəʊlt, -vɒlt (US) -voʊlt **-s** -s
megawatt ˈmeg.ə.wɒt (US) -wɑːt **-s** -s
Meghan ˈmeg.ən (US) ˈmeg-, ˈmiː.gən
megilp məˈgɪlp, mɪ- (US) mə-
megrim ˈmiː.grɪm, -grəm (US) -grɪm **-s** -z
Mehta ˈmeɪ.tə
Meier ˈmaɪ.əʳ (US) -ɚ
Meikle ˈmiː.kl̩
Meiklejohn ˈmɪk.l̩.dʒɒn, ˈmiː.kl̩- (US) -dʒɑːn
meios|is maɪˈəʊ.s|ɪs (US) -ˈoʊ- **-es** -iːz
Meir *English surname:* mɪəʳ (US) mɪr *Israeli surname:* meɪˈɪəʳ (US) meɪˈɪr, maɪ.ɚ
Meirionnydd mer.i.ɒn.ɪð (US) -ɑː.nɪθ
Meissen ˈmaɪ.sᵊn
Meistersinger ˈmaɪ.stəˌsɪŋ.əʳ, -ˌzɪŋ- (US) -stɚˌsɪŋ.ɚ, -ˌzɪŋ- **-s** -z
Mekka ˈmek.ə
Meknès mekˈnes
Mekong ˌmiːˈkɒŋ, ˌmeɪ- (US) ˌmeɪˈkɑːŋ, -kɔːŋ *stress shift:* ˌMekong ˈRiver
Mel mel
melamine ˈmel.ə.miːn, -mɪn (US) -miːn
melancholia ˌmel.ənˈkəʊ.li.ə, -əŋˈ- (US) -ənˈkoʊ-
melancholic ˌmel.ənˈkɒl.ɪk, -əŋˈ- (US) -ənˈkɑː.lɪk *stress shift:* ˌmelancholic ˈmood
melancholy ˈmel.ən.kᵊl.i, -əŋ-, -kɒl- (US) -ən.kɑː.li
Melanchthon məˈlæŋk.θɒn, mɪ-, melˈæŋk-, -θᵊn (US) məˈlæŋk.θᵊn
Melanesi|a ˌmel.əˈniː.zi|.ə, -ʒi-, ˈ-ʒ|ə (US) -ʒ|ə, -ʃ|ə **-an/s** -ən/z
mélang|e meɪˈlɑ̃ːnʒ, ˈ-- (US) meɪˈlɑ̃ːʒ, -ˈlɔ̃ːʒ, -ˈlɑːndʒ, -ˈlɔːndʒ **-es** -ɪz
Melanie ˈmel.ə.ni
mela|nin ˈmel.ə|.nɪn **-nism** -nɪ.zᵊm
melanom|a ˌmel.əˈnəʊ.m|ə (US) -ˈnoʊ- **-as** -əz **-ata** -ə.tə (US) -t̬ə
Melanthius məˈlænt.θi.əs, mɪ-, melˈænt-, -ɒs (US) məˈlænt.θi.əs
Melba ˈmel.bə **ˌMelba ˈtoast**
Melbourne ˈmel.bən, -bɔːn (US) -bɚn, -bɔːrn
Note: In Australia always /ˈmel.bən/.
Melchett ˈmel.tʃɪt
Melchior ˈmel.ki.ɔːʳ (US) -ɔːr
Melchizedek melˈkɪz.ə.dek
Melcombe ˈmel.kəm
meld meld **-s** -z **-ing** -ɪŋ **-ed** -ɪd
Meldrew ˈmel.druː
Meleager ˌmel.iˈeɪ.gəʳ (US) -dʒɚ
mêlée, melee ˈmel.eɪ, ˈmeɪ.leɪ, -ˈ- (US) ˈmeɪ.leɪ, -ˈ- **-s** -z
Melhuish ˈmel.ɪʃ, ˈmel.ju.ɪʃ, -hju-; melˈjuː.ɪʃ, -ˈhjuː-
Melibeus ˌmel.ɪˈbiː.əs, -əˈ- (US) -əˈ-
Melincourt ˈmel.ɪn.kɔːt, -ɪŋ- (US) -ɪn.kɔːrt
Melinda məˈlɪn.də, mɪ-, melˈɪn- (US) məˈlɪn-
melinite ˈmel.ɪ.naɪt
meliorable ˈmiː.li.ᵊr.ə.bl̩ (US) ˈmiːl.jɚ.ə-
melior|ate ˈmiː.li.ᵊr|.eɪt (US) ˈmiːl.jə.r|eɪt, ˈmiː.li.ə- **-ates** -eɪts **-ating** -eɪ.tɪŋ (US) -eɪ.t̬ɪŋ **-ated** -eɪ.tɪd (US) -eɪ.t̬ɪd
melioration ˌmiː.li.ᵊrˈeɪ.ʃᵊn (US) ˌmiːl.jəˈreɪ-, ˌmiː.li.əˈ- **-s** -z
meliorative ˈmiː.li.ᵊr.ə.tɪv (US) ˈmiːl.jɚ-
meliorator ˈmiː.li.ᵊr.eɪ.təʳ (US) ˈmiːl.jə.reɪ.t̬ɚ **-s** -z
Melissa məˈlɪs.ə, mɪ-, melˈɪs- (US) məˈlɪs-
Melita məˈliː.tə; ˈmel.ɪ- (US) ˈmel.ɪ.t̬ə; məˈliː-, -ˈlɪt̬.ə
Melksham ˈmelk.ʃəm
mellifluen|t mɪˈlɪf.lu.ən|t, mə-, melˈɪf- (US) məˈlɪf- **-ce** -*t*s
mellifluous mɪˈlɪf.lu.əs, mə-, melˈɪf- (US) məˈlɪf- **-ly** -li **-ness** -nəs, -nɪs
Mellin ˈmel.ɪn
Mellor ˈmel.əʳ, -ɔːʳ (US) -ɚ, -ɔːr
Mellors ˈmel.əz, -ɔːz (US) -ɚz, -ɔːrz
mellow ˈmel.əʊ (US) -oʊ **-er** -əʳ (US) -ɚ **-est** -ɪst, -əst **-ness** -nəs, -nɪs **-s** -z **-ing** -ɪŋ **-ed** -d
Melmoth ˈmel.məθ
Melmotte ˈmel.mɒt, -ˈ- (US) ˈmel.mɑːt
melodic məˈlɒd.ɪk, mɪ-, melˈɒd- (US) məˈlɑː.dɪk **-ally** -ᵊl.i, -li
melodious məˈləʊ.di.əs, mɪ-, melˈəʊ- (US) məˈloʊ- **-ly** -li **-ness** -nəs, -nɪs
melodist ˈmel.ə.dɪst **-s** -s
melodrama ˈmel.əʊˌdrɑː.mə (US) -oʊˌdrɑː.mə, -əˌ-, -ˌdræm.ə **-s** -z
melodramatic ˌmel.əʊ.drəˈmæt.ɪk (US) -oʊ.drəˈmæt̬-, ˌ-ə- **-s** -s **-ally** -ᵊl.i, -li
melodramatist ˌmel.əʊˈdræm.ə.tɪst (US) -oʊˈdrɑː.mə.t̬ɪst, -əˈ-, -ˈdræm.ə- **-s** -s
melod|y (M) ˈmel.ə.d|i **-ies** -iz
Meloids® ˈmel.ɔɪdz
melon ˈmel.ən **-s** -z
Melos ˈmiː.lɒs, ˈmel.ɒs (US) ˈmiː.lɑːs
Melpomene melˈpɒm.ə.ni, ˈ-ɪ-, -niː (US) -ˈpɑː.mə-
Melrose ˈmel.rəʊz (US) -roʊz
melt melt **-s** -s **-ing/ly** -ɪŋ/li (US) ˈmel.t̬ɪŋ/li **-ed** -ɪd (US) ˈmel.t̬ɪd **ˈmelting ˌpot**
meltdown ˈmelt.daʊn **-s** -z
Meltham ˈmel.θəm
Melton ˈmel.tᵊn
Meltonian® melˈtəʊ.ni.ən (US) -ˈtoʊ-
Melton Mowbray ˌmel.tənˈməʊ.breɪ, -təmˈ-, -bri (US) -tənˈmoʊ-
meltwater ˈmeltˌwɔː.təʳ (US) -ˌwɑː.t̬ɚ, -ˌwɔː- **-s** -z
Melville ˈmel.vɪl
Melvin, Melvyn ˈmel.vɪn
member ˈmem.bəʳ (US) -bɚ **-s** -z **-ship/s** -ʃɪp/s **ˌMember of ˈParliament**
membrane ˈmem.breɪn **-s** -z
membraneous memˈbreɪ.ni.əs
membranous ˈmem.brə.nəs
Memel ˈmeɪ.mᵊl
memento mɪˈmen.təʊ, memˈen-, məˈmen- (US) məˈmen.toʊ **-(e)s** -z

memento mori mɪˌmen.təʊˈmɒr.i, memˌen-, məˌmen-, -ˈmɔː.raɪ ⓤⓢ məˌmen.toʊˈmɔːr.iː, -aɪ
Memnon ˈmem.nɒn, -nən ⓤⓢ -nɑːn
memo ˈmem.əʊ ⓤⓢ -oʊ **-s** -z
memoir ˈmem.wɑːʳ ⓤⓢ -wɑːr, -wɔːr **-s** -z
memorabilia ˌmem.ᵊr.əˈbɪl.i.ə, -ˈbiː.li- ⓤⓢ -ˈbɪl.i-, ˈ-jə, -ˈbiː.li-, -ˈbiːl.jə
memorab|le ˈmem.ᵊr.ə.bl̩ **-ly** -li
memorand|um ˌmem.ᵊrˈæn.d|əm ⓤⓢ -əˈræn- **-a** -ə **-ums** -əmz
memorial məˈmɔː.ri.əl, mɪˈ-, memˈɔː- ⓤⓢ məˈmɔːr.i- **-s** -z
memorializ|e, -is|e məˈmɔː.ri.ə.laɪz, mɪˈ-, memˈɔː- ⓤⓢ məˈmɔːr.i- **-es** -ɪz **-ing** -ɪŋ **-ed** -d
memoriz|e, -is|e ˈmem.ᵊr.aɪz ⓤⓢ -ə.raɪz **-es** -ɪz **-ing** -ɪŋ **-ed** -d
memor|y ˈmem.ᵊr|.i, ˈ-r|i **-ies** -iz
Memphis ˈmemp.fɪs
memsahib ˈmemˌsɑː.hɪb, ˈ-sɑːb ⓤⓢ ˈmemˌsɑː.hɪb, ˈ-sɑːb; ˌmem.sɑːˈhiːb, -ˈɪb **-s** -z
men *(plur. of* **man***)* men **ˈmen's ˌroom**
menac|e ˈmen.ɪs, -əs ⓤⓢ -əs **-es** -ɪz **-ing/ly** -ɪŋ/li **-ed** -t
ménag|e menˈɑːʒ, meɪˈnɑːʒ, mə-, mɪ-, -ˈnæʒ, ˈ-- ⓤⓢ meɪˈnɑːʒ, mə- **-es** -ɪz
ménage à trois menˌɑːʒ.ɑːˈtrwɑː, meɪˌnɑːz-, mə-, mɪ-, -ˌnæʒ, ˌmen.ɑːz-, ˌmeɪ.nɑːʒ-, -ˌnæʒ ⓤⓢ meɪˌnɑːʒ-, mə-
menagerie məˈnædʒ.ᵊr.i, mɪ-, menˈædʒ-, -ˈæʒ- ⓤⓢ məˈnædʒ-, -ˈnæʒ- **-s** -z
Menai ˈmen.aɪ
Menander məˈnæn.dəʳ, mɪ-, menˈæn- ⓤⓢ məˈnæn.dɚ
menarche menˈɑː.ki, mɪˈnɑː-, mə-; ˈmen.ɑːk ⓤⓢ məˈnɑːr.ki, men-
Mencap ˈmen.kæp, ˈmeŋ- ⓤⓢ ˈmen-
Mencken ˈmeŋ.kən
mend mend **-s** -z **-ing** -ɪŋ **-ed** -ɪd **-er/s** -əʳ/z ⓤⓢ -ɚ/z
mendacious menˈdeɪ.ʃəs **-ly** -li **-ness** -nəs, -nɪs
mendacity menˈdæs.ə.ti, -ɪ.ti ⓤⓢ -ə.t̬i
Mendel ˈmen.dᵊl
Mendeleev ˌmen.dᵊlˈeɪ.ev, -dɪˈleɪ-, -ef, -əf ⓤⓢ -dəˈleɪ.əf
mendelevium ˌmen.dᵊlˈiː.vi.əm, -dɪˈliː- ⓤⓢ -dəˈliː-
Mendeleyev ˌmen.dᵊlˈeɪ.ev, -dɪˈleɪ-, -ef, -əf ⓤⓢ -dəˈleɪ.əf
Mendelian menˈdiː.li.ən
Mendelssohn *English surname:* ˈmen.dᵊl.sᵊn *German composer:* ˈmen.dᵊl.sᵊn, -səʊn ⓤⓢ -sᵊn, -soʊn, -zoʊn
Mendes ˈmen.dez, -des ⓤⓢ -ˈ-
mendican|cy ˈmen.dɪ.kən|t.si **-t/s** -t/s
mendicity menˈdɪs.ə.ti, -ɪ.ti ⓤⓢ -ə.t̬i
Mendip ˈmen.dɪp **-s** -s
Mendoza menˈdəʊ.zə ⓤⓢ -ˈdoʊ-, -sɑː
mene ˈmiː.ni
Menelaus ˌmen.ɪˈleɪ.əs, -ᵊlˈeɪ-
Menem ˈmen.em ⓤⓢ ˈmeɪn-
menfolk ˈmen.fəʊk ⓤⓢ -foʊk **-s** -s
menhir ˈmen.hɪəʳ ⓤⓢ -hɪr **-s** -z
menial ˈmiː.ni.əl, ˈ-njəl **-s** -z **-ly** -i
Ménière ˈmen.i.eəʳ, ˈmeɪ.ni-, ˌ--ˈ-; ˈmeɪ.njeəʳ, -ˈ- ⓤⓢ meɪˈnjer
meningeal menˈɪn.dʒi.əl, məˈnɪn-, mɪ-; ˌmen.ɪnˈdʒiː.əl, -ənˈ- ⓤⓢ məˈnɪn.dʒi-
meninges *(plur. of* **meninx***)* məˈnɪn.dʒiːz, mɪ-, menˈɪn- ⓤⓢ məˈnɪn-
meningitis ˌmen.ɪnˈdʒaɪ.tɪs, -ənˈ- ⓤⓢ -t̬ɪs
meningococcal məˌnɪn.dʒəʊˈkɒk.ᵊl, -ˌnɪŋ.gəʊˈ- ⓤⓢ -ˌnɪŋ.goʊˈkɑː.kᵊl
meningo|coccus məˌnɪn.dʒəʊ|ˈkɒk.əs, -ˌnɪŋ.gəʊˈ- ⓤⓢ -ˌnɪŋ.goʊ|ˈkɑː.kəs **-cocci** -ˈkɒk.saɪ, -aɪ, -iː ⓤⓢ -ˈkɑːk.saɪ, -ˈkɑː.kaɪ, -kiː
meninx ˈmen.ɪnks ⓤⓢ ˈmiː.nɪŋks, ˈmen.ɪŋks **meninges** məˈnɪn.dʒiːz, mɪ-, menˈɪn- ⓤⓢ məˈnɪn-
menisc|us məˈnɪs.k|əs, mɪ-, menˈɪs- ⓤⓢ məˈnɪs- **-uses** -ə.sɪz **-i** -aɪ, -iː
Menlo Park ˌmen.ləʊˈpɑːk ⓤⓢ -loʊˈpɑːrk
Mennonite ˈmen.ə.naɪt **-s** -s
Meno ˈmiː.nəʊ ⓤⓢ -noʊ
men-of-war *(plur. of* **man-of-war***)* ˌmen.əvˈwɔːʳ ⓤⓢ -ˈwɔːr
menopausal ˌmen.əʊˈpɔː.zᵊl, ˌmiː.nəʊˈ- ⓤⓢ ˈmen.ə.pɑː.zᵊl, -pɔː-
menopause ˈmen.əʊ.pɔːz, ˈmiː.nəʊ- ⓤⓢ ˈmen.ə.pɑːz, -pɔːz
menorah mɪˈnɔː.rə, mə- ⓤⓢ -ˈnɔːr.ə **-s** -z
Menorca menˈɔː.kə, məˈnɔː-, mɪ- ⓤⓢ məˈnɔːr.kə
Mensa ˈment.sə
menservants *(plur. of* **manservant***)* ˈmenˌsɜː.vᵊnts ⓤⓢ -ˌsɝː-
menses ˈment.siːz
Menshevik ˈmen.ʃə.vɪk, -ʃɪ- ⓤⓢ -ʃə.vɪk **-s** -s
mens rea ˌmenzˈreɪ.ə ⓤⓢ -ˈriː.ə
menstrual ˈment.strʊəl, -stru.əl ⓤⓢ -strəl, -stru.əl
menstru|ate ˈment.stru|.eɪt ⓤⓢ -stru-, -str|eɪt **-ates** -eɪts **-ating** -eɪ.tɪŋ ⓤⓢ -eɪ.t̬ɪŋ **-ated** -eɪ.tɪd ⓤⓢ -eɪ.t̬ɪd
menstruation ˌment.struˈeɪ.ʃᵊn ⓤⓢ -struˈeɪ-, -ˌstreɪ-
mensual ˈment.sju.əl, sjʊəl ⓤⓢ -ʃu.əl
mensurability ˌment.ʃᵊr.əˈbɪl.ə.ti, -ʃʊ.rəˈ-, -sjᵊr.əˈ-, -sjʊ.rəˈ-, -ɪ.ti ⓤⓢ -ʃɚ.əˈbɪl.ə.t̬i, -sɚ-
mensurable ˈment.ʃᵊr.ə.bl̩, -ʃʊ.rə-, -sjᵊr.ə-, -sjʊ.rə- ⓤⓢ -ʃɚ.ə-, -sɚ-
mensuration ˌment.ʃᵊrˈeɪ.ʃᵊn, -ʃʊˈreɪ-, -sjᵊrˈeɪ-, -sjʊˈreɪ- ⓤⓢ -ʃəˈreɪ-, -səˈ-
menswear ˈmenz.weəʳ ⓤⓢ -wer
-ment -mənt
mental ˈmen.tᵊl ⓤⓢ -t̬ᵊl **-ly** -i **ˌmental ˈage; ˈmental ˌhospital**
mentalism ˈmen.tᵊl.ɪ.zᵊm ⓤⓢ -t̬ᵊl-
mentalistic ˌmen.tᵊlˈɪs.tɪk ⓤⓢ -t̬ᵊlˈ- **-ally** -ᵊl.i, -li
mentalit|y menˈtæl.ə.t|i, -ɪ.t|i ⓤⓢ -ə.t̬|i **-ies** -iz
Menteith menˈtiːθ, mən-
menthol ˈment.θɒl, -θᵊl ⓤⓢ -θɔːl, -θɑːl, -θᵊl, -θoʊl
mentholated ˈment.θᵊl.eɪ.tɪd ⓤⓢ -t̬ɪd
mention ˈmen.tʃᵊn **-s** -z **-ing** -ɪŋ **-ed** -d **-able** -ə.bl̩, ˈmentʃ.nə-
Mentone menˈtəʊ.neɪ, -ni ⓤⓢ -ˈtoʊ.ni
mentor ˈmen.tɔːʳ, -təʳ ⓤⓢ -tɚ, -tɔːr **-s** -z **-ing** -ɪŋ
menu ˈmen.juː **-s** -z
menu-driven ˈmen.juːˌdrɪv.ᵊn, ˌmen.juːˈdrɪv- ⓤⓢ ˈmen.juːˌdrɪv-
Menuhin ˈmen.ju.ɪn, -hɪn ⓤⓢ -ɪn
Menzies ˈmen.zɪz, ˈmeŋ.ɪs, ˈmɪŋ- ⓤⓢ ˈmen.ziːz
Meopham ˈmep.əm
meow miːˈaʊ **-s** -z **-ing** -ɪŋ **-ed** -d
MEP ˌem.iːˈpiː **-s** -z
Mepham ˈmef.əm
Mephisto məˈfɪs.təʊ, mɪ-, mefˈɪs- ⓤⓢ məˈfɪs.toʊ
Mephistophelean, -lian ˌmef.ɪ.stəˈfiː.li.ən, ˌ-ə-, -stɒfˈɪl-; məˌfɪs.təˈ-, mɪ-, mefˌɪs-; ˌmef.ɪˌstɒf.əˈliː- ⓤⓢ ˌmef.ɪ.stəˈfiː.li-; məˌfɪs.təˈ-; ˌmef.əˌstɑː.fəˈliː-, -ˌstoʊ-
Mephistopheles ˌmef.ɪˈstɒf.ɪ.liːz, -ᵊl.iːz ⓤⓢ -əˈstɑː.fə.liːz
mephitic mɪˈfɪt.ɪk, mefˈɪt- ⓤⓢ məˈfɪt̬-
mephitis mɪˈfaɪ.tɪs, mefˈaɪ- ⓤⓢ məˈfaɪ.t̬ɪs
Merc mɜːk ⓤⓢ mɝːk **-s** -s
mercantile ˈmɜː.kᵊn.taɪl ⓤⓢ ˈmɝː-, -tiːl, -taɪl, -tɪl
mercantilism ˈmɜː.kᵊn.tɪ.lɪ.zᵊm, -taɪ-, -tᵊl.ɪ- ⓤⓢ ˈmɝː.kən.tiː-, -tɪ-, -taɪ-
Mercator mɜːˈkeɪ.təʳ, -tɔːʳ ⓤⓢ mɚˈkeɪ.t̬ɚ
Mercedes *English female name:* ˈmɜː.sɪ.diːz ⓤⓢ ˈmɝː-; mɚˈseɪ.diːz *trademark:* məˈseɪ.diːz, mɜː- ⓤⓢ mɚ-, mɝː-
Mercedes-Benz məˌseɪ.diːzˈbents, mɜː-, -ˈbenz ⓤⓢ mɚˌseɪ.diːzˈbenz, mɝː-, -ˈbents
mercenar|y ˈmɜː.sᵊn.ᵊr|.i, -sɪ.nᵊr-, -sᵊn.r|i ⓤⓢ ˈmɝː.sə.ner.i **-ies** -iz
mercer (M) ˈmɜː.səʳ ⓤⓢ ˈmɝː.sɚ **-s** -z
merceriz|e, -is|e ˈmɜː.sᵊr.aɪz ⓤⓢ ˈmɝː- **-es** -ɪz **-ing** -ɪŋ **-ed** -d

merchandise (*n.*) ˈmɜː.tʃᵊn.daɪs, -daɪs (US) ˈmɝː-
merchandiz|e, -ise (*v.*) ˈmɜː.tʃᵊn.daɪz (US) ˈmɝː- **-es** -ɪz **-ing** -ɪŋ **-ed** -d **-er/s** -əʳ/z (US) -ɚ/z
merchant ˈmɜː.tʃᵊnt (US) ˈmɝː- **-s** -s **-able** -ə.bl̩ ˌ**merchant** ˈ**bank**; ˌ**merchant** ˈ**navy**
merchant|man ˈmɜː.tʃᵊnt|.mən (US) ˈmɝː- **-men** -mən, -men
Merchison ˈmɜː.kɪ.sᵊn (US) ˈmɝː-
Merchiston ˈmɜː.tʃɪ.stᵊn (US) ˈmɝː-
Merci|a ˈmɜː.si|.ə, -ʃi|.ə (US) ˈmɝː.ʃə, ˈ-ʃi|.ə, -si- **-an** -ən
merciful ˈmɜː.sɪ.fᵊl, -fʊl (US) ˈmɝː- **-ly** -i **-ness** -nəs, -nɪs
merciless ˈmɜː.sɪ.ləs, -lɪs (US) ˈmɝː- **-ly** -li **-ness** -nəs, -nɪs
mercurial mɜːˈkjʊə.ri.əl, -ˈkjɔː- (US) mɝːˈkjʊr.i- **-s** -z **-ly** -i
mercuric mɜːˈkjʊə.rɪk, -ˈkjɔː- (US) mɝːˈkjʊr.ɪk
Mercurochrome® mɜːˈkjʊə.rə.krəʊm, -ˈkjɔː- (US) mɝːˈkjʊr.ə.kroʊm
mercurous ˈmɜː.kjᵊr.əs, -kjʊ.rəs (US) ˈmɝː.kjʊr.əs, -kjɚ-
mercury (M) ˈmɜː.kjᵊr.i, -kjʊ.ri (US) ˈmɝː.kjə.ri, -kjɚ-
Mercutio mɜːˈkjuː.ʃi.əʊ (US) mɝːˈkjuː.ʃi.oʊ
merc|y (M) ˈmɜː.s|i (US) ˈmɝː- **-ies** -iz ˈ**mercy** ˌ**killing**
mere mɪəʳ (US) mɪr **-s** -z
Meredith ˈmer.ə.dɪθ, ˈ-ɪ- *as if Welsh:* merˈed.ɪθ
merely ˈmɪə.li (US) ˈmɪr-
merest ˈmɪə.rɪst, -rəst (US) ˈmɪr.ɪst, -əst
meretricious ˌmer.ɪˈtrɪʃ.əs, -əˈ- (US) -əˈ- **-ly** -li **-ness** -nəs, -nɪs
merganser mɜːˈgænt.səʳ, -ˈgæn.zəʳ (US) mɝːˈgænt.sɚ **-s** -z
merg|e mɜːdʒ (US) mɝːdʒ **-es** -ɪz **-ing** -ɪŋ **-ed** -d
merger ˈmɜː.dʒəʳ (US) ˈmɝː.dʒɚ **-s** -z
Meribel ˈmer.i.bel
Mérida ˈmer.ɪ.də (US) -iː.dɑː
meridian məˈrɪd.i.ən, mɪ- (US) məˈrɪd- **-s** -z
meridional məˈrɪd.i.ə.nᵊl, mɪ- (US) məˈrɪd- **-ly** -i
Mérimée ˈmer.ɪ.meɪ (US) ˌmeɪ.riːˈmeɪ
meringue məˈræŋ **-s** -z
merino məˈriː.nəʊ (US) -noʊ **-s** -z
Merioneth ˌmer.iˈɒn.ɪθ, -neθ, -nəθ (US) -ˈɑː.nɪθ **-shire** -ʃəʳ, -ʃɪəʳ (US) -ʃɚ, -ˌʃɪr
meristem ˈmer.i.stem, ˈ-ə- (US) ˈ-ə- **-s** -z
meristematic ˌmer.i.stɪˈmæt.ɪk, ˌ-ə-, -stəˈ- (US) -ə.stəˈmæt̬- **-ally** -ᵊl.i, -li
mer|it ˈmer|.ɪt **-its** -ɪts **-iting** -ɪ.tɪŋ (US) -ɪ.t̬ɪŋ **-ited** -ɪ.tɪd (US) -ɪ.t̬ɪd

meritocrac|y ˌmer.ɪˈtɒk.rə.s|i, -əˈ- (US) -əˈtɑː.krə- **-ies** -iz
meritocratic ˌmer.ɪ.təˈkræt.ɪk
meritorious ˌmer.ɪˈtɔː.ri.əs, -əˈ- (US) -əˈtɔːr.i- **-ly** -li **-ness** -nəs, -nɪs
Merivale ˈmer.ɪ.veɪl
merl mɜːl (US) mɝːl **-s** -z
merle (M) mɜːl (US) mɝːl **-s** -z
merlin (M) ˈmɜː.lɪn (US) ˈmɝː- **-s** -z
merlot (M) ˈmeə.ləʊ, -ˈ- (US) mɝːˈloʊ, mer- **-s** -z
mermaid ˈmɜː.meɪd (US) ˈmɝː- **-s** -z
mer|man (M) ˈmɜː|.mæn (US) ˈmɝː- **-men** -men
Meroe ˈmer.əʊ.i (US) -oʊ-
Merope ˈmer.ə.pi
Merovingian ˌmer.əʊˈvɪn.dʒi.ən, ˈ-dʒᵊn (US) -oʊˈ-, -əˈ-
Merrick ˈmer.ɪk
Merrilies ˈmer.ɪ.liz, -ᵊl.iz
Merrill ˈmer.ᵊl, -ɪl
Merrimac ˈmer.ɪ.mæk, ˈ-ə-
Merriman ˈmer.i.mən
merriment ˈmer.i.mənt
Merritt ˈmer.ɪt
Merrivale ˈmer.i.veɪl
merr|y (M) ˈmer|.i **-ier** -i.əʳ (US) -i.ɚ **-iest** -i.ɪst, -i.əst **-ily** -ᵊl.i, -ɪ.li **-iness** -ɪ.nəs, -ɪ.nɪs
merry-andrew ˌmer.iˈæn.druː **-s** -z
Merrydown® ˈmer.i.daʊn
merry-go-round ˈmer.i.gəʊˌraʊnd (US) -goʊˌ- **-s** -z
merrymak|er ˈmer.iˌmeɪ.k|əʳ (US) -k|ɚ **-ers** -əz (US) -ɚz **-ing** -ɪŋ
Merryweather ˈmer.iˌweð.əʳ (US) -ɚ
Mersey ˈmɜː.zi (US) ˈmɝː- **-side** -saɪd **-sider/s** -ˌsaɪ.dəʳ/z
Merson ˈmɜː.sᵊn (US) ˈmɝː-
Merthyr ˈmɜː.θəʳ (US) ˈmɝː.θɚ
Merthyr Tydfil ˌmɜː.θəˈtɪd.vɪl (US) ˌmɝː.θɚˈ-
Merton ˈmɜː.tᵊn (US) ˈmɝː-
Mervyn ˈmɜː.vɪn (US) ˈmɝː-
Meryl ˈmer.ᵊl, -ɪl
mesa ˈmeɪ.sə **-s** -z
mésallianc|e mezˈæl.i.ənts, meɪˈzæl-, -ɑ̃ːns *as if French:* ˌmez.æl.i.ˈɑ̃ːns (US) meɪˈzæl.i.ᵊnts; ˌmeɪ.zəˈliː- **-es** -ɪz
mescal ˈmes.kæl, -ˈ- (US) -ˈ- **-s** -z
mescalin(e) ˈmes.kᵊl.ɪn, -iːn
mesdames (M) (*plur. of* **madame**) meɪˈdæm, -dæmz, ˈ-- (US) -ˈdɑːm, -ˈdæm
mesdemoiselles (M) (*plur. of* **mademoiselle**) ˌmeɪ.dᵊm.wəˈzel, -ˈzelz (US) ˌmeɪd.mwɑːˈzel
meseems mɪˈsiːmz
mesembryanthemum məˌzem.briˈænt.θɪ.məm, mɪ-, -θᵊm.əm (US) mesˌem-, mez- **-s** -z

mesh meʃ **-es** -ɪz **-ing** -ɪŋ **-ed** -t
Meshach, Meschak ˈmiː.ʃæk
Meshed ˈmeʃ.ed
mesial ˈmiː.zi.əl (US) ˈmiː-, ˈmez.i-, ˈmes-
Mesmer ˈmez.məʳ (US) -mɚ
mesmeric mezˈmer.ɪk
mesmer|ism ˈmez.mᵊr|.ɪ.zᵊm **-ist/s** -ɪst/s
mesmeriz|e, -is|e ˈmez.mᵊr.aɪz **-es** -ɪz **-ing** -ɪŋ **-ed** -d **-er/s** -əʳ/z (US) -ɚ/z
mesne miːn
meso- mes.əʊ-, mez-, miː.səʊ-, -zəʊ- (US) mez.oʊ-, mes-, -ə-, miː.soʊ-, -sə-
Note: Prefix. May carry either primary or secondary stress on the first syllable, e.g. **mesoderm** /ˈmes.əʊ.dɜːm (US) ˈmez.oʊ.dɜːrm/, **mesodermal** /ˌmes.əʊˈdɜː.mᵊl (US) ˌmez.oʊˈdɜːr-/.
mesoderm ˈmes.əʊ.dɜːm, ˈmez-, ˈmiː.səʊ-, -zəʊ- (US) ˈmez.oʊ.dɝːm, ˈmes-, ˈ-ə-
mesodermal ˌmes.əʊˈdɜː.mᵊl, ˌmez-, ˌmiː.səʊˈ-, -zəʊˈ- (US) ˌmez.oʊˈdɝː-, ˌmes-, -əˈ-
mesodermic ˌmes.əʊˈdɜː.mɪk, ˌmez-, ˌmiː.səʊˈ-, -zəʊˈ- (US) ˌmez.oʊˈdɝː-, ˌmes-, -əˈ-
mesolect ˈmes.əʊ.lekt, ˈmez-, ˈmiː.səʊ-, -zəʊ- (US) ˈmez.oʊ-, ˈmes-, -ə- **-s** -s
mesolectal ˌmes.əʊˈlek.tᵊl, ˌmez-, ˌmiː.səʊˈ-, -zəʊˈ- (US) ˌmez.oʊˈ-, ˌmes-, -ə-
mesomorph ˈmes.əʊ.mɔːf, ˈmez-, ˈmiː.səʊ-, -zəʊ- (US) ˈmez.oʊ.mɔːrf, ˈmes-, ˈ-ə- **-s** -s
meson ˈmiː.zɒn, ˈmeɪ-, -sɒn, ˈmes.ɒn, ˈmez- (US) ˈmez.ɑːn, ˈmes-, ˈmeɪ.sɑːn, ˈmiː-, -zɑːn **-s** -z
Mesopotami|a ˌmes.ə.pəˈteɪ.mi|.ə **-an/s** -ən/z
mesotron ˈmes.əʊ.trɒn, ˈmez-, ˈmiː.səʊ-, -zəʊ- (US) ˈmez.oʊ.trɑːn, ˈmes-, ˈ-ə- **-s** -z
Mesozoic ˌmes.əʊˈzəʊ.ɪk, ˌmiː.səʊˈ- (US) ˌmez.oʊˈzoʊ-, ˌmes-, -əˈ-
mesquite (M) mesˈkiːt, məˈskiːt, mɪ-; ˈmes.kɪt (US) məˈskiːt, mesˈkiːt
mess mes **-es** -ɪz **-ing** -ɪŋ **-ed** -t
messag|e ˈmes.ɪdʒ **-es** -ɪz **-ing** -ɪŋ **-ed** -d
messeigneurs (*plur. of* **monseigneur**) ˌmes.eɪˈnjɜː
messenger ˈmes.ɪn.dʒəʳ, -ᵊn- (US) -dʒɚ **-s** -z
Messerschmitt® ˈmes.ə.ʃmɪt (US) ˈ-ɚ-
Messiaen ˈmes.jɑ̃ːŋ, -i.ɑ̃ːŋ *as if French:* mesˈjɑ̃ːŋ (US) mesˈjɑ̃ːn
messiah (M) məˈsaɪ.ə, mɪ-, mesˈaɪ- (US) məˈsaɪ- **-s** -z
messianic ˌmes.iˈæn.ɪk

messieurs meɪ'sjɜːz, mes'jɜːz, 'mes.əz *as if French:* mes'jɜː (US) -ɚz
Messina mes'iː.nə, mə'siː-, mɪ- (US) mə-, mes'iː-
messmate 'mes.meɪt **-s** -s
Messrs. *(plur. of* **Mr***)* 'mes.əz (US) -ɚz
messuag|e 'mes.wɪdʒ, -ju.ɪdʒ (US) '-wɪdʒ **-es** -ɪz
mess|y 'mes|.i **-ier** -i.əʳ (US) -i.ɚ **-iest** -i.ɪst, -i.əst **-ily** -ɪ.li, -ᵊl.i **-iness** -ɪ.nəs, -ɪ.nɪs
mestiz|o mes'tiː.z|əʊ, mə'stiː-, mɪ- (US) mes'tiː.z|oʊ **-a** -ə **-os** -əʊz (US) -oʊz **-as** -əz
Mestre 'mes.treɪ
met *(from* **meet***)* met
meta- met.ə-; mə'tæ-, met'æ-, mɪ'tæ- (US) met̬.ə-; mə'tæ-, met'æ-
Note: Prefix. Normally carries primary or secondary stress on the first syllable, e.g. **metaplasm** /'met.ə,plæz.ᵊm (US) 'met̬-/, **metabolic** /,met.ə'bɒl.ɪk (US) ,met̬.ə'bɑː.lɪk/, or primary stress on the second syllable, e.g. **metabolism** /mə'tæb.ᵊl.ɪ.zᵊm/.
metabolic ,met.ə'bɒl.ɪk (US) ,met̬.ə'bɑː.lɪk **-ally** -ᵊl.i, -li
metabolism mə'tæb.ᵊl.ɪ.zᵊm, mɪ-, met'æb- (US) mə'tæb- **-s** -z
metaboliz|e, -is|e mə'tæb.ᵊl.aɪz, mɪ-, met'æb- (US) mə'- **-es** -ɪz **-ing** -ɪŋ **-ed** -d
metacarp|al ,met.ə'kɑː.p|ᵊl (US) ,met̬.ə'kɑːr- **-us** -əs
metacentre, -center 'met.ə,sen.təʳ (US) 'met̬.ə,sen.t̬ɚ **-s** -z
metagalax|y 'met.ə,gæl.ək.s|i (US) 'met̬- **-ies** -iz
metal 'met.ᵊl (US) 'met̬- **-s** -z **-ling** -ɪŋ **-led** -d **'metal de,tector**
metalanguage 'met.ᵊl,æŋ.gwɪdʒ (US) 'met̬-
metallic mə'tæl.ɪk, mɪ-, met'æl- (US) mə'tæl- **-ally** -ᵊl.i, -li
Metallica met'æl.ɪ.kə, mə'tæl-, mɪ-, -lə-
metalliferous ,met.ᵊl'ɪf.ᵊr.əs (US) ,met̬-
metallography ,met.ᵊl'ɒg.rə.fi (US) ,met̬.ᵊl'ɑː.grə-
metalloid 'met.ᵊl.ɔɪd (US) 'met̬-
metallurgic|al ,met.ᵊl'ɜː.dʒɪ.k|ᵊl (US) ,met̬.ᵊl'ɝː- **-ally** -ᵊl.i, -li
metallurgist met'æl.ə.dʒɪst, mə'tæl-, mɪ-; 'met.ᵊl.ɜː- (US) 'met̬.ᵊl.ɝː- **-s** -s
metallurgy met'æl.ə.dʒi, mə'tæl, mɪ-; 'met.ᵊl.ɜː- (US) 'met̬.ᵊl.ɝː-
metalwork 'met.ᵊl.wɜːk (US) 'met̬.ᵊl.wɝːk **-er/s** -əʳ/z (US) -ɚ/z
metamorphic ,met.ə'mɔː.fɪk (US) ,met̬.ə'mɔːr-
metamorphism ,met.ə'mɔː.fɪ.zᵊm (US) ,met̬.ə'mɔːr- **-s** -z
metamorphos|e ,met.ə'mɔː.fəʊz (US) ,met̬.ə'mɔːr.foʊz **-es** -ɪz **-ing** -ɪŋ **-ed** -d
metamorphos|is ,met.ə'mɔː.fə.s|ɪs; -mɔː'fəʊ- (US) ,met̬.ə'mɔːr.fə-; -mɔːr'foʊ- **-es** -iːz
metaphor 'met.ə.fəʳ, -fɔːʳ (US) 'met̬.ə.fɔːr, -fɚ **-s** -z
metaphoric ,met.ə'fɒr.ɪk (US) ,met̬.ə'fɔːr.ɪk **-al** -ᵊl **-ally** -ᵊl.i, -li
metaphysic|al ,met.ə'fɪz.ɪ.k|ᵊl (US) ,met̬- **-ally** -ᵊl.i, -li
metaphysician ,met.ə.fɪ'zɪʃ.ᵊn (US) ,met̬- **-s** -z
metaphysics ,met.ə'fɪz.ɪks (US) ,met̬-, 'met̬.ə,fɪz-
metaplasm 'met.ə,plæz.ᵊm (US) 'met̬-
metastas|is met'æs.tə.s|ɪs, mɪ'tæs-, mə'tæs- (US) mə'tæs- **-es** -iːz
metatarsal ,met.ə'tɑː.sᵊl (US) ,met̬.ə'tɑːr- **-s** -z
metatars|us ,met.ə'tɑː.s|əs (US) ,met̬.ə'tɑːr- **-i** -aɪ
metathes|is met'æθ.ə.s|ɪs, mɪ'tæθ-, mə-, '-ɪ- (US) mə'tæθ.ə- **-es** -iːz
Metaxa® met'æk.sə, mɪ'tæk-, mə- (US) mə-
Metayers mɪ'teɪəz, mə- (US) -'teɪɚz
Metcalfe 'met.kɑːf, -kəf (US) -kæf
met|e miːt **-es** -s **-ing** -ɪŋ (US) 'miː.t̬ɪŋ **-ed** -ɪd (US) 'miː.t̬ɪd
Metellus mɪ'tel.əs, met'el- (US) mɪ'tel-
metempsychosis ,met.emp.saɪ'kəʊ.sɪs, -əmp-, -sɪ'-; met,emp- (US) mɪ,temp.sɪ'koʊ-; ,met.əmp.saɪ'-
meteor 'miː.ti.əʳ, -ɔːʳ (US) -t̬i.ɚ, -ɔːr **-s** -z
meteoric ,miː.ti'ɒr.ɪk (US) -t̬i'ɔːr- **-ally** -ᵊl.i, -li
meteorite 'miː.ti.ᵊr.aɪt (US) -t̬i.ə.raɪt **-s** -s
meteorologic ,miː.ti.ᵊr.ə'lɒdʒ.ɪk (US) -t̬i.ɚ.ə'lɑː.dʒɪ- **-al** -ᵊl **-ally** -ᵊl.i, -li
meteorologist ,miː.ti.ᵊr'ɒl.ə.dʒɪst (US) -t̬i.ə'rɑːl- **-s** -s
meteorology ,miː.ti.ᵊr'ɒl.ə.dʒi (US) -ə'rɑː.lə-
met|er 'miː.t|əʳ (US) -t̬|ɚ **-ers** -əz (US) -ɚz **-ering** -ᵊr.ɪŋ **-ered** -əd (US) -ɚd
methadone 'meθ.ə.dəʊn (US) -doʊn
methane 'miː.θeɪn (US) 'meθ.eɪn
methanol 'meθ.ə.nɒl, 'miː.θə- (US) 'meθ.ə.nɑːl, -noʊl
metheglin meθ'eg.lɪn, mɪ'θeg-, mə- (US) mə'θeg-
Metheny mə'θiː.ni
methinks mɪ'θɪŋks
method 'meθ.əd **-s** -z
méthode champenoise meɪ,tɒd.ʃɑ̃ːm.pᵊn'wɑːz (US) -toʊd.ʃɑːm-
methodic mə'θɒd.ɪk, mɪ-, meθ'ɒd- (US) mə'θɑː.dɪk **-al** -ᵊl **-ally** -ᵊl.i, -li
Method|ism 'meθ.ə.d|ɪ.zᵊm **-ist/s** -ɪst/s
methodologi|cal ,meθ.ə.dᵊl'ɒdʒ.ɪ|kᵊl (US) -dᵊl'ɑː.dʒɪ- **-ally** -kᵊl.i, -kli
methodolog|y ,meθ.ə'dɒl.ə.dʒ|i (US) -'dɑː.lə- **-ies** -iz
methought mɪ'θɔːt (US) -'θɑːt, -'θɔːt
meths meθs
Methuen *surname:* 'meθ.ju.ən, -ɪn (US) mɪ'θjuː.ɪn, mə-, -'θuː-, -ən; 'meθ.juː-, -uː- *US town:* mɪ'θjuː.ɪn, mə-, -'θuː-, -ən
Methuselah mə'θjuː.zᵊl.ə, mɪ-, -'θuː- (US) mə'θuː-, -'θjuː-
Methven 'meθ.vən, -ven
methyl *commercial and general pronunciation:* 'meθ.ᵊl, -ɪl (US) -aɪl *chemists' pronunciation:* 'miː.θaɪl (US) 'meθ.aɪl
methylated 'meθ.ᵊl.eɪ.tɪd, -ɪ.leɪ- (US) -ɪ.leɪ.t̬ɪd **,methylated 'spirits**
methylene 'meθ.ᵊl.iːn, -ɪ.liːn (US) '-ɪ-
meti|cal ,met.ɪ'kæl (US) ,met̬- **-cais** -'kaɪʃ
meticulous mə'tɪk.jə.ləs, mɪ-, met'ɪk-, -jʊ- (US) mə'tɪk.jə-, -juː- **-ly** -li **-ness** -nəs, -nɪs
métier 'met.i.eɪ, 'meɪ.ti- (US) meɪ'tjeɪ **-s** -z
metonym 'met.ə.nɪm (US) 'met̬- **-s** -z
metonymy met'ɒn.ə.mi, mɪ'tɒn-, mə-, '-ɪ- (US) mə'tɑː.nə-
me-too ,miː'tuː **-ism** -ɪ.zᵊm
metope 'met.əʊp; -əʊ.pi (US) 'met̬.ə.pi; '-oʊp **-s** -s
metre 'miː.təʳ (US) -t̬ɚ **-s** -z
metric 'met.rɪk **-al** -ᵊl **-ally** -ᵊl.i, -li
metrication ,met.rɪ'keɪ.ʃᵊn, -rə'-
metrics 'met.rɪks
metro (M) 'met.rəʊ (US) -roʊ **-s** -z
metro- 'met.rəʊ-, met'rɒ- (US) 'met.roʊ-, -rə-; mə'trɑː-
Metro-Goldwyn-Mayer ,met.rəʊ,gəʊld.wɪn'meɪ.əʳ (US) -roʊ,goʊld.wɪn'meɪ.ɚ
Metroland 'met.rəʊ.lænd (US) -roʊ-
metronome 'met.rə.nəʊm (US) -noʊm **-s** -z
metronomic ,met.rə'nɒm.ɪk (US) -'nɑː.mɪk **-al** -ᵊl **-ally** -ᵊl.i, -li
Metropole 'met.rə.pəʊl (US) -poʊl
metropolis mə'trɒp.ə.lɪs, mɪ-, met'rɒp-, -ᵊl.ɪs (US) mə'trɑː.pᵊl- **-es** -ɪz
metropolitan ,met.rə'pɒl.ɪ.tᵊn, '-ə- (US) -'pɑː.lə- **-s** -z
-metry -mə.tri
mettle 'met.l̩ (US) 'met̬- **-some** -səm
Metz mets *as if French:* mes
meunière, meuniere ,mɜː.ni'eəʳ, -'njeəʳ, mə'-, '--- (US) mə'njer

Meursault ˈmɜː.səʊ (US) məˈsoʊ
Meuse mɜːz (US) mjuːz, mɜːz
Meux mjuːz, mjuːks, mjuː
Mevagissey ˌmev.əˈgɪs.i
mew (M) mjuː **-s** -z **-ing** -ɪŋ **-ed** -d
mewl mjuːl **-s** -z **-ing** -ɪŋ **-ed** -d
mews mjuːz
Mexborough ˈmeks.bᵊr.ə (US) -oʊ
Mexicali ˌmek.sɪˈkɑː.li, -ˈkæl.i (US) -ˈkæl.i
Mexican ˈmek.sɪ.kᵊn ˌ**Mexican** ˈ**wave**
Mexico ˈmek.sɪ.kəʊ (US) -koʊ ˌ**Mexico** ˈ**City**
Mey meɪ
Meyer ˈmaɪ.əʳ, ˈmeɪ-, meəʳ (US) ˈmaɪ.ɚ
Meyerbeer ˈmaɪ.ə.bɪəʳ, -beəʳ (US) -ɚ.bɪr, -ber
Meyers ˈmaɪ.əz, ˈmeɪ.əz, meəz (US) ˈmaɪ.ɚz
Meynell ˈmen.ᵊl, ˈmeɪ.nᵊl; meɪˈnel
Meyrick ˈmer.ɪk, ˈmeɪ.rɪk
mezzanine ˈmet.sə.niːn, ˈmez.ə- (US) ˈmez-, ˌ--ˈ- **-s** -z
mezzo ˈmet.səʊ, ˈmed.zəʊ (US) ˈmet.soʊ, ˈmed.zoʊ, ˈmez.oʊ **-s** -z
mezzo-soprano ˌmet.səʊ.səˈprɑː.nəʊ, ˌmed.zəʊ- (US) ˌmet.soʊ.səˈpræn.oʊ, -ˈprɑː.noʊ, ˌmed.zoʊ-, ˌmez.oʊ- **-s** -z
mezzotint ˈmet.səʊ.tɪnt, ˈmed.zəʊ- (US) ˈmet.soʊ-, ˈmed.zoʊ-, ˈmez.oʊ- **-s** -s
mg *(abbrev. for* **milligram/s)** *singular:* ˈmɪl.ɪ.græm *plural:* ˈmɪl.ɪ.græmz
MGM® ˌem.dʒiːˈem
Mgr. *(abbrev. for* **Monseigneur, Monsignor)** mɒnˈsiː.njəʳ, -njɔːʳ (US) mɑːnˈsiː.njɚ **-s.** -z
MHz *(abbrev. for* **megahertz)** ˈmeg.ə.hɜːts (US) -hɝːts
mi miː **-s** -z
MI5 ˌem.aɪˈfaɪv
MI6 ˌem.aɪˈsiks
Mia ˈmiː.ə
MIA ˌem.aɪˈeɪ
Miami maɪˈæm.i (US) -i, -ə
miaow ˌmiːˈaʊ, miˈaʊ (US) miˈaʊ, mjaʊ **-s** -z **-ing** -ɪŋ **-ed** -d
miasm|a miˈæz.m|ə, maɪ- (US) maɪ-, mi- **-as** -əz **-ata** -ə.tə (US) -ə.t̬ə **-al** -ᵊl
mic maɪk **-s** -s
mica ˈmaɪ.kə
micaceous maɪˈkeɪ.ʃəs
Micah ˈmaɪ.kə
Micawber mɪˈkɔː.bəʳ, mə- (US) -ˈkɑː.bɚ, -ˈkɔː-
mice *(plur. of* **mouse)** maɪs
Mich. *(abbrev. for* **Michigan)** ˈmɪʃ.ɪ.gən, ˈ-ə- (US) ˈ-ɪ-
Michael ˈmaɪ.kᵊl
Michaela mɪˈkaɪ.lə
Michaelmas ˈmɪk.ᵊl.məs
Michelangelo ˌmaɪ.kᵊlˈæn.dʒə.ləʊ, -dʒɪ- (US) -loʊ, ˌmɪk.ᵊl-
Micheldever ˈmɪtʃ.ᵊl.dev.əʳ (US) -ɚ
Michele, Michèle mɪˈʃel, miː-
Michelin® ˈmɪtʃ.ᵊl.ɪn, ˈmɪʃ- *as if French:* miːʃˈlæ̃ŋ (US) ˈmɪʃ.ə.lɪn, ˈmɪtʃ- **-s** -z
Note: In the UK, /miːʃˈlæ̃ŋ/ is used for the Guide, but not the tyres.
Michelle mɪˈʃel, miː-
Michelmore ˈmɪtʃ.ᵊl.mɔːʳ (US) -mɔːr
Michelson ˈmɪtʃ.ᵊl.sᵊn, ˈmɪk.ᵊl-, ˈmaɪ.kᵊl- (US) ˈmaɪ-, ˈmɪk.ᵊl-
Michie ˈmɪx.i, ˈmiː.xi, ˈmɪk.i (US) ˈmɪk.i
Michigan ˈmɪʃ.ɪ.gən, ˈ-ə- (US) ˈ-ɪ-
Michmash ˈmɪk.mæʃ
Michoacán ˌmɪtʃ.əʊ.əˈkæn (US) -ə.wɑːˈkɑːn
mick (M) mɪk
mickey (M) ˈmɪk.i ˌ**Mickey** ˈ**Finn**; ˌ**Mickey** ˈ**Mouse** (US) ˈ**Mickey** ˌ**Mouse**
mickey-mouse *(adj.)* ˌmɪk.iˈmaʊs (US) ˈ--ˌ- *stress shift, British only:* ˌmickey-mouse ˈjob
micra *(plur. of* **micron)** ˈmaɪ.krə
Micra® ˈmaɪ.krə
micro- maɪ.krəʊ- (US) maɪ.kroʊ-, maɪ.krə-
Note: Prefix. May carry primary or secondary stress, e.g. **microfiche** /ˈmaɪ.krəʊ.fiːʃ (US) -kroʊ-/, **microbiology** /ˌmaɪ.krəʊ.baɪˈɒl.ə.dʒi (US) -kroʊ.baɪˈɑː.lə-/.
micro ˈmaɪ.krəʊ (US) -kroʊ **-s** -z
microbe ˈmaɪ.krəʊb (US) -kroʊb **-s** -z
microbiologic|al ˌmaɪ.krəʊˌbaɪ.əˈlɒdʒ.ɪ.k|ᵊl (US) -kroʊˌbaɪ.əˈlɑː.dʒɪ- **-ally** -ᵊl.i (US) -li
microbiologist ˌmaɪ.krəʊ.baɪˈɒl.ə.dʒɪst (US) -kroʊ.baɪˈɑː.lə- **-s** -s
microbiolog|y ˌmaɪ.krəʊ.baɪˈɒl.ə.dʒ|i (US) -kroʊ.baɪˈɑː.lə- **-ist/s** -ɪst/s
microbrewer|y ˈmaɪ.krəʊˌbruː.ᵊr|.i (US) -kroʊ-, ˌ-r|i **-ies** -iz
microcephalic ˌmaɪ.krəʊ.sefˈæl.ɪk, -sɪˈfæl-, -kefˈæl-, -kɪˈfæl- (US) -kroʊ.səˈfæl-
microcephalous ˌmaɪ.krəʊˈsef.ᵊl.əs, -ˈkef- (US) -kroʊˈsef-
microchip ˈmaɪ.krəʊ.tʃɪp (US) -kroʊ-, -krə- **-s** -s
microcircuit ˈmaɪ.krəʊˌsɜː.kɪt (US) -kroʊˌsɝː- **-s** -s
microclimate ˈmaɪ.krəʊˌklaɪ.mɪt, -mət (US) -mɪt, -kroʊ- **-s** -s
microcomputer ˈmaɪ.krəʊ.kəmˌpjuː.təʳ (US) -kroʊ.kəmˌpjuː.t̬ɚ **-s** -z
microcop|y ˈmaɪ.krəʊˌkɒp|.i (US) -kroʊˌkɑː.p|i **-ies** -iz
microcosm ˈmaɪ.krəʊˌkɒz.ᵊm (US) -kroʊˌkɑː.zᵊm, -krəˌ- **-s** -z
microdot ˈmaɪ.krəʊ.dɒt (US) -kroʊ.dɑːt, -krə- **-s** -s
microeconomic ˌmaɪ.krəʊ.iː.kəˈnɒm.ɪk, -ek.əˈ- (US) -kroʊˌek.əˈnɑː.mɪk, -krəˌ-, -ˌiː.kəˈ- **-s** -s
microelectronics ˌmaɪ.krəʊˌɪl.ekˈtrɒn.ɪks, -ˌel-, -ˌel.ɪkˈ-, -ˌiː.lekˈ- (US) -kroʊ.ɪˌlekˈtrɑː.nɪks, -ˌiː.lekˈ-
microfich|e ˈmaɪ.krəʊ.fiːʃ (US) -kroʊ-, -krə- **-es** -ɪz
microfilm ˈmaɪ.krəʊ.fɪlm (US) -kroʊ-, -krə- **-s** -z **-ing** -ɪŋ **-ed** -d
microgram, microgramme ˈmaɪ.krəʊ.græm (US) -kroʊ- **-s** -z
microgroove ˈmaɪ.krəʊ.gruːv (US) -kroʊ- **-s** -z
microlight, microlite ˈmaɪ.krəʊ.laɪt (US) -kroʊ- **-s** -s
micromesh ˈmaɪ.krəʊ.meʃ (US) -kroʊ-
micrometer *measuring device:* maɪˈkrɒm.ɪ.təʳ, ˈ-ə- (US) -ˈkrɑː.mə.t̬ɚ
micrometre, micrometer *unit of measurement:* ˈmaɪ.krəʊˌmiː.təʳ (US) -kroʊˌmiː.t̬ɚ **-s** -z
micr|on ˈmaɪ.kr|ɒn, -kr|ᵊn (US) -kr|ɑːn **-ons** -ɒnz, -ᵊnz (US) -ɑːnz **-a** -ə
Micronesi|a ˌmaɪ.krəʊˈniː.zi|.ə, -ʒi|.ə, -ʒ|ə, -si|.ə, -ʃi|.ə, -ʃ|ə (US) -kroʊˈniː.ʒ|ə, -ʃ|ə **-an/s** -ən/z
microorganism ˌmaɪ.krəʊˈɔː.gᵊn.ɪ.zᵊm, ˈmaɪ.krəʊˌɔː- (US) ˌmaɪ.kroʊˈɔːr- **-s** -z
microphone ˈmaɪ.krə.fəʊn (US) -foʊn **-s** -z
microprocessor ˌmaɪ.krəʊˈprəʊ.ses.əʳ, ˈmaɪ.krəʊˌprəʊ- (US) ˈmaɪ.kroʊˌprɑː.ses.ɚ **-s** -z
micropyle ˈmaɪ.krəʊ.paɪl (US) -kroʊ-
microscope ˈmaɪ.krə.skəʊp (US) -skoʊp **-s** -s
microscopic ˌmaɪ.krəˈskɒp.ɪk (US) -ˈskɑː.pɪk **-al** -ᵊl **-ally** -ᵊl.i (US) -li
microscopy maɪˈkrɒs.kə.pi (US) -ˈkrɑː.skə-
microsecond ˈmaɪ.krəʊˌsek.ᵊnd (US) -kroʊˌ-, -krəˌ- **-s** -z
Microsoft® ˈmaɪ.krəʊ.sɒft (US) -kroʊ.sɑːft, -krə-
microsurgery ˌmaɪ.krəʊˈsɜː.dʒᵊr.i (US) -kroʊˈsɝː-, ˈmaɪ.kroʊˌsɝː-
microsurgical ˌmaɪ.krəʊˈsɜː.dʒɪ.kᵊl (US) -kroʊˈsɝː- *stress shift:* ˌmicrosurgical ˈgraft
microwav|e ˈmaɪ.krəʊ.weɪv (US) -kroʊ-, -krə- **-es** -z **-ing** -ɪŋ **-ed** -d **-eable** -ə.bl̩ ˌ**microwave** ˈ**oven**

mictur|ate 'mɪk.tj^{ə}r|.eɪt, -tjʊ.reɪt (US) -tʃuː-, -tʃə-, -tə- **-ates** -eɪts **-ating** -eɪ.tɪŋ (US) -eɪ.t̬ɪŋ **-ated** -eɪ.tɪd (US) -eɪ.t̬ɪd
micturation ˌmɪk.tj^{ə}r'eɪ.ʃ^{ə}n, -tjʊ'reɪ- (US) -tʃuː'reɪ-, -tʃə'-, -tə'- **-s** -z
micturition ˌmɪk.tj^{ə}r'ɪʃ.^{ə}n, -tjʊ'rɪʃ- (US) -tʃuː'-, -tʃə'-, -tə'-
mid mɪd
midair ˌmɪd'eə^{r}, mɪ'deə^{r} (US) ˌmɪd'er *stress shift:* ˌmidair 'crash
Midas 'maɪ.dəs, -dæs (US) -dəs
midday ˌmɪd'deɪ **-s** -z *stress shift:* ˌmidday 'sun
midden 'mɪd.^{ə}n **-s** -z
middle 'mɪd.l̩ **-s** -z ˌ**middle 'age**; ˌ**Middle 'Ages**; ˌ**middle 'class**; ˌ**Middle 'East**; ˌ**middle 'management**; ˌ**middle 'name**; ˌ**middle of 'nowhere**; '**middle ˌschool**
middle-aged ˌmɪd.l̩'eɪdʒd *stress shift, see compound:* ˌ**middle-aged 'spread**
middlebrow 'mɪd.l̩.braʊ **-s** -z
middle-class ˌmɪd.l̩'klɑːs (US) -'klæs *stress shift:* ˌmiddle-class 'values
middle distance *(n.)* ˌmɪd.l̩'dɪs.t^{ə}n*t*s
middle-distance *(adj.)* 'mɪd.l̩ˌdɪs.t^{ə}n*t*s
Middle-Earth ˌmɪd.l̩'ɜːθ (US) -'ɝːθ
Middle East ˌmɪd.l̩'iːst **-ern** -ən *stress shift:* ˌMiddle Eastern 'customs
Middleham 'mɪd.l̩.əm
middle|man 'mɪd.l̩|.mæn **-men** -men
Middlemarch 'mɪd.l̩.mɑːtʃ (US) -mɑːrtʃ
Middlemast 'mɪd.l̩.mɑːst, -mæst (US) -mæst
middlemost 'mɪd.l̩.məʊst (US) -moʊst
middle-of-the-road ˌmɪd.l̩.əv.ðə'rəʊd (US) -'roʊd
Middlesbro(ugh) 'mɪd.lz.brə
Middlesex 'mɪd.l̩.seks
Middleton 'mɪd.l̩.tən
middleweight 'mɪd.l̩.weɪt **-s** -s
Middlewich 'mɪd.l̩.wɪtʃ
middling 'mɪd.l̩.ɪŋ, 'mɪd.lɪŋ
Middx. *(abbrev. for* **Middlesex***)* 'mɪd.l̩.seks
midd|y 'mɪd|.i **-ies** -iz
Mideast ˌmɪd'iːst *stress shift:* ˌMideast 'town
midfield 'mɪd.fiːld, -'-
midfielder 'mɪdˌfiːl.də^{r}, ˌ-'-- (US) 'mɪdˌfiːl.dɚ, ˌ-'-- **-s** -z
Midgard 'mɪd.gɑːd (US) -gɑːrd
midg|e mɪdʒ **-es** -ɪz
midget 'mɪdʒ.ɪt **-s** -s
Midhurst 'mɪd.hɜːst (US) -hɝːst
MIDI *computer interface:* 'mɪd.i
midi *style of clothes:* 'mɪd.i **-s** -z
Midi *in France:* miː'diː, mɪd'iː (US) miː'di
Midian 'mɪd.i.ən **-ite/s** -aɪt/s
midland (M) 'mɪd.lənd **-s** -z
Midler 'mɪd.lə^{r} (US) -lɚ
mid-life ˌmɪd'laɪf *stress shift, see compound:* ˌ**mid-life 'crisis**
Midlothian ˌmɪd'ləʊ.ði.ən (US) -'loʊ-
midmorning ˌmɪd'mɔː.nɪŋ (US) -'mɔːr-
midnight 'mɪd.naɪt
mid-off ˌmɪd'ɒf (US) -'ɑːf **-s** -s
mid-on ˌmɪd'ɒn (US) -'ɑːn **-s** -z
midpoint 'mɪd.pɔɪnt **-s** -s
midriff 'mɪd.rɪf **-s** -s
midsection 'mɪd.sek.ʃ^{ə}n
midship|man 'mɪdˌʃɪp|.mən (US) 'mɪdˌ-, ˌmɪd'ʃɪp- **-men** -mən
midships 'mɪd.ʃɪps
midst mɪdst, mɪtst
midstream ˌmɪd'striːm
midsummer (M) ˌmɪd'sʌm.ə^{r}, '--- (US) -ɚ **-'s** -z *stress shift, see compounds:* ˌ**Midsummer 'Day**; ˌ**midsummer 'madness**; ˌ**Midsummer ˌNight's 'Dream**
midterm *(n.)* 'mɪd.tɜːm (US) -tɝːm *stress shift:* ˌmid-term 'crisis
mid-term *(adj.)* ˌmɪd'tɜːm (US) -'tɝːm
midtown 'mɪd.taʊn
midway ˌmɪd'weɪ, '--
Midway *island:* 'mɪd.weɪ
midweek ˌmɪd'wiːk *stress shift:* ˌmidweek 'news
Midwest ˌmɪd'west *stress shift:* ˌMidwest 'town
midwi|fe 'mɪd.waɪ|f **-ves** -vz
midwifery mɪd'wɪf.^{ə}r.i, 'mɪdˌwɪf.^{ə}r- (US) ˌmɪd'wɪf.ɚ-; 'mɪdˌwaɪf.ɚ-
midwinter ˌmɪd'wɪn.tə^{r} (US) -t̬ɚ *stress shift:* ˌmidwinter 'holiday
mien miːn **-s** -z
Miers maɪəz (US) maɪɚz
Mies van der Rohe ˌmiːz.væn.də'rəʊ.ə, ˌmiːs- (US) -dɚ'roʊ.ə
miff mɪf **-s** -s **-ing** -ɪŋ **-ed** -t
MiG, MIG mɪg **-s** -z
might maɪt
mightn't 'maɪ.t^{ə}nt
might|y 'maɪ.t|i (US) -t̬|i **-ier** -i.ə^{r} (US) -i.ɚ **-iest** -i.ɪst, -i.əst **-ily** -ɪ.li, -^{ə}l.i **-iness** -ɪ.nəs, -ɪ.nɪs
mignon 'miː.njɒn, ˌ-'- *as if French:* mɪ'njɔ̃ːŋ (US) ˌmiː'njɑːn, -'njɔ̃ːn
mignonette (M) ˌmɪn.jə'net, '--- (US) ˌ--'- **-s** -s
mignonne 'miː.njɒn, ˌ-'- *as if French:* mɪ'njɔːn (US) ˌmiː'njɑːn, -'njɔːn
migraine 'miː.greɪn, 'maɪ-, 'mɪg.reɪn (US) 'maɪ.greɪn **-s** -z
migrant 'maɪ.gr^{ə}nt **-s** -s
migra|te maɪ'greɪ|t, '-- (US) 'maɪ.greɪ|t **-tes** -ts **-ting** -tɪŋ (US) -t̬ɪŋ **-ted** -tɪd (US) -t̬ɪd **-tor/s** -tə^{r}/z (US) -t̬ɚ/z
migration maɪ'greɪ.ʃ^{ə}n **-s** -z
migratory 'maɪ.grə.t^{ə}r.i; maɪ'greɪ- (US) 'maɪ.grə.tɔːr-
Miguel mɪ'gel, miː-
mikado (M) mɪ'kɑː.dəʊ, mə- (US) mɪ'kɑː.doʊ **-s** -z
Mikardo mɪ'kɑː.dəʊ, mə- (US) mɪ'kɑːr.doʊ
mike (M) maɪk **-s** -s
Mikonos 'mɪk.ə.nɒs, -ɒn.ɒs (US) 'miː.kɑː.nɑːs
mil mɪl **-s** -z
milady mɪ'leɪ.di, mə-
Milan *in Italy:* mɪ'læn, mə-, -'lɑːn, 'mɪl.ən (US) mɪ'læn, -'lɑːn *in US:* 'maɪ.lən
Note: /'mɪl.ən/ is used for rhythm in Shakespeare's 'The Tempest'.
Milanese *from Milan:* ˌmɪl.ə'niːz, -'neɪz (US) -'niːz, -'niːs
Milanese *cookery term: as if Italian:* ˌmɪl.ə'neɪ.zeɪ, -æn'eɪ-, -zi (US) -ə'neɪz
Milburn 'mɪl.bɜːn, -bən (US) -bɚn
milch mɪltʃ (US) mɪltʃ
mild maɪld **-er** -ə^{r} (US) -ɚ **-est** -ɪst, -əst **-ly** -li **-ness** -nəs, -nɪs
Mildenhall 'mɪl.d^{ə}n.hɔːl (US) 'mɪl.d^{ə}n.hɔːl, -hɑːl
mildew 'mɪl.djuː (US) -duː, -djuː **-s** -z **-ing** -ɪŋ **-ed** -d
Mildmay 'maɪld.meɪ
Mildred 'mɪl.drəd, -drɪd, -dred
mile maɪl **-s** -z
mileag|e 'maɪ.lɪdʒ **-es** -ɪz
mileometer maɪ'lɒm.ɪ.tə^{r}, '-ə- (US) -'lɑː.mə.t̬ɚ **-s** -z
Miles maɪlz
Milesian maɪ'liː.zi.ən, mɪ-, -ʒi.ən, -ʒ^{ə}n (US) -ʒ^{ə}n, -ʃ^{ə}n **-s** -z
milestone 'maɪl.stəʊn (US) -stoʊn **-s** -z
Miletus maɪ'liː.təs, mɪ- (US) maɪ-
milfoil 'mɪl.fɔɪl **-s** -z
Milford 'mɪl.fəd (US) -fɚd
Milhaud 'miː.jəʊ, -əʊ *as if French:* miː'jəʊ (US) miː'joʊ
milieu 'miː.ljɜː, -'- (US) miːl'jɜː, mɪl-, -'juː, '-- **-s** -z
milieux *(alternative plur. of* **milieu***)* 'miː.ljɜː, -ljɜːz, -'- (US) miːl'jɜː, mɪl-, -'juː, -'jɜːz, -'juːz, '--
militancy 'mɪl.ɪ.t^{ə}n*t*.si, '-ə- (US) -tən*t*-
militant 'mɪl.ɪ.t^{ə}nt, '-ə- (US) -t̬ənt **-s** -s **-ly** -li
militarily 'mɪl.ɪ.t^{ə}r.^{ə}l.i, -ə-, ˌmɪl.ɪ'ter-, ˌmɪl.ɪ'tær-, -ə'- (US) ˌmɪl.ə'ter-
militar|ism 'mɪl.ɪ.t^{ə}r|.ɪ.z^{ə}m, '-ə- (US) -tɚ- **-ist/s** -ɪst/s
militaristic ˌmɪl.ɪ.t^{ə}r'ɪs.tɪk, ˌ-ə- (US) -tə'rɪs- **-ally** -^{ə}l.i, -li
militarization, -isa- ˌmɪl.ɪ.t^{ə}r.aɪ'zeɪ.ʃ^{ə}n, ˌ-ə-, -ɪ'- (US) -tɚ.ɪ'-

militariz|e, -is|e ˈmɪl.ɪ.tᵊr.aɪz, ˈ-ə- ⓤⓢ -tə.raɪz **-es** -ɪz **-ing** -ɪŋ **-ed** -d
military ˈmɪl.ɪ.tri, ˈ-ə-, -tᵊr.i ⓤⓢ -ter- **ˌmilitary poˈlice**
mili|tate ˈmɪl.ɪ|.teɪt, ˈ-ə- **-tates** -teɪts **-tating** -teɪ.tɪŋ ⓤⓢ -teɪ.t̬ɪŋ **-tated** -teɪ.tɪd ⓤⓢ -teɪ.t̬ɪd
militia mɪˈlɪʃ.ə, mə- **-s** -z **-man** -mən **-men** -mən, -men
milk mɪlk **-s** -s **-ing** -ɪŋ **-ed** -t **-er/s** -əʳ/z ⓤⓢ -ɚ/z **ˌmilk ˈchocolate** ⓤⓢ **ˈmilk ˌchocolate; ˈmilk ˌfloat; ˌmilk of magˈnesia; ˈmilk ˌround; ˈmilk ˌrun; ˈmilk ˌshake; ˈmilk ˌtooth; ˈmilking maˌchine; it's ˌno good ˌcrying over ˌspilt ˈmilk**
milkfish ˈmɪlk.fɪʃ **-es** -ɪz
milkmaid ˈmɪlk.meɪd **-s** -z
milk|man ˈmɪlk|.mən ⓤⓢ -mæn, -mən **-men** -mən, -men
milksop ˈmɪlk.sɒp ⓤⓢ -sɑːp **-s** -s
milkwort ˈmɪlk.wɜːt ⓤⓢ -wɝːt, -wɔːrt **-s** -s
milk|y ˈmɪl.k|i **-ier** -i.əʳ ⓤⓢ -i.ɚ **-iest** -i.ɪst, -i.əst **-ily** -ɪ.li, -ᵊl.i **-iness** -ɪ.nəs, -ɪ.nɪs **ˌMilky ˈWay**
mill (M) mɪl **-s** -z **-ing** -ɪŋ **-ed** -d
Millais ˈmɪl.eɪ, -ˈ- ⓤⓢ mɪˈleɪ
Millar ˈmɪl.əʳ ⓤⓢ -ɚ
Millard ˈmɪl.əd, -ɑːd ⓤⓢ -ɚd
Millay mɪˈleɪ
Millbank ˈmɪl.bæŋk
millboard ˈmɪl.bɔːd ⓤⓢ -bɔːrd
millefeuille(s) ˌmiːlˈfɔɪ, -ˈfɜː.jə ⓤⓢ -ˈfɝː.jə
millenarian ˌmɪl.əˈneə.ri.ən, -ɪˈ- ⓤⓢ -əˈner.i- **-s** -z
millenarianism ˌmɪl.əˈneə.ri.ə.nɪ.zᵊm, -ɪˈ- ⓤⓢ -əˈner.i-
millenary mɪˈlen.ᵊr.i, mə- ⓤⓢ ˈmɪl.ə.ner-
millenni|um mɪˈlen.i|.əm, mə- ⓤⓢ mɪ- **-ums** -əmz **-a** -ə **-al** -əl
millepede ˈmɪl.ɪ.piːd, ˈ-ə- **-s** -z
miller (M) ˈmɪl.əʳ ⓤⓢ -ɚ **-s** -z
millesimal mɪˈles.ɪ.mᵊl, mə-, ˈ-ə- ⓤⓢ mɪˈles.ə- **-ly** -i
millet (M) ˈmɪl.ɪt
milliard ˌmɪl.iˈɑːd; mɪlˈjɑːd ⓤⓢ ˈmɪl.jɚd, -jɑːrd **-s** -z
millibar ˈmɪl.ɪ.bɑːʳ ⓤⓢ -bɑːr **-s** -z
Millicent ˈmɪl.ɪ.sᵊnt, ˈ-ə-
milligram(me) ˈmɪl.ɪ.græm **-s** -z
millilitre, milliliter ˈmɪl.ɪˌliː.təʳ, ˈ-ə- ⓤⓢ -t̬ɚ **-s** -z
millimetre, millimeter ˈmɪl.ɪˌmiː.təʳ, ˈ-ə- ⓤⓢ -t̬ɚ **-s** -z
milliner ˈmɪl.ɪ.nəʳ, ˈ-ə- ⓤⓢ -nɚ **-s** -z
millinery ˈmɪl.ɪ.nᵊr.i, ˈ-ə- ⓤⓢ -ner-
Millington ˈmɪl.ɪŋ.tən
million ˈmɪl.jən, -i.ən ⓤⓢ ˈ-jən **-s** -z **a ˌchance in a ˈmillion**
millionaire ˌmɪl.jəˈneəʳ, -i.əˈ- ⓤⓢ ˌ-jəˈner, ˈmɪl.jə.ner **-s** -z
millionairess ˌmɪl.jə.neəˈres, ˌ-i.ə-; -ˈneə.rɪs, -res ⓤⓢ -jəˈner.ɪs **-es** -ɪz
millionfold ˈmɪl.jən.fəʊld, -i.ən- ⓤⓢ -jən.foʊld
millionth ˈmɪl.jənʈθ, -i.ənʈθ ⓤⓢ ˈ-jənʈθ **-s** -s
millipede ˈmɪl.ɪ.piːd, ˈ-ə- **-s** -z
millisecond ˈmɪl.ɪˌsek.ənd, ˈ-ə- **-s** -z
Millom ˈmɪl.əm
millpond ˈmɪl.pɒnd ⓤⓢ -pɑːnd **-s** -z
millrac|e ˈmɪl.reɪs **-es** -ɪz
Mills mɪlz
millstone ˈmɪl.stəʊn ⓤⓢ -stoʊn **-s** -z
Milltimber ˈmɪlˌtɪm.bəʳ ⓤⓢ -bɚ
Millwall ˈmɪl.wɔːl, -wəl; mɪlˈwɔːl
Millward ˈmɪl.wɔːd, -wəd ⓤⓢ -wɚd
Milman ˈmɪl.mən
Milne mɪln, mɪl
Milner ˈmɪl.nəʳ ⓤⓢ -nɚ
Milnes mɪlz, mɪlnz
Milngavie mɪlˈgaɪ, mʌl-
Milnrow ˈmɪln.rəʊ ⓤⓢ -roʊ
Milo ˈmaɪ.ləʊ, ˈmiː- ⓤⓢ ˈmaɪ.loʊ
milometer maɪˈlɒm.ɪ.təʳ, ˈ-ə- ⓤⓢ -ˈlɑː.mə.t̬ɚ **-s** -z
milord mɪˈlɔːd, mə- ⓤⓢ -ˈlɔːrd **-s** -z
Milos ˈmiː.lɒs ⓤⓢ -lɑːs
Milosevic mɪˈlɒs.ə.vɪtʃ ⓤⓢ -ˈlɑː.sə-
Milosz ˈmiː.lɒʃ ⓤⓢ -lɑːʃ
milquetoast ˈmɪlk.təʊst ⓤⓢ -toʊst **-s** -s
Milton ˈmɪl.tᵊn
Miltonic mɪlˈtɒn.ɪk ⓤⓢ -ˈtɑː.nɪk
Milton Keynes ˌmɪl.tᵊnˈkiːnz
Milwaukee mɪlˈwɔː.ki, -iː ⓤⓢ -ˈwɑː-, -ˈwɔː-
mim|e maɪm **-es** -z **-ing** -ɪŋ **-ed** -d **-er/s** -əʳ/z ⓤⓢ -ɚ/z
mimeo ˈmɪm.i.əʊ ⓤⓢ -oʊ **-s** -z **-ing** -ɪŋ **-ed** -d
mimeograph ˈmɪm.i.əʊ.grɑːf, -græf ⓤⓢ -ə.græf **-s** -s **-ing** -ɪŋ **-ed** -t
mimesis mɪˈmiː.sɪs, maɪ-
mimetic mɪˈmet.ɪk, maɪ-
mimic ˈmɪm.ɪk **-s** -s **-king** -ɪŋ **-ked** -t **-ker/s** -əʳ/z ⓤⓢ -ɚ/z
mimicry ˈmɪm.ɪ.kri
mimosa mɪˈməʊ.zə, -sə ⓤⓢ -ˈmoʊ.sə, -zə **-s** -z
mimulus ˈmɪm.jə.ləs, -jʊ- ⓤⓢ -jə-, -juː- **-es** -ɪz
mina ˈmaɪ.nə **-s** -z
minaret ˌmɪn.əˈret, ˈ--- **-s** -s
minatory ˈmɪn.ə.tᵊr.i, ˈmaɪ- ⓤⓢ ˈmɪn.ə.tɔːr-
minc|e mɪnts **-es** -ɪz **-ing/ly** -ɪŋ/li **-ed** -t **-er/s** -əʳ/z ⓤⓢ -ɚ/z **ˌmince ˈpie**
mincemeat ˈmɪnts.miːt **make ˈmincemeat of ˌsomeone**
Minch mɪntʃ **-es** -ɪz
mind maɪnd **-s** -z **-ing** -ɪŋ **-ed** -ɪd **ˈmind ˌreader; ˌmind's ˈeye; ˌgive someone a ˌpiece of one's ˈmind**
Mindanao ˌmɪn.dəˈnaʊ ⓤⓢ -ˈnaʊ, -ˈnɑː.oʊ
mind-blowing ˈmaɪndˌbləʊ.ɪŋ ⓤⓢ -ˌbloʊ- **-ly** -li
mind-boggling ˈmaɪndˌbɒg.l̩.ɪŋ, ˈmaɪm-, -ˌbɒg.lɪŋ ⓤⓢ ˈmaɪndˌbɑː.glɪŋ, -ˌbɑː.gl̩.ɪŋ **-ly** -li
minder ˈmaɪn.dəʳ ⓤⓢ -dɚ **-s** -z
mind-expanding ˈmaɪnd.ɪkˌspæn.dɪŋ, -ekˌ- ⓤⓢ -ekˌ-, -ɪkˌ-
mindful ˈmaɪnd.fᵊl, -fʊl **-ly** -i **-ness** -nəs, -nɪs
mindless ˈmaɪnd.ləs, -lɪs **-ly** -li **-ness** -nəs, -nɪs
mind-set ˈmaɪnd.set
Mindy ˈmɪn.di
min|e maɪn **-es** -z **-ing** -ɪŋ **-ed** -d
minefield ˈmaɪn.fiːld **-s** -z
Minehead ˈmaɪn.hed, ˌ-ˈ-
Minelli mɪˈnel.i, mə-
miner ˈmaɪ.nəʳ ⓤⓢ -nɚ **-s** -z
mineral ˈmɪn.ᵊr.ᵊl **-s** -z **ˈmineral ˌwater**
mineraliz|e, -is|e ˈmɪn.ᵊr.ᵊl.aɪz **-es** -ɪz **-ing** -ɪŋ **-ed** -d
mineralogical ˌmɪn.ᵊr.əˈlɒdʒ.ɪ.kᵊl ⓤⓢ -ˈlɑː.dʒɪ- **-ly** -i
mineralog|y ˌmɪn.ᵊrˈæl.ə.dʒ|i ⓤⓢ -əˈrɑː.lə-, -ˈræl.ə- **-ist/s** -ɪst/s
Minerva mɪˈnɜː.və ⓤⓢ məˈnɝː-
minestrone ˌmɪn.ɪˈstrəʊ.ni, -əˈ- ⓤⓢ -əˈstroʊ-
minesweep|er ˈmaɪnˌswiː.p|əʳ ⓤⓢ -p|ɚ **-ers** -əz ⓤⓢ -ɚz **-ing** -ɪŋ
Ming mɪŋ
Minghella mɪŋˈgel.ə
mingl|e ˈmɪŋ.gl̩ **-es** -z **-ing** -ɪŋ, ˈmɪŋ.glɪŋ **-ed** -d
mingogram ˈmɪŋ.gəʊ.græm, -əʊ- ⓤⓢ -gə- **-s** -z
mingograph® ˈmɪŋ.gəʊ.grɑːf, -əʊ-, -græf ⓤⓢ -gə.græf **-s** -s
Mingus ˈmɪŋ.gəs
ming|y ˈmɪn.dʒ|i **-ier** -i.əʳ ⓤⓢ -i.ɚ **-iest** -i.ɪst, -i.əst
mini (M®) ˈmɪn.i **-s** -z
miniature ˈmɪn.ə.tʃəʳ, ˈ-ɪ- ⓤⓢ ˈ-i.ə.tʃɚ, ˈ-ə.tʃɚ **-s** -z
miniaturist ˈmɪn.ə.tʃᵊr.ɪst, ˈ-ɪ-, -tjʊə.rɪst ⓤⓢ ˈ-i.ə.tʃɚ.ɪst, ˈ-ə.tʃɚ- **-s** -s
miniaturization, -isa- ˌmɪn.ə.tʃᵊr.aɪˈzeɪ.ʃᵊn, ˌ-ɪ- ⓤⓢ -i.ə.tʃɚ.ɪˈ-, -ə.tʃɚ- **-s** -z
miniaturiz|e, -is|e ˈmɪn.ə.tʃᵊr.aɪz, ˈ-ɪ- ⓤⓢ ˈ-i.ə.tʃɚ-, ˈ-ə.tʃɚ- **-es** -ɪz **-ing** -ɪŋ **-ed** -d
minibus ˈmɪn.ɪ.bʌs ⓤⓢ mɪn.i- **-es** -ɪz
minicab ˈmɪn.ɪ.kæb ⓤⓢ mɪn.i- **-s** -z
minicam ˈmɪn.ɪ.kæm ⓤⓢ mɪn.i- **-s** -z
minicomputer ˈmɪn.ɪ.kəmˌpjuː.təʳ,

ˌmɪn.ɪ.kəmˈpjuː- US mɪn.i-, -ˈpjuː.t̬ɚ **-s** -z
minim **(M)** ˈmɪn.ɪm **-s** -z
minimal ˈmɪn.ɪ.məl, ˈ-ə- **-ly** -i
minimal|ism ˈmɪn.ɪ.məl|.ɪ.zəm, ˈ-ə- **-ist/s** -ɪst/s
minimization ˌmɪn.ɪ.maɪˈzeɪ.ʃən, ˌ-ə-, -mɪˈ- US -mɪˈ-
minimiz|e, -is|e ˈmɪn.ɪ.maɪz, ˈ-ə- **-es** -ɪz **-ing** -ɪŋ **-ed** -d
minim|um ˈmɪn.ɪ.m|əm **-a** -ə **-ums** ˌ**minimum** ˈ**wage**
mining ˈmaɪ.nɪŋ
minion ˈmɪn.jən **-s** -z
minipill ˈmɪn.ɪ.pɪl
miniseries ˈmɪn.ɪˌsɪə.rɪz, -riːz US mɪn.i-, -ˌsɪr.iːz
minish ˈmɪn.ɪʃ **-es** -ɪz **-ing** -ɪŋ **-ed** -t
miniskirt ˈmɪn.ɪ.skɜːt US mɪn.i-, -skɝːt **-s** -s **-ed** -ɪd
minist|er ˈmɪn.ɪ.st|əʳ, ˈ-ə- US -st|ɚ **-ers** -əz US -ɚz **-ering** -ər.ɪŋ **-ered** -əd US -ɚd
ministerial ˌmɪn.ɪˈstɪə.ri.əl, -əˈ- US -ˈstɪr.i- **-ly** -i
ministration ˌmɪn.ɪˈstreɪ.ʃən, -əˈ- **-s** -z
ministr|y ˈmɪn.ɪ.str|i, ˈ-ə- **-ies** -iz
minivan ˈmɪn.i.væn US -i- **-s** -z
miniver **(M)** ˈmɪn.ɪ.vəʳ, ˈ-ə- US -vɚ
mink mɪŋk **-s** -s
minke ˈmɪŋ.ki, -kə US -kə **-s** -z
Minn. *(abbrev. for* **Minnesota***)* ˌmɪn.ɪˈsəʊ.tə, -əˈ- US -ˈsoʊ.t̬ə
Minneapolis ˌmɪn.iˈæp.əl.ɪs
Minnehaha ˌmɪn.iˈhɑː.hɑː
Minnelli mɪˈnel.i, mə-
minneola ˌmɪn.iˈəʊ.lə US -ˈoʊ- **-s** -z
minnesinger ˈmɪn.ɪˌsɪŋ.əʳ, -əˌ-, -gəʳ US -sɪŋ.ɚ **-s** -z
Minnesot|a ˌmɪn.ɪˈsəʊ.t|ə, -əˈ- US -ˈsoʊ.t̬|ə **-an/s** -ən/z
Minnie ˈmɪn.i
minnow ˈmɪn.əʊ US -oʊ **-s** -z
Minoan mɪˈnəʊ.ən, mə-, maɪ- US mɪ-
Minogue mɪˈnəʊg, mə- US -ˈnoʊg
Minolta® mɪˈnɒl.tə, mə-, -ˈnəʊl- US -ˈnoʊl-, -ˈnɑːl-
minor ˈmaɪ.nəʳ US -nɚ **-s** -z **-ing** -ɪŋ **-ed** -d
Minorca mɪˈnɔː.kə, mə- US -ˈnɔːr-
Minories ˈmɪn.ər.iz
minorit|y maɪˈnɒr.ə.t|i, mɪ-, mə-, -ɪ.t|i US maɪˈnɔːr.ə.t̬|i, mɪ- **-ies** -iz
Minos ˈmaɪ.nɒs US -nɑːs, -nəs
Minotaur ˈmaɪ.nə.tɔːʳ US ˈmɪn.ə.tɔːr **-s** -z
Minsk mɪntsk
Minsmere ˈmɪnz.mɪəʳ US -mɪr
minster **(M)** ˈmɪn.stəʳ US -stɚ **-s** -z
minstrel ˈmɪnt.strəl **-s** -z
minstrel|sy ˈmɪnt.strəl|.si **-sies** -siz
mint mɪnt **-s** -s **-ing** -ɪŋ US ˈmɪn.t̬ɪŋ **-ed** -ɪd US ˈmɪn.t̬ɪd **-age** -ɪdʒ US ˈmɪn.t̬ɪdʒ ˌ**mint con**ˈ**dition**; ˌ**mint** ˈ**julep**; ˌ**mint** ˈ**sauce** US ˈ**mint** ˌ**sauce**
Mintel ˈmɪn.tel
Minto ˈmɪn.təʊ US -toʊ
Mintoff ˈmɪn.tɒf US -tɑːf
minuet ˌmɪn.juˈet **-s** -s
minus ˈmaɪ.nəs **-es** -ɪz
minuscule ˈmɪn.ə.skjuːl, ˈ-ɪ- US ˈ-ɪ-; mɪˈnʌs.kjuːl **-s** -z
minu|te *very small:* maɪˈnjuː|t US -ˈnuː|t, -ˈnjuː|t **-test** -tɪst, -təst US -t̬ɪst, -t̬əst **-tely** -t.li **-teness** -t.nəs, -t.nɪs
minute *(n.) division of time, angle, memorandum:* ˈmɪn.ɪt **-s** -s
min|ute *(v.)* ˈmɪn|.ɪt **-utes** -ɪts **-uting** -ɪ.tɪŋ US -ɪ.t̬ɪŋ **-uted** -ɪ.tɪd US -ɪ.t̬ɪd
minute-gun ˈmɪn.ɪt.gʌn **-s** -z
minute-hand ˈmɪn.ɪt.hænd **-s** -z
minute|man **(M)** ˈmɪn.ɪt|.mæn **-men** -men
minuti|a maɪˈnjuː.ʃi|.ə, mɪ-, mə-, -ˈnuː-, -ti- US mɪˈnuː.ʃi-, -ˈnjuː-, ˈ-ʃ|ə **-ae** -iː, -aɪ
minx mɪŋks **-es** -ɪz
Miocene ˈmaɪ.əʊ.siːn US ˈ-oʊ-, ˈ-ə-
mios|is maɪˈəʊ.s|ɪs US -ˈoʊ- **-es** -iːz
miotic maɪˈɒt.ɪk US -ˈɑː.t̬ɪk **-s** -s
mips, MIPS mɪps
Mir mɪəʳ US mɪr
Mira ˈmaɪə.rə, ˈmɪr.ə US ˈmaɪ.rə
Mirabell ˈmɪr.ə.bel
miracle ˈmɪr.ə.kl̩, ˈ-ɪ- **-s** -z
miraculous mɪˈræk.jə.ləs, mə-, -jʊ- US mɪˈræk.jə.ləs, -juː- **-ly** -li **-ness** -nəs, -nɪs
mirag|e ˈmɪr.ɑːʒ; məˈrɑːʒ, mɪˈ- US mɪˈrɑːʒ, mə- **-es** -ɪz
Miramax ˈmɪr.ə.mæks
Miranda mɪˈræn.də US mə-, mɪ-
MIRAS ˈmaɪə.rəs, -ræs US ˈmaɪ-
mir|e maɪəʳ US maɪr **-es** **-ing** **-ed**
Mirfield ˈmɜː.fiːld US ˈmɝː-
Miriam ˈmɪr.i.əm
mirk|y ˈmɜː.k|i US ˈmɝː- **-ier** -i.əʳ US -i.ɚ **-iest** -i.ɪst, -i.əst **-ily** -ɪ.li, -əl.i **-iness** -ɪ.nəs, -ɪ.nɪs
Miró mɪˈrəʊ US miːˈroʊ
Mirren ˈmɪr.ən
mirr|or ˈmɪr|.əʳ US -ɚ **-ors** -əz US -ɚz **-oring** -ər.ɪŋ **-ored** -əd US -ɚd ˌ**mirror** ˈ**image**
mirth mɜːθ US mɝːθ
mirthful ˈmɜːθ.fəl, -fʊl US ˈmɝːθ- **-ly** -i **-ness** -nəs, -nɪs
mirthless ˈmɜːθ.ləs, -lɪs US ˈmɝːθ- **-ly** -li **-ness** -nəs, -nɪs
MIRV mɜːv US mɝːv **-s** -z **-ing** -ɪŋ **-ed** -d
mir|y ˈmaɪə.r|i **-ier** -i.əʳ US -i.ɚ **-iest** -i.ɪst, -i.əst **-iness** -ɪ.nəs, -ɪ.nɪs
mis- mɪs-
Note: Prefix. In words containing **mis-**, the prefix may either be unstressed, e.g. **misdeal** /mɪsˈdiːl/, or receive secondary stress, especially if the stem is stressed on its second syllable, e.g. **align** /əˈlaɪn/, **misalign** /ˌmɪs.əˈlaɪn/. There is sometimes a difference between nouns and verbs, e.g. **miscount**, noun /ˈmɪs.kaʊnt/, verb /mɪˈskaʊnt/. There are exceptions; see individual entries.
misadventure ˌmɪs.ədˈven.tʃəʳ US -tʃɚ **-s** -z
misalign ˌmɪs.əˈlaɪn **-s** -z **-ing** -ɪŋ **-d** -d
misalignment ˌmɪs.əˈlaɪn.mənt, -ˈlaɪm- US -ˈlaɪn- **-s** -s
misallianc|e ˌmɪs.əˈlaɪ.ənts **-es** -ɪz
misandry mɪˈsæn.dri; ˈmɪs.ən- US ˈmɪs.æn-
misanthrope ˈmɪs.ən.θrəʊp, ˈmɪz-, -æn- US -ən.θroʊp **-s** -s
misanthropic ˌmɪs.ənˈθrɒp.ɪk, ˌmɪz-, -ænˈ- US -ənˈθrɑː.pɪk **-al** -əl **-ally** -əl.i, -li
misanthrop|y mɪˈsæn.θrə.p|i, -ˈzæn- **-ist/s** -ɪst/s
misapplication ˌmɪs.æp.lɪˈkeɪ.ʃən, -ləˈ- **-s** -z
misappl|y ˌmɪs.əˈpl|aɪ **-ies** -aɪz **-ying** -aɪ.ɪŋ **-ied** -aɪd
misapprehend ˌmɪs.æp.rɪˈhend, -rəˈ- **-s** -z **-ing** -ɪŋ **-ed** -ɪd
misapprehension ˌmɪs.æp.rɪˈhen.tʃən, -rəˈ- **-s** -z
misappropri|ate ˌmɪs.əˈprəʊ.pri|.eɪt US -ˈproʊ- **-ates** -eɪts **-ating** -eɪ.tɪŋ US -eɪ.t̬ɪŋ **-ated** -eɪ.tɪd US -eɪ.t̬ɪd
misappropriation ˌmɪs.əˌprəʊ.priˈeɪ.ʃən US -ˌproʊ- **-s** -z
misbecoming ˌmɪs.bɪˈkʌm.ɪŋ, -bəˈ-
misbegotten ˌmɪs.bɪˈgɒt.ən, -bəˈ-, ˈmɪs.bɪˌgɒt-, -bəˌ- US ˌmɪs.bɪˈgɑː.tən
misbehav|e ˌmɪs.bɪˈheɪv, -bəˈ- **-es** -z **-ing** -ɪŋ **-ed** -d
misbehavio(u)r ˌmɪs.bɪˈheɪ.vjəʳ, -bəˈ- US -vjɚ **-s** -z
misbelief ˌmɪs.bɪˈliːf, -bəˈ-, ˈ--- US ˌ--ˈ-
misbeliev|e ˌmɪs.bɪˈliːv, -bəˈ-, ˈ--- US ˌ--ˈ- **-es** -z **-ing** -ɪŋ **-ed** -d **-er/s** -əʳ/z US -ɚ/z
misc. *(abbrev. for* **miscellaneous***)* ˌmɪs.əlˈeɪ.ni.əs
miscalcu|late mɪsˈkæl.kjə|.leɪt, -kjʊ-; ˌmɪsˈkæl- US -kjə-, -kjuː- **-lates** -leɪts **-lating** -leɪ.tɪŋ US -leɪ.t̬ɪŋ **-lated** -leɪ.tɪd US -leɪ.t̬ɪd
miscalculation ˌmɪs.kæl.kjəˈleɪ.ʃən, -kjʊˈ- US -kjəˈ-, -kjuːˈ- **-s** -z
miscall mɪˈskɔːl; ˌmɪsˈkɔːl US mɪsˈkɔːl, -ˈkɑːl; ˌmɪsˈkɔːl, -ˈkɑːl **-s** -z **-ing** -ɪŋ **-ed** -d

miscarriag|e ˈmɪsˌkær.ɪdʒ; -ˈ-- ⓤⓢ ˈmɪsˌker-, -ˌkær-; mɪˈsker-, -ˈskær-; ˌmɪsˈker-, -ˈkær- **-es** -ɪz
miscarr|y mɪˈskær|.i; ˌmɪsˈkær- ⓤⓢ ˈmɪsˌker-, -ˌkær-; mɪˈsker-, -ˈskær-; ˌmɪsˈker-, -ˈkær- **-ies** -iz **-ying** -i.ɪŋ **-ied** -id
miscast mɪˈskɑːst; ˌmɪsˈkɑːst ⓤⓢ mɪˈskæst; ˌmɪsˈkæst **-s** -s **-ing** -ɪŋ
miscegenation ˌmɪs.ɪ.dʒɪˈneɪ.ʃᵊn, ˌ-ə-, ˌ-e-, -dʒəˈ- ⓤⓢ -edʒ.əˈ-; -ɪ.dʒəˈ- **-al** -ᵊl
miscellanea ˌmɪs.ᵊlˈeɪ.ni.ə
miscellaneous ˌmɪs.ᵊlˈeɪ.ni.əs, -ɪˈleɪ- **-ly** -li **-ness** -nəs, -nɪs
miscellan|y mɪˈsel.ə.n|i ⓤⓢ ˈmɪs.ə.leɪ- **-ies** -iz
mischanc|e mɪsˈtʃɑːnts, ˌmɪs-, ˈ-- ⓤⓢ mɪsˈtʃænts, ˌmɪs-, ˈ-- **-es** -ɪz
mischief ˈmɪs.tʃɪf, -tʃiːf ⓤⓢ -tʃɪf **-s** -s
mischief-mak|er ˈmɪs.tʃɪfˌmeɪ.k|əʳ ⓤⓢ -k|ɚ **-ers** -əz ⓤⓢ -ɚz **-ing** -ɪŋ
mischievous ˈmɪs.tʃɪ.vəs, -tʃə- ⓤⓢ -tʃə- **-ly** -li **-ness** -nəs, -nɪs
miscibility ˌmɪs.ɪˈbɪl.ɪ.ti, -əˈ-, ˈ-ə- ⓤⓢ -əˈbɪl.ə.t̬i
miscible ˈmɪs.ɪ.bl̩, ˈ-ə- ⓤⓢ ˈ-ə-
misconceiv|e ˌmɪs.kənˈsiːv **-es** -z **-ing** -ɪŋ **-ed** -d
misconception ˌmɪs.kənˈsep.ʃᵊn **-s** -z
misconduct (*n.*) mɪˈskɒn.dʌkt; ˌmɪsˈkɒn-, -dəkt ⓤⓢ mɪˈskɑːn.dʌkt; ˌmɪsˈkɑːn-
misconduct (*v.*) ˌmɪs.kənˈdʌkt **-s** -s **-ing** -ɪŋ **-ed** -ɪd
misconstruction ˌmɪs.kənˈstrʌk.ʃᵊn **-s** -z
misconstru|e ˌmɪs.kənˈstruː, -kɒnˈ- ⓤⓢ -kənˈ- **-es** -z **-ing** -ɪŋ **-ed** -d
miscount (*n.*) ˈmɪs.kaʊnt **-s** -s
miscoun|t (*v.*) mɪˈskaʊn|t; **-ts** -ts **-ting** -tɪŋ ⓤⓢ -t̬ɪŋ **-ted** -tɪd ⓤⓢ -t̬ɪd
miscreant ˈmɪs.kri.ənt **-s** -s
miscu|e mɪˈskjuː; ˌmɪsˈkjuː ⓤⓢ mɪˈskjuː; ˌmɪsˈkjuː, ˈ-- **-es** -z **-ing** -ɪŋ **-ed** -d
misdeal mɪsˈdiːl, ˌ-ˈ- ⓤⓢ mɪsˈdiːl, ˌ-ˈ-, ˈ-- **-s** -z **-ing** -ɪŋ **misdealt** -ˈdelt, ˌ-ˈ- ⓤⓢ -ˈ-, ˌ-ˈ-, ˈ--
misdeed mɪsˈdiːd, ˌ-ˈ-, ˈ-- **-s** -z
misdemeano(u)r ˌmɪs.dɪˈmiː.nəʳ, -dəˈ- ⓤⓢ -nɚ, ˈ-ˌ--- **-s** -z
misdiagnos|e mɪsˈdaɪəg.nəʊz, ˌ-ˈ--- ⓤⓢ ˌmɪs.daɪ.əgˈnoʊs, -ˈnoʊz; -ˈ---, ˌ-ˈ---, -noʊz **-es** -ɪz **-ing** -ɪŋ **-ed** -d
misdiagnos|is ˌmɪs.daɪəgˈnəʊ.s|ɪs ⓤⓢ -ˈnoʊ-
misdirect ˌmɪs.dɪˈrekt, -dəˈ-, -daɪəˈ- ⓤⓢ -dəˈ-, -daɪˈ- **-s** -s **-ing** -ɪŋ **-ed** -ɪd
misdirection ˌmɪs.dɪˈrek.ʃᵊn, -dəˈ-, -daɪəˈ- ⓤⓢ -dəˈ-, -daɪˈ-
misdoing mɪsˈduː.ɪŋ, ˌmɪs- **-s** -z
mise-en-scène ˌmiːz.ɑ̃ːnˈseɪn, -ˈsen ⓤⓢ -ɑ̃ːnˈsen **mise-en-scènes** ˌmiːz.ɑ̃ːnˈseɪn, -ˈsen, -z ⓤⓢ -ɑ̃ːnˈsen, -z
miser ˈmaɪ.zəʳ ⓤⓢ -zɚ **-s** -z
miserab|le ˈmɪz.ᵊr.ə.b|l̩, ˈmɪz.rə- **-ly** -li **-leness** -l̩.nəs, -nɪs
miserere ˌmɪz.ᵊrˈeə.ri, -ˈɪə-, -reɪ ⓤⓢ -ˈrer.eɪ **-s** -z
misericord mɪˈzer.ɪ.kɔːd, mə-, ˈ-ə-; ˈmɪz.ᵊr.ɪ- ⓤⓢ -kɔːrd **-s** -z
miserl|y ˈmaɪ.zᵊl|.i ⓤⓢ -zɚ.l|i **-iness** -ɪ.nəs, -ɪ.nɪs
miser|y ˈmɪz.ᵊr|.i ⓤⓢ ˈ-r|i, ˈ-ɚ|.i **-ies** -iz
misfeasance mɪsˈfiː.zᵊnts ⓤⓢ ˌmɪs-
misfire (*n.*) mɪsˈfaɪəʳ, ˌmɪs-, ˈ-- ⓤⓢ ˈmɪs.faɪɚ
misfir|e (*v.*) mɪsˈfaɪəʳ, ˌmɪs- ⓤⓢ -ˈfaɪɚ **-es** -z **-ing** -ɪŋ **-ed** -d
misfit (*n.*) ˈmɪs.fɪt **-s** -s
misfortune mɪsˈfɔː.tʃuːn, ˌmɪs-, -tʃən, -tjuːn ⓤⓢ -ˈfɔːr.tʃən **-s** -z
misgiving mɪsˈgɪv.ɪŋ, ˌmɪs- **-s** -z
misgovern mɪsˈgʌv.ᵊn, ˌmɪs- ⓤⓢ -ɚn **-s** -z **-ing** -ɪŋ **-ed** -d **-ment** -mənt
misguided mɪsˈgaɪ.dɪd, ˌmɪs- **-ly** -li **-ness** -nəs, -nɪs
mishandl|e mɪsˈhæn.dl̩, ˌmɪs- **-es** -z **-ing** -ɪŋ, -ˈhænd.lɪŋ **-ed** -d
mishap ˈmɪs.hæp, -ˈ-, ˌ-ˈ- ⓤⓢ ˈmɪs.hæp **-s** -s
mis|hear mɪs|ˈhɪəʳ, ˌmɪs- ⓤⓢ -ˈhɪr **-hears** -ˈhɪəz ⓤⓢ -ˈhɪrz **-hearing** -ˈhɪə.rɪŋ ⓤⓢ -ˈhɪr.ɪŋ **-heard** -ˈhɜːd ⓤⓢ -ˈhɝːd
Mishima ˈmɪʃ.ɪ.mə; mɪˈʃiː- ⓤⓢ ˈmɪʃ.ɪ-, ˈmiː.ʃɪ-
mis|hit mɪs|ˈhɪt, ˌmɪs- **-hits** -ˈhɪts **-hitting** -ˈhɪt.ɪŋ ⓤⓢ -ˈhɪt̬.ɪŋ
mishmash ˈmɪʃ.mæʃ
misinform ˌmɪs.ɪnˈfɔːm ⓤⓢ -ˈfɔːrm **-s** -z **-ing** -ɪŋ **-ed** -d **-ant/s** -ənt/s **-er/s** -əʳ/z ⓤⓢ -ɚ/z
misinformation ˌmɪs.ɪn.fəˈmeɪ.ʃᵊn ⓤⓢ -fɚˈ-
misinter|pret ˌmɪs.ɪnˈtɜː|.prɪt ⓤⓢ -ˈtɝː- **-prets** -prɪts **-preting** -prɪ.tɪŋ ⓤⓢ -prɪ.t̬ɪŋ **-preted** -prɪ.tɪd ⓤⓢ -prɪ.t̬ɪd
misinterpretation ˌmɪs.ɪnˌtɜː.prɪˈteɪ.ʃᵊn, -prəˈ- ⓤⓢ -ˌtɝː.prɪˈ- **-s** -z
misjoinder mɪsˈdʒɔɪn.dəʳ, ˌmɪs- ⓤⓢ -dɚ
misjudg|e mɪsˈdʒʌdʒ, ˌmɪs- **-es** -ɪz **-ing** -ɪŋ **-ed** -d
misjudg(e)ment mɪsˈdʒʌdʒ.mənt, ˌmɪs- **-s** -s
Miskolc ˈmɪʃ.kəʊlts ⓤⓢ -koʊlts
mislay mɪˈsleɪ, ˌmɪsˈleɪ **-s** -z **-ing** -ɪŋ **mislaid** mɪˈsleɪd, ˌmɪsˈleɪd
mislead mɪˈsliːd, ˌmɪsˈliːd **-s** -z **-ing/ly** -ɪŋ/li **misled** mɪˈsled, ˌmɪsˈled
mismanag|e ˌmɪsˈmæn.ɪdʒ **-es** -ɪz **-ing** -ɪŋ **-ed** -d **-ement** -mənt
mismatch (*n.*) ˈmɪs.mætʃ; -ˈ-, ˌ-ˈ- **-es** -ɪz
mismatch (*v.*) mɪˈsmætʃ; ˌmɪsˈmætʃ, ˈ-- ⓤⓢ mɪˈsmætʃ; ˌmɪsˈmætʃ **-es** -ɪs **-ing** -ɪŋ **-ed** -t
misnomer mɪˈsnəʊ.məʳ; ˌmɪsˈnəʊ- ⓤⓢ mɪˈsnoʊ.mɚ, ˌmɪsˈnoʊ- **-s** -z
miso ˈmiː.səʊ ⓤⓢ -soʊ
misogynist mɪˈsɒdʒ.ᵊn.ɪst, maɪ-, mə- ⓤⓢ -ˈsɑːdʒ- **-s** -s
misogynistic mɪˌsɒdʒ.ᵊnˈɪs.tɪk, maɪ-, mə-, -dʒɪˈnɪs- ⓤⓢ -ˌɑː.dʒɪˈ-
misogyn|y mɪˈsɒdʒ.ɪ.n|i, maɪ-, mə- ⓤⓢ -sɑːdʒ-
misplac|e mɪˈspleɪs, ˌmɪsˈpleɪs **-es** -ɪz **-ing** -ɪŋ **-ed** -t **-ement** -mənt *stress shift:* ˌmisplaced ˈtrust
misprint (*n.*) ˈmɪs.prɪnt **-s** -s
misprin|t (*v.*) mɪˈsprɪn|t; ˌmɪsˈprɪn|t **-ts** -ts **-ting** -tɪŋ ⓤⓢ -t̬ɪŋ **-ted** -tɪd ⓤⓢ -t̬ɪd
misprision mɪˈsprɪʒ.ᵊn
mispronounc|e ˌmɪs.prəˈnaʊnts ⓤⓢ -prəˈ-, -proʊˈ- **-es** -ɪz **-ing** -ɪŋ **-ed** -t
mispronunciation ˌmɪs.prəˌnʌnt.siˈeɪ.ʃən ⓤⓢ -prəˌ-, -proʊˌ- **-s** -z
misquotation ˌmɪs.kwəʊˈteɪ.ʃᵊn ⓤⓢ -kwoʊˈ- **-s** -z
misquo|te mɪˈskwəʊ|t; ˌmɪsˈkwəʊ|t ⓤⓢ mɪˈskwoʊ|t; ˌmɪsˈkwoʊ|t **-tes** -ts **-ting** -tɪŋ ⓤⓢ -t̬ɪŋ **-ted** -tɪd ⓤⓢ -t̬ɪd
Misratah ˈmɪs.ræt.ɑː
misread mɪsˈriːd, ˌmɪs- **-s** -z **-ing** -ɪŋ *past tense:* mɪsˈred, ˌmɪs-
misrememb|er ˌmɪs.rɪˈmem.b|əʳ, -rəˈ- ⓤⓢ -b|ɚ **-ers** -əz ⓤⓢ -ɚz **-ering** -ᵊr.ɪŋ **-ered** -əd ⓤⓢ -ɚd
misre|port ˌmɪs.rɪ|ˈpɔːt ⓤⓢ -ˈpɔːrt **-ports** -ˈpɔːts ⓤⓢ -ˈpɔːrts **-porting** -ˈpɔː.tɪŋ ⓤⓢ -ˈpɔːr.t̬ɪŋ **-ported** -ˈpɔː.tɪd ⓤⓢ -ˈpɔːr.t̬ɪd
misrepre|sent ˌmɪs.rep.rɪ|ˈzent **-sents** -ˈzents **-senting** -ˈzen.tɪŋ ⓤⓢ -ˈzen.t̬ɪŋ **-sented** -ˈzen.tɪd ⓤⓢ -ˈzen.t̬ɪd
misrepresentation ˌmɪs.rep.rɪ.zenˈteɪ.ʃᵊn, -zᵊnˈ- ⓤⓢ -zenˈ- **-s** -z
misrule mɪsˈruːl, ˌmɪs-
miss (M) mɪs **-es** -ɪz **-ing** -ɪŋ **-ed** -t
Miss. (*abbrev. for* **Mississippi**) ˌmɪs.ɪˈsɪp.i ⓤⓢ -əˈ-, -ɪˈ-
missal ˈmɪs.ᵊl **-s** -z
missel thrush ˈmɪz.ᵊlˌθrʌʃ, ˈmɪs-
Missenden ˈmɪs.ᵊn.dən
misshapen mɪsˈʃeɪ.pᵊn, ˌmɪs-, mɪʃ-, ˌmɪʃ- **-ly** -li
missile ˈmɪs.aɪl ⓤⓢ -ᵊl **-s** -z
missing ˈmɪs.ɪŋ
mission ˈmɪʃ.ᵊn **-s** -z
missionar|y ˈmɪʃ.ᵊn.ᵊr|.i, ˈmɪʃ.nᵊr- ⓤⓢ ˈ-ᵊn.er- **-ies** -iz ˈ**missionary po**ˌ**sition**

missioner ˈmɪʃ.ən.əʳ ⓤⓢ -ɚ **-s** -z
missis ˈmɪs.ɪz
Mississippi ˌmɪs.ɪˈsɪp.i ⓤⓢ -əˈ-, -ɪˈ- **-an/s** -ən/z
missive ˈmɪs.ɪv **-s** -z
Missoula mɪˈzuː.lə
Missouri mɪˈzʊə.ri, -ˈsʊə- ⓤⓢ -ˈzʊr.i *locally:* -ə
misspell mɪsˈspel, ˌmɪs- **-s** -z **-ing/s** -ɪŋ/z **-ed** -t, -d **misspelt** mɪsˈspelt ⓤⓢ ˌmɪs-
misspend mɪsˈspend, ˌmɪs **-s** -z **-ing** -ɪŋ **misspent** mɪsˈspent, ˌmɪs- ˌ**misspent** ˈ**youth**
mis|state mɪsˈsteɪt, ˌmɪs- **-states** -ˈsteɪts **-stating** -ˈsteɪ.tɪŋ ⓤⓢ -ˈsteɪ.t̬ɪŋ **-stated** -ˈsteɪ.tɪd ⓤⓢ -ˈsteɪ.t̬ɪd **-statement/s** -ˈsteɪt.mənt/s
missus ˈmɪs.ɪz, -ɪs
miss|y ˈmɪs|.i **-ies** -iz
mist mɪst **-s** -s **-ing** -ɪŋ **-ed** -ɪd **-er/s** -əʳ/z, -ɚ/z
mistak|e mɪˈsteɪk **-es** -s **-ing** -ɪŋ **mistook** mɪˈstʊk
mistak(e)able mɪˈsteɪ.kə.bl̩
mistaken mɪˈsteɪ.kən **-ly** -li
mister (M) ˈmɪs.təʳ ⓤⓢ -tɚ
mistim|e mɪsˈtaɪm; ˌmɪs- **-es** -z **-ing** -ɪŋ **-ed** -d
mistle thrush ˈmɪs.l̩ˌθrʌʃ, ˈmɪz- ⓤⓢ ˈmɪs-
mistletoe ˈmɪs.l̩.təʊ, ˈmɪz- ⓤⓢ ˈmɪs.l̩.toʊ
mistook *(from* **mistake***)* mɪˈstʊk
mistral (M) ˈmɪs.trəl, -trɑːl; mɪˈstrɑːl ⓤⓢ mɪˈstrɑːl; ˈmɪs.trəl **-s** -z
mistransla|te ˌmɪs.trænˈsleɪ|t, -trɑːn-, -trən-; -trænzˈleɪ|t, -trɑːnzˈ-, -trənzˈ- ⓤⓢ ˌmɪsˈtræn.sleɪ|t, -ˈtrænz.leɪ|t; mɪs.trænˈsleɪ|t; -trænzˈleɪ|t **-tes** -ts **-ting** -tɪŋ ⓤⓢ -t̬ɪŋ **-ted** -tɪd ⓤⓢ -t̬ɪd
mistranslation ˌmɪs.trænˈsleɪ.ʃən, -trɑːnˈ-, -trənˈ-; -trænzˈleɪ-, -trænzˈ-, -trənzˈ- ⓤⓢ -trænˈsleɪ-; -trænzˈleɪ- **-s** -z
mistrea|t mɪsˈtriː|t; ˌmɪs- **-ts** -ts **-ting** -tɪŋ ⓤⓢ -t̬ɪŋ **-ted** -tɪd ⓤⓢ -t̬ɪd
mistreatment mɪsˈtriːt.mənt; ˌmɪs-
mistress ˈmɪs.trəs, -trɪs ⓤⓢ -trɪs **-es** -ɪz
mistrial mɪˈstraɪəl; ˌmɪsˈtraɪ- ⓤⓢ ˈmɪsˌtraɪ-; mɪˈstraɪ-; ˌmɪsˈtraɪ- **-s** -z
mistrust mɪˈstrʌst; ˌmɪsˈtrʌst ⓤⓢ ˌmɪsˈtrʌst; mɪˈstrʌst; ˈmɪs.trʌst **-s** -s **-ing** -ɪŋ **-ed** -ɪd
mistrustful mɪˈstrʌs*t*.fəl, ˌmɪsˈtrʌs*t*- **-ly** -li
mist|y (M) ˈmɪs.t|i **-ier** -i.əʳ ⓤⓢ -i.ɚ **-iest** -i.ɪst, -i.əst **-ily** -ɪ.li, -əl.i **-iness** -ɪ.nəs, -ɪ.nɪs
misunder|stand ˌmɪs.ʌn.də|ˈstænd ⓤⓢ -dɚˈ- **-stands** -ˈstændz **-standing/s** -ˈstæn.dɪŋ/z **-stood** -ˈstʊd
misuse *(n.)* ˌmɪsˈjuːs
misus|e *(v.)* ˌmɪsˈjuːz **-es** -ɪz **-ing** -ɪŋ **-ed** -d
MIT ˌem.aɪˈtiː *stress shift:* ˌMIT ˈgraduate
Mitcham ˈmɪtʃ.əm
Mitchel(l) ˈmɪtʃ.əl
Mitchison ˈmɪtʃ.ɪ.sən
Mitchum ˈmɪtʃ.əm
mite maɪt **-s** -s
mit|er ˈmaɪ.t|əʳ ⓤⓢ -t̬|ɚ **-ers** -əz ⓤⓢ -ɚz **-ering** -ər.ɪŋ **-ered** -əd ⓤⓢ -ɚd ˈ**miter** ˌ**box**; ˈ**miter** ˌ**joint**
Mitford ˈmɪt.fəd ⓤⓢ -fɚd
Mithr|a ˈmɪθ.r|ə **-as** -æs ⓤⓢ -əs, -æs
Mithraic mɪˈθreɪ.ɪk
Mithra|ism ˈmɪθ.reɪ|.ɪ.zəm; mɪˈθreɪ- ⓤⓢ ˈmɪθ.reɪ-, -rə- **-ist/s** -ɪst/s
Mithridates ˌmɪθ.rɪˈdeɪ.tiːz ⓤⓢ -rəˈ-
mitigable ˈmɪt.ɪ.gə.bl̩ ⓤⓢ ˈmɪt̬-
miti|gate ˈmɪt.ɪ|.geɪt ⓤⓢ ˈmɪt̬- **-gates** -geɪts **-gating** -geɪ.tɪŋ ⓤⓢ -geɪ.t̬ɪŋ **-gated** -geɪ.tɪd ⓤⓢ -geɪ.t̬ɪd **-gator/s** -geɪ.təʳ/z ⓤⓢ -geɪ.t̬ɚ/z
mitigation ˌmɪt.ɪˈgeɪ.ʃən ⓤⓢ ˌmɪt̬-
mitigatory ˈmɪt.ɪ.geɪ.tər.i ⓤⓢ ˈmɪt̬.ɪ.gə.tɔːr-
mitochondrial ˌmaɪ.təʊˈkɒn.dri.əl ⓤⓢ -toʊˈkɑːn-, -t̬əˈ-
mitochondri|on ˌmaɪ.təʊˈkɒn.dri|.ən ⓤⓢ -toʊˈkɑːn-, -t̬əˈ- **-a** -ə
mitosis maɪˈtəʊ.sɪs ⓤⓢ -ˈtoʊ-
mitrailleus|e ˌmɪt.raɪˈɜːz ⓤⓢ ˌmiː.treɪˈjɜːz **-es** -ɪz
mitral ˈmaɪ.trəl
mit|re ˈmaɪ.t|əʳ ⓤⓢ -t̬|ɚ **-res** -əz ⓤⓢ -ɚz **-ring** -ər.ɪŋ **-red** -əd ⓤⓢ -ɚd ˈ**mitre** ˌ**box**; ˈ**mitre** ˌ**joint**
Mitrovice ˌmɪt.rəʊˈvɪt.sə, ˈmɪt.rəʊ.vɪt.sə ⓤⓢ mɪt.rəˈviːt.sə, -roʊˈ-
Mitsubishi® ˌmɪt.sʊˈbɪʃ.i, -suːˈ- ⓤⓢ -suːˈ-
mitt mɪt **-s** -s
mitten ˈmɪt.ən **-s** -z
Mitterand, Mitterrand ˈmiː.tə.rɑ̃ːŋ ⓤⓢ ˈmiːt.ə.rɑːnd, ˈmɪt-
Mitylene ˌmɪt.əlˈiː.ni, -ɪˈliː- ⓤⓢ ˌmɪt̬.əˈliː-
mitz|vah ˈmɪts|.və ⓤⓢ ˈmɪts-; mɪtsˈvɑː **-vahs** -əz ⓤⓢ ˈmɪts.vəs; mɪtsˈvɑːz **-voth** -vɒt ⓤⓢ ˈmɪts.voʊt, -voʊs
Mivart ˈmaɪ.vət, -vɑːt ⓤⓢ -vɚt, -vɑːrt
mix *(n. v.)* mɪks **-es** -ɪz **-ing** -ɪŋ **-ed** -t ˌ**mixed** ˈ**bag**; ˌ**mixed** ˈ**blessing**; ˌ**mixed** ˈ**doubles**; ˌ**mixed** ˈ**farming**; ˌ**mixed** ˈ**grill**; ˌ**mixed** ˈ**marriage**; ˌ**mixed** ˈ**metaphor**
mix-and-match ˌmɪks.ənd̚ˈmætʃ, -əmˈ- ⓤⓢ -ənd̚- *stress shift:* ˌmix-and-match ˈclothes
mixed-ability ˌmɪkst.əˈbɪl.ə.ti, -ɪ.ti ⓤⓢ -ə.t̬i *stress shift:* ˌmixed-ability ˈstudents
mixed blessing ˌmɪkstˈbles.ɪŋ
mixed-up ˌmɪkstˈʌp *stress shift:* ˌmixed-up ˈkid
mixer ˈmɪk.səʳ ⓤⓢ -sɚ **-s** -z
mixture ˈmɪks.tʃəʳ ⓤⓢ -tʃɚ **-s** -z
mix-up ˈmɪks.ʌp **-s** -s
Mizpah ˈmɪz.pə
mizzen ˈmɪz.ən **-s** -z
mizzen-mast ˈmɪz.ənˌmɑːst, -əmˌ-, -ənˌmæst *nautical pronunciation:* -məst ⓤⓢ -ən.mæst **-s** -s
mizzl|e ˈmɪz.l̩ **-es** -z **-ing** -ɪŋ, ˈmɪz.lɪŋ **-ed** -d **-y** -i
ml *(abbrev. for* **millilitre/s***) singular:* ˈmɪl.ɪˌliː.təʳ, ˈ-ə- ⓤⓢ -t̬ɚ *plural:* -z
Mladic ˈmlæd.ɪtʃ ⓤⓢ məˈlæd.ɪtʃ
mm *(abbrev. for* **millimetre/s***) singular:* ˈmɪl.ɪˌmiː.təʳ, ˈ-ə- ⓤⓢ -t̬ɚ *plural:* -z
MMR ˌem.emˈɑːʳ ⓤⓢ -ɑːr
mnemonic nɪˈmɒn.ɪk, nə-, niː-, mnɪ-, mnə-, mniː- ⓤⓢ nɪˈmɑː.nɪk, niː- **-s** -s **-ally** -əl.i, -li

Pronouncing the letters MN

The consonant digraph **mn** is word or morpheme final and usually realised as /m/, that is, the **n** is silent, e.g.:

hymn /hɪm/
condemning /kənˈdem.ɪŋ/

However, in some cases the **n** is pronounced, particularly (as in the case of *condemnation*) where the vowel following the **n** is in a stressed syllable, e.g.:

hymnal /ˈhɪm.nəl/
condemnation /ˌkɒn.demˈneɪ.ʃən/ ⓤⓢ /ˌkɑːn-/

Mnemosyne nɪˈmɒz.ɪ.ni, nə-, niː-, mnɪ-, mnə-, mniː-, -ˈmɒs-, -ᵊn.i (US) nɪˈmɑː.sɪ-, niː-, -zɪ-

mo, mo' məʊ (US) moʊ

Mo. *(abbrev. for* **Missouri***)* mɪˈzʊə.ri, -ˈsʊə- (US) -ˈzʊr.i *locally:* -ə

Mo məʊ (US) moʊ

moa məʊə (US) moʊə **-s** -z

Moab ˈməʊ.æb (US) ˈmoʊ-

Moabite ˈməʊ.ə.baɪt (US) ˈmoʊ- **-s** -s

moan məʊn (US) moʊn **-s** -z **-ing/s** -ɪŋ/z **-ed** -d

moat (M) məʊt (US) moʊt **-s** -s **-ing** -ɪŋ (US) ˈmoʊ.t̬ɪŋ **-ed** -ɪd (US) ˈmoʊ.t̬ɪd

mob mɒb (US) mɑːb **-s** -z **-bing** -ɪŋ **-bed** -d

mobcap ˈmɒb.kæp (US) ˈmɑːb- **-s** -s

Moberly ˈməʊ.bᵊl.i (US) ˈmoʊ.bɚ.li

Mobil® ˈməʊ.bɪl, -bᵊl (US) ˈmoʊ.bᵊl, -bɪl

mobile *(adj.)* ˈməʊ.baɪl (US) ˈmoʊ.bᵊl, -bɪl, -baɪl ˌ**mobile ˈphone**; ˌ**mobile ˈhome**

mobile *(n.)* ˈməʊ.baɪl (US) ˈmoʊ.biːl **-s** -z

mobility məʊˈbɪl.ə.ti, -ɪ.ti (US) moʊˈbɪl.ə.t̬i

mobilization, -isa- ˌməʊ.bɪ.laɪˈzeɪ.ʃᵊn, -bᵊl.aɪ'-, -ɪ'- (US) -bᵊl.ɪ'- **-s** -z

mobiliz|e, -is|e ˈməʊ.bɪ.laɪz, -bᵊl.aɪz (US) -bə.laɪz **-es** -ɪz **-ing** -ɪŋ **-ed** -d

mobius, möbius (M) ˈməʊ.bi.əs *as if German:* ˈmɜː- (US) ˈmeɪ.bi.əs, ˈmoʊ-, ˈmiː- *as if German:* ˈmɜː- ˌ**Mobius ˈstrip**

mobster ˈmɒb.stəʳ (US) ˈmɑːb.stɚ **-s** -z

Mobutu məˈbuː.tuː

Moby Dick ˌməʊ.biˈdɪk (US) ˌmoʊ-

moccasin ˈmɒk.ə.sɪn (US) ˈmɑː.kə.sən, -sɪn **-s** -z

mocha *coffee, leather, etc.:* ˈmɒk.ə, ˈməʊ.kə (US) ˈmoʊ.kə

Mocha *Arabian seaport:* ˈməʊ.kə, ˈmɒk.ə (US) ˈmoʊ.kə

mock mɒk (US) mɑːk **-s** -s **-ing/ly** -ɪŋ/li **-ed** -t **-er/s** -əʳ/z (US) -ɚ/z

mockers ˈmɒk.əz (US) ˈmɑː.kɚz **put the ˈmockers on ˌsomething**

mocker|y ˈmɒk.ᵊr|.i (US) ˈmɑː.kɚ- **-ies** -iz

Mockett ˈmɒk.ɪt (US) ˈmɑː.kɪt

mockingbird ˈmɒk.ɪŋˌbɜːd (US) ˈmɑː.kɪŋˌbɝːd **-s** -z

mock-turtle ˌmɒkˈtɜː.tl̩ (US) ˌmɑːkˈtɝː.t̬l̩ *stress shift:* ˌmock-turtle ˈsoup

mock-up ˈmɒk.ʌp (US) ˈmɑːk- **-s** -s

mod (M) mɒd (US) mɑːd **-s** -z

MoD ˌem.əʊˈdiː (US) -oʊ'- *stress shift:* ˌMoD ˈcuts

modal ˈməʊ.dᵊl (US) ˈmoʊ- **-s** -z **-ly** -i ˌ**modal ˈverb**

modality məʊˈdæl.ə.ti, -ɪ.ti (US) moʊˈdæl.ə.t̬i

mod con ˌmɒdˈkɒn (US) ˌmɑːdˈkɑːn, ˈ-- **-s** -z

mode məʊd (US) moʊd **-s** -z

model ˈmɒd.ᵊl (US) ˈmɑː.dᵊl **-s** -z **-(l)ing** -ɪŋ, ˈmɒd.lɪŋ (US) ˈmɑːd- **-(l)ed** -d **-(l)er/s** -əʳ/z (US) -ɚ/z, ˈmɒd.ləʳ/z (US) ˈmɑːd.lɚ/z

modem ˈməʊ.dem, -dəm (US) ˈmoʊ.dəm, -dem **-s** -z

Modena ˈmɒd.ɪ.nə; mɒdˈeɪ.nə, məˈdeɪ- (US) ˈmoʊ.dᵊn.ə, ˈmɔː-, -ɑː

moderate *(n. adj.)* ˈmɒd.ᵊr.ət, -ɪt (US) ˈmɑː.dɚ- **-s** -s **-ly** -li **-ness** -nəs, -nɪs

moder|ate *(v.)* ˈmɒd.ᵊr|.eɪt (US) ˈmɑː.də.r|eɪt **-ates** -eɪts **-ating** -eɪ.tɪŋ (US) -eɪ.t̬ɪŋ **-ated** -eɪ.tɪd (US) -eɪ.t̬ɪd **-ator/s** -eɪ.təʳ/z (US) -eɪ.t̬ɚ/z

moderation ˌmɒd.ᵊrˈeɪ.ʃᵊn (US) ˌmɑː.dəˈreɪ- **-s** -z

moderato ˌmɒd.ᵊrˈɑː.təʊ (US) ˌmɑː.dəˈrɑː.toʊ **-s** -z

modern ˈmɒd.ᵊn (US) ˈmɑː.dɚn **-s** -z **-ly** -li **-ness** -nəs, -nɪs ˌ**modern ˈlanguages**

modern|ism (M) ˈmɒd.ᵊn|.ɪ.zᵊm (US) ˈmɑː.dɚ.n|ɪ- **-ist/s** -ɪst/s

modernistic ˌmɒd.ᵊnˈɪs.tɪk (US) ˌmɑː.dɚˈnɪs- **-ally** -ᵊl.i, -li

modernity mɒdˈɜː.nə.ti, məˈdɜː-, -ɪ.ti (US) mɑːˈdɝː.nə.t̬i, mə-, moʊ-

modernization, -isa- ˌmɒd.ᵊn.aɪˈzeɪ.ʃᵊn, -ɪ'- (US) ˌmɑː.dɚ.nɪ'- **-s** -z

moderniz|e, -is|e ˈmɒd.ᵊn.aɪz (US) ˈmɑː.dɚ.naɪz **-es** -ɪz **-ing** -ɪŋ **-ed** -d **-er/s**

modest ˈmɒd.ɪst (US) ˈmɑː.dɪst **-ly** -li **-y** -i

modicum ˈmɒd.ɪ.kəm, ˈ-ə- (US) ˈmɑː.dɪ- **-s** -z

modification ˌmɒd.ɪ.fɪˈkeɪ.ʃᵊn, ˌ-ə- (US) ˌmɑː.dɪ- **-s** -z

modi|fy ˈmɒd.ɪ|.faɪ (US) ˈmɑː.dɪ- **-fies** -faɪz **-fying** -faɪ.ɪŋ **-fied** -faɪd **-fier/s** -faɪ.əʳ/z (US) -faɪ.ɚ/z **-fiable** -faɪ.ə.bl̩

Modigliani ˌmɒd.ɪˈljɑː.ni (US) ˌmoʊ.diːlˈjɑː-

modish ˈməʊ.dɪʃ (US) ˈmoʊ- **-ly** -li **-ness** -nəs, -nɪs

modiste məʊˈdiːst (US) moʊ- **-s** -s

Modred ˈməʊ.drɪd (US) ˈmoʊ-

modular ˈmɒd.jə.ləʳ, ˈmɒdʒ-, -jʊ- (US) ˈmɑː.dʒə.lɚ

modularity ˌmɒd.jəˈlær.ə.ti, ˌmɒdʒ-, -jʊ'-, -ɪ.ti (US) ˌmɑː.dʒəˈler.ə.t̬i, -ˈlær-

modu|late ˈmɒd.jə|.leɪt, ˈmɒdʒ-, -jʊ- (US) ˈmɑː.dʒə- **-lates** -leɪts **-lating** -leɪ.tɪŋ (US) -leɪ.t̬ɪŋ **-lated** -leɪ.tɪd (US) -leɪ.t̬ɪd **-lator/s** -leɪ.təʳ/z (US) -leɪ.t̬ɚ/z

modulation ˌmɒd.jəˈleɪ.ʃᵊn, ˌmɒdʒ-, -jʊ'- (US) ˌmɑː.dʒə'- **-s** -z

module ˈmɒd.juːl, ˈmɒdʒ- (US) ˈmɑː.dʒuːl **-s** -z

modul|us ˈmɒd.jə.l|əs, -jʊ- (US) ˈmɑː.dʒə- **-uses** -ə.sɪz **-i** -aɪ

modus ˈməʊ.dəs (US) ˈmoʊ-

modus operandi ˌməʊ.dəsˌɒp.əˈræn.diː, ˌmɒd.əs-, -daɪ (US) ˌmoʊ.dəsˌoʊ.pəˈrɑːn.di, -ˌɑː-, -ˈræn-

modus vivendi ˌməʊ.dəs.vɪˈven.diː, ˌmɒd.əs-, -viː'-, -daɪ (US) ˌmoʊ.dəs.viːˈven.di

Moesia ˈmiː.si.ə, -ʃə, -zi.ə, -ʒə (US) -ʃi.ə, -ʃə

Moffat ˈmɒf.ət (US) ˈmɑː.fət

Moffett ˈmɒf.ət, -ɪt (US) ˈmɑː.fət

Mogadishu ˌmɒg.əˈdɪʃ.uː (US) ˌmoʊ.gɑːˈdiː.ʃuː, ˌmɑː-, -gə'-, -ˈdɪʃ.uː

Mogadon® ˈmɒg.ə.dɒn (US) ˈmɑː.gə.dɑːn

Mogador ˌmɒg.əˈdɔːʳ, ˈ--- (US) ˈmɑː.gə.dɔːr, ˌ--ˈ-

Moggach ˈmɒg.ək, -əx (US) ˈmɑː.gək

mogg|y, mogg|ie ˈmɒg|.i (US) ˈmɑː.g|i **-ies** -z

mogul (M) ˈməʊ.gᵊl, -gʊl, -gʌl (US) ˈmoʊ.gʌl, -gᵊl; moʊˈgʌl **-s** -z

mohair ˈməʊ.heəʳ (US) ˈmoʊ.her

Moham(m)ed məʊˈhæm.ɪd, -əd, -ed (US) moʊ-

Mohammedan məʊˈhæm.ɪ.dᵊn, ˈ-ə- (US) moʊ- **-s** -z **-ism** -ɪ.zᵊm

Mohave məʊˈhɑː.vi (US) moʊ-

Mohawk ˈməʊ.hɔːk (US) ˈmoʊ.hɑːk, -hɔːk **-s** -s

Mohegan məʊˈhiː.gᵊn, mə- (US) moʊ- **-s** -z

Mohican məʊˈhiː.kᵊn; ˈməʊ.ɪ- (US) moʊˈhiː- **-s** -z

Mohun məʊən; ˈməʊ.hən; muːn (US) muːn, ˈmoʊ.hən

moidore ˌmɔɪˈdɔːʳ, ˌməʊ.ɪ'-; ˈmɔɪ.dɔːʳ (US) ˈmɔɪ.dɔːr **-s** -z

Note: In John Masefield's poem 'Cargoes' the stress is on the last syllable.

moiet|y ˈmɔɪ.ə.t|i, ˈ-ɪ- (US) -ə.t̬|i **-ies** -iz

moil mɔɪl **-s** -z **-ing** -ɪŋ **-ed** -d

Moir mɔɪəʳ (US) mɔɪɚ

Moira ˈmɔɪə.rə (US) ˈmɔɪ-

moire mwɑːʳ, mwɔːʳ (US) mwɑːr, mɔːr **-s** -z

moiré ˈmwɑː.reɪ, ˈmwɔː- (US) mwɑːˈreɪ, mɔː-; ˈmɔː.reɪ

moist mɔɪst **-er** -əʳ (US) -ɚ **-est** -ɪst, -əst **-ly** -li **-ness** -nəs, -nɪs

moisten ˈmɔɪ.sᵊn **-s** -z **-ing** -ɪŋ, ˈmɔɪs.nɪŋ **-ed** -d

moisture ˈmɔɪs.tʃəʳ (US) -tʃɚ

moisturiz|e, -is|e ˈmɔɪs.tʃᵊr.aɪz (US) -tʃə.raɪz **-es** -ɪz **-ing** -ɪŋ **-ed** -d **-er/s** -əʳ/z (US) -ɚ/z

Moivre ˈmɔɪ.vəʳ (US) -vɚ

Mojave məʊˈhɑː.vi (US) moʊ-

moke məʊk (US) moʊk **-s** -s

molar ˈməʊ.ləʳ (US) ˈmoʊ.lɚ **-s** -z

molasses məʊˈlæs.ɪz, -əz (US) mə-

molassine ˈmɒl.ə.siːn, ˈməʊ.lə- (US) ˈmɑː.lə-, ˈmoʊ-

Mold məʊld (US) moʊld

mold məʊld (US) moʊld **-s** -z **-ing/s** -ɪŋ **-ed** -ɪd

Moldavi|a mɒlˈdeɪ.vi|.ə (US) mɑːl-, ˈ-vj|ə **-an/s** -ən/z

mold|er ˈməʊl.d|əʳ (US) ˈmoʊl.d|ɚ **-ers** -əz (US) -ɚz **-ering** -ᵊr.ɪŋ **-ered** -əd (US) -ɚd

Moldov|a mɒlˈdəʊ.v|ə (US) mɑːlˈdoʊ- **-an/s** -ən/z

mold|y ˈməʊl.d|i (US) ˈmoʊl- **-ier** -i.əʳ (US) -i.ɚ **-iest** -i.ɪst, -i.əst **-iness** -ɪ.nəs, -ɪ.nɪs

mole (M) məʊl (US) moʊl **-s** -z

Molech ˈməʊ.lek (US) ˈmoʊ-

molecular məʊˈlek.jə.ləʳ, mɒlˈek-, -jʊ- (US) məˈlek.jə.lɚ, moʊ-, -juː-

molecule ˈmɒl.ɪ.kjuːl, ˈməʊ.lɪ-, -lə- (US) ˈmɑː.lɪ.kjuːl **-s** -z

molehill ˈməʊl.hɪl (US) ˈmoʊl- **-s** -z **make a ˌmountain out of a ˈmole-hill**

Molesey ˈməʊl.zi (US) ˈmoʊl-

moleskin ˈməʊl.skɪn (US) ˈmoʊl- **-s** -z

molest məʊˈlest (US) mə-, moʊ- **-s** -s **-ing** -ɪŋ **-ed** -ɪd **-er/s** -əʳ/z (US) -ɚ/z

molestation ˌmɒl.esˈteɪ.ʃən, ˌməʊ.lesˈ- (US) ˌmoʊ.lesˈ-, ˌmɑː- **-s** -z

molester məʊˈles.təʳ (US) məˈles.tɚ, moʊ- **-s** -z

Molesworth ˈməʊlz.wəθ, -wɜːθ (US) ˈmoʊlz.wɚθ, -wɝːθ

Molière ˈmɒl.i.eəʳ, ˈməʊ.li- (US) ˌmoʊlˈjer

Moline məʊˈliːn (US) moʊ-

moll (M) mɒl (US) mɑːl

mollification ˌmɒl.ɪ.fɪˈkeɪ.ʃᵊn, ˌ-ə- (US) ˌmɑː.lə-

molli|fy ˈmɒl.ɪ|.faɪ, ˈ-ə- (US) ˈmɑː.lə- **-fies** -faɪz **-fying** -faɪ.ɪŋ **-fied** -faɪd

mollusc ˈmɒl.əsk, -ʌsk (US) ˈmɑː.ləsk **-s** -s

molluscan mɒlˈʌs.kᵊn, məˈlʌs- (US) mə-

molluscoid mɒlˈʌs.kɔɪd, məˈlʌs- (US) mə-

moll|y (M) ˈmɒl|.i (US) ˈmɑː.l|i **-ies** -iz

mollycoddl|e ˈmɒl.iˌkɒd.l̩ (US) ˈmɑː.liˌkɑː.dl̩ **-es** -z **-ing** -ɪŋ, -ˌkɒd.lɪŋ (US) -ˌkɑːd.lɪŋ **-ed** -d

Moloch ˈməʊ.lɒk (US) ˈmoʊ.lɑːk, ˈmɑː.lək

Molony məˈləʊ.ni (US) -ˈloʊ-

Molotov ˈmɒl.ə.tɒf (US) ˈmɑː.lə.tɔːf, ˈmoʊ-, -tɔːv **ˌMolotov ˈcocktail**

molt məʊlt (US) moʊlt **-s** -s **-ing** -ɪŋ (US) ˈmoʊl.t̬ɪŋ **-ed** -ɪd (US) ˈmoʊl.t̬ɪd **-er/s** -əʳ/z (US) ˈmoʊl.t̬ɚ/z

molten ˈməʊl.tᵊn (US) ˈmoʊl-

molto ˈmɒl.təʊ (US) ˈmoʊl.toʊ

Molton ˈməʊl.tᵊn (US) ˈmoʊl-

Moluccas məʊˈlʌk.əz (US) moʊ-, mə-

moly ˈməʊ.li (US) ˈmoʊ-

molybdenum məˈlɪb.də.nəm, -dɪ-, mɒlˈɪb-, məʊˈlɪb-; ˌmɒl.ɪbˈdiː.nəm (US) məˈlɪb.də-

Molyneux ˈmɒl.ɪ.njuːks, ˈmʌl-, ˈ-ə-, -njuː (US) ˈmʌl.ɪ.nuːks, -njuː, -nuː

mom (M) mɒm (US) mɑːm **-s** -z

Mombasa mɒmˈbæs.ə, -ˈbɑː.sə (US) mɑːmˈbɑː.sə, -ˈbæs.ə

moment ˈməʊ.mənt (US) ˈmoʊ- **-s** -s **ˌmoment of ˈtruth**

momenta *(plur. of* **momentum***)* məʊˈmen.tə (US) moʊˈmen.t̬ə, mə-

momentarily ˈməʊ.mən.tᵊr.ᵊl.i, -ɪ.li; ˌməʊ.mənˈter- (US) ˌmoʊ.mənˈter-, ˈmoʊ.mən.ter-

momentar|y ˈməʊ.mən.tᵊr|.i (US) ˈmoʊ.mən.ter- **-iness** -ɪ.nəs, -ɪ.nɪs

momentous məʊˈmen.təs (US) moʊˈmen.t̬əs, mə- **-ly** -li **-ness** -nəs, -nɪs

moment|um məʊˈmen.t|əm (US) moʊˈmen.t̬|əm, mə- **-ums** -əmz **-a** -ə

momma (M) ˈmɒm.ə (US) ˈmɑː.mə **-s** -z

momm|y ˈmɒm|.i (US) ˈmɑː.m|i **-ies** -iz

Mon *language:* məʊn, mɒn (US) moʊn

Mon. *(abbrev. for* **Monday***)* ˈmʌn.deɪ, -di

Note: Can be pronounced /mʌn/ in British English.

mona (M) ˈməʊ.nə (US) ˈmoʊ- **-s** -z **ˌMona ˈLisa**

Monaco ˈmɒn.ə.kəʊ, məˈnɑː- (US) ˈmɑː.nə.koʊ, məˈnɑː-

monad ˈmɒn.æd, ˈməʊ.næd (US) ˈmoʊ-, ˈmɑː.næd **-s** -z

Monadhliath ˌməʊ.nəˈliː.ə (US) ˌmoʊ-

monadic mɒnˈæd.ɪk, məʊˈnæd- (US) mə-, moʊ-

Monaghan ˈmɒn.ə.hən, -kən *as if Irish:* -xən (US) ˈmɑː.nə.gən

monarch ˈmɒn.ək (US) ˈmɑː.nɚk, -nɑːrk **-s** -s

monarch|al mɒnˈɑː.k|ᵊl, məˈnɑː- (US) məˈnɑːr-, moʊ- **-ic** -ɪk **-ical** -ɪ.kᵊl

monarch|ism ˈmɒn.ə.k|ɪ.zᵊm (US) ˈmɑː.nɚ-, -nɑːr- **-ist/s** -ɪst/s

monarchiz|e, -is|e ˈmɒn.ə.kaɪz (US) ˈmɑː.nɚ-, -nɑːr- **-es** -ɪz **-ing** -ɪŋ **-ed** -d

monarch|y ˈmɒn.ə.k|i (US) ˈmɑː.nɚ-, -nɑːr- **-ies** -iz

Monash ˈmɒn.æʃ (US) ˈmɑː.næʃ

monaster|y ˈmɒn.ə.stᵊr|.i, -str|i (US) ˈmɑː.nə.ster|.i **-ies** -iz

monastic məˈnæs.tɪk, mɒnˈæs- (US) mə-, moʊ- **-al** -ᵊl **-ally** -ᵊl.i, -li

monasticism məˈnæs.tɪ.sɪ.zᵊm, mɒnˈæs- (US) məˈnæs-, moʊ-

monatomic ˌmɒn.əˈtɒm.ɪk (US) ˌmɑː.nəˈtɑː.mɪk

monaural mɒnˈɔː.rᵊl (US) mɑːˈnɔːr.ᵊl

Monbiot ˈmɒn.bi.əʊ (US) -oʊ, ˈmɑːn.bi.oʊ

Monchen-Gladbach, Mönchen-Gladbach ˌmɜːn.ʃənˈglæd.bæk, ˌmʊn-, -kəŋˈ- (US) -kənˈglɑːt.bɑːk

Monck mʌŋk

Monckton ˈmʌŋk.tən

Moncrieff mənˈkriːf, məŋ-, mɒn-, mɒŋ- (US) mɑːn-, mən-; ˈmɑːn.kriːf

Mond mɒnd (US) mɑːnd

Mondale ˈmɒn.deɪl (US) ˈmɑːn-

Monday ˈmʌn.deɪ, -di **-s** -z

Mondeo® ˌmɒnˈdeɪ.əʊ (US) ˌmɑːnˈdeɪ.oʊ

Mondrian ˈmɒn.dri.æn, -ən (US) ˈmɑːn.dri.ɑːn, -ən

Monegasque ˌmɒn.ɪˈgæsk, -əˈ- (US) ˌmɑː.neɪˈ-

Monet ˈmɒn.eɪ *as if French:* -ˈ- (US) moʊˈneɪ, mə-

monetar|ism ˈmʌn.ɪ.tᵊr|.ɪ.zᵊm, ˈ-ə- (US) ˈmɑː.nə-, ˈmʌn.ə- **-ist/s** -ɪst/s

monetary ˈmʌn.ɪ.tᵊr.i, ˈ-ə-, -tri (US) ˈmɑː.nə.ter.i, ˈmʌn.ə-

monetiz|e, -is|e ˈmʌn.ɪ.taɪz, ˈ-ə- (US) ˈmɑː.nə-, ˈmʌn.ə- **-es** -ɪz **-ing** -ɪŋ **-ed** -d

mon|ey (M) ˈmʌn|.i **-eys** -z **-ies** -iz **-eyed** -id **-ied** -id **ˈmoney ˌbox; ˈmoney ˌchanger; ˈmoney ˌmarket; ˈmoney ˌorder; ˈmoney ˌsupply; ˌthrow good ˌmoney after ˈbad**

moneybag ˈmʌn.i.bæg **-s** -z

moneygrabb|ing ˈmʌn.iˌgræb|.ɪŋ **-er/s** -əʳ/z (US) -ɚ/z

money-grubb|er ˈmʌn.iˌgrʌb|.əʳ (US) -ɚ **-ers** -əz (US) -ɚz **-ing** -ɪŋ

moneylend|er ˈmʌn.iˌlen.d|əʳ (US) -d|ɚ **-ers** -əz (US) -ɚz **-ing** -ɪŋ

money-market ˈmʌn.iˌmɑː.kɪt (US) -ˌmɑːr- **-s** -s

money-off ˌmʌn.iˈɒf (US) -ˈɑːf

Moneypenny ˈmʌn.iˌpen.i

money-spinner ˈmʌn.iˌspɪn.əʳ (US) -ɚ **-s** -z

monger ˈmʌŋ.gəʳ (US) -gɚ, ˈmɑːŋ- **-s** -z

mongo ˈmɒŋ.gəʊ (US) ˈmɑːŋ.goʊ **-s** -z

mongol (M) ˈmɒŋ.gəl, -gɒl (US) ˈmɑːŋ-, ˈmɑːn-, -gəl, -goʊl **-s** -z **-oid** -ɔɪd

Mongoli|a mɒŋˈgəʊ.li|.ə (US) mɑːŋˈgoʊ-, mɑːn-, -ˈgoʊl.j|ə **-an/s** -ən/z

mongolism (M) ˈmɒŋ.gəl.ɪ.zəm, -gɒl- ⓤⓢ ˈmɑːŋ.gəl-, ˈmɑːn-
mongoos|e ˈmɒŋ.guːs, ˈmʌŋ- ⓤⓢ ˈmɑːŋ-, ˈmɑːn- **-es** -ɪz
mongrel ˈmʌŋ.grəl ⓤⓢ ˈmɑːŋ-, ˈmʌŋ- **-s** -z
Monica ˈmɒn.ɪ.kə ⓤⓢ ˈmɑː.nɪ-
monicker ˈmɒn.ɪ.kər ⓤⓢ ˈmɑː.nɪ.kɚ **-s** -z
Monier ˈmʌn.i.ər, ˈmɒn- ⓤⓢ ˈmɑː.ni.ɚ, ˈmʌn.i-
moniker ˈmɒn.ɪ.kər ⓤⓢ ˈmɑː.nɪ.kɚ **-s** -z
Monique mɒnˈiːk ⓤⓢ moʊ-, mə-
mon|ism ˈmɒn|.ɪ.zəm, ˈməʊ.n|ɪ- ⓤⓢ ˈmoʊ-, ˈmɑː- **-ist/s** -ɪst/s
monistic mɒnˈɪs.tɪk, məˈnɪs- ⓤⓢ moʊ-, mə- **-al** -əl
monition məʊˈnɪʃ.ən, mɒnˈɪʃ- ⓤⓢ moʊˈnɪʃ-, mə- **-s** -z
monit|or ˈmɒn.ɪ.t|ər, -ə- ⓤⓢ ˈmɑː.nə.t̬|ɚ **-ors** -əz ⓤⓢ -ɚz **-oring** -ər.ɪŋ **-ored** -əd ⓤⓢ -ɚd
monitorial ˌmɒn.ɪˈtɔː.ri.əl, -əˈ- ⓤⓢ ˌmɑː.nɪˈtɔːr.i-
monitory ˈmɒn.ɪ.tər.i, ˈ-ə- ⓤⓢ ˈmɑː.nɪ.tɔːr-
monk (M) mʌŋk **-s** -s **-ish** -ɪʃ
monkey ˈmʌŋ.ki **-s** -z **-ing** -ɪŋ **-ed** -d **ˈmonkey ˌbars; ˈmonkey ˌbusiness; ˈmonkey ˌwrench**
monkey-puzzle ˈmʌŋ.kiˌpʌz.l̩ **-s** -z
monkfish ˈmʌŋk.fɪʃ **-es** -ɪz
Monkhouse ˈmʌŋk.haʊs
Monkton ˈmʌŋk.tən
Monmouth ˈmɒn.məθ ⓤⓢ ˈmɑːn- **-shire** -ʃər, -ˌʃɪər ⓤⓢ -ʃɚ, -ˌʃɪr
mono- mɒn.əʊ-; məˈnɒ- ⓤⓢ mɑː.noʊ-, -nə-; məˈnɑː-
Note: Prefix. Normally either takes primary or secondary stress on the first syllable, e.g. **monotone** /ˈmɒn.ə.təʊn ⓤⓢ ˈmɑː.nə.toʊn/, **monotonic** /ˌmɒn.əˈtɒ.nɪk ⓤⓢ ˌmɑː.nəˈtɑː.nɪk/, or primary stress on the second syllable, e.g. **monotony** /məˈnɒt.ən.i ⓤⓢ -ˈnɑː.tən-/.

mono *monotype:* ˈməʊ.nəʊ, ˈmɒn.əʊ ⓤⓢ ˈmɑː.noʊ **-s** -z *in sound recording:* ˈmɒn.əʊ ⓤⓢ ˈmɑː.noʊ **-s** -z
monobasic ˌmɒn.əʊˈbeɪ.sɪk ⓤⓢ ˌmɑː.nəˈ-
monoceros məˈnɒs.ər.ɒs, mɒnˈɒs- ⓤⓢ məˈnɑː.sɚ-
monochloride ˌmɒn.əʊˈklɔː.raɪd ⓤⓢ ˌmɑː.noʊˈklɔːr.aɪd, -əˈ- **-s** -z
monochord ˈmɒn.əʊ.kɔːd ⓤⓢ ˈmɑː.nə.kɔːrd **-s** -z
monochromatic ˌmɒn.ə.krəʊˈmæt.ɪk ⓤⓢ ˌmɑː.nə.kroʊˈmæt̬-, -krə-
monochrome ˈmɒn.ə.krəʊm ⓤⓢ ˈmɑː.nə.kroʊm **-s** -z
monocle ˈmɒn.ə.kl̩ ⓤⓢ ˈmɑː.nə- **-s** -z
monoclonal ˌmɒn.əʊˈkləʊ.nəl ⓤⓢ ˌmɑː.nəˈkloʊ-, -noʊˈ-
monocotyledon ˌmɒn.əʊˌkɒt.ɪˈliː.dən, -əlˈiː- ⓤⓢ ˌmɑː.nəˌkɑː.təlˈiː-, -noʊˌ- **-s** -z
monoculture ˈmɒn.əʊˌkʌl.tʃər ⓤⓢ ˈmɑː.nəˌkʌl.tʃɚ, -noʊˌ-
monod|y ˈmɒn.ə.d|i ⓤⓢ ˈmɑː.nə- **-ies** -iz
monogamist məˈnɒg.ə.mɪst, mɒnˈɒg- ⓤⓢ məˈnɑː.gə- **-s** -s
monogamous məˈnɒg.ə.məs, mɒnˈɒg- ⓤⓢ məˈnɑː.gə-
monogamy məˈnɒg.ə.mi, mɒnˈɒg- ⓤⓢ məˈnɑː.gə-
monoglot ˈmɒn.ə.glɒt ⓤⓢ ˈmɑː.nə.glɑːt **-s** -s
monogram ˈmɒn.ə.græm ⓤⓢ ˈmɑː.nə- **-s** -z **-ming** -ɪŋ **-med** -d
monograph ˈmɒn.ə.grɑːf, -græf ⓤⓢ ˈmɑː.nə.græf **-s** -s
monographic ˌmɒn.əʊˈgræf.ɪk ⓤⓢ ˌmɑː.nəˈ-
monolingual ˌmɒn.əʊˈlɪŋ.gwəl ⓤⓢ ˌmɑː.nəˈ-, -noʊˈ- **-s** -z **-ly** -i
monolinguist ˌmɒn.əʊˈlɪŋ.gwɪst ⓤⓢ ˌmɑː.nəˈ-, -noʊˈ- **-s** -s
monolith ˈmɒn.əʊ.lɪθ ⓤⓢ ˈmɑː.nə- **-s** -s
monolithic ˌmɒn.əʊˈlɪθ.ɪk ⓤⓢ ˌmɑː.nəˈ-
monologue, monolog ˈmɒn.əl.ɒg ⓤⓢ ˈmɑː.nə.lɑːg, -lɔːg **-s** -z

monolog(u)ist ˈmɒn.əl.ɒg.ɪst, -ɒdʒ-; məˈnɒl.ə.gɪst, -dʒɪst ⓤⓢ ˈmɑː.nə.lɑːg.ɪst, -lɔːg.ɪst, məˈnɑː.lə.dʒɪst **-s** -s
monomani|a ˌmɒn.əʊˈmeɪ.ni|.ə ⓤⓢ ˌmɑː.noʊˈ-, -nəˈ- **-ac/s** -æk/s
mononuclear ˌmɒn.əʊˈnjuː.kli.ər ⓤⓢ ˌmɑː.noʊˈnuː.kli.ɚ, -ˈnjuː-
mononucleosis ˌmɒn.əʊˌnjuː.kliˈəʊ.sɪs ⓤⓢ ˌmɑː.noʊˌnuː.kliˈoʊ-, -ˌnjuː-
monophonic ˌmɒn.əʊˈfɒn.ɪk ⓤⓢ ˌmɑː.nəˈfɑː.nɪk, -noʊˈ-
monophthong ˈmɒn.əf.θɒŋ, ˈ-ə- ⓤⓢ ˈmɑː.nəf.θɑːŋ, -θɔːŋ **-s** -z
monophthong|al ˌmɒn.əfˈθɒŋ.g|əl, -əˈ- ⓤⓢ ˌmɑː.nəfˈθɑːŋ|.əl, -ˈθɔːŋ-, -g|əl **-ic** -ɪk
monophthongiz|e, -is|e ˈmɒn.əf.θɒŋ.gaɪz, ˈ-ə-, -aɪz ⓤⓢ ˈmɑː.nəf.θɑːŋ-, -θɔːŋ- **-es** -ɪz **-ing** -ɪŋ **-ed** -d
monoplane ˈmɒn.əʊ.pleɪn ⓤⓢ ˈmɑː.nə- **-s** -z
monopole ˈmɒn.ə.pəʊl ⓤⓢ ˈmɑː.nə.poʊl
monopolism məˈnɒp.əl.ɪ.zəm ⓤⓢ məˈnɑː.pə.lɪ-
monopolist məˈnɒp.əl.ɪst ⓤⓢ -ˈnɑː.pə.lɪst **-s** -s
monopolistic məˌnɒp.əlˈɪs.tɪk ⓤⓢ -ˌnɑː.pəˈlɪs- **-ally** -əl.i, -li
monopoliz|e, -is|e məˈnɒp.əl.aɪz ⓤⓢ -ˈnɑː.pə.laɪz **-es** -ɪz **-ing** -ɪŋ **-ed** -d **-er/s** -ər/z
monopol|y məˈnɒp.əl|.i ⓤⓢ -ˈnɑː.pəl- **-ies** -iz
monorail ˈmɒn.əʊ.reɪl ⓤⓢ ˈmɑː.nə-, -noʊ- **-s** -z
monosaccharide ˌmɒn.əʊˈsæk.ər.aɪd ⓤⓢ ˌmɑː.noʊˈsæk.ə.raɪd, -nəˈ- **-s** -z
monosodium ˌmɒn.əʊˈsəʊ.di.əm ⓤⓢ ˌmɑː.noʊˈsoʊ-, -nəˈ- *stress shift, see compound:* **ˌmonosodium ˈglutamate**
monosyllabic ˌmɒn.əʊ.sɪˈlæb.ɪk ⓤⓢ ˌmɑː.nə-, -noʊ- *stress shift:* ˌmonosyllabic ˈword **-ally** -əl.i, -li

Monophthong

A single vowel. The term is used only in contrast with the word DIPHTHONG, which originally meant a 'double sound'.

Examples for English

British English has 12 vowel monophthongs /ɪ e æ ʌ ɒ ʊ ə iː ɑː ɔː ɜː uː/, and US English has 11, or 12 if r-coloured SCHWA /ɚ/ is taken into account. In British English these are traditionally divided into short and long, with a length mark [ː] used to show that there is a difference in length as well as vowel quality. This convention is extended in this dictionary to US English vowels. Long vowels are permitted to appear in a stressed syllable without a CODA, whereas short vowels are not. It should be noted that the schwa vowel, /ə/, never appears in stressed syllables and has a different distribution to the other short vowels.

monosyllable 'mɒn.əʊˌsɪl.ə.bl̩ (US) 'mɑː.nəˌ-, -noʊˌ- **-s** -z

monothe|ism 'mɒn.əʊ.θiː|.ɪ.zᵊm, ˌmɒn.əʊ'θiː- (US) 'mɑː.noʊˌθiː-, -nəˌ- **-ist/s** -ɪst/s

monotheistic ˌmɒn.əʊ.θi'ɪs.tɪk (US) ˌmɑː.noʊ- *stress shift:* ˌmonotheistic 'culture

monoton|e 'mɒn.ə.təʊn (US) 'mɑː.nə.toʊn **-es** -z **-ing** -ɪŋ **-ed** -d

monotonic ˌmɒn.ə'tɒn.ɪk (US) ˌmɑː.nə'tɑː.nɪk *stress shift:* ˌmonotonic 'function

monotonous mə'nɒt.ᵊn.əs (US) -'nɑː.tᵊn- **-ly** -li **-ness** -nəs, -nɪs

monotony mə'nɒt.ᵊn.i (US) -'nɑː.tᵊn-

monotype (M®) 'mɒn.əʊ.taɪp, 'məʊ.nəʊ- (US) 'mɑː.noʊ-, -nə- **-s** -s

monovalen|ce ˌmɒn.əʊ'veɪ.lən|ts, 'mɒn.əʊˌveɪ- (US) ˌmɑː.noʊ'veɪ-, 'mɑː.noʊˌveɪ-, -nə'- **-t** -t

monoxide mə'nɒk.saɪd, mɒn'ɒk- (US) mə'nɑːk- **-s** -z

Monro(e) mən'rəʊ, mʌn'rəʊ, 'mʌn.rəʊ (US) mən'roʊ

Monrovia mɒn'rəʊ.vi.ə, mən- (US) mən'roʊ-

Mons mɒnz *as if French:* mɔ̃ːns (US) mõʊns

Monsanto® mɒn'sæn.təʊ

Monsarrat 'mɒnt.sᵊr.æt, ˌ--'- (US) ˌmɑːnt.sə'rɑːt, -'ræt

monseigneur ˌmɒn.sen'jɜːʳ (US) ˌmɑːn.sən'jɝː **-s** -z **messeigneurs** ˌmes.eɪ'njɜː (US) 'jɝː

monsieur (M) mə'sjɜːʳ, -'sjəʳ (US) -'sjɝː, -'sjɜː

Note: /mə'sjɜːʳ/ is the form of address in isolation. When attached to the surname /mə'sjəʳ/ is unstressed.

monsignor (M) mɒn'siː.njəʳ (US) mɑːn'siː.njɚ

Monson 'mʌnt.sᵊn

monsoon mɒn'suːn, mən- (US) mɑːn- **-s** -z

monster 'mɒnt.stəʳ (US) 'mɑːnt.stɚ **-s** -z

monstranc|e 'mɒnt.strənts (US) 'mɑːnt- **-es** -ɪz

monstrosit|y mɒn'strɒs.ə.t|i, mən-, -ɪ.t|i (US) mɑːn'strɑː.sə.t̬|i **-ies** -iz

monstrous 'mɒnt.strəs (US) 'mɑːnt- **-ly** -li **-ness** -nəs, -nɪs

Mont. *(abbrev. for* **Montana***)* mɒn'tæn.ə, -'tɑː.nə (US) mɑːn'tæn.ə

montag|e mɒn'tɑːʒ; '--, -tɪdʒ (US) 'mɑːn.tɑːʒ; moʊn'tɑːʒ **-es** -ɪz

Montagu(e) 'mɒn.tə.gjuː, -tɪ-, 'mʌn- (US) 'mɑːn-

Montaigne mɒn'teɪn (US) mɑːn-

Montana mɒn'tæn.ə, -'tɑː.nə (US) mɑːn'tæn.ə

Mont Blanc *as if French:* ˌmɔ̃ːm'blɑ̃ːŋ *as if French:* (US) mõʊm'blɑ̃ːŋ

montbretia mɒn'briː.ʃə, mɒm-, -ʃi.ə (US) mɑːnt'- **-s** -z

Mont Cenis ˌmɔ̃ːn.sə'niː (US) ˌmõʊn-

monte (M) 'mɒn.teɪ, -ti (US) 'mɑːn.t̬i

Monte Carlo ˌmɒnt.i'kɑː.ləʊ (US) ˌmɑːn.t̬i'kɑːr.loʊ

Montefiore ˌmɒn.ti.fi'ɔː.reɪ, -ri, -tə-, -'fjɔː- (US) ˌmɑːn.t̬i.fi'ɔːr.i

Montego® mɒn'tiː.gəʊ (US) mɑːn'tiː.goʊ

Montego Bay mɒnˌtiː.gəʊ'beɪ (US) mɑːnˌtiː.goʊ'-

monteith mɒn'tiːθ (US) mɑːn- **-s** -s

Monteith mən'tiːθ, mɒn- (US) mɑːn-

Montenegr|o ˌmɒn.tɪ'niː.gr|əʊ, -tə'-, -'neɪ- (US) ˌmɑːn.t̬ə'niː.gr|oʊ, -'neg.r|oʊ **-an/s** -ən/z

Monte Rosa ˌmɒn.tɪ'rəʊ.zə, -tə'- (US) ˌmɑːn.t̬ə'roʊ-

Monterrey ˌmɒn.tᵊr.eɪ, -tɪ'reɪ (US) ˌmɑːn.t̬ə'reɪ

Montesquieu ˌmɒn.tes'kjuː, -'kjɜː, '--- (US) 'mɑːn.t̬ə.skjuː

Montessori ˌmɒn.tes'ɔː.ri, -tɪ'sɔː- (US) ˌmɑːn.t̬ə'sɔːr.i

Monteverdi ˌmɒn.tɪ'vɜː.di, -tə'-, -'veə- (US) ˌmɑːn.t̬ə'ver

Montevideo ˌmɒn.tɪ.vɪ'deɪ.əʊ, -tə- (US) ˌmɑːn.t̬ə.və'deɪ.oʊ, -'vɪd.i.oʊ

Montezuma ˌmɒn.tɪ'zuː.mə, -tə'-, -'zjuː- (US) ˌmɑːn.t̬ə'zuː-

Montfort 'mɒnt.fət, -fɔːt (US) 'mɑːnt.fɚt, -fɔːrt

Montgomerie mənt'gʌm.ᵊr.i, mɒnt-, -'gɒm-, '-ri (US) mɑːnt'gʌm.ri, mənt-, '-ɚ.i

Montgomery mənt'gʌm.ᵊr.i, mɒnt-, -'gɒm-, -'ri (US) mɑːnt'gʌm.ri, mənt-, '-ɚ.i **-shire** -ʃəʳ, -ˌʃɪəʳ (US) -ʃɚ, -ˌʃɪr

month mʌntθ **-s** -s **-ly** -li **in a ˌmonth of 'Sundays**

Monticello ˌmɒn.tɪ'tʃel.əʊ (US) ˌmɑːn.tɪ'tʃel.oʊ, -'sel-

Montmorency ˌmɒnt.mᵊr'ent.si (US) ˌmɑːnt-

Montpelier *in US, London street:* mɒnt'piː.li.əʳ (US) mɑːnt'piːl.jɚ

Montpellier *in France:* mɔ̃ːm'pel.i.eɪ (US) ˌmõʊn.pəl'jeɪ *in names of streets, etc.:* mɒnt'pel.i.əʳ, mənt- (US) mɑːnt'pel.i.ɚ

Montreal ˌmɒn.tri'ɔːl (US) ˌmɑːn.tri'ɔːl, ˌmʌn-, -'ɑːl

Montreux mɒn'trɜː *as if French:* mɔ̃ːn- (US) mɑːn-

Montrose mɒn'trəʊz, mən- (US) mɑːn'troʊz

Mont-Saint-Michel ˌmɒntˌsæn.mɪ'ʃel, -ˌsæm- *as if French:* ˌmɔ̃ːn- *as if French:* (US) ˌmõʊnˌsæn.miː'ʃel

Montserrat *island in West Indies:* ˌmɒnt.sə'ræt, -ser'æt (US) ˌmɑːnt.sə'ræt *monastery in Spain:* ˌmɒnt.sə'rɑːt, -ser'ɑːt (US) ˌmɑːnt.sə'rɑːt

Monty 'mɒn.ti (US) 'mɑːn.t̬i, -ti

monument 'mɒn.jə.mənt, -jʊ- (US) 'mɑːn.jə-, -juː- **-s** -s

monumental ˌmɒn.jə'men.tᵊl, -jʊ'- (US) ˌmɑːn.jə'men.t̬ᵊl, -juː'- **-ly** -i

Monza 'mɒn.zə (US) 'mɔːnt.sɑː, 'moʊnt-, 'mɑː-

Monzie mə'niː, mɒn'iː (US) mɔːn'ziː, mɑːn-, '--

moo muː **-s** -z **-ing** -ɪŋ **-ed** -d

mooch muːtʃ **-es** -ɪz **-ing** -ɪŋ **-ed** -t **-er/s** -əʳ/z (US) -ɚ/z

moo-cow 'muː.kaʊ **-s** -z

mood muːd **-s** -z

mood|y (M) 'muː.d|i **-ier** -i.əʳ (US) -i.ɚ **-iest** -i.ɪst, -i.əst **-ily** -ɪ.li, -ᵊl.i **-iness** -ɪ.nəs, -ɪ.nɪs

Moog® məʊg, muːg (US) moʊg, muːg

moola(h) 'muː.lə

mooli 'muː.li

moon (M) muːn **-s** -z **-ing** -ɪŋ **-ed** -d **ˌover the 'moon**

moonbeam 'muːn.biːm, 'muːm- (US) 'muːn- **-s** -z

moonca|lf 'muːn.kɑː|f, 'muːŋ- (US) 'muːn.kæ|f **-ves** -vz

Mooney 'muː.ni

moonie (M) 'muː.ni **-s** -z

moon|light 'muːn|.laɪt **-lit** -lɪt **-lights** -laɪts **-lighting** -ˌlaɪ.tɪŋ (US) -ˌlaɪ.t̬ɪŋ **-lighted** -ˌlaɪ.tɪd (US) -ˌlaɪ.t̬ɪd

moonscape 'muːn.skeɪp **-s** -s

moonshine 'muːn.ʃaɪn

moonstone 'muːn.stəʊn (US) -stoʊn **-s** -z

moonstruck 'muːn.strʌk

moony 'muː.ni

moor (M) mɔːʳ, mʊəʳ (US) mʊr **-s** -z **-ing** -ɪŋ/z **-ed** -d

Moorall 'mɔː.rɔːl (US) 'mɔːr.ɔːl, -ᵊl

moorcock (M) 'mɔː.kɒk, 'mʊə- (US) 'mʊr.kɑːk **-s** -z

Moorcroft 'mɔː.krɒft, 'mʊə- (US) 'mʊr.krɑːft

Moore mɔːʳ, mʊəʳ (US) mʊr, mɔːr

Moorends 'mɔː.rendz, 'mʊə- (US) 'mʊr.endz

Moorfoot 'mɔː.fʊt, 'mʊə- (US) 'mʊr-

Moorgate 'mɔː.geɪt, 'mʊə-, -gɪt (US) 'mʊr-

Moorhead 'mɔː.hed, 'mʊə- (US) 'mʊr-, 'mɔːr-

moorhen 'mɔː.hen, 'mʊə- (US) 'mʊr- **-s** -z

Moorhouse 'mɔː.haʊs, 'mʊə- (US) 'mʊr-, 'mɔːr-

mooring 'mɔː.rɪŋ, 'mʊə- (US) 'mʊr.ɪŋ **-s** -z

Moorish 'mʊə.rɪʃ, 'mɔː- (US) 'mʊr.ɪʃ

moorland 'mɔː.lənd, 'mʊə-, -lænd (US) 'mʊr- **-s** -z

Note: The variant /-lænd/ is not used when the word is attributive.

moos|e muːs **-es** -ɪz

moot muːt **-s** -s **-ing** -ɪŋ US ˈmuː.t̬ɪŋ **-ed** -ɪd US ˈmuː.t̬ɪd

mop mɒp US mɑːp **-s** -s **-ping** -ɪŋ **-ped** -t

mop|e məʊp US moʊp **-es** -s **-ing/ly** -ɪŋ/li **-ed** -t

moped *(n.)* ˈməʊ.ped US ˈmoʊ- **-s** -z

mopoke ˈməʊ.pəʊk US ˈmoʊ.poʊk **-s** -s

moppet (M) ˈmɒp.ɪt US ˈmɑː.pɪt **-s** -s

Mopsy ˈmɒp.si US ˈmɑːp-

moquette mɒkˈet, məʊˈket US moʊ-

mor|a ˈmɔː.r|ə US ˈmɔːr|.ə, ˈmoʊ.r|ə **-ae** -iː, -aɪ **-as** -əz

Morag ˈmɔː.ræg US ˈmɔːr.æg

moraine mɒrˈeɪn, məˈreɪn US mə-, mɔː- **-s** -z

moral ˈmɒr.əl US ˈmɔːr- **-s** -z **-ly** -i

morale məˈrɑːl, mɒrˈɑːl US məˈræl, mɔː-

Morales mɒrˈɑː.lez, -les US məˈræl.ɪs, mɔːˈrɑː.lɪs

moralist ˈmɒr.əl.ɪst US ˈmɔːr- **-s** -s

moralistic ˌmɒr.əlˈɪs.tɪk US ˌmɔːr- **-ally** -əl.i, -li

morality məˈræl.ə.ti, mɒrˈæl-, -ɪ.ti US mɔːˈræl.ə.t̬i, mə- **moˈrality ˌplay**

moraliz|e, -is|e ˈmɒr.əl.aɪz US ˈmɔːr- **-es** -ɪz **-ing** -ɪŋ **-ed** -d **-er/s** -əʳ/z US -ɚ/z

Moran ˈmɔː.rən, ˈmɒr.ən; məˈræn, mɒrˈæn US mɔːˈræn, mə-; ˈmɔːr.ən

Morant məˈrænt, mɒrˈænt US mɔːˈrænt, mə-

Morar ˈmɔː.rəʳ US ˈmɔːr.ɚ

morass məˈræs, mɒrˈæs US məˈræs, mɔː- **-es** -ɪz

moratori|um ˌmɒr.əˈtɔː.ri|.əm, ˌmɔː.rəˈ- US ˌmɔːr.əˈtɔːr.i- **-ums** -əmz **-a** -ə

Moravi|a məˈreɪ.vi|.ə, mɒrˈeɪ- US mɔːˈreɪ-, mə- **-an/s** -ən/z

moray *eel:* ˈmɒr.eɪ, ˈmɔː.reɪ; məˈreɪ US ˈmɔːr.eɪ; mɔːˈreɪ, mə- **-s** -z

Moray ˈmʌr.i US ˈmɝː-

morbid ˈmɔː.bɪd US ˈmɔːr- **-ly** -li **-ness** -nəs, -nɪs

morbidity mɔːˈbɪd.ə.ti, -ɪ.ti US mɔːrˈbɪd.ə.t̬i

mordant ˈmɔː.dənt US ˈmɔːr- **-s** -s **-ly** -li

Mordaunt ˈmɔː.dənt, -daʊnt US ˈmɔːr-

Mordecai ˌmɔː.dɪˈkeɪ.aɪ, -dəˈ-, -ˈkaɪ.iː; ˈmɔː.dɪ.kaɪ, -də- US ˈmɔːr.də.kaɪ, ˈkeɪ.aɪ

Morden ˈmɔː.dən US ˈmɔːr-

mordent ˈmɔː.dənt US ˈmɔːr- **-s** -s

Mordor ˈmɔː.dɔːʳ US ˈmɔːr.dɔːr

Mordred ˈmɔː.drɪd, -drəd, -dred US ˈmɔːr.dred, -drəd

more (M) mɔːʳ US mɔːr

Morea mɒrˈiː.ə, məˈriː.ə, mɔː- US mɔːˈriː.ə

Moreau mɒrˈəʊ, məˈrəʊ US mɑːˈroʊ, mə-

Morecambe ˈmɔː.kəm US ˈmɔːr-

moreish ˈmɔː.rɪʃ US ˈmɔːr.ɪʃ

morel (M) mɒrˈel, məˈrel US mɔː-, mə- **-s** -z

morello məˈrel.əʊ, mɒrˈel- US məˈrel.oʊ **-s** -z

Morelos məˈrel.ɒs, mɔː- US mɔːˈrel.ɑːs

Moreno məˈriː.nəʊ, mɒrˈiː- US məˈriː.noʊ, mɔː-, -ˈren.oʊ

moreover mɔːˈrˈəʊ.vəʳ, məʳ- US mɔːrˈoʊ.vɚ, ˈ-ˌ--

mores ˈmɔː.reɪz, -riːz US ˈmɔːr.eɪz, -iːz

Moresby *surname:* ˈmɔːz.bi US ˈmɔːrz- *in Cumbria:* ˈmɒr.ɪs.bi US ˈmɔːr.ɪs-

Moreton ˈmɔː.tən US ˈmɔːr-

Morgan ˈmɔː.gən US ˈmɔːr-

morganatic ˌmɔː.gəˈnæt.ɪk US ˌmɔːr.gəˈnæt̬- **-ally** -əl.i US -li

Morgan le Fay ˌmɔː.gən.ləˈfeɪ US ˌmɔːr-

morgue mɔːg US mɔːrg **-s** -z

MORI ˈmɔː.ri, ˈmɒr.i US ˈmɔːr.i

Moriah mɒrˈaɪ.ə, mɔːˈraɪ.ə, mə- US mə-, mɔː-, moʊ-

Moriarty ˌmɒr.iˈɑː.ti US ˌmɔːr.iˈɑːr.t̬i

moribund ˈmɒr.ɪ.bʌnd, ˈmɔː.rɪ-, -bənd US ˈmɔːr.ɪ.bʌnd

Morison ˈmɒr.ɪ.sən, ˈ-ə- US ˈmɔːr.ɪ-

Morley ˈmɔː.li US ˈmɔːr-

Morlock ˈmɔː.lɒk US ˈmɔːr.lɑːk **-s** -s

Mormon ˈmɔː.mən US ˈmɔːr- **-s** -z **-ism** -ɪ.zəm

morn mɔːn US mɔːrn **-s** -z

mornay ˈmɔː.neɪ US mɔːrˈneɪ

morning ˈmɔː.nɪŋ US ˈmɔːr- **-s** -z **ˈmorning ˌcoat; ˈmorning ˌdress, ˌmorning ˈdress; ˈmorning ˌroom; ˈmorning ˌsickness; ˌmorning ˈstar**

morning-after ˌmɔː.nɪŋˈɑːf.təʳ US ˌmɔːr.nɪŋˈæf.tɚ **ˌmorning-ˈafter ˌpill**

Mornington ˈmɔː.nɪŋ.tən US ˈmɔːr-

Moroccan məˈrɒk.ən US -ˈrɑː.kən **-s** -z

Morocco, morocco məˈrɒk.əʊ US -ˈrɑː.koʊ **-s** -z

moron ˈmɔː.rɒn US ˈmɔːr.ɑːn **-s** -z

Moroni məˈrəʊ.ni US -ˈroʊ-, mɔː-

moronic mɔːˈrɒn.ɪk, mə-, mɒrˈɒn- US mɔːˈrɑː.nɪk, mə- **-ally** -əl.i, -li

morose məˈrəʊs, mɒrˈəʊs US məˈroʊs, mɔː- **-ly** -li **-ness** -nəs, -nɪs

Morpeth ˈmɔː.peθ, -pəθ US ˈmɔːr-

-morph -mɔːf US -mɔːrf

Note: Suffix. Normally not stressed, e.g. **ectomorph** /ˈek.təʊ.mɔːf US -tə.mɔːrf/.

morph mɔːf US mɔːrf **-s** -s **-ing** -ɪŋ **-ed** -t

morpheme ˈmɔː.fiːm US ˈmɔːr- **-s** -z

morphemic mɔːˈfiː.mɪk US mɔːr- **-ally** -əl.i, -li

morphemics mɔːˈfiː.mɪks US mɔːr-

Morpheus ˈmɔː.fi.əs, ˈ-fjəs US ˈmɔːr.fi.əs, ˈ-fjuːs

morphia ˈmɔː.fi.ə US ˈmɔːr-

morphine ˈmɔː.fiːn US ˈmɔːr-

morpho- mɔː.fəʊ-; mɔːˈfɒ- US mɔːr.foʊ-, -fə-; mɔːrˈfɑː-

Note: Prefix. Normally takes secondary stress on the first syllable, e.g. **morphologic** /ˌmɔː.fəˈlɒdʒ.ɪk US ˌmɔːr.fəˈlɑː.dʒɪk/, or primary stress on the second syllable, e.g **morphology** /mɔːˈfɒl.ə.dʒi US mɔːrˈfɑː.lə-/.

morphologic ˌmɔː.fəˈlɒdʒ.ɪk US ˌmɔːr.fəˈlɑː.dʒɪk **-al** -əl **-ally** -əl.i, -li

morpholog|y mɔːˈfɒl.ə.dʒ|i US mɔːrˈfɑː.lə- **-ies** -iz **-ist/s** -ɪst/s

morphophoneme ˌmɔː.fəʊˈfəʊ.niːm US ˌmɔːr.foʊˈfoʊ- **-s** -z

morphophonemic ˌmɔː.fəʊ.fəˈniː.mɪk US ˌmɔːr.foʊ- **-s** -s

morphophonology ˌmɔː.fəʊ.fəˈnɒl.ə.dʒi US ˌmɔːr.foʊ.fəˈnɑː.lə-

morphosyntactic ˌmɔː.fəʊ.sɪnˈtæk.tɪk US ˌmɔːr.foʊ- **-ally** -əl.i, -li

morphosyntax ˌmɔː.fəʊˈsɪn.tæks US ˌmɔːr.foʊ-

Morphy ˈmɔː.fi US ˈmɔːr-

Morrell ˈmʌr.əl, məˈrel

Morrill ˈmɒr.ɪl, -əl US ˈmɔːr-

morris (M) ˈmɒr.ɪs US ˈmɔːr- **-es** -ɪz **ˈmorris ˌdancing; ˈmorris ˌman**

Morrison ˈmɒr.ɪ.sən, ˈ-ə- US ˈmɔːr-

Morrissey ˈmɒr.ɪ.si, -ə- US ˈmɔːr-, ˈmɑːr-

Morristown ˈmɒr.ɪs.taʊn US ˈmɔːr-

morrow (M) ˈmɒr.əʊ US ˈmɑːr.oʊ, ˈmɔːr- **-s** -z

mors|e (M) mɔːs US mɔːrs **-es** -ɪz **ˌMorse ˈcode, ˈMorse ˌcode**

morsel ˈmɔː.səl US ˈmɔːr- **-s** -z

Morshead ˈmɔːz.hed US ˈmɔːrz-

mort (M) mɔːt US mɔːrt **-s** -s

mortadella ˌmɔː.təˈdel.ə US ˌmɔːr-

mortal ˈmɔː.təl US ˈmɔːr.t̬əl **-s** -z **-ly** -i **ˌmortal ˈsin**

mortalit|y (M) mɔːˈtæl.ə.t|i, -ɪ.t|i US mɔːrˈtæl.ə.t̬|i **-ies** -iz

mort|ar ˈmɔː.t|əʳ US ˈmɔːr.t|ɚ **-ars** -əz US -ɚz **-aring** -ər.ɪŋ **-ared** -əd US -ɚd

mortarboard ˈmɔː.tə.bɔːd US ˈmɔːr.t̬ɚ.bɔːrd **-s** -z

Morte d'Arthur(e) ˌmɔːtˈdɑː.θəʳ US ˌmɔːrtˈdɑːr.θɚ

mortgag|e ˈmɔː.gɪdʒ US ˈmɔːr- **-es** -ɪz **-ing** -ɪŋ **-ed** -d

mortgagee ˌmɔː.gɪˈdʒiː, -gəˈ- US ˌmɔːr- **-s** -z

mortgagor ˌmɔː.ɡɪˈdʒɔːʳ, -ɡəˈ-; ˈmɔː.ɡɪ.dʒəʳ, -ɡə- ⓊⓈ ˈmɔːr.ɡɪ.dʒɚ **-s** -z
mortic|e ˈmɔː.tɪs ⓊⓈ ˈmɔːr.t̬ɪs **-es** -ɪz **-ing** -ɪŋ **-ed** -t
mortician mɔːˈtɪʃ.ᵊn ⓊⓈ mɔːr- **-s** -z
mortification ˌmɔː.tɪ.fɪˈkeɪ.ʃᵊn, -tə- ⓊⓈ ˌmɔːr.t̬ə.fɪˈ-
morti|fy ˈmɔː.tɪ|.faɪ, -tə- ⓊⓈ ˈmɔːr.t̬ə- **-fies** -faɪz **-fying** -faɪ.ɪŋ **-fied** -faɪd
Mortimer ˈmɔː.tɪ.məʳ, -tə- ⓊⓈ ˈmɔːr.t̬ə.mɚ
mortis|e ˈmɔː.tɪs ⓊⓈ ˈmɔːr.t̬ɪs **-es** -ɪz **-ing** -ɪŋ **-ed** -t **ˈmortise ˌlock**
Mortlake ˈmɔːt.leɪk ⓊⓈ ˈmɔːrt-
Mortlock ˈmɔːt.lɒk ⓊⓈ ˈmɔːrt.lɑːk
mortmain ˈmɔːt.meɪn ⓊⓈ ˈmɔːrt-
Morton ˈmɔː.tᵊn ⓊⓈ ˈmɔːr-
mortuar|y ˈmɔː.tʃu.ᵊr|.i, -tjʊ-, -tjʊ.r|i, -tʃᵊr|.i ⓊⓈ ˈmɔːr.tʃu.er|.i **-ies** -iz
Morwenna mɔːˈwen.ə ⓊⓈ mɔːr-
mosaic (M) məʊˈzeɪ.ɪk ⓊⓈ moʊ- **-s** -s
Mosborough ˈmɒz.brə, -bᵊr.ə ⓊⓈ ˈmɑːz.bɚ.oʊ, -bᵊr.ə
Mosby ˈmɒz.bi ⓊⓈ ˈmoʊz-
Mosca ˈmɒs.kə ⓊⓈ ˈmɑːs-
Moscow ˈmɒs.kəʊ ⓊⓈ ˈmɑː.skaʊ, -skoʊ
Moseley ˈməʊz.li ⓊⓈ ˈmoʊz-
moselle (M) məʊˈzel ⓊⓈ moʊ- **-s** -z
Moses ˈməʊ.zɪz ⓊⓈ ˈmoʊ- **ˈMoses ˌbasket**
mosey ˈməʊ.zi ⓊⓈ ˈmoʊ- **-s** -z **-ing** -ɪŋ **-ed** -d
Mosimann ˈmɒs.ɪ.mən ⓊⓈ ˈmɑː.sɪ-
Moslem ˈmɒz.ləm, ˈmʊz-, -lem, -lɪm ⓊⓈ ˈmɑːz.lem, ˈmɑːs- **-s** -z
Mosley ˈməʊz.li, ˈmɒz- ⓊⓈ ˈmoʊz-
mosque mɒsk ⓊⓈ mɑːsk **-s** -s
mosquito (M) mɒsˈkiː.təʊ, məˈskiː- ⓊⓈ məˈskiː.t̬oʊ **-(e)s** -z **mosˈquito ˌnet**
moss (M) mɒs ⓊⓈ mɑːs **-es** -ɪz
Mossad ˈmɒs.æd ⓊⓈ moʊˈsɑːd
moss-grown ˈmɒs.ɡrəʊn ⓊⓈ ˈmɑːs.ɡroʊn
Mossley ˈmɒs.li ⓊⓈ ˈmɑːs-
Mossman *area of Sydney:* ˈmɒz.mən ⓊⓈ ˈmɑːz- *other senses:* ˈmɒs.mən ⓊⓈ ˈmɑːs-
Mossmorran mɒsˈmɒr.ən ⓊⓈ mɑːsˈmɔːr-
moss|y ˈmɒs|.i ⓊⓈ ˈmɑː.s|i **-ier** -i.əʳ ⓊⓈ -i.ɚ **-iest** -i.ɪst, -i.əst **-iness** -ɪ.nəs, -ɪ.nɪs
mos|t məʊs|t ⓊⓈ moʊs|t **-tly** -tli
Mostar ˈmɒs.tɑːʳ ⓊⓈ ˈmɑː.stɑːr
Mostyn ˈmɒs.tɪn ⓊⓈ ˈmɑː.stɪn
Mosul ˈməʊ.sᵊl ⓊⓈ moʊˈsuːl; ˈmoʊ.səl
mot məʊ ⓊⓈ moʊ **-s** -z
MoT, MOT ˌem.əʊˈtiː ⓊⓈ -oʊˈ- **-s** -z **-'s** -z **-'d** -d **-'ing** -ɪŋ **ˌMoT cerˈtificate, ˌMoˈT cerˌtificate; ˌMoT ˈtest, ˌMoˈT ˌtest**
mote məʊt ⓊⓈ moʊt **-s** -s
motel məʊˈtel ⓊⓈ moʊ- **-s** -z
motet məʊˈtet ⓊⓈ moʊ- **-s** -s
moth mɒθ ⓊⓈ mɑːθ **-s** -s
Mothaks® ˈmɒθ.æks ⓊⓈ ˈmɑː.θæks
mothball ˈmɒθ.bɔːl ⓊⓈ ˈmɑːθ-, -bɑːl **-s** -z **-ing** -ɪŋ **-ed** -d
moth-eaten ˈmɒθˌiː.tᵊn ⓊⓈ ˈmɑːθˌiː-
moth|er (M) ˈmʌð|.əʳ ⓊⓈ -ɚ **-ers** -əz ⓊⓈ -ɚz **-ering** -ᵊr.ɪŋ **-ered** -əd ⓊⓈ -ɚd **-erless** -ə.ləs, -les, -lɪs ⓊⓈ -ɚ- **ˈmother ˌcountry; ˌmother ˈhen; ˌmother ˈnature; ˌmother suˈperior; ˈMother's ˌDay; ˌmother ˈtongue**
motherboard ˈmʌð.ə.bɔːd ⓊⓈ -ɚ.bɔːrd **-s** -z
Mothercare® ˈmʌð.ə.keəʳ ⓊⓈ -ɚ.ker
motherfucker ˈmʌð.əˌfʌk.əʳ ⓊⓈ -ɚˌfʌk.ɚ **-s** -z
mother-fucking ˈmʌð.əˌfʌk.ɪŋ ⓊⓈ -ɚˌ-
motherhood ˈmʌð.ə.hʊd ⓊⓈ ˈ-ɚ-
mother-in-law ˈmʌð.ᵊr.ɪnˌlɔː ⓊⓈ -ɚ.ɪnˌlɑː, -ˌlɔː **mothers-in-law** ˈmʌð.əz- ⓊⓈ -ɚz-
motherland ˈmʌð.ə.lænd ⓊⓈ ˈ-ɚ- **-s** -z
motherl|y ˈmʌð.ᵊl|.i ⓊⓈ -ɚ.l|i **-iness** -ɪ.nəs, -ɪ.nɪs
mother-of-pearl ˌmʌð.əʳ.əvˈpɜːl ⓊⓈ -ɚ.əvˈpɝːl
mothersill ˈmʌð.ə.sɪl ⓊⓈ ˈ-ɚ-
Motherwell ˈmʌð.ə.wel ⓊⓈ ˈ-ɚ-
motif məʊˈtiːf ⓊⓈ moʊ- **-s** -s
motile ˈməʊ.taɪl ⓊⓈ ˈmoʊ.t̬ᵊl, -taɪl
motion (M) ˈməʊ.ʃᵊn ⓊⓈ ˈmoʊ- **-s** -z **-ing** -ɪŋ, ˈməʊʃ.nɪŋ ⓊⓈ ˈmoʊʃ- **-ed** -d **-less** -ləs, -lɪs **ˌmotion ˈpicture; ˈmotion ˌsickness**
moti|vate ˈməʊ.tɪ|.veɪt, -tə- ⓊⓈ ˈmoʊ.t̬ə- **-vates** -veɪts **-vating** -veɪ.tɪŋ ⓊⓈ -veɪ.t̬ɪŋ **-vated** -veɪ.tɪd ⓊⓈ -veɪ.t̬ɪd **-vator/s** -veɪ.təʳ/z ⓊⓈ -veɪ.t̬ɚ/z
motivation ˌməʊ.tɪˈveɪ.ʃᵊn, -təˈ- ⓊⓈ ˌmoʊ.t̬əˈ- **-al** -ᵊl
motive ˈməʊ.tɪv ⓊⓈ ˈmoʊ.t̬ɪv **-s** -z **-less** -ləs, -lɪs
mot juste ˌməʊˈʒuːst ⓊⓈ ˌmoʊ-
motley (M) ˈmɒt.li ⓊⓈ ˈmɑːt-
motocross ˈməʊ.təʊ.krɒs ⓊⓈ ˈmoʊ.t̬oʊ.krɑːs
mot|or ˈməʊ.t|əʳ ⓊⓈ ˈmoʊ.t̬|ɚ **-ors** -əz ⓊⓈ -ɚz **-oring** -ᵊr.ɪŋ **-ored** -əd ⓊⓈ -ɚd **ˈmotor ˌcar; ˈmotor ˌhome; ˈmotor ˌlodge; ˈmotor ˌscooter; ˈmotor ˌvehicle**
Motorail® ˈməʊ.tᵊr.eɪl ⓊⓈ ˈmoʊ.t̬ə.reɪl
motorbike ˈməʊ.tə.baɪk ⓊⓈ ˈmoʊ.t̬ɚ- **-s** -s
motorboat ˈməʊ.tə.bəʊt ⓊⓈ ˈmoʊ.t̬ɚ.boʊt **-s** -s
motorcade ˈməʊ.tə.keɪd ⓊⓈ ˈmoʊ.t̬ɚ- **-s** -z
motorcycle ˈməʊ.təˌsaɪ.kl̩ ⓊⓈ ˈmoʊ.t̬ɚ- **-s** -z
motorcyclist ˈməʊ.təˌsaɪ.klɪst, -kl̩.ɪst ⓊⓈ ˈmoʊ.t̬ɚ- **-s** -s
motorhome ˈməʊ.tə.həʊm ⓊⓈ ˈmoʊ.t̬ɚ.hoʊm **-s** -z
motorist ˈməʊ.tᵊr.ɪst ⓊⓈ ˈmoʊ.t̬ɚ- **-s** -s
motoriz|e, -is|e ˈməʊ.tᵊr.aɪz ⓊⓈ ˈmoʊ.t̬ə.raɪz **-es** -ɪz **-ing** -ɪŋ **-ed** -d
motor|man ˈməʊ.tə|.mæn ⓊⓈ ˈmoʊ.t̬ɚ-, -mən **-men** -men
motormou|th ˈməʊ.tə.maʊ|θ ⓊⓈ ˈmoʊ.t̬ɚ- **-ths** -ðz
Motorola ˌməʊ.təˈrəʊ.lə ⓊⓈ ˌmoʊ.t̬əˈroʊ.lə
motor-scooter ˈməʊ.təˌskuː.təʳ ⓊⓈ ˈmoʊ.t̬ɚˌskuː.t̬ɚ **-s** -z
motorway ˈməʊ.tə.weɪ ⓊⓈ ˈmoʊ.t̬ɚ- **-s** -z
Motown® ˈməʊ.taʊn ⓊⓈ ˈmoʊ-
Mott mɒt ⓊⓈ mɑːt
motte mɒt ⓊⓈ mɑːt **-s** -s
Mottistone ˈmɒt.ɪ.stᵊn, -stəʊn ⓊⓈ ˈmɑː.t̬ɪ.stᵊn, -stoʊn
mottl|e ˈmɒt.l̩ ⓊⓈ ˈmɑː.t̬l̩ **-es** -z **-ing** -ɪŋ **-ed** -d
motto ˈmɒt.əʊ ⓊⓈ ˈmɑː.t̬oʊ **-(e)s** -z
Mottram ˈmɒt.rəm ⓊⓈ ˈmɑː.trəm
moue muː **-s** -z
mouf(f)lon ˈmuː.flɒn ⓊⓈ -flɑːn **-s** -z
Moughton ˈməʊ.tᵊn ⓊⓈ ˈmoʊ-
Mouland ˈmuː.lænd, mʊˈlænd
mould məʊld ⓊⓈ moʊld **-s** -z **-ing/s** -ɪŋ/z **-ed** -ɪd
mould|er ˈməʊl.d|əʳ ⓊⓈ ˈmoʊl.d|ɚ **-ers** -əz ⓊⓈ -ɚz **-ering** -ᵊr.ɪŋ **-ered** -əd ⓊⓈ -ɚd
mould|y ˈməʊl.d|i ⓊⓈ ˈmoʊl- **-ier** -i.əʳ ⓊⓈ -i.ɚ **-iest** -i.ɪst, -i.əst **-iness** -ɪ.nəs, -ɪ.nɪs
Moule məʊl, muːl ⓊⓈ moʊl, muːl
Moulinex® ˈmuː.lɪ.neks, -lə-
Moulin Rouge ˌmuː.læ̃nˈruːʒ
Moulmein ˈmaʊl.meɪn ⓊⓈ mʊlˈmeɪn, moʊl-
Moulsford ˈməʊls.fəd, ˈməʊlz- ⓊⓈ ˈmoʊls.fɚd, ˈmoʊlz-
moult məʊlt ⓊⓈ moʊlt **-s** -s **-ing** -ɪŋ ⓊⓈ ˈmoʊl.t̬ɪŋ **-ed** -ɪd ⓊⓈ ˈmoʊl.t̬ɪd
Moulton ˈməʊl.tᵊn ⓊⓈ ˈmoʊl-
Moultrie ˈmɔːl.tri, ˈmuː-
mound (M) maʊnd **-s** -z
Mounsey ˈmaʊn.zi
mount (M) maʊnt **-s** -s **-ing** -ɪŋ ⓊⓈ ˈmaʊn.t̬ɪŋ **-ed** -ɪd ⓊⓈ ˈmaʊn.t̬ɪd
mountain ˈmaʊn.tɪn, -tən ⓊⓈ -tᵊn **-s** -z **ˈmountain ˌbike; ˈmountain ˌlion; make a ˌmountain out of a ˈmole-hill**

mountain-ash ˌmaʊn.tɪnˈæʃ, -tənˈ- ⓤⓢ -tᵊnˈ- **-es** -ɪz
mountaineer ˌmaʊn.tɪˈnɪəʳ, -təˈ- ⓤⓢ -tᵊnˈɪr **-s** -z **-ing** -ɪŋ
mountainous ˈmaʊn.tɪ.nəs, -tə- ⓤⓢ -tᵊn.əs
mountainside ˈmaʊn.tɪn.saɪd, -tən- ⓤⓢ -tᵊn- **-s** -z
mountaintop ˈmaʊn.tɪn.tɒp, -tən- ⓤⓢ -tᵊn.tɑːp **-s** -s
mountant ˈmaʊn.tənt **-s** -s
Mountbatten maʊntˈbæt.ᵊn
mountebank ˈmaʊn.tɪ.bæŋk, -tə- ⓤⓢ -t̬ə- **-s** -s
Mount Everest ˌmaʊntˈev.ᵊr.ɪst, -est
Mountford ˈmaʊnt.fəd ⓤⓢ -fɚd
Mountie ˈmaʊn.ti ⓤⓢ -t̬i **-s** -z
Mountjoy ˌmaʊntˈdʒɔɪ, ˈ--
Mountsorrel ˌmaʊntˈsɒr.əl ⓤⓢ -ˈsɔːr-
Mount Vernon ˌmaʊntˈvɜː.nən ⓤⓢ -ˈvɝː-
Mount|y ˈmaʊn.t|i ⓤⓢ -t̬|i **-ies** -iz
Moura ˈmʊə.rə ⓤⓢ ˈmʊr.ə
mourn mɔːn ⓤⓢ mɔːrn **-s** -z **-ing** -ɪŋ **-ed** -d **-er/s** -əʳ/z ⓤⓢ -ɚ/z
Mourne mɔːn ⓤⓢ mɔːrn
mournful ˈmɔːn.fᵊl, -fʊl ⓤⓢ ˈmɔːrn- **-ly** -i **-ness** -nəs, -nɪs
Mousa ˈmuː.zə
mouse *(n.)* maʊs **mice** maɪs
mous|e *(v.)* maʊs, maʊz ⓤⓢ maʊz **-es** -ɪz **-ing** -ɪŋ **-ed** -d
Mousehole ˈmaʊ.zᵊl
mouser ˈmaʊ.səʳ, -zəʳ ⓤⓢ -zɚ **-s** -z
mouse-trap ˈmaʊs.træp **-s** -s
mous|ey ˈmaʊ.s|i **-ier** -i.əʳ ⓤⓢ -i.ɚ **-iest** -i.ɪst, -i.əst
moussaka muˈsɑː.kə, ˈmuː.sæk.ə ⓤⓢ ˌmuˈsɑː.kə; ˌmuː.sɑːˈkɑː
mousse muːs
Moussec® ˌmuːˈsek
mousseline ˈmuː.slɪn, ˌmuːˈsliːn ⓤⓢ ˌmuːˈsliːn
Moussorgsky mʊˈsɔːg.ski, muː- ⓤⓢ muːˈsɔːrg-, mə-, -ˈzɔːrg-, -ˈsɔːrk-, -ˈzɔːrk-
moustach|e məˈstɑːʃ, mʊ- ⓤⓢ ˈmʌs.tæʃ; məˈstæʃ **-es** -ɪz
mous|y ˈmaʊ.s|i **-ier** -i.əʳ ⓤⓢ -i.ɚ **-iest** -i.ɪst, -i.əst
mou|th *(n.)* maʊ|θ **-ths** -ðz **ˈmouth ˌorgan; from the ˌhorse's ˈmouth; ˌdown in the ˈmouth**
mouth *(v.)* maʊð **-s** -z **-ing** -ɪŋ **-ed** -d
mouthful ˈmaʊθ.fʊl **-s** -z
mouthpiec|e ˈmaʊθ.piːs **-es** -ɪz
mouth-to-mouth ˌmaʊθ.təˈmaʊθ *stress shift, see compound:* **ˌmouth-to-mouth reˌsusciˈtation**
mouthwash ˈmaʊθ.wɒʃ ⓤⓢ -wɑːʃ, -wɔːʃ **-es** -ɪz

mouthwatering ˈmaʊθˌwɔː.tᵊr.ɪŋ ⓤⓢ -ˌwɑː.t̬ɚ-, -ˌwɔː- **-ly** -li
mouth|y ˈmaʊ.ð|i, -θ|i **-ier** -i.əʳ ⓤⓢ -i.ɚ **-iest** -i.ɪst, -i.əst
movability ˌmuː.vəˈbɪl.ə.ti, -ɪ.ti ⓤⓢ -ə.t̬i
movable ˈmuː.və.bl̩ **-s** -z **-ness** -nəs, -nɪs
movant ˈmuː.vənt **-s** -s
mov|e muːv **-es** -z **-ing/ly** -ɪŋ/li **-ed** -d **-er/s** -əʳ/z ⓤⓢ -ɚ/z **-eable** -ə.bl̩
movement ˈmuːv.mənt **-s** -s
movie ˈmuː.vi **-s** -z
moviegoer ˈmuː.viˌgəʊ.əʳ ⓤⓢ -ˌgoʊ.ɚ **-s** -z
moviegoing ˈmuː.viˌgəʊ.ɪŋ ⓤⓢ -ˌgoʊ-
moviemak|er ˈmuː.viˌmeɪ.k|əʳ ⓤⓢ -ɚ **-ers** -əz ⓤⓢ -ɚz **-ing** -ɪŋ
mow *(v.) cut down and stack:* məʊ ⓤⓢ moʊ **-s** -z **-ing** -ɪŋ **-ed** -d **-n** -n **-er/s** -əʳ/z ⓤⓢ -ɚ/z
mow *(n.) stack:* maʊ **-s** -z
mow *(n.) grimace:* maʊ ⓤⓢ moʊ, maʊ **-s** -z
Mowat, Mowatt maʊət, məʊət ⓤⓢ maʊət, moʊət
Mowbray ˈməʊ.breɪ, -bri ⓤⓢ ˈmoʊ-
Mowgli ˈmaʊ.gli
Mowlam ˈməʊ.ləm ⓤⓢ ˈmoʊ-
mown *(from* **mow** *v.)* məʊn ⓤⓢ moʊn
Moxon ˈmɒk.sᵊn ⓤⓢ ˈmɑːk-
moya (M) ˈmɔɪ.ə **-s** -z
Moyes mɔɪz
Moygashel *place:* mɔɪˈgæʃ.ᵊl *linen:* ˈmɔɪ.gə.ʃᵊl
Moynahan ˈmɔɪ.nə.hæn, -hən ⓤⓢ ˈmɔɪ.nə.hæn
Moynihan ˈmɔɪ.ni.ən, -hæn; -nə.hæn ⓤⓢ ˈmɔɪ.nɪ.hæn, -nə-
Mozambique ˌməʊ.zæmˈbiːk, -zəmˈ- ⓤⓢ ˌmoʊ-
Mozart ˈməʊt.sɑːt ⓤⓢ ˈmoʊt.sɑːrt
Mozartian ˌməʊtˈsɑː.ti.ən ⓤⓢ ˌmoʊtˈsɑːr.t̬i- **-s** -z
mozzarella ˌmɒt.səˈrel.ə ⓤⓢ ˌmɑːt-, ˌmoʊt-
MP ˌemˈpiː
mph ˌem.piːˈeɪtʃ
MPhil ˌemˈfɪl
Mr ˈmɪs.təʳ ⓤⓢ -tɚ
Mrs ˈmɪs.ɪz
ms, MS *(abbrev. for* **manuscript***)* ˌemˈes, ˈmæn.jə.skrɪpt, -jʊ-
MS *(abbrev. for* **multiple sclerosis***)* ˌemˈes
Ms mɪz, məz ⓤⓢ mɪz
Note: Used to avoid indicating a woman's marital status. The pronunciation is unstable in Britain.
MSc ˌem.esˈsiː
MS-DOS® ˌem.esˈdɒs ⓤⓢ -ˈdɑːs

MSS *(abbrev. for* **manuscripts***)* ˌem.esˈes, ˈmæn.jə.skrɪpts, -jʊ-
MTV ˌem.tiːˈviː
mu mjuː ⓤⓢ mjuː, muː
Mubarak mʊˈbɑː.rək, -ˈbær.æk, -ək ⓤⓢ muːˈbɑːr.ək
much mʌtʃ **-ly** -li
Muchalls ˈmʌk.ᵊlz, ˈmʌx-
muchness ˈmʌtʃ.nəs, -nɪs
mucilag|e ˈmjuː.sɪ.lɪdʒ, -sᵊl.ɪdʒ ⓤⓢ -sə.lɪdʒ **-es** -ɪz
mucilaginous ˌmjuː.sɪˈlædʒ.ɪ.nəs, -sᵊlˈædʒ-, ˈ-ə- ⓤⓢ -sɪˈlædʒ.ə-
muck mʌk **-s** -s **-ing** -ɪŋ **-ed** -t
muck|er ˈmʌk|.əʳ ⓤⓢ -ɚ **-ers** -əz ⓤⓢ -ɚz **-ering** -ᵊr.ɪŋ **-ered** -əd ⓤⓢ -ɚd
Muckle Flugga ˌmʌk.l̩ˈflʌg.ə
muckrak|e ˈmʌk.reɪk **-es** -s **-ing** -ɪŋ **-ed** -t **-er/s** -əʳ/z ⓤⓢ -ɚ/z
muck|y ˈmʌk|.i **-ier** -i.əʳ ⓤⓢ -i.ɚ **-iest** -i.ɪst, -i.əst **-iness** -ɪ.nəs, -ɪ.nɪs
muc(o)us ˈmjuː.kəs ˌ**mucous ˈmembrane**
mud mʌd **-s** -z
mudba|th ˈmʌd.bɑː|θ ⓤⓢ -bæ|θ **-ths** -ðz
Mud(d)eford ˈmʌd.ɪ.fəd ⓤⓢ -fɚd
muddl|e ˈmʌd.l̩ **-es** -z **-ing** -ɪŋ, ˈmʌd.lɪŋ **-ed** -d **-er/s** -əʳ/z ⓤⓢ -ɚ/z, ˈmʌd.ləʳ/z ⓤⓢ -lɚ/z
muddleheaded ˌmʌd.l̩ˈhed.ɪd, ˈmʌd.l̩ˌhed- ⓤⓢ ˈmʌd.l̩ˌhed- **-ness** -nəs, -nɪs
mudd|y ˈmʌd|.i **-ier** -i.əʳ ⓤⓢ -i.ɚ **-iest** -i.ɪst, -i.əst **-ily** -ɪ.li, -ᵊl.i **-iness** -ɪ.nəs, -ɪ.nɪs **-ies** -iz **-ying** -i.ɪŋ **-ied** -id
mudflap ˈmʌd.flæp **-s** -s
mudguard ˈmʌd.gɑːd ⓤⓢ -gɑːrd **-s** -z
Mudie ˈmjuː.di
mudlark ˈmʌd.lɑːk ⓤⓢ -lɑːrk **-s** -s
mudpack ˈmʌd.pæk **-s** -s
mudslide ˈmʌd.slaɪd **-s** -z
Mueller ˈmjuː.ləʳ, ˈmʊl.əʳ ⓤⓢ -ɚ
muesli ˈmjuːz.li, ˈmuːz- ⓤⓢ ˈmjuːz-, ˈmjuːs- **-s** -z
muezzin muˈez.ɪn, mju- ⓤⓢ mju-, mu- **-s** -z
muff mʌf **-s** -s **-ing** -ɪŋ **-ed** -t
muffin ˈmʌf.ɪn **-s** -z
muffl|e ˈmʌf.l̩ **-es** -z **-ing** -ɪŋ, ˈmʌf.lɪŋ **-ed** -d
muffler ˈmʌf.ləʳ ⓤⓢ -lɚ **-s** -z
mufti ˈmʌf.ti
mug mʌg **-s** -z **-ging/s** -ɪŋ/z **-ged** -d **ˈmug ˌshot**
Mugabe mʊˈgɑː.beɪ, -bi
mugger ˈmʌg.əʳ ⓤⓢ -ɚ **-s** -z
muggins (M) ˈmʌg.ɪnz **-es** -ɪz
Muggins ˈmʌg.ɪnz, ˈmjuː.gɪnz
Muggleton ˈmʌg.l̩.tᵊn ⓤⓢ -tən
Muggletonian ˌmʌg.l̩ˈtəʊ.ni.ən ⓤⓢ -ˈtoʊ- **-s** -z

mugg|y ˈmʌɡ|.i **-ier** -i.əʳ (US) -i.ɚ **-iest** -i.ɪst, -i.əst **-iness** -ɪ.nəs, -ɪ.nɪs

mugwump ˈmʌɡ.wʌmp **-s** -s

Muhhamad mʊˈhæm.əd, mə-, -ɪd, -ed

Muir mjʊəʳ, mjɔːʳ (US) mjʊr

Muirhead ˈmjʊə.hed, ˈmjɔː- (US) ˈmjʊr-

mujahideen (M) ˌmuː.dʒə.hedˈiːn, ˈmʊdʒ.ə-, ˈmuː.ʒə-, -ʒɑː-, -həˈdiːn (US) muːˌdʒɑː.həˈdiːn

Muji ˈmuː.dʒi

Mukden ˈmʊk.dən

Mukle ˈmjuː.kli

mukluk ˈmʌk.lʌk **-s** -s

mulatto mjuːˈlæt.əʊ, mjə-, mjʊ-, mə- (US) məˈlæt̬.oʊ, mjuː-, -ˈlɑː.t̬oʊ **-(e)s** -z

mulberr|y ˈmʌl.bᵊr|.i (US) -ˌber- **-ies** -iz

Mulcaster ˈmʌl.kæs.təʳ (US) -tɚ

mulch mʌltʃ **-es** -ɪz **-ing** -ɪŋ **-ed** -t

Mulciber ˈmʌl.sɪ.bəʳ (US) -bɚ

mulct mʌlkt **-s** -s **-ing** -ɪŋ **-ed** -ɪd

mulder ˈmʌl.dəʳ (US) -dɚ

Muldoon mʌlˈduːn

mule mjuːl **-s** -z

muleteer ˌmjuː.lɪˈtɪəʳ, -ləˈ- (US) -ləˈtɪr **-s** -z

mulga ˈmʊl.ɡə **-s** -z

Mulgrave ˈmʌl.ɡreɪv

Mulholland mʌlˈhɒl.ənd (US) -ˈhɑː.lənd

mulish ˈmjuː.lɪʃ **-ly** -li **-ness** -nəs, -nɪs

mull (M) mʌl **-s** -z **-ing** -ɪŋ **-ed** -d

mullah (M) ˈmʊl.ə, ˈmʌl.ə **-s** -z

Mullan, Mullen ˈmʌl.ən

mullein ˈmʌl.ɪn, -eɪn (US) -ɪn

mullet (M) ˈmʌl.ɪt, -ət **-s** -s

Mulligan ˈmʌl.ɪ.ɡən, ˈ-ə-

mulligatawny ˌmʌl.ɪ.ɡəˈtɔː.ni, ˌ-ə- (US) -ˈtɑː.ni, -ˈtɔː-

Mullinar, Mulliner ˈmʌl.ɪ.nəʳ (US) -nɚ

Mullinger ˈmʌl.ɪn.dʒəʳ, -ᵊn- (US) -dʒɚ

Mullins ˈmʌl.ɪnz

mullion (M) ˈmʌl.jən, ˈ-i.ən (US) ˈ-jən **-s** -z **-ed** -d

mullock ˈmʌl.ək

Mulready mʌlˈred.i

Mulroney mʌlˈrəʊ.ni (US) -ˈroʊ-

Multan ˌmʌlˈtɑːn (US) ˌmʊl-

multi- mʌl.ti-, -tɪ-, -tə- (US) mʌl.t̬i-, -t̬ə-, -taɪ-

Note: Prefix. Normally carries primary or secondary stress on the first syllable, e.g. **multiform** /ˈmʌl.ti.fɔːm (US) -t̬i.fɔːrm/, **multilingual** /ˌmʌl.tiˈlɪŋ.ɡwᵊl (US) -t̬iˈ-/.

multicolo(u)red ˌmʌl.tiˈkʌl.əd, ˈmʌl.tiˌkʌl- (US) ˌmʌl.t̬iˈkʌl.ɚd, ˈmʌl.t̬iˌkʌl-

multicultural ˌmʌl.tiˈkʌl.tʃᵊr.ᵊl (US) -t̬iˈ-, -taɪˈ- **-ly** -i **-ism** -ɪ.zᵊm *stress shift:* ˌmulticultural ˈfestival

multiethnic ˌmʌl.tiˈeθ.nɪk (US) -t̬iˈ- *stress shift:* ˌmultiethnic ˈbackground

multifarious ˌmʌl.tɪˈfeə.ri.əs (US) -t̬əˈfer.i- **-ly** -li **-ness** -nəs, -nɪs *stress shift:* ˌmultifarious ˈinfluences

multiform ˈmʌl.ti.fɔːm (US) -t̬i.fɔːrm

multigym ˈmʌl.ti.dʒɪm (US) -t̬i- **-s** -z

multilateral ˌmʌl.tiˈlæt.ᵊr.ᵊl (US) -t̬iˈlæt̬-, -taɪˈ- **-ly** -i *stress shift:* ˌmultilateral ˈtalks

multilingual ˌmʌl.tiˈlɪŋ.ɡwəl (US) -t̬iˈ- **-ly** -i *stress shift:* ˌmultilingual ˈpeople

multimedia ˌmʌl.tiˈmiː.di.ə (US) -t̬iˈ-

multimillionaire ˌmʌl.tiˌmɪl.jəˈneəʳ, -i.əˈ- (US) -t̬iˌmɪl.jəˈner, -taɪˌ-, ˌmʌl.t̬iˈmɪl.jə.ner, -taɪˈ- **-s** -z

multinational ˌmʌl.tiˈnæʃ.ᵊn.ᵊl, -ˈnæʃ.nᵊl (US) -t̬iˈ-, -taɪˈ- **-s** -z *stress shift:* ˌmultinational ˈcompany

multipartite ˌmʌl.tiˈpɑː.taɪt (US) -t̬iˈpɑːr- *stress shift:* ˌmultipartite ˈtreaty

multiplayer ˈmʌl.tɪˌpleɪ.əʳ, -tə- (US) -t̬iˌpleɪ.ɚ **-s** -z

multiple ˈmʌl.tɪ.pl̩, -tə- (US) -t̬ə- **-s** -z **ˌmultiple scleˈrosis**

multiple-choice ˌmʌl.tɪ.pl̩ˈtʃɔɪs, -tə- (US) -t̬ə- *stress shift:* ˌmultiple-choice ˈpaper

multiplex ˈmʌl.tɪ.pleks, -tə- (US) -t̬ə- **-es** -ɪz

multiplicand ˌmʌl.tɪ.plɪˈkænd, -tə- (US) -t̬ə- **-s** -z

multiplication ˌmʌl.tɪ.plɪˈkeɪ.ʃᵊn, -tə- (US) -t̬ə- **-s** -z

multiplicative ˌmʌl.tɪˈplɪk.ə.tɪv, -təˈ-; ˈmʌl.tɪ.plɪ.keɪ.tɪv (US) ˈmʌl.t̬ə.plɪ.keɪ.t̬ɪv; ˌmʌl.təˈplɪk.ə-

multiplicator ˈmʌl.tɪ.plɪ.keɪ.təʳ (US) -t̬ɚ **-s** -z

multiplicit|y ˌmʌl.tɪˈplɪs.ə.t|i, -təˈ-, -ɪ.t|i (US) -t̬əˈplɪs.ə.t̬|i **-ies** -iz

multipl|y ˈmʌl.tɪ.pl|aɪ, -tə- (US) -t̬ə- **-ies** -aɪz **-ying** -aɪ.ɪŋ **-ied** -aɪd **-ier/s** -aɪ.əʳ/z (US) -aɪ.ɚ/z

multiprocessing ˌmʌl.tiˈprəʊ.ses.ɪŋ (US) -t̬iˈprɑː-

multiprocessor ˌmʌl.tiˈprəʊ.ses.əʳ (US) -t̬iˈprɑː.ses.ɚ **-s** -z

multipurpose ˌmʌl.tiˈpɜː.pəs (US) -t̬iˈpɝː- *stress shift:* ˌmultipurpose ˈtool

multiracial ˌmʌl.tiˈreɪ.ʃᵊl, -ʃi.əl (US) -t̬iˈreɪ.ʃᵊl, -taɪˈ- *stress shift:* ˌmultiracial ˈarea

multiscreen ˌmʌl.tiˈskriːn *stress shift:* ˌmultiscreen ˈcinema

multi-storey ˌmʌl.tiˈstɔː.ri (US) -t̬iˈstɔːr.i *stress shift, see compound:* **ˌmulti-storey ˈcar park**

multi-tasking ˌmʌl.tiˈtɑː.skɪŋ, ˈmʌl.tiˌtɑː- (US) ˈmʌl.t̬iˌtæs.kɪŋ

multitude ˈmʌl.tɪ.tjuːd, -tə-, -tʃuːd (US) -t̬ə.tuːd, -tjuːd **-s** -z

multitudinous ˌmʌl.tɪˈtjuː.dɪ.nəs, -təˈ-, -ˈtʃuː-, -dᵊn.əs (US) -t̬əˈtuː.dᵊn-, -ˈtjuː- **-ly** -li **-ness** -nəs, -nɪs

multivalen|t ˌmʌl.tiˈveɪ.lən|t (US) -t̬iˈ- **-ce** -ts

multivitamin ˌmʌl.tiˈvɪt.ə.mɪn, -ˈvaɪ.tə- (US) -ˈvaɪ.t̬ə- **-s** -z

multum in parvo ˌmʊl.təm.ɪnˈpɑː.vəʊ, ˌmʌl- (US) -ˈpɑːr.voʊ

mum (M) mʌm **-s** -z

Mum and the Sothsegger ˌmʌm.ənd.ðəˈsɒθ.seɡ.əʳ, -ˈsəʊθ- (US) -ænd.ðəˈsɑːθ.seɡ.ɚ

mumbl|e ˈmʌm.bl̩ **-es** -z **-ing/ly** -ɪŋ/li, ˈ-blɪŋ/li **-ed** -d **-er/s** -əʳ/z (US) ˈ-bləʳ/z, ˈ-bl̩.ɚ/z (US) ˈ-blɚ/z

Mumbles ˈmʌm.bl̩z

mumbo-jumbo ˌmʌm.bəʊˈdʒʌm.bəʊ (US) -boʊˈdʒʌm.boʊ

Mumm mʌm *as if French:* mʊm

mumm|er ˈmʌm|.əʳ (US) -ɚ **-ers** -əz, -ɚz **-ery** -ᵊr.i

mummification ˌmʌm.ɪ.fɪˈkeɪ.ʃᵊn, ˌ-ə-

mummi|fy ˈmʌm.ɪ|.faɪ (US) ˈ-ə- **-fies** -faɪz **-fying** -faɪ.ɪŋ **-fied** -faɪd

mumm|y (M) ˈmʌm|.i **-ies** -iz

mump mʌmp **-s** -s **-ing** -ɪŋ **-ed** -t

mumpish ˈmʌm.pɪʃ **-ly** -li **-ness** -nəs, -nɪs

mumps mʌmps

mums|y ˈmʌm.z|i **-ily** -ɪ.li, -ᵊl.i **-iness** -ɪ.nəs, -ɪ.nɪs

Munby ˈmʌn.bi, ˈmʌm- (US) ˈmʌn-

munch mʌntʃ **-es** -ɪz **-ing** -ɪŋ **-ed** -t **-er/s** -əʳ/z (US) -ɚ/z

Munch mʊŋk **-s** -s

Munchausen, Münchausen, Münchhausen ˈmʌn.tʃaʊ.zᵊn, ˈmʊntʃ-, -haʊ-; mʌnˈtʃɔː.zᵊn (US) ˈmʌn.tʃaʊ.zᵊn, ˈmʊn-, -tʃɔː-

munchies (M®) ˈmʌn.tʃiz

munchkin ˈmʌntʃ.kɪn **-s** -z

Muncie ˈmʌn.tsi

mundane mʌnˈdeɪn, ˈ-- **-ly** -li

Munera Pulveris ˌmjuː.nᵊr.əˈpʊl.vᵊr.ɪs

mung mʌŋ **ˈmung ˌbean**

mungo (M) ˈmʌŋ.ɡəʊ (US) -ɡoʊ **-s** -z

Munich ˈmjuː.nɪk

municipal mjuːˈnɪs.ɪ.pᵊl, ˈ-ə- (US) ˈ-ə-

municipalit|y mjuːˌnɪs.ɪˈpæl.ə.t|i, -əˈ-, -ɪ.t|i; ˌmjuː.nɪ.sɪˈ-, -səˈ- (US) mjuːˌnɪs.əˈpæl.ə.t̬|i **-ies** -iz

municipaliz|e, -is|e mjuːˈnɪs.ɪ.pᵊl.aɪz, ˈ-ə- (US) ˈ-ə.pə.laɪz **-es** -ɪz **-ing** -ɪŋ **-ed** -d

munificen|ce mjuːˈnɪf.ɪ.sənt|s, ˈ-ə- ⓤⓢ ˈ-ə- **-t/ly** -t/li

muniment ˈmjuː.nɪ.mənt, -nə- ⓤⓢ -nə- **-s** -s

munition mjuːˈnɪʃ.ən **-s** -z

Munro mʌnˈrəʊ, mənˈ-; ˈmʌn.rəʊ ⓤⓢ mənˈroʊ

Munsey ˈmʌn.zi

Munster *in Ireland:* ˈmʌnt.stəʳ ⓤⓢ -stɚ

Münster *in Germany:* ˈmʊnt.stəʳ ⓤⓢ -stɚ, ˈmʌnt-

muntjak, muntjac ˈmʌnt.dʒæk, ˈmʌnt.ʃæk ⓤⓢ ˈmʌnt.dʒæk **-s** -s

Muppet ˈmʌp.ɪt **-s** -s

mural ˈmjʊə.rəl, ˈmjɔː- ⓤⓢ ˈmjʊr.əl **-s** -z

Murchie ˈmɜː.ki *in S. England also:* -tʃi ⓤⓢ ˈmɝː-

Murchison ˈmɜː.tʃɪ.sən, -kɪ- ⓤⓢ ˈmɝː.tʃɪ-

Murcia ˈmɜː.ʃi.ə *as if Spanish:* ˈmʊə.θi.ə ⓤⓢ ˈmɝː.ʃə, -ʃi.ə

Murcott ˈmɜː.kət ⓤⓢ ˈmɝː-

murd|er ˈmɜː.d|əʳ ⓤⓢ ˈmɝː.d|ɚ **-ers** -əz ⓤⓢ -ɚz **-ering** -ər.ɪŋ **-ered** -əd ⓤⓢ -ɚd

murderer ˈmɜː.dər.əʳ ⓤⓢ ˈmɝː.dɚ.ɚ **-s** -z

murderess ˈmɜː.dər.ɪs, -es, -əs; ˌmɜː.dəˈres ⓤⓢ ˈmɝː.dɚ.əs; ˌmɝː.dɚˈes **-es** -ɪz

murderous ˈmɜː.dər.əs ⓤⓢ ˈmɝː- **-ly** -li

Murdo ˈmɜː.dəʊ ⓤⓢ ˈmɝː.doʊ

Murdoch, Murdock ˈmɜː.dɒk ⓤⓢ ˈmɝː.dɑːk

Murdstone ˈmɜːd.stən ⓤⓢ ˈmɝːd-

Mure mjʊəʳ, mjɔːʳ ⓤⓢ mjʊr

muriate ˈmjʊə.ri.ət, ˈmjɔː-, -ɪt, -eɪt ⓤⓢ ˈmjʊr.i.eɪt, -ɪt

muriatic ˌmjʊə.riˈæt.ɪk, ˌmjɔː-, ˈmjʊə.ri.æt-, ˈmjɔː- ⓤⓢ ˌmjʊr.iˈæt̬-

Muriel ˈmjʊə.ri.əl, ˈmjɔː- ⓤⓢ ˈmjʊr.i-

Murillo mjʊˈrɪl.əʊ, mjʊə-, -jəʊ *as if Spanish:* mʊˈriː.jəʊ ⓤⓢ mjʊˈrɪl.oʊ, mə- **-s** -z

Murison ˈmjʊə.rɪ.sən, ˈmjɔː- ⓤⓢ ˈmjʊr.ɪ-

murk mɜːk ⓤⓢ mɝːk

murk|y ˈmɜː.k|i ⓤⓢ ˈmɝː- **-ier** -i.əʳ ⓤⓢ -i.ɚ **-iest** -i.ɪst, -i.əst **-ily** -ɪ.li, -əl.i **-iness** -ɪ.nəs, -ɪ.nɪs

Murmansk mɜːˈmæntsk, mə- ⓤⓢ mʊrˈmɑːntsk; ˈmɝː.mæntsk

murm|ur ˈmɜː.m|əʳ ⓤⓢ ˈmɝː.m|ɚ **-urs** -əz ⓤⓢ -ɚz **-uring/ly** -ər.ɪŋ/li **-ured** -əd ⓤⓢ -ɚd **-urer/s** -ər.əʳ/z ⓤⓢ -ɚ.ɚ/z

murph|y (M) ˈmɜː.f|i ⓤⓢ ˈmɝː- **-ies** -iz ˈ**Murphy's** ˌ**law**

murrain ˈmʌr.ɪn, -eɪn ⓤⓢ ˈmɝː.ɪn

Murray ˈmʌr.i ⓤⓢ ˈmɝː-, ˈmʌr-

Murrayfield ˈmʌr.i.fiːld

Murree ˈmʌr.i ⓤⓢ ˈmɝː-

Murrell ˈmʌr.əl; mʌrˈel, məˈrel ⓤⓢ ˈmɝː.əl; məˈrel

Murrie ˈmjʊə.ri ⓤⓢ ˈmjʊr.i

Murrumbidgee ˌmʌr.əmˈbɪdʒ.i ⓤⓢ ˌmɝː-

Murry ˈmʌr.i ⓤⓢ ˈmɝː-

Murtagh ˈmɜː.tə ⓤⓢ ˈmɝː.tɑː

Murtle ˈmɜː.tl̩ ⓤⓢ ˈmɝː.t̬l̩

Murton ˈmɜː.tən ⓤⓢ ˈmɝː-

Mururoa mʊ.rʊˈrəʊ.ə ⓤⓢ ˌmuː.ruːˈroʊ-

muscadet (M) ˈmʌs.kə.deɪ, ˌ--ˈ- ⓤⓢ ˈmʌs.kə.deɪ **-s** -z

muscat (M) ˈmʌs.kət, -kæt **-s** -s

muscatel ˌmʌs.kəˈtel **-s** -z

muscl|e ˈmʌs.l̩ **-es** -z **-ing** -ɪŋ, ˈmʌs.lɪŋ **-ed** -d

muscle-bound ˈmʌs.l̩ˌbaʊnd

muscle|man ˈmʌs.l̩|.mæn **-men** -men

muscl|y ˈmʌs.l|i, ˈmʌs.l̩|.i **-ier** -i.əʳ ⓤⓢ -i.ɚ **-iest** -i.ɪst, -i.əst

muscovado ˌmʌs.kəˈvɑː.dəʊ, -ˈveɪ- ⓤⓢ -doʊ

Muscovite ˈmʌs.kə.vaɪt **-s** -s

Muscovy ˈmʌs.kə.vi

muscular ˈmʌs.kjə.ləʳ, -kjʊ- ⓤⓢ -kjə.lɚ, -kjuː- **-ly** -li ˌ**muscular** ˈ**dystrophy**

muscularity ˌmʌs.kjəˈlær.ə.ti, -kjʊˈ-, -ɪ.ti ⓤⓢ -kjəˈler.ə.t̬i, -kjuːˈ-, -ˈlær-

musculature ˈmʌs.kjə.lə.tʃəʳ, -kjʊ-, -tjʊəʳ, -tʃʊəʳ ⓤⓢ -kjə.lə.tʃɚ, -kjuː- **-s** -z

mus|e (M) mjuːz **-es** -ɪz **-ing/s** -ɪŋ/z **-ingly** -ɪŋ.li **-ed** -d

musette mjuːˈzet **-s** -s

museum mjuːˈziː.əm, mjʊ- **-s** -z

Museveni ˌmuː.səˈveɪ.ni

Musgrave ˈmʌz.greɪv

mush mʌʃ **-es** -ɪz **-ing** -ɪŋ **-ed** -t

Musharraf mʊˈʃær.æf ⓤⓢ -ˈʃɑːr.əf

mushroom ˈmʌʃ.rʊm, -ruːm ⓤⓢ -ruːm, -rʊm **-s** -z **-ing** -ɪŋ **-ed** -d

mush|y ˈmʌʃ|.i **-ier** -i.əʳ ⓤⓢ -i.ɚ **-iest** -i.ɪst, -i.əst **-iness** -ɪ.nəs, -ɪ.nɪs

music ˈmjuː.zɪk ˈ**music** ˌ**centre**; ˈ**music** ˌ**hall**; ˈ**music** ˌ**stand**; ˈ**music** ˌ**stool**; ˈ**music** ˌ**video**; ˌ**face the** ˈ**music**

music|al ˈmjuː.zɪ.k|əl, -zə- **-als** -əlz **-ally** -əl.i, -li **-alness** -əl.nəs, -nɪs ˈ**musical** ˌ**box**; ˌ**musical** ˈ**chairs**

musicale ˌmjuː.zɪˈkɑːl, -ˈkæl ⓤⓢ -ˈkæl **-s** -z

musicality ˌmjuː.zɪˈkæl.ə.ti, -ɪ.ti ⓤⓢ -ə.t̬i

musician mjuːˈzɪʃ.ən **-s** -z **-ly** -li **-ship** -ʃɪp

musicolog|y ˌmjuː.zɪˈkɒl.ə.dʒ|i ⓤⓢ -ˈkɑː.lə- **-ist/s** -ɪst/s

Musil ˈmuː.zɪl, -sɪl

musk mʌsk **-y** -i ˈ**musk** ˌ**deer**; ˈ**musk** ˌ**rose**

musket ˈmʌs.kɪt **-s** -s **-ry** -ri

musketeer ˌmʌs.kɪˈtɪəʳ, -kəˈ- ⓤⓢ -kəˈtɪr **-s** -z

Muskett ˈmʌs.kɪt

Muskie ˈmʌs.ki

musk-ox ˈmʌsk.ɒks, ˌ-ˈ- ⓤⓢ ˈmʌsk.ɑːks **-en** -ən

muskrat ˈmʌsk.ræt, ˌ-ˈ- ⓤⓢ ˈ-- **-s** -s

Muslim ˈmʊz.lɪm, ˈmʊs-, -ləm ⓤⓢ ˈmʌz.ləm, ˈmʌs-, ˈmʊz-, ˈmʊs-, ˈmuːz-, ˈmuːz-, -lɪm **-s** -z

muslin ˈmʌz.lɪn **-s** -z

musquash ˈmʌs.kwɒʃ ⓤⓢ -kwɑːʃ

muss mʌs **-es** -ɪz **-ing** -ɪŋ **-ed** -t

mussel ˈmʌs.əl **-s** -z

Musselburgh ˈmʌs.l.bər.ə, -ˌbʌr.ə

Mussolini ˌmʊs.əˈliː.ni, ˌmʌs- ⓤⓢ ˌmuː.səˈ-

Mussorgsky mʊˈsɔːg.ski, mə-, -ˈzɔːg- ⓤⓢ məˈsɔːrg-, -ˈsɔːrk-, -ˈzɔːrg-, -ˈzɔːrk-

Mussulman ˈmʌs.əl.mən, -mæn **-s** -z

must (*n. adj.*) mʌst

must (*v.*) *strong form:* mʌst *weak forms:* məst, məs

Note: Weak form word. There are two senses of **must**: one is concerned with supposition, or making deductions, and in this sense it is usual for the strong form to be used (e.g. 'If he's late, he must be ill') The other sense is related to obligation: the word may be stressed, in which case it has the strong form (e.g. 'You must try harder'), or unstressed, in which case the pronunciation is either /məs/ before a consonant, or /məst/ before a vowel (e.g. 'Each of us must buy some' /ˈiːtʃ.əv.əs.məsˌbaɪ.sʌm/; 'You must always look first' /jʊ.məstˌɔːl.wɪz.lʊkˈfɜːst ⓤⓢ -ɑːl.weɪz.lʊkˈfɝːst/).

mustach|e məˈstɑːʃ, mʊ- ⓤⓢ ˈmʌs.tæʃ; məˈstæʃ **-es** -ɪz **-ed** -t

mustachio məˈstɑː.ʃi.əʊ, -ˈstæʃ.i- ⓤⓢ -ˈstæʃ.i.oʊ, -ˈstɑː.ʃi- **-s** -z **-ed** -d

mustang ˈmʌs.tæŋ **-s** -z

Mustapha ˈmʊs.tə.fə, ˈmʌs-, -fɑː, mʊˈstɑː.fə, mə- ⓤⓢ ˈmʊs.tɑː.fɑː *Egyptian:* mʊˈstɑː.fə, mə- ⓤⓢ ˈmʊs.tɑː.fɑː

Mustapha Kemal ˌmʊs.tə.fə.kemˈɑːl, -kɪˈmɑːl ⓤⓢ ˌmʊs.tɑː.fɑː.kemˈɑːl

mustard (M) ˈmʌs.təd ⓤⓢ -tɚd ˈ**mustard** ˌ**gas**; ˈ**mustard** ˌ**plaster**; **as** ˌ**keen as** ˈ**mustard**

Mustel ˈmʌs.təl

must|er ˈmʌs.t|əʳ ⓤⓢ -t|ɚ **-ers** -əz ⓤⓢ -ɚz **-ering** -ər.ɪŋ **-ered** -əd ⓤⓢ -ɚd

musth mʌst

Mustique muːˈstiːk

mustn't ˈmʌs.ənt

must|y 'mʌs.t|i **-ier** -i.əʳ ⓤⓢ -i.ɚ **-iest** -i.ɪst, -i.əst **-ily** -ɪ.li, -ᵊl.i **-iness** -ɪ.nəs, -ɪ.nɪs
Mut muːt
mutability ˌmjuː.tə'bɪl.ə.ti, -ɪ.ti ⓤⓢ -t̬ə'bɪl.ə.t̬i
mutable 'mjuː.tə.bl̩ ⓤⓢ -t̬ə-
mutant 'mjuː.tᵊnt **-s** -s
muta|te mjuː'teɪ|t ⓤⓢ '-- **-tes** -ts **-ting** -tɪŋ ⓤⓢ -t̬ɪŋ **-ted** -tɪd ⓤⓢ -t̬ɪd
mutation mjuː'teɪ.ʃᵊn **-s** -z
mutatis mutandis muːˌtɑː.tiːs.mu'tæn.diːs, mjuːˌteɪ.tiːs.mju'- ⓤⓢ muːˌtɑː.t̬ɪs.muː'tɑːn.dɪs, mjuːˌteɪ.t̬ɪs.mjuː'tæn.dɪs
mut|e mjuːt **-es** -s **-ely** -li **-eness** -nəs, -nɪs **-ing** -ɪŋ ⓤⓢ 'mjuː.t̬ɪŋ **-ed** -ɪd ⓤⓢ 'mjuː.t̬ɪd
mutil|ate 'mjuː.tɪ.l|eɪt, -tᵊl|.eɪt ⓤⓢ -t̬ᵊl- **-ates** -eɪts **-ating** -eɪ.tɪŋ ⓤⓢ -eɪ.t̬ɪŋ **-ated** -eɪ.tɪd ⓤⓢ -eɪ.t̬ɪd **-ator/s** -eɪ.təʳ/z ⓤⓢ -eɪ.t̬ɚ/z
mutilation ˌmjuː.tɪ'leɪ.ʃᵊn, -tᵊl'eɪ- ⓤⓢ -t̬ᵊl'- **-s** -z
mutineer ˌmjuː.tɪ'nɪəʳ, -tᵊn.ɪəʳ ⓤⓢ -tᵊn'ɪr **-s** -z
mutinous 'mjuː.tɪ.nəs, -tᵊn.əs ⓤⓢ -tᵊn- **-ly** -li **-ness** -nəs, -nɪs
mutin|y 'mjuː.tɪ.n|i, -tᵊ|n.i **-ies** -iz **-ying** -i.ɪŋ **-ied** -id
mutism 'mjuː.tɪ.zᵊm
mutt mʌt **-s** -s
mutt|er 'mʌt|.əʳ ⓤⓢ 'mʌt̬|.ɚ **-ers** -əz ⓤⓢ -ɚz **-ering/ly** -ᵊr.ɪŋ/li **-ered** -əd ⓤⓢ -ɚd **-erer/s** -ᵊr.əʳ/z ⓤⓢ -ɚ.ɚ/z **-erings** -ᵊr.ɪŋz ⓤⓢ -ɚ.ɪŋz
mutton (M) 'mʌt.ᵊn ˌ**mutton** ˌ**dressed as** '**lamb**
muttonchops 'mʌt.ᵊn.tʃɒps ⓤⓢ -tʃɑːps
muttonhead 'mʌt.ᵊn.hed **-s** -z
mutual 'mjuː.tʃu.əl, -tʃəl, -tju.əl ⓤⓢ -tʃu.əl **-s** -z **-ly** -i '**mutual** ˌ**fund**
mutuality ˌmjuː.tju'æl.ə.ti, -ɪ.ti ⓤⓢ -tʃu'æl.ə.t̬i
Muzak® 'mjuː.zæk
muzzl|e 'mʌz.l̩ **-es** -z **-ing** -ɪŋ, 'mʌz.l.ɪŋ **-ed** -d
muzzle-load|er 'mʌz.l̩ˌləʊ.d|əʳ ⓤⓢ -ˌloʊ.d|ɚ **-ers** -əz ⓤⓢ -ɚz **-ing** -ɪŋ
muzz|y 'mʌz|.i **-ier** -i.əʳ ⓤⓢ -i.ɚ **-iest** -i.ɪst, -i.əst **-iness** -ɪ.nəs, -ɪ.nɪs
Mwanza mə'wæn.zə ⓤⓢ 'mwɑːn.zɑː
my *normal form:* maɪ *occasional weak form:* mɪ
Note: Occasional weak form word. The strong form is used contrastively (e.g. 'My friends and your friends') or for emphasis (e.g. 'It's my turn'). Many speakers do not have a special weak form, and simply produce a brief, weakened pronunciation of /maɪ/. However, some speakers do use a weak form of **my** in common phrases. British English speakers may have the pronunciation /mi/ before a vowel (e.g. 'On my own' /ˌɒn.mi'əʊn/) and /mə/ before a consonant (e.g. 'On my back' /ˌɒn.mə'bæk/). For American English, the variant /mə/ may be used before a consonant, but /mi/ is not acceptable. In British English, there is also a special form of **my** used by lawyers in court, in phrases such as 'my Lord' or 'my learned friend', pronounced /mɪ/ or /mə/.
myalg|ia maɪ'æl.dʒ|ə, -i.ə **-ic** -ɪk
Myanmar 'mjæn.mɑːʳ ⓤⓢ mjɑːn'mɑːr
Myatt maɪət
myceli|um maɪ'siː.li|.əm **-a** -ə
Mycenae maɪ'siː.ni, -niː
Mycenaean ˌmaɪ.sɪ'niː.ən, -sᵊn'iː- ⓤⓢ -sə'niː-
mycolog|ist maɪ'kɒl.ə.dʒ|ɪst ⓤⓢ -'kɑː.lə- **-ists** -ɪsts **-y** -i
mycolog|y maɪ'kɒl.ə.dʒ|i ⓤⓢ -'kɑː.lə-
myelitis ˌmaɪə'laɪ.tɪs, ˌmaɪ.ɪ'-, maɪ'- ⓤⓢ ˌmaɪ.ə'laɪ.t̬ɪs
Myers maɪəz ⓤⓢ maɪɚz
Myerscough 'maɪə.skəʊ ⓤⓢ 'maɪɚ.skoʊ
Myfanwy mə'væn.wi, mɪ-, -'fæn-
Myingyan mjɪŋ'jɑːn
Mylar® 'maɪ.lɑːʳ ⓤⓢ -lɑːr
myna(h) 'maɪ.nə **-s** -z '**myna(h)** ˌ**bird**
mynheer maɪn'hɪəʳ, -'heəʳ ⓤⓢ mɪ'ner, -'nɪr; maɪn'her, -hɪr **-s** -z
Mynheer *form of address in S Africa:* mə'nɪəʳ ⓤⓢ -'ner, -'nɪr
Mynott 'maɪ.nət
myoelastic ˌmaɪ.əʊ.ɪ'læs.tɪk, -'lɑː.stɪk ⓤⓢ -oʊ.ɪ'læs.tɪk
myope 'maɪ.əʊp ⓤⓢ -oʊp **-s** -s
myopia maɪ'əʊ.pi.ə ⓤⓢ -'oʊ-
myopic maɪ'ɒp.ɪk ⓤⓢ -'ɑː.pɪk
myosin 'maɪ.əʊ.sɪn ⓤⓢ -oʊ-
myosis maɪ'əʊ.sɪs ⓤⓢ -'oʊ-
myosotis ˌmaɪ.əʊ'səʊ.tɪs ⓤⓢ -oʊ'soʊ.t̬ɪs
Myra 'maɪə.rə ⓤⓢ 'maɪ-
myriad 'mɪr.i.əd **-s** -z
myrmidon (M) 'mɜː.mɪ.dᵊn, -dɒn ⓤⓢ 'mɝː.mə.dɑːn, -dᵊn **-s** -z
myrrh mɜːʳ ⓤⓢ mɝː
Myrrha 'mɪr.ə
myrrhic 'mɜː.rɪk, 'mɪr.ɪk ⓤⓢ 'mɝː-
myrrhine 'mɜː.raɪn, 'mɪr.aɪn ⓤⓢ 'mɝː.iːn, -ɪn
myrtle (M) 'mɜː.tl̩ ⓤⓢ 'mɝː.t̬l̩ **-s** -z
myself maɪ'self, mɪ- ⓤⓢ maɪ-, mə-
Mysia 'mɪs.i.ə, 'mɪʃ.ə
Mysore 'maɪ.sɔːʳ ⓤⓢ -sɔːr
mysterious mɪ'stɪə.ri.əs ⓤⓢ -'stɪr.i- **-ly** -li **-ness** -nəs, -nɪs
myster|y 'mɪs.tᵊr|.i, '-tr|i **-ies** -iz '**mystery** ˌ**play**
mystic 'mɪs.tɪk **-s** -s
mystic|al 'mɪs.tɪ.k|ᵊl **-ally** -ᵊl.i, -li **-alness** -ᵊl.nəs, -nɪs
mysticism 'mɪs.tɪ.sɪ.zᵊm, -tə-
mystification ˌmɪs.tɪ.fɪ'keɪ.ʃᵊn, -tə-
mysti|fy 'mɪs.tɪ|.faɪ **-fies** -faɪz **-fying/ly** -faɪ.ɪŋ/li **-fied** -faɪd
mystique mɪ'stiːk
myth mɪθ **-s** -s
mythic 'mɪθ.ɪk **-al** -ᵊl **-ally** -ᵊl.i, -li
Mytholmroyd ˌmaɪ.ðᵊm'rɔɪd
mythologic ˌmɪθ.ᵊl'ɒdʒ.ɪk, ˌmaɪ.θᵊl'- ⓤⓢ ˌmɪθ.ə'lɑː.dʒɪk **-al** -ᵊl **-ally** -ᵊl.i, -li
mythologist mɪ'θɒl.ə.dʒɪst, maɪ- ⓤⓢ mɪ'θɑː.lə- **-s** -s
mythologiz|e, -is|e mɪ'θɒl.ə.dʒaɪz, maɪ- ⓤⓢ mɪ'θɑː.lə- **-es** -ɪz **-ing** -ɪŋ **-ed** -d
mytholog|y mɪ'θɒl.ə.dʒ|i, maɪ- ⓤⓢ -'θɑː.lə- **-ies** -iz
Mytilene ˌmɪt.ɪ'liː.ni, ˌmaɪ.tɪ'-, -tᵊl'iː-, -niː ⓤⓢ ˌmɪt.ᵊl'iː-
myxomatosis ˌmɪk.sə.mə'təʊ.sɪs ⓤⓢ -'toʊ-

Pronouncing the letter N

See also NG

The consonant letter **n** has two pronunciations: /n/ and /ŋ/.

In most contexts, it is realised as /n/, e.g.:

nail /neɪl/
mine /maɪn/

Preceding the letters **k**, **qu**, **x** and **c** realised as /k/, **n** is pronounced /ŋ/, e.g.:

bank /bæŋk/
anxious /ˈæŋk.ʃəs/

However, when **k** is silent, **n** is pronounced as /n/, e.g.:

unknown /ʌnˈnəʊn/ ⓤⓢ /-ˈnoʊn/

n (N) en **-'s** -z
N *(abbrev. for* **North***)* nɔːθ ⓤⓢ nɔːrθ *(abbrev. for* **Northerly***)* ˈnɔː.ðəl.i ⓤⓢ ˈnɔːr.ðɚ.li *(abbrev. for* **Northern***)* ˈnɔː.ðən ⓤⓢ ˈnɔːr.ðɚn
'n', 'n ən ˌ**fish 'n' 'chips**; ˌ**rock 'n' 'roll**
NAACP ˌen.dʌb.l̩ˌeɪ.siːˈpiː
NAAFI, Naafi ˈnæf.i
Naaman ˈneɪə.mən
naan nɑːn, næn ⓤⓢ nɑːn **-s** -z
Naas neɪs ⓤⓢ neɪs, nɑːs
nab næb **-s** -z **-bing** -ɪŋ **-bed** -d
nabe neɪb **-s** -z
Nabisco® nəˈbɪs.kəʊ, næbˈɪs- ⓤⓢ -koʊ
nablab ˈnæb.læb **-s** -z
Nablus ˈnɑː.bləs, ˈnæb.ləs ⓤⓢ ˈnɑː.bləs, ˈnæb.ləs ⓤⓢ -lʊs
nabob ˈneɪ.bɒb ⓤⓢ -bɑːb **-s** -z
nabobess ˌneɪ.bɒbˈes ⓤⓢ -bɑːˈbes **-es** -ɪz
Nabokov ˈnæb.ə.kɒf; nəˈbəʊ- ⓤⓢ nəˈbɑː.kɑːf; ˈnɑː.bə-, ˈnæb.ə-
Naboth ˈneɪ.bɒθ ⓤⓢ -bɑːθ
nacelle nəˈsel, næsˈel ⓤⓢ nəˈsel **-s** -z
nacho ˈnɑː.tʃəʊ, ˈnætʃ.əʊ ⓤⓢ ˈnɑː.tʃoʊ **-s** -z
NACNE ˈnæk.niː
NACODS ˈneɪ.kɒdz ⓤⓢ -kɑːdz
nacre ˈneɪ.kəʳ ⓤⓢ -kɚ
nacreous ˈneɪ.kri.əs
nacrite ˈneɪ.kraɪt
NACRO, Nacro ˈnæk.rəʊ ⓤⓢ -roʊ
Nader ˈneɪ.dəʳ ⓤⓢ -dɚ
Nadia ˈnɑː.di.ə, ˈneɪ- ⓤⓢ ˈnɑː-, ˈ-djə
Nadine neɪˈdiːn, nə-; ˈneɪ.diːn ⓤⓢ nəˈdiːn, neɪ-
nadir ˈneɪ.dɪəʳ, -dəʳ; ˈnæd.ɪəʳ ⓤⓢ ˈneɪ.dɚ, -dɪr **-s** -z
Nadir nædˈɪəʳ ⓤⓢ -ɪr
naev|us ˈniː.v|əs **-uses** -ə.sɪz **-i** -aɪ
naff næf
NAFTA, Nafta ˈnæf.tə
nag næg **-s** -z **-ging** -ɪŋ **-ged** -d **-ger/s** -əʳ/z ⓤⓢ -ɚ/z
Naga ˈnɑː.gə **-s** -z
Nagano ˈnæg.ə.nəʊ, ˈnɑː.gə- ⓤⓢ ˈnɑː.gə.noʊ
Nagasaki ˌnæg.əˈsɑː.ki, -ˈsæk.i ⓤⓢ ˌnɑː.gəˈsɑː.ki
Nagorno-Karabakh nəˌgɔː.nəʊˌkær.əˈbæk ⓤⓢ -ˌgɔːr.noʊ.kɑː.rɑːˈbɑːk
Nagoya nəˈgɔɪ.ə ⓤⓢ nɑːˈgɔː.jɑː, -ˈgɔɪ.ə
Nagpur ˌnægˈpʊəʳ ⓤⓢ ˌnɑːgˈpʊr
nah næː ⓤⓢ næː, nɑː
Note: This is an informal pronunciation of **no**; in the British accent described, its usage is often semi-comical.
Nahuatl ˈnɑː.wɑː.tl̩, -ˈ-- ⓤⓢ ˈnɑː.wɑː.t̬l̩ **-s** -z
Nahuatlan ˈnɑː.wɑː.tlən, nɑːˈwɑː- ⓤⓢ ˈnɑː.wɑː.t̬lən **-s** -z
Nahum ˈneɪ.həm, -hʌm ⓤⓢ -həm, -əm
naiad ˈnaɪ.æd ⓤⓢ ˈneɪ-, ˈnaɪ-, -əd **-s** -z
naif, naïf naɪˈiːf, nɑː- ⓤⓢ nɑː- **-s** -s
nail neɪl **-s** -z **-ing** -ɪŋ **-ed** -d **ˈnail ˌfile**; **ˈnail ˌpolish**; **ˈnail ˌscissors**; **ˈnail ˌvarnish**; ˌ**hit the ˌnail on the ˈhead**
nailbiting ˈneɪlˌbaɪ.tɪŋ ⓤⓢ -t̬ɪŋ **-ly** -li
nailbrush ˈneɪl.brʌʃ **-es** -ɪz
nailclipper ˈneɪlˌklɪp.əʳ ⓤⓢ -ɚ **-s** -z
Nailsea ˈneɪl.siː
Nailsworth ˈneɪlz.wəθ, -wɜːθ ⓤⓢ -wɚθ, -wɝːθ
Nain ˈneɪ.ɪn; neɪn
Naipaul ˈnaɪ.pɔːl ⓤⓢ -pɑːl, -pɔːl
naira ˈnaɪ.rə **-s** -z
Nairn(e) neən ⓤⓢ nern
Nairnshire ˈneən.ʃəʳ, -ˌʃɪəʳ ⓤⓢ ˈnern.ʃɚ, -ˌʃɪr
Nairobi naɪˈrəʊ.bi ⓤⓢ -ˈroʊ-
Naish næʃ, neɪʃ
naiv|e, naïv|e naɪˈiːv, nɑː- ⓤⓢ nɑː-, naɪ- **-ely** -li **-eness** -nəs, -nɪs
naiveté, naïveté nɑːˈiː.və.teɪ, naɪ-, -ˈiːv.teɪ ⓤⓢ ˌnɑː.iːvˈteɪ, ˌnaɪ-, -ˈ--
naivety, naïvety naɪˈiː.və.ti, nɑː- ⓤⓢ nɑːˈiː.və.t̬i, naɪ-
Nakasone ˌnæk.əˈsəʊ.neɪ, -ni ⓤⓢ ˌnɑːk.əˈsoʊ-
naked ˈneɪ.kɪd **-ly** -li **-ness** -nəs, -nɪs **the ˌnaked ˈeye**
naker ˈneɪ.kəʳ, ˈnæk.əʳ ⓤⓢ ˈneɪ.kɚ **-s** -z
Nakhon Ratchasima nəˌkɒn.rɑː.tʃɑːˈsiː.mə ⓤⓢ -ˌkɑːn-
NALGO ˈnæl.gəʊ ⓤⓢ -goʊ
Nam, 'Nam *(abbrev. for* **Vietnam***)* nɑːm, næm
Namangan ˌnæm.æŋˈgɑːn ⓤⓢ ˌnɑː.mən-, nə-
namby-pamby ˌnæm.biˈpæm.bi **-ism** -ɪ.zəm
nam|e neɪm **-es** -z **-ing** -ɪŋ **-ed** -d **-eless** -ləs, -lɪs
name-brand ˈneɪm.brænd **-s** -z
namedrop ˈneɪm.drɒp ⓤⓢ -drɑːp **-s** -s **-ping** -ɪŋ **-ped** -t **-per/s** -əʳ/z ⓤⓢ -ɚ/z
namely ˈneɪm.li
nameplate ˈneɪm.pleɪt **-s** -s
namesake ˈneɪm.seɪk **-s** -s
nametag ˈneɪm.tæg **-s** -z
Namibi|a nəˈmɪb.i|.ə, næmˈɪb- ⓤⓢ nəˈmɪb- **-an/s** -ən/z
Namier ˈneɪ.mɪəʳ, -mi.əʳ ⓤⓢ -mi.ɚ
Nampula næmˈpuː.lə
Namur næmˈʊəʳ ⓤⓢ -ˈʊr, nɑːˈmʊr
nan *bread:* nɑːn, næn ⓤⓢ næn, nɑːn **-s** -z
Nan *name:* næn
nana ˈnæn.ə ⓤⓢ ˈnæn.ə, ˈnɑː.nə, -nɑː **-s** -z
Nanaimo nəˈnaɪ.məʊ, nænˈaɪ- ⓤⓢ nəˈnaɪ.moʊ
Nanak ˈnɑː.nək
nance (N) nænts
nancy (N) *female name or effeminate man:* ˈnænt.si **ˈnancy ˌboy**
Nancy *in France:* ˈnɑ̃ːn.si; *as if French:* nɑ̃ːnˈsiː ⓤⓢ ˈnɑ̃ːn.si, ˈnænt-
NAND nænd
nandrolone ˈnæn.drə.ləʊn
Nanette nænˈet, nəˈnet
Nanjing nænˈdʒɪŋ
nankeen næŋˈkiːn, næn- ⓤⓢ næn-
Nank|in ˌnænˈk|ɪn, ˌnæŋ- ⓤⓢ ˌnæn-, ˌnɑːn- **-ing** -ɪŋ *stress shift:* ˌNankin ˈhighway
Nannie ˈnæn.i
nann|y (N) ˈnæn|.i **-ies** -iz **ˈnanny ˌgoat**
nanometre, nanometer ˈnæn.əʊˌmiː.təʳ; nænˈɒm.ɪ- ⓤⓢ ˈnæn.oʊˌmiː.t̬ɚ; nænˈɑː.mɪ-
Nanook ˈnæn.uːk ⓤⓢ -ʊk
nanosecond ˈnæn.əʊˌsek.ənd ⓤⓢ -oʊˌ-, -əˌ- **-s** -z

Names of people and places

It can be difficult to work out the pronunciation of some English words, and something like between ten to thirty percent of words in any text will have irregular spellings. Proper nouns for people and places can have really unexpected pronunciations. Here, we look at a few of the most interesting ones.

Examples

Family names are well known for having interesting realisations. This can be because some letters are not pronounced, but, in some cases, the way a word is written looks almost entirely different to the pronunciation, e.g.:

Cholmondeley /ˈtʃʌm.li/
Colquhoun /kəˈhuːn/
Dalziel /diːˈel; ˈdæl.ziːl/
Featherstonehawe /ˈfeð.ə.stᵊn.hɔː; ˈfæn.ʃɔː/ US /ˈfeð.ɚ.stᵊn.hɑː; ˈfæn.ʃɑː/
Quesnel /ˈkeɪ.nᵊl/

It is a similar situation for place names, e.g.:

Alnwick /ˈæn.ɪk/
Cirencester /ˈsaɪə.rᵊn.ses.təʳ; ˈsɪs.ɪ.təʳ/ US /ˈsaɪ.rᵊn.ses.tɚ/
Lympne /lɪm/
Woolfardisworthy /ˈwʊl.zᵊr.i; wʊlˈfɑː.dɪˌswɜː.ði/ US /ˈwʊl.zɚ.i; wʊlˈfɑːr.dɪˌswɝː.ði/
Worcester /ˈwʊs.təʳ/ US /-ɚ/

Welsh place names can be very difficult to decipher for people who do not know the rules that govern the spelling of Welsh. Although Welsh is written using the same alphabet as English, the values of the letters are frequently different, e.g.:

Llanrwst /*h*lænˈruːst/
Penmaenmawr /ˌpen.mənˈmaʊəʳ, -ˈmɔːʳ/ US /-ˈmaʊɚ, -ˈmɔːr/

There is some regularity amongst suffixes in some place names. The suffix *–ham* in British place names, for example, is usually pronounced /-əm/, as in *Birmingham*. However, in the North American place name *Birmingham*, *-ham* is pronounced /-hæm/. Another common suffix in British place names, *–cester*, is usually pronounced /-stəʳ US -stɚ/, e.g. as in *Worcester* above (although note also *Cirencester*, in which one possible realisation is /-ses.təʳ US –ses.tɚ/). Finally, the suffix *–wick* in e.g. *Warwick* is usually pronounced /-ɪk/ in British place names, although there are exceptions.

nanotechnology ˌnæn.əʊ.tekˈnɒl.ə.dʒi US -oʊ.tekˈnɑː.lə-
Nansen ˈnænt.sᵊn
Nantes nɑ̃ːnt US nɑ̃ːnt, nænts
Nantucket nænˈtʌk.ɪt
Nantwich ˈnænt.wɪtʃ *locally also:* -waɪtʃ
Naoise ˈniː.ʃə US -si, ˈneɪ-
Naomi ˈneɪ.ə.mi; neɪˈəʊ- US -ˈoʊ-; ˈneɪ.oʊ-
nap næp **-s** -s **-ping** -ɪŋ **-ped** -t
napalm ˈneɪ.pɑːm, ˈnæp.ɑːm US ˈneɪ.pɑːm **-s** -z **-ing** -ɪŋ **-ed** -d
Napa Valley ˌnæp.əˈvæl.i
nape neɪp **-s** -s
napery ˈneɪ.pᵊr.i
Naphtali ˈnæf.tə.laɪ
naphtha ˈnæf.θə, ˈnæp-
naphthalene ˈnæf.θə.liːn, ˈnæp-
naphthol ˈnæf.θɒl, ˈnæp- US -θɑːl
Napier ˈneɪ.pi.əʳ, nəˈpɪəʳ US ˈneɪ.pi.ɚ, nəˈpɪr
Napierian nəˈpɪə.ri.ən, neɪ- US -ˈpɪr.i-
napkin ˈnæp.kɪn **-s** -z **ˈnapkin ˌring**
Naples ˈneɪ.pl̩z
napoleon (N) nəˈpəʊ.li.ən US -ˈpoʊ- **-s** -z
Napoleonic nəˌpəʊ.liˈɒn.ɪk US -ˌpoʊ.liˈɑː.nɪk
napp|y ˈnæp|.i **-ies** -iz **ˈnappy ˌrash**
Napster ˈnæp.stəʳ US -stɚ
Narayan nəˈraɪ.ən US nɑːˈrɑː.jən
Narbonne nɑːˈbɒn US nɑːrˈbɑːn
Narborough ˈnɑː.bᵊr.ə US ˈnɑːr.bə.roʊ
narc nɑːk US nɑːrk **-s** -s
narcissi (*plur. of* **narcissus**) nɑːˈsɪs.aɪ US nɑːr-
narcissism ˈnɑː.sɪ.sɪ.zᵊm; nɑːˈsɪs.ɪ- US ˈnɑːr.sə.sɪ-
narcissist ˈnɑː.sɪ.sɪst; nɑːˈsɪs.ɪst US ˈnɑːr.sɪ- **-s** -s
narcissistic ˌnɑː.sɪˈsɪs.tɪk US ˌnɑːr-
narciss|us (N) nɑːˈsɪs|.əs US nɑːr- **-uses** -ə.sɪz **-i** -aɪ
narcolepsy ˈnɑː.kəʊ.lep.si US ˈnɑːr.kə-, -koʊ-
narcoleptic ˌnɑː.kəʊˈlep.tɪk US ˌnɑːr.kəˈ-, -koʊ- **-s** -s
narcos|is nɑːˈkəʊ.s|ɪs US nɑːrˈkoʊ- **-es** -iːz
narcotic nɑːˈkɒt.ɪk US nɑːrˈkɑːt̬- **-s** -s
nard nɑːd US nɑːrd
nares ˈneə.riːz US ˈner.iːz
Nares neəz US nerz
narghile, nargileh ˈnɑː.gɪ.leɪ, -gə-, -li US ˈnɑːr.gə- **-s** -z
nark nɑːk US nɑːrk **-s** -s **-ing** -ɪŋ **-ed** -t
nark|y ˈnɑː.k|i US ˈnɑːr- **-ier** -i.əʳ US -i.ɚ **-iest** -i.ɪst, -i.əst
Narnia ˈnɑː.ni.ə US ˈnɑːr-
Narragansett ˌnær.əˈgæn.sɪt US ˌnær-, ˌner-
narra|te nəˈreɪ|t, nærˈeɪ|t US ˈner.eɪ|t, ˈnær-; nəˈreɪ|t, nærˈeɪ|t **-tes** -ts **-ting** -tɪŋ US -t̬ɪŋ **-ted** -tɪd US -t̬ɪd
narration nəˈreɪ.ʃᵊn, nærˈeɪ- US nerˈeɪ-, nær- **-s** -z
narrative ˈnær.ə.tɪv US ˈner.ə.t̬ɪv, ˈnær- **-s** -z
narrator nəˈreɪ.təʳ, nærˈeɪ- US ˈner.eɪ.t̬ɚ, ˈnær-; nəˈreɪ-, nærˈeɪ- **-s** -z
narrow ˈnær.əʊ US ˈner.oʊ, ˈnær- **-s** -z **-er** -əʳ US -ɚ **-est** -ɪst, -əst **-ly** -li **-ness** -nəs, -nɪs **-ing** -ɪŋ **-ed** -d **ˈnarrow ˌboat**; **ˌnarrow ˈgauge**; *stress shift:* ˌnarrow gauge ˈrailway
narrowcast ˈnær.əʊˌkɑːst US ˈner.oʊˌkæst, ˈnær- **-s** -s **-ing** -ɪŋ **-ed** -ɪd **-er/s** -əʳ/z US -ɚ/z
narrow-minded ˌnær.əʊˈmaɪn.dɪd US ˌner.oʊˈ-, ˌnær- **-ly** -li **-ness** -nəs, -nɪs *stress shift:* ˌnarrow-minded ˈperson
narw(h)al ˈnɑː.wəl US ˈnɑːr- **-s** -z
nary ˈneə.ri US ˈner.i
NASA ˈnæs.ə

Nasal consonant

A consonant in which the air escapes only through the nose. For this to happen, two articulatory actions are necessary: firstly, the 'soft palate' (or 'velum') must be lowered to allow air to escape past it and, secondly, a closure must be made in the oral cavity to prevent air from escaping through it. The closure may be at any place of articulation from BILABIAL at the front of the oral cavity to 'uvular' at the back (in the latter case there is contact between the tip of the lowered soft palate and the raised back of the tongue).

Examples for English

English has three commonly found nasal consonants: bilabial, alveolar and velar, for which the symbols /m n ŋ/ are used. /ŋ/ cannot occur at the beginning of a syllable, e.g.:

map	/mæp/
nap	/næp/
sang	/sæŋ/

There is disagreement over the phonemic status of the velar nasal: some claim that it must be a phoneme since it can be placed in contrastive contexts like *sum/sun/sung*, while others state that the velar nasal is an ALLOPHONE of /n/ which occurs before /k/ and /g/.

In English we find 'nasal release' of PLOSIVE consonants: when a plosive is followed by a nasal consonant the usual articulation is to release the compressed air by lowering the soft palate. This is particularly noticeable when the plosive and the nasal are 'homorganic' (share the same place of articulation), as for example in *topmost*, *Putney*. The result is that no plosive release is heard from the speaker's mouth before the nasal consonant, e.g.:

topmost	ˈtɒp.məʊst	Ⓤⓢ ˈtɑːp.moʊst
Putney	ˈpʌt.ni	

Nasal release can also result in a SYLLABIC CONSONANT, e.g.:

button	ˈbʌt.n̩

Nasalisation

The addition of nasal escape of air to a sound which would not normally have it.

Examples for English

The best known examples of nasalisation in English are nasalised vowels. In most vowels the airflow escapes entirely through the mouth, but often, in a vowel preceding or following a nasal consonant, we find air escaping also through the nose.

This is a kind of coarticulation, e.g.:

pin	/pɪn/	[pʰɪ̃n]
man	/mæn/	[mæ̃n]
sing	/sɪŋ/	[sɪ̃ŋ]

Nasalised vowels are not phonemically contrastive in English.

In other languages

Nasalised vowels are phonemically contrastive in a number of languages, such as French, which has pairs of words such as *beau – bon* /bo – bõ/ and *mais – main* /mɛ – mɛ̃/.

nasal ˈneɪ.zᵊl **-s** -z **-ly** -i
nasalism ˈneɪ.zᵊl.ɪ.zᵊm
nasality neɪˈzæl.ə.ti, nə-, -ɪ.ti Ⓤⓢ neɪˈzæl.ə.t̬i
nasalization, -isa- ˌneɪ.zᵊl.aɪˈzeɪ.ʃᵊn, -ɪˈ- Ⓤⓢ -ɪˈ- **-s** -z
nasaliz|e, -is|e ˈneɪ.zᵊl.aɪz **-es** -ɪz **-ing** -ɪŋ **-ed** -d
Nasby ˈnæz.bi
nascen|t ˈnæs.ᵊn|t, ˈneɪ.sᵊn|t **-ce** -*t*s **-cy** -*t*.si
Nasdaq ˈnæz.dæk
Naseby ˈneɪz.bi
Nash(e) næʃ
Nashville ˈnæʃ.vɪl *locally:* -vəl
nasi goreng ˌnɑː.si.gəˈreŋ, -zi-, ˌnæs.i-
Nasmyth *name:* ˈneɪz.mɪθ, ˈneɪ.smɪθ, ˈnæz.mɪθ, ˈnæs- *in US:* ˈneɪ.smɪθ
nasopharyngeal ˌneɪ.zəʊ.fær.ɪnˈdʒiː.əl, -ᵊn-; -fᵊrˈɪn.dʒi.əl, -færˈ- Ⓤⓢ -zoʊ.fəˈrɪn- *stress shift:* ˌnasopharyngeal ˈport
nasopharynx ˌneɪ.zəʊˈfær.ɪŋks Ⓤⓢ -zoʊˈfer-, -ˈfær-
Nassau *in Bahamas and US:* ˈnæs.ɔː Ⓤⓢ -ɔː, -ɑː *German province:* ˈnæs.aʊ Ⓤⓢ ˈnɑː.saʊ *princely family:* ˈnæs.ɔː, -aʊ Ⓤⓢ ˈnɑː.saʊ
Nasser ˈnæs.əʳ, ˈnɑː.səʳ Ⓤⓢ ˈnæs.ɚ, ˈnɑː.sɚ
Nastase næsˈtɑː.zi, nəˈstɑː-, -zeɪ
nasturtium nəˈstɜː.ʃᵊm Ⓤⓢ -ˈstɝː-, næsˈtɝː- **-s** -z
nast|y ˈnɑː.st|i Ⓤⓢ ˈnæs.t|i **-ies** -iz **-ier** -i.əʳ Ⓤⓢ -i.ɚ **-iest** -i.ɪst, -i.əst **-ily** -ɪ.li, -ᵊl.i **-iness** -ɪ.nəs, -ɪ.nɪs
natal (*adj.*) ˈneɪ.tᵊl Ⓤⓢ -t̬ᵊl
Natal nəˈtæl, -ˈtɑːl
Natalie ˈnæt.ᵊl.i Ⓤⓢ ˈnæt̬-
Natasha nəˈtæʃ.ə
natation nəˈteɪ.ʃᵊn, neɪ- Ⓤⓢ neɪ-, nætˈeɪ-
natch nætʃ
NATFHE, Natfhe ˈnæt.fiː
Nathan ˈneɪ.θᵊn, -θæn Ⓤⓢ -θᵊn
Nathaniel nəˈθæn.jəl
nation ˈneɪ.ʃᵊn **-s** -z
national ˈnæʃ.ᵊn.ᵊl, ˈnæʃ.nᵊl **-s** -z **-ly** -i **ˌnational ˈanthem; ˌnational curˈriculum; ˌnational ˈdebt; ˌNational ˈFront; ˌNational ˈGuard; ˌNational ˈHealth ˌService; ˌnational ˈpark; ˌnational seˈcurity; ˌnational ˈservice; ˌNational ˈTrust**
national|ism ˈnæʃ.ᵊn.ᵊl|.ɪ.zᵊm, ˈnæʃ.nᵊl- **-ist/s** -ɪst/s
nationalistic ˌnæʃ.ᵊn.ᵊlˈɪs.tɪk, ˌnæʃ.nᵊlˈ- **-ally** -ᵊl.i, -li
nationalit|y ˌnæʃ.ᵊnˈæl.ə.t|i, ˌnæʃˈnæl-, -ɪ.t|i **-ies** -iz

nationalization, -isa- ˌnæʃ.ᵊn.ᵊl.aɪˈzeɪ.ʃᵊn, ˌnæʃ.nᵊl-, -ɪˈ- (US) -ɪˈ-
nationaliz|e, -is|e ˈnæʃ.ᵊn.ᵊl.aɪz, ˈnæʃ.nᵊl- **-es** -ɪz **-ing** -ɪŋ **-ed** -d
nationhood ˈneɪ.ʃᵊn.hʊd
nation-state ˌneɪ.ʃᵊnˈsteɪt (US) ˈ--- **-s** -s
nationwide ˌneɪ.ʃᵊnˈwaɪd *stress shift:* ˌnationwide ˈsearch
native ˈneɪ.tɪv (US) -t̬ɪv **-s** -z **-ly** -li **ˌNative Aˈmerican; ˌnative ˈspeaker**
nativit|y (N) nəˈtɪv.ə.t|i, -ɪ.t|i (US) -ə.t̬|i **-ies** -iz **naˈtivity ˌplay**
NATO, Nato ˈneɪ.təʊ (US) -t̬oʊ
natron ˈneɪ.trən, -trɒn (US) -trɑːn
NATSOPA nætˈsəʊ.pə (US) -ˈsoʊ-
natt|er ˈnæt|.əʳ (US) ˈnæt̬|.ɚ **-ers** -əz (US) -ɚz **-ering** -ᵊr.ɪŋ (US) -ɚ.ɪŋ **-ered** -əd (US) -ɚd **-erer/s** -ᵊr.əʳ/z, -ɚ.ɚ/z
natterjack ˈnæt.ə.dʒæk (US) ˈnæt̬.ɚ- **-s** -s
natt|y ˈnæt|.i (US) ˈnæt̬|.i **-ier** -i.əʳ (US) -i.ɚ **-iest** -i.ɪst, -i.əst **-ily** -ɪ.li, -ᵊl.i **-iness** -ɪ.nəs, -ɪ.nɪs
natural ˈnætʃ.ᵊr.ᵊl, -ʊ.rᵊl (US) -ɚ.əl, ˈ-rᵊl **-s** -z **-ly** -i **-ness** -nəs, -nɪs **ˌnatural ˈchildbirth; ˌnatural ˈgas; ˌnatural ˈhistory; ˌnatural reˈsources;** (US) **ˌnatural ˈresources; ˌnatural seˈlection**
natural|ism ˈnætʃ.ᵊr.ᵊl|.ɪ.zᵊm, -ʊr- (US) -ɚ.ᵊl-, ˈ-rᵊl- **-ist/s** -ɪst/s
naturalistic ˌnætʃ.ᵊr.ᵊlˈɪs.tɪk, -ʊr- (US) -ɚ.ᵊlˈ-, ˌ-rᵊlˈ- **-ally** -ᵊl.i, -li
naturalization, -isa- ˌnætʃ.ᵊr.ᵊl.aɪˈzeɪ.ʃᵊn, -ʊr-, -ɪˈ- (US) -ɚ.ᵊl.ɪˈ-, ˌ-rᵊl-
naturaliz|e, -is|e ˈnætʃ.ᵊr.ᵊl.aɪz, -ʊr- (US) -ɚ.ᵊl-, ˈ-rᵊl- **-es** -ɪz **-ing** -ɪŋ **-ed** -d
nature ˈneɪ.tʃəʳ (US) -tʃɚ **-s** -z **-d** -d **ˈnature reˌserve**
natur|ism ˈneɪ.tʃᵊr|.ɪ.zᵊm **-ist/s** -ɪst/s
naturopath ˈneɪ.tʃᵊr.əʊ.pæθ, -tʃʊr-, ˈnætʃ.ᵊr-, -ʊr- (US) ˈneɪ.tʃɚ.ə- **-s** -s
naturopathic ˌneɪ.tʃᵊr.əʊˈpæθ.ɪk, -tʃʊr-, ˌnætʃ.ᵊr- (US) ˌneɪ.tʃɚ.əˈ- **-ally** -ᵊl.i, -li
naturopathy ˌneɪ.tʃᵊrˈɒp.ə.θi, -tʃʊr-, ˌnætʃ.ᵊrˈ-, -ʊrˈ- (US) ˌneɪ.tʃəˈrɑː.pə-
NatWest® ˌnætˈwest *stress shift:* ˌNatWest ˈBank
Naugahyde® ˈnɔː.gə.haɪd (US) ˈnɑː.gə-, ˈnɔː-
naught nɔːt (US) nɑːt, nɔːt **-s** -s
Naughtie ˈnɒx.ti (US) ˈnɑːk-, ˈnɑːx-
naught|y ˈnɔː.t|i (US) ˈnɑː.t̬|i, ˈnɔː- **-ier** -i.əʳ (US) -i.ɚ **-iest** -i.ɪst, -i.əst **-ily** -ɪ.li, -ᵊl.i **-iness** -ɪ.nəs, -ɪ.nɪs
Nauru nɑːˈuː.ruː; naʊˈruː, nɑː-, ˈ-- (US) nɑːˈuː.ruː
Nauruan nɑːˈuː.ruː.ən; naʊˈruː-, nɑː- (US) nɑːˈuː.ruː- **-s** -z
nausea ˈnɔː.si.ə, -zi-, ˈ-ʒə (US) ˈnɑː.zi.ə, ˈnɔː-, ˈ-ʒə, ˈ-ʃə, ˈ-si.ə
nause|ate ˈnɔː.si|.eɪt, -zi-, ˈ-ʒ|eɪt (US) ˈnɑː.zi-, ˈnɔː-, -ʒi-, -ʃi-, -si- **-ates** -eɪts **-ating** -eɪ.tɪŋ (US) -eɪ.t̬ɪŋ **-ated** -eɪ.tɪd (US) -eɪ.t̬ɪd
nauseating ˈnɔː.si.eɪ.tɪŋ, -zi- (US) ˈnɑː.zi-, ˈnɔː-, -ʒi-, -ʃi-, -si- **-ly** -li
nauseous ˈnɔː.si.əs, -zi-, ˈ-ʃəs, ˈ-ʒəs (US) ˈnɑː.ʃəs, ˈnɔː-, ˈ-zi.əs **-ly** -li **-ness** -nəs, -nɪs
Nausicaa, Nausicaä nɔːˈsɪk.i.ə, -eɪ.ə (US) nɑː-, nɔː-
nautch nɔːtʃ (US) nɑːtʃ, nɔːtʃ **-es** -ɪz
nautic|al ˈnɔː.tɪ.k|ᵊl (US) ˈnɑː.t̬i-, ˈnɔː- **-ally** -ᵊl.i **ˌnautical ˈmile**
nautil|us ˈnɔː.tɪ.l|əs, ˈ-tᵊl- (US) ˈnɑː.t̬ɪ-, ˈnɔː- **-uses** -ə.sɪz **-i** -aɪ, -iː
Navajo, Navaho ˈnæv.ə.həʊ (US) -hoʊ, ˈnɑː.və- **-s** -z
naval ˈneɪ.vᵊl
Navan ˈneɪ.vᵊn
navarin ˈnæv.ᵊr.ɪn **-s** -z
Navarino ˌnæv.ᵊrˈiː.nəʊ (US) -əˈriː.noʊ
Navarre nəˈvɑːʳ (US) -ˈvɑːr
nave neɪv **-s** -z
navel ˈneɪ.vᵊl **-s** -z
navicular nəˈvɪk.jə.ləʳ, -jʊ- (US) -lɚ
navigability ˌnæv.ɪ.gəˈbɪl.ə.ti, -ɪ.ti (US) -ə.t̬i
navigable ˈnæv.ɪ.gə.bl̩ **-ness** -nəs, -nɪs
navi|gate ˈnæv.ɪ|.geɪt **-gates** -geɪts **-gating** -geɪ.tɪŋ (US) -geɪ.t̬ɪŋ **-gated** -geɪ.tɪd (US) -geɪ.t̬ɪd
navigation ˌnæv.ɪˈgeɪ.ʃᵊn **-al** -ᵊl
navigator ˈnæv.ɪ.geɪ.təʳ (US) -t̬ɚ **-s** -z
Navratilova nævˌræt.ɪˈləʊ.və, ˌnæv.rə- (US) ˌnæv.rə.tɪˈloʊ.və, ˌnɑːv-
navv|y ˈnæv|.i **-ies** -iz
nav|y ˈneɪ.v|i **-ies** -iz **ˌnavy ˈblue**
nawab (N) nəˈwɑːb (US) -ˈwɑːb, -ˈwɔːb **-s** -z
Nawanagar nəˈwɑː.nə.gəʳ (US) ˌnɑː.wəˈnʌg.ɚ; nəˈwɑː.nə.gɚ
Naxos ˈnæk.sɒs (US) -sɑːs, -soʊs
nay neɪ
Nayarit ˈnɑː.jɑː.rɪt
Naylor ˈneɪ.ləʳ (US) -lɚ
naysayer ˈneɪˌseɪ.əʳ (US) -ɚ **-s** -z
Nazarene ˌnæz.ᵊrˈiːn, ˈ--- (US) ˌnæz.əˈriːn, ˈ--- **-s** -z
Nazareth ˈnæz.ᵊr.əθ, -ɪθ
Nazarite ˈnæz.ᵊr.aɪt (US) -ə.raɪt **-s** -s
Naze neɪz
Nazeing ˈneɪ.zɪŋ
nazi (N) ˈnɑːt.si (US) ˈnɑːt-, ˈnæt- **-s** -z
nazism (N) ˈnɑːt.sɪ.zᵊm (US) ˈnɑːt-, ˈnæt-
NB ˌenˈbiː; ˌnəʊ.təˈbiː.ni, -tɑːˈben.eɪ (US) ˌenˈbiː; ˌnoʊ.t̬əˈben.eɪ, -tɑːˈ-, -ˈbiː.ni
NBA ˌen.biːˈeɪ, ˌem- (US) ˌen-
NBC ˌen.biːˈsiː, ˌem- (US) ˌen-
N.C. ˌenˈsiː
NCO ˌen.siːˈəʊ (US) -ˈoʊ **-s** -z
NCT ˌen.siːˈtiː
N.D. ˌenˈdiː
Ndebele ᵊn.dɪˈbel.i, -dəˈ-, -ˈbeɪ.li, -ˈbiː-, -leɪ (US) ᵊn.dəˈbel.eɪ, -ˈbiː.li **-s** -z
N'Djamena ᵊn.dʒɑːˈmeɪ.nə, -dʒæmˈeɪ- (US) -ˈdʒɑː.mə-
Ndola ᵊnˈdəʊ.lə (US) -ˈdoʊ-
NE *(abbrev. for* **northeast***)* ˌenˈiː, ˌnɔːθˈiːst (US) ˌenˈiː, ˌnɔːrθˈiːst
Neagh neɪ
Neagle ˈniː.gl̩
Neal(e) niːl
Neanderthal niˈæn.də.tɑːl, -θɔːl, -tᵊl (US) -dɚ.θɔːl, -tɑːl
neap niːp **-s** -s
Neapolis niˈæp.ə.lɪs
neapolitan (N) ˌniː.əˈpɒl.ɪ.tᵊn, nɪəˈ-, ˈ-ə- (US) ˌniː.əˈpɑː.lə- **-s** -z
near nɪəʳ (US) nɪr **-er** -əʳ (US) -ɚ **-est** -ɪst, -əst **-ness** -nəs, -nɪs **-s** -z **-ing** -ɪŋ **-ed** -d **ˌNear ˈEast; ˌnear ˈmiss; ˌnearest and ˈdearest**
nearby ˌnɪəˈbaɪ (US) ˌnɪr- *stress shift:* ˌnearby ˈtown
nearly ˈnɪə.li (US) ˈnɪr-
nearside ˌnɪəˈsaɪd (US) ˌnɪr- *stress shift:* ˌnearside ˈlane
nearsighted ˌnɪəˈsaɪ.tɪd (US) ˌnɪrˈsaɪ.t̬ɪd **-ness** -nəs, -nɪs *stress shift:* ˌnearsighted ˈvision
Neasden ˈniːz.dən
neat niːt **-er** -əʳ (US) ˈniː.t̬ɚ **-est** -ɪst, -əst (US) ˈniː.t̬ɪst, -t̬əst **-ly** -li **-ness** -nəs, -nɪs
neaten ˈniː.tᵊn **-s** -z **-ing** -ɪŋ **-ed** -d
'neath niːθ
Neath niːθ
Nebo ˈniː.bəʊ (US) -boʊ
Nebr. *(abbrev. for* **Nebraska***)* nɪˈbræs.kə, nebˈræs-, nəˈbræs- (US) nəˈbræs-
Nebrask|a nɪˈbræs.k|ə, nebˈræs-, nəˈbræs- (US) nəˈbræs- **-an** -ən
Nebuchadnezzar ˌneb.jə.kədˈnez.əʳ, -jʊ- (US) -ə.kədˈnez.ɚ, ˌneb.jə-
nebul|a ˈneb.jə.l|ə, -jʊ- (US) -jə- **-ae** -iː **-as** -əz **-ar** -əʳ (US) -ɚ **-ous** -əs
nebuliz|e, -is|e ˈneb.jə.laɪz, -jʊ- (US) -jə- **-es** -ɪs **-ing** -ɪŋ **-ed** -d **-er/s** -əʳ/z (US) -ɚ/z
nebulosity ˌneb.jəˈlɒs.ə.ti, -jʊˈ-, -ɪ.ti (US) -jəˈlɑː.sə.t̬i
nebulous ˈneb.jə.ləs, -jʊ- **-ly** -li **-ness** -nəs, -nɪs
NEC ˌen.iːˈsiː
necessarily ˈnes.ə.sᵊr.ᵊl.i, ˈ-ɪ-, -ɪ.li; ˌnes.əˈser-, -ɪˈ- (US) ˌnes.əˈser-; ˈnes.ə.ser-

necessar|y ˈnes.ə.sᵊr|.i, ˈ-ɪ-, -ser- (US) -ser- **-ies** -iz **-iness** -ɪ.nəs, -ɪ.nɪs
necessi|tate nəˈses.ɪ|.teɪt, nɪ-, ˈ-ə- (US) nə- **-tates** -teɪts **-tating** -teɪ.tɪŋ (US) -teɪ.t̬ɪŋ **-tated** -teɪ.tɪd (US) -teɪ.t̬ɪd
necessitous nəˈses.ɪ.təs, nɪ-, ˈ-ə- (US) nəˈses.ə.t̬əs **-ly** -li **-ness** -nəs, -nɪs
necessit|y nəˈses.ə.t|i, nɪ-, -ɪ.t|i (US) nəˈses.ə.t̬|i **-ies** -iz
neck nek **-s** -s **-ing** -ɪŋ **-ed** -t ˌ**neck and** ˈ**neck**; ˌ**neck of the** ˈ**woods**; ˌ**pain in the** ˈ**neck**; ˌ**up to one's** ˈ**neck**
Neckar ˈnek.əʳ *as if German:* -ɑːʳ (US) -ɚ *as if German:* -ɑːr
neckband ˈnek.bænd **-s** -z
neck|cloth ˈnek|.klɒθ (US) -klɑːθ **-cloths** -klɒθs, -klɒðz (US) -klɑːθs, -klɑːðz
necker|chief ˈnek.ə|.tʃɪf, -tʃiːf (US) ˈ-ɚ- **-chiefs** -tʃɪfs **-chieves** -tʃiːvz
necklac|e ˈnek.ləs, -lɪs **-es** -ɪz **-ing** -ɪŋ **-ed** -t
necklet ˈnek.lət, -lɪt **-s** -s
neckline ˈnek.laɪn **-s** -z
necktie ˈnek.taɪ **-s** -z
neckwear ˈnek.weəʳ (US) -wer
necro- nek.rəʊ-; nekˈrɒ- (US) nek.roʊ-, -rə-; nekˈrɑː-, nəˈkrɑː-
Note: Prefix. Normally takes either primary or secondary stress on the first syllable, e.g. **necrophile** /ˈnek.rəʊ.faɪl (US) -rə-/, **necrophilia** /ˌnek.rəʊˈfɪl.i.ə (US) -əˈ-/, or primary stress on the second syllable, e.g. **necrology** /nekˈrɒl.ə.dʒi (US) -ˈrɑː.lə-/.
necrolatry nekˈrɒl.ə.tri (US) -ˈrɑː.lə-, nəˈkrɑː-
necrological ˌnek.rəˈlɒdʒ.ɪ.kᵊl (US) -ˈlɑː.dʒɪ-
necrolog|y nekˈrɒl.ə.dʒ|i (US) -ˈrɑː.lə-, nəˈkrɑː- **-ies** -iz **-ist/s** -ɪst/s
necromanc|er ˈnek.rəʊ.mænt.s|əʳ (US) -rə.mænt.s|ɚ **-ers** -əz (US) -ɚz **-y** -i
necromantic ˌnek.rəʊˈmæn.tɪk (US) -rə- **-ally** -ᵊl.i, -li
necrophile ˈnek.rəʊ.faɪl (US) -rə- **-s** -z
necrophili|a ˌnek.rəʊˈfɪl.i|.ə (US) -əˈ-, -ˈfɪl.i|.ə, -ˈfiːl.j|ə **-ac/s** -æk/s
necrophilism nekˈrɒf.ɪ.lɪ.zᵊm, nɪˈkrɒf-, ˈ-ə- (US) nekˈrɑː.fə-, nəˈkrɑː-
necropol|is nekˈrɒp.ᵊl|.ɪs, nɪˈkrɒp- (US) nekˈrɑː-, nəˈkrɑː- **-ises** -ɪ.sɪz **-i** -aɪ
necrops|y ˈnek.rɒp.s|i (US) -rɑːp- **-ies** -iz
necrosis nekˈrəʊ.sɪs, nɪˈkrəʊ- (US) nekˈroʊ-, nəˈkroʊ-
nectar ˈnek.təʳ (US) -tɚ **-ous** -əs
nectarial nekˈteə.ri.ᵊl (US) -ˈter.i-
nectarine ˈnek.tᵊr.iːn, -ɪn (US) ˌnek.təˈriːn, ˈ--- **-s** -z
nectar|y ˈnek.tᵊr|.i **-ies** -iz
Ned ned
Nedd|y ˈned|.i **-ies** -iz
Neden ˈniː.dᵊn
née, nee neɪ
need niːd **-s** -z **-ing** -ɪŋ **-ed** -ɪd
needful ˈniːd.fᵊl, -fʊl **-ly** -i **-ness** -nəs, -nɪs
Needham ˈniː.dəm
needl|e (N) ˈniː.dl̩ **-es** -z **-ing** -ɪŋ, ˈniːd.lɪŋ **-ed** -d
needlecord ˈniː.dl̩.kɔːd (US) -kɔːrd
needlecraft ˈniː.dl̩.krɑːft (US) -kræft **-s** -s
needlepoint ˈniː.dl̩.pɔɪnt
needless ˈniːd.ləs, -lɪs **-ly** -li **-ness** -nəs, -nɪs
needle|woman ˈniː.dl̩|ˌwʊm.ən **-women** -ˌwɪm.ɪn
needlework ˈniː.dl̩.wɜːk (US) -wɝːk
needn't ˈniː.dᵊnt
needs (N) niːdz
need|y ˈniː.d|i **-ier** -i.əʳ (US) -i.ɚ **-iest** -i.ɪst, -i.əst **-ily** -ɪ.li, -ᵊl.i **-iness** -ɪ.nəs, -ɪ.nɪs
neep niːp **-s** -s
ne'er neəʳ (US) ner
ne'er-do-well ˈneə.duˌwel (US) ˈner- **-s** -z
Neeson ˈniː.sᵊn
nefarious nɪˈfeə.ri.əs, nə-, nefˈeə- (US) nəˈfer.i- **-ly** -li **-ness** -nəs, -nɪs
Nefertiti ˌnef.əˈtiː.ti (US) -ɚˈ-
Neff® nef
neg. *(abbrev. for* **negative***)* neg, ˈneg.ə.tɪv (US) neg, ˈneg.ə.t̬ɪv
nega|te nɪˈgeɪ|t, nə-, negˈeɪt (US) nɪˈgeɪ|t **-tes** -ts **-ting** -tɪŋ (US) -t̬ɪŋ **-ted** -tɪd (US) -t̬ɪd
negation nɪˈgeɪ.ʃᵊn, nə-, negˈeɪ- (US) nɪˈgeɪ- **-s** -z
negativ|e ˈneg.ə.tɪv (US) -t̬ɪv **-es** -z **-ely** -li **-eness** -nəs, -nɪs **-ing** -ɪŋ **-ed** -d ˌ**negative** ˈ**feedback**
negativ|ism ˈneg.ə.tɪ.v|ɪ.zᵊm (US) -t̬ɪ- **-ist/s** -ɪst/s
negativity ˌneg.əˈtɪv.ə.ti, -ɪ.ti (US) -ə.t̬i
Negeb ˈneg.eb
Negev ˈneg.ev
neglect nɪˈglekt, nə- (US) nɪ- **-s** -s **-ing** -ɪŋ **-ed** -ɪd
neglectful nɪˈglekt.fᵊl, nə-, -fʊl (US) nɪ- **-ly** -i **-ness** -nəs, -nɪs
negligé(s), negligee(s) ˈneg.lɪ.ʒeɪ, -lə-, -liː-, ˌ--ˈ- (US) ˌneg.ləˈʒeɪ, ˈ---
negligenc|e ˈneg.lɪ.dʒənts, -lə- **-es** -ɪz
negligent ˈneg.lɪ.dʒənt, -lə- **-ly** -li
negligibility ˌneg.lɪ.dʒəˈbɪl.ə.ti, -lə-, -ɪ.ti (US) -t̬i
negligi|ble ˈneg.lɪ.dʒə|bl̩, -lə-, -dʒɪ- (US) -dʒə- **-bly** -bli
negotiability nɪˌgəʊ.ʃi.əˈbɪl.ə.ti, nə-, ˌ-ʃəˈ-, -ɪ.ti (US) nɪˌgoʊ.ʃi.əˈbɪl.ə.t̬i, ˌ-ʃəˈ-
negotiable nɪˈgəʊ.ʃi.ə.bl̩, nə-, ˈ-ʃə- (US) nɪˈgoʊ.ʃi.ə-, ˈ-ʃə-
negoti|ate nɪˈgəʊ.ʃi|.eɪt, nə-, -si- (US) nɪˈgoʊ- **-ates** -eɪts **-ating** -eɪ.tɪŋ (US) -eɪ.t̬ɪŋ **-ated** -eɪ.tɪd (US) -eɪ.t̬ɪd **neˈgotiating** ˌ**table**
negotiation nɪˌgəʊ.ʃiˈeɪ.ʃᵊn, nə-, -siˈ- (US) nɪˌgoʊ- **-s** -z
negotiator nɪˈgəʊ.ʃi.eɪ.təʳ, nə-, -si- (US) nɪˈgoʊ.ʃi.eɪ.t̬ɚ, -si- **-s** -z
negotiatory nɪˈgəʊ.ʃi.eɪ.tᵊr.i, nə-, -si- (US) nɪˈgoʊ.ʃi.eɪ.t̬ɚ-
negress (N) ˈniː.grəs, -grɪs, -gres (US) -grɪs **-es** -ɪz
Negrillo nɪˈgrɪl.əʊ, nə-, negˈrɪl- (US) nəˈgrɪl.oʊ **-(e)s** -z
Negrito nɪˈgriː.təʊ, nə-, negˈriː- (US) nəˈgriː.t̬oʊ **-(e)s** -z
negritude ˈneg.rɪ.tjuːd, ˈniː.grɪ-, -grə- (US) -tuːd, -tjuːd
negro (N) *person:* ˈniː.grəʊ (US) -groʊ **-es** -z
Negro *river:* ˈneɪ.grəʊ, ˈneg.rəʊ (US) ˈneɪ.groʊ
negroid ˈniː.grɔɪd
negus (N) ˈniː.gəs **-es** -ɪz
Nehemiah ˌniː.*h*ɪˈmaɪ.ə, ˌneɪ-, -*h*əˈ- (US) ˌniː.əˈ-, -hɪˈ-
Nehru ˈneə.ruː (US) ˈneɪ-
neigh neɪ **-s** -z **-ing** -ɪŋ **-ed** -d
neighb|o(u)r ˈneɪ.b|əʳ (US) -bɚ **-o(u)rs** -əz (US) -ɚz **-o(u)ring** -ᵊr.ɪŋ
neighbo(u)rhood ˈneɪ.bə.hʊd (US) -bɚ- **-s** -z ˌ**neighbourhood** ˈ**watch**
neighbo(u)ring ˈneɪ.bᵊr.ɪŋ
neighbo(u)rl|y ˈneɪ.bᵊl|.i (US) -bɚ.l|i **-iness** -ɪ.nəs, -ɪ.nɪs
Neil(l) niːl
Neilson ˈniːl.sᵊn
Neisse ˈnaɪ.sə
neither ˈnaɪ.ðəʳ, ˈniː- (US) ˈniː.ðɚ, ˈnaɪ-
nekton ˈnek.tən (US) -tɑːn, -tən
Nell nel
Nellie ˈnel.i
nelly (N) ˈnel.i
Nelson ˈnel.sᵊn
Nelsonian nelˈsəʊ.ni.ən (US) -ˈsoʊ-
nematode ˈnem.ə.təʊd (US) -toʊd **-s** -z
Nembutal® ˈnem.bjə.tæl, -bjʊ-, -tɑːl (US) -bjə.tɑːl, -bjʊ-, -tɔːl
nem. con. ˌnemˈkɒn (US) -ˈkɑːn
Neme|a nɪˈmiː|.ə, nə-, nemˈiː-; ˈnem.i-, ˈniː.mi- (US) ˈniː.mi- **-an** -ən
nemesis (N) ˈnem.ə.sɪs, ˈ-ɪ- (US) ˈ-ə- **nemeses** ˈnem.ə.siːz
Nemo ˈniː.məʊ (US) -moʊ
nemophila nəˈmɒf.ɪ.lə, nɪ-, -ᵊl.ə (US) niːˈmɑː.fᵊl.ə, nə- **-s** -z
Nemtsov ˈnempt.sɒf (US) -sɑːv, -sɑːf
Nen nen
Nene *river:* niːn, nen
nene *goose:* ˈneɪ.neɪ
Nennius ˈnen.i.əs

neo-, Neo- niː.əʊ-; ni'ɒ- US ni.oʊ-, -ə-; ni'ɑː-
Note: Prefix. Normally either takes primary or secondary stress on the first syllable, e.g. **neonate** /'niː.əʊ.neɪt US -oʊ-/, **neonatal** /ˌniː.əʊ'neɪ.tᵊl US -oʊ'neɪ.t̬ᵊl/, or primary stress on the second syllable, e.g. **neologize** /ni'ɒl.ə.dʒaɪz ¯-'ɑː.lə-/.
neoclassic ˌniː.əʊ'klæs.ɪk US -oʊ'- **-al** -ᵊl
neoclassic|ism ˌniː.əʊ'klæs.ɪ.s|ɪ.zᵊm US -oʊ'- **-ist/s** -ɪst/s
neocolonial|ism ˌniː.əʊ.kə'ləʊ.ni.ᵊl|.ɪ.zᵊm, '-njᵊl- US -oʊ.kə'loʊ- **-ist/s** -ɪst/s
neodymium ˌniː.əʊ'dɪm.i.əm US -oʊ'-
neoimpressionism ˌniː.əʊ.ɪm'preʃ.ᵊnɪ.zᵊm US -oʊ-
neoimpressionist ˌniː.əʊ.ɪm'preʃ.ᵊn.ɪst US -oʊ- **-s** -s
Neo-Latin ˌniː.əʊ'læt.ɪn US -oʊ'læt.ᵊn
neolithic (N) ˌniː.əʊ'lɪθ.ɪk US -oʊ'-, -ə'-
neolog|ism ni'ɒl.ə.dʒ|ɪ.zᵊm US -'ɑː.lə- **-isms** -ɪ.zᵊmz **-y** -i
neologiz|e, -is|e ni'ɒl.ə.dʒaɪz US -'ɑː.lə- **-es** -ɪz **-ing** -ɪŋ **-ed** -d
neon 'niː.ɒn US -ɑːn ˌ**neon** '**light**
neonatal ˌniː.əʊ'neɪ.tᵊl US -oʊ'neɪ.t̬ᵊl, -ə'- **-ly** -i
neonate 'niː.əʊ.neɪt US -oʊ-, '-ə- **-s** -s
neophyte 'niː.əʊ.faɪt US -oʊ-, '-ə- **-s** -s
neoprene 'niː.əʊ.priːn US -oʊ-, '-ə-
Nepal nɪ'pɔːl, nə-, nep'ɔːl, -ɑːl US nə'pɔːl, -'pɑːl
Nepalese ˌnep.ᵊl'iːz, -ɔː'liːz US -ə'liːz, -'liːs
Nepali nɪ'pɔː.li, nə-, nep'ɔː-, -'ɑː- US nɪ'pɔː-, nep'ɔː-, -'ɑː- **-s** -z
nepenthe nɪ'pent.θi, nə-, nep'ent- US nɪ'pent-
nephew 'nef.juː, 'nev- US 'nef- **-s** -z
nephrite 'nef.raɪt
nephritic nɪ'frɪt.ɪk, nə-, nef'rɪt- US nɪ'frɪt̬-, nef'rɪt̬-
nephritis nɪ'fraɪ.tɪs, nə-, nef'raɪ- US nɪ'fraɪ.t̬ɪs, nef'raɪ-
Nephthys 'nef.tɪs US -θɪs
ne plus ultra ˌneɪ.plʊs'ʊl.trɑː, ˌniː-, -plʌs'-, -'ʌl-, -trə US -plʌs'ʌl.trə, -plʊs'-, -'ʊl-
Nepos 'niː.pɒs, 'nep.ɒs US 'niː.pɑːs, 'nep.ɑːs
nepotism 'nep.ə.tɪ.zᵊm, -ɒt.ɪ- US -ə.tɪ- **-ist/s** -ɪst/s
nepotistic nep.ə'tis.tik
Neptune 'nep.tjuːn, -tʃuːn US -tuːn, -tjuːn
neptunian (N) nep'tjuː.ni.ən, -'tʃuː- US -'tuː-, -'tjuː-
neptunium nep'tjuː.ni.əm, -'tʃuː- US -'tuː-, -'tjuː-
nerd nɜːd US nɝːd **-s** -z **-y** -i
nereid (N) 'nɪə.ri.ɪd US 'nɪr.i- **-s** -z
Nereus 'nɪə.ri.uːs, -əs US 'nɪr.i.əs, '-juːs
Neri 'nɪə.ri US 'nɪr.i, 'ner-, 'neɪ.ri
Nero 'nɪə.rəʊ US 'nɪr.oʊ, 'niː.roʊ
Neruda nə'ruː.də, ner'uː-
nerv|e nɜːv US nɝːv **-es** -z **-ing** -ɪŋ **-ed** -d '**nerve** ˌ**cell**; '**nerve** ˌ**centre**; '**nerve** ˌ**gas**; ˌ**get on** ˌ**someone's** '**nerves**
nerveless 'nɜːv.ləs, -lɪs US 'nɝːv- **-ly** -li **-ness** -nəs, -nɪs
nerve-racking, nerve-wracking 'nɜːvˌræk.ɪŋ US 'nɝːv-
nerves nɜːvz US nɝːvz
nervine 'nɜː.viːn US 'nɝː-, -vaɪn
nervous 'nɜː.vəs US 'nɝː- **-ly** -li **-ness** -nəs, -nɪs ˌ**nervous** '**breakdown**; '**nervous** ˌ**system**
nerv|y 'nɜː.v|i US 'nɝː- **-ier** -i.əʳ US -i.ɚ **-iest** -i.ɪst, -i.əst **-ily** -ɪ.li, -ᵊl.i **-iness** -ɪ.nəs, -ɪ.nɪs
Nesbit(t) 'nez.bɪt
Nescafé® 'nes.kə.feɪ, -kæf.eɪ US 'nes.kə.feɪ, -kæf.eɪ, ˌ--'-
nescien|ce 'nes.i.ən|ts US 'neʃ.ən|ts, '-i.ən|ts **-t** -t
Nesfield 'nes.fiːld
Nesquik® 'nes.kwɪk
ness (N) nes **-es** -ɪz
-ness *noun-forming suffix:* -nəs, -nɪs
Note: Suffix. When added to a stem to form a noun, **-ness** does not change the existing stress pattern, e.g. **happy** /'hæp.i/, **happiness** /'hæp.ɪ.nəs/.
-ness *in place names:* -'ness
Note: In place names, the suffix **-ness** normally takes primary stress, e.g. **Inverness** /ˌɪn.və'nes US -vɚ'-/. However, placenames containing **-ness** are subject to stress shift; see individual entries.
Nessie 'nes.i
nest nest **-s** -s **-ing** -ɪŋ **-ed** -ɪd '**nest** ˌ**egg**
Nesta 'nes.tə
nestl|e 'nes.l̩ **-es** -z **-ing** -ɪŋ, 'nes.lɪŋ **-ed** -d
Nestlé® 'nes.leɪ, -li, -l̩ US 'nes.li
nestling 'nest.lɪŋ **-s** -z
Neston 'nes.tᵊn
Nestor 'nes.tɔːʳ, -təʳ US -tɚ, -tɔːr
Nestorian nes'tɔː.ri.ən US -'tɔːr.i- **-s** -z
net (N) net **-s** -s **-ting** -ɪŋ US 'net̬.ɪŋ **-ted** -ɪd US 'net̬.ɪd
Netanyahu ˌnet.ən'jɑː.hu, -æn'- US ˌnet.ɑːn'jɑː.hu, -ən'-
netball 'net.bɔːl US -bɔːl, -bɑːl
netcronym 'net.krəʊ.nɪm, 'nek- US 'net.krə- **-s** -z
nether 'neð.əʳ US -ɚ **-most** -məʊst US -moʊst
Nether|land 'neð.ə|lənd, -ᵊl|.ənd US -ɚ|lənd **-lands** -ləndz **-lander/s** -lən.dəʳ/z US -lən.dɚ/z
netherworld 'neð.ə.wɜːld US -ɚ.wɝːld **-s** -z
netizen 'net.ɪ.zᵊn, -ə- US 'net̬- **-s** -z
Netley 'net.li
Netscape® 'net.skeɪp
netsuke 'net.skeɪ, -ski, '-sʊ.ki, -keɪ US -sʊ.ki, -sə.keɪ **-s** -z
Nettie, Netty 'net.i US 'net̬-
netting 'net.ɪŋ US 'net̬-
nettl|e 'net.l̩ US 'net̬- **-es** -z **-ing** -ɪŋ, 'net.lɪŋ **-ed** -d '**nettle** ˌ**rash**; ˌ**grasp the** '**nettle**
Nettlefold 'net.l̩.fəʊld US 'net̬.l̩.foʊld
nettlerash 'net.l̩.ræʃ US 'net̬-
Nettleship 'net.l̩.ʃɪp US 'net̬-
nettlesome 'net.l̩.səm US 'net̬-
network 'net.wɜːk US -wɝːk **-s** -s **-ing** -ɪŋ **-ed** -t
Neuchâtel ˌnɜː.ʃæt'el, -ʃə'tel; US ˌnuː.ʃə'tel, ˌnɜː-
Neufchâtel ˌnɜː.ʃæt'el, -ʃə'tel US ˌnuː.ʃə'tel, ˌnɜː-
neum(e) njuːm US nuːm, njuːm **-s** -z
neural 'njʊə.rᵊl, 'njɔː- US 'nʊr.əl, 'njʊr-, 'nɝː- ˌ**neural** '**network**
neuralg|ia njʊə'ræl.dʒ|ə, njɔː-, njᵊr'æl-, njʊ'ræl- US nʊ'ræl-, njʊ-, nə- **-ic** -ɪk
neurasthenia ˌnjʊə.rəs'θiː.ni.ə, ˌnjɔː- US ˌnʊr.æs'-, ˌnjʊr-
neurasthenic ˌnjʊə.rəs'θen.ɪk, ˌnjɔː- US ˌnʊr.æs'-, ˌnjʊr- **-s** -s
neuritis njʊə'raɪ.tɪs, njɔː-, njᵊr'aɪ-, njʊ'raɪ- US nʊ'raɪ.t̬ɪs, njʊ-
neuro- ˌnjʊə.rəʊ-, ˌnjɔː-, njʊə'rɒ-, njɔː'- US ˌnʊr.oʊ-, ˌnjʊr-, ˌ-ə-
Note: Prefix. Normally either takes primary or secondary stress on the first syllable, e.g. **neuron** /'njʊə.rɒn US 'nʊr.ɑːn/, **neurological** /ˌnjʊə.rə'lɒdʒ.ɪ.kᵊl US ˌnʊr.ə'lɑː.dʒɪ-/, or primary stress on the second syllable, e.g. **neurologist** /njʊə'rɒl.ə.dʒɪst US nʊ'rɑː.lə-/.
neurologi|cal ˌnjʊə.rə'lɒdʒ.ɪ|.kᵊl, ˌnjɔː- US ˌnʊr.ə'lɑː.dʒɪ-, ˌnjʊr- **-cally** -kᵊl.i, -kli
neurolog|ist njʊə'rɒl.ə.dʒ|ɪst, njɔː-, njᵊr'ɒl-, njʊ'rɒl- US nʊ'rɑː.lə-, njʊ- **-ist/s** -ɪst/s **-y** -i
neuron 'njʊə.rɒn, 'njɔː- US 'nʊr.ɑːn, 'njʊr- **-s** -z
neurone 'njʊə.rəʊn, 'njɔː- US 'nʊr.oʊn, 'njʊr- **-s** -z
neuroscien|ce ˌnjʊə.rəʊ'saɪ.ən|ts, ˌnjɔː-, 'njʊə.rəʊˌ-, 'njɔː- US ˌnʊr.oʊ'saɪ-, ˌnjʊr-, 'nʊr.oʊˌsaɪ-, 'njʊr- **-ces** -tsɪz **-tist/s** -tɪst/s

Neutral

A term used to describe lip configuration in speech sounds, in which the lips are neither rounded nor spread (see ROUNDING and SPREADING). The term 'unrounded' is also commonly used but can apply equally to spread lips.

Examples for English

The English vowels /ə/and /ɜː/are thought of as having a neutral lip configuration.

Neutralisation

The loss of contrast between PHONEMES.

Examples for English

In its simple form, the theory of the phoneme implies that two sounds that are in opposition to each other (e.g. /t/ and /d/ in English) are in this relationship in all contexts throughout the language. Closer study of phonemes has, however, shown that there are some contexts where the opposition no longer functions: for example, in a word like *still* /stɪl/, the /t/ is in a position (following /s/ and preceding a vowel) where voiced (LENIS) PLOSIVES do not occur. There is no possibility in English of the existence of a pair of words such as /stɪl/ and */sdɪl/, so in this context the opposition between /t/ and /d/ is 'neutralised'. One consequence of this is that one could equally well claim that the plosive in this word is a /d/, not a /t/. (See also ASPIRATION.)

neuros|is njʊə'rəʊ.sləs, njɔː-, njᵊr'əʊ-, njʊ'rəʊ- ⓤⓢ nʊ'roʊ-, njʊ-, nə- **-es** -iːz

neurosurgeon 'njʊə.rəʊˌsɜː.dʒᵊn, ˌnjɔː-, ˌ--'-- ⓤⓢ ˌnʊr.oʊ'sɝː-, ˌnjʊr- **-s** -z

neurosurg|ery ˌnjʊə.rəʊ'sɜː.dʒ|ᵊr.i, ˌnjɔː- ⓤⓢ ˌnʊr.oʊ'sɝː-, ˌnjʊr- **-ical** -ɪ.kᵊl

neurotic njʊə'rɒt.ɪk, njɔː-, njᵊr'ɒt-, njʊ'rɒt- ⓤⓢ nʊ'rɑː.t̬ɪk, njʊ-, nə- **-s** -s **-ally** -ᵊl.i, -li

neurotransmitter ˌnjʊə.rəʊ.trænz'mɪt.əʳ, '---ˌ--, ˌnjɔː- ⓤⓢ ˌnʊr.oʊ.træn'smɪt̬.ɚ, ˌnjʊr-, -trænz'mɪt̬- **-s** -z

neut|er 'njuː.t|əʳ ⓤⓢ 'nuː.t̬|ɚ, 'njuː- **-ers** -əz ⓤⓢ -ɚz **-ering** -ᵊr.ɪŋ **-ered** -əd ⓤⓢ -ɚd

neutral 'njuː.trᵊl ⓤⓢ 'nuː-, 'njuː- **-s** -z **-ly** -i **-ness** -nəs, -nɪs

neutralism 'njuː.trᵊl.ɪ.zᵊm ⓤⓢ 'nuː-, 'njuː-

neutralist 'njuː.trᵊl.ɪst ⓤⓢ 'nuː-, 'njuː- **-s** -s

neutrality njuː'træl.ə.ti, -ɪ.ti ⓤⓢ nuː'træl.ə.t̬i, njuː-

neutralization, -isa- ˌnjuː.trᵊl.aɪ'zeɪ.ʃᵊn, -ɪ'- ⓤⓢ ˌnuː.trᵊl.ɪ'-, ˌnjuː-

neutraliz|e, -is|e 'njuː.trᵊl.aɪz ⓤⓢ 'nuː-, 'njuː- **-es** -ɪŋ **-ing** -ɪz **-ed** -d

neutrino njuː'triː.nəʊ ⓤⓢ nuː'triː.noʊ, njuː- **-s** -z

neutron 'njuː.trɒn ⓤⓢ 'nuː.trɑːn, 'njuː- **-s** -z **'neutron ˌbomb**

Nev. *(abbrev. for* **Nevada***)* nə'vɑː.də, nɪ-, nev'ɑː- ⓤⓢ nə'væd.ə, -'vɑː.də

Neva 'neɪ.və, 'niː- ⓤⓢ 'niː-

Nevada nə'vɑː.də, nɪ-, nev'ɑː- ⓤⓢ nə'væd.ə, -'vɑː.də

Neve niːv

névé 'nev.eɪ ⓤⓢ neɪ'veɪ, '--

never 'nev.əʳ ⓤⓢ -ɚ

never-ending ˌnev.ᵊr'en.dɪŋ ⓤⓢ '-ɚ-

nevermore ˌnev.ə'mɔːʳ ⓤⓢ -ɚ'mɔːr

never-never ˌnev.ə'nev.əʳ ⓤⓢ ˌ-ɚ'nev.ɚ **on the ˌnever-'never; ˌnever-'never ˌland**

nevertheless ˌnev.ə.ðə'les ⓤⓢ ˌ-ɚ-

Nevey 'nev.i

Nevil 'nev.ᵊl, -ɪl ⓤⓢ -ᵊl

Nevill(e) 'nev.ᵊl, -ɪl ⓤⓢ -ᵊl

Nevin 'nev.ɪn

Nevinson 'nev.ɪn.sᵊn

Nevis *in Scotland:* 'nev.ɪs *in West Indies:* 'niː.vɪs

nev|us 'niː.v|əs **-uses** -ə.sɪz **-i** -aɪ

new njuː ⓤⓢ nuː, njuː **-er** -əʳ ⓤⓢ -ɚ **-est** -ɪst, -əst **-ish** -ɪʃ **-ly** -li **-ness** -nəs, -nɪs **ˌNew 'Age;** *stress shift:* ˌNew Age 'traveller; **ˌnew 'broom; ˌNew 'Brunswick; ˌNew Cale'donia; ˌNew 'Deal; ˌNew 'Delhi; ˌNew 'England** *stress shift:* ˌNew England 'coast; **ˌNew 'Forest** *stress shift:* ˌNew Forest 'ponies; **ˌNew 'Hampshire** *stress shift:* ˌNew Hampshire 'primary; **ˌNew 'Jersey** *stress shift:* ˌNew Jersey 'turnpike; **ˌnew 'man; ˌNew 'Mexico; ˌNew 'Quay** *stress shift:* ˌNew Quay 'harbour; **ˌNew ˌSouth 'Wales; ˌNew 'Testament; ˌNew 'Wave** *stress shift:* ˌNew Wave 'band; **ˌNew 'World** *stress shift:* ˌNew World 'Symphony; **ˌNew 'Year** *stress shift:* ˌNew Year 'party; **ˌNew ˌYear's 'Day; ˌNew ˌYear's 'Eve**

Newark 'njuː.ək ⓤⓢ 'nuː.ɚk, 'njuː-

Newbery 'njuː.bᵊr.i ⓤⓢ 'nuː.ber-, 'njuː-

newbie 'njuː.bi ⓤⓢ 'nuː-, 'njuː- **-s** -z

Newbiggin *place:* 'njuː.bɪ.gɪn ⓤⓢ 'nuː-, 'njuː- *surname:* 'njuː.bɪ.gɪn, -'bɪg.ɪn ⓤⓢ 'nuː-, 'njuː-, -'bɪg.ɪn

Newbold 'njuː.bəʊld ⓤⓢ 'nuː.boʊld, 'njuː-

Newbolt 'njuː.bəʊlt ⓤⓢ 'nuː.boʊlt, 'njuː-

newborn ˌnjuː'bɔːn ⓤⓢ 'nuː.bɔːrn, 'njuː- *stress shift, British only:* ˌnewborn 'baby

Newbridge 'njuː.brɪdʒ ⓤⓢ 'nuː-, 'njuː-

Newburg(h) *in the UK:* 'njuː.bᵊr.ə ⓤⓢ 'nuː-, 'njuː- *in the US:* 'njuː.bɜːg ⓤⓢ 'nuː.bɝːg, 'njuː-

Newburn 'njuː.bɜːn ⓤⓢ 'nuː.bɝːn, 'njuː-

Newbury 'njuː.bᵊr.i ⓤⓢ 'nuː.ber-, 'njuː-, -bɚ-

Newby 'njuː.bi ⓤⓢ 'nuː-, 'njuː-

Newcastle 'njuːˌkɑː.sl̩ ⓤⓢ 'nuːˌkæs.l̩, 'njuː-

Newcastle-under-Lyme ˌnjuː.kɑː.sl̩ˌʌn.dəˈlaɪm (US) ˌnuː.kæs.l̩ˌʌn.dɚˈ-, ˌnjuː-

Newcastle upon Tyne ˌnjuː.kɑː.sl̩.ə.pɒnˈtaɪn (US) ˌnuː.kæs.l̩.ə.pɑːn-, ˌnjuː-
Note: /njuːˈkæs.l̩/ is the local form.

Newcome ˈnjuː.kəm (US) ˈnuː-, ˈnjuː- **-s** -z

newcomer ˈnjuːˌkʌm.əʳ (US) ˈnuːˌkʌm.ɚ, ˈnjuː- **-s** -z

Newdigate ˈnjuː.dɪ.ɡeɪt, -ɡɪt, -ɡət (US) ˈnuː.dɪ.ɡeɪt, ˈnjuː-, -ɡət

Newe njuː (US) nuː, njuː

newel ˈnjuː.əl (US) ˈnuː.əl, ˈnjuː- **-s** -z **ˈnewel ˌpost**

Newell ˈnjuː.əl (US) ˈnuː.əl, ˈnjuː-

Newey ˈnjuː.i (US) ˈnuː-, ˈnjuː-

newfangled ˌnjuːˈfæŋ.ɡl̩d (US) ˌnuː-, ˌnjuː- *stress shift:* ˌnewfangled ˈways

new-fashioned ˌnjuːˈfæʃ.ᵊnd (US) ˈnuːˌfæʃ-, ˈnjuː-

new-found ˌnjuːˈfaʊnd (US) ˌnuː-, ˌnjuː- *stress shift:* ˌnew-found ˈlove

Newfoundland *place:* ˈnjuː.fᵊnd.lənd, -lænd; njuːˈfaʊnd-; ˌnjuː.fᵊndˈlænd (US) ˈnuː.fənd.lənd, ˈnjuː-, -lænd; ˌnuː.faʊndˈlænd, ˌnjuː-; nuːˈfaʊnd.lənd, njuː-, -lænd **-er/s** -əʳ/z (US) -ɚ/z
Note: /ˌnjuː.fᵊndˈlænd/ is the local form; it is also the nautical pronunciation in England.

Newfoundland *dog:* njuːˈfaʊnd.lənd (US) ˈnuː.fənd.lənd, ˈnjuː-, -lænd; nuːˈfaʊnd-, njuː- **-s** -z

Newgate ˈnjuː.ɡeɪt, -ɡɪt, -ɡət (US) ˈnuː.ɡeɪt, ˈnjuː-

Newham ˈnjuː.əm; njuːˈhæm (US) ˈnuː.əm, ˈnjuː-; nuːˈhæm, njuː-

Newhaven ˈnjuː.heɪ.vᵊn, -ˈ-- (US) ˈnuː.heɪ-, ˈnjuː-, -ˈ--

Newington ˈnjuː.ɪŋ.tən (US) ˈnuː-, ˈnjuː-

new-laid ˌnjuːˈleɪd (US) ˌnuː-, ˌnjuː- *stress shift:* ˌnew-laid ˈeggs

Newlands ˈnjuː.lənds (US) ˈnuː-, ˈnjuː-

newlywed ˈnjuː.li.wed (US) ˈnuː-, ˈnjuː- **-s** -z

Newman ˈnjuː.mən (US) ˈnuː-, ˈnjuː-

Newmarket ˈnjuː.mɑː.kɪt (US) ˈnuː.mɑːr-, ˈnjuː-

Newnes njuːnz (US) nuːnz, njuːnz

Newnham ˈnjuː.nəm (US) ˈnuː-, ˈnjuː-

New Orleans ˌnjuːˈɔː.li.ənz, ˈ-lɪənz, ˈ-lənz; -ɔːˈliːnz (US) ˌnuːˈɔːr.li.ənz, ˌnjuː-, ˈ-lənz; -ɔːrˈliːnz

Newport ˈnjuː.pɔːt (US) ˈnuː.pɔːrt, ˈnjuː-

Newport Pagnell ˌnjuː.pɔːtˈpæɡ.nᵊl (US) ˌnuː.pɔːrtˈ-, ˌnjuː-

Newquay ˈnjuː.ki (US) ˈnuː-, ˈnjuː-

New Rossington ˌnjuːˈrɒs.ɪŋ.tən (US) ˌnuːˈrɑː.sɪŋ-, ˌnjuː-

Newry ˈnjʊə.ri (US) ˈnʊr.i, ˈnjʊr-

news njuːz (US) nuːz, njuːz **ˈnews ˌagency**; **ˈnews ˌconference**

newsagent ˈnjuːzˌeɪ.dʒᵊnt (US) ˈnuːz-, ˈnjuːz- **-s** -s

newsboy ˈnjuːz.bɔɪ (US) ˈnuːz-, ˈnjuːz- **-s** -z

newsbreak ˈnjuːz.breɪk (US) ˈnuːz-, ˈnjuːz- **-s** -s

newscast ˈnjuːz.kɑːst (US) ˈnuːz.kæst, ˈnjuːz- **-s** -s **-ing** -ɪŋ **-er/s** -əʳ/z (US) -ɚ/z

newscopy ˈnjuːzˌkɒp.i (US) ˈnuːzˌkɑː.pi, ˈnjuːz-

newsdealer ˈnjuːzˌdiː.ləʳ (US) ˈnuːzˌdiː.lɚ, ˈnjuːz- **-s** -z

newsflash ˈnjuːz.flæʃ (US) ˈnuːz-, ˈnjuːz- **-es** -ɪz

newsgroup ˈnjuːz.ɡruːp (US) ˈnuːz-, ˈnjuːz- **-s** -s

newshound ˈnjuːz.haʊnd (US) ˈnuːz-, ˈnjuːz- **-s** -z

newsletter ˈnjuːzˌlet.əʳ (US) ˈnuːzˌlet̬.ɚ, ˈnjuːz- **-s** -z

news|man ˈnjuːz|.mən, -mæn (US) ˈnuːz-, ˈnjuːz- **-men** -men, -mən

newsmonger ˈnjuːzˌmʌŋ.ɡəʳ (US) ˈnuːzˌmʌŋ.ɡɚ, ˈnjuːz-, -ˌmɑːŋ- **-s** -z

newspaper ˈnjuːsˌpeɪ.pəʳ, ˈnjuːz- (US) ˈnuːzˌpeɪ.pɚ, ˈnjuːz- **-s** -z

newspeak (N) ˈnjuː.spiːk (US) ˈnuː-, ˈnjuː-

news|person ˈnjuːz|ˌpɜː.sᵊn (US) ˈnuːz|ˌpɝː-, ˈnjuːz- **-people** -ˌpiː.pl̩

newsprint ˈnjuːz.prɪnt (US) ˈnuːz-, ˈnjuːz-

newsreader ˈnjuːzˌriː.dəʳ (US) ˈnuːzˌriː.dɚ, ˈnjuːz- **-s** -z

newsreel ˈnjuːz.riːl (US) ˈnuːz-, ˈnjuːz- **-s** -z

newsroom ˈnjuːz.rʊm, -ruːm (US) ˈnuːz.ruːm, ˈnjuːz-, -rʊm **-s** -z

news-sheet ˈnjuːz.ʃiːt, ˈnjuːʒ- (US) ˈnuːz-, ˈnjuːz- **-s** -s

newsstand ˈnjuːz.stænd (US) ˈnuːz-, ˈnjuːz- **-s** -z

Newstead ˈnjuː.stɪd, -sted (US) ˈnuː-, ˈnjuː-

newsvendor ˈnjuːzˌven.dəʳ (US) ˈnuːzˌven.dɚ, ˈnjuːz- **-s** -z

news|woman ˈnjuːz|ˌwʊm.ən (US) ˈnuːz-, ˈnjuːz- **-women** -ˌwɪm.ɪn

newsworthy ˈnjuːzˌwɜː.ði (US) ˈnuːzˌwɝː-, ˈnjuːz-

news|y ˈnjuː.z|i (US) ˈnuː-, ˈnjuː- **-iness** -ɪ.nəs, -ɪ.nɪs

newt njuːt (US) nuːt, njuːt **-s** -s

New Testament ˌnjuːˈtes.tə.mənt (US) ˌnuː-, ˌnjuː-

newton (N) ˈnjuː.tᵊn (US) ˈnuː-, ˈnjuː-

Newtonian njuːˈtəʊ.ni.ən (US) nuːˈtoʊ-, njuː-

Newton-le-Willows ˌnjuː.tᵊn.liˈwɪl.əʊz (US) ˌnuː.tᵊn.liˈwɪl.oʊz, ˌnjuː-

Newtown ˈnjuː.taʊn (US) ˈnuː-, ˈnjuː-

Newtownabbey ˌnjuː.tᵊnˈæb.i (US) ˌnuː-, ˌnjuː-

Newtownards ˌnjuː.tᵊnˈɑːdz (US) ˌnuː.tᵊnˈɑːrdz, ˌnjuː-

Newtown St Boswells ˌnjuː.tᵊn.sᵊntˈbɒz.welz (US) ˌnuː.tᵊn.sᵊntˈbɑːz-, ˌnjuː-

New York ˌnjuːˈjɔːk (US) ˌnuːˈjɔːrk, ˌnjuː- **-er/s** -əʳ/z (US) -ɚ/z *stress shift, see compound:* **ˌNew York ˈCity**

New Zealand ˌnjuːˈziː.lənd (US) ˌnuː-, ˌnjuː- **-er/s** -əʳ/z (US) -ɚ/z

next nekst **ˌnext ˈdoor** *stress shift:* ˌnext door ˈneighbours; **ˌnext of ˈkin**

nexus ˈnek.səs **-es** -ɪz

Ng ɪŋ, əŋ, eŋ

Ngaio ˈnaɪ.əʊ *as if Maori:* ˈŋaɪ- (US) -oʊ

Pronouncing the letters NG

The main realisation for the consonant digraph **ng** is /ŋ/, e.g.:

sing /sɪŋ/
ringing /ˈrɪŋ.ɪŋ/

Other pronunciations are possible, one being /ŋɡ/, e.g.:

finger /ˈfɪŋ.ɡəʳ/ (US) /-ɡɚ/
English /ˈɪŋ.ɡlɪʃ/

In addition

In many words spelt **nge**, or where **ng** is followed by **i** or **y**, the pronunciation is /ndʒ/, e.g.:

change /tʃeɪndʒ/
engine /ˈen.dʒɪn/

Ngami ᵊŋ'gɑː.mi (US) ᵊn-, ᵊŋ-
ngultrum ᵊŋ'guːl.trəm (US) -'ʊl.trʊm; ən'gʌl.trəm, əŋ- **-s** -z
ngwee ᵊŋ'gweɪ (US) -'gwiː
N.H. ˌen'eɪtʃ
NHS ˌen.eɪtʃ'es
NI ˌen'aɪ
niacin 'naɪə.sɪn
Niagara naɪ'æg.ᵊr.ə (US) '-rə, '-ɚ.ə **Niˌagara 'Falls**
Niall 'naɪ.əl, naɪl, niːl
Niamey ni'ɑː.meɪ; nɪə'meɪ (US) ni'ɑː.meɪ; njɑː'meɪ
Niamh niːv, nɪəv
nib nɪb **-s** -z
nibbl|e 'nɪb.l̩ **-es** -z **-ing** -ɪŋ, 'nɪb.lɪŋ **-ed** -d **-er/s** -əʳ/z, -ɚ/z
Nibelung 'niː.bə.lʊŋ, -bɪ- (US) -bə- **-s** -z **-en** -ən
Nibelungenlied ˌniː.bə'lʊŋ.ənˌliːt, -ˌliːd
niblick 'nɪb.lɪk **-s** -s
NiCad® 'naɪ.kæd
Nicaea naɪ'siː.ə
NICAM 'naɪ.kæm
Nicaragu|a ˌnɪk.ᵊr'æg.ju|.ə, -'ɑː.gju-; -'ɑː.gw|ə, -'æg.w|ə (US) -ə'rɑː.gw|ə **-an/s** -ən/z
nic|e *(adj.)* naɪs **-er** -əʳ (US) -ɚ **-est** -ɪst, -əst **-ely** -li **-eness** -nəs, -nɪs
Nice *in France:* niːs
nicely 'naɪs.li
Nicene 'naɪ.siːn, -'- ˌ**Nicene 'Creed**
nicet|y 'naɪ.sə.t|i, -sɪ- (US) -sə.t̬|i **-ies** -iz
nich|e niːʃ (US) nɪtʃ, niːʃ **-es** -ɪz **-ed** -t
Nicholas 'nɪk.ᵊl.əs
Nichol(l) 'nɪk.ᵊl **-s** -z
Nicholson 'nɪk.ᵊl.sᵊn
nick (N) nɪk **-s** -s **-ing** -ɪŋ **-ed** -t **in the ˌnick of 'time**
nickel 'nɪk.l̩ **-s** -z **-(l)ing** -ɪŋ **-(l)ed** -d
nickel-and-dime ˌnɪk.ᵊl.ᵊn*d*'daɪm **-s** -z **-ing** -ɪŋ **-ed** -d
nickelodeon ˌnɪk.l̩'əʊ.di.ən (US) -'oʊ- **-s** -z
nicker 'nɪk.əʳ (US) -ɚ
Nicklaus 'nɪk.laʊs, -ləs (US) -ləs
Nickleby 'nɪk.l̩.bi
Nicklin 'nɪk.lɪn
nicknack 'nɪk.næk **-s** -s
nicknam|e 'nɪk.neɪm **-es** -z **-ing** -ɪŋ **-ed** -d
Nicobar 'nɪk.ə*ʊ*.bɑːʳ (US) -oʊ.bɑːr, ˌ--'-
Nicodemus ˌnɪk.ə*ʊ*'diː.məs (US) -ə'-
nicoise, niçoise niː'swɑːz, nɪ-
Nicola 'nɪk.ᵊl.ə
Nicolas 'nɪk.ᵊl.əs
Nicole nɪ'kəʊl, niː- (US) -'koʊl
Nicol(l) 'nɪk.ᵊl **-s** -z
Nicolson 'nɪk.ᵊl.sᵊn
Nicomachean ˌnaɪ.kɒm.ə'kiː.ən, naɪˌkɒm- (US) ˌnɪk.oʊ.mə'-; ˌnaɪ.kɑː.mə'-
Nicomachus naɪ'kɒm.ə.kəs (US) nɪ'kɑː.mə.kəs; ˌnaɪ.koʊ'mæk.əs
Nicosia ˌnɪk.ə*ʊ*'siː.ə (US) -ə'-, -oʊ'-
nicotine 'nɪk.ə.tiːn, ˌ--'-
nic|tate 'nɪk|.teɪt **-tates** -teɪts **-tating** -teɪ.tɪŋ (US) -teɪ.t̬ɪŋ **-tated** -teɪ.tɪd (US) -teɪ.t̬ɪd
nictation nɪk'teɪ.ʃᵊn
nicti|tate 'nɪk.tɪ|.teɪt (US) -tə- **-tates** -teɪts **-tating** -teɪ.tɪŋ (US) -teɪ.t̬ɪŋ **-tated** -teɪ.tɪd (US) -teɪ.t̬ɪd
nictitation ˌnɪk.tɪ'teɪ.ʃᵊn (US) -tə'-
niec|e niːs **-es** -ɪz
Niedersachsen 'niː.dəˌzæk.sᵊn *as if German:* -ˌzæx- (US) -dɚˌzɑːk-
Nielsen 'niːl.sᵊn
Niersteiner 'nɪə.staɪ.nəʳ *as if German:* -ʃtaɪ- (US) 'nɪr.staɪ.nɚ *as if German:* -ʃtaɪ-
Nietzsche 'niː.tʃə (US) -tʃə, -tʃi
niff nɪf **-s** -s **-ing** -ɪŋ **-ed** -t **-y** -i
nift|y 'nɪf.t|i **-ier** -i.əʳ (US) -i.ɚ **-iest** -i.ɪst, -i.əst **-ies** -iz **-ily** -ɪ.li
Nige naɪdʒ
Nigel 'naɪ.dʒᵊl
Nigella naɪ'dʒel.ə
Niger *river:* 'naɪ.dʒəʳ (US) -dʒɚ *country:* niː'ʒeəʳ (US) 'naɪ.dʒɚ **-ien/s** -i.ən/z
Nigeri|a naɪ'dʒɪə.ri|.ə (US) -'dʒɪr.i- **-an/s** -ən/z
niggard 'nɪg.əd (US) -ɚd **-s** -z
niggardl|y 'nɪg.əd.l|i (US) -ɚd- **-iness** -ɪ.nəs, -ɪ.nɪs
nigger 'nɪg.əʳ (US) -ɚ **-s** -z
niggl|e 'nɪg.l̩ **-es** -z **-ing** -ɪŋ, 'nɪg.lɪŋ **-ed** -d
niggl|y 'nɪg.l|i, 'nɪg.l̩|.i **-iness** -ɪ.nəs, -ɪ.nɪs
nigh naɪ
night naɪt **-s** -s ˌ**night 'blindness** (US) **'night ˌblindness; 'night ˌowl; ˌnight 'porter** (US) **'night ˌporter; 'night ˌschool; 'night ˌshift; ˌnight 'watchman**
nightcap 'naɪt.kæp **-s** -s
nightclothes 'naɪt.kləʊðz (US) -kloʊðz
nightclub 'naɪt.klʌb **-s** -z **-bing** -ɪŋ **-ber/s** -əʳ/z (US) -ɚ/z
nightdress 'naɪt.dres **-es** -ɪz
nightfall 'naɪt.fɔːl (US) -fɔːl, -fɑːl
nightgown 'naɪt.gaʊn **-s** -z
nighthawk 'naɪt.hɔːk (US) -hɑːk, -hɔːk **-s** -s
nightie 'naɪ.ti (US) -t̬i **-s** -z
nightingale (N) 'naɪ.tɪŋ.geɪl (US) -tᵊn-, -t̬ɪŋ- **-s** -z
nightjar 'naɪt.dʒɑːʳ (US) -dʒɑːr **-s** -z
nightlife 'naɪt.laɪf
night-light 'naɪt.laɪt **-s** -s
nightlong ˌnaɪt'lɒŋ (US) -'lɑːŋ, -'lɔːŋ *stress shift:* ˌnightlong 'vigil
nightly 'naɪt.li
nightmar|e 'naɪt.meəʳ (US) -mer **-es** -z **-ish** -ɪʃ **-ishly** -ɪʃ.li **-ishness** -ɪʃ.nəs, -ɪʃ.nɪs
nightshade 'naɪt.ʃeɪd
nightshirt 'naɪt.ʃɜːt (US) -ʃɝːt **-s** -s
nightspot 'naɪt.spɒt (US) -spɑːt **-s** -s
nightstand 'naɪt.stænd **-s** -z
nightstick 'naɪt.stɪk **-s** -s
nighttime 'naɪt.taɪm
nightwatch 'naɪt.wɒtʃ, ˌ-'- (US) 'naɪt.wɑːtʃ, -wɔːtʃ **-es** -ɪz
nightwear 'naɪt.weəʳ (US) -wer
nihil 'niː.hɪl, 'naɪ-, -hᵊl (US) 'naɪ.hɪl, 'niː-
nihil|ism 'niː.ɪ.l|ɪ.zᵊm, 'naɪ-, '-hɪ-, -ᵊl|.ɪ-, -hᵊl- (US) 'naɪ.ə.l|ɪ-, 'niː- **-ist/s** -ɪst/s **-istic** ˌ--'ɪs.tɪk
Nijinsky nɪ'dʒɪn*t*.ski, nə-, -'ʒɪn*t*- (US) nə'dʒɪn*t*-
Nijmegen 'naɪ.meɪ.gən, -'-- (US) '---
Nike *goddess:* 'naɪ.kiː *trademark:* 'naɪ.ki; naɪk (US) 'naɪ.ki
Nikita nɪ'kiː.tə (US) -t̬ə
Nikkei nɪ'keɪ (US) 'niː.keɪ *stress shift, see compound:* ˌ**Nikkei 'index**
Nikki 'nɪk.i
Nikon® 'nɪk.ɒn (US) 'naɪ.kɑːn, 'niː-
nil nɪl
nil desperandum ˌnɪl.des.pə'ræn.dəm, -pᵊr'æn-, -dʊm (US) -pə'ræn.dəm; -'rɑːn.dʊm
Nile naɪl
Nilgiri 'nɪl.gɪ.ri **-s** -z
nilometer naɪ'lɒm.ɪ.təʳ, -ə.təʳ (US) -'lɑː.mə.t̬ɚ **-s** -z
Nilotic naɪ'lɒt.ɪk (US) -'lɑː.t̬ɪk
Nilsen 'niːl.sᵊn, 'nɪl-
Nilsson 'niːl.sᵊn, 'nɪl-
nimbi *(plur. of* **nimbus***)* 'nɪm.baɪ
nimbl|e 'nɪm.bl̩ **-ler** -ləʳ, -l̩.əʳ (US) -lɚ, -l̩.ɚ **-lest** -lɪst, -ləst, -l̩.ɪst, -l̩.əst **-ly** -li **-leness** -l̩.nəs, -l̩.nɪs
nimb|us 'nɪm.b|əs **-uses** -ə.sɪz **-i** -aɪ
nimb|y, NIMB|Y 'nɪm.b|i **-ies** -iz
Nîmes niːm
nimiety nɪ'maɪə.ti, -'maɪ.ɪ.ti (US) -t̬i
nimini-piminy, niminy-piminy ˌnɪm.ɪ.ni'pɪm.ɪ.ni, ˌ-ə-, '-ə- (US) -ə.ni'pɪm.ə-
Nimmo 'nɪm.əʊ (US) -oʊ
Nimrod 'nɪm.rɒd (US) -rɑːd
Nin nɪn (US) nɪn, niːn
Nina 'niː.nə (US) 'niː-, 'naɪ-
nincompoop 'nɪŋ.kəm.puːp, 'nɪn- (US) 'nɪn-, 'nɪŋ- **-s** -s
nine naɪn **-s** -z **-fold** -fəʊld (US) -foʊld ˌ**dressed ˌup to the 'nines; ˌnine-to-'five; ˌnine days' 'wonder**
ninepenc|e 'naɪn.pən*t*s, 'naɪm- (US) 'naɪn- **-es** -ɪz
Note: See note under **penny**.
ninepenny 'naɪn.pᵊn.i, 'naɪm- (US) 'naɪn-

ninepin ˈnaɪn.pɪn, ˈnaɪm- US ˈnaɪn- **-s** -z

nineteen ˌnaɪnˈtiːn **-s** -z **-th/s** -tθ/s *stress shift:* ˌnineteen ˈyears **ˌnineteen to the ˈdozen**

ninetieth ˈnaɪn.ti.əθ, -ɪθ US -t̬i- **-s** -s

Ninette nɪˈnet, niː-

ninet|y ˈnaɪn.t|i US -t̬|i **-ies** -iz

ninetyfold ˈnaɪn.ti.fəʊld US -t̬i.foʊld

ninety-nine ˌnaɪn.tiˈnaɪn US -t̬iˈ- *stress shift:* ˌninety-nine ˈdays

Nineveh ˈnɪn.ɪ.və, ˈ-ə- US ˈ-ə-

ninish ˈnaɪ.nɪʃ

ninja ˈnɪn.dʒə **-s** -z **ˌNinja ˈwarriors**

ninn|y ˈnɪn|.i **-ies** -iz

Nintendo® nɪnˈten.dəʊ US -doʊ

ninth naɪntθ **-s** -s **-ly** -li

Ninus ˈnaɪ.nəs

Niobe ˈnaɪ.əʊ.bi US -oʊ-, ˈ-ə-

niobium naɪˈəʊ.bi.əm US -ˈoʊ-

nip (N) nɪp **-s** -s **-ping** -ɪŋ **-ped** -t **ˌnip and ˈtuck**

nipper ˈnɪp.əʳ US -ɚ **-s** -z

nipple ˈnɪp.l̩ **-s** -z

Nippon ˈnɪp.ɒn US -ɑːn; nɪˈpɑːn **-ese** -ˈiːz

nipp|y ˈnɪp|.i **-ier** -i.əʳ US -i.ɚ **-iest** -i.ɪst, -i.əst **-ily** -ɪ.li, -ᵊl.i **-iness** -ɪ.nəs, -ɪ.nɪs

NIREX, Nirex® ˈnaɪə.reks US ˈnaɪ-

nirvana (N) nɪəˈvɑː.nə, nɜː- US nɪr-, nɚ- **-s** -z

Nis, Nish niːʃ

Nisan ˈnaɪ.sæn *Jewish pronunciation:* ˈnɪs.ɑːn US niːˈsɑːn; ˈnɪs.ən

Nisbet(t) ˈnɪz.bɪt, -bət

nisei niːˈseɪ US niːˈseɪ, ˈ-- **-s** -z

Nish nɪʃ

nisi ˈnaɪ.saɪ, ˈniː-, -si US ˈnaɪ.saɪ

nisi prius ˌnaɪ.saɪˈpraɪ.əs, ˌniː-, -siˈ-, -ˈpriː- US ˌnaɪ.saɪˈpraɪ-

Nissan® ˈnɪs.æn US ˈniː.sɑːn

Nissen ˈnɪs.ᵊn **ˈNissen ˌhut**

nisus ˈnaɪ.səs

nit nɪt **-s** -s

niter ˈnaɪ.təʳ US -t̬ɚ

Nith nɪθ

nit-pick ˈnɪt.pɪk **-s** -s **-ing** -ɪŋ **-ed** -t **-er/s** -əʳ/z US -ɚ/z

nitrate ˈnaɪ.treɪt, -trɪt US -treɪt **-s** -s

nitre ˈnaɪ.təʳ US -t̬ɚ

nitric ˈnaɪ.trɪk **ˌnitric ˈacid**

nitrite ˈnaɪ.traɪt

nitro- ˌnaɪ.trəʊ- US ˌnaɪ.troʊ-, -trə-

nitrochalk ˈnaɪ.trəʊ.tʃɔːk, ˌ--ˈ- US ˈnaɪ.troʊ.tʃɔːk, -tʃɑːk

nitrogen ˈnaɪ.trə.dʒən, -trɪ- US -trə-

nitrogenous naɪˈtrɒdʒ.ɪ.nəs, -ᵊn.əs US -ˈtrɑː.dʒə.nəs

nitroglycerine, nitroglycerin ˌnaɪ.trəʊˈglɪs.ᵊr.iːn, -ɪn US -troʊˈ-, -trəˈ-

nitrous ˈnaɪ.trəs

nitty-gritty ˌnɪt.iˈgrɪt.i US ˌnɪt̬.iˈgrɪt̬-

nitwit ˈnɪt.wɪt **-s** -s

Niue ˈnjuː.eɪ, niˈuː- US niˈuː- **-an/s** -ᵊn/z

Nivea® ˈnɪv.i.ə

Niven ˈnɪv.ᵊn

nix nɪks **-es** -ɪz **-ing** -ɪŋ **-ed** -t

Nixdorf® ˈnɪks.dɔːf US -dɔːrf

nixie ˈnɪk.si **-s** -z

Nixon ˈnɪk.sᵊn

nizam (N) naɪˈzæm, nɪ-, -ˈzɑːm US nɪˈzɑːm; naɪˈzæm **-ate** -eɪt **-s** -z

Nizhni Novgorod ˌnɪʒ.niˈnɒv.gᵊr.ɒd US -ˈnɑːv.gə.rɑːd

N.J. ˌenˈdʒeɪ

Nkomo ᵊŋˈkəʊ.məʊ US -ˈkoʊ.moʊ, ᵊn-

Nkrumah ᵊŋˈkruː.mə US ᵊŋ-, ᵊn-

N.M. *(abbrev. for* **New Mexico***)* ˌenˈem

NME ˌen.emˈiː

N.Mex. *(abbrev. for* **New Mexico***)* ˌenˈmeks

NNE *(abbrev. for* **north-northeast***)* ˌnɔːθ.nɔːθˈiːst US ˌnɔːrθ.nɔːrθˈ- *nautical pronunciation:* ˌnɔː.nɔːrˈiːst US ˌnɔːr.nɔːrˈiːst

NNW *(abbrev. for* **north-northwest***)* ˌnɔːθ.nɔːθˈwest US ˌnɔːrθ.nɔːrθˈ- *nautical pronunciation:* ˌnɔː.nɔːˈ- US ˌnɔːr.nɔːrˈ-

no *(n. interj.)* nəʊ US noʊ **-es** -z

no *(adj.) normal form:* nəʊ US noʊ *weak form:* nə

Note: Occasional weak form word. The pronunciation of **no** is nearly always /nəʊ US noʊ/, but, particularly in British English, there is a weak form /nə/ in a few common expressions such as “no more do I” /nəˌmɔː.duːˈaɪ US -ˌmɔːr-/.

no. (N) *(abbrev. for* **number***)* ˈnʌm.bəʳ US -bɚ **nos.** -z

no-account ˈnəʊ.əˌkaʊnt US ˈnoʊ-

Noah ˈnəʊ.ə US ˈnoʊ- **ˌNoah's ˈark**

Noakes nəʊks US noʊks

Noam ˈnəʊ.əm, nəʊm US ˈnoʊ.əm, noʊm

nob nɒb US nɑːb **-s** -z

no-ball ˌnəʊˈbɔːl US ˈnoʊ-, -bɑːl **-s** -z **-ing** -ɪŋ **-ed** -d

nobbl|e ˈnɒb.l̩ US ˈnɑː.bl̩ **-es** -z **-ing** -ɪŋ, ˈnɒb.lɪŋ US ˈnɑː.blɪŋ **-ed** -d

nobb|y ˈnɒb|.i US ˈnɑː.b|i **-ier** -i.əʳ US -i.ɚ **-iest** -i.ɪst, -i.əst **-ily** -ɪ.li, -ᵊl.i **-iness** -ɪ.nəs, -ɪ.nɪs

Nobel nəʊˈbel US noʊ- *stress shift, see compound:* **ˌNobel ˈprize**

nobelium nəʊˈbiː.li.əm US noʊˈbel.i-

nobilit|y nəʊˈbɪl.ə.t|i, -ɪ.t|i US noʊˈbɪl.ə.t̬|i **-ies** -iz

nob|le (N) ˈnəʊ.b|l̩ US ˈnoʊ- **-les** -l̩z **-ler** -ləʳ, -l̩.əʳ **-lest** -lɪst, -ləst, -l̩.ɪst, -l̩.əst **-ly** -li **-leness** -l̩.nəs, -l̩.nɪs

noble|man ˈnəʊ.bl̩|.mən US ˈnoʊ- **-men** -mən

noble-minded ˌnəʊ.bl̩ˈmaɪn.dɪd US ˌnoʊ- **-ness** -nəs, -nɪs *stress shift:* ˌnoble-minded ˈperson

noblesse nəʊˈbles US noʊ-

noblesse oblige nəʊˌbles.əʊˈbliːʒ, ˌnəʊ.bles- US noʊˌbles.oʊˈ-

noble|woman ˈnəʊ.bl̩|ˌwʊm.ən US ˈnoʊ- **-women** -ˌwɪm.ɪn

nobod|y ˈnəʊ.bə.d|i, -bɒd|.i US ˈnoʊ.bɑː.d|i, -bʌd|.i, -bə.d|i **-ies** -iz

nock (N) nɒk US nɑːk

no-claim bonus ˌnəʊˈkleɪmˌbəʊ.nəs, ˌnəʊˌkleɪmˈbəʊ- US ˌnoʊˈkleɪmˌboʊ-, ˌnoʊˌkleɪmˈboʊ- **-es** -ɪz

no-claims bonus ˌnəʊˈkleɪmzˌbəʊ.nəs, ˌnəʊˌkleɪmzˈbəʊ- US ˌnoʊˈkleɪmzˌboʊ-, ˌnoʊˌkleɪmzˈboʊ- **-es** -ɪz

no-confidence ˌnəʊˈkɒn.fɪ.dᵊnts US ˌnoʊˈkɑːn-

noctambul|ism nɒkˈtæm.bjə.l|ɪ.zᵊm, -bjʊ- US nɑːkˈtæm.bjuː-, -bjə- **-ist/s** -ɪst/s

Noctes Ambrosianae ˌnɒk.teɪsˌæm.brəʊ.ziˈɑː.naɪ, -brɒs.iˈ- US ˌnɑːk.tiːz.æm.broʊ.siˈeɪ.ni

nocturnal nɒkˈtɜː.nᵊl US nɑːkˈtɝː- **-ly** -i

nocturn(e) ˈnɒk.tɜːn, ˌ-ˈ- US ˈnɑːk.tɝːn **-s** -z

nocuous ˈnɒk.ju.əs US ˈnɑːk- **-ly** -li

nod (N) nɒd US nɑːd **-s** -z **-ding** -ɪŋ **-ded** -ɪd

nodal ˈnəʊ.dᵊl US ˈnoʊ- **-ly** -i

nodding ˈnɒd.ɪŋ US ˈnɑː.dɪŋ

noddle ˈnɒd.l̩ US ˈnɑː.dl̩ **-s** -z

nodd|y (N) ˈnɒd|.i US ˈnɑː.d|i **-ies** -iz

node nəʊd US noʊd **-s** -z

nodul|ar ˈnɒd.jə.l|əʳ, -jʊ- US ˈnɑː.djuː.l|ɚ, -djə- **-ous** -əs

nodule ˈnɒd.juːl US ˈnɑː.djuːl **-s** -z

Noel, Noël *personal name:* nəʊəl US noʊəl *Christmas:* nəʊˈel US noʊ-

no-fault ˈnəʊ.fɔːlt, -fɒlt US ˈnoʊ.fɔːlt, -fɑːlt

no-fly ˌnəʊˈflaɪ US ˌnoʊ- *stress shift:* ˌno-fly ˈzone

no-frills ˌnəʊˈfrɪlz US ˌnoʊ- *stress shift:* ˌno-frills ˈservice

noggin ˈnɒg.ɪn US ˈnɑː.gɪn **-s** -z

no-go ˌnəʊˈgəʊ US ˌnoʊˈgoʊ *stress shift, see compound:* **ˌno-go ˈarea**

no-good ˌnəʊˈgʊd US ˌnoʊ- *stress shift:* ˌno-good ˈcheat

Noh nəʊ US noʊ

no-holds-barred ˌnəʊˌhəʊldzˈbɑːd US ˌnoʊˌhoʊldzˈbɑːrd *stress shift:* ˌno-holds-barred ˈcontest

no-hoper ˌnəʊˈhəʊ.pəʳ (US) ˌnoʊˈhoʊ.pɚ **-s** -z
nohow ˈnəʊ.haʊ (US) ˈnoʊ-
noir nwɑːʳ (US) nwɑːr
nois|e nɔɪz **-es** -ɪz **-ing** -ɪŋ **-ed** -d
noiseless ˈnɔɪz.ləs, -lɪs **-ly** -li **-ness** -nəs, -nɪs
noisemaker ˈnɔɪzˌmeɪ.kəʳ (US) -kɚ **-s** -z
noisette nwɑːˈzet **-s** -s
noisettes *(alternative plur. of* **noisette)** nwɑːˈzet
noisome ˈnɔɪ.səm **-ly** -li **-ness** -nəs, -nɪs
nois|y ˈnɔɪ.z|i **-ier** -i.əʳ (US) -i.ɚ **-iest** -i.ɪst, -i.əst **-ily** -ɪ.li, -ᵊl.i **-iness** -ɪ.nəs, -ɪ.nɪs
Nokes nəʊks (US) noʊks
Nokia ˈnɒk.i.ə (US) ˈnoʊ.ki-
Nokomis nəʊˈkəʊ.mɪs (US) noʊˈkoʊ-
Nolan ˈnəʊ.lən (US) ˈnoʊ-
noli me tangere ˌnəʊ.liˌmeɪˈtæŋ.gə.reɪ, ˈ-dʒə- (US) ˌnoʊ-
Noll nɒl (US) nɑːl
nolo contendere ˌnəʊ.ləʊ.kɒnˈten.dᵊr.i, -eɪ (US) ˌnoʊ.loʊ.kənˈ-
Nolte ˈnɒl.ti (US) ˈnoʊl.ti
noma ˈnəʊ.mə (US) ˈnoʊ- **-s** -z
nomad ˈnəʊ.mæd (US) ˈnoʊ- **-s** -z **-ism** -ɪ.zᵊm
nomadic nəʊˈmæd.ɪk (US) noʊ- **-ally** -ᵊl.i, -li
no-man's-land ˈnəʊ.mænz.lænd (US) ˈnoʊ-
nom(s) de guerre ˌnɔ̃ːn.dəˈgeəʳ, ˌnɒm- (US) ˌnɑːm.dəˈger
nom(s) de plume ˌnɔ̃ːn.dəˈpluːm, ˌnɒm- (US) ˌnɑːm.dəˈ-
-nome -nəʊm, -noʊm
Note: Suffix. Normally unstressed, e.g. **metronome** /ˈmet.rə.nəʊm (US) -noʊm/.
nomenclature nəʊˈmeŋ.klə.tʃəʳ; ˈnəʊ.men.kleɪ-, -mən- (US) ˈnoʊ.men.kleɪ.tʃɚ, -mən-; noʊˈmen.klə- **-s** -z
-nomic -ˈnɒm.ɪk, -ˈnəʊ.mɪk (US) -ˈnɑː.mɪk, -ˈnoʊ- **-s** -s
Note: Suffix. Words containing **-nomic** normally carry primary stress on the penultimate syllable, e.g. **ergonomic** /ˌɜː.gəˈnɒm.ɪk (US) ˌɜːr.gəˈnɑː.mɪk/.
nominal ˈnɒm.ɪ.nᵊl, -ᵊn.ᵊl (US) ˈnɑː.mə.nᵊl **-ly** -i
nomi|nate ˈnɒm.ɪ|.neɪt, ˈ-ə- (US) ˈnɑː.mə- **-nates** -neɪts **-nating** -neɪ.tɪŋ (US) -neɪ.t̬ɪŋ **-nated** -neɪ.tɪd (US) -neɪ.t̬ɪd **-nator/s** -neɪ.təʳ/z (US) -neɪ.t̬ɚ/z
nomination ˌnɒm.ɪˈneɪ.ʃᵊn, -əˈ- (US) ˌnɑː.məˈ- **-s** -z
nominative ˈnɒm.ɪ.nə.tɪv, -ᵊn.ə- (US) ˈnɑː.mə.nə.t̬ɪv **-s** -z
nominee ˌnɒm.ɪˈniː, -əˈ- (US) ˌnɑː.məˈ- **-s** -z
Nomura nəʊˈmʊə.rə, -ˈmjʊə- (US) noʊˈmuː.rə
-nomy -nə.mi
Note: Suffix. Words containing **-nomy** normally carry stress on the syllable preceding the suffix, e.g. **astronomy** /əˈstrɒn.ə.mi (US) -ˈstrɑː.nə-/.
non- ˌnɒn- (US) ˌnɑːn-
Note: Prefix. In words containing **non-**, the stress pattern of the stem to which it is added does not normally change, e.g. **verbal** /ˈvɜː.bᵊl (US) ˈvɜːr-/, **nonverbal** /ˌnɒnˈvɜː.bᵊl (US) ˌnɑːnˈvɜːr-/.
non nɒn (US) nɑːn
non-acceptance ˌnɒn.əkˈsep.tᵊnts, -ækˈ- (US) ˌnɑː.nəkˈ-
nonage ˈnəʊ.nɪdʒ, ˈnɒn.ɪdʒ (US) ˈnɑː.nɪdʒ, ˈnoʊ-, -neɪdʒ
nonagenarian ˌnəʊ.nə.dʒəˈneə.ri.ən, ˌnɒn.ə-, -dʒɪˈ- (US) ˌnɑː.nə.dʒəˈner.i-, ˌnoʊ- **-s** -z
nonaggression ˌnɒn.əˈgreʃ.ᵊn (US) ˌnɑː.nəˈ-
nonagon ˈnɒn.ə.gɒn, ˈnəʊ.nə- (US) ˈnɑː.nə.gɑːn, ˈnoʊ- **-s** -z
nonalcoholic ˌnɒn.æl.kəˈhɒl.ɪk (US) ˌnɑː.næl.kəˈhɑː.lɪk
nonalign|ed ˌnɒn.ᵊlˈaɪn|d (US) ˌnɑː.nəˈlaɪn|d **-ment** -mənt
non-appearance ˌnɒn.əˈpɪə.rᵊnts (US) ˌnɑː.nəˈpɪr.ᵊnts
nonary ˈnəʊ.nᵊr.i, ˈnɒn.ᵊr- (US) ˈnoʊ.nɚ-, ˈnɑː-
non-attendance ˌnɒn.əˈten.dənts (US) ˌnɑː.nəˈ-
nonbeliever ˌnɒn.bɪˈliː.vəʳ, ˌnɒm-, -bəˈ- (US) ˌnɑːn.bɪˈliː.vɚ, -bəˈ- **-s** -z
non-biological ˌnɒnˌbaɪəˈlɒdʒ.ɪ.kᵊl (US) ˌnɑːn.baɪəˈlɑː.dʒɪ-
nonc|e nɒnts (US) nɑːnts **-es** -ɪz ˈ**nonce** ˌ**word**
non-certifiable ˌnɒnˌsɜː.tɪˈfaɪ.ə.bl̩, -təˈ- (US) ˌnɑːnˌsɝː.t̬əˈ-
nonchalance ˈnɒn.tʃᵊl.ənts (US) ˌnɑːn.ʃəˈlɑːnts
nonchalant ˈnɒn.tʃᵊl.ənt (US) ˌnɑːn.ʃəˈlɑːnt **-ly** -li
non-collegiate ˌnɒn.kᵊlˈiː.dʒi.ət, ˌnɒŋ-, -kɒlˈ-, ˈ-dʒət (US) ˌnɑːn.kəˈliː.dʒɪt, -dʒi.ɪt **-s** -s
non-combatant ˌnɒnˈkɒm.bə.tᵊnt, ˌnɒŋ-, -ˈkʌm-; -kəmˈbæt.ᵊnt (US) ˌnɑːn.kəmˈbæt.ᵊnt; ˌnɑːnˈkɑːm.bə.tᵊnt **-s** -s
noncommercial ˌnɒn.kəˈmɜː.ʃᵊl, ˌnɒŋ- (US) ˌnɑːn.kəˈmɝː-
non-commissioned ˌnɒn.kəˈmɪʃ.ᵊnd, ˌnɒŋ- (US) ˌnɑːn- *stress shift, see compound:* ˌ**non-commissioned** ˈ**officer**
noncommitt|al ˌnɒn.kəˈmɪt|.ᵊl, ˌnɒŋ- (US) ˌnɑːn.kəˈmɪt̬- **-ally** -ᵊl.i *stress shift:* ˌnoncommittal ˈanswer
noncompetitive ˌnɒn.kəmˈpet.ə.tɪv, ˌnɒŋ-, ˈ-ɪ- (US) ˌnɑːn.kəmˈpet̬.ə.t̬ɪv **-ly** -li *stress shift:* ˌnoncompetitive ˈgames
non-compliance ˌnɒn.kəmˈplaɪ.ənts, ˌnɒŋ- (US) ˌnɑːn-
non compos mentis ˌnɒnˌkɒm.pəsˈmen.tɪs, ˌnɒŋ-, -pɒsˈ- (US) ˌnɑːnˌkɑːm.poʊsˈmen.t̬ɪs, -pəsˈ-
non-conducting ˌnɒn.kənˈdʌk.tɪŋ, ˌnɒŋ- (US) ˌnɑːn- *stress shift:* ˌnon-conducting ˈsubstance
nonconductor ˌnɒn.kənˈdʌk.təʳ, ˌnɒŋ- (US) ˌnɑːn.kənˈdʌk.tɚ **-s** -z
nonconform|ist ˌnɒn.kənˈfɔː.m|ɪst, ˌnɒŋ- (US) ˌnɑːn.kənˈfɔːr- **-ists** -ɪsts **-ism** -ɪ.zᵊm *stress shift:* ˌnonconformist ˈstance
nonconformity ˌnɒn.kənˈfɔː.mə.ti, ˌnɒŋ-, -mɪ- (US) ˌnɑːn.kənˈfɔːr.mə.t̬i
noncontiguous ˌnɒn.kənˈtɪg.ju.əs, ˌnɒŋ-, -kɒnˈ- (US) ˌnɑːn.kənˈ- **-ly** -li *stress shift:* ˌnoncontiguous ˈboundaries
noncontributory ˌnɒn.kənˈtrɪb.jə.tᵊr.i, ˌnɒŋ-, -jʊ- (US) ˌnɑːn.kənˈtrɪb.juː.tɔːr-, -jə- *stress shift:* ˌnoncontributory ˈaction
noncooperation ˌnɒn.kəʊˌɒp.ᵊrˈeɪ.ʃᵊn, ˌnɒŋ- (US) ˌnɑːn.koʊˌɑː.pəˈreɪ-
noncooperationist ˌnɒn.kəʊˌɒp.ᵊrˈeɪ.ʃᵊn.ɪst, ˌnɒŋ- (US) ˌnɑːn.koʊˌɑː.pəˈreɪ- **-s** -s *stress shift:* ˌnon-cooperationist ˈstance
noncorrosive ˌnɒn.kᵊrˈəʊ.sɪv, ˌnɒŋ-, -zɪv (US) ˌnɑːn.kəˈroʊ- *stress shift:* ˌnoncorrosive ˈacid
non-custodial ˌnɒn.kʌsˈtəʊ.di.əl, ˌnɒŋ- (US) ˌnɑːn.kʌsˈtoʊ- *stress shift:* ˌnon-custodial ˈsentence
nondairy ˌnɒnˈdeə.ri (US) ˌnɑːnˈder.i *stress shift:* ˌnondairy ˈproduct
non-delivery ˌnɒn.dɪˈlɪv.ᵊr.i, -dəˈ- (US) ˌnɑːn.dəˈ-, ˈ-ri
nondenominational ˌnɒn.dɪˌnɒm.ɪˈneɪ.ʃᵊn.ᵊl, -dəˌ-, -ˈneɪʃ.nᵊl (US) ˌnɑːn.dəˌnɑː.məˈ- *stress shift:* ˌnondenominational ˈpolicy
nondescript ˈnɒn.dɪ.skrɪpt, -də- (US) ˈnɑːn.dɪ-, ˌ--ˈ- **-s** -s
nondriver ˌnɒnˈdraɪ.vəʳ (US) ˌnɑːnˈdraɪ.vɚ **-s** -z
none *(adj. pron. adv.) not any:* nʌn

none (N) *(n.) church service:* nəʊn ⓤⓢ noʊn **-s** -z

nonentit|y ˌnɒnˈen.tə.t|i, nəˈnen-, -ɪ.t|i ⓤⓢ ˌnɑːˈnen.t̬ə.t̬|i **-ies** -iz

nones (N) nəʊnz ⓤⓢ noʊnz

non-essential ˌnɒn.ɪˈsen.*t*ʃᵊl ⓤⓢ ˌnɑː.nɪˈ- **-s** -z *stress shift:* ˌnon-essential ˈitem

nonesuch ˈnʌn.sʌtʃ **-es** -ɪz

nonet nəʊˈnet, nɒnˈet ⓤⓢ noʊˈnet **-s** -s

nonetheless ˌnʌn.ðəˈles

non-event ˌnɒn.ɪˈvent, ˈ--- ⓤⓢ ˌnɑː.nɪˈvent **-s** -s

non-existen|t ˌnɒn.ɪgˈzɪs.tᵊn|t, -egˈ-, -ɪkˈsɪs-, -ekˈ- ⓤⓢ ˌnɑː.nɪgˈzɪs-, -negˈ- **-ce** -*t*s *stress shift:* ˌnonexistent ˈmeans

nonfat ˌnɒnˈfæt ⓤⓢ ˌnɑːn- *stress shift:* ˌnonfat ˈsubstance

non-feasance ˌnɒnˈfiː.zᵊn*t*s ⓤⓢ ˌnɑːn-

nonfiction ˌnɒnˈfɪk.ʃᵊn ⓤⓢ ˌnɑːn-

nonflammab|le ˌnɒnˈflæm.ə.b|l̩ ⓤⓢ ˌnɑːn- *stress shift:* ˌnonflammable ˈclothing

nonillion nəʊˈnɪl.jən, nɒnˈɪl-, ˈ-i.ən ⓤⓢ noʊˈnɪl.jən **-s** -z

non-intervention ˌnɒn.ɪn.təˈven.*t*ʃᵊn ⓤⓢ ˌnɑː.nɪn.t̬ɚˈven*t*.ʃᵊn

non-interventionist ˌnɒn.ɪn.təˈven.*t*ʃᵊn.ɪst ⓤⓢ ˌnɑː.nɪn.tɚˈven*t*.ʃᵊn- **-s** -s *stress shift:* ˌnon-interventionist ˈpolicy

nonjudgmental ˌnɒn.dʒʌdʒˈmen.tᵊl ⓤⓢ ˌnɑːn.dʒʌdʒˈmen.t̬ᵊl **-ly** -i *stress shift:* ˌnonjudgmental ˈview

nonjuror ˌnɒnˈdʒʊə.rəʳ ⓤⓢ ˌnɑːnˈdʒʊr.ɚ, -ɔːr **-s** -z

nonlinear ˌnɒnˈlɪn.i.əʳ ⓤⓢ ˌnɑːnˈlɪn.i.ɚ *stress shift:* ˌnonlinear ˈtheory

non-member ˌnɒnˈmem.bəʳ, ˈ--- ⓤⓢ ˌnɑːnˈmem.bɚ, ˈ--- **-s** -z

non-nuclear ˌnɒnˈnjuː.kli.əʳ ⓤⓢ ˌnɑːnˈnuː.kli.ɚ, -ˈnjuː- *stress shift:* ˌnon-nuclear ˈpower

no-no ˈnəʊ.nəʊ ⓤⓢ ˈnoʊ.noʊ **-s** -z

non-observance ˌnɒn.əbˈzɜː.vᵊn*t*s ⓤⓢ ˌnɑː.nəbˈzɝː-

non obstante ˌnɒn.ɒbˈstæn.teɪ ⓤⓢ ˌnɑːn.əbˈstæn.ti, -ˈstɑːn-

non obstante verdicto ˌnɒn.ɒbˌstæn.teɪ.vəˈdɪk.təʊ ⓤⓢ ˌnɑːn.əbˌstæn.ti.vɚˈdɪk.toʊ, -ˌstɑːn-

nonoccurrence ˌnɒn.əˈkʌr.ᵊn*t*s ⓤⓢ ˌnɑː.nəˈkɝː-

no-nonsense ˌnəʊˈnɒn*t*.sᵊn*t*s ⓤⓢ ˌnoʊˈnɑːn*t*.sen*t*s *stress shift:* ˌno-nonsense ˈattitude

nonoperational ˌnɒn.ɒp.əˈreɪ.ʃᵊn.ᵊl, -ˈreɪʃ.nᵊl ⓤⓢ ˌnɑː.nɑː.pəˈreɪ.ʃᵊn.ᵊl, -ˈreɪʃ.nᵊl *stress shift:* ˌnonoperational ˈforces

nonpareil ˌnɒn.pəˈreɪl, ˌnɒm-, -ˈeɪ ⓤⓢ ˌnɑː.n.pəˈrel

non-payment ˌnɒnˈpeɪ.mənt, ˌnɒm- ⓤⓢ ˌnɑːn-

nonplaying ˌnɒnˈpleɪ.ɪŋ, ˌnɒm- ⓤⓢ ˌnɑːn- *stress shift:* ˌnonplaying ˈteam

nonplus ˌnɒnˈplʌs, ˌnɒm- ⓤⓢ ˌnɑːn- **-ses** -ɪz **-sing** -ɪŋ **-sed** -t

non-profit-making ˌnɒnˈprɒf.ɪtˌmeɪ.kɪŋ, ˌnɒm- ⓤⓢ ˌnɑːnˈprɑː.fɪt- *stress shift, see compound:* **ˌnon-profit-making ˌorganiˈsation**

nonproliferation ˌnɒn.prəˌlɪf.əˈreɪ.ʃᵊn, ˌnɒm- ⓤⓢ ˌnɑːn-

nonrefundable ˌnɒn.rɪˈfʌnd.ə.bl̩, -riːˈ- ⓤⓢ ˌnɑːn- *stress shift:* ˌnonrefundable ˈmoney

nonresident ˌnɒnˈrez.ɪ.dᵊnt, ˈ-ə- ⓤⓢ ˌnɑːn- **-s** -s

nonrestrictive ˌnɒn.rɪˈstrɪk.tɪv, -rəˈ- ⓤⓢ ˌnɑːn- *stress shift:* ˌnonrestrictive ˈclause

nonreturnable ˌnɒn.rɪˈtɜː.nə.bl̩, -rəˈ- ⓤⓢ ˌnɑːn.rɪˈtɝː- *stress shift:* ˌnonreturnable ˈgoods

nonsectarian ˌnɒn.sekˈteə.ri.ən ⓤⓢ ˌnɑːn.sekˈter.i- *stress shift:* ˌnonsectarian ˈviolence

nonsense ˈnɒn.sᵊn*t*s ⓤⓢ ˈnɑːn.sen*t*s, -sən*t*s **ˈnonsense ˌverse**

nonsensical ˌnɒnˈsen*t*.sɪ.kl̩ ⓤⓢ ˌnɑːn- **-ly** -i **-ness** -nəs, -nɪs

non sequitur ˌnɒnˈsek.wɪ.təʳ, ˌnəʊn-, -wə- ⓤⓢ ˌnɑːnˈsek.wɪ.t̬ɚ **-s** -z

nonskid ˌnɒnˈskɪd ⓤⓢ ˌnɑːn- *stress shift:* ˌnonskid ˈsurface

nonslip ˌnɒnˈslɪp ⓤⓢ ˌnɑːn- *stress shift:* ˌnonslip ˈsurface

nonsmok|er ˌnɒnˈsməʊ.k|əʳ ⓤⓢ ˌnɑːnˈsmoʊ.k|ɚ **-ers** -əz ⓤⓢ -ɚz **-ing** -ɪŋ

nonspecific ˌnɒn.spəˈsɪf.ɪk, -spɪˈ- ⓤⓢ ˌnɑːn- *stress shift:* ˌnonspecific ˈorder

nonstandard ˌnɒnˈstæn.dəd ⓤⓢ ˌnɑːnˈstæn.dɚd *stress shift:* ˌnonstandard ˈfitting

nonstarter ˌnɒnˈstɑː.təʳ ⓤⓢ ˌnɑːnˈstɑːr.t̬ɚ **-s** -z

nonstick ˌnɒnˈstɪk ⓤⓢ ˌnɑːn- *stress shift:* ˌnonstick ˈcoating

non-stop ˌnɒnˈstɒp ⓤⓢ ˌnɑːnˈstɑːp *stress shift:* ˌnon-stop ˈmusic

nonsuch (N) ˈnʌn.sʌtʃ

nonsui|t ˌnɒnˈsuː|t, -ˈsjuː|t ⓤⓢ ˌnɑːnˈsuː|t **-ts** -ts **-ting** -tɪŋ ⓤⓢ -t̬ɪŋ **-ted** -tɪd ⓤⓢ -t̬ɪd

nonswimmer ˌnɒnˈswɪm.əʳ ⓤⓢ ˌnɑːnˈswɪm.ɚ **-s** -z

nontrivial ˌnɒnˈtrɪv.i.əl ⓤⓢ ˌnɑːn- *stress shift:* ˌnontrivial ˈproblem

non-U ˌnɒnˈjuː ⓤⓢ ˌnɑːn- *stress shift:* ˌnon-U ˈaccent

nonunion ˌnɒnˈjuː.njən, ˈ-ni.ən ⓤⓢ ˌnɑːnˈjuː.njən *stress shift:* ˌnonunion ˈmembers

non-user ˌnɒnˈjuː.zəʳ ⓤⓢ ˌnɑːnˈjuː.zɚ *stress shift:* ˌnon-user ˈguide

nonverbal ˌnɒnˈvɜː.bᵊl ⓤⓢ ˌnɑːnˈvɝː- *stress shift:* ˌnonverbal ˈmessage

non-violen|t ˌnɒnˈvaɪə.lən|t ⓤⓢ ˌnɑːn- **-ly** -li **-ce** -*t*s *stress shift:* ˌnon-violent ˈpolicy

nonvoter ˌnɒnˈvəʊ.təʳ ⓤⓢ ˌnɑːnˈvoʊ.t̬ɚ **-s** -z

nonwhite ˌnɒnˈwaɪt ⓤⓢ ˌnɑːn- *stress shift:* ˌnonwhite ˈprejudice

noodle ˈnuː.dl̩ **-s** -z

nook nʊk **-s** -s **ˌnook and ˈcranny**

nooky, nookie ˈnʊk.i

noon nuːn **-s** -z

Noonan ˈnuː.nən

noonday ˈnuːn.deɪ

no one ˈnəʊ.wʌn ⓤⓢ ˈnoʊ-

noontide ˈnuːn.taɪd

noos|e nuːs **-es** -ɪz **-ing** -ɪŋ **-ed** -t

nope nəʊp ⓤⓢ noʊp

noplace ˈnəʊ.pleɪs ⓤⓢ ˈnoʊ-

nor *normal form:* nɔːʳ ⓤⓢ nɔːr *weak form:* nəʳ ⓤⓢ nɚ

Note: Occasional weak form word. The pronunciation is normally /nɔːʳ ⓤⓢ nɔːr/, but, particularly in British English, there is a weak form /nəʳ ⓤⓢ nɚ/, as in "no use to man nor beast" /nəʊˌjuːs.təˌmæn.nəˈbiːst ⓤⓢ noʊˌjuːs.təˌmæn.nɚˈ-/.

NORAD ˈnɔː.ræd ⓤⓢ ˈnɔːr.æd

noradrenalin(e) ˌnɔː.rəˈdren.ᵊl.ɪn, ˌnɒr.əˈ-, -iːn ⓤⓢ ˌnɔːr.əˈdren.ə.lɪn

Nora(h) ˈnɔː.rə ⓤⓢ ˈnɔːr.ə

Noraid ˈnɔː.reɪd ⓤⓢ ˈnɔːr.eɪd

Norden ˈnɔː.dᵊn ⓤⓢ ˈnɔːr-

Nordenfelt ˈnɔː.dᵊn.felt ⓤⓢ ˈnɔːr-

Nordic ˈnɔː.dɪk ⓤⓢ ˈnɔːr-

Nore nɔːʳ ⓤⓢ nɔːr

Norf. *(abbrev. for* **Norfolk***)* ˈnɔː.fək ⓤⓢ ˈnɔːr-, -fɔːk, -foʊk

Norfolk ˈnɔː.fək ⓤⓢ ˈnɔːr-, -fɔːk, -foʊk **ˌNorfolk ˈBroads**

Norgate ˈnɔː.geɪt, -gɪt ⓤⓢ ˈnɔːr-

Norham ˈnɒr.əm, ˈnɔː.rəm ⓤⓢ ˈnɔːr.əm

nori ˈnɒr.i, ˈnɔː.ri ⓤⓢ ˈnɔːr.i

Noriega ˌnɒr.iˈeɪ.gə ⓤⓢ ˌnɔːr-

Norland ˈnɔː.lənd ⓤⓢ ˈnɔːr-

norm nɔːm ⓤⓢ nɔːrm **-s** -z

Norma ˈnɔː.mə ⓤⓢ ˈnɔːr-

normal ˈnɔː.mᵊl ⓤⓢ ˈnɔːr- **-ly** -i

normalcy ˈnɔː.mᵊl.si ⓤⓢ ˈnɔːr-

normality nɔːˈmæl.ə.ti, -ɪ.ti ⓤⓢ nɔːrˈmæl.ə.t̬i

normalization, -isa- ˌnɔː.məl.aɪˈzeɪ.ʃən, -ɪˈ- ⓤⓢ ˌnɔːr.məl.ɪˈ-
normaliz|e, -is|e ˈnɔː.məl.aɪz ⓤⓢ ˈnɔːr- **-es** -ɪz **-ing** -ɪŋ **-ed** -d
normally ˈnɔː.məl.i ⓤⓢ ˈnɔːr-
Norman ˈnɔː.mən ⓤⓢ ˈnɔːr- **-s** -z **ˌNorman ˈconquest**
Normanby ˈnɔː.mən.bi, -məm- ⓤⓢ ˈnɔːr-
Normandy *in France:* ˈnɔː.mən.di ⓤⓢ ˈnɔːr- *in Surrey:* ˈnɔː.mən.di ⓤⓢ ˈnɔːr- *also locally:* nɔːˈmæn.di ⓤⓢ nɔːr-
Normanton ˈnɔː.mən.tən ⓤⓢ ˈnɔːr-
normative ˈnɔː.mə.tɪv ⓤⓢ ˈnɔːr.mə.t̬ɪv **-ly** -li
Norn nɔːn ⓤⓢ nɔːrn **-s** -z
Norodom Sihanouk ˌnɒr.ə.dɒmˈsiː.jæn.ʊk ⓤⓢ ˌnɔːr.ə.dɑːm-, -jɑː.nʊk
Norris ˈnɒr.ɪs ⓤⓢ ˈnɔːr-
Norrköping ˈnɔː.tʃɜː.pɪŋ ⓤⓢ ˈnɔːr-
Norroy ˈnɒr.ɔɪ ⓤⓢ ˈnɔːr- **-s** -z
Norse nɔːs ⓤⓢ nɔːrs **-man** -mən **-men** -mən, -men
north (N) nɔːθ ⓤⓢ nɔːrθ **ˌNorth Aˈmerica; ˌNorth Atˈlantic; ˌNorth Caroˈlina; ˌNorth Daˈkota; ˈNorth ˌIsland; ˌNorth Koˈrea; ˌnorth ˈpole; ˌNorth ˈSea**
Northallerton ˌnɔːˈθæl.ə.tən ⓤⓢ ˌnɔːrθˈæl.ɚ.t̬ən
Northampton ˌnɔːˈθæmp.tən, ˌnɔːθˈhæmp- *locally:* nəˈθæmp- ⓤⓢ ˌnɔːrˈθæmp-, ˌnɔːrθˈhæmp- **-shire** -ʃəʳ ⓤⓢ -ʃɚ, -ˌʃɪəʳ ⓤⓢ -ˌʃɪr
Northanger nɔːˈθæŋ.gəʳ, -əʳ; ˈnɔː.θæŋ-, ˈnɔːθ.hæŋ- ⓤⓢ nɔːrˈθæŋ.gɚ, -ɚ; ˈnɔːr.θæŋ-, ˈnɔːrθ.hæŋ-
Northants. *(abbrev. for* **Northamptonshire***)* ˈnɔː.θænts, -ˈ- ⓤⓢ ˈnɔːr.θænts, -ˈ-
North Baddesley ˌnɔːθˈbædz.li ⓤⓢ ˌnɔːrθ-
northbound ˈnɔːθ.baʊnd ⓤⓢ ˈnɔːrθ-
Northbrook ˈnɔːθ.brʊk ⓤⓢ ˈnɔːrθ-
Northcliffe ˈnɔːθ.klɪf ⓤⓢ ˈnɔːrθ-
Northcote ˈnɔːθ.kət, -kəʊt ⓤⓢ ˈnɔːrθ.kət, -koʊt
northeast (N) ˌnɔːθˈiːst ⓤⓢ ˌnɔːrθ- *nautical pronunciation:* ˌnɔːˈriːst ⓤⓢ ˌnɔːrˈiːst **-wards** -wədz ⓤⓢ -wɚdz *stress shift:* ˌnortheast ˈwind
northeaster ˌnɔːθˈiː.stəʳ ⓤⓢ ˌnɔːrθˈiː.stɚ *in nautical usage also:* ˌnɔːˈriː- ⓤⓢ ˌnɔːrˈiː- **-s** -z
northeasterl|y ˌnɔːθˈiː.stəl.|i ⓤⓢ ˌnɔːrθˈiː.stɚ.l|i *in nautical usage also:* ˌnɔːˈriː- ⓤⓢ ˌnɔːrˈiː- **-ies** -iz
northeastern (N) ˌnɔːθˈiː.stən ⓤⓢ ˌnɔːrθˈiː.stɚn *in nautical usage also:* ˌnɔːˈriː- ⓤⓢ ˌnɔːrˈiː- **-er/s** -əʳ/z ⓤⓢ -ɚ/z
northeastward ˌnɔːθˈiːst.wəd ⓤⓢ ˌnɔːrθˈiːst.wɚd *in nautical usage also:* ˌnɔːˈriː- ⓤⓢ ˌnɔːrˈiː- **-s** -z
Northen ˈnɔː.ðən ⓤⓢ ˈnɔːr-
northerl|y ˈnɔː.ðəl.|i ⓤⓢ ˈnɔːr.ðɚ.l|i **-ies** -iz
northern (N) ˈnɔː.ðən ⓤⓢ ˈnɔːr.ðɚn **-most** -məʊst, -məst ⓤⓢ -moʊst, -məst **ˌNorthern ˈIreland; ˌnorthern ˈlights; ˌNorthern ˈTerritory**
northerner (N) ˈnɔː.ðən.əʳ ⓤⓢ ˈnɔːr.ðɚ.nɚ **-s** -z
Northfield ˈnɔːθ.fiːld ⓤⓢ ˈnɔːrθ-
Northfleet ˈnɔːθ.fliːt ⓤⓢ ˈnɔːrθ-
northing ˈnɔː.θɪŋ ⓤⓢ ˈnɔːr-
Northland ˈnɔːθ.lənd ⓤⓢ ˈnɔːrθ.lænd, -lənd
North|man ˈnɔːθ|.mən ⓤⓢ ˈnɔːrθ- **-men** -mən, -men
north-northeast ˌnɔːθ.nɔːθˈiːst ⓤⓢ ˌnɔːrθ.nɔːrθˈ- *in nautical usage also:* ˌnɔː.nɔːˈriːst ⓤⓢ ˌnɔːr.nɔːrˈiːst
north-northwest ˌnɔːθ.nɔːθˈwest ⓤⓢ ˌnɔːrθ.nɔːrθˈ- *in nautical usage also:* ˌnɔː.nɔːˈ- ⓤⓢ ˌnɔːr.nɔːrˈ-
Northolt ˈnɔː.θəʊlt ⓤⓢ ˈnɔːr.θoʊlt
North-South ˌnɔːθˈsaʊθ ⓤⓢ ˌnɔːrθ- **ˌNorth-ˌSouth diˈvide**
Northumberland nɔːˈθʌmb.əl.ənd, nə- ⓤⓢ nɔːrˈθʌm.bɚ.lənd
Northumbri|a nɔːˈθʌm.bri|.ə ⓤⓢ nɔːr- **-an/s** -ən/z
northward ˈnɔːθ.wəd ⓤⓢ ˈnɔːrθ.wɚd **-s** -z **-ly** -li
northwest (N) ˌnɔːθˈwest ⓤⓢ ˌnɔːrθ- *nautical pronunciation:* ˌnɔːˈwest ⓤⓢ ˌnɔːr- **-wards** -wədz ⓤⓢ -wɚdz *stress shift, see compound:* **ˌNorthwest ˈTerritories**
northwesterl|y ˌnɔːθˈwes.təl.|i ⓤⓢ ˌnɔːrθˈwes.tɚ.l|i *in nautical usage also:* ˌnɔː- ⓤⓢ ˌnɔːr- **-ies** -iz
northwestern (N) ˌnɔːθˈwes.tən ⓤⓢ ˌnɔːrθˈwes.tɚn *in nautical usage also:* ˌnɔː- ⓤⓢ ˌnɔːr- **-er/s** -əʳ/z ⓤⓢ -ɚ/z
northwestward ˌnɔːθˈwest.wəd ⓤⓢ ˌnɔːrθˈwest.wɚd *in nautical usage also:* ˌnɔː- ⓤⓢ ˌnɔːr-
Northwich ˈnɔːθ.wɪtʃ ⓤⓢ ˈnɔːrθ-
Northwood ˈnɔːθ.wʊd ⓤⓢ ˈnɔːrθ-
Norton ˈnɔː.tən ⓤⓢ ˈnɔːr-
Norton Radstock ˌnɔː.tənˈræd.stɒk ⓤⓢ ˌnɔːr.tənˈræd.stɑːk
Norway ˈnɔː.weɪ ⓤⓢ ˈnɔːr-
Norwegian nɔːˈwiː.dʒən ⓤⓢ nɔːr- **-s** -z
Norwich *in England:* ˈnɒr.ɪdʒ, -ɪtʃ ⓤⓢ ˈnɔːr.ɪtʃ, -wɪtʃ *in US:* ˈnɔː.wɪtʃ ⓤⓢ ˈnɔːr-
Norwood ˈnɔː.wʊd ⓤⓢ ˈnɔːr-
nos. (N) *(abbrev. for* **numbers***)* ˈnʌm.bəz ⓤⓢ -bɚz
nos|e nəʊz ⓤⓢ noʊz **-es** -ɪz **-ing** -ɪŋ **-ed** -d **ˈnose ˌring; ˌcut off one's ˌnose to ˌspite one's ˈface; ˌkeep one's ˌnose to the ˈgrindstone; ˌlook down one's ˈnose at; ˌpay through the ˈnose (for); ˌpoke one's ˈnose (into)**
nosebag ˈnəʊz.bæg ⓤⓢ ˈnoʊz- **-s** -z
nosebleed ˈnəʊz.bliːd ⓤⓢ ˈnoʊz- **-s** -z
nosediv|e ˈnəʊz.daɪv ⓤⓢ ˈnoʊz- **-es** -z **-ing** -ɪŋ **-ed** -d
no-see-um ˌnəʊˈsiː.əm ⓤⓢ ˌnoʊ- **-s** -z
nosegay ˈnəʊz.geɪ ⓤⓢ ˈnoʊz- **-s** -z
nos|ey ˈnəʊ.z|i ⓤⓢ ˈnoʊ- **-ier** -i.əʳ ⓤⓢ -i.ɚ **-iest** -i.ɪst, -i.əst **-ily** -ɪ.li, -əl.i **-iness** -ɪ.nəs, -ɪ.nɪs
Nosferatu ˌnɒs.fəˈrɑː.tuː ⓤⓢ ˌnɑːs-
nosh nɒʃ ⓤⓢ nɑːʃ **-es** -ɪz **-ing** -ɪŋ **-ed** -t
no-show ˌnəʊˈʃəʊ ⓤⓢ ˈnoʊ.ʃoʊ *stress shift, British only:* ˌno-show ˈpassenger
nosh-up ˈnɒʃ.ʌp ⓤⓢ ˈnɑːʃ- **-s** -s
nostalg|ia nɒsˈtæl.dʒ|ə, -dʒ|i.ə ⓤⓢ nɑːˈstæl.dʒ|ə, nə-, nɔː-, -dʒ|i.ə **-ic** -ɪk **-ically** -ɪ.kəl.i, -ɪ.kli
Nostradamus ˌnɒs.trəˈdeɪ.məs, -ˈdɑː- ⓤⓢ ˌnoʊ.strəˈdɑː-, ˌnɑː.strəˈdeɪ-
nostril ˈnɒs.trəl, -trɪl ⓤⓢ ˈnɑː.strəl **-s** -z
Nostromo nɒsˈtrəʊ.məʊ ⓤⓢ nɑːˈstroʊ.moʊ
nostrum ˈnɒs.trəm ⓤⓢ ˈnɑː.strəm **-s** -z
nos|y ˈnəʊ.z|i ⓤⓢ ˈnoʊ- **-ier** -i.əʳ ⓤⓢ -i.ɚ **-iest** -i.ɪst, -i.əst **-ily** -ɪ.li, -əl.i **-iness** -ɪ.nəs, -ɪ.nɪs
nosy parker ˌnəʊ.ziˈpɑː.kəʳ ⓤⓢ ˌnoʊ.ziˈpɑːr.kɚ **-s** -z
not nɒt ⓤⓢ nɑːt
nota bene ˌnəʊ.tɑːˈben.eɪ, -təˈbiː.ni ⓤⓢ ˌnoʊ.t̬əˈben.eɪ, -tɑːˈ-, -ˈbiː.ni
notabilit|y ˌnəʊ.təˈbɪl.ə.t|i, -ɪ.t|i ⓤⓢ ˌnoʊ.t̬əˈbɪl.ə.t̬|i **-ies** -iz
notab|le ˈnəʊ.tə.b|l̩ ⓤⓢ ˈnoʊ.t̬ə- **-ly** -li **-leness** -l̩.nəs, -nɪs
notarial nəʊˈteə.ri.əl ⓤⓢ noʊˈter.i- **-ly** -i
notariz|e, -is|e ˈnəʊ.tər.aɪz ⓤⓢ ˈnoʊ.t̬ə.raɪz **-es** -ɪz **-ing** -ɪŋ **-ed** -d
notar|y ˈnəʊ.tər|.i ⓤⓢ ˈnoʊ.t̬ɚ- **-ies** -iz
nota|te nəʊˈteɪ|t ⓤⓢ ˈnoʊ.teɪ|t **-tes** -ts **-ting** -tɪŋ ⓤⓢ -t̬ɪŋ **-ted** -tɪd ⓤⓢ -t̬ɪd
notation nəʊˈteɪ.ʃən ⓤⓢ noʊ- **-s** -z
notch nɒtʃ ⓤⓢ nɑːtʃ **-es** -ɪz **-ing** -ɪŋ **-ed** -t
not|e nəʊt ⓤⓢ noʊt **-es** -s **-ing** -ɪŋ ⓤⓢ ˈnoʊ.t̬ɪŋ **-ed** -ɪd ⓤⓢ ˈnoʊ.t̬ɪd
notebook ˈnəʊt.bʊk ⓤⓢ ˈnoʊt- **-s** -s
notelet ˈnəʊt.lət, -lɪt ⓤⓢ ˈnoʊt- **-s** -s
notepad ˈnəʊt.pæd ⓤⓢ ˈnoʊt- **-s** -z
notepaper ˈnəʊtˌpeɪ.pəʳ ⓤⓢ ˈnoʊtˌpeɪ.pɚ
noteworth|y ˈnəʊtˌwɜː.ð|i

US ˈnoʊtˌwɝː- **-ily** -ɪ.li, -əl.i **-iness** -ɪ.nəs, -ɪ.nɪs
not-for-profit ˌnɒt.fəˈprɒf.ɪt US ˌnɑːt.fɚˈprɑː.fɪt
nothing ˈnʌθ.ɪŋ **-s** -z **-ness** -nəs, -nɪs
notic|e ˈnəʊ.tɪs US ˈnoʊ.t̬ɪs **-es** -ɪz **-ing** -ɪŋ **-ed** -t
noticeab|le ˈnəʊ.tɪ.sə.bl̩ US ˈnoʊ.t̬ɪ- **-ly** -li
notice-board ˈnəʊ.tɪs.bɔːd US ˈnoʊ.t̬ɪs.bɔːrd **-s** -z
notifiable ˈnəʊ.tɪ.faɪ.ə.bl̩, -tə-, ˌnəʊ.tɪˈfaɪ-, -təˈ- US ˈnoʊ.t̬ə.faɪ-
notification ˌnəʊ.tɪ.fɪˈkeɪ.ʃən, -tə- US ˌnoʊ.t̬ə- **-s** -z
noti|fy ˈnəʊ.tɪ.faɪ, -tə- US ˈnoʊ.t̬ə- **-fies** -faɪz **-fying** -faɪ.ɪŋ **-fied** -faɪd
notion ˈnəʊ.ʃən US ˈnoʊ- **-s** -z
notional ˈnəʊ.ʃən.əl, ˈnəʊʃ.nəl US ˈnoʊ.ʃən.əl, ˈnoʊʃ.nəl **-ly** -i
notoriety ˌnəʊ.tərˈaɪ.ə.ti US ˌnoʊ.t̬əˈraɪ.ə.t̬i
notorious nəʊˈtɔː.ri.əs US noʊˈtɔːr.i- **-ly** -li **-ness** -nəs, -nɪs
Notre Dame *in France:* ˌnəʊ.trəˈdɑːm, ˌnɒt.rəˈ- US ˌnoʊ.trəˈ-, ˌnoʊ.t̬ɚˈ-, -ˈdeɪm *in the US:* ˌnəʊ.trəˈdeɪm US ˌnoʊ.t̬ɚˈ-
Nottingham ˈnɒt.ɪŋ.əm US ˈnɑː.t̬ɪŋ- **-shire** -ʃəʳ, -ˌʃɪəʳ US -ʃɚ, -ˌʃɪr
Notting Hill ˌnɒt.ɪŋˈhɪl US ˌnɑː.t̬ɪŋˈ- *stress shift, see compound:* ˌ**Notting Hill ˈGate**
Notts. *(abbrev. for* **Nottinghamshire***)* nɒts US nɑːts
notwithstanding ˌnɒt.wɪθˈstæn.dɪŋ, -wɪðˈ- US ˌnɑːt-
Nouakchott nuˈɑːk.ʃɒt US ˈnwɑːk.ʃɑːt, -ˈ-
nougat ˈnuː.gɑː, ˈnʌg.ət US ˈnuː.gət **nougats** ˈnuː.gɑːz, ˈnʌg.əts US ˈnuː.gəts
nought nɔːt US nɑːt, nɔːt **-s** -s ˌ**noughts and ˈcrosses**
noumen|on ˈnuː.mə.n|ən, ˈnaʊ-, -mɪ-, -n|ɒn US ˈnuː.mə.n|ɑːn **-a** -ə **-al** -əl
noun naʊn **-s** -z
nourish ˈnʌr.ɪʃ US ˈnɝː- **-es** -ɪz **-ing** -ɪŋ **-ed** -t **-ment** -mənt
nourishing ˈnʌr.ɪ.ʃɪŋ US ˈnɝː-
nous naʊs US nuːs, naʊs
nouveau(x) ˈnuː.vəʊ, -ˈ- US nuːˈvoʊ, ˈ--
nouveau(x) riche(s) ˌnuː.vəʊˈriːʃ US -voʊˈ-
nouveau roman ˌnuː.vəʊ.rəʊˈmɑ̃ːŋ US -voʊ.roʊˈmɑːn
nouvelle cuisine ˌnuː.vel.kwɪˈziːn, nuːˌvel-, -kwəˈ-, -kwiː- US nuːˌvel-
nouvelle vague (N) ˌnuː.velˈvɑːg
Nov. *(abbrev. for* **November***)* nɒv, nəʊˈvem.bəʳ US noʊˈvem.bɚ

nov|a (N) ˈnəʊ.v|ə US ˈnoʊ- **-ae** -iː **-as** -əz
Nova Scotia ˌnəʊ.vəˈskəʊ.ʃə US ˌnoʊ.vəˈskoʊ-
novation nəʊˈveɪ.ʃən US noʊ-
Novaya Zemlya ˌnɒv.ə.jə.zemˈljɑː, ˌ-ɑː- US ˌnɔː.vɑː.jɑː-, ˌnoʊ-
novel ˈnɒv.əl US ˈnɑː.vəl **-istic** --ˈɪs.tɪk **-s** -z
novelette ˌnɒv.əlˈet US ˌnɑː.vəlˈ- **-s** -s
novelist ˈnɒv.əl.ɪst US ˈnɑː.və- **-s** -s
novelization, -isation ˌnɒv.əl.aɪˈzeɪ.ʃən, -ɪˈ- US ˌnɑː.vəl.ɪˈ- **-s** -z
noveliz|e, -is|e ˈnɒv.əl.aɪz US ˈnɑː.və.laɪz **-es** -ɪz **-ing** -ɪŋ **-ed** -d
novel|la nəʊˈvel|.ə US noʊ- **-las** -əz **-le** -eɪ
Novello nəˈvel.əʊ US -oʊ
novelt|y ˈnɒv.əl.t|i US ˈnɑː.vəl.t̬|i **-ies** -iz
November nəʊˈvem.bəʳ US noʊˈvem.bɚ **-s** -z
novena nəʊˈviː.nə US noʊ- **-s** -z
Novgorod ˈnɒv.gə.rɒd US ˈnɔːv.gə.rɑːd, ˈnɑːv-, -rɑːt
Novial ˈnəʊ.vi.əl US ˈnoʊ-
novic|e ˈnɒv.ɪs US ˈnɑː.vɪs **-es** -ɪz
novitiate nəʊˈvɪʃ.i.ət, nɒvˈɪʃ-, -eɪt, -ɪt US noʊˈvɪʃ.ɪt, ˈ-i.ɪt, -eɪt **-s** -s
Novocaine® ˈnəʊ.vəʊ.keɪn, ˈnɒv.əʊ- US ˈnoʊ.və-
Novosibirsk ˌnəʊ.vəʊ.sɪˈbɪəsk, ˌnɒv.əʊ-, -səˈ- US ˌnoʊ.və.sɪˈbɪrsk, -səˈ-
Novotna nəʊˈvɒt.nə, ˈnɒv.ɒt.nə US nəˈvɑːt.nə
Novum Organum ˌnəʊ.vəmˈɔː.gə.nəm, -ɔːˈgɑː.nəm US ˌnoʊ.vəmˈɔːr.gə.nəm; -ɔːrˈgæn-
now naʊ
NOW naʊ
nowadays ˈnaʊ.ə.deɪz, ˈnaʊə-
Nowell *personal name:* nəʊəl; ˈnəʊ.el US noʊəl; ˈnoʊ.el *Christmas:* nəʊˈel US noʊ-
nowhere ˈnəʊ.hweəʳ US ˈnoʊ.hwer
no-win ˌnəʊˈwɪn US ˌnoʊ- *stress shift, see compound:* ˌ**no-win situˈation**
nowise ˈnəʊ.waɪz US ˈnoʊ-
nowt naʊt
noxious ˈnɒk.ʃəs US ˈnɑːk- **-ly** -li **-ness** -nəs, -nɪs
Noye nɔɪ
Noyes nɔɪz
nozzle ˈnɒz.l̩ US ˈnɑː.zl̩ **-s** -z
nr *(abbrev. for* **near***)* nɪəʳ US nɪr
NSPCC ˌen.es.piː.siːˈsiː
-n't -ənt
Note: Weak form suffix. This spelling represents a weak form of **not** which occurs after auxiliary verbs.

nth enθ
nu njuː US nuː, njuː
nuanc|e ˈnjuː.ɑːnts, -ɑ̃ːns, -ˈ- US ˈnuː.ɑːnts, ˈnjuː-, -ˈ- **-es** -ɪz
nub nʌb
nubble ˈnʌb.l̩ **-s** -z
nubbly ˈnʌb.li, -l̩.i
Nubi|a ˈnjuː.bi|.ə US ˈnuː-, ˈnjuː- **-an/s** -ən/z
nubile ˈnjuː.baɪl US ˈnuː.bɪl, ˈnjuː-, -baɪl, -bəl
nubility njuːˈbɪl.ə.ti, -ɪ.ti US nuːˈbɪl.ə.t̬i, njuː-
nuclear ˈnjuː.kli.əʳ US ˈnuː.kli.ɚ, ˈnjuː- ˌ**nuclear disˈarmament;** ˌ**nuclear ˈenergy;** ˌ**nuclear ˈfamily;** ˌ**nuclear ˈfusion;** ˌ**nuclear ˈindustry;** ˌ**nuclear reˈactor;** ˌ**nuclear ˈwinter**
nuclear-free ˌnjuː.kli.əˈfriː US ˌnuː.kli.ɚˈ-, ˌnjuː- *stress shift, British only, see compound:* ˌ**nuclear-free ˈzone** US ˌ**nuclear-ˈfree** ˌ**zone**
nucleic njuːˈkliː.ɪk, -ˈkleɪ- US nuːˈkliː-, njuː-, -ˈkleɪ- **nuˌcleic ˈacid**
nucleo- ˌnjuː.kli.əʊ- US ˌnuː.kli.oʊ-, ˌnjuː-, -ə-
nucleol|us njuːˈkliː.əl|.əs; ˌnjuː.kliˈəʊ.l|əs US nuːˈkliː.əl|.əs, njuː- **-i** -aɪ
nucleotide ˈnjuː.kli.əʊ.taɪd US ˈnuː.kli.oʊ-, ˈnjuː- **-s** -z
nucle|us ˈnjuː.kli|.əs US ˈnuː-, ˈnjuː- **-uses** -əs.ɪz **-i** -aɪ
nuclide ˈnjuː.klaɪd US ˈnuː-, ˈnjuː- **-s** -z
nude njuːd US nuːd, njuːd **-s** -z
nudg|e nʌdʒ **-es** -ɪz **-ing** -ɪŋ **-ed** -d
nud|ism ˈnjuː.dɪ|.zəm US ˈnuː-, ˈnjuː- **-ist/s** -ɪst/s
nudit|y ˈnjuː.də.t|i, -ɪ.t|i US ˈnuː.də.t̬|i, ˈnjuː-
Nuevo Leon nweɪ.vəʊ.leɪˈɒn US nuːˈeɪ.voʊ.leɪˈɑːn
Nuffield ˈnʌf.iːld
nugatory ˈnjuː.gə.tər.i; njuːˈgeɪ- US ˈnuː.gə.tɔːr-, ˈnjuː-
Nugent ˈnjuː.dʒənt US ˈnuː-, ˈnjuː-
nugg|et ˈnʌg|.ɪt **-ets** -ɪts **-ety** -ɪ.ti US -ɪ.t̬i
nuisanc|e ˈnjuː.sənts US ˈnuː-, ˈnjuː- **-es** -ɪz
Nuit nʌt US nʌt, nuːt
NUJ ˌen.juːˈdʒeɪ
nuk|e njuːk US nuːk, njuːk **-es** -s **-ing** -ɪŋ **-ed** -t
Nuku'alofa ˌnuː.kuː.əˈlɔː.fə
null nʌl ˌ**null and ˈvoid**
nullah ˈnʌl.ə **-s** -z
Nullarbor ˈnʌl.ə.bɔːʳ US -ɚ.bɔːr ˌ**Nullarbor ˈPlains**
nullification ˌnʌl.ɪ.fɪˈkeɪ.ʃən, ˌ-ə-

nulli|fy ˈnʌl.ɪ|.faɪ, ˈ-ə- **-fies** -faɪz **-fying** -faɪ.ɪŋ **-fied** -faɪd
nullipar|a nʌlˈɪp.ᵊr|.ə ⓤⓢ nʌl-, nəˈlɪp- **-ae** -iː **-as** -əz **-ous** -əs
nullit|y ˈnʌl.ə.t|i, -ɪ.t|i ⓤⓢ -ə.t̬|i **-ies** -iz
NUM ˌen.juːˈem
Numa Pompilius ˌnjuː.mə.pɒmˈpɪl.i.əs ⓤⓢ ˌnuː.mə.pɑːmˈ-, ˌnjuː-
numb nʌm **-ly** -li **-ness** -nəs, -nɪs **-s** -z **-ing** -ɪŋ **-ed** -d
numbat ˈnʌm.bæt **-s** -s
numb|er ˈnʌm.b|əʳ ⓤⓢ -b|ɚ **-ers** -əz ⓤⓢ -ɚz **-ering** -ᵊr.ɪŋ **-ered** -əd ⓤⓢ -ɚd **-erless** -ᵊl.əs, -ɪs ⓤⓢ -ɚ.ləs, -lɪs ˌ**number ˈone** *stress shift:* ˌnumber one ˈfan; ˌ**Number ˈ10/Ten** *stress shift:* ˌNumber 10/Ten ˈDowning Street
number-crunch ˈnʌm.bə.krʌntʃ ⓤⓢ -bɚ- **-es** -ɪz **-ing** -ɪŋ **-ed** -t **-er/s** -əʳ/z ⓤⓢ -ɚ/z
numberplate ˈnʌm.bə.pleɪt ⓤⓢ -bɚ- **-s** -s
Numbers ˈnʌm.bəz ⓤⓢ -bɚz
numbing ˈnʌm.ɪŋ **-ly** -li
numbskull ˈnʌm.skʌl **-s** -z
numerable ˈnjuː.mᵊr.ə.bḷ ⓤⓢ ˈnuː-, ˈnjuː-
numeracy ˈnjuː.mᵊr.ə.si ⓤⓢ ˈnuː-, ˈnjuː-
numeral ˈnjuː.mᵊr.ᵊl ⓤⓢ ˈnuː-, ˈnjuː- **-s** -z
numerate *(adj.)* ˈnjuː.mᵊr.ət, -ɪt ⓤⓢ ˈnuː-, ˈnjuː-
numer|ate *(v.)* ˈnjuː.mᵊr|.eɪt ⓤⓢ ˈnuː.mə.r|eɪt, ˈnjuː- **-ates** -eɪts **-ating** -eɪ.tɪŋ ⓤⓢ -eɪ.t̬ɪŋ **-ated** -eɪ.tɪd ⓤⓢ -eɪ.t̬ɪd
numeration ˌnjuː.mᵊrˈeɪ.ʃᵊn ⓤⓢ ˌnuː.məˈreɪ-, ˌnjuː-
numerative ˈnjuː.mᵊr.ə.tɪv ⓤⓢ ˈnuː.mɚ.ə.t̬ɪv, ˈnjuː- **-s** -z
numerator ˈnjuː.mᵊr.eɪ.təʳ ⓤⓢ ˈnuː.mə.reɪ.t̬ɚ, ˈnjuː- **-s** -z
numeric njuːˈmer.ɪk ⓤⓢ nuː-, njuː- **-s** -s
numerical njuːˈmer.ɪ.kḷ ⓤⓢ nuː-, njuː- **-ly** -i
numerologic|al ˌnjuː.mᵊr.əˈlɒdʒ.ɪ.k|ᵊl ⓤⓢ ˌnuː.mɚ.əˈlɑː.dʒɪ-, ˌnjuː- **-ally** -ᵊl.i, -li
numerolog|y ˌnjuː.mᵊrˈɒl.ə.dʒ|i ⓤⓢ ˌnuː.məˈrɑː.lə-, ˌnjuː- **-ist** -ɪst/s
numero uno ˌnuː.mᵊr.əʊˈuː.nəʊ ⓤⓢ ˌnuː.mə.roʊˈuː.noʊ, ˌnjuː-
numerous ˈnjuː.mᵊr.əs ⓤⓢ ˈnuː-, ˈnjuː- **-ly** -li **-ness** -nəs, -nɪs
Numidi|a njuːˈmɪd.i|.ə ⓤⓢ nuː-, njuː- **-an/s** -ən/z
numinous ˈnjuː.mɪ.nəs ⓤⓢ ˈnuː-, ˈnjuː-
numismatic ˌnjuː.mɪzˈmæt.ɪk ⓤⓢ ˌnuː.mɪzˈmæt̬.ɪk, ˌnjuː- **-s** -s **-ally** -ᵊl.i, -li
numismatist njuːˈmɪz.mə.tɪst ⓤⓢ nuː-, njuː- **-s** -s
numnah ˈnʌm.nə **-s** -z
numskull ˈnʌm.skʌl **-s** -z
nun (N) nʌn **-s** -z
Nunc Dimittis ˌnʊŋk.dɪˈmɪt.ɪs, ˌnʌŋk-, -daɪˈ-, -dəˈ- ⓤⓢ ˌnʊŋk.dɪˈmɪt̬- **-es** -ɪz
nunciature ˈnʌnt.si.ə.tjʊəʳ, -tʃəʳ ⓤⓢ -tjʊr, -tʃɚ
nuncio ˈnʌn.ʃi.əʊ, -ʃəʊ, ˈnʌnt.si- ⓤⓢ ˈnʌnt.si.oʊ, ˈnʊnt- **-s** -z
Nuneaton nʌnˈiː.tᵊn
Nuneham ˈnjuː.nəm ⓤⓢ ˈnuː-, ˈnjuː-
Nunn nʌn
nunner|y ˈnʌn.ᵊr|.i **-ies** -iz
NUPE *trades union:* ˈnjuː.pi ⓤⓢ ˈnuː-, ˈnjuː-
Nupe *language and people:* ˈnuː.peɪ **-s** -z
nuptial ˈnʌp.ʃᵊl, -tʃᵊl **-s** -z
Nuremberg ˈnjʊə.rəm.bɜːg, ˈnjɔː- ⓤⓢ ˈnʊr.əm.bɝːg, ˈnjʊr-
Nureyev ˈnjʊə.ri.ef; -reɪ-, njʊəˈreɪ-, -ev ⓤⓢ ˈnʊr.i.ef, nʊˈreɪ.jef
Nurofen® ˈnjʊə.rəʊ.fen, ˈnjɔː- ⓤⓢ nuːˈroʊ.fən, njʊˈ-
nurs|e nɜːs ⓤⓢ nɝːs **-es** -ɪz **-ing** -ɪŋ **-ed** -t
nurs(e)ling ˈnɜːs.lɪŋ ⓤⓢ ˈnɝːs- **-s** -z
nursemaid ˈnɜːs.meɪd ⓤⓢ ˈnɝːs- **-s** -z
nurser|y ˈnɜː.sᵊr|.i ⓤⓢ ˈnɝː- **-ies** -iz ˈ**nursery** ˌ**rhyme**; ˈ**nursery** ˌ**school**; ˈ**nursery** ˌ**slope**
nurserymaid ˈnɜː.sᵊr.i.meɪd ⓤⓢ ˈnɝː- **-s** -z
nursery|man ˈnɜː.sᵊr.i|.mən ⓤⓢ ˈnɝː- **-men** -mən
nursing ˈnɜː.sɪŋ ⓤⓢ ˈnɝː- ˈ**nursing** ˌ**home**; ˌ**nursing** ˈ**mother**
nurt|ure ˈnɜː.tʃ|əʳ ⓤⓢ ˈnɝː.tʃ|ɚ **-ures** -əz ⓤⓢ -ɚz **-uring** -ᵊr.ɪŋ **-ured** -əd ⓤⓢ -ɚd
NUS ˌen.juːˈes
nut *food:* nʌt **-s** -s **-ting** -ɪŋ **-ted** -ɪd
Nut *Egyptian goddess:* nʌt ⓤⓢ nʌt, nuːt
NUT *trades union:* ˌen.juːˈtiː
nu|tate njuː|ˈteɪt ⓤⓢ nuː-, njuː- **-tates** -ˈteɪts **-tating** -ˈteɪ.tɪŋ ⓤⓢ -ˈteɪ.t̬ɪŋ **-tated** -ˈteɪ.tɪd ⓤⓢ -ˈteɪ.t̬ɪd
nutation njuːˈteɪ.ʃᵊn ⓤⓢ nuː-, njuː- **-al** **-s** -z
nut-brown ˌnʌtˈbraʊn *stress shift:* ˌnut-brown ˈhair
nutcas|e ˈnʌt.keɪs **-es** -ɪz
nutcracker ˈnʌtˌkræk.əʳ ⓤⓢ -ɚ **-s** -z
nuthatch ˈnʌt.hætʃ **-es** -ɪz
nuthou|se ˈnʌt.haʊ|s **-ses** -zɪz
Nutkin ˈnʌt.kɪn
nutmeg ˈnʌt.meg **-s** -z
nutraceutical ˌnjuː.trəˈsjuː.tɪ.kᵊl, -ˈsuː-, -ˈkjuː- ⓤⓢ ˌnuː.trəˈsuː.t̬ɪ-, ˌnjuː-, -ˈsjuː- **-s** -z
Nutrasweet® ˈnjuː.trəˌswiːt ⓤⓢ ˈnuː-, ˈnjuː
nutria ˈnjuː.tri.ə ⓤⓢ ˈnuː-, ˈnjuː-
nutrient ˈnjuː.tri.ənt ⓤⓢ ˈnuː-, ˈnjuː-
nutriment ˈnjuː.trə.mənt, -trɪ- ⓤⓢ ˈnuː-, ˈnjuː- **-s** -s
nutrition njuːˈtrɪʃ.ᵊn ⓤⓢ nuː-, njuː- **-al** -ᵊl **-ally** -ᵊl.i
nutritionist njuːˈtrɪʃ.ᵊn.ɪst, -ˈtrɪʃ.nɪst ⓤⓢ nuː-, njuː- **-s** -s
nutritious njuːˈtrɪʃ.əs ⓤⓢ nuː-, njuː- **-ly** -li **-ness** -nəs, -nɪs
nutritive ˈnjuː.trə.tɪv, -trɪ- ⓤⓢ ˈnuː.trə.t̬ɪv, ˈnjuː-
nuts nʌts ˌ**nuts and** ˈ**bolts**
nutshell ˈnʌt.ʃel **-s** -z
Nutt nʌt
Nuttall ˈnʌt.ɔːl
nutter (N) ˈnʌt.əʳ ⓤⓢ ˈnʌt̬.ɚ
nutt|y ˈnʌt|.i ⓤⓢ ˈnʌt̬|.i **-ily** -ɪ.li **-iness** -ɪ.nəs, -ɪ.nɪs
nux vomica ˌnʌksˈvɒm.ɪ.kə ⓤⓢ -ˈvɑː.mɪ-
nuzzl|e ˈnʌz.ḷ **-es** -z **-ing** -ɪŋ, ˈnʌz.lɪŋ **-ed** -d
NVQ ˌen.viːˈkjuː
NW *(abbrev. for* **northwest***)* ˌenˈdʌb.ḷ.juː; ˌnɔːθˈwest ⓤⓢ ˌenˈdʌb.ḷ.juː; ˌnɔːrθ-
NY *(abbrev. for* **New York***)* ˌenˈwaɪ
Nyanja ˈnjæn.dʒə
Nyanza niˈæn.zə, naɪ-; ˈnjæn- ⓤⓢ ˈnjæn-, niˈæn-, naɪ-
Nyasa naɪˈæs.ə, ni-; ˈnjæs- ⓤⓢ naɪˈæs.ə; ˈnjɑː.sɑː
Nyasaland naɪˈæs.ə.lænd, ni-; ˈnjæs- ⓤⓢ naɪˈæs-; ˈnjɑː.sɑː.lænd
Nyerere njəˈreə.ri, nɪə-, -ˈrer.i ⓤⓢ njəˈrer-, ˌni.əˈ-
nylon ˈnaɪ.lɒn ⓤⓢ -lɑːn **-s** -z
Nyman ˈnaɪ.mən
Nymex ˈnaɪ.meks
nymph nɪmpf **-s** -s **-al** -ᵊl
nymphet, nymphette nɪmpˈfet; ˈnɪmp.fɪt, -fət, -fet ⓤⓢ ˈnɪmp.fət; nɪmpˈfet
nympho ˈnɪmp.fəʊ ⓤⓢ -foʊ **-s** -z
nymphomani|a ˌnɪmp.fəʊˈmeɪ.ni|.ə ⓤⓢ -foʊˈ-, -fəˈ-, -ˈnj|ə **-ac/s** -æk
Nyree ˈnaɪə.riː, -ri ⓤⓢ ˈnaɪ-
nystagmus nɪˈstæg.məs
NZ *(abbrev. for* **New Zealand***)* ˌenˈzed ⓤⓢ -ˈziː

Pronouncing the letter O

See also OA, OEU, OI/OY, OO, OU, OW

The vowel letter **o** has several pronunciations. The two most predictable strong pronunciations linked to spelling are: a monophthongal pronunciation, sometimes described as 'short' in British English /ɒ (US) ɑː ɔː/ and a diphthongal pronunciation, sometimes described as 'long' /əʊ (US) oʊ/. In the monophthongal pronunciation, the **o** is generally followed by a consonant which closes the syllable, or a double consonant before another vowel, e.g.:

cod	/kɒd/	(US) /kɑːd/
robbing	/ˈrɒb.ɪŋ/	(US) /ˈrɑː.bɪŋ/

The diphthongal pronunciation usually means the **o** is followed by a single consonant and then a vowel, e.g.:

code	/kəʊd/	(US) /koʊd/
robing	/ˈrəʊ.bɪŋ/	(US) /ˈroʊ.bɪŋ/

In many cases, the monophthongal pronunciation results from the above kind of spelling, e.g.:

gone	/gɒn/	(US) /gɑːn/
copy	/ˈkɒp.i/	(US) /ˈkɑː.pi/

Also, the 'long' pronunciation occasionally appears in words where the vowel is followed by a single consonant and no vowel, e.g.:

control	/kənˈtrəʊl/	(US) /-ˈtroʊl/

When **r** is followed by **o**, the strong pronunciation is one of several possibilities: /ɒ (US) ɔːr/, /ɔː (US) ɔːr /, /ʌ (US) ɝː/ or /ɜː (US) ɝː/, e.g.:

forest	/ˈfɒr.ɪst/	(US) /ˈfɔːr-/
foremost	/ˈfɔː.məʊst/	(US) /ˈfɔːr.moʊst/
borough	/ˈbʌr.ə/	(US) /ˈbɝː-/
word	/wɜːd/	(US) /wɝːd/

And exceptionally, /ʊ/, e.g.:

Worcester	/ˈwʊs.təʳ/	(US) /-tɚ/

In addition

There are other vowel sounds associated with the letter **o**, e.g.:

/ʌ/	colour	/ˈkʌl.əʳ/	(US) /-ɚ/
/uː/	move	/muːv/	
/ʊ/	woman	/ˈwʊm.ən/	
/wʌ/	once	/wʌnts/	
/ɜː (US) ɝː/	colonel	/ˈkɜː.nᵊl/	(US) /ˈkɝː-/

And, exceptionally:

/ɪ/	women	/ˈwɪm.ɪn/

In weak syllables

The vowel letter **o** is realised with the vowel /ə/ in weak syllables, /ɚ/ in American English when followed by an **r**, and may also be elided in British English, due to compression or realisation as a syllabic consonant, e.g.:

observe	/əbˈzɜːv/	(US) /-ˈzɝːv/
forget	/fəˈget/	(US) /fɚ-/
factory	/ˈfæk.tᵊr.i/, /-tri/	

o *the letter:* əʊ (US) oʊ **-'s** -z **-es** -z

O (interjection) əʊ (US) oʊ

o' *(abbrev. for* **of***) weak form only:* ə

Note: This spelling is used to represent a weak form of **of** in archaic and slang expressions and names, for example "pint o' bitter" /ˌpaɪnt.əˈbɪt.əʳ (US) -ˈbɪt̬.ɚ/, "will-o'-the-wisp" /ˌwɪl.ə.ðəˈwɪsp/.

O. *(abbrev. of* **Ohio***)* əʊ; əʊˈhaɪ.əʊ (US) oʊ; oʊˈhaɪ.oʊ, ə-

Oadby ˈəʊd.bi (US) ˈoʊd-

oaf əʊf (US) oʊf **-s** -s

oafish ˈəʊ.fɪʃ (US) ˈoʊ- **-ly** -li **-ness** -nəs, -nɪs

Oahu əʊˈɑː.huː (US) oʊ-

oak əʊk (US) oʊk **-s** -s **-en** -ᵊn **-y** -i

oak-apple ˈəʊkˌæp.l̩ (US) ˈoʊk- **-s** -z

Oakdale ˈəʊk.deɪl (US) ˈoʊk-

Oakeley ˈəʊk.li (US) ˈoʊk-

Oakengates ˈəʊ.kᵊn.geɪts, -kᵊŋ-, ˌ--ˈ- (US) ˈoʊk.ᵊn.geɪts, ˌ--ˈ-

Oakes əʊks (US) oʊks

Oakey ˈəʊ.ki (US) ˈoʊ-

Oakham ˈəʊ.kəm (US) ˈoʊ-

Oakhampton ˌəʊkˈhæmp.tən (US) ˈoʊkˌhæmp- *stress shift, British only:* ˌOakhampton ˈcentre

Oakland ˈəʊk.lənd (US) ˈoʊk- **-s** -z

Oakleigh, Oakley ˈəʊk.li (US) ˈoʊk-

Oaks əʊks (US) oʊks

oakum ˈəʊ.kəm (US) ˈoʊ-

Oakworth ˈəʊk.wəθ, -wɜːθ (US) ˈoʊk.wɚθ, -wɝːθ

OAP ˌəʊ.eɪˈpiː (US) ˌoʊ- **-s** -z

OAPEC ˌəʊˈeɪ.pek (US) ˌoʊ-

oar ɔːʳ (US) ɔːr **-s** -z **-ing** -ɪŋ **-ed** -d **ˌstick one's ˈoar in**

oarlock ˈɔɪ.lɒk (US) ˈɔːr.lɑːk **-s** -s

oars|man ˈɔːz|.mən (US) ˈɔːrz- **-men** -mən **-woman** -ˌwʊm.ən **-women** -ˌwɪm.ɪn

OAS ˌəʊ.eɪ.ˈes (US) ˌoʊ-

oas|is (O) əʊˈeɪ.s|ɪs (US) oʊ- **-es** -iːz

oast əʊst (US) oʊst **-s** -s

oasthou|se ˈəʊst.haʊ|s (US) ˈoʊst- **-ses** -zɪz

oat əʊt (US) oʊt **-s** -s

oatcake ˈəʊt.keɪk (US) ˈoʊt- **-s** -s

oaten ˈəʊ.tᵊn (US) ˈoʊ-

Oates əʊts (US) oʊts

oa|th əʊ|θ (US) oʊ|θ **-ths** -ðz, -θs

Oatlands ˈəʊt.ləndz (US) ˈoʊt-

oatmeal ˈəʊt.miːl (US) ˈoʊt-

oats əʊts (US) oʊts

Oaxaca wəˈhɑː.kə, wɑː- (US) wɑːˈhɑː.kɑː, wə-, -kə

Ob ɒb (US) ɑːb, ɑːp

Obadiah ˌəʊ.bəˈdaɪə (US) ˌoʊ-

Oban ˈəʊ.bᵊn (US) ˈoʊ-

obbligat|o ˌɒb.lɪˈgɑː.t|əʊ, -ləˈ- (US) ˌɑː.blɪˈgɑː.t̬|oʊ **-os** -əʊz (US) -oʊz **-i** -iː

obduracy ˈɒb.djᵊr.ə.si, -djʊ.rə- (US) ˈɑːb.dʊr.ə-, -djʊr-

obdurate ˈɒb.djᵊr.ət, -djʊ.rət, -rɪt, -reɪt (US) ˈɑːb.dʊr.ɪt, -djʊr- **-ly** -li **-ness** -nəs, -nɪs

obduration ˌɒb.djᵊrˈeɪ.ʃᵊn, -djʊˈreɪ- (US) ˌɑːb.dʊrˈeɪ, -djʊrˈ-

OBE ˌəʊ.biːˈiː (US) ˌoʊ- **-s** -z

obeah (O) ˈəʊ.bi.ə (US) ˈoʊ-

obedience əʊˈbiː.di.ənts (US) oʊ-, ə-, ˈ-djənts

Pronouncing the letters OA

The vowel digraph **oa** has two main strong pronunciations: /əʊ (US) oʊ/ and /ɔː (US) ɑː/, e.g.:

road	/rəʊd/	(US) /roʊd/
broad	/brɔːd/	(US) /brɑːd/

When the digraph is followed by an **r** in the spelling, the strong pronunciation is /ɔː (US) ɔːr/, e.g.:

board	/bɔːd/	(US) /bɔːrd/
soar	/sɔːʳ/	(US) /sɔːr/

In addition

Another vowel sound associated with the digraph **oa** is /əʊə, (US) oʊə/, e.g.:

coalescence	/kəʊə'les.ənts/	(US) /koʊə-/

In weak syllables

The vowel digraph **oa** is realised with the vowel /ə/ in weak syllables and with /ɚ/ in American English when followed by an **r**, e.g.:

cupboard	/'kʌb.əd/	(US) /-ɚd/

obedient əʊ'biː.di.ənt (US) oʊ-, ə-, '-djənt **-ly** -li
obeisanc|e əʊ'beɪ.sənts (US) oʊ-, -'biː- **-es** -ɪz
obelisk 'ɒb.əl.ɪsk, -ɪ.lɪsk (US) 'ɑː.bəl.ɪsk **-s** -s
obel|us 'ɒb.əl|.əs, -ɪ.l|əs (US) 'ɑː.bəl|.əs, 'oʊ- **-i** -aɪ
Oberammergau ˌəʊ.bə'ræm.ə.gaʊ (US) ˌoʊ.bɚ'ɑː.mɚ-
Oberland 'əʊ.bə.lænd (US) 'oʊ.bɚ-
Oberlin 'əʊ.bə.lɪn (US) 'oʊ.bɚ-
Oberon 'əʊ.bər.ɒn, -ən (US) 'oʊ.bə.rɑːn, -bɚ.ən
obese əʊ'biːs (US) oʊ- **-ness** -nəs, -nɪs
obesity əʊ'biː.sə.ti, -sɪ- (US) oʊ'biː.sə.t̬i
obey əʊ'beɪ (US) oʊ-, ə- **-s** -z **-ing** -ɪŋ **-ed** -d **-er/s** -əʳ/z (US) -ɚ/z
obfus|cate 'ɒb.fʌs|.keɪt, -fə.s|keɪt (US) 'ɑːb.fə-; ɑːb'fʌs|.keɪt **-cates** -keɪts **-cating** -keɪ.tɪŋ (US) -keɪ.t̬ɪŋ **-cated** -keɪ.tɪd (US) -keɪ.t̬ɪd
obfuscation ˌɒb.fʌs'keɪ.ʃən, -fə'skeɪ- (US) ˌɑːb.fə'skeɪ- **-s** -z
obfuscatory ˌɒb.fʌs'keɪ.tər.i, -fə'skeɪ- (US) ɑːb'fʌs.kə.tɔːr-, əb-
obi 'əʊ.bi (US) 'oʊ- **-s** -z
Obi *river in Siberia:* 'əʊ.bi (US) 'oʊ-
Obie 'əʊ.bi (US) 'oʊ- **-s** -z
obit 'ɒb.ɪt; əʊ'bɪt (US) 'oʊ-, -'- **-s** -s
obiter dict|um ˌɒb.ɪ.tə'dɪk.t|ʊm, ˌəʊ.bɪ-, -təm (US) ˌoʊ.bɪ.t̬ɚ'dɪk-, ˌɑː- **-a** -ə
obituarist əʊ'bɪtʃ.ʊə.rɪst, ɒb'ɪtʃ-, -'ɪt.jʊə-, -jə-, -jʊ- (US) oʊ'bɪtʃ.u.ɚ.ɪst, ə- **-s** -s
obituar|y əʊ'bɪtʃ.ʊə.r|i, ɒb'ɪtʃ-, -'ɪt.jʊə-, -jə-, -jʊ- (US) oʊ'bɪtʃ.u.er|.i, ə- **-ies** -iz
object (*n.*) 'ɒb.dʒɪkt, -dʒekt (US) 'ɑːb- **-s** -s 'object ˌlesson
object (*v.*) əb'dʒekt **-s** -s **-ing** -ɪŋ **-ed** -ɪd **-or/s** -əʳ/z (US) -ɚ/z
objecti|fy əb'dʒek.tɪ|.faɪ, ɒb-, -tə- (US) əb'dʒek.tə- **-fies** -faɪz **-fying** -faɪ.ɪŋ **-fied** -faɪd
objection əb'dʒek.ʃən **-s** -z
objectionab|le əb'dʒek.ʃən.ə.b|l̩, -'dʒekʃ.nə- **-ly** -li
objective əb'dʒek.tɪv, ɒb- (US) əb- **-s** -z **-ly** -li **-ness** -nəs, -nɪs
objectivism əb'dʒek.tɪ.vɪ.zəm, ɒb- (US) əb'dʒek.tə-
objectivity ˌɒb.dʒɪk'tɪv.ə.ti, -dʒek-, -ɪ.ti (US) ˌɑːb.dʒek'tɪv.ə.t̬i
objectless 'ɒb.dʒɪkt.ləs, -dʒekt-, -lɪs (US) 'ɑːb.dʒɪkt-
objet(s) d'art ˌɒb.ʒeɪ'dɑːʳ (US) ˌɑːb.ʒeɪ'dɑːr
objet(s) trouvé(s) ˌɒb.ʒeɪ.truː'veɪ (US) ˌɑːb-
objur|gate 'ɒb.dʒə|.geɪt, -dʒɜː- (US) 'ɑːb.dʒɚ-, əb'dʒɝː- **-gates** -geɪts **-gating** -geɪ.tɪŋ (US) -geɪ.t̬ɪŋ **-gated** -geɪ.tɪd (US) -geɪ.t̬ɪd
objurgation ˌɒb.dʒə'geɪ.ʃən, -dʒɜː'- (US) ˌɑːb.dʒɚ'- **-s** -z
objurgatory ɒb'dʒɜː.gə.tər.i, əb-; ˌɒb.dʒə'geɪ-, -dʒɜː'- (US) əb'dʒɝː.gə.tɔːr-
oblate (*adj.*) 'ɒb.leɪt; -'-, əʊ'bleɪt (US) 'ɑː.bleɪt, -'- **-ly** -li **-ness** -nəs, -nɪs
oblate (*n.*) 'ɒb.leɪt (US) 'ɑː.bleɪt **-s** -s
oblation əʊ'bleɪ.ʃən, ɒb'leɪ- (US) ə'bleɪ-, oʊ-, ɑː- **-s** -z
obligat|e 'ɒb.lɪ.geɪt (US) 'ɑː.blɪ- **-es** -s **-ing** -ɪŋ **-ed** -ɪd
obligation ˌɒb.lɪ'geɪ.ʃən, -lə'- (US) ˌɑː.blə'- **-s** -z
obligat|o ˌɒb.lɪ'gɑː.t|əʊ, -lə'- (US) ˌɑː.blɪ'gɑː.t̬|oʊ **-os** -əʊz (US) -oʊz **-i** -iː
obligator|y ə'blɪg.ə.tər|.i, ɒb'lɪg-; ˌɒb.lɪ'geɪ-, -lə'- (US) ə'blɪg.ə.tɔːr-; 'ɑː.blə.gə- **-ily** -əl.i, -ɪ.li **-iness** -ɪ.nəs, -ɪ.nɪs
oblig|e ə'blaɪdʒ (US) ə-, oʊ- **-es** -ɪz **-ing/ly** -ɪŋ/li **-ingness** -ɪŋ.nəs, -nɪs **-ed** -d
obliged ə'blaɪdʒd (US) ə-, oʊ-
obligee ˌɒb.lɪ'dʒiː, -lə'- (US) ˌɑː.blə'- **-s** -z
obliging ə'blaɪ.dʒɪŋ (US) ə-, oʊ-
obligor ˌɒb.lɪ'gɔːʳ, -lə'- (US) ˌɑː.blə'gɔːr, '--- **-s** -z
oblique əʊ'bliːk (US) oʊ-, ə-, -'blaɪk **-ly** -li **-ness** -nəs, -nɪs
Note: The US form /-'blaɪk/ is associated with military usage.
obliquit|y əʊ'blɪk.wə.t|i, -wɪ- (US) ə'blɪk.wə.t̬|i **-ies** -iz
obliter|ate ə'blɪt.ər|.eɪt (US) -'blɪt̬.ə.r|eɪt, oʊ- **-ates** -eɪts **-ating** -eɪ.tɪŋ (US) -eɪ.t̬ɪŋ **-ated** -eɪ.tɪd (US) -eɪ.t̬ɪd
obliteration əˌblɪt.ər'eɪ.ʃən (US) -ˌblɪt̬.ə'reɪ-, oʊ- **-s** -z
oblivion ə'blɪv.i.ən
oblivious ə'blɪv.i.əs **-ly** -li **-ness** -nəs, -nɪs
oblong 'ɒb.lɒŋ (US) 'ɑːb.lɑːŋ, -lɔːŋ **-s** -z
obloquy 'ɒb.lə.kwi (US) 'ɑːb-
obnoxious əb'nɒk.ʃəs, ɒb- (US) əb'nɑːk-, ɑːb- **-ly** -li **-ness** -nəs, -nɪs
oboe 'əʊ.bəʊ (US) 'oʊ.boʊ **-s** -z
oboe d'amore ˌəʊ.bəʊ.dæm'ɔː.reɪ, -də'mɔː-, -riː (US) ˌoʊ.boʊ.də'mɔːr.eɪ
oboist 'əʊ.bəʊ.ɪst (US) 'oʊ.boʊ- **-s** -s
obol 'ɒb.ɒl, 'əʊ.bɒl, -bəl (US) 'ɑː.bəl, 'oʊ- **-s** -z
Obote əʊ'bəʊ.teɪ, ɒb'əʊ-, -ti (US) oʊ'boʊ-
O'Boyle əʊ'bɔɪl (US) oʊ-
O'Brady əʊ'breɪ.di, -'brɔː- (US) oʊ'breɪ-
O'Brien, O'Bryan əʊ'braɪən (US) oʊ-
obscene əb'siːn, ɒb- (US) əb-, ɑːb- **-ly** -li **-ness** -nəs, -nɪs
obscenit|y əb'sen.ə.t|i, ɒb-, -ɪ.t|i (US) əb'sen.ə.t̬|i, ɑːb- **-ies** -iz
obscurant ɒb'skjʊə.rənt, əb- (US) ɑːb'skjʊr.ənt, əb-
obscurant|ism ˌɒb.skjʊə'ræn.t|ɪ.zəm;

ɒb'skjʊə.rən-, əb- US ɑːb'skjʊr.ən-, əb- **-ist/s** -ɪst/s

obscuration ˌɒb.skjʊə'reɪ.ʃᵊn, -skjə'- US ˌɑːb.skjʊ'- **-s** -z

obscur|e əb'skjʊəʳ, -'skjɔːʳ US əb'skjʊr, ɑːb- **-er** -əʳ US -ɚ **-est** -ɪst, -əst **-ely** -li **-eness** -nəs, -nɪs **-es** -z **-ing** -ɪŋ **-ed** -d

obscurit|y əb'skjʊə.rə.t|i, -'skjɔː, -rɪ- US əb'skjʊr.ə.t̬|i, ɑːb- **-ies** -iz

obse|crate 'ɒb.sɪ|.kreɪt, -sə- US 'ɑːb.sɪ- **-crates** -kreɪts **-crating** -kreɪ.tɪŋ US -kreɪ.t̬ɪŋ **-crated** -kreɪ.tɪd US -kreɪ.t̬ɪd

obsecration ˌɒb.sɪ'kreɪ.ʃᵊn, -sə'- US ˌɑːb.sə'- **-s** -z

obsequies 'ɒb.sɪ.kwiz, -sə-; ɒb'siː- US 'ɑːb.sɪ-

obsequious əb'siː.kwi.əs, ɒb- US əb-, ɑːb- **-ly** -li **-ness** -nəs, -nɪs

observab|le əb'zɜː.və.b|l̩ US -'zɝː- **-ly** -li **-leness** -l̩.nəs, -nɪs

observanc|e əb'zɜː.vᵊn*t*s US -'zɝː- **-es** -ɪz

observant əb'zɜː.vᵊnt US -'zɝː- **-ly** -li

observation ˌɒb.zə'veɪ.ʃᵊn US ˌɑːb.zɚ'-, -sɚ'- **-s** -z

observational ˌɒb.zə'veɪ.ʃᵊn.ᵊl, -veɪʃ.nᵊl US ˌɑːb.zɚ'-, -sɚ'- **-ly** -i

observator|y əb'zɜː.və.tr|i, -tᵊr|.i US -'zɝː.və.tɔːr- **-ies** -iz

observ|e əb'zɜːv US -'zɝːv **-es** -z **-ing/ly** -ɪŋ/li **-ed** -d

observer (O) əb'zɜː.vəʳ US -'zɝː.vɚ **-s** -z

obsess əb'ses, ɒb- US əb- **-es** -ɪz **-ing** -ɪŋ **-ed** -t

obsession əb'seʃ.ᵊn, ɒb- US əb- **-s** -s **-al** -ᵊl

obsessive əb'ses.ɪv, ɒb- US əb- **-s** **-ly** -li **-ness** -nəs, -nɪs

obsidian ɒb'sɪd.i.ən, əb- US əb-, ɑːb-

obsolescence ˌɒb.sə'les.ᵊn*t*s, -sᵊl'es- US ˌɑːb-

obsolescent ˌɒb.sə'les.ᵊnt, -sᵊl'es- US ˌɑːb- **-ly** -li

obsolete 'ɒb.sᵊl.iːt US ˌɑːb.sᵊl'iːt **-ly** -li **-ness** -nəs, -nɪs

obstacle 'ɒb.stə.kl̩, -stɪ- US 'ɑːb.stə- **-s** -z **'obstacle ˌcourse**

obstetric ɒb'stet.rɪk, əb- US əb-, ɑːb- **-al** -ᵊl **-s** -s

obstetrician ˌɒb.stə'trɪʃ.ᵊn, -stɪ'-, -stet'rɪʃ- US ˌɑːb.stə'trɪʃ- **-s** -z

obstinac|y 'ɒb.stɪ.nə.s|i, -stᵊn.ə- US 'ɑːb.stə.nə- **-ies** -iz

obstinate 'ɒb.stɪ.nət, -stᵊn.ət, -ɪt US 'ɑːb.stə.nət **-ly** -li **-ness** -nəs, -nɪs

obstreperous əb'strep.ᵊr.əs, ɒb- US əb-, ɑːb- **-ly** -li **-ness** -nəs, -nɪs

obstruct əb'strʌkt **-s** -s **-ing** -ɪŋ **-ed** -ɪd **-or/s** -əʳ/z US -ɚ/z

obstruction əb'strʌk.ʃᵊn **-s** -z

obstructionism əb'strʌk.ʃᵊn.ɪ.zᵊm

obstructionist əb'strʌk.ʃᵊn.ɪst **-s** -s

obstructive əb'strʌk.tɪv **-ly** -li **-ness** -nəs, -nɪs

obstruent 'ɒb.stru.ənt US 'ɑːb- **-s** -s

obtain əb'teɪn **-s** -z **-ing** -ɪŋ **-ed** -d **-er/s** -əʳ/z US -ɚ/z **-able** -ə.bl̩

obtrud|e əb'truːd, ɒb- US əb-, ɑːb- **-es** -z **-ing** -ɪŋ **-ed** -ɪd **-er/s** -əʳ/z US -ɚ/z

obtrusion əb'truː.ʒᵊn, ɒb- US əb-, ɑːb- **-s** -z

obtrusive əb'truː.sɪv, ɒb-, -zɪv US əb-, ɑːb- **-ly** -li **-ness** -nəs, -nɪs

obtu|rate 'ɒb.tjʊə|.reɪt, -tjə- US 'ɑːb.tə-, -tjə-, -tʊ-, -tjʊ- **-rates** -reɪts **-rating** -reɪ.tɪŋ US -reɪ.t̬ɪŋ **-rated** -reɪ.tɪd US -reɪ.t̬ɪd **-rator/s** -reɪ.təʳ/z US -reɪ.t̬ɚ/z

obturation ˌɒb.tjʊə'reɪ.ʃᵊn, -tjə'- US ˌɑːb.tə'-, -tjə'-, -tʊ'-, -tjʊ'- **-s** -z

obtuse əb'tjuːs, ɒb- US ɑːb'tuːs, əb-, -'tjuːs **-ly** -li **-ness** -nəs, -nɪs

obvers|e (*adj.*) 'ɒb.vɜːs US ɑːb'vɝːs, əb-; 'ɑːb.vɝːs

obvers|e (*n.*) 'ɒb.vɜːs US 'ɑːb.vɝːs **-es** -ɪz

obversely 'ɒb.vɜː.sli US ɑːb'vɝː-

ob|vert ɒb|'vɜːt, əb- US ɑːb|'vɝːt, əb- **-verts** -'vɜːts US -'vɝːts **-verting** -'vɜː.tɪŋ US -'vɝː.t̬ɪŋ **-verted** -'vɜː.tɪd US -'vɝː.t̬ɪd

obvi|ate 'ɒb.vi|.eɪt US 'ɑːb- **-ates** -eɪts **-ating** -eɪ.tɪŋ US -eɪ.t̬ɪŋ **-ated** -eɪ.tɪd US -eɪ.t̬ɪd

obviative 'ɒb.vi.ə.tɪv US 'ɑːb.vi.eɪ.t̬ɪv

obvious 'ɒb.vi.əs US 'ɑːb- **-ly** -li **-ness** -nəs, -nɪs

O'Byrne əʊ'bɜːn US oʊ'bɝːn

O'Callaghan əʊ'kæl.ə.hən, -gən, -hæn US oʊ'kæl.ə.hən, -hæn

ocarina ˌɒk.ᵊr'iː.nə US ˌɑː.kə'riː- **-s** -z

O'Casey əʊ'keɪ.si US oʊ-

occam (O) 'ɒk.əm US 'ɑː.kəm

occasion ə'keɪ.ʒᵊn **-s** -z **-ing** -ɪŋ **-ed** -d **ˌrise to the ocˈcasion**

occasional ə'keɪ.ʒᵊn.ᵊl, -'keɪʒ.nᵊl **-ly** -i

occasional|ism ə'keɪ.ʒᵊn.ᵊl|.ɪ.zᵊm, -'keɪʒ.nᵊl- **-ist/s** -ɪst/s

occident (O) 'ɒk.sɪ.dᵊnt, -sə- US 'ɑːk.sə.dənt, -sɪ-, -dent

occidental (O) ˌɒk.sɪ'den.tᵊl, -sə'- US ˌɑːk.sə'den.t̬ᵊl, -sɪ'- **-s** -z

occidental|ism (O) ˌɒk.sɪ'den.tᵊl|.ɪ.zᵊm, -sə'- US ˌɑːk.sə'den.t̬ᵊl-, -sɪ'- **-ist/s** -ɪst/s

occidentaliz|e, -is|e ˌɒk.sɪ'den.tᵊl.aɪz, -sə'- US ˌɑːk.sə'den.t̬ᵊl-, -sɪ'- **-es** -ɪz **-ing** -ɪŋ **-ed** -d

occipita (*from* **occiput**) ɒk'sɪp.ɪ.tə US ɑːk'sɪp.ɪ.t̬ə

occipital ɒk'sɪp.ɪ.tᵊl, '-ə- US ɑːk'sɪp.ɪ.t̬ᵊl **-ly** -i

occiput 'ɒk.sɪ.pʌt, -pət US ɑːk- **-s** -s **occipita** ɒk'sɪp.ɪ.tə US ɑːk'sɪp.ɪ.t̬ə

Occleve 'ɒk.liːv US 'ɑːk-

occlud|e ə'kluːd, ɒk'luːd US ə'kluːd, ɑː- **-es** -z **-ing** -ɪŋ **-ed** -ɪd

occlusal ə'kluː.zᵊl, ɒk'luː- US ə'kluː-, ɑː-

occlusion ə'kluː.ʒᵊn, ɒk'luː- US ə'kluː-, ɑː- **-s** -z

occlusive ə'kluː.sɪv, ɒk'luː- US ə'kluː-, ɑː- **-s** -z

occult (*adj.*) 'ɒk.ʌlt; ə'kʌlt, ɒk'ʌlt US ə'kʌlt; 'ɑː.kʌlt **-ly** -li **-ness** -nəs, -nɪs

occul|t (*v.*) ɒk'ʌl|t, ə'kʌl|t US ə- **-ts** -ts **-ting** -tɪŋ US -t̬ɪŋ **-ted** -tɪd US -t̬ɪd

occultation ˌɒk.ᵊl'teɪ.ʃᵊn, -ʌl'- US ˌɑː.kʌl'- **-s** -z

occult|ism 'ɒk.ᵊl.t|ɪ.zᵊm, -ʌl-; ɒk'ʌl-, ə'kʌl- US ə'kʌl-; 'ɑː.kʌl- **-ist/s** -ɪst/s

occupancy 'ɒk.jə.pən*t*.si, -jʊ- US 'ɑː.kjə-, -kjʊ-

occupant 'ɒk.jə.pənt, -jʊ- US 'ɑː.kjə-, -kjʊ- **-s** -s

occupation ˌɒk.jə'peɪ.ʃᵊn, -jʊ'- US ˌɑː.kjə'-, -kjʊ'- **-s** -z

occupational ˌɒk.jə'peɪ.ʃᵊn.ᵊl, -jʊ'-, -'peɪʃ.nᵊl US ˌɑː.kjə'-, -kjʊ'- **-ly** -i *stress shift, see compound:* **ˌoccupational 'therapy**

occupier 'ɒk.jə.paɪ.əʳ, -jʊ- US 'ɑː.kjə.paɪ.ɚ, -kjʊ- **-s** -z

occup|y 'ɒk.jə.p|aɪ, -jʊ- US 'ɑː.kjuː-, -kjə- **-ies** -aɪz **-ying** -aɪ.ɪŋ **-ied** -aɪd

occur ə'kɜːʳ US -'kɝː **-s** -z **-ring** -ɪŋ **-red** -d

occurrenc|e ə'kʌr.ᵊn*t*s US -'kɝː- **-es** -ɪz

ocean 'əʊ.ʃᵊn US 'oʊ- **-s** -z **a ˌdrop in the 'ocean**

oceanfront 'əʊ.ʃᵊn.frʌnt US 'oʊ- **-s** -s

ocean-going 'əʊ.ʃᵊnˌgəʊ.ɪŋ US 'oʊ.ʃᵊnˌgoʊ-

Oceani|a ˌəʊ.ʃi'eɪ.ni|.ə, -si'-, -'ɑː- US ˌoʊ.ʃi'æn.i-, -'ɑː.ni-, -'eɪ- **-an/s** -ən/z

oceanic (O) ˌəʊ.ʃi'æn.ɪk, -si'- US ˌoʊ.ʃi'-

oceanographic ˌəʊ.ʃᵊn.əʊ'græf.ɪk, -ʃi.ᵊn- US ˌoʊ.ʃə.noʊ'-, -ʃi.ə- **-ally** -ᵊl.i, -li

oceanograph|y ˌəʊ.ʃᵊn'ɒg.rə.f|i, -ʃi.ᵊn'- US ˌoʊ.ʃə'nɑː.grə-, -ʃi.ə'- **-er/s** -əʳ/z US -ɚ/z

oceanolog|y ˌəʊ.ʃᵊn'ɒl.ə.dʒ|i, -ʃi.ᵊn'- US ˌoʊ.ʃə'nɑː.lə-, -ʃi.ə'- **-ist/s** -ɪst/s

Oceanus əʊ'siː.ə.nəs, -'ʃiː- US oʊ'siː-

ocell|us əʊ'sel|.əs US oʊ- **-i** -aɪ, -iː

ocelot 'ɒs.ᵊl.ɒt, 'əʊ.sᵊl-, -sɪ.lɒt US 'ɑː.sə.lɑːt, 'oʊ-, -lət **-s** -s

och ɒx US ɑːk *as if Scots:* ɑːx

oche ˈɒk.i (US) ˈɑː.ki **-s** -z
ocher ˈəʊ.kəʳ (US) ˈoʊ.kɚ **-ous** -əs
Ochil(l) ˈəʊ.kəl, -xəl (US) ˈoʊ.tʃɪl, ˈɑː-, -kəl
Ochiltree *in Scott's 'Antiquary':* ˈəʊ.kɪl.triː, -xɪl-, ˈɒk.ɪl-, ˈɒx-, -əl- (US) ˈoʊ.kɪl-, ˈɑː-, -tʃɪl- *in US:* ˈəʊ.kɪl.triː (US) ˈoʊ-
och|re ˈəʊ.k|əʳ (US) ˈoʊ.k|ɚ **-res** -əz (US) -ɚz **-reing** -ər.ɪŋ **-red** -əd (US) -ɚd
ochreous ˈəʊ.kri.əs, -kər- (US) ˈoʊ-
ochry ˈəʊ.kər.i (US) ˈoʊ-
Ochterlony ˌɒk.təˈləʊ.ni, ˌɒx- (US) ˌɑːk.tɚˈloʊ-
ocker, okker ˈɒk.əʳ (US) ˈɑː.kɚ **-s** -z
Ockham ˈɒk.əm (US) ˈɑː.kəm
Ockley ˈɒk.li (US) ˈɑːk-
O'Clery əʊˈklɪə.ri (US) oʊˈklɪr.i
o'clock əˈklɒk (US) -ˈklɑːk
O'Connell əʊˈkɒn.əl (US) oʊˈkɑː.nəl
O'Connor əʊˈkɒn.əʳ (US) oʊˈkɑː.nɚ
Ocracoke ˈəʊ.krə.kəʊk (US) ˈoʊ.krə.koʊk
Oct. *(abbrev. for* **October***)* ɒkt; ɒkˈtəʊ.bəʳ (US) ɑːkˈtoʊ.bɚ
octa- ɒk.tə-; ɒkˈtæ- (US) ɑːk-; ɑːkˈtæ-
Note: Prefix. Normally either takes primary or secondary stress on the first syllable, e.g. **octagon** /ˈɒk.tə.gən (US) ˈɑːk.tə.gɑːn/, **octahedron** /ˌɒk.təˈhiː.drən (US) ˌɑːk.təˈhiː.drən/, or primary stress on the second syllable, e.g. **octagonal** /ɒkˈtæg.ən.əl ˉɑːk-/.
octagon ˈɒk.tə.gən (US) ˈɑːk.tə.gɑːn **-s** -z
octagonal ɒkˈtæg.ən.əl (US) ɑːk- **-ly** -i
octahedr|on ˌɒk.təˈhiː.dr|ən, -ˈhed.r|ən (US) ˈɑːk.təˈhiː.dr|ən **-ons** -ənz **-a** -ə **-al** -əl
octal ˈɒk.təl (US) ˈɑːk-
octane ˈɒk.teɪn (US) ˈɑːk-
octant ˈɒk.tənt (US) ˈɑːk- **-s** -s
Octateuch ˈɒk.tə.tjuːk (US) ˈɑːk.tə.tuːk, -tjuːk
octave *musical term:* ˈɒk.tɪv, -teɪv (US) ˈɑːk- **-s** -z
octave *ecclesiastical term:* ˈɒk.teɪv, -tɪv (US) ˈɑːk.tɪv, -teɪv **-s** -z
Octavi|a ɒkˈteɪ.vi|.ə, -ˈtɑː- (US) ɑːkˈteɪ- **-an** -ən
Octavius ɒkˈteɪ.vi.əs, -ˈtɑː- (US) ɑːkˈteɪ-
octavo ɒkˈtɑː.vəʊ, -ˈteɪ- (US) ɑːkˈteɪ.voʊ, -ˈtɑː- **-s** -z
octennial ɒkˈten.i.əl (US) ɑːk- **-ly** -i
octet(te) ɒkˈtet (US) ɑːk- **-s** -s
octillion ɒkˈtɪl.jən, -i.ən (US) ɑːkˈtɪl.jən **-s** -z
octo- ɒk.təʊ- (US) ɑːk.toʊ-, -tə-
Note: Prefix. Normally takes primary or secondary stress on the first syllable, e.g. **octosyllable** /ˈɒk.təʊˌsɪl.ə.bl̩ (US) ˈɑːk.toʊ-/, **octosyllabic** /ˌɒk.təʊ.sɪˈlæb.ɪk (US) ˌɑːk.toʊ-/.
October ɒkˈtəʊ.bəʳ (US) ɑːkˈtoʊ.bɚ **-s** -z
octodecimo ˌɒk.təʊˈdes.ɪ.məʊ (US) ˌɑːk.toʊˈdes.ɪ.moʊ **-s** -z
octogenarian ˌɒk.təʊ.dʒəˈneə.ri.ən, -dʒɪˈ- (US) ˌɑːk.toʊ.dʒɪˈner.i-, -tə- **-s** -z
octop|us ˈɒk.tə.p|əs, -p|ʊs (US) ˈɑːk.tə.p|əs **-uses** -ə.sɪz, -ʊ.sɪz (US) -ə.sɪz **-i** -aɪ
octoroon ˌɒk.təˈruːn (US) ˌɑːk- **-s** -z
octosyllabic ˌɒk.təʊ.sɪˈlæb.ɪk, -səˈ- (US) ˌɑːk.toʊ-, -tə- *stress shift:* ˌoctosyllabic ˈmeter
octosyllable ˈɒk.təʊˌsɪl.ə.bl̩ (US) ˈɑːk.toʊˌ-, -təˌ- **-s** -z
octroi ˈɒk.trwɑː, -trɔɪ (US) ˈɑːk.trɔɪ **-s** -z
octuple ˈɒk.tjə.pl̩, -tjʊ-; ɒkˈtjuː- (US) ˈɑːk.tə-; ɑːkˈtuː-
ocular ˈɒk.jə.ləʳ, -jʊ- (US) ˈɑː.kjə.lɚ, -kjʊ- **-ly** -li
oculist ˈɒk.jə.lɪst, -jʊ- (US) ˈɑː.kjə-, -kjʊ- **-s** -s
O'Curry əʊˈkʌr.i (US) oʊˈkɝː-
od (O) ɒd (US) ɑːd **-s** -z
OD ˌəʊˈdiː (US) ˌoʊ- **-'s** -z **-'ing** -ɪŋ **-'d** -d
odalisque, odalisk ˈɒd.əl.ɪsk, ˈəʊ.dəl- (US) ˈoʊ.dəl- **-s** -s
O'Daly əʊˈdeɪ.li (US) oʊ-
Odam ˈəʊ.dəm (US) ˈoʊ-
odd ɒd (US) ɑːd **-er** -əʳ (US) -ɚ **-est** -ɪst, -əst **-ly** -li **-ness** -nəs, -nɪs ˌ**odd man ˈout**
oddball ˈɒd.bɔːl (US) ˈɑːd-, -bɑːl **-s** -z
Oddbins® ˈɒd.bɪnz (US) ˈɑːd-
odd bod ˈɒd.bɒd (US) ˈɑːd.bɑːd **-s** -z
Oddfellow ˈɒdˌfel.əʊ (US) ˈɑːdˌfel.oʊ **-s** -z
Oddie ˈɒd.i (US) ˈɑː.di
oddish ˈɒd.ɪʃ (US) ˈɑː.dɪʃ
oddit|y ˈɒd.ɪ.t|i, -ə.t|i (US) ˈɑː.də.t̬|i **-ies** -iz
odd-job |man ˌɒdˈdʒɒb|.mæn (US) ˈɑːd.dʒɑːb- **-men** -men
oddment ˈɒd.mənt (US) ˈɑːd- **-s** -s
odds ɒdz (US) ɑːdz ˌ**odds and ˈends**
odds-on ˌɒdzˈɒn (US) ˌɑːdzˈɑːn *stress shift:* ˌodds-on ˈfavourite
ode əʊd (US) oʊd **-s** -z
O'Dea əʊˈdeɪ (US) oʊ-
Odell əʊˈdel; ˈəʊ.dəl (US) oʊˈdel
Odense ˈəʊ.dən*t*.sə (US) ˈoʊ.dən*t*-, -θən*t*-
Odeon® ˈəʊ.di.ən (US) ˈoʊ-
Oder ˈəʊ.dəʳ (US) ˈoʊ.dɚ
Oder-Neisse Line ˌəʊ.dəˈnaɪ.səˌlaɪn (US) ˌoʊ.dɚˈ-
Odessa əʊˈdes.ə (US) oʊ-
Odets əʊˈdets (US) oʊ-
Odette əʊˈdet (US) oʊ-
ode|um əʊˈdiː|.əm; ˈəʊ.di- (US) oʊˈdiː-; ˈoʊ.di- **-a** -ə **-ums** -əmz
Odgers ˈɒdʒ.əz (US) ˈɑː.dʒɚz
Odham ˈɒd.əm (US) ˈɑː.dəm
Odiham ˈəʊ.dɪ.əm, -həm (US) ˈoʊ-
Odile əʊˈdiːl (US) oʊ-
Odin ˈəʊ.dɪn (US) ˈoʊ-
odious ˈəʊ.di.əs (US) ˈoʊ- **-ly** -li **-ness** -nəs, -nɪs
odium ˈəʊ.di.əm (US) ˈoʊ-
Odling ˈɒd.lɪŋ (US) ˈɑːd-
Odlum ˈɒd.ləm (US) ˈɑːd-
Odo ˈəʊ.dəʊ (US) ˈoʊ.doʊ
Odoacer ˌɒd.əʊˈeɪ.səʳ, ˌəʊ.dəʊˈ- (US) ˌoʊ.doʊˈeɪ.sɚ
O'Doherty əʊˈdəʊ.ə.ti, -ˈdɒ.hə.ti, -ˈdɒx.ə- (US) oʊˈdɔːr.t̬i, -ˈdɑː.hɚ-
odometer əʊˈdɒm.ɪ.təʳ, ɒdˈɒm-, -ə.təʳ (US) oʊˈdɑː.mə.t̬ɚ **-s** -z
O'Donnell əʊˈdɒn.əl (US) oʊˈdɑː.nəl
odontolog|y ˌɒd.ɒnˈtɒl.ə.dʒ|i, ˌəʊ.dɒnˈ- (US) ˌoʊ.dɑːnˈtɑː.lə- **-ist/s** -ɪst/s
odor ˈəʊ.dəʳ (US) ˈoʊ.dɚ **-s** -z **-ed** -d **-less** -ləs, -lɪs
odoriferous ˌəʊ.dərˈɪf.ər.əs, ˌɒd.ərˈ- (US) ˌoʊ.dəˈrɪf.ɚ.əs **-ly** -li **-ness** -nəs, -nɪs
odorous ˈəʊ.dər.əs (US) ˈoʊ- **-ly** -li **-ness** -nəs, -nɪs
odour ˈəʊ.dəʳ (US) ˈoʊ.dɚ **-s** -z **-ed** -d **-less** -ləs, -lɪs
O'Dowd əʊˈdaʊd (US) oʊ-
odsbodikins ˌɒdzˈbɒd.ɪ.kɪnz (US) ˌɑːdzˈbɑːd-
O'Dwyer əʊˈdwaɪəʳ (US) oʊˈdwaɪɚ
Ody ˈəʊ.di (US) ˈoʊ-
Odysseus əˈdɪs.juːs, ɒdˈɪs-, əʊˈdɪs-, -ˈ-i.əs (US) oʊˈdɪs.i.əs, ˈ-juːs
odyssey (O) ˈɒd.ɪ.si, ˈ-ə- (US) ˈɑː.dɪ-
OECD ˌəʊ.iː.siːˈdiː (US) ˌoʊ-
oecumenic ˌiː.kjuˈmen.ɪk (US) ˌek.jəˈ-, -jʊˈ- **-al** -əl *stress shift:* ˌoecumenic ˈservice
oedema ɪˈdiː.mə, iː- (US) ɪ- **-ta** -tə (US) -t̬ə
oedematous ɪˈdiː.mə.təs, iː-, -ˈdem.ə- (US) ɪˈdem.ə.t̬əs
oedipal (O) ˈiː.dɪ.pəl, -də- (US) ˈed.ɪ-, ˈiː.dɪ-
Oedipus ˈiː.dɪ.pəs, -də- (US) ˈed.ɪ-, ˈiː.dɪ- ˈ**Oedipus** ˌ**complex**
OEEC ˌəʊ.iː.iːˈsiː (US) ˌoʊ-
Oenomaus ˌiː.nəʊˈmeɪ.əs (US) -nəˈ-, -noʊˈ-
Oenone iːˈnəʊ.niː, ɪ-, -ni (US) iːˈnoʊ-
oenophile ˈiː.nəʊ.faɪl (US) -nə- **-s** -z
o'er *(contracted form of* **over***)* ɔəʳ, ɔːʳ, əʊəʳ (US) ɔːr, oʊɚ
oes *(plur. of* **O***)* əʊz (US) oʊz
oesophageal ɪˌsɒf.əˈdʒiː.əl, iː-, ə-; ˌiː.sɒf- (US) ɪˌsɑː.fəˈ-; ˌiː.sɑː-
oesopha|gus iːˈsɒf.ə|.gəs, ɪ-, ə- (US) ɪˈsɑː.fə-, iː- **-guses** -gə.sɪz **-gi** -gaɪ, -dʒaɪ

Pronouncing the letters OEU

The vowel letter combination **oeu** (a chiefly British spelling) has two possible pronunciations: /uː/ and /ɜː/, e.g.:

manoeuvre /məˈnuː.vəʳ/ (US) /-vɚ/
oeuvre /ˈɜː.vrə/

It should be noted that more recent borrowings from French, like *oeuvre* above, usually have the latter pronunciation (see, for example, *cri de coeur, hors d'oeuvre*).

oestrogen ˈiː.strəʊ.dʒən, ˈes.trəʊ- (US) ˈes.trə-, -dʒen
oestrus ˈiː.strəs (US) ˈes.trəs **-es** -ɪz
oeuvre ˈɜː.vrə **-s** -z
of *strong form:* ɒv (US) ɑːv *weak form:* əv
Note: Weak form word. The strong form is usually found only in final position (e.g. "She's the one I'm fond of"), though it can occur initially in some forms such as "Of the ten who set out, only three returned". Elsewhere the weak form /əv/ is used.
O'Faolain, O'Faoláin əʊˈfeɪ.lən, -ˈfæl.ən (US) oʊ-
off ɒf (US) ɑːf
Offa ˈɒf.ə (US) ˈɑː.fə ˌ**Offa's** ˈ**Dyke**
offal ˈɒf.əl (US) ˈɑː.fəl
Offaly ˈɒf.əl.i (US) ˈɑː.fəl.i
off-bail ˌɒfˈbeɪl (US) ˌɑːf- **-s** -z
Note: Also ˈ-- when in contrast with **leg-bail**.
offbeat (*adj.*) ˌɒfˈbiːt (US) ˌɑːfˈbiːt
offbeat (*n.*) ˈɒf.biːt (US) ˈɑːf- **-s** -s
off-bye ˌɒfˈbaɪ (US) ˌɑːf- **-s** -z
Note: Also ˈ-- when in contrast with **leg-bye**.
off-chance ˈɒf.tʃɑːnts (US) ˈɑːf.tʃænts ˌ**on the** ˈ**off-**ˌ**chance**
off-colo(u)r ˌɒfˈkʌl.əʳ (US) ˌɑːfˈkʌl.ɚ
offcut ˈɒf.kʌt (US) ˈɑːf- **-s** -s
off-drive ˈɒf.draɪv (US) ˈɑːf- **-s** -z
Offenbach ˈɒf.ən.bɑːk, -əm- (US) ˈɑː.fən.bɑːk, ˈɔː-
offenc|e əˈfents **-es** -ɪz **-eless** -ləs, -lɪs
offend əˈfend **-s** -z **-ing** -ɪŋ **-ed** -ɪd **-er/s** -əʳ/z (US) -ɚ/z
offens|e əˈfents (US) ə-; *especially in sport:* ˈɑː.fents **-es** -ɪz **-eless** -ləs, -lɪs
offensive əˈfent.sɪv (US) ə-; *especially in sport:* ˈɑː-, ˈʌf.ent- **-s** -z **-ly** -li **-ness** -nəs, -nɪs
off|er ˈɒf|.əʳ (US) ˈɑː.f|ɚ **-ers** -əz (US) -ɚz **-ering/s** -ər.ɪŋ/z **-ered** -əd (US) -ɚd **-erer/s** -ər.əʳ/z (US) -ɚ.ɚ/z **-erable** -ər.ə.bl̩
offertor|y ˈɒf.ə.tər|.i (US) ˈɑː.fɚ.tɔːr-, ˈɔː- **-ies** -iz
off-hand ˌɒfˈhænd (US) ˌɑːf-
off-handed ˌɒfˈhæn.dɪd (US) ˌɑːf- **-ly** -li **-ness** -nəs, -nɪs
offic|e ˈɒf.ɪs (US) ˈɑː.fɪs **-es** -ɪz ˈ**office** ˌ**block**; ˈ**office** ˌ**hours**, ˌ**office** ˈ**hours**
office-bearer ˈɒf.ɪsˌbeə.rəʳ (US) ˈɑː.fɪsˌber.ɚ **-s** -z
office-boy ˈɒf.ɪsˌbɔɪ (US) ˈɑː.fɪs- **-s** -z
officer ˈɒf.ɪ.səʳ (US) ˈɑː.fɪ.sɚ **-s** -z
official əˈfɪʃ|.əl (US) ə-, oʊ- **-s** -z **-ly** -i **-ism** -ɪ.zəm **of**ˌ**ficial re**ˈ**ceiver**; **Of**ˌ**ficial** ˈ**Secrets** ˌ**Act**
officialdom əˈfɪʃ.əl.dəm (US) ə-
officialese əˌfɪʃ.əlˈiːz, əˈfɪʃ.əl.iːz (US) əˌfɪʃ.əlˈiːz
officiant əˈfɪʃ.i.ənt, ɒfˈɪʃ- (US) əˈfɪʃ.ənt, -i.ənt **-s** -s
offici|ate əˈfɪʃ.i|.eɪt **-ates** -eɪts **-ating** -eɪ.tɪŋ (US) -eɪ.t̬ɪŋ **-ated** -eɪ.tɪd (US) -eɪ.t̬ɪd
officinal ˌɒf.ɪˈsaɪ.nəl; ɒfˈɪs.ɪ.nəl (US) əˈfɪs.ɪ-; ˌɑː.fɪˈsaɪ-
officious əˈfɪʃ.əs **-ly** -li **-ness** -nəs, -nɪs
offing ˈɒf.ɪŋ (US) ˈɑː.fɪŋ **-s** -z
offish ˈɒf.ɪʃ (US) ˈɑː.fɪʃ
off-key ˌɒfˈkiː (US) ˌɑːf- *stress shift:* ˌoff-key ˈsinging
off-licenc|e ˈɒfˌlaɪ.sənts (US) ˌɑːfˈlaɪ- **-es** -ɪz
offline ˌɒfˈlaɪn (US) ˌɑːf- *stress shift:* ˌoff-line ˈprinter
off-load ˌɒfˈləʊd (US) ˈɑːf.loʊd **-s** -z **-ing** -ɪŋ **-ed** -ɪd
Offor ˈɒf.əʳ (US) ˈɑː.fɚ
off-peak ˌɒfˈpiːk (US) ˌɑːf- *stress shift:* ˌoff-peak ˈtravel
off-piste ˌɒfˈpiːst (US) ˌɑːf- *stress shift:* ˌoff-piste ˈskiing
off-print ˈɒf.prɪnt (US) ˈɑːf- **-s** -s
off-putting ˌɒfˈpʊt.ɪŋ (US) ˈɑːfˌpʊt̬- *stress shift, British only:* ˌoff-putting ˈhabit
offscreen ˌɒfˈskriːn (US) ˌɑːf- *stress shift:* ˌoffscreen ˈlife
off|set (*v.*) *compensate:* ˌɒf|ˈset (US) ˌɑːf- **-sets** -ˈsets **-setting** -ˈset.ɪŋ (US) -ˈset̬.ɪŋ
offse|t (*n. v.*) ˈɒf.se|t (US) ˈɑːf-, -ˈ- **-ts** -ts **-tting** -tɪŋ (US) -t̬ɪŋ
offshoot ˈɒf.ʃuːt (US) ˈɑːf- **-s** -s
offshore ˌɒfˈʃɔːʳ (US) ˌɑːfˈʃɔːr *stress shift:* ˌoffshore ˈsavings
offside ˌɒfˈsaɪd (US) ˌɑːf- *stress shift:* ˌoffside ˈrule
offspring ˈɒf.sprɪŋ (US) ˈɑːf- **-s** -z
offstage ˌɒfˈsteɪdʒ (US) ˌɑːf- *stress shift:* ˌoffstage ˈwhisper
off-street ˌɒfˈstriːt (US) ˌɑːf- *stress shift:* ˌoff-street ˈshops
off-the-cuff ˌɒf.ðəˈkʌf (US) ˌɑːf- *stress shift:* ˌoff-the-cuff ˈcomment
off-the-peg ˌɒf.ðəˈpeg (US) ˌɑːf- *stress shift:* ˌoff-the-peg ˈsuit
off-the-rack ˌɒf.ðəˈræk (US) ˌɑːf- *stress shift:* ˌoff-the-rack ˈsuit
off-the-record ˌɒf.ðəˈrek.ɔːd (US) ˌɑːf.ðəˈrek.ɔːrd, -ˈrek.ɚd *stress shift:* ˌoff-the-record ˈquote
off-the-shelf ˌɒf.ðəˈʃelf (US) ˌɑːf- *stress shift:* ˌoff-the-shelf ˈgoods
off-the-wall ˌɒf.ðəˈwɔːl (US) ˌɑːf.ðəˈwɔːl, -ˈwɔːl *stress shift:* ˌoff-the-wall ˈcomedy
off-white ˌɒfˈ*h*waɪt (US) ˌɑːf- *stress shift:* ˌoff-white ˈdrapes
Ofgas, OFGAS ˈɒf.gæs (US) ˈɑːf-
O'Flaherty əʊˈfleə.ti, -ˈflæ.hə-, -ˈflɑː.ə-, -ˈflɑː- (US) oʊˈfler.t̬i, -ˈflæ.hɚ-
O'Flynn əʊˈflɪn (US) oʊ-
Ofsted ˈɒf.sted (US) ˈɑːf-
oft ɒft (US) ɑːft
Oftel, OFTEL ˈɒf.tel (US) ˈɑːf-
often ˈɒf.ən, -tən (US) ˈɑː.fən, ˈɑːf.tən **-times** -taɪmz **as** ˌ**often as** ˈ**not**
often|er ˈɒf.ən|.əʳ, -tən-, ˈɒf.n|əʳ (US) ˈɑː.fən|.ɚ, ˈɑːf.tən-, ˈɑːf.n|ɚ **-est** -ɪst
ofttimes ˈɒf*t*.taɪmz (US) ˈɑːf*t*-
Ofwat, OFWAT ˈɒf.wɒt (US) ˈɑːf.wɑːt
Og ɒg (US) ɑːg, ɔːg
ogam ˈɒg.əm (US) ˈɑː.gəm
ogamic ɒgˈæm.ɪk (US) ɑːˈgæm-, ɔː-, oʊ-
Ogbomosho ˌɒg.bəˈməʊ.ʃəʊ (US) ˌɑːg.bəˈmoʊ.ʃoʊ
Ogden ˈɒg.dən (US) ˈɑːg-, ˈɔːg-
ogee ˈəʊ.dʒiː, -ˈ- (US) ˈoʊ.dʒiː, -ˈ- **-s** -z
ogham ˈɒg.əm (US) ˈɑː.gəm, ˈɔː-
oghamic ɒgˈæm.ɪk (US) ɑːˈgæm-, ɔː-, oʊ-
Ogilby ˈəʊ.gəl.bi (US) ˈoʊ-
Ogilvie, Ogilvy ˈəʊ.gəl.vi (US) ˈoʊ-
ogival əʊˈdʒaɪ.vəl, -ˈgaɪ- (US) oʊˈdʒaɪ-
ogive ˈəʊ.dʒaɪv, -gaɪv, -ˈ- (US) ˈoʊ.dʒaɪv, -gaɪv, -ˈ- **-s** -z

Pronouncing the letters OI, OY

The vowel letter digraphs **oi** and **oy** are similar in that their most common pronunciation is /ɔɪ/, e.g.:

boy	/bɔɪ/
boil	/bɔɪl/

When followed by an **r** in the spelling, **oi** is pronounced as /waɪə, Ⓤⓢ waɪɚ/ or /wɑː, Ⓤⓢ wɑːr/, e.g.:

choir	/kwaɪəʳ/	Ⓤⓢ /kwaɪɚ/
reservoir	/ˈrez.əv.wɑːʳ/	Ⓤⓢ /-ɚv.wɑːr/

In addition

There are other vowel sounds associated with the digraph **oi**. In the following examples, the pronunciation is due to the addition of the inflection -ing to words ending in **o**, e.g.:

/əʊ.ɪ Ⓤⓢ oʊ.ɪ/	going	/ˈgəʊ.ɪŋ/	Ⓤⓢ /ˈgoʊ-/
/uː.ɪ/	doing	/ˈduː.ɪŋ/	

In words borrowed from French, the pronunciation of **oi** may be /wɑː/, e.g.:

Bois	/bɔɪs, bwɑː/
foie gras	/ˌfwɑːˈgrɑː/

In weak syllables

The vowel digraph **oi** is realised with the vowel /ə/ in weak syllables, e.g.:

tortoise	/ˈtɔː.təs/	Ⓤⓢ /ˈtɔːr.t̬əs/
connoisseur	/ˌkɒn.əˈsɜːʳ/	Ⓤⓢ /ˌkɑː.nəˈsɝː/

ogl|e (O) ˈəʊ.gl̩ Ⓤⓢ ˈoʊ-, ˈɑː- **-es** -z **-ing** -ɪŋ, ˈəʊ.glɪŋ Ⓤⓢ ˈoʊ-, ˈɑː- **-ed** -d **-er/s** -əʳ/z Ⓤⓢ -ɚ/z, ˈəʊ.gləʳ/z Ⓤⓢ ˈoʊ.glɚ/z, ˈɑː-

Ogleby ˈəʊ.gl̩.bi Ⓤⓢ ˈoʊ-

Oglethorpe ˈəʊ.gl̩.θɔːp Ⓤⓢ ˈoʊ.gl̩.θɔːrp

Ogmore ˈɒg.mɔːʳ Ⓤⓢ ˈɑːg.mɔːr, ˈɔːg-

Ogoni əˈgəʊ.ni, ɒgˈ- Ⓤⓢ oʊˈ- **-land** -lænd

Ogpu ˈɒg.puː Ⓤⓢ ˈɑːg-, ˈɔːg-

O'Grady əʊˈgreɪ.di Ⓤⓢ oʊ-

og|re ˈəʊ.g|əʳ Ⓤⓢ ˈoʊ.g|ɚ **-res** -əz Ⓤⓢ -ɚz **-reish** -ᵊr.ɪʃ

ogress ˈəʊ.grəs, -rɪs Ⓤⓢ ˈoʊ- **-es** -ɪz

Ogwr ˈɒg.ʊəʳ Ⓤⓢ ˈɑː.gʊr

oh əʊ Ⓤⓢ oʊ

O'Hagan əʊˈheɪ.gᵊn Ⓤⓢ oʊ-

O'Halloran əʊˈhæl.ᵊr.ən Ⓤⓢ oʊ-

O'Hanlon əʊˈhæn.lən Ⓤⓢ oʊ-

O'Hara əʊˈhɑː.rə Ⓤⓢ oʊˈher.ə, -ˈhær-

O'Hare əʊˈheəʳ Ⓤⓢ oʊˈher

O'Hea əʊˈheɪ Ⓤⓢ oʊ-

Ohio əʊˈhaɪ.əʊ Ⓤⓢ oʊˈhaɪ.oʊ, ə- **-an/s** -ən/z

ohm (O) əʊm Ⓤⓢ oʊm **-s** -z

OHMS ˌəʊ.eɪtʃ.emˈes Ⓤⓢ ˌoʊ-

oho əʊˈhəʊ Ⓤⓢ oʊˈhoʊ

oick ɔɪk **-s** -s

-oid -ɔɪd

Note: Suffix. Does not normally change the stress pattern of the stem, e.g. **human** /ˈhjuː.mən/, **humanoid** /ˈhjuː.mə.nɔɪd/.

oik ɔɪk **-s** -s

oil ɔɪl **-s** -z **-ing** -ɪŋ **-ed** -d **-er/s** -əʳ/z Ⓤⓢ -ɚ/z **ˈoil ˌcan; ˈoil ˌfield; ˈoil ˌpaint; ˈoil ˌpainting; ˈoil ˌslick; ˈoil ˌwell; ˌpour ˌoil on ˌtroubled ˈwaters; ˌburn the ˌmidnight ˈoil**

oil|cloth ˈɔɪl|.klɒθ Ⓤⓢ -klɑːθ **-cloths** -klɒθs, -klɒðz Ⓤⓢ -klɑːθs, -klɑːðz

oil|man ˈɔɪl|.mæn Ⓤⓢ -mæn, -mən **-men** -men

oil-rig ˈɔɪl.rɪg **-s** -z

oilseed ˈɔɪl.siːd

oilskin ˈɔɪl.skɪn **-s** -z

oil|y ˈɔɪ.l|i **-ier** -i.əʳ Ⓤⓢ -i.ɚ **-iest** -i.ɪst, -i.əst **-iness** -ɪ.nəs, -ɪ.nɪs

oink ɔɪnk **-s** -s **-ing** -ɪŋ **-ed** -t

ointment ˈɔɪnt.mənt **-s** -s

Oisin ˈɔɪ.zɪn Ⓤⓢ ˈɑː.ʃən, əˈʃiːn

Oistrakh ˈɔɪ.strɑːk *as if Russian:* -strɑːx

Ojai ˈəʊ.haɪ Ⓤⓢ ˈoʊ-

Ojibwa(y) əʊˈdʒɪb.weɪ, ɒdʒˈɪb-, -wə Ⓤⓢ oʊˈdʒɪb.weɪ, -wə **-s** -z

OK əʊˈkeɪ Ⓤⓢ oʊ-, ə- **-s** -z **-ing** -ɪŋ **-ed** -d *stress shift:* ˌOK ˈperson

O'Kane əʊˈkeɪn Ⓤⓢ oʊ-

okapi əʊˈkɑː.pi Ⓤⓢ oʊ- **-s** -z

Okara ɒkˈɑː.rə Ⓤⓢ əˈkɑːr.ə

Okavango, Okovango ˌɒk.əˈvæŋ.gəʊ Ⓤⓢ ˌoʊ.kəˈvæŋ.goʊ

okay əʊˈkeɪ Ⓤⓢ oʊ-, ə- **-s** -z **-ing** -ɪŋ **-ed** -d *stress shift:* ˌokay ˈperson

Okeechobee ˌəʊ.kɪˈtʃəʊ.bi, -kiːˈ- Ⓤⓢ ˌoʊ.kɪˈtʃoʊ-, -kiːˈ-

O'Keef(f)e əʊˈkiːf Ⓤⓢ oʊ-

Okehampton ˌəʊkˈhæm*p*.tᵊn Ⓤⓢ ˈoʊkˌhæm*p*- *stress shift, British only:* ˌOkehampton ˈcentre

O'Kelly əʊˈkel.i Ⓤⓢ oʊ-

okeydoke ˌəʊ.kiˈdəʊk Ⓤⓢ ˌoʊ.kiˈdoʊk **-y** -i

Okhotsk əʊˈkɒtsk, ɒkˈɒtsk Ⓤⓢ oʊˈkɑːtsk

Okie ˈəʊ.ki Ⓤⓢ ˈoʊ- **-s** -z

Okinawa ˌɒk.ɪˈnɑː.wə, ˌəʊ.kɪˈ- Ⓤⓢ ˌoʊ.kəˈnɑː.wə, -kɪ-

okker, ocker ˈɒk.əʳ Ⓤⓢ ˈɑː.kɚ **-s** -z

Okla. *(abbrev. for* **Oklahoma***)* ˌəʊ.kləˈhəʊ.mə Ⓤⓢ ˌoʊ.kləˈhoʊ-

Oklahom|a ˌəʊ.kləˈhəʊ.m|ə Ⓤⓢ ˌoʊ.kləˈhoʊ- **-an/s** -ən/z

Okovango, Okavango ˌɒk.əˈvæŋ.gəʊ Ⓤⓢ ˌoʊ.kəˈvæŋ.goʊ

okra ˈɒk.rə, ˈəʊ.krə Ⓤⓢ ˈoʊ-

Okri ˈɒk.ri Ⓤⓢ ˈɑː.kri

Olaf, Olav ˈəʊ.læf, -ləf Ⓤⓢ ˈoʊ.ləf, -lɑːf

Olave ˈɒl.ɪv, -əv, -eɪv Ⓤⓢ ˈoʊ.ləf, -lɑːf, -ləv

Olcott ˈɒl.kət Ⓤⓢ ˈɑːl-

old əʊld Ⓤⓢ oʊld **-er** -əʳ Ⓤⓢ -ɚ **-est** -ɪst **-ness** -nəs, -nɪs **ˌOld ˈBailey; ˈold boy; ˌOld ˈEnglish; ˌOld ˌEnglish ˈsheepdog; ˌOld ˈFaithful; ˌOld ˈGlory; ˌold ˈguard; ˌold ˈhand; ˌold ˈhat; ˌold ˈlady; ˌold ˈmaid; ˌold ˈman; ˌold ˈmaster; ˈold ˌschool; ˌOld ˈTestament; as ˌold as the ˈhills**

old-age *(adj.)* ˈəʊldˌeɪdʒ Ⓤⓢ ˈoʊld- *(n.)* ˌəʊldˈeɪdʒ Ⓤⓢ ˌoʊld-

old-age pension ˌəʊld.eɪdʒˈpen.*t*ʃᵊn Ⓤⓢ ˌoʊld- **-s** -z **-er/s** -əʳ/z Ⓤⓢ -ɚ/z

Oldbuck ˈəʊl*d*.bʌk Ⓤⓢ ˈoʊl*d*-

Oldbury ˈəʊl*d*.bᵊr.i Ⓤⓢ ˈoʊl*d*ˌber-, -bɚ.i

Oldcastle ˈəʊl*d*ˌkɑː.sl̩ Ⓤⓢ ˈoʊl*d*ˌkæs.l̩

olden ˈəʊl.dᵊn Ⓤⓢ ˈoʊl-

Oldenburg ˈəʊl.dᵊn.bɜːg, -dᵊm- Ⓤⓢ ˈoʊl.dᵊn.bɝːg

olde worlde ˌəʊl.diˈwɜːl.di Ⓤⓢ ˌoʊl.diˈwɝːl-

Note: Joking imitation of spelling.

old-fashioned ˌəʊl*d*ˈfæʃ.ᵊnd Ⓤⓢ ˌoʊl*d*- *stress shift:* ˌold-fashioned ˈways

Oldfield ˈəʊl*d*.fiːld Ⓤⓢ ˈoʊl*d*-

old-fog(e)yish ˌəʊl*d*ˈfəʊ.gi.ɪʃ Ⓤⓢ ˌoʊl*d*ˈfoʊ-

Oldham ˈəʊl.dəm Ⓤⓢ ˈoʊl-

oldie ˈəʊl.di Ⓤⓢ ˈoʊl- **-s** -z

oldish ˈəʊl.dɪʃ Ⓤⓢ ˈoʊl-

Oldrey ˈəʊl.dri Ⓤⓢ ˈoʊl-

Oldsmobile® 'əʊldz.mə.biːl ⓤⓢ 'oʊldz-
oldster 'əʊld.stəʳ ⓤⓢ 'oʊld.stɚ **-s** -z
old-time ˌəʊld'taɪm ⓤⓢ ˌoʊld'- *stress shift:* ˌold-time 'dancing
old-timer ˌəʊld'taɪ.məʳ ⓤⓢ 'oʊldˌtaɪ.mɚ **-s** -z
old wives' tale ˌəʊld'waɪvzˌteɪl ⓤⓢ ˌoʊld-
old-world ˌəʊld'wɜːld ⓤⓢ ˌoʊld'wɝːld *stress shift:* ˌold-world 'values
olé əʊ'leɪ ⓤⓢ oʊ-
oleaginous ˌəʊ.li'ædʒ.ɪ.nəs, '-ə- ⓤⓢ ˌoʊ- **-ly** -li **-ness** -nəs, -nɪs
oleander (O) ˌəʊ.li'æn.dəʳ ⓤⓢ ˌoʊ.li'æn.dɚ, 'oʊ.liˌæn- **-s** -z
O'Leary əʊ'lɪə.ri ⓤⓢ oʊ'lɪr.i
oleaster ˌəʊ.li'æs.təʳ ⓤⓢ ˌoʊ.li'æs.tɚ **-s** -z
oleograph 'əʊ.li.əʊ.grɑːf, 'ɒl.i-, -græf ⓤⓢ 'oʊ.li.oʊ.græf, -ə- **-s** -s
O level 'əʊˌlev.əl ⓤⓢ 'oʊ- **-s** -z
olfactory ɒl'fæk.tər.i ⓤⓢ ɑːl-, oʊl-
Olga 'ɒl.gə ⓤⓢ 'ɑːl-, 'ɔːl-, 'oʊl-
Oliffe 'ɒl.ɪf ⓤⓢ 'ɑː.lɪf
oligarch 'ɒl.ɪ.gɑːk ⓤⓢ 'ɑː.lɪ.gɑːrk, 'oʊ- **-s** -s
oligarchal ˌɒl.ɪ'gɑː.kəl ⓤⓢ ˌɑː.lɪ'gɑːr-, ˌoʊ- *stress shift:* ˌoligarchal 'state
oligarchic ˌɒl.ɪ'gɑː.kɪk ⓤⓢ ˌɑː.lɪ'gɑːr-, ˌoʊ- *stress shift:* ˌoligarchic 'state
oligarch|y 'ɒl.ɪ.gɑː.k|i ⓤⓢ 'ɑː.lɪ.gɑːr-, 'oʊ- **-ies** -iz
Oligocene 'ɒl.ɪ.gəʊ.siːn; ɒl'ɪg.əʊ- ⓤⓢ 'ɑː.lɪ.goʊ-, 'oʊ-
oligopol|y ˌɒl.ɪ'gɒp.əl|.i ⓤⓢ ˌɑː.lɪ'gɑː.pəl-, ˌoʊ- **-ies** -iz
olio 'əʊ.li.əʊ ⓤⓢ 'oʊ.li.oʊ **-s** -z
Oliphant 'ɒl.ɪ.fənt, '-ə- ⓤⓢ 'ɑː.lɪ-
olivaceous ˌɒl.ɪ'veɪ.ʃəs ⓤⓢ ˌɑː.lɪ'-
olive (O) 'ɒl.ɪv; ⓤⓢ 'ɑː.lɪv **-s** -z **'olive ˌbranch; ˌolive 'green; ˌolive 'oil, 'olive ˌoil**
oliver (O) 'ɒl.ɪ.vəʳ, '-ə- ⓤⓢ 'ɑː.lɪ.vɚ **-s** -z
Oliverian ˌɒl.ɪ'vɪə.ri.ən, -ə'- ⓤⓢ ˌɑː.lɪ'ver.i-
Olivet 'ɒl.ɪ.vet, '-ə-, -vɪt, -vət ⓤⓢ 'ɑː.lɪ.vet, -lə-
Olivetti® ˌɒl.ɪ'vet.i, -ə'- ⓤⓢ ˌɑː.lə'veţ.i
Olivia ɒl'ɪv.i.ə, ə'lɪv-, əʊ- ⓤⓢ oʊ-, ə-
Olivier ə'lɪv.i.eɪ, ɒl'ɪv-, -ə ⓤⓢ oʊ'lɪv.i.eɪ
olivine 'ɒl.ɪ.viːn, '-ə-, ˌ--'- ⓤⓢ 'ɑː.lə.viːn **-s** -z
olla podrida ˌɒl.jə.pɒd'riː.də, -pə'driː- ⓤⓢ ˌɑː.lə.poʊ'-, -pə'- **-s** -z
Ollendorf 'ɒl.ən.dɔːf, -ɪn- ⓤⓢ 'ɑː.lən.dɔːrf
Ollerton 'ɒl.ə.tən ⓤⓢ 'ɑː.lɚ-
Olley, Ollie 'ɒl.i ⓤⓢ 'ɑː.li
Olliffe 'ɒl.ɪf ⓤⓢ 'ɑː.lɪf
Ollivant 'ɒl.ɪ.vənt, -vænt ⓤⓢ 'ɑː.lɪ-
Olmstead 'ɒm.sted ⓤⓢ 'oʊm-, 'ɑːm-, -stəd
Olney 'əʊl.ni, 'əʊ- ⓤⓢ 'oʊl-, 'oʊ-, 'ɑːl-
-olog|y -'ɒl.ə.dʒ|i ⓤⓢ -'ɑː.lə.dʒ|i **-ies** -iz
Note: Suffix. Normally takes primary stress as shown, e.g. **biology** /baɪ'ɒl.ə.dʒi ⓤⓢ -'ɑː.lə-/, **pharmacology** /ˌfɑː.mə'kɒl.ə.dʒi ⓤⓢ ˌfɑːr.mə'kɑː.lə-/.
oloroso ˌɒl.ə'rəʊ.səʊ, ˌəʊ.lə'-, -zəʊ ⓤⓢ ˌoʊ.loʊ'roʊ.soʊ, -lə'- **-s** -z
Olsen, Olson 'əʊl.sən ⓤⓢ 'oʊl-
Olver 'ɒl.vəʳ, 'əʊl- ⓤⓢ 'ɑː.lvɚ
Olwen 'ɒl.wen, -wɪn ⓤⓢ 'ɑːl-
Olympi|a əʊ'lɪm.pi|.ə ⓤⓢ oʊ-, ə- **-an** -ən
Olympiad əʊ'lɪm.pi.æd ⓤⓢ oʊ-, ə- **-s** -z
Olympic əʊ'lɪm.pɪk ⓤⓢ oʊ-, ə- **-s** -s **OˌIympic 'Games**
Olympus əʊ'lɪm.pəs ⓤⓢ oʊ-, ə-
Olynthus əʊ'lɪnt.θəs ⓤⓢ oʊ-, ə-
om (O) əʊm, ɒm ⓤⓢ oʊm
Omagh 'əʊ.mə, -mɑː ⓤⓢ 'oʊ-
Omaha 'əʊ.mə.hɑː ⓤⓢ 'oʊ-, -hɔː
O'Malley əʊ'mæl.i, -'meɪ.li ⓤⓢ oʊ-
Oman əʊ'mɑːn ⓤⓢ oʊ-
Omar 'əʊ.mɑːʳ ⓤⓢ 'oʊ.mɑːr
Omar Khayyám ˌəʊ.mɑː.kaɪ'æm, -'ɑːm ⓤⓢ ˌoʊ.mɑːr.kaɪ'jɑːm, -'æm
ombre 'ɒm.bəʳ ⓤⓢ 'ɑːm.bɚ
ombuds|man 'ɒm.bʊdz|.mən, -bʌdz-, -bədz-, -mæn ⓤⓢ 'ɑːm.bədz-, -bʌdz-; ɑːm'bʌdz- **-men** -mən, -men
Omdurman ˌɒm.dɜː'mɑːn, -də'-, -'mæn; 'ɒm.də.mən ⓤⓢ ˌɑːm.dʊr'mɑːn
O'Meara əʊ'mɑː.rə, -'mɪə- ⓤⓢ oʊ'mɪr.ə, -'mɑːr-
omega (O) 'əʊ.mɪ.gə, -meg.ə ⓤⓢ oʊ'meɪ.gə, -'meg.ə, -'miː.gə; 'oʊ.meg- **-s** -z
omelet, omelette 'ɒm.lət, -lɪt, -let ⓤⓢ 'ɑːm.lət, -lɪt; 'ɑː.mə- **-s** -s
omen 'əʊ.mən, -men ⓤⓢ 'oʊ- **-s** -z **-ed** -d
omer (O) 'əʊ.məʳ ⓤⓢ 'oʊ.mɚ **-s** -z
omertà ˌəʊ.mə'tɑː ⓤⓢ ˌoʊ.mer'tɑː
omicron əʊ'maɪ.krɒn, -krən; 'ɒm.ɪ- ⓤⓢ 'oʊ.mɪ.krɑːn, 'ɑː- **-s** -z
ominous 'ɒm.ɪ.nəs, 'əʊ.mɪ-, -mə- ⓤⓢ 'ɑː.mə- **-ly** -li **-ness** -nəs, -nɪs
omissible əʊ'mɪs.ɪ.bl̩, '-ə- ⓤⓢ oʊ-
omission əʊ'mɪʃ.ən ⓤⓢ oʊ- **-s** -z
o|mit əʊ|'mɪt ⓤⓢ oʊ- **-mits** -'mɪts **-mitting** -'mɪt.ɪŋ ⓤⓢ -'mɪţ.ɪŋ **-mitted** -'mɪt.ɪd ⓤⓢ -'mɪţ.ɪd
ommatidi|um ˌɒm.ə'tɪd.i|.əm ⓤⓢ ˌɑː.mə'- **-a** -ə **-al** -əl
omni- ɒm.nɪ-, -nə-, -ni-; ɒm'nɪ- ⓤⓢ ɑːm.nɪ-, -nə-, -ni-; ɑːm'nɪ-
Note: Prefix. Normally takes either primary or secondary stress on the first syllable, e.g. **omnibus** /'ɒm.nɪ.bəs ⓤⓢ 'ɑːm-/, **omnipresent** /ˌɒm.nɪ'pres.ənt ⓤⓢ ˌɑːm-/, or primary stress on the second syllable, e.g. **omnipotent** /ɒm'nɪp.ə.tənt ⓤⓢ ɑːm'nɪ.pə.ţənt/.
omnibus 'ɒm.nɪ.bəs, -nə-, -bʌs ⓤⓢ 'ɑːm- **-es** -ɪz
omnifarious ˌɒm.nɪ'feə.ri.əs ⓤⓢ ˌɑːm.nɪ'fer.i-
omnificent ɒm'nɪf.ɪ.sənt ⓤⓢ ɑːm-
omnipotence ɒm'nɪp.ə.tənts ⓤⓢ ɑːm'nɪp.ə.ţənts
omnipotent ɒm'nɪp.ə.tənt ⓤⓢ ɑːm'nɪp.ə.ţənt **-ly** -li
omnipresen|t ˌɒm.nɪ'prez.ən|t, -nə'- ⓤⓢ ˌɑːm.nɪ'- **-ce** -ts
omniscience ɒm'nɪs.i.ənts, -'nɪʃ-, -'nɪʃ.ənts ⓤⓢ ɑːm'nɪʃ.ənts
omniscient ɒm'nɪs.i.ənt, -'nɪʃ-, -'nɪʃ.ənt ⓤⓢ ɑːm'nɪʃ.ənt **-ly** -li
omnium (O) 'ɒm.ni.əm ⓤⓢ 'ɑːm- **-s** -z
omnium gatherum ˌɒm.ni.əm'gæð.ər.əm ⓤⓢ ˌɑːm- **-s** -z
omnivore 'ɒm.nɪ.vɔːʳ, -nə- ⓤⓢ 'ɑːm.nɪ.vɔːr **-s** -z
omnivorous ɒm'nɪv.ər.əs ⓤⓢ ɑːm- **-ly** -li
Omond 'əʊ.mənd ⓤⓢ 'oʊ-
omphalos 'ɒmp.fəl.ɒs ⓤⓢ 'ɑːmp.fəl.əs, -ɑːs
Omri 'ɒm.raɪ ⓤⓢ 'ɑːm-
Omsk ɒmsk ⓤⓢ ɔːmsk, ɑːmsk
on (*n. adj. adv. prep.*) ɒn ⓤⓢ ɑːn, ɔːn
onager 'ɒn.ə.gəʳ ⓤⓢ 'ɑː.nə.gɚ **-s** -z
Onan 'əʊ.næn, -nən ⓤⓢ 'oʊ-
onan|ism 'əʊ.nə.n|ɪ.zəm, -næn|.ɪ- ⓤⓢ 'oʊ- **-ist/s** -ɪst/s
onanistic ˌəʊ.nə'nɪs.tɪk, -næn'ɪst- ⓤⓢ ˌoʊ-
Onassis əʊ'næs.ɪs ⓤⓢ oʊ-, -'nɑː.sɪs
on-board (*adj.*) 'ɒn.bɔːd ⓤⓢ 'ɑːn.bɔːrd
once wʌnts **ˌonce and for 'all**
once-over 'wʌntsˌəʊ.vəʳ, ˌ-'-- ⓤⓢ 'wʌntsˌoʊ.vɚ
oncer 'wʌnt.səʳ ⓤⓢ -sɚ **-s** -z
onco- ɒŋ.kəʊ-; ɒŋ'kɒ- ⓤⓢ ɑːn.koʊ-, ɑːŋ-, -kə-; ɑːn'kɑː-, ɑːŋ-
Note: Prefix. Normally either takes primary or secondary stress on the first syllable, e.g. **oncogene** /'ɒŋ.kəʊ.dʒiːn ⓤⓢ 'ɑːŋ.kə-/, **oncogenic** /ˌɒŋ.kəʊ'dʒen.ɪk ⓤⓢ ˌɑːŋ.kə-/, or primary stress on the second syllable, e.g. **oncology** /ɒŋ'kɒl.ə.dʒi ⓤⓢ ɑːŋ'kɑː.lə-/.
oncogene 'ɒŋ.kəʊ.dʒiːn ⓤⓢ 'ɑːn.kə-, 'ɑːŋ- **-s** -z
oncogenic ˌɒŋ.kəʊ'dʒen.ɪk ⓤⓢ ˌɑːn.kə'-, ˌɑːŋ-
oncologic ˌɒŋ.kəʊ'lɒdʒ.ɪk ⓤⓢ ˌɑːn.kə'lɑː.dʒɪk, ˌɑːŋ-
oncological ˌɒŋ.kəʊ'lɒdʒ.ɪ.kəl ⓤⓢ ˌɑːn.kə'lɑː.dʒɪ-, ˌɑːŋ-
oncologist ɒŋ'kɒl.ə.dʒɪst ⓤⓢ ɑːn'kɑː.lə-, ɑːŋ- **-s** -s

Onset

In the analysis of syllable structure (and occasionally in other areas), the first part of a syllable.

Examples for English

In English the onset may be zero (when no consonant precedes the vowel in a syllable), one consonant, or two, or three, e.g.:

in	/ɪn/	spin	/spɪn/
pin	/pɪn/	spring	/sprɪŋ/

There are many restrictions on what clusters of consonants may occur in onsets: for example, if an English syllable has a three-consonant onset, the first consonant must be /s/ and the last one must be one of /l r j w/.

oncology ɒŋˈkɒl.ə.dʒi ⓤⓢ ɑːnˈkɑː.lə-, ɑːŋ-
oncoming ˈɒnˌkʌm.ɪŋ, ˈɒŋ- ⓤⓢ ˈɑːn-, ˈɔːn-
Ondaatje ɒnˈdɑː.tʃə ⓤⓢ ɑːnˈdɑː.tʃe
on-drive ˈɒn.draɪv ⓤⓢ ˈɑːn-, ˈɔːn- **-s** -z
one wʌn **-s** -z
O'Neal əʊˈniːl ⓤⓢ oʊ-
one-armed ˌwʌnˈɑːmd ⓤⓢ -ˈɑːrmd ˌ**one-armed** ˈ**bandit**
one-eyed ˌwʌnˈaɪd *stress shift:* ˌone-eyed ˈpirate
Onega ɒnˈeɪ.gə, əʊˈneɪ-, -ˈnjeg.ə; *old fashioned:* ˈəʊ.nɪ.gə ⓤⓢ oʊnˈjeg.ə, -neɪ-
Onegin ɒnˈjeɪ.gɪn ⓤⓢ ɑːn-
one-horse ˌwʌnˈhɔːs ⓤⓢ -ˈhɔːrs *stress shift, see compound:* ˌ**one-horse** ˈ**town**
O'Neil(l) əʊˈniːl ⓤⓢ oʊ-
one-legged ˌwʌnˈleg.ɪd, -ˈlegd *stress shift:* ˌone-legged ˈtable
one-liner ˌwʌnˈlaɪ.nəʳ ⓤⓢ -nɚ **-s** -z
one-man ˌwʌnˈmæn, ˌwʌm- ⓤⓢ ˌwʌn- *stress shift, see compound:* ˌ**one-man** ˈ**band**
oneness ˈwʌn.nəs, -nɪs
one-night stand ˌwʌn.naɪtˈstænd
one-off ˌwʌnˈɒf, ˈ-- ⓤⓢ ˈwʌn.ɑːf **-s** -s
one-parent family ˌwʌn.peə.rᵊntˈfæm.ᵊl.i, ˌwʌm-, -ɪ.li ⓤⓢ ˌwʌn.per.ᵊntˈ-, -pær-
one-piece ˈwʌn.piːs, ˈwʌm- ⓤⓢ ˈwʌn-
oner ˈwʌn.əʳ ⓤⓢ -ɚ **-s** -z
onerous ˈəʊ.nᵊr.əs, ˈɒn.ᵊr- ⓤⓢ ˈɑː.nɚ-, ˈoʊ- **-ly** -li **-ness** -nəs, -nɪs
oneself wʌnˈself ˌ**keep one**ˌ**self to one**ˈ**self**
onesided ˌwʌnˈsaɪ.dɪd **-ly** -li **-ness** -nəs, -nɪs *stress shift:* ˌonesided ˈargument
Onesimus əʊˈnes.ɪ.məs, -ˈniː.sɪ-, -sə- ⓤⓢ oʊ-
one-stop ˌwʌnˈstɒp ⓤⓢ -ˈstɑːp *stress shift:* ˌone-stop ˈshop
onetime ˈwʌn.taɪm
one-to-one ˌwʌn.təˈwʌn, -tuˈ- ⓤⓢ -t̬əˈ-
one-track mind ˌwʌn.trækˈmaɪnd **-s** -z
one-upmanship ˌwʌnˈʌp.mən.ʃɪp
one-way ˌwʌnˈweɪ *stress shift, see compound:* ˌ**one-way** ˈ**street**
ongoing ˈɒnˌgəʊ.ɪŋ, ˈɒŋ-, ˌ-ˈ-- ⓤⓢ ˈɑːnˌgoʊ- **-s** -z
Onians əˈnaɪənz, əʊ- ⓤⓢ oʊ-
Onich ˈəʊ.nɪk, -nɪx ⓤⓢ ˈoʊ-
onion ˈʌn.jən **-s** -z **-y** -i
Onions ˈʌn.jənz, əʊˈnaɪənz ⓤⓢ ˈʌn.jənz
online ˌɒnˈlaɪn ⓤⓢ ˌɑːn-, ˌɔːn- *stress shift:* ˌonline ˈchat
onlook|er ˈɒnˌlʊk|.əʳ ⓤⓢ ˈɑːnˌlʊk|.ɚ, ˈɔːn- **-ers** -əz ⓤⓢ -ɚz **-ing** -ɪŋ
only ˈəʊn.li ⓤⓢ ˈoʊn-
Ono ˈəʊ.nəʊ ⓤⓢ ˈoʊ.noʊ
onomasiological ˌɒn.əʊˌmeɪ.si.əˈlɒdʒ.ɪ.kᵊl, -zi- ⓤⓢ ˌɑː.noʊˌmeɪ.si.əˈlɑː.dʒɪ-, -nəˌ-
onomasiology ˌɒn.əʊˌmeɪ.siˈɒl.ə.dʒi, -ziˈ- ⓤⓢ ˌɑː.noʊˌmeɪ.siˈɑː.lə, -nəˌ-
onomastic ˌɒn.əʊˈmæs.tɪk ⓤⓢ ˌɑː.noʊˈ-, -nəˈ- **-s** -s
onomatopoe|ia ˌɒn.əʊˌmæt.əˈpiː|.ə ⓤⓢ ˌɑː.noʊˌmæt̬.oʊˈ-, -nəˌ- **-ias** -əz **-ic** -ɪk
onrush ˈɒn.rʌʃ ⓤⓢ ˈɑːn-, ˈɔːn- **-ing** -ɪŋ
onscreen ˌɒnˈskriːn ⓤⓢ ˌɑːn-, ˌɔːn- *stress shift* ˌonscreen ˈdaughter
onset ˈɒn.set ⓤⓢ ˈɑːn-, ˈɔːn- **-s** -s
onshore ˌɒnˈʃɔːʳ ⓤⓢ ˈɑːn.ʃɔːr, ˈɔːn- *stress shift, British only:* ˌonshore ˈwind
onside ˌɒnˈsaɪd ⓤⓢ ˈɑːn.saɪd, ˈɔːn- *stress shift, British only:* ˌonside ˈplayer
onslaught ˈɒn.slɔːt ⓤⓢ ˈɑːn.slɑːt, ˈɔːn-, -slɔːt **-s** -s
Onslow ˈɒnz.ləʊ ⓤⓢ ˈɑːnz.loʊ
onstage ˌɒnˈsteɪdʒ ⓤⓢ ˌɑːn-, ˌɔːn- *stress shift:* ˌonstage ˈson
onstream ˌɒnˈstriːm ⓤⓢ ˌɑːn-, ˌɔːn- *stress shift:* ˌonstream ˈoilfield
Ontario ɒnˈteə.ri.əʊ ⓤⓢ ɑːnˈter.i.oʊ
onto ˈɒn.tuː, -tə, -tu ⓤⓢ ˈɑːn.tuː, ˈɔːn-, -tə, -tu
Note: The pronunciation /ˈɒn.tuː ⓤⓢ ˈɑːn-/ is only rarely heard. The usual pronunciation is /ˈɒn.tə ⓤⓢ ɑːn.tə/ before consonants, e.g. "onto ships" /ˌɒn.təˈʃɪps ⓤⓢ ɑːn.təˈ-/, and /ˈɒn.tu ⓤⓢ ˈɑːn-/ before vowels, e.g. "onto aircraft" /ˌɒn.tuˈeə.krɑːft ⓤⓢ ˌɑːn.tuˈer.kræft/.
ontogenesis ˌɒn.təʊˈdʒen.ə.sɪs, ˈ-ɪ- ⓤⓢ ˌɑːn.toʊˈdʒen.ə-
ontogenetic ˌɒn.təʊ.dʒəˈnet.ɪk, -dʒɪˈ- ⓤⓢ ˌɑːn.toʊ.dʒəˈnet̬- **-ally** -ᵊl.i, -li
ontogeny ɒnˈtɒdʒ.ə.ni, ˈ-ɪ- ⓤⓢ ɑːnˈtɑː.dʒə-
ontologic ˌɒn.təˈlɒdʒ.ɪk ⓤⓢ ˌɑːn.toʊˈlɑː.dʒɪk **-al** -ᵊl **-ally** -ᵊl.i, -li
ontolog|y ɒnˈtɒl.ə.dʒ|i ⓤⓢ ɑːnˈtɑː.lə- **-ist/s** -ɪst/s
onus ˈəʊ.nəs ⓤⓢ ˈoʊ-
onward ˈɒn.wəd ⓤⓢ ˈɑːn.wɚd, ˈɔːn- **-s** -z
onyx ˈɒn.ɪks ⓤⓢ ˈɑː.nɪks **-es** -ɪz
oodles ˈuː.dl̩z
oof uːf
ooh uː
oolite ˈəʊ.əʊ.laɪt ⓤⓢ ˈoʊ.ə- **-s** -s
oolitic ˌəʊ.əʊˈlɪt.ɪk ⓤⓢ ˌoʊ.əˈlɪt̬-
oolog|y əʊˈɒl.ə.dʒ|i ⓤⓢ oʊˈɑː.lə- **-ist/s** -ɪst/s
Oolong ˈuː.lɒŋ, ˌ-ˈ- ⓤⓢ ˈuː.lɑːŋ, -lɔːŋ
oompah ˈʊm.pɑː, ˈuːm-
oomph ʊmpf, uːmpf
oops uːps, ʊps
oops-a-daisy ˌʊps.əˈdeɪ.zi, ˌuːps-, ˌwʊps-, ˈʊps.əˌdeɪ-, ˈuːps-, ˈwʊps-
ooz|e uːz **-es** -ɪz **-ing** -ɪŋ **-ed** -d
ooz|y ˈuː.z|i **-ier** -i.əʳ ⓤⓢ -i.ɚ **-iest** -i.ɪst, -i.əst **-ily** -ɪ.li, -ᵊl.i **-iness** -ɪ.nəs, -ɪ.nɪs
op ɒp ⓤⓢ ɑːp **-s** -s
opacity əʊˈpæs.ə.ti, -ɪ.ti ⓤⓢ oʊˈpæs.ə.t̬i
opal ˈəʊ.pᵊl ⓤⓢ ˈoʊ- **-s** -z
opalescen|t ˌəʊ.pᵊlˈes.ᵊn|t ⓤⓢ ˌoʊ- **-ce** -*ts*
opaline (*adj.*) ˈəʊ.pᵊl.aɪn ⓤⓢ ˈoʊ.pᵊl.iːn, -aɪn, -ɪn
opaline (*n.*) ˈəʊ.pᵊl.iːn, -aɪn ⓤⓢ ˈoʊ- **-s** -z

Pronouncing the letters OO

The most common pronunciation for the vowel digraph **oo** is /uː/, e.g.:

boom	/buːm/

The realisation /ʊ/ is also quite common, e.g.:

book	/bʊk/
stood	/stʊd/

When followed by an **r** in the spelling, **oo** is pronounced as either /ɔː (US) ɔːr/ or /ʊə (US) ʊr/ e.g

door	/dɔːʳ/	(US) /dɔːr/
moor	/mɔːʳ, mʊəʳ/	(US) /mʊr/

It should be noted that, for many speakers, the form /mʊəʳ/ has dropped out of use in favour of /mɔːʳ/.

In addition

There are other vowel sounds associated with the digraph **oo**, e.g.:

/ʌ/	blood	/blʌd/	
/əʊ (US) oʊ/	brooch	/brəʊtʃ/	(US) /broʊtʃ/

opaque əʊˈpeɪk (US) oʊ- **-ly** -li **-ness** -nəs, -nɪs
op art ˈɒpˌɑːt (US) ˈɑːpˌɑːrt
op. cit. ˌɒpˈsɪt (US) ˌɑːp-
op|e əʊp (US) oʊp **-es** -s **-ing** -ɪŋ **-ed** -t
OPEC, Opec ˈəʊ.pek (US) ˈoʊ-
Opel® ˈəʊ.pᵊl (US) ˈoʊ-
open ˈəʊ.pᵊn (US) ˈoʊ- **-er** -əʳ (US) -ɚ **-est** -ɪst (US) -əst **-s** -z **-ing** -ɪŋ, ˈəʊp.nɪŋ (US) ˈoʊp- **-ed** -d **ˌopen ˈbook; ˈopen ˌday; ˌopen ˈhouse; ˌopen ˈmarket; ˌopen ˈprison; ˌopen ˈsesame; ˌOpen Uniˈversity; ˌopen ˈverdict**
open-air *(adj.)* ˌəʊ.pᵊnˈeəʳ (US) ˌoʊ.pᵊnˈer *stress shift:* ˌopen-air ˈconcert *(n.)* **open air** ˌəʊ.pᵊnˈeəʳ (US) ˌoʊ.pᵊnˈer
open-and-shut ˌəʊ.pᵊn.ənd ˈʃʌt (US) ˌoʊ- *stress shift:* ˌopen-and-shut ˈcase
opencast ˈəʊ.pᵊn.kɑːst, -pᵊŋ- (US) ˈoʊ.pᵊn.kæst
open-ended ˌəʊ.pᵊnˈend.ɪd (US) ˌoʊ- *stress shift:* ˌopen-ended ˈverdict
opener ˈəʊ.pᵊn.əʳ (US) ˈoʊ.pᵊn.ɚ **-s** -z
open-eyed ˌəʊ.pᵊnˈaɪd (US) ˌoʊ- *stress shift:* ˌopen-eyed ˈonlooker
open-handed ˌəʊ.pᵊnˈhæn.dɪd, ˈəʊ.pᵊnˌhæn- (US) ˈoʊ.pᵊnˌhæn-, ˌoʊ.pᵊnˈhæn- **-ness** -nəs, -nɪs *stress shift, British only:* ˌopen-handed ˈbenefactor
open-heart ˌəʊ.pᵊnˈhɑːt (US) ˌoʊ.pᵊnˈhɑːrt *stress shift, see compound:* **ˌopen-heart ˈsurgery**
open-hearted ˌəʊ.pᵊnˈhɑː.tɪd, ˈəʊ.pᵊnˌhɑː- (US) ˈoʊ.pᵊnˌhɑːr.t̬ɪd, ˌoʊ.pᵊnˈhɑːr- **-ly** -li **-ness** -nəs, -nɪs *stress shift, British only:* ˌopen-hearted ˈperson
opening ˈəʊp.nɪŋ, ˈəʊ.pᵊn.ɪŋ (US) ˈoʊp.nɪŋ, ˈoʊ.pᵊn.ɪŋ **-s** -z
opening time ˈəʊp.nɪŋˌtaɪm, ˈəʊ.pᵊn.ɪŋˌ- (US) ˈoʊp.nɪŋˌ-, ˈoʊ.pᵊn.ɪŋˌ-
openly ˈəʊ.pᵊn.li (US) ˈoʊ-
open-minded ˌəʊ.pᵊnˈmaɪn.dɪd, -pᵊmˈ-, ˈəʊ.pᵊnˌmaɪn-, -pᵊmˌ- (US) ˌoʊ.pᵊnˈmaɪn-, ˈoʊ.pᵊnˌmaɪn- **-ly** -li **-ness** -nəs, -nɪs *stress shift, British only:* ˌopen-minded ˈperson
open-mouthed ˌəʊ.pᵊnˈmaʊðd, -pᵊmˈ-, ˈəʊ.pᵊnˌmaʊðd (US) ˈoʊ.pᵊnˌmaʊðd, -ˌmaʊθt, ˌ--ˈ- *stress shift, British only:* ˌopen-mouthed ˈchildren
openness ˈəʊ.pᵊn.nəs, -nɪs (US) ˈoʊ-
open-plan ˌəʊ.pᵊnˈplæn, -pᵊmˈ- (US) ˌoʊ.pᵊn- *stress shift:* ˌopen-plan ˈoffices
open sesame ˌəʊ.pᵊnˈses.ə.mi (US) ˌoʊ-
Openshaw ˈəʊ.pᵊn.ʃɔː (US) ˈoʊ.pᵊn.ʃɑː, -ʃɔː
open-work ˈəʊ.pᵊn.wɜːk (US) ˈoʊ.pᵊn.wɝːk
opera ˈɒp.ᵊr.ə, ˈɒp.rə (US) ˈɑː.pᵊr.ə, ˈɑː.prə **-s** -z **ˈopera ˌhouse**
operability ˌɒp.ᵊr.əˈbɪl.ɪ.ti, -ə.ti (US) ˌɑː.pᵊr.əˈbɪl.ə.t̬i, ˌɑː.prəˈ-
operab|le ˈɒp.ᵊr.ə.bl̩ (US) ˈɑː.pᵊr.ə-, ˈɑː.prə- **-ly** -li
opéra bouffe ˌɒp.ᵊr.əˈbuːf (US) ˌɑː.pᵊr-, ˌɑː.prəˈ-
opera buffa ˌɒp.ᵊr.əˈbuː.fə (US) ˌɑː.pᵊr.əˈ-, ˌɑː.prəˈ-
opéra comique ˌɒp.ᵊr.ə.kɒmˈiːk (US) ˌɑː.pᵊr.ə.kɑːˈmiːk, ˌɑː.prə-
operant ˈɒp.ᵊr.ᵊnt (US) ˈɑː.pᵊr- **-s** -s
oper|ate ˈɒp.ᵊr|.eɪt (US) ˈɑː.pᵊr- **-ates** -eɪts **-ating** -eɪ.tɪŋ (US) -eɪ.t̬ɪŋ **-ated** -eɪ.tɪd (US) -eɪ.t̬ɪd **-ator/s** -eɪ.təʳ/z (US) -eɪ.t̬ɚ/z **ˈoperating ˌsystem; ˈoperating ˌtable**
operatic ˌɒp.ᵊrˈæt.ɪk (US) ˌɑː.pəˈræt̬- **-s** -s **-ally** -ᵊl.i, -li
operation ˌɒp.ᵊrˈeɪ.ʃᵊn (US) ˌɑː.pəˈreɪ- **-s** -z
operational ˌɒp.ᵊrˈeɪ.ʃᵊn.ᵊl, -ˈeɪʃ.nᵊl (US) ˌɑː.pəˈreɪ.ʃᵊn.ᵊl, -ˈreɪʃ.nᵊl **-ly** -i
operative ˈɒp.ᵊr.ə.tɪv, -eɪ- (US) ˈɑː.pɚ.ə.t̬ɪv, -pə.reɪ- **-ly** -li **-ness** -nəs, -nɪs
operetta ˌɒp.ᵊrˈet.ə (US) ˌɑː.pəˈret̬- **-s** -z
operettist ˌɒp.ᵊrˈet.ɪst (US) ˌɑː.pəˈret̬- **-s** -s
Ophelia əʊˈfiː.li.ə, ɒfˈiː- (US) oʊˈfiːl.jə
ophicleide ˈɒf.ɪ.klaɪd (US) ˈɑː.fɪ- **-s** -z
ophidian ɒfˈɪd.i.ən, əʊˈfɪd- (US) oʊ-
Ophir ˈəʊ.fəʳ (US) ˈoʊ.fɚ
Ophiuchus ɒfˈjuː.kəs, ˌɒf.iˈuː- (US) ˌɑː.fiˈjuː.kəs, ˌoʊ-
ophthalmia ɒfˈθæl.mi.ə, ɒp- (US) ɑːf-, ɑːp-
ophthalmic ɒfˈθæl.mɪk, ɒp- (US) ɑːf-, ɑːp-
ophthalmo- ɒfˌθæl.məʊ-, ɒp- (US) ɑːfˌθæl.moʊ-, ɑːp-, -mə-
ophthalmolog|y ˌɒf.θælˈmɒl.ə.dʒ|i, ɒp- (US) ˌɑːf.θælˈmɑː.lə-, ˌɑːp- **-ist/s** -ɪst/s
ophthalmoscope ɒfˈθæl.mə.skəʊp, ɒp- (US) ɑːfˈθæl.mə.skoʊp, ɑːp- **-s** -s
ophthalmoscopy ˌɒf.θælˈmɒs.kə.pi, ɒp- (US) ˌɑːf.θælˈmɑː.skə-, ˌɑːp-
opiate ˈəʊ.pi.ət, -ɪt, -eɪt (US) ˈoʊ.pi.ɪt, -eɪt **-s** -s
opiated ˈəʊ.pi.eɪ.tɪd (US) ˈoʊ.pi.eɪ.t̬ɪd
Opie ˈəʊ.pi (US) ˈoʊ-
opin|e əʊˈpaɪn (US) oʊ- **-es** -z **-ing** -ɪŋ **-ed** -d
opinion əˈpɪn.jən (US) ə-, oʊ- **-s** -z **oˈpinion ˌpoll**
opinionated əˈpɪn.jə.neɪ.tɪd (US) -t̬ɪd, oʊ-
opium ˈəʊ.pi.əm (US) ˈoʊ- **ˈopium ˌden**
Oporto əʊˈpɔː.təʊ (US) oʊˈpɔːr.toʊ
opossum əˈpɒs.əm (US) -ˈpɑː.səm **-s** -z
Oppenheim ˈɒp.ᵊn.haɪm (US) ˈɑː.pᵊn- **-er** -əʳ (US) -ɚ
oppidan ˈɒp.ɪ.dᵊn (US) ˈɑː.pɪ- **-s** -z
opponent əˈpəʊ.nənt (US) -ˈpoʊ- **-s** -s

opportune ˈɒp.ə.tjuːn, -tʃuːn, ˌ--ˈ- US ˌɑː.pɚˈtuːn, -ˈtjuːn **-ly** -li **-ness** -nəs, -nɪs

opportun|ism ˌɒp.əˈtjuː.n|ɪ.zᵊm, -ˈtʃuː-, ˈɒp.ə.tjuː-, -tʃuː- US ˌɑː.pɚˈtuː-, -ˈtjuː- **-ist/s** -ɪst/s

opportunistic ˌɒp.ə.tjuːˈnɪs.tɪk, -tʃuːˈ- US ˌɑː.pɚ.tuːˈ-, -tjuːˈ- **-ally** -ᵊl.i, -li

opportunit|y ˌɒp.əˈtjuː.nə.t|i, -ˈtʃuː-, -nɪ- US ˌɑː.pɚˈtuː.nə.t̬|i, -ˈtjuː- **-ies** -iz

oppos|e əˈpəʊz US -ˈpoʊz **-es** -ɪz **-ing** -ɪŋ **-ed** -d **-er/s** -əʳ/z US -ɚ/z **-able** -ə.bl̩

opposite ˈɒp.ə.zɪt, -sɪt US ˈɑː.pə- **-s** -s **-ly** -li **-ness** -nəs, -nɪs ˌ**opposite** ˈ**number**

opposition ˌɒp.əˈzɪʃ.ᵊn US ˌɑː.pəˈ- **-s** -z

oppress əˈpres **-es** -ɪz **-ing** -ɪŋ **-ed** -t

oppression əˈpreʃ.ᵊn **-s** -z

oppressive əˈpres.ɪv **-ly** -li **-ness** -nəs, -nɪs

oppressor əˈpres.əʳ US -ɚ **-s** -z

opprobrious əˈprəʊ.bri.əs US -ˈproʊ- **-ly** -li **-ness** -nəs, -nɪs

opprobrium əˈprəʊ.bri.əm US -ˈproʊ-

oppugn əˈpjuːn **-s** -z **-ing** -ɪŋ **-ed** -d **-er/s** -əʳ/z US -ɚ/z

Oprah ˈəʊ.prə US ˈoʊ-

Opren® ˈɒp.rᵊn, -ren US ˈɑː.prᵊn, -pren

opt ɒpt US ɑːpt **-s** -s **-ing** -ɪŋ **-ed** -ɪd

optative ˈɒp.tə.tɪv; ɒpˈteɪ- US ˈɑːp.tə.t̬ɪv **-s** -z

optic ˈɒp.tɪk US ˈɑːp- **-s** -s

optical ˈɒp.tɪ.kᵊl US ˈɑːp- **-ly** -i ˌ**optical** ˈ**fibre**; ˌ**optical il**ˈ**lusion**

optician ɒpˈtɪʃ.ᵊn US ɑːp- **-s** -z

optimal ˈɒp.tɪ.mᵊl US ˈɑːp- **-ly** -i

optime ˈɒp.tɪ.meɪ US ˈɑːp- **-s** -z

optim|ism ˈɒp.tɪ.m|ɪ.zᵊm, -tə- US ˈɑːp.tə- **-ist/s** -ɪst/s

optimistic ˌɒp.tɪˈmɪs.tɪk, -təˈ- US ˌɑːp.təˈ- **-al** -ᵊl **-ally** -ᵊl.i, -li

optimization ˌɒp.tɪ.maɪˈzeɪ.ʃᵊn, -tə-, -mɪ- US ˌɑːp.tə.mɪˈzeɪ- **-s** -z

optimiz|e, -is|e ˈɒp.tɪ.maɪz, -tə- US ˈɑːp.tə- **-es** -ɪz **-ing** -ɪŋ **-ed** -d

optim|um ˈɒp.tɪ.m|əm, -tə- US ˈɑːp.tə- **-ums** -əmz **-a** -ə

option ˈɒp.ʃᵊn US ˈɑːp- **-s** -z **-ing** -ɪŋ **-ed** -d

optional ˈɒp.ʃᵊn.ᵊl US ˈɑːp.ʃᵊn.ᵊl **-ly** -i

optometric ˌɒp.təʊˈmet.rɪk US ˌɑːp.təˈmet- **-s** -s

optometrist ɒpˈtɒm.ə.trɪst, ˈ-ɪ- US ɑːpˈtɑː.mə- **-s** -s

optometry ɒpˈtɒm.ɪ.tri, ˈ-ə- US ɑːpˈtɑː.mə-

Optrex® ˈɒp.treks US ˈɑːp-

opulence ˈɒp.jə.lənts, -jʊ- US ˈɑːp-

opulent ˈɒp.jə.lənt, -jʊ- US ˈɑːp- **-ly** -li

opus ˈəʊ.pəs, ˈɒp.əs US ˈoʊ.pəs **-es** -ɪz **opera** ˈɒp.ᵊr.ə US ˈoʊ.pɚ.ə, ˈɑː-, ˈ-prə

opuscule ɒpˈʌs.kjuːl, əʊˈpʌs- US oʊˈpʌs.kjuːl **-s** -z

or (*n.*) ɔːʳ US ɔːr

or (*conj.*) *normal form:* ɔːʳ US ɔːr *weak form:* əʳ US ɚ

Note: Occasional weak form word. The weak form /əʳ US ɚ/ is used in phrases such as "two or three pounds" /ˌtuː.əˌθriːˈpaʊndz US -ɚˌ-/.

orach|(e) ˈɒr.ɪtʃ US ˈɔːr.ətʃ **-es** -ɪz

oracle ˈɒr.ə.kl̩, ˈ-ɪ- US ˈɔːr.ə- **-s** -z

oracular ɒrˈæk.jə.ləʳ, ɔːˈræk-, ə-, -jʊ- US ɔːˈræk.juː.lɚ, ə-, -jə- **-ly** -li **-ness** -nəs, -nɪs

oracy ˈɔː.rə.si US ˈɔːr.ə-

Oradea ɒrˈɑː.di.ə US ɔːˈrɑː.djɑː

oral ˈɔː.rᵊl US ˈɔːr.əl **-s** -z **-ly** -i ˌ**oral** ˈ**sex**

Oran ɔːˈrɑːn, ə-, ɒrˈɑːn, -ˈæn US oʊˈrɑːn, -ˈræn

orang|e (O) ˈɒr.ɪndʒ, -əndʒ US ˈɔːr.ɪndʒ **-es** -ɪz ˌ**Orange** ˈ**Free** ˌ**State**; ˈ**orange** ˌ**juice**

orangeade ˌɒr.ɪndʒˈeɪd, -əndʒˈ- US ˌɔːr.ɪndʒˈ-

orange-blossom ˈɒr.ɪndʒˌblɒs.əm, -əndʒˌ- US ˈɔːr.ɪndʒˌblɑː.səm **-s** -z

Orange|man ˈɒr.ɪndʒ|.mən, -əndʒ-, -mæn US ˈɔːr.ɪndʒ **-men** -mən, -men

oranger|y ˈɒr.ɪn.dʒᵊr|.i, -ən-, ˈ-ɪndʒ.r|i US ˈɔːr.ɪndʒ.ri **-ies** -iz

orangoutan, orangutan, orangutang ɔːˌræŋ.uːˈtæn, ɒrˌæŋ-, əˌræŋ-, -əˈ-, -juːˈ-, -ˈtɑːn, -ˈtæŋ, ɔːˈræŋ.uː.tæn, ɒrˈæŋ-, əˈræŋ-, ˈ-ə-, ˈ-juː-, -tɑːn, -tæŋ US ɔːˈræŋ.ə.tæn, ə-, oʊ-, -tæŋ **-s** -s

ora|te ɔːˈreɪ|t, ɒrˈeɪ|t, əˈreɪ|t US ˈɔːr.eɪ|t; ɔːˈreɪ|t **-tes** -ts **-ting** -tɪŋ US -t̬ɪŋ **-ted** -tɪd US -t̬ɪd

oration əˈreɪ.ʃᵊn, ɒr- US ɔː- **-s** -z

orator ˈɒr.ə.təʳ US ˈɔːr.ə.t̬ɚ **-s** -z

oratorical ˌɒr.əˈtɒr.ɪ.kᵊl US ˌɔːr.əˈtɔːr- **-ly** -i

oratorio ˌɒr.əˈtɔː.ri.əʊ US ˌɔːr.əˈtɔːr.i.oʊ **-s** -z

orator|y (O) ˈɒr.ə.tᵊr|.i US ˈɔːr.ə.tɔːr- **-ies** -iz

orb ɔːb US ɔːrb **-s** -z **-ing** -ɪŋ **-ed** -d

Orbach ˈɔː.bæk US ˈɔːr-

orbed ɔːbd US ɔːrbd *in poetry generally:* ˈɔː.bɪd US ˈɔːr.bɪd

orbicular ɔːˈbɪk.jə.ləʳ, -jʊ- US ɔːrˈbɪk.juː.lɚ, -jə- **-ly** -li

Orbison ˈɔː.bɪ.sᵊn, -bə- US ˈɔːr-

or|bit ˈɔː|.bɪt US ˈɔːr- **-bits** -bɪts **-biting** -bɪ.tɪŋ US -bɪ.t̬ɪŋ **-bited** -bɪ.tɪd US -bɪ.t̬ɪd **-bital** -bɪ.tᵊl US -t̬ᵊl

orc ɔːk US ɔːrk **-s** -s

Orcadian ɔːˈkeɪ.di.ən US ɔːr- **-s** -z

orchard (O) ˈɔː.tʃəd US ˈɔːr.tʃɚd **-s** -z

Orchardson ˈɔː.tʃəd.sᵊn US ˈɔːr.tʃɚd-

Orchehill ˈɔː.tʃɪl US ˈɔːr-

orchestra ˈɔː.kɪ.strə, -kə-, -kes.trə US ˈɔːr.kɪ.strə, -kes.trə **-s** -z

orchestral ɔːˈkes.trᵊl US ɔːr-

orchest|rate ˈɔː.kɪ.st|reɪt, -kə-, -kes.t|reɪt US ˈɔːr.kɪ.st|reɪt, -kes.t|reɪt **-rates** -reɪts **-rating** -reɪ.tɪŋ US -reɪ.t̬ɪŋ **-rated** -reɪ.tɪd US -reɪ.t̬ɪd

orchestration ˌɔː.kɪˈstreɪ.ʃᵊn, -kəˈ-, -kesˈtreɪ- US ˌɔːr.kɪˈstreɪ-, -kesˈtreɪ- **-s** -z

orchestrion ɔːˈkes.tri.ən US ɔːr- **-s** -z

orchid ˈɔː.kɪd US ˈɔːr- **-s** -z

orchidaceous ˌɔː.kɪˈdeɪ.ʃəs US ˌɔːr-

orchil ˈɔː.tʃɪl, -kɪl US ˈɔːr-

orchis ˈɔː.kɪs US ˈɔːr- **-es** -ɪz

Orczy ˈɔːk.si, ˈɔːt- US ˈɔːrk-, ˈɔːrt-

Ord ɔːd US ɔːrd

ordain ɔːˈdeɪn US ɔːr- **-s** -z **-ing** -ɪŋ **-ed** -d **-er/s** -əʳ/z US -ɚ/z

Orde ɔːd US ɔːrd

ordeal ɔːˈdiːl, ˈ-- US ɔːrˈdiːl, ˈ-- **-s** -z

ord|er ˈɔː.d|əʳ US ˈɔːr.d|ɚ **-ers** -əz US -ɚz **-ering** -ᵊr.ɪŋ **-ered** -əd US -ɚd **-erless** -ᵊl.əs, -ɪs US -ɚ.ləs, -lɪs

orderl|y ˈɔː.dᵊl|.i US ˈɔːr.dɚ.l|i **-ies** -iz **-iness** -ɪ.nəs, -ɪ.nɪs

ordinaire ˌɔː.dɪˈneəʳ, -dᵊn.eəʳ, ˈ--- US ˌɔːr.dɪˈner

ordinal ˈɔː.dɪ.nᵊl, -dᵊn.ᵊl US ˈɔːr.dᵊn-, ˈɔːrd.nᵊl **-s** -z ˌ**ordinal** ˈ**number**

ordinanc|e ˈɔː.dɪ.nənts, -dᵊn.ənts US ˈɔːr.dᵊn-, ˈɔːrd.nənts **-es** -ɪz

ordinand ˈɔː.dɪ.nænd, -dᵊn.ænd, ˌ--ˈ- US ˈɔːr.dᵊn.ænd **-s** -z

ordinarily ˈɔː.dᵊn.ᵊr.ᵊl.i, -dɪ.nᵊr-, -ɪ.li; ˌɔː.dᵊnˈer.ɪ- US ˈɔːr.dᵊn.er.ᵊl.i, ˌɔːr.dᵊnˈer-

ordinariness ˈɔː.dᵊn.ᵊr.ɪ.nəs, -dɪ.nᵊr-, -nɪs US ˌɔːr.dᵊnˈer-

ordinar|y ˈɔː.dᵊn.ᵊr|.i, -dɪ.nᵊr- US ˈɔːr.dᵊn.er- **-ies** -iz

ordinate ˈɔː.dᵊn.ət, -dɪ.nət, -nɪt US ˈɔːr.dᵊn.ɪt, -eɪt **-s** -s

ordination ˌɔː.dɪˈneɪ.ʃᵊn, -dᵊnˈeɪ- US ˌɔːr.dᵊnˈeɪ- **-s** -z

ordnance ˈɔːd.nənts US ˈɔːrd- ˌ**Ordnance** ˈ**Survey**

ordure ˈɔː.djʊəʳ, -djəʳ US ˈɔːr.dʒɚ, -djʊr

Ore. (*abbrev. for* **Oregon**) ˈɒr.ɪ.gən, ˈ-ə-, -gɒn US ˈɔːr.ɪ.gən, -gɑːn

ore (O) ɔːʳ US ɔːr **-s** -z

öre, ore ˈɜː.rə US ˈɝː.ə

oread ˈɔː.ri.æd US ˈɔːr.i- **-s** -z

Örebro ˈɜː.rə.bruː US ˈɝː.ə-

O'Regan əʊˈriː.gən US oʊ-

oregano ˌɒr.ɪˈgɑː.nəʊ, -əˈ- US ɔːˈreg.ə.noʊ, ə-

Oregon ˈɒr.ɪ.gən, ˈ-ə-, -gɒn US ˈɔːr.ɪ.gən, -gɑːn
O'Reilly əʊˈraɪ.li US oʊ-
Oreo® ˈɔː.ri.əʊ US ˈɔːr.i.oʊ **-s** -z
Oresteia ˌɒr.ɪˈstaɪə, ˌɔː.rɪˈ-, -rəˈ-, -ˈsteɪə US ˌɔːr.esˈtiː.ə, -əˈstiː-
Orestes ɒrˈes.tiːz, ɔːˈres-, ə- US ɔː-
orfe ɔːf US ɔːrf
Orfeo ˈɔː.fi.əʊ *as if Italian:* ɔːˈfeɪ.əʊ US ˈɔːr.fi.oʊ, -feɪ-
Orff ɔːf US ɔːrf
Orford ˈɔː.fəd US ˈɔːr.fɚd
organ ˈɔː.gən US ˈɔːr- **-s** -z
organd|y, -|ie ˈɔː.gᵊn.d|i, ɔːˈgæn- US ˈɔːr.gən- **-ies** -iz
organelle ˌɔː.gᵊnˈel US ˌɔːr- **-s** -z
organ-grinder ˈɔː.gᵊnˌgraɪn.dəʳ, -gᵊŋˌ- US ˈɔːr.gᵊnˌgraɪn.dɚ **-s** -z
organic ɔːˈgæn.ɪk US ɔːr- **-s** -s **-al** -ᵊl **-ally** -ᵊl.i, -li
organism ˈɔː.gᵊn.ɪ.zᵊm US ˈɔːr- **-s** -z
organist ˈɔː.gᵊn.ɪst US ˈɔːr- **-s** -s
organizability, -isa- ˌɔː.gᵊnˌaɪ.zəˈbɪl.ə.ti, -ɪ.ti US ˌɔːr.gᵊnˌaɪ.zəˈbɪl.ə.t̬i
organization, -isa- ˌɔː.gᵊn.aɪˈzeɪ.ʃᵊn, -ɪˈ- US ˌɔːr.gᵊn.ɪˈ- **-s** -z
organizational, -isa- ˌɔː.gᵊn.aɪˈzeɪ.ʃᵊn.ᵊl, -ɪˈ- US ˌɔːr.gᵊn.ɪˈ- **-ly** -i
organiz|e, -is|e ˈɔː.gᵊn.aɪz US ˈɔːr- **-es** -ɪz **-ing** -ɪŋ **-ed** -d **-er/s** -əʳ/z US -ɚ/z **-able** -ə.bl̩
organ|on ˈɔː.gə.n|ɒn US ˈɔːr.gə.n|ɑːn **-ons** -ɒnz US -ɑːnz **-a** -ə
organophosphate ɔːˌgæn.əʊˈfɒs.feɪt, -fɪt, -fət; ˌɔːr.gᵊn.əʊ- US ɔːrˌgæn.oʊˈfɑːs.feɪt, -əˈ-; ˌɔːr.gᵊn.oʊ- **-s** -s
organum ˈɔː.gə.nəm US ˈɔːr- **-s** -z
organza ɔːˈgæn.zə US ɔːr-
orgasm ˈɔː.gæz.ᵊm US ˈɔːr- **-s** -z
orgasmic ɔːˈgæz.mɪk US ɔːr- **-ally** -ᵊl.i, -li
orgiastic ˌɔː.dʒiˈæs.tɪk US ˌɔːr- **-ally** -ᵊl.i, -li
org|y ˈɔː.dʒ|i US ˈɔːr- **-ies** -iz
Oriana ˌɒr.iˈɑː.nə, ˌɔː.riˈ- US ˌɔːr.iˈæn.ə
oriel (O) ˈɔː.ri.əl US ˈɔːr.i- **-s** -z
orient (O) *(n. adj.)* ˈɔː.ri.ənt, ˈɒr.i- US ˈɔːr.i- ˌ**Orient Ex'press**
ori|ent *(v.)* ˈɔː.ri|.ent, ˈɒr.i- US ˈɔːr.i- **-ents** -ents **-enting** -en.tɪŋ US -en.t̬ɪŋ **-ented** -en.tɪd US -en.t̬ɪd
oriental (O) ˌɔː.riˈen.tᵊl, ˌɒr.iˈ- US ˌɔːr.iˈ- **-s** -z
oriental|ism ˌɔː.riˈen.tᵊl|.ɪ.zᵊm, ˌɒr.iˈ- US ˌɔːr.iˈen.t̬ᵊl- **-ist/s** -ɪst/s
orientaliz|e, -is|e ˌɔː.riˈen.tᵊl.aɪz, ˌɒr.iˈ- US ˌɔːr.iˈen.t̬ᵊl- **-es** -ɪz **-ing** -ɪŋ **-ed** -d
orien|tate ˈɔː.ri.ən|.teɪt, ˈɒr.i-, -en- US ˈɔːr.i.en-, ˌɔːr.iˈen- **-tates** -teɪts **-tating** -teɪ.tɪŋ US -teɪ.t̬ɪŋ **-tated** -teɪ.tɪd US -teɪ.t̬ɪd
orientation ˌɔː.ri.enˈteɪ.ʃᵊn, ˌɒr.i- US ˌɔːr.i.enˈ- **-s** -z
orienteer ˌɔː.ri.ənˈtɪəʳ, ˌɒr.i-, -enˈ- US ˌɔːr.i.enˈtɪr **-s** -z
orienteering ˌɔː.ri.ənˈtɪə.rɪŋ, ˌɒr.i-, -enˈ- US ˌɔːr.i.enˈtɪr.ɪŋ
orific|e ˈɒr.ɪ.fɪs, ˈ-ə- US ˈɔːr.ə- **-es** -ɪz
oriflamme ˈɒr.ɪ.flæm, ˈ-ə- US ˈɔːr.ɪ- **-s** -z
origami ˌɒr.ɪˈgɑː.mi, -ˈgæm.i US ˌɔːr.ɪˈgɑː.mi
Origen ˈɒr.ɪ.dʒen, ˈ-ə- US ˈɔːr.ɪ.dʒən, -dʒen
origin ˈɒr.ɪ.dʒɪn, ˈ-ə-, -dʒən US ˈɔːr.ə.dʒɪn **-s** -z
original əˈrɪdʒ.ᵊn.ᵊl, ɒrˈɪdʒ-, -ɪ.nᵊl US əˈrɪdʒ.ɪ- **-s** -z **-ness** -nəs, -nɪs **oˌriginal 'sin**
originalit|y əˌrɪdʒ.ᵊnˈæl.ə.t|i, ɒrˌɪdʒ-, -ɪˈnæl-, -ɪ.t|i US əˌrɪdʒ.ɪˈnæl.ə.t̬|i **-ies** -iz
originally əˈrɪdʒ.ᵊn.ᵊl.i, ɒrˈɪdʒ-, -ɪ.nᵊl- US əˈrɪdʒ.ɪ-
origi|nate əˈrɪdʒ.ᵊn|.eɪt, ɒrˈɪdʒ-, -ɪ.n|eɪt US əˈrɪdʒ.ɪ- **-nates** -neɪts **-nating** -neɪ.tɪŋ US -neɪ.t̬ɪŋ **-nated** -neɪ.tɪd US -neɪ.t̬ɪd **-nator/s** -neɪ.təʳ/z US -neɪ.t̬ɚ/z **-native** -neɪ.tɪv US -neɪ.t̬ɪv
origination əˌrɪdʒ.ᵊnˈeɪ.ʃᵊn, ɒrˌɪdʒ-, -ɪˈneɪ- US əˌrɪdʒ.ɪˈ-
Orinoco ˌɒr.ɪˈnəʊ.kəʊ, -əˈ- US ˌɔːr.əˈnoʊ.koʊ
oriole ˈɔː.ri.əʊl US ˈɔːr.i.oʊl **-s** -z
Orion əˈraɪən, ɒrˈaɪən-, ɔːˈraɪən US oʊ-, ə-
O'Riordan əʊˈrɪə.dᵊn, -ˈraɪə- US oʊˈrɪr-
orison ˈɒr.ɪ.zᵊn, -ə- US ˈɔːr.ɪ.zᵊn, -sᵊn **-s** -z
Orissa ɒrˈɪs.ə, ɔːˈrɪs-, ə- US oʊ-, ɔː-
Oriya ɒrˈiː.ə US ɔːˈriː.ə
ork ɔːk US ɔːrk **-s** -s
Orkney ˈɔːk.ni US ˈɔːrk- **-s** -z
Orlan® ˈɔː.lᵊn, -læn US ˈɔːr.lɑːn
Orlando ɔːˈlæn.dəʊ US ɔːrˈlæn.doʊ
Orléans *in France:* ɔːˈlɪənz, ˈ-- *as if French:* ˌɔː.leɪˈɑ̃ːŋ US -ˈliː.ənz *as if French:* ˌɔːr.leɪˈɑ̃ːn
Orleans *in US:* ˈɔː.li.ənz, ˈ-lɪənz, ˈ-lənz; ɔːˈliːnz US ˈɔːr.li.ənz, ˈ-lənz; ɔːrˈliːnz
Orlon® ˈɔː.lɒn US ˈɔːr.lɑːn
Orly ˈɔː.li US ˈɔːr-
Orm(e) ɔːm US ɔːrm
ormer ˈɔː.məʳ US ˈɔːr.mɚ **-s** -z
Ormes ɔːmz US ɔːrmz
Ormiston ˈɔː.mɪ.stᵊn US ˈɔːr-
ormolu ˈɔː.mə.luː, -ljuː, ˌ--ˈ- US ˈɔːr.mə.luː
Ormond(e) ˈɔː.mənd US ˈɔːr-
Ormsby ˈɔːmz.bi US ˈɔːrmz-
Ormulum ˈɔː.mjə.ləm, -mjʊ- US ˈɔːr.mjuː-, -mjə-
ornament *(n.)* ˈɔː.nə.mənt US ˈɔːr- **-s** -s
orna|ment ˈɔː.nə|.ment US ˈɔːr- **-ments** -ments **-menting** -men.tɪŋ US -men.t̬ɪŋ **-mented** -men.tɪd US -men.t̬ɪd
ornamental ˌɔː.nəˈmen.tᵊl US ˌɔːr.nəˈmen.t̬ᵊl **-ly** -i
ornamentation ˌɔː.nə.menˈteɪ.ʃᵊn US ˌɔːr- **-s** -z
ornate ɔːˈneɪt US ɔːr- **-ly** -li **-ness** -nəs, -nɪs
ornery ˈɔː.nᵊr.i US ˈɔːr.nɚ-
ornithologic|al ˌɔː.nɪ.θəˈlɒdʒ.ɪ.k|ᵊl, -θᵊlˈɒdʒ-, -nə- US ˌɔːr.nə.θəˈlɑː.dʒɪ- **-ally** -ᵊl.i, -li
ornitholog|y ˌɔː.nɪˈθɒl.ə.dʒ|i, -nəˈ- US ˌɔːr.nəˈθɑː.lə- **-ist/s** -ɪst/s
orographic ˌɒr.əʊˈgræf.ɪk, ˌɔː.rəʊˈ- US ˌɔːr.oʊˈ- **-al** -ᵊl
orography ɒrˈɒg.rə.fi, ɔːˈrɒg- US ɔːˈrɑː.grə-
orological ˌɒr.əˈlɒdʒ.ɪ.kᵊl, ˌɔː.rəˈ- US ˌɔːr.əˈlɑː.dʒɪ-
orology ɒrˈɒl.ə.dʒi, ɔːˈrɒl- US ɔːˈrɑː.lə-
Oronsay ˈɒr.ᵊn.seɪ, -zeɪ US ˈɔːr-, -ɑːn-
Orontes ɒrˈɒn.tiːz, əˈrɒn- US oʊˈrɑːn-
Oroonoko ˌɒr.ʊˈnəʊ.kəʊ US ˌɔːr.ʊˈnoʊ.koʊ
Orosius əˈrəʊ.si.əs, ɒrˈəʊ- US ɔːˈroʊ.ʒi.əs
orotund ˈɒr.əʊ.tʌnd, ˈɔː.rəʊ- US ˈɔːr.ə-, -oʊ-, ˈ-ə-
O'Rourke əʊˈrɔːk US oʊˈrɔːrk
orphan ˈɔː.fᵊn US ˈɔːr- **-s** -z **-ing** -ɪŋ **-ed** -d
orphanag|e ˈɔː.fᵊn.ɪdʒ US ˈɔːr- **-es** -ɪz
Orphean ɔːˈfiː.ən; ˈɔː.fi- US ˈɔːr.fi.ən
Orpheus ˈɔː.fi.əs, -fjuːs US ˈɔːr.fi.əs, ˈ-fjuːs
orpiment ˈɔː.pɪ.mənt US ˈɔːr-
Orpington ˈɔː.pɪŋ.tən US ˈɔːr- **-s** -z
Orr ɔːʳ US ɔːr
Orrell ˈɒr.ᵊl US ˈɔːr-
orrer|y (O) ˈɒr.ᵊr|.i US ˈɔːr- **-ies** -iz
orris ˈɒr.ɪs US ˈɔːr-
Orsino ɔːˈsiː.nəʊ US ɔːrˈsiː.noʊ
Orson ˈɔː.sᵊn US ˈɔːr-
Ortega ɔːˈteɪ.gə US ɔːr-; ˌɔːr.t̬əˈgɑː
ortho- ɔː.θəʊ-; ɔːˈθɒ- US ɔːr.θoʊ-, -θə-; ɔːrˈθɑː-

Note: Prefix. Normally either takes primary or secondary stress on the first syllable, e.g. **orthodox** /ˈɔː.θə.dɒks US ˈɔːr.θə.dɑːks/, **orthogenic** /ˌɔː.θəʊˈdʒen.ɪk US ˌɔːr.θoʊ-/, or primary stress on

the second syllable, e.g. **orthography** /ɔː'θɒg.rə.fi (US) ɔːr'θɑː.grə-/.
orthochromatic ˌɔː.θəʊ.krəʊ'mæt.ɪk (US) ˌɔːr.θoʊ.kroʊ'mæţ-, -θə-
orthodontic ˌɔː.θəʊ'dɒn.tɪk (US) ˌɔːr.θoʊ'dɑːn.ţɪk, -θə'-
orthodontist ˌɔː.θəʊ'dɒn.tɪst (US) ˌɔːr.θoʊ'dɑːn.ţɪst, -θə'- **-s** -s
orthodox 'ɔː.θə.dɒks (US) 'ɔːr.θə.dɑːks
orthodox|y 'ɔː.θə.dɒk.s|i (US) 'ɔːr.θə.dɑːk- **-ies** -iz
orthoep|y 'ɔː.θəʊ.ep|.i; ɔː'θəʊ.ɪ.p|i; ˌɔː.θəʊ'ep|.i; (US) ɔːr'θoʊ.ə.p|i, 'ɔːr.θoʊ-, -ep|.i **-ist/s** -ɪst/s
orthogenic ˌɔː.θəʊ'dʒen.ɪk (US) ˌɔːr.θoʊ'-, -θə'-
orthogonal ɔː'θɒg.ᵊn.ᵊl (US) ɔːr'θɑː.gᵊn-
orthographer ɔː'θɒg.rə.fəʳ (US) ɔːr'θɑː.grə.fɚ **-s** -z
orthographic ˌɔː.θəʊ'græf.ɪk (US) ˌɔːr.θoʊ'-, -θə'- **-al** -ᵊl **-ally** -ᵊl.i, -li
orthograph|y ɔː'θɒg.rə.f|i (US) ɔː'θɑː.grə- **-ist/s** -ɪst/s
orthop(a)edic ˌɔː.θəʊ'piː.dɪk (US) ˌɔːr.θoʊ'-, -θə'- **-s** -s **-ally** -ᵊl.i, -li
orthop(a)ed|y ˌɔː.θəʊ'piː.d|i (US) ˌɔːr.θoʊ'-, -θə'- **-ist/s** -ɪst/s
orthopterous ɔː'θɒp.tᵊr.əs (US) ɔːr'θɑːp-
orthoptic ɔː'θɒp.tɪk (US) ɔːr'θɑːp-
Ortiz 'ɔː.tɪz, ɔː'tɪz, -'tiːz, -'tiːs (US) ɔːr'tiːz, -'tiːs
Ortler 'ɔːt.ləʳ (US) 'ɔːrt.lɚ
ortolan 'ɔː.tᵊl.ən, -æn (US) 'ɔːr.ţə.lən **-s** -z
Orton 'ɔː.tᵊn (US) 'ɔːr-
Oruro ɒr'ʊə.rəʊ (US) ɔː'rʊr.oʊ, -'ruː.roʊ
Orville 'ɔː.vɪl (US) 'ɔːr-
Orwell 'ɔː.wel, -wəl (US) 'ɔːr-
Orwellian ɔː'wel.i.ən (US) ɔːr-
-ory -ᵊr.i, -ri (US) -ɔːr.i, -ᵊr.i
Note: Suffix. When added to a free stem, **-ory** does not change the stress pattern of the word, e.g. **promise** /'prɒ.mɪs (US) 'prɑː.mɪs/, **promissory** /'prɒm.ɪs.ᵊr.i (US) 'prɑː.mɪ.sɔːr.i/. When added to a bound stem, stress may be one or two syllables before thesuffix, e.g. **olfactory** /ɒl'fæk.tᵊr.i (US) ɑːl-/.
oryx 'ɒr.ɪks (US) 'oʊ.rɪks, 'ɔːr.ɪks **-es** -ɪz
Osage ˌəʊ'seɪdʒ, '-- (US) ˌoʊ'seɪdʒ, '--
Osaka əʊ'sɑː.kə, 'ɔː.sə.kə (US) 'oʊ.sɑː.kɑː, oʊ'sɑː.kɑː
Osama əʊ'sɑː.mə, ɒs'-, ʊs'-
Osbaldiston(e) ˌɒz.bᵊl'dɪs.tᵊn (US) ˌɑːz-
Osbert 'ɒz.bət, -bɜːt (US) 'ɑːz.bɚt, -bɝːt
Osborn(e), Osbourne 'ɒz.bɔːn, -bən (US) 'ɑːz.bɔːrn, -bɚn
Oscan 'ɒs.kən (US) 'ɑːs- **-s** -z
Oscar 'ɒs.kəʳ (US) 'ɑː.skɚ **-s** -z
oscill|ate 'ɒs.ɪ.l|eɪt, -ᵊl|.eɪt (US) 'ɑː.sᵊl- **-ates** -eɪts **-ating** -eɪ.tɪŋ (US) -eɪ.ţɪŋ **-ated** -eɪ.tɪd (US) -eɪ.ţɪd **-ator/s** -eɪ.təʳ/z (US) -eɪ.ţɚ/z
oscillation ˌɒs.ɪ'leɪ.ʃᵊn, -ᵊl'eɪ- (US) ˌɑː.sᵊl'- **-s** -z
oscillatory 'ɒs.ɪ.lə.tᵊr.i, -ᵊl.eɪ-, -leɪ-; ˌɒs.ɪ'leɪ-, -ᵊl'eɪ- (US) 'ɑː.sᵊl.ə.tɔːr-
oscillogram ə'sɪl.ə.græm, ɒs'ɪl- (US) ə'sɪl- **-s** -z
oscillograph ə'sɪl.ə.grɑːf, ɒs'ɪl-, -græf (US) ə'sɪl.ə.græf **-s** -s
oscilloscope ə'sɪl.ə.skəʊp, ɒs'ɪl- (US) ə'sɪl.ə.skoʊp **-s** -s
osculant 'ɒs.kjə.lənt, -kjʊ- (US) 'ɑː.skjuː-, -skjə-
oscular 'ɒs.kjə.ləʳ, -kjʊ- (US) 'ɑː.skjuː.lɚ, -skjə-
oscu|late 'ɒs.kjə|.leɪt, -kjʊ- (US) 'ɑː.skjuː-, -skjə- **-lates** -leɪts **-lating** -leɪ.tɪŋ (US) -leɪ.ţɪŋ **-lated** -leɪ.tɪd (US) -leɪ.ţɪd
osculation ˌɒs.kjə'leɪ.ʃᵊn, -kjʊ'- (US) ˌɑː.skjuː'-, -skjə'- **-s** -z
osculator|y 'ɒs.kjə.lə.tᵊr|.i, -kjʊ-; ˌɒs.kjə'leɪ-, -kjʊ'- (US) 'ɑː.skjuː.lə.tɔːr-, -skjə- **-ies** -iz
Osgood 'ɒz.gʊd (US) 'ɑːz-
O'Shaughnessy əʊ'ʃɔː.nɪ.si, -nə- (US) oʊ'ʃɑː.nə-, -'ʃɔː-
O'Shea əʊ'ʃeɪ (US) oʊ-
Oshkosh 'ɒʃ.kɒʃ (US) 'ɑːʃ.kɑːʃ
Oshogbo ə'ʃɒg.bəʊ (US) oʊ'ʃɑːg.boʊ
osier 'əʊ.zi.əʳ, -ʒəʳ (US) 'oʊ.ʒɚ **-s** -z
Osijek 'ɒs.i.ek (US) ɔː'siː.ek
Osirian əʊ'saɪə.ri.ən, ɒs'aɪə- (US) oʊ'saɪ- **-s** -z
Osiris əʊ'saɪə.rɪs, ɒs'aɪə- (US) oʊ'saɪ-
-osis -ə.sɪs; -'əʊ.sɪs (US) -ə.sɪs; -'oʊ.sɪs
Note: Suffix. Words containing **-osis** either carry primary stress on the syllable preceeding the suffix, or on the suffix itself e.g. **metamorphosis** /ˌmet.ə'mɔː.fə.sɪs; -mɔː'fəʊ- (US) ˌmeţ.ə'mɔːr.fə-; -mɔːr'foʊ-/. See individual entries.
-osity -'ɒs.ə.ti, -ɪ.ti (US) -'ɑː.sə.ţi
Note: Suffix. Normally takes primary stress as shown, e.g. **curious** /'kjʊə.ri.əs (US) 'kjʊr.i-/, **curiosity** /ˌkjʊə.ri'ɒs.ə.ti (US) ˌkjʊr.i'ɑː.sə.ţi/.
Osler 'əʊz.ləʳ, 'əʊ.sləʳ (US) 'oʊz.lɚ, 'oʊ.slɚ
Oslo 'ɒz.ləʊ, 'ɒs- (US) 'ɑː.sloʊ, 'ɑːz-
Osman ɒz'mɑːn, ɒs-; '--, -mən (US) 'ɑːz.mən, 'ɑːs-
Osmanli ɒz'mæn.li, ɒs-, -'mɑːn- (US) ɑːs'mæn-, ɑːz- **-s** -z
osmium 'ɒz.mi.əm (US) 'ɑːz-
Osmond 'ɒz.mənd (US) 'ɑːz-
osmosis ɒz'məʊ.sɪs (US) ɑːz'moʊ-, ɑːs-
osmotic ɒz'mɒt.ɪk (US) ɑːz'mɑː.ţɪk, ɑːs- **-ally** -ᵊl.i, -li
osmund (O) 'ɒz.mənd (US) 'ɑːz-, 'ɑːs- **-s** -z
osmunda ɒz'mʌn.də (US) ɑːz-, ɑːs- **-s** -z
Osnaburg(h) 'ɒz.nə.bɜːg (US) 'ɑːz.nə.bɝːg
osprey 'ɒs.preɪ, -pri (US) 'ɑː.spri, -spreɪ **-s** -z
Ossa 'ɒs.ə (US) 'ɑː.sə
osseous 'ɒs.i.əs (US) 'ɑː.si-
Ossett 'ɒs.ɪt (US) 'ɑː.sɪt
Ossian 'ɒs.i.ən (US) 'ɑː.si-
ossicle 'ɒs.ɪ.kḷ (US) 'ɑː.sɪ- **-s** -z
ossicular ɒs'ɪk.jə.ləʳ, -jʊ- (US) ɑː'sɪk.jə.lɚ, -jʊ-
ossification ˌɒs.ɪ.fɪ'keɪ.ʃᵊn, ˌ-ə- (US) ˌɑː.sə.fɪ'-
ossifrag|e 'ɒs.ɪ.frɪdʒ, '-ə-, -freɪdʒ (US) 'ɑː.sə- **-es** -ɪz
ossi|fy 'ɒs.ɪ|.faɪ, '-ə- (US) 'ɑː.sə- **-fies** -faɪz **-fying** -faɪ.ɪŋ **-fied** -faɪd
Ossining 'ɒs.ɪn.ɪŋ (US) 'ɑː.sɪn-
osso buc(c)o ˌɒs.əʊ'buː.kəʊ (US) ˌɑː.soʊ'buː.koʊ, ˌoʊ-
Ossory 'ɒs.ᵊr.i (US) 'ɑː.sɚ-
ossuar|y 'ɒs.jʊə.r|i (US) 'ɑː.sjuː.er|.i **-ies** -iz
osteitis ˌɒs.ti'aɪ.tɪs (US) ˌɑː.sti'aɪ.ţɪs
Ostend ɒs'tend (US) ɑː'stend, '--
ostensibility ɒsˌtent.sɪ'bɪl.ə.ti, -sə'-, -ɪ.ti (US) ɑːˌstent.sə'bɪl.ə.ţi
ostensib|le ɒs'tent.sɪ.b|ḷ, -sə- (US) ɑː'stent.sə- **-ly** -li
ostentation ˌɒs.ten'teɪ.ʃᵊn, -tən'- (US) ˌɑː.stən'-
ostentatious ˌɒs.ten'teɪ.ʃəs, -tən'- (US) ˌɑː.stən'- **-ly** -li **-ness** -nəs, -nɪs
osteo- ˌɒs.ti.əʊ- (US) ˌɑː.sti.oʊ-, -ə-
osteoarthritis ˌɒs.ti.əʊ.ɑː'θraɪ.tɪs (US) ˌɑː.sti.oʊ.ɑːr'θraɪ.ţɪs
osteologic|al ˌɒs.ti.ə'lɒdʒ.ɪ.k|ᵊl (US) ˌɑː.sti.oʊ'lɑː.dʒɪ- **-ally** -ᵊl.i, -li
osteolog|y ˌɒs.ti'ɒl.ə.dʒ|i (US) ˌɑː.sti'ɑː.lə- **-ist/s** -ɪst/s
osteomyelitis ˌɒs.ti.əʊ.maɪ.ᵊl'aɪ.tɪs (US) ˌɑː.sti.oʊ.maɪ.ə'laɪ.ţɪs
osteopath 'ɒs.ti.əʊ.pæθ (US) 'ɑː.sti.oʊ-, -ə- **-s** -s
osteopathic ˌɒs.ti.əʊ'pæθ.ɪk (US) ˌɑː.sti.oʊ'-
osteopathy ˌɒs.ti'ɒp.ə.θi (US) ˌɑː.sti'ɑː.pə-
osteoporosis ˌɒs.ti.əʊ.pə'rəʊ.sɪs, -pɔː'- (US) ˌɑː.sti.oʊ.pə'roʊ-
Osterley 'ɒs.tᵊl.i (US) 'ɑː.stɚ.li
Ostia 'ɒs.ti.ə (US) 'ɑː.sti-
ostiar|y 'ɒs.ti.ər|.i (US) 'ɑː.sti.er- **-ies** -iz
osti|um (O) 'ɒs.ti|.əm (US) 'ɑː.sti- **-a** -ə
ostler 'ɒs.ləʳ (US) 'ɑː.slɚ **-s** -z
ostracism 'ɒs.trə.sɪ.zᵊm (US) 'ɑː.strə-

Pronouncing the letters OU

There are several pronunciation possibilities for the strong pronunciation of the vowel digraph **ou**, e.g.:

/aʊ/	cloud	/klaʊd/	
/əʊ (US) oʊ/	though	/ðəʊ/	(US) /ðoʊ/
/ʌ/	country	/ˈkʌn.tri/	
/ɔː (US) ɑː/	bought	/bɔːt/	(US) /bɑːt/
/uː/	soup	/suːp/	
/ʊ/	could	/kʊd/	

When followed by a **gh** in the spelling which is realised as /f/, it is usually pronounced /ɒ (US) ɑː/ or /ʌ/, e.g.:

cough	/kɒf/	(US) /kɑːf/
enough	/ɪˈnʌf/	

When followed by an **r** in the spelling, **ou** is pronounced as /ɔː (US) ɔːr/, /aʊə (US) aʊɚ/, /ɜː (US) ɝː/, /ʌ (US) ɝː/, and /ʊə (US) ʊr/, e.g.:

four	/fɔːʳ/	(US) /fɔːr/
flour	/flaʊəʳ/	(US) /flaʊɚ/
journey	/ˈdʒɜː.ni/	(US) /ˈdʒɝː-/
flourish	/ˈflʌr.ɪʃ/	(US) /ˈflɝː-/
tour	/tʊəʳ, stɔːʳ/	(US) /tʊr/

In weak syllables

The vowel digraph **ou** is realised with the vowel /ə/ in weak syllables, and may also not be pronounced at all in British English, due to compression, e.g.:

famous	/ˈfeɪ.məs/
favourite	/ˈfeɪ.vᵊr.ɪt, ˈfeɪv.rɪt/

ostraciz|e, -is|e ˈɒs.trə.saɪz (US) ˈɑː.strə- **-es** -ɪz **-ing** -ɪŋ **-ed** -d
Ostrava ˈɒs.trə.və (US) ˈɔː.strɑː.vɑː, ˈɑː-
ostrich ˈɒs.trɪtʃ (US) ˈɑː.strɪtʃ **-es** -ɪz
Ostrogoth ˈɒs.trəʊ.gɒθ (US) ˈɑː.strə.gɑːθ **-s** -s
O'Sullivan əʊˈsʌl.ɪ.vən, ˈ-ə- (US) oʊ-
Oswald ˈɒz.wəld (US) ˈɑːz-, -wɔːld
Oswaldtwistle ˈɒz.wəld,twɪs.l̩ (US) ˈɑːz.wɔːld-
Oswego ɒzˈwiː.gəʊ, ɒs- (US) ɑːˈswiː.goʊ **-s** -z
Oswestry ˈɒz.wə.stri, -wɪ- (US) ˈɑːz-
Otago əʊˈtɑː.gəʊ, ɒtˈɑː- (US) əˈtɑː.go, oʊ-
Otaheite ˌəʊ.tɑːˈheɪ.ti, -təˈ- (US) ˌoʊ.t̬əˈhiː.t̬i, -ˈheɪ-
otar|y ˈəʊ.tᵊr|.i (US) ˈoʊ.t̬ɚ- **-ies** -iz
OTB ˌəʊ.tiːˈbiː (US) ˌoʊ-
Otford ˈɒt.fəd (US) ˈɑːt.fɚd
Otfried ˈɒt.friːd (US) ˈɑːt-
Othello əʊˈθel.əʊ, ɒθˈel- (US) oʊˈθel.oʊ, ə-
other ˈʌð.əʳ (US) -ɚ **-s** -z **-ness** -nəs, -nɪs
otherwise ˈʌð.ə.waɪz (US) ˈ-ɚ-
otherworld|ly ˌʌð.əˈwɜːld|.li (US) -ɚˈwɝːld- **-liness** -lɪ.nəs, -nɪs
Othman ɒθˈmɑːn, ˈ-- (US) ˈɑːθ.mən, ʊθˈmɑːn
Othniel ˈɒθ.ni.əl (US) ˈɑːθ-
Otho ˈəʊ.θəʊ (US) ˈoʊ.θoʊ
-otic -ˈɒt.ɪk (US) -ˈɑː.t̬ɪk
Note: Suffix. Normally takes primary stress as shown, e.g **idiot** /ˈɪd.i.ət/, **idiotic** /ˌɪd.iˈɒt.ɪk (US) -ˈɑː.t̬ɪk/.
otiose ˈəʊ.ti.əʊz, -ʃi-, -əʊs (US) ˈoʊ.ʃi.oʊs, -t̬i- **-ly** -li **-ness** -nəs, -nɪs
otiosity ˌəʊ.tiˈɒs.ə.ti, -ʃiˈ-, -ɪ.ti (US) ˌoʊ.ʃiˈɑː.sə.t̬i, -t̬iˈ-
Otis ˈəʊ.tɪs (US) ˈoʊ.t̬ɪs
otitis əʊˈtaɪ.tɪs (US) oʊˈtaɪ.t̬ɪs
Otley ˈɒt.li (US) ˈɑːt-
otolaryngolog|y ˌəʊ.təʊˌlær.ɪŋˈgɒl.ə.dʒ|i, -ˌleə.rɪŋˈ- (US) ˌoʊ.t̬oʊˌler.ɪŋˈgɑː.lə-, -ˌlær- **-ist/s** -ɪst/s
otological ˌəʊ.təˈlɒdʒ.ɪ.kᵊl (US) ˌoʊ.t̬əˈlɑː.dʒɪ-
otolog|y əʊˈtɒl.ə.dʒ|i (US) oʊˈtɑː.lə- **-ist/s** -ɪst/s
otoscope ˈəʊ.tə.skəʊp (US) ˈoʊ.t̬oʊ.skoʊp, -t̬ə- **-s** -s
Otranto ɒtˈræn.təʊ, ˈɒt.rᵊn- (US) oʊˈtrɑːn.toʊ
O'Trigger əʊˈtrɪg.əʳ (US) oʊˈtrɪg.ɚ
OTT ˌəʊ.tiːˈtiː (US) ˌoʊ- *stress shift:* ˌOTT ˈspeech
Note: The letters OTT stand for "over-the-top"; see also that entry.
ottava rima ɒtˈɑː.vəˌriː.mə (US) oʊˈtɑː-
Ottaw|a ˈɒt.ə.w|ə (US) ˈɑː.t̬ə.w|ə, -w|ɑː, -w|ɔː **-as** -əz (US) -əz, -ɑːz, -ɔːz **-an/s** -ən/z
Ottaway ˈɒt.ə.weɪ (US) ˈɑː.t̬ə-
otter ˈɒt.əʳ (US) ˈɑː.t̬ɚ **-s** -z
Otterburn ˈɒt.ə.bɜːn (US) ˈɑː.t̬ɚ.bɝːn
Ottery ˈɒt.ᵊr.i (US) ˈɑː.t̬ɚ-
Ottley ˈɒt.li (US) ˈɑːt-
otto (O) ˈɒt.əʊ (US) ˈɑː.t̬oʊ
ottoman (O) ˈɒt.əʊ.mən (US) ˈɑː.t̬ə.mən **-s** -z
Ottoway ˈɒt.ə.weɪ (US) ˈɑː.t̬ə-
Otuel ˈɒt.juəl (US) ɔːˈtʊl, -ˈtuː.əl
Otway ˈɒt.weɪ (US) ˈɑːt-
Ouagadougou ˌwɑː.gəˈduː.guː, ˌwæg.əˈ- (US) ˌwɑː.gəˈ-
oubliette ˌuː.bliˈet **-s** -s
ouch aʊtʃ
Oudenarde ˈuː.də.nɑːd, -dɪ- (US) -dᵊn.ɑːrd; ˌuː.dəˈnɑːr.də
Oudh aʊd
Ougham ˈɔː.əm
ought ɔːt (US) ɑːt, ɔːt **-n't** -ᵊnt
Oughtershaw ˈaʊ.tə.ʃɔː (US) -t̬ɚ.ʃɑː, -ʃɔː
Oughterside ˈaʊ.tə.saɪd (US) -t̬ɚ-
Oughton ˈaʊ.tᵊn, ˈɔː.tᵊn
Oughtred ˈɔː.tred, -trɪd (US) ˈɔː-, ˈɑː-
ouguiya uːˈgwiː.ə, -ˈgiː-
Ouida ˈwiː.də
Ouija® ˈwiː.dʒə, -dʒɑː, -dʒi (US) -dʒə, -dʒi
Oujda uːdʒˈdɑː
Ould əʊld (US) oʊld
ounc|e aʊnts **-es** -ɪz
Oundle ˈaʊn.dl̩
our aʊəʳ, ɑːʳ (US) aʊɚ, aʊr, ɑːr **-s** -z
oursel|f ˌaʊəˈsel|f, ˌɑː- (US) ˌaʊɚ-, ˌaʊr-, ˌɑːr- **-ves** -vz
Ouse uːz
ousel ˈuː.zl̩ **-s** -z
Ouseley ˈuːz.li
Ousey ˈuː.zi
Ousley ˈaʊ.sli
oust aʊst **-s** -s **-ing** -ɪŋ **-ed** -ɪd **-er/s** -əʳ/z (US) -ɚ/z
Ouston ˈaʊ.stᵊn
out- aʊt-
Note: Prefix. Many compounds with beginning with **out-** have the stress pattern **ˈout**ˌ-; these are likely to undergo stress shift when a stressed syllable follows closely, especially in adjectives derived from verbs.

out aʊt **-s** -s **-ing** -ɪŋ Ⓤⓢ ˈaʊ.t̬ɪŋ **-ed** -ɪd Ⓤⓢ ˈaʊ.t̬ɪd
outag|e ˈaʊ.tɪdʒ Ⓤⓢ -t̬ɪdʒ **-es** -ɪz
out-and-out ˌaʊt.ənˈdaʊt *stress shift:* ˌout-and-out ˈscoundrel
outback ˈaʊt.bæk
outbalanc|e ˌaʊtˈbæl.ənts, aʊt- **-es** -ɪz **-ing** -ɪŋ **-ed** -t
outbid ˌaʊtˈbɪd, aʊt- **-s** -z **-ding** -ɪŋ
outboard ˈaʊt.bɔːd Ⓤⓢ -bɔːrd
outbound ˈaʊt.baʊnd
outbox ˈaʊt.bɒks Ⓤⓢ -bɑːks **-es** -ɪz
outbrav|e ˌaʊtˈbreɪv, aʊt- **-es** -z **-ing** -ɪŋ **-ed** -d
outbreak ˈaʊt.breɪk **-s** -s
outbuilding ˈaʊtˌbɪl.dɪŋ **-s** -z
outburst ˈaʊt.bɜːst Ⓤⓢ -bɝːst **-s** -s
outcast ˈaʊt.kɑːst Ⓤⓢ -kæst **-s** -s
outcast|e ˈaʊt.kɑːst Ⓤⓢ -kæst **-es** -s **-ing** -ɪŋ **-ed** -ɪd
outclass ˌaʊtˈklɑːs, aʊt- Ⓤⓢ -ˈklæs **-es** -ɪz **-ing** -ɪŋ **-ed** -t
outcome ˈaʊt.kʌm **-s** -z
outcrop ˈaʊt.krɒp Ⓤⓢ -krɑːp **-s** -s **-ping** -ɪŋ **-ped** -t
outcr|y ˈaʊt.kr|aɪ **-ies** -aɪz
out|date ˌaʊt|ˈdeɪt, aʊt- **-dates** -ˈdeɪts **-dating** -ˈdeɪ.tɪŋ Ⓤⓢ -ˈdeɪ.t̬ɪŋ **-dated** -ˈdeɪ.tɪd Ⓤⓢ -ˈdeɪ.t̬ɪd
outdated ˌaʊtˈdeɪ.tɪd, aʊt- Ⓤⓢ -t̬ɪd *stress shift:* ˌoutdated ˈclothes
outdistanc|e ˌaʊtˈdɪs.tənts, aʊt- **-es** -ɪz **-ing** -ɪŋ **-ed** -t
out|do ˌaʊt|ˈduː, aʊt- **-does** -ˈdʌz **-doing** -ˈduː.ɪŋ **-did** -ˈdɪd **-done** -ˈdʌn
outdoor ˌaʊtˈdɔːʳ, aʊt- Ⓤⓢ -ˈdɔːr **-s** -z *stress shift:* ˌoutdoor ˈsports
outer ˈaʊ.təʳ Ⓤⓢ -t̬ɚ **-most** -məʊst Ⓤⓢ -məst, -moʊst ˌ**outer** ˈ**space**
outerwear ˈaʊ.tə.weəʳ Ⓤⓢ -t̬ɚ.wer
outfac|e ˌaʊtˈfeɪs, aʊt- **-s** -ɪz **-ing** -ɪŋ **-ed** -t
outfall ˈaʊt.fɔːl **-s** -z
outfield ˈaʊt.fiːld **-s** -z **-er/s** -əʳ/z Ⓤⓢ -ɚ/z
out|fit ˈaʊt|.fɪt **-fits** -fɪts **-fitting** -ˌfɪt.ɪŋ Ⓤⓢ -ˌfɪt̬.ɪŋ **-fitted** -ˌfɪt.ɪd Ⓤⓢ -ˌfɪt̬.ɪd **-fitter/s** -ˌfɪt.əʳ/z Ⓤⓢ -ˌfɪt̬.ɚ/z
outflank ˌaʊtˈflæŋk, aʊt- **-s** -s **-ing** -ɪŋ **-ed** -t
outflow (*n.*) ˈaʊt.fləʊ Ⓤⓢ -floʊ **-s** -z
outflow (*v.*) ˌaʊtˈfləʊ, aʊt- Ⓤⓢ -ˈfloʊ **-s** -z **-ing** -ɪŋ **-ed** -d
outfox ˌaʊtˈfɒks, aʊt- Ⓤⓢ -ˈfɑːks **-es** -ɪz **-ing** -ɪŋ **-ed** -t
outgeneral ˌaʊtˈdʒen.ər.əl, aʊt- **-s** -z **-(l)ing** -ɪŋ **-(l)ed** -d
outgo (*n.*) ˈaʊt.gəʊ Ⓤⓢ -goʊ **-es** -z
out|go (*v.*) ˌaʊt|ˈgəʊ, aʊt- Ⓤⓢ -ˈgoʊ **-goes** -ˈgəʊz Ⓤⓢ -ˈgoʊz **-going** -ˈgəʊ.ɪŋ Ⓤⓢ -ˈgoʊ.ɪŋ **-went** -ˈwent **-gone** -ˈgɒn Ⓤⓢ -ˈgɑːn
outgoer ˈaʊtˌgəʊ.əʳ Ⓤⓢ -ˌgoʊ.ɚ **-s** -z
outgoing ˌaʊtˈgəʊ.ɪŋ, aʊt-, ˈ--- Ⓤⓢ ˈaʊt.goʊ- **-s** -z
out|grow (*v.*) ˌaʊt|ˈgrəʊ, aʊt- Ⓤⓢ -ˈgroʊ **-grows** -ˈgrəʊz Ⓤⓢ -ˈgroʊz **-growing** -ˈgrəʊ.ɪŋ Ⓤⓢ -ˈgroʊ.ɪŋ **-grew** -ˈgruː **-grown** -ˈgrəʊn Ⓤⓢ -ˈgroʊn
outgrowth ˈaʊt.grəʊθ Ⓤⓢ -groʊθ **-s** -s
outguess ˌaʊtˈges, aʊt- **-es** -ɪz **-ing** -ɪŋ **-ed** -t
outgun ˌaʊtˈgʌn, aʊt- **-s** -z **-ning** -ɪŋ **-ned** -d
out-Herod ˌaʊtˈher.əd, aʊt- **-s** -z **-ing** -ɪŋ **-ed** -ɪd
outhou|se ˈaʊt.haʊ|s **-ses** -zɪz
Outhwaite ˈuː.θweɪt, ˈəʊ-, ˈaʊ- Ⓤⓢ ˈuː-, ˈoʊ-, ˈaʊ-
outing ˈaʊ.tɪŋ Ⓤⓢ -t̬ɪŋ **-s** -z
Outlander ˈaʊtˌlæn.dəʳ Ⓤⓢ -dɚ **-s** -z
outlandish ˌaʊtˈlæn.dɪʃ, aʊt- **-ly** -li **-ness** -nəs, -nɪs
outlast ˌaʊtˈlɑːst, aʊt- Ⓤⓢ -ˈlæst **-s** -s **-ing** -ɪŋ **-ed** -ɪd
outlaw ˈaʊt.lɔː Ⓤⓢ -lɑː, -lɔː **-s** -z **-ing** -ɪŋ **-ed** -d **-ry** -ri
outlay (*n.*) ˈaʊt.leɪ **-s** -z
out|lay (*v.*) ˌaʊt|ˈleɪ, aʊt- **-lays** -ˈleɪz **-laying** -ˈleɪ.ɪŋ **-laid** -ˈleɪd
outlet ˈaʊt.let, -lət, -lɪt Ⓤⓢ -let, -lət **-s** -s
outlier ˈaʊtˌlaɪ.əʳ Ⓤⓢ -ɚ **-s** -z
outline (*n.*) ˈaʊt.laɪn **-s** -z
outlin|e (*v.*) ˈaʊt.laɪn, ˌ-ˈ-, aʊt- Ⓤⓢ ˈ-- **-es** -z **-ing** -ɪŋ **-ed** -d
outliv|e ˌaʊtˈlɪv, aʊt- **-es** -z **-ing** -ɪŋ **-ed** -d
outlook ˈaʊt.lʊk **-s** -s
outlying ˈaʊtˌlaɪ.ɪŋ, ˌ-ˈ--, aʊt- Ⓤⓢ ˈ-ˌ--
outmaneuv|er ˌaʊt.məˈnuː.v|əʳ Ⓤⓢ -v|ɚ **-ers** -əz Ⓤⓢ -ɚz **-ering** -ər.ɪŋ **-ered** -əd Ⓤⓢ -ɚd
outmanoeuv|re ˌaʊt.məˈnuː.v|əʳ Ⓤⓢ -v|ɚ **-res** -əz Ⓤⓢ -ɚz **-ring** -ər.ɪŋ **-red** -əd Ⓤⓢ -ɚd
outmarch ˌaʊtˈmɑːtʃ, aʊt- Ⓤⓢ -ˈmɑːrtʃ **-es** -ɪz **-ing** -ɪŋ **-ed** -t
outmatch ˌaʊtˈmætʃ, aʊt- **-es** -ɪz **-ing** -ɪŋ **-ed** -t
outmoded ˌaʊtˈməʊ.dɪd, aʊt- Ⓤⓢ -ˈmoʊ- *stress shift:* ˌoutmoded ˈclothes
outmost ˈaʊt.məʊst Ⓤⓢ -moʊst
outnumb|er ˌaʊtˈnʌm.b|əʳ, aʊt- Ⓤⓢ -bɚ **-ers** -əz Ⓤⓢ -ɚz **-ering** -ər.ɪŋ **-ered** -əd Ⓤⓢ -ɚd
out-of-date ˌaʊt.əvˈdeɪt Ⓤⓢ ˌaʊt̬- *stress shift:* ˌout-of-date ˈfoodstuffs
out-of-door ˌaʊt.əvˈdɔːʳ Ⓤⓢ ˌaʊt̬.əvˈdɔːr **-s** -z *stress shift:* ˌout-of-door ˈsports
out-of-pocket ˌaʊt.əvˈpɒk.ɪt Ⓤⓢ ˌaʊt̬.əvˈpɑː.kɪt *stress shift:* ˌout-of-pocket ˈpayment
out-of-state ˌaʊt.əvˈsteɪt Ⓤⓢ ˌaʊt̬- *stress shift:* ˌout-of-state ˈvisitors
out-of-the-way ˌaʊt.əv.ðəˈweɪ Ⓤⓢ ˌaʊt̬.əv.ðəˈ- *stress shift:* ˌout-of-the-way ˈplaces
outpac|e ˌaʊtˈpeɪs, aʊt- **-es** -ɪz **-ing** -ɪŋ **-ed** -t
outpatient ˈaʊtˌpeɪ.ʃənt **-s** -s
outperform ˌaʊt.pəˈfɔːm Ⓤⓢ -pɚˈfɔːrm **-s** -z **-ing** -ɪŋ **-ed** -d
outplacement ˈaʊtˌpleɪs.mənt
outplay ˌaʊtˈpleɪ, aʊt- **-s** -z **-ing** -ɪŋ **-ed** -d
outport ˈaʊt.pɔːt Ⓤⓢ -pɔːrt **-s** -s
outpost ˈaʊt.pəʊst Ⓤⓢ -poʊst **-s** -s
outpour (*n.*) ˈaʊt.pɔːʳ Ⓤⓢ -pɔːr **-s** -z
outpour (*v.*) ˌaʊtˈpɔːʳ, aʊt- Ⓤⓢ -ˈpɔːr **-s** -z **-ing** -ɪŋ **-ed** -d
outpouring ˈaʊtˌpɔː.rɪŋ, ˌ-ˈ--, aʊt- Ⓤⓢ ˈaʊtˌpɔːr.ɪŋ **-s** -z
out|put ˈaʊt|.pʊt **-puts** -pʊts **-putting** -ˌpʊt.ɪŋ Ⓤⓢ -ˌpʊt̬.ɪŋ **-putted** -ˌpʊt.ɪd Ⓤⓢ -ˌpʊt̬.ɪd
outrage (O) (*n.*) ˈaʊt.reɪdʒ
outrag|e (*v.*) ˈaʊt.reɪdʒ, ˌ-ˈ-, aʊt- Ⓤⓢ ˈ-- **-es** -ɪz **-ing** -ɪŋ **-ed** -d
outrageous ˌaʊtˈreɪ.dʒəs, aʊt- **-ly** -li **-ness** -nəs, -nɪs
Outram ˈuː.trəm
outrang|e ˌaʊtˈreɪndʒ, aʊt- **-es** -ɪz **-ing** -ɪŋ **-ed** -d
outrank ˌaʊtˈræŋk, aʊt- **-s** -s **-ing** -ɪŋ **-ed** -t
outré ˈuː.treɪ Ⓤⓢ -ˈ-
outreach (*n.*) ˈaʊt.riːtʃ **-es** -ɪz
outreach (*v.*) ˌaʊtˈriːtʃ, aʊt- **-es** -ɪz **-ing** -ɪŋ **-ed** -t
out|ride ˌaʊt|ˈraɪd, aʊt- **-rides** -ˈraɪdz **-riding** -ˈraɪ.dɪŋ **-rode** -ˈrəʊd Ⓤⓢ -ˈroʊd **-ridden** -ˈrɪd.ən
outrider ˈaʊtˌraɪ.dəʳ Ⓤⓢ -dɚ **-s** -z
outrigger ˈaʊtˌrɪg.əʳ Ⓤⓢ -ɚ **-s** -z
outright (*adj.*) ˈaʊt.raɪt (*adv.*) ˌaʊtˈraɪt, aʊt-
outrival ˌaʊtˈraɪ.vəl, aʊt- **-s** -z **-ling** -ɪŋ **-led** -d
out|run ˌaʊt|ˈrʌn, aʊt- **-runs** -ˈrʌnz **-running** -ˈrʌn.ɪŋ **-ran** -ˈræn
outrush ˈaʊt.rʌʃ **-es** -ɪz
out|sell ˌaʊt|ˈsel, aʊt- **-sells** -ˈselz **-selling** -ˈsel.ɪŋ **-sold** -ˈsəʊld Ⓤⓢ -ˈsoʊld
outset ˈaʊt.set **-s** -s
out|shine ˌaʊt|ˈʃaɪn, aʊt- **-shines** -ˈʃaɪnz **-shining** -ˈʃaɪ.nɪŋ **-shined** -ˈʃaɪnd **-shone** -ˈʃɒn Ⓤⓢ -ˈʃoʊn
outside ˌaʊtˈsaɪd, aʊt- **-s** -z *stress shift:* ˌoutside ˈtoilet
outsider ˌaʊtˈsaɪ.dəʳ, aʊt- Ⓤⓢ aʊtˈsaɪ.dɚ, ˈ--- **-s** -z *stress shift, British only:* ˌoutsider ˈdealing

outsiz|e ˌaʊtˈsaɪz, aʊt- **-es** -ɪz **-ed** -d *stress shift:* ˌoutsize ˈclothes
outskirts ˈaʊt.skɜːts (US) -skɝːts
out|smart ˌaʊtˈsmɑːt, aʊt- (US) -ˈsmɑːrt **-smarts** -ˈsmɑːts (US) -ˈsmɑːrts **-smarting** -ˈsmɑː.tɪŋ (US) -ˈsmɑːr.t̬ɪŋ **-smarted** -ˈsmɑː.tɪd (US) -ˈsmɑːr.t̬ɪd
outsourc|e ˈaʊt.sɔːs (US) -sɔːrs **-es** -ɪz **-ing** -ɪŋ **-ed** -t
Outspan® ˈaʊt.spæn **-s** -z
outspan ˌaʊtˈspæn, aʊt- **-s** -z **-ning** -ɪŋ **-ned** -d
outspend ˌaʊtˈspend, aʊt- **-s** -z **-ing** -ɪŋ **outspent** ˌaʊtˈspent, aʊt-
outspoken ˌaʊtˈspəʊ.kən, aʊt- (US) -ˈspoʊ- **-ly** -li **-ness** -nəs, -nɪs *stress shift:* ˌoutspoken ˈperson
outspread ˌaʊtˈspred (US) aʊt- **-s** -z **-ing** -ɪŋ *stress shift:* ˌoutspread ˈarms
outstanding *very good:* ˌaʊtˈstæn.dɪŋ, aʊt- **-ly** -li *sticking out:* ˈaʊtˌstæn.dɪŋ
outstar|e ˌaʊtˈsteəʳ, aʊt- (US) -ˈster **-es** -z **-ing** -ɪŋ **-ed** -d
outstation ˈaʊt.steɪ.ʃən **-s** -z **-ed** -d
outstay ˌaʊtˈsteɪ, aʊt- **-s** -z **-ing** -ɪŋ **-ed** -d
outstretch ˌaʊtˈstretʃ, aʊt- **-es** -ɪz **-ing** -ɪŋ **-ed** -t *stress shift:* ˌoutstretched ˈarms
outstrip ˌaʊtˈstrɪp, aʊt- **-s** -s **-ping** -ɪŋ **-ped** -t
outta ˈaʊ.t̬ə
Note: This is a form of **out of**, and is only used by British speakers when imitating American speakers.
outtake ˈaʊt.teɪk **-s** -s
out|vote ˌaʊtˈvəʊt, aʊt- (US) -ˈvoʊt **-votes** -ˈvəʊts (US) -ˈvoʊts **-voting** -ˈvəʊ.tɪŋ (US) -ˈvoʊ.t̬ɪŋ **-voted** -ˈvəʊ.tɪd (US) -ˈvoʊ.t̬ɪd
outward ˈaʊt.wəd (US) -wɚd **-s** -z **-ly** -li **-ness** -nəs, -nɪs
outward-bound ˌaʊt.wədˈbaʊnd (US) -wɚd- ˌ**Outward ˈBound ˌcourse**
out|wear ˌaʊtˈweəʳ, aʊt- (US) -ˈwer **-wears** -ˈweəz (US) -ˈwers **-wearing** -ˈweə.rɪŋ (US) -ˈwer.ɪŋ **-worn** -ˈwɔːn (US) -ˈwɔːrn
outweigh ˌaʊtˈweɪ, aʊt- **-s** -z **-ing** -ɪŋ **-ed** -d
outwent *(from* **outgo***)* ˌaʊtˈwent, aʊt-
out|wit ˌaʊtˈwɪt, aʊt- **-wits** -ˈwɪts **-witting** -ˈwɪt.ɪŋ (US) -ˈwɪt̬.ɪŋ **-witted** -ˈwɪt.ɪd (US) -ˈwɪt̬.ɪd
outwith ˌaʊtˈwɪθ, aʊt, -ˈwɪð
outwork *(n.)* ˈaʊt.wɜːk (US) -wɝːk **-s** -s
outwork *(v.)* ˌaʊtˈwɜːk, aʊt- (US) -ˈwɝːk **-s** -s **-ing** -ɪŋ **-ed** -t
out-worker ˈaʊtˌwɜː.kəʳ (US) -ˌwɝː.kɚ **-s** -z
outworn ˌaʊtˈwɔːn, aʊt- (US) -ˈwɔːrn
ouzel ˈuː.zəl **-s** -z
ouzo ˈuː.zəʊ (US) -zoʊ
ova *(plur. of* **ovum***)* ˈəʊ.və (US) ˈoʊ-
oval (O) ˈəʊ.vəl (US) ˈoʊ- **-s** -z **-ly** -i ˈ**Oval** ˌ**Office**, ˌ**Oval ˈOffice**
Ovaltine® ˈəʊ.vəl.tiːn (US) ˈoʊ-
ovari|an əʊˈveə.ri.ən (US) oʊˈver.i- **-al** -əl
ovariectomy əʊˌveə.riˈek.tə.mi (US) oʊˌver.iˈ-
ovariotomy əʊˌveə.riˈɒt.ə.mi (US) oʊˌver.iˈɑː.t̬ə-
ovar|y ˈəʊ.vər.i (US) ˈoʊ- **-ies** -iz
ovate *(n.) Welsh title:* ˈɒv.ət, -ɪt; ˈəʊ.veɪt (US) ˈoʊ.veɪt; ˈɑː.vət **-s** -s
ovate *(adj.) egg-shaped:* ˈəʊ.veɪt, -vɪt, -vət (US) ˈoʊ.veɪt
ovation əʊˈveɪ.ʃən (US) oʊ- **-s** -z ˌ**standing oˈvation**
oven ˈʌv.ən **-s** -z ˈ**oven** ˌ**glove**
ovenbird ˈʌv.ən.bɜːd, -əm- (US) -ən.bɝːd **-s** -s
ovenproof ˈʌv.ən.pruːf, -əm- (US) -ən-
oven-ready ˌʌv.ənˈred.i *stress shift:* ˌoven-ready ˈchicken
ovenware ˈʌv.ən.weəʳ (US) -wer
over- əʊ.vəʳ-, oʊ.vɚ-
Note: Prefix. Many compounds with **over-** have the stress pattern ˌ**over**ˈ-; these are likely to undergo stress shift when a stressed syllable follows, especially in adjectives derived from verbs.
over ˈəʊ.vəʳ (US) ˈoʊ.vɚ **-s** -z ˌ**over and ˈdone** ˌ**with**
over-abundan|ce ˌəʊ.vər.əˈbʌn.dən|ts (US) ˌoʊ.vɚ- **-t** -t
over-achiever ˌəʊ.vər.əˈtʃiː.vəʳ (US) ˌoʊ.vɚ.əˈtʃiː.vɚ, ˈoʊ.vɚ.əˌtʃiː- **-s** -z
overact ˌəʊ.vərˈækt (US) ˌoʊ.vɚˈ- **-s** -s **-ing** -ɪŋ **-ed** -ɪd
overactive ˌəʊ.vərˈæk.tɪv (US) ˌoʊ.vɚˈ- *stress shift:* ˌoveractive ˈgland
over-age ˌəʊ.vərˈeɪdʒ (US) ˌoʊ.vɚˈ- *stress shift:* ˌover-age ˈapplicant
overall (O) *(n. adj.)* ˈəʊ.vər.ɔːl (US) ˈoʊ- **-s** -z
overall *(adv.)* ˌəʊ.vərˈɔːl (US) ˌoʊ.vɚˈ-, -ˈɑːl
over-ambitious ˌəʊ.vər.æmˈbɪʃ.əs (US) ˌoʊ.vɚ- *stress shift:* ˌover-ambitious ˈpartner
over-anxiety ˌəʊ.vər.æŋ*g*ˈzaɪ.ə.ti (US) ˌoʊ.vɚ.æŋˈzaɪ.ə.t̬i
over-anxious ˌəʊ.vərˈæŋ*k*.ʃəs (US) ˌoʊ.vɚˈ- **-ly** -li *stress shift:* ˌover-anxious ˈparent
overarching ˌəʊ.vərˈɑː.tʃɪŋ (US) ˌoʊ.vɚˈɑːr-
overarm ˈəʊ.vər.ɑːm (US) ˈoʊ.vɚ.ɑːrm
overaw|e ˌəʊ.vərˈɔː (US) ˌoʊ.vɚˈɑː, -ˈɔː **-es** -z **-ing** -ɪŋ **-ed** -d
overbalanc|e ˌəʊ.vəˈbæl.ən*t*s (US) ˌoʊ.vɚˈ- **-es** -ɪz **-ing** -ɪŋ **-ed** -t
overbear ˌəʊ.vəˈbeəʳ (US) ˌoʊ.vɚˈber **-s** -z **-ing** -ɪŋ **over|bore** ˌəʊ.vəˈbɔːʳ (US) ˌoʊ.vɚˈbɔːr **-borne** -ˈbɔːn (US) -ˈbɔːrn
overbearing ˌəʊ.vəˈbeə.rɪŋ (US) ˌoʊ.vɚˈber.ɪŋ **-ly** -li **-ness** -nəs, -nɪs *stress shift:* ˌoverbearing ˈrelatives
overbid ˌəʊ.vəˈbɪd (US) ˌoʊ.vɚ- **-s** -z **-ding** -ɪŋ
overbid ˈəʊ.və.bɪd (US) ˈoʊ.vɚ- **s** -z
overbite ˈəʊ.və.baɪt (US) ˈoʊ.vɚ-
over|blow ˌəʊ.vəˈbləʊ (US) ˌoʊ.vɚˈbloʊ, ˈ--ˌ- **-blows** -ˈbləʊz (US) -ˈbloʊz, -bloʊz **-blowing** -ˈbləʊ.ɪŋ (US) -ˈbloʊ.ɪŋ, -ˌbloʊ.ɪŋ **-blew** -ˈbluː (US) -ˈbluː, -bluː **-blown** -ˈbləʊn (US) -ˈbloʊn, -bloʊn
overboard ˈəʊ.və.bɔːd, ˌ--ˈ- (US) ˈoʊ.vɚ.bɔːrd
overbook ˌəʊ.vəˈbʊk (US) ˌoʊ.vɚˈ- **-s** -s **-ing** -ɪŋ **-ed** -t
overbreadth ˌəʊ.vəˈbredθ, -ˈbretθ (US) ˌoʊ.vɚˈ-
overbrim ˌəʊ.vəˈbrɪm (US) ˌoʊ.vɚˈ- **-s** -z **-ming** -ɪŋ **-med** -d
overbuild ˌəʊ.vəˈbɪld (US) ˌoʊ.vɚˈ-, ˈ--- **-s** -z **-ing** -ɪŋ **overbuilt** ˌəʊ.vəˈbɪlt (US) ˌoʊ.vɚˈ-, ˈ---
overburden ˌəʊ.vəˈbɜː.dən (US) ˌoʊ.vɚˈbɝː- **-s** -z **-ing** -ɪŋ **-ed** -d
Overbury ˈəʊ.və.bər.i (US) ˈoʊ.vɚˌber-, -bɚ-
overcapacity ˌəʊ.və.kəˈpæs.ə.ti, -ɪ.ti (US) ˌoʊ.vɚ.kəˈpæs.ə.t̬i
over-careful ˌəʊ.vəˈkeə.fəl, -fʊl (US) ˌoʊ.vɚˈker- **-ly** -i **-ness** -nəs, -nɪs
overcast ˈəʊ.və.kɑːst, ˌ--ˈ- (US) ˈoʊ.vɚ.kæst, ˌoʊ.vɚˈkæst
over-cautious ˌəʊ.vəˈkɔː.ʃəs (US) ˌoʊ.vɚˈkɑː-, -ˈkɔː- *stress shift:* ˌover-cautious ˈperson
overcharg|e *(v.)* ˌəʊ.vəˈtʃɑːdʒ (US) ˌoʊ.vɚˈtʃɑːrdʒ, ˈ--- **-es** -ɪz **-ing** -ɪŋ **-ed** -d
overcloud ˌəʊ.vəˈklaʊd (US) ˌoʊ.vɚˈklaʊd **-s** -z **-ing** -ɪŋ **-ed** -ɪd
overcoat ˈəʊ.və.kəʊt (US) ˈoʊ.vɚ.koʊt **-s** -s
over|come ˌəʊ.vəˈkʌm (US) ˌoʊ.vɚˈ- **-comes** -ˈkʌmz **-coming** -ˈkʌm.ɪŋ **-came** -ˈkeɪm
overcompen|sate ˌəʊ.vəˈkɒm.pən.seɪt, -pen- (US) ˌoʊ.vɚˈkɑːm.pən- **-sates** -seɪts **-sating** -seɪ.tɪŋ (US) -seɪ.t̬ɪŋ **-sated** -seɪ.tɪd (US) -seɪ.t̬ɪd
overcompensation ˌəʊ.vəˌkɒm.pənˈseɪ.ʃən, -penˈ- (US) ˌoʊ.vɚˌkɑːm.pənˈ-

over-confidence ˌəʊ.vəˈkɒn.fɪ.d^{ə}nts, -fə- (US) ˌoʊ.vɚˈkɑːn.fə-
over-confident ˌəʊ.vəˈkɒn.fɪ.d^{ə}nt, -fə- (US) ˌoʊ.vɚˈkɑːn.fə- **-ly** -li *stress shift:* ˌover-confident ˈcandidate
over-cook ˌəʊ.vəˈkʊk (US) ˌoʊ.vɚˈ- **-s** -s **-ing** -ɪŋ **-ed** -t
overcrowd ˌəʊ.vəˈkraʊd (US) ˌoʊ.vɚˈ- **-s** -z **-ing** -ɪŋ **-ed** -ɪd *stress shift:* ˌovercrowded ˈroom
over-develop ˌəʊ.və.dɪˈvel.əp, -dəˈ- (US) ˌoʊ.vɚ.dɪˈ- **-s** -s **-ing** -ɪŋ **-ed** -t **-ment** -mənt *stress shift:* ˌoverdeveloped ˈmuscles
over|do ˌəʊ.və|ˈduː (US) ˌoʊ.vɚˈ- **-does** -ˈdʌz **-doing** -ˈduː.ɪŋ **-did** -ˈdɪd **-done** -ˈdʌn
overdone *over-cooked:* ˌəʊ.vəˈdʌn (US) ˌoʊ.vɚˈ- *stress shift:* ˌoverdone ˈchicken
overdos|e (*n.*) ˈəʊ.və.dəʊs (US) ˈoʊ.vɚ.doʊs **-es** -ɪz
overdos|e (*v.*) ˌəʊ.vəˈdəʊs (US) ˌoʊ.vɚˈdoʊs, ˈ--- **-es** -ɪz **-ing** -ɪŋ **-ed** -t
overdraft ˈəʊ.və.drɑːft (US) ˈoʊ.vɚ.dræft **-s** -s
overdraught ˈəʊ.və.drɑːft (US) ˈoʊ.vɚ.dræft **-s** -s
overdraw ˌəʊ.vəˈdrɔː (US) ˌoʊ.vɚˈdrɑː, -ˈdrɔː, ˈ--- **-s** -z **-ing** -ɪŋ **overdrew** ˌəʊ.vəˈdruː (US) ˌoʊ.vɚ-, ˈ--- **overdrawn** ˌəʊ.vəˈdrɔːn (US) ˌoʊ.vɚˈdrɑːn, -ˈdrɔːn, ˈ---
overdress (*v.*) ˌəʊ.vəˈdres (US) ˌoʊ.vɚˈ-, ˈ--- **-es** -ɪz **-ing** -ɪŋ **-ed** -t
overdress (*n.*) ˈəʊ.və.dres (US) ˈoʊ.vɚ- **-es** -ɪz
overdrive (*n.*) ˈəʊ.və.draɪv (US) ˈoʊ.vɚ-
over|drive (*v.*) ˌəʊ.və|ˈdraɪv (US) ˌoʊ.vɚˈ- **-drives** -ˈdraɪvz **-driving** -ˈdraɪ.vɪŋ **-drove** -ˈdrəʊv (US) -ˈdroʊv **-driven** -ˈdrɪv.^{ə}n
overdue ˌəʊ.vəˈdjuː (US) ˌoʊ.vɚˈduː, -ˈdjuː *stress shift:* ˌoverdue ˈpayment
over|eat ˌəʊ.v^{ə}r|ˈiːt (US) ˌoʊ.vɚˈ- **-eats** -ˈiːts **-eating** -ˈiː.tɪŋ (US) -ˈiː.ţɪŋ **-eaten** -ˈiː.t^{ə}n **-ate** -ˈet, -ˈeɪt (US) -ˈeɪt
over-emphasis ˌəʊ.v^{ə}rˈemp.fə.sɪs (US) ˌoʊ.vɚˈ-
over-emphasiz|e, -is|e ˌəʊ.v^{ə}rˈemp.fə.saɪz (US) ˌoʊ.vɚˈ- **-es** -ɪz **-ing** -ɪŋ **-ed** -d
overestimate (*n.*) ˌəʊ.v^{ə}rˈes.tɪ.mət, -tə-, -mɪt, -meɪt (US) ˌoʊ.vɚˈes.tɪ.mɪt **-s** -s
overesti|mate (*v.*) ˌəʊ.v^{ə}rˈes.tɪ|.meɪt, -tə- (US) ˌoʊ.vɚˈes.tə- **-mates** -meɪts **-mating** -meɪ.tɪŋ (US) -meɪ.ţɪŋ **-mated** -meɪ.tɪd (US) -meɪ.ţɪd
over-estimation ˌəʊ.v^{ə}rˌes.tɪˈmeɪ.ʃ^{ə}n, -təˈ- (US) ˌoʊ.vɚˌes.təˈ-
overex|cite ˌəʊ.v^{ə}r.ɪk|ˈsaɪt, -ekˈ- (US) ˌoʊ.vɚ- **-cites** -ˈsaɪts **-citing** -ˈsaɪ.tɪŋ (US) -ˈsaɪ.ţɪŋ **-cited** -ˈsaɪ.tɪd (US) -ˈsaɪ.ţɪd **-citement** -ˈsaɪt.mənt
overexer|t ˌəʊ.v^{ə}r.ɪgˈzɜː|t, -egˈ- (US) ˌoʊ.vɚ.ɪgˈzɝː|t, -egˈ- **-ts** -ts **-ting** -tɪŋ (US) -ţɪŋ **-ted** -tɪd (US) -ţɪd
overexertion ˌəʊ.v^{ə}r.ɪgˈzɜː.ʃ^{ə}n, -egˈ- (US) ˌoʊ.vɚ.ɪgˈzɝː-, -egˈ-
overexpos|e ˌəʊ.v^{ə}r.ɪkˈspəʊz, -ekˈ- (US) ˌoʊ.vɚ.ɪkˈspoʊz, -ekˈ- **-es** -ɪz **-ing** -ɪŋ **-ed** -d
over-exposure ˌəʊ.v^{ə}r.ɪkˈspəʊ.ʒə^{r}, -ekˈ- (US) ˌoʊ.vɚ.ɪkˈspoʊ.ʒɚ, -ekˈ-
overfatigu|e ˌəʊ.və.fəˈtiːg (US) ˌoʊ.vɚ- **-es** -z **-ing** -ɪŋ **-ed** -d
overfeed ˌəʊ.vəˈfiːd (US) ˌoʊ.vɚˈ- **-s** -z **-ing** -ɪŋ **overfed** ˌəʊ.vəˈfed (US) ˌoʊ.vɚˈ- *stress shift:* ˌoverfed ˈpets
overflow (*n.*) ˈəʊ.və.fləʊ (US) ˈoʊ.vɚ.floʊ **-s** -z
overflow (*v.*) ˌəʊ.vəˈfləʊ (US) ˌoʊ.vɚˈfloʊ **-s** -z **-ing** -ɪŋ **-ed** -d
over|fly ˌəʊ.və|ˈflaɪ (US) ˌoʊ.vɚˈ-, ˈ--- **-flies** -ˈflaɪz (US) -ˈflaɪz, -flaɪz **-flying** -ˈflaɪ.ɪŋ (US) -ˈflaɪ.ɪŋ, -flaɪ.ɪŋ **-flew** -ˈfluː (US) -ˈfluː, -fluː **-flown** -ˈfləʊn (US) -ˈfloʊn, -floʊn
over-fond ˌəʊ.vəˈfɒnd (US) ˌoʊ.vɚˈfɑːnd
over-generalization, -isa- ˌəʊ.vəˌdʒen.^{ə}r.^{ə}l.aɪˈzeɪ.ʃ^{ə}n, -ɪˈ- (US) ˌoʊ.vɚˌdʒen.ɚ.^{ə}l.ɪˈ-
overground ˈəʊ.və.graʊnd, ˌ--ˈ- (US) ˈoʊ.vɚ.graʊnd, ˌ--ˈ-
over|grow ˌəʊ.və|ˈgrəʊ (US) ˌoʊ.vɚˈgroʊ **-grows** -ˈgrəʊz (US) -ˈgroʊz **-growing** -ˈgrəʊ.ɪŋ (US) -ˈgroʊ.ɪŋ **-grew** -ˈgruː **-grown** -ˈgrəʊn (US) -ˈgroʊn
overgrowth ˈəʊ.və.grəʊθ (US) ˈoʊ.vɚ.groʊθ **-s** -s
overhand (*n. adj.*) ˈəʊ.və.hænd (US) ˈoʊ.vɚ- **-s** -z
overhang (*n.*) ˈəʊ.və.hæŋ (US) ˈoʊ.vɚ- **-s** -z
overhang (*v.*) ˌəʊ.vəˈhæŋ (US) ˌoʊ.vɚˈ-, ˈ--- **-s** -z **-ing** -ɪŋ **overhung** ˌəʊ.vəˈhʌŋ (US) ˌoʊ.vɚˈ-, ˈ---
over-hasty ˌəʊ.vəˈheɪ.sti (US) ˌoʊ.vɚˈ- *stress shift:* ˌover-hasty ˈchoice
overhaul (*n.*) ˈəʊ.və.hɔːl (US) ˈoʊ.vɚ.hɑːl, -hɔːl **-s** -z
overhaul (*v.*) ˌəʊ.vəˈhɔːl (US) ˌoʊ.vɚˈhɑːl, -ˈhɔːl, ˈ--- **-s** -z **-ing** -ɪŋ **-ed** -d
overhead (*n. adj.*) ˈəʊ.və.hed (US) ˈoʊ.vɚ- **-s** -z ˌ**overhead proˈjector**
overhead (*adv.*) ˌəʊ.vəˈhed (US) ˌoʊ.vɚˈ-
overhear ˌəʊ.vəˈhɪə^{r} (US) ˌoʊ.vɚˈhɪr **-s** -z **-ing** -ɪŋ **overheard** ˌəʊ.vəˈhɜːd (US) ˌoʊ.vɚˈhɝːd
over|heat ˌəʊ.və|ˈhiːt (US) ˌoʊ.vɚˈ- **-heats** -ˈhiːts **-heating** -ˈhiː.tɪŋ (US) -ˈhiː.ţɪŋ **-heated** -ˈhiː.tɪd (US) -ˈhiː.ţɪd
over-impress|ed ˌəʊ.v^{ə}r.ɪmˈpres|t (US) ˌoʊ.vɚ- **-ive** -ɪv
over-indulg|e ˌəʊ.v^{ə}r.ɪnˈdʌldʒ (US) ˌoʊ.vɚ- **-es** -ɪz **-ing** -ɪŋ **-ed** -d **-ence** -^{ə}nts
overjoyed ˌəʊ.vəˈdʒɔɪd (US) ˌoʊ.vɚˈ- *stress shift:* ˌoverjoyed ˈwinner
overkill ˈəʊ.və.kɪl (US) ˈoʊ.vɚ-
overladen ˌəʊ.vəˈleɪ.d^{ə}n (US) ˌoʊ.vɚˈ- *stress shift:* ˌoverladen ˈbasket
overlaid ˌəʊ.vəˈleɪd (US) ˌoʊ.vɚˈ-
overland (*adj.*) ˈəʊ.və.lænd (US) ˈoʊ.vɚ-
overland (*adv.*) ˌəʊ.vəˈlænd, ˈ--- (US) ˌoʊ.vɚˈlænd, ˈ---
overlap (*n.*) ˈəʊ.və.læp (US) ˈoʊ.vɚ- **-s** -s
overlap (*v.*) ˌəʊ.vəˈlæp (US) ˌoʊ.vɚˈ- **-s** -s **-ping** -ɪŋ **-ped** -t
overlay (*n.*) ˈəʊ.v^{ə}l.eɪ (US) ˈoʊ.vɚ.leɪ **-s** -z
overlay (*v.*) ˌəʊ.v^{ə}lˈeɪ (US) ˌoʊ.vɚˈleɪ **-s** -z **-ing** -ɪŋ **overlaid** ˌəʊ.v^{ə}lˈeɪd (US) ˌoʊ.vɚˈleɪd
overleaf ˌəʊ.v^{ə}lˈiːf (US) ˈoʊ.vɚ.liːf
overload (*n.*) ˈəʊ.v^{ə}l.əʊd (US) ˈoʊ.vɚ.loʊd **-s** -z
overload (*v.*) ˌəʊ.v^{ə}lˈəʊd (US) ˌoʊ.vɚˈloʊd, ˈ--- **-s** -z **-ing** -ɪŋ **-ed** -ɪd
overlock ˈəʊ.v^{ə}l.ɒk (US) ˈoʊ.vɚ.lɑːk **-s** -s **-ing** -ɪŋ **-ed** -t
overlong ˌəʊ.vəˈlɒŋ (US) ˌoʊ.vɚˈlɑːŋ, -ˈlɔːŋ
overlook (*v.*) ˌəʊ.vəˈlʊk (US) ˌoʊ.vɚˈ- **-s** -s **-ing** -ɪŋ **-ed** -t
overlook (*n.*) ˈəʊ.və.lʊk (US) ˈoʊ.vɚ- **-s** -s
overlord ˈəʊ.və.lɔːd (US) ˈoʊ.vɚ.lɔːrd **-s** -z
overly ˈəʊ.v^{ə}l.i (US) ˈoʊ.vɚ.li
overlying ˌəʊ.v^{ə}lˈaɪ.ɪŋ (US) ˌoʊ.vɚˈlaɪ- *stress shift:* ˌoverlying ˈstructure
overman (*v.*) ˌəʊ.vəˈmæn (US) ˌoʊ.vɚˈ- **-s** -z **-ning** -ɪŋ **-ned** -d
over|man (*n.*) ˈəʊ.və|.mæn (US) ˈoʊ.vɚ- **-men** -men
overmantel ˈəʊ.vəˌmæn.t^{ə}l (US) ˈoʊ.vɚˌmæn.ţ^{ə}l **-s** -z
overmast|er ˌəʊ.vəˈmɑː.st|ə^{r} (US) ˌoʊ.vɚˈmæs.tɚ **-ers** -əz (US) -ɚz **-ering** -^{ə}r.ɪŋ **-ered** -əd (US) -ɚd
overmatch ˌəʊ.vəˈmætʃ (US) ˌoʊ.vɚ-, ˈ--- **-es** -ɪz **-ing** -ɪŋ **-ed** -t
overmuch ˌəʊ.vəˈmʌtʃ, ˈ--- (US) ˌoʊ.vɚˈ-, ˈ---
overnight ˌəʊ.vəˈnaɪt (US) ˌoʊ.vɚˈ- *stress shift:* ˌovernight ˈsleeper
overoptimistic ˌəʊ.v^{ə}rˌɒp.tɪˈmɪs.tɪk, -təˈ- (US) ˌoʊ.vɚˌɑːp.təˈ- **-ally** -^{ə}l.i, -li *stress shift:* ˌoveroptimistic ˈoutlook

overpass (*n.*) 'əʊ.və.pɑːs (US) 'oʊ.vɚ.pæs **-es** -ɪz

over|pay ˌəʊ.və|'peɪ (US) ˌoʊ.vɚ'-, '--|- **-pays** -'peɪz **-paying** -'peɪ.ɪŋ **-paid** -'peɪd **-payment/s** -'peɪ.mənt/s

overplay ˌəʊ.və'pleɪ (US) ˌoʊ.vɚ- **-s** -z **-ing** -ɪŋ **-ed** -d

overplus 'əʊ.və.plʌs (US) 'oʊ.vɚ- **-es** -ɪz

overpopu|late ˌəʊ.və'pɒp.jə|.leɪt, -jʊ- (US) ˌoʊ.vɚ'pɑː.pjə-, -pjʊ- **-lates** -leɪts **-lating** -leɪ.tɪŋ (US) -leɪ.t̬ɪŋ **-lated** -leɪ.tɪd (US) -leɪ.t̬ɪd

overpopulation ˌəʊ.vəˌpɒp.jə'leɪ.ʃən, -jʊ'- (US) ˌoʊ.vɚˌpɑː.pjə'-, -pjʊ'-

overpower ˌəʊ.və'paʊəʳ (US) ˌoʊ.vɚ'paʊɚ **-s** -z **-ing/ly** -ɪŋ/li **-ed** -d

overpriced ˌəʊ.və'praɪst (US) ˌoʊ.vɚ- *stress shift:* ˌoverpriced 'goods

overprint (*n.*) 'əʊ.və.prɪnt (US) 'oʊ.vɚ- **-s** -s

overprin|t (*v.*) ˌəʊ.və'prɪn|t, '--- (US) ˌoʊ.vɚ'-, '--- **-ts** -ts **-ting** -tɪŋ (US) -t̬ɪŋ **-ted** -tɪd (US) -t̬ɪd

overproduc|e ˌəʊ.və.prə'djuːs (US) ˌoʊ.vɚ.proʊ'duːs, -'djuːs, 'oʊ.vɚ.proʊˌduːs, -ˌdjuːs **-es** -ɪz **-ing** -ɪŋ **-ed** -t

overproduction ˌəʊ.və.prə'dʌk.ʃən (US) ˌoʊ.vɚ-

overprotect ˌəʊ.və.prə'tekt (US) ˌoʊ.vɚ- **-s** -s **-ing** -ɪŋ **-ed** -ɪd

overprotective ˌəʊ.və.prə'tek.tɪv (US) ˌoʊ.vɚ- *stress shift:* ˌoverprotective 'parent

overqualified ˌəʊ.və'kwɒl.ɪ.faɪd, '-ə- (US) ˌoʊ.vɚ'kwɑː.lɪ-, 'oʊ.vɚˌkwɑː.lɪ- *stress shift, British only:* ˌoverqualified 'applicant

overra|te ˌəʊ.vəʳ'eɪ|t (US) ˌoʊ.vɚ'reɪ|t, '--- **-tes** -ts **-ting** -tɪŋ (US) -t̬ɪŋ **-ted** -tɪd (US) -t̬ɪd

overreach (*n.*) 'əʊ.vəʳ'iːtʃ (US) 'oʊ.vɚ.riːtʃ **-es** -ɪz

overreach (*v.*) ˌəʊ.vəʳ'iːtʃ (US) ˌoʊ.vɚ'riːtʃ, '--- **-es** -ɪz **-ing** -ɪŋ **-ed** -t

overreact ˌəʊ.vəʳ.i'ækt (US) ˌoʊ.vɚ.ri'- **-s** -s **-ing** -ɪŋ **-ed** -ɪd

overreaction ˌəʊ.vəʳ.i'æk.ʃən (US) -oʊ.vɚ.ri'-

overrid|e ˌəʊ.vəʳ'aɪd (US) ˌoʊ.vɚ'raɪd **-es** -z **-ing** -ɪŋ **overrode** ˌəʊ.vəʳ'əʊd (US) ˌoʊ.vɚ'roʊd **overridden** ˌəʊ.vəʳ'ɪd.ən (US) ˌoʊ.vɚ'rɪd-

overrider 'əʊ.vəʳˌaɪ.dəʳ (US) 'oʊ.vɚˌraɪ.dɚ **-s** -z

overripe ˌəʊ.vəʳ'aɪp (US) ˌoʊ.vɚ'raɪp **-ness** -nəs, -nɪs *stress shift:* ˌoverripe 'fruit

overripen ˌəʊ.vəʳ'aɪ.pən (US) ˌoʊ.vɚ'raɪ- **-s** -z **-ing** -ɪŋ, -vəʳ'aɪp.nɪŋ (US) -vɚ'raɪp- **-ed** -d

overrul|e ˌəʊ.vəʳ'uːl (US) ˌoʊ.vɚ'ruːl **-es** -z **-ing** -ɪŋ **-ed** -d

overrun (*v.*) ˌəʊ.vəʳ'ʌn (US) ˌoʊ.vɚ'rʌn **-s** -z **-ning** -ɪŋ **overran** ˌəʊ.vəʳ'æn (US) ˌoʊ.vɚ'ræn

overrun (*n.*) 'əʊ.vəʳ.ʌn (US) 'oʊ.vɚ- **-s** -z

over-scrupulous ˌəʊ.və'skruː.pjə.ləs, -pjʊ- (US) ˌoʊ.vɚ'skruː.pjə- **-ly** -li **-ness** -nəs, -nɪs *stress shift:* ˌover-scrupulous 'person

oversea ˌəʊ.və'siː (US) ˌoʊ.vɚ'-, 'oʊ.vɚ.siː **-s** -z *stress shift:* ˌoverseas 'applicant

over|see ˌəʊ.və|'siː (US) ˌoʊ.vɚ'- **-sees** -'siːz **-seeing** -'siː.ɪŋ **-saw** -'sɔː (US) -'sɑː, -'sɔː **-seen** -'siːn

overseer 'əʊ.vəˌsiː.əʳ (US) 'oʊ.vɚˌsiː.ɚ, -ˌsɪr **-s** -z

over|sell ˌəʊ.və|'sel (US) -vɚ- **-sells** -selz **-selling** -sel.ɪŋ **-sold** -səʊld (US) -soʊld

oversensitive ˌəʊ.və'sen*t*.sɪ.tɪv, -sə- (US) ˌoʊ.vɚ'sen*t*.sə.t̬ɪv *stress shift:* ˌoversensitive 'person

oversensitivity ˌəʊ.vəˌsen*t*.sɪ'tɪv.ə.ti, -sə'-, -ɪ.ti (US) ˌoʊ.vɚˌsen*t*.sə'tɪv.ə.t̬i

oversew 'əʊ.və.səʊ, ˌ--'- (US) 'oʊ.vɚ.soʊ, ˌ--'- **-s** -z **-ing** -ɪŋ **-ed** -d **-n** -n

oversexed ˌəʊ.və'sekst (US) ˌoʊ.vɚ'- *stress shift:* ˌoversexed 'person

overshadow ˌəʊ.və'ʃæd.əʊ (US) ˌoʊ.vɚ'ʃæd.oʊ **-s** -z **-ing** -ɪŋ **-ed** -d

overshoe 'əʊ.və.ʃuː (US) 'oʊ.vɚ- **-s** -z

overshoot (*n.*) 'əʊ.və.ʃuːt (US) 'oʊ.vɚ-

overshoot (*v.*) ˌəʊ.və'ʃuːt (US) ˌoʊ.vɚ'- **-s** -s **-ing** -ɪŋ **overshot** ˌəʊ.və'ʃɒt (US) ˌoʊ.vɚ'ʃɑːt

overside (*adv.*) 'əʊ.və.saɪd (US) 'oʊ.vɚ-

oversight 'əʊ.və.saɪt (US) 'oʊ.vɚ- **-s** -s

oversimplification ˌəʊ.vəˌsɪm.plɪ.fɪ'keɪ.ʃən, -plə- (US) ˌoʊ.vɚˌsɪm.plə- **-s** -z

oversimpli|fy ˌəʊ.və'sɪm.plɪ|.faɪ, -plə- (US) ˌoʊ.vɚ'sɪm.plə-, '--ˌ--- **-fies** -faɪz **-fying** -faɪ.ɪŋ **-fied** -faɪd

oversize ˌəʊ.və'saɪz (US) ˌoʊ.vɚ'-, '--- **-d** -d *stress shift:* ˌoversize 'clothes

oversleep ˌəʊ.və'sliːp (US) ˌoʊ.vɚ'- **-s** -s **-ing** -ɪŋ **overslept** ˌəʊ.və'slept (US) ˌoʊ.vɚ'-

oversold (*from* **oversell**) ˌəʊ.və'səʊld (US) ˌoʊ.vɚ'soʊld *stress shift:* ˌoversold 'concept

overspend ˌəʊ.və'spend (US) ˌoʊ.vɚ'-, '--- **-s** -z **-ing** -ɪŋ **overspent** ˌəʊ.və'spent (US) ˌoʊ.vɚ'-, '---

overspill 'əʊ.və.spɪl (US) 'oʊ.vɚ-

overspread ˌəʊ.və'spred (US) ˌoʊ.vɚ'-, '--- **-s** -z **-ing** -ɪŋ

overstaff ˌəʊ.və'stɑːf (US) ˌoʊ.vɚ'stæf **-s** -s **-ing** -ɪŋ **-ed** -t

over|state ˌəʊ.və|'steɪt (US) ˌoʊ.vɚ'- **-states** -'steɪts **-stating** -'steɪ.tɪŋ (US) -'steɪ.t̬ɪŋ **-stated** -'steɪ.tɪd (US) -'steɪ.t̬ɪd *stress shift:* ˌoverstated 'argument

overstatement ˌəʊ.və'steɪt.mənt, 'əʊ.vəˌsteɪt- (US) ˌoʊ.vɚ'steɪt, 'oʊ.vɚˌsteɪt **-s** -s

overstay ˌəʊ.və'steɪ (US) ˌoʊ.vɚ'-, '--- **-s** -z **-ing** -ɪŋ **-ed** -d

overstep ˌəʊ.və'step (US) ˌoʊ.vɚ'- **-s** -s **-ping** -ɪŋ **-ped** -t

overstimu|late ˌəʊ.və'stɪm.jə|.leɪt, -jʊ- (US) ˌoʊ.vɚ'stɪm.jə-, -jʊ- **-lates** -leɪts **-lating** -leɪ.tɪŋ (US) -leɪ.t̬ɪŋ **-lated** -leɪ.tɪd (US) -leɪ.t̬ɪd

overstock ˌəʊ.və'stɒk (US) ˌoʊ.vɚ'stɑːk **-s** -s **-ing** -ɪŋ **-ed** -t

overstrain (*n.*) 'əʊ.və.streɪn, ˌ--'- (US) ˌoʊ.vɚ'-, '---

overstrain (*v.*) ˌəʊ.və'streɪn (US) ˌoʊ.vɚ'- **-s** -z **-ing** -ɪŋ **-ed** -d

Overstrand 'əʊ.və.strænd (US) 'oʊ.vɚ-

overstretch ˌəʊ.və'stretʃ (US) ˌoʊ.vɚ'- **-es** -ɪz **-ing** -ɪŋ **-ed** -t

overstrung *in state of nervous tension:* ˌəʊ.və'strʌŋ (US) ˌoʊ.vɚ'- *of piano:* 'əʊ.və.strʌŋ (US) 'oʊ.vɚ-

oversubscrib|e ˌəʊ.və.səb'skraɪb (US) ˌoʊ.vɚ- **-es** -z **-ing** -ɪŋ **-ed** -d

oversubscription ˌəʊ.və.səb'skrɪp.ʃən (US) ˌoʊ.vɚ-

oversupp|ly ˌəʊ.və.sə'pl|aɪ (US) ˌoʊ.vɚ- **-ies** -aɪz

overt əʊ'vɜːt; 'əʊ.vɜːt (US) oʊ'vɝːt, '-- **-ly** -li **-ness** -nəs, -nɪs

over|take ˌəʊ.və|'teɪk (US) ˌoʊ.vɚ'- **-takes** -'teɪks **-taking** -'teɪ.kɪŋ **-took** -'tʊk **-taken** -'teɪ.kən, -kəŋ (US) -kən

overtask ˌəʊ.və'tɑːsk (US) ˌoʊ.vɚ'tæsk **-s** -s **-ing** -ɪŋ **-ed** -t

overtax ˌəʊ.və'tæks (US) ˌoʊ.vɚ'- **-es** -ɪz **-ing** -ɪŋ **-ed** -t

over-the-counter ˌəʊ.və.ðə'kaʊn.təʳ (US) ˌoʊ.vɚ.ðə'kaʊn.t̬ɚ *stress shift:* ˌover-the-counter 'sales

over-the-top ˌəʊ.və.ðə'tɒp (US) ˌoʊ.vɚ.ðə'tɑːp *stress shift:* ˌover-the-top 'speech

Note: See also **OTT**.

overthrow (*n.*) 'əʊ.və.θrəʊ (US) 'oʊ.vɚ.θroʊ **-s** -z

overthrow (*v.*) ˌəʊ.və'θrəʊ (US) ˌoʊ.vɚ'θroʊ, '--- **-s** -z **-ing** -ɪŋ **overthrew** ˌəʊ.və'θruː (US) ˌoʊ.vɚ'-, '--- **overthrown** ˌəʊ.və'θrəʊn (US) ˌoʊ.vɚ'θroʊn, '---

Pronouncing the letters OW

There are two common pronunciations of the vowel digraph **ow**: /əʊ (US) oʊ/ and /aʊ/, e.g.:

blow	/bləʊ/	(US) /bloʊ/
brown	/braʊn/	

In addition

A less common realisation is /ɒ (US) ɑː/, e.g.:

knowledge	/ˈnɒl.ɪdʒ/	(US) /ˈnɑː.lɪdʒ/

overthrust ˈəʊ.və.θrʌst (US) ˈoʊ.vɚ- **-s** -s
overtime ˈəʊ.və.taɪm (US) ˈoʊ.vɚ-
overtir|e ˌəʊ.vəˈtaɪəʳ (US) ˌoʊ.vɚˈtaɪɚ **-es** -z **-ing** -ɪŋ **-ed** -d
overtone ˈəʊ.və.təʊn (US) ˈoʊ.vɚ.toʊn **-s** -z
overtop ˌəʊ.vəˈtɒp (US) ˌoʊ.vɚˈtɑːp **-s** -s **-ping** -ɪŋ **-ped** -t
Overtoun ˈəʊ.və.tᵊn (US) ˈoʊ.vɚ-
Overtown ˈəʊ.və.tᵊn (US) ˈoʊ.vɚ-
over-trump ˌəʊ.vəˈtrʌmp (US) ˌoʊ.vɚˈ- **-s** -s **-ing** -ɪŋ **-ed** -t
overture ˈəʊ.və.tjʊəʳ, -tjəʳ, -tʃʊəʳ, -tʃəʳ (US) ˈoʊ.vɚ.tʃɚ, -tʃʊr **-s** -z
overturn *(n.)* ˈəʊ.və.tɜːn (US) ˈoʊ.vɚ.tɝːn **-s** -z
overturn *(v.)* ˌəʊ.vəˈtɜːn (US) ˌoʊ.vɚˈtɝːn **-s** -z **-ing** -ɪŋ **-ed** -d
overus|e *(v.)* ˌəʊ.vəˈjuːz (US) ˌoʊ.vɚˈ- **-es** -ɪz **-ing** -ɪŋ **-ed** -d
overuse *(n.)* ˌəʊ.vəˈjuːs (US) ˌoʊ.vɚˈ-
overval|ue ˌəʊ.vəˈvæl|.juː (US) ˌoʊ.vɚˈ- **-ues** -juːz **-uing** -juː.ɪŋ **-ued** -juːd
overview ˈəʊ.və.vjuː (US) ˈoʊ.vɚ- **-s** -z
overweening ˌəʊ.vəˈwiː.nɪŋ (US) ˌoʊ.vɚˈ-, ˈoʊ.vɚˌwiː- **-ly** -li *stress shift:* ˌoverweening ˈpride
overweight *(n.)* ˈəʊ.və.weɪt (US) ˈoʊ.vɚ- **-s** -s
overweight *(adj.)* ˌəʊ.vəˈweɪt (US) ˌoʊ.vɚˈ-, ˈ--- *stress shift, British only:* ˌoverweight ˈperson
overweigh|t *(v.)* ˌəʊ.vəˈweɪ|t (US) ˌoʊ.vɚˈ-, ˈ--- **-ts** -ts **-ting** -tɪŋ (US) -t̬ɪŋ **-ted** -tɪd (US) -t̬ɪd
overwhelm ˌəʊ.vəˈhwelm (US) ˌoʊ.vɚˈ- **-s** -z **-ing/ly** -ɪŋ/li **-ed** -d
overwind ˌəʊ.vəˈwaɪnd (US) ˌoʊ.vɚˈ-, ˈ--- **-s** -z **-ing** -ɪŋ **overwound** ˌəʊ.vəˈwaʊnd (US) ˌoʊ.vɚˈ-, ˈ---
overwint|er ˌəʊ.vəˈwɪn.t|əʳ (US) ˌoʊ.vɚˈwɪn.t̬|ɚ **-ers** -əz (US) -ɚz **-ering** -ᵊr.ɪŋ **-ered** -əd (US) -ɚd
overwork *(n.)* ˈəʊ.və.wɜːk (US) ˈoʊ.vɚ.wɝːk
overwork *(v.)* ˌəʊ.vəˈwɜːk (US) ˌoʊ.vɚˈwɝːk, ˈ--- **-s** -s **-ing** -ɪŋ **-ed** -t **-er/s** -əʳ/z (US) -ɚ/z *stress shift:* ˌoverworked ˈeditor
overwrit|e ˌəʊ.vᵊrˈaɪt (US) ˌoʊ.vɚˈraɪt **-es** -s **-ing** -ɪŋ **overwrote** ˌəʊ.vᵊrˈəʊt (US) ˌoʊ.vɚˈroʊt **overwritten** ˌəʊ.vᵊrˈɪt.ᵊn (US) ˌoʊ.vɚˈrɪt-
overwrought ˌəʊ.vᵊrˈɔːt (US) ˌoʊ.vɚˈrɑːt, -ˈrɔːt *stress shift:* ˌoverwrought ˈperson
overzealous ˌəʊ.vəˈzel.əs (US) ˌoʊ.vɚˈ- *stress shift:* ˌoverzealous ˈfollower
Ovett ˈəʊ.vet, -ˈ- (US) ˈoʊ.vet, -ˈ-
Ovid *Latin poet:* ˈɒv.ɪd (US) ˈɑː.vɪd *US surname:* ˈəʊ.vɪd (US) ˈoʊ-
Ovidian əʊˈvɪd.i.ən, ɒvˈɪd- (US) oʊˈvɪd-
Oviedo ˌɒv.iˈeɪ.dəʊ (US) oʊˈvjeɪ.doʊ, -ðoʊ
oviform ˈəʊ.vɪ.fɔːm (US) ˈoʊ.vɪ.fɔːrm
ovine ˈəʊ.vaɪn (US) ˈoʊ-
Ovingdean ˈɒv.ɪŋ.diːn (US) ˈɑː.vɪŋ-
Ovingham ˈɒv.ɪn.dʒəm (US) ˈɑː.vɪn-
Ovington *in North Yorkshire, street in London:* ˈɒv.ɪŋ.tən (US) ˈɑː.vɪŋ- *in Norfolk, surname:* ˈəʊ.vɪŋ.tən (US) ˈoʊ-
oviparous əʊˈvɪp.ᵊr.əs (US) oʊ- **-ly** -li **-ness** -nəs, -nɪs
ovoid ˈəʊ.vɔɪd (US) ˈoʊ- **-s** -z
ovular ˈɒv.jə.ləʳ, ˈəʊ.vjə-, -vjʊ- (US) ˈɑː.vjuː.lɚ, ˈoʊ-, -vjə-
ovu|late ˈɒv.jə|.leɪt, ˈəʊ.vjə- (US) ˈɑː.vjuː-, ˈoʊ-, -vjə- **-lates** -leɪts **-lating** -leɪ.tɪŋ (US) -leɪ.t̬ɪŋ **-lated** -leɪ.tɪd (US) -leɪ.t̬ɪd
ovulation ˌɒv.jəˈleɪ.ʃᵊn, ˌəʊ.vjəˈ-, -vjʊˈ- (US) ˌɑː.vjuːˈ-, ˌoʊ-, -vjəˈ-
ovule ˈɒv.juːl, ˈəʊ.vjuːl (US) ˈɑː-, ˈoʊ- **-s** -z
ov|um ˈəʊ.v|əm (US) ˈoʊ- **-a** -ə
Owbridge ˈəʊ.brɪdʒ (US) ˈoʊ-
ow|e əʊ (US) oʊ **-es** -z **-ing** -ɪŋ **-ed** -d
Owen ˈəʊ.ɪn (US) ˈoʊ- **-s** -z
Ower aʊəʳ (US) aʊɚ
Owers əʊəz, aʊəz (US) oʊɚz, aʊɚz
owing *(from* **owe***)* ˈəʊ.ɪŋ (US) ˈoʊ-
owl aʊl **-s** -z
owler|y ˈaʊ.lᵊr|.i **-ies** -iz
Owles əʊlz, aʊlz, uːlz (US) oʊlz, aʊlz, uːlz
owlet ˈaʊ.lət, -lɪt, -let (US) -lɪt **-s** -s
Owlett ˈaʊ.lɪt, -let (US) -lɪt
owlish ˈaʊ.lɪʃ **-ly** -li **-ness** -nəs, -nɪs
own əʊn (US) oʊn **-s** -z **-ing** -ɪŋ **-ed** -d **-er/s** -əʳ/z (US) -ɚ/z ˌ**own** ˈ**goal**
own-brand ˌəʊnˈbrænd, ˌəʊm-, ˈ-- (US) ˌoʊnˈ-, ˈ-- **-s** -z **-ing** -ɪŋ
owner-driver ˌəʊ.nəˈdraɪ.vəʳ (US) ˌoʊ.nɚˈdraɪ.vɚ **-s** -z *stress shift:* ˌowner-driver ˈtaxi
owner-occup|ier ˌəʊ.nəʳˈɒk.jə.p|aɪ.əʳ, -jʊ- (US) ˌoʊ.nɚˈɑː.kjuː.p|aɪ.ɚ, -kjə- **-iers** -aɪ.əz (US) -aɪ.ɚz **-ied** -aɪd
ownership ˈəʊ.nə.ʃɪp (US) ˈoʊ.nɚ-
own-label ˌəʊnˈleɪ.bᵊl (US) ˌoʊn-
Owsley ˈaʊz.li
owt aʊt, əʊt (US) aʊt, oʊt
ox ɒks (US) ɑːks **-en** -ᵊn
oxalate ˈɒk.sə.leɪt, -lɪt, -lət (US) ˈɑːk.sə.leɪt **-s** -s
oxalic ɒkˈsæl.ɪk (US) ɑːkˈ-
oxalis ɒkˈsɑː.lɪs, -ˈsæl.ɪs, -ˈseɪ.lɪs; ˈɒk.sə.lɪs (US) ˈɑːk.sə.lɪs; ɑːkˈsæl.ɪs
oxbow ˈɒks.bəʊ (US) ˈɑːks.boʊ **-s** -z
Oxbridge ˈɒks.brɪdʒ (US) ˈɑːks-
Oxbrow ˈɒks.braʊ (US) ˈɑːks-
oxen *(plur. of* **ox***)* ˈɒk.sᵊn (US) ˈɑːk-
Oxenden ˈɒk.sᵊn.dən (US) ˈɑːk-
Oxenford ˈɒk.sᵊn.fɔːd, -fəd (US) ˈɑːk.sən.fɔːrd, -fɚd
Oxenham ˈɒk.sᵊn.əm (US) ˈɑːk-
Oxenhope ˈɒk.sᵊn.həʊp (US) ˈɑːk.sᵊn.hoʊp
oxer ˈɒk.səʳ (US) ˈɑːk.sɚ **-s** -z
oxeye ˈɒks.aɪ (US) ˈɑːk.saɪ **-s** -z **-d** -d
Oxfam ˈɒks.fæm (US) ˈɑːks-
Oxford ˈɒks.fəd (US) ˈɑːks.fɚd **-shire** -ʃəʳ, -ˌʃɪəʳ (US) -ʃɚ, -ˌʃɪr
oxidant ˈɒk.sɪ.dᵊnt, -sə- (US) ˈɑːk.sɪ- **-s** -s
oxi|date ˈɒk.sɪ|.deɪt, -sə- (US) ˈɑːk.sɪ- **-dates** -deɪts **-dating** -deɪ.tɪŋ (US) -deɪ.t̬ɪŋ **-dated** -deɪ.tɪd (US) -deɪ.t̬ɪd
oxidation ˌɒk.sɪˈdeɪ.ʃᵊn, -səˈ- (US) ˌɑːk.sɪˈ-
oxide ˈɒk.saɪd (US) ˈɑːk- **-s** -z
oxidization, -isa- ˌɒk.sɪ.daɪˈzeɪ.ʃᵊn, -sə-, -dɪˈ- (US) ˌɑːk.sɪ.dɪˈ-
oxidiz|e, -is|e ˈɒk.sɪ.daɪz, -sə- (US) ˈɑːk.sɪ- **-es** -ɪz **-ing** -ɪŋ **-ed** -d **-er/s** -əʳ/z (US) -ɚ/z **-able** -ə.bl̩
Oxley ˈɒk.sli (US) ˈɑːk-
oxlip ˈɒk.slɪp (US) ˈɑːk- **-s** -s
oxo (O®) ˈɒk.səʊ (US) ˈɑːk.soʊ
Oxon. ˈɒk.sᵊn, -sɒn (US) ˈɑːk.sᵊn, -sɑːn

Oxonian ɒk'səʊ.ni.ən (US) ɑːk'soʊ- **-s** -z

Oxshott 'ɒk.ʃɒt (US) 'ɑːk.ʃɑːt

oxtail 'ɒks.teɪl (US) 'ɑːks- **-s** -z ˌ**oxtail** '**soup**

Oxted 'ɒk.stɪd (US) 'ɑːk-

ox-tongue 'ɒks.tʌŋ (US) 'ɑːks- **-s** -z

Oxus 'ɒk.səs (US) 'ɑːk-

oxy- ɒk.sɪ-, -si-; ɒk'sɪ (US) ɑːk.sɪ-, -si-; ɑːk'sɪ-

Note: Prefix. Normally either takes primary or secondary stress on the first syllable, e.g. **oxygen** /'ɒk.sɪ.dʒən (US) 'ɑːk-/, **oxychloride** /ˌɒk.sɪ'klɔː.raɪd (US) ˌɑːk.sɪ'klɔːr.aɪd/, or primary stress on the second syllable, e.g. **oxygenous** /ɒk'sɪdʒ.ᵊn.əs (US) ɑːk-/.

oxyacetylene ˌɒk.si.ə'set.ᵊl.iːn, -ɪ.liːn, -lɪn (US) ˌɑːk.si.ə'seṭ.ᵊl.iːn, -ɪn

oxychloride ˌɒk.sɪ'klɔː.raɪd (US) ˌɑːk.sɪ'klɔːr.aɪd **-s** -z

oxygen 'ɒk.sɪ.dʒən, -sə- (US) 'ɑːk.sɪ-

oxyge|nate 'ɒk.sɪ.dʒə|.neɪt, -sə-, -dʒɪ-; (US) 'ɑːk.sɪ.dʒə- **-nates** -neɪts **-nating** -neɪ.tɪŋ (US) -neɪ.ṭɪŋ **-nated** -neɪ.tɪd (US) -neɪ.ṭɪd

oxygenation ˌɒk.sɪ.dʒə'neɪ.ʃᵊn, -sə-, -dʒɪ'-; (US) ˌɑːk.sɪ.dʒə'-

oxygeniz|e, -is|e 'ɒk.sɪ.dʒə.naɪz, -sə- (US) 'ɑːk.sɪ- **-es** -ɪz **-ing** -ɪŋ **-ed** -d

oxygenous ɒk'sɪdʒ.ᵊn.əs, -ɪ.nəs (US) ɑːk-

oxyhaemoglobin ˌɒk.siˌhiː.məʊ'gləʊ.bɪn (US) ˌɑːk.siˌhiː.mə'gloʊ-, -moʊ'-

oxyhydrogen ˌɒk.si'haɪ.drə.dʒən, -drɪ- (US) ˌɑːk.si'haɪ.drə-

oxymoron ˌɒk.sɪ'mɔː.rɒn, -rᵊn (US) ˌɑːk.sɪ'mɔːr.ɑːn **-s** -z

oxytone 'ɒk.sɪ.təʊn (US) 'ɑːk.sɪ.toʊn **-s** -z

oyer 'ɔɪ.əʳ (US) -ɚ ˌ**oyer and** '**terminer**

oyes, oyez əʊ'jes, -'jez, -'jeɪ, '-- (US) 'oʊ.jes, -jez, -jeɪ

oyster (O) 'ɔɪ.stəʳ (US) -stɚ **-s** -z

oyster-catcher 'ɔɪ.stəˌkætʃ.əʳ (US) -stɚˌkætʃ.ɚ **-s** -z

Oystermouth 'ɔɪ.stə.maʊθ (US) -stɚ-

oz. *(abbrev. for* **ounce/s**) *singular:* aʊnts *plural:* 'aʊnt.sɪz

Oz ɒz (US) ɑːz

Ozalid® 'əʊ.zᵊl.ɪd, 'ɒz.ᵊl- (US) 'ɑː.zᵊl- **-s** -z

Ozanne əʊ'zæn (US) oʊ-

Ozarks 'əʊ.zɑːks (US) 'oʊ.zɑːrks

ozokerite əʊ'zəʊ.kᵊr.ɪt, ɒz'əʊ-, ə'zəʊ- (US) oʊ'zoʊ.kə.raɪt; ˌoʊ.zoʊ'kɪr.aɪt

ozone 'əʊ.zəʊn (US) 'oʊ.zoʊn '**ozone** ˌ**layer**

ozone-friendly ˌəʊ.zəʊn'frend.li (US) ˌoʊ.zoʊn'- *stress shift:* ˌozone-friendly 'chemicals

ozonic əʊ'zɒn.ɪk (US) oʊ'zɑː.nɪk

ozoniferous ˌəʊ.zəʊ'nɪf.ᵊr.əs (US) ˌoʊ.zə'-

ozonosphere əʊ'zɒn.ə.sfɪəʳ, -'zəʊ.nə- (US) oʊ'zoʊ.nə.sfɪr

Ozymandias ˌɒz.ɪ'mæn.di.əs, -æs (US) ˌɑː.zi-

Ozzie 'ɒz.i (US) 'ɑː.zi

Pronouncing the letter P

See also PH

The consonant letter **p** is most often realised as /p/, e.g.:

pen /pen/

In addition

p can be silent. There are three combinations in which this can occur: **pn**, **ps** and **pt**.

p is silent in **pn** and **ps** when word initial, e.g.:

pneumatic /njuːˈmæt.ɪk/ ⓊⓈ /nuːˈmæt̬-/
psalm /sɑːm/

pt can be silent word initially and word finally, e.g.:

pterodactyl /ˌter.əʊˈdæk.tɪl/ ⓊⓈ /ˌter.əˈdæk.təl/
receipt /rɪˈsiːt/

In addition

p can be silent in other instances, e.g.:

corps /kɔːʳ/ ⓊⓈ /kɔːr/
cupboard /ˈkʌb.əd/ ⓊⓈ /-ɚd/
raspberry /ˈrɑːz.bᵊr.i/ ⓊⓈ /ˈræzˌber.i/

p (P) piː -'s -z ˌp's and ˈq's
pa pɑː -s -z
PA ˌpiːˈeɪ
Pa. *(abbrev. for* **Pennsylvania***)* ˌpent.sɪlˈveɪ.ni.ə, -sᵊlˈ-, ˈ-njə ⓊⓈ -sᵊlˈveɪ.njə, ˈ-ni.ə
pa'anga pɑːˈæŋ.gə, -ə ⓊⓈ -ˈɑːŋ.gə, ˈpɑːŋ-
pabulum ˈpæb.jə.ləm, -jʊ-
pac|e *(n. v.)* peɪs -es -ɪz -ing -ɪŋ -ed -t -er/s -əʳ/z ⓊⓈ -ɚ/z ˌput someone ˌthrough their ˈpaces
pace *(prep.)* ˈpeɪ.si, ˈpɑː.tʃeɪ, -keɪ
pacemaker ˈpeɪsˌmeɪ.kəʳ ⓊⓈ -kɚ -s -z
pace|man ˈpeɪ.smæn, -smən -men -men
pace-setter ˈpeɪsˌset.əʳ ⓊⓈ -ˌset̬.ɚ -s -z
Pachmann ˈpɑːk.mən, -mɑːn
pachyderm ˈpæk.ɪ.dɜːm ⓊⓈ -ə.dɝːm -s -z
pachydermatous ˌpæk.ɪˈdɜː.mə.təs ⓊⓈ -əˈdɝː.mə.t̬əs
pacific (P) pəˈsɪf.ɪk -ally -ᵊl.i, -li
pacification ˌpæs.ɪ.fɪˈkeɪ.ʃᵊn, ˌ-ə- ⓊⓈ ˌ-ə- -s -z
pacificatory pəˈsɪf.ɪ.kə.tᵊr.i, pæsˈɪf-, ˌpæs.ɪ.fɪˈkeɪ-, ˌ-ə-; ˈ-ə- ⓊⓈ pəˈsɪf.ɪ.kə.tɔːr-
pacificist pəˈsɪf.ɪ.sɪst, pæsˈɪf- ⓊⓈ pəˈsɪf- -s -s
pacifism ˈpæs.ɪ.fɪ.zᵊm, ˈ-ə- ⓊⓈ ˈ-ə-
pacifist ˈpæs.ɪ.fɪst, ˈ-ə- ⓊⓈ ˈ-ə- -s -s
paci|fy ˈpæs.ɪ|.faɪ, ˈ-ə- ⓊⓈ ˈ-ə- -fies -faɪz -fying -faɪ.ɪŋ -fied -faɪd -fier/s -faɪ.əʳ/z ⓊⓈ -faɪ.ɚ/z
Pacino pəˈtʃiː.nəʊ ⓊⓈ -noʊ
pack pæk -s -s -ing -ɪŋ -ed -t -er/s -əʳ/z ⓊⓈ -ɚ/z ˈpack ˌice; ˈpacking ˌcase
packag|e ˈpæk.ɪdʒ -es -ɪz -ing -ɪŋ -ed -d ˌpackage ˈholiday; ˈpackage ˌstore
Packard ˈpæk.ɑːd ⓊⓈ -ɚd
packed pækt
Packer ˈpæk.əʳ ⓊⓈ -ɚ
packet ˈpæk.ɪt -s -s
packhors|e ˈpæk.hɔːs ⓊⓈ -hɔːrs -es -ɪz
packing|house ˈpæk.ɪŋ|.haʊs -houses -haʊ.zɪz
pack|man ˈpæk|.mən, -mæn -men -mən ⓊⓈ -mən, -men
Pac-man® ˈpæk.mæn
pact pækt -s -s
pactum ˈpæk.təm
pac|y ˈpeɪ.s|i -ier -i.əʳ ⓊⓈ -i.ɚ -iest -i.ɪst
pad pæd -s -z -ding -ɪŋ -ded -ɪd ˌpadded ˈcell
Padang ˈpɑː.dɑːŋ ⓊⓈ pɑːˈdɑːŋ
Paddington ˈpæd.ɪŋ.tən
paddl|e ˈpæd.l̩ -es -z -ing -ɪŋ, ˈpæd.lɪŋ -ed -d -er/s -əʳ/z, ˈpæd.ləʳ/z ⓊⓈ ˈpæd.l̩.ɚ/z, ˈpæd.lɚ/z ˈpaddle ˌsteamer; ˈpaddle ˌwheel
paddleboard ˈpæd.l̩.bɔːd ⓊⓈ -bɔːrd -s -z
paddling-pool ˈpæd.l̩.ɪŋ.puːl, ˈ-lɪŋ-
paddock (P) ˈpæd.ək -s -s
padd|y (P) ˈpæd|.i -ies -iz
paddyfield ˈpæd.i.fiːld -s -z
paddywagon ˈpæd.iˌwæg.ᵊn
Paderewski ˌpæd.ᵊrˈef.ski, -ᵊrˈev- ⓊⓈ ˌpæd.əˈ-, ˌpɑː.dəˈ-
Padiham ˈpæd.i.əm
padlock ˈpæd.lɒk ⓊⓈ -lɑːk -s -s -ing -ɪŋ -ed -t
Padraic ˈpɑː.drɪk, ˈpæt.rɪk ⓊⓈ ˈpɑː.drɪk, -drɪg
Padraic Colum ˌpɑː.drɪkˈkɒl.əm, ˌpæt.rɪk- ⓊⓈ ˌpɑː.drɪkˈkɑː.ləm, -drɪgˈ-
Padraig ˈpɑː.drɪg
padre ˈpɑː.dreɪ, -dri -s -z
padrone pædˈrəʊ.neɪ, pəˈdrəʊ-, -ni ⓊⓈ pəˈdroʊ- -s -z
Padstow ˈpæd.stəʊ ⓊⓈ -stoʊ
Padu|a ˈpæd.ju|.ə ⓊⓈ ˈpædʒ.uː-, ˈpæd.juː- -an/s -ən/z
paean ˈpiː.ən -s -z
paederast ˈpiː.dᵊr.æst, ˈped.ᵊr- ⓊⓈ ˈped.ə.ræst -s -s -y -i
paediatric ˌpiː.diˈæt.rɪk -s -s
paediatrician ˌpiː.di.əˈtrɪʃ.ᵊn -s -z
paedophile ˈpiː.dəʊ.faɪl ⓊⓈ ˈped.oʊ-, ˈpiː.doʊ-, -də- -s -z
paedophili|a ˌpiː.dəʊˈfɪl.i|.ə ⓊⓈ ˌped.oʊˈfiː.li-, ˌpiː.doʊˈ-, -dəˈ-, -ˈfiːl.j|ə -ac/s -æk/s
paella paɪˈel.ə ⓊⓈ pɑːˈjel-, -ˈeɪ.jɑː -s -z
paeon ˈpiː.ən -s -z
paeonic piːˈɒn.ɪk ⓊⓈ -ˈɑː.nɪk
paeon|y ˈpiː.ə.n|i -ies -iz
pagan ˈpeɪ.gᵊn -s -z
Pagani pəˈgɑː.ni ⓊⓈ pə-, pɑː-
Paganini ˌpæg.əˈniː.ni
paganism ˈpeɪ.gᵊn.ɪ.zᵊm
paganiz|e, -is|e ˈpeɪ.gᵊn.aɪz -es -ɪz -ing -ɪŋ -ed -d
pag|e (P) peɪdʒ -es -ɪz -ing -ɪŋ -ed -d
pageant ˈpædʒ.ənt -s -s
pageantry ˈpædʒ.ən.tri
pageboy ˈpeɪdʒ.bɔɪ
pager ˈpeɪ.dʒəʳ ⓊⓈ -dʒɚ -s -z
Paget ˈpædʒ.ɪt
paginal ˈpædʒ.ɪ.nᵊl, ˈpeɪ.dʒɪ- ⓊⓈ ˈpædʒ.ə-
pagin|ate ˈpædʒ.ɪ.n|eɪt, ˈpeɪ.dʒɪ-, -dʒᵊn|.eɪt ⓊⓈ ˈpædʒ.ᵊn- -ates -eɪts -ating -eɪ.tɪŋ ⓊⓈ -eɪ.t̬ɪŋ -ated -eɪ.tɪd ⓊⓈ -eɪ.t̬ɪd
pagination ˌpædʒ.ɪˈneɪ.ʃᵊn, ˌpeɪ.dʒɪ-, -dʒᵊnˈeɪ- ⓊⓈ ˌpædʒ.ᵊnˈeɪ- -s -z
Paglia pɑː.li.ə ⓊⓈ ˈpæg.liː.ə, ˈpeɪg.liː.ə
Pagliacci ˌpæl.iˈɑː.tʃi, -ˈætʃ.i ⓊⓈ pɑːˈjɑː.tʃi
Pagnell ˈpæg.nəl
pagoda pəˈgəʊ.də ⓊⓈ -ˈgoʊ- -s -z
Pagones pəˈgəʊ.nez ⓊⓈ -ˈgoʊ-
pah pɑː
Pahang pəˈhʌŋ, -ˈhæŋ ⓊⓈ -ˈhɑːŋ, pɑː-
Note: Usually pronounced /pəˈhʌŋ/ in Malaya.

Palatal

A palatal consonant is one in which the tongue makes contact with or approaches the highest part of the hard palate. The hard palate is mainly composed of a thin layer of bone and is dome-shaped, as you can feel by exploring it with the tip of your tongue.

Examples for English

In English, the only phoneme described as palatal is /j/, e.g.:

yes	/jes/	
beautiful	/ˈbjuː.tɪ.fəl/	US /-t̬ə-/

However, phonetically a voiceless palatal fricative [ç] can also occur for the consonants in the sequence /hjuː/, e.g.:

huge	/hjuːdʒ/	[çʉːdʒ̊]
Hugh, Huw	/hjuː/	[çʉː]

paid *(from* **pay***)* peɪd
Paige peɪdʒ
Paignton ˈpeɪn.tən US -tᵊn
pail peɪl **-s** -z **-ful/s** -fʊl/z
paillass|e ˈpæl.i.æs, ˌ--ˈ- US pælˈjæs, ˈ-- **-es** -ɪz
paillette pælˈjet, ˌpæl.iˈet US ˌpælˈjet, ˈpɑː.jet **-s** -s
pain peɪn **-s** -z **-ing** -ɪŋ **-ed** -d **ˌpain in the ˈneck; be at ˌpains to ˈdo something**
Pain(e) peɪn
painful ˈpeɪn.fᵊl, -fʊl **-ly** -i **-ness** -nəs, -nɪs
painkill|er ˈpeɪnˌkɪl|.əʳ, ˈpeɪŋ- US ˈpeɪnˌkɪl|.ɚ **-ers** -əz US -ɚz **-ing** -ɪŋ
painless ˈpeɪn.ləs, -lɪs **-ly** -li **-ness** -nəs, -nɪs
painstaking ˈpeɪnzˌteɪ.kɪŋ, ˈpeɪns- US ˈpeɪnz- **-ly** -li
Painswick ˈpeɪnz.wɪk
paint peɪnt **-s** -s **-ing/s** -ɪŋ/z US ˈpeɪn.t̬ɪŋ **-ed** -ɪd US ˈpeɪn.t̬ɪd **-er/s** -əʳ/z US ˈpeɪn.t̬ɚ/z **ˌpainted ˈlady**
paintball ˈpeɪnt.bɔːl US -bɔːl, -bɑːl **-ing** -ɪŋ **-er/s** -əʳ/z US -ɚ/z
paintbox ˈpeɪnt.bɒks US -bɑːks **-es** -ɪz
paintbrush ˈpeɪnt.brʌʃ **-es** -ɪz
Painter ˈpeɪn.təʳ US -t̬ɚ
painterly ˈpeɪn.tᵊl.i US -t̬ɚ.li
paintwork ˈpeɪnt.wɜːk US -wɝːk
paint|y ˈpeɪn.t|i US -t̬|i **-ier** -i.əʳ US -i.ɚ **-iest** -i.ɪst, -i.əst
pair peəʳ US per **-s** -z **-ing** -ɪŋ **-ed** -d
pais|a ˈpaɪ.s|ɑː **-e** -eɪ **-as** -ɑːz
paisley (P) ˈpeɪz.li
pajama pəˈdʒɑː.mə US -ˈdʒɑː-, -ˈdʒæm.ə **-s** -z
pak-choi ˌpækˈtʃɔɪ, ˌbɒk-, ˌpɑːk- US ˌbɑːkˈtʃɔɪ
Pakeman ˈpeɪk.mən
Pakenham ˈpæk.ᵊn.əm
Paki ˈpæk.i **-s** -z
Pakistan ˌpɑː.kɪˈstɑːn, ˌpæk.ɪˈ-, -ˈstæn US ˈpæk.ɪ.stæn, ˈpɑː.kɪ.stɑːn; ˌpæk.ɪˈstæn, ˌpɑː.kɪˈstɑːn
Pakistani ˌpɑː.kɪˈstɑː.ni, ˌpæk.ɪˈ- **-s** -z
pakora pəˈkɔː.rə US -ˈkɔːr.ə
pal pæl **-s** -z
palac|e ˈpæl.ɪs, -əs US -əs **-es** -ɪz
paladin ˈpæl.ə.dɪn **-s** -z
palaeo- ˌpæl.i.əʊ-, ˌpeɪ.li.əʊ- US ˌpeɪ.li.oʊ-, -ə-
palaeobotany ˌpæl.i.əʊˈbɒt.ᵊn.i, ˌpeɪ.li- US ˌpeɪ.li.oʊˈbɑː.tᵊn-
Palaeocene ˈpæl.i.əʊ.siːn, ˈpeɪ.li- US ˈpeɪ.li.oʊ-, -ə-
palaeographic ˌpæl.i.əʊˈgræf.ɪk, ˌpeɪ.li- US ˌpeɪ.li.oʊˈ-, -əˈ-
palaeograph|y ˌpæl.iˈɒg.rə.f|i, ˌpeɪ.li- US ˌpeɪ.liˈɑː.grə- **-er/s** -əʳ/z US -ɚ/z
palaeolithic (P) ˌpæl.i.əʊˈlɪθ.ɪk, ˌpeɪ.li- US ˌpeɪ.li.oʊˈ-, -əˈ-
palaeontological ˌpæl.iˌɒn.təˈlɒdʒ.ɪ.kᵊl, ˌpeɪ.li- US ˌpeɪ.liˌɑːn.təˈlɑː.dʒɪ-
palaeontolog|y ˌpæl.i.ɒnˈtɒl.ə.dʒ|i, ˌpeɪ.li- US ˌpeɪ.li.ɑːnˈtɑː.lə- **-ist/s** -ɪsts
palaeotype ˈpæl.i.əʊ.taɪp, ˈpeɪ.li- US ˈpeɪ.li.oʊ-, -ə-
Palaeozoic ˌpæl.i.əʊˈzəʊ.ɪk, ˌpeɪ.li- US ˌpeɪ.li.oʊˈzoʊ-, -ə-
Palamedes ˌpæl.əˈmiː.diːz
palamino ˌpæl.əˈmiː.nəʊ US -noʊ **-s** -z
Palamon ˈpæl.ə.mən, -mɒn US -mən, -mɑːn
palanquin ˌpæl.əŋˈkiːn US -ənˈ- **-s** -z
palatab|le ˈpæl.ə.tə.b|l̩, ˈ-ɪ- US -ə.t̬ə- **-ly** -li **-leness** -l̩.nəs, -nɪs
palatal ˈpæl.ə.tᵊl US -t̬ᵊl **-s** -z
palatalization, -isa- ˌpæl.ə.tᵊl.aɪˈzeɪ.ʃᵊn, pəˌlæt.ᵊl-, -ɪˈ- US ˌpæl.ə.t̬ᵊl.ɪˈ- **-s** -z
palataliz|e, -is|e ˈpæl.ə.tᵊl.aɪz, pəˈlæt.ᵊl- US ˈpæl.ə.t̬ə.laɪz **-es** -ɪz **-ing** -ɪŋ **-ed** -d
palate ˈpæl.ət, -ɪt US -ət **-s** -s
palatial pəˈleɪ.ʃᵊl US -ʃᵊl **-ly** -i
palatinate (P) pəˈlæt.ɪ.nət, -ᵊn.ət, -ɪt US -ᵊn.eɪt, -ɪt **-s** -s
palatine (P) ˈpæl.ə.taɪn US -taɪn, -tɪn **-s** -z
palatogram ˈpæl.ə.təʊ.græm, pəˈlæt.əʊ- US ˈpæl.ə.toʊ-, -t̬ə- **-s** -z
palatography ˌpæl.əˈtɒg.rə.fi US -ˈtɑː.grə-
palav|er pəˈlɑː.v|əʳ US -ˈlæv|.ɚ, -ˈlɑː.v|ɚ **-ers** -əz US -ɚz **-ering** -ᵊr.ɪŋ **-ered** -əd US -ɚd
palazzo pəˈlæt.səʊ, -sə; -ˈlæd.zəʊ, -zə US pəˈlɑːt.soʊ, pɑː- **paˌlazzo ˈpants**
pal|e peɪl **-er** -əʳ US -ɚ **-est** -ɪst, -əst **-ely** -li **-eness** -nəs, -nɪs **-es** -z **-ing** -ɪŋ **-ed** -d **ˌpale ˈale; beˌyond the ˈpale**
palefac|e ˈpeɪl.feɪs **-es** -ɪz
paleo- ˌpæl.i.əʊ-, ˌpeɪ.li.əʊ- US ˈpeɪ.li.oʊ-, -ə-
paleobotany ˌpæl.i.əʊˈbɒt.ᵊn.i, ˌpeɪ.li- US ˌpeɪ.li.oʊˈbɑː.tᵊn-
Paleocene ˈpæl.i.əʊ.siːn, ˈpeɪ.li- US ˈpeɪ.li.oʊ-, -ə-
paleographic ˌpæl.i.əʊˈgræf.ɪk, ˌpeɪ.li- US ˌpeɪ.li.oʊˈ-, -əˈ-
paleograph|y ˌpæl.iˈɒg.rə.f|i, ˌpeɪ.li- US ˌpeɪ.liˈɑː.grə- **-er/s** -əʳ/z US -ɚ/z
paleolithic (P) ˌpæl.i.əʊˈlɪθ.ɪk, ˌpeɪ.li- US ˌpeɪ.li.oʊˈ-, -əˈ-
paleontological ˌpæl.iˌɒn.təˈlɒdʒ.ɪ.kᵊl, ˌpeɪ.li- US ˌpeɪ.liˌɑːn.təˈlɑː.dʒɪ-
paleontolog|y ˌpæl.i.ɒnˈtɒl.ə.dʒ|i, ˌpeɪ.li- US ˌpeɪ.li.ɑːnˈtɑː.lə- **-ist/s** -ɪst/s
paleotype ˈpæl.i.əʊ.taɪp, ˈpeɪ.li- US ˈpeɪ.li.oʊ-, -ə-
Palermo pəˈlɜː.məʊ, -ˈleə- US -ˈler.moʊ
Palestine ˈpæl.ə.staɪn, ˈ-ɪ- US -ə.staɪn
Palestinian ˌpæl.əˈstɪn.i.ən, -ɪˈ- US -əˈstɪn- **-s** -z
Palestrina ˌpæl.əˈstriː.nə, -ɪˈ- US -əˈstriː-
palette ˈpæl.ət, -ɪt, -et US -ɪt **-s** -s **ˈpalette ˌknife**
Paley ˈpeɪ.li
palfrey (P) ˈpɔːl.fri, ˈpɒl- US ˈpɔːl-, ˈpɑːl- **-s** -z

Palato-alveolar

Palato-aleolar sounds are made between the upper teeth and the front part of the palate.

In the description of English, this term has been largely replaced by POST-ALVEOLAR.

In other languages

It has been proposed that there is a difference between palato-alveolar and 'alveolo-patatal' that can be reliably distinguished, though others argue that factors other than place of articulation are usually involved. The latter sounds are placed further forward in the mouth than the former: an example of an alveolo-palatal consonant is that of Polish /ɕ/ in *Kasia* (compare /ʃ/ in *kasza*).

Palgrave ˈpɔː.l.greɪv, ˈpæl- (US) ˈpæl-, ˈpɔːl-
Pali ˈpɑː.li
palimony ˈpæl.ɪ.mə.ni, ˈ-ə- (US) -ə.moʊ-
palimpsest ˈpæl.ɪmp.sest, -əm*p*- (US) -ɪm*p*- **-s** -s
Palin ˈpeɪ.lɪn
palindrome ˈpæl.ɪn.drəʊm, -ən- (US) -ɪn.droʊm **-s** -z
palindromic ˌpæl.ɪnˈdrɒm.ɪk, -ənˈ- (US) -ɪnˈdrɑː.mɪk, -ˈdroʊ-
paling ˈpeɪ.lɪŋ **-s** -z
palingenesis ˌpæl.ɪnˈdʒen.ə.sɪs, ˈ-ɪ- (US) ˈ-ə-
palinode ˈpæl.ɪ.nəʊd, ˈ-ə- (US) -ə.noʊd **-s** -z
palisad|e (P) ˌpæl.ɪˈseɪd, -əˈ- (US) -əˈ-, ˈ--- **-es** -z **-ing** -ɪŋ **-ed** -ɪd
palish ˈpeɪ.lɪʃ
Palk pɔːlk, pɒlk (US) pɔːlk, pɔːk
pall pɔːl **-s** -z **-ing** -ɪŋ **-ed** -d
palladi|an (P) pəˈleɪ.di|.ən **-um/s** -əm/z
Pallas ˈpæl.əs, -æs
pall-bearer ˈpɔːlˌbeə.rəʳ (US) -ˌber.ɚ, ˈpɑːl- **-s** -z
pallet ˈpæl.ɪt, -ət (US) -ɪt **-s** -s
palliass|e ˈpæl.i.æs, ˌ--ˈ- (US) pælˈjæs, ˈ-- **-es** -ɪz
palli|ate ˈpæl.i|.eɪt **-ates** -eɪts **-ating** -eɪ.tɪŋ (US) -eɪ.t̬ɪŋ **-ated** -eɪ.tɪd (US) -eɪ.t̬ɪd
palliation ˌpæl.iˈeɪ.ʃᵊn
palliative ˈpæl.i.ə.tɪv (US) -t̬ɪv **-s** -z
pallid ˈpæl.ɪd **-est** -ɪst, -əst **-ly** -li **-ness** -nəs, -nɪs
Palliser ˈpæl.ɪ.səʳ (US) -sɚ
palli|um ˈpæl.i|.əm **-ums** -əmz **-a** -ə
Pall Mall ˌpælˈmæl, ˌpelˈmel (US) ˌpælˈmæl, ˌpelˈmel, ˌpɔːlˈmɔːl *stress shift:* ˌPall Mall ˈClub
pall-mall ˌpælˈmæl (US) ˌpælˈmæl, ˌpelˈmel, ˌpɑːlˈmɑːl
pallor ˈpæl.əʳ (US) -ɚ
pally ˈpæl.i
palm pɑːm **-s** -z **-ing** -ɪŋ **-ed** -d ˌ**Palm** ˈ**Beach**; ˌ**Palm** ˈ**Springs**; ˌ**Palm** ˈ**Sunday**; ˌ**grease one's** ˈ**palm**
Palma ˈpæl.mə, ˈpɑː-, ˈpɑːl- (US) ˈpɑːl.mɑː
palmar ˈpæl.məʳ, -mɑːʳ (US) -mɚ, ˈpɑː*l*-
palma|te ˈpæl.meɪ|t, ˈpɑː-, -mɪ|t (US) ˈpæl.meɪ|t, ˈpɑːl-, ˈpɑː- **-ted** -tɪd (US) -t̬ɪd
palmer (P) ˈpɑː.məʳ (US) -mɚ **-s** -z
Palmerston ˈpɑː.mə.stᵊn (US) -mɚ-
palmist ˈpɑː.mɪst **-s** -s
palmistry ˈpɑː.mɪ.stri
palm-oil ˈpɑːm.ɔɪl, ˌ-ˈ- (US) ˈpɑːm.ɔɪl
Palmolive® pɑːˈmɒl.ɪv (US) -ˈmɑː.lɪv
palmtop ˈpɑːm.tɒp (US) -tɑːp **-s** -s
palm|y ˈpɑː.m|i **-ier** -i.əʳ (US) -i.ɚ **-iest** -i.ɪst, -i.əst
palmyra (P) pælˈmaɪə.rə -ˈmɪə.rə (US) -ˈmaɪ- **-s** -z
Palo Alto ˌpæl.əʊˈæl.təʊ (US) -oʊˈæl.t̬oʊ
Palomar ˈpæl.əʊ.mɑːʳ (US) -ə.mɑːr
palomino ˌpæl.əˈmiː.nəʊ (US) -noʊ, -oʊˈ- **-s** -z
palooka pəˈluː.kə **-s** -z
palpability ˌpæl.pəˈbɪl.ə.ti, ˈ-ɪ- (US) -ə.t̬i
palpab|le ˈpæl.pə.b|l̩ **-ly** -li **-leness** -l̩.nəs, -nɪs
palpa|te (*v.*) pælˈpeɪ|t (US) ˈ-- **-tes** -ts **-ting** -tɪŋ (US) -t̬ɪŋ **-ted** -tɪd (US) -t̬ɪd
palpate (*adj.*) ˈpæl.peɪt (US) -peɪt, -pɪt
palpation pælˈpeɪ.ʃᵊn
palpi|tate ˈpæl.pɪ|.teɪt (US) -pə- **-tates** -teɪts **-tating** -teɪ.tɪŋ (US) -teɪ.t̬ɪŋ **-tated** -teɪ.tɪd (US) -teɪ.t̬ɪd
palpitation ˌpæl.pɪˈteɪ.ʃᵊn (US) -pəˈ- **-s** -z
palsgrave (P) ˈpɔːlz.greɪv (US) ˈpɔːlz-, ˈpælz- **-s** -z
pals|y ˈpɔːl.z|i, ˈpɒl- (US) ˈpɔːl-, ˈpɑːl- **-ies** -iz **-ied** -id
palt|er ˈpɔːl.t|əʳ, ˈpɒl- (US) ˈpɔːl.t̬|ɚ, ˈpɑːl- **-ers** -əz (US) -ɚz **-ering** -ᵊr.ɪŋ **-ered** -əd (US) -ɚd **-erer/s** -ᵊr.əʳ/z (US) -ɚ.ɚ/z
Paltrow ˈpæl.trəʊ, ˈpɒl- (US) ˈpæl.troʊ, ˈpɑːl-
paltr|y ˈpɔːl.tr|i, ˈpɒl- (US) ˈpɔːl-, ˈpɑːl- **-ier** -i.əʳ (US) -i.ɚ **-iest** -i.ɪst, -i.əst **-ily** -ɪ.li, -ᵊl.i **-iness** -ɪ.nəs, -ɪ.nɪs
Pam pæm
Pamela ˈpæm.ᵊl.ə, -ɪ.lə (US) -ᵊl.ə
Pamir pəˈmɪəʳ (US) pɑːˈmɪr **-s** -z
Pampa ˈpæm.pə **-s** -z
pampas ˈpæm.pəs (US) ˈpæm.pəz, ˈpɑːm-, -pəs ˈ**pampas** ˌ**grass**
pamp|er ˈpæm.p|əʳ (US) -p|ɚ **-ers** -əz (US) -ɚz **-ering** -ᵊr.ɪŋ **-ered** -əd (US) -ɚd **-erer/s** -ᵊr.əʳ/z (US) -ɚ.ɚ/z
Pampers® ˈpæm.pəz (US) -pɚz
pamphlet ˈpæm.flɪt, -flət (US) -flɪt **-s** -s
pamphleteer ˌpæm.fləˈtɪəʳ, -flɪˈ- (US) -flɪˈtɪr **-s** -z **-ing** -ɪŋ
Pamphyli|a pæmˈfɪl.i|.ə **-an/s** -ən/z
Pamplona pæmˈpləʊ.nə (US) pæmˈploʊ.nə, pɑːm-, -nɑː
pan (P) pæn **-s** -z **-ning** -ɪŋ **-ned** -d
panacea ˌpæn.əˈsiː.ə **-s** -z
panach|e pəˈnæʃ, pænˈæʃ-, -ˈɑːʃ (US) pəˈnæʃ, -ˈnɑːʃ **-es** -ɪz
Panadol® ˈpæn.ə.dɒl (US) -dɑːl
panama (P) ˌpæn.əˈmɑː, ˈ--- (US) ˈ---, -mɔː **-s** -z ˌ**Panama Ca**ˈ**nal**; ˌ**Panama** ˈ**City**; ˌ**panama** ˈ**hat**
Panamanian ˌpæn.əˈmeɪ.ni.ən **-s** -z
Pan-American ˌpæn.əˈmer.ɪ.kən **-ism** -ɪ.zᵊm
Panasonic ˌpæn.əˈsɒn.ɪk (US) -ˈsɑː.nɪk
panatel(l)a ˌpæn.əˈtel.ə **-s** -z
pancake ˈpæn.keɪk, ˈpæŋ- (US) ˈpæn- **-s** -s ˈ**Pancake** ˌ**Day**
pancetta pænˈtʃet.ə (US) -ˈtʃet̬-
panchromatic ˌpæn.krəʊˈmæt.ɪk, ˌpæŋ- (US) ˌpæn.kroʊˈmæt̬-
Pancras ˈpæŋ.krəs
pancreas ˈpæŋ.kri.əs, -æs (US) ˈpæn.kri.əs, ˈpæŋ- **-es** -ɪz
pancreatic ˌpæŋ.kriˈæt.ɪk (US) ˌpæn.kriˈæt̬-, ˌpæŋ-
panda ˈpæn.də **-s** -z ˈ**panda** ˌ**car**
pandanus pænˈdeɪ.nəs, -ˈdæn.əs **-es** -ɪz
pandect ˈpæn.dekt **-s** -s
pandemic pænˈdem.ɪk **-s** -s
pandemonium (P) ˌpæn.dəˈməʊ.ni.əm, -dɪˈ- (US) -dəˈmoʊ- **-s** -z
pand|er ˈpæn.d|əʳ (US) -ɚ **-ers** -əz (US) -ɚz **-ering** -ᵊr.ɪŋ **-ered** -əd (US) -ɚd

pandialectal ˌpænˌdaɪəˈlek.tᵊl
pandit (P) ˈpæn.dɪt **-s** -s
pandora (P) pænˈdɔː.rə (US) -ˈdɔːr.ə **-s** -z
Panˌdora's ˈbox
pandowd|y pænˈdaʊ.d|i **-ies** -iz
pane peɪn **-s** -z
panegyric ˌpæn.əˈdʒɪr.ɪk, -ɪˈ- (US) -əˈ-, -ˈdʒaɪ.rɪk **-s** -s **-al** -ᵊl
panegyrist ˌpæn.əˈdʒɪr.ɪst, -ɪˈ-, ˈpæn.ə.dʒɪr-, -ˈɪ- (US) ˌpæn.əˈdʒɪr-, -ˈdʒaɪ.rɪst **-s** -s
panegyriz|e, -is|e ˈpæn.ə.dʒɪ.raɪz, ˈ-ɪ-, -dʒᵊr.aɪz (US) -dʒə.raɪz **-es** -ɪz **-ing** -ɪŋ **-ed** -d
panel ˈpæn.ᵊl **-s** -z **-(l)ing/s** -ɪŋ/z **-(l)ed** -d **ˈpanel ˌbeater**
panel(l)ist ˈpæn.ᵊl.ɪst **-s** -s
panettone ˌpæn.əˈtəʊ.neɪ, -ni (US) -ɪˈtoʊ- **-s** -z
pan-|fry ˈpæn|.fraɪ **-fries** -fraɪz **-frying** -fraɪ.ɪŋ **-fried** -fraɪd
panful ˈpæn.fʊl **-s** -z
pang pæŋ **-s** -z
panga ˈpæŋ.gə **-s** -z
Pangbourne ˈpæŋ.bɔːn, -bən (US) -bɔːrn
Pangloss ˈpæŋ.glɒs, ˈpæn- (US) ˈpæn.glɑːs
panglossian (P) pæŋˈglɒs.i.ən, pæn- (US) pænˈglɑː.si-
pangolin ˈpæŋ.gəʊ.lɪn; pæŋˈgəʊ- (US) ˈpæn.goʊ-, ˈpæŋ-, -gə-; pænˈgoʊ-, pæŋ- **-s** -z
panhandl|e ˈpænˌhæn.dl̩ **-es** -z **-ing** -ɪŋ, -ˌhænd.lɪŋ **-ed** -d **-er/s** -əʳ/z (US) -ɚ/z, -ˌhænd.ləʳ/z (US) -lɚ/z
panic ˈpæn.ɪk **-s** -s **-king** -ɪŋ **-ked** -t **ˈpanic ˌbutton; ˈpanic ˌstations**
panicky ˈpæn.ɪ.ki
panicle ˈpæn.ɪ.kl̩ **-s** -z
panic-stricken ˈpæn.ɪkˌstrɪk.ᵊn
Panini ˈpɑː.nɪ.niː, -ni (US) pɑːˈniː.ni
panjandr|um pænˈdʒæn.dr|əm, pən- (US) pæn- **-ums** -əmz **-a** -ə
Pankhurst ˈpæŋk.hɜːst (US) -hɝːst
panlectal ˌpænˈlek.tᵊl
panne pæn
pannier ˈpæn.i.əʳ (US) ˈ-jɚ, ˈ-i.ɚ **-s** -z
pannikin ˈpæn.ɪ.kɪn, ˈ-ə- (US) ˈ-ɪ- **-s** -z
Pannill ˈpæn.ɪl
panopl|y ˈpæn.ə.pl|i **-ies** -iz **-ied** -id
panorama ˌpæn.ᵊrˈɑː.mə (US) -əˈræm.ə, -ˈrɑː.mə **-s** -z
panoramic ˌpæn.ᵊrˈæm.ɪk, -ˈɑː.mɪk (US) -əˈræm.ɪk, -ˈrɑː.mɪk **-ally** -ᵊl.i (US) -li
panpipe ˈpæn.paɪp, ˈpæm- (US) ˈpæn- **-s** -s
Pan-Slavism ˌpænˈslɑː.vɪ.zᵊm, -ˈslæv.ɪ-
pans|y ˈpæn.z|i **-ies** -iz
pant pænt **-s** -s **-ing/ly** -ɪŋ/li (US) ˈpæn.t̬ɪŋ/li **-ed** -ɪd (US) ˈpæn.t̬ɪd
Pantagruel ˌpæn.tə.gruˈel; ˈpæn.tə.gru.əl, pænˈtæg.ru.əl (US) ˌpæn.t̬ə.gruˈel; -ˈgruː.əl; pænˈtæg.ru.el
pantaloon ˌpæn.tᵊlˈuːn, ˈ--- (US) ˌpæn.t̬ᵊlˈuːn, ˈ--- **-s** -z
pantechnicon pænˈtek.nɪ.kən **-s** -z
panthe|ism ˈpænt.θi|.ɪ.zᵊm **-ist/s** -ɪst/s
pantheistic ˌpænt.θiˈɪs.tɪk **-al** -ᵊl
pantheon (P) ˈpænt.θi.ən (US) -ɑːn, -ən **-s** -z
panther ˈpænt.θəʳ (US) -θɚ **-s** -z
pantie girdle ˈpæn.tiˌgɜː.dl̩ (US) -t̬iˌgɝː- **-s** -z
panties ˈpæn.tiz (US) -t̬iz
pantihose ˈpæn.ti.həʊz (US) -t̬i.hoʊz
pantile ˈpæn.taɪl **-s** -z
panto ˈpæn.təʊ (US) -toʊ **-s** -z
pantograph ˈpæn.təʊ.grɑːf, -græf (US) -t̬ə.græf **-s** -s
pantographic ˌpæn.təʊˈgræf.ɪk (US) -t̬əˈ- **-al** -ᵊl
pantomim|e ˈpæn.tə.maɪm (US) -t̬ə- **-es** -z **-ist/s** -ɪst/s
pantomimic ˌpæn.təʊˈmɪm.ɪk (US) -t̬əˈ- **-al** -ᵊl **-ally** -ᵊl.i, -li
pantr|y ˈpæn.tr|i **-ies** -iz
pants pænts
pantsuit ˈpænt.suːt, -sjuːt (US) -suːt **-s** -s
pantyhose ˈpæn.ti.həʊz (US) -t̬i.hoʊz
pantyliner ˈpæn.tiˌlaɪ.nəʳ (US) -t̬iˌlaɪ.nɚ **-s** -z
Panza ˈpæn.zə
panzer ˈpænt.səʳ, ˈpæn.zəʳ (US) ˈpæn.zɚ, ˈpɑːnt.sɚ **-s** -z
pap pæp **-s** -s
papa pəˈpɑː (US) ˈpɑː.pə; pəˈpɑː **-s** -z
papac|y (P) ˈpeɪ.pə.s|i **-ies** -iz
papal ˈpeɪ.pᵊl
papal|ism ˈpeɪ.pᵊl|.ɪ.zᵊm **-ist/s** -ɪst/s
Papandreou ˌpæp.ænˈdreɪ.uː
paparazz|o ˌpæp.ᵊrˈæt.s|əʊ (US) ˌpɑː.pɑːˈrɑːt.s|oʊ **-i** -i
papaw ˈpɔː.pɔː, pəˈpɔː (US) pɔːˈpɑː, -ˈɔː, ˈpɑː-, ˈpɔː- **-s** -z
papaya pəˈpaɪ.ə (US) -ˈpaɪ.ə, -ˈpɑː.jə **-s** -z
Papeete ˌpɑː.piˈeɪ.ti, -ˈiː-; pəˈpiː.ti (US) ˌpɑː.piˈeɪ.teɪ; pəˈpiː.ti
pap|er ˈpeɪ.p|əʳ (US) -ɚ **-ers** -əz (US) -ɚz **-ering** -ᵊr.ɪŋ **-ered** -əd (US) -ɚd **-erer/s** -ᵊr.əʳ/z (US) -ɚ.ɚ/z **-ery** -ᵊr.i **ˌpaper ˈbag; ˈpaper ˌboy; ˈpaper ˌchase; ˈpaper ˌclip; ˈpaper ˌknife; ˌpaper ˈmoney; ˈpaper ˌround; ˌpaper ˈtiger; ˈpaper ˌtrail**
paperback ˈpeɪ.pə.bæk (US) -pɚ- **-s** -s
paperbark ˈpeɪ.pə.bɑːk (US) -pɚ.bɑːrk **-s** -s
paperhang|er ˈpeɪ.pəˌhæŋ|.əʳ (US) -pɚˌhæŋ|.ɚ **-ers** -əz (US) -ɚz **-ing** -ɪŋ
paperless ˈpeɪ.pə.ləs, -lɪs (US) -pɚ-
paperweight ˈpeɪ.pə.weɪt (US) -pɚ- **-s** -s
paperwork ˈpeɪ.pə.wɜːk (US) -pɚ.wɝːk
Paphlagoni|a ˌpæf.ləˈgəʊ.ni|.ə (US) -ˈgoʊ- **-an/s** -ən/z
Paphos ˈpæf.ɒs (US) ˈpeɪ.fɑːs
papier-mâché ˌpæp.i.eɪˈmæʃ.eɪ, ˌpeɪ.pəˈ- (US) ˌpeɪ.pɚ.məˈʃeɪ, ˌpæp.jeɪ-
papill|a pəˈpɪl|.ə **-ae** -iː
papillary pəˈpɪl.ᵊr.i (US) ˈpæp.ə.ler-; pəˈpɪl.ɚ-
papillote ˈpæp.ɪ.lɒt, -ləʊt, -jɒt (US) -ə.loʊt, ˈpɑː.pə-, -joʊt **-s** -s
papist (P) ˈpeɪ.pɪst **-s** -s
papistry ˈpeɪ.pɪ.stri
papoos|e pəˈpuːs (US) pæpˈuːs, pəˈpuːs **-es** -ɪz
Papp pæp
papp|us (P) ˈpæp|.əs **-i** -aɪ
pappy ˈpæp.i
paprika ˈpæp.rɪ.kə; pəˈpriː- (US) pæpˈriː-, pəˈpriː-
Papu|a ˈpæp.u|.ə, ˈpɑː.pu-, -pju- (US) ˈpæp.ju|.ə, pɑːˈpuː- **-an/s** -ən/z **ˌPapua New ˈGuinea**
Papworth ˈpæp.wəθ, -wɜːθ (US) -wɚθ, -wɝːθ
papyr|us pəˈpaɪə.r|əs (US) -ˈpaɪ- **-i** -aɪ **-uses** -ə.sɪz
par (P) pɑːʳ (US) pɑːr
para- pær.ə-; pəˈræ- (US) per.ə-, pær.ə-; pəˈræ-
Note: Prefix. Normally either carries primary or secondary stress on the first syllable, e.g. **parachute** /ˈpær.ə.ʃuːt (US) ˈper-/, **parabolic** /ˌpær.əˈbɒl.ɪk (US) ˌper.əˈbɑː.lɪk/, or primary stress on the second syllable, e.g. **paraboloid** /pəˈræb.ᵊl.ɔɪd (US) -ə.lɔɪd/.
para *paratrooper, paramilitary:* ˈpær.ə (US) ˈper.ə, ˈpær- **-s** -z
para *Turk or Yugoslav monetary unit:* ˈpɑː.rə (US) ˈpɑː.rɑː, -ˈ- **-s** -z
Pará *Brazilian river:* pəˈrɑː
parable ˈpær.ə.bl̩ (US) ˈper-, ˈpær- **-s** -z
parabola pəˈræb.ᵊl.ə **-s** -z
parabolic ˌpær.əˈbɒl.ɪk (US) ˌper.əˈbɑː.lɪk, ˌpær- **-al** -ᵊl **-ally** -ᵊl.i, -li
paraboloid pəˈræb.ᵊl.ɔɪd (US) -ə.lɔɪd **-s** -z
Paracelsus ˌpær.əˈsel.səs (US) ˌper-, ˌpær-
paracetamol ˌpær.əˈsiː.tə.mɒl, -ˈset.ə- (US) ˌper.əˈsiː.t̬ə.mɑːl, ˌpær-, -ˈset̬.ə-, -moʊl **-s** -z
para|chute ˈpær.ə|.ʃuːt (US) ˈper-, ˈpær- **-chutes** -ʃuːts **-chuting** -ˌʃuː.tɪŋ (US) -ˌʃuː.t̬ɪŋ **-chuted** -ˌʃuː.tɪd (US) -ˌʃuː.t̬ɪd
parachutist ˈpær.əˌʃuː.tɪst (US) ˈper.əˌʃuː.t̬ɪst, ˈpær- **-s** -s

Paraclete ˈpær.ə.kliːt US ˈper-, ˈpær-
parad|e pəˈreɪd **-es** -z **-ing** -ɪŋ **-ed** -ɪd
paˈrade ˌground
paradigm ˈpær.ə.daɪm US ˈper-, ˈpær-, -dɪm **-s** -z
paradigmatic ˌpær.ə.dɪɡˈmæt.ɪk US ˌper.ə.dɪɡˈmæt̬-, ˌpær- **-al** -ᵊl **-ally** -ᵊl.i, -li
paradisal ˌpær.əˈdaɪ.sᵊl, -zᵊl US ˌper.əˈdaɪ-, ˌpær-
paradis|e (P) ˈpær.ə.daɪs US ˈper-, ˈpær-, -daɪz **-es** -ɪz
paradisiac ˌpær.əˈdɪs.i.æk, -ˈdɪz- US ˌper.əˈdɪs-, ˌpær-
paradisiacal ˌpær.ə.dɪˈsaɪ.ə.kᵊl, -dəˈ-, -ˈzaɪ- US ˌper.ə.dɪˈ-, ˌpær-
Paradiso ˌpær.əˈdiː.səʊ US ˌper.əˈdiː.soʊ, ˌpær-
parador ˈpær.ə.dɔːʳ US ˈper.ə.dɔːr, ˈpær- **paradores** ˌpær.əˈdɔː.reɪs, -rɪs US ˌper.əˈdɔːr.əs, ˌpær-, -ˈdɔːrz
parados ˈpær.ə.dɒs US ˈper.ə.dɑːs, ˈpær- **-es** -ɪz
paradox ˈpær.ə.dɒks US ˈper.ə.dɑːks, ˈpær- **-es** -ɪz
paradoxic|al ˌpær.əˈdɒk.sɪ.k|ᵊl US ˌper.əˈdɑːk-, ˌpær- **-ally** -ᵊl.i, -li **-alness** -ᵊl.nəs, -nɪs
paraffin ˈpær.ə.fɪn, -fiːn, ˌ--ˈ- US ˈper.ə.fɪn, ˈpær-
paraffine ˌpær.əˈfiːn US ˈper.ə.fɪn, ˈpær-, -fiːn
paragliding ˈpær.əˌɡlaɪ.dɪŋ US ˈper.ə-, ˈpær-
paragoge ˌpær.əˈɡəʊ.dʒi US ˈper.ə.ɡoʊ-, ˈpær- **-s** -z
paragogic ˌpær.əˈɡɒdʒ.ɪk US ˌper.əˈɡɑː.dʒɪk, ˌpær-
paragon ˈpær.ə.ɡən US ˈper.ə.ɡɑːn, ˈpær-, -ɡən **-s** -z
paragraph ˈpær.ə.ɡrɑːf, -ɡræf US ˈper.ə.ɡræf, ˈpær- **-s** -s **-ing** -ɪŋ **-ed** -t
Paraguay ˈpær.ə.ɡwaɪ, -ɡweɪ, ˌ--ˈ- US ˈper.ə.ɡweɪ, ˈpær-, -ɡwaɪ
Paraguayan ˌpær.əˈɡwaɪ.ən, -ˈɡweɪ- US ˌper.əˈɡweɪ-, ˌpær-, -ˈɡwaɪ-
parakeet ˌpær.əˈkiːt, ˈ--- US ˈper.ə.kiːt, ˈpær- **-s** -s
paraldehyde pəˈræl.dɪ.haɪd, pærˈæl-, -də- US pəˈræl.də-
paralexia ˌpær.əˈlek.si.ə US ˌper-, ˌpær-
paralinguistic ˌpær.ə.lɪŋˈɡwɪs.tɪk US ˌper-, ˌpær- **-s** -s **-ally** -ᵊl.i, -li
parallax ˈpær.ə.læks US ˈper-, ˈpær- **-es** -ɪz
parallel ˈpær.ə.lel, -ᵊl.əl US ˈper-, ˈpær- **-s** -z **-ing** -ɪŋ **-ed** -d **-ism** -ɪ.zᵊm
ˌparallel ˈbars
parallelepiped ˌpær.ə.lelˈep.ɪ.ped, -ᵊl.əˈlep-; ˌpær.əˌlel.əˈpaɪ- US ˌper.əˌlel.əˈpaɪ-, ˌpær-, -ˈpɪp.əd, -ed **-s** -z
parallelogram ˌpær.əˈlel.ə.ɡræm US ˌper-, ˌpær- **-s** -z
Paralympics ˌpær.əˈlɪm.pɪks US ˌper-, ˌpær-
paralys|e, -lyz|e ˈpær.ᵊl.aɪz US ˈper-, ˈpær- **-es** -ɪz **-ing** -ɪŋ **-ed** -d **-er/s** -əʳ/z US -ɚ/z
paralys|is pəˈræl.ə.s|ɪs, pᵊrˈæl-, ˈ-ɪ- US ˈ-ə- **-es** -iːz
paralytic ˌpær.əˈlɪt.ɪk US ˌper.əˈlɪt̬-, ˌpær- **-s** -s
paralyzation ˌpær.ᵊl.aɪˈzeɪ.ʃᵊn US ˌper.ə.lɪˈ-, ˌpær-
Paramaribo ˌpær.əˈmær.ɪ.bəʊ US ˌper.əˈmer.ɪ.boʊ, ˌpær-, -ˈmær-
paramatta (P) ˌpær.əˈmæt.ə US ˌper.əˈmæt̬-, ˌpær-
paramecium ˌpær.əˈmiː.si.əm US ˌper-, ˌpær-, -ʃi-
paramedic ˌpær.əˈmed.ɪk US ˌper.əˈmed-, ˌpær-, ˈper.əˌmed-, ˈpær- **-s** -s **-al** -ᵊl
parameter pəˈræm.ɪ.təʳ, pᵊrˈæm-, ˈ-ə- US -ə.t̬ɚ **-s** -z
parametric ˌpær.əˈmet.rɪk US ˌper-, ˌpær- **-ally** -ᵊl.i, -li
paramilitar|y ˌpær.əˈmɪl.ɪ.tᵊr|.i, ˈ-ə- US ˌper.əˈmɪl.ə.ter-, ˌpær- **-ies** -iz
paramount (P) ˈpær.ə.maʊnt US ˈper-, ˈpær- **-ly** -li
paramour ˈpær.ə.mʊəʳ, -mɔːʳ US ˈper.ə.mʊr, ˈpær- **-s** -z
Paraná pær.ænˈɑː
paranoi|a ˌpær.əˈnɔɪ|.ə US ˌper-, ˌpær- **-ac** -æk
paranoid ˈpær.ᵊn.ɔɪd US ˈper.ə.nɔɪd, ˈpær-
paranormal ˌpær.əˈnɔː.mᵊl US ˌper.əˈnɔːr-, ˌpær- **-ly** -i
parape|t ˈpær.ə.pɪ|t, -pe|t, -pə|t US ˈper.ə.pe|t, ˈpær-, -pə|t **-ts** -ts **-ted** -tɪd US -t̬ɪd
paraphernalia ˌpær.ə.fəˈneɪ.li.ə US ˌper.ə.fɚˈneɪl.jə, ˌpær-, -ˈneɪ.li.ə
paraphras|e ˈpær.ə.freɪz US ˈper-, ˈpær- **-es** -ɪz **-ing** -ɪŋ **-ed** -d
paraphrastic ˌpær.əˈfræs.tɪk US ˌper-, ˌpær- **-ally** -ᵊl.i, -li
parapleg|ia ˌpær.əˈpliː.dʒ|ə, -dʒi|.ə US ˌper-, ˌpær- **-ic/s** -ɪk
paraprax|is ˌpær.əˈpræk.s|ɪs US ˌper-, ˌpær- **-es** -ɪz
parapsychologic ˌpær.əˌsaɪ.kəˈlɒdʒ.ɪk, -kᵊlˈɒdʒ- US ˌper.ə.saɪ.kəˈlɑː.dʒɪk, ˌpær- **-al** -ᵊl **-ally** -ᵊl.i, -li
parapsycholog|y ˌpær.ə.saɪˈkɒl.ə.dʒ|i, -psaɪˈ- US ˌper.ə.saɪˈkɑː.lə-, ˌpær- **-ist/s** -ɪst/s
Paraquat® ˈpær.ə.kwɒt, -kwæt US ˈper.ə.kwɑːt, ˈpær-
parasang ˈpær.ə.sæŋ US ˈper-, ˈpær- **-s** -z
parascend|ing ˈpær.əˌsen.d|ɪŋ US ˈper-, ˈpær- **-er/s** -əʳ/z US -ɚ/z
parasite ˈpær.ə.saɪt US ˈper-, ˈpær- **-s** -s
parasitic ˌpær.əˈsɪt.ɪk US ˌper.əˈsɪt̬-, ˌpær- **-al** -ᵊl **-ally** -ᵊl.i, -li **-alness** -ᵊl.nəs, -nɪs
parasitolog|y ˌpær.ə.saɪˈtɒl.ə.dʒ|i, -sɪˈ- US ˌper.ə.saɪˈtɑː.lə-, ˌpær-, -sɪˈ- **-ist/s** -ɪst/s
parasol ˈpær.ə.sɒl, ˌ--ˈ- US ˈper.ə.sɔːl, ˈpær-, -sɑːl **-s** -z
paratactic ˌpær.əˈtæk.tɪk US ˌper-, ˌpær-
parataxis ˌpær.əˈtæk.sɪs US ˌper-, ˌpær-
parathyroid ˌpær.əˈθaɪə.rɔɪd US ˌper.əˈθaɪ-, ˌpær-
paratone ˈpær.ə.təʊn US ˈper.ə.toʊn, ˈpær- **-s** -z
paratroop ˈpær.ə.truːp US ˈper-, ˈpær- **-s** -s **-er/s** -əʳ/z US -ɚ/z
paratyphoid ˌpær.əˈtaɪ.fɔɪd US ˌper-, ˌpær-
paravane ˈpær.ə.veɪn US ˈper-, ˈpær- **-s** -z
parboil ˈpɑː.bɔɪl US ˈpɑːr- **-s** -z **-ing** -ɪŋ **-ed** -d
parcel ˈpɑː.sᵊl US ˈpɑːr- **-s** -z **-(l)ing** -ɪŋ **-(l)ed** -d **ˈparcel ˌpost**
parch pɑːtʃ US pɑːrtʃ **-es** -ɪz **-ing** -ɪŋ **-ed** -t **-edness** -t.nəs, -nɪs
Parcheesi® pɑːˈtʃiː.zi US pɑːr-
parchment (P) ˈpɑːtʃ.mənt US ˈpɑːrtʃ- **-s** -s
pard pɑːd US pɑːrd **-s** -z
pardner ˈpɑːd.nəʳ US ˈpɑːd.nəʳ, ˈpɑːrd.nɚ **-s**
Pardoe ˈpɑː.dəʊ US ˈpɑːr.doʊ
pardon ˈpɑː.dᵊn US ˈpɑːr- **-s** -z **-ing** -ɪŋ **-ed** -d **-er/s** -əʳ/z US -ɚ/z
pardonab|le ˈpɑː.dᵊn.ə.b|l̩ US ˈpɑːr- **-ly** -li **-leness** -l̩.nəs, -nɪs
par|e peəʳ US per **-es** -z **-ing** -ɪŋ **-ed** -d
paregoric ˌpær.ɪˈɡɒr.ɪk, -əˈ- US ˌper.əˈɡɔːr.ɪk, ˌpær-
paren|t ˈpeə.rᵊn|t US ˈper.ᵊn|t, ˈpær- **-ts** -ts **-tage** -tɪdʒ US -t̬ɪdʒ
parental pəˈren.tᵊl US -t̬ᵊl **-ly** -i
parenthes|is pəˈrent.θə.s|ɪs, -θɪ- US -θə- **-es** -iːz
parenthesiz|e, -is|e pəˈrent.θə.saɪz, -θɪ- US -θə- **-es** -ɪz **-ing** -ɪŋ **-ed** -d
parenthetic ˌpær.ᵊnˈθet.ɪk, -enˈ- US ˌper.ᵊnˈθet̬-, ˌpær- **-al** -ᵊl **-ally** -ᵊl.i, -li
parenthood ˈpeə.rᵊnt.hʊd US ˈper.ᵊnt-, ˈpær-
parenting ˈpeə.rᵊn.tɪŋ US ˈper.ᵊn.t̬ɪŋ, ˈpær-

parentless ˈpeə.rᵊnt.ləs, -lɪs Ⓤⓢ ˈper.ᵊnt-, ˈpær-

parent-teacher ˌpeə.rᵊntˈtiː.tʃəʳ Ⓤⓢ ˌper.ᵊntˈtiː.tʃɚ, ˌpær- **ˌparent-ˈteacher associˌation**

pareo pɑːˈreɪ.əʊ Ⓤⓢ -oʊ **-s** -z

paresis pəˈriː.sɪs; ˈpær.ə- Ⓤⓢ pəˈriː-; ˈper.ə-, ˈpær-

paretic pəˈret.ɪk Ⓤⓢ -ˈreţ-, -ˈriː.ţɪk

pareu pɑːˈreɪ.uː **-s** -z

par excellence ˌpɑːʳˈek.sᵊl.ɑ̃ːns, -sel-, -ɑːnts, ˌpɑːʳ.ek.sᵊlˈɑ̃ːns, -selˈ-, -ˈɑːnts Ⓤⓢ ˌpɑːrˌek.səˈlɑːnts

parfait ˌpɑːˈfeɪ, ˈ-- Ⓤⓢ pɑːrˈfeɪ **-s** -z

Parfitt ˈpɑː.fɪt Ⓤⓢ ˈpɑːr-

parfum ˈpɑː.fʌm Ⓤⓢ pɑːrˈfʌm

par|get ˈpɑː|.dʒɪt Ⓤⓢ ˈpɑːr- **-gets** -dʒɪts **-get(t)ing** -dʒɪ.tɪŋ Ⓤⓢ -dʒɪ.ţɪŋ **-get(t)ed** -dʒɪ.tɪd Ⓤⓢ -dʒɪ.ţɪd

Pargiter ˈpɑː.dʒɪ.təʳ Ⓤⓢ ˈpɑːr.dʒɪ.ţɚ

parheli|on pɑːˈhiː.li|.ən, -ɒn Ⓤⓢ pɑːrˈhiː-, -ˈhiːl.j|ən **-a** -ə

pariah pəˈraɪə, ˈpær.i.ə Ⓤⓢ pəˈraɪə **-s** -z

Parian ˈpeə.ri.ən Ⓤⓢ ˈper.i-, ˈpær- **-s** -z

parietal pəˈraɪə.tᵊl, -ˈraɪ.ɪ- Ⓤⓢ -ˈraɪə-

paring ˈpeə.rɪŋ Ⓤⓢ ˈper.ɪŋ, ˈpær- **-s** -z

Paris ˈpær.ɪs Ⓤⓢ ˈper-, ˈpær-

parish (P) ˈpær.ɪʃ Ⓤⓢ ˈper-, ˈpær- **-es** -ɪz **ˌparish ˈpriest**

parishioner pəˈrɪʃ.ᵊn.əʳ Ⓤⓢ -ɚ **-s** -z

Parisian pəˈrɪz.i.ən, -ˈrɪʒ.ᵊn Ⓤⓢ -ˈrɪʒ-, -ˈriː.ʒᵊn **-s** -z

parisyllabic ˌpær.ɪ.sɪˈlæb.ɪk, ˌ-ə-, -sᵊlˈæb- Ⓤⓢ ˌper-, ˌpær-

parity ˈpær.ə.ti, -ɪ.ti Ⓤⓢ ˈper.ə.ţi, ˈpær-

park (P) pɑːk Ⓤⓢ pɑːrk **-s** -s **-ing** -ɪŋ **-ed** -t **ˈparking ˌlot; ˈparking ˌmeter; ˈparking ˌspace; ˈparking ˌticket; ˌpark-and-ˈride**

parka ˈpɑː.kə Ⓤⓢ ˈpɑːr- **-s** -z

Parke pɑːk Ⓤⓢ pɑːrk **-s** -s

Parker ˈpɑː.kəʳ Ⓤⓢ ˈpɑːr.kɚ

Parkestone ˈpɑːk.stən Ⓤⓢ ˈpɑːrk-

Parkhurst ˈpɑːk.hɜːst Ⓤⓢ ˈpɑːrk.hɝːst

parkin (P) ˈpɑː.kɪn Ⓤⓢ ˈpɑːr-

parking meter ˈpɑː.kɪŋˌmiː.təʳ Ⓤⓢ ˈpɑːr.kɪŋˌmiː.ţɚ **-s** -z

Parkinson ˈpɑː.kɪn.sᵊn Ⓤⓢ ˈpɑːr- **-ism** -ɪ.zᵊm **ˈParkinson's diˌsease**

parkland ˈpɑːk.lænd Ⓤⓢ ˈpɑːrk-

Parkman ˈpɑːk.mən Ⓤⓢ ˈpɑːrk-

Parks pɑːks Ⓤⓢ pɑːrks

Parkstone ˈpɑːk.stən Ⓤⓢ ˈpɑːrk-

parkway ˈpɑːk.weɪ Ⓤⓢ ˈpɑːrk- **-s** -z

park|y ˈpɑː.k|i Ⓤⓢ ˈpɑːr- **-ier** -i.əʳ Ⓤⓢ -i.ɚ **-iest** -i.ɪst, -i.əst

parlance ˈpɑː.lənts Ⓤⓢ ˈpɑːr-

parlay (*v.*) ˈpɑː.li Ⓤⓢ ˈpɑːr.leɪ, -li; pɑːrˈleɪ **-s** -z **-ing** -ɪŋ **-ed** -d

parlay (*n.*) ˈpɑː.li Ⓤⓢ ˈpɑːr.leɪ, -li **-s** -z

Parlement of Foules ˌpɑː.lə.mənt.əvˈfuːlz Ⓤⓢ ˌpɑːr-

parley (P) ˈpɑː.li Ⓤⓢ ˈpɑːr- **-s** -z **-ing** -ɪŋ **-ed** -d

parliament (P) ˈpɑː.lə.mənt, -lɪ-, -li.ə- Ⓤⓢ ˈpɑːr.lə- **-s** -s

parliamentarian (P) ˌpɑː.lə.menˈteə.ri.ən, -lɪ-, -li.ə-, -mənˈ- Ⓤⓢ ˌpɑːr.lə.menˈter.i- **-s** -z

parliamentary ˌpɑː.ləˈmen.tᵊr.i, -lɪˈ-, -li.əˈ- Ⓤⓢ ˌpɑːr.ləˈmen.ţɚ-, ˈ-tri

parlo(u)r ˈpɑː.ləʳ Ⓤⓢ ˈpɑːr.lɚ **-s** -z **ˈparlo(u)r ˌcar; ˈparlo(u)r ˌgame; ˈparlo(u)r ˌmaid**

parlous ˈpɑː.ləs Ⓤⓢ ˈpɑːr- **-ly** -li

Parma ˈpɑː.mə Ⓤⓢ ˈpɑːr- **ˌParma ˈham**

Parmar ˈpɑː.məʳ Ⓤⓢ ˈpɑːr.mɚ

Parmenter ˈpɑː.mɪn.təʳ, -mən- Ⓤⓢ ˈpɑːr.mən.tɚ

Parmesan ˈpɑː.mɪˌzæn, ˌ--ˈ-, -əˈ- Ⓤⓢ ˈpɑːr.mə.zɑːn, -zən, -zæn, -ʒɑːn

Parminter ˈpɑː.mɪn.təʳ Ⓤⓢ ˈpɑːr.mɪn.tɚ

Parmiter ˈpɑː.mɪ.təʳ Ⓤⓢ ˈpɑːr.mɪ.ţɚ

Parnassian pɑːˈnæs.i.ən Ⓤⓢ pɑːr-

Parnassus pɑːˈnæs.əs Ⓤⓢ pɑːr-

Parnell pɑːˈnel; ˈpɑː.nᵊl Ⓤⓢ pɑːrˈnel; ˈpɑːr.nᵊl

parochial pəˈrəʊ.ki.əl Ⓤⓢ -ˈroʊ- **-ly** -i **-ism** -ɪ.zᵊm

parodist ˈpær.ə.dɪst Ⓤⓢ ˈper-, ˈpær- **-s** -s

parod|y ˈpær.ə.d|i Ⓤⓢ ˈper-, ˈpær- **-ies** -iz **-ying** -i.ɪŋ **-ied** -id

parol ˈpær.əl; pəˈrəʊl Ⓤⓢ -ˈroʊl, ˈper.ᵊl, ˈpær-

parol|e pəˈrəʊl Ⓤⓢ -ˈroʊl **-es** -z **-ing** -ɪŋ **-ed** -d

Parolles pəˈrɒl.ɪz, -ɪs, -iːz, -es, -ez Ⓤⓢ pəˈrɑː.ləs

paronomazia, -sia ˌpær.ə.nəˈmeɪ.zi.ə, -si.ə, ˈ-ʒə Ⓤⓢ ˌper.ə.noʊˈmeɪ.ʒə, ˌpær-, ˈ-ʒi.ə

paronym ˈpær.ə.nɪm Ⓤⓢ ˈper-, ˈpær- **-s** -z

paronymy pəˈrɒn.ɪ.mi, pærˈɒn-, ˈ-ə- Ⓤⓢ pəˈrɑːn-

Paros ˈpær.ɒs Ⓤⓢ ˈper.ɑːs, ˈpær-, ˈpɑːr-

parotid pəˈrɒt.ɪd Ⓤⓢ -ˈrɑː.ţɪd **-s** -z

paroxysm ˈpær.ək.sɪ.zᵊm, -ɒk-; pəˈrɒk- Ⓤⓢ ˈper.ək-, ˈpær- **-s** -z

paroxysmal ˌpær.əkˈsɪz.mᵊl, -ɒkˈ- Ⓤⓢ ˌper.əkˈ-, ˌpær-

paroxytone pəˈrɒk.sɪ.təʊn, pærˈɒk- Ⓤⓢ perˈɑːk.sɪ.toʊn, pær- **-s** -z

parquet ˈpɑː.keɪ, -ki Ⓤⓢ pɑːrˈkeɪ **-s** -z

parquetry ˈpɑː.kɪ.tri, -kə- Ⓤⓢ ˈpɑːr.kə-

parr (P) pɑːʳ Ⓤⓢ pɑːr

parrakeet ˌpær.əˈkiːt, ˈ--- Ⓤⓢ ˈper.ə.kiːt, ˈpær- **-s** -s

Parramatta ˌpær.əˈmæt.ə Ⓤⓢ ˌper.əˈmæţ-, ˌpær-

Parratt ˈpær.ət Ⓤⓢ ˈper-, ˈpær-

Parret ˈpær.ɪt Ⓤⓢ ˈper-, ˈpær-

parricidal ˌpær.ɪˈsaɪ.dᵊl, -əˈ- Ⓤⓢ ˌper.əˈ-, ˌpær-

parricide ˈpær.ɪ.saɪd, ˈ-ə- Ⓤⓢ ˈper.ə-, ˈpær- **-s** -z

Parrish ˈpær.ɪʃ Ⓤⓢ ˈper-, ˈpær-

parrot (P) ˈpær.ət Ⓤⓢ ˈper-, ˈpær- **-s** -s **-ing** -ɪŋ **-ed** -ɪd

parrot-fashion ˈpær.ətˌfæʃ.ᵊn Ⓤⓢ ˈper-, ˈpær-

parr|y (P) ˈpær|.i Ⓤⓢ ˈper-, ˈpær- **-ies** -iz **-ying** -i.ɪŋ **-ied** -id

pars|e pɑːz Ⓤⓢ pɑːrs **-es** -ɪz **-ing** -ɪŋ **-ed** -d **-er/s** -əʳ/z Ⓤⓢ -ɚ/z

Parsi, Parsee ˌpɑːˈsiː, ˈ-- Ⓤⓢ ˈpɑːr.siː, -ˈ- **-s** -z

Parsifal ˈpɑː.sɪ.fᵊl, -sə-, -fɑːl, -fæl Ⓤⓢ ˈpɑːr.sə.fᵊl, -fɑːl

parsimonious ˌpɑː.sɪˈməʊ.ni.əs, -səˈ- Ⓤⓢ ˌpɑːr.səˈmoʊ- **-ly** -li **-ness** -nəs, -nɪs

parsimony ˈpɑː.sɪ.mə.ni, -sə- Ⓤⓢ ˈpɑːr.sə.moʊ-

parsley ˈpɑː.sli Ⓤⓢ ˈpɑːr-

parsnip ˈpɑː.snɪp Ⓤⓢ ˈpɑːr- **-s** -z

parson ˈpɑː.sᵊn Ⓤⓢ ˈpɑːr- **-s** -z **ˌparson's ˈnose**

parsonag|e ˈpɑː.sᵊn.ɪdʒ Ⓤⓢ ˈpɑːr- **-es** -ɪz

Parsons ˈpɑː.sᵊnz Ⓤⓢ ˈpɑːr-

part pɑːt Ⓤⓢ pɑːrt **-s** -s **-ing** -ɪŋ Ⓤⓢ ˈpɑːr.ţɪŋ **-ed** -ɪd Ⓤⓢ ˈpɑːr.ţɪd **ˌpart and ˈparcel; ˌpart exˈchange; ˌparting ˈshot** Ⓤⓢ **ˈparting ˌshot; ˌpart of ˈspeech**

partak|e pɑːˈteɪk Ⓤⓢ pɑːr- **-es** -s **-ing** -ɪŋ **partook** pɑːˈtʊk Ⓤⓢ pɑːr- **partak|en** pɑːˈteɪ.k|ᵊn Ⓤⓢ pɑːr- **-er/s** -əʳ/z Ⓤⓢ -ɚ/z

parterre pɑːˈteəʳ Ⓤⓢ pɑːrˈter **-s** -z

Parthenia pɑːˈθiː.ni.ə Ⓤⓢ pɑːr-

parthenogenesis ˌpɑː.θə.nəʊˈdʒen.ɪ.sɪs, -θɪ-, ˈ-ə- Ⓤⓢ ˌpɑːr.θə.noʊˈdʒen.ə-

Parthenon ˈpɑː.θᵊn.ən, -θɪ.nən, -nɒn Ⓤⓢ ˈpɑːr.θə.nɑːn, -nən **-s** -z

Parthenope pɑːˈθen.ə.pi Ⓤⓢ pɑːr-

Parthi|a ˈpɑː.θi|.ə Ⓤⓢ ˈpɑːr- **-an/s** -ən/z

partial ˈpɑː.ʃᵊl Ⓤⓢ ˈpɑːr- **-ly** -i

partiality ˌpɑː.ʃiˈæl.ə.ti, -ɪ.ti Ⓤⓢ ˌpɑːr.ʃiˈæl.ə.ţi

participant pɑːˈtɪs.ɪ.pᵊnt, ˈ-ə- Ⓤⓢ pɑːrˈtɪs.ə-, pɚ- **-s** -s

partici|pate pɑːˈtɪs.ɪ|.peɪt, ˈ-ə- Ⓤⓢ pɑːrˈtɪs.ə-, pɚ- **-pates** -peɪts **-pating** -peɪ.tɪŋ Ⓤⓢ -peɪ.ţɪŋ **-pated** -peɪ.tɪd Ⓤⓢ -peɪ.ţɪd **-pator/s** -peɪ.təʳ/z Ⓤⓢ -peɪ.ţɚ/z

participation pɑːˌtɪs.ɪˈpeɪ.ʃᵊn, ˌpɑː.tɪ.sɪˈ-, -səˈ- Ⓤⓢ pɑːrˌtɪs.əˈ-, pɚ- **-s** -z

participatory pɑːˈtɪs.ɪ.pə.tᵊr.i, ˈ-ə-; ˌpɑː.tɪ.sɪˈpeɪ-, -səˈ- Ⓤⓢ pɑːrˈtɪs.ə.pəˌtɔːr-, pɚ-

participial ˌpɑː.tɪˈsɪp.i.əl, -təˈ- (US) ˌpɑːr.tɪˈ- **-ly** -i

participle pɑːˈtɪs.ɪ.pl̩, ˈ-ə- (US) ˈpɑːr.tɪ.sɪ- **-s** -z

particle ˈpɑː.tɪ.kl̩, -tə- (US) ˈpɑːr.t̬ə- **-s** -z

particleboard ˈpɑː.tɪ.kl̩ˌbɔːd (US) ˈpɑːr.t̬ɪ.kl̩ˌbɔːrd

particolo(u)red ˈpɑː.tiˌkʌl.əd, ˌpɑː.tiˈkʌl- (US) ˈpɑːr.t̬iˌkʌl.ɚd

particular pəˈtɪk.jə.ləʳ, -jʊ- (US) pɚˈtɪk.jə.lɚ, -juː- **-s** -z **-ly** -li

particularit|y pəˌtɪk.jəˈlær.ə.t|i, -jʊˈ-, -ɪ.t|i (US) pɚˌtɪk.jəˈler.ə.t̬|i, -juːˈ-, -ˈlær- **-ies** -iz

particulariz|e, -is|e pəˈtɪk.jə.lᵊr.aɪz, -jʊ- (US) pɚˈtɪk.jə.lə.raɪz, -juː- **-es** -ɪz **-ing** -ɪŋ **-ed** -d

parting ˈpɑː.tɪŋ (US) ˈpɑːr.t̬ɪŋ **-s** -z

Partington ˈpɑː.tɪŋ.tən (US) ˈpɑːr.t̬ɪŋ-

partisan ˌpɑː.tɪˈzæn, -təˈ-, ˈ--- (US) ˈpɑːr.t̬ɪ.zən, -zæn **-s** -z **-ship/s** -ʃɪp/s

partita pɑːˈtiː.tə (US) pɑːrˈtiː.t̬ə

partite ˈpɑː.taɪt (US) ˈpɑːr-

partition pɑːˈtɪʃ.ᵊn, pə- (US) pɑːr- **-s** -z **-ing** -ɪŋ **-ed** -d

partitive ˈpɑː.tɪ.tɪv, -tə- (US) ˈpɑːr.t̬ə.t̬ɪv **-ly** -li

partly ˈpɑːt.li (US) ˈpɑːrt-

partn|er ˈpɑːt.n|əʳ (US) ˈpɑːrt.n|ɚ **-ers** -əz (US) -ɚz **-ering** -ᵊr.ɪŋ **-ered** -əd (US) -ɚd

partnership ˈpɑːt.nə.ʃɪp (US) ˈpɑːrt.nɚ- **-s** -s

Parton ˈpɑː.tᵊn (US) ˈpɑːr-

partook *(from* **partake***)* pɑːˈtʊk (US) pɑːr-

partridg|e (P) ˈpɑː.trɪdʒ (US) ˈpɑːr- **-es** -ɪz

part-singing ˈpɑːtˌsɪŋ.ɪŋ (US) ˈpɑːrt-

part-song ˈpɑːt.sɒŋ (US) ˈpɑːrt.sɑːŋ, -sɔːŋ **-s** -z

part-tim|e ˌpɑːtˈtaɪm (US) ˌpɑːrt-, ˈ-- **-er/s** -əʳ/z (US) -ɚ/z *stress shift, British only:* ˌpart-time ˈjob

parturition ˌpɑː.tjʊəˈrɪʃ.ᵊn, -tjᵊrˈɪʃ- (US) ˌpɑːr.tuːˈrɪʃ-, -tjuːˈ-, -t̬əˈ-, -tʃəˈ- **-s** -z

partway ˌpɑːtˈweɪ (US) ˌpɑːrt- *stress shift:* ˌpartway ˈthere

part|y ˈpɑː.t|i (US) ˈpɑːr.t̬|i **-ies** -iz **-ying** -i.ɪŋ **-ied** -id ˈ**party ˌpiece**; ˌ**party ˈwall**

partygoer ˈpɑː.tiˌgəʊ.əʳ (US) ˈpɑːr.t̬iˌgoʊ.ɚ **-s** -z

party line *in politics:* ˌpɑː.tiˈlaɪn (US) ˌpɑːr.t̬iˈ-

party line *telephone:* ˈpɑː.ti.laɪn (US) ˈpɑːr.t̬i-

party poop|er ˈpɑː.tiˌpuː.p|əʳ (US) ˈpɑːr.t̬iˌpuː.p|ɚ **-ers** -əz (US) -ɚz **-ing** -ɪŋ

party-spirit ˌpɑː.tiˈspɪr.ɪt (US) ˌpɑːr.t̬iˈ-

parvenu(e) ˈpɑː.və.njuː, -nuː (US) ˈpɑːr.və.nuː, -njuː **-s** -z

Parzival ˈpɑːt.sɪ.fɑːl (US) ˈpɑːrt-

pas *singular:* pɑː *plural:* pɑːz, pɑː

Pasadena ˌpæs.əˈdiː.nə

Pascal, PASCAL pæsˈkæl, -ˈkɑːl; (US) pæsˈkæl, pɑːˈskæl, ˈ--

paschal ˈpæs.kᵊl, ˈpɑː.skᵊl (US) ˈpæs.kᵊl

pas de deux ˌpɑː.dəˈdɜː

pasha (P) ˈpɑː.ʃə, ˈpæʃ.ə; pəˈʃɑː **-s** -z

pashmina pæʃˈmiː.nə **-s** -z

Pashtun pæʃˈtuːn, ˈpɑːʃ-

Pasiphae pəˈsɪf.i.iː, -eɪ (US) ˈ-ə.i

paso doble ˌpæs.əʊˈdəʊ.bleɪ (US) ˌpɑː.soʊˈdoʊ-

Pasolini ˌpæs.əʊˈliː.ni (US) -oʊˈ-

pasquinade ˌpæs.kwɪˈneɪd, -kwəˈ- (US) -kwɪˈ- **-s** -z

pass pɑːs (US) pæs **-es** -ɪz **-ing** -ɪŋ **-ed** -t **-er/s** -əʳ/z (US) -ɚ/z ˈ**pass deˌgree**; ˈ**pass ˌlaw**

passab|le ˈpɑː.sə.b|l̩ (US) ˈpæs.ə- **-ly** -li **-leness** -l̩.nəs, -nɪs

passacaglia ˌpæs.əˈkɑː.li.ə, -ˈkæl.jə (US) ˌpɑː.səˈkɑːl.jə, ˌpæs.əˈ-, -ˈkæl- **-s** -z

passag|e ˈpæs.ɪdʒ **-es** -ɪz **-ing** -ɪŋ **-ed** -d

passageway ˈpæs.ɪdʒ.weɪ

passant *in heraldry:* ˈpæs.ᵊnt *in chess:* pæsˈɑ̃ːŋ, pɑːˈsɑːŋ (US) ˈpæs.ənt

Passat® pæsˈæt, -ɑːt (US) pəˈsɑːt, pæsˈɑːt

passbook ˈpɑːs.bʊk (US) ˈpæs- **-s** -s

Passe pæs

passé(e) pæsˈeɪ, pɑːˈseɪ, ˈ-- (US) pæsˈeɪ, ˈ--; pɑːˈseɪ

passenger ˈpæs.ᵊn.dʒəʳ, -ɪn- (US) -ᵊn.dʒɚ **-s** -z

passe-partout ˌpæs.pəˈtuː, ˌpɑːs-, -pɑːˈ-, ˈ--- (US) ˌpæs.pɑːrˈ-, ˌpɑːs- **-s** -z

passer-by ˌpɑː.səˈbaɪ (US) ˌpæs.ɚˈ- **passers-by** ˌpɑː.səzˈbaɪ (US) ˌpæs.ɚzˈ-

passerine ˈpæs.ə.raɪn, -riːn (US) -ə.raɪn, -ɚ.ɪn

Passfield ˈpæs.fiːld, ˈpɑːs- (US) ˈpæs-

passibility ˌpæs.ɪˈbɪl.ə.ti, -əˈ-, -ɪ.ti (US) -ɪˈbɪl.ə.t̬i

passible ˈpæs.ɪ.bl̩, ˈ-ə- (US) ˈ-ɪ-

passim ˈpæs.ɪm

passing note ˈpɑː.sɪŋˌnəʊt (US) ˈpæs.ɪŋˌnoʊt **-s** -s

passion (P) ˈpæʃ.ᵊn **-s** -z ˈ**passion ˌplay**

passionate ˈpæʃ.ᵊn.ət, -ɪt (US) -ə.nɪt **-ly** -li **-ness** -nəs, -nɪs

passionflower ˈpæʃ.ᵊnˌflaʊəʳ (US) -ˌflaʊɚ **-s** -z

passionfruit ˈpæʃ.ᵊn.fruːt **-s** -s

Passiontide ˈpæʃ.ᵊn.taɪd

passive ˈpæs.ɪv **-ly** -li **-ness** -nəs, -nɪs ˌ**passive ˈsmoking**

passivity pæsˈɪv.ə.ti, pəˈsɪv-, -ɪ.ti (US) pæsˈɪv.ə.t̬i

passivization, -isa- ˌpæs.ɪ.vaɪˈzeɪ.ʃᵊn, ˌ-ə-, -vɪˈ- (US) -ɪ.vɪˈ-

passiviz|e, -is|e ˈpæs.ɪ.vaɪz, ˈ-ə- (US) ˈ-ɪ- **-es** -ɪz **-ing** -ɪŋ **-ed** -d

pass-key ˈpɑːs.kiː (US) ˈpæs- **-s** -z

Passmore ˈpɑːs.mɔːʳ, ˈpæs- (US) ˈpæs.mɔːr

Passover ˈpɑːsˌəʊ.vəʳ (US) ˈpæsˌoʊ.vɚ **-s** -z

passport ˈpɑːs.pɔːt (US) ˈpæs.pɔːrt **-s** -s

password ˈpɑːs.wɜːd (US) ˈpæs.wɝːd **-s** -z

past pɑːst (US) pæst ˌ**past parˈticiple**; (US) ˌ**past ˈparticiple**; ˌ**past ˈperfect**; ˌ**past ˈtense**

pasta ˈpæs.tə, ˈpɑː.stə (US) ˈpɑː.stə

past|e peɪst **-es** -s **-ing** -ɪŋ **-ed** -ɪd

pasteboard ˈpeɪs*t*.bɔːd (US) -bɔːrd

pastel ˈpæs.tᵊl, -tel; pæsˈtel (US) pæsˈtel **-s** -z

pastelist ˈpæs.tᵊl.ɪst (US) pæsˈtel-; ˈpæs.tᵊl- **-s** -s

pastern ˈpæs.tɜːn, -tən (US) -tɚn **-s** -z

Pasternak ˈpæs.tə.næk (US) -tɚ-

paste-up ˈpeɪst.ʌp **-s** -s

Pasteur pæsˈtɜːʳ, pɑːˈstɜːʳ (US) pæsˈtɝː, pɑːˈstɝː

pasteurization, -isa- ˌpæs.tʃᵊr.aɪˈzeɪ.ʃᵊn, ˌpɑːs-, -tjᵊr-, -tᵊr-, -ɪˈ- (US) ˌpæs.tʃɚ.ɪˈ-, -tɚ-

pasteuriz|e, -is|e ˈpæs.tʃᵊr.aɪz, ˈpɑːs-, -tjᵊr-, -tᵊr- (US) ˈpæs.tʃə.raɪz, -tə- **-es** -ɪz **-ing** -ɪŋ **-ed** -d

pastich|e pæsˈtiːʃ, ˈ-- (US) pæsˈtiːʃ, pɑːˈstiːʃ **-es** -ɪz

pastille ˈpæs.tᵊl, -tɪl, -tiːl; pæsˈtiːl (US) pæsˈtiːl **-s** -z

pastime ˈpɑːs.taɪm (US) ˈpæs- **-s** -z

pastis pæsˈtiːs

past-master ˌpɑːstˈmɑː.stəʳ, ˈ-ˌ-- (US) ˈpæstˌmæs.tɚ, ˌ-ˈ-- **-s** -z

Paston ˈpæs.tᵊn

pastor ˈpɑː.stəʳ (US) ˈpæs.tɚ **-s** -z

pastoral ˈpɑː.stᵊr.ᵊl, ˈpæs.tᵊr- (US) ˈpæs- **-s** -z

pastorale ˌpæs.tᵊrˈɑːl, -ˈæl, -ˈɑː.leɪ (US) -təˈrɑːl, -ˈræl, -ˈrɑː.leɪ **-s** -z

pastoralism ˈpɑː.stᵊr.ᵊl.ɪ.zᵊm, ˈpæs.tᵊr- (US) ˈpæs-

pastorate ˈpɑː.stᵊr.ət, -ɪt (US) ˈpæs.tɚ.ɪt **-s** -s

pastrami pæsˈtrɑː.mi, pəˈstrɑː- (US) pə-

pastr|y ˈpeɪ.str|i **-ies** -iz

pastrycook ˈpeɪ.stri.kʊk **-s** -s

pasturage ˈpɑː.stjʊ.rɪdʒ, -tjᵊr.ɪdʒ, -tʃᵊr- (US) ˈpæs.tʃɚ.ɪdʒ, -tjɚ-

past|ure ˈpɑːs.tʃ|əʳ (US) ˈpæs.tʃ|ɚ, -tj|ɚ **-ures** -əz (US) -ɚz **-uring** -ᵊr.ɪŋ **-ured** -əd (US) -ɚd

pastureland ˈpɑː.stʃə.lænd Ⓤⓢ ˈpæs.tʃɚ-, -tjɚ-
past|y (*n.*) ˈpæs.t|i *for the Cornish kind also:* ˈpɑː.st|i Ⓤⓢ ˈpæs.t|i **-ies** -iz
past|y (*adj.*) ˈpeɪ.st|i **-ier** -i.əʳ Ⓤⓢ -i.ɚ **-iest** -i.ɪst, -i.əst **-ily** -ɪ.li, -əl.i **-iness** -ɪ.nəs, -ɪ.nɪs
pat **(P)** pæt **-s** -s **-ting** -ɪŋ Ⓤⓢ ˈpæt̬.ɪŋ **-ted** -ɪd Ⓤⓢ ˈpæt̬.ɪd
pat-a-cake ˈpæt.ə.keɪk Ⓤⓢ ˈpæt̬- **-s** -s
Patagoni|a ˌpæt.əˈgəʊ.ni|.ə Ⓤⓢ ˌpæt̬.əˈgoʊ-, ˈ-nj|ə **-an/s** -ən/z
Pataki pəˈtɑːk.i, -ˈtæk-
Patara ˈpæt.ər.ə
patch pætʃ **-es** -ɪz **-ing** -ɪŋ **-ed** -t
patchouli, patchouly pəˈtʃuː.li; ˈpætʃ.ʊ.li, -əl.i Ⓤⓢ ˈpætʃ.uː.li; pəˈtʃuː-
patchwork ˈpætʃ.wɜːk Ⓤⓢ -wɝːk **-s** -s ˌ**patchwork** ˈ**quilt**
patch|y ˈpætʃ|.i **-ier** -i.əʳ Ⓤⓢ -i.ɚ **-iest** -i.ɪst, -i.əst **-ily** -ɪ.li, -əl.i **-iness** -ɪ.nəs, -ɪ.nɪs
pate peɪt **-s** -s
pâté ˈpæt.eɪ, -ˈ- Ⓤⓢ pɑːˈteɪ, pætˈeɪ
pâté de foie ˌpæt.eɪ.dəˈfwɑː Ⓤⓢ pɑːˌteɪ-, pætˌeɪ-
pâté de foie gras ˌpæt.eɪ.dəˌfwɑːˈgrɑː Ⓤⓢ pɑːˌteɪ-, pætˌeɪ-
Patel pəˈtel, -ˈteɪl
Pateley ˈpeɪt.li
patell|a pəˈtel|.ə **-as** -əz **-ae** -iː **-ar** -əʳ Ⓤⓢ -ɚ
paten ˈpæt.ən **-s** -z
paten|t ˈpeɪ.tən|t, ˈpæt.ən|t Ⓤⓢ ˈpæt-, ˈpeɪ.tən|t **-ts** -ts **-ting** -tɪŋ Ⓤⓢ -t̬ɪŋ **-ted** -tɪd Ⓤⓢ -t̬ɪd **-table** -tə.bl̩ Ⓤⓢ -t̬ə.bl̩ ˌ**patent** ˈ**leather**
Note: For British English, /ˈpæt.ənt/ in **letters patent**; otherwise /ˈpeɪ.tənt/ seems the more usual. For American English, the usual pronunciation is /ˈpæt.ənt/, except for the meanings **open, obvious,** where /ˈpeɪ.tənt/ is the normal form.
patentee ˌpeɪ.tənˈtiː, ˌpæt.ənˈ- Ⓤⓢ ˌpæt.ənˈtiː **-s** -z
patently ˈpeɪ.tənt.li Ⓤⓢ ˈpeɪ-, ˈpæt.ənt-
pater **(P)** ˈpeɪ.təʳ, ˈpɑː- Ⓤⓢ ˈpɑː.t̬ɚ **-s** -z
Note: This word is never used to mean **father** in the U.S..
paterfamilias ˌpeɪ.tə.fəˈmɪl.i.æs, ˌpæt.ə-, -əs Ⓤⓢ ˌpeɪ.t̬ɚ.fəˈmɪl.i.əs, ˌpɑː.t̬ɚ-, ˌpæt̬.ɚ-
paternal pəˈtɜː.nəl Ⓤⓢ -ˈtɝː- **-ly** -li
paternal|ism pəˈtɜː.nəl|.ɪ.zəm Ⓤⓢ -ˈtɝː- **-ist/s** -ɪst/s
paternalistic pəˌtɜː.nəlˈɪs.tɪk Ⓤⓢ -ˌtɝː- **-ally** -əl.i, -li
paternity pəˈtɜː.nə.ti, -nɪ- Ⓤⓢ -ˈtɝː.nə.t̬i **paˈternity** ˌ**leave; paˈternity** ˌ**suit; paˈternity** ˌ**test**

Paternoster *Lord's prayer:* ˌpæt.əˈnɒs.təʳ Ⓤⓢ ˌpɑː.t̬ɚˈnɔː.stɚ, -ˈnoʊ- **-s** -z
Paternoster *Square:* ˈpæt.əˌnɒs.təʳ Ⓤⓢ ˌpɑː.t̬ɚˈnɔː.stɚ, ˌpæt.ɚˈ-, ˌpeɪ.tɚˈ-, -ˈnɑː-
Paterson ˈpæt.ə.sən Ⓤⓢ ˈpæt̬.ɚ-
Pateshall ˈpæt.ə.ʃəl, ˈ-ɪ- Ⓤⓢ ˈpæt̬-
Patey ˈpeɪ.ti Ⓤⓢ -t̬i
pa|th pɑː|θ Ⓤⓢ pæ|θ **-ths** -ðz Ⓤⓢ -θs, -ðz ˌ**lead someone** ˌ**up/**ˌ**down the** ˌ**garden** ˈ**path**
path. pæθ
-path -pæθ
Note: Suffix. Normally unstressed, e.g. **psychopath** /ˈsaɪ.kəʊ.pæθ Ⓤⓢ -kə-/.
Pathan pəˈtɑːn Ⓤⓢ pəˈtɑːn, pətˈhɑːn **-s** -z
Pathé ˈpæθ.eɪ
pathetic pəˈθet.ɪk Ⓤⓢ -ˈθet̬- **-ally** -əl.i, -li
pathfinder **(P)** ˈpɑːθˌfaɪn.dəʳ Ⓤⓢ ˈpæθˌfaɪn.dɚ **-s** -z
-pathic -ˈpæθ.ɪk
Note: Suffix. Words containing **-pathic** normally carry primary stress on the penultimate syllable, e.g. **psychopathic** /ˌsaɪ.kəʊˈpæθ.ɪk Ⓤⓢ -kəˈ-/.
pathless ˈpɑːθ.ləs, -lɪs Ⓤⓢ ˈpæθ-
patho- pæθ.əʊ-; pəˈθɒ-, pæθˈɒ- Ⓤⓢ pæθ.ə-; pəˈθɑː-, pæθˈɑː-
Note: Prefix. Normally either carries primary or secondary stress on the first syllable, e.g. **pathogen** /ˈpæθ.əʊ.dʒen Ⓤⓢ -ə-/, **pathogenic** /ˌpæθ.əʊˈdʒen.ɪk Ⓤⓢ -əˈ-/, or primary stress on the second syllable, e.g. **pathology** /pəˈθɒl.ə.dʒi Ⓤⓢ -ˈθɑː.lə-/.
pathogen ˈpæθ.əʊ.dʒən, -dʒen Ⓤⓢ -ə.dʒən **-s** -z
pathogenesis ˌpæθ.əʊˈdʒen.ə.sɪs, ˈ-ɪ- Ⓤⓢ ˈ-ə-
pathogenic ˌpæθ.əʊˈdʒen.ɪk Ⓤⓢ -əˈ- **-ally** -əl.i, -li
pathologic ˌpæθ.əˈlɒdʒ.ɪk Ⓤⓢ -ˈlɑː.dʒɪk **-al** -əl **-ally** -əl.i, -li
patholog|y pəˈθɒl.ə.dʒ|i, pæθˈɒl- Ⓤⓢ pəˈθɑː.lə- **-ist/s** -ɪst/s
pathos ˈpeɪ.θɒs Ⓤⓢ -θɑːs
pathway ˈpɑːθ.weɪ Ⓤⓢ ˈpæθ- **-s** -z
-pathy -pə.θi
Note: Suffix. Normally unstressed, e.g. **telepathy** /təˈlep.ə.θi/.
patience **(P)** ˈpeɪ.ʃənts
patient ˈpeɪ.ʃənt **-s** -s **-ly** -li
patina ˈpæt.ɪ.nə, -ən.ə; pəˈtiː.nə Ⓤⓢ ˈpæt.ən.ə; pəˈtiː.nə
patio ˈpæt.i.əʊ Ⓤⓢ ˈpæt̬.i.oʊ, ˈpɑː.t̬i- **-s** -z
patisserie pəˈtiː.sər.i, pætˈɪs- **-s** -z

Patman ˈpæt.mən
Patmore ˈpæt.mɔːʳ Ⓤⓢ -mɔːr
Patmos ˈpæt.mɒs Ⓤⓢ -məs, ˈpɑːt-, -mɑːs
Patna ˈpæt.nə, ˈpʌt- Ⓤⓢ ˈpʌt-, ˈpæt-
patois *singular:* ˈpæt.wɑː *plural:* -z
Paton ˈpeɪ.tən
Patou ˈpæt.uː *as if French:* -ˈ-
Patras pəˈtræs; ˈpæt.rəs
patrial ˈpeɪ.tri.əl, ˈpæt.ri- Ⓤⓢ ˈpeɪ.tri-
patriarch ˈpeɪ.tri.ɑːk, ˈpæt.ri- Ⓤⓢ ˈpeɪ.tri.ɑːrk **-s** -s **-y** -i **-ies** -iz
patriarch|al ˌpeɪ.triˈɑː.k|əl, ˌpæt.riˈ- Ⓤⓢ ˌpeɪ.triˈɑːr- **-ic** -ɪk
patriarchate ˈpeɪ.tri.ɑː.kɪt, ˈpæt.ri-, -keɪt, -kət Ⓤⓢ ˈpeɪ.tri.ɑːr.kɪt, -keɪt **-s** -s
Patricia pəˈtrɪʃ.ə Ⓤⓢ -ˈtrɪʃ-, -ˈtriː.ʃə
patrician pəˈtrɪʃ.ən **-s** -z
patriciate pəˈtrɪʃ.i.ət, -ˈtrɪʃ.ət Ⓤⓢ -ˈtrɪs.i-, -ɪt, -eɪt Ⓤⓢ -trɪʃ.i.ɪt, -eɪt; -ˈtrɪʃ.ɪt
patricide ˈpæt.rɪ.saɪd, ˈpeɪ.trɪ-, -trə- Ⓤⓢ ˈpæt.rə- **-s** -z
Patrick ˈpæt.rɪk
patrilineal ˌpæt.rɪˈlɪn.i.əl, -rəˈ- Ⓤⓢ ˌpæt.rəˈ-
patrimonial ˌpæt.rɪˈməʊ.ni.əl, -rəˈ- Ⓤⓢ ˌpæt.rəˈmoʊ- **-ly** -i
patrimon|y ˈpæt.rɪ.mə.n|i, -rə- Ⓤⓢ -rə.moʊ- **-ies** -iz
patriot ˈpeɪ.tri.ət, ˈpæt.ri- Ⓤⓢ ˈpeɪ-, -ɑːt **-s** -s
patriotic ˌpæt.riˈɒt.ɪk, ˌpeɪ.triˈ- Ⓤⓢ ˌpeɪ.triˈɑː.t̬ɪk **-ally** -əl.i, -li
patriotism ˈpeɪ.tri.ə.tɪ.zəm, ˈpæt.ri- Ⓤⓢ ˈpeɪ.tri-
patristic pəˈtrɪs.tɪk **-s** -s **-al** -əl
Patroclus pəˈtrɒk.ləs Ⓤⓢ -ˈtroʊ.kləs; ˈpæt.roʊ-
patrol pəˈtrəʊl Ⓤⓢ -ˈtroʊl **-s** -z **-ling** -ɪŋ **-led** -d
patrolcar pəˈtrəʊl.kɑːʳ Ⓤⓢ -ˈtroʊl.kɑːr **-s** -z
patrol|man pəˈtrəʊl|.mən, -mæn Ⓤⓢ -ˈtroʊl- **-men** -mən, -men
patron ˈpeɪ.trən, ˈpæt.rən Ⓤⓢ ˈpeɪ.trən **-s** -z
patronage ˈpæt.rən.ɪdʒ, ˈpeɪ.trən- Ⓤⓢ ˈpeɪ.trən-, ˈpæt.rən-
patronal pəˈtrəʊ.nəl, pætˈrəʊ- Ⓤⓢ ˈpeɪ.trən.əl, ˈpæt.rən-; pəˈtroʊ.nəl
patroness ˌpeɪ.trəˈnes, ˌpæt.rəˈ-; ˈpeɪ.trən.es, ˈpæt.rən-, -ɪs, -əs Ⓤⓢ ˈpeɪ.trə.nɪs **-es** -ɪz
patroniz|e, -is|e ˈpæt.rən.aɪz Ⓤⓢ ˈpeɪ.trən-, ˈpæt.rən- **-es** -ɪz **-ing/ly** -ɪŋ/li **-ed** -d
patronymic ˌpæt.rəˈnɪm.ɪk Ⓤⓢ -rəˈ-, -roʊˈ- **-s** -s
patroon pəˈtruːn **-s** -z
pats|y **(P)** ˈpæt.s|i **-ies** -iz

patten **(P)** ˈpæt.ᵊn **-s** -z
patt|er ˈpæt|.əʳ (US) ˈpæt̬|.ɚ **-ers** -əz (US) -ɚz **-ering** -ᵊr.ɪŋ **-ered** -əd (US) -ɚd
Patterdale ˈpæt.ə.deɪl (US) ˈpæt̬.ɚ-
pattern ˈpæt.ᵊn (US) ˈpæt̬.ɚn **-s** -z **-ing** -ɪŋ **-ed** -d
Patterson ˈpæt.ə.sᵊn (US) ˈpæt̬.ɚ-
Patteson ˈpæt.ɪ.sᵊn, ˈ-ə- (US) ˈpæt̬-
Patti(e) ˈpæt.i (US) ˈpæt̬-
Pattison ˈpæt.ɪ.sᵊn (US) ˈpæt̬-
Patton ˈpæt.ᵊn
patt|y ˈpæt|.i (US) ˈpæt̬- **-ies** -iz
paucity ˈpɔː.sə.ti, -sɪ- (US) ˈpɑː.sə.t̬i, ˈpɔː-
Paul pɔːl (US) pɔːl, pɑːl **-'s** -z ˌ**Paul** ˈ**Jones**
Paula ˈpɔː.lə (US) ˈpɑː-, ˈpɔː-
Paulding ˈpɔːl.dɪŋ (US) ˈpɑːl-, ˈpɔːl-
Paulette pɔːˈlet (US) pɑː-, pɔː-
Pauley ˈpɔː.li (US) ˈpɑː-, ˈpɔː-
Pauli ˈpɔː.li, ˈpaʊ- (US) ˈpaʊ-, ˈpɔː-
Paulin ˈpɔː.lɪn (US) ˈpɑː-, ˈpɔː-
Pauline *scholar of St Paul's school, relating to St Paul:* ˈpɔː.laɪn (US) ˈpɑː.laɪn, ˈpɔː-, -liːn **-s** -z
Pauline *female name:* ˈpɔː.liːn, -ˈ- (US) pɑːˈliːn, pɔː-
Pauling ˈpɔː.lɪŋ (US) ˈpɑː-, ˈpɔː-
Paulinus pɔːˈlaɪ.nəs (US) pɑː-, pɔː-
Paulus ˈpɔː.ləs (US) ˈpɑː-, ˈpɔː-
Pauncefote ˈpɔːnts.fʊt, -fət (US) ˈpɑːnts-, ˈpɔːnts-
paunch pɔːntʃ (US) pɑːntʃ, pɔːntʃ **-es** -ɪz **-y** -i **-iness** -ɪ.nəs, -ɪ.nɪs
pauper ˈpɔː.pəʳ (US) ˈpɑː.pɚ, ˈpɔː- **-s** -z
pauperism ˈpɔː.pᵊr.ɪ.zᵊm (US) ˈpɑː-, ˈpɔː-
pauperization, -isa- ˌpɔː.pᵊr.aɪˈzeɪ.ʃᵊn, -ɪˈ- (US) ˌpɑː.pɚ.ɪˈ-, ˌpɔː-
pauperiz|e, -is|e ˈpɔː.pᵊr.aɪz (US) ˈpɑː-, ˈpɔː- **-es** -ɪz **-ing** -ɪŋ **-ed** -d
Pausanias pɔːˈseɪ.ni.æs, -əs (US) pɑːˈseɪ.ni.əs, pɔː-
paus|e pɔːz (US) pɑːz, pɔːz **-es** -ɪz **-ing** -ɪŋ **-ed** -d
pavan(e) ˈpæv.ᵊn; pəˈvæn, -ˈvɑːn (US) pəˈvɑːn, -ˈvæn **-s** -z
Pavarotti ˌpæv.əˈrɒt.i (US) -ˈrɔː.t̬i, ˌpɑː.və-
pav|e peɪv **-es** -z **-ing** -ɪŋ **-ed** -d **-er/s** -əʳ/z (US) -ɚ/z ˈ**paving** ˌ**stone**
pavé ˈpæv.eɪ, -ˈ- (US) pævˈeɪ, ˈ-- **-s** -z
pavement ˈpeɪv.mənt **-s** -s
Pavia pəˈviː.ə, pɑː-, pɑːˈviː.ɑː
pavid ˈpæv.ɪd
pavilion pəˈvɪl.jən, ˈ-i.ən (US) ˈ-jən **-s** -z **-ing** -ɪŋ **-ed** -d
pavio(u)r ˈpeɪ.vjəʳ (US) -vjɚ **-s** -s
Pavitt ˈpæv.ɪt
Pavlov ˈpæv.lɒf, -lɒv (US) -lɔːv, -lɔːf
pavlova pævˈləʊ.və (US) pɑːvˈloʊ-, pæv- **-s** -z
Pavlova ˈpæv.lə.və, ˈpɑːv-; pævˈləʊ- (US) pɑːvˈloʊ-, pæv-
Pavlovian pævˈləʊ.vi.ən (US) pɑːvˈloʊ-, pæv-
paw *(n. v.)* pɔː (US) pɑː, pɔː **-s** -z **-ing** -ɪŋ **-ed** -d
pawk|y ˈpɔː.k|i (US) ˈpɑː-, ˈpɔː- **-ier** -i.əʳ (US) -i.ɚ **-iest** -i.ɪst, -i.əst **-ily** -ɪ.li, -ᵊl.i **-iness** -ɪ.nəs, -ɪ.nɪs
pawl pɔːl (US) pɑːl, pɔːl **-s** -z
pawn pɔːn (US) pɑːn, pɔːn **-s** -z **-ing** -ɪŋ **-ed** -d
pawnbrok|er ˈpɔːnˌbrəʊ.k|əʳ, ˈpɔːm- (US) ˈpɑːnˌbroʊ.k|ɚ, ˈpɔːn- **-ers** -əz (US) -ɚz **-ing** -ɪŋ
Pawnee ˌpɔːˈniː (US) ˌpɑː-, ˌpɔː- **-s** -z
pawnshop ˈpɔːn.ʃɒp (US) ˈpɑːn.ʃɑːp, ˈpɔːn- **-s** -s
pawpaw ˈpɔː.pɔː (US) ˈpɑː.pɑː; ˈpɔː.pɔː **-s** -z
Pawtucket pɔːˈtʌk.ɪt (US) pɑː-, pɔː-
pax pæks
Paxman ˈpæk.smən
Paxo® ˈpæk.səʊ (US) -soʊ
Paxos ˈpæk.sɒs (US) -sɑːs
Paxton ˈpæk.stᵊn
pay peɪ **-s** -z **-ing** -ɪŋ **paid** peɪd **payer/s** ˈpeɪ.əʳ/z (US) -ɚ/z ˈ**pay** ˌ**packet**
payable ˈpeɪ.ə.bl̩
payback ˈpeɪ.bæk
paybed ˈpeɪ.bed
paycheck, -cheque ˈpeɪ.tʃek
payday ˈpeɪ.deɪ **-s** -z
PAYE ˌpiː.eɪ.waɪˈiː
payee peɪˈiː **-s** -z
payload ˈpeɪ.ləʊd (US) -loʊd **-s** -z
paymaster ˈpeɪˌmɑː.stəʳ (US) -ˌmæs.tɚ **-s** -z ˌ**paymaster** ˈ**general**
payment ˈpeɪ.mənt **-s** -s
Payne peɪn
paynim **(P)** ˈpeɪ.nɪm
Paynter ˈpeɪn.təʳ (US) -t̬ɚ
payoff ˈpeɪ.ɒf (US) -ɑːf **-s** -s
payola peɪˈəʊ.lə (US) -ˈoʊ-
payout ˈpeɪ.aʊt **-s** -s
payphone ˈpeɪ.fəʊn (US) -foʊn
payroll ˈpeɪ.rəʊl (US) -roʊl **-s** -z
payslip ˈpeɪ.slɪp
paytrain ˈpeɪ.treɪn **-s** -z
Paz pæz (US) pɑːz, pɑːs
pazazz pəˈzæz
PBS ˌpiː.biːˈes
PC ˌpiːˈsiː
PE ˌpiːˈiː
pea piː **-s** -z
Peabody ˈpiːˌbɒd.i (US) -ˌbɑː.di
peac|e **(P)** piːs **-es** -ɪz ˈ**Peace** ˌ**Corps**; ˈ**peace** ˌ**offering**; ˈ**peace** ˌ**pipe**
peaceab|le ˈpiː.sə.bl̩ **-ly** -li **-leness** -l̩.nəs, -nɪs
peaceful ˈpiːs.fᵊl, -fʊl **-ly** -i **-ness** -nəs, -nɪs
Peacehaven ˈpiːsˌheɪ.vᵊn
peacekeep|er ˈpiːsˌkiː.p|əʳ (US) -ɚ **-ers** -əz (US) -ɚz **-ing** -ɪŋ
peacekeeping ˈpiːsˌkiː.pɪŋ
peacemaker ˈpiːsˌmeɪ.kəʳ (US) -kɚ **-s** -z
peacenik ˈpiːs.nɪk **-s** -s
peacetime ˈpiːs.taɪm
Peacey ˈpiː.si
peach piːtʃ **-es** -ɪz **-ing** -ɪŋ **-ed** -t **-er/s** -əʳ/z (US) -ɚ/z
Peachey ˈpiː.tʃi
Peachum ˈpiː.tʃəm
peach|y ˈpiː.tʃ|i **-ier** -i.əʳ (US) -i.ɚ **-iest** -i.ɪst, -i.əst **-iness** -ɪ.nəs, -ɪ.nɪs
peacock **(P)** ˈpiː.kɒk (US) -kɑːk **-s** -s
pea-green ˌpiːˈgriːn *stress shift:* ˌpea-green ˈboat
peahen ˈpiː.hen, ˌ-ˈ- (US) ˈ-- **-s** -z
pea-jacket ˈpiːˌdʒæk.ɪt **-s** -s
peak **(P)** piːk **-s** -s **-ing** -ɪŋ **-ed** -t ˈ**Peak** ˌ**District**; ˌ**peak** ˈ**time** *stress shift:* ˌpeak time ˈtraffic
Peake piːk
peaky ˈpiː.ki
peal piːl **-s** -z **-ing** -ɪŋ **-ed** -d
Peall piːl
pean *alternative spelling of* **paean**: ˈpiː.ən **-s** -z
pean *in heraldry:* piːn
peanut ˈpiː.nʌt **-s** -s ˌ**peanut** ˈ**butter** (US) ˈ**peanut** ˌ**butter**
pear peəʳ (US) per **-s** -z
Pear *surname:* pɪəʳ (US) pɪr
Pearce pɪəs (US) pɪrs
Peard pɪəd (US) pɪrd
pearl **(P)** pɜːl (US) pɝːl **-s** -z **-ing** -ɪŋ **-ed** -d ˌ**Pearl** ˈ**Harbor**
pearlite ˈpɜː.laɪt (US) ˈpɝː-
pearly ˈpɜː.li (US) ˈpɝː- ˌ**pearly** ˈ**gates**; ˌ**pearly** ˈ**king**; ˌ**pearly** ˈ**queen**
pearmain ˈpɜː.meɪn, ˈpeə- (US) ˈper- **-s** -z
Pearman ˈpɪə.mən (US) ˈpɪr-
Pears pɪəz, peəz (US) pɪrs, perz
Note: /peəz (US) perz/ in **Pears' soap**; /pɪəz (US) pɪrz/ for the singer.
Pearsall ˈpɪə.sɔːl, -sᵊl (US) ˈpɪr-, -sɑːl
Pearse pɪəs (US) pɪrs
pear-shaped ˈpeə.ʃeɪpt (US) ˈper-
Pearson ˈpɪə.sᵊn (US) ˈpɪr-
Peart pɪət (US) pɪrt
Peary ˈpɪə.ri (US) ˈpɪr.i
peasant ˈpez.ᵊnt **-s** -s
peasantry ˈpez.ᵊn.tri
Peascod ˈpes.kəd (US) -kəd, -kɑːd
pease **(P)** piːz
Peaseblossom ˈpiːzˌblɒs.ᵊm (US) -ˌblɑː.sᵊm
peasecod ˈpiːz.kɒd (US) -kɑːd **-s** -z
pease-pudding ˌpiːzˈpʊd.ɪŋ, ˌpiːs-
peashooter ˈpiːˌʃuː.təʳ (US) -t̬ɚ **-s** -z

pea-souper ˌpiːˈsuː.pə^{r} (US) ˈpiːˌsuː.pɚ, ˌ-ˈ-- **-s** -z

peat piːt ˈ**peat** ˌ**bog**

peat|y ˈpiː.t|i (US) -t̬|i **-ier** -i.ə^{r} (US) -i.ɚ **-iest** -i.ɪst, -i.əst **-iness** -ɪ.nəs, -ɪ.nɪs

pebble ˈpeb.l̩ **-s** -z

pebbledash ˈpeb.l̩.dæʃ **-es** -ɪz **-ing** -ɪŋ **-ed** -t

pebbly ˈpeb.l̩.i, ˈpeb.li

pecan ˈpiː.kæn, -k^{ə}n; pɪˈkæn (US) pɪˈkɑːn, piː-, -ˈkæn; ˈpiː.kɑːn, -kæn **-s** -z ˌ**pecan** ˈ**pie**

peccability ˌpek.əˈbɪl.ə.ti, -ɪ.ti (US) -ə.t̬i

peccable ˈpek.ə.bl̩

peccadillo ˌpek.əˈdɪl.əʊ (US) -oʊ **-(e)s** -z

peccant ˈpek.^{ə}nt **-ly** -li

peccar|y ˈpek.^{ə}r|.i **-ies** -iz

peccavi pekˈɑː.viː *old-fashioned:* -ˈkeɪ.vaɪ (US) peɪˈkɑː.vi **-s** -z

Pechey ˈpiː.tʃi

Pechili ˈpetʃ.ɪ.li

peck (P) pek **-s** -s **-ing** -ɪŋ **-ed** -t **-er/s** -ə^{r}/z (US) -ɚ/z ˈ**pecking** ˌ**order**

Peckham ˈpek.əm

Peckinpah ˈpek.ɪn.pɑː

peckish ˈpek.ɪʃ **-ly** -li **-ness** -nəs, -nɪs

Peckitt ˈpek.ɪt

Pecksniff ˈpek.snɪf

Pecock ˈpek.ɒk (US) -ɑːk

pecorino (P) ˌpek.^{ə}rˈiː.nəʊ (US) -əˈriː.noʊ

Pecos ˈpeɪ.kəs, -kɒs (US) -kəs, -koʊs

Pécs petʃ (US) peɪtʃ

pect|in ˈpek.t|ɪn **-ic** -ɪk **-inous** -ɪ.nəs

pectoral ˈpek.t^{ə}r.^{ə}l **-s** -z ˈ**pectoral** ˌ**muscle**

pecu|late ˈpek.jə|.leɪt **-lates** -leɪts **-lating** -leɪ.tɪŋ (US) -leɪ.t̬ɪŋ **-lated** -leɪ.tɪd (US) -leɪ.t̬ɪd **-lator/s** -leɪ.tə^{r}/z (US) -leɪ.t̬ɚ/z

peculation ˌpek.jəˈleɪ.ʃ^{ə}n, -jʊˈ- **-s** -z

peculiar pɪˈkjuː.li.ə^{r}, pə- (US) pɪˈkjuːl.jɚ, piː- **-s** -z **-ly** -li

peculiarit|y pɪˌkjuː.liˈær.ə.t|i, pə-, -ɪ.t|i (US) pɪˌkjuː.liˈer.ə.t̬|i, piː-, -ˈær- **-ies** -iz

pecuniar|y pɪˈkjuː.nj^{ə}r|.i, -ni.ə.r|i (US) pɪˈkjuː.ni.er-, piː- **-ily** -^{ə}l.i, -ɪ.li

pedagogic ˌped.əˈgɒdʒ.ɪk, -ˈgɒg-, -ˈgəʊ.dʒɪk (US) -ˈgɑː-, -ˈgoʊ- **-s** -s **-al** -^{ə}l **-ally** -^{ə}l.i, -li *stress shift:* ˌpedagogic ˈfunction

pedagogue ˈped.ə.gɒg (US) -gɑːg, -gɔːg **-s** -z

pedagogy ˈped.ə.gɒdʒ.i, -gɒg-, -gəʊ.dʒi (US) -gɑː.dʒi, -goʊ-

pedal *(n. v.)* ˈped.^{ə}l **-s** -z **-(l)ing** -ɪŋ **-(l)ed** -d ˈ**pedal** ˌ**pushers**

pedal *(adj.) of the foot:* ˈpiː.d^{ə}l, ˈped.^{ə}l *in geometry:* ˈped.^{ə}l

pedalo ˈped.^{ə}l.əʊ (US) -oʊ **-(e)s** -z

pedant ˈped.^{ə}nt **-s** -s

pedantic pɪˈdæn.tɪk, pə-, pedˈæn-, pəˈdæn- (US) pedˈæn- **-al** -^{ə}l **-ally** -^{ə}l.i, -li

pedantism ˈped.^{ə}n.tɪ.z^{ə}m, pɪˈdæn-, pedˈæn-

pedantr|y ˈped.^{ə}n.tr|i **-ies** -iz

peddl|e ˈped.l̩ **-es** -z **-ing** -ɪn, ˈped.lɪŋ **-ed** -d **-er/s** -ə^{r}/z (US) -ɚ/z, ˈped.lə^{r}/z **-er/z** (US) -ɚ/z

Peden ˈpiː.d^{ə}n (US) ˈpiː.d^{ə}n, ˈpeɪ-

pederast ˈped.^{ə}r.æst, ˈpiː.d^{ə}r- (US) ˈped.ə.ræst **-s** -s **-y** -i

pedestal ˈped.ɪ.st^{ə}l, ˈ-ə- **-s** -z

pedestrian pɪˈdes.tri.ən, pə- (US) pə- **-s** -z **-ism** -ɪ.z^{ə}m **peˌdestrian** ˈ**crossing**

pedestrianiz|e, -is|e pɪˈdes.tri.ə.naɪz, pə- (US) pə- **-es** -ɪz **-ing** -ɪŋ **-ed** -d

pediatric ˌpiː.diˈæt.rɪk **-s** -s

pediatrician ˌpiː.di.əˈtrɪʃ.^{ə}n **-s** -z

pedicel ˈped.ɪ.sel, ˈ-ə- **-s** -z

pedicle ˈped.ɪ.kl̩, ˈ-ə- **-s** -z

pedicure ˈped.ɪ.kjʊə^{r}, ˈ-ə-, -kjɔː^{r} (US) -ɪ.kjʊr **-s** -z

pedigree ˈped.ɪ.griː, ˈ-ə- **-s** -z **-d** -d

pediment ˈped.ɪ.mənt, ˈ-ə- **-s** -s

pedimental ˌped.ɪˈmen.t^{ə}l, -əˈ- (US) -t̬^{ə}l

pedimented ˈped.ɪ.men.tɪd, ˈ-ə-, -mən- (US) -men.t̬ɪd

pedlar ˈped.lə^{r} (US) -lɚ **-s** -z

pedometer pɪˈdɒm.ɪ.tə^{r}, pə-, pedˈɒm-, ˈ-ə- (US) pɪˈdɑː.mə.t̬ɚ, pə- **-s** -z

pedophile ˈpiː.dəʊ.faɪl (US) ˈped.oʊ-, ˈpiː.doʊ-, -də- **-s** -z

pedophili|a ˌpiː.dəʊˈfɪl.i|.ə (US) ˌped.oʊˈfiː.li-, ˌpiː.doʊˈ-, -dəˈ-, -ˈfiːl.j|ə **-ac/s** -æk

Pedro ˈped.rəʊ, ˈpiː.drəʊ (US) ˈpeɪ.droʊ, ˈped.roʊ

Note: The pronunciation /ˈpiː.drəʊ/ is generally used in Shakespeare's 'Much Ado.'

peduncle pɪˈdʌŋ.kl̩, pə-, pedˈʌŋ- (US) pɪˈdʌŋ-; ˈpiː.dʌŋ- **-s** -z

pee piː **-s** -z **-ing** -ɪŋ **-d** -d

Peeb|les ˈpiː.b|l̩z **-les-shire** -l̩z.ʃə^{r}, -l̩ʒ.ʃə^{r}, -l̩.ʃə^{r}, -ˌʃɪə^{r} (US) -ʃɚ, -ˌʃɪr

peek (P) piːk **-s** -s **-ing** -ɪŋ **-ed** -t

peekaboo ˈpiː.kə.buː

peel (P) piːl **-s** -z **-ing/s** -ɪŋ/z **-ed** -d

Peele piːl

peeler ˈpiː.lə^{r} (US) -lɚ **-s** -z

peep (P) piːp **-s** -s **-ing** -ɪŋ **-ed** -t **-er/s** -ə^{r}/z (US) -ɚ/z

peepal ˈpiː.p^{ə}l **-s** -z

peep-bo ˈpiːp.bəʊ, -əʊ, ˌ-ˈ- (US) ˈpiːp.boʊ, -oʊ, ˌ-ˈ-

peep-hole ˈpiːp.həʊl (US) -hoʊl **-s** -z

peeping Tom ˌpiː.pɪŋˈtɒm (US) -ˈtɑːm **-s** -z

peepshow ˈpiːp.ʃəʊ (US) -ʃoʊ **-s** -z

peep-toe ˈpiːp.təʊ (US) -toʊ **-d** -d

peepul ˈpiː.p^{ə}l **-s** -z

peer pɪə^{r} (US) pɪr **-s** -z **-ing** -ɪŋ **-ed** -d

peerag|e ˈpɪə.rɪdʒ (US) ˈpɪr.ɪdʒ **-es** -ɪz

peeress pɪəˈres; ˈpɪə.rəs, -rɪs, -res (US) ˈpɪr.ɪs **-es** -ɪz

peergroup ˈpɪə.gruːp (US) ˈpɪr- **-s** -s

peerless (P) ˈpɪə.ləs, -lɪs (US) ˈpɪr- **-ly** -li **-ness** -nəs, -nɪs

peev|e piːv **-es** -z **-ing** -ɪŋ **-ed** -d

peevish ˈpiː.vɪʃ **-ly** -li **-ness** -nəs, -nɪs

peewee ˈpiː.wiː **-s** -z

peewit ˈpiː.wɪt **-s** -s

peg (P) peg **-s** -z **-ging** -ɪŋ **-ged** -d

Pegasus ˈpeg.ə.səs

Pegeen pegˈiːn

Pegge peg

Peggotty ˈpeg.ə.ti (US) -t̬i

Peggy ˈpeg.i

Pegram, Pegrum ˈpiː.grəm

Pegu pegˈuː

Pei peɪ

peignoir ˈpeɪ.nwɑː^{r}, -nwɔː^{r} (US) peɪnˈwɑːr, pen-, ˈ-- **-s** -z

Peile piːl

Peiping ˌpeɪˈpɪŋ

Peirce pɪəs (US) pɪrs, pɝːs

pejoration ˌpiː.dʒ^{ə}rˈeɪ.ʃ^{ə}n, ˌpedʒ.^{ə}rˈ- (US) ˌpedʒ.əˈreɪ-, ˌpiː.dʒəˈ-

pejorative pɪˈdʒɒr.ə.tɪv, pə-, ˈpiː.dʒ^{ə}r- (US) pɪˈdʒɔːr.ə.t̬ɪv; ˈpedʒ.ə.reɪ-, ˈpiː.dʒə- **-s** -z **-ly** -li

peke piːk **-s** -s

Pekin ˌpiːˈkɪn (US) ˈ--

pekines|e (P) ˌpiː.kɪˈniːz, -k^{ə}nˈiːz (US) ˌpiː.kəˈniːz, -ˈniːs **-es** -ɪz

Peking ˌpiːˈkɪŋ *stress shift, see compound:* ˌ**Peking** ˈ**duck**

pekinges|e (P) ˌpiː.kɪŋˈiːz, -kɪˈniːz, -k^{ə}nˈiːz (US) -kɪŋˈiːz, -ˈiːs **-es** -ɪz

pekoe ˈpiː.kəʊ (US) -koʊ

pelagic pəˈlædʒ.ɪk, pɪ-, pelˈædʒ- (US) pəˈlædʒ-, pɪ-

pelargonium ˌpel.əˈgəʊ.ni.əm, -ɑːˈ- (US) -ɑːrˈgoʊ- **-s** -z

Pelasgian pelˈæz.gi.ən, pɪˈlæz-, pə-, -dʒi- (US) pəˈlæz.dʒi- **-s** -z

Pelé ˈpel.eɪ, -ˈ- (US) ˈpel.eɪ

pelerine ˈpel.^{ə}r.iːn (US) -ə.riːn **-s** -z

Peleus ˈpiː.ljuːs, ˈpel.juːs, -jəs, -i.əs (US) ˈpiː.li.əs, ˈpiːl.juːs

pelf pelf

pelham (P) ˈpel.əm

Pelias ˈpiː.li.æs, ˈpel.i-, -əs (US) -əs

pelican ˈpel.ɪ.k^{ə}n, ˈ-ə- **-s** -z ˌ**pelican** ˈ**crossing**

peliss|e pelˈiːs, pɪˈliːs, pə- (US) pəˈliːs **-es** -ɪz

pellagr|a pəˈlæg.r|ə, pelˈæg- (US) pəˈleɪ.gr|ə, -ˈlæg.r|ə **-ous** -əs

Pelleas, Pelléas ˈpel.eɪ.æs, ˈ-i- (US) ˈ-i-

Pelles ˈpel.iːz

pellet ˈpel.ɪt, -ət **-s** -s

Pelley ˈpel.i

pellicle ˈpel.ɪ.kl̩, ˈ-ə- **-s** -z
pellitory ˈpel.ɪ.tᵊr.i, ˈ-ə- US -tɔːr-
pell-mell ˌpelˈmel
pellucid pɪˈluː.sɪd, pə-, pelˈuː-, -ˈjuː- US pəˈluː.sɪd **-ly** -li **-ness** -nəs, -nɪs
Pelman ˈpel.mən **-ism** -ɪ.zᵊm
pelmet ˈpel.mɪt, -mət **-s** -s
Peloponnese ˈpel.ə.pə.niːz, -niːs, ˌpel.ə.pəˈniːs, -ˈniːz US ˌpel.ə.pəˈniːz, -ˈniːs
Peloponnesian ˌpel.ə.pəˈniː.ʃᵊn, -ʃi.ən, ˈ-ʒᵊn US -ʒən, -ʃən **-s** -z
Peloponnesus ˌpel.ə.pəˈniː.səs
Pelops ˈpiː.lɒps US -lɑːps
pelota pəˈlɒt.ə, pɪ-, pelˈɒt-, -ˈəʊ.tə US pəˈloʊ.t̬ə
Pelsall ˈpel.sɔːl
pelt pelt **-s** -s **-ing** -ɪŋ US ˈpel.t̬ɪŋ **-ed** -ɪd US ˈpel.t̬ɪd
Peltier effect ˈpel.ti.eɪ.ɪˌfekt US ˈpel.tjeɪ.ɪˌ-, -əˌ-, -iːˌ-
pelv|is ˈpel.v|ɪs **-ises** -ɪ.sɪz **-es** -iːz **-ic** -ɪk
Pemba ˈpem.bə
Pemberton ˈpem.bə.tᵊn US -bɚ-
Pembridge ˈpem.brɪdʒ
Pembroke ˈpem.brʊk, -brək US -brʊk, -broʊk **-shire** -ʃəʳ, -ˌʃɪəʳ US -ʃɚ, -ˌʃɪr
Pembury ˈpem.bᵊr.i
pemmican ˈpem.ɪ.kən
pen (P) pen **-s** -z **-ning** -ɪŋ **-ned** -d **ˈpen ˌfriend; ˈpen ˌname; ˈpen ˌpal; ˈpen ˌpusher**
penal ˈpiː.nᵊl **-ly** -i **ˈpenal ˌcolony**
penaliz|e, -is|e ˈpiː.nᵊl.aɪz US ˈpiː-, ˈpen.ᵊl- **-es** -ɪz **-ing** -ɪŋ **-ed** -d
penalt|y ˈpen.ᵊl.t|i US -t̬|i **-ies** -iz **ˈpenalty ˌbox**
penanc|e ˈpen.ənts **-es** -ɪz
pen-and-ink ˌpen.ənd̍ˈɪŋk *stress shift:* ˌpen-and-ink ˈdrawing
Penang penˈæŋ, pɪˈnæŋ, pə- US pɪˈnæŋ, penˈæŋ
Penarth penˈɑːθ, pəˈnɑːθ US penˈɑːrθ
penates penˈɑː.teɪz, pɪˈnɑː-, pə-, -ˈneɪ-, -tiːz US pəˈneɪ.t̬iːz, -ˈnɑː-
pence *(plur. of* **penny***)* pents
Note: See **penny**.
penchant ˈpɑ̃ːŋ.ʃɑ̃ːŋ US ˈpen.tʃənt **-s** -z
pencil ˈpent.sᵊl **-s** -z **-(l)ing** -ɪŋ **-(l)ed** -d **ˈpencil ˌcase; ˈpencil ˌsharpener**
Pencoed penˈkɔɪd, peŋ- US pen-
pendant ˈpen.dənt **-s** -s
penden|cy ˈpen.dən|t.si **-t** -t
Pendennis penˈden.ɪs
pendente lite penˌden.tiˈlaɪ.ti
Pender ˈpen.dəʳ US -dɚ
Pendine penˈdaɪn
pending ˈpen.dɪŋ
Pendle ˈpen.dl̩
Pendlebury ˈpen.dl̩.bᵊr.i US -ˌber-, -bɚ-
Pendleton ˈpen.dl̩.tən
pendragon (P) penˈdræg.ən **-s** -z
pendulous ˈpen.djᵊl.əs, -dʒʊ.ləs, -dʒᵊl.əs US -dʒə.ləs, -djə-, -də-, -dʒʊ- **-ly** -li **-ness** -nəs, -nɪs
pendulum ˈpen.djᵊl.əm, -djʊ.ləm, -dʒᵊl.əm US -dʒə.ləm, -djə-, -də-, -dʒʊ- **-s** -z
Penelope pəˈnel.ə.pi, pɪ- US pə-
penetrability ˌpen.ɪ.trəˈbɪl.ə.ti, ˌ-ə-, -ɪ.ti US -ə.t̬i
penetrab|le ˈpen.ɪ.trə.b|l̩, ˈ-ə- **-ly** -li **-leness** -l̩.nəs, -nɪs
penetralia ˌpen.ɪˈtreɪ.li.ə, -əˈ-
pene|trate ˈpen.ɪ|.treɪt, ˈ-ə- **-trates** -treɪts **-trating/ly** -treɪ.tɪŋ/li US -treɪ.t̬ɪŋ/li **-trated** -treɪ.tɪd US -treɪ.t̬ɪd
penetration ˌpen.ɪˈtreɪ.ʃᵊn, -əˈ- **-s** -z
penetrative ˈpen.ɪ.trə.tɪv, ˈ-ə-, -treɪ- US -treɪ.t̬ɪv **-ly** -li **-ness** -nəs, -nɪs
Penfold ˈpen.fəʊld US -foʊld
penful ˈpen.fʊl **-s** -z
Penge pendʒ
penguin ˈpeŋ.gwɪn US ˈpeŋ-, ˈpen- **-s** -z
Penhaligon penˈhæl.ɪ.gᵊn
penholder ˈpenˌhəʊl.dəʳ US -ˌhoʊl.dɚ **-s** -z
penicillin ˌpen.ɪˈsɪl.ɪn, -əˈ-
penicillium ˌpen.ɪˈsɪl.i.əm, -əˈ-
Penicuik ˈpen.ɪ.kʊk
penile ˈpiː.naɪl US -naɪl, -nɪl
peninsul|a (P) pəˈnɪnt.sjə.l|ə, pɪ-, penˈɪnt-, -sjʊ-, -ʃə-, -ʃʊ- US pəˈnɪnt.sə-, -sjə-, -ˈnɪn.tʃə- **-as** -əz **-ar** -əʳ US -ɚ
penis ˈpiː.nɪs **-es** -ɪz **ˈpenis ˌenvy**
Penistone ˈpen.ɪ.stᵊn
penitence ˈpen.ɪ.tᵊnts, ˈ-ə-
penitent ˈpen.ɪ.tᵊnt, ˈ-ə- **-s** -s **-ly** -li
penitential ˌpen.ɪˈten.tʃᵊl, -əˈ- US -ʃᵊl **-ly** -i
penitentiar|y ˌpen.ɪˈten.tʃᵊr|.i, -əˈ- US -tʃə.riː **-ies** -iz
penkni|fe ˈpen.naɪ|f **-ves** -vz
Penkridge ˈpeŋ.krɪdʒ
penlight ˈpen.laɪt **-s** -s
Penmaenmawr ˌpen.mənˈmaʊəʳ, -ˈmɔːʳ US -ˈmaʊɚ, -ˈmɔːr
pen|man ˈpen|.mən, ˈpem- US ˈpen- **-men** -mən
Penman ˈpen.mən, ˈpem- US ˈpen-
penmanship ˈpen.mən.ʃɪp, ˈpem- US ˈpen-
Penn pen
Penn. *(abbrev. for* **Pennsylvania***)* pen, ˌpent.sɪlˈveɪ.ni.ə, -sᵊlˈ-, ˈ-njə US ˌpent.sᵊlˈveɪ.njə, ˈ-ni.ə, pen
Note: The form /pen/ is especially used when referring to university names.
pennant (P) ˈpen.ənt **-s** -s
penne ˈpen.eɪ, -i US -i, -eɪ
penn|i ˈpen|.i **-is** -ɪs **-ia** -i.ə
penniless ˈpen.i.ləs, -lɪs
Pennine ˈpen.aɪn **-s** -z
Pennington ˈpen.ɪŋ.tən
pennon ˈpen.ən **-s** -z
Pennsylvani|a ˌpent.sɪlˈveɪ.ni|.ə, -sᵊlˈ-, ˈ-nj|ə US -sᵊlˈveɪ.nj|ə, ˈ-ni.ə **-an/s** -ən/z **ˌPennsylˌvania ˈDutch**
penn|y (P) ˈpen|.i **-ies** -iz **pence** pents **ˌpenny arˈcade; ˌpenny ˈblack; ˌpenny ˈdreadful; ˌpenny ˈfarthing**
Note: After decimalization of the currency in Britain, the pronunciation of compounds with **penny, pence** (now abbreviated to **p**) changed. Formerly, compounds from **1/2d** to **11d** invariably had /-pᵊn.i, -pᵊnts/, e.g. see entries under **half-penny,** fourpence**, etc..** With the extension of **-pence** compounds beyond **11p**, e.g. **12p**, the reduced forms have more or less disappeared. Instead, the full forms /ˈpen.i/ and /pents/, or commonly /piː/, are used, e.g. **4p** (/ˈfɔː.pᵊnts/) is /ˌfɔːˈpents/ or /-ˈpiː/; **12p** is /ˌtwelvˈpents/ or /-ˈpiː/.
penny-pinch|ing ˈpen.iˌpɪn.tʃ|ɪŋ **-er/s** -əʳ/z US -ɚ/z
pennyroyal ˌpen.iˈrɔɪəl US ˈpen.iˌrɔɪ.əl, ˌpen.iˈrɔɪ-
pennyweight ˈpen.i.weɪt **-s** -s
pennywort ˈpen.i.wɜːt US -wɝːt, -wɔːrt
pennyworth ˈpen.i.wəθ, -wɜːθ, ˈpen.əθ US ˈpen.i.wɚθ, -wɝːθ **-s** -s
Penobscot penˈɒb.skɒt, pəˈnɒb- US pəˈnɑːb.skɑːt, penˈɑːb-, -skət
penological ˌpiː.nəˈlɒdʒ.ɪ.kᵊl US -ˈlɑː.dʒɪ-
penolog|y piːˈnɒl.ə.dʒ|i, pɪ- US piːˈnɑː.lə- **-ist/s** -ɪst/s
Penrhyn penˈrɪn
Penrith *town in Cumbria:* penˈrɪθ, ˈ-- *surname:* ˈpen.rɪθ
Penrose *surname:* ˈpen.rəʊz, -ˈ- US ˈpen.roʊz, -ˈ- *place in Cornwall:* penˈrəʊz US -ˈroʊz
Penryn penˈrɪn
Pensacola ˌpent.səˈkəʊ.lə US -ˈkoʊ-
Pensarn penˈsɑːn US -ˈsɑːrn
penseroso ˌpent.səˈrəʊ.zəʊ, -səʊ US -ˈroʊ.soʊ
Penshurst ˈpenz.hɜːst US -hɝːst
pension *(n. v.) monetary allowance, etc.:* ˈpen.tʃᵊn **-s** -z **-ing** -ɪŋ **-ed** -d
pension *(n.) boarding house, board:* ˈpɑ̃ːn.sjɔ̃ːŋ, -ˈ- US pɑ̃ːnˈsjõʊŋ, ˌpɑːnˈsjoʊn **-s** -z
pensionable ˈpen.tʃᵊn.ə.bl̩ US -ʃᵊn-
pensioner ˈpen.tʃᵊn.əʳ US -ʃᵊn.ɚ **-s** -z

pensive ˈpent.sɪv **-ly** -li **-ness** -nəs, -nɪs

penta- pen.tə-; penˈtæ- (US) pen.t̬ə-; penˈtæ-

Note: Prefix. Normally either takes primary or secondary stress on the first syllable, e.g. **pentagon** /ˈpen.tə.gᵊn (US) -t̬ə.gɑːn/, **pentatonic** /ˌpen.təˈtɒn.ɪk (US) -t̬əˈtɑː.nɪk/, or primary stress on the second syllable, e.g. **pentagonal** /penˈtæg.ᵊn.ᵊl/.

pentad ˈpen.tæd **-s** -z

pentagon (P) ˈpen.tə.gᵊn, -gɒn (US) -t̬ə.gɑːn **-s** -z

pentagonal penˈtæg.ᵊn.ᵊl **-ly** -i

pentagram ˈpen.tə.græm (US) -t̬ə- **-s** -z

pentahedr|on ˌpen.təˈhiː.dr|ən, -dr|ɒn (US) -t̬əˈhiː.dr|ən **-ons** -ənz, -ɒnz (US) -ənz **-a** -ə **-al** -ᵊl

pentameter penˈtæm.ɪ.təʳ, ˈ-ə- (US) -ə.t̬ɚ **-s** -z

pentangle ˈpen.tæŋ.gl̩ **-s** -z

Pentateuch ˈpen.tə.tjuːk (US) -t̬ə.tuːk, -tjuːk

pentathlete penˈtæθ.liːt **-s** -s

pentathlon penˈtæθ.lɒn, -lən (US) -lɑːn, -lən

pentatonic ˌpen.təˈtɒn.ɪk (US) -t̬əˈtɑː.nɪk *stress shift:* ˌpentatonic ˈscale

Pentax® ˈpen.tæks

Pentecost ˈpen.tɪ.kɒst, -tə- (US) -t̬ɪ.kɑːst **-s** -s

Pentecostal ˌpen.tɪˈkɒs.tᵊl, -təˈ- (US) -t̬ɪˈkɑː.stᵊl **-ism** -ɪ.zᵊm **-ist/s** -ɪst/s *stress shift:* ˌPentecostal ˈfeast

Pentel® ˈpen.tel

Penthesilea ˌpent.θes.ɪˈliː.ə, -θə.sɪˈ-, -səˈ-, -ˈleɪ- (US) -θə.səˈliː-

penthou|se (P) ˈpent.haʊ|s **-ses** -zɪz

pentiment|o ˌpen.tɪˈmen.t|əʊ (US) -t̬ɪˈmen.t|oʊ **-i** -iː

Pentium® ˈpen.ti.əm (US) -t̬i-

Pentland ˈpent.lənd **-s** -z

Pentonville ˈpen.tən.vɪl

Pentothal® ˈpen.tə.θæl, -θɔːl (US) -t̬ə.θɔːl, -θɑːl

pentstemon pentˈstem.ən, pen-, -ˈstiː.mən; ˈpent.stɪ.mən, -stə- (US) pentˈstiː-; ˈpent.stə-

pent-up ˌpentˈʌp *stress shift:* ˌpent-up ˈanger

pentyl ˈpen.taɪl, -tɪl (US) -tɪl, -t̬ᵊl

penult pəˈnʌlt, pɪ-, penˈʌlt (US) ˈpiː.nʌlt; pɪˈnʌlt **-s** -s

penultimate pəˈnʌl.tɪ.mət, pɪ-, penˈʌl-, -tə-, -mɪt (US) pɪˈnʌl.t̬ə.mət **-s** -s **-ly** -li

penumbr|a pəˈnʌm.br|ə, pɪ-, penˈʌm- (US) pɪˈnʌm- **-as** -əz **-ae** -iː **-al** -ᵊl

penurious pəˈnjʊə.ri.əs, pɪ-, penˈjʊə-, -ˈjɔː- (US) pəˈnʊr.i-, penˈʊr-, -ˈjʊr- **-ly** -li **-ness** -nəs, -nɪs

penury ˈpen.jə.ri, -jʊ- (US) -jʊ.ri, -jɚ.i

Pen-y-Ghent ˌpen.iˈgent

Penzance penˈzænts, pən- *locally:* pənˈzɑːnts (US) penˈzænts

peon *Indian servant:* pjuːn; ˈpiː.ən; peɪˈɒn (US) ˈpiː.ɑːn, ˈpeɪ-, -ən **-s** -z *in US:* ˈpiː.ən (US) -ɑːn, -ən **-s** -z

peon|y ˈpiː.ə.n|i **-ies** -iz

peopl|e ˈpiː.pl̩ **-es** -z **-ing** -ɪŋ, ˈpiːp.lɪŋ **-ed** -d

Peoria piːˈɔː.ri.ə (US) -ˈɔːr.i-

Peover ˈpiː.vəʳ (US) -vɚ

pep pep **-s** -s **-ping** -ɪŋ **-ped** -t ˈ**pep** ˌ**pill**; ˈ**pep** ˌ**talk**

PEP pep, ˌpiː.iːˈpiː

Pepin ˈpep.ɪn

peplum ˈpep.ləm **-s** -z

pepp|er (P) ˈpep|.əʳ (US) -ɚ **-ers** -əz (US) -ɚz **-ering** -ᵊr.ɪŋ **-ered** -əd (US) -ɚd ˈ**pepper** ˌ**pot**

pepperbox ˈpep.ə.bɒks (US) -ɚ.bɑːks **-es** -ɪz

peppercorn ˈpep.ə.kɔːn (US) -ɚ.kɔːrn **-s** -z

peppermint ˈpep.ə.mɪnt (US) -ɚ-, -mənt **-s** -s

pepperoni ˌpep.əˈrəʊ.ni (US) -ˈroʊ-

pepper|y ˈpep.ᵊr|.i **-iness** -ɪ.nəs, -ɪ.nɪs

pepp|y ˈpep|.i **-ier** -i.əʳ (US) -i.ɚ **-iest** -i.ɪst, -i.əst **-iness** -ɪ.nəs, -ɪ.nɪs **-ily** -ɪ.li, -ᵊl.i

Pepsi® ˈpep.si

Pepsi-Cola® ˌpep.siˈkəʊ.lə (US) -ˈkoʊ-

pepsin ˈpep.sɪn

Pepsodent® ˈpep.səʊ.dent, -sə.dᵊnt (US) -soʊ.dent, -sə-

peptic ˈpep.tɪk

Pepto-Bismol® ˌpep.təʊˈbɪz.mɒl (US) -toʊˈbɪz.mɑːl, -tə-

peptone ˈpep.təʊn (US) -toʊn **-s** -z

Pepys ˈpep.ɪs; piːps, peps

Note: The pronunciation in the family of the present Lord Cottenham is /ˈpep.ɪs/. Samuel Pepys is generally referred to as /piːps/.

per *strong form:* pɜːʳ (US) pɝː *weak form:* pəʳ (US) pɚ

Note: This word has a weak form /pəʳ (US) pɚ/, which is almost always used in the phrases **per cent**, **per annum**. It is also used in phrases such as **per capita**, **per centimetre**, **per head**, but the strong form /pɜːʳ (US) pɜːr/ is more usual.

peradventure pə.rədˈven.tʃəʳ, ˌpɜː.rədˈ-, ˌper.ədˈ- (US) ˌpɝː.ədˈven.tʃɚ, ˌper-

Perak ˈpeə.rə, ˈpɪə.rə; pəˈræk, pɪ-, perˈæk (US) ˈpeɪ.ræk, -rɑːk; ˈper.ə, ˈpɪr-

Note: English speakers who have lived in Malaysia pronounce /ˈpeə.rə (US) ˈper.ə/ or /ˈpɪə.rə (US) ˈpɪr.ə/.

perambu|late pəˈræm.bjə|.leɪt, -bjʊ- **-lates** -leɪts **-lating** -leɪ.tɪŋ (US) -leɪ.t̬ɪŋ **-lated** -leɪ.tɪd (US) -leɪ.t̬ɪd

perambulation pəˌræm.bjəˈleɪ.ʃᵊn, -bjʊˈ- **-s** -z

perambulator pəˈræm.bjə.leɪ.təʳ, -bjʊ- (US) -t̬ɚ **-s** -z

per annum pəʳˈæn.əm (US) pɚ-

percale pəˈkeɪl, -ˈkɑːl (US) pɚˈkeɪl

per capita pəˈkæp.ɪ.tə, ˌpɜː- (US) pɚˈkæp.ɪ.t̬ə

perceivab|le pəˈsiː.və.b|l̩, pɜː- (US) pɚ- **-ly** -li

perceiv|e pəˈsiːv (US) pɚ- **-es** -z **-ing** -ɪŋ **-ed** -d

percener ˈpɜː.sᵊn.əʳ (US) ˈpɝː.sᵊn.ɚ **-s** -z

per cent, percent pəˈsent (US) pɚ-

percentag|e pəˈsen.tɪdʒ (US) pɚˈsen.t̬ɪdʒ **-es** -ɪz

percentile pəˈsen.taɪl (US) pɚˈsen-, -t̬ᵊl **-s** -z

percept ˈpɜː.sept (US) ˈpɝː- **-s** -s

perceptibility pəˌsep.təˈbɪl.ə.ti, -tɪˈ-, -ɪ.ti (US) pɚˌsep.təˈbɪl.ə.t̬i

perceptib|le pəˈsep.tə.b|l̩, -tɪ- (US) pɚˈsep.tə- **-ly** -li **-leness** -l̩.nəs, -nɪs

perception pəˈsep.ʃᵊn (US) pɚ- **-s** -z

perceptive pəˈsep.tɪv (US) pɚ- **-ly** -li **-ness** -nəs, -nɪs

perceptual pəˈsep.tʃu.əl, -tju- (US) -tʃu-, pɚˈsep.tju- **-ly** -i

Perceval ˈpɜː.sɪ.vᵊl, -sə- (US) ˈpɝː-

perch pɜːtʃ (US) pɝːtʃ **-es** -ɪz **-ing** -ɪŋ **-ed** -t

perchance pəˈtʃɑːnts, ˌpɜː- (US) pɚˈtʃænts

Percheron ˈpɜː.ʃə.rɒn (US) ˈpɝː.tʃə.rɑːn **-s** -z

percipien|t pəˈsɪp.i.ən|t (US) pɚ- **-ce** -ts

Percival(e) ˈpɜː.sɪ.vᵊl, -sə- (US) ˈpɝː-

percol|ate ˈpɜː.kᵊl|.eɪt (US) ˈpɝː- **-ates** -eɪts **-ating** -eɪ.tɪŋ (US) -eɪ.t̬ɪŋ **-ated** -eɪ.tɪd (US) -eɪ.t̬ɪd

percolation ˌpɜː.kᵊlˈeɪ.ʃᵊn (US) ˌpɝː- **-s** -z

percolator ˈpɜː.kᵊl.eɪ.təʳ (US) ˈpɝː.kᵊl.eɪ.t̬ɚ **-s** -z

per contra ˌpɜːˈkɒn.trə (US) pɚˈkɑːn-

per curiam ˌpɜːˈkjʊə.ri.æm, -ˈkjɔː- (US) pɚˈkjʊr.i-

percuss pəˈkʌs, pɜː- (US) pɚ- **-es** -ɪz **-ing** -ɪŋ **-ed** -t

percussion pəˈkʌʃ.ᵊn, pɜː- (US) pɚ- **-s** -z **-ist/s** -ɪst/s

percussive pəˈkʌs.ɪv, pɜː- (US) pɚ-

percutaneous ˌpɜː.kjuːˈteɪ.ni.əs, -kjʊˈ- (US) ˌpɝː.kjuːˈ- **-ly** -li

Percy ˈpɜː.si (US) ˈpɝː-

per diem ˌpɜː'diː.em, -'daɪ- (US) ˌpɝː-
Perdita 'pɜː.dɪ.tə (US) 'pɝː.dɪ.t̬ə; pɚ'diː-
perdition pə'dɪʃ.ᵊn, pɜː- (US) pɚ-
perdu(e) 'pɜː.djuː (US) pɚ'duː, -'djuː
père, pere peəʳ (US) per
peregrin 'per.ɪ.grɪn, '-ə- **-s** -z
peregri|nate 'per.ɪ.grɪ|.neɪt, '-ə-, -grə- (US) -ə.grɪ- **-nates** -neɪts **-nating** -neɪ.tɪŋ (US) -neɪ.t̬ɪŋ **-nated** -neɪ.tɪd (US) -neɪ.t̬ɪd
peregrination ˌper.ɪ.grɪ'neɪ.ʃᵊn, ˌ-ə-, -grə'- (US) -ə.grɪ'- **-s** -z
peregrine (P) *(n. adj.)* 'per.ɪ.grɪn, '-ə-, -griːn (US) -grɪn, -griːn, -graɪn **-s** -z **ˌperegrine 'falcon**
Perelman 'per.ᵊl.mən, 'pɜːl- (US) 'pɝːl-
peremptor|y pə'remp.tᵊr|.i, pɪ-; 'per.ᵊmp- (US) pə'remp- **-ily** -ᵊl.i, -ɪ.li **-iness** -ɪ.nəs, -ɪ.nɪs
Note: /'per.ᵊmp-/ is more usual in British English when the word is used as a legal term. Otherwise /pə'remp-/ and /pɪ-/ are commoner.
perennial pᵊr'en.i.əl, pɪ'ren- (US) pə'ren- **-s** -z **-ly** -i
Peres 'per.ez
perestroika ˌper.ə'strɔɪ.kə, -ɪ'-
Perez 'per.es (US) 'per.ez, -es, -əz, -əs
Pérez de Cuéllar ˌper.es.də'kweɪ.jɑː (US) ˌper.ez.deɪ'kweɪ.jɑːr, ˌ-əz-, ˌ-es-
perfec|t *(n. adj.)* 'pɜː.fɪk|t (US) 'pɝː- **-ts** -ts **-tly** -*t*.li **-tness** -*t*.nəs, -nɪs **ˌperfect 'pitch; ˌperfect 'tense**
perfect *(v.)* pə'fekt, pɜː- (US) pɝː-, pɚ- **-s** -s **-ing** -ɪŋ **-ed** -ɪd
perfectibility pəˌfek.tɪ'bɪl.ə.ti, pɜː-, -tə'-, -ɪ.ti (US) pɚˌfek.tə'bɪl.ə.t̬i
perfectible pə'fek.tə.bᵊl, pɜː-, -tɪ- (US) pɚ-
perfection pə'fek.ʃᵊn (US) pɚ- **-s** -z **-ist/s** -ɪst/s **-ism** -ɪ.zᵊm
perfective pə'fek.tɪv (US) pɚ- **-ly** -li **-ness** -nəs, -nɪs
perfervid pɜː'fɜː.vɪd, pə- (US) pɚ'fɝː-
perfidious pə'fɪd.i.əs, pɜː- (US) pɚ- **-ly** -li **-ness** -nəs, -nɪs
perfid|y 'pɜː.fɪ.d|i, -fə- (US) 'pɝː.fə- **-ies** -iz
perforable 'pɜː.fᵊr.ə.bl̩ (US) 'pɝː-
perforate *(adj.)* 'pɜː.fᵊr.ɪt, -ət, -eɪt (US) 'pɝː.fɚ.ɪt, -fə.reɪt
perfor|ate *(v.)* 'pɜː.fᵊr|.eɪt (US) 'pɝː.fə.r|eɪt **-ates** -eɪts **-ating** -eɪ.tɪŋ (US) -eɪ.t̬ɪŋ **-ated** -eɪ.tɪd (US) -eɪ.t̬ɪd **-ator/s** -eɪ.təʳ/z (US) -eɪ.t̬ɚ/z
perforation ˌpɜː.fᵊr'eɪ.ʃᵊn (US) ˌpɝː.fə'reɪ- **-s** -z
perforce pə'fɔːs, pɜː- (US) pɚ'fɔːrs
perform pə'fɔːm (US) pɚ'fɔːrm **-s** -z **-ing** -ɪŋ **-ed** -d **-er/s** -əʳ/z (US) -ɚ/z **-able** -ə.bl̩
performanc|e pə'fɔː.mənts (US) pɚ'fɔːr- **-es** -ɪz **per'formance ˌart, perˌformance 'art; perˌformance re'lated; perˌformance reˌlated 'pay**
performative pə'fɔː.mə.tɪv (US) pɚ'fɔːr.mə.t̬ɪv **-s** -z
perfume *(n.)* 'pɜː.fjuːm (US) 'pɝː-, -'- **-s** -z
perfum|e *(v.)* pə'fjuːm, pɜː-; 'pɜː.fjuːm (US) pɚ'fjuːm **-es** -z **-ing** -ɪŋ **-ed** -d
perfumed 'pɜː.fjuːmd (US) pɚ'fjuːmd
perfum|er pə'fjuː.m|əʳ, pɜː- (US) pɚ'fjuː.m|ɚ **-ers** -əz (US) -ɚz **-ery** -ᵊr.i
perfunctor|y pə'fʌŋ*k*.tᵊr|.i, pɜː- (US) pɚ- **-ily** -ᵊl.i, -ɪ.li **-iness** -ɪ.nəs, -ɪ.nɪs
Pergam|um 'pɜː.gə.m|əm (US) 'pɝː- **-us** -əs
pergola 'pɜː.gᵊl.ə (US) 'pɝː- **-s** -z
Pergolese ˌpɜː.gəʊ'leɪ.zi, ˌpeə-, -zeɪ (US) ˌper.goʊ'leɪ.zi, -si
Perham 'per.əm
perhaps pə'hæps; præps (US) pɚ'hæps, -'æps
Note: In British English, /pə'hæps/ is more usual in formal speech, and colloquially when the word is said in isolation or used parenthetically (as in **You know, perhaps, ...**). /præps/ is common in other situations, especially initially (e.g. in **Perhaps we shall, perhaps it is a mistake**).
peri- per.ɪ-, -i-; pə'rɪ-, per'ɪ-
Note: Prefix. Normally either takes primary or secondary stress on the first syllable, e.g. **periscope** /'per.ɪ.skəʊp (US) -skoʊp/, **periscopic** /ˌper.ɪ'skɒp.ɪk (US) -'skɑː.pɪk/, or primary stress on the second syllable, e.g. **peripheral** /pə'rɪf.ᵊr.ᵊl/.
peri 'pɪə.ri (US) 'piː-, 'pɪr.i **-s** -z
perianth 'per.i.æn*t*θ **-s** -s
pericarditis ˌper.ɪ.kɑː'daɪ.tɪs (US) -kɑːr'daɪ.t̬ɪs
pericardi|um ˌper.ɪ'kɑː.di|.əm (US) -'kɑːr- **-a** -ə
pericarp 'per.ɪ.kɑːp, '-ə- (US) -ɪ.kɑːrp **-s** -s
Pericles 'per.ɪ.kliːz, '-ə- (US) -ɪ.kliːz
peridot 'per.ɪ.dɒt (US) -dɑːt **-s** -s
perigee 'per.ɪ.dʒiː, '-ə- (US) '-ɪ- **-s** -z
perihели|on ˌper.ɪ'hiː.li|.ən (US) -'hiː.li.ən, -'hiːl.jən **-a** -ə
peril 'per.ᵊl, -ɪl (US) -ᵊl **-s** -z
perilous 'per.ᵊl.əs, -ɪ.ləs (US) -ᵊl.əs **-ly** -li **-ness** -nəs, -nɪs
perilune 'per.ɪ.luːn, -ljuːn (US) -luːn **-s** -z
Perim 'per.ɪm (US) pə'rɪm
perimeter pə'rɪm.ɪ.təʳ, pɪ-, per'ɪm-, '-ə- (US) pə'rɪm.ə.t̬ɚ **-s** -z
perinatal ˌper.ɪ'neɪ.tᵊl (US) -t̬ᵊl
perine|um ˌper.ɪ'niː|.əm **-a** -ə **-al** -ᵊl
period 'pɪə.ri.əd (US) 'pɪr.i- **-s** -z **'period ˌpiece**
periodic ˌpɪə.ri'ɒd.ɪk (US) ˌpɪr.i'ɑː.dɪk *stress shift, see compound:* **ˌperiodic 'table**
periodic|al ˌpɪə.ri'ɒd.ɪ.k|ᵊl (US) ˌpɪr.i'ɑː.dɪ- **-als** -ᵊlz **-ally** -ᵊl.i, -li
periodicit|y ˌpɪə.ri.ə'dɪs.ə.t|i, -ɒd'ɪs-, -ɪ.t|i (US) ˌpɪr.i.oʊ'dɪs.ə.t̬|i, -ə'- **-ies** -iz
periodontal ˌper.i.əʊ'dɒn.tᵊl (US) -oʊ'dɑːn.t̬ᵊl, -ə'- **-ly** -i
periodont|ic ˌper.i.əʊ'dɒn.t|ɪk (US) -oʊ'dɑːn.t̬|ɪk, -ə'- **-ics** -ɪks **-ist/s** -ɪst/s
peripatetic ˌper.ɪ.pə'tet.ɪk, ˌ-ə- (US) -'tet̬- **-ally** -ᵊl.i, -li *stress shift:* ˌperipatetic 'teacher
peripheral pə'rɪf.ᵊr.ᵊl, pɪ-, per'ɪf- (US) pə'rɪf- **-s** -z **-ly** -i
peripher|y pə'rɪf.ᵊr|.i, pɪ-, per'ɪf- (US) pə'rɪf- **-ies** -iz
periphras|is pə'rɪf.rə.s|ɪs, pɪ-, per'ɪf- (US) pə'rɪf **-es** -iːz
periphrastic ˌper.ɪ'fræs.tɪk, -ə'- **-ally** -ᵊl.i, -li
periscope 'per.ɪ.skəʊp, '-ə- (US) -ɪ.skoʊp **-s** -s
periscopic ˌper.ɪ'skɒp.ɪk, -ə'- (US) -ɪ'skɑː.pɪk
perish 'per.ɪʃ **-es** -ɪz **-ing/ly** -ɪŋ/li **-ed** -t **-er/s** -əʳ/z (US) -ɚ/z
perishability ˌper.ɪ.ʃə'bɪl.ə.ti, -ɪ.ti (US) -ə.t̬i
perishab|le 'per.ɪ.ʃə.bl̩ **-ly** -li **-leness** -l̩.nəs, -nɪs
perispomenon ˌper.ɪ'spəʊ.mɪ.nən, -mə-, -nɒn (US) -'spoʊ.mɪ.nɑːn
peristalsis ˌper.ɪ'stæl.sɪs, -ə'- (US) -ɪ'stɑːl-, -'stæl-
peristaltic ˌper.ɪ'stæl.tɪk, -ə'- (US) -ɪ'stɑːl.t̬ɪk, -'stæl-
peristyle 'per.ɪ.staɪl, '-ə- (US) '-ɪ- **-s** -z
peritone|um ˌper.ɪ.təʊ'niː|.əm, ˌ-ə- (US) -'toʊ.ni-, -tə- **-ums** -əmz **-a** -ə
peritonitis ˌper.ɪ.təʊ'naɪ.tɪs, ˌ-ə- (US) -ɪ.toʊ'naɪ.t̬ɪs
Perivale 'per.ɪ.veɪl, '-ə- (US) '-ɪ-
periwig 'per.ɪ.wɪg, '-ə- (US) '-ɪ- **-s** -z
periwinkle 'per.ɪˌwɪŋ.kl̩, '-ə- (US) -ɪˌ- **-s** -z
perj|ure 'pɜː.dʒ|əʳ (US) 'pɝː.dʒ|ɚ **-ures** -əz (US) -ɚz **-uring** -ᵊr.ɪŋ **-ured** -əd (US) -ɚd **-urer/s** -ᵊr.əʳ/z (US) -ɚ.ɚ/z
perjur|y 'pɜː.dʒᵊr|.i (US) 'pɝː- **-ies** -iz
perk pɜːk (US) pɝːk **-s** -s **-ing** -ɪŋ **-ed** -t
Perkin 'pɜː.kɪn (US) 'pɝː- **-s** -z
Perks pɜːks (US) pɝːks
perk|y 'pɜː.k|i (US) 'pɝː- **-ier** -i.əʳ (US) -i.ɚ **-iest** -i.ɪst, -i.əst **-ily** -ɪ.li, -ᵊl.i **-iness** -ɪ.nəs, -ɪ.nɪs

Perlis ˈpɜː.lɪs ⓤⓢ ˈpɝː-
perlite ˈpɜː.laɪt ⓤⓢ ˈpɝː-
Perlman ˈpɜːl.mən ⓤⓢ ˈpɝːl-
perlocutionary ˌpɜː.ləˈkjuː.ʃən.ər.i, -lɒkˈjuː- ⓤⓢ ˌpɝː.loʊˈkjuː-
perm pɜːm ⓤⓢ pɝːm **-s** -z **-ing** -ɪŋ **-ed** -d
Perm *city in Eastern Europe:* pɜːm, peəm ⓤⓢ perm
permafrost ˈpɜː.mə.frɒst ⓤⓢ ˈpɝː.mə.frɑːst
permanenc|e ˈpɜː.mən.ənts ⓤⓢ ˈpɝː- **-es** -ɪz **-y** -i **-ies** -iz
permanent ˈpɜː.mən.ənt ⓤⓢ ˈpɝː- **-ly** -li
permanganate pɜːˈmæŋ.gə.neɪt, pə-, -nɪt, -nət ⓤⓢ pɚˈmæŋ.gə.neɪt
permeability ˌpɜː.mi.əˈbɪl.ə.ti, -ɪ.ti ⓤⓢ ˌpɝː.mi.əˈbɪl.ə.t̬i
permeab|le ˈpɜː.mi.ə.bl̩ ⓤⓢ ˈpɝː- **-ly** -li **-leness** -l̩.nəs, -nɪs
perme|ate ˈpɜː.mi|.eɪt ⓤⓢ ˈpɝː- **-ates** -eɪts **-ating** -eɪ.tɪŋ ⓤⓢ -eɪ.t̬ɪŋ **-ated** -eɪ.tɪd ⓤⓢ -eɪ.t̬ɪd
permeation ˌpɜː.miˈeɪ.ʃən ⓤⓢ ˌpɝː-
permissib|le pəˈmɪs.ə.bl|̩, ˈ-ɪ- ⓤⓢ pɚˈmɪs.ə- **-ly** -li **-leness** -l̩.nəs, -nɪs
permission pəˈmɪʃ.ən ⓤⓢ pɚ- **-s** -z
permissive pəˈmɪs.ɪv ⓤⓢ pɚ- **-ly** -li **-ness** -nəs, -nɪs **perˌmissive soˈciety**
permit (*n.*) ˈpɜː.mɪt ⓤⓢ ˈpɝː-; pɚˈmɪt **-s** -s
per|mit (*v.*) pə|ˈmɪt ⓤⓢ pɚ- **-mits** -ˈmɪts **-mitting** -ˈmɪt.ɪŋ ⓤⓢ -ˈmɪt̬.ɪŋ **-mitted** -ˈmɪt.ɪd ⓤⓢ -ˈmɪt̬.ɪd
permutation ˌpɜː.mjʊˈteɪ.ʃən, -mjuːˈ-, -mjəˈ- ⓤⓢ ˌpɝː.mjuːˈ- **-s** -z
per|mute pə|ˈmjuːt ⓤⓢ pɚ- **-mutes** -ˈmjuːts **-muting** -ˈmjuː.tɪŋ ⓤⓢ -ˈmjuː.t̬ɪŋ **-muted** -ˈmjuː.tɪd ⓤⓢ -ˈmjuː.t̬ɪd **-mutable** -ˈmjuː.tə.bl̩ ⓤⓢ -ˈmjuː.t̬ə.bl̩
Pernambuco ˌpɜː.næmˈbuː.kəʊ, -nəmˈ-, -ˈbjuː- ⓤⓢ ˌpɝː.nəmˈbuː.koʊ
pernicious pəˈnɪʃ.əs, pɜː- ⓤⓢ pɚ- **-ly** -li **-ness** -nəs, -nɪs
pernicket|y pəˈnɪk.ə.t|i, -ɪ.t|i ⓤⓢ pɚˈnɪk.ə.t̬|i **-iness** -ɪ.nəs, -ɪ.nɪs
Pernod® ˈpɜː.nəʊ, ˈpeə- ⓤⓢ perˈnoʊ
Perón, Peron pəˈrɒn, perˈɒn, pɪˈrɒn ⓤⓢ perˈoʊn, pəˈroʊn
peror|ate ˈper.ər|.eɪt, -ɒr- ⓤⓢ -ə.r|eɪt, -oʊ- **-ates** -eɪts **-ating** -eɪ.tɪŋ ⓤⓢ -eɪ.t̬ɪŋ **-ated** -eɪ.tɪd ⓤⓢ -eɪ.t̬ɪd
peroration ˌper.ərˈeɪ.ʃən, -ɒrˈ- ⓤⓢ ˌper.əˈreɪ-, -oʊˈ- **-s** -z
Perot pəˈrəʊ, perˈəʊ ⓤⓢ pəˈroʊ
Perowne pəˈrəʊn, pɪ-, perˈəʊn ⓤⓢ pəˈroʊn
peroxide pəˈrɒk.saɪd ⓤⓢ pəˈrɑːk- **-s** -z
perpend (*v.*) pəˈpend, pɜː- ⓤⓢ pɚ- **-s** -z **-ing** -ɪŋ **-ed** -ɪd
perpend (*n.*) ˈpɜː.pənd ⓤⓢ ˈpɝː- **-s** -z
perpendicular ˌpɜː.pənˈdɪk.jʊ.lər, -kjə- ⓤⓢ ˌpɝː.pənˈdɪk.juː.lɚ, -jə- **-s** -z **-ly** -li
perpendicularity ˌpɜː.pənˌdɪk.jəˈlær.ə.ti, -jʊˈ-, -ɪ.ti ⓤⓢ ˌpɝː.pənˌdɪk.juːˈler.ə.t̬i, -jəˈ-, -ˈlær-
perpe|trate ˈpɜː.pɪ|.treɪt, -pə- ⓤⓢ ˈpɝː.pə|.treɪt **-trates** -treɪts **-trating** -treɪ.tɪŋ ⓤⓢ -treɪ.t̬ɪŋ **-trated** -treɪ.tɪd ⓤⓢ -treɪ.t̬ɪd **-trator/s** -treɪ.tər/z ⓤⓢ -treɪ.t̬ɚ/z
perpetration ˌpɜː.pɪˈtreɪ.ʃən, -pəˈ- ⓤⓢ ˌpɝː.pəˈ- **-s** -z
perpetual pəˈpetʃ.u.əl, -ˈpet.ju- ⓤⓢ pɚˈpetʃ.u- **-ly** -i
perpetu|ate pəˈpetʃ.u|.eɪt, pɜː-, -ˈpet.ju- ⓤⓢ pɚˈpetʃ.u- **-ates** -eɪts **-ating** -eɪ.tɪŋ ⓤⓢ -eɪ.t̬ɪŋ **-ated** -eɪ.tɪd ⓤⓢ -eɪ.t̬ɪd
perpetuation pəˌpetʃ.uˈeɪ.ʃən, pɜː-, -ˌpet.juˈ- ⓤⓢ ˌpɚ.petʃ.uˈ- **-s** -z
perpetuit|y ˌpɜː.pɪˈtjuː.ə.t|i, -pəˈ-, -ɪ.t|i ⓤⓢ ˌpɝː.pəˈtuː.ə.t̬|i, -ˈtjuː- **-ies** -iz
perpetuum mobile pəˌpetʃ.u.ʊmˈməʊ.bɪ.leɪ, pɜː-, -ˌpet.ju-, -əmˈ- ⓤⓢ pɚˌpetʃ.ə.wəmˈmoʊ-
Perpignan ˈpɜː.piː.njɑ̃ː, ˈpeə-, ˌ--ˈ- ⓤⓢ ˌper.piːˈnjɑ̃ːŋ
perplex pəˈpleks ⓤⓢ pɚ- **-es** -ɪz **-ing/ly** -ɪŋ/li **-ed** -t **-edly** -ɪd.li, -t.li **-edness** -ɪd.nəs, -t.nəs, -nɪs
perplexit|y pəˈplek.sə.t|i, -ɪ.t|i ⓤⓢ pɚˈplek.sə.t̬|i **-ies** -iz
perquisite ˈpɜː.kwɪ.zɪt, -kwə- ⓤⓢ ˈpɝː.kwɪ- **-s** -s
per quod ˌpɜːˈkwɒd ⓤⓢ ˌpɝːˈkwɑːd
Perrault ˈper.əʊ, -ˈ- ⓤⓢ perˈoʊ
Perrett ˈper.ɪt
Perrier® ˈper.i.eɪ ⓤⓢ -eɪ, ˌ--ˈ-
perrin (P) ˈper.ɪn
perr|y (P) ˈper|.i **-ies** -iz
Perse pɜːs ⓤⓢ pɝːs
per se ˌpɜːˈseɪ ⓤⓢ ˌpɝː-
perse|cute ˈpɜː.sɪ|.kjuːt, -sə- ⓤⓢ ˈpɝː.sɪ- **-cutes** -kjuːts **-cuting** -kjuː.tɪŋ ⓤⓢ -kjuː.t̬ɪŋ **-cuted** -kjuː.tɪd ⓤⓢ -kjuː.t̬ɪd **-cutor/s** -kjuː.tər/z ⓤⓢ -kjuː.t̬ɚ/z
persecution ˌpɜː.sɪˈkjuː.ʃən, -səˈ- ⓤⓢ ˌpɝː.sɪˈ- **-s** -z
Persephone pɜːˈsef.ən.i, pə- ⓤⓢ pɚ-
Persepolis pɜːˈsep.əl.ɪs, pə- ⓤⓢ pɚ-
Perseus ˈpɜː.si.əs, ˈ-sjuːs ⓤⓢ ˈpɝː-
persever|ate pəˈsev.ər|.eɪt, pɜː- ⓤⓢ pɚˈsev.ə.r|eɪt **-ates** -eɪts **-ating** -eɪ.tɪŋ ⓤⓢ -eɪ.t̬ɪŋ **-ated** -eɪ.tɪd ⓤⓢ -eɪ.t̬ɪd
perseveration pəˌsev.ərˈeɪ.ʃən, pɜː- ⓤⓢ pɚˌsev.əˈreɪ-
persever|e ˌpɜː.sɪˈvɪər, -səˈ- ⓤⓢ ˌpɝː.səˈvɪr **-es** -z **-ing/ly** -ɪŋ/li **-ed** -d **-ance** -ənts
Pershing ˈpɜː.ʃɪŋ ⓤⓢ ˈpɝː-
Pershore ˈpɜː.ʃɔːr ⓤⓢ ˈpɝː.ʃɔːr
Persi|a ˈpɜː.ʒ|ə, -ʃ|ə ⓤⓢ ˈpɝː.ʒ|ə, -ʃ|ə **-an/s** -ən/z
persiflage ˈpɜː.sɪ.flɑːʒ, ˈpeə-, -sə-, ˌ--ˈ- ⓤⓢ ˈpɝː.sɪ-
Persil® ˈpɜː.sɪl, -səl ⓤⓢ ˈpɝː-
persimmon (P) pəˈsɪm.ən, pɜː- ⓤⓢ pɚ- **-s** -z
persist pəˈsɪst ⓤⓢ pɚ- **-s** -s **-ing/ly** -ɪŋ/li **-ed** -ɪd
persisten|ce pəˈsɪs.tənt|s ⓤⓢ pɚ- **-cy** -si
persistent pəˈsɪs.tənt ⓤⓢ pɚ- **-ly** -li
persnickety pəˈsnɪk.ə.ti, -ɪ.ti ⓤⓢ pɚˈsnɪk.ə.t̬i
person ˈpɜː.sən ⓤⓢ ˈpɝː- **-s** -z
person|a pəˈsəʊ.n|ə, pɜː- ⓤⓢ pɚˈsoʊ- **-ae** -iː, -aɪ
personable ˈpɜː.sən.ə.bl̩ ⓤⓢ ˈpɝː-
personag|e ˈpɜː.sən.ɪdʒ ⓤⓢ ˈpɝː- **-es** -ɪz
personal ˈpɜː.sən.əl, ˈpɜːs.nəl ⓤⓢ ˈpɝː.sən.əl, ˈpɝːs.nəl **-ly** -i **ˌpersonal asˈsistant; ˈpersonal ˌcolumn; ˌpersonal comˈputer; ˌpersonal ˈhygiene; ˌpersonal ˈstereo**
personalit|y ˌpɜː.sənˈæl.ə.t|i, -ɪ.t|i ⓤⓢ ˌpɝː.sənˈæl.ə.t̬|i **-ies** -iz
personalization, -isa- ˌpɜː.sən.əl.aɪˈzeɪ.ʃən, -ɪˈ- ⓤⓢ ˌpɝː.sən.əlˈɪ-
personaliz|e, is|e ˈpɜː.sən.əl.aɪz ⓤⓢ ˈpɝː- **-es** -ɪz **-ing** -ɪŋ **-ed** -d
personalt|y ˈpɜː.sən.əl.t|i ⓤⓢ ˈpɝː.sən.əl.t̬|i **-ies** -iz
persona non grata pəˌsəʊ.nə.nɒnˈgrɑː.tə, pɜː-, -nəʊnˈ- ⓤⓢ pɚˌsoʊ.nə.nɑːnˈgrɑː.t̬ə, -ˈgræt̬.ə
person|ate ˈpɜː.sən|.eɪt ⓤⓢ ˈpɝː- **-ates** -eɪts **-ating** -eɪ.tɪŋ ⓤⓢ -eɪ.t̬ɪŋ **-ated** -eɪ.tɪd ⓤⓢ -eɪ.t̬ɪd **-ator/s** -eɪ.tər/z ⓤⓢ -eɪ.t̬ɚ/z
personation ˌpɜː.sənˈeɪ.ʃən ⓤⓢ ˌpɝː- **-s** -s
personification pəˌsɒn.ɪ.fɪˈkeɪ.ʃən, pɜː-, ˌ-ə- ⓤⓢ pɚˌsɑː.nɪ- **-s** -z
personi|fy pəˈsɒn.ɪ|.faɪ, pɜː-, ˈ-ə- ⓤⓢ pɚˈsɑː.nɪ- **-fies** -faɪz **-fying** -faɪ.ɪŋ **-fied** -faɪd
personnel ˌpɜː.sənˈel ⓤⓢ ˌpɝː- **-s** -z **personˈnel ˌmanager**
perspective pəˈspek.tɪv, pɜː- ⓤⓢ pɚ- **-s** -z **-ly** -li
Perspex® ˈpɜː.speks ⓤⓢ ˈpɝː-
perspicacious ˌpɜː.spɪˈkeɪ.ʃəs, -spəˈ- ⓤⓢ ˌpɝː.spɪˈ- **-ly** -li **-ness** -nəs, -nɪs
perspicacity ˌpɜː.spɪˈkæs.ə.ti, -spəˈ-, -ɪ.ti ⓤⓢ ˌpɝː.spɪˈkæs.ə.t̬i
perspicuity ˌpɜː.spɪˈkjuː.ə.ti, -ɪ.ti ⓤⓢ ˌpɝː.spɪˈkjuː.ə.t̬i

perspicuous pə'spɪk.ju.əs, pɜː- (US) pɚ- **-ly** -li **-ness** -nəs, -nɪs
perspiration ˌpɜː.spᵊr'eɪ.ʃᵊn (US) ˌpɝː.spə'reɪ-
perspir|e pə'spaɪəʳ (US) pɚ'spaɪɚ **-es** -z **-ing** -ɪŋ **-ed** -d
per stirpes ˌpɜː'stɜː.piːz (US) pɚ'stɝː-
persuad|e pə'sweɪd (US) pɚ- **-es** -z **-ing** -ɪŋ **-ed** -ɪd **-er/s** -əʳ/z (US) -ɚ/z
persuasion pə'sweɪ.ʒᵊn (US) pɚ- **-s** -z
persuasive pə'sweɪ.sɪv, -zɪv (US) pɚ'sweɪ.sɪv **-ly** -li **-ness** -nəs, -nɪs
pert pɜːt (US) pɝːt **-er** -əʳ (US) 'pɝː.t̬ɚ **-est** -ɪst, -əst (US) 'pɝː.t̬ɪst, -t̬əst **-ly** -li **-ness** -nəs, -nɪs
pertain pə'teɪn, pɜː- (US) pɚ- **-s** -z **-ing** -ɪŋ **-ed** -d
Perth pɜːθ (US) pɝːθ **-shire** -ʃəʳ, -ˌʃɪəʳ (US) -ʃɚ, -ˌʃɪr
pertinacious ˌpɜː.tɪ'neɪ.ʃəs, -tə'- (US) ˌpɝː.tᵊn'eɪ- **-ly** -li **-ness** -nəs, -nɪs
pertinacity ˌpɜː.tɪ'næs.ə.ti, -tə'-, -ɪ.ti (US) ˌpɝː.tᵊn'æs.ə.t̬i
pertinen|ce 'pɜː.tɪ.nən*t*|s, -tə- (US) 'pɝː.tᵊn.ᵊn*t*|s **-cy** -si
pertinent 'pɜː.tɪ.nənt, -tə- (US) 'pɝː.tᵊn.ᵊnt **-ly** -li
perturb pə'tɜːb, pɜː- (US) pɚ'tɝːb **-s** -z **-ing** -ɪŋ **-ed** -d **-er/s** -əʳ/z **-able** -ə.bl̩
perturbation ˌpɜː.tə'beɪ.ʃᵊn, -tɜː'- (US) ˌpɝː.t̬ɚ'- **-s** -z
pertussis pə'tʌs.ɪs, pɜː- (US) pɚ-
Pertwee 'pɜː.twiː (US) 'pɝː-
Peru pə'ruː, pɪ- (US) pə-
Perugia pə'ruː.dʒə, pɪ-, per'uː-, -dʒi.ə (US) per'uː.dʒɑː, -dʒi.ə
Perugino ˌper.u'dʒiː.nəʊ (US) -noʊ
peruke pə'ruːk, pɪ-, per'uːk (US) pə'ruːk **-s** -s
perusal pə'ruː.zᵊl, pɪ- (US) pə'ruː- **-s** -z
perus|e pə'ruːz, pɪ- (US) pə'ruːz **-es** -ɪz **-ing** -ɪŋ **-ed** -d **-er/s** -əʳ/z (US) -ɚ/z
Peruvian pə'ruː.vi.ən, pɪ-, per'uː- (US) pə'ruː- **-s** -z
pervad|e pə'veɪd, pɜː- (US) pɚ- **-es** -z **-ing** -ɪŋ **-ed** -ɪd
pervasion pə'veɪ.ʒᵊn, pɜː- (US) pɚ-
pervasive pə'veɪ.sɪv, pɜː-, -zɪv (US) pɚ'veɪ.sɪv **-ly** -li **-ness** -nəs, -nɪs
perverse pə'vɜːs, pɜː- (US) pɚ'vɝːs **-ly** -li **-ness** -nəs, -nɪs
perversion pə'vɜː.ʃᵊn, pɜː-, -ʒᵊn (US) pɚ'vɝː.ʒᵊn, -ʃᵊn **-s** -z
perversit|y pə'vɜː.sə.t|i, pɜː-, -ɪ.t|i (US) pɚ'vɝː.sə.t̬|i **-ies** -iz
pervert (*n.*) 'pɜː.vɜːt (US) 'pɝː.vɝːrt **-s** -s
per|vert (*v.*) pə|'vɜːt, pɜː- (US) pɚ|'vɝːt **-verts** -'vɜːts (US) -'vɝːts **-verting** -'vɜː.tɪŋ (US) -'vɝː.t̬ɪŋ **-verted** -'vɜː.tɪd (US) -'vɝː.t̬ɪd **-verter/s** -'vɜː.təʳ/z (US) -'vɝː.t̬ɚ/z
pervious 'pɜː.vi.əs (US) 'pɝː- **-ly** -li **-ness** -nəs, -nɪs
pesante pez'æn.teɪ (US) pes'ɑːn-
Pescadores ˌpes.kə'dɔː.rɪz (US) -'dɔːr.iːz, -ɪs
peseta pə'seɪ.tə, pɪ-, pes'eɪ- (US) pə'seɪ.t̬ə **-s** -z
pesewa pɪ'seɪ.wɑː (US) 'pes.ə.wɑː; peɪ'seɪ- **-s** -z
Peshawar pə'ʃɔː.əʳ, peʃ'ɔː-, -'ɑː-, -wə (US) peʃ'ɑː.wɚ, pə'ʃɑː-
peshwari peʃ'wɑː.ri
pesk|y 'pes.k|i **-ier** -i.əʳ (US) -i.ɚ **-iest** -i.ɪst, -i.əst **-ily** -ɪ.li, -ᵊl.i **-iness** -ɪ.nəs, -ɪ.nɪs
peso 'peɪ.səʊ (US) -soʊ **-s** -z
pessar|y 'pes.ᵊr|.i **-ies** -iz
pessim|ism 'pes.ɪ.m|ɪ.zᵊm, '-ə- (US) '-ə- **-ist/s** -ɪst/s
pessimistic ˌpes.ɪ'mɪs.tɪk, -ə'- (US) -ə'- **-al** -ᵊl **-ally** -ᵊl.i, -li
pest (P) pest **-s** -s
Pestalozzi ˌpes.tə'lɒt.si (US) -'lɑːt-
pest|er 'pes.t|əʳ (US) -t|ɚ **-ers** -əz (US) -ɚz **-ering/ly** -ᵊr.ɪŋ/li **-ered** -əd (US) -ɚd **-erer/s** -ᵊr.əʳ/z (US) -ɚ.ɚ/z
pesticide 'pes.tɪ.saɪd (US) -tə- **-s** -z
pestiferous pes'tɪf.ᵊr.əs **-ly** -li **-ness** -nəs, -nɪs
pestilenc|e 'pes.tɪ.lən*t*s, -tᵊl.ən*t*s (US) -tᵊl- **-es** -ɪz
pestilent 'pes.tɪ.lənt, -tᵊl.ənt (US) -tᵊl- **-ly** -li
pestilential ˌpes.tɪ'len.*t*ʃᵊl, -tə'- (US) -tə'len*t*.ʃᵊl **-ly** -i
pestl|e 'pes.l̩, -tl̩ **-es** -z **-ing** -ɪŋ, 'pes.lɪŋ, 'pest.lɪŋ **-ed** -d
pesto 'pes.təʊ (US) -toʊ
pestolog|y pes'tɒl.ə.dʒ|i (US) -'tɑː.lə- **-ist/s** -ɪst/s
pet pet **-s** -s **-ting** -ɪŋ (US) 'pet̬.ɪŋ **-ted** -ɪd (US) 'pet̬.ɪd
petal 'pet.ᵊl (US) 'pet̬- **-s** -z **-(l)ed** -d
pétanque peɪ'tɑ̃ːŋk
petard pet'ɑːd, pɪ'tɑːd, pə-; 'pet.ɑːd (US) pɪ'tɑːrd **-s** -z ˌ**hoist by one's** ˌ**own pe'tard**
Pete piːt
pet|er (P) 'piː.t|əʳ (US) -t̬|ɚ **-ers** -əz (US) -ɚz **-ering** -ᵊr.ɪŋ **-ered** -əd (US) -ɚd ˌ**Peter 'Pan**
Peterborough, -boro' 'piː.tə.bᵊr.ə, -ˌbʌr.ə (US) -t̬ɚˌbɚ.oʊ, -ə
Peterhead ˌpiː.tə'hed (US) -t̬ɚ'- *stress shift:* ˌPeterhead 'resident
Peterhouse 'piː.tə.haʊs (US) -t̬ɚ-
Peterlee ˌpiː.tə'liː, '--- (US) ˌpiː.t̬ɚ'liː, '---
Peters 'piː.təz (US) -t̬ɚz
Petersburg 'piː.təz.bɜːg (US) -t̬ɚz.bɝːg
Petersfield 'piː.təz.fiːld (US) -t̬ɚz-
petersham (P) 'piː.tə.ʃᵊm (US) -t̬ɚ- **-s** -z
Peterson, Petersen 'piː.tə.sᵊn (US) -t̬ɚ-
Pethick 'peθ.ɪk
petiole 'pet.i.əʊl, 'piː.ti- (US) 'pet̬.i.oʊl **-s** -z
petit(s) bourgeois ˌpet.i'bɔː.ʒwɑː, -'bʊə- (US) pəˌtiː.bʊr'ʒwɑː; ˌpet̬.i-
petite bourgeoisie pəˌtiːtˌbɔː.ʒwɑː'zi, -ˌbʊə- (US) -ˌbʊr-
petit bourgeoisie ˌpet.iˌbɔː.ʒwɑː'ziː, -ˌbʊə- (US) pəˌtiː.bʊr-; ˌpet̬.i-
petite pə'tiːt
petit four ˌpet.i'fɔːʳ, -fʊəʳ (US) ˌpet̬.i'fɔːr **-s** -z
petition pə'tɪʃ.ᵊn, pɪ- (US) pə- **-s** -z **-ing** -ɪŋ **-ed** -d **-er/s** -əʳ/z
petit mal ˌpet.i'mæl (US) pəˌtiː'mɑːl, -'mæl; ˌpet̬.i'-
petit point ˌpet.i'pɔɪnt (US) 'pet̬.iˌpɔɪnt
petit(s) pois ˌpet.i'pwɑː (US) pəˌtiː'-, ˌpet̬.i'-
Peto 'piː.təʊ (US) -toʊ
Petra 'pet.rə (US) 'piː.trə, 'pet.rə
Petrarch 'pet.rɑːk (US) 'piː.trɑːrk, 'pet.rɑːrk
Petrarchan pet'rɑː.kᵊn, pə'trɑː-, pɪ- (US) pɪ'trɑːr-
Petre 'piː.təʳ (US) -t̬ɚ
petrel 'pet.rᵊl **-s** -z
petri dish 'pet.riˌdɪʃ (US) 'piː.tri- **-es** -ɪz
Petrie 'piː.tri
petrifaction ˌpet.rɪ'fæk.ʃᵊn, -rə'-
petrification ˌpet.rɪ.fɪ'keɪ.ʃᵊn, -rə-
petri|fy 'pet.rɪ|.faɪ, -rə- **-fies** -faɪz **-fying** -faɪ.ɪŋ **-fied** -faɪd
petrochem|ical ˌpet.rəʊ'kem|.ɪ.kᵊl **-istry** -ɪ.stri
petrodollar 'pet.rəʊˌdɒl.əʳ (US) -roʊˌdɑː.lɚ **-s** -z
Petrograd 'pet.rəʊ.græd, -grɑːd (US) -rə.græd
petrol 'pet.rᵊl '**petrol** ˌ**pump;** '**petrol** ˌ**station**
petrolatum ˌpet.rə'leɪ.təm (US) -t̬əm
petrol-bomb 'pet.rᵊl.bɒm (US) -bɑːm **-s** -z **-ing** -ɪŋ **-ed** -d
petroleum pə'trəʊ.li.əm, pɪ- (US) pə'troʊ- **pe**ˌ**troleum 'jelly**
petrolog|y pet'rɒl.ə.dʒ|i, pə'trɒl-, pɪ- (US) pə'trɑː.lə- **-ist/s** -ɪst/s
Petruchio pɪ'truː.ki.əʊ, pə-, pet'ruː-, -tʃi- (US) pɪ'truː.ki.oʊ, pə-, -tʃi-
Petrushka pɪ'truːʃ.kə, pə-, pet'ruːʃ-
Pett pet
petticoat 'pet.ɪ.kəʊt (US) 'pet̬.ɪ.koʊt **-s** -s
pettifogg|ing 'pet.ɪˌfɒg|.ɪŋ (US) 'pet̬.ɪˌfɑː.g|ɪŋ, -ˌfɔː- **-er/s** -əʳ/z (US) -ɚ/z
Pettigrew 'pet.ɪ.gruː (US) 'pet̬-
pettish 'pet.ɪʃ (US) 'pet̬- **-ly** -li **-ness** -nəs, -nɪs
Pettit 'pet.ɪt (US) 'pet̬-

Pronouncing the letters PH

The consonant digraph **ph** is usually pronounced as /f/, e.g.:

photo	/ˈfəʊ.təʊ/	(US) /ˈfoʊ.t̬oʊ/
alphabet	/ˈæl.fə.bet/	

However, the realisation /v/ can occur in some words, e.g.:

nephew	/ˈnef.juː, ˈnev-/
Stephen	/ˈstiː.vᵊn/

In addition

A much less common realisation of the consonant digraph **ph** is /p/, e.g.:

shepherd	/ˈʃep.əd/	(US) /-ɚd/

Pharyngeal

Descriptive of a sound made by constricting the muscles of the pharynx (and usually also some of the LARYNX muscles) to create an obstruction to the airflow from the lungs.

Examples for English

English does not have any pharyngeal phonemes.

In other languages

The best known language that has pharyngeal consonants is Arabic, most dialects of which have voiced and voiceless fricatives.

pettitoes ˈpet.ɪ.təʊz (US) ˈpet̬.ɪ.toʊz
pett|y ˈpet|.i (US) ˈpet̬- **-ier** -i.əʳ (US) -i.ɚ **-iest** -i.ɪst, -i.əst **-ily** -ɪ.li, -ᵊl.i **-iness/es** -ɪ.nəs/ɪz, -ɪ.nɪs/ɪz ˌ**petty ˈcash**; ˌ**petty ˈofficer**
petty bourgeois ˌpet.iˈbɔː.ʒwɑː, -ˈbʊə- (US) ˌpet̬.i.bʊrˈʒwɑː
petty bourgeoisie ˌpet.iˌbɔː.ʒwɑːˈzi, -ˌbʊə- (US) ˌpet̬.iˌbʊr-
Petula pɪˈtjuː.lə, pə-, petˈjuː- (US) pəˈtuː-, -ˈtjuː-
petulan|ce ˈpet.jə.lənt|s, -jʊ-, ˈpetʃ.ə-, ˈ-ʊ- (US) ˈpetʃ.ə- **-cy** -si
petulant ˈpet.jə.lənt, -jʊ-, ˈpetʃ.ə-, ˈ-ʊ- (US) ˈpetʃ.ə- **-ly** -li
petunia pɪˈtjuː.ni.ə, pə- (US) pəˈtuː.njə, -ˈtjuː-, ˈ-ni.ə **-s** -z
Petworth ˈpet.wəθ, -wɜːθ (US) -wɚθ, -wɝːθ
Peugeot® ˈpɜː.ʒəʊ (US) pɜːˈʒoʊ, puː-, pjuː- **-s** -z
Pevensey ˈpev.ᵊn.zi
Peveril ˈpev.ᵊr.ɪl
Pevsner ˈpevz.nəʳ (US) -nɚ
pew pjuː **-s** -z
pewit ˈpiː.wɪt (US) ˈpiː-, ˈpjuː.ɪt **-s** -s
pewter ˈpjuː.təʳ (US) -t̬ɚ
Peynell ˈpeɪ.nᵊl, -nel
peyote peɪˈəʊ.ti (US) -ˈoʊ.t̬i **-s** -z
Peyton ˈpeɪ.tᵊn
Pfeiffer ˈfaɪ.fəʳ, ˈpfaɪ- (US) -fɚ
pfennig ˈ*p*fen.ɪg (US) ˈfen- **-s** -z
pH ˌpiːˈeɪtʃ
Phaedo ˈfiː.dəʊ, ˈfaɪ- (US) ˈfiː.doʊ
Phaedra ˈfiː.drə, ˈfaɪ- (US) ˈfiː-, ˈfed.rə
Phaedrus ˈfiː.drəs, ˈfaɪ- (US) ˈfiː-
Phaer feɪəʳ (US) feɪɚ, fer
Phaethon ˈfeɪ.ə.θən, ˈ-ɪ- (US) -ə.θɑːn, -θən
phaeton *carriage:* ˈfeɪ.tᵊn, -tɒn (US) ˈfeɪ.ə.t̬ən, ˈfeɪ.tᵊn **-s** -z
Phaeton *Greek mythology:* ˈfeɪ.ə.tᵊn, ˈ-ɪ- (US) -ə.tɑːn
phagocyte ˈfæg.əʊ.saɪt (US) -oʊ-, -ə- **-s** -s
phagocytosis ˌfæg.əʊ.saɪˈtəʊ.sɪs (US) -oʊ.saɪˈtoʊ-, ˌ-ə-
phalang|e ˈfæl.ændʒ; fəˈlændʒ (US) feɪˈlændʒ, fə-; ˈfæl.əndʒ **-es** -ɪz
phalanges *(alternative plur. of* **phalanx***)* fælˈæn.dʒiːz, fəˈlæn- (US) fə-, feɪ-
phalangist (P) fælˈæn.dʒɪst, fəˈlæn- (US) fə-, feɪ- **-s** -s
phalanster|y ˈfæl.ən.stᵊr|.i (US) -ster- **-ies** -iz
phalanx ˈfæl.æŋ*k*s (US) ˈfeɪ.læŋks, ˈfæl.æŋks **-es** -ɪz **phalanges** fælˈæn.dʒiːz, fəˈlæn- (US) fə-, feɪ-
Phalaris ˈfæl.ə.rɪs
phalarope ˈfæl.ə.rəʊp (US) -roʊp **-s** -s
phallic ˈfæl.ɪk
phallicism ˈfæl.ɪ.sɪ.zᵊm
phall|us ˈfæl|.əs **-uses** -ə.sɪz **-i** -aɪ
phanerogam ˈfæn.ᵊr.əʊ.gæm, fəˈner- (US) ˈfæn.ə.roʊ-, -ɚ.ə-; fəˈner.oʊ-, ˈ-ə- **-s** -z
phanerogamic ˌfæn.ᵊr.əʊˈgæm.ɪk, fəˌner- (US) ˌfæn.ə.roʊˈ-, -ɚ.əˈ-, fəˌner.oʊˈ-, -əˈ-
phanerogamous ˌfæn.ᵊrˈɒg.ə.məs (US) -əˈrɑː.gə-
phantasm ˈfæn.tæz.ᵊm **-s** -z
phantasmagoria ˌfæn.tæz.məˈgɔː.ri.ə, -təz-, -ˈgɒr.i- (US) -ˈgɔːr.i-
phantasmagoric ˌfæn.tæz.məˈgɒr.ɪk, -təz- (US) -ˈgɔːr.ɪk **-al** -ᵊl
phantasm|al fænˈtæz.m|ᵊl **-ally** -ᵊl.i **-ic** -ɪk
phantas|y ˈfæn.tə.s|i (US) -t̬ə- **-ies** -iz
phantom ˈfæn.təm (US) -t̬əm **-s** -z
pharaoh (P) ˈfeə.rəʊ (US) ˈfer.oʊ, ˈfær-, ˈfeɪ.roʊ **-s** -z
pharisaic (P) ˌfær.ɪˈseɪ.ɪk, -əˈ- (US) ˌfer.ɪˈ-, ˌfær- **-al** -ᵊl **-ally** -ᵊl.i, -li **-alness** -ᵊl.nəs, -nɪs
pharisaism (P) ˈfær.ɪ.seɪ.ɪ.zᵊm, ˈ-ə- (US) ˈfer.ɪ-, ˈfær-
pharisee (P) ˈfær.ɪ.siː, ˈ-ə- (US) ˈfer.ɪ-, ˈfær- **-s** -z
pharmaceutic ˌfɑː.məˈsjuː.tɪk, -ˈsuː-, -ˈkjuː- (US) ˌfɑːr.məˈsuː.t̬ɪ-, -ˈsjuː- **-al/s** -ᵊl/z **-ally** -ᵊl.i, -li **-s** -s
pharmacist ˈfɑː.mə.sɪst (US) ˈfɑːr- **-s** -s
pharmacolog|y ˌfɑː.məˈkɒl.ə.dʒ|i (US) ˌfɑːr.məˈkɑː.lə- **-ist/s** -ɪst/s
pharmacop(o)ei|a ˌfɑː.mə.kəˈpiː|.ə, -kəʊˈ- (US) ˌfɑːr.məˈkoʊ- **-as** -əz **-al** -ᵊl
pharmac|y ˈfɑː.mə.s|i (US) ˈfɑːr- **-ies** -iz
Pharos ˈfeə.rɒs, ˈfær.ɒs (US) ˈfer.ɑːs
pharyngal fəˈrɪŋ.gᵊl, færˈɪŋ- (US) fəˈrɪŋ-
pharyngeal ˌfær.ɪnˈdʒiː.əl; fəˈrɪn.dʒi.əl, færˈɪn- (US) fəˈrɪn.dʒi-; ˌfer.ɪnˈdʒiː-, ˌfær-

pharynges *(plur. of* **pharynx***)* fær'ɪn.dʒiːz, fə'rɪn- ⓤⓢ fə-
pharyngitis ˌfær.ɪn'dʒaɪ.tɪs ⓤⓢ ˌfer.ɪn'dʒaɪ.t̬ɪs, ˌfær-
pharynx 'fær.ɪŋks **-es** -ɪz **pharynges** fær'ɪn.dʒiːz, fə'rɪn- ⓤⓢ fə-
phas|e feɪz **-es** -ɪz **-ing** -ɪŋ **-ed** -d
phas|is 'feɪ.s|ɪs ⓤⓢ -s|ɪs, -z|ɪs **-es** -iːz
phatic 'fæt.ɪk ⓤⓢ 'fæt̬-
PhD ˌpiː.eɪtʃ'diː **-'s** -z
pheasant 'fez.ᵊnt **-s** -s
Phebe 'fiː.bi
Phelps felps
phenacetin fɪ'næs.ɪ.tɪn, fə-, fen'æs-, '-ə- ⓤⓢ fɪ'næs.ə-, -tən
Phenic|ia fɪ'nɪʃ|.ə, fə-, fiː-, -'niː.ʃ|ə, -ɪl.ə ⓤⓢ fə'nɪʃ|.ə, -'niː.ʃ|ə **-ian/s** -ᵊn/z
pheno- ˌfiː.nəʊ- ⓤⓢ ˌfiː.noʊ-, -nə-
phenobarbitone ˌfiː.nəʊ'bɑː.bɪ.təʊn, -bə- ⓤⓢ -noʊ'bɑːr.bɪ.toʊn, -nə'-
phenol 'fiː.nɒl ⓤⓢ -noʊl, -nɔːl, -nɑːl
phenolphthalein ˌfiː.nɒlf'θæl.iːn, -nɒl'-, -'θeɪ.li-, -i.ɪn ⓤⓢ -noʊl'θæl.iːn, -noʊlf'-, -iː.ɪn
phenom fɪ'nɒm, fə- ⓤⓢ -'nɑːm **-s** -z
phenomenologic|al fɪˌnɒm.ɪ.nə'lɒdʒ.ɪ.k|ᵊl, fə-, ˌ-ə- ⓤⓢ fəˌnɑː.mə.nə'lɑː.dʒɪ- **-ally** -ᵊl.i, -li
phenomenology fɪˌnɒm.ɪ'nɒl.ə.dʒi, fə-, -ə'- ⓤⓢ fəˌnɑː.mə'nɑː.lə-
phenomen|on fɪ'nɒm.ɪ.n|ən, fə-, '-ə- ⓤⓢ fə'nɑː.mə.n|ɑːn, -n|ən **-a** -ə **-al** -ᵊl **-ally** -ᵊl.i
phenotype 'fiː.nəʊ.taɪp ⓤⓢ -noʊ-, -nə-
pheromonal 'fer.ə.məʊ.nᵊl ⓤⓢ ˌfer.ə'moʊ-
pheromon|e 'fer.ə.məʊn ⓤⓢ -moʊn **-es** -s
phew ɸː, pɸː, fjuː
Note: Expression of surprise, or exclamation indicating that the speaker is hot. It may be a non-verbal exclamation, or have a spelling-based pronunciation /fjuː/.
phi faɪ **-s** -z
phial faɪəl **-s** -z
Phi Beta Kappa ˌfaɪˌbiː.tə'kæp.ə ⓤⓢ -ˌbeɪ.t̬ə'-, -ˌbiː-
Phidias 'faɪ.di.æs, 'fɪd.i- ⓤⓢ 'fɪd.i.əs
Phidippides faɪ'dɪp.ɪ.diːz
Phil fɪl
Philadelphi|a ˌfɪl.ə'del.fi|.ə ⓤⓢ -fi|.ə, -fj|ə **-an/s** -ən/z
philand|er fɪ'læn.d|əʳ, fə- ⓤⓢ fɪ'læn.d|ɚ **-ers** -əz ⓤⓢ -ɚz **-ering** -ᵊr.ɪŋ **-ered** -əd ⓤⓢ -ɚd **-erer/s** -ᵊr.əʳ/z ⓤⓢ -ɚ.ɚ/z
philanthrope 'fɪl.ən.θrəʊp, -æn- ⓤⓢ -ən.θroʊp **-s** -s
philanthropic ˌfɪl.ən'θrɒp.ɪk ⓤⓢ -æn'-, -ən'θrɑː.pɪk **-al** -ᵊl **-ally** -ᵊl.i, -li
philanthrop|y fɪ'lænt.θrə.p|i, fə- ⓤⓢ fə-, fɪ-, -θroʊ- **-ist/s** -ɪst/s
Philaster fɪ'læs.təʳ ⓤⓢ -tɚ
philatelic ˌfɪl.ə'tel.ɪk *stress shift:* ˌphilatelic 'club
philatel|y fɪ'læt.ᵊl|.i, fə- ⓤⓢ -'læt̬- **-ist/s** -ɪst/s
Philbrick 'fɪl.brɪk
Philby 'fɪl.bi
-phile, -phil -faɪl ⓤⓢ -faɪl, -fɪl
Note: Suffix. Normally unstressed, e.g. **francophile** /'fræŋ.kəʊ.faɪl ⓤⓢ -koʊ-/.
Philemon fɪ'liː.mɒn, faɪ-, fə-, -mən ⓤⓢ fɪ'liː.mən, faɪ-
Philharmonia ˌfɪl.*h*ɑː'məʊ.ni.ə, -ə'- ⓤⓢ -hɑːr'moʊ-, -ɚ'-
philharmonic (P) ˌfɪl.*h*ɑː'mɒn.ɪk, -ə'- ⓤⓢ -hɑːr'mɑː.nɪk, -ɚ'- **-s** -s *stress shift:* ˌphilharmonic 'orchestra
philhellene fɪl'hel.iːn, '--- ⓤⓢ fɪl'hel- **-s** -z
philhellenic ˌfɪl.hel'iː.nɪk, -hə'liː-, -'len.ɪk ⓤⓢ -hə'len-
philhellenism fɪl'hel.ɪ.nɪ.zᵊm, '-ə- ⓤⓢ '-ə-
-philia -'fɪl.i.ə ⓤⓢ -'fɪl.i.ə, '-jə
Note: Suffix. Words containing **-philia** are normally stressed on /-'fɪl-/, e.g. **haemophilia** /ˌhiː.mə'fɪl.i.ə ⓤⓢ -moʊ'-/.
-philiac -'fɪl.i.æk
Note: Suffix. Words containing **-philiac** are normally stressed on the antepenultimate syllable, e.g. **haemophiliac** /ˌhiː.mə'fɪl.i.æk ⓤⓢ -moʊ'-/.
Philip 'fɪl.ɪp **-s** -s
Philippa 'fɪl.ɪ.pə, '-ə-
Philippi fɪ'lɪp.aɪ, fə-; 'fɪl.ɪ.paɪ, '-ə- ⓤⓢ fɪ'lɪp.aɪ
Philippian fɪ'lɪp.i.ən, fə- **-s** -z
philippic fɪ'lɪp.ɪk, fə- **-s** -s
Philippine 'fɪl.ɪ.piːn, '-ə-, -paɪn, ˌ--'- ⓤⓢ 'fɪl.ə.piːn **-s** -z
Philippoussis ˌfɪl.ɪ'puː.sɪs, -ə'-
Philipps 'fɪl.ɪps
Philistia fɪ'lɪs.ti.ə, fə- ⓤⓢ fə-
philistine (P) 'fɪl.ɪ.staɪn, '-ə- ⓤⓢ 'fɪl.ɪ.stiːn, -staɪn; fɪ'lɪs.tɪn, -tiːn **-s** -z
philistinism 'fɪl.ɪ.stɪ.nɪ.zᵊm, '-ə- ⓤⓢ 'fɪl.ɪ.stiː-, -staɪ-; fɪ'lɪs.tɪ-
Phillimore 'fɪl.ɪ.mɔːʳ ⓤⓢ -mɔːr
Phillip(p)s 'fɪl.ɪps
Phillpot 'fɪl.pɒt ⓤⓢ -pɑːt **-s** -s
phillumenist fɪ'luː.mə.nɪst, fə-, -'ljuː-, -mɪ- ⓤⓢ -'luː.mə- **-s** -s
philo- fɪl.əʊ-; fɪ'lɒ-, fə- ⓤⓢ fɪl.oʊ-, -ə-; fɪ'lɑː-, fə-
Note: Prefix. Normally either takes primary or secondary stress on the first syllable, e.g. **philosophic** /ˌfɪl.ə'sɒf.ɪk ⓤⓢ -'sɑː.fɪk/, or primary stress on the second syllable, e.g. **philosophy** /fɪ'lɒs.ə.fi ⓤⓢ -'lɑː.sə-/.
Philoctetes ˌfɪl.ək'tiː.tiːz, -ɒk'- ⓤⓢ -ək'-, -ɑːk'-
philodendron ˌfɪl.ə'den.drən **-s** -z
philologic ˌfɪl.ə'lɒdʒ.ɪk ⓤⓢ -'lɑː.dʒɪk **-al** -ᵊl **-ally** -ᵊl.i, -li
philolog|y fɪ'lɒl.ə.dʒ|i, fə- ⓤⓢ fɪ'lɑː.lə- **-ist/s** -ɪst/s
Philomel 'fɪl.əʊ.mel ⓤⓢ -oʊ- **-s** -z
Philomela ˌfɪl.əʊ'miː.lə ⓤⓢ -oʊ'-
Philomena ˌfɪl.əʊ'miː.nə ⓤⓢ -oʊ'-
philosopher fɪ'lɒs.ə.fəʳ, fə- ⓤⓢ -'lɑː.sə.fɚ **-s** -z
philosophic ˌfɪl.ə'sɒf.ɪk ⓤⓢ -ə'sɑː.fɪk, -oʊ'- **-al** -ᵊl **-ally** -ᵊl.i, -li *stress shift:* ˌphilosophic 'view
philosoph|ism fɪ'lɒs.ə.f|ɪ.zᵊm, fə- ⓤⓢ -'lɑː.sə- **-ist/s** -ɪst/s
philosophiz|e, -is|e fɪ'lɒs.ə.faɪz, fə- ⓤⓢ -'lɑː.sə- **-es** -ɪz **-ing** -ɪŋ **-ed** -d
philosoph|y fɪ'lɒs.ə.f|i, fə- ⓤⓢ -'lɑː.sə- **-ies** -iz
Philostratus fɪ'lɒs.trə.təs, fə- ⓤⓢ fɪ'lɑː.strə.t̬əs
Philotas 'fɪl.ə.tæs
Philpot 'fɪl.pɒt ⓤⓢ -pɑːt
Philpotts 'fɪl.pɒts ⓤⓢ -pɑːts
philtre, philter 'fɪl.təʳ ⓤⓢ -t̬ɚ **-s** -z
Phineas 'fɪn.i.əs, -æs ⓤⓢ -əs
Phipps fɪps
phiz (P) fɪz
Phizackerley fɪ'zæk.ᵊl.i, fə- ⓤⓢ -ɚ.li
phizog 'fɪz.ɒg ⓤⓢ -ɑːg
phlebitic flɪ'bɪt.ɪk, fleb'ɪt- ⓤⓢ fliː'bɪt̬.ɪk, flɪ-
phlebitis flɪ'baɪ.tɪs, fleb'aɪ- ⓤⓢ fliː'baɪ.t̬ɪs, flɪ-
phlebotomy flɪ'bɒt.ə.mi, fleb'ɒt- ⓤⓢ fliː'bɑː.t̬ə-, flɪ-
Phlegethon 'fleg.ɪ.θɒn, '-ə-, -θən ⓤⓢ -ɪ.θɑːn, 'fledʒ-
phlegm flem **-s** -z
phlegmatic fleg'mæt.ɪk ⓤⓢ -'mæt̬- **-al** -ᵊl **-ally** -ᵊl.i, -li
phloem 'fləʊ.em, -ɪm ⓤⓢ 'floʊ.em
phlogistic flɒdʒ'ɪs.tɪk, flɒg-, flə'dʒɪs-, flə'gɪs- ⓤⓢ floʊ'dʒɪs-
phlogiston flɒdʒ'ɪs.tən, flɒg-, flə'dʒɪs-, flə'gɪs-, -tɒn ⓤⓢ floʊ'dʒɪs.tɑːn, -tən
phlox flɒks ⓤⓢ flɑːks **-es** -ɪz
Phnom Penh ˌnɒm'pen, pəˌnɒm- ⓤⓢ ˌnɑːm-
-phobe -fəʊb ⓤⓢ -foʊb
Note: Suffix. Normally unstressed, e.g. **technophobe** /'tek.nəʊ.fəʊb ⓤⓢ -nə.foʊb/.
phob|ia 'fəʊ.b|i.ə ⓤⓢ 'foʊ- **-ias** -i.əz **-ic** -ɪk
-phobia -'fəʊ.bi.ə ⓤⓢ -'foʊ.bi.ə

Phone

A unit at the phonetic level in the study of speech. The term PHONEME is very widely used for a contrastive unit of sound in language. However, a term is also needed for a unit at the phonetic level, since there is not always a one-to-one correspondence between units at the two levels.

Examples for English

The English word *can't* is phonemically /kɑːnt/ in British English and /kænt/ in US English (4 phonemic units), but may be pronounced [kɑ̃ːt] or [kæ̃t] with the nasal consonant phoneme absorbed into the preceding vowel as NASALISATION (3 phonetic units).

Phoneme

A fundamental unit of phonology, usually said to be the smallest unit of speech. It has been defined and used in many different ways.

Examples for English

Virtually all theories of phonology hold that spoken language can be broken down into a string of sound units (phonemes), and that each language has a small, relatively fixed set of these phonemes. Most phonemes can be put into groups; for example, in English we can identify a group of PLOSIVE phonemes /p t k b d g/, a group of voiceless FRICATIVES /f θ s ʃ h/, and so on.

An important question in phoneme theory is how the analyst can establish what the phonemes of a language are.

The most widely accepted view is that phonemes are 'contrastive' and one must find cases where the difference between two words is dependent on the difference between two phonemes. For example, we can prove that the difference between *pin* and *pan* depends on the vowel, and that /ɪ/ and /æ/ are different phonemes.

Pairs of words that differ in just one phoneme are known as 'minimal pairs'. We can establish the same fact about /p/ and /b/ by citing *pin* and *bin*.

Tests like these are called 'commutation tests' and can only be carried out when a provisional list of possible phonemes has been established, so some basic phonetic analysis must precede this stage.

Note: Suffix. Words containing -**phobia** are normally stressed on the antepenultimate syllable, e.g. **arachnophobia** /əˌræk.nəʊˈfəʊ.bi.ə ⓤⓢ -ˈfoʊ-/.

-phobic -ˈfəʊ.bɪk ⓤⓢ -ˈfoʊ.bɪk

Note: Suffix. Words containing -**phobic** are normally stressed on the penultimate syllable, e.g. **claustrophobic** /ˌklɔː.strəˈfəʊ.bɪk ⓤⓢ ˌklɑː.strəˈfoʊ-/.

Phocian ˈfəʊ.ʃi.ən, -si- ⓤⓢ ˈfoʊ.si- **-s** -z

Phocion ˈfəʊ.si.ən, -ɒn ⓤⓢ ˈfoʊ.si.ɑːn

Phocis ˈfəʊ.sɪs ⓤⓢ ˈfoʊ-

Phoebe ˈfiː.bi

Phoebus ˈfiː.bəs

Phoenic|ia fɪˈnɪʃ|.ə, fə-, fiː-, -ˈniː.ʃ|ə, -i|.ə ⓤⓢ fəˈnɪʃ|.ə, -ˈniː.ʃ|ə **-ian/s** -ən/z

phoenix (P) ˈfiː.nɪks **-es** -ɪz

phon fɒn ⓤⓢ fɑːn **-s** -z

phonaesthesia ˌfəʊ.nɪsˈθiː.zi.ə, -niːsˈ-, -nəsˈ-, -ʒi.ə, -ʒə ⓤⓢ ˌfoʊ.nɪsˈθiː.ʒə, -niːsˈ-, -nəsˈ-

pho|nate fəʊ|ˈneɪt ⓤⓢ ˈfoʊ|.neɪt **-nates** -ˈneɪts ⓤⓢ -neɪts **-nating** -ˈneɪ.tɪŋ ⓤⓢ -neɪ.t̬ɪŋ **-nated** -ˈneɪ.tɪd ⓤⓢ -neɪ.t̬ɪd

phonation fəʊˈneɪ.ʃən ⓤⓢ foʊ-

phonatory ˈfəʊ.nə.tər.i, fəʊˈneɪ- ⓤⓢ ˈfoʊ.nə.tɔːr-

phon|e fəʊn ⓤⓢ foʊn **-es** -z **-ing** -ɪŋ **-ed** -d ˈ**phone** ˌ**book**; ˈ**phone** ˌ**booth**; ˈ**phone** ˌ**box**; ˈ**phone** ˌ**call**

phonecard ˈfəʊn.kɑːd, ˈfəʊŋ- ⓤⓢ ˈfoʊn.kɑːrd **-s** -z

phone-in ˈfəʊn.ɪn ⓤⓢ ˈfoʊn- **-s** -z

phonematic ˌfəʊ.nɪˈmæt.ɪk, -niːˈ- ⓤⓢ ˌfoʊ.nɪˈmæt̬- **-s** -s **-ally** -əl.i, -li

phoneme ˈfəʊ.niːm ⓤⓢ ˈfoʊ- **-s** -z

phonemic fəʊˈniː.mɪk ⓤⓢ foʊ-, fə- **-s** -s **-ally** -əl.i, -li

phonemicist fəʊˈniː.mɪ.sɪst, -mə- ⓤⓢ foʊ-, fə- **-s** -s

phone-tapping ˈfəʊnˌtæp.ɪŋ ⓤⓢ ˈfoʊn-

phonetic fəʊˈnet.ɪk ⓤⓢ foʊˈnet̬-, fə- **-ally** -əl.i, -li **-s** -s

phonetician ˌfəʊ.nɪˈtɪʃ.ən, ˌfɒn.ɪˈ-, -əˈ- ⓤⓢ ˌfoʊ.nəˈ- **-s** -z

phoneticiz|e, -is|e fəʊˈnet.ɪ.saɪz, ˈ-ə- ⓤⓢ foʊˈnet̬-, fə- **-es** -ɪz **-ing** -ɪŋ **-ed** -d

phonetist ˈfəʊ.nɪ.tɪst, -nə-, -net.ɪst ⓤⓢ ˈfoʊ.nə.t̬ɪst **-s** -s

phon|ey ˈfəʊ.n|i ⓤⓢ ˈfoʊ- **-ier** -i.ər ⓤⓢ -i.ɚ **-iest** -i.ɪst, -i.əst **-ily** -ɪ.li, -əl.i **-eys** -iz **-iness** -ɪ.nəs, -ɪ.nɪs

phonic ˈfɒn.ɪk ⓤⓢ ˈfɑː.nɪk

phonics ˈfɒn.ɪks ⓤⓢ ˈfɑː.nɪks

phono- fəʊ.nəʊ-, fɒn.əʊ-; fəʊˈnɒ- ⓤⓢ foʊ.nə-, fɑː-, -noʊ-; foʊˈnɑː-, fə-

Note: Prefix. Normally either takes primary or secondary stress on the first syllable, e.g. **phonogram** /ˈfəʊ.nə.græm ⓤⓢ ˈfoʊ.nə-/, **phonographic** /ˌfəʊ.nəˈgræf.ɪk ⓤⓢ ˌfoʊ.nəˈ-/, or primary stress on the second syllable, e.g. **phonology** /fəʊˈnɒl.ə.dʒi ⓤⓢ fəˈnɑː.lə-/.

phonogram ˈfəʊ.nə.græm ⓤⓢ ˈfoʊ- **-s** -z

phonograph ˈfəʊ.nə.grɑːf, -græf ⓤⓢ ˈfoʊ.nə.græf **-s** -s

phonographer fəʊˈnɒg.rə.fər ⓤⓢ foʊˈnɑː.grə.fɚ, fə- **-s** -z

phonographic ˌfəʊ.nəˈgræf.ɪk ⓤⓢ ˌfoʊˈ- **-al** -əl **-ally** -əl.i, -li *stress shift:* ˌphonographic ˈsystem

phonographist fəʊˈnɒg.rə.fɪst ⓤⓢ foʊˈnɑː.grə-, fə- **-s** -s

phonography fəʊˈnɒg.rə.fi ⓤⓢ foʊˈnɑː.grə-, fə-

phonological ˌfəʊ.nəˈlɒdʒ.ɪ.kəl, ˌfɒn.əˈ-, -əlˈɒdʒ- ⓤⓢ ˌfoʊ.nəˈlɑː.dʒɪ-, -noʊˈ- **-ly** -i *stress shift:* ˌphonological ˈtheory

Phonetics

The scientific study of speech. It has a long history, going back certainly to well over two thousand years ago. The central concerns in phonetics are the discovery of how speech sounds are produced, how they are used in spoken language, how we can record speech sounds with written symbols and how we hear and recognise different sounds.

In the first of these areas, when we study the production of speech sounds we can observe what speakers do ('articulatory' observation) and we can try to feel what is going on inside our vocal tract ('kinaesthetic' observation). The second area is where phonetics overlaps with PHONOLOGY: usually in phonetics we are only interested in sounds that are used in meaningful speech, and phoneticians are interested in discovering the range and variety of sounds used in this way in all the known languages of the world. This is sometimes known as 'linguistic phonetics'. Thirdly, there has always been a need for agreed conventions for using phonetic symbols that represent speech sounds; the International Phonetic Association has played a very important role in this. Finally, the 'auditory' aspect of speech is very important. The ear is capable of making fine discrimination between different sounds, and sometimes it is not possible to define in articulatory terms precisely what the difference is. A good example of this is in vowel classification. While it is important to know the position and shape of the tongue and lips, it is often very important to have been trained in an agreed set of standard auditory qualities that vowels can be reliably related to (see CARDINAL VOWEL). Another important area is acoustic phonetics which studies the physical properties of speech sounds.

Phonology

The study of the sound systems of languages.

The most basic activity in phonology is 'phonemic analysis', in which the objective is to establish what the PHONEMES are and arrive at the 'phonemic inventory' of the language. Very few phonologists have ever believed that this would be an adequate analysis of the sound system of a language: it is necessary to go beyond this. One can look at 'suprasegmental' phonology – the study of STRESS, RHYTHM and INTONATION. One can go beyond the phoneme and look into the detailed characteristics of each unit in terms of 'distinctive features'. The way in which sounds can combine in a language is studied in 'phonotactics' and in the analysis of syllable structure.

For some phonologists the most important area is the relationships between the different phonemes – how they form groups, the nature of the contrasts between them and how those oppositions may be neutralised (see NEUTRALISATION). For others, the most important activity is to discover the rules which affect the phonemes of the language and the way they are produced, and to express these rules as economically as possible.

phonologist fəʊˈnɒl.ə.dʒɪst (US) fəˈnɑː.lə-, foʊ- **-s** -s

phonolog|y fəʊˈnɒl.ə.dʒ|i (US) fəˈnɑː.lə-, foʊ- **-ies** -iz

phonotactic ˌfəʊ.nəʊˈtæk.tɪk, ˌfɒn.əʊˈ- (US) ˌfoʊ.nəˈ-, -noʊˈ- **-s** -s **-ally** -ᵊl.i, -li *stress shift:* ˌphonotactic ˈrules

phonotype ˈfəʊ.nəʊ.taɪp (US) ˈfoʊ.nə-, -noʊ- **-s** -s

phon|y ˈfəʊ.n|i (US) ˈfoʊ- **-ier** -i.əʳ (US) -i.ɚ **-iest** -i.ɪst, -i.əst **-ily** -ɪ.li, -ᵊl.i **-ies** -iz **-iness** -ɪ.nəs, -ɪ.nɪs

phosgene ˈfɒz.dʒiːn, ˈfɒs- (US) ˈfɑːs-, ˈfɑːz-

phosphate ˈfɒs.feɪt, -fɪt, -fət (US) ˈfɑːs.feɪt **-s** -s

phosphene ˈfɒs.fiːn (US) ˈfɑːs-, ˈfɑːz- **-s** -z

phosphide ˈfɒs.faɪd (US) ˈfɑːs- **-s** -z

phosphite ˈfɒs.faɪt (US) ˈfɑːs- **-s** -s

phospho- ˌfɒs.fəʊ- (US) ˌfɑːs.foʊ-, -fə-

phosphor ˈfɒs.fəʳ (US) ˈfɑːs.fɚ, -fɔːr **-s** -z

phosphoresc|e ˌfɒs.fᵊrˈes (US) ˌfɑːs.fəˈres **-es** -ɪz **-ing** -ɪŋ **-ed** -t

phosphorescence ˌfɒs.fᵊrˈes.ᵊn*t*s (US) ˌfɑːs.fəˈres-

phosphorescent ˌfɒs.fᵊrˈes.ᵊnt (US) ˌfɑːs.fəˈres- *stress shift:* ˌphosphorescent ˈink

phosphoric fɒsˈfɒr.ɪk (US) fɑːsˈfɔːr-

phosphorous ˈfɒs.fᵊr.əs (US) ˈfɑːs-; fɑːsˈfɔːr-

phosphorus ˈfɒs.fᵊr.əs (US) ˈfɑːs-

phossy ˈfɒs.i (US) ˈfɑː.si

photic ˈfəʊ.tɪk (US) ˈfoʊ.t̬ɪk

photo ˈfəʊ.təʊ (US) ˈfoʊ.t̬oʊ **-s** -z **ˌphoto ˈfinish**

photocall ˈfəʊ.təʊ.kɔːl (US) ˈfoʊ.t̬oʊ- **-s** -z

photocell ˈfəʊ.təʊ.sel (US) ˈfoʊ.t̬oʊ- **-s** -z

photochemical ˌfəʊ.təʊˈkem.ɪ.kᵊl (US) ˌfoʊ.t̬oʊ-

photochrome ˈfəʊ.təʊ.krəʊm (US) ˈfoʊ.t̬oʊ.kroʊm **-s** -z

photocompos|e ˌfəʊ.təʊ.kəmˈpəʊz (US) ˌfoʊ.t̬oʊ.kəmˈpoʊz **-es** -ɪz **-ing** -ɪŋ **-ed** -d

photocomposition ˌfəʊ.təʊˌkɒm.pəˈzɪʃ.ᵊn (US) ˌfoʊ.t̬oʊˌkɑːm.pəˈ- **-s** -z

photocopier ˈfəʊ.təʊˌkɒp.i.əʳ, ˌfəʊ.təʊˈkɒp.i.əʳ (US) ˈfoʊ.t̬oʊˌkɑː.pi.ɚ, -t̬əˌ- **-s** -z

photocop|y ˈfəʊ.təʊˌkɒp|.i (US) ˈfoʊ.t̬oʊˌkɑː.p|i, -t̬əˌ- **-ies** -iz **-ying** -i.ɪŋ **-ied** -id

photoelectric ˌfəʊ.təʊ.ɪˈlek.trɪk (US) ˌfoʊ.t̬oʊ- *stress shift:* ˌphotoelectric ˈcell

photo-essay ˈfəʊ.təʊˌes.eɪ (US) ˌfoʊ.t̬oʊ- **-s** -z

Photofit® ˈfəʊ.təʊ.fɪt (US) ˈfoʊ.t̬oʊ-

photogenic ˌfəʊ.təʊˈdʒen.ɪk, -ˈdʒiː.nɪk US ˌfoʊ.t̬oʊˈdʒen.ɪk, -t̬əˈ- *stress shift:* ˌphotogenic ˈperson

photogrammetr|ist ˌfəʊ.təʊˈɡræm.ə.tr|ɪst, ˈ-ɪ- US ˌfoʊ.t̬oʊ- **-ists** -ɪsts **-y** -i

photograph ˈfəʊ.tə.ɡrɑːf, -ɡræf US ˈfoʊ.t̬oʊ.ɡræf, -t̬ə- **-s** -s **-ing** -ɪŋ **-ed** -t

photographer fəˈtɒɡ.rə.fəʳ US -ˈtɑː.ɡrə.fɚ **-s** -z

photographic ˌfəʊ.təˈɡræf.ɪk US ˌfoʊ.t̬əˈ- **-al** -ᵊl **-ally** -ᵊl.i, -li *stress shift:* ˌphotographic ˈmodel

photography fəˈtɒɡ.rə.fi US -ˈtɑː.ɡrə-

photogravure ˌfəʊ.təʊ.ɡrəˈvjʊəʳ, -ˈvjɔːʳ US ˌfoʊ.t̬oʊ.ɡrəˈvjʊr, -t̬ə- **-s** -z

photojournal|ism ˌfəʊ.təʊˈdʒɜː.nᵊl|.ɪ.zᵊm US ˌfoʊ.t̬oʊˈdʒɝː- **-ist/s** -ɪst/s

photomontag|e ˌfəʊ.təʊ.mɒnˈtɑːʒ US ˌfoʊ.t̬oʊ.mɑːnˈ- **-es** -ɪz

photon ˈfəʊ.tɒn US ˈfoʊ.tɑːn **-s** -z

photo-opportunit|y ˌfəʊ.təʊˌɒp.əˈtjuː.nə.t|i, -ˈtʃuː-, -nɪ- US ˌfoʊ.t̬oʊˌɑː.pɚˈtuː.nə.t̬|i, -ˈtjuː- **-ies** -iz

photosensitive ˌfəʊ.təʊˈsent.sɪ.tɪv, -sə- US ˌfoʊ.t̬oʊˈsent.sə-

photosensitivity ˌfəʊ.təʊˌsent.sɪˈtɪv.ə.ti, -səˈ-, -ə.ti US ˌfoʊ.t̬oʊˌsent.səˈt̬ɪv.ə.t̬i

photosensitiz|e, -is|e ˌfəʊ.təʊˈsent.sɪ.taɪz US ˌfoʊ.t̬oʊˈsent.sə- **-es** -ɪz **-ing** -ɪŋ **-ed** -d

photosphere ˈfəʊ.təʊ.sfɪəʳ US ˈfoʊ.t̬oʊ.sfɪr **-s** -z

photo|stat® ˈfəʊ.təʊ|.stæt US ˈfoʊ.t̬oʊ-, -t̬ə- **-stats** -stæts **-statting** -stæt.ɪŋ US -stæt̬.ɪŋ **-statted** -stæt.ɪd US -stæt̬.ɪd

photostatic ˌfəʊ.təʊˈstæt.ɪk US ˌfoʊ.t̬oʊˈstæt̬.ɪk, -t̬əˈ- *stress shift:* ˌphotostatic ˈcopy

photosynthesis ˌfəʊ.təʊˈsɪnt.θə.sɪs, -θɪ- US ˌfoʊ.t̬oʊˈ-, -t̬əˈ-

photosynthesiz|e, -is|e ˌfəʊ.təʊˈsɪnt.θə.saɪz, -θɪ- US ˌfoʊ.t̬oʊˈ-, -t̬əˈ- **-es** -ɪz **-ing** -ɪŋ **-ed** -d

photosynthetic ˌfəʊ.təʊ.sɪnˈθet.ɪk US ˌfoʊ.t̬oʊ.sɪnˈθet̬-, -t̬ə- **-ally** -ᵊl.i, -li

phototropic ˌfəʊ.təʊˈtrɒp.ɪk US ˌfoʊ.t̬oʊˈtrɑː.pɪk, -t̬əˈ-, -ˈtroʊ- **-ally** -ᵊl.i US -li

phototropism fəʊˈtɒt.rə.pɪ.zᵊm; ˌfəʊ.təʊˈtrəʊ- US foʊˈtɑː.trə- **-s** -z

phrasal ˈfreɪ.zᵊl **-s** -z ˌ**phrasal** ˈ**verb**

phras|e freɪz **-es** -ɪz **-ing** -ɪŋ **-ed** -d ˈ**phrase** ˌ**book**

phraseologic ˌfreɪ.zi.əˈlɒdʒ.ɪk US -ˈlɑː.dʒɪk **-al** -ᵊl **-ally** -ᵊl.i, -li

phraseolog|y ˌfreɪ.ziˈɒl.ə.dʒ|i US -ˈɑː.lə- **-ies** -iz

phrenetic frəˈnet.ɪk, frɪ-, frenˈet- US frɪˈnet̬-, frə- **-al** -ᵊl **-ally** -ᵊl.i, -li

phrenic ˈfren.ɪk

phrenologic|al ˌfren.ᵊlˈɒdʒ.ɪ.k|ᵊl US -əˈlɑː.dʒɪ- **-ally** -ᵊl.i, -li

phrenolog|y frɪˈnɒl.ə.dʒ|i, frə-, frenˈɒl- US frɪˈnɑː.lə-, frə- **-ist/s** -ɪst/s

Phryg|ia ˈfrɪdʒ|.i.ə **-ian/s** -i.ən/z US -i.ən/z, -jən/z

Phryne ˈfraɪ.ni

phthalic ˈθæl.ɪk, ˈfθæl-, ˈθeɪ.lɪk US ˈθæl-, ˈfθæl-

phthisis ˈθaɪ.sɪs, ˈfθaɪ- US ˈθaɪ-, ˈtaɪ-, ˈfθaɪ-

Phuket ˌpuːˈket

phut fʌt

phylacter|y fɪˈlæk.tᵊr|.i **-ies** -iz

Phyllis ˈfɪl.ɪs

phyllo ˈfaɪ.ləʊ, ˈfiː-, ˈfɪl.əʊ US ˈfiː.loʊ, ˈfaɪ- ˌ**phyllo** ˈ**pastry** US ˈ**phyllo** ˌ**pastry**

phylloxer|a fɪˈlɒk.sᵊr|.ə; ˌfɪl.ɒkˈsɪə.r|ə US fɪˈlɑːk.sɚ|.ə; ˌfɪl.ɑːkˈsɪr- **-ae** -iː **-as** -əz

phyl|um ˈfaɪ.l|əm **-a** -ə

physiatric ˌfɪz.iˈæt.rɪk **-s** -s **-al** -ᵊl

physiatricist ˌfɪz.iˈæt.rɪ.sɪst, -rə- **-s** -s

physic ˈfɪz.ɪk **-s** -s **-king** -ɪŋ **-ked** -t

physic|al ˈfɪz.ɪ.k|ᵊl **-als** -ᵊlz **-ally** -ᵊl.i, -li ˌ**physical eduˈcation**; ˌ**physical** ˈ**therapy**

physicality ˌfɪz.ɪˈkæl.ə.ti, -ɪ.ti US -ə.t̬i

physician fɪˈzɪʃ.ᵊn, fə- US fɪ- **-s** -z

physicist ˈfɪz.ɪ.sɪst, ˈ-ə- US ˈ-ɪ- **-s** -s

physio- fɪz.i.əʊ-; ˌfɪz.iˈɒ- US fɪz.i.oʊ-, -ə-; ˌfɪz.iˈɑː-

Note: Prefix. Normally either takes primary or secondary stress on the first syllable, e.g. **physiologic** /ˌfɪz.i.əˈlɒdʒ.ɪk US -ˈlɑː.dʒɪk/, or secondary stress on the first syllable with primary stress on the third syllable, e.g. **physiology** /ˌfɪz.iˈɒl.ə.dʒi US -ˈɑː.lə-/.

physio ˈfɪz.i.əʊ US -oʊ **-s** -z

physiognomic ˌfɪz.i.əˈnɒm.ɪk US -ɑːɡˈnɑː.mɪk, -əˈ- **-al** -ᵊl **-ally** -ᵊl.i, -li

physiognomist ˌfɪz.iˈɒn.ə.mɪst US -ˈɑːɡ.nə- **-s** -s

physiognom|y ˌfɪz.iˈɒn.ə.m|i US -ˈɑːɡ.nə- **-ies** -iz

physiographic ˌfɪz.i.əʊˈɡræf.ɪk US -oʊˈ-, -əˈ- **-al** -ᵊl

physiograph|y ˌfɪz.iˈɒɡ.rə.f|i US -ˈɑː.ɡrə- **-er/s** -əʳ/z US -ɚ/z

physiologic ˌfɪz.i.əˈlɒdʒ.ɪk US -ˈlɑː.dʒɪk **-al** -ᵊl **-ally** -ᵊl.i, -li

physiolog|y ˌfɪz.iˈɒl.ə.dʒ|i US -ˈɑː.lə- **-ist/s** -ɪst/s

physiotherap|y ˌfɪz.i.əʊˈθer.ə.p|i US -oʊˈ-, -əˈ- **-ist/s** -ɪst/s

physique fɪˈziːk, fə- US fɪ-

phytoplankton ˌfaɪ.təʊˈplæŋk.tən, -tɒn US -t̬oʊˈplæŋk.tən

pi paɪ **-s** -z

Piaf ˈpiː.æf, -ˈ- US ˈpiː.ɑːf, -ˈ-

piaff|e piˈæf, pjæf US pjæf **-es** -s **-ing** -ɪŋ **-ed** -t

Piaget piˈæʒ.eɪ, -ˈɑː.ʒeɪ US ˌpiː.əˈʒeɪ, pjɑːˈ-

pia mater ˌpaɪ.əˈmeɪ.təʳ, ˌpiː- US -ˈmeɪ.t̬ɚ, -ˈmɑː-

pianissimo ˌpiː.əˈnɪs.ɪ.məʊ, -ænˈɪs-, pjɑːˈnɪs-, ˌpiː.ɑːˈ-, pjænˈɪs-, pjəˈnɪs- US ˌpiː.əˈnɪs.ɪ.moʊ **-s** -z

Note: Among British professional musicians, /pjɑːˈnɪs-, ˌpɪ.ɑːˈ-, ˌpiː.əˈ-/ appear to be the most frequently used forms.

pianist ˈpiː.ə.nɪst, ˈpjɑː.nɪst, ˈpjæn.ɪst, piˈæn- US ˈpiː.ᵊn.ɪst; piˈæn-, ˈpjæn- **-s** -s

Note: British professional musicians generally pronounce /ˈpiː.ə.nɪst/.

piano *instrument:* piˈæn.əʊ, ˈpjæn-, ˈpjɑː.nəʊ, piˈɑː- US piˈæn.oʊ, ˈpjæn- **-s** -z **pi**ˌ**ano acˈcordion**; **piˈano** ˌ**bar**; **piˈano** ˌ**stool**

Note: The forms /ˈpjɑː.nəʊ, piˈɑː-/ are frequent among British professional musicians.

piano *softly:* ˈpjɑː.nəʊ, piˈɑː- US -noʊ **-s** -z

pianoforte piˌæn.əʊˈfɔː.teɪ, ˌpjæn-, ˌpjɑː.nəʊˈ-, piˌɑː-, -ti US piˌæn.oʊˈfɔːr.teɪ, -ti; -ˈæn.oʊ.fɔːrt **-s** -z

Pianola® ˌpiː.əˈnəʊ.lə, pjænˈəʊ-, ˌpiː.ænˈ- US ˌpiː.əˈnoʊ-, -ænˈoʊ- **-s** -z

piastre, piaster piˈæs.təʳ, -ˈɑː.stəʳ US -ˈæs.tɚ **-s** -z

piazza piˈæt.sə, -ˈɑːt- US -ˈɑːt.sə, -sɑː, -ˈɑː.zə, -ˈæt.sə, -ˈæz.ə **-s** -z

pibroch ˈpiː.brɒk, -brɒx US -brɑːk **-s** -s

pica ˈpaɪ.kə

picador ˈpɪk.ə.dɔːʳ US -dɔːr **-s** -z

picadores *(alternative plur. of* **picador***)* ˌpɪk.əˈdɔː.riːz US -ˈdɔːr.iːz

picaninn|y ˌpɪk.əˈnɪn|.i, ˈpɪk.ə.nɪ.n|i US ˈpɪk- **-ies** -iz

Picardy ˈpɪk.ə.di, ˈ-ɑː- US ˈ-ɚ-, ˈ-ɑːr-

picaresque ˌpɪk.ᵊrˈesk US -ɚˈ-

picaroon ˌpɪk.əˈruːn **-s** -z **-ing** -ɪŋ **-ed** -d

Picasso pɪˈkæs.əʊ US -ˈkɑː.soʊ, -ˈkæs.oʊ

picayun|e ˌpɪk.əˈjuːn, -eɪˈ-, -iˈ- US ˈpɪk.ə.juːn, ˌ--ˈ- **-es** -z **-ish** -ɪʃ

Piccadilly ˌpɪk.əˈdɪl.i *stress shift, see compound:* ˌ**Piccadilly** ˈ**Circus**

piccalilli ˌpɪk.əˈlɪl.i (US) ˈpɪk.ə.lɪl-

piccaninn|y ˌpɪk.əˈnɪn|.i, ˈpɪk.ə.nɪ.n|i (US) ˈpɪk- **-ies** -iz

piccolo ˈpɪk.ə.ləʊ (US) -loʊ **-s** -z

pick pɪk **-s** -s **-ing** -ɪŋ **-ed** -t **-er/s** -əʳ/z (US) -ɚ/z

pickaback ˈpɪk.ə.bæk

pickaninn|y ˌpɪk.əˈnɪn|.i, ˈpɪk.ə.nɪ.n|i (US) ˈpɪk- **-ies** -iz

pickax|(e) ˈpɪk.æks **-es** -ɪz **-ing** -ɪŋ **-ed** -t

pickerel ˈpɪk.ᵊr.ᵊl **-s** -z

Pickering ˈpɪk.ᵊr.ɪŋ

pick|et ˈpɪk|.ɪt **-ets** -ɪts **-eting** -ɪ.tɪŋ (US) -ɪ.t̬ɪŋ **-eted** -ɪ.tɪd (US) -ɪ.t̬ɪd **-er/s** -ɪ.təʳ/z (US) -ɪ.t̬ɚ/z ˈ**picket** ˌ**line**

Pickford ˈpɪk.fəd (US) -fɚd

pickings ˈpɪk.ɪŋz

pickl|e ˈpɪk.l̩ **-es** -z **-ing** -ɪŋ, ˈpɪk.lɪŋ **-ed** -d

Pickles ˈpɪk.l̩z

picklock ˈpɪk.lɒk (US) -lɑːk **-s** -s

pick-me-up ˈpɪk.mi.ʌp **-s** -s

pickpocket ˈpɪkˌpɒk.ɪt (US) -ˌpɑː.kɪt **-s** -s

pickup ˈpɪk.ʌp **-s** -s ˈ**pick-up** ˌ**truck**

Pickwick ˈpɪk.wɪk ˌ**Pickwick** ˈ**Papers** (US) ˈ**Pickwick** ˌ**Papers**

Pickwickian pɪkˈwɪk.i.ən

pick|y ˈpɪk|.i **-ier** -i.əʳ (US) -i.ɚ **-iest** -i.ɪst, -i.əst **-iness** -ɪ.nəs, -ɪ.nɪs

picnic ˈpɪk.nɪk **-s** -s **-king** -ɪŋ **-ked** -t **-ker/s** -əʳ/z (US) -ɚ/z

picot ˈpiː.kəʊ; -ˈ-, pɪˈkəʊ (US) ˈpiː.koʊ, -ˈ-

picotee ˌpɪk.əˈtiː (US) ˌpɪk.əˈtiː, ˈ--- **-s** -z

picric ˈpɪk.rɪk

Pict pɪkt **-s** -s

Pictish ˈpɪk.tɪʃ

pictogram ˈpɪk.təʊ.græm (US) -toʊ-, -tə- **-s** -z

pictograph ˈpɪk.təʊ.grɑːf, -græf (US) -toʊ.græf, -tə- **-s** -s

Picton ˈpɪk.tən

pictorial pɪkˈtɔː.ri.əl (US) -ˈtɔːr.i- **-ly** -i

pict|ure ˈpɪk.tʃ|əʳ (US) -tʃ|ɚ **-ures** -əz (US) -ɚz **-uring** -ᵊr.ɪŋ **-ured** -əd (US) -ɚd ˈ**picture** ˌ**book**; ˌ**picture** ˈ**postcard**; ˌ**picture** ˈ**window**

picturesque ˌpɪk.tʃᵊrˈesk **-ly** -li **-ness** -nəs, -nɪs

piddl|e ˈpɪd.l̩ **-es** -z **-ing** -ɪŋ, ˈpɪd.lɪŋ **-ed** -d **-er/s** -əʳ/z (US) -ɚ/z, ˈpɪd.ləʳ/z (US) -lɚ/z

piddling (*adj.*) ˈpɪd.l̩.ɪŋ, ˈpɪd.lɪŋ

pidgin (P) ˈpɪdʒ.ɪn **-s** -z

Pidsley ˈpɪdz.li

pie paɪ **-s** -z ˈ**pie** ˌ**chart**; **as** ˌ**easy as** ˈ**pie**; **have a** ˌ**finger in** ˌ**every** ˈ**pie**; **to** ˌ**eat** ˌ**humble** ˈ**pie**; ˌ**pie in the** ˈ**sky**

piebald ˈpaɪ.bɔːld (US) -bɔːld, -bɑːld **-s** -z

piec|e piːs **-es** -ɪz **-ing** -ɪŋ **-ed** -t ˈ**piece** ˌ**rate**; ˌ**piece of** ˈ**cake**

pièce(s) de résistance piˌes.də.rez.ɪˈstɑ̃ns, ˌpjes-, -rɪ.zɪˈ-, -rə- (US) ˌpjes.dəˌreɪ.ziːˈstɑ̃ːns

piecemeal ˈpiːs.miːl

piecework ˈpiːs.wɜːk (US) -wɝːk

piecrust ˈpaɪ.krʌst **-s** -s

pied paɪd ˌ**pied** ˈ**piper**

pied(s)-à-terre ˌpjeɪd.ɑːˈteəʳ, ˌpjed- (US) -ˈter

piedmont (P) ˈpiːd.mənt, -mɒnt (US) -mɑːnt

piedmontese (P) ˌpiːd.mənˈtiːz, -mɒnˈ- (US) -mɑːnˈ-

pie-eyed ˌpaɪˈaɪd *stress shift:* ˌpie-eyed ˈreveller

pier pɪəʳ (US) pɪr **-s** -z

pierc|e (P) pɪəs (US) pɪrs **-es** -ɪz **-ing/ly** -ɪŋ/li **-ed** -t **-er/s** -əʳ/z (US) -ɚ/z **-eable** -ə.bl̩

Piercy ˈpɪə.si (US) ˈpɪr-

pierglass ˈpɪə.glɑːs (US) ˈpɪr.glæs **-es** -ɪz

pierhead ˈpɪə.hed (US) ˈpɪr- **-s** -z

Pierian paɪˈer.i.ən, -ˈɪə.ri-, pi- (US) paɪˈɪr.i-

Pierpoint ˈpɪə.pɔɪnt (US) ˈpɪr-

Pierpont ˈpɪə.pɒnt, -pənt (US) ˈpɪr.pɑːnt

Pierre *name:* piˈeəʳ (US) piːˈer

Pierre *place in US:* pɪəʳ (US) pɪr

Pierrepont ˈpɪə.pɒnt, -pənt (US) ˈpɪr.pɑːnt

pierrot (P) ˈpɪə.rəʊ, ˈpjer.əʊ (US) ˌpiː.əˈroʊ **-s** -z

Piers pɪəz (US) pɪrz

Pierson ˈpɪə.sᵊn (US) ˈpɪr-

Piesporter ˈpiːz.pɔː.təʳ (US) -pɔːr.t̬ɚ

pietà ˌpiː.etˈɑː, -eɪˈtɑː, ˈ--- (US) ˌpiː.eɪˈtɑː, ˌpjeɪˈ- **-s** -z

Pietermaritzburg ˌpiː.təˈmær.ɪts.bɜːg (US) -t̬ɚˈmer.ɪts.bɝːg

piet|ism ˈpaɪə.t|ɪ.zᵊm, ˈpaɪ.ɪ- (US) ˈpaɪə- **-ist/s** -ɪst/s

pietistic ˌpaɪəˈtɪs.tɪk

piet|y ˈpaɪə.t|i, ˈpaɪ.ɪ- (US) ˈpaɪə.t̬|i **-ies** -iz

piezoelectric piˌet.səʊ.ɪˈlek.trɪk; ˌpiː.zəʊ-; paɪˌiː.zəʊ-; ˌpaɪ.ɪ- (US) paɪˌiː.zoʊ-; piːˌeɪ- **-al** -ᵊl

piezoelectricity piˌet.səʊˌel.ɪkˈtrɪs.ə.ti; ˌpiː.zəʊ-; paɪˌiː.zəʊ-; ˌpaɪ.ɪ-; -ˌiː.lekˈ-; -ɪˌlekˈ-; -ɪ.ti; (US) paɪˌiː.zoʊˌiː.lekˈtrɪs.ə.t̬i, -iːˌlekˈ-; piˌeɪ-

piffl|e ˈpɪf.l̩ **-es** -z **-ing** -ɪŋ, ˈpɪf.lɪŋ **-ed** -d

pig pɪg **-s** -z **-ging** -ɪŋ **-ged** -d ˈ**pig** ˌ**iron**; ˌ**make a** ˌ**pig's** ˈ**ear of**

pigeon ˈpɪdʒ.ən, -ɪn (US) -ən **-s** -z

pigeonhol|e (*n. v.*) ˈpɪdʒ.ən.həʊl, -ɪn- (US) -ən.hoʊl **-es** -z **-ing** -ɪŋ **-ed** -d

pigeon-toed ˌpɪdʒ.ənˈtəʊd, -ɪn- (US) ˈpɪdʒ.ən.toʊd *stress shift, British only:* ˌpigeon-toed ˈwalk

pigger|y ˈpɪg.ᵊr|.i **-ies** -iz

piggish ˈpɪg.ɪʃ **-ly** -li **-ness** -nəs, -nɪs

Piggott ˈpɪg.ət

pigg|y ˈpɪg|.i **-ies** -iz **-ier** -i.əʳ (US) -i.ɚ **-iest** -i.ɪst, -i.əst

piggyback ˈpɪg.i.bæk

piggybank ˈpɪg.i.bæŋk **-s** -s

pigheaded ˌpɪgˈhed.ɪd **-ly** -li **-ness** -nəs, -nɪs *stress shift:* ˌpigheaded ˈperson

piglet ˈpɪg.lət, -lɪt (US) -lɪt **-s** -s

pigment (*n.*) ˈpɪg.mənt **-s** -s

pigmen|t (*v.*) pɪgˈmen|t, ˈpɪg.mən|t (US) ˈpɪg.mən|t **-ts** -ts **-ting** -tɪŋ (US) -t̬ɪŋ **-ted** -tɪd (US) -t̬ɪd

pigmentation ˌpɪg.mənˈteɪ.ʃᵊn, -menˈ- **-s** -z

pigm|y ˈpɪg.m|i **-ies** -iz

pignut ˈpɪg.nʌt **-s** -s

Pigott ˈpɪg.ət

pigpen ˈpɪg.pen **-s** -z

pigskin ˈpɪg.skɪn **-s** -z

pig-sticking ˈpɪgˌstɪk.ɪŋ

pigst|y ˈpɪg.st|aɪ **-ies** -aɪz

pigswill ˈpɪg.swɪl

pigtail ˈpɪg.teɪl **-s** -z

Pikachu ˈpɪk.ə.tʃuː (US) ˈpiː.kə-

pike (P) paɪk **-s** -s ˌ**Pike's** ˈ**Peak**

pikelet ˈpaɪ.klət, -klɪt (US) -lɪt **-s** -s

piker ˈpaɪ.kəʳ (US) -kɚ **-s** -z

pikestaff ˈpaɪk.stɑːf (US) -stæf **-s** -s

pilaf(f) ˈpɪl.æf, ˈpiː.læf, -ˈ- (US) piːˈlɑːf, ˈ-- **-s** -s

pilaster pɪˈlæs.təʳ, pə- (US) pɪˈlæs.tɚ **-s** -z

Pilate ˈpaɪ.lət

Pilatus pɪˈlɑː.təs (US) pɪ-; piːˈlɑː.tʊs

pilau ˈpɪl.aʊ, ˈpiː.laʊ, -ˈ- (US) pɪˈlɔː, piː-, -ˈlaʊ, -ˈlɑː **-s** -z

pilchard ˈpɪl.tʃəd (US) -tʃɚd **-s** -z

pil|e paɪl **-es** -z **-ing** -ɪŋ **-ed** -d

pile-driv|er ˈpaɪlˌdraɪ.v|əʳ (US) -v|ɚ **-ers** -əz (US) -ɚz **-ing** -ɪŋ

pile-up ˈpaɪl.ʌp **-s** -s

pilf|er ˈpɪl.f|əʳ (US) -f|ɚ **-ers** -əz (US) -ɚz **-ering** -ᵊr.ɪŋ **-ered** -əd (US) -ɚd **-erer/s** -ᵊr.əʳ/z (US) -ɚ.ɚ/z

pilferage ˈpɪl.fᵊr.ɪdʒ

pilferous ˈpɪl.fᵊr.əs

Pilger ˈpɪl.dʒəʳ (US) -dʒɚ

pilgrim ˈpɪl.grɪm **-s** -z ˌ**Pilgrim** ˈ**Father**

pilgrimag|e ˈpɪl.grɪ.mɪdʒ, -grə- **-es** -ɪz

piling ˈpaɪ.lɪŋ **-s** -z

Pilkington ˈpɪl.kɪŋ.tən

pill pɪl **-s** -z **-ing** -ɪŋ **-ed** -d

pillag|e ˈpɪl.ɪdʒ **-es** -ɪz **-ing** -ɪŋ **-ed** -d **-er/s** -əʳ/z (US) -ɚ/z

pillar ˈpɪl.əʳ (US) -ɚ **-s** -z **-ed** -d **from** ˌ**pillar to** ˈ**post**

pillar-box ˈpɪl.ə.bɒks (US) -ɚ.bɑːks **-es** -ɪz

pillbox ˈpɪl.bɒks (US) -bɑːks **-es** -ɪz

pillion ˈpɪl.i.ən (US) ˈ-jən **-s** -z

pillock ˈpɪl.ək **-s** -s

pillor|y ˈpɪl.ᵊr|.i **-ies** -iz **-ying** -i.ɪŋ **-ied** -id

pillow ˈpɪl.əʊ US -oʊ **-s** -z **-ing** -ɪŋ **-ed** -d **ˈpillow ˌslip; ˈpillow ˌtalk**

pillowcas|e ˈpɪl.əʊ.keɪs US -oʊ- **-es** -ɪz

Pillsbury ˈpɪlz.bᵊr.i US -ˌber-

pilocarpine ˌpaɪ.ləʊˈkɑː.pɪn, -paɪn US ˌpaɪ.loʊˈkɑːr.piːn, ˌpɪl.oʊˈ-, -pɪn

pi|lot ˈpaɪ|.lət **-lots** -ləts **-loting** -lə.tɪŋ US -lə.t̬ɪŋ **-loted** -lə.tɪd US -lə.t̬ɪd **-lotage** -lə.tɪdʒ US -lə.t̬ɪdʒ **ˈpilot ˌlight**

Pilsen ˈpɪl.zᵊn, -sᵊn

pilsener (P) ˈpɪlz.nəʳ, ˈpɪl.snəʳ, -sᵊn.əʳ US ˈpɪlz.nɚ, ˈpɪl.snɚ

Pilsworth ˈpɪlz.wəθ, -wɜːθ US -wɚθ, -wɝːθ

Piltdown ˈpɪlt.daʊn

pilule ˈpɪl.juːl **-s** -z

pimento pɪˈmen.təʊ US -toʊ **-s** -z

pimiento pɪˈmjen.təʊ, -ˈmen- US -toʊ **-s** -z

Pimlico ˈpɪm.lɪ.kəʊ US -koʊ

Pimm pɪm **-'s** -z

pimp pɪmp **-s** -s **-ing** -ɪŋ **-ed** -t

pimpernel ˈpɪm.pə.nel, -nᵊl US -pɚ- **-s** -z

pimple ˈpɪm.pl̩ **-s** -z **-d** -d

pimpl|y ˈpɪm.pl̩|.i, ˈ-pl|i US ˈ-pl|i **-iness** -ɪ.nəs, -ɪ.nɪs

pin pɪn **-s** -z **-ning** -ɪŋ **-ned** -d **ˈpin ˌmoney; ˈpin ˌtuck; ˌpins and ˈneedles**

PIN pɪn **ˈPIN ˌnumber**

piña colada ˌpiː.nə.kəʊˈlɑː.də, -njə- US -njə.koʊˈ- **-s** -z

pinafore (P) ˈpɪn.ə.fɔːʳ US -fɔːr **-s** -z **ˈpinafore ˌdress**

piñata pɪnˈjɑː.tə US -t̬ə **-s** -z

pinball ˈpɪn.bɔːl, ˈpɪm- US ˈpɪn-, -bɑːl **-s** -z **ˈpinball maˌchine**

pince-nez *singular:* ˌpæ̃nsˈneɪ, ˌpæntsˈ-, ˌpɪntsˈ-, ˈ-ˌ- *plural:* -ˈneɪz

pincer ˈpɪnt.səʳ US -sɚ **-s** -z

pinch pɪntʃ **-es** -ɪz **-ing** -ɪŋ **-ed** -t **-er/s** -əʳ/z US -ɚ/z **ˌtake something with a ˌpinch of ˈsalt**

pinchbeck ˈpɪntʃ.bek **-s** -s

Pinches ˈpɪn.tʃɪz

pinch-hit ˈpɪntʃ.hɪt **-s** -s **-ting** -ɪŋ US -ˌhɪt̬.ɪŋ

Pinckney ˈpɪŋk.ni

pincushion ˈpɪnˌkʊʃ.ᵊn, ˈpɪŋ- US ˈpɪn- **-s** -z

Pindar ˈpɪn.dəʳ US -dɚ

Pindaric pɪnˈdær.ɪk US -ˈdær-, -ˈder- **-s** -s

Pindus ˈpɪn.dəs

pin|e paɪn **-es** -z **-ing** -ɪŋ **-ed** -d **ˈpine ˌcone; ˈpine ˌkernel; ˈpine ˌmarten; ˈpine ˌneedle; ˈpine ˌnut**

pineal ˈpɪn.i.əl; paɪˈniː- US ˈpɪn.i-

pineapple ˈpaɪ.næp.l̩ **-s** -z

Pinel pɪˈnel US pɪ-, ˌpiː-

Pinero pɪˈnɪə.rəʊ, -ˈneə- US -ˈnɪr.oʊ

piner|y ˈpaɪ.nᵊr|.i **-ies** -iz

pinetum paɪˈniː.təm US -t̬əm

pinewood (P) ˈpaɪn.wʊd **-s** -z

ping pɪŋ **-s** -z **-ing** -ɪŋ **-ed** -d **-er/s** -əʳ/z US -ɚ/z

ping-pong ˈpɪŋˌpɒŋ US -ˌpɑːŋ, -ˌpɔːŋ

pinhead ˈpɪn.hed **-s** -z **-ed** -ɪd

pinhole ˈpɪn.həʊl US -hoʊl **-s** -z **ˌpinhole ˈcamera**

pinion ˈpɪn.jən **-s** -z **-ing** -ɪŋ **-ed** -d

pink (P) pɪŋk **-s** -s **-ing** -ɪŋ **-ed** -t **-er** **-est** **ˌpink ˈgin; ˌpink ˈslip; ˈpinking ˌshears**

Pinker ˈpɪŋ.kəʳ US -kɚ

Pinkerton ˈpɪŋ.kə.tən US -kɚ.t̬ən

pink-eye ˈpɪŋk.aɪ **-d** -d

pinkie ˈpɪŋ.ki **-s** -z

pinkish ˈpɪŋ.kɪʃ

pinko ˈpɪŋ.kəʊ US -koʊ **-(e)s** -z

pink|y ˈpɪŋ.k|i **-ies** -iz

pinnac|e ˈpɪn.ɪs, -əs **-es** -ɪz

pinnacl|e ˈpɪn.ə.kl̩, ˈ-ɪ- **-es** -z **-ing** -ɪŋ, ˈpɪn.ə.klɪŋ, ˈ-ɪ- **-ed** -d

pinnate ˈpɪn.eɪt, -ɪt, -ət US -eɪt, -ɪt

pinner (P) ˈpɪn.əʳ US -ɚ **-s** -z

pinn|y ˈpɪn|.i **-ies** -iz

Pinocchio pɪˈnəʊ.ki.əʊ, -ˈnɒk.i- US pəˈnoʊ.ki.oʊ, pɪ-

Pinochet ˈpɪn.əʊ.ʃeɪ US ˈpiː.noʊ.ʃet, -ʃeɪ

pinoc(h)le ˈpiː.nʌk.l̩, -nɒk- US -nʌk-, -nɑː.kl̩

pinot ˈpiː.nəʊ, -ˈ- US piːˈnoʊ **-s** -z

Pinot Blanc ˌpiː.nəʊˈblɑ̃ːŋ US -noʊˈ-

Pinot Noir ˌpiː.nəʊˈnwɑːʳ US -noʊˈnwɑːr

pin|point ˈpɪn|.pɔɪnt, ˈpɪm- US ˈpɪn- **-points** -pɔɪnts **-pointing** -ˌpɔɪn.tɪŋ US -ˌpɔɪn.t̬ɪŋ **-pointed** -ˌpɔɪn.tɪd US -ˌpɔɪn.t̬ɪd

pinprick ˈpɪn.prɪk, ˈpɪm- US ˈpɪn- **-s** -s

Pinsent ˈpɪnt.sənt

pinstripe ˈpɪn.straɪp **-s** -s **-d** -t

pint paɪnt **-s** -s

pinta *pint of milk:* ˈpaɪn.tə US -t̬ə **-s** -z

pinta (P) *disease:* ˈpɪn.tə, ˈpiːn- US ˈpɪn.t̬ə, -tɑː

pintado pɪnˈtɑː.dəʊ US -doʊ **-(e)s** -z

pintail ˈpɪn.teɪl **-s** -z

Pinter ˈpɪn.təʳ US -t̬ɚ

Pinteresque ˌpɪn.tᵊrˈesk US -t̬ɚˈ-

pinto ˈpɪn.təʊ US -t̬oʊ **-(e)s** -z **ˈpinto bean**

pint-pot ˈpaɪnt.pɒt, ˌ-ˈ- US ˈpaɪnt.pɑːt **-s** -s

pint-size ˈpaɪnt.saɪz **-d** -d

pin-up ˈpɪn.ʌp **-s** -s

pinwheel ˈpɪn.hwiːl **-s** -z

pinxit ˈpɪŋk.sɪt

Pinxton ˈpɪŋk.stᵊn

Pioline ˌpiː.əʊˈliːn US ˌpiː.oʊˈliːn

pioneer (P) ˌpaɪəˈnɪəʳ US -ˈnɪr **-s** -z **-ing** -ɪŋ **-ed** -d

pious ˈpaɪ.əs **-ly** -li **-ness** -nəs, -nɪs

pip (P) pɪp **-s** -s **-ping** -ɪŋ **-ped** -t

pipal ˈpiː.pᵊl **-s** -z

pip|e (P) paɪp **-es** -s **-ing** -ɪŋ **-ed** -t **-er/s** -əʳ/z US -ɚ/z **ˈpipe ˌcleaner; ˈpipe ˌdream; ˌpipe of ˈpeace**

pipeclay ˈpaɪp.kleɪ

pipeline ˈpaɪp.laɪn **-s** -z

Piper ˈpaɪ.pəʳ US -pɚ

pipette pɪˈpet US paɪ-, pɪ- **-s** -s

piping ˈpaɪ.pɪŋ

pipistrel(le) ˌpɪp.ɪˈstrel, -əˈ-, ˈ--- US ˌpɪp.ɪˈstrel **-s** -z

pipit ˈpɪp.ɪt **-s** -s

pipkin ˈpɪp.kɪn **-s** -z

Pippa ˈpɪp.ə

pippin ˈpɪp.ɪn **-s** -z

pipsqueak ˈpɪp.skwiːk **-s** -s

piquancy ˈpiː.kənt.si

piquant ˈpiː.kənt, -kɑːnt **-ly** -li

piqu|e piːk **-es** -s **-ing** -ɪŋ **-ed** -t

piqué ˈpiː.keɪ US -ˈ-

piquet *card game:* piːˈket, -ˈkeɪ; ˈpɪk.et, -eɪ US piːˈkeɪ, -ˈket

piquet *soldiers:* ˈpɪk.ɪt **-s** -s

Piquet *racing driver:* ˈpiː.keɪ

pirac|y ˈpaɪə.rə.s|i US ˈpaɪ- **-ies** -iz

Piraeus paɪˈriː.əs, pɪˈreɪ-, pə- US paɪˈriː-

Pirandello ˌpɪr.ᵊnˈdel.əʊ US -oʊ

piranha pɪˈrɑː.nə, pə-, -njə US pəˈrɑː.njə, pɪ-, -nə **-s** -z

pira|te ˈpaɪə.rə|t, -rɪt US ˈpaɪ.rə|t **-tes** -ts **-ting** -tɪŋ US -t̬ɪŋ **-ted** -tɪd US -t̬ɪd

piratical paɪəˈræt.ɪ.kᵊl, pə-, pɪ- US paɪˈræt̬- **-ly** -i

Pirbright ˈpɜː.braɪt US ˈpɝː-

Pirelli® pɪˈrel.i, pə-

Pirie ˈpɪr.i

pirogue pɪˈrəʊg, pə- US -ˈroʊg **-s** -z

pirou|ette ˌpɪr.u|ˈet **-ettes** -ˈets **-etting** -ˈet.ɪŋ US -ˈet̬.ɪŋ **-etted** -ˈet.ɪd US -ˈet̬.ɪd *stress shift:* ˌpirouetting ˈdancer

Pisa ˈpiː.zə

pis aller ˌpiːzˈæl.eɪ, ˌ--ˈ- US -ælˈeɪ **-s** -z

Piscator pɪˈskeɪ.təʳ US -ˈskɑː.tɔːr

piscatorial ˌpɪs.kəˈtɔː.ri.əl US -ˈtɔːr.i-

piscatory ˈpɪs.kə.tᵊr.i US -tɔːr-

Piscean ˈpaɪ.si.ən, ˈpɪs.i-, ˈpɪs.ki-; pɪˈsiː- US ˈpaɪ.sɪ-, ˈpɪs.i-

Pisces ˈpaɪ.siːz, ˈpɪs.iːz, ˈpɪs.kiːz US ˈpaɪ.siːz, ˈpɪs.iːz

pisciculture ˈpɪs.ɪˌkʌl.tʃəʳ US -tʃɚ

piscin|a pɪˈsiː.n|ə **-as** -əz **-ae** -iː

piscine ˈpɪs.aɪn, ˈpɪsk-, ˈpaɪ.saɪn US ˈpaɪ.siːn, ˈpɪs.iːn-, -aɪn, -ɪn

Piscis| Austrinus ˌpɪs.ɪs|.ɒsˈtraɪ.nəs, ˌ-kɪs-, -ɔːˈstraɪ- US ˌpaɪ.sɪs|.ɔːˈ-, ˌpɪs.ɪs-, -ɑːˈ- **-Australis** -ɒsˈtrɑː.lɪs, -ɔːˈstrɑː- US -ɔːˈstreɪ-, -ɑːˈ-

Pitch

An auditory sensation which places sounds on a scale from low to high.

When we hear a regularly vibrating sound such as a note played on a musical instrument, or a vowel produced by the human voice, we hear a high pitch if the rate of vibration is high and a low pitch if the rate of vibration is low. Many speech sounds are voiceless (e.g. [s]), and cannot give rise to a sensation of pitch in this way. The pitch sensation that we receive from a voiced sound corresponds quite closely to the frequency of vibration of the vocal folds. However, we usually refer to this vibration frequency as 'fundamental frequency' (which we can measure) in order to distinguish it from the subjective impression of pitch.

Pitch is used in many languages as an essential component of the pronunciation of a word, so that a change of pitch may cause a change in meaning: these are called 'tone languages'. In most languages (whether or not they are tone languages) pitch plays a central role in **INTONATION**.

Pisgah 'pɪz.gə, -gɑː ⓤⓢ -gə
pish pɪʃ
Pisidia paɪ'sɪd.i.ə ⓤⓢ pɪ-
Pisistratus paɪ'sɪs.trə.təs, pɪ-
pismire 'pɪs.maɪəʳ ⓤⓢ -maɪɚ, 'pɪz- **-s** -z
piss pɪs **-es** -ɪz **-ing** -ɪŋ **-ed** -t **'piss ˌartist -er/s** -əʳ/z ⓤⓢ -ɚ/z
pissant 'pɪs.ᵊnt ⓤⓢ -ænt **-s** -s
Pissarro pɪ'sɑː.rəʊ ⓤⓢ -'sɑːr.oʊ
pissed pɪst **ˌpissed as a 'newt; ˌpissed as a 'fart**
pissoir 'pɪs.wɑːʳ, 'piː.swɑːʳ ⓤⓢ piː'swɑːr **-s** -z
pisspot 'pɪs.pɒt ⓤⓢ -pɑːt **-s** -s
piss-take 'pɪs.teɪk **-s** -s
piss-up 'pɪs.ʌp **-s** -s
pistachio pɪ'stɑː.ʃi.əʊ, -'stæʃ.i- ⓤⓢ -'stæʃ.i.oʊ, -'stɑː.ʃi- **-s** -z
piste piːst **-s** -s
pistil 'pɪs.tɪl, -tᵊl **-s** -z
pistol 'pɪs.tᵊl **-s** -z
pistole pɪ'stəʊl; 'pɪs.təʊl ⓤⓢ pɪ'stoʊl **-s** -z
pistol-whip 'pɪs.tᵊl.*h*wɪp **-s** -s **-ping** -ɪŋ **-ped** -t
piston 'pɪs.tᵊn **-s** -z **'piston ˌrod**
pit pɪt **-s** -s **-ting** -ɪŋ ⓤⓢ 'pɪt̬.ɪŋ **-ted** -ɪd ⓤⓢ 'pɪt̬.ɪd **ˌpit bull 'terrier; 'pit ˌpony; 'pit ˌstop**
pita 'pɪt.ə ⓤⓢ 'piː.t̬ə **'pita ˌbread**
pit-a-pat ˌpɪt.ə'pæt, '--- ⓤⓢ 'pɪt̬.ə.pæt
Pitcairn *surname:* pɪt'keən ⓤⓢ -'kern *island:* pɪt'keən, '-- ⓤⓢ pɪt'kern, '--
pitch pɪtʃ **-es** -ɪz **-ing** -ɪŋ **-ed** -t **'pitch ˌpipe**
pitch-and-putt ˌpɪtʃ.ᵊnd'pʌt
pitch-and-toss ˌpɪtʃ.ᵊnd'tɒs ⓤⓢ -'tɑːs
pitch-black ˌpɪtʃ'blæk *stress shift:* ˌpitch-black 'night
pitchblende 'pɪtʃ.blend
pitch-dark ˌpɪtʃ'dɑːk ⓤⓢ -'dɑːrk *stress shift:* ˌpitch-dark 'night
pitcher (P) 'pɪtʃ.əʳ ⓤⓢ -ɚ **-s** -z **'pitcher ˌplant**
pitchfork 'pɪtʃ.fɔːk ⓤⓢ -fɔːrk **-s** -s **-ing** -ɪŋ **-ed** -t
pitch|man 'pɪtʃ|.mən, -mæn **-men** -mən, -men
pitchpine 'pɪtʃ.paɪn **-s** -z
pitchy 'pɪtʃ.i
piteous 'pɪt.i.əs ⓤⓢ 'pɪt̬- **-ly** -li **-ness** -nəs, -nɪs
pitfall 'pɪt.fɔːl ⓤⓢ -fɔːl, -fɑːl **-s** -z
pith pɪθ **-s** -s **-ing** -ɪŋ **-ed** -t **-less** -ləs, -lɪs **ˌpith 'helmet** ⓤⓢ **'pith ˌhelmet**
pithead 'pɪt.hed **-s** -z
pithecanthrop|us ˌpɪθ.ɪ.kæn'θrəʊ.p|əs; -'kæn*t*.θrə- ⓤⓢ -'kæn*t*.θroʊ-, -θrə-; -kæn'θroʊ- **-i** -aɪ
Pither 'paɪ.θəʳ, -ðəʳ ⓤⓢ -θɚ, -ðɚ
pith|y 'pɪθ|.i **-ier** -i.əʳ ⓤⓢ -i.ɚ **-iest** -i.ɪst, -i.əst **-ily** -ɪ.li, -ᵊl.i **-iness** -ɪ.nəs, -ɪ.nɪs
pitiab|le 'pɪt.i.ə.b|l̩ ⓤⓢ 'pɪt̬- **-ly** -li **-leness** -l̩.nəs, -nɪs
pitiful 'pɪt.i.fᵊl, -fʊl ⓤⓢ 'pɪt̬- **-ly** -i **-ness** -nəs, -nɪs
pitiless 'pɪt.i.ləs, -lɪs ⓤⓢ 'pɪt̬- **-ly** -li **-ness** -nəs, -nɪs
Pitlochry pɪt'lɒk.ri, -'lɒx- ⓤⓢ -'lɑː.kri
pit|man (P) 'pɪt|.mən **-men** -mən, -men
piton 'piː.tɒn, -tɔ̃ːŋ ⓤⓢ -tɑːn **-s** -z
Pitsea 'pɪt.siː, -si
Pitt pɪt
pitta 'pɪt.ə ⓤⓢ 'pɪt̬- **'pitta ˌbread**
pittanc|e 'pɪt.ᵊn*t*s ⓤⓢ 'pɪt- **-es** -ɪz
Pittaway 'pɪt.ə.weɪ ⓤⓢ 'pɪt̬-
pitted 'pɪt.ɪd ⓤⓢ 'pɪt̬-
pitter-patter 'pɪt.əˌpæt.əʳ, ˌpɪt.ə'pæt- ⓤⓢ 'pɪt̬.ɚˌpæt̬.ɚ
Pittman 'pɪt.mən
Pitts pɪts
Pittsburgh 'pɪts.bɜːg ⓤⓢ -bɝːg
pituitary pɪ'tjuː.ɪ.tᵊr.i, '-ə- ⓤⓢ -'tuː.ə.ter-, pə-, -'tjuː- **pi'tuitary ˌgland**
pit|y 'pɪt|.i ⓤⓢ 'pɪt̬- **-ies** -iz **-ying/ly** -i.ɪŋ/li **-ied** -id
pityriasis ˌpɪt.ɪ'raɪə.sɪs, -ə'- ⓤⓢ ˌpɪt̬.ɪ'-
Pius paɪəs
piv|ot 'pɪv|.ət **-ots** -əts **-oting** -ə.tɪŋ ⓤⓢ -ə.t̬ɪŋ **-oted** -ə.tɪd ⓤⓢ -ə.t̬ɪd
pivotal 'pɪv.ə.tᵊl ⓤⓢ -t̬ᵊl **-ly** -i
pix pɪks
pixel 'pɪk.sᵊl, -sel **-s** -z
pix|ie, -|y 'pɪk.s|i **-ies** -iz
pixilated 'pɪk.sɪ.leɪ.tɪd, -sə- ⓤⓢ -t̬ɪd
Pizarro pɪ'zɑː.rəʊ ⓤⓢ -'zɑːr.oʊ
pizazz pɪ'zæz, pə- ⓤⓢ pɪ-
pizza 'piːt.sə, 'pɪt- ⓤⓢ 'piːt- **-s** -z
pizzazz pɪ'zæz, pə- ⓤⓢ pɪ-
pizzeria ˌpiːt.sə'riː.ə, ˌpɪt- ⓤⓢ ˌpiːt- **-s** -z
Pizzey 'pɪt.si; 'pɪz.i
pizzicat|o ˌpɪt.sɪ'kɑː.t|əʊ ⓤⓢ -t|oʊ **-os** -əʊz ⓤⓢ -oʊz **-i** -iː
placability ˌplæk.ə'bɪl.ə.ti, -ɪ.ti ⓤⓢ -ə.t̬i, ˌpleɪ.kə'-
placab|le 'plæk.ə.b|l̩ ⓤⓢ 'plæk.ə-, 'pleɪ.kə- **-ly** -li **-leness** -l̩.nəs, -nɪs
placard (*n.*) 'plæk.ɑːd ⓤⓢ -ɑːrd, -ɚd
placard (*v.*) 'plæk.ɑːd ⓤⓢ -ɑːrd, -ɚd; plə'kɑːrd, plæk'ɑːrd **-s** -z **-ing** -ɪŋ **-ed** -ɪd
placa|te plə'keɪ|t, pleɪ- ⓤⓢ 'pleɪ.keɪ|t, 'plæk.eɪ|t; pleɪ'keɪ|t **-tes** -ts **-ting** -tɪŋ ⓤⓢ -t̬ɪŋ **-ted** -tɪd ⓤⓢ -t̬ɪd
placatory plə'keɪ.tᵊr.i, pleɪ'- ⓤⓢ 'pleɪ.kə.tɔːr-, 'plæk.ə-
plac|e pleɪs **-es** -ɪz **-ing** -ɪŋ **-ed** -t **-er/s** -əʳ/z ⓤⓢ -ɚ/z **'place ˌsetting**
placebo plə'siː.bəʊ, plæs'iː- ⓤⓢ plə'siː.boʊ **-s** -z **pla'cebo efˌfect**
placekick 'pleɪs.kɪk **-s** -s **-ing** -ɪŋ **-ed** -t
place|man 'pleɪs|.mən **-men** -mən
placement 'pleɪs.mənt **-s** -s
placent|a plə'sen.t|ə, plæs'en- ⓤⓢ plə'sen.t̬|ə **-as** -əz **-ae** -iː
placet 'pleɪ.set, -sɪt **-s** -s
placid (P) 'plæs.ɪd **-ly** -li **-ness** -nəs, -nɪs
placidity plə'sɪd.ə.ti, plæs'ɪd-, -ɪ.ti ⓤⓢ plə'sɪd.ə.t̬i
placket 'plæk.ɪt **-s** -s
plagal 'pleɪ.gᵊl
plag|e plɑːʒ **-es** -ɪz
plagiarism 'pleɪ.dʒᵊr.ɪ.zᵊm, -dʒi.ə.rɪ- ⓤⓢ -dʒɚ.ɪ-, -dʒi.ɚ- **-s** -z
plagiarist 'pleɪ.dʒᵊr.ɪst, -dʒi.ə.rɪst ⓤⓢ -dʒɚ.ɪst, -dʒi.ɚ- **-s** -s

plagiaristic ˌpleɪ.dʒᵊrˈɪs.tɪk, -dʒi.əˈrɪs- (US) -dʒəˈrɪs-, -dʒi.əˈ-
plagiariz|e, -is|e ˈpleɪ.dʒᵊr.aɪz, -dʒi.ə.raɪz (US) -dʒə.raɪz, -dʒi.ə- **-es** -ɪz **-ing** -ɪŋ **-ed** -d
plagiar|y ˈpleɪ.dʒᵊr|.i, -dʒi.ə.r|i (US) -dʒɚ|.i, -dʒi.ɚ- **-ies** -iz
plagu|e pleɪg **-es** -z **-ing** -ɪŋ **-ed** -d **-er/s** -əʳ/z (US) -ɚ/z
plagu|y ˈpleɪ.g|i **-ily** -ɪ.li, -ᵊl.i **-iness** -ɪ.nəs, -ɪ.nɪs
plaice pleɪs
plaid plæd **-s** -z **-ed** -ɪd
Plaid Cymru ˌplaɪdˈkʌm.ri
plain pleɪn **-s** -z **-er** -əʳ (US) -ɚ **-est** -ɪst, -əst **-ly** -li **-ness** -nəs, -nɪs **ˌplain ˈclothes; ˌplain ˈsailing**
plainchant ˈpleɪn.tʃɑːnt (US) -tʃænt **-s** -s **-ing** -ɪŋ **-ed** -ɪd
plainsong ˈpleɪn.sɒŋ (US) -sɑːŋ, -sɔːŋ
plain-spoken ˌpleɪnˈspəʊ.kᵊn (US) -ˈspoʊ-, ˈ-ˌ-- **-ness** -nəs, -nɪs *stress shift:* ˌplain-spoken ˈperson
plaint pleɪnt **-s** -s
plaintiff ˈpleɪn.tɪf (US) -t̬ɪf **-s** -s
plaintive ˈpleɪn.tɪv (US) -t̬ɪv **-ly** -li **-ness** -nəs, -nɪs
Plaistow ˈplæs.təʊ, ˈplɑː.stəʊ (US) ˈplæs.toʊ, ˈplɑː.stoʊ
Note: The local pronunciation is /ˈplɑː.stəʊ/.
plait plæt **-s** -s **-ing** -ɪŋ (US) ˈplæt̬.ɪŋ **-ed** -ɪd (US) ˈplæt̬.ɪd
plan plæn **-s** -z **-ning** -ɪŋ **-ned** -d **-ner/s** -əʳ/z (US) -ɚ/z **ˈplanning perˌmission**
planchet ˈplɑːn.tʃɪt (US) ˈplæn-, -tʃet **-s** -s
planchette plɑ̃ːnˈʃet, plɑːn- (US) plænˈʃet **-s** -s
Planck plæŋk
plan|e pleɪn **-es** -z **-ing** -ɪŋ **-ed** -d **ˈplane ˌtree**
planer (P) ˈpleɪ.nəʳ (US) -nɚ **-s** -z
planet ˈplæn.ɪt **-s** -s
planetari|um ˌplæn.ɪˈteə.ri|.əm, -əˈ- (US) -ɪˈter.i- **-ums** -əmz **-a** -ə
planetary ˈplæn.ɪ.tᵊr.i, ˈ-ə- (US) -ɪ.ter-
plangent ˈplæn.dʒᵊnt **-ly** -li
planimeter plænˈɪm.ɪ.təʳ, pləˈnɪm-, ˈ-ə- (US) pləˈnɪm.ə.t̬ɚ, pleɪ- **-s** -z
planimetric ˌplæn.ɪˈmet.rɪk (US) ˌpleɪ.nɪˈ-, ˌplæn.ɪˈ-
planimetry plænˈɪm.ɪ.tri, pləˈnɪm-, ˈ-ə- (US) pləˈnɪm-, pleɪ-
plank plæŋk **-s** -s **-ing** -ɪŋ **-ed** -t
plankton ˈplæŋk.tən, -tɒn (US) -tən
plant (P) (*n. v.*) plɑːnt (US) plænt **-s** -s **-ing** -ɪŋ (US) ˈplæn.t̬ɪŋ **-ed** -ɪd (US) ˈplæn.t̬ɪd **-er/s** -əʳ/z (US) ˈplæn.t̬ɚ/z
Plantagenet plænˈtædʒ.ᵊn.ɪt, -ɪn-, -ət, -et (US) -ə.nɪt **-s** -s
plantain ˈplæn.teɪn, ˈplɑːn-, -tɪn (US) ˈplæn.tɪn, -tᵊn **-s** -z
plantation plænˈteɪ.ʃᵊn, plɑːn- (US) plæn- **-s** -z
Plantin ˈplæn.tɪn, ˈplɑːn- (US) ˈplɑːn.tæn, ˈplæn-
plantocrac|y plɑːnˈtɒk.rə.s|i (US) plænˈtɑː.krə- **-ies** -iz
plaque plɑːk, plæk (US) plæk **-s** -s
plash plæʃ **-es** -ɪz **-ing** -ɪŋ **-ed** -t **-y** -i
plasm ˈplæz.ᵊm
plasm|a ˈplæz.m|ə **-ic** -ɪk
plasmolysis plæzˈmɒl.ə.sɪs, ˈ-ɪ- (US) -ˈmɑː.lɪ-
Plassey ˈplæs.i
plast|er ˈplɑː.st|əʳ (US) ˈplæs.t|ɚ **-ers** -əz (US) -ɚz **-ering** -ᵊr.ɪŋ **-ered** -əd (US) -ɚd **-erer/s** -ᵊr.əʳ/z (US) -ɚ.ɚ/z **ˌplaster ˈcast; ˌplaster of ˈParis**
plasterboard ˈplɑː.stə.bɔːd (US) ˈplæs.tɚ.bɔːrd
plastic ˈplæs.tɪk, ˈplɑː.stɪk (US) ˈplæs.tɪk **-s** -s **ˌplastic ˈbullet; ˌplastic ˈmoney; ˌplastic ˈsurgeon; ˌplastic ˈsurgery**
Plasticine® ˈplæs.tə.siːn, ˈplɑː.stə-, -stɪ- (US) ˈplæs.tɪ-
plasticity plæsˈtɪs.ə.ti, plɑːˈstɪs-, -ɪ.ti (US) plæsˈtɪs.ə.t̬i
plasticiz|e, -is|e ˈplæs.tɪ.saɪz, ˈplɑː.stɪ-, -stə- (US) ˈplæs.tɪ- **-es** -ɪz **-ing** -ɪŋ **-ed** -d **-er/s** -əʳ/z (US) -ɚ/z
plastid ˈplæs.tɪd **-s** -z
Plata ˈplɑː.tə (US) -tɑː
Plataea pləˈtiː.ə
platan ˈplæt.ᵊn **-s** -z
plat(s) du jour ˌplɑː.djuˈʒʊəʳ, -dʊˈ-, -dəˈ- (US) -ˈʒʊr
plat|e (P) (*n. v.*) pleɪt **-es** -s **-ing** -ɪŋ (US) ˈpleɪ.t̬ɪŋ **-ed** -ɪd (US) ˈpleɪ.t̬ɪd **ˌplate tecˈtonics**
plateau ˈplæt.əʊ; -ˈ-, pləˈtəʊ (US) plætˈoʊ **-s** -z **-x** -z **-ing** **-ed**
plateful ˈpleɪt.fʊl **-s** -z
plate-glass ˌpleɪtˈglɑːs (US) -ˈglæs **ˌplate-glass ˈwindow**
platelayer ˈpleɪtˌleɪ.əʳ (US) -ɚ **-s** -z
platelet ˈpleɪt.lət, -lɪt **-s** -s
platen ˈplæt.ᵊn **-s** -z
platform ˈplæt.fɔːm (US) -fɔːrm **-s** -z **-ing** -ɪŋ **-ed** -d **ˌplatform ˈshoes**
Plath plæθ
Platignum® plætˈɪg.nəm, pləˈtɪg- (US) plə-
platiniz|e, -is|e ˈplæt.ɪ.naɪz, -ᵊn.aɪz (US) -ᵊn- **-es** -ɪz **-ing** -ɪŋ **-ed** -d
platinum ˈplæt.ɪ.nəm, -ᵊn.əm (US) ˈplæt.nəm **ˌplatinum ˈblond(e)**
platitude ˈplæt.ɪ.tjuːd, ˈ-ə-, -tʃuːd (US) ˈplæt̬.ə.tuːd, -tjuːd **-s** -z
platitudinarian ˌplæt.ɪˌtjuː.dɪˈneə.ri.ən, -əˌ-, -ˌtʃuː-, -dəˈ- (US) ˌplæt̬.əˌtuː.dɪˈner.i-, -ˌtjuː- **-s** -z
platitudinous ˌplæt.ɪˈtjuː.dɪ.nəs, -əˈ-, -ˈtʃuː-, -dᵊn.əs (US) ˌplæt̬.əˈtuː.dᵊn-, -ˈtjuː- **-ly** -li
Plato ˈpleɪ.təʊ (US) -t̬oʊ
platonic pləˈtɒn.ɪk, plætˈɒn- (US) pləˈtɑː.nɪk, pleɪ- **-al** -ᵊl **-ally** -ᵊl.i, -li
Platon|ism ˈpleɪ.tᵊn|.ɪ.zᵊm **-ist/s** -ɪst/s
platoon pləˈtuːn **-s** -z
Platt plæt **-s** -s
platter ˈplæt.əʳ (US) ˈplæt̬.ɚ **-s** -z
platyp|us ˈplæt.ɪ.p|əs, ˈ-ə- (US) ˈplæt̬.ɪ- **-uses** -ə.sɪz **-i** -aɪ
plaudit ˈplɔː.dɪt (US) ˈplɑː-, ˈplɔː- **-s** -s
plausibility ˌplɔː.zɪˈbɪl.ə.ti, -zəˈ-, -ɪ.ti (US) ˌplɑː.zəˈbɪl.ə.t̬i, ˌplɔː-
plausib|le ˈplɔː.zɪ.b|l̩, -zə- (US) ˈplɑː.zə-, ˈplɔː- **-ly** -li **-leness** -l̩.nəs, -nɪs
Plautus ˈplɔː.təs (US) ˈplɑː.t̬əs, ˈplɔː-
play pleɪ **-s** -z **-ing** -ɪŋ **-ed** -d **-er/s** -əʳ/z (US) -ɚ/z **ˌplay on ˈwords; ˌplay the ˈfield; ˈplaying ˌcard; ˈplaying ˌfield**
playable ˈpleɪ.ə.bl̩
play-act ˈpleɪ.ækt **-s** -z **-ing** -ɪŋ **-ed** -ɪd **-or/s** -əʳ/z (US) -ɚ/z
playback ˈpleɪ.bæk
playbill ˈpleɪ.bɪl **-s** -z
playboy ˈpleɪ.bɔɪ **-s** -z
Play-Doh® ˈpleɪ.dəʊ (US) -doʊ
player (P) ˈpleɪ.əʳ (US) -ɚ **-s** -z
Playfair ˈpleɪ.feəʳ (US) -fer
playfellow ˈpleɪˌfel.əʊ (US) -oʊ **-s** -z
playful ˈpleɪ.fᵊl, -fʊl **-ly** -i **-ness** -nəs, -nɪs
playgoer ˈpleɪˌgəʊ.əʳ (US) -ˌgoʊ.ɚ **-s** -z
playground ˈpleɪ.graʊnd **-s** -z
playgroup ˈpleɪ.gruːp **-s** -s
playhou|se ˈpleɪ.haʊ|s **-ses** -zɪz
playlet ˈpleɪ.lət, -lɪt **-s** -s
playlist ˈpleɪ.lɪst **-s** -s
playmate ˈpleɪ.meɪt **-s** -s
play-off ˈpleɪ.ɒf (US) -ɑːf **-s** -s
playpen ˈpleɪ.pen **-s** -z
playroom ˈpleɪ.rʊm, -ruːm (US) -ruːm, -rʊm **-s** -z
playschool ˈpleɪ.skuːl **-s** -z
PlayStation® ˈpleɪˌsteɪ.ʃᵊn **-s** -z
playsuit ˈpleɪ.suːt, -sjuːt (US) -suːt **-s** -s
Playtex® ˈpleɪ.teks
plaything ˈpleɪ.θɪŋ **-s** -z
playtime ˈpleɪ.taɪm **-s** -z
playwright ˈpleɪ.raɪt **-s** -s
plaza (P) ˈplɑː.zə (US) ˈplɑː-, ˈplæz.ə **-s** -z
plc ˌpiː.elˈsiː
plea pliː **-s** -z
plea-bargain ˈpliːˌbɑː.gɪn, -gən (US) -ˌbɑːr.gən **-s** -z **-ing** -ɪŋ **-ed** -d
plead pliːd **-s** -z **-ing/ly** -ɪŋ/li **-ed** -ɪd **pled** pled **pleader/s** ˈpliː.dəʳ/z (US) -dɚ/z
pleading ˈpliː.dɪŋ **-s** -z

Plosive

A sound produced by forming a complete obstruction to the flow of air out of the mouth and nose. Normally, this results in a build-up of compressed air inside the chamber formed by the closure. When the closure is released, there is a small explosion that causes a sharp noise.

Examples for English

British English and US English have six plosive consonants, /p t k/ (voiceless) and /b d g/ (voiced).

In syllable-initial position, sounds in the voiceless group /p t k/ are strongly aspirated (see ASPIRATION), and in final position GLOTTALISATION of these sounds causes a shortening of the preceding vowel. Sounds in the voiced group /b d g/ tend to be 'devoiced' at the beginning and ends of words. At the ends of words, the pairs of sounds /p b/, /t d/ and /k g/ can sound very similar due to this, and one must listen to the length of the vowel to work out which consonant is being produced.

The basic plosive consonant type can be of many different forms: plosives may have any place of articulation, may be voiced or voiceless and may have an 'egressive' (breathing out) or 'ingressive' (breathing in) airflow. The airflow may be from the lungs ('pulmonic'), from the larynx ('glottalic') or generated in the mouth ('velaric'). We find great variation in the release of the plosive.

pleasance **(P)** ˈplez.ᵊnts
pleas|ant ˈplez|.ᵊnt **-anter** -ᵊn.təʳ ⓤⓢ -ᵊn.t̬ɚ **-antest** -ᵊn.tɪst, -ᵊn.təst ⓤⓢ -ᵊn.t̬ɪst, -ᵊn.t̬əst **-antly** -ᵊnt.li **-antness** -ᵊnt.nəs, -ᵊnt.nɪs
pleasantr|y ˈplez.ᵊn.tr|i **-ies** -iz
pleas|e pliːz **-es** -ɪz **-ing/ly** -ɪŋ/li **-ed** -d
pleasurab|le ˈpleʒ.ᵊr.ə.b|l̩ **-ly** -li **-leness** -l̩.nəs, -nɪs
pleasure ˈpleʒ.əʳ ⓤⓢ -ɚ **-s** -z **-ing** -ɪŋ **-ed** -d **ˈpleasure ˌprinciple**
pleat pliːt **-s** -s **-ing** -ɪŋ ⓤⓢ ˈpliː.t̬ɪŋ **-ed** -ɪd ⓤⓢ ˈpliː.t̬ɪd
pleb pleb **-s** -z **-by** -i
plebe pliːb **-s** -z
plebeian pləˈbiː.ən, plɪ- ⓤⓢ plɪ-, plə- **-s** -z
plebiscite ˈpleb.ɪ.sɪt, ˈ-ə-, -saɪt ⓤⓢ -ə.saɪt, -sɪt **-s** -s
plectr|um ˈplek.tr|əm **-ums** -əmz **-a** -ə
pled *(past of* **plead)** pled
pledg|e pledʒ **-es** -ɪz **-ing** -ɪŋ **-ed** -d **-er/s** -əʳ/z ⓤⓢ -ɚ/z
Pledger ˈpledʒ.əʳ ⓤⓢ -ɚ
-plegia -ˈpliː.dʒi.ə, -dʒə
Note: Suffix. Words containing **-plegia** are always stressed on the syllable **-ple-**, e.g. **paraplegia** /ˌpær.əˈpliː.dʒə ⓤⓢ ˌper-/.
-plegic -ˈpliː.dʒɪk
Note: Suffix. Words containing **-plegic** are always stressed on the penultimate syllable, e.g. **paraplegic** /ˌpær.əˈpliː.dʒɪk ⓤⓢ ˌper-/.
Pleiad ˈplaɪ.æd, -əd, ˈpliː-, ˈpleɪ- ⓤⓢ ˈpliː.æd, ˈplaɪ-, -jæd, -əd **-s** -z **-es** -iːz
Pléiade ˈpleɪ.ɑːd, -æd, -ˈ- **-s** -z
Pleistocene ˈplaɪ.stəʊ.siːn ⓤⓢ -stoʊ-, -stə-
plenar|y ˈpliː.nᵊr|.i ⓤⓢ ˈpliː-, ˈplen.ɚ- **-ily** -ᵊl.i, -ɪ.li
plenipotentiar|y ˌplen.ɪ.pəʊˈten*t*.ʃᵊr|.i, -ʃi.ᵊr- ⓤⓢ ˌplen.ɪ.poʊˈten*t*.ʃi.er-, -pəˈ-, ˈ-ʃɚ- **-ies** -iz
plenitude ˈplen.ɪ.tjuːd ⓤⓢ -tuːd, -tjuːd
plenteous ˈplen.ti.əs ⓤⓢ -t̬i- **-ly** -li **-ness** -nəs, -nɪs
plentiful ˈplen.tɪ.fᵊl, -fʊl ⓤⓢ -t̬ɪ- **-ly** -i **-ness** -nəs, -nɪs
plenty ˈplen.ti ⓤⓢ -t̬i
plen|um ˈpliː.n|əm ⓤⓢ ˈpliː-, ˈplen|.əm **-ums** -əmz **-a** -ə
pleonasm ˈpliː.əʊ.næz.ᵊm ⓤⓢ -oʊ-, ˈ-ə- **-s** -z
pleonastic ˌpliː.əʊˈnæs.tɪk ⓤⓢ -oʊˈ-, -əˈ- **-al** -ᵊl **-ally** -ᵊl.i, -li
plesiosaur ˈpliː.si.əʊ.sɔːʳ ⓤⓢ -oʊ.sɔːr, -ə- **-s** -z
Plessey® ˈples.i
plethora ˈpleθ.ᵊr.ə; pleθˈɔː.rə, pləˈθɔː-, plɪ- ⓤⓢ ˈpleθ.ɚ.ə
plethoric pleθˈɒr.ɪk, plə-, plɪ- ⓤⓢ pləˈθɔːr-
pleur|a ˈplʊə.r|ə, ˈplɔː- ⓤⓢ ˈplʊr|.ə **-ae** -iː **-as** -əz **-al** -ᵊl
pleurisy ˈplʊə.rə.si, ˈplɔː-, -rɪ- ⓤⓢ ˈplʊr.ə-
pleuritic plʊəˈrɪt.ɪk, plɔː- ⓤⓢ plʊˈrɪt̬-
pleuro-pneumonia ˌplʊə.rəʊ.njuːˈməʊ.ni.ə, ˌplɔː- ⓤⓢ ˌplʊr.oʊ.nuːˈmoʊ.njə, -njuːˈ-
plexiglass (P®)ˈplek.si.glɑːs ⓤⓢ -sɪ.glæs
plexus ˈplek.səs **-es** -ɪz
Pleyel ˈpleɪ.el, ˈplaɪ- ⓤⓢ ˈplaɪ- **-s** -z
pliability ˌplaɪ.əˈbɪl.ə.ti, -ɪ.ti ⓤⓢ -ə.t̬i
pliab|le ˈplaɪ.ə.b|l̩ **-ly** -li **-leness** -l̩.nəs, -nɪs
pliancy ˈplaɪ.ᵊn*t*.si
pliant ˈplaɪ.ᵊnt **-ly** -li **-ness** -nəs, -nɪs
plié ˈpliː.eɪ, -ˈ- ⓤⓢ -ˈ- **-s** -z
pliers plaɪəz ⓤⓢ plaɪɚz
plight plaɪt **-s** -s **-ing** -ɪŋ ⓤⓢ ˈplaɪ.t̬ɪŋ **-ed** -ɪd ⓤⓢ ˈplaɪ.t̬ɪd
plimsoll (P) ˈplɪm*p*.sᵊl, -sɒl ⓤⓢ -səl, -sɑːl, -sɔːl **-s** -z **ˈPlimsoll ˌline**
Plinlimmon plɪnˈlɪm.ən
plinth plɪn*t*θ **-s** -s
Pliny ˈplɪn.i
Pliocene ˈplaɪ.əʊ.siːn ⓤⓢ -oʊ-, ˈ-ə-
PLO ˌpiː.elˈəʊ ⓤⓢ -ˈoʊ
plod plɒd ⓤⓢ plɑːd **-s** -z **-ding** -ɪŋ **-ded** -ɪd **-der/s** -əʳ/z ⓤⓢ -ɚ/z
Ploesti, Ploiesti pləʊˈjeʃ.ti ⓤⓢ plɔː-, -ˈjeʃt.i
Plomer ˈpluː.məʳ, ˈplʌm.əʳ ⓤⓢ -ɚ
Plomley ˈplʌm.li
plonk *(n. v.)* plɒŋk ⓤⓢ plʌŋk, plɑːŋk **-s** -s **-ing** -ɪŋ **-ed** -t
plonker ˈplɒŋ.kəʳ ⓤⓢ ˈplʌŋ.kɚ **-s** -z
plop plɒp ⓤⓢ plɑːp **-s** -s **-ping** -ɪŋ **-ped** -t
plosion ˈpləʊ.ʒᵊn ⓤⓢ ˈploʊ- **-s** -z
plosive ˈpləʊ.sɪv, -zɪv ⓤⓢ ˈploʊ.sɪv **-s** -z
plot plɒt ⓤⓢ plɑːt **-s** -s **-ting** -ɪŋ ⓤⓢ ˈplɑː.t̬ɪŋ **-ted** -ɪd ⓤⓢ ˈplɑː.t̬ɪd **-ter/s** -əʳ/z ⓤⓢ ˈplɑː.t̬ɚ/z
plough (P) plaʊ **-s** -z **-ing** -ɪŋ **-ed** -d **-er/s** -əʳ/z ⓤⓢ -ɚ/z **-able** -ə.bl̩
ploughboy ˈplaʊ.bɔɪ **-s** -z
plough|man ˈplaʊ|.mən **-men** -mən, -men **ˌploughman's ˈlunch**
ploughshare ˈplaʊ.ʃeəʳ ⓤⓢ -ʃer **-s** -z
Plovdiv ˈplɒv.dɪv, -dɪf ⓤⓢ ˈplɔːv.dɪf
plover ˈplʌv.əʳ ⓤⓢ -ɚ **-s** -z
plow plaʊ **-s** -z **-ing** -ɪŋ **-ed** -d **-er/s** -əʳ/z ⓤⓢ -ɚ/z **-able** -ə.bl̩
plowboy ˈplaʊ.bɔɪ **-s** -z
Plowden ˈplaʊ.dᵊn
plow|man (P) ˈplaʊ|.mən **-men** -mən, -men
Plowright ˈplaʊ.raɪt
plowshare ˈplaʊ.ʃeəʳ ⓤⓢ -ʃer **-s** -z
ploy plɔɪ **-s** -z
pluck (P) plʌk **-s** -s **-ing** -ɪŋ **-ed** -t

pluck|y ˈplʌk|.i **-ier** -i.əʳ US -i.ɚ **-iest** -i.ɪst, -i.əst **-ily** -ɪ.li, -ᵊl.i **-iness** -ɪ.nəs, -ɪ.nɪs
plug plʌg **-s** -z **-ging** -ɪŋ **-ged** -d
plughole ˈplʌg.həʊl US -hoʊl **-s** -z
plug-in ˈplʌg.ɪn **-s** -z
plum plʌm **-s** -z ˌ**plum** ˈ**pudding**
plumag|e ˈpluː.mɪdʒ **-es** -ɪz
plumb (P) plʌm **-s** -z **-ing** -ɪŋ **-ed** -d
plumbago plʌmˈbeɪ.gəʊ US -goʊ **-s** -z
Plumbe plʌm
plumber ˈplʌm.əʳ US -ɚ **-s** -z
plumbic ˈplʌm.bɪk
plumbing ˈplʌm.ɪŋ
plumb-line ˈplʌm.laɪn **-s** -z
plumbous ˈplʌm.bəs
plum|e pluːm **-es** -z **-ing** -ɪŋ **-ed** -d
Plummer ˈplʌm.əʳ US -ɚ
plumm|et ˈplʌm|.ɪt **-ets** -ɪts **-eting** -ɪ.tɪŋ US -ɪ.t̬ɪŋ **-eted** -ɪ.tɪd US -ɪ.t̬ɪd
plummy ˈplʌm.i
plump plʌmp **-er** -əʳ US -ɚ **-est** -ɪst, -əst **-ly** -li **-ness** -nəs, -nɪs **-s** -z **-ing** -ɪŋ **-ed** -t
Plumpton ˈplʌm*p*.tən
Plum(p)tre ˈplʌm*p*.triː
Plumridge ˈplʌm.rɪdʒ
Plumstead ˈplʌm*p*.stɪd, -sted
plumule ˈpluː.mjuːl **-s** -z
plund|er ˈplʌn.d|əʳ US -d|ɚ **-ers** -əz US -ɚz **-ering** -ᵊr.ɪŋ **-ered** -əd US -ɚd **-erer/s** -ᵊr.əʳ/z US -ɚ.ɚ/z **-erous** -ᵊr.əs
plung|e plʌndʒ **-es** -ɪz **-ing** -ɪŋ **-ed** -d
plunger ˈplʌn.dʒəʳ US -dʒɚ **-s** -z
plunk plʌŋk **-s** -s **-ing** -ɪŋ **-ed** -t
Plunket(t) ˈplʌŋ.kɪt
pluperfect ˌpluːˈpɜː.fɪkt, -fekt US ˈpluːˌpɝː.fɪkt, ˌ-ˈ-- **-s** -s *stress shift, British only:* ˌpluperfect ˈtense
plural ˈplʊə.rᵊl, ˈplɔː- US ˈplʊr.ᵊl **-s** -z **-ly** -i
plural|ism ˈplʊə.rᵊl|.ɪ.zᵊm, ˈplɔː- US ˈplʊr.ᵊl- **-ist/s** -ɪst/s
pluralistic ˌplʊə.rᵊlˈɪs.tɪk US ˌplʊr.ᵊlˈ- **-ally** -ᵊl.i, -li *stress shift:* ˌpluralistic ˈsystem
pluralit|y plʊəˈræl.ə.t|i, plɔː-, -ɪ.t|i US plʊˈræl.ə.t̬|i **-ies** -iz
pluraliz|e, -is|e ˈplʊə.rᵊl.aɪz, ˈplɔː- US ˈplʊr.ᵊl- **-es** -ɪz **-ing** -ɪŋ **-ed** -d
plurisegmental ˌplʊə.rɪ.segˈmen.tᵊl, ˌplɔː- US ˌplʊr.ɪ.segˈmen.t̬ᵊl *stress shift:* ˌplurisegmental ˈitem
plus plʌs **-(s)es** -ɪz
plus-fours ˌplʌsˈfɔːz US -ˈfɔːrz
plush plʌʃ **-er** **-est** **-es** -ɪz **-y** -i
Plutarch ˈpluː.tɑːk US -tɑːrk
Pluto ˈpluː.təʊ US -t̬oʊ
plutocracy pluːˈtɒk.rə.si US -ˈtɑː.krə-
plutocrat ˈpluː.təʊ.kræt US -t̬ə-, -toʊ- **-s** -s
plutocratic ˌpluː.təʊˈkræt.ɪk US -toʊˈkræt̬-, -t̬əˈ- **-ally** -ᵊl.i, -li *stress shift:* ˌplutocratic ˈgovernment
plutonian (P) pluːˈtəʊ.ni.ən US -ˈtoʊ-
plutonic (P) pluːˈtɒn.ɪk US -ˈtɑː.nɪk
plutonium pluːˈtəʊ.ni.əm US -ˈtoʊ-
pluvi|al ˈpluː.vi|.əl **-ous** -əs
pluviometer ˌpluː.viˈɒm.ɪ.təʳ, ˈ-ə- US -ˈɑː.mə.t̬ɚ **-s** -z
pl|y pl|aɪ **-ies** -aɪz **-ying** -aɪ.ɪŋ **-ied** -aɪd
Plymouth ˈplɪm.əθ ˌ**Plymouth** ˈ**Brethren;** ˌ**Plymouth** ˈ**Rock**
Plynlimon Fawr plɪnˌlɪm.ənˈvaʊəʳ US -ˈvaʊr
plywood ˈplaɪ.wʊd
p.m. ˌpiːˈem
PM ˌpiːˈem
PMS ˌpiː.emˈes
PMT ˌpiː.emˈtiː
pneumatic njuːˈmæt.ɪk US nuːˈmæt̬-, njuː- **-s** -s **-al** -ᵊl **-ally** -ᵊl.i, -li **pneu**ˌ**matic** ˈ**drill**
pneumatolog|y ˌnjuː.məˈtɒl.ə.dʒ|i US ˌnuː.məˈtɑː.lə-, ˌnjuː- **-ist/s** -ɪst/s
pneumoconios|is ˌnjuː.məʊˌkəʊ.niˈəʊ.s|ɪs, -ˌkɒn.iˈ- US ˌnuː.moʊˌkoʊ.niˈoʊ-, ˌnjuː-, -məˌ- **-es** -iːz
pneumonia njuːˈməʊ.ni.ə US nuːˈmoʊ.njə, njuː-
pneumonic njuːˈmɒn.ɪk US nuːˈmɑː.nɪk, njuː-
Pnom Penh ˌnɒmˈpen, pəˌnɒm- US ˌnɑːm-
po (P) pəʊ US poʊ **-es** -z
PO ˌpiːˈəʊ US -ˈoʊ ˈ**PO** ˌ**box**
poach pəʊtʃ US poʊtʃ **-es** -ɪz **-ing** -ɪŋ **-ed** -t **-er/s** -əʳ/z US -ɚ/z
Pocahontas ˌpɒk.əˈhɒn.təs, -tæs US ˌpoʊ.kəˈhɑːn.t̬əs
pochard ˈpəʊ.tʃəd, ˈpɒtʃ.əd US ˈpoʊ.tʃɚd, -kɚd **-s** -z
pochette pɒʃˈet US poʊˈʃet **-s** -s
pock pɒk US pɑːk **-s** -s **-ed** -t
pock|et ˈpɒk|.ɪt US ˈpɑː.k|ɪt **-ets** -ɪts **-eting** -ɪ.tɪŋ US -ɪ.t̬ɪŋ **-eted** -ɪ.tɪd US -ɪ.t̬ɪd **-etable** -ɪ.tə.bl̩ US -ɪ.t̬ə.bl̩ **-etful/s** -ɪt.fʊl/z ˈ**pocket** ˌ**money**
pocketbook ˈpɒk.ɪt.bʊk US ˈpɑː.kɪt- **-s** -s
pocket-handkerchie|f ˌpɒk.ɪtˈhæŋ.kə.tʃiː|f, -tʃɪ|f US ˌpɑː.kɪtˈhæŋ.kɚ- **-fs** -fs **-ves** -vz
pocketknif|e ˈpɒk.ɪt.naɪ|f US ˈpɑː.kɪt- **-ves** -vz
pocket-size ˈpɒk.ɪt.saɪz US ˈpɑː.kɪt- **-d** -d
Pocklington ˈpɒk.lɪŋ.tən US ˈpɑː.klɪŋ-
pockmark ˈpɒk.mɑːk US ˈpɑːk.mɑːrk **-s** -s **-ing** -ɪŋ **-ed** -t
poco ˈpəʊ.kəʊ US ˈpoʊ.koʊ
Pocock ˈpəʊ.kɒk US ˈpoʊ.kɑːk
pococurante ˌpəʊ.kəʊ.kjʊəˈræn.teɪ, -ti US ˌpoʊ.koʊ.kuːˈræn.t̬i, -kjuːˈ-, -ˈrɑːn- **-s** -z
pod pɒd US pɑːd **-s** -z **-ding** -ɪŋ **-ded** -ɪd
podagra pəʊˈdæg.rə, pɒdˈæg-, ˈpɒd.ə.grə US pəˈdæg.rə; ˈpɑː.də.grə
podg|y ˈpɒdʒ|.i US ˈpɑː.dʒ|i **-ier** -i.əʳ US -i.ɚ **-iest** -i.ɪst, -i.əst **-ily** -ɪ.li, -ᵊl.i **-iness** -ɪ.nəs, -ɪ.nɪs
podiatric ˌpəʊ.diˈæt.rɪk, ˌpɒd.iˈ- US ˌpoʊ-
podiatr|y pəʊˈdaɪ.ə.tr|i, pɒdˈaɪ- US pəˈdaɪ-, poʊ- **-ist/s** -ɪst/s
podi|um ˈpəʊ.di|.əm US ˈpoʊ- **-ums** -əmz **-a** -ə
Podunk ˈpəʊ.dʌŋk US ˈpoʊ-
Poe pəʊ US poʊ
Poel pəʊəl; ˈpəʊ.el, -ɪl US poʊəl; ˈpoʊ.el, -ɪl
poem ˈpəʊ.ɪm, -em; pəʊəm US poʊəm **-s** -z
Poema Morale pəʊˌeɪ.mə.mɒrˈɑː.leɪ, -mɔːˈrɑː- US poʊˌeɪ.mə.mɔːrˈɑː-
poesy ˈpəʊ.ɪ.zi, -ez.i; ˈpəʊə.zi US ˈpoʊə.si, -zi
poet ˈpəʊ.ɪt, -et; pəʊət US poʊət **-s** -s ˌ**poet** ˈ**laureate**
poetaster ˌpəʊ.ɪˈtæs.təʳ, ˌpəʊəˈ- US ˈpoʊə.tæs.tɚ **-s** -z
poetess ˌpəʊ.ɪˈtes, ˌpəʊəˈ-; ˈpəʊ.ɪ.tɪs, ˈpəʊə.tɪs, -tes US ˈpoʊ.ɪ.t̬ɪs **-es** -ɪz
poetic pəʊˈet.ɪk US poʊˈet̬- **-al** -ᵊl **-ally** -ᵊl.i, -li **po**ˌ**etic** ˈ**justice**
poeticism pəʊˈet.ɪ.sɪ.zᵊm, ˈ-ə- US poʊˈet̬.ə-
poeticiz|e, -is|e pəʊˈet.ɪ.saɪz, ˈ-ə- US poʊˈet̬.ə- **-es** -ɪz **-ing** -ɪŋ **-ed** -d **-er/s** -əʳ/z US -ɚ/z
poetiz|e, -is|e ˈpəʊ.ɪ.taɪz, ˈpəʊə.taɪz US ˈpoʊə- **-es** -ɪz **-ing** -ɪŋ **-ed** -d **-er/s** -əʳ/z US -ɚ/z
poetry ˈpəʊ.ɪ.tri, ˈpəʊə.tri US ˈpoʊə-
po-faced ˌpəʊˈfeɪst US ˌpoʊ- *stress shift:* ˌpo-faced ˈperson
Pogner ˈpəʊg.nəʳ US ˈpoʊg.nɚ
pogo ˈpəʊ.gəʊ US ˈpoʊ.goʊ **-s** -z **-ing** -ɪŋ **-ed** -d ˈ**pogo** ˌ**stick**
pogrom ˈpɒg.rəm, -rɒm US ˈpoʊ.grəm, -grɑːm; pəˈgrɑːm **-s** -z
poignancy ˈpɔɪ.njən*t*.si, -nən*t*- US -njən*t*.si
poignant ˈpɔɪ.njənt, -nənt US -njənt **-ly** -li
poikilotherm pɔɪˈkɪl.əʊ.θɜːm US -ə.θɝːm, ˈ-oʊ-
poikilotherm|ic ˌpɔɪ.kɪ.ləʊˈθɜː.m|ɪk US -ləˈθɝː-, -loʊˈ- **-al** -ᵊl **-ism** -ɪ.zᵊm
Poindexter ˈpɔɪn.dek.stəʳ US -stɚ
poinsettia ˌpɔɪn*t*ˈset.i.ə US -ˈset̬-, ˈ-ə **-s** -z

point pɔɪnt **-s** -s **-ing** -ɪŋ US ˈpɔɪn.t̬ɪŋ **-ed** -ɪd US ˈpɔɪn.t̬ɪd **-er/s** -əʳ/z US ˈpɔɪn.t̬ɚ/z ˌ**point of ˌno reˈturn**; ˌ**point of ˈorder**; ˌ**point of ˈview**

point-blank ˌpɔɪntˈblæŋk *stress shift:* ˌpoint-blank ˈrange

point-duty ˈpɔɪntˌdjuː.ti US -ˌduː.t̬i, -ˌdjuː-

pointed ˈpɔɪn.tɪd US -t̬ɪd **-ly** -li **-ness** -nəs, -nɪs

Pointe-Noire ˌpwɑ̃ːntˈnwɑːʳ US -ˈnwɑːr

pointill|ism ˈpɔɪn.tɪ.l|ɪ.zᵊm, ˈpwæ̃n.tiː.j|ɪ.zᵊm US ˈpwæn.tə.l|ɪ-, -tiː.j|ɪ- **-ist/s** -ɪst/s

pointless ˈpɔɪnt.ləs, -lɪs **-ly** -li **-ness** -nəs, -nɪs

point-of-sale ˌpɔɪnt.əvˈseɪl

Pointon ˈpɔɪn.tən US -tᵊn

points|man ˈpɔɪnts|.mən **-men** -mən, -men

point-to-point ˌpɔɪnt.təˈpɔɪnt *stress shift:* ˌpoint-to-point ˈchampion

point|y ˈpɔɪn.t|i US -t̬|i **-ier** -i.əʳ US -i.ɚ **-iest** -i.ɪst, -i.əst

Poirot ˈpwɑː.rəʊ, -ˈ- US pwɑːˈroʊ

pois|e pɔɪz **-es** -ɪz **-ing** -ɪŋ **-ed** -d

poison ˈpɔɪ.zᵊn **-s** -z **-ing** -ɪŋ **-ed** -d **-er/s** -əʳ/z US -ɚ/z ˌ**poison ˈivy**; ˌ**poison ˈoak**; ˈ**poison ˌpill**

poisonous ˈpɔɪ.zᵊn.əs **-ly** -li **-ness** -nəs, -nɪs

poison-pen letter ˌpɔɪ.zᵊnˈpenˌlet.əʳ US -ˌlet̬.ɚ **-s** -z

Poitier ˈpwɒt.i.eɪ, ˈpwæt-, ˈpwɑː.ti- US ˈpwɑː.ti.eɪ, -tjeɪ

Poitiers ˈpwɑː.ti.eɪ, ˈpwɒt.i-, ˈpwæt.i-, ˌ--ˈ- US pwɑːˈtjeɪ, -tiˈeɪ

pok|e pəʊk US poʊk **-es** -s **-ing** -ɪŋ **-ed** -t

Pokémon® ˈpəʊ.kə.mɒn, -kɪ-, ˈpɒk- US ˈpoʊ.keɪ.mɑːn, -kiː-

poker ˈpəʊ.kəʳ US ˈpoʊ.kɚ **-s** -z ˈ**poker ˌface**

pok|ey ˈpəʊ.k|i US ˈpoʊ- **-eys** -iz **-ies** -iz

pokie ˈpəʊ.ki US ˈpoʊ- **-s** -z

pok|y ˈpəʊ.k|i US ˈpoʊ- **-ier** -i.əʳ US -i.ɚ **-iest** -i.ɪst, -i.əst **-ily** -ɪ.li, -ᵊl.i **-iness** -ɪ.nəs, -ɪ.nɪs

Pola(c)k ˈpəʊ.læk US ˈpoʊ- **-s** -s

Poland ˈpəʊ.lənd US ˈpoʊ-

Polanski pəʊˈlænt.ski, pɒlˈænt- US pəˈlænt-, poʊ-

polar ˈpəʊ.ləʳ US ˈpoʊ.lɚ **-s** -z ˌ**polar ˈbear**, ˈ**polar ˌbear** US ˈ**polar ˌbear**

Polaris pəʊˈlɑː.rɪs, -ˈlær.ɪs, -ˈleə.rɪs US pəˈler.ɪs, poʊ-, -ˈlær-

Note: In British English, the rocket and submarine are usually pronounced with /-ˈlɑː-/.

polariscope pəʊˈlær.ɪ.skəʊp, ˈ-ə- US poʊˈler.ɪ.skoʊp, -ˈlær- **-s** -s

polarity pəʊˈlær.ə.ti, -ɪ.ti US poʊˈler.ə.t̬i, -ˈlær-

polarization, -isa- ˌpəʊ.lᵊr.aɪˈzeɪ.ʃᵊn, -ɪˈ- US ˌpoʊ.lɚ.ɪˈ-

polariz|e, -is|e ˈpəʊ.lᵊr.aɪz US ˈpoʊ.lə.raɪz **-es** -ɪz **-ing** -ɪŋ **-ed** -d **-er/s** -əʳ/z US -ɚ/z

Polaroid® ˈpəʊ.lᵊr.ɔɪd US ˈpoʊ.lə.rɔɪd **-s** -z

polder ˈpɒl.dəʳ, ˈpəʊl- US ˈpoʊl.dɚ **-s** -z

pole pəʊl US poʊl **-s** -z ˈ**Pole ˌStar**; ˈ**pole ˌvault**

Pole *inhabitant of Poland:* pəʊl US poʊl **-s** -z

Pole *surname:* pəʊl, puːl US poʊl, puːl

poleax|(e) ˈpəʊl.æks US ˈpoʊl- **-es** -ɪz **-ing** -ɪŋ **-ed** -t

polecat ˈpəʊl.kæt US ˈpoʊl- **-s** -s

polemic pəˈlem.ɪk, pɒlˈem- US pəˈlem- **-s** -s **-al** -ᵊl **-ally** -ᵊl.i, -li

polemicist pəˈlem.ɪ.sɪst, pɒlˈem- US pəˈlem- **-s** -s

polemiciz|e, -is|e pəˈlem.ɪ.saɪz, pɒlˈem- US pəˈlem.ɪ.saɪz **-es** -ɪz **-ing** -ɪŋ **-ed** -d

polenta pəʊˈlen.tə US poʊˈlen.t̬ə, pə-

polestar ˈpəʊl.stɑːʳ US ˈpoʊl.stɑːr **-s** -z

Polesworth ˈpəʊlz.wəθ, -wɜːθ US ˈpoʊlz.wɚθ, -wɝːθ

pole-vaul|t ˈpəʊl.vɔːl|t, -vɒl|t US ˈpoʊl.vɑːl|t, -vɔːl|t **-ts** -ts **-ting** -tɪŋ US -t̬ɪŋ **-ted** -tɪd US -t̬ɪd **-ter/s** -təʳ/z US -t̬ɚ/z

polic|e pəˈliːs, pliːs US pəˈliːs, poʊ-, pliːs **-es** -ɪz **-ing** -ɪŋ **-ed** -t **poˈlice ˌcar**; **poˌlice ˈconstable**; **poˈlice ˌforce**; **poˈlice ˌofficer, poˌlice ˈofficer**; **poˌlice ˈstate** US **poˈlice ˌstate**; **poˈlice ˌstation**

police|man pəˈliːs|.mən, ˈpliːs- US pəˈliːs-, poʊ-, pliːs- **-men** -mən

police|woman pəˈliːs|ˌwʊm.ən, ˈpliːs- US pəˈliːs-, poʊ-, pliːs- **-women** -ˌwɪm.ɪn

polic|y ˈpɒl.ə.s|i, ˈ-ɪ- US ˈpɑː.lə- **-ies** -iz

policyholder ˈpɒl.ə.siˌhəʊl.dəʳ, ˈ-ɪ- US ˈpɑː.lə.siˌhoʊl.dɚ **-s** -z

policymaker ˈpɒl.ə.siˌmeɪ.kəʳ, -ɪ- US ˈpɑː.lə.siˌmeɪ.kɚ **-s** -z

polio ˈpəʊ.li.əʊ US ˈpoʊ.li.oʊ

poliomyelitis ˌpəʊl.i.əʊ.maɪəˈlaɪ.tɪs, -maɪ.ɪˈ-, -elˈaɪ- US ˌpoʊ.li.oʊˌmaɪəˈlaɪ.t̬ɪs

polish (*n. v.*) ˈpɒl.ɪʃ US ˈpɑː.lɪʃ **-es** -ɪz **-ing** -ɪŋ **-ed** -t **-er/s** -əʳ/z US -ɚ/z

Polish (*adj.*) *of Poland:* ˈpəʊ.lɪʃ US ˈpoʊ-

politburo (P) ˈpɒl.ɪtˌbjʊə.rəʊ, pɒlˈɪt-, -ˌbjɔː-; -bjəˌrəʊ, -bjʊˌ- US ˈpɑː.lɪtˌbjʊr.oʊ, ˈpoʊ-; poʊˈlɪt-, pə- **-s** -z

po|lite pəlˈlaɪt US pə-, poʊ- **-litest** -ˈlaɪ.tɪst, -ˈlaɪ.təst US -ˈlaɪ.t̬ɪst, -ˈlaɪ.t̬əst **-litely** -ˈlaɪt.li **-liteness** -ˈlaɪt.nəs, -ˈlaɪt.nɪs

politic ˈpɒl.ə.tɪk, ˈ-ɪ- US ˈpɑː.lə- **-s** -s

politic|al pəˈlɪt.ɪ.k|ᵊl, ˈ-ə- US -ˈlɪt̬.ə-, poʊ- **-ally** -ᵊl.i, -li **poˌlitical ˈprisoner**; **poˌlitical ˈscience**

politician ˌpɒl.ɪˈtɪʃ.ᵊn, -əˈ- US ˌpɑː.ləˈ- **-s** -z

politiciz|e, -cis|e pəˈlɪt.ɪ.saɪz, ˈ-ə- US -ˈlɪt̬.ə-, poʊ- **-es** -ɪz **-ing** -ɪŋ **-ed** -d

politick ˈpɒl.ə.tɪk, ˈ-ɪ- US ˈpɑː.lə- **-s** -s **-ing** -ɪŋ **-ed** -t **-er/s** -əʳ/z US -ɚ/z

politico- pəˌlɪt.ɪ.kəʊ- US pəˌlɪt̬.ɪ.koʊ-, poʊ-, -kə-

politico pəˈlɪt.ɪ.kəʊ US -ˈlɪt̬.ɪ.koʊ, poʊ- **-s** -z

polity ˈpɒl.ə.ti, -ɪ.ti US ˈpɑː.lə.t̬i

Polixenes pɒlˈɪk.sə.niːz, pəˈlɪk-, -sɪ- US pəˈlɪk.sə-

Polk pəʊk US poʊk

polka ˈpɒl.kə US ˈpoʊl- **-s** -z ˈ**polka ˌdot**

poll (*n. v.*) pəʊl US poʊl **-s** -z **-ing** -ɪŋ **-ed** -d ˈ**poll ˌtax**; ˈ**polling ˌbooth**; ˈ**polling ˌstation**

pollard ˈpɒl.əd, -ɑːd US ˈpɑː.lɚd **-s** -z **-ing** -ɪŋ **-ed** -ɪd

Pollard ˈpɒl.ɑːd US ˈpɑː.lɚd

pollen (P) ˈpɒl.ən, -ɪn US ˈpɑː.lən **-s** -z ˈ**pollen ˌcount**

polli|nate ˈpɒl.ə|.neɪt, ˈ-ɪ- US ˈpɑː.lə- **-nates** -neɪts **-nating** -neɪ.tɪŋ US -neɪ.t̬ɪŋ **-nated** -neɪ.tɪd US -neɪ.t̬ɪd

pollination ˌpɒl.əˈneɪ.ʃᵊn, -ɪˈ- US ˌpɑː.ləˈ-

Pollock ˈpɒl.ək US ˈpɑː.lək

pollster ˈpəʊl.stəʳ US ˈpoʊl.stɚ **-s** -z

pollutant pəˈluː.tᵊnt, -ˈljuː- US -ˈluː- **-s** -s

pollu|te pəˈluː|t, -ˈljuː|t US -luː|t **-tes** -ts **-ting** -tɪŋ US -t̬ɪŋ **-ted** -tɪd US -t̬ɪd **-ter/s** -təʳ/z US -t̬ɚ/z

pollution pəˈluː.ʃᵊn, -ˈljuː- US -ˈluː- **-s** -z

Pollux ˈpɒl.əks US ˈpɑː.ləks

Polly ˈpɒl.i US ˈpɑː.li

pollyanna (P) ˌpɒl.iˈæn.ə US ˌpɑː.liˈ- **-s** -z

Polmont ˈpəʊl.mənt US ˈpoʊl.mɑːnt

polo (P) ˈpəʊ.ləʊ US ˈpoʊ.loʊ ˈ**polo ˌneck**

polonais|e ˌpɒl.əˈneɪz US ˌpɑː.ləˈ-, ˌpoʊ- **-es** -ɪz

polonium pəˈləʊ.ni.əm US -ˈloʊ-

Polonius pəˈləʊ.ni.əs, pɒlˈəʊ- US pəˈloʊ-

polon|y pəˈləʊ.n|i US -ˈloʊ- **-ies** -iz

Pol Pot ˌpɒlˈpɒt US ˌpɑːlˈpɑːt

Polson ˈpəʊl.sᵊn US ˈpoʊl-

poltergeist ˈpɒl.tə.gaɪst, ˈpəʊl- US ˈpoʊl.t̬ɚ- **-s** -s

poltroon pɒlˈtruːn US pɑːl- **-s** -z **-ery** -ᵊr.i

Polwarth *in Scotland:* ˈpəʊl.wəθ ⓤⓢ ˈpoʊl.wɚθ *surname:* ˈpɒl.wəθ ⓤⓢ ˈpɑːl.wɚθ
poly- pɒl.i-, -ɪ-; pəˈlɪ- ⓤⓢ pɑː.li-, -lɪ-, -lə-; pəˈlɪ-
Note: Prefix. Many compounds with **poly-** have the stress pattern ˈ**poly**ˌ-; these are likely to undergo stress shift when a stressed syllable follows. The prefix may also be stressed on the second syllable, e.g. **polygonal** /pəˈlɪg.ᵊn.ᵊl/.
poly ˈpɒl.i ⓤⓢ ˈpɑː.li **-s** -z
polyamide ˌpɒl.iˈæm.aɪd, -ˈeɪ.maɪd ⓤⓢ ˌpɑː.liˈ- **-s** -z
polyandrous ˌpɒl.iˈæn.drəs ⓤⓢ ˌpɑː.liˈ-
polyandry ˈpɒl.i.æn.dri, ˌpɒl.iˈæn- ⓤⓢ ˈpɑː.liˌæn-, ˌpɑː.liˈæn-
polyanth|us ˌpɒl.iˈænt.θ|əs ⓤⓢ ˌpɑː.liˈ- **-uses** -ə.sɪz **-i** -aɪ
polybag ˈpɒl.i.bæg, ˌ--ˈ- ⓤⓢ ˈpɑː.li.bæg **-s** -z
Polybius pəˈlɪb.i.əs, pɒlˈɪb- ⓤⓢ pəˈlɪb-, poʊ-
polycarbonate ˌpɒl.ɪˈkɑː.bə.neɪt, -iˈ-, -nət, -nɪt ⓤⓢ ˌpɑː.lɪˈkɑːr.bə.nɪt, -liˈ-, -neɪt **-s** -s
Polycarp ˈpɒl.ɪ.kɑːp, -i- ⓤⓢ ˈpɑː.lɪ.kɑːrp, -li-
Polycell® ˈpɒl.ɪ.sel, -i- ⓤⓢ ˈpɑː.lɪ-, -li-
polyclinic ˌpɒl.ɪˈklɪn.ɪk ⓤⓢ ˌpɑː.lɪˈ- **-s** -s
polycotton ˌpɒl.ɪˈkɒt.ᵊn, -iˈ- ⓤⓢ ˌpɑː.lɪˈkɑː.tᵊn, -liˈ-
Polycrates pəˈlɪk.rə.tiːz, pɒlˈɪk- ⓤⓢ pəˈlɪk-
Polydor® ˈpɒl.i.dɔːʳ ⓤⓢ ˈpɑː.lɪ.dɔːr, -li-
polyester ˌpɒl.iˈes.təʳ ⓤⓢ ˌpɑː.liˈes.tɚ, ˈpɑː.li.es-
polyethylene ˌpɒl.iˈeθ.ɪ.liːn, ˈ-ə- ⓤⓢ ˌpɑː.liˈeθ.ə-
Polyfilla® ˈpɒl.ɪˌfɪl.ə, -i- ⓤⓢ ˈpɑː.lɪˌ-, -liˌ-
polygam|y pəˈlɪg.ə.m|i, pɒlˈɪg- ⓤⓢ pəˈlɪg-, -li- **-ist/s** -ɪst/s **-ous** -əs
polyglot ˈpɒl.ɪ.glɒt, -i- ⓤⓢ ˈpɑː.lɪ.glɑːt, -li- **-s** -s
polygon ˈpɒl.ɪ.gɒn, -gən ⓤⓢ ˈpɑː.lɪ.gɑːn **-s** -z
polygonal pəˈlɪg.ᵊn.ᵊl, pɒlˈɪg- ⓤⓢ pəˈlɪg- **-ly** -i
polygonum pəˈlɪg.ᵊn.əm, pɒlˈɪg- ⓤⓢ pəˈlɪg-
Polygram® ˈpɒl.i.græm ⓤⓢ ˈpɑː.lɪ-
polygraph ˈpɒl.ɪ.grɑːf, -i-, -græf ⓤⓢ ˈpɑː.lɪ.græf, -li- **-s** -s
polyhedr|on ˌpɒl.ɪˈhiː.dr|ᵊn, -iˈ-, -ˈhed.r|ᵊn ⓤⓢ ˌpɑː.lɪˈhiː-, -li- **-ons** -ᵊnz **-a** -ə **-al** -ᵊl
polylectal ˌpɒl.ɪˈlek.tᵊl, -iˈ- ⓤⓢ ˌpɑː.lɪˈ-, -liˈ-
polymath ˈpɒl.ɪ.mæθ, -i- ⓤⓢ ˈpɑː.lɪ-, -li- **-s** -s
polymer ˈpɒl.ɪ.məʳ ⓤⓢ ˈpɑː.lɪ.mɚ **-s** -z
polymeras|e ˈpɒl.ɪ.mᵊr.eɪs, -eɪz ⓤⓢ ˈpɑː.lɪ.mə.reɪz, -reɪs **-es** -ɪz
polymeric ˌpɒl.ɪˈmer.ɪk ⓤⓢ ˌpɑː.lɪ- **-ally** -ᵊl.i, -li
polymerism pəˈlɪm.ᵊr.ɪ.zᵊm, pɒlˈɪm-; ˈpɒl.ɪ.mᵊr- ⓤⓢ pəˈlɪm.ɚ-; ˈpɑː.lɪ.mɚ-
polymerization, -isa- ˌpɒl.ɪ.mᵊr.aɪˈzeɪ.ʃᵊn, -lə-, -ɪˈ- ⓤⓢ ˌpɑː.lɪ.mɚ.ɪˈ-
polymeriz|e, -is|e ˈpɒl.ɪ.mᵊr.aɪz, ˈ-ə- ⓤⓢ ˈpɑː.lɪ.mə.raɪz **-es** -ɪz **-ing** -ɪŋ **-ed** -d
polymerous pəˈlɪm.ᵊr.əs, pɒlˈɪm- ⓤⓢ pəˈlɪm-
polymorph|ic ˌpɒl.ɪˈmɔː.f|ɪk, -i- ⓤⓢ ˌpɑː.lɪˈmɔːr-, -iˈ- **-ism** -ɪ.zᵊm **-ous** -əs
Polynesi|a ˌpɒl.ɪˈniː.ʒ|ə, -zi|.ə, -ʒi|.ə, -si|.ə, -ʃi|.ə, -ʃ|ə ⓤⓢ ˌpɑː.ləˈniː.ʒ|ə, -ʃ|ə **-an/s** -ən/z
polynomial ˌpɒl.ɪˈnəʊ.mi.əl ⓤⓢ ˌpɑː.liˈnoʊ- **-s** -z
Poly-Olbion ˌpɒl.iˈɒl.bi.ən ⓤⓢ ˌpɑː.liˈɑːl-
polyp ˈpɒl.ɪp ⓤⓢ ˈpɑː.lɪp **-s** -s **-ous** -əs
polypeptide ˌpɒl.ɪˈpep.taɪd, -i- ⓤⓢ ˌpɑː.lɪˈ-, -liˈ- **-s** -z
Polyphemus ˌpɒl.ɪˈfiː.məs, -əˈ- ⓤⓢ ˌpɑː.lɪˈ-
polyphon|ic ˌpɒl.ɪˈfɒn|.ɪk, -əˈ-, -iˈ- ⓤⓢ ˌpɑː.lɪˈfɑː.n|ɪk, -liˈ- **-ous** -əs
polyphony pəˈlɪf.ᵊn.i, pɒlˈɪf- ⓤⓢ pəˈlɪf-
polypody ˈpɒl.ɪ.pəʊ.di, -i- ⓤⓢ ˈpɑː.lɪ.poʊ-, -li-
polyp|us ˈpɒl.ɪ.p|əs, ˈ-ə- ⓤⓢ ˈpɑː.lɪ- **-i** -aɪ
polysaccharide ˌpɒl.ɪˈsæk.ᵊr.aɪd, -i-, -ɪd ⓤⓢ ˌpɑː.lɪˈsæk.ə.raɪd, -liˈ-
polysemous pəˈlɪs.ɪ.məs, pɒlˈɪs-; ˌpɒl.ɪˈsiː- ⓤⓢ ˌpɑː.lɪˈsiː-; pəˈlɪs.ə-
polysemy pəˈlɪs.ɪ.mi; ˌpɒl.ɪˈsiː.mi, ˈpɒl.ɪ.siː- ⓤⓢ ˈpɑː.lɪ.siː-; pəˈlɪs.ə-
polystyrene ˌpɒl.ɪˈstaɪə.riːn, -iˈ- ⓤⓢ ˌpɑː.lɪˈstaɪ-, -liˈ-
polysyllabic ˌpɒl.ɪ.sɪˈlæb.ɪk, -i-, -səˈ- ⓤⓢ ˌpɑː.lɪ.sɪˈ-, -li- **-al** -ᵊl **-ally** -ᵊl.i, -li
polysyllable ˌpɒl.ɪˈsɪl.ə.bl̩, ˈpɒl.ɪˌsɪl-, -i- ⓤⓢ ˈpɑː.lɪˌsɪl-, -liˌ- **-s** -z
polysyndeton ˌpɒl.ɪˈsɪn.də.tən, -iˈ-, -dɪ- ⓤⓢ ˌpɑː.lɪˈsɪn.də.tɑːn, -liˈ-, -tən
polysynthesis ˌpɒl.ɪˈsɪnt.θə.sɪs, -iˈ-, -θɪ- ⓤⓢ ˌpɑː.lɪˈ-, -liˈ-
polysynthetic ˌpɒl.ɪ.sɪnˈθet.ɪk, -i- ⓤⓢ ˌpɑː.lɪ.sɪnˈθet̬.ɪk, -li-
polysystemic ˌpɒl.ɪ.sɪˈstiː.mɪk, -i-, -səˈ- ⓤⓢ ˌpɑː.lɪ-, -li-
polytechnic ˌpɒl.ɪˈtek.nɪk ⓤⓢ -iˈ-, ˌpɑː.lɪˈ-, -liˈ- **-s** -s
polythe|ism ˈpɒl.ɪ.θiː|.ɪ.zᵊm, ˌpɒl.ɪˈθiː-, -i- ⓤⓢ ˈpɑː.lɪ.θiː-, ˌpɑː.liˈθiː, -li- **-ist/s** -ɪst/s
polytheistic ˌpɒl.ɪ.θiˈɪs.tɪk; -ˈθiː.ɪ.stɪk, -i- ⓤⓢ ˌpɑː.lɪ.θiˈɪs.tɪk, -li-
polythene ˈpɒl.ɪ.θiːn, ˈ-ə- ⓤⓢ ˈpɑː.lɪ-
polyunsaturate ˌpɒl.i.ʌnˈsætʃ.ᵊr.eɪt, -ˈsæt.jᵊr-, -ət ⓤⓢ ˌpɑː.li.ʌnˈsætʃ.ə.reɪt **-s** -s
polyunsaturated ˌpɒl.i.ʌnˈsætʃ.ᵊr.eɪ.tɪd, -ˈsæt.jᵊr- ⓤⓢ ˌpɑː.li.ʌnˈsætʃ.ə.reɪ.t̬ɪd
polyurethane ˌpɒl.ɪˈjʊə.rə.θeɪn, -ˈjɔː-, -iˈ-, -rɪ- ⓤⓢ ˌpɑː.lɪˈjʊr.ə-, -liˈ-
polyvalent ˌpɒl.ɪˈveɪ.lənt, -iˈ- ⓤⓢ ˌpɑː.lɪˈ-, ˈpɑː.lɪ.veɪ-, -liˈ-
polyvinyl ˌpɒl.ɪˈvaɪ.nᵊl, -iˈ-, -nɪl ⓤⓢ ˌpɑː.lɪˈvaɪ.nəl, -liˈ-
Polyxen|a pəˈlɪk.sɪ.n|ə, pɒlˈɪk-, -sə- ⓤⓢ pəˈlɪk-; ˌpoʊ.lɪkˈsiː- **-us** -əs
Polzeath pɒlˈzeθ ⓤⓢ pɑːl-
pom (P) pɒm ⓤⓢ pɑːm **-s** -z
pomace ˈpʌm.ɪs ⓤⓢ ˈpʌm-, ˈpɑː.mɪs
pomade pəʊˈmeɪd, pɒmˈeɪd, -ˈɑːd ⓤⓢ pɑːˈmeɪd, poʊ-, ˈpɑː.meɪd, -mɑːd **-s** -z
Pomagne® pəˈmeɪn, pɒmˈeɪn ⓤⓢ pɑːˈmeɪn, pə-
pomander pəˈmæn.dəʳ, pɒmˈæn- ⓤⓢ ˈpoʊ.mæn.dɚ; -ˈ--, pə- **-s** -z
pomatum pəˈmeɪ.təm, -ˈmɑː- ⓤⓢ -t̬əm, poʊ- **-s** -z
pome pəʊm ⓤⓢ poʊm **-s** -z
pomegranate ˈpɒm.ɪˌgræn.ɪt, -əˌ- ⓤⓢ ˈpɑːmˌgræn-, ˈpʌmˌ-, ˈpɑː.məˌ-, ˈpʌm.əˌ- **-s** -s
pomelo ˈpɒm.ɪ.ləʊ, ˈ-ə-; pəˈmel.oʊ ⓤⓢ ˈpɑː.mə.loʊ **-s** -z
Pomerania ˌpɒm.əˈreɪ.ni.ə ⓤⓢ ˌpɑː.məˈ-
Pomeranian ˌpɒm.əˈreɪ.ni.ən ⓤⓢ ˌpɑː.məˈ- *stress shift:* ˌPomeranian ˈdog
Pomeroy ˈpɒm.ə.rɔɪ, ˈpəʊm.rɔɪ ⓤⓢ ˈpɑː.mə.rɔɪ, ˈpɑːm.rɔɪ
pomfret *fish:* ˈpɒm.frɪt ⓤⓢ ˈpɑːm-, ˈpʌm- **-s** -s
Pomfret ˈpʌm.frɪt, ˈpɒm- ⓤⓢ ˈpʌm-, ˈpɑːm- ˈ**Pomfret** ˌ**cake**
pommel (*n.*) ˈpɒm.ᵊl ⓤⓢ ˈpʌm.ᵊl, ˈpɑː.mᵊl **-s** -z
pommel (*v.*) ˈpʌm.ᵊl, ˈpɒm- ⓤⓢ ˈpʌm-, ˈpɑː.mᵊl **-s** -z **-(l)ing** -ɪŋ **-(l)ed** -d
pomm|ie, pomm|y (P) ˈpɒm|.i ⓤⓢ ˈpɑː.m|i **-ies** -iz
Pomona pəˈməʊ.nə, pɒmˈəʊ- ⓤⓢ pəˈmoʊ-
pomp pɒmp ⓤⓢ pɑːmp **-s** -s
pompadour (P) ˈpɒm.pə.dʊəʳ, ˈpɔ̃ːm-, -dɔːʳ ⓤⓢ ˈpɑːm.pə.dɔːr, -dʊr **-s** -z
Pompeian pɒmˈpeɪ.ən, -ˈpiː- ⓤⓢ pɑːmˈpeɪ-
Pompeii pɒmˈpeɪ.i, -ˈpeɪ ⓤⓢ pɑːm-
Pompey ˈpɒm.pi ⓤⓢ ˈpɑːm-, -peɪ
Pompidou ˈpɒm.pɪ.duː ⓤⓢ ˈpɑːm- ˈ**Pompidou** ˌ**Centre**

pompom ˈpɒm.pɒm (US) ˈpɑːm.pɑːm **-s** -z

pompon ˈpɒm.pɒn, -pɒŋ, ˈpɔ̃ːm.pɔ̃ːŋ (US) ˈpɑːm.pɑːn **-s** -z

pomposity pɒmˈpɒs.ə.ti, -ɪ.ti (US) pɑːmˈpɑː.sə.t̬i

pompous ˈpɒm.pəs (US) ˈpɑːm- **-ly** -li **-ness** -nəs, -nɪs

ponc|e pɒnts (US) pɑːnts **-es** -ɪz **-(e)y** -i

poncho ˈpɒn.tʃəʊ (US) ˈpɑːn.tʃoʊ **-s** -z

pond (P) pɒnd (US) pɑːnd **-s** -z

pond|er ˈpɒn.d|əʳ (US) ˈpɑːn.d|ɚ **-ers** -əz (US) -ɚz **-ering/ly** -ᵊr.ɪŋ/li **-ered** -əd (US) -ɚd

ponderability ˌpɒn.dᵊr.əˈbɪl.ə.ti, -ɪ.ti (US) ˌpɑːn.dɚ.əˈbɪl.ə.t̬i

ponderable ˈpɒn.dᵊr.ə.bl̩ (US) ˈpɑːn.dɚ- **-ness** -nəs, -nɪs

ponderous ˈpɒn.dᵊr.əs (US) ˈpɑːn- **-ly** -li **-ness** -nəs, -nɪs

Ponders ˈpɒn.dəz (US) ˈpɑːn.dɚz

Pondicherry ˌpɒn.dɪˈtʃer.i, -ˈʃer- (US) ˌpɑːn.dɪˈtʃer-

pondweed ˈpɒnd.wiːd (US) ˈpɑːnd-

pong pɒŋ (US) pɑːŋ, pɔːŋ **-s** -z **-ing** -ɪŋ **-ed** -d

pongee ˌpɒnˈdʒiː, ˌpʌn- (US) ˌpɑːnˈdʒiː; ˈpɑːn.dʒi

poniard ˈpɒn.jəd, -jɑːd (US) ˈpɑː.njɚd **-s** -z **-ing** -ɪŋ **-ed** -ɪd

pons asinorum ˌpɒnzˌæs.ɪˈnɔː.rəm, -rʊm (US) ˌpɑːnzˌæs.ɪˈnɔːr.əm

Ponsonby ˈpʌnt.sᵊn.bi, ˈpɒnt-, -sᵊm- (US) ˈpɑːnt.sᵊn-, ˈpʌnt-

Pontardawe ˌpɒn.təˈdaʊ.i, -eɪ (US) ˌpɑːn.t̬ɚ-

Pontardulais ˌpɒn.təˈdɪl.əs, -ˈdʌl-, -aɪs (US) ˌpɑːn.t̬ɚ-

Pontefract ˈpɒn.tɪ.frækt (US) ˈpɑːn.t̬ɪ- ˈ**Pontefract** ˌ**cake**

Ponteland pɒnˈtiː.lənd (US) pɑːn-

Pontiac ˈpɒn.ti.æk (US) ˈpɑːn.t̬i- **-s** -s

pontifex (P) ˈpɒn.tɪ.feks (US) ˈpɑːn.t̬ɪ- **pontifices** pɒnˈtɪf.ɪ.siːz (US) pɑːn-

pontiff ˈpɒn.tɪf (US) ˈpɑːn.t̬ɪf **-s** -s

pontific pɒnˈtɪf.ɪk (US) pɑːn- **-al/s** -ᵊl/z **-ally** -ᵊl.i, -li

pontificate *(n.) pope:* pɒnˈtɪf.ɪ.kət, ˈ-ə-, -kɪt, -keɪt (US) pɑːnˈtɪf.ɪ.kət, -keɪt **-s** -s

pontifi|cate *(v.) give opinions:* pɒnˈtɪf.ɪ|.keɪt, ˈ-ə- (US) pɑːn- **-cates** -keɪts **-cating** -keɪ.tɪŋ, -keɪ.t̬ɪŋ **-cated** -keɪ.tɪd (US) -keɪ.t̬ɪd

pontification ˌpɒn.tɪ.fɪˈkeɪ.ʃᵊn, -tə- (US) ˌpɑːn.tɪ-, -t̬ə- **-s** -z

Pontine ˈpɒn.taɪn (US) ˈpɑːn.tiːn, -taɪn

Ponting ˈpɒn.tɪŋ (US) ˈpɑːn.t̬ɪŋ

Pontins® ˈpɒn.tɪnz (US) ˈpɑːn-

Pontius ˈpɒn.ti.əs, -tʃi.əs, ˈ-ʃəs (US) ˈpɑːn.tʃəs, ˈ-t̬i.əs ˌ**Pontius** ˈ**Pilate**

Pont l'Évêque ˌpɔ̃ːn.leɪˈvek (US) ˌpɑ̃ːnt.ləˈvek

Pontllanfraith ˌpɒnt.ɬlænˈvraɪθ, -θlænˈ- (US) ˌpɑːnt.θlænˈ-

pontoon pɒnˈtuːn (US) pɑːn- **-s** -z

Pont|us ˈpɒn.t|əs (US) ˈpɑːn.t̬|əs **-ic** -ɪk

Pontyclun ˌpɒn.tɪˈklɪn, -tə- (US) ˌpɑːn.t̬ɪ-

Pontypool ˌpɒn.tɪˈpuːl, -tə- (US) ˌpɑːn.t̬ɪ-

Pontypridd ˌpɒn.tɪˈpriːð, -tə- (US) ˌpɑːn.t̬ɪ-

pon|y ˈpəʊ.n|i (US) ˈpoʊ- **-ies** -iz ˈ**pony** ˌ**trekking**

ponytail ˈpəʊ.ni.teɪl (US) ˈpoʊ- **-s** -z

pooch puːtʃ **-es** -ɪz

pood puːd **-s** -z

poodle ˈpuː.dl̩ **-s** -z

poof pʊf, puːf (US) puːf, pʊf **-s** -s

poofter ˈpʊf.təʳ, ˈpuːf- (US) ˈpuːf.tɚ **-s** -z

poofy ˈpʊf.i, ˈpuː.fi (US) ˈpuː.fi

poo(h) (P) *exclamation:* pˌu, phuː, puː *other senses:* puː

Note: /puː/ is the pronunciation for A.A. Milne's character "Winnie the Pooh".

Pooh-Bah ˌpuːˈbɑː, ˈ-- (US) ˈ--

pooh-pooh ˌpuːˈpuː **-s** -z **-ing** -ɪŋ **-ed** -d

Pook puːk

pool puːl **-s** -z **-ing** -ɪŋ **-ed** -d

Poole puːl

Pooley ˈpuː.li

poolroom ˈpuːl.rʊm, -ruːm (US) -ruːm, -rʊm **-s** -z

poon puːn **-s** -z

Poona ˈpuː.nə, -nɑː (US) -nə

poontang ˈpuːn.tæŋ

poop puːp **-s** -s **-ing** -ɪŋ **-ed** -t ˈ**poop** ˌ**deck**

pooper ˈpuː.pəʳ (US) -pɚ **-s** -z

pooper-scooper ˈpuː.pəˌskuː.pəʳ (US) -pɚˌskuː.pɚ **-s** -z

poop-scoop ˈpuːp.skuːp **-s** -s

poor (P) pɔːʳ, pʊəʳ (US) pʊr **-er** -əʳ (US) -ɚ **-est** -ɪst, -əst **-ly** -li **-ness** -nəs, -nɪs ˈ**poor** ˌ**box**; ˈ**poor** ˌ**law**; ˌ**poor re**ˈ**lation**; ˌ**poor** ˈ**white**

Poore pɔːʳ, pʊəʳ (US) pʊr

poorhou|se ˈpɔː.haʊ|s, ˈpʊə- (US) ˈpʊr- **-ses** -zɪz

poorly ˈpɔː.li, ˈpʊə- (US) ˈpʊr-

Pooter ˈpuː.təʳ (US) -t̬ɚ **-ish** -ɪʃ

poove puːv **-s** -z

pop pɒp (US) pɑːp **-s** -s **-ping** -ɪŋ **-ped** -t **-per/s** -əʳ/z (US) -ɚ/z ˈ**pop** ˌ**art**; ˈ**pop** ˌ**music** (US) ˌ**pop** ˈ**music**; ˈ**pop** ˌ**star**

popadom, -dum ˈpɒp.ə.dəm (US) ˈpɑː.pə- **-s** -z

popcorn ˈpɒp.kɔːn (US) ˈpɑːp.kɔːrn

pop-down ˈpɒp.daʊn (US) ˈpɑːp-

pope (P) pəʊp (US) poʊp **-s** -s **-dom/s** -dəm/z

popery ˈpəʊ.pᵊr.i (US) ˈpoʊ-

Popeye ˈpɒp.aɪ (US) ˈpɑː.paɪ

pop-eyed ˌpɒpˈaɪd (US) ˈpɑːpˌaɪd *stress shift, British only:* ˌpop-eyed ˈmonster

pop-gun ˈpɒp.gʌn (US) ˈpɑːp- **-s** -z

Popham ˈpɒp.əm (US) ˈpɑː.pəm

popinjay ˈpɒp.ɪn.dʒeɪ (US) ˈpɑː.pɪn- **-s** -z

popish ˈpəʊ.pɪʃ (US) ˈpoʊ- **-ly** -li **-ness** -nəs, -nɪs

poplar (P) ˈpɒp.ləʳ (US) ˈpɑː.plɚ **-s** -z

poplin ˈpɒp.lɪn (US) ˈpɑː.plɪn **-s** -z

Popocatépetl ˌpɒp.əʊˌkæt.ɪˈpet.l̩, ˌpəʊ.pəʊ-, -əˈ-, ˌpəʊ.pəʊˈkæt.ɪ.pet-, ˌpɒp.əʊˈ-, ˈ-ə- (US) ˌpoʊ.pəˈkæt.ə.pet̬.l̩; ˌpɑː.pɑː.kɑːˈteɪ-

popover ˈpɒpˌəʊ.vəʳ (US) ˈpɑːˌpoʊ.vɚ **-s** -z

poppa ˈpɒp.ə (US) ˈpɑː.pə **-s** -z

poppadom, -dum ˈpɒp.ə.dəm (US) ˈpɑː.pə- **-s** -z

popper (P) ˈpɒp.əʳ (US) ˈpɑː.pɚ **-s** -z

Popperian pɒpˈɪə.ri.ən (US) pɑːˈpɪr.i-

poppet ˈpɒp.ɪt (US) ˈpɑː.pɪt **-s** -s

popping creas|e ˈpɒp.ɪŋˌkriːs (US) ˈpɑː.pɪŋˌ- **-es** -ɪz

poppl|e ˈpɒp.l̩ (US) ˈpɑː.pl̩ **-es** -z **-ing** -ɪŋ, ˈpɒp.lɪŋ (US) ˈpɑː.plɪŋ **-ed** -d

Popplewell ˈpɒp.l̩.wel (US) ˈpɑː.pl̩-

popp|y (P) ˈpɒp|.i (US) ˈpɑː.p|i **-ies** -iz ˈ**Poppy** ˌ**Day**

poppycock ˈpɒp.ɪ.kɒk (US) ˈpɑː.pɪ.kɑːk

popsicle (P®) ˈpɒp.sɪ.kl̩ (US) ˈpɑːp- **-s** -z

pop|sy, pop|sie ˈpɒp|.si (US) ˈpɑːp- **-sies** -siz

populace ˈpɒp.jə.ləs, -jʊ-, -lɪs (US) ˈpɑː.pjə.lɪs, -pjʊ-, -ləs

popular ˈpɒp.jə.ləʳ, -jʊ- (US) ˈpɑː.pjə.lɚ, -pjʊ- **-ly** -li

popularity ˌpɒp.jəˈlær.ə.ti, -jʊˈ-, -ɪ.ti (US) ˌpɑː.pjəˈler.ə.t̬i, -pjʊˈ-, -ˈlær-

popularization, -isa- ˌpɒp.jə.lᵊr.aɪˈzeɪ.ʃᵊn, -jə-, -ɪˈ- (US) ˌpɑː.pjə.lɚ.ɪˈ-, -pjʊ-

populariz|e, -is|e ˈpɒp.jə.lᵊr.aɪz, -jʊ- (US) ˈpɑː.pjə.lə.raɪz, -pjʊ- **-es** -ɪz **-ing** -ɪŋ **-ed** -d

popu|late ˈpɒp.jə|.leɪt, -jʊ- (US) ˈpɑː.pjə-, -pjʊ- **-lates** -leɪts **-lating** -leɪ.tɪŋ (US) -leɪ.t̬ɪŋ **-lated** -leɪ.tɪd (US) -leɪ.t̬ɪd

population ˌpɒp.jəˈleɪ.ʃᵊn, -jʊˈ- (US) ˌpɑː.pjəˈ-, -pjʊˈ- **-s** -z **popu**ˈ**lation ex**ˌ**plosion**

popul|ism ˈpɒp.jə.l|ɪ.zᵊm, -jʊ- (US) ˈpɑː.pjə-, -pjʊ- **-ist/s** -ɪst/s

populous ˈpɒp.jə.ləs, -jʊ- (US) ˈpɑː.pjə-, -pjʊ- **-ly** -li **-ness** -nəs, -nɪs

pop-up ˈpɒp.ʌp (US) ˈpɑːp-

porcelain ˈpɔː.sᵊl.ɪn (US) ˈpɔːr-, ˈ-slɪn **-s** -z

porch pɔːtʃ (US) pɔːrtʃ **-es** -ɪz

Porchester ˈpɔː.tʃɪ.stəʳ, -tʃə- (US) ˈpɔːr.tʃɪ.stɚ, -tʃə-

porcine ˈpɔː.saɪn (US) ˈpɔːr-, -sɪn

porcin|o pɔːˈtʃiː.n|əʊ US pɔːrˈtʃiː.n|oʊ **-i** -iː

porcupine ˈpɔː.kjə.paɪn, -kjʊ- US ˈpɔːr- **-s** -z

por|e pɔːʳ US pɔːr **-es** -z **-ing** -ɪŋ **-ed** -d

porg|y *fish:* ˈpɔː.dʒ|i US ˈpɔːr.g|i **-ies** -iz

Porgy *name:* ˈpɔː.gi US ˈpɔːr-

pork pɔːk US pɔːrk **-er/s** -əʳ/z US -ɚ/z **-y** -i ˌ**pork** ˈ**pie**

porkpie hat ˌpɔːk.paɪˈhæt US ˌpɔːrk- **-s** -s

Porlock ˈpɔː.lɒk US ˈpɔːr.lɑːk

porn pɔːn US pɔːrn

porno ˈpɔː.nəʊ US ˈpɔːr.noʊ

pornographic ˌpɔː.nəˈgræf.ɪk US ˌpɔːr-

pornograph|y pɔːˈnɒg.rə.f|i US pɔːrˈnɑː.grə- **-er/s** -əʳ/z US -ɚ/z

porosity pɔːˈrɒs.ə.ti, -ɪ.ti US pɔːˈrɑː.sə.t̬i, pə-

porous ˈpɔː.rəs US ˈpɔːr.əs **-ly** -li **-ness** -nəs, -nɪs

porphyria pɔːˈfɪr.i.ə, -ˈfaɪ.ri- US pɔːrˈfɪr.i-

porphyrin ˈpɔː.fᵊr.ɪn, -fɪ.rɪn US ˈpɔːr.fɚ.ɪn

porphyry (P) ˈpɔː.fᵊr.i, -fɪ.ri US ˈpɔːr.fɚ.i

porpois|e ˈpɔː.pəs US ˈpɔːr- **-es** -ɪz

porridge ˈpɒr.ɪdʒ US ˈpɔːr-

porringer ˈpɒr.ɪn.dʒəʳ US ˈpɔːr.ɪn.dʒɚ **-s** -z

Porritt ˈpɒr.ɪt US ˈpɔːr-

Porsch|e® pɔːʃ, ˈpɔː.ʃ|ə US pɔːrʃ, ˈpɔːr.ʃ|ə **-es** -iz, -əz

Porsena ˈpɔː.sɪ.nə, -sᵊn.ə US ˈpɔːr-

Porson ˈpɔː.sᵊn US ˈpɔːr-

port pɔːt US pɔːrt **-s** -s **-ing** -ɪŋ US ˈpɔːr.t̬ɪŋ **-ed** -ɪd US ˈpɔːr.t̬ɪd ˌ**Port** ˈ**Moresby;** ˌ**port of** ˈ**call;** ˌ**port of** ˈ**entry;** ˌ**Port** ˈ**Stanley;** ˌ**Port** ˈ**Talbot**

portability ˌpɔː.təˈbɪl.ə.ti, -ɪ.ti US ˌpɔːr.t̬əˈbɪl.ə.t̬i

portable ˈpɔː.tə.bl̩ US ˈpɔːr.t̬ə- **-ness** -nəs, -nɪs

Portadown ˌpɔː.təˈdaʊn US ˌpɔːr.t̬əˈ-

portage ˈpɔː.tɪdʒ US ˈpɔːr.t̬ɪdʒ

Portakabin® ˈpɔː.təˌkæb.ɪn US ˈpɔːr.t̬əˌ- **-s** -z

portal (P) ˈpɔː.tᵊl US ˈpɔːr.t̬ᵊl **-s** -z

portament|o ˌpɔː.təˈmen.t|əʊ US ˌpɔːr.t̬əˈmen.t|oʊ **-i** -iː

Port-au-Prince ˌpɔː.təʊˈprɪnts US ˌpɔːr.toʊˈ-

Portchester ˈpɔː.tʃɪ.stəʳ, -tʃə- US ˈpɔːr.tʃə.stɚ, -tʃɪ-

portcullis ˌpɔːtˈkʌl.ɪs US ˌpɔːrt- **-es** -ɪz

Porte pɔːt US pɔːrt

portend pɔːˈtend US pɔːr- **-s** -z **-ing** -ɪŋ **-ed** -ɪd

portent ˈpɔː.tent, -tᵊnt US ˈpɔːr.tent **-s** -s

portentous pɔːˈten.təs US pɔːrˈten.t̬əs **-ly** -li **-ness** -nəs, -nɪs

Porteous ˈpɔː.ti.əs US ˈpɔːr.t̬i-

porter (P) ˈpɔː.təʳ US ˈpɔːr.t̬ɚ **-s** -z **-age** -ɪdʒ

porterhou|se ˈpɔː.tə.haʊ|s US ˈpɔːr.t̬ɚ- **-ses** -zɪz

Porteus ˈpɔː.ti.əs US ˈpɔːr.t̬i-

portfolio ˌpɔːtˈfəʊ.li.əʊ US ˌpɔːrtˈfoʊ.li.oʊ **-s** -z

Porthcawl ˌpɔːθˈkɔːl, -ˈkaʊl US ˌpɔːrθˈkɑːl, -ˈkɔːl, -ˈkaʊl

porthole ˈpɔːt.həʊl US ˈpɔːrt.hoʊl **-s** -z

Portia ˈpɔː.ʃə, -ʃi.ə US ˈpɔːr.ʃə

portico ˈpɔː.tɪ.kəʊ US ˈpɔːr.t̬ɪ.koʊ **-(e)s** -z

portière ˌpɔː.tiˈeəʳ US ˌpɔːrˈtjer, -tiˈer, ˌ-ˈtɪr **-s** -z

Portillo pɔːˈtɪl.əʊ US pɔːrˈtɪl.oʊ

portion ˈpɔː.ʃᵊn US ˈpɔːr- **-s** -z **-ing** -ɪŋ **-ed** -d

Portishead ˈpɔː.tɪs.hed US ˈpɔːr.t̬ɪs-

Portland ˈpɔːt.lənd US ˈpɔːrt- ˌ**Portland ce**ˈ**ment;** ˌ**Portland** ˈ**stone**

portl|y ˈpɔːt.l|i US ˈpɔːrt- **-ier** -i.əʳ US -i.ɚ **-iest** -i.ɪst, -i.əst **-iness** -ɪ.nəs, -ɪ.nɪs

Portmadoc ˌpɔːtˈmæd.ək US ˌpɔːrt-

Portman ˈpɔːt.mən US ˈpɔːrt-

portmanteau pɔːtˈmæn.təʊ US pɔːrtˈmæn.toʊ, ˌ--ˈ- **-s** -z **-x** -z

Portmeirion ˌpɔːtˈmer.i.ən US ˌpɔːrt-

Pôrto Alegre ˌpɔː.təʊ.əˈleg.ri US ˌpɔːr.tu.əˈleg.rə

Portobello ˌpɔː.təˈbel.əʊ US ˌpɔːr.t̬əˈbel.oʊ, -t̬oʊˈ- *stress shift, see compound:* ˌ**Portobello** ˈ**Road**

Porto-Novo ˌpɔː.təʊˈnəʊ.vəʊ US ˌpɔːr.t̬oʊˈnoʊ.voʊ

Porto Rico ˌpɔː.təʊˈriː.kəʊ US ˌpɔːr.t̬oʊˈriː.koʊ, -t̬əˈ-

portrai|t ˈpɔː.trɪ|t, -trət, -treɪ|t US ˈpɔːr.trɪ|t, -treɪ|t **-ts** -ts **-tist/s** -tɪst/s US -t̬ɪst/s

portraiture ˈpɔː.trɪ.tʃə, -trə-, -tjʊəʳ US ˈpɔːr.trɪ.tʃɚ

portray pɔːˈtreɪ, pə- US pɔːr- **-s** -z **-ing** -ɪŋ **-ed** -d **-er/s** -əʳ/z US -ɚ/z

portrayal pɔːˈtreɪ.əl, pə- US pɔːr- **-s** -z

Portrush ˌpɔːtˈrʌʃ US ˌpɔːrt-

Port Said ˌpɔːtˈsaɪd, -sɑːˈiːd US ˌpɔːrt.sɑːˈiːd, -ɪd

Port Salut ˌpɔː.səˈluː, -sælˈuː US ˌpɔːr.sælˈuː

Portsea ˈpɔːt.si, -siː US ˈpɔːrt-

Portslade ˌpɔːtˈsleɪd US ˌpɔːrt-

Portsmouth ˈpɔːt.sməθ US ˈpɔːrt-

Portstewart ˌpɔːtˈstjuː.ət US ˌpɔːrtˈstuː.ɚt, -ˈstjuː-

Portugal ˈpɔː.tʃə.gᵊl, -tʃʊ-, -tjə-, -tjʊ- US ˈpɔːr.tʃə-

Portuguese ˌpɔː.tʃəˈgiːz, -tʃʊˈ-, -tjəˈ-, -tjʊˈ- US ˌpɔːr.tʃəˈ-, -ˈgiːs, ˈ--- *stress shift, British only, see compound:* ˌ**Portuguese** ˌ**man-of-**ˈ**war**

pos|e pəʊz US poʊz **-es** -ɪz **-ing** -ɪŋ **-ed** -d

Poseidon pəˈsaɪ.dᵊn, pɒsˈaɪ- US poʊˈsaɪ-, pə-

poser ˈpəʊ.zəʳ US ˈpoʊ.zɚ **-s** -z

poseur pəʊˈzɜːʳ US poʊˈzɝː **-s** -z

posh pɒʃ US pɑːʃ **-er** -əʳ US -ɚ **-est** -ɪst, -əst

pos|it ˈpɒz|.ɪt US ˈpɑː.z|ɪt **-its** -ɪts **-iting** -ɪ.tɪŋ US -ɪ.t̬ɪŋ **-ited** -ɪ.tɪd US -ɪ.t̬ɪd

position pəˈzɪʃ.ᵊn **-s** -z **-ing** -ɪŋ **-ed** -d

positional pəˈzɪʃ.ᵊn.ᵊl

positive ˈpɒz.ə.tɪv, ˈ-ɪ- US ˈpɑː.zə.t̬ɪv **-s** -z **-ly** -li **-ness** -nəs, -nɪs ˌ**positive discrimi**ˈ**nation**

positiv|ism ˈpɒz.ɪ.tɪ.v|ɪ.zᵊm, ˈ-ə- US ˈpɑː.zɪ.t̬ɪ- **-ist/s** -ɪst/s

positron ˈpɒz.ɪ.trɒn, -trən US ˈpɑː.zɪ.trɑːn **-s** -z

posse ˈpɒs.i US ˈpɑː.si **-s** -z

possess pəˈzes **-es** -ɪz **-ing** -ɪŋ **-ed** -t **-or/s** -əʳ/z US -ɚ/z

possession pəˈzeʃ.ᵊn **-s** -z

possessive pəˈzes.ɪv **-s** -z **-ly** -li **-ness** -nəs, -nɪs **pos**ˌ**sessive** ˈ**adjective; pos**ˌ**sessive** ˈ**pronoun**

possessory pəˈzes.ᵊr.i

posset ˈpɒs.ɪt US ˈpɑː.sɪt **-s** -s

possibilit|y ˌpɒs.əˈbɪl.ə.t|i, -ɪˈ-, -ɪ.t|i US ˌpɑː.səˈbɪl.ə.t̬|i **-ies** -iz

possib|le ˈpɒs.ə.b|l̩, ˈ-ɪ- US ˈpɑː.sə- **-ly** -li

possum ˈpɒs.əm US ˈpɑː.səm **-s** -z

post pəʊst US poʊst **-s** -s **-ing** -ɪŋ **-ed** -ɪd ˈ**post** ˌ**office**

postag|e ˈpəʊ.stɪdʒ US ˈpoʊ- **-es** -ɪz ˈ**postage** ˌ**stamp;** ˌ**postage and** ˈ**packing**

postal ˈpəʊ.stᵊl US ˈpoʊ- ˈ**postal** ˌ**order**

postbag ˈpəʊst.bæg US ˈpoʊst- **-s** -z

postbellum ˌpəʊstˈbel.əm US ˌpoʊst- *stress shift:* ˌpostbellum ˈbuilding

postbox ˈpəʊst.bɒks US ˈpoʊst.bɑːks **-es** -ɪz

postcard ˈpəʊst.kɑːd US ˈpoʊst.kɑːrd **-s** -z

post-chaise ˈpəʊst.ʃeɪz, ˌ-ˈ- US ˈpoʊst.ʃeɪz, ˌ-ˈ- **-s** -ɪz

postcode ˈpəʊst.kəʊd US ˈpoʊst.koʊd **-s** -z

postda|te ˌpəʊstˈdeɪ|t, ˈ-- US ˌpoʊstˈdeɪ|t, ˈ-- **-tes** -ts **-ting** -tɪŋ US -t̬ɪŋ **-ted** -tɪd US -t̬ɪd

post-diluvian ˌpəʊst.dɪˈluː.vi.ən, -daɪˈ-, -ˈljuː- US ˌpoʊst.dɪˈluː-

postdoctoral ˌpəʊstˈdɒk.tᵊr.ᵊl US ˌpoʊstˈdɑːk- *stress shift:* ˌpostdoctoral ˈcontract

poster ˈpəʊ.stəʳ US ˈpoʊ.stɚ **-s** -z ˈ**poster** ˌ**paint**

Postalveolar

Descriptive of sounds made between the upper teeth and the front part of the palate.

Examples for English

British and US English have two sets of sounds referred to postalveolar, the fricatives /ʃ ʒ/ and the affricates /tʃ dʒ/.

These are also referred to as PALATO-ALVEOLAR, e.g.:

pressure	/ˈpreʃ.əʳ/	(US)	/-ɚ/
pleasure	/ˈpleʒ.əʳ/	(US)	/-ɚ/
church	/tʃɜːtʃ/	(US)	/tʃɝːtʃ/
judge	/dʒʌdʒ/		

poste restante ˌpəʊst.resˈtɑ̃ːⁿt, ˌ-ˈ-- (US) ˌpoʊst.resˈtɑːnt

posterior pɒsˈtɪə.ri.əʳ (US) pɑːˈstɪr.i.ɚ, poʊ-, pə- **-ly** -li

posteriority pɒsˌtɪə.riˈɒr.ə.ti, ˌpɒs.tɪə-, -ɪ.ti (US) pɑːˌstɪr.iˈɔːr.ə.t̬i, poʊ-

posterit|y pɒsˈter.ə.t|i, -ɪ.t|i (US) pɑːˈster.ə- **-ies** -iz

postern ˈpɒs.tən, ˈpəʊ.stən, -stɜːn (US) ˈpoʊ.stɚn, ˈpɑː- **-s** -z

post-free ˌpəʊstˈfriː (US) ˌpoʊst- *stress shift:* ˌpost-free ˈsystem

Postgate ˈpəʊst.geɪt, -gɪt (US) ˈpoʊst.geɪt

postglacial ˌpəʊstˈgleɪ.si.əl, -ʃᵊl, -ˈglæs.i.əl (US) ˌpoʊstˈgleɪ.ʃᵊl *stress shift:* ˌpostglacial ˈperiod

postgraduate ˌpəʊstˈgrædʒ.u.ət, -ˈgræd.ju-, -ɪt (US) ˌpoʊstˈgrædʒ.u.wɪt, ˈ-ə-; ˈ-u.eɪt **-s** -s *stress shift:* ˌpostgraduate ˈstudent

posthaste ˌpəʊstˈheɪst (US) ˌpoʊst-

post hoc ˌpəʊstˈhɒk (US) ˌpoʊstˈhɑːk, -ˈhoʊk

posthumous ˈpɒs.tjə.məs, -tjʊ- (US) ˈpɑːs.tʃə.məs, -tʃʊ- **-ly** -li

Posthumus ˈpɒs.tjʊ.məs, ˈpɒst.hjʊ- (US) ˈpɑːs.tjuː-, -tʃuː-

postich|e pɒsˈtiːʃ (US) pɑːˈstiːʃ, pɔː- **-es** -ɪz

postie ˈpəʊ.sti (US) ˈpoʊ- **-s** -z

postil ˈpɒs.tɪl (US) ˈpɑː.stɪl **-s** -z

postil(l)ion pəˈstɪl.i.ən, pɒsˈtɪl-, ˈ-jən (US) poʊˈstɪl.jən, pɑː- **-s** -z

Post-impression|ism ˌpəʊst.ɪmˈpreʃ.ᵊn|.ɪ.zᵊm (US) ˌpoʊst- **-ist/s** -ɪst/s

posting ˈpəʊ.stɪŋ (US) ˈpoʊ- **-s** -z

Post-it® ˈpəʊst.ɪt (US) ˈpoʊst-

Postlethwaite ˈpɒs.l̩.θweɪt (US) ˈpɑː.sl̩-

post|man ˈpəʊst|.mən (US) ˈpoʊst- **-men** -mən **-woman** -ˌwʊm.ən **-women** -ˌwɪm.ɪn ˌ**postman's** ˈ**knock**

postmark ˈpəʊst.mɑːk (US) ˈpoʊst.mɑːrk **-s** -s **-ing** -ɪŋ **-ed** -t

postmaster ˈpəʊstˌmɑː.stəʳ (US) ˈpoʊstˌmæs.tɚ **-s** -z ˌ**Postmaster** ˈ**General**

post-meridian ˌpəʊst.məˈrɪd.i.ən (US) ˌpoʊst-

postmistress ˈpəʊst.mɪs.trəs, -trɪs (US) ˈpoʊst- **-es** -ɪz

postmodern ˌpəʊstˈmɒd.ən (US) ˌpoʊstˈmɑː.dɚn **-ism** -ɪ.zᵊm **-ist/s** -ɪst/s *stress shift:* ˌpostmodern ˈartists

postmortem ˌpəʊstˈmɔː.tem, -təm (US) ˌpoʊstˈmɔːr.t̬əm **-s** -z

postnatal ˌpəʊstˈneɪ.tᵊl (US) ˌpoʊstˈneɪ.t̬ᵊl *stress shift, see compound:* ˌ**postnatal de**ˈ**pression**

postoperative ˌpəʊstˈɒp.ᵊr.ə.tɪv (US) ˌpoʊstˈɑː.pɚ.ə.t̬ɪv

postpaid ˌpəʊstˈpeɪd (US) ˌpoʊst- *stress shift:* ˌpostpaid ˈenvelope

post partum ˌpəʊstˈpɑː.təm (US) ˌpoʊstˈpɑːr.t̬əm

postpon|e pəʊstˈpəʊn, pəs- (US) poʊstˈpoʊn **-es** -z **-ing** -ɪŋ **-ed** -d **-ement/s** -mənt/s

postposition ˌpəʊst.pəˈzɪʃ.ᵊn, ˈpəʊst.pəˌzɪʃ- (US) ˌpoʊst.pəˈzɪʃ- **-s** -z

postpositional ˌpəʊst.pəˈzɪʃ.ᵊn.ᵊl (US) ˌpoʊst- *stress shift:* ˌpostpositional ˈparticle

postpositive ˌpəʊstˈpɒz.ə.tɪv, ˈ-ɪ- (US) ˌpoʊstˈpɑː.zə.t̬ɪv *stress shift:* ˌpostpositive ˈadjective

postscript ˈpəʊst.skrɪpt (US) ˈpoʊst- **-s** -s

post-structuralism ˌpəʊstˈstrʌk.tʃᵊr.ᵊl.ɪ.zᵊm, -tʃʊ.rᵊl- (US) ˌpoʊstˈstrʌk.tʃɚ-

post-traumatic stress disorder ˌpəʊst.trɔːˌmæt.ɪkˈstres.dɪˌsɔː.dəʳ, -ˌzɔː- (US) ˌpoʊst.trɑːˌmæt̬.ɪkˈstres.dɪˌsɔːr.dɚ, -trɔːˌ-

postulant ˈpɒs.tjə.lənt, -tjʊ- (US) ˈpɑːs.tʃə-, ˈpɑː.stjə- **-s** -s

postulate (*n.*) ˈpɒs.tjə.lət, -tjʊ-, -lɪt, -leɪt (US) ˈpɑːs.tʃə.lɪt, -tʃʊ-, ˈpɑː.stjə-, -stjʊ-, -leɪt **-s** -s

postu|late (*v.*) ˈpɒs.tjə|.leɪt, -tjʊ- (US) ˈpɑːs.tʃə-, ˈpɑː.stjə- **-lates** -leɪts **-lating** -leɪ.tɪŋ (US) -leɪ.t̬ɪŋ **-lated** -leɪ.tɪd (US) -leɪ.t̬ɪd

postulation ˌpɒs.tjəˈleɪ.ʃᵊn, -tjʊˈ- (US) ˌpɑːs.tʃəˈ-, ˌpɑː.stjəˈ- **-s** -z

post|ure ˈpɒs.tʃ|əʳ (US) ˈpɑːs.tʃ|ɚ **-ures** -əz (US) -ɚz **-uring** -ᵊr.ɪŋ **-ured** -əd (US) -ɚd

postviral ˌpəʊstˈvaɪə.rᵊl (US) ˌpoʊstˈvaɪ- *stress shift, see compound:* ˌ**postviral fa**ˈ**tigue** ˌ**syndrome**

post-war ˌpəʊstˈwɔːʳ (US) ˌpoʊstˈwɔːr *stress shift:* ˌpost-war ˈpolitics

pos|y ˈpəʊ.z|i (US) ˈpoʊ- **-ies** -iz

pot pɒt (US) pɑːt **-s** -s **-ting** -ɪŋ (US) ˈpɑː.t̬ɪŋ **-ted** -ɪd (US) ˈpɑː.t̬ɪd **-er/s** -əʳ/z (US) ˈpɑː.t̬ɚ/z ˌ**pot** ˈ**luck**; ˈ**pot** ˌ**plant**; ˌ**potted** ˈ**plant**; ˈ**potting** ˌ**shed**

potable ˈpəʊ.tə.bl̩ (US) ˈpoʊ.t̬ə- **-s** -z

potag|e pɒtˈɑːʒ, pəʊˈtɑːʒ, ˈ-- (US) poʊˈtɑːʒ **-es** -ɪz

potash ˈpɒt.æʃ (US) ˈpɑːt-

potassium pəˈtæs.i.əm (US) pə-, poʊ-

potation pəʊˈteɪ.ʃᵊn (US) poʊ- **-s** -z

potato pəˈteɪ.təʊ (US) -t̬oʊ **-es** -z **po**ˈ**tato** ˌ**chip**; **po**ˌ**tato** ˈ**crisp**

pot-au-feu ˌpɒt.əʊˈfɜː (US) ˌpɑːt.oʊˈ-

pot-bell|y pɒtˈbel|.i, ˈ-ˌ-- (US) ˈpɑːtˌbel- **-ied** -id

potboiler ˈpɒtˌbɔɪ.ləʳ (US) ˈpɑːtˌbɔɪ.lɚ **-s** -z

potbound (*adj.*) ˈpɒt.baʊnd (US) ˈpɑːt-

poteen pɒtˈiːn, pəʊˈtiːn, -ˈtʃiːn (US) poʊˈtiːn

Potemkin pəˈtemp.kɪn, pɒtˈemp-, pəˈtjɒm.kɪn (US) poʊˈtemp-, pə-

potency ˈpəʊ.tᵊnt.si (US) ˈpoʊ-

potent ˈpəʊ.tᵊnt (US) ˈpoʊ- **-ly** -li

potentate ˈpəʊ.tᵊn.teɪt (US) ˈpoʊ- **-s** -s

potential pəʊˈten.tʃᵊl (US) poʊ-, pə- **-s** -z **-ly** -i

potentialit|y pəʊˌten.tʃiˈæl.ə.t|i, -ɪ.t|i (US) poʊˌten.tʃiˈæl.ə.t̬|i, pə- **-ies** -iz

potentilla ˌpəʊ.tᵊnˈtɪl.ə (US) ˌpoʊ- **-s** -z

potentiometer pəʊˌten.tʃiˈɒm.ɪ.təʳ, ˈ-ə- (US) poʊˌten.tʃiˈɑː.mə.t̬ɚ, pə- **-s** -z

potheen pɒtˈiːn, pəʊˈtiːn, -tʃiːn, -θiːn, ˈpɒθ.iːn (US) poʊˈθiːn, -ˈtiːn

poth|er ˈpɒð|.əʳ (US) ˈpɑː.ð|ɚ **-ers** -əz (US) -ɚz **-ering** -ᵊr.ɪŋ **-ered** -əd (US) -ɚd

pot-herb ˈpɒt.hɜːb (US) ˈpɑːt.hɝːb **-s** -z

pothole ˈpɒt.həʊl (US) ˈpɑːt.hoʊl **-s** -z
pothol|ing ˈpɒtˌhəʊ.l|ɪŋ (US) ˈpɑːtˌhoʊ- **-er/s** -əʳ/z (US) -ɚ/z
pothook ˈpɒt.hʊk (US) ˈpɑːt- **-s** -s
pothou|se ˈpɒt.haʊ|s (US) ˈpɑːt- **-ses** -zɪz
pot-hunter ˈpɒtˌhʌn.təʳ (US) ˈpɑːtˌhʌn.t̬ɚ **-s** -z
potion ˈpəʊ.ʃᵊn (US) ˈpoʊ- **-s** -z
Potiphar ˈpɒt.ɪ.fɑːʳ, ˈ-ə-, -fəʳ (US) ˈpɑː.t̬ə.fɚ
Potomac pəˈtəʊ.mæk, -mək (US) -ˈtoʊ.mək
potometer pəʊˈtɒm.ɪ.təʳ, ˈ-ə- (US) pəˈtɑː.mə.t̬ɚ
Potosi *in Bolivia:* ˌpɒt.əʊˈsiː (US) ˌpɔː.tɔːˈ-
Potosi *in US:* pəˈtəʊ.si (US) -ˈtoʊ-
potpourri ˌpəʊ.pəˈriː, -pʊˈ- (US) ˌpoʊ.pʊˈriː, -pəˈ-; ˈpoʊ.pʊr.i, -pɚ- **-s** -z
pot-roast ˈpɒt.rəʊst (US) ˈpɑːt.roʊst **-s** -s **-ing** -ɪŋ **-ed** -ɪd
Potsdam ˈpɒts.dæm (US) ˈpɑːts-
potsherd ˈpɒt.ʃɜːd (US) ˈpɑːt.ʃɝːd **-s** -z
potshot ˈpɒt.ʃɒt, ˌ-ˈ- (US) ˈpɑːt.ʃɑːt **-s** -s
Pott pɒt (US) pɑːt
pottage ˈpɒt.ɪdʒ (US) ˈpɑː.t̬ɪdʒ
potted ˈpɒt.ɪd (US) ˈpɑː.t̬ɪd
pott|er (P) ˈpɒt|.əʳ (US) ˈpɑː.t̬|ɚ **-ers** -əz (US) -ɚz **-ering** -ᵊr.ɪŋ **-ered** -əd (US) -ɚd **-erer/s** -ᵊr.əʳ/z (US) -ɚ.ɚ/z
potter|y (P) ˈpɒt.ᵊr|.i (US) ˈpɑː.t̬ɚ- **-ies** -iz
pottle ˈpɒt.l̩ (US) ˈpɑː.t̬l̩ **-s** -z
Potts pɒts (US) pɑːts
pott|y ˈpɒt|.i (US) ˈpɑː.t̬|i **-ier** -i.əʳ (US) -i.ɚ **-iest** -i.ɪst, -i.əst **-iness** -ɪ.nəs, -ɪ.nɪs
pouch paʊtʃ **-es** -ɪz **-ing** -ɪŋ **-ed** -t
pouf *(derog. for homosexual)* pʊf, puːf (US) puːf **-s** -s
pouffe, pouf, pouff *(seat, headdress)* puːf **-s** -s
Poughill ˈpɒf.ɪl, ˈpʌf-, ˈpaʊ- (US) ˈpɑː.fɪl, ˈpʌf.ɪl, ˈpaʊ-
Poughkeepsie pəˈkɪp.si (US) pə-, poʊ-
Poulenc ˈpuː.læ̃ŋk (US) puːˈlæ̃ŋk
Poulson ˈpəʊl.sᵊn, ˈpuːl- (US) ˈpoʊl-, ˈpuːl-
poult *chicken:* pəʊlt (US) poʊlt **-s** -s
poult *silk material:* puːlt (US) puːlt, puː
Poulter ˈpəʊl.təʳ (US) ˈpoʊl.t̬ɚ
poulterer ˈpəʊl.tᵊr.əʳ (US) ˈpoʊl.t̬ɚ.ɚ **-s** -z
poultic|e ˈpəʊl.tɪs (US) ˈpoʊl.t̬ɪs **-es** -ɪz **-ing** -ɪŋ **-ed** -t
Poultney ˈpəʊlt.ni (US) ˈpoʊlt-
Poulton ˈpəʊl.tᵊn (US) ˈpoʊl-
Poulton-le-Fylde ˌpəʊl.tᵊn.ləˈfaɪld, -lɪˈ- (US) ˌpoʊl-
poultry ˈpəʊl.tri (US) ˈpoʊl-
poultry|man ˈpəʊl.tri|.mən, -mæn (US) ˈpoʊl- **-men** -mən, -men
pounc|e paʊn*t*s **-es** -ɪz **-ing** -ɪŋ **-ed** -t
Pouncefoot ˈpaʊn*t*s.fʊt
pound (P) paʊnd **-s** -z **-ing** -ɪŋ **-ed** -ɪd **-er/s** -əʳ/z (US) -ɚ/z ˌ**pound** ˈ**sterling**
poundag|e ˈpaʊn.dɪdʒ **-es** -ɪz
Pounds paʊndz
Pount(e)ney ˈpaʊnt.ni
Poupart ˈpəʊ.pɑːt, ˈpuː- (US) ˌpuːˈpɑːrt
Pouparts ˈpuː.pɑːts (US) ˌpuːˈpɑːrts
pour pɔːʳ (US) pɔːr **-s** -z **-ing** -ɪŋ **-ed** -d **-er/s** -əʳ/z (US) -ɚ/z
pourboire ˈpʊə.bwɑːʳ, ˈpɔː- (US) pʊrˈbwɑːr **-s** -z
pourparler ˌpʊəˈpɑː.leɪ, ˌpɔː- (US) ˌpʊr.pɑːrˈleɪ **-s** -z
poussin (P) ˈpuː.sæ̃ŋ (US) puːˈsæ̃*n* **-s** -z
pout paʊt **-s** -s **-ing** -ɪŋ (US) ˈpaʊ.t̬ɪŋ **-ed** -ɪd (US) ˈpaʊ.t̬ɪd
poverty ˈpɒv.ə.ti (US) ˈpɑː.vɚ.t̬i ˈ**poverty** ˌ**trap**
poverty-stricken ˈpɒv.ə.tiˌstrɪk.ᵊn (US) ˈpɑː.vɚ.t̬iˌ-
Povey ˈpəʊ.vi; pəˈveɪ (US) ˈpoʊ.vi; pəˈveɪ
Pow paʊ
POW ˌpiː.əʊˈdʌb.l̩.juː (US) -oʊˈ- **-'s** -z
powd|er ˈpaʊ.d|əʳ (US) -d|ɚ **-ers** -əz (US) -ɚz **-ering** -ᵊr.ɪŋ **-ered** -əd (US) -ɚd ˌ**powder** ˈ**blue**; ˈ**powder** ˌ**keg**; ˈ**powder** ˌ**puff**; ˈ**powder** ˌ**room**
powder|y ˈpaʊ.dᵊr|.i **-iness** -ɪ.nəs, -ɪ.nɪs
Powell paʊəl, pəʊəl; ˈpaʊ.ɪl, ˈpəʊ-, -el (US) paʊəl, poʊəl
power (P) paʊəʳ (US) paʊɚ **-s** -z **-ing** -ɪŋ **-ed** -d ˈ**power** ˌ**base**; ˈ**power** ˌ**cut**; ˌ**power of at**ˈ**torney**; ˌ**power** ˈ**politics**; ˈ**power** ˌ**station**; ˌ**power** ˈ**steering**
powerboat ˈpaʊə.bəʊt (US) ˈpaʊɚ.boʊt **-s** -s
powerful ˈpaʊə.fᵊl, -fʊl (US) ˈpaʊɚ- **-ly** -i **-ness** -nəs, -nɪs
Powergen ˈpaʊə.dʒen (US) ˈpaʊɚ-
powerhou|se ˈpaʊə.haʊ|s (US) ˈpaʊɚ- **-ses** -zɪz
powerless ˈpaʊə.ləs, -lɪs (US) ˈpaʊɚ- **-ly** -li **-ness** -nəs, -nɪs
powerpack ˈpaʊə.pæk (US) ˈpaʊɚ- **-s** -s
powerpoint ˈpaʊə.pɔɪnt (US) ˈpaʊɚ- **-s** -s
Powerscourt ˈpɔːz.kɔːt, ˈpaʊəz- (US) ˈpaʊɚz.kɔːrt
Powicke ˈpəʊ.ɪk (US) ˈpoʊ-
Powis *place in Scotland, square in London:* ˈpaʊ.ɪs *surname:* ˈpəʊ.ɪs, ˈpaʊ- (US) ˈpoʊ-, ˈpaʊ-
Powles pəʊlz (US) poʊlz
Powlett ˈpɔː.lɪt (US) ˈpɑː-, ˈpɔː-
Pownall ˈpaʊ.nᵊl
powwow *(n. v.)* ˈpaʊ.waʊ **-s** -z **-ing** -ɪŋ **-ed** -d
Powys ˈpəʊ.ɪs, ˈpaʊ.ɪs (US) ˈpoʊ-, ˈpaʊ-
pox pɒks (US) pɑːks
poxy ˈpɒk.si (US) ˈpɑːk-
Poyner ˈpɔɪ.nəʳ (US) -nɚ
Poynings ˈpɔɪ.nɪŋz
Poynter ˈpɔɪn.təʳ (US) -t̬ɚ
Poynton ˈpɔɪn.tən
Poznan ˈpɒz.næn (US) ˈpoʊz-, -nɑːn
PR ˌpiːˈɑːʳ (US) -ˈɑːr
practicability ˌpræk.tɪ.kəˈbɪl.ə.ti, -ɪ.ti (US) -ə.t̬i
practicab|le ˈpræk.tɪ.kə.b|l̩ **-ly** -li **-leness** -l̩.nəs, -nɪs
practical ˈpræk.tɪ.kᵊl **-ness** -nəs, -nɪs ˌ**practical** ˈ**joke**
practicalit|y ˌpræk.tɪˈkæl.ə.t|i, -ɪ.t|i (US) -ə.t̬|i **-ies** -iz
practically ˈpræk.tɪ.kᵊl.i (US) -tɪ.kli
practic|e ˈpræk.tɪs **-es** -ɪz **-ing** -ɪŋ **-ed** -t
practician prækˈtɪʃ.ᵊn **-s** -z
practis|e ˈpræk.tɪs **-es** -ɪz **-ing** -ɪŋ **-ed** -t ˌ**practise what one** ˈ**preaches**
practitioner prækˈtɪʃ.ᵊn.əʳ (US) -ɚ **-s** -z
Prada® ˈprɑː.də
Prado ˈprɑː.dəʊ (US) -doʊ
praecox ˈpriː.kɒks, ˈpraɪ- (US) ˈpriː.kɑːks
Praed preɪd
prae|nomen ˌpriː|ˈnəʊ.men, ˌpraɪ- (US) ˌpriː|ˈnoʊ- **-nomens** -ˈnəʊ.mənz (US) -ˈnoʊ- **-nomina** -ˈnɒm.ɪ.nə, -ˈnəʊ.mɪ- (US) -ˈnɑː-, -ˈnoʊ-
praepostor ˌpriːˈpɒs.təʳ (US) -ˈpɑː.stɚ **-s** -z
praesidi|um prɪˈsɪd.i|.əm, prə-, praɪ- **-ums** -əmz **-a** -ə
Praeterita ˌpriːˈter.ɪ.tə, prɪ-, praɪ- (US) prɪˈter.ɪ.t̬ə
praetor ˈpriː.təʳ, ˈpraɪ-, -tɔːʳ (US) ˈpriː.t̬ɚ **-s** -z **-ship/s** -ʃɪp/s
praetori|al priːˈtɔː.ri|.əl, praɪˈ- (US) -ˈtɔːr- **-an** -ən
pragmatic prægˈmæt.ɪk (US) -ˈmæt̬- **-s** -s **-al** -ᵊl **-ally** -ᵊl.i, -li
pragmat|ism ˈpræg.mə.t|ɪ.zᵊm **-ist/s** -ɪst/s
Prague prɑːg
Praia ˈpraɪ.ə (US) ˈprɑː.jə
prairie (P) ˈpreə.ri (US) ˈprer.i **-s** -z ˈ**prairie** ˌ**dog**; ˌ**prairie** ˈ**oyster**
prais|e preɪz **-es** -ɪz **-ing** -ɪŋ **-ed** -d **-er/s** -əʳ/z
praiseworth|y ˈpreɪzˌwɜː.ð|i (US) -ˌwɝː- **-iness** -ɪ.nəs, -ɪ.nɪs
Prakrit ˈprɑː.krɪt
praline ˈprɑː.liːn (US) ˈprɑː-, ˈpreɪ- **-s** -z
Prall prɔːl (US) prɔːl, prɑːl
pram *baby carriage:* præm **-s** -z
pram *flat-bottomed boat:* prɑːm **-s** -z
pranc|e (P) prɑːn*t*s (US) præn*t*s **-es** -ɪz **-ing** -ɪŋ **-ed** -t **-er/s** -əʳ/z (US) -ɚ/z
prandial ˈpræn.di.əl
prang præŋ **-s** -z **-ing** -ɪŋ **-ed** -d
prank præŋk **-s** -s **-ing** -ɪŋ **-ed** -t

prank|ish ˈpræŋ.klɪʃ **-some** -səm
prankster ˈpræŋk.stəʳ ⓤⓢ -stɚ **-s** -z
praseodymium ˌpreɪ.zi.əʊˈdɪm.i.əm, ˌpraɪ.zəʊˈ- ⓤⓢ ˌpreɪ.zi.oʊˈ-, -si-
prat præt **-s** -s
Pratchett ˈprætʃ.ɪt
prat|e preɪt **-es** -s **-ing** -ɪŋ **-ed** -ɪd **-er/s** -əʳ/z ⓤⓢ -ɚ/z
pratfall ˈpræt.fɔːl **-s** -z
pratincole ˈpræt.ɪŋ.kəʊl, ˈpreɪ.tɪŋ- ⓤⓢ ˈpræt.ɪn.koʊl, ˈpreɪ.tɪn-, -tᵊn-, -ɪŋ- **-s** -z
pratique ˈpræt.iːk, -ɪk, prætˈiːk ⓤⓢ prætˈiːk; ˈpræt̬.ɪk **-s** -s
Pratt præt
prattl|e ˈpræt.l̩ ⓤⓢ ˈpræt̬- **-es** -z **-ing** -ɪŋ, ˈpræt.lɪŋ **-ed** -d **-er/s** -əʳ/z, ˈpræt.ləʳ/z ⓤⓢ ˈpræt̬.l̩.ɚ/z, ˈpræt.lɚ/z
Pravda ˈprɑːv.də
prawn prɔːn ⓤⓢ prɑːn, prɔːn **-s** -z ˌ**prawn** ˈ**cocktail**; ˌ**prawn** ˈ**cracker**
prax|is ˈpræk.s|ɪs **-es** -iːz
Praxiteles prækˈsɪt.ᵊl.iːz, -tɪ.liːz ⓤⓢ -ˈsɪt̬.ᵊl.iːz
pray (P) preɪ **-s** -z **-ing** -ɪŋ **-ed** -d
prayer *person who prays:* ˈpreɪ.əʳ ⓤⓢ -ɚ **-s** -z
prayer *supplication:* preəʳ ⓤⓢ prer **-s** -z ˈ**prayer** ˌ**mat**; ˈ**prayer** ˌ**meeting**; ˈ**prayer** ˌ**rug**; ˈ**prayer** ˌ**wheel**
prayer-book ˈpreə.bʊk ⓤⓢ ˈprer- **-s** -s
prayerful ˈpreə.fᵊl, -fʊl ⓤⓢ ˈprer- **-ly** -i **-ness** -nəs, -nɪs
prayerless ˈpreə.ləs, -lɪs ⓤⓢ ˈprer- **-ly** -li **-ness** -nəs, -nɪs
praying mant|is ˌpreɪ.ɪŋˈmæn.t|ɪs ⓤⓢ -t̬|ɪs **-ises** -ɪ.sɪz **-es** -iːz
pre- priː-, prɪ-, pri-, prə-
Note: Prefix. In words containing **pre-** where the stem is free, and the meaning is **beforehand**, it generally takes secondary stress, e.g. **pre-eminence** /ˌpriːˈem.ɪ.nənts/. Attached to bound stems the pronunciation is normally /prɪ-/ or /prə-/ for British English and /prɪ-/ or /priː-/ for American English, e.g. **prefer** /prɪˈfɜː ⓤⓢ priːˈfɜːr/. There are exceptions; see individual entries.
preach priːtʃ **-es** -ɪz **-ing** -ɪŋ **-ed** -t **-er/s** -əʳ/z ⓤⓢ -ɚ/z ˌ**preach to the con**ˈ**verted**
preachi|fy ˈpriː.tʃɪ|.faɪ **-fies** -faɪz **-fying** -faɪ.ɪŋ **-fied** -faɪd
preach|y ˈpriː.tʃ|i **-ily** -ɪ.li, -ᵊl.i **-iness** -ɪ.nəs, -ɪ.nɪs
Preager ˈpreɪ.gəʳ ⓤⓢ -gɚ
preamble ˈpriː.æm.bl̩, priˈæm- **-s** -z
preamplifier priˈæm.plɪ.faɪ.əʳ ⓤⓢ -plə.faɪ.ɚ **-s** -z
prearrang|e ˌpriː.əˈreɪndʒ **-es** -ɪz **-ing** -ɪŋ **-ed** -d
Prebble ˈpreb.l̩
prebend ˈpreb.ənd **-s** -z
prebendar|y ˈpreb.ᵊn.dᵊr|.i, -ᵊm-, -ᵊn.der- **-ies** -ɪz
Precambrian ˌpriːˈkæm.bri.ən
precancerous ˌpriːˈkænt.sᵊr.əs *stress shift:* ˌprecancerous ˈtissue
precarious prɪˈkeə.ri.əs, prə- ⓤⓢ prɪˈker.i-, priː- **-ly** -li **-ness** -nəs, -nɪs
precast ˌpriːˈkɑːst ⓤⓢ ˈpriː.kæst, ˌ-ˈ- *stress shift, British only:* ˌprecast ˈconcrete
preca|tory ˈprek.ə|.tᵊr.i ⓤⓢ -tɔːr- **-tive** -tɪv ⓤⓢ -t̬ɪv
precaution prɪˈkɔː.ʃᵊn, prə- ⓤⓢ prɪˈkɑː-, priː-, -ˈkɔː- **-s** -z
precautionary prɪˈkɔː.ʃᵊn.ᵊr.i, prə- ⓤⓢ prɪˈkɑː.ʃᵊn.er-, priː-, -ˈkɔː-
preced|e priːˈsiːd, prɪ- ⓤⓢ prɪ-, priː- **-es** -z **-ing** -ɪŋ **-ed** -ɪd
precedenc|e ˈpres.ɪ.dᵊnts, ˈpriː.sɪ- ⓤⓢ ˈpres.ə.dents; prɪˈsiː.dᵊnts, priː- **-y** -i
precedent (*n.*) ˈpres.ɪ.dᵊnt ⓤⓢ ˈ-ə- **-s** -s **-ed** -ɪd
precedent (*adj.*) prɪˈsiː.dᵊnt, ˈpres.ɪ.dənt ⓤⓢ prɪˈsiː.dᵊnt, priː-, ˈpres.ə.dənt **-ly** -li
precentor ˌpriːˈsen.təʳ, prɪ- ⓤⓢ priːˈsen.t̬ɚ **-s** -z
precept ˈpriː.sept **-s** -s
preceptor prɪˈsep.təʳ ⓤⓢ priːˈsep.tɚ, prɪ- **-s** -z
preceptor|y prɪˈsep.tᵊr|.i ⓤⓢ prɪ-, priː- **-ies** -iz
precession prɪˈseʃ.ᵊn, prə- ⓤⓢ prɪ-, priː- **-s** -z
precinct ˈpriː.sɪŋkt **-s** -s
preciosity ˌpres.iˈɒs.ə.ti, ˌpreʃ-, -ɪ.ti ⓤⓢ ˌpreʃ.iˈɑː.sə.t̬i, ˌpres-
precious (P) ˈpreʃ.əs **-ly** -li **-ness** -nəs, -nɪs ˌ**precious** ˈ**metal**; ˌ**precious** ˈ**stone**
precipic|e ˈpres.ɪ.pɪs, ˈ-ə- ⓤⓢ ˈ-ə- **-es** -ɪz
precipitanc|e prɪˈsɪp.ɪ.tᵊnts, prə-, ˈ-ə- ⓤⓢ prɪ-, priː- **-y** -i
precipitate (*n.*) prɪˈsɪp.ɪ.teɪt, prə-, ˈ-ə-, -tət, -tɪt ⓤⓢ prɪˈsɪp.ɪ.tɪt, priː-, -teɪt **-s** -s
precipitate (*adj.*) prɪˈsɪp.ɪ.tət, prə-, ˈ-ə-, -tɪt ⓤⓢ prɪˈsɪp.ɪ.tɪt, priː-, -teɪt **-ly** -li **-ness** -nəs, -nɪs
precipi|tate (*v.*) prɪˈsɪp.ɪ|.teɪt, prə-, ˈ-ə- ⓤⓢ prɪˈsɪp.ɪ-, priː- **-tates** -teɪts **-tating** -teɪ.tɪŋ ⓤⓢ -teɪ.t̬ɪŋ **-tated** -teɪ.tɪd ⓤⓢ -teɪ.t̬ɪd
precipitation prɪˌsɪp.ɪˈteɪ.ʃᵊn, prə-, -əˈ- ⓤⓢ prɪˌsɪp.ɪˈ-, priː- **-s** -z
precipitous prɪˈsɪp.ɪ.təs, prə-, ˈ-ə- ⓤⓢ prɪˈsɪp.ɪ.t̬əs, priː- **-ly** -li **-ness** -nəs, -nɪs
précis *singular:* ˈpreɪ.siː ⓤⓢ ˈpreɪ.siː, -ˈ- **-ing** -ɪŋ **-ed** -d *plural:* -z
precise prɪˈsaɪs, prə- ⓤⓢ prɪ-, priː- **-ly** -li **-ness** -nəs, -nɪs
precision prɪˈsɪʒ.ᵊn, prə- ⓤⓢ prɪ-, priː-
preclassical ˌpriːˈklæs.ɪ.kᵊl *stress shift:* ˌpreclassical ˈmusic
preclud|e prɪˈkluːd ⓤⓢ prɪ-, priː- **-es** -z **-ing** -ɪŋ **-ed** -ɪd
preclu|sion prɪˈkluː|.ʒᵊn ⓤⓢ prɪ-, priː- **-sive** -sɪv
precocious prɪˈkəʊ.ʃəs, prə- ⓤⓢ prɪˈkoʊ-, priː- **-ly** -li **-ness** -nəs, -nɪs
precocity prɪˈkɒs.ə.ti, prə-, -ɪ.ti ⓤⓢ prɪˈkɑː.sə.t̬i, priː-
precognition ˌpriː.kɒgˈnɪʃ.ᵊn ⓤⓢ -kɑːgˈ-
preconceiv|e ˌpriː.kənˈsiːv **-es** -z **-ing** -ɪŋ **-ed** -d
preconception ˌpriː.kənˈsep.ʃᵊn **-s** -z
precon|cert ˌpriː.kən|ˈsɜːt ⓤⓢ -ˈsɝːt **-certs** -ˈsɜːts ⓤⓢ -ˈsɝːts **-certing** -ˈsɜː.tɪŋ ⓤⓢ -ˈsɝː.t̬ɪŋ **-certed** -ˈsɜː.tɪd ⓤⓢ -ˈsɝː.t̬ɪd
precondition ˌpriː.kənˈdɪʃ.ᵊn **-s** -z **-ing** -ɪŋ **-ed** -d
precook ˌpriːˈkʊk **-s** -s **-ing** -ɪŋ **-ed** -t
precursor ˌpriːˈkɜː.səʳ, prɪ- ⓤⓢ prɪˈkɝː.sɚ, priː- **-s** -z **-y** -i
preda|te ˌpriːˈdeɪ|t ⓤⓢ ˌpriːˈdeɪ|t, ˈ-- **-tes** -ts **-ting** -tɪŋ ⓤⓢ -t̬ɪŋ **-ted** -tɪd ⓤⓢ -t̬ɪd *stress shift:* ˌpredated ˈcheque
predation prɪˈdeɪ.ʃᵊn, prə- ⓤⓢ prɪ-, priː- **-s** -z
predator ˈpred.ə.təʳ, ˈ-ɪ- ⓤⓢ -də.t̬ɚ
predator|y ˈpred.ə.tᵊr|.i ⓤⓢ -tɔːr- **-ily** -ᵊl.i, -ɪ.li **-iness** -ɪ.nəs, -ɪ.nɪs
predeceas|e ˌpriː.dɪˈsiːs, -dəˈ- ⓤⓢ -diːˈ-, -dɪˈ- **-es** -ɪz **-ing** -ɪŋ **-ed** -t
predecessor ˈpriː.dɪˌses.əʳ, -də-, ˌpriː.dɪˈses-, -dəˈ- ⓤⓢ ˈpred.ə.ses.ɚ, ˈpriː.də-; ˌpred.əˈses- **-s** -z
predesti|nate (*v.*) ˌpriːˈdes.tɪ|.neɪt, prɪ-, -tə- ⓤⓢ ˌpriːˈdes.tə- **-nates** -neɪts **-nating** -neɪ.tɪŋ ⓤⓢ -neɪ.t̬ɪŋ **-nated** -neɪ.tɪd ⓤⓢ -neɪ.t̬ɪd
predestinate (*adj.*) ˌpriːˈdes.tɪ.nət, prɪ-, -tə- ⓤⓢ ˌpriːˈdes.tə.nɪt
predestination ˌpriː.des.tɪˈneɪ.ʃᵊn, prɪˌdes- ⓤⓢ priː-, -təˈ-, priːˌdes.təˈ-
predestin|e ˌpriːˈdes.tɪn, prɪ- ⓤⓢ ˌpriː- **-es** -z **-ing** -ɪŋ **-ed** -d
predetermination ˌpriː.dɪˌtɜː.mɪˈneɪ.ʃᵊn, -dəˌ-, -məˈ- ⓤⓢ -dɪˌtɝː.məˈ-
predetermin|e ˌpriː.dɪˈtɜː.mɪn, -dəˈ-, -mən ⓤⓢ -dɪˈtɝː.mən **-es** -z **-ing** -ɪŋ **-ed** -d *stress shift:* ˌpredetermined ˈpath

Prefixes

A prefix is an element placed at the beginning of a word to modify or alter its meaning. In general, prefixes do not alter the original pronunciation of the word stem on to which they are affixed, though they may attract secondary stress.

A narrow definition of *prefix* would apply only in the case of words where removal of the prefix would leave a free-standing word (for example, 'unfit' is 'un' + 'fit'), but many treatments of English word stress also treat as prefixes such elements as 'con' in 'contain' or 'in' in 'insert', where 'tain' and 'sert' do not exist independently as words.

Examples

Some examples of words containing unstressed prefixes follow, e.g.:

admire	/əd'maɪəʳ/	(US) /-'maɪɚ/
contain	/kən'teɪn/	
desist	/dɪ'sɪst/	
undo	/ʌn'duː/	

A prefix may attract secondary stress if it is affixed to a word beginning with an unstressed syllable (e.g. another prefix), e.g.:

undivided	/ˌʌn.dɪ'vaɪ.dɪd/	
unforseen	/ˌʌn.fɔː'siːn/	(US) /-fɔːr'-/

A prefix may be stressed to avoid a clash of two stressed syllables in stress-shift situations, e.g.:

unfair dismissal	/ˌʌn.feə dɪ'smɪs.əl/
	(US) /-fer-/

In homographic noun/verb pairs containing prefixes, the prefix is usually stressed in the nominal form and unstressed in the verbal form (see the panel on HOMOGRAPHS), e.g.:

insert	(*n.*)	/'ɪn.sɜːt/	(US) /-sɝːt/
	(*v.*)	/ɪn'sɜːt/	(US) /-'sɝːt/
record	(*n.*)	/'rek.ɔːd/	(US) /-ɚd/
	(*v.*)	/rɪ'kɔːd/	(US) /-'kɔːrd/

predeterminer ˌpriː.dɪ'tɜː.mɪ.nəʳ, -də'-, -mə- (US) -dɪ'tɝː.mə.nɚ

predicability ˌpred.ɪ.kə'bɪl.ə.ti, -ɪ.ti (US) -ə.t̬i

predicable 'pred.ɪ.kə.bl̩

predicament prɪ'dɪk.ə.mənt, prə- (US) prɪ-, priː- **-s** -s

predicate (*n.*) 'pred.ɪ.kət, 'priː.dɪ-, -də-, -kɪt, -keɪt (US) 'pred.ɪ.kɪt, '-ə- **-s** -s

predi|cate (*v.*) 'pred.ɪ|.keɪt, '-ə- (US) '-ɪ- **-cates** -keɪts **-cating** -keɪ.tɪŋ (US) -keɪ.t̬ɪŋ **-cated** -keɪ.tɪd (US) -keɪ.t̬ɪd

predication ˌpred.ɪ'keɪ.ʃən, -ə'- (US) -ɪ'- **-s** -z

predicative prɪ'dɪk.ə.tɪv, prə- (US) prɪ'dɪk.ə.t̬ɪv, priː- **-ly** -li

predicatory 'pred.ɪ.keɪ.tər.i, '-ə-, ˌpred.ɪ'keɪ-, -ə'- (US) 'pred.ɪ.kə.tɔːr-

predict prɪ'dɪkt, prə- (US) prɪ-, priː- **-s** -s **-ing** -ɪŋ **-ed** -ɪd **-or/s** -əʳ/z (US) -ɚ/z

predictability prɪˌdɪk.tə'bɪl.ɪ.ti, prə- (US) prɪˌdɪk.tə'bɪl.ə.t̬i, priː-

predictab|le prɪ'dɪk.tə.b|l̩, prə- (US) prɪ-, priː- **-ly** -li

prediction prɪ'dɪk.ʃən, prə- (US) prɪ-, priː- **-s** -z

predictive prɪ'dɪk.tɪv **-ly** -li

predilection ˌpriː.dɪ'lek.ʃən, -də'- (US) ˌpred.əl'ek-, ˌpriː.dəl'- **-s** -z

predispos|e ˌpriː.dɪ'spəʊz, -də'- (US) -dɪ'spoʊz **-es** -ɪz **-ing** -ɪŋ **-ed** -d

predisposition ˌpriː.dɪ.spə'zɪʃ.ən, priːˌdɪs.pə'- **-s** -z

predominance prɪ'dɒm.ɪ.nənts, prə-, '-ə- (US) prɪ'dɑː.mə-, priː-

predominant prɪ'dɒm.ɪ.nənt, prə-, '-ə- (US) prɪ'dɑː.mə-, priː- **-ly** -li

predomi|nate prɪ'dɒm.ɪ|.neɪt, prə-, '-ə- (US) prɪ'dɑː.mə-, priː- **-nates** -neɪts **-nating** -neɪ.tɪŋ (US) -neɪ.t̬ɪŋ **-nated** -neɪ.tɪd (US) -neɪ.t̬ɪd

predomination prɪˌdɒm.ɪ'neɪ.ʃən, prə-, -ə'- (US) prɪˌdɑː.mə'-, priː-

Preece priːs

pre-eclampsia ˌpriː.ɪ'klæm*p*.si.ə

preemie 'priː.mi **-s** -z

pre-eminence ˌpriː'em.ɪ.nən*t*s, pri-, '-ə-

pre-eminent ˌpriː'em.ɪ.nənt, pri-, '-ə- **-ly** -li

pre-empt ˌpriː'em*p*t, pri- **-s** -s **-ing** -ɪŋ **-ed** -ɪd

pre-emption ˌpriː'em*p*.ʃən, pri-

pre-emptive ˌpriː'em*p*.tɪv, pri- **pre-ˌemptive 'strike**

preen priːn **-s** -z **-ing** -ɪŋ **-ed** -d

pre-exist ˌpriː.ɪg'zɪst, -eg'-; -ɪk'sɪst, -ek'- (US) -ɪg'zɪst, -eg'- **-s** -s **-ing** -ɪŋ **-ed** -ɪd **-ence** -ən*t*s **-ent** -ənt *stress shift:* ˌpre-existing 'rule

prefab 'priː.fæb **-s** -z

prefabri|cate ˌpriː'fæb.rɪ|.keɪt, -rə- **-cates** -keɪts **-cating** -keɪ.tɪŋ (US) -keɪ.t̬ɪŋ **-cated** -keɪ.tɪd (US) -keɪ.t̬ɪd

pre-fabrication ˌpriː.fæb.rɪ'keɪ.ʃən, priːˌfæb-, -rə'- (US) ˌpriː.fæb-

prefac|e 'pref.ɪs, -əs (US) -ɪs **-es** -ɪz **-ing** -ɪŋ **-ed** -t

prefatorial ˌpref.ə'tɔː.ri.əl (US) -'tɔːr.i- **-ly** -i

prefatory 'pref.ə.tər.i (US) -tɔːr-

prefect 'priː.fekt **-s** -s

prefecture 'priː.fek.tʃəʳ, -tʃʊəʳ, -tjʊəʳ (US) -tʃɚ **-s** -z

prefer prɪ'fɜːʳ, prə- (US) priː'fɝː, prɪ- **-s** -z **-ring** -ɪŋ **-red** -d

preferability ˌpref.ər.ə'bɪl.ə.ti, -ɪ.ti (US) -ə.t̬i

preferab|le 'pref.ər.ə.b|l̩ **-ly** -li **-leness** -l̩.nəs, -nɪs

preferenc|e 'pref.ər.ən*t*s **-es** -ɪz

preferential ˌpref.ə'ren.*t*ʃəl **-ly** -i

preferment prɪ'fɜː.mənt, prə- (US) priː'fɝː-, prɪ- **-s** -s

prefigurative priː'fɪg.ər.ə.tɪv (US) -jɚ- **-ly** -li **-ness** -nəs, -nɪs

prefig|ure priː'fɪg|.əʳ (US) -j|ɚ **-ures** -əz (US) -ɚz **-uring** -ər.ɪŋ **-ured** -əd (US) -ɚd

prefigurement priː'fɪg.ə.mənt (US) -jɚ-, -jʊr- **-s** -s

prefix (*n.*) 'priː.fɪks **-es** -ɪz

prefix (*v.*) ˌpriː'fɪks, '-- (US) 'priː.fɪks, ˌ-'- **-es** -ɪz **-ing** -ɪŋ **-ed** -t

preggers 'preg.əz (US) -ɚz

pregnable 'preg.nə.bl̩

pregnanc|y 'preg.nən*t*.s|i **-ies** -ɪz

pregnant 'preg.nənt **-ly** -li

pre|heat ˌpriː|'hiːt **-heats** -'hiːts **-heating** -'hiː.tɪŋ (US) -'hiː.t̬ɪŋ **-heated** -'hiː.tɪd (US) -'hiː.t̬ɪd *stress shift:* ˌpreheated 'meal

prehensible prɪ'hen*t*.sə.bl̩, -sɪ- (US) priː-

prehensile prɪ'hen*t*.saɪl, ˌpriː- (US) priː'hen*t*.sɪl, -səl

prehistoric ˌpriː.*h*ɪ'stɒr.ɪk (US) -hɪ'stɔːr-

-ally -ᵊl.i, -li *stress shift:* ˌprehistoric ˈmonster
prehistory ˌpriːˈhɪs.tᵊr.i
prejudg|e ˌpriːˈdʒʌdʒ **-es** -ɪz **-ing** -ɪŋ **-ed** -d **-(e)ment** -mənt
prejudic|e ˈpredʒ.ə.dɪs, ˈ-ʊ- **-es** -ɪz **-ing** -ɪŋ **-ed** -t
prejudicial ˌpredʒ.əˈdɪʃ.ᵊl, -ʊˈ- **-ly** -i
prelac|y ˈprel.ə.s|i **-ies** -iz
prelate ˈprel.ɪt, -ət ⓤⓢ -ɪt **-s** -s
preliminar|y prɪˈlɪm.ɪ.nᵊr|.i, prə-, -ᵊn.ᵊr- ⓤⓢ prɪˈlɪm.ə.ner-, priː- **-ies** -iz **-ily** -ᵊl.i, -ɪ.li
prelims ˈpriː.lɪmz, ˌ-ˈ-; prɪ- ⓤⓢ ˈpriː.lɪms; ˌpriːˈlɪmz, prɪ-
prelud|e ˈprel.juːd ⓤⓢ ˈprel-, -uːd; ˈpreɪ.luːd, ˈpriː- **-es** -z **-ing** -ɪŋ **-ed** -ɪd
premarital ˌpriːˈmær.ɪ.tᵊl ⓤⓢ -ˈmer.ə.t̬ᵊl, -ˈmær- **-ly** -i *stress shift, see compound:* ˌ**premarital** ˈ**sex**
premature ˈprem.ə.tʃəʳ, ˈpriː.mə-, -tjʊəʳ, -tʃʊəʳ, -tjɔːʳ, -tʃɔːʳ; ˌ--ˈ- ⓤⓢ ˌpriː.məˈtʊr, -ˈtjʊr, -ˈtʃʊr **-ly** -li **-ness** -nəs, -nɪs *stress shift, British only:* ˌpremature ˈaging
premed ˌpriːˈmed **-s** -z *stress shift:* ˌpremed ˈscience
premedical ˌpriːˈmed.ɪ.kᵊl, ˈ-ə- *stress shift:* ˌpremedical ˈscience
premedication ˌpriː.med.ɪˈkeɪ.ʃᵊn, -əˈ-
premedi|tate ˌpriːˈmed.ɪ|.teɪt, prɪ-, ˈ-ə- ⓤⓢ priːˈmed.ɪ- **-tates** -teɪts **-tating** -teɪ.tɪŋ ⓤⓢ -teɪ.t̬ɪŋ **-tated/ly** -teɪ.tɪd/li ⓤⓢ -teɪ.t̬ɪd/li
premeditation ˌpriː.med.ɪˈteɪ.ʃᵊn, prɪˌmed-, priː-, -əˈ- ⓤⓢ priː-
premenstrual ˌpriːˈment.stru.əl ⓤⓢ -strəl **-ly** -i *stress shift, see compounds:* ˌ**premenstrual** ˈ**tension**; ˌ**premenstrual** ˈ**syndrome**
premier ˈprem.i.əʳ, ˈpriː.mi- ⓤⓢ prɪˈmɪr, -ˈmjɪr; ˈpriː.miː.ɚ **-s** -z **-ship/s** -ʃɪp/s
premièr|e ˈprem.i.eəʳ, ˌ--ˈ- ⓤⓢ prɪˈmɪr, premˈɪr, -ˈjer, -ˈjɪr **-es** -z **-ing -ed**
Preminger ˈprem.ɪn.dʒəʳ, ˈpreɪ.mɪŋ.əʳ ⓤⓢ ˈprem.ɪn.dʒɚ
premis|e (*n.*) ˈprem.ɪs **-s** -ɪz
premis|e (*v.*) prɪˈmaɪz, ˈprem.ɪs ⓤⓢ ˈprem.ɪs **-es** -ɪz **-ing** -ɪŋ **-ed** prɪˈmaɪzd, ˈprem.ɪst ⓤⓢ ˈprem.ɪst
premium ˈpriː.mi.əm **-s** -z ˈ**premium** ˌ**bond**
premmie ˈprem.i **-s** -z
premodification ˌpriː.mɒd.ɪ.fɪˈkeɪ.ʃᵊn, priːˌmɒd-, -ə- ⓤⓢ ˌpriː.mɑː.dɪ.fɪˈ-
premodif|y priːˈmɒd.ɪ.f|aɪ ⓤⓢ -ˈmɑː.dɪ- **-ies** -aɪz **-ying** -aɪ.ɪŋ **-ied** -aɪd
premolar ˌpriːˈməʊ.ləʳ ⓤⓢ -ˈmoʊ.lɚ **-s** -z *stress shift:* ˌpremolar ˈteeth
premonition ˌprem.əˈnɪʃ.ᵊn, ˌpriː.məˈ- **-s** -z
premonitorily prɪˈmɒn.ɪ.tᵊr.ᵊl.i, -ɪ.li ⓤⓢ priːˈmɑː.nə.tɔːr-, -ˌmɑː.nəˈtɔːr-
premonitory prɪˈmɒn.ɪ.tᵊr.i ⓤⓢ priːˈmɑː.nə.tɔːr-
prenatal ˌpriːˈneɪ.tᵊl ⓤⓢ -t̬ᵊl **-ly** -i *stress shift:* ˌprenatal ˈcare
Prendergast ˈpren.də.gɑːst, -gæst ⓤⓢ -dɚ.gæst
prentic|e (P) ˈpren.tɪs ⓤⓢ -t̬ɪs **-es** -ɪz
Prentis(s) ˈpren.tɪs ⓤⓢ -t̬ɪs
prenuptial ˌpriːˈnʌp.*t*ʃᵊl *stress shift, see compound:* ˌ**prenuptial** **a**ˈ**greement**
preoccupation priːˌɒk.jəˈpeɪ.ʃᵊn, prɪ-, ˌpriː.ɒk-, -jʊˈ- ⓤⓢ priːˌɑː.kjuːˈ-, -kjəˈ- **-s** -z
preoccup|y ˌpriːˈɒk.jə.p|aɪ, pri- ⓤⓢ priːˈɑː.kjuː-, -kjə- **-ies** -aɪz **-ying** -aɪ.ɪŋ **-ied** -aɪd
preordain ˌpriː.ɔːˈdeɪn ⓤⓢ -ɔːrˈ- **-s** -z **-ing** -ɪŋ **-ed** -d *stress shift:* ˌpreordained ˈdestiny
prep prep **-s** -s **-ping** -ɪŋ **-ped** -t ˈ**prep** ˌ**school**
prepackag|e ˌpriːˈpæk.ɪdʒ **-es** -ɪz **-ing** -ɪŋ **-ed** -d *stress shift:* ˌprepackaged ˈgoods
prepaid (*from* **prepay**) ˌpriːˈpeɪd *stress shift:* ˌprepaid ˈpostage
preparation ˌprep.ᵊrˈeɪ.ʃᵊn ⓤⓢ -əˈreɪ- **-s** -z
preparative prɪˈpær.ə.tɪv, prə- ⓤⓢ prɪˈper.ə.t̬ɪv, priː-, -ˈpær- **-ly** -li
preparator|y prɪˈpær.ə.tᵊr|.i, prə- ⓤⓢ prɪˈper.ə.tɔːr-, priː-, -ˈpær-; ˈprep.ɚ.ə- **-ily** -ᵊl.i, -ɪ.li **pre**ˈ**paratory** ˌ**school**
prepar|e prɪˈpeəʳ, prə- ⓤⓢ prɪˈper, priː- **-es** -z **-ing** -ɪŋ **-ed** -d **-edly** -d.li, -ɪd.li **-edness** -d.nəs, -nɪs, -ɪd.nəs, -nɪs **-er/s** -əʳ/z ⓤⓢ -ɚ/z
prepay ˌpriːˈpeɪ **-s** -z **-ing** -ɪŋ **prepaid** ˌpriːˈpeɪd *stress shift:* ˌprepaid ˈpostage
prepayment ˌpriːˈpeɪ.mənt **-s** -s
prepense prɪˈpen*t*s **-ly** -li
preponderance prɪˈpɒn.dᵊr.ᵊn*t*s, prə- ⓤⓢ prɪˈpɑːn-, priː-
preponderant prɪˈpɒn.dᵊr.ᵊnt, prə- ⓤⓢ prɪˈpɑːn-, priː- **-ly** -li
preponder|ate prɪˈpɒn.dᵊr|.eɪt, prə- ⓤⓢ prɪˈpɑːn.də.r|eɪt, priː- **-ates** -eɪts **-ating/ly** -eɪ.tɪŋ/li ⓤⓢ -eɪ.t̬ɪŋ/li **-ated** -eɪ.tɪd ⓤⓢ -eɪ.t̬ɪd
preponderation prɪˌpɒn.dᵊrˈeɪ.ʃᵊn, prə-, priː- ⓤⓢ prɪˌpɑːn.dəˈreɪ-, priː-
preposition ˌprep.əˈzɪʃ.ᵊn **-s** -z
prepositional ˌprep.əˈzɪʃ.ᵊn.ᵊl, ˈ-nᵊl ⓤⓢ -əˈ- **-ly** -i *stress shift, see compound:* ˌ**prepositional** ˈ**phrase**
prepositive prɪˈpɒz.ə.tɪv, priː-, ˈ-ɪ- ⓤⓢ prɪˈpɑː.zə.t̬ɪv, priː- *stress shift:* ˌprepositive ˈadjective
prepossess ˌpriː.pəˈzes **-es** -ɪz **-ing/ly** -ɪŋ/li **-ed** -t
prepossession ˌpriː.pəˈzeʃ.ᵊn **-s** -z
preposterous prɪˈpɒs.tᵊr.əs, prə- ⓤⓢ prɪˈpɑː.stɚ-, priː- **-ly** -li **-ness** -nəs, -nɪs
prepp|y, prepp|ie ˈprep|.i **-ies** -iz **-ier** -i.əʳ ⓤⓢ -i.ɚ **-iest** -i.ɪst, -i.əst **-iness** -ɪ.nəs, -ɪ.nɪs
prepubescen|t ˌpriː.pjuːˈbes.ᵊn|t **-ce** -*t*s
prepuc|e ˈpriː.pjuːs **-es** -ɪz
prequel ˈpriː.kwəl **-s** -z
Pre-Raphaelite ˌpriːˈræf.i.ᵊl.aɪt, -eɪ-, -ˈræf.ᵊl-, -ɪ.laɪt ⓤⓢ -ˈræf.i.ᵊl-, -ˈreɪ.fi- **-s** -s ˌ**Pre-**ˌ**Raphaelite** ˈ**Brotherhood**
prerecord ˌpriː.rɪˈkɔːd, -rəˈ- ⓤⓢ -rɪˈkɔːrd **-s** -z **-ing** -ɪŋ **-ed** -ɪd
prerequisite ˌpriːˈrek.wɪ.zɪt, -wə- **-s** -s
prerogative prɪˈrɒg.ə.tɪv, prə- ⓤⓢ -ˈrɑː.gə.t̬ɪv **-s** -z
presag|e (*n.*) ˈpres.ɪdʒ **-es** -ɪz
presag|e (*v.*) ˈpres.ɪdʒ; prɪˈseɪdʒ, prə- ⓤⓢ prɪˈseɪdʒ; ˈpres.ɪdʒ **-es** -ɪz **-ing** -ɪŋ **-ed** -d
presbyopia ˌprez.biˈəʊ.pi.ə ⓤⓢ -ˈoʊ-, ˌpres-
presbyter ˈprez.bɪ.təʳ ⓤⓢ -t̬ɚ, ˈpres- **-s** -z
presbyterian (P) ˌprez.bɪˈtɪə.ri.ən, -bəˈ- ⓤⓢ -bɪˈtɪr.i-, ˌpres- **-s** -z **-ism** -ɪ.zᵊm
presbyter|y ˈprez.bɪ.tᵊr|.i, -bə- ⓤⓢ -bɪ.ter-, ˈpres- **-ies** -iz
Prescel(l)y prɪˈsel.i, prə-, presˈel-
preschool ˈpriː.skuːl, ˌ-ˈ- ⓤⓢ ˈ--
preschooler ˈpriːˌskuː.ləʳ ⓤⓢ -lɚ **-s** -z
prescience ˈpres.i.ən*t*s, ˈpreʃ- ⓤⓢ ˈpreʃ.ᵊn*t*s, ˈpriː.ʃᵊn*t*s, -ʃi.ən*t*s
prescient ˈpres.i.ənt, ˈpreʃ- ⓤⓢ ˈpreʃ.ᵊnt, ˈpriː.ʃᵊnt, -ʃi.ənt **-ly** -li
prescind prɪˈsɪnd, prə-, priː- ⓤⓢ prɪ-, priː- **-s** -z **-ing** -ɪŋ **-ed** -ɪd
Prescot(t) ˈpres.kət, -kɒt ⓤⓢ -kət, -kɑːt
prescrib|e prɪˈskraɪb, prə- ⓤⓢ prɪ-, priː- **-es** -z **-ing** -ɪŋ **-ed** -d **-er/s** -əʳ/z ⓤⓢ -ɚ/z
prescript ˈpriː.skrɪpt **-s** -s
prescription prɪˈskrɪp.ʃᵊn, prə- ⓤⓢ prɪ-, priː- **-s** -z
prescriptive prɪˈskrɪp.tɪv, prə-, priː- ⓤⓢ prɪ-, priː- **-ly** -li
prescriptiv|ism prɪˈskrɪp.tɪ.v|ɪ.zᵊm, prə-, priː- ⓤⓢ prɪ-, priː- **-ist/s** -ɪst/s
pre-season ˌpriːˈsiː.zᵊn *stress shift:* ˌpre-season ˈsale
Preseli prɪˈsel.i, prə-, priː-
presenc|e ˈprez.ᵊn*t*s **-es** -ɪz ˌ**presence of** ˈ**mind**
present (*n.*) *ordinary senses:* ˈprez.ᵊnt **-s** -s

present (*n.*) *military term:* prɪˈzent, prə- **-s** -s
present (*adj.*) ˈprez.ᵊnt **-ly** -li ˌ**present parˈticiple** ⓤⓢ ˌ**present ˈparticiple**; ˌ**present ˈperfect**; ˌ**present ˈtense**
pre|sent (*v.*) prɪ|ˈzent, prə- ⓤⓢ prɪ-, priː- **-sents** -ˈzents **-senting** -ˈzen.tɪŋ ⓤⓢ -ˈzen.t̬ɪŋ **-sented** -ˈzen.tɪd ⓤⓢ -ˈzen.t̬ɪd
presentab|le prɪˈzen.tə.b|l̩, prə- ⓤⓢ prɪˈzen.t̬ə-, priː- **-ly** -li **-leness** -l̩.nəs, -nɪs
presentation ˌprez.ᵊnˈteɪ.ʃᵊn, -enˈ- ⓤⓢ -ᵊnˈ-, ˌpriː.zᵊnˈ- **-s** -z **-al**
present-day ˌprez.ᵊntˈdeɪ *stress shift:* ˌpresent-day ˈfashions
presenter prɪˈzen.təʳ, prə- ⓤⓢ prɪˈzen.t̬ɚ, priː- **-s** -z
presentient prɪˈsen*t*.ʃi.ənt, -ʃᵊnt ⓤⓢ priː-, prɪ-
presentiment prɪˈzen.tɪ.mənt ⓤⓢ prɪ-, priː- **-s** -s
presently ˈprez.ᵊnt.li
preservation ˌprez.əˈveɪ.ʃᵊn ⓤⓢ -ɚˈ- **-s** -z **-ist/s** -ɪst/s **preserˈvation ˌorder**
preservative prɪˈzɜː.və.tɪv, prə- ⓤⓢ prɪˈzɝː.və.t̬ɪv, priː- **-s** -z
preserv|e prɪˈzɜːv, prə- ⓤⓢ prɪˈzɝːv, priː- **-es** -z **-ing** -ɪŋ **-ed** -d **-er/s** -əʳ/z ⓤⓢ -ɚ/z **-able** -ə.bl̩
pre|set priː|ˈset **-sets** -ˈsets **-setting** -ˈset.ɪŋ ⓤⓢ -ˈset̬.ɪŋ *stress shift:* ˌpreset ˈchannel
pre|shrink ˌpriːˈʃrɪŋk **-shrinks** -ˈʃrɪŋks **-shrinking** -ˈʃrɪŋ.kɪŋ **-shrank** -ˈʃræŋk **-shrunk** -ˈʃrʌŋk **-shrunken** -ˈʃrʌŋ.kᵊn *stress shift:* ˌpreshrunk ˈjeans
presid|e prɪˈzaɪd, prə- ⓤⓢ prɪ-, priː- **-es** -z **-ing** -ɪŋ **-ed** -ɪd
presidenc|y ˈprez.ɪ.dᵊn*t*.s|i **-ies** -iz
president ˈprez.ɪ.dᵊnt **-s** -s
presidential ˌprez.ɪˈden.*t*ʃᵊl *stress shift:* ˌpresidential ˈsuite
presidi|um prɪˈsɪd.i|.əm, prə- **-ums** -əmz **-a** -ə
Presley ˈprez.li ⓤⓢ ˈpres-, ˈprez-
pre|sort ˌpriː|ˈsɔːt ⓤⓢ -ˈsɔːrt **-sorts** -ˈsɔːts ⓤⓢ -ˈsɔːrts **-sorting** -ˈsɔː.tɪŋ ⓤⓢ -ˈsɔːr.t̬ɪŋ **-sorted** -ˈsɔː.tɪd ⓤⓢ -ˈsɔːr.t̬ɪd
press pres **-es** -ɪz **-ing/ly** -ɪŋ/li **-ed** -t **-er/s** -əʳ/z ⓤⓢ -ɚ/z ˈ**press ˌagent**; ˈ**press ˌbaron**; ˈ**press ˌconference**; ˈ**press ˌcutting**; ˈ**press ˌoffice**; ˈ**press reˌlease**
pressgang ˈpres.gæŋ **-s** -z **-ing** -ɪŋ **-ed** -d
pressie ˈprez.i **-s** -z
pression ˈpreʃ.ᵊn
press|man ˈpres|.mæn, -mən **-men** -mən, -men
pressrun ˈpres.rʌn
press-stud ˈpres.stʌd **-s** -s
press-up ˈpres.ʌp **-s** -s
pressur|e ˈpreʃ.əʳ ⓤⓢ -ɚ **-es** -z **-ing** -ɪŋ **-ed** -d ˈ**pressure ˌcooker**; ˈ**pressure ˌgroup**
pressuriz|e, -is|e ˈpreʃ.ᵊr.aɪz ⓤⓢ -ə.raɪz **-es** -ɪz **-ing** -ɪŋ **-ed** -d
Prestage ˈpres.tɪdʒ
Prestatyn presˈtæt.ɪn, prɪˈstæt-
Presteign presˈtiːn
Prestel® ˈpres.tel
prestidigitation ˌpres.tɪˌdɪdʒ.ɪˈteɪ.ʃᵊn ⓤⓢ -təˌ-
prestidigitator ˌpres.tɪˈdɪdʒ.ɪ.teɪ.təʳ ⓤⓢ -təˈdɪdʒ.ə.teɪ.t̬ɚ **-s** -z
prestige presˈtiːʒ ⓤⓢ -ˈtiːdʒ
Prestige *surname:* ˈpres.tɪdʒ
prestigious presˈtɪdʒ.əs, prɪˈstɪdʒ-, prə-, -i.əs ⓤⓢ presˈtɪdʒ.əs, -ˈtiː.dʒəs **-ly** -li **-ness** -nəs, -nɪs
prestissimo presˈtɪs.ɪ.məʊ, ˈ-ə- ⓤⓢ -ə.moʊ
presto (P) ˈpres.təʊ ⓤⓢ -toʊ **-s** -z
Preston ˈpres.tᵊn
Prestonpans ˌpres.tᵊnˈpænz, -tᵊmˈ- ⓤⓢ -tᵊnˈ-
prestressed ˌpriːˈstrest
Prestwich ˈpres.twɪtʃ
Prestwick ˈpres.twɪk
Prestwood ˈpres.twʊd
presumab|ly prɪˈzjuː.mə.b|li, prə-, -ˈzuː- ⓤⓢ prɪˈzuː.mə-, priː- **-le** -l̩
presum|e prɪˈzjuːm, prə-, -ˈzuːm ⓤⓢ prɪˈzuːm, priː- **-es** -z **-ing/ly** -ɪŋ/li **-ed** -d
presumption prɪˈzʌmp.ʃᵊn, prə- ⓤⓢ prɪ-, priː- **-s** -z
presumptive prɪˈzʌmp.tɪv, prə- ⓤⓢ prɪ-, priː- **-ly** -li
presumptuous prɪˈzʌmp.tʃu.əs, prə-, -tju-, -tʃəs ⓤⓢ prɪˈzʌmp.tʃuː.əs, priː-, -tʃə.wəs **-ly** -li **-ness** -nəs, -nɪs
presuppos|e ˌpriː.səˈpəʊz ⓤⓢ -ˈpoʊz **-es** -ɪz **-ing** -ɪŋ **-ed** -d
presupposition ˌpriː.sʌp.əˈzɪʃ.ᵊn **-s** -z
prêt-à-porter ˌpret.ɑːˈpɔː.teɪ ⓤⓢ -pɔːrˈteɪ
pre-tax ˌpriːˈtæks *stress shift:* ˌpretax ˈprofit
preteen ˌpriːˈtiːn **-s** -z *stress shift:* ˌpreteen ˈyears
pretenc|e prɪˈten*t*s, prə- ⓤⓢ ˈpriː.ten*t*s; prɪˈten*t*s **-es** -ɪz
pretend prɪˈtend, prə- ⓤⓢ prɪ-, priː- **-s** -z **-ing** -ɪŋ **-ed** -ɪd **-er/s** -əʳ/z ⓤⓢ -ɚ/z
pretens|e prɪˈten*t*s, prə- ⓤⓢ ˈpriː.ten*t*s; prɪˈten*t*s **-es** -ɪz
pretension prɪˈten.*t*ʃᵊn, prə- ⓤⓢ prɪ-, priː- **-s** -z
pretentious prɪˈten.*t*ʃəs, prə- ⓤⓢ prɪ-, priː- **-ly** -li **-ness** -nəs, -nɪs
preterit(e) ˈpret.ᵊr.ɪt, -ət ⓤⓢ ˈpret̬.ɚ.ɪt **-s** -s
pretermission ˌpriː.təˈmɪʃ.ᵊn ⓤⓢ -t̬ɚˈ-
preter|mit ˌpriː.tə|ˈmɪt ⓤⓢ -t̬ɚˈ- **-mits** -ˈmɪts **-mitting** -ˈmɪt.ɪŋ ⓤⓢ -ˈmɪt̬.ɪŋ **-mitted** -ˈmɪt.ɪd ⓤⓢ -ˈmɪt̬.ɪd
preternatural ˌpriː.təˈnætʃ.ᵊr.ᵊl, -ʊ.rᵊl ⓤⓢ -t̬ɚˈnætʃ.ɚ.ᵊl, ˈ-rᵊl **-ly** -i **-ness** -nəs, -nɪs *stress shift:* ˌpreternatural ˈhappening
pretext ˈpriː.tekst **-s** -s
pretor ˈpriː.təʳ ⓤⓢ -t̬ɚ **-s** -z **-ship/s** -ʃɪp/s
Pretori|a prɪˈtɔː.ri|.ə, prə- ⓤⓢ prɪˈtɔːr.i-, priː- **-us** -əs
pretori|al prɪˈtɔː.ri|.əl, prə- ⓤⓢ prɪˈtɔːr.i-, priː- **-an** -ən
prettification ˌprɪt.ɪ.fɪˈkeɪ.ʃᵊn, ˌ-ə- ⓤⓢ ˌprɪt̬-
prettif|y ˈprɪt.ɪ.f|aɪ ⓤⓢ ˈprɪt̬- **-ies** -aɪz **-ying** -aɪ.ɪŋ **-ied** -aɪd
prett|y (*adj. adv.*) ˈprɪt|.i ⓤⓢ ˈprɪt̬- **-ier** -i.əʳ ⓤⓢ -i.ɚ **-iest** -i.ɪst, -i.əst **-ily** -ɪ.li, -ᵊl.i **-iness** -ɪ.nəs, -ɪ.nɪs
Pretty *surname:* ˈprɪt.i, ˈpret- ⓤⓢ ˈprɪt̬-, ˈpret̬-
Pret(t)yman ˈprɪt.ɪ.mən ⓤⓢ ˈprɪt̬-
pretty-pretty ˈprɪt.iˌprɪt.i ⓤⓢ ˈprɪt̬.iˌprɪt̬.i
pretzel ˈpret.sᵊl **-s** -z
prevail prɪˈveɪl, prə- ⓤⓢ prɪ-, priː- **-s** -z **-ing** -ɪŋ **-ed** -d
prevalence ˈprev.ᵊl.ən*t*s ⓤⓢ -ə.lən*t*s
prevalent ˈprev.ᵊl.ənt ⓤⓢ -ə.lənt **-ly** -li
prevari|cate prɪˈvær.ɪ|.keɪt, prə-, ˈ-ə- ⓤⓢ prɪˈver.ɪ-, -ˈvær- **-cates** -keɪts **-cating** -keɪ.tɪŋ ⓤⓢ -keɪ.t̬ɪŋ **-cated** -keɪ.tɪd ⓤⓢ -keɪ.t̬ɪd **-cator/s** -keɪ.təʳ/z ⓤⓢ -keɪ.t̬ɚ/z
prevarication prɪˌvær.ɪˈkeɪ.ʃᵊn, prə-, -əˈ- ⓤⓢ prɪˌver-, -ˌvær- **-s** -z
pre|vent *hinder:* prɪ|ˈvent, prə- ⓤⓢ prɪ-, priː- **-vents** -ˈvents **-venting** -ˈven.tɪŋ ⓤⓢ -ˈven.t̬ɪŋ **-vented** -ˈven.tɪd ⓤⓢ -ˈven.t̬ɪd **-venter/s** -ˈven.təʳ/z ⓤⓢ -ˈven.t̬ɚ/z **-ventable** -ˈven.tə.bl̩ ⓤⓢ -ˈven.t̬ə.bl̩
pre|vent *go before:* ˌpriː|ˈvent, prɪ- ⓤⓢ priː-, prɪ- **-vents** -ˈvents **-venting** -ˈven.tɪŋ ⓤⓢ -ˈven.t̬ɪŋ **-vented** -ˈven.tɪd ⓤⓢ -ˈven.t̬ɪd
preventability prɪˌven.təˈbɪl.ə.ti, prə-, -ɪ.ti ⓤⓢ prɪˌven.t̬əˈbɪl.ə.t̬i, priː-
preventative prɪˈven.tə.tɪv, prə- ⓤⓢ prɪˈven.t̬ə.t̬ɪv, priː- **-s** -z
prevention prɪˈven.*t*ʃᵊn, prə- ⓤⓢ prɪ-, priː-
preventive prɪˈven.tɪv, prə- ⓤⓢ prɪˈven.t̬ɪv, priː- **-ly** -li **-ness** -nəs, -nɪs
preverbal ˌpriːˈvɜː.bᵊl ⓤⓢ -ˈvɝː- *stress shift:* ˌpreverbal ˈstate
preview ˈpriː.vjuː **-s** -z **-ing** -ɪŋ **-ed** -d
Previn ˈprev.ɪn

previous 'priː.vi.əs, '-vjəs (US) -vi.əs -ly -li -ness -nəs, -nɪs

prevision ˌpriː'vɪʒ.ən, prɪ- (US) priː-

prevocalic ˌpriː.vəʊ'kæl.ɪk (US) -voʊ'- -ally -əl.i, -li *stress shift:* ˌprevocalic 'consonant

Prevost 'prev.əʊ, 'prev.əʊst, prev'əʊ (US) 'preɪ.voʊ, 'prev.oʊ

pre-war ˌpriː'wɔːr (US) -'wɔːr *stress shift:* ˌpre-war 'politics

Prewett 'pruː.ɪt

prey preɪ -s -z -ing -ɪŋ -ed -d

prezzie 'prez.i -s -z

Priam praɪəm, 'praɪ.æm

priapic praɪ'æp.ɪk, -'eɪ.pɪk

priapism 'praɪ.ə.pɪ.zəm

priapus (P) praɪ'eɪ.pəs; 'praɪ.ə.pəs -es -ɪz

pric|e (P) praɪs -es -ɪz -ing -ɪŋ -ed -t 'price ˌtag; 'price ˌwar

price-cutting 'praɪsˌkʌt.ɪŋ (US) -ˌkʌt̬-

priceless 'praɪ.sləs, -slɪs -ness -nəs, -nɪs

pric|ey 'praɪ.s|i -ier -i.ər (US) -i.ɚ -iest -i.ɪst, -i.əst -ily -ɪ.li, -əl.i -iness -ɪ.nəs, -ɪ.nɪs

prick prɪk -s -s -ing/s -ɪŋ/z -ed -t -er/s -ər/z (US) -ɚ/z

prickl|e 'prɪk.l̩ -es -z -ing -ɪŋ, 'prɪk.lɪŋ -ed -d

prickl|y 'prɪk.l|i, -l̩|.i (US) '-li -ier -i.ər (US) -i.ɚ -iest -ɪ.ɪst, -i.əst -iness -ɪ.nəs, -ɪ.nɪs ˌprickly 'pear

prid|e (P) praɪd -es -z -ing -ɪŋ -ed -ɪd ˌpride of 'place

Prideaux 'prɪd.əʊ, 'priː.dəʊ (US) 'prɪd.oʊ

Pridham 'prɪd.əm

prie-dieu ˌpriː'djɜː, '-- (US) 'priː.djɜː prie-dieus ˌpriː'djɜːz, -'djɜː, '-- (US) 'priː.djɜːz

prie-dieux *(alternative plur. of* **prie-dieu***)* ˌpriː'djɜːz, -'djɜː, '-- (US) 'priː.djɜːz

priest (P) priːst -s -s

priestess ˌpriː'stes; 'priː.stəs, -stɪs (US) 'priː.stɪs -es -ɪz

priesthood 'priːst.hʊd

Priestland 'priːst.lənd

Priestley 'priːst.li

priestl|y 'priːst.l|i -iness -ɪ.nəs, -ɪ.nɪs

prig prɪg -s -z -gery -ər.i

priggish 'prɪg.ɪʃ -ly -li -ness -nəs, -nɪs

prim (P) prɪm -mer -ər (US) -ɚ -mest -ɪst, -əst -ly -li -ness -nəs, -nɪs -s -z -ming -ɪŋ -med -d

prima ballerina ˌpriː.mə.bæl.ər'iː.nə (US) -ə'riː- -s -z

primac|y 'praɪ.mə.s|i -ies -iz

prima donna ˌpriː.mə'dɒn.ə (US) -'dɑː.nə, ˌprɪm.ə'- -s -z

primaeval ˌpraɪ'miː.vəl

prima facie ˌpraɪ.mə'feɪ.ʃi, -ʃiː, '-ʃi.iː, '-si, -siː, '-si.iː (US) '-ʃi.ː, '-ʃiː, -ʃə

Primakov 'priː.mə.kɒf, ˌ--'- (US) 'priː.mə.kɔːf, -kɑːf

primal 'praɪ.məl ˌprimal 'therapy

primarily praɪ'mer.əl.i, -'meə.rəl-, -ɪ.li; 'praɪ.mər.əl-, -ɪ.li (US) praɪ'mer.əl.i, 'praɪ.mer-

primar|y 'praɪ.mər|.i (US) -mer-, -mɚ- -ies -iz -iness -ɪ.nəs, -ɪ.nɪs ˌprimary 'colour (US) 'primary ˌcolor; 'primary ˌschool; ˌprimary 'stress

primate *archbishop:* 'praɪ.meɪt, -mɪt, -mət (US) -mɪt -s -s

primate *higher mammal:* 'praɪ.meɪt -s -s

primateship 'praɪ.mət.ʃɪp, -mɪt-, -meɪt- (US) -mɪt- -s -s

prim|e (P) praɪm -es -z -ing -ɪŋ -ed -d ˌprime 'minister; ˌprime 'mover; 'prime ˌtime, ˌprime 'time

primer *thing that primes:* 'praɪ.mər (US) -mɚ -s -z *elementary school book:* 'praɪ.mər, 'prɪm.ər (US) 'prɪm.ɚ -s -z

primer *printing type:* 'prɪm.ər (US) -ɚ

primetime 'praɪm.taɪm

primeval praɪ'miː.vəl

primipar|a praɪ'mɪp.ər|.ə -as -əz -ae -iː

primiparous praɪ'mɪp.ər.əs

primitive 'prɪm.ɪ.tɪv, '-ə- (US) -ɪ.t̬ɪv -ly -li -ness -nəs, -nɪs

primitiv|ism 'prɪm.ɪ.tɪ.v|ɪ.zəm, '-ə- (US) -ɪ.t̬ɪ- -ist/s -ɪst/s

primo 'priː.məʊ (US) -moʊ

primogenitor ˌpraɪ.məʊ'dʒen.ɪ.tər, ˌpriː-, '-ə- (US) ˌpraɪ.moʊ'dʒen.ɪ.tɚ, -mə'- -s -z

primogeniture ˌpraɪ.məʊ'dʒen.ɪ.tʃər, '-ə-, -tʃʊər, -tjʊər (US) ˌpraɪ.moʊ'dʒen.ɪ.tʃɚ, -mə'-

primordial praɪ'mɔː.di.əl (US) -'mɔːr- -s -z -ly -i

primp prɪmp -s -s -ing -ɪŋ -ed -t, prɪmt

primros|e (P) 'prɪm.rəʊz (US) -roʊz -es -ɪz ˌprimrose 'path

primula 'prɪm.jə.lə, -jʊ- -s -z

primum mobile ˌpraɪ.məm'məʊ.bɪ.li, ˌpriː-, -mʊm'-, -bəl.i, -eɪ (US) ˌpraɪ.məm'moʊ.bəl.i, ˌpriː-, -eɪ -s -z

primus (P®) 'praɪ.məs -es -ɪz

princ|e (P) prɪnts -es -ɪz ˌprince 'charming; ˌprince 'consort; ˌPrince 'Edward ˌIsland (US) ˌPrince ˌEdward 'Island; ˌPrince of 'Wales; ˌprince 'regent

princedom 'prɪnts.dəm -s -z

princeling 'prɪnts.lɪŋ -s -z

princel|y 'prɪnts.l|i -ier -i.ər (US) -i.ɚ -iest -i.ɪst, -i.əst -iness -ɪ.nəs, -ɪ.nɪs

Princes Risborough ˌprɪnt.sɪz'rɪz.bər.ə (US) -bɚ.oʊ

princess (P) prɪn'ses, 'prɪnt.ses, -ɪs, -əs (US) 'prɪnt.sɪs, -ses -es -ɪz ˌprincess 'royal

Princeton 'prɪnt.stən

Princetown 'prɪnts.taʊn

princip|al (P) 'prɪnt.sə.p|əl, -sɪ- (US) -sə- -als -əlz -ally -əl.i, -li -alness -əl.nəs, -nɪs ˌprincipal 'boy

principalit|y ˌprɪnt.sɪ'pæl.ə.t|i, -sə'-, -ɪ.t|i (US) -sə'pæl.ə.t̬|i -ies -iz

principalship 'prɪnt.sə.pəl.ʃɪp, -sɪ- (US) -sə- -s -s

principate 'prɪnt.sɪ.pət, -sə-, -pɪt, -peɪt (US) -sə.peɪt, -pɪt -s -s

Principia prɪn'sɪp.i.ə

principle 'prɪnt.sə.pl̩, -sɪ- (US) -sə- -s -z -d -d

Pring prɪŋ

Pringle 'prɪŋ.gl̩

Prinknash 'prɪn.ɪdʒ

Prinsep 'prɪnt.sep

print prɪnt -s -s -ing/s -ɪn/z (US) 'prɪn.t̬ɪŋ/z -ed -ɪd (US) 'prɪn.t̬ɪd 'print ˌrun; 'printing ˌpress

printable 'prɪn.tə.bl̩ (US) -t̬ə-

printer 'prɪn.tər (US) -t̬ɚ -s -z

printmak|ing 'prɪntˌmeɪ.k|ɪŋ -er/s -ər/z (US) -ɚ/z

printout 'prɪnt.aʊt -s -s

printwheel 'prɪnt.*h*wiːl -s -z

prior (P) praɪər (US) praɪɚ -s -z

prioress 'praɪə.rəs, -rɪs, -res; ˌpraɪə'res (US) 'praɪɚ.ɪs -es -ɪz

prioritiz|e, -is|e praɪ'ɒr.ɪ.taɪz, '-ə- (US) -'ɔːr.ə- -es -ɪz -ing -ɪŋ -ed -d

priorit|y praɪ'ɒr.ə.t|i, -ɪ.t|i (US) -'ɔːr.ə.t̬|i -ies -iz

prior|y 'praɪə.r|i -ies -iz

Priscian 'prɪʃ.i.ən (US) '-ən, -i.ən

Priscilla prɪ'sɪl.ə, prə- (US) prɪ-

pris|e praɪz -es -ɪz -ing -ɪŋ -ed -d

prism 'prɪz.əm -s -z

prismatic prɪz'mæt.ɪk (US) -'mæt̬- -al -əl -ally -əl.i, -li

prison 'prɪz.ən -s -z 'prison ˌcamp; ˌprison 'visitor

prisoner 'prɪz.ən.ər, '-nər (US) 'prɪz.ən.ɚ, '-nɚ -s -z ˌprisoner of 'conscience; ˌprisoner of 'war

priss|y 'prɪs|.i -ier -i.ər (US) -i.ɚ -iest -i.ɪst, -i.əst -ily -ɪ.li, -əl.i -iness -ɪ.nəs, -ɪ.nɪs

Pristina 'prɪʃ.tɪ.nə

pristine 'prɪs.tiːn, -taɪn (US) -tiːn; prɪ'stiːn

Pritchard 'prɪtʃ.əd, -ɑːd (US) -ɚd

Pritchett 'prɪtʃ.ɪt, -ət

prithee 'prɪð.i, -iː

privacy 'prɪv.ə.si, 'praɪ.və- (US) 'praɪ-

private 'praɪ.vɪt, -vət (US) -vət -s -s -ly -li -ness -nəs, -nɪs ˌprivate de'tective; ˌprivate 'enterprise; ˌprivate 'eye;

ˌprivate ˈmember's ˌbill; ˌprivate ˈsector Ⓤⓢ ˈprivate ˌsector; ˌprivate ˈschool
privateer ˌpraɪ.vəˈtɪəʳ, -vɪˈ- Ⓤⓢ -vəˈtɪr **-s** -z
privation praɪˈveɪ.ʃən **-s** -z
privative ˈprɪv.ə.tɪv **-ly** -li
privatization, -isa- ˌpraɪ.vɪ.taɪˈzeɪ.ʃən, -və-, -tɪˈ- Ⓤⓢ -və.tɪˈ- **-s** -z
privatiz|e, -is|e ˈpraɪ.vɪ.taɪz, -və- Ⓤⓢ -və- **-es** -ɪz **-ing** -ɪŋ **-ed** -d
privet ˈprɪv.ɪt **-s** -s ˈ**privet** ˌ**hedge**, ˌprivet ˈhedge
privileg|e ˈprɪv.əl.ɪdʒ, -ɪ.lɪdʒ Ⓤⓢ -əl.ɪdʒ, ˈ-lɪdʒ **-es** -ɪz **-ed** -d
privity ˈprɪv.ə.ti, -ɪ.ti Ⓤⓢ -ə.t̬i
priv|y ˈprɪv|.i **-ies** -iz **-ily** -ɪ.li, -əl.i ˌPrivy ˈCouncil; ˌPrivy ˈPurse; ˌPrivy ˈSeal
priz|e praɪz **-es** -ɪz **-ing** -ɪŋ **-ed** -d ˈ**prize** ˌ**day**
prize|-fight ˈpraɪz|.faɪt **-fights** -faɪts **-fighter/s** -ˌfaɪ.təʳ/z Ⓤⓢ -ˌfaɪ.t̬ɚ/z
prizewinn|er ˈpraɪzˌwɪn|.əʳ Ⓤⓢ -ɚ **-ers** -əz Ⓤⓢ -ɚz **-ing** -ɪŋ
Prizren ˈprɪz.rɪn Ⓤⓢ ˈpriːz.rən
pro- prəʊ- Ⓤⓢ proʊ-, prə-
Note: Prefix. In words containing **pro-** where the stem is free and the meaning is **in favour of**, it generally takes secondary stress, e.g. **pro-choice** /ˌprəʊˈtʃɔɪs Ⓤⓢ ˌproʊ-/. Attached to bound stems, the pron is normally /prəʊ- Ⓤⓢ proʊ-, prə-/, e.g. **probation** /prəʊˈbeɪ.ʃən Ⓤⓢ proʊ-/. There are exceptions; see individual entries.
PRO ˌpiː.ɑːˈrəʊ Ⓤⓢ -ɑːrˈoʊ
pro prəʊ Ⓤⓢ proʊ **-s** -z ˌ**pros and** ˈ**cons**
proactive ˌprəʊˈæk.tɪv Ⓤⓢ ˌproʊ- **-ly** -li
pro-am ˌprəʊˈæm Ⓤⓢ ˌproʊ-
probabilistic ˌprɒb.ə.bəlˈɪs.tɪk, -bɪˈlɪs- Ⓤⓢ ˌprɑː.bə.bəlˈɪs-
probabilit|y ˌprɒb.əˈbɪl.ə.t|i, -ɪ.t|i Ⓤⓢ ˌprɑː.bəˈbɪl.ə.t̬|i **-ies** -iz
probab|le ˈprɒb.ə.b|l̩ Ⓤⓢ ˈprɑː.bə- **-ly** -li
proba|te ˈprəʊ.beɪ|t, -bɪ|t Ⓤⓢ ˈproʊ.beɪ|t **-tes** -ts **-ting** -tɪŋ Ⓤⓢ -t̬ɪŋ **-ted** -tɪd Ⓤⓢ -t̬ɪd
probation prəʊˈbeɪ.ʃən Ⓤⓢ proʊ- **-s** -z **proˈbation** ˌ**officer**
probationary prəʊˈbeɪ.ʃən.ər.i, -ˈbeɪʃ.nər- Ⓤⓢ proʊˈbeɪ.ʃən.er-
probationer prəʊˈbeɪ.ʃən.əʳ, -ˈbeɪʃ.nəʳ Ⓤⓢ proʊˈbeɪ.ʃən.ɚ, -ˈbeɪʃ.nɚ **-s** -z
probative ˈprəʊ.bə.tɪv Ⓤⓢ ˈproʊ.bə.t̬ɪv
prob|e prəʊb Ⓤⓢ proʊb **-es** -z **-ing** -ɪŋ **-ed** -d
Probert ˈprəʊ.bət, ˈprɒb.ət Ⓤⓢ ˈproʊ.bɚt, ˈprɑː.bɚt
probity ˈprəʊ.bə.ti, -ɪ.ti Ⓤⓢ ˈproʊ.bə.t̬i
problem ˈprɒb.ləm, -lem, -lɪm Ⓤⓢ ˈprɑː.bləm **-s** -z ˈ**problem** ˌ**child**; ˈ**problem** ˌ**page**
problematic ˌprɒb.ləˈmæt.ɪk, -lɪˈ-, -lemˈæt- Ⓤⓢ ˌprɑː.bləˈmæt̬- **-al** -əl **-ally** -əl.i, -li *stress shift:* ˌproblematic ˈstate
pro bono ˌprəʊˈbəʊ.nəʊ Ⓤⓢ ˌproʊˈboʊ.noʊ
proboscis prəʊˈbɒs.ɪs Ⓤⓢ proʊˈbɑː.sɪs **-es** -iːz
Probus ˈprəʊ.bəs Ⓤⓢ ˈproʊ-
Probyn ˈprəʊ.bɪn Ⓤⓢ ˈproʊ-
procedural prəˈsiː.dʒər.əl, prəʊ-, -djʊ.rəl, -djər.əl Ⓤⓢ prəˈsiː.dʒɚ.əl, proʊ-
procedure prəʊˈsiː.dʒəʳ, -djəʳ Ⓤⓢ prəˈsiː.dʒɚ, proʊ- **-s** -z
proceed (*v.*) prəʊˈsiːd Ⓤⓢ proʊ-, prə- **-s** -z **-ing/s** -ɪŋ/z **-ed** -ɪd
proceeds (*n.*) ˈprəʊ.siːdz Ⓤⓢ ˈproʊ-
pro-celebrity ˌprəʊ.səˈleb.rɪ.ti, -sɪˈ-, -rə- Ⓤⓢ ˌproʊ.səˈleb.rə.t̬i *stress shift:* ˌpro-celebrity ˈgolf
proc|ess (*n.*) ˈprəʊ.s|es, -s|ɪs Ⓤⓢ ˈprɑː.s|es, -s|əs **-esses** -es.ɪz, -ɪ.sɪz Ⓤⓢ -es.ɪz, -ə.sɪz
process (*v.*) *go in a procession:* prəʊˈses Ⓤⓢ prə-, proʊ- **-es** -ɪz **-ing** -ɪŋ **-ed** -t
process (*v.*) *treat by a process:* ˈprəʊ.ses, -sɪs Ⓤⓢ ˈprɑː.ses, -səs **-es** -ɪz **-ing** -ɪŋ **-ed** -t **-or/s** -əʳ/z Ⓤⓢ -ɚ/z
procession prəˈseʃ.ən Ⓤⓢ prə-, proʊ- **-s** -z
processional prəˈseʃ.ən.əl Ⓤⓢ prə-, proʊ- **-s** -z
pro-choice ˌprəʊˈtʃɔɪs Ⓤⓢ ˌproʊ-
proclaim prəʊˈkleɪm Ⓤⓢ proʊ-, prə- **-s** -z **-ing** -ɪŋ **-ed** -d **-er/s** -əʳ/z Ⓤⓢ -ɚ/z
proclamation ˌprɒk.ləˈmeɪ.ʃən Ⓤⓢ ˌprɑː.kləˈ- **-s** -z
proclitic prəʊˈklɪt.ɪk Ⓤⓢ proʊˈklɪt̬- **-s** -s
proclivit|y prəʊˈklɪv.ə.t|i, -ɪ.t|i Ⓤⓢ proʊˈklɪv.ə.t̬|i **-ies** -iz
proconsul prəʊˈkɒn*t*.səl Ⓤⓢ proʊˈkɑːn*t*- **-s** -z
proconsul|ar prəʊˈkɒn*t*.sjə.l|əʳ, -sjʊ- Ⓤⓢ proʊˈkɑːn*t*.səl|.ɚ **-ate/s** -ət/s, -ɪt/s, -eɪt/s Ⓤⓢ -ɪt/s
proconsulship prəʊˈkɒn*t*.səl.ʃɪp Ⓤⓢ proʊˈkɑːn*t*- **-s** -s
procrasti|nate prəʊˈkræs.tɪ|.neɪt Ⓤⓢ proʊˈkræs.tə-, prə- **-nates** -neɪts **-nating** -neɪ.tɪŋ Ⓤⓢ -neɪ.t̬ɪŋ **-nated** -neɪ.tɪd Ⓤⓢ -neɪ.t̬ɪd **-nator/s** -neɪ.təʳ/z Ⓤⓢ -neɪ.t̬ɚ/z
procrastination prəʊˌkræs.tɪˈneɪ.ʃən Ⓤⓢ proʊˌkræs.təˈ-, prə- **-s** -z
procreant ˈprəʊ.kri.ənt Ⓤⓢ ˈproʊ-
procrea|te ˈprəʊ.kri.eɪ|t, ˌ--ˈ- Ⓤⓢ ˈproʊ.kri.eɪ|t **-tes** -ts **-ting** -tɪŋ Ⓤⓢ -t̬ɪŋ **-ted** -tɪd Ⓤⓢ -t̬ɪd
procreation ˌprəʊ.kriˈeɪ.ʃən Ⓤⓢ ˌproʊ-
procreative ˈprəʊ.kri.eɪ.tɪv, -ə-, ˌprəʊ.kriˈeɪ- Ⓤⓢ ˈproʊ.kri.eɪ.t̬ɪv
Procrust|es prəʊˈkrʌs.t|iːz Ⓤⓢ proʊ- **-ean** -i.ən
Procter ˈprɒk.təʳ Ⓤⓢ ˈprɑːk.tɚ
proctor (P) ˈprɒk.təʳ Ⓤⓢ ˈprɑːk.tɚ **-s** -z **-ing** -ɪŋ **-ed** -d
proctorial prɒkˈtɔː.ri.əl Ⓤⓢ prɑːkˈtɔːr.i-
procumbent prəʊˈkʌm.bənt Ⓤⓢ proʊ-
procuration ˌprɒk.jʊəˈreɪ.ʃən, -jəˈ- Ⓤⓢ ˌprɑː.k.juːˈ-, -jəˈ- **-s** -z
procurator ˈprɒk.jʊə.reɪ.təʳ, -jə- Ⓤⓢ ˈprɑː.kjə.reɪ.t̬ɚ, -kjʊ- **-s** -z
procurator-fiscal, (PF) ˌprɒk.jʊə.reɪ.təˈfɪs.kəl, -jə- Ⓤⓢ ˌprɑː.kjə.reɪ.t̬ɚˈ-, -kjʊ- **-s** -z
procur|e prəˈkjʊəʳ, -kjɔːʳ Ⓤⓢ proʊˈkjʊr, prə- **-es** -z **-ing** -ɪŋ **-ed** -d **-er/s** -əʳ/z Ⓤⓢ -ɚ/z **-able** -ə.bl̩
procurement prəˈkjʊə.mənt, -ˈkjɔː- Ⓤⓢ proʊˈkjʊr-, prə-
procuress prəˈkjʊə.res, -ˈkjɔː-, -rɪs; ˈprɒk.jə-, -jʊ- Ⓤⓢ proʊˈkjʊr.ɪs, prə- **-es** -ɪz
Procyon ˈprəʊ.si.ən Ⓤⓢ ˈproʊ.si.ɑːn
prod prɒd Ⓤⓢ prɑːd **-s** -z **-ding** -ɪŋ **-ded** -ɪd
prodd|y ˈprɒd|.i Ⓤⓢ ˈprɑː.d|i **-ies** -iz
Prodi ˈprəʊ.di Ⓤⓢ ˈproʊ-
prodigal ˈprɒd.ɪ.gəl Ⓤⓢ ˈprɑː.dɪ- **-s** -z **-ly** -i **-ness** -nəs, -nɪs ˌ**prodigal** ˈ**son**
prodigality ˌprɒd.ɪˈgæl.ə.ti, -ɪ.ti Ⓤⓢ ˌprɑː.dɪˈgæl.ə.t̬i
prodigaliz|e, -is|e ˈprɒd.ɪ.gəl.aɪz Ⓤⓢ ˈprɑː.dɪ- **-es** -ɪz **-ing** -ɪŋ **-ed** -d
prodigious prəˈdɪdʒ.əs Ⓤⓢ prə-, proʊ- **-ly** -li **-ness** -nəs, -nɪs
prodig|y ˈprɒd.ɪ.dʒ|i, ˈ-ə- Ⓤⓢ ˈprɑː.də- **-ies** -iz
produce (*n.*) ˈprɒd.juːs, ˈprɒdʒ.uːs Ⓤⓢ ˈprɑː.duːs, ˈproʊ-, -djuːs
produc|e (*v.*) prəˈdjuːs, -ˈdʒuːs Ⓤⓢ -ˈduːs, proʊ-, -ˈdjuːs **-es** -ɪz **-ing** -ɪŋ **-ed** -t **-er/s** -əʳ/z Ⓤⓢ -ɚ/z
producible prəˈdjuː.sə.bl̩, -sɪ- Ⓤⓢ -ˈduː.sə-, proʊ-, -ˈdjuː-
product ˈprɒd.ʌkt, -əkt Ⓤⓢ ˈprɑː.dʌkt, -dəkt **-s** -s
production prəˈdʌk.ʃən Ⓤⓢ prə-, proʊ- **-s** -z **proˈduction** ˌ**line**
productional prəˈdʌk.ʃən.əl Ⓤⓢ prə-, proʊ-
productive prəˈdʌk.tɪv Ⓤⓢ prə-, proʊ- **-ly** -li **-ness** -nəs, -nɪs
productivity ˌprɒd.ʌkˈtɪv.ə.ti, -əkˈ-, -ɪ.ti Ⓤⓢ ˌproʊ.dəkˈtɪv.ə.t̬i, ˌprɑː-; proʊˌdʌkˈ-, prə-
proem ˈprəʊ.em Ⓤⓢ ˈproʊ- **-s** -z
prof prɒf Ⓤⓢ prɑːf **-s** -s

profanation ˌprɒf.əˈneɪ.ʃən US ˌprɑː.fəˈ- -s -z

profan|e prəˈfeɪn US proʊ-, prə- -est -ɪst, -əst -ely -li -eness -nəs, -nɪs -es -z -ing -ɪŋ -ed -d -er/s -əʳ/z US -ɚ/z

profanit|y prəˈfæn.ə.t|i, -ɪ.t|i US proʊˈfæn.ə.ţ|i, prə- -ies -iz

profess prəˈfes US prə-, proʊ- -es -ɪz -ing -ɪŋ -ed -t -edly -ɪd.li

profession prəˈfeʃ.ən US prə-, proʊ- -s -z

professional prəˈfeʃ.ən.əl US prə-, proʊ- -s -z

professionalism prəˈfeʃ.ən.əl.ɪ.zəm US prə-, proʊ-

professionally prəˈfeʃ.ən.əl.i, ˈ-nəl.i US prə-, proʊ-

professor prəˈfes.əʳ US -ɚ, proʊ- -s -z

professorate prəˈfes.ər.ət, -eɪt US -ɚ.ət, proʊ- -s -s

professorial ˌprɒf.ɪˈsɔː.ri.əl, -əˈ-, -esˈɔː- US ˌproʊ.fəˈsɔːr.i-, ˌprɑː- -ly -i *stress shift:* ˌprofessorial ˈduties

professoriat(e) ˌprɒf.ɪˈsɔː.ri.ət, -əˈ-, -esˈɔː-, -ɪt US ˌproʊ.fəˈsɔːr.i.ət, ˌprɑː- -s -s

professorship prəˈfes.ə.ʃɪp US ˈ-ɚ-, proʊ- -s -s

proff|er ˈprɒf|.əʳ US ˈprɑː.f|ɚ -ers -əz US -ɚz -ering -ər.ɪŋ -ered -əd US -ɚd

proficiency prəˈfɪʃ.ənt.si US prə-, proʊ-

proficient prəˈfɪʃ.ənt US prə-, proʊ- -ly -li

profil|e ˈprəʊ.faɪl US ˈproʊ- -es -z -ing -ɪŋ -ed -d

prof|it (*n. v.*) ˈprɒf|.ɪt US ˈprɑː.f|ɪt -its -ɪts -iting -ɪ.tɪŋ US -ɪ.ţɪŋ -ited -ɪ.tɪd US -ɪ.ţɪd ˌprofit and ˈloss; ˈprofit ˌmargin

profitability ˌprɒf.ɪ.təˈbɪl.ɪ.ti, ˌ-ə-, -ə.ti US ˌprɑː.fɪ.ţəˈbɪl.ə.ţi

profitab|le ˈprɒf.ɪ.tə.b|l̩, ˈ-ə- US ˈprɑː.fɪ.ţə- -ly -li -leness -l̩.nəs, -nɪs

profiteer ˌprɒf.ɪˈtɪəʳ, -əˈ- US ˌprɑː.fɪˈtɪr -s -z -ing -ɪŋ -ed -d

profiterole prɒfˈɪt.ər.əʊl, prəˈfɪt-; ˈprɒf.ɪ.tər-, ˌprɒf.ɪ.tərˈəʊl US prəˈfɪt.ə.roʊl -s -z

profitless ˈprɒf.ɪt.ləs, -lɪs US ˈprɑː.fɪt-

profitmaking ˈprɒf.ɪtˌmeɪ.kɪŋ US ˈprɑː.fɪt-

profit-sharing ˈprɒf.ɪtˌʃeə.rɪŋ US ˈprɑː.fɪtˌʃer.ɪŋ

profligacy ˈprɒf.lɪ.gə.si US ˈprɑː.flɪ-

profligate ˈprɒf.lɪ.gət, -gɪt US ˈprɑː.flɪ.gɪt -s -s -ly -li -ness -nəs, -nɪs

pro forma ˌprəʊˈfɔː.mə US ˌproʊˈfɔːr-

profound prəˈfaʊnd US prə-, proʊ- -er -əʳ US -ɚ -est -ɪst, -əst -ly -li -ness -nəs, -nɪs

Profumo prəˈfjuː.məʊ US -moʊ

profundit|y prəˈfʌn.də.t|i, -ɪ.t|i US proʊ-, prə- -ies -iz

profus|e prəˈfjuːs US prə-, proʊ- -est -ɪst, -əst -ely -li -eness -nəs, -nɪs

profusion prəˈfjuː.ʒən US prə-, proʊ- -s -z

prog prɒg US prɑːg, prɔːg -s -z -ging -ɪŋ -ged -d

progenitor prəʊˈdʒen.ɪ.təʳ, ˈ-ə- US proʊˈdʒen.ə.ţɚ, prə- -s -z

progeniture prəʊˈdʒen.ɪ.tʃəʳ, ˈ-ə-, -tjʊəʳ, -tjəʳ US proʊˈdʒen.ə.tʃɚ, prə-

progen|y ˈprɒdʒ.ə.n|i, ˈ-ɪ- US ˈprɑː.dʒə- -ies -iz

progesterone prəʊˈdʒes.tər.əʊn US proʊˈdʒes.tə.roʊn

progestogen prəʊˈdʒes.tə.dʒɪn, -dʒən US proʊˈdʒes.tə.dʒən, -dʒen -s -z

prognathic prɒgˈnæθ.ɪk US prɑːg-, -ˈneɪ.θɪk

prognathism ˈprɒg.nə.θɪ.zəm; prɒgˈnæθ.ɪ- US ˈprɑːg.nə.θɪ-; prɑːgˈneɪ-

prognathous prɒgˈneɪ.θəs; ˈprɒg.nə.θəs US ˈprɑːg.nə-; prɑːgˈneɪ-

prognos|is prɒgˈnəʊ.s|ɪs US prɑːgˈnoʊ- -es -iːz

prognostic prɒgˈnɒs.tɪk, prəg- US prɑːgˈnɑː.stɪk

prognosti|cate prɒgˈnɒs.tɪ|.keɪt, prəg- US prɑːgˈnɑː.stɪ- -cates -keɪts -cating -keɪ.tɪŋ US -keɪ.ţɪŋ -cated -keɪ.tɪd US -keɪ.ţɪd -cator/s -keɪ.təʳ/z US -keɪ.ţɚ/z

prognostication prəgˌnɒs.tɪˈkeɪ.ʃən, prɒg- US prɑːgˌnɑː.stɪˈ- -s -z

program ˈprəʊ.græm US ˈproʊ-, -grəm -s -z -ing -ɪŋ -ed -d -er/s -əʳ/z US -ɚ/z

programmable prəʊˈgræm.ə.bl̩; ˈprəʊ.græm- US ˈproʊ.græm.ə-, -grə.mə-

programmatic ˌprəʊ.grəˈmæt.ɪk US ˌproʊ.grəˈmæţ-

programm|e ˈprəʊ.græm US ˈproʊ-, -grəm -es -z -ing -ɪŋ -ed -d -er/s -əʳ/z US -ɚ/z

progress (*n.*) ˈprəʊ.gres US ˈprɑː- ˈprogress reˌport

progress (*v.*) prəʊˈgres US prə-, proʊ- -es -ɪz -ing -ɪŋ -ed -t

progression prəʊˈgreʃ.ən US prə-, proʊ- -s -z

progressional prəʊˈgreʃ.ən.əl, ˈ-nəl US prə-, proʊ-

progressionist prəʊˈgreʃ.ən.ɪst US prə-, proʊ- -s -s

progressist prəʊˈgres.ɪst US ˈprɑː.gres-, ˈproʊ-; prəˈgres- -s -s

progressive prəʊˈgres.ɪv US prə-, proʊ- -s -z -ly -li -ness -nəs, -nɪs

progressiv|ism prəʊˈgres.ɪ.v|ɪ.zəm US prə-, proʊ- -ist/s -ɪst/s

prohib|it prəʊˈhɪb|.ɪt US proʊ-, prə- -its -ɪts -iting -ɪ.tɪŋ US -ɪ.ţɪŋ -ited -ɪ.tɪd US -ɪ.ţɪd

prohibition (P) ˌprəʊ.*h*ɪˈbɪʃ.ən US ˌproʊ- -s -z

prohibition|ism ˌprəʊ.*h*ɪˈbɪʃ.ən|.ɪ.zəm US ˌproʊ- -ist/s -ɪst/s

prohibitive prəʊˈhɪb.ə.tɪv US proʊˈhɪb.ə.ţɪv, prə- -ly -li

prohibitory prəʊˈhɪb.ɪ.tər.i US proʊˈhɪb.ə.tɔːr-, prə-

project (*n.*) ˈprɒdʒ.ekt, -ɪkt US ˈprɑː.dʒekt, -dʒɪkt -s -s

project (*v.*) prəʊˈdʒekt US prə-, proʊ- -s -s -ing -ɪŋ -ed -ɪd

projectile prəʊˈdʒek.taɪl US prəˈdʒek.təl, proʊ- -s -z

projection prəʊˈdʒek.ʃən US prə-, proʊ- -s -z -ist/s -ɪst/s

projective prəʊˈdʒek.tɪv US prə-, proʊ- -ly -li

projector prəʊˈdʒek.təʳ US prəˈdʒek.tɚ, proʊ- -s -z

Prokofiev prəˈkɒf.i.ef US proʊˈkɔː.fi.ef, prə-, -ˈkoʊ-

prolactin prəʊˈlæk.tɪn US proʊ-

prolaps|e ˈprəʊ.læps, -ˈ- US ˈproʊ- -es -ɪz -ing -ɪŋ -ed -t

prolate ˈprəʊ.leɪt, ˌ-ˈ- US ˈproʊ.leɪt

prole prəʊl US proʊl -s -z

prolegomen|on ˌprəʊ.lɪˈgɒm.ɪ.n|ən, -ləˈ-, -legˈɒm-, ˈ-ə-, -ɒn US ˌproʊ.lɪˈgɑː.mə.n|ɑːn, -n|ən -a -ə

proleps|is prəʊˈlep.s|ɪs, -ˈliːp- US proʊˈlep- -es -iːz

proleptic prəʊˈlep.tɪk, -ˈliːp- US proʊˈlep- -ally -əl.i, -li

proletarian ˌprəʊ.lɪˈteə.ri.ən, -ləˈ-, -letˈeə- US ˌproʊ.ləˈter.i-, -ˈtær- -s -z -ism -ɪ.zəm

proletariat ˌprəʊ.lɪˈteə.ri.ət, -ləˈ-, -letˈeə-, -æt US ˌproʊ.ləˈter.i.ət, -ˈtær-

pro-life ˌprəʊˈlaɪf US ˌproʊ-

prolifer|ate prəʊˈlɪf.ər|.eɪt US proʊˈlɪf.ə.r|eɪt, prə- -ates -eɪts -ating -eɪ.tɪŋ US -eɪ.ţɪŋ -ated -eɪ.tɪd US -eɪ.ţɪd

proliferation prəʊˌlɪf.ərˈeɪ.ʃən US proʊˌlɪf.əˈreɪ-, prə- -s -z

prolific prəʊˈlɪf.ɪk US proʊ-, prə- -ally -əl.i, -li -ness -nəs, -nɪs

prolix ˈprəʊ.lɪks US proʊˈlɪks, ˈ--

prolixity prəʊˈlɪk.sə-, -sɪ- US proʊˈlɪk.sə.ţi, prə-

prolix|ly prəʊˈlɪk.s|li, ˈ--- US proʊˈlɪk.s|li, prə- -ness -nəs, -nɪs

prolocutor prəʊˈlɒk.jə.təʳ, -jʊ- ⓤⓢ proʊˈlɑː.kjə.t̬ɚ, -kjʊ- **-s** -z

prolog, PROLOG ˈprəʊ.lɒg ⓤⓢ ˈproʊ.lɑːg, -lɔːg **-s** -z

prologu|e ˈprəʊ.lɒg ⓤⓢ ˈproʊ.lɑːg, -lɔːg **-es** -z **-ing** -ɪŋ **-ed** -d

prolong prəʊˈlɒŋ ⓤⓢ proʊˈlɑːŋ, prə-, -ˈlɔːŋ **-s** -z **-ing** -ɪŋ **-ed** -d

prolongation ˌprəʊ.lɒŋˈgeɪ.ʃᵊn, ˌprɒl.ɒŋˈ- ⓤⓢ ˌproʊ.lɑːŋˈ-, -lɔːŋˈ- **-s** -z

prom (P) prɒm ⓤⓢ prɑːm **-s** -z

promenad|e ˌprɒm.əˈnɑːd, -ɪˈ- ⓤⓢ ˌprɑː.məˈneɪd, -ˈnɑːd **-es** -z **-ing** -ɪŋ **-ed** -ɪd **-er/s** -əʳ/z ⓤⓢ -ɚ/z *stress shift:* ˌpromenade ˈconcert

Note: A British pronunciation /ˌprɒm.əˈneɪd, -ɪˈ-/ also exists, used chiefly in square dancing.

Promethean prəʊˈmiː.θi.ən ⓤⓢ proʊ-, prə-

Prometheus prəʊˈmiː.θi.uːs, -əs ⓤⓢ proʊˈmiː.θi.əs, prə-, -uːs

promethium prəʊˈmiː.θi.əm ⓤⓢ proʊ-

prominenc|e ˈprɒm.ɪ.nənts, ˈ-ə- ⓤⓢ ˈprɑː.mə- **-es** -ɪz

prominent ˈprɒm.ɪ.nənt, ˈ-ə- ⓤⓢ ˈprɑː.mə- **-ly** -li

promiscuity ˌprɒm.ɪˈskjuː.ə.ti, -əˈ-, -ɪ.ti ⓤⓢ ˌprɑː.mɪˈskjuː.ə.t̬i, ˌproʊ-

promiscuous prəˈmɪs.kju.əs, prɒmˈɪs- ⓤⓢ prəˈmɪs-, proʊ- **-ly** -li **-ness** -nəs, -nɪs

promis|e ˈprɒm.ɪs ⓤⓢ ˈprɑː.mɪs **-es** -ɪz **-ing/ly** -ɪŋ/li **-ed** -t ˌ**promised** ˈ**land** ⓤⓢ ˈ**promised** ˌ**land**

promissory ˈprɒm.ɪ.sᵊr.i; prəˈmɪs.ᵊr- ⓤⓢ ˈprɑː.mɪ.sɔːr- ˌ**promissory** ˈ**note** ⓤⓢ ˈ**promissory** ˌ**note**

promo ˈprəʊ.məʊ ⓤⓢ ˈproʊ.moʊ **-s** -z

promontor|y ˈprɒm.ən.tᵊr|.i ⓤⓢ ˈprɑː.mən.tɔːr- **-ies** -iz

pro|mote prə|ˈməʊt ⓤⓢ -ˈmoʊt **-motes** -ˈməʊts ⓤⓢ -ˈmoʊts **-moting** -ˈməʊ.tɪŋ ⓤⓢ -ˈmoʊ.t̬ɪŋ **-moted** -ˈməʊ.tɪd ⓤⓢ -ˈmoʊ.t̬ɪd **-moter/s** -ˈməʊ.təʳ/z ⓤⓢ -ˈmoʊ.t̬ɚ/z

promotion prəˈməʊ.ʃᵊn ⓤⓢ -ˈmoʊ-, proʊ- **-s** -z

promotional prəˈməʊ.ʃᵊn.ᵊl ⓤⓢ -ˈmoʊ-, proʊ- **-ly** -i

promotive prəˈməʊ.tɪv ⓤⓢ -ˈmoʊ.t̬ɪv, proʊ-

prompt prɒmpt ⓤⓢ prɑːmpt **-s** -s **-est** -ɪst, -əst **-ly** -li **-ness** -nəs, -nɪs **-ing/s** -ɪŋ/z **-ed** -ɪd **-er/s** -əʳ/z ⓤⓢ -ɚ/z

promptitude ˈprɒmp.tɪ.tjuːd ⓤⓢ ˈprɑːmp.tɪ.tuːd

promul|gate ˈprɒm.ᵊl|.geɪt, -ʌl- ⓤⓢ ˈprɑː.mᵊl-; proʊˈmʌl- **-gates** -geɪts **-gating** -geɪ.tɪŋ ⓤⓢ -geɪ.t̬ɪŋ **-gated** -geɪ.tɪd ⓤⓢ -geɪ.t̬ɪd **-gator/s** -geɪ.təʳ/z ⓤⓢ -geɪ.t̬ɚ/z

promulgation ˌprɒm.ᵊlˈgeɪ.ʃᵊn, -ʌlˈ- ⓤⓢ ˌprɑː.məlˈ- **-s** -z

prone prəʊn ⓤⓢ proʊn **-ly** -li **-ness** -nəs, -nɪs

prong prɒŋ ⓤⓢ prɑːŋ, prɔːŋ **-s** -z **-ing** -ɪŋ **-ed** -d

pronghorn ˈprɒŋ.hɔːn ⓤⓢ ˈprɑːŋ.hɔːrn, ˈprɔːŋ- **-s** -z

pronominal prəʊˈnɒm.ɪ.nᵊl, -ᵊn.ᵊl ⓤⓢ proʊˈnɑː.mə- **-ly** -i

pronominalization prəʊˌnɒm.ɪ.nᵊl.aɪˈzeɪ.ʃᵊn, -ᵊn.ᵊl-, -ɪˈ- ⓤⓢ proʊˌnɑː.mɪ.nᵊl.ɪˈ- **-s** -z

pronominaliz|e, -is|e prəʊˈnɒm.ɪ.nᵊl.aɪz, -ᵊn.ᵊl- ⓤⓢ proʊˈnɑː.mɪ.nᵊl- **-es** -ɪz **-ing** -ɪŋ **-ed** -d

pronoun ˈprəʊ.naʊn ⓤⓢ ˈproʊ- **-s** -z

pronounc|e prəˈnaʊnts ⓤⓢ prə-, proʊ- **-es** -ɪz **-ing** -ɪŋ **-ed** -t **-edly** -t.li, -ɪd.li **-er/s** -əʳ/z ⓤⓢ -ɚ/z **-eable/ness** -ə.bl̩/nəs, -nɪs

pronouncement prəʊˈnaʊnt.smənt ⓤⓢ prə-, proʊ- **-s** -s

pronto ˈprɒn.təʊ ⓤⓢ ˈprɑːn.t̬oʊ

pronunciamento prəʊˌnʌnt.si.əˈmen.təʊ, -ʃi- ⓤⓢ proʊˌnʌnt.si.əˈmen.toʊ, prə- **-(e)s** -z

pronunciation prəˌnʌnt.siˈeɪ.ʃᵊn ⓤⓢ prə-, proʊ- **-s** -z

proof pruːf **-s** -s **-ing** -ɪŋ **-ed** -t

proofread ˈpruːf.riːd **-s** -z **-ing** -ɪŋ **-er/s** -əʳ/z ⓤⓢ -ɚ/z *past tense:* ˈpruːf.red

Proops pruːps

prop prɒp ⓤⓢ prɑːp **-s** -s **-ping** -ɪŋ **-ped** -t

propaedeutic ˌprəʊ.piːˈdjuː.tɪk ⓤⓢ ˌproʊ.pɪˈduː.t̬ɪk, -ˈdjuː- **-al** -ᵊl **-s** -s

propaganda ˌprɒp.əˈgæn.də ⓤⓢ ˌprɑː.pəˈ-

propagand|ism ˌprɒp.əˈgæn.d|ɪ.zᵊm ⓤⓢ ˌprɑː.pəˈ- **-ist/s** -ɪst/s

propagandiz|e, -is|e ˌprɒp.əˈgæn.daɪz ⓤⓢ ˌprɑː.pəˈ- **-es** -ɪz **-ing** -ɪŋ **-ed** -d

propa|gate ˈprɒp.ə|.geɪt ⓤⓢ ˈprɑː.pə- **-gates** -geɪts **-gating** -geɪ.tɪŋ ⓤⓢ -geɪ.t̬ɪŋ **-gated** -geɪ.tɪd ⓤⓢ -geɪ.t̬ɪd **-gator/s** -geɪ.təʳ/z ⓤⓢ -geɪ.t̬ɚ/z

propagation ˌprɒp.əˈgeɪ.ʃᵊn ⓤⓢ ˌprɑː.pəˈ

propane ˈprəʊ.peɪn ⓤⓢ ˈproʊ-

proparoxytone ˌprəʊ.pᵊrˈɒk.sɪ.təʊn, -pærˈ-, ˈ-ə-, -tən ⓤⓢ ˌproʊ.pəˈrɑːk.sɪ.toʊn, -pærˈ- **-s** -z

propel prəˈpel **-s** -z **-ling** -ɪŋ **-led** -d **pro**ˌ**pelling** ˈ**pencil**

propellant, propellent prəˈpel.ənt **-s** -s

propeller, propellor prəˈpel.əʳ ⓤⓢ -ɚ **-s** -z

propene ˈprəʊ.piːn ⓤⓢ ˈproʊ-

propensit|y prəʊˈpent.sə.t|i, -ɪ.t|i ⓤⓢ prəˈpent.sə.t̬|i, proʊ- **-ies** -iz

proper ˈprɒp.əʳ ⓤⓢ ˈprɑː.pɚ ˌ**proper** ˈ**noun**

properly ˈprɒp.ᵊl.i, ˈ-li ⓤⓢ ˈprɑː.pɚ.li

Propertius prəʊˈpɜː.ʃəs, -ʃi.əs ⓤⓢ proʊˈpɝː-

propert|y ˈprɒp.ə.t|i ⓤⓢ ˈprɑː.pɚ.t̬|i **-ies** -iz **-ied** -id

prophec|y (*n.*) ˈprɒf.ə.s|i, ˈ-ɪ- ⓤⓢ ˈprɑː.fə- **-ies** -iz

prophes|y (*v.*) ˈprɒf.ə.s|aɪ, ˈ-ɪ- ⓤⓢ ˈprɑː.fə- **-ies** -aɪz **-ying** -aɪ.ɪŋ **-ied** -aɪd **-ier/s** -aɪ.əʳ/z ⓤⓢ -aɪ.ɚ/z

prophet ˈprɒf.ɪt ⓤⓢ ˈprɑː.fɪt **-s** -s

prophetess ˌprɒf.ɪˈtes; ˈprɒf.ɪ.tɪs, -tes ⓤⓢ ˈprɑː.fɪ.t̬əs **-es** -ɪz

prophetic prəʊˈfet.ɪk ⓤⓢ prə-, proʊ- **-al** -ᵊl **-ally** -ᵊl.i, -li

prophylactic ˌprɒf.ɪˈlæk.tɪk, -əˈ- ⓤⓢ ˌproʊ.fəˈ-, ˌprɑː- **-s** -s **-ally** -ᵊl.i, -li *stress shift:* ˌprophylactic ˈmedicine

prophylax|is ˌprɒf.ɪˈlæk.s|ɪs, -əˈ- ⓤⓢ ˌproʊ.fəˈ-, ˌprɑː- **-es** -iːz

propinquity prəʊˈpɪŋ.kwə.ti, prɒpˈɪŋ-, -kwɪ- ⓤⓢ proʊˈpɪŋ.kwə.t̬i, -ˈpɪn-

propiti|ate prəˈpɪʃ.i|.eɪt ⓤⓢ proʊ-, prə- **-ates** -eɪts **-ating** -eɪ.tɪŋ ⓤⓢ -eɪ.t̬ɪŋ **-ated** -eɪ.tɪd ⓤⓢ -eɪ.t̬ɪd **-ator/s** -eɪ.təʳ/z ⓤⓢ -eɪ.t̬ɚ/z

propitiation prəˌpɪʃ.iˈeɪ.ʃᵊn ⓤⓢ proʊ-, prə- **-s** -z

propitiatory prəˈpɪʃ.i.ə.tᵊr.i, -ˈpɪʃ.ə-, -eɪ.tᵊr-; prəʊˌpɪʃ.iˈeɪ- ⓤⓢ proʊˈpɪʃ.i.ə.tɔːr-, prə-

propitious prəˈpɪʃ.əs ⓤⓢ prə-, proʊ- **-ly** -li **-ness** -nəs, -nɪs

propjet ˈprɒp.dʒet ⓤⓢ ˈprɑːp- **-s** -s

Pro-Plus® ˌprəʊˈplʌs ⓤⓢ ˌproʊ-

proponent prəʊˈpəʊ.nənt ⓤⓢ prəˈpoʊ-, proʊ- **-s** -s

proportion prəˈpɔː.ʃᵊn ⓤⓢ -ˈpɔːr- **-s** -z **-ing** -ɪŋ **-ed** -d

proportionab|le prəˈpɔː.ʃᵊn.ə.b|l̩ ⓤⓢ -ˈpɔːr- **-ly** -li **-leness** -l̩.nəs, -nɪs

proportional prəˈpɔː.ʃᵊn.ᵊl, -ˈpɔːʃ.nᵊl ⓤⓢ -ˈpɔːr.ʃᵊn.ᵊl, -ˈpɔːrʃ.nᵊl **-ly** -i **pro**ˌ**portional** ˌ**represen**ˈ**tation**

proportionality prəˌpɔː.ʃᵊnˈæl.ə.ti, -ɪ.ti ⓤⓢ -ˌpɔːr.ʃᵊnˈæl.ə.t̬i

proportionate prəˈpɔː.ʃᵊn.ət, -ˈpɔːʃ.nət, -nɪt ⓤⓢ -ˈpɔːr.ʃᵊn.ɪt, -ˈpɔːrʃ.nɪt **-ly** -li **-ness** -nəs, -nɪs

proposal prəˈpəʊ.zᵊl ⓤⓢ -ˈpoʊ- **-s** -z

propos|e prəˈpəʊz ⓤⓢ -ˈpoʊz **-es** -ɪz **-ing** -ɪŋ **-ed** -d **-er/s** -əʳ/z ⓤⓢ -ɚ/z

proposition ˌprɒp.əˈzɪʃ.ᵊn ⓤⓢ ˌprɑː.pəˈ- **-s** -z **-ing** -ɪŋ **-ed** -d

propound prəˈpaʊnd ⓤⓢ prə-, proʊ- **-s** -z **-ing** -ɪŋ **-ed** -ɪd **-er/s** -əʳ/z ⓤⓢ -ɚ/z

propranolol prəʊˈpræn.ə.lɒl ⓤⓢ proʊˈpræn.oʊ.lɔːl, ˈ-ə-, -loʊl
proprietary prəˈpraɪə.tᵊr.i ⓤⓢ -ter-
proprietor prəˈpraɪə.təʳ ⓤⓢ proʊˈpraɪə.t̬ɚ, prə- **-s** -z **-ship/s** -ʃɪp/s
proprietorial prəˌpraɪəˈtɔː.ri.əl ⓤⓢ -ˈtɔːr.i-, proʊ- **-ly** -i
proprietress prəˈpraɪə.trɪs, -tres ⓤⓢ proʊ-, -trɪs, -trəs **-es** -ɪz
propriet|y prəˈpraɪə.t|i ⓤⓢ -t̬|i, proʊ- **-ies** -iz
propriocep|tion ˌprəʊ.pri.əʊˈsep|.ʃᵊn, ˌprɒp.ri- ⓤⓢ ˌproʊ.pri.oʊˈ-, -əˈ- **-tive** -tɪv
propul|sion prəˈpʌl|.ʃᵊn ⓤⓢ prə-, proʊ- **-sive** -sɪv
propylae|um (P) ˌprɒp.ɪˈliː|.əm, -əˈ- ⓤⓢ ˌprɑː.pəˈ- **-a** -ə
propylene ˈprɒp.ɪ.liːn, ˈ-ə- ⓤⓢ ˈproʊ.pə-
pro rata ˌprəʊˈrɑː.tə, -ˈreɪ- ⓤⓢ ˌproʊˈreɪ.t̬ə, -ˈrɑː-
prorogation ˌprəʊ.rəʊˈgeɪ.ʃᵊn, ˌprɒr.əʊˈ- ⓤⓢ ˌproʊ.roʊˈ- **-s** -z
prorogu|e prəʊˈrəʊg ⓤⓢ proʊˈroʊg **-es** -z **-ing** -ɪŋ **-ed** -d
prosaic prəʊˈzeɪ.ɪk ⓤⓢ proʊ- **-al** -ᵊl **-ally** -ᵊl.i, -li **-ness** -nəs, -nɪs
prosceni|um prəʊˈsiː.ni|.əm ⓤⓢ proʊ- **-ums** -əmz **-a** -ə **proˌscenium ˈarch**
prosciutto prəʊˈʃuː.təʊ ⓤⓢ proʊˈʃuː.t̬oʊ
proscrib|e prəʊˈskraɪb ⓤⓢ proʊ- **-es** -z **-ing** -ɪŋ **-ed** -d **-er/s** -əʳ/z ⓤⓢ -ɚ/z
proscription prəʊˈskrɪp.ʃᵊn ⓤⓢ proʊ- **-s** -z
proscriptive prəʊˈskrɪp.tɪv ⓤⓢ proʊ-
pro se ˌprəʊˈseɪ ⓤⓢ ˌproʊ-
pros|e prəʊz ⓤⓢ proʊz **-es** -ɪz **-ing** -ɪŋ **-ed** -d **-er/s** -əʳ/z ⓤⓢ -ɚ/z
prose|cute ˈprɒs.ɪ|.kjuːt, ˈ-ə- ⓤⓢ ˈprɑː.sɪ- **-cutes** -kjuːts **-cuting** -kjuː.tɪŋ ⓤⓢ -kjuː.t̬ɪŋ **-cuted** -kjuː.tɪd ⓤⓢ -kjuː.t̬ɪd **ˌprosecuting atˈtorney**
prosecution ˌprɒs.ɪˈkjuː.ʃᵊn, -əˈ- ⓤⓢ ˌprɑː.sɪˈ- **-s** -z *stress shift:* ˌprosecution ˈwitness
prosecutor ˈprɒs.ɪ.kjuː.təʳ, ˈ-ə- ⓤⓢ ˈprɑː.sɪ.kjuː.t̬ɚ **-s** -z
prosecutorial ˌprɒs.ɪ.kjuːˈtɔː.ri.əl ⓤⓢ ˌprɑː.sɪ.kjuːˈtɔːr.i-
prosecutrix ˈprɒs.ɪ.kjuː.trɪks, ˈ-ə-; ˌprɒs.ɪˈkjuː-, -əˈ- ⓤⓢ ˈprɑː.sɪ.kjuː-, ˌprɑː.sɪˈkjuː- **-es** -ɪz
proselyte ˈprɒs.ə.laɪt, ˈ-ɪ- ⓤⓢ ˈprɑː.sə- **-s** -s
proselytism ˈprɒs.ᵊl.ɪ.tɪ.zᵊm, -ɪ.lɪ-, -lə- ⓤⓢ ˈprɑː.sə.lɪ-, -laɪ-
proselytiz|e, -is|e ˈprɒs.ᵊl.ɪ.taɪz, -ɪ.lɪ-, -lə- ⓤⓢ ˈprɑː.sə.lɪ- **-es** -ɪz **-ing** -ɪŋ **-ed** -d
Proserpina prəˈsɜː.pɪ.nə, prɒsˈsɜː- ⓤⓢ proʊˈsɝː-
Proserpine ˈprɒs.ə.paɪn ⓤⓢ ˈprɑː.sɚ-; proʊˈsɝː.pɪ.niː
prosit ˈprəʊ.zɪt, -sɪt; prəʊst ⓤⓢ ˈproʊ.sɪt, -zɪt; proʊst
prosodic prəˈsɒd.ɪk ⓤⓢ proʊˈsɑː.dɪk, prə- **-al** -ᵊl **-ally** -ᵊl.i, -li
prosodist ˈprɒs.ə.dɪst, ˈprɒz- ⓤⓢ ˈprɑː.sə-, -zə- **-s** -s
prosod|y ˈprɒs.ə.d|i, ˈprɒz- ⓤⓢ ˈprɑː.sə-, -zə- **-ies** -iz
prospect (P) (*n.*) ˈprɒs.pekt ⓤⓢ ˈprɑː.spekt **-s** -s
prospect (*v.*) prəˈspekt, prɒsˈpekt; ˈprɒs.pekt ⓤⓢ ˈprɑː.spekt **-s** -s **-ing** -ɪŋ **-ed** -ɪd
prospective prəˈspek.tɪv, prɒsˈpek- ⓤⓢ prəˈspek-, proʊ-, prɑː- **-ly** -li **-ness** -nəs, -nɪs
prospector prəˈspek.təʳ, prɒsˈpek- ⓤⓢ ˈprɑː.spek.tɚ **-s** -z
prospectus prəˈspek.təs ⓤⓢ prə-, proʊ-, prɑː- **-es** -ɪz
prosp|er ˈprɒs.p|əʳ ⓤⓢ ˈprɑː.sp|ɚ **-ers** -əz ⓤⓢ -ɚz **-ering** -ᵊr.ɪŋ **-ered** -əd ⓤⓢ -ɚd
prosperity prɒsˈper.ə.ti, prəˈsper-, -ɪ.ti ⓤⓢ prɑːˈsper.ə.t̬i
Prospero ˈprɒs.pᵊr.əʊ ⓤⓢ ˈprɑː.spə.roʊ
prosperous ˈprɒs.pᵊr.əs ⓤⓢ ˈprɑː.spɚ- **-ly** -li **-ness** -nəs, -nɪs
Prosser ˈprɒs.əʳ ⓤⓢ ˈprɑː.sɚ
Prost prɒst ⓤⓢ proʊst
prostaglandin ˌprɒs.təˈglæn.dɪn ⓤⓢ ˌprɑː.stəˈ- **-s** -z
prostate ˈprɒs.teɪt ⓤⓢ ˈprɑː.steɪt **-s** -s **ˈprostate ˌgland**
prostatic prɒsˈtæt.ɪk, prəˈstæt- ⓤⓢ proʊˈstæt̬.ɪk, prɑː-
prosthes|is *grammatical term:* ˈprɒs.θɪ.s|ɪs, -θə-; ˈprɑːs.θə- **-es** -iːz *medical term:* ˈprɒs.θə.s|ɪs, -θɪ-; prɒsˈθiː- ⓤⓢ ˈprɑːs.θə.s|ɪs; prɑːsˈθiː- **-es** ⓤⓢ -iːz
prosthetic prɒsˈθet.ɪk ⓤⓢ prɑːsˈθet̬- **-s** -s
prosthetist prɒsˈθiː.tɪst, prəs- ⓤⓢ ˈprɑːs.θɪ.tɪst **-s** -s
prostitu|te ˈprɒs.tɪ.tjuː|t, -tə-, -tʃuː|t ⓤⓢ ˈprɑː.stə.tuː|t, -tjuː|t **-tes** -ts **-ting** -tɪŋ ⓤⓢ -t̬ɪŋ **-ted** -tɪd ⓤⓢ -t̬ɪd
prostitution ˌprɒs.tɪˈtjuː.ʃᵊn, -təˈ-, -ˈtʃuː.ʃᵊn ⓤⓢ -ˈtʃuː-, ˌprɑː.stəˈtuː- **-s** -z
prostrate (*adj.*) ˈprɒs.treɪt, -ˈ- ⓤⓢ ˈprɑː.streɪt
prostra|te (*v.*) prɒsˈtreɪ|t, prəˈstreɪ|t ⓤⓢ ˈprɑː.streɪ|t **-tes** -ts **-ting** -tɪŋ ⓤⓢ -t̬ɪŋ **-ted** -tɪd ⓤⓢ -t̬ɪd
prostration prɒsˈtreɪ.ʃᵊn, prəˈstreɪ- ⓤⓢ prɑːˈstreɪ- **-s** -z
pros|y ˈprəʊ.z|i ⓤⓢ ˈproʊ- **-ier** -i.əʳ ⓤⓢ -i.ɚ **-iest** -i.ɪst, -i.əst **-ily** -ɪ.li, -ᵊl.i **-iness** -ɪ.nəs, -ɪ.nɪs
protactinium ˌprəʊ.tækˈtɪn.i.əm ⓤⓢ ˌproʊ-
protagonist prəʊˈtæg.ᵊn.ɪst ⓤⓢ proʊ- **-s** -s
Protagoras prəʊˈtæg.ᵊr.æs, -ɒr-, -əs ⓤⓢ proʊˈtæg.ɚ.əs
pro tanto ˌprəʊˈtæn.təʊ ⓤⓢ ˌproʊˈtæn.toʊ, -ˈtɑːn-
protas|is ˈprɒt.ə.s|ɪs ⓤⓢ ˈprɑː.t̬ə- **-es** -iːz
protean prəʊˈtiː.ən; ˈprəʊ.ti- ⓤⓢ ˈproʊ-; proʊˈtiː-
protease ˈprəʊ.ti.eɪz, -eɪs ⓤⓢ ˈproʊ.t̬i- **-s** -z
protect prəˈtekt ⓤⓢ prə-, proʊ- **-s** -s **-ing/ly** -ɪŋ/li **-ed** -ɪd **-or/s** -əʳ/z ⓤⓢ -ɚ/z
protection prəˈtek.ʃᵊn ⓤⓢ prə-, proʊ- **-s** -z
protection|ism prəˈtek.ʃᵊn|.ɪ.zᵊm ⓤⓢ prə-, proʊ- **-ist/s** -ɪst/s
protective prəˈtek.tɪv ⓤⓢ prə-, proʊ- **-ly** -li **-ness** -nəs, -nɪs
protectorate prəˈtek.tᵊr.ət, -ɪt ⓤⓢ -ɪt, proʊ- **-s** -s
protectress prəˈtek.trəs, -trɪs ⓤⓢ -trɪs, proʊ- **-es** -ɪz
protégé(e), protege(e) ˈprɒt.ɪ.ʒeɪ, ˈprəʊ.tɪ-, -tə-, -teʒ.eɪ, -teɪ.ʒeɪ ⓤⓢ ˈproʊ.t̬ə.ʒeɪ, ˌ--ˈ- **-s** -z
protein ˈprəʊ.tiːn ⓤⓢ ˈproʊ- **-s** -z
pro tem ˌprəʊˈtem ⓤⓢ ˌproʊˈtem
protest (*n.*) ˈprəʊ.test ⓤⓢ ˈproʊ.test **-s** -s
protest (*v.*) prəʊˈtest ⓤⓢ proʊˈtest, prə-; ˈproʊ.test **-s** -s **-ing/ly** -ɪŋ/li **-ed** -ɪd **-er/s** -əʳ/z ⓤⓢ -ɚ/z **-or/s** -əʳ/z ⓤⓢ -ɚ/z
protestant (P) ˈprɒt.ɪ.stᵊnt, ˈ-ə- ⓤⓢ ˈprɑː.t̬ə- **-s** -s **-ism** -ɪ.zᵊm
protestantiz|e, -is|e ˈprɒt.ɪ.stən.taɪz, ˈ-ə- ⓤⓢ ˈprɑː.t̬ə- **-es** -ɪz **-ing** -ɪŋ **-ed** -d
protestation ˌprɒt.esˈteɪ.ʃᵊn; ˌprəʊ.tesˈ-, -tɪˈsteɪ-, -təˈ- ⓤⓢ ˌprɑː.t̬esˈteɪ-, ˌproʊ-, -t̬əˈsteɪ- **-s** -z
Proteus ˈprəʊ.ti.uːs, -əs ⓤⓢ ˈproʊ.t̬i.əs
prothalami|on ˌprəʊ.θᵊlˈeɪ.mi|.ən ⓤⓢ ˌproʊ.θəˈleɪ-, -ɑːn **-um** -əm **-a** -ə
Protheroe ˈprɒð.ᵊr.əʊ ⓤⓢ ˈprɑː.ðə.roʊ
prothes|is ˈprɒθ.ɪ.s|ɪs, ˈ-ə- ⓤⓢ ˈprɑː.θə- **-es** -iːz
protium ˈprəʊ.ti.əm ⓤⓢ ˈproʊ.t̬i-
proto- prəʊ.təʊ- ⓤⓢ proʊ.t̬oʊ-, -t̬ə-
Note: Prefix. Normally takes primary or secondary stress on the first syllable, e.g. **prototype** /ˈprəʊ.təʊ.taɪp ⓤⓢ ˈproʊ.tə-/, **prototypic** /ˌprəʊ.təʊˈtɪp.ɪk ⓤⓢ ˌproʊ.t̬əˈ-/.

protocol 'prəʊ.tə.kɒl (US) 'proʊ.t̬ə.kɔːl, -t̬oʊ-, -kɑːl **-s** -z

proton (P®) 'prəʊ.tɒn (US) 'proʊ.tɑːn **-s** -z

protoplasm 'prəʊ.təʊ.plæz.ᵊm (US) 'proʊ.t̬ə-, -t̬oʊ-

prototype 'prəʊ.təʊ.taɪp (US) 'proʊ.t̬ə-, -t̬oʊ- **-s** -s

prototypic ˌprəʊ.təʊ'tɪp.ɪk (US) ˌproʊ.t̬ə'-, -t̬oʊ'- **-al** -ᵊl

protozo|a ˌprəʊ.təʊ'zəʊ|.ə (US) ˌproʊ.t̬ə'zoʊ-, -t̬oʊ'- **-an/s** -ən/z **-on** -ɒn (US) -ɑːn **-ic** -ɪk

protract prəʊ'trækt (US) proʊ-, prə- **-s** -s **-ing** -ɪŋ **-ed/ly** -ɪd/li **-ile** -aɪl (US) -ᵊl

protraction prəʊ'træk.ʃᵊn (US) proʊ-, prə- **-s** -z

protractor prəʊ'træk.təʳ (US) proʊ-, prə- **-s** -z

protrud|e prəʊ'truːd (US) proʊ-, prə- **-es** -z **-ing** -ɪŋ **-ed** -ɪd

protrusion prəʊ'truː.ʒᵊn (US) proʊ-, prə- **-s** -z

protrusive prəʊ'truː.sɪv (US) proʊ-, prə- **-ly** -li **-ness** -nəs, -nɪs

protuberanc|e prəʊ'tjuː.bᵊr.ᵊnts (US) proʊ'tuː-, prə-, -'tjuː- **-es** -ɪz

protuberant prəʊ'tjuː.bᵊr.ᵊnt (US) proʊ'tuː-, prə-, -'tjuː- **-ly** -li

proud praʊd **-er** -əʳ (US) -ɚ **-est** -ɪst, -əst **-ly** -li **-ness** -nəs, -nɪs

Proudfoot 'praʊd.fʊt

Proudhon 'pruː.dɒn (US) -dɑːn, -doʊn

Proudie 'praʊ.di

Proulx pruː

Proust pruːst

Proustian 'pruː.sti.ən

Prout praʊt

provab|le 'pruː.və.b|l̩ **-ly** -li **-leness** -l̩.nəs, -nɪs

prov|e pruːv **-es** -z **-ing** -ɪŋ **-ed** -d **-er/s** -əʳ/z (US) -ɚ/z

proven 'pruː.vᵊn, 'prəʊ- (US) 'pruː-

provenance 'prɒv.ᵊn.ənts, -ɪ.nənts (US) 'prɑː.vᵊn.ᵊnts

Provençal(e), Provencal(e) ˌprɒv.ɑ̃ːn'sɑːl, -ɔ̃ːn-, -vənt'- (US) ˌproʊ.vɑːn'-, ˌprɑː-, -vən'-

Provence prɒv'ɑ̃ːns, prə'vɑ̃ːns, -'vɔ̃ːns, -'vɑːnts (US) prɑː'vɑ̃ːnts, proʊ-

provender 'prɒv.ɪn.dəʳ, -ᵊn- (US) 'prɑː.vᵊn.dɚ

proverb (P) 'prɒv.ɜːb (US) 'prɑː.vɝːb **-s** -z

proverbial prəʊ'vɜː.bi.əl (US) prə'vɝː-, proʊ- **-ly** -i

provid|e prəʊ'vaɪd (US) prə-, proʊ- **-es** -z **-ing** -ɪŋ **-ed** -ɪd **-er/s** -əʳ/z (US) -ɚ/z

providen|ce (P) 'prɒv.ɪ.dᵊn|ts (US) 'prɑː.və- **-t/ly** -t/li

providential ˌprɒv.ɪ'den.tʃᵊl (US) ˌprɑː.və'- **-ly** -i

provinc|e 'prɒv.ɪnts (US) 'prɑː.vɪnts **-es** -ɪz

provincial prəʊ'vɪn.tʃᵊl (US) prə'vɪnt.ʃᵊl, proʊ- **-s** -z **-ly** -i

provincialism prəʊ'vɪn.tʃᵊl.ɪ.zᵊm (US) prə'vɪnt.ʃᵊl-, proʊ- **-s** -z

provinciality prəʊˌvɪn.tʃi'æl.ə.ti, -ɪ.ti (US) prəˌvɪnt.ʃi'æl.ə.t̬i, proʊ-

provincializ|e, -is|e prəʊ'vɪn.tʃᵊl.aɪz (US) prə'vɪnt.ʃᵊl-, proʊ- **-es** -ɪz **-ing** -ɪŋ **-ed** -d

provision prəʊ'vɪʒ.ᵊn (US) prə-, proʊ- **-s** -z **-ing** -ɪŋ **-ed** -d

provisional prəʊ'vɪʒ.ᵊn.ᵊl, '-nᵊl (US) prə-, proʊ-, prə'vɪʒ.ᵊn.ᵊl **-ly** -i

proviso prəʊ'vaɪ.zəʊ (US) prə'vaɪ.zoʊ, proʊ- **-(e)s** -z

provisor prəʊ'vaɪ.zəʳ (US) prə'vaɪ.zɚ, proʊ- **-s** -z

provisor|y prəʊ'vaɪ.zᵊr|.i (US) prə-, proʊ- **-ily** -ᵊl.i, -ɪ.li

Provo 'prəʊ.vəʊ (US) 'proʊ.voʊ **-s** -z

provocation ˌprɒv.ə'keɪ.ʃᵊn (US) ˌprɑː.və'- **-s** -z

provocative prə'vɒk.ə.tɪv (US) -'vɑː.kə.t̬ɪv, proʊ- **-ly** -li

provok|e prə'vəʊk (US) -'voʊk, proʊ- **-es** -s **-ing/ly** -ɪŋ/li **-ed** -t

provost 'prɒv.əst (US) 'proʊ.voʊst, -vəst; 'prɑː.vəst; *also in the US military:* 'proʊ.voʊ **-s** -s ˌ**provost 'marshal**

provostship 'prɒv.əst.ʃɪp (US) 'proʊ.voʊst-, -vəst-; 'prɑː.vəst- **-s** -s

prow praʊ **-s** -z

prowess 'praʊ.ɪs, -es; praʊ'es (US) 'praʊ.ɪs

prowl praʊl **-s** -z **-ing** -ɪŋ **-ed** -d **-er/s** -əʳ/z (US) -ɚ/z

Prowse praʊs, praʊz

prox. prɒks, 'prɒk.sɪ.məʊ, -sə- (US) 'prɑːk.sə.moʊ

proximal 'prɒk.sɪ.mᵊl, -sə- (US) 'prɑːk.sə- **-ly** -i

proximate 'prɒk.sɪ.mət, -sə-, -mɪt (US) 'prɑːk.sə.mət **-ly** -li

proxime access|it ˌprɒk.sɪ.meɪ.æk'ses|.ɪt, -ək'-, -ə'kes- (US) ˌprɑːk.səm.æk'ses.ət, -sɪm- **-erunt** -ə.rʊnt

proximit|y prɒk'sɪm.ə.t|i, -ɪ.t|i (US) prɑːk'sɪm.ə.t̬|i **-ies** -iz

proximo 'prɒk.sɪ.məʊ, -sə- (US) 'prɑːk.sə.moʊ

prox|y 'prɒk.s|i (US) 'prɑːk- **-ies** -iz

Prozac® 'prəʊ.zæk (US) 'proʊ-

prud|e pruːd **-es** -z **-ery** -ᵊr.i

prudence (P) 'pruː.dᵊnts

prudent 'pruː.dᵊnt **-ly** -li

prudential pruː'den.tʃᵊl (US) -'dent.ʃᵊl **-ly** -i

Prudhoe 'prʌd.həʊ, 'pruː.dəʊ, 'pruːd.həʊ (US) 'pruːd.hoʊ, 'pruː.doʊ, 'prʌd.hoʊ

prudish 'pruː.dɪʃ **-ly** -li **-ness** -nəs, -nɪs

Prufrock 'pruː.frɒk (US) -frɑːk

prun|e pruːn **-es** -z **-ing** -ɪŋ **-ed** -d

prunella (P) pruː'nel.ə **-s** -z

prurience 'prʊə.ri.ənts (US) 'prʊr.i-

prurient 'prʊə.ri.ənt (US) 'prʊr.i- **-ly** -li

prurigo prʊə'raɪ.gəʊ (US) prʊ'raɪ.goʊ

pru|ritus prʊə|'raɪ.təs (US) prʊ|'raɪ.t̬əs **-ritic** -'rɪt.ɪk (US) -'rɪt̬-

Prussia 'prʌʃ.ə

Prussian 'prʌʃ.ᵊn **-s** -z ˌ**Prussian 'blue**

prussiate 'prʌʃ.i.ət, 'prʌʃ.ət, -ɪt (US) 'prʌs.i.eɪt, 'prʌʃ-, -ɪt **-s** -s

prussic acid ˌprʌs.ɪk'æs.ɪd

Pruth pruːt

pr|y pr|aɪ **-ies** -aɪz **-ying/ly** -aɪ.ɪŋ/li **-ied** -aɪd **-yer/s** -aɪ.əʳ/z (US) -aɪ.ɚ/z

Pryce praɪs

Pryde praɪd

Pryke praɪk

Prynne prɪn

Pryor praɪəʳ (US) praɪɚ

Przewalski pʃə'væl.ski, -'vɑːl- (US) pʃə'vɑːl- **Przeˌwalski's 'horse**

PS ˌpiː'es **-'s** -ɪz

psalm (P) sɑːm **-s** -z **-ist/s** -ɪst/s

psalmodic sæl'mɒd.ɪk (US) sɑː'mɑː.dɪk, sæl-

psalmod|y 'sæl.mə.d|i, 'sɑː.mə- (US) 'sɑː-, 'sæl- **-ist/s** -ɪst/s

psalter 'sɔːl.təʳ, 'sɒl- (US) 'sɔːl.t̬ɚ, 'sɑːl- **-s** -z

psalt(e)r|y 'sɔːl.tᵊr|.i, 'sɒl- (US) 'sɔːl.tɚ-, 'sɑːl- **-ies** -iz

Note: In the following words beginning with **ps-**, the form with /p/ is rare.

psepholog|y psɪ'fɒl.ə.dʒ|i, psə-, psef'ɒl- (US) siː'fɑː.lə- **-ist/s** -ɪst/s

pseud sjuːd, suːd (US) suːd **-s** -z

pseudo- ˌsjuː.dəʊ-, ˌsuː- (US) ˌsuː.doʊ-

pseudo 'sjuː.dəʊ, 'suː- (US) 'suː.doʊ **-s** -z

pseudonym 'sjuː.də.nɪm, 'suː- (US) 'suː.dᵊn.ɪm **-s** -z

pseudonymity ˌsjuː.də'nɪm.ə.ti, ˌsuː-, -ɪ.ti (US) ˌsuː.dᵊn'ɪm.ə.t̬i

pseudonymous sjuː'dɒn.ɪ.məs, suː- (US) suː'dɑː.nɪ-

pseudopodi|um ˌsjuː.də'pəʊ.di|.əm, ˌsuː- (US) ˌsuː.doʊ'poʊ- **-a** -ə

Pseudoxia Epidemica sjuːˌdɒk.si.ə.ep.ɪ'dem.ɪ.kə, suː- (US) suːˌdɑːk.si-

pshaw (*interj.*) pɸː, pʃɔː (US) pʃɔː, pʃɑː

Note: Sound of derision or protest: the spelling was probably originally intended to represent a voiceless bilabial affricate (a more polite version of the bilabial trill known as a "raspberry" in British English

and also as a “Bronx Cheer” in American English), but it is usually now given a spelling-based pronunciation.
psi psaɪ, saɪ ⓤⓢ saɪ, psiː
Psion 'psaɪ.ɒn ⓤⓢ -ɑːn
psittacosis ˌpsɪt.ə'kəʊ.sɪs ⓤⓢ ˌsɪt.ə'koʊ-
Psmith smɪθ
psoriasis psə'raɪə.sɪs, psɒr'aɪə-, psɔː'raɪə-, psʊ- ⓤⓢ sə'raɪə-, soʊ-
psych saɪk **-s** -s **-ing** -ɪŋ **-ed** -t
psych|e (*v.*) saɪk **-es** -s **-ing** -ɪŋ **-ed** -t
psyche (*n.*) 'saɪ.ki, -kiː **-s** -s
psychedelia ˌsaɪ.kɪ'diː.li.ə, -kə'- ⓤⓢ -kə'diː.li.ə, -'diːl.jə
psychedelic ˌsaɪ.kɪ'del.ɪk, -kə'- ⓤⓢ -kə'- **-ally** -əl.i, -li *stress shift:* ˌpsychedelic 'colours
psychiatric ˌsaɪ.ki'æt.rɪk **-al** -əl **-ally** -əl.i, -li *stress shift:* ˌpsychiatric 'nurse
psychiatr|y saɪ'kaɪə.tr|i, sɪ-, sə- ⓤⓢ saɪ-, sɪ- **-ist/s** -ɪst/s
psychic 'saɪ.kɪk **-al** -əl **-ally** -əl.i, -li
psycho- saɪ.kəʊ-; saɪ'kɒ- ⓤⓢ saɪ.koʊ-, -kə-; saɪ'kɑː-
Note: Prefix. Normally either takes primary or secondary stress on the first syllable, e.g. **psychodrama** /'saɪ.kəʊˌdrɑː.mə ⓤⓢ -koʊˌ-/, **psychodramatic** /ˌsaɪ.kəʊ.drə'mæt.ɪk ⓤⓢ -koʊ.drə'mæt̬.ɪk/, or primary stress on the second syllable, e.g. **psychotic** /saɪ'kɒt.ɪk ⓤⓢ -'kɑː.t̬ɪk/.
psycho 'saɪ.kəʊ ⓤⓢ -koʊ **-s** -z
psychoanalys|e ˌsaɪ.kəʊ'æn.əl.aɪz ⓤⓢ -koʊ'æn.ə.laɪz **-es** -ɪz **-ing** -ɪŋ **-ed** -d
psychoanalysis ˌsaɪ.kəʊ.ə'næl.ə.sɪs, '-ɪ- ⓤⓢ -koʊ-
psychoanalyst ˌsaɪ.kəʊ'æn.əl.ɪst ⓤⓢ -koʊ'æn.ə.lɪst **-s** -s
psychoanalytic ˌsaɪ.kəʊˌæn.əl'ɪt.ɪk ⓤⓢ -koʊˌæn.ə'lɪt̬.ɪk **-al** -əl **-ally** -əl.i, -li *stress shift:* ˌpsychoanalytic 'counselling
psychoanalyz|e ˌsaɪ.kəʊ'æn.əl.aɪz ⓤⓢ -koʊ'æn.ə.laɪz **-es** -ɪz **-ing** -ɪŋ **-ed** -d
psychobabble 'saɪ.kəʊˌbæb.l̩ ⓤⓢ -koʊˌ-
psychodrama 'saɪ.kəʊˌdrɑː.mə ⓤⓢ -koʊˌ-, -ˌdræm.ə **-s** -z
psychodramatic ˌsaɪ.kəʊ.drə'mæt.ɪk ⓤⓢ -koʊ.drə'mæt̬-
psychokinesis ˌsaɪ.kəʊ.kaɪ'niː.sɪs, -kɪ'- ⓤⓢ -koʊ.kɪ'-, -kaɪ'-
psychokinetic ˌsaɪ.kəʊ.kɪ'net.ɪk, -kaɪ'- ⓤⓢ -koʊ- *stress shift:* ˌpsychokinetic 'powers
psycholinguist ˌsaɪ.kəʊ'lɪŋ.gwɪst ⓤⓢ -koʊ'- **-s** -s
psycholinguistic ˌsaɪ.kəʊ.lɪŋ'gwɪs.tɪk ⓤⓢ -koʊ- **-s** -s **-ally** -əl.i, -li *stress shift:* ˌpsycholinguistic 'process
psychologic ˌsaɪ.kə'lɒdʒ.ɪk ⓤⓢ -'lɑː.dʒɪk *stress shift:* ˌpsychologic 'warfare
psychological ˌsaɪ.kəl'ɒdʒ.ɪ.kəl ⓤⓢ -kə'lɑː.dʒɪ- **-ly** -i *stress shift, see compound:* **ˌpsychological 'warfare**
psychologiz|e, -is|e saɪ'kɒl.ə.dʒaɪz ⓤⓢ -'kɑː.lə- **-es** -ɪz **-ing** -ɪŋ **-ed** -d
psycholog|y saɪ'kɒl.ə.dʒ|i ⓤⓢ -'kɑː.lə- **-ist/s** -ɪst/s
psychometric ˌsaɪ.kəʊ'met.rɪk ⓤⓢ -koʊ'- **-s** -s *stress shift:* ˌpsychometric 'measurement
psychometr|y saɪ'kɒm.ɪ.tr|i, '-ə- ⓤⓢ -'kɑː.mə- **-ist/s** -ɪst/s
psychopath 'saɪ.kəʊ.pæθ ⓤⓢ -kə-, -koʊ- **-s** -s
psychopathic ˌsaɪ.kəʊ'pæθ.ɪk ⓤⓢ -kə'-, -koʊ'- **-ally** -əl.i, -li *stress shift:* ˌpsychopathic 'tendencies
psychopatholog|y ˌsaɪ.kəʊ.pæθ'ɒl.ə.dʒ|i ⓤⓢ -koʊ.pæθ'ɑː.lə- **-ist/s** -ɪst/s
psychophysical ˌsaɪ.kəʊ'fɪz.ɪ.kəl, '-ə- ⓤⓢ -koʊ'- **-ly** -li *stress shift:* ˌpsychophysical 'stimulus
psychosexual ˌsaɪ.kəʊ'sek.ʃʊəl, -sjʊəl ⓤⓢ -ʃu.əl **-ly** -i *stress shift:* ˌpsychosexual 'aspects
psychos|is saɪ'kəʊ.s|ɪs ⓤⓢ -'koʊ- **-es** -iːz
psychosocial ˌsaɪ.kəʊ'səʊ.ʃəl ⓤⓢ -koʊ'soʊ- *stress shift:* ˌpsychosocial 'problems
psychosomatic ˌsaɪ.kəʊ.səʊ'mæt.ɪk ⓤⓢ -koʊ.soʊ'mæt̬- **-ally** -əl.i, -li *stress shift:* ˌpsychosomatic 'symptoms
psychotherap|y ˌsaɪ.kəʊ'θer.ə.p|i ⓤⓢ -koʊ'- **-ist/s** -ɪst/s
psychotic saɪ'kɒt.ɪk ⓤⓢ -'kɑː.t̬ɪk **-ally** -əl.i, -li
pt *(abbrev. for* **pint***)* paɪnt
PTA ˌpiː.tiː'eɪ
Ptah tɑː, ptɑː, pə'tɑː ⓤⓢ pə'tɑː
ptarmigan 'tɑː.mɪ.gən, -mə- ⓤⓢ 'tɑːr-
pterodactyl ˌter.əʊ'dæk.tɪl, -təl ⓤⓢ -ə'dæk.təl, -oʊ'- **-s** -z
pterosaur 'ter.əʊ.sɔːr ⓤⓢ -ə.sɑːr, -oʊ-, -sɔːr **-s** -z
PTO ˌpiː.tiː'əʊ ⓤⓢ -'oʊ
Ptolemaeus ˌtɒl.ə'miː.əs, -ɪ'-, -'meɪ- ⓤⓢ ˌtɑː.lə'meɪ-, -'miː-
Ptolema|ic ˌtɒl.ə'meɪ|.ɪk, -ɪ'- ⓤⓢ ˌtɑː.lə'- **-ist** -ɪst
Ptolemy 'tɒl.ə.mi, '-ɪ- ⓤⓢ 'tɑː.lə-
ptomaine 'təʊ.meɪn; təʊ'meɪn ⓤⓢ 'toʊ.meɪn
Pty *(abbrev. for* **Proprietary***)* prə'praɪə.tər.i ⓤⓢ proʊ-, prə-
ptyalin 'taɪə.lɪn
pub pʌb **-s** -z **-by** -i
pub-crawl 'pʌb.krɔːl ⓤⓢ -krɑːl, -krɔːl **-s** -z **-ing** -ɪŋ **-ed** -d **-er/s** -ər/z ⓤⓢ -ɚ/z
puberty 'pjuː.bə.ti ⓤⓢ -bɚ.t̬i
pubes *slang for pubic hair:* pjuːbz
pubes *plural of* **pubis***:* 'pjuː.biːz
pubescen|ce pjuː'bes.ən|ts, pjʊ- **-t** -t
pubic 'pjuː.bɪk **ˌpubic 'hair** ⓤⓢ **'pubic ˌhair**
pub|is 'pjuː.b|ɪs **-es** -iːz
public 'pʌb.lɪk **-ly** -li **ˌpublic con'venience; ˌpublic 'enemy; ˌpublic 'house; ˌpublic o'pinion; ˌpublic re'lations; ˌpublic 'school; ˌpublic 'sector** ⓤⓢ **'public ˌsector;** *stress shift, British only:* ˌpublic sector 'services; **ˌpublic 'speaking; ˌpublic 'transport**
public-address system ˌpʌb.lɪk.ə'dresˌsɪs.təm **-s** -z
publican 'pʌb.lɪ.kən **-s** -z
publication ˌpʌb.lɪ'keɪ.ʃən, -lə'- **-s** -z
publicist 'pʌb.lɪ.sɪst, -lə- **-s** -s
publicity pʌb'lɪs.ə.ti, pə'blɪs-, -ɪ.ti ⓤⓢ -ə.t̬i
publiciz|e, -is|e 'pʌb.lɪ.saɪz, -lə- **-es** -ɪz **-ing** -ɪŋ **-ed** -d
public-spirited ˌpʌb.lɪk'spɪr.ɪ.tɪd, '-ə- ⓤⓢ -ə.t̬ɪd **-ness** -nəs, -nɪs *stress shift:* ˌpublic-spirited 'policies
publish 'pʌb.lɪʃ **-es** -ɪz **-ing** -ɪŋ **-ed** -t **-er/s** -ər/z ⓤⓢ -ɚ/z
Publius 'pʌb.li.əs
Puccini pʊ'tʃiː.ni ⓤⓢ puː-
puce pjuːs
puck (P) pʌk **-s** -s
puck|er 'pʌk|.ər ⓤⓢ -ɚ **-ers** -əz ⓤⓢ -ɚz **-ering** -ər.ɪŋ **-ered** -d ⓤⓢ -ɚd
puckish 'pʌk.ɪʃ **-ly** -li **-ness** -nəs, -nɪs
pud pʊd **-s** -z
pudding 'pʊd.ɪŋ **-s** -z **the ˌproof of the ˌpudding is ˌin the 'eating**
puddl|e 'pʌd.l̩ **-es** -z **-ing** -ɪŋ, 'pʌd.lɪŋ **-ed** -d **-er/s** -ər/z ⓤⓢ -ɚ/z, 'pʌd.lər/z ⓤⓢ -lɚ/z
pudend|um pjuː'den.d|əm, pjʊ- ⓤⓢ pjuː- **-a** -ə
pudg|y 'pʌdʒ|.i **-ier** -i.ər ⓤⓢ -i.ɚ **-iest** -i.ɪst, -i.əst **-iness** -ɪ.nəs, -ɪ.nɪs
Pudsey 'pʌd.zi *locally:* 'pʊt.si
Puebla 'pweb.lə, pu'eb- ⓤⓢ 'pweb.lɑː
pueblo (P) 'pweb.ləʊ, pu'eb- ⓤⓢ 'pweb.loʊ **-s** -z
puerile 'pjʊə.raɪl, 'pjɔː- ⓤⓢ 'pjuː.ɚ.ɪl, 'pjʊr.ɪl, -aɪl **-ly** -li
puerilit|y pjʊə'rɪl.ə.t|i, pjɔː-, -ɪ.t|i ⓤⓢ ˌpjuː.ə'rɪl.ə.t̬|i, pjʊ'- **-ies** -iz
puerperal pju'ɜː.pər.əl ⓤⓢ -'ɝː-
Puerto Ric|o ˌpwɜː.təʊ'riː.k|əʊ, ˌpweə- ⓤⓢ ˌpwer.t̬ə'riː.koʊ, -toʊ'-, ˌpɔːr.t̬ə'- **-an/s** -ən/z

Puerto Vallarta ˌpwɜː.təʊ.vælˈɑː.tə *as if Spanish:* ˌpweə.təʊ.vaɪˈ- (US) ˌpwer.toʊ.vɑːˈjɑːr.t̬ə, -tɑː

puff pʌf **-s** -s **-ing** -ɪŋ **-ed** -t **-er/s** -əʳ/z (US) -ɚ/z ˈ**puff** ˌ**adder**; ˌ**puff** ˈ**pastry**

puffball ˈpʌf.bɔːl (US) -bɔːl, -bɑːl **-s** -z ˌ**puffball** ˈ**skirt**

puffed sleeve ˌpʌf*t*ˈsliːv **-s** -z

puffery ˈpʌf.ᵊr.i (US) -ɚ-

puffin (P) ˈpʌf.ɪn **-s** -z

puff|y ˈpʌf|.i **-ier** -i.əʳ (US) -i.ɚ **-iest** -i.ɪst, -i.əst **-ily** -ɪ.li, -ᵊl.i **-iness** -ɪ.nəs, -ɪ.nɪs

pug pʌɡ **-s** -z

pug(g)aree ˈpʌɡ.ᵊr.i **-s** -z

puggree ˈpʌɡ.ri **-s** -z

Pugh pjuː

pugil|ism ˈpjuː.dʒɪ.l|ɪ.zᵊm, -dʒə- **-ist/s** -ɪst/s

pugilistic ˌpjuː.dʒɪˈlɪs.tɪk, -dʒəˈ- **-ally** -ᵊl.i, -li *stress shift:* ˌpugilistic ˈattitude

Pugin ˈpjuː.dʒɪn

pugnacious pʌɡˈneɪ.ʃəs **-ly** -li **-ness** -nəs, -nɪs

pugnacity pʌɡˈnæs.ə.ti, -ɪ.ti (US) -ə.t̬i

pug-nos|e ˌpʌɡˈnəʊz (US) ˈpʌɡ.noʊz **-es** -ɪz **-ed** -d *stress shift, British only:* ˌpug-nose ˈface

puisne ˈpjuː.ni

puissan|ce *power:* ˈpjuː.ɪ.sᵊn|ts, ˈpwɪs.ᵊn|*t*s *sometimes in poetry:* pjuˈɪ.sᵊn|*t*s **-t** -t

puissance *in show-jumping:* ˈpwiː.sɑ̃ːns, -sɑːnts, -sᵊnts

puk|e pjuːk **-es** -s **-ing** -ɪŋ **-ed** -t

pukka ˈpʌk.ə

pul puːl **-s** -z **-i** -iː

pula ˈpjuː.lə, ˈpuː- (US) ˈpuː.lɑː

Pulaski pəˈlæs.ki, pjuː- (US) pə-, pʊlˈæs-

pulchritude ˈpʌl.krɪ.tjuːd, -krə- (US) -tuːd, -tjuːd

pulchritudinous ˌpʌl.krɪˈtjuː.dɪ.nəs, -krəˈ-, -dᵊn.əs (US) -ˈtuː.dᵊn-, -ˈtjuː-

pul|e pjuːl **-es** -z **-ing** -ɪŋ **-ed** -d

Puleston ˈpʊl.ɪ.stᵊn *locally also:* ˈpɪl.sᵊn

Pulham ˈpʊl.əm

Pulitzer *US publisher:* ˈpʊl.ɪt.səʳ (US) ˈpʊl.ɪt.sɚ, ˈpjuː.lɪt- *prize at Columbia University:* ˈpjuː.lɪt.səʳ (US) ˈpʊl.ɪt.sɚ, ˈpjuː.lɪt- ˈ**Pulitzer** ˌ**prize**, ˌ**Pulitzer** ˈ**prize**

pull pʊl **-s** -z **-ing** -ɪŋ **-ed** -d **-er/s** -əʳ/z (US) -ɚ/z

pullback ˈpʊl.bæk **-s** -s

pull-down ˈpʊl.daʊn

pullet ˈpʊl.ɪt, -ət **-s** -s

pulley ˈpʊl.i **-s** -z

pullman (P) ˈpʊl.mən **-s** -z

pullout ˈpʊl.aʊt **-s** -s

pullover ˈpʊl.əʊ.vəʳ (US) -oʊ.vɚ **-s** -z

pullu|late ˈpʌl.jə|.leɪt, -jʊ- **-lates** -leɪts **-lating** -leɪ.tɪŋ (US) -leɪ.t̬ɪŋ **-lated** -leɪ.tɪd (US) -leɪ.t̬ɪd

pullulation ˌpʌl.jəˈleɪ.ʃᵊn, -jʊˈ-

pull-up ˈpʊl.ʌp **-s** -s

pulmonary ˈpʌl.mə.nᵊr.i, ˈpʊl- (US) -ner-

pulmonic pʌlˈmɒn.ɪk, pʊl- (US) -ˈmɑː.nɪk

pulp pʌlp **-s** -s **-ing** -ɪŋ **-ed** -t

pulpi|fy ˈpʌl.pɪ|.faɪ **-fies** -faɪz **-fying** -faɪ.ɪŋ **-fied** -faɪd

pulpit ˈpʊl.pɪt (US) ˈpʊl-, ˈpʌl- **-s** -s

pulp|y ˈpʌl.p|i **-ier** -i.əʳ (US) -i.ɚ **-iest** -i.ɪst, -i.əst **-iness** -ɪ.nəs, -ɪ.nɪs

pulsar ˈpʌl.sɑːʳ, -səʳ (US) -sɑːr, -sɚ **-s** -z

pul|sate pʌlˈ|seɪt (US) ˈ-- **-sates** -ˈseɪts (US) -seɪts **-sating** -ˈseɪ.tɪŋ (US) -seɪ.t̬ɪŋ **-sated** -ˈseɪ.tɪd (US) -seɪ.t̬ɪd

pulsatile ˈpʌl.sə.taɪl (US) -tɪl, -taɪl

pulsation pʌlˈseɪ.ʃᵊn **-s** -z

pulsative ˈpʌl.sə.tɪv (US) -t̬ɪv

pulsatory ˈpʌl.sə.tᵊr.i, pʌlˈseɪ- (US) ˈpʌl.sə.tɔːr-

puls|e pʌls **-es** -ɪz **-ing** -ɪŋ **-ed** -t

Pulteney *surname:* ˈpʌlt.ni, ˈpəʊlt-, ˈpʊlt- (US) ˈpʌlt-, ˈpoʊlt-, ˈpʊlt-

Pulteney *bridge in Bath:* ˈpʌlt.ni

pulverization, -isa- ˌpʌl.vᵊr.aɪˈzeɪ.ʃᵊn, -ɪˈ- (US) -ɪˈ- **-s** -z

pulveriz|e, -is|e ˈpʌl.vᵊr.aɪz (US) -və.raɪz **-es** -ɪz **-ing** -ɪŋ **-ed** -d

puma ˈpjuː.mə (US) ˈpjuː-, ˈpuː- **-s** -z

Pumblechook ˈpʌm.bl̩.tʃʊk

pumic|e ˈpʌm.ɪs **-es** -ɪz **-ing** -ɪŋ **-ed** -t ˈ**pumice** ˌ**stone**

pummel ˈpʌm.ᵊl **-s** -z **-(l)ing** -ɪŋ **-(l)ed** -d

pump pʌmp **-s** -s **-ing** -ɪŋ **-ed** -t **-er/s** -əʳ/z (US) -ɚ/z ˈ**pump** ˌ**room**

pumpernickel ˈpʌm.pə.nɪk.l̩ (US) -pɚ,-

pumpkin ˈpʌmp.kɪn **-s** -z ˌ**pumpkin** ˈ**pie**

pun pʌn **-s** -z **-ning** -ɪŋ **-ned** -d **-ner/s** -əʳ/z (US) -ɚ/z

punch (P) pʌn*t*ʃ (US) pʌntʃ **-es** -ɪz **-ing** -ɪŋ **-ed** -t **-er/s** -əʳ/z (US) -ɚ/z

Punch-and-Judy ˌpʌn*t*ʃ.ᵊn*d*ˈdʒuː.di (US) ˌpʌntʃ- ˌ**Punch-and-**ˈ**Judy** ˌ**show**

punchbag ˈpʌn*t*ʃ.bæɡ (US) ˈpʌntʃ- **-s** -z

punchball ˈpʌn*t*ʃ.bɔːl (US) ˈpʌntʃ.bɔːl, -bɑːl **-s** -z

punchbowl ˈpʌn*t*ʃ.bəʊl (US) ˈpʌntʃ.boʊl **-s** -z

punch-drunk ˈpʌn*t*ʃ.drʌŋk (US) ˈpʌntʃ-

puncheon ˈpʌn.*t*ʃᵊn (US) -tʃᵊn **-s** -z

punchinello (P) ˌpʌn.*t*ʃɪˈnel.əʊ, -*t*ʃəˈ- (US) -tʃəˈnel.oʊ

punchline ˈpʌn*t*ʃ.laɪn (US) ˈpʌntʃ- **-s** -z

punch-up ˈpʌn*t*ʃ.ʌp (US) ˈpʌntʃ- **-s** -s

punch|y ˈpʌn.*t*ʃ|i (US) -tʃ|i **-ier** -i.əʳ (US) -i.ɚ **-iest** -i.ɪst, -i.əst **-ily** -ɪ.li, -ᵊl.i **-iness** -ɪ.nəs, -ɪ.nɪs

punctilio pʌŋkˈtɪl.i.əʊ (US) -oʊ **-s** -z

punctilious pʌŋkˈtɪl.i.əs **-ly** -li **-ness** -nəs, -nɪs

punctual ˈpʌŋk.tʃu.əl, -tʃʊəl, -tju.əl, -tjʊəl (US) ˈpʌŋk.tʃu.əl **-ly** -i

punctuality ˌpʌnk.tʃuˈæl.ə.ti, -tjuˈ-, -ɪ.ti (US) -ə.t̬i

punctu|ate ˈpʌŋk.tʃu|.eɪt, -tju- (US) -tʃu- **-ates** -eɪts **-ating** -eɪ.tɪŋ (US) -eɪ.t̬ɪŋ **-ated** -eɪ.tɪd (US) -eɪ.t̬ɪd **-ator/s** -eɪ.təʳ/z (US) -eɪ.t̬ɚ/z

punctuation ˌpʌŋk.tʃuˈeɪ.ʃᵊn, -tjuˈ- (US) -tʃuˈ- **-s** -z

punct|ure ˈpʌŋk.tʃ|əʳ (US) -tʃ|ɚ **-ures** -əz (US) -ɚz **-uring** -ᵊr.ɪŋ **-ured** -əd (US) -ɚd

pundit ˈpʌn.dɪt **-s** -s

Pune pjuːn

pungency ˈpʌn.dʒᵊn*t*.si

pungent ˈpʌn.dʒᵊnt **-ly** -li

Punic ˈpjuː.nɪk

puniness ˈpjuː.nɪ.nəs, -nɪs (US) -ni-

punish ˈpʌn.ɪʃ **-es** -ɪz **-ing/ly** -ɪŋ/li **-ed** -t **-er/s** -əʳ/z (US) -ɚ/z **-able/ness** -ə.bl̩/nəs, -nɪs

punishment ˈpʌn.ɪʃ.mənt **-s** -s

puni|tive ˈpjuː.nə|.tɪv, -nɪ- (US) -nə|.t̬ɪv **-tively** -tɪv.li (US) -t̬ɪv.li **-tory** -tᵊr.i (US) -tɔːr.i

Punjab ˌpʌnˈdʒɑːb, ˌpʊn-, ˈ-- (US) pʌnˈdʒɑːb; ˈpʌn.dʒɑːb, -dʒæb **-i** -iː, -i

Punjabi pʌnˈdʒɑː.biː, pʊn-, -bi (US) pʌn-

punk pʌŋk **-s** -s **-y** -i **-ier** -i.əʳ (US) -i.ɚ **-iest** -i.ɪst, -i.əst ˌ**punk** ˈ**rock**; ˌ**punk** ˈ**rocker**

punkah ˈpʌŋ.kə **-s** -z

punnet ˈpʌn.ɪt **-s** -s

Punshon ˈpʌn.ʃᵊn

punster ˈpʌn.stəʳ (US) -stɚ **-s** -z

punt *boat:* pʌnt **-s** -s **-ing** -ɪŋ (US) ˈpʌn.t̬ɪŋ **-ed** -ɪd (US) ˈpʌn.t̬ɪd

punt *currency:* pʊnt **-s** -s

punter ˈpʌn.təʳ (US) -t̬ɚ **-s** -z

Punto® ˈpʊn.təʊ, ˈpʌn- (US) -toʊ

pun|y ˈpjuː.n|i **-ier** -i.əʳ (US) -i.ɚ **-iest** -i.ɪst, -i.əst **-iness** -ɪ.nəs, -ɪ.nɪs

pup pʌp **-s** -s **-ping** -ɪŋ **-ped** -t

pup|a ˈpjuː.p|ə **-ae** -iː **-as** -əz **-al** -ᵊl

pupil ˈpjuː.pᵊl, -pɪl (US) -pᵊl **-s** -z

pupil(l)age ˈpjuː.pɪ.lɪdʒ, -pᵊl.ɪdʒ (US) -pᵊl.ɪdʒ

pupillary ˈpjuː.pɪ.lᵊr.i, -pᵊl.ᵊr- (US) -pᵊl.er-

puppet ˈpʌp.ɪt **-s** -s ˌ**puppet** ˈ**government**

puppeteer ˌpʌp.ɪˈtɪəʳ, -əˈ- (US) -əˈtɪr **-s** -z

pupp|y ˈpʌp|.i **-ies** -iz ˈ**puppy** ˌ**dog**; ˈ**puppy** ˌ**fat**; ˈ**puppy** ˌ**love**

Purbeck ˈpɜː.bek (US) ˈpɝː-

purblind ˈpɜː.blaɪnd (US) ˈpɝː- **-ness** -nəs, -nɪs

Purcell ˈpɜː.sel, -sᵊl; pɜːˈsel (US) ˈpɝː.sᵊl, -ˈ-

purchas|e ˈpɜː.tʃəs, -tʃɪs (US) ˈpɝː.tʃəs

-es -ɪz -ing -ɪŋ -ed -t -er/s -əʳ/z ⓤⓢ -ɚ/z -able -ə.bl̩
purdah ˈpɜː.də, -dɑː ⓤⓢ ˈpɝː.də
Purdie, Purdy ˈpɜː.di ⓤⓢ ˈpɝː-
pur|e pjʊəʳ, pjɔːʳ ⓤⓢ pjʊr -er -əʳ ⓤⓢ -ɚ -est -ɪst, -əst -ely -li -eness -nəs, -nɪs
purebred ˈpjʊə.bred, ˈpjɔː- ⓤⓢ ˈpjʊr- -s -z
purée, puree ˈpjʊə.reɪ, ˈpjɔː- ⓤⓢ pjʊˈreɪ; ˈpjʊr.eɪ -s -z -ing -ɪŋ -d -d
purfl|e ˈpɜː.fl̩ ⓤⓢ ˈpɝː- -es -z -ing -ɪŋ, ˈ-flɪŋ -ed -d
purfling ˈpɜː.flɪŋ ⓤⓢ ˈpɝː- -s -z
purgation pɜːˈgeɪ.ʃən ⓤⓢ pɝː- -s -z
purgative ˈpɜː.gə.tɪv ⓤⓢ ˈpɝː.gə.t̬ɪv -s -z
purgatorial ˌpɜː.gəˈtɔː.ri.əl ⓤⓢ ˌpɝː.gəˈtɔːr.i-
Purgatorio ˌpɜː.gəˈtɔː.ri.əʊ ⓤⓢ ˌpɝː.gəˈtɔːr.i.oʊ
purgator|y (P) ˈpɜː.gə.tər|.i, -tr|i ⓤⓢ ˈpɝː.gə.tɔːr- -ies -iz
purg|e pɜːdʒ ⓤⓢ pɝːdʒ -es -ɪz -ing -ɪŋ -ed -d
purification ˌpjʊə.rɪ.fɪˈkeɪ.ʃən, ˌpjɔː-, -rə- ⓤⓢ ˌpjʊr.ə- -s -z
purificatory ˌpjʊə.rɪ.fɪˈkeɪ.tər.i, ˌpjɔː-, -rə-; ⓤⓢ pjʊˈrɪf.ɪ.kəˌtɔːr-
puri|fy ˈpjʊə.rɪ|.faɪ, ˈpjɔː-, -rə- ⓤⓢ ˈpjʊr.ə- -fies -faɪz -fying -faɪ.ɪŋ -fied -faɪd -fier/s -faɪ.əʳ/z ⓤⓢ -faɪ.ɚ/z
Purim ˈpʊə.rɪm, ˈpjʊə- ⓤⓢ ˈpʊr.ɪm; puːˈriːm
purism ˈpjʊə.rɪ.zəm, ˈpjɔː- ⓤⓢ ˈpjʊr.ɪ-
purist ˈpjʊə.rɪst, ˈpjɔː- ⓤⓢ ˈpjʊr.ɪst -s -s
puristic pjʊəˈrɪs.tɪk, pjɔː- ⓤⓢ pjʊ- -al -əl
puritan (P) ˈpjʊə.rɪ.tən, ˈpjɔː- ⓤⓢ ˈpjʊr.ɪ- -s -z -ism -ɪ.zəm
puritanic ˌpjʊə.rɪˈtæn.ɪk, ˌpjɔː- ⓤⓢ ˌpjʊr.ɪˈ- -al -əl -ally -əl.i, -li
purity ˈpjʊə.rə.ti, ˈpjɔː-, -rɪ- ⓤⓢ ˈpjʊr.ɪ.t̬i, ˈ-ə-
Purkinje pɜːˈkɪn.ji ⓤⓢ pɝː-
Purkiss ˈpɜː.kɪs ⓤⓢ ˈpɝː-
purl pɜːl ⓤⓢ pɝːl -s -z -ing -ɪŋ -ed -d
Purley ˈpɜː.li ⓤⓢ ˈpɝː-
purlieu ˈpɜː.ljuː ⓤⓢ ˈpɝːl.juː, ˈpɝː.luː -s -z
purlin(e) ˈpɜː.lɪn ⓤⓢ ˈpɝː- -s -z
purloin pɜːˈlɔɪn, ˈ-- ⓤⓢ pɚˈlɔɪn; ˈpɝː.lɔɪn -s -z -ing -ɪŋ -ed -d
purloiner pɜːˈlɔɪ.nəʳ ⓤⓢ pɚˈlɔɪ.nɚ -s -z
Purnell pɜːˈnel ⓤⓢ pɝː-
purpl|e ˈpɜː.pl̩ ⓤⓢ ˈpɝː- -er -əʳ, ˈpɜː.pləʳ ⓤⓢ ˈpɝː.plɚ -est -ɪst, -əst, ˈpɜː.plɪst, -pləst, -pləst ⓤⓢ ˈpɝː- -es -z -ing -ɪŋ, ˈpɜː.plɪŋ ⓤⓢ ˈpɝː- -ed -d ˌPurple ˈHeart
purplish ˈpɜː.pl̩.ɪʃ, -plɪʃ ⓤⓢ ˈpɝː-
purpor|t pəˈpɔː|t, pɜː-; ˈpɜː.pə|t, -pɔː|t ⓤⓢ pɝːˈpɔːr|t, ˈ-- -ts -ts -ting -tɪŋ ⓤⓢ -t̬ɪŋ -ted/ly -tɪd/li ⓤⓢ -t̬ɪd/li
purpos|e ˈpɜː.pəs ⓤⓢ ˈpɝː- -es -ɪz -ing -ɪŋ -ed -t
purpose-built ˌpɜː.pəsˈbɪlt ⓤⓢ ˌpɝː- *stress shift:* ˌpurpose-built ˈresidence
purposeful ˈpɜː.pəs|.fəl, -fʊl ⓤⓢ ˈpɝː- -ly -i -ness -nəs, -nɪs
purposeless ˈpɜː.pəs.ləs, -lɪs ⓤⓢ ˈpɝː- -ly -li -ness -nəs, -nɪs
purposely ˈpɜː.pə.sli ⓤⓢ ˈpɝː-
purposive ˈpɜː.pə.sɪv ⓤⓢ ˈpɝː- -ly -li -ness -nəs, -nɪs
purpura ˈpɜː.pjʊ.rə, -pjə- ⓤⓢ ˈpɝː.pɚ.ə, -pjɚ-, -pʊ.rə
purr pɜːʳ ⓤⓢ pɝː -s -z -ing -ɪŋ -ed -d
purs|e pɜːs ⓤⓢ pɝːs -es -ɪz -ing -ɪŋ -ed -t
purser ˈpɜː.səʳ ⓤⓢ ˈpɝː.sɚ -s -z
purse-string ˈpɜːs.strɪŋ ⓤⓢ ˈpɝːs- -s -z
purslane ˈpɜː.slɪn, -slən, -sleɪn ⓤⓢ ˈpɝː.slɪn, -sleɪn
pursuance pəˈsjuː.ənts, pɜː-, -ˈsu- ⓤⓢ pɚˈsuː-
pursuant pəˈsjuː.ənt, pɜː-, -ˈsu- ⓤⓢ pɚˈsuː- -ly -li
pursu|e pəˈsjuː, pɜː-, -ˈsuː ⓤⓢ pɚˈsuː -es -z -ing -ɪŋ -ed -d -er/s -əʳ/z ⓤⓢ -ɚ/z
pursuit pəˈsjuːt, pɜː-, -ˈsuːt ⓤⓢ pɚˈsuːt -s -s
pursuivant ˈpɜː.sɪ.vənt, -sə- ⓤⓢ ˈpɝː.sɪ-, -swɪ- -s -s
Purton ˈpɜː.tən ⓤⓢ ˈpɝː-
purulency ˈpjʊə.rʊ.lənt.si, -rjʊ-, -rə- ⓤⓢ ˈpjʊr.ə-, -jə-
purulent ˈpjʊə.rʊ.lənt, -rjʊ-, -rə- ⓤⓢ ˈpjʊr.ə-, -rjə- -ly -li
Purver ˈpɜː.vəʳ ⓤⓢ ˈpɝː.vɚ
Purves ˈpɜː.vɪs ⓤⓢ ˈpɝː-
purvey pəˈveɪ, pɜː- ⓤⓢ pɚ- -s -z -ing -ɪŋ -ed -d
purvey|ance pəˈveɪ|.ənts, pɜː- ⓤⓢ pɚ- -or/s -əʳ/z ⓤⓢ -ɚ/z
purview ˈpɜː.vjuː ⓤⓢ ˈpɝː- -s -z
pus pʌs
Pusan ˌpuːˈsæn ⓤⓢ -ˈsɑːn
Pusey ˈpjuː.zi -ism -ɪ.zəm -ite/s -aɪt/s
push pʊʃ -es -ɪz -ing -ɪŋ/li -ed -t -er/s -əʳ/z ⓤⓢ -ɚ/z
pushball ˈpʊʃ.bɔːl ⓤⓢ -bɔːl, -bɑːl
pushbike ˈpʊʃ.baɪk -s -s
push-button ˈpʊʃˌbʌt.ən -s -z
push-cart ˈpʊʃ.kɑːt ⓤⓢ -kɑːrt -s -s
pushchair ˈpʊʃ.tʃeəʳ ⓤⓢ -tʃer -s -z
pushdown ˈpʊʃ.daʊn
pushful ˈpʊʃ.fəl, -fʊl -ness -nəs, -nɪs
Pushkin ˈpʊʃ.kɪn
pushover ˈpʊʃˌəʊ.vəʳ ⓤⓢ -ˌoʊ.vɚ -s -z
pushpin ˈpʊʃ.pɪn -s -z
push|-start ˈpʊʃ|.stɑːt ⓤⓢ -stɑːrt -starts -stɑːts ⓤⓢ -stɑːrts -starting -ˌstɑː.tɪŋ ⓤⓢ -ˌstɑːr.t̬ɪŋ -started -ˌstɑː.tɪd ⓤⓢ -ˌstɑːr.t̬ɪd
Pushtu ˈpʌʃ.tuː, ˌ-ˈ- ⓤⓢ ˈpʌʃ.tuː
pushup ˈpʊʃ.ʌp -s -s
push|y ˈpʊʃ|.i -ier -i.əʳ ⓤⓢ -i.ɚ -iest -i.ɪst, -i.əst -iness -ɪ.nəs, -ɪ.nɪs
pusillanimity ˌpjuː.sɪ.ləˈnɪm.ə.ti, -zɪ-, -lænˈɪm-, -ɪ.ti ⓤⓢ -sɪ.ləˈnɪm.ə.t̬i
pusillanimous ˌpjuː.sɪˈlæn.ɪ.məs, -zɪˈ-, ˈ-ə- ⓤⓢ -sɪˈlæn.ə- -ly -li -ness -nəs, -nɪs
puss pʊs -es -ɪz
puss|y ˈpʊs|.i -ies -iz ˌpussy ˈwillow
pussycat ˈpʊs.i.kæt -s -s
pussy|foot ˈpʊs.i|.fʊt -foots -fʊts -footing -ˌfʊt.ɪŋ ⓤⓢ -ˌfʊt̬.ɪŋ -footed -ˌfʊt.ɪd ⓤⓢ -ˌfʊt̬.ɪd -footer/s -ˌfʊt.əʳ/z ⓤⓢ -ˌfʊt̬.ɚ/z
pustular ˈpʌs.tjə.ləʳ, -tjʊ- ⓤⓢ -tʃə.lɚ, -tjə-, -tjʊ-
pustu|late ˈpʌs.tjə|.leɪt, -tjʊ- ⓤⓢ -tjuː-, -tjə-, -tʃə- -lated -leɪ.tɪd ⓤⓢ -leɪ.t̬ɪd
pustulation ˌpʌs.tjəˈleɪ.ʃən, -tjʊˈ- ⓤⓢ -tʃəˈ-, -tjəˈ-, -tjʊˈ- -s -z
pustule ˈpʌs.tjuːl ⓤⓢ -tʃuːl, -tjuːl -s -z
pustulous ˈpʌs.tjə.ləs, -tjʊ- ⓤⓢ -tʃə-, -tjə-, -tjʊ-
put pʊt -s -s -ting -ɪŋ ⓤⓢ ˈpʊt̬.ɪŋ
putative ˈpjuː.tə.tɪv ⓤⓢ -t̬ə.t̬ɪv -ly -li
put-down ˈpʊt.daʊn -s -z
Putin ˈpuː.tɪn, ˈpjuː- ⓤⓢ ˈpuː.tɪn, ˈpuːt.n̩
Putnam ˈpʌt.nəm
Putney ˈpʌt.ni
put-on ˈpʊt.ɒn ⓤⓢ -ɑːn -s -z
putrefaction ˌpjuː.trɪˈfæk.ʃən, -trəˈ- ⓤⓢ -trəˈ-
putre|fy ˈpjuː.trɪ|.faɪ, -trə- ⓤⓢ -trə- -fies -faɪz -fying -faɪ.ɪŋ -fied -faɪd
putrescenc|e pjuːˈtres.ən|ts -t -t
putrid ˈpjuː.trɪd -ly -li -ness -nəs, -nɪs
putridity pjuːˈtrɪd.ə.ti, -ɪ.ti ⓤⓢ -ə.t̬i
putsch pʊtʃ -es -ɪz
putt (P) pʌt -s -s -ing -ɪŋ ⓤⓢ ˈpʌt̬.ɪŋ -ed -ɪd ⓤⓢ ˈpʌt̬.ɪd -er/s -əʳ/z ⓤⓢ ˈpʌt̬.ɚ/z ˈputting ˌgreen
puttee ˈpʌt.i, -iː-; pʌtˈiː ⓤⓢ pʌtˈiː, ˈ-- -s -z
Puttenham ˈpʌt.ən.əm
putter *(from* **putt***)* ˈpʌt.əʳ ⓤⓢ ˈpʌt̬.ɚ -s -z -ing -ed
putter *(from* **put***)* ˈpʊt.əʳ ⓤⓢ ˈpʊt̬.ɚ -s -z
putti *(plur. of* **putto***)* ˈpʊt.i, -iː ⓤⓢ ˈpuː.ti, -tiː
Puttick ˈpʌt.ɪk ⓤⓢ ˈpʌt̬-
Puttnam ˈpʌt.nəm
putt|o ˈpʊt|.əʊ ⓤⓢ ˈpuː.t|oʊ -i -i, -iː
putt|y ˈpʌt|.i ⓤⓢ ˈpʌt̬- -ies -iz -ying -i.ɪŋ -ied -id
putz pʌts -es -ɪz
puzzl|e ˈpʌz.l̩ -es -z -ing/ly -ɪŋ/li, ˈ-lɪŋ/li -ed -d
puzzlement ˈpʌz.l̩.mənt

puzzler ˈpʌz.ləʳ, -l̩.əʳ ⓊⓈ ˈ-lɚ, -l̩.ɚ **-s** -z
PVC ˌpiː.viːˈsiː
Pwllheli pʊθˈlel.i *as if Welsh:* pʊˈɬel.i
PWR ˌpiːˌdʌb.l̩.juˈɑːʳ ⓊⓈ -ˈɑːr
pya pjɑː, piˈɑː ⓊⓈ pjɑː **-s** -z
pyaemia paɪˈiː.mi.ə
Pybus ˈpaɪ.bəs
Pye paɪ
pygmaean pɪgˈmiː.ən
Pygmalion pɪgˈmeɪ.li.ən ⓊⓈ -ˈmeɪl.jən, -ˈmeɪ.li.ən
pygm|y ˈpɪg.m|i **-ies** -iz
pyjama pɪˈdʒɑː.mə, pə- ⓊⓈ pəˈdʒɑː-, -ˈdʒæm.ə **-s** -z
Pyke paɪk
Pylades ˈpɪl.ə.diːz, ˈpaɪ.lə-
Pyle paɪl
pylon ˈpaɪ.lɒn, -lən ⓊⓈ -lɑːn, -lən **-s** -z
pylor|us paɪˈlɔː.r|əs ⓊⓈ -ˈlɔːr|.əs, pɪ- **-i** -aɪ **-ic** -ɪk
Pym pɪm
Pynchon ˈpɪn.*t*ʃən ⓊⓈ ˈpɪn.tʃən
Pyongyang ˌpjɒŋˈjæŋ ⓊⓈ ˌpjʌŋˈjɑːŋ, ˌpjɑːŋ-, -ˈjæŋ
pyorrhoea ˌpaɪəˈrɪə ⓊⓈ -ˈriː.ə
pyracantha ˌpaɪə.rəˈkæn*t*.θə ⓊⓈ ˌpaɪ-, ˌpɪr.əˈ- **-s** -z
pyramid ˈpɪr.ə.mɪd **-s** -z **ˈpyramid ˌselling, ˌpyramid ˈselling**
pyramidal pɪˈræm.ɪ.dəl, pə-, ˈ-ə- ⓊⓈ pɪˈræm.ɪ-, pə-, ˈ-ə-; ˌpɪr.əˈmɪd.əl **-ly** -i
Pyramus ˈpɪr.ə.məs
pyre paɪəʳ ⓊⓈ paɪɚ **-s** -z
Pyrene paɪəˈriː.ni ⓊⓈ paɪˈriːn
Pyren|ees ˌpɪr.əˈn|iːz, -ɪˈ- ⓊⓈ -əˈ- **-ean** -iː.ən
pyrethrin paɪəˈriː.θrɪn ⓊⓈ paɪ-, -ˈreθ.rɪn
pyrethrum paɪəˈriː.θrəm ⓊⓈ paɪ-, -ˈreθ.rəm **-s** -z
pyretic paɪəˈret.ɪk, pɪ- ⓊⓈ paɪˈret̬-
Pyrex® ˈpaɪə.reks ⓊⓈ ˈpaɪ-
pyriform ˈpɪr.ɪ.fɔːm ⓊⓈ -fɔːrm
pyrite ˈpaɪə.raɪt ⓊⓈ ˈpaɪ-
pyrites paɪəˈraɪ.tiːz, pɪ-, pə- ⓊⓈ paɪˈraɪ.tiːz, pɪ-; ˈpaɪ.raɪts
pyritic paɪəˈrɪt.ɪk ⓊⓈ paɪˈrɪt̬-
pyro- paɪə.rəʊ-; paɪəˈrɒ-; ⓊⓈ paɪ.roʊ-, -rə-; paɪˈrɑː-
Note: Prefix. Normally either takes primary or secondary stress on the first syllable, e.g. **pyromania** /ˌpaɪə.rəʊˈmeɪ.ni.ə ⓊⓈ ˌpaɪ.roʊˈ-/, or primary stress on the second syllable, e.g. **pyrolysis** /paɪəˈrɒl.ə.sɪs ⓊⓈ paɪˈrɑː.lə-/.
pyrocanthus ˌpaɪə.rəʊˈkæn.θəs ⓊⓈ ˌpaɪ.roʊ-
pyrogallic ˌpaɪə.rəʊˈgæl.ɪk ⓊⓈ ˌpaɪ.roʊˈ-, -ˈgɑː.lɪk
pyrolysis (P) paɪəˈrɒl.ə.sɪs, ˈ-ə- ⓊⓈ paɪˈrɑː.lə-
pyromani|a ˌpaɪə.rəʊˈmeɪ.ni|.ə ⓊⓈ ˌpaɪ.roʊˈ-, ˈ-nj|ə **-ac** -æk
pyromet|er paɪəˈrɒm.ɪ.t|əʳ, ˈ-ə- ⓊⓈ paɪˈrɑː.mə.t̬|ɚ **-ers** -əz ⓊⓈ -ɚz **-ry** -ri
pyrometric ˌpaɪə.rəʊˈmet.rɪk ⓊⓈ ˌpaɪ.roʊˈ-, -rəˈ- **-ally** -əl.i, -li *stress shift:* ˌpyrometric ˈmeasurement
pyrotechnic ˌpaɪə.rəʊˈtek.nɪk ⓊⓈ ˌpaɪ.roʊˈ-, -rəˈ- **-al** -əl **-ally** -əl.i, -li **-s** -s *stress shift:* ˌpyrotechnic ˈsubstance
Pyrrh|a ˈpɪr|.ə **-us** -əs
pyrrhic (P) ˈpɪr.ɪk **-s** -s **ˌPyrrhic ˈvictory**
Pytchley ˈpaɪtʃ.li
Pythagoras paɪˈθæg.ər.əs, -ɒr-, -æs ⓊⓈ pɪˈθæg.ɚ.əs **Pyˌthagorasˈ ˈtheorem**
Pythagorean paɪˌθæg.ərˈiː.ən, ˌpaɪ.θæg-, -ɒrˈ- ⓊⓈ pɪˌθæg.əˈriː- **-s** -z
Pythian ˈpɪθ.i.ən
Pythias ˈpɪθ.i.æs ⓊⓈ -əs
python ˈpaɪ.θən ⓊⓈ -θɑːn, -θən **-s** -z
Pythonesque ˌpaɪ.θənˈesk
pythoness ˈpaɪ.θən.es, -ɪs ⓊⓈ ˈpaɪ-, ˈpɪθ.ən-, -ɪs **-es** -ɪz
pythonic paɪˈθɒn.ɪk ⓊⓈ -ˈθɑː.nɪk, pɪ-
pyx pɪks **-es** -ɪz

Pronouncing the letter Q

In general, the consonant letter **q** is followed by **u** and pronounced /kw/ or /k/, e.g.:

queen	/kwiːn/	
antiquated	/ˈæn.tɪ.kweɪ.tɪd/	US /ˈæn.t̬ə.kweɪ.t̬ɪd/
quay	/kiː/	
antique	/ænˈtiːk/	

In words borrowed from Arabic, **q** is not always followed by **u**, e.g.:

Qatar	/ˈkʌt.ɑːʳ ,kəˈtɑːʳ/	US /ˈkɑː.tɑːr, kəˈtɑːr/

q (Q) kjuː **-'s** -z
Qaddafi, Qadhafi gəˈdɑː.fi, -ˈdæf.i US kəˈdɑː-
Qantas® ˈkwɒn.təs, -tæs US ˈkwɑːn.təs
Qatar ˈkʌt.ɑːʳ, ˈkæt-, ˈgæt-; kəˈtɑːʳ, gætˈɑːʳ, kæt- US ˈkɑː.tɑːr; kəˈtɑːr
QC ˌkjuːˈsiː **-'s** -z
q.e.d., QED ˌkjuː.iːˈdiː
qintar kɪnˈtɑːʳ, ˈ-- US kɪnˈtɑːr **-s** -z
qt ˌkjuːˈtiː
Q-Tip® ˈkjuː.tɪp **-s** -s
qua kweɪ, kwɑː
quack kwæk **-s** -s **-ing** -ɪŋ **-ed** -t **-ery** -ᵊr.i **-ish** -ɪʃ
quad kwɒd US kwɑːd **-s** -z
Quadragesim|a ˌkwɒd.rəˈdʒes.ɪ.m|ə, ˈ-ə- US ˌkwɑː.drəˈ-, -ˈdʒeɪ.zɪ- **-al** -ᵊl
quadrangle ˈkwɒd.ræŋ.gl̩, kwɒdˈræŋ- US ˈkwɑː.dræŋ- **-s** -z
quadrangular kwɒdˈræŋ.gjə.ləʳ, kwəˈdræŋ-, -gjʊ- US kwɑːˈdræŋ.gjə.lɚ, -gjʊ-
quadrant ˈkwɒd.rᵊnt US ˈkwɑː.drᵊnt **-s** -s
quadraphonic ˌkwɒd.rəˈfɒn.ɪk US ˌkwɑː.drəˈfɑː.nɪk **-ally** -ᵊl.i, -li **-s** -s *stress shift:* ˌquadraphonic ˈsound
quadraphony kwɒdˈrɒf.ᵊn.i, kwəˈdrɒf-, -ˈdræf-; ˈkwɒd.rə.fɒn- US kwɑːˈdræf.ᵊn-
quadrate (*n. adj.*) ˈkwɒd.rət, -rɪt, -reɪt US ˈkwɑː.drɪt, -dreɪt **-s** -s
quadra|te (*v.*) kwɒdˈreɪ|t, kwəˈdreɪ|t US kwɑːˈdreɪ|t **-tes** -ts **-ting** -tɪŋ US -t̬ɪŋ **-ted** -tɪd US -t̬ɪd
quadratic kwɒdˈræt.ɪk, kwəˈdræt- US kwɑːˈdræt̬- **-s** -s **quadˌratic eˈquation**
quadrature ˈkwɒd.rə.tʃəʳ, -rɪ-, -tjʊəʳ US ˈkwɑː.drə.tʃɚ
quadric ˈkwɒd.rɪk US ˈkwɑː.drɪk **-s** -s
quadri|ga kwɒdˈriː|.gə, kwəˈdriː-, -ˈdraɪ- US kwɑːˈdraɪ- **-gae** -dʒiː US -giː, -dʒiː **-gas** -gəz
quadrilateral ˌkwɒd.rɪˈlæt.ᵊr.ᵊl, -rəˈ-, ˈ-rᵊl US ˌkwɑː.drɪˈlæt̬- **-s** -z *stress shift:* ˌquadrilateral ˈshape
quadrilingual ˌkwɒd.rɪˈlɪŋ.gwəl, -rəˈ- US ˌkwɑː.drɪˈ- *stress shift:* ˌquadrilingual ˈnation
quadrille kwəˈdrɪl, kwɒdˈrɪl US kwəˈdrɪl, kwɑː- **-s** -z
quadrillion kwɒdˈrɪl.jən, kwəˈdrɪl-, ˈ-i.ən US kwɑːˈdrɪl.jən **-s** -z
quadriplegia ˌkwɒd.rɪˈpliː.dʒə, -rəˈ-, ˈ-dʒi.ə US ˌkwɑː.drɪˈpliː-
quadriplegic ˌkwɒd.rɪˈpliː.dʒɪk, -rəˈ- US ˌkwɑː.drɪˈ- **-s** -s *stress shift:* ˌquadriplegic ˈstate
quadrisyllabic ˌkwɒd.rɪ.sɪˈlæb.ɪk, -rə-, -səˈ- US ˌkwɑː.drɪ- *stress shift:* ˌquadrisyllabic ˈword
quadrisyllable ˌkwɒd.rɪˈsɪl.ə.bl̩ US ˈkwɑː.drɪˌsɪl- **-s** -z
quadroon kwɒdˈruːn, kwəˈdruːn US kwɑːˈdruːn **-s** -z
quadrophonic ˌkwɒd.rəˈfɒn.ɪk US ˌkwɑː.drəˈfɑː.nɪk **-ally** -ᵊl.i, -li **-s** -s *stress shift:* ˌquadrophonic ˈsound
quadrophony kwɒdˈrɒf.ᵊn.i, kwəˈdrɒf-; ˈkwɒd.rə.fɒn- US kwɑːˈdræf.ᵊn-
quadrumana kwɒdˈruː.mə.nə, kwəˈdruː- US kwɑːˈdruː-
quadrumanous kwɒdˈruː.mə.nəs, kwəˈdruː- US kwɑːˈdruː-
quadruped ˈkwɒd.rə.ped, -rʊ- US ˈkwɑː.drʊ-, -drə- **-s** -z
quadrupl|e ˈkwɒd.rʊp.l̩, -ruː.pl̩; kwɒdˈruː.pl̩, kwəˈdruː- US kwɑːˈdruː.pl̩, kwə-, -ˈdrʊp.l̩; ˈkwɑː.druː.pl̩, -drʊ-, -drə- **-es** -z **-y** -i **-ing** -ɪŋ **-ed** -d
quadruplet kwɒdˈrʊ.plət, -plɪt, -plet; ˈkwɒd.ruː- US kwɑːˈdruː.plɪt; ˈkwɑː.druː-, -drə-; kwɑːˈdrʌp.lɪt **-s** -s
quadruplicate (*n. adj.*) kwɒdˈruː.plɪ.kət, kwəˈdruː-, -plə-, -kɪt, -keɪt US kwɑːˈdruː.plɪ.kɪt, -keɪt **-s** -s
quadrupli|cate (*v.*) kwɒdˈruː.plɪ|.keɪt, kwəˈdruː- US kwɑːˈdruː- **-cates** -keɪts **-cating** -keɪ.tɪŋ US -keɪ.t̬ɪŋ **-cated** -keɪ.tɪd US -keɪ.t̬ɪd
quaestor ˈkwiː.stəʳ, ˈkwaɪ-, -stɔːʳ US ˈkwes.tɚ, ˈkwiː.stɚ **-s** -z
quaff kwɒf, kwɑːf US kwɑːf, kwæf, kwɔːf **-s** -s **-ing** -ɪŋ **-ed** -t **-er/s** -əʳ/z US -ɚ/z
quag kwɒg, kwæg US kwæg, kwɑːg **-s** -z
quagga ˈkwæg.ə, ˈkwɒg- US ˈkwæg-, ˈkwɑː.gə **-s** -z
Quaglino's® kwægˈliː.nəʊz US -noʊz
quagmire ˈkwɒg.maɪəʳ, ˈkwæg- US ˈkwæg.maɪɚ, ˈkwɑːg- **-s** -z
quail (Q) kweɪl **-s** -z **-ing** -ɪŋ **-ed** -d
Quain kweɪn
quaint kweɪnt **-er** -əʳ US ˈkweɪn.t̬ɚ **-est** -ɪst, -əst US ˈkweɪn.t̬ɪst, -t̬əst **-ly** -li **-ness** -nəs, -nɪs
quak|e kweɪk **-es** -s **-ing** -ɪŋ **-ed** -t
Quaker ˈkweɪ.kəʳ US -kɚ **-s** -z
qualification ˌkwɒl.ɪ.fɪˈkeɪ.ʃᵊn, ˌ-ə- US ˌkwɑː.lɪ- **-s** -z
qualificative ˈkwɒl.ɪ.fɪ.kə.tɪv, ˈ-ə- US ˈkwɑː.lɪ.fɪ.keɪ.t̬ɪv **-s** -z
qualificatory ˌkwɒl.ɪ.fɪˈkeɪ.tᵊr.i, ˌ-ə- US ˈkwɑː.lɪ.fə.kə.tɔːr-
quali|fy ˈkwɒl.ɪ|.faɪ, ˈ-ə- US ˈkwɑː.lɪ- **-fies** -faɪz **-fying** -faɪ.ɪŋ **-fied** -faɪd **-fier/s** -faɪ.əʳ/z US -faɪ.ɚ/z
qualitative ˈkwɒl.ɪ.tə.tɪv, -teɪ- US ˈkwɑː.lɪ.teɪ.t̬ɪv **-ly** -li
qualit|y ˈkwɒl.ə.t|i, -ɪ.t|i US ˈkwɑː.lə.t̬|i **-ies** -iz **ˈquality conˌtrol; ˈquality ˌtime**
qualm kwɑːm, kwɔːm US kwɑːm **-s** -z
qualmish ˈkwɑː.mɪʃ, ˈkwɔː- US ˈkwɑː- **-ly** -li **-ness** -nəs, -nɪs
quandar|y (Q) ˈkwɒn.dᵊr|.i, -dr|i US ˈkwɑːn- **-ies** -iz
quango ˈkwæŋ.gəʊ US -goʊ **-s** -z
Quant kwɒnt US kwɑːnt
quanta (*plur. of* **quantum**) ˈkwɒn.tə US ˈkwɑːn.t̬ə
quantal ˈkwɒn.tᵊl US ˈkwɑːn.t̬ᵊl
quantic ˈkwɒn.tɪk US ˈkwɑːn.t̬ɪk **-s** -s
quantifiable ˈkwɒn.tɪ.faɪ.ə.bl̩, -tə-, ˌkwɒn.tɪˈfaɪ-, -təˈ- US ˈkwɑːn.t̬ə.faɪ-
quantification ˌkwɒn.tɪ.fɪˈkeɪ.ʃᵊn, -tə- US ˌkwɑːn.t̬ə-
quanti|fy ˈkwɒn.tɪ|.faɪ, -tə- US ˈkwɑːn.t̬ə- **-fies** -faɪz **-fying**

-faɪ.ɪŋ **-fied** -faɪd **-fier/s** -faɪ.əʳ/z
(US) -faɪ.ɚ/z
quantitative ˈkwɒn.tɪ.tə.tɪv, -teɪ-
(US) ˈkwɑːn.t̬ə.teɪ.t̬ɪv **-ly** -li
quantit|y ˈkwɒn.tə.t|i, -tɪ-
(US) ˈkwɑːn.t̬ə.t̬|i **-ies** -iz ˌ**quantity sur'veyor, 'quantity surˌveyor**
quantiz|e, -is|e ˈkwɒn.taɪz (US) ˈkwɑːn- **-es** -ɪz **-ing** -ɪŋ **-ed** -d
Quantock ˈkwɒn.tək, -tɒk
(US) ˈkwɑːn.t̬ək, -tɑːk
quant|um *amount:* ˈkwɒn.t|əm
(US) ˈkwɑːn.t̬|əm **-a** -ə ˌ**quantum 'jump;** ˌ**quantum 'leap;** ˌ**quantum me'chanics; 'quantum ˌtheory**
quantum *in Latin phrases:* ˈkwæn.tʊm, ˈkwɒn-, -təm (US) ˈkwɑːn.t̬əm, -tʊm
quantum meruit ˌkwæn.tʊmˈmer.u.ɪt, ˌkwɒn-, -təmˈ- (US) ˌkwɑːn.tʊmˈ-, -t̬əmˈ-
quarantin|e ˈkwɒr.ən.tiːn, -taɪn
(US) ˈkwɔːr.ən.tiːn, ˈkwɑːr- **-es** -z **-ing** -ɪŋ **-ed** -d
quare clausim fregit
ˌkwɑː.reɪˌklaʊ.səmˈfreɪ.gɪt
(US) ˌkwɑːr.iˌklaʊ.səmˈfreɪ.gət, -gɪt
Quaritch ˈkwɒr.ɪtʃ (US) ˈkwɑːr-
quark *in physics:* kwɑːk, kwɔːk
(US) kwɑːrk, kwɔːrk **-s** -s
quark *soft cheese:* kwɑːk (US) kwɑːrk, kwɔːrk
Quarles kwɔːlz (US) kwɔːrlz, kwɑːrlz
Quarmby ˈkwɔːm.bi (US) ˈkwɔːrm-
quarrel ˈkwɒr.əl (US) ˈkwɔːr-, ˈkwɑːr- **-s** -z **-(l)ing** -ɪŋ **-(l)ed** -d **-(l)er/s** -əʳ/z (US) -ɚ/z
quarrelsome ˈkwɒr.əl.səm (US) ˈkwɔːr-, ˈkwɑːr- **-ly** -li **-ness** -nəs, -nɪs
quarr|y ˈkwɒr|.i (US) ˈkwɔːr-, ˈkwɑːr- **-ies** -iz **-ying** -i.ɪŋ **-ied** -id **'quarry ˌtile,** ˌ**quarry 'tile**
quarry|man ˈkwɒr.i|.mən, -mæn
(US) ˈkwɔːr-, ˈkwɑːr- **-men** -mən, -men
quart *measurement:* kwɔːt, kɔː-
(US) kwɔːrt **-s** -s
quart *in card games, fencing:* kɑːt
(US) kɑːrt **-s** -s **-ing** -ɪŋ (US) ˈkɑːr.t̬ɪŋ **-ed** -ɪd (US) ˈkɑːr.t̬ɪd
quartan ˈkwɔː.tən (US) ˈkwɔːr-
quarte (*n. v.*) *in card games, fencing:* kɑːt (US) kɑːrt **-s** -s **-ing** -ɪŋ
(US) ˈkɑːr.t̬ɪŋ **-ed** -ɪd (US) ˈkɑːr.t̬ɪd
quart|er ˈkwɔː.t|əʳ, kɔː- (US) ˈkwɔːr.t̬|ɚ **-ers** -əz (US) -ɚz **-ering/s** -ər.ɪŋ/z **-ered** -əd (US) -ɚd **-erage** -ər.ɪdʒ **'quarter ˌday; 'quarter ˌnote; 'Quarter ˌSessions; 'quarter ˌtone**
quarterback ˈkwɔː.tə.bæk
(US) ˈkwɔːr.t̬ɚ- **-s** -s
quarterdeck ˈkwɔː.tə.dek
(US) ˈkwɔːr.t̬ɚ- **-s** -s
quarterfinal ˌkwɔː.təˈfaɪ.nəl
(US) ˌkwɔːr.t̬ɚˈ- **-s** -z
quarterfinalist ˌkwɔː.təˈfaɪ.nəl.ɪst
(US) ˌkwɔːr.t̬ɚˈ- **-s** -s
quarterl|y ˈkwɔː.təl|.i (US) ˈkwɔːr.t̬ɚ.l|i **-ies** -iz
Quartermain(e) ˈkwɔː.tə.meɪn
(US) ˈkwɔːr.t̬ɚ-
quartermaster ˈkwɔː.təˌmɑː.stəʳ
(US) ˈkwɔːr.t̬ɚˌmæs.tɚ **-s** -z
quartern ˈkwɔː.tən (US) ˈkwɔːr.t̬ɚn **-s** -z
quarter|staff ˈkwɔː.tə|.stɑːf
(US) ˈkwɔːr.t̬ɚ|.stæf **-aves** -steɪvz
quartet(te) kwɔːˈtet (US) kwɔːr- **-s** -s
quartic ˈkwɔː.tɪk (US) ˈkwɔːr.t̬ɪk **-s** -s
quartile ˈkwɔː.taɪl (US) ˈkwɔːr-, -t̬ɪl, -t̬əl **-s** -z
quarto ˈkwɔː.təʊ (US) ˈkwɔːr.t̬oʊ **-s** -z
quartus **(Q)** ˈkwɔː.təs (US) ˈkwɔːr.t̬əs
quartz ˈkwɔːts (US) ˈkwɔːrts
quasar ˈkweɪ.zɑːʳ, -sɑːʳ (US) -zɑːr, -sɑːr **-s** -z
quash kwɒʃ (US) kwɑːʃ, kwɔːʃ **-es** -ɪz **-ing** -ɪŋ **-ed** -t
quasi- kweɪ.zaɪ-, kwɑː-, -saɪ-, -zi-
(US) kweɪ.saɪ-, -zaɪ-; kwɑː.zi-, -si-
Note: Prefix. Words beginning with **quasi-** are normally hyphenated, with **quasi-** taking secondary stress on the first syllable, e.g. **quasi-stellar** /ˌkweɪ.zaɪˈstel.əʳ (US) -saɪˈstel.ɚ/.
quasi ˈkweɪ.zaɪ, ˈkwɑː-, -saɪ, -zi
(US) ˈkweɪ.saɪ, -zaɪ; ˈkwɑː.zi, -si
quasi in rem ˌkweɪ.zi.ɪnˈrem
(US) ˌkwɑː-, -ənˈ-
Quasimodo ˌkwɑː.ziˈməʊ.dəʊ, ˌkwɒz.iˈ-, ˌkwæz-
(US) ˌkwɑː.ziˈmoʊ.doʊ
quassia ˈkwɒʃ.ə, -i.ə (US) ˈkwɑː.ʃə, ˈ-ʃi.ə
quatercentenar|y
ˌkwæt.ə.senˈtiː.nər|.i, ˌkwɔː.tə-, ˌkwɒt.ə-, ˌkweɪ.tə-, -ˈten.ər-
(US) ˌkwɑː.t̬ɚ.senˈten.ɚ|.i; -ˈsen.tən.er- **-ies** -iz
Quatermain ˈkwɔː.tə.meɪn
(US) ˈkwɑː.t̬ɚ-
quaternar|y **(Q)** kwəˈtɜː.nər|.i, kwɒtˈɜː- (US) ˈkwɑː.t̬ɚ.ner-; kwəˈtɝː.nɚ- **-ies** -iz
quaternion kwəˈtɜː.ni.ən, kwɒtˈɜː-
(US) kwəˈtɝː-, kwɑː- **-s** -z
quatorzain kəˈtɔː.zeɪn, kætˈɔː-; ˈkæt.ə- (US) kəˈtɔːr-, kætˈɔːr-; ˈkæt̬.ɚ- **-s** -z
quatrain ˈkwɒt.reɪn, -rən
(US) ˈkwɑː.treɪn, -ˈ- **-s** -z
quatrefoil ˈkæt.rə.fɔɪl, ˈ-ə-
(US) ˈkæt̬.ɚ.fɔɪl, -rə- **-s** -z
quatrillion kwɒtˈrɪl.jən, kwəˈtrɪl-, ˈ-i.ən (US) kwɑːˈtrɪl-, kwə- **-s** -z
quattrocento **(Q)** ˌkwæt.rəʊˈtʃen.təʊ, ˌkwɒt- (US) ˌkwɑː.troʊˈtʃen.toʊ
quav|er ˈkweɪ.v|əʳ (US) -v|ɚ **-ers** -əz
(US) -ɚz **-ering/ly** -ər.ɪŋ/li **-ered** -əd
(US) -ɚd
quay kiː (US) kiː, keɪ, kweɪ **-s** -z **-age** -ɪdʒ
Quay *place name:* kiː *surname:* kweɪ
Quayle kweɪl
quayside ˈkiː.saɪd
quean kwiːn **-s** -z
queas|y ˈkwiː.z|i **-ier** **-iest** **-ily** -ɪ.li **-iness** -ɪ.nəs, -ɪ.nɪs
Quebec kwɪˈbek, kwə-, kɪ-, kə- *as if French:* kebˈek (US) kwiːˈbek, kwɪ-, kɪ- *as if French:* kebˈek
Quebecois, Québecois ˌkeɪ.bekˈwɑː, ˌkeb.ekˈ-, -ɪˈkwɑː, -əˈ-
(US) ˌkeɪ.bekˈwɑː
Quechu|a ˈketʃ.u|.ə, -w|ə (US) -w|ɑː, -w|ə **-an/s** -ən/z
queen kwiːn **-s** -z **-ing** -ɪŋ **-ed** -d ˌ**Queen's 'Counsel;** ˌ**Queen's 'English;** ˌ**queen's 'evidence;** ˌ**Queen 'Mother**
Queenborough ˈkwiːn.bər.ə, ˈkwiːm-
(US) ˈkwiːn.bɚ.oʊ
Queenie ˈkwiː.ni
queenlike ˈkwiːn.laɪk
queenl|y ˈkwiːn.l|i **-ier** -i.əʳ (US) -i.ɚ **-iest** -i.ɪst, -i.əst **-iness** -ɪ.nəs, -ɪ.nɪs
Queens kwiːnz
Queensberry ˈkwiːnz.bər.i (US) -ˌber.i, -bɚ- ˌ**Queensberry 'rules**
Queensbury ˈkwiːnz.bər.i
Queensferry ˈkwiːnzˌfer.i
Queensland ˈkwiːnz.lənd, -lænd
Queenstown ˈkwiːnz.taʊn
Queensway ˈkwiːnz.weɪ
queer kwɪəʳ (US) kwɪr **-s** -z **-ing** -ɪŋ **-ed** -d **-er** -əʳ (US) -ɚ **-est** -ɪst (US) -əst **-ly** -li **-ness** -nəs, -nɪs **-ish** -ɪʃ **'queer ˌstreet**
quell kwel **-s** -z **-ing** -ɪŋ **-ed** -d
quench kwentʃ **-es** -ɪz **-ing** -ɪŋ **-ed** -t **-er/s** -əʳ/z (US) -ɚ/z **-able** -ə.bl̩
quenelle kəˈnel, kɪ- (US) kə- **-s** -z
Quen(n)ell kwɪˈnel, kwə-, ˈkwen.əl
(US) kwəˈnel, ˈkwen.əl
Quentin ˈkwen.tɪn (US) -tən
Querétaro kəˈreɪ.tər.əʊ (US) -ˈret.ə.roʊ; kɚ.əˈtɑːr.oʊ
quern kwɜːn (US) kwɝːn **-s** -z
querulous ˈkwer.ʊ.ləs, -jʊ-, ˈ-ə-
(US) ˈkwer.jə.ləs, -jʊ-, ˈ-ə-, ˈ-ʊ- **-ly** -li **-ness** -nəs, -nɪs
quer|y ˈkwɪə.r|i (US) ˈkwɪr|.i **-ies** -iz **-ying** -i.ɪŋ **-ied** -id
quesadilla ˌkeɪ.səˈdiː.jə, -ljə (US) -jə **-s** -z
Quesnel ˈkeɪ.nəl
quest kwest **-s** -s **-ing** -ɪŋ **-ed** -ɪd
Quested ˈkwes.tɪd
question ˈkwes.tʃən, ˈkweʃ-
(US) ˈkwes.tʃən, -tjən **-s** -z **-ing/ly** -ɪŋ/li **-ed** -d **-er/s** -əʳ/z (US) -ɚ/z **'question ˌmark; 'question ˌtime;** ˌ**out of the 'question**

questionab|le ˈkwes.tʃə.nə.b|l̩, ˈkweʃ- US ˈkwes.tʃə-, -tjə- **-ly** -li **-leness** -l̩.nəs, -nɪs
questionar|y ˈkwes.tʃə.nᵊr|.i, ˈkweʃ- US ˈkwes.tʃə.ner-, -tjə- **-ies** -iz
question-master ˈkwes.tʃənˌmɑː.stəʳ, ˈkweʃ-, -tʃəmˌ- US ˈkwes.tʃənˌmæs.tɚ, -tjənˌ- **-s** -z
questionnaire ˌkwes.tʃəˈneəʳ, ˌkweʃ-, ˌkes-, ˈ---- US ˌkwes.tʃəˈner, -tjəˈ- **-s** -z
Quetta ˈkwet.ə US ˈkwet̬-
quetzal ˈkwet.sᵊl US ketˈsɑːl **-s** -z **quetzales** kwetˈsɑː.les US ket-
Quetzalcoatl ˌket.sᵊl.kəʊˈæt.ᵊl US -sɑːl.koʊˈɑː.t̬ᵊl
queue kjuː **-s** -z **-ing** -ɪŋ **-d** -d
queue-jump ˈkjuː.dʒʌmp **-s** -s **-ing** -ɪŋ **-ed** -t **-er/s** -əʳ/z US -ɚ/z
Quex kweks
Quezon City ˌkeɪ.zɒnˈsɪt.i, -sɒnˈ- US ˌkeɪ.sɑːnˈsɪt̬-
quibbl|e ˈkwɪb.l̩ **-es** -z **-ing** -ɪŋ, ˈkwɪb.lɪŋ **-ed** -d **-er/s** -əʳ/z, ˈkwɪb.ləʳ/z US ˈkwɪb.l̩.ɚ/z, ˈ-lɚ/z
Quibell ˈkwaɪ.bᵊl, ˈkwɪb.ᵊl; kwɪˈbel, kwaɪˈbel
Note: Baron Quibell of Scunthorpe pronounced /ˈkwaɪ.bᵊl/.
quich|e kiːʃ **-es** -ɪz
quick (Q) kwɪk **-er** -əʳ US -ɚ **-est** -ɪst, -əst **-ly** -li **-ness** -nəs, -nɪs ˌ**quick** ˈ**march**; ˈ**quick** ˌ**time**
quick-change ˌkwɪkˈtʃeɪndʒ *stress shift:* ˌquick-change ˈtyres
Quicke kwɪk
quicken ˈkwɪk.ᵊn **-s** -z **-ing** -ɪŋ **-ed** -d
quickfire ˈkwɪk.faɪəʳ US -faɪɚ
quick-freez|e ˌkwɪkˈfriːz, ˈ-- US ˈkwɪk.friːz **-es** -ɪz **-ing** -ɪŋ **quick-froze** ˌkwɪkˈfrəʊz, ˈ-- US ˈkwɪk.froʊz **quick frozen** -ən **quick-freezer/s** ˌkwɪkˈfriː.zəʳ/z, ˈ-ˌ-- US ˈkwɪkˌfriː.zɚ/z
quickie ˈkwɪk.i **-s** -z
quicklime ˈkwɪk.laɪm
Quickly ˈkwɪk.li
quicksand ˈkwɪk.sænd **-s** -z
quickset ˈkwɪk.set
quicksilver ˈkwɪkˌsɪl.vəʳ US -vɚ
quickstep ˈkwɪk.step **-s** -s
quick-tempered ˌkwɪkˈtem.pəd US -pɚd, ˈ-ˌ-- *stress shift, British only:* ˌquick-tempered ˈperson
quick-witted ˌkwɪkˈwɪt.ɪd US -ˈwɪt̬-, ˈ-ˌ-- **-ly** -li **-ness** -nəs, -nɪs *stress shift, British only:* ˌquick-witted ˈperson
quid kwɪd **-s** -z
quidditch ˈkwɪd.ɪtʃ
quiddit|y ˈkwɪd.ɪ.t|i, -ə.t|i US -ə.t̬|i **-ies** -iz
quid pro quo ˌkwɪd.prəʊˈkwəʊ US -proʊˈkwoʊ **-s** -z
quiescence kwiˈes.ᵊnts US kwaɪ-, kwi-
quiescent kwiˈes.ᵊnt US kwaɪ-, kwi- **-ly** -li
quiet kwaɪət **-er** -əʳ US ˈkwaɪə.t̬ɚ **-est** -ɪst, -əst US ˈkwaɪə.t̬ɪst, -əst **-ly** -li **-ness** -nəs, -nɪs **-s** -s **-ing** -ɪŋ US ˈkwaɪə.t̬ɪŋ **-ed** -ɪd US ˈkwaɪə.t̬ɪd
quieten ˈkwaɪə.tᵊn **-s** -z **-ing** -ɪŋ **-ed** -d
quiet|ism ˈkwaɪə.t|ɪ.zᵊm, ˈkwaɪ.ɪ- US ˈkwaɪə.t|ɪ- **-ist/s** -ɪst/s
quietude ˈkwaɪə.tjuːd, ˈkwaɪ.ɪ- US ˈkwaɪə.tuːd, -tjuːd
quietus kwaɪˈiː.təs, -ˈeɪ- US -ˈiː.t̬əs
quiff kwɪf **-s** -s
Quigg kwɪg
Quiggin ˈkwɪg.ɪn
Quigley ˈkwɪg.li
quill kwɪl **-s** -z **-ing** -ɪŋ **-ed** -d
Quiller-Couch ˌkwɪl.əˈkuːtʃ US -ɚˈ-
Quilliam ˈkwɪl.i.əm
Quilp kwɪlp
quilt kwɪlt **-s** -s **-ing** -ɪŋ US ˈkwɪl.t̬ɪŋ **-ed** -ɪd US ˈkwɪl.t̬ɪd
Quilter ˈkwɪl.təʳ US -t̬ɚ
quin (Q) kwɪn **-s** -z
Quinault *North American people:* ˈkwɪn.ᵊlt, -ɔːlt US kwɪˈnɑːlt *French dramatist:* ˈkiː.nəʊ US kɪˈnoʊ
quinc|e (Q) kwɪn*t*s **-es** -ɪz
quincentenar|y ˌkwɪn.senˈtiː.nᵊr|.i, -ˈten.ᵊr-, -ˈtɪn- US kwɪnˈsen.tə.ner|.i; ˌkwɪn.senˈten.ɚ- **-ies** -iz
Quincey ˈkwɪn*t*.si
quincunx ˈkwɪn.kʌŋks, ˈkwɪŋ- US ˈkwɪn- **-es** -ɪz
Quincy ˈkwɪn*t*.si
quindecagon kwɪnˈdek.ə.gᵊn US -gɑːn **-s** -z
quinella kwɪˈnel.ə
quingentenar|y ˌkwɪn.dʒenˈtiː.nᵊr|.i, -ˈten.ᵊr-, -ˈtɪn- **-ies** -iz
quinine ˈkwɪn.iːn, -ˈ-; kwə- US ˈkwaɪ.naɪn
Quink® kwɪŋk
Quinn kwɪn
Quinney ˈkwɪn.i
quinquagenarian ˌkwɪŋ.kwə.dʒəˈneə.ri.ən, -kwɪ-, -dʒɪˈ- US ˌkwɪn.kwə.dʒəˈner.i-, ˌkwɪŋ- **-s** -z
Quinquagesima ˌkwɪŋ.kwəˈdʒes.ɪ.mə, -kwɪˈ-, ˈ-ə- US ˌkwɪn.kwəˈdʒeɪ.zɪ-, ˌkwɪŋ-, -ˈdʒes.ɪ-
quinquennial kwɪŋˈkwen.i.əl US kwɪn-, kwɪŋ-
quinquennium kwɪŋˈkwen.i.əm US kwɪn-, kwɪŋ- **-s** -z
quinsy ˈkwɪn.zi
quint *organ stop:* kwɪnt **-s** -s *in piquet:* kɪnt, kwɪnt *old fashioned:* kent **-s** -s *US for quintuplet:* kwɪnt **-s** -s
quintain ˈkwɪn.tɪn **-s** -z
quintal ˈkwɪn.tᵊl US -t̬ᵊl **-s** -z
Quintana Roo kɪn.tɑː.nəˈrəʊ.əʊ US -ˈroʊ.oʊ
quintessence kwɪnˈtes.ᵊnts
quintessential ˌkwɪn.tɪˈsen.*t*ʃᵊl, -təˈ- US -teˈsen*t*.ʃəl **-ly** -i
quintet, quintette kwɪnˈtet **-s** -s
quintic ˈkwɪn.tɪk US -t̬ɪk **-s** -s
Quintilian kwɪnˈtɪl.i.ən US ˈ-jən, -i.ən
quintillion kwɪnˈtɪl.jən, ˈ-i.ən US ˈ-jən **-s** -z
Quintin ˈkwɪn.tɪn US -tɪn, -tᵊn
Quinton ˈkwɪn.tən US -tᵊn
quintupl|e ˈkwɪn.tjʊ.pl̩, -tjuː-; kwɪnˈtjuː- US kwɪnˈtuː-, -ˈtjuː-; ˈkwɪn.t̬ə- **-es** -z **-ing** -ɪŋ **-ed** -d
quintuplet ˈkwɪn.tjʊ.plət, -plɪt, -plet; kwɪnˈtjuː- US kwɪnˈtʌp.lɪt, -ˈtuː.plɪt, -ˈtjuː-; ˈkwɪn.tə.plet **-s** -s
quintus (Q) ˈkwɪn.təs US -t̬əs
quip kwɪp **-s** -s **-ping** -ɪŋ **-ped** -t
quire kwaɪəʳ US kwaɪɚ **-s** -z
Quirey *in England, surname:* ˈkwaɪə.ri US ˈkwaɪ- *in Ireland:* ˈkwɪə.ri US ˈkwɪr.i
Quirinal ˈkwɪr.ɪ.nᵊl, -ᵊn.ᵊl US ˈkwɪr.ɪ.nᵊl; kwɪˈraɪ-
Quirinus kwɪˈraɪ.nəs
quirk (Q) kwɜːk US kwɝːk **-s** -s
quirk|y ˈkwɜː.k|i US ˈkwɝː- **-ier** -i.əʳ US -i.ɚ **-iest** -i.ɪst, -i.əst **-ily** -ɪ.li, -ᵊl.i **-iness** -ɪ.nəs, -ɪ.nɪs
quisling ˈkwɪz.lɪŋ **-s** -z
quit kwɪt **-s** -s **-ting** -ɪŋ US ˈkwɪt̬.ɪŋ **-ted** -ɪd US ˈkwɪt̬.ɪd
quitclaim ˈkwɪt.kleɪm **-s** -s
quite kwaɪt
Quito ˈkiː.təʊ US -t̬oʊ, -toʊ
quit-rent ˈkwɪt.rent **-s** -s
quits kwɪts
quittanc|e ˈkwɪt.ᵊn*t*s **-es** -ɪz
quitter ˈkwɪt.əʳ US ˈkwɪt̬.ɚ **-s** -z
quiv|er ˈkwɪv|.əʳ US -ɚ **-ers** -əz US -ɚz **-ering/ly** -ᵊr.ɪŋ/li **-ered** -əd US -ɚd
Quiverful ˈkwɪv.ə.fʊl US ˈ-ɚ-
qui vive ˌkiːˈviːv
Quixote ˈkwɪk.sət, -səʊt; kɪˈhəʊ.ti, -teɪ US kɪˈhoʊ.t̬i, -teɪ; ˈkwɪk.sət
quixotic kwɪkˈsɒt.ɪk US -ˈsɑː.t̬ɪk **-ally** -ᵊl.i, -li
quiz kwɪz **-zes** -ɪz **-zing** -ɪŋ **-zed** -d
quiz-master ˈkwɪzˌmɑː.stəʳ US -ˌmæs.tɚ **-s** -z
quizzic|al ˈkwɪz.ɪ.k|ᵊl **-ally** -ᵊl.i, -li
quod kwɒd US kwɑːd **-s** -z **-ding** -ɪŋ **-ded** -ɪd
quod erat demonstrandum ˌkwɒdˌer.ætˌdem.ənˈstræn.dəm US ˌkwɑːd-, -ˈstrɑːn-
quodlibet ˈkwɒd.lɪ.bet US ˈkwɑːd.lə- **-s** -s

quoin kɔɪn, kwɔɪn **-s** -z **-ing** -ɪŋ **-ed** -d
quoit kɔɪt, kwɔɪt **-s** -s
quokka 'kwɒk.ə ⓤⓢ 'kwɑː.kə **-s** -z
quondam 'kwɒn.dæm, -dəm ⓤⓢ 'kwɑːn.dəm, -dæm
Quonset® 'kwɒnt.sɪt, -sət, -set ⓤⓢ 'kwɑːnt- **'Quonset ˌhut**
quorate 'kwɔː.reɪt, -rət, -rɪt ⓤⓢ 'kwɔːr.ɪt, -eɪt
Quorn® kwɔːn ⓤⓢ kwɔːrn
quorum 'kwɔː.rəm ⓤⓢ 'kwɔːr.əm **-s** -z
quota 'kwəʊ.tə ⓤⓢ 'kwoʊ.t̬ə **-s** -z **-ing** -ɪŋ **-ed** -d
quotable 'kwəʊ.tə.bl̩ ⓤⓢ 'kwoʊ.t̬ə-
quotation kwəʊ'teɪ.ʃən ⓤⓢ kwoʊ- **-s** -z **quo'tation ˌmark**
quot|e kwəʊt ⓤⓢ kwoʊt **-es** -s **-ing** -ɪŋ ⓤⓢ 'kwoʊ.t̬ɪŋ **-ed** -ɪd ⓤⓢ 'kwoʊ.t̬ɪd
quoth kwəʊθ ⓤⓢ kwoʊθ **-a** -ə
quotidian kwəʊ'tɪd.i.ən, kwɒt'ɪd- ⓤⓢ kwoʊ'tɪd-
quotient 'kwəʊ.ʃənt ⓤⓢ 'kwoʊ- **-s** -s
quo warranto ˌkwəʊ.wɒr'æn.təʊ ⓤⓢ ˌkwoʊ.wə'ræn.toʊ, -'rɑːn-, -wɔː'-
Qur'an, Quran kɒr'ɑːn, kɔː'rɑːn, kʊ-, kə- ⓤⓢ kə'rɑːn, kɔː-, kʊ-, -'ræn
qursh 'kuː.əʃ; kʊəʃ ⓤⓢ 'kuː.ɚʃ; kʊrʃ
Quy kwaɪ
q.v. ˌkjuː'viː, ˌwɪtʃ'siː, ˌkwɒd'vɪd.eɪ ⓤⓢ ˌkjuː'viː, ˌwɪtʃ'siː, ˌkwɑːd'vɪd.eɪ
qwerty, QWERTY 'kwɜː.ti ⓤⓢ 'kwɝː.t̬i

Pronouncing the letter R

See also RRH

In British English, **r** is pronounced only where it appears before a vowel. In American English, **r** is pronounced in all positions, e.g.:

red	/red/	
bore	/bɔːʳ/	(US) /bɔːr/
boring	/ˈbɔː.rɪŋ/	/ˈbɔːr.ɪŋ/

See the discussion at LIAISON for comments concerning 'linking r' in British English.

In addition

In the word *iron*, **r** is not pronounced in British English but colours the vowel in the second syllable in US English, e.g.:

iron	/aɪən/	(US) /ˈaɪ.ɚn, aɪrn/

r (R) ɑːʳ (US) ɑːr **-'s** -z
Ra rɑː
Rabat rəˈbɑːt, rɑː-, -ˈbæt (US) rəˈbɑːt, rɑː-
rabbet ˈræb.ɪt **-s** -s **-ing** -ɪŋ **-ed** -ɪd
rabbi ˈræb.aɪ **-s** -z
rabbinate ˈræb.ɪ.nət, ˈ-ə-, -nɪt, -neɪt (US) -ɪ.nɪt, -neɪt **-s** -s
rabbinic rəˈbɪn.ɪk, ræbˈɪn- (US) rəˈbɪn- **-al** -ᵊl **-ally** -ᵊl.i, -li
rabb|it ˈræb|.ɪt **-its** -ɪts **-iting** -ɪ.tɪŋ (US) -ɪ.t̬ɪŋ **-ited** -ɪ.tɪd (US) -ɪ.t̬ɪd **ˈrabbit ˌhole; ˈrabbit ˌhutch; ˈrabbit ˌwarren**
rabble ˈræb.l̩ **-s** -z
rabble-rous|er ˈræb.l̩ˌraʊ.z|əʳ (US) -z|ɚ **-ers** -əz (US) -ɚz **-ing** -ɪŋ
Rabelais ˈræb.ᵊl.eɪ (US) ˌræb.əˈleɪ, ˈ---
Rabelaisian ˌræb.ᵊlˈeɪ.zi.ən, -ʒᵊn (US) -əˈleɪ.ʒᵊn, ˈ-zi.ən
rabid ˈræb.ɪd, ˈreɪ.bɪd (US) ˈræb.ɪd **-ly** -li **-ness** -nəs, -nɪs
rabies ˈreɪ.biːz, -biz
Rabin ˈreɪ.bɪn *Israeli politician:* ræbˈiːn (US) rɑːˈbiːn
Rabindranath Tagore rəˌbɪn.drə.nɑːt.təˈgɔːʳ, -nɑːθ- (US) -ˌben.drə.nɑːt.təˈgɔːr, -nɑːθ-
Rabinowitz rəˈbɪn.ə.wɪts, ræbˈɪn-, -vɪts
Raby ˈreɪ.bi
RAC ˌɑːʳ.eɪˈsiː (US) ˌɑːr-
Racal® ˈreɪ.kᵊl, -kɔːl
raccoon rəˈkuːn, rækˈuːn (US) rækˈuːn, rəˈkuːn **-s** -z
rac|e reɪs **-es** -ɪz **-ing** -ɪŋ **-ed** -t **-er/s** -əʳ/z (US) -ɚ/z **ˌrace reˈlations** (US) **ˈrace ˌrelations**
racecar ˈreɪs.kɑːʳ (US) -kɑːr **-s** -z
racecours|e ˈreɪs.kɔːs (US) -kɔːrs **-es** -ɪz
racegoer ˈreɪsˌgəʊ.əʳ (US) -ˌgoʊ.ɚ **-s** -z
racehors|e ˈreɪs.hɔːs (US) -ˌhɔːrs **-es** -ɪz
raceme ˈræs.iːm, ˈreɪ.siːm; rəˈsiːm, ræsˈiːm (US) reɪˈsiːm, rə- **-s** -z
race-meeting ˈreɪsˌmiː.tɪŋ (US) -t̬ɪŋ **-s** -z
racemic rəˈsiː.mɪk, ræsˈiː-, reɪˈsiː-, -ˈsem.ɪk (US) reɪˈsiː-, rə-
racetrack ˈreɪs.træk **-s** -s
Rachael, Rachel ˈreɪ.tʃᵊl
Rachelle rəˈʃel; ˈreɪ.tʃᵊl
rachitis rəˈkaɪ.tɪs, rækˈaɪ- (US) -t̬ɪs
Rachman ˈræk.mən
Rachmaninoff, Rachmaninov rækˈmæn.ɪ.nɒf, ræxˈ- (US) rɑːkˈmɑːn.ɪ.nɔːf
rachmanism (R) ˈræk.mə.nɪ.zᵊm
racial ˈreɪ.ʃᵊl, -ʃi.əl (US) ˈ-ʃᵊl **-ly** -i
racial|ism ˈreɪ.ʃᵊl|.ɪ.zᵊm, -ʃi.ᵊl- (US) ˈ-ʃᵊl- **-ist/s** -ɪst/s
Racine *English personal name, city in US:* rəˈsiːn (US) rə-, reɪ- *French author:* ræsˈiːn, rəˈsiːn (US) rɑːˈsiːn, rə-
rac|ism ˈreɪ.s|ɪ.zᵊm **-ist/s** -ɪst/s
rack ræk **-s** -s **-ing** -ɪŋ **-ed** -t
rack|et ˈræk|.ɪt **-ets** -ɪts **-eting** -ɪ.tɪŋ (US) -ɪ.t̬ɪŋ **-eted** -ɪ.tɪd (US) -ɪ.t̬ɪd **-ety** -ə.ti, -ɪ.ti (US) -ə.t̬i
racketball ˈræk.ɪt.bɔːl (US) -bɔːl, -bɑːl
racketeer ˌræk.ɪˈtɪəʳ, -əˈ- (US) -əˈtɪr **-s** -z **-ing** -ɪŋ **-ed** -d
Rackham ˈræk.əm
rack|-rent ˈræk|.rent **-rents** -rents **-renter/s** -ˌren.təʳ/z (US) -ˌren.t̬ɚ/z
raclette rækˈlet
raconteur ˌræk.ɒnˈtɜːʳ, -ɔ̃ːnˈ- (US) -ɑːnˈtɝː, -ənˈ- **-s** -z
racoon rəˈkuːn, rækˈuːn (US) rækˈuːn, rəˈkuːn **-s** -z
racquet ˈræk.ɪt **-s** -s
racquetball ˈræk.ɪt.bɔːl (US) -bɔːl, -bɑːl
rac|y ˈreɪ.s|i **-ier** -i.əʳ (US) -i.ɚ **-iest** -i.ɪst, -i.əst **-ily** -ɪ.li, -ᵊl.i **-iness** -ɪ.nəs, -ɪ.nɪs
rad ræd **-s** -z
RADA ˈrɑː.də
radar ˈreɪ.dɑːʳ (US) -dɑːr
Radcliffe ˈræd.klɪf
raddled ˈræd.l̩d
Radetzky rəˈdet.ski, rædˈet- (US) rɑːˈdet-, rə-
Radford ˈræd.fəd (US) -fɚd
radial ˈreɪ.di.əl **-ly** -i
radian ˈreɪ.di.ən **-s** -z
radianc|e ˈreɪ.di.ənts **-es** -ɪz
radiant ˈreɪ.di.ənt **-s** -s **-ly** -li
radi|ate ˈreɪ.di|.eɪt **-ates** -eɪts **-ating** -eɪ.tɪŋ (US) -eɪ.t̬ɪŋ **-ated** -eɪ.tɪd (US) -eɪ.t̬ɪd
radiation ˌreɪ.diˈeɪ.ʃᵊn **-s** -z **radiˈation ˌsickness**
radiator ˈreɪ.di.eɪ.təʳ (US) -t̬ɚ **-s** -z
radic|al ˈræd.ɪ.k|ᵊl **-als** -ᵊlz **-ally** -ᵊl.i, -li **-alness** -ᵊl.nəs, -ᵊl.nɪs **-alism** -ᵊl.ɪ.zᵊm **ˌradical ˈchic; ˌradical ˈsign**
radicaliz|e, -is|e ˈræd.ɪ.kᵊl.aɪz **-es** -ɪz **-ing** -ɪŋ **-ed** -d
radicchio rəˈdɪk.i.əʊ, rædˈɪk- (US) rəˈdiː.ki.oʊ, rɑː-, ˈ-kjoʊ **-s** -z
Radice rəˈdiː.tʃi, -tʃeɪ
radicle ˈræd.ɪ.kl̩ **-s** -z
radii *(plur. of* **radius***)* ˈreɪ.di.aɪ
radio *(n.v.)* ˈreɪ.di.əʊ (US) -oʊ **-s** -z **-ing** -ɪŋ **-ed** -d **ˌradio aˈlarm; ˈradio ˌcar; ˌradio ˈtelescope; ˈradio ˌwave**
radioactive ˌreɪ.di.əʊˈæk.tɪv (US) -oʊˈ- **-ly** -li *stress shift:* ˌradioactive ˈwaste
radioactivity ˌreɪ.di.əʊ.ækˈtɪv.ə.ti, -ɪ.ti (US) -oʊ.ækˈtɪv.ə.t̬i
radiocarbon ˌreɪ.di.əʊˈkɑː.bᵊn (US) -oʊˈkɑːr-
radiogenic ˌreɪ.di.əʊˈdʒen.ɪk (US) -oʊˈ- *stress shift:* ˌradiogenic ˈoutput
radiogram ˈreɪ.di.əʊ.græm (US) -oʊ- **-s** -z
radiograph ˈreɪ.di.əʊ.grɑːf, -græf (US) -oʊ.græf **-s** -s
radiograph|y ˌreɪ.diˈɒg.rə.f|i (US) -ˈɑː.grə- **-er/s** -əʳ/z (US) -ɚ/z
Radiohead ˈreɪ.di.əʊ.hed (US) -oʊ-
radioisotope ˌreɪ.di.əʊˈaɪ.sə.təʊp (US) -oʊˈaɪ.sə.toʊp **-s** -s
radiolo|cate ˌreɪ.di.əʊ.ləʊ|ˈkeɪt (US) -oʊ.loʊˈ- **-cates** -ˈkeɪts **-cating** -ˈkeɪ.tɪŋ (US) -ˈkeɪ.t̬ɪŋ **-cated** -ˈkeɪ.tɪd (US) -ˈkeɪ.t̬ɪd
radiolocation ˌreɪ.di.əʊ.ləʊˈkeɪ.ʃᵊn (US) -oʊ.loʊˈ-
radiolog|y ˌreɪ.diˈɒl.ə.dʒ|i (US) -ˈɑː.lə- **-ist/s** -ɪst/s
radiometer ˌreɪ.diˈɒm.ɪ.təʳ, ˈ-ə- (US) -ˈɑː.mə.t̬ɚ **-s** -z

radionics ˌreɪ.di'ɒn.ɪks (US) -'ɑː.nɪks
radiopag|e ˌreɪ.di.əʊ'peɪdʒ, 'reɪ.di.əʊ.peɪdʒ (US) 'reɪ.di.oʊ- **-es** -ɪz **-ing** -ɪŋ **-ed** -d **-er/s** -əʳ/z (US) -ɚ/z
radiophone 'reɪ.di.əʊ.fəʊn (US) -oʊ.foʊn **-s** -z
radiophonic ˌreɪ.di.əʊ'fɒn.ɪk (US) -oʊ'fɑː.nɪk
radiotelegram ˌreɪ.di.əʊ'tel.ɪ.græm, '-ə- (US) -oʊ'tel.ə- **-s** -z
radiotelegraph ˌreɪ.di.əʊ'tel.ɪ.grɑːf, '-ə-, -græf (US) -oʊ'tel.ə.græf **-s** -s
radiotelephone ˌreɪ.di.əʊ'tel.ɪ.fəʊn, '-ə- (US) -oʊ'tel.ə.foʊn **-s** -z
radiotherap|y ˌreɪ.di.əʊ'θer.ə.p|i (US) -oʊ'- **-ist/s** -ɪst/s
radish 'ræd.ɪʃ **-es** -ɪz
radium 'reɪ.di.əm
radi|us 'reɪ.di|.əs **-i** -aɪ
rad|ix 'reɪ.d|ɪks, 'ræd- **-ixes** -ɪk.sɪz **-ices** -ɪ.siːz (US) 'ræd.ə.siːz, 'reɪ.də-
Radlett 'ræd.lɪt, -lət
Radley 'ræd.li
Radnor 'ræd.nəʳ, -nɔːʳ (US) -nɚ, -nɔːr **-shire** -ʃəʳ, -ˌʃɪəʳ (US) -ʃɚ, -ˌʃɪr
radon 'reɪ.dɒn (US) -dɑːn
Radovan 'ræd.ə.væn
Radox® 'reɪ.dɒks (US) -dɑːks
Rae reɪ
Raeburn 'reɪ.bɜːn (US) -bɝːn **-s** -z
Raf ræf
RAF ˌɑːʳ.eɪ'ef; ræf (US) ˌɑːr-;
Rafferty 'ræf.ə.ti (US) -ɚ.t̬i
raffia 'ræf.i.ə
raffish 'ræf.ɪʃ **-ly** -li **-ness** -nəs, -nɪs
raffl|e 'ræf.l̩ **-es** -z **-ing** -ɪŋ, 'ræf.lɪŋ **-ed** -d 'raffle ˌticket
Raffles 'ræf.l̩z
Rafsanjani ˌræf.sɑːn'dʒɑː.ni, -sæn'-, -'dʒæn.i; -dʒɑː'niː (US) ˌrɑːf.sɑːn'dʒɑː.ni; ˌrʌf.sən'dʒæn.i
raft rɑːft (US) ræft **-s** -s **-ing** -ɪŋ **-ed** -ɪd
rafter 'rɑːf.təʳ (US) 'ræf.tɚ **-s** -z **-ed** -d
rag ræg **-s** -z **-ging** -ɪŋ **-ged** -d ˌrag 'doll; 'rag ˌtrade
raga 'rɑː.gə; rɑːg (US) 'rɑː.gə **-s** -z
ragamuffin 'ræg.əˌmʌf.ɪn **-s** -z
rag-and-bone|-man ˌræg.ᵊnd'bəʊn|.mæn, -ᵊm'- (US) -ᵊnd'boʊn- **-men** -men
ragbag 'ræg.bæg **-s** -z
rag|e reɪdʒ **-es** -ɪz **-ing/ly** -ɪŋ/li **-ed** -d
ragga 'ræg.ə
ragged 'ræg.ɪd **-er** -əʳ (US) -ɚ **-est** -ɪst, -əst **-ly** -li **-ness** -nəs, -nɪs **-y** -i
raggle-taggle 'ræg.l̩ˌtæg.l̩, ˌræg.l̩'tæg-
raglan (R) 'ræg.lən ˌraglan 'sleeve
ragout ræg'uː, '-- (US) ræg'uː **-s** -z
ragtag 'ræg.tæg
ragtime 'ræg.taɪm
ragweed 'ræg.wiːd
ragwort 'ræg.wɜːt (US) -wɝːt, -wɔːrt **-s** -s
Rahman 'rɑː.mən
rah-rah 'rɑː.rɑː
raid reɪd **-s** -z **-ing** -ɪŋ **-ed** -ɪd **-er/s** -əʳ/z (US) -ɚ/z
Raikes reɪks
rail reɪl **-s** -z **-ing** -ɪŋ **-ed** -d
railcard 'reɪl.kɑːd (US) -kɑːrd **-s** -z
railhead 'reɪl.hed **-s** -z
railing 'reɪ.lɪŋ **-s** -z
railler|y 'reɪ.lᵊr|.i **-ies** -iz
railroad 'reɪl.rəʊd (US) -roʊd **-s** -z **-ing** -ɪŋ **-ed** -ɪd
Railtrack® 'reɪl.træk
railway 'reɪl.weɪ **-s** -z
railway|man 'reɪl.weɪ|.mən, -mæn **-men** -mən, -men
raiment 'reɪ.mənt
rain reɪn **-s** -z **-ing** -ɪŋ **-ed** -d **-less** -ləs, -lɪs 'rain ˌforest; ˌtake a 'rain ˌcheck; come ˌrain or 'shine
rainbow 'reɪn.bəʊ, 'reɪm- (US) 'reɪn.boʊ **-s** -z ˌrainbow 'trout
rainbow-colo(u)red 'reɪn.bəʊˌkʌl.əd, 'reɪm- (US) 'reɪn.boʊˌkʌl.ɚd
raincoat 'reɪn.kəʊt, 'reɪŋ- (US) 'reɪn.koʊt **-s** -s
raindrop 'reɪn.drɒp (US) -drɑːp **-s** -s
Raine reɪn
Rainey 'reɪ.ni
rainfall 'reɪn.fɔːl (US) -fɔːl, -fɑːl
Rainford 'reɪn.fəd (US) -fɚd
rainforest 'reɪnˌfɒr.ɪst (US) -ˌfɔːr- **-s** -s
rain-gaug|e 'reɪn.geɪdʒ, 'reɪŋ- (US) 'reɪn- **-es** -ɪz
Rainier *prince of Monaco:* 'reɪ.ni.eɪ (US) reɪ'nɪr, rə-; ren'jeɪ
Rainier *Mount:* 'reɪ.ni.əʳ; reɪ'nɪəʳ, rə- (US) rə'nɪr, reɪ-
rainmak|ing 'reɪnˌmeɪ.k|ɪŋ, 'reɪm- (US) 'reɪn- **-er/s** -əʳ/z (US) -ɚ/z
rainproof 'reɪn.pruːf, 'reɪm- (US) 'reɪn-
rainstorm 'reɪn.stɔːm (US) -stɔːrm **-s** -z
rainwater 'reɪnˌwɔː.təʳ (US) -ˌwɑː.t̬ɚ, -ˌwɔː-
Rainworth 'reɪn.wəθ, -wɜːθ (US) -wɝːθ, -wɚθ
rain|y 'reɪ.n|i **-ier** -i.əʳ (US) -i.ɚ **-iest** -i.ɪst, -i.əst **-iness** -ɪ.nəs, -ɪ.nɪs ˌsave something for a ˌrainy 'day
Raisa raɪ'iː.sə, raɪ (US) rɑː-
rais|e reɪz **-es** -ɪz **-ing** -ɪŋ **-ed** -d
raisin 'reɪ.zᵊn **-s** -z
raison d'être ˌreɪ.zɔ̃ːŋ'de.trə, -zɒn'- (US) ˌreɪ.zoʊn'det, ˌrez.ɑːn'-, -'det.rə
raj (R) rɑːdʒ, rɑːʒ (US) rɑːdʒ
raja(h) (R) 'rɑː.dʒə (US) -dʒə, -dʒɑː **-s** -z
Rajasthan ˌrɑː.dʒə'stɑːn (US) -dʒɑː'-
Rajasthani ˌrɑː.dʒə'stɑː.ni (US) -dʒɑː'-
Rajiv rɑː'dʒiːv *stress shift:* ˌRajiv 'Ghandi
Rajput 'rɑː.dʒ.pʊt (US) -puːt
Rajputana ˌrɑː.dʒ.pʊ'tɑː.nə (US) -puː'-
rak|e reɪk **-es** -s **-ing** -ɪŋ **-ed** -t
rakee 'rɑː.ki, 'ræk.i; rɑː'kiː
rake-off 'reɪk.ɒf (US) -ɑːf **-s** -s
raki 'rɑː.ki, 'ræk.i; rɑː'kiː
rakish 'reɪ.kɪʃ **-ly** -li **-ness** -nəs, -nɪs
rale rɑːl, ræl (US) rɑːl **-s** -z
Rale(i)gh 'rɔː.li, 'rɑː-, 'ræl.i (US) 'rɑː.li, 'rɔː-

Note: The family of the late Sir Walter Raleigh pronounced /'rɔː.li (US) 'rɑː-, rɔː-/. Raleigh bicycles are generally called /'ræl.i/ in Britain and /'rɑː.li/ in the United States. When used as the name of a ship, the British English pronunciation is /'ræl.i/.

rallentand|o ˌræl.en'tæn.d|əʊ, -ən'-, -ɪn'- (US) ˌrɑː.lən'tɑːn.d|oʊ **-os** -əʊz (US) -oʊz **-i** -i
rall|y 'ræl|.i **-ies** -iz **-ying** -i.ɪŋ **-ied** -id 'rally ˌdriver
rallycross 'ræl.i.krɒs (US) -krɑːs
Ralph rælf, reɪf
Ralph Cross ˌrɑːlf'krɒs, ˌrælf- (US) ˌrælf'krɑːs
Ralston 'rɔːl.stᵊn
ram (R) ræm **-s** -z **-ming** -ɪŋ **-med** -d **-mer/s** -əʳ/z (US) -ɚ/z
RAM ræm
Ramad(h)an ˌræm.ə'dæn, ˌrɑː.mə'-, -'dɑːn, '--- (US) ˌræm.ə'dɑːn, ˌrɑː.mə'-
Ramage 'ræm.ɪdʒ
Rama(h) 'rɑː.mə
Ramallah rə'mɑː.lə, -'mæl-
Ramaphosa ˌræm.ə'pəʊ.zə (US) -'poʊ-
Ramayana rɑː'maɪ.ə.nə, rə-, -'mɑː- (US) rɑː'mɑː.jə-
Rambert 'rɑ̃ː*m*.beə, -'- (US) rɑːm'ber
rambl|e 'ræm.bl̩ **-es** -z **-ing** -ɪŋ, 'ræm.blɪŋ **-ed** -d
rambler (R) 'ræm.bləʳ (US) -blɚ **-s** -z
rambling 'ræm.blɪŋ, -bl̩.ɪŋ **-s** -z **-ly** -li
Rambo 'ræm.bəʊ (US) -boʊ
Ramboesque ˌræm.bəʊ'esk (US) -boʊ'-
Rambouillet ˌrɑ̃ː*m*.buː'jeɪ, -'-- (US) ˌræm.bui'jeɪ
rambunctious ræm'bʌŋ*k*.ʃəs **-ly** -li **-ness** -nəs, -nɪs
rambutan ræm'buː.tᵊn; ˌræm.bʊ'tæn, -'tɑːn (US) ræm'buː.tᵊn **-s** -z
ramekin, ramequin 'ræm.ɪ.kɪn, '-ə-, '-kɪn (US) '-ə.kɪn **-s** -z
Rameses 'ræm.ɪ.siːz, '-ə-
ramification ˌræm.ɪ.fɪ'keɪ.ʃᵊn, ˌ-ə- **-s** -z
rami|fy 'ræm.ɪ|.faɪ, '-ə- **-fies** -faɪz **-fying** -faɪ.ɪŋ **-fied** -faɪd
Ramillies 'ræm.ɪ.liz
Ramirez rə'mɪə.rez (US) -'mɪr.ez, -'miː.reɪs, rɑː'mɪr.ez, -'miː.reθ
ramjet 'ræm.dʒet **-s** -s

Ramos 'rɑː.mɒs (US) 'reɪ.moʊs, rɑː'moʊs
ramp ræmp **-s** -s **-ing** -ɪŋ **-ed** -t
rampag|e (*n.*) 'ræm.peɪdʒ, -'- (US) 'ræm.peɪdʒ **-es** -ɪz (*v.*) ræm'peɪdʒ, '-- **-es** -ɪz **-ing** -ɪŋ **-ed** -d
rampageous ræm'peɪ.dʒəs **-ly** -li **-ness** -nəs, -nɪs
rampant 'ræm.pənt **-ly** -li
rampart 'ræm.pɑːt, -pət (US) -pɑːrt, -pɚt **-s** -s
rampion 'ræm.pi.ən **-s** -z
Rampling 'ræm.plɪŋ
Ramprakash 'ræm.prə.kæʃ
Rampton 'ræm*p*.tən
ram-raid 'ræm.reɪd **-s** -z **-er/s** -əʳ/z (US) -ɚ/z **-ing** -ɪŋ
ramrod 'ræm.rɒd (US) -rɑːd **-s** -z
Ramsaran 'rɑːm*p*.sᵊr.ən
Ramsay 'ræm.zi
Ramsbottom 'ræmz,bɒt.əm (US) -,bɑː.t̬əm
Ramsden 'ræmz.dən
Ramses 'ræm.siːz
Ramsey 'ræm.zi
Ramsgate 'ræmz.geɪt, -gɪt
ramshackle 'ræm,ʃæk.l̩
ran *(from* **run***)* ræn
Ranariddh ,ræn.ə'rɪt
rance ræn*t*s
Rance *surname:* rɑːn*t*s (US) ræn*t*s
ranch rɑːn*t*ʃ, ræn*t*ʃ (US) ræn*t*ʃ **-es** -ɪz **-ing** -ɪŋ **-ed** -t **-er/s** -əʳ/z (US) -ɚ/z **'ranch ,house**
ranchero rɑːn'tʃeə.rəʊ, ræn- (US) ræn'tʃer.oʊ **-s** -z
rancid 'ræn*t*.sɪd **-ness** -nəs, -nɪs
rancidity ræn'sɪd.ə.ti, -ɪ.ti (US) -ə.t̬i
rancorous 'ræŋ.kᵊr.əs **-ly** -li
ranco(u)r 'ræŋ.kəʳ (US) -kɚ
rand (R) *South African money and region:* rænd, rɑːnd, rɑːnt, rɒnt (US) rænd, rɑːnd, rɑːnt *strip, border:* rænd **-s** -z
Randall, Randell 'ræn.dᵊl
Randalstown 'ræn.dᵊlz.taʊn
R and B ,ɑːʳ.ᵊn*d*'biː, -ᵊm'- (US) ,ɑːr-
R and D ,ɑːʳ.ᵊn*d*'diː (US) ,ɑːr-
Randi 'ræn.di
Randle 'ræn.dl̩
Randolph 'ræn.dɒlf, -dᵊlf (US) -dɑːlf, -dᵊlf
random 'ræn.dəm **-ly** -li **-ness** -nəs, -nɪs
random-access ,ræn.dəm'æk.ses *stress shift:* ,random-access 'memory
randomization, -isa- ,ræn.dəm.aɪ'zeɪ.ʃᵊn, -ɪ'- (US) -ɪ'-
randomiz|e, -is|e 'ræn.də.maɪz **-es** -ɪz **-ing** -ɪŋ **-ed** -d
R and R ,ɑːʳ.ᵊn*d*'ɑːʳ (US) ,ɑːr.ᵊn*d*'ɑːr
rand|y (R) 'ræn.d|i **-ier** -i.əʳ (US) -i.ɚ **-iest** -i.ɪst, -i.əst **-ily** -ɪ.li, -ᵊl.i **-iness** -ɪ.nəs, -ɪ.nɪs
ranee (R) 'rɑː.niː, ,-'- (US) 'rɑː.niː **-s** -z
Ranelagh 'ræn.ɪ.lə, -ᵊl.ə, -ɔː (US) -ᵊl.ə
rang *(from* **ring***)* ræŋ
rang|e reɪndʒ **-es** -ɪz **-ing** -ɪŋ **-ed** -d
range-finder 'reɪndʒ,faɪn.dəʳ (US) -dɚ **-s** -z
ranger (R) 'reɪn.dʒəʳ (US) -dʒɚ **-s** -z
Rangoon ,ræŋ'guːn (US) ,ræn-, ,ræŋ- *stress shift:* ,Rangoon 'streets
rang|y 'reɪn.dʒ|i **-ier** -i.əʳ (US) -i.ɚ **-iest** -i.ɪst, -i.əst **-iness** -ɪ.nəs, -ɪ.nɪs
rani 'rɑː.niː, ,-'- (US) 'rɑː.niː **-s** -z
rank (R) ræŋk **-s** -s **-ing** -ɪŋ **-ed** -t **-ly** -li **-ness** -nəs, -nɪs **,rank and 'file**
Rankin(e) 'ræŋ.kɪn
rankl|e 'ræŋ.kl̩ **-es** -z **-ing** -ɪŋ, 'ræŋ.klɪŋ **-ed** -d
Rannoch 'ræn.ək, -əx (US) -ək
Ranoe 'rɑː.nəʊ (US) -noʊ
ransack 'ræn.sæk **-s** -s **-ing** -ɪŋ **-ed** -t **-er/s** -əʳ/z (US) -ɚ/z
ransom (R) 'ræn*t*.sᵊm **-s** -z **-ing** -ɪŋ **-ed** -d **-er/s** -əʳ/z (US) -ɚ/z
Ransome 'ræn*t*.səm
rant rænt **-s** -s **-ing/ly** -ɪŋ/li (US) 'ræn.t̬ɪŋ/li **-ed** -ɪd (US) 'ræn.t̬ɪd **-er/s** -əʳ/z (US) 'ræn.t̬ɚ/z
Rantzen 'rænt.sᵊn
Ranulph 'ræn.ʌlf, -ᵊlf
ranuncul|us rə'nʌŋ.kjə.l|əs, ræn'ʌŋ-, -kjʊ- (US) rə'nʌŋ- **-uses** -ə.sɪz **-i** -aɪ
Ranworth 'ræn.wəθ, -wɜːθ (US) -wɚθ, -wɝːθ
rap ræp **-s** -s **-ping** -ɪŋ **-ped** -t **-per/s** -əʳ/z (US) -ɚ/z
rapacious rə'peɪ.ʃəs **-ly** -li **-ness** -nəs, -nɪs
rapacity rə'pæs.ə.ti, -ɪ.ti (US) -ə.t̬i
rap|e reɪp **-es** -s **-ing** -ɪŋ **-ed** -t **-ist/s** -ɪst/s
Raphael *angel:* 'ræf.eɪ.əl; ,ræf.ɑː'el; 'ræf.eɪl; 'reɪ.fi.əl; *and in Jewish usage:* 'reɪ.fᵊl (US) 'ræf.i.əl; ,rɑː.fi'el; 'reɪ.fi.el *modern name:* 'reɪ.fᵊl, 'ræf.eɪl *Italian artist:* 'ræf.eɪ.əl, -fi.əl, -feɪl (US) 'ræf.i.əl; ,rɑː.fi'el; 'reɪ.fi.el
rapid 'ræp.ɪd **-est** -ɪst, -əst **-ly** -li **-ness** -nəs, -nɪs **-s** -z **,rapid 'eye ,movement; ,rapid 'transit**
rapid-fire ,ræp.ɪd'faɪəʳ (US) -'faɪɚ *stress shift:* ,rapid-fire 'shooting
rapidity rə'pɪd.ə.ti, ræp'ɪd-, -ɪ.ti (US) rə'pɪd.ə.t̬i
rapier 'reɪ.pi.əʳ (US) -pi.ɚ, '-pjɚ **-s** -z
rapine 'ræp.aɪn, -ɪn (US) -ɪn
rapparee ,ræp.ᵊr'iː (US) -ə'riː **-s** -z
rappel (US) ræp'el **-s** (US) -z **-ling** (US) -ɪŋ **-led** (US) -d
rapport ræp'ɔːʳ, rə'pɔːʳ; 'ræp.ɔːʳ (US) ræp'ɔːr, rə'pɔːr
rapporteur ,ræp.ɔː'tɜːʳ (US) -ɔːr'tɝː **-s** -z
rapprochement ræp'rɒʃ.mɑ̃ːŋ, -'rəʊʃ- (US) ,ræp.roːʃ'mɑ̃ːŋ, -roʊʃ'- **-s** -z
rapscallion ræp'skæl.jən, '-i.ən (US) '-jən **-s** -z
rapt ræpt
rapture 'ræp.tʃəʳ (US) -tʃɚ **-s** -z **-d** -d
rapturous 'ræp.tʃᵊr.əs **-ly** -li
Rapunzel rə'pʌn.zᵊl
Raquel rə'kel, ræk'el
rara avis ,rɑː.rə'æv.ɪs, ,reə-, -'eɪ.vɪs (US) ,rer.ə'eɪ.vɪs
rare reəʳ (US) rer **-r** -əʳ (US) -ɚ **-st** -ɪst, -əst **-ly** -li **-ness** -nəs, -nɪs **,rare 'earth**
rarebit 'reə.bɪt (US) 'rer- **-s** -s
Note: The pronunciation /'ræb.ɪt/ is very often used in British English in the phrase **Welsh rarebit**.
rarefaction ,reə.rɪ'fæk.ʃᵊn, -rə'- (US) ,rer.ə'-
rarefication ,reə.rɪ.fɪ'keɪ.ʃᵊn, -rə- (US) ,rer.ə-
rare|fy 'reə.rɪ|.faɪ, -rə- (US) 'rer.ə- **-fies** -faɪz **-fying** -faɪ.ɪŋ **-fied** -faɪd
raring (*adj.*) 'reə.rɪŋ (US) 'rer.ɪŋ
rarit|y 'reə.rə.t|i, -ɪ.t|i (US) 'rer.ə.t̬|i **-ies** -iz
Rarotonga ,reə.rəʊ'tɒŋ.gə, ,rær.əʊ'- (US) ,rɑːr.oʊ'tɔːŋ.gə, ,rer.ə'-
Ras al Khaimah ,rɑːs.æl'kaɪ.mə
rascal 'rɑː.skᵊl (US) 'ræs.kᵊl **-s** -z
rascalit|y rɑː'skæl.ə.t|i, -ɪ.t|i (US) ræs'kæl.ə.t̬|i **-ies** -iz
rascally 'rɑː.skᵊl.i (US) 'ræs.kᵊl-
ras|e reɪz **-es** -ɪz **-ing** -ɪŋ **-ed** -d
rash ræʃ **-es** -ɪz **-er** -əʳ (US) -ɚ **-est** -ɪst, -əst **-ly** -li **-ness** -nəs, -nɪs
rasher 'ræʃ.əʳ (US) -ɚ **-s** -z
Rashid ræʃ'iːd (US) ræʃ-, rɑː'ʃiːd
rasp rɑːsp (US) ræsp **-s** -s **-ing** -ɪŋ **-ed** -t
raspberr|y 'rɑːz.bᵊr|.i, 'rɑːs- (US) 'ræz,ber|.i, -bɚ- **-ies** -iz
Rasputin ræs'pjuː.tɪn, -'puː- (US) -'pjuː-
rasp|y 'rɑː.sp|i (US) 'ræsp|.i **-iness** -ɪ.nəs, -ɪ.nɪs
Rasselas 'ræs.ɪ.ləs (US) '-ə-, -læs
Rasta 'ræs.tə (US) 'rɑː.stə, 'ræs.tə **-s** -z
Rastafarian ,ræs.tə'feə.ri.ən (US) ,rɑː.stə'fer.i-, ,ræs.tə'-, -'fɑːr- **-s** -z **-ism** -ɪ.zᵊm
Rasta|man 'ræs.tə|.mæn (US) 'rɑː.stə-, 'ræs.tə- **-men** -men
rat ræt **-s** -s **-ting** -ɪŋ (US) 'ræt̬.ɪŋ **-ted** -ɪd (US) 'ræt̬.ɪd **'rat ,race; 'rat ,trap**
rata 'reɪ.tə (US) 'rɑː.t̬ə **-s** -z
rata *(in* **pro rata***)* 'rɑː.tə, 'reɪ- (US) -t̬ə
ratability ,reɪ.tə'bɪl.ə.ti, -ɪ.ti (US) -t̬ə'bɪl.ə.t̬i
ratab|le 'reɪ.tə.bl̩ (US) -t̬ə- **-ly** -li
ratafia ,ræt.ə'fiː.ə **-s** -z
rataplan ,ræt.ə'plæn (US) 'ræt̬.ə.plæn
rat-a-tat ,ræt.ə'tæt, '--- (US) ,ræt̬-, '---

ratatouille ˌræt.əˈtwiː, -ˈtuː.i (US) -ˈtuː.i, ˌrɑː.tɑːˈ-
ratbag ˈræt.bæg **-s** -z
rat-catcher ˈrætˌkætʃ.ə^{r} (US) -ɚ **-s** -z
ratchet ˈrætʃ.ɪt **-s** -s **-ing** **-ed**
Ratcliff(e) ˈræt.klɪf
rat|e reɪt **-es** -s **-ing** -ɪŋ (US) ˈreɪ.t̬ɪŋ **-ed** -ɪd (US) ˈreɪ.t̬ɪd ˌ**rate of exˈchange**
rateab|le ˈreɪ.tə.b|l̩ (US) -t̬ə- **-ly** -li ˌ**rateable ˈvalue**
rate-cap ˈreɪt.kæp **-s** -s **-ping** -ɪŋ **-ped** -t
ratel ˈreɪ.t^{ə}l, ˈrɑː-, -tel (US) ˈreɪ.t̬^{ə}l, ˈrɑː- **-s** -z
ratepayer ˈreɪtˌpeɪ.ə^{r} (US) -ɚ **-s** -z
Rath ræθ
Rathbone ˈræθ.bəʊn, -bən (US) -boʊn, -bən
rather (*adv.*) ˈrɑː.ðə^{r} (US) ˈræð.ɚ *British only, old-fashioned:* ˌrɑːˈðɜː^{r}
Rather ˈræð.ə^{r} (US) ˈræð.ɚ
Rathfarnham ræθˈfɑː.nəm (US) -ˈfɑːr-
Rathlin ˈræθ.lɪn
ratification ˌræt.ɪ.fɪˈkeɪ.ʃ^{ə}n, ˌ-ə- (US) ˌræt̬.ə- **-s** -z
rati|fy ˈræt.ɪ|.faɪ, ˈ-ə- (US) ˈræt̬.ə- **-fies** -faɪz **-fying** -faɪ.ɪŋ **-fied** -faɪd **-fier/s** -faɪ.ə^{r}/z (US) -faɪ.ɚ/z
rating ˈreɪ.tɪŋ (US) -t̬ɪŋ **-s** -z
ratio ˈreɪ.ʃi.əʊ (US) -oʊ, ˈ-ʃoʊ **-s** -z
ratioci|nate ˌræt.iˈɒs.ɪ|.neɪt, ˌræʃ-, -ˈəʊ.sɪ-, -sə- (US) ˌræʃ.iˈɑː.sə- **-nates** -neɪts **-nating** -neɪ.tɪŋ (US) -neɪ.t̬ɪŋ **-nated** -neɪ.tɪd (US) -neɪ.t̬ɪd
ratiocination ˌræt.i.ɒs.ɪˈneɪ.ʃ^{ə}n, ˌræʃ-, -əʊ.sɪˈ-, -səˈ- (US) ˌræʃ.i.ɑː.səˈ- **-s** -z
ratio decidendi ˌræt.i.əʊˌdeɪ.sɪˈden.di (US) ˌræt̬.i.oʊˌ-, ˌrɑː.t̬i-
ratio legis ˌræt.i.əʊˈleɪ.gɪs (US) ˌræt̬.i.oʊˈleg.ɪs, ˌrɑː.t̬i-
ration ˈræʃ.^{ə}n (US) ˈræʃ.^{ə}n, ˈreɪ- **-s** -z **-ing** -ɪŋ **-ed** -d
rational ˈræʃ.^{ə}n.^{ə}l, ˈ-n^{ə}l **-ly** -i
rationale ˌræʃ.əˈnɑːl, -ˈnæl, -ˈnɑː.leɪ (US) -əˈnæl **-s** -z
rational|ism ˈræʃ.^{ə}n.^{ə}l|.ɪ.z^{ə}m, ˈ-n^{ə}l- **-ist/s** -ɪst/s
rationalistic ˌræʃ.^{ə}n.^{ə}lˈɪs.tɪk, ˌ-n^{ə}lˈ- **-ally** -^{ə}l.i, -li
rationality ˌræʃ.^{ə}nˈæl.ə.ti, -ɪ.ti (US) -ə.t̬i
rationalization, -isa- ˌræʃ.^{ə}n.^{ə}l.aɪˈzeɪ.ʃ^{ə}n, ˌ-n^{ə}l-, -ɪˈ- (US) -ɪˈ-
rationaliz|e, -is|e ˈræʃ.^{ə}n.^{ə}l.aɪz, ˈ-n^{ə}l- (US) -^{ə}n.^{ə}.laɪz, ˈ-nə- **-es** -ɪz **-ing** -ɪŋ **-ed** -d
Ratisbon ˈræt.ɪz.bɒn, -ɪs-, -əz-, -əs- (US) -ɪz.bɑːn, -ɪs-
ratline ˈræt.lɪn **-s** -z
Ratner ˈræt.nə^{r} (US) -nɚ **-'s** -z
rat-race ˈræt.reɪs
rat-tail ˈræt.teɪl **-s** -z **-ed** -d
rattan rəˈtæn, rætˈæn **-s** -z
Rattigan ˈræt.ɪ.gən, ˈ-ə- (US) ˈræt̬-
rattl|e (R) ˈræt.l̩ (US) ˈræt̬- **-es** -z **-ing** -ɪŋ, ˈræt.lɪŋ **-ed** -d **-er/s** -ə^{r}/z (US) -ɚ/z, ˈræt.lə^{r}/z (US) -lɚ/z
rattlesnake ˈræt.l̩.sneɪk (US) ˈræt̬- **-s** -s
rattling ˈræt.lɪŋ, -l̩.ɪŋ (US) ˈræt.lɪŋ, ˈræt̬.l̩.ɪŋ
ratt|y (R) ˈræt|.i (US) ˈræt̬- **-ier** -i.ə^{r} (US) -i.ɚ **-iest** -i.ɪst, -i.əst **-ily** -ɪ.li, -^{ə}l.i **-iness** -ɪ.nəs, -ɪ.nɪs
raucous ˈrɔː.kəs (US) ˈrɑː-, ˈrɔː- **-ly** -li **-ness** -nəs, -nɪs
raunch|y ˈrɔːn.tʃ|i (US) ˈrɑːn.tʃ|i, ˈrɔːn- **-ier** -i.ə^{r} (US) -i.ɚ **-iest** -i.ɪst, -i.əst **-ily** -ɪ.li, -^{ə}l.i **-iness** -ɪ.nəs, -ɪ.nɪs
Raunds rɔːndz (US) rɑːndz, rɔːndz
Rauschenberg ˈraʊ.ʃ^{ə}n.bɜːg (US) -bɝːg
ravag|e ˈræv.ɪdʒ **-es** -ɪz **-ing** -ɪŋ **-ed** -d **-er/s** -ə^{r}/z (US) -ɚ/z
Ravana rəˈvɑː.nə (US) ˈrɑː.və-; rəˈvɑː-
rav|e reɪv **-es** -z **-ing/s** -ɪŋ/z **-ed** -d
ravel ˈræv.^{ə}l **-s** -z **-(l)ing** -ɪŋ **-(l)ed** -d
Ravel *French composer:* rævˈel (US) rəˈvel, rɑː-
ravelin ˈræv.^{ə}l.ɪn **-s** -z
raven (R) (*n.*) ˈreɪ.v^{ə}n **-s** -z
raven (*v.*) ˈræv.^{ə}n **-s** -z **-ing** -ɪŋ **-ed** -d
Ravening ˈreɪ.v^{ə}n.ɪŋ, ˈræv.^{ə}n-
Ravenna rəˈven.ə, rævˈen- (US) rə-, rɑː-
ravenous ˈræv.^{ə}n.əs, -ɪ.nəs (US) -^{ə}n.əs **-ly** -li **-ness** -nəs, -nɪs
Ravensbourne ˈreɪ.v^{ə}nz.bɔːn (US) -bɔːrn
Ravenshead ˈreɪ.v^{ə}nz.hed
Ravenshoe ˈreɪ.v^{ə}nz.həʊ (US) -hoʊ
raver ˈreɪ.və^{r} (US) -vɚ **-s** -z
Raverat ˈrɑː.v^{ə}r.ɑː (US) -və.rɑː
rave-up ˈreɪv.ʌp **-s** -s
ravin ˈræv.ɪn
ravine rəˈviːn **-s** -z
raving ˈreɪ.vɪŋ **-s** -z
ravioli ˌræv.iˈəʊ.li (US) -ˈoʊ-
ravish ˈræv.ɪʃ **-es** -ɪz **-ing/ly** -ɪŋ/li **-ed** -t **-er/s** -ə^{r}/z (US) -ɚ/z **-ment** -mənt
raw rɔː (US) rɑː, rɔː **-er** -ə^{r} (US) -ɚ **-est** -ɪst, -əst **-ly** -li **-ness** -nəs, -nɪs ˌ**raw ˈdeal;** ˌ**raw maˈterial**
Rawalpindi ˌrɑː.wəlˈpɪn.di, ˌrɔːlˈpɪn- (US) ˌrɑː.wəlˈ-
Rawdon ˈrɔː.d^{ə}n (US) ˈrɑː-, ˈrɔː-
rawhid|e ˈrɔː.haɪd (US) ˈrɑː-, ˈrɔː- **-es** -z **-ing** -ɪŋ **-ed** -ɪd
Rawlings ˈrɔː.lɪŋz (US) ˈrɑː-, ˈrɔː-
Rawlins ˈrɔː.lɪnz (US) ˈrɑː-, ˈrɔː-
Rawlinson ˈrɔː.lɪn.s^{ə}n (US) ˈrɑː-, ˈrɔː-
Rawlplug® ˈrɔːl.plʌg (US) ˈrɑːl-, ˈrɔːl-
Rawmarsh ˈrɔː.mɑːʃ (US) ˈrɑː.mɑːrʃ, ˈrɔː-
Rawnsley ˈrɔːnz.li (US) ˈrɑːnz-, ˈrɔː-
Rawtenstall ˈrɒt.^{ə}n.stɔːl, ˈrɔː.t^{ə}n- (US) ˈrɑː.t^{ə}n-, ˈrɔː-
ray (R) reɪ **-s** -z
Ray-Bans® ˈreɪ.bænz
Raybould ˈreɪ.bəʊld (US) -boʊld
Rayburn ˈreɪ.bɜːn (US) -bɝːn
Rayleigh ˈreɪ.li
Rayment ˈreɪ.mənt
Raymond ˈreɪ.mənd
Rayner ˈreɪ.nə^{r} (US) -nɚ
Raynes reɪnz
Raynsford ˈreɪnz.fəd (US) -fɚd
rayon ˈreɪ.ɒn, -ən (US) -ɑːn
raz|e reɪz **-es** -ɪz **-ing** -ɪŋ **-ed** -d
razoo rəˈzuː (US) rə-, rɑː-
razor ˈreɪ.zə^{r} (US) -zɚ **-s** -z ˈ**razor** ˌ**blade**
razorback ˈreɪ.zə.bæk (US) -zɚ- **-s** -s
razorbill ˈreɪ.zə.bɪl (US) -zɚ- **-s** -z
razor-blade ˈreɪ.zə.bleɪd (US) -zɚ- **-s** -z
razor-shell ˈreɪ.zə.ʃel (US) -zɚ- **-s** -z
razzamat(t)azz ˌræz.ə.məˈtæz, ˈræz.ə.mə.tæz (US) ˈræz.ə.mə.tæz
razzia ˈræz.i.ə **-s** -z
razzle ˈræz.l̩ ˌ**on the ˈrazzle**
razzle-dazzle ˌræz.l̩ˈdæz.l̩, ˈræz.l̩ˌdæz- (US) ˌræz.l̩ˈdæz-
razzmatazz ˌræz.məˈtæz, ˈ--- (US) ˈræz.mə.tæz
RC (*abbrev. for* **Roman Catholic**) ˌɑːˈsiː; ˌrəʊ.mənˈkæθ.^{ə}l.ɪk, -məŋˈ-, ˈ-lɪk (US) ˌɑːr-; ˌroʊ.mənˈkæθ.^{ə}l.ɪk, ˈ-lɪk
Rd (*abbrev. for* **Road**) rəʊd (US) roʊd
re- *prefix denoting repetition:* ˌriː-, rɪ-, ri-, rə-
Note: Prefix. In compounds containing **re-** where the stem is free and the meaning is “again”, it is normally pronounced /ˌriː-/, e.g. **re-read** /ˌriːˈriːd/. Many such compounds are likely to undergo stress shift, especially in adjectives derived from verbs, e.g. ˈ**rearˌrange**, ˈ**rearranged** ˌ**furniture**. Attached to bound stems the pronunciation is normally /rɪ-, ri-/ or /rə-/, e.g. **refer** /rɪˈfɜː^{r} (US) -ˈfɜːr/. There are exceptions; see individual entries.
re *note in Tonic Sol-fa:* reɪ **-s** -z
re (prep.) *with regard to:* riː
RE (*abbrev. for* **Religious Education**) ˌɑː^{r}ˈiː (US) ˌɑːr-
Rea reɪ, rɪə, riː
reach riːtʃ **-es** -ɪz **-ing** -ɪŋ **-ed** -t
reach-me-down ˈriːtʃ.mi.daʊn **-s** -z
react riˈækt **-s** -s **-ing** -ɪŋ **-ed** -ɪd
reactant riˈæk.t^{ə}nt (US) -tənt **-s** -s
reaction riˈæk.ʃ^{ə}n **-s** -z
reactionar|y riˈæk.ʃ^{ə}n.^{ə}r|.i (US) -er- **-ies** -iz
reacti|vate riˈæk.tɪ|.veɪt, ˌriː-, -tə- (US) -tə- **-vates** -veɪts **-vating** -veɪ.tɪŋ (US) -veɪ.t̬ɪŋ **-vated** -veɪ.tɪd (US) -veɪ.t̬ɪd
reactivation ˌriː.æk.tɪˈveɪ.ʃ^{ə}n, riˌæk-, -təˈ- (US) riˌæk-

reactive ri'æk.tɪv **-ly** -li
reactor ri'æk.təʳ ⓤⓢ -tɚ **-s** -z
read (R) *present tense:* riːd **-s** -z **-ing** -ɪŋ
past tense: red
readability ˌriː.də'bɪl.ə.ti, -ɪ.ti ⓤⓢ -ə.t̬i
readab|le 'riː.də.bl̩ **-ly** -li **-leness** -l̩.nəs, -nɪs
re-address ˌriː.ə'dres **-es** -ɪz **-ing** -ɪŋ **-ed** -t
Reade riːd
reader (R) 'riː.dəʳ ⓤⓢ -dɚ **-s** -z
readership 'riː.də.ʃɪp ⓤⓢ -dɚ- **-s** -s
readies 'red.iz
reading (*n.*) 'riː.dɪŋ **-s** -z
Reading 'red.ɪŋ
readjust ˌriː.ə'dʒʌst **-s** -s **-ing** -ɪŋ **-ed** -ɪd
readjustment ˌriː.ə'dʒʌst.mənt **-s** -s
readmission ˌriː.əd'mɪʃ.ən **-s** -z
read|mit ˌriː.əd'mɪt **-mits** -'mɪts **-mitting** -'mɪt.ɪŋ ⓤⓢ -'mɪt̬.ɪŋ **-mitted** -'mɪt.ɪd ⓤⓢ -'mɪt̬.ɪd **-mittance** -'mɪt.ənts
readout 'riː.daʊt **-s** -s
read|y 'red|.i **-ier** -i.əʳ ⓤⓢ -i.ɚ **-iest** -i.ɪst, -i.əst **-ily** -ɪ.li, -əl.i **-iness** -ɪ.nəs, -ɪ.nɪs **-ies** -iz **-ying** -i.ɪŋ **-ied** -id ˌ**ready** '**money**
ready-made ˌred.i'meɪd *stress shift:* ˌready-made 'meal
ready-to-wear ˌred.i.tə'weəʳ ⓤⓢ -'wer, 'red.i.təˌwer *stress shift, British only:* ˌready-to-wear 'suit
reaffirm ˌriː.ə'fɜːm ⓤⓢ -'fɝːm **-s** -z **-ing** -ɪŋ **-ed** -d
reafforest ˌriː.ə'fɒr.ɪst ⓤⓢ -'fɔːr.ɪst **-s** -s **-ing** -ɪŋ **-ed** -ɪd
reafforestation ˌriː.əˌfɒr.ɪ'steɪ.ʃən, -ə'- ⓤⓢ -ˌfɔːr.ɪ'-
Reagan 'reɪ.gən, 'riː-
Note: The former US president is normally /'reɪ-/.
Reaganomics ˌreɪ.gən'ɒm.ɪks ⓤⓢ -'ɑː.mɪks
reagent ˌriː'eɪ.dʒənt **-s** -s
real (*adj.*) rɪəl ⓤⓢ riːl, 'riː.əl '**real** **e**ˌ**state**; ˌ**real** '**life**
real *monetary unit:* reɪ'ɑːl ⓤⓢ reɪ'ɑːl; 'reɪ.əl **-s** -z
realia ri'eɪ.li.ə, -'ɑː- ⓤⓢ ri'eɪ-; reɪ'ɑː-
realign ˌriː.ə'laɪn **-s** -z **-ing** -ɪŋ **-ed** -d **-ment/s** -mənt/s
real|ism 'rɪə.l|ɪ.zəm ⓤⓢ 'riː-, 'riː.ə- **-ist/s** -ɪst/s
realistic ˌrɪə'lɪs.tɪk ⓤⓢ ˌriː.ə'- **-ally** -əl.i, -li
realit|y ri'æl.ə.t|i, -ɪ.t|i ⓤⓢ -ə.t̬|i **-ies** -iz
realization, -isa- ˌrɪə.laɪ'zeɪ.ʃən, -lɪ'- ⓤⓢ ˌriː.ə.lɪ'- **-s** -z
realiz|e, -is|e 'rɪə.laɪz ⓤⓢ 'riː.ə- **-es** -ɪz **-ing** -ɪŋ **-ed** -d **-able** -ə.bl̩
real-life ˌrɪəl'laɪf ⓤⓢ ˌriː.əl'- *stress shift:* ˌreal-life 'drama
reallo|cate ri'æl.ə.keɪt **-cates** -keɪts **-cating** -keɪ.tɪŋ ⓤⓢ -keɪ.t̬ɪŋ **-cated** -keɪ.tɪd ⓤⓢ -keɪ.t̬ɪd
reallocation ˌriː.æl.ə'keɪ.ʃən, riˌæl- ⓤⓢ ˌriː.æl-
really 'rɪə.li ⓤⓢ 'riː.ə-, 'riː.li
realm relm **-s** -z
realpolitik reɪ'ɑːl.pɒl.ɪˌtiːk, -ə- ⓤⓢ -poʊ.lɪˌ- **-s** -s
real-time 'rɪəl.taɪm ⓤⓢ 'riː.əl-
realtor (R®) 'riːl.təʳ, 'rɪəl-, -tɔːʳ ⓤⓢ 'riː.əl.t̬ɚ, -tɔːr **-s** -z
realty 'rɪəl.ti ⓤⓢ 'riː.əl.t̬i
ream riːm **-s** -z **-ing** -ɪŋ **-ed** -d
reamer 'riː.məʳ ⓤⓢ -mɚ **-s** -z
reap riːp **-s** -s **-ing** -ɪŋ **-ed** -t **-er/s** -əʳ/z ⓤⓢ -ɚ/z
reappear ˌriː.ə'pɪəʳ ⓤⓢ -'pɪr **-s** -z **-ing** -ɪŋ **-ed** -d
reappearanc|e ˌriː.ə'pɪə.rənts ⓤⓢ -'pɪr.ənts **-es** -ɪz
reapplication ˌriː.æp.lɪ'keɪ.ʃən, riˌæp-, -lə'- ⓤⓢ ˌriː.æp- **-s** -z
reappl|y ˌriː.ə'pl|aɪ **-ies** -aɪz **-ying** -aɪ.ɪŋ **-ied** -aɪd
reap|point ˌriː.ə|'pɔɪnt **-points** -'pɔɪnts **-pointing** -'pɔɪn.tɪŋ ⓤⓢ -'pɔɪn.t̬ɪŋ **-pointed** -'pɔɪn.tɪd ⓤⓢ -'pɔɪn.t̬ɪd **-pointment/s** -'pɔɪnt.mənt/s
reappraisal ˌriː.ə'preɪ.zəl **-s** -z
reapprais|e ˌriː.ə'preɪz **-es** -ɪz **-ing** -ɪŋ **-ed** -d
rear rɪəʳ ⓤⓢ rɪr **-s** -z **-ing** -ɪŋ **-ed** -d ˌ**bring up the** '**rear**
rear-admiral ˌrɪəʳ'æd.mər.əl, -mɪ.rəl ⓤⓢ ˌrɪr- **-s** -z
rearguard 'rɪə.gɑːd ⓤⓢ 'rɪr.gɑːrd **-s** -z ˌ**rearguard** '**action**
rearm ˌriː'ɑːm ⓤⓢ -'ɑːrm **-s** -z **-ing** -ɪŋ **-ed** -d
rearmament ri'ɑː.mə.mənt, ˌriː- ⓤⓢ -'ɑːr-
rearmost 'rɪə.məʊst ⓤⓢ 'rɪr.moʊst
rearrang|e ˌriː.ə'reɪndʒ **-es** -ɪz **-ing** -ɪŋ **-ed** -d **-ement/s** -mənt/s
rearview ˌrɪə'vjuː ⓤⓢ ˌrɪr- *stress shift, see compound:* ˌ**rearview** '**mirror**
rearward 'rɪə.wəd ⓤⓢ 'rɪr.wɚd **-s** -z
reason 'riː.zən **-s** -z **-ing/s** -ɪŋ/z **-ed** -d **-er/s** -əʳ/z ⓤⓢ -ɚ/z
reasonab|le 'riː.zən.ə.bl|̩ **-ly** -li **-leness** -l̩.nəs, -nɪs
reassembl|e ˌriː.ə'sem.bl̩ **-es** -z **-ing** -ɪŋ, ˌriː.ə'sem.blɪŋ **-ed** -d
reas|sert ˌriː.ə|'sɜːt ⓤⓢ -'sɝːt **-serts** -'sɜːts ⓤⓢ -'sɝːts **-serting** -'sɜː.tɪŋ ⓤⓢ -'sɝː.t̬ɪŋ **-serted** -'sɜː.tɪd ⓤⓢ -'sɝː.t̬ɪd
reassess ˌriː.ə'ses **-es** -ɪz **-ing** -ɪŋ **-ed** -t **-ment/s** -mənt/s
reassign ˌriː.ə'saɪn **-s** -z **-ing** -ɪŋ **-ed** -d
reassuranc|e ˌriː.ə'ʃʊə.rənts, -'ʃɔː- ⓤⓢ -'ʃʊr.ənts, -'ʃɝː- **-es** -ɪz
reassur|e ˌriː.ə'ʃʊəʳ, -'ʃɔːʳ ⓤⓢ -'ʃʊr, -'ʃɝː **-es** -z **-ing/ly** -ɪŋ/li **-ed** -d
Réaumur 'reɪ.əʊ.mjʊəʳ, -məʳ ⓤⓢ -ə.mjʊr, '-oʊ-
reawaken ˌriː.ə'weɪ.kən **-s** -z **-ing** -ɪŋ **-ed** -d
Reay reɪ
rebarbative rɪ'bɑː.bə.tɪv, rə- ⓤⓢ rɪ'bɑːr.bə.t̬ɪv **-ly** -li
rebate (*n.*) *discount:* 'riː.beɪt; rɪ'beɪt, rə- ⓤⓢ 'riː.beɪt **-s** -s
reba|te (*v.*) *deduct:* rɪ'beɪ|t, rə-; 'riː.beɪ|t ⓤⓢ 'riː.beɪ|t, rɪ'beɪ|t **-tes** -ts **-ting** -tɪŋ ⓤⓢ -t̬ɪŋ **-ted** -tɪd ⓤⓢ -t̬ɪd
reba|te (*v.*) *in masonry and woodworking:* 'ræb.ɪ|t, 'riː.beɪ|t ⓤⓢ 'riː.beɪ|t, 'ræb.ɪ|t **-tes** -ts **-ting** -tɪŋ ⓤⓢ -t̬ɪŋ **-ted** -tɪd ⓤⓢ -t̬ɪd
Rebecca rɪ'bek.ə, rə-
rebec(k) 'riː.bek, 'reb.ek **-s** -s
Rebekah rɪ'bek.ə, rə-
rebel (*n.*) 'reb.əl **-s** -z
rebel (*v.*) rɪ'bel, rə- **-s** -z **-ling** -ɪŋ **-led** -d
rebellion rɪ'bel.i.ən, rə-, '-jən ⓤⓢ '-jən **-s** -z
rebellious rɪ'bel.i.əs, rə- ⓤⓢ rɪ'bel.jəs **-ly** -li **-ness** -nəs, -nɪs
rebirth ˌriː'bɜːθ ⓤⓢ -'bɝːθ **-s** -s
rebirthing ˌriː'bɜː.θɪŋ ⓤⓢ -'bɝː-
reborn ˌriː'bɔːn ⓤⓢ -'bɔːrn
rebound (*n.*) 'riː.baʊnd **-s** -z ˌ**on the** '**rebound**
rebound (*adj.*) *of books, etc.:* ˌriː'baʊnd
rebound (*v.*) rɪ'baʊnd, ˌriː- ⓤⓢ 'riː.baʊnd-; ˌriː'baʊnd, rɪ- **-s** -z **-ing** -ɪŋ **-ed** -ɪd
rebrand ˌriː'brænd **-s** -z **-ing** -ɪŋ **-ed** -ɪd
Rebuck 'riː.bʌk
rebuff rɪ'bʌf, rə- **-s** -s **-ing** -ɪŋ **-ed** -t
rebuild ˌriː'bɪld **-s** -z **-ing** -ɪŋ **rebuilt** ˌriː'bɪlt
rebuk|e rɪ'bjuːk, rə- **-es** -s **-ing/ly** -ɪŋ/li **-ed** -t
rebus 'riː.bəs **-es** -ɪz
re|but rɪ|'bʌt **-buts** -'bʌts **-butting** -'bʌt.ɪŋ ⓤⓢ -'bʌt̬.ɪŋ **-butted** -'bʌt.ɪd ⓤⓢ -'bʌt̬.ɪd
rebuttable rɪ'bʌt|.ə.bl̩ ⓤⓢ -'bʌt̬-
rebutt|al rɪ'bʌt|.əl ⓤⓢ -'bʌt̬- **-er/s** -əʳ/z ⓤⓢ -ɚ/z
recalcitran|t rɪ'kæl.sɪ.trən|t, rə-, -sə- ⓤⓢ -sɪ- **-ts** -ts **-ce** -ts
recall (*v.*) rɪ'kɔːl, rə- ⓤⓢ rɪ-, rə-; 'riː.kɔːl, -kɑːl **-s** -z **-ing** -ɪŋ **-ed** -d
recall (*n.*) rɪ'kɔːl, rə-; 'riː.kɔːl ⓤⓢ 'riː.kɔːl, -kɑːl **-s** -z
re|cant rɪ|'kænt **-cants** -'kænts **-canting** -'kæn.tɪŋ ⓤⓢ -'kæn.t̬ɪŋ **-canted** -'kæn.tɪd ⓤⓢ -'kæn.t̬ɪd
recantation ˌriː.kæn'teɪ.ʃən **-s** -z

recap *(n.) recapitulation:* ˈriː.kæp **-s** -s

recap *(v.) recapitulate:* ˈriː.kæp; ˌriːˈkæp, rɪ-, rə- (US) ˈriː.kæp **-s** -s **-ping** -ɪŋ **-ped** -t

recap *(n.) a recapped tyre:* ˈriː.kæp **-s** -s

recap *(v.) retread a tyre:* ˌriːˈkæp (US) ˌriːˈkæp, ˈ-- **-s** -s **-ping** -ɪŋ **-ped** -t

recapitu|late ˌriː.kəˈpɪt.jə|.leɪt, -jʊ-, -ˈpɪtʃ.ə-, ˈ-ʊ- (US) -ˈpɪtʃ.ə- **-lates** -leɪts **-lating** -leɪ.tɪŋ (US) -leɪ.t̬ɪŋ **-lated** -leɪ.tɪd (US) -leɪ.t̬ɪd

recapitulation ˌriː.kəˌpɪt.jəˈleɪ.ʃᵊn, -jʊˈ-, -ˌpɪtʃ.əˈ-, -ʊˈ- (US) -ˌpɪtʃ.əˈ- **-s** -z

recapitulatory ˌriː.kəˈpɪt.jə.lə.tᵊr.i, -jʊ-, -ˈpɪtʃ.ə-, ˈ-ʊ-, -leɪ- (US) -ˈpɪtʃ.ə.lə.tɔːr-

recapt|ure ˌriːˈkæp.tʃ|əʳ (US) -tʃ|ɚ **-ures** -əz (US) -ɚz **-uring** -ᵊr.ɪŋ **-ured** -əd (US) -ɚd

recast ˌriːˈkɑːst (US) -ˈkæst **-s** -s **-ing** -ɪŋ

recce (R) ˈrek.i **-s** -z **-ing** -ɪŋ **-(e)d** -d

reced|e rɪˈsiːd, rə-, ˌriː- **-es** -z **-ing** -ɪŋ **-ed** -ɪd

re|ceipt rɪ|ˈsiːt, rə- **-ceipts** -ˈsiːts **-ceipting** -ˈsiː.tɪŋ (US) -ˈsiː.t̬ɪŋ **-ceipted** -ˈsiː.tɪd (US) -ˈsiː.t̬ɪd

receiv|e rɪˈsiːv, rə- **-es** -z **-ing** -ɪŋ **-ed** -d **-er/s** -əʳ/z (US) -ɚ/z **-able** -ə.bl̩ **ReˌceivedpronunciˈationˌonthereˈceivingˌendReˌceived pronunciˈation; ˌon the reˈceiving ˌend (of)**

receivership rɪˈsiː.və.ʃɪp, rə- (US) -vɚ-

recency ˈriː.sᵊn*t*.si

recension rɪˈsen*t*.ʃᵊn, rə- **-s** -z

recent ˈriː.sᵊnt **-ly** -li **-ness** -nəs, -nɪs

receptacle rɪˈsep.tə.kl̩, rə- **-s** -z

reception rɪˈsep.ʃᵊn, rə- **-s** -z

receptionist rɪˈsep.ʃᵊn.ɪst, rə- **-s** -s

receptive rɪˈsep.tɪv, rə- **-ly** -li **-ness** -nəs, -nɪs

receptivity ˌriː.sepˈtɪv.ə.ti, ˌrɪs.epˈ-, ˌres.epˈ-, -ɪ.ti (US) riːˌsepˈtɪv.ə.t̬i, rɪ-

receptor rɪˈsep.təʳ, rə- (US) -tɚ **-s** -z

recess rɪˈses, rə-; ˈriː.ses (US) ˈriː.ses; rɪˈses **-es** -ɪz

recession rɪˈseʃ.ᵊn, rə- **-s** -z

recessional rɪˈseʃ.ᵊn.ᵊl, rə- **-s** -z

recessive rɪˈses.ɪv, rə- **-ly** -li **-ness** -nəs, -nɪs

Rechabite ˈrek.ə.baɪt

recharg|e *(v.)* ˌriːˈtʃɑːdʒ, rɪ- (US) ˌriːˈtʃɑːrdʒ **-es** -ɪz **-ing** -ɪŋ **-ed** -d **-able** -ə.bl̩ **-er/s** -əʳ/z (US) -ɚ/z

recharge *(n.)* ˈriː.tʃɑːdʒ (US) -tʃɑːrdʒ

recherché rəˈʃeə.ʃeɪ (US) -ˈʃer-, --ˈ-

rechristen ˌriːˈkrɪs.ᵊn **-s** -z **-ing** -ɪŋ **-ed** -d

recidivism rɪˈsɪd.ɪ.vɪ.zᵊm, rə-, ˈ-ə- (US) ˈ-ə-

recidivist rɪˈsɪd.ɪ.vɪst, rə-, ˈ-ə- (US) ˈ-ə- **-s** -s

Recife resˈiː.fə (US) rəˈsiː-, resˈiː

recipe ˈres.ɪ.pi, ˈ-ə-, -piː **-s** -z

recipient rɪˈsɪp.i.ənt, rə- **-s** -s

reciproc|al rɪˈsɪp.rə.k|ᵊl, rə- **-als** -ᵊlz **-ally** -ᵊl.i, -li **-alness** -ᵊl.nəs, -nɪs

recipro|cate rɪˈsɪp.rə|.keɪt, rə- **-cates** -keɪts **-cating** -keɪ.tɪŋ (US) -keɪ.t̬ɪŋ **-cated** -keɪ.tɪd (US) -keɪ.t̬ɪd

reciprocation rɪˌsɪp.rəˈkeɪ.ʃᵊn, rə-

reciprocity ˌres.ɪˈprɒs.ə.ti, -ɪ.ti (US) -ˈprɑː.sə.t̬i

recis(s)ion rɪˈsɪʒ.ᵊn, rə-

recital rɪˈsaɪ.tᵊl, rə- (US) -t̬ᵊl **-s** -z

recitation ˌres.ɪˈteɪ.ʃᵊn **-s** -z

recitative *(adj.) relating to* **recital***:* rɪˈsaɪ.tə.tɪv (US) ˈres.ɪ.teɪ.t̬ɪv; rɪˈsaɪ.t̬ə-

recitative *(n. adj.) in music:* ˌres.ɪ.təˈtiːv (US) -təˈ- **-s** -z

re|cite rɪ|ˈsaɪt, rə- **-cites** -ˈsaɪts **-citing** -ˈsaɪ.tɪŋ (US) -ˈsaɪ.t̬ɪŋ **-cited** -ˈsaɪ.tɪd (US) -ˈsaɪ.t̬ɪd **-citer/s** -ˈsaɪ.təʳ/z (US) -ˈsaɪ.t̬ɚ/z

reck rek **-s** -s **-ing** -ɪŋ **-ed** -t

reckless ˈrek.ləs, -lɪs **-ly** -li **-ness** -nəs, -nɪs

reckon ˈrek.ᵊn **-s** -z **-ing/s** -ɪŋ/z **-ed** -d **-er/s** -əʳ/z (US) -ɚ/z

reclaim rɪˈkleɪm, ˌriː- **-s** -z **-ing** -ɪŋ **-ed** -d

reclaimable rɪˈkleɪ.mə.bl̩, ˌriː-

reclamation ˌrek.ləˈmeɪ.ʃᵊn **-s** -z

reclin|e rɪˈklaɪn, rə- **-es** -z **-ing** -ɪŋ **-ed** -d

recliner rɪˈklaɪ.nəʳ, rə- (US) -nɚ **-s** -z

reclus|e rɪˈkluːs, rə- (US) ˈrek.luːs; rɪˈkluːs **-es** -ɪz **-ive** -ɪv

recognition ˌrek.əgˈnɪʃ.ᵊn **-s** -z

recognizab|le, -isa- ˈrek.əg.naɪ.zə.b|l̩, ˌrek.əgˈnaɪ- (US) ˈrek.əg.naɪ- **-ly** -li

recognizanc|e, -isa- rɪˈkɒg.nɪ.zᵊn*t*s, rə-, -ˈkɒn.ɪ- (US) -ˈkɑːg.nɪ-, -ˈkɑː- **-es** -ɪz

recogniz|e, -is|e ˈrek.əg.naɪz **-es** -ɪz **-ing** -ɪŋ **-ed** -d

recoil *(n.)* ˈriː.kɔɪl; rɪˈkɔɪl, rə- **-s** -z

recoil *(v.)* rɪˈkɔɪl, rə- **-s** -z **-ing** -ɪŋ **-ed** -d

recollect ˌrek.ᵊlˈekt, ˈ--- (US) ˌrek.əˈlekt **-s** -s **-ing** -ɪŋ **-ed** -ɪd

recollection ˌrek.ᵊlˈek.ʃᵊn (US) -əˈlek- **-s** -z

recombinant ˌriːˈkɒm.bɪ.nənt, rɪ-, rə-, -bə- (US) -ˈkɑːm.bə-

recommenc|e ˌriː.kəˈmen*t*s, ˌrek.əˈ- **-es** -ɪz **-ing** -ɪŋ **-ed** -t

recommend ˌrek.əˈmend **-s** -z **-ing** -ɪŋ **-ed** -ɪd **-able** -ə.bl̩

recommendation ˌrek.ə.menˈdeɪ.ʃᵊn, -mənˈ- (US) -mənˈ- **-s** -z

recompens|e ˈrek.əm.pen*t*s **-es** -ɪz **-ing** -ɪŋ **-ed** -t

recompos|e ˌriː.kəmˈpəʊz (US) -ˈpoʊz **-es** -ɪz **-ing** -ɪŋ **-ed** -d

recon ˈriː.kɒn (US) -kɑːn

reconcilab|le ˈrek.ᵊn.saɪ.lə.b|l̩, ˌrek.ᵊnˈsaɪ- (US) ˌrek.ᵊnˈsaɪ- **-ly** -li

reconcil|e ˈrek.ᵊn.saɪl **-es** -z **-ing** -ɪŋ **-ed** -d **-er/s** -əʳ/z (US) -ɚ/z

reconciliation ˌrek.ᵊnˌsɪl.iˈeɪ.ʃᵊn **-s** -z

recondite ˈrek.ᵊn.daɪt; rɪˈkɒn-, rə- (US) ˈrek.ᵊn-; rɪˈkɑːn-, rə-

recondition ˌriː.kᵊnˈdɪʃ.ᵊn **-s** -z **-ing** -ɪŋ **-ed** -d

reconduct ˌriː.kᵊnˈdʌkt **-s** -s **-ing** -ɪŋ **-ed** -ɪd

reconnaissanc|e rɪˈkɒn.ɪ.sᵊn*t*s, rə-, ˈ-ə- (US) -ˈkɑː.nə-, -zᵊn*t*s **-es** -ɪz

reconnoit|er ˌrek.əˈnɔɪ.t|əʳ (US) ˌriː.kəˈnɔɪ.t̬|ɚ, ˌrek.əˈ- **-ers** -əz (US) -ɚz **-ering** -ᵊr.ɪŋ **-ered** -əd (US) -ɚd

reconnoit|re ˌrek.əˈnɔɪ.t|əʳ (US) ˌriː.kəˈnɔɪ.t̬|ɚ, ˌrek.əˈ- **-res** -əz (US) -ɚz **-ring** -ᵊr.ɪŋ **-red** -əd (US) -ɚd

reconqu|er ˌriːˈkɒŋ.k|əʳ (US) -ˈkɑːŋ.k|ɚ **-ers** -əz (US) -ɚz **-ering** -ᵊr.ɪŋ **-ered** -əd (US) -ɚd

reconquest ˌriːˈkɒŋ.kwest (US) -ˈkɑːŋ- **-s** -s

reconsid|er ˌriː.kᵊnˈsɪd|.əʳ (US) -ɚ **-ers** -əz (US) -ɚz **-ering** -ᵊr.ɪŋ **-ered** -əd (US) -ɚz

reconsideration ˌriː.kᵊnˌsɪd.ᵊrˈeɪ.ʃᵊn (US) -əˈreɪ-

reconstitu|te ˌriːˈkɒn.stɪ.tjuː|t, -stə-, -tʃuː|t (US) -ˈkɑːn.stə.tuː|t, -tjuː|t **-tes** -ts **-ting** -tɪŋ (US) -t̬ɪŋ **-ted** -tɪd (US) -t̬ɪd

reconstitution ˌriːˌkɒn*t*.stɪˈtjuː.ʃᵊn, -stəˈ-, -ˈtʃuː- (US) -ˌkɑːn*t*.stəˈtuː-, -ˈtjuː- **-s** -z

reconstruct ˌriː.kᵊnˈstrʌkt **-s** -s **-ing** -ɪŋ **-ed** -ɪd **-ive** -ɪv

reconstruction ˌriː.kᵊnˈstrʌk.ʃᵊn **-s** -z

reconven|e ˌriː.kənˈviːn **-es** -z **-ing** -ɪŋ **-ed** -d

reconversion ˌriː.kᵊnˈvɜː.ʃᵊn, -ʒᵊn (US) -ˈvɝː.ʒᵊn, -ʃᵊn **-s** -z

recon|vert ˌriː.kᵊn|ˈvɜːt (US) -ˈvɝːt **-verts** -ˈvɜːts (US) -ˈvɝːts **-verting** -ˈvɜː.tɪŋ (US) -ˈvɝː.t̬ɪŋ **-verted** -ˈvɜː.tɪd (US) -ˈvɝː.t̬ɪd

reconvey ˌriː.kᵊnˈveɪ **-s** -z **-ing** -ɪŋ **-ed** -d

record *(n.)* ˈrek.ɔːd (US) -ɚd **-s** -z **ˈrecord ˌplayer**

record *(v.)* rɪˈkɔːd, rə- (US) -ˈkɔːrd **-s** -z **-ing/s** -ɪŋ/z **-ed** -ɪd **-able** -ə.bl̩ **reˌcorded deˈlivery**

record-break|ing ˈrek.ɔːdˌbreɪ.k|ɪŋ (US) -ɚdˌ- **-er/s** -əʳ/z (US) -ɚ/z

recorder rɪˈkɔː.dəʳ, rə- (US) -ˈkɔːr.dɚ **-s** -z

recordist rɪˈkɔː.dɪst, rə- (US) -ˈkɔːr- **-s** -s

recount *(n.)* ˈriː.kaʊnt, ˌ-ˈ- (US) ˈriː.kaʊnt **-s** -s

re|count *(v.) count again:* ˌriː|ˈkaʊnt **-counts** -ˈkaʊnts **-counting** -ˈkaʊn.tɪŋ (US) -ˈkaʊn.t̬ɪŋ **-counted** -ˈkaʊn.tɪd (US) -ˈkaʊn.t̬ɪd

re|count (*v.*) *narrate:* rɪˈkaʊnt, rə- **-counts** -ˈkaʊnts **-counting** -ˈkaʊn.tɪŋ (US) -ˈkaʊn.t̬ɪŋ **-counted** -ˈkaʊn.tɪd (US) -ˈkaʊn.t̬ɪd

recoup rɪˈkuːp, rə-, ˌriː- (US) rɪ-, rə- **-s** -s **-ing** -ɪŋ **-ed** -t **-ment** -mənt

recourse rɪˈkɔːs, rə- (US) ˈriː.kɔːrs; rɪˈkɔːrs

recov|er *get back, come back to health, etc.:* rɪˈkʌv|.əʳ, rə- (US) -ɚ **-ers** -əz (US) -ɚz **-ering** -ᵊr.ɪŋ **-ered** -əd (US) -ɚd **-erable** -ᵊr.ə.bl̩

recov|er *cover again:* ˌriːˈkʌv|.əʳ (US) -ɚ **-ers** -əz (US) -ɚz **-ering** -ᵊr.ɪŋ **-ered** -əd (US) -ɚd

recover|y rɪˈkʌv.ᵊr|.i, rə- (US) -ɚ|.i, ˈ-r|i **-ies** -iz

recreant ˈrek.ri.ənt **-s** -s **-ly** -li

recre|ate *create anew:* ˌriː.kriˈ|eɪt **-ates** -ˈeɪts **-ating** -ˈeɪ.tɪŋ (US) -ˈeɪ.t̬ɪŋ **-ated** -ˈeɪ.tɪd (US) -ˈeɪ.t̬ɪd

recre|ate *refresh:* ˈrek.ri.|eɪt **-ates** -eɪts **-ating** -eɪ.tɪŋ (US) -eɪ.t̬ɪŋ **-ated** -eɪ.tɪd (US) -eɪ.t̬ɪd **-ative** -eɪ.tɪv (US) -eɪ.t̬ɪv

recreation *creating anew:* ˌriː.kriˈeɪ.ʃᵊn **-s** -z

recreation *refreshment, amusement:* ˌrek.riˈeɪ.ʃᵊn **-s** -z **-al** -ᵊl

recrimi|nate rɪˈkrɪm.ɪ|.neɪt, rə-, ˈ-ə- (US) ˈ-ə- **-nates** -neɪts **-nating** -neɪ.tɪŋ (US) -neɪ.t̬ɪŋ **-nated** -neɪ.tɪd (US) -neɪ.t̬ɪd **-nator/s** -neɪ.təʳ/z (US) -neɪ.t̬ɚ/z

recrimination rɪˌkrɪm.ɪˈneɪ.ʃᵊn, rə-, -əˈ- (US) -əˈ- **-s** -z

recriminatory rɪˈkrɪm.ɪ.nə.tᵊr.i, rə-, ˈ-ə- (US) -ə.nə.tɔːr-

recross ˌriːˈkrɒs (US) -ˈkrɑːs **-es** -ɪz **-ing** -ɪŋ **-ed** -t

recrudesc|e ˌriː.kruːˈdes, ˌrek.ruːˈ- (US) ˌriː.kruːˈ- **-es** -ɪz **-ing** -ɪŋ **-ed** -t

recrudescen|ce ˌriː.kruːˈdes.ᵊn|*t*s, ˌrek.ruːˈ- (US) ˌriː.kruːˈ- **-t** -t

re|cruit rɪˈkruːt, rə- **-cruits** -ˈkruːts **-cruiting** -ˈkruː.tɪŋ (US) -ˈkruː.t̬ɪŋ **-cruited** -ˈkruː.tɪd (US) -ˈkruː.t̬ɪd **-cruiter/s** -ˈkruː.təʳ/z (US) -ˈkruː.t̬ɚ/z **-cruitment** -ˈkruːt.mənt

rectal ˈrek.tᵊl **-ly** -i

rectangle ˈrek.tæŋ.gl̩ **-s** -z

rectangular rekˈtæŋ.gjə.ləʳ, -gjʊ- (US) -gjə.lɚ **-ly** -li

rectification ˌrek.tɪ.fɪˈkeɪ.ʃᵊn, -tə- (US) -tə- **-s** -z

recti|fy ˈrek.tɪ|.faɪ, -tə- (US) -tə- **-fies** -faɪz **-fying** -faɪ.ɪŋ **-fied** -faɪd **-fier/s** -faɪ.əʳ/z (US) -faɪ.ɚ/z **-fiable** -faɪ.ə.bl̩

rectiline|al ˌrek.tɪˈlɪn.i|.əl, -təˈ- (US) -təˈ- **-ar** -əʳ (US) -ɚ

rectitude ˈrek.tɪ.tjuːd, -tə-, -tʃuːd (US) -tə.tuːd, -tjuːd

recto ˈrek.təʊ (US) -toʊ

rector ˈrek.təʳ (US) -tɚ **-s** -z

rectorate ˈrek.tᵊr.ət, -ɪt, -eɪt (US) -ɪt **-s** -s

rectorial rekˈtɔː.ri.əl (US) -ˈtɔːr.i-

rectorship ˈrek.tə.ʃɪp (US) -tɚ- **-s** -s

rector|y ˈrek.tᵊr|.i **-ies** -iz

rect|um ˈrek.t|əm **-ums** -əmz **-a** -ə

rect|us ˈrek.t|əs **-i** -aɪ

Reculver rɪˈkʌl.vəʳ, rə- (US) -vɚ **-s** -z

recumben|ce rɪˈkʌm.bən|*t*s, rə- **-cy** -si

recumbent rɪˈkʌm.bənt, rə- **-ly** -li

recuper|ate rɪˈkjuː.pᵊr|.eɪt, rə-, -ˈkuː- (US) -ˈkuː.pə.r|eɪt, -ˈkjuː- **-ates** -eɪts **-ating** -eɪ.tɪŋ (US) -eɪ.t̬ɪŋ **-ated** -eɪ.tɪd (US) -eɪ.t̬ɪd

recuperation rɪˌkjuː.pᵊrˈeɪ.ʃᵊn, rə-, -ˌkuː- (US) -ˌkuː.pəˈreɪ-, -ˌkjuː-

recuperative rɪˈkjuː.pᵊr.ə.tɪv, rə-, -ˈkjuː- (US) -ˈkuː.pɚ.ə.t̬ɪv, -ˈkjuː-

recur rɪˈkɜːʳ, rə- (US) -ˈkɝː **-s** -z **-ring** -ɪŋ **-red** -d

recurrenc|e rɪˈkʌr.ᵊn*t*s, rə- (US) -ˈkɝː- **-es** -ɪz

recurrent rɪˈkʌr.ənt, rə- (US) -ˈkɝː- **-ly** -li

recursive rɪˈkɜː.sɪv, ˌriː- (US) -ˈkɝː- **-s** -z **-ly** -li

recurved ˌriːˈkɜːvd, rɪ-, rə- (US) -ˈkɝːvd

recusan|cy ˈrek.jʊ.zᵊn*t*|.si, -jə-; rɪˈkjuː-, rə- (US) ˈrek.jʊ-; rɪˈkjuː-, rə- **-ce** -s

recusant ˈrek.jʊ.zᵊnt, -jə-; rɪˈkjuː-, rə- (US) ˈrek.jʊ-; rɪˈkjuː-, rə- **-s** -s

recycl|e ˌriːˈsaɪ.kl̩ **-es** -z **-ing** -ɪŋ, ˈ-klɪŋ **-ed** -d **-able** -ə.bl̩, ˈ-klə.bl̩

red (R) red **-s** -z **-der** -əʳ (US) -ɚ **-dest** -ɪst, -əst **-ness** -nəs, -nɪs **ˌred aˈlert; ˌred ˈcard; ˌred ˈcarpet; ˌRed ˈCrescent; ˌRed ˈCross; ˌred ˈherring; ˌRed ˈIndian; ˌRed ˈSea; ˌred ˈtape; in the ˈred; ˌsee ˈred; ˌnot worth a ˌred ˈcent; ˌreds under the ˈbed**

redact rɪˈdækt, rə- **-s** -s **-ing** -ɪŋ **-ed** -ɪd **-or/s** -əʳ/z (US) -ɚ/z

redaction rɪˈdæk.ʃᵊn, rə- **-s** -z

red-blooded ˌredˈblʌd.ɪd **-ness** -nəs, -nɪs *stress shift:* ˌred-blooded ˈmale

Redbourn ˈred.bɔːn (US) ˈred.bɔːrn

redbreast ˈred.brest **-s** -s

redbrick ˈred.brɪk, ˌ-ˈ- (US) ˈred.brɪk **ˌredbrick uniˈversity**

Redbridge ˈred.brɪdʒ

redbud ˈred.bʌd **-s** -z

redcap ˈred.kæp **-s** -s

Redcar ˈred.kɑːʳ *locally:* -kə (US) ˈred.kɑːr

Redcliffe, Redclyffe ˈred.klɪf

redcoat ˈred.kəʊt (US) -koʊt **-s** -s

redcurrant ˈredˌkʌr.ənt **-s** -s

Reddaway ˈred.ə.weɪ

redden ˈred.ᵊn **-s** -z **-ing** -ɪŋ **-ed** -d

Redding ˈred.ɪŋ

reddish ˈred.ɪʃ **-ness** -nəs, -nɪs

Redditch ˈred.ɪtʃ

reddle ˈred.l̩

redecor|ate ˌriːˈdek.ᵊr|.eɪt (US) -ə.r|eɪt **-ates** -eɪts **-ating** -eɪ.tɪŋ (US) -eɪ.t̬ɪŋ **-ated** -eɪ.tɪd (US) -eɪ.t̬ɪd

redeem rɪˈdiːm, rə- **-s** -z **-ing** -ɪŋ **-ed** -d **-able** -ə.bl̩

redeemer (R) rɪˈdiː.məʳ, rə- (US) -mɚ **-s** -z

redefin|e ˌriː.dɪˈfaɪn, -dəˈ- **-es** -z **-ing** -ɪŋ **-ed** -d

redeliv|er ˌriː.dɪˈlɪv|.əʳ, -dəˈ- (US) -ɚ **-ers** -əz (US) -ɚz **-ering** -ᵊr.ɪŋ **-ered** -əd (US) -ɚd **-ery** -ᵊr.i

redemption (R) rɪˈdem*p*.ʃᵊn, rə- **-s** -z

redemptive rɪˈdem*p*.tɪv, rə-

re-deploy ˌriː.dɪˈplɔɪ, -dəˈ- **-s** -z **-ing** -ɪŋ **-ed** -d **-ment/s** -mənt/s

redesign ˌriː.dɪˈzaɪn, -dəˈ- **-s** -z **-ing** -ɪŋ **-ed** -d

redevelop ˌriː.dɪˈvel.əp, -dəˈ- **-s** -s **-ing** -ɪŋ **-ed** -t **-ment/s** -mənt/s

red-eye ˈred.aɪ **-s** -z

Redfern ˈred.fɜːn (US) -fɝːn

Redfield ˈred.fiːld

Redford ˈred.fəd (US) -fɚd

Redgrave ˈred.greɪv, ˈreg- (US) ˈred-

red-handed ˌredˈhæn.dɪd

redhead (R) ˈred.hed **-s** -z

Redheugh ˈred.hjuːf, -juːf, -jəf

Redhill ˌredˈhɪl, ˈ--

red-hot ˌredˈhɒt (US) -ˈhɑːt *stress shift:* ˌred-hot ˈpoker

re-dial ˌriːˈdaɪəl (US) -ˈdaɪəl **-s** -z **-ling** -ɪŋ **-led** -d

Rediffusion® ˌriː.dɪˈfjuː.ʒᵊn, -dəˈ-

redintegration rɪˌdɪn.tɪˈgreɪ.ʃᵊn, redˌɪn-, -təˈ- (US) redˌɪn.t̬əˈ-, rɪˌdɪn-

redirect ˌriː.dɪˈrekt, -daɪ-, -də- (US) -dɪˈ-, -daɪˈ- **-s** -s **-ing** -ɪŋ **-ed** -ɪd

rediscov|er ˌriː.dɪˈskʌv|.əʳ (US) -ɚ **-ers** -əz (US) -ɚz **-ering** -ᵊr.ɪŋ **-ered** -əd (US) -ɚd **-ery** -ᵊr.i

redistribu|te ˌriː.dɪˈstrɪb.juː|t, -jʊ|t, -dəˈ-; -strɪˈbjuː|t, -stəˈ- (US) ˌriː.dɪˈstrɪb.juː|t, -jʊ|t **-tes** -ts **-ting** -tɪŋ (US) -t̬ɪŋ **-ted** -tɪd (US) -t̬ɪd

redistribution ˌriː.dɪ.strɪˈbjuː.ʃᵊn, -strəˈ- **-s** -z

redivid|e ˌriː.dɪˈvaɪd, -dəˈ- **-es** -z **-ing** -ɪŋ **-ed** -ɪd

redivivus ˌred.ɪˈvaɪ.vəs, -əˈ-, -ˈviː-

Redknapp ˈred.næp

red-letter day ˌredˈlet.əˌdeɪ (US) -ˈlet̬.ɚˌ- **-s** -z

red-light district ˌredˈlaɪtˌdɪs.trɪkt (US) ˈred.laɪtˌ- **-s** -s

Redman ˈred.mən, ˈreb- (US) ˈred.mæn

Redmond ˈred.mənd

redneck ˈred.nek **-s** -s

re|-do ˌriːˈ|duː **-does** -ˈdʌz **-doing** -ˈduː.ɪŋ **-did** -ˈdɪd **-done** -ˈdʌn

redolen|t ˈred.ᵊl.ən|t, -əʊ.lən|t (US) -ᵊl.ən|t **-ce** -*t*s

redoubl|e ˌriːˈdʌb.l̩, rɪ- **-es** -z **-ing** -ɪŋ, ˌriːˈdʌb.lɪŋ, rɪˈdʌb- **-ed** -d
redoubt rɪˈdaʊt, rə- **-s** -s
redoubtab|le rɪˈdaʊ.tə.b|l̩, rə- Ⓤⓢ -t̬ə- **-ly** -li
redound rɪˈdaʊnd, rə- **-s** -z **-ing** -ɪŋ **-ed** -ɪd
Redpath ˈred.pɑːθ, ˈreb- Ⓤⓢ ˈred.pæθ
redraft ˌriːˈdrɑːft Ⓤⓢ -ˈdræft **-s** -s **-ing** -ɪŋ **-ed** -ɪd
re-draw ˌriːˈdrɔː Ⓤⓢ -ˈdrɑː, -ˈdrɔː **-s** -z **-ing** -ɪŋ **re-drew** ˌriːˈdruː **re-drawn** ˌriːˈdrɔːn Ⓤⓢ -ˈdrɑːn, -ˈdrɔːn
redress (*v.*) rɪˈdres, rə- **-es** -ɪz **-ing** -ɪŋ **-ed** -t
redress (*n.*) rɪˈdres, rə-; ˈriː.dres Ⓤⓢ ˈriː.dres
Redriff ˈred.rɪf
Redruth ˌredˈruːθ, ˈ--
redshank ˈred.ʃæŋk **-s** -s
redskin (R) ˈred.skɪn **-s** -z
redstart ˈred.stɑːt Ⓤⓢ -stɑːrt **-s** -s
reduc|e rɪˈdjuːs, rə- Ⓤⓢ -ˈduːs, -ˈdjuːs **-es** -ɪz **-ing** -ɪŋ **-ed** -t **-er/s** -əʳ/z Ⓤⓢ -ɚ/z
reducibility rɪˌdjuː.səˈbɪl.ə.ti, rə-, -sɪˈ-, -ɪ.ti Ⓤⓢ -ˌduː.səˈbɪl.ə.t̬i, -ˌdjuː-
reducible rɪˈdjuː.sə.bl̩, rə-, -sɪ- Ⓤⓢ -ˈduː.sə-, -ˈdjuː-
reductio ad absurdum rɪˌdʌk.ti.əʊ.æd.æbˈsɜː.dəm, rə-, -ʃi-, -əbˈ- Ⓤⓢ -ti.oʊ.æd.æbˈsɝː-, ˈ-ʃi-
reduction rɪˈdʌk.ʃᵊn, rə- **-s** -z
reduction|ism rɪˈdʌk.ʃᵊn|.ɪ.zᵊm **-ist/s** -ɪst/s
reductionistic rɪˌdʌk.ʃᵊnˈɪs.tɪk, rə-
reductive rɪˈdʌk.tɪv, rə-
redundan|cy rɪˈdʌn.dənt|.si, rə- **-cies** -siz **-ce** -s
redundant rɪˈdʌn.dənt, rə- **-ly** -li
redupli|cate rɪˈdjuː.plɪ|.keɪt, rə-, ˌriː-, -ˈdʒuː-, -plə- Ⓤⓢ -ˈduː.plə-, -ˈdjuː- **-cates** -keɪts **-cating** -keɪ.tɪŋ Ⓤⓢ -keɪ.t̬ɪŋ **-cated** -keɪ.tɪd Ⓤⓢ -keɪ.t̬ɪd
reduplication rɪˌdjuː.plɪˈkeɪ.ʃᵊn, rə-, ˌriː-, -ˌdʒuː-, -pləˈ- Ⓤⓢ -ˌduː.pləˈ-, -ˌdjuː- **-s** -z
reduplicative rɪˈdjuː.plɪ.kə.tɪv, rə-, -ˈdʒuː-, -plə-, -keɪ- Ⓤⓢ -ˈduː.plə.keɪ.t̬ɪv, -ˈdju-
redwing ˈred.wɪŋ **-s** -z
redwood (R) ˈred.wʊd **-s** -z
Reebok® ˈriː.bɒk Ⓤⓢ -bɑːk **-s** -s
Reece riːs
re-echo ˌriːˈek.əʊ, ri- Ⓤⓢ -oʊ **-es** -z **-ing** -ɪŋ **-ed** -d
reed (R) riːd **-s** -z
re-ed|it ˌriːˈed|.ɪt **-its** -ɪts **-iting** -ɪ.tɪŋ Ⓤⓢ -ɪ.t̬ɪŋ **-ited** -ɪ.tɪd Ⓤⓢ -ɪ.t̬ɪd
re-edition ˌriː.ɪˈdɪʃ.ᵊn, -əˈ- **-s** -z
re-edu|cate ˌriːˈedʒ.ʊ|.keɪt, ˈ-ə-, -ˈed.jʊ-, -jə- Ⓤⓢ -ˈedʒ.ʊ-, ˈ-ə- **-cates** -keɪts **-cating** -keɪ.tɪŋ Ⓤⓢ -keɪ.t̬ɪŋ **-cated** -keɪ.tɪd Ⓤⓢ -keɪ.t̬ɪd
re-education ˌriːˌedʒ.ʊˈkeɪ.ʃᵊn, -əˈ-, -ˌed.jʊˈ-, -jəˈ- Ⓤⓢ -ˌedʒ.ʊˈ-, -əˈ-
reed-warbler ˈriːdˌwɔː.bləʳ, ˌ-ˈ-- Ⓤⓢ ˈriːdˌwɔːr.blɚ **-s** -z
reed|y ˈriː.d|i **-ier** -i.əʳ Ⓤⓢ -i.ɚ **-iest** -i.ɪst, -i.əst **-iness** -ɪ.nəs, -ɪ.nɪs
reef riːf **-s** -s **-ing** -ɪŋ **-ed** -t **ˈreef ˌknot**
reefer ˈriː.fəʳ Ⓤⓢ -fɚ **-s** -z
reek riːk **-s** -s **-ing** -ɪŋ **-ed** -t
Reekie ˈriː.ki
reel riːl **-s** -z **-ing** -ɪŋ **-ed** -d
re-elect ˌriː.ɪˈlekt, -əˈ- **-s** -s **-ing** -ɪŋ **-ed** -ɪd
re-election ˌriː.ɪˈlek.ʃᵊn, -əˈ- **-s** -z
reel-to-reel ˌriːl.təˈriːl, -tʊˈ-
re-embark ˌriː.ɪmˈbɑːk, -emˈ- Ⓤⓢ -ˈbɑːrk **-s** -s **-ing** -ɪŋ **-ed** -t
re-embarkation ˌriː.ɪm.bɑːˈkeɪ.ʃᵊn, -em-; riˌem- Ⓤⓢ ˌriː.ɪm.bɑːrˈ-, -em- **-s** -z
re-enact ˌriː.ɪˈnækt, -əˈ-, -enˈækt **-s** -s **-ing** -ɪŋ **-ed** -ɪd **-ment/s** -mənt/s
reenforc|e ˌriː.ɪnˈfɔːs, -ənˈ- Ⓤⓢ -ˈfɔːrs **-es** -ɪz **-ing** -ɪŋ **-ed** -t
re-engag|e ˌriː.ɪŋˈgeɪdʒ, -eŋˈ-, -ɪnˈ-, -enˈ- Ⓤⓢ -ɪnˈ-, -enˈ- **-es** -ɪz **-ing** -ɪŋ **-ed** -d **-ement/s** -mənt/s
re-enlist ˌriː.ɪnˈlɪst, -enˈ- **-s** -s **-ing** -ɪŋ **-ed** -ɪd
re-ent|er ˌriːˈen.t|əʳ, ri- Ⓤⓢ -t̬|ɚ **-ers** -əz Ⓤⓢ -ɚz **-ering** -ᵊr.ɪŋ **-ered** -əd Ⓤⓢ -ɚd
re-entr|y ˌriːˈen.tr|i, ri- **-ies** -iz
Rees(e) riːs
re-establish ˌriː.ɪˈstæb.lɪʃ, -esˈtæb- **-es** -ɪz **-ing** -ɪŋ **-ed** -t **-ment** -mənt
reeve (R) riːv **-s** -z
Reeves riːvz
re-examination ˌriː.ɪgˌzæm.ɪˈneɪ.ʃᵊn, -egˌ-, -əˈ- **-s** -z
re-examin|e ˌriː.ɪgˈzæm.ɪn, -egˈ- **-es** -z **-ing** -ɪŋ **-ed** -d
re-expor|t (*v.*) ˌriː.ɪkˈspɔː|t, -ekˈ- Ⓤⓢ -ˈspɔːr|t; -ˈek.spɔːr|t **-ts** -ts **-ting** -tɪŋ Ⓤⓢ -t̬ɪŋ **-ted** -tɪd Ⓤⓢ -t̬ɪd
ref (R) ref **-s** -s
refac|e ˌriːˈfeɪs **-es** -ɪz **-ing** -ɪŋ **-ed** -t
refashion ˌriːˈfæʃ.ᵊn **-s** -z **-ing** -ɪŋ **-ed** -d
refection rɪˈfek.ʃᵊn, rə-
refector|y rɪˈfek.tᵊr|.i, rə-, ˈref.ɪk- Ⓤⓢ rɪˈfek-, rə- **-ies** -iz
refer rɪˈfɜːʳ, rə- Ⓤⓢ -ˈfɝː **-s** -z **-ring** -ɪŋ **-red** -d
referable rɪˈfɜː.rə.bl̩, rə-; ˈref.ᵊr- Ⓤⓢ rɪˈfɝː.ə-, rə-; ˈref.ɚ-
referee ˌref.ᵊrˈiː Ⓤⓢ -əˈriː **-s** -z **-ing** -ɪŋ **-d** -d
referenc|e ˈref.ᵊr.ᵊnts, ˈ-rᵊnts **-es** -ɪz ˈ**reference ˌbook**; ˈ**reference ˌlibrary**
referend|um ˌref.ᵊrˈen.d|əm Ⓤⓢ -əˈren- **-ums** -əmz **-a** -ə
referent ˈref.ᵊr.ənt, ˈ-rᵊnt **-s** -s
referential ˌref.ᵊrˈen.tʃᵊl Ⓤⓢ -əˈrent.ʃᵊl **-ly** -i
referral rɪˈfɜː.rᵊl, rə- Ⓤⓢ -ˈfɝː.ᵊl **-s** -z
refill (*n.*) ˈriː.fɪl **-s** -z
refill (*v.*) ˌriːˈfɪl **-s** -z **-ing** -ɪŋ **-ed** -d
refin|e rɪˈfaɪn, rə- **-es** -z **-ing** -ɪŋ **-ed** -d **-er/s** -əʳ/z Ⓤⓢ -ɚ/z **-ement/s** -mənt/s
refiner|y rɪˈfaɪ.nᵊr|.i, rə- **-ies** -iz
refit (*n.*) ˈriː.fɪt, ˌ-ˈ-
re|fit (*v.*) ˌriː|ˈfɪt **-fits** -ˈfɪts **-fitting** -ˈfɪt.ɪŋ Ⓤⓢ -ˈfɪt̬.ɪŋ **-fitted** -ˈfɪt.ɪd Ⓤⓢ -ˈfɪt̬.ɪd
re|flate ˌriː|ˈfleɪt **-flates** -ˈfleɪts **-flating** -ˈfleɪ.tɪŋ Ⓤⓢ -ˈfleɪ.t̬ɪŋ **-flated** -ˈfleɪ.tɪd Ⓤⓢ -ˈfleɪ.t̬ɪd
reflation ˌriːˈfleɪ.ʃᵊn
reflationary ˌriːˈfleɪ.ʃᵊn.ᵊr.i Ⓤⓢ -er-
reflect rɪˈflekt, rə- **-s** -s **-ing** -ɪŋ **-ed** -ɪd **-or/s** -əʳ/z Ⓤⓢ -ɚ/z
reflection rɪˈflek.ʃᵊn, rə- **-s** -z
reflective rɪˈflek.tɪv, rə- **-ly** -li **-ness** -nəs, -nɪs
reflex ˈriː.fleks **-es** -ɪz
reflexed rɪˈflekst, ˌriː-; ˈriː.flekst
reflexive rɪˈflek.sɪv, rə- **-ly** -li **-ness** -nəs, -nɪs
reflexolog|y ˌriː.flekˈsɒl.ə.dʒ|i Ⓤⓢ -ˈsɑː.lə- **-ist/s** -ɪst/s
re|float ˌriː|ˈfləʊt Ⓤⓢ -ˈfloʊt **-floats** -ˈfləʊts Ⓤⓢ -ˈfloʊts **-floating** -ˈfləʊ.tɪŋ Ⓤⓢ -ˈfloʊ.t̬ɪŋ **-floated** -ˈfləʊ.tɪd Ⓤⓢ -ˈfloʊ.t̬ɪd
refluent ˈref.lu.ənt
reflux ˈriː.flʌks **-es** -ɪz
reforest ˌriːˈfɒr.ɪst Ⓤⓢ -ˈfɔːr.ɪst **-s** -s **-ing** -ɪŋ **-ed** -ɪd
reforestation ˌriː.fɒr.ɪˈsteɪ.ʃᵊn, -əˈ- Ⓤⓢ -fɔːr.ɪˈ-
reform (*n. v.*) *make better, become better, etc.:* rɪˈfɔːm, rə- Ⓤⓢ -ˈfɔːrm **-s** -z **-ing** -ɪŋ **-ed** -d **-er/s** -əʳ/z Ⓤⓢ -ɚ/z **-able** -ə.bl̩ **reˈform ˌschool**
re-form (*v.*) *form again:* ˌriːˈfɔːm Ⓤⓢ -ˈfɔːrm **-s** -z **-ing** -ɪŋ **-ed** -d
reformation (R) ˌref.əˈmeɪ.ʃᵊn, -ɔːˈ- Ⓤⓢ -ɚˈ- **-s** -z
reformative rɪˈfɔː.mə.tɪv, rə- Ⓤⓢ -ˈfɔːr.mə.t̬ɪv
reformator|y rɪˈfɔː.mə.tᵊr|.i, rə- Ⓤⓢ -ˈfɔːr.mə.tɔːr- **-ies** -iz
reformist rɪˈfɔː.mɪst, rə- Ⓤⓢ -ˈfɔːr-
refract rɪˈfrækt, rə- **-s** -s **-ing** -ɪŋ **-ed** -ɪd **-or/s** -əʳ/z Ⓤⓢ -ɚ/z **-ive** -ɪv
refraction rɪˈfræk.ʃᵊn, rə- **-s** -z
refractor|y rɪˈfræk.tᵊr|.i, rə- **-ily** -ᵊl.i, -ɪ.li **-iness** -ɪ.nəs, -ɪ.nɪs
refrain rɪˈfreɪn, rə- **-s** -z **-ing** -ɪŋ **-ed** -d
refresh rɪˈfreʃ, rə- **-es** -ɪz **-ing/ly** -ɪŋ/li **-ed** -t **-er/s** -əʳ/z Ⓤⓢ -ɚ/z **reˈfresher ˌcourse**
refreshment rɪˈfreʃ.mənt, rə- **-s** -s

refried *stress shift, see compound:* ˌriːˈfraɪd ˌ**refried** ˈ**beans**
refriger|ate rɪˈfrɪdʒ.ᵊr|.eɪt, rə- ⓤⓢ -ə.r|eɪt **-ates** -eɪts **-ating** -eɪ.tɪŋ ⓤⓢ -eɪ.t̬ɪŋ **-ated** -eɪ.tɪd ⓤⓢ -eɪ.t̬ɪd
refrigeration rɪˌfrɪdʒ.ᵊrˈeɪ.ʃᵊn, rə- ⓤⓢ -əˈreɪ-
refrigerator rɪˈfrɪdʒ.ᵊr.eɪ.təʳ, rə- ⓤⓢ -ə.reɪ.t̬ɚ **-s** -z
reft reft
re-fuel ˌriːˈfjuː.əl, -ˈfjʊəl ⓤⓢ -ˈfjuː.əl, -ˈfjuːl **-s** -z **-ling** -ɪŋ **-led** -d
refug|e ˈref.juːdʒ **-es** -ɪz
refugee ˌref.jʊˈdʒiː, -jəˈ- ⓤⓢ ˌref.jʊˈdʒiː, -jəˈ-; ˈref.jʊ.dʒi, -jə- **-s** -z
refulgen|ce rɪˈfʌl.dʒən|ts, rə- ⓤⓢ -ˈfʌl-, -ˈfʊl- **-t/ly** -t/li
refund (*n.*) ˈriː.fʌnd **-s** -z
refund (*v.*) ˌriːˈfʌnd, rɪ-, rə-; ˈriː.fʌnd ⓤⓢ ˌriːˈfʌnd, rɪ-, rə- **-s** -z **-ing** -ɪŋ **-ed** -ɪd
refurbish ˌriːˈfɜː.bɪʃ ⓤⓢ -ˈfɝː- **-es** -ɪz **-ing** -ɪŋ **-ed** -t **-ment/s** -mənt/s
refurnish ˌriːˈfɜː.nɪʃ ⓤⓢ -ˈfɝː- **-es** -ɪz **-ing** -ɪŋ **-ed** -t
refusal rɪˈfjuː.zᵊl, rə- **-s** -z
refuse (*n. adj.*) ˈref.juːs
refus|e (*v.*) rɪˈfjuːz, rə- **-es** -ɪz **-ing** -ɪŋ **-ed** -d **-able** -ə.bl̩
refusenik rɪˈfjuːz.nɪk, rə- **-s** -s
refutability ˌref.jʊ.təˈbɪl.ə.ti, -jə-, -ɪ.ti; rɪˌfjuː-, rə- ⓤⓢ rɪˌfjuː.t̬əˈbɪl.ə.t̬i; ˌref.jə.t̬əˈ-
refutab|le ˈref.jʊ.tə.b|l̩, -jə-; rɪˈfjuː-, rə- ⓤⓢ rɪˈfjuː.t̬ə-, rə-; ˈref.jə- **-ly** -li
refutation ˌref.jʊˈteɪ.ʃᵊn, -jəˈ- **-s** -z
re|fute rɪ|ˈfjuːt, rə- **-futes** -ˈfjuːts **-futing** -ˈfjuː.tɪŋ ⓤⓢ -ˈfjuː.t̬ɪŋ **-futed** -ˈfjuː.tɪd ⓤⓢ -ˈfjuː.t̬ɪd
Reg redʒ
-reg *car numberplate:* -ˌredʒ
Note: Used in the UK to refer to the year of registration of a car, which is indicated on the numberplate by a letter, e.g. **an F-reg**.
regain rɪˈgeɪn, ˌriː- **-s** -z **-ing** -ɪŋ **-ed** -d
regal ˈriː.gᵊl **-ly** -i
regal|e rɪˈgeɪl, rə- **-es** -z **-ing** -ɪŋ **-ed** -d
regalia rɪˈgeɪ.li.ə, rə- ⓤⓢ -ˈgeɪl.jə, -ˈgeɪ.li.ə
Regan ˈriː.gᵊn
regard rɪˈgɑːd, rə- ⓤⓢ -ˈgɑːrd **-s** -z **-ing** -ɪŋ **-ed** -ɪd **-ant** -ᵊnt
regardful rɪˈgɑːd.fᵊl, rə-, -fʊl ⓤⓢ -ˈgɑːrd- **-ly** -i **-ness** -nəs, -nɪs
regardless rɪˈgɑːd.ləs, rə-, -lɪs ⓤⓢ -ˈgɑːrd- **-ly** -li **-ness** -nəs, -nɪs
regatta rɪˈgæt.ə, rə- ⓤⓢ -ˈgɑː.t̬ə, -ˈgæt̬.ə **-s** -z
regenc|y (R) ˈriː.dʒᵊnt.s|i **-ies** -iz
regenerat|e (*adj.*) rɪˈdʒen.ᵊr.ət, rə-, -ɪt, -eɪt ⓤⓢ -ɪt **-ive** -ɪv
regener|ate (*v.*) rɪˈdʒen.ᵊr|.eɪt, rə-, ˌriː- ⓤⓢ -ə.r|eɪt **-ates** -eɪts **-ating** -eɪ.tɪŋ ⓤⓢ -eɪ.t̬ɪŋ **-ated** -eɪ.tɪd ⓤⓢ -eɪ.t̬ɪd
regeneration rɪˌdʒen.ᵊrˈeɪ.ʃᵊn, rə-, ˌriː.dʒen- ⓤⓢ -əˈreɪ- **-s** -z
Regensburg ˈreɪ.gᵊnz.bɜːg ⓤⓢ -bɝːg
regent (R) ˈriː.dʒᵊnt **-s** -s
regentship ˈriː.dʒᵊnt.ʃɪp **-s** -s
reggae ˈreg.eɪ
Reggie ˈredʒ.i
Reggio ˈredʒ.i.əʊ ⓤⓢ -oʊ
regicidal ˌredʒ.ɪˈsaɪ.dᵊl, -əˈ-
regicide ˈredʒ.ɪ.saɪd, ˈ-ə- **-s** -z
regime, régime reɪˈʒiːm, rɪ-, rə-, reʒˈiːm; ˈreɪ.ʒiːm ⓤⓢ rəˈʒiːm, rɪ-, reɪ- **-s** -z
regimen ˈredʒ.ɪ.mən, ˈ-ə-, -men ⓤⓢ ˈ-ə- **-s** -z
regiment (*n.*) ˈredʒ.ɪ.mənt, ˈ-ə- ⓤⓢ ˈ-ə- **-s** -s
regimen|t (*v.*) ˈredʒ.ɪ.men|t, ˈ-ə-, ˌ--ˈ- ⓤⓢ ˈredʒ.ə.men|t **-ts** -ts **-ting** -tɪŋ ⓤⓢ -t̬ɪŋ **-ted** -tɪd ⓤⓢ -t̬ɪd
regimental ˌredʒ.ɪˈmen.tᵊl, -əˈ- ⓤⓢ -əˈmen.t̬ᵊl **-s** -z *stress shift:* ˌregimental ˈcolours
regimentation ˌredʒ.ɪ.menˈteɪ.ʃᵊn, -ə-, -mənˈ- ⓤⓢ -ə.mənˈ-, -menˈ-
Regina rɪˈdʒaɪ.nə, rə- ⓤⓢ -ˈdʒaɪ-, -ˈdʒiː-
Note: In the US, /-ˈdʒiː-/ is especially suitable for the female name.
Reginald ˈredʒ.ɪ.nᵊld
region ˈriː.dʒᵊn **-s** -z
regional ˈriː.dʒᵊn.ᵊl **-ly** -i
regional|ism ˈriː.dʒᵊn.ᵊl|.ɪ.zᵊm **-ist/s** -ɪst/s
regionalistic ˌriː.dʒᵊn.ᵊlˈɪs.tɪk
Regis ˈriː.dʒɪs
regist|er ˈredʒ.ɪ.st|əʳ, ˈ-ə- ⓤⓢ -st|ɚ **-ers** -əz ⓤⓢ -ɚz **-ering** -ᵊr.ɪŋ **-ered** -əd ⓤⓢ -ɚd ˌ**registered** ˈ**mail**
registrant ˈredʒ.ɪ.strənt, ˈ-ə- **-s** -s
registrar ˌredʒ.ɪˈstrɑːʳ, -əˈ-, ˈ--- ⓤⓢ ˈredʒ.ɪ.strɑːr, ˌ--ˈ- **-s** -z
registrar|y ˈredʒ.ɪ.strᵊr|.i, ˈ-ə- ⓤⓢ -ɪ.strer- **-ies** -iz
registration ˌredʒ.ɪˈstreɪ.ʃᵊn, -əˈ- **-s** -z **regiˈstration** ˌ**number**
registr|y ˈredʒ.ɪ.str|i, ˈ-ə- **-ies** -iz ˈ**registry** ˌ**office**
Regius ˈriː.dʒi.əs, -dʒəs
regn|al ˈreg.n|ᵊl **-ant** -ənt
regress (*n.*) ˈriː.gres
regress (*v.*) rɪˈgres, ˌriː-, rə- **-es** -ɪz **-ing** -ɪŋ **-ed** -t
regression rɪˈgreʃ.ᵊn, ˌriː-, rə- **-s** -z
regressive rɪˈgres.ɪv, ˌriː-, rə- **-ly** -li **-ness** -nəs, -nɪs
re|gret rɪ|ˈgret, rə- **-grets** -ˈgrets **-gretting** -ˈgret.ɪŋ ⓤⓢ -ˈgret̬.ɪŋ **-gretted** -ˈgret.ɪd ⓤⓢ -ˈgret̬.ɪd
regretful rɪˈgret.fᵊl, rə-, -fʊl **-ly** -i
regrettab|le rɪˈgret.ə.b|l̩, rə- ⓤⓢ -ˈgret̬- **-ly** -li
regroup ˌriːˈgruːp **-s** -s **-ing** -ɪŋ **-ed** -t
regular ˈreg.jə.ləʳ, -jʊ- ⓤⓢ -lɚ **-s** -z **-ly** -li
regularity ˌreg.jəˈlær.ə.ti, -jʊˈ-, -ɪ.ti ⓤⓢ -ˈler.ə.t̬i, -ˈlær-
regularization, -isa- ˌreg.jə.lᵊr.aɪˈzeɪ.ʃᵊn, -jʊ-, -ɪˈ- ⓤⓢ -ɪˈ-
regulariz|e, -is|e ˈreg.jə.lᵊr.aɪz, -jʊ- ⓤⓢ -lə.raɪz **-es** -ɪz **-ing** -ɪŋ **-ed** -d
regu|late ˈreg.jə|.leɪt, -jʊ- **-lates** -leɪts **-lating** -leɪ.tɪŋ ⓤⓢ -leɪ.t̬ɪŋ **-lated** -leɪ.tɪd ⓤⓢ -leɪ.t̬ɪd **-lator/s** -leɪ.təʳ/z ⓤⓢ -leɪ.t̬ɚ/z
regulation ˌreg.jəˈleɪ.ʃᵊn, -jʊˈ- **-s** -z
regulative ˈreg.jə.lə.tɪv, -jʊ-, -leɪ- ⓤⓢ -leɪ.t̬ɪv, -lə-
regulatory ˈreg.jə.lə.tᵊr.i, -jʊ-, ˌreg.jəˈleɪ-, -jəˈ- ⓤⓢ ˈreg.jə.lə.tɔːr-, -jʊ-
regul|us (R) ˈreg.jə.l|əs, -jʊ- **-uses** -ə.sɪz **-i** -aɪ
regurgi|tate rɪˈgɜː.dʒɪ|.teɪt, rə-, ˌriː-, -dʒə- ⓤⓢ -ˈgɝː.dʒə- **-tates** -teɪts **-tating** -teɪ.tɪŋ ⓤⓢ -teɪ.t̬ɪŋ **-tated** -teɪ.tɪd ⓤⓢ -teɪ.t̬ɪd
regurgitation rɪˌgɜː.dʒɪˈteɪ.ʃᵊn, rə-, ˌriː-, -dʒəˈ- ⓤⓢ -ˌgɝː.dʒəˈ-
rehab ˈriː.hæb **-s** -z **-bing** -ɪŋ **-bed** -d
rehabili|tate ˌriː.həˈbɪl.ɪ|.teɪt, -əˈ-, ˈ-ə- ⓤⓢ ˈ-ə- **-tates** -teɪts **-tating** -teɪ.tɪŋ ⓤⓢ -teɪ.t̬ɪŋ **-tated** -teɪ.tɪd ⓤⓢ -teɪ.t̬ɪd
rehabilitation ˌriː.həˌbɪl.ɪˈteɪ.ʃᵊn, -əˌ-, -əˈ- ⓤⓢ -əˈ- **-s** -z
Rehan ˈriː.ən, ˈreɪ- ⓤⓢ ˈriː-
rehash (*n.*) ˈriː.hæʃ, ˌ-ˈ- **-es** -ɪz
rehash (*v.*) ˌriːˈhæʃ **-es** -ɪz **-ing** -ɪŋ **-ed** -t
rehear ˌriːˈhɪəʳ ⓤⓢ -ˈhɪr **-s** -z **-ing** -ɪŋ **reheard** ˌriːˈhɜːd ⓤⓢ -ˈhɝːd
rehearsal rɪˈhɜː.sᵊl, rə- ⓤⓢ -ˈhɝː- **-s** -z
rehears|e rɪˈhɜːs, rə- ⓤⓢ -ˈhɝːs **-es** -ɪz **-ing** -ɪŋ **-ed** -t
re|heat ˌriː|ˈhiːt **-heats** -ˈhiːts **-heating** -ˈhiː.tɪŋ ⓤⓢ -ˈhiː.t̬ɪŋ **-heated** -ˈhiː.tɪd ⓤⓢ -ˈhiː.t̬ɪd **-heater/s** -ˈhiː.təʳ/z ⓤⓢ -ˈhiː.t̬ɚ/z
Rehnquist ˈren.kwɪst, ˈreŋ-
rehoboam (R) ˌriː.əˈbəʊ.əm, -həˈ- ⓤⓢ -həˈboʊ- **-s** -z
re-hous|e ˌriːˈhaʊz **-es** -ɪz **-ing** -ɪŋ **-ed** -d
rehy|drate ˌriː.haɪ|ˈdreɪt ⓤⓢ -ˈhaɪ|.dreɪt **-drates** -ˈdreɪts ⓤⓢ -dreɪts **-drating** -ˈdreɪ.tɪŋ ⓤⓢ -dreɪ.t̬ɪŋ **-drated** -ˈdreɪ.tɪd ⓤⓢ -dreɪ.t̬ɪd
rehydration ˌriː.haɪˈdreɪ.ʃᵊn
Reich raɪk *as if German:* raɪx
Reichstag ˈraɪk.stɑːg *as if German:* ˈraɪx-, -tɑːk ⓤⓢ ˈraɪk.stɑːg *as if German:* ˈraɪx-

Reid riːd
reification ˌreɪ.ɪ.fɪˈkeɪ.ʃən, ˌriː-, ˌ-ə- (US) ˌ-ə-
rei|fy ˈreɪ.ɪ|.faɪ, ˈriː-, ˈ-ə- (US) ˈriː.ə- **-fies** -faɪz **-fying** -faɪ.ɪŋ **-fied** -faɪd
Reigate ˈraɪ.geɪt, -gɪt
reign *(n. v.)* reɪn **-s** -z **-ing** -ɪŋ **-ed** -d ˌ**reign of ˈterror**
Reigny ˈreɪ.ni
Reill(e)y ˈraɪ.li
reimburs|e ˌriː.ɪmˈbɜːs, -əmˈ- (US) -ˈbɝːs **-es** -ɪz **-ing** -ɪŋ **-ed** -t **-ement/s** -mənt/s
re-im|port ˌriː.ɪm|ˈpɔːt (US) -ˈpɔːrt, -ˈ-- **-ports** -ˈpɔːts (US) -ˈpɔːrts **-porting** -ˈpɔː.tɪŋ (US) -ˈpɔːr.t̬ɪŋ **-ported** -ˈpɔː.tɪd (US) -ˈpɔːr.t̬ɪd
reimpos|e ˌriː.ɪmˈpəʊz (US) -ˈpoʊz **-es** -ɪz **-ing** -ɪŋ **-ed** -d
reimpression ˌriː.ɪmˈpreʃ.ən **-s** -z
Reims riːmz
rein reɪn **-s** -z **-ing** -ɪŋ **-ed** -d
reincarnate *(adj.)* ˌriː.ɪnˈkɑː.nət, -ɪŋˈ-, -nɪt, -neɪt (US) -ɪnˈkɑːr.nɪt, -neɪt
reincarna|te *(v.)* ˌriː.ɪn.kɑːˈneɪ|t, -ɪŋ-, ˌriːˈɪn.kɑː.neɪ|t, -ˈɪŋ- (US) ˌriː.ɪnˈkɑːr.neɪ|t **-tes** -ts **-ting** -tɪŋ (US) -t̬ɪŋ **-ted** -tɪd (US) -t̬ɪd
reincarnation ˌriː.ɪn.kɑːˈneɪ.ʃən, -ɪŋ- (US) -ɪn.kɑːrˈ- **-s** -z
reindeer ˈreɪn.dɪəʳ (US) -dɪr
reinforc|e ˌriː.ɪnˈfɔːs (US) -ˈfɔːrs **-es** -ɪz **-ing** -ɪŋ **-ed** -t **-ement/s** -mənt/s
Reinhard(t) ˈraɪn.hɑːt (US) -hɑːrt
reinstal|l ˌriː.ɪnˈstɔːl (US) -stɔːl, -stɑːl **-(l)s** -z **-(l)ing** -ɪŋ **-(l)ed** -d **-ment** -mənt
rein|state ˌriː.ɪn|ˈsteɪt **-states** -ˈsteɪts **-stating** -ˈsteɪ.tɪŋ (US) -ˈsteɪ.t̬ɪŋ **-stated** -ˈsteɪ.tɪd (US) -ˈsteɪ.t̬ɪd **-statement** -ˈsteɪt.mənt
reinsur|e ˌriː.ɪnˈʃʊəʳ, -ˈʃɔːʳ (US) -ˈʃʊr **-es** -z **-ing** -ɪŋ **-ed** -d **-ance/s** -ənts/ɪz
reintroduc|e ˌriː.ɪn.trəˈdjuːs, -ˈdʒuːs (US) -ˈduːs, -ˈdjuːs **-es** -ɪz **-ing** -ɪŋ **-ed** -t
reintroduction ˌriː.ɪn.trəˈdʌk.ʃən **-s** -z
rein|vent ˌriː.ɪn|ˈvent **-vents** -ˈvents **-venting** -ˈven.tɪŋ (US) -ˈven.t̬ɪŋ **-vented** -ˈven.tɪd (US) -ˈven.t̬ɪd
reinvention ˌriː.ɪnˈven.*t*ʃən (US) -ˈvent.ʃən
reinvest ˌriː.ɪnˈvest **-s** -s **-ing** -ɪŋ **-ed** -ɪd
reinvigor|ate ˌriː.ɪnˈvɪg.ər|.eɪt (US) -ə.r|eɪt **-ates** -eɪts **-ating** -eɪ.tɪŋ (US) -eɪ.t̬ɪŋ **-ated** -eɪ.tɪd (US) -eɪ.t̬ɪd
reinvigoration ˌriː.ɪn.vɪ.gərˈeɪ.ʃən (US) -gəˈreɪ-
reissu|e ˌriːˈɪʃ.uː, -ˈɪs.juː (US) -ˈɪʃ.juː, -uː **-es** -z **-ing** -ɪŋ **-ed** -d
reiter|ate riˈɪt.ər|.eɪt (US) -ˈɪt̬.ə.r|eɪt **-ates** -eɪts **-ating** -eɪ.tɪŋ (US) -eɪ.t̬ɪŋ **-ated** -eɪ.tɪd (US) -eɪ.t̬ɪd
reiteration riˌɪt.ərˈeɪ.ʃən (US) -ˌɪt̬.əˈreɪ- **-s** -z
reiterative riˈɪt.ər.ə.tɪv, -eɪ- (US) -ˈɪt̬.ə.reɪ.t̬ɪv, ˈ-ɚ.ə- **-ly** -li **-ness** -nəs, -nɪs
Reith riːθ
reject *(n.)* ˈriː.dʒekt **-s** -s
reject *(v.)* rɪˈdʒekt, rə- **-s** -s **-ing** -ɪŋ **-ed** -ɪd **-or/s** -əʳ/z (US) -ɚ/z
rejection rɪˈdʒek.ʃən, rə- **-s** -z
rejig ˌriːˈdʒɪg **-s** -z **-ging** -ɪŋ **-ged** -d
rejoic|e rɪˈdʒɔɪs, rə- **-es** -ɪz **-ing/ly** -ɪŋ/li **-ed** -t
rejoin *answer:* rɪˈdʒɔɪn, rə- **-s** -z **-ing** -ɪŋ **-ed** -d
rejoin *join again:* ˌriːˈdʒɔɪn, rɪ- **-s** -z **-ing** -ɪŋ **-ed** -d
rejoinder rɪˈdʒɔɪn.dəʳ, rə- (US) -dɚ **-s** -z
rejuven|ate rɪˈdʒuː.vən|.eɪt, -vɪ.n|eɪt (US) -və- **-ates** -eɪts **-ating** -eɪ.tɪŋ (US) -eɪ.t̬ɪŋ **-ated** -eɪ.tɪd (US) -eɪ.t̬ɪd
rejuvenation rɪˌdʒuː.vənˈeɪ.ʃən, rə-, -vɪˈneɪ- (US) -vəˈ-
rejuvenescen|ce ˌriː.dʒuː.vənˈes.ən|*t*s, rɪˌdʒuː-, -vɪˈnes- (US) rɪˌdʒuː.vəˈ- **-t** -t
rekindl|e ˌriːˈkɪn.dl̩ **-es** -z **-ing** -ɪŋ, ˌriːˈkɪnd.lɪŋ **-ed** -d
re-label ˌriːˈleɪ.bəl **-s** -z **-ling** -ɪŋ, -ˈleɪ.blɪŋ **-led** -d
relaid *(past of* **relay** *= lay again)* riːˈleɪd, rɪ-, rə-
relapse *(n.)* rɪˈlæps, rə-; ˈriː.læps
relaps|e *(v.)* rɪˈlæps, rə- **-es** -ɪz **-ing** -ɪŋ **-ed** -t
re|late (R) rɪ|ˈleɪt, rə- **-lates** -ˈleɪts **-lating** -ˈleɪ.tɪŋ (US) -ˈleɪ.t̬ɪŋ **-lated** -ˈleɪ.tɪd (US) -ˈleɪ.t̬ɪd **-later/s** -ˈleɪ.təʳ/z (US) -ˈleɪ.t̬ɚ/z
relation rɪˈleɪ.ʃən, rə- **-s** -z
relational rɪˈleɪ.ʃən.əl, rə-
relationship rɪˈleɪ.ʃən.ʃɪp, rə- **-s** -s
relatival ˌrel.əˈtaɪ.vəl
relative ˈrel.ə.tɪv (US) -t̬ɪv **-s** -z **-ly** -li ˌ**relative ˈclause**; ˌ**relative ˈpronoun**
relativ|ism ˈrel.ə.tɪ.v|ɪ.zəm (US) -t̬ɪ- **-ist/s** -ɪst/s
relativistic ˌrel.ə.tɪˈvɪs.tɪk (US) -t̬ɪˈ-
relativity ˌrel.əˈtɪv.ə.ti, -ɪ.ti (US) -ə.t̬i
relaunch *(n.)* ˈriː.lɔːn*t*ʃ (US) -lɑːn*t*ʃ **-es** -ɪz
relaunch *(v.)* ˌriːˈlɔːn*t*ʃ (US) -ˈlɑːn*t*ʃ, -ˈlɔːn*t*ʃ **-es** -ɪz **-ing** -ɪŋ **-ed** -t
relax rɪˈlæks, rə- **-es** -ɪz **-ing** -ɪŋ **-ed** -t **-ant/s** -ənt/s
relaxation ˌriː.lækˈseɪ.ʃən **-s** -z
relay *(n.)* ˈriː.leɪ, rɪˈleɪ, rə- (US) ˈriː.leɪ **-s** -z ˈ**relay** ˌ**race**
relay *(v.) lay again:* ˌriːˈleɪ **-s** -z **-ing** -ɪŋ **relaid** ˌriːˈleɪd
relay *(v.) send, broadcast:* ˈriː.leɪ, rɪˈleɪ, rə-, riː- **-s** -z **-ing** -ɪŋ **-ed** -d
releas|e rɪˈliːs, rə- **-es** -ɪz **-ing** -ɪŋ **-ed** -t
rele|gate ˈrel.ɪ|.geɪt, ˈ-ə- (US) ˈ-ə- **-gates** -geɪts **-gating** -geɪ.tɪŋ (US) -geɪ.t̬ɪŋ **-gated** -geɪ.tɪd (US) -geɪ.t̬ɪd
relegation ˌrel.ɪˈgeɪ.ʃən, -əˈ- (US) -əˈ-
re|lent rɪ|ˈlent, rə- **-lents** -ˈlents **-lenting** -ˈlen.tɪŋ (US) -ˈlen.t̬ɪŋ **-lented** -ˈlen.tɪd (US) -ˈlen.t̬ɪd
relentless rɪˈlent.ləs, rə-, -lɪs **-ly** -li **-ness** -nəs, -nɪs
Relenza rɪˈlen.zə
re|-let ˌriː|ˈlet **-lets** -ˈlets **-letting** -ˈlet.ɪŋ (US) -ˈlet̬.ɪŋ
relevan|ce ˈrel.ə.vən*t*|s, ˈ-ɪ- (US) ˈ-ə- **-cy** -si
relevant ˈrel.ə.vənt, ˈ-ɪ- (US) ˈ-ə- **-ly** -li
reliability rɪˌlaɪ.əˈbɪl.ə.ti, rə-, -ɪ.ti (US) -ə.t̬i
reliab|le rɪˈlaɪ.ə.b|l̩, rə- **-ly** -li **-leness** -l̩.nəs, -nɪs
relian|ce rɪˈlaɪ.ən|*t*s, rə- **-t** -t
reliant rɪˈlaɪ.ənt, rə-
relic ˈrel.ɪk **-s** -s
relict ˈrel.ɪkt **-s** -s
reliction rɪˈlɪk.ʃən
relief rɪˈliːf, rə- **-s** -s **reˈlief** ˌ**map**
reliev|e rɪˈliːv, rə- **-es** -z **-ing** -ɪŋ **-ed** -d **-able** -ə.bl̩
relievo rɪˈliː.vəʊ (US) -voʊ
Religio Laici rɪˌlɪg.i.əʊˈlɑː.ɪ.siː, rə-, -kiː (US) rɪˌlɪdʒ.i.oʊˈleɪ.ə-
religion rɪˈlɪdʒ.ən, rə- **-s** -z
religion|ism rɪˈlɪdʒ.ən|.ɪ.zəm, rə- **-ist/s** -ɪst/s
religiosity rɪˌlɪdʒ.iˈɒs.ə.ti, rə-, -ɪ.ti (US) -ˈɑː.sə.t̬i
religious rɪˈlɪdʒ.əs, rə- **-ly** -li **-ness** -nəs, -nɪs
relin|e ˌriːˈlaɪn **-es** -z **-ing** -ɪŋ **-ed** -d
relinquish rɪˈlɪŋ.kwɪʃ, rə- **-es** -ɪz **-ing** -ɪŋ **-ed** -t **-ment** -mənt
reliquar|y ˈrel.ɪ.kwər|.i (US) -ə.kwer- **-ies** -ɪz
relish ˈrel.ɪʃ **-es** -ɪz **-ing** -ɪŋ **-ed** -t
reliv|e ˌriːˈlɪv **-es** -z **-ing** -ɪŋ **-ed** -d
reload ˌriːˈləʊd (US) -ˈloʊd **-s** -z **-ing** -ɪŋ **-ed** -ɪd
relo|cate ˌriː.ləʊ|ˈkeɪt (US) -ˈloʊ|.keɪt **-cates** -ˈkeɪts (US) -keɪts **-cating** -ˈkeɪ.tɪŋ (US) -keɪ.t̬ɪŋ **-cated** -ˈkeɪ.tɪd (US) -keɪ.t̬ɪd
relocation ˌriː.ləʊˈkeɪ.ʃən (US) -loʊˈ-
reluctance rɪˈlʌk.tənts, rə-
reluctant rɪˈlʌk.tənt, rə- **-ly** -li
reluctivity ˌrel.ʌkˈtɪv.ə.ti, ˌriː.lʌkˈ-; rɪˌlʌkˈ-, rə-, -ɪ.ti (US) ˌrel.əkˈtɪv.ə.t̬i
re|ly rɪ|ˈlaɪ, rə- **-lies** -ˈlaɪz **-lying** -ˈlaɪ.ɪŋ **-lied** -ˈlaɪd
REM, rem ˌɑːʳ.iːˈem; rem (US) ˌɑːr.iːˈem; rem
remain rɪˈmeɪn, rə- **-s** -z **-ing** -ɪŋ **-ed** -d
remainder rɪˈmeɪn.dəʳ, rə- (US) -dɚ **-s** -z **-ing** -ɪŋ **-ed** -d

remak|e (*v.*) ˌriːˈmeɪk **-es** -s **-ing** -ɪŋ **remade** ˌriːˈmeɪd
re-make (*n.*) ˈriː.meɪk **-s** -s
remand rɪˈmɑːnd, rə- US -ˈmænd **-s** -z **-ing** -ɪŋ **-ed** -ɪd **reˈmand ˌhome**
remanence ˈrem.ə.nənts
remark rɪˈmɑːk, rə- US -ˈmɑːrk **-s** -s **-ing** -ɪŋ **-ed** -t
remarkab|le rɪˈmɑː.kə.bl̩, rə- US -ˈmɑːr- **-ly** -li **-leness** -l̩.nəs, -nɪs
Remarque rɪˈmɑːk, rə- US -ˈmɑːrk
remarriag|e ˌriːˈmær.ɪdʒ US -ˈmer-, -ˈmær- **-es** -ɪz
remarr|y ˌriːˈmær|.i US -ˈmer-, -ˈmær- **-ies** -iz **-ying** -i.ɪŋ **-ied** -id
rematch ˈriː.mætʃ **-es** -ɪz
Rembrandt ˈrem.brænt, -brənt US -brænt, -brɑːnt **-s** -s
REME ˈriː.mi
remediable rɪˈmiː.di.ə.bl̩, rə-
remedial rɪˈmiː.di.əl, rə- **-ly** -i
remediation rɪˌmiː.diˈeɪ.ʃᵊn, rə-
remed|y ˈrem.ə.d|i, ˈ-ɪ- **-ies** -iz **-ying** -i.ɪŋ **-ied** -id
rememb|er rɪˈmem.b|əʳ, rə- US -b|ɚ **-ers** -əz US -ɚz **-ering** -ᵊr.ɪŋ **-ered** -əd US -ɚd
remembranc|e rɪˈmem.brᵊnts, rə- **-es** -ɪz **-er/s** -əʳ/z US -ɚ/z **Reˈmembrance ˌDay**
re-militariz|e, -is|e ˌriːˈmɪl.ɪ.tᵊr.aɪz, ˈ-ə- US -t̬ə.raɪz **-es** -ɪz **-ing** -ɪŋ **-ed** -d
remind rɪˈmaɪnd, rə- **-s** -z **-ing** -ɪŋ **-ed** -ɪd **-er/s** -əʳ/z US -ɚ/z
Remington ˈrem.ɪŋ.tən **-s** -z
reminisc|e ˌrem.ɪˈnɪs, -əˈ- US -əˈ- **-es** -ɪz **-ing** -ɪŋ **-ed** -t
reminiscenc|e ˌrem.ɪˈnɪs.ᵊnts, -əˈ- US -əˈ- **-es** -ɪz
reminiscent ˌrem.ɪˈnɪs.ᵊnt, -əˈ- US -əˈ-
remiss rɪˈmɪs, rə- **-ly** -li **-ness** -nəs, -nɪs
remission rɪˈmɪʃ.ᵊn, rə- **-s** -z
remit (*n.*) ˈriː.mɪt; rɪˈmɪt, rə-, riː- US rɪˈmɪt, rə- **-s** -s
re|mit (*v.*) rɪ|ˈmɪt, rə- **-mits** -ˈmɪts **-mitting** -ˈmɪt.ɪŋ US -ˈmɪt̬.ɪŋ **-mitted** -ˈmɪt.ɪd US -ˈmɪt̬.ɪd **-mitter/s** -ˈmɪt.əʳ/z US -ˈmɪt̬.ɚ/z
remittal rɪˈmɪt.ᵊl, rə- US -ˈmɪt̬- **-s** -z
remittanc|e rɪˈmɪt.ᵊnts, rə- **-es** -ɪz
remittitur rɪˈmɪt.ɪ.tʊəʳ, rə-, -tɜːʳ US rəˈmɪt̬.ə.t̬ɚ
remix (*n.*) ˈriː.mɪks **-es** -ɪz
remix (*v.*) ˌriːˈmɪks **-es** -ɪz **-ing** -ɪŋ -t
remnant ˈrem.nənt **-s** -s
remodel ˌriːˈmɒd.ᵊl US -ˈmɑː.dᵊl **-s** -z **-(l)ing** -ɪŋ **-(l)ed** -d
remold (*v.*) ˌriːˈməʊld US -ˈmoʊld **-s** -z **-ing** -ɪŋ **-ed** -ɪd
remold (*n.*) ˈriː.məʊld US -moʊld **-s** -z
remonetiz|e, -is|e ˌriːˈmʌn.ɪ.taɪz, ˈ-ə- US -ˈmɑː.nə-, -ˈmʌn.ə- **-es** -ɪz **-ing** -ɪŋ **-ed** -d
remonstranc|e rɪˈmɒnt.strᵊnts, rə- US -ˈmɑːnt- **-es** -ɪz
remonstrant rɪˈmɒnt.strᵊnt, rə- US -ˈmɑːnt- **-ly** -li
remon|strate ˈrem.ən|.streɪt; rɪˈmɒnt-, rə- US rɪˈmɑːnt-, rə-; ˈrem.ənt- **-strates** -streɪts **-strating** -streɪ.tɪŋ US -streɪ.t̬ɪŋ **-strated** -streɪ.tɪd US -streɪ.t̬ɪd
remonstrative rɪˈmɒnt.strə.tɪv, rə- US -ˈmɑːnt.strə.t̬ɪv **-ly** -li
remorse rɪˈmɔːs, rə- US -ˈmɔːrs
remorseful rɪˈmɔːs.fᵊl, rə-, -fʊl US -ˈmɔːrs- **-ly** -i
remorseless rɪˈmɔː.sləs, rə-, -lɪs US -ˈmɔːrs- **-ly** -li **-ness** -nəs, -nɪs
remortgag|e ˌriːˈmɔː.gɪdʒ US -ˈmɔːr- **-es** -ɪz **-ing** -ɪŋ **-ed** -d
remote rɪˈməʊt, rə- US -ˈmoʊt **-ly** -li **-ness** -nəs, -nɪs **reˌmote conˈtrol**
remould (*v.*) ˌriːˈməʊld US -ˈmoʊld **-s** -z **-ing** -ɪŋ **-ed** -ɪd
remould (*n.*) ˈriː.məʊld US -moʊld **-s** -z
remount (*n.*) ˈriː.maʊnt, ˌ-ˈ- US ˈriː.maʊnt **-s** -s
re|mount (*v.*) ˌriː|ˈmaʊnt **-mounts** -ˈmaʊnts **-mounting** -ˈmaʊn.tɪŋ US -ˈmaʊn.t̬ɪŋ **-mounted** -ˈmaʊn.tɪd US -ˈmaʊn.t̬ɪd
removability rɪˌmuː.vəˈbɪl.ə.ti, rə-, -ɪ.ti US -ə.t̬i
removal rɪˈmuː.vᵊl, rə- **-s** -z **reˈmoval ˌvan**
remov|e rɪˈmuːv, rə- **-es** -z **-ing** -ɪŋ **-ed** -d **-er/s** -əʳ/z US -ɚ/z **-able** -ə.bl̩
Remploy® ˈrem.plɔɪ
remuner|ate rɪˈmjuː.nᵊr|.eɪt, rə- US -nə.r|eɪt **-ates** -eɪts **-ating** -eɪ.tɪŋ US -eɪ.t̬ɪŋ **-ated** -eɪ.tɪd US -eɪ.t̬ɪd
remuneration rɪˌmjuː.nᵊrˈeɪ.ʃᵊn, rə- US -nəˈreɪ- **-s** -z
remunerative rɪˈmjuː.nᵊr.ə.tɪv, rə- US -nə.reɪ.t̬ɪv, -nɚ.ə-
Remus ˈriː.məs
renaissance (R) rəˈneɪ.sᵊnts, rɪ-, ˌren.eɪˈsɑ̃ːns, -ˈsɑːnts US ˌren.əˈsɑːnts, -ˈzɑːnts, ˈ--- **Reˌnaissance ˈman**
renal ˈriː.nᵊl
renam|e ˌriːˈneɪm **-es** -z **-ing** -ɪŋ **-ed** -d
renascen|t rɪˈneɪ.sᵊn|t, rə-, -ˈnæs.ᵊn|t US -ˈnæs.ᵊn|t, -ˈneɪ.sᵊn|t **-ce** -*ts*
Renault® ˈren.əʊ US rəˈnoʊ, -ˈnɔːlt **-s** -z
rend rend **-s** -z **-ing** -ɪŋ **-ed** -ɪd **rent** rent
Rendell ˈren.dᵊl
rend|er ˈren.d|əʳ US -d|ɚ **-ers** -əz US -ɚz **-ering/s** -ᵊr.ɪŋ/z **-ered** -əd US -ɚd
rendezvous *singular:* ˈrɒn.dɪ.vuː, -deɪ- US ˈrɑːn.deɪ-, -diː-, -dɪ- **-ing** -ɪŋ **-ed** -d *plural:* -z
rendition renˈdɪʃ.ᵊn **-s** -z
Renee, Renée ˈren.eɪ; rəˈneɪ; ˈriː.ni US rəˈneɪ
renegade ˈren.ɪ.geɪd, ˈ-ə- US ˈ-ə- **-s** -z
renegoti|ate ˌriː.nɪˈgəʊ.ʃi|.eɪt, -nəˈ- US -nəˈgoʊ- **-ates** -eɪts **-ating** -eɪ.tɪŋ US -eɪ.t̬ɪŋ **-ated** -eɪ.tɪd US -eɪ.t̬ɪd
renegotiation ˌriː.nɪˌgəʊ.ʃiˈeɪ.ʃᵊn, -nəˌ- US -nəˌgoʊ- **-s** -z
reneg(u)|e rɪˈniːg, rə-, -ˈneɪg, -ˈneg US -ˈnɪg, -ˈneg, -ˈniːg **-es** -z **-ing** -ɪŋ **-ed** -d
renew rɪˈnjuː, rə- US rɪˈnuː, -ˈnjuː **-s** -z **-ing** -ɪŋ **-ed** -d **-able/s** -ə.bl̩/z
renewal rɪˈnjuː.əl, rə-, -ˈnjʊəl US -ˈnuː.əl, -ˈnjuː- **-s** -z
Renfrew ˈren.fruː **-shire** -ʃəʳ, -ˌʃɪəʳ US -ʃɚ, -ˌʃɪr
renin ˈriː.nɪn US ˈriː.nɪn, ˈren.ən
renminbi renˈmɪn.bi US ˈren.mɪn-
Rennes ren
rennet ˈren.ɪt
Rennie ˈren.i
Rennies® ˈren.iz
rennin ˈren.ɪn
Reno ˈriː.nəʊ US -noʊ
Renoir rənˈwɑːʳ; ˈren.wɑːʳ, ˌ-ˈ- US rənˈwɑːr, ˈren.wɑːr
renounc|e rɪˈnaʊnts, rə- **-es** -ɪz **-ing** -ɪŋ **-ed** -t **-ement** -mənt
reno|vate ˈren.ə|.veɪt **-vates** -veɪts **-vating** -veɪ.tɪŋ US -veɪ.t̬ɪŋ **-vated** -veɪ.tɪd US -veɪ.t̬ɪd **-vator/s** -veɪ.təʳ/z US -veɪ.t̬ɚ/z
renovation ˌren.əˈveɪ.ʃᵊn **-s** -z
renown rɪˈnaʊn, rə- **-ed** -d
Renshaw ˈren.ʃɔː US -ʃɑː, -ʃɔː
rent rent **-s** -s **-ing** -ɪŋ US ˈren.t̬ɪŋ **-ed** -ɪd US ˈren.t̬ɪd **-er/s** -əʳ/z US ˈren.t̬ɚ/z
rent-a-crowd ˈrent.ə.kraʊd US ˈrent̬-
rental ˈren.tᵊl US -t̬ᵊl **-s** -z
rent-free ˌrentˈfriː *stress shift:* ˌrent-free ˈflat
rentier ˈrɑːn.ti.eɪ US -ˈtjeɪ **-s** -z
Rentokil® ˈren.təʊ.kɪl US -t̬ə-, -toʊ-
Renton ˈren.tən US -tᵊn
rent-roll ˈrent.rəʊl US -roʊl **-s** -z
renunciation rɪˌnʌnt.siˈeɪ.ʃᵊn, rə- **-s** -z
renvoi renˈvɔɪ
Renwick ˈren.ɪk, -wɪk
Note: For US names, /ˈren.wɪk/ is the likely pronunciation.
reoccupation riːˌɒk.jəˈpeɪ.ʃᵊn, ri-, -jʊˈ- US -ˌɑː.kjəˈ-, -kjʊˈ- **-s** -z
reoccup|y ˌriːˈɒk.jə.p|aɪ, ri-, -jʊ- US -ˈɑː.kjə-, -kjʊ- **-ies** -aɪz **-ying** -aɪ.ɪŋ **-ied** -aɪd
reoffend ˌriː.əˈfend **-s** -z **-ing** -ɪŋ **-ed** -ɪd **-er/s** -əʳ/z US -ɚ/z
reopen ˌriːˈəʊ.pᵊn, ri-, -pᵊm US -ˈoʊ.pᵊn **-s** -z **-ing** -ɪŋ **-ed** -d

reorganization, -isa- riːˌɔː.gᵊn.aɪˈzeɪ.ʃᵊn, ri-, -ɪˈ- (US) -ˌɔːr.gᵊn.ɪˈ-; ˌriː.ɔːr- **-s** -z

reorganiz|e, -is|e ˌriːˈɔː.gᵊn.aɪz, ri- (US) -ˈɔːr- **-es** -ɪz **-ing** -ɪŋ **-ed** -d

reori|ent ˌriːˈɔː.ri|.ənt, ri- (US) -ˈɔːr.i- **-ents** -ənts **-enting** -ən.tɪŋ (US) -ən.t̬ɪŋ **-ented** -ən.tɪd (US) -ən.t̬ɪd

reorien|tate ˌriːˈɔː.ri.ən|.teɪt, -ˈɒr.i-, -en- (US) ˌriːˈɔːr.i.en-, -ən- **-tates** -teɪts **-tating** -teɪ.tɪŋ (US) -teɪ.t̬ɪŋ **-tated** -teɪ.tɪd (US) -teɪ.t̬ɪd

reorientation riːˌɔː.ri.ənˈteɪ.ʃᵊn, -ˌɒr.i-, -enˈ- (US) -ˌɔːr.i.enˈ-, -ənˈ-

rep rep **-s** -s

repackag|e ˌriːˈpæk.ɪdʒ **-s** -ɪz **-ing** -ɪŋ **-ed** -d

repaid *(from* **repay**, *pay back)* rɪˈpeɪd, rə-, ˌriː- ˌriːˈpeɪd

repair rɪˈpeəʳ, rə- (US) -ˈper **-s** -z **-ing** -ɪŋ **-ed** -d **-er/s** -əʳ/z (US) -ɚ/z

repairable rɪˈpeə.rə.bl̩, rə- (US) -ˈper.ə-

reparability ˌrep.ᵊr.əˈbɪl.ə.ti, -ɪ.ti (US) -ə.t̬i

reparable ˈrep.ᵊr.ə.bl̩

reparation ˌrep.ᵊrˈeɪ.ʃᵊn (US) -əˈreɪ- **-s** -z

repartee ˌrep.ɑːˈtiː (US) -ɑːrˈ-, -ɚˈ-, -ˈteɪ

repass ˌriːˈpɑːs (US) -ˈpæs **-es** -ɪz **-ing** -ɪŋ **-ed** -t

repast rɪˈpɑːst, rə- (US) -ˈpæst **-s** -s

repatri|ate riːˈpæt.ri|.eɪt, rɪ- (US) -ˈpeɪ.tri- **-ates** -eɪts **-ating** -eɪ.tɪŋ (US) -eɪ.t̬ɪŋ **-ated** -eɪ.tɪd (US) -eɪ.t̬ɪd

repatriation ˌriː.pæt.riˈeɪ.ʃᵊn; rɪˌpæt- (US) rɪˌpeɪ.triˈ-

repay *pay back:* rɪˈpeɪ, rə-, ˌriː- **-s** -z **-ing** -ɪŋ **repaid** rɪˈpeɪd, rə-, ˌriː-

repay *pay again:* ˌriːˈpeɪ **-s** -z **-ing** -ɪŋ **repaid** ˌriːˈpeɪd

repayable rɪˈpeɪ.ə.bl̩, ˌriː-

repayment rɪˈpeɪ.mənt, ˌriː- **-s** -s

repeal rɪˈpiːl, rə- **-s** -z **-ing** -ɪŋ **-ed** -d

re|peat rɪ|ˈpiːt, rə- **-peats** -ˈpiːts **-peating** -ˈpiː.tɪŋ (US) -ˈpiː.t̬ɪŋ **-peated/ly** -ˈpiː.tɪd/li (US) -ˈpiː.t̬ɪd/li **-peater/s** -ˈpiː.təʳ/z (US) -ˈpiː.t̬ɚ/z

repeatability rɪˌpiː.təˈbɪl.ɪ.ti, rə-, -ə.ti (US) -t̬əˈbɪl.ə.t̬i

repêchage, repechage ˈrep.ə.ʃɑːʒ, ˈ-ɪ-, ˌ--ˈ- (US) ˌrep.əˈʃɑːʒ; rəˌpeʃˈ-

repel rɪˈpel, rə- **-s** -z **-ling** -ɪŋ **-led** -d

repellent, repellant rɪˈpel.ᵊnt, rə- **-s** -s

re|pent rɪ|ˈpent, rə- **-pents** -ˈpents **-penting** -ˈpen.tɪŋ (US) -ˈpen.t̬ɪŋ **-pented** -ˈpen.tɪd (US) -ˈpen.t̬ɪd

repentanc|e rɪˈpen.tən*t*s, rə- (US) -tᵊnts **-es** -ɪz

repentant rɪˈpen.tənt, rə- (US) -tᵊnt **-ly** -li

repercussion ˌriː.pəˈkʌʃ.ᵊn (US) -pɚˈ-, ˌrep.ɚˈ- **-s** -z

repertoire ˈrep.ə.twɑːʳ (US) -ɚ.twɑːr, ˈ-ə- **-s** -z

repertor|y ˈrep.ə.tᵊr|.i (US) -ɚ.tɔːr-, ˈ-ə- **-ies** -iz

répétiteur rɪˌpet.ɪˈtɜːʳ, rə- (US) ˌreɪ.peɪˈtiː.tɚ **-s** -z

repetition ˌrep.ɪˈtɪʃ.ᵊn, -əˈ- (US) -əˈ- **-s** -z

repetitious ˌrep.ɪˈtɪʃ.əs, -əˈ- (US) -əˈ- **-ly** -li **-ness** -nəs, -nɪs

repetitive rɪˈpet.ə.tɪv, rə-, ˈ-ɪ- (US) -ˈpet̬.ə.t̬ɪv **-ly** -li **-ness** -nəs, -nɪs **reˌpetitive ˈstrain ˌinjury; reˌpetitive ˈmotion ˌinjury**

rephras|e ˌriːˈfreɪz **-es** -ɪz **-ing** -ɪŋ **-ed** -d

repin|e rɪˈpaɪn, rə- **-es** -z **-ing** -ɪŋ **-ed** -d

replac|e rɪˈpleɪs, rə-, ˌriː- **-es** -ɪz **-ing** -ɪŋ **-ed** -t

replaceable rɪˈpleɪ.sə.bl̩, rə-, ˌriː-

replacement rɪˈpleɪs.mənt, rə-, ˌriː- **-s** -s

re|plant ˌriː|ˈplɑːnt (US) -ˈplænt **-plants** -ˈplɑːnts (US) -ˈplænts **-planting** -ˈplɑːn.tɪŋ (US) -ˈplæn.t̬ɪŋ **-planted** -ˈplɑːn.tɪd (US) -ˈplæn.t̬ɪd

replay *(n.)* ˈriː.pleɪ **-s** -z

replay *(v.)* ˌriːˈpleɪ **-s** -z **-ing** -ɪŋ **-ed** -d

replenish rɪˈplen.ɪʃ, rə- **-es** -ɪz **-ing** -ɪŋ **-ed** -t **-ment** -mənt

replete rɪˈpliːt **-ness** -nəs, -nɪs

repletion rɪˈpliː.ʃᵊn

replevin rɪˈplev.ɪn, rə-

replevy rɪˈplev.i, rə-

replica ˈrep.lɪ.kə, -lə- (US) -lɪ- **-s** -z

replicable ˈrep.lɪ.kə.bl̩, -lə- (US) -lɪ-

repli|cate ˈrep.lɪ|.keɪt, -lə- (US) -lɪ- **-cates** -keɪts **-cating** -keɪ.tɪŋ (US) -keɪ.t̬ɪŋ **-cated** -keɪ.tɪd (US) -keɪ.t̬ɪd

replication ˌrep.lɪˈkeɪ.ʃᵊn, -ləˈ- (US) -ləˈ- **-s** -z

repl|y rɪˈpl|aɪ, rə- **-ies** -aɪz **-ying** -aɪ.ɪŋ **-ied** -aɪd

repo ˈriː.pəʊ (US) -poʊ **-s** -z

re|point ˌriː|ˈpɔɪnt **-points** -ˈpɔɪnts **-pointing** -ˈpɔɪn.tɪŋ (US) -ˈpɔɪn.t̬ɪŋ **-pointed** -ˈpɔɪn.tɪd (US) -ˈpɔɪn.t̬ɪd

repolish ˌriːˈpɒl.ɪʃ (US) -ˈpɑː.lɪʃ **-es** -ɪz **-ing** -ɪŋ **-ed** -t

repopu|late ˌriːˈpɒp.jə|.leɪt, rɪˈ-, -jʊ- (US) -ˈpɑː.pjə-, -pjʊ- **-lates** -leɪts **-lating** -leɪ.tɪŋ (US) -leɪ.t̬ɪŋ **-lated** -leɪ.tɪd (US) -leɪ.t̬ɪd

re|port rɪ|ˈpɔːt, rə- (US) -ˈpɔːrt **-ports** -ˈpɔːts (US) -ˈpɔːrts **-porting** -ˈpɔː.tɪŋ (US) -ˈpɔːr.t̬ɪŋ **-ported/ly** -ˈpɔː.tɪd/li (US) -ˈpɔːr.t̬ɪd/li **reˌported ˈspeech**

reportage ˌrep.ɔːˈtɑːʒ; rɪˈpɔː.tɪdʒ, rə- (US) rɪˈpɔːr.t̬ɪdʒ, rə-; ˌrep.ɚˈtɑːʒ

reporter rɪˈpɔː.təʳ, rə- (US) -ˈpɔːr.t̬ɚ **-s** -z

repos|e rɪˈpəʊz, rə- (US) -ˈpoʊz **-es** -ɪz **-ing** -ɪŋ **-ed** -d

reposeful rɪˈpəʊz.fᵊl, rə-, -fʊl (US) -ˈpoʊz- **-ly** -i

reposition ˌriː.pəˈzɪʃ.ᵊn **-s** -z **-ing** -ɪŋ **-ed** -d

repositor|y rɪˈpɒz.ɪ.tᵊr|.i, rə- (US) -ˈpɑː.zɪ.tɔːr- **-ies** -iz

repossess ˌriː.pəˈzes **-es** -ɪz **-ing** -ɪŋ **-ed** -t

repossession ˌriː.pəˈzeʃ.ᵊn **-s** -z

repoussé rəˈpuː.seɪ, rɪ- (US) rəˌpuːˈseɪ

reprehend ˌrep.rɪˈhend, -rəˈ- (US) -rɪˈ- **-s** -z **-ing** -ɪŋ **-ed** -ɪd

reprehensib|le ˌrep.rɪˈhen*t*.sə.bl|̩, -rəˈ-, -sɪ- (US) -sə- **-ly** -li

reprehension ˌrep.rɪˈhen.*t*ʃᵊn, -rəˈ-

repre|sent ˌrep.rɪ|ˈzent, -rəˈ- (US) -rɪˈ- **-sents** -ˈzents **-senting** -ˈzen.tɪŋ (US) -ˈzen.t̬ɪŋ **-sented** -ˈzen.tɪd (US) -ˈzen.t̬ɪd

representation ˌrep.rɪ.zenˈteɪ.ʃᵊn, -rə-, -zᵊnˈ- (US) -rɪ.zenˈ- **-s** -z

representational ˌrep.rɪ.zenˈteɪ.ʃᵊn.ᵊl, -rə-, -zᵊnˈ- (US) -rɪ.zenˈ- **-ly** -i

representative ˌrep.rɪˈzen.tə.tɪv, -rəˈ- (US) -rɪˈzen.t̬ə.t̬ɪv **-s** -z **-ly** -li

repress rɪˈpres, rə- **-es** -ɪz **-ing** -ɪŋ **-ed** -t **-ible** -ə.bl̩, -ɪ.bl̩

repression rɪˈpreʃ.ᵊn, rə- **-s** -z

repressive rɪˈpres.ɪv, rə- **-ly** -li **-ness** -nəs, -nɪs

repriev|e rɪˈpriːv, rə- **-es** -z **-ing** -ɪŋ **-ed** -d

reprimand *(n.)* ˈrep.rɪ.mɑːnd, -rə- (US) -rə.mænd **-s** -z

reprimand *(v.)* ˈrep.rɪ.mɑːnd, -rə-, ˌ--ˈ- (US) ˈrep.rə.mænd, ˌ--ˈ- **-s** -z **-ing** -ɪŋ **-ed** -ɪd

reprint *(n.)* ˈriː.prɪnt, ˌ-ˈ- (US) ˈriː.prɪnt **-s** -s

re|print *(v.)* ˌriː|ˈprɪnt **-prints** -ˈprɪnts **-printing** -ˈprɪn.tɪŋ (US) -ˈprɪn.t̬ɪŋ **-printed** -ˈprɪn.tɪd (US) -ˈprɪn.t̬ɪd

reprisal rɪˈpraɪ.zᵊl, rə- **-s** -z

repris|e *(n. v.) in music:* rɪˈpriːz, rə- **-es** -ɪz **-ing** -ɪŋ **-ed** -d *legal term:* rɪˈpraɪz, rə-, -ˈpriːz (US) -ˈpraɪz **-es** -ɪz **-ing** -ɪŋ **-ed** -d

repro ˈriː.prəʊ (US) -proʊ **-s** -z

reproach rɪˈprəʊtʃ, rə- (US) -ˈproʊtʃ **-es** -ɪz **-ing** -ɪŋ **-ed** -t **-able** -ə.bl̩

reproachful rɪˈprəʊtʃ.fᵊl, rə-, -fʊl (US) -ˈproʊtʃ- **-ly** -i **-ness** -nəs, -nɪs

reprobate *(n. adj.)* ˈrep.rə*ʊ*.beɪt, -bɪt (US) -rə.beɪt, -bɪt **-s** -s

repro|bate *(v.)* ˈrep.rə*ʊ*|.beɪt (US) -rə- **-bates** -beɪts **-bating** -beɪ.tɪŋ (US) -beɪ.t̬ɪŋ **-bated** -beɪ.tɪd (US) -beɪ.t̬ɪd

reprobation ˌrep.rə*ʊ*ˈbeɪ.ʃᵊn (US) -rəˈ-

reprocess ˌriːˈprəʊ.ses, -sɪs (US) -ˈprɑː.ses, -səs **-es** -ɪz **-ing** -ɪŋ **-ed** -t

reproduc|e ˌriː.prəˈdjuːs, -ˈdʒuːs (US) -ˈduːs, -ˈdjuːs **-es** -ɪz **-ing** -ɪŋ **-ed** -t **-er/s** -əʳ/z (US) -ɚ/z

reproduction ˌriː.prəˈdʌk.ʃᵊn **-s** -z

reproductive ˌriː.prəˈdʌk.tɪv **-ness** -nəs, -nɪs

reprogram ˌriːˈprəʊ.græm (US) -ˈproʊ- **-s** -z **-(m)ing** -ɪŋ **-(m)ed** -d

reprographic ˌriː.prəʊˈgræf.ɪk, ˌrep.rəʊˈ- (US) ˌriː.proʊˈ-, -prəˈ- **-s** -s

reprograph|y rɪˈprɒg.rə.f|i, riː- (US) -ˈprɑː.grə- **-er/s** -əʳ/z (US) -ɚ/z

reproof rɪˈpruːf, rə- **-s** -s

re-proof (*v.*) ˌriːˈpruːf **-s** -s **-ing** -ɪŋ **-ed** -t

reproval rɪˈpruː.vᵊl, rə- **-s** -z

reprov|e rɪˈpruːv, rə- **-es** -z **-ing/ly** -ɪŋ/li **-ed** -d **-er/s** -əʳ/z (US) -ɚ/z

reptile ˈrep.taɪl (US) -taɪl, -tᵊl **-s** -z

reptilian repˈtɪl.i.ən (US) -i.ən, ˈ-jən **-s** -z

Repton ˈrep.tən

republic (R) rɪˈpʌb.lɪk, rə- **-s** -s

republican (R) rɪˈpʌb.lɪ.kən, rə- **-s** -z **-ism** -ɪ.zᵊm

republication ˌriːˌpʌb.lɪˈkeɪ.ʃᵊn, -ləˈ- (US) ˌriː.pʌb.lɪˈ- **-s** -z

republish ˌriːˈpʌb.lɪʃ **-es** -ɪz **-ing** -ɪŋ **-ed** -t

repudi|ate rɪˈpjuː.di|.eɪt, rə- **-ates** -eɪts **-ating** -eɪ.tɪŋ (US) -eɪ.t̬ɪŋ **-ated** -eɪ.tɪd (US) -eɪ.t̬ɪd **-ater/s** -eɪ.təʳ/z (US) -eɪ.t̬ɚ/z

repudiation rɪˌpjuː.diˈeɪ.ʃᵊn, rə-

repugnance rɪˈpʌg.nənts, rə-

repugnant rɪˈpʌg.nənt, rə- **-ly** -li

repuls|e rɪˈpʌls, rə- **-es** -ɪz **-ing** -ɪŋ **-ed** -t

repulsion rɪˈpʌl.ʃᵊn, rə-

repulsive rɪˈpʌl.sɪv, rə- **-ly** -li **-ness** -nəs, -nɪs

reputability ˌrep.jə.təˈbɪl.ə.ti, -jʊ-, -ɪ.ti (US) -t̬əˈbɪl.ə.t̬i

reputab|le ˈrep.jə.tə.b|l̩, -jʊ- (US) -t̬ə- **-ly** -li

reputation ˌrep.jəˈteɪ.ʃᵊn, -jʊˈ- **-s** -z

re|pute rɪ|ˈpjuːt, rə- **-puted/ly** -ˈpjuː.tɪd/li (US) -ˈpjuː.t̬ɪd/li

request rɪˈkwest, rə- **-s** -s **-ing** -ɪŋ **-ed** -ɪd

requiem ˈrek.wi.əm, -em **-s** -z ˌ**requiem** ˈ**mass**

requiescat ˌrek.wiˈes.kæt (US) ˌreɪ.kwiˈ-, ˌrek.wiˈ-, -kɑːt

requir|e rɪˈkwaɪəʳ, rə- (US) -ˈkwaɪɚ **-es** -z **-ing** -ɪŋ **-ed** -d

requirement rɪˈkwaɪə.mənt, rə- (US) -ˈkwaɪɚ- **-s** -s

requisite ˈrek.wɪ.zɪt, -wə- **-s** -s **-ly** -li **-ness** -nəs, -nɪs

requisition ˌrek.wɪˈzɪʃ.ᵊn, -wəˈ- **-s** -z **-ing** -ɪŋ **-ed** -d

re|quite rɪ|ˈkwaɪt, rə- **-quites** -ˈkwaɪts **-quiting** -ˈkwaɪ.tɪŋ (US) -ˈkwaɪ.t̬ɪŋ **-quited** -ˈkwaɪ.tɪd (US) -ˈkwaɪ.t̬ɪd **-quital** -ˈkwaɪ.tᵊl (US) -ˈkwaɪ.t̬ᵊl

re-read *present tense:* ˌriːˈriːd **-s** -z **-ing** -ɪŋ *past tense:* ˌriːˈred

reredos ˈrɪə.dɒs (US) ˈrɪr.dɑːs **-es** -ɪz

rereleas|e (*v.*) ˌriː.rɪˈliːs **-es** -ɪz **-ing** -ɪŋ **-ed** -t

rereleas|e (*n.*) ˈriː.rɪ.liːs **-s** -es

rerou|te ˌriːˈruː|t (US) -ˈruː|t, -ˈraʊ|t **-tes** -ts **-ting** -tɪŋ (US) -t̬ɪŋ **-ted** -tɪd (US) -t̬ɪd

rerun (*v.*) ˌriːˈrʌn **-s** -z **-ning** -ɪŋ **reran** ˌriːˈræn

rerun (*n.*) ˈriː.rʌn **-s** -z

res reɪz, reɪs, riːz (US) reɪs, riːz

resale ˈriː.seɪl, ˌ-ˈ- (US) ˈriː.seɪl **-s** -z

reschedul|e ˌriːˈʃed.juːl, -ˈʃedʒ.uːl (US) -ˈskedʒ.uːl, -əl **-es** -z **-ing** -ɪŋ **-ed** -d

rescind rɪˈsɪnd, rə- **-s** -z **-ing** -ɪŋ **-ed** -ɪd

rescission rɪˈsɪʒ.ᵊn, rə-

rescript ˈriː.skrɪpt **-s** -s

rescu|e ˈres.kjuː **-es** -z **-ing** -ɪŋ **-ed** -d **-er/s** -əʳ/z (US) -ɚ/z

research (*n.*) rɪˈsɜːtʃ, rə-, ˈriː.sɜːtʃ (US) ˈriː.sɝːtʃ; rɪˈsɝːtʃ, rə- **-es** -ɪz

research (*v.*) rɪˈsɜːtʃ, rə- (US) -ˈsɝːtʃ; ˈriː.sɝːtʃ **-es** -ɪz **-ing** -ɪŋ **-ed** -t **-er/s** -əʳ/z (US) -ɚ/z

re|seat ˌriː|ˈsiːt **-seats** -ˈsiːts **-seating** -ˈsiː.tɪŋ (US) -ˈsiː.t̬ɪŋ **-seated** -ˈsiː.tɪd (US) -ˈsiː.t̬ɪd

resection ˌriːˈsek.ʃᵊn, rɪ- **-s** -z

reseda ˈres.ɪ.də, ˈrez-, ˈ-ə-; rɪˈsiː.də, rə- (US) rɪˈsiː.də, rə-, -ˈsed.ə **-s** -z

reselect ˌriː.sɪˈlekt, -səˈ- **-s** -s **-ing** -ɪŋ **-ed** -ɪd

reselection ˌriː.sɪˈlek.ʃᵊn, -səˈ-

resell ˌriːˈsel **-s** -z **-ing** -ɪŋ **resold** ˌriːˈsəʊld (US) -ˈsoʊld

resemblanc|e rɪˈzem.blənts, rə- **-es** -ɪz

resembl|e rɪˈzem.bl̩, rə- **-es** -z **-ing** -ɪŋ, -ˈzem.blɪŋ **-ed** -d

re|sent rɪ|ˈzent, rə- **-sents** -ˈzents **-senting** -ˈzen.tɪŋ (US) -ˈzen.t̬ɪŋ **-sented** -ˈzen.tɪd (US) -ˈzen.t̬ɪd

resentful rɪˈzent.fᵊl, rə-, -fʊl **-ly** -li

resentment rɪˈzent.mənt, rə-

reservation ˌrez.əˈveɪ.ʃᵊn (US) -ɚˈ- **-s** -z

reserv|e rɪˈzɜːv, rə- (US) -ˈzɝːv **-es** -z **-ing** -ɪŋ **-ed** -d

reservedly rɪˈzɜː.vɪd.li, rə- (US) -ˈzɝː-

reservist rɪˈzɜː.vɪst, rə- (US) -ˈzɝː- **-s** -s

reservoir ˈrez.əv.wɑːʳ (US) -ɚv.wɑːr, -wɔːr, ˈ-ɚ.vɔːr, ˈ-ə- **-s** -z

re|set ˌriː|ˈset **-sets** -ˈsets **-setting/s** -ˈset.ɪŋ/z (US) -ˈset̬.ɪŋ/z

resettle ˌriːˈset.l̩ **-s** -z **-ing** -ɪŋ **-ed** -d **-ment** -mənt

res gestae ˌreɪsˈges.taɪ, ˌreɪz-, ˌriːz-, -ˈdʒes-, -tiː

reshap|e ˌriːˈʃeɪp **-es** -s **-ing** -ɪŋ **-ed** -t

reship ˌriːˈʃɪp **-s** -s **-ping** -ɪŋ **-ped** -t **-ment/s** -mənt/s

reshuffle (*n.*) ˌriːˈʃʌf.l̩, ˈ-ˌ-- (US) ˌriːˈʃʌf- **-s** -z

reshuffl|e (*v.*) ˌriːˈʃʌf.l̩ **-es** -z **-ing** -ɪŋ, -ˈʃʌf.lɪŋ **-ed** -d

resid|e rɪˈzaɪd, rə- **-es** -z **-ing** -ɪŋ **-ed** -ɪd

residenc|e ˈrez.ɪ.dᵊnts **-es** -ɪz

residenc|y ˈrez.ɪ.dᵊnt.s|i **-ies** -iz

resident ˈrez.ɪ.dᵊnt **-s** -s

residential ˌrez.ɪˈden.tʃᵊl

residual rɪˈzɪd.ju.əl, rə-, -ˈzɪdʒ.u- (US) -ˈzɪdʒ- **-ly** -i

residuary rɪˈzɪd.ju.əri, rə-, -ˈzɪdʒ.ʊə- (US) -ˈzɪdʒ.u.er-

residue ˈrez.ɪ.djuː, ˈ-ə-, -dʒuː (US) -ə.duː, -djuː **-s** -z

residu|um rɪˈzɪd.ju|.əm, rə-, -ˈzɪdʒ.u- (US) -ˈzɪdʒ- **-a** -ə

resign rɪˈzaɪn, rə- **-s** -z **-ing** -ɪŋ **-ed** -d **-edly** -ɪd.li

resignation ˌrez.ɪgˈneɪ.ʃᵊn, -əgˈ- (US) -ɪgˈ- **-s** -z

resilien|ce rɪˈzɪl.i.ənt|s, rə-, -ˈsɪl- (US) -ˈzɪl.jənt|s, ˈ-i.ənt|s **-cy** -si

resilient rɪˈzɪl.i.ənt, rə-, -ˈsɪl- (US) -ˈzɪl.jənt, ˈ-i.ənt **-ly** -li

resin ˈrez.ɪn **-s** -z **-ous** -əs

res ipsa loquitur ˌreɪsˌɪp.sɑːˈlɒk.wɪ.tʊəʳ, ˌreɪz-, ˌriːz-, -səˈ-, -təʳ (US) ˌreɪsˌɪp.səˈlɑː.wɪ.tʊr

resist rɪˈzɪst, rə- **-s** -s **-ing** -ɪŋ **-ed** -ɪd **-or/s** -əʳ/z (US) -ɚ/z

resistanc|e rɪˈzɪs.tᵊnts, rə- **-es** -ɪz

resistant rɪˈzɪs.tᵊnt, rə- **-ly** -li

resistivity ˌriː.zɪˈstɪv.ə.ti, ˌrez.ɪˈ-, -ɪ.ti (US) ˌriː.zɪˈstɪv.ə.t̬i; rɪˌzɪsˈtɪv-

resistless rɪˈzɪst.ləs, rə-, -lɪs

resistor rɪˈzɪs.təʳ, rə- (US) -tɚ **-s** -z

resit (*n.*) ˈriː.sɪt **-s** -s

re|sit (*v.*) ˌriː|ˈsɪt **-sits** -ˈsɪts **-sitting** -ˈsɪt.ɪŋ (US) -ˈsɪt̬.ɪŋ **resat** ˌriːˈsæt

res judicata ˌreɪsˌdʒuː.dɪˈkɑː.tə, ˌreɪz-, ˌriːz-, -dəˈ- (US) ˌreɪs-, ˌreɪz-, ˌriːz-, ˌriːs-

reskill ˌriːˈskɪl **-s** -z **-ing** -ɪŋ **-ed** -d

resnoid ˈrez.nɔɪd **-s** -z

resol|e ˌriːˈsəʊl (US) -ˈsoʊl **-es** -z **-ing** -ɪŋ **-ed** -d

resoluble rɪˈzɒl.jə.bl̩, rə-, -jʊ-; ˈrez.ᵊl- (US) rɪˈzɑːl.jə-, rə-, -jʊ-; ˈrez.ᵊl-

resolute ˈrez.ᵊl.uːt, -juːt (US) -ə.luːt **-ly** -li **-ness** -nəs, -nɪs

resolution ˌrez.ᵊlˈuː.ʃᵊn, -ˈjuː- (US) -əˈluː- **-s** -z

resolvability rɪˌzɒl.vəˈbɪl.ə.ti, rə-, -ɪ.ti (US) -ˌzɑːl.vəˈbɪl.ə.t̬i

resolv|e rɪˈzɒlv, rə- (US) -ˈzɑːlv **-es** -z **-ing** -ɪŋ **-ed** -d **-able** -ə.bl̩

resonanc|e ˈrez.ᵊn.ənts **-es** -ɪz

resonant ˈrez.ᵊn.ənt **-ly** -li

reson|ate ˈrez.ᵊn|.eɪt **-ates** -eɪts **-ating** -eɪ.tɪŋ (US) -eɪ.t̬ɪŋ **-ated** -eɪ.tɪd (US) -eɪ.t̬ɪd

resonator ˈrez.ᵊn.eɪ.təʳ (US) -t̬ɚ **-s** -z

resorb rɪˈzɔːb, rə-, -ˈsɔːb (US) -ˈsɔːrb, -ˈzɔːrb **-s** -z **-ing** -ɪŋ **-ed** -d

resorp|tion rɪˈsɔːp|.ʃᵊn, rə-, -ˈzɔːp- ⓤⓢ -ˈsɔːrp-, -ˈzɔːrp- **-tive** -tɪv
re|sort (*n. v.*) rɪ|ˈzɔːt, rə- ⓤⓢ -ˈzɔːrt **-sorts** -ˈzɔːts ⓤⓢ -ˈzɔːrts **-sorting** -ˈzɔː.tɪŋ ⓤⓢ -ˈzɔːr.t̬ɪŋ **-sorted** -ˈzɔː.tɪd ⓤⓢ -ˈzɔːr.t̬ɪd
re|-sort (*v.*) *sort again:* ˌriː|ˈsɔːt ⓤⓢ -ˈsɔːrt **-sorts** -ˈsɔːts ⓤⓢ -ˈsɔːrts **-sorting** -ˈsɔː.tɪŋ ⓤⓢ -ˈsɔːr.t̬ɪŋ **-sorted** -ˈsɔː.tɪd ⓤⓢ -ˈsɔːr.t̬ɪd
resound rɪˈzaʊnd, rə- **-s** -z **-ing** -ɪŋ **-ed** -ɪd
resourc|e rɪˈzɔːs, rə-, -ˈsɔːs; ˈriː.sɔːs ⓤⓢ ˈriː.sɔːrs, -zɔːrs; rɪˈsɔːrs, rə-, -ˈzɔːrs **-es** -ɪz **-ing** -ɪŋ **-ed** -t
resourceful rɪˈzɔːs.fᵊl, rə-, -ˈsɔːs-, -fʊl ⓤⓢ -ˈsɔːrs-, -ˈzɔːrs- **-ly** -i **-ness** -nəs, -nɪs
respect rɪˈspekt, rə- **-s** -s **-ing** -ɪŋ **-ed** -ɪd **-er/s** -əʳ/z ⓤⓢ -ɚ/z
respectability rɪˌspek.təˈbɪl.ə.ti, rə-, -ɪ.ti ⓤⓢ -ə.t̬i
respectab|le rɪˈspek.tə.b|l̩, rə- **-ly** -li **-leness** -l̩.nəs, -nɪs
respectful rɪˈspekt.fᵊl, rə-, -fʊl **-ly** -i **-ness** -nəs, -nɪs
respective rɪˈspek.tɪv, rə- **-ly** -li
Respighi resˈpiː.gi, rɪˈspiː-, rə-
respirable ˈres.pɪ.rə.bl̩, rɪˈspaɪə-, rə- ⓤⓢ ˈres.pɚ.ə.bl̩; rɪˈspaɪ-, rə-
respiration ˌres.pᵊrˈeɪ.ʃᵊn, -pɪˈreɪ- ⓤⓢ -pəˈreɪ- **-s** -z
respirator ˈres.pᵊr.eɪ.təʳ, -pɪ.reɪ- ⓤⓢ -pə.reɪ.t̬ɚ **-s** -z
respiratory rɪˈspɪr.ə.tᵊr.i, -ˈspaɪə.rə-, rə-, resˈpaɪə-, ˈres.pɪ.rə-, -reɪ- ⓤⓢ ˈres.pɚ.ə.tɔːr-; rɪˈspaɪ.rə-, rə-
respir|e rɪˈspaɪəʳ, rə- ⓤⓢ -ˈspaɪɚ **-es** -z **-ing** -ɪŋ **-ed** -d
respi|te ˈres.paɪ|t, -pɪ|t ⓤⓢ -pɪ|t **-tes** -ts **-ting** -tɪŋ ⓤⓢ -t̬ɪŋ **-ted** -tɪd ⓤⓢ -t̬ɪd
resplenden|ce rɪˈsplen.dənt|s, rə- **-cy** -si
resplendent rɪˈsplen.dənt, rə- **-ly** -li
respond rɪˈspɒnd, rə- ⓤⓢ -ˈspɑːnd **-s** -z **-ing** -ɪŋ **-ed** -ɪd **-er/s** -əʳ/z ⓤⓢ -ɚ/z
respondeat resˈpɒn.deɪ.æt, rɪs-, -di- ⓤⓢ resˈpɑːn.di.ət
respondent rɪˈspɒn.dənt, rə- ⓤⓢ -ˈspɑːn- **-s** -s
respons|e rɪˈspɒnts, rə- ⓤⓢ -ˈspɑːnts **-es** -ɪz
responsibilit|y rɪˌspɒnt.səˈbɪl.ə.t|i, rə-, -sɪˈ-, -ɪ.t|i ⓤⓢ -ˌspɑːnt.səˈbɪl.ə.t̬|i **-ies** -iz
responsib|le rɪˈspɒnt.sə.b|l̩, rə-, -sɪ- ⓤⓢ -ˈspɑːnt.sə- **-ly** -li **-leness** -l̩.nəs, -nɪs
responsive rɪˈspɒnt.sɪv, rə- ⓤⓢ -ˈspɑːnt- **-ly** -li **-ness** -nəs, -nɪs
respray (*n.*) ˈriː.spreɪ **-s** -z
respray (*v.*) ˌriːˈspreɪ **-s** -z **-ing** -ɪŋ **-ed** -d
rest rest **-s** -s **-ing** -ɪŋ **-ed** -ɪd ˈ**rest** ˌ**home**; ˈ**rest** ˌ**room**; ˈ**resting** ˌ**place**
re|start ˌriː|ˈstɑːt ⓤⓢ -ˈstɑːrt **-starts** -ˈstɑːts ⓤⓢ -ˈstɑːrts **-starting** -ˈstɑː.tɪŋ ⓤⓢ -ˈstɑːr.t̬ɪŋ **-started** -ˈstɑː.tɪd ⓤⓢ -ˈstɑːr.t̬ɪd
re|state ˌriː|ˈsteɪt **-states** -ˈsteɪts **-stating** -ˈsteɪ.tɪŋ ⓤⓢ -ˈsteɪ.t̬ɪŋ **-stated** -ˈsteɪ.tɪd ⓤⓢ -ˈsteɪ.t̬ɪd
re-statement ˌriːˈsteɪt.mənt **-s** -s
restaur|ant ˈres.tᵊr|.ɔ̃ːŋ, -ɑ̃ːŋ, -ɑːŋ, -ɒnt, -ənt, ˈ-tr|ɔ̃ːŋ, -tr|ɑ̃ːŋ, -tr|ɑːŋ, -tr|ɒnt, -tr|ənt ⓤⓢ -tə.r|ɑːnt, -tɚ|.ənt, ˈ-tr|ɑːnt, -tr|ənt **-ants** -ɔ̃ːŋz, -ɑ̃ːŋz, -ɑːŋz, -ɒŋz, -ɒnts, -ənts ⓤⓢ -ɑːnts, -ənts ˈ**restaurant** ˌ**car**
restaurateur ˌres.tɒr.əˈtɜːʳ, -tər-, -tɔː.rəˈ- ⓤⓢ -tɚ.əˈtɝː, -ˈtʊr **-s** -z
restful ˈrest.fᵊl, -fʊl **-ly** -i **-ness** -nəs, -nɪs
restitution ˌres.tɪˈtjuː.ʃᵊn ⓤⓢ -ˈtuː-, -ˈtjuː-
restive ˈres.tɪv **-ly** -li **-ness** -nəs, -nɪs
restless ˈrest.ləs, -lɪs **-ly** -li **-ness** -nəs, -nɪs
restock ˌriːˈstɒk ⓤⓢ -ˈstɑːk **-s** -s **-ing** -ɪŋ **-ed** -t
restoration (R) ˌres.tᵊrˈeɪ.ʃᵊn ⓤⓢ -təˈreɪ- **-s** -z
restorative rɪˈstɒr.ə.tɪv, rə-, resˈtɒr-, -ˈtɔː.rə- ⓤⓢ rɪˈstɔːr.ə.t̬ɪv, rə- **-s** -z
restor|e rɪˈstɔːʳ, rə- ⓤⓢ -ˈstɔːr **-es** -z **-ing** -ɪŋ **-ed** -d **-er/s** -əʳ/z ⓤⓢ -ɚ/z **-able** -ə.bl̩
restrain rɪˈstreɪn, rə- **-s** -z **-ing** -ɪŋ **-ed** -d **-er/s** -əʳ/z ⓤⓢ -ɚ/z
restraint rɪˈstreɪnt, rə- **-s** -s
restrict rɪˈstrɪkt, rə- **-s** -s **-ing** -ɪŋ **-ed** -ɪd
restriction rɪˈstrɪk.ʃᵊn, rə- **-s** -z
restrictionism rɪˈstrɪk.ʃᵊn.ɪ.zᵊm, rə-
restrictive rɪˈstrɪk.tɪv, rə- **-ly** -li **-ness** -nəs, -nɪs **re**ˌ**strictive** ˈ**practice**
restroom ˈrest.rʊm, -ruːm ⓤⓢ -ruːm, -rʊm **-s** -z
restruct|ure ˌriːˈstrʌk.tʃ|əʳ ⓤⓢ -tʃ|ɚ **-ures** -əz ⓤⓢ -ɚz **-uring** -ᵊr.ɪŋ **-ured** -əd ⓤⓢ -ɚd
re|sult rɪ|ˈzʌlt, rə- **-sults** -ˈzʌlts **-sulting** -ˈzʌl.tɪŋ ⓤⓢ -ˈzʌl.t̬ɪŋ **-sulted** -ˈzʌl.tɪd ⓤⓢ -ˈzʌl.t̬ɪd **-sultant/s** -ˈzʌl.tᵊnt/s
resultative rɪˈzʌl.tə.tɪv, rə- ⓤⓢ -t̬ə.t̬ɪv
resum|e rɪˈzjuːm, rə-, -ˈzuːm ⓤⓢ -ˈzuːm **-es** -z **-ing** -ɪŋ **-ed** -d
résumé, resumé ˈrez.juː.meɪ, ˈreɪ.zuː-, -zjʊ-, -zʊ-; rɪˈzjuː-, rə- ⓤⓢ ˈrez.ʊ.meɪ, ˈ-ə-, ˌ--ˈ- **-s** -z
resumption rɪˈzʌmp.ʃᵊn, rə- **-s** -z
resumptive rɪˈzʌmp.tɪv, rə-
resurfac|e ˌriːˈsɜː.fɪs, -fəs ⓤⓢ -ˈsɝː- **-es** -ɪz **-ing** -ɪŋ **-ed** -t
resurgenc|e rɪˈsɜː.dʒənts, rə- ⓤⓢ -ˈsɝː- **-es** -ɪz
resurgent rɪˈsɜː.dʒənt, rə- ⓤⓢ -ˈsɝː-
resurrect ˌrez.ᵊrˈekt ⓤⓢ -əˈrekt **-s** -s **-ing** -ɪŋ **-ed** -ɪd
resurrection (R) ˌrez.ᵊrˈek.ʃᵊn ⓤⓢ -əˈrek- **-s** -z
resusci|tate rɪˈsʌs.ɪ|.teɪt, rə-, ˈ-ə- ⓤⓢ ˈ-ə- **-tates** -teɪts **-tating** -teɪ.tɪŋ ⓤⓢ -teɪ.t̬ɪŋ **-tated** -teɪ.tɪd ⓤⓢ -teɪ.t̬ɪd **-tator/s** -teɪ.təʳ/z ⓤⓢ -teɪ.t̬ɚ/z
resuscitation rɪˌsʌs.ɪˈteɪ.ʃᵊn, rə-, -əˈ- ⓤⓢ -əˈ- **-s** -z
retail (*n. adj.*) ˈriː.teɪl, ˌ-ˈ- ⓤⓢ ˈriː.teɪl ˌ**retail** ˈ**price**
retail (*v.*) *sell:* ˈriː.teɪl, ˌ-ˈ- ⓤⓢ ˈriː.teɪl; rɪˈteɪl **-s** -z **-ing** -ɪŋ **-ed** -d **-er/s** -əʳ/z ⓤⓢ -ɚ/z
retail (*v.*) *tell:* rɪˈteɪl, rə-, ˌriː- **-s** -z **-ing** -ɪŋ **-ed** -d
retain rɪˈteɪn, rə- **-s** -z **-ing** -ɪŋ **-ed** -d **-er/s** -əʳ/z ⓤⓢ -ɚ/z
retake (*n.*) ˈriː.teɪk **-s** -s
re|take (*v.*) ˌriːˈteɪk **-takes** -ˈteɪks **-taking** -ˈteɪ.kɪŋ **-took** -ˈtʊk **-taken** -ˈteɪ.kᵊn
retali|ate rɪˈtæl.i|.eɪt, rə- **-ates** -eɪts **-ating** -eɪ.tɪŋ ⓤⓢ -eɪ.t̬ɪŋ **-ated** -eɪ.tɪd ⓤⓢ -eɪ.t̬ɪd
retaliation rɪˌtæl.iˈeɪ.ʃᵊn, rə-
retaliatory rɪˈtæl.i.ə.tᵊr.i, rə-, -eɪ-; rɪˌtæl.iˈeɪ-, rə- ⓤⓢ rɪˈtæl.i.ə.tɔːr-, rə-, ˈ-jə-
retard (*v.*) rɪˈtɑːd, rə- ⓤⓢ -ˈtɑːrd **-s** -z **-ing** -ɪŋ **-ed** -ɪd
retard (*n.*) ˈriː.tɑːd ⓤⓢ -tɑːrd **-s** -z
retardant rɪˈtɑː.dənt, rə- ⓤⓢ -ˈtɑːr- **-s** -s
retardation ˌriː.tɑːˈdeɪ.ʃᵊn ⓤⓢ -tɑːrˈ- **-s** -z
retch retʃ, riːtʃ ⓤⓢ retʃ **-es** -ɪz **-ing** -ɪŋ **-ed** -t
retell ˌriːˈtel **-s** -z **-ing** -ɪŋ **retold** ˌriːˈtəʊld ⓤⓢ -ˈtoʊld
retention rɪˈten.tʃᵊn, rə-
retentive rɪˈten.tɪv, rə- ⓤⓢ -t̬ɪv **-ly** -li **-ness** -nəs, -nɪs
Retford ˈret.fəd ⓤⓢ -fɚd
rethink (*v.*) ˌriːˈθɪŋk **-s** -s **-ing** -ɪŋ **rethought** ˌriːˈθɔːt ⓤⓢ -ˈθɑːt, -ˈθɔːt
rethink (*n.*) ˈriː.θɪŋk **-s** -s
reticence ˈret.ɪ.sᵊnts, ˈ-ə- ⓤⓢ ˈret̬.ə-
reticent ˈret.ɪ.sᵊnt, ˈ-ə- ⓤⓢ ˈret̬.ə- **-ly** -li
reticle ˈret.ɪ.kl̩ ⓤⓢ ˈret̬.ɪ- **-s** -z
reticulate (*adj.*) rɪˈtɪk.jə.lət, rə-, retˈɪk-, -jʊ-, -lɪt, -leɪt ⓤⓢ rɪˈtɪk.jə.lɪt, rə-, -jʊ-, -leɪt
reticu|late (*v.*) rɪˈtɪk.jə|.leɪt, rə-, retˈɪk-, -jʊ- ⓤⓢ rɪˈtɪk-, rə- **-lates** -leɪts **-lating** -leɪ.tɪŋ ⓤⓢ -leɪ.t̬ɪŋ **-lated** -leɪ.tɪd ⓤⓢ -leɪ.t̬ɪd
reticulation rɪˌtɪk.jəˈleɪ.ʃᵊn, rə-, retˌɪk-, -jʊˈ- ⓤⓢ rɪˌtɪk-, rə- **-s** -z
reticule ˈret.ɪ.kjuːl, ˈ-ə- ⓤⓢ ˈret̬.ə- **-s** -z

Retroflex

In a retroflex articulation the tip of the tongue is curled upward and backward.

Examples for English

The /r/ sound of some British and American accents is sometimes described as being retroflex, though in BBC pronunciation the degree of retroflexion is relatively small.

In US English and some accents of south-west England it is common for vowels preceding /r/ (e.g. /ɑː/ in *car*, or /ɜː/ in *bird*) to be affected by the consonant so that they have a retroflex quality for most of their duration. This 'r-colouring' is most common in back or central vowels where the forward part of the tongue is relatively free to change shape.

In other languages

Other languages have retroflex consonants with a more noticeable auditory quality, the best known examples being the great majority of the languages of the Indian sub-continent. The sound of retroflex consonants is fairly familiar to English listeners, since first-generation immigrants from India and Pakistan tend to carry the retroflex quality into their pronunciation of English consonants which are alveolar in BBC pronunciation.

retin|a 'ret.ɪ.n|ə ⓤⓢ -ən|.ə **-as** -əz **-ae** -iː **-al** -əl
retinue 'ret.ɪ.njuː ⓤⓢ -ən.uː, -juː **-s** -z
retir|e rɪ'taɪər, rə- ⓤⓢ -'taɪɚ **-es** -z **-ing** -ɪŋ **-ed** -d **-ant/s** -ənts
retiree rɪˌtaɪə'riː, rə- ⓤⓢ rɪ'taɪ.riː, rə- **-s** -z
retirement rɪ'taɪə.mənt, rə- ⓤⓢ -'taɪɚ- **re'tirement ˌage; re'tirement ˌhome**
retold *(from* **retell***)* ˌriː'təʊld ⓤⓢ -'toʊld
re|tort rɪ|'tɔːt, rə- ⓤⓢ -'tɔːrt **-torts** -'tɔːts ⓤⓢ -'tɔːrts **-torting** -'tɔː.tɪŋ ⓤⓢ -'tɔːr.t̬ɪŋ **-torted** -'tɔː.tɪd ⓤⓢ -'tɔːr.t̬ɪd
retouch ˌriː'tʌtʃ **-es** -ɪz **-ing** -ɪŋ **-ed** -t
retrac|e rɪ'treɪs, ˌriː- **-es** -ɪz **-ing** -ɪŋ **-ed** -t
retract rɪ'trækt, rə- **-s** -s **-ing** -ɪŋ **-ed** -ɪd **-or/s** -ər/z ⓤⓢ -ɚ/z
retractable rɪ'træk.tə.bl̩, rə-
retractation ˌriː.træk'teɪ.ʃən
retraction rɪ'træk.ʃən, rə- **-s** -z
retrain ˌriː'treɪn **-s** -z **-ing** -ɪŋ **-ed** -d
retransla|te ˌriː.træn'sleɪ|t, -trɑːn'-, -trænz'leɪ|t, -trɑːnz'-, -trən'sleɪ|t, -trənz'leɪ|t ⓤⓢ ˌriː'træn.sleɪ|t, -'trænz.leɪ|t, ˌ--'- **-tes** -ts **-ting** -tɪŋ ⓤⓢ -t̬ɪŋ **-ted** -tɪd ⓤⓢ -t̬ɪd
retranslation ˌriː.træn'sleɪ.ʃən, -trɑːn'-, -trænz'leɪ-, -trɑːnz'-, -trən'sleɪ-, -trənz'leɪ- ⓤⓢ -træn'sleɪ-, -trænz'leɪ- **-s** -z
retread *(n.)* 'riː.tred **-s** -z
retread *(v.)* ˌriː'tred **-s** -z **-ing** -ɪŋ **retrod** ˌriː'trɒd ⓤⓢ -'trɑːd
re|treat rɪ|'triːt, rə- **-treats** -'triːts **-treating** -'triː.tɪŋ ⓤⓢ -'triː.t̬ɪŋ **-treated** -'triː.tɪd ⓤⓢ -'triː.t̬ɪd
retrench rɪ'trentʃ, rə- ⓤⓢ -'trentʃ **-es** -ɪz **-ing** -ɪŋ **-ed** -t **-ment/s** -mənt/s
retrial ˌriː'traɪəl, '-- ⓤⓢ 'riː.traɪəl, ˌ-'- **-s** -z
retribution ˌret.rɪ'bjuː.ʃən, -rə'- ⓤⓢ -rə'-
retribu|tive rɪ'trɪb.jə|.tɪv, rə-, -jʊ-, -t̬ɪv **-tory** -tər.i ⓤⓢ -tɔːr-
retrievab|le rɪ'triː.və.b|l̩, rə- **-ly** -li **-leness** -l̩.nəs, -nɪs
retrieval rɪ'triː.vəl, rə-
retriev|e rɪ'triːv, rə- **-es** -z **-ing** -ɪŋ **-ed** -d **-er/s** -ər/z ⓤⓢ -ɚ/z
retrim ˌriː'trɪm **-s** -z **-ming** -ɪŋ **-med** -d
retro- ret.rəʊ- ⓤⓢ ret.roʊ-, -rə-
Note: Prefix. Normally takes primary or secondary stress on the first syllable, e.g. **retrograde** /'ret.rəʊ.greɪd ⓤⓢ -rə-/, **retroact** /ˌret.rəʊ'ækt ⓤⓢ -roʊ'-/.
retro 'ret.rəʊ ⓤⓢ -roʊ
retroact ˌret.rəʊ'ækt ⓤⓢ -roʊ'- **-s** -s **-ing** -ɪŋ **-ed** -ɪd
retroaction ˌret.rəʊ'æk.ʃən ⓤⓢ -roʊ'-
retroactive ˌret.rəʊ'æk.tɪv ⓤⓢ -roʊ'- **-ly** -li *stress shift:* ˌretroactive 'laws
retroced|e ˌret.rəʊ'siːd ⓤⓢ -roʊ'-, -rə'- **-es** -z **-ing** -ɪŋ **-ed** -ɪd
retrocession ˌret.rəʊ'seʃ.ən ⓤⓢ -roʊ'-, -rə'- **-s** -z
retroflex 'ret.rəʊ.fleks ⓤⓢ -rə- **-ed** -t
retroflexion ˌret.rəʊ'flek.ʃən ⓤⓢ -rə'-
retrograde 'ret.rəʊ.greɪd ⓤⓢ -rə-, -roʊ-
retrogress ˌret.rəʊ'gres ⓤⓢ 'ret.rə.gres, -roʊ-, ˌ--'- **-es** -ɪz **-ing** -ɪŋ **-ed** -t **-ive/ly** -ɪv/li
retrogression ˌret.rəʊ'greʃ.ən ⓤⓢ -rə'-, -roʊ'-
retro-rocket 'ret.rəʊˌrɒk.ɪt ⓤⓢ -roʊˌrɑː.kɪt **-s** -s
retrospect 'ret.rəʊ.spekt ⓤⓢ -rə- **-s** -s
retrospection ˌret.rəʊ'spek.ʃən ⓤⓢ -rə'- **-s** -z
retrospective ˌret.rəʊ'spek.tɪv ⓤⓢ -rə'- **-s** -z **-ly** -li *stress shift:* ˌretrospective 'view
retroussé rə'truː.seɪ, rɪ- ⓤⓢ rəˌtruː'seɪ, retˌruː-
retroversion ˌret.rəʊ'vɜː.ʃən, -ʒən ⓤⓢ -roʊ'vɝː.ʒən, -rə'-, -ʃən **-s** -z
retrovert *(n.)* 'ret.rəʊ.vɜːt ⓤⓢ -roʊ.vɝːt, -rə- **-s** -s
retro|vert *(v.)* ˌret.rəʊ|'vɜːt ⓤⓢ -roʊ|'vɝːt, -rə- **-verts** -'vɜːts ⓤⓢ -'vɝːts **-verting** -'vɜː.tɪŋ ⓤⓢ -'vɝː.t̬ɪŋ **-verted** -'vɜː.tɪd ⓤⓢ -'vɝː.t̬ɪd
retrovirus 'ret.rəʊ.vaɪə.rəs, ˌret.rəʊ'vaɪə- ⓤⓢ 'ret.roʊˌvaɪ- **-es** -ɪz
retr|y ˌriː'tr|aɪ **-ies** -aɪz **-ying** -aɪ.ɪŋ **-ied** -aɪd
retsina ret'siː.nə, 'ret.sɪ.nə
returf ˌriː'tɜːf ⓤⓢ -'tɝːf **-s** -s **-ing** -ɪŋ **-ed** -t
return rɪ'tɜːn, rə- ⓤⓢ -'tɝːn **-s** -z **-ing** -ɪŋ **-ed** -d **-able** -ə.bl̩ **-er/s** -ər/z ⓤⓢ -ɚ/z
returnee rɪˌtɜː'niː, rə-, -'tɜː.niː ⓤⓢ rɪˌtɝː'niː, rə- **-s** -z
Reuben 'ruː.bən, -bɪn ⓤⓢ -bən
reunification ˌriː.juː.nɪ.fɪ'keɪ.ʃən, riːˌjuː-, -nə- ⓤⓢ riːˌjuː.nə- **-s** -z
reuni|fy ˌriː'juː.nɪ|.faɪ, -nə- ⓤⓢ -nə- **-fies** -faɪ **-fying** -faɪ.ɪŋ **-fied** -faɪd
reunion ˌriː'juː.ni.ən ⓤⓢ '-njən **-s** -z
Réunion ˌriː'juː.ni.ən; *as if French:* ˌreɪ.uː'njɔ̃ːŋ ⓤⓢ ˌriː'juːn.jən
reu|nite ˌriː.juː|'naɪt **-nites** -'naɪts **-niting** -'naɪ.tɪŋ ⓤⓢ -'naɪ.t̬ɪŋ **-nited** -'naɪ.tɪd ⓤⓢ -'naɪ.t̬ɪd
reusable ˌriː'juː.zə.bl̩
re-use *(n.)* ˌriː'juːs, '-- ⓤⓢ ˌriː'juːs
re-us|e *(v.)* ˌriː'juːz **-es** -ɪz **-ing** -ɪŋ **-ed** -d
Reuter 'rɔɪ.tər ⓤⓢ -t̬ɚ **-s** -z
Rev. *(abbrev. for* **Reverend***)* 'rev.ər.ənd, rev
rev *(n. v.)* rev **-s** -z **-ving** -ɪŋ **-ved** -d **'rev ˌcounter**
revalu|e riː'væl.juː, ˌriː- **-es** -z **-ing** -ɪŋ **-ed** -d
revamp *(v.)* ˌriː'væmp **-s** -s **-ing** -ɪŋ **-ed** -t

revamp (*n.*) ˈriː.væmp **-s** -s
revanch|ist rɪˈvæntʃ|.ɪst **-ists** -ɪsts **-ism** -ɪ.zᵊm
Revd (*abbrev. for* **Reverend**) ˈrev.ᵊr.ᵊnd
reveal rɪˈviːl, rə- **-s** -z **-ing** -ɪŋ **-ed** -d **-er/s** -əʳ/z (US) -ɚ/z **-able** -ə.bl̩
revealing rɪˈviː.lɪŋ **-ly** -li
reveille rɪˈvæl.i, rə-, -ˈvel- (US) ˈrev.ᵊl.i **-s** -z
revel ˈrev.ᵊl **-s** -z **-(l)ing** -ɪŋ **-(l)ed** -d **-(l)er/s** -əʳ/z (US) -ɚ/z
revelation (R) ˌrev.ᵊlˈeɪ.ʃᵊn **-s** -z
revelatory ˌrev.əˈleɪ.tᵊr.i (US) ˈrev.ə.lə.tɔːr.i
Revell ˈrev.ᵊl
revelr|y ˈrev.ᵊl.r|i **-ies** -iz
Revelstoke ˈrev.ᵊl.stəʊk (US) -stoʊk
revendication rɪˌven.dɪˈkeɪ.ʃᵊn, rə-, -dəˈ- (US) -dəˈ- **-s** -z
reveng|e rɪˈvendʒ, rə- **-es** -ɪz **-ing** -ɪŋ **-ed** -d
revengeful rɪˈvendʒ.fᵊl, rə-, -fʊl **-ly** -i **-ness** -nəs, -nɪs
revenue ˈrev.ᵊn.juː, -ɪ.njuː (US) ˈrev.ə.nuː, -njuː **-s** -z
reverber|ate rɪˈvɜː.bᵊr|.eɪt, rə- (US) -ˈvɝː.bə.r|eɪt **-ates** -eɪts **-ating** -eɪ.tɪŋ (US) -eɪ.t̬ɪŋ **-ated** -eɪ.tɪd (US) -eɪ.t̬ɪd **-ator/s** -eɪ.təʳ/z (US) -eɪ.t̬ɚ/z
reverberation rɪˌvɜː.bᵊrˈeɪ.ʃᵊn, rə- (US) -ˌvɝː.bəˈreɪ- **-s** -z
reverberatory rɪˈvɜː.bᵊr.ə.tᵊr.i, rə-, -reɪ- (US) -ˈvɝː.bɚ.ə.tɔːr-
rever|e (R) rɪˈvɪəʳ, rə- (US) -ˈvɪr **-es** -z **-ing** -ɪŋ **-ed** -d
reverenc|e ˈrev.ᵊr.ᵊnts, ˈ-rᵊnts **-es** -ɪz **-ing** -ɪŋ **-ed** -t
reverend (R) ˈrev.ᵊr.ᵊnd, ˈ-rᵊnd **-s** -z
reverent ˈrev.ᵊr.ᵊnt, ˈ-rᵊnt **-ly** -li
reverential ˌrev.ᵊrˈen.tʃᵊl (US) -əˈrent.ʃᵊl **-ly** -i
reverie ˈrev.ᵊr.i (US) -ə.ri **-s** -z
revers *singular:* rɪˈvɪəʳ, rə-, -ˈveəʳ (US) -ˈvɪr, -ˈver *plural:* -z
reversal rɪˈvɜː.sᵊl, rə- (US) -ˈvɝː- **-s** -z
revers|e rɪˈvɜːs, rə- (US) -ˈvɝːs **-es** -ɪz **-ing** -ɪŋ **-ed** -t
reversibility rɪˌvɜː.səˈbɪl.ə.ti, rə-, -sɪˈ-, -ɪ.ti (US) -ˌvɝː.səˈbɪl.ə.t̬i
reversible rɪˈvɜː.sə.bl̩, rə-, -sɪ- (US) -ˈvɝː.sə-
reversion rɪˈvɜː.ʃᵊn, rə- (US) -ˈvɝː.ʒᵊn, -ʃᵊn **-s** -z
reversionary rɪˈvɜː.ʃᵊn.ᵊr.i, rə-, -ʒᵊn- (US) -ˈvɝː.ʒᵊn.er-, -ʃᵊn-
re|vert rɪ|ˈvɜːt, rə- (US) -ˈvɝːt **-verts** -ˈvɜːts (US) -ˈvɝːts **-verting** -ˈvɜː.tɪŋ (US) -ˈvɝː.t̬ɪŋ **-verted** -ˈvɜː.tɪd (US) -ˈvɝː.t̬ɪd
reverter rɪˈvɜː.təʳ, rə- (US) -ˈvɝː.t̬ɚ
re|vet rɪ|ˈvet, rə- **-vets** -ˈvets **-vetting** -ˈvet.ɪŋ (US) -ˈvet̬.ɪŋ **-vetted** -ˈvet.ɪd (US) -ˈvet̬.ɪd **-vetment/s** -ˈvet.mənt/s
review rɪˈvjuː, rə- **-s** -z **-ing** -ɪŋ **-ed** -d **-er/s** -əʳ/z (US) -ɚ/z
revil|e rɪˈvaɪl, rə- **-es** -z **-ing** -ɪŋ **-ed** -d **-er/s** -əʳ/z (US) -ɚ/z
revis|e rɪˈvaɪz, rə- **-es** -ɪz **-ing** -ɪŋ **-ed** -d **-er/s** -əʳ/z (US) -ɚ/z **Reˌvised ˈVersion, Reˈvised ˌVersion**
revision rɪˈvɪʒ.ᵊn, rə- **-s** -z
revision|ism rɪˈvɪʒ.ᵊn|.ɪ.zᵊm, rə- **-ist/s** -ɪst/s
revis|it ˌriːˈvɪz|.ɪt **-its** -ɪts **-iting** -ɪ.tɪŋ (US) -ɪ.t̬ɪŋ **-ited** -ɪ.tɪd (US) -ɪ.t̬ɪd
revisualiz|e, -is|e ˌriːˈvɪz.ju.ᵊl.aɪz, -ˈvɪʒ-, -u- (US) -ˈvɪʒ.u- **-es** -ɪz **-ing** -ɪŋ **-ed** -d
revitaliz|e, is|e ˌriːˈvaɪ.tᵊl.aɪz (US) -t̬ᵊl- **-es** -ɪz **-ing** -ɪŋ **-ed** -d
revival rɪˈvaɪ.vᵊl, rə- **-s** -z
revival|ism rɪˈvaɪ.vᵊl|.ɪ.zᵊm, rə- **-ist/s** -ɪst/s
reviv|e rɪˈvaɪv, rə- **-es** -z **-ing** -ɪŋ **-ed** -d
revivi|fy ˌriːˈvɪv.ɪ|.faɪ, rɪ- **-fies** -faɪz **-fying** -faɪ.ɪŋ **-fied** -faɪd
reviviscence ˌrev.ɪˈvɪs.ᵊnts, ˌriː.vaɪˈ- (US) ˌrev.əˈ-
Revlon® ˈrev.lɒn (US) -lɑːn
revocability ˌrev.ə.kəˈbɪl.ə.ti, -ɪ.ti (US) -ə.t̬i
revocable ˈrev.ə.kə.bl̩ *when applied to letters of credit:* rɪˈvəʊ.kə.bl̩, rə- (US) -ˈvoʊ-
revocation ˌrev.əʊˈkeɪ.ʃᵊn (US) -əˈ- **-s** -z
revok|e rɪˈvəʊk, rə- (US) -ˈvoʊk **-es** -s **-ing** -ɪŋ **-ed** -t
re|volt rɪ|ˈvəʊlt, rə- (US) -ˈvoʊlt **-volts** -ˈvəʊlts (US) -ˈvoʊlts **-volting** -ˈvəʊl.tɪŋ (US) -ˈvoʊl.t̬ɪŋ **-volted** -ˈvəʊl.tɪd (US) -ˈvoʊl.t̬ɪd
revolution ˌrev.ᵊlˈuː.ʃᵊn, -ˈjuː- (US) -əˈluː- **-s** -z
revolutionar|y ˌrev.ᵊlˈuː.ʃᵊn.ᵊr|.i, -ˈjuː- (US) -əˈluː.ʃᵊn.er- **-ies** -iz
revolutionist ˌrev.ᵊlˈuː.ʃᵊn.ɪst, -ˈjuː- (US) -əˈluː- **-s** -s
revolutioniz|e, -is|e ˌrev.ᵊlˈuː.ʃᵊn.aɪz, -ˈjuː- (US) -əˈluː- **-es** -ɪz **-ing** -ɪŋ **-ed** -d
revolv|e rɪˈvɒlv, rə- (US) -ˈvɑːlv **-es** -z **-ing** -ɪŋ **-ed** -d **reˌvolving ˈdoor; reˌvolving ˈcredit; reˌvolving ˈfund**
revolver rɪˈvɒl.vəʳ, rə- (US) -ˈvɑːl.vɚ **-s** -z
revue rɪˈvjuː, rə- **-s** -z
revulsion rɪˈvʌl.ʃᵊn, rə- **-s** -z
reward rɪˈwɔːd, rə- (US) -ˈwɔːrd **-s** -z **-ing** -ɪŋ **-ed** -ɪd
rewind ˌriːˈwaɪnd **-s** -z **-ing** -ɪŋ **rewound** ˌriːˈwaʊnd
rewir|e ˌriːˈwaɪəʳ (US) -ˈwaɪɚ **-es** -z **-ing** -ɪŋ **-ed** -d
reword ˌriːˈwɜːd (US) -ˈwɝːd **-s** -z **-ing** -ɪŋ **-ed** -ɪd
rework ˌriːˈwɜːk **-s** -s **-ing** -ɪŋ **-ed** -t
rewrite (*n.*) ˈriː.raɪt **-s** -s
re|write (*v.*) ˌriː|ˈraɪt **-writes** -ˈraɪts **-writing** -ˈraɪ.tɪŋ (US) -ˈraɪ.t̬ɪŋ **-wrote** ˌriːˈrəʊt (US) -ˈroʊt **-written** ˌriːˈrɪt.ᵊn
Rex reks
Reyes raɪz, reɪz
Reykjavik ˈreɪ.kjə.vɪk, ˈrek.jə-, -viːk (US) ˈreɪ.kjə.viːk, -vɪk
reynard ˈren.ɑːd, ˈreɪ.nɑːd, -nəd (US) ˈren.ɚd, ˈreɪ.nɚd, -nɑːrd **-s** -z
Reynard ˈren.əd, -ɑːd, ˈreɪ.nɑːd (US) -nɑːrd, ˈreɪ.nɚd, ˈren.ɚd
Reynold ˈren.ᵊld **-s** -z
rezon|e ˌriːˈzəʊn (US) -ˈzoʊn **-es** -z **-ing** -ɪŋ **-ed** -d
Rh (*abbrev. for* **rhesus**) ˈriː.səs
Rhadamanthus ˌræd.əˈmænt.θəs
Rhaeti|a ˈriː.ʃi|.ə, ˈ-ʃ|ə (US) -ʃ|ə, ˈ-ʃi|.ə **-an** -ən
Rhaetic ˈriː.tɪk (US) -t̬ɪk
Rhaeto-Roman|ce ˌriː.təʊ.rəʊˈmæn|ts (US) -t̬oʊ.roʊˈ- **-ic** -ɪk
rhapsodic ræpˈsɒd.ɪk (US) -ˈsɑː.dɪk **-al** -ᵊl **-ally** -ᵊl.i, -li
rhapsodiz|e, -is|e ˈræp.sə.daɪz **-es** -ɪz **-ing** -ɪŋ **-ed** -d
rhapsod|y ˈræp.sə.d|i **-ies** -iz
rhea (R) ˈriː.ə, rɪə (US) ˈriː.ə **-s** -z
Rhea Silvia ˌriː.əˈsɪl.vi.ə, ˌrɪəˈ- (US) ˌriː.əˈ-
Rheims riːmz
Rhenish ˈren.ɪʃ
rhenium ˈriː.ni.əm
rheostat ˈriː.əʊ.stæt (US) -oʊ-, ˈ-ə- **-s** -s
rhesus ˈriː.səs **-es** -ɪz **ˈrhesus ˌfactor; ˌrhesus ˈmonkey, ˈrhesus ˌmonkey**
rhetoric ˈret.ᵊr.ɪk (US) ˈret̬-
rhetoric|al rɪˈtɒr.ɪ.k|ᵊl, rə- (US) -ˈtɔːr.ɪ- **-ally** -ᵊl.i, -li **rheˌtorical ˈquestion**
rhetorician ˌret.ᵊrˈɪʃ.ᵊn, -ɒrˈ- (US) ˌret̬.əˈrɪʃ- **-s** -z
Rhett ret
rheum ruːm
rheumatic ruːˈmæt.ɪk (US) -ˈmæt̬- **-s** -s **-ky** -i
rheumatism ˈruː.mə.tɪ.zᵊm
rheumatoid ˈruː.mə.tɔɪd **ˌrheumatoid arthˈritis**
rheumatolog|y ˌruː.məˈtɒl.ə.dʒ|i (US) -ˈtɑː.lə- **-ist/s** -ɪst/s
rheumy ˈruː.mi
Rhiannon riˈæn.ən
Rhine raɪn **-land** -lænd, -lənd
Rhineland-Palatinate ˌraɪn.lænd.pəˈlæt.ɪ.nɪt, -lənd-, -nət, -neɪt (US) -lænd.pəˈlæt.ᵊn.eɪt, -lənd-, -ɪt
rhinestone ˈraɪn.stəʊn (US) -stoʊn **-s** -z
rhinitis ˌraɪˈnaɪ.tɪs (US) -t̬ɪs

Rhotic

In rhotic varieties of English pronunciation the /r/ PHONEME is found in all phonological contexts.

Examples for English

In BBC pronunciation, /r/ is only found before vowels, and never before consonants or before a pause (see also LIAISON), e.g.:

red	/red/
around	/ə'raʊnd/
there is	/ðər ɪz/

In US English and other rhotic accents, on the other hand, /r/ may occur before consonants and before a pause, e.g.:

cart	/kɑːt/	US /kɑːrt/
car	/kɑːʳ/	US /kɑːr/

While the BBC accent is non-rhotic, many accents of the British Isles are rhotic, including most of the south and west of England, much of Wales and all of Scotland and Ireland. Most speakers of American English speak with a rhotic accent, but there are non-rhotic areas including the Boston area, lower-class New York and the Deep South.

Rhyme/Rime

In the phonological analysis of the syllable, this is a way of referring to the vowel in the middle of the syllable forming its 'peak' plus any sounds following the peak within the syllable (the CODA).

Examples for English

In the word *spoon* the rhyme (or rime) is /uːn/, in *tea* it is /iː/ and in *strengths* it is /eŋθs/ or /eŋkθs/.

Note

The spelling "rhyme" also refers to a pair of lines that end with the same sequence of sounds in verse. If we examine the sound sequences that must match each other, we find that these consist of the vowel and any final consonants of the last syllable: thus *moon* and *June* rhyme, and the initial consonants of these two words are not important (of course, we do find longer-running rhymes than this in verse, e.g. *ability* rhyming with *senility*).

rhino- raɪ.nəʊ-; raɪ'nɒ- US raɪ.noʊ-, -nə-; raɪ'nɑː-
Note: Prefix. Normally either takes primary or secondary stress on the first syllable, e.g. **rhinoplasty** /'raɪ.nəʊ.plæs.ti US -noʊ-/, or primary stress on the second syllable, e.g. **rhinoceros** /raɪ'nɒs.ᵊr.əs US -'nɑː.sɚ-/.
rhino 'raɪ.nəʊ US -noʊ **-s** -z
rhinoceri *(alternative plur. of* **rhinoceros***)* raɪ'nɒs.ᵊr.aɪ US -'nɑː.sə.raɪ
rhinoceros raɪ'nɒs.ᵊr.əs US -'nɑː.sɚ- **-es** -ɪz
rhinolog|y raɪ'nɒl.ə.dʒ|i US -'nɑː.lə- **-ist/s** -ɪst/s
rhinoplasty 'raɪ.nəʊ.plæs.ti US -noʊ-, -nə-
rhinoscope 'raɪ.nəʊ.skəʊp US -skoʊp **-s** -s
rhinoscopy raɪ'nɒs.kə.pi US -'nɑː.skə-
rhizome 'raɪ.zəʊm US -zoʊm **-s** -z
rho rəʊ US roʊ
Rhoads rəʊdz US roʊdz
Rhoda 'rəʊ.də US 'roʊ-
Rhode Island *state in US:* ˌrəʊd'aɪ.lənd US ˌroʊd- **-er/s** -əʳ/z US -ɚ/z *stress shift, see compound:* ˌ**Rhode Island 'Red**
Rhodes rəʊdz US roʊdz ˌ**Rhodes 'scholar**
Rhodesi|a rəʊ'diː.ʒ|ə, -ʃ|ə US roʊ-, '-ʒi|.ə **-an** -ən
Rhodian 'rəʊ.di.ən US 'roʊ- **-s** -z
rhodium 'rəʊ.di.əm US 'roʊ-
rhododendron ˌrəʊ.də'den.drən, -dɪ'- US ˌroʊ.də'- **-s** -z
rhomb rɒm US rɑːm*b* **-s** -z
rhomboid 'rɒm.bɔɪd US 'rɑːm- **-s** -z
rhomb|us 'rɒm.b|əs US 'rɑːm- **-uses** -ə.sɪz **-i** -aɪ
Rhona 'rəʊ.nə US 'roʊ-
Rhonda 'rɒn.də US 'rɑːn-
Rhondda 'rɒn.də, -ðə US 'rɑːn-
Rhone rəʊn US roʊn
Rhosllanerchrugog ˌrəʊs.*h*læn.ə'krɪg.ɒg, -θlæn- US ˌroʊs.*h*læn.ə'kriː.gɑːg
rhotacism 'rəʊ.tə.sɪ.zᵊm US 'roʊ.t̬ə-
rhotacization, -isa- ˌrəʊ.tə.saɪ'zeɪ.ʃᵊn, -tɪ- US ˌroʊ.t̬ə.sɪ'- **-s** -z
rhotaciz|e, -is|e 'rəʊ.tə.saɪz US 'roʊ.t̬ə- **-es** -ɪz **-ing** -ɪŋ **-ed** -d
rhotic 'rəʊ.tɪk US 'roʊ.t̬ɪk **-s** -s
rhoticity rəʊ'tɪs.ɪ.ti, -ə.ti US roʊ'tɪs.ə.t̬i
rhubarb 'ruː.bɑːb US -bɑːrb
Rhuddlan 'rɪð.lən, -læn
rhumb rʌm US rʌm*b* **-s** -z
Rhyl rɪl
rhym|e raɪm **-es** -z **-ing** -ɪŋ **-ed** -d **-er/s** -əʳ/z US -ɚ/z
rhymester 'raɪm.stəʳ US -stɚ **-s** -z
Rhymney 'rʌm.ni
Rhys *Welsh name:* riːs *family name of Baron Dynevor:* raɪs
Rhys-Jones ˌriːs'dʒəʊnz US -'dʒoʊnz
rhythm 'rɪð.ᵊm, 'rɪθ- US 'rɪð- **-s** -z ˌ**rhythm and 'blues**; '**rhythm** ˌ**method**
rhythmic 'rɪð.mɪk, 'rɪθ- US 'rɪð- **-al** -ᵊl **-ally** -ᵊl.i US -li
RI ˌɑːʳ'aɪ US ˌɑːr-
ria 'riː.ə, rɪə US 'riː.ə **-s** -z
rial ri'ɑːl; 'raɪ.əl, 'raɪ.əl; US 'riː.ɔːl, -ɑːl **-s** -z
Note: The usual pronunciation for the Saudi Arabian currency is /ri'ɑːl US 'riː.ɔːl/.
rialto (R) ri'æl.təʊ US -toʊ **-s** -z
rib rɪb **-s** -z **-bing** -ɪŋ **-bed** -d '**rib** ˌ**cage**
ribald 'rɪb.ᵊld, 'raɪ.bᵊld, -bɔːld US 'rɪb.ᵊld, 'raɪ.bɔːld **-s** -z **-ry** -ri
riband 'rɪb.ənd **-s** -z
Ribbentrop 'rɪb.ᵊn.trɒp US -trɑːp
Ribble 'rɪb.l̩
ribbon 'rɪb.ᵊn **-s** -z
Ribena® raɪ'biː.nə
riboflavin ˌraɪ.bəʊ'fleɪ.vɪn,

Rhythm

The way events in speech are distributed in time.

Examples for English

Obvious examples of vocal rhythms are chanting as part of games or physical activities. In conversational speech the rhythms are vastly more complicated, but it is clear that the timing of speech is not random. An extreme view (though a quite common one) is that English speech has a rhythm that allows us to divide it up into more or less equal intervals of time called 'feet', each of which begins with a stressed syllable: this is called the 'stress-timed rhythm hypothesis', e.g.:

London	'london
a return to London	a re | 'turn to | 'london
a day return to London	a | 'day re | 'turn to | 'london

Languages where the length of each syllable remains more or less the same as that of its neighbours whether or not it is stressed are called 'syllable-timed'.

Most evidence from the study of real speech suggests that such rhythms only exist in very careful, controlled speaking, but it appears from psychological research that listeners' brains tend to hear timing regularities even where there is little or no physical regularity.

'raɪ.bəʊ.fleɪ- (US) 'raɪ.bə.fleɪ.vɪn, ˌraɪ.bə'fleɪ-, -boʊ'-
ribosomal ˌraɪ.bəʊ'səʊ.məl (US) -bə'soʊ-
ribosome 'raɪ.bəʊ.səʊm (US) -bə.soʊm **-s** -z
Rica 'riː.kə
Ricardo rɪ'kɑː.dəʊ (US) -'kɑːr.doʊ
Ricci 'riː.tʃi
Riccio 'rɪtʃ.i.əʊ, 'rɪt.si- (US) 'rɪt.ʃi.oʊ; 'riːt.ʃoʊ
ric|e (R) raɪs **-es** -ɪz **-ing** -ɪŋ **-ed** -t **'rice ˌpaper; ˌrice 'pudding**
Rice Krispies® ˌraɪs'krɪs.piz
rich (R) rɪtʃ **-es** -ɪz **-er** -ər (US) -ɚ **-est** -ɪst, -əst **-ly** -li **-ness** -nəs, -nɪs
Richard 'rɪtʃ.əd (US) -ɚd **-s** -z
Richardson 'rɪtʃ.əd.sən (US) -ɚd-
Richelieu 'riː.ʃəl.jɜː, 'rɪʃ.əl-, -juː (US) 'rɪʃ.luː, 'riːʃ-, '-ə.luː
Riches 'rɪtʃ.ɪz
Richey, Richie 'rɪtʃ.i
Richler 'rɪtʃ.lər (US) -lɚ
Richmond 'rɪtʃ.mənd
Richter 'rɪk.tə, 'rɪx- (US) 'rɪk.tɚ **'Richter ˌscale**
Richthofen 'rɪk.təʊ.fən, 'rɪx- (US) -toʊ-
rick rɪk **-s** -s **-ing** -ɪŋ **-ed** -d
Rickard 'rɪk.ɑːd (US) -ɑːrd **-s** -z
rickets 'rɪk.ɪts
Rickett 'rɪk.ɪt
Ricketts 'rɪk.ɪts
rickettsi|a rɪ'ket.si|.ə **-ae** -iː **-as** -əz
ricket|y 'rɪk.ə.t|i, -ɪ.t|i (US) -ə.t̬|i **-ier** -i.ər (US) -i.ɚ **-iest** -i.ɪst, -i.əst **-ily** -ɪ.li, -əl.i **-iness** -ɪ.nəs, -ɪ.nɪs
Rickmansworth 'rɪk.mənz.wəθ, -wɜːθ (US) -wɚθ, -wɝːθ
rickshaw 'rɪk.ʃɔː (US) -ʃɑː, -ʃɔː **-s** -z
Ricky 'rɪk.i
Rico 'riː.kəʊ (US) -koʊ
ricoch|et 'rɪk.ə.ʃ|eɪ, -ɒʃ|.eɪ, -et, ˌ--'- (US) 'rɪk.ə.ʃ|eɪ, ˌ--'- **-ets** -eɪz, -ets (US) -eɪz **-eting** -eɪ.ɪŋ, -et.ɪŋ (US) -eɪ.ɪŋ **-eted** -eɪd, -et.ɪd (US) -eɪd
ricotta rɪ'kɒt.ə, rə- (US) -'kɑː.t̬ə
rictus 'rɪk.təs
rid rɪd **-s** -z **-ding** -ɪŋ
Ridd rɪd
riddance 'rɪd.ənts
Riddell 'rɪd.əl; rɪ'del
-ridden -ˌrɪd.ən
Ridding 'rɪd.ɪŋ
riddl|e 'rɪd.l̩ **-es** -z **-ing** -ɪŋ, 'rɪd.lɪŋ **-ed** -d
rid|e (R) raɪd **-es** -z **-ing** -ɪŋ **rode** rəʊd (US) roʊd **ridden** 'rɪd.ən
rid|er (R) 'raɪ.d|ər (US) -d|ɚ **-ers** -əz (US) -ɚz **-erless** -əl.əs, -ɪs, -es (US) -ɚ.ləs, -lɪs, -les
ridg|e (R) rɪdʒ **-es** -ɪz **-ed** -d
ridgepole 'rɪdʒ.pəʊl (US) -poʊl **-s** -z
Ridg(e)way 'rɪdʒ.weɪ
ridicul|e 'rɪd.ɪ.kjuːl, '-ə- **-es** -z **-ing** -ɪŋ **-ed** -d
ridiculous rɪ'dɪk.jə.ləs, rə-, -jʊ- **-ly** -li **-ness** -nəs, -nɪs
Riding 'raɪ.dɪŋ **-s** -z
Ridley 'rɪd.li
Ridout 'rɪd.aʊt, 'raɪ.daʊt
Ridpath 'rɪd.pɑːθ (US) -pæθ
riel 'riː.əl (US) ri'el
Rienzi ri'en.zi, -'ent.si (US) -'en.zi
Riesling 'riː.slɪŋ, 'riːz.lɪŋ (US) 'riːz-, 'riː.slɪŋ
Rievaulx 'riː.vəʊ, -vəʊz, 'rɪv.əz (US) 'riː.voʊ, -voʊz; 'rɪv.əz
Note: /'riː.vəʊ (US) -voʊ/ is the usual local pronunciation.
rife raɪf
riff rɪf **-s** -s
riffl|e 'rɪf.l̩ **-es** -z **-ing** -ɪŋ, 'rɪf.lɪŋ **-ed** -d
riff-raff 'rɪf.ræf
Rifkind 'rɪf.kɪnd
rifl|e 'raɪ.fl̩ **-es** -z **-ing** -ɪŋ, 'raɪ.flɪŋ **-ed** -d **'rifle ˌrange**
rift rɪft **-s** -s **-ing** -ɪŋ **-ed** -ɪd **ˌrift 'valley, 'rift ˌvalley**
rig rɪg **-s** -z **-ging** -ɪŋ **-ged** -d
Riga 'riː.gə
rigamarole 'rɪg.ə.mə.rəʊl (US) -roʊl **-s**
rigatoni ˌrɪg.ə'təʊ.ni (US) -'toʊ-
Rigby 'rɪg.bi
Rigel 'raɪ.gəl, -dʒəl (US) -dʒəl, -gəl
Rigg rɪg
rigger 'rɪg.ər (US) -ɚ **-s** -z
rigging (*n.*) 'rɪg.ɪŋ **-s** -z
right (R) raɪt **-s** -s **-ly** -li **-ness** -nəs, -nɪs **-ing** -ɪŋ (US) 'raɪ.t̬ɪŋ **-ed** -ɪd (US) 'raɪ.t̬ɪd **'right ˌangle; ˌright 'wing**
rightabout 'raɪt.əˌbaʊt (US) 'raɪt̬-
right angle (*n.*) 'raɪtˌæŋ.gl̩ (US) 'raɪt- **-s** -z
right-angled (*adj.*) 'raɪtˌæŋ.gl̩d (US) 'raɪt-, ˌ-'--
righteous 'raɪ.tʃəs, -ti.əs (US) -tʃəs **-ly** -li **-ness** -nəs, -nɪs
rightful 'raɪt.fəl, -fʊl **-ly** -i **-ness** -nəs, -nɪs
right-hand ˌraɪt'hænd (US) ˌraɪt'hænd, '-- *stress shift, British only, see compound:* **ˌright-hand 'man**
right-handed ˌraɪt'hæn.dɪd *stress shift:* ˌright-handed 'player
right(h)o ˌraɪt'əʊ (US) -'oʊ
right|ism (R) 'raɪ.t|ɪ.zəm (US) -t̬|ɪ- **-ist/s** -ɪst/s
rightist 'raɪ.tɪst **-s** -s
right-minded ˌraɪt'maɪn.dɪd **-ly** -li **-ness** -nəs, -nɪs *stress shift:* ˌright-minded 'person
right-of-way ˌraɪt.əv'weɪ (US) ˌraɪt.əv'weɪ, '--ˌ- **rights-of-way** ˌraɪts- (US) ˌraɪts-, '--ˌ-
right-on ˌraɪt'ɒn (US) -'ɑːn *stress shift:* ˌright-on 'speaker
right-wing (*adj.*) ˌraɪt'wɪŋ **-er/s** -ər/s (US) -ɚ/z *stress shift:* ˌright-wing 'policies

righty-ho ˌraɪ.ti'həʊ ⓤⓢ -t̬i'hoʊ
rigid 'rɪdʒ.ɪd **-ly** -li **-ness** -nəs, -nɪs
rigidity rɪ'dʒɪd.ə.ti, -ɪ.ti ⓤⓢ -ə.t̬i
rigmarole 'rɪg.mᵊr.əʊl ⓤⓢ -mə.roʊl **-s** -z
Rigoletto ˌrɪg.əʊ'let.əʊ ⓤⓢ -ə'let.oʊ
rigor 'rɪg.əʳ ⓤⓢ -ɚ
rigor mortis ˌrɪg.ə'mɔː.tɪs, ˌraɪ.gɔː'- ⓤⓢ ˌrɪg.ɚ'mɔːr.t̬ɪs, ˌraɪ.gɔːr'-
rigorous 'rɪg.ᵊr.əs **-ly** -li **-ness** -nəs, -nɪs
rigour 'rɪg.əʳ ⓤⓢ -ɚ **-s** -z
rig-out 'rɪg.aʊt
Rig-Veda ˌrɪg'veɪ.də ⓤⓢ -'veɪ-, -'viː-
Rijeka ri'ek.ə ⓤⓢ -'jek-, -'ek-
Rikki-Tiki-Tavi ˌrɪk.iˌtɪk.iˈtɑː.vi, -'teɪ- ⓤⓢ -'tɑː-, -'tæv.i
ril|e raɪl **-es** -z **-ing** -ɪŋ **-ed** -d
Riley 'raɪ.li
rilievo ˌrɪl.i'eɪ.vəʊ ⓤⓢ -voʊ, -'jeɪ-
Rilke 'rɪl.kə
rill rɪl **-s** -z
rim rɪm **-s** -z **-ming** -ɪŋ **-med** -d **-less** -ləs, -lɪs
Rimbaud 'ræ̃m.bəʊ ⓤⓢ ræm'boʊ
rime raɪm **-s** -z
Rimington 'rɪm.ɪŋ.tən
Rimini 'rɪm.ɪ.ni, '-ə- ⓤⓢ '-ə-
Rimsky-Korsakov ˌrɪm*p*.ski'kɔː.sə.kɒf, -kɒv ⓤⓢ -'kɔːr.sə.kɔːf
Rinaldo rɪ'næl.dəʊ ⓤⓢ rɪ'nɑːl.doʊ, -næl-
rind raɪnd **-s** -z
Rind rɪnd
rinderpest 'rɪn.də.pest ⓤⓢ -dɚ-
ring *(n. v.) encircle, put a ring on, etc.:* rɪŋ **-s** -z **-ing** -ɪŋ **-ed** -d **'ring ˌbinder, ˌring 'binder; 'ring ˌfinger; 'ring ˌroad; ˌrun 'rings round ˌsomeone**
ring *(n. v.) sound, etc.:* rɪŋ **-s** -z **-ing** -ɪŋ **rang** ræŋ **rung** rʌŋ **-er/s** -əʳ/z ⓤⓢ -ɚ/z
ringgit 'rɪŋ.gɪt **-s** -s
ringleader 'rɪŋˌliː.dəʳ ⓤⓢ -dɚ **-s** -z
ring|let 'rɪŋ|.lɪt, -lət ⓤⓢ -lɪt **-lets** -lɪts, -ləts ⓤⓢ -lɪts **-leted** -lɪ.tɪd, -lə.tɪd ⓤⓢ -lɪ.t̬ɪd
ringmaster 'rɪŋˌmɑː.stəʳ ⓤⓢ -ˌmæs.tɚ **-s** -z
Ringo 'rɪŋ.gəʊ ⓤⓢ -goʊ
ringpull 'rɪŋ.pʊl **-s** -z
Ringshall 'rɪŋ.ʃᵊl
ringside 'rɪŋ.saɪd **ˌringside 'seat**
ring-tailed 'rɪŋ.teɪld
Ringwood 'rɪŋ.wʊd
ringworm 'rɪŋ.wɜːm ⓤⓢ -wɝːm
rink rɪŋk **-s** -s
rinky-dink 'rɪŋ.ki.dɪŋk
rins|e rɪn*t*s **-es** -ɪz **-ing** -ɪŋ **-ed** -t
Rintoul 'rɪn.tuːl, -'-
Rio 'riː.əʊ ⓤⓢ -oʊ
Rio de Janeiro ˌriː.əʊ.də.dʒə'nɪə.rəʊ, -deɪ-, -dɪ-, -ʒə'-, -'neə- ⓤⓢ -oʊ.deɪ.ʒə'ner.oʊ, -diː-, -də-, -dʒə'-, -'nɪr-
Rio Grande ˌriː.əʊ'grænd, -'græn.di, -deɪ ⓤⓢ -oʊ'grænd, -'græn.di, -'grɑːn.deɪ
rioja (R) ri'ɒk.ə, -'ɒx-, -'əʊ.kə ⓤⓢ -'ɔː.hɑː, -'oʊ-
riot raɪət **-s** -s **-ing** -ɪŋ ⓤⓢ 'raɪə.t̬ɪŋ **-ed** -ɪd ⓤⓢ 'raɪə.t̬ɪd **-er/s** -əʳ/z ⓤⓢ 'raɪə.t̬ɚ/z **'riot poˌlice; ˌread someone the 'riot act**
riotous 'raɪə.təs ⓤⓢ -t̬əs **-ly** -li **-ness** -nəs, -nɪs
rip rɪp **-s** -s **-ping** -ɪŋ **-ped** -t
RIP ˌɑːʳ.aɪ'piː ⓤⓢ ˌɑːr-
riparian raɪ'peə.ri.ən, rɪ- ⓤⓢ rɪ'per.i-, raɪ-
ripcord 'rɪp.kɔːd ⓤⓢ -kɔːrd **-s** -z
rip|e raɪp **-er** -əʳ ⓤⓢ -ɚ **-est** -ɪst, -əst **-ely** -li **-eness** -nəs, -nɪs
ripen 'raɪ.pᵊn **-s** -z **-ing** -ɪŋ **-ed** -d
ripien|o ˌrɪp.i'eɪ.n|əʊ, rɪ'pjeɪ- ⓤⓢ rɪ'pjeɪ.n|oʊ **-os** -əʊz ⓤⓢ -oʊz **-i** -iː
Ripley 'rɪp.li
Ripman 'rɪp.mən
rip-off 'rɪp.ɒf ⓤⓢ -ɑːf **-s** -s
Ripon 'rɪp.ən
ripost|e, ripost rɪ'pɒst, -'pəʊst ⓤⓢ -'poʊst **-(e)s** -s **-ing** -ɪŋ **-ed** -ɪd
ripper 'rɪp.əʳ ⓤⓢ -ɚ **-s** -z
ripping 'rɪp.ɪŋ **-ly** -li
rippl|e 'rɪp.l̩ **-es** -z **-ing** -ɪŋ, 'rɪp.lɪŋ **-ed** -d
Rippon 'rɪp.ᵊn
rip-roaring ˌrɪp'rɔː.rɪŋ ⓤⓢ -'rɔːr.ɪŋ *stress shift:* ˌrip-roaring 'wave
ripsnort|ing ˌrɪp'snɔː.t|ɪŋ ⓤⓢ -'snɔːr.t̬|ɪŋ **-er/s** -əʳ/z ⓤⓢ -ɚ/z *stress shift:* ˌripsnorting 'finish
riptide 'rɪp.taɪd **-s** -z
Ripuarian ˌrɪp.ju'eə.ri.ən ⓤⓢ -'er.i-
Rip van Winkle ˌrɪp.væn'wɪŋ.kl̩
Risborough, -boro' 'rɪz.bᵊr.ə ⓤⓢ -bɚ.oʊ
Risca 'rɪs.kə
ris|e raɪz **-es** -ɪz **-ing** -ɪŋ **rose** rəʊz ⓤⓢ roʊz **risen** 'rɪz.ᵊn
riser 'raɪ.zəʳ ⓤⓢ -zɚ **-s** -z
Rishton 'rɪʃ.tᵊn
risibility ˌrɪz.ə'bɪl.ə.ti, ˌraɪ.zə'-, -zɪ'-, -ɪ.ti ⓤⓢ ˌrɪz.ə'bɪl.ə.t̬i
risib|le 'rɪz.ə.bl|̩, 'raɪ.zə-, -zɪ- ⓤⓢ 'rɪz.ə- **-ly** -li
rising 'raɪ.zɪŋ **-s** -z
risk rɪsk **-s** -s **-ing** -ɪŋ **-ed** -t
risk|y 'rɪs.k|i **-ier** -i.əʳ ⓤⓢ -i.ɚ **-iest** -i.ɪst, -i.əst **-iness** -ɪ.nəs, -ɪ.nɪs
Risley 'rɪz.li
risotto rɪ'zɒt.əʊ, -'sɒt- ⓤⓢ -'zɑː.t̬oʊ, -'sɑː- **-s** -z
risqué 'rɪs.keɪ, 'riː.skeɪ ⓤⓢ rɪ'skeɪ
rissole 'rɪs.əʊl ⓤⓢ -oʊl **-s** -z
Rita 'riː.tə ⓤⓢ -t̬ə
Ritalin® 'rɪt.ᵊl.ɪn ⓤⓢ 'rɪt̬-, 'rɪd.l̩n
ritardando ˌrɪt.ɑː'dæn.dəʊ ⓤⓢ ˌriː.tɑːr'dɑːn.doʊ **-s** -z
Ritchie 'rɪtʃ.i
rite raɪt **-s** -s **ˌrite of 'passage**
ritornell|o ˌrɪt.ɔː'nel|.əʊ, -ᵊn'el- ⓤⓢ -ɚ'nel|.oʊ, -ɔːr'- **-os** -əʊz ⓤⓢ -oʊz **-i** -iː
Ritson 'rɪt.sᵊn
ritual 'rɪt.ju.əl, 'rɪtʃ.u- ⓤⓢ 'rɪtʃ- **-s** -z **-ly** -li
ritual|ism 'rɪt.ju.ᵊl|.ɪ.zᵊm, 'rɪtʃ.u- ⓤⓢ 'rɪtʃ- **-ist/s** -ɪst/s
ritualistic ˌrɪt.ju.ᵊl'ɪs.tɪk, ˌrɪtʃ.u- ⓤⓢ ˌrɪtʃ- **-ally** -ᵊl.i, -li
rituali|z|e, -is|e 'rɪt.ju.ᵊl.aɪz, 'rɪtʃ.u- ⓤⓢ 'rɪtʃ- **-es** -ɪz **-ing** -ɪŋ **-ed** -d
Ritz rɪts
ritz|y 'rɪt.s|i **-ier** -i.əʳ ⓤⓢ -i.ɚ **-iest** -i.ɪst, -i.əst **-iness** -ɪ.nəs, -ɪ.nɪs
rival 'raɪ.vᵊl **-s** -z **-(l)ing** -ɪŋ **-(l)ed** -d
rivalr|y 'raɪ.vᵊl.r|i **-ies** -iz
riv|e raɪv **-es** -z **-ing** -ɪŋ **-ed** -d
riven 'rɪv.ᵊn
river (R) 'rɪv.əʳ ⓤⓢ -ɚ **-s** -z **'river ˌbank, ˌriver 'bank; 'river ˌbed, ˌriver 'bed; ˌsell someone ˌdown the 'river**
Rivera rɪ'veə.rə ⓤⓢ -'ver.ə
riverboat 'rɪv.ə.bəʊt ⓤⓢ -ɚ.boʊt **-s** -s
Rivers 'rɪv.əz ⓤⓢ -ɚz
riverside (R) 'rɪv.ə.saɪd ⓤⓢ '-ɚ-
riv|et 'rɪv|.ɪt, -ət ⓤⓢ -ɪt **-ets** -ɪts, -əts ⓤⓢ -ɪts **-eting** -ɪ.tɪŋ, -ə.tɪŋ ⓤⓢ -ɪ.t̬ɪŋ **-eted** -ɪ.tɪd, -ə.tɪd ⓤⓢ -ɪ.t̬ɪd **-eter/s** -ɪ.təʳ/z, -ə.təʳ/z ⓤⓢ -ɪ.t̬ɚ/z
Riviera ˌrɪv.i'eə.rə ⓤⓢ -'er.ə
Rivington 'rɪv.ɪŋ.tən **-s** -z
rivulet 'rɪv.jə.lət, -jʊ-, -lɪt, -let ⓤⓢ -lɪt **-s** -s
Rix rɪks
Riyadh 'riː.æd; -ɑːd, -'- ⓤⓢ riː'jɑːd
riyal ri'ɑːl, -'æl; 'riː.ɑːl, -æl ⓤⓢ riː'jɑːl, -'jɔːl, -'ɑːl, -'ɔːl **-s** -z
Rizla® 'rɪz.lə
Rizzio 'rɪt.si.əʊ ⓤⓢ -oʊ
RN *(abbrev. for* **Royal Navy***)* ˌɑːʳ'en; ˌrɔɪəl'neɪ.vi ⓤⓢ ˌɑːr'en; ˌrɔɪəl'neɪ.vi
roach (R) rəʊtʃ ⓤⓢ roʊtʃ **-es** -ɪz
road rəʊd ⓤⓢ roʊd **-s** -z **'road ˌhog; 'road ˌrage; 'road ˌtax**
roadblock 'rəʊd.blɒk ⓤⓢ 'roʊd.blɑːk **-s** -s
roadhou|se 'rəʊd.haʊ|s ⓤⓢ 'roʊd- **-ses** -zɪz
roadie 'rəʊ.di ⓤⓢ 'roʊ- **-s** -z
roadrunner 'rəʊdˌrʌn.əʳ ⓤⓢ 'roʊdˌrʌn.ɚ **-s** -z
roadshow 'rəʊd.ʃəʊ ⓤⓢ 'roʊd.ʃoʊ **-s** -z
roadside 'rəʊd.saɪd ⓤⓢ 'roʊd-
roadstead 'rəʊd.sted ⓤⓢ 'roʊd- **-s** -z
roadster 'rəʊd.stəʳ ⓤⓢ 'roʊd.stɚ **-s** -z

road-test ˈrəʊd.test US ˈroʊd- **-s** -s **-ing** -ɪŋ **-ed** -ɪd

roadway ˈrəʊd.weɪ US ˈroʊd- **-s** -z

roadworks ˈrəʊd.wɜːks US ˈroʊd.wɝːks

roadworth|y ˈrəʊdˌwɜː.ð|i US ˈroʊdˌwɝː- **-iness** -ɪ.nəs, -ɪ.nɪs

Roald rəʊəld US roʊəld

roam rəʊm US roʊm **-s** -z **-ing** -ɪŋ **-ed** -d

roan (R) rəʊn US roʊn **-s** -z

Roanoke ˈrəʊə.nəʊk, ˈrəʊ-, ˌrəʊəˈnəʊk US ˈroʊə.noʊk

roar rɔːʳ US rɔːr **-s** -z **-ing** -ɪŋ **-ed** -d

roast rəʊst US roʊst **-s** -s **-ing** -ɪŋ **-ed** -ɪd **-er/s** -əʳ/z US -ɚ/z

rob (R) rɒb US rɑːb **-s** -z **-bing** -ɪŋ **-bed** -d

Robards ˈrəʊ.bɑːdz US ˈroʊ.bɑːrdz

Robb rɒb US rɑːb

robber ˈrɒb.əʳ US ˈrɑː.bɚ **-s** -z

robber|y ˈrɒb.ər|.i US ˈrɑː.bɚ|.i, ˈ-br|i **-ies** -iz

Robbins ˈrɒb.ɪnz US ˈrɑː.bɪnz

rob|e rəʊb US roʊb **-es** -z **-ing** -ɪŋ **-ed** -d

Robens ˈrəʊ.bɪnz US ˈroʊ-

Roberson ˈrəʊ.bə.sən, ˈrɒb.ə- US ˈroʊ.bɚ-, ˈrɑː-

Note: In **Roberson's medium** the usual pronunciation is /ˈrɒb.ə- US ˈrɑː.bɚ-/.

Robert ˈrɒb.ət US ˈrɑː.bɚt **-s** -s

Roberta rəʊˈbɜː.tə, rɒbˈɜː- US rəˈbɝː.t̬ə, roʊ-

Roberto rəʊˈbɜː.təʊ, rɒbˈɜː- US rəˈbɝː.t̬oʊ, roʊ-, -toʊ

Robertson ˈrɒb.ət.sən US ˈrɑː.bɚt-

Robeson ˈrəʊb.sən US ˈroʊb-

Robespierre ˈrəʊbz.pjeəʳ, -pɪəʳ, ˈrəʊb.spjeəʳ, -spɪəʳ US ˌroʊbzˈpjer, -ˈpɪr, -piˈer

robin (R) ˈrɒb.ɪn US ˈrɑː.bɪn **-s** -z **ˌRobin ˈHood,** US **ˈRobin ˌHood; ˌRobin Hood's ˈBay**

Robina rɒbˈiː.nə, rəʊˈbiː- US rəˈbiː-, roʊ-

Robins ˈrəʊ.bɪnz, ˈrɒb.ɪnz US ˈrɑː.bɪnz, ˈroʊ-

Robinson ˈrɒb.ɪn.sən US ˈrɑː.bɪn- **ˌRobinson ˈCrusoe**

robot ˈrəʊ.bɒt US ˈroʊ.bɑːt, -bət **-s** -s

Robotham ˈrəʊ.bɒθ.əm, -bɒt- US ˈroʊ.bɑː.θəm, -bɑː.t̬əm

robotic rəʊˈbɒt.ɪk US roʊˈbɑː.t̬ɪk **-s** -s

Rob Roy ˌrɒbˈrɔɪ US ˌrɑːb-

Robsart ˈrɒb.sɑːt US ˈrɑːb.sɑːrt

Robson ˈrɒb.sən US ˈrɑːb-

robust rəʊˈbʌst US roʊ-, ˈ-- **-ly** -li **-ness** -nəs, -nɪs

Roby ˈrəʊ.bi US ˈroʊ-

Robyn ˈrɒb.ɪn US ˈrɑː.bɪn

Rocha ˈrɒʃ.ə US ˈrɑː.ʃə

Rochdale ˈrɒtʃ.deɪl US ˈrɑːtʃ-

Roche rəʊtʃ, rəʊʃ, rɒʃ US roʊtʃ, roʊʃ, rɑːʃ

Rochester ˈrɒtʃ.ɪ.stəʳ, ˈ-ə- US ˈrɑː.tʃə.stɚ, -tʃes.tɚ

rochet ˈrɒtʃ.ɪt US ˈrɑː.tʃɪt **-s** -s

Rochford ˈrɒtʃ.fəd US ˈrɑːtʃ.fɚd

rock (R) rɒk US rɑːk **-s** -s **-ing** -ɪŋ **-ed** -t **-er/s** -əʳ/z US -ɚ/z **ˈrock ˌcake; ˈrock ˌclimbing; ˈrock ˌgarden; ˈrock ˌsalmon; ˈrock ˌsalt; ˈrocking ˌchair; ˈrocking ˌhorse**

rockabilly ˈrɒk.əˌbɪl.i US ˈrɑː.kəˌ-

rock-and-roll ˌrɒk.ənˈrəʊl US ˌrɑːk.ənˈroʊl **-er/s** -əʳ/z US -ɚ/z *stress shift:* ˌrock-and-roll ˈmusic

rock-bottom ˌrɒkˈbɒt.əm US ˌrɑːkˈbɑː.t̬əm *stress shift:* ˌrock-bottom ˈlevel

rockbound ˈrɒk.baʊnd US ˈrɑːk-

Rockefeller ˈrɒk.əˌfel.əʳ, -ɪˌ- US ˈrɑː.kəˌfel.ɚ **ˈRockefeller ˌCenter** US **ˌRockefeller ˈCenter**

rocker|y ˈrɒk.ər|.i US ˈrɑː.kɚ- **-ies** -iz

rock|et ˈrɒk|.ɪt US ˈrɑː.k|ɪt **-ets** -ɪts **-eting** -ɪ.tɪŋ US -ɪ.t̬ɪŋ **-eted** -ɪ.tɪd US -ɪ.t̬ɪd **ˈrocket ˌbase; ˈrocket ˌrange**

rocketry ˈrɒk.ɪ.tri, ˈ-ə- US ˈrɑː.kɪ-, -kə-

rockfall ˈrɒk.fɔːl US ˈrɑːk-, -fɑːl **-s** -z

Rockhampton rɒkˈhæmp.tən US rɑːk-

Rockies ˈrɒk.iz US ˈrɑː.kiz

Rockingham ˈrɒk.ɪŋ.əm US ˈrɑː.kɪŋ-

rockmelon ˈrɒkˌmel.ən US ˈrɑːk- **-s** -z

Rockne ˈrɒk.ni US ˈrɑːk-

rock 'n' roll ˌrɒk.ənˈrəʊl US ˌrɑːk.ənˈroʊl **-er/s** -əʳ/z US -ɚ/z *stress shift:* ˌrock 'n' roll ˈmusic

rockros|e ˈrɒk.rəʊz US ˈrɑːk.roʊz **-es** -ɪz

Rockwell ˈrɒk.wel, -wəl US ˈrɑː.kwel, -kwəl

rock|y (R) ˈrɒk|.i US ˈrɑː.k|i **-ier** -i.əʳ US -i.ɚ **-iest** -i.ɪst, -i.əst **-iness** -ɪ.nəs, -ɪ.nɪs **ˌRocky ˈMountains**

rococo rəʊˈkəʊ.kəʊ US rəˈkoʊ.koʊ; ˌroʊ.kəˈkoʊ

rod (R) rɒd US rɑːd **-s** -z **make a ˌrod for one's ˌown ˈback; ˌrule someone with a ˌrod of ˈiron**

Roddick ˈrɒd.ɪk US ˈrɑː.dɪk

rode *(from* **ride***)* rəʊd US roʊd

Roden ˈrəʊ.dən US ˈroʊ-

rodent ˈrəʊ.dənt US ˈroʊ- **-s** -s

rodeo rəʊˈdeɪ.əʊ; ˈrəʊ.di- US ˈroʊ.di.oʊ; roʊˈdeɪ.oʊ **-s** -z

Roderic(k) ˈrɒd.ər.ɪk US ˈrɑː.dɚ-

Rodger ˈrɒdʒ.əʳ US ˈrɑː.dʒɚ **-s** -z

Rodgers ˈrɒdʒ.əz US ˈrɑː.dʒɚz

Rodin ˈrəʊ.dæ̃ŋ US roʊˈdæ̃n

Roding ˈrəʊ.dɪŋ *locally sometimes:* ˈruː.dɪŋ, -ðɪŋ US ˈroʊ.dɪŋ, ˈruː-, -ðɪŋ

Rodman ˈrɒd.mən, ˈrɒb- US ˈrɑːd-

Rodmell ˈrɒd.məl US ˈrɑːd-

Rodney ˈrɒd.ni US ˈrɑːd-

rodomontad|e ˌrɒd.ə.mɒnˈteɪd, ˌrəʊ.də-, -ˈtɑːd US ˌrɑː.də.mənˈteɪd, ˌroʊ-, -ˈtɑːd **-es** -z **-ing** -ɪŋ **-ed** -ɪd

Rodriguez rɒdˈriː.gez US rɑːˈdriː.ges, -geɪs, -geɪz, -gəz

Rodway ˈrɒd.weɪ US ˈrɑːd-

roe (R) rəʊ US roʊ **-s** -z

Roebling ˈrəʊ.blɪŋ US ˈroʊ-

roebuck (R) ˈrəʊ.bʌk US ˈroʊ- **-s** -s

Roedean ˈrəʊ.diːn US ˈroʊ-

Roehampton rəʊˈhæmp.tən US roʊ- *stress shift:* ˌRoehampton ˈCollege

roentgen (R) ˈrɒn.tjən, ˈrɜːn-, ˈrɒnt.gən, ˈrɜːn- US ˈrent.gən, ˈrɜːnt-, ˈrʌnt-, ˈren.tʃən, ˈrɜːn-, ˈrʌn- **-s** -z

Roethke ˈret.kə US ˈret-, ˈreθ-, -ki

rogation (R) rəʊˈgeɪ.ʃən US roʊ- **-s** -z

rogatory ˈrɒg.ə.tər.i, -tri US ˈrɑː.gə.tɔːr-

rog|er (R) ˈrɒdʒ|.əʳ US ˈrɑː.dʒ|ɚ **-ers** -əz US -ɚz **-ering** -ər.ɪŋ **-ered** -əd US -ɚz

Roget ˈrɒʒ.eɪ, ˈrəʊ.ʒeɪ US ˌroʊˈʒeɪ, ˈ-- **ˌRoget's Theˈsaurus**

rogue rəʊg US roʊg **-s** -z **ˌrogue's ˈgallery**

roguer|y ˈrəʊ.gər|.i US ˈroʊ- **-ies** -iz

roguish ˈrəʊ.gɪʃ US ˈroʊ- **-ly** -li **-ness** -nəs, -nɪs

roil rɔɪl **-s** -z **-ing** -ɪŋ **-ed** -d

roist|er ˈrɔɪ.st|əʳ US -st|ɚ **-ers** -əz US -ɚz **-ering** -ər.ɪŋ **-ered** -əd US -ɚd **-erer/s** -ər.əʳ/z US -ɚ.ɚ/z

Rokeby ˈrəʊk.bi US ˈroʊk-

Roker ˈrəʊ.kəʳ US ˈroʊ.kɚ

Roland ˈrəʊ.lənd US ˈroʊ-

role, rôle rəʊl US roʊl **-s** -z **ˈrole ˌmodel**

roleplay ˈrəʊl.pleɪ US ˈroʊl- **-s** -z **-ing** -ɪŋ **-ed** -d

Rolex® ˈrəʊ.leks US ˈroʊ-

Rolf(e) rɒlf, rəʊf US rɑːlf

roll rəʊl US roʊl **-s** -z **-ing** -ɪŋ **-ed** -d **ˈroll ˌbar; ˈroll ˌcall; ˈrolling ˌpin; ˈrolling ˌstock; ˌrolling ˈstone; ˌRolling ˈStones**

Rollason ˈrɒl.ə.sən US ˈrɑː.lə-

roller ˈrəʊ.ləʳ US ˈroʊ.lɚ **-s** -z **ˈroller ˌblind; ˈroller ˌcoaster, ˌroller ˈcoaster**

Rollerblade® ˈrəʊ.lə.bleɪd US ˈroʊ.lɚ- **-s** -z

roller|-skate ˈrəʊ.lə|.skeɪt US ˈroʊ.lɚ- **-skates** -skeɪts **-skating** -skeɪ.tɪŋ US -skeɪ.t̬ɪŋ **-skated** -skeɪ.tɪd US -skeɪ.t̬ɪd

Rolleston ˈrəʊl.stən US ˈroʊl-

rollicking ˈrɒl.ɪ.kɪŋ US ˈrɑː.lɪ- **-ly** -li

Rollins ˈrɒl.ɪnz US ˈrɑː.lɪnz

rollmop ˈrəʊl.mɒp US ˈroʊl.mɑːp **-s** -s

rollneck ˈrəʊl.nek US ˈroʊl- **-s** -s

Rollo ˈrɒl.əʊ US ˈrɑː.loʊ

roll-on ˈrəʊl.ɒn US ˈroʊl.ɑːn **-s** -z

roll-out ˈrəʊl.aʊt US ˈroʊl- **-s** -s

rollover ˈrəʊˌləʊ.vəʳ, ˈroʊˌloʊ.vɚ **-s** -z

Rolls rəʊlz ⓤⓢ roʊlz
Rolls-Royc|e® ˌrəʊlz'rɔɪs ⓤⓢ ˌroʊlz- **-es** -ɪz *stress shift:* ˌRolls-Royce 'engine
roll-top 'rəʊl.tɒp ⓤⓢ 'roʊl.tɑːp **-s** -s
Rolo® 'rəʊ.ləʊ ⓤⓢ 'roʊ.loʊ
Rolodex® 'rəʊ.lə.deks ⓤⓢ 'roʊ-
Rolph rɒlf ⓤⓢ rɑːlf
roly-pol|y ˌrəʊ.li'pəʊ.l|i ⓤⓢ ˌroʊ.li'poʊ- **-ies** -iz *stress shift:* ˌroly-poly 'pudding
ROM rɒm ⓤⓢ rɑːm
Romagna rəʊ'mɑː.njə ⓤⓢ roʊ'-
Romaic rəʊ'meɪ.ɪk ⓤⓢ roʊ-
romaine rəʊ'meɪn ⓤⓢ rə-, roʊ- **roˌmaine 'lettuce, ˌromaine 'lettuce**
Roman 'rəʊ.mən ⓤⓢ 'roʊ- **-s** -z **ˌRoman 'candle; ˌRoman 'Catholic; ˌRoman Ca'tholicism; ˌRoman 'Empire; ˌRoman 'holiday; ˌRoman 'nose; ˌRoman 'numeral**
roman(s) à clef rəʊˌmɑ̃ːn.ɑː'kleɪ ⓤⓢ roʊ-
roman(s) à thèse rəʊˌmɑ̃ːn.ɑː'teɪz ⓤⓢ roʊ-
romanc|e (R) rəʊ'mænts; 'rəʊ.mænts ⓤⓢ roʊ'mænts, '-- **-es** -ɪz **-ing** -ɪŋ **-ed** -t **-er/s** -əʳ/z ⓤⓢ -ɚ/z
Romanes *surname:* rəʊ'mɑː.nɪz, -nɪs, -nes ⓤⓢ roʊ'mɑː.nɪz *gypsy language:* 'rɒm.ə.nes, -nɪs ⓤⓢ 'rɑː.mə-
Romanesque ˌrəʊ.mᵊn'esk ⓤⓢ ˌroʊ- *stress shift:* ˌRomanesque 'church
roman fleuve rəʊˌmɑ̃ːŋ'flɜːv ⓤⓢ roʊ-
Romani|a rʊ'meɪ.ni|.ə, rəʊ-, ruː- ⓤⓢ roʊ-, ruː-, '-nj|ə **-an/s** -ən/z
Romanic rəʊ'mæn.ɪk ⓤⓢ roʊ-
Roman|ism 'rəʊ.mᵊn|.ɪ.zᵊm ⓤⓢ 'roʊ- **-ist/s** -ɪst/s
romanization, -isa- ˌrəʊ.mᵊn.aɪ'zeɪ.ʃᵊn, -ɪ'- ⓤⓢ ˌroʊ.mᵊn.ɪ'- **-s** -z
romaniz|e, -is|e 'rəʊ.mᵊn.aɪz ⓤⓢ 'roʊ- **-es** -ɪz **-ing** -ɪŋ **-ed** -d
Romanov 'rəʊ.mᵊn.ɒf, -nɒv ⓤⓢ 'roʊ.mə.nɔːf; roʊ'mɑː-
Romans(c)h rəʊ'mænʃ, rʊ- ⓤⓢ roʊ'mɑːnʃ, -'mænʃ
romantic (R) rəʊ'mæn.tɪk ⓤⓢ roʊ'mæn.t̬ɪk **-ally** -ᵊl.i, -li
romantic|ism (R) rəʊ'mæn.tɪ.s|ɪ.zᵊm, -tə- ⓤⓢ roʊ'mæn.t̬ə- **-ist/s** -ɪst/s
romanticization, -isa- rəʊˌmæn.tɪ.saɪ'zeɪ.ʃᵊn, -tə-, -sɪ'- ⓤⓢ roʊˌmæn.t̬ə.sɪ'-
romanticiz|e, -is|e rəʊ'mæn.tɪ.saɪz, -tə- ⓤⓢ roʊ'mæn.t̬ə- **-es** -ɪz **-ing** -ɪŋ **-ed** -d
Roman|y 'rəʊ.mə.n|i, 'rɒm.ə- ⓤⓢ 'rɑː.mə-, 'roʊ- **-ies** -iz
romaunt rəʊ'mɔːnt ⓤⓢ roʊ'mɑːnt, -'mɔːnt **-s** -s
Rombauer 'rɒm.baʊəʳ ⓤⓢ 'rɑːm.baʊɚ

Rome rəʊm ⓤⓢ roʊm
Romeo 'rəʊ.mi.əʊ; rəʊ'meɪ- ⓤⓢ 'roʊ.mi.oʊ **-s** -z
Romero rəʊ'meə.rəʊ ⓤⓢ roʊ'mer.oʊ, rə-
Romford 'rɒm.fəd, 'rʌm- ⓤⓢ 'rɑːm.fɚd
romic (R) 'rəʊ.mɪk ⓤⓢ 'roʊ-
Romiley 'rɒm.ᵊl.i, -ɪ.li ⓤⓢ 'rɑː.mᵊl.i
Romilly 'rɒm.ᵊl.i, -ɪ.li ⓤⓢ 'rɑː.mᵊl.i
Romish 'rəʊ.mɪʃ ⓤⓢ 'roʊ-
Rommel 'rɒm.ᵊl ⓤⓢ 'rɑː.mᵊl
Romney 'rɒm.ni, 'rʌm- ⓤⓢ 'rɑːm-, 'rʌm- **-s** -z
Romola 'rɒm.ᵊl.ə ⓤⓢ 'rɑː.mᵊl-
romp rɒmp ⓤⓢ rɑːmp **-s** -s **-ing** -ɪŋ **-ed** -t
romper 'rɒm.pəʳ ⓤⓢ 'rɑːm.pɚ **-s** -z **'romper ˌsuit**
Romsey 'rʌm.zi, 'rɒm- ⓤⓢ 'rɑːm-
Romulus 'rɒm.jʊ.ləs, -jə- ⓤⓢ 'rɑː.mjə-, -mjʊ-
Ronald 'rɒn.ᵊld ⓤⓢ 'rɑː.nᵊld
Ronaldshay 'rɒn.ᵊld.ʃeɪ ⓤⓢ 'rɑː.nᵊld-
Ronaldsway 'rɒn.ᵊldz.weɪ ⓤⓢ 'rɑː.nᵊldz-
Ronan 'rəʊ.nən ⓤⓢ 'roʊ-
Ronay 'rəʊ.neɪ ⓤⓢ 'roʊ-
ron|deau 'rɒn|.dəʊ ⓤⓢ 'rɑːn|.doʊ **-deaus** -dəʊz, -dəʊ ⓤⓢ -doʊz **-deaux** -dəʊ ⓤⓢ -doʊ
rondel 'rɒn.dᵊl ⓤⓢ 'rɑːn-, -del **-s** -z
rondo 'rɒn.dəʊ ⓤⓢ 'rɑːn.doʊ **-s** -z
roneo (R®) 'rəʊ.ni.əʊ ⓤⓢ 'roʊ.ni.oʊ **-s** -z **-ing** -ɪŋ **-ed** -d
Ronnie 'rɒn.i ⓤⓢ 'rɑː.ni
Ronson 'rɒnt.sᵊn ⓤⓢ 'rɑːnt-
Ronstadt 'rɒn.stæt ⓤⓢ 'rɑːn-
röntgen, rontgen (R) 'rɒn.tjən, 'rɜːn-, 'rɒnt.gən, 'rɜːnt- ⓤⓢ 'rent.gən, 'rɜːnt-, 'rʌnt-, 'ren.tʃən, 'rɜːn-, 'rʌn- **-s** -z
röntgenogram 'rɒn.tʃən.ə.græm, 'rɜːn-, 'rɒnt.gən-, 'rɜːnt- ⓤⓢ 'rent.gə.nə-, 'rɜːnt-, 'rʌnt-, 'ren.tʃə-, 'rɜːn-, 'rʌn-, -dʒə- **-s** -z
Ronuk 'rɒn.ək ⓤⓢ 'rɑː.nək
roo ruː **-s** -z
rood ruːd **-s** -z **'rood ˌscreen**
roo|f *(n.)* ruː|f ⓤⓢ ruː|f, rʊ|f **-fs** -fs **-ves** -vz **'roof ˌgarden; 'roof ˌrack**
roof *(v.)* ruːf ⓤⓢ ruːf, rʊf **-s** -s **-ing** -ɪŋ **-ed** -t
roofer 'ruː.fəʳ ⓤⓢ -fɚ, 'rʊf.ɚ **-s** -z
rooftop 'ruːf.tɒp ⓤⓢ -tɑːp, 'rʊf- **-s** -s
rook rʊk **-s** -s **-ing** -ɪŋ **-ed** -t
Rooke rʊk **-s** -s
rooker|y 'rʊk.ᵊr|.i **-ies** -iz
rookie 'rʊk.i **-s** -z
room (R) ruːm, rʊm **-s** -z **-ing -ed -er/s** -əʳ/z ⓤⓢ -ɚ/z **'room ˌservice; 'rooming ˌhouse**
roomful 'ruːm.fʊl, 'rʊm- **-s** -z
roommate 'ruːm.meɪt, 'rʊm- **-s** -s

Rooms ruːmz
room|y 'ruː.m|i, 'rʊm|.i **-ier** -i.əʳ ⓤⓢ -i.ɚ **-iest** -i.ɪst, -i.əst **-ily** -ɪ.li, -ᵊl.i **-iness** -ɪ.nəs, -ɪ.nɪs
Rooney 'ruː.ni
Roosevelt 'rəʊ.zə.velt, 'ruː-, -sə-; 'ruːs.velt ⓤⓢ 'roʊ.zə.velt, 'ruː-, -vəlt; 'roʊz.velt
Note: /'rəʊ.zə.velt ⓤⓢ 'roʊ-/ is the pronunciation used in the families of the late presidents of the U.S.A..
roost (R) ruːst **-s** -s **-ing** -ɪŋ **-ed** -ɪd
rooster 'ruː.stəʳ ⓤⓢ -stɚ **-s** -z
root (R) ruːt **-s** -s **-ing** -ɪŋ ⓤⓢ 'ruː.t̬ɪŋ **-ed** -ɪd ⓤⓢ 'ruː.t̬ɪd **-less/ness** -ləs/nəs, -lɪs/nɪs **'root ˌbeer, ˌroot 'beer; 'root caˌnal; 'root ˌvegetable, ˌroot 'vegetable**
Rootham 'ruː.təm ⓤⓢ -t̬əm
rootstock 'ruːt.stɒk ⓤⓢ -stɑːk **-s** -s
rop|e rəʊp ⓤⓢ roʊp **-es** -s **-ing** -ɪŋ **-ed** -t **ˌrope 'ladder**
Roper 'rəʊ.pəʳ ⓤⓢ 'roʊ.pɚ
rop|ey, rop|y 'rəʊ.p|i ⓤⓢ 'roʊ- **-ier** -i.əʳ ⓤⓢ -i.ɚ **-iest** -i.ɪst, -i.əst **-iness** -ɪ.nəs, -ɪ.nɪs
Roquefort 'rɒk.fɔːʳ ⓤⓢ 'roʊk.fɚt
roquet 'rəʊ.ki, -keɪ ⓤⓢ roʊ'keɪ **-s** -z **-ing** -ɪŋ **-ed** -d
Rorke rɔːk ⓤⓢ rɔːrk
Rorqual 'rɔː.kwᵊl, -kᵊl ⓤⓢ 'rɔːr.kwᵊl **-s** -z
Rorschach 'rɔː.ʃɑːk, -ʃæk ⓤⓢ 'rɔːr.ʃɑːk
rort rɔːt ⓤⓢ rɔːrt **-s** -s **-ing** -ɪŋ, 'rɔːr.t̬ɪŋ **-ed** -ɪd ⓤⓢ 'rɔːr.t̬ɪd
Rory 'rɔː.ri ⓤⓢ 'rɔːr.i
Ros *(abbrev. for* **Rosalind***)* rɒz ⓤⓢ rɑːz
Ros *surname:* rɒs ⓤⓢ rɑːs
Rosa 'rəʊ.zə ⓤⓢ 'roʊ-
rosaceous rəʊ'zeɪ.ʃəs ⓤⓢ roʊ-
Rosalba rəʊ'zæl.bə, rɒz'æl- ⓤⓢ roʊ'zɑːl-, -bɑː
Rosalie 'rəʊ.zᵊl.i, 'rɒz.ᵊl- ⓤⓢ 'roʊ.zə.li, 'rɑː-
Rosalind 'rɒz.ᵊl.ɪnd ⓤⓢ 'rɑː.zə.lɪnd
Rosaline 'rɒz.ᵊl.aɪn, -iːn ⓤⓢ 'rɑː.zə.lɪn, -laɪn
Rosalynde 'rɒz.ᵊl.ɪnd ⓤⓢ 'rɑː.zə.lɪnd
Rosamond 'rɒz.ə.mənd ⓤⓢ 'rɑː.zə-, 'roʊ-
Rosario rəʊ'sɑː.ri.əʊ ⓤⓢ roʊ'zɑːr.i.oʊ, -sɑːr-
rosarium rəʊ'zeə.ri.əm ⓤⓢ roʊ'zer.i- **-s** -z
rosar|y 'rəʊ.zᵊr|.i ⓤⓢ 'roʊ- **-ies** -iz
Roscius 'rɒʃ.i.əs, 'rɒs-; 'rɒs.ki.əs ⓤⓢ 'rɑː.ʃi-, '-ʃəs
Roscoe 'rɒs.kəʊ ⓤⓢ 'rɑː.skoʊ
Roscommon rɒs'kɒm.ən ⓤⓢ rɑː'skɑː.mən
ros|e (R) rəʊz ⓤⓢ roʊz **-es** -ɪz **'rose ˌbush; 'rose ˌgarden; 'rose ˌwater; ˌrose 'window**

rose *(from* **rise)** rəʊz (US) roʊz
rosé 'rəʊ.zeɪ, -'- (US) roʊ'zeɪ
Roseanne rəʊ'zæn (US) roʊ-
roseate 'rəʊ.zi.ət, -ɪt, -eɪt (US) 'roʊ.zi.ɪt, -eɪt
Roseau rəʊ'zəʊ (US) roʊ'zoʊ
Rosebery 'rəʊz.bᵊr.i (US) 'roʊzˌber-
rosebud 'rəʊz.bʌd (US) 'roʊz- **-s** -z
rose-colo(u)red 'rəʊzˌkʌl.əd (US) 'roʊzˌkʌl.ɚd
rosehip 'rəʊz.hɪp (US) 'roʊz- **-s** -s
rosella rəʊ'zel.ə (US) roʊ-, rə- **-s** -z
rosemary (R) 'rəʊz.mᵊr.i (US) 'roʊz.mer-
Rosenberg 'rəʊ.zᵊn.bɜːg, -zᵊm- (US) 'roʊ.zᵊn.bɝːg
Rosencrantz 'rəʊ.zᵊn.krænts, -zᵊŋ- (US) 'roʊ-
Rosenkavalier ˌrəʊ.zᵊn.kæv.ə'lɪəʳ, -zᵊŋ-, 'rəʊ.zᵊnˌkæv.ə.lɪə, ˌroʊ- (US) 'roʊ-
Rosenkranz (US) 'rəʊ.zᵊn.kræn*t*s, -zᵊŋ- (US) 'roʊ.zᵊn-
Rosenthal 'rəʊ.zᵊn.tɑːl, -θɔːl (US) 'roʊ.zᵊn.θɑːl, -θɔːl, -tɑːl, -tɔːl
roseola rəʊ'ziː.ᵊl.ə; ˌrəʊ.zi'əʊ.lə (US) roʊ'ziː.ᵊl.ə; ˌroʊ.zi'oʊ.lə
Rosetta rəʊ'zet.ə (US) roʊ'zet̬- **Roˌsetta 'Stone** (US) **Ro'setta ˌStone**
rosette rəʊ'zet (US) roʊ- **-s** -s
rosewood 'rəʊz.wʊd (US) 'roʊz-
Rosh Hashana ˌrɒʃ.hæʃ'ɑː.nə, -hə'ʃɑː- (US) ˌroʊʃ.hə'ʃɔː.nə, ˌrɑːʃ-, -'ʃɑː-
Rosicrucian ˌrəʊ.zɪ'kruː.ʃᵊn, ˌrɒz.ɪ'-, -ʃi.ən (US) ˌroʊ.zə'kruː.ʃən, ˌrɑː- **-s** -z
Rosie 'rəʊ.zi (US) 'roʊ-
Rosier 'rəʊ.zɪəʳ, -zi.əʳ (US) 'roʊ.ʒɚ; roʊ'zɪr
rosin 'rɒz.ɪn (US) 'rɑː.zən
Rosina rəʊ'ziː.nə (US) roʊ-
Roslin 'rɒz.lɪn (US) 'rɑːz-
Ross rɒs (US) rɑːs
Rossall 'rɒs.ᵊl (US) 'rɑː.sᵊl
Ross|e rɒs (US) rɑːs **-er** -əʳ (US) -ɚ
Rossellini ˌrɒs.ə'liː.ni (US) ˌrɑː.sə'-
Rossetti rə'zet.i, rɒz'et-, rə'set-, rɒs'et- (US) roʊ'zet̬-, rə-, -'set̬-
Rossini rɒs'iː.ni, rə'siː- (US) roʊ'siː-, rɑː-
Rossiter 'rɒs.ɪ.təʳ, '-ə- (US) 'rɑː.sə.t̬ɚ
Rosslare ˌrɒs'leəʳ (US) rɑː'sler *stress shift:* ˌRosslare 'streets
Rosslyn 'rɒs.lɪn (US) 'rɑː.slɪn
Ross-on-Wye ˌrɒs.ɒn'waɪ (US) ˌrɑːs.ɑːn'- *stress shift:* ˌRoss-on-Wye 'streets
rost|er 'rɒs.t|əʳ (US) 'rɑː.st|ɚ **-ers** -əz (US) -ɚz **-ering** -ᵊr.ɪŋ **-ered** -əd (US) -ɚd
Rostock 'rɒs.tɒk (US) 'rɑː.stɑːk
Rostov 'rɒs.tɒv (US) 'rɑː.stɑːf; rə'stɔːf
Rostrevor rɒs'trev.əʳ (US) rɑː'strev.ɚ
Rostropovich ˌrɒs.trə'pəʊ.vɪtʃ (US) ˌrɑː.strə'poʊ.viːtʃ, -strɑː'pɔː-
rostr|um 'rɒs.tr|əm (US) 'rɑː.str|əm **-ums** -əmz **-a** -ə
ros|y (R) 'rəʊ.z|i (US) 'roʊ- **-ier** -i.əʳ (US) -i.ɚ **-iest** -i.ɪst, -i.əst **-ily** -ɪ.li, -ᵊl.i **-iness** -ɪ.nəs, -ɪ.nɪs
Rosyth rɒs'aɪθ, rə'saɪθ (US) rɑː'saɪθ, rə-
rot rɒt (US) rɑːt **-s** -s **-ting** -ɪŋ (US) 'rɑː.t̬ɪŋ **-ted** -ɪd (US) 'rɑː.t̬ɪd
rota 'rəʊ.tə (US) 'roʊ.t̬ə **-s** -z
Rotarian rəʊ'teə.ri.ən (US) roʊ'ter.i- **-s** -z
rotar|y 'rəʊ.tᵊr|.i (US) 'roʊ.t̬ɚ- **-ies** -iz **'Rotary ˌClub**
rotatable rəʊ'teɪ.tə.bl̩ (US) 'roʊ.teɪ.t̬ə-
rota|te rəʊ'teɪ|t (US) 'roʊ.teɪ|t, -'- **-tes** -ts **-ting** -tɪŋ (US) -t̬ɪŋ **-ted** -tɪd (US) -t̬ɪd **-tor/s** -təʳ/z (US) -t̬ɚ/z
rotation rəʊ'teɪ.ʃᵊn (US) roʊ- **-s** -z
rotatory 'rəʊ.tə.tᵊr.i; rəʊ'teɪ- (US) 'roʊ.tə.tɔːr-
ROTC ˌɑːʳ.əʊˌtiː'siː; ˌrɒt'siː (US) ˌɑːr.oʊ.tiː'siː; 'rɑːt.si
rote rəʊt (US) roʊt
rotgut 'rɒt.gʌt (US) 'rɑːt-
Roth rɒθ, rəʊθ (US) rɑːθ
Rothamsted 'rɒθ.ᵊm.sted (US) 'rɑː.θəm-
Rothenstein 'rəʊ.θᵊn.staɪn, -tᵊn-; 'rɒθ.ᵊn- (US) 'rɑː.θən-, 'roʊ-
Rother 'rɒð.əʳ (US) 'rɑː.ðɚ
Rotherfield 'rɒð.ə.fiːld (US) 'rɑː.ðɚ-
Rotherham 'rɒð.ᵊr.əm (US) 'rɑː.ðɚ-
Rotherhithe 'rɒð.ə.haɪð (US) 'rɑː.ðɚ-
Rothermere 'rɒð.ə.mɪəʳ (US) 'rɑː.ðɚ.mɪr
Rotherston 'rɒð.ə.stᵊn (US) 'rɑː.ðɚ-
Rotherwick 'rɒð.ᵊr.ɪk, -ə.wɪk (US) 'rɑː.ðɚ.ɪk, -wɪk
Rothes 'rɒθ.ɪs (US) 'rɑː.θɪs
Rothesay 'rɒθ.si, -seɪ (US) 'rɑːθ-
Rothko 'rɒθ.kəʊ (US) 'rɑːθ.koʊ
Rothman 'rɒθ.mən (US) 'rɑːθ-
Rothschild 'rɒθ.tʃaɪld, 'rɒs-, 'rɒθs- (US) 'rɑːθ-, 'rɔːθ-, 'rɑːθs-, 'rɔːθs-
Rothwell 'rɒθ.wel, -wəl (US) 'rɑːθ.wel, -wəl
roti 'rəʊ.ti (US) roʊ'tiː **-s** -z
rotisserie rəʊ'tɪs.ᵊr.i, -'tiː.sᵊr- (US) roʊ'tɪs.ɚ- **-s** -z
rotogravure ˌrəʊ.təʊ.grə'vjʊəʳ (US) ˌroʊ.t̬ə.grə'vjʊr; 'roʊ.t̬əˌgreɪ.vjɚ
rotor 'rəʊ.təʳ (US) 'roʊ.t̬ɚ **-s** -z
Rotorua ˌrəʊ.tə'ruː.ə (US) ˌroʊ.t̬ə'-
roto|vate 'rəʊ.tə|.veɪt (US) 'roʊ.t̬ə- **-vates** -veɪts **-vating** -veɪ.tɪŋ (US) -veɪ.t̬ɪŋ **-vated** -veɪ.tɪd (US) -veɪ.t̬ɪd
rotovator (R®) 'rəʊ.tə.veɪ.təʳ (US) 'roʊ.t̬ə.veɪ.t̬ɚ **-s** -z
rotten 'rɒt.ᵊn (US) 'rɑː.tᵊn **-est** -ɪst **-ly** -li **-ness** -nəs, -nɪs **ˌrotten 'borough**
rottenstone 'rɒt.ᵊn.stəʊn (US) 'rɑː.tᵊn.stoʊn
rotter 'rɒt.əʳ (US) 'rɑː.t̬ɚ **-s** -z
Rotterdam 'rɒt.ə.dæm, ˌ--'- (US) 'rɑː.t̬ɚ.dæm
Rottingdean 'rɒt.ɪŋ.diːn, ˌ--'- (US) 'rɑː.t̬ɪŋ.diːn
rottweiler (R) 'rɒt.waɪ.ləʳ, -vaɪ- (US) 'rɑːt.waɪ.lɚ, 'rɔːt.vaɪ- **-s** -z
rotund rəʊ'tʌnd; 'rəʊ.tʌnd (US) roʊ- **-ity** -ə.ti, -ɪ.ti (US) -ə.t̬i **-ness** -nəs, -nɪs
rotunda (R) rəʊ'tʌn.də (US) roʊ- **-s** -z
rouble 'ruː.bl̩ **-s** -z
Rouch raʊtʃ
roué 'ruː.eɪ, -'- (US) ru'eɪ; 'ruː.eɪ **-s** -z
Rouen 'ruː.ɑ̃ː*ŋ*, -ɑːŋ, -'- (US) ru'ɑ̃ː*ŋ*, -'ɑːn
roug|e ruːʒ **-es** -ɪz **-ing** -ɪŋ **-ed** -d
rough rʌf **-s** -s **-er** -əʳ (US) -ɚ **-est** -ɪst, -əst **-ly** -li **-ness** -nəs, -nɪs **-ing** -ɪŋ **-ed** -t **ˌrough 'diamond; 'rough ˌstuff; ˌrough 'trade; take the ˌrough with the 'smooth**
roughage 'rʌf.ɪdʒ
rough-and-ready ˌrʌf.ᵊnd'red.i *stress shift:* ˌrough-and-ready 'treatment
rough-and-tumble ˌrʌf.ᵊnd'tʌm.bl̩ *stress shift:* ˌrough-and-tumble 'games
roughcast 'rʌf.kɑːst (US) -kæst
roughen 'rʌf.ᵊn **-s** -z **-ing** -ɪŋ, 'rʌf.nɪŋ **-ed** -d
rough-hew ˌrʌf'hjuː **-s** -z **-ing** -ɪŋ **-ed** -d **-n** -n *stress shift:* ˌrough-hewn 'stone
roughhous|e 'rʌf.haʊs **-es** -ɪz **-ing** -ɪŋ **-ed** -t
roughish 'rʌf.ɪʃ
roughneck 'rʌf.nek **-s** -s
roughrider 'rʌfˌraɪ.dəʳ (US) -dɚ **-s** -z
roughshod 'rʌf.ʃɒd (US) -ʃɑːd **ˌride 'roughshod over**
rough-spoken ˌrʌf'spəʊ.kᵊn (US) -'spoʊ- *stress shift:* ˌrough-spoken 'person
Rough Tor ˌraʊ'tɔːʳ (US) -'tɔːr
roulade ruː'lɑːd **-s** -z
roulette ruː'let
Roulston 'rəʊl.stᵊn (US) 'roʊl-
Roumani|a rʊ'meɪ.ni|.ə, rʊ-, rəʊ- (US) ruː-, roʊ-, '-nj|ə **-an/s** -ən/z
round (R) raʊnd **-s** -z **-er** -əʳ (US) -ɚ **-est** -ɪst, -əst **-ly** -li **-ness** -nəs, 'raʊn.nəs, -nɪs **-ish** -ɪʃ **-ing** -ɪŋ **-ed** -ɪd **ˌround 'robin; ˌRound 'Table** (US) **'Round ˌTable; ˌround 'trip**
roundabout 'raʊnd.əˌbaʊt **-s** -s
roundel 'raʊn.dᵊl **-s** -z
roundelay 'raʊn.dɪ.leɪ, -dᵊl.eɪ (US) -də.leɪ **-s** -z
rounders 'raʊn.dəz (US) -dɚz
roundhand 'raʊnd.hænd
Roundhay 'raʊn.deɪ, 'raʊnd.heɪ
Roundhead 'raʊnd.hed **-s** -z
roundhou|se 'raʊnd.haʊ|s **-ses** -zɪz
round-shouldered ˌraʊnd'ʃəʊl.dəd (US) -'ʃoʊl.dɚd *stress shift:* ˌround-shouldered 'person

Rounding

A term used to describe lip configuration in speech sounds.

Examples for English

Practically any vowel or consonant may be produced with different amounts of lip-rounding. The lips are rounded by muscles that act rather like a draw-string round the neck of a bag, bringing the edges of the lips towards each other. Except in unusual cases, this results not only in the mouth opening adopting a round shape, but also in a protrusion or "pushing forward" of the lips. In theory, any vowel position (defined in terms of height and frontness/backness) may be produced rounded or unrounded, though we do not necessarily find all possible vowels in natural languages. BBC English has four rounded vowel monophthongs, while US English has three:

pot	/pɒt/	(US) /pɑːt/	(unrounded)
put	/pʊt/		
core	/kɔːʳ/	(US) /kɔːr/	
coo	/kuː/		

Consonants, too, may have rounded lips (in [w], the basic consonantal articulation itself consists of lip-rounding): this lip-rounding in consonants is regarded as a 'secondary articulation', and it is usual to refer to it as 'labialisation'. In British English, it is common to find /ʃ/, /tʃ/ and /r/ with lip-rounding.

In other languages

Swedish is described as having a rounded vowel without lip protrusion.

rounds|man ˈraʊndz|.mən **-men** -mən
round-table ˌraʊndˈteɪ.bl̩ (US) ˈ-ˌ-- *stress shift:* ˌround-table ˈconference
round-the-clock ˌraʊnd.ðəˈklɒk (US) -ˈklɑːk *stress shift:* ˌround-the-clock ˈvigil
round-up ˈraʊnd.ʌp **-s** -s
roundworm ˈraʊnd.wɜːm (US) -wɝːm **-s** -z
Rourke rɔːk (US) rɔːrk
Rous raʊs
rous|e raʊz **-es** -ɪz **-ing/ly** -ɪŋ/li **-ed** -d
Rouse raʊs, ruːs
Rousseau ˈruː.səʊ, -ˈ- (US) ruːˈsoʊ
Roussillon ˌruː.siˈjɔ̃ŋ, ˈ--- (US) -ˈjõʊn
roustabout ˈraʊst.əˌbaʊt **-s** -s
rout raʊt **-s** -s **-ing** -ɪŋ (US) ˈraʊ.t̬ɪŋ **-ed** -ɪd (US) ˈraʊ.t̬ɪd
rout|e ruːt (US) ruːt, raʊt **-es** -s **-(e)ing/s** -ɪŋ/z (US) ˈruː.t̬ɪŋ, ˈraʊ- **-ed** -ɪd (US) ˈruː.t̬ɪd, ˈraʊ- **ˈroute ˌmarch**
Routh raʊθ
routine ruːˈtiːn **-s** -z
Routledge ˈraʊt.lɪdʒ, -ledʒ, ˈrʌt-
Routley ˈraʊt.li
roux (R) ruː
rov|e rəʊv (US) roʊv **-es** -z **-ing** -ɪŋ **-ed** -d **-er/s** -əʳ/z (US) -ɚ/z
Rover® ˈrəʊ.vəʳ (US) ˈroʊ.vɚ **-s** -z
row *(n.v.) quarrel:* raʊ **-s** -z **-ing** -ɪŋ **-ed** -d
row *(n.v.) all other senses:* rəʊ (US) roʊ **-s** -z **-ing** -ɪŋ **-ed** -d **ˈrow ˌhouse; ˈrowing ˌboat**
Rowallan rəʊˈæl.ən (US) roʊ-
rowan *tree:* rəʊən, raʊən; ˈrəʊ.æn (US) roʊən, raʊən **-s** -z
Note: More commonly /raʊən/ in Scotland.
Rowan *name:* rəʊən, raʊən (US) roʊən, raʊən
rowanberr|y ˈrəʊən,ber|.i, ˈrəʊəm- (US) ˈroʊən- **-ies** -iz
Rowant raʊənt
row-boat ˈrəʊ.bəʊt (US) ˈroʊ.boʊt **-s** -s
Rowbottom, Rowbotham ˈrəʊˌbɒt.əm (US) ˈroʊˌbɑː.t̬əm
Rowden ˈraʊ.dən
rowd|y ˈraʊ.d|i **-ies** -iz **-ier** -i.əʳ (US) -i.ɚ **-iest** -i.ɪst, -i.əst **-ily** -ɪ.li, -əl.i **-iness** -ɪ.nəs, -ɪ.nɪs **-yism** -i.ɪ.zəm
Rowe rəʊ (US) roʊ
rowel raʊəl **-s** -z
Rowell raʊəl
Rowena rəʊˈiː.nə (US) roʊ-, -ˈwiː-
Rowenta® rəʊˈen.tə (US) roʊˈen.t̬ə
rower ˈrəʊ.əʳ (US) ˈroʊ.ɚ **-s** -z
Rowland ˈrəʊ.lənd (US) ˈroʊ- **-s** -z
Rowlandson ˈrəʊ.lənd.sən (US) ˈroʊ-
Rowles rəʊlz (US) roʊlz
Rowley ˈrəʊ.li, ˈraʊ- (US) ˈroʊ-, ˈraʊ-
Rowling ˈrəʊ.lɪŋ, ˈraʊ- (US) ˈroʊ-
Rowlinson ˈrəʊ.lɪn.sən (US) ˈroʊ-
rowlock ˈrɒl.ək, ˈrəʊ.lɒk, ˈrʌl.ək (US) ˈrɑː.lək, ˈrʌl.ək, ˈroʊ.lɑːk **-s** -s
Rowney ˈrəʊ.ni, ˈraʊ- (US) ˈroʊ-, ˈraʊ-
Rowntree ˈraʊn.triː **ˌRowntree ˈMackintosh®**
Rowridge ˈraʊ.rɪdʒ
Rowse raʊs
Rowton ˈraʊ.tən, ˈrɔː-
Roxana rɒkˈsɑː.nə, -ˈsæn.ə (US) rɑːkˈsæn-
Roxanne rɒkˈsæn (US) rɑːk-
Roxburgh(e) ˈrɒks.bər.ə (US) ˈrɑːks- **-shire** -ʃəʳ, -ˌʃɪəʳ (US) -ʃɚ, -ˌʃɪr
Roxy ˈrɒk.si (US) ˈrɑːk-
Roy rɔɪ
royal ˈrɔɪəl **-s** **-ly** -i **ˌRoyal ˈAir ˌForce; ˌroyal ˈblue; ˌroyal ˈfamily; ˌRoyal ˈHighness; ˌroyal ˈjelly; ˌRoyal ˈMail; ˌRoyal ˈNavy**
royal|ism ˈrɔɪə.l|ɪ.zəm **-ist/s** -ɪst/s
royalt|y ˈrɔɪəl.t|i (US) -t̬|i **-ies** -iz
Royce rɔɪs
Royle rɔɪl
Royston ˈrɔɪ.stən
Royton ˈrɔɪ.tən
RP ˌɑːˈpiː (US) ˌɑːr-
rpm (R) ˌɑː.piːˈem (US) ˌɑːr-
RSA ˌɑːʳ.esˈeɪ (US) ˌɑːr-
RSC ˌɑːʳ.esˈsiː (US) ˌɑːr-
RSPB ˌɑːʳ.esˌpiːˈbiː (US) ˌɑːr-
RSPCA ˌɑːʳ.esˌpiː.siːˈeɪ (US) ˌɑːr-
RSVP ˌɑːʳ.es.viːˈpiː (US) ˌɑːr-
Rt. Hon. *(abbrev. for* **Right Honourable***)* ˌraɪtˈɒn.ər.ə.bl̩ (US) -ˈɑː.nɚ.ə- *stress shift:* ˌRt. Hon. ˈmember
Ruabon ruˈæb.ən

Pronouncing the letters RRH

The consonant letter combination **rrh** behaves like the letter **r**, e.g.:

myrrh	/mɜːʳ/	(US) /mɝːr/
diarrh(o)ea	/ˌdaɪəˈrɪə/	(US) /-ˈriː.ə/

Ruanda ru'æn.də US -'ɑːn-

rub rʌb **-s** -z **-bing** -ɪŋ **-bed** -d

Rubáiyát 'ruː.baɪ.jæt, -beɪ- US ˌruː.baɪ'jɑːt, -biː'-, '---

rubato ruː'bɑː.təʊ, rʊ- US ruː'bɑː.toʊ **-s** -z

rubb|er 'rʌb|.əʳ US -ɚ **-ers** -əz US -ɚz **-ery** -ᵊr.i ˌ**rubber 'band**; '**rubber ˌplant**

rubberiz|e, -is|e 'rʌb.ᵊr.aɪz US -ə.raɪz **-es** -ɪz **-ing** -ɪŋ **-ed** -d

rubberneck 'rʌb.ə.nek US '-ɚ- **-s** -s **-ing** -ɪŋ **-ed** -t **-er/s** -əʳ/z US -ɚ/z

rubber-stamp ˌrʌb.ə'stæmp US -ɚ'- **-s** -s **-ing** -ɪŋ **-ed** -t *stress shift:* ˌrubber-stamped 'document

rubbish 'rʌb.ɪʃ **-es** -ɪz **-ing** -ɪŋ **-ed** -t **-y** -i

rubble 'rʌb.l̩

Rubbra 'rʌb.rə

rubefacient ˌruː.bɪ'feɪ.ʃi.ənt, '-ʃᵊnt US -bə'feɪ.ʃᵊnt

Rube Goldberg ˌruːb'gəʊl*d*.bɜːg US -'goʊld.bɝːg

rubella ruː'bel.ə, rʊ- US ruː-

Ruben 'ruː.bɪn, -bən US -bən

Rubenesque ˌruː.bɪ'nesk, -bᵊn'esk US -bə'nesk

Rubens 'ruː.bənz, -bɪnz US -bənz

rubeola ruː'biː.əʊ.lə, rʊ-; ˌruː.bi'əʊ.lə US ruː'bi.ᵊl.ə; ˌruː.bi'oʊ.lə

Rubicon 'ruː.bɪ.kᵊn, -kɒn US -kɑːn

rubicund 'ruː.bɪ.kənd, -kʌnd US -bə.kʌnd, -bɪ-, -kənd

rubidium ruː'bɪd.i.əm, rʊ- US ruː-

Rubik 'ruː.bɪk ˌ**Rubik's 'Cube**

Rubinstein 'ruː.bɪn.staɪn, -bən- US -bɪn-

ruble 'ruː.bl̩ **-s** -z

rubric 'ruː.brɪk **-s** -s

rub|y (R) 'ruː.b|i **-ies** -iz

RUC ˌɑː.juː'siː US ˌɑːr-

ruch|e ruːʃ **-es** -ɪz **-ing** -ɪŋ **-ed** -t

ruck rʌk **-s** -s **-ing** -ɪŋ **-ed** -t

rucksack 'rʌk.sæk, 'rʊk- **-s** -s

ruckus 'rʌk.əs

ruction 'rʌk.ʃᵊn **-s** -z

rudd (R) rʌd **-s** -z

rudd|er 'rʌd|.əʳ US -ɚ **-ers** -əz US -ɚz **-erless** -ᵊl.əs, -ɪs US -ɚ.ləs, -lɪs

Rudderham 'rʌd.ᵊr.əm

Ruddigore 'rʌd.ɪ.gɔːʳ US -gɔːr

ruddl|e 'rʌd.l̩ **-es** -z **-ing** -ɪŋ, 'rʌd.lɪŋ **-ed** -d

Ruddlington 'rʌd.lɪŋ.tən

Ruddock 'rʌd.ək

rudd|y 'rʌd|.i **-ier** -i.əʳ US -i.ɚ **-iest** -i.ɪst, -i.əst **-ily** -ɪ.li, -ᵊl.i **-iness** -ɪ.nəs, -ɪ.nɪs

rud|e ruːd **-er** -əʳ US -ɚ **-est** -ɪst, -əst **-ely** -li **-eness** -nəs, -nɪs

Rudge rʌdʒ

Rudi 'ruː.di

rudiment 'ruː.dɪ.mənt, -də- US -də- **-s** -s

rudimentary ˌruː.dɪ'men.tᵊr.i, -də'-, '-tri US -də'- *stress shift:* ˌrudimentary 'knowledge

Rudolf, Rudolph 'ruː.dɒlf US -dɑːlf

Rudy 'ruː.di

Rudyard *first name:* 'rʌd.jəd, -jɑːd US -jɚd, -jɑːrd

Rudyard *in Staffordshire:* 'rʌdʒ.əd US -ɚd

rue ruː **-s** -z **-ing** -ɪŋ **-d** -d

rueful 'ruː.fᵊl, -fʊl **-ly** -i **-ness** -nəs, -nɪs

ruff rʌf **-s** -s **-ing** -ɪŋ **-ed** -t

ruffian 'rʌf.i.ən **-s** -z **-ly** -li **-ism** -ɪ.zᵊm

ruffl|e 'rʌf.l̩ **-es** -z **-ing** -ɪŋ, 'rʌf.lɪŋ **-ed** -d

rufiyaa 'ruː.fi.jɑː

rufous 'ruː.fəs

Rufus 'ruː.fəs

rug rʌg **-s** -z

Rugbeian rʌg'biː.ən **-s** -z

rugby (R) 'rʌg.bi ˌ**Rugby 'League**; ˌ**Rugby 'Union**

Rugeley 'ruːdʒ.li, 'ruːʒ-

rugged 'rʌg.ɪd **-ly** -li **-ness** -nəs, -nɪs

rugger 'rʌg.əʳ US -ɚ

rugrat (R) 'rʌg.ræt **-s** -s

Ruhr rʊəʳ US rʊr

ruin 'ruː.ɪn **-s** -z **-ing** -ɪŋ **-ed** -d

ruination ˌruː.ɪ'neɪ.ʃᵊn, rʊɪ'- US ˌruː.ə'-

ruinous 'ruː.ɪ.nəs US 'ruː.ə- **-ly** -li **-ness** -nəs, -nɪs

Ruislip 'raɪ.slɪp, 'raɪz.lɪp

Ruiz ru'iːθ US ru'iːθ; ruː'iːs

rul|e (R) ruːl **-es** -z **-ing** -ɪŋ **-ed** -d **-er/s** -əʳ/z US -ɚ/z

rulebook 'ruːl.bʊk **-s** -s

ruling 'ruː.lɪŋ **-s** -z ˌ**ruling 'class** US '**ruling ˌclass**

rum rʌm **-mer** -əʳ US -ɚ **-mest** -ɪst, -əst

Rumani|a rʊ'meɪ.ni|.ə, rəʊ-, ruː- US roʊ-, ruː-, '-nj|ə **-an/s** -ənz

rumba 'rʌm.bə **-s** -z

Rumbelow 'rʌm.bə.ləʊ, -bɪ- US -loʊ

rumbl|e 'rʌm.bl̩ **-es** -z **-ing/s** -ɪŋ/z, 'rʌm.blɪŋ/z **-ed** -d

Rumbold 'rʌm.bəʊld US -boʊld

rumbustious rʌm'bʌs.ti.əs, '-tʃəs US -tʃəs **-ness** -nəs, -nɪs

Rumelia ruː'miː.li.ə US -li.ə, -'miːl.jə

rumen 'ruː.men, -mɪn, -mən US -mən **-s** -z **rumina** 'ruː.mɪ.nə, -mə- US -mə-

Rumford 'rʌm.fəd US -fɚd

ruminant 'ruː.mɪ.nənt, -mə- US -mə- **-s** -s

rumi|nate 'ruː.mɪ|.neɪt, -mə- US -mə- **-nates** -neɪts **-nating** -neɪ.tɪŋ US -neɪ.t̬ɪŋ **-nated** -neɪ.tɪd US -neɪ.t̬ɪd

rumination ˌruː.mɪ'neɪ.ʃᵊn, -mə'- US -mə'- **-s** -z

ruminative 'ruː.mɪ.nə.tɪv, -mə-, -neɪ- US -mə.neɪ.t̬ɪv

rummag|e 'rʌm.ɪdʒ **-es** -ɪz **-ing** -ɪŋ **-ed** -d '**rummage ˌsale**

rumm|y 'rʌm|.i **-ier** -i.əʳ US -i.ɚ **-iest** -i.ɪst, -i.əst **-ily** -ɪ.li, -ᵊl.i **-iness** -ɪ.nəs, -ɪ.nɪs

rumo(u)r 'ruː.məʳ US -mɚ **-s** -z **-ed** -d

rumo(u)r-mong|er 'ruː.məˌmʌŋ.g|əʳ US -mɚˌmʌŋ.g|ɚ, -ˌmɑːŋ- **-ers** -əz US -ɚz **-ering** -ᵊr.ɪŋ

rump rʌmp **-s** -s ˌ**rump 'steak**

Rumpelstiltskin ˌrʌm.pᵊl'stɪlt.skɪn

rumpl|e 'rʌm.pl̩ **-es** -z **-ing** -ɪŋ, 'rʌm.plɪŋ **-ed** -d

Rumpole 'rʌm.pəʊl US -poʊl

rumpus 'rʌm.pəs **-es** -ɪz

rum-runner 'rʌmˌrʌn.əʳ US -ɚ **-s** -z

Rumsfeld 'rʌmz.felt US -feld

run rʌn **-s** -z **-ning** -ɪŋ **ran** ræn ˌ**running 'water**; ˌ**take a** ˌ**running 'jump**; '**running ˌshoe**

runabout 'rʌn.əˌbaʊt **-s** -s

runagate 'rʌn.əˌgeɪt **-s** -s

runaround 'rʌn.ᵊrˌaʊnd

runaway 'rʌn.əˌweɪ **-s** -z

runcible 'rʌn*t*.sɪ.bl̩, -sə- US -sə-

Runcie 'rʌn*t*.si

Runciman 'rʌn*t*.sɪ.mən

Runcorn 'rʌŋ.kɔːn US -kɔːrn

run-down *(adj.)* ˌrʌn'daʊn *stress shift:* ˌrun-down 'area

rundown *(n.)* 'rʌn.daʊn **-s** -z

rune (R) ruːn **-s** -z

rung rʌŋ **-s** -z

rung *(from* **ring)** rʌŋ

Runham 'rʌn.əm

runic (R) 'ruː.nɪk

run-in 'rʌn.ɪn **-s** -z

runnel 'rʌn.ᵊl **-s** -z

runner 'rʌn.əʳ US -ɚ **-s** -z ˌ**runner 'bean**, '**runner ˌbean**

runner-up ˌrʌn.əʳ'ʌp US -ɚ'- **runners-up** ˌrʌn.əz'- US -ɚz'- *stress shift:* ˌrunner-up 'prizes

running-board 'rʌn.ɪŋ.bɔːd US -bɔːrd **-s** -z

runn|y 'rʌn|.i **-ier** -i.əʳ US -i.ɚ **-iest** -i.ɪst, -i.əst **-iness** -ɪ.nəs, -ɪ.nɪs

Runnymede 'rʌn.i.miːd

runoff 'rʌn.ɒf US -ɑːf **-s** -s

run-of-the-mill ˌrʌn.əv.ðə'mɪl *stress shift:* ˌrun-of-the-mill 'job

runt rʌnt **-s** -s **-y** -i US 'rʌn.t̬i

Runton 'rʌn.tən US -tᵊn

runway 'rʌn.weɪ **-s** -z

Runyon 'rʌn.jən

rupee ruː'piː US 'ruː.piː, -'- **-s** -z

Rupert 'ruː.pət US -pɚt

rupiah ruː'piː.ə **-s** -z

rupt|ure 'rʌp.tʃ|əʳ US -tʃ|ɚ **-ures** -əz US -ɚz **-uring** -ᵊr.ɪŋ **-ured** -əd US -ɚd

rural ˈrʊə.rəl ⓊⓈ ˈrʊr.əl **-ly** -i
ruridecanal ˌrʊə.rɪ.dɪˈkeɪ.nəl, -rə- ⓊⓈ ˌrʊr.ɪ.dəˈ-; -ˈdek.ə.næl
Ruritani|a ˌrʊə.rɪˈteɪ.ni|.ə, -rəˈ- ⓊⓈ ˌrʊr.ɪˈ- **-an** -ən
Rusbridger ˈrʌsˌbrɪdʒ.əʳ ⓊⓈ -ɚ
rus|e ruːz ⓊⓈ ruːz, ruːs **-es** -ɪz
rusé ˈruː.zeɪ ⓊⓈ ruːˈzeɪ
Rusedski rʊˈset.ski, -ˈsed-, -ˈzet-, -ˈzed-
rush (R) rʌʃ **-es** -ɪz **-ing** -ɪŋ **-ed** -t **-er/s** -əʳ/z ⓊⓈ -ɚ/z **ˈrush ˌhour**
Rushall ˈrʌʃ.əl
Rushden ˈrʌʃ.dən
Rushdie ˈrʊʃ.di, ˈrʌʃ-
Rushforth ˈrʌʃ.fɔːθ, -fəθ ⓊⓈ -fɔːrθ, -fɚθ
rushlight ˈrʌʃ.laɪt **-s** -s
Rushmere ˈrʌʃ.mɪəʳ ⓊⓈ -mɪr
Rushmore ˈrʌʃ.mɔːʳ ⓊⓈ -mɔːr
Rusholme ˈrʌʃ.əm, -həʊm ⓊⓈ -əm, -hoʊm
Rushton ˈrʌʃ.tən
Rushworth ˈrʌʃ.wəθ, -wɜːθ ⓊⓈ -wɚθ, -wɝːθ
rushy ˈrʌʃ.i
rusk (R) rʌsk **-s** -s
Ruskin ˈrʌs.kɪn
Rusper ˈrʌs.pəʳ ⓊⓈ -pɚ
Russell ˈrʌs.əl
russet ˈrʌs.ɪt **-s** -s
Russia ˈrʌʃ.ə
Russian ˈrʌʃ.ən **-s** -z **ˌRussian rouˈlette**
russianism (R) ˈrʌʃ.ən.ɪ.zəm **-s** -z
russianiz|e, -is|e (R) ˈrʌʃ.ən.aɪz **-es** -ɪz **-ing** -ɪŋ **-ed** -d
Russo- ˌrʌs.əʊ- ⓊⓈ ˌrʌs.oʊ-, ˌ-ə-
Russo ˈrʌs.əʊ ⓊⓈ -oʊ
rust (R) rʌst **-s** -s **-ing** -ɪŋ **-ed** -ɪd
rustbelt ˈrʌst.belt
rustbucket ˈrʌstˌbʌk.ɪt **-s** -s
rustic ˈrʌs.tɪk **-s** -s **-ally** -əl.i, -li
rusti|cate ˈrʌs.tɪ|.keɪt ⓊⓈ -tə- **-cates** -keɪts **-cating** -keɪ.tɪŋ ⓊⓈ -keɪ.t̬ɪŋ **-cated** -keɪ.tɪd ⓊⓈ -keɪ.t̬ɪd
rustication ˌrʌs.tɪˈkeɪ.ʃən ⓊⓈ -təˈ-
rusticity rʌsˈtɪs.ə.ti, -ɪ.ti ⓊⓈ -ə.t̬i
rustl|e ˈrʌs.l̩ **-es** -z **-ing** -ɪŋ, ˈrʌs.lɪŋ **-ed** -d **-er/s** -əʳ/z ⓊⓈ -ɚ/z, ˈrʌs.ləʳ/z ⓊⓈ -lɚ/z
rustproof ˈrʌst.pruːf
Rustum ˈrʌs.təm
rust|y (R) ˈrʌs.t|i **-ier** -i.əʳ ⓊⓈ -i.ɚ **-iest** -i.ɪst, -i.əst **-iness** -ɪ.nəs, -ɪ.nɪs
Ruswarp ˈrʌs.əp, ˈrʌz- ⓊⓈ -ɚp
rut rʌt **-s** -s **-ting** -ɪŋ ⓊⓈ ˈrʌt̬.ɪŋ **-ted** -ɪd ⓊⓈ ˈrʌt̬.ɪd
rutabaga ˌruː.təˈbeɪ.gə, ˌrʊt.əˈ-, ˈruː.təˌbeɪ-, ˈrʊt.əˌ- ⓊⓈ ˌruː.t̬əˈbeɪ-, ˈruː.t̬əˌbeɪ- **-s** -z
Rutgers ˈrʌt.gəz ⓊⓈ -gɚz
Ruth, ruth ruːθ
Ruthenia ruːˈθiː.ni.ə ⓊⓈ -ni.ə, ˈ-njə
Ruthenian ruːˈθiː.ni.ən ⓊⓈ -ni.ən, ˈ-njən **-s** -z
ruthenium ruːˈθiː.ni.əm
Rutherford ˈrʌð.ə.fəd ⓊⓈ -ɚ.fɚd, ˈrʌθ-
rutherfordium ˌrʌð.əˈfɔː.di.əm ⓊⓈ -ɚˈfɔːr-
Rutherglen ˈrʌð.ə.glen ⓊⓈ ˈ-ɚ-
ruthful ˈruːθ.fəl, -fʊl **-ly** -li **-ness** -nəs, -nɪs
Ruthin ˈrɪθ.ɪn, ˈruː.θɪn
ruthless ˈruːθ.ləs, -lɪs **-ly** -li **-ness** -nəs, -nɪs
Ruthven *personal name:* ˈruːθ.vən, ˈrɪv.ən *Baron, place in Tayside region:* ˈrɪv.ən *place in Grampian region, loch in Highland region:* ˈrʌθ.vən
Ruthwell ˈrʌθ.wəl *locally:* ˈrɪð.əl
rutilant ˈruː.tɪ.lənt ⓊⓈ -təl.ənt
rutile ˈruː.taɪl ⓊⓈ -tiːl, -taɪl
rutin ˈruː.tɪn, -tən ⓊⓈ -tən
Rutland ˈrʌt.lənd
Rutledge ˈrʌt.lɪdʒ
Rutskoi ˌrʊtˈskɔɪ, ˌruːt-
Rutter ˈrʌt.əʳ ⓊⓈ ˈrʌt̬.ɚ
Rutterford ˈrʌt.ə.fəd ⓊⓈ ˈrʌt̬.ɚ.fɚd
rutt|y ˈrʌt|.i ⓊⓈ ˈrʌt̬- **-ier** -i.əʳ ⓊⓈ -i.ɚ **-iest** -i.ɪst, -i.əst **-iness** -ɪ.nəs, -ɪ.nɪs
Ruysdael ˈraɪz.dɑːl, ˈriːz-, -deɪl ⓊⓈ ˈraɪs.dɑːl, ˈraɪz-, ˈrɔɪs-
Ruyter ˈraɪ.təʳ ⓊⓈ ˈrɔɪ.t̬ɚ, ˈraɪ-
RV ˌɑːˈviː ⓊⓈ ˌɑːr-
Rwanda ruˈæn.də ⓊⓈ -ˈɑːn- **-n/s** -n/z
Ryan raɪən
Rydal ˈraɪ.dəl
Ryde raɪd
Ryder ˈraɪ.dəʳ ⓊⓈ -dɚ **ˌRyder ˈCup**
rye (R) raɪ **ˈrye ˌbread; ˈrye ˌgrass**
Ryecroft ˈraɪ.krɒft ⓊⓈ -krɑːft
Ryle raɪl
Rylstone ˈrɪl.stən, -stəʊn ⓊⓈ -stən, -stoʊn
Ryman ˈraɪ.mən
Rymer ˈraɪ.məʳ ⓊⓈ -mɚ
ryot raɪət **-s** -s
Ryswick ˈrɪz.wɪk
Ryton ˈraɪ.tən
Ryukyu riˈuː.kjuː ⓊⓈ -ˈjuː-, -ˈuː-
Ryvita® raɪˈviː.tə ⓊⓈ -t̬ə

Pronouncing the letter S

See also SC, SCH, SH

The consonant letter **s** has five realisations: /s z ʃ ʒ/ and silent. The most obvious of these is /s/, e.g.:

sack	/sæk/	
case	/keɪs/	

/z/ is a very common realisation of **s**, but it is not usually word-initial, e.g.:

rise	/raɪz/	
losing	/ˈluː.zɪŋ/	

It particularly occurs in the verb form of homographs, and in words ending **sm**.

close (v.)	/kləʊz/	(US) /kloʊz/
use (v.)	/juːz/	
spasm	/ˈspæz.əm/	

In suffixes *-sion*, *-sure*, *-sia* and their derivatives, **s** is realised as /tʃ/ or /ʒ/, e.g.:

Asia	/ˈeɪ.ʃə, -ʒə/	(US) /ˈeɪ.ʒə/
insure	/ɪnˈʃʊəʳ/	(US) /ɪnˈʃʊr/
tension	/ˈten.*t*ʃᵊn/	(US) /ˈten*t*.ʃᵊn/
treasure	/ˈtreʒ.əʳ/	(US) /-ɚ/
persuasion	/pəˈsweɪ.ʒᵊn/	(US) /pɚ-/

In addition

s can be silent. This usually happens in word final position, where the word is a borrowing from French, e.g.:

debris	/ˈdeɪ.briː/	(US) /dəˈbriː/

The grammatical inflections -(e)s, -'s

There are three possible ways of pronouncing the grammatical inflections *-(e)s* and *-'s*. Following /s z ʃ ʒ tʃ/ and /dʒ/ the inflection is realised as /ɪz/, e.g.:

horses	/ˈhɔː.sɪz/	(US) /ˈhɔːr-/
rises	/ˈraɪ.zɪz/	

Following all other voiceless consonant sounds the inflection is realised as /s/, e.g.:

laughs	/lɑːfs/	(US) /læfs/
shapes	/ʃeɪps/	

Following all other voiced consonant sounds and after vowel sounds, the inflection is realised as /z/, e.g.:

John's	/dʒɒnz/	(US) /dʒɑːnz/
plays	/pleɪz/	

s (S) es **-'s** -ɪz

S *(abbrev. for* **south***)* saʊθ

Saab® sɑːb

Saarbrücken ˌsɑːˈbrʊk.ᵊn *as if German:* ˌzɑː- (US) ˈsɑːrˌbrʊk- *as if German:* ˈzɑːr-

Saarland ˈsɑː.lænd *as if German:* ˈzɑː- (US) ˈsɑːr- *as if German:* ˈzɑːr-

Saatchi ˈsɑː.tʃi

Saba *in Arabia:* ˈsɑː.bə, ˈseɪ- (US) ˈseɪ.bə, ˈsɑː- *in West Indies:* ˈseɪ.bə, ˈsɑː- (US) ˈsɑː.bə

Sabaean səˈbiː.ən, sæbˈiː- (US) səˈbiː-

Sabah ˈsɑː.bɑː

Sabaoth sæbˈeɪ.ɒθ, səˈbeɪ-, ˈsæb.eɪ.ɒθ, -əθ (US) ˈsæb.eɪ.ɑːθ, -ə.ɔːθ; səˈbeɪ.ɔːθ

Sabatini ˌsæb.əˈtiː.ni

Sabbatarian ˌsæb.əˈteə.ri.ən (US) -ˈter.i- **-s** -z **-ism** -ɪ.zᵊm

Sabbath ˈsæb.əθ **-s** -s

sabbatical səˈbæt.ɪ.kᵊl (US) -ˈbæt̬-

Sabena® səˈbiː.nə, sæbˈiː-

sab|er ˈseɪ.b|əʳ (US) -b|ɚ **-ers** -əz (US) -ɚz **-ering** -ᵊr.ɪŋ **-ered** -əd (US) -ɚd

Sabin ˈseɪ.bɪn, ˈsæb.ɪn (US) ˈseɪ.bɪn

Sabine *Italian people:* ˈsæb.aɪn, ˈseɪ.baɪn (US) ˈseɪ.baɪn **-s** -z *surname:* ˈsæb.aɪn, ˈseɪ.baɪn, -bɪn (US) ˈseɪ- *river, lake, pass in US:* səˈbiːn, sæbˈiːn (US) səˈbiːn

sable ˈseɪ.bl̩ **-s** -z

sabot ˈsæb.əʊ, -ˈ- (US) sæbˈoʊ, ˈ-- **-s** -z

sabotag|e ˈsæb.ə.tɑː*d*ʒ (US) -tɑːʒ, ˌ--ˈ- **-es** -ɪz **-ing** -ɪŋ **-ed** -d

saboteur ˌsæb.əˈtɜːʳ, ˈ--- (US) ˌsæb.əˈtɝː, -ˈtʊr **-s** -z

sabra (S) ˈsɑː.brə

sab|re ˈseɪ.b|əʳ (US) -b|ɚ **-res** -əz (US) -ɚz **-ring** -ᵊr.ɪŋ **-red** -əd (US) -ɚd **ˈsabre ˌrattling**

sabretach|e ˈsæb.ə.tæʃ (US) ˈseɪ.bɚ-, ˈsæb.ɚ- **-es** -ɪz

sabre-toothed ˌseɪ.bəˈtuːθt (US) ˈseɪ.bɚ.tuːθt *stress shift, British only, see compound:* **ˌsabre-toothed ˈtiger**

Sabrina səˈbriː.nə

sabulous ˈsæb.jə.ləs, -jʊ-

sac sæk **-s** -s

saccade sækˈɑːd, səˈkɑːd, -ˈkeɪd (US) sækˈɑːd, səˈkɑːd **-s** -z

Note: In British psychology, /sækˈeɪd, səˈkeɪd/ is the usual pronunciation.

saccharide ˈsæk.ᵊr.aɪd, -ɪd (US) -ə.raɪd **-s** -z

saccharin(e) *(n.)* ˈsæk.ᵊr.ɪn, -iːn (US) -ɪn, -ən

saccharine *(adj.)* ˈsæk.ᵊr.ɪn, -aɪn, -iːn (US) -ɚ.ɪn, -ə.raɪn

sacerdotal ˌsæs.əˈdəʊ.tᵊl (US) -ɚˈdoʊ.t̬ᵊl, ˌsæk- **-ly** -i

sachem ˈseɪ.tʃəm, -tʃem (US) -tʃəm **-s** -z

sachet ˈsæʃ.eɪ (US) -ˈ- **-s** -z

Sacheverell səˈʃev.ᵊr.ᵊl, sæʃˈev-

Sachs sæks

sack sæk **-s** -s **-ing/s** -ɪŋ/z **-ed** -t

sackbut ˈsæk.bʌt, -bət (US) -bʌt **-s** -s

sackcloth ˈsæk.klɒθ (US) -klɑːθ **ˌsackcloth and ˈashes**

sackful ˈsæk.fʊl **-s** -z **sacksful** ˈsæks.fʊl

sacking ˈsæk.ɪŋ

sackload ˈsæk.ləʊd (US) -loʊd

Sackville-West ˌsæk.vɪlˈwest

sacral ˈseɪ.krᵊl

sacrament (S) ˈsæk.rə.mənt **-s** -s

sacramental ˌsæk.rəˈmen.tᵊl (US) -t̬ᵊl **-ly** -i **-ism** -ɪ.zᵊm

Sacramento ˌsæk.rəˈmen.təʊ (US) -t̬oʊ

sacred ˈseɪ.krɪd **-ly** -li **-ness** -nəs, -nɪs **ˌsacred ˈcow**

sacrific|e ˈsæk.rɪ.faɪs, -rə- (US) -rə- **-es** -ɪz **-ing** -ɪŋ **-ed** -t

sacrificial ˌsæk.rɪˈfɪʃ.ᵊl, -rəˈ- (US) -rəˈ- **-ly** -i

sacrilege ˈsæk.rɪ.lɪdʒ, -rə- (US) -rə-

sacrilegious ˌsæk.rɪˈlɪdʒ.əs, -rəˈ- (US) -rəˈ- **-ly** -li **-ness** -nəs, -nɪs

sacristan ˈsæk.rɪ.stᵊn, -rə- (US) -rɪ- **-s** -z

Sacriston ˈsæk.rɪ.stᵊn, -rə- (US) -rɪ-

sacrist|y ˈsæk.rɪ.st|i, -rə- (US) -rɪ- **-ies** -iz

sacrosanct ˈsæk.rə*ʊ*.sæŋ*k*t (US) -roʊ- **-ity** -ə.ti, -ɪ.ti (US) -ə.t̬i

sacr|um ˈseɪ.kr|əm, ˈsæk.r|əm **-a** -ə

sad sæd **-der** -əʳ (US) -ɚ **-dest** -ɪst, -əst **-ly** -li **-ness** -nəs, -nɪs

Sadat səˈdæt, sædˈæt (US) səˈdɑːt, sɑː-, -ˈdæt

Saddam səˈdæm, sædˈæm; ˈsæd.əm (US) sɑːˈdɑːm, sə-, sædˈæm, səˈdæm

sadden ˈsæd.ᵊn **-s** -z **-ing** -ɪŋ **-ed** -d

saddhu ˈsɑː.duː **-s** -z

saddl|e ˈsæd.l̩ **-es** -z **-ing** -ɪŋ, ˈsæd.lɪŋ **-ed** -d ˈ**saddle** ˌ**horse**; ˈ**saddle** ˌ**sore**

saddleback ˈsæd.l̩.bæk

saddlebag ˈsæd.l̩.bæg **-s** -z

saddle|cloth ˈsæd.l̩|.klɒθ (US) -klɑːθ **-cloths** -klɒθs, -klɒðz (US) -klɑːθs, -klɑːðz

saddler ˈsæd.ləʳ, -l̩.əʳ (US) ˈ-lɚ, -l̩.ɚ **-s** -z **-y** -i

Sadducee ˈsæd.jʊ.siː, -jə- (US) ˈsædʒ.ʊ-, ˈsæd.jʊ- **-s** -z

Sade sɑːd (US) sɑːd, sæd

sadhu ˈsɑː.duː **-s** -z

Sadie ˈseɪ.di

sad|ism ˈseɪ.d|ɪ.zᵊm (US) ˈsæd|.ɪ-, ˈseɪ.d|ɪ- **-ist/s** -ɪst/s

sadistic səˈdɪs.tɪk, sædˈɪs- (US) səˈdɪs-, seɪ-, sædˈɪs- **-ally** -ᵊl.i, -li

Sadleir ˈsæd.ləʳ (US) -lɚ

Sadler ˈsæd.ləʳ (US) -lɚ

sadomasoch|ism ˌseɪ.dəʊˈmæs.ə.k|ɪ.zᵊm, -ˈmæz- (US) ˌsæd.oʊˈ-, ˌseɪ.doʊˈ- **-ist/s** -ɪst/s

sadomasochistic ˌseɪ.dəʊˌmæs.əˈkɪs.tɪk, -ˌmæz- (US) ˌsæd.oʊˌ-, ˌseɪ.doʊˌ-

Sadova ˈsɑː.dəʊ.ə, -və (US) -doː.vɑː, sɑːˈdoː-

sae, SAE ˌes.eɪˈiː

safari səˈfɑː.ri (US) -ˈfɑːr.i **-s** -z **sa**ˈ**fari** ˌ**park**; **sa**ˈ**fari** ˌ**suit**

saf|e seɪf **-es** -s **-er** -əʳ (US) -ɚ **-est** -ɪst, -əst **-ely** -li **-eness** -nəs, -nɪs ˈ**safe** ˌ**house**,; ˌ**safe** ˈ**house** (US) ˈ**safe** ˌ**house**; ˌ**safe** ˈ**sex**

safe-break|er ˈseɪfˌbreɪ.k|əʳ (US) -k|ɚ **-s** -z **-ing** -ɪŋ

safe-conduct ˌseɪfˈkɒn.dʌkt, -dəkt (US) -ˈkɑːn.dʌkt **-s** -s

safe-crack|er ˈseɪfˌkræk|.əʳ (US) -ɚ **-s** -z **-ing** -ɪŋ

safe-deposit ˈseɪf.dɪˌpɒz.ɪt, -dəˌ- (US) -dɪˈpɑː.zɪt **-s** -s ˈ**safe-de**ˌ**posit** ˌ**box**, ˌ**safe-de**ˈ**posit** ˌ**box** (US) ˈ**safe-de**ˌ**posit** ˌ**box**

safeguard ˈseɪf.gɑːd (US) -gɑːrd **-s** -z **-ing** -ɪŋ **-ed** -ɪd

safekeeping ˌseɪfˈkiː.pɪŋ

safety ˈseɪf.ti ˈ**safety** ˌ**belt**; ˈ**safety** ˌ**curtain**; ˈ**safety** ˌ**lamp**; ˈ**safety** ˌ**match**; ˈ**safety** ˌ**net**; ˈ**safety** ˌ**pin**; ˈ**safety** ˌ**razor**; ˈ**safety** ˌ**valve**

Safeway® ˈseɪf.weɪ

Saffell səˈfel

safflower ˈsæf.laʊəʳ (US) -laʊɚ **-s** -z

saffron (S) ˈsæf.rən, -rɒn (US) -rən

Safin ˈsɑː.fɪn

sag sæg **-s** -z **-ging** -ɪŋ **-ged** -d

saga ˈsɑː.gə **-s** -z

sagacious səˈgeɪ.ʃəs **-ly** -li **-ness** -nəs, -nɪs

sagacity səˈgæs.ə.ti, -ɪ.ti (US) -ə.t̬i

Sagan *English name:* ˈseɪ.gən *French name:* səˈgɑ̃ːŋ, sægˈɑ̃ːŋ (US) ˈseɪ.gᵊn; sɑːˈgɑ̃ːn

sag|e (S) seɪdʒ **-es** -ɪz **-ely** -li **-eness** -nəs, -nɪs

sagg|y ˈsæg|.i **-ier** -i.əʳ (US) -i.ɚ **-iest** -i.ɪst, -i.əst **-iness** -i.nəs, -i.nɪs

sagitt|a (S) səˈdʒɪt|.ə, -ˈgɪt- (US) -ˈdʒɪt̬- **-ae** -iː, -aɪ

sagittal ˈsædʒ.ɪ.tᵊl (US) -ə.t̬ᵊl **-ly** -i

Sagittarian ˌsædʒ.ɪˈteə.ri.ən, ˌsæg-, -əˈ-, -ˈtɑː- (US) ˌsædʒ.əˈter.i- **-s** -z

Sagittarius ˌsædʒ.ɪˈteə.ri.əs, ˌsæg-, -əˈ-, -ˈtɑː- (US) ˌsædʒ.əˈter.i-

sago ˈseɪ.gəʊ (US) -goʊ

Sahara səˈhɑː.rə (US) -ˈher.ə, -ˈhær-, -ˈhɑːr-

Sahel sɑːˈhel, sə- (US) sɑː-

sahib (S) sɑːb; ˈsɑː.*h*ɪb (US) ˈsɑː.*h*ɪb, -*h*iːb, -ˈ- **-s** -z

said *(from* **say***)* sed

Said *(in* **Port Said***)* saɪd, seɪd, sɑːˈiːd (US) sɑːˈiːd

Saigon saɪˈgɒn (US) -ˈgɑːn, ˈ--

Saigonese ˌsaɪ.gɒnˈiːz, -gᵊnˈ- (US) -gɑːˈniːz, -gəˈ- *stress shift:* ˌSaigonese ˈexports

sail seɪl **-s** -z **-ing/s** -ɪŋ/z **-ed** -d ˈ**sailing** ˌ**boat**; ˈ**sailing** ˌ**ship**

sailboard ˈseɪl.bɔːd (US) -bɔːrd **-s** -z **-ing** -ɪŋ **-er/s** -əʳ/z (US) -ɚ/z

sailboat ˈseɪl.bəʊt (US) -boʊt **-s** -s

sailcloth ˈseɪl.klɒθ (US) -klɑːθ

sailor ˈseɪ.ləʳ (US) -lɚ **-s** -z ˈ**sailor** ˌ**suit**

sailplane ˈseɪl.pleɪn **-s** -z

sainfoin ˈsæn.fɔɪn, ˈseɪn- (US) ˈseɪn-, ˈsæn-

Sainsbury ˈseɪnz.bᵊr.i (US) -bɚ-, -ber- **-'s** -z

saint (S) *strong form:* seɪnt **-s** -s **-ed** -ɪd **-hood** -hʊd *weak forms:* sᵊnt, sɪnt

Note: The weak forms are usual in British English for the names of saints (and places containing the word **Saint**), while the strong form is used when the word occurs on its own. For example, "This would try the patience of a saint" would have the strong form, while **St. John, St. Cecilia** (saints' names), **St. Alban's, St. Helen's** (placenames) have the weak forms. In American English, the strong form is usually used in all cases. When **Saint** occurs in British family names (e.g. **St. Clair**) the pronunciation is variable and individual names should be checked in their dictionary entries.

Saint-Etienne ˌsæ̃*n*t.eɪˈtjen

Saint Laurent ˌsæ̃*n*.lɔːˈrɑ̃ːŋ, -ləˈ- (US) -lɑːˈrɑːnt, -ləˈ-

saintl|y ˈseɪnt.l|i **-ier** -i.əʳ (US) -i.ɚ **-iest** -i.ɪst, -i.əst **-iness** -ɪ.nəs, -ɪ.nɪs

Saint-Saëns ˌsæ̃*n*ˈsɑ̃ːŋ, -ˈsɑ̃ː*n*s

Saintsbury ˈseɪn*t*s.bᵊr.i

saith *(from* **say***)* seθ, seɪθ

sake *cause, purpose:* seɪk **-s** -s

sake *drink:* ˈsɑː.ki, ˈsæk.i (US) ˈsɑː.ki

Sakhalin ˈsæk.ə.liːn, ˈsɑː.kə-, -lɪn *as if Russian:* ˌsæx.əˈliːn (US) ˈsæk.ə.liːn

Sakharov ˈsæk.ə.rɒf, -rɒv *as if Russian:* ˈsæx- (US) ˈsɑː.kə.rɔːf, ˈsæk.ə-, -rɑːf

saki (S) ˈsɑː.ki

salaam səˈlɑːm, sælˈɑːm (US) səˈlɑːm **-s** -z **-ing** -ɪŋ **-ed** -d

salability ˌseɪ.ləˈbɪl.ə.ti, -ɪ.ti (US) -ə.t̬i

salable ˈseɪ.lə.bl̩

salacious səˈleɪ.ʃəs **-ly** -li **-ness** -nəs, -nɪs

salacity səˈlæs.ə.ti, -ɪ.ti (US) -ə.t̬i

salad ˈsæl.əd **-s** -z ˈ**salad** ˌ**bar**; ˈ**salad** ˌ**cream**, ˌ**salad** ˈ**cream** (US) ˈ**salad** ˌ**cream**; ˈ**salad** ˌ**days**; ˈ**salad** ˌ**dressing**; ˈ**salad** ˌ**onion**

Saladin ˈsæl.ə.dɪn

Salamanca ˌsæl.əˈmæŋ.kə

salamander ˈsæl.ə.mæn.dəʳ (US) -dɚ **-s** -z

salami səˈlɑː.mi **-s** -z

Salamis ˈsæl.ə.mɪs

sal ammoniac ˌsæl.əˈməʊ.ni.æk (US) -ˈmoʊ-

salariat səˈleə.ri.æt

salar|y ˈsæl.ᵊr|.i **-ies** -iz **-ied** -id

Salcombe ˈsɔːl.kəm, ˈsɒl- (US) ˈsɔːl-, ˈsɑːl-

sale (S) seɪl **-s** -z ˌ**sale or re**ˈ**turn**; ˌ**sale of** ˈ**work**; ˈ**sales** ˌ**tax**

saleability ˌseɪ.ləˈbɪl.ə.ti, -ɪ.ti (US) -ə.t̬i

saleable ˈseɪ.lə.bl̩

Salem ˈseɪ.ləm, -lem (US) -ləm

Salerno səˈlɜː.nəʊ, -ˈleə- (US) -ˈlɝː.noʊ; sɑːˈler-

Salesbury ˈseɪlz.bᵊr.i

salesclerk ˈseɪlz.klɑːk (US) -klɝːk **-s** -s

salesgirl ˈseɪlz.gɜːl (US) -gɝːl **-s** -z

sales|man ˈseɪlz|.mən **-men** -mən, -men

salesmanship ˈseɪlz.mən.ʃɪp

sales|person ˈseɪlz|ˌpɜː.sᵊn (US) -ˌpɝː- **-people** -ˌpiː.pl̩

salesroom ˈseɪlz.rʊm, -ruːm (US) -ruːm, -rʊm **-s** -z

salestalk ˈseɪlz.tɔːk (US) -tɑːk, -tɔːk

sales|woman ˈseɪlzˌwʊm.ən **-women** -ˌwɪm.ɪn
Salford ˈsɔːl.fəd, ˈsɒl- (US) ˈsɔːl.fɚd, ˈsɑːl-
Salfords ˈsæl.fədz (US) -fɚdz
Salian ˈseɪ.li.ən **-s** -z
Salic, Salique ˈsæl.ɪk, ˈseɪ.lɪk
salicylate səˈlɪs.ɪ.leɪt, sælˈɪs-, -əl.eɪt (US) səˈlɪs.ə.leɪt; ˌsæl.əˈsɪl.eɪt, -ɪt **-s** -s
salicylic ˌsæl.ɪˈsɪl.ɪk, -əˈ- *stress shift, see compound:* (US) -əˈ- ˌ**salicylic** ˈ**acid**
salienc|e ˈseɪ.li.ən*t*s **-y** -i
salient ˈseɪ.li.ənt (US) ˈseɪl.jənt, ˈseɪ.li.ənt **-s** -s **-ly** -li
Salieri ˌsæl.iˈeə.ri (US) -ˈer.i
saline *(adj.)* ˈseɪ.laɪn, ˈsæl.aɪn (US) ˈseɪ.liːn, -laɪn
saline *(n.)* ˈseɪ.laɪn, ˈsæl.aɪn (US) ˈseɪ.liːn, -laɪn; səˈliːn
Saline *in Fife:* ˈsæl.ɪn *in US:* səˈliːn
Salinger ˈsæl.ɪn.dʒəʳ, ˈseɪ.lɪn- (US) ˈsæl.ɪn.dʒɚ
salinity səˈlɪn.ə.ti, -ɪ.ti (US) -ə.ţi
Salisbury ˈsɔːlz.bər.i, ˈsɒlz- (US) ˈsɔːlz-, ˈsɑːlz-, -ber- ˌ**Salisbury** ˈ**Plain**
saliva səˈlaɪ.və
salivary ˈsæl.ɪ.vər.i, ˈ-ə-; səˈlaɪ- (US) ˈsæl.ə.ver- **saˈlivary** ˌ**gland,** ˈ**salivary** ˌ**gland**
sali|vate ˈsæl.ɪ|.veɪt, ˈ-ə- (US) ˈ-ə- **-vates** -veɪts **-vating** -veɪ.tɪŋ (US) -veɪ.ţɪŋ **-vated** -veɪ.tɪd (US) -veɪ.ţɪd **-vation** ˌ--ˈveɪ.ʃən
Salk sɔːlk ˈ**Salk** ˌ**vaccine**
sallet ˈsæl.ɪt, -ət (US) -ɪt **-s** -s
Sallis ˈsæl.ɪs
sallow ˈsæl.əʊ (US) -oʊ **-er -est -s** -z **-y** -i **-ness** -nəs, -nɪs
Sallust ˈsæl.əst
sall|y (S) ˈsæl|.i **-ies** -iz **-ying** -i.ɪŋ **-ied** -id ˌ**Sally** ˈ**Army**
Sally Lunn ˌsæl.iˈlʌn **-s** -z
salmagundi ˌsæl.məˈgʌn.di
Salman ˈsæl.mæn, -mən
salmi ˈsæl.mi **-s** -z
salmon ˈsæm.ən
Salmon *surname:* ˈsæm.ən, ˈsæl.mən, ˈsɑː- *river, etc. in Canada & US:* ˈsæm.ən *biblical name:* ˈsæl.mɒn, -mən (US) -mən
salmonberr|y ˈsæm.ən.bər|.i, ˈ-əm- (US) -ˌber- **-ies** -iz
Salmond ˈsæm.ənd
salmonella ˌsæl.məˈnel.ə
Salome səˈləʊ.mi, -meɪ (US) -ˈloʊ-; ˈsæl.ə.meɪ
Salomon ˈsæl.ə.mən (US) ˈsɑːl-
salon ˈsæl.ɔ̃ːŋ, -lɒn (US) səˈlɑːn; ˈsæl.ɑːn **-s** -z
Salonika, Salonica səˈlɒn.ɪ.kə, ˌsæl.əˈniː- (US) səˈlɑː.nə-; ˌsæl.əˈnaɪ-, -ˈniː-
saloon səˈluːn **-s** -z **saˌloon** ˈ**bar; saˈloon** ˌ**car**
Salop ˈsæl.əp
Salopian səˈləʊ.pi.ən (US) -ˈloʊ- **-s** -z
Salpeter ˈsæl.piː.təʳ (US) -ţɚ
salpingitis ˌsæl.pɪnˈdʒaɪ.tɪs, -təs (US) -ţɪs
salsa ˈsæl.sə (US) ˈsɑːl-
salsify ˈsæl.sɪ.fi, -sə-, -faɪ (US) -sə-
salt, SALT (S) sɔːlt, sɒlt (US) sɔːlt, sɑːlt **-s** -s **-ing** -ɪŋ (US) ˈsɔːl.ţɪŋ **-ed** -ɪd (US) ˈsɔːl.ţɪd **-ness** -nəs, -nɪs ˈ**salt** ˌ**cellar;** ˌ**Salt** ˌ**Lake** ˈ**City;** ˈ**salt** ˌ**marsh;** ˈ**salt** ˌ**shaker; rub** ˌ**salt into someone's** ˈ**wounds;** ˌ**salt of the** ˈ**earth;** ˌ**take something with a** ˌ**pinch/grain of** ˈ**salt**
Saltaire sɔːlˈteəʳ, sɒl- (US) sɑːlˈter
saltant ˈsæl.tənt, ˈsɔːl-, ˈsɒl- (US) ˈsæl.tənt
Saltash ˈsɔːl.tæʃ, ˈsɒl- (US) ˈsɑːl-
saltation sælˈteɪ.ʃən **-s** -z
Saltburn ˈsɔːlt.bɜːn, ˈsɒlt- (US) ˈsɔːlt.bɝːn, ˈsɑːlt-
Saltcoats ˈsɔːlt.kəʊts, ˈsɒlt- (US) ˈsɔːlt.koʊts, ˈsɑːlt-
Saltdean ˈsɔːlt.diːn, ˈsɒlt- (US) ˈsɔːlt-, ˈsɑːlt-
Salter ˈsɔːl.təʳ, ˈsɒl- (US) ˈsɔːl.ţɚ, ˈsɑːl-
Salterton ˈsɔːl.tə.tən, ˈsɒl- (US) ˈsɔːl.ţɚ.tən, ˈsɑːl-
Saltfleetby ˈsɔːltˌfliːt.bi, ˈsɒlt- *locally also:* ˈsɒl.ə.bi (US) ˈsɔːltˌfliːt.bi, ˈsɑːlt-
Salting ˈsɔːl.tɪŋ, ˈsɒl- (US) ˈsɔːl.ţɪŋ, ˈsɑːl-
saltire ˈsɔːl.taɪəʳ, ˈsɒl-, ˈsæl- (US) ˈsɔːl.tɪr, ˈsɑːl-, ˈsæl-, -taɪɚ **-s** -z
Saltmarsh ˈsɔːlt.mɑːʃ, ˈsɒlt- (US) ˈsɔːlt.mɑːrʃ, ˈsɑːlt-
Salto ˈsæl.təʊ (US) ˈsɑːl.toʊ
Saltoun ˈsɔːl.tən, ˈsɒlt- (US) ˈsɔːl.tən, ˈsɑːl-
saltpan ˈsɔːlt.pæn, ˈsɒlt- (US) ˈsɔːlt-, ˈsɑːlt- **-s** -z
saltpetre, saltpeter ˌsɔːltˈpiː.təʳ, ˌsɒlt-, ˈ--- (US) ˈsɔːltˌpiː.ţɚ, ˈsɑːlt-
saltwater ˈsɔːltˌwɔː.təʳ, ˈsɒlt- (US) ˈsɔːltˌwɑː.ţɚ, ˈsɑːlt-, -ˌwɔː-
salt|y ˈsɔːl.t|i, ˈsɒl- (US) ˈsɔːl.ţ|i, ˈsɑːl- **-ier** -i.əʳ (US) -i.ɚ **-iest** -i.ɪst, -i.əst **-iness** -ɪ.nəs, -ɪ.nɪs
salubrious səˈluː.bri.əs, -ˈljuː- (US) -ˈluː- **-ly** -li **-ness** -nəs, -nɪs
salubrity səˈluː.brə.ti, -ˈljuː-, -brɪ- (US) -ˈluː.brə.ţi
Salusbury ˈsɔːlz.bər.i
Salut *(in* **Port Salut***)* səˈluː
salutar|y ˈsæl.jə.tər|.i, -jʊ- (US) -ter- **-ily** -əl.i, -ɪ.li **-iness** -ɪ.nəs, -ɪ.nɪs
salutation ˌsæl.jəˈteɪ.ʃən, -jʊˈ- **-s** -z
salu|te səˈluː|t, -ˈljuː|t (US) -ˈluː|t **-tes** -ts **-ting** -tɪŋ (US) -ţɪŋ **-ted** -tɪd (US) -ţɪd
salvable ˈsæl.və.bl̩
Salvador ˈsæl.və.dɔːʳ, ˌ--ˈ- (US) ˈsæl.və.dɔːr **-an/s** -ən/z
Salvadorean, Salvadorian ˌsæl.vəˈdɔː.ri.ən (US) -ˈdɔːr.i- **-s** -z
salvag|e ˈsæl.vɪdʒ **-es** -ɪz **-ing** -ɪŋ **-ed** -d **-eable** -ə.bl̩ **-er/s** -əʳ/z (US) -ɚ/z
Salvarsan® ˈsæl.və.sən, -sæn (US) -vɚ-
salvation sælˈveɪ.ʃən **-s** -z **Salˌvation** ˈ**Army**
salvation|ism sælˈveɪ.ʃən|.ɪ.zəm **-ist/s** -ɪst/s
salv|e *anoint, soothe:* sælv, sɑːv (US) sæv, sɑːv **-es** -z **-ing** -ɪŋ **-ed** -d
salv|e *save ship, cargo:* sælv **-es** -z **-ing** -ɪŋ **-ed** -d
Salve *Catholic antiphon:* ˈsæl.veɪ **-s** -z
salver ˈsæl.vəʳ (US) -vɚ **-s** -z
salvia ˈsæl.vi.ə **-s** -z
salvo ˈsæl.vəʊ (US) -voʊ **-(e)s** -z **-ing** -ɪŋ **-ed** -d
sal volatile ˌsæl.vəʊˈlæt.əl.i, -vɒlˈæt- (US) -voʊˈlæţ.əl-
Salyut səˈljuːt, sælˈjuːt (US) ˈsæl.juːt
Salzburg ˈsælts.bɜːg, ˈsɑːlts- (US) ˈsɔːlz.bɝːg, ˈsɑːlz-
Sam sæm ˌ**Sam** ˌ**Browne** ˈ**belt**
Samantha səˈmæn*t*.θə
Samara səˈmɑː.rə (US) -ˈmɑːr.ə, -ˈmær-
Samaria səˈmeə.ri.ə (US) -ˈmer.i-, -ˈmær-
Samaritan səˈmær.ɪ.tən (US) -ˈmer.ə-, -ˈmær- **-s** -z ˌ**good Saˈmaritan**
samarium səˈmeə.ri.əm (US) -ˈmer.i-, -ˈmær-
Samarkand ˌsæm.ɑːˈkænd, -əˈ-, ˈ--- (US) ˈsæm.ɚ.kænd, ˌ--ˈ-
samarskite səˈmɑː.skaɪt (US) -ˈmɑːr-; ˈsæm.ɚ-
samba ˈsæm.bə (US) ˈsɑːm-, ˈsæm- **-s** -z **-ing** -ɪŋ **-ed** -d
sambo (S) ˈsæm.bəʊ (US) -boʊ **-s** -z
same seɪm **-y** -i **-ness** -nəs, -nɪs
S. America *(abbrev. for* **South America***)* ˌsaʊθ.əˈmer.ɪ.kə
samite ˈseɪ.maɪt, ˈsæm.aɪt (US) ˈsæm.aɪt, ˈseɪ.maɪt
samizdat ˌsæm.ɪzˈdæt, ˈ--- (US) ˈsɑː.mɪz.dɑːt, ˌ--ˈ-
Sammy ˈsæm.i
Samnite ˈsæm.naɪt **-s** -s
Samo|a səˈməʊ|ə, sɑː- (US) səˈmoʊ|ə **-an/s** -ən/z
Samos ˈseɪ.mɒs, ˈsæm- (US) -mɑːs; ˈsæm.oʊs
samosa səˈməʊ.sə, sæmˈəʊ-, -zə (US) səˈmoʊ.sə **-s** -z
Samothrace ˈsæm.əʊ.θreɪs (US) ˈ-ə-, -oʊ-
samovar ˈsæm.ə.vɑːʳ, ˌ--ˈ- (US) ˈsæm.ə.vɑːr; ˌsɑː.məˈvɑːr **-s** -z
Samoyed *people:* ˌsæm.ɔɪˈed; -ˈ--, -ɪd (US) ˈsæm.ə.jed; səˈmɔɪ.ed **-s** -z *dog:* səˈmɔɪ.ed, -ɪd (US) ˈsæm.ə.jed; səˈmɔɪ.ed **-s** -z

sampan ˈsæm.pæn **-s** -z
Samper ˈsæm.pəʳ (US) -pɚ
samphire ˈsæm*p*.faɪəʳ (US) -faɪɚ
sampl|e ˈsɑːm.pl̩ (US) ˈsæm- **-es** -z **-ing** -ɪŋ, ˈsɑːm.plɪŋ (US) ˈsæm- **-ed** -d
sampler ˈsɑːm.pləʳ (US) ˈsæm.plɚ **-s** -z
Sampras ˈsæm.prəs, -præs
Sampson ˈsæm*p*.sᵊn
Samson ˈsæm*p*.sᵊn
Samsonite® ˈsæm*p*.sᵊn.aɪt
Samsung® ˈsæm.sʌŋ, -sʊŋ
Samuel ˈsæm.jʊəl, -ju.əl (US) -ju.əl, -jʊl **-s** -z
samurai (S) ˈsæm.ʊ.raɪ, -jʊ- (US) -ə.raɪ **-s** -z
San Antonio ˌsæn.ænˈtəʊ.ni.əʊ (US) -ˈtoʊ.ni.oʊ
sanatari|um ˌsæn.əˈteə.ri|.əm (US) -ˈter.i- **-ums** -əmz **-a** -ə
Sanatogen® səˈnæt.ə.dʒᵊn, -dʒen (US) -ˈnæt̬-
sanatori|um ˌsæn.əˈtɔː.ri|.əm (US) -ˈtɔːr.i- **-ums** -əmz **-a** -ə
Sancerre sænˈseəʳ, sɑ̃ːn- (US) sɑːnˈser
Sanchez ˈsæn.tʃez
Sancho Panza ˌsæn.tʃəʊˈpæn.zə (US) ˌsɑːn.tʃoʊˈpɑːn-
San Cristóbal ˌsæn.krɪˈstəʊ.bæl, ˌsæŋ- (US) ˌsæn.krɪˈstoʊ.bəl, -bɑːl
sanctification ˌsæŋ*k*.tɪ.fɪˈkeɪ.ʃᵊn, -tə-
sancti|fy ˈsæŋ*k*.tɪ|.faɪ, -tə- **-fies** -faɪz **-fying** -faɪ.ɪŋ **-fied** -faɪd
sanctimonious ˌsæŋ*k*.tɪˈməʊ.ni.əs, -təˈ- (US) -ˈmoʊ- **-ly** -li **-ness** -nəs, -nɪs
sanction ˈsæŋ*k*.ʃᵊn **-s** -z **-ing** -ɪŋ **-ed** -d
sanctity ˈsæŋ*k*.tə.ti, -tɪ- (US) -tə.t̬i
sanctuar|y ˈsæŋ*k*.tʃʊə.r|i, -tʃᵊ.r|i, -tjʊə.r|i, -tjᵊr|.i (US) -tʃu.er|.i **-ies** -iz
sanct|um ˈsæŋ*k*.t|əm **-ums** -əmz **-a** -ə ˌ**inner ˈsanctum**
Sanctus ˈsæŋ*k*.təs **-es** -ɪz
sand *on beach:* sænd **-s** -z **-ing** -ɪŋ **-ed** -ɪd **-er/s** -əʳ/z (US) -ɚ/z ˈ**sand** ˌ**dollar**; ˈ**sand** ˌ**trap**; ˌ**bury one's** ˌ**head in the** ˈ**sand,** ˌ**bury one's** ˈ**head in the** ˌ**sand** (US) ˌ**bury one's** ˌ**head in the** ˈ**sand**
Sand *French novelist:* sɑ̃ːnd (US) sænd, sɑ̃ːnd
sandal ˈsæn.dᵊl **-s** -z
sandalwood ˈsæn.dᵊl.wʊd
Sanday ˈsæn.deɪ, -di
Sandbach ˈsæn*d*.bætʃ, ˈsæm- (US) ˈsæn*d*-
sandbag ˈsæn*d*.bæg, ˈsæm- (US) ˈsæn*d*- **-s** -z **-ging** -ɪŋ **-ged** -d **-ger/s** -əʳ/z (US) -ɚ/z
sandbank ˈsæn*d*.bæŋk, ˈsæm- (US) ˈsæn*d*- **-s** -s
sandbar ˈsæn*d*.bɑːʳ, ˈsæm- (US) ˈsæn*d*.bɑːr **-s** -z
sandblast ˈsæn*d*.blɑːst, ˈsæm- (US) ˈsæn*d*.blæst **-s** -s **-ing** -ɪŋ **-ed** -ɪd **-er/s** -əʳ/z (US) -ɚ/z
sandbox ˈsæn*d*.bɒks, ˈsæm- (US) -bɑːks **-es** -ɪz
sandboy ˈsæn*d*.bɔɪ, ˈsæm- (US) ˈsæn*d*- **-s** -z ˌ**happy as a** ˈ**sandboy**
Sandburg ˈsæn*d*.bɜːg (US) -bɝːg
sandcastle ˈsæn*d*ˌkɑː.sl̩, ˈsæŋ- (US) ˈsæn*d*ˌkæs.l̩ **-s** -z
sanderling ˈsæn.dᵊl.ɪŋ (US) -dɚ.lɪŋ **-s** -z
Sanders ˈsɑːn.dəz (US) ˈsæn.dɚz
Sanderson ˈsɑːn.də.sᵊn (US) ˈsæn.dɚ-
Sanderstead ˈsɑːn.də.sted, -stɪd (US) ˈsæn.dɚ-
sandfl|y ˈsænd.fl|aɪ **-ies** -aɪz
Sandford ˈsæn*d*.fəd, -fɔːd; ˈsæn.əd (US) ˈsæn*d*.fɚd, -fɔːrd
Sandgate ˈsæn*d*.geɪt, ˈsæŋ-, -gɪt (US) ˈsæn*d*-
sandhi ˈsæn.diː, ˈsʌn-; ˈsænd.hiː, ˈsʌnd- (US) ˈsæn.di, ˈsɑːn-, ˈsʌn-
sandhopper ˈsændˌhɒp.əʳ (US) -ˌhɑː.pɚ **-s** -z
Sandhurst ˈsænd.hɜːst (US) -hɝːst
San Diego ˌsæn.diˈeɪ.gəʊ (US) -goʊ
Sandinista ˌsæn.dəˈnɪs.tə, -dɪˈ- (US) -ˈniː.stə **-s** -z
Sanditon ˈsæn.dɪ.tᵊn (US) -t̬ən
Sandling ˈsænd.lɪŋ
sand|man ˈsæn*d*|.mæn, ˈsæm- (US) ˈsæn*d*- **-men** -men
San Domingo ˌsæn.dəˈmɪŋ.gəʊ, -dəʊˈ-, -dɒmˈɪŋ- (US) -dəˈmɪŋ.goʊ, -doʊˈ-
Sandown ˈsæn.daʊn
sandpail ˈsæn*d*.peɪl, ˈsæm- (US) ˈsæn*d*- **-s** -z
sandpap|er ˈsæn*d*ˌpeɪ.p|əʳ, ˈsæm- (US) ˈsæn*d*ˌpeɪ.p|ɚ **-ers** -əz (US) -ɚz **-ering** -ᵊr.ɪŋ **-ered** -əd (US) -ɚd
sandpiper ˈsæn*d*ˌpaɪ.pəʳ, ˈsæm- (US) ˈsæn*d*ˌpaɪ.pɚ **-s** -z
sandpit ˈsæn*d*.pɪt, ˈsæm- (US) ˈsæn*d*- **-s** -s
Sandra ˈsæn.drə, ˈsɑːn- (US) ˈsæn-
Sandringham ˈsæn.drɪŋ.əm
Sands sændz
sandstone ˈsæn*d*.stəʊn (US) -stoʊn
sandstorm ˈsæn*d*.stɔːm (US) -stɔːrm **-s** -z
sand|wich ˈsæn|.wɪdʒ, ˈsæm-, -wɪtʃ (US) ˈsæn*d*|.wɪtʃ **-wiches** -wɪdʒ.ɪz, -wɪtʃ.ɪz (US) -wɪtʃ.ɪz **-wiching** -wɪdʒ.ɪŋ, -wɪtʃ.ɪŋ (US) -wɪtʃ.ɪŋ **-wiched** -wɪdʒd, -wɪtʃt (US) -wɪtʃt ˈ**sandwich** ˌ**board**; ˈ**sandwich** ˌ**course**
Note: Some British speakers use /-wɪtʃ/ in the uninflected form and /-wɪdʒ/ in the inflected forms of this word.
Sandwich *in Kent:* ˈsæn*d*.wɪtʃ, ˈsæm-, -wɪdʒ (US) ˈsænd.wɪtʃ
sandwich|man ˈsæn*d*.wɪdʒ|.mæn, ˈsæm-, -wɪtʃ- (US) ˈsæn*d*.wɪtʃ- **-men** -men
Sandwick ˈsæn*d*.wɪk
sand|y (S) ˈsæn.d|i **-ier** -i.əʳ (US) -i.ɚ **-iest** -i.ɪst, -i.əst **-iness** -ɪ.nəs, -ɪ.nɪs
Sandys sændz
san|e seɪn **-er** -əʳ (US) -ɚ **-est** -ɪst, -əst **-ely** -li **-eness** -nəs, -nɪs
San Fernando ˌsæn.fəˈnæn.dəʊ (US) -fɚˈnæn.doʊ
Sanford ˈsæn.fəd (US) -fɚd
sanforiz|e, -is|e ˈsæn.fᵊr.aɪz (US) -fə.raɪz **-es** -ɪz **-ing** -ɪŋ **-ed** -d
San Francisco ˌsæn.frənˈsɪs.kəʊ, -frænˈ- (US) -koʊ
sang *(from* **sing***)* sæŋ
Sanger ˈsæŋ.gəʳ, -əʳ (US) -ɚ
sang-froid ˌsɑ̃ːŋˈfrwɑː (US) ˌsɑ̃ːŋ-, ˌsɑːn-
sangria ˈsæŋ.gri.ə, sæŋˈgriː- (US) sænˈgriː-, sæŋ-
Sangster ˈsæŋ*k*.stəʳ (US) -stɚ
sanguinar|y ˈsæŋ.gwɪ.nᵊr|.i, -gwə- (US) -gwɪ.ner- **-ily** -ᵊl.i, -ɪ.li **-iness** -ɪ.nəs, -ɪ.nɪs
sanguine ˈsæŋ.gwɪn **-ly** -li **-ness** -nəs, -nɪs
sanguineous sæŋˈgwɪn.i.əs
sanitari|um ˌsæn.ɪˈteə.ri|.əm, -əˈ- (US) -ˈter.i- **-ums** -əmz **-a** -ə
sanitar|y ˈsæn.ɪ.tᵊr|.i, -tr|i (US) -ter|.i **-ily** -ᵊl.i, -ɪ.li **-iness** -ɪ.nəs, -ɪ.nɪs ˈ**sanitary** ˌ**towel**; ˈ**sanitary** ˌ**napkin**
sanitation ˌsæn.ɪˈteɪ.ʃᵊn, -əˈ- **saniˈtation** ˌ**worker**
sanitization, -isa- ˌsæn.ɪ.taɪˈzeɪ.ʃᵊn, ˌ-ə-, -tɪˈ- (US) -tɪˈ-
sanitiz|e, -is|e ˈsæn.ɪ.taɪz, ˈ-ə- **-es** -ɪz **-ing** -ɪŋ **-ed** -d
sanitori|um ˌsæn.əˈtɔː.ri|.əm, -ɪˈ- (US) -ˈtɔːr.i- **-ums** -əmz **-a** -ə
sanity ˈsæn.ə.ti, -ɪ.ti (US) -ə.t̬i
San José ˌsæn.həʊˈzeɪ, -əʊˈ- (US) -hoʊˈ-, -əˈ-
San Juan ˌsænˈ*h*wɑːn (US) -ˈhwɑːn, -ˈwɔːn
sank *(from* **sink***)* sæŋk
Sankey ˈsæŋ.ki
San Marino ˌsæn.məˈriː.nəʊ, ˌsæm- (US) ˌsæn.məˈriː.noʊ
San Miguel ˌsæn.mɪˈgel, ˌsæm- (US) ˌsæn-
San Pedro Sula sænˌped.rəʊˈsuː.lə, sæm- (US) sænˌpiː.droʊˈ-, -ˌped.roʊˈ-
San Remo ˌsænˈreɪ.məʊ, -ˈriː- (US) -ˈriː.moʊ, -ˈreɪ-
sans *English word:* sænz *in French phrases:* sɑ̃ːŋ (US) sænz, sɑ̃ːn
San Salvador ˌsænˈsæl.və.dɔːʳ, -ˌsæl.vəˈdɔːʳ (US) -ˈsæl.və.dɔːr
sans-culotte ˌsænz.kjʊˈlɒt (US) -kuːˈlɑːt, -kjuːˈ- **-s** -s
San Sebastian ˌsæn.sɪˈbæs.ti.ən, -səˈ- (US) -sɪˈbæs.tʃən
Sanskrit ˈsæn.skrɪt

sanskritic (S) sæn'skrɪt.ɪk ⓤⓢ -'skrɪt̬-
sans serif ˌsæn'ser.ɪf
Santa 'sæn.tə ⓤⓢ -t̬ə **-s** -z
Santa Ana ˌsæn.tə'æn.ə ⓤⓢ -t̬ə'-
Santa Claus ˌsæn.tə'klɔːz, '--ˌ- ⓤⓢ 'sæn.t̬əˌklɑːz, -ˌklɔːz **-es** -ɪz
Santa Cruz ˌsæn.tə'kruːz ⓤⓢ 'sæn.t̬ə.kruːz, ˌ--'-
Santa Fe ˌsæn.tə'feɪ ⓤⓢ 'sæn.t̬ə.feɪ, ˌ--'-
Santa Marta ˌsæn.tə'mɑː.tə ⓤⓢ -t̬ə'mɑːr.t̬ə
Santander ˌsæn.tən'deəʳ, -tæn'-; ⓤⓢ ˌsɑːn.tɑːn'der
Santayana ˌsæn.taɪ'ɑː.nə ⓤⓢ -t̬i'æn-, -'ɑː.nə
Santer 'sæn.təʳ, sɑ̃ː'teə ⓤⓢ sɑːn.t̬ɚ
Santiago ˌsæn.ti'ɑː.gəʊ ⓤⓢ -t̬i'ɑː.goʊ, ˌsɑːn-
Santley 'sænt.li
Santo Domingo ˌsæn.təʊ.dəʊ'mɪŋ.gəʊ, -dɒm'ɪŋ- ⓤⓢ -toʊ.də'mɪŋ.goʊ, ˌsɑːn-, -doʊ'-
Sanyo® 'sæn.jəʊ ⓤⓢ -joʊ
Saône səʊn ⓤⓢ soʊn
São Paulo saʊm'paʊ.ləʊ, saʊ- ⓤⓢ sɑ̃ʊ'paʊ.lu, -loʊ
São Tomé ˌsaʊn.tə'meɪ, ˌsaʊ- ⓤⓢ ˌsɑ̃ʊ.toʊ'-, -tə'-
sap sæp **-s** -s **-ping** -ɪŋ **-ped** -t
sapele (S) sæp'ɪl.i, sə'pɪl-, -'piː.li ⓤⓢ sə'piː.li **saˌpele ma'hogany**
sapien|ce 'seɪ.pi.ən|ts, 'sæp.i- ⓤⓢ 'seɪ.pi- **-t/ly** -t/li
sapiens 'sæp.i.enz, -seɪ.pi-
Sapir sə'pɪəʳ, sæp'ɪəʳ; 'seɪ.pɪəʳ ⓤⓢ sæp'ɪr, sə'pɪr
sapless 'sæp.ləs, -lɪs **-ness** -nəs, -nɪs
sapling 'sæp.lɪŋ **-s** -z
saponaceous ˌsæp.əʊ'neɪ.ʃəs ⓤⓢ -ə'- **-ness** -nəs, -nɪs
saponification səˌpɒn.ɪ.fɪ'keɪ.ʃᵊn, sæpˌɒn-, ˌ-ə- ⓤⓢ səˌpɑː.nə-
saponi|fy sə'pɒn.ɪ|.faɪ, sæp'ɒn-, '-ə- ⓤⓢ sə'pɑː.nə- **-fies** -faɪz **-fying** -faɪ.ɪŋ **-fied** -faɪd
sapper 'sæp.əʳ ⓤⓢ -ɚ **-s** -z
sapphic (S) 'sæf.ɪk **-s** -s
Sapphira sə'faɪə.rə, sæf'aɪə- ⓤⓢ sə'faɪ-
sapphire 'sæf.aɪəʳ ⓤⓢ -aɪɚ **-s** -z
sapph|ism (S) 'sæf|.ɪ.zᵊm **-ist/s** -ɪst/s
Sappho 'sæf.əʊ ⓤⓢ -oʊ
Sapporo sə'pɔː.rəʊ, sæp'ɔː-, -'ɒr.əʊ ⓤⓢ sə'pɔːr.oʊ, sɑː-
sapp|y 'sæp|.i **-iness** -ɪ.nəs, -ɪ.nɪs
saprogenic ˌsæp.rəʊ'dʒen.ɪk ⓤⓢ -rə'-
saprophyte 'sæp.rəʊ.faɪt ⓤⓢ -rə- **-s** -s
sapwood 'sæp.wʊd
Sara 'sɑː.rə, 'seə- ⓤⓢ 'ser.ə, 'sær-
saraband(e) 'sær.ə.bænd, ˌ--'- ⓤⓢ 'sær.ə.bænd, 'ser- **-s** -z
Saracen 'sær.ə.sən, -sɪn, -sen ⓤⓢ -sən, 'ser-, 'sær- **-s** -z
Saracenic ˌsær.ə'sen.ɪk ⓤⓢ ˌser-, ˌsær-
Saragossa ˌsær.ə'gɒs.ə ⓤⓢ -'gɑː.sə, ˌser-, ˌsær-
Sarah 'seə.rə ⓤⓢ 'ser.ə, 'sær-
Sarajevo ˌsær.ə'jeɪ.vəʊ ⓤⓢ -voʊ, ˌser-, ˌsær-
Saran® sə'ræn **Sa'ran ˌwrap**
Sarandon 'sær.ən.dən ⓤⓢ sə'ræn.dən
Sarasate ˌsær.ə'sɑː.teɪ ⓤⓢ ˌsɑːr.ɑː'sɑː.teɪ
Saratoga ˌsær.ə'təʊ.gə ⓤⓢ ˌser.ə'toʊ-, ˌsær-
Sarawak sə'rɑː.wæk, -wək, -wə ⓤⓢ -'rɑː.wɑːk
Sarawakian ˌsær.ə'wæk.i.ən ⓤⓢ ˌser.ə'wɑː.ki-, ˌsær- **-s** -z
sarcasm 'sɑː.kæz.ᵊm ⓤⓢ 'sɑːr- **-s** -z
sarcastic sɑː'kæs.tɪk ⓤⓢ sɑːr- **-ally** -ᵊl.i, -li
sarcenet 'sɑːs.net, -nət, -nɪt ⓤⓢ 'sɑːr.snet
sarcoma sɑː'kəʊ.mə ⓤⓢ sɑːr'koʊ- **-s** -z **-ta** -tə **-tous** -təs
sarcopha|gus sɑː'kɒf.ə|.gəs ⓤⓢ sɑːr'kɑː.fə- **-guses** -gə.sɪz **-gi** -gaɪ, -dʒaɪ
Sardanapalus ˌsɑː.də'næp.ᵊl.əs; -nə'pɑː.ləs ⓤⓢ ˌsɑːr.də'næp.ᵊl.əs; -nə'peɪ.ləs
sardine *fish:* sɑː'diːn ⓤⓢ sɑːr- **-s** -z
sardine *stone:* 'sɑː.daɪn ⓤⓢ 'sɑːr.dɪn, -daɪn
Sardini|a sɑː'dɪn.i|.ə ⓤⓢ sɑːr-, '-j|ə **-an/s** -ən/z
Sardis 'sɑː.dɪs ⓤⓢ 'sɑːr-
sardius 'sɑː.di.əs ⓤⓢ 'sɑːr- **-es** -ɪz
sardonic sɑː'dɒn.ɪk ⓤⓢ sɑːr'dɑː.nɪk **-ally** -ᵊl.i, -li
sardonyx 'sɑː.dᵊn.ɪks; sɑː'dɒn- ⓤⓢ sɑːr'dɑː.nɪks; 'sɑːr.də- **-es** -ɪz
Sargant 'sɑː.dʒᵊnt ⓤⓢ 'sɑːr-
sargasso (S) sɑː'gæs.əʊ ⓤⓢ sɑːr'gæs.oʊ **-(e)s** -z **Sarˌgasso 'Sea**
sarge sɑːdʒ ⓤⓢ sɑːrdʒ
Sargeant, Sargent 'sɑː.dʒᵊnt ⓤⓢ 'sɑːr-
Sargeson 'sɑː.dʒɪ.sᵊn ⓤⓢ 'sɑːr-
Sargon 'sɑː.gɒn ⓤⓢ 'sɑːr.gɑːn
sari 'sɑː.ri ⓤⓢ 'sɑːr.i **-s** -z
Sark sɑːk ⓤⓢ sɑːrk
sark|y 'sɑː.k|i ⓤⓢ 'sɑːr- **-ier** -i.əʳ ⓤⓢ -i.ɚ **-iest** -i.ɪst, -i.əst
Sarmati|a sɑː'meɪ.ʃi|.ə, '-ʃ|ə ⓤⓢ sɑːr'meɪ.ʃ|ə, -ʃi|.ə **-an/s** -ən/z
sarnie 'sɑː.ni ⓤⓢ 'sɑːr- **-s** -z
sarong sə'rɒŋ, sɑː-, sær'ɒŋ ⓤⓢ sə'rɔːŋ, -'rɑːŋ **-s** -z
Saro-Wiwa ˌsær.əʊ'wiː.wə, -wɑː ⓤⓢ ˌsær.oʊ'wiː.wɑː, ˌsɑːr-
Saroyan sə'rɔɪən
sarsaparilla ˌsɑː.spᵊr'ɪl.ə, -sə.pᵊr'- ⓤⓢ ˌsɑːr.sə.pə'rɪl-, ˌsɑːr.spə'- *popularly:* ˌsæs.pə'-
sarsenet 'sɑːs.net, -nət, -nɪt ⓤⓢ 'sɑːr.snet
Sarton 'sɑː.tᵊn ⓤⓢ 'sɑːr-
Sartor 'sɑː.tɔːʳ, -təʳ ⓤⓢ 'sɑːr.tɔːr, -t̬ɚ
sartorial sɑː'tɔː.ri.əl ⓤⓢ sɑːr'tɔːr.i-
Sartre 'sɑː.trə ⓤⓢ 'sɑːr-; sɑːrt
Sarum 'seə.rəm ⓤⓢ 'ser.əm
SAS ˌes.eɪ'es
SASE ˌes.eɪ.es'iː
sash sæʃ **-es** -ɪz **-ed** -t **ˌsash 'window**
Sasha 'sæʃ.ə ⓤⓢ 'sɑː.ʃə, 'sæʃ.ə
sashay 'sæʃ.eɪ, -'- ⓤⓢ sæʃ'eɪ **-s** -z **-ing** -ɪŋ **-ed** -d
sashimi sæʃ'iː.mi, sə'ʃiː- ⓤⓢ sɑː'ʃiː.mi
Saskatchewan sə'skætʃ.ɪ.wən, sæs'kætʃ-, '-ə-, -wɒn ⓤⓢ sæs'kætʃ.ə.wɑːn, -wən **-er/s** -əʳ/z ⓤⓢ -ɚ/z
saskatoon (S) ˌsæs.kə'tuːn
Saskia 'sæs.ki.ə
sasquatch (S) 'sæs.kwɒtʃ, -kwætʃ ⓤⓢ -kwɑːtʃ, -kwætʃ **-es** -ɪz
sass sæs
sassafras 'sæs.ə.fræs **-es** -ɪz
Sassenach 'sæs.ə.næk, -næx, -nək, -nəx ⓤⓢ -næk **-s** -s
Sassoon sə'suːn, sæs'uːn ⓤⓢ sæs'uːn, sə'suːn
sass|y 'sæs|.i **-ier** -i.əʳ ⓤⓢ -i.ɚ **-iest** -i.ɪst, -i.əst
sat *(from* **sit***)* sæt
Sat. *(abbrev. for* **Saturday***)* 'sæt.ə.deɪ, -di ⓤⓢ 'sæt̬.ɚ-
SAT sæt ⓤⓢ es.eɪ'tiː **-s** -z
Satan 'seɪ.tᵊn **-ism** -ɪ.zᵊm **-ist/s** -ɪst/s
satang sæt'æŋ ⓤⓢ sɑː'tæŋ **-s** -z
satanic sə'tæn.ɪk, seɪ'tæn- **-ally** -ᵊl.i ⓤⓢ -li
satay, saté 'sæt.eɪ, 'sɑː.teɪ ⓤⓢ sɑː'teɪ **-s** -z **ˌsatay 'sauce** ⓤⓢ **'satay ˌsauce**
satchel 'sætʃ.ᵊl **-s** -z
Satchwell 'sætʃ.wel
sateen sæt'iːn, sə'tiːn **-s** -z
satellite 'sæt.ᵊl.aɪt, -ɪ.laɪt ⓤⓢ 'sæt̬.ᵊl.aɪt **-s** -s **'satellite ˌdish; ˌsatellite 'television** ⓤⓢ **'satellite ˌtelevision**
sati 'sɑː.tiː **-s** -z
satiable 'seɪ.ʃi.ə.bl̩, '-ʃə.bl̩ ⓤⓢ -ʃə-, -ʃi.ə-
sati|ate *(v.)* 'seɪ.ʃi|.eɪt **-ates** -eɪts **-ating** -eɪ.tɪŋ ⓤⓢ -eɪ.t̬ɪŋ **-ated** -eɪ.tɪd ⓤⓢ -eɪ.t̬ɪd
satiate *(adj.)* 'seɪ.ʃi.ət, -ɪt, -eɪt ⓤⓢ -ɪt
satiation ˌseɪ.ʃi'eɪ.ʃᵊn
Satie 'sæt.i, 'sɑː.ti, -'- ⓤⓢ sɑː'tiː
satiety sə'taɪ.ə.ti, -'taɪ.ɪ-; 'seɪ.ʃə.ti, -ʃi.ə- ⓤⓢ sə'taɪ.ə.t̬i
satin 'sæt.ɪn ⓤⓢ -ᵊn **-s** -z **-y** -i

satinette, satinet ˌsæt.ɪˈnet (US) -ᵊnˈet

satinwood ˈsæt.ɪn.wʊd (US) -ᵊn-

satire ˈsæt.aɪəʳ (US) -aɪɚ **-s** -z

satiric|al səˈtɪr.ɪ.k|ᵊl, ˈ-ə- (US) ˈ-ɪ- **-ally** -ᵊl.i, -li

satirist ˈsæt.ᵊr.ɪst, -ɪ.rɪst (US) ˈsæţ.ɚ.ɪst **-s** -s

satiriz|e, -is|e ˈsæt.ᵊr.aɪz, -ɪ.raɪz (US) ˈsæţ.ə.raɪz **-es** -ɪz **-ing** -ɪŋ **-ed** -d

satisfaction ˌsæt.ɪsˈfæk.ʃᵊn, -əsˈ- (US) ˌsæţ-

satisfactor|y ˌsæt.ɪsˈfæk.tᵊr|.i, -əsˈ-, -tr|i (US) ˌsæţ- **-ily** -ᵊl.i, -ɪ.li **-iness** -ɪ.nəs, -ɪ.nɪs

satis|fy ˈsæt.ɪs|.faɪ (US) -əs-, ˈsæţ- **-fies** -faɪz **-fying** -faɪ.ɪŋ **-fied** -faɪd

satrap ˈsæt.ræp, -rəp (US) ˈseɪ.træp, ˈsæt.ræp **-s** -s **-y** -i **-ies** -iz

satsuma ˌsætˈsuː.mə; -sʊ- (US) ˈsæt.sə.mɑː; sɑːtˈsuː.mə **-s** -z

satur|ate (*v.*) ˈsætʃ.ᵊr|.eɪt, -ʊ.r|eɪt, -tjᵊr|.eɪt, -tjʊ.r|eɪt (US) ˈsætʃ.ə.r|eɪt **-ates** -eɪts **-ating** -eɪ.tɪŋ (US) -eɪ.ţɪŋ **-ated** -eɪ.tɪd (US) -eɪ.ţɪd ˌsaturated ˈfat

saturate (*adj.*) ˈsætʃ.ᵊr.eɪt, -ʊ.reɪt, ˈsæt.jᵊr.eɪt, -jʊ.reɪt (US) ˈsætʃ.ɚ.ɪt

saturation ˌsætʃ.ᵊrˈeɪ.ʃᵊn, -tʃʊˈreɪ-, -tjᵊrˈeɪ-, -tjʊˈreɪ- (US) ˌsætʃ.əˈreɪ- satuˈration ˌpoint

Saturday ˈsæt.ə.deɪ, -di (US) ˈsæţ.ɚ- **-s** -z

Saturn ˈsæt.ən, -ɜːn (US) ˈsæţ.ɚn

saturnalia (S) ˌsæt.əˈneɪ.li.ə, -ɜːˈ- (US) ˌsæţ.ɚˈ-, -ˈneɪl.jə **-n** -n **-s** -z

saturnian (S) sætˈɜː.ni.ən, səˈtɜː- (US) səˈtɝː-

saturnine ˈsæt.ə.naɪn (US) ˈsæţ.ɚ-

satyr ˈsæt.əʳ (US) ˈseɪ.ţɚ, ˈsæţ.ɚ **-s** -z

satyriasis ˌsæt.ᵊrˈaɪə.sɪs (US) ˌseɪ.ţəˈraɪə.sɪs, ˌsæţ-

satyric səˈtɪr.ɪk (US) seɪ-, sə-

sauc|e sɔːs (US) sɑːs, sɔːs **-es** -ɪz **-ing** -ɪŋ **-ed** -d ˈsauce ˌboat

saucepan ˈsɔːs.pən (US) ˈsɑːs-, ˈsɔːs- **-s** -z

saucer ˈsɔː.səʳ (US) ˈsɑː.sɚ, ˈsɔː- **-s** -z

Sauchiehall ˌsɔː.kɪˈhɔːl, ˌsɒk.ɪˈ-, ˈ--- (US) ˌsɑː.kiˈ-, ˌsɔː-

sauc|y ˈsɔː.s|i (US) ˈsɑː-, ˈsɔː- **-ier** -i.əʳ (US) -i.ɚ **-iest** -i.ɪst, -i.əst **-ily** -ɪ.li, -ᵊl.i **-iness** -ɪ.nəs, -ɪ.nɪs

Saudi ˈsaʊ.di, ˈsɔː- (US) ˈsaʊ-, ˈsɔː-, ˈsɑː- **-s** -z ˌSaudi Aˈrabia

sauerbraten ˈsaʊəˌbrɑː.tᵊn (US) ˈsaʊɚ-

sauerkraut ˈsaʊə.kraʊt (US) ˈsaʊɚ-

Saul sɔːl (US) sɔːl, sɑːl

Sault St. Marie ˌsuː.seɪnt.məˈriː

sauna ˈsɔː.nə, ˈsaʊ- (US) ˈsaʊ-, ˈsɔː-, ˈsɑː- **-s** -z

Saunders ˈsɔːn.dəz, ˈsɑːn- (US) ˈsɑːn.dɚz, ˈsɔːn-

Saunderson ˈsɔːn.də.sᵊn, ˈsɑːn- (US) ˈsɑːn.dɚ-, ˈsɔːn-

saunt|er ˈsɔːn.t|əʳ (US) ˈsɑːn.ţ|ɚ, ˈsɔːn- **-ers** -əz (US) -ɚz **-ering** -ᵊr.ɪŋ **-ered** -əd (US) -ɚd **-erer/s** -ə.rəʳ/z (US) -ɚ.ɚ/z

saurian ˈsɔː.ri.ən (US) ˈsɑːr.i-, ˈsɔːr- **-s** -z

sausag|e ˈsɒs.ɪdʒ (US) ˈsɑː.sɪdʒ, ˈsɔː- **-es** -ɪz ˈsausage ˌdog; ˈsausage maˌchine; ˌsausage ˈroll (US) ˈsausage ˌroll

Saussure səʊˈsjʊəʳ, -ˈsʊəʳ (US) soʊˈsʊr

sauté ˈsəʊ.teɪ, ˈsɔː- (US) sɔːˈteɪ, soʊ-, sɑː- **-s** -z **-ing** -ɪŋ **-(e)d** -d

Sauternes, Sauterne səʊˈtɜːn, -ˈteən (US) soʊˈtɝːn, sɔː-, sɑː-

Sauvage ˈsæv.ɪdʒ; səʊˈvɑːʒ (US) ˈsæv.ɪdʒ; soʊˈvɑːʒ

Sauvignon ˈsəʊ.viː.njɔ̃ːŋ, -vɪ-, -njɒn, ˌ--ˈ- (US) ˌsoʊ.viːˈnjõʊn, ˈ--- ˌSauvignon ˈBlanc

savag|e (S) ˈsæv.ɪdʒ **-es** -ɪz **-est** -ɪst, -əst **-ely** -li **-eness** -nəs, -nɪs **-ery** -ᵊr.i, -ri **-ing** -ɪŋ **-ed** -d

savanna(h) (S) səˈvæn.ə **-s** -z

savant ˈsæv.ənt (US) sævˈɑːnt; səˈvænt; ˈsæv.ənt **-s** -s

sav|e seɪv **-es** -z **-ing/s** -ɪŋ **-ed** -d **-er/s** -əʳ/z (US) -ɚ/z **-(e)able** -ə.bl̩

saveloy ˈsæv.ə.lɔɪ, ˈ-ɪ-, ˌ--ˈ- (US) ˈsæv.ə.lɔɪ **-s** -z

Savels ˈsæv.ᵊlz

Savernake ˈsæv.ə.næk (US) ˈ-ɚ-

Savery ˈsæv.ᵊr.i

Savile ˈsæv.ɪl, -ᵊl ˌSavile ˈRow

Savill(e) ˈsæv.ɪl, -ᵊl

saving ˈseɪ.vɪŋ **-s** -z ˌsaving ˈgrace; ˈsavings acˌcount; ˈsavings ˌbank; ˈsavings ˌbond; ˈsavings cerˌtificate; ˈsavings ˌstamp

savio(u)r (S) ˈseɪ.vjəʳ (US) -vjɚ **-s** -z

Savlon® ˈsæv.lɒn (US) -lɑːn

savoir faire ˌsæv.wɑːˈfeəʳ (US) -wɑːrˈfer, -wɑːˈ-

savoir vivre ˌsæv.wɑːˈviː.vrə (US) -wɑːrˈ-, -wɑːˈ-

Savonarola ˌsæv.ᵊn.əˈrəʊ.lə (US) -ˈroʊ-

sav|or ˈseɪ.v|əʳ (US) -v|ɚ **-ors** -əz (US) -ɚz **-oring** -ᵊr.ɪŋ **-ored** -əd (US) -ɚd **-orless** -ə.ləs, -lɪs (US) -ɚ.ləs, -lɪs

savory (S) ˈseɪ.vᵊr.i **-ies** -iz **-iness** -ɪ.nəs, -ɪ.nɪs

sav|our ˈseɪ.v|əʳ (US) -v|ɚ **-ours** -əz (US) -ɚz **-ouring** -ᵊr.ɪŋ **-oured** -əd (US) -ɚd **-ourless** -ə.ləs, -lɪs (US) -ɚ.ləs, -lɪs

savour|y ˈseɪ.vᵊr|.i **-ies** -iz **-iness** -ɪ.nəs, -ɪ.nɪs

savoy (S) səˈvɔɪ **-s** -z saˌvoy ˈcabbage

Savoyard səˈvɔɪ.ɑːd; ˌsæv.ɔɪˈɑːd (US) səˈvɔɪ.ɚd; ˌsæv.ɔɪˈɑːrd **-s** -z

savvy ˈsæv.i

saw sɔː (US) sɑː, sɔː **-s** -z **-ing** -ɪŋ **-ed** -d **-n** -n

saw (*from* **see**) sɔː (US) sɑː, sɔː

saw|bones *singular:* ˈsɔː|.bəʊnz (US) ˈsɑː|.boʊnz, ˈsɔː- *plural:* ˈsɔː|.bəʊnz (US) ˈsɑː|.boʊnz, ˈsɔː- **-boneses** -ˌbəʊn.zɪz (US) -ˌboʊn-

Sawbridgeworth ˈsɔː.brɪdʒ.wɜːθ *old-fashioned:* ˈsæp.swəθ (US) ˈsɑː.brɪdʒ.wɝːθ, ˈsɔː-

sawbuck ˈsɔː.bʌk (US) ˈsɑː-, ˈsɔː- **-s** -s

sawd|er ˈsɔː.d|əʳ (US) ˈsɑː.d|ɚ, ˈsɔː- **-ers** -əz (US) -ɚz **-ering** -ᵊr.ɪŋ **-ered** -əd (US) -ɚd

sawdust ˈsɔː.dʌst (US) ˈsɑː-, ˈsɔː-

sawfish ˈsɔː.fɪʃ (US) ˈsɑː-, ˈsɔː-

sawfl|y ˈsɔː.fl|aɪ (US) ˈsɑː-, ˈsɔː- **-ies** -aɪz

sawhors|e ˈsɔː.hɔːs (US) ˈsɑː.hɔːrs, ˈsɔː- **-es** -ɪz

sawmill ˈsɔː.mɪl (US) ˈsɑː-, ˈsɔː- **-s** -z

sawn (*from* **saw**) sɔːn (US) sɑːn, sɔːn

Sawney ˈsɔː.ni (US) ˈsɑː-, ˈsɔː- **-s** -z

sawn-off ˌsɔːnˈɒf (US) ˌsɑːnˈɑːf, ˌsɔːn- *stress shift, see compound:* ˌ**sawn-off** ˈ**shotgun**

Sawoniuk səˈvɒn.i.ʊk (US) -vɑːn-

Sawston ˈsɔːs.tᵊn (US) ˈsɑːz-, ˈsɔːz-

sawtooth ˈsɔː.tuːθ (US) ˈsɑː-, ˈsɔː- **-ed** -t

Sawtry ˈsɔː.tri (US) ˈsɑː-, ˈsɔː-

sawyer (S) ˈsɔː.jəʳ, ˈsɔɪ.əʳ (US) ˈsɑː.jɚ, ˈsɔː-, ˈsɔɪ.ɚ **-s** -z

sax sæks **-es** -ɪz

Saxe-Coburg-Gotha ˌsæksˌkəʊ.bɜːgˈgəʊ.θə, -tə (US) -ˌkoʊ.bɝːgˈgoʊ-

saxhorn ˈsæks.hɔːn (US) -hɔːrn **-s** -z

saxifrag|e ˈsæk.sɪ.frɪdʒ, -sə-, -freɪdʒ (US) -sə.frɪdʒ **-es** -ɪz

Saxmundham sæksˈmʌn.dəm

Saxon ˈsæk.sᵊn **-s** -z

Saxone® ˈsæk.səʊn, -ˈ- (US) -ˈsoʊn

saxony (S) ˈsæk.sᵊn.i

saxophone ˈsæk.sə.fəʊn (US) -foʊn **-s** -z

saxophonist sækˈsɒf.ᵊn.ɪst (US) ˈsæk.sə.foʊ.nɪst **-s** -s

say seɪ **says** sez **saying** ˈseɪ.ɪŋ **said** sed

Sayce seɪs

SAYE ˌes.eɪ.waɪˈiː

sayer (S) ˈseɪəʳ (US) ˈseɪɚ **-s** -z

saying ˈseɪ.ɪŋ **-s** -z

Sayle seɪl

say-so ˈseɪ.səʊ (US) -soʊ

SC (*abbrev. for* **South Carolina**) ˌsaʊθ.kær.ᵊlˈaɪ.nə (US) -ker.əˈlaɪ-, -kær-

scab skæb **-s** -z **-by** -i **-biness** -ɪ.nəs, -ɪ.nɪs **-bing** -ɪŋ **-bed** -d

scabbard ˈskæb.əd (US) -ɚd **-s** -z

scabies ˈskeɪ.biːz, -biz

scabious ˈskeɪ.bi.əs **-es** -ɪz

scabrous ˈskeɪ.brəs (US) ˈskæb.rəs, ˈskeɪ.brəs **-ly** -li **-ness** -nəs, -nɪs

Scacchi ˈskæk.i

scad skæd **-s** -z

Pronouncing the letters SC

The consonant digraph **sc** has two main pronunciations: /s/ and /sk/.

It is normally pronounced /s/ before the letters **e**, **i** or **y**, e.g.:

scene	/siːn/	
science	/saɪənts/	
scythe	/saɪð/	
coalesce	/ˌkəʊ.əˈles/	(US) /ˌkoʊ-/

However, the realisation /sk/ can occur before **e**, and /tʃ/ is possible before **i**, e.g.:

sceptic	/ˈskep.tɪk/	
conscious	/ˈkɒn.tʃəs/	(US) /ˈkɑːnt.ʃəs/

In other cases, /sk/ is the usual pronunciation in word initial position, and /s/ in the combination **–scle**, e.g.:

scale	/skeɪl/	
Scotland	/ˈskɒt.lənd/	(US) /ˈskɑːt-/
muscle	/ˈmʌs.l̩/	

Scafell ˌskɔːˈfel *stress shift, see compound:* ˌ**Scafell** ˈ**Pike**
scaffold ˈskæf.əʊld, -ᵊld (US) -ᵊld, -oʊld **-s** -z
scaffolding ˈskæf.ᵊl.dɪŋ **-s** -z
scag skæg
Scala ˈskɑː.lə
scalable ˈskeɪ.lə.bl̩
scalar ˈskeɪ.ləʳ, -lɑːʳ (US) -lɚ, -lɑːr
scalawag ˈskæl.ə.wæg, ˈ-ɪ- (US) ˈ-ə- **-s** -z
Scalby ˈskæl.bi
scald skɔːld (US) skɑːld, skɔːld **-s** -z **-ing** -ɪŋ **-ed** -ɪd
scal|e skeɪl **-es** -z **-ing** -ɪŋ **-ed** -d **-less** -ləs, -lɪs **-er/s** -əʳ/z (US) -ɚ/z
scalene ˈskeɪ.liːn; -ˈ-, skælˈiːn (US) ˈskeɪ.liːn, -ˈ-
scales (S) skeɪlz ˌ**tip the** ˈ**scales**
Scaliger ˈskæl.ɪ.dʒəʳ (US) -dʒɚ
scallion ˈskæl.i.ən, ˈ-jən (US) ˈ-jən **-s** -z
scallop ˈskæl.əp, ˈskɒl- (US) ˈskɑː.ləp, ˈskæl.əp **-s** -s **-ing** -ɪŋ **-ed** -t
scallywag ˈskæl.i.wæg **-s** -z
scalp skælp **-s** -s **-ing** -ɪŋ **-ed** -t **-er/s** -əʳ/z (US) -ɚ/z
scalpel ˈskæl.pᵊl **-s** -z
scal|y ˈskeɪ.l|i **-ier** -i.əʳ (US) -i.ɚ **-iest** -i.ɪst, -i.əst **-iness** -ɪ.nəs, -ɪ.nɪs
scam skæm **-s** -z
Scammell ˈskæm.ᵊl
scamp skæmp **-s** -s **-ing** -ɪŋ **-ed** -t **-ish** -ɪʃ
scamp|er ˈskæm.p|əʳ (US) -p|ɚ **-ers** -əz (US) -ɚz **-ering** -ᵊr.ɪŋ **-ered** -əd (US) -ɚd
scampi ˈskæm.pi
scan skæn **-s** -z **-ning** -ɪŋ **-ned** -d
scandal ˈskæn.dᵊl **-s** -z
scandalization, -isa- ˌskæn.dᵊl.aɪˈzeɪ.ʃᵊn (US) -ɪˈ-
scandaliz|e, -is|e ˈskæn.dᵊl.aɪz (US) -də.laɪz **-es** -ɪz **-ing** -ɪŋ **-ed** -d
scandalmong|er ˈskæn.dᵊlˌmʌŋ.g|əʳ (US) -ˌmɑːŋ.g|ɚ, -ˌmʌŋ- **-ers** -əz (US) -ɚz **-ering** -ᵊr.ɪŋ
scandalous ˈskæn.dᵊl.əs **-ly** -li **-ness** -nəs, -nɪs
scandent ˈskæn.dənt
Scandian ˈskæn.di.ən
Scandinavi|a ˌskæn.dɪˈneɪ.vi|.ə, -dəˈ- (US) -vi|.ə, ˈ-vj|ə **-an/s** -ən/z
scandium ˈskæn.di.əm
Scania® ˈskæn.i.ə, ˈ-jə
Scanlan, Scanlon ˈskæn.lən
Scannell ˈskæn.ᵊl; skəˈnel
scanner ˈskæn.əʳ (US) -ɚ **-s** -z
scansion ˈskæn.ʃᵊn **-s** -z
scant skænt **-ly** -li **-ness** -nəs, -nɪs
scant|y ˈskæn.t|i (US) -t̬|i **-ier** -i.əʳ (US) -i.ɚ **-iest** -i.ɪst, -i.əst **-ily** -ɪ.li, -ᵊl.i **-iness** -ɪ.nəs, -ɪ.nɪs
Scapa Flow ˌskɑː.pəˈfləʊ, ˌskæp.əˈ- (US) -ˈfloʊ
scape skeɪp **-s** -s
-scape -skeɪp
Note: Suffix. Normally unstressed, e.g. **landscape** /ˈlænd.skeɪp/.
scapegoat ˈskeɪp.gəʊt (US) -goʊt **-s** -s **-ing** -ɪŋ **-ed** -ɪd
scapegrac|e ˈskeɪp.greɪs **-es** -ɪz
scapul|a ˈskæp.jə.l|ə, -jʊ- **-as** -əz **-ae** -iː **-ar/s** -əʳ
scar (S) skɑːʳ (US) skɑːr **-s** -z **-ring** -ɪŋ **-red** -d ˈ**scar** ˌ**tissue**
scarab ˈskær.əb (US) ˈsker-, ˈskær- **-s** -z
scarabae|us ˌskær.əˈbiː|.əs (US) ˌsker-, ˌskær- **-uses** -ə.sɪz **-i** -aɪ
scaramouch(e) (S) ˈskær.ə.muːʃ, -muːtʃ, -maʊtʃ, ˌ--ˈ- (US) ˈsker.ə.muːʃ, ˈskær-, -muːtʃ **-(e)s** -ɪz
Scarborough, Scarboro' ˈskɑː.bᵊr.ə (US) ˈskɑːr.bɚ.oʊ, -ə
Scarbrough ˈskɑː.brə (US) ˈskɑːr-, -broʊ
scarc|e skeəs (US) skers **-er** -əʳ (US) -ɚ **-est** -ɪst, -əst **-ely** -li **-eness** -nəs, -nɪs
scarcity ˈskeə.sə.ti, -sɪ- (US) ˈsker.sə.t̬i
Scardino skɑːˈdiː.nəʊ (US) skɑːrˈdiː.noʊ
scar|e skeəʳ (US) sker **-es** -z **-ing** -ɪŋ **-ed** -d **-er/s** -əʳ/z (US) -ɚ/z ˈ**scare** ˌ**story**
scarecrow ˈskeə.krəʊ (US) ˈsker.kroʊ **-s** -z
scaredy-cat ˈskeə.di.kæt (US) ˈsker- **-s** -s
scaremong|er ˈskeəˌmʌŋ.g|əʳ (US) ˈskerˌmɑːŋ.g|ɚ, -ˌmʌŋ- **-ers** -əz (US) -ɚz **-ering** -ᵊr.ɪŋ
scar|ey ˈskeə.r|i (US) ˈsker|.i **-ier** -i.əʳ (US) -i.ɚ **-iest** -i.ɪst, -i.əst **-ily** -ɪ.li **-iness** -ɪ.nəs, -ɪ.nɪs
scar|f (*n.*) skɑː|f (US) skɑːr|f **-ves** -vz **-fs** -fs
scarf (*v.*) skɑːf (US) skɑːrf **-s** -s **-ing** -ɪŋ **-ed** -t
Scarfe skɑːf (US) skɑːrf
Scargill ˈskɑː.gɪl (US) ˈskɑːr-
scarification ˌskær.ɪ.fɪˈkeɪ.ʃᵊn, ˌskeə.rɪ-, -rə- (US) ˌsker.ə.fɪˈ-, ˌskær-
scari|fy ˈskær.ɪ|.faɪ, ˈskeə.rɪ-, -rə- (US) ˈsker.ə-, ˈskær- **-fies** -faɪz **-fying** -faɪ.ɪŋ **-fied** -faɪd
scarlatina ˌskɑː.ləˈtiː.nə, -lɪˈ- (US) ˌskɑːr.ləˈ-
Scarlatti skɑːˈlæt.i (US) skɑːrˈlɑː.t̬i
scarlet (S) ˈskɑː.lət, -lɪt (US) ˈskɑːr- ˌ**scarlet** ˈ**fever**; ˌ**scarlet** ˈ**pimpernel**; ˌ**scarlet** ˈ**woman**
Scarlett ˈskɑː.lət, -lɪt (US) ˈskɑːr-
Scarman ˈskɑː.mən (US) ˈskɑːr-
scarp skɑːp (US) skɑːrp **-s** -s **-ing** -ɪŋ **-ed** -t
scarper ˈskɑː.pəʳ (US) ˈskɑːr.pɚ **-s** -z **-ing** -ɪŋ **-ed** -d
scarves (*plur. of* **scarf**) skɑːvz (US) skɑːrvs
scar|y ˈskeə.r|i (US) ˈsker|.i **-ier** -i.əʳ (US) -i.ɚ **-iest** -i.ɪst, -i.əst **-ily** -ɪ.li, -ᵊl.i **-iness** -ɪ.nəs, -ɪ.nɪs
Scase skeɪs
scat skæt **-s** -s **-ting** -ɪŋ (US) ˈskæt̬.ɪŋ **-ted** -ɪd (US) ˈskæt̬.ɪd
scath|e skeɪð **-es** -z **-ing** -ɪŋ/li **-ed** -d **-eless** -ləs, -lɪs
scathing ˈskeɪ.ðɪŋ **-ly** -li
scatological ˌskæt.əˈlɒdʒ.ɪ.kᵊl (US) ˌskæt̬.əˈlɑː.dʒɪ-
scatolog|y skætˈɒl.ə.dʒ|i (US) -ˈɑː.lə-, skəˈtɑː- **-ist/s** -ɪst/s
scatt|er ˈskæt|.əʳ (US) ˈskæt̬|.ɚ **-ers** -əz (US) -ɚz **-ering** -ᵊr.ɪŋ **-ered** -əd (US) -ɚd
scatterbrain ˈskæt.ə.breɪn (US) ˈskæt̬.ɚ- **-s** -z **-ed** -d

Pronouncing the letters SCH

The consonant letter combination **sch** has several possible pronunciations, the most common being /sk/, e.g.:

school /skuːl/
scheme /skiːm/

Other possible realisations are /ʃ/ and /s/.

schedule /ˈʃed.juːl/ (US) /ˈsked-/
schism /ˈskɪz.ᵊm, ˈsɪz-/

For words of German origin, the pronunciation is /ʃ/, e.g.:

schmalz /ʃmɔːlts/

In addition

When the three letters come together due to the addition of a prefix, the pronunciation is /s.tʃ/, e.g.:

mischance /ˈmɪs.tʃɑːnts/ (US) /-tʃænts/

scatt|y ˈskæt|.i (US) ˈskæṭ|.i **-ier** -i.əʳ (US) -i.ɚ **-iest** -i.ɪst, -i.əst **-iness** -ɪ.nəs, -ɪ.nɪs
scaup skɔːp (US) skɑːp, skɔːp **-s** -s
scaveng|e ˈskæv.ɪndʒ, -ᵊndʒ **-es** -ɪz **-ing** -ɪŋ **-ed** -d **-er/s** -əʳ/z (US) -ɚ/z
Scawfell ˌskɔːˈfel (US) ˌskɑː-, ˌskɔː- *stress shift, see compound:* ˌ**Scawfell** ˈ**Pike**
scena ˈʃeɪ.nə (US) **-s** -z
scenario sɪˈnɑː.ri.əʊ, sə-, senˈɑː- (US) səˈner.i.oʊ, -ˈnær-, -ˈnɑːr- **-s** -z
scenarist ˈsiː.nᵊr.ɪst (US) səˈner-, -ˈnær-, -ˈnɑːr- **-s** -s
scene siːn **-s** -z
scenery ˈsiː.nᵊr.i
sceneshifter ˈsiːnˌʃɪf.təʳ (US) -tɚ **-s** -z
scenic ˈsiː.nɪk, ˈsen.ɪk (US) ˈsiː- **-ally** -ᵊl.i, -li ˌ**scenic** ˈ**railway**
scent sent **-s** -s **-ing** -ɪŋ (US) ˈsen.ṭɪŋ **-ed** -ɪd (US) ˈsen.ṭɪd
scepter ˈsep.təʳ (US) -tɚ **-s** -z **-ed** -əd ˌ**scepter'd** ˈ**isle**
sceptic ˈskep.tɪk **-s** -s **-al** -ᵊl **-ally** -ᵊl.i, -li
scepticism ˈskep.tɪ.sɪ.zᵊm, -tə-
sceptre ˈsep.təʳ (US) -tɚ **-s** -z **-d** -d
schadenfreude ˈʃɑː.dᵊnˌfrɔɪ.də
Schaefer ˈʃeɪ.fəʳ (US) -fɚ
Schama ˈʃɑː.mə
schedul|e ˈʃed.juːl, ˈʃedʒ.uːl, -ᵊl; ˈsked.juːl, ˈskedʒ.uːl, -ᵊl (US) ˈskedʒ.uːl, -u.əl, -ᵊl **-es** -z **-ing** -ɪŋ **-ed** -d
Scheherazade ʃɪˌher.əˈzɑː.də, ʃə-, -ˌhɪə.rəˈ-, -ˈzɑːd (US) ʃəˌher.əˈzɑːd, -ˈzɑː.də
Scheldt skelt, ʃelt (US) skelt
schema ˈskiː.mə **-s** -z **schemata** ˈskiː.mə.tə; skɪˈmɑː.tə (US) skiːˈmɑː.ṭə; ˈskiː.mə.ṭə
schematic skiːˈmæt.ɪk, skɪ- (US) skiːˈmæṭ-, skə- **-ally** -ᵊl.i, -li
schematiz|e, -is|e ˈskiː.mə.taɪz **-es** -ɪz **-ing** -ɪŋ **-ed** -d
schem|e skiːm **-es** -z **-ing/ly** -ɪŋ/li **-ed** -d **-er/s** -əʳ/z (US) -ɚ/z
Schenectady skɪˈnek.tə.di, skə- (US) skə-
scherzand|o skeətˈsæn.d|əʊ, skɜːt- (US) skertˈsɑːn.d|oʊ, -ˈsæn- **-os** -əʊz (US) -oʊz **-i** -i
scherz|o ˈskeət.s|əʊ, ˈskɜːt- (US) ˈskert.s|oʊ **-os** -əʊz (US) -oʊz **-i** -i
Schiaparelli ˌskæp.əˈrel.i, ˌskjæp-, ˌʃæp- (US) ˌskæp-, ˌʃæp-, ˌskjɑː.pɑːˈ-
Schiedam skɪˈdæm, ˈskɪd.æm (US) skɪˈdɑːm
Schiffer ˈʃɪf.əʳ (US) -ɚ
Schiller ˈʃɪl.əʳ (US) -ɚ
schilling (S) ˈʃɪl.ɪŋ **-s** -z
Schindler ˈʃɪnd.ləʳ (US) -lɚ
schipperke (S) ˈʃɪp.ə.ki, ˈskɪ-; ˈʃɪp.ək (US) ˈskɪp.ɚ.ki **schipperkes** ˈʃɪp.ə.kiz, ˈskɪ-; ˈʃɪp.əks (US) ˈskɪp.ɚ.kiz
schism ˈskɪz.əm, ˈsɪz- (US) ˈskɪz-, ˈsɪz- **-s** -z
schismatic skɪzˈmæt.ɪk, sɪz- (US) skɪzˈmæṭ-, sɪz- **-al** -ᵊl **-ally** -ᵊl.i, -li
schist ʃɪst **-s** -s **-ose** -əʊs (US) -oʊs
schizo ˈskɪt.səʊ (US) -soʊ **-s** -z
schizoid ˈskɪt.sɔɪd
schizophrenia ˌskɪt.səʊˈfriː.ni.ə, ˌskɪd.zəʊˈ- (US) ˌskɪt.səˈ-, -soʊˈ-, -ˈfren.i-
schizophrenic ˌskɪt.səʊˈfren.ɪk, ˌskɪd.zəʊˈ-, -ˈfriː.nɪk (US) ˌskɪt.səˈ-, -soʊˈ- **-ally** -ᵊl.i, -li **-s** -s
Schlegel ˈʃleɪ.gᵊl
schlemiel ʃləˈmiːl **-s** -z
schlep(p) ʃlep **-s** -s **-ping** -ɪŋ **-ped** -t
Schlesinger ˈʃlez.ɪn.dʒəʳ, ˈʃles- (US) ˈʃlees.ɪŋ.ɚ; ˈʃlez.ɪn.dʒɚ, ˈʃleɪ.zɪŋ-
Schleswig-Holstein ˌʃlez.vɪgˈhəʊl.staɪn, ˌʃles-, -wɪgˈ- (US) -wɪgˈhoʊl-, ˌʃles.vɪgˈ-, -ˈhɔːl.ʃtaɪn
schlock ʃlɒk (US) ʃlɑːk **-s** -s
schlockmeister ˈʃlɒkˌmaɪ.stəʳ (US) ˈʃlɑːkˌmaɪ.stɚ **-s** -z
schmal(t)z ʃmɔːlts, ʃmɒlts, ʃmælts (US) ʃmɑːlts, ʃmɔːlts **-y** -i **-ier** -i.əʳ (US) -i.ɚ **-iest** -i.ɪst, -i.əst
Schmidt ʃmɪt
schmo ʃməʊ (US) ʃmoʊ **-es** -z
schmooz|e ʃmuːz **-es** -ɪz **-ing** -ɪŋ **-ed** -d
schmuck ʃmʌk **-s** -s
Schnabel ʃnɑː.bᵊl
schnap(p)s ʃnæps (US) ʃnɑːps, ʃnæps
schnauzer ˈʃnaʊt.səʳ (US) ˈʃnaʊ.zɚ **-s** -z
Schneider ˈʃnaɪ.dəʳ (US) -dɚ
schnitzel ˈʃnɪt.sᵊl **-s** -z
Schnitzler ˈʃnɪt.sləʳ (US) -slɚ
schnorkel ˈʃnɔː.kᵊl (US) ˈʃnɔːr- **-s** -z
schnozzle ˈʃnɒz.l̩ (US) ˈʃnɑː.zl̩ **-s** -z
Schoen ʃəʊn, ʃɜːn (US) ʃoʊn, ʃɜːrn
Schoenberg ˈʃɜːn.bɜːg, -beəg (US) ˈʃɜːrn.bɝːg, ˈʃoʊn-
Schofield ˈskəʊ.fiːld (US) ˈskoʊ-
scholar ˈskɒl.əʳ (US) ˈskɑː.lɚ **-s** -z **-ly** -li
scholarship ˈskɒl.ə.ʃɪp (US) ˈskɑː.lɚ- **-s** -s
scholastic skəˈlæs.tɪk, skɒlˈæs- (US) skəˈlæs- **-ally** -ᵊl.i, -li
scholasticism skəˈlæs.tɪ.sɪ.zᵊm, skɒlˈæs- (US) skəˈlæs.tə-
Scholes skəʊlz (US) skoʊlz
scholiast ˈskəʊ.li.æst (US) ˈskoʊ-, -əst **-s** -s
scholi|um ˈskəʊ.li|.əm (US) ˈskoʊ- **-a** -ə
Scholl ʃɒl, ʃəʊl, skɒl (US) ʃoʊl
Schönberg ˈʃɜːn.bɜːg, -beəg (US) ˈʃɜːrn.bɝːg, ˈʃoʊn-
school skuːl **-s** -z **-ing** -ɪŋ **-ed** -d ˌ**school** ˈ**leaver**; ˌ**school** ˈ**tie**
schoolbag ˈskuːl.bæg **-s** -z
schoolbook ˈskuːl.bʊk **-s** -s
schoolboy ˈskuːl.bɔɪ **-s** -z **-ish** -ɪʃ
school|child ˈskuːl|.tʃaɪld **-children** -ˌtʃɪl.drᵊn
schooldays ˈskuːl.deɪz
schoolgirl ˈskuːl.gɜːl (US) -gɝːl **-s** -z **-ish** -ɪʃ
schoolhou|se ˈskuːl.haʊ|s **-ses** -zɪz
schoolkid ˈskuːl.kɪd **-s** -z
schoolmarm ˈskuːl.mɑːm (US) -mɑːrm **-s** -z **-ish** -ɪʃ
schoolmaster ˈskuːlˌmɑː.stəʳ (US) -ˌmæs.tɚ **-s** -z
schoolmate ˈskuːl.meɪt **-s** -s
schoolmistress ˈskuːlˌmɪs.trɪs, -trəs **-es** -ɪz

Schwa

An unstressed central vowel.

Examples for English

One of the most noticeable features of English pronunciation is the phonetic difference between stressed and unstressed syllables. In most languages, any of the vowels of the language can occur in any syllable whether that syllable is stressed or not. In English, however, a syllable which bears no stress is more likely to have one of a small number of weak vowels. The most common weak vowel is one which never occurs in a stressed syllable, the schwa vowel (symbolised ə), which is generally described as being unrounded, central (i.e. between front and back) and mid (i.e. between close and open), e.g.:

appease /ə'piːz/
syllable /'sɪl.ə.bl̩/
China /'tʃaɪ.nə/
mother /'mʌð.əʳ/ (US) /'mʌð.ɚ/

Statistically, schwa is reported to be the most frequently occurring vowel of English (over 10% of all vowels).

schoolroom 'skuːl.rʊm, -ruːm (US) -ruːm, -rʊm **-s** -z
schoolteacher 'skuːlˌtiː.tʃəʳ (US) -tʃɚ **-s** -z
schooltime 'skuːl.taɪm
schoolwork 'skuːl.wɜːk (US) -wɝːk
schoolyard 'skuːl.jɑːd (US) -jɑːrd
schooner 'skuː.nəʳ (US) -nɚ **-s** -z
Schopenhauer 'ʃəʊ.pᵊn.haʊ.əʳ, 'ʃɒp.ᵊn- (US) 'ʃoʊ.pᵊn.haʊ.ɚ
schottisch|e ʃɒt'iːʃ, ʃə'tiːʃ (US) 'ʃɑː.t̬ɪʃ **-es** -ɪz
Schreiner 'ʃraɪ.nəʳ (US) -nɚ
Schrödinger 'ʃrɜː.dɪŋ.əʳ (US) 'ʃroʊ.dɪŋ.ɚ, 'ʃrɜːr-
Schroeder 'ʃrɜː.dəʳ (US) 'ʃroʊ.dɚ, 'ʃreɪ-
schtuck ʃtʊk
Schubert 'ʃuː.bət, -bɜːt (US) -bɚt
Schultz ʃʊlts
Schumacher 'ʃuːˌmæk.əʳ (US) -mɑːk.ɚ, -mæk-
Schuman 'ʃuː.mən
Schumann 'ʃuː.mən, -mæn, -mɑːn (US) -mɑːn, -mən
schuss ʃʊs, ʃuːs **-es** -ɪz **-ing** -ɪŋ **-ed** -t
Schuster 'ʃʊs.tə, 'ʃuː.stəʳ (US) -stɚ
schwa ʃwɑː **-s** -z
Schwabe ʃwɑːb, 'ʃwɑː.bə
Schwann ʃwɒn *as if German:* ʃvæn (US) ʃvɑːn, ʃwɑːn
Schwartz ʃwɔːts *as if German:* ʃvɑːts (US) ʃwɔːrts
Schwarzenegger 'ʃwɔːts.ᵊn.eg.əʳ (US) 'ʃwɔːrts.ᵊn.eg.ɚ
Schwarzkopf 'ʃvɑːts.kɒpf, 'ʃwɑːts-, 'ʃwɔːts- (US) 'ʃwɔːrts.kɑːpf
Schwarzwald 'ʃvɑːts.væld, 'ʃwɑːts-, -wæld (US) 'ʃvɑːrts.vɑːlt
Schweitzer 'ʃwaɪt.səʳ *as if German:* 'ʃvaɪt- (US) 'ʃwaɪt.sɚ *as if German:* 'ʃvaɪt-
Schweizer 'ʃwaɪt.səʳ *as if German:* 'ʃvaɪt- (US) 'ʃwaɪt.sɚ *as if German* 'ʃvaɪt-
Schweppes® ʃweps
Schwerin ʃveə'riːn, ʃweə- (US) ʃver'iːn, ʃveɪ'riːn
sciatic saɪ'æt.ɪk (US) -'æt̬-
sciatica saɪ'æt.ɪ.kə (US) -'æt̬-
scienc|e saɪənts **-es** -ɪz ˌ**science 'fiction**; '**science ˌpark**
scientific ˌsaɪən'tɪf.ɪk **-ally** -ᵊl.i, -li
scientist 'saɪən.tɪst (US) -t̬ɪst **-s** -s
scientologist (S) ˌsaɪən'tɒl.ə.dʒɪst (US) -'tɑː.lə- **-s** -s
Scientology® ˌsaɪən'tɒl.ə.dʒi (US) -'tɑː.lə-
sci-fi 'saɪˌfaɪ
scilicet 'saɪ.lɪ.set, 'sɪl.ɪ- (US) 'sɪl.ɪ-
Scillonian sɪ'ləʊ.ni.ən (US) -'loʊ- **-s** -z
Scill|y 'sɪl|.i **-ies** -ɪz '**Scilly ˌIsles**
scimitar 'sɪm.ɪ.təʳ, '-ə-, -tɑːʳ (US) -ə.t̬ɚ, -tɑːr **-s** -z
scintilla sɪn'tɪl.ə
scintill|ate 'sɪn.tɪ.l|eɪt, -tᵊl|.eɪt (US) -t̬ᵊl|.eɪt **-ates** -eɪts **-ating** -eɪ.tɪŋ (US) -eɪ.t̬ɪŋ **-ated** -eɪ.tɪd (US) -eɪ.t̬ɪd
scintillation ˌsɪn.tɪ'leɪ.ʃᵊn, -tᵊl'eɪ- (US) -t̬ᵊl'eɪ- **-s** -z
sciol|ism 'saɪ.əʊ.l|ɪ.zᵊm (US) '-ə- **-ist/s** -ɪst/s
scion saɪən **-s** -z
Scipio 'skɪp.i.əʊ, 'sɪp- (US) 'sɪp.i.oʊ
scire facias ˌsaɪə.ri'feɪ.ʃi.æs, -əs (US) ˌsaɪ.ri'feɪ.ʃi.æs
scirocco ʃɪ'rɒk.əʊ, sɪ-, sə- (US) ʃɪ'rɑː.koʊ, sə- **-s** -z
scission 'sɪʒ.ᵊn, 'sɪʃ- **-s** -z
sciss|or 'sɪz|.əʳ (US) -ɚ **-ors** -əz (US) -ɚz **-oring** -ᵊr.ɪŋ **-ored** -əd (US) -ɚd
scissors 'sɪz.əz (US) -ɚz
scissors-and-paste ˌsɪz.əz.ᵊnd'peɪst (US) -ɚz-
scler|a 'sklɪə.r|ə (US) 'sklɪr|.ə **-as** -əz **-ae** -iː
scleros|is sklə'rəʊ.s|ɪs, sklɪ-, skler'əʊ-, sklɪə'rəʊ- (US) sklɪ'roʊ- **-es** -iːz
sclerotic sklə'rɒt.ɪk, sklɪ-, skler'ɒt-, sklɪə'rɒt- (US) sklɪ'rɑː.t̬ɪk
scoff skɒf (US) skɑːf **-s** -s **-ing/ly** -ɪŋ/li **-ed** -t **-er/s** -əʳ/z (US) -ɚ/z
scofflaw 'skɒf.lɔː (US) 'skɑːf.lɑː, -lɔː **-s** -z
Scofield 'skəʊ.fiːld (US) 'skoʊ-
Scoggin 'skɒg.ɪn (US) 'skɑː.gɪn **-s** -z
scold skəʊld (US) skoʊld **-s** -z **-ing/s** -ɪŋ/z **-ed** -ɪd
scoliosis ˌskɒl.i'əʊ.sɪs (US) ˌskoʊ.li'oʊ-, ˌskɑː-
scollop 'skɒl.əp (US) 'skɑː.ləp **-s** -s **-ing** -ɪŋ **-ed** -t
sconc|e skɒnts (US) skɑːnts **-es** -ɪz **-ing** -ɪŋ **-ed** -t
scone skɒn, skəʊn (US) skoʊn, skɑːn **-s** -z
Scone skuːn ˌ**Stone of 'Scone**
scoop skuːp **-s** -s **-ing** -ɪŋ **-ed** -t
scoot skuːt **-s** -s **-ing** -ɪŋ (US) 'skuː.t̬ɪŋ **-ed** -ɪd (US) 'skuː.t̬ɪd
scooter 'skuː.təʳ (US) -t̬ɚ **-s** -z
scope skəʊp (US) skoʊp **-s** -s
-scope -skəʊp (US) -skoʊp
Note: Suffix. Normally unstressed, e.g. **microscope** /'maɪ.krə.skəʊp (US) -skoʊp/.
-scopic -'skɒp.ɪk (US) -'skɑː.pɪk
Note: Suffix. Words containing **-scopic** normally carry primary stress on the penultimate syllable, e.g. **microscopic** /ˌmaɪ.krə'skɒp.ɪk (US) -'skɑː.pɪk/.
scopolamine skə'pɒl.ə.miːn, -mɪn; ˌskəʊ.pə'læm.ɪn (US) skə'pɑː.lə.miːn, skoʊ-, -mɪn
-scopy -skə.pi
Note: Suffix. Words containing **-scopy** normally carry primary stress on the antepenultimate syllable, e.g. **microscopy** /maɪ'krɒs.kə.pi (US) -'krɑː.skə-/.
scorbutic skɔː'bjuː.tɪk (US) skɔːr'bjuː.t̬ɪk
scorch skɔːtʃ (US) skɔːrtʃ **-es** -ɪz **-ing/ly** -ɪŋ/li **-ed** -t **-er/s** -əʳ/z (US) -ɚ/z ˌ**scorched 'earth**

scor|e skɔːʳ US skɔːr **-es** -z **-ing** -ɪŋ **-ed** -d **-er/s** -əʳ/z US -ɚ/z **-less** -ləs, -lɪs

scoreboard ˈskɔː.bɔːd US ˈskɔːr.bɔːrd **-s** -z

scorecard ˈskɔː.kɑːd US ˈskɔːr.kɑːrd **-s** -z

scorekeeper ˈskɔːˌkiː.pəʳ US ˈskɔːrˌkiː.pɚ **-s** -z

score-line ˈskɔː.laɪn US ˈskɔːr- **-s** -z

scoresheet ˈskɔː.ʃiːt US ˈskɔːr- **-s** -s

scoria ˈskɔː.ri.ə, ˈskɒr.i- US ˈskɔːr.i-

scoriaceous ˌskɔː.riˈeɪ.ʃəs, ˌskɒr.iˈ- US ˌskɔːr.iˈ-

scorn skɔːn US skɔːrn **-s** -z **-ing** -ɪŋ **-ed** -d

scornful ˈskɔːn.fᵊl, -fʊl US ˈskɔːrn- **-ly** -i **-ness** -nəs, -nɪs

Scorpi|o ˈskɔː.pi|.əʊ US ˈskɔːr.pi|.oʊ **-os** -əʊz US -oʊz **-an/s** -ən/z

scorpion ˈskɔː.pi.ən US ˈskɔːr- **-s** -z

Scorsese skɔːˈseɪ.zi, -zeɪ US skɔːrˈseɪ.zi

scot (S) skɒt US skɑːt **-s** -s

scotch (S) skɒtʃ US skɑːtʃ **-es** -ɪz **-ing** -ɪŋ **-ed** -t **ˌScotch ˈbroth; ˌScotch ˈegg; ˌScotch ˈmist; ˌScotch ˈpine; ˌScotch ˈtape®**

Scotch|man ˈskɒtʃ|.mən US ˈskɑːtʃ- **-men** -mən

Scotch|woman ˈskɒtʃ|ˌwʊm.ən US ˈskɑːtʃ- **-women** -ˌwɪm.ɪn

scoter ˈskəʊ.təʳ US ˈskoʊ.t̬ɚ **-s** -z

scot-free ˌskɒtˈfriː US ˌskɑːt-

scotia (S) ˈskəʊ.ʃə US ˈskoʊ-

Scotland ˈskɒt.lənd US ˈskɑːt- **ˌScotland ˈYard**

Scots skɒts US skɑːts **ˌScots ˈpine**

Scots|man ˈskɒts|.mən US ˈskɑːts- **-men** -mən

Scots|woman ˈskɒts|ˌwʊm.ən US ˈskɑːts- **-women** -ˌwɪm.ɪn

Scott skɒt US skɑːt

Scotticism ˈskɒt.ɪ.sɪ.zᵊm US ˈskɑː.t̬ɪ- **-s** -z

Scotticiz|e, -is|e ˈskɒt.ɪ.saɪz US ˈskɑː.t̬ɪ- **-es** -ɪz **-ing** -ɪŋ **-ed** -d

scottie (S) ˈskɒt.i US ˈskɑː.ti

Scottish ˈskɒt.ɪʃ US ˈskɑː.t̬ɪʃ **-ness** -nəs, -nɪs **ˌScottish ˈterrier**

scoundrel ˈskaʊn.drəl **-s** -z **-ly** -i

scour skaʊəʳ US skaʊɚ **-s** -z **-ing** -ɪŋ **-ed** -d **-er/s** -əʳ/z US -ɚ/z **ˈscouring ˌpad**

scourg|e skɜːdʒ US skɝːdʒ **-es** -ɪz **-ing** -ɪŋ **-ed** -d

Scous|e skaʊs **-er/s** -əʳ/z US -ɚ/z

scout skaʊt **-s** -s **-ing** -ɪŋ US ˈskaʊ.t̬ɪŋ **-ed** -ɪd US ˈskaʊ.t̬ɪd **-er/s** -əʳ/z US ˈskaʊ.t̬ɚ/z **ˌscout's ˈhono(u)r**

scoutmaster ˈskaʊtˌmɑː.stəʳ US -ˌmæs.tɚ **-s** -z

scow skaʊ **-s** -z

scowl skaʊl **-s** -z **-ing/ly** -ɪŋ/li **-ed** -d

scrabbl|e (S®) ˈskræb.l̩ **-es** -z **-ing** -ɪŋ, ˈskræb.lɪŋ **-ed** -d

scrag skræg **-s** -z **-ging** -ɪŋ **-ged** -d

scrag-end ˌskrægˈend **-s** -z

scraggly ˈskræg.l̩.i **-ier** -i.əʳ US -i.ɚ **-iest** -i.ɪst **-iness** -ɪ.nəs, -ɪ.nɪs

scragg|y ˈskrægl.i **-ier** -i.əʳ US -i.ɚ **-iest** -i.ɪst, -i.əst **-iness** -ɪ.nəs, -ɪ.nɪs

scram skræm **-s** -z **-ming** -ɪŋ **-med** -d

scrambl|e ˈskræm.bl̩ **-es** -z **-ing** -ɪŋ, ˈskræm.blɪŋ **-ed** -d **ˌscrambled ˈeggs**

scramjet ˈskræm.dʒet **-s** -s

scran skræn **-s** -z

scrap skræp **-s** -s **-ping** -ɪŋ **-ped** -t **-per/s** -əʳ/z US -ɚ/z **ˈscrap ˌheap; ˈscrap ˌmerchant; ˌscrap ˈmetal** US **ˈscrap ˌmetal**

scrapbook ˈskræp.bʊk **-s** -s

scrap|e skreɪp **-es** -s **-ing/s** -ɪŋ/z **-ed** -t **-er/s** -əʳ/z US -ɚ/z

scraperboard ˈskreɪ.pə.bɔːd US -pɚ.bɔːrd **-s** -z

scrapie ˈskreɪ.pi US ˈskreɪ-, ˈskræp.i

scrapple ˈskræp.l̩

scrapp|y ˈskræp|.i **-ier** -i.əʳ US -i.ɚ **-iest** -i.ɪst, -i.əst **-ily** -ɪ.li, -ᵊl.i **-iness** -ɪ.nəs, -ɪ.nɪs

scrapyard ˈskræp.jɑːd US -jɑːrd **-s** -z

scratch skrætʃ **-es** -ɪz **-ing** -ɪŋ **-ed** -t **-er/s** -əʳ/z US -ɚ/z **ˈscratch ˌpad; ˈscratch ˌpaper**

scratchcard ˈskrætʃ.kɑːd US -kɑːrd **-s** -z

scratchpad ˈskrætʃ.pæd **-s** -z

scratch|y ˈskrætʃ|.i **-ier** -i.əʳ US -i.ɚ **-iest** -i.ɪst, -i.əst **-ily** -ɪ.li, -ᵊl.i **-iness** -ɪ.nəs, -ɪ.nɪs

scrawl skrɔːl US skrɑːl, skrɔːl **-s** -z **-ing** -ɪŋ **-ed** -d

scrawl|y ˈskrɔː.l|i US ˈskrɑː-, ˈskrɔː- **-ier** -i.əʳ US -i.ɚ **-iest** -i.ɪst, -i.əst **-iness** -ɪ.nəs, -ɪ.nɪs

scrawn|y ˈskrɔː.n|i US ˈskrɑː-, ˈskrɔː- **-ier** -i.əʳ US -i.ɚ **-iest** -i.ɪst, -i.əst **-iness** -ɪ.nəs, -ɪ.nɪs

scray skreɪ **-s** -z

scream skriːm **-s** -z **-ing/ly** -ɪŋ **-ed** -d **-er/s** -əʳ/z US -ɚ/z

scree skriː **-s** -z

screech skriːtʃ **-es** -ɪz **-ing** -ɪŋ **-ed** -t **-er/s** -əʳ/z US -ɚ/z **ˈscreech ˌowl**

screed skriːd **-s** -z

screen skriːn **-s** -z **-ing/s** -ɪŋ **-ed** -d **ˈscreen ˌprinting; ˈscreen ˌtest**

screenplay ˈskriːn.pleɪ, ˈskriːm- US ˈskriːn- **-s** -z

screensaver ˈskriːnˌseɪ.vəʳ US -vɚ **-s** -z

screenwriter ˈskriːnˌraɪ.təʳ US -t̬ɚ **-s** -z

screw skruː **-s** -z **-ing** -ɪŋ **-ed** -d **ˌscrew ˈcap** US **ˈscrew ˌcap; ˌscrew ˈtop** US **ˈscrew ˌtop; ˌscrewed ˈup**

screwball ˈskruː.bɔːl US -bɔːl, -bɑːl **-s** -z

screwdriver ˈskruːˌdraɪ.vəʳ US -vɚ **-s** -z

screw|y ˈskruː|.i **-ier** -i.əʳ US -i.ɚ **-iest** -i.ɪst, -i.əst **-iness** -ɪ.nəs, -ɪ.nɪs

Scriabin ˈskrɪə.bɪn, skriˈæb.ɪn US skriˈɑː.bɪn

scribal ˈskraɪ.bᵊl

scribbl|e ˈskrɪb.l̩ **-es** -z **-ing** -ɪŋ, ˈskrɪb.lɪŋ **-ed** -d **-er/s** -əʳ/z, ˈskrɪb.ləʳ/z US ˈ-l̩.ɚ/z, ˈ-lɚ/z

scribe skraɪb **-s** -z

Scriblerus skrɪˈblɪə.rəs US -ˈbler.əs, -ˈblɪr-

Scribner ˈskrɪb.nəʳ US -nɚ

scrim skrɪm

scrimmag|e ˈskrɪm.ɪdʒ **-es** -ɪz **-ing** -ɪŋ **-ed** -d

scrimp skrɪmp **-s** -s **-ing** -ɪŋ **-ed** -t **-er/s** -əʳ/z US -ɚ/z

scrimshaw ˈskrɪm.ʃɔː US -ʃɑː, -ʃɔː **-s** -z **-ing** -ɪŋ **-ed** -d

scrip skrɪp **-s** -s

script skrɪpt **-s** -s **-ing** -ɪŋ **-ed** -ɪd

scriptori|um skrɪpˈtɔː.ri|.əm US -ˈtɔːr.i- **-ums** -əmz **-a** -ə

scriptural ˈskrɪp.tʃᵊr.ᵊl, -tʃʊ.rᵊl US -tʃɚ.ᵊl **-ly** -i

scripture (S) ˈskrɪp.tʃəʳ US -tʃɚ **-s** -z

scriptwriter ˈskrɪptˌraɪ.təʳ US -t̬ɚ **-s** -z

Scriven ˈskrɪv.ᵊn

scrivener (S) ˈskrɪv.ᵊn.əʳ, ˈ-nəʳ US ˈ-ᵊn.ɚ, ˈ-nɚ **-s** -z

scrofula ˈskrɒf.jʊ.lə US ˈskrɑː.fjə-

scrofulous ˈskrɒf.jʊ.ləs US ˈskrɑː.fjə- **-ly** -li **-ness** -nəs, -nɪs

scroll skrəʊl US skroʊl **-s** -z **-ing** -ɪŋ **-ed** -d

scrooge (S) skruːdʒ **-s** -ɪz

Scroope skruːp

Scrope skruːp, skrəʊp US skruːp, skroʊp

scrot|um ˈskrəʊ.t|əm US ˈskroʊ.t̬|əm **-ums** -əmz **-a** -ə **-al** -ᵊl

scroung|e skraʊndʒ **-es** -ɪz **-ing** -ɪŋ **-ed** -d **-er/s** -əʳ/z US -ɚ/z

scrub skrʌb **-s** -z **-bing** -ɪŋ **-bed** -d **ˈscrubbing ˌbrush; ˈscrub ˌbrush**

scrubber ˈskrʌb.əʳ US -ɚ **-s** -z

scrubb|y ˈskrʌb|.i **-ier** -i.əʳ US -i.ɚ **-iest** -i.ɪst, -i.əst **-iness** -ɪ.nəs, -ɪ.nɪs

scrubland ˈskrʌb.lənd, -lænd US -lænd **-s** -z

scruff skrʌf **-s** -s

scruff|y ˈskrʌf|.i **-ier** -i.əʳ US -i.ɚ **-iest** -i.ɪst, -i.əst **-iness** -ɪ.nəs, -ɪ.nɪs **-ily** -ɪ.li, -ᵊl.i

scrum skrʌm **-s** -z

scrum-|half ˌskrʌm|ˈhɑːf US -ˈhæf **-halfs** -ˈhɑːfs US -ˈhæfs **-halves** -ˈhɑːvz US -ˈhævz

scrummag|e ˈskrʌm.ɪdʒ **-es** -ɪz **-ing** -ɪŋ **-ed** -d **-er/s** -əʳ/z US -ɚ/z

scrummy ˈskrʌm.i **-ier** -i.əʳ (US) -i.ɚ **-iest** -i.ɪst **-iness** -ɪ.nəs, -ɪ.nɪs
scrump skrʌmp **-s** -s **-ing** -ɪŋ **-ed** -t
scrumptious ˈskrʌmp.ʃəs, -tʃəs
scrumpy ˈskrʌm.pi
scrunch skrʌntʃ **-es** -ɪz **-ing** -ɪŋ **-ed** -t **-y** -i
scrupl|e ˈskruː.pl̩ **-es** -z **-ing** -ɪŋ, ˈskruː.plɪŋ **-ed** -d
scrupulosity ˌskruː.pjəˈlɒs.ə.ti, -pjʊˈ-, -ɪ.ti (US) -ˈlɑː.sə.t̬i
scrupulous ˈskruː.pjə.ləs, -pjʊ- **-ly** -li **-ness** -nəs, -nɪs
scrutator skruːˈteɪ.təʳ (US) -t̬ɚ **-s** -z
scrutineer ˌskruː.tɪˈnɪəʳ, -tənˈɪəʳ (US) -tənˈɪr **-s** -z
scrutiniz|e, -is|e ˈskruː.tɪ.naɪz, -tən.aɪz (US) -tən.aɪz **-es** -ɪz **-ing** -ɪŋ **-ed** -d
scrutin|y ˈskruː.tɪ.n|i, -tən|.i (US) -tən|.i **-ies** -iz
Scruton ˈskruː.tən
scr|y skr|aɪ **-ies** -aɪz **-ying** -aɪ.ɪŋ **-ied** -aɪd
Scrymgeour ˈskrɪm.dʒəʳ (US) -dʒɚ
scuba ˈskuː.bə, ˈskjuː- (US) ˈskuː- ˈ**scuba** ˌ**diving**
scud (S) skʌd **-s** -z **-ding** -ɪŋ **-ded** -ɪd
Scudamore ˈskjuː.də.mɔːʳ (US) ˈskuː.də.mɔːr
scuff skʌf **-s** -s **-ing** -ɪŋ **-ed** -t
scuffl|e ˈskʌf.l̩ **-es** -z **-ing** -ɪŋ, ˈskʌf.lɪŋ **-ed** -d
scull skʌl **-s** -z **-ing** -ɪŋ **-ed** -d **-er/s** -əʳ/z (US) -ɚ/z
sculler|y ˈskʌl.ər|.i **-ies** -iz ˈ**scullery** ˌ**maid**
scullion (S) ˈskʌl.i.ən (US) ˈ-jən **-s** -z
Scully ˈskʌl.i
sculpsit ˈskʌlp.sɪt
sculpt skʌlpt **-s** -s **-ing** -ɪŋ **-ed** -ɪd
sculptor ˈskʌlp.təʳ (US) -tɚ **-s** -z
sculpt|ure ˈskʌlp.tʃ|əʳ (US) -tʃ|ɚ **-ures** -əz (US) -ɚz **-uring** -ər.ɪŋ **-ured** -əd (US) -ɚd **-ural** -ər.əl
scum skʌm **-s** -z **-ming** -ɪŋ **-med** -d **-my** -i
scumbag ˈskʌm.bæg **-s** -z
Scunthorpe ˈskʌn.θɔːp (US) -θɔːrp
scupper ˈskʌp.əʳ (US) -ɚ **-s** -z **-ing** -ɪŋ **-ed** -d
scurf skɜːf (US) skɝːf **-y** -i **-iness** -ɪ.nəs, -ɪ.nɪs
scurrility skʌrˈɪl.ə.ti, skəˈrɪl-, -ɪ.ti (US) skəˈrɪl.ə.t̬i
scurrilous ˈskʌr.ə.ləs, ˈ-ɪ- (US) ˈskɝː- **-ly** -li **-ness** -nəs, -nɪs
scurr|y ˈskʌr|.i (US) ˈskɝː- **-ies** -iz **-ying** -i.ɪŋ **-ied** -id
scurv|y ˈskɜː.v|i (US) ˈskɝː- **-ier** -i.əʳ (US) -i.ɚ **-iest** -i.ɪst, -i.əst **-ily** -ɪ.li, -əl.i **-iness** -ɪ.nəs, -ɪ.nɪs
Scutari ˈskuː.tər.i; skuːˈtɑː.ri, skʊ- (US) ˈskuː.t̬ɚ.i, -tɑː-
scutcheon ˈskʌtʃ.ən **-s** -z
scutt|er ˈskʌt|.əʳ (US) ˈskʌt̬|.ɚ **-ers** -əz (US) -ɚz **-ering** -ər.ɪŋ **-ered** -əd (US) -ɚd
scuttl|e ˈskʌt.l̩ (US) ˈskʌt̬- **-es** -z **-ing** -ɪŋ, ˈskʌt.lɪŋ **-ed** -d
scuttlebutt ˈskʌt.l̩.bʌt **-s** -s
scut|um ˈskjuː.t|əm (US) -t̬|əm **-ums** -əmz **-a** -ə
scuzz|y ˈskʌz|.i **-ier** -i.əʳ (US) -i.ɚ **-iest** -i.ɪst, -i.əst **-iness** -ɪ.nəs, -ɪ.nɪs
Scylla ˈsɪl.ə
scyth|e saɪð **-es** -z **-ing** -ɪŋ **-ed** -d
Scythi|a ˈsɪð.i|.ə, ˈsɪθ- (US) ˈsɪθ-, ˈsɪð- **-an/s** -ən/z
S.D. *(abbrev. for* **South Dakota***)* ˌsaʊθ.dəˈkəʊ.tə (US) -ˈkoʊ.t̬ə
S.D.I. ˌes.diːˈaɪ
SDP ˌes.diːˈpiː
SE *(abbrev. for* **southeast***)* ˌesˈiː, ˌsaʊθˈiːst
sea siː **-s** -z ˌ**sea** ˈ**breeze** (US) ˈ**sea** ˌ**breeze**; ˈ**sea** ˌ**captain**; ˈ**sea** ˌ**change**; ˈ**sea** ˌ**cow**; ˈ**sea** ˌ**elephant**; ˈ**sea** ˌ**fog**; ˌ**sea** ˈ**green**; ˈ**sea** ˌ**horse**; ˈ**sea** ˌ**legs**; ˈ**sea** ˌ**level**; ˈ**sea** ˌ**lion**; ˈ**sea** ˌ**power**; ˈ**sea** ˌ**serpent**; ˈ**sea** ˌ**slug**; ˈ**sea** ˌ**snail**; ˈ**sea** ˌ**urchin**; **between the** ˌ**devil and the** ˌ**deep** ˌ**blue** ˈ**sea**
seabed ˈsiː.bed, -ˈ-
seabird ˈsiː.bɜːd (US) -bɝːd **-s** -z
seaboard ˈsiː.bɔːd (US) -bɔːrd
seaborne ˈsiː.bɔːn (US) -bɔːrn
Seabright ˈsiː.braɪt
seadog ˈsiː.dɒg (US) -dɑːg, -dɔːg **-s** -z
seafar|er ˈsiːˌfeə.r|əʳ (US) -ˌfer|.ɚ **-ers** -əz (US) -ɚz **-ing** -ɪŋ
seafood ˈsiː.fuːd
Seaford ˈsiː.fəd, -fɔːd (US) -fɚd, -fɔːrd
Seaforth ˈsiː.fɔːθ (US) -fɔːrθ **-s** -s
seafront ˈsiː.frʌnt **-s** -s
Seager ˈsiː.gəʳ (US) -gɚ
seagoing ˈsiːˌgəʊ.ɪŋ (US) -ˌgoʊ-
Seagram® ˈsiː.grəm
seagull ˈsiː.gʌl **-s** -z
Seaham ˈsiː.əm
seakale ˈsiː.keɪl, ˌ-ˈ- (US) ˈsiː.keɪl
seal siːl **-s** -z **-ing** -ɪŋ **-ed** -d ˈ**sealing** ˌ**wax**
sealant ˈsiː.lənt **-s** -s
sealer ˈsiː.ləʳ (US) -lɚ **-s** -z
sealskin ˈsiːl.skɪn **-s** -z
Sealyham ˈsiː.li.əm **-s** -z
seam siːm **-s** -z **-ing** -ɪŋ **-ed** -d **-less/ly** -ləs/li, -lɪs/li
sea|man (S) ˈsiː|.mən **-men** -mən, -men **-manship** -mən.ʃɪp **-manlike** -mən.laɪk
Seamas ˈʃeɪ.məs
seamer ˈsiː.məʳ (US) -mɚ **-s** -z
seamstress ˈsemp.strɪs, ˈsiːmp-, -strəs (US) ˈsiːmp- **-es** -ɪz
Seamus ˈʃeɪ.məs
seamy ˈsiː.mi **-ier** -i.əʳ (US) -i.ɚ **-iest** -i.ɪst, -i.əst **-iness** -ɪ.nəs, -ɪ.nɪs
Sean ʃɔːn (US) ʃɑːn, ʃɔːn
seanc|e, séance ˈseɪ.ɑ̃ːnts (US) ˈseɪ.ɑːnts **-es** -ɪz
sea-pink ˈsiː.pɪŋk
seaplane ˈsiː.pleɪn **-s** -z
seaport ˈsiː.pɔːt (US) -pɔːrt **-s** -s
sear sɪəʳ (US) sɪr **-s** -z **-ing/ly** -ɪŋ **-ed** -d
search sɜːtʃ (US) sɝːtʃ **-es** -ɪz **-ing/ly** -ɪŋ/li **-ed** -t **-er/s** -əʳ/z (US) -ɚ/z **-able** -ə.bl̩ ˈ**search** ˌ**party**; ˈ**search** ˌ**warrant**
searchlight ˈsɜːtʃ.laɪt (US) ˈsɝːtʃ- **-s** -s
Searle sɜːl (US) sɝːl
Sears sɪəz (US) sɪrz
Seascale ˈsiː.skeɪl
seascape ˈsiː.skeɪp **-s** -s
seashell ˈsiː.ʃel **-s** -z
seashore ˈsiː.ʃɔːʳ, ˌ-ˈ- (US) ˈsiː.ʃɔːr **-s** -z
seasick ˈsiː.sɪk **-ness** -nəs, -nɪs
seaside ˈsiː.saɪd
season ˈsiː.zən **-s** -z **-ing** -ɪŋ **-ed** -d ˌ**Season's** ˈ**Greetings**; ˈ**season** ˌ**ticket** (US) ˌ**season** ˈ**ticket**
seasonab|le ˈsiː.zən.ə.b|l̩, ˈsiːz.nə- **-ly** -li **-leness** -l̩.nəs, -nɪs
seasonal ˈsiː.zən.əl **-ly** -i
seasonality ˌsiː.zənˈæl.ə.ti, -ɪ.ti (US) -ə.t̬i
seasoning ˈsiː.zən.ɪŋ **-s** -z
seat siːt **-s** -s **-ing** -ɪŋ (US) ˈsiː.t̬ɪŋ **-ed** -ɪd (US) ˈsiː.t̬ɪd **-er/s** -əʳ/z (US) -ɚ/z ˈ**seat** ˌ**belt**
SEATO ˈsiː.təʊ (US) -t̬oʊ
Seaton ˈsiː.tən
Seaton Delavel ˌsiː.tənˈdel.ə.vəl
Seattle siˈæt.l̩ (US) -ˈæt̬-
seawall ˌsiːˈwɔːl, ˈ-- (US) ˈsiː.wɔːl, -wɑːl **-s** -z
seaward ˈsiː.wəd (US) -wɚd
seawater ˈsiːˌwɔː.təʳ (US) -ˌwɑː.t̬ɚ, -ˌwɔː-
seaway ˈsiː.weɪ **-s** -z
seaweed ˈsiː.wiːd
seaworth|y ˈsiːˌwɜː.ð|i (US) -ˌwɝː- **-iness** -ɪ.nəs, -ɪ.nɪs
sebaceous sɪˈbeɪ.ʃəs, sebˈeɪ- (US) səˈbeɪ- **se**ˈ**baceous** ˌ**gland**
Sebastian sɪˈbæs.ti.ən, səˈbæs-, sebˈæs- (US) səˈbæs.tʃən
Sebastopol sɪˈbæs.tə.pɒl, sə-, sebˈæs-, pəl (US) sɪˈbæs.tə.poʊl
seborrhea ˌseb.əˈriː.ə, -ˈrɪə (US) -ˈriː.ə
sebum ˈsiː.bəm
sec sek **-s** -s
secant ˈsiː.kənt, ˈsek.ənt (US) ˈsiː.kənt, -kænt **-s** -s
secateurs ˌsek.əˈtɜːz; ˈ---, -təz (US) ˈsek.ə.tɚz
seced|e sɪˈsiːd, siː-, sə- (US) sɪ- **-es** -z **-ing** -ɪŋ **-ed** -ɪd **-er/s** -əʳ/z (US) -ɚ/z
secession sɪˈseʃ.ən, sə- **-s** -z **-ist/s** -ɪst/s

secludle sɪˈkluːd, sə- **-es** -z **-ing** -ɪŋ **-ed** -ɪd
seclusion sɪˈkluː.ʒᵊn, sə-
Secombe ˈsiː.kəm
second (*n. adj. v.*) *most senses:* ˈsek.ᵊnd **-s** -z **-ly** -li **-ing** -ɪŋ **-ed** -ɪd **-er/s** -əʳ/z ⓤⓢ -ɚ/z ˌ**second** ˈ**best**; ˌ**Second** ˈ**Coming**; ˌ**second** ˈ**cousin**; ˌ**second** ˈ**fiddle**; ˌ**second** ˈ**nature**; ˌ**second** ˈ**person**; *stress shift:* ˌsecond person ˈsingular; ˌ**second** ˈ**reading**; ˌ**second** ˈ**sight**; ˌ**second** ˈ**thoughts**; ˌ**second** ˈ**wind**; ˌ**Second** ˌ**World** ˈ**War**
second (*v.*) *to release for temporary service:* sɪˈkɒnd, sə- ⓤⓢ -ˈkɑːnd **-s** -z **-ing** -ɪŋ **-ed** -ɪd **-ment/s**
secondarly ˈsek.ᵊn.dᵊr|.i, -dr|i ⓤⓢ -der|.i **-ies** -iz **-ily** -ᵊl.i, -ɪ.li ˌ**secondary** ˈ**modern**; ˈ**secondary** ˌ**school**
second-class ˌsek.ᵊndˈklɑːs ⓤⓢ -ˈklæs ˌ**second-class** ˈ**citizen**
second-generation ˌsek.ᵊnˌdʒen.ᵊrˈeɪ.ʃᵊn ⓤⓢ -əˈreɪ-
second-guess ˌsek.ᵊndˈges **-es** -ɪz **-ing** -ɪŋ **-ed** -t
secondhand ˌsek.ᵊndˈhænd *stress shift:* ˌsecondhand ˈbooks
Secondi *town in Ghana:* ˌsek.ənˈdiː *surname:* sɪˈkɒn.di, sə- ⓤⓢ -ˈkɑːn-
secondment sɪˈkɒnd.mənt, sə- ⓤⓢ -ˈkɑːnd-
secondo sekˈɒn.dəʊ, sɪˈkɒn- ⓤⓢ sɪˈkɑːn.doʊ **-s** -z
second|-rate ˌsek.ᵊnd|ˈreɪt **-rater/s** -ˈreɪ.təʳ/z ⓤⓢ -ˈreɪ.t̬ɚ/z
secrecy ˈsiː.krə.si, -krɪ-
secret ˈsiː.krət, -krɪt **-s** -s **-ly** -li ˌ**secret** ˈ**agent**; ˌ**secret poˈlice**; ˌ**secret** ˈ**service**
secretarial ˌsek.rəˈteə.ri.əl, -rɪˈ- ⓤⓢ -rəˈter.i-
secretariat ˌsek.rəˈteə.ri.ət, -rɪˈ-, -æt ⓤⓢ -rəˈter.i.ət **-s** -s
secretarly ˈsek.rə.tᵊr|.i, -rɪ-, -tr|i ⓤⓢ -rə.ter|.i **-ies** -iz **-yship/s** -i.ʃɪp/s ˌ**Secretary of** ˈ**State**
secretary-general, (**S G**) ˌsek.rə.tᵊr.iˈdʒen.ᵊr.ᵊl, -rɪ- ⓤⓢ -rə.ter.iˈ- **-s** -z **secretaries-general** ˌsek.rə.tᵊr.izˈ-, -rɪ- ⓤⓢ -rə.ter.izˈ-
se|crete sɪ|ˈkriːt, siː-, sə- ⓤⓢ sɪ- **-cretes** -ˈkriːts **-creting** -ˈkriː.tɪŋ ⓤⓢ -ˈkriː.t̬ɪŋ **-creted** -ˈkriː.tɪd ⓤⓢ -ˈkriː.t̬ɪd
secretion sɪˈkriː.ʃᵊn, siː-, sə- ⓤⓢ sɪ- **-s** -z
secretive *inclined to secrecy:* ˈsiː.krə.tɪv, -krɪ- ⓤⓢ -krə.t̬ɪv **-ly** -li **-ness** -nəs, -nɪs
secretive *of secretion:* sɪˈkriː.tɪv, sə- ⓤⓢ -t̬ɪv
sect sekt **-s** -s
sectarian sekˈteə.ri.ən ⓤⓢ -ˈter.i- **-s** -z **-ism** -ɪ.zᵊm
sectarly ˈsek.tᵊr|.i **-ies** -iz
section ˈsek.ʃᵊn **-s** -z **-ing** -ɪŋ **-ed** -d
sectional ˈsek.ʃᵊn.ᵊl **-ly** -i
sectional|ism ˈsek.ʃᵊn.ᵊl|.ɪ.zᵊm **-ist/s** -ɪst/s
sectionaliz|e, -is|e ˈsek.ʃᵊn.ᵊl.aɪz ⓤⓢ -ə.laɪz **-es** -ɪz **-ing** -ɪŋ **-ed** -d
sector ˈsek.təʳ ⓤⓢ -tɚ **-s** -z
secular ˈsek.jə.ləʳ, -jʊ- ⓤⓢ -lɚ **-ly** -li
secular|ism ˈsek.jə.lᵊr|.ɪ.zᵊm, -jʊ- **-ist/s** -ɪst/s
secularity ˌsek.jəˈlær.ə.ti, -jʊˈ-, -ɪ.ti ⓤⓢ -ˈler.ə.t̬i, -ˈlær-
secularization, -isa- ˌsek.jə.lᵊr.aɪˈzeɪ.ʃᵊn, -jʊ-, -ɪˈ- ⓤⓢ -ɪˈ-
securalriz|e, -is|e ˈsek.jə.lᵊr.aɪz, -jʊ- ⓤⓢ -lə.raɪz **-es** -ɪz **-ing** -ɪŋ **-ed** -d
secur|e sɪˈkjʊəʳ, sə-, -ˈkjɔːʳ ⓤⓢ -ˈkjʊr **-er** -əʳ ⓤⓢ -ɚ **-est** -ɪst, -əst **-ely** -li **-es** -z **-ing** -ɪŋ **-ed** -d **-able** -rə.bl̩
Securicor® sɪˈkjʊə.rɪ.kɔːʳ, sə-, -ˈkjɔː-, -rə- ⓤⓢ -ˈkjʊr.ə.kɔːr
securitly sɪˈkjʊə.rə.t|i, sə-, -ˈkjɔː-, -ɪ.t|i ⓤⓢ -ˈkjʊr.ə.t̬|i **-ies** -iz **seˈcurity** ˌ**guard**; **Seˈcurity** ˌ**Council**; **seˈcurity** ˌ**risk**
sedan (**S**) sɪˈdæn, sə- **seˌdan** ˈ**chair** ⓤⓢ **seˈdan** ˌ**chair**
se|date (*v.*) sɪ|ˈdeɪt, sə- **-dates** -ˈdeɪts **-dating** -ˈdeɪ.tɪŋ ⓤⓢ -ˈdeɪ.t̬ɪŋ **-dated** -ˈdeɪ.tɪd ⓤⓢ -ˈdeɪ.t̬ɪd
sedate (*adj.*) sɪˈdeɪt, sə- **-ly** -li **-ness** -nəs, -nɪs
sedation sɪˈdeɪ.ʃᵊn, sə-
sedative ˈsed.ə.tɪv ⓤⓢ -t̬ɪv **-s** -z
Sedbergh *public school:* ˈsed.bəʳ, -bɜːg ⓤⓢ -bɜːg, -bɚ *name of town:* ˈsed.bəʳ ⓤⓢ -bɚ
Sedding ˈsed.ɪŋ
Seddon ˈsed.ᵊn
sedentarly ˈsed.ᵊn.tᵊr|.i, -tr|i ⓤⓢ -ter|.i **-ily** -ᵊl.i, -ɪ.li **-iness** -ɪ.nəs, -ɪ.nɪs
sedg|e sedʒ **-es** -ɪz ˈ**sedge** ˌ**warbler**, ˌ**sedge** ˈ**warbler** ⓤⓢ ˈ**sedge** ˌ**warbler**
Sedgefield ˈsedʒ.fiːld
Sedgemoor ˈsedʒ.mɔːʳ, -mʊəʳ ⓤⓢ -mʊr, -mɔːr
Sedgley ˈsedʒ.li
Sedgwick ˈsedʒ.wɪk
sedilia sedˈiː.li.ə, sɪˈdiː-, sə-, -ˈdaɪ- ⓤⓢ sɪˈdɪl.i.ə, ˈ-jə
sediment ˈsed.ɪ.mənt, ˈ-ə- ⓤⓢ ˈ-ə- **-s** -s **-ation** ˌ--menˈteɪ.ʃᵊn
sedimentary ˌsed.ɪˈmen.tᵊr.i, -əˈ-, ˈ-tri
sedition sɪˈdɪʃ.ᵊn, sə- **-s** -z
seditious sɪˈdɪʃ.əs, sə- **-ly** -li **-ness** -nəs, -nɪs
Sedlescombe ˈsed.l̩z.kəm
Sedley ˈsed.li
seduc|e sɪˈdjuːs, sə-, -ˈdʒuːs ⓤⓢ -ˈduːs, -ˈdjuːs **-es** -ɪz **-ing** -ɪŋ **-ed** -t **-er/s** -əʳ/z ⓤⓢ -ɚ/z
seduction sɪˈdʌk.ʃᵊn, sə- **-s** -z
seductive sɪˈdʌk.tɪv, sə- **-ly** -li **-ness** -nəs, -nɪs
seductress sɪˈdʌk.trɪs, -trəs **-es** -ɪz
sedulous ˈsed.jʊ.ləs, -jə-, ˈsedʒ.ʊ-, ˈ-ə- ⓤⓢ ˈsedʒ.ə-, ˈ-ʊ- **-ly** -li **-ness** -nəs, -nɪs
sedum ˈsiː.dəm **-s** -z
see (**S**) siː **-s** -z **-ing** -ɪŋ **saw** sɔː ⓤⓢ sɑː, sɔː **seen** siːn
Seebeck ˈsiː.bek
seed siːd **-s** -z **-ing** -ɪŋ **-ed** -ɪd ˌ**go to** ˈ**seed**; ˈ**seed poˌtato**, ˌ**seed poˈtato**
seedbed ˈsiːd.bed **-s** -z
seedcake ˈsiːd.keɪk **-s** -s
seedcas|e ˈsiːd.keɪs **-es** -ɪz
seedless ˈsiːd.ləs, -lɪs
seedling ˈsiːd.lɪŋ **-s** -z
seeds|man ˈsiːdz|.mən **-men** -mən, -men
seedtime ˈsiːd.taɪm **-s** -z
seed|y ˈsiː.d|i **-ier** -i.əʳ ⓤⓢ -i.ɚ **-iest** -i.ɪst, -i.əst **-ily** -ɪ.li, -ᵊl.i **-iness** -ɪ.nəs, -ɪ.nɪs
Seeger ˈsiː.gəʳ ⓤⓢ -gɚ
seek siːk **-s** -s **-ing** -ɪŋ **sought** sɔːt ⓤⓢ sɑːt, sɔːt **seeker/s** ˈsiː.kəʳ/z ⓤⓢ -kɚ/z
Seel(e)y ˈsiː.li
seem siːm **-s** -z **-ing/ly** -ɪŋ/li **-ed** -d
seeml|y ˈsiːm.l|i **-ier** -i.əʳ ⓤⓢ -i.ɚ **-iest** -i.ɪst, -i.əst **-iness** -ɪ.nəs, -ɪ.nɪs
seen (*from* **see**) siːn
seep siːp **-s** -s **-ing** -ɪŋ **-ed** -t
seepage ˈsiː.pɪdʒ
seer *prophet:* ˈsiː.əʳ, sɪəʳ ⓤⓢ sɪr, ˈsiː.ɚ **-s** -z
seer *Indian weight:* sɪəʳ ⓤⓢ siːr, sɪr **-s** -z
seersucker ˈsɪəˌsʌk.əʳ ⓤⓢ ˈsɪrˌsʌk.ɚ
seesaw ˈsiː.sɔː ⓤⓢ -sɑː, -sɔː **-s** -z **-ing** -ɪŋ **-ed** -d
seeth|e siːð **-es** -z **-ing** -ɪŋ **-ed** -d
see-through ˈsiː.θruː
Sefton ˈsef.tᵊn ⓤⓢ -tən
Sega® ˈseɪ.gə, ˈsiː-
Segal ˈsiː.gəl
segment (*n.*) ˈseg.mənt **-s** -s
segmen|t (*v.*) segˈmen|t, səg-, sɪg- ⓤⓢ ˈseg.men|t, -ˈ-- **-ts** -ts **-ting** -tɪŋ ⓤⓢ -t̬ɪŋ **-ted** -tɪd ⓤⓢ -t̬ɪd
segmental segˈmen.tᵊl, səg-, sɪg- ⓤⓢ segˈmen.t̬ᵊl
segmentation ˌseg.menˈteɪ.ʃᵊn, -mənˈ-
segn|o ˈsen.j|əʊ, ˈseɪ.nj|əʊ ⓤⓢ ˈseɪ.nj|oʊ **-i** -i
Segovia sɪˈgəʊ.vi.ə, sə-, segˈəʊ- ⓤⓢ sɪˈgoʊ-, sə-
segregate (*n.*) ˈseg.rɪ.gət, -rə-, -geɪt, -gɪt ⓤⓢ -rə.gɪt

segre|gate (*v.*) ˈseg.rɪ|.geɪt, -rə- (US) -rə- **-gates** -geɪts **-gating** -geɪ.tɪŋ (US) -geɪ.t̬ɪŋ **-gated** -geɪ.tɪd (US) -geɪ.t̬ɪd
segregation ˌseg.rɪˈgeɪ.ʃən, -rəˈ- (US) -rəˈ-
segu|e ˈseg.weɪ, ˈseɪ.gweɪ, -gwi **-es** -z **-ing** -ɪŋ **-d** -d
seguidilla ˌseg.ɪˈdiː.jə, -li.ə (US) -əˈdiː.jə, ˌseɪ.gəˈ-, -ˈdiːl- **-s** -z
seich|e seɪʃ (US) seɪʃ, siːtʃ **-es** -ɪz
Seidlitz ˈsed.lɪts
seigneur senˈjɜːr, seɪˈnjɜːr; ˈseɪ.njər (US) seɪˈnjɝː, senˈjɝː **-s** -z **-ial** -i.əl
seignior *lord:* ˈseɪ.njər (US) ˈseɪ.njɚ; seɪˈnjɔːr **-s** -z
Seignior *surname:* ˈsiː.njər (US) -njɚ
seignior|y ˈseɪ.njər|.i (US) ˈseɪ- **-ies** -iz
Seiko® ˈseɪ.kəʊ (US) -koʊ
sein|e *net:* seɪn **-es** -z **-ing** -ɪŋ **-ed** -d
Seine *river in France:* seɪn, sen
Seinfeld ˈsaɪn.feld
Seir ˈsiː.ər (US) -ɚ
seis|e siːz **-es** -ɪz **-ing** -ɪŋ **-ed** -d
seisin ˈsiː.zɪn **-s** -z
seismic ˈsaɪz.mɪk (US) ˈsaɪz-, ˈsaɪs-
seismo- saɪz.məʊ-; saɪzˈmɒ- (US) saɪz.moʊ-, saɪs-, -mə-; saɪzˈmɑː-, saɪs-
Note: Prefix. Normally takes either primary or secondary stress on the first syllable, e.g. **seismograph** /ˈsaɪz.məʊ.grɑːf (US) -mə.græf/, **seismographic** /ˌsaɪz.məʊˈgræf.ɪk (US) -məˈ-/, or primary stress on the second syllable, e.g. **seismographer** /saɪzˈmɒg.rə.fər (US) -ˈmɑː.grə.fɚ/.
seismograph ˈsaɪz.məʊ.grɑːf, -græf (US) -mə.græf, ˈsaɪs-, -moʊ- **-s** -s
seismograph|er saɪzˈmɒg.rə.f|ər (US) -ˈmɑː.grə.f|ɚ, saɪs- **-ers** -əz (US) -ɚz **-y** -i
seismographic ˌsaɪz.məʊˈgræf.ɪk (US) -məˈ-, saɪs-, -moʊˈ-
seismologic|al ˌsaɪz.məˈlɒdʒ.ɪ.k|əl (US) -məˈlɑː.dʒɪ-, saɪs- **-ally** -əl.i (US) -li
seismolog|y saɪzˈmɒl.ə.dʒ|i (US) -ˈmɑː.lə-, seɪs- **-ist/s** -ɪst/s
seismometer saɪzˈmɒm.ɪ.tər, ˈ-ə- (US) -ˈmɑː.mə.t̬ɚ, saɪs- **-s** -z
seizable ˈsiː.zə.bl̩
seiz|e siːz **-es** -ɪz **-ing** -ɪŋ **-ed** -d
seizin ˈsiː.zɪn **-s** -z
seizure ˈsiː.ʒər (US) -ʒɚ **-s** -z
sejant ˈsiː.dʒənt
Sejanus sɪˈdʒeɪ.nəs, sə-, sedʒˈeɪ- (US) sɪˈdʒeɪ-
Sekhmet ˈsek.met
Sekondi-Takoradi ˌsek.ənˌdiː.tɑː.kəˈrɑː.di
selah ˈsiː.lə, -lɑː (US) ˈsiː.lə, ˈsel.ə, -ɑː **-s** -z
Selangor səˈlæŋ.ər, sɪ-, -ɔːr (US) selˈɑːŋ.gɔːr
Selassie səˈlæs.i (US) -ˈlæs-, -ˈlɑː.si
Selborne ˈsel.bɔːn, -bən (US) -bɔːrn, -bɚn
Selby ˈsel.bi
Selden ˈsel.dən
seldom ˈsel.dəm
select sɪˈlekt, sə- (US) sə- **-ness** -nəs, -nɪs **-s** -s **-ing** -ɪŋ **-ed** -ɪd **seˌlect comˈmittee**
selection sɪˈlek.ʃən, sə- (US) sə- **-s** -z
selective sɪˈlek.tɪv, sə- (US) sə- **-ly** -li **-ness** -nəs, -nɪs
selectivity ˌsɪl.ekˈtɪv.ə.ti, ˌsel-, ˌsiː.lekˈ-, -ɪ.ti; səˌlekˈ-, sɪ- (US) səˌlekˈtɪv.ə.t̬i, sɪ-; ˌsiː.lekˈ-
selector sɪˈlek.tər, sə- (US) səˈlek.tɚ **-s** -z
Selena sɪˈliː.nə, sə-
selenite *substance:* ˈsel.ɪ.naɪt, ˈ-ə- (US) ˈ-ə-
Selenite *inhabitant of moon:* sɪˈliː.naɪt, sə- (US) sɪˈliː-, sə-; ˈsel.ə- **-s** -s
selenium sɪˈliː.ni.əm, sə- (US) sə-
Seles ˈsel.ez, -əs
Seleuci|a sɪˈljuː.ʃi|.ə, sə-, -ˈluː-, -si- (US) səˈluː.ʃi-, ˈ-ʃ|ə **-an/s** -ən/z
Seleucid sɪˈljuː.sɪd, sə-, -ˈluː- (US) səˈluː- **-s** -z
Seleucus sɪˈljuː.kəs, sə-, -ˈluː- (US) səˈluː-
self- self-
Note: Many compounds beginning with **self-** have the stress pattern **ˌself'-**; these are likely to undergo stress shift when a stressed syllable follows closely, especially in adjectives or adjectives derived from verbs.
sel|f sel|f **-ves** -vz
self-abuse ˌself.əˈbjuːs
self-addressed ˌself.əˈdrest
self-appointed ˌself.əˈpɔɪn.tɪd (US) -t̬ɪd
self-assurance ˌself.əˈʃʊə.rənts (US) -ˈʃʊr.ənts
self-assured ˌself.əˈʃʊəd (US) -ˈʃʊrd
self-catering ˌselfˈkeɪ.tər.ɪŋ (US) -t̬ɚ-
self-centred, self-centered ˌselfˈsen.təd (US) -t̬ɚd **-ly** -li **-ness** -nəs, -nɪs
self-command ˌself.kəˈmɑːnd (US) -ˈmænd
self-confessed ˌself.kənˈfest
self-conscious ˌselfˈkɒn.tʃəs (US) -ˈkɑːnt.ʃəs **-ly** -li **-ness** -nəs, -nɪs
self-contained ˌself.kənˈteɪnd **-ly** -li **-ness** -nəs, -nɪs **-ment** -mənt
self-control ˌself.kənˈtrəʊl (US) -ˈtroʊl **-led** -d
self-critic|al ˌselfˈkrɪt.ɪ.k|əl (US) -ˈkrɪt̬- **-ally** -əl.i, -li
self-deception ˌself.dɪˈsep.ʃən
self-defence, self-defense ˌself.dɪˈfents
self-denial ˌself.dɪˈnaɪ.əl
self-denying ˌself.dɪˈnaɪ.ɪŋ
self-destruct ˌself.dɪˈstrʌkt **-s** -s **-ing** -ɪŋ **-ed** -ɪd **-ive** -ɪv **-ion** -ʃən
self-determination ˌself.dɪˌtɜː.mɪˈneɪ.ʃən (US) -ˌtɝː-
self-discipline ˌselfˈdɪs.ɪ.plɪn, ˈ-ə- **-d** -d
self-drive ˌselfˈdraɪv
self-effac|ing ˌself.ɪˈfeɪ.s|ɪŋ **-ingly** -ɪŋ.li **-ement** -mənt
self-employed ˌself.ɪmˈplɔɪd, -emˈ-
self-esteem ˌself.ɪˈstiːm, -əˈ-
self-evident ˌselfˈev.ɪ.dənt
self-explanatory ˌself.ɪkˈsplæn.ə.tər.i, -ekˈ-, ˈ-ɪ- (US) -tɔːr-
self-fulfilling ˌself.fʊlˈfɪl.ɪŋ
self-governing ˌselfˈgʌv.ən.ɪŋ (US) -ɚ.nɪŋ
self-government ˌselfˈgʌv.ən.mənt, -əm-, -və.mənt (US) -ɚn.mənt
self-heal ˌselfˈhiːl
self-help ˌselfˈhelp
self-image ˌselfˈɪm.ɪdʒ **-s** -ɪz
self-importan|ce ˌself.ɪmˈpɔː.tən|ts (US) -ˈpɔːr- **-t/ly** -t/li
self-imposed ˌself.ɪmˈpəʊzd (US) -ˈpoʊzd
self-indulgen|ce ˌself.ɪnˈdʌl.dʒən|ts **-t/ly** -t/li
self-inflicted ˌself.ɪnˈflɪk.tɪd
self-interest ˌselfˈɪn.trəst, -trəst; -tər.əst, -est, -ɪst (US) -ˈɪn.trɪst, -trəst, -trest; -t̬ɚ.ɪst, -əst, -est
selfish ˈsel.fɪʃ **-ly** -li **-ness** -nəs, -nɪs
selfless ˈsel.fləs, -flɪs **-ly** -li **-ness** -nəs, -nɪs
self-made ˌselfˈmeɪd
self-pity ˌselfˈpɪt.i (US) -ˈpɪt̬-
self-portrait ˌselfˈpɔː.trɪt, -trət, -treɪt (US) -ˈpɔːr.trɪt, -treɪt **-s** -s
self-possessed ˌself.pəˈzest
self-possession ˌself.pəˈzeʃ.ən
self-preservation ˌselfˌprez.əˈveɪ.ʃən (US) -ɚˈ-
self-proclaimed ˌself.prəʊˈkleɪmd (US) -proʊˈ-, -prəˈ-
self-raising ˌselfˈreɪ.zɪŋ **ˌself-raising ˈflour, selfˌ-raising ˈflour**
self-relian|ce ˌself.rɪˈlaɪ.ən|ts, -rəˈ- **-t** -t
self-respect ˌself.rɪˈspekt, -rəˈ-
self-respecting ˌself.rɪˈspek.tɪŋ, -rəˈ-
self-restraint ˌself.rɪˈstreɪnt, -rəˈ-
Selfridge ˈsel.frɪdʒ **-'s** -ɪz
Selfridges® ˈsel.frɪdʒ.ɪz
self-righteous ˌselfˈraɪ.tʃəs, -tjəs (US) -tʃəs **-ly** -li **-ness** -nəs, -nɪs
self-rising ˌselfˈraɪ.zɪŋ **ˌself-rising ˈflour, selfˌ-rising ˈflour**

self-rul|e ˌselfˈruːl **-ing** -ɪŋ
self-sacrific|e ˌselfˈsæk.rɪ.faɪs, -rə- **-ing/ly** -ɪŋ/li
selfsame ˈself.seɪm
self-satisfaction ˌselfˌsæt.ɪsˈfæk.ʃᵊn ⓤⓢ -ˌsæt̬-
self-satisfied ˌselfˈsæt.ɪs.faɪd ⓤⓢ -ˈsæt̬-
self-service ˌselfˈsɜː.vɪs ⓤⓢ -ˈsɝː-
self-starter ˌselfˈstɑː.təʳ ⓤⓢ -ˈstɑːr.t̬ɚ **-s** -z
self-styled ˌselfˈstaɪld
self-sufficien|cy ˌself.səˈfɪʃ.ᵊn|*t*.si **-t** -t
self-taught ˌselfˈtɔːt ⓤⓢ -ˈtɑːt, -ˈtɔːt
self-will ˌselfˈwɪl **-ed** -d
self-winding ˌselfˈwaɪn.dɪŋ
Selhurst ˈsel.hɜːst ⓤⓢ -hɝːst
Selina səˈliː.nə
Selkirk ˈsel.kɜːk ⓤⓢ -kɝːk
sell (S) sel **-s** -z **-ing** -ɪŋ **sold** səʊld ⓤⓢ soʊld **seller/s** ˈsel.əʳ/z ⓤⓢ -ɚ/z
Sellafield ˈsel.ə.fiːld
Sellar ˈsel.əʳ ⓤⓢ -ɚ
sell-by ˈsel.baɪ ˈ**sell-by** ˌ**date**
Sellers ˈsel.əz ⓤⓢ -ɚz
sellotap|e ˈsel.*əʊ*.teɪp ⓤⓢ -oʊ- **-es** -s **-ing** -ɪŋ **-ed** -t
sellout ˈsel.aʊt **-s** -s
Selma ˈsel.mə
Selous səˈluː
Selsey ˈsel.si
Selston ˈsel.stᵊn
seltzer (S) ˈselt.səʳ ⓤⓢ -sɚ **-s** -z
selva ˈsel.və **-s** -z
selvag|e, selvedg|e ˈsel.vɪdʒ **-es** -ɪz
selves *(plur. of* **self***)* selvz
Selwyn ˈsel.wɪn
Selznick ˈselz.nɪk
semantic sɪˈmæn.tɪk, sə-, semˈæn-, siːˈmæn- ⓤⓢ səˈmæn.t̬ɪk, sɪ- **-s** -s **-ally** -ᵊl.i, -li
semanticism sɪˈmæn.tɪ.sɪ.zᵊm, sə-, semˈæn-, siːˈmæn- ⓤⓢ səˈmæn.t̬ə-, sɪ-
semanticist sɪˈmæn.tɪ.sɪst, sə-, semˈæn-, siːˈmæn-, -tə- ⓤⓢ səˈmæn.t̬ə-, sɪ- **-s** -s
semanticiz|e, -is|e sɪˈmæn.tɪ.saɪz, sə-, semˈæn-, siːˈmæn-, -tə- ⓤⓢ səˈmæn.t̬ə-, sɪ- **-es** -ɪz **-ing** -ɪŋ **-ed** -d
semaphore ˈsem.ə.fɔːʳ ⓤⓢ -fɔːr **-s** -z **-ing** -ɪŋ **-ed** -d
semaphoric ˌsem.əˈfɒr.ɪk ⓤⓢ -ˈfɔːr- **-ally** -ᵊl.i, -li
semasiology sɪˌmeɪ.siˈɒl.ə.dʒi, sə-, semˌeɪ-, -ziˈ- ⓤⓢ sɪˌmeɪ.siˈɑː.lə-
sematology ˌsem.əˈtɒl.ə.dʒi, ˌsiː.məˈ- ⓤⓢ -ˈtɑː.lə-
semblanc|e ˈsem.blən*t*s **-es** -ɪz
seme siːm **-s** -z
Semele ˈsem.ɪ.li ⓤⓢ ˈ-ə-
sememe ˈsiː.miːm ⓤⓢ ˈsem.iːm **-s** -z
sememic sɪˈmiː.mɪk, sə- ⓤⓢ sə-, sɪ- **-s** -s
semen ˈsiː.mən, -men ⓤⓢ -mən
semester sɪˈmes.təʳ, sə- ⓤⓢ səˈmes.tɚ **-s** -z
semi- sem.ɪ-, -i- ⓤⓢ sem.ɪ-, -i-, -aɪ-, -ə-
Note: Many compounds beginning with **semi-** have the stress pattern ˈ**semi**ˌ-; these are likely to undergo stress shift when a stressed syllable follows closely, especially in adjectives and adjectives derived from verbs.
semi *house:* ˈsem.i **-s** -z
semiautomatic ˌsem.i.ɔː.təˈmæt.ɪk ⓤⓢ -ɑː.t̬əˈmæt̬.ɪk, ˌ-aɪ-, -ɔː- **-s** -s
semiautonomous ˌsem.i.ɔːˈtɒn.ə.məs ⓤⓢ -ɑːˈtɑː.nə-, ˌ-aɪ-, -ɔːˈ-
semibreve ˈsem.ɪ.briːv, -i- **-s** -z
semicircle ˈsem.ɪˌsɜː.kl̩, -iˌ- ⓤⓢ -ˌsɝː-, -aɪˌ- **-s** -z
semicircular ˌsem.ɪˈsɜː.kjə.ləʳ, -iˈ-, -kjʊ- ⓤⓢ -ˈsɝː.kjə.lɚ, -aiˈ-
semicolon ˌsem.ɪˈkəʊ.lən, ˈsem.ɪˌkəʊ-, -lɒn ⓤⓢ ˈsem.ɪˌkoʊ.lən **-s** -z
semiconductivity ˌsem.ɪˌkɒn.dʌkˈtɪv.ə.ti, -iˌ-, -ɪ.ti ⓤⓢ -ˌkɑːn.dʌkˈtɪv.ə.t̬i, -aɪˌ-
semiconduc|tor ˌsem.ɪ.kənˈdʌk|.təʳ, -i- ⓤⓢ -tɚ, -aɪ- **-tors** -təz ⓤⓢ -tɚz **-ting** -tɪŋ
semiconscious ˌsem.ɪˈkɒn.*t*ʃəs, -iˈ- ⓤⓢ -ˈkɑːn-, -aɪˈ- **-ness** -nəs, -nɪs
semidesert ˌsem.ɪˈdez.ət, -iˈ- ⓤⓢ -ɚt, -aɪˈ- **-s** -s
semidetached ˌsem.ɪ.dɪˈtætʃt, -i- ⓤⓢ -ɪ-, -i-, ˌ-aɪ-
semifinal ˌsem.ɪˈfaɪ.nᵊl, -iˈ- ⓤⓢ -ɪˈ-, -iˈ-, -aɪˈ- **-s** -z
semifinalist ˌsem.ɪˈfaɪ.nᵊl.ɪst, -iˈ- ⓤⓢ -ɪˈ-, -iˈ-, -aɪˈ- **-s** -s
semiformal ˌsem.ɪˈfɔː.mᵊl, -iˈ- ⓤⓢ -ˈfɔːr-, -aɪˈ-
Sémillon ˌseɪ.miːˈjɔ̃ː*ŋ* ⓤⓢ -ˈjõʊ*n*, ˌsem.iːˈ-
seminal ˈsem.ɪ.nᵊl, ˈsiː.mɪ-, -mə- ⓤⓢ ˈsem.ə- **-ly** -i
seminar ˈsem.ɪ.nɑːʳ, ˈ-ə- ⓤⓢ -ə.nɑːr **-s** -z
seminarist ˈsem.ɪ.nᵊr.ɪst ⓤⓢ ˌsem.ɪˈner- **-s** -s
seminar|y ˈsem.ɪ.nᵊr|.i ⓤⓢ -ner- **-ies** -iz
seminiferous ˌsem.ɪˈnɪf.ᵊr.əs
Seminole ˈsem.ɪ.nəʊl ⓤⓢ -noʊl **-s** -z
semiolog|y ˌsem.iˈɒl.ə.dʒ|i, ˌsiː.miˈ- ⓤⓢ ˌsiː.miˈɑː.lə-, ˌsem.iˈ- **-ist/s** -ɪst/s
semiotic ˌsem.iˈɒt.ɪk, ˌsiː.miˈ- ⓤⓢ ˌsiː.miˈɑː.t̬ɪk, ˌsem.iˈ- **-s** -s
Semipalatinsk ˌsem.i.pælˈæt.ɪnsk ⓤⓢ -pəˈlɑː-
semiprecious ˌsem.ɪˈpreʃ.əs, -iˈ- ⓤⓢ -ɪˈ-, -iˈ-, -aɪˈ-
semiprofessional ˌsem.ɪ.prəˈfeʃ.ᵊn.ᵊl, -i- ⓤⓢ -ɪ.prəˈ-, -i-, ˌ-aɪ-, -proʊˈ-
semiquaver ˈsem.ɪˌkweɪ.vəʳ, -iˌ- ⓤⓢ -ɪˌ-, -iˌ-, -vɚ **-s** -z
Semiramide ˌsem.ɪˈrɑː.mɪ.deɪ, -ˈræm.ɪ-, ˈ-ə-, -di
Semiramis semˈɪr.ə.mɪs, sɪˈmɪr- ⓤⓢ sɪˈmɪr-
semiretired ˌsem.ɪ.rɪˈtaɪəd, -i- ⓤⓢ -taɪrd, ˌ-aɪ-
semiretirement ˌsem.ɪ.rɪˈtaɪə.mənt, -i- ⓤⓢ -ˈtaɪr-, ˌ-aɪ-
semiskilled ˌsem.ɪˈskɪld, -iˈ- ⓤⓢ -ɪˈ-, -iˈ-, -aɪˈ-
semiskimmed ˌsem.ɪˈskɪmd, -iˈ- ⓤⓢ -ɪˈ-, -iˈ-, -aɪˈ-
Semite ˈsiː.maɪt, ˈsem.aɪt ⓤⓢ ˈsem.aɪt **-s** -s
Semitic sɪˈmɪt.ɪk, sə-, semˈɪt- ⓤⓢ səˈmɪt̬-
Semitism ˈsem.ɪ.tɪ.zᵊm, ˈ-ə- ⓤⓢ ˈ-ə-
semitone ˈsem.ɪ.təʊn, -i- ⓤⓢ -toʊn, -aɪ- **-s** -z
semitrailer ˈsem.ɪˌtreɪ.ləʳ, -iˌ- ⓤⓢ -lɚ, -aɪˌ- **-s** -z
semitropical ˌsem.ɪˈtrɒp.ɪ.kᵊl, -iˈ- ⓤⓢ -ˈtrɑː.pɪ-, -aɪˈ-
semivowel ˈsem.ɪˌvaʊəl **-s** -z
semolina ˌsem.ᵊlˈiː.nə ⓤⓢ -əˈliː-
semology semˈɒl.ə.dʒi, siːˈmɒl- ⓤⓢ semˈɑː.lə-, siːˈmɑː-
Semon ˈsiː.mən
Sempill ˈsem.pᵊl
sempiternal ˌsem.pɪˈtɜː.nᵊl ⓤⓢ -ˈtɝː- **-ly** -i
Semple ˈsem.pl̩
semplice ˈsem.plɪ.tʃeɪ
sempre ˈsem.preɪ
sempstress ˈsem*p*.strɪs, -strəs ⓤⓢ -strɪs **-es** -ɪz
Semtex® ˈsem.teks
sen sen
senary ˈsiː.nᵊr.i
senate (S) ˈsen.ɪt, -ət ⓤⓢ -ɪt **-s** -s
senator (S) ˈsen.ə.təʳ, ˈ-ɪ- ⓤⓢ -ə.t̬ɚ **-s** -z
senatorial ˌsen.əˈtɔː.ri.əl ⓤⓢ -ˈtɔːr.i- **-ly** -i
send send **-s** -z **-ing** -ɪŋ **sent** sent **sender/s** ˈsen.dəʳ/z ⓤⓢ -dɚ/z
Sendai ˈsen.daɪ
Sendak ˈsen.dæk
send-off ˈsend.ɒf ⓤⓢ -ɑːf **-s** -s
send-up ˈsend.ʌp **-s** -s
sene ˈseɪ.neɪ
Seneca ˈsen.ɪ.kə **-s** -z
Senegal ˌsen.ɪˈɡɔːl ⓤⓢ ˌsen.ɪˈɡɔːl, -ˈɡɑːl; ˈsen.ə.ɡᵊl
Senegalese ˌsen.ɪ.ɡəˈliːz, -ɡɔːˈ- ⓤⓢ -ɡəˈ-
Senegambia ˌsen.ɪˈɡæm.bi.ə
senescen|ce sɪˈnes.ᵊn|*t*s, sə-, senˈes- ⓤⓢ səˈnes- **-t** -t

seneschal 'sen.ɪ.ʃᵊl US '-ə- **-s** -z
Senghenydd ˌseŋ'hen.ɪð
Senghor 'seŋ.gɔːʳ *as if French:* 'sæ̃ŋ- US sæ̃n'gɔːr
senhor (S) sen'jɔːʳ US -'jɔːr, seɪ'njɔːr **-s** -z **-es** -z *stress shift:* ˌSenhor So'ares
senhora (S) sen'jɔː.rə US -'jɔːr.ə, seɪ'njɔːr- **-s** -z
senhorita (S) ˌsen.jɔː'riː.tə, -jə'- US ˌsen.jə'riː.t̬ə, ˌseɪ.njə'-, -njɔː'- **-s** -z
senile 'siː.naɪl US 'siː-, 'sen.aɪl
senility sɪ'nɪl.ə.ti, sə-, sen'ɪl-, -ɪ.ti US sə'nɪl.ə.t̬i
senior (S) 'siː.ni.əʳ, 'njəʳ US -njɚ **-s** -z ˌ**senior** '**citizen**
seniorit|y ˌsiː.ni'ɒr.ə.t|i, -ɪ.t|i US siː'njɔːr.ə.t̬|i **-ies** -iz
seniti 'sen.ɪ.ti US -ə.t̬i
Senlac 'sen.læk
senna (S) 'sen.ə
Sennacherib sen'æk.ə.rɪb, sɪ'næk-, sə- US sə'næk.ɚ.ɪb
sennet 'sen.ɪt, -ət US -ɪt
sennight 'sen.aɪt US -aɪt, -ɪt **-s** -s
señor, senor (S) sen'jɔːʳ US -'jɔːr, seɪ'njɔːr **-s** -z *stress shift:* ˌSeñor 'Lopez
señora, senora (S) sen'jɔː.rə US -'jɔːr.ə, seɪ'njɔːr- **-s** -z
señorita, senorita (S) ˌsen.jɔː'riː.tə, -jə'- US ˌsen.jə'riː.t̬ə, ˌseɪ.njə'-, -njɔː'- *stress shift:* ˌSeñorita 'Lopez
sensate 'sen.seɪt US -seɪt, -sɪt **-ly** -li
sensation sen'seɪ.ʃᵊn, sᵊn- US sen- **-s** -z
sensational sen'seɪ.ʃᵊn.ᵊl, sᵊn-, -'seɪʃ.nᵊl US sen- **-ly** -i
sensational|ism sen'seɪ.ʃᵊn.ᵊl|.ɪ.zᵊm, sᵊn-, -'seɪʃ.nᵊl- US sen- **-ist/s** -ɪst/s
sensationaliz|e, -is|e ˌsen'seɪ.ʃᵊn.ᵊl.aɪz **-es** -ɪz **-ing** -ɪŋ **-ed** -d
sens|e sents **-es** -ɪz **-ing** -ɪŋ **-ed** -d ˌ**sense of** '**humo(u)r**
senseless 'sent.sləs, -slɪs **-ly** -li **-ness** -nəs, -nɪs
sensibilit|y ˌsent.sɪ'bɪl.ə.t|i, -sə'-, -ɪ.t|i US -sə'bɪl.ə.t̬|i **-ies** -iz
sensib|le 'sent.sɪ.b|l̩, -sə- US -sə- **-ly** -li
sensitive 'sent.sɪ.tɪv, -sə- US -sə.t̬ɪv **-s** -z **-ly** -li **-ness** -nəs, -nɪs
sensitivit|y ˌsent.sɪ'tɪv.ə.t|i, -sə'-, -ɪ.t|i US -sə'tɪv.ə.t̬|i **-ies** -iz
sensitization, -isa- ˌsent.sɪ.taɪ'zeɪ.ʃᵊn, -sə-, -tɪ'- US -sə.tɪ'-
sensitiz|e, -is|e 'sent.sɪ.taɪz, -sə- US -sə- **-es** -ɪz **-ing** -ɪŋ **-ed** -d
Sensodyne® 'sent.səʊ.daɪn US -soʊ-, -sə-
sensor 'sent.səʳ US -sɚ **-s** -z
sensorial sent'sɔː.ri.əl US -'sɔːr.i- **-ly** -i
sensor|y 'sent.sᵊr|.i **-ily** -ᵊl.i, -ɪ.li
sensual 'sent.sjʊəl, -sju.əl, -ʃʊəl, -ʃu.əl US -ʃu.əl **-ly** -i **-ness** -nəs, -nɪs
sensual|ism 'sent.sjʊə.l|ɪ.zᵊm, -sju.ᵊl|.ɪ-, -ʃʊə.l|ɪ-, -ʃu.ᵊl|.ɪ- US -ʃu.ə.l|ɪ- **-ist/s** -ɪst/s
sensuality ˌsent.sju'æl.ə.ti, -ʃu'-, -ɪ.ti US -ʃu'æl.ə.t̬i
sensuous 'sent.sjʊəs, -sju.əs, -ʃʊəs, -ʃu.əs US -ʃu.əs **-ly** -li **-ness** -nəs, -nɪs
Sensurround® 'sent.sə.raʊnd
sent *(from* **send***)* sent
sentenc|e 'sen.tənts US -t̬ənts, -tᵊnts **-es** -ɪz **-ing** -ɪŋ **-ed** -t
sentential sen'ten.tʃᵊl, sən- US sen'tent.ʃᵊl **-ly** -li
sententious sen'ten.tʃəs, sən- US sen'tent.ʃəs **-ly** -li **-ness** -nəs, -nɪs
sentience 'sen.tʃᵊnts, -tʃi.ənts US 'sent.ʃᵊnts, -ʃi.ənts
sentient 'sen.tʃᵊnt, -tʃi.ənt US 'sent.ʃᵊnt, -ʃi.ənt **-ly** -li
sentiment 'sen.tɪ.mənt, -tə- US -t̬ə- **-s** -s
sentimental ˌsen.tɪ'men.tᵊl, -tə'- US -t̬ə'men.t̬ᵊl **-ly** -i **-ism** -ɪ.zᵊm **-ist/s** -ɪst/s
sentimentality ˌsen.tɪ.men'tæl.ə.ti, -tə-, -mən-, -ɪ.ti US -t̬ə.men'tæl.ə.t̬i
sentimentalization, -isa- ˌsen.tɪ.men.tᵊl.aɪ'zeɪ.ʃᵊn, -ˌmen-, -tə-, -ɪ'- US -t̬əˌmen.t̬ᵊl.ɪ'-
sentimentaliz|e, -is|e ˌsen.tɪ'men.tᵊl.aɪz, -tə'- US -t̬ə'men.t̬ə.laɪz **-es** -ɪz **-ing** -ɪŋ **-ed** -d
sentinel 'sen.tɪ.nᵊl, -tə- US -t̬ɪ-, -tᵊn.ᵊl **-s** -z
sentr|y 'sen.tr|i **-ies** -iz '**sentry** ˌ**box**
sentry-go 'sen.tri.gəʊ US -goʊ
senza 'sent.sə
Seoul səʊl US soʊl
sepal 'sep.əl, 'siː.pəl US 'siː.pᵊl **-s** -z
separability ˌsep.ᵊr.ə'bɪl.ə.ti, -ɪ.ti US -ə.t̬i
separab|le 'sep.ᵊr.ə.b|l̩ **-ly** -li **-leness** -l̩.nəs, -l̩.nɪs
separate *(adj.)* 'sep.ᵊr.ət, -ɪt, '-rət, -rɪt US -ɚ.ɪt, '-rɪt **-ly** -li **-ness** -nəs, -nɪs
separ|ate *(v.)* 'sep.ᵊr|.eɪt US -ə.r|eɪt **-ates** -eɪts **-ating** -eɪ.tɪŋ US -eɪ.t̬ɪŋ **-ated** -eɪ.tɪd US -eɪ.t̬ɪd **-ator/s** -eɪ.təʳ/z US -eɪ.t̬ɚ/z
separates 'sep.ᵊr.əts, -ɪts, '-rəts, '-rɪts US -ɚ.ɪts, '-rɪts
separation ˌsep.ᵊr'eɪ.ʃᵊn US -ə'reɪ- **-s** -z
separat|ism 'sep.ᵊr.ə.t|ɪ.zᵊm, '-rə- **-ist/s** -ɪst/s
Sephardi sə'fɑː.di, sef'ɑː- US sə'fɑːr.di; -ˌfɑːr'diː **Sephardim** sə'fɑː.dɪm, sef'ɑː- US sə'fɑːr.dɪm; -ˌfɑːr'diːm
Sephardic sə'fɑː.dɪk, sef'ɑː- US sə'fɑːr-
sepia 'siː.pi.ə
sepoy 'siː.pɔɪ **-s** -z
seppuku sep'uː.kuː
seps|is 'sep.s|ɪs **-es** -iːz
Sept. *(abbrev. for* **September***)* sep'tem.bəʳ, səp-, sɪp- US sep'tem.bɚ
September sep'tem.bəʳ, səp-, sɪp- US sep'tem.bɚ **-s** -z
Septembrist sep'tem.brɪst, səp-, sɪp- US sep- **-s** -s
septennial sep'ten.i.əl
septet, septette sep'tet **-s** -s
septic 'sep.tɪk ˌ**septic** '**tank,** '**septic** ˌ**tank** US '**septic** ˌ**tank**
septic(a)emia ˌsep.tɪ'siː.mi.ə US -tə'-
septillion sep'tɪl.jən **-s** -z
Septimus 'sep.tɪ.məs
septuagenarian ˌsep.tjʊə.dʒɪ'neə.ri.ən, -tʃʊə-, -dʒə'- US -tu.ə.dʒə'ner.i-, -tju- **-s** -z
Septuagesima ˌsep.tjʊə'dʒes.ɪ.mə, -tʃʊə'-, '-ə- US -tu.ə'dʒes.ɪ-, -tju-, -'dʒeɪ.zɪ-
Septuagint 'sep.tjʊə.dʒɪnt, -tʃʊə- US -tu.ə-, -tju-
sept|um 'sep.t|əm **-ums** -əmz **-a** -ə
septuple 'sep.tjʊ.pl̩, -tjuː- US sep'tʌp.əl; 'tuː.pəl
septuplet sep'tjuː.plət, -plɪt, 'sep.tjʊ.plət, -plɪt US -'tuː- **-s** -s
sepulcher 'sep.ᵊl.kə US -kɚ **-s** -z
sepulchral sɪ'pʌl.krᵊl, sə-, sep'ʌl- US sə'pʌl- **-ly** -i
sepulchre 'sep.ᵊl.kəʳ US -kɚ **-s** -z
sepulture 'sep.ᵊl.tʃəʳ, -ˌtjʊəʳ US -tʃɚ
sequel 'siː.kwᵊl **-s** -z
sequel|a sɪ'kwiː.l|ə, sə- US sɪ'kwiː-, -'kwel|.ə **-ae** -iː
sequenc|e 'siː.kwənts US -kwənts, -kwents **-es** -ɪz **-ing** -ɪŋ **-ed** -t
sequential sɪ'kwen.tʃᵊl US -'kwent.ʃᵊl **-ly** -i
sequest|er sɪ'kwes.t|əʳ, sə- US sɪ'kwes.t|ɚ **-ers** -əz US -ɚz **-ering** -ᵊr.ɪŋ **-ered** -əd US -ɚd
seques|trate sɪ'kwes|.treɪt, sə-; 'siː.kwə.s|treɪt US sɪ'kwes|.treɪt; 'siː.kwə.s|treɪt, 'sek.wə- **-trates** -treɪts **-trating** -treɪ.tɪŋ US -treɪ.t̬ɪŋ **-trated** -treɪ.tɪd US -treɪ.t̬ɪd
sequestration ˌsiː.kwes'treɪ.ʃᵊn, ˌsek.wes'-, -wə'streɪ-, -wɪ'- US ˌsiː.kwə'streɪ-, ˌsek.wə'-; sɪˌkwes'treɪ- **-s** -z
sequin 'siː.kwɪn **-s** -z **-(n)ed** -d
sequoia sɪ'kwɔɪə, sek'wɔɪə US sɪ'kwɔɪə **-s** -z
seraglio ser'ɑː.li.əʊ, sɪ'rɑː-, sə-, -'ɑːl.jəʊ US sɪ'ræl.joʊ, -'rɑːl- **-s** -z
serai ser'aɪ, sə'raɪ US sɪ'reɪ.i, sə- **-s** -z

seraph (S) 'ser.əf -s -s -im -ɪm
seraphic ser'æf.ɪk, sɪ'ræf-, sə- ⓤⓢ sə'ræf- -al -əl -ally -əl.i, -li
Serapis 'ser.ə.pɪs, sə'reɪ-
Serb sɜːb ⓤⓢ sɝːb -s -z
Serbi|a 'sɜː.bi|.ə ⓤⓢ 'sɝː- -an/s -ən/z
Serbo-Croat ˌsɜː.bəʊ'krəʊ.æt ⓤⓢ ˌsɝː.boʊ'kroʊ- -s -s
Serbo-Croatian ˌsɜː.bəʊ.krəʊ'eɪ.ʃən ⓤⓢ ˌsɝː.boʊ.kroʊ'- -s -z
sere sɪər ⓤⓢ sɪr -s -z
Serena sə'riː.nə, sɪ-, -'reɪ- ⓤⓢ sə'riː-
serenad|e ˌser.ə'neɪd, -ɪ'- ⓤⓢ -ə'- -es -z -ing -ɪŋ -ed -ɪd
serenata ˌser.ɪ'nɑː.tə, -ə'- ⓤⓢ -ə'nɑː.t̬ə -s -z
serendipit|y ˌser.ən'dɪp.ə.t|i, -en'-, -ɪ.t|i ⓤⓢ -ən'dɪp.ə.t̬|i -ous -əs
seren|e sɪ'riːn, sə- ⓤⓢ sə- -est -ɪst, -əst -ely -li
Serengeti ˌser.ən'get.i, -əŋ'-, -ɪn'-, -ɪŋ'- ⓤⓢ -ən'get̬-
serenity sɪ'ren.ɪ.ti, sə-, -ə.ti ⓤⓢ sə'ren.ə.t̬i
serf sɜːf ⓤⓢ sɝːf -s -s -dom -dəm
serg|e (S) sɜːdʒ ⓤⓢ sɝːdʒ -es -ɪz
sergeant (S) 'sɑː.dʒənt ⓤⓢ 'sɑːr- -s -s ˌsergeant 'major
sergeant-at-arms, ˌsɑː.dʒənt.ət'ɑːmz ⓤⓢ ˌsɑːr.dʒənt.ət'ɑːrmz **sergeants-at-arms** ˌsɑː.dʒənts- ⓤⓢ ˌsɑːr.dʒənts-
Sergei 'seə.geɪ, 'sɜː-, -'- ⓤⓢ 'ser.geɪ, 'sɝː-
serial 'sɪə.ri.əl ⓤⓢ 'sɪr.i- -s -z 'serial ˌkiller; 'serial ˌnumber
serialization, -isa- ˌsɪə.ri.əl.aɪ'zeɪ.ʃən, -ɪ'- ⓤⓢ ˌsɪr.i.əl.ɪ'- -s -z
serializ|e, -is|e 'sɪə.ri.əl.aɪz ⓤⓢ 'sɪr.i.ə.laɪz -es -ɪz -ing -ɪŋ -ed -d
seriatim ˌsɪə.ri'eɪ.tɪm, ˌser.i'-, -'ɑː- ⓤⓢ ˌsɪr.i'eɪ.t̬ɪm
series 'sɪə.riːz, -rɪz ⓤⓢ 'sɪr.iːz, 'siː.riːz
serif 'ser.ɪf -s -s
Serifos 'ser.ɪ.fɒs ⓤⓢ sə'raɪ.fəs; 'ser.ɪ.fɑːs
serin 'ser.ɪn -s -z
seringa sɪ'rɪŋ.gə, sə- ⓤⓢ sə- -s -z
Seringapatam səˌrɪŋ.gə.pə'tɑːm, sɪ-, -'tæm
seriocomic ˌsɪə.ri.əʊ'kɒm.ɪk ⓤⓢ ˌsir.i.oʊ'kɑː.mɪk -ally -əl.i, -li
serious 'sɪə.ri.əs ⓤⓢ 'sɪr.i- -ly -li -ness -nəs, -nɪs
serjeant (S) 'sɑː.dʒənt ⓤⓢ 'sɑːr- -s -s ˌserjeant-at-'arms
Serjeantson 'sɑː.dʒənt.sən ⓤⓢ 'sɑːr-
sermon 'sɜː.mən ⓤⓢ 'sɝː- -s -z
sermonette ˌsɜː.mə'net ⓤⓢ ˌsɝː- -s -s
sermoniz|e, -is|e 'sɜː.mə.naɪz ⓤⓢ 'sɝː- -es -ɪz -ing -ɪŋ -ed -d
serolog|y sɪ'rɒl.ə.dʒ|i, sɪə- ⓤⓢ sɪ'rɑː.lə- -ist/s -ɪst/s
seronegative ˌsɪə.rəʊ'neg.ə.tɪv ⓤⓢ ˌsɪr.oʊ'neg.ə.t̬ɪv
seropositive ˌsɪə.rəʊ'pɒz.ɪ.tɪv, '-ə- ⓤⓢ ˌsɪr.oʊ'pɑː.zə.t̬ɪv
Serota sə'rəʊ.tə, sɪ- ⓤⓢ -'roʊ.t̬ə
serotonin ˌser.ə'təʊ.nɪn, ˌsɪə.rə'- ⓤⓢ ˌser.ə'toʊ-, ˌsɪr-
serous 'sɪə.rəs ⓤⓢ 'sɪr.əs
Serpell 'sɜː.pəl ⓤⓢ 'sɝː-
Serpens 'sɜː.penz, -pənz ⓤⓢ 'sɝː-
serpent 'sɜː.pənt ⓤⓢ 'sɝː- -s -s
serpentine (S) 'sɜː.pən.taɪn ⓤⓢ 'sɝː-
SERPS, Serps sɜːps ⓤⓢ sɝːps
serrate 'ser.ɪt, -eɪt, -ət ⓤⓢ -eɪt, -ɪt
serrated sɪ'reɪ.tɪd, sə-, ser'eɪ- ⓤⓢ 'ser.eɪ.t̬ɪd
serration sɪ'reɪ.ʃən, sə-, ser'eɪ- ⓤⓢ sə'reɪ-, ser'eɪ- -s -z
serried 'ser.id ˌserried 'ranks
ser|um 'sɪə.r|əm ⓤⓢ 'sɪr|.əm -ums -əmz -a -ə
servant 'sɜː.vənt ⓤⓢ 'sɝː- -s -s
serv|e sɜːv ⓤⓢ sɝːv -es -z -ing -ɪŋ -ed -d -er/s -ər/z ⓤⓢ -ɚ/z
server|y 'sɜː.vər|.i ⓤⓢ 'sɝː- -ies -iz
servic|e (S) 'sɜː.vɪs ⓤⓢ 'sɝː- -es -ɪz -ing -ɪŋ -ed -t 'service ˌcharge; 'service ˌstation
serviceability ˌsɜː.vɪ.sə'bɪl.ə.ti, -ɪ.ti ⓤⓢ ˌsɝː.vɪ.sə'bɪl.ə.t̬i
serviceab|le 'sɜː.vɪ.sə.b|l̩ ⓤⓢ 'sɝː- -ly -li -leness -l̩.nəs, -l̩.nɪs
service|man 'sɜː.vɪs|.mən, -mæn ⓤⓢ 'sɝː- -men -mən
service|woman 'sɜː.vɪs|ˌwʊm.ən ⓤⓢ 'sɝː- -women -wɪm.ɪn
serviette ˌsɜː.vi'et, -s ⓤⓢ ˌsɝː-
servile 'sɜː.vaɪl ⓤⓢ 'sɝː.vəl, -vaɪl -ly -li
servility sɜː'vɪl.ə.ti, -ɪ.ti ⓤⓢ sɝː'vɪl.ə.t̬i
serving 'sɜː.vɪŋ ⓤⓢ 'sɝː- -s -z
serving-spoon 'sɜː.vɪŋ.spuːn ⓤⓢ 'sɝː- -s -z
servitor 'sɜː.vɪ.tər ⓤⓢ 'sɝː.və.t̬ɚ -s -z
servitude 'sɜː.vɪ.tjuːd, -tʃuːd ⓤⓢ 'sɝː.və.tuːd, -tjuːd
servo 'sɜː.vəʊ ⓤⓢ 'sɝː.voʊ -s -z
servomechanism 'sɜː.vəʊˌmek.ə.nɪ.zəm, ˌsɜː.vəʊ'mek- ⓤⓢ ˌsɝː.voʊ'mek- -s -z
servomotor 'sɜː.vəʊˌməʊ.tər ⓤⓢ 'sɝː.voʊˌmoʊ.t̬ɚ -s -z
sesame (S) 'ses.ə.mi -s -z 'sesame ˌseed
Sesotho ses'uː.tuː, sɪ'suː-, sə-, -'səʊ.θəʊ ⓤⓢ ses'uː.tuː, sɪ'suː-, sə-, -'soʊ.θoʊ
sesqui- 'ses.kwɪ-
sesquicentennial ˌses.kwɪ.sen'ten.i.əl, -sən'- ⓤⓢ -sen'-
sesquipedalian ˌses.kwɪ.pɪ'deɪ.li.ən, -pə'-, -ped'eɪ- ⓤⓢ -pə'deɪ-, -'deɪl.jən
sessile 'ses.aɪl ⓤⓢ -ɪl, -aɪl
session 'seʃ.ən -s -z
sessional 'seʃ.ən.əl -s -z
sesterc|e 'ses.tɜːs, -təs ⓤⓢ -tɝːs -es -ɪz
sesterti|um ses'tɜː.ti|.əm, -ʃi- ⓤⓢ -'tɝː.ʃi-, '-ʃ|əm -a -ə
sestet ses'tet ⓤⓢ ses'tet, '-- -s -s
set set -s -s -ting -ɪŋ ⓤⓢ 'set̬.ɪŋ ˌset 'book; ˌset 'piece; ⓤⓢ 'set ˌpiece; ˌset 'point ⓤⓢ 'set ˌpoint
setaceous sɪ'teɪ.ʃəs, sə- ⓤⓢ sɪ- -ly -li
setback 'set.bæk -s -s
Setchell 'setʃ.əl
Setebos 'set.ɪ.bɒs ⓤⓢ 'set̬.ə.bɑːs
Seth seθ
set-off 'set.ɒf ⓤⓢ -ɑːf -s -s
seton (S) 'siː.tən -s -z
setsquare 'set.skweər ⓤⓢ -skwer -s -z
sett set -s -s
settee set'iː -s -z
setter (S) 'set.ər ⓤⓢ 'set̬.ɚ -s -z
setting 'set.ɪŋ ⓤⓢ 'set̬.ɪŋ -s -z
settl|e (S) 'set.l̩ ⓤⓢ 'set̬- -es -z -ing -ɪŋ, 'set.lɪŋ -ed -d
settlement 'set.l̩.mənt ⓤⓢ 'set̬- -s -s
settler 'set.l̩.ər, '-lər ⓤⓢ 'set.lɚ, 'set̬.l̩.ɚ -s -z
set-to 'set.tuː
Setúbal sə'tuː.bəl, set'uː-
setup 'set.ʌp ⓤⓢ 'set̬- -s -s
Seurat 'sɜː.rɑː, -'- ⓤⓢ sɜː'rɑː
Seuss sjuːs ⓤⓢ suːs
Sevastopol sə'væst.ə.pɒl ⓤⓢ -poʊl
Seve 'sev.i
seven 'sev.ən -s -z -fold -fəʊld ⓤⓢ -foʊld ˌseven 'seas
sevenish 'sev.ən.ɪʃ
Sevenoaks 'sev.ən.əʊks ⓤⓢ -oʊks
seven|pence 'sev.ən|.pənts, -əm- ⓤⓢ -ən- -penny -pən.i
Note: See note under **penny**.
seventeen ˌsev.ən'tiːn -s -z -th/s -tθ/s
seventh 'sev.əntθ -s -s -ly -li ˌseventh 'heaven
sevent|y 'sev.ən.t|i ⓤⓢ -t̬|i -ies -iz -ieth/s -i.əθ/s, -i.ɪθ/s
seventy-eight, 78 ˌsev.ən.ti'eɪt ⓤⓢ -t̬i'- -s -s
sev|er 'sev|.ər ⓤⓢ -ɚ -ers -əz ⓤⓢ -ɚz -ering -ər.ɪŋ -ered -əd ⓤⓢ -ɚd
several 'sev.ər.əl, '-rəl -ly -i
severalty 'sev.ər.əl.ti, '-rəl-
severance 'sev.ər.ənts 'severance ˌpay
sever|e sɪ'vɪər, sə- ⓤⓢ sə'vɪr -er -ər ⓤⓢ -ɚ -est -ɪst, -əst -ely -li -eness -nəs, -nɪs
severit|y sɪ'ver.ə.t|i, sə-, -ɪ.t|i ⓤⓢ sə'ver.ə.t̬|i -ies -iz
Severn 'sev.ən ⓤⓢ -ɚn
Severus sɪ'vɪə.rəs, sə- ⓤⓢ sə'vɪr.əs

Pronouncing the letters SH

The consonant digraph **sh** is most commonly pronounced /ʃ/, e.g.:

sheep /ʃiːp/

In addition

When the two letters come together due to the addition of a prefix, the pronunciation is /s.h/, or /s/ alone with a silent **h**, e.g.:

mishap /ˈmɪs.hæp/
dishonest /dɪsˈɒn.ɪst/ US /-ˈɑː.nɪst/

seviche sevˈiːʃ
Sevier ˈsev.i.əʳ US -ɚ; səˈvɪr
Seville səˈvɪl, sɪ-, sevˈɪl; ˈsev.ɪl, -ᵊl *stress shift, see compound:* US səˈvɪl **ˌSeville ˈorange**
Sèvres ˈseɪ.vrə, -vəʳ US -vrə
sew səʊ US soʊ **-s** -z **-ing** -ɪŋ **-ed** -d **-n** -n
sewage ˈsuː.ɪdʒ, ˈsjuː- US ˈsuː-
Sewanee səˈwɒn.i US -ˈwɑː.ni, -ˈwɔː-
Seward ˈsiː.wəd US ˈsuː.ɚd; ˈsiː.wɚd
Sewell ˈsjuː.əl, sjʊəl US ˈsuː.əl
sewer *one who sews:* ˈsəʊ.əʳ US ˈsoʊ.ɚ **-s** -z
sewer *drain:* sʊəʳ, sjʊəʳ US ˈsuː.ɚ **-s** -z
sewerage ˈsʊə.rɪdʒ, ˈsjʊə- US ˈsuː.ɚ.ɪdʒ
sewing ˈsəʊ.ɪŋ US ˈsoʊ- **ˈsewing maˌchine**
sewn *(from* **sew***)* səʊn US soʊn
sex seks **-es** -ɪz **-ing** -ɪŋ **-ed** -t **ˈsex apˌpeal**; **ˈsex ˌchange**; **ˈsex ˌkitten**; **ˈsex ˌobject**
sexagenarian ˌsek.sə.dʒɪˈneə.ri.ən, -dʒəˈ- US -dʒɪˈner.i- **-s** -z
Sexagesi|ma ˌsek.səˈdʒes.ɪ|.mə US -ˈdʒes.ɪ|.mə, -ˈdʒeɪ.zɪ-
sexagesimal ˌsek.səˈdʒes.ɪ.mᵊl, ˈ-ə-
sex|ism ˈsek.s|ɪ.zᵊm **-ist/s** -ɪst/s
sexless ˈsek.sləs, -slɪs **-ness** -nəs, -nɪs
sexolog|y sekˈsɒl.ə.dʒ|i US -ˈsɑː.lə- **-ist/s** -ɪst/s
sexploitation ˌsek.splɔɪˈteɪ.ʃᵊn
sexpot ˈseks.pɒt US -pɑːt **-s** -s
sext sekst
sextant ˈsek.stᵊnt **-s** -s
sextet, sextette sekˈstet **-s** -s
sextillion sekˈstɪl.jən, -i.ən US ˈ-jən **-s** -z
sexto ˈsek.stəʊ US -stoʊ **-s** -z
sexton (S) ˈsek.stᵊn **-s** -z
sextuple ˈsek.stjʊ.pl̩, -stjə-; sekˈstjuː- US sekˈstuː-, -ˈstjuː-; ˈsek.stə.pl̩
sextuplet ˈsek.stjʊ.plet, -stjə-; -plət, -plɪt, sekˈstjuː- US sekˈstʌp.lɪt, -ˈstuː.plɪt, -ˈstjuː-; ˈsek.stə- **-s** -s
sexual ˈsek.ʃʊəl, -ʃu.əl, -sjʊəl, -sju.əl US -ʃu.əl **-ly** -i **ˌsexual ˈintercourse**; **ˌsexual reˈlations**; **ˌsexual reproˈduction**
sexuality ˌsek.ʃuˈæl.ə.ti, -sjuˈ-, -ɪ.ti US -ʃuˈæl.ə.t̬i
sex|y ˈsek.s|i **-ier** -i.əʳ US -i.ɚ **-iest** -i.ɪst, -i.əst **-ily** -ɪ.li, -ᵊl.i **-iness** -ɪ.nəs, -ɪ.nɪs
Sey seɪ
Seychelles seɪˈʃelz, ˈ-- US seɪˈʃelz, -ˈʃel
Seymour ˈsiː.mɔːʳ, ˈseɪ-, -məʳ US -mɔːr
Note: /ˈseɪ-/ chiefly in families of Scottish origin.
Sfax sfæks US sfɑːks
sferics ˈsfer.ɪks US ˈsfɪr-, ˈsfer-
sforzando sfɔːtˈsæn.dəʊ US sfɔːrtˈsɑːn.doʊ
sgian-dhu ˌskiː.ənˈduː, ˌskɪənˈ- US ˌskiː.ənˈ- **-s** -z
sgraffit|o sgræfˈiː.t|əʊ US skræfˈiː.t|oʊ, zgrɑːˈfiː- **-i** -i
Sgt. *(abbrev. for* **Sergeant***)* ˈsɑː.dʒᵊnt US ˈsɑːr-
sh, shh, ssh ʃ
Note: Used to command silence.
Shabbat ʃəˈbæt
shabb|y ˈʃæb|.i **-ier** -i.əʳ US -i.ɚ **-iest** -i.ɪst, -i.əst **-ily** -ɪ.li, -ᵊl.i **-iness** -ɪ.nəs, -ɪ.nɪs
Shabuoth ˈʃæb.u.ɒt US ˌʃɑː.vuːˈɑːt; ʃəˈvuː.oʊt, -oʊθ
shack ʃæk **-s** -s
shackl|e (S) ˈʃæk.l̩ **-es** -z **-ing** -ɪŋ, ˈʃæk.lɪŋ **-ed** -d
Shackleton ˈʃæk.l̩.tən
shad ʃæd **-s** -z
Shadbolt ˈʃæd.bəʊlt US -boʊlt
shaddock (S) ˈʃæd.ək
shad|e ʃeɪd **-es** -z **-ing** -ɪŋ **-ed** -ɪd
shadoof ʃædˈuːf, ʃəˈduːf US ʃɑː- **-s** -s
shadow ˈʃæd.əʊ US -oʊ **-s** -z **-ing** -ɪŋ **-ed** -d **-y** -i **-iness** -ɪ.nəs, -ɪ.nɪs
shadowbox ˈʃæd.əʊ.bɒks US -oʊ.bɑːks **-es** -ɪz **-ing** -ɪŋ **-ed** -t
shadowless ˈʃæd.əʊ.ləs, -lɪs US -oʊ-
Shadrach, Shadrak ˈʃæd.ræk
Note: Some Jews pronounce /-rɑːx/.
Shadwell ˈʃæd.wel, -wəl
shad|y ˈʃeɪ.d|i **-ier** -i.əʳ US -i.ɚ **-iest** -i.ɪst, -i.əst **-ily** -ɪ.li, -ᵊl.i **-iness** -ɪ.nəs, -ɪ.nɪs
Shaffer ˈʃæf.əʳ US ˈʃeɪ.fɚ, ˈʃæf.ɚ
shaft ʃɑːft US ʃæft **-s** -s **-ing** -ɪŋ **-ed** -ɪd
Shaftesbury ˈʃɑːfts.bᵊr.i US ˈʃæftsˌber-, ˈʃɑːfts-, -bɚ-
shag ʃæg **-s** -z **-ging** -ɪŋ **-ged** -d
shagg|y ˈʃæg|.i **-ier** -i.əʳ US -i.ɚ **-iest** -i.ɪst, -i.əst **-ily** -ɪ.li, -ᵊl.i **-iness** -ɪ.nəs, -ɪ.nɪs **ˌshaggy ˈdog ˌstory**
shagreen ʃægˈriːn, ʃəˈgriːn US ʃə-
shah (S) ʃɑː **-s** -z
Shairp ʃeəp, ʃɑːp US ʃerp, ʃɑːrp
shak|e ʃeɪk **-es** -s **-ing** -ɪŋ **shook** ʃʊk **shaken** ˈʃeɪ.kᵊn
shakedown ˈʃeɪk.daʊn **-s** -z
shaken *(from* **shake***)* ˈʃeɪ.kᵊn
shakeout ˈʃeɪk.aʊt **-s** -s
shaker (S) ˈʃeɪ.kəʳ US -kɚ **-s** -z **-ism** -ɪ.zᵊm
Shakespear(e) ˈʃeɪk.spɪəʳ US -spɪr
Shakespearean ˌʃeɪkˈspɪə.ri.ən US -ˈspɪr.i- **-s** -z
Shakespeareana ʃeɪkˌspɪə.riˈɑː.nə, ˌʃeɪk- US ˌʃeɪk.spɪr.i.æn.ə, -ˈɑː.nə
Shakespearian ʃeɪkˈspɪə.ri.ən US -ˈspɪr.i- **-s** -z
Shakespeariana ʃeɪkˌspɪə.riˈɑː.nə, ˌʃeɪk.spɪə- US ˌʃeɪk.spɪr.iˈæn.ə, -ˈɑː.nə
shake-up ˈʃeɪk.ʌp **-s** -s
shako ˈʃæk.əʊ, ˈʃeɪ.kəʊ, ˈʃɑː- US ˈʃæk.oʊ, ˈʃeɪ.koʊ, ˈʃɑː- **-(e)s** -z
shak|y ˈʃeɪ.k|i **-ier** -i.əʳ US -i.ɚ **-iest** -i.ɪst, -i.əst **-ily** -ɪ.li, -ᵊl.i **-iness** -ɪ.nəs, -ɪ.nɪs
shale ʃeɪl
shall *strong form:* ʃæl *weak form:* ʃᵊl
Note: Weak form word. The strong form is used for strong insistence or prediction (e.g. "You **shall** go to the ball, Cinderella"), and in final position (e.g. "And so you **shall**"). The weak form is used elsewhere (e.g. "What shall we do today?" /ˌwɒt.ʃᵊl.wiˌduː.təˈdeɪ US ˌwɑːt-/). American English uses 'shall' much less frequently than British English.
shallop ˈʃæl.əp **-s** -s

shallot **(S)** ʃə'lɒt (US) -'lɑːt; 'ʃæl.ət **-s** -s
shallow **(S)** 'ʃæl.əʊ (US) -oʊ **-s** -z **-er** -ə^r (US) -ɚ **-est** -ɪst, -əst **-ly** -li **-ness** -nəs, -nɪs
shalom ʃæl'ɒm, ʃə'lɒm, -'ləʊm (US) ʃɑː'loʊm, ʃə-
shalt *(from* **shall***) strong form:* ʃælt *weak form:* ʃ^əlt
shal|y 'ʃeɪ.l|i **-iness** -ɪ.nəs, -ɪ.nɪs
sham ʃæm **-s** -z **-ming** -ɪŋ **-med** -d **-mer/s** -ə^r/z (US) -ɚ/z
shaman 'ʃeɪm.ən, 'ʃæ.mən, 'ʃɑː- (US) 'ʃɑː.mən, 'ʃeɪ-, 'ʃæm.ən **-s** -z **-ist/s** **-ism** -ɪ.z^əm
shamateur ˌʃæm.ə'tɜː^r (US) -'tɝː **-s** -z **-ism** -ɪ.z^əm
shambl|e 'ʃæm.bl̩ **-es** -z **-ing** -ɪŋ, '-blɪŋ **-ed** -d
shambles *(n.)* 'ʃæm.bl̩z
shambolic ʃæm'bɒl.ɪk (US) -'bɑː.lɪk
sham|e ʃeɪm **-es** -z **-ing** -ɪŋ **-ed** -d
shamefaced ˌʃeɪm'feɪst (US) '-- *stress shift, British only:* ˌshamefaced 'person
shamefaced|ness ˌʃeɪm'feɪst|.nəs, -'feɪ.sɪd-, -nɪs (US) 'ʃeɪm.feɪst-; ˌʃeɪm'feɪ.sɪd- **-ly** -li
shameful 'ʃeɪm.f^əl, -fʊl **-ly** -i **-ness** -nəs, -nɪs
shameless 'ʃeɪm.ləs, -lɪs **-ly** -li **-ness** -nəs, -nɪs ˌ**shameless** '**hussy**
Shamir ʃæm'ɪə^r, ʃə'mɪə^r (US) ʃə'mɪr, ʃæm'ɪr
shamm|y 'ʃæm.i **-ies** -iz
shampoo ʃæm'puː **-(e)s** -z **-ing** -ɪŋ **-ed** -d
shamrock **(S)** 'ʃæm.rɒk (US) -rɑːk
Shan ʃɑːn (US) ʃɑːn, ʃæn
Shana 'ʃɑː.nə (US) 'ʃeɪ-, 'ʃɑː-
shand|y **(S)** 'ʃæn.d|i **-ies** -iz
Shane ʃɑːn, ʃɔːn, ʃeɪn (US) ʃeɪn
shanghai *(v.)* ˌʃæŋ'haɪ (US) 'ʃæŋ.haɪ, -'- **-s** -z **-ing** -ɪŋ **-ed** -d *stress shift, British only:* ˌShanghai 'trader
Shanghai ˌʃæŋ'haɪ (US) ˌʃæŋ-, ˌʃɑːŋ-, '--
Shangri-la ˌʃæŋ.gri'lɑː
shank ʃæŋk **-s** -s ˌ**shank's** '**pony**, ˌ**shanks's** '**pony**
Shankill 'ʃæŋ.kɪl
Shanklin 'ʃæŋ.klɪn
Shanks ʃæŋks
Shanna 'ʃæn.ə
Shannon 'ʃæn.ən
shan't ʃɑːnt (US) ʃænt
shantung *silk material:* ˌʃæn'tʌŋ
Shantung ˌʃæn'dʌŋ, -tʌŋ, -dʊŋ, -tʊŋ (US) ˌʃæn'-, ˌʃɑːn'-
shant|y 'ʃæn.t|i (US) -t̬|i **-ies** -iz
shantytown 'ʃæn.ti.taʊn (US) -t̬i- **-s** -z
shap|e ʃeɪp **-es** -s **-ing** -ɪŋ **-ed** -t
SHAPE ʃeɪp
shapeless 'ʃeɪp.ləs, -lɪs **-ly** -li **-ness** -nəs, -nɪs
shapel|y 'ʃeɪ.pl|i **-ier** -i.ə^r (US) -i.ɚ **-iest** -i.ɪst, -i.əst **-iness** -ɪ.nəs, -ɪ.nɪs
Shapiro ʃə'pɪə.rəʊ (US) -'pɪr.oʊ
shard ʃɑːd (US) ʃɑːrd **-s** -z
shar|e ʃeə^r (US) ʃer **-es** -z **-ing** -ɪŋ **-ed** -d
sharecropp|er 'ʃeəˌkrɒp|.ə^r (US) 'ʃerˌkrɑː.p|ɚ **-ers** -əz (US) -ɚz **-ing** -ɪŋ
sharehold|er 'ʃeəˌhəʊl.d|ə^r (US) 'ʃerˌhoʊl.d|ɚ **-ers** -əz (US) -ɚz **-ing/s** -ɪŋ/z
share-out 'ʃeə^r.aʊt (US) 'ʃer- **-s** -s
shareware 'ʃeə.weə^r (US) 'ʃer.wer
sharia(h) ʃə'riː.ə
Sharif ʃə'riːf, ʃɑː-, ʃær'iːf
Sharjah 'ʃɑː.dʒɑː, -ʒɑː, -dʒə (US) 'ʃɑːr.dʒɑː
shark ʃɑːk (US) ʃɑːrk **-s** -s
sharkskin 'ʃɑːk.skɪn (US) 'ʃɑːrk-
Sharman 'ʃɑː.mən (US) 'ʃɑːr-
Sharon *female name & fruit:* 'ʃær.ən, 'ʃɑː.rən, 'ʃeə-, -rɒn (US) 'ʃer.ən, 'ʃær- *Israeli politician:* ʃə'rəʊn, -'rɒn (US) -'roʊn
sharp **(S)** ʃɑːp (US) ʃɑːrp **-s** -s **-er** -ə^r (US) -ɚ **-est** -ɪst, -əst **-ly** -li **-ness** -nəs, -nɪs ˌ**sharp** '**end**, '**sharp** ˌ**end**; ˌ**sharp** '**practice**
Sharpe ʃɑːp (US) ʃɑːrp
sharpen 'ʃɑː.p^ən (US) 'ʃɑːr- **-s** -z **-ing** -ɪŋ, -ɪŋ **-ed** -d
sharpener 'ʃɑː.p^ən.ə^r (US) 'ʃɑːr.p^ən.ɚ **-s** -z
sharper 'ʃɑː.pə^r (US) 'ʃɑːr.pɚ **-s** -z
Sharpeville 'ʃɑːp.vɪl (US) 'ʃɑːrp-
sharp-eyed ˌʃɑːp'aɪd (US) ˌʃɑːrp-
sharpish 'ʃɑː.pɪʃ (US) 'ʃɑːr-
Sharples 'ʃɑː.pl̩z (US) 'ʃɑːr-
sharp-set ˌʃɑːp'set (US) 'ʃɑːrp.set *stress shift, British only:* ˌsharp-set 'features
sharpshooter 'ʃɑːpˌʃuː.tə^r (US) 'ʃɑːrpˌʃuː.t̬ɚ **-s** -z
sharp-sighted ˌʃɑːp'saɪ.tɪd (US) 'ʃɑːrpˌsaɪ.t̬ɪd *stress shift, British only:* ˌsharp-sighted 'person
sharp-witted ˌʃɑːp'wɪt.ɪd (US) 'ʃɑːrpˌwɪt̬- *stress shift, British only:* ˌsharp-witted 'person
shashlik ʃɑːʃ'lɪk, ʃæʃ-, '-- (US) 'ʃɑːʃ- **-s** -s
Shasta 'ʃæs.tə
Shastri 'ʃæs.tri (US) 'ʃɑː.stri
shat *(from* **shit***)* ʃæt
Note: This past tense form is rarely used in American English.
Shatner 'ʃæt.nə^r (US) -nɚ
Shatt-al-Arab ˌʃæt.æl'ær.əb (US) -əl'er-, -'ær-
shatt|er 'ʃæt|.ə^r (US) 'ʃæt̬|.ɚ **-ers** -əz (US) -ɚz **-ering** -^ər.ɪŋ **-ered** -əd (US) -ɚd
shatterproof 'ʃæt.ə.pruːf (US) 'ʃæt̬.ɚ-
Shaughnessy 'ʃɔː.nə.si (US) 'ʃɑː-, 'ʃɔː-
Shaula 'ʃaʊ.lə (US) 'ʃoʊ-, 'ʃɔː-
Shaun ʃɔːn (US) ʃɑːn, ʃɔːn
Shauna 'ʃɔː.nə (US) 'ʃɑː-, 'ʃɔː-
shav|e ʃeɪv **-es** -z **-ing** -ɪŋ **-ed** -d '**shaving** ˌ**brush**; '**shaving** ˌ**cream**; '**shaving** ˌ**foam**
shaven 'ʃeɪ.v^ən
shaver 'ʃeɪ.və^r (US) -vɚ **-s** -z
Shavian 'ʃeɪ.vi.ən
shaving 'ʃeɪ.vɪŋ **-s** -z
shaw **(S)** ʃɔː (US) ʃɑː, ʃɔː **-s** -z
shawl ʃɔːl (US) ʃɑːl, ʃɔːl **-s** -z
shawm ʃɔːm (US) ʃɑːm, ʃɔːm **-s** -z
Shawn ʃɔːn (US) ʃɑːn, ʃɔːn
Shawna 'ʃɔː.nə (US) 'ʃɑː-, 'ʃɔː-
Shawnee ʃɔː'niː (US) ʃɑː-, ʃɔː- **-s** -z
shay ʃeɪ **-s** -z
Shayler 'ʃeɪ.lə, -lɚ
she *normal form:* ʃiː *freq. weak form:* ʃi
Note: Weak form word. The strong form, /ʃiː/ is used mainly contrastively (e.g. “I wouldn’t go, so SHE went”) or emphatically (e.g. “What does SHE want?”). The weak form is /ʃi/ (e.g. “off she went”, /ˌɒf.ʃi'went (US) ˌɑːf-/).
shea ʃɪə, 'ʃiː.ə, ʃiː (US) ʃiː, ʃeɪ **-s** -z
Shea ʃeɪ
shea|f ʃiː|f **-ves** -vz
Sheaffer 'ʃeɪ.fə^r (US) -fɚ
shear ʃɪə^r (US) ʃɪr **-s** -z **-ing** -ɪŋ **-ed** -d **shorn** ʃɔːn (US) ʃɔːrn
Sheard ʃeəd, ʃɪəd, ʃɜːd (US) ʃerd, ʃɪrd, ʃɝːd
shearer **(S)** 'ʃɪə.rə^r (US) 'ʃɪr.ɚ **-s** -z
Shearman 'ʃɪə.mən, 'ʃɜː.mən (US) 'ʃɪr-, 'ʃɝː-
Shearn ʃɪən, ʃɜːn (US) ʃɪrn, ʃɝːn
shears **(S)** ʃɪəz (US) ʃɪrz
Shearson 'ʃɪə.s^ən (US) 'ʃɪr-
shearwater 'ʃɪəˌwɔː.tə^r (US) 'ʃɪrˌwɑː.t̬ɚ, -ˌwɔː- **-s** -z
shea|th ʃiː|θ **-ths** -ðz, -θs
sheath|e ʃiːð **-es** -z **-ing** -ɪŋ **-ed** -d
sheaves *(plur. of* **sheaf***)* ʃiːvz
Sheba 'ʃiː.bə
shebang ʃɪ'bæŋ, ʃə-
she-bear 'ʃiː.beə^r (US) -ber **-s** -z
shebeen ʃɪ'biːn, ʃə-, ʃeb'iːn (US) ʃɪ'biːn **-s** -z
she-cat 'ʃiː.kæt **-s** -s
Shechem 'ʃiː.kem, 'ʃek.em; *as if Jewish:* ʃə'xem (US) 'ʃiː.kəm, 'ʃek.əm
shed ʃed **-s** -z **-ding** -ɪŋ
she-devil 'ʃiːˌdev.^əl **-s** -z
Shee ʃiː
sheen **(S)** ʃiːn
Sheena 'ʃiː.nə
sheen|y 'ʃiː.n|i **-ies** -iz

sheep ʃiːp ˈ**sheep's ˌeyes; ˌseparate the ˌsheep from the ˈgoats**
sheep-dip ˈʃiːp.dɪp
sheepdog ˈʃiːp.dɒg US -dɑːg, -dɔːg **-s** -z
sheepfold ˈʃiːp.fəʊld US -foʊld **-s** -z
sheepish ˈʃiː.pɪʃ **-ly** -li **-ness** -nəs, -nɪs
sheepshank ˈʃiːp.ʃæŋk **-s** -s
Sheepshanks ˈʃiːp.ʃæŋks
sheepshear|ing ˈʃiːpˌʃɪə.r|ɪŋ US -ˌʃɪr|.ɪŋ **-er/s** -əʳ/z US -ɚ/z
sheepskin ˈʃiːp.skɪn **-s** -z
sheer ʃɪəʳ US ʃɪr **-s** -z **-ing** -ɪŋ **-ed** -d
Sheerness ˌʃɪəˈnes US ˈʃɪr.nes
sheet ʃiːt **-s** -s **-ing** -ɪŋ US ˈʃiː.t̬ɪŋ ˈ**sheet ˌanchor; ˌsheet ˈlightning;** US ˈ**sheet ˌlightning; ˌsheet ˈmetal; ˈsheet ˌmusic; ˌwhite as a ˈsheet**
Sheffield ˈʃef.iːld *locally:* -ɪld US -iːld
Shefford ˈʃef.əd US -ɚd
she-goat ˈʃiː.gəʊt US -goʊt **-s** -s
sheik(h) ʃeɪk, ʃiːk, ʃek, ʃex US ʃiːk, ʃeɪk **-s** -s **-dom/s** -dəm/z
sheila (S) ˈʃiː.lə
shekel ˈʃek.ᵊl **-s** -z
Shekinah ʃekˈaɪ.nə, ʃɪˈkaɪ- US ʃəˈkiː-, -ˈkaɪ-
Shelagh ˈʃiː.lə
Shelby ˈʃel.bi
Sheldon ˈʃel.dᵊn
Sheldonian ʃelˈdəʊ.ni.ən US -ˈdoʊ-
sheldrake ˈʃel.dreɪk **-s** -s
Sheldrick ˈʃel.drɪk
shelduck ˈʃel.dʌk **-s** -s
shel|f ʃel|f **-ves** -vz
Shelfield ˈʃel.fiːld
shelf-life ˈʃelf.laɪf **-lives** -laɪvz
Shelford ˈʃel.fəd US -fɚd
shell (S) ʃel **-s** -z **-ing** -ɪŋ **-ed** -d ˈ**shell ˌshock; ˈshell ˌsuit**
shellac ʃəˈlæk, ʃelˈæk; ˈʃel.æk US ʃəˈlæk **-s** -s **-king** -ɪŋ **-ked** -t
Shelley ˈʃel.i
shellfish ˈʃel.fɪʃ
Shelta ˈʃel.tə US -t̬ə
shelt|er ˈʃel.t|əʳ US -t̬|ɚ **-ers** -əz US -ɚz **-ering** -ᵊr.ɪŋ **-ered** -əd US -ɚd
shelt|ie, shelt|y ˈʃel.t|i US -t̬|i **-ies** -iz
Shelton ˈʃel.tən US -tᵊn
shelv|e ʃelv **-es** -z **-ing** -ɪŋ **-ed** -d
Shem ʃem
shemozzle ʃɪˈmɒz.l̩, ʃə- US -ˈmɑː.zl̩ **-s** -z
Shenandoah ˌʃen.ənˈdəʊə US -ˈdoʊə
shenanigan ʃɪˈnæn.ɪ.gən, ʃə- **-s** -z
Shennan ˈʃen.ən
Shenstone ˈʃen.stən
Shenyang ˌʃenˈjæŋ US ˌʃʌnˈjɑːŋ
Shepard ˈʃep.əd US -ɚd
shepherd (S) ˈʃep.əd US -ɚd **-s** -z **-ing** -ɪŋ **-ed** -ɪd ˌ**shepherd's ˈpie**
shepherdess ˌʃep.əˈdes; ˈ---, -dɪs US ˈʃep.ɚ.dɪs **-es** -ɪz
Sheppard ˈʃep.əd US -ɚd
Shepperton ˈʃep.ə.tᵊn US -ɚ.t̬ən
Sheppey ˈʃep.i
Shepreth ˈʃep.rəθ
Shepshed ˈʃep.ʃed
Shepton Mallet ˌʃep.tənˈmæl.ɪt
Sheraton ˈʃer.ə.tᵊn US -t̬ən, -tᵊn
sherbet, sherbert ˈʃɜː.bət US ˈʃɝː-, -bɚt
Note: Both pronunciations are possible for both variants in American English, even though only one is spelt with an **r**.
Sherborne ˈʃɜː.bən, -bɔːn US ˈʃɝː.bɔːrn, -bɚn
Sherbrooke ˈʃɜː.brʊk US ˈʃɝː-
sherd ʃɜːd US ʃɝːd **-s** -z
Shere ʃɪəʳ US ʃɪr
Shergar ˈʃɜː.gɑːʳ, ˈʃeə- US ˈʃɝː.gɑːr, ˈʃer-
Sheridan ˈʃer.ɪ.dᵊn
sheriff (S) ˈʃer.ɪf **-s** -s
Sheringham ˈʃer.ɪŋ.əm
sherlock (S) ˈʃɜː.lɒk US ˈʃɝː.lɑːk
Sherman ˈʃɜː.mən US ˈʃɝː-
Sherpa ˈʃɜː.pə US ˈʃɝː- **-s** -z
Sherrin ˈʃer.ɪn
sherr|y (S) ˈʃer|.i **-ies** -iz
Sherwood ˈʃɜː.wʊd US ˈʃɝː- ˌ**Sherwood ˈForest**
she's *(from* **she is** *or* **she has***) strong form:* ʃiːz *weak form:* ʃɪz
Note: The use of the strong form /ʃiːz/ and the weak form /ʃɪz/ is parallel to the two forms of **she**.
Shetland ˈʃet.lənd **-s** -z **-er/s** -əʳ/z US -ɚ/z ˈ**Shetland ˌIslands; ˌShetland ˈpony**
Shevardnadze ˌʃev.ədˈnɑːd.zeɪ, -zə US -ɚdˈnɑːrd.ziː
Shevington ˈʃev.ɪŋ.tən
shew ʃəʊ US ʃoʊ **-s** -z **-ing** -ɪŋ **-ed** -d **-n** -n
shewbread ˈʃəʊ.bred US ˈʃoʊ-
Shewell ʃʊəl, ˈʃuː.əl US ˈʃuː.əl
shewn *(from* **shew***)* ʃəʊn US ʃoʊn
she-wol|f ˈʃiː.wʊl|f **-ves** -vz
shh, sh, ssh ʃ
Note: Used to command silence.
Shia(h) ˈʃiː.ə ˌ**Shia ˈMuslim**
shiatsu ʃiˈæt.su US -ˈɑːt-
shibboleth (S) ˈʃɪb.ᵊl.eθ, -əθ, -ɪθ US -ə.leθ, -ləθ **-s** -s
shickered ˈʃɪk.əd US -ɚd
shield (S) ʃiːld **-s** -z **-ing** -ɪŋ **-ed** -ɪd
shieling ˈʃiː.lɪŋ **-s** -z
Shiels ʃiːlz
Shifnal ˈʃɪf.nᵊl
shift ʃɪft **-s** -s **-ing** -ɪŋ **-ed** -ɪd ˈ**shift ˌstick**
shiftless ˈʃɪft.ləs, -lɪs **-ly** -li **-ness** -nəs, -nɪs
shiftwork ˈʃɪft.wɜːk US -wɝːk **-er/s** -əʳ/z US -ɚ/z
shift|y ˈʃɪf.t|i **-ier** -i.əʳ US -i.ɚ **-iest** -i.ɪst, -i.əst **-ily** -ɪ.li, -ᵊl.i **-iness** -ɪ.nəs, -ɪ.nɪs
Shiism ˈʃiː.ɪ.zᵊm
Shiite ˈʃiː.aɪt **-s** -s
shikari ʃɪˈkɑː.ri, -ˈkær.i US -ˈkɑːr.i **-s** -z
Shikoku ʃɪˈkəʊ.kuː US -ˈkɑː-, ʃiː-, -ˈkɔː-
shiksa ˈʃɪk.sə **-s** -z
shikse ˈʃɪk.sə **-s** -z
Shildon ˈʃɪl.dᵊn
Shillan ʃɪˈlæn
shillela(g)h (S) ʃɪˈleɪ.lə, -li US -li, -lə **-s** -z
Shilleto, Shillito ˈʃɪl.ɪ.təʊ US -toʊ
shilling ˈʃɪl.ɪŋ **-s** -z
shilly-shall|y ˈʃɪl.iˌʃæl|.i, ˌʃɪl.iˈʃæl- US ˈʃɪl.iˌʃæl- **-ies** -iz **-ying** -i.ɪŋ **-ied** -id
Shiloh ˈʃaɪ.ləʊ US -loʊ
Shilton ˈʃɪl.tᵊn
shimm|er ˈʃɪm|.əʳ US -ɚ **-ers** -əz US -ɚz **-ering** -ᵊr.ɪŋ **-ered** -əd US -ɚd
shimm|y ˈʃɪm|.i **-ies** -iz **-ying** -i.ɪŋ **-ied** -id
shin ʃɪn **-s** -z **-ning** -ɪŋ **-ned** -d
shinbone ˈʃɪn.bəʊn, ˈʃɪm- US ˈʃɪn.boʊn **-s** -z
shindig ˈʃɪn.dɪg **-s** -z
shind|y ˈʃɪn.d|i **-ies** -iz
shin|e ʃaɪn **-es** -z **-ing** -ɪŋ **-ed** -d **shone** ʃɒn US ʃoʊn, ʃɑːn
shiner ˈʃaɪ.nəʳ US -nɚ **-s** -z
shingle ˈʃɪŋ.gl̩ **-s** -z
shingly ˈʃɪŋ.gli, -gl̩.i
shinn|y ˈʃɪn|.i **-ies** -iz **-ying** -i.ɪŋ **-ied** -id
shinsplints ˈʃɪn.splɪnts
Shinto ˈʃɪn.təʊ US -toʊ **-ism** -ɪ.zᵊm **-ist/s** -ɪst/s
Shinwell ˈʃɪn.wəl, -wel
shin|y ˈʃaɪ.n|i **-ier** -i.əʳ US -i.ɚ **-iest** -i.ɪst, -i.əst **-iness** -ɪ.nəs, -ɪ.nɪs
ship ʃɪp **-s** -s **-ping** -ɪŋ **-ped** -t **-per/s** -əʳ/z US -ɚ/z
-ship -ʃɪp
Note: Suffix. Normally unstressed, e.g. **kinship** /ˈkɪn.ʃɪp/.
shipboard ˈʃɪp.bɔːd US -bɔːrd
shipbroker ˈʃɪpˌbrəʊ.kəʳ US -ˌbroʊ.kɚ **-s** -z
shipbuild|er ˈʃɪpˌbɪl.d|əʳ US -d|ɚ **-ers** -əz US -ɚz **-ing** -ɪŋ
Shiplake ˈʃɪp.leɪk
Shipley ˈʃɪp.li
shipload ˈʃɪp.ləʊd US -loʊd **-s** -z
Shipman ˈʃɪp.mən
shipmaster ˈʃɪpˌmɑː.stəʳ US -ˌmæs.tɚ **-s** -z
shipmate ˈʃɪp.meɪt **-s** -s
shipment ˈʃɪp.mənt **-s** -s
Shipp ʃɪp
shipping ˈʃɪp.ɪŋ ˈ**shipping ˌclerk**
shipshape ˈʃɪp.ʃeɪp
Shipston ˈʃɪp.stən

Shipton ˈʃɪp.tən

shipway ˈʃɪp.weɪ -s -z

shipwreck ˈʃɪp.rek -s -s -ing -ɪŋ -ed -t

shipwright (S) ˈʃɪp.raɪt -s -s

shipyard ˈʃɪp.jɑːd (US) -jɑːrd -s -z

Shiraz ʃɪəˈrɑːz, ʃɪ-, -ˈræz (US) ʃiː-

shire ʃaɪəʳ (US) ʃaɪɚ -s -z ˈshire ˌhorse

-shire -ʃəʳ, -ˌʃɪəʳ (US) -ʃɚ, -ˌʃɪr

Note: Suffix. Does not normally change the stress pattern of the stem to which it is added, e.g. **Lincoln** /ˈlɪŋ.kən/, **Lincolnshire** /ˈlɪŋ.kən.ʃəʳ (US) -ʃɚ/. There is a free choice between the unstressed variant and that with secondary stress in all names ending **-shire**.

Shirebrook ˈʃaɪə.brʊk (US) ˈʃaɪɚ-

Shiremoor ˈʃaɪə.mɔːʳ, -mʊəʳ (US) ˈʃaɪɚ.mɔːr, -mʊr

shirk ʃɜːk (US) ʃɝːk -s -s -ing -ɪŋ -ed -t -er/s -əʳ/z (US) -ɚ/z

Shirley ˈʃɜː.li (US) ˈʃɝː-

shirr ʃɜːʳ (US) ʃɝː -s -z -ing -ɪŋ -ed -d

shirt (S) ʃɜːt (US) ʃɝːt -s -s

shirtdress ˈʃɜːt.dres (US) ˈʃɝːt- -es -ɪz

shirt-front ˈʃɜːt.frʌnt (US) ˈʃɝːt- -s -s

shirting ˈʃɜː.tɪŋ (US) ˈʃɝː.t̬ɪŋ

shirt-sleev|es ˈʃɜːt.sliːv|z, -ˈ- (US) ˈʃɝːt- -ed -d

shirt-tail ˈʃɜːt.teɪl (US) ˈʃɝːt- -s -z

shirtwaist ˈʃɜːt.weɪst (US) ˈʃɝːt- -s -s

shirtwaister ˈʃɜːtˌweɪ.stəʳ, ˌ-ˈ-- (US) ˈʃɝːtˌweɪ.stɚ -s -z

shirt|y ˈʃɜː.t|i (US) ˈʃɝː.t̬|i -ier -i.əʳ (US) -i.ɚ -iest -i.ɪst, -i.əst -iness -ɪ.nəs, -ɪ.nɪs

Shishak ˈʃaɪ.ʃæk, -ʃək *rarely:* ˈʃɪʃ.æk, -ək (US) ˈʃaɪ.ʃɑːk, -ʃæk

shish kebab ˈʃiːʃ.kɪˌbæb, -kəˌ-, ˌ--ˈ- (US) ˈʃɪʃ.kəˌbɑːb -s -z

shit ʃɪt -s -s -ting -ɪŋ (US) ˈʃɪt̬.ɪŋ **shat** ʃæt

Note: The past tense form **shat** is rarely used in American English, the normal past tense being **shit**.

shite ʃaɪt -s -s

shitfaced ˈʃɪt.feɪst

shithouse ˈʃɪt.haʊs

shitless ˈʃɪt.ləs, -lɪs

shitt|y ˈʃɪt|.i (US) ˈʃɪt̬|.i -ier -i.əʳ (US) -i.ɚ -iest -i.ɪst, -i.əst -iness -ɪ.nəs, -ɪ.nɪs

Shiva ˈʃiː.və, ˈʃɪv.ə (US) ˈʃiː.və

shiv|er ˈʃɪv|.əʳ (US) -ɚ -ers -əz (US) -ɚz -ering/ly -ᵊr.ɪŋ/li -ered -əd (US) -ɚd

shiver|y ˈʃɪv.ᵊr|.i -iness -ɪ.nəs, -ɪ.nɪs

shlemiel ʃləˈmiːl -s -z

shlep ʃlep -s -s -ping -ɪŋ -ped -t

shlock ʃlɒk (US) ʃlɑːk -s -s

shlockmeister ˈʃlɒkˌmaɪ.stəʳ (US) ˈʃlɑːkˌmaɪ.stɚ -s -z

Shloer® ʃlɜːʳ (US) ʃlɝː

shmal(t)z ʃmɔːlts, ʃmɒlts, ʃmælts (US) ʃmɑːlts, ʃmɔːlts -y -i -ier -i.əʳ (US) -i.ɚ -iest -i.ɪst, -i.əst

shmooz|e ʃmuːz -es -ɪz -ing -ɪŋ -ed -d -er/s -əʳ/z (US) -ɚ/z

shmuck ʃmʌk -s -s

shoal ʃəʊl (US) ʃoʊl -s -z

shock ʃɒk (US) ʃɑːk -s -s -ing -ɪŋ -ed -t -er/s -əʳ/z (US) -ɚ/z ˈshock abˌsorber; ˈshock ˌtreatment; ˈshock ˌwave

shocking ˈʃɒk.ɪŋ (US) ˈʃɑː.kɪŋ -ly -li

shockproof ˈʃɒk.pruːf (US) ˈʃɑːk-

shodd|y ˈʃɒd|.i (US) ˈʃɑː.d|i -ier -i.əʳ (US) -i.ɚ -iest -i.ɪst, -i.əst -ily -ɪ.li, -ᵊl.i -iness -ɪ.nəs, -ɪ.nɪs

shoe ʃuː -s -z -ing -ɪŋ **shod** ʃɒd (US) ʃɑːd ˈshoe ˌleather

shoeblack ˈʃuː.blæk -s -s

Shoeburyness ˌʃuː.bᵊr.iˈnes

shoehorn ˈʃuː.hɔːn (US) -hɔːrn -s -z -ing -ɪŋ -ed -d

shoelac|e ˈʃuː.leɪs -es -ɪz

shoeless ˈʃuː.ləs, -lɪs

shoemaker (S) ˈʃuːˌmeɪ.kəʳ (US) -kɚ -s -z

shoeshine ˈʃuː.ʃaɪn -s -z

shoestring ˈʃuː.strɪŋ

shoetree ˈʃuː.triː -s -z

shogun ˈʃəʊ.gʌn, -guːn, -gən (US) ˈʃoʊ.gʌn, -gʊn, -guːn -s -s

Sholokhov ˈʃɒl.ə.kɒf (US) ˈʃɔː.lə.kɔːf

Shona *female name:* ˈʃəʊ.nə (US) ˈʃoʊ- *African language & people:* ˈʃɒ.nə, ˈʃɔː-, ˈʃəʊ- (US) ˈʃoʊ-

shone *(from* **shine***)* ʃɒn (US) ʃoʊn

shonk|y ˈʃɒŋ.ki (US) ˈʃɑːŋ- -ier i.əʳ (US) i.ɚ -iest i.ɪst, i.əst

shoo ʃuː -s -z -ing -ɪŋ -ed -d

shoofl|y ˈʃuː.fl|aɪ -ies -aɪz

shoo-in ˈʃuː.ɪn -s -z

shook *(from* **shake***)* ʃʊk

shook-up ˌʃʊkˈʌp

shoot ʃuːt -s -s -ing -ɪŋ (US) ˈʃuː.t̬ɪŋ **shot** ʃɒt (US) ʃɑːt ˌshoot the ˈbreeze

shooter (S) ˈʃuː.təʳ (US) -t̬ɚ -s -z

shooting ˈʃuː.tɪŋ (US) -t̬ɪŋ -s -z ˈshooting ˌgallery; ˌshooting ˈstar, ˈshooting ˌstar; (US) ˌshooting ˈstar; ˈshooting ˌstick

shoot-out ˈʃuːt.aʊt -s -s

shop ʃɒp (US) ʃɑːp -s -s -ping -ɪŋ -ped -t -per/s -əʳ/z (US) -ɚ/z ˈshop asˌsistant; ˌshop ˈsteward; (US) ˈshop ˌsteward; ˌshop ˈwindow

shopaholic ˌʃɒp.əˈhɒl.ɪk (US) ˌʃɑː.pəˈhɑː.lɪk -s -s

shopfloor ˌʃɒpˈflɔːʳ (US) ˌʃɑːpˈflɔːr

shopfront ˌʃɒpˈfrʌnt, ˈ-- (US) ˈʃɑːp.frʌnt -s -s

shopgirl ˈʃɒp.gɜːl (US) ˈʃɑːp.gɝːl -s -z

shopkeeper ˈʃɒpˌkiː.pəʳ (US) ˈʃɑːpˌkiː.pɚ -s -z

shoplift ˈʃɒp.lɪft (US) ˈʃɑːp- -s -s -ing -ɪŋ -ed -ɪd

shop-lifter ˈʃɒpˌlɪf.təʳ (US) ˈʃɑːpˌlɪf.tɚ -s -z

shopping ˈʃɒp.ɪŋ ˈshopping ˌcentre/ˌcenter; ˈshopping ˌlist; ˈshopping ˌmall

shop-soiled ˈʃɒp.sɔɪld (US) ˈʃɑːpˌsɔɪld

shoptalk ˈʃɒp.tɔːk (US) ˈʃɑːp.tɑːk, -tɔːk

shopwalker ˈʃɒpˌwɔː.kəʳ (US) ˈʃɑːpˌwɔː.kɚ, -ˌwɑː- -s -z

shopworn ˈʃɒp.wɔːn (US) ˈʃɑːp.wɔːrn

shor|e ʃɔːʳ (US) ʃɔːr -es -z -ing -ɪŋ -ed -d

Shoreditch ˈʃɔː.dɪtʃ (US) ˈʃɔːr-

Shoreham ˈʃɔː.rəm (US) ˈʃɔːr.əm

shoreline ˈʃɔː.laɪn (US) ˈʃɔːr-

shoreward ˈʃɔː.wəd (US) ˈʃɔːr.wɚd

shorn *(from* **shear***)* ʃɔːn (US) ʃɔːrn

Shorncliffe ˈʃɔːn.klɪf (US) ˈʃɔːrn-

short (S) ʃɔːt (US) ʃɔːrt -s -s -er -əʳ (US) ˈʃɔːr.t̬ɚ -est -ɪst, -əst (US) ˈʃɔːr.t̬ɪst, -t̬əst -ly -li -ness -nəs, -nɪs -ing -ɪŋ -ed -ɪd ˌshort ˌback and ˈsides; ˌshort ˈshrift; ˌshort ˈstory; the ˌshort ˌend of the ˈstick; the ˌlong and the ˈshort of it

shortag|e ˈʃɔː.tɪdʒ (US) ˈʃɔːr.t̬ɪdʒ -es -ɪz

shortbread ˈʃɔːt.bred (US) ˈʃɔːrt- -s -z

shortcake ˈʃɔːt.keɪk (US) ˈʃɔːrt- -s -s

short-chang|e ˌʃɔːtˈtʃeɪndʒ (US) ˌʃɔːrt- -es -ɪz -ing -ɪŋ -ed -d

short-cir|cuit ˌʃɔːtˈsɜː|.kɪt (US) ˌʃɔːrtˈsɝː- -cuits -kɪts -cuiting -kɪ.tɪŋ (US) -kɪ.t̬ɪŋ -cuited -kɪ.tɪd (US) -kɪ.t̬ɪd

shortcoming ˈʃɔːtˌkʌm.ɪŋ, ˌ-ˈ-- (US) ˈʃɔːrtˌkʌm- -s -z

shortcrust ˈʃɔːt.krʌst (US) ˈʃɔːrt- -s -s ˌshortcrust ˈpastry

shortcut ˈʃɔːt.kʌt (US) ˈʃɔːrt- -s -s

short-dated ˌʃɔːtˈdeɪ.tɪd (US) ˌʃɔːrtˈdeɪ.t̬ɪd

short-eared ˌʃɔːtˈɪəd (US) ˈʃɔːrt.ɪrd *stress shift, British only:* ˌshort-eared ˈrabbit

shorten ˈʃɔː.tᵊn (US) ˈʃɔːr- -s -z -ing -ɪŋ, ˈʃɔːt.nɪŋ (US) ˈʃɔːr.tᵊn.ɪŋ, ˈʃɔːrt.nɪŋ -ed -d

shortening ˈʃɔːt.nɪŋ; ˈʃɔː.tᵊn.ɪŋ (US) ˈʃɔːrt.nɪŋ; ˈʃɔːr.tᵊn.ɪŋ

shortfall ˈʃɔːt.fɔːl (US) ˈʃɔːrt-, -fɑːl -s -z

shorthand ˈʃɔːt.hænd (US) ˈʃɔːrt- ˌshorthand ˈtypist

short-handed ˌʃɔːtˈhæn.dɪd (US) ˌʃɔːrt- *stress shift:* ˌshort-handed ˈvessel

short-haul ˈʃɔːt.hɔːl, ˌ-ˈ- (US) ˈʃɔːrt.hɑːl, -hɔːl, ˌ-ˈ-

shorthorn ˈʃɔːt.hɔːn (US) ˈʃɔːrt.hɔːrn -s -z

shortlist ˈʃɔːt.lɪst (US) ˈʃɔːrt- -s -s -ing -ɪŋ -ed -ɪd

short-lived ˌʃɔːtˈlɪvd (US) ˈʃɔːrt.laɪvd, -lɪvd *stress shift, British only:* ˌshort-lived ˈglory

short-order ˈʃɔːtˌɔː.dəʳ, ˌ-ˈ-- (US) ˈʃɔːrtˌɔːr.dɚ

short-range ˌʃɔːt'reɪndʒ (US) ˌʃɔːrt- *stress shift:* ˌshort-range 'missile

shortsighted ˌʃɔːt'saɪ.tɪd (US) 'ʃɔːrtˌsaɪ.t̬ɪd **-ly** -li **-ness** -nəs, -nɪs *stress shift, British only:* ˌshort-sighted 'person

short-staffed ˌʃɔːt'stɑːft (US) ˌʃɔːrt'stæft *stress shift:* ˌshort-staffed 'bar

shortstop 'ʃɔːt.stɒp (US) 'ʃɔːrt.stɑːp **-s** -s

short-tempered ˌʃɔːt'tem.pəd (US) ˌʃɔːrt'tem.pɚd *stress shift:* ˌshort-tempered 'person

short-term ˌʃɔːt'tɜːm (US) 'ʃɔːrt.tɝːm **-ism** -ɪ.zᵊm *stress shift, British only:* ˌshort-term 'plans

shortwave 'ʃɔːt.weɪv (US) 'ʃɔːrt- **-s** -z

short-winded ˌʃɔːt'wɪn.dɪd (US) 'ʃɔːrtˌwɪn-, ˌ-'-- *stress shift, British only:* ˌshort-winded 'story

short|y 'ʃɔː.t|i (US) 'ʃɔːr.t̬|i **-ies** -iz

Shostakovich ˌʃɒs.tə'kəʊ.vɪtʃ (US) ˌʃɑː.stə'koʊ-

shot ʃɒt (US) ʃɑːt **-s** -s **'shot ˌput; 'shot ˌputter**

shotgun 'ʃɒt.gʌn (US) 'ʃɑːt- **-s** -z **ˌshotgun 'wedding**

Shotton 'ʃɒt.ᵊn (US) 'ʃɑː.tᵊn

Shotts ʃɒts (US) ʃɑːts

should *strong form:* ʃʊd *weak forms:* ʃəd, ʃd, ʃt

Note: Weak form word. The strong form is used for emphatic pronunciation (e.g. "He **should** have asked first"), or for contrast (e.g. "Don't tell me what I should or shouldn't do"). It is also used in final position (e.g. "We both should"). The most usual weak form is /ʃəd/, as in "When should it arrive?" /ˌwen.ʃəd.ɪt.ə'raɪv/, but in rapid speech we also find /ʃd/ before voiced sounds (e.g. "I should go now" /ˌaɪ.ʃd'gəʊ.naʊ (US) -'goʊ-/) and /ʃt/ before voiceless sounds (e.g. "You should try to finish" /ju.ʃtˌtraɪ.tə'fɪn.ɪʃ (US) -t̬ə'-/).

should|er 'ʃəʊl.d|əʳ (US) 'ʃoʊl.d|ɚ **-ers** -əz (US) -ɚz **-ering** -ᵊr.ɪŋ **-ered** -əd (US) -ɚd **'shoulder ˌbag; 'shoulder ˌblade; 'shoulder ˌpad; 'shoulder ˌstrap; a 'shoulder to ˌcry on, a ˌshoulder to 'cry on** (US) **a ˌshoulder to 'cry on**

shouldn't 'ʃʊd.ᵊnt

shout ʃaʊt **-s** -s **-ing** -ɪŋ (US) 'ʃaʊ.t̬ɪŋ **-ed** -ɪd (US) 'ʃaʊ.t̬ɪd

shov|e *(n. v.)* ʃʌv **-es** -z **-ing** -ɪŋ **-ed** -d

shove-halfpenny ˌʃʌv'heɪp.ni

shovel (S) 'ʃʌv.ᵊl **-s** -z **-(l)ing** -ɪŋ, 'ʃʌv.lɪŋ **-(l)ed** -d **-(l)er/s** -əʳ/z, 'ʃʌv.ləʳ/z (US) '-l̩.ɚ/z, '-lɚ/z **-ful/s** -fʊl/z

show ʃəʊ (US) ʃoʊ **-s** -z **-ing** -ɪŋ **-ed** -d **-n** -n **'show ˌbusiness; ˌshow 'trial, 'show ˌtrial**

showbiz 'ʃəʊ.bɪz (US) 'ʃoʊ-

showboat 'ʃəʊ.bəʊt (US) 'ʃoʊ.boʊt **-s** -s **-ing** -ɪŋ

showbread 'ʃəʊ.bred (US) 'ʃoʊ-

showcas|e 'ʃəʊ.keɪs (US) 'ʃoʊ- **-es** -ɪz **-ing** -ɪŋ **-ed** -t

showdown 'ʃəʊ.daʊn (US) 'ʃoʊ- **-s** -z

shower *fall of rain etc.:* ʃaʊəʳ (US) ʃaʊɚ **-s** -z **-ing** -ɪŋ **-ed** -d **-y** -i

shower *one who shows:* 'ʃəʊ.əʳ (US) 'ʃoʊ.ɚ **-s** -z

shower-ba|th 'ʃaʊə.bɑː|θ (US) 'ʃaʊɚ.bæ|θ **-ths** -ðz

showerhead 'ʃaʊə.hed (US) 'ʃaʊɚ- **-s** -z

showerproof 'ʃaʊə.pruːf (US) 'ʃaʊɚ-

showgirl 'ʃəʊ.gɜːl (US) 'ʃoʊ.gɝːl **-s** -z

showjump 'ʃəʊ.dʒʌmp (US) 'ʃoʊ- **-s** -s **-ing** -ɪŋ **-er/s** -əʳ/z (US) -ɚ/z

show|man 'ʃəʊ|.mən (US) 'ʃoʊ- **-men** -mən, -men

showmanship 'ʃəʊ.mən.ʃɪp (US) 'ʃoʊ-

shown *(from* **show***)* ʃəʊn (US) ʃoʊn

show-off 'ʃəʊ.ɒf (US) 'ʃoʊ.ɑːf

showpiec|e 'ʃəʊ.piːs (US) 'ʃoʊ- **-es** -ɪz

showplac|e 'ʃəʊ.pleɪs (US) 'ʃoʊ- **-es** -ɪz

showroom 'ʃəʊ.rʊm, -ruːm (US) 'ʃoʊ.ruːm, -rʊm **-s** -z

showstopp|er 'ʃəʊˌstɒp|.əʳ (US) 'ʃoʊˌstɑː.p|ɚ **-ers** -əz (US) -ɚz **-ing** -ɪŋ

show|y 'ʃəʊ|.i (US) 'ʃoʊ- **-ier** -i.əʳ (US) -i.ɚ **-iest** -i.ɪst, -i.əst **-ily** -ɪ.li, -ᵊl.i **-iness** -ɪ.nəs, -ɪ.nɪs

shoyu 'ʃɔɪ.juː (US) 'ʃoʊ.juː

shrank *(from* **shrink***)* ʃræŋk

shrapnel 'ʃræp.nᵊl

shred ʃred **-s** -z **-ding** -ɪŋ **-ded** -ɪd **-der/s** -əʳ/z (US) -ɚ/z

Shredded Wheat® ˌʃred.ɪd'*h*wiːt **-s** -s

shrew ʃruː **-s** -z

shrewd ʃruːd **-er** -əʳ (US) -ɚ **-est** -ɪst, -əst **-ly** -li **-ness** -nəs, -nɪs

shrewish 'ʃruː.ɪʃ **-ly** -li **-ness** -nəs, -nɪs

Shrewsbury *in the UK:* 'ʃrəʊz.bᵊr.i, 'ʃruːz-, '-bri (US) 'ʃruːzˌber.i, 'ʃroʊz-, -bɚ-

Note: /'ʃrəʊz / is the most widely used pronunciation, but /'ʃruːz-/ or /'ʃuːz-/ is more usually used by many local people.

Shrewsbury *in the US:* 'ʃruːz.bᵊr.i (US) -ˌber-, -bɚ-

shriek ʃriːk **-s** -s **-ing** -ɪŋ **-ed** -t

shrift ʃrɪft

shrike ʃraɪk **-s** -s

shrill ʃrɪl **-er** -əʳ (US) -ɚ **-est** -ɪst, -əst **-y** -i, -li **-ness** -nəs, -nɪs

shrimp ʃrɪmp **-s** -s **-ing** -ɪŋ **-er/s** -əʳ/z (US) -ɚ/z

Shrimpton 'ʃrɪmp.tən

shrine ʃraɪn **-s** -z

shriner (S) 'ʃraɪ.nəʳ (US) -nɚ **-s** -z

shrink ʃrɪŋk **-s** -s **-ing/ly** -ɪŋ/li **shrank** ʃræŋk **shrunk** ʃrʌŋk **shrunken** 'ʃrʌŋ.kən **ˌshrinking 'violet**

shrinkage 'ʃrɪŋ.kɪdʒ

shrink-wrap 'ʃrɪnk.ræp, -'- **-s** -s **-ping** -ɪŋ **-ped** -t

shriv|e (S) ʃraɪv **-es** -z **-ing** -ɪŋ **shrove** ʃrəʊv (US) ʃroʊv **shriven** 'ʃrɪv.ᵊn

shrivel 'ʃrɪv.ᵊl **-s** -z **-(l)ing** -ɪŋ, 'ʃrɪv.lɪŋ **-(l)ed** -d

shriven *(from* **shrive***)* 'ʃrɪv.ᵊn

shroff ʃrɒf (US) ʃrɑːf **-s** -s **-ing** -ɪŋ **-ed** -t

Shropshire 'ʃrɒp.ʃəʳ, -ˌʃɪəʳ (US) 'ʃrɑːp.ʃɚ, -ˌʃɪr

shroud ʃraʊd **-s** -z **-ing** -ɪŋ **-ed** -ɪd **-less** -ləs, -lɪs

shrove *(from* **shrive***)* ʃrəʊv (US) ʃroʊv

Shrove ʃrəʊv (US) ʃroʊv **ˌShrove 'Tuesday**

Shrovetide 'ʃrəʊv.taɪd (US) 'ʃroʊv-

shrub ʃrʌb **-s** -z

shrubber|y 'ʃrʌb.ᵊr|.i **-ies** -iz

shrubby 'ʃrʌb.i

shrug ʃrʌg **-s** -z **-ging** -ɪŋ **-ged** -d

shrunk *(from* **shrink***)* ʃrʌŋk **-en** -ᵊn

shtick ʃtɪk

shuck ʃʌk **-s** -s **-ing** -ɪŋ **-ed** -d

Shuckburgh 'ʃʌk.bᵊr.ə (US) -bɝːg, -bɚ.ə

shudd|er 'ʃʌd|.əʳ (US) -ɚ **-ers** -əz (US) -ɚz **-ering** -ᵊr.ɪŋ **-ered** -əd (US) -ɚd

shuffl|e 'ʃʌf.l̩ **-es** -z **-ing** -ɪŋ, 'ʃʌf.lɪŋ **-ed** -d **-er/s** -əʳ/z, 'ʃʌf.ləʳ/z (US) '-l̩.ɚ/z, '-lɚ/z

shuffleboard 'ʃʌf.l̩.bɔːd (US) -bɔːrd **-s** -z

shufti 'ʃʊf.ti, 'ʃʌf- **-s** -z

Shulamite 'ʃuː.lə.maɪt

shun ʃʌn **-s** -z **-ning** -ɪŋ **-ned** -d

shunt ʃʌnt **-s** -s **-ing** -ɪŋ (US) 'ʃʌn.t̬ɪŋ **-ed** -ɪd (US) 'ʃʌn.t̬ɪd **-er/s** -əʳ/z (US) 'ʃʌn.t̬ɚ/z

shush ʃʊʃ, ʃʌʃ **-es** -ɪz **-ing** -ɪŋ **-ed** -t

shut ʃʌt **-s** -s **-ting** -ɪŋ (US) 'ʃʌt̬.ɪŋ

shutdown 'ʃʌt.daʊn **-s** -z

Shute ʃuːt

shut-eye 'ʃʌt.aɪ (US) 'ʃʌt̬-

shutout 'ʃʌt.aʊt **-s** -z

shutt|er 'ʃʌt|.əʳ (US) 'ʃʌt̬|.ɚ **-ers** -əz (US) -ɚz **-ering** -ᵊr.ɪŋ **-ered** -əd (US) -ɚd

shuttle 'ʃʌt.l̩ (US) 'ʃʌt̬- **-s** -z **-ling** -ɪŋ **-ed** -d **ˌshuttle di'plomacy**

shuttlecock 'ʃʌt.l̩.kɒk (US) 'ʃʌt̬.l̩.kɑːk **-s** -s

Shuttleworth 'ʃʌt.l̩.wəθ, -wɜːθ (US) 'ʃʌt̬.l̩.wɚθ, -wɝːθ

shwa ʃwɑː **-s** -z

sh|y ʃaɪ **-ies** -aɪz **-yer** -aɪ.əʳ (US) -aɪ.ɚ **-yest** -aɪ.ɪst, -aɪ.əst **-yly** -aɪ.li **-yness** -aɪ.nəs, -nɪs **-ying** -aɪ.ɪŋ **-ied** -aɪd
shylock (S) ˈʃaɪ.lɒk (US) -lɑːk
shyster ˈʃaɪ.stəʳ (US) -stɚ **-s** -z
si siː
Sialkot siˈæl.kɒt (US) -ˈɑːl.koʊt
Siam ˌsaɪˈæm, ˈ-- (US) saɪˈæm
Siamese ˌsaɪ.əˈmiːz (US) -ˈmiːz, -ˈmiːs *stress shift, see compounds:* **ˌSiamese ˈcat; ˌSiamese ˈtwins**
Sian, Siân ʃɑːn
Sibbald ˈsɪb.əld
Sibelius sɪˈbeɪ.li.əs (US) -li.əs, -ˈbeɪl.jəs
Siberi|a saɪˈbɪə.ri|.ə (US) -ˈbɪr.i- **-an/s** -ən/z
sibilan|ce ˈsɪb.ɪ.lᵊn|*t*s, -ᵊl.ᵊn|*t*s (US) -ᵊl.ᵊn|*t*s **-t/s** -t/s
sibilation ˌsɪb.ɪˈleɪ.ʃᵊn (US) -ᵊlˈeɪ-, -əˈleɪ **-s** -z
Sibley ˈsɪb.li
sibling ˈsɪb.lɪŋ **-s** -z **ˌsibling ˈrivalry**
sibyl (S) ˈsɪb.ᵊl, -ɪl (US) -ᵊl **-s** -z
sibylline ˈsɪb.ə.laɪn, ˈ-ɪ-; sɪˈbɪl.aɪn (US) ˈsɪb.ə.laɪn, -liːn, -lɪn
sic sɪk, siːk
Sichuan ˌsɪtʃˈwɑːn (US) ˈ-ˌ-
Sicilian sɪˈsɪl.jən, sə-, -i.ən **-s** -z
Sicil|y ˈsɪs.ɪ.l|i, -ᵊl|.i (US) -ᵊl|.i **-ies** -iz
sick sɪk **-er** -əʳ (US) -ɚ **-est** -ɪst, -əst **-ness** -nəs, -nɪs **ˈsick ˌbay; ˌsick ˈbuilding ˌsyndrome; ˈsick ˌleave; ˈsick ˌpay**
sickbed ˈsɪk.bed **-s** -z
sicken ˈsɪk.ᵊn **-s** -z **-ing/ly** -ɪŋ, ˈsɪk.nɪŋ **-ed** -d
Sickert ˈsɪk.ət (US) -ɚt
sickle ˈsɪk.l̩ **-s** -z **ˌsickle-cell aˈn(a)emia**
sickl|y ˈsɪk.l|i **-ier** -i.əʳ (US) -i.ɚ **-iest** -i.ɪst, -i.əst **-iness** -ɪ.nəs, -ɪ.nɪs
sickness ˈsɪk.nəs, -nɪs
sicko ˈsɪk.əʊ (US) -oʊ **-s** -z
sick-out ˈsɪk.aʊt **-s** -s
sickroom ˈsɪk.rʊm, -ruːm (US) -ruːm, -rʊm **-s** -z
sic transit gloria mundi ˌsɪkˌtræn.zɪtˌglɔː.ri.əˈmʊn.di, ˌsiːk-, -ˌtræn*t*.sɪt-, -ˌtrɑːn.zɪt-, -ˌtrɑːn*t*.sɪt- (US) ˌsɪkˌtræn.sɪtˌglɔːr.i.əˈmʌn.di
Sid sɪd
Sidcup ˈsɪd.kʌp, -kəp
Siddeley ˈsɪd.ᵊl.i
Siddharta sɪˈdɑː.tə (US) -ˈdɑːr.t̬ə
Siddons ˈsɪd.ᵊnz
sid|e saɪd **-es** -z **-ing** -ɪŋ **-ed** -ɪd **ˈside ˌarm; ˌside by ˈside; ˈside ˌdish; ˈside ˌdrum; ˈside efˌfect; ˈside ˌissue; ˈside ˌsalad; ˈside ˌstreet; ˌknow which ˌside one's ˌbread is ˈbuttered (on), ˌknow which ˌside one's ˈbread is ˌbuttered (on); ˌlaugh on the ˌother ˌside of one's ˈface; ˌlook on the ˈbright ˌside (of things)**
sidebar ˈsaɪd.bɑːʳ (US) -bɑːr **-s** -z
sideboard ˈsaɪd.bɔːd (US) -bɔːrd **-s** -z
Sidebotham ˈsaɪdˌbɒt.əm (US) -ˌbɑː.t̬əm
Sidebottom ˈsaɪdˌbɒt.əm, ˈsiːd-, ˌsɪd.ɪ.bəˈtəʊm (US) ˈsaɪdˌbɑː.t̬əm, ˈsiːd-; ˌsɪd.ɪ.bəˈtoʊm
sideburn ˈsaɪd.bɜːn (US) -bɝːn **-s** -z
sidecar ˈsaɪd.kɑːʳ (US) -kɑːr **-s** -z
sidedish ˈsaɪd.dɪʃ **-es** -ɪz
sidekick ˈsaɪd.kɪk **-s** -s
sidelight ˈsaɪd.laɪt **-s** -s
sidelin|e ˈsaɪd.laɪn **-es** -z **-ing** -ɪŋ **-ed** -d
sidelong ˈsaɪd.lɒŋ (US) -lɑːŋ, -lɔːŋ
sidereal saɪˈdɪə.ri.əl, sɪ- (US) saɪˈdɪr.i-
siderite ˈsaɪ.dᵊr.aɪt, ˈsɪd.ᵊr- (US) ˈsɪd.ə.raɪt
Sidery ˈsaɪ.dᵊr.i
sidesaddle ˈsaɪdˌsæd.l̩ **-s** -z
sideshow ˈsaɪd.ʃəʊ (US) -ʃoʊ **-s** -z
sideslip ˈsaɪd.slɪp **-s** -s **-ping** -ɪŋ **-ped** -t
sides|man ˈsaɪdz|.mən **-men** -mən, -men
sidespin ˈsaɪd.spɪn
sidesplitting ˈsaɪdˌsplɪt.ɪŋ (US) -ˌsplɪt̬-
sidestep ˈsaɪd.step **-s** -s **-ping** -ɪŋ **-ped** -t
sidestroke ˈsaɪd.strəʊk (US) -stroʊk **-s** -s
sideswip|e ˈsaɪd.swaɪp **-es** -s **-ing** -ɪŋ **-ed** -t
sidetrack ˈsaɪd.træk **-s** -s **-ing** -ɪŋ **-ed** -t
sidewalk ˈsaɪd.wɔːk (US) -wɑːk, -wɔːk **-s** -s
sideways ˈsaɪd.weɪz
sidewinder ˈsaɪdˌwaɪn.dəʳ (US) -dɚ **-s** -z
Sidgwick ˈsɪdʒ.wɪk
siding ˈsaɪ.dɪŋ **-s** -z
Sidlaw ˈsɪd.lɔː (US) -lɑː, -lɔː
sidl|e ˈsaɪ.dl̩ **-es** -z **-ing** -ɪŋ, ˈsaɪd.lɪŋ **-ed** -d
Sidmouth ˈsɪd.məθ
Sidney ˈsɪd.ni
Sidon ˈsaɪ.dᵊn, -dɒn (US) -dᵊn
Sidonian saɪˈdəʊ.ni.ən, sɪ- (US) saɪˈdoʊ.ni.ən **-s** -z
Sidonie sɪˈdəʊ.ni (US) -ˈdoʊ-
sieg|e siːdʒ **-es** -ɪz **ˈsiege menˌtality**
Siegfried ˈsiːg.friːd *as if German:* ˈziːg (US) ˈsɪg-, ˈsiːg-
Sieg Heil ˌsiːgˈhaɪl *as if German:* ˌziːk-
Sieglinde siːˈglɪn.də *as if German:* ziː- (US) siː-, ziː-, sɪ-
Siegmund ˈsiːg.mʊnd *as if German:* ˈziːg-, -mənd (US) ˈsɪg-, ˈsiːg-
Siemens ˈsiː.mənz *as if German:* ˈziː- **ˌSiemens-ˈNixdorf®**
Siena siˈen.ə
Sienese ˌsi.enˈiːz, -əˈniːz (US) -əˈniːz, -ˈniːs
sienna siˈen.ə
sierra (S) siˈer.ə, -ˈeə.rə; (US) siˈer.ə **-s** -z
Sierra Leone siˌer.ə.liˈəʊn, -ˌeə.rə-, -ˈəʊ.ni (US) siˌer.ə.liˈoʊn
Sierra Madre siˌer.əˈmɑː.dreɪ, -ˌeə.rəˈ-; (US) siˌer.əˈ-
Sierra Nevada siˌer.ə.nəˈvɑː.də, -ˈeə.rə-; (US) siˌer.ə.nəˈvæd.ə, -ˈvɑː.də
siesta siˈes.tə **-s** -z
siev|e sɪv **-es** -z **-ing** -ɪŋ **-ed** -d
sift sɪft **-s** -s **-ing** -ɪŋ **-ed** -ɪd **-er/s** -əʳ/z (US) -ɚ/z
sigh saɪ **-s** -z **-ing** -ɪŋ **-ed** -d
sight saɪt **-s** -s **-ing/s** -ɪŋ/s (US) ˈsaɪ.t̬ɪŋ/s **-ed** -ɪd (US) ˈsaɪ.t̬ɪd **-less/ness** -ləs, -lɪs **ˌsight unˈseen**
sightl|y ˈsaɪt.l|i **-iness** -ɪ.nəs, -ɪ.nɪs
sightread *present tense:* ˈsaɪt.riːd **-s** -z **-ing** -ɪŋ *past tense:* ˈsaɪt.red
sightreader ˈsaɪtˌriː.dəʳ (US) -dɚ **-s** -z
sightscreen ˈsaɪt.skriːn **-s** -z
sightsee ˈsaɪt.siː **-s** -z **-ing** -ɪŋ
sight-seeing ˈsaɪtˌsiː.ɪŋ
sightseer ˈsaɪtˌsiː.əʳ (US) -ɚ **-s** -z
Sigismond, Sigismund ˈsɪg.ɪs.mənd, ˈsɪdʒ-, -ɪz- (US) -ɪs-
sigma (S) ˈsɪg.mə **-s** -z
Sigmund ˈsɪg.mənd *as if German:* ˈzɪg-
sign saɪn **-s** -z **-ing/s** -ɪŋ/s **-ed** -d **-er/s** -əʳ/z (US) -ɚ/z **-age** -ɪdʒ **ˈsign ˌlanguage; ˌsign of the ˈtimes**
signal ˈsɪg.nᵊl **-s** -z **-(l)y** -i **-(l)ing** -ɪŋ **-(l)ed** -d **-(l)er/s** -əʳ/z (US) -ɚ/z **ˈsignal ˌbox**
signaliz|e, -is|e ˈsɪg.nᵊl.aɪz (US) -nə.laɪz **-es** -ɪz **-ing** -ɪŋ **-ed** -d
signal|man ˈsɪg.nᵊl|.mən, -mæn **-men** -mən, -men
signator|y ˈsɪg.nə.tᵊr|.i (US) -tɔːr- **-ies** -iz
signature ˈsɪg.nə.tʃəʳ, -nɪ- (US) -nə.tʃɚ **-s** -z **ˈsignature ˌtune**
signboard ˈsaɪn.bɔːd, ˈsaɪm- (US) ˈsaɪn.bɔːrd **-s** -z
signer ˈsaɪ.nəʳ (US) -nɚ **-s** -z
signet ˈsɪg.nɪt, -nət **-s** -s **ˈsignet ˌring**
significance sɪgˈnɪf.ɪ.kən*t*s, ˈ-ə- (US) ˈ-ə-
significant sɪgˈnɪf.ɪ.kənt, ˈ-ə- (US) ˈ-ə- **-ly** -li **sigˌnificant ˈother**
signification ˌsɪg.nɪ.fɪˈkeɪ.ʃᵊn, -nə- (US) -nə-
significative sɪgˈnɪf.ɪ.kə.tɪv, ˈ-ə-, -keɪ- (US) -keɪ.t̬ɪv **-ly** -li **-ness** -nəs, -nɪs
signi|fy ˈsɪg.nɪ|.faɪ, -nə- (US) -nə- **-fies** -faɪz **-fying** -faɪ.ɪŋ **-fied** -faɪd **-fier/s** -faɪ.əʳ/z (US) -faɪ.ɚ/z
signor (S) ˈsiː.njɔːʳ (US) siːˈnjɔːr **-s** -z
signora (S) siːˈnjɔː.r|ə (US) -ˈnɔːr|.ə **-az** -əz **-ez** -eɪz
signorina (S) ˌsiː.njɔːˈriː.nə, -njəˈ-
signpost ˈsaɪn.pəʊst, ˈsaɪm- (US) ˈsaɪn.poʊst **-s** -s **-ing** -ɪŋ **-ed** -ɪd
Sigourney sɪˈgɔː.ni, sə- (US) -ˈgɔːr-
Sigurd *English first name:* ˈsiː.gɜːd, ˈsɪg.ɜːd (US) ˈsɪg.ɚd *Scandinavian name:* ˈsɪg.ʊəd, -ɜːd (US) ˈsɪg.ɚd

Sikes saɪks
Sikh siːk **-s** -s **-ism** -ɪ.zᵊm
Sikkim ˈsɪk.ɪm, sɪˈkɪm (US) ˈsɪk.ɪm
Sikorsky sɪˈkɔː.ski (US) -ˈkɔːr-
silage ˈsaɪ.lɪdʒ
Silas ˈsaɪ.ləs, -læs (US) -ləs
Silchester ˈsɪl.tʃɪ.stəʳ, -tʃə-, -tʃes.təʳ (US) -tʃes.tɚ
Sileby ˈsaɪl.bi
silenc|e ˈsaɪ.lənts **-es** -ɪz **-ing** -ɪŋ **-ed** -t
silencer ˈsaɪ.lənt.səʳ (US) -sɚ **-s** -z
silent ˈsaɪ.lənt **-ly** -li **-ness** -nəs, -nɪs ˌ**silent maˈjority**; ˌ**silent ˈpartner**
Silenus saɪˈliː.nəs, sɪ-, -ˈleɪ- (US) saɪˈliː-
Silesi|a saɪˈliː.zi|.ə, sɪ-, -ʒi|.ə, ˈ-ʒ|ə, -si|.ə, -ʃi|.ə, ˈ-ʃ|ə (US) saɪˈliː.ʃ|ə, sɪ-, -ʒ|ə **-an/s** -ən/z
silex ˈsaɪ.leks
silhouett|e ˌsɪl.uˈet, ˈ--- (US) ˌsɪl.uˈet **-es** -s **-ing** -ɪŋ **-ed** -ɪd
silica ˈsɪl.ɪ.kə ˌ**silica ˈgel** (US) ˈ**silica** ˌ**gel**
silicate ˈsɪl.ɪ.keɪt, ˈ-ə-, -kət, -kɪt (US) -ɪ.keɪt, -kɪt
silicon ˈsɪl.ɪ.kən, ˈ-ə- (US) ˈ-ɪ-, -kɑːn ˌ**silicon ˈchip** (US) ˈ**silicon** ˌ**chip**; ˌ**Silicon ˈValley**
silicone ˈsɪl.ɪ.kəʊn, ˈ-ə- (US) -ɪ.koʊn
silicosis ˌsɪl.ɪˈkəʊ.sɪs, -əˈ- (US) -ɪˈkoʊ-
silicotic ˌsɪl.ɪˈkɒt.ɪk, -əˈ- (US) -ɪˈkɑː.t̬ɪk **-s** -s
silk (S) sɪlk **-s** -s **-en** -ᵊn
Silkin ˈsɪl.kɪn
silk-screen ˈsɪlk.skriːn **-s** -z **-ing** -ɪŋ **-ed** -d ˌ**silk-screen ˈprinting**
silkworm ˈsɪlk.wɜːm (US) -wɝːm **-s** -z
silk|y ˈsɪl.k|i **-ier** -i.əʳ (US) -i.ɚ **-iest** -i.ɪst, -i.əst **-iness** -ɪ.nəs, -ɪ.nɪs
sill (S) sɪl **-s** -z
sillabub ˈsɪl.ə.bʌb, -bəb (US) -bʌb **-s** -z
Sillery ˈsɪl.ᵊr.i
Sillitoe ˈsɪl.ɪ.təʊ (US) -toʊ
Silloth ˈsɪl.əθ
sill|y ˈsɪl|.i **-ies** -iz **-ier** -i.əʳ (US) -i.ɚ **-iest** -i.ɪst, -i.əst **-ily** -ɪ.li, -ᵊl.i **-iness** -ɪ.nəs, -ɪ.nɪs
silly-bill|y ˌsɪl.iˈbɪl|.i **-ies** -iz
silo ˈsaɪ.ləʊ (US) -loʊ **-s** -z
Siloam saɪˈləʊ.əm, sɪ-, -æm (US) sɪˈloʊ.əm, saɪ-
Silsden ˈsɪlz.dən
silt sɪlt **-s** -s **-ing** -ɪŋ (US) ˈsɪl.t̬ɪŋ **-ed** -ɪd (US) ˈsɪl.t̬ɪd **-y** -i (US) ˈsɪl.t̬i
Silurian saɪˈlʊə.ri.ən, sɪ-, -ˈljʊə-, -ˈljɔː- (US) sɪˈlʊr.i-, saɪ-
Silva ˈsɪl.və
silvan ˈsɪl.vən
Silvanus sɪlˈveɪ.nəs
silv|er (S) ˈsɪl.v|əʳ (US) -v|ɚ **-ers** -əz (US) -ɚz **-ering** -ᵊr.ɪŋ **-ered** -əd (US) -ɚd **-ery** -ᵊr.i **-eriness** -ᵊr.ɪ.nəs, -nɪs ˌ**silver ˈbirch**; ˌ**silver ˈfoil** (US) ˈ**silver** ˌ**foil**; ˌ**silver ˈlining**; ˌ**silver ˈnitrate**; ˌ**silver ˈpaper**; ˌ**silver ˈplate**; (US) ˈ**silver** ˌ**plate**; ˌ**silver ˈscreen**; ˌ**silver ˈspoon**; ˌ**silver ˈwedding**
silverfish ˈsɪl.və.fɪʃ (US) -vɚ- **-es** -ɪz
Silverman ˈsɪl.və.mən (US) -vɚ-
Silvers ˈsɪl.vəz (US) -vɚz
silverside ˈsɪl.və.saɪd (US) -vɚ- **-s** -z
silversmith ˈsɪl.və.smɪθ (US) -vɚ- **-s** -s
Silverstone ˈsɪl.və.stəʊn, -stən (US) -vɚ.stoʊn, -stən
silver-tongued ˌsɪl.vəˈtʌŋd (US) -vɚˈ- *stress shift:* ˌsilver-tongued ˈdevil
Silvertown ˈsɪl.və.taʊn (US) -vɚ- **-s** -z
silverware ˈsɪl.və.weəʳ (US) -vɚ.wer
Silvester sɪlˈves.təʳ (US) -tɚ
Silvia ˈsɪl.vi.ə
Silvikrin® ˈsɪl.vɪ.krɪn, -və-
Sim sɪm
Simca® ˈsɪm.kə **-s** -z
Simcox ˈsɪm.kɒks (US) -kɑːks
Simenon ˈsiː.mə.nɔ̃ːŋ, ˈsɪm.ə-, -nɒn (US) ˈsiː.mə.noʊn, -nɔ̃ːn
Simeon ˈsɪm.i.ən
simian ˈsɪm.i.ən **-s** -z
similar ˈsɪm.ɪ.ləʳ, ˈ-ə- (US) -ə.lɚ **-ly** -li
similarit|y ˌsɪm.ɪˈlær.ə.t|i, -əˈ-, -ɪ.t|i (US) -əˈler.ə.t̬|i, -ˈlær- **-ies** -iz
simile ˈsɪm.ɪ.li, -ᵊl.i (US) -ə.li **-s** -z
similitude sɪˈmɪl.ɪ.tjuːd, ˈ-ə-, -tʃuːd (US) səˈmɪl.ə.tuːd, -tjuːd **-s** -z
Simla ˈsɪm.lə
simm|er ˈsɪm|.əʳ (US) -ɚ **-ers** -əz (US) -ɚz **-ering** -ᵊr.ɪŋ **-ered** -əd (US) -ɚd
Simmonds ˈsɪm.əndz
Simmons ˈsɪm.ənz
Simms sɪmz
simnel (S) ˈsɪm.nᵊl **-s** -z ˈ**simnel** ˌ**cake**
Simon ˈsaɪ.mən
Simond ˈsaɪ.mənd, ˈsɪm.ənd
Simonds ˈsɪm.əndz
Simone sɪˈməʊn, sə- (US) -ˈmoʊn
simoniacal ˌsaɪ.məʊˈnaɪə.kᵊl (US) -məˈ-, ˌsɪm.əˈ-
Simons ˈsaɪ.mənz
simony ˈsaɪ.mə.ni, ˈsɪm.ə-
simoom sɪˈmuːm (US) sɪ-, saɪ- **-s** -z
simpatico sɪmˈpæt.ɪ.kəʊ (US) -ˈpæt̬.ɪ.koʊ
simp|er ˈsɪm.p|əʳ (US) -p|ɚ **-ers** -əz (US) -ɚz **-ering/ly** -ᵊr.ɪŋ **-ered** -əd (US) -ɚd
Simpkin ˈsɪmp.kɪn **-s** -z **-son** -sən
simp|le ˈsɪm.p|l̩ **-ler** -ləʳ (US) -lɚ **-lest** -lɪst, -ləst **-ly** -li **-leness** -l̩.nəs, -nɪs
simplehearted ˌsɪm.pl̩ˈhɑː.tɪd (US) -ˈhɑːr.t̬ɪd *stress shift:* ˌsimplehearted ˈperson
simple-minded ˌsɪm.pl̩ˈmaɪn.dɪd *stress shift:* ˌsimple-minded ˈperson
simpleton ˈsɪm.pl̩.tᵊn (US) -tən **-s** -z
simplex ˈsɪm.pleks **-es** -ɪz
simplicity sɪmˈplɪs.ə.ti, -ɪ.ti (US) -ə.t̬i
simplification ˌsɪm.plɪ.fɪˈkeɪ.ʃᵊn, -plə- (US) -plə- **-s** -z
simpli|fy ˈsɪm.plɪ|.faɪ (US) -plə- **-fies** -faɪz **-fying** -faɪ.ɪŋ **-fied** -faɪd
simplistic sɪmˈplɪs.tɪk **-ally** -ᵊl.i, -li
Simplon ˈsæ̃m.plɔ̃ːŋ, ˈsæm-, ˈsɪm-, -plən (US) ˈsɪm.plɑːn; ˈsæ̃m.plɔ̃ːn
simply ˈsɪm.pli
Simpson ˈsɪmp.sən
Sims sɪmz
Simson ˈsɪmp.sən
simulacr|um ˌsɪm.jəˈleɪ.kr|əm, -jʊˈ-, -ˈlæk.r|əm (US) -ˈleɪ-, -ˈlæk.r|əm **-ums** -əmz **-a** -ə
simu|late ˈsɪm.jə|.leɪt, -jʊ- **-lates** -leɪts **-lating** -leɪ.tɪŋ (US) -leɪ.t̬ɪŋ **-lated** -leɪ.tɪd (US) -leɪ.t̬ɪd
simulation ˌsɪm.jəˈleɪ.ʃᵊn, -jʊˈ- **-s** -z
simulator ˈsɪm.jə.leɪ.təʳ, -jʊ- (US) -t̬ɚ **-s** -z ˈ**flight** ˌ**simulator**
simulcast ˈsɪm.ᵊl.kɑːst (US) ˈsaɪ.mᵊl.kæst, ˈsɪm.ᵊl- **-s** -s **-ing** -ɪŋ
simultaneity ˌsɪm.ᵊl.təˈneɪ.ə.ti, ˌsaɪ.mᵊl-, -ˈniː-, -ɪ.ti (US) ˌsaɪ.mᵊl.təˈniː.ə.t̬i, ˌsɪm.ᵊl-
simultaneous ˌsɪm.ᵊlˈteɪ.ni.əs, ˌsaɪ.mᵊlˈ- (US) ˌsaɪ.mᵊlˈteɪ.njəs, ˌsɪm.ᵊlˈ-, -ni.əs **-ly** -li **-ness** -nəs, -nɪs
sin (*n. v.*) *do wrong:* sɪn **-s** -z **-ning** -ɪŋ **-ned** -d **-ner/s** -əʳ/z (US) -ɚ/z ˈ**sin** ˌ**bin**
sin *in trigonometry:* saɪn
Sinai ˈsaɪ.naɪ, -ni.aɪ, -neɪ- (US) ˈsaɪ.naɪ
sinapism ˈsɪn.ə.pɪ.zᵊm **-s** -z
Sinatra sɪˈnɑː.trə
Sinbad ˈsɪn.bæd, ˈsɪm- (US) ˈsɪn-
since sɪnts
sincer|e sɪnˈsɪəʳ, sᵊn- (US) sɪnˈsɪr **-er** -əʳ (US) -ɚ **-est** -ɪst, -əst **-ely** -li **-eness** -nəs, -nɪs
sincerity sɪnˈser.ə.ti, sᵊn-, -ɪ.ti (US) sɪnˈser.ə.t̬i
Sinclair ˈsɪŋ.kleəʳ, ˈsɪn-, -kləʳ; sɪŋˈkleəʳ, sɪn- (US) sɪnˈkler, ˈ--
Sind sɪnd
Sindbad ˈsɪnd.bæd
Sindh sɪnd
Sindhi ˈsɪn.diː, -di
Sindlesham ˈsɪn.dl̩.ʃəm
Sindy® ˈsɪn.di ˈ**Sindy** ˌ**doll**
sine saɪn **-s** -z
Sinead, Sinéad ʃɪˈneɪd, -ˈneəd (US) -ˈneɪd
sinecure ˈsaɪ.nɪ.kjʊəʳ, ˈsɪn.ɪ-, -kjɔːʳ (US) ˈsaɪ.nə.kjʊr, ˈsɪn.ə- **-s** -z
sine die ˌsaɪ.nɪˈdaɪ.iː, -ɪ; ˌsɪn.ɪˈdiː.eɪ (US) ˌsaɪ.niˈdaɪ.i, ˌsɪn.eɪˈdiː.eɪ
Sinel ˈsɪn.ᵊl
sine qua non ˌsɪn.i.kwɑːˈnəʊn, ˌsaɪ.ni.kweɪˈnɒn (US) ˌsɪn.eɪ.kwɑːˈnoʊn, ˌsaɪ.ni.kweɪˈnɑːn **-s** -z

sinew ˈsɪn.juː **-s** -z **-y** -i
sinfonia sɪnˈfəʊ.ni.ə; ˌsɪn.fəʊˈniː- ⓤⓢ ˌsɪn.fəˈniː-; sɪnˈfoʊ.ni- **-s** -z
sinfonia concertante sɪnˌfəʊ.ni.əˌkɒn*t*.ʃəˈtæn.teɪ ⓤⓢ ˌsɪn.fəˌniː.əˌkɑːn*t*.sɚˈtɑːn.teɪ, -ˌkɑːn.tʃɚˈ-; sɪnˌfoʊ.ni-
sinfonietta ˌsɪn.fəʊ.niˈet.ə, -fɒn.iˈ- ⓤⓢ -fəˈnjet̬-, -foʊˈ- **-s** -z
sinful ˈsɪn.fᵊl, -fʊl **-ly** -i **-ness** -nəs, -nɪs
sing sɪŋ **-s** -z **-ing** -ɪŋ **sang** sæŋ **sung** sʌŋ **singer/s** ˈsɪŋ.əʳ/z ⓤⓢ -ɚ/z
singable ˈsɪŋ.ə.bl̩
sing-along ˈsɪŋ.ə.lɒŋ ⓤⓢ -lɑːŋ **-s** -z
Singapore ˌsɪŋ.əˈpɔːʳ, -gəˈ-, ˈ--- ⓤⓢ ˈsɪŋ.ə.pɔːr, -gə-
Singaporean ˌsɪŋ.ə.pɔːˈriː.ən, -gə-; -ˈpɔː.ri- ⓤⓢ ˌsɪŋ.ə.pɔːˈriː-, -gə-; -ˈpɔːr.i- **-s** -z
sing|e sɪndʒ **-es** -ɪz **-eing** -ɪŋ **-ed** -d
Singer ˈsɪŋ.əʳ, -gəʳ ⓤⓢ -ɚ, -gɚ
Singh sɪŋ
Singhalese ˌsɪŋ.*h*əˈliːz, -gəˈ- ⓤⓢ -gəˈliːz, -ˈliːs
sing|le (S) ˈsɪŋ.gl̩ **-les** -l̩z **-ling** -ɪŋ, -sɪŋ.glɪŋ **-led** -d **-ly** -li **-leness** -l̩.nəs, -nɪs ˌ**single** ˈ**bed** ⓤⓢ ˈ**single** ˌ**bed**; ˌ**single** ˈ**currency**; ˌ**single** ˈ**file**; ˌ**single** ˈ**figures**
single-breasted ˌsɪŋ.gl̩ˈbres.tɪd *stress shift:* ˌsingle-breasted ˈjacket
single-decker ˌsɪŋ.gl̩ˈdek.əʳ ⓤⓢ -ɚ **-s** -z *stress shift:* ˌsingle-decker ˈbus
single-handed ˌsɪŋ.gl̩ˈhæn.dɪd **-ly** -li **-ness** -nəs, -nɪs *stress shift:* ˌsingle-handed ˈcrossing
single-hearted ˌsɪŋ.gl̩ˈhɑː.tɪd ⓤⓢ ˈsɪŋ.gl̩ˌhɑːr.t̬ɪd **-ly** -li **-ness** -nəs, -nɪs *stress shift, British only:* ˌsingle-hearted ˈlove
single-minded ˌsɪŋ.gl̩ˈmaɪn.dɪd ⓤⓢ ˈsɪŋ.gl̩ˌmaɪn- **-ly** -li **-ness** -nəs, -nɪs *stress shift, British only:* ˌsingle-minded ˈperson
singlestick ˈsɪŋ.gl̩.stɪk **-s** -s
singlet ˈsɪŋ.glɪt, -glət **-s** -s
singleton (S) ˈsɪŋ.gl̩.tən ⓤⓢ -t̬ən, -tən **-s** -z
singly ˈsɪŋ.gli
singsong ˈsɪŋ.sɒŋ ⓤⓢ -sɑːŋ, -sɔːŋ **-s** -z
singular ˈsɪŋ.gjə.ləʳ, -gjʊ- ⓤⓢ -lɚ **-s** -z **-ly** -li
singularit|y ˌsɪŋ.gjəˈlær.ə.t|i, -gjʊˈ-, -ɪ.t|i ⓤⓢ -ˈler.ə.t̬|i, -ˈlær- **-ies** -iz
Sinhalese ˌsɪŋ.*h*əˈliːz, ˌsɪn- ⓤⓢ ˌsɪn.*h*əˈliːz, -ˈliːs
Sinim ˈsɪn.ɪm, ˈsaɪ.nɪm
sinister ˈsɪn.ɪ.stəʳ ⓤⓢ -stɚ
sinistral ˈsɪn.ɪ.strᵊl **-ly** -i
Sinitic saɪˈnɪt.ɪk, sɪ- ⓤⓢ -ˈnɪt̬-
sink sɪŋk **-s** -s **-ing** -ɪŋ **sank** sæŋk **sunk** sʌŋk **sunken** ˈsʌŋ.kᵊn
sinker ˈsɪŋ.kəʳ ⓤⓢ -kɚ **-s** -z
sinless ˈsɪn.ləs, -lɪs **-ly** -li **-ness** -nəs, -nɪs
sinner ˈsɪn.əʳ ⓤⓢ -ɚ **-s** -z
Sinn Fein ˌʃɪnˈfeɪn **-er/s** -əʳ/z ⓤⓢ -ɚ/z
sinologue ˈsɪn.ə.lɒg, ˈsaɪ.nə-, -ləʊg ⓤⓢ ˈsaɪ.nə.lɑːg, ˈsɪn.ə-, -lɔːg **-s** -z
sinolog|y saɪˈnɒl.ə.dʒ|i, sɪ- ⓤⓢ -ˈnɑː.lə- **-ist/s** -ɪst/s
sinuosit|y ˌsɪn.juˈɒs.ə.t|i, -ɪ.t|i ⓤⓢ -ˈɑː.sə.t̬|i **-ies** -iz
sinuous ˈsɪn.ju.əs **-ly** -li **-ness** -nəs, -nɪs
sinus ˈsaɪ.nəs **-es** -ɪz
sinusitis ˌsaɪ.nəˈsaɪ.tɪs ⓤⓢ -t̬ɪs
sinusoid ˈsaɪ.nə.sɔɪd **-s** -z
Siobhan ʃɪˈvɔːn, ʃə- ⓤⓢ -ˈvɑːn, -ˈvɔːn
Sion ˈsaɪ.ən, ˈzaɪ- ⓤⓢ ˈsaɪ-
Sioux *singular:* suː, sjuː ⓤⓢ suː *plural:* suːz, sjuːz, suː, sjuː ⓤⓢ suːz, suː
sip sɪp **-s** -s **-ping** -ɪŋ **-ped** -t
siphon (*n. v.*) ˈsaɪ.fᵊn **-s** -z **-ing** -ɪŋ, ˈsaɪf.nɪŋ **-ed** -d
sir (S) *strong forms:* sɜːʳ ⓤⓢ sɝː *weak forms:* səʳ ⓤⓢ sɚ **-s** -z
Note: Weak form word. The strong form is used in various social situations. In school, it is often used by children to address a male teacher (e.g. “Sir, can I go now?”), and contrastively (e.g. “Dear Sir or Madam”). Similarly, in old-fashioned speech, the strong form would be used to begin addressing someone (e.g. “Sir, you are a scoundrel”). When it occurs utterance-finally in addressing someone, either form may be used, although the weak form is more common in military usage (e.g. “Ready to sail, sir”). In the title of a Knight (e.g. **Sir John Roberts**), the weak form is always used.
sirdar (S) ˈsɜː.dɑːʳ ⓤⓢ sɚˈdɑːr; ˈsɝː.dɑːr **-s** -z
sir|e saɪəʳ ⓤⓢ saɪɚ **-es** -z **-ing** -ɪŋ **-ed** -d
siren ˈsaɪə.rən, -rɪn ⓤⓢ ˈsaɪ.rən **-s** -z
Sirion ˈsɪr.i.ən
Sirius ˈsɪr.i.əs
sirloin ˈsɜː.lɔɪn ⓤⓢ ˈsɝː- **-s** -z
sirocco sɪˈrɒk.əʊ, sə- ⓤⓢ səˈrɑː.koʊ, ʃə- **-s** -z
Siros ˈsɪə.rɒs ⓤⓢ ˈsiː.rɑːs
sirrah ˈsɪr.ə
sirree, siree ˌsɜːˈriː, sə- ⓤⓢ sə-
sis sɪs
sisal ˈsaɪ.sᵊl ⓤⓢ ˈsaɪ-, ˈsɪs.ᵊl
Sisal *Mexican port:* sɪˈsɑːl ⓤⓢ ˈsiː.səl, ˈsɪs.ɑːl
Sisera ˈsɪs.ᵊr.ə
siskin (S) ˈsɪs.kɪn **-s** -z
Sisley ˈsɪz.li
Sissinghurst ˈsɪs.ɪŋ.hɜːst ⓤⓢ -hɝːst
Sisson ˈsɪs.ᵊn **-s** -z
siss|y ˈsɪs|.i **-ies** -iz
sist|er ˈsɪs.t|əʳ ⓤⓢ -t|ɚ **-ers** -əz ⓤⓢ -ɚz **-erly** -ᵊl.i ⓤⓢ -ɚ.li
sisterhood ˈsɪs.tə.hʊd ⓤⓢ -tɚ- **-s** -z
sister-in-law ˈsɪs.tᵊr.ɪn.lɔː ⓤⓢ -tɚ.ɪn.lɑː, -lɔː **sisters-in-law** -təz- ⓤⓢ -tɚz-
Sistine ˈsɪs.tiːn, -taɪn ⓤⓢ -tiːn, -ˈ- ˌ**Sistine** ˈ**Chapel**
sistrum ˈsɪs.trəm **-s** -z
Sisulu sɪˈsuː.luː
Sisyphean, Sisyphian ˌsɪs.ɪˈfiː.ən, -əˈ- ⓤⓢ -əˈ-
Sisyphus ˈsɪs.ɪ.fəs, ˈ-ə- ⓤⓢ ˈ-ə-
sit sɪt **-s** -s **-ting** -ɪŋ/z ⓤⓢ ˈsɪt̬.ɪŋ/z **sat** sæt ˌ**Sitting** ˈ**Bull**; ˌ**sit on the** ˈ**fence**
Sita ˈsɪt.ə, ˈsiː.tə ⓤⓢ ˈsiː.tɑː
sitar sɪˈtɑːʳ; ˈsɪt.ɑːʳ ⓤⓢ sɪˈtɑːr
sitcom ˈsɪt.kɒm ⓤⓢ -kɑːm **-s** -z
sit-down ˈsɪt.daʊn
sit|e saɪt **-es** -s **-ing** -ɪŋ **-ed** -ɪd
sit-in ˈsɪt.ɪn ⓤⓢ ˈsɪt̬- **-s** -z
sitter ˈsɪt.əʳ ⓤⓢ ˈsɪt̬.ɚ **-s** -z
sitting ˈsɪt.ɪŋ ⓤⓢ ˈsɪt̬- **-s** -z ˌ**sitting** ˈ**duck**; ˈ**sitting** ˌ**room**; ˌ**sitting** ˈ**target**; ˌ**sitting** ˈ**tenant**
Sittingbourne ˈsɪt.ɪŋ.bɔːn ⓤⓢ ˈsɪt̬.ɪŋ.bɔːrn
situate (*adj.*) ˈsɪt.ju.eɪt, ˈsɪtʃ.u-, -ɪt, -ət ⓤⓢ ˈsɪtʃ.u.ɪt, -eɪt
situ|ate (*v.*) ˈsɪt.ju|.eɪt, ˈsɪtʃ.u- ⓤⓢ ˈsɪtʃ.u- **-ates** -eɪts **-ating** -eɪ.tɪŋ ⓤⓢ -eɪ.t̬ɪŋ **-ated** -eɪ.tɪd ⓤⓢ -eɪ.t̬ɪd
situation ˌsɪt.juˈeɪ.ʃᵊn, ˌsɪtʃ.uˈ- ⓤⓢ ˌsɪtʃ.uˈ- **-s** -z ˌ**situation** ˈ**comedy**
sit-up ˈsɪt.ʌp **-s** -s
Sitwell ˈsɪt.wəl, -wel
Siva ˈʃiː.və, ˈsiː-, ˈsɪv.ə, ˈʃɪv- ⓤⓢ ˈʃiː.və, ˈsiː-
Siward ˈsjuː.əd ⓤⓢ -ɚd, ˈsuː-
six sɪks **-es** -ɪz **-fold** -fəʊld ⓤⓢ -foʊld
sixer ˈsɪk.səʳ ⓤⓢ -sɚ **-s** -z
sixish ˈsɪk.sɪʃ
six-pack ˈsɪks.pæk **-s** -s
six|pence ˈsɪks|.pən*t*s **-pences** -pən*t*.sɪz **-penny** -pᵊn.i
Note: See note under **penny**.
six-shooter ˈsɪksˌʃuː.təʳ, ˈsɪkʃ-, ˌ-ˈ-- ⓤⓢ ˈsɪksˌʃuː.t̬ɚ **-s** -z
sixte sɪkst
sixteen ˌsɪkˈstiːn **-s** -z **-th/s** -θ/s **-thly** -θ.li *stress shift, British only:* ˌsixteen ˈdays **six**ˈ**teenth** ˌ**note**
sixteenmo, 16mo sɪkˈstiːn.məʊ ⓤⓢ -moʊ **-s** -z
sixth sɪksθ ⓤⓢ sɪkstθ **-s** -s **-ly** -li ˈ**sixth** ˌ**form**; ˌ**sixth form** ˈ**college**; ˌ**sixth** ˈ**sense**
Sixtus ˈsɪk.stəs
sixt|y ˈsɪk.st|i **-ies** -iz **-ieth/s** -i.əθs, -i.ɪθ/s

sixty-nine, 69 ˌsɪk.stiˈnaɪn
sizar ˈsaɪ.zəʳ ⓤⓢ -zɚ **-s** -z **-ship/s** -ʃɪp/s
siz|e saɪz **-es** -ɪz **-ing** -ɪŋ **-ed** -d
sizeab|le, sizab|le ˈsaɪ.zə.bl̩ **-ly** -li **-leness** -l̩.nəs, -nɪs
Sizer ˈsaɪ.zəʳ ⓤⓢ -zɚ
Sizewell ˈsaɪz.wəl, -wel
sizzl|e ˈsɪz.l̩ **-es** -z **-ing** -ɪŋ, ˈsɪz.lɪŋ **-ed** -d
sizzler ˈsɪz.ləʳ, -l̩.əʳ ⓤⓢ ˈ-lɚ, -l̩.ɚ **-s** -z
sjambok ˈʃæm.bɒk, -bʌk ⓤⓢ -bɑːk, -bʌk **-s** -s **-ing** -ɪŋ **-ed** -t
ska skɑː
Skagerrak ˈskæg.ə.ræk
Skara Brae ˌskær.əˈbreɪ
skat skæt
skat|e skeɪt **-es** -s **-ing** -ɪŋ ⓤⓢ ˈskeɪ.t̬ɪŋ **-ed** -ɪd ⓤⓢ ˈskeɪ.t̬ɪd **-er/s** -əʳ/z ⓤⓢ ˈskeɪ.t̬ɚ/z
skateboard ˈskeɪt.bɔːd ⓤⓢ -bɔːrd **-s** -z **-er/s** -əʳ/z ⓤⓢ -ɚ/z **-ing** -ɪŋ
skating-rink ˈskeɪ.tɪŋ.rɪŋk **-s** -s
skean dhu ˌskiː.ənˈduː, ˌskiːnˈ- ⓤⓢ ˌskiːn-, ˌʃkiːn- **-s** -z
Skeat skiːt
skedaddl|e skɪˈdæd.l̩ **-es** -z **-ing** -ɪŋ, -ˈdæd.lɪŋ **-ed** -d
Skeels skiːlz
Skeggs skegz
Skegness ˌskegˈnes *stress shift:* ˌSkegness ˈbeach
skein skeɪn **-s** -z
skeletal ˈskel.ɪ.təl, ˈ-ə-; skɪˈliː-, skə- ⓤⓢ ˈskel.ə.t̬əl **-ly** -i
skeleton ˈskel.ɪ.tən, ˈ-ə- ⓤⓢ ˈ-ə- **-s** -z **ˈskeleton ˌkey; ˌskeleton in the ˈcupboard; ˌskeleton in the ˈcloset**
Skelmanthorpe ˈskel.mən.θɔːp ⓤⓢ -θɔːrp
Skelmersdale ˈskel.məz.deɪl ⓤⓢ -mɚz-
skelter ˈskel.təʳ ⓤⓢ -t̬ɚ
Skelton ˈskel.tən
skeptic ˈskep.tɪk **-s** **-al** -əl **-ally** -əl.i, -li
skepticism ˈskep.tɪ.sɪ.zəm, -tə- ⓤⓢ -tə-
sketch sketʃ **-es** -ɪz **-ing** -ɪŋ **-ed** -t **-able** -ə.bl̩ **-er/s** -əʳ/z ⓤⓢ -ɚ/z
sketchbook ˈsketʃ.bʊk **-s** -s
Sketchley ˈsketʃ.li
sketchpad ˈsketʃ.pæd **-s** -z
sketch|y ˈsketʃ|.i **-ier** -i.əʳ ⓤⓢ -i.ɚ **-iest** -i.ɪst, -i.əst **-ily** -ɪ.li, -əl.i **-iness** -ɪ.nəs, -ɪ.nɪs
skew skjuː **-s** -z **-ing** -ɪŋ **-ed** -d
skewbald ˈskjuː.bɔːld ⓤⓢ -bɑːld, -bɔːld
skewer skjʊəʳ ⓤⓢ ˈskjuː.ɚ, ˈskjuː.ɚ **-s** -z **-ing** -ɪŋ **-ed** -d
skew-whiff ˌskjuːˈ*h*wɪf
Skey skiː
ski skiː **-s** -z **-ing** -ɪŋ **-ed** -d **ˈski ˌlift; ˈski ˌpants**
skibob ˈskiː.bɒb ⓤⓢ -bɑːb **-s** -z **-bing** -ɪŋ **-bed** -d
skid skɪd **-s** -z **-ding** -ɪŋ **-ded** -ɪd **-dy** -i ˌ**skid ˈrow**
Skiddaw ˈskɪd.ɔː *locally:* -ə ⓤⓢ ˈskɪd.ɑː, -ɔː
Skidmore ˈskɪd.mɔːʳ ⓤⓢ -mɔːr
skidpan ˈskɪd.pæn **-s** -z
skier ˈskiː.əʳ ⓤⓢ -ɚ **-s** -z
skiff skɪf **-s** -s
skiffle ˈskɪf.l̩
ski-jump ˈskiː.dʒʌmp **-s** -s **-ing** -ɪŋ **-ed** -t **-er/s** -əʳ/z ⓤⓢ -ɚ/z
skilful ˈskɪl.fəl, -fʊl **-ly** -i **-ness** -nəs, -nɪs
skill skɪl **-s** -z **-ed** -d
skillet ˈskɪl.ɪt **-s** -s
skilly ˈskɪl.i
skim skɪm **-s** -z **-ming** -ɪŋ **-med** -d **-mer/s** -əʳ/z ⓤⓢ -ɚ/z
skimp skɪmp **-s** -s **-ing** -ɪŋ/li **-ed** -t
skimp|y ˈskɪm.p|i **-ier** -i.əʳ ⓤⓢ -i.ɚ **-iest** -i.ɪst, -i.əst **-ily** -ɪ.li, -əl.i **-iness** -ɪ.nəs, -ɪ.nɪs
skin skɪn **-s** -z **-ning** -ɪŋ **-ned** -d **-less** -ləs, -lɪs **by the ˌskin of one's ˈteeth**
skincare ˈskɪn.keəʳ, ˈskɪŋ- ⓤⓢ -ker
skin-deep ˌskɪnˈdiːp ⓤⓢ ˌskɪnˈdiːp, ˈ-- *stress shift, British only:* ˌskin-deep ˈwound
skin-div|ing ˈskɪnˌdaɪ.v|ɪŋ **-er/s** -əʳ/z ⓤⓢ -ɚ/z
skinflint ˈskɪn.flɪnt **-s** -s
skinful ˈskɪn.fʊl **-s** -z
skinhead ˈskɪn.hed **-s** -z
skink skɪŋk **-s** -s
skinner (S) ˈskɪn.əʳ ⓤⓢ -ɚ **-s** -z
skinn|y ˈskɪn|.i **-ier** -i.əʳ ⓤⓢ -i.ɚ **-iest** -i.ɪst, -i.əst **-iness** -ɪ.nəs, -ɪ.nɪs
skinny-dip ˈskɪn.i.dɪp **-s** -s **-ping** -ɪŋ **-ped** -t
skint skɪnt
skintight ˈskɪn.taɪt
skip skɪp **-s** -s **-ping** -ɪŋ **-ped** -t
skipjack ˈskɪp.dʒæk **-s** -s
skipper ˈskɪp.əʳ ⓤⓢ -ɚ **-s** -z **-ing** -ɪŋ **-ed** -d
skipping-rope ˈskɪp.ɪŋ.rəʊp ⓤⓢ -roʊp **-s** -s
Skipton ˈskɪp.tən
skirl skɜːl ⓤⓢ skɝːl **-s** -z
skirmish ˈskɜː.mɪʃ ⓤⓢ ˈskɝː- **-es** -ɪz **-ing** -ɪŋ **-ed** -t **-er/s** -əʳ/z ⓤⓢ -ɚ/z
skirt skɜːt ⓤⓢ skɝːt **-s** -s **-ing** -ɪŋ/z ⓤⓢ ˈskɝː.t̬ɪŋ/s **-ed** -ɪd ⓤⓢ ˈskɝː.t̬ɪd
skirting ˈskɜː.tɪŋ ⓤⓢ ˈskɝː.t̬ɪŋ **-s** -z
skirting-board ˈskɜː.tɪŋ.bɔːd ⓤⓢ ˈskɝː.t̬ɪŋ.bɔːrd **-s** -z
skit skɪt **-s** -s
skitter ˈskɪt.əʳ ⓤⓢ ˈskɪt̬.ɚ **-s** -z **-ing** -ɪŋ **-ed** -d
skittish ˈskɪt.ɪʃ ⓤⓢ ˈskɪt̬- **-ly** -li **-ness** -nəs, -nɪs
skittle ˈskɪt.l̩ ⓤⓢ ˈskɪt̬- **-s** -z
skiv|e skaɪv **-es** -z **-ing** -ɪŋ **-ed** -d **-er/s** -əʳ/z ⓤⓢ -ɚ/z
skivv|y ˈskɪv|.i **-ies** -iz
Skoda® ˈskəʊ.də ⓤⓢ ˈskoʊ-
Skol® skɒl, skəʊl ⓤⓢ skoʊl, skɑːl
Skopje ˈskɔː.pjeɪ, ˈskɒp.jeɪ ⓤⓢ ˈskɔː.pjeɪ, ˈskɑː-
Skrimshire ˈskrɪm.ʃəʳ, -ˌʃaɪəʳ ⓤⓢ -ʃɚ, -ˌʃaɪɚ
Skrine skriːn
skua ˈskjuː.ə, skjʊə ⓤⓢ ˈskjuː.ə **-s** -z
skulk skʌlk **-s** -s **-ing** -ɪŋ **-ed** -t
skull skʌl **-s** -z ˌ**skull and ˈcrossbones**
skullcap ˈskʌl.kæp **-s** -s
skul(l)duggery skʌlˈdʌg.ər.i
skunk skʌŋk **-s** -s
sk|y (S®) sk|aɪ **-ies** -aɪz **-ying** -aɪ.ɪŋ **-ied** -aɪd **-ier/s** -aɪ.əʳ/z ⓤⓢ -aɪ.ɚ/z
sky-blue ˌskaɪˈbluː *stress shift:* ˌsky-blue ˈfabric
skycap (S) ˈskaɪ.kæp **-s** -s
skydiv|er ˈskaɪˌdaɪ.v|əʳ ⓤⓢ -v|ɚ **-ers** -əz ⓤⓢ -ɚz **-ing** -ɪŋ
Skye skaɪ
sky-high ˌskaɪˈhaɪ *stress shift:* ˌsky-high ˈprices
skyjack ˈskaɪ.dʒæk **-s** -s **-ing** -ɪŋ **-ed** -t **-er/s** -əʳ/z ⓤⓢ -ɚ/z
skylark ˈskaɪ.lɑːk ⓤⓢ -lɑːrk **-s** -s **-ing** -ɪŋ **-ed** -t **-er/s** -əʳ/z ⓤⓢ -ɚ/z
skylight ˈskaɪ.laɪt **-s** -s
skyline ˈskaɪ.laɪn **-s** -z
skyrock|et ˈskaɪˌrɒk|.ɪt ⓤⓢ -ˌrɑː.k|ɪt **-ets** -ɪts **-eting** -ɪ.tɪŋ ⓤⓢ -ɪ.t̬ɪŋ **-eted** -ɪ.tɪd ⓤⓢ -ɪ.t̬ɪd
skyscape ˈskaɪ.skeɪp **-s** -s
skyscraper ˈskaɪˌskreɪ.pəʳ ⓤⓢ -pɚ **-s** -z
skyward ˈskaɪ.wəd ⓤⓢ -wɚd **-s** -z
skywriting ˈskaɪˌraɪ.tɪŋ ⓤⓢ -t̬ɪŋ
slab slæb **-s** -z **-bing** -ɪŋ **-bed** -d
slack slæk **-s** -s **-er** -əʳ ⓤⓢ -ɚ **-est** -ɪst, -əst **-ly** -li **-ness** -nəs, -nɪs **-ing** -ɪŋ **-ed** -t **-er/s** -əʳ/z ⓤⓢ -ɚ/z
slacken ˈslæk.ən **-s** -z **-ing** -ɪŋ, ˈslæk.nɪŋ **-ed** -d
Slade sleɪd
slag slæg **-s** -z **-ging** -ɪŋ **-ged** -d **-gy** -i
slagheap ˈslæg.hiːp **-s** -s
slain *(from* **slay***)* sleɪn
slainte ˈslɑːn.tʃə, -tjə
Slaithwaite ˈslæθ.wət, -weɪt *locally also:* ˈslaʊ.ɪt
slak|e sleɪk **-es** -s **-ing** -ɪŋ **-ed** -t
slalom ˈslɑː.ləm **-s** -z
slam slæm **-s** -z **-ming** -ɪŋ **-med** -d
slam-bang ˌslæmˈbæŋ *stress shift:* ˌslam-bang ˈclatter
slam-dunk ˌslæmˈdʌŋk, ˈ-- **-s** -s **-ing** -ɪŋ **-ed** -t
slammer ˈslæm.əʳ ⓤⓢ -ɚ **-s** -z
sland|er ˈslɑːn.d|əʳ ⓤⓢ ˈslæn.d|ɚ **-ers** -əz ⓤⓢ -ɚz **-ering** -ər.ɪŋ **-ered** -əd ⓤⓢ -ɚd **-erer/s** -ər.əʳ/z ⓤⓢ -ɚ.ɚ/z

slanderous ˈslɑːn.dᵊr.əs, ˈ-drəs (US) ˈslæn.dɚ.əs, ˈ-drəs -ly -li -ness -nəs, -nɪs
slang slæŋ -s -z -ing -ɪŋ -ed -d -y -i -ier -i.əʳ (US) -i.ɚ -iest -i.ɪst, -i.əst -ily -ɪ.li, -ᵊl.i -iness -ɪ.nəs, -ɪ.nɪs ˈslanging ˌmatch
slant slɑːnt (US) slænt -s -s -ing/ly -ɪŋ/li (US) ˈslæn.t̬ɪŋ/li -ed -ɪd (US) ˈslæn.t̬ɪd
slantways ˈslɑːnt.weɪz (US) ˈslænt-
slantwise ˈslɑːnt.waɪz (US) ˈslænt-
slap slæp -s -s -ping -ɪŋ -ped -t ˌslap and ˈtickle
slap-bang ˌslæpˈbæŋ *stress shift:* ˌslap-bang ˈcentral
slapdash ˈslæp.dæʃ, ˌ-ˈ-
slaphappy ˌslæpˈhæp.i (US) ˈ-ˌ-- *stress shift, British only:* ˌslaphappy ˈstate
slapstick ˈslæp.stɪk -s -s
slap-up ˌslæpˈʌp (US) ˈ-- *stress shift, British only:* ˌslap-up ˈmeal
slash slæʃ -es -ɪz -ing -ɪŋ -ed -t -er/s -əʳ/z (US) -ɚ/z
slash-and-burn ˌslæʃ.ᵊndˈbɜːn, -ᵊmˈ- (US) -ᵊndˈbɝːn *stress shift:* ˌslash-and-burn ˈfarming
slat slæt -s -s -ted -ɪd
slat|e sleɪt -es -s -ing -ɪŋ (US) ˈsleɪ.t̬ɪŋ -ed -ɪd (US) ˈsleɪ.t̬ɪd -er/s -əʳ/z (US) ˈsleɪ.t̬ɚ/z
Slater ˈsleɪ.təʳ (US) -t̬ɚ
slath|er ˈslæð|.əʳ (US) -ɚ -ers -əz (US) -ɚz -ering -ᵊr.ɪŋ -ered -əd (US) -ɚd
Slatkin ˈslæt.kɪn
slattern ˈslæt.ən, -ɜːn (US) ˈslæt̬.ɚn -s -z -ly -li -liness -lɪ.nəs, -nɪs
Slattery ˈslæt.ᵊr.i (US) ˈslæt̬.ɚ-
slaty ˈsleɪ.ti (US) -t̬i
slaught|er (S) (*n. v.*) ˈslɔː.t|əʳ (US) ˈslɑː.t̬|ɚ, ˈslɔː- -ers -əz (US) -ɚz -ering -ᵊr.ɪŋ -ered -əd (US) -ɚd -erer/s -ᵊr.əʳ/z (US) -ɚ.ɚ/z -erous/ly -ᵊr.əs/li
slaughterhou|se ˈslɔː.tə.haʊ|s (US) ˈslɑː.t̬ɚ-, ˈslɔː- -ses -zɪz
Slav slɑːv (US) slɑːv, slæv -s -z
slav|e sleɪv -es -z -ing -ɪŋ -ed -d -er/s -əʳ/z (US) -ɚ/z ˈslave ˌdriver; ˌslave ˈlabour; ˈslave ˌtrade
slave-owner ˈsleɪvˌəʊ.nəʳ (US) -ˌoʊ.nɚ -s -z
slaver *slave-trader:* ˈsleɪ.vəʳ (US) -vɚ -s -z
slav|er (*n. v.*) *slobber:* ˈslæv|.əʳ, ˈsleɪ.v|əʳ (US) ˈslæv|.ɚ -ers -əz (US) -ɚz -ering -ᵊr.ɪŋ -ered -əd (US) -ɚd
slavery ˈsleɪ.vᵊr.i
slavey ˈsleɪ.vi, ˈslæv.i -s -z
Slavic ˈslɑː.vɪk, ˈslæv.ɪk
slavish ˈsleɪ.vɪʃ -ly -li -ness -nəs, -nɪs
Slavonic sləˈvɒn.ɪk, slævˈɒn- (US) sləˈvɑː.nɪk
slaw slɔː (US) slɑː, slɔː -s -z
slay sleɪ -s -z -ing/s -ɪŋ/z -ed slew sluː slain sleɪn slayer/s sleɪ.əʳ/z (US) -ɚ/z
Slazenger® ˈslæz.ᵊn.dʒəʳ (US) -dʒɚ
Sleaford ˈsliː.fəd (US) -fɚd
sleaze sliːz
sleazebag ˈsliːz.bæg -s -z
sleazeball ˈsliːz.bɔːl (US) -bɔːl, -bɑːl -s -z
sleaz|y ˈsliː.z|i -ier -i.əʳ (US) -i.ɚ -iest -i.ɪst, -i.əst -ily -ɪ.li, -ᵊl.i -iness -ɪ.nəs, -ɪ.nɪs
sled sled -s -z -ding -ɪŋ -ded -ɪd
sledg|e sledʒ -es -ɪz -ing -ɪŋ -ed -d
sledgehammer ˈsledʒˌhæm.əʳ (US) -ɚ -s -z -ing -ɪŋ -ed -d
sleek sliːk -er -əʳ (US) -ɚ -est -ɪst, -əst -ly -li -ness -nəs, -nɪs
sleep sliːp -s -s -ing -ɪŋ slept slept ˈsleeping ˌbag; ˌSleeping ˈBeauty; ˈsleeping ˌcar; ˈsleeping ˌdraught; ˈsleeping ˌpill; ˈsleeping ˌpartner; ˌsleeping poˈliceman; ˈsleeping ˌsickness
sleeper ˈsliː.pəʳ (US) -pɚ -s -z
sleepless ˈsliː.pləs, -plɪs -ly -li -ness -nəs, -nɪs
sleepout ˈsliːp.aʊt -s -s
sleepover ˈsliːpˌəʊ.vəʳ (US) -ˌoʊ.vɚ -s -z
sleepwalk|er ˈsliːpˌwɔː.k|əʳ (US) -ˌwɑː.k|ɚ, -ˌwɔː- -ers -əz (US) -ɚz -ing -ɪŋ
sleep|y ˈsliː.p|i -ier -i.əʳ (US) -i.ɚ -iest -i.ɪst, -i.əst -ily -ɪ.li, -ᵊl.i -iness -ɪ.nəs, -ɪ.nɪs
sleepyhead ˈsliː.pi.hed -s -z
sleet sliːt -s -s -ing -ɪŋ (US) ˈsliː.t̬ɪŋ -ed -ɪd (US) ˈsliː.t̬ɪd -y -i (US) ˈsliː.t̬i -iness -ɪ.nəs, -ɪ.nɪs (US) ˈsliː.t̬ɪ.nəs, -nɪs
sleeve sliːv -s -z -d -d -less -ləs, -lɪs
sleigh sleɪ -s -z -ing -ɪŋ -ed -d ˈsleigh ˌbells
sleight (S) slaɪt ˌsleight of ˈhand
Sleights slaɪts
slender ˈslen.dəʳ (US) -dɚ -er -əʳ (US) -ɚ -est -ɪst, -əst -ly -li -ness -nəs, -nɪs
slenderiz|e ˈslen.dᵊr.aɪz (US) -də.raɪz -es -ɪz -ing -ɪŋ -ed -d
slept (*from* **sleep**) slept
sleuth sluːθ, sljuːθ (US) sluːθ -s -s -ing -ɪŋ -ed -t
sleuthhound ˈsluːθ.haʊnd, ˈsljuːθ- (US) ˈsluːθ- -s -z
slew sluː -s -z -ing -ɪŋ -ed -d
slic|e slaɪs -es -ɪz -ing -ɪŋ -ed -t -er/s -əʳ/z (US) -ɚ/z ˌsliced ˈbread
slick slɪk -er -əʳ (US) -ɚ -est -ɪst, -əst -s -z -ing -ɪŋ -ly -li -ed -ness -nəs, -nɪs
slicker ˈslɪk.əʳ (US) -ɚ -s -z
slid (*from* **slide**) slɪd
slid|e slaɪd -es -z -ing -ɪŋ slid slɪd ˈslide proˌjector; ˈslide ˌrule; ˈslide ˌvalve; ˌsliding ˈdoor; ˌsliding ˈscale
slider ˈslaɪ.dəʳ (US) -dɚ -s -z
slight slaɪt -s -s -er -əʳ (US) ˈslaɪ.t̬ɚ -est -ɪst, -əst (US) ˈslaɪ.t̬ɪst, -t̬əst -ly -li -ness -nəs, -nɪs -ing/ly -ɪŋ/li (US) ˈslaɪ.t̬ɪŋ/li -ed -ɪd (US) ˈslaɪ.t̬ɪd
Sligo ˈslaɪ.gəʊ (US) -goʊ
slim (S) slɪm -mer/s -əʳ/z (US) -ɚ/z -mest -ɪst -est -əst -ly -li -ness -nəs, -nɪs -s -z -ming -ɪŋ -med -d ˈSlim diˌsease
Slimbridge ˈslɪm.brɪdʒ
slim|e slaɪm -es -z -ing -ɪŋ -ed -d
slimline ˈslɪm.laɪn
slim|y ˈslaɪ.m|i -ier -i.əʳ (US) -i.ɚ -iest -i.ɪst, -i.əst -ily -ɪ.li, -ᵊl.i -iness -ɪ.nəs, -ɪ.nɪs
sling slɪŋ -s -z -ing -ɪŋ slung slʌŋ
slingback ˈslɪŋ.bæk -s -s
slingshot ˈslɪŋ.ʃɒt (US) -ʃɑːt -s -s
slink slɪŋk -s -s -ing -ɪŋ slunk slʌŋk
slink|y ˈslɪŋ.k|i -ier -i.əʳ (US) -i.ɚ -iest -i.ɪst, -i.əst
slip slɪp -s -s -ping -ɪŋ -ped -t ˌslipped ˈdisc; ˈslip ˌroad; ˈslip ˌstitch; ˌgive someone the ˈslip
slipcas|e ˈslɪp.keɪs -es -ɪz
slipcover ˈslɪpˌkʌv.əʳ (US) -ɚ -s -z
slipknot ˈslɪp.nɒt (US) -nɑːt -s -s
slip-on ˈslɪp.ɒn (US) -ɑːn -s -z
slipover ˈslɪpˌəʊ.vəʳ (US) -ˌoʊ.vɚ -s -z
slippag|e ˈslɪp.ɪdʒ -es -ɪz
slipper ˈslɪp.əʳ (US) -ɚ -s -z -ing -ɪŋ -ed -d
slipper|y ˈslɪp.ᵊr|.i -ier -i.əʳ (US) -i.ɚ -iest -i.ɪst, -i.əst -ily -ɪ.li, -ᵊl.i -iness -ɪ.nəs, -ɪ.nɪs ˌslippery ˈslope
slipp|y ˈslɪp|.i -ier -i.əʳ (US) -i.ɚ -iest -i.ɪst, -i.əst -iness -ɪ.nəs, -ɪ.nɪs
slipshod ˈslɪp.ʃɒd (US) -ʃɑːd
slipstream ˈslɪp.striːm -s -z -ing -ɪŋ -ed -d
slip-up ˈslɪp.ʌp -s -s
slipway ˈslɪp.weɪ -s -z
slit slɪt -s -s -ting -ɪŋ (US) ˈslɪt̬.ɪŋ
slith|er ˈslɪð|.əʳ (US) -ɚ -ers -əz (US) -ɚz -ering -ᵊr.ɪŋ -ered -əd (US) -ɚd -ery -ᵊr.i
sliv|er ˈslɪv|.əʳ (US) -ɚ -ers -əz (US) -ɚz -ering -ᵊr.ɪŋ -ered -əd (US) -ɚd
slivovitz ˈslɪv.ə.vɪts, ˈsliː.və- (US) ˈslɪv.ə-
Sloan sləʊn (US) sloʊn
Sloan|e sləʊn (US) sloʊn -es -z -ey -i -ier -i.əʳ (US) -ɚ -iest -i.ɪst, -əst ˌSloane ˈRanger; ˌSloane ˈSquare
slob slɒb (US) slɑːb -s -z -bing -ɪŋ -bed -d -bish -ɪʃ
slobb|er ˈslɒb|.əʳ (US) ˈslɑː.b|ɚ -ers -əz (US) -ɚz -ering -ᵊr.ɪŋ -ered -əd (US) -ɚd -erer/s -ə.rəʳ/z (US) -ɚ.ɚ/z
slobber|y ˈslɒb.ᵊr|.i (US) ˈslɑː.bɚ- -iness -ɪ.nəs, -ɪ.nɪs
Slobodan ˈslɒb.ə.dæn, sləˈbɒd.ən (US) ˈslɑːbə-
Slocombe ˈsləʊ.kəm (US) ˈsloʊ-
Slocum ˈsləʊ.kəm (US) ˈsloʊ-
sloe sləʊ (US) sloʊ -s -z ˌsloe ˈgin

slog slɒg (US) slɑːg, slɔːg **-s** -z **-ging** -ɪŋ **-ged** -d **-ger/s** -əʳ/z (US) -ɚ/z
slogan ˈsləʊ.gən (US) ˈsloʊ- **-s** -z
sloganeer ˌsləʊ.gəˈnɪəʳ (US) ˌsloʊ.gəˈnɪr **-s** -z **-ing/s** -ɪŋ/z **-ed** -d
sloganiz|e, -is|e ˈsləʊ.gə.naɪz (US) ˈsloʊ- **-es** -ɪz **-ing** -ɪŋ **-ed** -d **-er/s** -əʳ/z (US) -ɚ/z
sloop sluːp **-s** -s
slop slɒp (US) slɑːp **-s** -s **-ping** -ɪŋ **-ped** -t
slop|e sləʊp (US) sloʊp **-es** -s **-ing** -ɪŋ/li **-ed** -t **-er/s** -əʳ/z (US) -ɚ/z
Sloper ˈsləʊ.pəʳ (US) ˈsloʊ.pɚ
slopp|y ˈslɒp|.i (US) ˈslɑː.p|i **-ier** -i.əʳ (US) -i.ɚ **-iest** -i.ɪst, -i.əst **-ily** -ɪ.li, -ᵊl.i **-iness** -ɪ.nəs, -ɪ.nɪs ˌ**sloppy** ˈ**joe**
slosh slɒʃ (US) slɑːʃ **-es** -ɪz **-ing** -ɪŋ **-ed** -t
slosh|y ˈslɒʃ|.i (US) ˈslɑː.ʃ|i **-ier** -i.əʳ (US) -i.ɚ **-iest** -i.ɪst, -i.əst **-iness** -ɪ.nəs, -ɪ.nɪs
slot slɒt (US) slɑːt **-s** -s **-ting** -ɪŋ (US) ˈslɑː.t̬ɪŋ **-ted** -ɪd (US) ˈslɑː.t̬ɪd
sloth sləʊθ (US) slɑːθ, slɔːθ, sloʊθ **-s** -s
slothful ˈsləʊθ.fᵊl, -fʊl (US) ˈslɑːθ-, ˈslɔːθ-, ˈsloʊθ- **-ly** -i **-ness** -nəs, -nɪs
slot-machine ˈslɒt.məˌʃiːn (US) ˈslɑːt- **-s** -z
slouch slaʊtʃ **-es** -ɪz **-ing/ly** -ɪŋ/li **-ed** -t
slough (*n.*) *bog:* slaʊ (US) sluː, slaʊ **-s** -z **-y** -i
slough (*v.*) *skin:* slʌf **-s** -s **-ing** -ɪŋ **-ed** -t
Slough slaʊ
Slovak ˈsləʊ.væk (US) ˈsloʊ.vɑːk, -væk **-s** -s
Slovaki|a sləʊˈvæk.i|.ə, -ˈvɑː.ki- (US) sloʊˈvɑː.ki-, -ˈvæk.i- **-an/s** -ən/z
sloven ˈslʌv.ᵊn **-s** -z
Slovene sləʊˈviːn; ˈsləʊ.viːn (US) ˈsloʊ.viːn **-s** -z
Sloveni|a sləʊˈviː.ni|.ə, ˈ-nj|ə (US) sloʊ- **-an/s** -ən/z
slovenl|y ˈslʌv.ᵊn.l|i **-iness** -ɪ.nəs, -ɪ.nɪs
slow sləʊ (US) sloʊ **-er** -əʳ (US) -ɚ **-est** -ɪst, -əst **-ly** -li **-ness** -nəs, -nɪs **-s** -z **-ing** -ɪŋ **-ed** -d ˌ**slow** ˈ**motion**
slowcoach ˈsləʊ.kəʊtʃ (US) ˈsloʊ.koʊtʃ **-es** -ɪz
slowdown ˈsləʊ.daʊn (US) ˈsloʊ- **-s** -z
slowpoke ˈsləʊ.pəʊk (US) ˈsloʊ.poʊk **-s** -s
slow-witted ˌsləʊˈwɪt.ɪd (US) ˌsloʊˈwɪt̬-
slowworm ˈsləʊ.wɜːm (US) ˈsloʊ.wɝːm **-s** -z
slub slʌb **-s** -z **-bing** -ɪŋ **-bed** -d
sludg|e slʌdʒ **-y** -i
slu|e sluː **-s** -z **-ing** -ɪŋ **-ed** -d
slug slʌg **-s** -z **-ging** -ɪŋ **-ged** -d
slugabed ˈslʌg.ə.bed **-s** -z
sluggard ˈslʌg.əd (US) -ɚd **-s** -z **-ly** -li
sluggish ˈslʌg.ɪʃ **-ly** -li **-ness** -nəs, -nɪs
sluic|e sluːs **-es** -ɪz **-ing** -ɪŋ **-ed** -t ˈ**sluice** ˌ**gate**
sluiceway ˈsluːs.weɪ **-s** -z
slum slʌm **-s** -z **-ming** -ɪŋ **-med** -d **-mer/s** -əʳ/z (US) -ɚ/z
slumb|er ˈslʌm.b|əʳ (US) -b|ɚ **-ers** -əz (US) -ɚz **-ering** -ᵊr.ɪŋ **-ered** -əd (US) -ɚd **-erer/s** -ᵊr.əʳ/z (US) -ɚ.ɚ/z ˈ**slumber** ˌ**party**
slumm|y ˈslʌm|.i **-ier** -i.əʳ (US) -i.ɚ **-iest** -i.ɪst, -i.əst **-iness** -ɪ.nəs, -ɪ.nɪs
slump slʌmp **-s** -s **-ing** -ɪŋ **-ed** -t
slung (*from* **sling**) slʌŋ
slunk (*from* **slink**) slʌŋk
slur slɜːʳ (US) slɝː **-s** -z **-ring** -ɪŋ **-red** -d
slurp slɜːp (US) slɝːp **-s** -s **-ing** -ɪŋ **-ed** -t
slurr|y ˈslʌr|.i (US) ˈslɝː- **-ies** -iz
slush slʌʃ **-y** -i **-ier** -i.əʳ (US) -i.ɚ **-iest** -i.ɪst, -i.əst **-iness** -ɪ.nəs, -ɪ.nɪs ˈ**slush** ˌ**fund**
slut slʌt **-s** -s **-ty** -i
sluttish ˈslʌt.ɪʃ (US) ˈslʌt̬- **-ly** -li **-ness** -nəs, -nɪs
Sluys slɔɪs
sly slaɪ **-er** -əʳ (US) -ɚ **-est** -ɪst, -əst **-ly** -li **-ness** -nəs, -nɪs
slyboots ˈslaɪ.buːts
SM ˌesˈem
smack smæk **-s** -s **-ing/s** -ɪŋ/z **-ed** -t **-er/s** -əʳ/z (US) -ɚ/z
smacker ˈsmæk.əʳ (US) -ɚ **-s** -z
smackeroo ˌsmæk.ᵊrˈuː (US) -əˈruː **-s** -z
Smale smeɪl
small (S) smɔːl (US) smɔːl, smɑːl **-s** -z **-er** -əʳ (US) -ɚ **-est** -ɪst, -əst **-ness** -nəs, -nɪs **-ish** -ɪʃ ˈ**small** ˌ**ad**, ˌ**small** ˈ**ad**; ˌ**small** ˈ**arm**; ˌ**small** ˈ**beer**; ˌ**small** ˈ**change**; ˈ**small** ˌ**fry**; ˈ**small** ˌ**hours** (US) ˌ**small** ˈ**hours**; ˌ**small po**ˈ**tatoes**; ˌ**small** ˈ**print**,; ˈ**small** ˌ**print**; (US) ˌ**small** ˈ**print**; ˌ**small** ˈ**screen**; ˈ**small** ˌ**talk**
small-claims ˌsmɔːlˈkleɪmz (US) ˌsmɔːl-, ˌsmɑːl- ˌ**small**-ˈ**claims** ˌ**court**, ˌ**small-claims** ˈ**court**
Smalley ˈsmɔː.li (US) ˈsmɔː-, ˈsmɑː-
small-hold|er ˈsmɔːlˌhəʊl.d|əʳ (US) -ˌhoʊl.dɚ, ˈsmɑːl- **-ers** -əz (US) -ɚz **-ing/s** -ɪŋ/z
smallish ˈsmɔː.lɪʃ (US) ˈsmɔː-, ˈsmɑː-
small-minded ˌsmɔːlˈmaɪn.dɪd (US) ˌsmɔːl-, ˌsmɑːl- **-ly** -li **-ness** -nəs, -nɪs *stress shift:* ˌsmall-minded ˈperson
smallpox ˈsmɔːl.pɒks (US) -pɑːks, ˈsmɑːl-
small-scale ˌsmɔːlˈskeɪl (US) ˈ--, ˈsmɑːl- *stress shift, British only:* ˌsmall-scale ˈproject
small-tim|e ˌsmɔːlˈtaɪm (US) ˈ--, ˈsmɑːl- **-er/s** -əʳ/z (US) -ɚ/z
small-town ˈsmɔːl.taʊn (US) ˈsmɔːl-, ˈsmɑːl-
Smallwood ˈsmɔːl.wʊd (US) ˈsmɔːl-, ˈsmɑːl-
smalt smɔːlt, smɒlt (US) smɔːlt, smɑːlt
smarm smɑːm (US) smɑːrm **-s** -z **-ing** -ɪŋ **-ed** -d
smarm|y ˈsmɑː.m|i (US) ˈsmɑːr- **-ily** -ɪli, -ᵊli **-iness** -ɪ.nəs, -ɪ.nɪs
smart (S) smɑːt (US) smɑːrt **-s** -s **-er** -əʳ (US) ˈsmɑːr.t̬ɚ **-est** -ɪst, -əst (US) ˈsmɑːr.t̬ɪst, -t̬əst **-ly** -li **-ness** -nəs, -nɪs **-ing** -ɪŋ (US) ˈsmɑːr.t̬ɪŋ **-ed** -ɪd (US) ˈsmɑːr.t̬ɪd ˈ**smart** ˌ**alec(k)** (US) ˌ**smart** ˈ**alec(k)**; ˈ**smart** ˌ**card**; ˌ**smart** ˈ**money**; ˈ**smart** ˌ**set**
smartarse ˈsmɑːt.ɑːs (US) ˈsmɑːrt.ɑːrs
smartass ˈsmɑːt.ɑːs, -æs (US) ˈsmɑːrt.æs
smarten ˈsmɑː.tᵊn (US) ˈsmɑːr- **-s** -z **-ing** -ɪŋ, ˈsmɑːt.nɪŋ (US) ˈsmɑːrt- **-ed** -d
Smarties® ˈsmɑː.tiz (US) ˈsmɑːr.t̬iz
smartish ˈsmɑː.tɪʃ (US) ˈsmɑːr.t̬ɪʃ
smarty-pants ˈsmɑː.ti.pænts (US) ˈsmɑːr.t̬i-
smash smæʃ **-es** -ɪz **-ing** -ɪŋ **-ed** -t **-er/s** -əʳ/z (US) -ɚ/z ˌ**smash** ˈ**hit**
smash-and-grab ˌsmæʃ.ᵊndˈgræb, -ᵊŋˈ- (US) -ᵊndˈ- **-s** -z *stress shift:* ˌsmash-and-grab ˈraid
smattering ˈsmæt.ᵊr.ɪŋ (US) ˈsmæt̬- **-s** -z
smear smɪəʳ (US) smɪr **-s** -z **-ing** -ɪŋ **-ed** -d **-y** -i **-iness** -ɪ.nəs, -ɪ.nɪs ˈ**smear** **cam**ˌ**paign**; ˈ**smear** ˌ**test**
Smeaton ˈsmiː.tᵊn
Smedley ˈsmed.li
Smeeth smiːð, smiːθ
smegma ˈsmeg.mə
smell smel **-s** -z **-ing** -ɪŋ **smelt** -t **smelled** -t, -d ˈ**smelling** ˌ**salts**
smell|y ˈsmel|.i **-ier** -i.əʳ (US) -i.ɚ **-iest** -i.ɪst, -i.əst **-iness** -ɪ.nəs, -ɪ.nɪs
smelt smelt **-s** -s **-ing** -ɪŋ (US) ˈsmel.t̬ɪŋ **-ed** -ɪd (US) ˈsmel.t̬ɪd **-er/s** -əʳ/z (US) -ɚ/z
Smetana ˈsmet.ᵊn.ə
Smethwick ˈsmeð.ɪk
smew smjuː **-s** -z
smidgen, smidgin, smidgeon ˈsmɪdʒ.ᵊn, -ɪn **-s** -z
Smieton ˈsmiː.tᵊn
Smike smaɪk
smilax ˈsmaɪ.læks **-es** -ɪz
smil|e smaɪl **-es** -z **-ing/ly** -ɪŋ/li **-ed** -d
Smiles smaɪlz
smil|ey (S) ˈsmaɪ.l|i **-ier** -i.əʳ (US) -i.ɚ **-iest** -i.ɪst, -i.əst
Smillie ˈsmaɪ.li
smirch smɜːtʃ (US) smɝːtʃ **-es** -ɪz **-ing** -ɪŋ **-ed** -t
smirk smɜːk (US) smɝːk **-s** -s **-ing** -ɪŋ **-ed** -t **-er/s** -əʳ/z (US) -ɚ/z
Smirke smɜːk (US) smɝːk
Smirnoff® ˈsmɜː.nɒf (US) ˈsmɝː.nɔːf, ˈsmɪr-, -nɑːf
smit (*from* **smite**) smɪt
smit|e smaɪt **-es** -s **-ing** -ɪŋ (US) ˈsmaɪ.t̬ɪŋ **smote** sməʊt (US) smoʊt **smit** smɪt **smitten** ˈsmɪt.ᵊn

smith (S) smɪθ **-s** -s
Smithells 'smɪð.ᵊlz
smithereens ˌsmɪð.ᵊr'iːnz ⓤⓢ -ə'riːnz
Smithers 'smɪð.əz ⓤⓢ -ɚz
Smithfield 'smɪθ.fiːld
Smithson 'smɪθ.sᵊn
Smithsonian smɪθ'səʊ.ni.ən ⓤⓢ -'soʊ-
smith|y 'smɪð|.i, 'smɪθ- ⓤⓢ 'smɪθ-, 'smɪð- **-ies** -iz
smitten *(from* **smite***)* 'smɪt.ᵊn
smock smɒk ⓤⓢ smɑːk **-s** -s **-ing** -ɪŋ **-ed** -t
smog smɒg ⓤⓢ smɑːg, smɔːg
smogg|y 'smɒg|.i ⓤⓢ 'smɑː.g|i, 'smɔː- **-ier** -i.əʳ ⓤⓢ -i.ɚ **-iest** -i.ɪst, -i.əst
smok|e sməʊk ⓤⓢ smoʊk **-es** -s **-ing** -ɪŋ **-ed** -t **-er/s** -əʳ/z ⓤⓢ -ɚ/z **'smoke aˌlarm; ˌsmoke and 'mirrors; 'smoke ˌscreen; 'smoking comˌpartment; 'smoking ˌjacket; 'smoking ˌroom; ˌgo up in 'smoke; there's ˌno ˌsmoke without 'fire**
smokehou|se 'sməʊk.haʊ|s ⓤⓢ 'smoʊk- **-ses** -zɪz
smokeless 'sməʊk.ləs, -lɪs ⓤⓢ 'smoʊk-
smokestack 'sməʊk.stæk ⓤⓢ 'smoʊk- **-s** -s **'smokestack ˌindustry**
Smokies 'sməʊ.kiz ⓤⓢ 'smoʊ-
smoko 'sməʊ.kəʊ ⓤⓢ 'smoʊ.koʊ **-s** -z
smok|y 'sməʊ.k|i ⓤⓢ 'smoʊ- **-ier** -i.əʳ ⓤⓢ -i.ɚ **-iest** -i.ɪst, -i.əst **-ily** -ɪ.li, -ᵊl.i **-iness** -ɪ.nəs, -ɪ.nɪs
smold|er 'sməʊl.d|əʳ ⓤⓢ 'smoʊl.d|ɚ **-ers** -əz ⓤⓢ -ɚz **-ering** -ᵊr.ɪŋ **-ered** -əd ⓤⓢ -ɚd
Smollett 'smɒl.ɪt ⓤⓢ 'smɑː.lɪt
smolt sməʊlt ⓤⓢ smoʊlt
smooch smuːtʃ **-es** -ɪz **-ing** -ɪŋ **-ed** -t **-y** -i
smooth *(adj.)* smuːð **-er** -əʳ ⓤⓢ -ɚ **-est** -ɪst, -əst **-ly** -li **-ness** -nəs, -nɪs
smoothbore 'smuːð.bɔːʳ ⓤⓢ -bɔːr **-s** -z
smooth|(e) *(v.)* smuːð **-(e)s** -z **-ing** -ɪŋ **-ed** -d
smooth|ie, smooth|y 'smuː.ð|i **-ies** -iz
smorgasbord 'smɔː.gəs.bɔːd ⓤⓢ 'smɔːr.gəs.bɔːrd **-s** -z
smote *(from* **smite***)* sməʊt ⓤⓢ smoʊt
smoth|er 'smʌð|.əʳ ⓤⓢ -ɚ **-ers** -əz ⓤⓢ -ɚz **-ering** -ᵊr.ɪŋ **-ered** -əd ⓤⓢ -ɚd
smould|er 'sməʊl.d|əʳ ⓤⓢ 'smoʊl.d|ɚ **-ers** -əz ⓤⓢ -ɚz **-ering** -ᵊr.ɪŋ **-ered** -əd ⓤⓢ -ɚd
smudg|e smʌdʒ **-es** -ɪz **-ing** -ɪŋ **-ed** -d **-y** -i **-ier** -i.əʳ ⓤⓢ -i.ɚ **-iest** -i.ɪst, -i.əst **-ily** -ɪ.li, -ᵊl.i **-iness** -ɪ.nəs, -ɪ.nɪs
smug smʌg **-ly** -li **-ness** -nəs, -nɪs **-ger** -əʳ ⓤⓢ -gɚ **-gest** -ɪst, -gəst
smuggl|e 'smʌg|.l̩ **-es** -z **-ing** -ɪŋ, 'smʌg.lɪŋ **-ed** -d
smuggler 'smʌg.ləʳ, '-l̩.əʳ ⓤⓢ '-lɚ, '-l̩.ɚ **-s** -z
smut smʌt **-s** -s **-ty** -i ⓤⓢ 'smʌt̬.i **-tier** -i.əʳ ⓤⓢ 'smʌt̬.i.ɚ **-tiest** -i.ɪst, -i.əst ⓤⓢ 'smʌt̬.i.ɪst, -i.əst **-tily** -ɪ.li, -ᵊl.i ⓤⓢ 'smʌt̬.ɪ.li, -ᵊl.i **-tiness** -ɪ.nəs, -ɪ.nɪs ⓤⓢ 'smʌt̬.ɪ.nəs, -ɪ.nɪs
Smylie 'smaɪ.li
Smyrna 'smɜː.nə ⓤⓢ 'smɝː-
Smyth smɪθ, smaɪθ
Smythe smaɪð, smaɪθ
snack snæk **-s** -s **-ing** -ɪŋ **-ed** -d **'snack ˌbar**
Snaefell ˌsneɪ'fel
snaffl|e 'snæf.l̩ **-es** -z **-ing** -ɪŋ, 'snæf.lɪŋ **-ed** -d
snafu snæf'uː ⓤⓢ snæf'uː, '-- **-es** -z **-ing** -ɪŋ **-ed** -d
snag snæg **-s** -z **-ging** -ɪŋ **-ged** -d
Snagge snæg
snail sneɪl **-s** -z **-like** -laɪk **'snail's ˌpace**
snak|e sneɪk **-es** -s **-ing** -ɪŋ **-ed** -t **'snake ˌcharmer; ˌsnakes and 'ladders; ˌsnake in the 'grass** ⓤⓢ **'snake in the ˌgrass**
snakebite 'sneɪk.baɪt **-s** -s
snakeskin 'sneɪk.skɪn
snak|y 'sneɪ.k|i **-iness** -ɪ.nəs, -ɪ.nɪs
snap snæp **-s** -s **-ping** -ɪŋ **-ped** -t **'snap ˌfastener**
snapdragon 'snæpˌdræg.ən **-s** -z
Snape sneɪp
snapper 'snæp.əʳ ⓤⓢ -ɚ **-s** -z
snappish 'snæp.ɪʃ **-ly** -li **-ness** -nəs, -nɪs
Snapple® 'snæp.l̩
snapp|y 'snæp|.i **-ier** -i.əʳ ⓤⓢ -i.ɚ **-iest** -i.ɪst, -i.əst **-ily** -ɪ.li, -ᵊl.i **-iness** -ɪ.nəs, -ɪ.nɪs
snapshot 'snæp|.ʃɒt ⓤⓢ -ʃɑːt
snar|e sneəʳ ⓤⓢ sner **-es** -z **-ing** -ɪŋ **-ed** -d **'snare ˌdrum**
snark snɑːk ⓤⓢ snɑːrk **-s** -s
snarl snɑːl ⓤⓢ snɑːrl **-s** -z **-ing** -ɪŋ **-ed** -d
snarl-up 'snɑːl.ʌp ⓤⓢ 'snɑːrl- **-s** -s
snatch snætʃ **-es** -ɪz **-ing** -ɪŋ **-ed** -t **-er/s** -əʳ/z ⓤⓢ -ɚ/z
snatch|y 'snætʃ|.i **-ier** -i.əʳ ⓤⓢ -i.ɚ **-iest** -i.ɪst, -i.əst **-ily** -ɪ.li, -ᵊl.i
snazz|y 'snæz|.i **-ier** -i.əʳ ⓤⓢ -i.ɚ **-iest** -i.ɪst, -i.əst **-ily** -ɪ.li, -ᵊl.i **-iness** -ɪ.nəs, -ɪ.nɪs
sneak sniːk **-s** -s **-ing/ly** -ɪŋ/li **-ed** -t **-y** -i **-ier** -i.əʳ ⓤⓢ -i.ɚ **-iest** -i.ɪst, -i.əst **-ily** -ɪ.li, -ᵊl.i **-iness** -ɪ.nəs, -ɪ.nɪs **ˌsneak 'preview; 'sneak ˌthief, ˌsneak 'thief** ⓤⓢ **'sneak ˌthief**
sneaker 'sniː.kəʳ ⓤⓢ -kɚ **-s** -z
sneakers 'sniː.kəz ⓤⓢ -kɚz
sneaky 'sniː.ki **-ier** -i.əʳ ⓤⓢ -i.ɚ **-iest** -i.ɪst, -i.əst **-iness** -ɪ.nəs, -ɪ.nɪs
Snedden 'sned.ᵊn
sneer snɪəʳ ⓤⓢ snɪr **-s** -z **-ing/ly** -ɪŋ/li **-ed** -d
sneez|e sniːz **-es** -ɪz **-ing** -ɪŋ **-ed** -d
Snelgrove 'snel.grəʊv ⓤⓢ -groʊv
snell (S) snel **-s** -z
Sneyd sniːd
snib snɪb **-s** -z
snick snɪk **-s** -s **-ing** -ɪŋ **-ed** -t
snick|er 'snɪk|.əʳ ⓤⓢ -ɚ **-ers** -əz ⓤⓢ -ɚz **-ering** -ᵊr.ɪŋ **-ered** -əd ⓤⓢ -ɚd
Snickers® 'snɪk.əz ⓤⓢ -ɚz
snickersnee ˌsnɪk.ə'sniː, '--- ⓤⓢ 'snɪk.ɚ.sniː **-s** -z
snide snaɪd **-ly** -li **-ness** -nəs, -nɪs
sniff snɪf **-s** -s **-ing** -ɪŋ **-ed** -t **-y** -i **-ier** -i.əʳ ⓤⓢ -i.ɚ **-iest** -i.ɪst, -i.əst **-ily** -ɪ.li, -ᵊl.i **-iness** -ɪ.nəs, -ɪ.nɪs
sniffer 'snɪf.əʳ ⓤⓢ -ɚ **-s** -z **'sniffer ˌdog**
sniffl|e 'snɪf.l̩ **-es** -z **-ing** -ɪŋ, 'snɪf.lɪŋ **-ed** -d
snifter 'snɪf.təʳ ⓤⓢ -tɚ **-s** -z
snigg|er 'snɪg|.əʳ ⓤⓢ -ɚ **-ers** -əz ⓤⓢ -ɚz **-ering** -ᵊr.ɪŋ **-ered** -əd ⓤⓢ -ɚd **-erer/s** -ə.rəʳ/z ⓤⓢ -ɚ.ɚ/z
snip snɪp **-s** -s **-ping** -ɪŋ **-ped** -t **-per/s** -əʳ/z ⓤⓢ -ɚ/z
snip|e snaɪp **-es** -s **-ing** -ɪŋ **-ed** -t **-er/s** -əʳ/z ⓤⓢ -ɚ/z
snipp|et 'snɪp|.ɪt **-ets** -ɪts **-ety** -ɪ.ti ⓤⓢ -ɪ.t̬i
snit snɪt **-s** -s
snitch snɪtʃ **-es** -ɪz **-ing** -ɪŋ **-ed** -t
snivel 'snɪv.ᵊl **-s** -z **-(l)ing** -ɪŋ, 'snɪv.lɪŋ **-(l)ed** -d **-(l)er/s** -əʳ/z, 'snɪv.ləʳ/z ⓤⓢ '-ᵊl.ɚ/z, '-lɚ/z
snob snɒb ⓤⓢ snɑːb **-s** -z **-bism** -ɪ.zᵊm
snobbery 'snɒb.ᵊr.i ⓤⓢ 'snɑː.bɚ-
snobbish 'snɒb.ɪʃ ⓤⓢ 'snɑː.bɪʃ **-ly** -li **-ness** -nəs, -nɪs
snobb|y 'snɒb|.i ⓤⓢ 'snɑː.b|i **-ier** -i.əʳ ⓤⓢ -i.ɚ **-iest** -i.ɪst, -i.əst
SNOBOL 'snəʊ.bɒl ⓤⓢ 'snoʊ.bɔːl, -bɑːl
Snodgrass 'snɒd.grɑːs ⓤⓢ 'snɑːd.græs
Snodland 'snɒd.lənd ⓤⓢ 'snɑːd-
snoek snʊk, snuːk **-s** -s
snog snɒg ⓤⓢ snɑːg, snɔːg **-s** -z **-ging** -ɪŋ **-ged** -d
snood snuːd, snʊd ⓤⓢ snuːd **-s** -z **-ed** -ɪd
Snoody 'snuː.di
snook snuːk ⓤⓢ snʊk, snuːk **-s** -s
snooker 'snuː.kəʳ ⓤⓢ 'snʊk.ɚ **-s** -z **-ing** -ɪŋ **-ed** -d
snoop snuːp **-s** -s **-ing** -ɪŋ **-ed** -t **-er/s** -əʳ/z ⓤⓢ -ɚ/z
Snoopy® 'snuː.pi
snoot|y 'snuː.t|i ⓤⓢ -t̬|i **-ily** -ɪ.li, -ᵊl.i **-iness** -ɪ.nəs, -ɪ.nɪs **-ier** -i.əʳ ⓤⓢ -i.ɚ **-iest** -i.ɪst, -i.əst
snooz|e snuːz **-es** -ɪz **-ing** -ɪŋ **-ed** -d **-er/s** -əʳ/z ⓤⓢ -ɚ/z
snor|e snɔːʳ ⓤⓢ snɔːr **-es** -z **-ing** -ɪŋ **-ed** -d **-er/s** -əʳ/z ⓤⓢ -ɚ/z
snorkel 'snɔː.kᵊl ⓤⓢ 'snɔːr- **-s** -z **-(l)ing** -ɪŋ **-(l)ed** -d **-(l)er/s** -əʳ/z ⓤⓢ -ɚ/z

snort snɔːt (US) snɔːrt **-s** -s **-ing** -ɪŋ (US) ˈsnɔːr.t̬ɪŋ **-ed** -ɪd (US) ˈsnɔːr.t̬ɪd

snorter ˈsnɔː.təʳ (US) ˈsnɔːr.t̬ɚ **-s** -z

snort|y ˈsnɔː.t|i (US) ˈsnɔːr.t̬|i **-ier** -i.əʳ (US) -i.ɚ **-iest** -i.ɪst, -i.əst **-ily** -ɪ.li, -ᵊl.i **-iness** -ɪ.nəs, -ɪ.nɪs

snot snɒt (US) snɑːt **-ty** -i (US) ˈsnɑː.t̬i

snout (S) snaʊt **-s** -s

snow (S) snəʊ (US) snoʊ **-s** -z **-ing** -ɪŋ **-ed** -d **-er/s** ˈ**snow** ˌ**blindness**; ˈ**snow** ˌ**goose**; ˌ**Snow** ˈ**White**

snowball ˈsnəʊ.bɔːl (US) ˈsnoʊ.bɔːl, -bɑːl **-s** -z **-ing** -ɪŋ **-ed** -d

snowberr|y ˈsnəʊ.bᵊr|.i, -br|i (US) ˈsnoʊˌber|.i **-ies** -iz

snowblower ˈsnəʊˌbləʊ.əʳ (US) ˈsnoʊˌbloʊ.ɚ **-s** -z

snowboard ˈsnəʊ.bɔːd (US) ˈsnoʊ.bɔːrd **-s** -z **-ing** -ɪŋ **-ed** -ɪd **-er/s** -əʳ/z (US) -ɚ/z

snowbound ˈsnəʊ.baʊnd (US) ˈsnoʊ-

snowcap ˈsnəʊ.kæp (US) ˈsnoʊ- **-s** -s **-ped** -t

Snowden, Snowdon ˈsnəʊ.dᵊn (US) ˈsnoʊ-

Snowdonia snəʊˈdəʊ.ni.ə (US) snoʊˈdoʊ-

snowdrift ˈsnəʊ.drɪft (US) ˈsnoʊ- **-s** -s

snowdrop ˈsnəʊ.drɒp (US) ˈsnoʊ.drɑːp **-s** -s

snowfall ˈsnəʊ.fɔːl (US) ˈsnoʊ-, -fɑːl **-s** -z

snowfield ˈsnəʊ.fiːld (US) ˈsnoʊ- **-s** -z

snowflake ˈsnəʊ.fleɪk (US) ˈsnoʊ- **-s** -s

snow|man ˈsnəʊ|.mæn (US) ˈsnoʊ- **-men** -men

snowmobile ˈsnəʊ.məˌbiːl (US) ˈsnoʊ.moʊˌ- **-s** -z

snowplough, snowplow ˈsnəʊ.plaʊ (US) ˈsnoʊ- **-s** -z **-ing** -ɪŋ **-ed** -d

snowshoe ˈsnəʊ.ʃuː (US) ˈsnoʊ- **-s** -z

snowstorm ˈsnəʊ.stɔːm (US) ˈsnoʊ.stɔːrm **-s** -z

snowsuit ˈsnəʊ.suːt, -sjuːt (US) ˈsnoʊ.suːt **-s** -s

snow-white ˌsnəʊˈ*h*waɪt (US) ˌsnoʊ- *stress shift:* ˌsnow-white ˈhair

snow|y ˈsnəʊ|.i (US) ˈsnoʊ- **-ier** -i.əʳ (US) -i.ɚ **-iest** -i.ɪst, -i.əst **-ily** -ɪ.li, -ᵊl.i **-iness** -ɪ.nəs, -ɪ.nɪs ˌ**snowy** ˈ**owl**

SNP ˌes.enˈpiː, -emˈ- (US) -enˈ-

snr (S) *(abbrev. for* **senior***)* ˈsiː.ni.əʳ, -njəʳ (US) -njɚ

snub snʌb **-s** -z **-bing** -ɪŋ **-bed** -d

snub-nosed ˌsnʌbˈnəʊzd (US) ˈsnʌb.noʊzd *stress shift, British only:* ˌsnub-nosed ˈbullet

snuck snʌk

snuff snʌf **-s** -s **-ing** -ɪŋ **-ed** -t **-er/s** -əʳ/z (US) -ɚ/z ˈ**snuff** ˌ**box**

snuffl|e ˈsnʌf.l̩ **-es** -z **-ing** -ɪŋ, ˈsnʌf.lɪŋ **-ed** -d **-er/s** -əʳ/z, ˈsnʌf.ləʳ/z (US) ˈ-l̩.ɚ/z, ˈ-lɚ/z **-y** -i

snug snʌg **-ger** -əʳ (US) -ɚ **-gest** -ɪst, -əst **-ly** -li **-ness** -nəs, -nɪs

snugger|y ˈsnʌg.ᵊr|.i **-ies** -iz

snuggl|e ˈsnʌg.l̩ **-es** -z **-ing** -ɪŋ, ˈsnʌg.lɪŋ **-ed** -d

Snyder ˈsnaɪ.dəʳ (US) -dɚ

so *normal forms:* səʊ (US) soʊ *occasional weak form:* sə ˌ**so** ˈ**long,** ˈ**so** ˌ**long**

Note: Weak form word. The weak form is used only rarely, and only in casual speech before adjectives and adverbs (e.g. “Not so bad” /ˌnɒt.səˈbæd (US) ˌnɑːt-/, “Don't go so fast” /ˌdəʊnt.gəʊ.səˈfɑːst (US) ˌdoʊnt.goʊ.səˈfæst/).

soak səʊk (US) soʊk **-s** -s **-ing** -ɪŋ **-ed** -t

soakaway ˈsəʊk.əˌweɪ (US) ˈsoʊk- **-s** -z

Soames səʊmz (US) soʊmz

so-and-so ˈsəʊ.ən*d*.səʊ (US) ˈsoʊ.ən*d*.soʊ **-(')s** -z

Soane səʊn (US) soʊn **-s** -z

soap səʊp (US) soʊp **-s** -s **-ing** -ɪŋ **-ed** -t **-y** -i **-ier** -i.əʳ (US) -i.ɚ **-iest** -i.ɪst, -i.əst **-ily** -ɪ.li, -ᵊl.i **-iness** -ɪ.nəs, -ɪ.nɪs

soapbox ˈsəʊp.bɒks (US) ˈsoʊp.bɑːks **-es** -ɪz

soap opera ˈsəʊpˌɒp.ᵊr.ə, ˌ-rə (US) ˈsoʊpˌɑː.pɚ.ə, ˌ-prə **-s** -z

soapstone ˈsəʊp.stəʊn (US) ˈsoʊp.stoʊn

soapsuds ˈsəʊp.sʌdz (US) ˈsoʊp-

soar (S) sɔːʳ (US) sɔːr **-s** -z **-ing** -ɪŋ **-ed** -d

soaraway ˈsɔː.rə.weɪ (US) ˈsɔːr.ə-

Soares səʊˈɑː.rɪz (US) soʊˈɑːr.ɪz

sob sɒb (US) sɑːb **-s** -z **-bing** -ɪŋ **-bed** -d ˈ**sob** ˌ**story**

SOB ˌes.əʊˈbiː (US) -oʊˈ-

Sobel ˈsəʊ.bel (US) ˈsoʊ-

sob|er ˈsəʊ.b|əʳ (US) ˈsoʊ.b|ɚ **-erer** -ᵊr.əʳ (US) -ɚ.ɚ **-erest** -ᵊr.ɪst, -ᵊr.əst **-erly** -ᵊl.i (US) -ɚ.li **-erness** -ə.nəs, -ə.nɪs (US) -ɚ.nəs, -ɚ.nɪs **-ers** -əz (US) -ɚz **-ering/ly** -ᵊr.ɪŋ/li **-ered** -əd (US) -ɚd

Sobers ˈsəʊ.bəz (US) ˈsoʊ.bɚz

sobersides ˈsəʊ.bə.saɪdz (US) ˈsoʊ.bɚ-

sobriety səʊˈbraɪ.ɪ.ti, ˈ-ə- (US) səˈbraɪ.ə.t̬i, soʊ-

sobriquet ˈsəʊ.brɪ.keɪ (US) ˈsoʊ-, -ket, ˌ--ˈ- **-s** -z

so-called ˌsəʊˈkɔːld (US) ˌsoʊˈkɑːld, -ˈkɔːld *stress shift:* ˌso-called ˈfriend

soc(c)age ˈsɒk.ɪdʒ (US) ˈsɑː.kɪdʒ

soccer ˈsɒk.əʳ (US) ˈsɑː.kɚ

sociability ˌsəʊ.ʃəˈbɪl.ə.ti, -ɪ.ti (US) ˌsoʊ.ʃəˈbɪl.ə.t̬i

sociab|le ˈsəʊ.ʃə.b|l̩ (US) ˈsoʊ- **-ly** -li **-leness** -l̩.nəs, -nɪs

social ˈsəʊ.ʃᵊl (US) ˈsoʊ- **-s** -z **-ly** -i ˌ**social** ˈ**climber** (US) ˈ**social** ˌ**climber**; ˌ**social** **de**ˈ**mocracy**; ˌ**social** ˈ**democrat**; ˈ**social** ˌ**life**; ˌ**social** ˈ**science** (US) ˈ**social** ˌ**science**; ˌ**social** ˈ**secretary**; ˌ**social** **se**ˈ**curity**; ˌ**social** ˈ**service** (US) ˈ**social** ˌ**service**; ˈ**social** ˌ**work**

social|ism ˈsəʊ.ʃᵊl|.ɪ.zᵊm (US) ˈsoʊ- **-ist/s** -ɪst/s

socialistic ˌsəʊ.ʃᵊlˈɪs.tɪk (US) ˌsoʊ.ʃəˈlɪs-

socialite ˈsəʊ.ʃᵊl.aɪt (US) ˈsoʊ.ʃə.laɪt **-s** -s

socialization, -isa- ˌsəʊ.ʃᵊl.aɪˈzeɪ.ʃᵊn (US) ˌsoʊ.ʃᵊl.ɪˈ-

socializ|e, -is|e ˈsəʊ.ʃᵊl.aɪz (US) ˈsoʊ.ʃə.laɪz **-es** -ɪz **-ing** -ɪŋ **-ed** -d

societal səˈsaɪ.ə.tᵊl (US) -t̬ᵊl

societ|y (S) səˈsaɪ.ə.t|i (US) -t̬|i **-ies** -iz

Socinian səʊˈsɪn.i.ən (US) soʊ- **-s** -z

Socinus səʊˈsaɪ.nəs (US) soʊ-

socio- səʊ.ʃi.əʊ-, -si-; ˌsəʊ.ʃiˈɒ-, -siˈ- (US) soʊ.si.oʊ-, -ʃi-, -ə-; ˌsoʊ.siˈɑː-, -ʃiˈ-

Note: Prefix. Normally either takes primary or secondary stress on the first syllable, e.g. **sociopath** /ˈsəʊ.ʃi.əʊ.pæθ (US) ˈsoʊ.si.ə-/, **sociopolitical** /ˌsəʊ.ʃi.əʊ.pəˈlɪt.ɪ.kᵊl (US) ˌsoʊ.si.oʊ.pəˈlɪt̬-/, or secondary stress on the first syllable andprimary stress on the third syllable, e.g. **sociology** /ˌsəʊ.ʃiˈɒl.ə.dʒi (US) ˌsoʊ.siˈɑː.lə-/.

sociobiolog|y ˌsəʊ.ʃi.əʊ.baɪˈɒl.ə.dʒ|i, -si- (US) ˌsoʊ.si.oʊ.baɪˈɑː.lə-, -ʃi- **-ist/s** -ɪst/s

sociocultural ˌsəʊ.ʃi.əʊˈkʌl.tʃᵊr.əl, -si- (US) ˌsoʊ.si.oʊ-, -ʃi- **-ly** -i

socioeconomic ˌsəʊ.ʃi.əʊˌiː.kəˈnɒm.ɪk, -si-, -ˌek.əˈ- (US) ˌsoʊ.si.oʊˌek.əˈnɑː.mɪk, -ʃi-, -ˌiː.kəˈ-

sociolinguist ˌsəʊ.ʃi.əʊˈlɪŋ.gwɪst, -si- (US) ˌsoʊ.si.oʊˈ-, -ʃi- **-s** -s

sociolinguistic ˌsəʊ.ʃi.əʊ.lɪŋˈgwɪs.tɪk, -si- (US) ˌsoʊ.si.oʊ-, -ʃi- **-s** -s

sociologic|al ˌsəʊ.ʃi.əˈlɒdʒ.ɪ.k|ᵊl, -si- (US) ˌsoʊ.si.əˈlɑː.dʒɪ-, -ʃi- **-ally** -ᵊl.i, -li

sociologist ˌsəʊ.ʃiˈɒl.ə.dʒ|ɪst, -siˈ- (US) ˌsoʊ.siˈɑː.lə-, -ʃiˈ- **-s** -s

sociolog|y ˌsəʊ.ʃiˈɒl.ə.dʒ|i, -siˈ- (US) ˌsoʊ.siˈɑː.lə-, -ʃiˈ- **-ist/s** -ɪst/s

sociopath ˈsəʊ.ʃi.əʊ.pæθ, -si- (US) ˈsoʊ.si.ə-, -ʃi- **-s** -s

sociopolitical ˌsəʊ.ʃi.əʊ.pᵊlˈɪt.ɪ.kᵊl, -si- (US) ˌsoʊ.si.oʊ.pəˈlɪt̬-, -ʃi-

socioreligious ˌsəʊ.ʃi.əʊ.rɪˈlɪdʒ.əs, -si-, -rəˈ- (US) ˌsoʊ.si.oʊ-, -ʃi-

sock sɒk (US) sɑːk **-s** -s **-ing** -ɪŋ **-ed** -t

sockdolager, sockdologer sɒkˈdɒl.ə.dʒəʳ (US) sɑːkˈdɑː.lə.dʒɚ **-s** -z

sock|et ˈsɒk|.ɪt (US) ˈsɑː.k|ɪt **-ets** -ɪts **-eted** -ɪ.tɪd (US) -ɪ.t̬ɪd

Socotra səʊˈkəʊ.trə, sɒkˈəʊ- (US) soʊˈkoʊ-

Socrates ˈsɒk.rə.tiːz (US) ˈsɑː.krə-

Soft palate

The rear part of the roof of the mouth.

Most of the roof of the mouth consists of 'hard palate', which has bone beneath the skin. Towards the back of the mouth, the layer of bone comes to an end but the layer of soft tissue continues for some distance, ending eventually in a loose appendage that can easily be seen by looking in a mirror. This dangling object is the 'uvula', and the layer of soft tissue attached to it is called the soft palate (it is also sometimes known as the 'velum'). In normal breathing the velum is allowed to hang down so that air may pass above it and escape through the nose, but for most speech sounds it is lifted up and pressed against the upper back wall of the throat so that no air can escape through the nose. This is necessary for a PLOSIVE, for example, so that air may be compressed within the vocal tract. However, for NASAL consonants (e.g., [m], [n]) the soft palate must be lowered since air should escape only through the nose in these sounds.

In nasalised vowels (such vowels are found in considerable numbers in French, for example) the soft palate is lowered and air escapes through the mouth and the nose together.

socratic (S) sɒk'ræt.ɪk, səʊ'kræt- ⓤⓢ sə'kræţ-, soʊ- **-ally** -əl.i, -li

sod sɒd ⓤⓢ sɑːd **-s** -z **-ding** -ɪŋ **-ded** -ɪd **ˌsod's 'law, 'sod's ˌlaw**

soda 'səʊ.də ⓤⓢ 'soʊ- **-s** -z **'soda ˌbiscuit; 'soda ˌbread; 'soda ˌcracker; 'soda ˌfountain; 'soda ˌpop; 'soda ˌsiphon; 'soda ˌwater**

sodalit|y səʊ'dæl.ə.t|i, -ɪ.t|i ⓤⓢ soʊ'dæl.ə.ţ|i **-ies** -iz

sodden 'sɒd.ən ⓤⓢ 'sɑː.dən **-ness** -nəs, -nɪs **-s** -z **-ing** -ɪŋ **-ed** -d

sodding 'sɒd.ɪŋ ⓤⓢ 'sɑː.dɪŋ

sodium 'səʊ.di.əm ⓤⓢ 'soʊ-

Sodom 'sɒd.əm ⓤⓢ 'sɑː.dəm

sodomiz|e, -is|e 'sɒd.ə.maɪz ⓤⓢ 'sɑː.də- **-es** -ɪz **-ing** -ɪŋ **-ed** -d

sodom|y 'sɒd.ə.m|i ⓤⓢ 'sɑː.də- **-ite/s** -aɪt/s

Sodor 'səʊ.dəʳ ⓤⓢ 'soʊ.dɚ

Soeharto sʊ'hɑː.təʊ ⓤⓢ -'hɑːr.ţoʊ

soever səʊ'ev.əʳ ⓤⓢ soʊ'ev.ɚ

sofa 'səʊ.fə ⓤⓢ 'soʊ- **-s** -z

sofabed 'səʊ.fə.bed ⓤⓢ 'soʊ- **-s** -z

Sofala səʊ'fɑː.lə ⓤⓢ soʊ-, sə-

soffit 'sɒf.ɪt ⓤⓢ 'sɑː.fɪt **-s** -s

Sofia 'sɒf.i.ə, 'səʊ.fi- ⓤⓢ 'soʊ.fi-; soʊ'fiː-

soft sɒft ⓤⓢ sɑːft **-s** -s **-er** -əʳ ⓤⓢ -ɚ **-est** -ɪst, -əst **-ly** -li **-ness** -nəs, -nɪs **ˌsoft 'copy; ˌsoft 'drink** ⓤⓢ **'soft ˌdrink; ˌsoft 'fruit; ˌsoft 'furnishings; ˌsoft 'landing; ˌsoft 'option; ˌsoft 'sell; 'soft ˌspot, ˌsoft 'spot** ⓤⓢ **'soft ˌspot; ˌsoft 'target; 'soft ˌtouch, ˌsoft 'touch**

softback 'sɒf*t*.bæk ⓤⓢ 'sɑːf*t*- **-s** -s

softball 'sɒf*t*.bɔːl ⓤⓢ 'sɑːft-, -bɑːl

soft-boil ˌsɒft'bɔɪl ⓤⓢ ˌsɑːft- **-s** -z **-ing** -ɪŋ **-ed** -d

soft-centred ˌsɒft'sen.təd ⓤⓢ ˌsɑːft'sen.tɚd

soft-core 'sɒft.kɔːʳ ⓤⓢ 'sɑːft.kɔːr

softcover ˌsɒft'kʌv.əʳ ⓤⓢ 'sɑːft.kʌv.ɚ **-s** -z

soften 'sɒf.ən ⓤⓢ 'sɑː.fən **-s** -z **-ing** -ɪŋ, 'sɒf.nɪŋ ⓤⓢ 'sɑːf- **-ed** -d

softener 'sɒf.ən.əʳ, '-nəʳ ⓤⓢ 'sɑː.fən.ɚ, 'sɑːf.nɚ **-s** -z

softhearted ˌsɒft'hɑː.tɪd ⓤⓢ 'sɑːft ˌhɑːr.ţɪd **-ly** -li **-ness** -nəs, -nɪs *stress shift, British only:* ˌsofthearted 'person

soft|ie 'sɒf.t|i ⓤⓢ 'sɑːf- **-ies** -iz

softish 'sɒf.tɪʃ ⓤⓢ 'sɑːf-

softly-softly ˌsɒft.li'sɒft.li ⓤⓢ ˌsɑːft.li'sɑːft-

soft-pedal ˌsɒf*t*'ped.əl ⓤⓢ ˌsɑːf*t*- **-s** -z **-(l)ing** -ɪŋ, -'ped.lɪŋ **-(l)ed** -d

soft-soap ˌsɒf*t*'səʊp ⓤⓢ ˌsɑːf*t*'soʊp **-s** -s **-ing** -ɪŋ **-ed** -t

soft-spoken ˌsɒf*t*'spəʊ.kən ⓤⓢ ˌsɑːft'spoʊ- *stress shift:* ˌsoft-spoken 'person

software 'sɒf*t*.weəʳ ⓤⓢ 'sɑːf*t*.wer

softwood 'sɒf*t*.wʊd ⓤⓢ 'sɑːf*t*- **-s** -z

soft|y 'sɒf.t|i ⓤⓢ 'sɑːf- **-ies** -iz

SOGAT 'səʊ.gæt ⓤⓢ 'soʊ-

sogg|y 'sɒg|.i ⓤⓢ 'sɑː.g|i **-ily** -ɪ.li, -əl.i **-ier** -i.əʳ ⓤⓢ -i.ɚ **-iest** -i.ɪst, -i.əst **-iness** -ɪ.nəs, -ɪ.nɪs

soh səʊ ⓤⓢ soʊ **-s** -z

Soham 'səʊ.əm ⓤⓢ 'soʊ-

Soho 'səʊ.həʊ; ⓤⓢ 'soʊ.hoʊ

soi-disant ˌswɑː.diː'zɑ̃ː*ŋ*, ˌ-'-- ⓤⓢ ˌswɑː.diː'zɑ̃ː*n*

soigné(e) 'swɑː.njeɪ, -'- ⓤⓢ swɑː'njeɪ

soil sɔɪl **-s** -z **-ing** -ɪŋ **-ed** -d **'soil ˌpipe**

soirée, soiree 'swɑː.reɪ, 'swɒr.eɪ, -'- ⓤⓢ swɑː'reɪ **-s** -z

soixante-neuf ˌswæs.ɑ̃ː*n*t'nɜːf, ˌswʌs- ⓤⓢ ˌswɑː.sɑ̃ː*n*t'nɜːf

sojourn 'sɒdʒ.ɜːn, 'sʌdʒ-, -ən ⓤⓢ 'soʊ.dʒɝːn, -'- **-s** -z **-ing** -ɪŋ **-ed** -d **-er/s** -əʳ/z ⓤⓢ -ɚ/z

Sokoto 'səʊ.kə.təʊ, ˌ--'- ⓤⓢ 'soʊ.koʊ.toʊ, ˌ--'-; sə'koʊ-

sol (S) sɒl ⓤⓢ soʊl, sɑːl **-s** -z

sola 'səʊ.lə ⓤⓢ 'soʊ-

solac|e 'sɒl.əs, -ɪs ⓤⓢ 'sɑː.lɪs **-es** -ɪz **-ing** -ɪŋ **-ed** -t

solanum səʊ'leɪ.nəm, -'lɑː- ⓤⓢ soʊ'leɪ-

solar 'səʊ.ləʳ ⓤⓢ 'soʊ.lɚ **ˌsolar 'energy; ˌsolar 'panel; ˌsolar 'plexus; 'solar ˌsystem**

solari|um səʊ'leə.ri.əm ⓤⓢ soʊ'ler.i-, sə- **-ums** -z **-a** -ə

solati|um səʊ'leɪ.ʃi|.əm ⓤⓢ soʊ- **-ums** -əmz **-a** -ə

sold *(from* **sell)** səʊld ⓤⓢ soʊld

sold|er 'səʊl.d|əʳ, 'sɒl- ⓤⓢ 'sɑː.d|ɚ **-ers** -əz ⓤⓢ -ɚz **-ering** -ər.ɪŋ **-ered** -əd ⓤⓢ -ɚd **'soldering ˌiron**

soldi|er 'səʊl.dʒ|əʳ ⓤⓢ 'soʊl.dʒ|ɚ **-ers** -əz ⓤⓢ -ɚz **-ering** -ər.ɪŋ **-ered** -əd ⓤⓢ -ɚd **ˌsoldier of 'fortune**

soldierly 'səʊl.dʒəl.i ⓤⓢ 'soʊl.dʒɚ.li

soldiery 'səʊl.dʒər.i ⓤⓢ 'soʊl-

sol|e (S) səʊl ⓤⓢ soʊl **-es** -z **-ely** -li **-ing** -ɪŋ **-ed** -d

solecism 'sɒl.ɪ.sɪ.zəm, '-ə-, -es.ɪ- ⓤⓢ 'sɑː.lə- **-s** -z

solemn 'sɒl.əm ⓤⓢ 'sɑː.ləm **-ly** -li **-ness** -nəs, -nɪs

solemnif|y sə'lem.nɪ.f|aɪ, sɒl'em- ⓤⓢ sə'lem- **-ies** -z **-ying** -ɪŋ **-ied** -d

solemnit|y sə'lem.nə.t|i, sɒl'em-, -nɪ- ⓤⓢ sə'lem.nə.ţ|i **-ies** -z

solemnization, -isa- ˌsɒl.əm.naɪ'zeɪ.ʃən, -nɪ'- ⓤⓢ ˌsɑː.ləm.nɪ'- **-s** -z

solemniz|e, -is|e 'sɒl.əm.naɪz ⓤⓢ 'sɑː.ləm- **-es** -ɪz **-ing** -ɪŋ **-ed** -d

solenoid 'səʊ.lə.nɔɪd, 'sɒl.ə-, '-ɪ- ⓤⓢ 'soʊ.lə-, 'sɑː- **-s** -z

Solent 'səʊ.lənt ⓤⓢ 'soʊ-

sol-fa (S) ˌsɒl'fɑː, '-- ⓤⓢ ˌsoʊl-

solfegg|io sɒl'fedʒ|.i.əʊ ⓤⓢ soʊl'fedʒ|.i.oʊ; sɑːl'fedʒ|.oʊ **-i** -iː

solferino (S) ˌsɒl.fər'iː.nəʊ ⓤⓢ ˌsoʊl.fə'riː.noʊ, ˌsɑːl-

solic|it sə'lɪs|.ɪt **-its** -ɪts **-iting** -ɪ.tɪŋ ⓤⓢ -ɪ.ţɪŋ **-ited** -ɪ.tɪd ⓤⓢ -ɪ.ţɪd

solicitation səˌlɪs.ɪˈteɪ.ʃən **-s** -z
solicitor səˈlɪs.ɪ.tər, ˈ-ə- ⓤⓢ -t̬ɚ **-s** -z
soˌlicitor ˈgeneral
solicitous səˈlɪs.ɪ.təs ⓤⓢ -t̬əs **-ly** -li **-ness** -nəs, -nɪs
solicitude səˈlɪs.ɪ.tjuːd, -tʃuːd ⓤⓢ -tuːd, -tjuːd
solid ˈsɒl.ɪd ⓤⓢ ˈsɑː.lɪd **-s** -z **-est** -ɪst, -əst **-ly** -li **-ness** -nəs, -nɪs
solidarity (S) ˌsɒl.ɪˈdær.ə.ti, -ɪ.ti ⓤⓢ ˌsɑː.ləˈder.ə.t̬i, -ˈdær-
solidifiable səˈlɪd.ɪ.faɪ.ə.bl̩, sɒlˈɪd- ⓤⓢ səˈlɪd-
solidification səˌlɪd.ɪ.fɪˈkeɪ.ʃən, sɒlˌɪd- ⓤⓢ səˌlɪd.ə-
solidi|fy səˈlɪd.ɪ.|faɪ, sɒlˈɪd- ⓤⓢ səˈlɪd.ə- **-fies** -faɪz **-fying** -faɪ.ɪŋ **-fied** -faɪd
solidity səˈlɪd.ə.ti, sɒlˈɪd-, -ɪ.ti ⓤⓢ səˈlɪd.ə.t̬i
solid-state ˌsɒl.ɪdˈsteɪt ⓤⓢ ˌsɑː.lɪdˈ- *stress shift, see compound:* **ˌsolid-state ˈphysics**
solid|us ˈsɒl.ɪ.d|əs ⓤⓢ ˈsɑː.lɪ- **-i** -aɪ, -iː
Solihull ˌsəʊ.lɪˈhʌl, ˌsɒl.ɪˈ- ⓤⓢ ˌsoʊ.lɪˈ- *stress shift:* ˌSolihull ˈresidents
soliloquiz|e, -is|e səˈlɪl.ə.kwaɪz, sɒlˈɪl- ⓤⓢ səˈlɪl- **-es** -ɪz **-ing** -ɪŋ **-ed** -d
soliloqu|y səˈlɪl.ə.kw|i, sɒlˈɪl- ⓤⓢ səˈlɪl- **-ies** -iz
solipsism ˈsɒl.ɪp.sɪ.zəm, ˈsəʊ.lɪp- ⓤⓢ ˈsɑː.lɪp-, ˈsoʊ- **-s** -z
solipsist ˈsɒl.ɪp.sɪst ⓤⓢ ˈsɑː.lɪp- **-s** -s **-ic** -ɪk
solitaire ˌsɒl.ɪˈteər, ˈ--- ⓤⓢ ˈsɑː.lə.ter **-s** -z
solitar|y ˈsɒl.ɪ.tər|.i, ˈ-ə-, -tr|i ⓤⓢ ˈsɑː.lə.ter|.i **-ies** -iz **-ily** -əl.i, -ɪ.li **-iness** -ɪ.nəs, -ɪ.nɪs **ˌsolitary conˈfinement**
solitude ˈsɒl.ɪ.tjuːd, ˈ-ə-, -tʃuːd ⓤⓢ ˈsɑː.lə.tuːd, -tjuːd **-s** -z
Solloway ˈsɒl.ə.weɪ ⓤⓢ ˈsɑː.lə-
solo ˈsəʊ.ləʊ ⓤⓢ ˈsoʊ.loʊ **-s** -z
soloist ˈsəʊ.ləʊ.ɪst ⓤⓢ ˈsoʊ.loʊ- **-s** -s
Solomon ˈsɒl.ə.mən ⓤⓢ ˈsɑː.lə- **ˈSolomon ˌIslands**
Solon ˈsəʊ.lɒn, -lən ⓤⓢ ˈsoʊ.lən, -lɑːn
so-long ˌsəʊˈlɒŋ; sə- ⓤⓢ ˌsoʊˈlɑːŋ, sə-, -ˈlɔːŋ
solstic|e ˈsɒl.stɪs ⓤⓢ ˈsɑːl- **-es** -ɪz
Solti ˈʃɒl.ti ⓤⓢ ˈʃoʊl.tiː
solubility ˌsɒl.jəˈbɪl.ə.ti, -jʊˈ-, -ɪ.ti ⓤⓢ ˌsɑːl.jəˈbɪl.ə.t̬i, -jʊˈ-
soluble ˈsɒl.jə.bl̩, -jʊ- ⓤⓢ ˈsɑːl-
solus ˈsəʊ.ləs ⓤⓢ ˈsoʊ-
solution səˈluː.ʃən, -ˈljuː- ⓤⓢ -ˈluː- **-s** -z
solvability ˌsɒl.vəˈbɪl.ə.ti, -ɪ.ti ⓤⓢ ˌsɑːl.vəˈbɪl.ə.t̬i
solv|e sɒlv ⓤⓢ sɑːlv **-es** -z **-ing** -ɪŋ **-ed** -d **-able** -ə.bl̩
solvency ˈsɒl.vənt.si ⓤⓢ ˈsɑːl-
solvent ˈsɒl.vənt ⓤⓢ ˈsɑːl- **ˈsolvent aˌbuse**
Solway ˈsɒl.weɪ ⓤⓢ ˈsɑːl-
Solzhenitsyn ˌsɒl.ʒəˈnɪt.sɪn ⓤⓢ ˌsoʊl.ʒəˈniːt-
som|a ˈsəʊ.m|ə ⓤⓢ ˈsoʊ- **-ata** -ə.tə ⓤⓢ -ə.t̬ə
Somali səˈmɑː.li ⓤⓢ soʊ-, sə- **-s** -z
Somali|a səˈmɑː.li|.ə ⓤⓢ soʊ-, sə- **-an/s** -ən/z
somatic səʊˈmæt.ɪk ⓤⓢ soʊˈmæt̬-
somatostatin ˌsəʊ.mə.təˈstæt.ɪn ⓤⓢ səˌmæt̬.əˈstæt.ən; ˌsoʊ.mə.t̬əˈ-
somatotropin səʊˌmæt.əˈtrəʊ.pɪn; ˌsəʊ.mə.təˈ- ⓤⓢ səˌmæt̬.əˈtroʊ.pən; ˌsoʊ.mə.t̬əˈ-
sombl|er ˈsɒm.b|ər ⓤⓢ ˈsɑːm.b|ɚ **-erest** -ər.ɪst, -ər.əst **-erly** -ə.li ⓤⓢ -ɚ.li **-erness** -ə.nəs, -ə.nɪs ⓤⓢ -ɚ.nəs, -ɚ.nɪs
sombr|e ˈsɒm.b|ər ⓤⓢ ˈsɑːm.b|ɚ **-est** -ər.ɪst, -ər.əst **-ely** -ə.li **-eli** -ɚ.li **-eness** -ə.nəs, -ə.nɪs ⓤⓢ -ɚ.nəs, -ɚ.nɪs
sombrero sɒmˈbreə.rəʊ ⓤⓢ sɑːmˈbrer.oʊ, səm- **-s** -z
some *strong form:* sʌm *weak form:* səm
Note: Weak form word. There are two grammatical functions for this word, one being the determiner, as in "some apples, some bananas", etc., where a weak form is used, the other being a quantifier, as in "some were tired and some were hungry", where the strong form is usual. In final position, the strong form is used (e.g. "I want some").
-some -səm
Note: Suffix. Does not normally change the stress pattern of the word to which it is added, e.g. **trouble** /ˈtrʌb.l̩/, **troublesome** /ˈtrʌb.l̩.səm/.
somebody ˈsʌm.bə.di, -ˌbɒd.i ⓤⓢ -ˌbɑː.di, -ˌbʌd.i, -bə.di
someday ˈsʌm.deɪ
somehow ˈsʌm.haʊ
someone ˈsʌm.wʌn
someplace ˈsʌm.pleɪs
Somerfield® ˈsʌm.ə.fiːld ⓤⓢ -ɚ-
Somers ˈsʌm.əz ⓤⓢ -ɚz
somersault ˈsʌm.ə.sɔːlt, -sɒlt ⓤⓢ -ɚ.sɑːlt, -sɔːlt **-s** -s **-ing** -ɪŋ **-ed** -ɪd
Somerset ˈsʌm.ə.set, -sɪt ⓤⓢ ˈ-ɚ- **-shire** -ʃər, -ˌʃɪər ⓤⓢ -ʃɚ, -ʃɪr
Somerton ˈsʌm.ə.tən ⓤⓢ -ɚ.t̬ən
Somervell ˈsʌm.ə.vɪl, -vel ⓤⓢ ˈ-ɚ-
Somerville ˈsʌm.ə.vɪl ⓤⓢ ˈ-ɚ-
something ˈsʌmp.θɪŋ
sometime ˈsʌm.taɪm
sometimes ˈsʌm.taɪmz
someway ˈsʌm.weɪ
somewhat ˈsʌm.hwɒt ⓤⓢ -hwɑːt, -hwʌt, -hwət
somewhere ˈsʌm.hweər ⓤⓢ -hwer
Somme sɒm ⓤⓢ sʌm
sommelier sɒmˈel.i.ər, sʌm-, -eɪ; ˈsʌm.əl.jeɪ, ˈsɒm- ⓤⓢ ˌsʌm.əlˈjeɪ **-s** -z
somnambul|ism sɒmˈnæm.bjə.l|ɪ.zəm, -bjʊ- ⓤⓢ sɑːmˈnæm- **-ist/s** -ɪst/s
somniferous sɒmˈnɪf.ər.əs ⓤⓢ sɑːm-
somnolen|ce ˈsɒm.nəl.ən|ts ⓤⓢ ˈsɑːm- **-t/ly** -t/li
Sompting ˈsɒmp.tɪŋ, ˈsʌmp-
son (S) sʌn **-s** -z **ˌson of a ˈbitch**; **ˌson of a ˈgun**
sonagram ˈsəʊ.nə.græm, ˈsɒn.ə- ⓤⓢ ˈsɑː.nə-, ˈsoʊ- **-s** -z
sonagraph (S®) ˈsəʊ.nə.grɑːf, ˈsɒn.ə-, -græf ⓤⓢ ˈsɑː.nə.græf, ˈsoʊ- **-s** -s
sonant ˈsəʊ.nənt ⓤⓢ ˈsoʊ- **-s** -s
sonar ˈsəʊ.nɑːr ⓤⓢ ˈsoʊ.nɑːr
sonata səˈnɑː.tə ⓤⓢ -t̬ə **-s** -z
sonatina ˌsɒn.əˈtiː.nə ⓤⓢ ˌsɑː.nəˈ- **-s** -z
Sondheim ˈsɒnd.haɪm ⓤⓢ ˈsɑːnd-
son et lumière ˌsɒn.eɪˈluː.mjeər, ˌsɔːn-, -luːˈmjeər ⓤⓢ ˌsɑːn.eɪˈluː.mjer, ˌsɔːn-
song sɒŋ ⓤⓢ sɑːŋ, sɔːŋ **-s** -z **ˌsong and ˈdance**; **ˈsong ˌthrush**
songbird ˈsɒŋ.bɜːd ⓤⓢ ˈsɑːŋ.bɝːd, ˈsɔːŋ- **-s** -z
songbook ˈsɒŋ.bʊk ⓤⓢ ˈsɑːŋ-, ˈsɔːŋ- **-s** -s
songfest ˈsɒŋ.fest ⓤⓢ ˈsɑːŋ-, ˈsɔːŋ- **-s** -s
songster ˈsɒŋk.stər ⓤⓢ ˈsɑːŋk.stɚ, ˈsɔːŋk- **-s** -z
songwrit|er ˈsɒŋˌraɪ.t|ər ⓤⓢ ˈsɑːŋˌraɪ.t̬|ɚ, ˈsɔːŋ- **-ers** -əz ⓤⓢ -ɚz **-ing** -ɪŋ
Sonia ˈsɒn.jə, ˈsəʊ.njə ⓤⓢ ˈsɑː.njə, ˈsoʊ-
sonic ˈsɒn.ɪk ⓤⓢ ˈsɑː.nɪk **ˌsonic ˈboom**
son-in-law ˈsʌn.ɪn.lɔː ⓤⓢ -lɑː, -lɔː **sons-in-law** ˈsʌnz-
sonnet ˈsɒn.ɪt ⓤⓢ ˈsɑː.nɪt **-s** -s
sonneteer ˌsɒn.ɪˈtɪər, -əˈ- ⓤⓢ ˌsɑː.nəˈtɪr **-s** -z
Sonning ˈsɒn.ɪŋ, ˈsʌn- ⓤⓢ ˈsɑː.nɪŋ, ˈsʌn.ɪŋ
sonn|y ˈsʌn|.i **-ies** -iz
sonogram ˈsəʊ.nə.græm, ˈsɒn.ə- ⓤⓢ ˈsɑː.nə-, ˈsoʊ- **-s** -z
sonograph ˈsəʊ.nə.grɑːf, ˈsɒn.ə-, -græf ⓤⓢ ˈsɑː.nə.græf, ˈsoʊ- **-s** -s
sonometer səʊˈnɒm.ɪ.tər, ˈ-ə- ⓤⓢ səˈnɑː.mə.t̬ɚ, soʊ- **-s** -z
Sonora səˈnɔː.rə ⓤⓢ -ˈnɔːr.ə
sonorant ˈsɒn.ər.ənt, ˈsəʊ.nər- ⓤⓢ ˈsɑː.nɚ-, ˈsoʊ-; səˈnɔːr-, soʊ- **-s** -s
sonorit|y səʊˈnɒr.ə.t|i, -ɪ.t|i ⓤⓢ səˈnɔːr.ə.t̬|i, soʊ- **-ies** -iz
sonorous ˈsɒn.ər.əs; səˈnɔː.rəs ⓤⓢ səˈnɔːr.əs, soʊ-; ˈsɑː.nɚ-, ˈsoʊ- **-ly** -li

sonsie, sonsy ˈsɒn*t*.si (US) ˈsɑːn*t*-
Sontag ˈsɒn.tæg (US) ˈsɑːn-
Sony® ˈsəʊ.ni, ˈsɒn.i (US) ˈsoʊ.ni
Sonya ˈsɒn.jə, ˈsəʊ.njə (US) ˈsɑː.njə, ˈsoʊ-
soon suːn **-er** -əʳ (US) -ɚ **-est** -ɪst, -əst ˌ**sooner or ˈlater**
soot sʊt (US) sʊt, suːt
sooth suːθ
sooth|e suːð **-es** -z **-ing/ly** -ɪŋ/li **-ed** -d
soothsayer ˈsuːθˌseɪ.əʳ (US) -ɚ **-s** -z
soot|y (S) ˈsʊt|.i (US) ˈsʊt̬-, ˈsuː.t̬|i **-ier** -i.əʳ (US) -i.ɚ **-iest** -i.ɪst, -i.əst **-iness** -ɪ.nəs, -ɪ.nɪs
sop sɒp (US) sɑːp **-s** -s **-ping** -ɪŋ **-ped** -t
Sophia səʊˈfiː.ə, -ˈfaɪ- (US) soʊ-
Sophie ˈsəʊ.fi (US) ˈsoʊ-
soph|ism ˈsɒf|.ɪ.zᵊm (US) ˈsɑː.f|ɪ- **-isms** -ɪ.zᵊmz **-ist/s** -ɪst/s
sophister ˈsɒf.ɪ.stəʳ (US) ˈsɑː.fɪ.stɚ **-s** -z
sophistic səʊˈfɪs.tɪk (US) sə- **-al** -ᵊl **-ally** -ᵊl.i, -li
sophisti|cate (*v.*) səˈfɪs.tɪ|.keɪt (US) -tə- **-cates** -keɪts **-cating** -keɪ.tɪŋ (US) -keɪ.t̬ɪŋ **-cated** -keɪ.tɪd (US) -keɪ.t̬ɪd
sophisticate (*n.*) səˈfɪs.tɪ.kət, -kɪt, -keɪt (US) -tə.kɪt **-s** -s
sophistication səˌfɪs.tɪˈkeɪ.ʃᵊn (US) -təˈ-
sophistr|y ˈsɒf.ɪ.str|i (US) ˈsɑː.fɪ- **-ies** -iz
Sophoclean ˌsɒf.əˈkliː.ən (US) ˌsɑː.fəˈ-
Sophocles ˈsɒf.ə.kliːz (US) ˈsɑː.fə-
sophomore ˈsɒf.ə.mɔːʳ (US) ˈsɑː.fə.mɔːr **-s** -z
sophomoric ˌsɒf.əˈmɒr.ɪk (US) ˌsɑː.fəˈmɔːr-
Sophy ˈsəʊ.fi (US) ˈsoʊ-
soporific ˌsɒp.ᵊrˈɪf.ɪk, ˌsəʊ.pᵊrˈ- (US) ˌsɑː.pəˈrɪf-, ˌsoʊ- **-ally** -ᵊl.i, -li
sopping ˈsɒp.ɪŋ (US) ˈsɑː.pɪŋ ˌ**sopping ˈwet**
sopp|y ˈsɒp|.i (US) ˈsɑː.p|i **-ier** -i.əʳ (US) -i.ɚ **-iest** -i.ɪst, -i.əst **-iness** -ɪ.nəs, -ɪ.nɪs **-ily** -ɪ.li
sopranino ˌsɒp.rəˈniː.nəʊ (US) ˌsoʊ.prəˈniː.noʊ **-s** -z
sopran|o səˈprɑː.n|əʊ (US) -ˈpræn|.oʊ, -ˈprɑː.n|oʊ **-os** -əʊz (US) -oʊz **-i** -iː
Sopwith ˈsɒp.wɪθ (US) ˈsɑːp- **-s** -s
sorbet ˈsɔː.beɪ (US) ˈsɔːr.beɪ; sɔːrˈbət **-s** -s
sorbic ˈsɔː.bɪk (US) ˈsɔːr- ˌ**sorbic ˈacid**
sorbitol ˈsɔː.bɪ.tɒl (US) ˈsɔːr.bɪ.tɑːl, -tɔːl, -toʊl
Sorbonne sɔːˈbɒn (US) sɔːrˈbɑːn, -ˈbʌn
sorcer|y ˈsɔː.sᵊr|.i (US) ˈsɔːr- **-ies** -iz **-er/s** -əʳ/z (US) -ɚ/z **-ess/es** -ɪs/ɪz, -es/ɪz
Sorcha ˈsɔː.ʃə
Sordello sɔːˈdel.əʊ (US) sɔːrˈdel.oʊ
sordid ˈsɔː.dɪd (US) ˈsɔːr- **-ly** -li **-ness** -nəs, -nɪs
sordin|o sɔːˈdiː.n|əʊ (US) sɔːrˈdiː.n|oʊ **-i** -iː
sor|e sɔːʳ (US) sɔːr **-es** -z **-er** -əʳ (US) -ɚ **-est** -ɪst, -əst **-ely** -li **-eness** -nəs, -nɪs
sorghum ˈsɔː.gəm (US) ˈsɔːr-
Soroptimist səˈrɒp.tɪ.mɪst, -tə- (US) -ˈrɑːp.tɪ- **-s** -s
sororit|y səˈrɒr.ə.t|i, sɒrˈɒr-, -ɪ.t|i (US) səˈrɔːr.ə.t̬|i **-ies** -iz
sorrel ˈsɒr.ᵊl (US) ˈsɔːr-
Sorrento səˈren.təʊ (US) -toʊ
sorrow ˈsɒr.əʊ (US) ˈsɑːr.oʊ **-s** -z **-ing/ly** -ɪŋ/li **-ed** -d **-er/s** -əʳ/z (US) -ɚ/z
sorrow|ful ˈsɒr.əʊ|.fᵊl, -fʊl (US) ˈsɑːr.ə- **-fully** -fᵊl.i, -fli, -fʊl.i **-fulness** -fᵊl.nəs, -fʊl.nəs, -nɪs
sorr|y ˈsɒr|.i (US) ˈsɑːr- **-ier** -i.əʳ (US) -i.ɚ **-iest** -i.ɪst, -i.əst **-ily** -ᵊl.i, -ɪ.li **-iness** -ɪ.nəs, -ɪ.nɪs
sort sɔːt (US) sɔːrt **-s** -s **-ing** -ɪŋ (US) ˈsɔːr.t̬ɪŋ **-ed** -ɪd (US) ˈsɔːr.t̬ɪd **-er/s** -əʳ/z (US) ˈsɔːr.t̬ɚ/z
sortie ˈsɔː.ti (US) ˈsɔːr.tiː, ˌ-ˈ- **-s** -z
sortilege ˈsɔː.tɪ.lɪdʒ (US) ˈsɔːr.t̬ᵊl.ɪdʒ, -edʒ
SOS ˌes.əʊˈes (US) -oʊˈ-
so-so ˈsəʊ.səʊ, ˌ-ˈ- (US) ˈsoʊ.soʊ, ˌ-ˈ-
sostenuto ˌsɒs.təˈnuː.təʊ, -tɪˈ-, -ˈnjuː- (US) ˌsɑː.stəˈnuː.t̬oʊ, ˌsoʊ-
sot sɒt (US) sɑːt **-s** -s
Sotheby ˈsʌð.ə.bi **-'s** -z
Sothern ˈsʌð.ᵊn (US) -ɚn
Sotho ˈsuː.tuː, ˈsəʊ.təʊ (US) ˈsoʊ.toʊ **-s** -z
sottish ˈsɒt.ɪʃ (US) ˈsɑː.t̬ɪʃ **-ly** -li **-ness** -nəs, -nɪs
sotto voce ˌsɒt.əʊˈvəʊ.tʃeɪ (US) ˌsɑː.t̬oʊˈvoʊ-
sou suː **-s** -z
soubise suːˈbiːz
soubrette suːˈbret, sʊ- (US) suː- **-s** -s
soubriquet ˈsuː.brɪ.keɪ, ˈsoʊ-, -brə- (US) ˈsuː.brə-, -ket **-s** -z
souchong ˌsuːˈ*t*ʃɒŋ, ˈ-- (US) ˈsuː.tʃɑːŋ, -ʃɑːŋ
souffle ˈsuː.fl̩ **-s** -z
soufflé ˈsuː.fleɪ (US) suːˈfleɪ, ˈ-- **-s** -z **-ed** -d
sough saʊ, sʌf **-s** saʊz, sʌfs **-ing** ˈsaʊ.ɪŋ, ˈsʌf.ɪŋ **-ed** saʊd, sʌft
sought *(from* **seek***)* sɔːt (US) sɑːt, sɔːt
sought-after ˈsɔːtˌɑːf.təʳ (US) ˈsɑːtˌæf.tɚ, ˈsɔːt-
souk suːk **-s** -s
soul səʊl (US) soʊl **-s** -z ˈ**soul ˌfood**; ˈ**soul ˌmate**
Soulbury ˈsəʊl.bᵊr.i (US) ˈsoʊl-, -ber.i
soul-destroying ˈsəʊl.dɪˌstrɔɪ.ɪŋ (US) ˈsoʊl-
soulful ˈsəʊl.fᵊl, -fʊl (US) ˈsoʊl- **-ly** -i **-ness** -nəs, -nɪs
soulless ˈsəʊl.ləs, -lɪs (US) ˈsoʊl- **-ly** -li **-ness** -nəs, -nɪs
soulmate ˈsəʊl.meɪt (US) ˈsoʊl- **-s** -s
soul-searching ˈsəʊlˌsɜː.tʃɪŋ (US) ˈsoʊlˌsɝː-
sound saʊnd **-s** -z **-er** -əʳ (US) -ɚ **-est** -ɪst, -əst **-ly** -li **-ness** -nəs, -nɪs **-ing/s** -ɪŋ/z **-ed** -ɪd ˈ**sound ˌbarrier**; ˈ**sound ˌbite**; ˈ**sound ˌbox**; ˈ**sound efˌfect**
soundbite ˈsaʊn*d*.baɪt, ˈsaʊm- (US) ˈsaʊn*d*- **-s** -s
soundboard ˈsaʊn*d*.bɔːd, ˈsaʊm- (US) ˈsaʊn*d*.bɔːrd **-s** -z
soundless ˈsaʊnd.ləs, -lɪs **-ly** -li
soundproof ˈsaʊn*d*.pruːf, ˈsaʊm- (US) ˈsaʊn*d*- **-s** -s **-ing** -ɪŋ **-ed** -t
soundtrack ˈsaʊn*d*.træk **-s** -s
soundwave ˈsaʊnd.weɪv **-s** -z
soup suːp **-s** -s **-y** -i **-ed** -t ˈ**soup ˌkitchen**; ˌ**souped ˈup**
soupçon ˈsuːp.sɔ̃ː*ŋ*, -sɒŋ, -sɒn (US) suːpˈsõʊn, suː-, -ˈsɑːn, ˈ-- **-s** -z
soupspoon ˈsuːp.spuːn **-s** -z
sour saʊəʳ (US) saʊɚ **-er** -əʳ (US) -ɚ **-est** -ɪst, -əst **-ly** -li **-ness** -nəs, -nɪs **-s** -z **-ing** -ɪŋ **-ed** -d ˌ**sour ˈcream**; ˌ**sour ˈgrapes**
sourc|e sɔːs (US) sɔːrs **-es** -ɪz **-ing** -ɪŋ **-ed** -t
sourdine sʊəˈdiːn (US) sʊr- **-s** -z
sourdough ˈsaʊə.dəʊ (US) ˈsaʊɚ.doʊ
sourpuss ˈsaʊə.pʊs (US) ˈsaʊɚ- **-es** -ɪz
Sousa ˈsuː.zə (US) -zə, -sə
sousaphone ˈsuː.zə.fəʊn (US) -zə.foʊn, -sə- **-s** -z
sous-chef ˈsuː.ʃef **-s** -s
sous|e saʊs **-es** -ɪz **-ing** -ɪŋ **-ed** -t
Sousse suːs
soutane suːˈtɑːn (US) -ˈtæn, -ˈtɑːn **-s** -z
Souter ˈsuː.təʳ (US) -t̬ɚ
south (S) (*n. adj. adv.*) saʊθ ˌ**South ˈAfrica**; ˌ**South Aˈmerica**; ˌ**South Caroˈlina**; ˌ**South Daˈkota**; ˌ**South ˈIsland** (US) ˈ**South ˌIsland**; ˌ**South Koˈrea**; ˌ**south ˈpole**; ˌ**South ˈSeas**
Southall *place in London:* ˈsaʊ.θɔːl, -ðɔːl (US) -θɔːl, -θɑːl, -ðɔːl, -ðɑːl *surname:* ˈsʌð.ɔːl, -ᵊl (US) -ɔːl, -ɑːl, -ᵊl
Southam ˈsaʊ.θəm
Southampton saʊˈθæm*p*.tən, saʊθˈhæm*p*-
southbound ˈsaʊθ.baʊnd
Southbourne ˈsaʊθ.bɔːn (US) -bɔːrn
Southdown ˈsaʊθ.daʊn
southeast (S) ˌsaʊθˈiːst *in nautical usage also:* ˌsaʊ- **-wards** -wədz (US) -wɚdz *stress shift:* ˌsoutheast ˈwind
south-easter ˌsaʊθˈiː.stəʳ (US) -stɚ *in nautical usage also:* ˌsaʊ- **-s** -z
southeasterl|y ˌsaʊθˈiː.stᵊl.i (US) -stɚ.li *in nautical usage also:* ˌsaʊ- **-ies** -iz
southeastern (S) ˌsaʊθˈiː.stən (US) -stɚn *in nautical usage also:* ˌsaʊ- **-er/s** -əʳ/z (US) -ɚ/z *stress shift:*

ˌsoutheastern ˈwind
southeastward ˌsaʊθˈiːst.wəd (US) -wɚd **-s** -z
Southend ˌsaʊθˈend *stress shift:* ˌSouthend ˈpier
souther|ly ˈsʌð.əl|.i (US) -ɚ.l|i **-ies** -iz
southern (S) ˈsʌð.ən (US) -ɚn **-most** -ən.məʊst, -əm.məʊst (US) -ɚn.moʊst ˌ**Southern** ˈ**Cross**
southerner (S) ˈsʌð.ən.əʳ (US) -ɚ.nɚ **-s** -z
southernwood ˈsʌð.ən.wʊd (US) -ɚn-
Southey ˈsaʊ.ði, ˈsʌð.i
Southgate ˈsaʊθ.geɪt, -gɪt
Southon ˈsaʊ.ðən
southpaw ˈsaʊθ.pɔː (US) -pɑː, -pɔː **-s** -z
Southport ˈsaʊθ.pɔːt (US) -pɔːrt
southron (S) ˈsʌð.rən **-s** -z
Southsea ˈsaʊθ.siː, -si
south-southeast ˌsaʊθ.saʊθˈiːst *in nautical usage also:* ˌsaʊ.saʊˈ-
south-southwest ˌsaʊθ.saʊθˈwest *in nautical usage also:* ˌsaʊ.saʊˈ-
southward ˈsaʊθ.wəd (US) -wɚd **-s** -z **-ly** -li
Southwark ˈsʌð.ək (US) -ɚk
Southwell *surname:* ˈsaʊθ.wəl, -wel; ˈsʌð.əl *town in Nottinghamshire:* ˈsaʊθ.wəl *locally:* ˈsʌð.əl
Note: Viscount Southwell is /sʌð.əl/
southwest (S) ˌsaʊθˈwest *in nautical usage also:* ˌsaʊ- **-wards** -wədz (US) -wɚdz *stress shift:* ˌsouthwest ˈwind
south-wester ˌsaʊθˈwes.təʳ (US) -tɚ *in nautical usage also:* ˌsaʊ- **-s** -z
south-westerl|y ˌsaʊθˈwes.təl|.i (US) -tɚ.l|i *in nautical usage also:* ˌsaʊ- **-ies** -iz
southwestern (S) ˌsaʊθˈwes.tən (US) -tɚn *in nautical usage also:* ˌsaʊ- **-er/s** -əʳ/z (US) -ɚ/z *stress shift:* ˌsouthwestern ˈwind
south-westward ˌsaʊθˈwest.wəd (US) -wɚd *in nautical usage also:* ˌsaʊ- **-s** -z
Southwick *in West Sussex:* ˈsaʊθ.wɪk *in Northamptonshire:* ˈsʌð.ɪk *in Hampshire:* ˈsʌð.ɪk, ˈsaʊθ.wɪk
Southwold ˈsaʊθ.wəʊld (US) -woʊld
Soutter ˈsuː.təʳ (US) -t̬ɚ
souvenir ˌsuː.vənˈɪəʳ, -vɪˈnɪəʳ, ˈ--- (US) ˌsuː.vəˈnɪr, ˈ--- **-s** -z
sou'wester ˌsaʊˈwes.təʳ (US) -tɚ **-s** -z
Souza ˈsuː.zə
sovereign ˈsɒv.ər.ɪn, ˈ-rɪn (US) ˈsɑːv.rən, -ɚ.ən **-s** -z **-ly** -li
sovereignty ˈsɒv.rən.ti, -rɪn- (US) ˈsɑːv.rən.t̬i, -ɚ.ən-
soviet (S) ˈsəʊ.vi.ət, ˈsɒv.i- (US) ˈsoʊ.vi.et, -ɪt; ˌ--ˈ- **-s** -s **-ism** -ɪ.zəm ˌ**Soviet** ˈ**Union**
sovran ˈsɒv.rən (US) ˈsɑːv- **-s** -z
sow *(n.) pig, metal, channel for metal:* saʊ **-s** -z
sow *(v.) plant seed:* səʊ (US) soʊ **-s** -z **-ing** -ɪŋ **-ed** -d **-n** -n **-er/s** -əʳ/z (US) -ɚ/z
Sowerby *in North Yorkshire:* ˈsaʊə.bi (US) ˈsaʊɚ- *in West Yorkshire, surname:* ˈsəʊə.bi, ˈsaʊə- (US) ˈsoʊɚ-, ˈsaʊɚ-
Soweto səˈwet.əʊ, -ˈweɪ.təʊ (US) -ˈwet̬.oʊ, -ˈweɪ.t̬oʊ
sox sɒks (US) sɑːks
soy sɔɪ ˌ**soy** ˈ**sauce** (US) ˈ**soy** ˌ**sauce**
soya ˈsɔɪ.ə ˈ**soya** ˌ**bean**
soybean ˈsɔɪ.biːn **-s** -z
Soyinka sɔɪˈɪŋ.kə
Soyuz sɔːˈjʊz, səˈjuːz (US) ˈsɑː.juːz, ˈsɔɪ.jʊz
sozzled ˈsɒz.l̩d (US) ˈsɑː.zl̩d
spa (S) spɑː **-s** -z
spac|e speɪs **-es** -ɪz **-ing** -ɪŋ **-ed** -t ˈ**space** ˌ**age**; ˈ**space** ˌ**bar**; ˈ**space** ˌ**shuttle**; ˈ**space** ˌ**station**; ˈ**space** ˌ**suit**; ˈ**space** ˌ**walk**
spacecraft ˈspeɪs.krɑːft (US) -kræft **-s** -s
spaced-out ˌspeɪstˈaʊt *stress shift:* ˌspaced-out ˈperson
spacelab ˈspeɪs.læb **-s** -z
space|man ˈspeɪs|.mæn, -mən **-men** -men, -mən
spaceship ˈspeɪs.ʃɪp, ˈspeɪʃ- (US) ˈspeɪs- **-s** -s
space-time ˌspeɪsˈtaɪm *stress shift:* ˌspace-time conˈtinuum
spacewalk ˈspeɪs.wɔːk (US) -wɔːk, -wɑːk **-s** -s **-ing** -ɪŋ **-ed** -t **-er/s** -əʳ/z (US) -ɚ/z
spac|ey ˈspeɪ.s|i **-ier** -i.əʳ (US) -i.ɚ **-iest** -i.ɪst, -i.əst **-iness** -ɪ.nəs, -ɪ.nɪs
spacious ˈspeɪ.ʃəs **-ly** -li **-ness** -nəs, -nɪs
spade speɪd **-s** -z **-ful/s** -fʊl/z ˌ**call a** ˌ**spade a** ˈ**spade**
spadework ˈspeɪd.wɜːk (US) -wɝːk
spaghetti spəˈget.i (US) -ˈget̬- **spa**ˌ**ghetti bologˈnese**
spahi ˈspɑː.hiː, -iː (US) -hiː **-s** -z
Spain speɪn
spake *(archaic past tense of* **speak***)* speɪk
Spalding ˈspɔːl.dɪŋ, ˈspɒl- (US) ˈspɔːl-, ˈspɑːl-
spall spɔːl (US) spɔːl, spɑːl **-s** -z **-ing** -ɪŋ **-ed** d
spam (S) spæm **-s** -z **-ming** -ɪŋ **-med** -d
span spæn **-s** -z **-ning** -ɪŋ **-ned** -d
Spandau ˈspæn.daʊ
spandex ˈspæn.deks
spandrel ˈspæn.drəl **-s** -z
spangl|e ˈspæŋ.gl̩ **-es** -z **-ing** -ɪŋ, ˈspæŋ.glɪŋ **-ed** -d
spangly ˈspæŋ.gli, -gl̩.i
Spaniard ˈspæn.jəd (US) -jɚd **-s** -z
spaniel ˈspæn.jəl **-s** -z
Spanish ˈspæn.ɪʃ ˌ**Spanish** ˈ**fly**; ˌ**Spanish** ˈ**omelette**; ˌ**Spanish** ˈ**onion**; ˌ**Spanish Saˈhara**
spank spæŋk **-s** -s **-ing** -ɪŋ **-ed** -t **-er/s** -əʳ/z (US) -ɚ/z
spanking ˈspæŋ.kɪŋ **-s** -z
spanner ˈspæn.əʳ (US) -ɚ **-s** -z
spar spɑːʳ (US) spɑːr **-s** -z **-ring** -ɪŋ **-red** -d ˈ**sparring** ˌ**match**; ˈ**sparring** ˌ**partner**
spar|e speəʳ (US) sper **-ely** -li **-eness** -nəs, -nɪs **-es** -z **-ing** -ɪŋ/li **-ed** -d ˌ**spare** ˈ**part**; ˌ**spare** ˈ**rib**; ˌ**spare** ˈ**tyre**
sparing ˈspeə.rɪŋ (US) ˈsper.ɪŋ **-ly** -li
spark (S) spɑːk (US) spɑːrk **-s** -s **-ing** -ɪŋ **-ed** -t ˈ**spark** ˌ**plug**; ˈ**sparking** ˌ**plug**
Sparkes spɑːks (US) spɑːrks
sparkl|e ˈspɑː.kl̩ (US) ˈspɑːr- **-es** -z **-ing** -ɪŋ, ˈspɑː.klɪŋ (US) ˈspɑːr- **-ed** -d **-y** -i, ˈspɑː.kli (US) ˈspɑːr- ˌ**sparkling** ˈ**wine**
sparkler ˈspɑː.kləʳ (US) ˈspɑːr.klɚ **-s** -z
spark|y ˈspɑː.k|i (US) ˈspɑːr.k|i **-ier** -i.əʳ (US) -i.ɚ **-iest** -i.ɪst, -i.əst **-iness** -ɪ.nəs, -ɪ.nɪs **-ily** -ɪ.li
sparrow (S) ˈspær.əʊ (US) ˈsper.oʊ, ˈspær- **-s** -z
sparrowhawk ˈspær.əʊ.hɔːk (US) ˈsper.oʊ.hɑːk, ˈspær-, -hɔːk **-s** -s
spars|e spɑːs (US) spɑːrs **-er** -əʳ (US) -ɚ **-est** -ɪst, -əst **-ely** -li **-eness** -nəs, -nɪs **-ity** -ə.ti, -ɪ.ti (US) -ə.t̬i
Spar|ta ˈspɑː|.tə (US) ˈspɑːr|.t̬ə **-tan/s** -tən/z
Spartacus ˈspɑː.tə.kəs (US) ˈspɑːr.t̬ə-
spartan ˈspɑː.tən (US) ˈspɑːr-
spasm ˈspæz.əm **-s** -z
spasmodic spæzˈmɒd.ɪk (US) -ˈmɑː.dɪk **-ally** -əl.i, -li
spastic ˈspæs.tɪk **-s** -s
spasticity spæsˈtɪs.ə.ti, -ɪ.ti (US) -ə.t̬i
spat spæt **-s** -s **-ting** -ɪŋ **-ted** -ɪd
spatchcock ˈspætʃ.kɒk (US) -kɑːk **-s** -s **-ing** -ɪŋ **-ed** -t
spate speɪt **-s** -s
spatial ˈspeɪ.ʃəl **-ly** -i
spatt|er ˈspæt|.əʳ (US) ˈspæt̬|.ɚ **-ers** -əz (US) -ɚz **-ering** -ər.ɪŋ **-ered** -əd (US) -ɚd
spatul|a ˈspæt.jə.l|ə, -jʊ-, ˈspætʃ.ə-, ˈ-ʊ- (US) ˈspætʃ.ə- **-ae** -iː **-as** -əz
spatulate ˈspæt.jə.lət, -jʊ-, ˈspætʃ.ə-, ˈ-ʊ-, -lɪt, -leɪt (US) ˈspætʃ.ə.lɪt, -leɪt
spavin ˈspæv.ɪn **-ed** -d
spawn spɔːn (US) spɑːn, spɔːn **-s** -z **-ing** -ɪŋ **-ed** -d
spay speɪ **-s** -z **-ing** -ɪŋ **-ed** -d
Speaight speɪt
speak spiːk **-s** -s **-ing** -ɪŋ **spoke** spəʊk (US) spoʊk **spoken** ˈspəʊ.kən (US) ˈspoʊ- **speaker/s** ˈspiː.kəʳ/z (US) -kɚ/z
speakeas|y ˈspiːkˌiː.z|i **-ies** -iz
speakerphone ˈspiː.kə.fəʊn (US) -kɚ.foʊn **-s** -z

Spean spɪən, ˈspiː.ən (US) ˈspiː.ən
spear spɪəʳ (US) spɪr **-s** -z **-ing** -ɪŋ **-ed** -d
spearhead ˈspɪə.hed (US) ˈspɪr- **-s** -z **-ing** -ɪŋ **-ed** -ɪd
spear|man (S) ˈspɪə|.mən (US) ˈspɪr- **-men** -mən, -men
spearmint ˈspɪə.mɪnt (US) ˈspɪr-
spec spek
speci|al ˈspeʃ|.ᵊl **-als** -ᵊlz **-ally** -ᵊl.i, -li **-alness** -ᵊl.nəs, -ᵊl.nɪs **ˈSpecial ˌBranch**; **ˌspecial deˈlivery**; **ˌspecial efˈfects**
special|ism ˈspeʃ.ᵊl.ɪ|.zᵊm, ˈ-lɪ- (US) ˈ-ᵊl.ɪ- **-s** -z
specialist ˈspeʃ.ᵊl.ɪst **-s** -s
specialit|y ˌspeʃ.iˈæl.ə.t|i, -ɪ.t|i (US) -ə.t̬|i **-ies** -iz
specialization, -isa- ˌspeʃ.ᵊl.aɪˈzeɪ.ʃᵊn, -ɪˈ- (US) -ɪˈ-
specializ|e, -is|e ˈspeʃ.ᵊl.aɪz (US) -ə.laɪz **-es** -ɪz **-ing** -ɪŋ **-ed** -d
specialt|y ˈspeʃ.ᵊl.t|i (US) -t̬|i **-ies** -iz
specie ˈspiː.ʃiː, -ʃi (US) -ʃiː, -siː
species ˈspiː.ʃiːz, -ʃɪz, -siːz, -sɪz (US) -ʃiːz, -siːz **-ism** -ɪ.zᵊm
specific spəˈsɪf.ɪk, spɪ- (US) spə- **-s** -s **-ally** -ᵊl.i, -li **speˌcific ˈgravity**
specification ˌspes.ɪ.fɪˈkeɪ.ʃᵊn, ˌ-ə- (US) ˌ-ə- **-s** -z
specificity ˌspes.ɪˈfɪs.ə.ti, -ɪ.ti (US) -əˈfɪs.ə.t̬i
speci|fy ˈspes.ɪ|.faɪ, ˈ-ə- (US) ˈ-ə- **-fies** -faɪz **-fying** -faɪ.ɪŋ **-fied** -faɪd **-fiable** -faɪ.ə.bl̩
specimen ˈspes.ə.mɪn, ˈ-ɪ-, -mən (US) -ə.mən **-s** -z
specious ˈspiː.ʃəs **-ly** -li **-ness** -nəs, -nɪs
speck spek **-s** -s **-ed** -t
speckle ˈspek.l̩ **-s** -z **-d** -d
speckless ˈspek.ləs, -lɪs
specs speks
spectacle ˈspek.tə.kl̩, -tɪ- **-s** -z **-d** -d
spectacular spekˈtæk.jə.ləʳ, -jʊ- (US) -lɚ **-ly** -li
spectat|e spekˈteɪt **-es** -s **-ing** -ɪŋ **-ed** -ɪd
spectator (S) spekˈteɪ.təʳ (US) -t̬ɚ **-s** -z **specˌtator ˈsport, specˈtator ˌsport**
specter ˈspek.təʳ (US) -tɚ **-s** -z
spectral ˈspek.trᵊl
spectre ˈspek.təʳ (US) -tɚ **-s** -z
spectrogram ˈspek.trəʊ.græm (US) -trə- **-s** -z
spectrograph ˈspek.trəʊ.grɑːf, -græf (US) -trə.græf **-s** -s
spectrographic ˌspek.trəʊˈgræf.ɪk (US) -trəˈ- *stress shift:* ˌspectrographic ˈsection
spectrography spekˈtrɒg.rə.fi (US) -ˈtrɑː.grə-
spectrometer spekˈtrɒm.ɪ.təʳ, ˈ-ə- (US) -ˈtrɑː.mə.t̬ɚ **-s** -z
spectroscope ˈspek.trə.skəʊp (US) -trə.skoʊp **-s** -s
spectroscopic ˌspek.trəˈskɒp.ɪk (US) -ˈskɑː.pɪk **-al** -ᵊl **-ally** -ᵊl.i, -li *stress shift:* ˌspectroscopic ˈpicture
spectroscop|ist spekˈtrɒs.kə.p|ɪst (US) -ˈtrɑː.skə- **-ists** -ɪsts **-y** -i
spectr|um ˈspek.tr|əm **-a** -ə **-ums** -əmz
specu|late ˈspek.jə|.leɪt, -jʊ- **-lates** -leɪts **-lating** -leɪ.tɪŋ (US) -leɪ.t̬ɪŋ **-lated** -leɪ.tɪd (US) -leɪ.t̬ɪd **-lator/s** -leɪ.təʳ/z (US) -leɪ.t̬ɚ/z
speculation ˌspek.jəˈleɪ.ʃᵊn, -jʊˈ- **-s** -z
speculative ˈspek.jə.lə.tɪv, -jʊ-, -leɪ- (US) -leɪ.t̬ɪv, -lə- **-ly** -li **-ness** -nəs, -nɪs
specul|um ˈspek.jə.l|əm, -jʊ- **-a** -ə **-ar** -əʳ (US) -ɚ
sped *(from* **speed***)* sped
speech spiːtʃ **-es** -ɪz **ˈspeech ˌday**; **ˈspeech imˌpediment**; **ˌspeech ˈsynthesiser**
speechification ˌspiː.tʃɪ.fɪˈkeɪ.ʃᵊn, -tʃə- (US) -tʃə- **-s** -z
speechi|fy ˈspiː.tʃɪ|.faɪ, -tʃə- (US) -tʃə- **-fies** -faɪz **-fying** -faɪ.ɪŋ **-fied** -faɪd **-fier/s** -faɪ.əʳ/z (US) -faɪ.ɚ/z
speechless ˈspiːtʃ.ləs, -lɪs **-ly** -li **-ness** -nəs, -nɪs
speed (S) spiːd **-s** -z **-ing** -ɪŋ **-ed** -ɪd **sped** sped **ˈspeed ˌbump**; **ˈspeed ˌlimit**; **ˈspeed ˌtrap**
speedboat ˈspiːd.bəʊt (US) -boʊt **-s** -s
speed-cop ˈspiːd.kɒp (US) -kɑːp **-s** -s
speedo ˈspiː.dəʊ (US) -doʊ **-s** -z
speedometer spiːˈdɒm.ɪ.təʳ, spɪ-, -mə- (US) -ˈdɑː.mə.t̬ɚ **-s** -z
speed-read ˈspiːd.riːd **-s** -z **-ing** -ɪŋ *past tense:* ˈspiːd.red
speed|skate ˈspiːd|.skeɪt **-skating** -ˌskeɪ.tɪŋ (US) -t̬ɪŋ **-skater/s** -ˌskeɪ.təʳ/z (US) -t̬ɚ/z
speedway ˈspiːd.weɪ **-s** -z
speedwell (S) ˈspiːd.wel, -wᵊl **-s** -z
Speedwriting® ˈspiːdˌraɪ.tɪŋ (US) -t̬ɪŋ
speed|y ˈspiː.d|i **-ier** -i.əʳ (US) -i.ɚ **-iest** -i.ɪst, -i.əst **-ily** -ᵊl.i, -ɪ.li **-iness** -ɪ.nəs, -ɪ.nɪs
Speen spiːn
Speer speəʳ *as if German:* ʃpeəʳ (US) spɪr *as if German:* ʃper
Speight speɪt
Speirs spɪəz (US) spɪrz
speiss spaɪs
Speke spiːk
speleological ˌspiː.li.əˈlɒdʒ.ɪ.kᵊl, ˌspel.i- (US) -ˈlɑː.dʒɪ-
speleolog|y ˌspiː.liˈɒl.ə.dʒ|i, ˌspel.iˈ- (US) ˌspiː.liˈɑː.lə- **-ist/s** -ɪst/s
spell spel **-s** -z **-ing/s** -ɪŋ/z **-ed** -d, -t **spelt** -t **speller/s** ˈspel.əʳ/z (US) -ɚ/z **ˈspelling ˌbee**
spell|bind ˈspel|.baɪnd **-binds** -baɪndz **-binding** -baɪn.dɪŋ **-bound** -baʊnd **-binder/s** -ˌbaɪn.dəʳ/z (US) -ˌbaɪn.dɚ/z
spellbound ˈspel.baʊnd
spelt *(from* **spell***)* spelt
spelt|er ˈspel.t|əʳ (US) -t̬|ɚ **-ers** -əz (US) -ɚz **-ering** -ᵊr.ɪŋ **-ered** -əd (US) -ɚd
spelunk|er spəˈlʌŋ.k|əʳ (US) -k|ɚ; ˈspiː.lʌŋ- **-er/s** -ᵊr.əʳ/z (US) -ɚ.ɚ/z **-ing** -ɪŋ
spenc|e (S) spen*t*s **-es** -ɪz
spencer (S) ˈspen*t*.səʳ (US) -sɚ **-s** -z
spend spend **-s** -z **-ing** -ɪŋ **spent** -t **spender/s** ˈspen.dəʳ/z (US) -dɚ/z
Spender ˈspen.dəʳ (US) -dɚ
spendthrift ˈspen*d*.θrɪft **-s** -s
Spengler ˈspeŋ.gləʳ (US) -glɚ
Spenlow ˈspen.ləʊ (US) -loʊ
Spennymoor ˈspen.i.mɔːʳ, -mʊəʳ (US) -mɔːr, -mʊr
Spens spenz
Spenser ˈspen*t*.səʳ (US) -sɚ
Spenserian spenˈsɪə.ri.ən (US) -ˈsɪr.i-
spent *(from* **spend***)* spent
sperm spɜːm (US) spɝːm **-s** -z **ˈsperm ˌbank**; **ˈsperm ˌwhale**
spermaceti ˌspɜː.məˈset.i, -ˈsiː.ti (US) ˌspɝː.məˈsiː.ti, -ˈset.i
spermatozo|on ˌspɜː.mə.təʊˈzəʊ|.ɒn, -ən (US) ˌspɝː.mə.t̬əˈzoʊ|.ɑːn, -ən **-a** -ə
spermicidal ˌspɜː.mɪˈsaɪ.dᵊl (US) ˌspɝː.məˈ-
spermicide ˈspɜː.mɪ.saɪd (US) ˈspɝː.mə- **-s** -z
Sperrin ˈsper.ɪn
spew spjuː **-s** -z **-ing** -ɪŋ **-ed** -d
Spey speɪ
Spezia ˈspet.si.ə, ˈsped.zi- (US) ˈspet.si.ɑː
Spezzia ˈspet.si.ə
sphagnum ˈsfæg.nəm ˌ**sphagnum ˈmoss**
sphene spiːn, sfiːn (US) sfiːn **-s** -z
sphere sfɪəʳ (US) sfɪr **-s** -z
spheric ˈsfer.ɪk (US) ˈsfɪr-, ˈsfer- **-s** -s **-al** -ᵊl **-ally** -ᵊl.i, -li
spheroid ˈsfɪə.rɔɪd (US) ˈsfɪr.ɔɪd, ˈsfer- **-s** -z
spheroidal sfɪəˈrɔɪ.dᵊl, sferˈɔɪ- (US) sfɪˈrɔɪ-, sferˈɔɪ-
spherometer sfɪəˈrɒm.ɪ.təʳ, sferˈɒm-, ˈ-ə- (US) sfɪˈrɑː.mə.tɚ, sferˈɑː- **-s** -z
sphincter ˈsfɪŋ*k*.təʳ (US) -tɚ **-s** -z
sphinx sfɪŋks **-es** -ɪz
sphragistics sfrəˈdʒɪs.tɪks
sphygmomanometer ˌsfɪg.məʊ.məˈnɒm.ɪ.təʳ, ˈ-ə- (US) -moʊ.məˈnɑː.mə.t̬ɚ **-s** -z
spic spɪk **-s** -s
spi|ca (S) ˈspaɪ|.kə **-cae** -siː **-cas** -kəz
spiccato spɪˈkɑː.təʊ (US) -t̬oʊ
spic|e (S) spaɪs **-es** -ɪz **-ing** -ɪŋ **-ed** -t

spiceberr|y ˈspaɪs.bᵊr|.i, -br|i (US) -ˌber|.i **-ies** -iz
Spicer ˈspaɪ.səʳ (US) -sɚ
spick spɪk **ˌspick and ˈspan**
spicule ˈspɪk.juːl, ˈspaɪ.kjuːl (US) ˈspɪk.juːl **-s** -z
spic|y ˈspaɪ.s|i **-ier** -i.əʳ (US) -i.ɚ **-iest** -i.ɪst, -i.əst **-ily** -ɪ.li, -ᵊl.i **-iness** -ɪ.nəs, -ɪ.nɪs
spid|er ˈspaɪ.d|əʳ (US) -dɚ **-ers** -əz (US) -ɚz **-ery** -ᵊr.i **ˈspider ˌmonkey; ˈspider ˌplant**
spidergram ˈspaɪ.də.græm (US) -dɚ- **-s** -z
spiderweb ˈspaɪ.də.web (US) -dɚ- **-s** -z
spiel ʃpiːl, spiːl (US) spiːl, ʃpiːl
Spielberg ˈspiːl.bɜːg (US) -bɝːg
spiffing ˈspɪf.ɪŋ **-ly** -li
spiff|y ˈspɪf|.i **-ier** -i.əʳ (US) -i.ɚ **-iest** -i.ɪst, -i.əst
spigot ˈspɪg.ət **-s** -s
spik spɪk **-s** -s
spik|e spaɪk **-es** -s **-ing** -ɪŋ **-ed** -t
spikenard ˈspaɪk.nɑːd, ˈspaɪ.kə- (US) ˈspaɪk.nɑːrd, -nɚd
Spikins ˈspaɪ.kɪnz
spik|y ˈspaɪ.k|i **-ier** -i.əʳ (US) -i.ɚ **-iest** -i.ɪst, -i.əst **-iness** -ɪ.nəs, -ɪ.nɪs
spill spɪl **-s** -z **-ing** -ɪŋ **-ed** -d **spilt** -t
spillag|e ˈspɪl.ɪdʒ **-es** -ɪz
spiller (S) ˈspɪl.əʳ (US) -ɚ **-s** -z
spillikin ˈspɪl.ɪ.kɪn **-s** -z
Spilling ˈspɪl.ɪŋ
spillover ˈspɪl.əʊ.vəʳ (US) -oʊ.vɚ **-s** -z
spilt *(from* **spill***)* spɪlt
spin spɪn **-s** -z **-ning** -ɪŋ **span** spæn **spun** spʌn **spinner/s** ˈspɪn.əʳ/z (US) -ɚ/z **ˌspin ˈbowling** (US) **ˈspin ˌbowling; ˈspin ˌdoctor; ˈspinning ˌwheel**
spina bifida ˌspaɪ.nəˈbɪf.ɪ.də, -ˈbaɪ.fɪ- (US) -ˈbɪf.ɪ-
spinach ˈspɪn.ɪtʃ, -ɪdʒ (US) -ɪtʃ
spinal ˈspaɪ.nᵊl **ˈspinal ˌcord, ˌspinal ˈcord** (US) **ˈspinal ˌcord**
spindl|e ˈspɪn.dl̩ **-es** -z **-y** -i, ˈspɪnd.li
spindle-legged ˌspɪn.dl̩ˈlegd (US) ˈspɪn.dl̩.legd, -ˌleg.ɪd *stress shift, British only:* ˌspindle-legged ˈchair
spindrift ˈspɪn.drɪft
spin-dr|y ˌspɪnˈdr|aɪ, ˈ-- (US) ˈspɪn.dr|aɪ **-ies** -aɪz **-ying** -aɪ.ɪŋ **-ied** -aɪd **-ier/s** -aɪ.əʳ/z (US) -aɪ.ɚ/z
spine spaɪn **-s** -z **-d** -d
spine-chill|ing ˈspaɪn,tʃɪl|.ɪŋ **-ingly** -ɪŋ.li **-er/s** -əʳ/z (US) -ɚ/z
spinel spɪˈnel (US) spɪˈnel; ˈspɪn.ᵊl
spineless ˈspaɪn.ləs, -lɪs **-ly** -li **-ness** -nəs, -nɪs
spinet spɪˈnet; ˈspɪn.et, -ɪt (US) ˈspɪn.ɪt **-s** -s
spinifex ˈspɪn.ɪ.feks, ˈ-ə-
Spink spɪŋk **-s** -s
spinnaker ˈspɪn.ə.kəʳ, ˈ-ɪ- (US) -ə.kɚ **-s** -z
spinney ˈspɪn.i **-s** -z
spinoff ˈspɪn.ɒf (US) -ɑːf **-s** -s
spinose ˈspaɪ.nəʊs, -ˈ- (US) ˈspaɪ.noʊs
spinous ˈspaɪ.nəs
Spinoza spɪˈnəʊ.zə (US) -ˈnoʊ-
spinster ˈspɪn*t*.stəʳ (US) -stɚ **-s** -z **-hood** -hʊd **-ish** -ɪʃ
spin|y ˈspaɪ.n|i **-iness** -ɪ.nəs, -ɪ.nɪs
Spion Kop ˌspaɪ.ənˈkɒp, -əŋˈ- (US) -ənˈkɑːp
spiraea spaɪˈriː.ə, -ˈrɪə (US) -ˈriː.ə **-s** -z
spiral ˈspaɪə.rᵊl (US) ˈspaɪ- **-s** -z **-ly** -i **-(l)ing** -ɪŋ **-(l)ed** -d **ˌspiral ˈstaircase**
spirant ˈspaɪə.rᵊnt (US) ˈspaɪ- **-s** -s
spire spaɪəʳ (US) spaɪɚ **-s** -z **-d** -d
spirea spaɪˈrɪə, -ˈriː.ə (US) -ˈriː.ə **-s** -z
spiri|t ˈspɪr.ɪ|t, -ə|t **-ts** -ts **-ting** -tɪŋ (US) -t̬ɪŋ **-ted/ly** -tɪd/li (US) -t̬ɪd/li **ˈspirit ˌlamp; ˈspirit ˌlevel**
spiritism ˈspɪr.ɪ.tɪ.zᵊm (US) -t̬ɪ-
spiritless ˈspɪr.ɪt.ləs, -lɪs **-ly** -li **-ness** -nəs, -nɪs
spiritual ˈspɪr.ɪ.tʃu.əl, ˈ-ə-, -tju- (US) -tʃu- **-s** -z **-ly** -i
spiritual|ism ˈspɪr.ɪ.tʃu.ᵊl|.ɪ.zᵊm, ˈ-ə-, -tju- (US) -tʃu- **-ist/s** -ɪst/s
spiritualistic ˌspɪr.ɪ.tʃu.ᵊlˈɪs.tɪk, ˌ-ə-, -tju- (US) -tʃu-
spiritualit|y ˌspɪr.ɪ.tʃuˈæl.ə.t|i, ˌ-ə-, -tjuˈ-, -ɪ.t|i (US) -tʃuˈæl.ə.t̬|i **-ies** -iz
spirituous ˈspɪr.ɪ.tʃu.əs, -tju.əs (US) -tʃu-
spiritus ˈspɪr.ɪ.təs, ˈ-ə- (US) -t̬əs
spirogyra ˌspaɪə.rəʊˈdʒaɪə.rə (US) ˌspaɪ.roʊˈdʒaɪ-
spirt spɜːt (US) spɝːt **-s** -s **-ing** -ɪŋ (US) ˈspɝː.t̬ɪŋ **-ed** -ɪd (US) ˈspɝː.t̬ɪd
spit *(n. v.)* spɪt **-s** -s **-ting** -ɪŋ (US) ˈspɪt̬.ɪŋ **-ted** -ɪd (US) ˈspɪt̬.ɪd **spat** spæt **ˌspitting ˈimage; ˌspit and ˈpolish**
Spitalfields ˈspɪt.ᵊl.fiːldz (US) ˈspɪt̬-
spitball ˈspɪt.bɔːl (US) -bɔːl, -bɑːl **-s** -z
spit|e spaɪt **-es** -s **-ing** -ɪŋ (US) ˈspaɪ.t̬ɪŋ **-ed** -ɪd (US) ˈspaɪ.t̬ɪd
spiteful ˈspaɪt.fᵊl, -fʊl **-ly** -i **-ness** -nəs, -nɪs
spitfire (S) ˈspɪt,faɪəʳ (US) -ˌfaɪɚ **-s** -z
Spithead ˌspɪtˈhed *stress shift:* ˌSpithead ˈcoastline
Spitsbergen ˈspɪts,bɜː.gən, ˌ-ˈ-- (US) ˈspɪts,bɝː-
spittle ˈspɪt.l̩ (US) ˈspɪt̬-
spittoon spɪˈtuːn **-s** -z
Spitz spɪts
spiv spɪv **-s** -z **-vy** -i
splash splæʃ **-es** -ɪz **-ing** -ɪŋ **-ed** -t **-er/s** -əʳ/z (US) -ɚ/z **ˈsplash ˌguard**
splashback ˈsplæʃ.bæk **-s** -s
splashboard ˈsplæʃ.bɔːd (US) -bɔːrd **-s** -z
splashdown ˈsplæʃ.daʊn **-s** -z
splash|y ˈsplæʃ|.i **-iness** -ɪ.nəs, -ɪ.nɪs
splat splæt **-s** -s **-ting** -ɪŋ **-ted** -ɪd
splatt|er ˈsplæt|.əʳ (US) ˈsplæt̬|.ɚ **-ers** -əz (US) -ɚz **-ering** -ᵊr.ɪŋ **-ered** -əd (US) -ɚd
splay spleɪ **-s** -z **-ing** -ɪŋ **-ed** -d
splayfooted ˌspleɪˈfʊt.ɪd (US) ˈspleɪˌfʊt̬- *stress shift, British only:* ˌsplayfooted ˈwalk
spleen spliːn **-s** -z **-ful** -fᵊl, -fʊl **-fully** -fᵊl.i, -fʊ.li
splendid ˈsplen.dɪd **-ly** -li **-ness** -nəs, -nɪs
splendiferous splenˈdɪf.ᵊr.əs **-ly** -li **-ness** -nəs, -nɪs
splendo(u)r ˈsplen.dəʳ (US) -dɚ **-s** -z
splenetic spləˈnet.ɪk, splɪ- (US) splɪˈnet̬- **-s** -s **-ally** -ᵊl.i, -li
splic|e splaɪs **-es** -ɪz **-ing** -ɪŋ **-ed** -t
spliff splɪf **-s** -s
splint splɪnt **-s** -s **-ing** -ɪŋ (US) ˈsplɪn.t̬ɪŋ **-ed** -ɪd (US) ˈsplɪn.t̬ɪd
splint|er ˈsplɪn.t|əʳ (US) -t̬|ɚ **-ers** -əz (US) -ɚz **-ering** -ᵊr.ɪŋ **-ered** -əd (US) -ɚd **-ery** -ᵊr.i **ˈsplinter ˌgroup**
split (S) splɪt **-s** -s **-ting** -ɪŋ (US) ˈsplɪt̬.ɪŋ **-ter/s** -əʳ/z (US) ˈsplɪt̬.ɚ/z **ˌsplit deˈcision; ˌsplit ˈends; ˌsplit ˈhairs; ˌsplit inˈfinitive; ˌsplit ˈpea; ˌsplit persoˈnality; ˌsplit ˈscreen** *stress shift:* ˌsplit screen ˈpicture; **ˌsplit ˈsecond;** *stress shift:* ˌsplit second ˈtiming
split-level ˌsplɪtˈlev.ᵊl *stress shift:* ˌsplit-level ˈflat
splodg|e splɒdʒ (US) splɑːdʒ **-es** -ɪz
splodg|y ˈsplɒdʒ|.i (US) ˈsplɑː.dʒ|i **-ier** -i.əʳ (US) -i.ɚ **-iest** -i.ɪst, -i.əst **-iness** -ɪ.nəs, -ɪ.nɪs
splosh splɒʃ (US) splɑːʃ **-es** -ɪz **-ing** -ɪŋ **-ed** -t
splotch splɒtʃ (US) splɑːtʃ **-es** -ɪz **-y** -i
splurg|e splɜːdʒ (US) splɝːdʒ **-es** -ɪz **-ing** -ɪŋ **-ed** -d
splutt|er ˈsplʌt|.əʳ (US) ˈsplʌt̬|.ɚ **-ers** -əz (US) -ɚz **-ering** -ᵊr.ɪŋ **-ered** -əd (US) -ɚd
Spock spɒk (US) spɑːk
Spode spəʊd (US) spoʊd
Spofforth ˈspɒf.əθ (US) ˈspɑː.fɚθ
Spohr spɔːʳ *as if German:* ʃpɔːʳ (US) spɔːr *as if German:* ʃpɔːr
spoil spɔɪl **-s** -z **-ing** -ɪŋ **-ed** -d, -t **-t** -t **-er/s** -əʳ/z (US) -ɚ/z **-age** -ɪdʒ
spoilsport ˈspɔɪl.spɔːt (US) -spɔːrt **-s** -s
spoke *of wheel:* spəʊk (US) spoʊk **-s** -s
spok|e *(from* **speak***)* spəʊk (US) spoʊk **-en** -ᵊn
spokes|man ˈspəʊks|.mən (US) ˈspoʊks- **-men** -mən
spokes|person ˈspəʊks|ˌpɜː.sᵊn (US) ˈspoʊks|ˌpɝː- **-persons** -ˌpɜː.sᵊnz (US) -ˌpɝː- **-people** -ˌpiː.pl̩

Spreading

A term used to describe lip positions in speech, produced by pulling the corners of the mouth away from each other, as in a smile.

Phonetics books tend to be rather inconsistent about this, sometimes implying that any sound that is not rounded has spread lips, but elsewhere treating lip-spreading as being different from NEUTRAL lip shape. Vowels with spreading are often referred to as 'unrounded'.

Examples for English

The English vowel /iː/ is thought of as having strong lip-spreading, while /ɪ/ has spreading to a lesser degree.

spokes|woman 'spəʊksˌwʊm.ən (US) 'spoʊks- **-women** -ˌwɪm.ɪn

spoliation ˌspəʊ.li'eɪ.ʃ^{ə}n (US) ˌspoʊ-

spoliator 'spəʊ.li.eɪ.tə^{r} (US) 'spoʊ.li.eɪ.t̬ɚ **-s** -z

spondee 'spɒn.diː, -di (US) 'spɑːn- **-s** -z

spondulicks spɒn'duː.lɪks (US) spɑːn'duː-

spondylitis ˌspɒn.dɪ'laɪ.tɪs, -də'- (US) ˌspɑːn.də'laɪ.t̬ɪs

spong|e spʌndʒ **-es** -ɪz **-(e)ing** -ɪŋ **-ed** -d **-er/s** -ə^{r}/z (US) -ɚ/z **'sponge ˌbag; 'sponge ˌcake; ˌsponge 'finger**

spongiform 'spʌn.dʒɪ.fɔːm (US) -fɔːrm

spong|y 'spʌn.dʒ|i **-ier** -i.ə^{r} (US) -i.ɚ **-iest** -i.ɪst, -i.əst **-iness** -ɪ.nəs, -ɪ.nɪs

sponson 'spɒnt.sən (US) 'spɑːnt- **-s** -z

spons|or 'spɒnt.s|ə^{r} (US) 'spɑːnt.s|ɚ **-ors** -əz (US) -ɚz **-oring** -^{ə}r.ɪŋ **-ored** -əd (US) -ɚd **-orship** -ə.ʃɪp (US) -ɚ.ʃɪp

spontaneity ˌspɒn.tə'neɪ.ə.ti, -'niː.ə.ti, -ɪ.ti (US) ˌspɑːn.t^{ə}n'eɪ.ə.t̬i, -'iː-

spontaneous spɒn'teɪ.ni.əs, spən- (US) spɑːn- **-ly** -li **-ness** -nəs, -nɪs **sponˌtaneous com'bustion**

spoof spuːf **-s** -s **-ing** -ɪŋ **-ed** -t

spook spuːk **-s** -s **-ing** -ɪŋ **-ed** -t **-ish** -ɪʃ

spook|y 'spuː.k|i **-ier** -i.ə^{r} (US) -i.ɚ **-iest** -i.ɪst, -i.əst **-ily** -ɪ.li, -^{ə}l.i **-iness** -ɪ.nəs, -ɪ.nɪs

spool spuːl **-s** -z **-ing** -ɪŋ **-ed** -d

spoon spuːn **-s** -z **-ing** -ɪŋ **-ed** -d

spoonbill 'spuːn.bɪl, 'spuːm- (US) 'spuːn- **-s** -z **-ed** -d

Spooner 'spuː.nə^{r} (US) -nɚ

spoonerism 'spuː.n^{ə}r.ɪ.z^{ə}m **-s** -z

spoon|-feed 'spuːn|.fiːd **-feeds** -fiːdz **-feeding** -ˌfiː.dɪŋ **-fed** -fed

spoonful 'spuːn.fʊl, -f^{ə}l **-s** -z **spoonsful** 'spuːnz-

spoon|y 'spuː.n|i **-ier** -i.ə^{r} (US) -i.ɚ **-iest** -i.ɪst, -i.əst **-ily** -ɪ.li, -^{ə}l.i **-iness** -ɪ.nəs, -ɪ.nɪs

spoor spɔː^{r}, spʊə^{r} (US) spʊr **-s** -z **-ing** -ɪŋ **-ed** -d

Sporades 'spɒr.ə.diːz (US) 'spɔːr-

sporadic spə'ræd.ɪk, spɒr'æd- (US) spə'ræd-, spɔː- **-ally** -^{ə}l.i, -li

sporangi|um spə'ræn.dʒi|.əm (US) spə-, spoʊ- **-a** -ə

spore spɔː^{r} (US) spɔːr **-s** -z

sporran 'spɒr.ən (US) 'spɔːr-, 'spɑːr- **-s** -z

sport spɔːt (US) spɔːrt **-s** -s **-ing** -ɪŋ (US) 'spɔːr.t̬ɪŋ **-ed** -ɪd (US) 'spɔːr.t̬ɪd **'sports ˌcar; 'sports ˌday; 'sports ˌjacket**

sportive 'spɔː.tɪv (US) 'spɔːr.t̬ɪv **-ly** -li **-ness** -nəs, -nɪs

sportscast 'spɔːts.kɑːst (US) 'spɔːrts.kæst **-s** -s **-ing** -ɪŋ **-er/s** -ə^{r}/z (US) -ɚ/z

sports|man 'spɔːts|.mən (US) 'spɔːrts- **-men** -mən

sportsman|like 'spɔːts.mən|.laɪk (US) 'spɔːrts- **-ship** -ʃɪp

sports|person 'spɔːts|ˌpɜː.s^{ə}n (US) 'spɔːrts|ˌpɝː- **-persons** -ˌpɜː.s^{ə}nz (US) -ˌpɝː- **-people** -ˌpiː.pl̩

sportswear 'spɔːts.weə^{r} (US) 'spɔːrts.wer

sports|woman 'spɔːts|ˌwʊm.ən (US) 'spɔːrts- **-women** -ˌwɪm.ɪn

sport|y 'spɔː.t|i (US) 'spɔːr.t̬|i **-ier** -i.ə^{r} (US) -i.ɚ **-iest** -i.ɪst, -i.əst **-ily** -ɪ.li, -^{ə}l.i **-iness** -ɪ.nəs, -ɪ.nɪs

spot spɒt (US) spɑːt **-s** -s **-ting** -ɪŋ (US) 'spɑː.t̬ɪŋ **-ted** -ɪd (US) 'spɑː.t̬ɪd **ˌspotted 'dick; ˌknock (the) 'spots off**

spot-check ˌspɒt'tʃek, '-- (US) 'spɑːt.tʃek **-s** -s **-ing** -ɪŋ **-ed** -t

spotless 'spɒt.ləs, -lɪs (US) 'spɑːt- **-ly** -li **-ness** -nəs, -nɪs

spotlight 'spɒt.laɪt (US) 'spɑːt- **-s** -s **-ing** -ɪŋ **-ed** -ɪd **spotlit** -lɪt

spot-on ˌspɒt'ɒn (US) spɑːt'ɑːn

Spottiswoode 'spɒt.ɪs.wʊd, -ɪz-; 'spɒt.swʊd (US) 'spɑː.t̬ɪs-, 'spɑːt.swʊd

spott|y 'spɒt|.i (US) 'spɑː.t̬|i **-ier** -i.ə^{r} (US) -i.ɚ **-iest** -i.ɪst, -i.əst **-iness** -ɪ.nəs, -ɪ.nɪs

spous|e spaʊs **-es** -ɪz

spout spaʊt **-s** -s **-ing** -ɪŋ (US) 'spaʊ.t̬ɪŋ **-ed** -ɪd (US) 'spaʊ.t̬ɪd **-er/s** -ə^{r}/z (US) 'spaʊ.t̬ɚ/z

Spragge spræg

Sprague spreɪg

sprain spreɪn **-s** -z **-ing** -ɪŋ **-ed** -d

sprang (*from* **spring**) spræŋ

Sprange spreɪndʒ

Sprangle 'spræŋ.gl̩

sprat (S) spræt **-s** -s

Spratt spræt

sprawl sprɔːl (US) sprɑːl, sprɔːl **-s** -z **-ing** -ɪŋ **-ed** -d **-er/s** -ə^{r}/z (US) -ɚ/z

sprawl|y 'sprɔː.l|i (US) 'sprɑː-, 'sprɔː- **-ier** -i.ə^{r} (US) -i.ɚ **-iest** -i.ɪst, -i.əst **-iness** -ɪ.nəs, -ɪ.nɪs

spray spreɪ **-s** -z **-ing** -ɪŋ **-ed** -d **-er/s** -ə^{r}/z (US) -ɚ/z **'spray ˌgun**

spraycan 'spreɪ.kæn **-s** -z

spread spred **-s** -z **-ing** -ɪŋ **-er/s** -ə^{r}/z (US) -ɚ/z

spread-eagl|e ˌspred'iː.gl̩ (US) 'spredˌiː- **-es** -z **-ing** -ɪŋ, -'iː.glɪŋ (US) -ˌiː.glɪŋ **-ed** -d

spreadsheet 'spred.ʃiːt **-s** -s

sprechgesang (S) 'ʃprek.gə.sæŋ *as if German:* 'ʃprex.gə.zæŋ (US) 'ʃprek.gə.sɑːŋ

spree spriː **-s** -z

sprig sprɪg **-s** -z

Sprigg sprɪg **-s** -z

sprightl|y 'spraɪt.l|i **-ier** -i.ə^{r} (US) -i.ɚ **-iest** -i.ɪst, -i.əst **-iness** -ɪ.nəs, -ɪ.nɪs

spring (S) sprɪŋ **-s** -z **-ing** -ɪŋ **sprang** spræŋ **sprung** sprʌŋ **springer/s** 'sprɪŋ.ə^{r}/z (US) -ɚ/z **ˌspring 'balance, 'spring ˌbalance** (US) **'spring ˌbalance; ˌspring 'chicken; ˌspring 'fever; ˌspring 'greens; ˌspring 'onion; ˌspring 'roll** (US) **'spring ˌroll**

springboard 'sprɪŋ.bɔːd (US) -bɔːrd **-s** -z

springbok (S) 'sprɪŋ.bɒk (US) -bɑːk **-s** -s

spring-clean ˌsprɪŋ'kliːn **-s** -z **-ing** -ɪŋ **-ed** -d

spring|e sprɪndʒ **-es** -ɪz

Springell 'sprɪŋ.^{ə}l, -g^{ə}l

springer (S) 'sprɪŋ.ə^{r} (US) -ɚ **ˌspringer 'spaniel**

Springfield 'sprɪŋ.fiːld

springlike 'sprɪŋ.laɪk

Springsteen 'sprɪŋ.stiːn

springtime 'sprɪŋ.taɪm

spring|y 'sprɪŋ|.i **-ier** -i.ə^{r} (US) -i.ɚ **-iest** -i.ɪst, -i.əst **-ily** -ɪ.li, -^{ə}l.i **-iness** -ɪ.nəs, -ɪ.nɪs

sprinkl|e ˈsprɪŋ.kl̩ -es -z -ing -ɪŋ, ˈsprɪŋ.klɪŋ -ed -d -er/s -əʳ/z, ˈsprɪŋ.kləʳ/z (US) ˈ-kl̩.ɚ/z, ˈ-klɚ/z
sprinkling ˈsprɪŋ.klɪŋ, ˈ-kl̩.ɪŋ -s -z
sprint sprɪnt -s -s -ing -ɪŋ (US) ˈsprɪn.t̬ɪŋ -ed -ɪd (US) ˈsprɪn.t̬ɪd -er/s -əʳ/z (US) ˈsprɪn.t̬ɚ/z
sprit sprɪt -s -s
sprite spraɪt -s -s
spritsail ˈsprɪt.sᵊl, -seɪl (US) -seɪl, -sᵊl -s -z
spritz sprɪts -es -ɪz -ing -ɪŋ -ed -t
spritzer ˈsprɪt.səʳ (US) -sɚ -s -z
sprocket ˈsprɒk.ɪt (US) ˈsprɑː.kɪt -s -s
sprog sprɒg (US) sprɑːg, sprɔːg -s -z -ging -ɪŋ -ged -d
Sproule sprəʊl (US) sproʊl, sproʊl
sprout spraʊt -s -s -ing -ɪŋ (US) ˈspraʊ.t̬ɪŋ -ed -ɪd (US) ˈspraʊ.t̬ɪd
spruc|e spruːs -es -ɪz -er -əʳ (US) -ɚ -est -ɪst, -əst -ely -li -eness -nəs, -nɪs -ing -ɪŋ -ed -t
sprue spruː -s -z
sprung *(from* **spring***)* sprʌŋ
spry (S) spraɪ -er -əʳ (US) -ɚ -est -ɪst, -əst -ness -nəs, -nɪs
spud spʌd -s -z
spu|e spjuː -es -z -ing -ɪŋ -ed -d
spum|e spjuːm -es -z -ing -ɪŋ -ed -d -y -i
spun *(from* **spin***)* spʌn
spunk spʌŋk -y -i -ier -i.əʳ (US) -i.ɚ -iest -i.ɪst, -i.əst -iness -ɪ.nəs, -ɪ.nɪs
spur spɜːʳ (US) spɝː -s -z -ring -ɪŋ -red -d on the ˌspur of the ˈmoment
spurg|e spɜːdʒ (US) spɝːdʒ -es -ɪz
Spurgeon ˈspɜː.dʒᵊn (US) ˈspɝː-
spurious ˈspjʊə.ri.əs, ˈspjɔː- (US) ˈspjʊr.i- -ly -li -ness -nəs, -nɪs
spurn (S) spɜːn (US) spɝːn -s -z -ing -ɪŋ -ed -d
Spurr spɜːʳ (US) spɝː
Spurrier ˈspʌr.i.əʳ (US) ˈspɝː.i.ɚ
spurt spɜːt (US) spɝːt -s -s -ing -ɪŋ (US) ˈspɝː.t̬ɪŋ -ed -ɪd (US) ˈspɝː.t̬ɪd
sputnik (S) ˈspʌt.nɪk, ˈspʊt-
sputt|er ˈspʌt|.əʳ (US) ˈspʌt̬|.ɚ -ers -əz (US) -ɚz -ering -ᵊr.ɪŋ -ered -əd (US) -ɚd -erer/s -ᵊr.əʳ/z (US) -ɚ.ɚ/z
sput|um ˈspjuː|.təm (US) -t̬əm -a -ə
sp|y sp|aɪ -ies -aɪz -ying -aɪ.ɪŋ -ied -aɪd
spyglass ˈspaɪ.glɑːs (US) -glæs -es -ɪz
spyhole ˈspaɪ.həʊl (US) -hoʊl -s -z
spymaster ˈspaɪˌmɑː.stəʳ (US) -ˌmæs.tɚ -s -z
sq *(abbrev. for* **square***)* skweəʳ (US) skwer
squab skwɒb (US) skwɑːb -s -z ˌsquab ˈpie
squabbl|e ˈskwɒb.l̩ (US) ˈskwɑː.bl̩ -es -z -ing -ɪŋ, ˈskwɒb.lɪŋ (US) ˈskwɑː.blɪŋ -ed -d -er/s -əʳ/z, ˈskwɒb.ləʳ/z (US) ˈskwɑː.bl̩.ɚ/z, ˈ-blɚ/z
squad skwɒd (US) skwɑːd -s -z ˈsquad ˌcar
squadd|y, squadd|ie ˈskwɒd|.i (US) ˈskwɑː.d|i -ies -iz
squadron ˈskwɒd.rᵊn (US) ˈskwɑː.drən -s -z
squalid ˈskwɒl.ɪd (US) ˈskwɑː.lɪd -est -ɪst, -əst -ly -li -ness -nəs, -nɪs
squall skwɔːl (US) skwɔːl, skwɑːl -s -z -ing -ɪŋ -ed -d -y -i
squalor ˈskwɒl.əʳ (US) ˈskwɑː.lɚ
squam|a ˈskweɪ.m|ə, ˈskwɑː- -ae -iː
squamate ˈskweɪ.meɪt, ˈskwɑː-
squam|ose ˈskweɪ.m|əʊs, ˈskwɑː- (US) -m|oʊs -ous/ness -əs/nəs, -nɪs
squand|er ˈskwɒn.d|əʳ (US) ˈskwɑːn.d|ɚ -ers -əz (US) -ɚz -ering -ᵊr.ɪŋ -ered -əd (US) -ɚd -erer/s -ᵊr.əʳ/z (US) -ɚ.ɚ/z
squar|e skweəʳ (US) skwer -es -z -er -əʳ (US) -ɚ -est -ɪst, -əst -ely -li -eness -nəs, -nɪs -ing -ɪŋ -ed -d ˈsquare ˌdance; ˌsquare ˈdeal; ˌsquare ˈfoot; ˌsquare ˈleg; ˌsquare ˈmeal; ˌSquare ˈMile; ˌsquare ˈone; ˌsquare ˈroot
squarish ˈskweə.rɪʃ (US) ˈskwer.ɪʃ
squash skwɒʃ (US) skwɑːʃ -es -ɪz -ing -ɪŋ -ed -t
squash|y ˈskwɒʃ|.i (US) ˈskwɑː.ʃ|i -ier -i.əʳ (US) -i.ɚ -iest -i.ɪst, -i.əst -iness -ɪ.nəs, -ɪ.nɪs
squat skwɒt (US) skwɑːt -ly -li -ness -nəs, -nɪs -s -s -ting -ɪŋ (US) ˈskwɑː.t̬ɪŋ -ted -ɪd (US) ˈskwɑː.t̬ɪd -ter/s -əʳ/z (US) ˈskwɑː.t̬ɚ/z
squaw skwɔː (US) skwɑː, skwɔː -s -z
squawk skwɔːk (US) skwɑːk, skwɔːk -s -s -ing -ɪŋ -ed -t
squeak skwiːk -s -s -ing -ɪŋ -ed -t -er/s -əʳ/z (US) -ɚ/z
squeak|y ˈskwiː.k|i -ier -i.əʳ (US) -i.ɚ -iest -i.ɪst, -i.əst -ily -ɪ.li, -ᵊl.i -iness -ɪ.nəs, -ɪ.nɪs
squeaky-clean ˌskwiː.kiˈkliːn
squeal skwiːl -s -z -ing -ɪŋ -ed -d -er/s -əʳ/z (US) -ɚ/z
squeamish ˈskwiː.mɪʃ -ly -li -ness -nəs, -nɪs
squeegee ˈskwiː.dʒiː, ˌ-ˈ- (US) ˈskwiː.dʒiː -s -z -ing -ɪŋ -d -d
Squeers skwɪəz (US) skwɪrz
squeez|e skwiːz -es -ɪz -ing -ɪŋ -ed -d -er/s -əʳ/z (US) -ɚ/z -able -ə.bl̩ -y -i
squeeze-box ˈskwiːz.bɒks (US) -bɑːks -es -ɪz
squelch skweltʃ -es -ɪz -ing -ɪŋ -ed -t -y -i
squib skwɪb -s -z
squid skwɪd -s -z
squidg|y ˈskwɪdʒ|.i -ier -i.əʳ (US) -i.ɚ -iest -i.ɪst, -i.əst -iness -ɪ.nəs, -ɪ.nɪs
squiff|y ˈskwɪf|.i -ed -t -ier -i.əʳ (US) -i.ɚ -iest -i.ɪst, -i.əst -iness -ɪ.nəs, -ɪ.nɪs
squiggl|e ˈskwɪg|.l̩ -es -z -ing -ɪŋ, ˈskwɪg.lɪŋ -ed -d -y -i
squilgee ˈskwɪl.dʒiː, ˌ-ˈ- (US) ˈskwɪl.dʒiː -s -z -ing -ɪŋ -d -d
squill skwɪl -s -z
squinch skwɪntʃ -es -ɪz -ing -ɪŋ -ed -t
squint skwɪnt -s -s -ing -ɪŋ (US) ˈskwɪn.t̬ɪŋ -ed -ɪd (US) ˈskwɪn.t̬ɪd -y -i
squirarch|y ˈskwaɪə.rɑː.k|i (US) ˈskwaɪɚ.ɑːr- -ies -iz
squir|e (S) skwaɪəʳ (US) skwaɪɚ -es -z -ing -ɪŋ -ed -d
squirearch|y ˈskwaɪə.rɑː.k|i (US) ˈskwaɪɚ.ɑːr- -ies -iz
Squires skwaɪəz (US) skwaɪɚz
squirm skwɜːm (US) skwɝːm -s -z -ing -ɪŋ -ed -d -y -i
squirrel ˈskwɪr.ᵊl (US) ˈskwɝː- -s -z -(l)ing -ɪŋ -(l)ed -d
squirt skwɜːt (US) skwɝːt -s -s -ing -ɪŋ (US) ˈskwɝː.t̬ɪŋ -ed -ɪd (US) ˈskwɝː.t̬ɪd -er/s -əʳ/z (US) -ɚ/z
squish skwɪʃ -es -ɪz -ing -ɪŋ -ed -t -y -i
sr (S) *(abbrev. for* **senior***)* ˈsiː.ni.əʳ, -njəʳ (US) -njɚ
Srebrenica ˌsreb.rəˈniːt.sə, ˌʃreb-, -tʃə
Sri Lank|a ˌsriːˈlæŋ.kə, ˌsrɪ-, ˌʃriː- (US) -ˈlɑːŋ- -an/s -ən/z
Srinagar srɪˈnʌg.əʳ, sriː-, ʃrɪ-, ʃriː-, -ˈnɑː.gəʳ (US) ˌsriːˈnʌg.ɚ
SS *Nazi unit:* ˌesˈes *stress shift:* ˌSS ˈofficer
SS *(abbrev. for* **steamship***)* ˌesˈes *stress shift:* ˌSS ˌGreat ˈBritian
SSE *(abbrev. for* **south-southeast***)* ˌes.esˈiː, ˌsaʊθ.saʊθˈiːst *in nautical usage also:* ˌsaʊ.saʊ-
ssh, sh, shh ʃ
Note: Used to command silence
SSW *(abbrev. for* **south-southwest***)* ˌes.esˈdʌb.l̩.juː, -ju, ˌsaʊθ.saʊθˈwest (US) ˌes,esˈdʌb.l̩.juː, -jə, ˌsaʊθ.saʊθˈwest *in nautical usage also:* ˌsaʊ.saʊ-
St. *(abbrev. for* **Street***)* striːt
St. *(abbrev. for* **Saint***)* sᵊnt, sɪnt, seɪnt (US) seɪnt
Note: See panel information at **Saint**.
st *(abbrev. for* **stone***)* stəʊn (US) stoʊn
stab stæb -s -z -bing/s -ɪŋ/z -bed -d
Stabat Mater ˌstɑː.bætˈmɑː.təʳ, -bətˈ- (US) -bɑːtˈmɑː.tɚ -s -z
St. Abb's sᵊntˈæbz, sɪnt- (US) seɪnt-
stability stəˈbɪl.ə.ti, -ɪ.ti (US) -ə.t̬i
stabilization, -isa- ˌsteɪ.bᵊl.aɪˈzeɪ.ʃᵊn, -bɪ.laɪ-, -lɪˈ- (US) -bᵊl.ɪˈ-
stabiliz|e, -is|e ˈsteɪ.bᵊl.aɪz, -bɪ.laɪz (US) -bə.laɪz -es -ɪz -ing -ɪŋ -ed -d -er/s -əʳ/z (US) -ɚ/z

stabl|e 'steɪ.bl̩ **-es** -z **-y** -i, 'steɪ.bli **-eness** -nəs, -nɪs **-ing** -ɪŋ, 'steɪ.blɪŋ **-ed** -d ˌ**stable 'door; 'stable ˌlad**
stablemate 'steɪ.bl̩.meɪt **-s** -s
stabling 'steɪ.bl̩.ɪŋ, '-blɪŋ
stablish 'stæb.lɪʃ **-es** -ɪz **-ing** -ɪŋ **-ed** -t
staccato stə'kɑː.təʊ ⓤⓢ -t̬oʊ **-s** -z
Stacey, Stacie 'steɪ.si
stack stæk **-s** -s **-ing** -ɪŋ **-ed** -t
Stacpoole 'stæk.puːl
Stacy 'steɪ.si
stadi|um 'steɪ.di|.əm **-ums** -əmz **-a** -ə
staff stɑːf ⓤⓢ stæf **-s** -s **-ing** -ɪŋ **-ed** -t **'staff ˌnurse; 'staff ˌsergeant**
Staffa 'stæf.ə
staffer 'stɑː.fəʳ ⓤⓢ 'stæf.ɚ **-s** -z
Stafford 'stæf.əd ⓤⓢ -ɚd **-shire** -ʃəʳ, -ˌʃɪəʳ ⓤⓢ -ʃɚ, -ˌʃɪr
staffroom 'stɑːf.rʊm, -ruːm ⓤⓢ 'stæf.ruːm, -rʊm **-s** -z
Staffs. *(abbrev. for* **Staffordshire***)* stæfs
stag stæg **-s** -z **'stag ˌnight**
stag|e steɪdʒ **-es** -ɪz **-ing** -ɪŋ **-ed** -d ˌ**stage 'door; 'stage ˌfright**
stagecoach 'steɪdʒ.kəʊtʃ ⓤⓢ -koʊtʃ **-es** -ɪz
stagecraft 'steɪdʒ.krɑːft ⓤⓢ -kræft
stagehand 'steɪdʒ.hænd **-s** -z
stage-manag|e ˌsteɪdʒ'mæn.ɪdʒ, '-ˌ-- ⓤⓢ 'steɪdʒˌmæn- **-es** -ɪz **-ing** -ɪŋ **-ed** -d **-ment** -mənt
stage-manager ˌsteɪdʒ'mæn.ə.dʒəʳ, '-ɪ- ⓤⓢ 'steɪdʒˌmæn.ə.dʒɚ
stager 'steɪ.dʒəʳ ⓤⓢ -dʒɚ **-s** -z
stage-struck 'steɪdʒ.strʌk
stag|ey 'steɪ.dʒ|i **-ier** -i.əʳ ⓤⓢ -i.ɚ **-iest** -i.ɪst, -i.əst **-iness** -ɪ.nəs, -ɪ.nɪs
stagflation stæg'fleɪ.ʃᵊn
stagg|er 'stæg|.əʳ ⓤⓢ -ɚ **-ers** -əz ⓤⓢ -ɚz **-ering/ly** -ᵊr.ɪŋ **-ered** -əd ⓤⓢ -ɚd **-erer/s** -ᵊr.əʳ/z ⓤⓢ -ɚ.ɚ/z
staghound 'stæg.haʊnd **-s** -z
staging 'steɪ.dʒɪŋ **-s** -z
Stagirite 'stædʒ.ɪ.raɪt ⓤⓢ '-ə- **-s** -s
stagnancy 'stæg.nən*t*.si
stagnant 'stæg.nənt **-ly** -li
stagna|te stæg'neɪ|t, '-- ⓤⓢ 'stæg.neɪ|t **-tes** -ts **-ting** -tɪŋ ⓤⓢ -t̬ɪŋ **-ted** -tɪd ⓤⓢ -t̬ɪd
stagnation stæg'neɪ.ʃᵊn
St. Agnes sᵊnt'æg.nɪs, sɪnt-, seɪnt- ⓤⓢ seɪnt-
stag|y 'steɪ.dʒ|i **-ier** -i.əʳ ⓤⓢ -i.ɚ **-iest** -i.ɪst, -i.əst **-ily** -ɪ.li, -ᵊl.i **-iness** -ɪ.nəs, -ɪ.nɪs
staid steɪd **-ly** -li **-ness** -nəs, -nɪs
stain steɪn **-s** -z **-ing** -ɪŋ **-ed** -d **-er/s** -əʳ/z ⓤⓢ -ɚ/z ˌ**stained 'glass**
Stainer *English name:* 'steɪ.nəʳ ⓤⓢ -nɚ *German name:* 'staɪ.nəʳ *as if German:* 'ʃtaɪ- ⓤⓢ -nɚ

Staines steɪnz
Stainforth 'steɪn.fəθ ⓤⓢ -fɚθ
stainless 'steɪn.ləs, -lɪs **-ly** -li **-ness** -nəs, -nɪs ˌ**stainless 'steel**
stair steəʳ ⓤⓢ ster **-s** -z
staircas|e 'steə.keɪs ⓤⓢ 'ster- **-es** -ɪz
stair-rod 'steə.rɒd ⓤⓢ 'ster.rɑːd **-s** -z
stairway 'steə.weɪ ⓤⓢ 'ster- **-s** -z
stairwell 'steə.wel ⓤⓢ 'ster- **-s** -z
Staithes steɪðz
stak|e steɪk **-es** -s **-ing** -ɪŋ **-ed** -t
stakeholder 'steɪkˌhəʊl.dəʳ ⓤⓢ -ˌhoʊl.dɚ **-s** -z
stakeout 'steɪk.aʊt **-s** -s
Stakhanov|ite stæk'æn.ə.v|aɪt ⓤⓢ stə'kɑː.nə- **-ites** -aɪts **-ism** -ɪ.zᵊm
Stakis 'stæk.ɪs
stalactite 'stæl.ək.taɪt ⓤⓢ stə'læk-; 'stæl.ək- **-s** -s
stalag 'stæl.æg ⓤⓢ 'stɑː.lɑːg, 'stæl.æg **-s** -z
stalagmite 'stæl.əg.maɪt ⓤⓢ stə'læg-; 'stæl.əg- **-s** -s
St. Albans sᵊnt'ɔːl.bənz, sɪnt-, -'ɒl- ⓤⓢ seɪnt'ɔːl-, -'ɑːl-
Stalbridge 'stɔːl.brɪdʒ ⓤⓢ 'stɔːl-
St. Aldate's sᵊnt'ɔːl.deɪts, sɪnt-, -'ɒl-, -dɪts *old-fashioned:* -'əʊldz ⓤⓢ seɪnt'ɔːl.deɪts, -'ɑːl-
stal|e steɪl **-er** -əʳ ⓤⓢ -ɚ **-est** -ɪst, -əst **-ely** -li **-eness** -nəs, -nɪs
stale|mate 'steɪl|.meɪt **-mates** -meɪts **-mating** -meɪ.tɪŋ ⓤⓢ -meɪ.t̬ɪŋ **-mated** -meɪ.tɪd ⓤⓢ -meɪ.t̬ɪd
Stalin 'stɑː.lɪn, 'stæl.ɪn **-ism** -ɪ.zᵊm
Stalingrad 'stɑː.lɪn.græd, 'stæl.ɪn-, -grɑːd ⓤⓢ 'stɑː.lɪn.græd, 'stæl.ɪn-
stalin|ism (S) 'stɑː.lɪ.n|ɪ.zᵊm, 'stæl.ɪ- ⓤⓢ 'stɑː.lɪ- **-ist/s** -ɪsts
stalk stɔːk ⓤⓢ stɔːk, stɑːk **-s** -s **-ing** -ɪŋ **-ed** -t **-er/s** -əʳ/z ⓤⓢ -ɚ/z
stalking-hors|e 'stɔː.kɪŋ.hɔːs ⓤⓢ -hɔːrs, 'stɑː- **-es** -ɪz
Stalky 'stɔː.ki ⓤⓢ 'stɔː-, 'stɑː-
stall stɔːl ⓤⓢ stɔːl, stɑːl **-s** -z **-ing** -ɪŋ **-ed** -d
stallage 'stɔː.lɪdʒ
stallholder 'stɔːlˌhəʊl.dəʳ ⓤⓢ 'stɔːlˌhoʊl.dɚ, 'stɑːl- **-s** -z
stallion 'stæl.jən, -i.ən ⓤⓢ '-jən **-s** -z
Stallone stə'ləʊn, stæl'əʊn ⓤⓢ stə'loʊn
stalwart 'stɔːl.wət, 'stɒl- ⓤⓢ 'stɔːl.wɚt, 'stɑːl- **-s** -s **-ly** -li **-ness** -nəs, -nɪs
Stalybridge 'steɪ.lɪ.brɪdʒ
Stamboul stæm'buːl ⓤⓢ stɑːm-
St. Ambrose sᵊnt'æm.brəʊz, sɪnt-, -brəʊs ⓤⓢ seɪnt'æm.broʊz, -broʊs
stamen 'steɪ.men, -mən **-s** -z
Stamford 'stæm*p*.fəd ⓤⓢ -fɚd
stamina 'stæm.ɪ.nə, '-ə- ⓤⓢ '-ə-

stamm|er 'stæm|.əʳ ⓤⓢ -ɚ **-ers** -əz ⓤⓢ -ɚz **-ering** -ᵊr.ɪŋ **-ered** -əd ⓤⓢ -ɚd **-erer/s** -ᵊr.əʳ/z ⓤⓢ -ɚ.ɚ/z
stamp (S) stæmp **-s** -s **-ing** -ɪŋ **-ed** -t **-er/s** -əʳ/z ⓤⓢ -ɚ/z **'stamp ˌalbum; 'stamp colˌlector; 'stamp ˌduty; 'stamping ˌground**
stamped|e stæm'piːd **-es** -z **-ing** -ɪŋ **-ed** -ɪd
Stanbury 'stæn.bᵊr.i, 'stæm-, '-bri ⓤⓢ 'stæn.ber.i, -bɚ-
stanc|e stæn*t*s, stɑːn*t*s ⓤⓢ stæn*t*s **-es** -ɪz
stanch stɑːn*t*ʃ ⓤⓢ stɑːntʃ, stɔːntʃ, stæntʃ **-es** -ɪz **-ing** -ɪŋ **-ed** -t
stanchion 'stɑːn.*t*ʃᵊn, 'stæn- ⓤⓢ 'stæn- **-s** -z **-ing** -ɪŋ **-ed** -d
stand stænd **-s** -z **-ing** -ɪŋ **stood** stʊd
stand-alone 'stænd.əˌləʊn, -ᵊlˌəʊn ⓤⓢ -əˌloʊn
standard 'stæn.dəd ⓤⓢ -dɚd **-s** -z ˌ**standard deviˈation; 'standard ˌlamp; ˌstandard of 'living; 'standard ˌtime**
standard-bearer 'stæn.dədˌbeə.rəʳ ⓤⓢ -dɚdˌber.ɚ **-s** -z
standardization, -isa- ˌstæn.də.daɪ'zeɪ.ʃᵊn, -dɪ'- ⓤⓢ -dɚ.dɪ'-
standardiz|e, -is|e 'stæn.də.daɪz ⓤⓢ -dɚ- **-es** -ɪz **-ing** -ɪŋ **-ed** -d
standby 'stæn*d*.baɪ, 'stæm- ⓤⓢ 'stæn*d*- **-s** -z
stand-in 'stænd.ɪn **-s** -z
standing 'stæn.dɪŋ **-s** -z ˌ**standing 'joke; ˌstanding 'order; 'standing ˌroom**
standish (S) 'stæn.dɪʃ **-es** -ɪz
standoff 'stænd.ɒf ⓤⓢ -ɑːf **-s** -s
standoffish ˌstænd'ɒf.ɪʃ ⓤⓢ -'ɑː.fɪʃ **-ly** -li **-ness** -nəs, -nɪs
standout 'stænd.aʊt **-s** -s
standpipe 'stæn*d*.paɪp, 'stæm- ⓤⓢ 'stæn*d*- **-s** -s
standpoint 'stæn*d*.pɔɪnt, 'stæm- ⓤⓢ 'stæn*d*- **-s** -s
St. Andrew sᵊnt'æn.druː, sɪnt- ⓤⓢ seɪnt- **-(')s** -z **St. ˌAndrew's 'cross**
standstill 'stæn*d*.stɪl **-s** -z
stand-up 'stænd.ʌp
Staneydale 'steɪ.ni.deɪl
Stanfield 'stæn.fiːld
Stanford 'stæn.fəd ⓤⓢ -fɚd
Stanford-Binet ˌstæn.fəd'biː.neɪ, ˌstæm-; -bɪ'neɪ ⓤⓢ ˌstæn.fɚd.bɪ'neɪ
Stanford le Hope ˌstæn.fəd.lɪ'həʊp ⓤⓢ -fɚd.lɪ'hoʊp
stanhope (S) 'stæn.əp, -həʊp ⓤⓢ -hoʊp, -əp **-s** -s
staniel 'stæn.jəl, -i.əl ⓤⓢ '-jəl **-s** -z
Stanis|las 'stæn.ɪ.s|læs, '-ə-, -s|ləs, -s|lɑːs ⓤⓢ -s|lɑːs **-laus** -s|lɔːs

Stanislavski ˌstæn.ɪˈslæv.ski, -ˈslæf- (US) -əˈslɑːv-, -ˈslɑːf- **Staniˈslavski ˌmethod**

stank *(from* **stink***)* stæŋk

Stanley ˈstæn.li **ˈStanley ˌknife**

Stanmore ˈstæn.mɔːʳ, ˈstæm- (US) ˈstæn.mɔːr

Stannard ˈstæn.əd (US) -ɚd

stannar|y ˈstæn.ᵊr|.i **-ies** -iz

St. Anne sᵊntˈæn, sɪnt- (US) seɪnt- **-ˈs** -z

stann|ic ˈstæn|.ɪk **-ous** -əs

Stansfield ˈstænz.fiːld, ˈstænts-

Stansted ˈstænt.sted, -stɪd, -stəd **ˌStansted ˈAirport**

Stansted Mountfitchet ˌstænt.sted.maʊntˈfɪtʃ.ɪt, -stɪd-, -stəd

St. Anthony sᵊntˈæn.tə.ni, sɪnt- (US) seɪntˈæn.tᵊn.i, -θə.ni

Stanton ˈstæn.tən, ˈstɑːn- (US) ˈstæn.tᵊn

stanza ˈstæn.zə **-s** -z

stapes ˈsteɪ.piːz

staphylo|coccus ˌstæf.ɪ.ləʊ|ˈkɒk.əs, -ᵊl.əʊ- (US) -ə.loʊ|ˈkɑː.kəs **-cocci** -ˈkɒk.saɪ, -aɪ, -iː (US) -ˈkɑːk.saɪ, -aɪ **-coccal** -ˈkɒk.ᵊl (US) -ˈkɑː.kᵊl **-coccic** -ˈkɒk.ɪk (US) -ˈkɑː.kɪk

stapl|e (S) ˈsteɪ.pl̩ **-es** -z **-ing** -ɪŋ, ˈsteɪ.plɪŋ **-ed** -d

Stapleford ˈsteɪ.pl̩.fəd (US) -fɚd

stapler ˈsteɪ.pləʳ (US) -plɚ **-s** -z

Stapleton ˈsteɪ.pl̩.tən (US) -t̬ən

Stapley ˈstæp.li, ˈsteɪ.pli

star stɑːʳ (US) stɑːr **-s** -z **-ring** -ɪŋ **-red** -d **ˌStars and ˈBars; ˌstar ˈchamber; ˌStar of ˈDavid; ˈstar ˌsign; ˌStars and ˈStripes; ˈstar ˌwars**

starboard ˈstɑː.bəd, -bɔːd (US) ˈstɑːr.bɚd, -bɔːrd

Note: The nautical pronunciation is /ˈstɑː.bəd (US) -bɚd/.

Starbuck ˈstɑː.bʌk (US) ˈstɑːr- **-s** -s

starch stɑːtʃ (US) stɑːrtʃ **-es** -ɪz **-ing** -ɪŋ **-ed** -t **-y** -i **-ier** -i.əʳ (US) -i.ɚ **-iest** -i.ɪst, -i.əst **-iness** -ɪ.nəs, -ɪ.nɪs **-ily** -ɪ.li

starch-reduced ˌstɑːtʃ.rɪˈdjuːst, -rəˈ-, -ˈdʒuːst, ˈ--ˌ- (US) ˈstɑːrtʃ.rɪˌduːst, -ˌdjuːst

star-crossed ˈstɑː.krɒst (US) ˈstɑːr.krɑːst **ˌstar-crossed ˈlovers**

stardom ˈstɑː.dəm (US) ˈstɑːr-

stardust ˈstɑː.dʌst (US) ˈstɑːr-

star|e steəʳ (US) ster **-es** -z **-ing/ly** -ɪŋ/li **-ed** -d **-er/s** -əʳ/z (US) -ɚ/z

starfish ˈstɑː.fɪʃ (US) ˈstɑːr- **-es** -ɪz

stargaz|e ˈstɑː.geɪz (US) ˈstɑːr- **-es** -ɪz **-ing** -ɪŋ **-er/s** -əʳ/z (US) -ɚ/z

stark (S) stɑːk (US) stɑːrk **-ly** -li **-ness** -nəs, -nɪs **ˌstark ˈnaked; ˌstark ˌraving ˈmad**

starkers ˈstɑː.kəz (US) ˈstɑːr.kɚz

Starks stɑːks (US) stɑːrks

star|less ˈstɑː|.ləs, -lɪs (US) ˈstɑːr-

starlet ˈstɑː.lət, -lɪt (US) ˈstɑːr- **-s** -s

starlight ˈstɑː.laɪt (US) ˈstɑːr-

starling (S) ˈstɑː.lɪŋ (US) ˈstɑːr- **-s** -z

starlit ˈstɑː.lɪt (US) ˈstɑːr-

Starr stɑːʳ (US) stɑːr

starr|y ˈstɑː.r|i (US) ˈstɑːr|.i **-iness** -ɪ.nəs, -ɪ.nɪs

starry-eyed ˌstɑː.riˈaɪd (US) ˈstɑː.riˌaɪd *stress shift, British only:* ˌstarry-eyed ˈfan

star-spangled ˈstɑːˌspæŋ.gl̩d (US) ˈstɑːr- **ˌstar-ˌspangled ˈbanner**

starstruck ˈstɑː.strʌk (US) ˈstɑːr-

star-studded ˈstɑːˌstʌd.ɪd (US) ˈstɑːr-

start (S) stɑːt (US) stɑːrt **-s** -s **-ing** -ɪŋ (US) ˈstɑːr.t̬ɪŋ **-ed** -ɪd (US) ˈstɑːr.t̬ɪd **-er/s** -əʳ/z (US) ˈstɑːr.t̬ɚ/z **ˈstarting ˌblock; ˈstarting ˌpoint**

startl|e ˈstɑː.tl̩ (US) ˈstɑːr.t̬l̩ **-es** -z **-ing/ly** -ɪŋ, ˈstɑːt.lɪŋ (US) ˈstɑːrt- **-ed** -d **-er/s** -əʳ/z, ˈstɑːt.ləʳ/z (US) ˈstɑːr.t̬l̩.ɚ/z, ˈstɑːrt.lɚ/z

Start-rite® ˈstɑːt.raɪt (US) ˈstɑːrt-

start-up ˈstɑːt.ʌp (US) ˈstɑːrt- **-s** -s

starvation stɑːˈveɪ.ʃᵊn (US) stɑːr- **starˌvation ˈwages**

starv|e stɑːv (US) stɑːrv **-es** -z **-ing** -ɪŋ **-ed** -d

starveling ˈstɑːv.lɪŋ (US) ˈstɑːrv- **-s** -z

St. Asaph sᵊntˈæs.əf, sɪnt- (US) seɪnt-

stash stæʃ **-es** -ɪz **-ing** -ɪŋ **-ed** -t

Stasi ˈstɑː.zi *as if German:* ˈʃtɑː-

stas|is ˈsteɪ.s|ɪs (US) ˈsteɪ-, ˈstæs|.ɪs **-es** -iːz

stat|e steɪt **-es** -s **-ing** -ɪŋ (US) ˈsteɪ.t̬ɪŋ **-ed/ly** -ɪd (US) ˈsteɪ.t̬ɪd **ˈState ˌDepartment; ˌstate of eˈmergency; ˈstate ˌschool; ˌstate ˈtrooper**

statecraft ˈsteɪt.krɑːft (US) -kræft

statehood ˈsteɪt.hʊd

stateless ˈsteɪt.ləs, -lɪs **-ness** -nəs, -nɪs

statel|y ˈsteɪt.l|i **-ier** -i.əʳ (US) -i.ɚ **-iest** -i.ɪst, -i.əst **-iness** -ɪ.nəs, -ɪ.nɪs **ˌstately ˈhome**

statement ˈsteɪt.mənt **-s** -s

Staten Island ˌstæt.ᵊnˈaɪ.lənd

state-of-the-art ˌsteɪt.əv.ðiˈɑːt (US) -ˈɑːrt *stress shift:* ˌstate-of-the-art ˈgadget

state-owned ˌsteɪtˈəʊnd (US) -ˈoʊnd *stress shift:* ˌstate owned ˈbusiness

stateroom ˈsteɪt.rʊm, -ruːm (US) -ruːm, -rʊm **-s** -z

States steɪts

stateside ˈsteɪt.saɪd

states|man ˈsteɪts|.mən **-men** -mən

statesman|like ˈsteɪts.mən|.laɪk **-ly** -li **-ship** -ʃɪp

states|woman ˈsteɪts|ˌwʊm.ən **-women** -ˌwɪm.ɪn

statewide ˈsteɪt.waɪd

Statham ˈsteɪ.θəm, -ðəm (US) -ðəm, -θəm, -t̬əm; ˈstæt̬.əm

St. Athan sᵊntˈæθ.ᵊn, sɪnt- (US) seɪnt-

static ˈstæt.ɪk (US) ˈstæt̬- **-s** -s **-al** -ᵊl **-ally** -ᵊl.i, -li

static|e ˈstæt.ɪs, -ɪ.s|i (US) ˈstæt̬.ə.s|i, -ɪs **-es** -ɪz, -iz

station ˈsteɪ.ʃᵊn **-s** -z **-ing** -ɪŋ, ˈsteɪʃ.nɪŋ **-ed** -d **ˈstation ˌwagon; ˌstations of the ˈcross**

stationar|y ˈsteɪ.ʃᵊn.ᵊr|.i, ˈsteɪʃ.nᵊr- (US) ˈsteɪ.ʃə.ner- **-ily** -ᵊl.i, -ɪ.li **-iness** -ɪ.nəs, -ɪ.nɪs

stationer ˈsteɪ.ʃᵊn.əʳ, ˈsteɪʃ.nəʳ (US) -ʃᵊn.ɚ, ˈsteɪʃ.nɚ **-s** -z

stationery ˈsteɪ.ʃᵊn.ᵊr.i, ˈsteɪʃ.nᵊr- (US) ˈsteɪ.ʃə.ner-

stationmaster ˈsteɪ.ʃᵊnˌmɑː.stəʳ (US) -ˌmæs.tɚ **-s** -z

stat|ism ˈsteɪ.t|ɪ.zᵊm (US) -t̬|ɪ- **-ist/s** -ɪst/s

statistic stəˈtɪs.tɪk, stætˈɪs- (US) stəˈtɪs- **-s** -s **-al** -ᵊl **-ally** -ᵊl.i, -li

statistician ˌstæt.ɪˈstɪʃ.ᵊn, -əˈ- (US) -ɪˈ- **-s** -z

Statius ˈsteɪ.ʃəs

stative ˈsteɪ.tɪv (US) -t̬ɪv

stator ˈsteɪ.təʳ (US) -t̬ɚ **-s** -z

statuary ˈstætʃ.u.ᵊr.i, ˈstæt.ju- (US) ˈstætʃ.u.er-

statue ˈstætʃ.uː, ˈstæt.juː (US) ˈstætʃ.uː **-s** -z

statuesque ˌstæt.juˈesk, ˌstætʃ.uˈ- (US) ˌstætʃ.uˈ-

statuette ˌstæt.juˈet, ˌstætʃ.uˈ- (US) ˌstætʃ.uˈ- **-s** -s

stature ˈstætʃ.əʳ, ˈstæt.jəʳ (US) ˈstætʃ.ɚ **-s** -z

status ˈsteɪ.təs (US) stæ.t̬əs **-es** -ɪz **ˈstatus ˌsymbol**

status quo ˌsteɪ.təsˈkwəʊ, ˌstæt.əsˈ- (US) ˌstæt̬.əsˈkwoʊ, ˌsteɪ.t̬əsˈ-

statute ˈstæt.juːt, ˈstætʃ.uːt (US) ˈstætʃ.uːt **-s** -s **ˈstatute ˌbook**

statutory ˈstæt.jə.tᵊr.i, -jʊ-, ˈstætʃ.ə-, ˈ-ʊ- (US) ˈstætʃ.ə.tɔːr-, ˈ-ʊ- **ˌstatutory ˈrape**

St. Augustine sᵊnt.ɔːˈgʌs.tɪn, sɪnt-, ˌsent-, ˌseɪnt-, -əˈ-; (US) seɪntˈɔː.gə.stiːn, -ˈɑː-

staunch stɔːntʃ (US) stɔːntʃ, stɑːntʃ **-er** -əʳ (US) -ɚ **-est** -ɪst, -əst **-ly** -li **-ness** -nəs, -nɪs **-es** -ɪz **-ing** -ɪŋ **-ed** -t

Staunton *English surname:* ˈstɔːn.tən (US) ˈstɑːn.tᵊn, ˈstɔːn- *towns in US:* ˈstæn.tən (US) -tᵊn

St. Austell sᵊntˈɔː.stᵊl, sɪnt- *locally:* -ˈɔː.sᵊl (US) seɪntˈɑː.stᵊl, -ˈɔː-

Stavanger stəˈvæŋ.əʳ, stævˈæŋ- (US) stəˈvɑːŋ.ɚ, stɑː-

stav|e steɪv **-es** -z **-ing** -ɪŋ **-ed** -d **stove** stəʊv (US) stoʊv

Staveley ˈsteɪv.li
stay steɪ **-s** -z **-ing** -ɪŋ **-ed** -d **-er/s** -əʳ/z (US) -ɚ/z
stay-at-home ˈsteɪ.ət.həʊm (US) -hoʊm
staysail ˈsteɪ.seɪl *nautical pronunciation:* -sᵊl **-s** -z
St. Bartholomew sᵊnt.bɑːˈθɒl.ə.mjuː, sɪnt-, -bəˈ- (US) ˌseɪnt.bɑːrˈθɑː.lə- **-'s** -z
St. Bees sᵊn*t*ˈbiːz, sɪn*t*- (US) seɪnt-
St. Bernard sᵊn*t*ˈbɜː.nəd, sɪn*t*- (US) ˌseɪnt.bɚˈnɑːrd **-s** -z
St. Blaize sᵊn*t*ˈbleɪz, sɪn*t*- (US) seɪnt-
St. Blazey sᵊn*t*ˈbleɪ.zi, sɪn*t*- (US) seɪnt-
St. Bride's sᵊn*t*ˈbraɪdz, sɪn*t*- (US) seɪnt-
St. Bruno sᵊn*t*ˈbruː.nəʊ, sɪn*t*- (US) seɪntˈbruː.noʊ
St. Catherine, St. Catharine sᵊn*t*ˈkæθ.ᵊr.ɪn, sɪn*t*-, sᵊŋˈ-, ˈ-rɪn (US) seɪnt- **-'s** -z
St. Cecilia sᵊnt.sɪˈsɪl.i.ə, sɪnt-, -ˈsiː.li.ə, ˈ-ljə (US) ˌseɪnt.sɪˈsiːl.jə
St. Christopher sᵊn*t*ˈkrɪs.tə.fəʳ, sɪn*t*-, sᵊŋ- (US) seɪntˈkrɪs.tə.fɚ **-s** -z
St. Clair *surname:* ˈsɪŋ.kleəʳ, ˈsɪn- (US) seɪntˈkler *place in US:* sᵊn*t*ˈkleəʳ, sɪn*t*-, sᵊŋ- (US) seɪntˈkler
St. Columb sᵊn*t*ˈkɒl.əm, sɪn*t*- (US) seɪntˈkɑː.ləm
STD ˌes.tiːˈdiː **STˈD ˌcode**
St. David sᵊn*t*ˈdeɪ.vɪd, sɪn*t*- (US) seɪnt- **-'s** -z
stead (S) sted
steadfast ˈsted.fɑːst, -fəst (US) -fæst, -fəst **-ly** -li **-ness** -nəs, -nɪs
steading ˈsted.ɪŋ **-s** -z
Steadman ˈsted.mən
stead|y ˈsted|.i **-ier** -i.əʳ (US) -i.ɚ **-iest** -i.ɪst, -i.əst **-ily** -ɪ.li, -ᵊl.i **-iness** -ɪ.nəs, -ɪ.nɪs **-ies** -iz **-ying** -i.ɪŋ **-ied** -id ˌ**steady ˈstate;** ˌ**steady ˈstate** ˌ**theory**
steak steɪk **-s** -s ˌ**steak tarˈtare;** ˌ**steak and** ˌ**kidney ˈpie**
steakhou|se ˈsteɪk.haʊ|s **-ses** -zɪz
steal stiːl **-s** -z **-ing** -ɪŋ **stole** stəʊl (US) stoʊl **stolen** ˈstəʊ.lᵊn (US) ˈstoʊ- **stealer/s** ˈstiː.ləʳ/z (US) -lɚ/z
stealth stelθ
stealth|y ˈstel.θ|i **-ier** -i.əʳ (US) -i.ɚ **-iest** -i.ɪst, -i.əst **-ily** -ɪ.li, -ᵊl.i **-iness** -ɪ.nəs, -ɪ.nɪs
steam stiːm **-s** -z **-ing** -ɪŋ **-ed** -d **-er/s** -əʳ/z (US) -ɚ/z ˈ**steam** ˌ**engine;** ˈ**steam** ˌ**iron;** ˈ**steam** ˌ**power**
steamboat ˈstiːm.bəʊt (US) -boʊt **-s** -s
steam-hammer ˈstiːmˌhæm.əʳ (US) -ɚ **-s** -z
steamroll ˈstiːm.rəʊl (US) -roʊl **-s** -z **-ing** -ɪŋ **-ed** -d
steamroll|er ˈstiːmˌrəʊ.l|əʳ (US) -ˌroʊ.l|ɚ **-ers** -əz (US) -ɚz **-ering** -ᵊr.ɪŋ **-ered** -əd (US) -ɚd
steamship ˈstiːm.ʃɪp **-s** -s
steam|y ˈstiː.m|i **-ier** -i.əʳ (US) -i.ɚ **-iest** -i.ɪst, -i.əst **-iness** -ɪ.nəs, -ɪ.nɪs
stearic stiˈær.ɪk (US) stiˈær-; ˈstɪr-
stearin ˈstɪə.rɪn (US) ˈstiː.ɚ.ɪn; ˈstɪr-
Stearn(e) stɜːn (US) stɝːn **-s** -z
steatite ˈstɪə.taɪt (US) ˈstiː.ə-
steatolysis stɪəˈtɒl.ə.sɪs, ˈ-ɪ- (US) ˌstiː.əˈtɑː.lə-
steatopygia ˌstɪə.təʊˈpɪdʒ.i.ə, -ˈpaɪ.dʒi-, ˈ-dʒə (US) ˌstiː.æt.əˈpaɪ.dʒi.ə, -ˈpɪdʒ.i-
steatopygous ˌstɪə.təʊˈpaɪ.gəs; stɪəˈtɒp.ɪ- (US) ˌstiː.æt.əˈpaɪ-
Stedman ˈsted.mən
St. Edmunds sᵊntˈed.məndz, sɪnt- (US) seɪnt-
steed stiːd **-s** -z
steel (S) stiːl **-s** -z **-ing** -ɪŋ **-ed** -d ˌ**steel ˈwool**
Steele stiːl
steel-plated ˌstiːlˈpleɪ.tɪd (US) ˈ-ˌ-- *stress shift, British only:* ˌsteel-plated ˈhull
steelworker ˈstiːlˌwɜː.kəʳ (US) ˌwɝː.kɚ **-s** -z
steelworks ˈstiːl.wɜːks (US) -wɝːks
steel|y ˈstiː.l|i **-ier** -i.əʳ (US) -i.ɚ **-iest** -i.ɪst, -i.əst **-iness** -ɪ.nəs, -ɪ.nɪs
steelyard ˈstiːl.jɑːd, ˈstɪl.jəd (US) ˈstiːl.jɑːrd, ˈstɪl.jɚd **-s** -z
steenbok ˈstiːn.bɒk, ˈsteɪn- (US) -bɑːk **-s** -s
Steenson ˈstiːn*t*.sən
steep stiːp **-s** -s **-er** -əʳ (US) -ɚ **-est** -ɪst, -əst **-ly** -li **-ness** -nəs, -nɪs **-ing** -ɪŋ **-ed** -t
steepen ˈstiː.pᵊn **-s** -z **-ing** -ɪŋ, ˈstiːp.nɪŋ **-ed** -d
steeple ˈstiː.pl̩ **-s** -z **-d** -d
steeplechas|e ˈstiː.pl̩.tʃeɪs **-es** -ɪz **-ing** -ɪŋ **-er/s** -əʳ/z (US) -ɚ/z
steeplejack ˈstiː.pl̩.dʒæk **-s** -s
steer stɪəʳ (US) stɪr **-s** -z **-ing** -ɪŋ **-ed** -d **-er/s** -əʳ/z (US) -ɚ/z ˈ**steering** ˌ**gear;** ˈ**steering com**ˌ**mittee;** ˈ**steering** ˌ**wheel**
steerage ˈstɪə.rɪdʒ (US) ˈstɪr.ɪdʒ
steers|man ˈstɪəz|.mən (US) ˈstɪrz- **-men** -mən
steev|e stiːv **-es** -z **-ing** -ɪŋ **-ed** -d
Steevens ˈstiː.vᵊnz
Stefanie ˈstef.ᵊn.i
Steiger ˈstaɪ.gəʳ (US) -gɚ
stein *beer mug:* staɪn *as if German:* ʃtaɪn **-s** -z
Stein *surname:* staɪn, stiːn *as if German:* ʃtaɪn
Steinbeck ˈstaɪn.bek, ˈstaɪm- (US) ˈstaɪn-
steinbock ˈstaɪn.bɒk, ˈstaɪm- (US) ˈstaɪn.bɑːk **-s** -s
Steinbrenner ˈstaɪnˌbren.əʳ, ˈstaɪm- (US) ˈstaɪnˌbren.ɚ
Steinem ˈstaɪ.nəm
Steiner ˈstaɪ.nəʳ (US) -nɚ
Steinway® ˈstaɪn.weɪ **-s** -z
stel|e *monument:* ˈstiː.l|i; stiːl (US) ˈstiː.l|i **-ae** -iː **-es** ˈstiː.liz; stiːlz (US) ˈstiː.liz *in architecture or botany:* ˈstiː.l|i; stiːl (US) stiːl; ˈstiː.l|i **-ae** -iː **-es** ˈstiː.liz; stiːlz (US) stiːlz; ˈstiː.liz
St. Elian sᵊntˈiː.li.ən, sɪnt- (US) seɪnt-
St. Elias sᵊnt.ɪˈlaɪ.əs, sɪnt-, -æs (US) ˌseɪnt.ɪˈlaɪ.əs
Stella ˈstel.ə ˌ**Stella ˈArtois®** *as if French:* ˌ**Stella Arˈtois**
stellar ˈstel.əʳ (US) -ɚ
St. Elmo sᵊntˈel.məʊ, sɪnt- (US) seɪntˈel.moʊ **-'s** -z **St.** ˌ**Elmo's ˈfire**
stem stem **-s** -z **-ming** -ɪŋ **-med** -d
stemple ˈstem.pl̩ **-s** -z
Sten sten ˈ**Sten** ˌ**gun**
stench sten*t*ʃ (US) stentʃ **-es** -ɪz
stencil ˈsten*t*.sᵊl, -ɪl (US) -sᵊl **-s** -z **-(l)ing** -ɪŋ **-(l)ed** -d
Stendhal ˈstɑ̃ːn.dɑːl, -ˈ- (US) ˈsten-, ˈstæn-
Stenhouse ˈsten.haʊs
Stenhousemuir ˌsten.haʊsˈmjʊəʳ, -əsˈ-, -ˈmjɔːʳ (US) -ˈmjʊɚ
Stenness ˈsten.əs
steno ˈsten.əʊ (US) -oʊ **-s** -z
stenograph ˈsten.əʊ.grɑːf, -græf (US) -ə.græf **-s** -s
stenograph|er stəˈnɒg.rə.f|əʳ, stenˈɒg- (US) stəˈnɑː.grə.f|ɚ **-ers** -əz (US) -ɚ **-y** -i
stenotyp|e ˈsten.əʊ.taɪp (US) ˈ-ə- **-ing** -ɪŋ **-ist/s** -ɪst/s
stentorian stenˈtɔː.ri.ən (US) -ˈtɔːr.i-
step step **-s** -s **-ping** -ɪŋ **-ped** -t **-per/s** -əʳ/z (US) -ɚ/z ˌ**step aeˈrobics;** ˈ**step** ˌ**dance;** ˌ**step by ˈstep**
stepbrother ˈstepˌbrʌ.ðəʳ (US) -ðɚ **-s** -z
step|child ˈstep|.tʃaɪld **-children** -ˌtʃɪl.drᵊn
stepdad ˈstep.dæd **-s** -z
stepdaughter ˈstepˌdɔː.təʳ (US) -ˌdɑː.t̬ɚ, -ˌdɔː- **-s** -z
stepfather ˈstepˌfɑː.ðəʳ (US) -ðɚ **-s** -z
Stephanie ˈstef.ᵊn.i
Stephano ˈstef.ᵊn.əʊ (US) -ə.noʊ
stephanotis ˌstef.əˈnəʊ.tɪs (US) -ˈnoʊ.t̬ɪs
Stephen ˈstiː.vᵊn **-s** -z
Stephenson ˈstiː.vᵊn.sᵊn
stepladder ˈstepˌlæd.əʳ (US) -ɚ **-s** -z
stepmother ˈstepˌmʌð.əʳ (US) -ɚ **-s** -z
stepmum ˈstep.mʌm **-s** -z
Stepney ˈstep.ni
stepparent ˈstepˌpeə.rᵊnt (US) -ˌper.ᵊnt, -ˌpær- **-s** -s
steppe step **-s** -s
Steppenwolf ˈstep.ᵊn.wʊlf
stepping-stone ˈstep.ɪŋ.stəʊn (US) -stoʊn **-s** -z

stepsister ˈstepˌsɪs.təʳ ⓤⓢ -tɚ **-s** -z
stepson ˈstep.sʌn **-s** -z
Steptoe ˈstep.təʊ ⓤⓢ -toʊ
-ster -stəʳ ⓤⓢ -stɚ
Note: Suffix. Does not normally change the stress pattern of the word to which it is added, e.g. **prank** /præŋk/, **prankster** /ˈpræŋk.stəʳ ⓤⓢ -stɚ/.
stereo- ster.i.əʊ-, stɪə.ri-; ˌster.iˈɒ-, ˌstɪə.riˈ- ⓤⓢ ster.i.oʊ-, stɪr-, -ə-; ˌster.iˈɑː-, ˌstɪr-
Note: Prefix. Normally either takes primary or secondary stress on the first syllable, e.g. **stereoscope** /ˈster.i.əʊ.skəʊp ⓤⓢ -ə.skoʊp/, **stereophonic** /ˌster.i.əʊˈfɒn.ɪk ⓤⓢ -əˈfɑː.nɪk/, or secondary stress on the first syllable and primary stress on the third syllable, e.g. **stereophony** /ˌster.iˈɒf.ᵊn.i ⓤⓢ -ˈɑː.fᵊn-/.
stereo ˈster.i.əʊ, ˈstɪə.ri- ⓤⓢ ˈster.i.oʊ, ˈstɪr- **-s** -z
stereophonic ˌster.i.əʊˈfɒn.ɪk, ˌstɪə.ri- ⓤⓢ ˌster.i.əˈfɑː.nɪk, ˌstɪr-
stereophony ˌster.iˈɒf.ᵊn.i, ˌstɪə.riˈ- ⓤⓢ ˌster.iˈɑː.fᵊn-, ˌstɪr-
stereopticon ˌster.iˈɒp.tɪ.kən, ˌstɪə.riˈ- ⓤⓢ ˌster.iˈɑːp-, ˌstɪr-, -kɑːn **-s** -z
stereoscope ˈster.i.ə.skəʊp, ˈstɪə.ri- ⓤⓢ ˈster.i.ə.skoʊp, ˈstɪr- **-s** -s
stereoscopic ˌster.i.əˈskɒp.ɪk, ˌstɪə.ri- ⓤⓢ ˌster.i.əˈskɑː.pɪk, ˌstɪr- **-al** -ᵊl **-ally** -ᵊl.i, -li
stereoscopy ˌster.iˈɒs.kə.pi, ˌstɪə.riˈ- ⓤⓢ ˌster.iˈɑː.skə-, ˌstɪr-
stereotyp|e ˈster.i.əʊ.taɪp, ˈstɪə.ri- ⓤⓢ ˈster.i.ə-, ˈstɪr- **-es** -s **-ing** -ɪŋ **-ed** -t
stereotypic|al ˌster.i.əʊˈtɪp.ɪ.k|ᵊl, ˌstɪə.ri- ⓤⓢ ˌster.i.əˈ-, ˌstɪr- **-ally** -ᵊl.i, -li
sterile ˈster.aɪl ⓤⓢ -ᵊl
sterility stəˈrɪl.ə.ti, sterˈɪl-, -ɪ.ti ⓤⓢ stəˈrɪl.ə.t̬i
sterilization, -isa- ˌster.ᵊl.aɪˈzeɪ.ʃᵊn, -ɪ.laɪˈ-, -lɪˈ- ⓤⓢ -ᵊl.ɪˈ- **-s** -z
sterilizle, -is|e ˈster.ᵊl.aɪz, -ɪ.laɪz ⓤⓢ -ə.laɪz **-es** -ɪz **-ing** -ɪŋ **-ed** -d **-er/s** -əʳ/z ⓤⓢ -ɚ/z
sterling (S) ˈstɜː.lɪŋ ⓤⓢ ˈstɝː-
stern (S) *(adj.)* stɜːn ⓤⓢ stɝːn **-er** -əʳ ⓤⓢ -ɚ **-est** -ɪst, -əst **-ly** -li **-ness** -nəs, -nɪs
Sterne stɜːn ⓤⓢ stɝːn
stern|um ˈstɜː.n|əm ⓤⓢ ˈstɝː- **-ums** -əmz **-a** -ə
steroid ˈster.ɔɪd, ˈstɪə.rɔɪd ⓤⓢ ˈster-, ˈstɪr- **-s** -z
stertorous ˈstɜː.tᵊr.əs ⓤⓢ ˈstɝː.t̬ɚ- **-ly** -li **-ness** -nəs, -nɪs
stet stet **-s** -s **-ting** -ɪŋ ⓤⓢ ˈstet̬.ɪŋ **-ted** -ɪd ⓤⓢ ˈstet̬.ɪd
stethoscope ˈsteθ.ə.skəʊp ⓤⓢ -skoʊp **-s** -s
stethoscopic ˌsteθ.əˈskɒp.ɪk ⓤⓢ -ˈskɑː.pɪk **-al** -ᵊl **-ally** -ᵊl.i, -li
stethoscopy steθˈɒs.kə.pi ⓤⓢ -ˈɑː.skə-
Stetson® ˈstet.sᵊn
Steve stiːv
stevedore ˈstiː.və.dɔːʳ, -vɪ- ⓤⓢ -və.dɔːr **-s** -z
Steven ˈstiː.vᵊn **-s** -z
Stevenage ˈstiː.vᵊn.ɪdʒ
Stevenson ˈstiː.vᵊn.sᵊn
Stevenston ˈstiː.vᵊn.stᵊn
Stevie ˈstiː.vi
stew stjuː ⓤⓢ stuː, stjuː **-s** -z **-ing** -ɪŋ **-ed** -d
steward (S) ˈstjuː.əd, stjʊəd ⓤⓢ ˈstuː.ɚd, ˈstjuː- **-s** -z **-ing** -ɪŋ **-ed** -ɪd
stewardess ˈstjuː.ə.dɪs, ˈstjʊə-, -dəs, -des; ˌstjuː.əˈdes ⓤⓢ ˈstuː.ɚ.dɪs, ˈstjuː- **-es** -ɪz
stewardship ˈstjuː.əd.ʃɪp, ˈstjʊəd- ⓤⓢ ˈstuː.ɚd-, ˈstjuː-
Stewart stjʊət, ˈstjuː.ət ⓤⓢ ˈstuː.ɚt, ˈstjuː-, stʊrt
Stewarton ˈstjʊə.tᵊn, ˈstjuː.ə- ⓤⓢ ˈstuː.ɚ-, ˈstjuː-, stʊr.tᵊn
Steyn staɪn
Steyne stiːn
Steyning ˈsten.ɪŋ
St. Fagans sᵊn*t*ˈfæg.ᵊnz, sɪn*t*- ⓤⓢ seɪntˈfæg-, -ˈfeɪ.gᵊnz
St. Francis sᵊn*t*ˈfrɑːn*t*.sɪs, sɪn*t*- ⓤⓢ seɪntˈfræn*t*-
stg. *(abbrev. for* **sterling***)* ˈstɜː.lɪŋ ⓤⓢ ˈstɝː-
St. Gall sᵊn*t*ˈgæl, sɪn*t*-, -gɑːl, -gɔːl ⓤⓢ seɪnt-
St. Gallen sᵊn*t*ˈgæl.ən, sɪn*t*- ⓤⓢ seɪntˈgɑː.lən
St. George sᵊn*t*ˈdʒɔːdʒ, sɪn*t*- ⓤⓢ seɪntˈdʒɔːrdʒ **-'s** -ɪz
St. Giles sᵊn*t*ˈdʒaɪlz, sɪn*t*- ⓤⓢ seɪnt- **-'s** -ɪz
St. Godric sᵊn*t*ˈgɒd.rɪk, sɪn*t*- ⓤⓢ seɪntˈgɑː.drɪk
St. Gotthard sᵊn*t*ˈgɒt.əd, sɪn*t*-, -ɑːd ⓤⓢ seɪntˈgɑː.t̬ɚd
St. Helen sᵊntˈhel.ən, sɪnt-, -ɪn ⓤⓢ seɪntˈhel.ən **-s** -z
St. Helena *Saint:* sᵊntˈhel.ə.nə, sɪnt-, ˈ-ɪ- ⓤⓢ ˌseɪnt.həˈliː-; seɪntˈhel.ə- *island:* ˌsent.*h*ɪˈliː.nə, ˌsɪnt-, sᵊnt-, -*h*əˈ- ⓤⓢ ˌseɪnt.həˈ-; seɪntˈhel.ə-
St. Helier sᵊntˈhel.i.əʳ, sɪnt- ⓤⓢ seɪntˈhel.jɚ **-s** -z
Stich stɪx *as if German:* ʃtiːx
stichomythia ˌstɪk.əʊˈmɪθ.i.ə ⓤⓢ -əˈ-, -oʊˈ- **-s** -z
stick stɪk **-s** -s **-ing** -ɪŋ **stuck** stʌk **ˈstick ˌinsect; ˈsticking ˌplaster; ˈstick ˌshift; get (ˌhold of) the ˌwrong ˌend of the ˈstick**
sticker ˈstɪk.əʳ ⓤⓢ -ɚ **-s** -z
stick-in-the-mud ˈstɪk.ɪn.ðəˌmʌd **-s** -z
stickjaw ˈstɪk.dʒɔː ⓤⓢ -dʒɑː, -dʒɔː **-s** -z
stickleback ˈstɪk.l̩.bæk **-s** -s
stickler ˈstɪk.ləʳ, -l̩.ɚ ⓤⓢ ˈ-lɚ, -l̩.ɚ **-s** -z
stick-on ˈstɪk.ɒn ⓤⓢ -ɑːn
stickpin ˈstɪk.pɪn
stick-up ˈstɪk.ʌp **-s** -s
stick|y ˈstɪk|.i **-ier** -i.əʳ ⓤⓢ -i.ɚ **-iest** -i.ɪst, -i.əst **-ily** -ɪ.li, -ᵊl.i **-iness** -ɪ.nəs, -ɪ.nɪs
stickybeak ˈstɪk.i.biːk **-s** -s
stiff stɪf **-er** -əʳ ⓤⓢ -ɚ **-est** -ɪst, -əst **-ing** -ɪŋ **-ed** -t **-ly** -li **-ness** -nəs, -nɪs **ˌstiff ˌupper ˈlip**
stiffen ˈstɪf.ᵊn **-s** -z **-ing** -ɪŋ, ˈstɪf.nɪŋ **-ed** -d
Stiffkey ˈstɪf.ki *old-fashioned local pronunciation:* ˈstjuː.ki, ˈstuː-
stiff-necked ˌstɪfˈnekt ⓤⓢ ˈstɪf.nekt *stress shift:* ˌstiff-necked ˈpride
stifl|e ˈstaɪ.fl̩ **-es** -z **-ing/ly** -ɪŋ/li, ˈstaɪ.flɪŋ/li **-ed** -d
Stiggins ˈstɪg.ɪnz
stigma ˈstɪg.mə **-s** -z **-tism** -tɪ.zᵊm
stigmata *(alternative plur. of* **stigmata***)* stɪgˈmɑː.tə ⓤⓢ -t̬ə, -ˈmæt̬.ə
stigmatic stɪgˈmæt.ɪk ⓤⓢ -ˈmæt̬-
stigmatization, -isa- ˌstɪg.mə.taɪˈzeɪ.ʃᵊn, -tɪˈ- ⓤⓢ -t̬ɪˈ-
stigmatiz|e, -is|e ˈstɪg.mə.taɪz **-es** -ɪz **-ing** -ɪŋ **-ed** -d
stilbene ˈstɪl.biːn
stilbestrol stɪlˈbiː.strəl, -ˈbes.trəl ⓤⓢ -ˈbes.trɔːl, -troʊl
stile staɪl **-s** -z
stiletto stɪˈlet.əʊ ⓤⓢ -ˈlet̬.oʊ **-(e)s** -z
still (S) stɪl **-s** -z **-er** -əʳ ⓤⓢ -ɚ/z **-est** -ɪst, -əst **-ness** -nəs, -nɪs **-ing** -ɪŋ **-ed** -d **ˌstill ˈlife** *stress shift:* ˌstill life ˈpainting
stillbirth ˈstɪl.bɜːθ ⓤⓢ -bɝːθ **-s** -s
stillborn ˈstɪl.bɔːn ⓤⓢ ˈstɪl.bɔːrn
Stillson ˈstɪl.sᵊn **ˈStillson ˌwrench®**
stilly ˈstɪl.i
stilt stɪlt **-s** -s
stilted ˈstɪl.tɪd ⓤⓢ -t̬ɪd **-ly** -li **-ness** -nəs, -nɪs
Stilton ˈstɪl.tᵊn **-s** -z
Stimpson ˈstɪmp.sᵊn
Stimson ˈstɪm*p*.sᵊn
stimulant ˈstɪm.jə.lənt, -jʊ- **-s** -s
stimu|late ˈstɪm.jə|.leɪt, -jʊ- **-lates** -leɪts **-lating** -leɪ.tɪŋ ⓤⓢ -leɪ.t̬ɪŋ **-lated** -leɪ.tɪd ⓤⓢ -leɪ.t̬ɪd **-lator/s** -leɪ.təʳ/z ⓤⓢ -leɪ.t̬ɚ/z
stimulation ˌstɪm.jəˈleɪ.ʃᵊn, -jʊˈ- **-s** -z

stimulative ˈstɪm.jə.lə.tɪv, -jʊ-, -leɪ- ⓤⓢ -leɪ.t̬ɪv
stimul|us ˈstɪm.jə.l|əs, -jʊ- **-i** -aɪ, -iː
stim|y ˈstaɪ.m|i **-ies** -iz **-ying** -i.ɪŋ **-ied** -id
sting stɪŋ **-s** -z **-ing** -ɪŋ **stung** stʌŋ **stinger/s** ˈstɪŋ.əʳ/z ⓤⓢ -ɚ/z ˈ**stinging** ˌ**nettle**
stingo ˈstɪŋ.gəʊ ⓤⓢ -goʊ **-s** -z
stingray ˈstɪŋ.reɪ **-s** -z
sting|y ˈstɪn.dʒ|i **-ier** -i.əʳ ⓤⓢ -i.ɚ **-iest** -i.ɪst, -i.əst **-ily** -ɪ.li, -əl.i **-iness** -ɪ.nəs, -ɪ.nɪs
stink stɪŋk **-s** -s **-ing** -ɪŋ **stank** stæŋk **stunk** stʌŋk
stink-bomb ˈstɪŋk.bɒm ⓤⓢ -bɑːm **-s** -z
stinker ˈstɪŋ.kəʳ ⓤⓢ -kɚ **-s** -z
stinkpot ˈstɪŋk.pɒt ⓤⓢ -pɑːt **-s** -s
stint stɪnt **-s** -s **-ing** -ɪŋ ⓤⓢ ˈstɪn.t̬ɪŋ **-ed** -ɪd ⓤⓢ ˈstɪn.t̬ɪd
stipend ˈstaɪ.pend, -pənd **-s** -z
stipendiar|y staɪˈpen.di.ər|.i, stɪ- ⓤⓢ staɪˈpen.di.er- **-ies** -iz
stippl|e ˈstɪp.l̩ **-es** -z **-ing** -ɪŋ, ˈstɪp.lɪŋ **-ed** -d **-er/s** -əʳ/z ⓤⓢ -ɚ/z
stipu|late ˈstɪp.jə|.leɪt, -jʊ- **-lates** -leɪts **-lating** -leɪ.tɪŋ ⓤⓢ -leɪ.t̬ɪŋ **-lated** -leɪ.tɪd ⓤⓢ -leɪ.t̬ɪd
stipulation ˌstɪp.jəˈleɪ.ʃən, -jʊˈ- **-s** -z
stipule ˈstɪp.juːl **-s** -z
stir stɜːʳ ⓤⓢ stɝː **-s** -z **-ring/ly** -ɪŋ/li **-red** -d **-rer/s** -əʳ/z ⓤⓢ -ɚ/z
stir|-fry ˈstɜː|ˌfraɪ ⓤⓢ ˈstɝː- **-fries** -ˈfraɪz ⓤⓢ -fraɪz **-frying** -ˈfraɪ.ɪŋ ⓤⓢ -ˌfraɪ.ɪŋ **-fried** -ˈfraɪd ⓤⓢ -fraɪd *stress shift, British only:* ˌstir-fried ˈvegetables
Stirling ˈstɜː.lɪŋ ⓤⓢ ˈstɝː- **-shire** -ʃəʳ, -ˌʃɪəʳ ⓤⓢ -ʃɚ, -ˌʃɪr
stirp|s stɜːp|s ⓤⓢ stɝːp|s **-es** -iːz, -eɪz
stirrup ˈstɪr.əp ⓤⓢ ˈstɝː-, ˈstɪr- **-s** -s ˈ**stirrup** ˌ**pump**
stitch stɪtʃ **-es** -ɪz **-ing** -ɪŋ **-ed** -t
St. Ivel sənt ˈaɪ.vəl, sɪnt- ⓤⓢ seɪnt-
St. Ives sənt ˈaɪvz, sɪnt- ⓤⓢ seɪnt-
St. James sən*t*ˈdʒeɪmz, sɪnt- ⓤⓢ seɪnt- **-'s** -ɪz
St. Joan sən*t*ˈdʒəʊn, sɪn*t*- ⓤⓢ seɪntˈdʒoʊn
St. John *Saint, place:* sən*t*ˈdʒɒn, sɪn*t*- ⓤⓢ seɪntˈdʒɑːn **-'s** -z *surname:* ˈsɪn.dʒən ⓤⓢ seɪntˈdʒɑːn **-'s** -z
St. Joseph sən*t*ˈdʒəʊ.zɪf, sɪn*t*-, -zəf ⓤⓢ seɪntˈdʒoʊ.zəf, -səf
St. Kilda sən*t*ˈkɪl.də, sɪn*t*- ⓤⓢ seɪnt-
St. Kitts sən*t*ˈkɪts, sɪnt- ⓤⓢ seɪnt-
St. Kitts-Nevis sən*t*ˌkɪtsˈniː.vɪs, sɪnt- ⓤⓢ seɪnt-
St. Laurent *Yves:* ˌsæ̃n.lɔːˈrɑ̃ːŋ, -ləˈ- ⓤⓢ -lɔːˈrɑːn *place in Canada:* ˌsæn.lɔːˈrɒ̃ŋ, -ləˈ-, -ˈrɑːnt ⓤⓢ ˌsæ̃.lɔːˈrɑːn, ˌsæn.lɔːˈrent

St. Lawrence sən*t*ˈlɒr.ənts, sɪn*t*- ⓤⓢ seɪntˈlɔːr- **St.** ˌ**Lawrence** ˈ**Seaway**
St. Leger *surname:* sən*t*ˈledʒ.əʳ, sɪnt-; ˈsel.ɪn.dʒəʳ ⓤⓢ seɪntˈledʒ.ɚ; ˈsel.ɪn.dʒɚ
Note: Most people bearing this name (including the Irish families) pronounce /sən*t*ˈledʒ.əʳ ⓤⓢ seɪnt-/. But there are members of the Doncaster family who pronounce /ˈsel.ɪn.dʒəʳ ⓤⓢ -dʒɚ/.
St. Leger *race:* sən*t*ˈledʒ.əʳ, sɪnt- ⓤⓢ seɪntˈledʒ.ɚ
St. Leonards sən*t*ˈlen.ədz, sɪnt- ⓤⓢ seɪntˈlen.ɚdz *city in Quebec:* sænˈleɪ.əʊ.nɑːʳ, -oʊ.nɑːr
St. Levan sən*t*ˈlev.ən, sɪnt- ⓤⓢ seɪnt-
St. Louis *city in US:* sən*t*ˈluː.ɪs, sɪnt- ⓤⓢ seɪnt-, -i *sometimes locally:* sænt- *places in Canada:* sən*t*ˈluː.i, sɪn*t*-, -ɪs ⓤⓢ seɪnt-
St. Lucia sən*t*ˈluː.ʃə, sɪnt-, -ʃi.ə, -si.ə ⓤⓢ seɪntˈluː.ʃi.ə, -si-, ˈ-ʃə
St. Ludger sən*t*ˈluː.dʒəʳ, sɪnt- ⓤⓢ seɪntˈluː.dʒɚ
St. Luke sən*t*ˈluːk, sɪnt- ⓤⓢ seɪnt-
St. Malo sən*t*ˈmɑː.ləʊ, sɪn*t*-, sæ̃n- *as if French:* ˌsæ̃n.mɑːˈləʊ ⓤⓢ ˌsæn.mɑːˈloʊ
St. Margaret sən*t*ˈmɑː.gər.ɪt, sɪn*t*-, ˈ-grɪt ⓤⓢ seɪntˈmɑːr.grət **-'s** -s
St. Mark sən*t*ˈmɑːk, sɪn*t*- ⓤⓢ seɪntˈmɑːrk **-'s** -s
St. Martin sən*t*ˈmɑː.tɪn, sɪn*t*- ⓤⓢ seɪntˈmɑːr.tən **-'s** -z
St. Mary sən*t*ˈmeə.ri, sɪn*t*- ⓤⓢ seɪntˈmer.i **-'s** -z
St. Mary Axe sən*t*ˌmeə.riˈæks, sɪn*t*- ⓤⓢ seɪntˌmer.iˈ-
Note: The old form /ˌsɪm.ər.iˈæks/ is used in Gilbert and Sullivan's opera 'The Sorcerer'.
St. Marylebone sən*t*ˈmær.əl.ə.bən, sɪn*t*-, -ɪ.lə- ⓤⓢ seɪntˈmer.əl.ə.boʊn
St. Mary-le-Bow sən*t*ˌmeə.ri.ləˈbəʊ, sɪn*t*- ⓤⓢ seɪntˌmer.i.ləˈboʊ
St. Matthew sən*t*ˈmæθ.juː, sɪn*t*- ⓤⓢ seɪnt-
St. Mawes sən*t*ˈmɔːz, sɪn*t*- ⓤⓢ seɪntˈmɑːz, -ˈmɔːz
St. Michael sən*t*ˈmaɪ.kəl, sɪn*t*- ⓤⓢ seɪnt- **-'s** -z
St. Moritz ˌsæn.məˈrɪts, ˌsæm-; sən*t*ˈmɒr.ɪts, sɪnt- ⓤⓢ ˌsæn.məˈrɪts, ˌseɪnt-, -mɔːˈ-
St. Neots sən*t*ˈniː.əts, sɪn*t*-, -niːts ⓤⓢ seɪnt-
St. Nicholas sən*t*ˈnɪk.əl.əs, sɪnt-, ˈ-ləs ⓤⓢ seɪnt-
stoat stəʊt ⓤⓢ stoʊt **-s** -s
Stobart ˈstəʊ.bɑːt ⓤⓢ ˈstoʊ.bɑːrt

stochastic stɒkˈæs.tɪk, stəˈkæs- ⓤⓢ stoʊˈkæs-, stə-
stock stɒk ⓤⓢ stɑːk **-s** -s **-ing** -ɪŋ **-ed** -t ˈ**stock** ˌ**car**; ˈ**stock** ˌ**cube**; ˈ**stock** **ex**ˌ**change**; ˈ**stock** ˌ**market**
stockad|e stɒkˈeɪd ⓤⓢ stɑːˈkeɪd **-es** -z **-ing** -ɪŋ **-ed** -ɪd
stockbreed|er ˈstɒkˌbriː.d|əʳ ⓤⓢ ˈstɑːkˌbriː.d|ɚ **-ers** -əz ⓤⓢ -ɚz **-ing** -ɪŋ
Stockbridge ˈstɒk.brɪdʒ ⓤⓢ ˈstɑːk-
stockbrok|er ˈstɒkˌbrəʊ.k|əʳ ⓤⓢ ˈstɑːkˌbroʊ.k|ɚ **-ers** -əʳz ⓤⓢ -ɚz **-ing** -ɪŋ ˈ**stockbroker** ˌ**belt**
stockfish ˈstɒk.fɪʃ ⓤⓢ ˈstɑːk-
Stockhausen ˈstɒkˌhaʊ.zən *as if German:* ˈʃtɒk- ⓤⓢ ˈstɑːk-
stockholder ˈstɒkˌhəʊl.dəʳ ⓤⓢ ˈstɑːkˌhoʊl.dɚ **-s** -z
Stockholm ˈstɒk.həʊm ⓤⓢ ˈstɑːk.hoʊlm, -hoʊm
stockinet(te) ˌstɒk.ɪˈnet ⓤⓢ ˌstɑː.kɪˈ-
stocking ˈstɒk.ɪŋ ⓤⓢ ˈstɑː.kɪŋ **-s** -z **-ed** -d ˈ**stocking** ˌ**cap**; ˈ**stocking** ˌ**filler**; ˈ**stocking** ˌ**stitch**; **in one's** ˌ**stocking/ed** ˈ**feet**
stock-in-trade ˌstɒk.ɪnˈtreɪd ⓤⓢ ˌstɑːk-
stockist ˈstɒk.ɪst ⓤⓢ ˈstɑː.kɪst **-s** -s
stockjobb|er ˈstɒkˌdʒɒb|.əʳ ⓤⓢ ˈstɑːkˌdʒɑː.b|ɚ **-ers** -əz ⓤⓢ -ɚz **-ing** -ɪŋ
stock|man (S) ˈstɒk.mən ⓤⓢ ˈstɑːk- **-men** -men, -mən
stockpil|e ˈstɒk.paɪl ⓤⓢ ˈstɑːk- **-es** -z **-ing** -ɪŋ **-ed** -d
Stockport ˈstɒk.pɔːt ⓤⓢ ˈstɑːk.pɔːrt
stockpot ˈstɒk.pɒt ⓤⓢ ˈstɑːk.pɑːt **-s** -s
stockroom ˈstɒk.rʊm, -ruːm ⓤⓢ ˈstɑːk.ruːm, -rʊm **-s** -z
Stocksbridge ˈstɒks.brɪdʒ ⓤⓢ ˈstɑːks-
stock-still ˌstɒkˈstɪl ⓤⓢ ˌstɑːk-
stocktaking ˈstɒkˌteɪ.kɪŋ ⓤⓢ ˈstɑːk-
Stockton ˈstɒk.tən ⓤⓢ ˈstɑːk-
Stockton-on-Tees ˌstɒk.tən.ɒnˈtiːz ⓤⓢ ˌstɑːk.tən.ɑːnˈ-
Stockwell ˈstɒk.wel, -wəl ⓤⓢ ˈstɑːk-
stock|y ˈstɒk|.i ⓤⓢ ˈstɑː.k|i **-ier** -i.əʳ ⓤⓢ -i.ɚ **-iest** -i.ɪst, -i.əst **-iness** -ɪ.nəs, -ɪ.nɪs **-ily** -ɪ.li
stockyard ˈstɒk.jɑːd ⓤⓢ ˈstɑːk.jɑːrd **-s** -z
Stoddard ˈstɒd.əd, -ɑːd ⓤⓢ ˈstɑː.dɚd
Stoddart ˈstɒd.ət, -ɑːt ⓤⓢ ˈstɑː.dɚt
stodg|e stɒdʒ ⓤⓢ stɑːdʒ **-es** -ɪz **-ing** -ɪŋ **-ed** -d **-y** -i **-ier** -i.əʳ ⓤⓢ -i.ɚ **-iest** -i.ɪst, -i.əst **-iness** -ɪ.nəs, -ɪ.nɪs
stoep stuːp **-s** -s
Stogumber *in Somerset:* stəʊˈgʌm.bəʳ; ˈstɒg.əm- ⓤⓢ stoʊˈgʌm.bɚ; ˈstɑː.gəm- *character in Shaw's 'Saint Joan':* ˈstɒg.əm.bəʳ ⓤⓢ ˈstɑː.gəm.bɚ, ˈstɔː-

Stogursey stəʊˈgɜː.zi ⓤⓢ stoʊˈgɝː-

stoic (S) ˈstəʊ.ɪk ⓤⓢ ˈstoʊ- **-s** -s **-al** -ᵊl **-ally** -ᵊl.i, -li

stoicism (S) ˈstəʊ.ɪ.sɪ.zᵊm, ˈ-ə- ⓤⓢ ˈstoʊ.ɪ-

stok|e (S) stəʊk ⓤⓢ stoʊk **-es** -s **-ing** -ɪŋ **-ed** -t **-er/s** -əʳ/z ⓤⓢ -ɚ/z

Stoke Courcy stəʊˈgɜː.zi ⓤⓢ stoʊˈgɝː-

Stoke d'Abernon ˌstəʊkˈdæb.ᵊn.ən ⓤⓢ ˌstoʊkˈdæb.ɚ.nən

stokehold ˈstəʊk.həʊld ⓤⓢ ˈstoʊk.hoʊld **-s** -z

stokehole ˈstəʊk.həʊl ⓤⓢ ˈstoʊk.hoʊl **-s** -z

Stoke Mandeville ˌstəʊkˈmæn.də.vɪl, ˈ-dɪ- ⓤⓢ ˌstoʊk-

Stoke on Trent ˌstəʊk.ɒnˈtrent ⓤⓢ ˌstoʊk.ɑːnˈ-

Stoke Poges ˌstəʊkˈpəʊ.dʒɪz ⓤⓢ ˌstoʊkˈpoʊ-

stoker (S) ˈstəʊ.kəʳ ⓤⓢ ˈstoʊ.kɚ **-s** -z

STOL stɒl, ˈes.tɒl ⓤⓢ stɑːl, ˈes.tɑːl

St. Olaves, St. Olave's sᵊntˈɒl.ɪvz, sɪnt-, -əvz ⓤⓢ seɪntˈɑː.lɪvz, -ləvz

stole (S) stəʊl ⓤⓢ stoʊl **-s** -z

stol|e *(from* **steal***)* stəʊl ⓤⓢ stoʊl **-en** -ən

stolid ˈstɒl.ɪd ⓤⓢ ˈstɑː.lɪd **-est** -ɪst, -əst **-ly** -li

stolidity stɒlˈɪd.ə.ti, stəˈlɪd-, -ɪ.ti ⓤⓢ stəˈlɪd.ə.t̬i

Stoll stəʊl, stɒl ⓤⓢ stoʊl, stɑːl

stollen ˈstɒl.ən *as if German:* ˈʃtɒl- ⓤⓢ ˈstoʊ.lən *as if German:* ˈʃtoʊ- **-s** -z

stolon ˈstəʊ.lɒn, -lən ⓤⓢ ˈstoʊ.lɑːn, -lən **-s** -z

stoma ˈstəʊ.mə ⓤⓢ ˈstoʊ- **-s** -z **-ta** -tə

stomach ˈstʌm.ək **-s** -s **-ing** -ɪŋ **-ed** -t **ˈstomach ˌpump**

stomachache ˈstʌm.ək.eɪk **-s** -s

stomacher ˈstʌm.ə.kəʳ ⓤⓢ -kɚ **-s** -z

stomachic stəʊˈmæk.ɪk, stɒmˈæk-; ˈstʌm.ə.kɪk ⓤⓢ stəˈmæk.ɪk

stomati|tis ˌstəʊ.məˈtaɪ|.tɪs, ˌstɒm.əˈ- ⓤⓢ ˌstoʊ.məˈtaɪ|.t̬ɪs, ˌstɑː- **-tides** -tɪ.diːz **-tises** -tɪ.siːz, -tɪ.ziːz

stomatoscope stəʊˈmæt.ə.skəʊp, stɒmˈæt- ⓤⓢ stoʊˈmæt̬.ə.skoʊp, stɑː- **-s** -s

stomp stɒmp ⓤⓢ stɑːmp **-s** -s **-ing** -ɪŋ **-ed** -t

ston|e (S) stəʊn ⓤⓢ stoʊn **-es** -z **-ing** -ɪŋ **-ed** -d **-y** -i **ˈStone ˌAge; kill ˌtwo ˌbirds with ˌone ˈstone; leave ˌno ˌstone unˈturned; a ˈstone's ˌthrow, a ˌstone's ˈthrow**

stone-blind ˌstəʊnˈblaɪnd, ˌstəʊm- ⓤⓢ ˌstoʊn- **-ness** -nəs, -nɪs

stonechat ˈstəʊn.tʃæt ⓤⓢ ˈstoʊn- **-s** -s

stone-cold ˌstəʊnˈkəʊld, ˌstəʊŋ- ⓤⓢ ˌstoʊnˈkoʊld *stress shift, see compound:* **ˌstone-cold ˈsober**

stonecrop ˈstəʊn.krɒp, ˈstəʊŋ- ⓤⓢ ˈstoʊn.krɑːp **-s** -s

stonecutter ˈstəʊnˌkʌt.əʳ, ˈstəʊŋ- ⓤⓢ ˈstoʊnˌkʌt̬.ɚ **-s** -z

stone-dead ˌstəʊnˈded ⓤⓢ ˌstoʊn-

stone-deaf ˌstəʊnˈdef ⓤⓢ ˌstoʊn- **-ness** -nəs, -nɪs

stonefish ˈstəʊn.fɪʃ ⓤⓢ ˈstoʊn- **-es** -ɪz

stoneground ˌstəʊnˈgraʊnd, ˌstəʊŋ- ⓤⓢ ˌstoʊn-

Stonehaven ˈstəʊnˌheɪ.vᵊn ⓤⓢ ˈstoʊn-

Stonehenge ˌstəʊnˈhendʒ ⓤⓢ ˈstoʊn.hendʒ

Stonehouse ˈstəʊn.haʊs ⓤⓢ ˈstoʊn-

stonemason ˈstəʊnˌmeɪ.sᵊn, ˈstəʊm- ⓤⓢ ˈstoʊn- **-s** -z

stonewall (S) ˌstəʊnˈwɔːl ⓤⓢ ˈstoʊn- **-s** -z **-ing** -ɪŋ **-ed** -d **-er/s** -əʳ/z ⓤⓢ -ɚ/z

stoneware ˈstəʊn.weəʳ ⓤⓢ ˈstoʊn.wer

stone-washed ˌstəʊnˈwɒʃt ⓤⓢ ˌstoʊnˈwɑːʃt *stress shift, British only:* ˌstonewashed ˈjeans

stonework ˈstəʊn.wɜːk ⓤⓢ ˈstoʊn.wɝːk

Stoney ˈstəʊ.ni ⓤⓢ ˈstoʊ-

stonking ˈstɒŋ.kɪŋ ⓤⓢ ˈstɑːŋ- **-ly** -li

Stonor ˈstəʊ.nəʳ, ˈstɒn.əʳ ⓤⓢ ˈstoʊ.nɚ, ˈstɑː.nɚ

ston|y ˈstəʊ.n|i ⓤⓢ ˈstoʊ- **-ier** -i.əʳ ⓤⓢ -i.ɚ **-iest** -i.ɪst, -i.əst **-ily** -ɪ.li, -ᵊl.i **-iness** -ɪ.nəs, -ɪ.nɪs **ˌstony ˈbroke**

stony-hearted ˌstəʊ.niˈhɑː.tɪd ⓤⓢ ˈstoʊ.niˌhɑːr.t̬ɪd **-ness** -nəs, -nɪs

Stony Stratford ˌstəʊ.niˈstræt.fəd ⓤⓢ ˌstoʊ.niˈstræt.fɚd

stood *(from* **stand***)* stʊd

stoog|e stuːdʒ **-es** -ɪz **-ing** -ɪŋ **-ed** -d

stook stuːk, stʊk **-s** -s

stool stuːl **-s** -z **ˈstool ˌpigeon; ˌfall beˌtween two ˈstools**

stoop stuːp **-s** -s **-ing** -ɪŋ **-ed** -t **-er/s** -əʳ/z ⓤⓢ -ɚ/z

stop stɒp ⓤⓢ stɑːp **-s** -s **-ping** -ɪŋ **-ped** -t **-per/s** -əʳ/z ⓤⓢ -ɚ/z **ˈstop ˌvolley**

stopcock ˈstɒp.kɒk ⓤⓢ ˈstɑːp.kɑːk **-s** -s

Stopes stəʊps ⓤⓢ stoʊps

Stopford ˈstɒp.fəd ⓤⓢ ˈstɑːp.fɚd

stopgap ˈstɒp.gæp ⓤⓢ ˈstɑːp- **-s** -s

stop-go ˌstɒpˈgəʊ ⓤⓢ ˌstɑːpˈgoʊ

stoplight ˈstɒp.laɪt ⓤⓢ ˈstɑːp- **-s** -s

stopover ˈstɒpˌəʊ.vəʳ ⓤⓢ ˈstɑːpˌoʊ.vɚ **-s** -z

stoppag|e ˈstɒp.ɪdʒ ⓤⓢ ˈstɑː.pɪdʒ **-es** -ɪz

Stoppard ˈstɒp.ɑːd, -əd ⓤⓢ ˈstɑː.pɚd

stopper ˈstɒp.əʳ ⓤⓢ ˈstɑː.pɚ **-s** -z **-ing** -ɪŋ **-ed** -d

stop-press ˌstɒpˈpres ⓤⓢ ˌstɑːp-

stopwatch ˈstɒp.wɒtʃ ⓤⓢ ˈstɑːp.wɑːtʃ, -wɔːtʃ **-es** -ɪz

storage ˈstɔː.rɪdʒ ⓤⓢ ˈstɔːr.ɪdʒ **ˈstorage ˌheater**

stor|e stɔːʳ ⓤⓢ stɔːr **-es** -z **-ing** -ɪŋ **-ed** -d **-able** -ə.bl̩ **ˈstore ˌbrand; ˈstore deˌtective, ˌstore deˈtective**

storefront ˈstɔː.frʌnt ⓤⓢ ˈstɔːr- **-s** -s

storehou|se ˈstɔː.haʊ|s ⓤⓢ ˈstɔːr- **-ses** -zɪz

storekeep|er ˈstɔːˌkiː.p|əʳ ⓤⓢ ˈstɔːrˌkiː.p|ɚ **-ers** -əz ⓤⓢ -ɚz **-ing** -ɪŋ

storeroom ˈstɔː.rʊm, -ruːm ⓤⓢ ˈstɔːr.ruːm, -rʊm **-s** -z

storey (S) ˈstɔː.ri ⓤⓢ ˈstɔːr.i **-s** -z **-ed** -d

storiated ˈstɔː.ri.eɪ.tɪd ⓤⓢ ˈstɔːr.i.eɪ.t̬ɪd

stork stɔːk ⓤⓢ stɔːrk **-s** -s

storm (S) stɔːm ⓤⓢ stɔːrm **-s** -z **-ing** -ɪŋ **-ed** -d **ˈstorm ˌcloud; ˈstorm ˌlantern; ˈstorm ˌpetrel; ˈstorm ˌtrooper; ˈstorm ˌwindow; a ˌstorm in a ˈteacup**

stormbound ˈstɔːm.baʊnd ⓤⓢ ˈstɔːrm-

Stormont ˈstɔː.mɒnt, -mənt ⓤⓢ ˈstɔːr.mɑːnt, -mənt

Stormonth ˈstɔː.mənθ, -mʌnθ ⓤⓢ ˈstɔːr-

stormproof ˈstɔːm.pruːf ⓤⓢ ˈstɔːrm-

storm|y ˈstɔː.m|i ⓤⓢ ˈstɔːr- **-ier** -i.əʳ ⓤⓢ -i.ɚ **-iest** -i.ɪst, -i.əst **-ily** -ɪ.li, -ᵊl.i **-iness** -ɪ.nəs, -ɪ.nɪs

Stornoway ˈstɔː.nə.weɪ ⓤⓢ ˈstɔːr-

Storr stɔːʳ ⓤⓢ stɔːr **-s** -z

Storrington ˈstɒr.ɪŋ.tən ⓤⓢ ˈstɔːr-

Stort stɔːt ⓤⓢ stɔːrt

Stortford ˈstɔːt.fəd, ˈstɔː- ⓤⓢ ˈstɔːrt.fɚd, ˈstɔːr-

Storthing ˈstɔː.tɪŋ ⓤⓢ ˈstɔːr.t̬ɪŋ

stor|y (S) ˈstɔː.r|i ⓤⓢ ˈstɔːr|.i **-ies** -iz **-ied** -id

storyboard ˈstɔː.ri.bɔːd ⓤⓢ ˈstɔːr.i.bɔːrd **-s** -z

storybook ˈstɔː.ri.bʊk ⓤⓢ ˈstɔːr.i- **-s** -s

storyline ˈstɔː.ri.laɪn ⓤⓢ ˈstɔːr.i- **-s** -z

storytell|er ˈstɔː.riˌtel|.əʳ ⓤⓢ ˈstɔːr.iˌtel|.ɚ **-ers** -əʳz ⓤⓢ -ɚz **-ing** -ɪŋ

St. Osyth sᵊntˈəʊ.zɪθ, sɪnt-, -sɪθ ⓤⓢ seɪntˈoʊ-

Stotfold ˈstɒt.fəʊld ⓤⓢ ˈstɑːt.foʊld

Stothard ˈstɒð.əd ⓤⓢ ˈstɑː.ðɚd

stotink|a stɒtˈɪŋ.k|ə ⓤⓢ stoʊˈtɪŋ- **-i** -iː

Stoughton *in West Sussex, Leicestershire and US:* ˈstəʊ.tᵊn ⓤⓢ ˈstoʊ- *in Somerset:* ˈstɔː.tᵊn ⓤⓢ ˈstɔː-, ˈstɑː- *in Surrey:* ˈstaʊ.tᵊn *surname:* ˈstɔː.tᵊn, ˈstaʊ-, ˈstəʊ- ⓤⓢ ˈstɔː-, ˈstɑː-, ˈstaʊ-, ˈstoʊ-
Note: /ˈstəʊ.tᵊn ⓤⓢ ˈstoʊ-/ in **Hodder & Stoughton**, the publishers.

stoup stuːp **-s** -s

Stour *in Suffolk, Essex:* stʊəʳ ⓤⓢ stʊr *in Kent:* stʊəʳ, staʊəʳ ⓤⓢ stʊr, staʊɚ *in Hampshire:* staʊəʳ, stʊəʳ ⓤⓢ staʊɚ, stʊr *in Warwickshire, Hereford &*

Worcestershire and Oxfordshire: stauəʳ, stəuəʳ (US) stauɚ, stoʊɚ *in Dorset:* stauəʳ (US) stauɚ
Stourbridge *in West Midlands:* ˈstauə.brɪdʒ, ˈstəuə- (US) ˈstauɚ-, ˈstoʊɚ- *Common in Cambridge:* ˈstauə.brɪdʒ (US) ˈstauɚ-
Stourhead ˈstɔː.hed, ˈstauə- (US) ˈstɔːr-, ˈstauɚ-
Stourmouth ˈstauə.mauθ, ˈstuə- (US) ˈstauɚ-, ˈstur-
Stourport ˈstauə.pɔːt, ˈstuə- (US) ˈstauɚ.pɔːrt, ˈstur-
Stourton *surname:* ˈstɜː.tᵊn (US) ˈstɝː- *in Hereford & Worcestershire:* ˈstɔː.tᵊn (US) ˈstɔːr- *in Wiltshire:* ˈstɜː.tᵊn, ˈstɔː- (US) ˈstɝː-, ˈstɔːr-
stout (S) staut **-s** -s **-er** -əʳ (US) ˈstau.t̬ɚ **-est** -ɪst, -əst (US) ˈstau.t̬ɪst, -t̬əst **-ly** -li **-ness** -nəs, -nɪs
stout-hearted ˌstautˈhɑː.tɪd (US) -ˈhɑːr.t̬ɪd **-ly** -li **-ness** -nəs, -nɪs
stoutish ˈstau.tɪʃ (US) -t̬ɪʃ
stove stəuv (US) stouv **-s** -z
stovepipe ˈstəuv.paɪp (US) ˈstouv- **-s** -s
stovetop ˈstəuv.tɒp (US) ˈstouv.tɑːp **-s** -s
stow (S) stəu (US) stou **-s** -z **-ing** -ɪŋ **-ed** -d **-age** -ɪdʒ
stowaway ˈstəu.əˌweɪ (US) ˈstou- **-s** -z
Stowe stəu (US) stou
Stowers stauəz (US) stauɚz
Stowey ˈstəu.i (US) ˈstou-
Stowmarket ˈstəuˌmɑː.kɪt (US) ˈstouˌmɑːr-
Stow-on-the-Wold ˌstəu.ɒn.ðəˈwəuld (US) ˌstou.ɑːn.ðəˈwould
St. Pancras sᵊn*t*ˈpæŋ.krəs, sɪn*t*-, sᵊm- (US) seɪnt-, -ˈpæn-
St. Patrick sᵊn*t*ˈpæt.rɪk, sɪn*t*-, sᵊm- (US) seɪnt- **St. ˈPatrick's ˌDay**
St. Paul sᵊn*t*ˈpɔːl, sɪn*t*-, sᵊm- (US) seɪntˈpɑːl, -ˈpɔːl **-'s** -z
St. Peter sᵊn*t*ˈpiː.təʳ, sɪn*t*-, sᵊm- (US) seɪntˈpiː.t̬ɚ **-'s** -z
St. Petersburg sᵊn*t*ˈpiː.təz.bɜːg, sɪn*t*-, sᵊm- (US) seɪntˈpiː.t̬ɚz.bɝːg
Strabane strəˈbæn
strabismus strəˈbɪz.məs, stræbˈɪz- (US) strəˈbɪz-
Strabo ˈstreɪ.bəu (US) -bou
Strabolgi strəˈbəu.gi (US) -ˈbou-
Strachan strɔːn; ˈstræk.ən (US) strɑːn, strɔːn; ˈstræk.ən
Strachey ˈstreɪ.tʃi (US) -ki, -tʃi
Strad stræd **-s** -z
Strada® ˈstrɑː.də **-s** -z
straddl|e ˈstræd.l̩ **-es** -z **-ing** -ɪŋ, ˈstræd.lɪŋ **-ed** -d
Stradivari ˌstræd.ɪˈvɑː.ri, -əˈ- (US) ˌstrɑː.diˈvɑːr.i **-s** -z
Stradivarius ˌstræd.ɪˈveə.ri.əs, -əˈ-, -ˈvɑː- (US) -əˈver.i- **-es** -ɪz
straf|e streɪf, strɑːf (US) streɪf **-es** -s **-ing/s** -ɪŋ/z **-ed** -t
Strafford ˈstræf.əd (US) -ɚd
straggl|e ˈstræg.l̩ **-es** -z **-ing** -ɪŋ, ˈstræg.lɪŋ **-ed** -d **-er/s** -əʳ/z, ˈstræg.ləʳ/z (US) ˈ-l̩.ɚ/z, ˈ-lɚ/z
straggl|y ˈstræg.l̩|.i, ˈ-l|i **-iness** -ɪ.nəs, -ɪ.nɪs
Strahan strɔːn, strɑːn
straight streɪt **-er** -əʳ (US) ˈstreɪ.t̬ɚ **-est** -ɪst, -əst (US) ˈstreɪ.t̬ɪst, -t̬əst **-ness** -nəs, -nɪs **ˌstraight ˈface; ˌstraight and ˈnarrow**
straightaway ˌstreɪt.əˈweɪ (US) ˌstreɪt̬-
straightedg|e ˈstreɪt.edʒ (US) ˈstreɪt̬- **-es** -ɪz
straighten ˈstreɪ.tᵊn **-s** -z **-ing** -ɪŋ, ˈstreɪt.nɪŋ **-ed** -d
straight-|faced ˌstreɪtˈfeɪst **-facedly** -ˈfeɪ.sɪd.li *stress shift:* ˌstraight-faced ˈspeaker
straightforward ˌstreɪtˈfɔː.wəd (US) -ˈfɔːr.wɚd **-ly** -li **-ness** -nəs, -nɪs
straightjacket ˈstreɪtˌdʒæk.ɪt **-s** -s **-ing** -ɪŋ **-ed** -ɪd
straightlaced ˌstreɪtˈleɪst (US) ˈ-- **-ly** -ˈleɪ.sɪd.li **-ness** -nəs, -nɪs *stress shift, British only:* ˌstraightlaced ˈteacher
straightway ˈstreɪt.weɪ
strain (S) streɪn **-s** -z **-ing** -ɪŋ **-ed** -d **-er/s** -əʳ/z (US) -ɚ/z
strait (S) streɪt **-s** -s **-ened** -ᵊnd
straitjacket ˈstreɪtˌdʒæk.ɪt **-s** -s **-ing** -ɪŋ **-ed** -ɪd
straitlaced ˌstreɪtˈleɪst (US) ˈ-- **-ly** -ˈleɪ.sɪd.li **-ness** -nəs, -nɪs *stress shift, British only:* ˌstraitlaced ˈteacher
Straker ˈstreɪ.kəʳ (US) -kɚ
strand (S) strænd **-s** -z **-ing** -ɪŋ **-ed** -ɪd
Strang stræŋ
strang|e (S) streɪndʒ **-er** -əʳ (US) -ɚ **-est** -ɪst, -əst **-ely** -li **-eness** -nəs, -nɪs
stranger ˈstreɪn.dʒəʳ (US) -dʒɚ **-s** -z
Strangeways ˈstreɪndʒ.weɪz
Strangford ˈstræŋ.fəd (US) -fɚd
strangl|e ˈstræŋ.gl̩ **-es** -z **-ing** -ɪŋ, ˈstræŋ.glɪŋ **-ed** -d **-er/s** -əʳ/z (US) -ɚ/z
stranglehold ˈstræŋ.gl̩.həuld (US) -hould **-s** -z
strangu|late ˈstræŋ.gjə|.leɪt, -gjʊ- **-lates** -leɪts **-lating** -leɪ.tɪŋ (US) -leɪ.t̬ɪŋ **-lated** -leɪ.tɪd (US) -leɪ.t̬ɪd
strangulation ˌstræŋ.gjəˈleɪ.ʃᵊn, -gjʊˈ- **-s** -z
Strangways ˈstræŋ.weɪz
Stranraer strænˈrɑːʳ, strən- (US) -ˈrɑːr
strap stræp **-s** -s **-ping** -ɪŋ **-ped** -t **-per/s** -əʳ/z (US) -ɚ/z **-py** -i
strap|hang ˈstræp|.hæŋ **-hangs** -hæŋz **-hanging** -ˌhæŋ.ɪŋ **-hung** -hʌŋ **-hanger/s** -ˌhæŋ.əʳ/z (US) -ɚ/z
strapless ˈstræp.ləs, -lɪs
Strasb(o)urg ˈstræz.bɜːg, -buəg, -bɔːg (US) ˈstrɑːs.burg, ˈstrɑːz-; ˈstræs.bɝːg
strata *(plur. of* **stratum***)* ˈstrɑː.tə, ˈstreɪ- (US) ˈstreɪ.t̬ə, ˈstræt̬.ə
stratagem ˈstræt.ə.dʒəm, ˈ-ɪ-, -dʒɪm, -dʒem (US) ˈstræt̬.ə.dʒəm **-s** -z
strategic strəˈtiː.dʒɪk, strætˈiː- (US) strəˈtiː- **-al** -ᵊl **-ally** -ᵊl.i, -li **Straˌtegic DeˈfenceIˌnitiative**
strategist ˈstræt.ə.dʒɪst, ˈ-ɪ- (US) ˈstræt̬.ə- **-s** -s
strateg|y ˈstræt.ə.dʒ|i, ˈ-ɪ- (US) ˈstræt̬.ə- **-ies** -iz
Stratford ˈstræt.fəd (US) -fɚd
Stratford-atte-Bowe ˌstræt.fədˌæt.ɪˈbəu, -ˈbəu.i; -ˌæt.əˈbəu.ə (US) -fɚdˌæt̬.əˈbou
Stratford-upon-Avon ˌstræt.fəd.ə.pɒnˈeɪ.vᵊn (US) -fɚd.ə.pɑːnˈ-, -vɑːn
strath stræθ **-s** -s
Strathaven ˈstreɪ.vᵊn
Strathavon stræθˈɑːn
Strathclyde stræθˈklaɪd *stress shift:* ˌStrathclyde ˈcampus
Strathcona stræθˈkəu.nə (US) -ˈkou-
Strathearn stræθˈɜːn (US) -ˈɝːn
Strathmore stræθˈmɔːʳ (US) -ˈmɔːr
strathspey (S) stræθˈspeɪ **-s** -z
stratification ˌstræt.ɪ.fɪˈkeɪ.ʃᵊn, ˌ-ə- (US) ˌstræt̬.ə-
strati|fy ˈstræt.ɪ|.faɪ, ˈ-ə- (US) ˈstræt̬.ə- **-fies** -faɪz **-fying** -faɪ.ɪŋ **-fied** -faɪd
stratocruiser ˈstræt.əˌkruː.zəʳ (US) ˈstræt̬.əˌkruː.zɚ **-s** -z
Straton ˈstræt.ᵊn
stratosphere ˈstræt.əuˌsfɪəʳ (US) ˈstræt̬.ə.sfɪr **-s** -z
stratospheric ˌstræt.əuˈsfer.ɪk (US) ˌstræt̬.əˈsfɪr-, -ˈsfer-
Stratton ˈstræt.ᵊn
strat|um ˈstrɑː.t|əm, ˈstreɪ- (US) ˈstreɪ.t̬|əm, ˈstræt̬|.əm **-a** -ə
stratus ˈstreɪ.təs, ˈstrɑː- (US) ˈstreɪ.t̬əs, ˈstræt̬.əs
Straus(s) straus *as if German:* ʃtraus
Stravinsky strəˈvɪn*t*.ski
straw (S) strɔː (US) strɑː, strɔː **-s** -z **-y** -i **ˌstraw ˈpoll** (US) **ˈstraw ˌpoll; ˌstraw ˈvote** (US) **ˈstraw ˌvote; ˌclutch at ˈstraws; the ˌstraw that ˌbreaks the ˌcamel's ˈback**
strawberr|y ˈstrɔː.bᵊr|.i, -br|i (US) ˈstrɑːˌber|.i, ˈstrɔː- **-ies** -iz **ˌstrawberry ˈblonde; ˈstrawberry ˌmark**
strawboard ˈstrɔː.bɔːd (US) ˈstrɑː.bɔːrd, ˈstrɔː-

Stress

A property of syllables which makes them stand out as more noticeable than others.

Examples for English

Stress is a large topic, which cannot be covered in its entirety here. However, some examples follow.

The position of stress can change the meaning or word class of a word, and so forms part of the phonological composition of the word, e.g.:

import (n)	/ˈɪm.pɔːt/	(US) /-pɔːrt/
import (v)	/ɪmˈpɔːt/	(US) /-ˈpɔːrt/
record (n)	/ˈrek.ɔːd/	(US) /-ɚd/
record (v)	/rɪˈkɔːd/	(US) /-ˈkɔːrd/

It is necessary to consider what factors make a syllable count as stressed. It seems likely that stressed syllables are produced with greater effort than unstressed, and that this effort is manifested in the air pressure generated in the lungs for producing the syllable and also in the articulatory movements in the vocal tract. These effects of stress produce in turn various audible results: one is 'pitch prominence', in which the stressed syllable stands out from its context (for example, being higher if its unstressed neighbours are low in PITCH, or lower if those neighbours are high; often a pitch glide such as a fall or rise is used to give greater pitch prominence). Another effect of stress is that stressed syllables tend to be longer – this is very noticeable in English, less so in some other languages. Also, stressed syllables tend to be louder than unstressed, though experiments have shown that differences in loudness alone are not very noticeable to most listeners. It has been suggested by many writers that the term 'accent' should be used to refer to some of the manifestations of stress (particularly pitch prominence), but the word, though widely used, has never acquired a distinct meaning of its own.

One of the areas in which there is little agreement is that of 'levels' of stress. Some descriptions of languages manage with just two levels (stressed and unstressed), while others use more. In English, one can argue that if one takes the word *indicator* as an example, the first syllable is the most strongly stressed, the third syllable is the next most strongly stressed and the second and fourth syllables are weakly stressed, or unstressed. This gives us three levels: it is possible to argue for more, though this rarely seems to give any practical benefit.

Stress shift

A change in the position of the stress in a word when that word is combined with others in a phrase.

Examples for English

The RHYTHM of English prefers patterns in which two stressed syllables do not come together. In order to avoid this, stress in some polysyllabic words may move to an earlier syllable when combined with another in a phrase, e.g.:

Heathrow	/hiːθˈrəʊ/	(US) /-ˈroʊ/
Heathrow Airport	/ˌhiːθ.rəʊ ˈeə.pɔːt/	(US) /-roʊ ˈer.pɔːrt/
academic	/ˌæk.əˈdem.ɪk/	
academic dress	/ˌæk.ə.dem.ɪk ˈdres/	

In this dictionary, words which change their stress in this way are shown with an example demonstrating the stress shift.

stray (S) streɪ **-s** -z **-ing** -ɪŋ **-ed** -d

streak striːk **-s** -s **-ing** -ɪŋ **-ed** -t

streak|y ˈstriː.k|i **-ier** -i.əʳ (US) -i.ɚ **-iest** -i.ɪst, -i.əst **-iness** -ɪ.nəs, -ɪ.nɪs **ˌstreaky ˈbacon**

stream striːm **-s** -z **-ing** -ɪŋ **-ed** -d

streamer ˈstriː.məʳ (US) -mɚ **-s** -z

streamlet ˈstriːm.lət, -lɪt (US) -lɪt **-s** -s

streamlin|e ˈstriːm.laɪn **-es** -z **-ing** -ɪŋ **-ed** -d

stream-of-consciousness ˌstriːm.əvˈkɒn.*t*ʃəs.nəs, -nɪs (US) -ˈkɑːn*t*.ʃəs-

Streatham ˈstret.əm (US) ˈstreṭ-

Streatley ˈstriːt.li

Streep striːp

street (S) striːt **-s** -s **ˈstreet ˌcred; ˌstreet crediˈbility** (US) **ˈstreet crediˌbility; ˌstreet ˈtheatre/ˈtheater** (US) **ˈstreet ˌtheatre/ˌtheater; ˈstreet ˌvalue**

streetcar ˈstriːt.kɑːʳ (US) -kɑːr **-s** -z

streetlight ˈstriːt.laɪt **-s** -s

streetwalk|er ˈstriːtˌwɔː.k|əʳ (US) -ˌwɑː.k|ɚ, -ˌwɔː- **-ers** -əz (US) -ɚz **-ing** -ɪŋ

streetwise ˈstriːt.waɪz

St. Regis sᵊntˈriː.dʒɪs, sɪnt- (US) seɪnt-

Streisand ˈstraɪ.zænd, -sənd, -sænd

strength streŋ*k*θ **-s** -s

strengthen ˈstreŋ*k*.θᵊn **-s** -z **-ing** -ɪŋ, ˈstreŋ*k*θ.nɪŋ **-ed** -d **-er/s** -əʳ/z, ˈstreŋ*k*θ.nəʳ/z (US) ˈstreŋ*k*.θᵊn.ɚ/z, ˈstreŋ*k*θ.nɚ/z

strenuous ˈstren.ju.əs **-ly** -li **-ness** -nəs, -nɪs

strep strep **ˌstrep ˈthroat**

strepto|coccus ˌstrep.təʊ|ˈkɒk.əs (US) -tə|ˈkɑː.kəs **-cocci** -ˈkɒk.saɪ, -aɪ, -iː (US) -ˈkɑːk.saɪ, -aɪ **-coccal** -ˈkɒk.ᵊl (US) -ˈkɑː.kᵊl **-coccic** -ˈkɒk.ɪk (US) -ˈkɑː.kɪk

streptomycin ˌstrep.təʊˈmaɪ.sɪn (US) -təˈ-

stress stres **-es** -ɪz **-ing** -ɪŋ **-ed** -t

stressful ˈstres.fʊl, -fᵊl **-ly** -i **-ness** -nəs, -nɪs

stressless ˈstres.ləs, -lɪs **-ness** -nəs, -nɪs

stretch stretʃ **-es** -ɪz **-ing** -ɪŋ **-ed** -t **ˌstretch(ed) ˈlimo**

stretcher ˈstretʃ.əʳ (US) -ɚ **-s** -z **-ing** -ɪŋ **-ed** -d

stretcher-bearer ˈstretʃ.əˌbeə.rəʳ (US) -ɚˌber.ɚ **-s** -z

stretchmark ˈstretʃ.mɑːk ⓤⓢ -mɑːrk **-s** -s

stretch|y ˈstretʃ|.i **-ier** -i.əʳ ⓤⓢ -i.ɚ **-iest** -i.ɪst, -i.əst

Stretford ˈstret.fəd ⓤⓢ -fɚd

Strevens ˈstrev.ᵊnz

strew struː **-s** -z **-ing** -ɪŋ **-ed** -d **-n** -n

strewth struːθ

stri|a ˈstraɪ|.ə **-ae** -iː

stri|ate (*v.*) ˈstri|.eɪt **-ates** -eɪts **-ating** -eɪ.tɪŋ ⓤⓢ -eɪ.t̬ɪŋ **-ated** -eɪ.tɪd ⓤⓢ -eɪ.t̬ɪd **striˌated ˈmuscle**

striation straɪˈeɪ.ʃᵊn **-s** -z

stricken *(from* **strike***)* ˈstrɪk.ᵊn

Strickland ˈstrɪk.lənd

strict strɪkt **-er** -əʳ ⓤⓢ -ɚ **-est** -ɪst, -əst **-ly** -li **-ness** -nəs, -nɪs

stricture ˈstrɪk.tʃəʳ ⓤⓢ -tʃɚ **-s** -z

strid|e straɪd **-es** -z **-ing** -ɪŋ **strode** strəʊd ⓤⓢ stroʊd **stridden** ˈstrɪd.ᵊn

stridency ˈstraɪ.dᵊn*t*.si

strident ˈstraɪ.dᵊnt **-ly** -li

StrideRite® ˈstraɪd.raɪt

stridu|late ˈstrɪd.jə|.leɪt, -jʊ- ⓤⓢ ˈstrɪdʒ.ə-, ˈ-ʊ- **-lates** -leɪts **-lating** -leɪ.tɪŋ ⓤⓢ -leɪ.t̬ɪŋ **-lated** -leɪ.tɪd ⓤⓢ -leɪ.t̬ɪd **-lation/s** ˌ--ˈleɪ.ʃᵊn/z

strife straɪf

strigil ˈstrɪdʒ.ɪl **-s** -z

strik|e straɪk **-es** -s **-ing/ly** -ɪŋ/li **struck** strʌk **stricken** ˈstrɪk.ᵊn **striker/s** ˈstraɪ.kəʳ/z ⓤⓢ -kɚ/z **ˈstrike ˌpay; ˌstrike while the ˌiron's ˈhot**

strikebound ˈstraɪk.baʊnd

strikebreak|er ˈstraɪkˌbreɪ.k|əʳ ⓤⓢ -k|ɚ **-ers** -əz ⓤⓢ -ɚz **-ing** -ɪŋ

strikeout ˈstraɪ.kaʊt **-s** -s

strike-pay ˈstraɪk.peɪ

strim strɪm **-s** -z **-ming** -ɪŋ **-med** -d

Strimmer® ˈstrɪm.əʳ ⓤⓢ -ɚ

Strindberg ˈstrɪn*d*.bɜːg, ˈstrɪm- ⓤⓢ ˈstrɪn*d*.bɝːg

string strɪŋ **-s** -z **-ing** -ɪŋ **-ed** -d **strung** strʌŋ **stringer/s** ˈstrɪŋ.əʳ/z ⓤⓢ -ɚ/z **ˌstring ˈbean; ˌstring quarˈtet**

stringency ˈstrɪn.dʒən*t*.si

stringendo strɪnˈdʒen.dəʊ ⓤⓢ -doʊ

stringent ˈstrɪn.dʒənt **-ly** -li

stringer (S) ˈstrɪŋ.əʳ ⓤⓢ -ɚ

Stringfellow ˈstrɪŋˌfel.əʊ ⓤⓢ -oʊ

string-pull|ing ˈstrɪŋˌpʊl|.ɪŋ **-er/s** -əʳ/z ⓤⓢ -ɚ/z

string|y ˈstrɪŋ|.i **-ier** -i.əʳ ⓤⓢ -i.ɚ **-iest** -i.ɪst, -i.əst **-iness** -ɪ.nəs, -ɪ.nɪs

strip strɪp **-s** -s **-ping** -ɪŋ **-ped** -t **-per/s** -əʳ/z ⓤⓢ -ɚ/z **ˌstrip carˈtoon; ˈstrip ˌclub; ˈstrip ˌlight; ˌstrip ˈpoker**

strip|e straɪp **-es** -s **-ing** -ɪŋ **-ed** -t **-(e)y** -i **-iness** -ɪ.nəs, -ɪ.nɪs

striplight ˈstrɪp.laɪt **-s** -s **-ing** -ɪŋ

stripling ˈstrɪp.lɪŋ **-s** -z

strippagram ˈstrɪp.ə.græm **-s** -z

strip-search ˌstrɪpˈsɜːtʃ, ˈ-- ⓤⓢ ˈstrɪp.sɝːtʃ **-es** -ɪz **-ing** -ɪŋ **-ed** -t

stripteas|e ˈstrɪp.tiːz, ˌ-ˈ- **-er/s** -əʳ/z ⓤⓢ -ɚ/z

striv|e straɪv **-es** -z **-ing/s** -ɪŋ/z **-ed** -d **strove** strəʊv ⓤⓢ stroʊv **striven** ˈstrɪv.ᵊn **striver/s** ˈstraɪ.vəʳ/z ⓤⓢ -vɚ/z

strobe strəʊb ⓤⓢ stroʊb **-s** -z **ˈstrobe ˌlight**

stroboscope ˈstrəʊ.bə.skəʊp, ˈstrɒb.ə- ⓤⓢ ˈstroʊ.bə.skoʊp, ˈstrɑː- **-s** -s

stroboscopic ˌstrəʊ.bəˈskɒp.ɪk, ˌstrɒb.əˈ- ⓤⓢ ˌstroʊ.bəˈskɑː.pɪk, ˌstrɑː-

stroboscopy strəʊˈbɒs.kə.pi, strɒbˈɒs- ⓤⓢ strəˈbɑː.skə-

strode *(from* **stride***)* strəʊd ⓤⓢ stroʊd

stroganoff ˈstrɒg.ə.nɒf ⓤⓢ ˈstrɔː.gə.nɔːf, ˈstroʊ- **-s** -s

strok|e strəʊk ⓤⓢ stroʊk **-es** -s **-ing** -ɪŋ **-ed** -t

strokeplay ˈstrəʊk.pleɪ ⓤⓢ ˈstroʊk-

stroll strəʊl ⓤⓢ stroʊl **-s** -z **-ing** -ɪŋ **-ed** -d **-er/s** -əʳ/z ⓤⓢ -ɚ/z

Stromberg ˈstrɒm.bɜːg ⓤⓢ ˈstrɑːm.bɝːg

Stromboli ˈstrɒm.bᵊl.i, -bʊ.li, -bəʊ-; strɒmˈbəʊ.li ⓤⓢ ˈstrɑːm.bə-, -ˈboʊ.li

Stromness ˈstrɒm.nes, ˈstrʌm- ⓤⓢ ˈstrɑːm-, ˈstrʌm-

St. Ronan sᵊntˈrəʊ.nən, sɪnt- ⓤⓢ seɪntˈroʊ-

strong (S) strɒŋ ⓤⓢ strɑːŋ, strɔːŋ **-er** -gəʳ ⓤⓢ -gɚ **-est** -gɪst, -gəst **-ly** -li **-ish** -ɪʃ **ˌstrong ˈlanguage; ˈstrong ˌroom; ˈstrong ˌpoint**

strong-arm ˈstrɒŋ.ɑːm ⓤⓢ ˈstrɑːŋ.ɑːrm, ˈstrɔːŋ- **-s** -z **-ing** -ɪŋ **-ed** -d

strongbox ˈstrɒŋ.bɒks ⓤⓢ ˈstrɑːŋ.bɑːks, ˈstrɔːŋ- **-es** -ɪz

stronghold ˈstrɒŋ.həʊld ⓤⓢ ˈstrɑːŋ.hoʊld, ˈstrɔːŋ- **-s** -z

strong|man ˈstrɒŋ|.mæn **-men** -men

strong-minded ˌstrɒŋˈmaɪn.dɪd ⓤⓢ ˈstrɑːŋ-, ˈstrɔːŋ- **-ly** -li **-ness** -nəs, -nɪs *stress shift:* ˌstrong-minded ˈperson

strong-willed ˌstrɒŋˈwɪld **-ness** -nəs, -nɪs *stress shift:* ˌstrong-willed ˈchild

stronti|a ˈstrɒn.ti|.ə, -*t*ʃi-, ˈ-*t*ʃ|ə, -tj|ə ⓤⓢ ˈstrɑːn*t*.ʃi.|ə, ˈ-ʃ|ə **-an** -ən **-um** -əm

Strood struːd

strop strɒp ⓤⓢ strɑːp **-s** -s **-ping** -ɪŋ **-ped** -t

strophe ˈstrəʊ.fi, ˈstrɒf.i ⓤⓢ ˈstroʊ.fi **-s** -z

strophic ˈstrɒf.ɪk, ˈstrəʊ.fɪk ⓤⓢ ˈstrɑː.fɪk, ˈstroʊ-

stropp|y ˈstrɒp|.i ⓤⓢ ˈstrɑː.p|i **-ier** -i.əʳ ⓤⓢ -i.ɚ **-iest** -i.ɪst, -i.əst **-iness** -ɪ.nəs, -ɪ.nɪs

Stroud straʊd

Note: *As a surname, the pronunciation* /struːd/ *is sometimes heard.*

strove *(from* **strive***)* strəʊv ⓤⓢ stroʊv

strow strəʊ ⓤⓢ stroʊ **-s** -z **-ing** -ɪŋ **-ed** -d **-n** -n

struck *(from* **strike***)* strʌk

structural ˈstrʌk.tʃᵊr.ᵊl **-ly** -i **ˌstructural engiˈneer**

structural|ism ˈstrʌk.tʃᵊr.ᵊl|.ɪ.zᵊm **-ist/s** -ɪst/s

structur|e ˈstrʌk.tʃəʳ ⓤⓢ -tʃɚ **-es** -z **-ing** -ɪŋ **-ed** -d

strudel ˈstruː.dᵊl *as if German:* ˈʃtruː- **-s** -z

struggl|e ˈstrʌg.l̩ **-es** -z **-ing** -ɪŋ, ˈstrʌg.lɪŋ **-ed** -d **-er/s** -əʳ/z, ˈstrʌg.ləʳ/z ⓤⓢ ˈ-l̩.ɚ/z, ˈ-lɚ/z

strum strʌm **-s** -z **-ming** -ɪŋ **-med** -d **-mer/s** -əʳ/z ⓤⓢ -ɚ/z

strumpet ˈstrʌm.pɪt **-s** -s

strung *(from* **string***)* strʌŋ **ˌstrung ˈout**

strung-up ˌstrʌŋˈʌp

strut strʌt **-s** -s **-ting** -ɪŋ ⓤⓢ ˈstrʌt̬.ɪŋ **-ted** -ɪd ⓤⓢ ˈstrʌt̬.ɪd

struth struːθ

Struthers ˈstrʌð.əz ⓤⓢ -ɚz

Strutt strʌt

Struwwelpeter ˌstruː.əlˈpiː.təʳ, ˈstruː.əlˌpiː-; ˌstruːlˈpiː-, ˈ-ˌ-- ⓤⓢ ˈstruː.əlˌpiː.t̬ɚ

strychnine ˈstrɪk.niːn, -nɪn ⓤⓢ -naɪn, -nɪn, -niːn

St. Salvator's sᵊn*t*.sælˈveɪ.təz, sɪnt- ⓤⓢ seɪntˈsæl.və.tɔːrz

St. Simon sᵊn*t*ˈsaɪ.mən, sɪn*t*- ⓤⓢ seɪnt-

St. Swithin sᵊn*t*ˈswɪð.ɪn, sɪn*t*- ⓤⓢ seɪnt-

St. Thomas sᵊn*t*ˈtɒm.əs, sɪn*t*- ⓤⓢ seɪntˈtɑː.məs **-'s** -ɪz

St. Trinian's sᵊntˈtrɪn.i.ənz

St. Tropez ˌsæ̃n.trəʊˈpeɪ ⓤⓢ ˌsæ̃n.trɔːˈpeɪ, -troʊˈ-

Stuart stjʊət, ˈstjuː.ət ⓤⓢ ˈstuː.ɚt, ˈstjuː-, stʊrt **-s** -s

stub stʌb **-s** -z **-bing** -ɪŋ **-bed** -d

Stubbings ˈstʌb.ɪŋz

Stubbington ˈstʌb.ɪŋ.tən

stubbl|e ˈstʌb.l̩ **-y** -i, ˈstʌb.li

stubborn ˈstʌb.ən ⓤⓢ -ɚn **-er** -əʳ ⓤⓢ -ɚ **-est** -ɪst, -əst **-ly** -li **-ness** -nəs, -nɪs

Stubbs stʌbz

stubb|y ˈstʌb|.i **-ier** -i.əʳ ⓤⓢ -i.ɚ **-iest** -i.ɪst, -i.əst **-iness** -ɪ.nəs, -ɪ.nɪs **-ies** -iz

stucco ˈstʌk.əʊ ⓤⓢ -oʊ **-(e)s** -z **-ing** -ɪŋ **-ed** -d

stuck *(from* **stick***)* stʌk

stuck-up ˌstʌkˈʌp
Stucley ˈstjuː.kli ⓊⓈ ˈstuː-, ˈstjuː-
stud stʌd **-s** -z **-ding** -ɪŋ **-ded** -ɪd ˌ**stud ˈpoker**
studding-sail ˈstʌd.ɪŋ.seɪl *nautical pronunciation:* ˈstʌnt.səl **-s** -z
Studebaker ˈstjuː.dɪˌbeɪ.kəʳ ⓊⓈ ˈstuː.dəˌbeɪ.kɚ, ˈstjuː-
student ˈstjuː.dənt ⓊⓈ ˈstuː-, ˈstjuː- **-s** -s ˌ**student ˈgrant**; ˌ**student ˈloan**; ˌ**student ˈteacher**; ˌ**student ˈunion**
studentship ˈstjuː.dənt.ʃɪp ⓊⓈ ˈstuː-, ˈstjuː- **-s** -s
studio ˈstjuː.di.əʊ ⓊⓈ ˈstuː.di.oʊ, ˈstjuː- **-s** -z ˌ**studio ˈflat** ⓊⓈ ˈ**studio** ˌ**flat**
studious ˈstjuː.di.əs ⓊⓈ ˈstuː-, ˈstjuː- **-ly** -li **-ness** -nəs, -nɪs
Studley ˈstʌd.li
stud|y ˈstʌd|.i **-ies** -iz **-ying** -i.ɪŋ **-ied** -id
stuff stʌf **-s** -s **-ing** -ɪŋ **-ed** -t ˌ**stuffed ˈshirt**
stuffing ˈstʌf.ɪŋ **-s** -z
stuff|y ˈstʌf|.i **-ier** -i.əʳ ⓊⓈ -i.ɚ **-iest** -i.ɪst, -i.əst **-iness** -ɪ.nəs, -ɪ.nɪs **-ily** -ɪ.li
stultification ˌstʌl.tɪ.fɪˈkeɪ.ʃən, -tə- ⓊⓈ -t̬ə-
stulti|fy ˈstʌl.tɪ|.faɪ, -tə- ⓊⓈ -t̬ə- **-fies** -faɪz **-fying** -ˌfaɪ.ɪŋ **-fied** -faɪd
stum stʌm
stumbl|e ˈstʌm.bl̩ **-es** -z **-ing** -ɪŋ, ˈstʌm.blɪŋ **-ed** -d **-er/s** -əʳ/z, ˈstʌm.bləʳ/z ⓊⓈ ˈ-bl̩.ɚ/z, ˈ-blɚ/z ˈ**stumbling** ˌ**block**
stumm ʃtʊm
stump stʌmp **-s** -s **-ing** -ɪŋ **-ed** -t **-y** -i **-ier** -i.əʳ ⓊⓈ -i.ɚ **-iest** -i.ɪst, -i.st **-iness** -ɪ.nəs, -ɪ.nɪs
stun stʌn **-s** -z **-ning/ly** -ɪŋ/li **-ned** -d ˈ**stun** ˌ**gun**
stung *(from* **sting)** stʌŋ
stunk *(from* **stink)** stʌŋk
stunner ˈstʌn.əʳ ⓊⓈ -ɚ **-s** -z
stunt stʌnt **-s** -s **-ing** -ɪŋ ⓊⓈ ˈstʌn.t̬ɪŋ **-ed** -ɪd ⓊⓈ ˈstʌn.t̬ɪd
stunt|man ˈstʌnt|.mæn **-men** -men
stunt|woman ˈstʌnt|ˌwʊm.ən **-women** -ˌwɪm.ɪn
stupa ˈstuː.pə **-s** -z
stupe stjuːp ⓊⓈ stuːp, stjuːp **-s** -s
stupefaction ˌstjuː.pɪˈfæk.ʃən ⓊⓈ ˌstuː.pəˈ-, ˌstjuː-
stupe|fy ˈstjuː.pɪ|.faɪ ⓊⓈ ˈstuː.pə-, ˈstjuː- **-fies** -faɪz **-fying/ly** -ˌfaɪ.ɪŋ **-fied** -faɪd
stupendous stjuːˈpen.dəs ⓊⓈ stuː-, stjuː- **-ly** -li **-ness** -nəs, -nɪs
stupid ˈstjuː.pɪd ⓊⓈ ˈstuː-, ˈstjuː- **-er** -əʳ ⓊⓈ -ɚ **-est** -ɪst, -əst **-ly** -li **-ness** -nəs, -nɪs
stupidit|y stjuːˈpɪd.ə.t|i, -ɪ.t|i ⓊⓈ stuːˈpɪd.ə.t̬|i, stjuː- **-ies** -iz
stupor ˈstjuː.pəʳ ⓊⓈ ˈstuː.pɚ, ˈstjuː-
sturd|y ˈstɜː.d|i ⓊⓈ ˈstɝː- **-ier** -i.əʳ ⓊⓈ -i.ɚ **-iest** -i.ɪst, -i.əst **-ily** -ɪ.li, -əl.i **-iness** -ɪ.nəs, -ɪ.nɪs
sturgeon (S) ˈstɜː.dʒən ⓊⓈ ˈstɝː- **-s** -z
Sturminster ˈstɜː.mɪnt.stəʳ ⓊⓈ ˈstɝː.mɪnt.stɚ
Sturm und Drang ˌʃtʊəm.ʊntˈdræŋ, ˌstʊərm- ⓊⓈ ˌʃtʊrm.ʊntˈdrɑːŋ
Sturtevant ˈstɜː.tɪ.vənt, -tə-, -vænt ⓊⓈ ˈstɝː.t̬ə-
stutt|er ˈstʌt|.əʳ ⓊⓈ ˈstʌt̬|.ɚ **-ers** -əz ⓊⓈ -ɚz **-ering** -ər.ɪŋ **-ered** -əd ⓊⓈ -ɚd **-erer/s** -ər.əʳ/z ⓊⓈ -ɚ.ɚ/z
Stuttgart ˈʃtʊt.gɑːt, ˈstʊt- ⓊⓈ ˈstʌt.gɑːrt, ˈstʊt-, ˈʃtʊt-
Stuyvesant ˈstaɪ.vɪ.sənt, -və- ⓊⓈ -və-
St. Valentine sənt ˈvæl.ən.taɪn ⓊⓈ seɪnt- **St. ˈValentine's** ˌ**Day**
St. Vincent sənˈvɪnt.sənt, sɪnt- ⓊⓈ seɪnt-
St. Vitus sənˈvaɪ.təs, sɪnt- ⓊⓈ seɪntˈvaɪ.t̬əs **-'s** -ɪz **St.** ˌ**Vitus's ˈdance** ⓊⓈ **St.** ˈ**Vitus's** ˌ**dance**
st|y st|aɪ **-ies** -aɪz
Styal staɪəl
stye staɪ **-s** -z
stygian (S) ˈstɪdʒ.i.ən ⓊⓈ -i.ən, ˈ-ən
styl|e staɪl **-es** -z **-ing** -ɪŋ **-ed** -d
styleless ˈstaɪl.ləs, -lɪs **-ly** -li **-ness** -nəs, -nɪs
Styles staɪlz
stylet ˈstaɪ.lət, -lɪt ⓊⓈ -lɪt **-s** -s
stylish ˈstaɪ.lɪʃ **-ly** -li **-ness** -nəs, -nɪs
stylist ˈstaɪ.lɪst **-s** -s
stylistic staɪˈlɪs.tɪk **-s** -s **-ally** -əl.i, -li
stylite ˈstaɪ.laɪt **-s** -s
Stylites staɪˈlaɪ.tiːz ⓊⓈ -t̬iːz
stylization, -isa- ˌstaɪ.laɪˈzeɪ.ʃən, -lɪˈ- ⓊⓈ -lɪˈ-
styliz|e, -is|e ˈstaɪ.laɪz **-es** -ɪz **-ing** -ɪŋ **-ed** -d
stylograph ˈstaɪ.ləʊ.grɑːf, -græf ⓊⓈ -lə.græf **-s** -s
stylographic ˌstaɪ.ləʊˈgræf.ɪk ⓊⓈ -ləˈ-
styl|us ˈstaɪ.l|əs **-uses** -ə.sɪz **-i** -aɪ
stym|ie ˈstaɪ.m|i **-ies** -iz **-ying** -i.ɪŋ **-ied** -id
styptic ˈstɪp.tɪk ˌ**styptic ˈpencil**
styrax ˈstaɪə.ræks ⓊⓈ ˈstaɪ- **-es** -ɪz
Styrofoam® ˈstaɪə.rəʊ.fəʊm ⓊⓈ -rə.foʊm
Styron ˈstaɪə.rən
Styx stɪks
suable ˈsuː.ə.bl̩, ˈsjuː- ⓊⓈ ˈsuː-
Suak|im ˈsuː.ɑː.k|ɪm, ˈswɑː.k|ɪm ⓊⓈ ˈswɑː- **-in** -ɪn
suasion ˈsweɪ.ʒən
sua sponte ˌsuː.ɑːˈspɒn.teɪ ⓊⓈ ˌswɑːˈspɑːn.teɪ
suav|e swɑːv **-er** -əʳ ⓊⓈ -ɚ **-est** -ɪst, -əst **-ely** -li **-eness** -nəs, -nɪs
suavity ˈswɑː.və.ti, ˈsweɪ-, ˈswæv.ə-, -ɪ.ti ⓊⓈ ˈswɑː.və.t̬i, ˈswæv.ə-
sub- sʌb-
sub sʌb **-s** -z **-bing** -ɪŋ **-bed** -d
subacid sʌbˈæs.ɪd, ˌsʌb-
subacute ˌsʌb.əˈkjuːt
subalpine sʌbˈæl.paɪn, ˌsʌb- ⓊⓈ -paɪn, -pɪn
subaltern ˈsʌb.əl.tən ⓊⓈ səbˈɔːl.tɚn, -ˈɑːl- **-s** -z
subaqua sʌbˈæk.wə, ˌsʌb- ⓊⓈ -ˈɑː.kwə, -ˈæk.wə
subarctic sʌbˈɑːk.tɪk, ˌsʌb- ⓊⓈ -ˈɑːrk-
Subaru® ˌsuː.bərˈuː, ˈ--- ⓊⓈ ˈsuː.bə.ruː **-s** -z
subatomic ˌsʌb.əˈtɒm.ɪk ⓊⓈ -ˈtɑː.mɪk ˌ**subatomic ˈparticles**
sub-bass ˌsʌbˈbeɪs ⓊⓈ ˈ-- **-es** -ɪz
Subbuteo® səˈbjuː.ti.əʊ, sʌbˈjuː-, -ˈuː- ⓊⓈ sʌbˈjuː.t̬i.oʊ
subclass ˈsʌb.klɑːs ⓊⓈ -klæs **-es** -ɪz
subclassification sʌbˌklæs.ɪ.fɪˈkeɪ.ʃən, ˌsʌb.klæs-, -ə- ⓊⓈ ˌsʌb.klæs- **-s** -z
subclassi|fy sʌbˈklæs.ɪ|.faɪ, ˌsʌb-, ˈ-ə- ⓊⓈ ˈ-ə- **-fies** -faɪz **-fying** -faɪ.ɪŋ **-fied** -faɪd
subclinical sʌbˈklɪn.ɪ.kəl, ˌsʌb-
subcommittee ˈsʌb.kəˌmɪt.i, ˌsʌb.kəˈmɪt.i ⓊⓈ -ˌmɪt̬- **-s** -z
subcompact ˌsʌbˈkɒm.pækt ⓊⓈ -ˈkɑːm- **-s** -s
subconscious sʌbˈkɒn.tʃəs, ˌsʌb- ⓊⓈ -ˈkɑːnt.ʃəs **-ly** -li **-ness** -nəs, -nɪs
subcontinent sʌbˈkɒn.tɪ.nənt, ˌsʌb- ⓊⓈ ˈsʌbˌkɑːn.tən.ənt, ˌsʌbˈkɑːn-
subcontinental ˌsʌb.kɒn.tɪˈnen.təl, -təˈ- ⓊⓈ -kɑːn.t̬ənˈen.t̬əl **-ly** -i
subcontract *(v.)* ˌsʌb.kənˈtrækt ⓊⓈ sʌbˈkɑːn.trækt **-s** -s **-ing** -ɪŋ **-ed** -ɪd **-or/s** -əʳ/z ⓊⓈ -ɚ/z
subcontract *(n.)* ˈsʌbˌkɒn.trækt ⓊⓈ -ˌkɑːn-, -ˈkɑːn- **-s** -s
subculture ˈsʌbˌkʌl.tʃəʳ ⓊⓈ -tʃɚ **-s** -z
subcutaneous ˌsʌb.kjuːˈteɪ.ni.əs
subdean sʌbˈdiːn, ˌsʌb- **-s** -z
subdivid|e ˌsʌb.dɪˈvaɪd, -dəˈ-, ˈ--ˌ- **-es** -z **-ing** -ɪŋ **-ed** -ɪd
subdivision ˌsʌb.dɪˈvɪʒ.ən, -dəˈ-, ˈsʌb.dɪˌvɪʒ-, -dəˌ- ⓊⓈ ˌsʌb.dɪˈvɪʒ.ən, ˈsʌb.dɪˌvɪʒ- **-s** -z
subdominant sʌbˈdɒm.ɪ.nənt, ˌsʌb- ⓊⓈ -ˈdɑː.mə- **-s** -s
subdu|e səbˈdjuː ⓊⓈ -ˈduː, -ˈdjuː **-es** -z **-ing** -ɪŋ **-ed** -d **-er/s** -əʳ/z ⓊⓈ -ɚ/z **-able** -ə.bl̩
subed|it sʌbˈed|.ɪt, ˌsʌb- **-its** -ɪts **-iting** -ɪ.tɪŋ ⓊⓈ -ɪ.t̬ɪŋ **-ited** -ɪ.tɪd ⓊⓈ -ɪ.t̬ɪd
subeditor sʌbˈed.ɪ.təʳ, ˈsʌbˌed- ⓊⓈ sʌbˈed.ɪ.t̬ɚ **-s** -z **-ship/s** -ʃɪp/s
subentr|y ˈsʌbˌen.tr|i, ˌ-ˈ-- **-ies** -iz

subfamil|y 'sʌbˌfæm.əl|.i, -ɪ.l|i ⓤⓢ -əl|.i **-ies** -iz
subfusc 'sʌb.fʌsk, -'-
subgroup 'sʌb.gruːp **-s** -s
subhead sʌb'hed, ˌsʌb- ⓤⓢ 'sʌb.hed **-s** -z
subheading 'sʌbˌhed.ɪŋ, -'-- ⓤⓢ 'sʌbˌhed- **-s** -z
subhuman sʌb'hjuː.mən, ˌsʌb- **-s** -z
subito 'suː.bɪ.təʊ, 'sʊb.ɪ- ⓤⓢ -t̬oʊ
subjacency sʌb'dʒeɪ.sənt.si, səb- ⓤⓢ sʌb-
subjacent sʌb'dʒeɪ.sənt, səb- ⓤⓢ sʌb-
subject (*n. adj.*) 'sʌb.dʒɪkt, -dʒekt **-s** -s **'subject ˌmatter**
subject (*v.*) səb'dʒekt, sʌb-; 'sʌb.dʒekt, -dʒɪkt ⓤⓢ səb'dʒekt **-s** -s **-ing** -ɪŋ **-ed** -ɪd
subjection səb'dʒek.ʃən
subjective səb'dʒek.tɪv, sʌb- ⓤⓢ səb- **-ly** -li **-ness** -nəs, -nɪs
subjectivism səb'dʒek.tɪ.vɪ.zəm, sʌb- ⓤⓢ səb-
subjectivity ˌsʌb.dʒek'tɪv.ə.ti, -dʒɪk-, -ɪ.ti ⓤⓢ -ə.t̬i
subjoin sʌb'dʒɔɪn, ˌsʌb- ⓤⓢ səb- **-s** -z **-ing** -ɪŋ **-ed** -d
sub judice ˌsʌb'dʒuː.dɪ.si, ˌsʊb-, -də-, -seɪ; ⓤⓢ ˌsʌb'dʒuː.də.si
subju|gate 'sʌb.dʒə|.geɪt, -dʒʊ- **-gates** -geɪts **-gating** -geɪ.tɪŋ ⓤⓢ -geɪ.t̬ɪŋ **-gated** -geɪ.tɪd ⓤⓢ -geɪ.t̬ɪd **-gator/s** -geɪ.təʳ/z ⓤⓢ -geɪ.t̬ɚ/s
subjugation ˌsʌb.dʒə'geɪ.ʃən, -dʒʊ'-
subjunct 'sʌb.dʒʌŋkt **-s** -s
subjunctive səb'dʒʌŋk.tɪv **-s** -z
subleas|e (*n.*) 'sʌb.liːs **-s** -ɪz
subleas|e (*v.*) sʌb'liːs, ˌsʌb- **-es** -ɪz **-ing** -ɪŋ **-ed** -t
sublessee ˌsʌb.les'iː **-s** -z
sublessor ˌsʌb.les'ɔːʳ ⓤⓢ -'ɔːr; sʌb'les.ɔːr **-s** -z
suble|t sʌb'le|t, ˌsʌb- ⓤⓢ sʌb'le|t, ˌsʌb-, '-- **-ts** -ts **-tting** -tɪŋ ⓤⓢ -t̬ɪŋ
sublieutenanc|y ˌsʌb.lef'ten.ənt.s|i, -ləf- ⓤⓢ -luː- **-ies** -iz
sublieutenant ˌsʌb.lef'ten.ənt, -ləf'- ⓤⓢ -luː'- **-s** -s
sublimate (*n.*) 'sʌb.lɪ.mət, -lə-, -mɪt, -meɪt ⓤⓢ -meɪt, -mɪt **-s** -s
subli|mate (*v.*) 'sʌb.lɪ|.meɪt, -lə- **-mates** -meɪts **-mating** -meɪ.tɪŋ ⓤⓢ -meɪ.t̬ɪŋ **-mated** -meɪ.tɪd ⓤⓢ -meɪ.t̬ɪd
sublimation ˌsʌb.lɪ'meɪ.ʃən, -lə'-
sublim|e sə'blaɪm **-ely** -li **-eness** -nəs, -nɪs **-es** -z **-ing** -ɪŋ **-ed** -d
subliminal sʌb'lɪm.ɪ.nəl, sə'blɪm-, -ən.əl ⓤⓢ sʌb'lɪm.ən- **-ly** -i
sublimity sə'blɪm.ə.ti, -ɪ.ti ⓤⓢ -ə.t̬i
submachine gun ˌsʌb.mə'ʃiːnˌgʌn, -'ʃiːŋˌ- ⓤⓢ -'ʃiːnˌ- **-s** -z
submarin|e ˌsʌb.mər'iːn, '--- ⓤⓢ 'sʌb.mə.riːn, ˌ--'- **-es** -z **-ing** -ɪŋ **-ed** -d
submariner sʌb'mær.ɪ.nəʳ, ˌsʌb-, -ən.əʳ ⓤⓢ ˌsʌb.mə'riː.nɚ, 'sʌb.məˌriː-; sʌb'mer.ən.ɚ, -'mær- **-s** -z
submerg|e səb'mɜːdʒ, sʌb- ⓤⓢ -'mɝːdʒ **-es** -ɪz **-ing** -ɪŋ **-ed** -d **-ence** -ənts
submers|e səb'mɜːs, sʌb'- ⓤⓢ səb'mɝːs **-es** -ɪz **-ing** -ɪŋ **-ed** -t
submersible səb'mɜː.sə.bl̩, sʌb-, -sɪ- ⓤⓢ -'mɝː.sə- **-s** -z
submersion səb'mɜː.ʃən, sʌb- ⓤⓢ -'mɝː.ʒən, -ʃən **-s** -z
submission səb'mɪʃ.ən **-s** -z
submissive səb'mɪs.ɪv **-ly** -li **-ness** -nəs, -nɪs
sub|mit səb|'mɪt **-mits** -'mɪts **-mitting** -'mɪt.ɪŋ ⓤⓢ -'mɪt̬.ɪŋ **-mitted** -'mɪt.ɪd ⓤⓢ -'mɪt̬.ɪd
submultiple sʌb'mʌl.tɪ.pl̩, ˌsʌb- ⓤⓢ -t̬ə- **-s** -z
subnormal sʌb'nɔː.məl, ˌsʌb- ⓤⓢ -'nɔːr- **-ly** -i
subnormality ˌsʌb.nɔː'mæl.ə.ti, -ɪ.ti ⓤⓢ -nɔːr.mæl.ə.t̬i
subnuclear sʌb'njuː.kli.əʳ, ˌsʌb- ⓤⓢ -'nuː.kli.ɚ, -'njuː-
suboctave 'sʌbˌɒk.tɪv ⓤⓢ -ˌɑːk- **-s** -z
suborbital sʌb'ɔː.bɪ.təl, ˌsʌb- ⓤⓢ -'ɔːr.bə.t̬əl
subordinate (*n. adj.*) sə'bɔː.dən.ət, -dɪ.nət, -'bɔːd.nət, -nɪt ⓤⓢ -'bɔːr.dən.ɪt **-s** -s **-ly** -li
subordin|ate (*v.*) sə'bɔː.dɪ.n|eɪt ⓤⓢ -'bɔːr.dən|.eɪt **-ates** -eɪts **-ating** -eɪ.tɪŋ ⓤⓢ -eɪ.t̬ɪŋ **-ated** -eɪ.tɪd ⓤⓢ -eɪ.t̬ɪd
subordination səˌbɔː.dɪ'neɪ.ʃən ⓤⓢ -ˌbɔːr.dən'eɪ-
subordinative sə'bɔː.dɪ.nə.tɪv, -dən.ə- ⓤⓢ -'bɔːr.dən.eɪ.t̬ɪv, -dɪ.nə-
suborn sə'bɔːn, sʌb'ɔːn ⓤⓢ sə'bɔːrn **-s** -z **-ing** -ɪŋ **-ed** -d **-er/s** -əʳ/z ⓤⓢ -ɚ/z
subornation ˌsʌb.ɔː'neɪ.ʃən ⓤⓢ -ɔːr'-
Subotica sə'bɒt.ɪ.tʃə, sʊ- ⓤⓢ 'suː.bɔː.tiːt.sə, -bə-
subplot 'sʌb.plɒt ⓤⓢ -plɑːt **-s** -s
subpoena səb'piː.nə, sʌb-, sə- ⓤⓢ sə- **-s** -z **-ing** -ɪŋ **-ed** -d
subpostmaster ˌsʌb'pəʊstˌmɑː.stəʳ ⓤⓢ -'poʊstˌmæs.tɚ **-s** -z
subpostmistress ˌsʌb'pəʊstˌmɪs.trəs, -trɪs ⓤⓢ -'poʊst- **-es** -ɪz
subpostoffice ˌsʌb'pəʊstˌɒf.ɪs ⓤⓢ -'poʊstˌɑː.fɪs **-s** -ɪz
subprefect sʌb'priː.fekt, ˌsʌb- **-s** -s
subprogram ˌsʌb'prəʊ.græm ⓤⓢ 'sʌbˌproʊ-, -grəm **-s** -z
subrogation ˌsʌb.rəʊ'geɪ.ʃən ⓤⓢ -roʊ'-, -rə'-
subrogee ˌsʌb.rəʊ'giː ⓤⓢ -roʊ'-, -rə'- **-s** -z
subrogor ˌsʌb.rəʊ'gɔːʳ ⓤⓢ 'sʌb.rə.gɔːr **-s** -z
sub rosa ˌsʌb'rəʊ.zə, -zɑː ⓤⓢ -'roʊ.zə
subroutine 'sʌb.ruːˌtiːn **-s** -z
subscrib|e səb'skraɪb **-es** -z **-ing** -ɪŋ **-ed** -d **-er/s** -əʳ/z ⓤⓢ -ɚ/z
subscript 'sʌb.skrɪpt
subscription səb'skrɪp.ʃən **-s** -z
subsection 'sʌbˌsek.ʃən **-s** -z
subsequent 'sʌb.sɪ.kwənt, -sə- ⓤⓢ -sɪ- **-ly** -li
subserv|e səb'sɜːv, sʌb- ⓤⓢ səb'sɝːv **-es** -z **-ing** -ɪŋ **-ed** -d
subservien|ce səb'sɜː.vi.ənt|s, sʌb- ⓤⓢ səb'sɝː- **-cy** -si
subservient səb'sɜː.vi.ənt, sʌb- ⓤⓢ səb'sɝː- **-ly** -li
subset 'sʌb.set **-s** -s
subsid|e səb'saɪd **-es** -z **-ing** -ɪŋ **-ed** -ɪd
subsidence səb'saɪ.dənts; 'sʌb.sɪ.dənts, -sə- **-s** -ɪz
subsidiarity səbˌsɪd.i'ær.ə.ti, -ɪ.ti ⓤⓢ -'er.ə.t̬i, -'ær-
subsidiar|y səb'sɪd.i.ər|.i ⓤⓢ -er-, -ɚ- **-ies** -iz **-ily** -əl.i, -ɪ.li
subsidization ˌsʌb.sɪ.daɪ'zeɪ.ʃən, -sə- ⓤⓢ -dɪ'- **-s** -z
subsidiz|e, -is|e 'sʌb.sɪ.daɪz, -sə- ⓤⓢ -sə- **-es** -ɪz **-ing** -ɪŋ **-ed** -d
subsid|y 'sʌb.sɪ.d|i, -sə- ⓤⓢ -sə- **-ies** -iz
sub silentio ˌsʌb.sɪ'len.ti.əʊ ⓤⓢ ˌsʌb.sɪ'len.ti.oʊ, -'lent.ʃi-
subsist səb'sɪst **-s** -s **-ing** -ɪŋ **-ed** -ɪd
subsistence səb'sɪs.tənts **sub'sistence ˌlevel**
subsoil 'sʌb.sɔɪl **-s** -z
subsonic sʌb'sɒn.ɪk, ˌsʌb- ⓤⓢ -'sɑː.nɪk
subspecies 'sʌbˌspiː.ʃiːz, -ʃɪz, -siːz, -sɪz ⓤⓢ -ʃiːz, -siːz
substanc|e 'sʌb.stənts **-es** -ɪz **-less** -ləs, -lɪs
substandard sʌb'stæn.dəd, ˌsʌb- ⓤⓢ -dɚd
substantial səb'stæn.tʃəl, -'stɑːn- ⓤⓢ -'stænt.ʃəl **-ly** -i **-ness** -nəs, -nɪs
substantiality səbˌstæn.tʃi'æl.ə.ti, -ˌstɑːn-, -ɪ.ti ⓤⓢ -ˌstænt.ʃi'æl.ə.t̬i
substanti|ate səb'stæn.tʃi|.eɪt, -'stɑːn-; -'stænt.si-, -'stɑːnt- ⓤⓢ -'stænt.ʃi- **-ates** -eɪts **-ating** -eɪ.tɪŋ ⓤⓢ -eɪ.t̬ɪŋ **-ated** -eɪ.tɪd ⓤⓢ -eɪ.t̬ɪd
substantiation səbˌstæn.tʃi'eɪ.ʃən, -ˌstɑːn-, -ˌstænt.si'-, -ˌstɑːnt- ⓤⓢ -ˌstænt.ʃi'-
substantival ˌsʌb.stən'taɪ.vəl
substantive (*n.*) 'sʌb.stən.tɪv ⓤⓢ -t̬ɪv **-s** -z
substantive (*adj.*) 'sʌb.stən.tɪv; səb'stæn- ⓤⓢ -t̬ɪv **-s** -z **-ly** -li **-ness** -nəs, -nɪs

Note: In British English, generally /səb'stæn.tɪv/ when applied to rank, pay, etc.

substation 'sʌbˌsteɪ.ʃᵊn **-s** -z

substitutable 'sʌb.stɪ.tjuː.tə.bl̩, ˌsʌb.stɪ'tjuː- US 'sʌb.stə.tuː.t̬ə-, -tjuː-

substitu|te 'sʌb.stɪ.tjuː|t US -stə.tuː|t, -tjuː|t **-tes** -ts **-ting** -tɪŋ US -t̬ɪŋ **-ted** -tɪd US -t̬ɪd

substitution ˌsʌb.stɪ'tjuː.ʃᵊn US -stə'tuː-, -'tjuː- **-s** -z

substitutional ˌsʌb.stɪ'tjuː.ʃᵊn.ᵊl, -'tjuːʃ.nᵊl US -stə'tuː.ʃᵊn.ᵊl, -'tjuː- **-ly** -i

substitutive 'sʌb.stɪ.tjuː.tɪv US -stə.tuː.t̬ɪv, -tjuː-

substrate 'sʌb.streɪt **-s** -s

substratosphere sʌb'stræt.əʊˌsfɪəʳ, -'strɑː.təʊ- US -'stræt.ə.sfɪr **-s** -z

substrat|um sʌb'strɑː.t|əm, -'streɪ-, '-ˌ-- US 'sʌbˌstreɪ.t̬|əm, -ˌstræt̬|.əm **-a** -ə

substructure 'sʌbˌstrʌk.tʃəʳ US -tʃɚ **-s** -z

subsum|e səb'sjuːm US -'suːm **-es** -z **-ing** -ɪŋ **-ed** -d

subsystem 'sʌbˌsɪs.təm, -tɪm US -təm **-s** -z

subtangent sʌb'tæn.dʒᵊnt, ˌsʌb- **-s** -s

subtenancy sʌb'ten.ənt.si, ˌsʌb-, 'sʌbˌten- US sʌb'ten-, ˌsʌb-

subtenant sʌb'ten.ᵊnt, ˌsʌb-, '-ˌ-- US 'sʌbˌten- **-s** -s

subtend səb'tend, sʌb- **-s** -z **-ing** -ɪŋ **-ed** -ɪd

subterfug|e 'sʌb.tə.fjuːdʒ US -tɚ- **-es** -ɪz

subterrane|an ˌsʌb.tᵊr'eɪ.ni|.ən US -tə'reɪ- **-ous** -əs

subtext 'sʌb.tekst **-s** -s

subtil(e) 'sʌt.ᵊl US 'sʌt̬.ᵊl; 'sʌb.tɪl

subtility sʌb'tɪl.ə.ti, -ɪ.ti US -ə.t̬i

subtiliz|e, -is|e 'sʌt.ᵊl.aɪz, -ɪ.laɪz US 'sʌt̬.ᵊl.aɪz, 'sʌb.tɪ.laɪz **-es** -ɪz **-ing** -ɪŋ **-ed** -d

subtilty 'sʌt.ᵊl.ti, -ɪl- US 'sʌt̬.ᵊl.t̬i, 'sʌb.tɪl-

subtitl|e 'sʌbˌtaɪ.tl̩, -'-- US 'sʌbˌtaɪ.t̬l̩ **-es** -z **-ing** -ɪŋ **-ed** -d

subtl|e 'sʌt.l̩ US 'sʌt̬- **-er** -əʳ, 'sʌt.ləʳ US 'sʌt̬.l̩.ɚ, 'sʌt.lɚ **-est** -ɪst, -əst, 'sʌt.lɪst, -ləst US 'sʌt̬.l̩.ɪst, -əst, 'sʌt.lɪst, -ləst **-y** -i **-eness** -nəs, -nɪs

subtlet|y 'sʌt.l̩.t|i US 'sʌt̬.l̩.t̬|i **-ies** -iz

subtopia sʌb'təʊ.pi.ə US -'toʊ-

subtotal 'sʌbˌtəʊ.tᵊl, -'--, ˌ-'-- US 'sʌbˌtoʊ.t̬ᵊl **-s** -s **-(l)ing** -ɪŋ **-(l)ed** -d

subtract səb'trækt **-s** -s **-ing** -ɪŋ **-ed** -ɪd

subtraction səb'træk.ʃᵊn **-s** -z

subtrahend 'sʌb.trə.hend **-s** -z

subtropic sʌb'trɒp.ɪk US -'trɑː.pɪk **-s** -s

subtropical sʌb'trɒp.ɪ.kᵊl, ˌsʌb- US -'trɑː.pɪ-

suburb 'sʌb.ɜːb US -ɝːb **-s** -z

suburban sə'bɜː.bᵊn US -'bɝː-

suburbanite sə'bɜː.bᵊn.aɪt US -'bɝː- **-s** -s

suburbanization, -isa- səˌbɜː.bᵊn.aɪ'zeɪ.ʃᵊn US -ˌbɝː-, -ɪ'-

suburbaniz|e, -is|e sə'bɜː.bᵊn.aɪz US -'bɝː- **-es** -ɪz **-ing** -ɪŋ **-ed** -d

suburbia sə'bɜː.bi.ə US -'bɝː-

subvariet|y 'sʌb.vᵊrˌaɪ.ə.t|i US -vəˌraɪ.ə.t̬|i **-ies** -iz

subvention səb'ven.*t*ʃᵊn, sʌb- US -'ven*t*.ʃᵊn **-s** -z

subversion səb'vɜː.ʃᵊn, sʌb-, -ʒᵊn US -'vɝː.ʒᵊn, -ʃᵊn

subversive səb'vɜː.sɪv, sʌb- US -'vɝː- **-ly** -li **-ness** -nəs, -nɪs

sub|vert sʌb|'vɜːt, səb- US -'vɝːt **-verts** -'vɜːts US -'vɝːts **-verting** -'vɜː.tɪŋ US -'vɝː.t̬ɪŋ **-verted** -'vɜː.tɪd US -'vɝː.t̬ɪd

subway 'sʌb.weɪ **-s** -z

subzero sʌb'zɪə.rəʊ, ˌsʌb- US -'zɪr.oʊ, -'ziː.roʊ

succeed sək'siːd **-s** -z **-ing** -ɪŋ **-ed** -ɪd

succès de scandale sjuːkˌseɪ.dəˌskɑ̃ː*n*'dɑːl *as if French:* sʊk-

success sək'ses **-es** -ɪz **suc'cess ˌstory**

successful sək'ses.fᵊl, -fʊl **-ly** -li **-ness** -nəs, -nɪs

succession sək'seʃ.ᵊn **-s** -z

successive sək'ses.ɪv **-ly** -li

successor sək'ses.əʳ US -ɚ **-s** -z

succinct sək'sɪŋ*k*t, sʌk- **-ly** -li **-ness** -nəs, -nɪs

succ|or 'sʌk|.əʳ US -ɚ **-ors** -əz US -ɚz **-oring** -ᵊr.ɪŋ **-ored** -əd US -ɚd

succory 'sʌk.ᵊr.i

succotash 'sʌk.ə.tæʃ

Succoth 'sʌk.əs, 'sʊk-; sʊ'kɒt US 'sʊk.əs; 'suː.kɔːt

succ|our 'sʌk|.əʳ US -ɚ **-ours** -əz US -ɚz **-ouring** -ᵊr.ɪŋ **-oured** -əd US -ɚd

succub|a 'sʌk.jə.b|ə, -jʊ- **-ae** -iː

succub|us 'sʌk.jə.b|əs, -jʊ- **-i** -aɪ

succulence 'sʌk.jə.lən*t*s, -jʊ-

succulent 'sʌk.jə.lənt, -jʊ- **-ly** -li

succumb sə'kʌm **-s** -z **-ing** -ɪŋ **-ed** -d

such *usual form:* sʌtʃ *occasional weak form:* sətʃ

such-and-such 'sʌtʃ.ᵊn.sʌtʃ

Suchard® 'suː.ʃɑːd, -ʃɑː US -ʃɑːrd

suchlike 'sʌtʃ.laɪk

suck sʌk **-s** -s **-ing** -ɪŋ **-ed** -t **'sucking ˌpig**

sucker 'sʌk.əʳ US -ɚ **-s** -z

suckl|e 'sʌk.l̩ **-es** -z **-ing** -ɪŋ, 'sʌk.lɪŋ **-ed** -d

suckling (S) 'sʌk.lɪŋ, '-l̩.ɪŋ **-s** -z

sucre *currency:* 'suː.kreɪ **-s** -z

Sucre *in Bolivia:* 'suː.kreɪ

sucrose 'suː.krəʊs, 'sjuː-, -krəʊz US 'suː.kroʊs

suction 'sʌk.ʃᵊn **'suction ˌpad; 'suction ˌpump**

Sudan suː'dɑːn, sʊ-, -'dæn US suː'dæn

Sudanese ˌsuː.dᵊn'iːz

Sudanic suː'dæn.ɪk, sʊ- US suː-

sudarium sjuː'deə.ri.əm, suː- US suː'der.i- **-s** -z

sudatory 'sjuː.də.tᵊr.i, 'suː- US 'suː.də.tɔːr-

Sudbury 'sʌd.bᵊr.i, 'sʌb- US 'sʌd.ber-, -bɚ-

sudd sʌd

sudden 'sʌd.ᵊn **-est** -ɪst, -əst **-ly** -li **-ness** -nəs, -nɪs ˌ**sudden 'death**

Sudetenland sʊ'deɪ.tᵊn.lænd US suː-

sudorific ˌsjuː.dᵊr'ɪf.ɪk, ˌsuː-, -dɒr'- US ˌsuː.də'rɪf- **-s** -s

suds sʌdz

suds|y 'sʌd.z|i **-ier** -i.əʳ US -i.ɚ **-iest** -i.ɪst, -i.əst **-iness** -ɪ.nəs, -ɪ.nɪs

su|e (S) suː, sjuː US suː **-es** -z **-ing** -ɪŋ **-ed** -d

suede sweɪd

su|et 'suː|.ɪt, 'sjuː- US 'suː- **-ety** -ɪ.ti US -ɪ.t̬i ˌ**suet 'pudding**

Suetonius swɪ'təʊ.ni.əs, swiː-, ˌsjuː.ɪ'-, ˌsuː-, -iː'- US swiː'toʊ-, swɪ-

Suez 'suː.ɪz, 'sjuː- US suː'ez, '-- ˌ**Suez Ca'nal**

suff|er 'sʌf|.əʳ US -ɚ **-ers** -əz US -ɚz **-ering/s** -ᵊr.ɪŋ/z **-ered** -əd US -ɚd **-erer/s** -ᵊr.əʳ/z US -ɚ.ɚ/z **-erable** -ᵊr.ə.bl̩ **-erance** -ᵊr.ᵊn*t*s

suffic|e sə'faɪs **-es** -ɪz **-ing** -ɪŋ **-ed** -t

sufficiency sə'fɪʃ.ᵊn*t*.si

sufficient sə'fɪʃ.ᵊnt **-ly** -li

suffix (*v.*) 'sʌf.ɪks; sə'fɪks, sʌf'ɪks US 'sʌf.ɪks; sə'fɪks **-es** -ɪz **-ing** -ɪŋ **-ed** -t

suffix (*n.*) 'sʌf.ɪks **-es** -ɪz

suffo|cate 'sʌf.ə|.keɪt **-cates** -keɪts **-cating/ly** -keɪ.tɪŋ/li US -keɪ.t̬ɪŋ/li **-cated** -keɪ.tɪd US -keɪ.t̬ɪd

suffocation ˌsʌf.ə'keɪ.ʃᵊn

Suffolk 'sʌf.ək

suffragan 'sʌf.rə.gən **-s** -z

suffrag|e 'sʌf.rɪdʒ **-es** -ɪz

suffragette ˌsʌf.rə'dʒet **-s** -s

suffragist 'sʌf.rə.dʒɪst **-s** -s

suffus|e sə'fjuːz, sʌf'juːz US sə'fjuːz **-es** -ɪz **-ing** -ɪŋ **-ed** -d

suffusion sə'fjuː.ʒᵊn, sʌf'juː- US sə'fjuː- **-s** -z

Suf|i 'suː.f|i **-is** -iz **-ism** -ɪ.zᵊm **-ic** -ɪk

sug|ar 'ʃʊg|.əʳ US -ɚ **-ars** -əz US -ɚz **-aring** -ᵊr.ɪŋ **-ared** -əd US -ɚd **'sugar ˌbeet; 'sugar ˌdaddy**

Suffixes

A suffix is an element placed at the end of a word to modify or alter its meaning. Unlike PREFIXES, it is possible for a suffix to alter the original pronunciation of the word stem on to which they are affixed. This depends on whether the suffix is stress-neutral, pre-stressed or stress-attracting.

Examples

Some suffixes do not change the pronunciation of the word stem. These are known as 'stress-neutral' suffixes. Some words containing stress-neutral suffixes follow:

eleventh /ɪˈlev.ənθ/
dramatise /ˈdræm.ə.taɪz/ (US) /ˈdrɑː.mə-/
fatherhood /ˈfɑː.ðə.hʊd/ (US) /-ðɚ-/
happily /ˈhæp.ɪ.li/

A suffix which attracts stress is known as 'stress-attracting'. Some words containing stress-attracting suffixes follow:

engineer /ˌen.dʒɪˈnɪəʳ/ (US) /-ˈnɪr/
Japanese /ˌdʒæp.əˈniːz/
nineteen /ˌnaɪnˈtiːn/

A 'pre-stressed' suffix is one in which the affixation of the suffix causes stress to be assigned to a syllable before it. There are a number of different types of pre-stressed suffixes. Here is an example where the stress falls on the syllable immediately before the suffix:

despotic /dɪˈspɒt.ɪk/ (US) /desˈpɑː.t̬ɪk/

In other words, the stress falls two syllables ahead of the suffix:

insecticide /ɪnˈsek.tɪ.saɪd/

There are also 'mixed' pre-stressed suffixes where the stress may fall either one or two syllables before the suffix.

The suffix *–ation* is actually a combination of the stress-neutral *–ate* and the pre-stressed suffix *–ion*. In words containing *–ation*, the strongest stress is always on the penultimate syllable, e.g.:

condemnation /ˌkɒn.demˈneɪ.ʃən/ (US) /ˌkɑːn-/

sugarcane ˈʃʊg.ə.keɪn (US) ˈ-ɚ- **-s** -z
sugarloa|f ˈʃʊg.ə.ləʊ|f (US) -ɚ.loʊ|f **-ves** -vz ˌ**Sugarloaf ˈMountain**
sugarplum ˈʃʊg.ə.plʌm (US) ˈ-ɚ- **-s** -z
sugar|y ˈʃʊg.ər|.i **-iest** -i.ɪst, -i.əst **-iness** -ɪ.nəs, -ɪ.nɪs
suggest səˈdʒest (US) səg- **-s** -s **-ing** -ɪŋ **-ed** -ɪd
suggestibility səˌdʒes.təˈbɪl.ə.ti, -tɪˈ-, -ɪ.ti (US) səgˌdʒes.təˈbɪl.ə.t̬i
suggestible səˈdʒes.tə.bl̩, -tɪ- (US) səgˈdʒes.tə-
suggestion səˈdʒes.tʃən, -ˈdʒeʃ- (US) səgˈdʒes- **-s** -z
suggestive səˈdʒes.tɪv (US) səgˈdʒes- **-ly** -li **-ness** -nəs, -nɪs
Suharto sʊˈhɑː.təʊ (US) -ˈhɑːr.t̬oʊ
suicidal ˌsuː.ɪˈsaɪ.dəl, ˌsjuː- (US) ˌsuː.əˈ- **-ly** -i
suicide ˈsuː.ɪ.saɪd, ˈsjuː- (US) ˈsuː.ə- **-s** -z
sui generis ˌsjuː.iːˈdʒen.ər.ɪs, ˌsuː-, -aɪˈ-, -ˈgen- (US) ˌsuː.iːˈdʒen-, -aɪˈ-
sui juris ˌsjuː.iːˈdʒʊə.rɪs, ˌsuː-, -aɪˈ-, -ˈdʒɔː- (US) ˌsuː.iːˈdʒʊr.ɪs, -aɪˈ-
suit suːt, sjuːt (US) suːt **-s** -s **-ing/s** -ɪŋ/z (US) ˈsuː.t̬ɪŋ/z **-ed** -ɪd (US) ˈsuː.t̬ɪd
suitability ˌsuː.təˈbɪl.ə.ti, ˌsjuː-, -ɪ.ti (US) ˌsuː.t̬əˈbɪl.ə.t̬i
suitab|le ˈsuː.tə.bl̩|, ˈsjuː- (US) ˈsuː.t̬ə- **-ly** -li **-leness** -l̩.nɪs, -nəs
suitcas|e ˈsuːt.keɪs, ˈsjuːt- (US) ˈsuːt- **-es** -ɪz
suite swiːt **-s** -s
suitor ˈsuː.təʳ, ˈsjuː- (US) ˈsuː.t̬ɚ **-s** -z
sukiyaki ˌsuː.kiˈjæk.i (US) -ˈjɑː.ki, ˌsʊk.iˈ-
Sukkot(h) ˈsʊk.ɒt
Sukkur ˈsʊk.ʊə (US) ˈsʊk.ʊr, -ɚ
Sulawesi ˌsuː.ləˈweɪ.si, -læˈ- (US) -lɑːˈ-
sulcal ˈsʌl.kəl
sulcalization, -isa- ˌsʌl.kəl.aɪˈzeɪ.ʃən, -lɪˈ- (US) -lɪˈ-
sulcaliz|e, -is|e ˈsʌl.kəl.aɪz **-es** -ɪz **-ing** -ɪŋ **-ed** -d
sulcate ˈsʌl.keɪt, -kɪt, -kət (US) -keɪt
Suleiman ˌsʊl.eɪˈmɑːn, ˌsuː.leɪˈ-, -lɪˈ-, ˈ--- (US) ˈsuː.leɪ.mɑːn, -lə-
sulfanilamide ˌsʌl.fəˈnɪl.ə.maɪd (US) -maɪd, -mɪd
sulfate ˈsʌl.feɪt, -fɪt, -fət (US) -feɪt **-s** -s
sulf|ide ˈsʌl.f|aɪd **-ides** -aɪdz **-ite/s** -aɪt/s
sulfonamide sʌlˈfɒn.ə.maɪd (US) -ˈfɑː.nə-, -mɪd **-s** -z
sulfur ˈsʌl.fəʳ (US) -fɚ
sulfureous sʌlˈfjʊə.ri.əs, -ˈfjɔː- (US) -ˈfjʊr.i-
sulfuretted ˈsʌl.fjʊ.ret.ɪd, -fjʊə-, -fə- (US) -fjə.ret̬-, -fə-, -fjʊ-
sulfuric sʌlˈfjʊə.rɪk, -ˈfjɔː- (US) -ˈfjʊr.ɪk **sulˌfuric ˈacid**
sulfurous ˈsʌl.fər.əs, -fjʊ.rəs (US) -fɚ-; sʌlˈfjʊr.əs
sulfury ˈsʌl.fər.i
Suliman ˌsʊl.ɪˈmɑːn, ˈ--- (US) ˈsuː.leɪ.mɑːn, -lə-
sulk sʌlk **-s** -s **-ing** -ɪŋ **-ed** -t **-y** -i **-ier** -i.əʳ (US) -i.ɚ **-iest** -i.ɪst, -i.əst **-ily** -ɪ.li, -əl.i **-iness** -ɪ.nəs, -ɪ.nɪs
Sulla ˈsʌl.ə, ˈsʊl- (US) ˈsʌl-
sullen ˈsʌl.ən **-est** -ɪst, -əst **-ly** -li **-ness** -nəs, -nɪs
Sullivan ˈsʌl.ɪ.vən
Sullom Voe ˌsuː.ləmˈvəʊ, ˌsʌl.əmˈ- (US) -ˈvoʊ
sull|y (S) ˈsʌl|.i **-ies** -iz **-ying** -i.ɪŋ **-ied** -id
sulphanilamide ˌsʌl.fəˈnɪl.ə.maɪd (US) -maɪd, -mɪd
sulphate ˈsʌl.feɪt, -fɪt, -fət (US) -feɪt **-s** -s
sulph|ide ˈsʌl.f|aɪd **-ides** -aɪdz **-ite/s** -aɪt/s
sulphonamide sʌlˈfɒn.ə.maɪd (US) -ˈfɑː.nə-, -mɪd **-s** -z
sulphur ˈsʌl.fəʳ (US) -fɚ
sulphureous sʌlˈfjʊə.ri.əs, -ˈfjɔː- (US) -ˈfjʊr.i-
sulphuretted ˈsʌl.fjʊ.ret.ɪd, -fjʊə-, -fə- (US) -fjə.ret̬-, -fə-, -fjʊ-
sulphuric sʌlˈfjʊə.rɪk, -ˈfjɔː- (US) -ˈfjʊr.ɪk **sulˌphuric ˈacid**
sulphurous ˈsʌl.fər.əs, -fjʊ.rəs (US) -fɚ.əs; sʌlˈfjʊr.əs
sulphury ˈsʌl.fər.i
sultan (S) ˈsʌl.tən **-s** -z
sultana *kind of raisin:* səlˈtɑː.nə, sʌl- (US) sʌlˈtæn.ə, -ˈtɑː.nə **-s** -z
sultana (S) *sultan's wife, mother, etc.:* sʌlˈtɑː.nə, sʊl- (US) sʌlˈtæn.ə, -ˈtɑː.nə **-s** -z
sultanate ˈsʌl.tə.nət, -neɪt, -nɪt (US) -tən.ɪt, -eɪt **-s** -s
sultr|y ˈsʌl.tr|i **-ier** -i.əʳ (US) -i.ɚ **-iest** -i.ɪst, -i.əst **-ily** -əl.i, -ɪ.li **-iness** -ɪ.nəs, -ɪ.nɪs

Sulu ˈsuː.luː

sum sʌm **-s** -z **-ming** -ɪŋ **-med** -d ˌ**sum ˈtotal**

sumac(h) ˈʃuː.mæk, ˈsuː-, ˈsjuː- US ˈsuː.mæk, ˈʃʊm.æk **-s** -s

Sumatr|a sʊˈmɑː.tr|ə, sjʊ- US suː- **-an/s** -ən/z

Sumburgh ˈsʌm.bᵊr.ə

Sumerian sʊˈmɪə.ri.ən, suː-, sjʊ-, sjuː-, -ˈmeə- US suːˈmɪr.i-, -ˈmer-

summa cum laude ˌsʊm.ɑː.kʊmˈlaʊ.deɪ US -əˌ-, -di; ˌsʌm.əˌkʌmˈlɔː.di

summariz|e, is|e ˈsʌm.ᵊr.aɪz US -ə.raɪz **-es** -ɪz **-ing** -ɪŋ **-ed** -d

summar|y ˈsʌm.ᵊr|.i **-ies** -iz **-ily** -ᵊl.i, -ɪ.li **-iness** -ɪ.nəs, -ɪ.nɪs

summat ˈsʌm.ət

summation sʌmˈeɪ.ʃᵊn, səˈmeɪ- US səˈmeɪ- **-s** -z

summer (S) ˈsʌm.əʳ US -ɚ **-s** -z **-ing** -ɪŋ **-ed** -d **-like** -laɪk ˌ**summer ˈpudding; ˈsummer ˌschool; ˈSummer ˌTime**

Summerfield ˈsʌm.ə.fiːld US ˈ-ɚ- **-s** -z

summerhou|se ˈsʌm.ə.haʊ|s US ˈ-ɚ- **-ses** -zɪz

Summers ˈsʌm.əz US -ɚz

summertime ˈsʌm.ə.taɪm US ˈ-ɚ-

Summerville ˈsʌm.ə.vɪl US ˈ-ɚ-

summery ˈsʌm.ᵊr.i

summing-up ˌsʌm.ɪŋˈʌp **summings-up** ˌsʌm.ɪŋzˈ-

summit ˈsʌm.ɪt **-s** -s

summiteer ˌsʌm.ɪˈtɪəʳ US -tɪɚ **-s** -z

summon ˈsʌm.ən **-s** -z **-ing** -ɪŋ **-ed** -d **-er/s** -əʳ/z US -ɚ/z

summons ˈsʌm.ənz **-es** -ɪz **-ing** -ɪŋ **-ed** -d

Sumner ˈsʌm.nəʳ US -nɚ

sumo ˈsuː.məʊ US -moʊ **ˈsumo ˌwrestler, ˌsumo ˈwrestler; ˌsumo ˈwrestling, ˈsumo ˌwrestling**

sump sʌmp **-s** -s

sumpter (S) ˈsʌmp.təʳ US -tɚ **-s** -z

sumptuary ˈsʌmp.tjʊə.ri, -tjʊ-, -tʃʊə-, -tʃʊ- US -tʃu.er.i

sumptuous ˈsʌmp.tʃu.əs, -tju- US -tʃu- **-ly** -li **-ness** -nəs, -nɪs

sun (S) sʌn **-s** -z **-ning** -ɪŋ **-ned** -d ˌ**Sun ˈCity; ˈsun ˌdeck; ˈsun ˌhat; ˈsun ˌlounge**

Sun. *(abbrev. for* **Sunday***)* ˈsʌn.deɪ, -di

sunbaked ˈsʌn.beɪkt, ˈsʌm- US ˈsʌn-

sunba|th ˈsʌn.bɑː|θ, ˈsʌm- US ˈsʌn.bæ|θ **-ths** -ðz

sunbath|e ˈsʌn.beɪð, ˈsʌm- US ˈsʌn- **-es** -z **-ing** -ɪŋ **-ed** -d **-er/s** -əʳ/z US -ɚ/z

sunbeam (S) ˈsʌn.biːm, ˈsʌm- US ˈsʌn- **-s** -z

sunbed ˈsʌn.bed, ˈsʌm- US ˈsʌn- **-s** -z

sun-belt ˈsʌn.belt, ˈsʌm- **-s** -s

sunblind ˈsʌn.blaɪnd, ˈsʌm- US ˈsʌn- **-s** -z

sunblock ˈsʌn.blɒk, ˈsʌm- US ˈsʌn.blɑːk **-s** -s

sun-bonnet ˈsʌnˌbɒn.ɪt, ˈsʌm- US ˈsʌnˌbɑː.nɪt **-s** -s

sunburn ˈsʌn.bɜːn, ˈsʌm- US ˈsʌn.bɝːn **-s** -z **-ed** -d **-t** -t

sunburst ˈsʌn.bɜːst, ˈsʌm- US ˈsʌn.bɝːst **-s** -s

Sunbury ˈsʌn.bᵊr.i, ˈsʌm- US ˈsʌn-, -beri

Sunda ˈsʌn.də

sundae ˈsʌn.deɪ US -di, -deɪ **-s** -z

Sundanese ˌsʌn.dəˈniːz

Sunday ˈsʌn.deɪ, -di **-s** -z ˌ**Sunday ˈbest; ˈSunday ˌschool; in a ˌmonth of ˈSundays**

sund|er ˈsʌn.d|əʳ US -d|ɚ **-ers** -əz US -ɚz **-ering** -ᵊr.ɪŋ **-ered** -əd US -ɚd

Sunderland ˈsʌn.dᵊl.ənd US -dɚ.lənd

sundial ˈsʌn.daɪl **-s** -z

sundown ˈsʌn.daʊn

sundowner ˈsʌnˌdaʊ.nəʳ US -nɚ **-s** -z

sundrenched ˈsʌn.drentʃt

sundress ˈsʌn.dres **-es** -ɪz

sun-dried ˈsʌn.draɪd

sundr|y ˈsʌn.dr|i **-ies** -iz

sunfish ˈsʌn.fɪʃ

sunflower ˈsʌn.flaʊəʳ US -flaʊɚ **-s** -z **ˈsunflower ˌseed**

sung *(from* **sing***)* sʌŋ

Sung sʊŋ, sʌŋ US sʊŋ

sunglasses ˈsʌnˌglɑː.sɪz, ˈsʌŋ- US ˈsʌnˌglæs.ɪs

sunk *(from* **sink***)* sʌŋk

sunken *(from* **sink***)* ˈsʌŋ.kən

sunkissed ˈsʌn.kɪst, ˈsʌŋ-

sunlamp ˈsʌn.læmp **-s** -s

sunless ˈsʌn.ləs, -lɪs

sun|light ˈsʌn|.laɪt **-lit** -lɪt

sunlounger ˈsʌnˌlaʊn.dʒəʳ US -dʒɚ **-s** -z

Sunn|i ˈsʊn|.i, ˈsʌn- US ˈsʊn- **-ite/s** -aɪt/s **-ism** -ɪ.zᵊm ˌ**Sunni ˈMuslim**

Sunningdale ˈsʌn.ɪŋ.deɪl

sunn|y ˈsʌn|.i **-ier** -i.əʳ US -i.ɚ **-iest** -i.ɪst, -i.əst **-iness** -ɪ.nəs, -ɪ.nɪs ˌ**sunny-side ˈup**

Sunnyside ˈsʌn.i.saɪd

sunproof ˈsʌn.pruːf, ˈsʌm- US ˈsʌn-

sunray ˈsʌn.reɪ **-s** -z

sunris|e ˈsʌn.raɪz **-es** -ɪz

sunroo|f ˈsʌn.ruː|f US -ruː|f, -rʊ|f **-fs** -fs **-ves** -vz

sunscreen ˈsʌn.skriːn **-s** -z **-ing** -ɪŋ

sunset ˈsʌn.set **-s** -s

sunshade ˈsʌn.ʃeɪd **-s** -z

sunshin|e ˈsʌn.ʃaɪn **-y** -i

sunspot ˈsʌn.spɒt US -spɑːt **-s** -s

sunstroke ˈsʌn.strəʊk US -stroʊk **-s** -s

suntan ˈsʌn.tæn **-s** -z **-ned** -d

suntrap ˈsʌn.træp **-s** -s

sunup ˈsʌn.ʌp **-s** -s

sun-worship ˈsʌnˌwɜː.ʃɪp US -ˌwɝː- **-per/s** -əʳ/z US -ɚ/z

suo nomine ˌsuː.əʊˈnəʊ.mɪ.neɪ, ˌsjuː-, -ˈnɒm.ɪ- US ˌsuː.oʊˈnoʊ.mɪ-, -ˈnɑː-

sup sʌp **-s** -s **-ping** -ɪŋ **-ped** -t

super- ˈsuː.pəʳ-, ˈsjuː- US ˈsuː.pɚ-

super ˈsuː.pəʳ, ˈsjuː- US ˈsuː.pɚ **-s** -z

superab|le ˈsuː.pᵊr.ə.b|l̩, ˈsjuː- US ˈsuː- **-ly** -li **-leness** -l̩.nəs, -nɪs

superabundan|ce ˌsuː.pᵊr.əˈbʌn.dən|ts, ˌsjuː- US ˌsuː- **-t/ly** -t/li

superannu|ate ˌsuː.pᵊrˈæn.ju|.eɪt, ˌsjuː- US ˌsuː- **-ates** -eɪts **-ating** -eɪ.tɪŋ US -eɪ.t̬ɪŋ **-ated** -eɪ.tɪd US -eɪ.t̬ɪd

superannuation ˌsuː.pᵊrˌæn.juˈeɪ.ʃᵊn, ˌsjuː- US ˌsuː- **-s** -z

superb suːˈpɜːb, sjuː-, sʊ-, sjʊ- US səˈpɝːb, sʊ-, suː- **-ly** -li **-ness** -nəs, -nɪs

Superbowl ˈsuː.pə.bəʊl, ˈsjuː- US ˈsuː.pɚ.boʊl

superbug ˈsuː.pə.bʌg, ˈsjuː- US ˈsuː.pɚ- **-s** -z

supercargo ˈsuː.pəˌkɑː.gəʊ, ˈsjuː- US ˈsuː.pɚˌkɑːr.goʊ **-es** -z

supercharg|e ˈsuː.pə.tʃɑːdʒ, ˈsjuː- US ˈsuː.pɚ.tʃɑːrdʒ **-es** -ɪz **-ing** -ɪŋ **-ed** -d

supercharger ˈsuː.pəˌtʃɑː.dʒəʳ, ˈsjuː- US ˈsuː.pɚˌtʃɑːr.dʒɚ **-s** -z

superchip ˈsuː.pə.tʃɪp, ˈsjuː- US ˈsuː.pɚ- **-s** -s

supercilious ˌsuː.pəˈsɪl.i.əs, ˌsjuː- US ˌsuː.pɚˈ- **-ly** -li **-ness** -nəs, -nɪs

supercomputer ˈsuː.pə.kəmˌpjuː.təʳ, ˈsjuː- US ˈsuː.pɚ.kəmˌpjuː.t̬ɚ **-s** -z

superconductivity ˌsuː.pəˌkɒn.dʌkˈtɪv.ə.ti, ˌsjuː-, -dəkˈ-, -ɪ.ti US ˌsuː.pɚˌkɑːn.dʌkˈtɪv.ə.t̬i

superconduct|or ˈsuː.pə.kənˌdʌk.t|əʳ, ˈsjuː- US ˈsuː.pɚ.kənˌdʌk.t|ɚ **-ors** -əz US -ɚz **-ing** -ɪŋ

supercool ˌsuː.pəˈkuːl, ˌsjuː- US ˌsuː.pɚˈ- **-s** -z **-ing** -ɪŋ **-ed** -d

Superdrug® ˈsuː.pə.drʌg, ˈsjuː- US ˈsuː.pɚ-

super-duper ˌsuː.pəˈduː.pəʳ, ˌsjuː- US ˌsuː.pɚˈduː.pɚ

superego ˌsuː.pᵊrˈiː.gəʊ, ˌsjuː-, -ˈeg.əʊ US ˌsuː.pɚˈiː.goʊ **-s** -z

supererogation ˌsuː.pᵊrˌer.əʊˈgeɪ.ʃᵊn, ˌsjuː- US ˌsuː.pɚˌer.əˈ-

supererogatory ˌsuː.pᵊr.erˈɒg.ə.tᵊr.i, ˌsjuː-, -ɪˈrɒg- US ˌsuː.pɚ.ɪˈrɑː.gə.tɔːr-

superfici|al ˌsuː.pəˈfɪʃ|.ᵊl, ˌsjuː- US ˌsuː.pɚˈ- **-ally** -ᵊl.i **-alness** -ᵊl.nəs, -nɪs

superficialit|y ˌsuː.pəˌfɪʃ.iˈæl.ə.t|i, ˌsjuː-, -ɪ.t|i ⓤⓢ ˌsuː.pɚˌfɪʃ.iˈæl.ə.t̬|i **-ies** -iz
superficies ˌsuː.pəˈfɪʃ.iːz, ˌsjuː-, -i.iːz ⓤⓢ ˌsuː.pɚˈfɪʃ.i.iːz, ˈ-iːz
superfine ˌsuː.pəˈfaɪn, ˌsjuː-, ˈ--- ⓤⓢ ˈsuː.pɚ.faɪn, ˌ--ˈ-
superfix ˈsuː.pə.fɪks, ˈsjuː- ⓤⓢ ˈsuː.pɚ-
superfluit|y ˌsuː.pəˈfluː.ə.t|i, ˌsjuː-, -ɪ.t|i ⓤⓢ ˌsuː.pɚˈfluː.ə.t̬|i **-ies** -iz
superfluous suːˈpɜː.flu.əs, sjuː-, sʊ-, sjʊ- ⓤⓢ -ˈpɝː- **-ly** -li **-ness** -nəs, -nɪs
superglottal ˌsuː.pəˈglɒt.ᵊl, ˌsjuː- ⓤⓢ ˌsuː.pɚˈglɑː.t̬ᵊl
Superglue® ˈsuː.pə.gluː, ˈsjuː- ⓤⓢ ˈsuː.pɚ-
supergrass ˈsuː.pə.grɑːs, ˈsjuː- ⓤⓢ ˈsuː.pɚ.græs **-es** -ɪz
supergravity ˌsuː.pəˈgræv.ə.ti, ˌsjuː-, -ɪ.ti ⓤⓢ ˌsuː.pɚˈgræv.ə.t̬i
supergun ˈsuː.pə.gʌn, ˈsjuː- ⓤⓢ ˈsuː.pɚ- **-s** -z
superhead ˈsuː.pə.hed, ˈsjuː-, ˈsuː.pɚ- **-s** -z
superheat (*v.*) ˌsuː.pəˈhiːt, ˌsjuː- ⓤⓢ ˌsuː.pɚˈ- **-s** -s **-ing** -ɪŋ **-ed** -ɪd
superheat (*n.*) ˈsuː.pə.hiːt, ˈsjuː- ⓤⓢ ˈsuː.pɚ-
superhero ˈsuː.pəˌhɪə.rəʊ, ˈsjuː-, ˌsuː.pəˈhɪə.rəʊ ⓤⓢ ˈsuː.pɚ- **-es** -z
superheterodyne ˌsuː.pəˈhet.ᵊr.əʊ.daɪn, ˌsjuː- ⓤⓢ ˌsuː.pɚˈhet̬.ə.roʊ.daɪn **-s** -z
superhighway ˌsuː.pəˈhaɪ.weɪ, ˌsjuː-, ˈsuː.pəˌhaɪ.weɪ ⓤⓢ ˈsuː.pɚ- **-s** -z **ˌinformation ˈsuperˌhighway, ˌinformation ˌsuperˈhighway**
superhuman ˌsuː.pəˈhjuː.mən, ˌsjuː- ⓤⓢ ˌsuː.pɚˈ- **-ly** -li **-ness** -nəs, -nɪs
superimpos|e ˌsuː.pᵊr.ɪmˈpəʊz, ˌsjuː- ⓤⓢ ˌsuː.pɚ.ɪmˈpoʊz **-es** -ɪz **-ing** -ɪŋ **-ed** -d
superintend ˌsuː.pᵊr.ɪnˈtend, ˌsjuː- ⓤⓢ ˌsuː.pɚ- **-s** -z **-ing** -ɪŋ **-ed** -ɪd **-ence** -ənts
superintendenc|y ˌsuː.pᵊr.ɪnˈten.dᵊn*t*.s|i, ˌsjuː- ⓤⓢ ˌsuː.pɚ- **-ies** -iz
superintendent ˌsuː.pᵊr.ɪnˈten.dənt, ˌsjuː- ⓤⓢ ˌsuː.pɚ- **-s** -s
superior (S) suːˈpɪə.ri.əʳ, sjuː-, sʊ-, sjʊ-, sə- ⓤⓢ səˈpɪr.i.ɚ, sʊ- **-s** -z
superiorit|y suːˌpɪə.riˈɒr.ə.t|i, sjuː-, sʊ-, sjʊ-, sə-, -ɪ.t|i ⓤⓢ səˌpɪr.iˈɔːr.ə.t̬|i, sʊ- **-ies** -iz
superlative suːˈpɜː.lə.tɪv, sjuː-, sʊ-, sjʊ- ⓤⓢ səˈpɝː.lə.t̬ɪv, sʊ-, suː- **-s** -z **-ly** -li **-ness** -nəs, -nɪs
Superleague ˈsuː.pə.liːg, ˈsjuː- ⓤⓢ ˈsuː.pɚ **-s** -z

super|man (S) ˈsuː.pə|.mæn, ˈsjuː- ⓤⓢ ˈsuː.pɚ- **-men** -men
supermarket ˈsuː.pəˌmɑː.kɪt, ˈsjuː- ⓤⓢ ˈsuː.pɚˌmɑːr- **-s** -s
supermodel ˈsuː.pəˌmɒd.ᵊl, ˈsjuː- ⓤⓢ ˈsuː.pɚˌmɑː.dᵊl **-s** -z
supernal suːˈpɜː.nᵊl, sjuː-, sʊ-, sjʊ- ⓤⓢ səˈpɝː-, sʊ-, suː-
supernatural ˌsuː.pəˈnætʃ.ᵊr.ᵊl, ˌsjuː-, ˌsjʊ.pəˈ-, ˌsʊ-, -ʊ.rᵊl ⓤⓢ ˌsuː.pɚˈnætʃ.ɚ.ᵊl **-ly** -i **-ness** -nəs, -nɪs
supernormal ˌsuː.pəˈnɔː.mᵊl, ˌsjuː- ⓤⓢ ˌsuː.pɚˈnɔːr-
supernov|a ˌsuː.pəˈnəʊ.v|ə, ˌsjuː- ⓤⓢ ˌsuː.pɚˈnoʊ- **-ae** -iː **-as** -əz
supernumerar|y ˌsuː.pəˈnjuː.mᵊr.ᵊr|.i, ˌsjuː- ⓤⓢ ˌsuː.pɚˈnuː.mə.rer|.i, -ˈnjuː- **-ies** -iz
superoctave ˈsuː.pᵊrˌɒk.tɪv, ˈsjuː- ⓤⓢ ˈsuː.pɚˌɑːk- **-s** -z
superordinate ˌsuː.pᵊrˈɔː.dᵊn.ət, ˌsjuː-, -dɪ.nət, -nɪt, -neɪt ⓤⓢ ˌsuː.pɚˈɔːr.dᵊn.ɪt **-s** -s
superpos|e ˌsuː.pəˈpəʊz, ˌsjuː- ⓤⓢ ˌsuː.pɚˈpoʊz **-es** -ɪz **-ing** -ɪŋ **-ed** -d
superposition ˌsuː.pə.pəˈzɪʃ.ᵊn, ˌsjuː- ⓤⓢ ˌsuː.pɚ- **-s** -z
superpower ˈsuː.pəˌpaʊəʳ, ˈsjuː- ⓤⓢ ˈsuː.pɚˌpaʊɚ **-s** -z
superpriorit|y ˌsuː.pə.praɪˈɒr.ə.t|i, ˌsjuː-, -ɪ.t|i ⓤⓢ ˌsuː.pɚ.praɪˈɔːr.ə.t̬|i **-ies** -iz
supersaver ˈsuː.pəˌseɪ.vəʳ, ˈsjuː- ⓤⓢ ˈsuː.pɚˌseɪ.vɚ **-s** -z
superscrib|e ˌsuː.pəˈskraɪb, ˌsjuː-, ˈ--- ⓤⓢ ˈsuː.pɚ.skraɪb **-es** -z **-ing** -ɪŋ **-ed** -d
superscript ˈsuː.pə.skrɪpt, ˈsjuː- ⓤⓢ ˈsuː.pɚ-
superscription ˌsuː.pəˈskrɪp.ʃᵊn, ˌsjuː- ⓤⓢ ˌsuː.pɚˈ- **-s** -z
supersed|e ˌsuː.pəˈsiːd, ˌsjuː- ⓤⓢ ˌsuː.pɚˈ- **-es** -z **-ing** -ɪŋ **-ed** -ɪd
supersession ˌsuː.pəˈseʃ.ᵊn, ˌsjuː- ⓤⓢ ˌsuː.pɚˈ-
supersonic ˌsuː.pəˈsɒn.ɪk, ˌsjuː- ⓤⓢ ˌsuː.pɚˈsɑː.nɪk **-s** -z **-ally** -ᵊl.i, -li
superstar ˈsuː.pə.stɑːʳ, ˈsjuː- ⓤⓢ ˈsuː.pɚ.stɑːr **-s** -z **-dom** -dəm
superstate ˈsuː.pə.steɪt, ˈsjuː- ⓤⓢ ˈsuː.pɚ- **-s** -s
superstition ˌsuː.pəˈstɪʃ.ᵊn, ˌsjuː- ⓤⓢ ˌsuː.pɚˈ- **-s** -z
superstitious ˌsuː.pəˈstɪʃ.əs, ˌsjuː- ⓤⓢ ˌsuː.pɚˈ- **-ly** -li **-ness** -nəs, -nɪs
superstore ˈsuː.pə.stɔːʳ, ˈsjuː- ⓤⓢ ˈsuː.pɚ.stɔːr **-s** -z
superstring ˈsuː.pə.strɪŋ, ˈsjuː- ⓤⓢ ˈsuː.pɚ- **-s** -z
superstructure ˈsuː.pəˌstrʌk.tʃəʳ, ˈsjuː- ⓤⓢ ˈsuː.pɚˌstrʌk.tʃɚ **-s** -z

supertanker ˈsuː.pəˌtæŋ.kəʳ, ˈsjuː- ⓤⓢ ˈsuː.pɚˌtæŋ.kɚ **-s** -z
supertax ˈsuː.pə.tæks, ˈsjuː-, ˌ--ˈ- ⓤⓢ ˈsuː.pɚ.tæks **-es** -ɪz
supertitle ˈsuː.pəˌtaɪ.tl̩, ˈsjuː- ⓤⓢ ˈsuː.pɚ- **-s** -z
supertonic ˌsuː.pəˈtɒn.ɪk, ˌsjuː- ⓤⓢ ˌsuː.pɚˈtɑː.nɪk **-s** -s
superven|e ˌsuː.pəˈviːn, ˌsjuː- ⓤⓢ ˌsuː.pɚˈ- **-es** -z **-ing** -ɪŋ **-ed** -d
supervis|e ˈsuː.pə.vaɪz, ˈsjuː- ⓤⓢ ˈsuː.pɚ- **-es** -ɪz **-ing** -ɪŋ **-ed** -d
supervision ˌsuː.pəˈvɪʒ.ᵊn, ˌsjuː- ⓤⓢ ˌsuː.pɚˈ- **-s** -z
supervisor ˈsuː.pə.vaɪ.zəʳ, ˈsjuː- ⓤⓢ ˈsuː.pɚ.vaɪ.zɚ **-s** -z
supervisory ˌsuː.pəˈvaɪ.zᵊr.i, ˌsjuː-, ˈsuː.pə.vaɪ-, ˈsjuː- ⓤⓢ ˌsuː.pɚˈvaɪ.zɚ-
super|woman ˈsuː.pə|ˌwʊm.ən, ˈsjuː- ⓤⓢ ˈsuː.pɚˌ- **-women** -ˌwɪm.ɪn
supine (*n.*) ˈsuː.paɪn, ˈsjuː- ⓤⓢ ˈsuː- **-s** -z
supine (*adj.*) ˈsuː.paɪn, ˈsjuː-, -ˈ- ⓤⓢ suːˈpaɪn, ˈ-- **-ly** -li **-ness** -nəs, -nɪs
supper ˈsʌp.əʳ ⓤⓢ -ɚ **-s** -z **-less** -ləs, -lɪs
sup|plant səˈ|plɑːnt ⓤⓢ -ˈplænt **-plants** -ˈplɑːnts ⓤⓢ -ˈplænts **-planting** -ˈplɑːn.tɪŋ ⓤⓢ -ˈplæn.t̬ɪŋ **-planted** -ˈplɑːn.tɪd ⓤⓢ -ˈplæn.t̬ɪd **-planter/s** -ˈplɑːn.təʳ/z ⓤⓢ -ˈplæn.t̬ɚ/z
supp|le ˈsʌp|.l̩ **-leness** -l̩.nəs, -nɪs **-ly** -li, -l̩.i
supplement (*n.*) ˈsʌp.lɪ.mənt, -lə- ⓤⓢ -lə- **-s** -s
supple|ment (*v.*) ˈsʌp.lɪ|.ment, -lə-, ˌ--ˈ- ⓤⓢ ˈsʌp.lə- **-ments** -ments **-menting** -men.tɪŋ ⓤⓢ -men.t̬ɪŋ **-mented** -men.tɪd ⓤⓢ -men.t̬ɪd
supplemental ˌsʌp.lɪˈmen.tᵊl, -ləˈ- ⓤⓢ -ləˈmen.t̬ᵊl
supplementary ˌsʌp.lɪˈmen.tᵊr.i, -ləˈ-, ˈ-tri ⓤⓢ -ləˈmen.t̬ɚ.i *stress shift, see compound:* **ˌsupplementary ˈbenefit**
supplementation ˌsʌp.lɪ.menˈteɪ.ʃᵊn, -lə- ⓤⓢ -lə-
suppliant ˈsʌp.li.ənt **-s** -s **-ly** -li
supplicant ˈsʌp.lɪ.kənt, -lə- ⓤⓢ -lə- **-s** -s
suppli|cate ˈsʌp.lɪ|.keɪt, -lə- ⓤⓢ -lə- **-cates** -keɪts **-cating/ly** -keɪ.tɪŋ/li ⓤⓢ -keɪ.t̬ɪŋ/li **-cated** -keɪ.tɪd ⓤⓢ -keɪ.t̬ɪd
supplication ˌsʌp.lɪˈkeɪ.ʃᵊn, -ləˈ- ⓤⓢ -ləˈ- **-s** -z
supplicatory ˈsʌp.lɪ.kə.tᵊr.i, -lə-, -keɪ- ⓤⓢ -lə.kə.tɔːr-
supplier səˈplaɪ.əʳ ⓤⓢ -ɚ **-s** -z
suppl|y səˈpl|aɪ **-ies** -aɪz **-ying** -aɪ.ɪŋ **-ied** -aɪd **supˌply and deˈmand; supˈply ˌteacher**
supply-sid|e səˈplaɪ.saɪd **-er/s** -əʳ/z ⓤⓢ -ɚ/z

sup|port səˈpɔːt ⓤⓢ -ˈpɔːrt **-ports** -ˈpɔːts ⓤⓢ -ˈpɔːrts **-porting** -ˈpɔː.tɪŋ ⓤⓢ -ˈpɔːr.t̬ɪŋ **-ported** -ˈpɔː.tɪd ⓤⓢ -ˈpɔːr.t̬ɪd **-porter/s** -ˈpɔː.təʳ/z ⓤⓢ -ˈpɔːr.t̬ɚ/z

supportab|le səˈpɔː.tə.bl̩ ⓤⓢ -ˈpɔːr.t̬ə- **-ly** -li

supportive səˈpɔː.tɪv ⓤⓢ -ˈpɔːr.t̬ɪv

suppos|e səˈpəʊz ⓤⓢ -ˈpoʊz **-es** -ɪz **-ing** -ɪŋ **-ed** -d

supposedly səˈpəʊ.zɪd.li ⓤⓢ -ˈpoʊ-

supposition ˌsʌp.əˈzɪʃ.ᵊn **-s** -z

suppositional ˌsʌp.əˈzɪʃ.ᵊn.ᵊl, ˈ-nᵊl **-li** -i

supposititious səˌpɒz.ɪˈtɪʃ.əs, -əˈ- ⓤⓢ -ˌpɑː.zəˈ- **-ly** -li **-ness** -nəs, -nɪs

suppositor|y səˈpɒz.ɪ.tᵊr|.i, -ə-, -tr|i ⓤⓢ -ˈpɑː.zə.tɔːr|.i **-ies** -iz

suppress səˈpres **-es** -ɪz **-ing** -ɪŋ **-ed** -t **-or/s** -əʳ/z ⓤⓢ -ɚ/z **-ible** -ə.bl̩, -ɪ.bl̩

suppressant səˈpres.ᵊnt **-s** -s

suppression səˈpreʃ.ᵊn **-s** -z

suppu|rate ˈsʌp.jə|.reɪt, -jʊ- **-rates** -reɪts **-rating** -reɪ.tɪŋ ⓤⓢ -reɪ.t̬ɪŋ **-rated** -reɪ.tɪd ⓤⓢ -reɪ.t̬ɪd

suppuration ˌsʌp.jᵊrˈeɪ.ʃᵊn, -jʊˈreɪ- ⓤⓢ -jəˈreɪ-, -jʊˈ- **-s** -z

supra- ˈsuː.prə, ˈsjuː- ⓤⓢ ˈsuː.prə-

supradental ˌsuː.prəˈden.tᵊl, ˌsjuː- ⓤⓢ ˌsuː.prəˈden.t̬ᵊl

suprafix ˈsuː.prə.fɪks, ˈsjuː- ⓤⓢ ˈsuː-

supranational ˌsuː.prəˈnæʃ.ᵊn.ᵊl, ˌsjuː-, ˈ-nᵊl ⓤⓢ ˌsuː- **-ly** -li

suprarenal ˌsuː.prəˈriː.nᵊl, ˌsjuː-, ˈsuː.prəˌriː-, ˈsjuː- ⓤⓢ ˌsuː.prəˈriː

suprasegmental ˌsuː.prə.segˈmen.tᵊl, ˌsjuː- ⓤⓢ ˌsuː.prə.segˈmen.t̬ᵊl

supremacist suːˈprem.ə.sɪst, sjuː-, sʊ-, sjʊ- ⓤⓢ səˈ-, sʊ-, suː- **-s** -s

supremac|y suːˈprem.ə.s|i, sjuː-, sʊ-, sjʊ- ⓤⓢ sə-, sʊ-, suː- **-ies** -iz

supreme suːˈpriːm, sjuː-, sʊ-, sjʊ- ⓤⓢ sə-, sʊ-, suː- **-ly** -li **-ness** -nəs, -nɪs **SuˌpremeˈCourt; SuˌpremeˈSoviet**

supremo suːˈpriː.məʊ, sjuː-, sʊ-, sjʊ- ⓤⓢ suːˈpriː.moʊ, sʊ-, sə- **-s** -z

supt (S) *(abbrev. for* **superintendent***)* ˌsuː.pᵊr.ɪnˈten.dənt, ˌsjuː- ⓤⓢ ˌsuː.pɚ-

sura ˈsʊə.rə ⓤⓢ ˈsʊr.ə **-s** -z

surah ˈsjʊə.rə ⓤⓢ ˈsʊr.ə

surat sʊˈræt, sjuː- ⓤⓢ ˈsʊr.æt

Surat ˈsʊə.rət, ˈsuː-; sʊˈrɑːt, -ˈræt ⓤⓢ ˈsʊr.ət; səˈræt

Surbiton ˈsɜː.bɪ.tᵊn ⓤⓢ ˈsɝː.bɪ.t̬ən

surceas|e *(v.)* sɜːˈsiːs ⓤⓢ sɝː- **-es** -ɪz **-ing** -ɪŋ **-ed** -t

surceas|e *(n.)* sɜːˈsiːs ⓤⓢ sɝː-, ˈ-- **-es** -ɪz

surcharg|e *(n.)* ˈsɜː.tʃɑːdʒ, ˌ-ˈ- ⓤⓢ ˈsɝː.tʃɑːrdʒ **-es** -ɪz

surcharg|e *(v.)* ˈsɜː.tʃɑːdʒ, ˌ-ˈ- ⓤⓢ ˈsɝː.tʃɑːrdʒ, -ˈ- **-es** -ɪz **-ing** -ɪŋ **-ed** -d

surcingle ˈsɜː.sɪŋ.gl̩ ⓤⓢ ˈsɝː- **-s** -z

surcoat ˈsɜː.kəʊt ⓤⓢ ˈsɝː.koʊt **-s** -s

surd sɜːd ⓤⓢ sɝːd **-s** -z **-ity** -ə.ti, -ɪ.ti ⓤⓢ -ə.t̬i

sur|e ʃɔːʳ, ʃʊəʳ ⓤⓢ ʃʊr **-er** -əʳ ⓤⓢ -ɚ **-est** -ɪst, -əst **-ness** -nəs, -nɪs

surefire ˈʃɔːˌfaɪəʳ, ˈʃʊə- ⓤⓢ ˈʃʊrˌfaɪɚ

surefooted ˌʃɔːˈfʊt.ɪd, ˌʃʊə- ⓤⓢ ˈʃʊrˌfʊt̬.ɪd **-ly** -li **-ness** -nəs, -nɪs

surely ˈʃɔː.li, ˈʃʊə- ⓤⓢ ˈʃʊr-

suret|y ˈʃɔː.rə.t|i, ˈʃʊə- ⓤⓢ ˈʃʊr.ə.t̬|i, ˈ-t̬|i **-ies** -iz **-yship/s** -i.ʃɪp/s

surf sɜːf ⓤⓢ sɝːf **-s** -s **-ing** -ɪŋ **-ed** -t

surfac|e ˈsɜː.fɪs, -fəs ⓤⓢ ˈsɝː- **-es** -ɪz **-ing** -ɪŋ **-ed** -t **ˈsurface ˌmail; ˈsurface ˌstructure; ˌsurface ˈtension** ⓤⓢ **ˈsurface ˌtension**

surface-to-air ˌsɜː.fɪs.tuˈeəʳ ⓤⓢ ˌsɝː.fɪs.tuˈer **ˌsurface-to-air ˈmissile**

surface-to-surface ˌsɜː.fɪs.təˈsɜː.fɪs ⓤⓢ ˌsɝː.fɪs.təˈsɝːr- *stress shift:* ˌsurface-to-surface ˈmissile

surfactant sɜːˈfæk.tənt ⓤⓢ sɝː- **-s** -s

surfboard ˈsɜːf.bɔːd ⓤⓢ ˈsɝːf.bɔːrd **-s** -z **-er/s** -əʳ/z ⓤⓢ -ɚ/z

surfboat ˈsɜːf.bəʊt ⓤⓢ ˈsɝːf.boʊt **-s** -s

surfei|t ˈsɜː.fɪ|t, -ə|t ⓤⓢ ˈsɝː.fɪ|t **-ts** -ts **-ting** -tɪŋ ⓤⓢ -t̬ɪŋ **-ted** -tɪd ⓤⓢ -t̬ɪd

surfer ˈsɜː.fəʳ ⓤⓢ ˈsɝː.fɚ **-s** -z

surfing ˈsɜː.fɪŋ ⓤⓢ ˈsɝː-

surg|e sɜːdʒ ⓤⓢ sɝːdʒ **-es** -ɪz **-ing** -ɪŋ **-ed** -d

surgeon ˈsɜː.dʒᵊn ⓤⓢ ˈsɝː- **-s** -z

surger|y ˈsɜː.dʒᵊr|.i ⓤⓢ ˈsɝː- **-ies** -iz

surgic|al ˈsɜː.dʒɪ.k|ᵊl ⓤⓢ ˈsɝː- **-ally** -ᵊl.i, -li **ˌsurgical ˈspirit**

Suriname, Surinam ˌsʊə.rɪˈnæm, ˌsjʊə-, ˈ--- ⓤⓢ ˌsʊr.ɪˈnɑːm; ˈsʊr.ɪ.næm

Surinamese ˌsʊə.rɪ.næmˈiːz, ˌsjʊə-

surl|y ˈsɜː.l|i ⓤⓢ ˈsɝː- **-ier** -i.əʳ ⓤⓢ -i.ɚ **-iest** -i.ɪst, -i.əst **-ily** -ɪ.li, -ᵊl.i **-iness** -ɪ.nəs, -ɪ.nɪs

surmis|e *(n.)* ˈsɜː.maɪz; ˌ-ˈ-, sə- ⓤⓢ sɚˈmaɪz; ˈsɜːr.maɪz **-es** -ɪz

surmis|e *(v.)* sɜːˈmaɪz, sə-; ˈsɜː.maɪz ⓤⓢ sɚˈmaɪz **-es** -ɪz **-ing** -ɪŋ **-ed** -d

sur|mount səˈmaʊnt, sɜː- ⓤⓢ sɚ- **-mounts** -ˈmaʊnts **-mounting** -ˈmaʊn.tɪŋ ⓤⓢ -ˈmaʊn.t̬ɪŋ **-mounted** -ˈmaʊn.tɪd ⓤⓢ ˈmaʊn.t̬ɪd **-mountable** -ˈmaʊn.tə.bl̩ ⓤⓢ -ˈmaʊn.t̬ə.bl̩

surnam|e ˈsɜː.neɪm ⓤⓢ ˈsɝː- **-es** -z **-ing** -ɪŋ **-ed** -d

surpass səˈpɑːs, sɜː- ⓤⓢ sɚˈpæs **-es** -ɪz **-ing/ly** -ɪŋ/li **-ed** -t **-able** -ə.bl̩

surplic|e ˈsɜː.plɪs, -pləs ⓤⓢ ˈsɝː- **-es** -ɪz **-ed** -t

surplus ˈsɜː.pləs ⓤⓢ ˈsɝː-, -plʌs **-es** -ɪz **-age** -ɪdʒ

surpris|e səˈpraɪz ⓤⓢ sɚ- **-es** -ɪz **-ing/ly** -ɪŋ/li **-ed/ly** -ɪd/li, -d/li

surreal səˈrɪəl ⓤⓢ səˈriː.əl, -ˈriːl

surreal|ism səˈrɪə.lɪ|.zᵊm ⓤⓢ -ˈriː.ə-, -ˈriː.lɪ- **-ist/s** -ɪst/s

surrealistic səˌrɪəˈlɪs.tɪk ⓤⓢ -ˌriː.əˈ-, -ˌriːˈ-

surrend|er sᵊrˈen.d|əʳ ⓤⓢ səˈren.d|ɚ **-ers** -əz ⓤⓢ -ɚz **-ering** -ᵊr.ɪŋ **-ered** -əd ⓤⓢ -ɚd

surreptitious ˌsʌr.əpˈtɪʃ.əs, -ɪpˈ-, -epˈ- ⓤⓢ ˌsɝː.əpˈ- **-ly** -li **-ness** -nəs, -nɪs

Surrey, surrey ˈsʌr.i ⓤⓢ ˈsɝː-

surrogac|y ˈsʌr.ə.gə.s|i **-ies** -iz

surrogate ˈsʌr.ə.gɪt, -gət, -geɪt ⓤⓢ ˈsɝː.ə.gɪt, -geɪt **-s** -s **ˌsurrogate ˈmother**

surround səˈraʊnd **-s** -z **-ing/s** -ɪŋ/z **-ed** -ɪd **surˌround ˈsound**

sursum corda ˌsɜː.səmˈkɔː.də, -sʊmˈ- ⓤⓢ ˌsɝː.səmˈkɔːr-, -sʊmˈ-

surtax ˈsɜː.tæks ⓤⓢ ˈsɝː- **-es** -ɪz

Surtees ˈsɜː.tiːz ⓤⓢ ˈsɝː-

surtitl|e ˈsɜːˌtaɪ.tl̩ ⓤⓢ ˈsɝːˌtaɪ.t̬l̩ **-es** -z **-ing** -ɪŋ, -ˌtaɪt.lɪŋ **-ed** -d

Surtsey ˈsɜːt.si, -seɪ ⓤⓢ ˈsɝːt-

surveil səˈveɪ **-s** -z **-ing** -ɪŋ **-led** -d **-lant/s** -ənt/s

surveillance sɜːˈveɪ.lənts, sə- ⓤⓢ sɚ-, -ˈveɪl.jənts

survey *(n.)* ˈsɜː.veɪ; ˌ-ˈ-, sə- ⓤⓢ ˈsɝː.veɪ **-s** -z

survey *(v.)* səˈveɪ, sɜː-; ˈsɜː.veɪ ⓤⓢ sɚˈveɪ; ˈsɝː.veɪ **-s** -z **-ing** -ɪŋ **-ed** -d

surveyor səˈveɪ.əʳ ⓤⓢ sɚˈveɪ.ɚ **-s** -z

survival səˈvaɪ.vᵊl ⓤⓢ sɚ- **-s** -z **surˌvival of the ˈfittest**

survivalist səˈvaɪ.vᵊl.ɪst ⓤⓢ sɚ- **-s** -s

surviv|e səˈvaɪv ⓤⓢ sɚ- **-es** -z **-ing** -ɪŋ **-ed** -d **-able** -ə.bl̩

survivor səˈvaɪ.vəʳ ⓤⓢ sɚˈvaɪ.vɚ **-s** -z

Susan ˈsuː.zᵊn

Susanna(h) suːˈzæn.ə, sʊ-

susceptibilit|y səˌsep.təˈbɪl.ə.t|i, -tɪˈ-, -ɪ.t|i ⓤⓢ -təˈbɪl.ə.t̬|i **-ies** -iz

susceptib|le səˈsep.tə.b|l̩, -tɪ- ⓤⓢ -tə- **-ly** -li

susceptive səˈsep.tɪv

sushi ˈsuː.ʃi

Susie ˈsuː.zi

suspect *(n. adj.)* ˈsʌs.pekt **-s** -s

suspect *(v.)* səˈspekt **-s** -s **-ing** -ɪŋ **-ed** -ɪd

suspend səˈspend **-s** -z **-ing** -ɪŋ **-ed** -ɪd

suspender səˈspen.dəʳ ⓤⓢ -dɚ **-s** -z **suˈspender ˌbelt**

suspens|e səˈspents **-ible** -ə.bl̩, -ɪ.bl̩

suspensibility səˌspent.sɪˈbɪl.ə.ti, -səˈ-, -ɪ.ti ⓤⓢ -səˈbɪl.ə.t̬i

suspension səˈspen.tʃᵊn ⓤⓢ -ˈspent.ʃᵊn **-s** -z **suˈspension ˌbridge**

suspens|ive səˈspent.s|ɪv **-ory** -ᵊr.i

suspicion sə'spɪʃ.ᵊn **-s** -z
suspicious sə'spɪʃ.əs **-ly** -li **-ness** -nəs, -nɪs
suss sʌs **-es** -ɪz **-ing** -ɪŋ **-ed** -t
Sussex 'sʌs.ɪks
Susskind 'sʊs.kɪnd ⓤⓢ 'sʌs-
sustain sə'steɪn **-s** -z **-ing** -ɪŋ **-ed** -d **-er/s** -əʳ/z ⓤⓢ -ɚ/z **-able** -ə.bl̩
sustainability səˌsteɪ.nə'bɪl.ə.ti, -ɪ.ti ⓤⓢ -ə.ţi
sustenance 'sʌs.tɪ.nənts, -tᵊn.ənts ⓤⓢ -tᵊn.ənts
sustentation ˌsʌs.ten'teɪ.ʃᵊn, -tən'-
susurr|ate 'suː.sᵊr|.eɪt, 'sjuː- ⓤⓢ suː'sɝː|.eɪt, sʊ-, sə- **-ates** -eɪts **-ating** -eɪ.tɪŋ ⓤⓢ -eɪ.ţɪŋ **-ated** -eɪ.tɪd ⓤⓢ -eɪ.ţɪd
susurration ˌsuː.sᵊr'eɪ.ʃᵊn, ˌsjuː- ⓤⓢ ˌsuː.sə'reɪ- **-s** -z
Sutcliffe 'sʌt.klɪf
Sutherland 'sʌð.ᵊl.ənd ⓤⓢ -ɚ.lənd
Sutlej 'sʌt.lɪdʒ, -ledʒ ⓤⓢ -ledʒ
sutler 'sʌt.ləʳ ⓤⓢ -lɚ **-s** -z
Sutro 'suː.trəʊ ⓤⓢ -troʊ
suttee 'sʌt.iː, -'- ⓤⓢ sə'tiː; 'sʌt.iː **-s** -z
Sutton 'sʌt.ᵊn
Sutton Coldfield ˌsʌt.ᵊn'kəʊld.fiːld ⓤⓢ -'koʊld-
Sutton Hoo ˌsʌt.ᵊn'huː
sutur|e 'suː.tʃəʳ, 'sjuː-, -tjəʳ ⓤⓢ 'suː.tʃɚ **-es** -z **-ing** -ɪŋ **-ed** -d
Suva 'suː.və
Suzanne suː'zæn, sʊ-
suzerain 'suː.zᵊr.eɪn, 'sjuː- ⓤⓢ 'suː.zɚ.ɪn, -zə.raɪn **-s** -z
suzeraint|y 'suː.zᵊr.eɪn.t|i, 'sjuː-, -ᵊn- ⓤⓢ 'suː.zɚ.ɪn-, -zə.raɪn- **-ies** -iz
Suzuki® sə'zuː.ki, sʊ- **-s** -z
Suzy 'suː.zi
svarabhakti ˌsvʌr.ə'bʌk.ti, ˌsvɑː.rə'-, -'bæk-, -tiː ⓤⓢ ˌsvɑː.r.ɑː'bɑːk-
svelt|e svelt, sfelt **-ely** -li **-eness** -nəs, -nɪs
Svengali sveŋ'gɑː.li, sfeŋ- ⓤⓢ sven-, sfen- **-s** -z
Sverdlovsk sveəd'lɒvsk, -'lɒfsk; '--, -ləvsk, -ləfsk ⓤⓢ sverd'lɔːfsk
SW *(abbrev. for* **southwest***)* ˌes'dʌb.l̩.juː, saʊθ'west
swab swɒb ⓤⓢ swɑːb **-s** -z **-bing** -ɪŋ **-bed** -d **-ber/s** -əʳ/z ⓤⓢ -ɚ/z
Swabi|a 'sweɪ.bi|.ə **-an/s** -ən/z
swaddl|e 'swɒd.l̩ ⓤⓢ 'swɑː.dl̩ **-es** -z **-ing** -ɪŋ, 'swɒd.lɪŋ ⓤⓢ 'swɑːd- **-ed** -d **'swaddling ˌclothes**
Swadlincoat 'swɒd.lɪn.kəʊt, -lɪŋ- ⓤⓢ 'swɑːd.lɪn.koʊt
Swadling 'swɒd.lɪŋ ⓤⓢ 'swɑːd-
Swaffer 'swɒf.əʳ ⓤⓢ 'swɑː.fɚ
Swaffham 'swɒf.əm ⓤⓢ 'swɑː.fəm
swag swæg
swag|e sweɪdʒ **-es** -ɪz **-ing** -ɪŋ **-ed** -d
Swaggart 'swæg.ət ⓤⓢ -ɚt
swagg|er 'swæg|.əʳ ⓤⓢ -ɚ **-ers** -əz ⓤⓢ -ɚz **-ering/ly** -ᵊr.ɪŋ/li **-ered** -əd ⓤⓢ -ɚd **-erer/s** -ᵊr.əʳ/z ⓤⓢ -ɚ.ɚ/z **'swagger ˌstick**
swag|man 'swæg|.mæn, -mən **-men** -men, -mən
Swahili swɑː'hiː.li, swə- ⓤⓢ swɑː- **-s** -z
swain (S) sweɪn **-s** -z
swale (S) sweɪl
Swaledale 'sweɪl.deɪl
SWALK swɔːlk ⓤⓢ swɑːk, swɔːk
swallow 'swɒl.əʊ ⓤⓢ 'swɑː.loʊ **-s** -z **-ing** -ɪŋ **-ed** -d
swallowtail 'swɒl.əʊ.teɪl ⓤⓢ 'swɑː.loʊ- **-s** -z **-ed** -d
swam *(from* **swim***)* swæm
swami 'swɑː.mi **-(e)s** -z
swamp swɒmp ⓤⓢ swɑːmp, swɔːmp **-s** -s **-ing** -ɪŋ **-ed** -t **-y** -i **-ier** -i.əʳ ⓤⓢ -i.ɚ **-iest** -i.ɪst, -i.əst **-iness** -ɪ.nəs, -ɪ.nɪs
swampland 'swɒmp.lænd ⓤⓢ 'swɑːmp- **-s** -z
swan (S) swɒn ⓤⓢ swɑːn **-s** -z **-ning** -ɪŋ **-ned** -d **'swan ˌsong**
Swanage 'swɒn.ɪdʒ ⓤⓢ 'swɑː.nɪdʒ
Swanee 'swɒn.i ⓤⓢ 'swɑː.ni
swank swæŋk **-y** -i **-ier** -i.əʳ ⓤⓢ -i.ɚ **-iest** -i.ɪst, -i.əst **-ily** -ɪ.li, -ᵊl.i **-iness** -ɪ.nəs, -ɪ.nɪs
Swanley 'swɒn.li ⓤⓢ 'swɑːn-
Swann swɒn ⓤⓢ swɑːn
swanner|y 'swɒn.ᵊr|.i ⓤⓢ 'swɑː.nɚ- **-ies** -iz
Swanscombe 'swɒnz.kəm ⓤⓢ 'swɑːnz-
swansdown 'swɒnz.daʊn ⓤⓢ 'swɑːnz-
Swansea *in Wales:* 'swɒn.zi ⓤⓢ 'swɑːn- *in Tasmania:* 'swɒnt.si, -siː ⓤⓢ 'swɑːnt-
Swanson 'swɒnt.sən ⓤⓢ 'swɑːnt-
swan-upp|ing 'swɒnˌʌp|.ɪŋ ⓤⓢ 'swɑːn- **-er/s** -əʳ/z ⓤⓢ -ɚ/z
Swanwick 'swɒn.ɪk ⓤⓢ 'swɑː.nɪk
swap swɒp ⓤⓢ swɑːp **-s** -s **-ping** -ɪŋ **-ped** -t **'swap ˌshop**
Swapo, SWAPO 'swɑː.pəʊ, 'swɒp.əʊ ⓤⓢ 'swɑː.poʊ
sward swɔːd ⓤⓢ swɔːrd **-s** -z
swarf swɔːf ⓤⓢ swɔːrf
Swarfega® swɔː'fiː.gə ⓤⓢ swɔːr-
swarm swɔːm ⓤⓢ swɔːrm **-s** -z **-ing** -ɪŋ **-ed** -d
swart swɔːt ⓤⓢ swɔːrt
swarth|y 'swɔː.ð|i ⓤⓢ 'swɔːr-, -θ|i **-ier** -i.əʳ ⓤⓢ -i.ɚ **-iest** -i.ɪst, -i.əst **-ily** -ɪ.li, -ᵊl.i **-iness** -ɪ.nəs, -ɪ.nɪs
swash swɒʃ ⓤⓢ swɑːʃ **-es** -ɪz **-ing** -ɪŋ **-ed** -t
swashbuckl|er 'swɒʃˌbʌk.l|.əʳ, -l|əʳ ⓤⓢ 'swɑːʃˌbʌk.l|.ɚ, -l|ɚ **-ers** -əz ⓤⓢ -ɚz **-ing** -ɪŋ
swastika 'swɒs.tɪ.kə ⓤⓢ 'swɑː.stɪ- **-s** -z
swat swɒt ⓤⓢ swɑːt **-s** -s **-ting** -ɪŋ ⓤⓢ 'swɑː.ţɪŋ **-ted** -ɪd ⓤⓢ 'swɑː.ţɪd **-ter/s** -əʳ/z ⓤⓢ 'swɑː.ţɚ/s
swatch (S®) swɒtʃ ⓤⓢ swɑːtʃ **-es** -ɪz
swa|th swɒ|θ, swɔː|θ ⓤⓢ swɑː|θ, swɔː|θ **-ths** -θs, -ðz
swath|e sweɪð **-es** -z **-ing** -ɪŋ **-ed** -d
sway sweɪ **-s** -z **-ing** -ɪŋ **-ed** -d
Swazi 'swɑː.zi **-s** -z
Swaziland 'swɑː.zi.lænd
swear sweəʳ ⓤⓢ swer **-s** -z **-ing** -ɪŋ **swore** swɔːʳ ⓤⓢ swɔːr **sworn** swɔːn ⓤⓢ swɔːrn
swearword 'sweə.wɜːd ⓤⓢ 'swer.wɝːd **-s** -z
sweat swet **-s** -s **-ing** -ɪŋ ⓤⓢ 'sweţ.ɪŋ **-ed** -ɪd ⓤⓢ 'sweţ.ɪd
sweatband 'swet.bænd **-s** -z
sweater 'swet.əʳ ⓤⓢ 'sweţ.ɚ **-s** -z
sweatpants 'swet.pænts
sweatshirt 'swet.ʃɜːt ⓤⓢ -ʃɝːt **-s** -s
sweatshop 'swet.ʃɒp ⓤⓢ -ʃɑːp **-s** -s
sweat|y 'swet|.i ⓤⓢ 'sweţ- **-ier** -i.əʳ ⓤⓢ -i.ɚ **-iest** -i.ɪst, -i.əst **-iness** -ɪ.nəs, -ɪ.nɪs
swede (S) swiːd **-s** -z
Sweden 'swiː.dᵊn
Swedenborg 'swiː.dᵊn.bɔːg, -dᵊm- ⓤⓢ -dᵊn.bɔːrg
Swedenborgian ˌswiː.dᵊn'bɔː.dʒən, -dᵊm'-, -dʒi.ən, -gən, -gi.ən ⓤⓢ -dᵊn'bɔːr.dʒi.ən, -gi- **-s** -z
Swedish 'swiː.dɪʃ **ˌSwedish 'massage** ⓤⓢ **ˌSwedish mas'sage**
Sweeney 'swiː.ni
sweep swiːp **-s** -s **-ing/s** -ɪŋ **swept** swept **sweeper/s** 'swiː.pəʳ/z ⓤⓢ -pɚ/z
sweepstake 'swiːp.steɪk **-s** -s
sweet (S) swiːt **-s** -s **-er** -əʳ ⓤⓢ 'swiː.ţɚ **-est** -ɪst, -əst ⓤⓢ 'swiː.ţɪst, -ţəst **-ly** -li **-ness** -nəs, -nɪs **ˌsweet 'nothings; ˌsweet 'pea; ˌsweet po'tato** ⓤⓢ **'sweet poˌtato; ˌsweet 'tooth** ⓤⓢ **'sweet ˌtooth; ˌsweet 'William; ˌsweetness and 'light**
sweet-and-sour ˌswiːt.ᵊn'saʊəʳ ⓤⓢ -'saʊɚ
sweetbread 'swiːt.bred **-s** -z
sweetbrier 'swiːt.braɪəʳ ⓤⓢ -braɪɚ **-s** -z
sweetcorn 'swiːt.kɔːn ⓤⓢ -kɔːrn
sweeten 'swiː.tᵊn **-s** -z **-ing** -ɪŋ, 'swiːt.nɪŋ **-ed** -d **-er/s** -əʳ/z, 'swiːt.nəʳ/z ⓤⓢ 'swiː.tᵊn.ɚ/z, 'swiːt.nɚ/z
Sweetex® 'swiː.teks
sweetheart 'swiːt.hɑːt ⓤⓢ -hɑːrt **-s** -s
sweetie 'swiː.ti ⓤⓢ -ţi **-s** -z
sweeting (S) 'swiː.tɪŋ ⓤⓢ -ţɪŋ **-s** -z
sweetish 'swiː.tɪʃ ⓤⓢ -ţɪʃ
sweetmeal 'swiːt.miːl
sweetmeat 'swiːt.miːt **-s** -s

sweet-talk ˈswiːt.tɔːk US -tɑːk, -tɔːk **-s** -s **-ing** -ɪŋ **-ed** -t
sweet|y ˈswiː.t|i US -t̬|i **-ies** -iz
swell swel **-s** -z **-ing/s** -ɪŋ/z **-ed** -d **swollen** ˈswəʊ.lən US ˈswoʊ- ˌ**swelled** ˈ**head**
swelt|er ˈswel.t|əʳ US -t̬|ɚ **-ers** -əz US -ɚz **-ering/ly** -ᵊr.ɪŋ/li **-ered** -əd US -ɚd
swept *(from* **sweep***)* swept
swerv|e swɜːv US swɝːv **-es** -z **-ing** -ɪŋ **-ed** -d
Swettenham ˈswet.ᵊn.əm
swift (S) swɪft **-s** -s **-er** -əʳ US -ɚ **-est** -ɪst, -əst **-ly** -li **-ness** -nəs, -nɪs
Swiftsure ˈswɪft.ʃɔːʳ, -ʃʊəʳ US -ʃʊr
swig swɪɡ **-s** -z **-ging** -ɪŋ **-ged** -d
swill swɪl **-s** -z **-ing** -ɪŋ **-ed** -d **-er/s** -əʳ/z US -ɚ/z
swim swɪm **-s** -z **-ming/ly** -ɪŋ/li **swam** swæm **swum** swʌm **swimmer/s** ˈswɪm.əʳ/z US -ɚ/z ˈ**swimming** ˌ**bath(s)**; ˈ**swimming** ˌ**costume**; ˈ**swimming** ˌ**pool**
swimsuit ˈswɪm.suːt, -sjuːt US -suːt **-s** -s
swimwear ˈswɪm.weəʳ US -wer
Swinbourne ˈswɪn.bɔːn, ˈswɪm- US ˈswɪn.bɔːrn
Swinburne ˈswɪn.bɜːn, ˈswɪm-, -bən US ˈswɪn.bɝːn, -bɚn
swindl|e ˈswɪn.dl̩ **-es** -z **-ing** -ɪŋ, ˈswɪnd.lɪŋ **-ed** -d **-er/s** -əʳ/z, ˈswɪnd.ləʳ/z US ˈswɪn.dl̩.ɚ/z, ˈswɪnd.lɚ/z
Swindon ˈswɪn.dən
swine swaɪn **-s** -z
swineherd ˈswaɪn.hɜːd US -hɝːd **-s** -z
swing swɪŋ **-s** -z **-ing** -ɪŋ **swung** swʌŋ **swinger/s** ˈswɪŋ.əʳ/z US -ɚ/z ˌ**swing** ˈ**door**; ˌ**swings and** ˈ**roundabouts**
swingbridge swɪŋˈbrɪdʒ **-s** -ɪz
swingeing ˈswɪn.dʒɪŋ
swingl|e ˈswɪŋ.ɡl̩ **-es** -z **-ing** -ɪŋ, ˈswɪŋ.ɡlɪŋ **-ed** -d
swingometer swɪŋˈɒm.ɪ.təʳ, -ə.təʳ US ˈɑː.mə.t̬ɚ **-s** -z
swing-wing ˌswɪŋˈwɪŋ US ˈ-- *stress shift:* ˌswing-wing ˈplane
swinish ˈswaɪ.nɪʃ **-ly** -li **-ness** -nəs, -nɪs
Swinton ˈswɪn.tən US -tᵊn
swip|e swaɪp **-es** -s **-ing** -ɪŋ **-ed** -t **-er/s** -əʳ/z US -ɚ/z
swirl swɜːl US swɝːl **-s** -z **-ing** -ɪŋ **-ed** -d **-y** -i
swish swɪʃ **-es** -ɪz **-ing** -ɪŋ **-ed** -t
swish|y ˈswɪʃ|.i **-ier** -i.əʳ US -i.ɚ **-iest** -i.ɪst, -i.əst
Swiss swɪs ˌ**Swiss** ˈ**cheese**; ˌ**Swiss** ˈ**cheese** ˌ**plant**; ˌ**Swiss** ˈ**roll**
Swissair® swɪsˈeəʳ US -er
switch (S®) swɪtʃ **-es** -ɪz **-ing** -ɪŋ **-ed** -t
switchback ˈswɪtʃ.bæk **-s** -s
switchblade ˈswɪtʃ.bleɪd **-s** -z
switchboard ˈswɪtʃ.bɔːd US -bɔːrd **-s** -z
switchgear ˈswɪtʃ.ɡɪəʳ US -ɡɪr
Swithin ˈswɪð.ɪn, ˈswɪθ-
Switzerland ˈswɪt.sᵊl.ənd US -sɚ.lənd
swivel ˈswɪv.ᵊl **-s** -z **-(l)ing** -ɪŋ, ˈswɪv.lɪŋ **-(l)ed** -d ˌ**swivel** ˈ**chair**
swiz(z) swɪz **-es** -ɪz
swizzl|e ˈswɪz.l̩ **-es** -z **-ing** -ɪŋ, ˈswɪz.lɪŋ **-ed** -d **-er/s** -əʳ/z, ˈswɪz.ləʳ/z US ˈ-l̩.ɚ/z, ˈ-lɚ/z ˈ**swizzle** ˌ**stick**
swollen *(from* **swell***)* ˈswəʊ.lən US ˈswoʊ- ˌ**swollen** ˈ**head**
swoon swuːn **-s** -z **-ing** -ɪŋ **-ed** -d
swoop swuːp **-s** -s **-ing** -ɪŋ **-ed** -t
swoosh swuːʃ, swʊʃ **-es** -ɪz **-ing** -ɪŋ **-ed** -t
swop swɒp US swɑːp **-s** -s **-ping** -ɪŋ **-ped** -t
sword sɔːd US sɔːrd **-s** -z ˈ**sword** ˌ**dance**
Sworder ˈsɔː.dəʳ US ˈsɔːr.dɚ
swordfish ˈsɔːd.fɪʃ US ˈsɔːrd-
swordplay ˈsɔːd.pleɪ US ˈsɔːrd-
swords|man ˈsɔːdz|.mən US ˈsɔːrdz- **-men** -mən **-manship** -mən.ʃɪp
swordstick ˈsɔːd.stɪk US ˈsɔːrd- **-s** -s
sword-swallower ˈsɔːdˌswɒl.əʊ.əʳ US ˈsɔːrdˌswɑː.loʊ.ɚ **-s** -z
swore *(from* **swear***)* swɔːʳ US swɔːr
sworn *(from* **swear***)* swɔːn US swɔːrn
swot swɒt US swɑːt **-s** -s **-ting** -ɪŋ US ˈswɑː.t̬ɪŋ **-ted** -ɪd US ˈswɑː.t̬ɪd **-ter/s** -əʳ/z US ˈswɑː.t̬ɚ/z
swum *(from* **swim***)* swʌm
swung *(from* **swing***)* swʌŋ
Sybaris ˈsɪb.ᵊr.ɪs; sɪˈbɑːr- US ˈsɪb.ɚ.ɪs
sybarite ˈsɪb.ᵊr.aɪt US -ə.raɪt **-s** -s
sybaritic ˌsɪb.ᵊrˈɪt.ɪk US -əˈrɪt̬- **-ally** -ᵊl.i, -li
Sybil ˈsɪb.ɪl, -ᵊl US -ᵊl
Note: As a feminine name, /ˈsɪb.ᵊl/ is more common in British English; the /-ɪl/ ending is more usual for the soothsayer.
sycamore (S) ˈsɪk.ə.mɔːʳ US -mɔːr **-s** -z
syc|e saɪs **-es** -ɪz
sycophancy ˈsɪk.ə.fᵊnt.si, ˈsaɪ.kə-, -ˈfænt- US -fᵊnt-
sycophant ˈsɪk.ə.fænt, ˈsaɪ.kə-, -fənt US -fᵊnt **-s** -s
sycophantic ˌsɪk.əʊˈfæn.tɪk, ˌsaɪ.kəˈ- US -t̬ɪk
Sydenham ˈsɪd.ᵊn.əm, ˈ-nəm
Sydney ˈsɪd.ni
Sydneysider ˈsɪd.niˌsaɪ.dəʳ US -dɚ
syenite ˈsaɪ.ə.naɪt, ˈ-ɪ- US ˈ-ə-
Sykes saɪks
syllabar|y ˈsɪl.ə.bᵊr|.i US -ber- **-ies** -iz
syllabic sɪˈlæb.ɪk, sə- US sɪ- **-ally** -ᵊl.i, -li
syllabi|cate sɪˈlæb.ɪ|.keɪt, sə-, ˈ-ə- US sɪˈlæb.ə- **-cates** -keɪts **-cating** -keɪ.tɪŋ US -keɪ.t̬ɪŋ **-cated** -keɪ.tɪd US -keɪ.t̬ɪd
syllabication sɪˌlæb.ɪˈkeɪ.ʃᵊn, sə-, -əˈ- US sɪˌlæb.əˈ-
syllabicity ˌsɪl.əˈbɪs.ə.ti, -ɪ.ti US -ə.t̬i
syllabification sɪˌlæb.ɪ.fɪˈkeɪ.ʃᵊn, sə-, ˌ-ə- US sɪˌlæb.ə-
syllabi|fy sɪˈlæb.ɪ|.faɪ, sə-, ˈ-ə- US sɪˈlæb.ə- **-fies** -faɪz **-fying** -faɪ.ɪŋ **-fied** -faɪd
syllabism ˈsɪl.ə.bɪ.zᵊm
syllable ˈsɪl.ə.bl̩ **-s** -z
syllabub ˈsɪl.ə.bʌb
syllab|us ˈsɪl.ə.bl|əs **-uses** -əs.ɪz **-i** -aɪ
syllep|sis sɪˈlep|.sɪs, sə- US sɪ- **-tic** -tɪk
syllogism ˈsɪl.ə.dʒɪ.zᵊm **-s** -z
syllogistic ˌsɪl.əˈdʒɪs.tɪk **-ally** -ᵊl.i, -li
syllogiz|e, -is|e ˈsɪl.ə.dʒaɪz **-es** -ɪz **-ing** -ɪŋ **-ed** -d
sylph sɪlf **-s** -s
sylphlike ˈsɪlf.laɪk
sylvan ˈsɪl.vən
Sylvester sɪlˈves.təʳ US -tɚ
Sylvia ˈsɪl.vi.ə
symbiont ˈsɪm.baɪ.ɒnt, -bi- US -bi-, -baɪ-, -ɑːnt **-s** -s
symbiosis ˌsɪm.baɪˈəʊ.sɪs, -biˈ- US -bi-, -baɪ-, -ˈoʊ-
symbiotic ˌsɪm.baɪˈɒt.ɪk, -biˈ- US -bi-, -baɪ-, -ˈɑː.t̬ɪk
symbol ˈsɪm.bᵊl **-s** -z
symbolic sɪmˈbɒl.ɪk US -ˈbɑː.lɪk **-al** -ᵊl **-ally** -ᵊl.i, -li
symbolism ˈsɪm.bᵊl.ɪ.zᵊm
symbolist ˈsɪm.bᵊl.ɪst **-s** -s
symbolization, -isa- ˌsɪm.bᵊl.aɪˈzeɪ.ʃᵊn, -ɪˈ- US -ɪˈ-
symboliz|e, -is|e ˈsɪm.bᵊl.aɪz US -bə.laɪz **-es** -ɪz **-ing** -ɪŋ **-ed** -d
Syme saɪm
Symington ˈsaɪ.mɪŋ.tən, ˈsɪm.ɪŋ-
symmetric sɪˈmet.rɪk, sə- US sɪ- **-al** -ᵊl **-ally** -ᵊl.i, -li **-alness** -ᵊl.nəs, -nɪs
symmetry ˈsɪm.ə.tri, ˈ-ɪ- US ˈ-ə-
Symond ˈsaɪ.mənd
Symonds ˈsaɪ.məndz, ˈsɪm.əndz
Symonds Yat ˌsɪm.əndzˈjæt
Symons ˈsaɪ.mənz, ˈsɪm.ənz
sympathetic ˌsɪm.pəˈθet.ɪk US -ˈθet̬- **-al** -ᵊl **-ally** -ᵊl.i, -li
sympathiz|e, is|e ˈsɪm.pə.θaɪz **-es** -ɪz **-ing** -ɪŋ **-ed** d **-er/s** -əʳ/z US -ɚ/z
sympath|y ˈsɪm.pə.θ|i **-ies** -iz
symphonic sɪmˈfɒn.ɪk US -ˈfɑː.nɪk
symphon|y ˈsɪmp.fə.n|i **-ies** -iz ˈ**symphony** ˌ**orchestra** US ˌ**symphony** ˈ**orchestra**
symposi|um sɪmˈpəʊ.zi|.əm US -ˈpoʊ- **-ums** -əmz **-a** -ə
symptom ˈsɪmp.təm **-s** -z
symptomatic ˌsɪmp.təˈmæt.ɪk US -ˈmæt̬- **-ally** -ᵊl.i, -li

Syllabic consonant

A consonant which can stand alone as a syllable.

Examples for English

The great majority of syllables in all languages have a vowel at their centre, and may have one or more consonants preceding and following the vowel (though languages differ greatly in the possible occurrences of consonants in syllables). However, in a few cases we find syllables which contain nothing that could conventionally be classed as a vowel. In English, syllabic consonants appear to arise as a consequence of a weak vowel becoming lost, and some appear to have become obligatory in present-day speech, e.g.:

bottle /ˈbɒt.l̩/ (US) /ˈbɑː.t̬l̩/

In many other cases in English it appears to be possible either to pronounce /m n ŋ l r/ as syllabic consonants or to pronounce them with a preceding vowel, e.g.:

button /ˈbʌt.n̩/
orderly /ˈɔː.dl̩.i, -də.li/ (US) /ˈɔːr.dɚ.li/
history /ˈhɪs.tr̩.i, -tə.ri/ (US) /-tr̩.i, -tɚ-/

In this dictionary, the use of a superscript schwa (ᵊ) indicates the possibility of a syllabic consonant.

The matter is more confusing because of the fact that speakers do not agree in their intuitions about whether a consonant (particularly /l/) is syllabic or not: while most would agree that, for example, *cuddle* and *cycle* are disyllabic (i.e. contain two syllables), *cuddly* and *cycling* are disyllabic for some people (and therefore do not contain a syllabic consonant) while for others they are trisyllabic.

In other languages

For syllables not to contain a vowel is a normal state of affairs in some languages (consider the first syllables of the Czech names *Brno* and *Vltava*). In Japanese some consonants appear to be able to stand as syllables by themselves, according to the intuitions of native speakers who are asked to divide speech up into rhythmical beats.

Syllable

A fundamentally important unit - the most basic unit in speech. Here we are concerned with the phonological notion of the syllable.

Examples for English

Phonologists are interested in the structure of the syllable, since there appear to be interesting observations to be made about which phonemes may occur at the beginning, in the middle and at the end of syllables. In English, it is possible to have from zero to up to three consonants in the ONSET of a syllable, and from zero to up to four in the CODA.

The study of sequences of phonemes is called 'phonotactics', and it seems that the phonotactic possibilities of a language are determined by syllabic structure. This means that any sequence of sounds that a native speaker produces can be broken down into syllables without any segments being left over. For example, in *Their strengths triumphed frequently*, we find the rather daunting sequences of consonant phonemes /ŋθstr/ and /mftfr/, but using what we know of English phonotactics we can split these clusters into one part that belongs to the end of one syllable and another part that belongs to the beginning of another. Thus the first one can only be divided /ŋθ | str/ or /ŋθs | tr/ and the second can only be /mft | fr/.

Phonological treatments of syllable structure usually call the first part of a syllable the ONSET, the middle part the 'peak' and the end part the CODA. The combination of peak and coda is called the RHYME. Syllable breaks, however, may be problematic when approximants occur at syllable boundaries.

synaesthesia ˌsɪn.ɪsˈθiː.zi.ə, -iːsˈ-, -əsˈ-, -ʒə, -ʒi.ə (US) -ɪsˈθiː.ʒə, -ʒi.ə, -zi-

synagogue ˈsɪn.ə.gɒg (US) -gɑːg, -gɔːg **-s** -z

synaloepha ˌsɪn.ᵊlˈiː.fə (US) -əˈliː-

synapse ˈsaɪ.næps, ˈsɪn.æps; sɪˈnæps (US) ˈsɪn.æps; sɪˈnæps

synap|sis sɪˈnæp|.sɪs **-ses** -siːz **-tic/ally** -tɪk/.ᵊl.i, -tɪk/.li

sync(h) sɪŋk **-s** -s **-ing** -ɪŋ **-ed** -t

synchromesh ˈsɪŋ.krəʊ.meʃ, ˈsɪn-, ˌ--ˈ- (US) ˈsɪŋ.krə-, ˈsɪn-, -kroʊ- **-es** -ɪz

synchronic sɪŋˈkrɒn.ɪk, sɪn- (US) sɪnˈkrɑː.nɪk, sɪŋ-

synchronicity ˌsɪŋ.krəˈnɪs.ə.ti, ˌsɪn-, -krɒnˈɪs-, -ɪ.ti (US) -krəˈnɪs.ə.t̬i

synchronism ˈsɪŋ.krə.nɪ.zᵊm, ˈsɪn-

synchronistic ˌsɪŋ.krəˈnɪs.tɪk, ˌsɪn-

synchronization, -isa- ˌsɪŋ.krə.naɪˈzeɪ.ʃᵊn, ˌsɪn-, -nɪˈ- (US) -nɪˈ- **-s** -z

synchroniz|e, -is|e ˈsɪŋ.krə.naɪz, ˈsɪn- **-es** -ɪz **-ing** -ɪŋ **-ed** -d ˌ**synchronized ˈswimming**

synchronous ˈsɪŋ.krə.nəs, ˈsɪn- **-ly** -li **-ness** -nəs, -nɪs

synchrony ˈsɪŋ.krə.ni, ˈsɪn-

synchrotron ˈsɪŋ.krəʊ.trɒn, ˈsɪn- (US) -krə.trɑːn **-s** -z

synco|pate ˈsɪŋ.kə|.peɪt (US) ˈsɪŋ-, ˈsɪn- **-pates** -peɪts **-pating** -peɪ.tɪŋ (US) -peɪ.t̬ɪŋ **-pated** -peɪ.tɪd (US) -peɪ.t̬ɪd

syncopation ˌsɪn.kəˈpeɪ.ʃᵊn, ˌsɪŋ- (US) ˌsɪŋ-, ˌsɪn- **-s** -z

syncope ˈsɪŋ.kə.pi, ˈsɪn-

syncretic sɪŋˈkriː.tɪk, sɪn-, -ˈkret.ɪk (US) -ˈkreţ.ɪk
syncretism ˈsɪŋ.krɪ.tɪ.zᵊm, ˈsɪn- (US) -krə-
syndesis sɪnˈdiː.sɪs (US) ˈsɪn.də-; sɪnˈdiː-
syndetic sɪnˈdet.ɪk (US) -ˈdeţ-
syndic ˈsɪn.dɪk **-s** -s
syndical|ism ˈsɪn.dɪ.kᵊl|.ɪ.zᵊm **-ist/s** -ɪst/s
syndicate (*n.*) ˈsɪn.dɪ.kət, -kɪt (US) -də.kɪt **-s** -s
syndi|cate (*v.*) ˈsɪn.dɪ|.keɪt (US) -də- **-cates** -keɪts **-cating** -keɪ.tɪŋ (US) -keɪ.ţɪŋ **-cated** -keɪ.tɪd (US) -keɪ.ţɪd
syndication ˌsɪn.dɪˈkeɪ.ʃᵊn (US) -dəˈ-
syndrome ˈsɪn.drəʊm (US) -droʊm **-s** -z
syne saɪn
synecdoche sɪˈnek.də.ki
syneres|is sɪˈnɪə.rə.s|ɪs, -rɪ- (US) -ˈner.ə- **-es** -iːz
synergism ˈsɪn.ə.dʒɪ.zᵊm (US) ˈ-ɚ-
synerg|y ˈsɪn.ə.dʒ|i (US) ˈ-ɚ- **-ies** -iz
synesthesia ˌsɪn.ɪsˈθiː.zi.ə, -iːsˈ-, -əsˈ-, -ʒə, -ʒi.ə (US) -ɪsˈθiː.ʒə, -ʒi.ə, -zi-
Synge sɪŋ
synod ˈsɪn.əd, -ɒd (US) -əd **-s** -z **-al** -ᵊl
synodic sɪˈnɒd.ɪk (US) -ˈnɑː.dɪk **-al** -ᵊl **-ally** -ᵊl.i, -li
synonym ˈsɪn.ə.nɪm **-s** -z
synonymous sɪˈnɒn.ɪ.məs, ˈ-ə- (US) -ˈnɑː.nə- **-ly** -li
synonymy sɪˈnɒn.ɪ.mi, ˈ-ə- (US) -ˈnɑː.nə-
synops|is sɪˈnɒp.s|ɪs (US) -ˈnɑːp- **-es** -iːz
synoptic sɪˈnɒp.tɪk (US) -ˈnɑːp- **-s** -s **-al** -ᵊl **-ally** -ᵊl.i, -li
synovi|a saɪˈnəʊ.vi|.ə, sɪ- (US) sɪˈnoʊ- **-al** -ᵊl
synovitis ˌsaɪ.nəʊˈvaɪ.tɪs, ˌsɪn.əʊˈ- (US) ˌsaɪ.nəˈvaɪ.ţɪs, ˌsɪn.əˈ-
syntactic sɪnˈtæk.tɪk **-al** -ᵊl **-ally** -ᵊl.i, -li
syntagm ˈsɪn.tæm **-s** -z
syntagmatic ˌsɪn.tægˈmæt.ɪk (US) -ˈmæţ-
syntax ˈsɪn.tæks **-es** -ɪz
synthes|is ˈsɪnt.θə.s|ɪs, -θɪ- (US) -θə- **-es** -iːz
synthesiz|e, -is|e ˈsɪnt.θə.saɪz, -θɪ- (US) -θə- **-es** -ɪz **-ing** -ɪŋ **-ed** -d **-er/s** -əʳ/z (US) -ɚ/z
synthespian sɪnˈθes.pi.ən **-s** -z
synthetic sɪnˈθet.ɪk (US) -ˈθeţ- **-s** -s **-ally** -ᵊl.i, -li
syphilis ˈsɪf.ɪ.lɪs, -ᵊl.ɪs (US) -ᵊl.ɪs
syphilitic ˌsɪf.ɪˈlɪt.ɪk, -ᵊlˈɪt- (US) -əˈlɪţ-
syphon ˈsaɪ.fᵊn **-s** -z **-ing** -ɪŋ **-ed** -d
Syracusan ˌsaɪə.rəˈkjuː.zᵊn, ˌsɪr.əˈ- (US) ˌsɪr.əˈ-
Syracuse *in classical history:* ˈsaɪə.rə.kjuːz (US) ˈsɪr.ə- *modern town in Sicily:* ˈsaɪə.rə.kjuːz, ˈsɪr.ə- (US) ˈsɪr.ə- *town in US:* ˈsɪr.ə.kjuːs, -kjuːz
Syri|a ˈsɪr.i|.ə **-an/s** -ən/z
Syriac ˈsɪr.i.æk
syringa sɪˈrɪŋ.gə **-s** -z
syring|e sɪˈrɪndʒ, sə-; ˈsɪr.ɪndʒ (US) səˈrɪndʒ; ˈsɪr.ɪndʒ **-es** -ɪz **-ing** -ɪŋ **-ed** -d
syrinx ˈsɪr.ɪŋks **-es** -ɪz
syrophoenician ˌsaɪə.rəʊ.fɪˈnɪʃ.ᵊn, -fiːˈ-, -ʃi.ən, -si.ən (US) ˌsaɪ.roʊ.fiːˈnɪʃ.ᵊn, -fɪˈ-
syr|tis (S) ˈsɜː|.tɪs (US) ˈsɝː|.ţɪs **-tes** -tiːz
syrup ˈsɪr.əp (US) ˈsɪr-, ˈsɝː- **-s** -s **-y** -i
systaltic sɪˈstæl.tɪk (US) -ˈstɑːl.ţɪk, -ˈstæl-
system ˈsɪs.təm, -tɪm (US) -təm **-s** -z ˌ**systems** ˈ**analyst**
systematic ˌsɪs.təˈmæt.ɪk, -tɪˈ- (US) -təˈmæţ- **-ally** -ᵊl.i, -li
systematization, -isa- ˌsɪs.tə.mə.taɪˈzeɪ.ʃᵊn, -tɪ-, -tɪˈ- (US) -tə.mə.ţɪˈ-
systematiz|e, -is|e ˈsɪs.tə.mə.taɪz, -tɪ- (US) -tə- **-es** -ɪz **-ing** -ɪŋ **-ed** -d **-er/s** -əʳ/z (US) -ɚ/z
systemic sɪˈstem.ɪk, -ˈstiː.mɪk (US) -ˈstem.ɪk
systemiz|e ˈsɪs.tə.maɪz, -tɪ- (US) -tə- **-es** -ɪz **-ing** -ɪŋ **-ed** -d
systole ˈsɪs.tᵊl.i
systolic sɪˈstɒl.ɪk (US) -ˈɑː.lɪk
syzyg|y ˈsɪz.ɪ.dʒ|i, ˈ-ə- (US) ˈ-ə- **-ies** -iz
Szczecin ˈʃtʃet.ʃiːn
Szeged ˈseg.ed

Pronouncing the letter T

See also TH, TZ

The consonant letter **t** has several possible realisations. In word initial and final position, it is most often realised as /t/, e.g.:

tap	/tæp/
get	/get/

However, in consonant clusters /t/ may be elided, and it is silent in some words borrowed from French, e.g.:

castle	/ˈkɑː.sl̩/	ⓤⓢ /ˈkæs.l̩/
depot	/ˈdep.əʊ/	ⓤⓢ /ˈdiː.poʊ/

In US English, **t** is often pronounced as a voiced consonant in certain environments. The **t** must be at the end of a stressed syllable, preceded either by one of /n/, /l/, or /r/ or a vowel, and followed by an unstressed syllable, either beginning with a vowel or containing a syllabic consonant other than /n/. Such a pronunciation is shown in EPD as /t̬/.

When appearing between two vowels, **t** is most likely to be pronounced as a tap or flap, e.g.:

butter	/ˈbʌt.əʳ/	/ⓤⓢ ˈbʌt̬.ɚ/

Before a syllabic consonant, and following /n/ or /l/, **t** is pronounced as a brief voiced plosive rather than a tap or flap, e.g.:

little	/ˈlɪt.l̩/	ⓤⓢ /ˈlɪt̬-/
canter	/ˈkæn.təʳ/	ⓤⓢ /-t̬ɚ/

In careful speech, these words may be pronounced with a voiceless /t/, as in British English.

Another common pronunciation for **t** is /ʃ/ where it is followed by a suffix which begins with the letter **i**, e.g.:

negotiate	/nɪˈgəʊ.ʃi.eɪt/	ⓤⓢ /-ˈgoʊ-/
affection	/əˈfek.ʃᵊn/	

In addition

t can be pronounced as a GLOTTAL STOP either word finally or between two vowels.

t is also sometimes realised as /tʃ/, e.g.:

adventure	/ədˈven.tʃəʳ/	ⓤⓢ /-tʃɚ/
picture	/ˈpɪk.tʃəʳ/	ⓤⓢ /-tʃɚ/

Due to coalescence between /t/ and /j/ in British English and omission of /j/ in US English, syllables beginning with **tu** do not always sound the same, e.g.:

Tuesday	/ˈtʃuːz.deɪ/	ⓤⓢ /ˈtuːz-/

t (T) tiː -'s -z
ta *Tonic Sol-fa name for diminished seventh from the tonic:* tɔː ⓤⓢ tɑː **-s** -z
ta *syllable used in Tonic Sol-fa for counting time:* tɑː
ta *thank you:* tɑː
Note: This form is used in casual British English.
Taal tɑːl
tab tæb **-s** -z **-bing** -ɪŋ **-bed** -d
tabard 'tæb.ɑːd, -əd ⓤⓢ -ɚd **-s** -z
Tabasco® tə'bæs.kəʊ ⓤⓢ -koʊ
Tabatha 'tæb.ə.θə
tabbouleh tə'buː.lə, -li
tabb|y 'tæb|.i **-ies** -iz
tabernacle 'tæb.əˌnæk.l̩ ⓤⓢ -ɚˌ- **-s** -z
Taberner tə'bɜː.nəʳ; 'tæb.ᵊn.əʳ ⓤⓢ tə'bɝː.nɚ; 'tæb.ɚ.nɚ
tabes 'teɪ.biːz
Tabitha 'tæb.ɪ.θə, '-ə-
tabla 'tæb.lə ⓤⓢ 'tɑː.blə, -blɑː **-s** -z
tablature 'tæb.lə.tʃəʳ, -lɪ-, -tjʊəʳ ⓤⓢ -lə.tʃɚ **-s** -z
tabl|e (T) 'teɪ.bl̩ **-es** -z **-ing** -ɪŋ, 'teɪ.blɪŋ **-ed** -d **'table ˌlinen; 'table ˌmanners; 'table ˌtennis, ˌtable 'tennis; 'table ˌwine; ˌdrink someone ˌunder the 'table; ˌturn the 'tables on ˌsomeone**
tableau 'tæb.ləʊ ⓤⓢ -loʊ, -'- **-s** -z
tableaux *(alternative plur. of* **tableau***)* 'tæb.ləʊ, -ləʊz ⓤⓢ -loʊ, -loʊz, -'-
table|cloth 'teɪ.bl̩|.klɒθ ⓤⓢ -klɑːθ **-cloths** -klɒθs, -klɒðz ⓤⓢ -klɑːθs, -klɑːðz
table d'hôte ˌtɑː.bl̩'dəʊt, -blə'- ⓤⓢ -bl̩'doʊt, ˌtæb.l̩'-
table-hop 'teɪ.bl̩.hɒp ⓤⓢ -hɑːp **-s** -s **-ping** -ɪŋ **-ped** -t **-per/s** -əʳ/z ⓤⓢ -ɚ/z
tableland 'teɪ.bl̩.lænd **-s** -z
tablemat 'teɪ.bl̩.mæt **-s** -s
tablespoon 'teɪ.bl̩.spuːn **-s** -z
tablespoonful 'teɪ.bl̩ˌspuːn.fʊl **-s** -z
tablespoonsful *(alternative plur. of* **tablespoonful***)* 'teɪ.bl̩ˌspuːnz.fʊl
tablet 'tæb.lət, -lɪt ⓤⓢ -lɪt **-s** -s **ˌtablets of 'stone**
table-turning 'teɪ.bl̩ˌtɜː.nɪŋ ⓤⓢ -ˌtɝː-
tableware 'teɪ.bl̩.weəʳ ⓤⓢ -wer
tabloid 'tæb.lɔɪd **-s** -z
taboo tə'buː, tæb'uː **-s** -z **-ing** -ɪŋ **-ed** -d
tabor 'teɪ.bəʳ, -bɔːʳ ⓤⓢ -bɚ **-s** -z
Tabor 'teɪ.bɔːʳ, -bəʳ ⓤⓢ -bɚ
tabo(u)ret 'tæb.ᵊr.ɪt, -et ⓤⓢ ˌtæb.ə'ret, '--- **-s** -s
Tabriz tæb'riːz ⓤⓢ tɑː'briːz, tə-
tabular 'tæb.jə.ləʳ, -jʊ- ⓤⓢ -lɚ
tabula rasa ˌtæb.jə.lə'rɑː.sə, -jʊ-, -zə
tabulae rasae ˌtæb.jə.liː'rɑː.siː, -jʊ-, -ziː
tabu|late 'tæb.jə|.leɪt, -jʊ- **-lates** -leɪts **-lating** -leɪ.tɪŋ ⓤⓢ -leɪ.t̬ɪŋ **-lated** -leɪ.tɪd ⓤⓢ -leɪ.t̬ɪd **-lator/s** -leɪ.təʳ/z ⓤⓢ -leɪ.t̬ɚ/z
tabulation ˌtæb.jə'leɪ.ʃᵊn, -jʊ'- **-s** -z
tacet 'teɪ.set, 'tæs.et, -ɪt ⓤⓢ 'teɪ.set, 'tæs.et; 'tɑː.ket
tach|e tɑːʃ, tæʃ ⓤⓢ tætʃ **-es** -ɪz
tach|ism (T) 'tæʃ|.ɪ.zᵊm **-ist/s** -ɪst/s **-iste/s** -'iːst/s
tachograph 'tæk.əʊ.grɑːf, -græf ⓤⓢ -ə.græf **-s** -s
tachometer tæk'ɒm.ɪ.təʳ, '-ə- ⓤⓢ tæk'ɑː.mə.t̬ɚ, tə'kɑː- **-s** -z
tachycardia ˌtæk.ɪ'kɑː.di.ə ⓤⓢ -'kɑːr-
tachygraph 'tæk.ɪ.grɑːf, -græf ⓤⓢ -græf **-s** -s
tachygraph|y tæk'ɪ.grə.f|i, tə'kɪg- **-er/s** -əʳ/z ⓤⓢ -ɚ/z
tacit 'tæs.ɪt **-ly** -li **-ness** -nəs, -nɪs
taciturn 'tæs.ɪ.tɜːn ⓤⓢ -ə.tɝːn **-ly** -li
taciturnity ˌtæs.ɪ'tɜː.nə.ti, -nɪ- ⓤⓢ -ə'tɝː.nə.t̬i
Tacitus 'tæs.ɪ.təs ⓤⓢ -t̬əs
tack tæk **-s** -s **-ing** -ɪŋ **-ed** -t
tackl|e 'tæk.l̩ *nautical often:* 'teɪ.kl̩ **-es** -z **-ing** -ɪŋ, 'tæk.lɪŋ, 'teɪ.klɪŋ **-ed** -d

-er/s -əʳ/z, ˈtæk.ləʳ/z, ˈteɪ.kləʳ/z (US) ˈtæk.l̩.ɚ/z, ˈteɪ.kl̩.ɚ/z, ˈtæk.lɚ/z, ˈteɪ.klɚ/z
tack|y ˈtæk|.i **-ier** -i.əʳ (US) -i.ɚ **-iest** -i.ɪst, -i.əst **-ily** -ɪ.li, -əl.i **-iness** -ɪ.nəs, -ɪ.nɪs
taco ˈtæk.əʊ, ˈtɑː.kəʊ (US) ˈtɑː.koʊ **-s** -z
Tacoma təˈkəʊ.mə (US) -ˈkoʊ-
tact tækt
tactful ˈtækt.fəl, -fʊl **-ly** -i **-ness** -nəs, -nɪs
tactic ˈtæk.tɪk **-s** -s **-al** -əl **-ally** -əl.i, -li
tactician tækˈtɪʃ.ən **-s** -z
tactile ˈtæk.taɪl (US) -təl
tactless ˈtækt.ləs, -lɪs **-ly** -li **-ness** -nəs, -nɪs
tactual ˈtæk.tju.əl, -tʃu- (US) -tʃu- **-ly** -i
tad tæd **-s** -z
Tadcaster ˈtædˌkæs.təʳ, -kə.stəʳ (US) -ˌkæs.tɚ
Tadema ˈtæd.ɪ.mə, ˈ-ə-
Tadley ˈtæd.li
tadpole ˈtæd.pəʊl (US) -poʊl **-s** -z
Tadworth ˈtæd.wəθ, -wɜːθ (US) -wɚθ, -wɝːθ
Tadzhik ˈtɑː.dʒiːk, -ˈ- (US) ˌtɑːˈdʒɪk, -ˈdʒiːk
Tadzhikistan tɑːˌdʒɪk.ɪˈstɑːn, -ˌdʒiː.kɪˈ- (US) -ˈdʒɪk.ɪ.stæn, -ˈdʒiː.kɪ-, -stɑːn
Taegu ˌteɪˈguː (US) ˈtaɪ.guː, -ˈ-
Tae Kwon Do ˌtaɪˈkwɒn.dəʊ, ˌteɪ-, ˌ--ˈ- (US) ˌtaɪ.kwɑːnˈdoʊ, ˌ-ˈ--
tael teɪl **-s** -z
ta'en *(dialectal for* **taken***)* teɪn
Taff tæf
Taff-Ely ˌtæfˈiː.li
taffeta ˈtæf.ɪ.tə, ˈ-ə- (US) -ɪ.t̬ə
taffrail ˈtæf.reɪl, -rɪl, -rəl (US) -reɪl **-s** -z
Taff|y *Brit slang for Welsh:* ˈtæf|.i **-ies** -iz
taffy *US for toffee:* ˈtæf.i
Taft *surname* tæft, tɑːft (US) tæft *town in Iran:* tɑːft
tag tæg **-s** -z **-ging** -ɪŋ **-ged** -d **ˈtag ˌquestion**
Tagalog təˈgɑː.lɒg, -ləg (US) -lɑːg, -ləg
tagetes tædʒˈiː.tiːz
Taggart ˈtæg.ət (US) -ɚt
tagliatelle ˌtæl.jəˈtel.i (US) ˌtɑːl.jəˈ-
tagmeme ˈtæg.miːm **-s** -z
tagmemic tægˈmiː.mɪk **-s** -s
Tagore təˈgɔːʳ (US) -ˈgɔːr
Tagus ˈteɪ.gəs
tahini tɑːˈhiː.ni, tə- (US) tə-, tɑː-
Tahi|ti tɑːˈhiː|.ti, tə- (US) təˈhiː|.t̬i **-tian/s** -ʃən/z (US) -ʃən/z, -t̬i.ənz
Tahoe ˈtɑː.həʊ (US) -hoʊ
t'ai chi, tai chi ˌtaɪˈtʃiː, -ˈdʒiː (US) -ˈdʒiː, -ˈtʃiː
Taichung, T'ai-chung ˌtaɪˈtʃʊŋ
Taig taɪk, taɪx **-s** -s
taiga ˈtaɪ.gə, -gɑː (US) -gə
tail teɪl **-s** -z **-ing** -ɪŋ **-ed** -d **-less** -ləs, -lɪs **ˌtail ˈend; ˈtail ˌpipe; make ˌhead or ˈtail of; with one's ˌtail between one's ˈlegs**
tailback ˈteɪl.bæk **-s** -s
tailboard ˈteɪl.bɔːd (US) -bɔːrd **-s** -z
tailbone ˈteɪl.bəʊn (US) -boʊn **-s** -z
tailcoat ˌteɪlˈkəʊt, ˈ-- (US) ˈteɪl.koʊt **-s** -s
tail|gate ˈteɪl|.geɪt **-gates** -geɪts **-gating** -geɪ.tɪŋ (US) -geɪ.t̬ɪŋ **-gated** -geɪ.tɪd (US) -geɪ.t̬ɪd **-gater/s** -ˌgeɪ.təʳ/z (US) -ˌgeɪ.t̬ɚ/z
taille taɪ (US) teɪl
tail|or ˈteɪ.l|əʳ (US) -l|ɚ **-ors** -əz (US) -ɚz **-oring** -ər.ɪŋ **-ored** -əd (US) -ɚd
tailor-made ˌteɪ.ləˈmeɪd (US) -lɚˈ- **-s** -z *stress shift:* ˌtailor-made ˈsuit
tailpiec|e ˈteɪl.piːs **-es** -ɪz
tailpipe ˈteɪl.paɪp **-s** -s
tail-rhyme ˈteɪl.raɪm
tailspin ˈteɪl.spɪn **-s** -z
tailwind ˈteɪl.wɪnd **-s** -z
Taine teɪn
taint teɪnt **-s** -s **-ing** -ɪŋ (US) ˈteɪn.t̬ɪŋ **-ed** -ɪd (US) ˈteɪn.t̬ɪd **-less** -ləs, -lɪs
taipan ˈtaɪ.pæn (US) ˈ--, -ˈ- **-s** -z
Taipei ˌtaɪˈpeɪ
Taiping ˌtaɪˈpɪŋ
Tait teɪt
Taiwan ˌtaɪˈwɑːn, -ˈwæn (US) -ˈwɑːn
Taiwanese ˌtaɪ.wəˈniːz, -wɑːˈ- (US) -wəˈniːz, -ˈniːs
Ta'izz teɪˈiːz, tæ- (US) tæˈɪz
Tajik tɑːˈdʒiːk; ˈtɑː.dʒɪk **-s** -s
Tajikistan tɑːˈdʒiː.kɪˌstɑːn, -ˌstæn
Taj Mahal ˌtɑːdʒ.məˈhɑːl
taka ˈtɑː.kɑː
tak|e teɪk **-es** -s **-ing** -ɪŋ **took** tʊk **taken** ˈteɪ.kən **taker/s** ˈteɪ.kəʳ/z (US) -kɚ/z **ˌtake a ˈwalk; ˌtake a ˈhike**
takeaway ˈteɪk.ə.weɪ **-s** -z
take-home pay ˈteɪk.həʊmˌpeɪ, ˌ--ˈ- (US) ˈteɪk.hoʊmˌpeɪ
take-it-or-leave-it ˌteɪk.ɪt.ɔːˈliːv.ɪt, -əˈ- (US) -ɔːrˈ-, -ɚˈ-
take-off ˈteɪk.ɒf (US) -ɑːf **-s** -s
takeout ˈteɪk.aʊt **-s** -s
takeover ˈteɪkˌəʊ.vəʳ (US) -ˌoʊ.vɚ **-s** -z **ˈtakeover ˌbid**
take-up ˈteɪk.ʌp **-s** -s
taking ˈteɪ.kɪŋ **-s** -z **-ly** -li **-ness** -nəs, -nɪs
tala ˈtɑː.lɑː
Talbot ˈtɔːl.bət, ˈtɒl- (US) ˈtɔːl-, ˈtæl-
Note: Both pronunciations are current for **Port Talbot** in Wales.
talc tælk **-s** -s
Talcahuano ˌtæl.kəˈwɑː.nəʊ (US) ˌtɑːl.kɑːˈwɑː.noʊ, ˌtæl.kəˈ-
talcum powder ˈtæl.kəmˌpaʊ.dəʳ (US) -dɚ **-s** -z
tale teɪl **-s** -z
talebearer ˈteɪlˌbeə.rəʳ (US) -ˌber.ɚ **-s** -z
tal|ent ˈtæl|.ənt **-ents** -ənts **-ented** -ən.tɪd (US) -ən.t̬ɪd **-entless** -ənt.ləs, -lɪs **ˈtalent ˌcontest; ˈtalent ˌscout**
talent|-spot ˈtæl.ənt|.spɒt (US) -spɑːt **-spots** -spɒts (US) -spɑːts **-spotting** -ˌspɒt.ɪŋ (US) -ˌspɑː.t̬ɪŋ **-spotted** -ˌspɒt.ɪd (US) -ˌspɑː.t̬ɪd **-spotter/s** -ˌspɒt.əʳ/z (US) -ˌspɑː.t̬ɚ/z
tales *law:* ˈteɪ.liːz (US) ˈteɪ.liːz; teɪlz
tales|man ˈteɪ.liːz|.mən, ˈteɪlz-, -mæn (US) ˈteɪlz-, ˈteɪl.iːz- **-men** -mən, -men
taletell|er ˈteɪlˌtel|.əʳ (US) -ɚ **-er/s** -əʳ/z (US) -ɚ/z **-ing** -ɪŋ
Talfourd ˈtæl.fəd (US) -fɚd
Taliban ˈtæl.ɪ.bæn, ˈtɑː.lɪ-, -lə-, -bɑːn, ˌ--ˈ- (US) ˈtæl.ə.bæn, -bɑːn, ˈtɑːl-, -ɪ-
Taliesin ˌtæl.iˈes.ɪn, ˌ-ˈjes- (US) -iˈes.ɪn
talisman ˈtæl.ɪz.mən, -ɪs- **-s** -z
talismanic ˌtæl.ɪzˈmæn.ɪk, -ɪsˈ- **-ally** -əl.i, -li
talk tɔːk (US) tɔːk, tɑːk **-s** -s **-ing** -ɪŋ **-ed** -t **-er/s** -əʳ/z (US) -ɚ/z **ˌtalking ˈhead; ˈtalking ˌpoint; ˈtalk ˌshow; (to) ˌtalk ˈshop**
talkathon ˈtɔː.kə.θɒn (US) -θɑːn, ˈtɑː- **-s** -z
talkative ˈtɔː.kə.tɪv (US) -t̬ɪv, ˈtɑː- **-ly** -li **-ness** -nəs, -nɪs
talkback ˈtɔːk.bæk (US) ˈtɔːk-, ˈtɑːk- **-s** -s
talkie ˈtɔː.ki (US) ˈtɔː-, ˈtɑː- **-s** -z
talking-to ˈtɔː.kɪŋ.tuː (US) ˈtɔː-, ˈtɑː- **-s** -z
tall tɔːl **-er** -əʳ (US) -ɚ **-est** -ɪst, -əst **-ness** -nəs, -nɪs **ˌtall ˈstory**
tallage ˈtæl.ɪdʒ
Tallahassee ˌtæl.əˈhæs.i
tallboy ˈtɔːl.bɔɪ **-s** -z
Talleyrand ˈtæl.i.rænd
Tallin(n) ˈtæl.ɪn, -ˈ-, -ˈiːn (US) ˈtɑː.lɪn, ˈtæl.ɪn
Tallis ˈtæl.ɪs
tallish ˈtɔː.lɪʃ
tallow ˈtæl.əʊ (US) -oʊ **-y** -i
Tallulah təˈluː.lə
tall|y ˈtæl|.i **-ies** -iz **-ying** -i.ɪŋ **-ied** -id
tally-ho ˌtæl.iˈhəʊ (US) -ˈhoʊ **-s** -z
tally|man ˈtæl.i|.mən **-men** -mən, -men
Talman ˈtɔːl.mən
Talmud ˈtæl.mʊd, -məd, -mʌd (US) ˈtɑːl.mʊd, ˈtæl-, -məd
talmudic (T) tælˈmʊd.ɪk, -ˈmʌd-, -ˈmjuː.dɪk (US) tɑːlˈmʊd.ɪk, tæl- **-al** -əl
talmud|ism (T) ˈtæl.mʊd|.ɪ.zəm, -məd-, -mʌd- **-ist/s** -ɪst/s
talon ˈtæl.ən **-s** -z
Tal-y-llyn ˌtæl.iˈɬɪn, -əˈ-, -ˈθlɪn
tamable ˈteɪ.mə.bl̩
tamagotchi ˌtæm.əˈgɒtʃ.i (US) ˌtɑː.məˈgɑːtʃ.i, ˈtæm- **-s** -z

tamale *Mexican dish:* tə'mɑː.li, -leɪ
Tamale *in Ghana:* tə'mɑː.leɪ
Tamaqua tə'mɑː.kwə
Tamar *river in W. of England:* 'teɪ.məʳ, -mɑːʳ US -mɚ, -mɑːr
Tamar *biblical name:* 'teɪ.mɑːʳ, -məʳ US -mɑːr, -mɚ
Tamara tə'mɑː.rə, -'mær.ə; 'tæm.ᵊr.ə US tə'mɑːr.ə, -'mær-, -'mer-
tamarillo ˌtæm.ᵊr'ɪl.əʊ US -ə'rɪl.oʊ **-s** -z
tamarin 'tæm.ᵊr.ɪn US -ɚ.ɪn, -ə.ræn **-s** -z
tamarind 'tæm.ᵊr.ɪnd **-s** -z
tamarisk 'tæm.ᵊr.ɪsk **-s** -s
tambala tæm'bɑː.lə US tɑːm'bɑː.lɑː **-s** -z
tamber 'tæm.bəʳ US -bɚ **-s** -z
Tambo 'tæm.bəʊ US -boʊ
tambour 'tæm.bʊəʳ, -bɔːʳ, -bəʳ US -bʊr **-s** -z
tamboura tæm'bʊə.rə, -'bɔː- US tɑːm'bʊr.ə **-s** -z
tambourine ˌtæm.bᵊr'iːn US -bə'riːn **-s** -z
Tamburlaine 'tæm.bə.leɪn US -bɚ-
tam|e teɪm **-er/s** -əʳ/z US -ɚ/z **-est** -ɪst, -əst **-ely** -li **-eness** -nəs, -nɪs **-es** -z **-ing** -ɪŋ **-ed** -d
tameable 'teɪ.mə.bl̩
Tamerlane 'tæm.ə.leɪn US '-ɚ-
Tameside 'teɪm.saɪd
Tamil 'tæm.ɪl, -ᵊl US -ᵊl, 'tɑː.mᵊl, 'tʊm.ᵊl **-s** -z
Tamil Nadu ˌtæm.ɪl'nɑː.duː, -ᵊl- US -ᵊl'nɑː.duː, ˌtɑː.mᵊl'-, ˌtʊm.ᵊl'-, -nɑː'duː
Tammany 'tæm.ᵊn.i
Tammerfors 'tæm.ə.fɔːz US -ɚ.fɔːrz
Tammuz 'tæm.uːz, -ʊz US 'tɑː.mʊz
Tammy 'tæm.i
Tamora 'tæm.ᵊr.ə
tam-o'-shanter ˌtæm.ə'ʃæn.təʳ US 'tæm.əˌʃæn.t̬ɚ **-s** -z
tamoxifen tə'mɒk.sɪ.fen, tæm'ɒk-, -sə- US tə'mɑːk-, tæm'ɑːk-
tamp tæmp **-s** -s **-ing** -ɪŋ **-ed** -t **-er/s** -əʳ/z US -ɚ/z
Tampa 'tæm.pə
Tampax® 'tæm.pæks
tamp|er 'tæm.p|əʳ US -p|ɚ **-ers** -əz US -ɚz **-ering** -ᵊr.ɪŋ **-ered** -əd US -ɚd **-erer/s** -ə.rəʳ/z US -ɚ.ɚ/z
Tampere 'tæm.pᵊr.eɪ US 'tɑːm.pə.reɪ
tamper-evident ˌtæm.pᵊr'ev.ɪ.dᵊnt US -pɚ'-
tamper-proof 'tæm.pə.pruːf US -pɚ-
Tampico tæm'piː.kəʊ US -koʊ, tɑːm-
tampon 'tæm.pɒn US -pɑːn **-s** -z
Tamsin 'tæm.zɪn, -sɪn
Tamworth 'tæm.wəθ, -wɜːθ US -wɚθ, -wɝːθ

tan tæn **-s** -z **-ning** -ɪŋ **-ned** -d **-ner/s** -əʳ/z US -ɚ/z
Tancred 'tæŋ.kred, -krɪd US -krɪd
tandem 'tæn.dəm, -dem US -dəm **-s** -z
tandoori tæn'dʊə.ri, -'dɔː- US tɑːn'dʊr.i
Tandy 'tæn.di
Tanfield 'tæn.fiːld
tang tæŋ **-s** -z **-y** -i
Tang tæŋ US tɑːŋ
Tanga 'tæŋ.gə
Tanganyika ˌtæŋ.gə'njiː.kə, -gæn'jiː- US -gə'njiː-
tangenc|y 'tæn.dʒᵊnt.s|i **-ies** -iz
tangent 'tæn.dʒᵊnt **-s** -s
tangential tæn'dʒen.tʃᵊl US -'dʒent.ʃᵊl **-ly** -i **-ness** -nəs, -nɪs
tangerine ˌtæn.dʒᵊr'iːn, '--- US ˌtæn.dʒə'riːn, '--- **-s** -z
tangibility ˌtæn.dʒə'bɪl.ə.ti, -dʒɪ'-, -ɪ.ti US -dʒə'bɪl.ə.t̬i
tangib|le 'tæn.dʒə.b|l̩, -dʒɪ- US -dʒə- **-ly** -li **-leness** -l̩.nəs, -nɪs
Tangier tæn'dʒɪəʳ, '-- US tæn'dʒɪr **-s** -z
tangl|e 'tæŋ.gl̩ **-es** -z **-ing** -ɪŋ, 'tæŋ.glɪŋ **-ed** -d
Tanglewood 'tæŋ.gl̩.wʊd
tangly 'tæŋ.gli, '-gl̩.i
tango 'tæŋ.gəʊ US -goʊ **-s** -z **-ing** -ɪŋ **-ed** -d
tang|y 'tæŋ|.i **-ier** -i.əʳ US -i.ɚ **-iest** -i.ɪst, -i.əst **-iness** -ɪ.nəs, -ɪ.nɪs
Tangye 'tæŋ.gi
tanh θæn, tæntʃ
tank tæŋk **-s** -s **-age** -ɪdʒ **-er/s** -əʳ/z US -ɚ/z **'tank ˌtop; ˌtanked 'up**
tankard 'tæŋ.kəd US -kɚd **-s** -z
tankful 'tæŋk.fʊl **-s** -z
tanner (T) 'tæn.əʳ US -ɚ **-s** -z
tanner|y 'tæn.ᵊr|.i **-ies** -iz
Tannhäuser 'tænˌhɔɪ.zəʳ US 'tɑːnˌhɔɪ.zɚ, 'tæn-
tann|ic 'tæn|.ɪk **-in** -ɪn **ˌtannic 'acid**
tannin 'tæn.ɪn **-s** -z
Tannoy® 'tæn.ɔɪ
Tanqueray 'tæŋ.kᵊr.i, -eɪ US -kə.reɪ, -kɚ.i
tansy (T) 'tæn.zi
tantalization, -isa- ˌtæn.tᵊl.aɪ'zeɪ.ʃᵊn, -ɪ'- US -t̬ᵊl.ɪ'- **-s** -z
tantaliz|e, -is|e 'tæn.tᵊl.aɪz US -t̬ə.laɪz **-es** -ɪz **-ing/ly** -ɪŋ/li **-ed** -d **-er/s** -əʳ/z US -ɚ/z
tantalum 'tæn.tᵊl.əm US -t̬ᵊl- **-s** -z
tantalus (T) 'tæn.tᵊl.əs US -t̬ᵊl- **-es** -ɪz
tantamount 'tæn.tə.maʊnt US -t̬ə-
tantiv|y tæn'tɪv|.i **-ies** -iz
tanto 'tæn.təʊ US -toʊ
tantr|a (T) 'tæn.tr|ə, 'tʌn- US 'tʌn-, 'tɑːn-, 'tæn- **-ic** -ɪk
tantrum 'tæn.trəm **-s** -z
Tanya 'tæn.jə, 'tɑː.njə US 'tɑː.njə, 'tæn.jə

Tanzani|a ˌtæn.zə'niː|.ə; tæn'zeɪ.ni- US ˌtæn.zə'niː- **-an/s** -ən/z
Tao taʊ US daʊ, taʊ
Taoiseach 'tiː.ʃək, -ʃəx US -ʃək
Tao|ism 'taʊ|.ɪ.zᵊm, 'teɪ.əʊ- US 'daʊ|.ɪ-, 'taʊ- **-ist/s** -ɪst/s
tap tæp **-s** -s **-ping** -ɪŋ **-ped** -t **-per/s** -əʳ/z US -ɚ/z
tapas 'tæp.æs, -əs **'tapas ˌbar**
tap-danc|e 'tæpˌdɑːnts US -ˌdænts **-es** -ɪz **-ing** -ɪŋ **-ed** -t **-er/s** -əʳ/z US -ɚ/z
tap|e (T) teɪp **-es** -s **-ing** -ɪŋ **-ed** -t **'tape ˌdeck; 'tape ˌmeasure; 'tape reˌcorder**
tap|er 'teɪ.p|əʳ US -p|ɚ **-ers** -əz US -ɚz **-ering** -ᵊr.ɪŋ **-ered** -əd US -ɚd
tapestr|y 'tæp.ɪ.str|i, '-ə- US '-ə- **-ies** -iz
tapeworm 'teɪp.wɜːm US -wɝːm **-s** -z
tapioca ˌtæp.i'əʊ.kə US -'oʊ-
tapir 'teɪ.pəʳ, -pɪəʳ US -pɚ **-s** -z
tapis 'tæp.iː, -pi US -i, -ɪs; tæp'iː
Tapling 'tæp.lɪŋ
Tappertit 'tæp.ə.tɪt US '-ɚ-
tappet 'tæp.ɪt **-s** -s
taproom 'tæp.rʊm, -ruːm US -ruːm, -rʊm **-s** -z
tap-root 'tæp.ruːt **-s** -s
tapster 'tæp.stəʳ US -stɚ **-s** -z
tar tɑːʳ US tɑːr **-s** -z **-ring** -ɪŋ **-red** -d
Tara *literary location, place in Ireland:* 'tɑː.rə US 'ter.ə, 'tær- *female name:* 'tɑː.rə US 'tɑːr.ə
taradiddle 'tær.əˌdɪd.l̩ US 'ter-, 'tær- **-s** -z
taramasalata, taramosalata ˌtær.ə.mə.sə'lɑː.tə US ˌtɑːr.ɑː.mɑː.sɑː'lɑː.tɑː
Taransay 'tær.ən.seɪ
tarantella ˌtær.ᵊn'tel.ə US ˌter-, ˌtær- **-s** -z
Tarantino ˌtær.ᵊn'tiː.nəʊ US ˌter.ᵊn'tiː.noʊ, ˌtær-
Taranto tə'ræn.təʊ; US -toʊ; 'tɑːr.ɑːn-
tarantula tə'ræn.tjə.lə, -tjʊ-, -tʃə- US -tʃə-, -tʃʊ-, -tjʊ-, -t̬ə- **-s** -z
Tarawa tə'rɑː.wə US tə'rɑː-; 'tɑːr.ə-
taraxacum tə'ræk.sə.kəm
Tarbuck 'tɑː.bʌk US 'tɑːr-
Tardis 'tɑː.dɪs US 'tɑːr- **-es** -ɪz
tard|y 'tɑː.d|i US 'tɑːr- **-ier** -i.əʳ US -i.ɚ **-iest** -i.ɪst, -i.əst **-ily** -ɪ.li, -ᵊl.i **-iness** -ɪ.nəs, -ɪ.nɪs
tare teəʳ US ter **-s** -z
tar|get 'tɑː|.gɪt US 'tɑːr- **-gets** -gɪts **-geting** -gɪ.tɪŋ US -gɪ.t̬ɪŋ **-geted** -gɪ.tɪd US -gɪ.t̬ɪd **'target ˌpractice**
tariff 'tær.ɪf US 'ter-, 'tær- **-s** -s
Tariq 'tær.ɪk, 'tɑː.rɪk US 'tɑːr.ɪk
Tarka 'tɑː.kə US 'tɑːr-
Tarkington 'tɑː.kɪŋ.tən US 'tɑːr-
Tarleton 'tɑːl.tən, 'tɑː.lə- US 'tɑːrl.tən, 'tɑːr.lə-

Tap

A sound which resembles [t] or [d], being made by a complete closure between the tongue and the alveolar region, but which is very brief and is produced by a sharp upward throw of the tongue blade. As soon as contact is made, the effects of gravity and air pressure cause the tongue to fall again.

Examples for English

The tap sound (for which the phonetic symbol is [ɾ]) is noticeable in Scottish accents as the realisation of /r/, and in US English it is often heard as a (voiced) realisation of /t/ when it occurs after a stressed vowel and before an unstressed one, e.g.:

getting better ⓊⓈ /ˈget̬.ɪŋ ˈbet̬.ɚ/ [g̊eɾɪŋb̥eɾɚ]

In British English it used to be quite common to hear a tap for /r/ in careful or emphatic speech (e.g. *very* [v̥eɾɪ]), though this is less often heard now. It is increasingly common to hear the American-style tapped /t/ in England.

Several varieties of tap are possible: they may be voiced or voiceless. For instance, Scottish pre-pausal /r/ is often realised as a voiceless tap, as in *here* [hiɾ̥]. Taps may also be produced with the SOFT PALATE lowered, resulting in a nasalised tap which is sometimes heard in the US English pronunciation of words like *mental* [meɾ̃əɫ]. A closely related sound is the FLAP, and the TRILL also has some similar characteristics.

tarmac **(T®)** ˈtɑː.mæk ⓊⓈ ˈtɑːr- **-s** -s **-king** -ɪŋ **-ked** -t
tarmacadam ˌtɑː.məˈkæd.əm ⓊⓈ ˌtɑːr-
tarn tɑːn ⓊⓈ tɑːrn **-s** -z
tarnation tɑːˈneɪ.ʃən ⓊⓈ tɑːr-
tarnish ˈtɑː.nɪʃ ⓊⓈ ˈtɑːr- **-es** -ɪz **-ing** -ɪŋ **-ed** -t
tarot ˈtær.əʊ ⓊⓈ -oʊ, -ət, ˈter-; təˈroʊ **-s** -z ˈ**tarot** ˌ**card** ⓊⓈ **taˈrot** ˌ**card**
tarp tɑːp ⓊⓈ tɑːrp **-s** -s
tarpaulin tɑːˈpɔː.lɪn ⓊⓈ tɑːrˈpɑː-, -ˈpɔː-; ˈtɑːr.pə- **-s** -z
Tarpeian tɑːˈpiː.ən ⓊⓈ tɑːr-
tarpon ˈtɑː.pɒn ⓊⓈ ˈtɑːr.pən, -pɑːn **-s** -z
Tarquin ˈtɑː.kwɪn ⓊⓈ ˈtɑːr- **-s** -z
Tarquini|us tɑːˈkwɪn.i|.əs ⓊⓈ tɑːr- **-i** -aɪ, -iː
tarradiddle ˈtær.əˌdɪd.l̩ ⓊⓈ ˈter-, ˈtær- **-s** -z
tarragon ˈtær.ə.gən ⓊⓈ ˈter.ə.gɑːn, ˈtær-
Tarragona ˌtær.əˈgəʊ.nə ⓊⓈ ˌter.əˈgoʊ-, ˌtær-, ˌtɑːr.ɑːˈ-
tarrah təˈrɑː; trɑː
Tarrant ˈtær.ənt ⓊⓈ ˈter-, ˈtær-
Tarring ˈtær.ɪŋ ⓊⓈ ˈter-, ˈtær-
tarrock ˈtær.ək ⓊⓈ ˈter-, ˈtær- **-s** -s
tarry *(adj.) tarred, like tar:* ˈtɑː.ri ⓊⓈ ˈtɑːr.i
tarr|y *(v.) wait:* ˈtær|.i ⓊⓈ ˈter-, ˈtær- **-ies** -iz **-ying** -i.ɪŋ **-ied** -id **-ier/s** -i.əʳ/z ⓊⓈ -i.ɚ/z
Tarshish ˈtɑː.ʃɪʃ ⓊⓈ ˈtɑːr-
tars|us **(T)** ˈtɑː.s|əs ⓊⓈ ˈtɑːr- **-i** -aɪ
tart tɑːt ⓊⓈ tɑːrt **-s** -s **-ly** -li **-ness** -nəs, -nɪs
tartan ˈtɑː.tən ⓊⓈ ˈtɑːr- **-s** -z
tartar, tartare **(T)** ˈtɑː.təʳ ⓊⓈ ˈtɑːr.t̬ɚ **-s** -z ˌ**tartar** ˈ**sauce** ⓊⓈ ˈ**tartar** ˌ**sauce**
tartaric tɑːˈtær.ɪk ⓊⓈ tɑːr-, -ˈter-, -ˈtɑːr- **tar**ˌ**taric** ˈ**acid**
Tartar|us ˈtɑː.tər|.əs ⓊⓈ ˈtɑːr.t̬ɚ- **-y** -i
tartlet ˈtɑːt.lət, -lɪt ⓊⓈ ˈtɑːrt.lət, -lɪt **-s** -s
tartrazine ˈtɑː.trə.ziːn, -zɪn ⓊⓈ ˈtɑːr-
Tartu ˈtɑː.tu ⓊⓈ ˈtɑːr-
Tartuffe tɑːˈtʊf, -ˈtuːf ⓊⓈ tɑːr-
tart|y ˈtɑː.t|i ⓊⓈ ˈtɑːr.t̬|i **-ier** -i.əʳ ⓊⓈ -i.ɚ **-iest** -i.ɪst, -i.əst **-ily** -ɪ.li, -əl.i **-iness** -ɪ.nəs, -ɪ.nɪs
Tarzan ˈtɑː.zən, -zæn ⓊⓈ ˈtɑːr-
Tasha ˈtæʃ.ə
Tashkent tæʃˈkent ⓊⓈ tæʃ-, tɑːʃ-
Tashtego tæʃˈtiː.gəʊ ⓊⓈ -goʊ
task tɑːsk ⓊⓈ tæsk **-s** -s **-ing** -ɪŋ **-ed** -t ˈ**task** ˌ**force**
Tasker ˈtæs.kəʳ ⓊⓈ -kɚ
taskmaster ˈtɑːskˌmɑː.stəʳ ⓊⓈ ˈtæskˌmæs.tɚ **-s** -z
taskmistress ˈtɑːskˌmɪs.trəs, -trɪs ⓊⓈ ˈtæskˌmɪs.trɪs **-es** -ɪz
Tasman ˈtæz.mən
Tasmani|a tæzˈmeɪ.ni|.ə, -nj|ə **-an/s** -ən/z
Tass, TASS tæs
tassel ˈtæs.əl **-s** -z **-led** -d
tassie **(T)** ˈtæs.i
Tasso ˈtæs.əʊ ⓊⓈ -oʊ
tast|e teɪst **-es** -s **-ing** -ɪŋ **-ed** -ɪd **-er/s** -əʳ/z ⓊⓈ -ɚ/z **give someone a** ˌ**taste of their** ˌ**own** ˈ**medicine**
tastebud ˈteɪst.bʌd **-s** -z
tasteful ˈteɪst.fəl, -fʊl **-ly** -i **-ness** -nəs, -nɪs
tasteless ˈteɪst.ləs, -lɪs **-ly** -li **-ness** -nəs, -nɪs
tast|y ˈteɪ.st|i **-ier** -i.əʳ ⓊⓈ -i.ɚ **-iest** -i.ɪst, -i.əst **-ily** -ɪ.li, -əl.i **-iness** -ɪ.nəs, -ɪ.nɪs
tat tæt **-s** -s **-ting** -ɪŋ ⓊⓈ ˈtæt̬.ɪŋ **-ted** -ɪd ⓊⓈ ˈtæt̬.ɪd
ta-ta təˈtɑː, tætˈɑː ⓊⓈ tɑːˈtɑː
tatami təˈtɑː.mi, tɑː-, tætˈɑː- ⓊⓈ təˈtɑː- **-s** -z
Tatar ˈtɑː.təʳ ⓊⓈ -t̬ɚ **-s** -z
Tatchell ˈtætʃ.əl
Tate teɪt ˌ**Tate** ˈ**Gallery**
Tatham ˈteɪ.θəm, -ðəm; ˈtæt.əm
Tati ˈtæt.i, -ˈ- ⓊⓈ tɑːˈtiː
Tatiana ˌtæt.iˈɑː.nə ⓊⓈ ˌ-ˈjɑː.nə
tatler **(T®)** ˈtæt.ləʳ ⓊⓈ -lɚ **-s** -z
Tatra ˈtɑː.trə, ˈtæt.rə ⓊⓈ ˈtɑː.trə
tatter ˈtæt.əʳ ⓊⓈ ˈtæt̬.ɚ **-s** -z **-ed** -d
tatterdemalion ˌtæt.ə.dəˈmeɪ.li.ən, -dɪˈ-, -ˈmæl.i- ⓊⓈ ˌtæt̬.ɚ-
tattersall **(T)** ˈtæt.ə.sɔːl, -səl ⓊⓈ ˈtæt̬.ɚ.sɔːl, -sɑːl **-s** -z
tattl|e ˈtæt.l̩ ⓊⓈ ˈtæt̬- **-es** -z **-ing** -ɪŋ, ˈtæt.lɪŋ **-ed** -d **-er/s** -əʳ/z, ˈtæt.ləʳ/z ⓊⓈ ˈ-l̩.ɚ/z, ˈ-lɚ/z
tattletale ˈtæt.l̩.teɪl ⓊⓈ ˈtæt̬- **-s** -z
Tatton ˈtæt.ən
tattoo tætˈuː, təˈtuː ⓊⓈ tætˈuː **-s** -z **-ing** -ɪŋ **-ed** -d **-er/s** -əʳ/z ⓊⓈ -ɚ/z
tattooist tætˈuː.ɪst, təˈtuː- ⓊⓈ tætˈuː- **-s** -s
tatt|y ˈtæt|.i ⓊⓈ ˈtæt̬- **-ier** -i.əʳ ⓊⓈ -i.ɚ **-iest** -i.ɪst, -i.əst **-ily** -ɪ.li, -əl.i **-iness** -ɪ.nəs, -ɪ.nɪs
Tatum ˈteɪ.təm ⓊⓈ -t̬əm
tau taʊ, tɔː ⓊⓈ taʊ, tɔː, tɑː
Tauchnitz ˈtaʊk.nɪts *as if German:* ˈtaʊx-
taught *(from* **teach***)* tɔːt ⓊⓈ tɑːt, tɔːt
taun|t tɔːn|t ⓊⓈ tɑːn|t, tɔːn|t **-ts** -ts **-ting/ly** -tɪŋ/li ⓊⓈ -t̬ɪŋ/li **-ted** -tɪd ⓊⓈ -t̬ɪd **-ter/s** -təʳ/z ⓊⓈ -t̬ɚ/z
Taunton ˈtɔːn.tən *locally:* ˈtɑːn- ⓊⓈ ˈtɑːn.tən, ˈtɔːn-
taupe təʊp ⓊⓈ toʊp
Taupo ˈtaʊ.pəʊ ⓊⓈ ˈtoʊ.poʊ
Taurean ˈtɔː.ri.ən; tɔːˈriː- ⓊⓈ ˈtɔːr.i- **-s** -z

Taurus ˈtɔː.rəs US ˈtɔːr.əs
taut tɔːt US tɑːt, tɔːt **-er** -əʳ US -ɚ **-est** -ɪst, -əst **-ly** -li **-ness** -nəs, -nɪs
tauten ˈtɔː.tᵊn US ˈtɑː- **-s** -z **-ing** -ɪŋ **-ed** -d
tautologic ˌtɔː.təˈlɒdʒ.ɪk US ˌtɑː.t̬əˈlɑː.dʒɪ-, ˌtɔː- **-al** -ᵊl **-ally** -ᵊl.i, -li
tautologic|al ˌtɔː.təˈlɒdʒ.ɪk|.ᵊl US ˌtɑː.t̬əˈlɑː.dʒɪk-, ˌtɔː- **-ally** -ᵊl.i, -li
tautologism tɔːˈtɒl.ə.dʒɪ.zᵊm US tɑːˈtɑː.lə-, tɔːˈ- **-s** -z
tautologiz|e, -is|e tɔːˈtɒl.ə.dʒaɪz US tɑːˈtɑː.lə-, tɔː- **-es** -ɪz **-ing** -ɪŋ **-ed** -d
tautologous tɔːˈtɒl.ə.gəs US tɑːˈtɑː.lə-, tɔː-
tautolog|y tɔːˈtɒl.ə.dʒ|i US tɑːˈtɑː.lə-, tɔː- **-ies** -iz
Tavener ˈtæv.ᵊn.əʳ, -nəʳ US -ᵊn.ɚ, -nɚ
Taverham ˈteɪ.vᵊr.əm
tavern ˈtæv.ᵊn US -ɚn **-s** -z **-er/s** -əʳ/z US -ɚ/z
taverna təˈvɜː.nə, ˌtævˈɜː- US tɑːˈvɝː-, tə- **-s** -z
Tavistock ˈtæv.ɪ.stɒk, ˈ-ə- US -ə.stɑːk
taw tɔː US tɑː, tɔː **-s** -z **-ing** -ɪŋ **-ed** -d
tawdr|y ˈtɔː.dr|i US ˈtɑː-, ˈtɔː- **-ier** -i.əʳ US -i.ɚ **-iest** -i.ɪst, -i.əst **-ily** -ᵊl.i, -ɪ.li **-iness** -ɪ.nəs, -ɪ.nɪs
Tawe ˈtaʊ.i, -eɪ
Tawell tɔːl; ˈtɔː.əl US tɑːl, tɔːl, ˈtɑː.əl, ˈtɔː-
tawn|y ˈtɔː.n|i US ˈtɑː-, ˈtɔː- **-ier** -i.əʳ US -i.ɚ **-iest** -i.ɪst, -i.əst **-iness** -ɪ.nəs, -ɪ.nɪs ˌ**tawny** ˈ**owl**, ˈ**tawny** ˌ**owl**
tax tæks **-es** -ɪz **-ing/ly** -ɪŋ/li **-ed** -t **-er/s** -əʳ/z US -ɚ/z ˈ**tax e**ˌ**vasion**; ˈ**tax** ˌ**exile**; ˈ**tax** ˌ**haven**; ˈ**tax in**ˌ**spector**; ˈ**tax** ˌ**office**; ˈ**tax re**ˌ**turn**; ˈ**tax** ˌ**year**
taxability ˌtæk.səˈbɪl.ə.ti, -ɪ.ti US -ə.t̬i
taxable ˈtæk.sə.bl̩ **-ness** -nəs, -nɪs
taxation tækˈseɪ.ʃᵊn **-s** -z
tax-deductible ˌtæks.dɪˈdʌk.tə.bl̩, -dəˈ- *stress shift:* ˌtax-deductible ˈearnings
tax-deferred ˌtæks.dɪˈfɜːd US -ˈfɝːd *stress shift:* ˌtax-deferred ˈearnings
taxeme ˈtæk.siːm
taxemic tækˈsiː.mɪk
tax-exempt ˌtæks.ɪgˈzempt, -egˈ-; -ɪkˈsempt, -ekˈ- US -ɪgˈzempt, -egˈ- *stress shift:* ˌtax-exempt ˈearnings
tax-free ˌtæksˈfriː *stress shift:* ˌtax-free ˈbonus
tax|i (*v.*) ˈtæk.s|i **-i(e)s** -iz **-ying** -i.ɪŋ **-iing** -i.ɪŋ **-ied** -id ˈ**taxi** ˌ**rank**; ˈ**taxi** ˌ**stand**
taxicab ˈtæk.si.kæb **-s** -z
taxidermic ˌtæk.sɪˈdɜː.mɪk US -ˈdɝː-
taxidermist ˈtæk.sɪ.dɜː.mɪst, ˌtæk.sɪˈdɜː-; tækˈsɪd.ə- US ˈtæk.sɪ.dɝː- **-s** -s
taxidermy ˈtæk.sɪ.dɜː.mi US -dɝː-
taximeter ˈtæk.siˌmiː.təʳ US -t̬ɚ **-s** -z
tax|is (T) ˈtæk.s|ɪs **-es** -iːz
taxiway ˈtæk.si.weɪ **-s** -z
taxman ˈtæks.mæn **-men** -men
taxonomic ˌtæk.səˈnɒm.ɪk US -ˈnɑː.mɪk **-ally** -ᵊl.i, -li
taxonom|y tækˈsɒn.ə.m|i US -ˈsɑː.nə- **-ist/s** -ɪst/s
taxpayer ˈtæksˌpeɪ.əʳ US -ɚ **-s** -z
tay *syllable used in Tonic Sol-fa in counting time:* teɪ, te
Note: In the sequence 'tay fe' this may be pronounced /te/.
Tay teɪ
tayberr|y ˈteɪ.bᵊr|.i, ˈ-br|i, -ˌber|.i US -ˌber|.i **-ies** -iz
Taylor ˈteɪ.ləʳ US -lɚ
Taylorian teɪˈlɔː.ri.ən US -ˈlɔːr.i-
Taymouth ˈteɪ.maʊθ, -məθ
Tay-Sachs ˌteɪˈsæks US ˌ-ˈ-, ˈ-- ˌ**Tay-**ˈ**Sachs di**ˌ**sease**
Tayside ˈteɪ.saɪd
TB ˌtiːˈbiː
T-bar ˈtiː.bɑːʳ US -bɑːr **-s** -z
Tbilisi tə.bɪˈliː.si; təˈbɪl.ɪ- US təˌbɪl.iˈsiː; ˌtʌb.ɪˈliː.si; təˈbɪl.i-
T-bone ˈtiː.bəʊn US -boʊn **-s** -z ˌ**T-bone** ˈ**steak**
tbs., tbsp. (*abbrev. for* **tablespoon, tablespoonful**) ˈteɪ.bl̩.spuːn, ˈteɪ.bl̩ˌspuːn.fʊl
Tchad tʃæd
Tchaikovsky tʃaɪˈkɒf.ski, -ˈkɒv- US -ˈkɔːf-, -ˈkɑːv-
Tcherkasy tʃɜːˈkæs.i US tʃɝː-
TCP® ˌtiː.siːˈpiː
te *Tonic Sol-fa name for leading note:* tiː **-s** -z
tea tiː **-s** -z ˈ**tea** ˌ**bag**; ˈ**tea** ˌ**break**; ˈ**tea** ˌ**chest**; ˈ**tea** ˌ**cosy**; ˈ**tea** ˌ**dance**; ˈ**tea** ˌ**lady**; ˈ**tea** ˌ**leaf**; ˈ**tea** ˌ**party**; ˈ**tea** ˌ**set**; ˈ**tea** ˌ**shop**; ˈ**tea** ˌ**towel**; ˈ**tea** ˌ**tray**; ˈ**tea** ˌ**trolley**; ˈ**tea** ˌ**wagon**; **not for** ˌ**all the** ˌ**tea in** ˈ**China**
teabread ˈtiː.bred
tea-cadd|y ˈtiːˌkæd|.i **-ies** -iz
teacake ˈtiː.keɪk **-s** -s
teach tiːtʃ **-es** -ɪz **-ing/s** -ɪŋ/z **taught** tɔːt US tɑːt, tɔːt ˈ**teaching** ˌ**practice**
teachability ˌtiː.tʃəˈbɪl.ə.ti, -ɪ.ti US -ə.t̬i
teachable ˈtiː.tʃə.bl̩ **-ness** -nəs, -nɪs
teacher ˈtiː.tʃəʳ US -tʃɚ **-s** -z ˌ**teacher(s')** ˈ**training** ˌ**college**
teach-in ˈtiːtʃ.ɪn **-s** -z
tea|cloth ˈtiː|.klɒθ US -klɑːθ **-cloths** -klɒθs, -klɒðz US -klɑːθs, -klɑːðz
teacup ˈtiː.kʌp **-s** -s **-ful/s** -fʊl/z
Teague tiːg **-s** -z
teahou|se ˈtiː.haʊ|s **-ses** -zɪz
teak tiːk
teakettle ˈtiːˌket.l̩ US -ˌket̬- **-s** -z
teal tiːl **-s** -z
team tiːm **-s** -z **-ing** -ɪŋ **-ed** -d ˌ**team** ˈ**spirit**, ˈ**team** ˌ**spirit**
teammate ˈtiːm.meɪt **-s** -s
teamster (T) ˈtiːmp.stəʳ US -stɚ **-s** -z ˌ**Teamsters'** ˈ**Union** US ˈ**Teamsters'** ˌ**Union**
teamwork ˈtiːm.wɜːk US -wɝːk
teapot ˈtiː.pɒt US -pɑːt **-s** -s
teapoy ˈtiː.pɔɪ **-s** -z
tear (*n.*) *fluid from the eye:* tɪəʳ US tɪr **-s** -z ˈ**tear** ˌ**gas**
tear (*n. v.*) *pull apart, rush, a rent etc.:* teəʳ US ter **-s** -z **-ing** -ɪŋ **tore** tɔːʳ US tɔːr **torn** tɔːn US tɔːrn
tearaway ˈteə.rə.weɪ US ˈter.ə- **-s** -z
teardrop ˈtɪə.drɒp US ˈtɪr.drɑːp **-s** -s
tearful ˈtɪə.fᵊl, -fʊl US ˈtɪr- **-ly** -i **-ness** -nəs, -nɪs
teargas ˈtɪə.gæs US ˈtɪr- **-es** -ɪz **-sing** -ɪŋ **-sed** -t
tearjerker ˈtɪəˌdʒɜː.kəʳ US ˈtɪrˌdʒɝː.kɚ **-s** -z
tearless ˈtɪə.ləs, -lɪs US ˈtɪr- **-ly** -li **-ness** -nəs, -nɪs
tearoom ˈtiː.rʊm, -ruːm US -ruːm, -rʊm **-s** -z
tearstained ˈtɪə.steɪnd US ˈtɪr-
tear|y ˈtɪə.r|i US ˈtɪr|.i **-ily** -ɪ.li
teas|e tiːz **-es** -ɪz **-ing/ly** -ɪŋ/li **-ed** -d **-er/s** -əʳ/z US -ɚ/z
teasel ˈtiː.zᵊl **-s** -z **-(l)ing** -ɪŋ, ˈtiːz.lɪŋ **-(l)ed** -d
Teasmade® ˈtiːz.meɪd
teaspoon ˈtiː.spuːn **-s** -z
teaspoonful ˈtiː.spuːn.fʊl **-s** -z
teaspoonsful (*alternative plur. of* **teaspoonful**) ˈtiː.spuːnz.fʊl
tea-strainer ˈtiːˌstreɪ.nəʳ US -nɚ **-s** -z
teat tiːt **-s** -s
tea-table ˈtiːˌteɪ.bl̩ **-s** -z
teatime ˈtiː.taɪm
tea-tree ˈtiː.triː **-s** -z ˈ**tea-tree** ˌ**oil**
tea-urn ˈtiː.ɜːn US -ɝːn **-s** -z
teazel ˈtiː.zᵊl **-s** -z
teazle (T) ˈtiː.zᵊl **-s** -z
Tebay ˈtiː.beɪ *locally:* -bi
Tebbitt ˈteb.ɪt
tec tek **-s** -s
tech tek **-s** -s
techie ˈtek.i **-s** -z
technetium tekˈniː.ʃi.əm, -si-, ˈ-ʃəm US -ʃi.əm, ˈ-ʃəm
technic|al ˈtek.nɪ.k|ᵊl **-ally** -ᵊl.i, -li **-alness** -l̩.nəs, -nɪs ˈ**technical** ˌ**college**
technicalit|y ˌtek.nɪˈkæl.ə.t|i, -nəˈ-, -ɪ.t|i US -nəˈkæl.ə.t̬|i **-ies** -iz
technician tekˈnɪʃ.ᵊn **-s** -z
Technicolor® ˈtek.nɪˌkʌl.əʳ US -ɚ

technicolo(u)r 'tek.nɪˌkʌl.əʳ (US) -ɚ **-ed** -d
technics (T®) 'tek.nɪks
technique tek'niːk **-s** -s
techno- tek.nəʊ-; tek'nɒ- (US) 'tek.noʊ-, -nə-; tek'nɑː-
Note: Prefix. This may carry primary or secondary stress on the first syllable, e.g. **technophobe** /'tek.nə.fəʊb (US) -foʊb/, **technophobia** /ˌtek.nə'fəʊ.bi.ə (US) -'foʊ-/, or on the second syllable, e.g. **technology** /tek'nɒl.ə.dʒi (US) tek'nɑː-/.
technocrat 'tek.nəʊ.kræt (US) -nə- **-s** -s
technocratic ˌtek.nəʊ'kræt.ɪk (US) -nə'kræṭ-
technologic|al ˌtek.nə'lɒdʒ.ɪ.k|əl (US) -'lɑː.dʒɪ- **-ly** -əl.i, -li
technolog|y tek'nɒl.ə.dʒ|i (US) -'nɑː.lə- **-ist/s** -ɪst/s **-ies**
technophobe 'tek.nəʊ.fəʊb (US) -nə.foʊb **-s** -z
technophob|ia ˌtek.nəʊ'fəʊ.b|i.ə (US) -nə'foʊ- **-ic** -ɪk
tech|y 'tetʃ|.i **-ier** -i.əʳ (US) -i.ɚ **-iest** -i.ɪst, -i.əst **-ily** -ɪ.li, -əl.i **-iness** -ɪ.nəs, -ɪ.nɪs
Teck tek
tectonic tek'tɒn.ɪk (US) -'tɑː.nɪk **-s** -s **tecˌtonic 'plates**
ted (T) ted **-s** -z **-ding** -ɪŋ **-ded** -ɪd **-der/s** -əʳ/z (US) -ɚ/z
Teddington 'ted.ɪŋ.tən
tedd|y (T) 'ted|.i **-ies** -iz **'teddy ˌbear; ˌTeddy Bear's 'Picnic; 'teddy ˌboy**
Te Deum ˌteɪ'deɪ.ʊm, ˌtiː'diː.əm; **-s** -z
tedious 'tiː.di.əs (US) -di.əs, -dʒəs **-ly** -li **-ness** -nəs, -nɪs
tedium 'tiː.di.əm
tee tiː **-s** -z **-ing** -ɪŋ **-d** -d
tee-hee ˌtiː'hiː **-s** -z
teem tiːm **-s** -z **-ing** -ɪŋ **-ed** -d
teen tiːn **-s** -z
teenage 'tiːn.eɪdʒ **-d** -d
teenager 'tiːnˌeɪ.dʒəʳ (US) -dʒɚ **-s** -z
teens|y 'tiːn.z|i **-ier** -i.əʳ (US) -i.ɚ **-iest** -i.ɪst, -i.əst
teensy-weensy ˌtiːn.zi'wiːn.zi, ˌtiːnt.si'wiːnt.si *stress shift:* ˌteensy-weensy 'house
teen|y 'tiː.n|i **-iest** -i.ɪst, -i.əst
teenybopper 'tiː.niˌbɒp.əʳ (US) -ˌbɑː.pɚ **-s** -z
teeny-weeny ˌtiː.ni'wiː.ni *stress shift:* ˌteeny-weeny 'house
teepee 'tiː.piː **-s** -z
Tees tiːz
Teesdale 'tiːz.deɪl
teeshirt 'tiː.ʃɜːt (US) -ʃɝːt **-s** -s
tee-square 'tiː.skweəʳ, ˌ-'- (US) 'tiː.skwer **-s** -z
Teesside 'tiː.saɪd, 'tiːz-
teet|er 'tiː.t|əʳ (US) -ṭ|ɚ **-ers** -əz (US) -ɚz **-ering** -ər.ɪŋ **-ered** -əd (US) -ɚd
teeter-tott|er ˌtiː.tə'tɒt|.əʳ (US) -ṭɚ'tɑː.ṭ|ɚ **-ers** -əz (US) -ɚz **-ering** -ər.ɪŋ **-ered** -əd (US) -ɚd
teeth *(plur. of* **tooth***)* tiːθ **ˌgrit one's 'teeth; ˌset someone's 'teeth on ˌedge**
teeth|e tiːð **-es** -z **-ing** -ɪŋ **-ed** -d **'teething ˌring; 'teething ˌtroubles**
teetotal ˌtiː'təʊ.təl (US) -'toʊ.ṭəl, '-ˌ-- **-ism** -ɪ.zəm
teetotal(l)er ˌtiː'təʊ.təl.əʳ, -'təʊt.ləʳ (US) -'toʊ.ṭəl.ɚ, -'toʊt.lɚ, 'tiːˌtoʊ.ṭəl.ɚ, -ˌtoʊt.lɚ **-s** -z
teetotum ˌtiː'təʊ.təm, '---; ˌtiː.təʊ'tʌm (US) ˌtiː'toʊṭ.əm **-s** -z
TEFL 'tef.l̩
Teflon® 'tef.lɒn (US) -lɑːn
Tegucigalpa tegˌuː.sɪ'gæl.pə (US) -sə'gæl.pɑː, -'gɑːl-
tegument 'teg.jʊ.mənt, -jə- **-s** -s
Tehran, Teheran teə'rɑːn, -'ræn; ˌte.həʳ'ɑːn, ˌteɪ.əʳ'-, -'æn (US) teɪ'ɑːn, tə'rɑːn, teə-, -'ræn
Tehuantepec tə'wɑːn.tə.pek (US) -ṭə-
Teifi 'taɪ.vi
Teign tɪn, tiːn
Teignbridge 'tɪn.brɪdʒ, 'tiːn-, 'tɪm-, 'tiːm- (US) 'tɪn-, 'tiːn-
Teignmouth 'tɪn.məθ, 'tiːn-, 'tɪm-, 'tiːm- *locally also:* 'tɪŋ- (US) 'tɪn-, 'tiːn-
Teignton 'teɪn.tən (US) -tən
Teiresias taɪə'riː.si.əs (US) taɪ-
Te Kanawa teɪ'kɑː.nə.wə, tɪ-
tel. *(abbrev. for* **telephone***)* 'tel.ɪ.fəʊn (US) -ə.foʊn
telaesthesia ˌtel.əs'θiː.zi.ə, -ɪs'-, -iːs'-, -ʒi-, '-ʒə (US) ˌtel.əs'θiː.ʒə
telaesthetic ˌtel.əs'θet.ɪk, -ɪs'-, -iːs'- (US) -'θeṭ- **-s** -s **-ally** -əl.i, -li
telamon (T) 'tel.ə.mən, -mɒn (US) -mən, -mɑːn **-s** -z
TelAutograph® tel'ɔː.tə.grɑːf, -græf (US) -'ɑː.ṭə.græf, -'ɔː-
Tel Aviv ˌtel.ə'viːv, -æv'iːv, -'ɪv (US) -ə'viːv, -ɑː'-
tele- tel.ɪ-; tɪ'le-, tə- (US) 'tel.ə-; tɪ'le-, tə-, tel.ɪ-
Note: Prefix. This may carry primary or secondary stress on the first syllable, e.g. **telephone** /'tel.ɪ.fəʊn (US) 'tel.ə.foʊn/, **telegraphic** /ˌtel.ɪ'græf.ɪk (US) -ə'-/, or on the second syllable, e.g. **telephony** /tə'lef.ə.ni/.
tele 'tel.i **-s** -z
telebanking 'tel.ɪˌbæŋ.kɪŋ
telecamera 'tel.ɪˌkæm.ər.ə, ˌ-rə **-s** -z
telecast 'tel.ɪ.kɑːst (US) -kæst **-s** -s **-ing** -ɪŋ **-ed** -ɪd **-er/s** -əʳ/z (US) -ɚ/z
tele-cine ˌtel.ɪ'sɪn.i
telecom 'tel.ɪ.kɒm (US) -kɑːm **-s** -z
telecommunications ˌtel.ɪ.kəˌmjuː.nɪ'keɪ.ʃənz, -nə'-
telecom|mute ˌtel.ɪ.kə|'mjuːt (US) '---- **-mutes** -'mjuːts **-muting** -'mjuː.tɪŋ (US) -mjuː.ṭɪŋ **-muted** -'mjuː.tɪd (US) -mjuː.ṭɪd **-muter/s** -'mjuː.təʳ/z (US) -mjuː.ṭɚ/z
teleconferenc|e ˌtel.ɪ'kɒn.fər.ənts (US) 'tel.ɪˌkɑːn- **-es** -ɪz
telecottag|e 'tel.ɪˌkɒt.ɪdʒ (US) -ˌkɑː.ṭɪdʒ **-ing** -ɪŋ
telefilm 'tel.ɪ.fɪlm (US) '-ə- **-s** -z
telegenic ˌtel.ɪ'dʒen.ɪk (US) -ə'-
telegram 'tel.ɪ.græm **-s** -z **-ming** -ɪŋ **-med** -d
telegramese ˌtel.ɪ.græm'iːz
telegraph 'tel.ɪ.grɑːf, -græf (US) -græf **-s** -s **-ing** -ɪŋ **-ed** -t **'telegraph ˌpole; 'telegraph ˌwire**
telegrapher tɪ'leg.rə.fəʳ, tel'eg-, tə'leg- (US) tə'leg.rə.fɚ **-s** -z
telegraphese ˌtel.ɪ.grɑː'fiːz, -græf'iːz, -grə'fiːz (US) -græf'iːz, -grə'fiːz
telegraphic ˌtel.ɪ'græf.ɪk (US) -ə'- **-ally** -əl.i, -li
telegraph|y tɪ'leg.rə.f|i, tel'eg-, tə'leg- (US) tə'leg- **-ist/s** -ɪst/s
teleki|nesis ˌtel.ɪ.kɪ|'niː.sɪs, ˌ-ə-, -kaɪ'- (US) -kɪ'- **-netic** -'net.ɪk (US) -'neṭ-
Telemachus tɪ'lem.ə.kəs, tel'em-, tə'lem- (US) tə'lem-
Telemann 'teɪ.lə.mæn (US) -mɑːn
telemark 'tel.ɪ.mɑːk, '-ə- (US) -ə.mɑːrk **-s** -s **-ing** -ɪŋ **-ed** -t
telemarketing ˌtel.ɪ'mɑː.kɪ.tɪŋ, -kə-, 'tel.ɪˌmɑː- (US) 'tel.əˌmɑːr.kə.ṭɪŋ
Telemessag|e® 'tel.ɪˌmes.ɪdʒ **-es** -ɪz
telemet|er tə'lem.ɪ.t|əʳ, '-ə-; 'tel.ɪˌmiː- (US) 'tel.əˌmiː.ṭ|ɚ; tə'lem.ə- **-ers** -əz (US) -ɚz **-ering** -ər.ɪŋ **-ered** -əd (US) -ɚd
telemetric ˌtel.ɪ'met.rɪk (US) -ə'- **-ally** -əl.i, -li
telemetry tɪ'lem.ɪ.tri, tə-, '-ə- (US) tə'lem.ə-
teleological ˌtel.i.ə'lɒdʒ.ɪ.kəl, ˌtiː.li- (US) ˌtiː.li.ə'lɑː.dʒɪ-, ˌtel.i-
teleolog|y ˌtel.i'ɒl.ə.dʒ|i, ˌtiː.li'- (US) ˌtiː.li'ɑː.lə-, ˌtel.i'- **-ist/s** -ɪst/s
telepathic ˌtel.ɪ'pæθ.ɪk (US) -ə'- **-ally** -əl.i, -li
telepathiz|e, -is|e tɪ'lep.ə.θaɪz, tel'ep-, tə'lep- (US) tə'lep- **-es** -ɪz **-ing** -ɪŋ **-ed** -d
telepath|y tɪ'lep.ə.θ|i, tel'ep-, tə'lep- (US) tə'lep- **-ist/s** -ɪst/s
telephon|e 'tel.ɪ.fəʊn (US) -ə.foʊn **-es** -z **-ing** -ɪŋ **-ed** -d **-er/s** -əʳ/z (US) -ɚ/z **'telephone ˌbooth; 'telephone ˌbook; 'telephone ˌbox; 'telephone ˌcall; 'telephone diˌrectory; 'telephone ˌnumber; 'telephone ˌpole**

telephonic ˌtel.ɪˈfɒn.ɪk, -əˈ- (US) -əˈfɑː.nɪk **-ally** -ᵊl.i, -li
telephonist tɪˈlef.ᵊn.ɪst, telˈef-, təˈlef- (US) təˈlef- **-s** -s
telephony tɪˈlef.ᵊn.i, telˈef-, təˈlef- (US) təˈlef-
telephoto ˌtel.ɪˈfəʊ.təʊ (US) ˈtel.ə.foʊ.t̬oʊ **-s** -z *stress shift, see compound:* ˌ**telephoto** ˈ**lens**
telephotography ˌtel.ɪ.fəˈtɒg.rə.fi (US) -ə.fəˈtɑː.grə-
teleprinter ˈtel.ɪˌprɪn.təʳ (US) -əˌprɪn.t̬ɚ **-s** -z
TelePrompTer® ˈtel.ɪˌprɒmp.təʳ (US) -əˌprɑːmp.tɚ **-s** -z
telerecord (*n.*) ˈtel.ɪˌrek.ɔːd (US) -ɚd **-s** -z
telerecord (*v.*) ˈtel.ɪ.rɪˌkɔːd, -rəˌ-, ˌtel.ɪ.rɪˈkɔːd, -rəˈ- (US) ˈtel.ɪ.rɪˌkɔːrd, -rə-, ˌtel.ɪ.rɪˈkɔːrd, -rəˈ- **-s** -z **-ing/s** -ɪŋ/z **-ed** -ɪd
telesales ˈtel.ɪ.seɪlz
telescop|e ˈtel.ɪ.skəʊp (US) -ə.skoʊp **-es** -s **-ing** -ɪŋ **-ed** -t
telescopic ˌtel.ɪˈskɒp.ɪk (US) -əˈskɑː.pɪk **-ally** -ᵊl.i, -li
telescreen ˈtel.ɪ.skriːn **-s** -z
teleshopping ˈtel.ɪˌʃɒp.ɪŋ, ˌtel.ɪˈʃɒp- (US) ˈtel.əˌʃɑː.pɪŋ
telesthesia ˌtel.əsˈθiː.zi.ə, -ɪsˈ-, -iːsˈ-, -ʒi-, ˈ-ʒə- (US) ˌtel.əsˈθiː.ʒə
telesthetic ˌtel.əsˈθet.ɪk, -ɪsˈ-, -iːsˈ- (US) -ˈθet̬- **-s** -s **-ally** -ᵊl.i, -li
Teletex® ˈtel.ɪ.teks
teletext ˈtel.ɪ.tekst (US) ˈ-ə- **-s** -s
telethon ˈtel.ɪ.θɒn (US) -ə.θɑːn **-s** -z
Teletype® ˈtel.ɪ.taɪp (US) ˈ-ə- **-s** -s
Teletypesetter® ˌtel.ɪˈtaɪpˌset.əʳ (US) -əˈtaɪpˌset̬.ɚ **-s** -z
televangel|ism ˌtel.ɪˈvæn.dʒə.l|ɪ.zᵊm, -dʒɪ- **-ist/s** -ɪst/s
teleview ˈtel.ɪ.vjuː (US) ˈ-ə- **-s** -z **-ing** -ɪŋ **-ed** -d **-er/s** -əʳ/z (US) -ɚ/z
televis|e ˈtel.ɪ.vaɪz (US) ˈ-ə- **-es** -ɪz **-ing** -ɪŋ **-ed** -d
television ˈtel.ɪ.vɪʒ.ᵊn, ˌtel.ɪˈvɪʒ- (US) ˈtel.ə.vɪʒ- **-s** -z ˈ**television** ˌ**set**, **tele**ˈ**vision** ˌ**set**
televisor ˈtel.ɪ.vaɪ.zəʳ (US) -ə.vaɪ.zɚ **-s** -z
televisual ˌtel.ɪˈvɪʒ.u.əl, -ˈvɪz.ju- (US) -əˈvɪʒ.u- **-ly** -i
telework|ing ˈtel.ɪˌwɜː.k|ɪŋ (US) -ˌwɝː- **-er/s** -əʳ/z (US) -ɚ/z
telex ˈtel.eks **-es** -ɪz **-ing** -ɪŋ **-ed** -t
Telfer ˈtel.fəʳ (US) -fɚ
Telford ˈtel.fəd (US) -fɚd
telic ˈtel.ɪk (US) ˈtiː.lɪk, ˈtel.ɪk
tell (T) tel **-s** -z **-ing/ly** -ɪŋ/li **told** təʊld (US) toʊld
teller (T) ˈtel.əʳ (US) -ɚ **-s** -z
telling-off ˌtel.ɪŋˈɒf (US) -ˈɑːf **tellings-off** ˌtel.ɪŋzˈɒf (US) -ˈɑːf
telltale ˈtel.teɪl **-s** -z
tellurian telˈʊə.ri.ən, təˈlʊə-, tɪ-, -ˈljʊə- (US) telˈʊr.i-, təˈlʊr- **-s** -z
telluric telˈʊə.rɪk, təˈlʊə-, tɪ-, -ˈljʊə- (US) telˈʊr.ɪk, təˈlʊr-
tellurium telˈʊə.ri.əm, təˈlʊə-, tɪ-, -ˈljʊə- (US) telˈʊr.i-, təˈlʊr-
tell|y ˈtel|.i **-ies** -iz
Telstar® ˈtel.stɑːʳ (US) -stɑːr
Telugu ˈtel.ə.guː, ˈ-ʊ- (US) ˈ-ə-
temerity tɪˈmer.ə.ti, tə-, temˈer-, -ɪ.ti (US) təˈmer.ə.t̬i
temp temp **-s** -s **-ing** -ɪŋ **-ed** -t
Tempe ˈtem.pi
tempeh ˈtem.peɪ **-s** -z
temp|er ˈtem.p|əʳ (US) -p|ɚ **-ers** -əz (US) -ɚz **-ering** -ᵊr.ɪŋ **-ered** -əd (US) -ɚd **-erer/s** -ᵊr.əʳ/z (US) -ɚ.ɚ/z
tempera ˈtem.pᵊr.ə
temperable ˈtem.pᵊr.ə.bl̩, -prə.bl̩
temperament ˈtem.pᵊr.ə.mənt, -prə.mənt **-s** -s
temperamental ˌtem.pᵊr.əˈmen.tᵊl, -prəˈ- (US) -t̬ᵊl **-ly** -i
temperance ˈtem.pᵊr.ᵊnts, ˈ-prənts
temperate ˈtem.pᵊr.ət, ˈ-prət, -prɪt **-ly** -li **-ness** -nəs, -nɪs
temperature ˈtem.prə.tʃəʳ, -prɪ-, -pᵊr.ə-, -ɪ- (US) -pɚ.ə.tʃɚ, ˈ-prə-, -pɚ-, -pə- **-s** -z
-tempered -ˈtem.pəd (US) -pɚd **-ly** -li
Temperley ˈtem.pᵊl.i (US) -pɚ.li
tempest ˈtem.pɪst, -pəst **-s** -s
tempestuous temˈpes.tju.əs, -tʃu- (US) -tʃu-, -tʃə.wəs **-ly** -li **-ness** -nəs, -nɪs
Templar ˈtem.pləʳ, -plɑːʳ (US) -plɚ **-s** -z
template ˈtem.pleɪt, -plɪt (US) -plɪt **-s** -s
temple (T) ˈtem.pl̩ **-s** -z
templet ˈtem.plɪt, -plət (US) -plɪt **-s** -s
Templeton ˈtem.pl̩.tən
temp|o ˈtem.p|əʊ (US) -p|oʊ **-os** -əʊz (US) -oʊz **-i** -iː
temporal ˈtem.pᵊr.ᵊl **-ly** -i
temporality ˌtem.pᵊrˈæl.ə.ti, -ɪ.ti (US) -pəˈræl.ə.t̬i
temporar|y ˈtem.pᵊr.ᵊr|.i, -prᵊr- (US) -pə.rer|.i **-ies** -iz **-ily** -ᵊl.i, -ɪ.li **-iness** -ɪ.nəs, -ɪ.nɪs
temporization, -isa- ˌtem.pᵊr.aɪˈzeɪ.ʃᵊn, -ɪˈ- (US) -ɪˈ-
temporiz|e, -is|e ˈtem.pᵊr.aɪz (US) -pə.raɪz **-es** -ɪz **-ing/ly** -ɪŋ/li **-ed** -d **-er/s** -əʳ/z (US) -ɚ/z
tempt tempt **-s** -s **-ing** -ɪŋ **-ed** -ɪd **-er/s** -əʳ/z (US) -ɚ/z
temptation tempˈteɪ.ʃᵊn **-s** -z
tempting ˈtemp.tɪŋ **-ly** -li **-ness** -nəs, -nɪs
temptress ˈtemp.trəs, -trɪs (US) -trɪs **-es** -ɪz
tempura ˈtem.pᵊr.ə; temˈpʊə.rə (US) ˈtem.pʊ.rɑː; temˈpʊr.ə
tempus fugit ˌtem.pəsˈfjuː.dʒɪt, -pʊsˈ-, -gɪt (US) -pəsˈfjuː.dʒɪt
ten ten **-s** -z ˌ**Ten Com**ˈ**mandments**
tenability ˌten.əˈbɪl.ə.ti, -ɪ.ti (US) -ə.t̬i
tenable ˈten.ə.bl̩ **-ness** -nəs, -nɪs
tenacious tɪˈneɪ.ʃəs, tə-, tenˈeɪ- (US) təˈneɪ- **-ly** -li **-ness** -nəs, -nɪs
tenacity tɪˈnæs.ə.ti, tə-, tenˈæs-, -ɪ.ti (US) təˈnæs.ə.t̬i
tenanc|y ˈten.ənt.s|i **-ies** -iz
tenant ˈten.ənt **-s** -s **-ing** -ɪŋ **-ed** -ɪd
tenantry ˈten.ən.tri
Tenbury ˈten.bᵊr.i, ˈtem- (US) ˈten.ber-, -bɚ-
Tenby ˈten.bi, ˈtem- (US) ˈten-
tench tentʃ
tend tend **-s** -z **-ing** -ɪŋ **-ed** -ɪd
tendencious tenˈden.tʃəs (US) -ˈdent.ʃəs **-ly** -li **-ness** -nəs, -nɪs
tendenc|y ˈten.dənt.s|i **-ies** -iz
tendentious tenˈden.tʃəs (US) -ˈdent.ʃəs **-ly** -li **-ness** -nəs, -nɪs
tend|er ˈten.d|əʳ (US) -d|ɚ **-ers** -əz (US) -ɚz **-erer** -ᵊr.əʳ (US) -ɚ.ɚ **-erest** -ᵊr.ɪst, -əst **-erly** -ᵊl.i (US) -ɚ.li **-erness** -ə.nəs, -nɪs (US) -ɚ.nəs, -nɪs **-ering** -ᵊr.ɪŋ **-ered** -əd (US) -ɚd
tender|foot ˈten.də|.fʊt (US) -dɚ- **-foots** -s **-feet** -fiːt
tender-hearted ˌten.dəˈhɑː.tɪd, ˈten.dəˌhɑː- (US) ˈten.dɚˌhɑːr.t̬ɪd, ˌten.dɚˈhɑːr- **-ly** -li **-ness** -nəs, -nɪs *stress shift, British only:* ˌtender-hearted ˈperson
tenderization, -isa- ˌten.dᵊr.aɪˈzeɪ.ʃᵊn, -ɪˈ- (US) -ɪˈ-
tenderiz|e, -is|e ˈten.dᵊr.aɪz (US) -də.raɪz **-es** -ɪz **-ing** -ɪŋ **-ed** -d **-er/s** -əʳ/z (US) -ɚ/z
tenderloin ˈten.dᵊl.ɔɪn (US) -dɚ.lɔɪn **-s** -z
tendinitis ˌten.dɪˈnaɪ.tɪs, -dəˈ-
tendon ˈten.dən **-s** -z
tendonitis ˌten.dəˈnaɪ.tɪs (US) -t̬ɪs
tendril ˈten.drᵊl, -drɪl (US) -drᵊl **-s** -z
Tenebrae ˈten.ɪ.briː, ˈ-ə-, -breɪ, -braɪ (US) -ə.breɪ, -briː
tenebrous ˈten.ɪ.brəs, ˈ-ə- (US) ˈ-ə-
tenement ˈten.ə.mənt, ˈ-ɪ- (US) ˈ-ə- **-s** -s
Tenerif(f)e ˌten.ᵊrˈiːf (US) -əˈriːf
tenet ˈten.ɪt **-s** -s
tenfold ˈten.fəʊld (US) -foʊld
ten-gallon hat ˌtenˌgæl.ənˈhæt, ˌteŋ- (US) ˌten- **-s** -s
Tengu ˈteŋ.gu **-s** -z
Teniers ˈten.i.əz, ˈ-jəz (US) -i.ɚz, ˈ-jɚz; təˈnɪrz
Tenison ˈten.ɪ.sᵊn
Tenko ˈteŋ.kəʊ (US) -koʊ

Tense

See LAX.

Tenn. *(abbrev. for* **Tennessee***)* ˌten.əˈsiː, -ɪˈ- ⓤⓢ ˌten.ɪˈsiː *regionally:* ˈten.ɪ.si, -ə-
Tennant ˈten.ənt
tenner ˈten.əʳ ⓤⓢ -ɚ **-s** -z
Tennessee ˌten.əˈsiː, -ɪˈ- ⓤⓢ ˌten.ɪˈsiː *regionally:* ˈten.ɪ.si, -ə-
Tenniel ˈten.i.əl, ˈ-jəl
tennis ˈten.ɪs ˈ**tennis** ˌ**ball**; ˈ**tennis** ˌ**court**; ˌ**tennis** ˈ**elbow**; ˈ**tennis** ˌ**racket**
Tennyson ˈten.ɪ.sᵊn
tenon ˈten.ən **-s** -z
tenor ˈten.əʳ ⓤⓢ -ɚ **-s** -z
tenour ˈten.əʳ ⓤⓢ -ɚ
ten|pence ˈten|.pənts, ˈtem- ⓤⓢ ˈten- **-penny** -pᵊn.i
tenpin ˈten.pɪn, ˈtem- ⓤⓢ ˈten- **-s** -z ˌ**tenpin** ˈ**bowling**
tenpins ˈten.pɪnz, ˈtem- ⓤⓢ ˈten-
tens|e ten*t*s **-es** -ɪz **-er** -əʳ ⓤⓢ -ɚ **-est** -ɪst, -əst **-ing** -ɪŋ **-ed** -t **-ely** -li **-eness** -nəs, -nɪs
tensile ˈten*t*.saɪl ⓤⓢ -sɪl, -saɪl
tension ˈten.*t*ʃᵊn ⓤⓢ ˈten*t*.ʃᵊn **-s** -z
tensity ˈten*t*.sə.ti, -sɪ- ⓤⓢ -sə.t̬i
tensor ˈten*t*.səʳ ⓤⓢ -sɚ **-s** -z
tent tent **-s** -s **-ing** -ɪŋ ⓤⓢ ˈten.t̬ɪŋ **-ed** -ɪd ⓤⓢ ˈten.t̬ɪd
tentacle ˈten.tə.kl̩, -tɪ- ⓤⓢ -t̬ə- **-s** -z
tentacular tenˈtæk.jə.ləʳ, -jʊ- ⓤⓢ -lɚ
tentative ˈten.tə.tɪv ⓤⓢ -t̬ə.t̬ɪv **-s** -z **-ly** -li
tenter ˈten.təʳ ⓤⓢ -t̬ɚ **-s** -z
Tenterden ˈten.tə.dᵊn ⓤⓢ -t̬ɚ-
tenterhook ˈten.tə.hʊk ⓤⓢ -t̬ɚ- **-s** -s
tenth ten*t*θ **-s** -s **-ly** -li
tentpegging ˈtentˌpeg.ɪŋ
Tentsmuir ten*t*sˈmjʊəʳ ⓤⓢ -ˈmjʊr
tenu|is ˈten.ju|.ɪs **-es** -iːz, -eɪz
tenuity tenˈjuː.ə.ti, təˈnjuː-, tɪ-, -ɪ.ti ⓤⓢ təˈnuː.ə.t̬i, -ˈnjuː-
tenuous ˈten.ju.əs **-ly** -li **-ness** -nəs, -nɪs
tenur|e ˈten.jəʳ, -jʊəʳ ⓤⓢ -jɚ, -jʊr **-es** -z **-ed** -d
tepal ˈtiː.pᵊl, ˈtep.ᵊl
tepee ˈtiː.piː **-s** -z
tepid ˈtep.ɪd **-est** -ɪst, -əst **-ly** -li **-ness** -nəs, -nɪs
tepidity tepˈɪd.ə.ti, -ɪ.ti ⓤⓢ təˈpɪd.ə.t̬i
tequila təˈkiː.lə, tɪ- ⓤⓢ tə- **-s** -z **te**ˌ**quila** ˈ**sunrise**
ter *three times:* tɜːʳ ⓤⓢ tɝː, ter
Ter *river in Essex:* tɑːʳ ⓤⓢ tɑːr
teraph ˈter.əf **-im** -ɪm
terbium ˈtɜː.bi.əm ⓤⓢ ˈtɝː-
tercel *hawk:* ˈtɜː.sᵊl ⓤⓢ ˈtɝː- **-s** -z
Tercel *car:* ˈtɜː.sel ⓤⓢ tɚˈsel
tercentenar|y ˌtɜː.senˈtiː.nᵊr|.i, -ˈten.ᵊr-; tɜːˈsen.tɪ.nᵊr- ⓤⓢ tɚˈsen.tᵊn.er-; ˌtɝː.senˈten.ɚ- **-ies** -iz
tercentennial ˌtɜː.senˈten.i.əl ⓤⓢ ˌtɝː-
tercet ˈtɜː.sɪt, -set ⓤⓢ ˈtɝː.sɪt; tɚˈset **-s** -s
terebene ˈter.ə.biːn, ˈ-ɪ- ⓤⓢ ˈ-ə-
terebinth ˈter.ə.bɪn*t*θ, ˈ-ɪ- ⓤⓢ ˈ-ə- **-s** -s
Terence ˈter.ᵊn*t*s
Teresa təˈriː.zə, tɪ-, -ˈreɪ-, terˈiː- ⓤⓢ təˈriː.sə, -zə, -ˈreɪ-
tergiver|sate ˈtɜː.dʒɪ.vɜː|.seɪt, -və- ⓤⓢ ˈtɝː.dʒɪ.vɚ- **-sates** -seɪts **-sating** -seɪ.tɪŋ ⓤⓢ -seɪ.t̬ɪŋ **-sated** -seɪ.tɪd ⓤⓢ -seɪ.t̬ɪd
tergiversation ˌtɜː.dʒɪ.vɜːˈseɪ.ʃᵊn, -vəˈ- ⓤⓢ ˌtɝː.dʒɪ.vɚ-
teriyaki ˌter.iˈæk.i ⓤⓢ -ˈjɑː.ki
Terling ˈtɑː.lɪŋ, ˈtɜː- ⓤⓢ ˈtɑːr-, ˈtɝː-
term tɜːm ⓤⓢ tɝːm **-s** -z **-ing** -ɪŋ **-ed** -d **-ly** -li
termagant **(T)** ˈtɜː.mə.gənt ⓤⓢ ˈtɝː- **-s** -s **-ly** -li
terminab|le ˈtɜː.mɪ.nə.bl|̩, -mə- ⓤⓢ ˈtɝː- **-ly** -li **-leness** -l̩.nəs, -nɪs
terminal ˈtɜː.mɪ.nᵊl, -mə- ⓤⓢ ˈtɝː- **-s** -z **-ly** -i
termi|nate ˈtɜː.mɪ|.neɪt, -mə- ⓤⓢ ˈtɝː- **-nates** -neɪts **-nating** -neɪ.tɪŋ ⓤⓢ -neɪ.t̬ɪŋ **-nated** -neɪ.tɪd ⓤⓢ -neɪ.t̬ɪd **-nator/s** -neɪ.təʳ/z ⓤⓢ -neɪ.t̬ɚ/z
termination ˌtɜː.mɪˈneɪ.ʃᵊn, -məˈ- ⓤⓢ ˌtɝː- **-s** -z
terminative ˈtɜː.mɪ.nə.tɪv, -mə-, -neɪ- ⓤⓢ ˈtɝː.mɪ.neɪ.t̬ɪv, -mə- **-ly** -li
terminer ˈtɜː.mɪ.nəʳ, -mə- ⓤⓢ ˈtɝː.mɪ.nɚ, -mə-
terminologic|al ˌtɜː.mɪ.nəˈlɒdʒ.ɪ.k|ᵊl, -mə- ⓤⓢ ˌtɝː.mɪ.nəˈlɑː.dʒɪ-, -mə- **-ally** -ᵊl.i, -li
terminolog|y ˌtɜː.mɪˈnɒl.ə.dʒ|i, -məˈ- ⓤⓢ ˌtɝː.mɪˈnɑː.lə-, -məˈ- **-ies** -iz
termin|us ˈtɜː.mɪ.n|əs, -mə- ⓤⓢ ˈtɝː- **-i** -aɪ **-uses** -ə.sɪz
termite ˈtɜː.maɪt ⓤⓢ ˈtɝː- **-s** -s
termtime ˈtɜːm.taɪm ⓤⓢ ˈtɝːm-
tern tɜːn ⓤⓢ tɝːn **-s** -z
ternary ˈtɜː.nᵊr.i ⓤⓢ ˈtɝː-
Ternate tɜːˈnɑː.ti ⓤⓢ tɝːˈnɑː.teɪ
Terpsichore tɜːpˈsɪk.ᵊr.i ⓤⓢ tɝːp-
terpsichorean ˌtɜːp.sɪ.kᵊrˈiː.ən, -kɒrˈ- ⓤⓢ ˌtɝːp.sɪ.kəˈriː-; ˌtɝːp.sɪˈkɔːr.i-
terra ˈter.ə
terrac|e ˈter.ɪs, -əs **-es** -ɪz **-ing** -ɪŋ **-ed** -t
terracotta ˌter.əˈkɒt.ə ⓤⓢ -ˈkɑː.t̬ə
terra firma ˌter.əˈfɜː.mə ⓤⓢ -ˈfɝː-
terrain təˈreɪn, tɪ-, terˈeɪn; ˈter.eɪn ⓤⓢ terˈeɪn, təˈreɪn; ˈter.eɪn **-s** -z
terra incognita ˌter.ə.ɪŋˈkɒg.nɪ.tə, -ɪnˈ-; -kɒgˈniː.tə- ⓤⓢ -ɪnˈkɑːg.niː.t̬ə, -nɪ- **terrae incognitae** ˌter.i.ɪŋˈkɒg.nɪ.ti, -ɪnˈ-; -kɒgˈniː.ti ⓤⓢ -ɪnˈkɑːg.niː.t̬i, -nɪ-
Terramycin® ˌter.əˈmaɪ.sɪn
Terrance ˈter.ᵊn*t*s
terrapin ˈter.ə.pɪn **-s** -z
terrari|um təˈreə.ri|.əm, terˈeə-, tɪˈreə- ⓤⓢ təˈrer.i- **-ums** -əmz **-a** -ə
terrazzo terˈæt.səʊ, təˈræt-, tɪ- ⓤⓢ təˈrɑːt.soʊ, terˈɑːt-; təˈræz.oʊ **-s** -z
Terrell ˈter.ᵊl
Terrence ˈter.ᵊn*t*s
terrestrial təˈres.tri.əl, terˈes-, tɪˈres- ⓤⓢ təˈres- **-s** -z **-ly** -i **-ness** -nəs, -nɪs
terret ˈter.ɪt **-s** -s
Terri ˈter.i
terrib|le ˈter.ə.bl|̩, ˈ-ɪ- ⓤⓢ ˈ-ə- **-ly** -li **-leness** -l̩.nəs, -nɪs
terricolous təˈrɪk.ᵊl.əs, terˈɪk-, tɪˈrɪk- ⓤⓢ terˈɪk-, təˈrɪk-
terrier ˈter.i.əʳ ⓤⓢ -ɚ **-s** -z
terrific təˈrɪf.ɪk, tɪ- ⓤⓢ tə- **-ally** -ᵊl.i, -li
terri|fy ˈter.əl.faɪ, ˈ-ɪ- ⓤⓢ ˈ-ə- **-fies** -faɪz **-fying/ly** -faɪ.ɪŋ/li **-fied** -faɪd
terrine terˈiːn, təˈriːn; ˈter.iːn ⓤⓢ terˈiːn **-s** -z
territorial ˌter.ɪˈtɔː.ri.əl, -əˈ- ⓤⓢ -əˈtɔːr.i- **-s** -z **-ly** -i *stress shift, see compounds:* ˌ**Territorial** ˈ**Army**, **Terri**ˌ**torial** ˈ**Army**; **terri**ˌ**torial** ˈ**waters**
territorializ|e, -is|e ˌter.ɪˈtɔː.ri.ᵊl.aɪz, -əˈ- ⓤⓢ -əˈtɔːr.i- **-es** -ɪz **-ing** -ɪŋ **-ed** -d
territor|y ˈter.ɪ.tᵊr|.i, ˈ-ə-, -tr|i ⓤⓢ -ə.tɔːr|.i **-ies** -iz
terror ˈter.əʳ ⓤⓢ -ɚ **-s** -z
terror|ism ˈter.ᵊr|.ɪ.zᵊm **-ist/s** -ɪst/s
terrorization, -isa-, ˌter.ᵊr.aɪˈzeɪ.ʃᵊn, -ɪˈ- ⓤⓢ -ɪˈ-
terroriz|e, -is|e ˈter.ᵊr.aɪz ⓤⓢ -ə.raɪz **-es** -ɪz **-ing** -ɪŋ **-ed** -d **-er/s** -əʳ/z ⓤⓢ -ɚ/z
terror-stricken ˈter.əˌstrɪk.ᵊn ⓤⓢ -ɚˌ-
terror-struck ˈter.ə.strʌk ⓤⓢ ˈ-ɚ-
terr|y **(T)** ˈter|.i **-ies** -iz ˌ**terry** ˈ**nappy**; ˌ**terry** ˈ**towelling**
ters|e tɜːs ⓤⓢ tɝːs **-er** -əʳ ⓤⓢ -ɚ **-est** -ɪst, -əst **-ely** -li **-eness** -nəs, -nɪs
tertian ˈtɜː.ʃᵊn, -ʃi.ən ⓤⓢ ˈtɝː.ʃᵊn
tertiary ˈtɜː.ʃᵊr.i, -ʃi.ᵊr- ⓤⓢ ˈtɝː.ʃi.er-, -ʃɚ.i ˌ**tertiary edu**ˈ**cation**
tertium quid ˌtɜː.ti.əmˈkwɪd, ˌ-ʃəmˈ-, -ʃi.əmˈ- ⓤⓢ ˌtɝː.ʃi.əmˈ-; ˌter.ti.ʊmˈ-
Tertius ˈtɜː.ʃəs, -ʃi.əs, -ti-
Tertullian tɜːˈtʌl.i.ən, ˈ-jən ⓤⓢ tɚ-
terylene **(T®)** ˈter.ə.liːn, ˈ-ɪ- ⓤⓢ ˈ-ɪ-
terza rima ˌteət.səˈriː.mə, ˌtɜːt- ⓤⓢ ˌtert-
Tesco® ˈtes.kəʊ ⓤⓢ -koʊ **-'s** -z
TESL ˈtes.l̩
tesla **(T)** ˈtes.lə
TESOL ˈtiː.sɒl ⓤⓢ -sɑːl; ˈtes.ᵊl
Tess tes

Tessa, TESSA 'tes.ə
tesse(l)l|ate 'tes.ᵊl|.eɪt, -ɪ.l|eɪt (US) -ə.l|eɪt **-ates** -eɪts **-ating** -eɪ.tɪŋ (US) -eɪ.t̬ɪŋ **-ated** -eɪ.tɪd (US) -eɪ.t̬ɪd
tessellation ˌtes.ᵊl'eɪ.ʃᵊn, -ɪ'leɪ- (US) -ə'leɪ- **-s** -z
tessitura ˌtes.ɪ'tʊə.rə, -ə'-, -'tjʊə-, -'tɔː-, -'tjɔː- (US) -ɪ'tʊr.ə
test (T) test **-s** -s **-ing** -ɪŋ **-ed** -ɪd **-able** -ə.bl̩ **-er/s** -əʳ/z (US) -ɚ/z **'test ˌcard; 'test ˌcase; 'test ˌmatch**
testace|an tes'teɪ.ʃ|ᵊn, -ʃi|.ən (US) '-ʃ|ən **-ous** -əs
testacy 'tes.tə.si
testament (T) 'tes.tə.mənt **-s** -s
testament|ary ˌtes.tə'men.t|ᵊr.i (US) -t̬ɚ- **-al** -ᵊl
testate 'tes.teɪt, -tɪt (US) -teɪt **-s** -s
testator tes'teɪ.təʳ (US) 'tes.teɪ.t̬ɚ, -'-- **-s** -z
testatri|x tes'teɪ.trɪ|ks **-ces** -siːz
test-bed 'test.bed **-s** -z
test-|drive 'test|.draɪv **-drives** -draɪvz **-driving** -ˌdraɪ.vɪŋ **-drove** -drəʊv (US) -droʊv **-driven** -ˌdrɪv.ᵊn
testes *(plur. of* **testis)** 'tes.tiːz
testicle 'tes.tɪ.kl̩, -tə- **-s** -z
testicular tes'tɪk.jə.ləʳ, -jʊ- (US) -lɚ
testification ˌtes.tɪ.fɪ'keɪ.ʃᵊn, -tə- **-s** -z
testi|fy 'tes.tɪ|.faɪ, -tə- **-fies** -faɪz **-fying** -faɪ.ɪŋ **-fied** -faɪd **-fier/s** -faɪ.əʳ/z (US) -faɪ.ɚ/z
testimonial ˌtes.tɪ'məʊ.ni.əl, -tə'- (US) -'moʊ- **-s** -z
testimonializ|e, -is|e ˌtes.tɪ'məʊ.ni.ᵊl.aɪz, -tə'- (US) -'moʊ.ni.ə.laɪz **-es** -ɪz **-ing** -ɪŋ **-ed** -d
testimon|y 'tes.tɪ.mə.n|i, -tə- (US) -moʊ.n|i **-ies** -iz
test|is 'tes.t|ɪs **-es** -iːz
Teston 'tiː.sᵊn
testosterone tes'tɒs.tᵊr.əʊn (US) -'tɑː.stə.roʊn
test-tube 'test.tjuːb, -tʃuːb (US) -tuːb, -tjuːb **-s** -z ˌ**test-tube 'baby** (US) **'test-tube ˌbaby**
testud|o tes'tjuː.d|əʊ, -'tuː- (US) -'tuː.d|oʊ, -'tjuː- **-os** -əʊz (US) -oʊz **-ines** -dɪ.niːz, -neɪz (US) -dɪ.niːz
test|y 'tes.t|i **-ier** -i.əʳ (US) -i.ɚ **-iest** -i.ɪst, -i.əst **-ily** -ɪ.li, -ᵊl.i **-iness** -ɪ.nəs, -ɪ.nɪs
tetanus 'tet.ᵊn.əs
Tetbury 'tet.bᵊr.i (US) -ber-, -bɚ-
tetch|y 'tetʃ|.i **-ier** -i.əʳ (US) -i.ɚ **-iest** -i.ɪst, -i.əst **-ily** -ɪ.li, -ᵊl.i **-iness** -ɪ.nəs, -ɪ.nɪs
tête-à-tête ˌteɪt.ɑː'teɪt, ˌtet.ə'tet (US) ˌteɪt.ə'teɪt, ˌtet.ə'tet **-s** -s
teth|er 'teð|.əʳ (US) -ɚ **-ers** -əz (US) -ɚz **-ering** -ᵊr.ɪŋ **-ered** -əd (US) -ɚd
Tetley 'tet.li
Tétouan tet'wɑːn (US) tet'wɑːn; 'teɪ.twɑːn
Tetovo tet'əʊ.vəʊ (US) -'oʊ.voʊ
tetrachord 'tet.rə.kɔːd (US) -kɔːrd **-s** -z
tetrad 'tet.ræd, -rəd (US) -ræd **-s** -z
tetragon 'tet.rə.gən (US) -gɑːn **-s** -z
tetrahedr|on ˌtet.rə'hiː.dr|ᵊn, -'hed.r|ᵊn (US) -'hiː- **-ons** -ᵊnz **-a** -ə **-al** -ᵊl
tetralog|y tet'ræl.ə.dʒ|i, tə'træl- (US) tet'rɑː.lə- **-ies** -iz
tetrameter tet'ræm.ɪ.təʳ, '-ə- (US) -ə.t̬ɚ **-s** -z
tetrarch 'tet.rɑːk (US) -rɑːrk **-s** -s **-y** -i **-ies** -iz
tetrasyllabic ˌtet.rə.sɪ'læb.ɪk, -sə'- (US) -sɪ'-
tetrasyllable 'tet.rəˌsɪl.ə.bl̩, ˌtet.rə'sɪl- **-s** -z
tetrathlon tet'ræθ.lɒn, tɪ'træθ-, tə-, -lən (US) tet'ræθ.lɑːn
Tettenhall 'tet.ᵊn.hɔːl
tetter 'tet.əʳ (US) 'tet̬.ɚ
Teucer 'tjuː.səʳ (US) 'tuː.sɚ, 'tjuː-
Teuton 'tjuː.tᵊn (US) 'tuː-, 'tjuː- **-s** -z
Teutonic tjuː'tɒn.ɪk (US) tuː'tɑː.nɪk, tjuː-
teutonization, -isa- ˌtjuː.tᵊn.aɪ'zeɪ.ʃᵊn, -ɪ'- (US) ˌtuː.tᵊn.ɪ'-, ˌtjuː-
teutoniz|e, -is|e 'tjuː.tᵊn.aɪz (US) 'tuː-, 'tjuː- **-es** -ɪz **-ing** -ɪŋ **-ed** -d
Teviot *river:* 'tiː.vi.ət *Lord:* 'tev.i.ət
Teviotdale 'tiː.vi.ət.deɪl
Tewfik 'tjuː.fɪk (US) 'tuː-, 'tjuː-
Tewkesbury 'tjuːks.bᵊr.i (US) 'tuːks.ber-, 'tjuːks-, -bɚ-
Tex. *(abbrev. for* **Texas)** 'tek.səs
Texaco® 'tek.sə.kəʊ (US) -sɪ.koʊ, -sə-
Texan 'tek.sᵊn **-s** -z
Texas 'tek.səs
Texel 'tek.sᵊl
Tex-Mex ˌteks'meks *stress shift:* ˌTex-Mex 'food
text tekst **-s** -s **-ing** -ɪŋ **-ed** -ɪd
textbook 'tekst.bʊk **-s** -s
textile 'tek.staɪl (US) -staɪl, -stɪl **-s** -z
textual 'teks.tju.əl (US) -tʃu- **-ly** -i
textural 'teks.tʃᵊr.ᵊl
textur|e 'teks.tʃəʳ (US) -tʃɚ **-es** -z **-ing** -ɪŋ **-ed** -d
Tey teɪ
Teynham 'ten.əm, 'teɪ.nəm
Note: The former is appropriate for Baron Teynham.
-th -θ
Note: Suffix. Not a syllable in itself, and does not affect the word stress, e.g. **tenth** /tentθ/.
Thacker 'θæk.əʳ (US) -ɚ
Thackeray 'θæk.ᵊr.i, '-ri
Thackley 'θæk.li
Thaddeus 'θæd.i.əs; θæd'iː-
Thai taɪ **-s** -z
Thailand 'taɪ.lænd, -lənd
Thake θeɪk
thalam|us 'θæl.ə.m|əs **-i** -aɪ, -iː
thalassotherapy θəˌlæs.əʊ'θer.ə.pi, θælˌæs- (US) -ə'-
Thalben 'θæl.bən, 'θɔːl-
thaler 'tɑː.ləʳ (US) -lɚ **-s** -z
Thales 'θeɪ.liːz
Thali|a *of the three Graces:* θə'laɪ|.ə **-an** -ən *Greek Muse:* 'θæl.i.ə, '-jə (US) 'θeɪ.li.ə, 'θeɪl.jə
thalidomide θə'lɪd.ə.maɪd, θæl'ɪd- (US) θə'lɪd-
thallium 'θæl.i.əm
Thame teɪm
Thames *in England, Canada, New Zealand:* temz *in Connecticut:* θeɪmz, teɪmz, temz
Thamesmead 'temz.miːd
than *strong form:* ðæn *weak forms:* ðᵊn, ðən, ðn̩
Note: Weak form word. The strong form /ðæn/ is rarely used; it is sometimes found in emphatic utterances such as 'The Queen, than whom no-one is richer...', but it normally has the weak pronunciation /ðən/, e.g. 'faster than sound', /ˌfɑː.stə.ðən'saʊnd (US) -stɚ-/, or in rapid speech /ðn̩/, e.g. 'better than ever', /ˌbet.ə.ðn̩'ev.ə (US) ˌbet̬.ɚ.ðn̩'ev.ɚ/.
Thanatos 'θæn.ə.tɒs (US) -tɑːs
thane (T) θeɪn **-s** -z
Thanet 'θæn.ɪt
thank θæŋk **-s** -s **-ing** -ɪŋ **-ed** -t **-er/s** -əʳ/z (US) -ɚ/z
thankful 'θæŋk.fᵊl, -fʊl **-ly** -i **-ness** -nəs, -nɪs
thankless 'θæŋ.kləs, -klɪs **-ly** -li **-ness** -nəs, -nɪs
thanksgiving (T) ˌθæŋks'gɪv.ɪŋ (US) ˌ-'--, '-ˌ-- **-s** -z **Thanks'giving ˌDay** (US) **Thanks'giving ˌDay** (US) **'Thanksgiving ˌDay**
thankworth|y 'θæŋkˌwɜː.ð|i (US) -ˌwɝː- **-iness** -ɪ.nəs, -ɪ.nɪs
thank-you 'θæŋk.ju **-s** -z **'thank-you ˌletter**
Note: Although the most common abbreviation for 'thank you' is 'thanks', the pronunciation /kjuː/ is also heard in British English, usually with high pitch, in casual speech.
Thant θænt
that *(adj., demonstr. pron., adv.)* ðæt
Note: Weak form word. When used demonstratively it is always

Pronouncing the letters TH

The consonant digraph **th** is most commonly pronounced /θ/ or /ð/. In initial position, /ð/ occurs mostly in function or grammar words like determiners and conjunctions, e.g.:

the	/ðə/	
that	/ðæt, ðət/	

In content words like nouns and main verbs, /θ/ most usually appears in initial position, e.g.:

theme	/θiːm/	
think	/θɪŋk/	

At the ends of words, it is more difficult to predict which realisation will occur. However, /ð/ is more common here than /θ/, and is highly likely in verbs. For example, before **e** or the grammatical inflection *-ing*, the pronunciation is usually /ð/, e.g.:

loathe	/ləʊð/	(US) /loʊð/
loath	/ləʊθ, ləʊð/	
bathe	/beɪð/	
bath	/bɑːθ/	(US) /bæθ/

Note that the verb *bathe* and *bath* when used as a verb both have the same spelling for the present participle, *bathing*, but different pronunciations.

In addition

In some names and a few other words, **th** is pronounced as /t/, e.g.:

Thames	/temz/	
thyme	/taɪm/	

The suffix *-th* when applied to numbers is always pronounced /θ/, e.g.:

eighth	/eɪtθ/	
sixteenth	/sɪkˈstiːnθ/	

When the two letters come together due to the addition of a prefix, the pronunciation is /t.h/, e.g.:

lighthouse	/ˈlaɪt.haʊs/	
sweetheart	/ˈswiːt.hɑːt/	(US) /-hɑːrt/

Occasionally, **th** may be silent, e.g.:

asthma	/ˈæsθ.mə, ˈæs-/	(US) /ˈæz-/

pronounced with its strong form /ðæt/, e.g. 'that's final', 'I like **that** one'.

that (*relative pron.*) *strong form:* ðæt *weak form:* ðət *weak form:* ðt

Note: The strong form is seldom used, except in very deliberate speech or when the word is said in isolation.

that (*conj.*) *strong form:* ðæt *weak form:* ðət

Note: The strong form is rarely used.

thataway ˈðæt.əˌweɪ (US) ˈðæt̬-

thatch θætʃ **-es** -ɪz **-ing** -ɪŋ **-ed** -t **-er/s** -əʳ/z (US) -ɚ/z

Thatcham ˈθætʃ.əm

Thatch|er ˈθætʃ|.əʳ (US) -ɚ **-erism** -əʳ.ɪ.zᵊm **-erite/s** -əʳ.aɪt/s (US) -ə.raɪt/s

thaumaturg|e ˈθɔː.mə.tɜːdʒ (US) -tɝːdʒ, ˈθɑː- **-es** -ɪz

thaumaturgic ˌθɔː.məˈtɜː.dʒɪk (US) -ˈtɝː-, ˌθɑː-

thaumaturg|y ˈθɔː.mə.tɜː.dʒ|i (US) -tɝː-, ˈθɑː- **-ist/s** -ɪst/s

thaw (T) θɔː (US) θɑː, θɔː **-s** -z **-ing** -ɪŋ **-ed** -d

the *strong form:* ðiː *weak form before vowels:* ði; *weak form before consonants:* ðə

Note: Weak form word. The strong form /ðiː/ is used for emphasis, e.g. 'This is **the** place to eat' or contrast, e.g. 'It's not **a** solution, but **the** solution'. Weak forms are /ðə/ before consonants, e.g 'the cat' /ðəˈkæt/ and /ði/ before vowels, e.g. 'the apple' /ðiˈæp.l̩/.

Thea θɪə, ˈθiː.ə (US) ˈθiː.ə

Theakston ˈθiːk.stən **-'s** -z

theatre, theater ˈθɪə.təʳ, ˈθiː.ə-; θiˈet.əʳ (US) ˈθiː.ə.t̬ɚ **-s** -z

theatregoer, theatergoer ˈθɪə.təˌgəʊ.əʳ, ˈθiː.ə-; θiˈet.əˌ- (US) ˈθiː.ə.t̬ɚˌgoʊ.ɚ **-s** -z

theatreland, theaterland ˈθɪə.tə.lænd, ˈθiː.ə-; θiˈet.ə- (US) ˈθiː.ə.t̬ɚ-

theatric|al θiˈæt.rɪ.k|ᵊl **-als** -ᵊlz **-ally** -ᵊl.i, -li **-alness** -ᵊl.nəs, -nɪs **-alism** -ᵊl.ɪ.zᵊm

theatricality θiˌæt.rɪˈkæl.ə.ti, -ɪ.ti (US) -ə.t̬i

theatrics θiˈæt.rɪks

Thebaid ˈθiː.beɪ.ɪd, -bi-

Theban ˈθiː.bən **-s** -z

thebe ˈtiː.beɪ

Thebes θiːbz

thee *normal form:* ðiː *occasional weak form:* ði

theft θeft **-s** -s

thegn θeɪn **-s** -z

their *normal form:* ðeəʳ (US) ðer *occasional weak form when a vowel follows:* ðəʳ (US) ðɚ

Note: The weak form is found in commonly-used phrases such as 'on their own' /ˌɒn.ðəʳˈəʊn (US) ˌɑːn.ðɚˈoʊn/.

theirs ðeəz (US) ðerz

the|ism ˈθiː|.ɪ.zᵊm **-ist/s** -ɪst/s

theistic θiːˈɪs.tɪk **-al** -ᵊl

Thelma ˈθel.mə

Thelwall ˈθel.wɔːl

Thelwell ˈθel.wəl, -wel

them *strong form:* ðem *weak forms:* ðəm, ðm *occasional weak forms:* əm, ᵊm

Note: Weak form word. The strong form /ðem/ is used for contrast, e.g. 'them and us' or for emphasis, e.g. 'look at **them**'. The weak form is usually /ðəm/, e.g. 'leave them alone' /ˌliːv.ðəm.əˈləʊn (US) -ˈloʊn/, or in rapid, casual speech /ðm/, e.g. 'run them out', /ˌrʌn.ðmˈaʊt/.

thematic θɪˈmæt.ɪk, θiː- (US) θiːˈmæt̬- **-ally** -ᵊl.i, -li

them|e θiːm **-es** -z **-ing** -ɪŋ **-ed** -d **ˈtheme ˌpark**

Themistocles θɪˈmɪs.tə.kliːz, θemˈɪs-, θəˈmɪs- (US) θəˈmɪs-

themselves ðəmˈselvz (US) ðəm-, ðem-

then ðen

thence ðen*t*s

thenceforth ˌðen*t*sˈfɔːθ (US) -ˈfɔːrθ

thenceforward ˌðen*t*sˈfɔː.wəd (US) -ˈfɔːr.wɚd

theo- θiː.əʊ-, θɪə-; θi'ɒ- US θi.oʊ-, -ə-, θi'ɑː-
Note: Prefix. Normally stressed on the second syllable, e.g. **theology** /θi'ɒl.ə.dʒi US θi'ɑː-/, but may also carry secondary stress on the first syllable with primary stress on the third syllable, e.g. **theological** /ˌθiː.ə'lɒdʒ.ɪ.kḷ US -'lɑː.dʒ-/. This prefix is not present in 'theory' and related words.
Theo 'θiː.əʊ US -oʊ
Theobald 'θiː.ə.bɔːld, 'θɪə- *formerly:* 'θɪb.əld, 'tɪb- US 'θiː.ə.bɔːld, -bɑːld; 'tɪb.əld
Theobalds *in Hertfordshire:* 'θiː.ə.bɔːldz, 'θɪə- US 'θiː.ə-, -bɑːldz *road in London:* 'θiː.ə.bɔːldz, 'θɪə- *formerly:* 'tɪb.əldz US 'θiː.ə.bɔːldz, -bɑːldz; 'tɪb.əldz
theocrac|y θi'ɒk.rə.s|i US -'ɑː.krə- **-ies** -iz
theocratic ˌθiː.əʊ'kræt.ɪk, ˌθɪə'- US ˌθiː.ə'kræt̬- **-al** -əl
Theocritus θi'ɒk.rɪ.təs US -'ɑː.krə.t̬əs
theodicy θi'ɒd.ɪ.si, '-ə- US -'ɑː.də-
theodolite θi'ɒd.əl.aɪt US -'ɑː.də.laɪt **-s** -s
Theodora ˌθiː.ə'dɔː.rə, ˌθɪə'- US ˌθiː.ə'dɔːr.ə
Theodore 'θiː.ə.dɔːr, 'θɪə- US 'θiː.ə.dɔːr
Theodoric θi'ɒd.ər.ɪk US -'ɑː.dɚ-
Theodosi|a ˌθiː.ə'dəʊ.si|.ə, ˌθɪə'- US ˌθiː.oʊ'doʊ.ʃi|.ə, -ə'-, '-ʃ|ə **-us** -əs
theologian ˌθiː.ə'ləʊ.dʒən, ˌθɪə'-, -dʒi.ən US ˌθiː.ə'loʊ.dʒən, -dʒi.ən **-s** -z
theologic ˌθiː.ə'lɒdʒ.ɪk, ˌθɪə'- US ˌθiː.ə'lɑː.dʒɪk **-al** -əl **-ally** -əl.i, -li
theologi|cal ˌθiː.ə'lɒdʒ.ɪ|.kəl, ˌθɪə'- US ˌθiː.ə'lɑː.dʒɪ- **-cally** -kəl.i, -kli
theologiz|e, -is|e θi'ɒl.ə.dʒaɪz US -'ɑː.lə- **-es** -ɪz **-ing** -ɪŋ **-ed** -d
theolog|y θi'ɒl.ə.dʒ|i US -'ɑː.lə- **-ist/s** -ɪst/s
Theophilus θi'ɒf.ɪ.ləs, -əl.əs US -'ɑː.fəl-
Theophrastus ˌθiː.əʊ'fræs.təs, ˌθɪə'- US ˌθiː.oʊ'-, -ə'-
theorbo θi'ɔː.bəʊ US -'ɔːr.boʊ **-s** -z
theorem 'θɪə.rəm, -rem, -rɪm US 'θiː.ɚ.əm, 'θɪr.əm, -em **-s** -z
theoretic θɪə'ret.ɪk, ˌθiː.ə'- US ˌθiː.ə'ret̬- **-al** -əl **-ally** -əl.i, -li
theoreti|cal θɪə'ret.ɪ|.kəl, ˌθiː.ə'- US ˌθiː.ə'ret̬- **-cally** -kəl.i, -kli
theoretician ˌθɪə.rə'tɪʃ.ən, ˌθiː.ə-, -rɪ'-, -ret'ɪʃ- US ˌθiː.ə.rə'tɪʃ-, ˌθɪr.ə'- **-s** -z
theorist 'θɪə.rɪst, 'θiː.ə- US 'θiː.ɚ.ɪst, 'θɪr.ɪst **-s** -s
theoriz|e, -is|e 'θɪə.raɪz, 'θiː.ə- US 'θiː.ə-, 'θɪr.aɪz **-es** -ɪz **-ing** -ɪŋ **-ed** -d **-er/s** -ər/z US -ɚ/z
theor|y 'θɪə.r|i, 'θiː.ə- US 'θiː.ə-, 'θɪr|.i **-ies** -iz
theosophic ˌθiː.ə'sɒf.ɪk, ˌθɪə'- US ˌθiː.ə'sɑː.fɪk **-al** -əl **-ally** -əl.i, -li
theosophiz|e, -is|e θi'ɒs.ə.faɪz US -'ɑː.sə- **-es** -ɪz **-ing** -ɪŋ **-ed** -d
theosoph|y θi'ɒs.ə.f|i US -'ɑː.sə- **-ist/s** -ɪst/s **-ism** -ɪ.zəm
Thera 'θɪə.rə US 'θɪr.ə
therapeutic ˌθer.ə'pjuː.tɪk US -t̬ɪk **-s** -s **-ally** -əl.i, -li
therapeutist ˌθer.ə'pjuː.tɪst US -t̬ɪst **-s** -s
therap|y 'θer.ə.p|i **-ies** -iz **-ist/s** -ɪst/s
Theravada ˌθer.ə'vɑː.də
there *strong form:* ðeər US ðer *weak form:* ðər US ðɚ *alternative weak form before vowels:* ðər US ðɚ
Note: Weak form word. The weak forms occur only when 'there' is used existentially as in 'there is', 'there are', 'there was', 'there won't be', etc. The strong form /ðeər US ðer/ is also used in such expressions, and is the normal pronunciation for 'there' as a place adverbial, e.g. 'there it is'.
thereabout 'ðeə.rə.baʊt, ˌ--'- US 'ðer.ə.baʊt, ˌ--'- **-s** -s
Note: The form /ˌðeər.ə'baʊts US ˌðer-/ is always used in the expression 'there or thereabouts'.
thereafter ˌðeə'rɑːf.tər US ˌðer'æf.tɚ
thereat ˌðeə'ræt US ˌðer-
thereby ˌðeə'baɪ US ˌðer-
there'd ðeəd US ðerd
therefor ˌðeə'fɔːr US ˌðer'fɔːr
therefore 'ðeə.fɔːr US 'ðer.fɔːr
therefrom ˌðeə'frɒm US ˌðer'frʌm, -'frɑːm
therein ˌðeə'rɪn US ˌðer'ɪn
thereinafter ˌðeə.rɪn'ɑːf.tər US ˌðer.ɪn'æf.tɚ
thereinto ˌðeə'rɪn.tuː US ˌðer'ɪn-
there'll ðeəl *weak form:* ðəl, ðḷ US ðerl
Note: See note for 'there'.
thereof ˌðeə'rɒv US ˌðer'ɑːv, -'ʌv
thereon ˌðeə'rɒn US ˌðer'ɑːn
there's (= **there is, there has**) *strong form:* ðeəz US ðerz *weak form:* ðəz US ðɚz
Note: See note for 'there'.
Theresa tɪ'riː.zə, tə- US tə'riː.sə, -zə
thereto ˌðeə'tuː US ˌðer-
theretofore ˌðeə.tuː'fɔːr US ˌðer.t̬ə'fɔːr, '---
thereunder ˌðeə'rʌn.dər US ˌðer'ʌn.dɚ
thereunto ˌðeə'rʌn.tuː, ˌ--'- US ˌðer'ʌn.tuː, ˌ--'-
thereupon ˌðeə.rə'pɒn, '--- US ˌðer.ə'pɑːn, '---
there've *strong forms:* 'ðeər.əv US 'ðer- *weak forms:* ðər.əv, ðəv US ðɚ.əv
therewith ˌðeə'wɪð, -'wɪθ US ˌðer-
therewithal ˌðeə.wɪð'ɔːl, -wɪθ'- *when used as a noun:* '--- US ˌðer-, '---
therm θɜːm US θɝːm **-s** -z
thermal 'θɜː.məl US 'θɝː- **-ly** -i
thermic 'θɜː.mɪk US 'θɝː- **-ally** -əl.i, -li
Thermidor 'θɜː.mɪ.dɔːr US 'θɝː.mə.dɔːr
thermion 'θɜː.mi.ən US 'θɝː- **-s** -z
thermionic ˌθɜː.mi'ɒn.ɪk US ˌθɝː.mi'ɑː.nɪk **-s** -s
thermistor θɜː'mɪs.tər US 'θɝː.mɪ.stɚ, θɚ'mɪs.tɚ **-s** -z
Thermit® 'θɜː.mɪt US 'θɝː-
thermite 'θɜː.maɪt US 'θɝː-
thermo- θɜː.məʊ-; θə'mɒ- US θɝː.moʊ-, -mə-, θɚ'mɑː-
Note: Prefix. There may be primary or secondary stress on the first syllable, e.g. **thermocouple** /'θɜː.məˌkʌp.ḷ US 'θɜːr.mə-/, **thermometric** /ˌθɜː.məʊ'met.rɪk US ˌθɜːr.moʊ'-/, or on the second syllable, e.g. **thermometer** /θə'mɒm.ɪ.tə US θɚ'mɑː.mə.t̬ɚ/.
thermocouple 'θɜː.məʊˌkʌp.ḷ US 'θɝː.moʊ-, -mə- **-s** -z
thermodynamic ˌθɜː.məʊ.daɪ'næm.ɪk, -dɪ'- US ˌθɝː.moʊ.daɪ'-, -mə- **-s** -s **-ally** -əl.i, -li
thermoelectric ˌθɜː.məʊ.ɪ'lek.trɪk, -ə'- US ˌθɝː.moʊ- **-ally** -əl.i, -li
thermoelectricity ˌθɜː.məʊ.ɪˌlek'trɪs.ə.ti, -əˌ-, -ˌiː.lek'-, -'trɪz-, -ɪ.ti US ˌθɝː.moʊˌiː.lek'trɪs.ə.t̬i
thermograph 'θɜː.məʊ.grɑːf, -græf US 'θɝː.moʊ.græf, -mə- **-s** -s
thermometer θə'mɒm.ɪ.tər, '-ə- US θɚ'mɑː.mə.t̬ɚ **-s** -z
thermometric ˌθɜː.məʊ'met.rɪk US ˌθɝː.moʊ'-, -mə'- **-al** -əl **-ally** -əl.i, -li
thermonuclear ˌθɜː.məʊ'njuː.kli.ər US ˌθɝː.moʊ'nuː.kli.ɚ, -mə'-, -'njuː-
thermopile 'θɜː.məʊ.paɪl US 'θɝː.moʊ-, -mə- **-s** -z
thermoplastic ˌθɜː.məʊ'plæs.tɪk, -'plɑː.stɪk US ˌθɝː.moʊ'plæs.tɪk, -mə'- **-s** -s
Thermopylae θɜː'mɒp.ɪ.liː, θə-, -əl.iː, -i, -aɪ US θɚ'mɑː.pə.liː
Thermos® 'θɜː.mɒs, -məs US 'θɝː.məs **-es** -ɪz **'Thermos ˌflask**
thermosetting 'θɜː.məʊˌset.ɪŋ US 'θɝː.moʊˌset̬-, -məˌ-
thermostat 'θɜː.mə.stæt US 'θɝː.mə- **-s** -s **-(t)ing** -ɪŋ **-(t)ed** -ɪd
thermostatic ˌθɜː.mə'stæt.ɪk US ˌθɝː.mə'stæt̬-

Theroux θəˈruː
Thersites θɜːˈsaɪ.tiːz, θə- ⓤⓢ θɚˈsaɪ-
thesaur|us θɪˈsɔː.r|əs, θiː-, θə- ⓤⓢ θɪˈsɔːr|.əs **-i** -aɪ **-uses** -ə.sɪz
these *(plur. of* **this***)* ðiːz
Theseus *in Greek legend:* ˈθiː.sjuːs, -sjəs, -si.əs ⓤⓢ -si.əs, -sjuːs *Shakespearian character, and as name of ship:* ˈθiː.sjəs, -si.əs
Thesiger ˈθes.ɪ.dʒəʳ ⓤⓢ -dʒɚ
thes|is *dissertation:* ˈθiː.s|ɪs **-es** -iːz
thesis *metrical term:* ˈθes.ɪs, ˈθiː.sɪs ⓤⓢ ˈθiː.sɪs
thespian (T) ˈθes.pi.ən **-s** -z
Thespis ˈθes.pɪs
Thessalonian ˌθes.əlˈəʊ.ni.ən ⓤⓢ -əˈloʊ- **-s** -z
Thessalonika ˌθes.əlˈɒn.ɪ.kə ⓤⓢ -əˈlɑː.nɪ-
Thessaly ˈθes.əl.i
theta ˈθiː.tə ⓤⓢ ˈθeɪ.t̬ə, ˈθiː- **-s** -z
Thetford ˈθet.fəd ⓤⓢ -fɚd
Thetis *Greek:* ˈθet.ɪs ⓤⓢ ˈθet̬- *otherwise:* ˈθiː.tɪs ⓤⓢ -t̬ɪs
thews θjuːz
they ðeɪ
they'd ðeɪd
Theydon Bois ˌθeɪ.dənˈbɔɪz
they'd've ˈðeɪ.dəv
they'll ðeɪl
they're ðeəʳ ⓤⓢ ðer
they've ðeɪv
thiamin(e) ˈθaɪə.miːn, -mɪn ⓤⓢ -mɪn, -miːn
thick θɪk **-er** -əʳ ⓤⓢ -ɚ **-est** -ɪst, -əst **-ly** -li **-ness/es** -nəs/ɪz, -nɪs/ɪz **as ˌthick as ˈthieves; as ˌthick as ˌtwo ˌshort ˈplanks; ˌgive someone a ˌthick ˈear; through ˌthick and ˈthin**
thicken ˈθɪk.ən **-s** -z **-ing** -ɪŋ, ˈθɪk.nɪŋ **-ed** -d **-er/s** -əʳ/z ⓤⓢ -ɚ/z
thicket ˈθɪk.ɪt **-s** -s
thickhead ˈθɪk.hed **-s** -z
thickheaded ˌθɪkˈhed.ɪd ⓤⓢ ˈ-ˌ--, ˌ-ˈ-- **-ness** -nəs, -nɪs *stress shift, British only:* ˌthickheaded ˈfool
thickish ˈθɪk.ɪʃ
thicko ˈθɪk.əʊ ⓤⓢ -oʊ **-s** -z
thickset ˌθɪkˈset ⓤⓢ ˈ--, ˌ-ˈ- *stress shift, British only:* ˌthickset ˈman
thick-skinned ˌθɪkˈskɪnd ⓤⓢ ˈ--, ˌ-ˈ- *stress shift, British only:* ˌthick-skinned ˈman
thick-skulled ˌθɪkˈskʌld ⓤⓢ ˈ--, ˌ-ˈ- *stress shift, British only:* ˌthick-skulled ˈidiot
thick-witted ˌθɪkˈwɪt.ɪd ⓤⓢ ˈθɪkˌwɪt̬.ɪd, ˌ-ˈ-- *stress shift, British only:* ˌthick-witted ˈfool
thie|f θiː|f **-ves** -vz
Thiès tjez ⓤⓢ tjes
thiev|e θiːv **-es** -z **-ing** -ɪŋ **-ed** -d **-ery** -ər.i
thievish ˈθiː.vɪʃ **-ly** -li **-ness** -nəs, -nɪs
thigh θaɪ **-s** -z
thighbone ˈθaɪ.bəʊn ⓤⓢ -boʊn **-s** -z
thill θɪl **-s** -z
thimble ˈθɪm.bl̩ **-s** -z **-ful/s** -fʊl/z
thimblerig ˈθɪm.bl̩.rɪg **-s** -z **-ging** -ɪŋ **-ged** -d
Thimbu ˈθɪm.buː
Thimphu ˈθɪmp.fuː
thin θɪn **-ner** -əʳ ⓤⓢ -ɚ **-nest** -ɪst, -əst **-ly** -li **-ness** -nəs, -nɪs **-s** -z **-ning** -ɪŋ **-ned** -d **into ˌthin ˈair**
thine ðaɪn
thing θɪŋ **-s** -z
thingamabob ˈθɪŋ.ə.məˌbɒb ⓤⓢ -ˌbɑːb **-s** -z
thingamajig ˈθɪŋ.ə.məˌdʒɪg **-s** -z
thingam|y ˈθɪŋ.ə.m|i **-ies** -iz
thingie ˈθɪŋ.i **-s** -z
thingumabob ˈθɪŋ.ə.məˌbɒb ⓤⓢ -ˌbɑːb **-s** -z
thingumajig ˈθɪŋ.ə.məˌdʒɪg **-s** -z
thingumm|y ˈθɪŋ.ə.m|i **-ies** -iz
thing|y ˈθɪŋ|.i **-ies** -z
think θɪŋk **-s** -s **-ing/ly** -ɪŋ/li **thought** θɔːt ⓤⓢ θɑːt, θɔːt **thinker/s** ˈθɪŋ.kəʳ/z ⓤⓢ -kɚ/z **ˈthink ˌtank**
thinkable ˈθɪŋ.kə.bl̩
thinktank ˈθɪŋkˌtæŋk **-s** -s
Thinn θɪn
thinnish ˈθɪn.ɪʃ
thin-skinned ˌθɪnˈskɪnd ⓤⓢ ˈ-- *stress shift, British only:* ˌthin-skinned ˈperson
third θɜːd ⓤⓢ θɝːd **-s** -z **-ly** -li **ˌthird ˈclass; ˌthird diˈmension; ˌthird ˈparty; ˌthird ˈperson; ˌThird ˈWorld; ˌgive someone the ˌthird deˈgree**
third-degree ˌθɜːd.dɪˈgriː, -dəˈ- ⓤⓢ ˌθɝːd- *stress shift, see compound:* **ˌthird-degree ˈburn**
thirdhand ˌθɜːdˈhænd ⓤⓢ ˌθɝːd- *stress shift:* ˌthirdhand ˈgossip
third-ra|te ˌθɜːdˈreɪ|t ⓤⓢ ˌθɝːd- **-ter/s** -təʳ/z ⓤⓢ -t̬ɚ/z *stress shift:* ˌthird-rate ˈdrama
Thirsk θɜːsk ⓤⓢ θɝːsk
thirst θɜːst ⓤⓢ θɝːst **-s** -s **-ing** -ɪŋ **-ed** -ɪd
thirst|y ˈθɜː.st|i ⓤⓢ ˈθɝː- **-ier** -i.əʳ ⓤⓢ -i.ɚ **-iest** -i.ɪst, -i.əst **-ily** -ɪ.li, -əl.i **-iness** -ɪ.nəs, -ɪ.nɪs
thirteen θɜːˈtiːn ⓤⓢ θɝː- **-s** -z *stress shift:* ˌthirteen ˈpounds
thirteenth θɜːˈtiːntθ ⓤⓢ θɝː- **-s** -s *stress shift:* ˌthirteenth ˈplace
thirtieth ˈθɜː.ti.əθ ⓤⓢ ˈθɝː.t̬i- **-s** -s
thirt|y ˈθɜː.t|i ⓤⓢ ˈθɝː.t̬|i **-ies** -iz **ˈthirty ˌsomething; ˌThirty ˌYearsˈ ˈWar**
thirtyfold ˈθɜː.ti.fəʊld ⓤⓢ ˈθɝː.t̬i.foʊld
this ðɪs *occasional weak form:* ðəs **ˌthis, ˌthat, and the ˈother**
Note: Some speakers use a weak form /ðəs/ in 'this morning, afternoon, evening'.
Thisbe ˈθɪz.bi
Thiselton ˈθɪs.l̩.tən
thistle ˈθɪs.l̩ **-s** -z
thistledown ˈθɪs.l̩.daʊn
thistly ˈθɪs.l̩.i, ˈ-li
thither ˈðɪð.əʳ ⓤⓢ ˈθɪð.ɚ, ˈðɪð- **-ward/s** -wəd/z ⓤⓢ -wɚd/z
tho' ðəʊ ⓤⓢ ðoʊ
Thoday ˈθəʊ.deɪ ⓤⓢ ˈθoʊ-
thole θəʊl ⓤⓢ θoʊl **-s** -z
Thom tɒm ⓤⓢ tɑːm
Thomas ˈtɒm.əs ⓤⓢ ˈtɑː.məs
Thomasin ˈtɒm.ə.sɪn ⓤⓢ ˈtɑː.mə-
Thomond ˈθəʊ.mənd ⓤⓢ ˈθoʊ-
Thompson ˈtɒmp.sən ⓤⓢ ˈtɑːmp-
Thompstone ˈtɒmp.stəʊn ⓤⓢ ˈtɑːmp.stoʊn
Thomson ˈtɒmp.sən ⓤⓢ ˈtɑːmp-
-thon -θɒn, -θən ⓤⓢ -θɑːn
Note: Suffix. Normally unstressed, e.g. /ˈmær.ə.θən ⓤⓢ ˈmer.ə.θɑːn/.
thong θɒŋ ⓤⓢ θɑːŋ, θɔːŋ **-s** -z
Thor θɔːʳ ⓤⓢ θɔːr
Thora ˈθɔː.rə ⓤⓢ ˈθɔːr.ə
thoraces *(alternative plur. of* **thorax***)* ˈθɔː.rə.siːz
thoracic θɔːˈræs.ɪk, θɒrˈæs-, θəˈræs- ⓤⓢ θɔːˈræs-, θə-
thorax ˈθɔː.ræks ⓤⓢ ˈθɔːr.æks **-es** -ɪz
Thorburn ˈθɔː.bɜːn ⓤⓢ ˈθɔːr.bɚn
Thoreau θɔːˈrəʊ, θə-; ˈθɔː.rəʊ ⓤⓢ θəˈroʊ, θɔː-; ˈθɔːr.oʊ
thorium ˈθɔː.ri.əm ⓤⓢ ˈθɔːr.i-
thorn (T) θɔːn ⓤⓢ θɔːrn **-s** -z **a ˌthorn in one's ˈflesh/side**
Thornaby ˈθɔː.nə.bi ⓤⓢ ˈθɔːr-
Thornbury ˈθɔːn.bər.i, ˈθɔːm- ⓤⓢ ˈθɔːrn.ber-, -bɚ-
thornbush ˈθɔːn.bʊʃ, ˈθɔːm- ⓤⓢ ˈθɔːrn- **-es** -ɪz
Thorndike ˈθɔːn.daɪk ⓤⓢ ˈθɔːrn-
Thorne θɔːn ⓤⓢ θɔːrn
Thorneycroft ˈθɔː.nɪ.krɒft ⓤⓢ ˈθɔːr.nɪ.krɑːft
Thornhill ˈθɔːn.hɪl ⓤⓢ ˈθɔːrn-
thornless ˈθɔːn.ləs, -lɪs ⓤⓢ ˈθɔːrn-
Thornton ˈθɔːn.tən ⓤⓢ ˈθɔːrn.tən
thorn|y ˈθɔː.n|i ⓤⓢ ˈθɔːr- **-ier** -i.əʳ ⓤⓢ -i.ɚ **-iest** -i.ɪst, -i.əst **-ily** -ɪ.li, -əl.i **-iness** -ɪ.nəs, -ɪ.nɪs
Thorold ˈθɒr.əld, ˈθʌr- ⓤⓢ ˈθɔːr-, ˈθɝː-
thorough ˈθʌr.ə ⓤⓢ ˈθɝː.oʊ, -ə **-ly** -li **-ness** -nəs, -nɪs
thoroughbass ˈθʌr.ə.beɪs ⓤⓢ ˈθɝː.oʊ-, ˈ-ə-
thoroughbred ˈθʌr.ə.bred ⓤⓢ ˈθɝː.oʊ-, ˈ-ə- **-s** -z

thoroughfare ˈθʌr.ə.feəʳ (US) ˈθɝː.oʊ.fer, ˈ-ə- **-s** -z
thoroughgoing ˌθʌr.əˈgəʊ.ɪŋ (US) ˌθɝː.oʊˈgoʊ-, -əˈ-
thorough-paced ˌθʌr.əˈpeɪst (US) ˈθɝː.oʊ.peɪst, ˈ-ə-
Thorowgood ˈθʌr.ə.gʊd (US) ˈθɝː.oʊ-
Thorpe θɔːp (US) θɔːrp
Thorrowgood ˈθʌr.ə.gʊd (US) ˈθɝː-
those *(plur. of* **that***)* ðəʊz (US) ðoʊz
Thoth θəʊθ, təʊt, θɒθ (US) θoʊθ, toʊt
thou *you:* ðaʊ
thou *(abbrev. for* **thousand***)* θaʊ
though ðəʊ (US) ðoʊ
thought *(from* **think***)* θɔːt (US) θɑːt, θɔːt **-s** -s
thoughtful ˈθɔːt.fəl, -fʊl (US) ˈθɑːt-, ˈθɔːt- **-ly** -i **-ness** -nəs, -nɪs
thoughtless ˈθɔːt.ləs, -lɪs (US) ˈθɑːt-, ˈθɔːt- **-ly** -li **-ness** -nəs, -nɪs
thought-out ˌθɔːtˈaʊt (US) ˌθɑːt̬-, ˌθɔːt̬-
thought-provoking ˈθɔːt.prəˌvəʊ.kɪŋ (US) ˈθɑːt.prəˌvoʊ-, ˈθɔːt-
Thouless ˈθaʊ.les, -lɪs
thous|and ˈθaʊ.z|ənd **-ands** -əndz ˌ**Thousand** ˌ**Island** ˈ**dressing**
thousandfold ˈθaʊ.zənd.fəʊld (US) -foʊld
thousandth ˈθaʊ.zəndθ **-s** -s
Thrace θreɪs
Thracian ˈθreɪ.ʃən, -ʃi.ən (US) ˈ-ʃən **-s** -z
thrall θrɔːl (US) θrɔːl, θrɑːl **-s** -z **-ing** -ɪŋ **-ed** -d
thral(l)dom ˈθrɔːl.dəm (US) ˈθrɔːl-, ˈθrɑːl-
thrash θræʃ **-es** -ɪz **-ing** -ɪŋ **-ed** -t **-er/s** -əʳ/z (US) -ɚ/z
thread θred **-s** -z **-ing** -ɪŋ **-ed** -ɪd
threadbare ˈθred.beəʳ (US) -ber
Threadneedle ˌθredˈniː.dl̩, ˈ-ˌ--
thread|y ˈθred|.i **-iness** -ɪ.nəs, -ɪ.nɪs
threat θret **-s** -s
threaten ˈθret.ən **-s** -z **-ing/ly** -ɪŋ/li, ˈθret.nɪŋ/li **-ed** -d
three θriː **-s** -z
three-cornered ˌθriːˈkɔː.nəd (US) -ˈkɔːr- *stress shift:* ˌthree-cornered ˈhat
three-D, 3-D ˌθriːˈdiː *stress shift:* ˌthree-D ˈglasses
three-day ˌθriːˈdeɪ ˌ**three-day eˈvent**; ˌ**three-day ˈweek**
three-decker ˌθriːˈdek.əʳ (US) ˈθriːˌdek.ɚ **-s** -z
three-dimensional ˌθriː.dɪˈmen.*t*ʃən.əl, -daɪˈ-, -ˈment*ʃ*.nəl (US) -dəˈment.ʃən.əl
threefold ˈθriː.fəʊld (US) -foʊld
threeish ˈθriː.ɪʃ
three-legged ˌθriːˈlegd, -ˈleg.ɪd (US) ˈθriː.legd, -ˌleg.ɪd *stress shift:* ˌthree-legged ˈstool ˌthree-ˈlegged ˌrace
three-line ˌθriːˈlaɪn *stress shift, see compound:* ˌ**three-line ˈwhip**
three|pence ˈθre|p.ən*t*s, ˈθrɪ|p-, ˈθrʌ|p-, ˈθrʊ|p- **-pences** -pən*t*.sɪz **-penny** -pən.i, -p.ni
Note: See note for **penny**.
three-piece ˌθriːˈpiːs *stress shift, see compound:* ˌ**three-piece ˈsuite**
three-ply ˈθriː.plaɪ, ˌ-ˈ-
three-point ˌθriːˈpɔɪnt *stress shift, see compound:* ˌ**three-point ˈturn**
three-quarter ˌθriːˈkwɔː.təʳ (US) -ˈkwɔːr.t̬ɚ **-s** -z *stress shift:* ˌthree-quarter ˈlength
three-ring ˌθriːˈrɪŋ *stress shift, see compound:* ˌ**three-ring ˈcircus**
three Rs θriːˈɑːz (US) -ˈɑːrz
threescore ˌθriːˈskɔːʳ (US) ˈθriː.skɔːr *stress shift:* ˌthreescore ˈyears ˌ**threescore** ˌ**years and ˈten**
threesome ˈθriː.səm **-s** -z
three-star ˌθriːˈstɑːʳ (US) -ˈstɑːr *stress shift:* ˌthree-star hoˈtel
threnod|y ˈθren.ə.d|i, ˈθriː.nə- (US) ˈθren.ə- **-ies** -iz
thresh θreʃ **-es** -ɪz **-ing** -ɪŋ **-ed** -t **-er/s** -əʳ/z (US) -ɚ/z ˈ**threshing maˌchine**
thresher (T®) ˈθreʃ.əʳ (US) -ɚ **-s** -z
threshold ˈθreʃ.*h*əʊld (US) -*h*oʊld **-s** -z
threw *(from* **throw***)* θruː
thrice θraɪs
thrift θrɪft ˈ**thrift** ˌ**shop**
thriftless ˈθrɪft.ləs, -lɪs **-ly** -li **-ness** -nəs, -nɪs
thrift|y ˈθrɪf.t|i **-ier** -i.əʳ (US) -i.ɚ **-iest** -i.ɪst, -i.əst **-ily** -ɪ.li, -əl.i **-iness** -ɪ.nəs, -ɪ.nɪs
thrill θrɪl **-s** -z **-ing/ly** -ɪŋ/li **-ed** -d **-er/s** -əʳ/z (US) -ɚ/z
Thring θrɪŋ
thrip θrɪp **-s** -s
thriv|e θraɪv **-es** -z **-ing** -ɪŋ **-ed** -d **throve** θrəʊv (US) θroʊv **thriven** ˈθrɪv.ən
thro' θruː
throat θrəʊt (US) θroʊt **-s** -s **-ed** -ɪd (US) ˈθroʊ.t̬ɪd
throat|y ˈθrəʊ.t|i (US) ˈθroʊ.t̬|i **-ier** -i.əʳ (US) -i.ɚ **-iest** -i.ɪst, -i.əst **-ily** -ɪ.li, -əl.i **-iness** -ɪ.nəs, -ɪ.nɪs
throb θrɒb (US) θrɑːb **-s** -z **-bing/ly** -ɪŋ/li **-bed** -d
throes θrəʊz (US) θroʊz
Throgmorton θrɒgˈmɔː.tən, ˈ--- (US) θrɑːgˈmɔːr-, θrɔːg-, ˈ---
thrombin ˈθrɒm.bɪn (US) ˈθrɑːm-
thrombos|is θrɒmˈbəʊ.s|ɪs (US) θrɑːmˈboʊ- **-es** -iːz
thromb|us ˈθrɒm.b|əs (US) ˈθrɑːm- **-i** -aɪ
thron|e θrəʊn (US) θroʊn **-es** -z **-ing** -ɪŋ **-ed** -d
throng θrɒŋ (US) θrɑːŋ, θrɔːŋ **-s** -z **-ing** -ɪŋ **-ed** -d
throstle ˈθrɒs.l̩ (US) ˈθrɑː.sl̩ **-s** -z
throttl|e ˈθrɒt.l̩ (US) ˈθrɑː.t̬l̩ **-es** -z **-ing** -ɪŋ, ˈθrɒt.lɪŋ (US) ˈθrɑːt- **-ed** -d
through θruː ˌ**through and ˈthrough**
Througham ˈθrʌf.əm
throughout θruˈaʊt
throughput ˈθruː.pʊt **-s** -s
throughway ˈθruː.weɪ **-s** -z
throve *(from* **thrive***)* θrəʊv (US) θroʊv
throw θrəʊ (US) θroʊ **-s** -z **-ing** -ɪŋ **threw** θruː **thrown** θrəʊn (US) θroʊn **thrower/s** ˈθrəʊ.əʳ/z (US) ˈθroʊ.ɚ/z
throwaway ˈθrəʊ.ə.weɪ (US) ˈθroʊ-
throwback ˈθrəʊ.bæk (US) ˈθroʊ- **-s** -s
thru θruː
thrum θrʌm **-s** -z **-ming** -ɪŋ **-med** -d
thrush θrʌʃ **-es** -ɪz
thrust θrʌst **-s** -s **-ing** -ɪŋ
thruway ˈθruː.weɪ **-s** -z
Thucydides θjuːˈsɪd.ɪ.diːz, θjʊ-, ˈ-ə- (US) θuːˈsɪd.ə-
thud θʌd **-s** -z **-ding** -ɪŋ **-ded** -ɪd
thug θʌg **-s** -z
thuggery ˈθʌg.ər.i
thuggish ˈθʌg.ɪʃ **-ly** -li **-ness** -nəs, -nɪs
thuja ˈθuː.jə (US) ˈθuː-, ˈθjuː- **-s** -z
Thule *Northernmost region of the world:* ˈθjuː.liː, ˈθuː-, -li; θuːl (US) ˈθuː.li, ˈθjuː-, ˈtuː-, ˈtjuː- *Eskimo settlement:* ˈtuː.li (US) ˈθuː-, ˈθjuː-
thulium ˈθuː.li.əm (US) ˈθuː-, ˈθjuː-
thumb θʌm **-s** -z **-ing** -ɪŋ **-ed** -d ˌ**thumb** ˈ**index**
thumbnail ˈθʌm.neɪl **-s** -z ˌ**thumbnail** ˈ**sketch**
thumbprint ˈθʌm.prɪnt **-s** -s
thumbscrew ˈθʌm.skruː **-s** -z
thumbs-down ˌθʌmzˈdaʊn
thumbstall ˈθʌm.stɔːl (US) -stɔːl, -stɑːl **-s** -z
thumbs-up ˌθʌmzˈʌp
thumbtack ˈθʌm.tæk **-s** -s
Thummim ˈθʌm.ɪm *in Jewish usage also:* ˈθʊm-, ˈtʊm-
thump θʌmp **-s** -s **-ing** -ɪŋ **-ed** -t **-er/s** -əʳ/z (US) -ɚ/z
Thun tuːn
thund|er ˈθʌn.d|əʳ (US) -d|ɚ **-ers** -əz (US) -ɚz **-ering/ly** -ər.ɪŋ/li **-ered** -əd (US) -ɚd **-erer/s** -ər.əʳ/z (US) -ɚ.ɚ/z
Thunderball ˈθʌn.də.bɔːl (US) -dɚ-, -bɑːl
thunderbird (T) ˈθʌn.də.bɜːd (US) -dɚ.bɝːd **-s** -z
thunderbolt ˈθʌn.də.bəʊlt (US) -dɚ.boʊlt **-s** -s
thunderclap ˈθʌn.də.klæp (US) -dɚ- **-s** -s
thundercloud ˈθʌn.də.klaʊd (US) -dɚ- **-s** -z
thunderfl|y ˈθʌn.də.fl|aɪ (US) -dɚ- **-ies** -aɪz
thunderhead ˈθʌn.də.hed (US) -dɚ- **-s** -z
thunderous ˈθʌn.dər.əs **-ly** -li

thunderstorm 'θʌn.də.stɔːm (US) -dɚ.stɔːrm **-s** -z
thunderstruck 'θʌn.də.strʌk (US) -dɚ-
thunder|y 'θʌn.dᵊr|.i **-iness** -ɪ.nəs, -ɪ.nɪs
Thur. *(abbrev. for* **Thursday***)* 'θɜːz.deɪ, -di (US) 'θɝːz-
Note: This abbreviation may also be pronounced /θɜːʳ/ in British English.
Thurber 'θɜː.bəʳ (US) 'θɝː.bɚ
Thurcroft 'θɜː.krɒft (US) 'θɝː.krɑːft
thurible 'θjʊə.rɪ.bl̩, 'θjɔː-, -rə- (US) 'θɝː.ə-, 'θʊr-, 'θjʊr- **-s** -z
Thuringi|a θjʊə'rɪn.dʒi|.ə, tʊə-, -'rɪŋ.gi|.ə (US) θʊ'rɪn.dʒi|.ə, θjʊ-, '-dʒ|ə **-an/s** -ən/z
Thurloe, Thurlow 'θɜː.ləʊ (US) 'θɝː.loʊ
Thurman 'θɜː.mən (US) θɝː-
Thurnscoe 'θɜːnz.kəʊ (US) 'θɝːnz.koʊ
Thuron tʊə'rɒn, tə- (US) -'rɑːn
Thurs. *(abbrev. for* **Thursday***)* 'θɜːz.deɪ, -di (US) 'θɝːz-
Note: This abbreviation may also be pronounced /θɜːz/in British English.
Thursday 'θɜːz.deɪ, -di (US) 'θɝːz- **-s** -z
Thurso 'θɜː.səʊ, -zəʊ (US) 'θɝː.soʊ, -zoʊ
Thurston 'θɜː.stᵊn (US) 'θɝː-
thus ðʌs
thwack θwæk **-s** -s **-ing** -ɪŋ **-ed** -t
Thwackum 'θwæk.əm
thwaite (T) θweɪt **-s** -s
thwart *of a boat:* θwɔːt (US) θwɔːrt *in nautical usage also:* θɔːt (US) θɔːrt **-s** -s
thwart *(v.)* θwɔːt (US) θwɔːrt **-s** -s **-ing** -ɪŋ (US) 'θwɔːr.t̬ɪŋ **-ed** -ɪd (US) 'θwɔːr.t̬ɪd
thy ðaɪ
thyme taɪm **-s** -z
thymine 'θaɪ.miːn (US) -miːn, -mɪn
thymol 'θaɪ.mɒl (US) -mɔːl, -moʊl
thymus 'θaɪ.məs **-es** -ɪz
Thynne θɪn
thyroid 'θaɪ.rɔɪd **-s** -z **'thyroid ˌgland**
thyroxin θaɪ'rɒk.siːn, -sɪn (US) -'rɑːk-
Thyrsis 'θɜː.sɪs (US) 'θɝː-
thyself ðaɪ'self
Tia Maria® ˌtiː.ə.mə'riː.ə
Tiananmen Square tiˌæn.ən.mɪn'skweəʳ, -men'- (US) ˌtjɑː.nɑːn.mɪn'skwer; tiˌæn.ən
Tianjin ˌtjen'dʒɪn
tiara ti'ɑː.rə (US) -'er.ə, -'ær-, -'ɑːr- **-s** -z **-ed** -d
Tibbitts 'tɪb.ɪts
Tibbs tɪbz
Tiber 'taɪ.bəʳ (US) -bɚ
Tiberias taɪ'bɪə.ri.æs, -əs (US) -'bɪr.i.əs
Tiberius taɪ'bɪə.ri.əs (US) -'bɪr.i-
Tibet tɪ'bet
Tibetan tɪ'bet.ᵊn **-s** -s
tibi|a 'tɪb.i|.ə, 'taɪ.bi- (US) 'tɪb.i- **-ae** -iː **-as** -əz
Tibullus tɪ'bʌl.əs, -'bʊl-
tic tɪk **-s** -s
tic douloureux ˌtɪk.duː.lᵊr'ɜː (US) -lʊ'ruː
tic|e taɪs **-es** -ɪz **-ing** -ɪŋ **-ed** -t
Ticehurst 'taɪs.hɜːst (US) -hɝːst
Tichborne 'tɪtʃ.bɔːn, -bən (US) -bɔːrn, -bɚn
Ticino tɪ'tʃiː.nəʊ (US) -noʊ
tick tɪk **-s** -s **-ing** -ɪŋ **-ed** -t **-er/s** -əʳ/z (US) -ɚ/z ˌ**ticking 'off**
tickertape 'tɪk.ə.teɪp (US) '-ɚ- ˌ**tickertape re'ception; 'tickertape ˌparade**
tick|et 'tɪk|.ɪt **-ets** -ɪts **-eting** -ɪ.tɪŋ (US) -ɪ.t̬ɪŋ **-eted** -ɪ.tɪd (US) -ɪ.t̬ɪd **'ticket ˌoffice**
tickety-boo ˌtɪk.ɪ.ti'buː, ˌ-ə- (US) -ə.t̬i'-
ticking 'tɪk.ɪŋ **-s** -z
ticking-off ˌtɪk.ɪŋ'ɒf (US) -'ɑːf **tickings-off** ˌtɪk.ɪŋz'ɒf (US) -'ɑːf
tickl|e 'tɪk.l̩ **-es** -z **-ing** -ɪŋ, 'tɪk.lɪŋ **-ed** -d **-er/s** -əʳ/z, 'tɪk.ləʳ/z (US) '-l̩.ɚ/z, '-lɚ/z
Tickler 'tɪk.ləʳ (US) -lɚ
ticklish 'tɪk.lɪʃ, '-l̩.ɪʃ **-ly** -li **-ness** -nəs, -nɪs
tickl|y 'tɪk.l̩|.i, '-l|i **-ier** -i.əʳ (US) -i.ɚ **-iest** -i.ɪst, -i.əst **-iness** -ɪ.nəs, -ɪ.nɪs
ticktacktoe ˌtɪkˌtæk'təʊ (US) -'toʊ
ticktock 'tɪk.tɒk (US) -tɑːk **-s** -s
tic-tac-toe ˌtɪkˌtæk'təʊ (US) -'toʊ
tidal 'taɪ.dᵊl **'tidal ˌwave, ˌtidal 'wave**
tidbit 'tɪd.bɪt **-s** -s
tiddledywink 'tɪd.l̩.di.wɪŋk **-s** -s
tiddler 'tɪd.l̩.əʳ, '-ləʳ (US) '-lɚ, '-l̩.ɚ **-s** -z
Tiddles 'tɪd.l̩z
tiddl|y 'tɪd.l|i, '-l̩|.i **-ier** -i.əʳ (US) -i.ɚ **-iest** -i.ɪst, -i.əst **-iness** -ɪ.nəs, -ɪ.nɪs
tiddlywink 'tɪd.l̩.i.wɪŋk, '-li- (US) '-li-, '-l̩.i- **-s** -s
tid|e taɪd **-es** -z **-ing** -ɪŋ **-ed** -ɪd
tideland 'taɪd.lænd **-s** -z
tidemark 'taɪd.mɑːk (US) -mɑːrk **-s** -s
tidewater 'taɪdˌwɔː.təʳ (US) -ˌwɑː.t̬ɚ, -ˌwɔː-
tideway 'taɪd.weɪ
tidings 'taɪ.dɪŋz
Tidworth 'tɪd.wəθ, -wɜːθ (US) -wɚθ, -wɝːθ
tid|y 'taɪ.d|i **-ies** -iz **-ier** -i.əʳ (US) -i.ɚ **-iest** -i.ɪst, -i.əst **-ily** -ɪ.li, -ᵊl.i **-iness** -ɪ.nəs, -ɪ.nɪs **-ying** -i.ɪŋ **-ied** -id
tie taɪ **-s** -z **tying** 'taɪ.ɪŋ **tieing** 'taɪ.ɪŋ **tied** taɪd ˌ**tied 'house**
tie-break 'taɪ.breɪk **-s** -s **-er/s** -əʳ/z (US) -ɚ/z
tie-dy|e 'taɪ.daɪ **-es** -z **-ing** -ɪŋ **-ed** -d
tie-in 'taɪ.ɪn **-s** -z
Tientsin ˌtjent'sɪn
tiepin 'taɪ.pɪn **-s** -z
Tiepolo ti'ep.ᵊl.əʊ (US) -ə.loʊ
tier *one who ties:* 'taɪ.əʳ (US) -ɚ **-s** -z
tier *set of seats in theatre, etc.:* tɪəʳ (US) tɪr **-s** -z **-ed** -d
tierc|e *in music, fencing, cash:* tɪəs (US) tɪrs **-es** -ɪz
tierc|e *in cards:* tɜːs, tɪəs (US) tɪrs **-es** -ɪz
tiercel 'tɜː.sᵊl, 'tɪə- (US) 'tɪr- **-s** -z
Tierra del Fuego tiˌer.ə.del'fweɪ.gəʊ, ˌtjer.ə-, -fu'eɪ- (US) tiˌer.ə.del'fweɪ.goʊ
tiff tɪf **-s** -s **-ing** -ɪŋ **-ed** -t
tiffany (T) 'tɪf.ᵊn.i
tiffin (T) 'tɪf.ɪn **-s** -z
Tiflis 'tɪf.lɪs
tig tɪg **-s** -z
tig|e tiːʒ **-es** -ɪz
tiger 'taɪ.gəʳ (US) -gɚ **-s** -z **'tiger ˌlily; 'tiger ˌmoth**
tigerish 'taɪ.gᵊr.ɪʃ **-ly** -li **-ness** -nəs, -nɪs
Tigger 'tɪg.əʳ (US) -ɚ
Tiggy-Winkle 'tɪg.iˌwɪŋ.kl̩
Tighe taɪ
tight taɪt **-er** -əʳ (US) 'taɪ.t̬ɚ **-est** -ɪst, -əst (US) 'taɪ.t̬ɪst, -t̬əst **-ly** -li **-ness** -nəs, -nɪs
tighten 'taɪ.tᵊn **-s** -z **-ing** -ɪŋ, 'taɪt.nɪŋ **-ed** -d **-er/s** -əʳ/z, 'taɪt.nəʳ/z (US) 'taɪ.tᵊn.ɚ/z, 'taɪt.nɚ/z
tightfisted ˌtaɪt'fɪs.tɪd (US) '-ˌ--, ˌ-'-- **-ly** -li **-ness** -nəs, -nɪs *stress shift, British only:* ˌtightfisted 'miser
tightknit ˌtaɪt'nɪt (US) '--, ˌ-'- *stress shift, British only:* ˌtightknit 'group
tight-lipped ˌtaɪt'lɪpt (US) '--, ˌ-'- *stress shift, British only:* ˌtight-lipped 'speaker
tightrope 'taɪt.rəʊp (US) -roʊp **'tightrope ˌwalker**
tights taɪts
tightwad 'taɪt.wɒd (US) 'wɑːd **-s** -z
Tiglath-pileser ˌtɪg.læθ.paɪ'liː.zəʳ, -pɪ'-, -pə'- (US) -zɚ
tigon 'taɪ.gən **-s** -z
Tigré 'tiː.greɪ
tigress 'taɪ.gres, -grɪs (US) -grɪs **-es** -ɪz
Tigris 'taɪ.grɪs
Tijuana tɪ'*h*wɑː.nə, ˌtiː.ə'- (US) ˌtiː.ə'wɑː-, tiː'*h*wɑː-
tike taɪk **-s** -s
tikka 'tɪk.ə, 'tiː.kə
tilbur|y (T) 'tɪl.bᵊr|.i (US) -ber-, -bɚ- **-ies** -iz
tilde 'tɪl.də, -di, -deɪ; tɪld (US) 'tɪl.də **-s** -z
til|e taɪl **-es** -z **-ing** -ɪŋ **-ed** -d **-er/s** -əʳ/z (US) -ɚ/z
Tilehurst 'taɪl.hɜːst (US) -hɝːst
till (T) tɪl **-s** -z **-ing** -ɪŋ **-ed** -d **-er/s** -əʳ/z (US) -ɚ/z **-able** -ə.bl̩ **-age** -ɪdʒ
tiller 'tɪl.əʳ (US) -ɚ **-s** -z
Tilley 'tɪl.i
Tillicoultry ˌtɪl.ɪ'kuː.tri, -ə'-

Tilling ˈtɪl.ɪŋ **-s** -z
Tillotson ˈtɪl.ət.sᵊn
Tilly ˈtɪl.i
tilt tɪlt **-s** -s **-ing** -ɪŋ US ˈtɪl.t̬ɪŋ **-ed** -ɪd US ˈtɪl.t̬ɪd **-er/s** -əʳ/z US ˈtɪl.t̬ɚ/z
tilth tɪlθ
tilt-yard ˈtɪlt.jɑːd US -jɑːrd **-s** -z
Tim tɪm
Timaeus taɪˈmiː.əs, tɪ- US taɪˈ-
timbal ˈtɪm.bᵊl **-s** -z
timbale tæmˈbɑːl; tɪmˈ-, ˈtɪm.bᵊl, tɪmˈbɑːl US ˈtɪm.bᵊl; tɪmˈbɑːl, tæm- **-s** -z
timb|er ˈtɪm.b|əʳ US -b|ɚ **-ers** -əz US -ɚz **-ering** -ᵊr.ɪŋ **-ered** -əd US -ɚd
Timberlake ˈtɪm.bə.leɪk US -bɚ-
timberland (T®) ˈtɪm.bə.lænd US -bɚ- **-s** -z
timberline ˈtɪm.bə.laɪn US -bɚ-
timbre ˈtæ̃m.brə, ˈtæm-, -bəʳ; ˈtɪm.bəʳ US ˈtæm.bɚ, ˈtɪm- **-s** -z
timbrel ˈtɪm.brᵊl **-s** -z
Timbuktu, Timbuctoo ˌtɪm.bʌkˈtuː, -bəkˈ- US -bʌkˈ-
tim|e taɪm **-es** -z **-ing** -ɪŋ **-ed** -d **-er/s** -əʳ/z US -ɚ/z **ˌtime and a ˈhalf; ˌtime and ˈmotion; ˌtime after ˈtime; since ˌtime immeˈmorial; ˈtime ˌbomb; ˈtime ˌcapsule; ˌtime ˈoff; ˈtime ˌswitch; ˈtime ˌwarp; ˈtime ˌzone; ˌfall on ˌhard ˈtimes**
time-consuming ˈtaɪm.kənˌsjuː.mɪŋ, -ˌsuː- US -ˌsuː-
time-hono(u)red ˈtaɪmˌɒn.əd, ˌ-ˈ-- US ˈtaɪmˌɑː.nɚd
timekeep|er ˈtaɪmˌkiː.p|əʳ US -p|ɚ **-ers** -əz US -ɚz **-ing** -ɪŋ
time-lapse ˈtaɪm.læps **-s** -ɪz **ˌtime-lapse phoˈtography**
timeless ˈtaɪm.ləs, -lɪs **-ly** -li **-ness** -nəs, -nɪs
time-lock ˈtaɪm.lɒk US -lɑːk **-s** -s
timel|y ˈtaɪm.l|i **-ier** -i.əʳ US -i.ɚ **-iest** -i.ɪst, -i.əst **-iness** -ɪ.nəs, -ɪ.nɪs
timeous ˈtaɪ.məs
time-out ˌtaɪmˈaʊt, ˈ-- **time-outs** ˌtaɪmˈaʊts, ˈ-- **times-out** ˌtaɪmzˈaʊt, ˈ--
timepiec|e ˈtaɪm.piːs **-es** -ɪz
time-saving ˈtaɪmˌseɪ.vɪŋ
timescale ˈtaɪm.skeɪl
timeserv|er ˈtaɪmˌsɜː.v|əʳ US -ˌsɝː.v|ɚ **-ers** -əz US -ɚz **-ing** -ɪŋ
timeshar|e ˈtaɪm.ʃeəʳ US -ʃer **-es** -z **-er/s** -əʳ/z US -ɚ/z **-ing** -ɪŋ
timesheet ˈtaɪm.ʃiːt **-s** -s
time-switch ˈtaɪm.swɪtʃ **-es** -ɪz
timetabl|e ˈtaɪmˌteɪ.bl̩ **-es** -z **-ing** -ɪŋ, -ˌteɪ.blɪŋ **-ed** -d
timework ˈtaɪm.wɜːk US -wɝːk **-er/s** -əʳ/z US -ɚ/z
timeworn ˈtaɪm.wɔːn US -wɔːrn
Timex® ˈtaɪ.meks
timid ˈtɪm.ɪd **-est** -ɪst, -əst **-ly** -li **-ness** -nəs, -nɪs
timidity tɪˈmɪd.ə.ti, -ɪ.ti US -ə.t̬i
Timisoara ˌtɪm.ɪˈʃwɑː.rə US ˌtiː.miːˈʃwɑːr.ə
Timmins ˈtɪm.ɪnz
Timms tɪmz
Timon ˈtaɪ.mən, -mɒn US -mən
Timor ˈtiː.mɔːʳ, ˈtaɪ- US -mɔːr; tiːˈmɔːr
timorous ˈtɪm.ᵊr.əs **-ly** -li **-ness** -nəs, -nɪs
Timotheus tɪˈməʊ.θi.əs US -ˈmoʊ-, taɪ-, -ˈmɑː-
Timothy ˈtɪm.ə.θi
timpan|i, timpan|y ˈtɪm.pə.n|i **-ist/s** -ɪst/s
Timpson ˈtɪmp.sᵊn
tin tɪn **-s** -z **-ning** -ɪŋ **-ned** -d **ˌtin ˈcan; ˌtin ˈgod; ˈtin ˌopener; ˌtin ˌpan ˈalley**
Tina ˈtiː.nə
tinctorial tɪŋkˈtɔː.ri.əl US -ˈtɔːr.i-
tinct|ure ˈtɪŋk.tʃ|əʳ US -tʃ|ɚ **-ures** -əz US -ɚz **-uring** -ᵊr.ɪŋ **-ured** -əd US -ɚd
Tindal(l), Tindale ˈtɪn.dᵊl
tinder ˈtɪn.dəʳ US -dɚ
tinderbox ˈtɪn.də.bɒks US -dɚ.bɑːks **-es** -ɪz
tine taɪn **-s** -z
tinfoil ˈtɪn.fɔɪl, ˌ-ˈ- US ˈtɪn.fɔɪl
ting tɪŋ
ting|e tɪndʒ **-es** -ɪz **-(e)ing** -ɪŋ **-ed** -d
Tingey ˈtɪŋ.gi
tingl|e ˈtɪŋ.gl̩ **-es** -z **-ing** -ɪŋ, ˈtɪŋ.glɪŋ **-ed** -d
tingly ˈtɪŋ.gli, ˈ-gl̩.i
tink|er ˈtɪŋ.k|əʳ US -k|ɚ **-ers** -əz US -ɚz **-ering** -ᵊr.ɪŋ **-ered** -əd US -ɚd **ˌtinker's ˈcuss; ˌtinker's ˈdamn**
Tinkerbell ˈtɪŋ.kə.bel US -kɚ-
Tinkertoy® ˈtɪŋ.kə.tɔɪ US -kɚ-
tinkl|e ˈtɪŋ.kl̩ **-es** -z **-ing/s** -ɪŋ/z, ˈtɪŋ.klɪŋ/z **-ed** -d
Tinnevelly tɪˈnev.ᵊl.i; ˌtɪn.ɪˈvel.i
tinnitus ˈtɪn.ɪ.təs, ˈ-ə- US tɪˈnaɪ.t̬əs; ˈtɪn.ɪ-
tinn|y ˈtɪn|.i **-ies** -iz **-ier** -i.əʳ US -i.ɚ **-iest** -i.ɪst, -i.əst **-ily** -ɪ.li, -ᵊl.i **-iness** -ɪ.nəs, -ɪ.nɪs
Tinos ˈtiː.nɒs US -nɑːs
tinplate ˈtɪn.pleɪt, ˈtɪm-, ˌ-ˈ- US ˈtɪn.pleɪt **-d** -ɪd
tin-pot ˈtɪn.pɒt, ˈtɪm- US ˈtɪn.pɑːt **ˌtin-pot dicˈtator**
tinsel ˈtɪnt.sᵊl **-ly** -i **ˈtinsel ˌtown**
Tinseltown ˈtɪnt.sᵊl.taʊn
tint tɪnt **-s** -s **-ing** -ɪŋ US ˈtɪn.t̬ɪŋ **-ed** -ɪd US ˈtɪn.t̬ɪd **-er/s** -əʳ/z US ˈtɪn.t̬ɚ/z
Tintagel tɪnˈtædʒ.ᵊl
Tintern ˈtɪn.tən, -tɜːn US -tɚn, -tɝːn
Tintin ˈtin.tɪn
tintinnabulation ˌtɪn.tɪˌnæb.jəˈleɪ.ʃᵊn, -jʊˈ- **-s** -z
tintinnabul|um ˌtɪn.tɪˈnæb.jə.l|əm, -jʊ- **-a** -ə **-ar** -əʳ US -ɚ **-ary** -ᵊr.i **-ous** -əs
Tintoretto ˌtɪn.tᵊrˈet.əʊ, -tɒrˈ- US -təˈret̬.oʊ **-s** -z
tin|y ˈtaɪ.n|i **-ier** -i.əʳ US -i.ɚ **-iest** -i.ɪst, -i.əst **-iness** -ɪ.nəs, -ɪ.nɪs
-tion -ʃᵊn
Note: Suffix. Words containing **-tion** are normally stressed on the penultimate syllable, e.g. **fruition** /fruˈɪʃ.ᵊn/.
Tio Pepe® ˌtiː.əʊˈpep.eɪ, -i US -oʊˈ-
-tious -ʃəs
Note: Suffix. Words containing **-tious** are normally stressed on the penultimate syllable, e.g. **propitious** /prəˈpɪʃ.əs/.
tip tɪp **-s** -s **-ping** -ɪŋ **-ped** -t **-per/s** -əʳ/z US -ɚ/z
tipcat ˈtɪp.kæt
tipi ˈtiː.piː **-s** -z
Tipo® ˈtiː.pəʊ US -poʊ
tip-off ˈtɪp.ɒf US -ɑːf **-s** -s
Tippell ˈtɪp.ᵊl
Tipperary ˌtɪp.ᵊrˈeə.ri US -əˈrer.i
tippet ˈtɪp.ɪt **-s** -s
Tippett ˈtɪp.ɪt
Tipp-Ex® ˈtɪp.eks
Tippex ˈtɪp.eks **-es** -ɪz **-ing** -ɪŋ **-ed** -t
tippl|e ˈtɪp.l̩ **-es** -z **-ing** -ɪŋ, ˈtɪp.lɪŋ **-ed** -d **-er/s** -əʳ/z, ˈtɪp.ləʳ/z US ˈ-l̩.ɚ/z, ˈ-lɚ/z
tip|staff ˈtɪp|.stɑːf US -stæf **-staves** -steɪvz
tipster ˈtɪp.stəʳ US -stɚ **-s** -z
tips|y ˈtɪp.s|i **-ier** -i.əʳ US -i.ɚ **-iest** -i.ɪst, -i.əst **-ily** -ɪ.li, -ᵊl.i **-iness** -ɪ.nəs, -ɪ.nɪs
tipto|e ˈtɪp.təʊ US -toʊ **-es** -z **-(e)ing** -ɪŋ **-ed** -d
Tipton ˈtɪp.tᵊn
tiptop ˌtɪpˈtɒp US ˈtɪp.tɑːp *stress shift:* ˌtiptop ˈshape
Tiptree ˈtɪp.triː
tirade taɪˈreɪd, tɪ-, -ˈrɑːd US ˈtaɪ.reɪd, -ˈ- **-s** -z
tiramisu ˌtɪr.ə.mɪˈsuː US -ˈmiː.suː
Tirana, Tiranë tɪˈrɑː.nə US tɪ-, tiː-
tirass|e tɪˈræs **-es** -ɪz
tir|e taɪəʳ US taɪɚ **-es** -z **-ing** -ɪŋ **-ed** -d
tired taɪəd US taɪɚd **-ly** -li **-ness** -nəs, -nɪs
Tiree taɪˈriː
tireless ˈtaɪə.ləs, -lɪs US ˈtaɪɚ- **-ly** -li **-ness** -nəs, -nɪs
Tiresias taɪəˈriː.si.æs, -ˈres.i-, -əs, ˈ-sjəs US taɪˈriː.si.əs
tiresome ˈtaɪə.səm US ˈtaɪɚ- **-ly** -li **-ness** -nəs, -nɪs
Tirney ˈtɜː.ni US ˈtɝː-
tiro ˈtaɪə.rəʊ US ˈtaɪ.roʊ **-s** -z

Tirol tɪˈrəʊl; ˈtɪr.əʊl ⓤⓢ tɪˈroʊl, -ˈrɑːl; ˈtɪr.oʊl, ˈtaɪ.roʊl, -rɑːl
Tirolean ˌtɪr.əʊˈliː.ən ⓤⓢ tɪˈroʊ.li-, taɪ-; ˌtɪr.əˈliː-
Tirolese ˌtɪr.əʊˈliːz ⓤⓢ -əˈliːz, -ˈliːs
Tiruchchirappalli ˌtɪr.əˌtʃɪr.əˈpʌl.i; tɪˌruː.tʃɪˈrɑː.pəl- ⓤⓢ ˌtɪr.ə.tʃɪˈrɑː.pəl-; -ˌtʃɪr.əˈpuː.li, -ˈpʌl.i
'tis tɪz
tisane tɪˈzæn, tiː-, -ˈsæn ⓤⓢ tɪˈzæn **-s** -z
Tishbite ˈtɪʃ.baɪt **-s** -s
Tissaphernes ˌtɪs.əˈfɜː.niːz ⓤⓢ -ˈfɝː-
Tissot ˈtiː.səʊ ⓤⓢ tiːˈsoʊ
tissue ˈtɪʃ.uː, ˈtɪs.juː ⓤⓢ ˈtɪʃ.uː **-s** -z **ˈtissue ˌpaper**
tit tɪt **-s** -s **ˌtit for ˈtat**
titan (T) ˈtaɪ.tən **-s** -z
Titania tɪˈtɑː.njə, taɪ-, -ˈteɪ-, -ni.ə ⓤⓢ tɪˈteɪ.ni.ə, taɪ-, -ˈtɑː-
titanic (T) taɪˈtæn.ɪk, tɪ- **-ally** -əl.i, -li
titanium tɪˈteɪ.ni.əm, taɪ- ⓤⓢ taɪ-, tɪ-
titbit ˈtɪt.bɪt **-s** -s
titch tɪtʃ
Titchmarsh ˈtɪtʃ.mɑːʃ ⓤⓢ -mɑːrʃ
titch|y ˈtɪtʃ|.i **-ier** -i.əʳ ⓤⓢ -i.ɚ **-iest** -i.ɪst, -i.əst
tith|e taɪð **-es** -z **-ing** -ɪŋ **-ed** -d
tithing ˈtaɪ.ðɪŋ **-s** -z
Tithonus tɪˈθəʊ.nəs, taɪ- ⓤⓢ -ˈθoʊ-
Titian ˈtɪʃ.ən, -i.ən ⓤⓢ -ən **-s** -z
Titicaca ˌtɪt.ɪˈkɑː.kɑː, -kə ⓤⓢ ˌtɪt.ɪ-, ˌtiː.tɪˈ-
titill|ate ˈtɪt.ɪ.l|eɪt, -əl|.eɪt ⓤⓢ -əl|.eɪt **-ates** -eɪts **-ating** -eɪ.tɪŋ ⓤⓢ -eɪ.t̬ɪŋ **-ated** -eɪ.tɪd ⓤⓢ -eɪ.t̬ɪd
titillation ˌtɪt.ɪˈleɪ.ʃən, -əlˈeɪ- ⓤⓢ -əlˈeɪ- **-s** -z
titi|vate ˈtɪt.ɪ|.veɪt, ˈ-ə- ⓤⓢ ˈtɪt̬.ə- **-vates** -veɪts **-vating** -veɪ.tɪŋ ⓤⓢ -veɪ.t̬ɪŋ **-vated** -veɪ.tɪd ⓤⓢ -veɪ.t̬ɪd
titivation ˌtɪt.ɪˈveɪ.ʃən, -əˈ- ⓤⓢ ˌtɪt̬.əˈ- **-s** -z
title ˈtaɪ.tl̩ ⓤⓢ -t̬l̩ **-s** -z **-ing** -ɪŋ **-d** -d **-less** -ləs, -lɪs **ˈtitle ˌdeed**
titleholder ˈtaɪ.tl̩ˌhəʊl.dəʳ ⓤⓢ -ˌhoʊl.dɚ **-s** -z
titling ˈtaɪt.lɪŋ, ˈtaɪ.tl̩.ɪŋ ⓤⓢ ˈtaɪt.lɪŋ, ˈtaɪ.t̬l̩.ɪŋ **-s** -z
Titmarsh ˈtɪt.mɑːʃ ⓤⓢ -mɑːrʃ
tit|mouse ˈtɪt|.maʊs **-mice** -maɪs
Tito ˈtiː.təʊ ⓤⓢ -t̬oʊ, -toʊ
Titograd ˈtiː.təʊ.græd ⓤⓢ -t̬oʊ-, -grɑːd
titration taɪˈtreɪ.ʃən, tɪ- ⓤⓢ taɪ-
titt|er ˈtɪt|.əʳ ⓤⓢ ˈtɪt̬|.ɚ **-ers** -əz ⓤⓢ -ɚz **-ering** -ər.ɪŋ **-ered** -əd ⓤⓢ -ɚd **-erer/s** -ər.əʳ/z ⓤⓢ -ɚ.ɚ/z
tittle ˈtɪt.l̩ ⓤⓢ ˈtɪt̬- **-s** -z
tittle-tattle ˈtɪt.l̩ˌtæt.l̩ ⓤⓢ ˈtɪt̬.l̩ˌtæt̬-
titular ˈtɪt.jə.ləʳ, -jʊ- ⓤⓢ ˈtɪtʃ.ə.lɚ, ˈ-ʊ-, ˈtɪt.jə-, -jʊ- **-s** -z **-ly** -li
titular|y ˈtɪt.jə.lər|.i, -jʊ- ⓤⓢ ˈtɪtʃ.ə.ler-, ˈ-ʊ-, ˈtɪt.jə-, -jʊ- **-ies** -iz
Titus ˈtaɪ.təs ⓤⓢ -t̬əs
Tiverton ˈtɪv.ə.tən ⓤⓢ -ɚ.t̬ən
Tivoli ˈtɪv.əl.i
Tivy ˈtaɪ.vi
Tizard ˈtɪz.əd ⓤⓢ -ɚd
Tizer® ˈtaɪ.zəʳ ⓤⓢ -zɚ
tizz tɪz **-es** -ɪz
tizz|y ˈtɪz|.i **-ies** -iz
T-junction ˈtiːˌdʒʌŋk.ʃən **-s** -z
Tlaxcala tləˈskɑː.lə, tlæsˈkɑː- ⓤⓢ tlɑːˈskɑː.lə
Tlemcen tlemˈsen
TM ˌtiːˈem
tmesis ˈtmiː.sɪs, ˈmiː-; təˈmiː- ⓤⓢ təˈmiː-, ˈmiː-
TN *(abbrev. for* **Tennessee***)* ten.əˈsiː, -ɪˈ- ⓤⓢ ˈten.ə.siː *regionally:* ˈten.ɪ.si, -ə-
TNT ˌtiː.enˈtiː
to *(adv.)* tuː
Note: This form of **to** is found in expressions such as 'to and fro'.
to *(prep.) strong form:* tuː *weak forms:* tʊ, tu, tə ⓤⓢ tə, t̬ə, tu
Note: Weak form word. The strong form /tuː/ is used contrastively, e.g. 'the letter was **to** him, not **from** him', and sometimes in final position, e.g. 'I don't want to', though the /u/ vowel is more often used in this context. The weak form /tə/ is used before consonants, e.g. 'to cut' /təˈkʌt/, while the pronunciation /tu/ is used before vowels in British English, e.g. 'to eat' /tuˈiːt/. In American English, the schwa form is usual before both vowels and consonants, so the latter is /təˈiːt/.
toad təʊd ⓤⓢ toʊd **-s** -z
toadflax ˈtəʊd.flæks ⓤⓢ ˈtoʊd-
toad-in-the-hole ˌtəʊd.ɪn.ðəˈhəʊl ⓤⓢ ˌtoʊd.ɪn.ðəˈhoʊl
toadstool ˈtəʊd.stuːl ⓤⓢ ˈtoʊd- **-s** -z
toad|y ˈtəʊ.d|i ⓤⓢ ˈtoʊ- **-ies** -iz **-ying** -i.ɪŋ **-ied** -id
Toal təʊl ⓤⓢ toʊl
to-and-fro ˌtuː.əndˈfrəʊ ⓤⓢ -ˈfroʊ
toast təʊst ⓤⓢ toʊst **-s** -s **-ing** -ɪŋ **-ed** -ɪd **-er/s** -əʳ/z ⓤⓢ -ɚ/z **-y** **ˈtoasting ˌfork; ˈtoast ˌrack**
toastmaster ˈtəʊst*ˌ*mɑː.stəʳ ⓤⓢ ˈtoʊst*ˌ*mæs.tɚ **-s** -z
tobacco təˈbæk.əʊ ⓤⓢ -oʊ **-s** -z
tobacconist təˈbæk.ən.ɪst **-s** -s
Tobagan təʊˈbeɪ.gən ⓤⓢ tə- **-s** -z
Tobago təʊˈbeɪ.gəʊ ⓤⓢ toʊˈbeɪ.goʊ, tə-
Tobagonian ˌtəʊ.bəˈgəʊ.ni.ən ⓤⓢ ˌtoʊ.bəˈgoʊ- **-s** -z
to-be təˈbiː
Tobermory ˌtəʊ.bəˈmɔː.ri ⓤⓢ ˌtoʊ.bɚˈmɔːr.i
Tobias təʊˈbaɪ.əs ⓤⓢ toʊ-, tə-
Tobin ˈtəʊ.bɪn ⓤⓢ ˈtoʊ-
Tobit ˈtəʊ.bɪt ⓤⓢ ˈtoʊ-
Toblerone® ˈtəʊ.blə.rəʊn ⓤⓢ ˈtoʊ.blə.roʊn
toboggan təˈbɒg.ən ⓤⓢ -ˈbɑː.gən **-s** -z **-ing** -ɪŋ **-ed** -d **-er/s** -əʳ/z ⓤⓢ -ɚ/z
Tobruk təˈbrʊk ⓤⓢ tə-, toʊ-
tob|y (T) ˈtəʊ.b|i ⓤⓢ ˈtoʊ- **-ies** -iz **ˈtoby ˌjug**
toccata təˈkɑː.tə, tɒkˈɑː- ⓤⓢ təˈkɑː.t̬ə **-s** -z
Toc H ˌtɒkˈeɪtʃ ⓤⓢ ˌtɑːk-
Tocharian tɒkˈeə.ri.ən, təʊˈkeə-, -ˈkɑː- ⓤⓢ toʊˈker.i-, -ˈkær-, -ˈkɑːr-
Tocqueville ˈtɒk.vɪl, ˈtəʊk- ⓤⓢ ˈtoʊk-, ˈtɑːk-
tocsin ˈtɒk.sɪn ⓤⓢ ˈtɑːk- **-s** -z
tod (T) tɒd ⓤⓢ tɑːd **-s** -z
today təˈdeɪ, tʊ- ⓤⓢ tə-, tʊ-, tu-
Todd tɒd ⓤⓢ tɑːd
toddl|e ˈtɒd.l̩ ⓤⓢ ˈtɑː.dl̩ **-es** -z **-ing** -ɪŋ, ˈtɒd.lɪŋ ⓤⓢ ˈtɑːd- **-ed** -d **-er/s** -əʳ/z, ˈtɒd.ləʳ/z ⓤⓢ ˈtɑːd.l̩.ɚ/z, ˈ-lɚ/z
todd|y ˈtɒd|.i ⓤⓢ ˈtɑː.d|i **-ies** -iz
Todhunter ˈtɒdˌhʌn.təʳ, -*h*ən.təʳ ⓤⓢ ˈtɑːdˌhʌn.t̬ɚ, -*h*ən.t̬ɚ
Todmorden ˈtɒd.mə.dən, -ˌmɒː.dən ⓤⓢ ˈtɑːd.mɚ.dən, -ˌmɔːr.dən
to-do təˈduː, tʊ- **-s** -z
toe təʊ ⓤⓢ toʊ **-s** -z **-ing** -ɪŋ **-d** -d **ˈtoe ˌcap; ˌtoe the ˈline; ˌtread on someone's ˈtoes**
toea ˈtəʊ.ɑː ⓤⓢ ˈtoʊ-
TOEFL ˈtəʊ.fl̩ ⓤⓢ ˈtoʊ-
toehold ˈtəʊ.həʊld ⓤⓢ ˈtoʊ.hoʊld **-s** -z
toenail ˈtəʊ.neɪl ⓤⓢ ˈtoʊ- **-s** -z
toerag ˈtəʊ.ræg ⓤⓢ ˈtoʊ- **-s** -z
toff tɒf ⓤⓢ tɑːf **-s** -s
toffee ˈtɒf.i ⓤⓢ ˈtɑː.fi **-s** -z **ˈtoffee ˌapple, ˌtoffee ˈapple**
toffee-nosed ˈtɒf.i.nəʊzd ⓤⓢ ˈtɑː.fi.noʊzd
toff|y ˈtɒf|.i ⓤⓢ ˈtɑː.f|i **-ies** -iz
Tofts tɒfts ⓤⓢ tɑːfts
tofu ˈtəʊ.fuː ⓤⓢ ˈtoʊ-
tog tɒg ⓤⓢ tɑːg, tɔːg **-s** -z **-ging** -ɪŋ **-ged** -d
toga ˈtəʊ.gə ⓤⓢ ˈtoʊ- **-s** -z **-ed** -d
together təˈgeð.əʳ ⓤⓢ -ɚ **-ness** -nəs, -nɪs
toggery ˈtɒg.ər.i ⓤⓢ ˈtɑː.gɚ-, ˈtɔː-
toggl|e ˈtɒg.l̩ ⓤⓢ ˈtɑː.gl̩, ˈtɔː- **-es** -z **-ing** -ɪŋ **-ed** -d
Togo ˈtəʊ.gəʊ ⓤⓢ ˈtoʊ.goʊ **-land** -lænd
Togolese ˌtəʊ.gəʊˈliːz ⓤⓢ ˌtoʊ.goʊˈ-, -ˈliːs *stress shift:* ˌTogolese ˈpeople
Toibin təʊˈbiːn ⓤⓢ ˈtɔɪ.bɪn
toil tɔɪl **-s** -z **-ing** -ɪŋ **-ed** -d **-er/s** -əʳ/z ⓤⓢ -ɚ/z

Tone

An identifiable movement or level of PITCH that is used in a linguistically contrastive way.

Examples for English

In English, tone forms the central part of INTONATION, and the difference between, for example, a rising and a falling tone on a particular word may cause a different interpretation of the sentence in which it occurs, e.g.:

- it was ˋcold (meaning 'it was cold')
- it was ˊcold (meaning 'was it cold?')

There are often recognised as being at least five tones in English: a fall, a rise, a fall-rise, a rise-fall and a level tone.

Meanings are frequently ascribed to each tone; the scope of this panel does not allow us to discuss this further.

In intonation, tone may be spread over many syllables. E.g., in:

- hisˇ car could have broken down (in which the pitch movement falls on *car* and rises on *down*)

In other languages

In some languages (known as 'tone languages') the linguistic function of tone is to change the meaning of a word: in Mandarin Chinese, for example, [ma] said on a high pitch means *mother* while [ma] said on a low rising tone means *hemp*. It is usual to identify tones as being a property of individual syllables.

toile twɑːl, twɔːl ⓤⓢ twɑːl **-s** -z
toilet ˈtɔɪ.lət **-s** -s ˈ**toilet** ˌ**bag**; ˈ**toilet** ˌ**paper**; ˈ**toilet** ˌ**roll**; ˈ**toilet** ˌ**training**; ˈ**toilet** ˌ**water**
toiletr|y ˈtɔɪ.lɪ.tr|i, -lə- **-ies** -iz
toilette twɑːˈlet **-s** -s
toilsome ˈtɔɪl.səm **-ly** -li **-ness** -nəs, -nɪs
toilworn ˈtɔɪl.wɔːn ⓤⓢ -wɔːrn
to-ing and fro-ing ˌtuː.ɪŋ.ənd'frəʊ.ɪŋ ⓤⓢ -ˈfroʊ- **to-ings and fro-ings** ˌtuː.ɪŋz.ənd'frəʊ.ɪŋz ⓤⓢ -ˈfroʊ-
tokay (T) təʊˈkeɪ, -ˈkaɪ, ˈ--; tɒkˈaɪ, -ˈeɪ ⓤⓢ toʊˈkeɪ
Tokelau ˈtəʊ.kə.laʊ, ˈtɒk.ə- ⓤⓢ ˈtoʊ.kə-
token ˈtəʊ.kᵊn ⓤⓢ ˈtoʊ- **-s** -z **-ism** -ɪ.zᵊm
Tokharian tɒkˈeə.ri.ən, təʊˈkeə-, -ˈkɑː- ⓤⓢ toʊˈker.i-, -ˈkær-
Toklas ˈtɒk.ləs, ˈtəʊk-, -læs ⓤⓢ ˈtoʊk.ləs
Tokley ˈtəʊ.kli ⓤⓢ ˈtoʊ-
Tokyo ˈtəʊ.ki.əʊ ⓤⓢ ˈtoʊ.ki.oʊ
Toland ˈtəʊ.lənd ⓤⓢ ˈtoʊ-
told *(from* **tell***)* təʊld ⓤⓢ toʊld
toledo *blade:* təˈliː.dəʊ, tɒlˈiː- ⓤⓢ təˈliː.doʊ **-s** -z
Toledo *in Spain:* tɒlˈeɪ.dəʊ, təˈleɪ-, -ˈliː- ⓤⓢ təˈliː.doʊ, -ˈleɪ- *in US:* təˈliː.dəʊ ⓤⓢ -doʊ
tolerability ˌtɒl.ᵊr.əˈbɪl.ə.ti, -ɪ.ti ⓤⓢ ˌtɑː.lɚ.əˈbɪl.ə.t̬i
tolerab|le ˈtɒl.ᵊr.ə.b|l̩ ⓤⓢ ˈtɑː.lɚ- **-ly** -li **-leness** -l̩.nəs, -nɪs
tolerance ˈtɒl.ᵊr.ᵊnts ⓤⓢ ˈtɑː.lɚ-
tolerant ˈtɒl.ᵊr.ᵊnt ⓤⓢ ˈtɑː.lɚ- **-ly** -li
toler|ate ˈtɒl.ᵊr|.eɪt ⓤⓢ ˈtɑː.lə.r|eɪt **-ates** -eɪts **-ating** -eɪ.tɪŋ ⓤⓢ -eɪ.t̬ɪŋ **-ated** -eɪ.tɪd ⓤⓢ -eɪ.t̬ɪd
toleration ˌtɒl.ᵊrˈeɪ.ʃᵊn ⓤⓢ ˌtɑː.ləˈreɪ-
Tolkien ˈtɒl.kiːn, -ˈ- ⓤⓢ ˈtoʊl.kiːn, ˈtɑːl-
toll təʊl ⓤⓢ toʊl **-s** -z **-ing** -ɪŋ **-ed** -d **-er/s** -əʳ/z ⓤⓢ -ɚ/z ˈ**toll** ˌ**bridge**; ˈ**toll** ˌ**call**
toll|booth ˈtɒl.buːθ, ˈtəʊl-, -buːð ⓤⓢ ˈtoʊl- **-booths** -buːθs, -buːðz
Tollemache ˈtɒl.mæʃ, -mɑːʃ ⓤⓢ ˈtɑːl-
Tollesbury ˈtəʊlz.bᵊr.i ⓤⓢ ˈtoʊlz.ber-, -bɚ-
Tolleshunt ˈtəʊlz.hʌnt ⓤⓢ ˈtoʊlz-
Tolley ˈtɒl.i ⓤⓢ ˈtɑː.li
toll-free ˌtəʊlˈfriː, ˌtoʊl- *stress shift:* ˌtoll-free ˈcall
tollgate ˈtəʊl.geɪt ⓤⓢ ˈtoʊl- **-s** -s
tollhou|se ˈtəʊl.haʊ|s ⓤⓢ ˈtoʊl- **-ses** -zɪz
Tolpuddle ˈtɒlˌpʌd.l̩ *locally also:* -ˌpɪd- ⓤⓢ ˈtɑːl-
Tolstoy ˈtɒl.stɔɪ ⓤⓢ ˈtɑːl-, ˈtoʊl-
Toltec ˈtɒl.tek ⓤⓢ ˈtɑːl-, ˈtoʊl- **-s** -s
tolu (T) tɒlˈuː, təʊˈluː, -ˈljuː ⓤⓢ toʊˈluː
toluene ˈtɒl.ju.iːn ⓤⓢ ˈtɑːl-
Tolworth ˈtɒl.wəθ, -wɜːθ ⓤⓢ ˈtɑːl.wɚθ, -wɝːθ
tom (T) tɒm ⓤⓢ tɑːm **-s** -z ˌ**Tom** ˈ**Collins**; ˌ**Tom**, ˌ**Dick and** ˈ**Harry**; ˌ**Tom and** ˈ**Jerry**; ˌ**Tom** ˈ**Thumb**
tomahawk ˈtɒm.ə.hɔːk ⓤⓢ ˈtɑː.mə.hɑːk, -hɔːk **-s** -s **-ing** -ɪŋ **-ed** -t
Tomalin ˈtɒm.ᵊl.ɪn ⓤⓢ ˈtɑː.mᵊl-
toman təʊˈmɑːn ⓤⓢ toʊ-, tə- **-s** -z
tomato təˈmɑː.təʊ ⓤⓢ -ˈmeɪ.t̬oʊ **-es** -z
tomb tuːm **-s** -z
tombola tɒmˈbəʊ.lə ⓤⓢ tɑːmˈboʊ-, ˈtɑːm.bᵊl.ə **-s** -z
tomboy ˈtɒm.bɔɪ ⓤⓢ ˈtɑːm- **-s** -z
tombstone (T) ˈtuːm.stəʊn ⓤⓢ -stoʊn **-s** -z
tomcat ˈtɒm.kæt ⓤⓢ ˈtɑːm- **-s** -s
tome təʊm ⓤⓢ toʊm **-s** -z
Tomelty ˈtʌm.ᵊl.ti ⓤⓢ -t̬i
tomfool ˌtɒmˈfuːl ⓤⓢ ˌtɑːm- **-s** -z **-ery** -ᵊr.i ⓤⓢ -ɚ.i
Tomintoul ˌtɒm.ɪnˈtaʊl, -ənˈ- ⓤⓢ ˌtɑːm-
Tomkins ˈtɒmp.kɪnz ⓤⓢ ˈtɑːmp-
Tomlinson ˈtɒm.lɪn.sən ⓤⓢ ˈtɑːm-
tomm|y, tomm|ie (T) ˈtɒm|.i ⓤⓢ ˈtɑː.m|i **-ies** -iz ˈ**tommy** ˌ**gun**
tommy-gun ˈtɒm.i.gʌn ⓤⓢ ˈtɑː.mi- **-s** -z
tommyrot ˈtɒm.i.rɒt, ˌ--ˈ- ⓤⓢ ˈtɑː.mi.rɑːt
tomogram ˈtəʊ.mə.græm, ˈtɒm.ə- ⓤⓢ ˈtoʊ.mə- **-s** -z
tomography təˈmɒg.rə.fi ⓤⓢ toʊˈmɑː.grə-, tə-
tomorrow təˈmɒr.əʊ, tʊ- ⓤⓢ -ˈmɑːr.oʊ **-s** -z **to**ˌ**morrow after**ˈ**noon**; **to**ˌ**morrow** ˈ**evening**; **to**ˌ**morrow** ˈ**morning**; **to**ˌ**morrow** ˈ**night**
Tompion ˈtɒm.pi.ən ⓤⓢ ˈtɑːm-
Tompkins ˈtɒmp.kɪnz ⓤⓢ ˈtɑːmp-
Tomsk tɒmpsk ⓤⓢ tɑːmpsk
tomtit ˈtɒm.tɪt, ˌ-ˈ- ⓤⓢ ˌtɑːmˈtɪt, ˈ-- **-s** -s
tom-tom ˈtɒm.tɒm ⓤⓢ ˈtɑːm.tɑːm **-s** -z
ton *weight:* tʌn **-s** -z
ton *fashion:* tɔ̃ːŋ ⓤⓢ tõʊn
tonal ˈtəʊ.nᵊl ⓤⓢ ˈtoʊ-
tonalit|y təʊˈnæl.ə.t|i, -ɪ.t|i ⓤⓢ toʊˈnæl.ə.t̬|i, tə- **-ies** -iz
Tonbridge ˈtʌn.brɪdʒ, ˈtʌm- ⓤⓢ ˈtʌn-
ton|e təʊn ⓤⓢ toʊn **-es** -z **-ing** -ɪŋ **-ed** -d
tone-deaf ˌtəʊnˈdef ⓤⓢ ˈtoʊn-, ˌ-ˈ- **-ness** -nəs, -nɪs *stress shift, British only:* ˌtone-deaf ˈperson
toneless ˈtəʊn.ləs, -lɪs ⓤⓢ ˈtoʊn- **-ly** -li **-ness** -nəs, -nɪs
tonematic ˌtəʊ.nɪˈmæt.ɪk ⓤⓢ ˌtoʊ.nɪˈmæt̬.ɪk **-s** -s
toneme ˈtəʊ.niːm ⓤⓢ ˈtoʊ- **-s** -z
tonemic təʊˈniː.mɪk ⓤⓢ toʊ-, tə- **-s** -s
toner (T) ˈtəʊ.nəʳ ⓤⓢ ˈtoʊ.nɚ **-s** -z

Tone unit

A unit of speech consisting of one or more syllables or feet.

Examples for English

A tone unit must contain a tonic syllable, that is, a syllable on which a pitch movement begins. Only one tonic syllable is allowed in an English tone unit. The tone unit may also contain a 'head' (from the first stressed syllable up to the tonic syllable), a 'pre-head' (any unstressed syllables preceding the head) and a 'tail' (all syllables after the tonic syllable). The tonic syllable is underlined in each of the examples which follow:

- ` yes
  tonic
- ˈJoe said ` yes
  head + tonic
- and then ˈJoe said ` yes
  pre-head + head + tonic
- and then ˈJoe said ` yes to me
  pre-head + head + tonic + tail

As each of the non-tonic elements is optional, it is possible to have any combination together with the tonic syllable, e.g.:

- was it ˇyou
  pre-head + tonic
- it was ˇyesterday
  pre-head + tonic + tail
- ˇnow I understand
  tonic + tail

In the study of **INTONATION** it is usual to divide speech into larger units than syllables. If one studies only short sentences said in isolation it may be sufficient to make no subdivision of the utterance, but in longer utterances there must be some points at which the analyst marks a break between the end of one pattern and the beginning of the next. These breaks divide speech into 'tone-units', and are called 'tone-unit boundaries', e.g.:

| the ˇlast time I saw her | was ` yesterday |

If the study of intonation is part of phonology, these boundaries should be identifiable with reference to their effect on pronunciation rather than to grammatical information about word and clause boundaries; statistically, however, we find that in most cases tone-unit boundaries do fall at obvious syntactic boundaries, and it would be rather odd to divide two tone-units in the middle of a phrase. The most obvious factor to look for in trying to establish boundaries is the presence of a pause, and in slow careful speech (e.g. in lectures, sermons and political speeches) this may be done quite regularly. However, it seems that we detect tone-unit boundaries even when the speaker does not make a pause, if there is an identifiable break or discontinuity in the rhythm or in the intonation pattern.

There is evidence that we use a larger number of shorter tone-units in informal conversational speech, and fewer, longer tone units in formal styles.

tonetic təʊˈnet.ɪk (US) toʊˈnet̬-, tə- **-s** -s
ton|ey ˈtəʊ.n|i (US) ˈtoʊ- **-ier** -i.ə^{r} (US) -i.ɚ **-iest** -i.ɪst, -i.əst
tonga *cart, medicinal bark:* ˈtɒŋ.gə (US) ˈtɑːŋ-, ˈtɔːŋ- **-s** -z
Tong|a *Pacific islands:* ˈtɒŋ|.ə, -g|ə (US) ˈtɑːŋ-, ˈtɔːŋ- **-an/s** -^{ə}n/z
Tong|a *East Africa:* ˈtɒŋ.g|ə (US) ˈtɑːŋ-, ˈtɔːŋ- **-as** -əz **-an** -ən
Tongking ˌtɒŋˈkɪŋ (US) ˌtɑːŋ-, ˌtɔːŋ-
tongs tɒŋz (US) tɑːŋz, tɔːŋz
tongu|e tʌŋ **-es** -z **-ing** -ɪŋ **-ed** -d **-eless** -ləs, -lɪs **ˌtongue and ˈgroove; ˈtongue ˌtwister; ˌbite one's ˈtongue;**
tongue-in-cheek ˌtʌŋ.ɪnˈtʃiːk *stress shift:* ˌtongue-in-cheek ˈarticle
tongue-lashing ˈtʌŋˌlæʃ.ɪŋ **-s** -z
tongue-tied ˈtʌŋ.taɪd
Toni ˈtəʊ.ni (US) ˈtoʊ-
tonic ˈtɒn.ɪk (US) ˈtɑː.nɪk **-s** -s **-ally** -^{ə}l.i, -li
tonicity təʊˈnɪs.ə.ti, -ɪ.ti (US) toʊˈnɪs.ə.t̬i, tə-
tonic-solfa, ˌtɒn.ɪk.sɒlˈfɑː (US) ˌtɑː.nɪk.soʊlˈfɑː, -sɑːlˈ-
tonight təˈnaɪt
tonka bean ˈtɒŋ.kə.biːn (US) ˈtɑːŋ-, ˈtɔːŋ- **-s** -z
Tonks tɒŋks (US) tɑːŋks, tɔːŋks
tonnag|e ˈtʌn.ɪdʒ **-es** -ɪz
tonne tʌn **-s** -z
tonsil ˈtɒn*t*.s^{ə}l, -sɪl (US) ˈtɑːn*t*.s^{ə}l **-s** -z
tonsillectom|y ˌtɒn*t*.s^{ə}lˈek.tə.m|i, -sɪˈlek- (US) ˌtɑːn*t*.səˈlek- **-ies** -iz
tonsil(l)itis ˌtɒn*t*.s^{ə}lˈaɪ.tɪs, -sɪˈlaɪ- (US) ˌtɑːn*t*.səˈlaɪ.t̬ɪs
tonsorial tɒnˈsɔː.ri.əl (US) tɑːnˈsɔːr.i-
tonsure ˈtɒn.*t*ʃə^{r}, ˈtɒn*t*.ʃʊə^{r}, -ˌsjʊə^{r} (US) ˈtɑːn*t*.ʃɚ **-s** -z **-d** -d
tontine ˈtɒn.tiːn, -taɪn; tɒnˈtiːn (US) ˈtɑːn.tiːn, -ˈ-
Tonto ˈtɒn.təʊ (US) ˈtɑːn.t̬oʊ
ton-up ˌtʌnˈʌp *stress shift:* ˌton-up ˈbike
ton|y (T) ˈtəʊ.n|i (US) ˈtoʊ- **-ier** -i.ə^{r} (US) -i.ɚ **-iest** -i.ɪst, -i.əst **ˈTony Aˌward**
Tonya ˈtɒn.jə (US) ˈtɑːn-
Tonypandy ˌtɒn.iˈpæn.di (US) ˌtɑː.niˈ-
Tonyrefail ˌtɒn.iˈrev.aɪl (US) ˌtɑː.niˈ-
too tuː
toodle-oo ˌtuː.dl̩ˈuː
toodle-pip ˌtuː.dl̩ˈpɪp
took *(from* **take***)* tʊk
Tooke tʊk
tool tuːl **-s** z **-ing** ɪŋ **-ed** -d
toolbox ˈtuːl.bɒks (US) -bɑːks **-es** -ɪz
Toole tuːl
Tooley ˈtuː.li
toolmaker ˈtuːlˌmeɪ.kə^{r} (US) -kɚ **-s** -z
toonie ˈtuː.ni **-s** -z
toot tuːt **-s** -s **-ing** -ɪŋ (US) ˈtuː.t̬ɪŋ **-ed** -ɪd (US) ˈtuː.t̬ɪd **-er/s** -ə^{r}/z (US) ˈtuː.t̬ɚ/z
tooth tuːθ **-s** -s **-ing** -ɪŋ **-ed** -t **teeth** tiːθ **ˈtooth ˌfairy; ˈtooth ˌpowder; ˌtooth and ˈnail; ˌlong in the ˈtooth**
toothache ˈtuːθ.eɪk
toothbrush ˈtuːθ.brʌʃ **-es** -ɪz **-ing** -ɪŋ
toothless ˈtuːθ.ləs, -lɪs **-ly** -li **-ness** -nəs, -nɪs
toothpaste ˈtuːθ.peɪst **-s** -s
toothpick ˈtuːθ.pɪk **-s** -s
toothsome ˈtuːθ.səm **-ly** -li **-ness** -nəs, -nɪs
tooth|y ˈtuː.θ|i **-ier** -i.ə^{r} (US) -i.ɚ **-iest** -i.ɪst, -i.əst **-ily** -ɪ.li, -^{ə}l.i **-iness** -ɪ.nəs, -ɪ.nɪs
Tooting ˈtuː.tɪŋ (US) -t̬ɪŋ
tootl|e ˈtuː.tl̩ (US) -t̬l̩ **-es** -z **-ing** -ɪŋ, ˈtuːt.lɪŋ **-ed** -d

toots|y, toots|ie ˈtʊt.s|i, ˈtuːt- US ˈtʊt- **-ies** -iz

Toowoomba təˈwʊm.bə, tʊ-

top tɒp US tɑːp **-s** -s **-ping** -ɪŋ **-ped** -t ˌ**top ˈbrass**; ˌ**top ˈdog**; ˌ**top ˈdrawer**; ˌ**top ˈgear**; ˌ**top ˈhat** US ˈ**top** ˌ**hat**; ˌ**top ˈsecret**; **at the** ˌ**top of one's ˈvoice**; ˌ**off the** ˌ**top of one's ˈhead**; **on** ˌ**top of the ˈworld**

topaz ˈtəʊ.pæz US ˈtoʊ- **-es** -ɪz

top-class ˌtɒpˈklɑːs US ˌtɑːpˈklæs *stress shift:* ˌtop-class ˈmodel

topcoat ˈtɒp.kəʊt US ˈtɑːp.koʊt **-s** -s

top-down ˌtɒpˈdaʊn US ˌtɑːp- *stress shift:* ˌtop-down ˈprocessing

top-dress ˌtɒpˈdres, ˈ-- US ˈtɑːp.dres **-es** -ɪz **-ing** -ɪŋ **-ed** -t

top|e təʊp US toʊp **-es** -s **-ing** -ɪŋ **-ed** -t **-er/s** -ər/z US -ɚ/z

topee ˈtəʊ.piː, -pi; toʊˈpiː US toʊˈpiː, ˈ-- **-s** -z

Topeka təʊˈpiː.kə US tə-

top-flight ˌtɒpˈflaɪt US ˈtɑːp.flaɪt, ˌ-ˈ- *stress shift:* ˌtop-flight ˈsurgeon

topgallant ˌtɒpˈgæl.ənt US ˌtɑːp- *nautical pronunciation:* təˈgæl-

Topham ˈtɒp.əm US ˈtɑː.pəm

top-heav|y ˌtɒpˈhev|.i US ˈtɑːpˌhev- **-iness** -ɪ.nəs, -ɪ.nɪs *stress shift:* ˌtop-heavy ˈcargo

Tophet(h) ˈtəʊ.fet US ˈtoʊ-

top-hole ˌtɒpˈhəʊl US ˌtɑːpˈhoʊl

topi ˈtəʊ.piː, -pi; toʊˈpiː US toʊˈpiː, ˈ-- **-s** -z

topiary ˈtəʊ.pjər.i, -pi.ər- US ˈtoʊ.pi.er-

topic ˈtɒp.ɪk US ˈtɑː.pɪk **-s** -s **-al** -əl **-ally** -əl.i, -li

topicalit|y ˌtɒp.ɪˈkæl.ə.t|i, -ɪ.t|i US ˌtɑː.pɪˈkæl.ə.t̬|i **-ies** -iz

topknot ˈtɒp.nɒt US ˈtɑːp.nɑːt **-s** -s

Toplady ˈtɒpˌleɪ.di US ˈtɑːp-

topless ˈtɒp.ləs, -lɪs US ˈtɑːp- **-ness** -nəs, -nɪs

top-level ˌtɒpˈlev.əl US ˈtɑːpˌlev- *stress shift, British only:* ˌtop-level ˈleak

topmast ˈtɒp.mɑːst US ˈtɑːp.mæst *nautical pronuciation:* -məst **-s** -s

topmost ˈtɒp.məʊst US ˈtɑːp-

top-notch ˌtɒpˈnɒtʃ US ˌtɑːpˈnɑːtʃ, ˌ-ˈ- *stress shift:* ˌtop-notch ˈperson

topographic ˌtɒp.əʊˈgræf.ɪk US ˌtɑː.pəˈ- **-al** -əl **-ally** -əl.i, -li

topograph|y tɒpˈɒg.rə.f|i, təˈpɒg- US təˈpɑː.grə- **-er/s** -ər/z US -ɚ/z

topologic|al ˌtɒp.əlˈɒdʒ.ɪ.k|əl US ˌtɑː.pəˈlɑː.dʒɪ- **-ally** -əl.i, -li

topolog|y tɒpˈɒl.ə.dʒ|i, təˈpɒl- US təˈpɑː.lə- **-ies** -iz **-ist/s** -ɪst/s

toponymy tɒpˈɒn.ɪ.mi, təˈpɒn-, ˈ-ə- US təˈpɑː.nə-, toʊ-

top|os ˈtɒp|.ɒs US ˈtoʊ.p|oʊs, -ɑːs **-oi** -ɔɪ

topper ˈtɒp.ər US ˈtɑː.pɚ **-s** -z

topping (T) ˈtɒp.ɪŋ US ˈtɑː.pɪŋ **-s** -z **-ly** -li

toppl|e ˈtɒp.l̩ US ˈtɑː.pl̩ **-es** -z **-ing** -ɪŋ, ˈtɒp.lɪŋ US ˈtɑː.plɪŋ **-ed** -d

top-ranking ˌtɒpˈræŋ.kɪŋ US ˌtɑːp- *stress shift:* ˌtop-ranking ˈamateur

topsail ˈtɒp.seɪl US ˈtɑːp- *nautical pronunciation:* -səl **-s** -z

Topsham ˈtɒp.səm US ˈtɑːp-

topside ˈtɒp.saɪd US ˈtɑːp-

topsoil ˈtɒp.sɔɪl US ˈtɑːp- **-s** -z

topspin ˈtɒp.spɪn US ˈtɑːp-

topsy-turv|y ˌtɒp.siˈtɜː.v|i US ˌtɑːp.siˈtɝː- **-ily** -ɪ.li, -əl.i **-yness** -ɪ.nəs, -nɪs **-iness** -ɪ.nəs, -nɪs **-ydom** -ɪ.dəm

top-up ˈtɒp.ʌp, ˌ-ˈ- US ˈtɑːp.ʌp, ˌ-ˈ- **-s** -s

toque təʊk US toʊk **-s** -s

tor tɔːr US tɔːr **-s** -z

Torah ˈtɔː.rə *with some Jews:* ˈtəʊ.rɑː, ˌ-ˈ-, ˌtɔː- US ˈtɔːr.ə; tɔːˈrɑː; ˈtoʊ.rə

Torbay ˌtɔːˈbeɪ US ˌtɔːr- *stress shift:* ˌTorbay ˈguesthouse

torch tɔːtʃ US tɔːrtʃ **-es** -ɪz **-ing** -ɪŋ **-ed** -t ˈ**torch** ˌ**song**

torchlight ˈtɔːtʃ.laɪt US ˈtɔːrtʃ-

torchon ˈtɔː.ʃən, -ʃɒn US ˈtɔːr.ʃɑːn

tore *(from* **tear***)* tɔːr US tɔːr

toreador ˈtɒr.i.ə.dɔːr US ˈtɔːr.i.ə.dɔːr **-s** -z

Torfaen ˌtɔːˈveɪn US ˌtɔːr-

torment *(n.)* ˈtɔː.ment US ˈtɔːr- **-s** -s

tormen|t *(v.)* tɔːˈmen|t US tɔːr-, ˈ-- **-ts** -ts **-ting/ly** -tɪŋ/li US -t̬ɪŋ/li **-ted** -tɪd US -t̬ɪd

tormentor, tormenter tɔːˈmen.tər US tɔːrˈmen.t̬ɚ, ˈ--- **-s** -z

torn *(from* **tear***)* tɔːn US tɔːrn

tornado tɔːˈneɪ.dəʊ US tɔːrˈneɪ.doʊ **-(e)s** -z

Toronto təˈrɒn.təʊ US -ˈrɑːn.t̬oʊ

torpedo tɔːˈpiː.dəʊ US tɔːrˈpiː.doʊ **-es** -z **-ing** -ɪŋ **-ed** -d

Torpenhow ˈtɔː.pən.haʊ, trɪˈpen.ə *locally:* trə- US ˈtɔːr.pen.haʊ

torpid ˈtɔː.pɪd US ˈtɔːr- **-s** -z **-ly** -li **-ness** -nəs, -nɪs

torpidity tɔːˈpɪd.ə.ti, -ɪ.ti US tɔːrˈpɪd.ə.t̬i

Torpoint ˌtɔːˈpɔɪnt US ˌtɔːr-

torpor ˈtɔː.pər US ˈtɔːr.pɚ

Torquay ˌtɔːˈkiː US ˌtɔːr- *stress shift:* ˌTorquay ˈguesthouse

torque tɔːk US tɔːrk **-s** -s

Torquemada ˌtɔː.kɪˈmɑː.də, -kemˈɑː-, -kwɪˈmɑː-, -kwemˈɑː- US ˌtɔːr.kəˈmɑː-, -kwə-

torr tɔːr US tɔːr

Torrance ˈtɒr.ənts US ˈtɔːr-

torrefaction ˌtɒr.ɪˈfæk.ʃən, -əˈ- US ˌtɔːr.əˈ-

torre|fy ˈtɒr.ɪ|.faɪ, ˈ-ə- US ˈtɔːr.ə- **-fies** -faɪz **-fying** -faɪ.ɪŋ **-fied** -faɪd

Torremolinos ˌtɒr.ɪ.məˈliː.nɒs, ˌ-ə- US ˌtɔːr.ə.məˈliː.nɑːs, -əs

Torrens ˈtɒr.ənz US ˈtɔːr-

torrent ˈtɒr.ənt US ˈtɔːr- **-s** -s

torrential təˈren.*t*ʃəl, tɒrˈen- US tɔːˈren*t*.ʃəl, tə- **-ly** -i

torrentiality təˌren.*t*ʃiˈæl.ə.ti, tɒrˌen-, -ɪ.ti US tɔːˌren*t*.ʃiˈæl.ə.t̬i, tə-

Torres ˈtɒr.ɪs, ˈtɔː.rɪs, -rɪz US ˈtɔːr.ɪz, -ɪs

Torricelli ˌtɒr.ɪˈtʃel.i US ˌtɔːr.əˈ- **-an** -ən

torrid ˈtɒr.ɪd US ˈtɔːr.ɪd **-ly** -li **-ness** -nəs, -nɪs

Torridge ˈtɒr.ɪdʒ US ˈtɔːr-

Torrington ˈtɒr.ɪŋ.tən US ˈtɔːr-

torsion ˈtɔː.ʃən US ˈtɔːr-

torso ˈtɔː.səʊ US ˈtɔːr.soʊ **-s** -z

tort tɔːt US tɔːrt **-s** -s

torte ˈtɔː.tə; tɔːt US tɔːrt; ˈtɔːr.tə **-s** -z

Tortelier tɔːˈtel.i.eɪ US tɔːr-

tortellini ˌtɔː.təlˈiː.ni US ˌtɔːr.t̬əˈliː-

tortelloni ˌtɔː.təlˈəʊ.ni US ˌtɔːr.t̬əˈloʊ-

tortfeasor ˌtɔːtˈfiː.zər US ˌtɔːrtˈfiː.zɚ **-s** -z

tortilla tɔːˈtiː.ə, -jə; -ˈtɪl.ə US tɔːrˈtiː.jə **torˈtilla** ˌ**chip**

tortious ˈtɔː.ʃəs US ˈtɔːr- **-ly** -li

tortois|e ˈtɔː.təs US ˈtɔːr.t̬əs **-es** -ɪz

tortoiseshell ˈtɔː.təʃ.ʃel, -tə.ʃel US ˈtɔːr.t̬əs.ʃel

tortuosity ˌtɔː.tʃuˈɒs.ə.ti, -tjuˈ-, -ɪ.ti US ˌtɔːr.tʃuˈɑː.sə.t̬i

tortuous ˈtɔː.tʃu.əs, -tju- US ˈtɔːr.tʃu- **-ly** -li **-ness** -nəs, -nɪs

tort|ure ˈtɔː.tʃ|ər US ˈtɔːr.tʃ|ɚ **-ures** -əz US -ɚz **-uring/ly** -ər.ɪŋ/li **-ured** -əd US -ɚd **-urer/s** -ər.ər/z US -ɚ.ɚ/z ˈ**torture** ˌ**chamber**

torturous ˈtɔː.tʃər.əs US ˈtɔːr- **-ly** -li **-ness** -nəs, -nɪs

tor|us ˈtɔː.r|əs US ˈtɔːr|.əs **-i** -aɪ

Torvill ˈtɔː.vɪl US ˈtɔːr-

tor|y (T) ˈtɔː.r|i US ˈtɔːr|.i **-ies** -iz **-yism** -i.ɪ.zəm ˈ**Tory** ˌ**party**

Tosca ˈtɒs.kə US ˈtɑː.skə

Toscanini ˌtɒs.kəˈniː.ni US ˌtɑː.skəˈ-

tosh tɒʃ US tɑːʃ

Toshiba® təˈʃiː.bə, tɒʃˈiː- US toʊˈʃiː.bə, tə-

toss tɒs US tɑːs **-es** -ɪz **-ing** -ɪŋ **-ed** -t **-er/s** -ər/z US -ɚ/z ˌ**argue the ˈtoss**

tosspot ˈtɒs.pɒt US ˈtɑːs.pɑːt **-s** -s

toss-up ˈtɒs.ʌp US ˈtɑːs- **-s** -s

tostad|a tɒsˈtɑː.d|ə US toʊˈstɑː- **-as** -əz **-o** -əʊ US -oʊ **-os** -əʊz US -oʊz

tot tɒt US tɑːt **-s** -s **-ting** -ɪŋ US ˈtɑː.t̬ɪŋ **-ted** -ɪd US ˈtɑː.t̬ɪd

total (T) ˈtəʊ.təl US ˈtoʊ.t̬əl **-s** -z **-ly** -i

-(l)ing -ɪŋ, -ɪŋ -(l)ed -d ˌ**total** ˈ**recall,** ˌ**total re**ˈ**call**
totalitarian təʊˌtæl.ɪˈteə.ri.ən, -əˈ-; ˌtəʊ.tæl- Ⓤⓢ toʊˌtæl.əˈter.i-, ˌtoʊ.tæl- **-ism** -ɪ.zᵊm
totalit|y təʊˈtæl.ə.t|i, -ɪ.t|i Ⓤⓢ toʊˈtæl.ə.t̬|i **-ies** -iz
totalizator, -isa- ˈtəʊ.tᵊl.aɪ.zeɪ.təʳ, -ɪ- Ⓤⓢ ˈtoʊ.t̬ᵊl.ɪ.zeɪ.t̬ɚ **-s** -z
totaliz|e, -is|e ˈtəʊ.tᵊl.aɪz Ⓤⓢ ˈtoʊ.t̬ə.laɪz **-es** -ɪz **-ing** -ɪŋ **-ed** -d **-er/s** -əʳ/z Ⓤⓢ -ɚ/z
tot|e təʊt Ⓤⓢ toʊt **-es** -s **-ing** -ɪŋ **-ed** -ɪd ˈ**tote** ˌ**bag**
totem ˈtəʊ.təm Ⓤⓢ ˈtoʊ.t̬əm **-s** -z **-ism** -ɪ.zᵊm ˈ**totem** ˌ**pole**
totemic təʊˈtem.ɪk Ⓤⓢ toʊ- **-ally** -ᵊl.i, -li
t'other, tother ˈtʌð.əʳ Ⓤⓢ -ɚ
Tothill ˈtɒt.*h*ɪl Ⓤⓢ ˈtɑː.tɪl, ˈtɑːt.hɪl
Totnes ˈtɒt.nɪs, -nəs Ⓤⓢ ˈtɑːt-
Totten ˈtɒt.ᵊn Ⓤⓢ ˈtɑː.tᵊn
Tottenham ˈtɒt.ᵊn.əm, ˈ-nəm Ⓤⓢ ˈtɑː.tᵊn.əm ˌ**Tottenham Court** ˈ**Road;** ˌ**Tottenham** ˈ**Hotspur**
tott|er ˈtɒt|.əʳ Ⓤⓢ ˈtɑː.t̬|ɚ **-ers** -əz Ⓤⓢ -ɚz **-ering/ly** -ᵊr.ɪŋ/li **-ered** -əd Ⓤⓢ -ɚd **-erer/s** -ᵊr.əʳ/z Ⓤⓢ -ɚ.ɚ/z **-ery** -ᵊr.i
Totteridge ˈtɒt.ᵊr.ɪdʒ Ⓤⓢ ˈtɑː.t̬ɚ-
Tottington ˈtɒt.ɪŋ.tən Ⓤⓢ ˈtɑː.t̬ɪŋ-
Totton ˈtɒt.ᵊn Ⓤⓢ ˈtɑː.tᵊn
totty ˈtɒt.i Ⓤⓢ ˈtɑː.t̬i
toucan ˈtuː.kæn, -kən Ⓤⓢ -kæn, -kɑːn, -kən; tuːˈkæn, -ˈkɑːn **-s** -z
touch tʌtʃ **-es** -ɪz **-ing** -ɪŋ **-ed** -t ˌ**touch and** ˈ**go**
touchable ˈtʌtʃ.ə.bl̩
touchdown ˈtʌtʃ.daʊn **-s** -z
touché ˈtuː.ʃeɪ, -ˈ- Ⓤⓢ tuːˈʃeɪ
touching ˈtʌtʃ.ɪŋ **-ly** -li **-ness** -nəs, -nɪs
touchline ˈtʌtʃ.laɪn **-s** -z
touchpaper ˈtʌtʃˌpeɪ.pəʳ Ⓤⓢ -pɚ
touchstone (T) ˈtʌtʃ.stəʊn Ⓤⓢ -stoʊn **-s** -z
touch-tone ˈtʌtʃ.təʊn Ⓤⓢ -toʊn
touch-typ|e ˈtʌtʃ.taɪp **-es** -s **-ing** -ɪŋ **-ed** -t **-ist/s** -ɪst/s
touchwood ˈtʌtʃ.wʊd
touch|y ˈtʌtʃ|.i **-ier** -i.əʳ Ⓤⓢ -i.ɚ **-iest** -i.ɪst, -i.əst **-ily** -ɪ.li, -ᵊl.i **-iness** -ɪ.nəs, -ɪ.nɪs
tough tʌf **-s** -s **-er** -əʳ Ⓤⓢ -ɚ **-est** -ɪst, -əst **-ly** -li **-ness** -nəs, -nɪs
toughen ˈtʌf.ᵊn **-s** -z **-ing** -ɪŋ, ˈtʌf.nɪŋ **-ed** -d
tough|ie, tough|y ˈtʌf|.i **-ies** -z
Toulon tuːˈlɔ̃ːŋ Ⓤⓢ -ˈlõʊn, -ˈlɑːn
Toulouse tuːˈluːz
Toulouse-Lautrec ˌtuː.luːz.ləʊˈtrek, tuːˌluːz- Ⓤⓢ tuːˌluːz.loʊˈ-, -ˌluːs-, -ləˈ-
toupée, toupee ˈtuː.peɪ, -ˈ- Ⓤⓢ tuːˈpeɪ **-s** -z
tour tʊəʳ, tɔːʳ Ⓤⓢ tʊr **-s** -z **-ing** -ɪŋ **-ed** -d **-er/s** -əʳ/z Ⓤⓢ -ɚ/z ˈ**tour** ˌ**operator**
Touraine tʊˈreɪn Ⓤⓢ -ˈreɪn, -ˈren
tourbillion tʊəˈbɪl.i.ən, ˈ-jən Ⓤⓢ tʊrˈbɪl.jən **-s** -z
tour de force ˌtʊə.dəˈfɔːs, ˌtɔː- Ⓤⓢ ˌtʊr.dəˈfɔːrs **tours de force** ˌtʊəz-, ˌtɔːz- Ⓤⓢ ˌtʊrz-
Tour de France ˌtʊə.dəˈfrɑːn*t*s, ˌtɔː- Ⓤⓢ ˌtʊr-
Tourette syndrome tʊəˈretˌsɪn.drəʊm, tɔː- Ⓤⓢ tʊˈretˌsɪn.droʊm
tourism ˈtʊə.rɪ.zᵊm, ˈtɔː- Ⓤⓢ ˈtʊr.ɪ-
tourist ˈtʊə.rɪst, ˈtɔː- Ⓤⓢ ˈtʊr.ɪst **-s** -s ˈ**tourist at**ˌ**traction;** ˈ**tourist** ˌ**class;** ˌ**tourist infor**ˈ**mation office**
touristic tʊəˈrɪs.tɪk, tɔː- Ⓤⓢ tʊˈrɪs- **-ally** -ᵊl.i, -li
touristy ˈtʊə.rɪ.sti, ˈtɔː- Ⓤⓢ ˈtʊr.ɪ-
tourmaline ˈtʊə.mə.liːn, ˈtɜː-, ˈtɔː-, -lɪn Ⓤⓢ ˈtʊr.mə.lɪn, -liːn
Tournai ˈtʊə.neɪ, -ˈ- Ⓤⓢ tʊrˈneɪ
tournament ˈtʊə.nə.mənt, ˈtɔː-, ˈtɜː- Ⓤⓢ ˈtɝː-, ˈtʊr- **-s** -s
tournedos (*sing.*) ˈtʊə.nə.dəʊ, ˈtɔː-, ˈtɜː- Ⓤⓢ ˈtʊr.nə.doʊ, ˌ--ˈ- (*plur.*) -z
Tourneur ˈtɜː.nəʳ Ⓤⓢ ˈtɝː.nɚ
tourney ˈtʊə.ni, ˈtɔː- Ⓤⓢ ˈtɝː-, ˈtʊr- **-s** -z
tourniquet ˈtʊə.nɪ.keɪ, ˈtɔː-, ˈtɜː- Ⓤⓢ ˈtɝː.nɪ.kɪt, ˈtʊr-, -ket **-s** -z
tournure ˈtʊə.njʊəʳ, ˈtɔː-, -ˈ- Ⓤⓢ ˈtɝː.njʊr **-s** -z
Tours *French town:* tʊəʳ Ⓤⓢ tʊr *English musical composer:* tʊəz, tɔːz Ⓤⓢ tʊrz
tousl|e ˈtaʊ.zl̩ **-es** -z **-ing** -ɪŋ, ˈtaʊz.lɪŋ **-ed** -d
tout taʊt **-s** -s **-ing** -ɪŋ Ⓤⓢ ˈtaʊ.t̬ɪŋ **-ed** -ɪd Ⓤⓢ ˈtaʊ.t̬ɪd
Tout *in* **Belle Tout** *in East Sussex:* tuːt *surname:* taʊt
tout court ˌtuːˈkʊəʳ, -ˈkɔːʳ Ⓤⓢ -ˈkʊr
tout de suite ˌtuːtˈswiːt
Tovey ˈtəʊ.vi, ˈtʌv.i Ⓤⓢ ˈtoʊ.vi, ˈtʌv.i
tow (T) təʊ Ⓤⓢ toʊ **-s** -z **-ing** -ɪŋ **-ed** -d
towage ˈtəʊ.ɪdʒ Ⓤⓢ ˈtoʊ-
toward (*adj.*) ˈtəʊ.əd; tɔːd Ⓤⓢ tɔːrd; ˈtoʊ.ɚd **-ly** -li **-ness** -nəs, -nɪs
toward (*prep.*) təˈwɔːd, tʊ-; twɔːd, tɔːd Ⓤⓢ tɔːrd, twɔːrd; ˈtoʊ.ɚd; təˈwɔːrd **-s** -z
towaway ˈtəʊ.ə.weɪ Ⓤⓢ ˈtoʊ- **-s** -z
towbar ˈtəʊ.bɑːʳ Ⓤⓢ ˈtoʊ.bɑːr **-s** -z
Towcester ˈtəʊ.stəʳ Ⓤⓢ ˈtoʊ.stɚ
towel taʊəl **-s** -z **-(l)ing** -ɪŋ **-(l)ed** -d ˌ**throw in the** ˈ**towel**
towelette ˌtaʊəˈlet Ⓤⓢ ˌtaʊə- **-s** -s
tower (T) taʊəʳ Ⓤⓢ taʊɚ **-s** -z **-ing/ly** -ɪŋ/li **-ed** -d ˈ**tower** ˌ**block;** ˌ**Tower** ˈ**Hamlets;** ˌ**Tower of** ˈ**London;** ˌ**tower of** ˈ**strength**
towhead ˈtəʊ.hed Ⓤⓢ ˈtoʊ- **-s** -z **-ed** -ɪd
Towle təʊl Ⓤⓢ toʊl
Towler ˈtaʊ.ləʳ Ⓤⓢ -lɚ
town taʊn **-s** -z ˌ**town** ˈ**centre;** ˌ**town** ˈ**crier;** ˌ**town** ˈ**hall;** ˈ**town** ˌ**house;** ˌ**town** ˈ**planning;** ˌ**paint the** ˌ**town** ˈ**red**
Towne taʊn **-s** -z
townee taʊˈniː, ˈ-- **-s** -z
townie ˈtaʊ.ni **-s** -z
townscape ˈtaʊn.skeɪp **-s** -s
Townsend ˈtaʊn.zend
townsfolk ˈtaʊnz.fəʊk Ⓤⓢ -foʊk
Townshend ˈtaʊn.zend
township ˈtaʊn.ʃɪp **-s** -s
towns|man ˈtaʊnz|.mən **-men** -mən, -men
townspeople ˈtaʊnzˌpiː.pl̩
Townsville ˈtaʊnz.vɪl
towns|woman ˈtaʊnz|ˌwʊm.ən **-women** -ˌwɪm.ɪn
town|y ˈtaʊ.n|i **-ies** -iz
towpa|th ˈtəʊ.pɑː|θ Ⓤⓢ ˈtoʊ.pæ|θ **-ths** -ðz Ⓤⓢ -θs, -ðz
towrope ˈtəʊ.rəʊp Ⓤⓢ ˈtoʊ.roʊp **-s** -z
Towton ˈtaʊ.tᵊn
Towy ˈtaʊ.i
Towyn ˈtaʊ.ɪn
tox(a)emia tɒkˈsiː.mi.ə Ⓤⓢ tɑːk-
toxic ˈtɒk.sɪk Ⓤⓢ ˈtɑːk- **-al** -ᵊl **-ally** -ᵊl.i, -li ˌ**toxic** ˈ**shock** ˌ**syndrome;** ˌ**toxic** ˈ**waste**
toxicity tɒkˈsɪs.ə.ti, -ɪ.ti Ⓤⓢ tɑːkˈsɪs.ə.t̬i
toxicological ˌtɒk.sɪ.kᵊlˈɒdʒ.ɪ.kᵊl Ⓤⓢ ˌtɑːk.sɪ.kəˈlɑː.dʒɪ-
toxicolog|y ˌtɒk.sɪˈkɒl.ə.dʒ|i Ⓤⓢ ˌtɑːk.sɪˈkɑː.lə- **-ist/s** -ɪst/s
toxin ˈtɒk.sɪn Ⓤⓢ ˈtɑːk- **-s** -z
toxophilite tɒkˈsɒf.ɪ.laɪt, -ᵊl.aɪt Ⓤⓢ tɑːkˈsɑː.fə.laɪt **-s** -s
toxoplasmosis ˌtɒk.səʊ.plæzˈməʊ.sɪs Ⓤⓢ ˌtɑːk.soʊ.plæzˈmoʊ-
Toxteth ˈtɒk.steθ, -stəθ Ⓤⓢ ˈtɑːk-
toy tɔɪ **-s** -z **-ing** -ɪŋ **-ed** -d
Toya(h) ˈtɔɪ.ə
toyboy ˈtɔɪ.bɔɪ **-s** -z
Toye tɔɪ
Toynbee ˈtɔɪn.biː, ˈtɔɪm- Ⓤⓢ ˈtɔɪn-
Toyota® tɔɪˈəʊ.tə, tɔːˈjəʊ- Ⓤⓢ tɔɪˈjoʊ.t̬ə, -ˈoʊ-
toyshop ˈtɔɪ.ʃɒp Ⓤⓢ -ʃɑːp **-s** -s
Tozer ˈtəʊ.zəʳ Ⓤⓢ ˈtoʊ.zɚ
trac|e treɪs **-es** -ɪz **-ing** -ɪŋ **-ed** -t **-er/s** -əʳ/z Ⓤⓢ -ɚ/z ˈ**trace** ˌ**element;** ˈ**tracing** ˌ**paper**
traceab|le ˈtreɪ.sə.b|l̩ **-ly** -li **-leness** -l̩.nəs, -nɪs
tracer|y ˈtreɪ.sᵊr|.i **-ies** -iz
Tracey ˈtreɪ.si
trache|a trəˈkiː|.ə; ˈtreɪ.ki- Ⓤⓢ ˈtreɪ.ki- **-as** -əz **-ae** -iː

tracheal trə'kiː.əl; 'treɪ.ki- (US) 'treɪ.ki-

tracheotomy ˌtræk.i'ɒt.ə.mi (US) ˌtreɪ.ki'ɑː.t̬ə-

trachoma trə'kəʊ.mə, træk'əʊ- (US) trə'koʊ-

Traci 'treɪ.si

tracing 'treɪ.sɪŋ **-s** -z

track træk **-s** -s **-ing** -ɪŋ **-ed** -t **-er/s** -əʳ/z (US) -ɚ/z **ˌtrack and 'field; 'track eˌvent; 'track ˌrecord, ˌtrack 'record** (US) **'track ˌrecord; keep 'track of ˌsomeone/something; ˌoff the ˌbeaten 'track**

trackless 'træk.ləs, -lɪs

trackpad 'træk.pæd **-s** -z

tracksuit 'træk.suːt, -sjuːt (US) -suːt **-s** -s **-ed** -ɪd

tract trækt **-s** -s

tractability ˌtræk.tə'bɪl.ə.ti, -ɪ.ti (US) -ə.t̬i

tractab|le 'træk.tə.b|l̩ **-ly** -li **-leness** -l̩.nəs, -nɪs

Tractarian træk'teə.ri.ən (US) -'ter.i- **-s** -z **-ism** -ɪ.zᵊm

tractate 'træk.teɪt **-s** -s

tractile 'træk.taɪl (US) -tɪl, -taɪl

traction 'træk.ʃᵊn **'traction ˌengine**

tractor 'træk.təʳ (US) -tɚ **-s** -z

Tracy 'treɪ.si

trad træd **ˌtrad 'jazz**

trad|e treɪd **-es** -z **-ing** -ɪŋ **-ed** -ɪd **-er/s** -əʳ/z (US) -ɚ/z **'trade ˌbook; ˌTrades Des'cription ˌAct; 'trading eˌstate; 'trade ˌfair; 'trade ˌgap; 'trade ˌname; 'trading ˌpost; 'trade ˌprice; 'trade ˌroute; ˌtrade 'secret; ˌtrade(s) 'union** (US) **'trade(s) ˌunion; 'trade ˌwind**

trade-in 'treɪd.ɪn **-s** -z

trademark 'treɪd.mɑːk (US) -mɑːrk **-s** -s **-ing** -ɪŋ **-ed** -t

trade-off 'treɪd.ɒf (US) -ɑːf **-s** -s

Tradescant trə'des.kənt

tradescantia ˌtræd.ɪ'skæn.ti.ə, ˌtreɪ.dɪ'-, -des'kæn-, -də'skæn- (US) ˌtræd.es'kænt.ʃi.ə, '-ʃə **-s** -z

tradesfolk 'treɪdz.fəʊk (US) -foʊk

trades|man 'treɪdz|.mən **-men** -mən

tradespeople 'treɪdzˌpiː.pl̩

tradition trə'dɪʃ.ᵊn **-s** -z

traditional trə'dɪʃ.ᵊn.ᵊl, -'dɪʃ.nᵊl **-ly** -i

traditional|ism trə'dɪʃ.ᵊn.ᵊl|.ɪ.zᵊm, '-nᵊl- **-ist/s** -ɪst/s

traduc|e trə'djuːs, -'dʒuːs (US) -'duːs, -'djuːs **-es** -ɪz **-ing** -ɪŋ **-ed** -t **-er/s** -əʳ/z (US) -ɚ/z **-ement** -mənt

Trafalgar *in Spain:* trə'fæl.gəʳ *archaic and poetical:* ˌtræf.ᵊl'gɑːʳ (US) trə'fæl.gɚ

Trafalgar *Square:* trə'fæl.gəʳ (US) -gɚ *Viscount:* trə'fæl.gəʳ (US) -gɚ *House near Salisbury:* ˌtræf.ᵊl'gɑːʳ; trə'fæl.gəʳ (US) ˌtræf.ᵊl'gɑːr; trə'fæl.gɚ

traffic 'træf.ɪk **-s** -s **-king** -ɪŋ **-ked** -t **-ker/s** -əʳ/z (US) -ɚ/z **'traffic ˌcalming; 'traffic ˌcircle; 'traffic ˌjam; 'traffic ˌlight; 'traffic ˌwarden**

trafficator 'træf.ɪ.keɪ.təʳ (US) -t̬ɚ **-s** -z

Trafford 'træf.əd (US) -ɚd

tragacanth 'træg.ə.kænθ, 'trædʒ-, -sæntθ (US) -kæntθ

tragedian trə'dʒiː.di.ən **-s** -z

traged|y 'trædʒ.ə.d|i, '-ɪ- (US) '-ə- **-ies** -iz

Trager 'treɪ.gəʳ (US) -gɚ

tragic 'trædʒ.ɪk **-al** -ᵊl **-ally** -ᵊl.i, -li

tragicomed|y ˌtrædʒ.ɪ'kɒm.ə.d|i, '-ɪ- (US) -'kɑː.mə- **-ies** -iz

tragicomic ˌtrædʒ.ɪ'kɒm.ɪk (US) -'kɑː.mɪk **-al** -ᵊl **-ally** -ᵊl.i, -li

tra|gus 'treɪ|.gəs **-gi** -gaɪ, -dʒaɪ (US) -dʒaɪ

Traherne trə'hɜːn (US) -'hɝːn

trail treɪl **-s** -z **-ing** -ɪŋ **-ed** -d **-er/s** -əʳ/z (US) -ɚ/z

trailblaz|er 'treɪlˌbleɪ.z|əʳ (US) -z|ɚ **-ers** -əz (US) -ɚz **-ing** -ɪŋ

train treɪn **-s** -z **-ing/s** -ɪŋ/z **-ed** -d **-er/s** -əʳ/z (US) -ɚ/z **'training ˌcollege; 'training ˌcourse; 'train ˌset; 'training ˌshoe; 'train ˌspotter**

trainbearer 'treɪnˌbeə.rəʳ, 'treɪm- (US) 'treɪnˌber.ɚ **-s** -z

trainee ˌtreɪ'niː **-s** -z **-ship/s** -ʃɪp/s

Trainor 'treɪ.nəʳ (US) -nɚ

traips|e treɪps **-es** -ɪz **-ing** -ɪŋ **-ed** -t

trait treɪt, treɪ (US) treɪt **traits** treɪz, treɪts (US) treɪts

traitor 'treɪ.təʳ (US) -t̬ɚ **-s** -z

traitoress 'treɪ.tᵊr.ɪs, -əs (US) -t̬ɚ- **-es** -ɪz

traitorous 'treɪ.tᵊr.əs (US) -t̬ɚ- **-ly** -li **-ness** -nəs, -nɪs

traitress 'treɪ.trəs, -trɪs (US) -trɪs **-es** -ɪz

Trajan 'treɪ.dʒᵊn

trajector|y trə'dʒek.tᵊr|.i, '-tr|i (US) -tɚ|.i **-ies** -iz

Tralee trə'liː

tram træm **-s** -z

tramcar 'træm.kɑːʳ (US) -kɑːr **-s** -z

tramline 'træm.laɪn **-s** -z

trammel 'træm.ᵊl **-s** -z **-(l)ing** -ɪŋ **-(l)ed** -d

tramontane trə'mɒn.teɪn (US) trə'mɑːn-; træm'ɑːn-; ˌtræm.ɑːn'teɪn

tramp træmp **-s** -s **-ing** -ɪŋ **-ed** -t **-er/s** -əʳ/z (US) -ɚ/z

trampl|e 'træm.pl̩ **-es** -z **-ing** -ɪŋ, 'træm.plɪŋ **-ed** -d **-er/s** -əʳ/z, 'træm.pləʳ/z (US) '-pl̩.ɚ/z, '-plɚ/z

trampolin|e 'træm.pᵊl.iːn, -ɪn; ˌtræm.pᵊl'iːn (US) 'træm.pə.liːn, -pᵊl.ɪn; ˌtræm.pə'liːn **-es** -z **-ing** -ɪŋ **-ist/s** -ɪst/s

tramway 'træm.weɪ **-s** -z

tranc|e trɑːnts (US) trænts **-es** -ɪz

tranch|e trɑːntʃ, trɔːntʃ, træntʃ (US) trɑːntʃ **-es** -ɪz

Tranent trə'nent

Tranmere træn.mɪəʳ (US) -mɪə

trann|y, trann|ie 'træn|.i **-ies** -iz

tranquil 'træŋ.kwɪl (US) 'træŋ-, 'træn- **-ly** -i **-ness** -nəs, -nɪs

tranquil(l)ity træŋ'kwɪl.ə.ti, -ɪ.ti (US) -ə.t̬i, træn-

tranquil(l)ization, -isa- ˌtræŋ.kwɪ.laɪ'zeɪ.ʃᵊn, -kwə-, -lɪ'- (US) -kwə.lɪ'-, ˌtræn-

tranquil(l)iz|e, -is|e 'træŋ.kwɪ.laɪz, -kwə- (US) 'træŋ-, 'træn- **-es** -ɪz **-ing/ly** -ɪŋ/li **-ed** -d **-er/s** -əʳ/z (US) -ɚ/z

trans- trænts-, trɑːnts-, trænz-, trɑːnz- (US) trænts-, trænz-

Note: Prefix. May carry primary or secondary stress, or be unstressed; see individual entries.

transact træn'zækt, trɑːn-, -'sækt (US) træn- **-s** -s **-ing** -ɪŋ **-ed** -ɪd **-or/s** -əʳ/z (US) -ɚ/z

transaction træn'zæk.ʃᵊn, trɑːn-, -'sæk- (US) træn- **-s** -z

transalpine træn'zæl.paɪn, trɑːn- (US) træn-

transatlantic ˌtræn.zət'læn.tɪk, ˌtrɑːn- (US) ˌtrænt.sæt'-, ˌtræn.zæt'- *stress shift:* ˌtransatlantic 'yacht

transcend træn'send, trɑːn- (US) træn- **-s** -z **-ing** -ɪŋ **-ed** -ɪd

transcenden|ce træn'sen.dənt|s, trɑːn- (US) træn- **-cy** -si

transcendent træn'sen.dənt, trɑːn- (US) træn- **-ly** -li

transcendental ˌtrænt.sen'den.tᵊl, ˌtrɑːnt-, -sᵊn'- (US) ˌtrænt.sen'den.t̬ᵊl **-ly** -i **ˌtranscendental medi'tation**

transcendental|ism ˌtrænt.sen'den.tᵊl|.ɪ.zᵊm, ˌtrɑːnt-, -sᵊn'- (US) ˌtrænt.sen'den.t̬ᵊl- **-ist/s** -ɪst/s

transcontinental ˌtrænsˌkɒn.tɪ'nen.tᵊl, ˌtrɑːns-, -tə'- (US) ˌtræntsˌkɑːn.tᵊn'en-, ˌtrænz-

transcrib|e træn'skraɪb, trɑːn- (US) træn- **-es** -z **-ing** -ɪŋ **-ed** -d **-er/s** -əʳ/z (US) -ɚ/z

transcript 'trænt.skrɪpt, 'trɑːnt- (US) 'trænt- **-s** -s

transcription træn'skrɪp.ʃᵊn, trɑːn- (US) træn- **-s** -z

transducer trænz'djuː.səʳ, trɑːnz-, trænts-, trɑːnts- (US) trænts'duː.sɚ, trænz-, -'djuː- **-s** -z

transept 'trænt.sept, 'trɑːnt- (US) 'trænt- **-s** -s

transexual træn'sek.ʃuəl, trɑːn-, -ʃu.əl, -sjuəl, -sju.əl (US) træn'sek.ʃu.əl **-s** -z **-ism** -ɪ.zᵊm

transexuality trænˌsek.ʃuˈæl.ɪ.ti, -sju-, -ə.ti (US) -ʃuˈæl.ə.t̬i

transfer (*n.*) ˈtræn*t*s.fɜːʳ, ˈtrɑːn*t*s- (US) ˈtræn*t*s.fɝː **-s** -z

transfer (*v.*) træn*t*sˈfɜːʳ, trɑːn*t*s- (US) træn*t*sˈfɝː, ˈ-- **-s** -z **-ring** -ɪŋ **-red** -d **-rer/s** -əʳ/z (US) -ɚ/z

transferability ˌtræn*t*s.fᵊr.əˈbɪl.ə.ti, ˌtrɑːn*t*s-, -ɪ.ti; træn*t*sˌfɜː.rəˈ-, trɑːn*t*s- (US) træn*t*sˌfɝː.əˈbɪl.ə.t̬i

transferable træn*t*sˈfɜː.rə.bl̩, trɑːn*t*s-; ˈtræn*t*s.fᵊr.ə-, ˈtrɑːn*t*s- (US) træn*t*sˈfɝː.ə-

transferee ˌtræn*t*s.fɜːˈriː, ˌtrɑːn*t*s-, -fəˈ- (US) ˌtræn*t*s.fəˈriː **-s** -z

transferenc|e træn*t*sˈfɜː.rᵊn*t*s, trɑːn*t*s-; ˈtræn*t*s.fᵊr.ᵊn*t*s, ˈtrɑːn*t*s- (US) træn*t*sˈfɝː-; ˈtræn*t*s.fɚ- **-es** -ɪz

transfiguration (T) ˌtræn*t*s.fɪ.gᵊrˈeɪ.ʃᵊn, ˌtrɑːn*t*s-, -fɪg.jᵊrˈeɪ-; træn*t*sˌfɪg.ᵊrˈ-, trɑːn*t*s-, -jᵊrˈ- (US) ˌtræn*t*s.fɪg.jəˈreɪ-, træn*t*sˌfɪg-, -jʊˈ- **-s** -z

transfig|ure træn*t*sˈfɪg|.əʳ, trɑːn*t*s- (US) træn*t*sˈfɪg.j|ɚ **-ures** -əz (US) -ɚz **-uring** -ᵊr.ɪŋ **-ured** -əd (US) -ɚd **-urement/s** -ə.mənt/s (US) -ɚ.mənt/s

transfinite træn*t*sˈfaɪ.naɪt, trɑːn*t*s- (US) træn*t*s-

transfix træn*t*sˈfɪks, trɑːn*t*s- (US) træn*t*s- **-es** -ɪz **-ing** -ɪŋ **-ed** -t

transfixion træn*t*sˈfɪk.ʃᵊn, trɑːn*t*s- (US) træn*t*s- **-s** -z

transform træn*t*sˈfɔːm, trɑːn*t*s- (US) træn*t*sˈfɔːrm **-s** -z **-ing** -ɪŋ **-ed** -d **-er/s** -əʳ/z (US) -ɚ/z **-able** -ə.bl̩

transformation ˌtræn*t*s.fəˈmeɪ.ʃᵊn, ˌtrɑːn*t*s-, -fɔːˈ- (US) ˌtræn*t*s.fɚˈ-, -fɔːrˈ- **-s** -z

transformational ˌtræn*t*s.fəˈmeɪ.ʃᵊn.ᵊl, ˌtrɑːn*t*s-, -ˈmeɪʃ.nᵊl (US) ˌtræn*t*s.fɚˈ-, -fɔːrˈ- *stress shift, see compound:* **ˌtransformational ˈgrammar**

transfusable træn*t*sˈfjuː.zə.bl̩, trɑːn*t*s- (US) træn*t*s-

transfus|e træn*t*sˈfjuːz, trɑːn*t*s- (US) træn*t*s- **-es** -ɪz **-ing** -ɪŋ **-ed** -d **-er/s** -əʳ/z (US) -ɚ/z

transfusible træn*t*sˈfjuː.zə.bl̩, trɑːn*t*s-, -zɪ- (US) træn*t*s-

transfusion træn*t*sˈfjuː.ʒᵊn, trɑːn*t*s- (US) træn*t*s- **-s** -z

transgenic trænzˈdʒen.ɪk, trɑːnz- (US) trænz-

transgress trænzˈgres, trɑːnz-, træn*t*s-, trɑːn*t*s- (US) træn*t*s-, trænz- **-es** -ɪz **-ing** -ɪŋ **-ed** -t **-or/s** -əʳ/z (US) -ɚ/z

transgression trænzˈgreʃ.ᵊn, trɑːnz-, træn*t*s-, trɑːn*t*s- (US) træn*t*s-, trænz- **-s** -z

tranship træn*t*sˈʃɪp, trɑːn*t*s-, trænz-, trɑːnz-, træn-, trɑːn- (US) træn- **-s** -s **-ping** -ɪŋ **-ped** -t **-ment/s** -mənt/s

transhuman|ce træn*t*sˈhjuː.mən|*t*s, trɑːn*t*s- (US) træn*t*s-, trænz- **-t** -t

transien|ce ˈtræn.zi.ən*t*|s, ˈtrɑːn-; ˈtræn*t*.si-, ˈtrɑːn*t*- (US) ˈtræn*t*.ʃᵊn*t*|s, -si.ən*t*|s; ˈtræn.ʒᵊn*t*|s, -zi.ən*t*|s **-cy** -si

transient ˈtræn.zi.ənt, ˈtrɑːn-; ˈtræn*t*.si.ənt, ˈtrɑːn*t*- (US) ˈtræn*t*.ʃᵊnt, -si.ənt; ˈtræn.ʒᵊnt, -zi.ənt **-ly** -li **-ness** -nəs, -nɪs

transilient trænˈsɪl.i.ənt, trɑːn-, -ˈzɪl-, ˈ-jənt (US) træn-

transistor trænˈzɪs.təʳ, trɑːn-, -ˈsɪs- (US) trænˈzɪs.tɚ, -ˈsɪs- **-s** -z **tranˌsistor ˈradio, ˌtransistor ˈradio**

transistoriz|e, -is|e trænˈzɪs.tᵊr.aɪz, trɑːn-, -ˈsɪs- (US) trænˈzɪs.tə.raɪz, -ˈsɪs- **-es** -ɪz **-ing** -ɪŋ **-ed** -d

transit ˈtræn*t*.sɪt, ˈtrɑːn*t*-; ˈtræn.zɪt, ˈtrɑːn- (US) ˈtræn*t*.sɪt; ˈtræn.zɪt **-s** -s **ˈtransit ˌlounge**

transition trænˈzɪʃ.ᵊn, trɑːn-, trən-, -ˈsɪʒ- (US) trænˈzɪʃ-, -ˈsɪʃ-, -ˈsɪʒ- **-s** -z

transitional trænˈzɪʃ.ᵊn.əl, trɑːn-, trən-, -ˈsɪʒ-, ˈ-nᵊl (US) trænˈzɪʃ-, -ˈsɪʃ-, -ˈsɪʒ- **-li** -i

transitive ˈtræn*t*.sə.tɪv, ˈtrɑːn*t*-, -sɪ-; ˈtræn.zə-, ˈtrɑːn-, -zɪ- (US) ˈtræn*t*.sə.t̬ɪv; ˈtræn.zə- **-ly** -li **-ness** -nəs, -nɪs

transitivity ˌtræn*t*.səˈtɪv.ɪ.ti, ˌtrɑːn*t*-, -sɪˈ-; ˌtræn.zəˈ-, ˌtrɑːn-, -zɪˈ- (US) ˌtræn*t*.səˈtɪv.ə.t̬i; ˌtræn.zəˈ-

transitor|y ˈtræn*t*.sɪ.tᵊr|.i, ˈtrɑːn*t*-, -sə-; ˈtræn.zɪ-, ˈtrɑːn-, -zə- (US) ˈtræn*t*.sə.tɔːr-; ˈtræn.zə- **-ily** -ᵊl.i, -ɪ.li **-iness** -ɪ.nəs, -ɪ.nɪs

Transkei ˌtræn*t*ˈskaɪ, ˌtrɑːn*t*-; ˌtrænzˈkaɪ, ˌtrɑːnz- (US) trænˈskeɪ, -ˈskaɪ

transla|te trænzˈleɪ|t, trɑːnz-; træn*t*ˈsleɪ|t, trɑːn*t*- (US) trænˈsleɪ|t, ˈ--; trænzˈleɪ|t, ˈ-- **-tes** -ts **-ting** -tɪŋ (US) -t̬ɪŋ **-ted** -tɪd (US) -t̬ɪd **-tor/s** -təʳ/z (US) -t̬ɚ/z **-table** -tə.bl̩ (US) -t̬ə.bl̩

translation trænzˈleɪ.ʃᵊn, trɑːnz-; træn*t*ˈsleɪ-, trɑːn*t*- (US) trænˈsleɪ-; trænzˈleɪ- **-s** -z

translative trænzˈleɪ.tɪv, trɑːnz-; træn*t*ˈsleɪ-, trɑːn*t*- (US) trænˈsleɪ.t̬ɪv; trænzˈleɪ-

translatory trænzˈleɪ.tᵊr.i, trɑːnz-; træn*t*ˈsleɪ-, trɑːn*t*- (US) trænˈsleɪ.t̬ɚ-; trænzˈleɪ-

transliter|ate trænzˈlɪt.ᵊr|.eɪt, trɑːnz-; træn*t*ˈslɪt-, trɑːn*t*- (US) trænˈslɪt̬.ə.r|eɪt; trænzˈlɪt̬- **-ates** -eɪts **-ating** -eɪ.tɪŋ (US) -eɪ.t̬ɪŋ **-ated** -eɪ.tɪd (US) -eɪ.t̬ɪd **-ator/s** -eɪ.təʳ/z (US) -eɪ.t̬ɚ/z

transliteration ˌtrænz.lɪ.tᵊrˈeɪ.ʃᵊn, ˌtrɑːnz-; trænzˌlɪt.ᵊrˈ-, trɑːnz-; ˌtræn*t*.slɪ.tᵊr-, ˌtrɑːn*t*-; trænˌslɪt.ᵊrˈ-, trɑːn- (US) trænˌslɪt̬.əˈreɪ-; trænzˌlɪt̬- **-s** -z

translocation ˌtrænz.ləʊˈkeɪ.ʃᵊn, ˌtrɑːnz- (US) ˌtrænz.loʊ-

translucenc|e trænzˈluː.sᵊn*t*s, trɑːnz-, -ˈljuː-; trænˈsluː-, trɑːn-; trænsˈljuː-, trɑːns- (US) trænˈsluː-; trænzˈluː- **-y** -i

translucent trænzˈluː.sᵊnt, trɑːnz-, -ˈljuː-; trænˈsluː-, trɑːn-; trænsˈljuː-, trɑːns- (US) trænˈsluː-; trænzˈluː- **-ly** -li

transmigra|te ˌtrænz.maɪˈgreɪ|t, ˌtrɑːnz-; ˌtræn*t*.smaɪˈ-, ˌtrɑːn*t*- (US) ˌtræn*t*ˈsmaɪ.greɪ|t; ˌtrænzˈmaɪ- **-tes** -ts **-ting** -tɪŋ (US) -t̬ɪŋ **-ted** -tɪd (US) -t̬ɪd **-tor/s** -təʳ/z (US) -t̬ɚ/z

transmigration ˌtrænz.maɪˈgreɪ.ʃᵊn, ˌtrɑːnz-; ˌtræn*t*.smaɪˈ-, ˌtrɑːn*t*- (US) ˌtræn*t*.smaɪˈ-; ˌtrænz.maɪˈ- **-s** -z

transmigratory trænzˈmaɪ.grə.tᵊr.i, trɑːnz-; trænˈsmaɪ-, trɑːn- (US) trænˈsmaɪ.grə.tɔːr-; trænzˈmaɪ-

transmissibility trænzˌmɪs.əˈbɪl.ə.ti, trɑːnz-, -ɪˈ-, -ɪ.ti; trænˌsmɪs-, trɑːn-; ˌtrænz.mɪ.səˈ-, ˌtrɑːnz-, -sɪˈ-; ˌtræn*t*.smɪ-, ˌtrɑːn*t*- (US) ˌtræn*t*.smɪs.əˈbɪl.ə.t̬i; ˌtrænz.mɪs-

transmissible trænzˈmɪs.ə.bl̩, trɑːnz-, ˈ-ɪ-; trænˈsmɪs-, trɑːn- (US) trænˈsmɪs-; trænzˈmɪs-

transmission trænzˈmɪʃ.ᵊn, trɑːnz-; trænˈsmɪʃ-, trɑːn- (US) trænˈsmɪʃ-; trænzˈmɪʃ- **-s** -z

transmi|t trænzˈmɪ|t, trɑːnz-; trænˈsmɪ|t, trɑːn- (US) trænˈsmɪ|t; trænzˈmɪ|t **-ts** -ts **-tting** -tɪŋ (US) -t̬ɪŋ **-tted** -tɪd (US) -t̬ɪd **-tter/s** -təʳ/z (US) -t̬ɚ/z

transmittal trænzˈmɪt.ᵊl, trɑːnz-; trænˈsmɪt-, trɑːn- (US) trænˈsmɪt̬-; trænzˈmɪt̬- **-s** -z

transmittanc|e trænzˈmɪt.ᵊn*t*s, trɑːnz-; trænˈsmɪt-, trɑːn- (US) trænˈsmɪt̬-; trænzˈmɪt̬- **-es** -ɪz

transmogrification ˌtrænz.mɒg.rɪ.fɪˈkeɪ.ʃᵊn, ˌtrɑːnz-, trænzˌmɒg-, trɑːnz-, -rə-; ˌtræn*t*.smɒg-, ˌtrɑːn*t*-, trænˌsmɒg-, trɑːn- (US) trænˌsmɑː.grə-; trænzˌmɑːg-

transmogri|fy trænzˈmɒg.rɪ|.faɪ, trɑːnz-, -rə-; trænˈsmɒg-, trɑːn- (US) trænˈsmɑː.grə-; trænzˈmɑː- **-fies** -faɪz **-fying** -faɪ.ɪŋ **-fied** -faɪd

transmutability trænzˌmjuː.təˈbɪl.ə.ti, trɑːnz-, træn*t*s-, trɑːn*t*s-, ˌtrænz.mjuː-, ˌtrɑːnz-, ˌtræn*t*s-, ˌtrɑːn*t*s-, -ɪ.ti ⓤⓢ ˌtræn*t*s.mjuː.t̬əˈbɪl.ə.t̬i, ˌtrænz-

transmutation ˌtrænz.mjuːˈteɪ.ʃᵊn, ˌtrɑːnz-, ˌtræn*t*s-, ˌtrɑːn*t*s-, -mjʊˈ- ⓤⓢ ˌtræn*t*s-, ˌtrænz- **-s** -z

trans|mute trænz|ˈmjuːt, trɑːnz-, træn*t*s-, trɑːn*t*s- ⓤⓢ træn*t*s-, trænz- **-mutes** -ˈmjuːts **-muting** -ˈmjuː.tɪŋ ⓤⓢ -ˈmjuː.t̬ɪŋ **-muted** -ˈmjuː.tɪd ⓤⓢ -ˈmjuː.t̬ɪd **-muter/s** -ˈmjuː.təʳ/z ⓤⓢ -ˈmjuː.t̬ɚ/z **-mutable** -ˈmjuː.tə.bl̩ ⓤⓢ -ˈmjuː.t̬ə.bl̩

transnational trænzˈnæʃ.ᵊn.ᵊl, trɑːnz-, ˈ-nᵊl; trænˈsnæʃ-, trɑːn- ⓤⓢ trænˈsnæʃ-; trænzˈnæʃ-

transoceanic ˌtræn.zəʊ.ʃiˈæn.ɪk, -siˈ-; ˌtræn*t*.səʊ- ⓤⓢ ˌtræn*t*.soʊ.ʃiˈ-; ˌtræn.zoʊ-

transom ˈtræn*t*.səm **-s** -z

transpacific ˌtræn*t*.spəˈsɪf.ɪk, ˌtrɑːn*t*s-; ˌtrænz.pəˈ-, ˌtrɑːnz- ⓤⓢ ˌtræn*t*.spə-, ˌtrænz-

transparenc|y trænˈspær.ᵊn*t*.s|i, trɑːn-, trən-, -ˈspeə.rᵊn*t*-; trænzˈpær.ᵊn*t*-, trɑːnz-, trənz-, -ˈpeə.rᵊn*t*- ⓤⓢ trænˈsper.ᵊn*t*-, -ˈspær- **-ies** -iz

transparen|t træn*t*ˈspær.ᵊn|t, trɑːn*t*-, trən*t*-, -speə.rᵊn|t; trænzˈpær.ᵊn|t, trɑːnz-, trənz-, -ˈpeə.rᵊn|t ⓤⓢ trænˈsper.ᵊn|t, -ˈspær- **-tly** -t.li **-tness** -t.nəs, -t.nɪs **-ce** -*t*s

transpiration ˌtræn*t*.spɪˈreɪ.ʃᵊn, ˌtrɑːn*t*-, -spəˈ- ⓤⓢ ˌtræn*t*-

transpir|e trænˈspaɪəʳ, trɑːn- ⓤⓢ trænˈspaɪɚ **-es** -z **-ing** -ɪŋ **-ed** -d

transplan|t (*v.*) trænˈsplɑːn|t, trɑːn- ⓤⓢ trænˈsplæn|t; ˈtræn*t*.splæn|t **-ts** -ts **-ting** -tɪŋ ⓤⓢ -t̬ɪŋ **-ted** -tɪd ⓤⓢ -t̬ɪd **-table** -tə.bl̩ ⓤⓢ -t̬ə.bl̩

transplant (*n.*) ˈtræn*t*.splɑːnt, ˈtrɑːn- ⓤⓢ ˈtræn*t*.splænt **-s** -s

transplantation ˌtræn*t*.splɑːnˈteɪ.ʃᵊn, ˌtrɑːn*t*- ⓤⓢ ˌtræn*t*.splænˈ- **-s** -z

transponder trænˈspɒn.dəʳ, trɑːn- ⓤⓢ trænˈspɑːn.dɚ **-s** -z

transpontine træn*t*ˈspɒn.taɪn, trɑːn*t*-; trænzˈpɒn-, trɑːnz- ⓤⓢ trænˈspɑːn.taɪn, -tɪn, -tiːn

transport (*n.*) ˈtræn*t*.spɔːt, ˈtrɑːn*t*- ⓤⓢ ˈtræn*t*.spɔːrt **-s** -s **ˈtransport ˌcafe**

transpor|t (*v.*) trænˈspɔː|t, trɑːn- ⓤⓢ trænˈspɔːr|t, ˈ-- **-ts** -ts **-ting** -tɪŋ ⓤⓢ -t̬ɪŋ **-ted** -tɪd ⓤⓢ -t̬ɪd **-table** -tə.bl̩ ⓤⓢ -t̬ə.bl̩

transportability ˌtræn*t*.spɔː.təˈbɪl.ə.ti, ˌtrɑːn*t*-, trænˌspɔː-, trɑːn-, -ɪ.ti ⓤⓢ trænˌspɔːr.t̬əˈbɪl.ə.t̬i

transportation ˌtræn*t*.spɔːˈteɪ.ʃᵊn, ˌtrɑːn*t*-, -spəˈ- ⓤⓢ ˌtræn*t*.spɚˈ- **-s** -z

transporter trænˈspɔː.təʳ, trɑːn- ⓤⓢ trænˈspɔːr.t̬ɚ **-s** -z

transpos|e trænˈspəʊz, trɑːn- ⓤⓢ trænˈspoʊz **-es** -ɪz **-ing** -ɪŋ **-ed** -d **-er/s** -əʳ/z ⓤⓢ -ɚ/z **-able** -ə.bl̩ **-al/s** -ᵊl/z

transposition ˌtræn*t*.spəˈzɪʃ.ᵊn, ˌtrɑːn*t*- ⓤⓢ ˌtræn*t*- **-s** -z

transputer trænˈspjuː.təʳ, trɑːn-; trænzˈpjuː-, trɑːnz- ⓤⓢ trænˈspjuː.t̬ɚ **-s** -z

transsexual trænˈsek.ʃʊəl, trɑːn-, træn*t*s-, trɑːn*t*s-, -ʃu.əl, -sjʊəl, -sju.əl ⓤⓢ trænˈsek.ʃu.əl, træn*t*s- **-s** -z **-ism** -ɪ.zᵊm

transsexuality trænˌsek.ʃuˈæl.ɪ.ti, -sju-, -ə.ti ⓤⓢ -ʃuˈæl.ə.t̬i

transship træn*t*sˈʃɪp, trɑːn*t*s-, trænz-, trɑːnz-, træn-, trɑːn- ⓤⓢ træn*s*ˈʃɪp **-s** -s **-ping** -ɪŋ **-ped** -t **-ment/s** -mənt/s

Trans-Siberian ˌtræn*t*s.saɪˈbɪə.ri.ən, ˌtrɑːn*t*s-, ˌtrænz-, ˌtrɑːnz- ⓤⓢ ˌtræn*t*s.saɪˈbɪr.i-, ˌtrænz-

transubstanti|ate ˌtræn*t*.səbˈstæn.*t*ʃi|.eɪt, ˌtrɑːn*t*-, -ˈstɑːn-; -ˈstæn*t*.si-, -ˈstɑːn*t*- ⓤⓢ ˌtræn*t*.səbˈstæn*t*.ʃi- **-ates** -eɪts **-ating** -eɪ.tɪŋ ⓤⓢ -eɪ.t̬ɪŋ **-ated** -eɪ.tɪd ⓤⓢ -eɪ.t̬ɪd

transubstantiation ˌtræn*t*.səbˌstæn.*t*ʃiˈeɪ.ʃᵊn, ˌtrɑːn*t*-, -ˌstɑːn-; -ˌstæn*t*s.i-, -ˌstɑːn*t*- ⓤⓢ ˌtræn*t*.səbˌstæn*t*.ʃiˈ- **-s** -z

Transvaal ˈtrænz.vɑːl, ˈtrɑːnz-, ˈtræn*t*s-, ˈtrɑːn*t*s-, ˌ-ˈ- ⓤⓢ ˌtræn*t*sˈvɑːl, ˌtrænz-

Transvaaler ˈtrænzˌvɑː.ləʳ, ˈtrɑːnz-, ˈtræn*t*s-, ˈtrɑːn*t*s-, ˌ-ˈ-- ⓤⓢ ˌtræn*t*sˈvɑː.lɚ, ˌtrænz- **-s** -z

transversal trænzˈvɜː.sᵊl, trɑːnz-, træn*t*s-, trɑːn*t*s- ⓤⓢ træn*t*sˈvɝː-, trænz- **-s** -z

transverse trænzˈvɜːs, trɑːnz-, træn*t*s-, trɑːn*t*s- ⓤⓢ træn*t*sˈvɝːs, trænz- **-ly** -li *stress shift:* ˌtransverse ˈengine

transverse (*n.*) ˈtrænz.vɜːs, ˈtrɑːnz-, ˈtræn*t*s-, ˈtrɑːn*t*s-, ˌ-ˈ- ⓤⓢ ˈtræn*t*s-, ˈtrænz-

transvestism trænzˈves.tɪ.zᵊm, trɑːnz-, træn*t*s-, trɑːn*t*s- ⓤⓢ træn*t*s-, trænz-

transvestite trænzˈves.taɪt, trɑːnz-, træn*t*s-, trɑːn*t*s- ⓤⓢ træn*t*s-, trænz- **-s** -s

Transylvani|a ˌtræn*t*.sɪlˈveɪ.ni|.ə, ˌtrɑːn*t*-, -sᵊlˈ-, ˈ-nj|ə ⓤⓢ ˌtræn*t*- **-an/s** -ən

tranter (T) ˈtræn.təʳ ⓤⓢ -t̬ɚ **-s** -z

trap træp **-s** -s **-ping/s** -ɪŋ/z **-ped** -t **-per/s** -əʳ/z ⓤⓢ -ɚ/z

trapdoor ˌtræpˈdɔːʳ ⓤⓢ ˈtræp.dɔːr, ˌ-ˈ- **-s** -z *stress shift, British only:* ˌtrapdoor ˈspider

trapes treɪps **-es** -ɪz **-ing** -ɪŋ **-ed** -t

trapez|e trəˈpiːz ⓤⓢ træpˈiːz, trəˈpiːz **-es** -ɪz

trapezi|um trəˈpiː.zi|.əm **-ums** -əmz **-a** -ə

trapezoid ˈtræp.ɪ.zɔɪd **-s** -z

Trapp træp

trappings ˈtræp.ɪŋz

Trappist ˈtræp.ɪst **-s** -s

trapshoot|ing ˈtræpˌʃuː.t|ɪŋ **-er/s** -əʳ/z ⓤⓢ -ɚ/z

Traquair trəˈkweəʳ ⓤⓢ -ˈkwer

trash træʃ **-es** -ɪz **-ing** -ɪŋ **-ed** -t

trashcan ˈtræʃ.kæn **-s** -z

trash|man ˈtræʃ|.mæn, -mən **-men** -men, -mən

trash|y ˈtræʃ|.i **-ier** -i.əʳ ⓤⓢ -i.ɚ **-iest** -i.ɪst, -i.əst **-iness** -ɪ.nəs, -ɪ.nɪs

Trasimene ˈtræz.ɪ.miːn, ˈ-ə- ⓤⓢ ˈtrɑː.zɪ.miːn, -zə-

trattoria ˌtræt.ᵊrˈiː.ə ⓤⓢ ˌtrɑː.t̬əˈriː.ə, -tɔːˈ-; trɑːˈtɔːr.i- **-s** -z

traum|a ˈtrɔː.m|ə, ˈtraʊ- ⓤⓢ ˈtrɑː-, ˈtrɔː-, ˈtraʊ- **-as** -əz **-ata** -ə.tə ⓤⓢ -ə.t̬ə

traumatic trɔːˈmæt.ɪk, traʊ- ⓤⓢ trɑːˈmæt̬-, trɔː-, traʊ- **-ally** -ᵊl.i, -li

traumatism ˈtrɔː.mə.tɪ.zᵊm ⓤⓢ ˈtrɑː-, ˈtrɔː- **-s** -z

traumatization, -isa- ˌtrɔː.mə.taɪˈzeɪ.ʃᵊn, ˌtraʊ-, -tɪˈ- ⓤⓢ ˌtrɑː.mə.t̬ɪˈ-, ˌtrɔː-, ˌtraʊ-

traumatiz|e, -is|e ˈtrɔː.mə.taɪz, ˈtraʊ- ⓤⓢ ˈtrɑː-, ˈtrɔː-, ˈtraʊ- **-es** -ɪz **-ing** -ɪŋ **-ed** -d

travail ˈtræv.eɪl; trəˈveɪl ⓤⓢ trəˈveɪl; ˈtræv.eɪl **-s** -z **-ing** -ɪŋ **-ed** -d

Travancore ˌtræv.ᵊŋˈkɔːʳ ⓤⓢ -ˈkɔːr

travel ˈtræv.ᵊl **-s** -z **-(l)ing** -ɪŋ, ˈtræv.lɪŋ **-(l)ed** -d **ˈtravel ˌagency**; **ˈtravel ˌagent**; **ˈtravelling exˌpenses**; **ˌtravelling ˈsalesman**; **ˈtravel ˌsickness**

travelator ˈtræv.ᵊl.eɪ.təʳ ⓤⓢ -ə.leɪ.t̬ɚ **-s** -z

Travelcard ˈtræv.ᵊl.kɑːd ⓤⓢ -kɑːrd

travel(l)er ˈtræv.ᵊl.əʳ, ˈ-ləʳ ⓤⓢ ˈ-ᵊl.ɚ, ˈ-lɚ **-s** -z **ˈtravel(l)er's ˌcheque**

travelogue, travelog ˈtræv.ᵊl.ɒg ⓤⓢ -ə.lɑːg, -lɔːg **-s** -z

Travers ˈtræv.əz ⓤⓢ -ɚz

travers|e (*n. adj.*) ˈtræv.əs, -ɜːs; trəˈvɜːs, trævˈɜːs ⓤⓢ ˈtræv.ɚs, -ɝːs; trəˈvɝːs, trævˈɝːs **-es** -ɪz

travers|e (*v.*) trəˈvɜːs, trævˈɜːs; ˈtræv.ɜːs ⓤⓢ trəˈvɝːs, trævˈɝːs; ˈtræv.ɚs **-es** -ɪz **-ing** -ɪŋ **-ed** -t

travest|y ˈtræv.ə.st|i, ˈ-ɪ- ⓤⓢ ˈ-ɪ- **-ies** -iz **-ying** -i.ɪŋ **-ied** -id ˌ**travesty of ˈjustice**

Traviata ˌtræv.iˈɑː.tə (US) ˌtrɑː.viˈɑː.t̬ə
Travis ˈtræv.ɪs
travolator ˈtræv.əl.eɪ.təʳ (US) -t̬ɚ **-s** -z
Travolta trəˈvəʊl.tə, -ˈvɒl- (US) -ˈvoʊl.t̬ə
trawl trɔːl (US) trɑːl, trɔːl **-s** -z **-ing** -ɪŋ **-ed** -d
trawler ˈtrɔː.ləʳ (US) ˈtrɑː.lɚ, ˈtrɔː- **-s** -z
trawler|man ˈtrɔː.lə|.mən (US) ˈtrɑː.lɚ-, ˈtrɔː- **-men** -mən
tray treɪ **-s** -z
Traynor ˈtreɪ.nəʳ (US) -nɚ
treacherous ˈtretʃ.ər.əs **-ly** -li **-ness** -nəs, -nɪs
treacher|y ˈtretʃ.ər|.i **-ies** -iz
treacle ˈtriː.kl̩ **-s** -z ˌ**treacle ˈtart**
treacl|y ˈtriː.kl̩|.i, ˈ-kl|i **-iness** -ɪ.nəs, -ɪ.nɪs
tread tred **-s** -z **-ing** -ɪŋ **trod** trɒd (US) trɑːd **trodden** ˈtrɒd.ən (US) ˈtrɑː.dən **treader/s** ˈtred.əʳ/z (US) -ɚ/z ˌ**tread on someone's ˈtoes**
treadle ˈtred.l̩ **-s** -z
treadmill ˈtred.mɪl **-s** -z
Treadwell ˈtred.wel
treason ˈtriː.zən **-s** -z
treasonab|le ˈtriː.zən.ə.b|l̩, ˈtriːz.nə- **-ly** -li **-leness** -l̩.nəs, -nɪs
treasonous ˈtriː.zən.əs, ˈtriːz.nəs
treas|ure ˈtreʒ|.əʳ (US) -ɚ **-ures** -əz (US) -ɚz **-uring** -ər.ɪŋ **-ured** -əd (US) -ɚd ˈ**treasure ˌhunt**; ˈ**treasure ˌtrove**
treasure-hou|se ˈtreʒ.ə.haʊ|s (US) ˈ-ɚ- **-ses** -zɪz
treasurer ˈtreʒ.ər.əʳ (US) -ɚ **-s** -z
treasurership ˈtreʒ.ər.ə.ʃɪp (US) -ɚ- **-s** -s
treasure-trove ˈtreʒ.ə.trəʊv (US) ˈ-ɚ.troʊv
treasur|y (T) ˈtreʒ.ər|.i **-ies** -iz
treat triːt **-s** -s **-ing** -ɪŋ (US) ˈtriː.t̬ɪŋ **-ed** -ɪd (US) ˈtriː.t̬ɪd
treatable ˈtriː.tə.bl̩ (US) -t̬ə-
treatis|e ˈtriː.tɪz, -tɪs (US) -t̬ɪs **-es** -ɪz
treatment ˈtriːt.mənt **-s** -s
treat|y ˈtriː.t|i (US) -t̬|i **-ies** -iz
Trebizond ˈtreb.ɪ.zɒnd (US) -zɑːnd
trebl|e ˈtreb.l̩ **-es** -z **-y** -i, ˈtreb.li **-ing** -ɪŋ, ˈtreb.lɪŋ **-ed** -d
Treblinka trəˈblɪŋ.kə, trebˈlɪŋ- (US) trəˈblɪŋ-; trebˈliːŋ-
Trebor ˈtriː.bɔːʳ (US) -bɔːr
Tredegar trɪˈdiː.gəʳ, trə- (US) -gɚ
tree (T) triː **-s** -z **-ing** -ɪŋ **-d** -d ˈ**tree ˌfrog**; ˌ**Tree of ˈKnowledge**; ˈ**tree ˌsurgeon**; ˌ**bark up the ˌwrong ˈtree**
treecreeper ˈtriːˌkriː.pəʳ (US) -pɚ **-s** -z
treeless ˈtriː.ləs, -lɪs
treeline ˈtriː.laɪn
tree-lined ˈtriː.laɪnd
treetop ˈtriː.tɒp (US) -tɑːp **-s** -z
trefoil ˈtref.ɔɪl, ˈtriː.fɔɪl, ˈtrɪf.ɔɪl (US) ˈtriː.fɔɪl, ˈtref.ɔɪl **-s** -z
Trefor ˈtrev.əʳ (US) -ɚ
Trefusis trɪˈfjuː.sɪs, trə-
Tregear trɪˈgɪəʳ, trə- (US) -ˈgɪr
Treharne trɪˈhɑːn, trə-, -ˈhɜːn (US) -ˈhɑːrn, -ˈhɝːn
Treharris trɪˈhær.ɪs, trə- (US) -ˈher-, -ˈhær-
Treherne trɪˈhɜːn, trə- (US) -ˈhɝːn
trek trek **-s** -s **-king** -ɪŋ **-ked** -t **-ker/s** -əʳ/z (US) -ɚ/z
Trekkie ˈtrek.i **-s** -z
Trelawn(e)y trɪˈlɔː.ni, trə- (US) -ˈlɑː-, -ˈlɔː-
Treleaven trɪˈlev.ən, trə-
trellis ˈtrel.ɪs **-es** -ɪz **-ed** -t
trelliswork ˈtrel.ɪs.wɜːk (US) -wɝːk
Tremadoc trɪˈmæd.ək, trə-
Tremain, Tremayne trɪˈmeɪn, trə-
trembl|e ˈtrem.bl̩ **-es** -z **-ing/ly** -ɪŋ/li, ˈtrem.blɪŋ/li **-ed** -d **-er/s** -əʳ/z, ˈtrem.bləʳ/z (US) ˈ-l̩.ɚ/z, ˈ-lɚ/z
trembl|y ˈtrem.bl|i, ˈ-bl̩|.i **-ier** -i.əʳ (US) -i.ɚ **-iest** -i.ɪst, -i.əst **-iness** -ɪ.nəs, -ɪ.nɪs
tremendous trɪˈmen.dəs, trə- **-ly** -li **-ness** -nəs, -nɪs
tremolo ˈtrem.əl.əʊ (US) -ə.loʊ **-s** -z
tremor ˈtrem.əʳ (US) -ɚ **-s** -z
tremulant ˈtrem.jə.lənt, -jʊ- **-s** -s
tremulous ˈtrem.jə.ləs, -jʊ- **-ly** -li **-ness** -nəs, -nɪs
trench (T) trentʃ **-es** -ɪz **-ing** -ɪŋ **-ed** -t **-er/s** -əʳ/z (US) -ɚ/z ˈ**trench ˌcoat**; ˌ**trench ˈfoot**; ˌ**trench ˈwarfare**
trenchancy ˈtren.*t*ʃən*t*.si
trenchant ˈtren.*t*ʃənt **-ly** -li
Trenchard ˈtren.*t*ʃɑːd, -*t*ʃəd (US) -*t*ʃɑːrd, -*t*ʃɚd
trencher|man ˈtren.*t*ʃə|.mən (US) -*t*ʃɚ- **-men** -mən
trend trend **-s** -z **-ing** -ɪŋ **-ed** -ɪd
trendsett|er ˈtrendˌset|.əʳ (US) -ˌset̬|.ɚ **-s** -əʳ/z (US) -ɚ/z **-ing** -ɪŋ
trend|y ˈtren.d|i **-ies** -iz **-ier** -i.əʳ (US) -i.ɚ **-iest** -i.ɪst, -i.əst **-ily** -ɪ.li **-iness** -ɪ.nəs, -ɪ.nɪs
Trent trent
Trentham ˈtren.təm
Trenton ˈtren.tən (US) -tən
trepan trɪˈpæn, trə- **-s** -z **-ning** -ɪŋ **-ned** -d
trepang trɪˈpæŋ, trə- **-s** -z
trephin|e trɪˈfiːn, trefˈiːn, trəˈfiːn, -ˈfaɪn (US) trɪˈfaɪn, triː-, -ˈfiːn **-es** -z **-ing** -ɪŋ **-ed** -d
trepidation ˌtrep.ɪˈdeɪ.ʃən, -əˈ-
Tresilian trɪˈsɪl.i.ən, trə-, ˈ-jən
trespass (*v.*) ˈtres.pəs (US) -pæs, -pəs **-es** -ɪz **-ing** -ɪŋ **-ed** -t **-er/s** -əʳ/z (US) -ɚ/z
trespass (*n.*) ˈtres.pəs **-es** -ɪz
tress tres **-es** -ɪz **-ed** -t
trestle ˈtres.l̩ **-s** -z ˌ**trestle ˈtable**, ˈ**trestle ˌtable**
Trethowan trɪˈθəʊən, trə-, -ˈθaʊən, -ˈθɔː.ən (US) -ˈθoʊən, -ˈθaʊən, -ˈθɑː.ən, -ˈθɔː-
Trevelyan *in Cornwall:* trɪˈvɪl.jən, trə- (US) trɪˈvel-, -ˈvɪl- *in Northumbria:* trɪˈvel.jən, trə-
Treves triːvz
Trevethick trɪˈveθ.ɪk, trə-
Trevisa trɪˈviː.sə, trə-
Treviso trɪˈviː.səʊ, -zəʊ (US) -soʊ
Trevithick ˈtrev.ɪ.θɪk (US) -ə-
Trevor ˈtrev.əʳ (US) -ɚ
Trevor-Roper ˌtrev.əˈrəʊ.pəʳ (US) -ɚˈroʊ.pɚ
Trewin trɪˈwɪn, trə-
trews truːz
trey treɪ **-s** -z
tri- traɪ-, trɪ-, triː-
Note: Prefix. See individual entries for pronunciation and stressing.
triable ˈtraɪ.ə.bl̩ **-ness** -nəs, -nɪs
triad (T) ˈtraɪ.æd, -əd **-s** -z
triage ˈtriː.ɑːʒ; ˈtraɪ.ɪdʒ (US) ˈtriː.ɑːʒ
trial traɪəl **-s** -z **-(l)ing** -ɪŋ **-(l)ed** -d ˌ**trial and ˈerror**; ˌ**trials and tribuˈlations**; ˌ**trial ˈrun**
trialogue ˈtraɪ.ə.lɒg (US) -lɑːg, -lɔːg **-s** -z
triangle ˈtraɪ.æŋ.gl̩ **-s** -z **-d** -d
triangular traɪˈæŋ.gjə.ləʳ, -gjʊ- (US) -lɚ **-ly** -li
triangularity traɪˌæŋ.gjəˈlær.ə.ti, ˌtraɪ.æŋ-, -jʊˈ-, -ɪ.ti (US) traɪˌæŋ.gjəˈler.ə.t̬i, -gjʊˈ-, -ˈlær-
triangu|late traɪˈæŋ.gjə|.leɪt, -gjʊ- **-lates** -leɪts **-lating** -leɪ.tɪŋ (US) -leɪ.t̬ɪŋ **-lated** -leɪ.tɪd (US) -leɪ.t̬ɪd
triangulation traɪˌæŋ.gjəˈleɪ.ʃən, ˌtraɪ.æŋ-, -gjʊˈ- (US) traɪˌæŋ-
Triangulum traɪˈæŋ.gjə.ləm, -gjʊ-
Triassic traɪˈæs.ɪk
triathlete traɪˈæθ.liːt **-s** -s
triathlon traɪˈæθ.lɒn, -lən (US) -lɑːn, -lən **-s** -z
triatomic ˌtraɪ.əˈtɒm.ɪk (US) -ˈtɑː.mɪk
tribadism ˈtrɪb.ə.dɪ.zəm, ˈtraɪ.bə-
tribal ˈtraɪ.bəl **-ly** -i **-ism** -ɪ.zəm
tribalistic ˌtraɪ.bəlˈɪs.tɪk (US) -bəˈlɪs-
tribasic traɪˈbeɪ.sɪk
tribe traɪb **-s** -z
tribes|man ˈtraɪbz|.mən **-men** -mən, -men **-woman** -ˌwʊm.ən **-women** -ˌwɪm.ɪn
tribespeople ˈtraɪbzˌpiː.pl̩
tribrach ˈtraɪ.bræk, ˈtrɪb.ræk **-s** -s
tribrachic traɪˈbræk.ɪk, trɪ-
tribulation ˌtrɪb.jəˈleɪ.ʃən, -jʊˈ- **-s** -z
tribunal traɪˈbjuː.nəl, trɪ- **-s** -z
tribunate ˈtrɪb.jə.neɪt, -jʊ-, -nɪt, -nət (US) -nɪt, -neɪt **-s** -s
tribune (T) ˈtrɪb.juːn **-s** -z
tributar|y ˈtrɪb.jə.tər|.i, -jʊ-, -tr|i (US) -ter|.i **-ies** -iz

Trill

A speech sound produced by the rapid vibration of one of the vocal organs.

Examples

The parts of the body that are used in speaking (the 'vocal apparatus') include some 'wobbly bits' that can be made to vibrate. When this type of vibration is made as a speech sound, it is called a trill. The possibilities include a **BILABIAL** trill, where the lips vibrate (used as a mild insult, this is sometimes called "blowing a raspberry", or, in the US, a 'Bronx Cheer'), a tongue-tip trill which is produced in many languages for a sound represented alphabetically as **r**, and a uvular trill, which is a rather dramatic way of pronouncing a "uvular r" as found in French, German and many other European languages, most commonly used in acting and singing.

In British English, the trill most likely to occur is the **ALVEOLAR** trill, which is (perhaps confusingly) represented by the symbol [r], and is an allophone of the English phoneme /r/. However, it most frequently occurs in restricted contexts, such as singing.

tribute 'trɪb.juːt **-s** -s
trice traɪs
Tricel® 'traɪ.sel
triceps 'traɪ.seps **-es** -ɪz
trichin|a trɪ'kaɪ.n|ə, trə- **-ae** -iː **-as** -əz
Trichinopoly ˌtrɪtʃ.ɪ'nɒp.^{ə}l.i, -ə'- (US) -'nɑː.p^{ə}l-
trichinosis ˌtrɪk.ɪ'nəʊ.sɪs, -ə'- (US) -ɪ'noʊ-
trichloride traɪ'klɔː.raɪd (US) -'klɔːr.aɪd **-s** -z
tricholog|y trɪ'kɒl.ə.dʒ|i, trə- (US) -'kɑː.lə- **-ist/s** -ɪst/s
trichord 'traɪ.kɔːd (US) -kɔːrd **-s** -z
trichosis trɪ'kəʊ.sɪs, trə- (US) -'koʊ-
trichotomy trɪ'kɒt.ə.mi, trə- (US) -'kɑː.t̬ə-
Tricia 'trɪʃ.ə
Tricity® 'trɪs.ə.ti, -ɪ.ti (US) -ə.t̬i
trick trɪk **-s** -s **-ing** -ɪŋ **-ed** -t **-er/s** -ə^{r}/z (US) -ɚ/z ˌ**trick 'cyclist**; ˌ**trick or 'treat**
tricker|y 'trɪk.^{ə}r|.i **-ies** -iz
trickl|e 'trɪk.l̩ **-es** -z **-ing** -ɪŋ, 'trɪk.lɪŋ **-ed** -d '**trickle** ˌ**charger**
trickledown 'trɪk.l̩.daʊn
trickly 'trɪk.l̩.i, '-li
trickster 'trɪk.stə^{r} (US) -stɚ **-s** -z
tricks|y 'trɪk.s|i **-ier** -i.ə^{r} (US) -i.ɚ **-iest** -i.ɪst, -i.əst **-iness** -ɪ.nəs, -ɪ.nɪs
trick|y 'trɪk|.i **-ier** -i.ə^{r} (US) -i.ɚ **-iest** -i.ɪst, -i.əst **-ily** -ɪ.li, -^{ə}l.i **-iness** -ɪ.nəs, -ɪ.nɪs
tricolo(u)r 'trɪk.^{ə}l.ə^{r}; 'traɪˌkʌl.ə^{r} (US) 'traɪˌkʌl.ɚ **-s** -z
tricorn(e) 'traɪ.kɔːn (US) -kɔːrn
tricot 'triː.kəʊ, 'trɪk.əʊ (US) 'triː.koʊ **-s** -z
tricycl|e 'traɪ.sɪ.kl̩, -sə- **-es** -z **-ing** -ɪŋ, -klɪŋ **-ed** -d
trident (T) 'traɪ.d^{ə}nt **-s** -s
Tridentine traɪ'den.taɪn, trɪ-, trə-, -tiːn (US) traɪ'den.taɪn, -tiːn, -tɪn
tried *(from* **try***)* traɪd
triennial traɪ'en.i.əl, '-jəl **-ly** -i
trier 'traɪ.ə^{r} (US) -ɚ **-s** -z
Trier trɪə^{r} (US) trɪr
trierarch 'traɪ.^{ə}r.ɑːk (US) -ə.rɑːrk **-s** -s **-y** -i **-ies** -iz
tries *(from* **try***)* traɪz
Trieste tri'est; -'es.teɪ
triffid (T) 'trɪf.ɪd **-s** -z
trifid 'traɪ.fɪd
trifl|e 'traɪ.fl̩ **-es** -z **-ing/ly** -ɪŋ/li, 'traɪ.flɪŋ/li **-ed** -d **-er/s** -ə^{r}/z, 'traɪ.flə^{r}/z (US) '-fl̩.ɚ/z, '-flɚ/z
trifolium traɪ'fəʊ.li.əm (US) -'foʊ- **-s** -z
trifori|um traɪ'fɔː.ri|.əm (US) -'fɔːr.i- **-a** -ə
trig trɪg **-s** -z **-ging** -ɪŋ **-ged** -d
Trigg trɪg
trigg|er 'trɪg|.ə^{r} (US) -ɚ **-ers** -əz (US) -ɚz **-ering** -^{ə}r.ɪŋ **-ered** -əd (US) -ɚd
trigger-happy 'trɪg.əˌhæp.i (US) -ɚˌ-
triglyph 'traɪ.glɪf, 'trɪg.lɪf (US) 'traɪ.glɪf **-s** -s
trigon 'traɪ.gən, -gɒn (US) -gɑːn **-s** -z
trigonometric ˌtrɪg.ə.nəʊ'met.rɪk (US) -nə'- **-al** -^{ə}l **-ally** -^{ə}l.i, -li
trigonometr|y ˌtrɪg.ə'nɒm.ɪ.tr|i, '-ə- (US) -'nɑː.mə- **-ies** -iz
trigraph 'traɪ.grɑːf, -græf (US) -græf **-s** -s
trihedral traɪ'hiː.drəl
trike traɪk **-s** -s
trilateral traɪ'læt.^{ə}r.^{ə}l, '-r^{ə}l (US) -'læt̬.ɚ.^{ə}l, -'læt.r^{ə}l **-ly** -i **-ness** -nəs, -nɪs
trilb|y (T) 'trɪl.b|i **-ies** -iz
trilingual traɪ'lɪŋ.gw^{ə}l **-ly** -i
triliteral traɪ'lɪt.^{ə}r.^{ə}l, '-r^{ə}l (US) -'lɪt̬.ɚ.^{ə}l, -'lɪt.r^{ə}l
trill trɪl **-s** -z **-ing** -ɪŋ **-ed** -d
Trilling 'trɪl.ɪŋ
trillion 'trɪl.jən, -i.ən (US) '-jən **-s** -z **-th/s** -*t*.θ/s
trilobite 'traɪ.ləʊ.baɪt (US) -loʊ-, -lə- **-s** -s
trilog|y 'trɪl.ə.dʒ|i **-ies** -iz
trim (T) trɪm **-mer/s** -ə^{r}/z (US) -ɚ/z **-mest** -ɪst, -əst **-ly** -li **-ness** -nəs, -nɪs **-s** -z **-ming/s** -ɪŋ/z **-med** -d
trimaran 'traɪ.m^{ə}r.æn, ˌ--'- (US) 'traɪ.mə.ræn **-s** -z
Trimble 'trɪm.bl̩
trimester trɪ'mes.tə^{r}, traɪ- (US) traɪ'mes.tɚ, '--- **-s** -z
trimestral trɪ'mes.tr^{ə}l, traɪ- (US) traɪ-, '---
trimestrial trɪ'mes.tri.əl, traɪ- (US) traɪ-
trimeter 'trɪm.ɪ.tə^{r}, '-ə- (US) -ə.t̬ɚ **-s** -z
Trincomalee ˌtrɪŋ.kəʊ.m^{ə}l'iː (US) -koʊ.mə'liː
Trinculo 'trɪŋ.kjə.ləʊ, -kjʊ- (US) -loʊ
Trinder 'trɪn.də^{r} (US) -dɚ
trine (T) traɪn **-s** -z
Tring trɪŋ
Trinidad 'trɪn.ɪ.dæd, '-ə-, ˌ--'- (US) 'trɪn.ɪ.dæd ˌ**Trinidad and To'bago**
Trinidadian ˌtrɪn.ɪ'dæd.i.ən, -ə'-, -'deɪ.di- (US) -ɪ'dæd.i- **-s** -z
Trinitarian ˌtrɪn.ɪ'teə.ri.ən, -ə'- (US) -ɪ'ter.i- **-s** -z **-ism** -ɪ.z^{ə}m
trinitroglycerin(e) ˌtraɪ.naɪ.trəʊ'glɪs.^{ə}r.ɪn, traɪˌnaɪ-, -iːn (US) traɪˌnaɪ.troʊ'glɪs.ɚ.ɪn
trinitrotoluene ˌtraɪ.naɪ.trəʊ'tɒl.ju.iːn, traɪˌnaɪ- (US) traɪˌnaɪ.troʊ'tɑːl-
trinit|y (T) 'trɪn.ə.t|i, -ɪ.t|i (US) -ə.t̬|i **-ies** -iz
trinket 'trɪŋ.kɪt, -kət **-s** -s
trinomial traɪ'nəʊ.mi.əl (US) -'noʊ- **-s** -z
trio 'triː.əʊ (US) -oʊ **-s** -z
triode 'traɪ.əʊd (US) -oʊd **-s** -z
triolet 'triː.əʊ.let, 'traɪ-, 'trɪə.let, -lɪt, -lət (US) 'triː.ə-, 'traɪ- **-s** -s
trioxide traɪ'ɒk.saɪd (US) -'ɑːk- **-s** -z
trip trɪp **-s** -s **-ping/ly** -ɪŋ/li **-ped** -t **-per/s** -ə^{r}/z (US) -ɚ/z '**trip** ˌ**wire**
tripartite ˌtraɪ'pɑː.taɪt (US) -'pɑːr- **-ly** -li *stress shift:* ˌtripartite 'talks
tripe traɪp

Triphthong

A vowel glide with three distinguishable vowel qualities.

Examples for English

In British English there are said to be five triphthongs, formed by adding /ə/ to the diphthongs /eɪ aɪ ɔɪ aʊ əʊ/. US English treats most of these sequences differently, e.g.:

layer	/leɪəʳ/	(US) /ˈleɪ.ɚ/
liar	/laɪəʳ/	(US) /ˈlaɪ.ɚ/
loyal	/lɔɪəl/	(US) /ˈlɔɪ.əl/
power	/paʊəʳ/	(US) /paʊɚ/
mower	/məʊəʳ/	(US) /ˈmoʊ.ɚ/

There are many other examples of sequences of three vowel qualities, e.g. *play-off* /pleɪɒf/, *reopen* /riəʊpən/, so the five listed above must have some special characteristic. One possibility is that speakers feel them to be one syllable; this may be the case, but there does not seem to be any clear way of proving this. This is a matter which depends to some extent on the accent: many BBC speakers pronounce these sequences almost as pure vowels (prolongations of the first element of the triphthong), so that the word *Ireland*, for example, sounds like /ˈɑː.lənd/. In Lancashire and Yorkshire accents, on the other hand, the middle vowel (/ɪ/ or /ʊ/) is pronounced with such a close vowel quality that it would seem more appropriate to transcribe the triphthongs with /j/ or /w/ in the middle (e.g. *fire* /ˈfaj.ər/), emphasising the disyllabic aspect of their pronunciation.

triphibi|ous traɪˈfɪb.i|.əs **-an/s** -ən/z
triphthong ˈtrɪf.θɒŋ, ˈtrɪp- (US) -θɑːŋ, -θɔːŋ **-s** -z
triphthongal trɪfˈθɒŋ.gᵊl, trɪp- (US) -ˈθɑːŋ-, -ˈθɔːŋ- **-ly** -i
triplane ˈtraɪ.pleɪn **-s** -z
tripl|e ˈtrɪp.l̩ **-y** -i **-es** -z **-ing** -ɪŋ, ˈtrɪp.lɪŋ **-ed** -d ˈ**triple** ˌ**jump**, ˌ**triple** ˈ**jump**
triplet ˈtrɪp.lət, -lɪt **-s** -s
triplex (T®) ˈtrɪp.leks **-es** -ɪz
triplicate *(adj.)* ˈtrɪp.lɪ.kət, -lə-, -kɪt (US) -kɪt
tripli|cate *(v.)* ˈtrɪp.lɪ|.keɪt, -lə- **-cates** -keɪts **-cating** -keɪ.tɪŋ (US) -keɪ.t̬ɪŋ **-cated** -keɪ.tɪd (US) -keɪ.t̬ɪd
triploid ˈtrɪp.lɔɪd **-s** -z **-y** -i
tripod ˈtraɪ.pɒd (US) -pɑːd **-s** -z
Tripoli, tripoli ˈtrɪp.ᵊl.i
Tripolitania ˌtrɪp.ᵊl.ɪˈteɪ.ni.ə, -ɒl-; trɪˌpɒl- (US) ˌtrɪp.ᵊl.əˈ-; trɪˌpɑː.ləˈ-
tripos ˈtraɪ.pɒs (US) -pɑːs **-es** -ɪz
Tripp trɪp
triptych ˈtrɪp.tɪk **-s** -s
tripwire ˈtrɪp.waɪəʳ (US) -waɪɚ **-s** -z
trireme ˈtraɪ.riːm **-s** -z
trisect traɪˈsekt **-s** -s **-ing** -ɪŋ **-ed** -ɪd **-or/s** -əʳ/z (US) -ɚ/z
trisection traɪˈsek.ʃᵊn **-s** -z
Trisha ˈtrɪʃ.ə
Tristan ˈtrɪs.tən, -tæn (US) -tən, -tæn, -tɑːn
Tristan da Cunha ˌtrɪs.tən.dəˈkuː.nə, -njə
Tristram ˈtrɪs.trəm, -træm (US) -trəm
trisyllabic ˌtraɪ.sɪˈlæb.ɪk, -səˈ- (US) -sɪˈ- **-al** -ᵊl **-ally** -ᵊl.i, -li
trisyllable traɪˈsɪl.ə.bl̩ **-s** -z
trit|e traɪt **-er** -əʳ (US) ˈtraɪ.t̬ɚ **-est** -ɪst, -əst (US) ˈtraɪ.t̬ɪst, -t̬əst **-ely** -li **-eness** -nəs, -nɪs
tritium ˈtrɪt.i.əm, ˈ-jəm (US) ˈtrɪt̬.i.əm, ˈtrɪʃ-
triton (T) *sea god, mollusc:* ˈtraɪ.tɒn, -tᵊn (US) -tᵊn *physics:* ˈtraɪ.tɒn, -tᵊn (US) -tɑːn **-s** -z
tritone ˈtraɪ.təʊn (US) -toʊn **-s** -z
triumph (T®) ˈtraɪ.əm*p*f, -ʌm*p*f **-s** -s **-ing** -ɪŋ **-ed** -t
triumphal traɪˈʌm*p*.fᵊl **-ism** -ɪ.zᵊm **-ist/s** -ɪsts
triumphant traɪˈʌm*p*.fənt **-ly** -li
triumv|ir traɪˈʌm.v|əʳ, tri-, -ˈʊm-, -v|ɪəʳ, -v|ɜːʳ; ˈtraɪ.ʌm-, -əm- (US) traɪˈʌm.v|ɪr, -v|ɚ **-irs** -əz, -ɪəz, -ɜːz (US) -ɪrz, -ɚz **-iri** -ɪˌriː, -ᵊr.iː, -aɪ (US) -ɪˌraɪ
triumvirate traɪˈʌm.vɪ.rət, tri-, -vᵊr.ət, -ɪt (US) traɪˈʌm.vɪ.rɪt, -vɚ.ɪt **-s** -s
triumviri traɪˈʌm.vɪˌriː, tri-, -vᵊr.iː, -aɪ, ˈtraɪ.ʌm-, -əm- (US) traɪˈʌm.vɪˌraɪ, -və-
triune (T) ˈtraɪ.uːn (US) -juːn
trivalent traɪˈveɪ.lᵊnt; ˈtrɪv.ᵊl.ᵊnt (US) traɪˈveɪ.lᵊnt, ˌtraɪ-, ˈ---
trivet ˈtrɪv.ɪt **-s** -s
trivia ˈtrɪv.i.ə
trivial ˈtrɪv.i.əl **-ly** -i **-ness** -nəs, -nɪs ˌ**Trivial Pur**ˈ**suit®**
trivialit|y ˌtrɪv.iˈæl.ə.t|i, -ɪ.t|i (US) -ə.t̬|i **-ies** -iz
trivializ|e, -is|e ˈtrɪv.i.ᵊl.aɪz, ˈ-jᵊl- (US) -i.ᵊl- **-es** -ɪz **-ing** -ɪŋ **-ed** -d
trivi|um ˈtrɪv.i|.əm **-a** -ə
Trixie ˈtrɪk.si
trizonal traɪˈzəʊ.nᵊl (US) -ˈzoʊ-
Trizone ˈtraɪ.zəʊn (US) -zoʊn
Troad ˈtrəʊ.æd (US) ˈtroʊ-
Troas ˈtrəʊ.æs (US) ˈtroʊ-
Trocadero ˌtrɒk.əˈdɪə.rəʊ (US) ˌtrɑː.kəˈder.oʊ, ˌtroʊ-
trochaic trəʊˈkeɪ.ɪk, trɒkˈeɪ- (US) troʊˈkeɪ-
troch|e trəʊʃ (US) ˈtroʊ.ki **-es** -ɪz
trochee ˈtrəʊ.kiː, -ki (US) ˈtroʊ- **-s** -z
trod *(from* **tread***)* trɒd (US) trɑːd **-den** -ᵊn
Troed-y-rhiw ˌtrɔɪd.ə.riˈuː
trog trɒg (US) trɑːg, trɔːg **-s** -z **-ging** -ɪŋ **-ged** -d
troglodyte ˈtrɒg.ləʊ.daɪt (US) ˈtrɑː.glə- **-s** -s
troika ˈtrɔɪ.kə **-s** -z
troilism ˈtrɔɪ.lɪ.zᵊm
Troilus ˈtrɔɪ.ləs, ˈtrəʊ.ɪ.ləs (US) ˈtrɔɪ.ləs, ˈtroʊ.ə-
Trojan ˈtrəʊ.dʒᵊn (US) ˈtroʊ- **-s** -z ˌ**Trojan** ˈ**horse**; ˌ**Trojan** ˈ**War**
troll trəʊl, trɒl (US) troʊl **-s** -z **-ing** -ɪŋ **-ed** -d
trolley ˈtrɒl.i (US) ˈtrɑː.li **-s** -z
trolleybus ˈtrɒl.i.bʌs (US) ˈtrɑː.li- **-es** -ɪz
trollop ˈtrɒl.əp (US) ˈtrɑː.ləp **-s** -s
Trollope ˈtrɒl.əp (US) ˈtrɑː.ləp
Tromans ˈtrəʊ.mənz (US) ˈtroʊ-
trombone trɒmˈbəʊn (US) trɑːmˈboʊn, trəm-; ˈtrɑːm.boʊn **-s** -z
trombonist trɒmˈbəʊ.nɪst (US) trɑːmˈboʊ-, ˈ--- **-s** -s
tromp trɒmp (US) trɑːmp, trɔːmp **-s** -s **-ing** -ɪŋ **-ed** -d
trompe l'oeil ˌtrɒmpˈlɔɪ *as if French:* ˌtrɔ̃ːmpˈlɜː.i (US) ˌtrɔːmpˈlɔɪ **-s** -z
Trondheim ˈtrɒn*d*.haɪm (US) ˈtrɑːn.heɪm
Troon truːn
troop truːp **-s** -s **-ing** -ɪŋ **-ed** -t **-er/s** -əʳ/z (US) -ɚ/z ˈ**troop** ˌ**carrier**
trope trəʊp (US) troʊp **-s** -s
trophic ˈtrɒf.ɪk (US) ˈtrɑː.fɪk
troph|y ˈtrəʊ.f|i (US) ˈtroʊ- **-ies** -iz
tropic ˈtrɒp.ɪk (US) ˈtrɑː.pɪk **-s** -s **-al** -ᵊl **-ally** -ᵊl.i, -li ˌ**tropic of** ˈ**Cancer**; ˌ**tropic of** ˈ**Capricorn**

tropism ˈtrəʊ.pɪ.zᵊm US ˈtroʊ- **-s** -z
tropistic trəʊˈpɪs.tɪk US troʊ-
troppo ˈtrɒp.əʊ US ˈtrɑː.poʊ
Trossachs ˈtrɒs.əks, -æks, -əxs US ˈtrɑː.səks, -sæks
trot (T) trɒt US trɑːt **-s** -s **-ting** -ɪŋ US ˈtrɑː.t̬ɪŋ **-ted** -ɪd US ˈtrɑː.t̬ɪd
troth trəʊθ, trɒθ US trɑːθ, trɔːθ, troʊθ
Trotsky ˈtrɒt.ski US ˈtrɑːt- **-ist/s** -ɪst/s **-ite/s** -aɪt/s **-ism** -ɪ.zᵊm
Trotskyite ˈtrɒt.ski.aɪt US ˈtrɑːt- **-s** -s
Trott trɒt US trɑːt
trotter (T) ˈtrɒt.əʳ US ˈtrɑː.t̬ɚ **-s** -z
Trottiscliffe ˈtrɒz.li, ˈtrɒs- US ˈtrɑːz-, ˈtrɑːs-
troubadour ˈtruː.bə.dɔːʳ, -dʊəʳ US -dɔːr **-s** -z
troubl|e ˈtrʌb.l̩ **-es** -z **-ing/ly** -ɪŋ/li, ˈtrʌb.lɪŋ/li **-ed** -d **-er/s** -əʳ/z, ˈtrʌb.ləʳ/z US ˈ-l̩.ɚ/z, ˈ-lɚ/z ˌ**trouble and ˈstrife**; ˈ**trouble** ˌ**spot**
trouble-free ˌtrʌb.l̩ˈfriː *stress shift:* ˌtrouble-free ˈjourney
troublemaker ˈtrʌb.l̩ˌmeɪ.kəʳ US -kɚ **-s** -z
troubleshoot|er ˈtrʌb.l̩ˌʃuː.t|əʳ US -t̬|ɚ **-ers** -əz US -ɚz **-ing** -ɪŋ
troublesome ˈtrʌb.l̩.səm **-ly** -li **-ness** -nəs, -nɪs
troublous ˈtrʌb.ləs **-ly** -li **-ness** -nəs, -nɪs
Troubridge ˈtruː.brɪdʒ
trough trɒf US trɑːf, trɔːf **-s** -s
Note: Some bakers pronounce /traʊ/.
Troughton ˈtraʊ.tᵊn, ˈtrɔː-
trounc|e traʊnts **-es** -ɪz **-ing/s** -ɪŋ/z **-ed** -t
Troup truːp
troup|e truːp **-es** -s **-er/s** -əʳ/z US -ɚ/z
trouper ˈtruː.pəʳ US -pɚ **-s** -z
trouser ˈtraʊ.zəʳ US -zɚ ˈ**trouser** ˌ**press**; ˈ**trouser** ˌ**suit**
trousers ˈtraʊ.zəz US -zɚz
trousseau ˈtruː.səʊ, -ˈ- US ˈtruː.soʊ, -ˈ- **-s** -z **-x** -z
trout traʊt **-s** -s
trove trəʊv US troʊv
trover ˈtrəʊ.vəʳ US ˈtroʊ.vɚ
trow trəʊ, traʊ US troʊ
Trowbridge ˈtrəʊ.brɪdʒ US ˈtroʊ-
trowel traʊəl **-s** -z **-(l)ing** -ɪŋ **-(l)ed** -d
Trowell trəʊəl, traʊəl US troʊəl, traʊəl
troy (T) trɔɪ
truancy ˈtruː.ənt.si
truant ˈtruː.ənt **-s** -s **-ing** -ɪŋ **-ed** -ɪd
Trübner ˈtruːb.nəʳ US -nɚ
truc|e truːs **-es** -ɪz
trucial (T) ˈtruː.ʃᵊl US ˈ-ʃᵊl
truck trʌk **-s** -s **-ing** -ɪŋ **-ed** -t **-age** -ɪdʒ **-er/s** -əʳ/z US -ɚ/z ˈ**truck** ˌ**stop**
truckl|e ˈtrʌk.l̩ **-es** -z **-ing** -ɪŋ, ˈtrʌk.lɪŋ **-ed** -d ˈ**truckle** ˌ**bed**
truckload ˈtrʌk.ləʊd US -loʊd **-s** -z
truculen|ce ˈtrʌk.jə.lᵊnt|s, -jʊ- **-cy** -si
truculent ˈtrʌk.jə.lᵊnt, -jʊ- **-ly** -li
Trudeau ˈtruː.dəʊ US truːˈdoʊ, ˈ--
trudg|e trʌdʒ **-es** -ɪz **-ing** -ɪŋ **-ed** -d **-er/s** -əʳ/z US -ɚ/z
trudgen (T) ˈtrʌdʒ.ᵊn
Trudgill ˈtrʌd.gɪl
Trudy, Trudi ˈtruː.di
tru|e (T) truː **-er** -əʳ US -ɚ **-est** -ɪst, -əst **-ly** -li **-eness** -nəs, -nɪs
true-blue ˌtruːˈbluː **-s** -z *stress shift:* ˌtrue-blue ˈTory
trueborn ˈtruː.bɔːn US -bɔːrn
Truefitt ˈtruː.fɪt
truehearted ˌtruːˈhɑː.tɪd US ˈtruːˌhɑːr.t̬ɪd **-ness** -nəs, -nɪs *stress shift, British only:* ˌtruehearted ˈperson
true-life ˌtruːˈlaɪf *stress shift:* ˌtrue-life ˈstory
truelove ˈtruː.lʌv
Trueman ˈtruː.mən
Truffaut ˈtruː.fəʊ, ˈtrʊf.əʊ US truːˈfoʊ
truffle ˈtrʌf.l̩ **-s** -z **-d** -d
trug trʌg **-s** -z
truism ˈtruː.ɪ.zᵊm **-s** -z
Trujillo trʊˈhiː.jəʊ US truːˈhiː.joʊ
Truk trʌk, trʊk
truly ˈtruː.li
Truman ˈtruː.mən
Trumbull ˈtrʌm.bʊl US -bʊl, -bᵊl
trump (T) trʌmp **-s** -s **-ing** -ɪŋ **-ed** -t ˈ**trump** ˌ**card**, ˌ**trump** ˈ**card**
trumped-up ˌtrʌmptˈʌp *stress shift:* ˌtrumped-up ˈcharges
Trumper ˈtrʌm.pəʳ US -pɚ
trumpery ˈtrʌm.pᵊr.i
trum|pet ˈtrʌm|.pɪt US -pət **-pets** -pɪts US -pəts **-peting/s** -pɪ.tɪŋ/z US -pə.t̬ɪŋ/z **-peted** -pɪ.tɪd US -pə.t̬ɪd **-peter/s** -pɪ.təʳ/z US -pə.t̬ɚ/z ˌ**blow one's** ˌ**own** ˈ**trumpet**
trunca|te trʌŋˈkeɪ|t, ˈ-- US ˈtrʌŋ.keɪ|t, ˈtrʌn- **-tes** -ts **-ting** -tɪŋ US -t̬ɪŋ **-ted** -tɪd US -t̬ɪd
truncation trʌŋˈkeɪ.ʃᵊn US trʌŋ-, trʌn- **-s** -z
truncheon ˈtrʌn.tʃᵊn US ˈtrʌnt.ʃᵊn **-s** -z **-ing** -ɪŋ **-ed** -d
trundl|e ˈtrʌn.dl̩ **-es** -z **-ing** -ɪŋ, ˈtrʌnd.lɪŋ **-ed** -d **-er/s** -əʳ/z US -ɚ/z
trunk trʌŋk **-s** -s **-ful/s** -fʊl/z ˈ**trunk** ˌ**call**; ˈ**trunk** ˌ**road**
trunnion ˈtrʌn.i.ən, ˈ-jən US ˈ-jən **-s** -z **-ed** -d
Truro ˈtrʊə.rəʊ US ˈtrʊr.oʊ
Truscott ˈtrʌs.kət US -kət, -kɑːt
Truslove ˈtrʌs.lʌv
truss trʌs **-es** -ɪz **-ing** -ɪŋ **-ed** -t
trust trʌst **-s** -s **-ing/ly** -ɪŋ/li **-ed** -ɪd ˈ**trust** ˌ**fund**
trustee trʌsˈtiː **-s** -z
trusteeship trʌsˈtiː.ʃɪp **-s** -s
trustful ˈtrʌst.fᵊl, -fʊl **-ly** -i **-ness** -nəs, -nɪs
Trusthouse Forte® ˌtrʌst.haʊsˈfɔː.teɪ US -ˈfɔːr-
trustworth|y ˈtrʌstˌwɜː.ð|i US -ˌwɝː- **-iness** -ɪ.nəs, -ɪ.nɪs
trust|y ˈtrʌs.t|i **-ier** -i.əʳ US -i.ɚ **-iest** -i.ɪst, -i.əst **-ily** -ɪ.li, -ᵊl.i **-iness** -ɪ.nəs, -ɪ.nɪs
tru|th truː|θ **-ths** -ðz, -θs ˈ**truth** ˌ**drug**
truthful ˈtruːθ.fᵊl, -fʊl **-ly** -i **-ness** -nəs, -nɪs
tr|y tr|aɪ **-ies** -aɪz **-ying/ly** -aɪ.ɪŋ/li **-ied** -aɪd **-ier/s** -aɪ.əʳ/z US -aɪ.ɚ/z
Tryon traɪən
try-on ˈtraɪ.ɒn US -ɑːn **-s** -z
tryout ˈtraɪ.aʊt **-s** -s
trypanosome ˈtrɪp.ə.nəʊ.səʊm; trɪˈpæn.ə- US trɪˈpæn.ə.soʊm; ˈtrɪp.ə.noʊ- **-s** -z
trypanosomiasis ˌtrɪp.ə.nəʊ.səʊˈmaɪ.ə.sɪs; trɪˌpæn.əʊ- US trɪˌpæn.ə.soʊˈ-; ˌtrɪp.ə.noʊ-;
trypsin ˈtrɪp.sɪn
trypsinogen trɪpˈsɪn.ə.dʒᵊn US ˈ-oʊ-
tryst trɪst **-s** -s **-ing** -ɪŋ **-ed** -ɪd
Trystan ˈtrɪs.tæn, -tən
tsar (T) zɑːʳ, tsɑːʳ US zɑːr, tsɑːr **-s** -z
tsarevitch, tsarevich (T) ˈzɑː.rə.vɪtʃ, ˈtsɑː-, -rɪ- US ˈzɑːr.ə-, ˈtsɑːr- **-es** -ɪz
tsarina (T) zɑːˈriː.nə, tsɑː- **-s** -z
tsarism ˈzɑː.rɪ.zᵊm, ˈtsɑː- US ˈzɑːr.ɪ-, ˈtsɑːr-
tsarist ˈzɑː.rɪst, ˈtsɑː- US ˈzɑːr.ɪst, ˈtsɑːr- **-s** -s
TSB® ˌtiː.esˈbiː
tsetse ˈtet.si, ˈtset- US ˈtset-, ˈtsiːt-, ˈtet-, ˈtiːt- **-s** -z ˈ**tsetse** ˌ**fly**
T-shirt ˈtiː.ʃɜːt US -ʃɝːt **-s** -s
tsk *(interj.)* tɪsk
Note: This spelling represents the tongue click used (usually repeated) to indicate disapproval; it may be described as a voiceless affricated alveolar click, symbolized as [!Ús]. The transcription given above is only used in mock disapproval. See also **tut**.
tsp *(abbrev. for* **teaspoon, teaspoonful***)* ˈtiː.spuːn, ˈtiː.spuːn.fʊl
T-square ˈtiː.skweəʳ US -skwer **-s** -z
tsunam|i tsʊˈnɑː.m|i, sʊ-, -ˈnæm|.i US tsuːˈnɑː.m|i **-is** -iz **-ic** -ɪk
Tswana ˈtswɑː.nə, ˈswɑː- **-s** -z
TT ˌtiːˈtiː ˌ**TˈT** ˌ**races**
Tuamotu ˌtuː.əˈməʊ.tuː US -ˈmoʊ-

Tuareg ˈtwɑː.reg ⓊⓈ ˈtwɑːr.eg **-s** -z
tub tʌb **-s** -z **-bing** -ɪŋ **-bed** -d
tuba ˈtjuː.bə, ˈtʃuː- ⓊⓈ ˈtuː-, ˈtjuː- **-s** -z
tubb|y ˈtʌb|.i **-ier** -i.əʳ ⓊⓈ -i.ɚ **-iest** -i.ɪst, -i.əst **-iness** -ɪ.nəs, -ɪ.nɪs
tube tjuːb, tʃuːb ⓊⓈ tuːb, tjuːb **-s** -z
tubeless ˈtjuː.bləs, ˈtʃuː-, -blɪs ⓊⓈ ˈtuː-, ˈtjuː-
tuber ˈtjuː.bəʳ ⓊⓈ ˈtuː.bɚ, ˈtjuː- **-s** -z
tubercle ˈtjuː.bə.kl̩, -bɜː- ⓊⓈ ˈtuː.bɚ-, ˈtjuː- **-s** -z
tubercular tjuːˈbɜː.kjə.ləʳ, tjʊ-, -kjʊ- ⓊⓈ tuːˈbɝː.kjə.lɚ, tjuː-, tə-, -kjʊ-
tuberculin tjuːˈbɜː.kjə.lɪn, tjʊ-, -kjʊ- ⓊⓈ tuːˈbɝː-, tjuː-, tə-
tuberculization, -isa- tjuːˌbɜː.kjə.laɪˈzeɪ.ʃᵊn, tjʊ-, -kjʊ-, -lɪˈ- ⓊⓈ tuːˌbɝː.kjə.lɪˈ-, tjuː-, tə-, -kjʊ-
tuberculiz|e, -is|e tjuːˈbɜː.kjə.laɪz, tjʊ-, -kjʊ- ⓊⓈ tuːˈbɝː-, tjuː-, tə- **-es** -ɪz **-ing** -ɪŋ **-ed** -d
tuberculoid tjuːˈbɜː.kjə.lɔɪd, tjʊ-, -kjʊ- ⓊⓈ tuːˈbɝː-, tjuː-, tə-
tuberculosis tjuːˌbɜː.kjəˈləʊ.sɪs, tjʊ-, -kjʊ- ⓊⓈ tuːˌbɝː.kjəˈloʊ-, tjuː-, tə-, -kjʊ-
tuberculous tjuːˈbɜː.kjə.ləs, tjʊ-, -kjʊ- ⓊⓈ tuːˈbɝː-, tjuː-, tə-
tuberose *(n.)* ˈtjuː.bᵊr.əʊz ⓊⓈ ˈtuː.broʊz, ˈtjuː-, -bə.roʊz
tuberose *(adj.)* ˈtjuː.bᵊr.əʊs ⓊⓈ ˈtuː.bə.roʊs, ˈtjuː-
tuberous ˈtjuː.bᵊr.əs ⓊⓈ ˈtuː-, ˈtjuː-
tubful ˈtʌb.fʊl **-s** -z
tubiform ˈtjuː.bɪ.fɔːm, ˈtʃuː- ⓊⓈ ˈtuː.bɪ.fɔːrm, ˈtjuː-
tubing ˈtjuː.bɪŋ, ˈtʃuː- ⓊⓈ ˈtuː-, ˈtjuː- **-s** -z
Tübingen ˈtuː.bɪŋ.ən, ˈtjuː-
tub-thump|ing ˈtʌbˌθʌm.p|ɪŋ **-er/s** -əʳ/z ⓊⓈ -ɚ/z
Tubuai ˌtuː.buˈaɪ
tubular ˈtjuː.bjə.ləʳ, ˈtʃuː-, -bjʊ- ⓊⓈ ˈtuː.bjə.lɚ, ˈtjuː-, -bjʊ-
tubule ˈtjuː.bjuːl, ˈtʃuː- ⓊⓈ ˈtuː-, ˈtjuː- **-s** -z
TUC ˌtiː.juːˈsiː
tuck (T) tʌk **-s** -s **-ing** -ɪŋ **-ed** -t
tucker (T) ˈtʌk.əʳ ⓊⓈ -ɚ **-s** -z
tuck-shop ˈtʌk.ʃɒp ⓊⓈ -ʃɑːp **-s** -s
Tucson ˈtuː.sɒn ⓊⓈ ˈtuː.sɑːn
Tudjman ˈtʊdʒ.mən, ˈtʊdz-, ˈtʌdʒ-
Tudor ˈtjuː.dəʳ, ˈtʃuː- ⓊⓈ ˈtuː.dɚ, ˈtjuː- **-s** -z
Tue. *(abbrev. for* **Tuesday***)* ˈtjuːz.deɪ, ˈtʃuːz-, -di ⓊⓈ ˈtuːz-, ˈtjuːz-
Note: This abbreviation may also be pronounced /tjuː/ in British English.
Tues. *(abbrev. for* **Tuesday***)* ˈtjuːz.deɪ, ˈtʃuːz-, -di ⓊⓈ ˈtuːz-, ˈtjuːz-
Note: This abbreviation may also be pronounced /tjuːz/ in British English.
Tuesday ˈtjuːz.deɪ, ˈtʃuːz-, -di ⓊⓈ ˈtuːz-, ˈtjuːz- **-s** -z
tufa ˈtjuː.fə ⓊⓈ ˈtuː-, ˈtjuː-
tuffet ˈtʌf.ɪt, -ət **-s** -s
Tufnell ˈtʌf.nᵊl ˌ**Tufnell ˈPark**
tuft tʌft **-s** -s **-ing** -ɪŋ **-ed** -ɪd
tuft|y ˈtʌf.t|i **-ier** -i.əʳ ⓊⓈ -i.ɚ **-iest** -i.ɪst, -i.əst **-iness** -ɪ.nəs, -ɪ.nɪs
tug tʌg **-s** -z **-ging** -ɪŋ **-ged** -d **-ger/s** -əʳ/z ⓊⓈ -ɚ/z
tugboat ˈtʌg.bəʊt ⓊⓈ -boʊt **-s** -s
tug-of-love ˌtʌg.əvˈlʌv
tug-of-war ˌtʌg.əvˈwɔːʳ ⓊⓈ -ˈwɔːr **-s** -z **tugs-of-war** ˌtʌgz.əvˈwɔːʳ ⓊⓈ -ˈwɔːr
tugrik ˈtuː.griːk **-s** -s
Tuileries ˈtwiː.lᵊr.iː, -i ⓊⓈ -iː, -i, -iz
tuition tjuˈɪʃ.ᵊn ⓊⓈ tu-, tju- **-s** -z **-al** -ᵊl
Tuke tjuːk ⓊⓈ tuːk, tjuːk
tulip ˈtjuː.lɪp, ˈtʃuː- ⓊⓈ ˈtuː-, ˈtjuː- **-s** -s
Tull tʌl
tulle tjuːl ⓊⓈ tuːl **-s** -z
Tulloch ˈtʌl.ək, -əx ⓊⓈ -ək
Tully ˈtʌl.i
Tulsa ˈtʌl.sə
Tulse tʌls
tum tʌm **-s** -z
tumbl|e ˈtʌm.bl̩ **-es** -z **-ing** -ɪŋ, -blɪŋ **-ed** -d **-er/s** -əʳ/z ⓊⓈ -ɚ/z
tumbledown (T) ˈtʌm.bl̩.daʊn
tumble-drier, tumble-dryer ˌtʌm.bl̩ˈdraɪ.əʳ, ˈtʌm.bl̩ˌdraɪ- ⓊⓈ -ɚ **-s** -z
tumble-dr|y ˌtʌm.bl̩ˈdr|aɪ, ˈ--- **-ies** -aɪz **-ying** -aɪ.ɪŋ **-ied** -aɪd
tumbler ˈtʌm.bləʳ, ˈ-bl̩.əʳ ⓊⓈ ˈ-blɚ, ˈ-bl̩.ɚ **-s** -z **-ful/s** -fʊl/z
tumbleweed ˈtʌm.bl̩.wiːd
tumbrel ˈtʌm.brᵊl **-s** -z
tumbril ˈtʌm.brɪl, -brᵊl **-s** -z
tumefaction ˌtjuː.mɪˈfæk.ʃᵊn, -məˈ- ⓊⓈ ˌtuː.məˈ-, ˌtjuː-
tume|fy ˈtjuː.mɪ|.faɪ, -mə- ⓊⓈ ˈtuː.mə-, ˈtjuː- **-fies** -faɪz **-fying** -faɪ.ɪŋ **-fied** -faɪd
tumescen|t tjuːˈmes.ᵊn|t, tjʊ- ⓊⓈ tuː-, tjuː- **-ce** -*t*s
tumid ˈtjuː.mɪd ⓊⓈ ˈtuː-, ˈtjuː- **-ly** -li
tumidity tjuːˈmɪd.ə.ti, tjʊ-, -ɪ.ti ⓊⓈ tuːˈmɪd.ə.t̬i, tjuː-
Tummel ˈtʌm.ᵊl
tumm|y ˈtʌm|.i **-ies** -iz **ˈtummy ˌache; ˈtummy ˌbutton**
tumo(u)r ˈtjuː.məʳ, ˈtʃuː- ⓊⓈ ˈtuː.mɚ, ˈtjuː- **-s** -z
tumo(u)rous ˈtjuː.mᵊr.əs, ˈtʃuː- ⓊⓈ ˈtuː-, ˈtjuː-
tumult ˈtjuː.mʌlt, -məlt ⓊⓈ ˈtuː-, ˈtjuː- **-s** -s
tumultuous tjuːˈmʌl.tju.əs, tjʊ- ⓊⓈ tuːˈmʌl.tʃu.əs, tjuː-, tə-, -tʃə.wəs **-ly** -li **-ness** -nəs, -nɪs
tumul|us ˈtjuː.mjə.l|əs, -mju- ⓊⓈ ˈtuː-, ˈtjuː- **-i** -aɪ
tun tʌn **-s** -z
tuna ˈtjuː.nə, ˈtuː- ⓊⓈ ˈtuː-, ˈtjuː- **-s** -z **ˈtuna ˌfish**
Tunbridge ˈtʌn.brɪdʒ, ˈtʌm- ⓊⓈ ˈtʌn- ˌ**Tunbridge ˈWells**
tundra ˈtʌn.drə **-s** -z
tun|e tjuːn, tʃuːn ⓊⓈ tuːn, tjuːn **-es** -z **-ing** -ɪŋ **-ed** -d **-er/s** -əʳ/z ⓊⓈ -ɚ/z **ˈtuning ˌfork; ˈtuning ˌpeg; ˌchange one's ˈtune**
tuneful ˈtjuːn.fᵊl, ˈtʃuːn-, -fʊl ⓊⓈ ˈtuːn-, ˈtjuːn- **-ly** -i **-ness** -nəs, -nɪs
tuneless ˈtjuːn.ləs, ˈtʃuːn-, -lɪs ⓊⓈ ˈtuːn-, ˈtjuːn- **-ly** -li **-ness** -nəs, -nɪs
tunesmith ˈtjuːn.smɪθ, ˈtʃuːn- ⓊⓈ ˈtuːn-, ˈtjuːn- **-s** -s
tungsten ˈtʌŋ*k*.stən
tunic ˈtjuː.nɪk, ˈtʃuː- ⓊⓈ ˈtuː-, ˈtjuː- **-s** -s
tunicle ˈtjuː.nɪ.kl̩ ⓊⓈ ˈtuː-, ˈtjuː- **-s** -z
Tunis ˈtjuː.nɪs ⓊⓈ ˈtuː-, ˈtjuː-
Tunisi|a tjuːˈnɪz.i|.ə, tjʊ-, -ˈnɪs- ⓊⓈ tuːˈniː.ʒ|ə, tjuː-, -ˈnɪʒ|.ə, -ˈnɪʃ|.ə **-an/s** -ən/z
Tunnard ˈtʌn.əd ⓊⓈ -ɚd
tunnel ˈtʌn.ᵊl **-s** -z **-(l)ing** -ɪŋ **-(l)ed** -d **-(l)er/s** -əʳ/z ⓊⓈ -ɚ/z ˌ**tunnel ˈvision; ˌlight at the ˌend of the ˈtunnel**
Tunnicliff(e) ˈtʌn.ɪ.klɪf
tunn|y ˈtʌn|.i **-ies** -iz
Tunstall ˈtʌn*t*.stᵊl, -stɔːl
Tuoh(e)y ˈtuː.i, -hi
Tupman ˈtʌp.mən
tuppenc|e ˈtʌp.ᵊn*t*s, -ᵊm*p*s **-es** -ɪz
tuppenny ˈtʌp.ᵊn.i, ˈ-ni
tuppeny ˈtʌp.ᵊn.i, ˈ-ni
Tupperware® ˈtʌp.ə.weəʳ ⓊⓈ -ɚ.wer
tuque tjuːk ⓊⓈ tuːk, tjuːk **-s** -s
tu quoque ˌtuːˈkwəʊ.kwi, -ˈkwɒk.weɪ ⓊⓈ ˌtuːˈkwoʊ.kwi, ˌtjuː-, -kweɪ **-s** -z
Turandot ˈtʊə.rən.dɒt, ˈtjʊə-, -dəʊ ⓊⓈ ˈtʊr.ən.dɑːt, -doʊ
Turani|a tjʊəˈreɪ.ni|.ə ⓊⓈ tʊˈreɪ-, tjʊ-, -ˈrɑː- **-an/s** -ən/z
turban ˈtɜː.bən ⓊⓈ ˈtɝː- **-s** -z **-(n)ed** -d
turbid ˈtɜː.bɪd ⓊⓈ ˈtɝː- **-ly** -li **-ness** -nəs, -nɪs
turbidity tɜːˈbɪd.ə.ti, -ɪ.ti ⓊⓈ tɝːˈbɪd.ə.t̬i
turbine ˈtɜː.baɪn, -bɪn ⓊⓈ ˈtɝː.bɪn, -baɪn **-s** -z
turbo ˈtɜː.bəʊ ⓊⓈ ˈtɝː.boʊ **-s** -z
turbocharg|e ˈtɜː.bəʊ.tʃɑːdʒ ⓊⓈ ˈtɝː.boʊ.tʃɑːrdʒ **-es** -ɪz **-ing** -ɪŋ **-ed** -d **-er/s** -əʳ/z ⓊⓈ -ɚ/z
turbofan ˈtɜː.bəʊ.fæn ⓊⓈ ˈtɝː.boʊ- **-s** -z

turbo-jet ˈtɜː.bəʊ.dʒet, ˌ--ˈ- ⓤⓢ ˈtɝː.boʊ.dʒet **-s** -s
turbo-prop ˈtɜː.bəʊ.prɒp, ˌ--ˈ- ⓤⓢ ˈtɝː.boʊ.prɑːp **-s** -s
turbot ˈtɜː.bət ⓤⓢ ˈtɝː- **-s** -s
turbulence ˈtɜː.bjə.lənts, -jʊ- ⓤⓢ ˈtɝː-
turbulent ˈtɜː.bjə.lənt, -bjʊ- ⓤⓢ ˈtɝː- **-ly** -li
Turco- ˈtɜː.kəʊ- ⓤⓢ ˈtɝː.koʊ-, -kə-
Turcoman ˈtɜː.kəʊ.mən, -mæn, -mɑːn ⓤⓢ ˈtɝː.koʊ.mən, -kə- **-s** -z
turd tɜːd ⓤⓢ tɝːd **-s** -z
tureen tjʊˈriːn, tjə-, tə-, tʊ- ⓤⓢ tʊ-, tjʊ- **-s** -z
tur|f tɜːf ⓤⓢ tɝːf **-fs** -fs **-ves** -vz **-ing** -ɪŋ **-ed** -t **ˈturf acˌcountant**
turf (*v.*) tɜːf ⓤⓢ tɝːf **-s** -s **-ing** -ɪŋ **-ed** -t
Turgenev tɜːˈgeɪ.njev, tʊə-, -ˈgen.jev, -jef, -jɪf, -ev, -əv ⓤⓢ tʊrˈgeɪ.nəf, tɝː-, -gen-, -njef, -njev
turgescen|ce tɜːˈdʒes.ᵊn|ts **-t** -t
turgid ˈtɜː.dʒɪd ⓤⓢ ˈtɝː- **-ly** -li **-ness** -nəs, -nɪs
turgidity tɜːˈdʒɪd.ə.ti, -ɪ.ti ⓤⓢ tɝːˈdʒɪd.ə.t̬i
turgor ˈtɜː.gəʳ ⓤⓢ ˈtɝː.gɚ
Turin tjʊəˈrɪn ⓤⓢ tʊ-, tjʊ- *stress shift, see compound:* ˌ**Turin ˈShroud**
Turing ˈtjʊə.rɪŋ ⓤⓢ ˈtʊr.ɪŋ, ˈtjʊr-
Turk tɜːk ⓤⓢ tɝːk **-s** -s
Turkestan ˌtɜː.kɪˈstɑːn, -kəˈ-, -stæn ⓤⓢ ˈtɝː.kɪ.stæn, -stɑːn
turkey (T) ˈtɜː.ki ⓤⓢ ˈtɝː- **-s** -z
turkey-cock ˈtɜː.ki.kɒk ⓤⓢ ˈtɝː.ki.kɑːk **-s** -s
Turki ˈtɜː.kiː, -ki ⓤⓢ ˈtɝː-
Turkic ˈtɜː.kɪk ⓤⓢ ˈtɝː-
Turkington ˈtɜː.kɪŋ.tən ⓤⓢ ˈtɝː-
Turkish ˈtɜː.kɪʃ ⓤⓢ ˈtɝː- ˌ**Turkish ˈbath**; ˌ**Turkish deˈlight**
Turkmenia tɜːkˈmiː.ni.ə ⓤⓢ tɝːk-
Turkmenistan tɜːkˌmen.ɪˈstɑːn, -ˈstæn ⓤⓢ tɝːkˈmen.ɪ.stæn, -stɑːn
Turko- ˈtɜː.kəʊ- ⓤⓢ ˈtɝː.koʊ-, -kə-
Turkoman ˈtɜːk.əʊ.mən, -mæn, -mɑːn ⓤⓢ ˈtɝː.koʊ.mən, -kə- **-s** -z
Turku ˈtʊə.kuː, ˈtɜː- ⓤⓢ ˈtʊr-
Turley ˈtɜː.li ⓤⓢ ˈtɝː-
turmeric ˈtɜː.mᵊr.ɪk ⓤⓢ ˈtɝː-
turmoil ˈtɜː.mɔɪl ⓤⓢ ˈtɝː-
turn tɜːn ⓤⓢ tɝːn **-s** -z **-ing** -ɪŋ **-ed** -d **-er/s** -əʳ/z ⓤⓢ -ɚ/z **ˈturning ˌpoint**; ˌ**turn of ˈphrase**
turnabout ˈtɜːn.əˌbaʊt ⓤⓢ ˈtɝːn- **-s** -s
Turnage ˈtɜː.nɪdʒ ⓤⓢ tɝː-
turnaround ˈtɜːn.ᵊrˈaʊnd ⓤⓢ ˈtɝːn.ɚ- **-s** -z
Turnbull ˈtɜːn.bʊl, ˈtɜːm- ⓤⓢ ˈtɝːn-, -bᵊl
turncoat ˈtɜːn.kəʊt, ˈtɜːŋ- ⓤⓢ ˈtɝːn.koʊt **-s** -s
turned-on ˌtɜːndˈɒn ⓤⓢ ˌtɝːndˈɑːn
turner (T) ˈtɜː.nəʳ ⓤⓢ ˈtɝː.nɚ **-s** -z
turnery ˈtɜː.nᵊr.i ⓤⓢ ˈtɝː-
Turnham ˈtɜː.nəm ⓤⓢ ˈtɝː-
Turnhouse ˈtɜːn.haʊs ⓤⓢ ˈtɝːn-
turning ˈtɜː.nɪŋ ⓤⓢ ˈtɝː- **-s** -z
turning-point ˈtɜː.nɪŋ.pɔɪnt ⓤⓢ ˈtɝː- **-s** -s
turnip ˈtɜː.nɪp ⓤⓢ ˈtɝː- **-s** -s
turnkey ˈtɜːn.kiː, ˈtɜːŋ- ⓤⓢ ˈtɝːn- **-s** -z
turn-off ˈtɜːn.ɒf ⓤⓢ ˈtɝːn.ɑːf **-s** -s
turn-on ˈtɜːn.ɒn ⓤⓢ ˈtɝːn.ɑːn **-s** -z
turnout ˈtɜːn.aʊt ⓤⓢ ˈtɝːn- **-s** -s
turnover ˈtɜːnˌəʊ.vəʳ ⓤⓢ ˈtɝːnˌoʊ.vɚ **-s** -z
turnpike ˈtɜːn.paɪk, ˈtɜːm- ⓤⓢ ˈtɝːn- **-s** -s
turnround ˈtɜːn.raʊnd ⓤⓢ ˈtɝːn- **-s** -z
turnstile ˈtɜːn.staɪl ⓤⓢ ˈtɝːn- **-s** ⓤⓢ -z
turnstone ˈtɜːn.stəʊn ⓤⓢ ˈtɝːn.stoʊn **-s** -z
turntable ˈtɜːnˌteɪ.bl̩ ⓤⓢ ˈtɝːn- **-s** -z
turn-up ˈtɜːn.ʌp ⓤⓢ ˈtɝːn- **-s** -s
turpentine ˈtɜː.pᵊn.taɪn, -pᵊm- ⓤⓢ ˈtɝː.pᵊn-
Turpin ˈtɜː.pɪn ⓤⓢ ˈtɝː-
turpitude ˈtɜː.pɪ.tjuːd, -tʃuːd ⓤⓢ ˈtɝː.pɪ.tuːd, -tjuːd
turps tɜːps ⓤⓢ tɝːps
turquois|e ˈtɜː.kwɑːz, -kwɔɪz ⓤⓢ ˈtɝː.kwɔɪz, -kɔɪz **-es** -ɪz
turre|t ˈtʌr.ɪ|t, -ə|t ⓤⓢ ˈtɝː.ɪ|t **-ts** -ts **-ted** -tɪd ⓤⓢ -t̬ɪd
turtle ˈtɜː.tl̩ ⓤⓢ ˈtɝː.t̬l̩ **-s** -z
turtledove ˈtɜː.tl̩.dʌv ⓤⓢ ˈtɝː.t̬l̩- **-s** -z
turtleneck ˈtɜː.tl̩.nek ⓤⓢ ˈtɝː.t̬l̩- **-s** -s
Turton ˈtɜː.tᵊn ⓤⓢ ˈtɝː-
turves *(plur. of* **turf***)* tɜːvz ⓤⓢ tɝːvz
Tuscan ˈtʌs.kən **-s** -z
Tuscany ˈtʌs.kə.ni
tush (*interj.*) tʌʃ
tush *tooth:* tʌʃ **-es** -ɪz
tush *buttocks:* tʊʃ **-es** -ɪz
tusk tʌsk **-s** -s **-ed** -t
tusker ˈtʌs.kəʳ ⓤⓢ -kɚ **-s** -z
tussah ˈtʌs.ə
Tussaud *surname:* ˈtuː.səʊ ⓤⓢ tuːˈsoʊ
Tussaud's *exhibition:* tʊˈsɔːdz, tjʊ-, tə-, -ˈsəʊdz, -ˈsəʊz ⓤⓢ tʊˈsoʊz, tə-, -ˈsɑːd, -ˈsɔːd; ˈtuː.soʊz
Tusser ˈtʌs.əʳ ⓤⓢ -ɚ
tussl|e ˈtʌs.l̩ **-es** -z **-ing** -ɪŋ, ˈtʌs.lɪŋ **-ed** -d **-er/s** -əʳ/z ⓤⓢ -ɚ/z
tussock ˈtʌs.ək **-s** -s **-y** -i
tussore ˈtʌs.əʳ, -ɔːʳ ⓤⓢ -ɚ
tut tʌt **-s** -s **-ting** -ɪŋ ⓤⓢ ˈtʌt̬.ɪŋ **-ted** -ɪd ⓤⓢ ˈtʌt̬.ɪd
tut (*interj.*) tʌt
Note: This spelling represents the tongue click used (usually repeated - see **tut-tut**) to indicate disapproval; it may be described as a voiceless affricated alveolar click, symbolised as [ǃˢ].
Tutankhamen, Tutankhamon ˌtuː.tᵊnˈkɑː.mən, -təŋ-, -tæŋ-, -tɑːŋ-, -kɑːˈmuːn
Tutbury ˈtʌt.bᵊr.i ⓤⓢ -ber-, -bɚ-
tutee ˌtjuːˈtiː, ˌtʃuː- ⓤⓢ ˌtuː-, ˌtjuː- **-s** -z
tutelage ˈtjuː.tɪ.lɪdʒ, -tᵊl.ɪdʒ ⓤⓢ ˈtuː.t̬ᵊl.ɪdʒ, ˈtjuː-
tutelar ˈtjuː.tᵊl.əʳ ⓤⓢ ˈtuː.t̬ᵊl.ɚ, ˈtjuː-
tutelary ˈtjuː.tᵊl.ᵊr.i ⓤⓢ ˈtuː.t̬ᵊl.er.i, ˈtjuː-
Tutin ˈtjuː.tɪn ⓤⓢ ˈtuː-, ˈtjuː-
tut|or ˈtjuː.t|əʳ, ˈtʃuː- ⓤⓢ ˈtuː.t̬|ɚ, ˈtjuː- **-ors** -əz ⓤⓢ -ɚz **-oring** -ᵊr.ɪŋ **-ored** -əd ⓤⓢ -ɚd **-orage** -ᵊr.ɪdʒ
tutorial tjuːˈtɔː.ri.əl, tjʊ-, tʃuː-, tʃʊ- ⓤⓢ tuːˈtɔːr.i-, tjuː- **-s** -z **-ly** -i
tutorship ˈtjuː.tə.ʃɪp, ˈtʃuː- ⓤⓢ ˈtuː.t̬ɚ-, ˈtjuː- **-s** -s
Tutsi ˈtʊt.si **-s** -z
tutti ˈtʊt.i, ˈtuː.ti, -tiː ⓤⓢ ˈtuː.t̬i **-s** -z
tutti-frutti ˌtuː.tiˈfruː.ti, ˌtʊt.iˈ-, -ˈfrʊt.i ⓤⓢ ˌtuː.t̬iˈfruː.t̬i **-s** -z
Tuttle ˈtʌt.l̩ ⓤⓢ ˈtʌt̬-
tut|-tut ˌtʌt|ˈtʌt **-tuts** -ˈtʌts **-tutting** -ˈtʌt.ɪŋ ⓤⓢ -ˈtʌt̬.ɪŋ **-tutted** -ˈtʌt.ɪd ⓤⓢ -ˈtʌt̬.ɪd
tutu (T) ˈtuː.tuː **-s** -z
Tuvalu tuːˈvɑː.luː; ˈtuː.və- ⓤⓢ ˌtuː.vəˈluː; tuːˈvɑː.luː
tu-whit tu-whoo tʊˌhwɪt.tʊˈhwuː, tə-, -təˈ-
tux tʌks **-es** -ɪz
tuxedo (T) tʌkˈsiː.dəʊ ⓤⓢ -doʊ **-(e)s** -z
Tuxford ˈtʌks.fəd ⓤⓢ -fɚd
Tuzla ˈtʊz.lə, ˈtuːz- ⓤⓢ ˈtuːz.lɑː
TV ˌtiːˈviː **-s** -z ˌ**TV ˈdinner**; ˌ**TˈV ˌprogram(me)**
Twaddell ˈtwɒd.ᵊl; twɒdˈel ⓤⓢ twɑːˈdel; ˈtwɑː.dᵊl
twaddl|e ˈtwɒd.l̩ ⓤⓢ ˈtwɑː.dl̩ **-es** -z **-ing** -ɪŋ, ˈtwɒd.lɪŋ ⓤⓢ ˈtwɑːd- **-ed** -d **-er/s** -əʳ/z, ˈtwɒd.ləʳ/z ⓤⓢ ˈtwɑː.dl̩.ɚ/z, ˈtwɑːd.lɚ/z **-y** -i, ˈtwɒd.li ⓤⓢ ˈtwɑː.dl̩.i, ˈtwɑːd.li
twain (T) tweɪn
twang twæŋ **-s** -z **-ing** -ɪŋ **-ed** -d **-y** -i
Twank(e)y ˈtwæŋ.ki
'twas *strong form:* twɒz ⓤⓢ twɑːz *weak form:* twəz
twat twæt, twɒt ⓤⓢ twɑːt **-s** -s
tweak twiːk **-s** -s **-ing** -ɪŋ **-ed** -t
twee twiː
tweed (T) twiːd **-s** -z
Tweeddale ˈtwiːd.deɪl
Tweedie ˈtwiː.di
tweedl|e ˈtwiː.dl̩ **-es** -z **-ing** -ɪŋ, ˈtwiːd.lɪŋ **-ed** -d
Tweedledee ˌtwiː.dl̩ˈdiː
Tweedledum ˌtwiː.dl̩ˈdʌm
Tweedmouth ˈtwiːd.məθ, -maʊθ
Tweedsmuir ˈtwiːdz.mjʊəʳ, -mjɔːʳ ⓤⓢ -mjʊr, -mjʊɚ

tweed|y ˈtwiː.d|i **-ier** -i.əʳ (US) -i.ɚ **-iest** -i.ɪst, -i.əst **-iness** -ɪ.nəs, -ɪ.nɪs
'tween twiːn
tween|y ˈtwiː.n|i **-ies** -iz
tweet twiːt **-s** -s **-ing** -ɪŋ (US) ˈtwiː.t̬ɪŋ **-ed** -ɪd (US) ˈtwiː.t̬ɪd **-er/s** -əʳ/z (US) ˈtwiː.t̬ɚ/z
tweezers ˈtwiː.zəz (US) -zɚz
twelfth twelfθ **-s** -s **-ly** -li ˌ**Twelfth ˈNight** (US) ˈ**Twelfth** ˌ**Night**
twelve twelv **-s** -z
twelvemonth ˈtwelv.mʌntθ **-s** -s
twelvish ˈtwel.vɪʃ
twentieth ˈtwen.ti.ɪθ, -əθ (US) -t̬i- **-s** -s
twent|y ˈtwen.t|i (US) -t̬|i **-ies** -iz ˌ**twenty-**ˌ**twenty ˈvision**
twenty-first ˌtwen.tiˈfɜːst (US) -t̬iˈfɝːst *stress shift:* ˌtwenty-first ˈbirthday
twentyfold ˈtwen.ti.fəʊld (US) -t̬i.foʊld
Twentyman ˈtwen.ti.mən (US) -t̬i-
twenty-one ˌtwen.tiˈwʌn (US) -t̬iˈ- *stress shift:* ˌtwenty-one ˈyears
'twere *strong form:* twɜːʳ (US) twɝː *weak form:* twəʳ (US) twɚ
twerp twɜːp (US) twɝːp **-s** -s
Twi twiː
twice twaɪs
twice-told twaɪsˈtəʊld (US) -ˈtoʊld *stress shift:* ˌtwice-told ˈtale
Twickenham ˈtwɪk.ᵊn.əm, ˈ-nəm
twiddl|e ˈtwɪd.l̩ **-es** -z **-ing** -ɪŋ, ˈtwɪd.lɪŋ **-ed** -d ˌ**twiddle your ˈthumbs**
twiddl|y ˈtwɪd.l|i, -l̩|.i **-ier** -i.əʳ (US) -i.ɚ **-iest** -i.ɪst **iest** -i.əst
twig twɪg **-s** -z **-ging** -ɪŋ **-ged** -d
Twigg twɪg
twiggy (T) ˈtwɪg.i
twilight ˈtwaɪ.laɪt **-s** -s ˈ**twilight** ˌ**zone**
twilit ˈtwaɪ.lɪt
twill twɪl **-s** -z **-ing** -ɪŋ **-ed** -d **-y** -i
'twill *normal form:* twɪl *occasional weak form:* twᵊl
twin twɪn **-s** -z **-ning** -ɪŋ **-ned** -d ˌ**twin ˈbed**; ˈ**twin** ˌ**set**
twin|e twaɪn **-es** -z **-ing/ly** -ɪŋ/li **-ed** -d **-er/s** -əʳ/z (US) -ɚ/z
twing|e twɪndʒ **-es** -ɪz **-(e)ing** -ɪŋ **-ed** -d
Twingo ˈtwɪn.gəʊ, ˈtwɪŋ- (US) -goʊ
Twining ˈtwaɪ.nɪŋ
Twinkie® ˈtwɪŋ.ki **-s** -z
twinkl|e ˈtwɪŋ.kl̩ **-es** -z **-ing** -ɪŋ, ˈtwɪŋ.klɪŋ **-ed** -d **-er/s** -əʳ/z, ˈtwɪŋ.kləʳ/z (US) ˈ-kl.ɚ/z, ˈ-klɚ/z
Twinn twɪn
twinset ˈtwɪn.set **-s** -s
twin-track ˌtwɪnˈtræk *stress shift:* ˌtwin-track ˈrailway
twin-tub ˈtwɪn.tʌb **-s** -z
twirl twɜːl (US) twɝːl **-s** -z **-ing** -ɪŋ **-ed** -d **-y** -i
twirp twɜːp (US) twɝːp **-s** -s
twist (T) twɪst **-s** -s **-ing** -ɪŋ **-ed** -ɪd **-er/s** -əʳ/z (US) -ɚ/z
Twistington ˈtwɪs.tɪŋ.tən
twist|y ˈtwɪs.t|i **-ier** -i.əʳ (US) -i.ɚ **-iest** -i.ɪst, -i.əst **-iness** -ɪ.nəs, -ɪ.nɪs
twit twɪt **-s** -s **-ting/ly** -ɪŋ/li (US) ˈtwɪt̬.ɪŋ/li **-ted** -ɪd (US) ˈtwɪt̬.ɪd
twitch twɪtʃ **-es** -ɪz **-ing/s** -ɪŋ/z **-ed** -t **-er/s** -əʳ/z (US) -ɚ/z
twitch|y ˈtwɪtʃ|.i **-ier** -i.əʳ (US) -i.ɚ **-iest** -i.ɪst, -i.əst
twite twaɪt **-s** -s
twitt|er ˈtwɪt|.əʳ (US) ˈtwɪt̬|.ɚ **-ers** -əz (US) -ɚz **-ering** -ᵊr.ɪŋ (US) -ɚ.ɪŋ **-ered** -əd (US) -ɚd **-ery** -ᵊr.i (US) -ɚ.i
'twixt twɪkst
two tuː **-s** -z **put** ˌ**two and** ˌ**two toˈgether**
two-bit tuːˈbɪt (US) ˈ-- *stress shift, British only:* ˌtwo-bit ˈliar
two-by-four ˌtuː.baɪˈfɔːʳ, -bəˈ-, -bɪˈ- (US) ˈtuː.baɪ.fɔːr, -bə-
two-dimensional ˌtuː.dɪˈmen.tʃᵊn.ᵊl, -daɪˈ-, -ˈmentʃ.nᵊl (US) -dəˈ-, -dɪˈ-, -daɪˈ-
two-edged ˌtuːˈedʒd *stress shift:* ˌtwo-edged ˈsword
two-|faced ˌtuː|ˈfeɪst (US) ˈ-- **-facedly** -ˈfeɪ.sɪd.li; -ˈfeɪst.li (US) -feɪ.sɪd.li, -feɪst.li **-facedness** -ˈfeɪ.sɪd.nəs, -nɪs; -ˈfeɪst.nəs, -nɪs (US) -feɪ.sɪd.nəs, -nɪs; -feɪst.nəs, -nɪs *stress shift, British only:* ˌtwo-faced ˈliar
twofold ˈtuː.fəʊld (US) -foʊld
two-ish ˈtuː.ɪʃ
two-legged ˌtuːˈlegd; -ˈleg.ɪd (US) ˈtuː.legd; -ˌleg.ɪd *stress shift, British only:* ˌtwo-legged ˈcreature
twopenc|e ˈtʌp.ᵊnts, -ᵊmps **-es** -ɪz
Note: The British English pronunciation of **twopenny, twopence,** etc., date from the period before the introduction of decimal coinage in 1971. They remain in use to suggest a very small value (e.g. a twopenny-halfpenny bus ride).
twopenny ˈtʌp.ᵊn.i, ˈ-ni
twopenny-halfpenny ˌtʌp.niˈheɪp.ni, ˌtʌp.ᵊn.iˈheɪ.pᵊn.i
twopennyworth ˌtuːˈpen.i.wɜːθ, ˈ-əθ; ˈtʌp.ᵊn.i.wɜːθ, ˈ-ni-, -wəθ (US) -wɝːθ, -wɚθ **-s** -s
two-piece ˈtuː.piːs
two-ply ˈtuː.plaɪ
two-seater ˌtuːˈsiː.təʳ (US) -t̬ɚ, ˈ-ˌ-- **-s** -z *stress shift:* ˌtwo-seater ˈsportscar
twosome ˈtuː.səm **-s** -z
two-step ˈtuː.step **-s** -s
two-stroke ˈtuː.strəʊk (US) -stroʊk
two-time ˌtuːˈtaɪm, ˈ-- (US) ˈ-- **-s** -z **-ing** -ɪŋ **-ed** -d **-er/s** -əʳ/z (US) -ɚ/z
two-tone ˌtuːˈtəʊn, ˈ-- (US) ˈtuː.toʊn **-d** -d
two-way ˌtuːˈweɪ (US) ˈ-- *stress shift, British only:* ˌtwo-way ˈmirror
Twyford ˈtwaɪ.fəd (US) -fɚd
TX *(abbrev. for* **Texas***)* ˈtek.səs
Tybalt ˈtɪb.ᵊlt
Tyburn ˈtaɪ.bɜːn (US) -bɝːn
Tycho ˈtaɪ.kəʊ (US) -koʊ
tycoon taɪˈkuːn **-s** -z
Tydeus ˈtaɪ.djuːs, -djəs, -di.əs (US) ˈtaɪ.di.əs, ˈ-djəs
Tydfil ˈtɪd.vɪl
tyger ˈtaɪ.gəʳ (US) -gɚ
tying *(from* **tie***)* ˈtaɪ.ɪŋ
tyke taɪk **-s** -s
Tyldesley ˈtɪldz.li
Tyler ˈtaɪ.ləʳ (US) -lɚ
tympan|i ˈtɪm.pə.n|i **-ist/s** -ɪst/s
tympanic tɪmˈpæn.ɪk
tympan|um ˈtɪm.pᵊn|.əm **-ums** -əmz **-a** -ə
tympan|y ˈtɪm.pᵊn|.i **-ies** -iz
Tynan ˈtaɪ.nən
Tyndale, Tyndall ˈtɪn.dᵊl
Tyndrum ˈtaɪn.drʌm
Tyne taɪn ˌ**Tyne and ˈWear**
Tynemouth ˈtaɪn.məθ, ˈtaɪm-, -maʊθ; ˈtɪn.məθ, ˈtɪm- (US) ˈtaɪn-
Tynesid|e ˈtaɪn.saɪd **-er/s** -əʳ/z (US) -ɚ/z
Tynwald ˈtɪn.wəld
typ|e taɪp **-es** -s **-ing** -ɪŋ **-ed** -t ˈ**typing** ˌ**pool**
typecast ˈtaɪp.kɑːst (US) -kæst **-s** -s **-ing** -ɪŋ
Typee ˌtaɪˈpiː
typefac|e ˈtaɪp.feɪs **-es** -ɪz
typefounder ˈtaɪpˌfaʊn.dəʳ (US) -dɚ **-s** -z
typefoundr|y ˈtaɪpˌfaʊn.dr|i **-ies** -iz
typescript ˈtaɪp.skrɪpt **-s** -s
type|set ˈtaɪp|.set **-sets** -sets **-setting** -ˌset.ɪŋ (US) -ˌset̬.ɪŋ **-setter/s** -ˌset.əʳ/z (US) -ˌset̬.ɚ/z
typesetter ˈtaɪpˌset.əʳ (US) -ˌset̬.ɚ **-s** -z
type|write ˈtaɪp|.raɪt **-writes** -raɪts **-writing** -ˌraɪ.tɪŋ (US) -ˌraɪ.t̬ɪŋ **-wrote** -rəʊt (US) -roʊt **-written** -ˌrɪt.ᵊn
typewriter ˈtaɪpˌraɪ.təʳ (US) -t̬ɚ **-s** -z
typhoid ˈtaɪ.fɔɪd
typhonic taɪˈfɒn.ɪk (US) -ˈfɑː.nɪk
Typhoo® taɪˈfuː
typhoon taɪˈfuːn **-s** -z
typh|us ˈtaɪ.f|əs **-ous** -əs
typic|al ˈtɪp.ɪ.k|ᵊl **-ally** -ᵊl.i, -li **-alness** -ᵊl.nəs, -nɪs
typicality ˌtɪp.ɪˈkæl.ə.ti, -ɪ.ti (US) -ə.t̬i
typi|fy ˈtɪp.ɪ|.faɪ **-fies** -faɪz **-fying** -faɪ.ɪŋ **-fied** -faɪd
typist ˈtaɪ.pɪst **-s** -s
typo ˈtaɪ.pəʊ (US) -poʊ **-s** -z
typographic ˌtaɪ.pəʊˈgræf.ɪk (US) -pəˈ-, -poʊˈ- **-al** -ᵊl **-ally** -ᵊl.i, -li
typograph|y taɪˈpɒg.rə.f|i (US) -ˈpɑː.grə- **-er/s** -əʳ/z (US) -ɚ/z

Pronouncing the letters TZ

The consonant digraph **tz** is most commonly pronounced /ts/, e.g.:

chintz /tʃɪnts/
quartz /kwɔːts/ ⓤⓢ /kwɔːrts/

However, the /t/ is sometimes optional in British English, e.g.:

waltz /wɒl*t*s, wɔːl*t*s/ ⓤⓢ /wɑːlts, wɔːlts/

typolog|y taɪˈpɒl.ə.dʒ|i ⓤⓢ -ˈpɑː.lə- **-ies** -iz
tyrannic|al tɪˈræn.ɪ.k|əl, tə-, taɪ- ⓤⓢ tə-, tɪ-, taɪ- **-ally** -əl.i, -li **-alness** -əl.nəs, -nɪs
tyrannicide tɪˈræn.ɪ.saɪd, tə-, taɪ- ⓤⓢ tə-, tɪ-, taɪ- **-s** -z
tyranniz|e, -is|e ˈtɪr.ən.aɪz **-es** -ɪz **-ing** -ɪŋ **-ed** -d
tyrannosaur tɪˈræn.ə.sɔːr, tə-, taɪ- ⓤⓢ təˈræn.ə.sɔːr, tɪ-, taɪ- **-s** -z
tyrannosaurus tɪˌræn.əˈsɔː.rəs, tə-, taɪ- ⓤⓢ təˌræn.əˈsɔːr.əs, tɪ-, taɪ- **-es** -ɪz **tyˌrannoˌsaurus ˈrex**
tyrannous ˈtɪr.ən.əs **-ly** -li
tyrann|y ˈtɪr.ən|.i **-ies** -iz
tyrant ˈtaɪə.rənt ⓤⓢ ˈtaɪ- **-s** -s
tyre (T) taɪər ⓤⓢ taɪɚ **-s** -z
Tyrian ˈtɪr.i.ən **-s** -z
tyro ˈtaɪə.rəʊ ⓤⓢ ˈtaɪ.roʊ **-s** -z
Tyrol tɪˈrəʊl, tə-; ˈtɪr.əl ⓤⓢ tɪˈroʊl, taɪ-; ˈtɪr.oʊl, -ɑːl
Tyrolean ˌtɪr.əʊˈliː.ən; tɪˈrəʊ.li-, tə- ⓤⓢ tɪˈroʊ.li-, taɪ-; ˌtɪr.əˈliː-
Tyrolese ˌtɪr.əʊˈliːz ⓤⓢ -əˈliːz, -ˈliːs
Tyrolienne tɪˌrəʊ.liˈen, tə-; ˌtɪr.əʊ- ⓤⓢ tɪˈroʊ.li.ən; ˌtɪr.əˈliː-, ˌtaɪ.rəˈ- **-s** -z
Tyrone *in Ireland:* tɪˈrəʊn, tə- ⓤⓢ -ˈroʊn
Tyrone *person's name:* ˈtaɪə.rəʊn; taɪˈrəʊn, tɪ-, tə- ⓤⓢ ˈtaɪ.roʊn, ˌ-ˈ-
Tyrrell ˈtɪr.əl
Tyrrhenian tɪˈriː.ni.ən, tə- ⓤⓢ tɪ-
Tyrtaeus tɜːˈtiː.əs ⓤⓢ tɝː-
Tyrwhitt ˈtɪr.ɪt
Tyser ˈtaɪ.zər ⓤⓢ -zɚ
Tyson ˈtaɪ.sən
Tytler ˈtaɪt.lər ⓤⓢ -lɚ
Tyzack ˈtaɪ.zæk, ˈtɪz.æk, -ək
tzar (T) zɑːr, tsɑːr ⓤⓢ zɑːr, tsɑːr **-s** -z
tzarina (T) zɑːˈriː.nə, tsɑː- **-s** -z
tzar|ism ˈzɑː.r|ɪ.zəm, ˈtsɑː- ⓤⓢ ˈzɑːr.ɪ-, ˈtsɑːr- **-ist/s** -ɪst/s
tzetze ˈtet.si, ˈtset- ⓤⓢ ˈtset-, ˈtsiːt-, ˈtet-, ˈtiːt- **-s** -z **ˈtzetze ˌfly**

Pronouncing the letter U

See also UE, UI, UOU, UY

The vowel letter **u** has several strong pronunciations linked to spelling. 'Short' pronunciations include /ʌ/ and /ʊ/, and 'long' pronunciations include /uː/ and /juː/. In 'short' pronunciations pronounced /ʌ/, the **u** is generally followed by a consonant letter which ends the word, or a double consonant before another vowel. Words containing /ʊ/ which end with a consonant sound often have two consonant letters finally, a notable exception being *put* /pʊt/, e.g.:

tub	/tʌb/
tubby	/ˈtʌb.i/
bull	/bʊl/
bully	/ˈbʊl.i/

The 'long' pronunciations usually mean the **u** is followed by a single consonant letter and then a vowel, e.g.:

tube	/tjuːb/	(US) /tuːb/
tubing	/ˈtjuː.bɪŋ/	(US) /ˈtuː-/
supervise	/ˈsuː.pə.vaɪz/	(US) /-pɚ-/

In word initial position, the 'long' pronunciation is almost always pronounced /juː/, e.g.:

unique	/juːˈniːk/
useful	/ˈjuːs.fəl/

However, there are exceptions to these guidelines, e.g.:

study	/ˈstʌd.i/	
sugar	/ˈʃʊg.əʳ/	(US) /-ɚ/
truth	/truːθ/	

When **u** is followed by **r**, the strong pronunciation is one of several possibilities: /jʊə, jɔː (US) jʊr/, /ʊə, ɔː (US) ʊr/, /ɜː (US) ɝː/, or /ʌ (US) ɝː/, e.g.:

cure	/kjʊəʳ, kjɔːʳ/	(US) /kjʊr/
plural	/ˈplʊə.rəl, ˈplɔː-/	(US) /ˈplʊr.əl/
burn	/bɜːn/	(US) /bɝːn/
hurry	/ˈhʌr.i/	(US) /ˈhɝː.i/

In weak syllables

The vowel letter **u** is realised as one of /jə/, /jʊ/, /ə/ or /ʊ/ in weak syllables, e.g.:

failure	/ˈfeɪ.ljəʳ/	(US) /ˈfeɪl.jɚ/
accurate	/ˈæk.jə.rət, -jʊ-/	(US) /-jɚ.ət, -jʊ.rət/
status	/ˈsteɪ.təs/	(US) /ˈstæţ̬əs/
July	/dʒʊˈlaɪ/	

It may also result in a syllabic consonant, e.g.:

hopeful	/ˈhəʊp.fəl, -fʊl/	(US) /ˈhoʊp-/

u (U) juː **-'s** -z
UAE ˌjuː.eɪˈiː
UB40 ˌjuː.biːˈfɔː.ti (US) -ˈfɔːr.ţi **-s** -z
Ubbelohde ˈʌb.əl.əʊd (US) -oʊd
U-bend ˈjuː.bend **-s** -z
Übermensch ˈuː.bə.mentʃ (US) -bɚ- **-en** -ən
ubiquitarian (U) juːˌbɪk.wɪˈteə.ri.ən, ˌjuː.bɪ.kwɪˈ- (US) juːˌbɪk.wəˈter.i- **-s** -z
ubiquitous juːˈbɪk.wɪ.təs (US) -wə.ţəs **-ly** -li **-ness** -nəs, -nɪs
ubiquity juːˈbɪk.wə.ti, -wɪ- (US) -wə.ţi
U-boat ˈjuː.bəʊt (US) -boʊt **-s** -s
Ubu Roi ˌuː.buːˈrwɑː
UCAS, Ucas ˈjuː.kæs
UCATT ˈʌk.ət, ˈjuː.kæt
UCCA ˈʌk.ə
Uccello uːˈtʃel.əʊ (US) -oʊ
Uckfield ˈʌk.fiːld
UDA ˌjuː.diːˈeɪ
Udall ˈjuː.dəl (US) -dɔːl, -dɑːl, -dəl
udder ˈʌd.əʳ (US) -ɚ **-s** -z
Uddin ˈʌd.ɪn
Uddingston ˈʌd.ɪŋ.stən
UDI ˌjuː.diːˈaɪ
Udolpho uːˈdɒl.fəʊ, juː- (US) -ˈdɑːl.foʊ
udometer juːˈdɒm.ɪ.təʳ, ˈ-ə- (US) -ˈdɑː.mə.ţɚ **-s** -z
UDR ˌjuː.diːˈɑːʳ (US) -ˈɑːr
UEFA, Uefa juːˈeɪ.fə, -ˈiː-
Uffizi juːˈfɪt.si, uː-, -ˈfiːt-
UFO ˌjuː.efˈəʊ (US) -ˈoʊ **-('**)**s** -z
ufolog|y juːˈfɒl.ə.dʒ|i (US) -ˈfɑː.lə- **-ist/s** -ɪst/s
Ugand|a juːˈgæn.d|ə, jʊ- (US) juː-, uː- **-an/s** -ən/z
Ugaritic ˌuː.gəˈrɪt.ɪk, ˌjuː- (US) -gəˈrɪţ-
ugh ɜːx, ɜːh, ʌx, ʊɸ, ʊh, ɜːh, ʌg
Note: Used to indicate disgust.
ugli ˈʌg.li **-s** -z **ˈugli ˌfruit**
uglification ˌʌg.lɪ.fɪˈkeɪ.ʃən, -lə-
ugli|fy ˈʌg.lɪ|.faɪ **-fies** -faɪz **-fying** -faɪ.ɪŋ **-fied** -faɪd
ugl|y ˈʌg.l|i **-ier** -i.əʳ (US) -i.ɚ **-iest** -i.ɪst, -i.əst **-iness** -ɪ.nəs, -ɪ.nɪs **ˌugly ˈduckling**
Ugrian ˈuː.gri.ən, ˈjuː- **-s** -z
Ugric ˈuː.grɪk, ˈjuː-
UHF ˌjuː.eɪtʃˈef
uh-huh ʌˈhʌ, ˈʌ.hʌ
uhlan ˈuː.lɑːn, ˈjuː-, -lən; uːˈlɑːn, juː- **-s** -z
Uhland ˈuː.lənd, -lænd, -lɑːnd (US) -lɑːnt, -lɑːnd
UHT ˌjuː.eɪtʃˈtiː *stress shift, see compound:* **ˌUHT ˈmilk**
Uhu® ˈjuː.huː, ˈuː-
uh-uh ˈʌʔ.ʌʔ (US) ˈʌ̃ʔ.ʌ̃
Note: Used to indicate alarm or anxiety.
uhuru (U) uːˈhuː.ruː, -ˈhʊə-
Uig ˈuː.ɪg, ˈjuː-
Uist ˈjuː.ɪst
uitlander (U) ˈeɪtˌlæn.dəʳ, ˈɔɪt- (US) ˈɔɪtˌlæn.dɚ, ˈeɪt-, ˈaɪt- **-s** -z
UK ˌjuːˈkeɪ *stress shift:* ˌUK ˈcitizen
ukas|e juːˈkeɪz, -ˈkeɪs (US) juːˈkeɪz, -ˈkeɪs, ˈ-- **-es** -ɪz
uke juːk **-s** -s
ukelele ˌjuː.kəlˈeɪ.li (US) -kəˈleɪ- **-s** -z
Ukraine juːˈkreɪn (US) -ˈkreɪn, ˈjuː.kreɪn
ukulele ˌjuː.kəlˈeɪ.li (US) -kəˈleɪ- **-s** -z
ulan ˈuː.lɑːn, ˈjuː-, -lən; uːˈlɑːn, juː- **-s** -z
Ulan Bator uːˌlɑːnˈbɑː.tɔːʳ (US) ˌuː.lɑːnˈbɑː.tɔːr
Ulan-Ude uːˌlɑːn.uːˈdeɪ (US) uːˌlɑːn.uːˈdeɪ, uːˈlɑːn.uːˌdeɪ
ulcer ˈʌl.səʳ (US) -sɚ **-s** -z
ulcer|ate ˈʌl.sər|.eɪt (US) -sə.r|eɪt **-ates** -eɪts **-ating** -eɪ.tɪŋ (US) -eɪ.ţɪŋ **-ated** -eɪ.tɪd (US) -eɪ.ţɪd
ulceration ˌʌl.sərˈeɪ.ʃən (US) -səˈreɪ- **-s** -z
ulcerative ˈʌl.sər.ə.tɪv, -eɪ- (US) -sə.reɪ.ţɪv, -sɚ.ə-
ulcerous ˈʌl.sər.əs
ulema ˈuː.lɪ.mə, -lə-, -mɑː; ˌuː.lɪˈmɑː, -ləˈ- (US) ˌuː.ləˈmɑː, ˈ--- **-s** -z
Ulfilas ˈʊl.fɪ.læs, -fə-, -ləs (US) ˈʌl.fɪ.ləs
Ulgham ˈʌf.əm
ullage ˈʌl.ɪdʒ

Pronouncing the letters UE

The vowel digraph **ue** is most commonly pronounced as /juː/ or /uː/. The /j/ sound is not always present in US English where it is found in British English. In general, the /j/ is dropped in US English where it appears in British English following an alveolar consonant such as /t/, /d/ or /n/, e.g.:

cue	/kjuː/	
due	/djuː/	ⓊⓈ /duː/

Another possible pronunciation is /juː.ə/ or /jʊə/, e.g.:

dual	/ˈdjuː.əl, djʊəl/	ⓊⓈ /ˈduː.ᵊl/

In addition

Other sounds are associated with the digraph **ue**, e.g.:

/weɪ/	suede	/sweɪd/
/e/	guess	/ges/
/uː.ɪ/	suet, bluest	/ˈsuː.ɪt/, /ˈbluː.ɪst/
silent	league	/liːg/

Pronouncing the letters UI

There are several pronunciation possibilities for the vowel digraph **ui**. The most common is likely to be /uː/, e.g.:

fruit	/fruːt/

A similar pronunciation is /juː/ in British English, realised as /uː/ in US English, e.g.:

nuisance	/ˈnjuː.sᵊnts/	ⓊⓈ /ˈnuː-/
suit	/sjuːt, suːt/	ⓊⓈ /suːt/

In addition

Other sounds are associated with the digraph **ui**, e.g.:

/wiː/	suite	/swiːt/
/wɪ/	linguist	/ˈlɪŋ.gwɪst/
/ɪ/	build	/bɪld/
/aɪ/	guide	/gaɪd/
/u.ɪ/	fruition	/fruˈɪʃ.ᵊn/
/uː.ɪ/	ruin	/ˈruː.ɪn/

It should also be noted that **ui** may follow **q,** producing the sound /kwɪ/ or /kwaɪ/.

Ullah ˈʌl.ə
Ullapool ˈʌl.ə.puːl
Ullman(n) ˈʊl.mən, ˈʌl- ⓊⓈ ˈʌl-, ˈʊl-
Ullswater ˈʌlzˌwɔː.təʳ ⓊⓈ -ˌwɑː.t̬ɚ, -ˌwɔː-
Ulm ʊlm
uln|a ˈʌl.n|ə **-as** -əz **-ae** -iː **-ar** -əʳ ⓊⓈ -ɚ
Ulrica ˈʊl.rɪkə, ˈʌl-
Ulrich ˈʊl.rɪk *as if German:* -rɪx ⓊⓈ ˈʌl-, ˈʊl-
Ulrika ʊlˈriː.kə
Ulster, ulster ˈʌl.stəʳ ⓊⓈ -stɚ **-s** -z
Ulster|man ˈʌl.stə|.mən ⓊⓈ -stɚ- **-men** -mən
Ulster|woman ˈʌl.stəˌ|wʊm.ən ⓊⓈ -stɚ- **-women** -ˌwɪm.ɪn
ulterior ʌlˈtɪə.ri.əʳ ⓊⓈ -ˈtɪr.i.ɚ **-ly** -li **ulˌterior ˈmotive**
ultima ˈʌl.tɪ.mə, -tə- ⓊⓈ -t̬ɪ- **ˌultima ˈThule**
ultimate ˈʌl.tɪ.mət, -tə-, -mət ⓊⓈ -t̬ə.mɪt **-ly** -li
ultimat|um ˌʌl.tɪˈmeɪ.t|əm ⓊⓈ -t̬əˈmeɪ.t̬|əm **-ums** -əmz **-a** -ə
ultimo ˈʌl.tɪ.məʊ, -tə- ⓊⓈ -t̬ɪ.moʊ
ultra- ʌl.trə-
Note: Prefix. Normally takes primary or secondary stress on the first syllable, e.g. **ultrasound** /ˈʌl.trə.saʊnd/, **ultrasonic** /ˌʌl.trəˈsɒn.ɪk ⓊⓈ -ˈsɑː.nɪk/.
ultra ˈʌl.trə **-s** -z
ultra-high frequenc|y ˌʌl.trə,haɪˈfriː.kwənt.s|i **-ies** -iz
ultramarine ˌʌl.trə.məˈriːn *stress shift:* ˌultramarine ˈblue
ultramodern ˌʌl.trəˈmɒd.ən ⓊⓈ -ˈmɑː.dɚn **-ist/s** -ɪst/s *stress shift:* ˌultramodern ˈstyling
ultramontane ˌʌl.trəˈmɒn.teɪn, -mɒnˈteɪn ⓊⓈ -ˈmɑːn.teɪn, -mɑːnˈteɪn
ultramontanism (U) ˌʌl.trəˈmɒn.tə.nɪ.zᵊm, -tɪ-, -teɪ- ⓊⓈ -ˈmɑːn.tə-
ultrasonic ˌʌl.trəˈsɒn.ɪk ⓊⓈ -ˈsɑː.nɪk **-s** -s **-ally** -ᵊl.i, -li *stress shift:* ˌultrasonic ˈscanner
ultrasound ˈʌl.trə.saʊnd
ultraviolet ˌʌl.trəˈvaɪə.lət, -lɪt ⓊⓈ -lɪt *stress shift, see compound:* **ˌultraviolet ˈlight**
ultra vires ˌʌl.trəˈvaɪə.riːz, ˌʊl.trɑːˈvɪə.reɪz ⓊⓈ ˌʌl.trəˈvaɪ.riːz
ululant ˈjuː.ljə.lənt, ˈʌl.jə-, -jʊ- ⓊⓈ ˈjuːl.juː.lənt, ˈʌl-, -jə-
ulu|late ˈjuː.ljə|.leɪt, ˈʌl.jə-, -jʊ- ⓊⓈ ˈjuːl.juː-, ˈʌl-, -jə- **-lates** -leɪts **-lating** -leɪ.tɪŋ ⓊⓈ -leɪ.t̬ɪŋ **-lated** -leɪ.tɪd ⓊⓈ -leɪ.t̬ɪd
ululation ˌjuː.ljəˈleɪ.ʃᵊn, ˌʌl.jəˈ-, -jʊˈ- ⓊⓈ ˌjuːl.juːˈ-, ˌʌl-, -jəˈ- **-s** -z
Uluru uːˈluː.ruː; ˌʊl.əˈruː
Ulverston ˈʌl.və.stən ⓊⓈ -vɚ-
Ulyanovsk ʊlˈjɑː.nɒfsk ⓊⓈ uːlˈjɑː.nɔːfsk
Ulysses ˈjuː.lɪ.siːz; juːˈlɪs.iːz ⓊⓈ juːˈlɪs-
umbel ˈʌm.bəl, -bel **-s** -z
umbellifer ʌmˈbel.ɪ.fəʳ ⓊⓈ -fɚ **umbelliferae** ˌʌm.bᵊlˈɪf.ᵊr.iː, -belˈ- ⓊⓈ -bəˈlɪf.ə.riː
umbelliferous ˌʌm.bᵊlˈɪf.ᵊr.əs, -belˈ- ⓊⓈ -bəˈlɪf-
umber ˈʌm.bəʳ ⓊⓈ -bɚ **-s** -z
Umberto ʊmˈbeə.təʊ, -ˈbɜː- ⓊⓈ -ˈber.toʊ
umbilical ʌmˈbɪl.ɪ.kl̩, ˈ-ə-, ˌʌm.bɪˈlaɪ-, -bəˈ- ⓊⓈ ʌmˈbɪl.ɪ-, ˈ-ə- **umˌbilical ˈcord, ˌumbiˌlical ˈcord** ⓊⓈ **umˈbilical ˌcord**
umbilic|us ʌmˈbɪl.ɪ.k|əs, ˈ-ə-; ˌʌm.bɪˈlaɪ-, -bəˈ- **-uses** -ə.sɪz **-i** -aɪ
umbles ˈʌm.bl̩z

um|bo 'ʌm|.bəʊ US -boʊ **-bos** -bəʊz US -boʊz **-bones** -'bəʊ.neɪz US -'boʊ-

umbr|a 'ʌm.br|ə **-as** -əz **-ae** -iː **-al** -ᵊl

umbrage 'ʌm.brɪdʒ

umbrageous ʌm'breɪ.dʒəs **-ly** -li **-ness** -nəs, -nɪs

umbrated 'ʌm.breɪ.tɪd US -t̬ɪd

umbration ʌm'breɪ.ʃᵊn **-s** -z

umbrella ʌm'brel.ə **-s** -z

Umbri|a 'ʌm.bri|.ə **-an/s** -ən/z

Umbro® 'ʌm.brəʊ US -broʊ

Umfreville 'ʌm.frə.vɪl

umiak 'uː.mi.æk, -mjæk **-s** -s

umlaut 'ʊm.laʊt **-s** -s

umpirag|e 'ʌm.paɪ.ᵊr.ɪdʒ **-es** -ɪz

umpir|e 'ʌm.paɪəʳ US -paɪɚ **-es** -z **-ing** -ɪŋ **-ed** -d

umpteen ʌmp'tiːn **-th** -θ *stress shift:* ˌumpteen 'times

un- ʌn-

Note: Prefix. It may be unstressed, usually when a stressed syllable follows it and it is a frequently-used word, e.g. **unable** /ʌn'eɪ.bl̩/. Otherwise it will have secondary stress, e.g. **unadvisable** /ˌʌn.əd'vaɪ.zə.bl̩/. This syllable frequently becomes the main stress in the word through stress-shift, e.g. **unattended** /ˌʌn.ə'ten.dɪd/, **unattended parking** /ˌʌn.ə.ten.dɪd'pɑː.kɪŋ US -'pɑːr-/. There are so many such cases that individual examples are not given for each word.

'un ən **-s** -z

Note: Old-fashioned colloquial form for 'one', as in 'little 'un'.

UN ˌjuː'en

Una 'juː.nə, 'uː-

unabash|ed ˌʌn.ə'bæʃ|t **-edly** -ɪd.li

unabated ˌʌn.ə'beɪ.tɪd US -t̬ɪd **-ly** -li

unable ʌn'eɪ.bl̩, ˌʌn-

Unabomber 'juː.nəˌbɒm.əʳ US -ˌbɑː.mɚ

unabridged ˌʌn.ə'brɪdʒd

unaccented ˌʌn.ək'sen.tɪd, -æk'- US ʌn'æk.sen.t̬ɪd

unacceptability ˌʌn.ək.sep.tə'bɪl.ə.ti, -ɪ.ti US -ə.t̬i

unaccepta|ble ˌʌn.ək'sep.tə|.bl̩, -æk'- **-bly** -bli

unaccompanied ˌʌn.ə'kʌm.pə.nid, -'kʌmp.nid

unaccountability ˌʌn.əˌkaʊn.tə'bɪl.ɪ.ti, -ə.ti US -t̬ə'bɪl.ə.t̬i

unaccountab|le ˌʌn.ə'kaʊn.tə.bl|̩ US -t̬ə- **-ly** -li **-leness** -l̩.nəs, -nɪs

unaccounted ˌʌn.ə'kaʊn.tɪd US -t̬ɪd ˌ**unac'counted** ˌ**for**

unaccustomed ˌʌn.ə'kʌs.təmd **-ly** -li

unacknowledged ˌʌn.ək'nɒl.ɪdʒd US -'nɑː.lɪdʒd

unacquainted ˌʌn.ə'kweɪn.tɪd US -t̬ɪd

unadaptable ˌʌn.ə'dæp.tə.bl̩

unaddressed ˌʌn.ə'drest

unadopted ˌʌn.ə'dɒp.tɪd US -'dɑːp-

unadorned ˌʌn.ə'dɔːnd US -'dɔːrnd

unadulterated ˌʌn.ə'dʌl.tᵊr.eɪ.tɪd US -t̬ə.reɪ.t̬ɪd

unadvised ˌʌn.əd'vaɪzd

unadvisedly ˌʌn.əd'vaɪ.zɪd.li

unaffected ˌʌn.ə'fek.tɪd **-ly** -li **-ness** -nəs, -nɪs

unaffectionate ˌʌn.ə'fek.ʃᵊn.ət **-ly** -li

unafraid ˌʌn.ə'freɪd

unaided ʌn'eɪ.dɪd, ˌʌn-

unalienab|le ʌn'eɪ.li.ə.nə.bl|̩, ˌʌn-, '-ljə- US -li.ə-, -'eɪl.jə- **-ly** -li

unaligned ˌʌn.ə'laɪnd

unalloyed ˌʌn.ə'lɔɪd

unalterability ʌnˌɔːl.tᵊr.ə'bɪl.ɪ.ti, ˌʌn-, -ə.ti US -ˌɑːl.t̬ɚ.ə'bɪl.ə.t̬i, -ˌɔːl-

unalterab|le ʌn'ɔːl.tᵊr.ə.bl|̩, ˌʌn- US -'ɔːl.t̬ɚ-, -'ɑːl- **-ly** -li **-leness** -l̩.nəs US -nɪs

unaltered ʌn'ɔːl.təd, ˌʌn- US -t̬ɚd, -'ɑːl-

unambiguous ˌʌn.æm'bɪg.ju.əs **-ly** -li **-ness** -nəs, -nɪs

unambivalent ˌʌn.æm'bɪv.ᵊl.ənt **-ly** -li

un-American ˌʌn.ə'mer.ɪ.kən

unanalysab|le ʌnˌæn.ᵊl'aɪ.zə.bl|̩, ˌʌn-, -'æn.ᵊl.aɪ- US -ˌæn.ə'laɪ-, -'æn.ə.laɪ- **-ly** -li **-leness** -l̩.nəs, -nɪs

unanimity ˌjuː.nə'nɪm.ə.ti, -næn'ɪm-, -ɪ.ti US -nə'nɪm.ə.t̬i

unanimous juː'næn.ɪ.məs, '-ə- US '-ə- **-ly** -li **-ness** -nəs, -nɪs, -nəs

unannounced ˌʌn.ə'naʊntst

unanswerability ʌnˌɑːnt.sᵊr.ə'bɪl.ɪ.ti, ˌʌn-, -ə.ti US -ˌænt.sɚ.ə'bɪl.ə.t̬i

unanswerab|le ʌn'ɑːnt.sᵊr.ə.bl|̩, ˌʌn- US -'ænt- **-ly** -li

unanswered ʌn'ɑːnt.səd, ˌʌn- US -'ænt.sɚd

unappealing ˌʌn.ə'piː.lɪŋ **-ly** -li

unappeasable ˌʌn.ə'piː.zə.bl̩

unappeased ˌʌn.ə'piːzd

unappetizing, -ising ʌn'æp.ɪ.taɪ.zɪŋ, ˌʌn-, '-ə- US '-ə- **-ly** -li

unapplied ˌʌn.ə'plaɪd

unappreciated ˌʌn.ə'priː.ʃi.eɪ.tɪd US -t̬ɪd

unappreciative ˌʌn.ə'priː.ʃi.ə.tɪv US -t̬ɪv **-ly** -li

unapproachability ˌʌn.əˌprəʊ.tʃə'bɪl.ɪ.ti, -ə.ti US -ˌproʊ.tʃə'bɪl.ə.t̬i

unapproachab|le ˌʌn.ə'prəʊ.tʃə.bl|̩ US -'proʊ- **-ly** -bli **-leness** -bl̩.nəs, -nɪs

unappropriate ˌʌn.ə'prəʊ.pri.ət US -'proʊ- **-ly** -li **-ness** -nəs, -nɪs

unappropriated ˌʌn.ə'prəʊ.pri.eɪ.tɪd US -'proʊ.pri.eɪ.t̬ɪd

unapproved ˌʌn.ə'pruːvd

unapt ʌn'æpt **-ly** -li **-ness** -nəs, -nɪs

unarguab|le ʌn'ɑː.gju.ə.bl|̩ US -'ɑːr- **-ly** -li **-leness** -l̩.nəs, -nɪs

unarm ʌn'ɑːm, ˌʌn- US -'ɑːrm **-s** -z **-ing** -ɪŋ **-ed** -d ˌ**unarmed** '**combat**

unarticulated ˌʌn.ɑː'tɪk.jə.leɪ.tɪd, -jʊ- US -ɑːr'tɪk.jə.leɪ.t̬ɪd

unary 'juː.nᵊr.i

unasha|med ˌʌn.ə'ʃeɪ|md **-medly** -mɪd.li **-medness** -mɪd.nəs, -nɪs

unasked ʌn'ɑːskt, ˌʌn- US -'æskt

unaspirated ʌn'æs.pᵊr.eɪ.tɪd, ˌʌn- US -pə.reɪ.t̬ɪd

unassailability ˌʌn.əˌseɪ.lə'bɪl.ɪ.ti, -ə.ti US -ə.t̬i

unassailab|le ˌʌn.ə'seɪ.lə.bl|̩ **-ly** -li **-leness** -l̩.nəs, -nɪs

unassertive ˌʌn.ə'sɜː.tɪv US -'sɝː.t̬ɪv **-ly** -li **-ness** -nəs, -nɪs

unassigned ˌʌn.ə'saɪnd

unassimilated ˌʌn.ə'sɪm.ᵊl.eɪ.tɪd, -ɪ.leɪ- US -t̬ɪd

unassisted ˌʌn.ə'sɪs.tɪd

unassuageable ˌʌn.ə'sweɪ.dʒə.bl̩

unassuming ˌʌn.ə'sjuː.mɪŋ US, -'suː- US -'suː- **-ly** -li **-ness** -nəs, -nɪs

unattached ˌʌn.ə'tætʃt

unattainab|le ˌʌn.ə'teɪ.nə.bl|̩ **-ly** -li **-ness** -nəs, -nɪs

unattended ˌʌn.ə'ten.dɪd

unattested ˌʌn.ə'tes.tɪd

unattractive ˌʌn.ə'træk.tɪv **-ly** -li **-ness** -nəs, -nɪs

unauthenticated ˌʌn.ɔː'θen.tɪ.keɪ.tɪd US -ɑː'θen.t̬ɪ.keɪ.t̬ɪd, -ɔː'-

unauthorized, -ised ʌn'ɔː.θᵊr.aɪzd, ˌʌn- US -'ɑː.θə.raɪzd, -'ɔː-

unavailability ˌʌn.əˌveɪ.lə'bɪl.ɪ.ti, -ə.ti US -ə.t̬i

unavailable ˌʌn.ə'veɪ.lə.bl̩

unavailing ˌʌn.ə'veɪ.lɪŋ **-ly** -li **-ness** -nəs, -nɪs

unavenged ˌʌn.ə'ven*d*ʒd

unavoidab|le ˌʌn.ə'vɔɪ.də.bl|̩ **-ly** -li

unaware ˌʌn.ə'weəʳ US -'wer **-s** -z **-ly** -li **-ness** -nəs, -nɪs

unbalanc|e ʌn'bæl.ən*t*s, ˌʌn-, ʌm-, ˌʌm- US ʌn-, ˌʌn- **-es** -ɪz **-ing** -ɪŋ **-ed** -t

unbaptized ˌʌn.bæp'taɪzd, ˌʌm- US ʌn'bæp.taɪzd

unbar ʌn'bɑːʳ, ˌʌn-, ʌm-, ˌʌm- US ʌn'bɑːr, ˌʌn- **-s** -z **-ring** -ɪŋ **-red** -d

unbearab|le ʌn'beə.rə.bl|̩, ˌʌn-, ʌm-, ˌʌm- US ʌn'ber.ə-, -nəs, ˌʌn- **-ly** -li **-leness** -l̩.nəs, -nɪs

unbeatab|le ʌn'biː.tə.bl|̩, ˌʌn-, ʌm-, ˌʌm- US ʌn'biː.t̬ə-, ˌʌn- **-ly** -li

unbeaten ʌn'biː.tᵊn, ˌʌn-, ʌm-, ˌʌm- US ʌn-, ˌʌn-

unbecoming ˌʌn.bɪˈkʌm.ɪŋ, ˌʌm-, -bəˈ- ⓤⓢ ˌʌn- **-ly** -li **-ness** -nəs, -nɪs
unbegotten ˌʌn.bɪˈɡɒt.ᵊn, ˌʌm-, -bəˈ- ⓤⓢ ˌʌn.bɪˈɡɑː.tᵊn, -bəˈ-
unbeknown ˌʌn.bɪˈnəʊn, ˌʌm-, -bəˈ- ⓤⓢ ˌʌn.bɪˈnoʊn, -bəˈ- **-st** -tst
unbelief ˌʌn.bɪˈliːf, ˌʌm-, -bəˈ- ⓤⓢ ˌʌn-
unbelievab|le ˌʌn.bɪˈliː.və.b|l̩, ˌʌm-, -bəˈ- ⓤⓢ ˌʌn- **-ly** -li
unbeliever ˌʌn.bɪˈliː.vəʳ, ˌʌm-, -bəˈ- ⓤⓢ ˌʌn.bɪˈliː.vɚ, -bəˈ- **-s** -z
unbelieving ˌʌn.bɪˈliː.vɪŋ, ˌʌm-, -bəˈ- ⓤⓢ ˌʌn- **-ly** -li
un|bend ʌnˈbend, ˌʌn-, ʌm-, ˌʌm- ⓤⓢ ʌn-, ˌʌn- **-bends** -ˈbendz **-bending** -ˈben.dɪŋ **-bended** -ˈben.dɪd **-bent** -ˈbent
unbeneficed ʌnˈben.ɪ.fɪst, ˌʌn-, ʌm-, ˌʌm- ⓤⓢ ʌn-, ˌʌn-
unbias(s)ed ʌnˈbaɪəst, ˌʌn-, ʌm-, ˌʌm- ⓤⓢ ʌn-, ˌʌn- **-ness** -nəs, -nɪs
unbidden ʌnˈbɪd.ᵊn, ˌʌn-, ʌm-, ˌʌm- ⓤⓢ ʌn-, ˌʌn-
un|bind ʌn|ˈbaɪnd, ˌʌn-, ʌm-, ˌʌm- ⓤⓢ ʌn-, ˌʌn- **-binds** -ˈbaɪndz **-binding** -ˈbaɪn.dɪŋ **-bound** -ˈbaʊnd
unbleached ʌnˈbliːtʃt, ˌʌn-, ʌm-, ˌʌm- ⓤⓢ ʌn-, ˌʌn-
unblemished ʌnˈblem.ɪʃt, ˌʌn-, ʌm-, ˌʌm- ⓤⓢ ʌn-, ˌʌn-
unblinking ʌnˈblɪŋ.kɪŋ, ʌm- ⓤⓢ ʌn- **-ly** -li **-ness** -nəs, -nɪs
unblock ʌnˈblɒk, ʌm- ⓤⓢ ʌnˈblɑːk **-s** -s **-ing** -ɪŋ **-ed** -t **-er/s** -əʳ/z ⓤⓢ -ɚ/z
unblushing ʌnˈblʌʃ.ɪŋ, ˌʌn-, ʌm-, ˌʌm- ⓤⓢ ʌn-, ˌʌn- **-ly** -li
un|bolt ʌn|ˈbəʊlt, ˌʌn-, ʌm-, ˌʌm- ⓤⓢ ʌn|ˈboʊlt, ˌʌn- **-bolts** -ˈbəʊlts ⓤⓢ -ˈboʊlts **-bolting** -ˈbəʊl.tɪŋ ⓤⓢ -ˈboʊl.t̬ɪŋ **-bolted** -ˈbəʊl.tɪd ⓤⓢ -ˈboʊl.t̬ɪd
unborn ʌnˈbɔːn, ˈʌn-, ʌm-, ˌʌm- ⓤⓢ ʌnˈbɔːrn, ˌʌn- ˌ**unborn** ˈ**child**
unbosom ʌnˈbʊz.əm, ˌʌn-, ʌm-, ˌʌm- ⓤⓢ ʌn-, ˌʌn- **-s** -z **-ing** -ɪŋ **-ed** -d
unbound ʌnˈbaʊnd, ˌʌn-, ʌm-, ˌʌm- ⓤⓢ ʌn-, ˌʌn-
unbounded ʌnˈbaʊn.dɪd, ˌʌn-, ʌm-, ˌʌm- ⓤⓢ ʌn-, ˌʌn- **-ness** -nəs, -nɪs
unbowed ʌnˈbaʊd, ˌʌn-, ʌm-, ˌʌm- ⓤⓢ ʌn-, ˌʌn-
unbridled ʌnˈbraɪ.dl̩d, ˌʌn-, ʌm-, ˌʌm- ⓤⓢ ʌn-, ˌʌn-
unbroken ʌnˈbrəʊ.kᵊn, ˌʌn-, ʌm-, ˌʌm- ⓤⓢ ʌnˈbroʊ-, ˌʌn-
unbuckl|e ʌnˈbʌk.l̩, ˌʌn-, ʌm-, ˌʌm- ⓤⓢ ʌn-, ˌʌn- **-es** -z **-ing** -ɪŋ, -ˈbʌk.lɪŋ **-ed** -d
unbuilt ʌnˈbɪlt, ʌm- ⓤⓢ ʌn-
unburden ʌnˈbɜː.dᵊn, ˌʌn-, ʌm-, ˌʌm- ⓤⓢ ʌnˈbɝː-, ˌʌn- **-s** -z **-ing** -ɪŋ **-ed** -d
unburied ʌnˈber.id, ˌʌn-, ʌm-, ˌʌm- ⓤⓢ ʌn-, ˌʌn-
unbusiness-like ʌnˈbɪz.nɪs.laɪk, -nəs-, ˌʌn-, ʌm-, ˌʌm- ⓤⓢ ʌn-, ˌʌn-
unbutton ʌnˈbʌt.ᵊn, ˌʌn-, ʌm-, ˌʌm- ⓤⓢ ʌn-, ˌʌn- **-s** -z **-ing** -ɪŋ, -ˈbʌt.nɪŋ **-ed** -d
uncalculat|ed ʌnˈkæl.kjə.leɪ.t|ɪd, ʌŋ-, -kjʊ- ⓤⓢ ʌn- **-ing** -ɪŋ
uncalled-for ʌnˈkɔːld.fɔːʳ, ˌʌn-, ʌŋ-, ˌʌŋ- ⓤⓢ ʌnˈkɔːld.fɔːr, ˌʌn-, -ˈkɑːld-
uncann|y ʌnˈkæn|.i, ˌʌn-, ʌŋ-, ˌʌŋ- ⓤⓢ ʌn-, ˌʌn- **-ier** -i.əʳ ⓤⓢ -i.ɚ **-iest** -i.ɪst, -i.əst **-ily** -ɪ.li, -ᵊl.i **-iness** -ɪ.nəs, -ɪ.nɪs
uncanonical ˌʌn.kəˈnɒn.ɪ.kᵊl, ˌʌŋ- ⓤⓢ ˌʌn.kəˈnɑː.nɪ-
uncap ʌnˈkæp, ˌʌn-, ʌŋ-, ˌʌŋ- ⓤⓢ ʌn-, ˌʌn- **-s** -s **-ping** -ɪŋ **-ped** -t
uncared-for ʌnˈkeəd.fɔːʳ, ˌʌn-, ʌŋ-, ˌʌŋ- ⓤⓢ ʌnˈkerd.fɔːr, ˌʌn-
uncaring ʌnˈkeə.rɪŋ, ʌŋ- ⓤⓢ ʌn- **-ly** -li **-ness** -nəs, -nɪs
Uncas ˈʌŋ.kəs
uncatalog(u)ed ʌnˈkæt.ᵊl.ɒɡd, ˌʌn-, ʌŋ-, ˌʌŋ- ⓤⓢ ʌnˈkæt̬.ᵊl.ɑːɡd, ˌʌn-, -ɔːɡd
unceasing ʌnˈsiː.sɪŋ, ˌʌn- **-ly** -li **-ness** -nəs, -nɪs
uncensored ʌnˈsen*t*.səd, ˌʌn- ⓤⓢ -sɚd
unceremonious ʌnˌser.ɪˈməʊ.ni.əs, ˌʌn-, -əˈ- ⓤⓢ -ˈmoʊ- **-ly** -li **-ness** -nəs, -nɪs
uncertain ʌnˈsɜː.tᵊn, ˌʌn- ⓤⓢ -ˈsɝː- **-ly** -li
uncertaint|y ʌnˈsɜː.tᵊn.t|i, ˌʌn- ⓤⓢ -ˈsɝː.tᵊn.t̬|i **-ies** -iz
unchain ʌnˈtʃeɪn, ˌʌn- **-s** -z **-ing** -ɪŋ **-ed** -d
unchallenged ʌnˈtʃæl.ɪndʒd, ˌʌn-, -əndʒd
unchangeability ʌnˌtʃeɪn.dʒəˈbɪl.ɪ.ti, ˌʌn-, -ə.ti ⓤⓢ -ə.t̬i
unchangeab|le ʌnˈtʃeɪn.dʒə.b|l̩, ˌʌn- **-ly** -li **-leness** -l̩.nəs, -nɪs
unchanged ʌnˈtʃeɪndʒd, ˌʌn-
unchanging ʌnˈtʃeɪn.dʒɪŋ, ˌʌn-
uncharacteristic ˌʌn.kær.ək.tᵊrˈɪs.tɪk, ʌnˈkær-, ˌʌŋ- ⓤⓢ ʌnˌker.ɪk.təˈrɪs.tɪk, -ˌkær- **-ally** -ᵊl.i, -li
uncharged ʌnˈtʃɑːdʒd, ˌʌn- ⓤⓢ -ˈtʃɑːrdʒd
uncharitab|le ʌnˈtʃær.ɪ.tə.b|l̩, ˌʌn-, ˈ-ə- ⓤⓢ -ˈtʃer.ə.t̬ə-, -ˈtʃær- **-ly** -li **-leness** -l̩.nəs, -nɪs
uncharted ʌnˈtʃɑː.tɪd, ˌʌn- ⓤⓢ -ˈtʃɑːr.t̬ɪd **un**ˌ**charted** ˈ**waters**, ˌ**uncharted** ˈ**waters**
unchartered ʌnˈtʃɑː.təd, ˌʌn- ⓤⓢ -ˈtʃɑːr.t̬ɚd
unchaste ʌnˈtʃeɪst ⓤⓢ ˌʌn- **-ly** -li
unchastened ʌnˈtʃeɪ.sᵊnd, ˌʌn-
unchecked ʌnˈtʃekt, ˌʌn-
unchivalrous ʌnˈʃɪv.ᵊl.rəs **-ly** -li **-ness** -nəs, -nɪs
unchristian ʌnˈkrɪs.tʃən, ˌʌn-, ʌŋ-, ˌʌŋ-, -ˈkrɪʃ-, -ti.ən ⓤⓢ ʌnˈkrɪs-, ˌʌn-
uncial ˈʌn*t*.si.əl ⓤⓢ -ʃi-, ˈ-ʃᵊl **-s** -z
unciform ˈʌn*t*.sɪ.fɔːm ⓤⓢ -fɔːrm
uncinate ˈʌn.sɪ.nɪt, -neɪt, -nət
uncircumcised ʌnˈsɜː.kəm.saɪzd, ˌʌn- ⓤⓢ -ˈsɝː-
uncircumcision ʌnˌsɜː.kəmˈsɪʒ.ᵊn, ˌʌn- ⓤⓢ -ˌsɝː-
uncivil ʌnˈsɪv.ᵊl, -ɪl, ˌʌn- **-ly** -i
uncivilized, -ised ʌnˈsɪv.ᵊl.aɪzd, ˌʌn-, -ɪ.laɪzd
unclaimed ʌnˈkleɪmd, ˌʌn-, ʌŋ-, ˌʌŋ- ⓤⓢ ʌn-, ˌʌn-
unclamp ʌnˈklæmp, ʌŋ- ⓤⓢ ʌn- **-s** -s **-ing** -ɪŋ **-ed** -t
unclasp ʌnˈklɑːsp, ˌʌn-, ʌŋ-, ˌʌŋ- ⓤⓢ ʌnˈklæsp, ˌʌn- **-s** -s **-ing** -ɪŋ **-ed** -t
unclassified ʌnˈklæs.ɪ.faɪd, ˌʌn-, ʌŋ-, ˌʌŋ- ⓤⓢ ʌn-, ˌʌn-
uncle ˈʌŋ.kl̩ **-s** -z ˌ**Uncle** ˈ**Sam**; ˌ**Uncle** ˈ**Tom**
unclean ʌnˈkliːn, ˌʌn-, ʌŋ-, ˌʌŋ- ⓤⓢ ʌn-, ˌʌn- **-ly** -li **-ness** -nəs, -nɪs
uncleanl|y ʌnˈklen.l|i, ˌʌn-, ʌŋ-, ˌʌŋ- ⓤⓢ ʌn-, ˌʌn- **-iness** -ɪ.nəs, -ɪ.nɪs
unclear ʌnˈklɪəʳ, ˌʌn-, ʌŋ-, ˌʌŋ- ⓤⓢ ʌnˈklɪr, ˌʌn-
unclench ʌnˈklentʃ, ˌʌn-, ʌŋ-, ˌʌŋ- ⓤⓢ ʌnˈklentʃ, ˌʌn- **-es** -ɪz **-ing** -ɪŋ **-ed** -t
unclog ʌnˈklɒɡ, ʌŋ- ⓤⓢ ʌnˈklɑːɡ, -ˈklɔːɡ **-s** -z **-ging** -ɪŋ **-ged** -d
unclos|e ʌnˈkləʊz, ˌʌn-, ʌŋ-, ˌʌŋ- ⓤⓢ ʌnˈkloʊz, ˌʌn- **-es** -ɪz **-ing** -ɪŋ **-ed** -d
unclothed ʌnˈkləʊðd, ˌʌn-, ʌŋ-, ˌʌŋ- ⓤⓢ ʌnˈkloʊðd, ˌʌn-
unclouded ʌnˈklaʊ.dɪd, ˌʌn-, ʌŋ-, ˌʌŋ- ⓤⓢ ʌn-, ˌʌn-
uncluttered ʌnˈklʌt.əd, ˌʌn-, ʌŋ-, ˌʌŋ- ⓤⓢ ʌnˈklʌt̬.ɚd, ˌʌn-
uncoil ʌnˈkɔɪl, ˌʌn-, ʌŋ-, ˌʌŋ- ⓤⓢ ʌn-, ˌʌn- **-s** -z **-ing** -ɪŋ **-ed** -d
uncollected ˌʌn.kəˈlek.tɪd, ˌʌŋ- ⓤⓢ ˌʌn-
uncolo(u)red ʌnˈkʌl.əd, ˌʌn-, ʌŋ-, ˌʌŋ- ⓤⓢ ʌnˈkʌl.ɚd, ˌʌn-
uncomfortab|le ʌnˈkʌmpf.tə.b|l̩, ˌʌn-, ʌŋ-, ˌʌŋ-, -ˈkʌm*p*.fə.tə- ⓤⓢ ʌnˈkʌm*p*.fɚ.t̬ə-, ˌʌn-, -ˈkʌm*p*f.tə- **-ly** -li **-leness** -l̩.nəs, -nɪs
uncommercial ˌʌn.kəˈmɜː.ʃᵊl, ˌʌŋ- ⓤⓢ ˌʌn.kəˈmɝː-
uncommercialized, -ised ˌʌn.kəˈmɜː.ʃᵊl.aɪzd, ˌʌŋ- ⓤⓢ ˌʌn.kəˈmɝː-
uncommitted ˌʌn.kəˈmɪt.ɪd, ˌʌŋ- ⓤⓢ ˌʌn.kəˈmɪt̬-

uncommon ʌnˈkɒm.ən, ˌʌn-, ʌŋ-, ˌʌŋ- (US) ʌnˈkɑː.mən, ˌʌn- **-ly** -li **-ness** -nəs, -nɪs

uncommunicable ˌʌn.kəˈmjuː.nɪ.kə.bl̩, ˌʌŋ-, -nə- (US) ˌʌn-

uncommunicated ˌʌn.kəˈmjuː.nɪ.keɪ.tɪd, ˌʌŋ-, -nə- (US) ˌʌn.kəˈmjuː.nɪ.keɪ.t̬ɪd, -nə-

uncommunicative ˌʌn.kəˈmjuː.nɪ.kə.tɪv, ˌʌŋ-, -nə-, -keɪ- (US) ˌʌn.kəˈmjuː.nɪ.kə.t̬ɪv, -nə-, -keɪ- **-ness** -nəs, -nɪs

uncompetitive ˌʌn.kəmˈpet.ɪ.tɪv, ˌʌŋ-, ˈ-ə- (US) ˌʌn.kəmˈpet̬.ə.t̬ɪv **-ly** -li **-ness** -nəs, -nɪs

uncomplaining ˌʌn.kəmˈpleɪ.nɪŋ, ˌʌŋ- (US) ˌʌn- **-ly** -li

uncompleted ˌʌn.kəmˈpliː.tɪd, ˌʌŋ- (US) ˌʌn.kəmˈpliː.t̬ɪd

uncomplicated ˌʌnˈkɒm.plɪ.keɪ.tɪd, ˌʌŋ- (US) ʌnˈkɑːm.plɪ.keɪ.t̬ɪd

uncomplimentary ʌnˌkɒm.plɪˈmen.tᵊr.i, ˌʌn-, ʌŋ-, ˌʌŋ-, -pləˈ- (US) ʌnˌkɑːm.pləˈmen.t̬ɚ-, ˌʌn-

uncompounded ˌʌn.kəmˈpaʊn.dɪd, ˌʌŋ- (US) ˌʌn-

uncomprehending ˌʌn.kɒm.prɪˈhen.dɪŋ, ˌʌŋ- (US) ˌʌn.kɑːm- **-ly** -li

uncompromising ʌnˈkɒm.prə.maɪ.zɪŋ, ˌʌn-, ʌŋ-, ˌʌŋ- (US) ʌnˈkɑːm-, ˌʌn- **-ly** -li **-ness** -nəs, -nɪs

unconcealed ˌʌn.kənˈsiːld, ˌʌŋ- (US) ˌʌn-

unconcern ˌʌn.kənˈsɜːn, ˌʌŋ- (US) ˌʌn.kənˈsɝːn **-ed** -d **-edly** -d.li, -ɪd.li **-edness** -d.nəs, -nɪs, -ɪd.nəs, -nɪs

unconditional ˌʌn.kənˈdɪʃ.ᵊn.ᵊl, ˌʌŋ-, ˈ-nᵊl (US) ˌʌn- **-ly** -i ˌ**unconditional** ˈ**offer**

unconditioned ˌʌn.kənˈdɪʃ.ᵊnd, ˌʌŋ- (US) ˌʌn-

unconfined ˌʌn.kənˈfaɪnd, ˌʌŋ- (US) ˌʌn-

unconfirmed ˌʌn.kənˈfɜːmd, ˌʌŋ- (US) ˌʌn.kənˈfɝːmd

unconformit|y ˌʌn.kənˈfɔː.mə.t|i, ˌʌŋ-, -mɪ.t|i (US) ˌʌn.kənˈfɔːr.mə.t̬|i **-ies** -iz

uncongenial ˌʌn.kənˈdʒiː.ni.əl, ˌʌŋ- (US) ˌʌn-, -jəl

uncongeniality ˌʌn.kənˌdʒiː.niˈæl.ɪ.ti, ˌʌŋ-, -ə.ti (US) ˌʌn.kənˌdʒiː.niˈæl.ə.t̬i

unconnected ˌʌn.kəˈnek.tɪd, ˌʌŋ- (US) ˌʌn- **-ness** -nəs, -nɪs

unconquerab|le ʌnˈkɒŋ.kᵊr.ə.b|l̩, ˌʌn-, ʌŋ-, ˌʌŋ- (US) ʌnˈkɑːŋ-, ˌʌn- **-ly** -li

unconquered ʌnˈkɒŋ.kəd, ˌʌn-, ʌŋ-, ˌʌŋ- (US) ʌnˈkɑːŋ.kɚd, ˌʌn-

unconscionab|le ʌnˈkɒn.*t*ʃᵊn.ə.b|l̩, ˌʌn-, ʌŋ-, ˌʌŋ- (US) ʌnˈkɑːn-, ˌʌn- **-ly** -li **-leness** -l̩.nəs, -nɪs

unconscious ʌnˈkɒn.*t*ʃəs, ˌʌn-, ʌŋ-, ˌʌŋ- (US) ʌnˈkɑːn-, ˌʌn- **-ly** -li **-ness** -nəs, -nɪs

unconsecrated ʌnˈkɒn*t*.sɪ.kreɪ.tɪd, ˌʌn-, ʌŋ-, ˌʌŋ-, -sə- (US) ʌnˈkɑːn*t*.sə-, ˌʌn-

unconsidered ˌʌn.kənˈsɪd.əd, ˌʌŋ- (US) ˌʌn.kənˈsɪd.ɚd

unconstitutional ʌnˌkɒn*t*.stɪˈtjuː.ʃᵊn.ᵊl, ˌʌn-, ʌŋ-, ˌʌŋ-, -stəˈ-, -ˈtʃuː-, -ˈtjuːʃ.nᵊl, -ˈtʃuːʃ- (US) ʌnˌkɑːn*t*.stəˈtuː-, ˌʌn-, -ˈtjuː- **-ly** -i

unconstrain|ed ˌʌn.kənˈstreɪn|d, ˌʌŋ- (US) ˌʌn- **-edly** -d.li, -ɪd.li

uncontaminated ˌʌn.kənˈtæm.ɪ.neɪ.tɪd, ˌʌŋ-, ˈ-ə- (US) ˌʌn.kənˈtæm.ɪ.neɪ.t̬ɪd, ˈ-ə-

uncontestable ˌʌn.kənˈtes.tə.bl̩, ˌʌŋ- (US) ˌʌn-

uncontested ˌʌn.kənˈtes.tɪd, ˌʌŋ- (US) ˌʌn-

uncontradicted ʌnˌkɒn.trəˈdɪk.tɪd, ˌʌn-, ʌŋ-, ˌʌŋ- (US) ʌnˌkɑːn-, ˌʌn-

uncontrollab|le ˌʌn.kənˈtrəʊ.lə.b|l̩, ˌʌŋ- (US) ˌʌn.kənˈtroʊ- **-ly** -li **-leness** -l̩.nəs, -nɪs

uncontrolled ˌʌn.kənˈtrəʊld, ˌʌŋ- (US) ˌʌn.kənˈtroʊld

unconvention|al ˌʌn.kənˈven.*t*ʃᵊn|.ᵊl, ˌʌŋ-, -ˈven*t*ʃ.n|ᵊl (US) ˌʌn.kənˈven*t*.ʃᵊn|.ᵊl, -ˈven*t*ʃ.n|ᵊl **-ally** -ᵊl.i

unconventionalit|y ˌʌn.kənˌven.*t*ʃᵊnˈæl.ə.t|i, ˌʌŋ-, -ɪ.t|i (US) ˌʌn.kənˌven.*t*ʃᵊnˈæl.ə.t̬|i **-ies** -iz

unconverted ˌʌn.kənˈvɜː.tɪd, ˌʌŋ- (US) ˌʌn.kənˈvɝː.t̬ɪd

unconvertible ˌʌn.kənˈvɜː.tə.bl̩, ˌʌŋ-, -tɪ- (US) ˌʌn.kənˈvɝː.t̬ə-

unconvinced ˌʌn.kənˈvɪn*t*st, ˌʌŋ- (US) ˌʌn-

unconvincing ˌʌn.kənˈvɪn*t*.sɪŋ, ˌʌŋ- (US) ˌʌn- **-ly** -li

uncooked ʌnˈkʊkt, ˌʌn-, ʌŋ-, ˌʌŋ- (US) ʌn-, ˌʌn-

uncool ʌnˈkuːl, ˌʌn-, ʌŋ- (US) ʌn-, ˌʌn- **-ly** -li **-ness** -nəs, -nɪs

uncooperative ˌʌn.kəʊˈɒp.ᵊr.ə.tɪv, ˌʌŋ-, ˈ-rə- (US) ˌʌn.koʊˈɑː.pɚ.ə.t̬ɪv, ˈ-prə- **-ly** -li **-ness** -nəs, -nɪs

uncoordinated ˌʌn.kəʊˈɔː.dɪ.neɪ.tɪd, ˌʌŋ- (US) ˌʌn.koʊˈɔːr.dᵊn.eɪ.t̬ɪd

uncork ʌnˈkɔːk, ˌʌn-, ʌŋ-, ˌʌŋ- (US) ʌnˈkɔːrk, ˌʌn- **-s** -s **-ing** -ɪŋ **-ed** -t

uncorrected ˌʌn.kᵊrˈek.tɪd, ˌʌŋ- (US) ˌʌn.kəˈrek-

uncorroborated ˌʌn.kᵊrˈɒb.ᵊr.eɪ.tɪd, ˌʌŋ- (US) ˌʌn.kəˈrɑː.bə.reɪ.t̬ɪd

uncorrupt ˌʌn.kᵊrˈʌpt, ˌʌŋ- (US) ˌʌn.kəˈrʌpt **-ness** -nəs, -nɪs

uncorrupted ˌʌn.kᵊrˈʌp.tɪd, ˌʌŋ- (US) ˌʌn.kəˈrʌp-

uncountable ʌnˈkaʊn.tə.bl̩, ˌʌn-, ʌŋ-, ˌʌŋ- (US) ʌnˈkaʊn.t̬ə-, ˌʌn- **un**ˌ**countable** ˈ**noun**

uncounted ʌnˈkaʊn.tɪd, ˌʌn-, ʌŋ-, ˌʌŋ- (US) ʌnˈkaʊn.t̬ɪd, ˌʌn-

uncoupl|e ʌnˈkʌp.l̩, ˌʌn-, ʌŋ-, ˌʌŋ- (US) ʌn-, ˌʌn- **-es** -z **-ing** -ɪŋ, -ˈkʌp.lɪŋ **-ed** -d

uncouth ʌnˈkuːθ, ˌʌn-, ʌŋ-, ˌʌŋ- (US) ʌn-, ˌʌn- **-ly** -li **-ness** -nəs, -nɪs

uncov|er ʌnˈkʌv|.əʳ, ˌʌn-, ʌŋ-, ˌʌŋ- (US) ʌnˈkʌv|.ɚ, ˌʌn- **-ers** -əz (US) -ɚz **-ering** -ᵊr.ɪŋ **-ered** -əd (US) -ɚd

uncritic|al ʌnˈkrɪt.ɪ.k|ᵊl, ˌʌn-, ʌŋ-, ˌʌŋ- (US) ʌnˈkrɪt̬.ɪ-, ˌʌn- **-ally** -ᵊl.i, -li

uncrossed ʌnˈkrɒst, ˌʌn-, ʌŋ-, ˌʌŋ- (US) ʌnˈkrɑːst, ˌʌn-

uncrowned ʌnˈkraʊnd, ˌʌn-, ʌŋ-, ˌʌŋ- (US) ʌn-, ˌʌn- *stress shift, see compounds:* ˌ**uncrowned** ˈ**king**; ˌ**uncrowned** ˈ**queen**

uncrushable ʌnˈkrʌʃ.ə.bl̩, ˌʌn-, ʌŋ-, ˌʌŋ- (US) ʌn-, ˌʌn-

unction ˈʌŋk.ʃᵊn **-s** -z

unctuosity ˌʌŋk.tjuˈɒs.ə.ti, -tʃuˈ-, -ɪ.ti (US) -tʃuˈɑː.sə.t̬i

unctuous ˈʌŋk.tju.əs, -tʃu- (US) -tʃu-, ˈ-tʃəs **-ly** -li **-ness** -nəs, -nɪs

uncultivated ʌnˈkʌl.tɪ.veɪ.tɪd, ˌʌn-, ʌŋ-, ˌʌŋ-, -tə- (US) ʌnˈkʌl.t̬ə.veɪ.t̬ɪd, ˌʌn-

uncultured ʌnˈkʌl.tʃəd, ˌʌn-, ʌŋ-, ˌʌŋ- (US) ʌnˈkʌl.tʃɚd, ˌʌn-

uncurbed ʌnˈkɜːbd, ˌʌn-, ʌŋ-, ˌʌŋ- (US) ʌnˈkɝːbd, ˌʌn-

uncurl ʌnˈkɜːl, ˌʌn-, ʌŋ-, ˌʌŋ- (US) ʌnˈkɝːl, ˌʌn- **-s** -z **-ing** -ɪŋ **-ed** -d

uncut ʌnˈkʌt, ˌʌn-, ʌŋ-, ˌʌŋ- (US) ʌn-, ˌʌn-

undamaged ʌnˈdæm.ɪdʒd, ˌʌn-

undated *wavy:* ˈʌn.deɪ.tɪd (US) -t̬ɪd

undated *not dated:* ʌnˈdeɪ.tɪd, ˌʌn- (US) -t̬ɪd

undaunted ʌnˈdɔːn.tɪd, ˌʌn- (US) -ˈdɑːn.t̬ɪd, -ˈdɔːn- **-ly** -li **-ness** -nəs, -nɪs

undebated ˌʌn.dɪˈbeɪ.tɪd, -dəˈ- (US) -t̬ɪd

undeceiv|e ˌʌn.dɪˈsiːv, -dəˈ- **-es** -z **-ing** -ɪŋ **-ed** -d

undecided ˌʌn.dɪˈsaɪ.dɪd, -dəˈ- **-ly** -li **-ness** -nəs, -nɪs

undecipherab|le ˌʌn.dɪˈsaɪ.fᵊr.ə.b|l̩, -dəˈ- **-ly** -li

undecisive ˌʌn.dɪˈsaɪ.sɪv, -dəˈ-, -zɪv (US) -sɪv **-ly** -li **-ness** -nəs, -nɪs

undeclared ˌʌn.dɪˈkleəd, -dəˈ- (US) -ˈklerd

undefeated ˌʌn.dɪˈfiː.tɪd, -dəˈ- (US) -dɪˈfiː.t̬ɪd

undefended ˌʌn.dɪˈfen.dɪd, -dəˈ-

undefiled ˌʌn.dɪˈfaɪld, -dəˈ-
undefinab|le ˌʌn.dɪˈfaɪ.nə.bl̩, -dəˈ- **-ly** -li
undefined ˌʌn.dɪˈfaɪnd, -dəˈ-
unde|lete ˌʌn.dɪlˈliːt, -dəˈ- (US) -dɪˈ- **-letes** -ˈliːts **-leting** -ˈliː.tɪŋ (US) -ˈliː.t̬ɪŋ **-leted** -ˈliː.tɪd (US) -ˈliː.t̬ɪd
undelivered ˌʌn.dɪˈlɪv.əd, -dəˈ- (US) -ɚd
undemanding ˌʌn.dɪˈmɑːn.dɪŋ, -dəˈ- (US) -dɪˈmæn-
undemocratic ʌn.dem.əˈkræt.ɪk, ˌʌn- **-ally** -ᵊl.i, -li
undemonstrative ˌʌn.dɪˈmɒnt.strə.tɪv, -dəˈ- (US) -ˈmɑːnt.strə.t̬ɪv **-ly** -li **-ness** -nəs, -nɪs
undeniab|le ˌʌn.dɪˈnaɪ.ə.bl̩, -dəˈ- **-ly** -li
undenominational ˌʌn.dɪˌnɒm.ɪˈneɪ.ʃᵊn.ᵊl, -dəˌ-, -əˈ-, -ˈneɪʃ.nᵊl (US) -ˌnɑː.mɪˈ-, -məˈ- **-ism** -ɪ.zᵊm
under- ʌn.dəʳ- (US) ʌn.dɚ-
Note: Prefix. May receive primary stress, e.g. **undercarriage** /ˈʌn.dəˌkær.ɪdʒ (US) ˈʌn.dɚ-/, or secondary stress, e.g. **understand** /ˌʌn.dəˈstænd (US) -dɚˈ-/. Such secondary-stressed syllables may come to carry the strongest stress in the word through stress-shift, e.g. **understand** /ˌʌn.dəˈstænd (US) ˌʌn.dɚ-/, **understand problems** /ˌʌn.də.stændˈprɒb.ləmz (US) ˌʌn.dɚ.stændˈprɑː.bləmz/. Although /r/ is normally assigned to a following strong syllable in American English, when /ɚ/ is perceived to be morphemically linked to the preceding unit /r/ is retained as /ɚ/.
under ˈʌn.dəʳ (US) -dɚ **-s** -z ˌ**under** ˈ**way**
underachiev|e ˌʌn.dəʳ.əˈtʃiːv (US) -dɚ- **-es** -z **-ing** -ɪŋ **-ed** -d **-er/s** -əʳ/z (US) -ɚ/z **-ment/s** -mənt/s
underact ˌʌn.dəʳˈækt (US) -dɚˈ- **-s** -s **-ing** -ɪŋ **-ed** -ɪd
under-age ˌʌn.dəʳˈeɪdʒ (US) -dɚˈ- *stress shift:* ˌunder-age ˈdrinking
underarm ˈʌn.dəʳ.ɑːm (US) -dɚ.ɑːrm
underbell|y ˈʌn.dəˌbel|.i (US) -dɚˌ- **-ies** -iz
underbid ˌʌn.dəˈbɪd (US) -dɚˈ- **-s** -z **-ding** -ɪŋ **-der/s** -əʳ/z (US) -ɚ/z
underbred ˌʌn.dəˈbred (US) -dɚˈ- *stress shift:* ˌunderbred ˈstock
underbrush ˈʌn.də.brʌʃ (US) -dɚ-
underbudgeted ˌʌn.dəˈbʌdʒ.ɪ.tɪd, ˈ-ə- (US) -dɚˈbʌdʒ.ɪ.t̬ɪd
under|buy ˌʌn.dəlˈbaɪ (US) -dɚˈ- **-buys** -ˈbaɪz **-buying** -ˈbaɪ.ɪŋ **-bought** -ˈbɔːt (US) -ˈbɑːt, -ˈbɔːt
undercapitaliz|e, -is|e ˌʌn.dəˈkæp.ɪ.tᵊl.aɪz (US) -dɚˈ- **-es** -ɪz **-ing** -ɪŋ **-ed** -d
undercard ˈʌn.də.kɑːd (US) -dɚ.kɑːrd **-s** -z
undercarriag|e ˈʌn.dəˌkær.ɪdʒ (US) -dɚˌker-, -ˌkær- **-es** -ɪz
undercharg|e (*n.*) ˈʌn.dəˌtʃɑːdʒ, ˌ--ˈ- (US) ˈʌn.dɚ.tʃɑːrdʒ **-es** -ɪz
undercharg|e (*v.*) ˌʌn.dəˈtʃɑːdʒ (US) -dɚˈtʃɑːrdʒ **-es** -ɪz **-ing** -ɪŋ **-ed** -d
underclass ˈʌn.də.klɑːs (US) -dɚ.klæs **-es** -ɪz
under-clerk ˈʌn.də.klɑːk (US) -dɚ.klɝːk **-s** -s
underclothes ˈʌn.də.kləʊðz (US) -dɚ.kloʊðz, -kloʊz
underclothing ˈʌn.dəˌkləʊ.ðɪŋ (US) -dɚˌkloʊ-
undercoat ˈʌn.də.kəʊt (US) -dɚ.koʊt **-s** -s **-ing** -ɪŋ
undercook ˌʌn.dəˈkʊk (US) -dɚˈ- **-s** -s **-ing** -ɪŋ **-ed** -t
undercover ˌʌn.dəˈkʌv.əʳ (US) -dɚˈkʌv.ɚ *stress shift:* ˌundercover ˈagent
undercroft ˈʌn.də.krɒft (US) -dɚ.krɑːft **-s** -s
undercurrent ˈʌn.dəˌkʌr.ᵊnt (US) -dɚˌkɝː- **-s** -s
undercut (*n.*) ˈʌn.də.kʌt (US) -dɚ- **-s** -s
under|cut (*adj. v.*) ˌʌn.dəlˈkʌt (US) -dɚˈ- **-cuts** -ˈkʌts **-cutting** -ˈkʌt.ɪŋ (US) -ˈkʌt̬.ɪŋ
underdevelop|ed ˌʌn.də.dɪˈvel.əp|t, -dəˈ- (US) -dɚ- **-ment** -mənt *stress shift:* ˌunderdeveloped ˈbrain
under|do ˌʌn.dəlˈduː (US) -dɚˈ- **-does** -ˈdʌz **-doing** -ˈduː.ɪŋ **-did** -ˈdɪd **-done** -ˈdʌn
underdog ˈʌn.də.dɒg (US) -dɚ.dɑːg, -dɔːg **-s** -z
underdone ˌʌn.dəˈdʌn (US) -dɚˈ- *stress shift:* ˌunderdone ˈbeef
underdress ˌʌn.dəˈdres (US) -dɚˈ- **-es** -ɪz **-ing** -ɪŋ **-ed** -t
undereducated ˌʌn.dᵊrˈedʒ.ʊ.keɪ.tɪd, -ˈed.jʊ- (US) -dɚˈedʒ.ʊ.keɪ.t̬ɪd, ˈ-ə-
undereducation ˌʌn.dᵊr.edʒ.ʊˈkeɪ.ʃᵊn, -ed.jʊ- (US) -dɚ.edʒ.ʊ-, -ə-
underemployed ˌʌn.dᵊr.ɪmˈplɔɪd, -emˈ- (US) -dɚ- *stress shift:* ˌunderemployed ˈworkforce
underemployment ˌʌn.dᵊr.ɪmˈplɔɪ.mənt (US) -dɚ-
underestimate (*n.*) ˌʌn.dᵊrˈes.tɪ.mət, -tə-, -mɪt, -meɪt (US) -dɚˈes.tə.mɪt, -mət **-s** -s
underesti|mate (*v.*) ˌʌn.dᵊrˈes.tɪ|.meɪt, -tə- (US) -dɚˈes.tə- **-mates** -meɪts **-mating** -meɪ.tɪŋ (US) -meɪ.t̬ɪŋ **-mated** -meɪ.tɪd (US) -meɪ.t̬ɪd
underestimation ˌʌn.dᵊrˌes.tɪˈmeɪ.ʃᵊn, -təˈ- (US) -dɚˌes.təˈ- **-s** -z
under-expos|e ˌʌn.dᵊr.ɪkˈspəʊz, -ekˈ- (US) -dɚ.ɪkˈspoʊz, -ekˈ- **-es** -ɪz **-ing** -ɪŋ **-ed** -d
underexposure ˌʌn.dᵊr.ɪkˈspəʊ.ʒəʳ, -ekˈ- (US) -dɚ.ɪkˈspoʊ.ʒɚ, -ekˈ- **-s** -z
under-eye ˈʌn.dᵊr.aɪ
under|feed ˌʌn.dəlˈfiːd (US) -dɚˈ- **-feeds** -ˈfiːdz **-feeding** -ˈfiː.dɪŋ **-fed** -ˈfed *stress shift:* ˌunderfed ˈchickens
underfelt ˈʌn.də.felt (US) -dɚ- **-s** -s
underfinanced ˌʌn.dəˈfaɪ.næntst (US) -dɚˈ-
underfloor ˌʌn.dəˈflɔːʳ (US) -dɚˈflɔːr *stress shift:* ˌunderfloor ˈheating
underfoot ˌʌn.dəˈfʊt (US) -dɚˈ-
underfund ˌʌn.dəˈfʌnd (US) -dɚˈ- **-s** -z **-ing** -ɪŋ **-ed** -ɪd
undergarment ˈʌn.dəˌgɑː.mənt (US) -dɚˌgɑːr- **-s** -s
under|go ˌʌn.dəlˈgəʊ (US) -dɚlˈgoʊ **-goes** -ˈgəʊz (US) -ˈgoʊz **-going** -ˈgəʊ.ɪŋ (US) -ˈgoʊ.ɪŋ **-went** -ˈwent **-gone** -ˈgɒn (US) -ˈgɑːn *stress shift:* ˌundergo ˈtreatment
undergrad ˈʌn.də.græd (US) -dɚ- **-s** -z
undergraduate ˌʌn.dəˈgrædʒ.u.ət, -ˈgræd.ju-, -ɪt (US) -dɚˈgrædʒ.u.ət, -ə.wət **-s** -s *stress shift:* ˌundergraduate ˈhumour
underground (U) (*n. adj.*) ˈʌn.də.graʊnd (US) -dɚ- **-er/s** -əʳ/z (US) -ɚ/z
underground (*adv.*) ˌʌn.dəˈgraʊnd (US) -dɚˈ-
undergrown ˌʌn.dəˈgrəʊn (US) -dɚˈgroʊn *stress shift:* ˌundergrown ˈtrees
undergrowth ˈʌn.də.grəʊθ (US) -dɚ.groʊθ
underhand ˌʌn.dəˈhænd (US) -dɚˈ- **-ed/ly** -ɪd/li **-edness** -ɪd.nəs, -nɪs *stress shift:* ˌunderhand ˈtrick
Underhill ˈʌn.də.hɪl (US) -dɚ-
underhung ˌʌn.dəˈhʌŋ (US) -dɚˈ- *stress shift:* ˌunderhung ˈaxle
underinsured ˌʌn.dᵊr.ɪnˈʃʊəd, -ˈʃɔːd (US) -dɚ.ɪnˈʃʊrd
underlay (*n.*) ˈʌn.dᵊl.eɪ (US) -dɚ.leɪ **-s** -z
under|lay (*v.*) ˌʌn.dəlˈleɪ (US) -dɚˈ- **-lays** -ˈleɪz **-laying** -ˈleɪ.ɪŋ **-laid** -ˈleɪd
under|let ˌʌn.dəlˈlet (US) -dɚˈ- **-lets** -ˈlets **-letting** -ˈlet.ɪŋ (US) -ˈlet̬.ɪŋ
under|lie ˌʌn.dəlˈlaɪ (US) -dɚˈ- **-lies** -ˈlaɪz **-lying** -ˈlaɪ.ɪŋ **-lay** -ˈleɪ **-lain** -ˈleɪn
underline (*n.*) ˈʌn.dᵊl.aɪn (US) ˈʌn.dɚ.laɪn **-s** -z
underlin|e (*v.*) ˌʌn.dəˈlaɪn (US) -dɚˈ-, ˈ--- **-es** -z **-ing** -ɪŋ **-ed** -d
underling ˈʌn.dᵊl.ɪŋ (US) -dɚ.lɪŋ **-s** -z
underlip ˈʌn.dᵊl.ɪp (US) -dɚ.lɪp **-s** -s

underlying ˌʌn.dəˈlaɪ.ɪŋ US -dɚˈ-, ˈʌn.dɚˌlaɪ.ɪŋ *stress shift, British only:* ˌunderlying ˈcause

underman ˌʌn.dəˈmæn US -dɚˈ- **-s** -z **-ning** -ɪŋ **-ned** -d *stress shift:* ˌundermanned ˈindustry

undermentioned ˌʌn.dəˈmen.*t*ʃᵊnd US -dɚˈ- *stress shift:* ˌundermentioned ˈclause

undermin|e ˌʌn.dəˈmaɪn US -dɚˈ-, ˈ--- **-es** -z **-ing** -ɪŋ **-ed** -d **-er/s** -əʳ/z US -ɚ/z *stress shift, British only:* ˌundermine ˈconfidence

undermost ˈʌn.də.məʊst US -dɚ.moʊst

underneath ˌʌn.dəˈniːθ US -dɚˈ- *stress shift:* ˌunderneath ˈeverything

undernourish ˌʌn.dəˈnʌr.ɪʃ US -dɚˈnɝː- **-es** -ɪz **-ing** -ɪŋ **-ed** -t **-ment** -mənt

underpants ˈʌn.də.pænts US -dɚ-

underpass ˈʌn.də.pɑːs US -dɚ.pæs **-es** -ɪz

under|pay ˌʌn.də|ˈpeɪ US -dɚˈ- **-pays** -ˈpeɪz **-paying** -ˈpeɪ.ɪŋ **-paid** -ˈpeɪd *stress shift:* ˌunderpaid ˈstaff

underpayment ˌʌn.dəˈpeɪ.mənt US -dɚˈ- **-s** -s

underperform ˌʌn.də.pəˈfɔːm US -dɚ.pɚˈfɔːrm **-s** -z **-ing** -ɪŋ **-ed** -d **-er/s** -əʳ/z US -ɚ/z *stress shift:* ˌunderperforming ˈworker

underpin ˌʌn.dəˈpɪn US -dɚˈ-, ˈ--- **-s** -z **-ning** -ɪŋ **-ned** -d

underpinning ˈʌn.dəˌpɪn.ɪŋ US -dɚˌ- **-s** -z

underplay ˌʌn.dəˈpleɪ US -dɚˈ-, ˈ--- **-s** -z **-ing** -ɪŋ **-ed** -d

underpopulated ˌʌn.dəˈpɒp.jə.leɪ.tɪd, -pjʊ- US -dɚˈpɑː.pjə-, -pjʊ-

underpri|ce ˌʌn.dəˈpraɪ|s US -dɚˈ- **-ces** -sɪz **-ced** -st **-cing** -sɪŋ

underprivileged ˌʌn.dəˈprɪv.ᵊl.ɪdʒd, -vɪ.lɪdʒd US -dɚˈprɪv.ᵊl.ɪdʒd, ˈ-lɪdʒd

underproduc|e ˌʌn.də.prəˈdjuːs, -ˈdʒuːs US -dɚ.prəˈduːs, -ˈdjuːs **-es** -ɪz **-ing** -ɪŋ **-ed** -t

underproduction ˌʌn.də.prəˈdʌk.ʃᵊn US -dɚ-

underprop ˌʌn.dəˈprɒp US -dɚˈprɑːp **-s** -s **-ping** -ɪŋ **-ped** -t

under|rate ˌʌn.də|ˈreɪt US -dɚˈ- **-rates** -ˈreɪts **-rating** -ˈreɪ.tɪŋ US -ˈreɪ.t̬ɪŋ **-rated** -ˈreɪ.tɪd US -ˈreɪ.t̬ɪd

underrepresentation ˌʌn.dəˌrep.rɪ.zenˈteɪ.ʃᵊn US -dɚˌrep- **-s** -z

underrepresented ˌʌn.dəˌrep.rɪˈzen.tɪd, -rəˈ- US -dɚˌrep.rɪˈzen.t̬ɪd

underripe ˌʌn.dəˈraɪp US -dɚˈ- *stress shift:* ˌunderripe ˈfruit

under|run ˌʌn.də|ˈrʌn US -dɚˈ- **-runs** -ˈrʌnz **-running** -ˈrʌn.ɪŋ **-ran** -ˈræn

underscor|e (*v.*) ˌʌn.dəˈskɔːʳ US -dɚˈskɔːr, ˈ--- **-es** -z **-ing** -ɪŋ **-ed** -d

underscore (*n.*) ˈʌn.də.skɔːʳ US -dɚ.skɔːr **-s** -z

undersea ˌʌn.dəˈsiː US -dɚˈ- **-s** -z *stress shift:* ˌundersea ˈcable

underseal ˈʌn.də.siːl US -dɚ- **-s** -z **-ing** -ɪŋ **-ed** -d

undersecretar|y ˌʌn.dəˈsek.rə.tᵊr|.i, -rɪ-, -tr|i US -dɚˈsek.rə.ter- **-ies** -iz **-yship/s** -i.ʃɪp/s

under|sell ˌʌn.də|ˈsel US -dɚˈ- **-sells** -ˈselz **-selling** -ˈsel.ɪŋ **-sold** -ˈsəʊld US -ˈsoʊld

undersexed ˌʌn.dəˈsekst US -dɚˈ-

Undershaft ˈʌn.də.ʃɑːft US -dɚ.ʃæft

undersheriff ˈʌn.dəˌʃer.ɪf US -dɚˌ- **-s** -s

undershirt ˈʌn.də.ʃɜːt US -dɚ.ʃɝːt **-s** -s

under|shoot (*v.*) ˌʌn.də|ˈʃuːt US -dɚˈ- **-shoots** -ˈʃuːts **-shooting** -ˈʃuː.tɪŋ US -ˈʃuː.t̬ɪŋ **-shot** -ˈʃɒt US -ˈʃɑːt

undershoot (*n.*) ˈʌn.də.ʃuːt, ˌ--ˈ- US ˈʌn.dɚ.ʃuːt, ˌ--ˈ- **-s** -s

undershorts ˈʌn.də.ʃɔːts US -dɚˈʃɔːrts

undershot (*adj.*) ˌʌn.dəˈʃɒt US -ˈʃɑːt *stress shift:* ˌundershot ˈwheel

undershot (*from* **undershoot**) ˌʌn.dəˈʃɒt US -dɚˈʃɑːt

underside ˈʌn.də.saɪd US -dɚ- **-s** -z

undersigned ˈʌn.də.saɪnd, ˌ--ˈ- US ˈʌn.dɚ.saɪnd

undersized ˌʌn.dəˈsaɪzd US ˈʌn.dɚ.saɪzd *stress shift, British only:* ˌundersized ˈbelt

underskirt ˈʌn.də.skɜːt US -dɚ.skɝːt **-s** -s

underspend ˌʌn.dəˈspend US -dɚˈ- **-s** -z **-ing** -ɪŋ **underspent** ˌʌn.dəˈspent US -dɚˈ-

understaffed ˌʌn.dəˈstɑːft US -dɚˈstæft *stress shift:* ˌunderstaffed ˈschool

under|stand ˌʌn.də|ˈstænd US -dɚˈ- **-stands** -ˈstændz **-standing** -ˈstæn.dɪŋ **-stood** -ˈstʊd

understandab|le ˌʌn.dəˈstæn.də.b|l̩ US -dɚˈ- **-ly** -li

under|state ˌʌn.də|ˈsteɪt US -dɚˈ- **-states** -ˈsteɪts **-stating** -ˈsteɪ.tɪŋ US -ˈsteɪ.t̬ɪŋ **-stated** -ˈsteɪ.tɪd US -ˈsteɪ.t̬ɪd

understatement ˌʌn.dəˈsteɪt.mənt, ˈʌn.dəˌsteɪt- US ˌʌn.dɚˈsteɪt-, ˈʌn.dɚˌsteɪt- **-s** -s

understocked ˌʌn.dəˈstɒkt US -dɚˈstɑːkt *stress shift:* ˌunderstocked ˈshelves

understood (*from* **understand**) ˌʌn.dəˈstʊd US -dɚˈ- *stress shift:* ˌunderstood ˈplan

understrapper ˈʌn.dəˌstræp.əʳ US -dɚˌstræp.ɚ **-s** -z

understud|y ˈʌn.dəˌstʌd|.i US -dɚˌ- **-ies** -iz **-ying** -i.ɪŋ **-ied** -id

undersubscrib|e ˌʌn.də.səbˈskraɪb US -dɚ- **-es** -z **-ing** -ɪŋ **-ed** -d

under|take *agree or promise to do something:* ˌʌn.də|ˈteɪk US -dɚˈ- **-takes** -ˈteɪks **-taking** -ˈteɪ.kɪŋ **-took** -ˈtʊk **-taken** -ˈteɪ.kᵊn, -kᵊŋ US -kᵊn

undertaker *person who agrees to do something:* ˌʌn.dəˈteɪ.kəʳ US -dɚˈteɪ.kɚ **-s** -z *person who arranges funerals:* ˈʌn.dəˌteɪ.kəʳ US -dɚˌteɪ.kɚ **-s** -z

undertaking *enterprise, promise:* ˌʌn.dəˈteɪ.kɪŋ, ˈʌn.dəˌteɪ- US ˌʌn.dɚˈteɪ-, ˈʌn.dɚˌteɪ- **-s** -z *arranging funerals:* ˈʌn.dəˌteɪ.kɪŋ US -dɚˌ-

under-the-counter ˌʌn.də.ðəˈkaʊn.təʳ US -dɚ.ðəˈkaʊn.t̬ɚ *stress shift:* ˌunder-the-counter ˈdeal

underthings ˈʌn.də.θɪŋz US -dɚ-

undertint ˈʌn.də.tɪnt US -dɚ- **-s** -s

undertone ˈʌn.də.təʊn US -dɚ.toʊn **-s** -z

undertook (*from* **undertake**) ˌʌn.dəˈtʊk US -dɚˈ-

undertow ˈʌn.də.təʊ US -dɚ.toʊ **-s** -z

underused ˌʌn.dəˈjuːzd US -dɚˈ- *stress shift:* ˌunderused ˈpath

underutiliz|e, -is|e ˌʌn.dəˈjuː.tɪ.laɪz, -tᵊl.aɪz US -dɚˈjuː.t̬ᵊl.aɪz **-es** -ɪz **-ing** -ɪŋ **-ed** -d

undervaluation ˌʌn.dəˌvæl.juˈeɪ.ʃᵊn US -dɚˌ- **-s** -z

underval|ue ˌʌn.dəˈvæl|.juː US -dɚˈ- **-ues** -juːz **-uing** -juː.ɪŋ **-ued** -juːd *stress shift:* ˌundervalued ˈshares

underwater ˌʌn.dəˈwɔː.təʳ US -dɚˈwɑː.t̬ɚ, -ˈwɔː- *stress shift:* ˌunderwater ˈcamera

underway ˌʌn.dəˈweɪ US -dɚˈ-

underwear ˈʌn.də.weəʳ US -dɚ.wer

underweight ˌʌn.dəˈweɪt US -dɚˈ-, ˈ--- *stress shift:* ˌunderweight ˈbaggage

underwent (*from* **undergo**) ˌʌn.dəˈwent US -dɚˈ- *stress shift:* ˌunderwent ˈsurgery

underwhelm ˌʌn.dəˈ*h*welm US -dɚˈ- **-s** -z **-ing** -ɪŋ **-ed** -d

underwing ˈʌn.də.wɪŋ US -dɚ- **-s** -z

underwired ˌʌn.dəˈwaɪəd US -dɚˈwaɪɚd, ˈ--- *stress shift:* ˌunderwired ˈbra

underwood (U) ˈʌn.də.wʊd **underwood** US -dɚ- **-s** -z

underworld (U) ˈʌn.də.wɜːld
underworld (US) -dɚ.wɝːld
underwri|te ˌʌn.dᵊrˈraɪ|t, ˈ---
(US) ˈʌn.dɚ.raɪ|t **-tes** -ts **-ting** -tɪŋ
(US) -t̬ɪŋ **underwrote** ˌʌn.dᵊrˈəʊt, ˈ---
(US) ˈʌn.dɚ.roʊt **underwritten**
ˌʌn.dᵊrˈɪt.ᵊn, ˈʌn.dᵊrˌɪt-
(US) ˈʌn.dɚˌrɪt.ᵊn
underwriter ˈʌn.dᵊrˌaɪ.təʳ
(US) -dɚˌraɪ.t̬ɚ **-s** -z
undescended ˌʌn.dɪˈsen.dɪd
undescribab|le ˌʌn.dɪˈskraɪ.bə.b|l̩,
-dəˈ- **-ly** -li
undeserv|ed ˌʌn.dɪˈzɜːv|d, -dəˈ-
(US) -ˈzɝːv|d **-edly** -ɪd.li **-edness**
-ɪd.nəs, -nɪs
undeserving ˌʌn.dɪˈzɜː.vɪŋ, -dəˈ-
(US) -ˈzɝː- **-ly** -li
undesigning ˌʌn.dɪˈzaɪ.nɪŋ
undesirability ˌʌn.dɪˌzaɪə.rəˈbɪl.ə.ti,
-dəˌ-, -ɪ.ti (US) -ˌzaɪ.rəˈbɪl.ə.t̬i
undesirab|le ˌʌn.dɪˈzaɪə.rə.b|l̩, -dəˈ-
(US) -ˈzaɪ- **-ly** -li **-leness** -l̩.nəs, -nɪs
undetected ˌʌn.dɪˈtek.tɪd, -dəˈ-
undeterminable ˌʌn.dɪˈtɜː.mɪ.nə.bl̩,
-dəˈ-, -mə- (US) -ˈtɝː-
undeterminate ˌʌn.dɪˈtɜː.mɪ.nət,
-dəˈ-, -mə-, -nɪt (US) -ˈtɝː- **-ly** -li
-ness -nəs, -nɪs
undetermination
ˌʌn.dɪˌtɜː.mɪˈneɪ.ʃᵊn, -də-, -məˈ-
(US) -ˌtɝː-
undetermined ˌʌn.dɪˈtɜː.mɪnd, -dəˈ-
(US) -ˈtɝː-
undeterred ˌʌn.dɪˈtɜːd, -dəˈ- (US) -ˈtɝːd
undeveloped ˌʌn.dɪˈvel.əpt, -dəˈ-
undeviating ʌnˈdiː.vi.eɪ.tɪŋ, ˌʌn-
(US) -t̬ɪŋ **-ly** -li
undid *(from* **undo***)* ʌnˈdɪd, ˌʌn-
undies ˈʌn.diz
undigested ˌʌn.daɪˈdʒes.tɪd, -dɪˈ-, -dəˈ-
undignified ʌnˈdɪg.nɪ.faɪd, ˌʌn-, -nə-
undiluted ˌʌn.daɪˈluː.tɪd, -dɪˈ-, -ˈljuː-
(US) -ˈluː.t̬ɪd
undiminished ˌʌn.dɪˈmɪn.ɪʃt, -dəˈ-
undimmed ʌnˈdɪmd, ˌʌn-
undine (U) ˈʌn.diːn; ʌnˈdiːn, ʊn-
(US) ʌnˈdiːn; ˈʌn.diːn, -daɪn **-s** -z
undiplomatic ˌʌn.dɪp.ləˈmæt.ɪk
(US) -ˈmæt̬- **-ally** -ᵊl.i, -li
undiscerning ˌʌn.dɪˈsɜː.nɪŋ, -dəˈ-,
-ˈzɜː- (US) -ˈsɝː-, -ˈzɝː-
undischarged ˌʌn.dɪsˈtʃɑːdʒd
(US) -ˈtʃɑːrdʒd
undisciplined ʌnˈdɪs.ɪ.plɪnd, ˌʌn-, ˈ-ə-
undisclosed ˌʌn.dɪsˈkləʊzd (US) -ˈkloʊzd
undiscouraged ˌʌn.dɪˈskʌr.ɪdʒd
(US) -ˈskɝː-
undiscovered ˌʌn.dɪˈskʌv.əd (US) -ɚd
undiscussed ˌʌn.dɪˈskʌst
undisguised ˌʌn.dɪsˈgaɪzd, -dɪzˈ-
undismayed ˌʌn.dɪˈsmeɪd, -dəˈ-

undisputed ˌʌn.dɪˈspjuː.tɪd, -dəˈ-
(US) -t̬ɪd
undissolved ˌʌn.dɪˈzɒlvd, -ˈsɒlvd
(US) -ˈzɑːlvd
undistinguishab|le
ˌʌn.dɪˈstɪŋ.gwɪ.ʃə.b|l̩, -dəˈ- **-ly** -li
-leness -l̩.nəs, -nɪs
undistinguished ˌʌn.dɪˈstɪŋ.gwɪʃt, -dəˈ-
undistracted ˌʌn.dɪˈstræk.tɪd, -dəˈ-
undisturbed ˌʌn.dɪˈstɜːbd, -dəˈ-
(US) -ˈstɝːbd
undivided ˌʌn.dɪˈvaɪ.dɪd, -dəˈ- **-ly** -li
-ness -nəs, -nɪs
un|do ʌn|ˈduː, ˌʌn- **-does** -ˈdʌz **-doing**
-ˈduː.ɪŋ **-did** -ˈdɪd **-done** -ˈdʌn
-doer/s -ˈduː.əʳ/z (US) -ˈduː.ɚ/z
undock ʌnˈdɒk, ˌʌn- (US) -ˈdɑːk **-s** -s
-ing -ɪŋ **-ed** -t
undomesticated ˌʌn.dəˈmes.tɪ.keɪ.tɪd
(US) -t̬ɪd
undone *(from* **undo***)* ʌnˈdʌn, ˌʌn-
undoubted ʌnˈdaʊ.tɪd, ˌʌn- (US) -t̬ɪd
-ly -li
undreamed, undreamt ʌnˈdriːmd,
ˌʌnˈdrem*p*t **unˈdreamed ˌof**
undress ʌnˈdres, ˌʌn- **-es** -ɪz **-ing** -ɪŋ
-ed -t
undrinkable ʌnˈdrɪŋ.kə.bl̩, ˌʌn-
undrunk ʌnˈdrʌŋk
undue ʌnˈdjuː, ˌʌn- (US) -ˈduː, -ˈdjuː
undulant ˈʌn.djᵊl.ənt, -djʊ.lənt,
-dʒᵊl.ənt, -dʒʊ.lənt (US) -dʒᵊl.ənt,
-djᵊl-
undu|late ˈʌn.dj|ə|.leɪt, -djʊ-, -dʒə-,
-dʒʊ- (US) -dʒə-, -djə- **-lates** -leɪts
-lating/ly -leɪ.tɪŋ/li (US) -leɪ.t̬ɪŋ/li
-lated -leɪ.tɪd (US) -leɪ.t̬ɪd
undulation ˌʌn.djəˈleɪ.ʃᵊn, -djʊˈ-,
-dʒəˈ-, -dʒʊˈ- (US) -dʒəˈ-, -djəˈ-, -dəˈ-
-s -z
undulatory ˈʌn.djᵊl.ə.tᵊr.i, -djʊ.lə-,
-dʒᵊl.ə-, -dʒʊ.lə-, -tri;
ˌʌn.djəˈleɪ.tᵊr-, -djʊˈ-
(US) ˈʌn.dʒᵊl.ə.tɔːr.i, -djᵊl-, -dᵊl-
unduly ʌnˈdjuː.li, ˌʌn-, -ˈdʒuː-
(US) -ˈduː-, -ˈdjuː-
undutiful ʌnˈdjuː.tɪ.fᵊl, ˌʌn-, -ˈdʒuː-,
-fʊl (US) -ˈduː.t̬ɪ-, -ˈdjuː- **-ly** -i **-ness**
-nəs, -nɪs
undying ʌnˈdaɪ.ɪŋ, ˌʌn- **-ly** -li
unearned ʌnˈɜːnd, ˌʌn- (US) -ˈɝːnd
unearth ʌnˈɜːθ, ˌʌn- (US) -ˈɝːθ **-s** -s **-ing**
-ɪŋ **-ed** -t
unearthl|y ʌnˈɜːθ.l|i, ˌʌn- (US) -ˈɝːθ-
-iness -ɪ.nəs, -ɪ.nɪs
unease ʌnˈiːz, ˌʌn-
uneas|y ʌnˈiː.z|i, ˌʌn- **-ier** -i.əʳ (US) -i.ɚ
-iest -i.ɪst, -i.əst **-ily** -ɪ.li, -ᵊl.i **-iness**
-ɪ.nəs, -ɪ.nɪs
uneatable ʌnˈiː.tə.bl̩, ˌʌn- (US) -t̬ə- **-ness**
-nəs, -nɪs
uneaten ʌnˈiː.tᵊn, ˌʌn-

uneconomic ʌnˌiː.kəˈnɒm.ɪk, ˌʌn-,
-ˌek.əˈ- (US) -ˌek.əˈnɑː.mɪk, -ˌiː.kəˈ-
-al -ᵊl **-ally** -ᵊl.i, -li
unedifying ʌnˈed.ɪ.faɪ.ɪŋ, ˌʌn-
unedited ʌnˈed.ɪ.tɪd (US) -t̬ɪd
uneducated ʌnˈedʒ.ʊ.keɪ.tɪd, ˌʌn-,
ˈ-ə-, -ˈed.jʊ-, -jə- (US) -ˈedʒ.ʊ.keɪ.t̬ɪd,
ˈ-ə-
unelected ˌʌn.ɪˈlek.tɪd
unembarrassed ˌʌn.ɪmˈbær.əst, -emˈ-
(US) -emˈber-, -ɪmˈ-, -ˈbær-
unemotional ˌʌn.ɪˈməʊ.ʃᵊn.ᵊl
(US) -ˈmoʊ- **-ly** -i
unemphatic ˌʌn.ɪmˈfæt.ɪk, -emˈ-
(US) -ˈfæt̬- **-ally** -ᵊl.i, -li
unemployability ˌʌn.ɪmˌplɔɪ.əˈbɪl.ɪ.ti,
-emˌ-, -ə.ti (US) -ə.t̬i
unemployable ˌʌn.ɪmˈplɔɪ.ə.bl̩, -emˈ-
unemployed ˌʌn.ɪmˈplɔɪd, -emˈ-
unemployment ˌʌn.ɪmˈplɔɪ.mənt,
-emˈ- **unemˈployment ˌbenefit,**
ˌunemployment ˈbenefit
(US) **unemˈployment ˌbenefit**
unenclosed ˌʌn.ɪnˈkləʊzd, -ɪŋˈ-, -enˈ-,
-eŋˈ- (US) -ɪnˈkloʊzd, -enˈ-
unencumbered ˌʌn.ɪŋˈkʌm.bəd, -ɪnˈ-,
-eŋˈ-, -enˈ- (US) -ɪnˈkʌm.bɚd, -enˈ-
unending ʌnˈen.dɪŋ, ˌʌn- **-ly** -li
unendowed ˌʌn.ɪnˈdaʊd, -enˈ-
unendurab|le ˌʌn.ɪnˈdjʊə.rə.b|l̩, -enˈ-,
-ˈdjɔː- (US) -ˈdʊr.ə-, -ˈdjʊr-, -ˈdɝː-
-ly -li **-leness** -l̩.nəs, -nɪs
unenforceable ˌʌn.ɪnˈfɔː.sə.bl̩
(US) -ˈfɔːr-
unengaged ˌʌn.ɪŋˈgeɪdʒd, -ɪnˈ-, -eŋˈ-,
-enˈ- (US) -ɪnˈ-, -enˈ-
un-English ˌʌnˈɪŋ.glɪʃ **-ness** -nəs, -nɪs
unenlightened ˌʌn.ɪnˈlaɪ.tᵊnd, -enˈ-
unenterprising ʌnˈen.tə.praɪ.zɪŋ, ˌʌn-
(US) -t̬ɚ- **-ly** -li
unenthusiastic ˌʌn.ɪnˌθjuː.ziˈæs.tɪk,
-enˌ- (US) -ˌθuː-, -ˌθjuː- **-ally** -ᵊl.i, -li
unenviab|le ʌnˈen.vi.ə.b|l̩, ˌʌn- **-ly** -li
unequal ʌnˈiː.kwᵊl, ˌʌn- **-s** -z **-ly** -i
-ness -nəs, -nɪs **-(l)ed** -d
unequitab|le ʌnˈek.wɪ.tə.b|l̩, ˌʌn-,
-wə- (US) -t̬ə- **-ly** -li
unequivoc|al ˌʌn.ɪˈkwɪv.ə.k|ᵊl **-ally**
-ᵊl.i, -li **-alness** -ᵊl.nəs, -nɪs
unerring ʌnˈɜː.rɪŋ, ˌʌn- (US) -ˈɝː.ɪŋ, -ˈer-
-ly -li **-ness** -nəs, -nɪs
unescapable ˌʌn.ɪˈskeɪ.pə.bl̩
UNESCO, Unesco juːˈnes.kəʊ (US) -koʊ
unessential ˌʌn.ɪˈsen.*t*ʃᵊl
unethic|al ʌnˈeθ.ɪ.k|ᵊl **-ly** -ᵊl.i, -li **-ness**
-nəs, -nɪs
uneven ʌnˈiː.vᵊn, ˌʌn- **-ly** -li **-ness** -nəs,
-nɪs
uneventful ˌʌn.ɪˈvent.fᵊl, -fʊl **-ly** -i
-ness -nəs, -nɪs
unexampled ˌʌn.ɪgˈzɑːm.pl̩d, -egˈ-,
-ɪkˈsɑːm-, -ekˈ- (US) -ɪgˈzæm-, -egˈ-

unexceptionab|le ˌʌn.ɪkˈsep.ʃᵊn.ə.b|l̩, -ekˈ-, -ˈsepʃ.nə- **-ly** -li **-leness** -l̩.nəs (US) -nɪs

unexceptional ˌʌn.ɪkˈsep.ʃᵊn.ᵊl, -ekˈ-, -ˈsepʃ.nᵊl **-ly** -i

unexhausted ˌʌn.ɪɡˈzɔː.stɪd, -eɡˈ-, -ɪkˈsɔː-, -ekˈ- (US) -ɪɡˈzɑː-, -eɡˈ-, -ˈzɔː-

unexpected ˌʌn.ɪkˈspek.tɪd, -ekˈ- **-ly** -li **-ness** -nəs, -nɪs

unexpired ˌʌn.ɪkˈspaɪəd, -ekˈ- (US) -ˈspaɪɚd

unexplained ˌʌn.ɪkˈspleɪnd, -ekˈ-

unexplored ˌʌn.ɪkˈsplɔːd, -ekˈ- (US) -ˈsplɔːrd

unexposed ˌʌn.ɪkˈspəʊzd, -ekˈ- (US) -ˈspoʊzd

unexpressib|le ˌʌn.ɪkˈspres.ə.b|l̩, -ekˈ-, ˈ-ɪ- **-ly** -li

unexpressive ˌʌn.ɪkˈspres.ɪv, -ekˈ-

unexpurgated ʌnˈek.spə.ɡeɪ.tɪd, ˌʌn-, -spɜː- (US) -spɚ.ɡeɪ.t̬ɪd

unfading ʌnˈfeɪ.dɪŋ, ˌʌn- **-ly** -li

unfailing ʌnˈfeɪ.lɪŋ, ˌʌn- **-ly** -li **-ness** -nəs, -nɪs

unfair ʌnˈfeəʳ, ˌʌn- (US) -ˈfer **-ly** -li **-ness** -nəs, -nɪs ˌ**unfair disˈmissal**

unfaithful ʌnˈfeɪθ.fᵊl, ˌʌn-, -fʊl **-ly** -i **-ness** -nəs, -nɪs

unfaltering ʌnˈfɔːl.tᵊr.ɪŋ, ˌʌn-, -ˈfɒl- (US) -ˈfɑːl.t̬ɚ-, -ˈfɔːl- **-ly** -li

unfamiliar ˌʌn.fəˈmɪl.jəʳ, ˈ-i.əʳ (US) ˈ-jɚ **-ly** -li

unfamiliarity ˌʌn.fəˌmɪl.iˈær.ə.ti, -ɪ.ti (US) -ˈer.ə.t̬i, -ˈær-

unfashionab|le ʌnˈfæʃ.ᵊn.ə.b|l̩, ˌʌn-, ˈ-nə- **-ly** -li

unfasten ʌnˈfɑː.sᵊn, ˌʌn- (US) -ˈfæs- **-s** -z **-ing** -ɪŋ, -ˈfɑːs.nɪŋ (US) -ˈfæs.nɪŋ **-ed** -d

unfathomab|le ʌnˈfæð.ə.mə.b|l̩, ˌʌn- **-ly** -li **-leness** -l̩.nəs, -nɪs

unfathomed ʌnˈfæð.əmd, ˌʌn-

unfavo(u)rab|le ʌnˈfeɪ.vᵊr.ə.b|l̩, ˌʌn-, -ˈfeɪv.rə- **-ly** -li **-leness** -l̩.nəs, -nɪs

unfavo(u)rite ʌnˈfeɪ.vᵊr.ɪt, ˌʌn-, -ˈfeɪv.rɪt

unfazed ʌnˈfeɪzd

unfed ʌnˈfed, ˌʌn-

unfeeling ʌnˈfiː.lɪŋ, ˌʌn- **-ly** -li **-ness** -nəs, -nɪs

unfeigned ʌnˈfeɪnd, ˌʌn-

unfeigned|ly ʌnˈfeɪ.nɪd|.li, ˌʌn- **-ness** -nəs, -nɪs

unfelt ʌnˈfelt, ˌʌn-

unfermented ˌʌn.fəˈmen.tɪd, -fɜːˈ- (US) -fɚˈmen.t̬ɪd

unfertilized, -ised ʌnˈfɜː.tᵊl.aɪzd, ˌʌn-, -tɪ.laɪzd (US) -ˈfɝː.t̬ᵊl.aɪzd

unfett|er ʌnˈfet|.əʳ, ˌʌn- (US) -ˈfet̬|.ɚ **-ers** -əz (US) -ɚz **-ering** -ᵊr.ɪŋ **-ed** -əd (US) -ɚd

unfettered ʌnˈfet.əd (US) -ˈfet̬.ɚd

unfilial ʌnˈfɪl.i.əl, ˌʌn- **-ly** -i

unfinished ʌnˈfɪn.ɪʃt, ˌʌn- ˌ**unfinished ˈbusiness, unˌfinished ˈbusiness**

unfit (*adj.*) ʌnˈfɪt **-ly** -li **-ness** -nəs, -nɪs

un|fit (*v.*) ʌn|ˈfɪt, ˌʌn- **-fits** -ˈfɪts **-fitting/ly** -ˈfɪt.ɪŋ/li (US) -ˈfɪt̬.ɪŋ/li **-fitted** -ˈfɪt.ɪd (US) -ˈfɪt̬.ɪd

unfix ʌnˈfɪks, ˌʌn- **-es** -ɪz **-ing** -ɪŋ **-ed** -t

unflagging ʌnˈflæɡ.ɪŋ, ˌʌn- **-ly** -li

unflappab|le ʌnˈflæp.ə.b|l̩, ˌʌn- **-ly** -li

unflattering ʌnˈflæt.ᵊr.ɪŋ, ˌʌn- (US) -ˈflæt̬- **-ly** -li

unfledged ʌnˈfledʒd, ˌʌn-

unflinching ʌnˈflɪn.tʃɪŋ, ˌʌn- **-ly** -li **-ness** -nəs, -nɪs

unfold ʌnˈfəʊld, ˌʌn- (US) -ˈfoʊld **-s** -z **-ing** -ɪŋ **-ed** -ɪd

unforeseeable ˌʌn.fɔːˈsiː.ə.bl̩, -fəˈ- (US) -fɔːrˈ-, -fɚˈ-

unforeseen ˌʌn.fɔːˈsiːn, -fəˈ- (US) -fɔːrˈ-, -fɚˈ- ˌ**unforeseen ˈcircumstances**

unforgettab|le ˌʌn.fəˈɡet.ə.b|l̩ (US) -fɚˈɡet̬- **-ly** -li

unforgivable ˌʌn.fəˈɡɪv.ə.bl̩ (US) -fɚˈ-

unforgiven ˌʌn.fəˈɡɪv.ən (US) -fɚˈ-

unforgiving ˌʌn.fəˈɡɪv.ɪŋ (US) -fɚˈ- **-ly** -li **-ness** -nəs, -nɪs

unforgotten ˌʌn.fəˈɡɒt.ᵊn (US) -fɚˈɡɑː.tᵊn

unformatted ʌnˈfɔː.mæt.ɪd (US) -ˈfɔːr.mæt̬-

unformed ʌnˈfɔːmd, ˌʌn- (US) -ˈfɔːrmd

unforthcoming ˌʌn.fɔːθˈkʌm.ɪŋ (US) -fɔːrθ-

unfortified ʌnˈfɔː.tɪ.faɪd, ˌʌn- (US) -ˈfɔːr.t̬ɪ-

unfortunate ʌnˈfɔː.tʃᵊn.ət, ˌʌn-, -ɪt (US) -ˈfɔːr- **-ly** -li **-ness** -nəs, -nɪs

unfounded ʌnˈfaʊn.dɪd, ˌʌn-

unframed ʌnˈfreɪmd, ˌʌn-

un|freeze ʌn|ˈfriːz (US) ˌʌn- **-freezes** -ˈfriː.zɪz **-froze** -ˈfrəʊz (US) -ˈfroʊz **-frozen** -ˈfrəʊ.zᵊn (US) -ˈfroʊ.zᵊn

unfrequented ˌʌn.frɪˈkwen.tɪd (US) ʌnˈfriː.kwen.t̬ɪd, ˌʌn-

unfriend|ly ʌnˈfrend|.li, ˌʌn- **-liness** -lɪ.nəs, -lɪ.nɪs

unfrock ʌnˈfrɒk, ˌʌn- (US) -ˈfrɑːk **-s** -s **-ing** -ɪŋ **-ed** -t

unfruitful ʌnˈfruːt.fᵊl, ˌʌn-, -fʊl **-ly** -i **-ness** -nəs, -nɪs

unfulfilled ˌʌn.fʊlˈfɪld

unfunny ʌnˈfʌn.i, ˌʌn-

unfurl ʌnˈfɜːl, ˌʌn- (US) -ˈfɝːl **-s** -z **-ing** -ɪŋ **-ed** -d

unfurnished ʌnˈfɜː.nɪʃt, ˌʌn- (US) -ˈfɝː-

ungainl|y ʌnˈɡeɪn.l|i, ˌʌn-, ʌŋ-, ˌʌŋ- (US) ʌn-, ˌʌn- **-iest** -i.ɪst, -i.əst **-iness** -ɪ.nəs, -ɪ.nɪs

ungallant ʌnˈɡæl.ənt, ˌʌn.ɡəˈlænt, ʌŋ-, ˌʌŋ- (US) ʌnˈɡæl.ənt, ˌʌn.ɡəˈlænt, -ˈlɑːnt **-ly** -li

ungenerous ʌnˈdʒen.ᵊr.əs, ˌʌn- **-ly** -li

ungentlemanl|y ʌnˈdʒent.l̩.mən.l|i, ˌʌn- **-iness** -ɪ.nəs, -ɪ.nɪs

un-get-at-able ˌʌn.ɡetˈæt.ə.bl̩, ˌʌŋ- (US) ˌʌn.ɡet̬ˈæt̬-

ungird ʌnˈɡɜːd, ˌʌn-, ʌŋ-, ˌʌŋ- (US) ʌnˈɡɝːd, ˌʌn- **-s** -z **-ing** -ɪŋ **-ed** -ɪd

unglazed ʌnˈɡleɪzd, ˌʌn-, ʌŋ-, ˌʌŋ- (US) ʌn-, ˌʌn-

ungloved ʌnˈɡlʌvd, ˌʌn-, ʌŋ-, ˌʌŋ- (US) ʌn-, ˌʌn-

unglu|e ʌnˈɡluː, ˌʌn-, ʌŋ-, ˌʌŋ- (US) ʌn-, ˌʌn- **-es** -z **-ing** -ɪŋ **-ed** -d

ungodl|y ʌnˈɡɒd.l|i, ˌʌn-, ʌŋ-, ˌʌŋ- (US) ʌnˈɡɑːd.l|i, ˌʌn- **-ier** -i.əʳ (US) -i.ɚ **-iest** -i.ɪst, -i.əst **-iness** -ɪ.nəs, -ɪ.nɪs

Ungoed ˈʌŋ.ɡɔɪd

ungotten ʌnˈɡɒt.ᵊn, ˌʌn-, ʌŋ-, ˌʌŋ- (US) ʌnˈɡɑː.tᵊn, ˌʌn-

ungovernab|le ʌnˈɡʌv.ᵊn.ə.b|l̩, ˌʌn-, ʌŋ-, ˌʌŋ-, ˈ-nə- (US) ʌnˈɡʌv.ɚ.nə-, ˌʌn- **-ly** -li **-leness** -l̩.nəs (US) -nɪs

ungoverned ʌnˈɡʌv.ᵊnd, ˌʌn-, ʌŋ-, ˌʌŋ- (US) ʌnˈɡʌv.ɚnd, ˌʌn-

ungraceful ʌnˈɡreɪs.fᵊl, ˌʌn-, ʌŋ-, ˌʌŋ-, -fʊl (US) ʌn-, ˌʌn- **-ly** -i **-ness** -nəs, -nɪs

ungracious ʌnˈɡreɪ.ʃəs, ˌʌn-, ʌŋ-, ˌʌŋ- (US) ʌn-, ˌʌn- **-ly** -li **-ness** -nəs, -nɪs

ungrammatic|al ˌʌn.ɡrəˈmæt.ɪ.k|ᵊl, ˌʌŋ- (US) ˌʌn.ɡrəˈmæt̬- **-ally** -ᵊl.i, -li

ungrateful ʌnˈɡreɪt.fᵊl, ˌʌn-, ʌŋ-, ˌʌŋ-, -fʊl (US) ʌn-, ˌʌn- **-ly** -li **-ness** -nəs, -nɪs

ungrounded ʌnˈɡraʊn.dɪd, ˌʌn-, ʌŋ-, ˌʌŋ- (US) ʌn-, ˌʌn-

ungrudging ʌnˈɡrʌdʒ.ɪŋ, ˌʌn-, ʌŋ-, ˌʌŋ- (US) ʌn-, ˌʌn- **-ly** -li

unguarded ʌnˈɡɑː.dɪd, ˌʌn-, ʌŋ-, ˌʌŋ- (US) ʌnˈɡɑːr-, ˌʌn- **-ly** -li **-ness** -nəs, -nɪs

unguent ˈʌŋ.ɡwənt, -ɡju.ənt (US) -ɡwənt **-s** -s

unguided ʌnˈɡaɪ.dɪd, ˌʌn-, ʌŋ-, ˌʌŋ- (US) ʌn-, ˌʌn-

ungul|a ˈʌŋ.ɡjə.l|ə, -ɡjʊ- **-ae** -iː

ungulate ˈʌŋ.ɡjə.leɪt, -ɡjʊ-, -lət, -lɪt (US) -lɪt, -leɪt **-s** -s

unhallowed ʌnˈhæl.əʊd, ˌʌn- (US) -oʊd

unhampered ʌnˈhæm.pəd, ˌʌn- (US) -pɚd

unhand ʌnˈhænd, ˌʌn- **-s** -z **-ing** -ɪŋ **-ed** -ɪd

unhandy ʌnˈhæn.di, ˌʌn-

unhapp|y ʌnˈhæp|.i, ˌʌn- **-ier** -i.əʳ (US) -i.ɚ **-iest** -i.ɪst, -i.əst **-ily** -ɪ.li, -ᵊl.i **-iness** -ɪ.nɪs, -ɪ.nəs

unharmed ʌnˈhɑːmd, ˌʌn- (US) -ˈhɑːrmd

unharness ʌnˈhɑː.nɪs, ˌʌn- (US) -ˈhɑːr- **-es** -ɪz **-ing** -ɪŋ **-ed** -t

unhatched ʌnˈhætʃt, ˌʌn-

unhealth|y ʌnˈhel.θ|i, ˌʌn- **-ier** -i.əʳ (US) -i.ɚ **-iest** -i.ɪst, -i.əst **-ily** -ɪ.li, -ᵊl.i **-iness** -ɪ.nəs, -ɪ.nɪs

unheard ʌnˈhɜːd, ˌʌn- (US) -ˈhɝːd
unheard-of ʌnˈhɜːdˌɒv (US) -ˈhɝːdˌɑːv, -əv
unheeded ʌnˈhiː.dɪd, ˌʌn-
unheeding ʌnˈhiː.dɪŋ **-ly** -li
unhelpful ʌnˈhelp.fʊl, -fəl **-ly** -i **-ness** -nəs, -nɪs
unheralded ʌnˈher.əl.dɪd
unhesitating ʌnˈhez.ɪ.teɪ.tɪŋ, ˌʌn-, ˈ-ə- (US) -t̬ɪŋ **-ly** -li
unhing|e ʌnˈhɪndʒ, ˌʌn- **-es** -ɪz **-ing** -ɪŋ **-ed** -d
unhistoric ˌʌn.hɪˈstɒr.ɪk, -ɪˈ- (US) -hɪˈstɔːr- **-al** -əl
unhitch ʌnˈhɪtʃ, ˌʌn- **-es** -ɪz **-ing** -ɪŋ **-ed** -t
unhol|y ʌnˈhəʊ.l|i, ˌʌn- (US) -ˈhoʊ- **-iness** -ɪ.nəs, -ɪ.nɪs **unˌholy alˈliance**
unhook ʌnˈhʊk, ˌʌn- **-s** -s **-ing** -ɪŋ **-ed** -t
unhoped-for ʌnˈhəʊptˌfɔːr (US) -ˈhoʊptˌfɔːr
unhors|e ʌnˈhɔːs, ˌʌn- (US) -ˈhɔːrs **-es** -ɪz **-ing** -ɪŋ **-ed** -t
unhous|e ʌnˈhaʊz, ˌʌn- **-es** -ɪz **-ing** -ɪŋ **-ed** -d
unhuman ʌnˈhjuː.mən, ˌʌn-
unhung ʌnˈhʌŋ, ˌʌn-
unhurried ʌnˈhʌr.ɪd, ˌʌn- (US) -ˈhɝː- **-ly** -li **-ness** -nəs, -nɪs
unhurt ʌnˈhɜːt, ˌʌn- (US) -ˈhɝːt
uni- juː.nɪ-, -ni-
Note: Prefix. Normally takes primary or secondary stress on the first syllable, e.g. **unify** /ˈjuː.nɪ.faɪ (US) -nə-/, **unification** /ˌjuː.nɪ.fɪˈkeɪ.ʃən (US) -nə-/.
uni ˈjuː.ni **-s** -z
Uniate ˈjuː.ni.ət, -ɪt, -eɪt (US) -ɪt, -eɪt **-s** -s
unicameral ˌjuː.nɪˈkæm.ər.əl
UNICEF, Unicef ˈjuː.nɪ.sef
unicellular ˌjuː.nɪˈsel.jə.lər, -jʊ- (US) -jə.lɚ
unicorn ˈjuː.nɪ.kɔːn (US) -kɔːrn **-s** -z
unicycl|e ˈjuː.nɪˌsaɪ.kl̩ (US) -nə- **-es** -z **-ist/s** -ɪst/s
unidentified ˌʌn.aɪˈden.tɪ.faɪd (US) -t̬ə- **ˌunidentified ˌflying ˈobject**
unidimensional ˌjuː.nɪ.daɪˈmen.tʃən.əl, -dɪˈ-, -dəˈ- (US) -nə.dəˈment.ʃə-, -dɪˈ-, -daɪ-
unidiomatic ʌnˌɪd.i.əʊˈmæt.ɪk, ˌʌn- (US) -əˈmæt̬- **-ally** -əl.i, -li
unifiable ˈjuː.nɪ.faɪ.ə.bl̩ (US) -nə-
unification ˌjuː.nɪ.fɪˈkeɪ.ʃən, -nə- (US) -nə- **-s** -z
uniform ˈjuː.nɪ.fɔːm, -nə- (US) -nə.fɔːrm **-s** -z **-ed** -d **-ly** -li **-ness** -nəs, -nɪs
uniformity ˌjuː.nɪˈfɔː.mə.ti, -nəˈ-, -mɪ- (US) -nəˈfɔːr.mə.t̬i
uni|fy ˈjuː.nɪ|.faɪ, -nə- (US) -nə- **-fies** -faɪz **-fying** -faɪ.ɪŋ **-fied** -faɪd **-fier/s** -faɪ.ər/z (US) -faɪ.ɚ/z
Unigate® ˈjuː.nɪ.geɪt, -nə- (US) -nə-
unilateral ˌjuː.nɪˈlæt.ər.əl (US) -nəˈlæt̬- **-ly** -i **-ism** -ɪ.zəm **-ist/s** -ɪst/s
Unilever® ˈjuː.nɪ.liː.vər (US) -nə.liː.vɚ
unimaginab|le ˌʌn.ɪˈmædʒ.ɪ.nə.bl|l̩, -ən.ə- **-ly** -li **-leness** -l̩.nəs, -nɪs
unimaginative ˌʌn.ɪˈmædʒ.ɪ.nə.tɪv, -ən.ə- (US) -t̬ɪv **-ly** -li **-ness** -nəs, -nɪs
unimagined ˌʌn.ɪˈmædʒ.ɪnd, -ənd
unimpaired ˌʌn.ɪmˈpeəd (US) -ˈperd
unimpassioned ʌn.ɪmˈpæʃ.ənd
unimpeachab|le ˌʌn.ɪmˈpiː.tʃə.bl|l̩ **-ly** -li **-leness** -l̩.nəs, -nɪs
unimpeded ˌʌn.ɪmˈpiː.dɪd
unimportance ˌʌn.ɪmˈpɔː.tənts (US) -ˈpɔːr-
unimportant ˌʌn.ɪmˈpɔː.tənt (US) -ˈpɔːr- **-ly** -li
unimpressed ˌʌn.ɪmˈprest
unimpressive ˌʌn.ɪmˈpres.ɪv **-ly** -li
unimproved ʌn.ɪmˈpruːvd
uninflated ˌʌn.ɪnˈfleɪ.tɪd (US) -t̬ɪd
uninflected ˌʌn.ɪnˈflek.tɪd
uninfluenced ʌnˈɪn.flu.əntst, ˌʌn-, -fluəntst (US) -flu.əntst
uninformative ˌʌn.ɪnˈfɔː.mə.tɪv (US) -ˈfɔːr.mə.t̬ɪv **-ly** -li
uninformed ˌʌn.ɪnˈfɔːmd (US) -ˈfɔːrmd
uninhabitable ˌʌn.ɪnˈhæb.ɪ.tə.bl̩, ˈ-ə- (US) -t̬ə- **-ness** -nəs, -nɪs
uninhabited ˌʌn.ɪnˈhæb.ɪ.tɪd, ˈ-ə- (US) -t̬ɪd
uninhibited ˌʌn.ɪnˈhɪb.ɪ.tɪd, ˈ-ə- (US) -t̬ɪd **-ly** -li **-ness** -nəs, -nɪs
uninitiated ˌʌn.ɪˈnɪʃ.i.eɪ.tɪd (US) -t̬ɪd
uninjured ʌnˈɪn.dʒəd, ˌʌn- (US) -dʒɚd
uninspired ˌʌn.ɪnˈspaɪəd (US) -ˈspaɪɚd
uninspiring ˌʌn.ɪnˈspaɪə.rɪŋ (US) -ˈspaɪ- **-ly** -li
uninstall ˌʌn.ɪnˈstɔːl (US) -ˈstɔːl, -ˈstɑːl **-s** -z **-ing** -ɪŋ **-ed** -d
uninstructed ˌʌn.ɪnˈstrʌk.tɪd
uninsured ˌʌn.ɪnˈʃʊəd, -ˈʃɔːd (US) -ˈʃʊrd
unintelligent ˌʌn.ɪnˈtel.ɪ.dʒənt, ˈ-ə- **-ly** -li
unintelligibility ˌʌn.ɪnˌtel.ɪ.dʒəˈbɪl.ə.ti, ˌ-ə-, -dʒɪˈ-, -ɪ.ti (US) -ə.t̬i
unintelligib|le ˌʌn.ɪnˈtel.ɪ.dʒə.bl|l̩, ˈ-ə-, -dʒɪ- **-ly** -li
unintentional ˌʌn.ɪnˈten.tʃən.əl, -ˈtentʃ.nəl **-ly** -i
uninterest|ed ʌnˈɪn.trə.st|ɪd, ˌʌn-, -trɪ-, -tres.t|ɪd, -tər.ə.st|ɪd, -ɪ-, -es.t|ɪd (US) -trɪ.st|ɪd, -trə-, -tres.t|ɪd, -tɚ.es-, -ə.st|ɪd **-ing** -ɪŋ
uninterrupted ʌnˌɪn.tərˈʌp.tɪd, ˌʌn- (US) -təˈrʌp- **-ly** -li
uninvited ˌʌn.ɪnˈvaɪ.tɪd (US) -t̬ɪd
uninviting ʌn.ɪnˈvaɪ.tɪŋ (US) -t̬ɪŋ **-ly** -li **-ness** -nəs, -nɪs
union (U) ˈjuː.njən, -ni.ən (US) ˈ-njən **-s** -z **ˌUnion ˈJack**
union|ism (U) ˈjuː.njə.n|ɪ.zəm, -ni.ə- (US) -njə- **-ist/s** -ɪst/s
unionization, -isa- ˌjuː.njə.naɪˈzeɪ.ʃən, -ni.ə-, -ɪˈ- (US) -njə.nɪˈ-
unioniz|e, -is|e ˈjuː.njə.naɪz, -ni.ə- (US) -ˈnjə- **-es** -ɪz **-ing** -ɪŋ **-ed** -d
unipartite ˌjuː.nɪˈpɑː.taɪt (US) -ˈpɑːr-
unique juːˈniːk **-ly** -li **-ness** -nəs, -nɪs
Uniroyal® ˈjuː.nɪ.rɔɪəl
unisex ˈjuː.nɪ.seks (US) -nə-
unisexual ˌjuː.nɪˈsek.ʃʊəl, -sjʊəl (US) -nəˈsek.ʃu.əl
unison ˈjuː.nɪ.sən, -nə-, -zən (US) -nə- **-s** -z
unissued ʌnˈɪʃ.uːd, ˌʌn-, -ˈɪs.juːd (US) -ˈɪʃ.uːd
unit ˈjuː.nɪt **-s** -s **ˌunit ˈtrust**
UNITA, Unita juːˈniː.tə (US) -t̬ə
unitable juːˈnaɪ.tə.bl̩ (US) -t̬ə-
unitarian (U) ˌjuː.nɪˈteə.ri.ən (US) -ˈter.i- **-s** -z **-ism** -ɪ.zəm
unitary ˈjuː.nɪ.tər.i, -tri (US) -ter.i
u|nite juː|ˈnaɪt, jʊ- **-nites** -ˈnaɪts **-niting** -ˈnaɪ.tɪŋ (US) -ˈnaɪ.t̬ɪŋ **-nited/ly** -ˈnaɪ.tɪd/li (US) -ˈnaɪ.t̬ɪd/li **-niter/s** -ˈnaɪ.tər/z (US) -ˈnaɪ.t̬ɚ/z
United Arab Emirates juːˌnaɪ.tɪdˌær.əbˈem.ɪ.rəts, jʊ-, -ər.əts, -ɪts, -eɪts (US) -t̬ɪdˌer.əbˈem.ɚ.əts, -ˌær-; -ɪˈmɪr-
United Kingdom juːˌnaɪ.tɪdˈkɪŋ.dəm, jʊ- (US) -t̬ɪdˈ-
United Nations juːˌnaɪ.tɪdˈneɪ.ʃənz, jʊ- (US) -t̬ɪdˈ-
United Reformed Church juːˌnaɪ.tɪd.rɪˈfɔːmdˌtʃɜːtʃ, jʊ- (US) -t̬ɪd.rɪˈfɔːrmdˌtʃɝːtʃ
United States juːˌnaɪ.tɪdˈsteɪts, jʊ- (US) -t̬ɪdˈ- **Uˌnited ˌStates of Aˈmerica**
unit|y (U) ˈjuː.nə.t|i, -nɪ- (US) -nə.t̬|i **-ies** -iz
univalen|t ˌjuː.nɪˈveɪ.lən|t (US) -nəˈ-; juːˈnɪv.əl.ən|t **-ce** -ts
univalve ˈjuː.nɪ.vælv (US) -nə- **-s** -z
universal ˌjuː.nɪˈvɜː.səl, -nəˈ- (US) -nəˈvɝː- **-s** -z **-ly** -i **-ness** -nəs, -nɪs **-ism** -ɪ.zəm **-ist/s** -ɪst/s *stress shift:* ˌuniversal ˈjoint
universality ˌjuː.nɪ.vɜːˈsæl.ə.ti, -nə-, -ɪ.ti (US) -nə.vɝːˈsæl.ə.t̬i
universaliz|e, -is|e ˌjuː.nɪˈvɜː.səl.aɪz, -nəˈ- (US) -nəˈvɝː.sə.laɪz **-es** -ɪz **-ing** -ɪŋ **-ed** -d
univers|e ˈjuː.nɪ.vɜːs, -nə- (US) -nə.vɝːs **-es** -ɪz
universit|y ˌjuː.nɪˈvɜː.sə.t|i, -nəˈ-, -sɪ- (US) -nəˈvɝː.sə.t̬|i **-ies** -iz *stress shift:* ˌuniversity ˈgrant
univocal ˌjuː.nɪˈvəʊ.kəl (US) -ˈnɪv.ə- **-s** -z

Unix®, UNIX ˈjuː.nɪks
unjust ʌnˈdʒʌst, ˌʌn- **-ly** -li **-ness** -nəs, -nɪs
unjustifiab|le ʌnˌdʒʌs.tɪˈfaɪ.ə.b|l̩, ˌʌn.dʒʌs-, ˌʌnˌdʒʌs-, -təˈ- ⓤⓢ ʌnˌdʒʌs.tɪˈfaɪ.ə.b|l̩, ˌʌn-, -təˈ-, -ˈdʒʌs.tɪ.faɪ-, -tə- **-ly** -li **-leness** -l̩.nəs, -nɪs
unjustified ʌnˈdʒʌs.tɪ.faɪd, ˌʌn-, -tə- **-ly** -li
unkempt ʌnˈkempt, ˌʌn-, ʌŋ-, ˌʌŋ- ⓤⓢ ʌn-, ˌʌn-
unkept ʌnˈkept, ˌʌn-, ʌŋ-, ˌʌŋ- ⓤⓢ ʌn-, ˌʌn-
unkin|d ʌnˈkaɪn|d, ˌʌn-, ʌŋ-, ˌʌŋ- ⓤⓢ ʌn-, ˌʌn- **-der** -dəʳ ⓤⓢ -dɚ **-dest** -dɪst, -dəst **-dly** -d.li **-dness** -*d*.nɪs, -nəs
un|knot ʌn|ˈnɒt, ˌʌn- ⓤⓢ -ˈnɑːt **-knots** -ˈnɒts ⓤⓢ -ˈnɑːts **-knotting** -ˈnɒt.ɪŋ ⓤⓢ -ˈnɑː.t̬ɪŋ **-knotted** -ˈnɒt.ɪd ⓤⓢ -ˈnɑː.t̬ɪd
unknowable ʌnˈnəʊ.ə.bl̩, ˌʌn- ⓤⓢ -ˈnoʊ-
unknowing ʌnˈnəʊ.ɪŋ, ˌʌn- ⓤⓢ -ˈnoʊ- **-ly** -li **-ness** -nəs, -nɪs
unknown ʌnˈnəʊn, ˌʌn- ⓤⓢ -ˈnoʊn **-s** -z **ˌUnknown ˈSoldier; ˌunknown ˈquantity**
unlac|e ʌnˈleɪs, ˌʌn- **-es** -ɪz **-ing** -ɪŋ **-ed** -t
unlad|e ʌnˈleɪd ⓤⓢ ˌʌn- **-es** -z **-ing** -ɪŋ **-ed** -ɪd **-en** -ᵊn
unladylike ʌnˈleɪ.di.laɪk, ˌʌn-
unlamented ˌʌn.ləˈmen.tɪd ⓤⓢ -t̬ɪd
unlash ʌnˈlæʃ ⓤⓢ ˌʌn- **-es** -ɪz **-ing** -ɪŋ **-ed** -t
unlatch ʌnˈlætʃ ⓤⓢ ˌʌn- **-es** -ɪz **-ing** -ɪŋ **-ed** -t
unlawful ʌnˈlɔː.fᵊl, ˌʌn-, -fʊl ⓤⓢ -ˈlɑː-, -ˈlɔː- **-ly** -i **-ness** -nəs, -nɪs
unleaded ʌnˈled.ɪd, ˌʌn- **ˌunleaded ˈpetrol, unˌleaded ˈpetrol**
unlearn ʌnˈlɜːn, ˌʌn- ⓤⓢ -ˈlɝːn **-s** -z **-ing** -ɪŋ **-ed** -t, -d **-t** -t
unlearned ʌnˈlɜː.nɪd, ˌʌn- ⓤⓢ -ˈlɝː- **-ly** -li **-ness** -nəs, -nɪs
unleash ʌnˈliːʃ, ˌʌn- **-es** -ɪz **-ing** -ɪŋ **-ed** -t
unleavened ʌnˈlev.ᵊnd, ˌʌn- **ˌunleavened ˈbread, unˌleavened ˈbread**
unled ʌnˈled, ˌʌn-
unless ənˈles, ʌn-
unlettered ʌnˈlet.əd, ˌʌn- ⓤⓢ -ˈlet̬.ɚd
unliberated ʌnˈlɪb.ᵊr.eɪ.tɪd, ˌʌn- ⓤⓢ -ə.reɪ.t̬ɪd
unlicensed ʌnˈlaɪ.sᵊn*t*st, ˌʌn-
unlike ʌnˈlaɪk, ˌʌn-
unlikel|y ʌnˈlaɪ.kl|i, ˌʌn- **-ier** -i.əʳ ⓤⓢ -i.ɚ **-iest** -i.ɪst, -i.əst **-ihood** -ɪ.hʊd **-iness** -ɪ.nəs, -ɪ.nɪs
unlikeness ʌnˈlaɪk.nəs, ˌʌn-, -nɪs
unlimb|er ʌnˈlɪm.b|əʳ, ˌʌn- ⓤⓢ -b|ɚ **-ers** -əz ⓤⓢ -ɚz **-ering** -ᵊr.ɪŋ **-ered** -əd ⓤⓢ -ɚd
unlimited ʌnˈlɪm.ɪ.tɪd, ˌʌn- ⓤⓢ -t̬ɪd
unlink ʌnˈlɪŋk ⓤⓢ ˌʌn- **-s** -s **-ing** -ɪŋ **-ed** -t
unliquidated ʌnˈlɪk.wɪ.deɪ.tɪd, ˌʌn-, -wə- ⓤⓢ -wə.deɪ.t̬ɪd
unlisted ʌnˈlɪs.tɪd
unlit ʌnˈlɪt, ˌʌn-
unload ʌnˈləʊd, ˌʌn- ⓤⓢ -ˈloʊd **-s** -z **-ing** -ɪŋ **-ed** -ɪd **-er/s** -əʳ/z ⓤⓢ -ɚ/z
unlock ʌnˈlɒk, ˌʌn- ⓤⓢ -ˈlɑːk **-s** -s **-ing** -ɪŋ **-ed** -t
unlooked-for ʌnˈlʊkt,fɔːʳ, ˌʌn- ⓤⓢ -ˌfɔːr
unloos|e ʌnˈluːs, ˌʌn- **-es** -ɪz **-ing** -ɪŋ **-ed** -t
unloosen ʌnˈluː.sᵊn, ˌʌn- **-s** -z **-ing** -ɪŋ, -ˈluːs.nɪŋ **-ed** -d
unlovel|y ʌnˈlʌv.l|i, ˌʌn- **-iness** -ɪ.nəs, -ɪ.nɪs
unloving ʌnˈlʌv.ɪŋ, ˌʌn-
unluck|y ʌnˈlʌk|.i, ˌʌn- **-ier** -i.əʳ ⓤⓢ -i.ɚ **-iest** -i.ɪst, -i.əst **-ily** -ɪ.li, -ᵊl.i **-iness** -ɪ.nəs, -ɪ.nɪs
unmade ʌnˈmeɪd, ˌʌn-
un|make ʌn|ˈmeɪk, ˌʌn- **-makes** -ˈmeɪks **-making** -ˈmeɪ.kɪŋ **-made** -ˈmeɪd
unman ʌnˈmæn, ˌʌn- **-s** -z **-ning** -ɪŋ **-ned** -d
unmanageab|le ʌnˈmæn.ɪ.dʒə.b|l̩, ˌʌn-, ˈ-ə- **-ly** -li **-leness** -l̩.nəs, -nɪs
unmanl|y ʌnˈmæn.l|i, ˌʌn- **-iness** -ɪ.nəs, -ɪ.nɪs
unmannered ʌnˈmæn.əd ⓤⓢ -ɚd **-ly** -li
unmannerl|y ʌnˈmæn.ᵊl|.i, ˌʌn- ⓤⓢ -ɚ.l|i **-iness** -ɪ.nəs, -ɪ.nɪs
unmarked ʌnˈmɑːkt, ˌʌn- ⓤⓢ -ˈmɑːrkt
unmarriageable ʌnˈmær.ɪ.dʒə.bl̩, ˌʌn- ⓤⓢ -ˈmer-, -ˈmær-
unmarried ʌnˈmær.ɪd, ˌʌn- ⓤⓢ -ˈmer-, -ˈmær-
unmask ʌnˈmɑːsk, ˌʌn- ⓤⓢ -ˈmæsk **-s** -s **-ing** -ɪŋ **-ed** -t
unmatched ʌnˈmætʃt, ˌʌn-
unmeaning ʌnˈmiː.nɪŋ, ˌʌn-
unmeaning|ly ʌnˈmiː.nɪŋ|.li, ˌʌn- **-ness** -nəs, -nɪs
unmeasurable ʌnˈmeʒ.ᵊr.ə.bl̩, ˌʌn-
unmeasured ʌnˈmeʒ.əd, ˌʌn- ⓤⓢ -ɚd
unmentionable ʌnˈmen.*t*ʃᵊn.ə.bl̩, ˌʌn-, -ˈmen*t*ʃ.nə- ⓤⓢ -ˈmen*t*.ʃᵊn.ə-, -ˈmen*t*ʃ.nə- **-s** -z **-ness** -nəs, -nɪs
unmentioned ʌnˈmen.*t*ʃᵊnd, ˌʌn- ⓤⓢ -ˈmen*t*.ʃᵊnd
unmerciful ʌnˈmɜː.sɪ.fᵊl, ˌʌn-, -sə-, -fʊl ⓤⓢ -ˈmɝː- **-ly** -i **-ness** -nəs, -nɪs
unmerited ʌnˈmer.ɪ.tɪd, ˌʌn- ⓤⓢ -t̬ɪd
unmethodic|al ˌʌn.məˈθɒd.ɪ.k|ᵊl, -mɪˈ-, -meθˈɒd- ⓤⓢ -məˈθɑː.dɪ- **-ally** -ᵊl.i, -li
unmetred, unmetered ʌnˈmiː.təd ⓤⓢ -t̬ɚd
unmindful ʌnˈmaɪn*d*.fᵊl, ˌʌn-, -fʊl **-ly** -i **-ness** -nəs, -nɪs
unmissable ʌnˈmɪs.ə.bl̩
unmistakab|le ˌʌn.mɪˈsteɪ.kə.b|l̩ **-ly** -li **-leness** -l̩.nəs, -nɪs
unmitigated ʌnˈmɪt.ɪ.geɪ.tɪd, ˌʌn-, ˈ-ə- ⓤⓢ -ˈmɪt̬.ə.geɪ.t̬ɪd
unmixed ʌnˈmɪkst, ˌʌn-
unmodifiable ʌnˈmɒd.ɪ.faɪ.ə.bl̩, ˌʌn- ⓤⓢ -ˈmɑː.dɪ-
unmodified ʌnˈmɒd.ɪ.faɪd, ˌʌn- ⓤⓢ -ˈmɑː.dɪ-
unmolested ˌʌn.məʊˈles.tɪd ⓤⓢ -məˈ-
unmounted ʌnˈmaʊn.tɪd, ˌʌn- ⓤⓢ -t̬ɪd
unmourned ʌnˈmɔːnd, ˌʌn- ⓤⓢ -ˈmɔːrnd
unmov(e)able ʌnˈmuː.və.bl̩, ˌʌn-
unmoved ʌnˈmuːvd, ˌʌn-
unmuffl|e ʌnˈmʌf.l̩, ˌʌn- **-es** -z **-ing** -ɪŋ, -ˈmʌf.lɪŋ **-ed** -d
unmusic|al ʌnˈmjuː.zɪ.k|ᵊl, ˌʌn- **-ally** -ᵊl.i, -li
unmuzzl|e ʌnˈmʌz.l̩, ˌʌn- **-es** -z **-ing** -ˈmʌz.lɪŋ **-ed** -d
unnamed ʌnˈneɪmd, ˌʌn-
unnatural ʌnˈnætʃ.ᵊr.ᵊl, ˌʌn-, -ʊ.rᵊl ⓤⓢ -ɚ.əl, ˈ-rᵊl **-ly** -i **-ness** -nəs, -nɪs
unnavigable ʌnˈnæv.ɪ.gə.bl̩, ˌʌn-
unnecessarily ʌnˈnes.ə.sᵊr.ᵊl.i, ˌʌn-, ˈ-ɪ-, -ɪ.li; -ˌnes.əˈser-, -ɪˈ- ⓤⓢ -ˌnes.əˈser-; -ˈnes.ə.ser-
unnecessary ʌnˈnes.ə.sᵊr.i, ˌʌn-, ˈ-ɪ-, -ser- ⓤⓢ -ser-
unneighbo(u)rl|y ʌnˈneɪ.bᵊl|.i, ˌʌn- ⓤⓢ -bɚ.l|i **-iness** -ɪ.nəs, -ɪ.nɪs
unnerv|e ʌnˈnɜːv, ˌʌn- ⓤⓢ -ˈnɝːv **-es** -z **-ing/ly** -ɪŋ/li **-ed** -d
unnoticeab|le ʌnˈnəʊ.tɪ.sə.b|l̩, ˌʌn-, -tə- ⓤⓢ -ˈnoʊ.t̬ə- **-ly** -li
unnoticed ʌnˈnəʊ.tɪst, ˌʌn- ⓤⓢ -ˈnoʊ.t̬ɪst
unnumbered ʌnˈnʌm.bəd, ˌʌn- ⓤⓢ -bɚd
UNO ˈjuː.nəʊ ⓤⓢ -noʊ
uno (U) ˈuː.nəʊ, ˈjuː- ⓤⓢ -noʊ **ˌFiat ˈUno®**
unobjectionab|le ˌʌn.əbˈdʒek.ʃᵊn.ə.b|l̩, -ˈdʒekʃ.nə- **-ly** -li
unobliging ˌʌn.əˈblaɪ.dʒɪŋ **-ly** -li
unobliterated ˌʌn.əˈblɪt.ᵊr.eɪ.tɪd ⓤⓢ -ˈblɪt̬.ə.reɪ.t̬ɪd
unobservant ˌʌn.əbˈzɜː.vᵊnt ⓤⓢ -ˈzɝː- **-ly** -li
unobserv|ed ˌʌn.əbˈzɜːv|d ⓤⓢ -ˈzɝːv|d **-edly** -ɪd.li
unobstructed ˌʌn.əbˈstrʌk.tɪd
unobtainable ˌʌn.əbˈteɪ.nə.bl̩
unobtrusive ˌʌn.əbˈtruː.sɪv ⓤⓢ -əbˈ- **-ly** -li **-ness** -nəs, -nɪs
unoccupied ʌnˈɒk.jə.paɪd, ˌʌn-, -jʊ- ⓤⓢ -ˈɑː.kjə-

unoffending ˌʌn.əˈfen.dɪŋ

unoffensive ˌʌn.əˈfen*t*.sɪv

unofficial ˌʌn.əˈfɪʃ.ᵊl **-ly** -li

unopened ʌnˈəʊ.pᵊnd, ˌʌn- (US) -ˈoʊ-

unopposed ˌʌn.əˈpəʊzd (US) -ˈpoʊzd

unordained ˌʌn.ɔːˈdeɪnd (US) -ɔːr-

unordered ʌnˈɔː.dəd, ˌʌn- (US) -ˈɔːr.dɚd

unorganized, -ise- ʌnˈɔː.gᵊn.aɪzd, ˌʌn- (US) -ˈɔːr-

unorthodox ʌnˈɔː.θə.dɒks, ˌʌn- (US) -ˈɔːr.θə.dɑːks **-ly** -li

unorthodoxy ʌnˈɔː.θə.dɒk.si, ˌʌn- (US) -ˈɔːr.θə.dɑːk-

unostentatious ʌnˌɒs.tenˈteɪ.ʃəs, ˌʌn-, -tənˈ- (US) -ˌɑː.stənˈ- **-ly** -li **-ness** -nəs, -nɪs

unowned ʌnˈəʊnd, ˌʌn- (US) -ˈoʊnd

unpack ʌnˈpæk, ˌʌn-, ʌm-, ˌʌm- (US) ʌn-, ˌʌn- **-s** -s **-ing** -ɪŋ **-ed** -t **-er/s** -əʳ/z (US) -ɚ/z

unpaid ʌnˈpeɪd, ˌʌn-, ʌm-, ˌʌm- (US) ʌn-, ˌʌn-

unpaired ʌnˈpeəd, ˌʌn-, ʌm-, ˌʌm- (US) ʌnˈperd, ˌʌn-

unpalatability ʌnˌpæl.ə.təˈbɪl.ɪ.ti, ˌʌn-, ʌm-, ˌʌm-, -ɪ-, -ə.ti (US) ʌnˌpæl.ə.t̬əˈbɪl.ə.t̬i, ˌʌn-

unpalatab|le ʌnˈpæl.ə.tə.b|l̩, ˌʌn-, ʌm-, ˌʌm-, ˈ-ɪ- (US) ʌnˈpæl.ə.t̬ə-, ˌʌn- **-leness** -l̩.nəs, -nɪs

unparalleled ʌnˈpær.ᵊl.eld, ˌʌn-, ʌm-, ˌʌm- (US) ʌnˈper-, ˌʌn-, -ˈpær-

unpardonab|le ʌnˈpɑː.dᵊn.ə.b|l̩, ˌʌn-, ʌm-, ˌʌm-, -ˈpɑːd.nə- (US) ʌnˈpɑːr.dᵊn.ə-, ˌʌn-, -ˈpɑːrd.nə- **-leness** -l̩.nəs, -nɪs

unpardonab|ly ʌnˈpɑː.dᵊn.ə.b|li, ˌʌn-, ʌm-, ˌʌm-, -ˈpɑːd.nə- (US) ʌnˈpɑːr.dᵊn.ə-, ˌʌn-, -ˈpɑːrd.nə-

unparliamentary ʌnˌpɑː.ləˈmen.tᵊr.i, ˌʌn-, ʌm-, ˌʌm-, -lɪˈ-, -li.əˈ- (US) ʌnˌpɑːr.ləˈmen.t̬ɚ-, ˌʌn-, ˈ-tri

unpasteurized, -ised ʌnˈpæs.tʃᵊr.aɪzd, ˌʌn-, ʌm-, ˌʌm-, -ˈpɑːs-, -tjᵊr-, -tᵊr- (US) ʌnˈpæs.tʃə.raɪzd, ˌʌn-, -tə-

unpatriotic ʌnˌpæt.riˈɒt.ɪk, ˌʌn-, ʌm-, ˌʌm-, -ˌpeɪ.triˈ- (US) ʌnˌpeɪ.triˈɑː.t̬ɪk, ˌʌn- **-ally** -ᵊl.i, -li

unpaved ʌnˈpeɪvd, ˌʌn-, ʌm-, ˌʌm- (US) ʌn-, ˌʌn-

unpeeled ʌnˈpiːld, ˌʌn-, ʌm-, ˌʌm- (US) ʌn-, ˌʌn-

unperceiv|able ˌʌn.pəˈsiː.v|ə.bl̩, ˌʌm- (US) ˌʌn.pɚˈ- **-ed** -d

unperforated ʌnˈpɜː.fᵊr.eɪ.tɪd, ˌʌn-, ʌm-, ˌʌm- (US) ʌnˈpɝː.fə.reɪ.t̬ɪd, ˌʌn-

unperformed ˌʌn.pəˈfɔːmd, ˌʌm- (US) ˌʌn.pɚˈfɔːrmd

unpersuadable ˌʌn.pəˈsweɪ.də.bl̩, ˌʌm- (US) ˌʌn.pɚˈ-

unpersuaded ˌʌn.pəˈsweɪ.dɪd, ˌʌm- (US) ˌʌn.pɚˈ-

unpersuasive ˌʌn.pəˈsweɪ.sɪv, ˌʌm-, -zɪv (US) ˌʌn.pɚˈ-

unperturbable ˌʌn.pəˈtɜː.bə.bl̩, ˌʌm- (US) ˌʌn.pɚˈtɝː-

unperturbed ˌʌn.pəˈtɜːbd, ˌʌm- (US) ˌʌn.pɚˈtɝːbd

unphilosophic|al ʌnˌfɪl.əˈsɒf.ɪ.k|ᵊl (US) -ˈsɑː.fɪ- **-ally** -ᵊl.i, -li **-alness** -ᵊl.nəs, -nɪs

unpick ʌnˈpɪk, ˌʌn-, ʌm-, ˌʌm- (US) ʌn-, ˌʌn- **-s** -s **-ing** -ɪŋ **-ed** -t

unpiloted ʌnˈpaɪ.lə.tɪd, ˌʌn-, ʌm-, ˌʌm- (US) ʌnˈpaɪ.lə.t̬ɪd, ˌʌn-

unpin ʌnˈpɪn, ˌʌn-, ʌm-, ˌʌm- (US) ʌn-, ˌʌn- **-s** -z **-ning** -ɪŋ **-ned** -d

unpitying ʌnˈpɪt.i.ɪŋ, ˌʌn-, ʌm-, ˌʌm- (US) ʌnˈpɪt̬.i-, ˌʌn- **-ly** -li

unplaced ʌnˈpleɪst, ˌʌn-, ʌm-, ˌʌm- (US) ʌn-, ˌʌn-

unplanned ʌnˈplænd, ˌʌn-, ʌm-, ˌʌm- (US) ʌn-, ˌʌn-

unplayable ʌnˈpleɪ.ə.bl̩, ˌʌn-, ʌm-, ˌʌm- (US) ʌn-, ˌʌn-

unpleasant ʌnˈplez.ᵊnt, ˌʌn-, ʌm-, ˌʌm- (US) ʌn-, ˌʌn- **-ly** -li **-ness** -nəs, -nɪs

unpleasing ʌnˈpliː.zɪŋ, ˌʌn-, ʌm-, ˌʌm- (US) ʌn-, ˌʌn- **-ly** -li **-ness** -nəs, -nɪs

unplug ʌnˈplʌg, ˌʌn-, ʌm-, ˌʌm- (US) ʌn-, ˌʌn- **-s** -z **-ging** -ɪŋ **-ged** -d

unplumbed ʌnˈplʌmd, ˌʌn-, ʌm-, ˌʌm- (US) ʌn-, ˌʌm-

unpoetic|al ˌʌn.pəʊˈet.ɪ.k|ᵊl, ˌʌm- (US) ˌʌn.poʊˈet̬- **-ally** -ᵊl.i, -li **-alness** -ᵊl.nəs, -nɪs

unpolished ʌnˈpɒl.ɪʃt, ˌʌn-, ʌm-, ˌʌm- (US) ʌnˈpɑː.lɪʃt, ˌʌn-

unpolitical ˌʌn.pəˈlɪt.ɪ.kᵊl, ˌʌm- (US) ˌʌn.pəˈlɪt̬-

unpolluted ˌʌn.pəˈluː.tɪd, ˌʌm-, -ˈljuː- (US) ˌʌn.pəˈluː.t̬ɪd

unpopular ʌnˈpɒp.jə.ləʳ, ˌʌn-, ʌm-, ˌʌm-, -jʊ- (US) ʌnˈpɑː.pjə.lɚ, ˌʌn-

unpopularity ʌnˌpɒp.jəˈlær.ə.ti, ˌʌn-, ʌm-, ˌʌm-, -jʊˈ-, -ɪ.ti (US) ʌnˌpɑː.pjəˈler.ə.t̬i, ˌʌn-, -pjʊˈ-, -ˈlær-

unpractic|al ʌnˈpræk.tɪ.k|ᵊl, ˌʌn-, ʌm-, ˌʌm- (US) ʌn-, ˌʌn- **-ally** -ᵊl.i, -li

unpracticality ʌnˌpræk.tɪˈkæl.ə.ti, ˌʌn-, ʌm-, ˌʌm-, -təˈ-, -ɪ.ti (US) ʌnˌpræk.təˈkæl.ə.t̬i, ˌʌn-

unpractised, -iced ʌnˈpræk.tɪst, ˌʌn-, ʌm-, ˌʌm- (US) ʌn-, ˌʌn-

unprecedented ʌnˈpres.ɪ.dᵊn.tɪd, ˌʌn-, ʌm-, ˌʌm-, -ˈpriː.sɪ-, -den- (US) ʌnˈpres.ə.den.t̬ɪd, ˌʌn-

unpredictability ˌʌn.prɪˌdɪk.təˈbɪl.ɪ.ti, ˌʌm-, -prə-, -ɪ.ti (US) ˌʌn.prɪˌdɪk.təˈbɪl.ə.t̬i, -ˌpriː-

unpredictab|le ˌʌn.prɪˈdɪk.tə.b|l̩, ˌʌm-, -prəˈ- (US) ˌʌn.prɪˈ-, -priːˈ- **-ly** -li

unprejudiced ʌnˈpredʒ.ə.dɪst, ˌʌn-, ʌm-, ˌʌm-, ˈ-ʊ- (US) ʌnˈpredʒ.ə-, ˌʌn-

unpremeditated ˌʌn.priːˈmed.ɪ.teɪ.tɪd, ˌʌm-, -prɪˈ-, ˈ-ə- (US) ˌʌn.priːˈmed.ɪ.teɪ.t̬ɪd

unpre|pared ˌʌn.prɪ|ˈpeəd, ˌʌm-, -prəˈ- (US) ˌʌn.prɪ|ˈperd, -priːˈ- **-paredly** -ˈpeə.rɪd.li, -ˈpeəd.li (US) -ˈper.ɪd.li, -ˈperd.li **-paredness** -ˈpeə.rɪd.nəs, -ˈpeəd.nəs, -nɪs (US) -ˈper.ɪd.nəs, -ˈperd.nəs, -nɪs

unprepossessing ʌnˌpriː.pəˈzes.ɪŋ, ˌʌn-, ʌm-, ˌʌm- (US) ʌn-, ˌʌn- **-ly** -li

unpresentable ˌʌn.prɪˈzen.tə.bl̩, ˌʌm-, -prəˈ- (US) ˌʌn.prɪˈzen.t̬ə-, -priːˈ-

unpresuming ˌʌn.prɪˈzjuː.mɪŋ, ˌʌm-, -prəˈ-, -ˈzuː- (US) ˌʌn.prɪˈzuː-, -priːˈ-, -ˈzjuː-

unpretending ˌʌn.prɪˈten.dɪŋ, ˌʌm-, -prəˈ- (US) ˌʌn.prɪˈten.dɪŋ, -priːˈ- **-ly** -li

unpretentious ˌʌn.prɪˈten.*t*ʃəs, ˌʌm-, -prəˈ- (US) ˌʌn.prɪˈ-, -priːˈ- **-ly** -li **-ness** -nəs, -nɪs

unpreventable ˌʌn.prɪˈven.tə.bl̩, ˌʌm-, -prəˈ- (US) ˌʌn.prɪˈven.t̬ə-, -priːˈ-

unpriced ʌnˈpraɪst, ˌʌn-, ʌm-, ˌʌm- (US) ʌn-, ˌʌn-

unprincipled ʌnˈprɪn*t*.sə.pl̩d, ˌʌn-, ʌm-, ˌʌm-, -sɪ- (US) ʌn-, ˌʌn-

unprintable ʌnˈprɪn.tə.bl̩, ˌʌn-, ʌm-, ˌʌm- (US) ʌnˈprɪn.t̬ə-, ˌʌn-

unprinted ʌnˈprɪn.tɪd, ˌʌn-, ʌm-, ˌʌm- (US) ʌnˈprɪn.t̬ɪd, ˌʌn-

unproclaimed ˌʌn.prəʊˈkleɪmd, ˌʌm- (US) ˌʌn.proʊˈ-, -prəˈ-

unprocurable ˌʌn.prəˈkjʊə.rə.bl̩, ˌʌm-, -ˈkjɔː- (US) ˌʌn.prəˈkjʊr.ə-, -proʊˈ-

unproductive ˌʌn.prəˈdʌk.tɪv, ˌʌm- (US) ˌʌn- **-ly** -li **-ness** -nəs, -nɪs

unprofessional ˌʌn.prəˈfeʃ.ᵊn.ᵊl, ˌʌm-, -ˈfeʃ.nᵊl (US) ˌʌn- **-ly** -i **-ness** -nəs, -nɪs

unprofitab|le ʌnˈprɒf.ɪ.tə.b|l̩, ˌʌn-, ʌm-, ˌʌm-, ˈ-ə- (US) ʌnˈprɑː.fɪ.t̬ə-, ˌʌn- **-ly** -li **-leness** -l̩.nəs, -nɪs

Unprofor ˈʌn.prə.fɔːʳ, ˈʌm- (US) ˈʌn.prə.fɔːr

unprohibited ˌʌn.prəʊˈhɪb.ɪ.tɪd, ˌʌm-, ˈ-ə- (US) ˌʌn.proʊˈhɪb.ə.t̬ɪd, -prəˈ-

unpromising ʌnˈprɒm.ɪ.sɪŋ, ˌʌn-, ʌm-, ˌʌm-, ˈ-ə- (US) ʌnˈprɑː.mə-, ˌʌn- **-ly** -li

unprompted ʌnˈprɒm*p*.tɪd, ˌʌn-, ʌm-, ˌʌm- (US) ʌnˈprɑːm*p*-, ˌʌn-

unpronounceable ˌʌn.prəˈnaʊn*t*.sə.bl̩, ˌʌm- (US) ˌʌn-

unprop ʌnˈprɒp, ˌʌn-, ʌm-, ˌʌn- (US) ʌnˈprɑːp, ˌʌn- **-s** -s **-ping** -ɪŋ **-ped** -t

unpropitious ˌʌn.prəˈpɪʃ.əs, ˌʌm- US ˌʌn.prəˈ-, -proʊˈ- **-ly** -li **-ness** -nəs, -nɪs
unprotected ˌʌn.prəˈtek.tɪd, ˌʌm- US ˌʌn-
unproved ʌnˈpruːvd, ˌʌn-, ʌm-, ˌʌm- US ʌn-, ˌʌn-
unproven ʌnˈpruː.vᵊn, ˌʌn-, ʌm-, ˌʌm-, -ˈprəʊ- US ʌnˈpruː-, ˌʌn-
unprovided ˌʌn.prəˈvaɪ.dɪd, ˌʌm- US ˌʌn-
unprovok|ed ˌʌn.prəˈvəʊk|t, ˌʌm- US ˌʌn.prəˈvoʊk|t **-edly** -ɪd.li, -t.li
unpublished ʌnˈpʌb.lɪʃt, ˌʌn-, ʌm-, ˌʌm- US ʌn-, ˌʌn-
unpunctual ʌnˈpʌŋk.tʃu.əl, ˌʌn-, ʌm-, ˌʌm-, -tʃʊəl, -tju.əl, -tjʊəl US ʌnˈpʌŋk.tʃu.əl, ˌʌn- **-ly** -i
unpunctuality ʌnˌpʌŋk.tʃuˈæl.ə.ti, ˌʌn-, ʌm-, ˌʌm-, -tjuˈ-, -ɪ.ti US ʌnˌpʌŋk.tʃuˈæl.ə.t̬i, ˌʌn-
unpunished ʌnˈpʌn.ɪʃt, ˌʌn-, ʌm-, ˌʌm- US ʌn-, ˌʌn-
unputdownable ˌʌn.pʊtˈdaʊ.nə.bl̩, ˌʌm- US ˌʌn-
unqualified ʌnˈkwɒl.ɪ.faɪd, ˌʌn-, ʌŋ-, ˌʌŋ-, ˈ-ə- US ʌnˈkwɑː.lə-, ˌʌn-
unquenchable ʌnˈkwen.tʃə.bl̩, ˌʌn-, ʌŋ-, ˌʌŋ- US ʌn-, ˌʌn-
unquestionab|le ʌnˈkwes.tʃə.nə.bl|l̩, ˌʌn-, ʌŋ-, ˌʌŋ-, -ˈkweʃ- US ʌnˈkwes.tʃə-, ˌʌn-, -tjə- **-ly** -li **-leness** -l̩.nəs, -nɪs
unquestioned ʌnˈkwes.tʃənd, ˌʌn-, ʌŋ-, ˌʌŋ-, -ˈkweʃ- US ʌnˈkwes.tʃənd, ˌʌn-, -tjənd
unquestioning ʌnˈkwes.tʃə.nɪŋ, ˌʌn-, ʌŋ-, ˌʌŋ-, -ˈkweʃ- US ʌnˈkwes.tʃə-, ˌʌn-, -tjə- **-ly** -li
unquiet ʌnˈkwaɪət, ʌŋ- **-ly** -li **-ness** -nəs, -nɪs
unquote ʌnˈkwəʊt, ˌʌn-, ʌŋ-, ˌʌŋ- US ʌnˈkwoʊt, ˌʌn-
unravel ʌnˈræv.ᵊl, ˌʌn- **-s** -z **-(l)ing** -ɪŋ, -ˈræv.lɪŋ **-(l)ed** -d **-(l)er/s** -əʳ/z, -ɚ/z US -ˈræv.ləʳ/z, -lɚ/z
unread ʌnˈred, ˌʌn-
unreadable ʌnˈriː.də.bl̩, ˌʌn- **-ness** -nəs, -nɪs
unread|y ʌnˈred|.i, ˌʌn- **-ily** -ɪ.li, -ᵊl.i **-iness** -ɪ.nəs, -ɪ.nɪs
unreal ʌnˈrɪəl, ˌʌn- US -ˈriːl, -ˈriː.əl
unrealistic ˌʌn.rɪəˈlɪs.tɪk US ri.əˈ- **-ally** -ᵊl.i, -li
unrealit|y ˌʌn.riˈæl.ə.t|i, -ɪ.t|i US -ə.t̬|i **-ies** -iz
unreason ʌnˈriː.zᵊn, ˌʌn-
unreasonab|le ʌnˈriː.zᵊn.ə.bl|l̩, ˌʌn-, -ˈriːz.nə- **-ly** -li **-leness** -l̩.nəs, -nɪs
unreasoning ʌnˈriː.zᵊn.ɪŋ, ˌʌn-, -ˈriːz.nɪŋ
unreceived ˌʌn.rɪˈsiːvd, -rəˈ- US -rɪˈ-
unreciprocated ˌʌn.rɪˈsɪp.rə.keɪ.tɪd, -rəˈ- US -rɪˈsɪp.rə.keɪ.t̬ɪd
unreckoned ʌnˈrek.ᵊnd, ˌʌn-
unreclaimed ˌʌn.rɪˈkleɪmd
unrecognizable, -isa- ʌnˈrek.əg.naɪ.zə.bl̩, ˌʌn-, ˌʌn.rek.əgˈnaɪ- US ˌʌn.rek.əgˈnaɪ-, ʌnˈrek.əg.naɪ-, ˌʌn-
unrecognized, -ised ʌnˈrek.əg.naɪzd, ˌʌn-
unreconcilable ʌnˈrek.ᵊn.saɪ.lə.bl̩, ˌʌn-, ˌʌn.rek.ᵊnˈsaɪ-
unreconciled ʌnˈrek.ᵊn.saɪld, ˌʌn-
unreconstructed ˌʌn.riː.kənˈstrʌk.tɪd
unrecorded ˌʌn.rɪˈkɔː.dɪd, -rəˈ- US -rɪˈkɔːr-
unrecounted ˌʌn.rɪˈkaʊn.tɪd, -rəˈ- US -rɪˈkaʊn.t̬ɪd
unredeemable ˌʌn.rɪˈdiː.mə.bl̩, -rəˈ- US -rɪˈ-
unredeemed ˌʌn.rɪˈdiːmd, -rəˈ- US -rɪˈ-
unrefined ˌʌn.rɪˈfaɪnd, -rəˈ- US -rɪˈ-
unreflecting ˌʌn.rɪˈflek.tɪŋ, -rəˈ- US -rɪˈ-
unreformed ˌʌn.rɪˈfɔːmd, -rəˈ- US -rɪˈfɔːrmd
unrefuted ˌʌn.rɪˈfjuː.tɪd, -rəˈ- US -rɪˈfjuː.t̬ɪd
unregenerate ˌʌn.rɪˈdʒen.ᵊr.ət, -rəˈ-, -ɪt US -rəˈdʒen.ɚ.ɪt
unregistered ʌnˈredʒ.ɪ.stəd, ˌʌn- US -stɚd
unregulated ʌnˈreg.jə.leɪ.tɪd, -jʊ- US -t̬ɪd
unrehearsed ˌʌn.rɪˈhɜːst, -rəˈ- US -rɪˈhɝːst
unrelated ˌʌn.rɪˈleɪ.tɪd, -rəˈ- US -rɪˈleɪ.t̬ɪd
unrelaxed ˌʌn.rɪˈlækst, -rəˈ- US -rɪˈ-
unrelenting ˌʌn.rɪˈlen.tɪŋ, -rəˈ- US -rɪˈlen.t̬ɪŋ **-ly** -li **-ness** -nəs, -nɪs
unreliability ˌʌn.rɪ.laɪ.əˈbɪl.ɪ.ti, -rə-, -ə.ti US -rɪ.laɪ.əˈbɪl.ə.t̬i
unreliab|le ˌʌn.rɪˈlaɪ.ə.bl|l̩, -rəˈ- US -rɪˈ- **-ly** -li **-leness** -l̩.nəs, -nɪs
unreliev|ed ˌʌn.rɪˈliːv|d, -rəˈ- US -rɪˈ- **-edly** -ɪd.li
unremarkable ˌʌn.rɪˈmɑː.kə.bl̩, -rəˈ- US -ˈmɑːr-
unremembered ˌʌn.rɪˈmem.bəd, -rəˈ- US -rɪˈmem.bɚd
unremitting ˌʌn.rɪˈmɪt.ɪŋ, -rəˈ- US -rɪˈmɪt̬- **-ly** -li **-ness** -nəs, -nɪs
unremonstrative ˌʌn.rɪˈmɒnt.strə.tɪv, -rəˈ- US -rɪˈmɑːnt.strə.t̬ɪv
unremovable ˌʌn.rɪˈmuː.və.bl̩, -rəˈ- US -rɪˈ-
unremunerative ˌʌn.rɪˈmjuː.nᵊr.ə.tɪv, -rəˈ- US -rɪˈmjuː.nɚ.ə.t̬ɪv, -nə.reɪ-
unrepaired ˌʌn.rɪˈpeəd US -ˈperd
unrepeatable ˌʌn.rɪˈpiː.tə.bl̩, -rəˈ- US -rɪˈpiː.t̬ə-
unrepentant ˌʌn.rɪˈpen.tənt, -rəˈ- US -rɪˈpen.tᵊnt
unreplaceable ˌʌn.rɪˈpleɪs.ə.bl̩
unreported ˌʌn.rɪˈpɔː.tɪd, -rəˈ- US -rɪˈpɔːr.t̬ɪd
unrepresentative ˌʌn.rep.rɪˈzen.tə.tɪv US -t̬ə.t̬ɪv
unrepresented ˌʌn.rep.rɪˈzen.tɪd US -t̬ɪd
unrequested ˌʌn.rɪˈkwes.tɪd, -rəˈ- US -rɪˈ-
unrequited ˌʌn.rɪˈkwaɪ.tɪd, -rəˈ- US -rɪˈkwaɪ.t̬ɪd **ˌunrequited ˈlove**
unreserv|ed ˌʌn.rɪˈzɜːv|d, -rəˈ- US -rɪˈzɝːv|d **-edly** -ɪd.li **-edness** -ɪd.nəs, -nɪs
unresisting ˌʌn.rɪˈzɪs.tɪŋ, -rəˈ- US -rɪˈ- **-ly** -li
unresolved ˌʌn.rɪˈzɒlvd, -rəˈ- US -rɪˈzɑːlvd
unresponsive ˌʌn.rɪˈspɒnt.sɪv, -rəˈ- US -rɪˈspɑːnt- **-ly** -li **-ness** -nəs, -nɪs
unrest ʌnˈrest, ˌʌn- US ʌnˈrest, ˌʌn-, ˈ--
unrestful ʌnˈrest.fᵊl, ˌʌn-, -fʊl **-ly** -i **-ness** -nəs, -nɪs
unresting ʌnˈres.tɪŋ, ˌʌn-
unrestored ˌʌn.rɪˈstɔːd, -rəˈ- US -rɪˈstɔːrd
unrestrain|ed ˌʌn.rɪˈstreɪn|d, -rəˈ- US -rɪˈ- **-edly** -ɪd.li
unrestraint ˌʌn.rɪˈstreɪnt
unrestricted ˌʌn.rɪˈstrɪk.tɪd, -rəˈ- US -rɪˈ-
unretentive ˌʌn.rɪˈten.tɪv, -rəˈ- US -rɪˈten.t̬ɪv
unreveal|ed ˌʌn.rɪˈviːl|d, -rəˈ- US -rɪˈ- **-ing** -ɪŋ
unrevoked ˌʌn.rɪˈvəʊkt, -rəˈ- US -rɪˈvoʊkt
unrewarded ˌʌn.rɪˈwɔː.dɪd, -rəˈ- US -rɪˈwɔːr-
unriddl|e ʌnˈrɪd.l̩ **-es** -z **-ing** -ɪŋ **-ed** -d
unrighteous ʌnˈraɪ.tʃəs, -ti.əs US -tʃəs **-ly** -li **-ness** -nəs, -nɪs
unrightful ʌnˈraɪt.fᵊl, ˌʌn-, -fʊl **-ly** -i **-ness** -nəs, -nɪs
unripe ʌnˈraɪp, ˌʌn- **-ness** -nəs, -nɪs
unrivalled ʌnˈraɪ.vᵊld, ˌʌn-
unrob|e ʌnˈrəʊb, ˌʌn- US -ˈroʊb **-es** -z **-ing** -ɪŋ **-ed** -d
unroll ʌnˈrəʊl, ˌʌn- US -ˈroʊl **-s** -z **-ing** -ɪŋ **-ed** -d
unromantic ˌʌn.rəʊˈmæn.tɪk US -roʊˈmæn.t̬ɪk, -rəˈ- **-ally** -ᵊl.i, -li
unrounded ʌnˈraʊn.dɪd, ˌʌn-
unruffled ʌnˈrʌf.l̩d, ˌʌn-
unrul|y ʌnˈruː.l|i, ˌʌn- **-ier** -i.əʳ US -i.ɚ **-iest** -i.ɪst, -i.əst **-iness** -ɪ.nəs, -ɪ.nɪs
unsaddl|e ʌnˈsæd.l̩, ˌʌn- **-es** -z **-ing** -ɪŋ, -ˈsæd.lɪŋ **-ed** -d
unsafe ʌnˈseɪf, ˌʌn- **-ly** -li **-ness** -nəs, -nɪs
unsaid ʌnˈsed, ˌʌn-

unsal(e)able ʌn'seɪ.lə.bl̩, ˌʌn-
unsalted ʌn'sɔːl.tɪd, ˌʌn-, -'sɒl- US -'sɔːl.t̬ɪd, -sɑː-
unsanctified ʌn'sæŋk.tɪ.faɪd, ˌʌn-
unsanitary ʌn'sæn.ɪ.tᵊr.i, ˌʌn-, '-ə-, -tri US -'sæn.ə.ter.i
unsatisfactor|y ʌnˌsæt.ɪs'fæk.tᵊr|.i, ˌʌn.sæt-, ˌʌnˌsæt- US ʌnˌsæt̬-, ˌʌn- **-ily** -ᵊl.i, -ɪ.li **-iness** -ɪ.nəs, -ɪ.nɪs
unsatisf|ied ʌn'sæt.ɪs.f|aɪd, ˌʌn- US -'sæt̬- **-ying** -aɪ.ɪŋ
unsaturated ʌn'sætʃ.ᵊr.eɪ.tɪd, ˌʌn-, -tʃʊ.reɪ-, -tjᵊr.eɪ, -tjʊ.reɪ- US -'sætʃ.ə.reɪ.t̬ɪd **unˌsaturated 'fat**
unsavo(u)r|y ʌn'seɪ.vᵊr|.i, ˌʌn- **-iness** -ɪ.nəs, -ɪ.nɪs
un|say ʌn|'seɪ, ˌʌn- **-says** -'sez **-saying** -'seɪ.ɪŋ **-said** -'sed **-sayable** -'seɪ.ə.bl̩
unscathed ʌn'skeɪðd, ˌʌn-
unscented ʌn'sen.tɪd, ˌʌn- US -t̬ɪd
unscheduled ʌn'ʃed.juːld, ˌʌn-, -'ʃedʒ.uːld, -'sked.juːld, -'skedʒ.uːld, -ᵊld US -'skedʒ.ʊld, -uːld, -u.əld
unscholarly ʌn'skɒl.ə.li, ˌʌn- US -'skɑː.lɚ-
unschooled ʌn'skuːld, ˌʌn-
unscientific ˌʌn.saɪən'tɪf.ɪk **-ally** -ᵊl.i, -li
Unscom 'ʌn.skɒm US -skɑːm
unscrambl|e ʌn'skræm.bl̩, ˌʌn- **-es** -z **-ing** -ɪŋ, -'skræm.blɪŋ **-ed** -d
unscrew ʌn'skruː, ˌʌn- **-s** -z **-ing** -ɪŋ **-ed** -d
unscripted ʌn'skrɪp.tɪd, ˌʌn-
unscriptural ʌn'skrɪp.tʃᵊr.ᵊl, ˌʌn-, -tʃʊ.rᵊl US -tʃɚ.ᵊl **-ly** -i
unscrupulous ʌn'skruː.pjə.ləs, ˌʌn-, -pjʊ- US -pjə- **-ly** -li **-ness** -nəs, -nɪs
unseal ʌn'siːl, ˌʌn- **-s** -z **-ing** -ɪŋ **-ed** -d
unseasonab|le ʌn'siː.zᵊn.ə.bl|l̩, ˌʌn-, -'siːz.nə- **-ly** -li **-leness** -l̩.nəs, -nɪs
unseasoned ʌn'siː.zᵊnd, ˌʌn-
un|seat ʌn|'siːt, ˌʌn- **-seats** -'siːts **-seating** -'siː.tɪŋ US -'siː.t̬ɪŋ **-seated** -'siː.tɪd US -'siː.t̬ɪd
unseaworth|y ʌn'siːˌwɜː.ð|i, ˌʌn- US -ˌwɝː- **-iness** -ɪ.nəs, -ɪ.nɪs
unsectarian ˌʌn.sek'teə.ri.ən US -'ter.i-
unsecured ˌʌn.sɪ'kjʊəd, -sə'-, -'kjɔːd US -'kjʊrd
unseeded ʌn'siː.dɪd, ˌʌn-
unseeing ʌn'siː.ɪŋ, ˌʌn- **-ly** -li
unseeml|y ʌn'siːm.l|i US ˌʌn- **-iness** -ɪ.nəs, -ɪ.nɪs
unseen ʌn'siːn, ˌʌn-
unselfconscious ˌʌn.self'kɒn.tʃəs US -'kɑːn- **-ly** -li **-ness** -nəs, -nɪs
unselfish ʌn'sel.fɪʃ, ˌʌn- **-ly** -li **-ness** -nəs, -nɪs
unsensational ˌʌn.sen'seɪ.ʃᵊn.ᵊl, -sᵊn'-, -'seɪʃ.nᵊl
unsensitive ʌn'sent.sə.tɪv, ˌʌn-, -sɪ- US -sə.t̬ɪv **-ly** -li **-ness** -nəs, -nɪs
unsentimental ˌʌn.sen.tɪ'men.tᵊl US -t̬ᵊl **-ly** -i
unserviceable ʌn'sɜː.vɪ.sə.bl̩, ˌʌn- US -'sɝː-
unsettl|e ʌn'set.l̩, ˌʌn- US -'set̬- **-es** -z **-ing/ly** -ɪŋ/li, -'set.lɪŋ/li **-ness** -nəs, -nɪs
unsettled ʌn'set.l̩d US -'set̬-
unsevered ʌn'sev.əd, ˌʌn- US -ɚd
unshackl|e ʌn'ʃæk.l̩, ˌʌn- **-es** -z **-ing** -ɪŋ, -'ʃæk.lɪŋ **-ed** -d
unshak(e)able ʌn'ʃeɪ.kə.bl̩, ˌʌn-
unshaken ʌn'ʃeɪ.kᵊn, ˌʌn-
unshapely ʌn'ʃeɪ.pli, ˌʌn-
unshaven ʌn'ʃeɪ.vᵊn, ˌʌn-
unsheath|e ʌn'ʃiːð, ˌʌn- **-es** -z **-ing** -ɪŋ **-ed** -d
unship ʌn'ʃɪp, ˌʌn- **-s** -s **-ping** -ɪŋ **-ped** -t
unshockability ˌʌn.ʃɒk.ə'bɪl.ɪ.ti, -ˌʃɒk-, -ə.ti US -ʃɑː.kə'bɪl.ə.t̬i, -ˌʃɑː-
unshockable ʌn'ʃɒk.ə.bl̩, ˌʌn- US -'ʃɑː.kə-
unshod ʌn'ʃɒd, ˌʌn- US -'ʃɑːd
unshorn ʌn'ʃɔːn, ˌʌn- US -'ʃɔːrn
unshrinkable ʌn'ʃrɪŋ.kə.bl̩, ˌʌn-
unshrinking ʌn'ʃrɪŋ.kɪŋ, ˌʌn- **-ly** -li
unsighted ʌn'saɪ.tɪd, ˌʌn- US -t̬ɪd
unsightl|y ʌn'saɪt.l|i, ˌʌn- **-ier** -i.əʳ US -i.ɚ **-iest** -i.ɪst, -i.əst **-iness** -ɪ.nəs, -ɪ.nɪs
unsigned ʌn'saɪnd, ˌʌn-
unskilful ʌn'skɪl.fᵊl, ˌʌn-, -fʊl **-ly** -i
unskilled ʌn'skɪld, ˌʌn- **ˌunskilled 'worker**
unslaked ʌn'sleɪkt, ˌʌn-
unsliced ʌn'slaɪst
unsociability ˌʌn.səʊ.ʃə'bɪl.ɪ.ti, -ˌsəʊ-, -ə.ti US -soʊ.ʃə'bɪl.ə.t̬i, -ˌsoʊ-
unsociab|le ʌn'səʊ.ʃə.bl|l̩, ˌʌn- US -'soʊ- **-ly** -li **-leness** -l̩.nəs, -nɪs
unsocial ʌn'səʊ.ʃᵊl, ˌʌn- US -'soʊ- **-ly** -i **ˌunsocial 'hours, unˌsocial 'hours**
unsold ʌn'səʊld, ˌʌn- US -'soʊld
unsold|er ʌn'səʊl.d|əʳ, ˌʌn-, -'sɒl- US -'sɑː.d|ɚ **-ers** -əz US -ɚz **-ering** -ᵊr.ɪŋ **-ered** -əd US -ɚd
unsolicited ˌʌn.sə'lɪs.ɪ.tɪd US -t̬ɪd
unsolved ʌn'sɒlvd, ˌʌn- US -'sɑːlvd, -'sɔːlvd
unsophisticated ˌʌn.sə'fɪs.tɪ.keɪ.tɪd, -tə- US -tə.keɪ.t̬ɪd **-ly** -li **-ness** -nəs, -nɪs
unsophistication ˌʌn.səˌfɪs.tɪ'keɪ.ʃᵊn, -tə'-
unsorted ʌn'sɔː.tɪd, ˌʌn- US -'sɔːr.t̬ɪd
unsought ʌn'sɔːt, ˌʌn- US -'sɑːt, -'sɔːt
unsound ʌn'saʊnd, ˌʌn- **-ly** -li **-ness** -nəs, -nɪs
unsparing ʌn'speə.rɪŋ, ˌʌn- US -'sper.ɪŋ **-ly** -li **-ness** -nəs, -nɪs
unspeakab|le ʌn'spiː.kə.bl|l̩, ˌʌn- **-ly** -li
unspecified ʌn'spes.ɪ.faɪd, ˌʌn-, -'ə-
unspent ʌn'spent, ˌʌn-
unspoiled ʌn'spɔɪlt, ˌʌn-, -'spɔɪld US -'spɔɪld
unspoilt ʌn'spɔɪlt, ˌʌn-
unspoken ʌn'spəʊ.kᵊn, ˌʌn- US -'spoʊ-
unsporting ʌn'spɔː.tɪŋ, ˌʌn- US -'spɔːr.t̬ɪŋ **-ly** -li **-ness** -nəs, -nɪs
unsportsmanlike ʌn'spɔːts.mən.laɪk, ˌʌn- US -'spɔːrts-
unspotted ʌn'spɒt.ɪd, ˌʌn- US -'spɑː.t̬ɪd
Unst ʌntst
unstable ʌn'steɪ.bl̩, ˌʌn- **-ness** -nəs, -nɪs
unstack ʌn'stæk, ˌʌn- **-s** -s **-ing** -ɪŋ **-ed** -t
unstamped ʌn'stæmpt, ˌʌn-
unstarched ʌn'stɑːtʃt, ˌʌn- US -'stɑːrtʃt
unstated ʌn'steɪ.tɪd US -t̬ɪd
unstatesmanlike ʌn'steɪts.mən.laɪk, ˌʌn-
unsteadfast ʌn'sted.fɑːst, ˌʌn-, -fəst US -fæst, -fəst **-ly** -li **-ness** -nəs, -nɪs
unstead|y ʌn'sted|.i, ˌʌn- **-ier** -i.əʳ US -i.ɚ **-iest** -i.ɪst, -i.əst **-ily** -ɪ.li, -ᵊl.i **-iness** -ɪ.nəs, -ɪ.nɪs
unstick ʌn'stɪk, ˌʌn- **-s** -s **-ing** -ɪŋ **unstuck** ʌn'stʌk, ˌʌn-
unstinted ʌn'stɪn.tɪd, ˌʌn- US -t̬ɪd
unstinting ʌn'stɪn.tɪŋ, ˌʌn- US -t̬ɪŋ **-ly** -li
unstitch ʌn'stɪtʃ, ˌʌn- **-es** -ɪz **-ing** -ɪŋ **-ed** -t
unstop ʌn'stɒp, ˌʌn- US -'stɑːp **-s** -s **-ping** -ɪŋ **-ped** -t
unstoppab|le ʌn'stɒp.ə.bl|l̩, ˌʌn- US -'stɑː.pə- **-ly** -li
unstrap ʌn'stræp, ˌʌn- **-s** -s **-ping** -ɪŋ **-ped** -t
unstressed ʌn'strest, ˌʌn-
unstructured ʌn'strʌk.tʃəd US -tʃɚd
unstrung ʌn'strʌŋ, ˌʌn-
unstuck *(from* **unstick***)* ʌn'stʌk, ˌʌn- **ˌcome un'stuck**
unstudied ʌn'stʌd.ɪd, ˌʌn-
unstylish ʌn'staɪ.lɪʃ, ˌʌn- **-ly** -li
unsubmissive ˌʌn.səb'mɪs.ɪv **-ly** -li **-ness** -nəs, -nɪs
unsubstantial ˌʌn.səb'stæn.tʃᵊl, -'stɑːn- US -'stænt.ʃᵊl **-ly** -i
unsubstantiality ˌʌn.səbˌstæn.tʃi'æl.ə.ti, -ˌstɑːn-, -ɪ.ti US -ˌstænt.ʃi'æl.ə.t̬i
unsubstantiated ˌʌn.səb'stæn.tʃi.eɪ.tɪd, -'stɑːn- US -'stænt.ʃi.eɪ.t̬ɪd
unsuccess ˌʌn.sək'ses, '--- US ˌʌn.sək'ses
unsuccessful ˌʌn.sək'ses.fᵊl, -fʊl **-ly** -i **-ness** -nəs, -nɪs

unsuitability ˌʌn.suː.təˈbɪl.ə.ti, -sjuː-, ʌnˌsuː-, -ˌsjuː-, -ɪ.ti Ⓤⓢ ˌʌn.suː.t̬əˈbɪl.ə.t̬i, ʌnˌsuː-
unsuitab|le ʌnˈsuː.tə.b|l̩, ˌʌn-, -ˈsjuː- Ⓤⓢ -ˈsuː.t̬ə- **-ly** -li **-leness** -l̩.nəs, -nɪs
unsuited ʌnˈsuː.tɪd, ˌʌn-, -ˈsjuː- Ⓤⓢ -ˈsuː.t̬ɪd
unsullied ʌnˈsʌl.ɪd, ˌʌn-
unsung ʌnˈsʌŋ, ˌʌn-
unsupportab|le ˌʌn.səˈpɔː.tə.b|l̩ Ⓤⓢ -ˈpɔːr.t̬ə- **-ly** -li **-leness** -l̩.nəs, -nɪs
unsupported ˌʌn.səˈpɔː.tɪd Ⓤⓢ -ˈpɔːr.t̬ɪd
unsure ʌnˈʃɔːʳ, ˌʌn-, -ʃʊəʳ Ⓤⓢ -ˈʃʊr
unsurmountab|le ˌʌn.səˈmaʊn.tə.b|l̩ Ⓤⓢ -sɚˈmaʊn.t̬ə- **-ly** -li
unsurpassable ˌʌn.səˈpɑː.sə.bl̩ Ⓤⓢ -sɚˈpæs.ə-
unsurpassed ˌʌn.səˈpɑːst Ⓤⓢ -sɚˈpæst
unsurprising ʌn.səˈpraɪ.zɪŋ Ⓤⓢ -sɚ- **-ly** -li
unsusceptibility ˌʌn.səˌsep.təˈbɪl.ə.ti, -tɪˈ-, -ɪ.ti Ⓤⓢ -ə.t̬i
unsusceptible ˌʌn.səˈsep.tə.bl̩, -tɪ-
unsuspected ˌʌn.səˈspek.tɪd
unsuspecting ˌʌn.səˈspek.tɪŋ **-ly** -li **-ness** -nəs, -nɪs
unsuspicious ˌʌn.səˈspɪʃ.əs **-ly** -li **-ness** -nəs, -nɪs
unsustainable ˌʌn.səˈsteɪ.nə.bl̩
unsweetened ʌnˈswiː.tᵊnd, ˌʌn-
unswerving ʌnˈswɜː.vɪŋ, ˌʌn- Ⓤⓢ -ˈswɝː- **-ly** -li
Unsworth ˈʌnz.wəθ, -wɜːθ Ⓤⓢ -wɚθ, -wɝːθ
unsymmetric ˌʌn.sɪˈmet.rɪk, -səˈ- **-al** -ᵊl **-ally** -ᵊl.i, -li
unsymmetry ʌnˈsɪm.ɪ.tri, ˌʌn-, ˈ-ə-
unsympathetic ˌʌn.sɪm.pəˈθet.ɪk, -ˌsɪm- Ⓤⓢ -ˈθet̬- **-ally** -ᵊl.i, -li
unsystematic ˌʌn.sɪ.stəˈmæt.ɪk, -ˌsɪs.təˈ-, -tɪˈ- Ⓤⓢ -stəˈmæt̬- **-al** -ᵊl **-ally** -ᵊl.i, -li
untainted ʌnˈteɪn.tɪd, ˌʌn- Ⓤⓢ -t̬ɪd
untamable, untameable ʌnˈteɪ.mə.bl̩, ˌʌn-
untangl|e ʌnˈtæŋ.gl̩, ˌʌn- **-es** -z **-ing** -ɪŋ, -ˈtæŋ.glɪŋ **-ed** -d
untapped ʌnˈtæpt, ˌʌn-
untarnished ʌnˈtɑː.nɪʃt, ˌʌn- Ⓤⓢ -ˈtɑːr-
untaught ʌnˈtɔːt, ˌʌn- Ⓤⓢ -ˈtɑːt, -ˈtɔːt
untaxed ʌnˈtækst, ˌʌn-
unteachable ʌnˈtiː.tʃə.bl̩, ˌʌn-
untempered ʌnˈtem.pəd, ˌʌn- Ⓤⓢ -pɚd
untenability ˌʌn.ten.əˈbɪl.ɪ.ti, -ˌten-, -ə.ti Ⓤⓢ -ə.t̬i
untenable ʌnˈten.ə.bl̩, ˌʌn-
untenanted ʌnˈten.ən.tɪd, ˌʌn- Ⓤⓢ -t̬ɪd
unthankful ʌnˈθæŋk.fᵊl, ˌʌn-, -fʊl **-ly** -i **-ness** -nəs, -nɪs
unthinka|ble ʌnˈθɪŋ.kə|.bl̩, ˌʌn- **-bly** -bli
unthinking ʌnˈθɪŋ.kɪŋ, ˌʌn- **-ly** -li
unthought ʌnˈθɔːt Ⓤⓢ -ˈθɑːt, -ˈθɔːt
  unˈthought of
unthoughtful ʌnˈθɔːt.fᵊl, ˌʌn-, -fʊl Ⓤⓢ -ˈθɑːt-, -ˈθɔːt- **-ly** -i **-ness** -nəs, -nɪs
unthread ʌnˈθred, ˌʌn- **-s** -z **-ing** -ɪŋ **-ed** -ɪd
untid|y ʌnˈtaɪ.d|i, ˌʌn- **-ier** -i.əʳ Ⓤⓢ -i.ɚ **-iest** -i.ɪst, -i.əst **-ily** -ɪ.li, -ᵊl.i **-iness** -ɪ.nəs, -ɪ.nɪs **-ies** -iz **-ying** -i.ɪŋ **-ied** -id
un|tie ʌn|ˈtaɪ, ˌʌn- **-ties** -ˈtaɪz **-tying** -ˈtaɪ.ɪŋ **-tied** -ˈtaɪd
until ᵊnˈtɪl, ʌnˈtɪl
Note: There is an occasional weak form /ˈʌn.tɪl, -tᵊl/ in stress-shift environments (e.g. ˈuntil ˌdeath), but this is rare.
untimel|y ʌnˈtaɪm.l|i, ˌʌn- **-iness** -ɪ.nəs, -ɪ.nɪs
untinged ʌnˈtɪndʒd, ˌʌn-
untiring ʌnˈtaɪə.rɪŋ, ˌʌn- Ⓤⓢ -ˈtaɪ- **-ly** -li **-ness** -nəs, -nɪs
untitled ʌnˈtaɪ.tl̩d, ˌʌn- Ⓤⓢ -t̬l̩d
unto ˈʌn.tuː, -tu, -tə Ⓤⓢ -tuː, -t̬ə, -tu
untold ʌnˈtəʊld, ˌʌn- Ⓤⓢ -ˈtoʊld
untouchability ʌnˌtʌtʃ.əˈbɪl.ə.ti, ˌʌn-, -ɪ.ti Ⓤⓢ -ə.t̬i
untouchable ʌnˈtʌtʃ.ə.bl̩, ˌʌn- **-s** -z
untouched ʌnˈtʌtʃt, ˌʌn-
untoward ˌʌn.təˈwɔːd, -tʊˈ-; -ˈtəʊəd Ⓤⓢ -ˈtɔːrd, -təˈwɔːrd **-ly** -li **-ness** -nəs, -nɪs
untraceable ʌnˈtreɪ.sə.bl̩, ˌʌn-
untrained ʌnˈtreɪnd, ˌʌn-
untrammel(l)ed ʌnˈtræm.ᵊld, ˌʌn-
untransferable ˌʌn.træntsˈfɜː.rə.bl̩, -trɑːntsˈ-, ʌnˈtrænts.fɜː-, -ˈtrɑːnts- Ⓤⓢ ˌʌn.træntsˈfɝː.ə-, ʌnˈtrænts.fɚ-
untranslat|able ˌʌn.træntˈsleɪ.t|ə.bl̩, -trɑːntˈ-, -trᵊnˈ-; -trænzˈleɪ-, -trɑːnzˈ-, -trᵊnzˈ- Ⓤⓢ -trænˈsleɪ.t̬|ə-, -trænzˈleɪ- **-ed** -ɪd
untried ʌnˈtraɪd, ˌʌn-
untrimmed ʌnˈtrɪmd, ˌʌn-
untrodden ʌnˈtrɒd.ᵊn, ˌʌn- Ⓤⓢ -ˈtrɑː.dᵊn
untroubled ʌnˈtrʌb.l̩d, ˌʌn-
untrue ʌnˈtruː, ˌʌn- **-ness** -nəs, -nɪs
untruly ʌnˈtruː.li, ˌʌn-
untrustworth|y ʌnˈtrʌstˌwɜː.ð|i, ˌʌn- Ⓤⓢ -ˌwɝː- **-ily** -ɪ.li, -ᵊl.i **-iness** -ɪ.nəs, -ɪ.nɪs
untru|th ʌnˈtruː|θ, ˌʌn- **-ths** -ðz, -θs
untruthful ʌnˈtruːθ.fᵊl, ˌʌn-, -fʊl **-ly** -i **-ness** -nəs, -nɪs
untuck ʌnˈtʌk, ˌʌn- **-s** -s **-ing** -ɪŋ **-ed** -t
unturned ʌnˈtɜːnd, ˌʌn- Ⓤⓢ -ˈtɝːnd
  ˌleave no ˌstone unˈturned, leave ˌno ˌstone unˈturned
untutored ʌnˈtjuː.təd, ˌʌn- Ⓤⓢ -ˈtuː.t̬ɚd, -ˈtjuː-
untwist ʌnˈtwɪst, ˌʌn- **-s** -s **-ing** -ɪŋ **-ed** -ɪd
untypic|al ʌnˈtɪp.ɪ.k|ᵊl **-ly** -ᵊl.i, -li
unused *not made use of:* ʌnˈjuːzd, ˌʌn-
unused *not accustomed:* ʌnˈjuːst, ˌʌn-
unusual ʌnˈjuː.ʒᵊl, ˌʌn-, -ʒu.əl Ⓤⓢ -ʒu.əl, -ˈjuːʒ.wəl **-ly** -i **-ness** -nəs, -nɪs
unutterab|le ʌnˈʌt.ᵊr.ə.b|l̩, ˌʌn- Ⓤⓢ -ˈʌt̬- **-ly** -li **-leness** -l̩.nəs, -nɪs
unvariable ʌnˈveə.ri.ə.bl̩, ˌʌn- Ⓤⓢ -ˈver.i-
unvaried ʌnˈveə.rid, ˌʌn- Ⓤⓢ -ˈver.id, -ˈvær-
unvarnished ʌnˈvɑː.nɪʃt, ˌʌn- Ⓤⓢ -ˈvɑːr-
unvarying ʌnˈveə.ri.ɪŋ, ˌʌn- Ⓤⓢ -ˈver.i-, -ˈvær.i-
unveil ʌnˈveɪl, ˌʌn- **-s** -z **-ing** -ɪŋ **-ed** -d
unventilated ʌnˈven.tɪ.leɪ.tɪd, ˌʌn-, -tə- Ⓤⓢ -t̬ə.leɪ.t̬ɪd
unversed ʌnˈvɜːst, ˌʌn- Ⓤⓢ -ˈvɝːst
unvoiced ʌnˈvɔɪst, ˌʌn-
unwaged ʌnˈweɪdʒd, ˌʌn-
unwanted ʌnˈwɒn.tɪd, ˌʌn- Ⓤⓢ -ˈwɑːn.t̬ɪd
unwarlike ʌnˈwɔː.laɪk, ˌʌn- Ⓤⓢ -ˈwɔːr-
unwarmed ʌnˈwɔːmd, ˌʌn- Ⓤⓢ -ˈwɔːrmd
unwarned ʌnˈwɔːnd, ˌʌn- Ⓤⓢ -ˈwɔːrnd
unwarrantab|le ʌnˈwɒr.ᵊn.tə.b|l̩, ˌʌn- Ⓤⓢ -ˈwɔːr.ᵊn.t̬ə-, -ˈwɑːr- **-ly** -li **-leness** -l̩.nəs, -nɪs
unwarranted ʌnˈwɒr.ᵊn.tɪd, ˌʌn- Ⓤⓢ -ˈwɔːr.ᵊn.t̬ɪd, -ˈwɑːr-
unwar|y ʌnˈweə.r|i, ˌʌn- Ⓤⓢ -ˈwer|.i **-ily** -ɪ.li, -ᵊl.i **-iness** -ɪ.nəs, -ɪ.nɪs
unwashed ʌnˈwɒʃt, ˌʌn- Ⓤⓢ -ˈwɑːʃt, -ˈwɔːʃt
unwavering ʌnˈweɪ.vᵊr.ɪŋ, ˌʌn- **-ly** -li
unwearable ʌnˈweə.rə.bl̩, ˌʌn- Ⓤⓢ -ˈwer.ə-
unwearied ʌnˈwɪə.rid, ˌʌn- Ⓤⓢ -ˈwɪr.id
unwearying ʌnˈwɪə.ri.ɪŋ, ˌʌn- Ⓤⓢ -ˈwɪr.i-
unwed ʌnˈwed, ˌʌn-
unwelcome ʌnˈwel.kəm, ˌʌn-
unwell ʌnˈwel, ˌʌn-
unwholesome ʌnˈhəʊl.səm, ˌʌn- Ⓤⓢ -ˈhoʊl- **-ly** -li **-ness** -nəs, -nɪs
unwieldy|y ʌnˈwiːl.d|i, ˌʌn- **-ier** -i.əʳ Ⓤⓢ -i.ɚ **-iest** -i.ɪst, -i.əst **-ily** -ɪ.li, -ᵊl.i **-iness** -ɪ.nəs, -ɪ.nɪs
unwilling ʌnˈwɪl.ɪŋ, ˌʌn- **-ly** -li **-ness** -nəs, -nɪs
Unwin ˈʌn.wɪn
unwind ʌnˈwaɪnd, ˌʌn- **-s** -z **-ing** -ɪŋ
  unwound ʌnˈwaʊnd, ˌʌn-
unwise ʌnˈwaɪz, ˌʌn- **-ly** -li
unwish ʌnˈwɪʃ **-es** -ɪz **-ing** -ɪŋ **-ed** -t
  unˈwished ˌfor
unwitting ʌnˈwɪt.ɪŋ, ˌʌn- Ⓤⓢ -ˈwɪt̬- **-ly** -li

unwomanl|y ʌnˈwʊm.ən.l|i, ˌʌn- **-iness** -ɪ.nəs, -ɪ.nɪs

unwonted ʌnˈwəʊn.tɪd, ˌʌn- (US) -ˈwɔːn.t̬ɪd, -ˈwoʊn-, -ˈwɑːn-, -ˈwʌn- **-ly** -li **-ness** -nəs, -nɪs

unworkable ʌnˈwɜː.kə.bl̩, ˌʌn- (US) -ˈwɝː-

unworkmanlike ʌnˈwɜːk.mən.laɪk, ˌʌn- (US) -ˈwɝːk-

unworldl|y ʌnˈwɜːld.l|i, ˌʌn- (US) -ˈwɝːld- **-iness** -ɪ.nəs, -ɪ.nɪs

unworn ʌnˈwɔːn, ˌʌn- (US) -ˈwɔːrn

unworth|y ʌnˈwɜː.ð|i, ˌʌn- (US) -ˈwɝː- **-ily** -ɪ.li, -ᵊl.i **-iness** -ɪ.nəs, -ɪ.nɪs

unwound *(from* **unwind***)* ʌnˈwaʊnd, ˌʌn-

unwounded ʌnˈwuːn.dɪd, ˌʌn-

unwrap ʌnˈræp, ˌʌn- **-s** -s **-ping** -ɪŋ **-ped** -t

unwritten ʌnˈrɪt.ᵊn, ˌʌn- **ˌunwritten ˌconstiˈtution; ˌunwritten ˈlaw; ˌunwritten ˈrule**

unwrought ʌnˈrɔːt, ˌʌn- (US) -ˈrɑːt, -ˈrɔːt

unyielding ʌnˈjiːl.dɪŋ, ˌʌn- **-ly** -li **-ness** -nəs, -nɪs

unyok|e ʌnˈjəʊk, ˌʌn- (US) -ˈjoʊk **-es** -s **-ing** -ɪŋ **-ed** -t

unzip ʌnˈzɪp, ˌʌn- **-s** -s **-ping** -ɪŋ **-ped** -t

up- ʌp-

Note: Prefix. It is normally unstressed or receives secondary stress. It may carry the strongest stress in stress shift cases.

up ʌp **-s** -s **-ping** -ɪŋ **-ped** -t

up-and-coming ˌʌp.ᵊŋˈkʌm.ɪŋ, -ᵊndˈ- (US) -ᵊndˈ- *stress shift:* ˌup-and-coming ˈleader

up-and-down ˌʌp.ᵊndˈdaʊn *stress shift:* ˌup-and-down ˈmotion

up-and-up ˌʌp.ᵊndˈʌp

Upanishad ʊˈpʌn.ɪ.ʃəd, jʊ-, -ˈpæn-, -ʃæd (US) uːˈpæn.ɪ.ʃæd, juː-, -ˈpɑː.nɪ-, -ʃɑːd **-s** -z

upas ˈjuː.pəs **-es** -ɪz

upbeat *(adj.)* ʌpˈbiːt (US) ˈ-- *stress shift, British only:* ˌupbeat ˈending

upbeat *(n.)* ˈʌp.biːt **-s** -s

upbraid ʌpˈbreɪd, ˌʌp- **-s** -z **-ing** -ɪŋ **-ed** -ɪd

upbringing ˈʌpˌbrɪŋ.ɪŋ

upcast ˈʌp.kɑːst (US) -kæst **-s** -s

upchuck ˈʌp.tʃʌk **-s** -s **-ing** -ɪŋ **-ed** -t

upcoming ˈʌpˌkʌm.ɪŋ, -ˈ-- (US) ˈʌpˌkʌm-

Upcott ˈʌp.kət, -kɒt (US) -kət, -kɑːt

up-countr|y *(n. adj.)* ˌʌpˈkʌn.tr|i (US) ˈ--- **-ies** -iz *stress shift, British only:* ˌup-country ˈfarm

up-country *(adv.)* ʌpˈkʌn.tri

update *(n.)* ˈʌp.deɪt **-s** -s

up|date *(v.)* ʌp|ˈdeɪt, ˌʌp- **-dates** -ˈdeɪts **-dating** -ˈdeɪ.tɪŋ (US) -ˈdeɪ.t̬ɪŋ **-dated** -ˈdeɪ.tɪd (US) -ˈdeɪ.t̬ɪd

Updike ˈʌp.daɪk

upend ʌpˈend, ˌʌp- **-s** -z **-ing** -ɪŋ **-ed** -ɪd

up-front ʌpˈfrʌnt, ˌʌp- *stress shift:* ˌup-front ˈpayment

upgrad|e *(v.)* ʌpˈɡreɪd, ˌʌp- **-es** -z **-ing** -ɪŋ **-ed** -ɪd

upgrade *(n.)* ˈʌp.ɡreɪd **-s** -z

Upham ˈʌp.əm

upheaval ʌpˈhiː.vᵊl **-s** -z

upheav|e ʌpˈhiːv **-es** -z **-ing** -ɪŋ **-ed** -d

upheld *(from* **uphold***)* ʌpˈheld

uphill ʌpˈhɪl, ˌʌp- *stress shift:* ˌuphill ˈstruggle

up|hold ʌp|ˈhəʊld (US) -ˈhoʊld **-holds** -ˈhəʊldz (US) -ˈhoʊldz **-holding** -ˈhəʊl.dɪŋ (US) -ˈhoʊl.dɪŋ **-held** -ˈheld **-holder/s** -ˈhəʊl.dəʳ/z (US) -ˈhoʊl.dɚ/z

upholst|er ʌpˈhəʊl.st|əʳ, əp- (US) ʌpˈhoʊl.st|ɚ **-ers** -əz (US) -ɚz **-ering** -ᵊr.ɪŋ **-ered** -əd (US) -ɚd **-erer/s** -ᵊr.əʳ/z (US) -ɚ.ɚ/z **-ery** -ᵊr.i

Upjohn ˈʌp.dʒɒn (US) -dʒɑːn

upkeep ˈʌp.kiːp

upland ˈʌp.lənd (US) -lənd, -lænd **-s** -z **-er/s** -əʳ/z (US) -ɚ/z

uplift *(n.)* ˈʌp.lɪft

uplift *(v.)* ʌpˈlɪft, ˌʌp- **-s** -s **-ing** -ɪŋ **-ed** -ɪd

uplifting ʌpˈlɪf.tɪŋ, ˌʌp- *stress shift:* ˌuplifting ˈday

uplighter ˈʌpˌlaɪ.təʳ (US) -t̬ɚ **-s** -z

upload ʌpˈləʊd, ˈʌp.ləʊd (US) -loʊd **-s** -z **-ing** -ɪŋ **-ed** -ɪd

up-market ˌʌpˈmɑː.kɪt (US) ˈʌpˌmɑːr- *stress shift, British only:* ˌup-market ˈshop

Upminster ˈʌpˌmɪn*t*.stəʳ (US) -stɚ

upmost ˈʌp.məʊst (US) -moʊst

upon *strong form:* əˈpɒn (US) -ˈpɑːn *occasional weak form:* ə.pən

upper ˈʌp.əʳ (US) -ɚ **-s** -z **ˌupper ˈclass; ˌupper ˈcrust; ˌUpper ˈHouse; ˌstiff upper ˈlip; have the ˌupper ˈhand**

upper-case ˌʌp.əˈkeɪs (US) -ɚˈ- *stress shift, see compound:* **ˌupper-case ˈletters**

uppercut ˈʌp.ə.kʌt (US) ˈ-ɚ- **-s** -s

Uppermill ˈʌp.ə.mɪl (US) ˈ-ɚ-

uppermost ˈʌp.ə.məʊst (US) -ɚ.moʊst

Uppingham ˈʌp.ɪŋ.əm

uppish ˈʌp.ɪʃ **-ly** -li **-ness** -nəs, -nɪs

uppity ˈʌp.ɪ.ti (US) -t̬i **-ness** -nəs, -nɪs

Uppsala ʊpˈsɑː.lə, ʌp-, ˈ---; ˈʌp.sᵊl.ə, ˈʊp-, -sɑː.lɑː (US) ʌpˈsɑː.lɑː, ʊp-; ˈʌp.sᵊl.ə

uprais|e ʌpˈreɪz, ˌʌp- **-es** -ɪz **-ing** -ɪŋ **-ed** -d

uprear ʌpˈrɪəʳ, ˌʌp- (US) -ˈrɪr **-s** -z **-ing** -ɪŋ **-ed** -d

Uprichard juːˈprɪtʃ.ɑːd, -əd; ʌpˈrɪtʃ.əd (US) juːˈprɪtʃ.ɑːrd, -ɚd; ʌpˈrɪtʃ.ɚd

upright ˈʌp.raɪt **-s** -s **-ly** -li **-ness** -nəs, -nɪs

uprising ˈʌpˌraɪ.zɪŋ, -ˈ--, ˌ-ˈ-- (US) ˈʌpˌraɪ- **-s** -z

upriver ˌʌpˈrɪv.əʳ (US) -ɚ

uproar ˈʌp.rɔːʳ (US) -rɔːr **-s** -z

uproarious ʌpˈrɔː.ri.əs (US) -ˈrɔːr.i- **-ly** -li **-ness** -nəs, -nɪs

up|root ʌp|ˈruːt, ˌʌp- **-roots** -ˈruːts **-rooting** -ˈruː.tɪŋ (US) -ˈruː.t̬ɪŋ **-rooted** -ˈruː.tɪd (US) -ˈruː.t̬ɪd **-rooter/s** -ˈruː.təʳ/z (US) -ˈruː.t̬ɚ/z

upsadaisy ˌʌps.əˈdeɪ.zi, ˌʊps-

Upsala ʊpˈsɑː.lə, ʌp-, ˈ---; ˈʌp.sᵊl.ə, ˈʊp-, -sɑː.lɑː (US) ʌpˈsɑː.lɑː, ʊp-; ˈʌp.sᵊl.ə

upscale ˌʌpˈskeɪl

upset *(n.)* ˈʌp.set **-s** -s

upset *(adj.)* ʌpˈset, ˌʌp- *stress shift, see compound:* **ˌupset ˈstomach**

up|set *(v.)* ʌp|ˈset, ˌʌp- **-sets** -ˈsets **-setting** -ˈset.ɪŋ (US) -ˈset̬.ɪŋ

upshot ˈʌp.ʃɒt (US) -ʃɑːt

upside ˈʌp.saɪd **-s** -z **ˌupside ˈdown**

upsilon juːpˈsaɪ.lən, ʊp-, ʌp-, -lɒn; ˈjuːp.sɪl.ən, ˈʌp-, -ɒn (US) ˈʌp.sə.lɑːn, ˈuːp- **-s** -z

upstag|e *(v.)* ʌpˈsteɪdʒ, ˌʌp- **-es** -ɪz **-ing** -ɪŋ **-ed** -d *stress shift, British only:* ˌupstage ˈspeech

upstage *(adj.)* ʌpˈsteɪdʒ, ˌʌp- (US) ˈʌp.steɪdʒ

upstairs ʌpˈsteəz, ˌʌp- (US) -ˈsterz *stress shift:* ˌupstairs ˈwindow

upstanding ʌpˈstæn.dɪŋ, ˌʌp- **-ness** -nəs, -nɪs *stress shift:* ˌupstanding ˈsoldier

upstart ˈʌp.stɑːt (US) -stɑːrt **-s** -s

upstate ˌʌpˈsteɪt (US) ˈʌp-, -ˈ- *stress shift, British only:* ˌupstate ˈtown

upstream ʌpˈstriːm, ˌʌp- *stress shift:* ˌupstream ˈjourney

upstretched ʌpˈstretʃt, ˌʌp- *stress shift:* ˌupstretched ˈhands

Pronouncing the letters UOU

The vowel letter combination **uou** has only one possible pronunciation: /ju.ə/, e.g.:

ambiguous /æmˈbɪɡ.ju.əs/

upstroke ˈʌp.strəʊk (US) -stroʊk **-s** -s
upsurg|e ˈʌp.sɜːdʒ (US) -sɝːdʒ **-es** -ɪz
upswept ʌpˈswept, ˌʌp- *stress shift:* ˌupswept ˈwings
upswing (*n.*) ˈʌp.swɪŋ **-s** -z
upswing (*v.*) ʌpˈswɪŋ, ˌʌp- **-s** -z **-ing** -ɪŋ **upswung** ʌpˈswʌŋ, ˌʌp-
uptake ˈʌp.teɪk **-s** -s
up-tempo ˌʌpˈtem.pəʊ (US) -poʊ
upthrust ˈʌp.θrʌst **-s** -s
uptight ʌpˈtaɪt, ˌʌp- **-ness** -nəs, -nɪs *stress shift:* ˌuptight ˈperson
up|tilt ʌpˈ|tɪlt, ˌʌp- **-tilts** -ˈtɪlts **-tilting** -ˈtɪl.tɪŋ (US) -ˈtɪl.t̬ɪŋ **-tilted** -ˈtɪl.tɪd (US) -ˈtɪl.t̬ɪd
up-to-date ˌʌp.təˈdeɪt **-ness** -nəs, -nɪs *stress shift:* ˌup-to-date ˈmethod
Upton ˈʌp.tən
up-to-the-minute ˌʌp.tə.ðəˈmɪn.ɪt, -tʊ- *stress shift:* ˌup-to-the-minute ˈstyling
uptown ʌpˈtaʊn, ˌʌp- (US) ˈʌp.taʊn, ˌ-ˈ- *stress shift, British only:* ˌuptown ˈhouse
upturn (*v.*) ʌpˈtɜːn (US) -ˈtɝːn **-s** -z **-ing** -ɪŋ **-ed** -d
upturn (*n.*) ˈʌp.tɜːn (US) -tɝːn **-s** -z
upturned ʌpˈtɜːnd, ˌʌp- (US) -ˈtɝːnd *stress shift:* ˌupturned ˈboat
upward ˈʌp.wəd (US) -wɚd **-ly** -li **-s** -z ˌ**upwardly** ˈ**mobile**
upwind ʌpˈwɪnd
Ur ɜːʳ, ʊəʳ (US) ɝː, ʊr
uraemia jʊəˈriː.mi.ə, jə-, jɔː- (US) juːˈriː-, jʊ-
Ural ˈjʊə.rᵊl, ˈjɔː- (US) ˈjʊr.ᵊl **-s** -z ˌ**Ural** ˈ**Mountains**
uralite ˈjʊə.rᵊl.aɪt, ˈjɔː- (US) ˈjʊr.ə.laɪt
Urani|a jʊəˈreɪ.ni|.ə, jə-, jɔː- (US) jʊ- **-an** -ən
uranium jʊəˈreɪ.ni.əm, jə-, jɔː- (US) jʊ-, jə-
Uranus ˈjʊə.rᵊn.əs, ˈjɔː-; jʊəˈreɪ.nəs, jə- (US) ˈjʊr.ᵊn.əs; juːˈreɪ.nəs
urate ˈjʊə.reɪt, ˈjɔː-, -rɪt (US) ˈjʊr.eɪt **-s** -s
urban (U) ˈɜː.bᵊn **urban** (US) ˈɝː- **-ite/s** -aɪt/s ˌ**urban gueˈrilla**
Urbana ɜːˈbæn.ə, -ˈbɑː.nə (US) ɝːˈbæn.ə
urbane ɜːˈbeɪn (US) ɝː- **-ly** -li **-ness** -nəs, nɪs
urban|ism ˈɜː.bᵊn|.ɪ.zᵊm (US) ˈɝː- **-ist/s** -ɪst/s
urbanistic ˌɜː.bᵊnˈɪs.tɪk (US) ˌɝː- **-ally** -ᵊl.i, -li
urbanity ɜːˈbæn.ə.ti, -ɪ.ti (US) ɝːˈbæn.ə.t̬i
urbanization, -isa- ˌɜː.bᵊn.aɪˈzeɪ.ʃᵊn, -ɪˈ- (US) ˌɝː.bᵊn.ɪˈ-
urbaniz|e, -is|e ˈɜː.bᵊn.aɪz (US) ˈɝː- **-es** -ɪz **-ing** -ɪŋ **-ed** -d
Urbervilles ˈɜː.bə.vɪlz (US) ˈɝː-
urchin ˈɜː.tʃɪn (US) ˈɝː- **-s** -z
Urdu ˈʊə.duː, ˈɜː-, ˌ-ˈ- (US) ˈʊr.duː, ˈɝː-
Ure jʊəʳ (US) jʊr
-ure -əʳ (US) -ɚ
Note: Suffix. In words containing **-ure** where the stem is free, **-ure** does not normally affect the stress pattern of the word, e.g. **proceed** /prəʊˈsiːd (US) prə-/, **procedure** /prəʊˈsiː.dʒəʳ (US) prəˈsiː.dʒɚ/. Where the stem is bound, the word is normally stressed on the penultimate or antepenultimate syllable, e.g. **furniture** /ˈfɜː.nɪ.tʃəʳ (US) ˈfɝː.nɪ.tʃɚ/. Exceptions exist; see individual entries.
ure|a jʊəˈriː|.ə; ˈjʊə.ri-, ˈjɔː- (US) jʊˈriː-; ˈjʊr.i- **-al** -ᵊl
ureter jʊəˈriː.təʳ; ˈjʊə.rɪ-, -rə- (US) jʊˈriː.t̬ɚ **-s** -z
ureth|ra jʊəˈriː.θ|rə (US) jʊ- **-rae** -riː **-ras** -rəz
urethritis ˌjʊə.rəˈθraɪ.tɪs, ˌjɔː-, -rɪˈ- (US) ˌjʊr.əˈθraɪ.t̬ɪs
uretic jʊəˈret.ɪk, jə- (US) jʊˈret̬.ɪk **-s** -s
urg|e ɜːdʒ (US) ɝːdʒ **-es** -ɪz **-ing** -ɪŋ **-ed** -d **-er/s** -əʳ/z (US) -ɚ/z
urgency ˈɜː.dʒᵊnt.si (US) ˈɝː-
urgent ˈɜː.dʒᵊnt (US) ˈɝː- **-ly** -li
Uriah jʊəˈraɪə, jə- (US) jʊ-
uric ˈjʊə.rɪk, ˈjɔː- (US) ˈjʊr.ɪk
Uriel ˈjʊə.ri.əl, ˈjɔː- (US) ˈjʊr.i-
Urim ˈjʊə.rɪm, ˈjɔː-, ˈʊə- (US) ˈjʊr.ɪm
urinal jʊəˈraɪ.nᵊl, jə-; ˈjʊə.rɪ.nᵊl, ˈjɔː-, -rᵊn.ᵊl; (US) ˈjʊr.ᵊn.ᵊl **-s** -z
urinary ˈjʊə.rɪ.nᵊr.i, ˈjɔː-, -rᵊn.ᵊr- (US) ˈjʊr.ə.ner.i
urin|ate ˈjʊə.rɪ.n|eɪt, ˈjɔː-, -rᵊn|.eɪt (US) ˈjʊr.ə.n|eɪt **-ates** -eɪts **-ating** -eɪ.tɪŋ (US) -eɪ.t̬ɪŋ **-ated** -eɪ.tɪd (US) -eɪ.t̬ɪd
urination ˌjʊə.rɪˈneɪ.ʃᵊn, ˌjɔː-, -rᵊnˈeɪ- (US) ˌjʊr.əˈneɪ-
urine ˈjʊə.rɪn, ˈjɔː- (US) ˈjʊr.ɪn **-s** -z
uriniferous ˌjʊə.rɪˈnɪf.ᵊr.əs, ˌjɔː-, -rᵊnˈɪf- (US) ˌjʊr.əˈnɪf-
urinogenital ˌjʊə.rɪ.nəʊˈdʒen.ɪ.tᵊl, ˌjɔː-, ˈ-ə- (US) ˌjʊr.ə.noʊˈdʒen.ə.t̬ᵊl
Urmia ˈɜː.mi.ə, ˈʊə- (US) ˈʊr-
Urmston ˈɜːm.stᵊn (US) ˈɝːm-
urn ɜːn (US) ɝːn **-s** -z
uro- ˌjʊə.rəʊ-, ˌjɔː- (US) ˌjʊr.oʊ-, ˌ-ə-
urolog|y jʊəˈrɒl.ə.dʒ|i (US) jʊrˈɑː- **-ist/s** -ɪst/s
Urquhart ˈɜː.kət (US) ˈɝː.kɚt, -kɑːrt
Ursa ˈɜː.sə (US) ˈɝː- ˌ**Ursa** ˈ**Major**; ˌ**Ursa** ˈ**Minor**
ursine ˈɜː.saɪn (US) ˈɝː-, -sɪn
Ursula ˈɜː.sjə.lə, -sjʊ-, -ʃə-, -ʃʊ- (US) ˈɝː.sə.lə
Ursuline ˈɜː.sjə.laɪn, -sjʊ-, -ʃə-, -ʃʊ-, -lɪn (US) ˈɝː.sə.lɪn, -laɪn **-s** -z
urticaria ˌɜː.tɪˈkeə.ri.ə (US) ˌɝː.t̬ɪˈker.i-
Uruguay ˈjʊə.rə.gwaɪ, ˈʊr.ə-, ˈ-ʊ-, -gweɪ (US) ˈjʊr.ə.gweɪ, ˈʊr-, ˈuː.ruː-, -gwaɪ
Uruguayan ˌjʊə.rəˈgwaɪ.ən, ˌʊr.əˈ-, -ʊˈ-, -ˈgweɪ- (US) ˌjʊr.əˈgweɪ-, ˌʊr-, ˌuː.ruː-, -ˈgwaɪ- **-s** -z
urus ˈjʊə.rəs, ˈjɔː- (US) ˈjʊr.əs
us *strong form:* ʌs *weak forms:* əs, s
Note: Weak form word. The strong form is used mainly for contrast, e.g. 'a them and us attitude', or for emphasis, e.g. 'This land belongs to **us**'. The weak form is used when unstressed, and can occur in final position, e.g. 'They joined us' /ðeɪˈdʒɔɪnd.əs/.
US ˌjuːˈes
USA ˌjuː.esˈeɪ
usability ˌjuː.zəˈbɪl.ə.ti, -ɪ.ti (US) -ə.t̬i
usable ˈjuː.zə.bl̩
USAF ˌjuː.es.eɪˈef
usag|e ˈjuː.sɪdʒ, -zɪdʒ **-es** -ɪz
usanc|e ˈjuː.zᵊnts **-es** -ɪz
USDAW ˈʌs.dɔː, ˈʌz- (US) -dɑː, -dɔː
use (*n.*) juːs **uses** ˈjuː.sɪz
us|e (*v.*) *make use of:* juːz **-es** -ɪz **-ing** -ɪŋ **-ed** -d **-er/s** -əʳ/z (US) -ɚ/z
useab|le ˈjuː.zə.b|l̩ **-ly** -li **-leness** -l̩.nəs, -nɪs
used (*from* **use** *v.*) juːzd
used (*adj.*) *accustomed:* juːst, juːzd
used (*v.*) *was or were accustomed; when followed by* **to**: juːst *when not followed by* **to**: juːst, juːzd
usedn't *when followed by* **to**: ˈjuː.sᵊnt *when not followed by* **to**: ˈjuː.sᵊnt
Note: This form is rare in present-day English, especially in American English.
useful ˈjuːs.fᵊl, -fʊl **-ly** -i **-ness** -nəs, -nɪs
useless ˈjuː.sləs, -slɪs **-ly** -li **-ness** -nəs, -nɪs
usen't *when followed by* **to**: ˈjuː.sᵊnt *when not followed by* **to**: ˈjuː.sᵊnt
Note: See note for 'usedn't'.
user-friendl|y ˌjuː.zəˈfrend.l|i (US) -zɚˈ- **-iness** -ɪ.nəs, -ɪ.nɪs *stress shift:* ˌuser-friendly ˈproduct
uses (*plur. of* **use** *n.*) ˈjuː.sɪz
uses (*from* **use** *v.*) ˈjuː.zɪz
Ushant ˈʌʃ.ᵊnt
Ushaw ˈʌʃ.ə, -ɔː (US) -ə, -ɑː, -ɔː
ush|er (U) ˈʌʃ|.əʳ (US) -ɚ **-ers** -əz (US) -ɚz **-ering** -ᵊr.ɪŋ **-ered** -əd (US) -ɚd
usherette ˌʌʃ.ᵊrˈet **-s** -s
Usk ʌsk
USN ˌjuː.esˈen
usquebaugh ˈʌs.kwɪ.bɔː, -kwə- (US) -bɑː, -bɔː **-s** -z
Ussher ˈʌʃ.əʳ (US) -ɚ
USSR ˌjuː.es.esˈɑːʳ (US) -ˈɑːr

Uvular

A consonant sound made between the back of the tongue and a lump of soft tissue (uvula) which is in the back of the mouth, dangling from the end of the soft palate.

Examples for English

English does not have any examples of uvular sounds as phonemes, but sounds with this place of articulation are widely found in other languages.

In other languages

The voiceless uvular PLOSIVE [q] is found as the phoneme /q/ in many dialects of Arabic. Uvular FRICATIVES [χ ʁ] are found quite commonly: German, Hebrew, Dutch and Spanish, for example, have voiceless ones, and French, Arabic and Danish have voiced ones. The uvular NASAL [ɴ] is found in some Inuit languages. The uvula itself is active only when it vibrates in a uvular TRILL, [ʀ].

Pronouncing the letters UY

The vowel digraph **uy** has two possible pronunciations: /aɪ/ and, at the end of words where it is usually preceded by the letter **q**, /wi/, e.g.:

buy /baɪ/
soliloquy /səˈlɪl.ə.kwi/

An exceptional case is the word Gruyère, borrowed from French.

Gruyère /ˈgruː.jeəʳ; gruˈjeəʳ/ (US) /gruˈjer/

Ustinov ˈjuː.stɪ.nɒf, ˈuː-, -stə-, -nɒv (US) -nɑːf, -nɔːf, -nɑːv

usu. *(abbrev. for* **usual/ly***)* ˈjuː.ʒᵊl/i, -ʒu.əl- (US) -ʒu.əl-, ˈjuːʒ.wəl-

usual ˈjuː.ʒᵊl, -ʒu.əl (US) -ʒu.əl, ˈjuːʒ.wəl **-ly** -i **-ness** -nəs, -nɪs

usufruct ˈjuː.sjʊ.frʌkt, -zjʊ- (US) -zʊ-, -sʊ-, -zə-, -sə- **-s** -s

usurer ˈjuː.ʒᵊr.əʳ (US) -ɚ **-s** -z

usurious juːˈzjʊə.ri.əs, -ˈʒʊə-, -ˈzjɔː- (US) juːˈʒʊr.i- **-ly** -li **-ness** -nəs, -nɪs

usurp juːˈzɜːp, -ˈsɜːp (US) -ˈsɝːp, -ˈzɝːp **-s** -s **-ing** -ɪŋ **-ed** -t **-er/s** -əʳ/z (US) -ɚ/z

usurpation ˌjuː.zɜːˈpeɪ.ʃᵊn, -sɜːˈ- (US) -sɚˈ-, -zɚˈ- **-s** -z

usury ˈjuː.ʒᵊr.i (US) -ʒɚ.i

Ut. *(abbrev. for* **Utah***)* ˈjuː.tɑː (US) -tɔː, -tɑː

Utah ˈjuː.tɑː (US) -tɔː, -tɑː

Ute juːt **-s** -s

utensil juːˈtent.sᵊl, -sɪl (US) -sᵊl **-s** -z

uteri *(alternative plur. of* **uterus***)* ˈjuː.tᵊr.aɪ (US) -t̬ə.raɪ

uterine ˈjuː.tᵊr.aɪn (US) -t̬ɚ.ɪn, -t̬ə.raɪn

uterus ˈjuː.tᵊr.əs (US) -t̬ɚ- **-es** -ɪz

Uther ˈjuː.θəʳ (US) -θɚ

Utica ˈjuː.tɪ.kə (US) -t̬ɪ-

utilitarian ˌjuː.tɪ.lɪˈteə.ri.ən, -ləˈ-; juːˌtɪl.ɪˈ-, -əˈ- (US) juːˌtɪl.əˈter.i- **-s** -z **-ism** -ɪ.zᵊm

utilit|y juːˈtɪl.ə.t|i, -ɪ.t|i (US) -ə.t̬|i **-ies** -iz uˈtility ˌroom

utilization, -isa- ˌjuː.tᵊl.aɪˈzeɪ.ʃᵊn, -tɪ.laɪˈ-, -lɪˈ- (US) -t̬ᵊl.ɪˈ-

utiliz|e, -is|e ˈjuː.tɪ.laɪz, -tᵊl.aɪz (US) -t̬ᵊl.aɪz **-es** -ɪz **-ing** -ɪŋ **-ed** -d **-er/s** -əʳ/z (US) -ɚ/z **-able** -ə.bl̩

utmost ˈʌt.məʊst, -məst (US) -moʊst

utopi|a (U) juːˈtəʊ.pi|.ə (US) -ˈtoʊ- **-an/s** -ən/z

utopianism (U) juːˈtəʊ.pi.ə.nɪ.zᵊm (US) -ˈtoʊ-

Utrecht ˈjuː.trekt, -trext, -ˈ- (US) ˈjuː.trekt

utricle ˈjuː.trɪ.kl̩ **-s** -z

Utrillo juːˈtrɪl.əʊ, uː- (US) -oʊ

Utsira uːtˈsɪə.rə (US) -ˈsɪr.ə

Uttar Pradesh ˌʊt.ə.prəˈdeʃ, -ˈdeɪʃ (US) ˌuː.t̬ɚ-

utt|er ˈʌt|.əʳ (US) ˈʌt̬|.ɚ **-erly** -ᵊl.i (US) -ɚ.li **-erness** -ə.nəs, -nɪs (US) -ɚ- **-ers** -əz (US) -ɚz **-ering** -ᵊr.ɪŋ **-ered** -əd (US) -ɚd **-erer/s** -ᵊr.əʳ/z (US) -ɚ.ɚ/z **-erable** -ᵊr.ə.bl̩

utteranc|e ˈʌt.ᵊr.ᵊnts (US) ˈʌt̬- **-es** -ɪz

uttermost ˈʌt.ə.məʊst (US) ˈʌt̬.ɚ.moʊst

Uttley ˈʌt.li

Uttoxeter juːˈtɒk.sɪ.təʳ, ʌtˈɒk-, ˈʌk.sɪ- (US) juːˈtɑːk.sɪ.t̬ɚ, ʌt̬ˈɑːk-, ˈʌk.sɪ-
Note: The common pronunciation is /juːˈtɒk.sɪ.təʳ (US) -ˈtɑːk.sɪ.t̬ɚ/ or /ʌtˈɒk.sɪ.təʳ (US) -ˈɑːk.sɪ.t̬ɚ/. The former is more frequent, and is the pronunciation of most outsiders.

U-turn ˈjuː.tɜːn, ˌjuːˈtɜːn (US) ˈjuː.tɝːn, ˌ-ˈ- **-s** -z

UV ˌjuːˈviː *stress shift, see compound:* ˌ**UV** ˈ**light**

uvul|a ˈjuː.vjə.l|ə, -vjʊ- **-as** -z **-ae** -i

uvular ˈjuː.vjə.ləʳ, -vjʊ- (US) -lɚ

Uxbridge ˈʌks.brɪdʒ

uxorial ʌkˈsɔː.ri.əl (US) -ˈsɔːr.i-; ʌgˈzɔːr-

uxorious ʌkˈsɔː.ri.əs (US) -ˈsɔːr.i-; ʌgˈzɔːr- **-ly** -li **-ness** -nəs, -nɪs

Uzbek ˈʊz.bek, ˈʌz- **-s** -s

Uzbekistan ʊzˌbek.ɪˈstɑːn, ʌz- (US) -ˈstæn, -ˈstɑːn **-i/s** -i/z

Uzi® ˈuː.zi

Pronouncing the letter V

The consonant letter **v** is always realised as /v/ in English words, e.g.:

van	/væn/
love	/lʌv/

However, in words borrowed from German and Slavic languages, the pronunciation may be /f/, e.g.:

Volkswagen	/ˈfɒlksˌvɑː.gən, ˈvɒlks-/
	(US) /ˈfoʊlks-, ˈvoʊlks-/
Gorbachev	/ˈgɔː.bə.tʃɒf/
	(US) /ˈgɔːr.bə.tʃɑːf/

v (V) viː -**'s** -z ˈ**v** ˌ**sign**
v. *versus:* viː, ˈvɜː.səs (US) viː, ˈvɝː- *vide:* viː, siː, ˈviː.deɪ, ˈvaɪ.di (US) ˈviː.deɪ
Va. *(abbrev. for* **Virginia***)* vəˈdʒɪn.jə, vɜː-, -i.ə; ˌviːˈeɪ (US) vɚˈdʒɪn.jə; ˌviːˈeɪ
Vaal vɑːl
vac væk -**s** -s
vacanc|y ˈveɪ.kᵊnt.s|i -**ies** -iz
vacant ˈveɪ.kᵊnt -**ly** -li ˌ**vacant** ˈ**lot**
vaca|te vəˈkeɪ|t, veɪ- (US) ˈveɪ.keɪ|t, -ˈ- -**tes** -ts -**ting** -tɪŋ (US) -t̬ɪŋ -**ted** -tɪd (US) -t̬ɪd
vacation vəˈkeɪ.ʃᵊn (US) veɪ-, və- -**s** -z -**ing** -ɪŋ -**ed** -d -**er/s** -əʳ/z (US) -ɚ/z -**ist/s** -ɪst/s
vaccin|ate ˈvæk.sɪ.n|eɪt, -sᵊn|.eɪt (US) -sə.n|eɪt -**ates** -eɪts -**ating** -eɪ.tɪŋ (US) -eɪ.t̬ɪŋ -**ated** -eɪ.tɪd (US) -eɪ.t̬ɪd -**ator/s** -eɪ.təʳ/z (US) -eɪ.t̬ɚ/z
vaccination ˌvæk.sɪˈneɪ.ʃᵊn, -sᵊnˈeɪ- (US) -səˈneɪ- -**s** -z
vaccine ˈvæk.siːn, -sɪn (US) vækˈsiːn, ˈ-- -**s** -z
Vachel(l) ˈveɪ.tʃᵊl
Vacher ˈvæʃ.əʳ, ˈveɪ.tʃəʳ (US) ˈvæʃ.ɚ, ˈveɪ.tʃɚ
vacill|ate ˈvæs.ᵊl|.eɪt, -sɪ.l|eɪt (US) -ə.l|eɪt -**ates** -eɪts -**ating/ly** -eɪ.tɪŋ/li (US) -eɪ.t̬ɪŋ/li -**ated** -eɪ.tɪd (US) -eɪ.t̬ɪd -**ator/s** -eɪ.təʳ/z (US) -eɪ.t̬ɚ/z
vacillation ˌvæs.ᵊlˈeɪ.ʃᵊn, -ɪˈleɪ- (US) -əˈleɪ- -**s** -z
Václav ˈvæt.slæv (US) ˈvɑːt.slɑːf
vacuity vækˈjuː.ə.ti, vəˈkjuː-, -ɪ.ti (US) -ə.t̬i
vacuolar ˌvæk.juˈəʊ.ləʳ (US) ˈvæk.ju.wə.lɚ; ˌvæk.juˈoʊ-, -lɑːr
vacuole ˈvæk.ju.əʊl (US) -oʊl -**s** -z
vacuous ˈvæk.ju.əs -**ly** -li -**ness** -nəs, -nɪs
vacuum ˈvæk.juːm, -jʊm, -juəm (US) -juːm, -ju.əm, -jʊm, -jəm -**s** -z -**ing** -ɪŋ -**ed** -d ˈ**vacuum** ˌ**cleaner**; ˈ**vacuum** ˌ**flask**; ˈ**vacuum** ˌ**pump**
vacuum-packed ˌvæk.juːmˈpækt, -jʊmˈ-, -juəmˈ- (US) -ju.əmˈ-, -juːmˈ-, -jʊmˈ-, -jəmˈ-, ˈ---
vade-mecum ˌvɑː.deɪˈmeɪ.kəm, -kʊm; ˌveɪ.diˈmiː.kəm, -kʌm (US) ˌveɪ.diˈmiː.kəm, ˌvɑː-, -ˈmeɪ- -**s** -z
Vaduz vɑːˈduːts
vagabond ˈvæg.ə.bɒnd, -bənd (US) -bɑːnd -**s** -z -**ish** -ɪʃ -**ism** -ɪ.zᵊm
vagabondage ˈvæg.əˌbɒn.dɪdʒ (US) -ˌbɑːn-
vagar|y ˈveɪ.gᵊr|.i; vəˈgeə.r|i (US) ˈveɪ.gɚ.|i; vəˈger|.i -**ies** -iz
vagina vəˈdʒaɪ.nə -**s** -z
vaginal vəˈdʒaɪ.nᵊl; ˈvædʒ.ɪ-, -ᵊn.ᵊl (US) ˈvædʒ.ᵊn.ᵊl -**ly** -i
vaginismus ˌvædʒ.ɪˈnɪz.məs, -əˈ-, -ˈnɪs- (US) -əˈnɪz-
vagrancy ˈveɪ.grᵊnt.si
vagrant ˈveɪ.grᵊnt -**s** -s
vagu|e veɪg -**er** -əʳ (US) -ɚ -**est** -ɪst, -əst -**ely** -li -**eness** -nəs, -nɪs
vail (V) veɪl -**s** -z -**ing** -ɪŋ -**ed** -d
Vaile veɪl
vain veɪn -**er** -əʳ (US) -ɚ -**est** -ɪst, -əst -**ly** -li -**ness** -nəs, -nɪs
vainglorious ˌveɪnˈglɔː.ri.əs, ˌveɪŋˈ- (US) ˌveɪnˈglɔːr.i- -**ly** -li -**ness** -nəs, -nɪs
vainglory ˌveɪnˈglɔː.ri, ˌveɪŋ- (US) ˈveɪnˌglɔːr.i, ˌ-ˈ--
Vaishnav|a ˈveʃ.nə.v|ɑː -**ism** -ɪ.zᵊm
Val væl
Valais ˈvæl.eɪ
valanc|e ˈvæl.ənts (US) ˈvæl-, ˈveɪ.lᵊnts -**es** -ɪz -**ed** -t
Valdez vælˈdiːz
vale (V) *valley:* veɪl -**s** -z
vale *latin word meaning "goodbye":* ˈvɑː.leɪ, ˈveɪ.li, ˈvæl.eɪ (US) ˈveɪ.li, ˈvɑː.leɪ
valediction ˌvæl.ɪˈdɪk.ʃᵊn, -əˈ- (US) ˌvæl.əˈdɪk.ʃᵊn -**s** -z
valedictorian ˌvæl.ɪ.dɪkˈtɔː.ri.ən, ˌ-ə- (US) ˌvæl.ə.dɪkˈtɔːr.i- -**s** -z
valedictor|y ˌvæl.ɪˈdɪk.tᵊr|.i, -əˈ- (US) ˌvæl.əˈdɪk.tɚ- -**ies** -iz
valence ˈveɪ.lᵊnts
Valencia vəˈlent.si.ə
Valenciennes ˌvæl.ən.siˈen, -ɑ̃ːn-, -ɑːnt-, -ˈsjen (US) -siˈenz, -ˈsjenz; vəˌlent.siˈenz, -ˌlɑːnt-
valenc|y ˈveɪ.lənt.s|i -**ies** -iz
valentine (V) *person or card:* ˈvæl.ən.taɪn -**s** -z ˈ**Valentine's** ˌ**card**; ˈ**Valentine's** ˌ**Day**
Valentine *first name/surname:* ˈvæl.ən.taɪn, -tɪn (US) -taɪn
Valentinian ˌvæl.ənˈtɪn.i.ən
Valentino ˌvæl.ənˈtiː.nəʊ (US) -noʊ
valerian (V) vəˈlɪə.ri.ən, -ˈleə- (US) -ˈlɪr.i- -**s** -z
Valerie, Valery ˈvæl.ᵊr.i
Valerius vəˈlɪə.ri.əs, -ˈleə- (US) -ˈlɪr.i-
Valéry ˈvæl.eə.riː, ˌvæl.eəˈriː (US) ˌvæl.əˈriː, ˌvɑː.lerˈiː
valet ˈvæl.eɪ, -ɪt, -ət, -i (US) ˈvæl.ɪt; vəˈleɪ, vælˈeɪ; ˈvæl.eɪ **valets** ˈvæl.eɪz, -ɪts, -əts, -iz (US) ˈvæl.ɪts; vəˈleɪz, vælˈeɪz; ˈvæl.eɪz **valeting** ˈvæl.eɪ.ɪŋ, -ɪ.tɪŋ, -ə.tɪŋ, -i.ɪŋ (US) ˈvæl.ɪ.t̬ɪŋ; vəˈleɪ.ɪŋ, vælˈeɪ.ɪŋ; ˈvæl.eɪ.ɪŋ **valeted** ˈvæl.eɪd, -ɪ.tɪd, -ə.tɪd, ˈ-id (US) ˈvæl.ɪ.t̬ɪd; vəˈleɪd, vælˈeɪd; ˈvæl.eɪd ˈ**valet** ˌ**parking**
valetudinarian ˌvæl.ɪ.tjuː.dɪˈneə.ri.ən, ˌ-ə-, -tʃuː- (US) -əˌtuː.dəˈner.i-, -ˌtjuː- -**s** -z -**ism** -ɪ.zᵊm
Valhalla vælˈhæl.ə (US) vælˈhæl-, vɑːlˈhɑː.lə
valiant ˈvæl.i.ənt, ˈ-jənt (US) ˈ-jənt -**ly** -li -**ness** -nəs, -nɪs
valid ˈvæl.ɪd -**ly** -li -**ness** -nəs, -nɪs
vali|date ˈvæl.ɪ|.deɪt, ˈ-ə- (US) ˈ-ə- -**dates** -deɪts -**dating** -deɪ.tɪŋ (US) -deɪ.t̬ɪŋ -**dated** -deɪ.tɪd (US) -deɪ.t̬ɪd
validation ˌvæl.ɪˈdeɪ.ʃᵊn, -əˈ- (US) -əˈ- -**s** -z
validit|y vəˈlɪd.ə.t|i, vælˈɪd-, -ɪ.t|i (US) vəˈlɪd.ə.t̬|i -**ies** -iz
valis|e vəˈliːz, vælˈiːz, -ˈiːs (US) vəˈliːs, -ˈliːz -**es** -ɪz
Valium® ˈvæl.i.əm (US) ˈ-i.əm, ˈ-jəm -**s** -z
Valkyrie vælˈkɪə.ri, ˈvæl.kᵊr.i, -kɪ.ri (US) vælˈkɪr.i, ˈvæl.kɚ.i, -kɪ.ri -**s** -z
Valladolid ˌvæl.ə.dəʊˈlɪd, -dɒlˈɪd *as if Spanish:* ˌvaɪ.ɑː.dɒlˈiːd (US) -doʊˈlɪd
Vallance ˈvæl.ənts
Valletta vəˈlet.ə (US) vɑːˈlet.ɑː
valley ˈvæl.i -**s** -z
Vallone vəˈləʊn (US) -ˈloʊn

Valois ˈvæl.wɑː ⓤⓢ vɑːlˈwɑː; ˈvæl.wɑː
valor ˈvæl.əʳ ⓤⓢ -ɚ
valorization, -isa- ˌvæl.ᵊr.aɪˈzeɪ.ʃᵊn, -ɪˈ- ⓤⓢ -ɪˈ- **-s** -z
valoriz|e, -is|e ˈvæl.ᵊr.aɪz ⓤⓢ -ə.raɪz **-es** -ɪz **-ing** -ɪŋ **-ed** -d
valorous ˈvæl.ᵊr.əs **-ly** -li **-ness** -nəs, -nɪs
valour ˈvæl.əʳ ⓤⓢ -ɚ
Valparaiso ˌvæl.pᵊrˈaɪ.zəʊ, -ˈeɪ- ⓤⓢ -pəˈraɪ.zoʊ, -ˈreɪ-
Valpolicella ˌvæl.pɒl.ɪˈtʃel.ə ⓤⓢ ˌvɑːl.poʊ.lɪ-
vals|e vɑːls, væls, vɔːls ⓤⓢ vɑːls, vʌls **-es** -ɪz
valuab|le ˈvæl.ju.ə.bl̩, -jə.bl̩, -jʊ- **-les** -l̩z **-ly** -li **-leness** -l̩.nəs, -nɪs
valuat|e ˈvæl.ju.eɪt **-es** -s **-ing** -ɪŋ **-ed** -ɪd
valuation ˌvæl.juˈeɪ.ʃᵊn **-s** -z
valu|e ˈvæl.juː **-es** -z **-ing** -ɪŋ **-ed** -d **-er/s** -əʳ/z ⓤⓢ -ɚ/z ˈ**value** ˌ**judgment**; ˌ**family** ˈ**values**
value-added ˌvæl.juːˈæd.ɪd ˌ**value-**ˌ**added** ˈ**tax**, ˌ**value-**ˈ**added** ˌ**tax**
valueless ˈvæl.juː.ləs, -jʊ-, -lɪs
valve vælv **-s** -z
valvular ˈvæl.vjə.ləʳ, -vjʊ- ⓤⓢ -vjə.lɚ
valvule ˈvæl.vjuːl **-s** -z
vamoos|e vəˈmuːs, væmˈuːs ⓤⓢ væmˈuːs, vəˈmuːs **-es** -ɪz **-ing** -ɪŋ **-ed** -t
vamp væmp **-s** -s **-ing** -ɪŋ **-ed** -t
vampire ˈvæm.paɪəʳ ⓤⓢ -paɪɚ **-s** -z ˈ**vampire** ˌ**bat**
vampirism ˈvæm.paɪə.rɪ.zᵊm ⓤⓢ -paɪ-, -pɪ-
vampish ˈvæm.pɪʃ **-ly** -li **-ness** -nəs, -nɪs
van (V) væn **-s** -z
vanadium vəˈneɪ.di.əm
Van Allen vænˈæl.ən **Van** ˌ**Allen** ˈ**belt** ⓤⓢ **Van** ˈ**Allen** ˌ**belt**
Vanbrugh ˈvæn.brə, ˈvæm- ⓤⓢ ˈvæn.bruː
Note: **Sir John Vanbrugh**, the seventeenth-century dramatist and architect, is also sometimes referred to as /ˈvæn.bruː/ in British English.
Vance vænts, vɑːnts ⓤⓢ vænts
Vancouver vænˈkuː.vəʳ, væŋ- ⓤⓢ vænˈkuː.vɚ
V and A, V & A *(abbrev. for* **Victoria and Albert Museum***)* ˌviː.ənˈdeɪ
vandal (V) ˈvæn.dᵊl **-s** -z
vandalism ˈvæn.dᵊl.ɪ.zᵊm
vandaliz|e, -is|e ˈvæn.dᵊl.aɪz **-es** -ɪz **-ing** -ɪŋ **-ed** -d
Van de Graaff generator ˌvæn.dəˌɡrɑːfˈdʒen.ᵊ.reɪ.təʳ ⓤⓢ -t̬ɚ, -ˌɡræf- **-s** -z
Vanderbilt ˈvæn.də.bɪlt ⓤⓢ -dɚ-
Vanderbyl ˈvæn.də.bɪl ⓤⓢ -dɚ-
Vandermeer ˌvæn.dəˈmɪəʳ ⓤⓢ -dɚˈmɪr
van der Post ˌvæn.dəˈpɒst ⓤⓢ -dɚˈpɑːst
Van Diemen vænˈdiː.mən
Vandyke, Van Dyck vænˈdaɪk *stress shift, see compounds:* ˌ**Vandyke** ˈ**brown**; ˌ**Vandyke** ˈ**collar**
vane (V) veɪn **-s** -z **-d** -d
Vanessa vəˈnes.ə
Van Eyck vænˈaɪk **-s** -s
Vange vændʒ
Van Gogh vænˈɡɒf, væŋ-, -ˈɡɒk, -ˈɡɒx ⓤⓢ vænˈɡoʊ, -ˈɡɔːx
vanguard ˈvæn.ɡɑːd, ˈvæŋ- ⓤⓢ ˈvæn.ɡɑːrd **-s** -z
Van Helsing vænˈhel.sɪŋ ⓤⓢ væn-, vɑːn-
vanilla vəˈnɪl.ə **va**ˈ**nilla** ˌ**pod**
vanish ˈvæn.ɪʃ **-es** -ɪz **-ing** -ɪŋ **-ed** -t ˈ**vanishing** ˌ**cream**; ˈ**vanishing** ˌ**point**
Vanitory® ˈvæn.ɪ.tᵊr.i ˈ**Vanitory** ˌ**unit**
vanit|y ˈvæn.ə.t|i, -ɪ.t|i ⓤⓢ -ə.t̬|i **-ies** -iz ˈ**vanity** ˌ**case**; ˌ**Vanity** ˈ**Fair**; ˈ**vanity** ˌ**plates**; ˈ**vanity** ˌ**table**
vanquish ˈvæŋ.kwɪʃ ⓤⓢ ˈvæŋ-, ˈvæn- **-es** -ɪz **-ing** -ɪŋ **-ed** -t **-er/s** -əʳ/z ⓤⓢ -ɚ/z **-able** -ə.bl̩
Vansittart vænˈsɪt.ət, -ɑːt ⓤⓢ -ˈsɪt̬.ɚt
van Straubenzee ˌvæn.strɔːˈben.zi ⓤⓢ -strɑːˈ-, -strɔːˈ-
vantag|e ˈvɑːn.tɪdʒ ⓤⓢ ˈvæn.t̬ɪdʒ **-es** -ɪz ˈ**vantage** ˌ**point**
Vanuatu ˌvæn.uˈɑː.tuː, -ˈæt.uː ⓤⓢ vænˈwɑː.tuː
Vanunu vəˈnuː.nuː
Van Vechten vænˈvek.tən
Vanya ˈvɑː.njə, ˈvæn.jə ⓤⓢ ˈvɑː.njə
vapid ˈvæp.ɪd **-ly** -li **-ness** -nəs, -nɪs
vapidity væpˈɪd.ə.ti, vəˈpɪd-, -ɪ.ti ⓤⓢ væpˈɪd.ə.t̬i
vap|or ˈveɪ.p|əʳ ⓤⓢ -p|ɚ **-ors** -əz ⓤⓢ -ɚz **-ory** -ᵊr.i ˈ**vapor** ˌ**trail**
vaporett|o ˌvæp.ᵊrˈet|.əʊ ⓤⓢ -pəˈret̬|.oʊ **-os** -əʊz ⓤⓢ -oʊz **-i** -i
vaporization, -isa- ˌveɪ.pᵊr.aɪˈzeɪ.ʃᵊn, -ɪˈ- ⓤⓢ -ɪˈ- **-s** -z
vaporiz|e, -is|e ˈveɪ.pᵊr.aɪz ⓤⓢ -pə.raɪz **-es** -ɪz **-ing** -ɪŋ **-ed** -d **-er/s** -əʳ/z ⓤⓢ -ɚ/z
vaporosity ˌveɪ.pᵊrˈɒs.ə.ti, -ɪ.ti ⓤⓢ -pəˈrɑː.sə.t̬i
vaporous ˈveɪ.pᵊr.əs **-ly** -li **-ness** -nəs, -nɪs
vap|our ˈveɪ.p|əʳ ⓤⓢ -p|ɚ **-ours** -əz ⓤⓢ -ɚz **-oury** -ᵊr.i ˈ**vapour** ˌ**trail**
Varah ˈvɑː.rə ⓤⓢ ˈvɑːr.ə
Varden ˈvɑː.dᵊn ⓤⓢ ˈvɑːr-
varec ˈvær.ek, -ɪk ⓤⓢ ˈver-, ˈvær-
variability ˌveə.ri.əˈbɪl.ə.ti, -ɪ.ti ⓤⓢ ˌver.i.əˈbɪl.ə.t̬i, ˌvær-
variab|le ˈveə.ri.ə.bl̩ ⓤⓢ ˈver.i-, ˈvær- **-les** -l̩z **-ly** -li **-leness** -l̩.nəs, -nɪs
variance ˈveə.ri.ənts ⓤⓢ ˈver.i-, ˈvær-
variant ˈveə.ri.ənt ⓤⓢ ˈver.i-, ˈvær- **-s** -s
variate ˈveə.ri.ət, -ɪt ⓤⓢ ˈver.i.ɪt, ˈvær- **-s** -s
variation ˌveə.riˈeɪ.ʃᵊn ⓤⓢ ˌver.iˈ-, ˌvær- **-s** -z
varicella ˌvær.ɪˈsel.ə ⓤⓢ ˌver-, ˌvær-, -ə-
varices *(plur. of* **varix***)* ˈvær.ɪ.siːz, ˈveə.rɪ- ⓤⓢ ˈver.ə.siːz, ˈvær-
varicose ˈvær.ɪ.kəʊs ⓤⓢ ˈver.ə.koʊs, ˈvær- ˌ**varicose** ˈ**veins**
varicosity ˌvær.ɪˈkɒs.ə.ti, -ɪ.ti ⓤⓢ ˌver.ɪˈkɑː.sə.t̬i, ˌvær-
varied ˈveə.rɪd ⓤⓢ ˈver.ɪd, ˈvær- **-ly** -li
varie|gate ˈveə.rɪ|.ɡeɪt, -ri.ə- ⓤⓢ ˈver.i.ə-, ˈvær- **-gates** -ɡeɪts **-gating** -ɡeɪ.tɪŋ ⓤⓢ -ɡeɪ.t̬ɪŋ **-gated** -ɡeɪ.tɪd ⓤⓢ -ɡeɪ.t̬ɪd **-gator/s** -ɡeɪ.təʳ/z ⓤⓢ -ɡeɪ.t̬ɚ/z
variegation ˌveə.rɪˈɡeɪ.ʃᵊn, -ri.əˈ- ⓤⓢ ˌver.i.əˈ-, ˌvær- **-s** -z
varietal vəˈraɪə.tᵊl ⓤⓢ -t̬ᵊl
variet|y vəˈraɪə.t|i ⓤⓢ -t̬|i **-ies** -iz **va**ˈ**riety** ˌ**show**; **va**ˈ**riety** ˌ**store**
variform ˈveə.rɪ.fɔːm ⓤⓢ ˈver.ə.fɔːrm, ˈvær-
Varig® ˈvær.ɪɡ ⓤⓢ ˈver-, ˈvær-
variola vəˈraɪ.ə.lə
variole ˈveə.ri.əʊl ⓤⓢ ˈver.i.oʊl, ˈvær- **-s** -z
variorum ˌveə.riˈɔː.rəm, ˌvær- ⓤⓢ ˌver.iˈɔːr.əm, ˌvær-
various ˈveə.ri.əs ⓤⓢ ˈver.i-, ˈvær- **-ly** -li **-ness** -nəs, -nɪs
variphone ˈveə.rɪ.fəʊn ⓤⓢ ˈver.ɪ.foʊn, ˈvær- **-s** -z
varix ˈveə.rɪks ⓤⓢ ˈver.ɪks, ˈvær- **varices** ˈvær.ɪ.siːz, ˈveə.rɪ- ⓤⓢ ˈvær.ə-, ˈver-
varlet ˈvɑː.lət, -lɪt ⓤⓢ ˈvɑːr- **-s** -s
Varley ˈvɑː.li ⓤⓢ ˈvɑːr-
varmint ˈvɑː.mɪnt ⓤⓢ ˈvɑːr- **-s** -s
Varna ˈvɑː.nə ⓤⓢ ˈvɑːr-
Varney ˈvɑː.ni ⓤⓢ ˈvɑːr-
varnish ˈvɑː.nɪʃ ⓤⓢ ˈvɑːr- **-es** -ɪz **-ing** -ɪŋ **-ed** -t **-er/s** -əʳ/z ⓤⓢ -ɚ/z
Varro ˈvær.əʊ ⓤⓢ -oʊ, ˈver-
varsit|y ˈvɑː.sə.t|i, -ɪ.t|i ⓤⓢ ˈvɑːr.sə.t̬|i **-ies** -iz
Varuna værˈuː.nə ⓤⓢ vʌr-, vɑːˈruː-
var|y ˈveə.r|i ⓤⓢ ˈver|.i, ˈvær- **-ies** -iz **-ying/ly** -i.ɪŋ/li **-ied** -id
Vasari vəˈsɑː.ri ⓤⓢ vɑːˈsɑːr.i
Vasco da Gama ˌvæs.kəʊ.dəˈɡɑː.mə, -dɑːˈ- ⓤⓢ ˌvɑː.skoʊ-, -ˈɡæm.ə
vascular ˈvæs.kjə.ləʳ, -kjʊ- ⓤⓢ -kjə.lɚ
vascularity ˌvæs.kjəˈlær.ə.ti, -kjʊˈ-, -ɪ.ti ⓤⓢ -kjəˈler.ə.t̬i, -ˈlær-
vascul|um ˈvæs.kjə.l|əm, -kjʊ- ⓤⓢ -kjə- **-a** -ə

vas deferens ˌvæsˈdef.ə.renz, ˌvæz- (US) ˌvæsˈdef.ə.renz
vas|e vɑːz (US) veɪs, veɪz, vɑːz **-es** -ɪz
vasectom|y vəˈsek.tə.m|i, væsˈek- **-ies** -ɪz
Vaseline® ˈvæs.əl.iːn, -ɪ.liːn, ˌ--ˈ- (US) ˈvæs.ə.liːn, ˌ--ˈ-
Vashti ˈvæʃ.ti (US) ˈvɑːʃ.ti, -taɪ
vasoconstriction ˌveɪ.zəʊ.kənˈstrɪk.ʃən, ˌvæs.əʊ- (US) ˌvæs.oʊ-, ˌveɪ.zoʊ-
vasoconstrictor ˌveɪ.zəʊ.kənˈstrɪk.tər, ˌvæs.əʊ- (US) ˌvæs.oʊ-, ˌveɪ.zoʊ- **-s** -z
vasodilation ˌveɪ.zəʊ.daɪˈleɪ.ʃən, ˌvæs.əʊ- (US) ˌvæs.oʊ-, ˌveɪ.zoʊ-
vasodilator ˌveɪ.zəʊ.daɪˈleɪ.tər, ˌvæs.əʊ- (US) ˌvæs.oʊˈdaɪ.leɪ.t̬ɚ, ˌveɪ.zoʊ-, -dəˈ-; -daɪˈleɪ- **-s** -z
vasomotor ˌveɪ.zəʊˈməʊ.tər, ˌvæs.əʊ- (US) ˌvæs.oʊˈmoʊ.t̬ɚ, ˌveɪ.zoʊˈ-
vassal ˈvæs.əl **-s** -z
vassalage ˈvæs.əl.ɪdʒ
vast vɑːst (US) væst **-er** -ər (US) -ɚ **-est** -ɪst, -əst **-ly** -li **-ness/es** -nəs/ɪz, -nɪs/ɪz
Västerås ˌves.təˈrɔːs
vat væt **-s** -s **-ting** -ɪŋ (US) ˈvæt̬.ɪŋ **-ted** -ɪd (US) ˈvæt̬.ɪd
VAT ˌviː.eɪˈtiː, væt **-able** ˈvæt.ə.bl̩
Vathek ˈvæθ.ek, ˈvɑː.θek
vatic ˈvæt.ɪk (US) ˈvæt̬-
Vatican ˈvæt.ɪ.kən (US) ˈvæt̬- ˌ**Vatican ˈCity**
vatici|nate vəˈtɪs.ɪ|.neɪt, vætˈɪs- (US) ˈ-ə- **-nates** -neɪts **-nating** -neɪ.tɪŋ (US) -neɪ.t̬ɪŋ **-nated** -neɪ.tɪd (US) -neɪ.t̬ɪd
vaticination ˌvæt.ɪ.sɪˈneɪ.ʃən, ˌ-ə-; vəˌtɪs.ɪˈ-, vætˌɪs- (US) ˌvæt̬.ə.səˈ-; vəˌtɪs-, vætˌɪs- **-s** -z
vatu ˈvɑː.tuː **-s** -z
Vaucluse vəʊˈkluːz (US) voʊ-
Vaud vəʊ (US) voʊ
vaudeville ˈvɔː.də.vɪl, ˈvəʊ-; ˈvɔːd.vɪl, -vəl (US) ˈvɑːd.vɪl, ˈvɔːd-, ˈvoʊd-, ˈvɑː.də-, ˈvɔː-, ˈvoʊ- **-s** -z
vaudevillian ˌvɔː.dəˈvɪl.i.ən, ˌvəʊ-, ˌvɔːdˈvɪl- (US) ˌvɑːdˈvɪl-, ˌvɔːd-, ˌvoʊd-, ˌvɑː.dəˈ-, ˌvɔː-, ˌvoʊ- **-s** -z
Vaudin ˈvəʊ.dɪn (US) ˈvoʊ-
Vaudois (*sing.*) ˈvəʊ.dwɑː, -ˈ-, -dwɔː (US) voʊˈdwɑː (*plur.*) -z
Vaughan vɔːn (US) vɑːn, vɔːn
Vaughan Williams ˌvɔːnˈwɪl.jəmz, -i.əmz (US) ˌvɑːnˈ-, ˌvɔːnˈ-
Vaughn vɔːn (US) vɑːn, vɔːn
vault vɔːlt, vɒlt (US) vɑːlt, vɔːlt **-s** -s **-ing/s** -ɪŋ/z (US) ˈvɑːl.t̬ɪŋz, ˈvɔːl- **-ed** -ɪd (US) ˈvɑːl.t̬ɪd, ˈvɔːl- **-er/s** -ər/z (US) ˈvɑːl.t̬ɚ/z, -ˈvɔːl- ˈ**vaulting ˌhorse**
vaunt vɔːnt (US) vɑːnt, vɔːnt **-s** -s **-ing/ly** -ɪŋ/li (US) ˈvɑːn.t̬ɪŋ/li, ˈvɔːn- **-ed** -ɪd (US) ˈvɑːn.t̬ɪd, ˈvɔːn- **-er/s** -ər/z (US) ˈvɑːn.t̬ɚ/z, ˈvɔːn-
Vaux *English surname:* vɔːz, vɒks, vɔːks, vəʊks (US) vɔːks, vɑːks *in* **de Vaux**: *vəʊ* (US) *voʊ*
Vauxhall® ˈvɒk.sɔːl, ˈvɒks.hɔːl, -ˈ- (US) ˈvɑːks.hɔːl, ˈvɔːks-
vavaso(u)r (V) ˈvæv.ə.sʊər, -sɔːr (US) -sɔːr **-s** -z
VAX® væks
Vaz væz
VC ˌviːˈsiː **-s** -z
VCR ˌviː.siːˈɑːr (US) -ˈɑːr **-s** -z
VD ˌviːˈdiː
VDT ˌviː.diːˈtiː **-s** -z
VDU, vdu ˌviː.diːˈjuː **-s** -z
-'ve (*=* **have**) -v, -əv
veal viːl **-y** -i
Veblen ˈveb.lən
vector (*n.*) ˈvek.tər, -tɔːr (US) -tɚ **-s** -z
vect|or (*v.*) ˈvek.t|ər (US) -t|ɚ **-ors** -əz (US) -ɚz **-oring** -ər.ɪŋ **-ored** -əd (US) -ɚd
vectorial vekˈtɔː.ri.əl (US) -ˈtɔːr.i-
Veda ˈveɪ.də, ˈviː- **-s** -z
Vedanta vedˈɑːn.tə, vɪˈdɑːn-, və-, -ˈdæn- (US) vɪˈdɑːn-, -ˈdæn-
V-E Day ˌviːˈiː.deɪ
vedette vɪˈdet, və-, vedˈet (US) və- **-s** -s
Vedic ˈveɪ.dɪk, ˈviː-
veep (V) viːp
veer vɪər (US) vɪr **-s** -z **-ing/ly** -ɪŋ/li **-ed** -d
veg vedʒ ˌ**meat and two ˈveg**
Vega *star:* ˈviː.gə (US) ˈviː-, ˈveɪ- *Spanish dramatist:* ˈveɪ.gə
vegan ˈviː.gən **-s** -z **-ism** -ɪzəm
Vegas ˈveɪ.gəs
vegeburger ˈvedʒ.iˌbɜː.gər (US) -ˌbɝː.gɚ **-s** -z
Vegemite® ˈvedʒ.i.maɪt, ˈ-ə-
vegetable ˈvedʒ.tə.bl̩, ˈ-ə.tə-, ˈ-ɪ- (US) ˈvedʒ.tə-, -ə.t̬ə- **-s** -z
vegetal ˈvedʒ.ɪ.təl, ˈ-ə- (US) ˈ-ə-
vegetarian ˌvedʒ.ɪˈteə.ri.ən, -əˈ- (US) -əˈter.i- **-s** -z **-ism** -ɪ.zəm
vege|tate ˈvedʒ.ɪ|.teɪt, ˈ-ə- (US) ˈ-ə- **-tates** -teɪts **-tating** -teɪ.tɪŋ (US) -teɪ.t̬ɪŋ **-tated** -teɪ.tɪd (US) -teɪ.t̬ɪd
vegetation ˌvedʒ.ɪˈteɪ.ʃən, -əˈ- (US) -əˈ- **-s** -z
vegetative ˈvedʒ.ɪ.tə.tɪv, ˈ-ə-, -teɪ- (US) -ə.teɪ.t̬ɪv **-ly** -li
veggie ˈvedʒ.i **-s** -z
veggieburger ˈvedʒ.iˌbɜː.gər (US) ˌbɝː.gɚ **-s** -z
vegg|y ˈvedʒ|.i **-ies** -iz
vehemence ˈviː.ə.mənts, ˈ-ɪ-, -hɪ-, -hə-, ˈvɪə.mənts (US) ˈviː.ə-, -hə-
vehement ˈviː.ə.mənt, ˈ-ɪ-, -hɪ-, -hə-, ˈvɪə.mənt (US) ˈviː.ə-, -hə- **-ly** -li
vehicle ˈvɪə.kl̩, ˈviː.ɪ- (US) ˈviː.ə-, -hɪ- **-s** -z
vehicular vɪˈɪk.jə.lər, vɪˈhɪk-, və-, -jʊ- (US) viːˈhɪk.jə.lɚ, -jʊ-
veil veɪl **-s** -z **-ing/s** -ɪŋ/z **-ed** -d
Veil viːl (US) veɪ, viːl
vein veɪn **-s** -z **-ed** -d **-less** -ləs, -lɪs
vein|y ˈveɪ.n|i **-ier** -i.ər (US) -i.ɚ **-iest** -i.ɪst, -i.əst
Veitch viːtʃ
velar ˈviː.l|ər (US) -lɚ **-s** -z
velaric viːˈlær.ɪk, vɪ- (US) -ˈler-, -ˈlær-
velarization, -isa- ˌviː.lər.aɪˈzeɪ.ʃən, -ɪˈ- (US) -ɪˈ- **-s** -z
velariz|e, -is|e ˈviː.lər.aɪz (US) -lə.raɪz **-es** -ɪz **-ing** -ɪŋ **-ed** -d
Velasquez, Velazquez vɪˈlæs.kwɪz, velˈæs-, -kɪz, -kez, -kwɪθ (US) vəˈlɑː.skes, -ˈlæs.kes, -kwez
Velcro® ˈvel.krəʊ (US) -kroʊ

Velar

Velar consonant sounds are produced between the tongue and the SOFT PALATE, or 'velum'.

Examples for English

Velar sounds occurring as English phonemes are /k g/ and /ŋ/. The first two are PLOSIVES, and the last, a NASAL. Although /k g/ can occur syllable-initially and finally, /ŋ/ is restricted to syllable-final position only in English, e.g.:

cap	/kæp/
gap	/gæp/
sack	/sæk/
sag	/sæg/
sang	/sæŋ/

/k/ and /g/ are one of the pairs of consonants said to be distinguished from each other by being FORTIS or LENIS rather than voiced or voiceless.

Velarisation

A type of secondary articulation in which a constriction in the vocal tract is added to the primary constriction which gives a consonant its place of articulation.

Examples for English

In the case of English DARK L, the /l/ phoneme is articulated with its usual primary constriction in the alveolar region, while the back of the tongue is raised as for an [u] vowel creating a secondary constriction (see DARK L).

In other languages

Arabic has a number of consonant phonemes that are velarized, and are known as 'emphatic' consonants.

veldt, veld (V) velt US velt, felt **-s** -z
velic 'viː.lɪk
velleity vel'iː.ə.ti, və'liː-, -ɪ.ti US və'liː-
vellum 'vel.əm **-s** -z
veloce vɪ'ləʊ.tʃeɪ, vel'əʊ-, və'ləʊ- US veɪ'loʊ.tʃeɪ
velocipede vɪ'lɒs.ɪ.piːd, və-, '-ə- US və'lɑː.sə- **-s** -z
velocit|y vɪ'lɒs.ə.t|i, və-, -ɪ.t|i US və'lɑː.sə.t̬|i **-ies** -iz
velodrome 'vel.ə.drəʊm, 'viː.ləʊ- US 'vel.ə.droʊm **-s** -z
velour və'lʊəʳ US -'lʊr **-s** -z
velouté və'luː.teɪ **-s** -z
vel|um 'viː.l|əm **-a** -ə
velvet 'vel.vɪt, -vət **-s** -s
velveteen ˌvel.vɪ'tiːn, -və'-, '--- **-s** -z
velvet|y 'vel.vɪ.t|i, -və- US -və.t̬|i **-iness** -ɪ.nəs, -nɪs
Venables 'ven.ə.bl̩z
vena cava ˌviː.nə'keɪ.və, -'kɑː- US -'keɪ- **venae cavae** -niː'keɪ.viː, -'kɑː- US -'keɪ-
venal 'viː.nᵊl **-ly** US -i
venality viː'næl.ə.ti, vɪ-, -ɪ.ti US vɪ'næl.ə.t̬i
venation viː'neɪ.ʃᵊn
vend vend **-s** -z **-ing** -ɪŋ **-ed** -ɪd **-er/s** -əʳ/z US -ɚ/z 'vending maˌchine
Venda 'ven.də
vendee ven'diː **-s** -z
vendetta ven'det.ə US -'det̬- **-s** -z
vendor 'ven.dɔːʳ, -dəʳ US -dɚ, -dɔːr **-s** -z
veneer və'nɪəʳ, vɪ- US -'nɪr **-s** -z **-ing** -ɪŋ **-ed** -d
venerab|le 'ven.ᵊr.ə.b|l̩ **-ly** -li **-leness** -l̩.nəs, -nɪs
vener|ate 'ven.ᵊr|.eɪt US -ə.r|eɪt **-ates** -eɪts **-ating** -eɪ.tɪŋ US -eɪ.t̬ɪŋ **-ated** -eɪ.tɪd US -eɪ.t̬ɪd **-ator/s** -eɪ.təʳ/z US -eɪ.t̬ɚ/z
veneration ˌven.ᵊr'eɪ.ʃᵊn US -ə'reɪ-
venereal və'nɪə.ri.əl, vɪ- US və'nɪr.i- veˌnereal diˌsease
venery 'ven.ᵊr.i
Venetia və'niː.ʃi.ə, vɪ-, '-ʃə
Venetian, venetian və'niː.ʃᵊn, vɪ- US '-ʃᵊn **-s** -z veˌnetian 'blind
Venezuel|a ˌven.ɪ'zweɪ.l|ə, -ez'weɪ-, -ə'zweɪ- US -ə'zweɪ-, -'zwiː- **-an/s** -ən/z
veng|e vendʒ **-es** -ɪz **-ing** -ɪŋ **-ed** -d
vengeance 'ven.dʒᵊnts
vengeful 'vendʒ.fᵊl, -fʊl **-ly** -i **-ness** -nəs US -nɪs
Vengerov 'veŋ.gə.rɒf US -gɚ.ɑːf
veni, vidi, vici ˌveɪ.niːˌviː.diː'viː.kiː, ˌweɪ.niːˌwiː.diː'wiː.kiː
venial 'viː.ni.əl, '-njəl **-ly** -i **-ness** -nəs, -nɪs ˌvenial 'sin
veniality ˌviː.ni'æl.ə.ti, -ɪ.ti US -ə.t̬i
Venice 'ven.ɪs
venire və'nɪə.riː US -'naɪ-, -'nɪr.iː
venison 'ven.ɪ.sᵊn, '-ə-, -zᵊn
Venite vɪ'naɪ.ti, ven'aɪ-, -'niː- US və'niː- **-s** -z
Venn ven 'Venn ˌdiagram, ˌVenn 'diagram
Venner 'ven.əʳ US -ɚ
venom 'ven.əm **-s** -z **-ed** -d
venomous 'ven.ə.məs **-ly** -li **-ness** -nəs, -nɪs
venous 'viː.nəs **-ly** -li
vent vent **-s** -s **-ing** -ɪŋ US 'ven.t̬ɪŋ **-ed** -ɪd US 'ven.t̬ɪd
Vent-Axia® ˌvent'æk.si.ə
ventil|ate 'ven.tɪ.l|eɪt, -tᵊl|.eɪt US -t̬ə.l|eɪt **-ates** -eɪts **-ating** -eɪ.tɪŋ US -eɪ.t̬ɪŋ **-ated** -eɪ.tɪd US -eɪ.t̬ɪd
ventilation ˌven.tɪ'leɪ.ʃᵊn, -tᵊl'eɪ- US -t̬ə'leɪ-
ventilator 'ven.tɪ.leɪ.təʳ, -tᵊl.eɪ- US -t̬ə.leɪ.t̬ɚ **-s** -z
Ventnor 'vent.nəʳ US -nɚ
Ventolin® 'ven.təʊ.lɪn, -tᵊl.ɪn US -t̬ᵊl.ɪn, -toʊ.lɪn
ventral 'ven.trᵊl **-ly** -i
ventricle 'ven.trɪ.kl̩ **-s** -z
ventricular ven'trɪk.jə.ləʳ, -jʊ- US -jə.lɚ
ventriloquial ˌven.trɪ'ləʊ.kwi.əl, -trə'- US -trə'loʊ- **-ly** -i
ventriloquism ven'trɪl.ə.kwɪ.zᵊm
ventriloquist ven'trɪl.ə.kwɪst **-s** -s
ventriloquiz|e, -is|e ven'trɪl.ə.kwaɪz **-es** -ɪz **-ing** -ɪŋ **-ed** -d
ventriloquy ven'trɪl.ə.kwi
vent|ure 'ven.tʃ|əʳ US -tʃ|ɚ **-ures** -əz US -ɚz **-uring** -ᵊr.ɪŋ **-ured** -əd US -ɚd **-urer/s** -ᵊr.əʳ/z US -ɚ.ɚ/z ˌventure 'capital US 'venture ˌcapital; 'Venture ˌScout
venturesome 'ven.tʃə.səm US -tʃɚ- **-ly** -li **-ness** -nəs, -nɪs
venturi ven'tjʊə.ri, -'tʃʊə- US -'tʊr.i **-s** -z
venturous 'ven.tʃᵊr.əs **-ly** -li **-ness** -nəs, -nɪs
venue 'ven.juː **-s** -z
venul|ar 'ven.jʊ.l|əʳ, -jə- US -juː.l|ɚ, 'viː.njuː-, -njə- **-ose** -əʊs US -oʊs
venule 'ven.juːl US 'ven.juːl, 'viː.njuːl **-s** -z
Venus 'viː.nəs **-es** -ɪz ˌVenus' 'flytrap
Venusian vɪ'njuː.si.ən, və-, -zi.ən US vɪ'nuː.ʃᵊn, -ʒᵊn, -zi.ən **-s** -z
Vera 'vɪə.rə US 'vɪr.ə
veracious və'reɪ.ʃəs, vɪ-, ver'eɪ- US və'reɪ- **-ly** -li **-ness** -nəs, -nɪs
veracity və'ræs.ə.ti, vɪ-, ver'æs-, -ɪ.ti US və'ræs.ə.t̬i
Veracruz ˌvɪə.rə'kruːz, ˌver.ə'-, ˌveə.rə'- US ˌver.ə'-
veranda(h) və'ræn.də **-s** -z
verb vɜːb US vɝːb **-s** -z
verbal 'vɜː.bᵊl US 'vɝː- **-ly** -i
verbal|ism 'vɜː.bᵊl|.ɪ.zᵊm US 'vɝː- **-ist/s** -ɪst/s
verbalization ˌvɜː.bᵊl.aɪ'zeɪ.ʃᵊn, -ɪ'- US ˌvɝː.bᵊl.ɪ'-
verbaliz|e, -is|e 'vɜː.bᵊl.aɪz US 'vɝː.bə.laɪz **-es** -ɪz **-ing** -ɪŋ **-ed** -d
verbatim vɜː'beɪ.tɪm, və- US vɚ'beɪ.t̬ɪm, -t̬əm
verbena vɜː'biː.nə, və- US vɚ- **-s** -z
verbiage 'vɜː.bi.ɪdʒ US 'vɝː-
Verbier 'veə.bi.eɪ US 'ver-
verbose vɜː'bəʊs, və- US vɚ'boʊs **-ly** -li **-ness** -nəs, -nɪs
verbosity vɜː'bɒs.ə.ti, və-, -ɪ.ti US vɚ'bɑː.sə.t̬i
verboten vɜː'bəʊ.tᵊn *as if German:* fə'- US vɚ'boʊ-

Vercingetorix ˌvɜː.sɪnˈdʒet.ə.rɪks, -sᵊnˈ-, -ˈget- (US) ˌvɝː.sɪnˈdʒet̬.ɚ.ɪks, -ˈget̬-
verdancy ˈvɜː.dᵊnt.si (US) ˈvɝː-
verdant ˈvɜː.dᵊnt (US) ˈvɝː- **-ly** -li
Verde vɜːd (US) vɝːd
Verdi ˈveə.diː, -di (US) ˈver- **-an** -ən
verdict ˈvɜː.dɪkt (US) ˈvɝː- **-s** -s
verdigris ˈvɜː.dɪ.griːs, -griː (US) ˈvɝː.dɪ.griːs, -grɪs, -griː
Verdun vɜːˈdʌn, ˈ-- (US) verˈdʌn, ˌvɝː-
verdure ˈvɜː.djəʳ, -dʒəʳ, -djʊəʳ (US) ˈvɝː.dʒɚ
Vere vɪəʳ (US) vɪr
verg|e vɜːdʒ (US) vɝːdʒ **-es** -ɪz **-ing** -ɪŋ **-ed** -d
verger ˈvɜː.dʒəʳ (US) ˈvɝː.dʒɚ **-s** -z
Vergil ˈvɜː.dʒɪl (US) ˈvɝː- **-s** -z
Vergilian vɜːˈdʒɪl.i.ən, və- (US) vɝː-, ˈ-jən
verifiable ˈver.ɪ.faɪ.ə.bl̩, ˈ-ə-, ˌver.ɪˈfaɪ-, -əˈ- (US) ˈver.ə.faɪ-
verification ˌver.ɪ.fɪˈkeɪ.ʃᵊn, ˌ-ə- (US) ˌ-ə- **-s** -z
veri|fy ˈver.ɪ|.faɪ, ˈ-ə- (US) ˈ-ə- **-fies** -faɪz **-fying** -faɪ.ɪŋ **-fied** -faɪd **-fier/s** -faɪ.əʳ/z (US) -faɪ.ɚ/z
verily ˈver.ᵊl.i, -ɪ.li
verisimilitude ˌver.ɪ.sɪˈmɪl.ɪ.tjuːd, ˌ-ə-, -səˈ- (US) -ə.səˈmɪl.ə.tuːd, -tjuːd
verismo vəˈrɪz.moʊ
veritab|le ˈver.ɪ.tə.bl̩| (US) -ə.t̬ə- **-ly** -li
verit|y (V) ˈver.ə.t|i -ɪ.t|i (US) -ə.t̬|i **-ies** -iz
verjuice ˈvɜː.dʒuːs (US) ˈvɝː-
Verlaine veəˈlen, vɜː- (US) vɚˈleɪn, -ˈlen
Vermeer vəˈmɪəʳ, vɜː-, -ˈmeəʳ (US) vɚˈmɪr **-s** -z
vermeil ˈvɜː.meɪl, -mɪl (US) ˈvɝː.mɪl; vɚˈmeɪl
vermicelli ˌvɜː.mɪˈtʃel.i, -ˈsel- (US) ˌvɝː.məˈtʃel-, -ˈsel-
vermicide ˈvɜː.mɪ.saɪd (US) ˈvɝː.mə- **-s** -z
vermicular vɜːˈmɪk.jə.ləʳ, -jʊ- (US) vɚˈmɪk.jə.lɚ
vermiform ˈvɜː.mɪ.fɔːm (US) ˈvɝː.mə.fɔːrm ˌ**vermiform apˈpendix**
vermil(l)ion vəˈmɪl.jən, vɜː-, -i.ən (US) vɚˈmɪl.jən **-s** -z
vermin ˈvɜː.mɪn (US) ˈvɝː- **-ous** -əs
Vermont vəˈmɒnt, vɜː- (US) vɚˈmɑːnt
vermouth ˈvɜː.məθ, -muːθ; vɜːˈmuːθ, və- (US) vɚˈmuːθ **-s** -s
vernacular vəˈnæk.jə.ləʳ, vɜː-, -jʊ- (US) vɚˈnæk.jə.lɚ **-s** -z **-ly** -li
vernal ˈvɜː.nᵊl (US) ˈvɝː- **-ly** -i ˌ**vernal ˈequinox**
Verne vɜːn, veən (US) vɝːn
Verner *English surname:* ˈvɜː.nəʳ (US) ˈvɝː.nɚ *Danish grammarian:* ˈvɜː.nəʳ, ˈveə- (US) ˈvɝː.nɚ, ˈver-
Verney ˈvɜː.ni (US) ˈvɝː-
vernier ˈvɜː.ni.əʳ (US) ˈvɝː.ni.ɚ **-s** -z
Vernon ˈvɜː.nən (US) ˈvɝː-
Verona vəˈrəʊ.nə, vɪ-, verˈəʊ- (US) vəˈroʊ-
Veronal® ˈver.ə.nᵊl
Veronese *artist:* ˌver.əʊˈneɪ.zeɪ (US) -əˈneɪ.si, -zi
Veronese *(person) from Verona:* ˌver.əˈniːz, -əʊˈ- (US) -əˈniːz
veronica (V) vəˈrɒn.ɪ.kə, vɪ- verˈɒn- (US) vəˈrɑː.nɪ- **-s** -z
Verrazano ˌver.əˈzɑː.nəʊ (US) -noʊ *stress shift, see compound:* ˌ**Verrazano ˈNarrows**
verru|ca vəˈruː|.kə, vɪ-, verˈuː- (US) vəˈruː- **-cas** -kəz **-cae** -kiː, -kaɪ
verrucose vəˈruː.kəʊs, vɪ-, verˈuː- (US) ˈver.uː.koʊs, -jə-
Versace vəˈsɑː.tʃi, vɜː- (US) vɚ-
Versailles *in France:* veəˈsaɪ, vɜː- (US) vɝːˈsaɪ-, ver- *in US:* vɜːˈseɪlz (US) vɝː-
versant ˈvɜː.sᵊnt (US) ˈvɝː- **-s** -s
versatile ˈvɜː.sə.taɪl (US) ˈvɝː.sə.t̬ᵊl **-ly** -li **-ness** -nəs, -nɪs
versatility ˌvɜː.səˈtɪl.ə.ti, -ɪ.ti (US) ˌvɝː.səˈtɪl.ə.t̬i
vers de société ˌveə.dəˌsɒs.jeɪˈteɪ (US) ˌver.dɪ.soʊˈsiː.eɪ.teɪ; -dəˌsɑː.sjeɪˈteɪ
vers|e vɜːs (US) vɝːs **-es** -ɪz **-ed** -t
versicle ˈvɜː.sɪ.kl̩ (US) ˈvɝː- **-s** -z
versification ˌvɜː.sɪ.fɪˈkeɪ.ʃᵊn, -sə- (US) ˌvɝː.sə-
versificator ˈvɜː.sɪ.fɪ.keɪ.təʳ, -sə- (US) ˈvɝː.sə.fɪ.keɪ.t̬ɚ **-s** -z
versi|fy ˈvɜː.sɪ|.faɪ, -sə- (US) ˈvɝː.sə- **-fies** -faɪz **-fying** -faɪ.ɪŋ **-fied** -faɪd **-fier/s** -faɪ.əʳ/z (US) -faɪ.ɚ/z
version ˈvɜː.ʃᵊn, -ʒᵊn (US) ˈvɝː.ʒᵊn, -ʃᵊn **-s** -z
verso ˈvɜː.səʊ (US) ˈvɝː.soʊ **-s** -z
versus ˈvɜː.səs (US) ˈvɝː-
vert (V) vɜːt (US) vɝːt **-s** -s
vertebr|a ˈvɜː.tɪ.br|ə, -tə- (US) ˈvɝː.t̬ə- **-ae** -iː, -aɪ, -eɪ **-as** -əz
vertebral ˈvɜː.tɪ.brᵊl, -tə- (US) ˈvɝː.t̬ə- **-ly** -i ˌ**vertebral ˈcolumn**
vertebrata ˌvɜː.tɪˈbrɑː.tə, -təˈ-, -ˈbreɪ- (US) -ˈbreɪ.t̬ə, -ˈbrɑː-
vertebrate ˈvɜː.tɪ.breɪt, -tə-, -brət, -brɪt (US) ˈvɝː.tə.brɪt, -breɪt **-s** -s
ver|tex ˈvɜː|.teks (US) ˈvɝː- **-tices** -tɪ.siːz (US) -t̬ɪ- **-texes** -tek.sɪz
vertic|al ˈvɜː.tɪ.k|ᵊl, -tə- (US) ˈvɝː.t̬ə- **-ally** -ᵊl.i, -li **-alness** -ᵊl.nəs, -nɪs
vertiginous vɜːˈtɪdʒ.ɪ.nəs, ˈ-ə- (US) vɚˈtɪdʒ.ə- **-ly** -li
vertigo ˈvɜː.tɪ.gəʊ, -tə- (US) ˈvɝː.t̬ə.goʊ
Verulam ˈver.ʊ.ləm (US) -juː-
Verulamium ˌver.ʊˈleɪ.mi.əm (US) -juːˈ-
vervain ˈvɜː.veɪn (US) ˈvɝː-
verve vɜːv (US) vɝːv
Verwoerd fəˈvʊət, feə-, -ˈvɔːt (US) fɚ-ˈvɔːrt, -ˈvʊrt
Verwood ˈvɜː.wʊd (US) ˈvɝː-
very *(adj. adv.)* ˈver.i
Very *surname:* ˈvɪə.ri, ˈver.i (US) ˈvɪr.i, ˈver-
Vesalius vesˈeɪ.li.əs
Vesey ˈviː.zi
vesi|ca ˈves.ɪ|.kə; vɪˈsaɪ|.kə, və- (US) vɪˈsaɪ-, -ˈsiː- **-cae** -kiː
vesicle ˈves.ɪ.kl̩ **-s** -z
vesicular vɪˈsɪk.jə.ləʳ, vəˈ- (US) -lɚ
vesiculate vɪˈsɪk.jə.leɪt, vəˈ-
Vespa® ˈves.pə
Vespasian vesˈpeɪ.zi.ən, -ʒi-, ˈ-ʒᵊn (US) ˈ-ʒᵊn, -ʒi.ən
vesper (V) ˈves.pəʳ (US) -pɚ **-s** -z
vespertine ˈves.pə.taɪn (US) -pɚ.tɪn, -taɪn
Vespucci vesˈpuː.tʃi
vessel ˈves.ᵊl **-s** -z
vest vest **-s** -s **-ing** -ɪŋ **-ed** -ɪd ˌ**vested ˈinterest**
vesta (V) ˈves.tə **-s** -z
vestal ˈves.tᵊl **-s** -z ˌ**vestal ˈvirgin**
vestiar|y ˈvest.jə.r|i **-ies** -iz
vestibular vesˈtɪb.jə.ləʳ, -jʊ- (US) -jə.lɚ
vestibule ˈves.tɪ.bjuːl (US) -tə- **-s** -z **-d** -d
vestig|e ˈves.tɪdʒ **-es** -ɪz
vestigial vesˈtɪdʒ.i.əl, ˈ-əl **-ly** -i
vestiture ˈves.tɪ.tʃəʳ (US) -tʃɚ
vestment ˈvest.mənt **-s** -s
vest-pocket ˌvestˈpɒk.ɪt (US) -ˈpɑː.kɪt, ˈ-ˌ--
Vestris ˈves.trɪs
vestr|y ˈves.tr|i **-ies** -iz
vesture ˈves.tʃəʳ, -tjəʳ (US) -tʃɚ **-s** -z
vesuvian (V) vɪˈsuː.vi.ən və-, -ˈsjuː- (US) vəˈsuː- **-s** -z **-ite** -aɪt
Vesuvius vɪˈsuː.vi.əs, və-, -ˈsjuː- (US) vəˈsuː-
vet vet **-s** -s **-ting** -ɪŋ (US) ˈvet̬.ɪŋ **-ted** -ɪd (US) ˈvet̬.ɪd
vetch vetʃ **-es** -ɪz
veteran ˈvet.ᵊr.ᵊn, -rən (US) ˈvet̬.ɚ.ᵊn; ˈvet.rən **-s** -z ˈ**Veterans ˌDay**
veterinarian ˌvet.ᵊr.ɪˈneə.ri.ən, ˌ-rəˈ- (US) -ˈner.i- **-s** -z
veterinar|y ˈvet.ᵊr.ɪ.nᵊr|.i, ˈ-rə.nᵊr- (US) -ner- **-ies** -iz ˈ**veterinary ˌsurgeon**
veto ˈviː.təʊ (US) -t̬oʊ **-es** -z **-ing** -ɪŋ **-ed** -d **-er/s** -əʳ/z (US) -ɚ/z
Vevey ˈvev.eɪ, -i (US) vəˈveɪ
vex veks **-es** -ɪz **-ing** -ɪŋ **-ed** -t ˌ**vexed ˈquestion**
vexation vekˈseɪ.ʃᵊn **-s** -z
vexatious vekˈseɪ.ʃəs **-ly** -li **-ness** -nəs, -nɪs
vgc ˌviː.dʒiːˈsiː

VHF ˌviː.eɪtʃˈef
via vaɪə ⓤⓢ vaɪə, ˈviː.ə
viability ˌvaɪ.əˈbɪl.ə.ti, -ɪ.ti ⓤⓢ -ə.t̬i
viab|le ˈvaɪ.ə.bl̩ **-ly** -li
via dolorosa, (V D) ˌviː.əˌdɒl.əˈrəʊ.sə ⓤⓢ -ˌdɑː.ləˈroʊ-, -ˌdoʊ-
viaduct ˈvaɪə.dʌkt **-s** -s
Viagra vaɪˈæg.rə, vi-
vial vaɪəl ⓤⓢ ˈvaɪ.əl; vaɪl **-s** -z
Vialli viˈɑː.li
viand ˈvaɪ.ənd **-s** -z
viatic|um vaɪˈæt.ɪ.k|əm, vi- ⓤⓢ vaɪˈæt̬- **-ums** -əmz **-a** -ə
vibe vaɪb **-s** -z
vibrancy ˈvaɪ.brənt.si
vibrant ˈvaɪ.brənt **-ly** -li
vibraphone ˈvaɪ.brə.fəʊn ⓤⓢ -foʊn **-s** -z
vibra|te vaɪˈbreɪ|t ⓤⓢ ˈ-- **-tes** -ts **-ting** -tɪŋ ⓤⓢ -t̬ɪŋ **-ted** -tɪd ⓤⓢ -t̬ɪd
vibration vaɪˈbreɪ.ʃən **-s** -z
vibrational vaɪˈbreɪ.ʃən.əl, -ˈbreɪʃ.nəl
vibrative vaɪˈbreɪ.tɪv ⓤⓢ ˈvaɪ.brə.t̬ɪv
vibrato vɪˈbrɑː.təʊ ⓤⓢ -t̬oʊ **-s** -z
vibrator vaɪˈbreɪ.təʳ ⓤⓢ ˈvaɪ.breɪ.t̬ɚ **-s** -z
vibratory ˈvaɪ.brə.tər.i; vaɪˈbreɪ- ⓤⓢ ˈvaɪ.brə.tɔːr-
viburnum vaɪˈbɜː.nəm ⓤⓢ -ˈbɝː- **-s** -z
vic (V) vɪk **-s** -s
vicar ˈvɪk.əʳ ⓤⓢ -ɚ **-s** -z
vicarag|e ˈvɪk.ər.ɪdʒ **-es** -ɪz
vicarial vɪˈkeə.ri.əl, vaɪ-, və- ⓤⓢ -ˈker.i-, -ˈkær-
vicarious vɪˈkeə.ri.əs, vaɪ-, və- ⓤⓢ -ˈker.i-, -ˈkær- **-ly** -li **-ness** -nəs, -nɪs
vice- ˌvaɪs-
Note: Prefix. This usually receives secondary stress. It may carry the strongest stress in the word in stress shift cases.
vic|e (*n.*) vaɪs **-es** -ɪz **ˈvice ˌsquad**
vice (*prep.*) ˈvaɪ.si, -sə ⓤⓢ -sə, -si
vice-admiral ˌvaɪsˈæd.mər.əl, -mɪ.rəl **-s** -z *stress shift:* ˌvice-admiral's ˈflag
vice-chair|man ˌvaɪsˈtʃeəl.mən ⓤⓢ -ˈtʃer- **-men** -mən *stress shift:* ˌvice-chairman's ˈprivilege
vice-chancellor ˌvaɪsˈtʃɑːnt.səl.əʳ ⓤⓢ -ˈtʃænt- **-s** -z *stress shift:* ˌvice-chancellor's ˈsecretary
vice-consul ˌvaɪsˈkɒnt.səl ⓤⓢ -ˈkɑːnt- **-s** -z *stress shift:* ˌvice-consul's ˈpost
vice-consulate ˌvaɪsˈkɒnt.sjə.lət, -sjʊ-, -lɪt ⓤⓢ -ˈkɑːnt.sə.lət **-s** -s
vicegerent ˌvaɪsˈdʒer.ənt, -ˈdʒɪə.rənt ⓤⓢ -ˈdʒɪr.ənt **-s** -s
vice-presidenc|y ˌvaɪsˈprez.ɪ.dənt.s|i **-ies** -iz
vice-president ˌvaɪsˈprez.ɪ.dənt **-s** -s *stress shift:* ˌvice-president's ˈvote
vice-presidential ˌvaɪs.prez.ɪˈdent.ʃəl
vice-principal ˌvaɪsˈprɪnt.sə.pəl, -sɪ.pəl **-s** -z *stress shift:* ˌvice-principal's ˈoffice
viceregal ˌvaɪsˈriː.gəl *stress shift:* ˌviceregal ˈprivilege
vicereine ˌvaɪsˈreɪn, ˈ-- ⓤⓢ ˈvaɪs.reɪn **-s** -z
viceroy ˈvaɪs.rɔɪ **-s** -z
viceroyalt|y ˌvaɪsˈrɔɪ.əl.t|i ⓤⓢ -t̬|i **-ies** -iz
viceroyship ˈvaɪs.rɔɪ.ʃɪp **-s** -s
vice versa ˌvaɪ.siˈvɜː.sə, -səˈ-, ˌvaɪsˈ- ⓤⓢ ˌvaɪ.səˈvɝː-, ˌvaɪsˈ-
Vichy ˈviː.ʃiː, -ʃi, ˈvɪʃ.iː, -i
vichyssoise ˌviː.ʃiˈswɑːz, ˌvɪʃ.iˈ-
vicinage ˈvɪs.ɪ.nɪdʒ, ˈ-ə- ⓤⓢ ˈ-ə-
vicinity vɪˈsɪn.ə.ti, və-, vaɪ-, -ɪ.ti ⓤⓢ vəˈsɪn.ə.t̬i
vicious ˈvɪʃ.əs **-ly** -li **-ness** -nəs, -nɪs ˌ**vicious ˈcircle**
vicissitude vɪˈsɪs.ɪ.tjuːd, və-, vaɪs-, ˈ-ə- ⓤⓢ vɪˈsɪs.ə.tuːd, -tjuːd **-s** -z
Vick® vɪk
Vickers ˈvɪk.əz ⓤⓢ -ɚz
Vickery ˈvɪk.ər.i
Vicki, Vicky ˈvɪk.i
victim ˈvɪk.tɪm, -təm **-s** -z **-less** -ləs, -lɪs
victimization, -isa- ˌvɪk.tɪ.maɪˈzeɪ.ʃən, -tə-, -mɪˈ- ⓤⓢ -tə.mɪˈ-
victimiz|e, -is|e ˈvɪk.tɪ.maɪz, -tə- ⓤⓢ -tə- **-es** -ɪz **-ing** -ɪŋ **-ed** -d **-er/s** -əʳ/z ⓤⓢ -ɚ/z
victor (V) ˈvɪk.təʳ ⓤⓢ -tɚ **-s** -z
Victoria, victoria vɪkˈtɔː.ri.ə ⓤⓢ -ˈtɔːr.i- **-s** -z **Vicˌtoria ˈCross; Vicˈtoria ˌDay; Vicˌtoria ˈFalls; Vicˌtoria ˈsandwich**
Victorian, victorian vɪkˈtɔː.ri.ən ⓤⓢ -ˈtɔːr.i- **-s** -z **Vicˌtorian ˈvalues**
Victoriana ˌvɪk.tɔː.riˈɑː.nə, vɪkˌtɔː- ⓤⓢ vɪkˌtɔːr.iˈæn.ə
victorious vɪkˈtɔː.ri.əs ⓤⓢ -ˈtɔːr.i- **-ly** -li **-ness** -nəs, -nɪs
victor ludorum ˌvɪk.təˌluːˈdɔː.rəm ⓤⓢ -tɚ.luːˈdɔːr.əm **victores ludorum** vɪkˌtɔː.reɪsˌ- ⓤⓢ -ˌtɔːr.eɪs-
victor|y ˈvɪk.tər|.i, ˈ-tr|i **-ies** -iz
Victory-V® ˌvɪk.tər.iˈviː
victual ˈvɪt.əl ⓤⓢ ˈvɪt̬- **-s** -z **-(l)ing** -ɪŋ **-(l)ed** -d **-(l)er/s** -əʳ/z ⓤⓢ -ɚ/z
vicuña, vicuna vɪˈkjuː.nə, vaɪ-, və-, -ˈkuː-, -ˈkuː.njə ⓤⓢ vaɪˈkjuː.nə, vɪ-, -ˈkuː-, -ˈkuː.njə
Vidal vɪˈdɑːl, və-, -ˈdæl; ˈvaɪ.dəl ⓤⓢ vɪˈdæl, -ˈdɑːl
Note: The author Gore Vidal is normally /vɪˈdɑːl/; Vidal Sassoon is normally /vɪˈdæl/.
vide ˈvaɪ.diː, -di; ˈvɪd.eɪ ⓤⓢ ˈvaɪ.diː, -di; ˈviː.deɪ, ˈwiː-
videlicet vɪˈdiː.lɪ.set, vaɪ-, və-; -ˈdeɪ.lɪ.ket ⓤⓢ vɪˈdel.ə.sɪt, wɪ-
video ˈvɪd.i.əʊ ⓤⓢ -oʊ **-s** -z **-ing** -ɪŋ **-ed** -d **ˈvideo arˌcade; ˈvideo ˌcamera; ˈvideo ˌgame; ˌvideo ˈnasty; ˈvideo recˌorder**
videocassette ˌvɪd.i.əʊ.kəˈset, -kæsˈet ⓤⓢ -oʊ.kəˈset **-s** -s ˌ**video-casˈsette recˌorder**
videoconferenc|e ˌvɪd.i.əʊˈkɒn.fər.ənts ⓤⓢ ˈvɪd.i.oʊˌkɑːn.fɚ-, -frəns **-es** -ɪz **-ing** -ɪŋ
videodisc ˈvɪd.i.əʊ.dɪsk ⓤⓢ -oʊ- **-s** -s
videofit ˈvɪd.i.əʊ.fɪt ⓤⓢ -oʊ **-s** -s
video-link ˈvɪd.i.əʊ.lɪŋk ⓤⓢ -oʊ- **-s** -s **-ing** -ɪŋ **-ed** -t
Videophone® ˈvɪd.i.əʊ.fəʊn ⓤⓢ -oʊ.foʊn
videorecorder ˈvɪd.i.əʊ.rɪˌkɔː.dəʳ ⓤⓢ -oʊ.rɪˌkɔːr.dɚ **-s** -z
videorecording ˈvɪd.i.əʊ.rɪˌkɔː.dɪŋ, -rəˌ- ⓤⓢ -oʊ.rɪˌkɔːr-, -rəˌ- **-s** -z
videotap|e ˈvɪd.i.əʊ.teɪp ⓤⓢ -oʊ- **-es** -s **-ing** -ɪŋ **-ed** -t
videotext ˈvɪd.i.əʊ.tekst ⓤⓢ -oʊ- **-s** -s
vie vaɪ **vies** vaɪz **vying** ˈvaɪ.ɪŋ **vied** vaɪd
Vienna viˈen.ə
Viennese ˌvɪəˈniːz ⓤⓢ ˌviː.əˈ-
Vientiane ˌvjenˈtjɑːn
Vietcong, Viet Cong ˌvjetˈkɒŋ ⓤⓢ ˌviː.etˈkɑːŋ, -ˈkɔːŋ; viˌetˈ-; ˌvjetˈ- *stress shift:* ˌVietcong ˈfighters
Vietminh ˌvjetˈmɪn ⓤⓢ ˌviː.etˈ-; viˌetˈ-; ˌvjetˈ-
Vietnam, Viet Nam ˌvjetˈnæm, -ˈnɑːm ⓤⓢ ˌviː.etˈnɑːm, -ətˈ-, -ˈnæm; vɪˌetˈ-; ˌvjetˈ- *stress shift:* ˌVietnam ˈwar
Vietnamese ˌvjet.nəˈmiːz ⓤⓢ viˌet-; ˌvjet-, ˌviː.ət- *stress shift:* ˌVietnamese ˈpeople
view vjuː **-s** -z **-ing** -ɪŋ **-ed** -d **-er/s** -əʳ/z ⓤⓢ -ɚ/z **-able** -ə.bl̩ **-less** -ləs, -lɪs
viewfinder ˈvjuːˌfaɪn.dəʳ ⓤⓢ -dɚ **-s** -z
Viewpark ˈvjuː.pɑːk ⓤⓢ -pɑːrk
viewpoint ˈvjuː.pɔɪnt **-s** -s
Vigar ˈvaɪ.gəʳ ⓤⓢ -gɚ
Vigers ˈvaɪ.gəz ⓤⓢ -gɚz
vigil ˈvɪdʒ.ɪl, -əl ⓤⓢ -əl **-s** -z
vigilance ˈvɪdʒ.ɪ.ləns, -əl.ənts
vigilant ˈvɪdʒ.ɪ.lənt, -əl.ənt **-ly** -li
vigilant|e ˌvɪdʒ.ɪˈlæn.t|i, -əˈ- ⓤⓢ -t̬|i **-es** -iz **-ism** -ɪ.zəm
vig|nette vɪ|ˈnjet, -ˈnet ⓤⓢ -ˈnjet **-nettes** -ˈnjets, -ˈnets ⓤⓢ -ˈnjets **-netting** -ˈnjet.ɪŋ, -ˈnet- ⓤⓢ -ˈnjet̬.ɪŋ **-netted** -ˈnjet.ɪd, -ˈnet- ⓤⓢ -ˈnjet̬.ɪd **-nettist/s** -ˈnjet.ɪst/s ⓤⓢ -ˈnjet̬.ɪst/s
Vignoles ˈviː.njəʊlz, ˈvɪn.jəʊlz, -jəʊl, -jɒlz; vɪˈnjɒlz, -ˈnjəʊlz ⓤⓢ viːˈnjoʊl, -ˈnjoʊlz, ˈ--
Vigo ˈviː.gəʊ, ˈvaɪ- ⓤⓢ ˈviː.goʊ
vigor ˈvɪg.əʳ ⓤⓢ -ɚ

vigorous ˈvɪɡ.ᵊr.əs **-ly** -li **-ness** -nəs, -nɪs
vigour ˈvɪɡ.əʳ (US) -ɚ
viking (V) ˈvaɪ.kɪŋ **-s** -z
Vila ˈviː.lə
vil|e vaɪl **-er** -əʳ (US) -ɚ **-est** -ɪst, -əst **-ely** -li **-eness** -nəs, -nɪs
vilification ˌvɪl.ɪ.fɪˈkeɪ.ʃᵊn, ˌ-ə- (US) ˌ-ə-
vili|fy ˈvɪl.ɪ|.faɪ, ˈ-ə- (US) ˈ-ə- **-fies** -faɪz **-fying** -faɪ.ɪŋ **-fied** -faɪd **-fier/s** -faɪ.əʳ/z (US) -faɪ.ɚ/z
villa (V) *house:* ˈvɪl.ə **-s** -z
Villa *foreign name:* ˈviː.ə
villag|e ˈvɪl.ɪdʒ **-es** -ɪz
villager ˈvɪl.ɪ.dʒəʳ, ˈ-ə- (US) -ə.dʒɚ **-s** -z
villain ˈvɪl.ən *in historical sense also:* -ɪn, -eɪn (US) -ən **-s** -z
villainage ˈvɪl.ɪ.nɪdʒ, ˈ-ə- (US) ˈ-ə-
villainess ˌvɪl.əˈnes **-es** -ɪz
villainous ˈvɪl.ə.nəs **-ly** -li **-ness** -nəs, -nɪs
villain|y ˈvɪl.ə.n|i **-ies** -iz
Villa-Lobos ˌviː.əˈləʊ.bɒs, ˌviː.lə- (US) ˌviː.ləˈloʊ.bəs, -boʊs
villanelle ˌvɪl.əˈnel **-s** -z
-ville -vɪl, -viːl (US) -vɪl, -vəl
villein ˈvɪl.ɪn, -eɪn (US) -ən **-s** -z **-age** -ɪdʒ
villenage ˈvɪl.ə.nɪdʒ, -ɪ-
Villeneuve ˈviːl.nɜːv (US) vɪl.əˈnɜːv
Villette vɪˈlet
Villiers ˈvɪl.əz, -jəz, -i.əz (US) ˈ-ɚz, -jɚz
Villon ˈvɪl.ən *as if French:* viːˈjɔ̃ːŋ (US) viːˈjoʊn
vill|us ˈvɪl|.əs **-i** -aɪ
Vilna ˈvɪl.nə
Vilnius ˈvɪl.ni.əs (US) -ʊs, -əs
vim® (V) vɪm
Vimto® ˈvɪm*p*.təʊ (US) -toʊ
Viña del Mar ˌviː.njə.delˈmɑːʳ (US) -ˈmɑːr
vinaigrette ˌvɪn.ɪˈɡret, -eɪˈ- (US) -əˈ- **-s** -s
Vince vɪn*t*s
Vincennes *in France:* væ̃nˈsen, væn- (US) væn- *in Indiana:* vɪnˈsenz
Vincent ˈvɪn*t*.sᵊnt
Vinci ˈvɪn.tʃiː, -tʃi
vincul|um ˈvɪŋ.kjə.l|əm, -kjʊ- (US) -kjə- **-a** -ə **-ums** -əmz
vindaloo ˌvɪn.dᵊlˈuː (US) -dəˈluː **-s** -z
vin(s) de pays ˌvæ̃*n*.də.peɪˈiː, ˌvæn-
vindicability ˌvɪn.dɪ.kəˈbɪl.ə.ti, -ɪ.ti (US) -ə.t̬i
vindicable ˈvɪn.dɪ.kə.bl̩
vindi|cate ˈvɪn.dɪ|.keɪt (US) -də- **-cates** -keɪts **-cating** -keɪ.tɪŋ (US) -keɪ.t̬ɪŋ **-cated** -keɪ.tɪd (US) -keɪ.t̬ɪd **-cator/s** -keɪ.təʳ/z (US) -keɪ.t̬ɚ/z
vindication ˌvɪn.dɪˈkeɪ.ʃᵊn (US) -dəˈ-
vindicative ˈvɪn.dɪ.kə.tɪv, -keɪ-; vɪnˈdɪk.ə- (US) vɪnˈdɪk.ə.t̬ɪv; ˈvɪn.dɪ.keɪ-
vindictive vɪnˈdɪk.tɪv **-ly** -li **-ness** -nəs, -nɪs
vine vaɪn **-s** -z
vineg|ar ˈvɪn.ɪ.ɡ|əʳ, ˈ-ə- (US) -ə.ɡ|ɚ **-ars** -əz (US) -ɚz **-ary** -ᵊr.i
viner|y ˈvaɪ.nᵊr|.i **-ies** -iz
Viney ˈvaɪ.ni
vineyard ˈvɪn.jəd, -jɑːd (US) -jɚd **-s** -z
vingt-et-un ˌvæ̃*n*.teɪˈɜ̃ː*ŋ*, ˌvæn-, -ˈɜːn (US) ˌvæn.teɪˈɜːn
viniculture ˈvɪn.ɪˌkʌl.tʃəʳ, ˌvɪn.ɪˈkʌl- (US) ˈvɪn.ɪˌkʌl.tʃɚ
viniculturist ˌvɪn.ɪˈkʌl.tʃᵊr.ɪst, ˈvɪn.ɪˌkʌl- (US) ˌvɪn.ɪˈkʌl- **-s** -s
vino ˈviː.nəʊ (US) -noʊ
vin(s) ordinaire(s) ˌvæ̃*n*ˌɔː.dɪˈneəʳ, ˌvæn- (US) ˌvæ̃nˌɔːr.dᵊnˈer
vinous ˈvaɪ.nəs
vin(s) væ̃*ŋ*, væn
vintag|e ˈvɪn.tɪdʒ (US) -t̬ɪdʒ **-es** -ɪz ˌ**vintage** ˈ**year**
Vinter ˈvɪn.təʳ (US) -t̬ɚ
vintner ˈvɪnt.nəʳ (US) -nɚ **-s** -z
viny ˈvaɪ.ni
vinyl ˈvaɪ.nᵊl, -nɪl (US) -nᵊl
viol vaɪəl, vaɪl, vɪəl (US) vaɪəl **-s** -z
viola *flower:* ˈvaɪə.lə, ˈvaɪ.əʊ-, ˈviː.ə-, -əʊ-; vaɪˈəʊ-, viˈ- (US) ˈviː.ə.lə; vaɪˈoʊ- **-s** -z
viola *musical instrument:* viˈəʊ.lə (US) viˈoʊ- **-s** -z
Viola *female name:* ˈvaɪə.lə, ˈvaɪ.əʊ-, ˈviː.ə.lə; viˈəʊ-, vaɪ- (US) vaɪˈoʊ.lə, vi-; viː.ə-
violable ˈvaɪə.lə.bl̩
viola da gamba viˌəʊ.lə.dəˈɡæm.bə (US) -ˌoʊ.lə.dəˈɡɑːm- **-s** -z **viole da gamba** viˌəʊ.leɪ- (US) -ˌoʊ-
viola d'amore viˌəʊ.lə.dæmˈɔː.reɪ (US) -ˌoʊ.lə.dɑːˈmɔːr.eɪ, -ˌoʊ- **viole d'amore** viˌəʊ.leɪ-
vio|late *(v.)* ˈvaɪə|.leɪt, ˈvaɪ.əʊ- (US) ˈvaɪə- **-lates** -leɪts **-lating** -leɪ.tɪŋ (US) -leɪ.t̬ɪŋ **-lated** -leɪ.tɪd (US) -leɪ.t̬ɪd **-lator/s** -leɪ.təʳ/z (US) -leɪ.t̬ɚ/z
violate *(adj.)* ˈvaɪə.lɪt, ˈvaɪ.əʊ- (US) ˈvaɪə-
violation ˌvaɪəˈleɪ.ʃᵊn, ˌvaɪ.əʊˈ- (US) ˌvaɪəˈ- **-s** -z
violence ˈvaɪə.lᵊn*t*s
violent ˈvaɪə.lᵊnt **-ly** -li
violet (V) ˈvaɪə.lət, -lɪt (US) -lɪt **-s** -s
violin ˌvaɪəˈlɪn **-s** -z
violinist vaɪəˈlɪn.ɪst, ˌvaɪə- **-s** -s
violist *viola player:* viˈəʊ.lɪst (US) -ˈoʊ- **-s** -s *viol player:* ˈvaɪə.lɪst **-s** -s
violoncellist ˌvaɪə.lənˈtʃel.ɪst, ˌvɪə.lənˈ-, -lɪnˈ- (US) ˌviː.ə.lɑːnˈ-, ˌvaɪə.lɑːnˈ- **-s** -s
violoncello ˌvaɪə.lənˈtʃel.əʊ, ˌvɪə.lənˈ-, -lɪnˈ- (US) ˌviː.ə.lɑːnˈtʃel.oʊ, ˌvaɪə.lɑːnˈ- **-s** -z
violone ˈvaɪə.ləʊn, ˈvɪə-, ˌvɪəˈləʊ.neɪ (US) ˌviː.əˈloʊ- **-s** -z
VIP ˌviː.aɪˈpiː **-s** -z
vip|er ˈvaɪ.p|əʳ (US) -p|ɚ **-ers** -əz (US) -ɚz **-erish** -ᵊr.ɪʃ **-erous** -ᵊr.əs
virago (V) vɪˈrɑː.ɡəʊ, -ˈreɪ- (US) vəˈrɑː.ɡoʊ, -ˈreɪ-; ˈvɪr.ə- **-(e)s** -z
viral ˈvaɪə.rᵊl (US) ˈvaɪ-
vires ˈvaɪə.riːz (US) ˈvaɪ-
Virgil ˈvɜː.dʒɪl (US) ˈvɝː.dʒᵊl **-s** -z
Virgilian vɜːˈdʒɪl.i.ən, və- (US) vɝː-, ˈ-jən
virgin (V®) ˈvɜː.dʒɪn (US) ˈvɝː- **-s** -z ˌ**virgin** ˈ**birth**; ˈ**Virgin** ˌ**Islands** (US) ˌ**Virgin** ˈ**Islands**; ˌ**Virgin** ˈ**Mary**
virginal ˈvɜː.dʒɪ.nᵊl, -dʒᵊn.ᵊl (US) ˈvɝː- **-s** -z **-ly** -li
Virgini|a, virgini|a vəˈdʒɪn.j|ə, vɜː-, -i|.ə (US) vɚ- **-as** -əz **-an/s** -ən/z **vir**ˌ**ginia** ˈ**creeper**
virginity vəˈdʒɪn.ə.ti, vɜː-, -ɪ.ti (US) vɚˈdʒɪn.ə.t̬i
Virgo *constellation:* ˈvɜː.ɡəʊ, ˈvɪə- (US) ˈvɝː.ɡoʊ **-s** -z
Virgoan vɜːˈɡəʊ.ən (US) vɝːˈɡoʊ- **-s** -z
virgule ˈvɜː.ɡjuːl (US) ˈvɝː- **-s** -z
viridescen|t ˌvɪr.ɪˈdes.ᵊn|t (US) -əˈ- **-ce** -*t*s
viridian vɪˈrɪd.i.ən, və- (US) və-
virile ˈvɪr.aɪl (US) -ᵊl, -aɪl
virility vɪˈrɪl.ə.ti, və-, -ɪ.ti (US) vəˈrɪl.ə.t̬i
virolog|y vaɪəˈrɒl.ə.dʒ|i (US) vaɪˈrɑː.lə- **-ist/s** -ɪst/s
virtu vɜːˈtuː (US) vɚ-; ˈvɝː.tuː
virtual ˈvɜː.tʃu.əl, -tju-, ˈ-tʃʊəl, -tjʊəl (US) ˈvɝː.tʃu- **-ly** -i ˌ**virtual re**ˈ**ality**
virtue ˈvɜː.tjuː, -tʃuː (US) ˈvɝː.tʃuː **-s** -z
virtuosity ˌvɜː.tjuˈɒs.ə.ti, -tʃuˈ-, -ɪ.ti (US) ˌvɝː.tʃuˈɑː.sə.t̬i
virtuos|o ˌvɜː.tjuˈəʊ.s|əʊ, -tʃuˈ-, -z|əʊ (US) ˌvɝː.tʃuˈoʊ.s|oʊ **-os** -əʊz (US) -oʊz **-i** -i
virtuous ˈvɜː.tʃu.əs, -tju- (US) ˈvɝː.tʃu- **-ly** -li **-ness** -nəs, -nɪs
virulence ˈvɪr.ʊ.lᵊn*t*s, ˈ-ə-, -jʊ-, -jə- (US) -jə-, ˈ-ə-, -jʊ-
virulent ˈvɪr.ʊ.lᵊnt, ˈ-ə-, -jʊ-, -jə- (US) -jə-, ˈ-ə-, -jʊ- **-ly** -li
virus ˈvaɪə.rəs (US) ˈvaɪ- **-es** -ɪz
vis vɪs
visa (V®) ˈviː.zə (US) -zə, -sə **-s** -z **-ing** -ɪŋ **-ed** -d
visag|e ˈvɪz.ɪdʒ **-es** -ɪz
visagiste ˌvɪz.ɑːˈʒiːst **-s** -s
vis-à-vis ˌviːz.ɑːˈviː, ˌvɪz-, -əˈ-, -æˈ- (US) ˌviːz.əˈviː
viscera ˈvɪs.ᵊr|.ə
visceral ˈvɪs.ᵊr.ᵊl **-ly** -i
viscid ˈvɪs.ɪd
viscidity vɪˈsɪd.ə.ti, -ɪ.ti (US) -ə.t̬i
Visconti vɪˈskɒn.ti (US) -ˈskɑːn-

viscose ˈvɪs.kəʊs, -kəʊz (US) -koʊs, -koʊz
viscosity vɪˈskɒs.ə.ti, -ɪ.ti (US) -ˈskɑː.sə.t̬i
vis|count ˈvaɪ|.kaʊnt **-counts** -kaʊnts **-county** -kaʊn.ti (US) -kaʊn.t̬i **-counties** -kaʊn.tiz (US) -kaʊn.t̬iz
viscountc|y ˈvaɪ.kaʊnt.s|i **-ies** -iz
viscountess ˌvaɪ.kaʊnˈtes; ˈvaɪ.kaʊn.tɪs, -təs (US) ˈvaɪ.kaʊn.t̬ɪs **-es** -ɪz
viscous ˈvɪs.kəs **-ness** -nəs, -nɪs
visé ˈviː.zeɪ (US) ˈviː.zeɪ, -ˈ- **-s** -z **-ing** -ɪŋ **-d** -d
vis|e vaɪs **-es** -ɪz **-ing** -ɪŋ **-ed** -t
Vishnu ˈvɪʃ.nuː
visibility ˌvɪz.əˈbɪl.ə.ti, -ɪˈ-, -ɪ.ti (US) -əˈbɪl.ə.t̬i
visib|le ˈvɪz.ə.bl̩, ˈ-ɪ- (US) ˈ-ə- **-ly** -li **-leness** -l̩.nəs, -nɪs
Visigoth ˈvɪz.ɪ.gɒθ, ˈvɪs- (US) -ə.gɑːθ **-s** -s
Visigothic ˌvɪz.ɪˈgɒθ.ɪk, ˌvɪs- (US) -əˈgɑː.θɪk
vision ˈvɪʒ.ᵊn **-s** -z
visional ˈvɪʒ.ᵊn.ᵊl, ˈ-nᵊl (US) ˈvɪʒ.ᵊn.ᵊl **-ly** -i
visionar|y ˈvɪʒ.ᵊn.ᵊr|.i, -ᵊn.r|i (US) -ᵊn.er|.i **-ies** -iz
vis|it ˈvɪz|.ɪt **-its** -ɪts **-iting** -ɪ.tɪŋ (US) -ɪ.t̬ɪŋ **-ited** -ɪ.tɪd (US) -ɪ.t̬ɪd **ˈvisiting ˌcard; ˌvisiting proˈfessor**
visitant ˈvɪz.ɪ.tᵊnt (US) -t̬ənt **-s** -s
visitation ˌvɪz.ɪˈteɪ.ʃᵊn (US) -əˈ- **-s** -z
visitor ˈvɪz.ɪ.təʳ (US) -t̬ɚ **-s** -z **ˈvisitors' ˌbook**
vis major ˌvɪsˈmeɪ.dʒəʳ (US) -dʒɚ
visor ˈvaɪ.zəʳ (US) -zɚ **-s** -z
vista ˈvɪs.tə **-s** -z
Vistula ˈvɪs.tjʊ.lə (US) -tʃuː-
visual ˈvɪʒ.u.əl, ˈvɪz.ju- (US) ˈvɪʒ.u- **-s** -z **-ly** -i **ˌvisual ˈaid; ˌvisual diˈsplay ˌunit**
visualization, -isa- ˌvɪʒ.u.ᵊl.aɪˈzeɪ.ʃᵊn, ˌvɪz.ju-, -ɪˈ- (US) ˌvɪʒ.u.ᵊl.ɪˈ-
visualiz|e, -is|e ˈvɪʒ.u.ᵊl.aɪz, ˈvɪz.ju- (US) ˈvɪʒ.u.ə.laɪz **-es** -ɪz **-ing** -ɪŋ **-ed** -d **-er/s** -əʳ/z (US) -ɚ/z
vita *glass:* ˈvaɪ.tə (US) -t̬ə *aqua:* ˈviː.tə (US) -t̬ə
Vita ˈviː.tə (US) -t̬ə
vitae *curriculum:* ˈviː.taɪ, ˈvaɪ.tiː (US) ˈvaɪ.t̬iː, ˈviː-, -taɪ
vital ˈvaɪ.tᵊl (US) -t̬ᵊl **-ly** -i **ˌvital ˈsigns** (US) **ˈvital ˌsigns; ˌvital staˈtistics**
Vitalite® ˈvaɪ.tə.laɪt
vitality vaɪˈtæl.ə.ti, -ɪ.ti (US) -ə.t̬i
vitalization, -isa- ˌvaɪ.tᵊl.aɪˈzeɪ.ʃᵊn (US) -tᵊl.ɪˈ-
vitaliz|e, -is|e ˈvaɪ.tᵊl.aɪz (US) -t̬ə.laɪz **-es** -ɪz **-ing** -ɪŋ **-ed** -d
vitals ˈvaɪ.tᵊlz (US) -t̬ᵊlz
vitamin ˈvɪt.ə.mɪn, ˈvaɪ- (US) ˈvaɪ.t̬ə- **-s** -z **ˌvitamin ˈC**
VitBe® ˈvɪt.biː
vitellus vɪˈtel.əs (US) vɪ-, vaɪ-
Vitez ˈviː.tez
viti|ate ˈvɪʃ.i|.eɪt **-ates** -eɪts **-ating** -eɪ.tɪŋ (US) -eɪ.t̬ɪŋ **-ated** -eɪ.tɪd (US) -eɪ.t̬ɪd **-ator/s** -eɪ.təʳ/z (US) -eɪ.t̬ɚ/z
vitiation ˌvɪʃ.iˈeɪ.ʃᵊn
viticulture ˈvɪt.ɪˌkʌl.tʃəʳ, ˈvaɪ- (US) -t̬əˌkʌl.tʃɚ
vitiligo ˌvɪt.ɪˈlaɪ.gəʊ (US) ˌvɪt̬.ɪˈlaɪ.goʊ
vitreous ˈvɪt.ri.əs **-ness** -nəs, -nɪs
vitrescen|t vɪˈtres.ᵊn|t **-ce** -ts
vitric ˈvɪt.rɪk
vitrifaction ˌvɪt.rɪˈfæk.ʃᵊn (US) -rəˈ-
vitrification ˌvɪt.rɪ.fɪˈkeɪ.ʃᵊn, -rə- (US) -rə-
vitri|fy ˈvɪt.rɪ|.faɪ (US) -trə- **-fies** -faɪz **-fying** -faɪ.ɪŋ **-fied** -faɪd **-fiable** -faɪ.ə.bl̩
vitriol ˈvɪt.ri.əl, -ɒl (US) -əl, -ɔːl
vitriolic ˌvɪt.riˈɒl.ɪk (US) -ˈɑː.lɪk **-ally** -ᵊl.i, -li
vitro ˈviː.trəʊ (US) -troʊ
Vitruvius vɪˈtruː.vi.əs
vittles ˈvɪt.l̩z (US) ˈvɪt̬-
Vittoria vɪˈtɔː.ri.ə (US) -ˈtɔːr.i-
vituper|ate vɪˈtjuː.pᵊr|.eɪt, vaɪ- (US) vaɪˈtuː.pə.r|eɪt, vɪ-, -ˈtjuː- **-ates** -eɪts **-ating** -eɪ.tɪŋ (US) -eɪ.t̬ɪŋ **-ated** -eɪ.tɪd (US) -eɪ.t̬ɪd **-ator/s** -eɪ.təʳ/z (US) -eɪ.t̬ɚ/z
vituperation vɪˌtjuː.pᵊrˈeɪ.ʃᵊn, vaɪ- (US) vaɪˌtuː.pəˈreɪ-, vɪ-, -ˌtjuː- **-s** -z
vituperative vɪˈtjuː.pᵊr.ə.tɪv, vaɪ-, -eɪ- (US) vaɪˈtuː.pɚ.ə.t̬ɪv, vɪ-, -ˈtjuː-, -pə.reɪ- **-ly** -li
vituperatory vɪˈtjuː.pᵊr.ə.tᵊr.i, vaɪ- (US) vaɪˈtuː.pɚ.ə.tɔːr-, -tjuː-, -prə.tɔːr-
Vitus ˈvaɪ.təs (US) -t̬əs
viva *long live:* ˈviː.və
viva *examination:* ˈvaɪ.və (US) ˈvaɪ.və, ˈviː- **-s** -z **ˌviva ˈvoce**
Viva® ˈviː.və
vivace vɪˈvɑː.tʃeɪ (US) -tʃeɪ **-s** -z
vivacious vɪˈveɪ.ʃəs, vaɪ- **-ly** -li **-ness** -nəs, -nɪs
vivacity vɪˈvæs.ə.ti, vaɪ-, -ɪ.ti (US) -ə.t̬i
Vivaldi vɪˈvæl.di (US) -ˈvɑːl-
vivari|um vaɪˈveə.ri|.əm, vɪ- (US) vaɪˈver.i- **-ums** -əmz **-a** -ə
vivat ˈvaɪ.væt, ˈviː-
vive viːv
Vivendi® vɪˈven.di
Vivian ˈvɪv.i.ən
vivid ˈvɪv.ɪd **-ly** -li **-ness** -nəs, -nɪs
Vivien ˈvɪv.i.ən
Vivienne ˈvɪv.i.ən, ˌvɪv.iˈen
vivification ˌvɪv.ɪ.fɪˈkeɪ.ʃᵊn (US) ˌ-ə-
vivi|fy ˈvɪv.ɪ|.faɪ (US) ˈ-ə- **-fies** -faɪz **-fying** -faɪ.ɪŋ **-fied** -faɪd
viviparity ˌvɪv.ɪˈpær.ə.ti, -ɪ.ti (US) -əˈper.ə.t̬i, -ˈpær-
viviparous vɪˈvɪp.ᵊr.əs, vaɪ- (US) vaɪ- **-ly** -li **-ness** -nəs, -nɪs
vivisect ˌvɪv.ɪˈsekt, ˈ--- (US) ˈvɪv.ə.sekt **-s** -s **-ing** -ɪŋ **-ed** -ɪd **-or/s** -əʳ/z (US) -ɚ/z
vivisection ˌvɪv.ɪˈsek.ʃᵊn (US) -əˈ-, ˈvɪv.ə.sek-
vivisectionist ˌvɪv.ɪˈsek.ʃᵊn.ɪst (US) -əˈ- **-s** -s
vixen ˈvɪk.sᵊn **-s** -z
vixenish ˈvɪk.sᵊn.ɪʃ
Viyella® vaɪˈel.ə
viz. vɪz; vɪˈdiː.lɪ.set, vaɪ-; vɪˈdeɪ.lɪ.ket (US) vɪz; vɪˈdel.ɪ.set, wɪ-

Note: Many people in reading aloud substitute **namely** (/ˈneɪm.li/) for this word.

Vizetelly ˌvɪz.ɪˈtel.i
vizier vɪˈzɪəʳ, ˈvɪz.ɪəʳ; (US) vɪˈzɪr; ˈvɪz.jɚ **-s** -z
vizor ˈvaɪ.zəʳ (US) -zɚ **-s** -z
VJ-Day ˌviːˈdʒeɪ.deɪ
Vladimir ˈvlæd.ɪ.mɪəʳ, -məʳ, vlædˈiː.mɪəʳ (US) -ə.mɪr
Vladivostok ˌvlæd.ɪˈvɒs.tɒk (US) -ˈvɑː.stɑːk
V-neck ˌviːˈnek (US) ˈ-- **-s** -s **-ed** -t
vocab ˈvəʊ.kæb (US) ˈvoʊ-
vocable ˈvəʊ.kə.bl̩ (US) ˈvoʊ- **-s** -z
vocabular|y vəʊˈkæb.jə.lᵊr|.i, -jʊ- (US) voʊˈkæb.jə.ler-, -jʊ- **-ies** -iz
vocal ˈvəʊ.kᵊl (US) ˈvoʊ- **-s** -z **-ly** -i **ˌvocal ˈcords** (US) **ˈvocal ˌcords**
vocalic vəʊˈkæl.ɪk (US) voʊ-
vocalism ˈvəʊ.kᵊl.ɪ.zᵊm (US) ˈvoʊ-
vocalist ˈvəʊ.kᵊl.ɪst (US) ˈvoʊ- **-s** -s
vocality vəʊˈkæl.ə.ti, -ɪ.ti (US) voʊˈkæl.ə.t̬i
vocalization, -isa- ˌvəʊ.kᵊl.aɪˈzeɪ.ʃᵊn, -ɪˈ- (US) ˌvoʊ.kᵊl.ɪˈ- **-s** -z
vocaliz|e, -is|e ˈvəʊ.kᵊl.aɪz (US) ˈvoʊ.kə.laɪz **-es** -ɪz **-ing** -ɪŋ **-ed** -d **-er/s** -əʳ/z (US) -ɚ/z
vocation vəʊˈkeɪ.ʃᵊn (US) voʊ- **-s** -z
vocational vəʊˈkeɪ.ʃᵊn.ᵊl, -ˈkeɪʃ.nᵊl (US) voʊ- **-ly** -i
vocational|ism vəʊˈkeɪ.ʃᵊn.ᵊl|.ɪ.zᵊm, -ˈkeɪʃ.nᵊl- (US) voʊ- **-ist/s** -ɪst/s
vocative ˈvɒk.ə.tɪv (US) ˈvɑː.kə.t̬ɪv **-s** -z
voce *(in* **viva voce***)* ˈvəʊ.si, -tʃi, -tʃeɪ (US) ˈvoʊ.siː *(in* **sotto voce***)* ˈvəʊ.tʃi (US) ˈvoʊ.tʃi, -tʃeɪ
vocifer|ate vəʊˈsɪf.ᵊr|.eɪt (US) voʊˈsɪf.ə.r|eɪt **-ates** -eɪts **-ating** -eɪ.tɪŋ (US) -eɪ.t̬ɪŋ **-ated** -eɪ.tɪd (US) -eɪ.t̬ɪd **-ator/s** -eɪ.təʳ/z (US) -eɪ.t̬ɚ/z
vociferation vəʊˌsɪf.əˈreɪ.ʃᵊn (US) voʊ- **-s** -z
vociferous vəʊˈsɪf.ᵊr.əs (US) voʊ- **-ly** -li **-ness** -nəs, -nɪs
vocoid ˈvəʊ.kɔɪd (US) ˈvoʊ- **-s** -z

Vocal folds

An essential part of the larynx, performing a number of important linguistic functions. The term 'vocal cords' is also used.

The vocal folds may be firmly closed to produce what is sometimes called a GLOTTAL STOP, and while they are closed the larynx may be moved up or down move air out of or into the vocal tract; this is done in the production of 'ejective' and 'implosive' consonants. When brought into light contact with each other the vocal folds tend to vibrate if air is forced through them, producing VOICING, also called 'phonation'. This vibration can be made to vary in many ways, resulting in differences in such things as PITCH, loudness and voice quality. If a narrow opening is made between the vocal folds, friction noise can result and this is found in whispering and in the glottal fricative [h]. A more widely open glottis is found in most voiceless consonants.

Voice onset time

A measure of the timing of the start of voicing.

All languages distinguish between voiced and voiceless consonants, and PLOSIVES are the most common consonants to be distinguished in this way. However, this is not a simple matter of a plosive being either completely voiced or completely voiceless: the timing of the voicing in relation to the consonant articulation is very important. In one particular case this is so noticeable that it has for a long time been given its own name: ASPIRATION, in which the beginning of full voicing does not happen until some time after the release of the plosive (usually voiceless). This delay, or 'lag', has been the subject of much experimental investigation which has led to the development of a scientific measure of voice timing called voice onset time or V.O.T.. The onset of voicing in a plosive may lag behind the plosive release, or it may precede ('lead') it, resulting in a fully or partially voiced plosive. Both can be represented on the V.O.T. scale, one case having positive values and the other negative values.

Voicing

A term used to refer to the vibration of the VOCAL FOLDS. A sound made with this vibration is called *voiced*, and one without vibration is called *voiceless*. Most vowels in most languages are voiced, though voiceless vowels are found in some languages. Among consonants, it is very common to find pairs that are distinguished from each other by the presence or absence of voicing, but in English we find that consonants such as /b d g v ð z ʒ/, though frequently described as voiced (in contrast with the corresponding voiceless consonants /p t k f θ s ʃ/) often have little or no voicing. See FORTIS, LENIS, ONSET TIME. Whispering is speech that is entirely voiceless.

In other languages

Many pairs of consonants distinguished by the voiced-voiceless contrast are found in different languages. Welsh has voiced and voiceless LATERAL consonants, while Burmese has voiced and voiceless NASAL consonants.

Vodafone®, Vodaphone ˈvəʊ.də.fəʊn (US) ˈvoʊ.də.foʊn
vodka ˈvɒd.kə (US) ˈvɑːd- **-s** -z
Vogt *English surname:* vəʊkt (US) voʊkt
vogue (V®) vəʊg (US) voʊg
voic|e vɔɪs **-es** -ɪz **-ing** -ɪŋ **-ed** -t ˌ**Voice of Aˈmerica;** ˈ**voice** ˌ**box**
voiceless ˈvɔɪ.sləs, -slɪs **-ly** -li **-ness** -nəs, -nɪs
voicemail ˈvɔɪs.meɪl
voice-over ˈvɔɪsˌəʊ.vəʳ (US) -ˌoʊ.vɚ **-s** -z
voiceprint ˈvɔɪs.prɪnt **-s** -s
void vɔɪd **-s** -z **-ing** -ɪŋ **-ed** -ɪd **-able** -ə.bl̩ **-ance** -ᵊnts **-ness** -nəs, -nɪs
voilà vwælˈɑː, vwɒl-, vwɑːˈlɑː (US) vwɑːˈlɑː
voile vɔɪl
voir dire ˌvwɑːˈdɪəʳ (US) ˌvwɑːrˈdɪr
vol vɒl (US) vɑːl
volant ˈvəʊ.lənt (US) ˈvoʊ-
Volapük ˈvɒl.ə.puːk, ˈvəʊl-, -pʊk, ˌ--ˈ- (US) ˈvoʊ.lɑː-, ˈvɑː-
volatile *(adj)* ˈvɒl.ə.taɪl (US) ˈvɑː.lə.t̬ᵊl **-ness** -nəs, -nɪs
volatile *(in* **sal volatile***)* vəʊˈlæt.ə.li, vɒlˈæt- (US) voʊˈlæt.li
volatility ˌvɒl.əˈtɪl.ə.ti, -ɪ.ti (US) ˌvɑː.ləˈtɪl.ə.t̬i
volatilization, -isa- vɒlˌæt.ɪ.laɪˈzeɪ.ʃᵊn, vəʊˌlæt-, -ᵊl.aɪˈ-, -ɪˈ-; ˌvɒl.ə.tɪ.laɪˈ-, -tᵊl.aɪˈ-, -ɪˈ- (US) ˌvɑː.lə.tᵊl.ɪˈ-
volatiliz|e, -is|e vɒlˈæt.ɪ.laɪz, vəʊˈlæt-, -ᵊl.aɪz; ˈvɒl.ə.tɪ.laɪz, -tᵊl.aɪz (US) ˈvɑː.lə.tə.laɪz **-es** -ɪz **-ing** -ɪŋ **-ed** -d
vol-au-vent ˈvɒl.əʊ.vɑ̃ːŋ, ˌ--ˈ- (US) ˌvɔː.loʊˈvɑ̃ːn, ˌvoʊ- **-s** -z
volcanic vɒlˈkæn.ɪk (US) vɑːl- **-ally** -ᵊl.i, -li
volcanicity ˌvɒl.kəˈnɪs.ə.ti, -ɪ.ti (US) ˌvɑːl.kəˈnɪs.ə.t̬i
volcanism ˈvɒl.kə.nɪ.zᵊm (US) ˈvɑːl-
volcano vɒlˈkeɪ.nəʊ (US) vɑːlˈkeɪ.noʊ **-(e)s** -z
volcanology ˌvɒl.kəˈnɒl.ə.dʒi (US) ˌvɑːl.kəˈnɑː.lə-
vole vəʊl (US) voʊl **-s** -z

volenti non fit injuria vɒlˌen.tiːˌnəʊn.fɪt.ɪnˈjʊə.ri.ə, -ˈjɔː- (US) voʊˌlen.ti.nɑːnˌfɪt.ɪnˈdʒʊr.i.ə
volet ˈvɒl.eɪ (US) ˈvoʊ.leɪ, -ˈ- **-s** -z
Volga ˈvɒl.gə (US) ˈvɑːl-, ˈvoʊl-
Volgograd ˈvɒl.gəʊ.græd (US) ˈvɑːl.gə-, ˈvoʊl-
volition vəʊˈlɪʃ.ᵊn (US) voʊ-, və- **-al** -ᵊl
volitive ˈvɒl.ɪ.tɪv, ˈ-ə- (US) ˈvɑː.lə.t̬ɪv
volks|lied ˈfɒlks|.liːd, ˈvɒlks- *as if German:* -liːt (US) ˈfɔːlks|.liːt **-lieder** -ˌliː.dəʳ (US) -ˌliː.dɚ
volkstaat ˈfɒlk.ʃtɑːt (US) ˈfɔːlk- **-s** -s
Volkswagen® ˈfɒlksˌvɑː.gən, ˈvɒlks- (US) ˈfɔːlks-, ˈvɔːlks-, ˈvoʊks-, -ˌwɑː-, -ˌwæg.ᵊn **-s** -z
volley ˈvɒl.i (US) ˈvɑː.li **-s** -z **-ing** -ɪŋ **-ed** -d **-er/s** -əʳ/z (US) -ɚ/z
volleyball ˈvɒl.i.bɔːl (US) ˈvɑː.li-
Volos ˈvɒl.ɒs (US) ˈvɔː.lɑːs
volplan|e ˈvɒl.pleɪn (US) ˈvɑːl- **-es** -z **-ing** -ɪŋ **-ed** -d
Volpone vɒlˈpəʊ.neɪ, -ni (US) vɑːlˈpoʊ-
Volsci ˈvɒl.skiː, -saɪ (US) ˈvɑːl.saɪ, -skiː
Volscian ˈvɒl.ski.ən, -ʃi-, -si- (US) ˈvɑːl.ʃᵊn, -ski.ən
Volstead ˈvɒl.sted (US) ˈvɑːl-
Volsung ˈvɒl.sʊŋ (US) ˈvɑːl-
volt *electric unit:* vəʊlt, vɒlt (US) voʊlt **-s** -s
volt *movement of horse, movement in fencing:* vɒlt (US) voʊlt, vɑːlt, vɔːlt **-s** -s
Volta (V) *physicist:* ˈvɒl.tə, ˈvəʊl- (US) ˈvoʊl.t̬ə
Volta *lake and river:* ˈvɒl.tə (US) ˈvɑːl.t̬ə, ˈvɔːl-, ˈvoʊl-
volta *dance:* ˈvɒl.tə (US) ˈvɑːl- **-s** -z
voltag|e ˈvəʊl.tɪdʒ, ˈvɒl- (US) ˈvoʊl.t̬ɪdʒ **-es** -ɪz
voltaic vɒlˈteɪ.ɪk (US) vɑːl-, voʊl-
Voltaire vɒlˈteəʳ, ˈ-- (US) voʊlˈter, vɑːl-
voltameter vɒlˈtæm.ɪ.təʳ, vəʊl-, ˈ-ə- (US) voʊlˈtæm.ə.t̬ɚ, vɑːl- **-s** -z
volte ˈvɒl.teɪ, -ti (US) vɑːlt, voʊlt **-s** -z
volte-fac|e ˌvɒltˈfæs (US) ˌvɑːltˈfɑːs **-es** -ɪz
voltmeter ˈvəʊltˌmiː.təʳ, ˈvɒlt- (US) ˈvoʊltˌmiː.t̬ɚ **-s** -z
volubility ˌvɒl.jəˈbɪl.ə.ti, -jʊˈ-, -ɪ.ti (US) ˌvɑːl.jəˈbɪl.ə.t̬i, -jʊˈ-
volub|le ˈvɒl.jə.b|l̩, -jʊ- (US) ˈvɑːl- **-ly** -li **-leness** -l̩.nəs, -nɪs
volume ˈvɒl.juːm, -jʊm, -jəm (US) ˈvɑːl.juːm, -jəm **-s** -z
volumeter vɒlˈjuː.mɪ.təʳ, vəˈljuː-, -ˈluː-, -mə- (US) ˈvɑːl.jʊˌmiː.t̬ɚ **-s** -z
volumetric ˌvɒl.jəˈmet.rɪk, -jʊˈ- (US) ˌvɑːl- **-al** -ᵊl **-ally** -ᵊl.i, -li
voluminous vəˈluː.mɪ.nəs, vɒlˈuː-, -ˈjuː-, -mə- (US) vəˈluː.mə- **-ly** -li **-ness** -nəs, -nɪs
voluntar|y ˈvɒl.ən.tᵊr|.i, -tr|i (US) ˈvɑː.lᵊn.ter|.i **-ies** -iz **-ily** -ᵊl.i, -ɪ.li, ˌvɒl.ənˈteə.rᵊl.i, -ˈtær-, -ɪ.li **-iness** -ɪ.nəs, -ɪ.nɪs
volunteer ˌvɒl.ənˈtɪəʳ (US) ˌvɑː.lənˈtɪr **-s** -z **-ing** -ɪŋ **-ed** -d
voluptuar|y vəˈlʌp.tjʊə.r|i, -tʃʊə- (US) -tʃu.er|.i **-ies** -iz
voluptuous vəˈlʌp.tʃu.əs, -tju.əs (US) -tʃu- **-ly** -li **-ness** -nəs, -nɪs
volu|te vəʊˈluː|t, vɒlˈuː|t, -ˈjuː|t (US) vəˈluː|t **-tes** -ts **-ted** -tɪd (US) -t̬ɪd
volution vəʊˈluː.ʃᵊn, vɒlˈuː-, -ˈjuː- (US) vəˈluː- **-s** -z
Volvo® ˈvɒl.vəʊ (US) ˈvɑːl.voʊ **-s** -z
vom|it ˈvɒm|.ɪt (US) ˈvɑː.m|ɪt **-its** -ɪts **-iting** -ɪ.tɪŋ (US) -ɪ.t̬ɪŋ **-ited** -ɪ.tɪd (US) -ɪ.t̬ɪd
vomitor|y ˈvɒm.ɪ.tᵊr|.i, -tr|i (US) ˈvɑː.mə.tɔːr|.i **-ies** -iz
von (V) vɒn, fɒn (US) vɑːn, fɑːn
Vonnegut ˈvɒn.ɪ.gət (US) ˈvɑː.nə-
voodoo ˈvuː.duː **-s** -z **-ing** -ɪŋ **-ed** -d **-ist/s** -ɪst/s **-ism** -ɪ.zᵊm
Vooght vuːt
voracious vəˈreɪ.ʃəs, vɔː-, vɒrˈeɪ- (US) vɔːˈreɪ-, və- **-ly** -li **-ness** -nəs, -nɪs
voracity vəˈræs.ə.ti, vɔː-, vɒrˈæs-, -ɪ.ti (US) vɔːˈræs.ə.t̬i, və-
Vorderman ˈvɔː.də.mən (US) ˈvɔːr.dɚ-
Vorster ˈfɔː.stəʳ (US) ˈfɔːr.stɚ
vort|ex ˈvɔː.t|eks (US) ˈvɔːr- **-ices** -ɪ.siːz **-exes** -ek.sɪz
vortic|al ˈvɔː.tɪ.k|ᵊl (US) ˈvɔːr.t̬ɪ- **-ally** -ᵊl.i, -li
vortices *(plur. of* **vortex***)* ˈvɔː.tɪ.siːz (US) ˈvɔːr.t̬ɪ-
vortic|ism (V) ˈvɔː.tɪ.s|ɪ.zᵊm (US) ˈvɔːr.t̬ɪ- **-ist/s** -ɪst/s
Vortigern ˈvɔː.tɪ.gɜːn, -gən (US) ˈvɔːr.t̬ɪ.gɝːn
Vosges vəʊʒ (US) voʊʒ
Voss vɒs (US) vɑːs
votaress ˈvəʊ.tᵊr.es, -ɪs (US) ˈvoʊ.t̬ɚ.əs, ˈ-trəs **-es** -ɪz
votar|y ˈvəʊ.tᵊr|.i (US) ˈvoʊ.t̬ɚ- **-ies** -iz **-ist/s** -ɪst/s
vot|e vəʊt (US) voʊt **-es** -s **-ing** -ɪŋ (US) ˈvoʊ.t̬ɪŋ **-ed** -ɪd (US) ˈvoʊ.t̬ɪd **-er/s** -əʳ/z (US) ˈvoʊ.t̬ɚ/z **ˌvote of (ˌno) ˈconfidence; ˌvote of ˈthanks; ˌvote with one's ˈfeet**
voteless ˈvəʊt.ləs, -lɪs (US) ˈvoʊt-
votive ˈvəʊ.tɪv (US) ˈvoʊ.t̬ɪv **-ly** -li **-ness** -nəs, -nɪs
vouch vaʊtʃ **-es** -ɪz **-ing** -ɪŋ **-ed** -t
voucher ˈvaʊ.tʃəʳ (US) -tʃɚ **-s** -z **ˈvoucher ˌsystem**
vouchsaf|e ˌvaʊtʃˈseɪf, ˈ-- **-es** -s **-ing** -ɪŋ **-ed** -t
Vouvray ˈvuː.vreɪ (US) -ˈ-
vow vaʊ **-s** -z **-ing** -ɪŋ **-ed** -d
vowel vaʊəl **-s** -z **-(l)ing** -ɪŋ **-(l)ed** -d
Vowles vəʊlz, vaʊlz (US) voʊlz, vaʊlz
vox (V) vɒks (US) vɑːks
vox humana ˌvɒks.hjuːˈmɑː.nə (US) ˌvɑːks-, -ˈmeɪ- **-s** -z
vox pop ˌvɒksˈpɒp (US) ˌvɑːksˈpɑːp
vox populi ˌvɒksˈpɒp.jʊ.liː, -jə- (US) ˌvɑːksˈpɑː.pjuː.laɪ, -liː
voyag|e ˈvɔɪ.ɪdʒ **-es** -ɪz **-ing** -ɪŋ **-ed** -d
voyager ˈvɔɪ.ɪ.dʒəʳ, ˈvɔɪ.ə- (US) ˈvɔɪ.ɪ.dʒɚ **-s** -z
voyeur vwɑːˈjɜːʳ, vɔɪˈɜːʳ (US) vɔɪˈjɝː, vwɑː- **-s** -z
voyeurism vwɑːˈjɜː.rɪ.zᵊm, vɔɪˈɜː-, ˈvwɑː.jɜː-, ˈvɔɪ.ɜː- (US) vɔɪˈjɝː.ɪ-, vwɑː-; ˈvɔɪ.jɚ.ɪ-
voyeuristic ˌvɔɪ.əˈrɪ.stɪk, ˌvwɑː.jɜːˈ- (US) ˌvɔɪ.jəˈ-, ˌvwɑː- **-ally** -ᵊl.i, li
VP ˌviːˈpiː **-s** -z
vroom vruːm, vrʊm
vs. ˈvɜː.səs (US) ˈvɝː-
VSO ˌviː.esˈəʊ (US) -ˈoʊ
V/STOL ˈviːˌstɒl (US) -ˌstɑːl
Vt. *(abbrev. for* **Vermont***)* vəˈmɒnt, vɜː- (US) vɚˈmɑːnt
VTOL ˈviː.tɒl (US) -tɑːl
Vuillard ˈvuː.jɑː, -ˈ-
Vuitton® ˈvjuː.ɪ.tɔ̃ːŋ, ˈvwiː.tɒn (US) vwiːˈtɔ̃ːn
Vukovar ˈvʊk.ə.vəʳ, -vɑːʳ (US) -vɚ
Vulcan ˈvʌl.kən **-s** -z
vulcanite ˈvʌl.kə.naɪt
vulcanization, -isa- ˌvʌl.kə.naɪˈzeɪ.ʃᵊn, -nɪˈ- (US) -nɪˈ-
vulcaniz|e, -is|e ˈvʌl.kə.naɪz **-es** -ɪz **-ing** -ɪŋ **-ed** -d
vulgar (V) ˈvʌl.gəʳ (US) -gɚ **-ly** -li **ˌVulgar ˈLatin**
vulgarian vʌlˈgeə.ri.ən (US) -ˈger.i- **-s** -z
vulgarism ˈvʌl.gᵊr.ɪ.zᵊm **-s** -z
vulgarit|y vʌlˈgær.ə.t|i, -ɪ.t|i (US) -ˈger.ə.t̬|i, -ˈgær- **-ies** -iz
vulgarization, -isa- ˌvʌl.gᵊr.aɪˈzeɪ.ʃᵊn, -ɪˈ- (US) -ɪˈ-
vulgariz|e, -is|e ˈvʌl.gᵊr.aɪz (US) -gə.raɪz **-es** -ɪz **-ing** -ɪŋ **-ed** -d **-er/s** -əʳ/z (US) -ɚ/z
vulgate (V) ˈvʌl.geɪt, -gɪt, -gət (US) -geɪt, -gɪt
Vulliamy ˈvʌl.jə.mi
vulnerability ˌvʌl.nᵊr.əˈbɪl.ə.ti, ˌvʌn.ᵊr-, ˌvʌn.rəˈ-, -ɪ.ti (US) ˌvʌl.nɚ.əˈbɪl.ə.t̬i
vulnerab|le ˈvʌl.nᵊr.ə.b|l̩, ˈvʌn.ᵊr-, ˈvʌn.rə.b|l̩ (US) ˈvʌl.nɚ.ə- **-ly** -li **-leness** -l̩.nəs, -nɪs
Vulpecula vʌlˈpek.jə.lə, -jʊ-
vulpine ˈvʌl.paɪn (US) -paɪn, -pɪn
vulture ˈvʌl.tʃəʳ (US) -tʃɚ **-s** -z

Vowel

Definition

The class of sound which makes the least obstruction to the flow of air. They are almost always found at the centre of a syllable, and it is rare to find any sound other than a vowel which is able to stand alone as a whole syllable.

Examples for English

Here we examine the vowel monophthongs of English. In phonetic terms, each vowel has a number of properties that distinguish it from other vowels. These include the shape of the lips, which may be rounded (as for an [u] vowel), NEUTRAL (as for [ə]) or spread (as in a smile, or an [i] vowel – photographers traditionally ask their subjects to say *cheese* /tʃiːz/ so that they will seem to be smiling):

Unrounded	Rounded	(US) Unrounded	Rounded
iː	uː	iː	uː
ɪ	ʊ	ɪ	ʊ
e	ɔː	e	ɔː
æ	ɒ	æ	
ʌ		ʌ	
ɑː		ɑː	
ɜː		ɝː	
ə		ə ɚ	

Secondly, the front, the middle or the back of the tongue may be raised, giving different vowel qualities: the BBC English /æ/ vowel (*cat*) is a front vowel, while the /ɑː/ of *cart* is a back vowel:

Front	Central	Back	(US) Front	Central	Back
iː	ʌ	uː	iː	ʌ	uː
ɪ	ɜː	ʊ	ɪ	ɝː	ʊ
e	ə	ɔː	e	ə ɚ	ɔː
æ		ɒ	æ		ɑː
		ɑː			

The tongue (and the lower jaw) may be raised close to the roof of the mouth, or the tongue may be left low in the mouth with the jaw comparatively open. In British phonetics we talk about 'close' and 'open' vowels, whereas American phoneticians more often talk about 'high' and 'low' vowels. The meaning is clear in either case, e.g.:

Close	Mid	Open	(US) High	Mid	Low
iː	e	ʌ	iː	e	ʌ
ɪ	ɜː	ɒ	ɪ	ɝː	ɑː
uː	ə	ɑː	uː	ə ɚ	æ
ʊ	ɔː	æ	ʊ	ɔː	

Vowels also differ in other ways: they may be 'nasalised' (see NASALISATION) by being pronounced with the soft palate lowered as for [m n] or [ŋ]. Vowels may be voiced, as the great majority are, or voiceless: in English the first vowel in *perhaps* or *potato* is often voiceless. It is claimed that in some languages (including English) there is a distinction to be made between TENSE and LAX vowels, the former being made with greater force than the latter.

In other languages

Nasalisation is phonemically contrastive in French, where we find 'minimal pairs' such as *très* /tʀɛ/ (*very*) and *train* /tʀɛ̃/ (*train*), where the [˜] diacritic indicates nasality. Concerning voiceless vowels: in Portuguese, for example, unstressed vowels in the last syllable of a word are often voiceless. Less usual is the case of stressed voiceless vowels, but these are found in French: close vowels, particularly /i/ but also the close front rounded /y/, become voiceless for some speakers when they are word-final before a pause (for example *oui* [wi̥], *midi* [midi̥], and also *entendu* [ɑ̃tɑ̃dẙ]).

Vowel Reduction

The process by which an unstressed vowel may change to become like the mid central vowel 'schwa' /ə/. In the words 'photograph', 'photographic' and 'photography', the vowels in the first three syllables alternate between full vowels and /ə/ according to the position of stress, e.g.:

photograph	/ˈfəʊ.tə.grɑːf/	(US) /ˈfoʊ.t̬ə.græf/
photographic	/ˌfəʊ.təˈgræf.ɪk/	(US) /ˈfoʊ.t̬əˈ-/
photography	/fəˈtɒg.rəfi/	(US) /-ˈtɑː.grə/

Although the word 'man' is pronounced /mæn/, the reduced form can be seen in 'postman' /ˈpəʊs*t*.mən (US) ˈpoʊs*t*-/, 'chairman' /ˈtʃeə.mən (US) tʃer-/, etc.

Another example of vowel reduction is found in the alternation between /e/ and /ɪ/ in, for example, the first syllables of 'exhibition' /ˌek.sɪˈbɪʃ.ən/ and /ɪgˈzɪb.ɪt/.

vulturine ˈvʌl.tʃ^{ə}r.aɪn, -tʃʊ.raɪn, -tj^{ə}r.aɪn, -tjʊ.raɪn (US) -tʃə.raɪn, -rɪn

vulturous ˈvʌl.tʃ^{ə}r.əs, -tʃʊ.rəs, -tj^{ə}r.əs, -tjʊ.rəs (US) -tʃɚ.əs

vulv|a ˈvʌl.v|ə **-as** -əz **-ae** -iː

VW ˌviːˈdʌb.l̩.ju, -juː (US) -juː, -jə **-s** -z

Vye vaɪ

vying *(from* vie*)* ˈvaɪ.ɪŋ

Pronouncing the letter W

See also WH

The consonant letter **w** is most often realised as /w/, e.g.:

wet /wet/
swing /swɪŋ/

In addition

w can be silent. There are four conditions under which this can occur. In the spelling combination **wr, w** is not pronounced and the realisation is /r/. In some instances of **tw** when at the beginning of a word, the pronunciation is /t/. Some word-medial **sw** spellings are pronounced /s/. Finally, in (mostly) British place names ending *-wich*, **w** is not normally pronounced, although exceptions do exist. E.g.:

write /raɪt/
two /tuː/
answer /ˈɑːnt.səʳ/ ⓤⓢ /ˈæn .sɚ/
Greenwich /ˈgren.ɪdʒ/

The examples given above are for **w** in word or syllable-initial position. The letter **w** can also appear at the end of a word or syllable. These instances of **w** are covered at the panels for **aw** and **ow**.

In words borrowed from German, **w** may be pronounced /v/. Words borrowed from Slavic may have /v/ or /f/. E.g.:

Wagner /ˈwɑːg.nəʳ/ ⓤⓢ /-nɚ/
Krakow /ˈkræk.ɒv, -ɒf/ ⓤⓢ /ˈkrɑː.kʊf/

w (W) ˈdʌb.l̩.juː, -ju ⓤⓢ -juː, -jə **-'s** -z
W *(abbrev. for* **west***)* west
Waaf, WAAF wæf **-s** -s
Wabash ˈwɔː.bæʃ ⓤⓢ ˈwɔː-, ˈwɑː-
Wace weɪs
wacko ˈwæk.əʊ ⓤⓢ -oʊ **-s** -z
wack|y ˈwæk|.i **-ier** -i.əʳ ⓤⓢ -i.ɚ **-iest** -i.ɪst, -i.əst **-ily** -ɪ.li, -ᵊl.i **-iness** -ɪ.nəs, -ɪ.nɪs
Waco ˈweɪ.kəʊ ⓤⓢ -koʊ
wad wɒd ⓤⓢ wɑːd **-s** -z **-ding** -ɪŋ **-ded** -ɪd
Waddell wɒdˈel, ˈwɒd.ᵊl ⓤⓢ wɑːˈdel, ˈwɑː.dᵊl
wadding ˈwɒd.ɪŋ ⓤⓢ ˈwɑː.dɪŋ
Waddington ˈwɒd.ɪŋ.tən ⓤⓢ ˈwɑː.dɪŋ-
waddl|e ˈwɒd.l̩ ⓤⓢ ˈwɑː.dl̩ **-es** -z **-ing** -ɪŋ, ˈwɒd.lɪŋ ⓤⓢ ˈwɑːd- **-ed** -d **-er/s** -əʳ/z, ˈwɒd.ləʳ/z ⓤⓢ ˈwɑː.dl̩.ɚ/z, ˈwɑːd.lɚ/z
wadd|y (W) ˈwɒd|.i ⓤⓢ ˈwɑː.d|i **-ies** -iz
wad|e (W) weɪd **-es** -z **-ing** -ɪŋ **-ed** -ɪd
Wadebridge ˈweɪd.brɪdʒ
Wade-Giles ˌweɪdˈdʒaɪlz
wader ˈweɪ.dəʳ ⓤⓢ -dɚ **-s** -z
Wadey ˈweɪ.di
wadg|e wɒdʒ ⓤⓢ wɑːdʒ **-es** -ɪz
Wadham ˈwɒd.əm ⓤⓢ ˈwɑː.dəm
Wadhurst ˈwɒd.hɜːst ⓤⓢ ˈwɑːd.hɝːst
wadi ˈwɒd.i, ˈwæd-, ˈwɑː.di ⓤⓢ ˈwɑː.di **-s** -z
Wadi Halfa ˌwɒd.iˈhæl.fə, ˌwæd-, ˌwɑː.diˈ- ⓤⓢ ˌwɑː.diˈhɑːl.fə
Wadman ˈwɒd.mən ⓤⓢ ˈwɑːd-
Wad Medani ˌwɑːd.məˈdɑː.ni
Wadsworth ˈwɒdz.wəθ, -wɜːθ ⓤⓢ ˈwɑːdz.wɚθ, -wɝːθ
WAF, Waf wæf **-s** -s
Wafd wɒft, wæft, wɑːft ⓤⓢ wɑːft
waf|er ˈweɪ.f|əʳ ⓤⓢ -f|ɚ **-ers** -əz ⓤⓢ -ɚz **-ery** -ᵊr.i
wafer-thin ˌweɪ.fəˈθɪn ⓤⓢ -fɚˈ- *stress shift:* ˌwafer-thin ˈmints
waffl|e ˈwɒf.l̩ ⓤⓢ ˈwɑː.fl̩ **-es** -z **-ing** -ɪŋ, ˈwɒf.lɪŋ ⓤⓢ ˈwɑːf- **-ed** -d **-er/s** -əʳ/z, ˈwɒf.ləʳ/z ⓤⓢ ˈwɑː.fl̩.ɚ/z, ˈwɑːf.lɚ/z **-y** -i, ˈwɒf.li ⓤⓢ ˈwɑː.fl̩.i, ˈwɑːf.li
waffle-iron ˈwɒf.l̩ˌaɪən ⓤⓢ ˈwɑː.fl̩ˌaɪɚn **-s** -z
waft wɒft, wɑːft ⓤⓢ wɑːft, wæft **-s** -s **-ing** -ɪŋ **-ed** -ɪd
wag wæg **-s** -z **-ging** -ɪŋ **-ged** -d
wag|e weɪdʒ **-es** -ɪz **-ing** -ɪŋ **-ed** -d ˈ**wage** ˌ**packet**
wage-earner ˈweɪdʒˌɜː.nəʳ ⓤⓢ -ˌɝː.nɚ **-s** -z
wag|er ˈweɪ.dʒ|əʳ ⓤⓢ -dʒ|ɚ **-ers** -əz ⓤⓢ -ɚz **-ering** -ᵊr.ɪŋ **-ered** -əd ⓤⓢ -ɚd **-erer/s** -ᵊr.əʳ/z ⓤⓢ -ɚ.ɚ/z
wageworker ˈweɪdʒˌwɜː.kəʳ ⓤⓢ -ˌwɝː.kɚ **-s** -z
waggish ˈwæg.ɪʃ **-ly** -li **-ness** -nəs, -nɪs
waggl|e ˈwæg.l̩ **-es** -z **-ing** -ɪŋ, ˈwæg.lɪŋ **-ed** -d
waggon ˈwæg.ən **-s** -z
waggoner ˈwæg.ᵊn.əʳ ⓤⓢ -ɚ **-s** -z
waggonette ˌwæg.əˈnet **-s** -s
Waghorn ˈwæg.hɔːn ⓤⓢ -hɔːrn
Wagnall ˈwæg.nᵊl
Wagner *English name:* ˈwæg.nəʳ ⓤⓢ -nɚ *German composer:* ˈvɑːg.nəʳ ⓤⓢ -nɚ
Wagnerian vɑːgˈnɪə.ri.ən ⓤⓢ -ˈnɪr.i-, -ˈner- **-s** -z
wagon ˈwæg.ən **-s** -z
wagoner ˈwæg.ə.nəʳ ⓤⓢ -nɚ **-s** -z
wagonette ˌwæg.əˈnet **-s** -s
wagon-lit ˌvæg.ɔ̃ːnˈliː, ˌvɑːg-, -gɒnˈ-, ˈ--- ⓤⓢ ˌvɑː.gɔ̃ːnˈliː **-s** -z
Wagstaff ˈwæg.stɑːf ⓤⓢ -stæf
wagtail ˈwæg.teɪl **-s** -z
Wah(h)abi wəˈhɑː.bi, wɑː- **-s** -z
Wahlberg ˈwɑːl.bɜːg ⓤⓢ -bɝːg
waif weɪf **-s** -s
Waikiki ˌwaɪ.kiˈkiː, ˈ---
wail weɪl **-s** -z **-ing/ly** -ɪŋ/li **-ed** -d
wain (W) weɪn **-s** -z
Wain(e) weɪn
Wainfleet ˈweɪn.fliːt
wainsco|t ˈweɪn.skə|t, ˈwen-, -skɒ|t ⓤⓢ ˈweɪn.skə|t, -skɑː|t, -skoʊ|t **-ts** -ts **-t(t)ing** -tɪŋ ⓤⓢ -t̬ɪŋ **-t(t)ed** -tɪd ⓤⓢ -t̬ɪd
Wainwright ˈweɪn.raɪt
waist weɪst **-s** -s **-ed** -ɪd
waistband ˈweɪst.bænd **-s** -z
waistcoat ˈweɪst.kəʊt *old-fashioned:* ˈwes.kət, -kɪt ⓤⓢ ˈwes.kət, ˈweɪst.koʊt **-s** -s
waist-deep ˌweɪstˈdiːp *stress shift:* ˌwaist-deep ˈwater
waist-high ˌweɪstˈhaɪ *stress shift:* ˌwaist-high ˈwater
waistline ˈweɪst.laɪn **-s** -z
wait weɪt **-s** -s **-ing** -ɪŋ ⓤⓢ ˈweɪ.t̬ɪŋ **-ed** -ɪd ⓤⓢ ˈweɪ.t̬ɪd ˈ**waiting** ˌ**list**
Waite weɪt
waiter ˈweɪ.təʳ ⓤⓢ -t̬ɚ **-s** -z
waiting-room ˈweɪ.tɪŋ.rʊm, -ruːm ⓤⓢ -t̬ɪŋ.ruːm, -rʊm **-s** -z
wait|person ˈweɪt|ˌpɜː.sᵊn ⓤⓢ -ˌpɝː- **-people** -ˌpiː.pl̩
waitress ˈweɪ.trəs, -trɪs ⓤⓢ -trɪs **-es** -ɪz
Waitrose® ˈweɪ.trəʊz ⓤⓢ -troʊz
waiv|e weɪv **-es** -z **-ing** -ɪŋ **-ed** -d
waiver ˈweɪ.vəʳ ⓤⓢ -vɚ **-s** -z
Wajda ˈvaɪ.də
wak|e weɪk **-es** -s **-ing** -ɪŋ **-ed** -t **woke** wəʊk ⓤⓢ woʊk **woken** ˈwəʊ.kᵊn ⓤⓢ ˈwoʊ-
Wakefield ˈweɪk.fiːld
wakeful ˈweɪk.fᵊl, -fʊl **-ly** -i **-ness** -nəs, -nɪs

Wakeham ˈweɪ.kəm
Wakehurst ˈweɪk.hɜːst ⓤⓢ -hɝːst
Wakeling ˈweɪ.klɪŋ
Wakeman ˈweɪk.mən
waken ˈweɪ.kᵊn **-s** -z **-ing** -ɪŋ, ˈweɪk.nɪŋ **-ed** -d
wakey wakey ˌweɪ.kiˈweɪ.ki
Wakley ˈweɪ.kli
Wakonda wəˈkɒn.də ⓤⓢ wɑːˈkɑːn-
Wal wɒl, wɔːl ⓤⓢ wɑːl
Walachi|a wɒlˈeɪ.ki|.ə, wəˈleɪ- ⓤⓢ wɑːˈleɪ-, wə- **-an/s** -ən/z
Walberswick ˈwɔːl.bəz.wɪk, ˈwɒl- ⓤⓢ ˈwɔːl.bɚz-, ˈwɑːl-
Walbrook ˈwɔːl.brʊk, ˈwɒl- ⓤⓢ ˈwɔːl-, ˈwɑːl-
Walcott ˈwɔːl.kət, ˈwɒl-, -kɒt ⓤⓢ ˈwɔːl.kət, ˈwɑːl-, -kɑːt
Waldeck ˈwɔːl.dek, ˈwɒl- ⓤⓢ ˈwɔːl-, ˈvɑːl-
Waldegrave ˈwɔːl.greɪv, ˈwɒl-, -də.greɪv ⓤⓢ ˈwɔːl-, ˈwɑːl-
Note: Earl Waldegrave is /ˈwɔːl.greɪv, ˈwɒl- ⓤⓢ ˈwɔːl-, ˈwɑːl-/; the politician William Waldegrave is /ˈwɔːl.də.greɪv, ˈwɒl- ⓤⓢ ˈwɔːl-, ˈwɑːl-/.
Waldemar ˈvæl.də.mɑːʳ, ˈvɑːl-, ˈwɔːl-, -dɪ- ⓤⓢ ˈvɑːl.də.mɑːr
Walden ˈwɔːl.dᵊn, ˈwɒl- ⓤⓢ ˈwɔːl-, ˈwɑːl-
Waldheim ˈvɑːld.haɪm *as if German:* ˈvælt- ⓤⓢ ˈwɑːld- *as if German:* ˈvɑːlt-
Waldhere ˈwɑːldˌheə.rə ⓤⓢ ˈwɔːldˌher.ə, ˈwɑːld-
Waldo ˈwɔːl.dəʊ, ˈwɒl- ⓤⓢ ˈwɔːl.doʊ, ˈwɑːl-
Waldock ˈwɔːl.dɒk, ˈwɒl- ⓤⓢ ˈwɔːl.dɑːk, ˈwɑːl-
Waldorf ˈwɔːl.dɔːf, ˈwɒl- ⓤⓢ ˈwɔːl.dɔːrf, ˈwɑːl- **ˌWaldorf ˈsalad**
Waldron ˈwɔːl.drən, ˈwɒl- ⓤⓢ ˈwɔːl-, ˈwɑːl-
Waldstein *American name:* ˈwɔːld.staɪn, ˈwɒld- ⓤⓢ ˈwɔːld-, ˈwɑːld- *German name, Beethoven sonata:* ˈvæld.staɪn, ˈvɑːld-, ˈvɔːld-, ˈvɒld-, ˈwɔːld-, ˈwɒld-, -ʃtaɪn ⓤⓢ ˈvɑːlt.ʃtaɪn, ˈvɑːld-
wale weɪl **-s** -z
waler (W) ˈweɪ.ləʳ ⓤⓢ -lɚ **-s** -z
Waleran *Baron:* ˈwɔːl.rən, ˈwɒl- ⓤⓢ ˈwɔːl-, ˈwɑːl- *buildings in Borough High Street, London:* ˈwɒl.ᵊr.ən ⓤⓢ ˈwɑː.lɚ-, ˈwɔː-
Wales weɪlz
Walesa vɑːˈwent.sə, væˈ- ⓤⓢ wɑːˈlent.sə; vɑːˈwent.sɑː
Waley ˈweɪ.li
Walfish ˈwɔːl.fɪʃ, ˈwɒl- ⓤⓢ ˈwɔːl-, ˈwɑːl-
Walford ˈwɔːl.fəd, ˈwɒl- ⓤⓢ ˈwɔːl.fɚd, ˈwɑːl-
Walhalla vælˈhæl.ə ⓤⓢ wɑːlˈhɑː.lə; wælˈhæl.ə, væl-
Walham ˈwɒl.əm ⓤⓢ ˈwɑː.ləm
walk wɔːk ⓤⓢ wɑːk, wɔːk **-s** -s **-ing** -ɪŋ **-ed** -t **-er/s** -əʳ/z ⓤⓢ -ɚ/z **ˈwalking ˌstick**
walkabout ˈwɔː.kəˌbaʊt ⓤⓢ ˈwɑː-, ˈwɔː- **-s** -s
walkaway ˈwɔː.kə.weɪ ⓤⓢ ˈwɑː-, ˈwɔː-
Walkden ˈwɔːk.dən ⓤⓢ ˈwɑːk-, ˈwɔːk-
Walker ˈwɔː.kəʳ ⓤⓢ ˈwɑː.kɚ, ˈwɔː-
Walkern ˈwɔːl.kən, -kɜːn ⓤⓢ ˈwɔːl.kɚn, ˈwɑːl-, -kɝːn
walkies ˈwɔː.kiz ⓤⓢ ˈwɑː-, ˈwɔː-
walkie-talkie ˌwɔː.kiˈtɔː.ki ⓤⓢ ˌwɑː.kiˈtɑː-, ˌwɔː-, -ˈtɔː- **-s** -z
walk-in ˈwɔːk.ɪn ⓤⓢ ˈwɑːk-, ˈwɔːk-
Walkman® ˈwɔːk.mən ⓤⓢ ˈwɑːk-, ˈwɔːk- **-s** -z
walk-on ˈwɔːk.ɒn ⓤⓢ ˈwɑːk.ɑːn, ˈwɔːk- **-s** -z
walkout ˈwɔːk.aʊt ⓤⓢ ˈwɑːk-, ˈwɔːk- **-s** -s
walkover ˈwɔːkˌəʊ.vəʳ ⓤⓢ ˈwɑːkˌoʊ.vɚ, ˈwɔːk- **-s** -z
walkway ˈwɔːk.weɪ ⓤⓢ ˈwɑːk-, ˈwɔːk- **-s** -z
Walkyrie vælˈkɪə.ri; ˈvæl.kᵊr.i, -kɪ.ri ⓤⓢ wɑːlˈkɪr.i; ˈwɑːl.kɚ-, ˈvɑːl- **-s** -z
walky-talk|y ˌwɔː.kiˈtɔː.k|i ⓤⓢ ˌwɑː.kiˈtɑː-, ˌwɔː-, -ˈtɔː- **-ies** -iz
wall (W) wɔːl ⓤⓢ wɔːl, wɑːl **-s** -z **-ing** -ɪŋ **-ed** -d **ˈWall ˌStreet; ˌWall Street ˈJournal; ˌbang one's ˌhead against a ˌbrick ˈwall**
wallab|y (W) ˈwɒl.ə.b|i ⓤⓢ ˈwɑː.lə- **-ies** -iz
Wallace ˈwɒl.ɪs, -əs ⓤⓢ ˈwɑː.lɪs, -ləs
Wallach ˈwɒl.ək ⓤⓢ ˈwɑː.lək **-s** -s
Wallachi|a wɒlˈeɪ.ki|.ə, wəˈleɪ- ⓤⓢ wɑːˈleɪ- **-an/s** -an/z
walla(h) ˈwɒl.ə ⓤⓢ ˈwɑː.lɑː **-s** -z
Wallasey ˈwɒl.ə.si ⓤⓢ ˈwɑː.lə-
wallboard ˈwɔːl.bɔːd ⓤⓢ ˈwɔːl.bɔːrd, ˈwɑːl-
wallchart ˈwɔːl.tʃɑːt ⓤⓢ -tʃɑːrt, ˈwɑːl- **-s** -s
Waller ˈwɒl.əʳ ⓤⓢ ˈwɑː.lɚ
wallet ˈwɒl.ɪt ⓤⓢ ˈwɑː.lɪt **-s** -s
wall-eye ˈwɔːl.aɪ ⓤⓢ ˈwɔːl-, ˈwɑːl- **-s** -z **-d** -d
wallflower ˈwɔːl.flaʊəʳ ⓤⓢ -flaʊɚ, ˈwɑːl- **-s** -z
Wallingford ˈwɒl.ɪŋ.fəd ⓤⓢ ˈwɑː.lɪŋ.fɚd
Wallington ˈwɒl.ɪŋ.tən ⓤⓢ ˈwɑː.lɪŋ-
Wallis ˈwɒl.ɪs ⓤⓢ ˈwɑː.lɪs
Wallonia wəˈləʊ.ni.ə ⓤⓢ wɑːˈloʊ-
Walloon wɒlˈuːn, wəˈluːn ⓤⓢ wɑːˈluːn **-s** -z
wallop ˈwɒl.əp ⓤⓢ ˈwɑː.ləp **-s** -s **-ing/s** -ɪŋ/z **-ed** -t
wallow ˈwɒl.əʊ ⓤⓢ ˈwɑː.loʊ **-s** -z **-ing** -ɪŋ **-ed** -d **-er/s** -əʳ/z ⓤⓢ -ɚ/z
wallpap|er ˈwɔːlˌpeɪ.p|əʳ ⓤⓢ -p|ɚ, ˈwɑːl- **-ers** -əz ⓤⓢ -ɚz **-ering** -ᵊr.ɪŋ **-ered** -əd ⓤⓢ -ɚd
Wallsend ˈwɔːl.zend ⓤⓢ ˈwɔːl-, ˈwɑːl-
wall-to-wall ˌwɔːl.təˈwɔːl, -tuˈ- ⓤⓢ -t̬əˈ-, ˌwɑːl-, -ˈwɑːl
Wallwork ˈwɔːl.wɜːk, ˈwɒl- ⓤⓢ ˈwɔːl.wɝːk, ˈwɑːl-
wall|y (W) ˈwɒl|.i ⓤⓢ ˈwɑː.l|i **-ies** -iz
Wal-Mart® ˈwɒl.mɑːt ⓤⓢ ˈwɔːl.mɑːrt, ˈwɑːl-
Walmer ˈwɔːl.məʳ, ˈwɒl- ⓤⓢ ˈwɔːl.mɚ, ˈwɑːl-
Walm(e)sley ˈwɔːmz.li ⓤⓢ ˈwɑːmz-, ˈwɔːmz-
Walmisley ˈwɔːmz.li ⓤⓢ ˈwɑːmz-, ˈwɔːmz-
Walney ˈwɔːl.ni, ˈwɒl- ⓤⓢ ˈwɔːl-, ˈwɑːl-
walnut ˈwɔːl.nʌt, -nət ⓤⓢ ˈwɔːl-, ˈwɑːl- **-s** -s
Walpole ˈwɔːl.pəʊl, ˈwɒl- ⓤⓢ ˈwɔːl.poʊl, ˈwɑːl-
Walpurgis vælˈpʊə.gɪs, vɑːl-, -ˈpɜː- ⓤⓢ vɑːlˈpʊr.gɪs
walrus ˈwɔːl.rəs, ˈwɒl-, -rʌs ⓤⓢ ˈwɔːl.rəs, ˈwɑːl- **-es** -ɪz
Walsall ˈwɔːl.sɔːl, ˈwɒl-, -sᵊl ⓤⓢ ˈwɔːl.sɔːl, ˈwɑːl-, -sɑːl
Walsh wɒlʃ, wɔːlʃ ⓤⓢ wɔːlʃ, wɑːlʃ
Walsham ˈwɔːl.ʃəm *locally:* -səm ⓤⓢ ˈwɔːl-, ˈwɑːl-
Walsingham *surname:* ˈwɔːl.sɪŋ.əm, ˈwɒl- ⓤⓢ ˈwɔːl-, ˈwɑːl- *place:* ˈwɔːl.zɪŋ.əm, ˈwɒl-, -sɪŋ- ⓤⓢ ˈwɔːl-, ˈwɑːl-
Walt wɒlt, wɔːlt ⓤⓢ wɔːlt, wɑːlt
Walter *English name:* ˈwɒl.təʳ, ˈwɔːl- ⓤⓢ ˈwɔːl.t̬ɚ, ˈwɑːl- *German name:* ˈvɑːl.təʳ ⓤⓢ -t̬ɚ
Walter Mitty ˌwɒl.təˈmɪt.i, ˌwɔːl- ⓤⓢ ˌwɔːl.t̬ɚˈmɪt̬-, ˌwɑːl-
Walters ˈwɒl.təz, ˈwɔːl- ⓤⓢ ˈwɔːl.t̬ɚz, ˈwɑːl-
Waltham ***Great and Little****, in Essex:* ˈwɔːl.təm, ˈwɒl- ⓤⓢ ˈwɔːl-, ˈwɑːl-
Note: Some new residents pronounce /-θəm/. *other places:* ˈwɔːl.θəm, ˈwɒl- ⓤⓢ ˈwɔːl-, ˈwɑːl- **ˌWaltham ˈForest**
Walthamstow ˈwɒl.θəm.stəʊ, ˈwɔːl- ⓤⓢ ˈwɔːl.θəm.stoʊ, ˈwɑːl-
Walther ˈvɑːl.təʳ ⓤⓢ -t̬ɚ
Walton ˈwɒl.tᵊn, ˈwɔːl- ⓤⓢ ˈwɔːl-, ˈwɑːl-
Walton-on-the-Naze ˌwɒl.tᵊnˌɒn.ðəˈneɪz, ˌwɔːl- ⓤⓢ ˌwɔːl.tᵊnˌɑːn-, ˌwɑːl-
waltz wɒls, wɔːls, wɒlts, wɔːlts ⓤⓢ wɔːlts, wɑːlts **-es** -ɪz **-ing** -ɪŋ **-ed** -t **-er/s** -əʳ/z ⓤⓢ -ɚ/z

Walworth ˈwɒl.wəθ, ˈwɔːl-, -wɜːθ (US) ˈwɔːl.wɝːθ, ˈwɑːl-, -wɚθ
wampum ˈwɒm.pəm (US) ˈwɑːm-, ˈwɔːm- **-s** -z
WAN wæn
wan wɒn (US) wɑːn **-ner** -əʳ (US) -ɚ **-nest** -ɪst, -əst **-ly** -li **-ness** -nəs, -nɪs
Wanamaker ˈwɒn.ə.meɪ.kəʳ (US) ˈwɑː.nə.meɪ.kɚ
wand (W) wɒnd (US) wɑːnd **-s** -z
Wanda ˈwɒn.də (US) ˈwɑːn-
wand|er ˈwɒn.d|əʳ (US) ˈwɑːn.d|ɚ **-ers** -əz (US) -ɚz **-ering/s** -ᵊr.ɪŋ/z **-ered** -əd (US) -ɚd **-erer/s** -ᵊr.əʳ/z (US) -ɚ.ɚ/z
wanderlust ˈwɒn.də.lʌst, ˈvɑːn.də.lʊst (US) ˈwɑːn.dɚ.lʌst
Wandle ˈwɒn.dl̩ (US) ˈwɑːn-
Wandsworth ˈwɒn*dz*.wəθ (US) ˈwɑːn*dz*.wɚθ
wan|e weɪn **-es** -z **-ing** -ɪŋ **-ed** -d
Wang® wæŋ
Wanganui *in New Zealand:* ˌwɒŋ.əˈnuː.i, ˌwɒn.gə- (US) ˌwɔːŋ.gə-, ˌwɑːn-
Note: The first is the form always used by those of Polynesian descent.
wangl|e ˈwæŋ.gl̩ **-es** -z **-ing** -ɪŋ (US) ˈwæŋ.glɪŋ **-ed** -d
wank wæŋk **-s** -s **-ing** -ɪŋ **-ed** -t
wanker ˈwæŋ.kəʳ (US) -kɚ **-s** -z
Wann wɒn (US) wɑːn
wanna ˈwɒn.ə (US) ˈwɑː.nə
wannabe(e) ˈwɒn.ə.bi, -biː (US) ˈwɑː.nə- **-s** -z
Wansbeck ˈwɒnz.bek (US) ˈwɑːnz-
Wanstall ˈwɒn.stɔːl (US) ˈwɑːn.stɑːl, -stɔːl
Wanstead ˈwɒn*t*.sted, -stɪd (US) ˈwɑːn*t*-
wan|t wɒn|t (US) wɑːn|t, wɔːn|t, wʌn|t **-ts** -ts **-ting** -tɪŋ (US) -t̬ɪŋ **-ted** -tɪd (US) -t̬ɪd
Wantage ˈwɒn.tɪdʒ (US) ˈwɑːn.t̬ɪdʒ
wanton ˈwɒn.tən (US) ˈwɑːn.tᵊn **-ly** -li **-ness** -nəs, -nɪs
WAP, Wap wæp, wɒp (US) wɑːp, wæp
wapentake ˈwæp.ən.teɪk, ˈwɒp- (US) ˈwɑː.pən-, ˈwæp.ən- **-s** -s
wapiti ˈwɒp.ɪ.ti (US) ˈwɑː.pə.t̬i **-s** -z
Wapping ˈwɒp.ɪŋ (US) ˈwɑː.pɪŋ
Wappinger ˈwɒp.ɪn.dʒəʳ (US) ˈwɑː.pɪn.dʒɚ
war wɔːʳ (US) wɔːr **-s** -z **-ring** -ɪŋ **-red** -d ˈ**war** ˌ**crime;** ˈ**war** ˌ**dance;** ˈ**war** ˌ**game;** ˈ**war me**ˌ**morial;** ˌ**war of** ˈ**nerves;** ˈ**war** ˌ**paint;** ˈ**war** ˌ**widow**
Warbeck ˈwɔː.bek (US) ˈwɔːr-
warbl|e ˈwɔː.bl̩ (US) ˈwɔːr- **-es** -z **-ing** -ɪŋ, ˈ-blɪŋ (US) ˈwɔːr.bl̩.ɪŋ, ˈ-blɪŋ **-ed** -d
warbler ˈwɔː.bləʳ, -bl̩.əʳ (US) ˈwɔːr.blɚ, -bl̩.ɚ **-s** -z
Warburg ˈwɔː.bɜːg (US) ˈwɔːr.bɝːg
Warburton ˈwɔː.bə.tᵊn, -bɜː- (US) ˈwɔːr.bɚ-, -bɝː-
war-cr|y ˈwɔː.kr|aɪ (US) ˈwɔːr- **-ies** -aɪz
ward (W) wɔːd (US) wɔːrd **-s** -z **-ing** -ɪŋ **-ed** -ɪd
-ward -wəd (US) -wɚd
Note: Suffix. Normally unstressed, e.g. **homeward** /ˈhəʊm.wəd (US) ˈhoʊm.wɚd/.
warden (W) ˈwɔː.dᵊn (US) ˈwɔːr- **-s** -z
warder (W) ˈwɔː.dəʳ (US) ˈwɔːr.dɚ **-s** -z
Wardlaw ˈwɔːd.lɔː (US) ˈwɔːrd.lɑː, -lɔː
Wardle ˈwɔː.dl̩ (US) ˈwɔːr-
Wardour ˈwɔː.dəʳ (US) ˈwɔːr.dɚ
wardress *fem. warder:* ˈwɔː.drɪs, -drəs (US) ˈwɔːr.drɪs **-es** -ɪz
war-dress *war costume:* ˈwɔː.dres (US) ˈwɔːr- **-es** -ɪz
wardrobe ˈwɔː.drəʊb (US) ˈwɔːr.droʊb **-s** -z
wardroom ˈwɔːd.rʊm, -ruːm (US) ˈwɔːrd.ruːm, -rʊm **-s** -z
-wards -wədz (US) -wɚdz
Note: See note for **-ward**.
wardship ˈwɔːd.ʃɪp (US) ˈwɔːrd- **-s** -s
ware (W) weəʳ (US) wer **-s** -z
-ware -weəʳ (US) -wer
Note: Suffix. Normally unstressed, e.g. **tableware** /ˈteɪ.bl̩.weəʳ (US) -wer/.
Wareham ˈweə.rəm (US) ˈwer.əm
warehou|se *(n.)* ˈweə.haʊ|s (US) ˈwer- **-ses** -zɪz
warehou|se *(v.)* ˈweə.haʊ|z, -haʊ|s (US) ˈwer- **-ses** -zɪz, -sɪz **-sing** -zɪŋ, -sɪŋ **-sed** -zd, -st
warehouse|man ˈweə.haʊs|.mən (US) ˈwer- **-men** -mən
warfare ˈwɔː.feəʳ (US) ˈwɔːr.fer
warfarin ˈwɔː.fᵊr.ɪn (US) ˈwɔːr-
Wargrave ˈwɔː.greɪv (US) ˈwɔːr-
Warham ˈwɔː.rəm (US) ˈwɔːr.əm
warhead ˈwɔː.hed (US) ˈwɔːr- **-s** -z
Warhol ˈwɔː.həʊl (US) ˈwɔːr.hɔːl, -hoʊl
warhors|e ˈwɔː.hɔːs (US) ˈwɔːr.hɔːrs **-es** -ɪz
Waring ˈweə.rɪŋ (US) ˈwer.ɪŋ
warlike ˈwɔː.laɪk (US) ˈwɔːr-
Warlingham ˈwɔː.lɪŋ.əm (US) ˈwɔːr-
warlock (W) ˈwɔː.lɒk (US) ˈwɔːr- **-s** -s
warlord ˈwɔː.lɔːd (US) ˈwɔːr.lɔːrd **-s** -z
warm wɔːm (US) wɔːrm **-er** -əʳ (US) -ɚ **-est** -ɪst, -əst **-ly** -li **-ness** -nəs, -nɪs **-s** -z **-ing** -ɪŋ **-ed** -d
warm-blooded ˌwɔːmˈblʌd.ɪd (US) ˌwɔːrm- **-ness** -nəs, -nɪs *stress shift:* ˌwarm-blooded ˈanimal
warmer ˈwɔː.məʳ (US) ˈwɔːr.mɚ **-s** -z
warm-hearted ˌwɔːmˈhɑː.tɪd (US) ˌwɔːrmˈhɑːr.t̬ɪd **-ly** -li **-ness** -nəs, -nɪs *stress shift:* ˌwarm-hearted ˈperson
warming-pan ˈwɔː.mɪŋ.pæn (US) ˈwɔːr- **-s** -z
Warmington ˈwɔː.mɪŋ.tən (US) ˈwɔːr-
Warminster ˈwɔː.mɪn*t*.stəʳ (US) ˈwɔːr.mɪn*t*.stɚ
warmong|er ˈwɔːˌmʌŋ.g|əʳ (US) ˈwɑːrˌmʌŋ.g|ɚ, ˈwɔːr-, -ˌmɑːŋ- **-ers** -əz (US) -ɚz **-ering** -ᵊr.ɪŋ
warmth wɔːm*p*θ (US) wɔːrm*p*θ
warn wɔːn (US) wɔːrn **-s** -z **-ing/ly** -ɪŋ/li **-ed** -d
Warne wɔːn (US) wɔːrn
Warner ˈwɔː.nəʳ (US) ˈwɔːr.nɚ
warning ˈwɔː.nɪŋ (US) ˈwɔːr- **-s** -z
Warnock ˈwɔː.nɒk (US) ˈwɔːr.nɑːk
warp wɔːp (US) wɔːrp **-s** -s **-ing** -ɪŋ **-ed** -t
warpath ˈwɔː.pɑːθ (US) ˈwɔːr.pæθ
warr|ant ˈwɒr|.ᵊnt (US) ˈwɔːr-, ˈwɑːr- **-ants** -ᵊnts **-anting** -ᵊn.tɪŋ (US) -ᵊn.t̬ɪŋ **-anted** -ᵊn.tɪd (US) -ᵊn.t̬ɪd **-anter/s** -ᵊn.təʳ/z (US) -ᵊn.t̬ɚ/z ˈ**warrant** ˌ**officer**
warrantab|le ˈwɒr.ᵊn.tə.bl̩ (US) ˈwɔːr.ᵊn.t̬ə-, ˈwɑːr- **-ly** -li **-leness** -l̩.nəs, -nɪs
warrantee ˌwɒr.ᵊnˈtiː (US) ˌwɔːr-, ˌwɑːr- **-s** -z
warrantor ˈwɒr.ᵊn.tɔːʳ, -təʳ, ˌwɒr.ᵊnˈtɔːʳ (US) ˈwɔːr.ᵊn.tɔːr, ˈwɑːr-, -t̬ɚ **-s** -z
warrant|y ˈwɒr.ᵊn.t|i (US) ˈwɔːr.ᵊn.t̬|i, ˈwɑːr- **-ies** -iz
Warre wɔːʳ (US) wɔːr
warren (W) ˈwɒr.ᵊn, -ɪn (US) ˈwɔːr.ᵊn, ˈwɑːr- **-s** -z
Warrender ˈwɒr.ən.dəʳ, -ɪn- (US) ˈwɔːr.ən.dɚ, ˈwɑːr-, -ɪn-
Warrenpoint ˈwɒr.ən.pɔɪnt, -əm- (US) ˈwɔːr.ən-, ˈwɑːr-
Warrington ˈwɒr.ɪŋ.tən (US) ˈwɔːr-, ˈwɑːr-
warrior (W) ˈwɒr.i.əʳ (US) ˈwɔːr.jɚ, ˈwɑːr-, -i.ɚ **-s** -z
Warrnambool ˈwɔː.nəm.buːl (US) ˈwɔːr-
Warsaw ˈwɔː.sɔː (US) ˈwɔːr.sɑː, -sɔː ˌ**Warsaw** ˈ**Pact**
warship ˈwɔː.ʃɪp (US) ˈwɔːr- **-s** -s
Warsop ˈwɔː.sɒp (US) ˈwɔːr-
Warspite ˈwɔː.spaɪt (US) ˈwɔːr-
wart wɔːt (US) wɔːrt **-s** -s **-y** -i (US) ˈwɔːr.t̬i
warthog ˈwɔːt.hɒg (US) ˈwɔːrt.hɑːg, -hɔːg **-s** -z
wartime ˈwɔː.taɪm (US) ˈwɔːr-
Warton ˈwɔː.tᵊn (US) ˈwɔːr-
war-weary ˈwɔːˌwɪə.ri (US) ˈwɔːrˌwɪr.i
Warwick *in Britain:* ˈwɒr.ɪk (US) ˈwɔːr.ɪk, ˈwɑːr- **-shire** -ʃəʳ, -ˌʃɪəʳ (US) -ʃɚ, -ˌʃɪr *in US:* ˈwɔː.wɪk (US) ˈwɔːr-
war-worn ˈwɔː.wɔːn (US) ˈwɔːr.wɔːrn
war|y ˈweə.r|i (US) ˈwer|.i **-ier** -i.əʳ (US) -i.ɚ **-iest** -i.ɪst, -i.əst **-ily** -ᵊl.i, -ɪ.li **-iness** -ɪ.nəs, -ɪ.nɪs

was *(from* **be***) strong forms:* wɒz ⓤⓢ wɑːz, wʌz *weak forms:* wəz, wz
Note: Weak form word. The strong forms are used in contrastive contexts (e.g. 'I don't know whether it **was** or it **wasn't**), and for emphasis (e.g. 'I **was** right!'). The strong form is also usual in final position (e.g. 'That's where it was'). The weak forms are used elsewhere; the form /wz/ is found only in rapid, casual speech.
Wasbrough 'wɒz.brə ⓤⓢ 'wɑːz-
wash (W) wɒʃ ⓤⓢ wɑːʃ, wɔːʃ **-es** -ɪz **-ing** -ɪŋ **-ed** -t **-able** -ə.bl̩ **ˌwash and 'wear**
Wash. *(abbrev. for* **Washington***)* 'wɒʃ.ɪŋ.tən ⓤⓢ 'wɑː.ʃɪŋ-, 'wɔː-
washbasin 'wɒʃˌbeɪ.sᵊn ⓤⓢ 'wɑːʃ-, 'wɔːʃ- **-s** -z
washboard 'wɒʃ.bɔːd ⓤⓢ 'wɑːʃ.bɔːrd, 'wɔːʃ- **-s** -z
washbowl 'wɒʃ.bəʊl ⓤⓢ 'wɑːʃ.boʊl, 'wɔːʃ- **-s** -z
wash|cloth 'wɒʃ|.klɒθ ⓤⓢ 'wɑːʃ|.klɑːθ, 'wɔːʃ- **-cloths** -klɒθs, -klɒðz ⓤⓢ -klɑːθs, -klɑːðz
washday 'wɒʃ.deɪ ⓤⓢ 'wɑːʃ-, 'wɔːʃ- **-s** -z
washed-out ˌwɒʃt'aʊt ⓤⓢ ˌwɑːʃt-, ˌwɔːʃt- *stress shift:* ˌwashed-out 'colour
washed-up ˌwɒʃt'ʌp ⓤⓢ ˌwɑːʃt-, ˌwɔːʃt- *stress shift:* ˌwashed-up 'writer
washer 'wɒʃ.əʳ ⓤⓢ 'wɑː.ʃɚ, 'wɔː- **-s** -z
washer-dryer ˌwɒʃ.ə'draɪ.əʳ ⓤⓢ ˌwɑː.ʃɚ'draɪ.ɚ, ˌwɔː- **-s** -z
washer-up ˌwɒʃ.əʳ'ʌp ⓤⓢ ˌwɑː.ʃɚ-, ˌwɔː- **washers-up** ˌwɒʃ.əz'- ⓤⓢ ˌwɑː.ʃɚz'-, ˌwɔː-
washer|woman 'wɒʃ.ə|ˌwʊm.ən ⓤⓢ 'wɑː.ʃɚ-, 'wɔː- **-women** -ˌwɪm.ɪn
wash-hou|se 'wɒʃ.haʊ|s ⓤⓢ 'wɑːʃ-, 'wɔːʃ- **-ses** -zɪz
washing 'wɒʃ.ɪŋ ⓤⓢ 'wɑː.ʃɪŋ, 'wɔː- **'washing maˌchine; 'washing ˌpowder**
Washingborough 'wɒʃ.ɪŋˌbʌr.ə ⓤⓢ 'wɑː.ʃɪŋ.bɚ.oʊ, 'wɔː-
Washington 'wɒʃ.ɪŋ.tən ⓤⓢ 'wɑː.ʃɪŋ-, 'wɔː- **ˌWashington ˌD'C; ˌWashington 'State**
Washingtonian ˌwɒʃ.ɪŋ'təʊ.ni.ən ⓤⓢ ˌwɑː.ʃɪŋ'toʊ-, ˌwɔː- **-s** -z
washing-up ˌwɒʃ.ɪŋ'ʌp ⓤⓢ ˌwɑː.ʃɪŋ'-, ˌwɔː-
washout 'wɒʃ.aʊt ⓤⓢ 'wɑːʃ-, 'wɔːʃ- **-s** -s
washrag 'wɒʃ.ræg ⓤⓢ 'wɑːʃ-, 'wɔːʃ- **-s** -z
washroom 'wɒʃ.rʊm, -ruːm ⓤⓢ 'wɑːʃ.ruːm, 'wɔːʃ-, -rʊm **-s** -z
washstand 'wɒʃ.stænd ⓤⓢ 'wɑːʃ-, 'wɔːʃ- **-s** -z
wash-tub 'wɒʃ.tʌb ⓤⓢ 'wɑːʃ-, 'wɔːʃ- **-s** -z
wash|y 'wɒʃ|.i ⓤⓢ 'wɑː.ʃ|i, 'wɔː- **-ier** -i.əʳ ⓤⓢ -i.ɚ **-iest** -i.ɪst, -i.əst **-iness** -ɪ.nəs, -ɪ.nɪs
wasn't 'wɒz.ᵊnt ⓤⓢ 'wɑː.zᵊnt, 'wʌz-
wasp, WASP (W) wɒsp ⓤⓢ wɑːsp **-s** -s
waspish 'wɒs.pɪʃ ⓤⓢ 'wɑː.spɪʃ **-ly** -li **-ness** -nəs, -nɪs
wassail 'wɒs.eɪl, 'wæs-, -ᵊl ⓤⓢ 'wɑː.sᵊl, 'wæs.ᵊl, -eɪl; wɑː'seɪl **-s** -z
wassailing 'wɒs.ᵊl.ɪŋ, 'wæs-, -eɪ.lɪŋ ⓤⓢ 'wɑː.sᵊl.ɪŋ, 'wæs.ᵊl-, -eɪ.lɪŋ; wɑː'seɪ.lɪŋ
Wassell 'wæs.ᵊl
Wasson 'wɒs.ᵊn ⓤⓢ 'wɑː.sᵊn
wast *(from* **be***) strong forms:* wɒst ⓤⓢ wɑːst *weak form:* wəst
Wast wɒst ⓤⓢ wɑːst
wast|e weɪst **-es** -s **-ing** -ɪŋ **-ed** -ɪd **-er/s** -əʳ/z ⓤⓢ -ɚ/z **-age** -ɪdʒ **'waste ˌproduct, ˌwaste 'product**
wastebasket 'weɪst*t*ˌbɑː.skɪt ⓤⓢ -ˌbæs.kət **-s** -s
wasteful 'weɪst*t*.fᵊl, -fʊl **-ly** -i **-ness** -nəs, -nɪs
wasteland 'weɪst*t*.lænd **-s** -z
wastepaper ˌweɪst*t*'peɪ.pəʳ, '-ˌ-- ⓤⓢ 'weɪst*t*ˌpeɪ.pɚ **waste'paper ˌbasket, 'wastepaper ˌbasket; waste'paper ˌbin**
wastepipe 'weɪst*t*.paɪp **-s** -s
wastrel 'weɪ.strᵊl **-s** -z
Wastwater 'wɒstˌwɔː.təʳ ⓤⓢ 'wɑːstˌwɑː.t̬ɚ, -ˌwɔː-
Wat wɒt ⓤⓢ wɑːt
watch wɒtʃ ⓤⓢ wɑːtʃ, wɔːtʃ **-es** -ɪz **-ing** -ɪŋ **-ed** -t **-er/s** -əʳ/z ⓤⓢ -ɚ/z
watchable 'wɒtʃ.ə.bl̩ ⓤⓢ 'wɑː.tʃə-, 'wɔː-
watchamacallit 'wɒtʃ.ə.məˌkɔːl.ɪt ⓤⓢ 'wɑː.tʃə-, 'wɔː-, -ˌkɑːl- **-s** -s
watch-cas|e 'wɒtʃ.keɪs ⓤⓢ 'wɑːtʃ-, 'wɔːtʃ- **-es** -ɪz
watchdog 'wɒtʃ.dɒg ⓤⓢ 'wɑːtʃ.dɑːg, 'wɔːtʃ-, -dɔːg **-s** -z
Watchet 'wɒtʃ.ɪt ⓤⓢ 'wɑː.tʃɪt, 'wɔː-
watchful 'wɒtʃ.fᵊl, -fʊl ⓤⓢ 'wɑːtʃ-, 'wɔːtʃ- **-ly** -i **-ness** -nəs, -nɪs
watchmak|er 'wɒtʃˌmeɪ.k|əʳ ⓤⓢ 'wɑːtʃˌmeɪ.k|ɚ, 'wɔːtʃ- **-ers** -əz ⓤⓢ -ɚz **-ing** -ɪŋ
watch|man 'wɒtʃ|.mən ⓤⓢ 'wɑːtʃ-, 'wɔːtʃ- **-men** -mən, -men
watchstrap 'wɒtʃ.stræp ⓤⓢ 'wɑːtʃ-, 'wɔːtʃ- **-s** -s
watchtower (W) 'wɒtʃ.taʊəʳ ⓤⓢ 'wɑːtʃ.taʊɚ, 'wɔːtʃ- **-s** -z
watchword 'wɒtʃ.wɜːd ⓤⓢ 'wɑːtʃ.wɝːd, 'wɔːtʃ- **-s** -z
wat|er 'wɔː.t|əʳ ⓤⓢ 'wɑː.t̬|ɚ, 'wɔː- **-ers** -əz ⓤⓢ -ɚz **-ering** -ᵊr.ɪŋ **-ered** -əd ⓤⓢ -ɚd **'water ˌbed; 'water ˌbeetle; 'water ˌbottle; 'water ˌbuffalo,; ˌwater 'buffalo** ⓤⓢ **'water ˌbuffalo; 'water ˌcannon; ˌwater 'chestnut** ⓤⓢ **'water ˌchestnut; 'water ˌcloset; 'water ˌice; 'water ˌmain; 'water ˌmeadow; 'water ˌmill; 'water supˌply; 'water ˌtable; 'water ˌtower; ˌkeep one's ˌhead above 'water; ˌpour cold 'water on; like ˌwater off a ˌduck's 'back;** ⓤⓢ **like ˌwater off a 'duck's ˌback; ˌwater ˌunder the 'bridge**
water-borne 'wɔː.tə.bɔːn ⓤⓢ 'wɑː.t̬ɚ.bɔːrn, 'wɔː-
waterbuck 'wɔː.tə.bʌk ⓤⓢ 'wɑː.t̬ɚ-, 'wɔː-
Waterbur|y 'wɔː.tə.bᵊr|.i ⓤⓢ 'wɑː.t̬ɚ.ber-, 'wɔː-, -bɚ- **-ies** -iz
water-chute 'wɔː.tə.ʃuːt ⓤⓢ 'wɑː.t̬ɚ-, 'wɔː- **-s** -s
watercolo(u)r 'wɔː.təˌkʌl.əʳ ⓤⓢ 'wɑː.t̬ɚˌkʌl.ɚ, 'wɔː- **-s** -z
watercolo(u)rist 'wɔː.təˌkʌl.ᵊr.ɪst ⓤⓢ 'wɑː.t̬ɚ-, 'wɔː- **-s** -s
water-cooled ˌwɔː.tə'kuːld ⓤⓢ 'wɑː.t̬ɚ.kuːld, 'wɔː- *stress shift, British only:* ˌwater-cooled 'engines
watercours|e 'wɔː.tə.kɔːs ⓤⓢ 'wɑː.t̬ɚ.kɔːrs, 'wɔː- **-es** -ɪz
watercress 'wɔː.tə.kres ⓤⓢ 'wɑː.t̬ɚ-, 'wɔː-
water-divin|ing 'wɔː.tə.dɪˌvaɪ.n|ɪŋ, -dəˌ- ⓤⓢ 'wɑː.t̬ɚ-, 'wɔː- **-er/s** -əʳ/z ⓤⓢ -ɚ/z
watered-down ˌwɔː.təd'daʊn ⓤⓢ ˌwɑː.t̬ɚd'-, ˌwɔː- *stress shift:* ˌwatered-down 'rum
waterfall 'wɔː.tə.fɔːl ⓤⓢ 'wɑː.t̬ɚ.fɔːl, 'wɔː-, -fɑːl **-s** -z
water-finder 'wɔː.təˌfaɪn.dəʳ ⓤⓢ 'wɑː.t̬ɚˌfaɪn.dɚ, 'wɔː- **-s** -z
Waterford 'wɔː.tə.fəd ⓤⓢ 'wɑː.t̬ɚ.fɚd, 'wɔː-
waterfowl 'wɔː.tə.faʊl ⓤⓢ 'wɑː.t̬ɚ-, 'wɔː- **-s** -z **-er/s** -əʳ/z ⓤⓢ -ɚ/z
waterfront 'wɔː.tə.frʌnt ⓤⓢ 'wɑː.t̬ɚ-, 'wɔː- **-s** -s
Watergate 'wɔː.tə.geɪt ⓤⓢ 'wɑː.t̬ɚ-, 'wɔː-
waterhole 'wɔː.tə.həʊl ⓤⓢ 'wɑː.t̬ɚ.hoʊl, 'wɔː- **-s** -z
Waterhouse 'wɔː.tə.haʊs ⓤⓢ 'wɑː.t̬ɚ-, 'wɔː-
wateriness 'wɔː.tᵊr.ɪ.nəs, -nəs ⓤⓢ 'wɑː.t̬ɚ-, 'wɔː-
watering-can 'wɔː.tᵊr.ɪŋ.kæn ⓤⓢ 'wɑː.t̬ɚ-, 'wɔː- **-s** -z
watering-hole 'wɔː.tᵊr.ɪŋ.həʊl ⓤⓢ 'wɑː.t̬ɚ.ɪŋ.hoʊl, 'wɔː- **-s** -z

watering-plac|e ˈwɔː.tᵊr.ɪŋ.pleɪs (US) ˈwɑː.t̬ɚ-, ˈwɔː- **-es** -ɪz
waterless ˈwɔː.tᵊl.əs, -lɪs (US) ˈwɑː.t̬ɚ.ləs, ˈwɔː-
water-level ˈwɔː.tə,lev.ᵊl (US) ˈwɑː.t̬ɚ-, ˈwɔː- **-s** -z
water-lil|y ˈwɔː.tə,lɪl|.i (US) ˈwɑː.t̬ɚ-, ˈwɔː- **-ies** -iz
water-line ˈwɔː.tə.laɪn (US) ˈwɑː.t̬ɚ-, ˈwɔː- **-s** -z
waterlog ˈwɔː.tə.lɒg (US) ˈwɑː.t̬ɚ.lɑːg, ˈwɔː-, -lɔːg **-s** -z **-ging** -ɪŋ **-ged** -d
waterlogged ˈwɔː.tə.lɒgd (US) ˈwɑː.t̬ɚ.lɑːgd, ˈwɔː-, -lɔːgd
waterloo (W) ,wɔː.təˈluː (US) ˈwɑː.t̬ɚ-, ˈwɔː-, ,--ˈ- **-s** -z *stress shift, British only:* ,Waterloo ˈBridge
Waterlooville ,wɔː.təˈluː.vɪl, ,wɔː.tᵊl.uːˈvɪl (US) ,wɑː.t̬ɚ.luːˈ-, ,wɔː-, ˈwɑː.t̬ɚ.luː.vɪl
water|man (W) ˈwɔː.tə|.mən (US) ˈwɔː- (US) ˈwɑː.t̬ɚ- **-men** -mən, -men
watermark ˈwɔː.tə.mɑːk (US) ˈwɑː.t̬ɚ.mɑːrk, ˈwɔː- **-s** -s **-ing** -ɪŋ **-ed** -t
watermelon ˈwɔː.tə,mel.ən (US) ˈwɑː.t̬ɚ-, ˈwɔː- **-s** -z
watermill ˈwɔː.tə.mɪl (US) ˈwɑː.tɚ-, ˈwɔː- **-s** -z
water-nymph ˈwɔː.tə.nɪm*p*f (US) ˈwɑː.t̬ɚ-, ˈwɔː- **-s** -s
waterpolo ˈwɔː.tə,pəʊ.ləʊ (US) ˈwɑː.t̬ɚ,poʊ.loʊ, ˈwɔː-
waterproof ˈwɔː.tə.pruːf (US) ˈwɑː.t̬ɚ-, ˈwɔː- **-s** -s **-ing** -ɪŋ **-ed** -t
water-resistant ˈwɔː.tə.rɪ,zɪs.tənt, -rə- (US) ˈwɑː.t̬ɚ-, ˈwɔː-
Waters ˈwɔː.təz (US) ˈwɑː.t̬ɚz, ˈwɔː-
watershed ˈwɔː.tə.ʃed (US) ˈwɑː.t̬ɚ-, ˈwɔː- **-s** -z
Watership ˈwɔː.tə.ʃɪp (US) ˈwɑː.t̬ɚ-, ˈwɔː-
watersid|e ˈwɔː.tə.saɪd (US) ˈwɑː.t̬ɚ-, ˈwɔː- **-er/s** -əʳ/z (US) -ɚ/z
water-ski ˈwɔː.tə.skiː (US) ˈwɑː.t̬ɚ-, ˈwɔː- **-s** -z **-ing** -ɪŋ **-ed** -d **-er/s** -əʳ/z (US) -ɚ/z
watersport ˈwɔː.tə.spɔːt (US) ˈwɑː.t̬ɚ.spɔːrt, ˈwɔː- **-s** -s
waterspout ˈwɔː.tə.spaʊt (US) ˈwɑː.t̬ɚ-, ˈwɔː- **-s** -s
Waterstone ˈwɔː.tə.stəʊn (US) ˈwɑː.t̬ɚ.stoʊn, ˈwɔː-, -stən **'s** -z
watertight ˈwɔː.tə.taɪt (US) ˈwɑː.t̬ɚ-, ˈwɔː-
waterway ˈwɔː.tə.weɪ (US) ˈwɑː.t̬ɚ-, ˈwɔː- **-s** -z
waterwheel ˈwɔː.tə.*h*wiːl (US) ˈwɑː.t̬ɚ-, ˈwɔː- **-s** -z
waterwings ˈwɔː.tə.wɪŋz (US) ˈwɑː.tɚ-, ˈwɔː-
waterworks ˈwɔː.tə.wɜːks (US) ˈwɑː.t̬ɚ.wɝːks, ˈwɔː-
water|y ˈwɔː.tᵊr|.i, -tr|i (US) ˈwɑː.t̬ɚ|.i, ˈwɔː- **-iness** -ɪ.nəs, -ɪ.nɪs
Watford ˈwɒt.fəd (US) ˈwɑːt.fɚd
Wath upon Dearne ,wɒθ.ə,pɒnˈdɜːn, ,wæθ- (US) ,wɑːθ.ə,pɑːnˈdɝːn, ,wæθ-
Watkin ˈwɒt.kɪn (US) ˈwɑːt- **-s** -z
Watling ˈwɒt.lɪŋ (US) ˈwɑːt-
Watson ˈwɒt.sᵊn (US) ˈwɑːt-
watt (W) wɒt (US) wɑːt **-s** -s
wattag|e ˈwɒt.ɪdʒ (US) ˈwɑː.t̬ɪdʒ **-es** -ɪz
Watteau ˈwɒt.əʊ (US) wɑːˈtoʊ
Watters ˈwɔː.təz, ˈwɒt.əz (US) ˈwɑː.t̬ɚz, ˈwɔː-
Watterson ˈwɔː.tə.sᵊn, ˈwɒt.ə- (US) ˈwɑː.t̬ɚ-, ˈwɔː-
wattle ˈwɒt.l̩ (US) ˈwɑː.t̬l̩ **-s** -z **-d** -d
wattmeter ˈwɒt,miː.təʳ (US) ˈwɑːt,miː.t̬ɚ **-s** -z
Watton ˈwɒt.ᵊn (US) ˈwɑː.tᵊn
Wauchope ˈwɔː.kəp, ˈwɒx.əp (US) ˈwɑː.kəp, ˈwɔː-
Waugh wɔː, wɒx, wɒf, wɑːf (US) wɑː, wɔː
Note: /wɔː (US) wɑː, wɔː/ are the appropriate pronunciations for authors Auberon and Evelyn Waugh.
wav|e weɪv **-es** -z **-ing** -ɪŋ **-ed** -d **-eless** -ləs, -lɪs
waveband ˈweɪv.bænd **-s** -z
waveform ˈweɪv.fɔːm (US) -fɔːrm **-s** -z
wavelength ˈweɪv.leŋ*k*θ **-s** -s
wavelet ˈweɪv.lət, -lɪt **-s** -s
Wavell ˈweɪ.vᵊl
Waveney ˈweɪv.ni
wav|er ˈweɪ.v|əʳ (US) -v|ɚ **-ers** -əz (US) -ɚz **-ering/ly** -ᵊr.ɪŋ/li **-ered** -əd (US) -ɚd **-erer/s** -ᵊr.əʳ/z (US) -ɚ.ɚ/z
Waverley ˈweɪ.vᵊl.i (US) -vɚ.li
wav|y ˈweɪ.v|i **-ier** -i.əʳ (US) -i.ɚ **-iest** -i.ɪst, -i.əst **-ily** -ɪ.li, -ᵊl.i **-iness** -ɪ.nəs, -ɪ.nɪs
wax wæks **-es** -ɪz **-ing** -ɪŋ **-ed** -t **-en** -ᵊn
waxhead ˈwæks.hed **-s** -z
waxwing ˈwæks.wɪŋ **-s** -z
waxwork ˈwæks.wɜːk (US) -wɝːk **-s** -s
wax|y ˈwæk.s|i **-ier** -i.əʳ (US) -i.ɚ **-iest** -i.ɪst, -i.əst **-iness** -ɪ.nəs, -ɪ.nɪs
way (W) weɪ **-s** -z **,right of ˈway** (US) **ˈright of ,way; ,ways and ˈmeans**
waybill ˈweɪ.bɪl **-s** -z
wayfar|er ˈweɪ,feə.r|əʳ (US) -,fer|.ɚ **-ers** -əz (US) -ɚz **-ing** -ɪŋ
Wayland ˈweɪ.lənd
way|lay ,weɪ|ˈleɪ (US) ˈweɪ|.leɪ, -ˈ- **-lays** -ˈleɪz (US) -leɪz, -ˈleɪz **-laying** -ˈleɪ.ɪŋ (US) -,leɪ.ɪŋ, -ˈleɪ.ɪŋ **-laid** -ˈleɪd (US) -leɪd, -ˈleɪd **-layer/s** -ˈleɪ.əʳ/z (US) -,leɪ.ɚ/z, -ˈleɪ.ɚ/z
Wayman ˈweɪ.mən
Wayne weɪn
Waynflete ˈweɪn.fliːt
way-out *unusual and daring:* ,weɪˈaʊt *stress shift:* ,way-out ˈclothes
way out *exit:* ,weɪˈaʊt
-ways -weɪz, -wɪz
Note: Suffix. Normally unstressed, e.g. **lengthways** /ˈleŋ*k*θ.weɪz/.
wayside ˈweɪ.saɪd **,fall by the ˈwayside**
wayward ˈweɪ.wəd (US) -wɚd **-ly** -li **-ness** -nəs, -nɪs
wazoo wæzˈuː, wəˈzuː (US) wɑːˈzuː **-s** -z
wazzock ˈwæz.ək **-s** -s
WC ,dʌb.l̩.juːˈsiː, -jʊ- (US) -juːˈ-, -jəˈ- **-s** -z
we *strong form:* wiː *weak form:* wi
Note: Weak form word. The strong form is used contrastively (e.g. 'We, not they, will win it') or for emphasis (e.g. '**We** are the winners'). It is also used in final position (e.g. 'So are we'). The weak form is used elsewhere.
weak wiːk **-er** -əʳ (US) -ɚ **-est** -ɪst, -əst **-ly** -li **,weak at the ˈknees**
weaken ˈwiː.kᵊn **-s** -z **-ing** -ɪŋ, ˈwiːk.nɪŋ **-ed** -d
weak-kneed ,wiːkˈniːd (US) ˈwiːk.niːd *stress shift, British only:* ,weak-kneed ˈcoward
weakling ˈwiː.klɪŋ **-s** -z
weak-minded ,wiːkˈmaɪn.dɪd **-ness** -nəs, -nɪs *stress shift:* ,weak-minded ˈperson
weakness ˈwiːk.nəs, -nɪs **-es** -ɪz
weal wiːl **-s** -z
weald (W) wiːld **-s** -z
wealden (W) ˈwiːl.dᵊn
Wealdstone ˈwiːld.stəʊn (US) -stoʊn
wealth welθ
wealth|y ˈwel.θ|i **-ier** -i.əʳ (US) -i.ɚ **-iest** -i.ɪst, -i.əst **-ily** -ɪ.li, -ᵊl.i **-iness** -ɪ.nəs, -ɪ.nɪs
wean *child or baby:* weɪn **-s** -z
wean *withdraw mother's milk:* wiːn **-s** -z **-ing** -ɪŋ **-ed** -d
weaner ˈwiː.nəʳ (US) -nɚ **-s** -z
weanling ˈwiːn.lɪŋ **-s** -z
weapon ˈwep.ən **-s** -z **-less** -ləs, -lɪs **-ry** -ri
wear (*v.*) weəʳ (US) wer **-s** -z **-ing** -ɪŋ **wore** wɔːʳ (US) wɔːr **worn** wɔːn (US) wɔːrn **wearer/s** ˈweə.rəʳ/z (US) ˈwer.ɚ/z **,wear and ˈtear**
Wear *river:* wɪəʳ (US) wɪr
wearability ,weə.rəˈbɪl.ə.ti, -ɪ.ti (US) ,wer.əˈbɪl.ə.t̬i
wearable ˈweə.rə.bl̩ (US) ˈwer.ə-
Wearing ˈweə.rɪŋ (US) ˈwer.ɪŋ
wearisome ˈwɪə.rɪ.sᵊm (US) ˈwɪr.ɪ- **-ly** -li **-ness** -nəs, -nɪs
Wearmouth ˈwɪə.məθ, -maʊθ (US) ˈwɪr-

Weak form

A variant form of a word, used when it is unstressed.

Examples for English

A very important aspect of the dynamics of English pronunciation is that many very common words have not only a 'strong' or 'full' pronunciation (which is used when the word is said in isolation), but also one or more weak forms which are used when the word occurs in certain contexts. Words which have weak forms are, for the most part, function words such as conjunctions (e.g. and, but), articles (e.g. a, the), pronouns (e.g. she, he her), prepositions (e.g. for, to) and some auxiliary and modal verbs (e.g. do, must). Generally the strong form of such words is used when the word is being quoted (e.g. the word *and* is given its strong form in the sentence 'We use the word and to join clauses'), when it is being contrasted (e.g. *for* in 'There are arguments for and against') and when it is at the end of a sentence (e.g. *from* in 'Where did you get it from?'). Often the pronunciation of a weak-form word is so different from its strong form that if it were heard in isolation it would be impossible to recognise it: for example, *and* can become /n̩/ in *us and them, fish and chips*, and *of* can become /f/ or /v/ in *of course*. The reason for this is that to someone who knows the language well these words are usually highly predictable in their normal context.

Wearn wɜːn Ⓤⓢ wɝːn
wear|y 'wɪə.r|i Ⓤⓢ 'wɪr|.i **-ier** -i.əʳ Ⓤⓢ -i.ɚ **-iest** -i.ɪst, -i.əst **-ily** -ᵊl.i, -ɪ.li **-iness** -ɪ.nəs, -ɪ.nɪs **-ies** -iz **-ying** -i.ɪŋ **-ied** -id
weasel 'wiː.zᵊl **-s** -z
weaselly 'wiː.zᵊl.i, 'wiːz.li
weath|er 'weð|.əʳ Ⓤⓢ -ɚ **-ers** -əz Ⓤⓢ -ɚz **-ering** -ᵊr.ɪŋ **-ered** -əd Ⓤⓢ -ɚd **'weather ˌforecast; make ˌheavy 'weather of ˌsomething**
weather-beaten 'weð.əˌbiː.tᵊn Ⓤⓢ -ɚˌ-
weatherboard 'weð.ə.bɔːd Ⓤⓢ -ɚ.bɔːrd **-s** -z **-ing** -ɪŋ
weather-bound 'weð.ə.baʊnd Ⓤⓢ '-ɚ-
weathercock 'weð.ə.kɒk Ⓤⓢ -ɚ.kɑːk **-s** -s
weather-eye 'weð.əʳ.aɪ, ˌ--'- Ⓤⓢ 'weð.ɚ.aɪ **-s** -z **ˌkeep a 'weather-eye open for something**
weather-glass 'weð.ə.glɑːs Ⓤⓢ -ɚ.glæs **-es** -ɪz
Weatherhead 'weð.ə.hed Ⓤⓢ '-ɚ-
weatherly (W) 'weð.ᵊl.i Ⓤⓢ -ɚ.li
weather|man 'weð.ə|.mæn Ⓤⓢ '-ɚ- **-men** -men
weatherproof 'weð.ə.pruːf Ⓤⓢ '-ɚ-
weathership 'weð.ə.ʃɪp Ⓤⓢ '-ɚ- **-s** -s
weathervane 'weð.ə.veɪn Ⓤⓢ '-ɚ- **-s** -z
weather-wise 'weð.ə.waɪz Ⓤⓢ '-ɚ-
weather-worn 'weð.ə.wɔːn Ⓤⓢ -ɚ.wɔːrn
Weatly 'wiːt.li
weav|e wiːv **-es** -z **-ing** -ɪŋ **-ed** -d **wove** wəʊv Ⓤⓢ woʊv **woven** 'wəʊ.vᵊn Ⓤⓢ 'woʊ-
weaver (W) 'wiː.vəʳ Ⓤⓢ -vɚ **-s** -z
Weaverham 'wiː.və.hæm, -vᵊr.əm Ⓤⓢ -vɚ.hæm, -əm
web web **-s** -z
web-based 'web.beɪst
Webb(e) web
webbed webd **ˌwebbed 'feet**
Webber 'web.əʳ Ⓤⓢ -ɚ
webb|ing 'webl.ɪŋ **-y** -i
webcam 'web.kæm **-s** -z
webcast 'web.kɑːst Ⓤⓢ -kæst **-s** -s **-ing** -ɪŋ
Weber *English name:* 'web.əʳ, 'weɪ.bəʳ, 'wiː- Ⓤⓢ 'web.ɚ, 'weɪ.bɚ, 'wiː- *German composer:* 'veɪ.bəʳ Ⓤⓢ -bɚ
Webern 'veɪ.bɜːn Ⓤⓢ -bɚn
webfooted ˌweb'fʊt.ɪd, 'webˌfʊt̬.ɪd *stress shift, British only:* ˌwebfooted 'bird
webmaster 'webˌmɑː.stəʳ Ⓤⓢ -ˌmæs.tɚ **-s** -z
webpag|e 'web.peɪdʒ **-es** -ɪz
website 'web.saɪt **-s** -s
Webster 'web.stəʳ Ⓤⓢ -stɚ **-s** -z
we'd (= **we had, we would**) *strong form:* wiːd *weak form:* wid
Note: Weak form word. The weak form is used when the word is unstressed (e.g. 'We'd be silly to do it' /wid.bi'sɪl.i.təˌduː.ɪt/).
wed wed **-s** -z **-ding** -ɪŋ **-ded** -ɪd
Wed. *(abbrev. for* **Wednesday***)* 'wenz.deɪ, 'wed.ᵊnz-, -di Ⓤⓢ 'wenz.deɪ, -di
Note: This abbreviation may also be pronounced /wed/ in British English.
Weddell *surname:* wə'del, 'wed.ᵊl *Sea:* 'wed.ᵊl
Wedderburn 'wed.ə.bɜːn Ⓤⓢ -ɚ.bɝːn
wedding 'wed.ɪŋ **-s** -z **'wedding ˌbreakfast; 'wedding ˌcake; 'wedding ˌday; 'wedding ˌdress; 'wedding ˌmarch; 'wedding ˌring**
Wedekind 'veɪ.də.kɪnd, -kɪnt Ⓤⓢ -kɪnt, -kɪnd
wedg|e wedʒ **-es** -ɪz **-ing** -ɪŋ **-ed** -d **-ewise** -waɪz
wedge-shaped 'wedʒ.ʃeɪpt
Wedg(e)wood 'wedʒ.wʊd
wedlock 'wed.lɒk Ⓤⓢ -lɑːk
Wednesbury 'wenz.bᵊr.i *locally also:* 'wedʒ- Ⓤⓢ 'wenz.bɚ-
Wednesday 'wenz.deɪ, 'wed.nz-, -di Ⓤⓢ 'wenz.deɪ, -di **-s** -z
Wednesfield 'wenz.fiːld *locally also:* 'wedʒ- Ⓤⓢ 'wenz-
Weds. *(abbrev. for* **Wednesday***)* 'wenz.deɪ, 'wed.nz-, -di Ⓤⓢ 'wenz.deɪ, -di
Note: This abbreviation may also be pronounced /wedz/ in British English.
wee wiː
weed wiːd **-s** -z **-ing** -ɪŋ **-ed** -ɪd
weedkiller 'wiːdˌkɪl.əʳ Ⓤⓢ -ɚ **-s** -z
Weedon 'wiː.dᵊn
weed|y 'wiː.d|i **-ier** -i.əʳ Ⓤⓢ -i.ɚ **-iest** -i.ɪst, -i.əst **-iness** -ɪ.nəs, -ɪ.nɪs
week wiːk **-s** -s
weekday 'wiːk.deɪ **-s** -z
weekend ˌwiːk'end, '-- Ⓤⓢ 'wiːk.end **-s** -z *stress shift, British only:* ˌweekend 'traffic
weekender ˌwiːk'en.dəʳ Ⓤⓢ 'wiːk.ˌen.dɚ **-s** -z
Weekes wiːks
Weekl(e)y 'wiː.kli
weekl|y *(n. adv.)* 'wiː.kl|i **-ies** -iz
weeknight 'wiːk.naɪt **-s** -s
Weeks wiːks
Weelkes wiːlks
ween wiːn **-s** -z **-ing** -ɪŋ **-ed** -d
ween|y 'wiː.n|i **-ies** -iz **-ier** -i.əʳ Ⓤⓢ -i.ɚ **-iest** -i.ɪst, -i.əst
weenybopper 'wiː.niˌbɒp.əʳ Ⓤⓢ -ˌbɑː.pɚ **-s** -z
weep wiːp **-s** -s **-ing** -ɪŋ **wept** wept
weeper 'wiː.pəʳ Ⓤⓢ -pɚ **-s** -z
weepie 'wiː.pi **-s** -z
weep|y 'wiː.p|i **-ier** -i.əʳ Ⓤⓢ -i.ɚ **-iest** -i.ɪst, -i.əst **-ily** -ɪ.li, -ᵊl.i **-iness** -ɪ.nəs, -ɪ.nɪs

Weetabix® ˈwiː.tə.bɪks
weever ˈwiː.vəʳ ⓤⓢ -vɚ **-s** -z
weevil ˈwiː.vəl, -vɪl ⓤⓢ -vəl **-s** -z
wee-wee ˈwiː.wiː **-s** -z **-ing** -ɪŋ **-d** -d
weft weft
Weidenfeld ˈvaɪ.dən.felt, ˈwaɪ-
Weigall ˈwaɪ.gɔːl
weigela waɪˈdʒiː.lə, -ˈgiː- ⓤⓢ waɪˈgiː-, -ˈjiː-; ˈwaɪ.gə- **-s** -z
weigelia waɪˈdʒiː.li.ə, -ˈgiː- ⓤⓢ waɪˈgiː- **-s** -z
weigh weɪ **-s** -z **-ing** -ɪŋ **-ed** -d **-able** -ə.bl̩
weighbridg|e ˈweɪ.brɪdʒ **-es** -ɪz
weight weɪt **-s** -s **-ing** -ɪŋ ⓤⓢ ˈweɪ.t̬ɪŋ **-ed** -ɪd ⓤⓢ ˈweɪ.t̬ɪd **ˈweight ˌtraining**
weightless ˈweɪt.ləs, -lɪs **-ly** -li **-ness** -nəs, -nɪs
weightlift|ing ˈweɪtˌlɪf.t|ɪŋ **-er/s** -əʳ/z ⓤⓢ -ɚ/z
Weighton *in* ***Market Weighton,*** *Humberside* ˈwiː.tən
WeightWatchers® ˈweɪtˌwɒtʃ.əz ⓤⓢ -ˌwɑː.tʃɚz
weightwatch|ing ˈweɪtˌwɒtʃ|.ɪŋ ⓤⓢ -ˌwɑː.tʃ|ɪŋ **-er/s** -əʳ/z ⓤⓢ -ɚ/z
weight|y ˈweɪ.t|i ⓤⓢ -t̬|i **-ier** -i.əʳ ⓤⓢ -i.ɚ **-iest** -i.ɪst, -i.əst **-ily** -ɪ.li, -əl.i **-iness** -ɪ.nəs, -ɪ.nɪs
Weill *English surname:* wiːl, vaɪl *German composer:* vaɪl
Weimar ˈvaɪ.mɑːʳ ⓤⓢ -mɑːr
Weinberger ˈwaɪnˌbɜː.gəʳ, ˈwaɪm- ⓤⓢ ˈwaɪnˌbɝː.gɚ
weir (W) wɪəʳ **weir** ⓤⓢ wɪr **-s** -z
weird wɪəd ⓤⓢ wɪrd **-er** -əʳ ⓤⓢ -ɚ **-est** -ɪst, -əst **-ly** -li **-ness** -nəs, -nɪs
weirdo ˈwɪə.dəʊ ⓤⓢ ˈwɪr.doʊ **-s** -z
Weiss vaɪs
Weisshorn ˈvaɪs.hɔːn ⓤⓢ -hɔːrn
Weissmuller ˈvaɪsˌmʊl.əʳ, ˈwaɪs- ⓤⓢ ˈwaɪsˌmʌl.ɚ
Weland ˈweɪ.lənd, ˈwiː-
Welbeck ˈwel.bek
Welby ˈwel.bi
welch (W) (*v. adj.*) welt*ʃ* **-es** -ɪz **-ing** -ɪŋ **-ed** -t **-er/s** -əʳ/z ⓤⓢ -ɚ/z
Welcombe ˈwel.kəm
welcom|e ˈwel.kəm **-es** -z **-ing** -ɪŋ **-ed** -d
weld weld **-s** -z **-ing** -ɪŋ **-ed** -ɪd **-er/s** -əʳ/z ⓤⓢ -ɚ/z
Weldon ˈwel.dən
welfare ˈwel.feəʳ ⓤⓢ -fer **ˌwelfare ˈstate** ⓤⓢ **ˈwelfare ˌstate**
Welford ˈwel.fəd ⓤⓢ -fɚd
welkin ˈwel.kɪn
we'll *(=* **we will, we shall***) strong form:* wiːl *weak form:* wil
Note: Weak form word. The weak form is used when the word is unstressed (e.g. 'We'll write today' /wilˌraɪt.təˈdeɪ/).

well wel **-s** -z **-ing** -ɪŋ **-ed** -d **-ness** -nəs, -nɪs
well-advised ˌwel.ədˈvaɪzd *stress shift:* ˌwell-advised ˈaction
Welland ˈwel.ənd
well-appointed ˌwel.əˈpɔɪn.tɪd ⓤⓢ -t̬ɪd *stress shift:* ˌwell-appointed ˈoffice
well-balanced ˌwelˈbæl.ən*t*st *stress shift:* ˌwell-balanced ˈdiet
well-behaved ˌwel.bɪˈheɪvd, -bəˈ- *stress shift:* ˌwell-behaved ˈdog
well-being ˈwelˌbiː.ɪŋ, ˌ-ˈ--
well-born ˌwelˈbɔːn ⓤⓢ -ˈbɔːrn *stress shift:* ˌwell-born ˈlady
well-bred ˌwelˈbred *stress shift:* ˌwell-bred ˈchild
well-built ˌwelˈbɪlt *stress shift:* ˌwell-built ˈperson
Wellby ˈwel.bi
well-chosen ˌwelˈtʃəʊ.zən ⓤⓢ -ˈtʃoʊ- *stress shift:* ˌwell-chosen ˈwords
Wellcome ˈwel.kəm
well-conducted ˌwel.kənˈdʌk.tɪd *stress shift:* ˌwell-conducted ˈscheme
well-connected ˌwel.kəˈnek.tɪd *stress shift:* ˌwell-connected ˈperson
well-cooked ˌwelˈkʊkt *stress shift:* ˌwell-cooked ˈfood
well-disposed ˌwel.dɪˈspəʊzd ⓤⓢ -ˈspoʊzd *stress shift:* ˌwell-disposed ˈmanner
well-do|er ˈwelˌduː|.əʳ, ˌ-ˈ-- ⓤⓢ ˈwelˌduː|.ɚ **-ers** -əz ⓤⓢ -ɚz **-ing** -ɪŋ
Welldon ˈwel.dən
well-done ˌwelˈdʌn *stress shift:* ˌwell-done ˈfood
well-earned ˌwelˈɜːnd ⓤⓢ -ˈɝːnd *stress shift:* ˌwell-earned ˈrest
Weller ˈwel.əʳ ⓤⓢ -ɚ
Welles welz
Wellesley ˈwelz.li
well-fed ˌwelˈfed *stress shift:* ˌwell-fed ˈcat
well-formed ˌwelˈfɔːmd ⓤⓢ -ˈfɔːrmd *stress shift:* ˌwell-formed ˈsentence
well-found ˌwelˈfaʊnd *stress shift:* ˌwell-found ˈship
well-groomed ˌwelˈgruːmd *stress shift:* ˌwell-groomed ˈman
well-grounded ˌwelˈgraʊn.dɪd *stress shift:* ˌwell-grounded ˈargument
well-heeled ˌwelˈhiːld *stress shift:* ˌwell-heeled ˈowner
wellie ˈwel.i **-s** -z
well-informed ˌwel.ɪnˈfɔːmd ⓤⓢ -ˈfɔːrmd *stress shift:* ˌwell-informed ˈjournalist
Welling ˈwel.ɪŋ
Wellingborough ˈwel.ɪŋ.bər.ə ⓤⓢ -bɚ.oʊ
wellington (W) ˈwel.ɪŋ.tən **-s** -z **ˌwellington ˈboot** ⓤⓢ **ˈwellington ˌboot**
wellingtonia ˌwel.ɪŋˈtəʊ.ni.ə ⓤⓢ -ˈtoʊ- **-s** -z
well-intentioned ˌwel.ɪnˈten.*t*ʃənd *stress shift:* ˌwell-intentioned ˈaction
well-judged ˌwelˈdʒʌdʒd *stress shift:* ˌwell-judged ˈshot
well-known ˌwelˈnəʊn ⓤⓢ -ˈnoʊn *stress shift:* ˌwell-known ˈwriter
well-made ˌwelˈmeɪd *stress shift:* ˌwell-made ˈproduct
well-meaning ˌwelˈmiː.nɪŋ *stress shift:* ˌwell-meaning ˈaction
well-meant ˌwelˈment *stress shift:* ˌwell-meant ˈgesture
well-nigh ˌwelˈnaɪ *stress shift:* ˌwell-nigh imˈpossible
well-off ˌwelˈɒf ⓤⓢ -ˈɑːf *stress shift:* ˌwell-off ˈperson
well-ordered ˌwelˈɔː.dəd ⓤⓢ -ˈɔːr.dɚd *stress shift:* ˌwell-ordered ˈhousehold
well-proportioned ˌwel.prəˈpɔː.ʃənd ⓤⓢ -ˈpɔːr- *stress shift:* ˌwell-proportioned ˈroom
well-read ˌwelˈred *stress shift:* ˌwell-read ˈperson
well-rounded ˌwelˈraʊn.dɪd *stress shift:* ˌwell-rounded ˈcharacter
Wells welz
well-spoken ˌwelˈspəʊ.kən ⓤⓢ -ˈspoʊ- *stress shift:* ˌwell-spoken ˈperson
wellspring ˈwel.sprɪŋ **-s** -z
well-thumbed ˌwelˈθʌmd *stress shift:* ˌwell-thumbed ˈbook
well-timed ˌwelˈtaɪmd *stress shift:* ˌwell-timed ˈaction
well-to-do ˌwel.təˈduː *stress shift:* ˌwell-to-do ˈperson
well-versed ˌwelˈvɜːst ⓤⓢ -ˈvɝːst *stress shift:* ˌwell-versed ˈteacher
well-wisher ˈwelˌwɪʃ.əʳ, ˌ-ˈ-- ⓤⓢ ˈwelˌwɪʃ.ɚ **-s** -z
well-worn ˌwelˈwɔːn ⓤⓢ -ˈwɔːrn *stress shift:* ˌwell-worn ˈphrase
well|y ˈwel|.i **-ies** -iz
Welsch welt*ʃ*
welsh (W) welʃ **-es** -ɪz **-ing** -ɪŋ **-ed** -t **-er/s** -əʳ/z ⓤⓢ -ɚ/z **ˌWelsh ˈdresser; ˌWelsh ˈNationalists; ˌWelsh ˈrarebit**
Welsh|man ˈwelʃ|.mən **-men** -mən
Welshpool ˈwelʃ.puːl, ˌ-ˈ-
Welsh|woman ˈwelʃ|ˌwʊm.ən **-women** -ˌwɪm.ɪn
welt welt **-s** -s **-ing** -ɪŋ ⓤⓢ ˈwel.t̬ɪŋ **-ed** -ɪd ⓤⓢ ˈwel.t̬ɪd
weltanschauung (W) ˈvelt.ænˌʃaʊ.ʊŋ ⓤⓢ -ɑːn,-
welt|er ˈwel.t|əʳ ⓤⓢ -t̬|ɚ **-ers** -əz ⓤⓢ -ɚz **-ering** -ər.ɪŋ **-ered** -əd ⓤⓢ -ɚd
welterweight ˈwel.tə.weɪt ⓤⓢ -t̬ɚ- **-s** -s

weltschmerz **(W)** ˈvelt.ʃmeəts ⓤⓢ -ʃmerts
Welty ˈwel.ti ⓤⓢ -t̬i
Welwyn ˈwel.ɪn ˌ**Welwyn** ˌ**Garden** ˈ**City**
Wembley ˈwem.bli
Wemyss wiːmz
wen wen **-s** -z
Wenceslas ˈwen.sɪ.sləs, -sə-, -slæs ⓤⓢ -sɪ.slɑːs, -slɔːs
wench wentʃ **-es** -ɪz
wend wend **-s** -z **-ing** -ɪŋ **-ed** -ɪd
Wend wend, vend **-s** -z **-ic** -ɪk **-ish** -ɪʃ
Wendell ˈwen.dᵊl
Wenders ˈwen.dəz ⓤⓢ ˈven.dɚz
Wendover ˈwen.dəʊ.vəʳ ⓤⓢ -doʊ.vɚ
Wendy ˈwen.di ˈ**Wendy** ˌ**house**
Wengen ˈveŋ.ən
Wenger ˈveŋ.gəʳ ⓤⓢ -gɚ
Wengern Alp ˌveŋ.ənˈælp ⓤⓢ -ɚnˈ-
Wenham ˈwen.əm
Wenlock ˈwen.lɒk ⓤⓢ -lɑːk ˌ**Wenlock** ˈ**Edge**
Wensleydale ˈwenz.lɪ.deɪl
went *(from* **go***)* went
Wentworth ˈwent.wəθ, -wɜːθ ⓤⓢ -wɚθ, -wɝːθ
wept *(from* **weep***)* wept
we're *(=* **we are***)* wɪəʳ ⓤⓢ wɪr
were *(from* **be***)* *strong forms:* wɜːʳ ⓤⓢ wɝː *weak forms:* wəʳ ⓤⓢ wɚ
Note: Weak form word. The strong form is used for emphasis (e.g. 'You **were** a long time') and for contrast (e.g. 'what they were and what they might have been'). The strong form is also usual in final position (e.g. 'We didn't know where we were'). The weak form is used elsewhere.
weren't wɜːnt ⓤⓢ wɝːnt
werewol|f ˈweə.wʊl|f, ˈwɪə-, ˈwɜː- ⓤⓢ ˈwer-, ˈwɪr-, ˈwɝː- **-ves** -vz
Werner ˈwɜː.nəʳ *as if German:* ˈveə- ⓤⓢ ˈwɝː.nɚ *as if German:* ˈvɝː-
wert *(from* **be***)* *strong forms:* wɜːt ⓤⓢ wɝːt *weak forms:* wət ⓤⓢ wɚt
Note: Archaic form; see information at **were**.
Weser *German river:* ˈveɪ.zəʳ ⓤⓢ -zɚ
Note: /ˈwiː.zəʳ ⓤⓢ -zɚ/ is necessary for rhyme in Browning's 'Pied Piper', but this pronunciation is exceptional.
Wesker ˈwes.kəʳ ⓤⓢ -kɚ
Wesley ˈwez.li, ˈwes- ⓤⓢ ˈwes-, ˈwez-
Note: Most people bearing the name **Wesley** pronounce /ˈwes.li/, but in Britain the pronunciation is commonly /ˈwez.li/.
Wesleyan ˈwez.li.ən, ˈwes- ⓤⓢ ˈwes-, ˈwez- **-s** -z **-ism** -ɪ.zᵊm
Note: /ˈwes-/ appears to be the more usual pronunciation among Wesleyans; with those who are not Wesleyans /ˈwez-/ is probably the commoner form in British English. There exists also an old-fashioned pronunciation /wesˈliː.ən/.
Wessex ˈwes.ɪks
west **(W)** west ˌ**West** ˈ**Bank** *stress shift:* ˌWest Bank ˈsettlement; ˌ**West** ˈ**Coast**; *stress shift:* ˌWest Coast ˈsinger; ˈ**West** ˌ**Country**; ˌ**West** ˈ**End**; *stress shift:* ˌWest End ˈplay; ˌ**West** ˈ**Indian**; ˌ**West** ˈ**Indies**; ˌ**West** ˈ**Point**; ⓤⓢ ˈ**West** ˌ**Point**; ˌ**West** ˌ**Side** ˈ**Story** ⓤⓢ ˈ**West Side** ˌ**Story**; ˌ**West Vir**ˈ**ginia**
westbound ˈwest.baʊnd
Westbourne ˈwest.bɔːn, -bən ⓤⓢ -bɔːrn, -bɚn
West Bridgford ˌwestˈbrɪdʒ.fəd ⓤⓢ -fɚd
Westbrook ˈwest.brʊk
Westbury ˈwest.bᵊr.i
Westchester ˈwest.tʃes.təʳ ⓤⓢ -tɚ
Westcott ˈwest.kət
Westergate ˈwes.tə.geɪt ⓤⓢ -tɚ-
Westerham ˈwes.tᵊr.əm
westering ˈwes.tᵊr.ɪŋ
westerl|y ˈwes.tᵊl|.i ⓤⓢ -tɚ.l|i **-ies** -iz
western **(W)** ˈwes.tən ⓤⓢ -tɚn **-s** -z **-er/s** -əʳ/z ⓤⓢ -ɚ/z **-most** -məʊst ⓤⓢ -moʊst ˌ**Western Aus**ˈ**tralia**; ˈ**Western** ˌ**Isles**,; ˌ**Western** ˈ**Isles**
westernization, -isa- ˌwes.tᵊn.aɪˈzeɪ.ʃᵊn, -ɪˈ- ⓤⓢ -tɚ.nɪˈ-
westerniz|e, -is|e ˈwes.tən.aɪz ⓤⓢ -tɚ.naɪz **-es** -ɪz **-ing** -ɪŋ **-ed** -d
Westfield ˈwest.fiːld
Westgate ˈwest.geɪt, -gɪt
Westhill ˈwest.hɪl
Westhoughton ˌwestˈhɔː.tᵊn ⓤⓢ -ˈhɑː-, -ˈhɔː-
Westinghouse ˈwes.tɪŋ.haʊs
Westlake ˈwest.leɪk
Westland® ˈwest.lənd
Westlife ˈwest.laɪf
Westly ˈwest.li
Westmeath ˌwestˈmiːð
West Mersea ˌwestˈmɜː.zi ⓤⓢ -ˈmɝː-
Westminster westˈmɪnt.stəʳ, ˈ--- ⓤⓢ westˈmɪnt.stɚ, ˈ--- ˌ**Westminster** ˈ**Abbey**
Westmor(e)land ˈwest.mᵊl.ənd ⓤⓢ -mɔːr.lənd
west-northwest ˌwest.nɔːθˈwest ⓤⓢ -nɔːrθˈ- *nautical pronunciation:* -nɔːˈ- ⓤⓢ -nɔːrˈ-
Weston ˈwes.tən
Weston-super-Mare ˌwes.tənˌsuː.pəˈmeəʳ, -ˌsjuː-; -ˈsuː.pə.meəʳ, -ˈsjuː- ⓤⓢ -ˌsuː.pɚˈmer, -ˈsuː.pɚ.mer
Westphali|a ˌwestˈfeɪ.li|.ə, ˈ-lj|ə ⓤⓢ ˈ-li|.ə, -ˈfeɪl.j|ə **-an/s** -ən/z
Westray ˈwes.treɪ
Westside ˈwest.saɪd
west-southwest ˌwest.saʊθˈwest *nautical pronunciation:* -saʊˈ-
westward ˈwest.wəd ⓤⓢ -wɚd **-s** -z **-ly** -li
Westward Ho! ˌwest.wədˈhəʊ ⓤⓢ -wɚdˈhoʊ
Westwood ˈwest.wʊd
wet wet **-ter** -əʳ ⓤⓢ ˈwet̬.ɚ **-test** -ɪst, -əst ⓤⓢ ˈwet̬.ɪst, -əst **-s** -s **-ting** -ɪŋ ⓤⓢ ˈwet̬.ɪŋ **-ted** -ɪd ⓤⓢ ˈwet̬.ɪd **-ly** -li **-ness** -nəs, -nɪs ˌ**wet** ˈ**blanket**; ˈ**wet** ˌ**suit**; **(still)** ˌ**wet behind the** ˈ**ears**
wetback ˈwet.bæk **-s** -s
wether ˈweð.əʳ ⓤⓢ -ɚ **-s** -z
Wetherby ˈweð.ə.bi ⓤⓢ ˈ-ɚ-
wetland ˈwet.lənd ⓤⓢ -lænd **-s** -z
wet-look ˈwet.lʊk
wet-nurs|e ˈwet.nɜːs ⓤⓢ -nɝːs **-es** -ɪz
we've *(=* **we have***)* *strong form:* wiːv *weak form:* wiv
Note: Weak form word. The weak form is usually found when the word is unstressed, but the strong form may also be used in this situation.
Wexford ˈweks.fəd ⓤⓢ -fɚd
Wey weɪ
Weybridge ˈweɪ.brɪdʒ
Weyman ˈweɪ.mən
Weymouth ˈweɪ.məθ
whack *h*wæk **-s** -s **-ing/s** -ɪŋ/z **-ed** -t **-er/s** -əʳ/z ⓤⓢ -ɚ/z
whacko ˈ*h*wæk.əʊ ⓤⓢ -oʊ
whack|y ˈ*h*wæk|.i **-ier** -i.əʳ ⓤⓢ -i.ɚ **-iest** -i.ɪst, -i.əst **-ily** -ɪ.li, -ᵊl.i
whal|e **(W)** *h*weɪl **-es** -z **-ing** -ɪŋ **-er/s** -əʳ/z ⓤⓢ -ɚ/z ˌ**have a** ˈ**whale of a** ˌ**time**
whalebone ˈ*h*weɪl.bəʊn ⓤⓢ -boʊn
whale-oil ˈ*h*weɪl.ɔɪl
Whaley ˈ*h*weɪ.li
Whalley *surname:* ˈ*h*weɪ.li, ˈ*h*wɔː-, ˈ*h*wɒl.i ⓤⓢ ˈ*h*weɪ.li, ˈ*h*wɑː.li *abbey near Blackburn:* ˈ*h*wɔː.li ⓤⓢ ˈ*h*wɑː-
wham *h*wæm **-s** -z **-ming** -ɪŋ **-med** -d
whammo ˈ*h*wæm.əʊ ⓤⓢ -oʊ
whamm|y ˈ*h*wæm|.i **-ies** -iz
whamo ˈ*h*wæm.əʊ ⓤⓢ -oʊ
whang *h*wæŋ **-s** -z **-ing** -ɪŋ **-ed** -d
whangee ˌ*h*wæŋˈgiː, -ˈiː ⓤⓢ -ˈiː
whar|f *h*wɔː|f ⓤⓢ *h*wɔːr|f **-ves** -vz **-fs** -fs
wharfage ˈ*h*wɔː.fɪdʒ ⓤⓢ ˈ*h*wɔːr-
Wharfedale ˈ*h*wɔːf.deɪl ⓤⓢ ˈ*h*wɔːrf-
wharfinger ˈ*h*wɔː.fɪn.dʒəʳ ⓤⓢ ˈ*h*wɔːr.fɪn.dʒɚ **-s** -z
Wharton ˈ*h*wɔː.tᵊn ⓤⓢ ˈ*h*wɔːr-
what *h*wɒt ⓤⓢ *h*wʌt, *h*wɑːt
whatchamacallit ˈ*h*wɒtʃ.ə.məˌkɔː.lɪt ⓤⓢ ˈ*h*wʌtʃ-
what-d'you-call-it ˈ*h*wɒt.djʊˌkɔː.lɪt, -djəˌ-, -dʒʊˌ-, -dʒəˌ- ⓤⓢ ˈ*h*wʌt̬.i.jəˌkɔː-, ˈ*h*wʌtʃ.əˌ-, -ˌkɑː-

Pronouncing the letters WH

The consonant digraph **wh** is found in word or morpheme initial position in English, and usually pronounced as /w/ in British English and /hw/ in US English. The realisation /hw/ also occurs amongst some speakers of British English. In this dictionary, the transcription /hw/ is used to cover both variants, e.g.:

when	/hwen/	
where	/hweəʳ/	US /hwer/

Another realisation of the consonant digraph **wh** is /h/, e.g.:

who	/huː/	
wholesome	/ˈhəʊl.sᵊm/	US /ˈhoʊl-/

what-d'you-ma-call-it ˈhwɒt.djʊ.mə,kɔː.lɪt, -djə-, -dʒʊ-, -dʒə- US ˈhwʌt̬.i.jə.mə,kɔː-, -hwʌtʃ.ə-, -kɑː-
whate'er hwɒtˈeəʳ US hwʌtˈer, hwɑːt-
Whateley ˈhweɪt.li
whatever hwɒtˈev.əʳ US hwʌtˈev.ɚ, hwɑːt-
Whatley ˈhwɒt.li US ˈhwɑːt-
Whatman ˈhwɒt.mən US ˈhwɑːt-
Whatmough ˈhwɒt.məʊ US ˈhwɑːt.moʊ
whatnot ˈhwɒt.nɒt US ˈhwʌt.nɑːt, ˈhwɑːt- **-s** -s
what's-her-name ˈhwɒt.sᵊn.eɪm US ˈhwʌt.sɚ.neɪm, ˈhwɑːt-
what's-his-name ˈhwɒt.sɪz.neɪm US ˈhwʌt-, ˈhwɑːt-
whatsit ˈhwɒt.sɪt US ˈhwʌt- **-s** -s
whatsoe'er ,hwɒt.səʊˈeəʳ US ,hwʌt.soʊˈer, ,hwɑːt-
whatsoever ,hwɒt.səʊˈev.əʳ US ,hwʌt.soʊˈev.ɚ, ,hwɑːt-
wheal hwiːl **-s** -z
wheat hwiːt **-en** -ᵊn
wheatgerm ˈhwiːt.dʒɜːm US -dʒɝːm
Wheathampstead ˈhwiː.təmp.sted, ˈhwet.əmp-
Wheatley ˈhwiːt.li
wheatmeal ˈhwiːt.miːl
Wheaton ˈhwiː.tᵊn
Wheatstone ˈhwiːt.stᵊn, -stəʊn US -stoʊn, -stᵊn
wheedl|e ˈhwiː.dl̩ **-es** -z **-ing** -ɪŋ, ˈhwiːd.lɪŋ **-ed** -d **-er/s** -əʳ/z, ˈhwiːd.ləʳ/z US ˈhwiː.dl̩.əʳ/z, ˈhwiːd.lɚ/z
wheel hwiːl **-s** -z **-ing** -ɪŋ **-ed** -d ˈ**wheel** ,**clamp**
wheelbarrow ˈhwiːl,bær.əʊ US -,ber.oʊ, -,bær- **-s** -z
wheelbas|e ˈhwiːl.beɪs **-es** -ɪz
wheelchair ˈhwiːl.tʃeəʳ US -tʃer **-s** -z
wheeler (W) ˈhwiː.ləʳ US -lɚ **-s** -z
wheeler-dealer ,hwiː.ləˈdiː.ləʳ US -lɚˈdiː.lɚ **-s** -z
wheelhou|se ˈhwiːl.haʊ|s **-ses** -zɪz
wheelie ˈhwiː.li **-s** -z ˈ**wheelie** ,**bin**
Wheelock ˈhwiː.lək
wheelwright, wheelright (W) ˈhwiːl.raɪt **-s** -s
Wheen ˈhwiːn
wheez|e hwiːz **-es** -ɪz **-ing** -ɪŋ **-ed** -d **-y** -i **-ier** -i.əʳ US -i.ɚ **-iest** -i.ɪst, -i.əst **-iness** -ɪ.nəs, -ɪ.nɪs
Whelan ˈhwiː.lən
whelk welk US hwelk **-s** -s
whelm hwelm **-s** -z **-ing** -ɪŋ **-ed** -d
whelp hwelp **-s** -s **-ing** -ɪŋ **-ed** -t
when hwen
whence hwents
whene'er hwenˈeəʳ US -ˈer
whenever hwenˈev.əʳ, hwənˈ- US -ɚ
whensoever ,hwen.səʊˈev.əʳ US -soʊˈev.ɚ
where hweəʳ US hwer
whereabout ,hweə.rəˈbaʊt US ˈhwer.ə,-
whereabouts (*n.*) ˈhweə.rə.baʊts US ˈhwer.ə-
whereabouts *interrogation:* ,hweə.rəˈbaʊts US ,hwer.əˈ-
whereas hweəˈræz, hwər- US hwerˈæz, hwɚ-
whereat hweəˈræt, hwər- US hwerˈæt, hwɚ-
whereby hweəˈbaɪ US hwer-
where'er hweəˈreəʳ, hwə- US hwerˈer, hwɚ-
wherefore ˈhweə.fɔːʳ US ˈhwer.fɔːr **-s** -z
wherein hweəˈrɪn US hwerˈɪn
whereof hweəˈrɒv US hwerˈɑːv
whereon hweəˈrɒn US hwerˈɑːn
wheresoe'er ,hweə.səʊˈeəʳ US ,hwer.soʊˈer
wheresoever ,hweə.səʊˈev.əʳ US ,hwer.soʊˈev.ɚ
whereto hweəˈtuː US hwer-
whereunder hweəˈrʌn.dəʳ US hwerˈʌn.dɚ
whereunto ,hweə.rʌnˈtuː US ,hwer.ʌnˈ-
whereupon ,hweə.rəˈpɒn, ˈ--,- US ˈhwer.ə,pɑːn
wherever hweəˈrev.əʳ, hwər- US hwerˈev.ɚ, hwɚ-
wherewith hweəˈwɪθ, -ˈwɪð US hwer-
wherewithal (*n.*) ˈhweə.wɪ.ðɔːl US ˈhwer-, -θɔːl, -ðɑːl, -θɑːl
wherewithal (*adv.*) ,hweə.wɪˈðɔːl, ˈ--- US ˈhwer.wɪ.ðɔːl, -θɔːl, -ðɑːl, -θɑːl
Whernside ˈhwɜːn.saɪd US ˈhwɝːn-
wherr|y ˈhwer|.i **-ies** -iz
whet hwet **-s** -s **-ting** -ɪŋ US ˈhwet̬.ɪŋ **-ted** -ɪd US ˈhwet̬.ɪd
whether ˈhweð.əʳ US -ɚ
whetstone (W) ˈhwet.stəʊn US -stoʊn **-s** -z
whew ,y,u, fjuː
Note: This is an attempt at a symbolic representation of an interjection used to indicate that the speaker is either surprised, or suffering from the heat. The sound is related to a whistle (falling or rising-falling pitch), but in speech is more usually a whispered sound. The pronunciation /fjuː/ is an alternative based on the spelling.
Whewell ˈhjuː.əl, -el, -ɪl; hjʊəl US ˈhjuː.əl
whey hweɪ
which hwɪtʃ
whichever hwɪˈtʃev.əʳ US -ɚ
whick|er (W) ˈhwɪk|.əʳ US -ɚ **-ers** -əz US -ɚz **-ering** -ᵊr.ɪŋ **-ered** -əd US -ɚd
Whickham ˈhwɪk.əm
whiff hwɪf **-s** -s **-ing** -ɪŋ **-ed** -t
Whiffen ˈhwɪf.ɪn, -ən
Whig hwɪg **-s** -z
Whigg|ery ˈhwɪg|.ᵊr.i **-ism** -ɪ.zᵊm
Whiggish ˈhwɪg.ɪʃ
Whigham ˈhwɪg.əm
whil|e ˈhwaɪl **-es** -z **-ing** -ɪŋ **-ed** -d
whilst hwaɪlst
whim hwɪm **-s** -z
whimbrel ˈhwɪm.brᵊl **-s** -z
whimp|er ˈhwɪm.p|əʳ US -p|ɚ **-ers** -əz US -ɚz **-ering/ly** -ᵊr.ɪŋ/li **-ered** -əd US -ɚd
whimsic|al ˈhwɪm.zɪ.k|ᵊl, -sɪ- US -zɪ- **-ally** -ᵊl.i, -li **-alness** -ᵊl.nəs, -nɪs
whimsicality ,hwɪm.zɪˈkæl.ə.ti, -sɪˈ-, -ɪ.ti US -zɪˈkæl.ə.t̬i
whims|y ˈhwɪm.z|i **-ies** -iz
whin hwɪn **-s** -z
whinchat ˈhwɪn.tʃæt **-s** -s
whin|e hwaɪn **-es** -z **-ing/ly** -ɪŋ/li **-ed** -d **-er/s** -əʳ/z US -ɚ/z

whing|e *h*wɪndʒ **-es** -ɪz **-(e)ing** -ɪŋ **-ed** -d **-er/s** -əʳ/z (US) -ɚ/z
whinn|y ˈ*h*wɪn|.i **-ies** -iz **-ying** -i.ɪŋ **-ied** -id
whin|y ˈ*h*waɪ.n|i **-ier** -i.əʳ (US) -i.ɚ **-iest** -i.ɪst, -i.əst **-iness** -ɪ.nəs, -ɪ.nɪs
whip *h*wɪp **-s** -s **-ping/s** -ɪŋ/z **-ped** -t **have the ˌwhip ˈhand**
whipcord ˈ*h*wɪp.kɔːd (US) -kɔːrd
whiplash ˈ*h*wɪp.læʃ
whipp|er-in ˌ*h*wɪp|.əʳˈɪn (US) -ɚˈ- **-ers-in** -əzˈɪn (US) -ɚzˈ-
whippersnapper ˈ*h*wɪp.əˌsnæp.əʳ (US) -ɚˌsnæp.ɚ **-s** -z
whippet ˈ*h*wɪp.ɪt **-s** -s
whipping-boy ˈ*h*wɪp.ɪŋ.bɔɪ **-s** -z
Whippingham ˈ*h*wɪp.ɪŋ.əm
Whipple ˈ*h*wɪp.l̩
whippoorwill ˈ*h*wɪp.ə.wɪl, -ʊə-, -pʊə-, -pɔː- (US) ˈ-ɚ- **-s** -z
whip-round ˈ*h*wɪp.raʊnd **-s** -z
whipsaw ˈ*h*wɪp.sɔː (US) -sɑː, -sɔː **-s** -z
Whipsnade ˈ*h*wɪp.sneɪd
whir *h*wɜːʳ (US) *h*wɝː **-s** -z **-ring/s** -ɪŋ/z **-red** -d
whirl *h*wɜːl (US) *h*wɝːl **-s** -z **-ing** -ɪŋ **-ed** -d
whirligig ˈ*h*wɜː.lɪ.gɪg (US) ˈ*h*wɝː- **-s** -z
whirlpool ˈ*h*wɜːl.puːl (US) ˈ*h*wɝːl- **-s** -z
whirlwind ˈ*h*wɜːl.wɪnd (US) ˈ*h*wɝːl- **-s** -z
whirlybird ˈ*h*wɜː.lɪ.bɜːd (US) ˈ*h*wɝː.lɪ.bɝːd **-s** -z
whirr *h*wɜːʳ (US) *h*wɝː **-s** -z **-ing/s** -ɪŋ/z **-ed** -d
whisk *h*wɪsk **-s** -s **-ing** -ɪŋ **-ed** -t
Whiskas® ˈ*h*wɪs.kəz
whisker ˈ*h*wɪs.kəʳ (US) -kɚ **-s** -z **-ed** -d
whiskey ˈ*h*wɪs.ki **-s** -z
whisk|y ˈ*h*wɪs.k|i **-ies** -iz
whisp|er ˈ*h*wɪs.p|əʳ (US) -p|ɚ **-ers** -əz (US) -ɚz **-ering/s** -ᵊr.ɪŋ/z **-ered** -əd (US) -ɚd **-erer/s** -ᵊr.əʳ/z (US) -ɚ.ɚ/z
whist *h*wɪst ˈ**whist** ˌ**drive**
whistl|e ˈ*h*wɪs.l̩ **-es** -z **-ing** -ɪŋ, ˈ*h*wɪs.lɪŋ **-ed** -d ˌ**blow the** ˈ**whistle** ˌ**on**
whistle-blower ˈ*h*wɪs.l̩ˌbləʊ.əʳ (US) -ˌbloʊ.ɚ **-s** -z
whistler (W) ˈ*h*wɪs.ləʳ, -l̩.əʳ (US) ˈ-lɚ, -l̩.ɚ **-s** -z
whistle-stop ˈ*h*wɪs.l̩.stɒp (US) -stɑːp **-s** -s **-ping** -ɪŋ **-ped** -t ˌ**whistle-stop** ˈ**tour**
whit (W) *h*wɪt
Whitaker ˈ*h*wɪt.ə.kəʳ, ˈ-ɪ- (US) *h*wɪt̬.ə.kɚ
Whitbread ˈ*h*wɪt.bred
Whitburn ˈ*h*wɪt.bɜːn (US) -bɝːn
Whitby ˈ*h*wɪt.bi
Whitchurch ˈ*h*wɪt.tʃɜːtʃ (US) -tʃɝːtʃ
Whitcombe ˈ*h*wɪt.kəm
Whitcut ˈ*h*wɪt.kʌt
whit|e (W) *h*waɪt **-es** -s **-er** -əʳ (US) ˈ*h*waɪ.t̬ɚ **-est** -ɪst, -əst (US) ˈ*h*waɪ.t̬ɪst, -t̬əst **-ely** -li **-eness** -nəs, -nɪs **-ing** -ɪŋ (US) ˈ*h*waɪ.t̬ɪŋ **-ed** -ɪd (US) ˈ*h*waɪ.t̬ɪd ˌ**white** ˈ**elephant**; ˌ**white** ˈ**flag**; ˈ**white** ˌ**goods**; ˈ**White** ˌ**House**; ˌ**white** ˈ**knight**; ˌ**white** ˈ**lie**; ˈ**white** ˌ**man**; ˌ**white** ˈ**paper** (US) ˈ**white** ˌ**paper**; ˌ**white** ˈ**sauce**; (US) ˈ**white** ˌ**sauce**; ˌ**white** ˈ**trash**; ˌ**white** ˈ**wedding**; ˌ**white as a** ˈ**sheet**
whitebait ˈ*h*waɪt.beɪt
whitebeard ˈ*h*waɪt.bɪəd (US) -bɪrd **-s** -z **-ed** -ɪd
whiteboard ˈ*h*waɪt.bɔːd (US) -bɔːrd **-s** -z
whitecap ˈ*h*waɪt.kæp **-s** -s
Whitechapel ˈ*h*waɪtˌtʃæp.ᵊl
white-collar ˌ*h*waɪtˈkɒl.əʳ (US) -ˈkɑː.lɚ *stress shift:* ˌwhite-collar ˈworker
Whitefield ˈ*h*waɪt.fiːld, ˈ*h*wɪt-
whitefl|y ˈ*h*waɪt.fl|aɪ **-ies** -aɪz
Whitefriars ˈ*h*waɪt.fraɪəz, ˌ-ˈ- (US) ˈ*h*waɪt.fraɪɚz, ˌ-ˈ-
Whitehall ˈ*h*waɪt.hɔːl, ˌ-ˈ- (US) ˈ*h*waɪt.hɔːl, -hɑːl
Whitehaven ˈ*h*waɪtˌheɪ.vᵊn
whitehead (W) ˈ*h*waɪt.hed **-s** -z
Whitehorn ˈ*h*waɪt.hɔːn (US) -hɔːrn
Whitehorse ˈ*h*waɪt.hɔːs (US) -hɔːrs
white-hot ˌ*h*waɪtˈhɒt (US) -ˈhɑːt *stress shift:* ˌwhite-hot ˈmetal
Whitehouse ˈ*h*waɪt.haʊs
Whitelaw ˈ*h*waɪt.lɔː (US) -lɑː, -lɔː
Whiteley ˈ*h*waɪt.li
white-livered ˈ*h*waɪtˌlɪv.əd, ˌ-ˈ-- (US) -ɚd
whiten ˈ*h*waɪ.tᵊn **-s** -z **-ing** -ɪŋ, ˈ*h*waɪt.nɪŋ **-ed** -d
whitener ˈ*h*waɪt.nəʳ, ˈ*h*waɪ.tᵊn.əʳ (US) ˈ*h*waɪt.nɚ, ˈ*h*waɪ.tᵊn.ɚ **-s** -z
whiteout ˈ*h*waɪt.aʊt **-s** -s
Whiteread ˈ*h*waɪt.riːd
Whiteside ˈ*h*waɪt.saɪd
whitethorn ˈ*h*waɪt.θɔːn (US) -θɔːrn **-s** -z
whitethroat ˈ*h*waɪt.θrəʊt (US) -θroʊt **-s** -s
whitewash ˈ*h*waɪt.wɒʃ (US) -wɑːʃ **-es** -ɪz **-ing** -ɪŋ **-ed** -t **-er/s** -əʳ/z (US) -ɚ/z
whitewater (W) ˈ*h*waɪt.wɔː.təʳ (US) -wɑː.t̬ɚ, -wɔː- ˌ**whitewater** ˈ**rafting**
whitewood ˈ*h*waɪt.wʊd
whitey ˈ*h*waɪ.ti (US) -t̬i
Whitfield ˈ*h*wɪt.fiːld
Whitgift ˈ*h*wɪt.gɪft
whither ˈ*h*wɪð.əʳ (US) -ɚ
whithersoever ˌ*h*wɪð.ə.səʊˈev.əʳ (US) -ɚ.soʊˈev.ɚ
whiting (W) ˈ*h*waɪ.tɪŋ (US) -t̬ɪŋ **-s** -z
whitish ˈ*h*waɪ.tɪʃ (US) -t̬ɪʃ
Whitlam ˈ*h*wɪt.ləm
Whitley ˈ*h*wɪt.li
whitlow ˈ*h*wɪt.ləʊ (US) -loʊ **-s** -z
Whitman ˈ*h*wɪt.mən
Whitmarsh ˈ*h*wɪt.mɑːʃ (US) -mɑːrʃ
Whitmore ˈ*h*wɪt.mɔːʳ (US) -mɔːr
Whitney ˈ*h*wɪt.ni
Whitstable ˈ*h*wɪt.stə.bl̩
Whitstone ˈ*h*wɪt.stəʊn, -stᵊn (US) -stoʊn, -stᵊn
Whitsun ˈ*h*wɪt.sᵊn
Whitsunday ˌ*h*wɪtˈsʌn.deɪ, -di; -sᵊnˈdeɪ **-s** -z
Whitsuntide ˈ*h*wɪt.sᵊn.taɪd **-s** -z
Whittaker ˈ*h*wɪt.ə.kəʳ, ˈ-ɪ- (US) ˈ*h*wɪt̬.ə.kɚ
Whittall ˈ*h*wɪt.ᵊl, -ɔːl (US) ˈ*h*wɪt̬-
Whittier ˈ*h*wɪt.i.əʳ (US) ˈ*h*wɪt̬.i.ɚ
Whittingeham(e) ˈ*h*wɪt.ɪn.dʒəm (US) ˈ*h*wɪt̬-
Whittington ˈ*h*wɪt.ɪŋ.tən (US) ˈ*h*wɪt̬-
whittl|e (W) ˈ*h*wɪt.l̩ (US) ˈ*h*wɪt̬- **-es** -z **-ing** -ɪŋ, ˈ*h*wɪt.lɪŋ **-ed** -d
Whittlesey ˈ*h*wɪt.l̩.si (US) ˈ*h*wɪt̬-
Whitworth ˈ*h*wɪt.wəθ, -wɜːθ (US) -wɚθ, -wɝːθ
whit|y ˈ*h*waɪ.t|i (US) -t̬|i **-iness** -ɪ.nəs, -ɪ.nɪs
whiz, whiz|z *h*wɪz **-zes** -ɪz **-zing** -ɪŋ **-zed** -d ˌ**gee** ˈ**whiz(z)**; ˈ**whiz(z)** ˌ**kid**
whiz(z)-bang ˈ*h*wɪz.bæŋ **-s** -z
who *strong form:* huː *weak form:* *h*u ˌ**Who's** ˈ**Who**
Note: Weak form word. The weak form is only found in unstressed syllables, and the /h/ is frequently not pronounced. The strong form is also found in unstressed syllables.
WHO ˌdʌb.l̩.juːˌeɪtʃˈəʊ (US) ˌdʌb.l̩.juːˌeɪtʃˈoʊ, -jəˌ-
whoa *h*wəʊ (US) *h*woʊ
who'd huːd
whodun(n)it ˌhuːˈdʌn.ɪt **-s** -s
whoe'er huːˈeəʳ, hu- (US) -ˈer
whoever huːˈev.əʳ, hu- (US) -ɚ
whole həʊl (US) hoʊl **-ness** -nəs, -nɪs **go the** ˌ**whole** ˈ**hog**
wholefood ˈhəʊl.fuːd (US) ˈhoʊl- **-s** -z
wholegrain ˈhəʊl.greɪn (US) ˈhoʊl-
whole-hearted ˌhəʊlˈhɑː.tɪd (US) ˌhoʊlˈhɑːr.t̬ɪd **-ly** -li **-ness** -nəs, -nɪs *stress shift:* ˌwhole-hearted ˈeffort
wholemeal ˈhəʊl.miːl (US) ˈhoʊl-
wholesale ˈhəʊl.seɪl (US) ˈhoʊl-
wholesaler ˈhəʊlˌseɪ.ləʳ (US) ˈhoʊlˌseɪ.lɚ **-s** -z
wholesom|e ˈhəʊl.sᵊm (US) ˈhoʊl- **-est** -ɪst, -əst **-ely** -li **-eness** -nəs, -nɪs
wholewheat ˈhəʊl.*h*wiːt (US) ˌhoʊlˈ*h*wiːt
wholism ˈhəʊ.lɪ.zᵊm (US) ˈhoʊ-
wholistic həʊˈlɪs.tɪk (US) hoʊ-
who'll huːl
wholly ˈhəʊl.li, ˈhəʊ- (US) ˈhoʊl.li, ˈhoʊ-
whom huːm

whomever ˌhuːˈmev.əʳ, hʊˈ-
whomsoever ˌhuːm.səʊˈev.əʳ, ˌhʊm- (US) -soʊˈev.ɚ
whoop *h*wuːp, huːp **-s** -s **-ing** -ɪŋ **-ed** -t
whoopee (*n.*) ˈ*h*wʊp.i (US) ˈ*h*wuː.pi **ˈwhoopee ˌcushion** (*interj.*) *h*wʊˈpiː
Whoopi ˈ*h*wʊp.i (US) ˈ*h*wʊp.i, ˈ*h*wuː.pi
whooping-cough ˈhuː.pɪŋ.kɒf (US) -kɑːf, ˈhʊp.ɪŋ-, ˈwuː.pɪŋ-, ˈwʊp.ɪŋ-
whoops *h*wʊps (US) *h*wʊps, *h*wuːps
whoops-a-daisy ˈ*h*wʊps.əˌdeɪ.zi (US) ˈ*h*wʊps-, ˈ*h*wuːps-
whoosh *h*wʊʃ (US) *h*wʊʃ, *h*wuːʃ **-es** -ɪz **-ing** -ɪŋ **-ed** -t
whop *h*wɒp (US) *h*wɑːp **-s** -s **-ping/s** -ɪŋ/z **-ped** -t
whopper ˈ*h*wɒp.əʳ (US) ˈ*h*wɑː.pɚ **-s** -z
whopping ˈ*h*wɒp.ɪŋ (US) ˈ*h*wɑː.pɪŋ
whor|e hɔːʳ (US) hɔːr **-es** -z **-ing** -ɪŋ **-ed** -d
whoredom ˈhɔː.dəm (US) ˈhɔːr-
whorehou|se ˈhɔː.haʊ|s (US) ˈhɔːr- **-ses** -zɪz
whoreson ˈhɔː.sᵊn (US) ˈhɔːr- **-s** -z
Whorf *h*wɔːf (US) *h*wɔːrf
whorish ˈhɔː.rɪʃ (US) ˈhɔːr.ɪʃ
whorl *h*wɜːl (US) *h*wɝːl, *h*wɔːrl **-s** -z **-ed** -d
whortle ˈ*h*wɜː.tl̩ (US) ˈ*h*wɝː.t̬l̩ **-s** -z
whortleberr|y ˈ*h*wɜː.tl̩ˌber|.i, -bᵊr- (US) ˈ*h*wɝː.t̬l̩ˌber- **-ies** -iz
who's huːz
whose huːz
whoso ˈhuː.səʊ (US) -soʊ
whosoever ˌhuː.səʊˈev.əʳ (US) -soʊˈev.ɚ
who've huːv
why *h*waɪ **-s** -z
Whybrow ˈ*h*waɪ.braʊ
Whyle ˈ*h*waɪ.li
why'll *h*waɪl
Whymper ˈ*h*wɪm.pəʳ (US) -pɚ
why're ˈ*h*waɪ.əʳ (US) -ɚ
why's *h*waɪz
Whyte *h*waɪt
Whytt *h*waɪt
why've *h*waɪv, ˈ*h*waɪ.əv
WI ˌdʌb.l̩.juːˈaɪ
Wichita ˈwɪtʃ.ɪ.tɔː, ˈ-ə- (US) -ə.tɔː, -tɑː
wick (W) wɪk **-s** -s
wicked ˈwɪk.ɪd **-est** -ɪst, -əst **-ly** -li **-ness/es** -nəs/ɪz, -nɪs/ɪz
Wicken ˈwɪk.ᵊn
Wickens ˈwɪk.ɪnz
wicker (W) ˈwɪk.əʳ (US) -ɚ
wickerwork ˈwɪk.ə.wɜːk (US) -ɚ.wɝːk
wicket ˈwɪk.ɪt **-s** -s **ˈwicket ˌgate**
wicket-keeper ˈwɪk.ɪtˌkiː.pəʳ (US) -pɚ **-s** -z
Wickford ˈwɪk.fəd (US) -fɚd
Wickham ˈwɪk.əm
Wickliffe ˈwɪk.lɪf
Wicklow ˈwɪk.ləʊ (US) -loʊ
Widdecombe, Widdicombe ˈwɪd.ɪ.kəm
Widdowson ˈwɪd.əʊ.sᵊn (US) -oʊ-, ˈ-ə-
wid|e waɪd **-es** -z **-er** -əʳ (US) -ɚ **-est** -ɪst, -əst **-ely** -li **-eness** -nəs, -nɪs **ˈwide ˌboy**
wide-angle ˌwaɪdˈæŋ.gl̩ *stress shift:* ˌwide-angle ˈlens
wide-awake (*adj.*) ˌwaɪd.əˈweɪk
Widecombe ˈwɪd.ɪ.kəm
wide-eyed ˌwaɪdˈaɪd (US) ˈ-- *stress shift, British only:* ˌwide-eyed ˈstare
Widemouth ˈwɪd.məθ
widen ˈwaɪ.dᵊn **-s** -z **-ing** -ɪŋ, ˈwaɪd.nɪŋ **-ed** -d
Wideopen ˈwaɪdˌəʊ.pᵊn (US) -ˌoʊ-
widescreen ˈwaɪd.skriːn
widespread ˈwaɪd.spred
widgeon ˈwɪdʒ.ən, -ɪn **-s** -z
widget ˈwɪdʒ.ɪt **-s** -s
widish ˈwaɪ.dɪʃ
Widmerpool ˈwɪd.mə.puːl (US) -mɚ-
Widnes ˈwɪd.nəs, -nɪs
widow ˈwɪd.əʊ (US) -oʊ **-s** -z **-ed** -d
widower ˈwɪd.əʊ.əʳ (US) -oʊ.ɚ **-s** -z
widowhood ˈwɪd.əʊ.hʊd (US) -oʊ-
Widsith ˈwɪd.sɪθ
width wɪtθ, wɪdθ **-s** -s
wield wiːld **-s** -z **-ing** -ɪŋ **-ed** -ɪd
Wiener schnitzel ˌviː.nəˈʃnɪt.sᵊl (US) ˈviː.nɚˌʃnɪt- **-s** -z
Wiesbaden ˈviːsˌbɑː.dᵊn, ˈviːz-, ˌ-ˈ-- (US) ˈviːsˌbɑː-
Wiesenthal ˈwiː.zᵊn.tɑːl, ˈviː- (US) ˈwiː.zᵊn.tɑːl, ˈviː-, -θɔːl
wi|fe waɪ|f **-ves** -vz
wife|hood ˈwaɪf|.hʊd **-less** -ləs, -lɪs
wifelike ˈwaɪf.laɪk
wifely ˈwaɪ.fli
wife-swapping ˈwaɪfˌswɒp.ɪŋ (US) -ˌswɑː.pɪŋ
Wiffen ˈwɪf.ɪn
Wiffle ball® ˈwɪf.l̩ˌbɔːl (US) -ˌbɑːl, -ˌbɔːl
wig wɪg **-s** -z **-ging** -ɪŋ **-ged** -d
Wigan ˈwɪg.ən
wigeon ˈwɪdʒ.ən, -ɪn **-s** -z
Wiggin ˈwɪg.ɪn **-s** -z
wigging ˈwɪg.ɪŋ **-s** -z
wiggl|e ˈwɪg.l̩ **-es** -z **-ing** -ɪŋ, ˈwɪg.lɪŋ **-ed** -d
Wigglesworth ˈwɪg.l̩z.wəθ, -wɜːθ (US) -wɚθ, -wɝːθ
wiggly ˈwɪg.l̩.i, ˈwɪg.li
wight (W) waɪt **-s** -s
Wigley ˈwɪg.li
Wigmore ˈwɪg.mɔːʳ (US) -mɔːr
Wigram ˈwɪg.rəm
Wigston ˈwɪg.stən
Wigton ˈwɪg.tən
Wigtown ˈwɪg.taʊn, -tən
Wigtownshire ˈwɪg.tən.ʃəʳ, -ˌʃɪəʳ (US) -ʃɚ, -ˌʃɪr
wigwam ˈwɪg.wæm (US) -wɑːm **-s** -z
Wilberforce ˈwɪl.bə.fɔːs (US) -bɚ.fɔːrs
Wilbraham *surname:* ˈwɪl.brə.hæm, ˈ-brəm, ˈ-bri.əm (US) ˈ-brə.hæm, ˈ-brəm ***Great and Little in*** *Cambridgeshire:* ˈwɪl.brəm, -brə.hæm
Wilbur ˈwɪl.bəʳ (US) -bɚ
Wilbye ˈwɪl.bi
wilco ˈwɪl.kəʊ (US) -koʊ
Wilcox ˈwɪl.kɒks (US) -kɑːks
wild (W) waɪld **-s** -z **-er** -əʳ (US) -ɚ **-est** -ɪst, -əst **-ly** -li **-ness** -nəs, -nɪs **ˈwild ˌcard**; **ˈwild ˌchild**; **ˌWild ˈWest**; **ˌsow one's ˌwild ˈoats**
wild|cat ˈwaɪld|.kæt **-cats** -kæts **-catting** -ˌkæt.ɪŋ (US) -ˌkæt̬.ɪŋ **-catted** -ˌkæt.ɪd (US) -ˌkæt̬.ɪd **-catter/s** -ˌkæt.əʳ/z (US) -ˌkæt̬.ɚ/z **ˌwildcat ˈstrike**
Wilde waɪld
wildebeest ˈwɪl.dɪ.biːst, ˈvɪl-, -də- (US) -də- **-s** -s
Wilder ˈwaɪl.dəʳ (US) -dɚ
wilderness ˈwɪl.də.nəs, -nɪs (US) -dɚ- **-es** -ɪz
Wilderspin ˈwɪl.də.spɪn (US) -dɚ-
Wildfell ˈwaɪld.fel
wildfire ˈwaɪld.faɪəʳ (US) -faɪɚ
wildfowl ˈwaɪld.faʊl **-ing** -ɪŋ **-er/s** -əʳ/z (US) -ɚ/z
wild-goose chase ˌwaɪldˈguːsˌtʃeɪs
wilding (W) ˈwaɪl.dɪŋ **-s** -z
wildlife ˈwaɪld.laɪf **ˈwildlife ˌpark**
wil|e (W) waɪl **-es** -z **-ing** -ɪŋ **-ed** -d
Wiley ˈwaɪ.li
Wilfred, Wilfrid ˈwɪl.frɪd, -frəd (US) ˈwɪl-
wilful ˈwɪl.fᵊl, -fʊl **-ly** -i **-ness** -nəs, -nɪs
Wilhelmina ˌwɪl.helˈmiː.nə, -əˈ-
Wilkerson ˈwɪl.kə.sᵊn (US) -kɚ-
Wilkes wɪlks
Wilkie ˈwɪl.ki
Wilkin ˈwɪl.kɪn
Wilkins ˈwɪl.kɪnz
Wilkinson ˈwɪl.kɪn.sᵊn
Wilks wɪlks
will (W) (*n.*) wɪl **-s** -z
will (*transitive v.*) wɪl **-s** -z **-ing** -ɪŋ **-ed** -d
will (*auxil. v.*) *strong form:* wɪl *weak forms:* wᵊl, ᵊl
Note: Weak form word. The strong form is used for emphasis (e.g. 'I **will** do it') and contrast (e.g. 'I don't know if I will or not'). It is also the usual form of 'will' in final position (e.g. 'I think they both will'). Elsewhere the weak form (often speltin contracted form as **'ll**) is used.
Willard ˈwɪl.ɑːd, -əd (US) -ɚd
Willcocks, -cox ˈwɪl.kɒks (US) -kɑːks

Willenhall ˈwɪl.ən.hɔːl
Willes wɪlz
Willesden ˈwɪlz.dᵊn
Willett ˈwɪl.ɪt **-s** -s
willful ˈwɪl.fᵊl, -fʊl **-ly** -i **-ness** -nəs, -nɪs
William ˈwɪl.jəm, -i.əm (US) ˈ-jəm **-s** -z **-son** -sᵊn
willie (W) ˈwɪl.i **-s** -z
willing (W) ˈwɪl.ɪŋ **-ly** -li **-ness** -nəs, -nɪs
Willingdon ˈwɪl.ɪŋ.dən
Willington ˈwɪl.ɪŋ.tən
Willis ˈwɪl.ɪs
Willmott ˈwɪl.mɒt, -mət (US) -mɑːt, -mət
will-o'-the-wisp ˌwɪl.ə.ðəˈwɪsp, ˈwɪl.ə.ðə.wɪsp (US) ˌwɪl.ə.ðəˈwɪsp **-s** -s
Willoughby ˈwɪl.ə.bi
willow ˈwɪl.əʊ (US) -oʊ **-s** -z **-ing** -ɪŋ **-ed** -d
willowherb ˈwɪl.əʊ.hɜːb (US) -oʊ.*hɝː*b
willow-pattern ˈwɪl.əʊˌpæt.ᵊn (US) -oʊˌpæt̬.ɚn
willowy ˈwɪl.əʊ.i (US) -oʊ-
willpower ˈwɪl.paʊəʳ (US) -paʊɚ **-s** -z
Wills wɪlz
Willson ˈwɪl.sᵊn
Willsteed ˈwɪl.stiːd
will|y (W) ˈwɪl|.i **-ies** -iz
willy-nilly ˌwɪl.iˈnɪl.i
Wilma ˈwɪl.mə
Wilmcote ˈwɪlm.kəʊt (US) -koʊt, -kət
Wilmington ˈwɪl.mɪŋ.tən
Wilmot(t) ˈwɪl.mɒt, -mət (US) -mɑːt, -mət
Wilmslow ˈwɪlmz.ləʊ *locally:* ˈwɪmz.ləʊ (US) ˈwɪlmz.loʊ
Wilna ˈvɪl.nə
Wilno ˈwɪl.nəʊ (US) -noʊ
Wilsden ˈwɪlz.dᵊn
Wilshire ˈwɪl.ʃəʳ, -ˌʃɪəʳ (US) -ʃɚ, -ˌʃɪr
Wilson ˈwɪl.sᵊn
wilt *(from* **will**, *auxil. v.) normal form:* wɪlt *occasional weak form:* ᵊlt
Note: This archaic form is rarely used.
wilt wɪlt **-s** -s **-ing** -ɪŋ (US) ˈwɪl.t̬ɪŋ **-ed** -ɪd (US) ˈwɪl.t̬ɪd
Wilton ˈwɪl.tən (US) -tən, -tᵊn **-s** -z
Wilts. *(abbrev. for* **Wiltshire***)* wɪlts
Wiltshire ˈwɪlt.ʃəʳ, -ˌʃɪəʳ (US) -ʃɚ, -ˌʃɪr
wil|y ˈwaɪ.l|i **-ier** -i.əʳ (US) -i.ɚ **-iest** -i.ɪst, -i.əst **-iness** -ɪ.nəs, -ɪ.nɪs
wimble ˈwɪm.bl̩ **-s** -z
Wimbledon ˈwɪm.bl̩.dᵊn ˌ**Wimbledon ˈCommon**
Wimborne ˈwɪm.bɔːn (US) -bɔːrn
Wimms wɪmz
wimp wɪmp **-s** -s **-y** -i
WIMP wɪmp
Wimpey ˈwɪm.pi
wimpish ˈwɪm.pɪʃ **-ly** -li **-ness** -nəs, -nɪs
wimple ˈwɪm.pl̩ **-s** -z
Wimpole ˈwɪm.pəʊl (US) -poʊl
Wimpy® ˈwɪm.pi **-bar/s** -bɑːʳ/z (US) -bɑːr/z
Wimsey ˈwɪm.zi
win wɪn **-s** -z **-ning** -ɪŋ **won** wʌn **winner/s** ˈwɪn.əʳ/z (US) -ɚ/z
Winalot® ˈwɪn.ə.lɒt (US) -lɑːt
Wincanton wɪŋˈkæn.tən, wɪn- (US) wɪnˈkæn.tᵊn
winc|e wɪn*t*s **-es** -ɪz **-ing** -ɪŋ **-ed** -t
wincey ˈwɪn*t*.si
winceyette ˌwɪn*t*.siˈet
winch wɪn*t*ʃ **-es** -ɪz **-ing** -ɪŋ **-ed** -t
Winchelsea ˈwɪn.*t*ʃᵊl.si
Winchester ˈwɪn.tʃɪ.stəʳ, -tʃə- (US) -tʃes.tɚ, -tʃə.stɚ
Winchfield ˈwɪn*t*ʃ.fiːld
Winchilsea ˈwɪn.*t*ʃᵊl.si
Winchmore ˈwɪn*t*ʃ.mɔːʳ (US) -mɔːr
wind *(n.) air blowing:* wɪnd **-s** -z ˈ**wind** ˌ**tunnel**; **take the** ˌ**wind out of someone's** ˈ**sails**
wind *(v.) go round, roll round:* waɪnd **-s** -z **-ing** -ɪŋ **wound** waʊnd **-er/s** -əʳ/z (US) -ɚ/z
wind *(v.) blow horn:* waɪnd (US) waɪnd, wɪnd **-s** -z **-ing** -ɪŋ **-ed** -ɪd
wind *(v.) detect by scent, make unable to breathe:* wɪnd **-s** -z **-ing** -ɪŋ **-ed** -ɪd
windage ˈwɪn.dɪdʒ
windbag ˈwɪn*d*.bæg **-s** -z
windblown ˈwɪn*d*.bləʊn (US) -bloʊn
windbreak ˈwɪn*d*.breɪk **-s** -s **-er/s** -əʳ/z (US) -ɚ/z
windburn ˈwɪn*d*.bɜːn (US) -bɝːn **-ed** -t, -d **-t** -t
windcheater ˈwɪn*d*ˌtʃiː.təʳ (US) -t̬ɚ **-s** -z
wind-chest ˈwɪn*d*.tʃest **-s** -s
windchill ˈwɪn*d*.tʃɪl
wind-cone ˈwɪn*d*.kəʊn (US) -koʊn **-s** -z
Windermere ˈwɪn.də.mɪəʳ (US) -dɚ.mɪr
windfall ˈwɪn*d*.fɔːl (US) -fɔːl, -fɑːl **-s** -z
Windham ˈwɪn.dəm
Windhoek ˈwɪnd.hʊk, ˈwɪnt-, ˈvɪnt- (US) ˈvɪnt-
windhover ˈwɪndˌhɒv.əʳ (US) -ˌhʌv.ɚ, -ˌhɑː.vɚ **-s** -z
winding *in furnaces:* ˈwɪn.dɪŋ
winding *(n. adj.)* ˈwaɪn.dɪŋ **-s** -z **-ly** -li
winding-sheet ˈwaɪn.dɪŋ.ʃiːt **-s** -s
winding-up ˌwaɪn.dɪŋˈʌp
wind-instrument ˈwɪndˌɪn.strə.mənt, -strʊ- **-s** -s
windjammer ˈwɪn*d*ˌdʒæm.əʳ (US) -ɚ **-s** -z
windlass ˈwɪnd.ləs **-es** -ɪz
Windley ˈwɪnd.li
windmill ˈwɪn*d*.mɪl **-s** -z
Windolene® ˈwɪn.də*ʊ*.liːn (US) -doʊ-, -də-
window ˈwɪn.dəʊ (US) -doʊ **-s** -z ˈ**window** ˌ**box**; ˈ**window** ˌ**cleaner**; ˈ**window** ˌ**dressing**; ˈ**window** ˌ**seat**
windowpane ˈwɪn.dəʊ.peɪn (US) -doʊ- **-s** -z
window-shop ˈwɪn.dəʊ.ʃɒp (US) -doʊ.ʃɑːp **-s** -s **-ing** -ɪŋ **-ed** -t
windowsill ˈwɪn.dəʊ.sɪl (US) -doʊ- **-s** -z
windpipe ˈwɪn*d*.paɪp **-s** -s
windproof ˈwɪn*d*.pruːf
windrow ˈwɪn.drəʊ (US) -droʊ **-s** -z
Windrush ˈwɪn.drʌʃ
Windscale ˈwɪn*d*.skeɪl
windscreen ˈwɪn*d*.skriːn **-s** -z ˈ**windscreen** ˌ**wiper**
windshield ˈwɪn*d*.ʃiːld **-s** -z ˈ**windshield** ˌ**wiper**
windsock ˈwɪn*d*.sɒk (US) -sɑːk **-s** -s
Windsor ˈwɪn*d*.zəʳ (US) -zɚ ˌ**Windsor ˈCastle**; ˌ**Duke of ˈWindsor**; ˌ**Duchess of ˈWindsor**
windstorm ˈwɪnd.stɔːm (US) -stɔːrm **-s** -z
windsurf ˈwɪn*d*.sɜːf (US) -sɝːf **-s** -s **-ing** -ɪŋ **-ed** -t **-er/s** -əʳ/z (US) -ɚ/z
windswept ˈwɪn*d*.swept
wind-up ˈwaɪnd.ʌp **-s** -s
Windus ˈwɪn.dəs
windward (W) ˈwɪn*d*.wəd (US) -wɚd
wind|y ˈwɪn.d|i **-ier** -i.əʳ (US) -i.ɚ **-iest** -i.ɪst, -i.əst **-ily** -ɪ.li, -ᵊl.i **-iness** -ɪ.nəs, -ɪ.nɪs ˌ**Windy ˈCity**
win|e waɪn **-es** -z **-ing** -ɪŋ **-ed** -d ˈ**wine** ˌ**bar**; ˈ**wine** ˌ**bottle**; ˈ**wine** ˌ**cellar**; ˌ**wine ˈvinegar**
winebibber ˈwaɪnˌbɪb.əʳ (US) -ɚ **-s** -z
wineglass ˈwaɪn.glɑːs (US) -glæs **-es** -ɪz
winemaker ˈwaɪnˌmeɪ.kəʳ, ˈwaɪm- (US) ˈwaɪnˌmeɪ.kɚ **-s** -z
winer|y ˈwaɪ.nᵊr|.i **-ies** -iz
winey ˈwaɪ.ni
Winfrey ˈwɪn.fri
wing (W) wɪŋ **-s** -z **-ing** -ɪŋ **-ed** -d ˈ**wing** ˌ**nut**; ˌ**clip someone's ˈwings**
Wingate ˈwɪn.geɪt, ˈwɪŋ-, -gɪt (US) ˈwɪn-
wing-commander ˌwɪŋ.kəˈmɑːn.dəʳ (US) ˈwɪŋ.kəˌmæn.dɚ **-s** -z *stress shift, British only:* ˌwing-commander ˈSmith
winged wɪŋd
-winger -ˈwɪŋ.əʳ (US) -ɚ **-s** -z
Note: Suffix. Normally carries primary stress as shown, e.g. **left-winger** /ˌleftˈwɪŋ.əʳ (US) -ɚ/.
winger ˈwɪŋ.əʳ (US) -ɚ **-s** -z
Wingerworth ˈwɪŋ.ə.wəθ, -wɜːθ (US) -ɚ.wɚθ, -wɝːθ
Wingfield ˈwɪŋ.fiːld
wingspan ˈwɪŋ.spæn
Winifred ˈwɪn.ɪ.frɪd (US) ˈ-ə-
wink (W) wɪŋk **-s** -s **-ing** -ɪŋ **-ed** -t **-er/s** -əʳ/z (US) -ɚ/z
Winkfield ˈwɪŋk.fiːld
Winkie ˈwɪŋ.ki
winkle (W) ˈwɪŋ.kl̩ **-s** -z

winkle-picker ˈwɪŋ.kl̩ˌpɪk.əʳ (US) -ɚ **-s** -z

winnable ˈwɪn.ə.bl̩

winner ˈwɪn.əʳ (US) -ɚ **-s** -z

Winnie ˈwɪn.i

Winnie-the-Pooh ˌwɪn.i.ðəˈpuː

winning (W) ˈwɪn.ɪŋ **-s** -z **-ly** -li

winning-post ˈwɪn.ɪŋ.pəʊst (US) -poʊst **-s** -s

Winnipeg ˈwɪn.ɪ.peg

winnow ˈwɪn.əʊ (US) -oʊ **-s** -z **-ing** -ɪŋ **-ed** -d **-er/s** -əʳ/z (US) -ɚ/z

wino ˈwaɪ.nəʊ (US) -noʊ **-s** -z

Winona wɪˈnəʊ.nə (US) -ˈnoʊ-

Winsford ˈwɪnz.fəd, ˈwɪns- (US) -fɚd

Winslet ˈwɪndz.lɪt, -lət

Winslow ˈwɪnz.ləʊ (US) -loʊ

winsome ˈwɪn.səm **-ly** -li **-ness** -nəs, -nɪs

Winstanley *in Greater Manchester:* ˈwɪnt.stᵊn.li; wɪnˈstæn- *surname:* wɪnˈstæn.li; ˈwɪnt.stᵊn-

Winston ˈwɪn*t*.stᵊn

Winstone ˈwɪn*t*.stəʊn, -stᵊn (US) -stoʊn, -stən

wint|er (W) ˈwɪn.t|əʳ (US) -t̬|ɚ **-ers** -əz (US) -ɚz **-ering** -ᵊr.ɪŋ **-ered** -əd (US) -ɚd ˌ**winter ˈsports**; ˌ**Winter Oˈlympics**

Winterbottom ˈwɪn.təˌbɒt.əm (US) -t̬ɚˌbɑː.t̬əm

Winterbourne ˈwɪn.tə.bɔːn (US) -t̬ɚ.bɔːrn

Winters ˈwɪn.təz (US) -tɚz

Winterson ˈwɪn.tə.sᵊn (US) -t̬ɚ-

Winterthur ˈvɪn.tə.tʊəʳ (US) -t̬ɚ.tʊr

wintertime ˈwɪn.tə.taɪm (US) -t̬ɚ-

Winterton ˈwɪn.tə.tᵊn (US) -t̬ɚ.tən

Winthrop ˈwɪn.θrɒp, ˈwɪn*t*.θrəp (US) ˈwɪn*t*.θrəp

Winton ˈwɪn.tən (US) -tᵊn

Wintour ˈwɪn.təʳ (US) -t̬ɚ

wintr|y ˈwɪn.tr|i **-iness** -ɪ.nəs (US) -ɪ.nɪs

Winwick ˈwɪn.ɪk

Winwood ˈwɪn.wʊd

winy ˈwaɪ.ni

wip|e waɪp **-es** -s **-ing** -ɪŋ **-ed** -t **-er/s** -əʳ/z (US) -ɚ/z ˌ**wiped ˈout**

wipeout ˈwaɪp.aʊt **-s** -s

wir|e waɪəʳ (US) waɪɚ **-es** -z **-ing** -ɪŋ **-ed** -d

wire-cutter ˈwaɪəˌkʌt.əʳ (US) ˈwaɪɚˌkʌt̬.ɚ **-s** -z

wire|draw ˈwaɪə|.drɔː (US) ˈwaɪɚ|.drɑː, -drɔː **-draws** -drɔːz (US) -drɑːz, -drɔːz **-drawing** -ˌdrɔː.ɪŋ (US) -ˌdrɑː.ɪŋ, -ˌdrɔː- **-drew** -druː **-drawn** -drɔːn (US) -drɑːn, -drɔːn **-drawer/s** -ˌdrɔː.əʳ/z (US) -ˌdrɑː.ɚ/z, -ˌdrɔː-

wire-haired ˈwaɪə.heəd (US) ˈwaɪɚ.herd

wireless ˈwaɪə.ləs, -lɪs (US) ˈwaɪɚ- **-es** -ɪz

wiretap ˈwaɪə.tæp (US) ˈwaɪɚ- **-s** -s **-ping** -ɪŋ **-ped** -t

wireworm ˈwaɪə.wɜːm (US) ˈwaɪɚ.wɝːm **-s** -z

wiring ˈwaɪə.rɪŋ (US) ˈwaɪɚ.ɪŋ

Wirksworth ˈwɜːk.swəθ, -swɜːθ (US) ˈwɝːk.swɚθ, -swɝːθ

Wirral ˈwɪr.ᵊl

wir|y ˈwaɪə.r|i (US) ˈwaɪɚ|.i **-ier** -i.əʳ (US) -i.ɚ **-iest** -i.ɪst, -i.əst **-iness** -ɪ.nəs, -ɪ.nɪs

Wis. *(abbrev. for* **Wisconsin***)* wɪˈskɒn*t*.sɪn (US) -ˈskɑːn*t*.sən

Wisbech ˈwɪz.biːtʃ *locally:* -bɪtʃ

Wisbey ˈwɪz.bi

Wisconsin wɪˈskɒn*t*.sɪn (US) -ˈskɑːn*t*.sən

Wisden ˈwɪz.dən

wisdom ˈwɪz.dəm ˈ**wisdom ˌtooth**

wis|e (W) waɪz **-er** -əʳ (US) -ɚ **-est** -ɪst, -əst **-ely** -li **-eness** -nəs, -nɪs ˈ**wise ˌguy**; ˌ**three ˌwise ˈmen**

wiseacre ˈwaɪzˌeɪ.kəʳ (US) -kɚ **-s** -z

wisecrack ˈwaɪz.kræk **-s** -s

Wiseman ˈwaɪz.mən

wish wɪʃ **-es** -ɪz **-ing** -ɪŋ **-ed** -t **-er/s** -əʳ/z (US) -ɚ/z

Wishart ˈwɪʃ.ət (US) -ɚt

Wishaw ˈwɪʃ.ɔː (US) -ɑː, -ɔː

wishbone ˈwɪʃ.bəʊn (US) -boʊn **-s** -z

wishful ˈwɪʃ.fᵊl, -fʊl **-ly** -i **-ness** -nəs, -nɪs ˌ**wishful ˈthinking**

wishing-well ˈwɪʃ.ɪŋ.wel **-s** -z

wish-wash ˈwɪʃ.wɒʃ (US) -wɑːʃ, -wɔːʃ

wishy-washy ˈwɪʃ.iˌwɒʃ.i, ˌwɪʃ.iˈwɒʃ- (US) ˈwɪʃ.iˌwɑː.ʃi, -ˌwɔː-

wisp wɪsp **-s** -s

wisp|y ˈwɪs.p|i **-ier** -i.əʳ (US) -i.ɚ **-iest** -i.ɪst, -i.əst **-ily** -ɪ.li, -ᵊl.i **-iness** -ɪ.nəs, -ɪ.nɪs

wist wɪst

Wistar ˈwɪs.təʳ (US) -tɚ

wistaria wɪˈsteə.ri.ə, -ˈstɪə- (US) -ˈster.i-, -ˈstɪr- **-s** -z

Wister ˈwɪs.təʳ (US) -tɚ

wisteria wɪˈstɪə.ri.ə, -ˈsteə- (US) -ˈstɪr.i-, -ˈster- **-s** -z

wistful ˈwɪs*t*.fᵊl, -fʊl **-ly** -i **-ness** -nəs, -nɪs

wit wɪt **-s** -s

witch wɪtʃ **-es** -ɪz **-ing/ly** -ɪŋ/li **-ed** -t

witchcraft ˈwɪtʃ.krɑːft (US) -kræft

witchdoctor ˈwɪtʃˌdɒk.təʳ (US) -ˌdɑːk.tɚ **-s** -z

witcher|y ˈwɪtʃ.ᵊr|.i **-ies** -iz

witch-hazel ˈwɪtʃˌheɪ.zᵊl, ˌ-ˈ-- (US) ˈwɪtʃˌheɪ- **-s** -z

witch-hunt ˈwɪtʃ.hʌnt **-s** -s **-er/s** -əʳ/z (US) -ɚ/z

witching ˈwɪtʃ.ɪŋ ˈ**witching ˌhour**

witenagemot(e) ˌwɪt.ɪ.nə.gɪˈməʊt, -ᵊn.ə-, -gəˈ- (US) ˌwɪt.ᵊn.ə.gəˈmoʊt

with wɪð, wɪθ

Note: The pronunciation /wɪθ/ is most frequently found when followed by a voiceless consonant (e.g. 'with care' /wɪθˈkeə (US) -ˈker/).

withal wɪˈðɔːl (US) wɪˈðɔːl, -ˈðɑːl

Witham ˈwɪð.əm *town in Essex:* ˈwɪt.əm (US) ˈwɪt̬-

withdraw wɪðˈdrɔː, wɪθ- (US) -ˈdrɑː, -ˈdrɔː **-s** -z **-ing** -ɪŋ **withdrew** wɪðˈdruː, wɪθ- **withdrawn** wɪðˈdrɔːn, wɪθ- (US) -ˈdrɑːn, -ˈdrɔːn

withdrawal wɪðˈdrɔː.ᵊl, wɪθ- (US) -ˈdrɑː-, -ˈdrɔː- **-s** -z **withˈdrawal ˌmethod**; **withˈdrawal ˌsymptoms**

withe wɪθ, wɪð, waɪð **-s** -s, -z

with|er (W) ˈwɪð|.əʳ (US) -ɚ **-ers** -əz (US) -ɚz **-ering/ly** -ᵊr.ɪŋ/li **-ered** -əd (US) -ɚd

Withernsea ˈwɪð.ən.siː (US) -ɚn-

withers (W) *(n.)* ˈwɪð.əz (US) -ɚz

Witherspoon ˈwɪð.ə.spuːn (US) ˈ-ɚ-

with|hold wɪθ|ˈhəʊld, wɪð- (US) -ˈhoʊld **-holds** -ˈhəʊldz (US) -ˈhoʊldz **-holding** -ˈhəʊl.dɪŋ (US) -ˈhoʊl.dɪŋ **-held** -ˈheld **-holden** -ˈhəʊl.dᵊn (US) -ˈhoʊl.dᵊn **-holder/s** -ˈhəʊl.dəʳ/z (US) -ˈhoʊl.dɚ/z

within wɪˈðɪn; ˈwɪð.ɪn (US) wɪˈðɪn, -ˈθɪn

with-it ˈwɪð.ɪt (US) ˈwɪð-, ˈwɪθ-

withless ˈwɪt.ləs, -lɪs **-ly** -li **-ness** -nəs, -nɪs

without wɪˈðaʊt; ˈwɪð.aʊt (US) wɪˈðaʊt, -ˈθaʊt

withstand wɪðˈstænd, wɪθ- (US) wɪθ-, wɪð- **-s** -z **-ing** -ɪŋ **withstood** wɪðˈstʊd, wɪθ- (US) wɪθ-, wɪð-

with|y ˈwɪð|.i (US) ˈwɪð-, ˈwɪθ- **-ies** -iz

witless ˈwɪt.ləs, -lɪs **-ly** -li **-ness** -nəs, -nɪs

Witley ˈwɪt.li

witness *(n. v.)* ˈwɪt.nəs, -nɪs **-es** -ɪz **-ing** -ɪŋ **-ed** -t ˈ**witness ˌbox**

witney (W) ˈwɪt.ni

-witted -ˈwɪt.ɪd, -ˌwɪt.ɪd (US) -ˌwɪt̬.ɪd

Note: Suffix. May take either primary or secondary stress in British English, unless it is used attributively, in which case it always takes secondary stress, e.g. **quick-witted** /ˌkwɪkˈwɪt.ɪd/, ˈquick-witted ˌfox. Normally takes only secondary stress in American English.

Wittenberg ˈvɪt.ᵊn.bɜːg, -beəg *old-fashioned:* ˈwɪt.ᵊn.bɜːg (US) ˈwɪt.ᵊn.bɝːg, ˈvɪt-

witter ˈwɪt.əʳ (US) ˈwɪt̬- **-s** -z **-ing** -ɪŋ **-ed** -d **-er/s** -əʳ/z (US) -ɚ/z

Wittgenstein ˈvɪt.gən.ʃtaɪn, -staɪn

witticism ˈwɪt.ɪ.sɪ.zᵊm (US) ˈwɪt̬.ə- **-s** -z

wittingly ˈwɪt.ɪŋ.li (US) ˈwɪt̬-

witt|y ˈwɪt|.i (US) ˈwɪt̬- **-ier** -i.əʳ (US) -i.ɚ **-iest** -i.ɪst, -i.əst **-ily** -ɪ.li, -ᵊl.i **-iness** -ɪ.nəs, -ɪ.nɪs

Witwatersrand wɪtˈwɔː.təz.rænd, -raːnd, -raːnt; ˈwɪtˌwɔː-, ˈvɪtˌvaː.təz.rɒnt ⓤⓢ wɪtˈwɔː.t̬ɚz.rænd, -ˈwaː-
Wiveliscombe ˈwɪv.əl.ɪ.skəm, ˌwɪv.əˈlɪs.kəm *locally also:* ˈwɪl.skəm
Wivelsfield ˈwɪv.əlz.fiːld
Wivenhoe ˈwɪv.ən.həʊ ⓤⓢ -hoʊ
wivern ˈwaɪ.vən, -vɜːn ⓤⓢ -vɚn, -vɝːn **-s** -z
wives *(plur. of* **wife***)* waɪvz
wizard ˈwɪz.əd ⓤⓢ -ɚd **-s** -z **-ry** -ri
wizen ˈwɪz.ən **-ed** -d
wk *(abbrev. for* **week***)* wiːk
WNW *(abbrev. for* **west-northwest***)* ˌwest.nɔːθˈwest ⓤⓢ -nɔːrθˈ- *nautical pronunciation:* -nɔːˈ- ⓤⓢ -nɔːrˈ-
wo wəʊ ⓤⓢ woʊ
woad wəʊd ⓤⓢ woʊd
wobbl|e ˈwɒb.l̩ ⓤⓢ ˈwaː.bl̩ **-es** -z **-ing** -ɪŋ, ˈwɒb.lɪŋ ⓤⓢ ˈwaː.blɪŋ **-ed** -d **-er/s** -əʳ/z ⓤⓢ ˈwɒb.ləʳ/z, ˈwaː.bl̩.əʳ/z ⓤⓢ ˈwaː.blɚ/z
wobbl|y ˈwɒb.l̩|.i, ˈ-l|i ⓤⓢ ˈwaː.bl̩|.i, ˈ-bl|i **-iness** -ɪ.nəs, -ɪ.nɪs
Wobegon ˈwəʊ.bɪ.gɒn ⓤⓢ ˈwoʊ.bɪ.gaːn
Woburn *Abbey:* ˈwuː.bɜːn, -bən ⓤⓢ -bɝːn, -bɚn *street and square in London:* ˈwəʊ.bən, -bɜːn ⓤⓢ ˈwoʊ.bɚn, -bɝːn *village:* ˈwəʊ.bən, ˈwuː- ⓤⓢ ˈwoʊ.bɚn, ˈwuː-
Wodehouse ˈwʊd.haʊs
Woden ˈwəʊ.dən ⓤⓢ ˈwoʊ-
wodge wɒdʒ ⓤⓢ waːdʒ **-s** -ɪz
woe wəʊ ⓤⓢ woʊ **-s** -z
woebegone ˈwəʊ.bɪ.gɒn ⓤⓢ ˈwoʊ.bɪ.gaːn
woeful ˈwəʊ.fəl, -fʊl ⓤⓢ ˈwoʊ- **-ly** -i **-ness** -nəs, -nɪs
Woffington ˈwɒf.ɪŋ.tən ⓤⓢ ˈwaː.fɪŋ-
wog wɒg ⓤⓢ waːg, wɔːg **-s** -z
Wogan ˈwəʊ.gən ⓤⓢ ˈwoʊ-
wok wɒk ⓤⓢ waːk **-s** -s
woke *(from* **wake***)* wəʊk ⓤⓢ woʊk
woken *(from* **wake***)* ˈwəʊ.kən ⓤⓢ ˈwoʊ-
Woking ˈwəʊ.kɪŋ ⓤⓢ ˈwoʊ-
Wokingham ˈwəʊ.kɪŋ.əm ⓤⓢ ˈwoʊ-
Wolborough ˈwɒl.bər.ə ⓤⓢ ˈwaːl.bɚ.oʊ
Wolcot(t) ˈwʊl.kət ⓤⓢ ˈwʊl-, ˈwɔːl-
wold wəʊld ⓤⓢ woʊld **-s** -z
Woldingham ˈwəʊl.dɪŋ.əm ⓤⓢ ˈwoʊl-
Woledge ˈwʊl.ɪdʒ
wol|f **(W)** *(n.)* wʊl|f **-ves** -vz **a ˌwolf in ˌsheep's ˈclothing; keep the ˌwolf from, the ˈdoor, keep the ˈwolf from the ˌdoor**
wolf *(v.)* wʊlf **-s** -s **-ing** -ɪŋ **-ed** -t
wolf-cub ˈwʊlf.kʌb **-s** -z
Wolfe wʊlf
Wolfenden ˈwʊl.fən.dən
Wolff wʊlf, vɒlf ⓤⓢ wʊlf, vɔːlf
Wolfgang ˈwʊlf.gæŋ
wolfhound ˈwʊlf.haʊnd **-s** -z
wolfish ˈwʊl.fɪʃ **-ly** -li **-ness** -nəs, -nɪs
wolfram **(W)** ˈwʊl.frəm **-ite** -aɪt
Wolfson ˈwʊlf.sən
wolf-whistl|e ˈwʊlfˌhwɪs.l̩ **-es** -z **-ing** -ɪŋ, -ˌhwɪs.lɪŋ **-ed** -d
Wollard ˈwʊl.aːd ⓤⓢ -aːrd, -ɚd
Wollaston ˈwʊl.ə.stən
Wollaton ˈwʊl.ə.tən ⓤⓢ -tən
Wollongong ˈwʊl.ən.gɒŋ, -əŋ- ⓤⓢ -ən.gaːŋ
Wollstonecraft ˈwʊl.stən.kraːft ⓤⓢ -kræft, -kraːft
Wolmer ˈwʊl.məʳ ⓤⓢ -mɚ
Wolseley® ˈwʊlz.li
Wolsey ˈwʊl.zi
Wolsingham ˈwɒl.sɪŋ.əm ⓤⓢ ˈwaːl-
Wolstenholme ˈwʊl.stən.həʊm ⓤⓢ -hoʊm
Wolverhampton ˈwʊl.vəˌhæmp.tən, ˌwʊl.vəˈhæmp- ⓤⓢ ˈwʊl.vɚˌhæmp-
wolverine ˈwʊl.vər.iːn ⓤⓢ ˌwʊl.vəˈriːn, ˈ--- **-s** -z
Wolverton ˈwʊl.və.tən ⓤⓢ -vɚ-
wolves *(plur. of* **wolf***)* wʊlvz
Womad ˈwəʊ.mæd ⓤⓢ ˈwoʊ-
woman ˈwʊm.ən **women** ˈwɪm.ɪn **ˌwoman of the ˈworld**
woman-hat|er ˈwʊm.ənˌheɪ.t|əʳ ⓤⓢ -t̬|ɚ **-ers** -əz ⓤⓢ -ɚz **-ing** -ɪŋ
womanhood ˈwʊm.ən.hʊd
womanish ˈwʊm.ə.nɪʃ **-ly** -li **-ness** -nəs, -nɪs
womanist ˈwʊm.ə.nɪst **-s** -s
womaniz|e, -is|e ˈwʊm.ə.naɪz **-es** -ɪz **-ing** -ɪŋ **-ed** -d **-er/s** -əʳ/z ⓤⓢ -ɚ/z
womankind ˌwʊm.ənˈkaɪnd, -əŋˈ-, ˈ--- ⓤⓢ ˈwʊm.ən.kaɪnd
womanlike ˈwʊm.ən.laɪk
womanl|y ˈwʊm.ən.l|i **-iness** -ɪ.nəs, -ɪ.nɪs
womb wuːm **-s** -z
wombat ˈwɒm.bæt ⓤⓢ ˈwaːm- **-s** -s
Womble ˈwɒm.bl̩, ˈwʌm- ⓤⓢ ˈwaː.m-
Wombourne ˈwɒm.bɔːn ⓤⓢ ˈwaːm.bɔːrn
Wombwell *place in South Yorkshire:* ˈwʊm.wel, -wəl *surname:* ˈwʊm.wəl, ˈwʌm-, ˈwɒm- ⓤⓢ ˈwʊm-, ˈwʌm-, ˈwaːm-
women *(plur. of* **woman***)* ˈwɪm.ɪn **ˌWomen's ˈInstitute; ˌwomen's ˈlib; ˈwomen's ˌmovement; ˈwomen's ˌroom**
womenfolk ˈwɪm.ɪn.fəʊk ⓤⓢ -foʊk
womenkind ˌwɪm.ɪnˈkaɪnd, -ɪŋˈ-, ˈ--- ⓤⓢ ˈwɪm.ɪn.kaɪnd
womenswear ˈwɪm.ɪnz.weəʳ ⓤⓢ -wer
won *(from* **win***)* wʌn
won *Korean money:* wɒn ⓤⓢ waːn
wond|er **(W)** ˈwʌn.d|əʳ ⓤⓢ -d|ɚ **-ers** -əz ⓤⓢ -ɚz **-ering/ly** -ər.ɪŋ/li **-ered** -əd ⓤⓢ -ɚd **-erer/s** -ər.əʳ/z ⓤⓢ -ɚ.ɚ/z
wonder|ful ˈwʌn.də|.fəl, -fʊl ⓤⓢ -dɚ- **-fully** -fəl.i, -fʊl-, -fli **-fulness** -fəl.nəs, -fʊl-, -nɪs
wonderland **(W)** ˈwʌn.dəl.ænd ⓤⓢ -dɚ.lænd **ˌAlice in ˈWonderland**
wonderment ˈwʌn.də.mənt ⓤⓢ -dɚ-
wondrous ˈwʌn.drəs **-ly** -li **-ness** -nəs, -nɪs
wonk ˈwɒŋk ⓤⓢ ˈwaːŋk **-s** -s
wonk|y ˈwɒŋ.k|i ⓤⓢ ˈwaːŋ-, ˈwɔːŋ- **-ier** -i.əʳ ⓤⓢ -i.ɚ **-iest** -i.ɪst, -i.əst **-ily** -ɪ.li, -əl.i **-iness** -ɪ.nəs, -ɪ.nɪs
Wonsan ˌwɒnˈsæn ⓤⓢ ˌwaːnˈsaːn, ˌwʌn-
won|t *(n. adj.)* wəʊn|t ⓤⓢ wɔːn|t, waːn|t, woʊn|t, wʌn|t **-ted** -tɪd ⓤⓢ -t̬ɪd
won't wəʊnt ⓤⓢ woʊnt
wonton ˌwɒnˈtɒn ⓤⓢ ˈwaːn.taːn
woo wuː **-s** -z **-ing** -ɪŋ **-ed** -d **-er/s** -əʳ/z ⓤⓢ -ɚ/z
wood **(W)** wʊd **-s** -z **-ed** -ɪd **not see the ˌwood for the ˈtrees**
Woodall ˈwʊd.ɔːl ⓤⓢ -ɔːl, -aːl
Woodard ˈwʊd.aːd ⓤⓢ -ɚd
woodbine **(W)** ˈwʊd.baɪn **-s** -z
woodblock ˈwʊd.blɒk ⓤⓢ -blaːk **-s** -s
Woodbridge ˈwʊd.brɪdʒ
Woodbury ˈwʊd.bər.i ⓤⓢ -ber-, -bɚ-
wood-carv|er ˈwʊdˌkaː.v|əʳ ⓤⓢ -ˌkaːr.v|ɚ **-ers** -əz ⓤⓢ -ɚz **-ing/s** -ɪŋ/z
woodchuck ˈwʊd.tʃʌk **-s** -s
woodcock **(W)** ˈwʊd.kɒk ⓤⓢ -kaːk **-s** -s
woodcut ˈwʊd.kʌt **-s** -s
woodcutter ˈwʊdˌkʌt.əʳ ⓤⓢ -ˌkʌt̬.ɚ **-s** -z
wooden ˈwʊd.ən **-ly** -li **-ness** -nəs, -nɪs
wooden-headed ˌwʊd.ənˈhed.ɪd *stress shift:* ˌwooden-headed ˈperson
Woodfield ˈwʊd.fiːld
Woodford(e) ˈwʊd.fəd ⓤⓢ -fɚd
Woodgate ˈwʊd.geɪt, ˈwʊg- ⓤⓢ ˈwʊd-
Woodhead ˈwʊd.hed
Woodhouse ˈwʊd.haʊs
woodland ˈwʊd.lənd **-s** -z
Woodley ˈwʊd.li
wood-|louse ˈwʊd|.laʊs **-lice** -laɪs
wood|man **(W)** ˈwʊd|.mən **-men** -mən
wood-nymph ˈwʊd.nɪmpf **-s** -s
woodpecker ˈwʊdˌpek.əʳ ⓤⓢ -ɚ **-s** -z
wood-pigeon ˈwʊdˌpɪdʒ.ən, -ɪn **-s** -z
Woodroffe ˈwʊd.rɒf, -rʌf ⓤⓢ -raːf, -rʌf
Woodrow ˈwʊd.rəʊ ⓤⓢ -roʊ
woodruff **(W)** ˈwʊd.rʌf **-s** -s
Woods wʊdz
woodshed ˈwʊd.ʃed **-s** -z **-ing** -ɪŋ **-ed** -ɪd
Woodside ˌwʊdˈsaɪd, ˈ-- ⓤⓢ ˈwʊd.saɪd
woodsman ˈwʊdz.mən

Woodstock 'wʊd.stɒk (US) -stɑːk
Woodward 'wʊd.wəd (US) -wɚd
woodwind 'wʊd.wɪnd **-s** -z
woodwork 'wʊd.wɜːk (US) -wɝːk **-ing** -ɪŋ
woodworm 'wʊd.wɜːm (US) -wɝːm
wood|y (W) 'wʊd|.i **-ier** -i.əʳ (US) -i.ɚ **-iest** -i.ɪst, -i.əst **-iness** -ɪ.nəs, -ɪ.nɪs
woof *weaving:* wuːf (US) wuːf, wʊf **-s** -s
woof *dog's bark:* wʊf **-s** -s
Woof *surname:* wʊf
woofer 'wʊf.əʳ (US) -ɚ **-s** -z
woofter 'wʊf.təʳ (US) -tɚ **-s** -z
Wookey 'wʊk.i
wool wʊl **-s** -z
Woolacombe 'wʊl.ə.kəm
Wooldridge 'wʊl.drɪdʒ
woolen 'wʊl.ən **-s** -z
Wooler 'wʊl.əʳ (US) -ɚ
Woolf wʊlf
Woolfardisworthy *near Bideford, Devon:* 'wʊl.zᵊr.i, 'wʊl.fɑː.dɪˌswɜː.ði (US) 'wʊl.zɚ.i, 'wʊl.fɑːr.dɪ.swɝː.ði *near Crediton, Devon:* 'wʊl.fɑː.dɪˌswɜː.ði (US) -fɑːr.dɪˌswɝː-
Woolford 'wʊl.fəd (US) -fɚd
wool-gathering 'wʊlˌgæð.ᵊr.ɪŋ
Woollard 'wʊl.ɑːd (US) -ɚd
woollen 'wʊl.ən **-s** -z
Woolley 'wʊl.i
wooll|y 'wʊl|.i **-ies** -iz **-ier** -i.əʳ (US) -i.ɚ **-iest** -i.ɪst, -i.əst **-iness** -ɪ.nəs, -ɪ.nɪs
woolly-headed ˌwʊl.i'hed.ɪd (US) 'wʊl.iˌhed- *stress shift, British only:* ˌwoolly-headed 'person
Woolner 'wʊl.nəʳ (US) -nɚ
Woolnough 'wʊl.nəʊ (US) -noʊ
woolpack 'wʊl.pæk **-s** -s
woolsack 'wʊl.sæk **-s** -s
Woolsey 'wʊl.zi
Woolwich 'wʊl.ɪdʒ, -ɪtʃ
Woolworth 'wʊl.wəθ, -wɜːθ (US) -wɚθ, -wɝːθ **-'s** -s
wool|y 'wʊl|.i **-ier** -i.əʳ (US) -i.ɚ **-iest** -i.ɪst, -i.əst **-iness** -ɪ.nəs, -ɪ.nɪs
Woomera 'wʊm.ᵊr.ə, 'wuː.mᵊr-
Woorstead 'wʊs.tɪd, -təd (US) 'wʊs-, 'wɝː-
Woosley 'wuːz.li
Woosnam 'wuːz.nəm
Wooster 'wʊs.təʳ (US) -tɚ
Woot(t)on 'wʊt.ᵊn
wooz|y 'wuː.z|i **-ier** -i.əʳ (US) -i.ɚ **-iest** -i.ɪst, -i.əst **-ily** -ɪ.li, -ᵊl.i **-iness** -ɪ.nəs, -ɪ.nɪs
wop wɒp (US) wɑːp **-s** -z
Worboys 'wɔː.bɔɪz (US) 'wɔːr-
Worcester 'wʊs.təʳ (US) -tɚ **-shire** -ʃəʳ, -ˌʃɪəʳ (US) -ʃɚ, -ˌʃɪr ˌ**Worcester 'sauce**
Worcs. *(abbrev. for* **Worcestershire***)* 'wʊs.tə.ʃəʳ, -ˌʃɪəʳ (US) -tɚ.ʃɚ, -ˌʃɪr
word wɜːd (US) wɝːd **-s** -z **-ing/s** -ɪŋ/z **-ed** -ɪd **-less** -ləs, -lɪs **'word ˌorder; 'word ˌprocessor, ˌword 'processor; ˌeat one's 'words; get a ˌword in 'edgewise; put ˌwords in(to) someone's 'mouth** (US) **put 'words in(to) someone's ˌmouth**
wordbook 'wɜːd.bʊk (US) 'wɝːd- **-s** -s
Worde wɔːd (US) wɔːrd
word-formation 'wɜːd.fɔːˌmeɪ.ʃᵊn (US) 'wɝːd.fɔːrˌ-
word-for-word ˌwɜːd.fə'wɜːd (US) ˌwɝːd.fɚ'wɝːrd
wordless 'wɜːd.ləs, -lɪs (US) 'wɝːd- **-ly** -li **-ness** -nəs, -nɪs
word-of-mouth ˌwɜːd.əv'maʊθ (US) ˌwɝːd-
word-perfect ˌwɜːd'pɜː.fɪkt, -fekt (US) ˌwɝːd'pɝːr.fɪkt
wordplay 'wɜːd.pleɪ (US) 'wɝːd- **-s** -z
word processing 'wɜːdˌprəʊ.ses.ɪŋ, ˌ-'--- (US) 'wɝːdˌprɑː-, -ˌproʊ-
wordsmith 'wɜːd.smɪθ (US) 'wɝːd- **-s** -s
Wordsworth 'wɜːdz.wəθ, -wɜːθ (US) 'wɝːdz.wɚθ, -wɝːθ
Wordsworthian ˌwɜːdz'wɜː.θi.ən (US) ˌwɝːdz'wɝːr-
word|y 'wɜː.d|i (US) 'wɝː- **-ier** -i.əʳ (US) -i.ɚ **-iest** -i.ɪst, -i.əst **-ily** -ɪ.li, -ᵊl.i **-iness** -ɪ.nəs, -ɪ.nɪs
wore *(from* **wear***)* wɔːʳ (US) wɔːr
work wɜːk (US) wɝːk **-s** -s **-ing/s** -ɪŋ/z **-ed** -t **-er/s** -əʳ/z (US) -ɚ/z ˌ**working 'day** (US) **'working ˌday; ˌworking 'knowledge** (US) **'working ˌknowledge; ˌwork of 'art; ˌworking 'order** (US) **'working ˌorder**
workable 'wɜː.kə.bl̩ (US) 'wɝː- **-ness** -nəs, -nɪs
workaday 'wɜː.kə.deɪ (US) 'wɝː-
workaholic ˌwɜː.kə'hɒl.ɪk (US) ˌwɝː.kə'hɑː.lɪk **-s** -s
workaholism 'wɜː.kə.hɒl.ɪ.zᵊm (US) 'wɝː.kə.hɑː.lɪ-
workbag 'wɜːk.bæg (US) 'wɝːk- **-s** -z
workbasket 'wɜːkˌbɑː.skɪt (US) 'wɝːkˌbæs.kɪt **-s** -s
workbench 'wɜːk.bentʃ (US) 'wɝːk- **-es** -ɪz
workbook 'wɜːk.bʊk (US) 'wɝːk- **-s** -s
workbox 'wɜːk.bɒks (US) 'wɝːk.bɑːks **-es** -ɪz
workday 'wɜːk.deɪ (US) 'wɝːk- **-s** -z
worker 'wɜː.kəʳ (US) 'wɝː.kɚ **-s** -z
workfare 'wɜːk.feəʳ (US) 'wɝːk.fer
workforc|e 'wɜːk.fɔːs (US) 'wɝːk.fɔːrs **-es** -ɪz
workhors|e 'wɜːk.hɔːs (US) 'wɝːk.hɔːrs **-es** -ɪz
workhou|se 'wɜːk.haʊ|s (US) 'wɝːk- **-ses** -zɪz
working-class *(adj.)* ˌwɜː.kɪŋ'klɑːs (US) 'wɝː.kɪŋˌklæs *stress shift, British only:* ˌworking-class 'origins
working class *(n.)* ˌwɜː.kɪŋ'klɑːs (US) 'wɝː.kɪŋˌklæs **-es** -ɪz
Workington 'wɜː.kɪŋ.tən (US) 'wɝː-
workload 'wɜːk.ləʊd (US) 'wɝːk.loʊd **-s** -z
work|man (W) 'wɜːk|.mən (US) 'wɝːk- **-men** -mən
workman|like 'wɜːk.mən|.laɪk (US) 'wɝːk- **-ly** -li
workmanship 'wɜːk.mən.ʃɪp (US) 'wɝːk-
workmate 'wɜːk.meɪt (US) 'wɝːk- **-s** -s
workout 'wɜːk.aʊt (US) 'wɝːk- **-s** -s
workpeople 'wɜːkˌpiː.pl̩ (US) 'wɝːk-
workplac|e 'wɜːk.pleɪs (US) 'wɝːk- **-es** -ɪz
workroom 'wɜːk.rʊm, -ruːm (US) 'wɝːk.ruːm, -rʊm **-s** -z
workshop 'wɜːk.ʃɒp (US) 'wɝːk.ʃɑːp **-s** -s
work-shy 'wɜːk.ʃaɪ (US) 'wɝːk-
Worksop 'wɜːk.sɒp, -səp (US) 'wɝːk.sɑːp, -səp
workstation 'wɜːkˌsteɪ.ʃᵊn (US) 'wɝːk- **-s** -s
worktable 'wɜːkˌteɪ.bl̩ (US) 'wɝːk- **-s** -z
worktop 'wɜːk.tɒp (US) 'wɝːk.tɑːp **-s** -s
work-to-rule ˌwɜːk.tə'ruːl (US) ˌwɝːk- **-s** -z
world wɜːld (US) wɝːld **-s** -z ˌ**World 'Cup; ˌWorld 'Series; ˌWorld 'Service; ˌworld 'war; ˌWorld ˌWar 'I; ˌWorld ˌWar 'II; ˌWorld Wide 'Web; ˌout of this 'world**
world-class ˌwɜːld'klɑːs (US) 'wɝːld.klæs, ˌ-'- *stress shift, British only:* ˌworld-class 'sportsman
world-famous ˌwɜːld'feɪ.məs (US) 'wɝːldˌfeɪ-, ˌ-'-- *stress shift, British only:* ˌworld-famous 'actor
worldling 'wɜːld.lɪŋ (US) 'wɝːld- **-s** -z
worldl|y 'wɜːld.l|i (US) 'wɝːld- **-ier** -i.əʳ (US) -i.ɚ **-iest** -i.ɪst, -i.əst **-iness** -ɪ.nəs, -ɪ.nɪs
worldly-wise ˌwɜːld.li'waɪz (US) 'wɝːld.liˌwaɪz, ˌ--'- *stress shift, British only:* ˌworldly-wise 'person
worldview 'wɜːld.vjuː, ˌ-'- (US) 'wɝːld- **-s** -z
world-wear|y ˌwɜːld'wɪə.r|i, '-ˌ-- (US) 'wɝːldˌwɪr|.i **-ier** -i.əʳ (US) -i.ɚ **-iest** -i.ɪst, -i.əst **-ily** -ɪ.li, -ᵊl.i **-iness** -ɪ.nəs, -ɪ.nɪs *stress shift, British only:* ˌworld-weary 'attitude
worldwide ˌwɜːld'waɪd (US) 'wɝːld.waɪd, ˌ-'- *stress shift, British only:* ˌworldwide 'coverage
worm wɜːm (US) wɝːm **-s** -z **-ing** -ɪŋ **-ed** -d

WORM wɜːm (US) wɝːm
wormcast ˈwɜːm.kɑːst (US) ˈwɝːm.kæst -s -s
worm-eaten ˈwɜːmˌiː.tᵊn (US) ˈwɝːm-
wormhole ˈwɜːm.həʊl (US) ˈwɝːm.hoʊl -s -z
Worms vɔːmz, wɜːmz (US) wɝːmz, vɔːrmz
wormwood (W) ˈwɜːm.wʊd (US) ˈwɝːm- ˌ**Wormwood** ˈ**Scrubs**
worm|y ˈwɜː.m|i (US) ˈwɝː- **-iness** -ɪ.nəs, -ɪ.nɪs
worn *(from* **wear***)* wɔːn (US) wɔːrn
worn-out ˌwɔːnˈaʊt (US) ˌwɔːrn- *stress shift:* ˌworn-out ˈshoes
Worple ˈwɔː.pl̩ (US) ˈwɔːr-
Worplesdon ˈwɔː.pl̩z.dən (US) ˈwɔːr-
Worrall ˈwʌr.ᵊl, ˈwɒr- (US) ˈwɔːr-, ˈwɝː-
worrisome ˈwʌr.ɪ.səm (US) ˈwɝː.i- **-ly** -li
worr|y ˈwʌr|.i (US) ˈwɝː- **-ies** -iz **-ying/ly** -i.ɪŋ/li **-ied** -id **-ier/s** -i.əʳ/z (US) -i.ɚ/z ˈ**worry** ˌ**beads**
worrywart ˈwʌr.i.wɔːt (US) ˈwɝː.i.wɔːrt **-s** -s
Worsborough ˈwɜːz.bᵊr.ə (US) ˈwɝːz.bɚ.oʊ, -ə
worse wɜːs (US) wɝːs
worsen ˈwɜː.sᵊn (US) ˈwɝː- **-s** -z **-ing** -ɪŋ, ˈwɜːs.nɪŋ (US) ˈwɝːs- **-ed** -d
worse-off ˌwɜːsˈɒf (US) ˌwɝːsˈɑːf *stress shift:* ˌworse-off ˈcircumstances
Worsfold ˈwɜːs.fəʊld, ˈwɔːz- (US) ˈwɝːs.foʊld, ˈwɔːrz-
worship (W) ˈwɜː.ʃɪp (US) ˈwɝː- **-s** -s **-(p)ing** -ɪŋ **-(p)ed** -t **-(p)er/s** -əʳ/z (US) -ɚ/z
worshipful ˈwɜː.ʃɪp.fᵊl, -fʊl (US) ˈwɝː- **-ly** -i **-ness** -nəs, -nɪs
Worsley *surname:* ˈwɜː.sli, ˈwɜːz.li (US) ˈwɝː.sli, ˈwɝːz.li *place near Manchester:* ˈwɜː.sli (US) ˈwɝː-
worst wɜːst (US) wɝːst **-s** -s **-ing** -ɪŋ **-ed** -ɪd
worst-case ˌwɜːs*t*ˈkeɪs (US) ˌwɝːs*t*- *stress shift:* ˌworst-case sceˈnario
Worstead ˈwʊs.tɪd, -təd (US) ˈwʊs-, ˈwɝː.stɪd, -stəd
worsted *yarn, cloth:* ˈwʊs.tɪd, -təd (US) ˈwʊs-, ˈwɝː.stɪd, -stəd
worsted *(from* **worst***)* ˈwɜː.stɪd (US) ˈwɝː-
Worsthorne ˈwɜːs.θɔːn (US) ˈwɝːs.θɔːrn
Worswick ˈwɜː.sɪk (US) ˈwɝː-
wort wɜːt (US) wɝːt, wɔːrt **-s** -s
worth (W) wɜːθ (US) wɝːθ
Worthing ˈwɜː.ðɪŋ (US) ˈwɝː- **-ton** -tən
worthless ˈwɜːθ.ləs, -lɪs (US) ˈwɝːθ- **-ly** -li **-ness** -nəs, -nɪs
worthwhile ˌwɜːθˈ*h*waɪl (US) ˌwɝːθ- *stress shift:* ˌworthwhile ˈprogress
worth|y ˈwɜː.ð|i (US) ˈwɝː- **-ies** -iz **-ier** -i.əʳ (US) -i.ɚ **-iest** -i.ɪst, -i.əst **-ily** -ɪ.li (US) -ᵊl.i **-iness** -ɪ.nəs, -ɪ.nɪs
Wortley ˈwɜːt.li (US) ˈwɝːt-
wot wɒt (US) wɑːt
Wotan ˈwəʊ.tæn, ˈvəʊ- (US) ˈvoʊ.tɑːn
wotcha ˈwɒtʃ.ə (US) ˈwɑː.tʃə
wotcher ˈwɒt.ʃəʳ (US) ˈwɑː.tʃɚ
Wotherspoon ˈwɒð.ə.spuːn (US) ˈwɑː.ðɚ-
Wotton ˈwɒt.ᵊn, ˈwʊt- (US) ˈwɑː.tᵊn, ˈwʊt.ᵊn
Note: The place in Buckinghamshire is pronounced /ˈwʊt.ᵊn/.
would *(from* **will***) strong form:* wʊd *weak forms:* wəd, əd, d
Note: Weak form word. The strong form is used contrastively (e.g. 'I don't know if he would or he wouldn't') and emphatically (e.g. 'I certainly **would**'). The strong form is always used in final position, even when unstressed (e.g. 'I **knew** she would'). The weak forms are used elsewhere. The forms /əd/ and /d/ are usually represented in spelling as 'd (e.g 'John'd do it' /ˈdʒɒn.ədˌduː.ɪt (US) ˈdʒɑːn- /; 'I'd do it' /ˈaɪdˌduː.ɪt/).
would-be ˈwʊd.bi
wouldn't ˈwʊd.ᵊnt
wouldst wʊdst
wound *(n. v.)* wuːnd **-s** -z **-ing** -ɪŋ **-ed** -ɪd
wound *(from* **wind***, v.)* waʊnd
wov|e *(from* **weave***)* wəʊv (US) woʊv **-en** -ᵊn
wow waʊ **-s** -z **-ing** -ɪŋ **-ed** -d
wowser ˈwaʊ.zəʳ (US) -zɚ **-s** -z
Wozzeck ˈvɒt.sek (US) ˈvɑːt.sek
WP ˌdʌb.l̩.juːˈpiː
WPC ˌdʌb.l̩.juːˌpiːˈsiː, -jʊˌ- (US) -juːˌ-, -jəˌ- **-s** -z *stress shift:* ˌWPC ˈSmith
WRAC ræk, ˌdʌb.l̩.juːˌɑːʳˌeɪˈsiː, -ju- (US) ræk, -juːˌɑːr-, -jəˌ-
wrack ræk **-s** -s **-ing** -ɪŋ **-ed** -t
WRAF ræf; ˌdʌb.l̩.juːˌɑːʳ.eɪˈef (US) ræf; ˌdʌb.l̩.juːˌɑːr.eɪˈef
Wragg ræg
wraith reɪθ **-s** -s
wrangl|e ˈræŋ.gl̩ **-es** -z **-ing** -ɪŋ, ˈ-glɪŋ **-ed** -d **-er/s** -əʳ/z, ˈ-gləʳ/z (US) ˈ-gl̩.ɚ/z, ˈ-glɚ/z
wrangler (W®) ˈræŋ.gləʳ (US) -glɚ **-s** -z
wrap ræp **-s** -s **-ping/s** -ɪŋ/z **-ped** -t
wraparound ˈræp.ə.raʊnd **-s** -z
wrapper ˈræp.əʳ (US) -ɚ **-s** -z
wrapround ˈræp.raʊnd
wrass|e ræs **-es** -ɪz
wrath rɒθ, rɔːθ (US) ræθ, rɑːθ
Wrath *Cape:* rɔːθ, rɑːθ, ræθ (US) ræθ, rɑːθ
wrathful ˈrɒθ.fᵊl, ˈrɔːθ-, -fʊl (US) ˈræθ-, ˈrɑːθ- **-ly** -i **-ness** -nəs, -nɪs
Wratislaw ˈræt.ɪ.slɔː (US) ˈræt̬.ɪ.slɑː, -slɔː
Wraxall ˈræk.sɔːl
Wray reɪ
wreak riːk **-s** -s **-ing** -ɪŋ **-ed** -t
wrea|th riː|θ **-ths** -ðz, -θs
wreath|e riːð **-es** -z **-ing** -ɪŋ **-ed** -d
Wreay reɪ *locally:* rɪə
wreck rek **-s** -s **-ing** -ɪŋ **-ed** -t **-er/s** -əʳ/z (US) -ɚ/z
wreckag|e ˈrek.ɪdʒ **-es** -ɪz
Wrekin ˈriː.kɪn
wren (W) ren **-s** -z
wrench rentʃ **-es** -ɪz **-ing** -ɪŋ **-ed** -t
Wrenn ren
wrest rest **-s** -s **-ing** -ɪŋ **-ed** -ɪd
wrestl|e ˈres.l̩ **-es** -z **-ing** -ɪŋ, ˈres.lɪŋ **-ed** -d **-er/s** -əʳ/z, ˈres.ləʳ/z (US) ˈres.l̩.ɚ/z, ˈres.lɚ/z
wretch retʃ **-es** -ɪz
wretched ˈretʃ.ɪd **-ly** -li **-ness** -nəs, -nɪs
Wrexham ˈrek.səm
wriggl|e ˈrɪg.l̩ **-es** -z **-ing** -ɪŋ, ˈrɪg.lɪŋ **-ed** -d **-er/s** -əʳ/z, ˈrɪg.ləʳ/z (US) ˈrɪg.l̩.ɚ/z, ˈrɪg.lɚ/z
wright (W) raɪt **-s** -s
Wrigley ˈrɪg.li
wring rɪŋ **-s** -z **-ing** -ɪŋ **-er/s** -əʳ/z (US) -ɚ/z **wrung** rʌŋ
wringing-wet ˌrɪŋ.ɪŋˈwet *stress shift:* ˌwringing-wet ˈcloth
wrinkl|e ˈrɪŋ.kl̩ **-es** -z **-ing** -ɪŋ, ˈrɪŋ.klɪŋ **-ed** -d
wrinkl|y ˈrɪŋ.kl|i **-ies** -iz
Wriothesley ˈraɪəθ.sli
wrist rɪst **-s** -s
wristband ˈrɪs*t*.bænd **-s** -z
wristlet ˈrɪs*t*.lɪt, -lət **-s** -s
wristwatch ˈrɪst.wɒtʃ (US) -wɑːtʃ **-es** -ɪz
wristy ˈrɪs.ti
writ rɪt **-s** -s
writ *(=* **written***)* rɪt
writ|e raɪt **-es** -s **-ing/s** -ɪŋ/z (US) ˈraɪ.t̬ɪŋ/z **wrote** rəʊt (US) roʊt **written** ˈrɪt.ᵊn **writer/s** ˈraɪ.təʳ/z (US) ˈraɪ.t̬ɚ/z ˌ**writer's** ˈ**cramp**
writh|e raɪð **-es** -z **-ing** -ɪŋ **-ed** -d
writing ˈraɪ.tɪŋ (US) -t̬ɪŋ **-s** -z **see the** ˌ**writing on the** ˈ**wall**
writing-cas|e ˈraɪ.tɪŋ.keɪs (US) -t̬ɪŋ- **-es** -ɪz
writing-paper ˈraɪ.tɪŋˌpeɪ.pəʳ (US) -t̬ɪŋˌpeɪ.pɚ
written-off ˌrɪt.ᵊnˈɒf (US) -ˈɑːf
Writtle ˈrɪt.l̩ (US) ˈrɪt̬-
WRNS *(abbrev. for* **Women's Royal Navy Service***)* renz; ˌdʌb.l̩.juːˌɑːʳ.enˈes (US) renz; ˌdʌb.l̩.juːˌɑːr.enˈes
Wroclaw ˈvrɒt.slɑːf, -slæf, -swɑːf (US) ˈvrɑːt.slɑːf

wrong (W) rɒŋ ⓤⓢ rɑːŋ, rɔːŋ **-s** -z **-ly** -li **-ness** -nəs, -nɪs **-ing** -ɪŋ **-ed** -d
wrong-doer ˈrɒŋˌduː.əʳ, ˌ-ˈ-- ⓤⓢ ˈrɑːŋˌduː.ɚ, ˈrɔːŋ- **-s** -z
wrong-doing ˈrɒŋˌduː.ɪŋ, ˌ-ˈ-- ⓤⓢ ˈrɑːŋˌduː-, ˈrɔːŋ-
wrong|-foot ˌrɒŋ|ˈfʊt ⓤⓢ ˌrɑːŋ-, ˌrɔːŋ- **-foots** -ˈfʊts **-footing** -ˈfʊt.ɪŋ ⓤⓢ -ˈfʊt̬.ɪŋ **-footed** -ˈfʊt.ɪd ⓤⓢ -ˈfʊt̬.ɪd
wrongful ˈrɒŋ.fəl, -fʊl ⓤⓢ ˈrɑːŋ-, ˈrɔːŋ- **-ly** -i **-ness** -nəs, -nɪs
wrongheaded ˌrɒŋˈhed.ɪd ⓤⓢ ˌrɑːŋ-, ˌrɔːŋ-, ˈ-ˌ-- **-ly** -li **-ness** -nəs, -nɪs
wrote *(from* **write***)* rəʊt ⓤⓢ roʊt
wroth rəʊθ, rɔːθ, rɒθ ⓤⓢ rɔːθ, rɑːθ
Wrotham ˈruː.təm ⓤⓢ -t̬əm
Wrottesley ˈrɒt.sli ⓤⓢ ˈrɑːt-
wrought rɔːt ⓤⓢ rɑːt, rɔːt
wrought-iron ˌrɔːtˈaɪən ⓤⓢ ˌrɑːtˈaɪɚn, ˌrɔːt- *stress shift:* ˌwrought-iron ˈgate
Wroughton ˈrɔː.tən ⓤⓢ ˈrɑː-, ˈrɔː-
Wroxham ˈrɒk.səm ⓤⓢ ˈrɑːk-
wrung *(from* **wring***)* rʌŋ
W.R.V.S. ˌdʌb.l̩.juːˌɑːˌviːˈes, -jʊˌ- ⓤⓢ -juːˌɑːrˌ-, -jəˌ-
wry raɪ **wrier, wryer** ˈraɪ.əʳ ⓤⓢ -ɚ **wriest, wryest** ˈraɪ.ɪst, -əst **wryly** ˈraɪ.li **wryness** ˈraɪ.nəs, -nɪs
wryneck ˈraɪ.nek **-s** -s
Wrythe raɪð
WSW *(abbrev. for* **west southwest***)* ˌwest.saʊθˈwest *nautical pronunciation:* -saʊˈ-
wt *(abbrev. for* **weight***)* weɪt
Wuhan ˌwuːˈhæn ⓤⓢ -ˈhɑːn
Wulf wʊlf
Wulfila ˈwʊl.fɪ.lə
Wulfstan ˈwʊlf.stən ⓤⓢ -stæn, -stɑːn
wunder|kind ˈwʊn.də|.kɪnd, ˈvʊn- ⓤⓢ -dɚ|.kɪnt, ˈwʌn- **-kinder** -ˌkɪn.dəʳ ⓤⓢ -ˌkɪn.dɚ
Wurlitzer ˈwɜː.lɪt.səʳ, -lət- ⓤⓢ ˈwɝː.lət.sɚ **-s** -z
Württemberg ˈvɜː.təm.beəg; ˈwɜː.təm.bɜːg ⓤⓢ ˈwɝː.t̬əm.bɜːrg; ˈvɝː.təm.berk
Würzburg ˈvɜːts.bʊəg; ˈwɜːts.bɜːg ⓤⓢ ˈwɝːts.bɜːrg; ˈvɝːts.burk
wuss wʊs
Wuthering ˈwʌð.ər.ɪŋ ˌ**Wuthering ˈHeights**
W.Va. *(abbrev. for* **West Virginia***)* ˌwest.vəˈdʒɪn.jə, -vɜːˈ-, -i.ə ⓤⓢ -vɚˈ-
WVS ˌdʌb.l̩.juːˌviːˈes, -jʊˌ- ⓤⓢ -juːˌ-, -jəˌ-
Wyandotte ˈwaɪən.dɒt ⓤⓢ -dɑːt **-s** -s
Wyat(t) waɪət
Wych waɪtʃ, wɪtʃ
Wycherley ˈwɪtʃ.əl.i ⓤⓢ -ɚ.li
wych-hazel ˈwɪtʃˌheɪ.zəl, ˌ-ˈ-- ⓤⓢ ˈwɪtʃˌheɪ- **-s** -z
Wycliffe, Wyclif ˈwɪk.lɪf
Wycliffite ˈwɪk.lɪ.faɪt **-s** -s
Wycombe ˈwɪk.əm
Wye waɪ
Wygram ˈwaɪ.grəm
Wykeham ˈwɪk.əm **-ist/s** -ɪst/s
Wyld(e) waɪld
Wyl(l)ie ˈwaɪ.li
Wyman ˈwaɪ.mən
Wymondham *in Norfolk:* ˈwɪm.ən.dəm *locally:* ˈwɪn.dəm *in Leicestershire:* ˈwaɪ.mən.dəm
Wyndham ˈwɪn.dəm
Wynn(e) wɪn
Wynyard ˈwɪn.jəd, -jɑːd ⓤⓢ -jɚd, -jɑːrd
Wyo. *(abbrev. for* **Wyoming***)* waɪˈəʊ.mɪŋ ⓤⓢ -ˈoʊ-
Wyoming waɪˈəʊ.mɪŋ ⓤⓢ -ˈoʊ-
WYSIWYG ˈwɪz.i.wɪg
Wyss waɪs
Wystan ˈwɪs.tən
Wytch Farm ˌwɪtʃˈfɑːm ⓤⓢ -ˈfɑːrm
Wytham ˈwaɪ.təm ⓤⓢ -t̬əm
Wythenshawe ˈwɪð.ən.ʃɔː ⓤⓢ -ʃɑː, -ʃɔː
wyvern (W) ˈwaɪ.vən, -vɜːn ⓤⓢ -vɚn, -vɜːrn **-s** -z

Pronouncing the letter X

See also XC

The consonant letter **x**, which rarely occurs at the beginning of a word, has three main pronuncations: /ks gz/ and /kʃ/, e.g.:

box	/bɒks/	(US) /bɑːks/
examine	/ɪɡˈzæm.ɪn, ɪkˈsæm-/	(US) /ɪɡˈzæm-/
noxious	/ˈnɒk.ʃəs/	(US) /ˈnɑːk-/

When **x** does appear at the beginning of a word, it is almost always pronounced /z/, e.g.:

/z/	xylophone	/ˈzaɪ.lə.fəʊn/	(US) /-foʊn/

Another pronunciation associated with **x is** /eks/, e.g.:

/eks/	X-ray	/ˈeks.reɪ/	(US) /ˈek.sreɪ/

Pronouncing the letters XC

The consonant digraph **xc** has two pronunciations: /ks/ and /ksk/.

Before the vowel letters **i** or **e**, it is pronounced as /ks/, e.g.:

exceed /ɪkˈsiːd/

In other situations, **xc** is pronounced as /ksk/, e.g.:

exclaim /ɪksˈkleɪm/

x (X) eks **-'s** -ɪz

Xanadu ˈzæn.ə.duː, ˌ--ˈ- (US) ˈzæn.ə.duː, -djuː, ˌ--ˈ-

Xanthe ˈzænt.θi

Xanthipp|e zænˈθɪp|.i, zænˈtɪp- (US) zænˈtɪp- **-us** -əs

Xanthus ˈzænt.θəs

Xantia® ˈzæn.ti.ə (US) zænˈtiː-

Xavier ˈzæv.i.əʳ, -eɪ, ˈzeɪ.vi.əʳ, ˈ-vjəʳ (US) ˈzeɪ.vjɚ, ˈzæv.jɚ, -i.ɚ

X-certificate ˌeks.səˈtɪf.ɪ.kət, -sɜːˈ-, ˈ-ə-, -kɪt (US) -sɚˈ- **-s** -s

xebec ˈziː.bek **-s** -s

Xenia ˈzen.i.ə, ˈksen-, ˈziː.ni-, ˈksiː-, ˈ-njə (US) ˈziː.njə, ˈ-ni.ə

xeno- zen.əʊ-, ziː.nəʊ-; zɪˈnɒ- (US) zen.oʊ-, ziː.noʊ-, -nə-; zɪˈnɑː-

Note: Prefix. Normally either takes primary or secondary stress on the first syllable, e.g. **xenophobe** /ˈzen.əʊ.fəʊb (US) -ə.foʊb/, **xenophobia** /ˌzen.əʊˈfəʊ.bi.ə (US) -əˈfoʊ-/, or primary stress on the second syllable, e.g. **xenogamy** /zɪˈnɒɡ.ə.mi (US) -ˈnɑː.ɡə-/.

xenogamy zɪˈnɒɡ.ə.mi (US) -ˈnɑː.ɡə-

xenon ˈziː.nɒn (US) -nɑːn, ˈzen.ɑːn

xenophobe ˈzen.əʊ.fəʊb (US) -ə.foʊb, ˈziː.nə-, -noʊ- **-s** -z

xenophobia ˌzen.əʊˈfəʊ.bi.ə (US) -əˈfoʊ-, ˌziː.nəˈ-, -noʊˈ-

xenophobic ˌzen.əʊˈfəʊ.bɪk (US) -əˈfoʊ-, ˌziː.nə-, -noʊ- *stress shift:* ˌxenophobic ˈsentiment

Xenophon ˈzen.ə.fᵊn (US) -fən, -fɑːn

xerography zɪəˈrɒɡ.rə.fi, zerˈɒɡ- (US) zɪˈrɑː.ɡrə-

xerox® (X) (*n. v.*) ˈzɪə.rɒks (US) ˈzɪr.ɑːks, ˈziː.rɑːks **-es** -ɪz **-ing** -ɪŋ **-ed** -t

Xerxes ˈzɜːk.siːz (US) ˈzɝːk-

Xhosa ˈkɔː.sə, ˈkəʊ-, -zə (US) ˈkoʊ.sɑː, -zɑː

xi saɪ, ksaɪ (US) zaɪ, saɪ **-'s** -z

Xiaoping ˌʃaʊˈpɪŋ

Xinhua ˌʃɪnˈhwɑː *stress shift:* ˌXinhua ˈNews Agency

Xmas ˈkrɪst.məs, ˈeks.məs (US) ˈkrɪs-

X-rated ˈeksˌreɪ.tɪd (US) -t̬ɪd

X-ray ˈeks.reɪ, ˌ-ˈ- (US) ˈek.sreɪ **-s** -z **-ing** -ɪŋ **-ed** -d

xu suː

xylem ˈzaɪ.ləm, -lem (US) ˈzaɪ-

xylene ˈzaɪ.liːn

xylograph ˈzaɪ.ləʊ.ɡrɑːf, -ɡræf (US) -loʊ.ɡræf, -lə- **-s** -s

xylograph|y zaɪˈlɒɡ.rə.f|i (US) -ˈlɑː.ɡrə- **-er/s** -əʳ/z (US) -ɚ/z

xylonite ˈzaɪ.lə.naɪt

xylophone ˈzaɪ.lə.fəʊn (US) -foʊn **-s** -z

xylose ˈzaɪ.ləʊs, -ləʊz (US) -loʊs

xyster ˈzɪs.t əʳ (US) -tɚ

Pronouncing the letter Y

The consonant letter **y** is special in that it can act as both vowel and consonant. At the beginning of a word, it most often behaves as a consonant and, when doing so, is pronounced as /j/, e.g.:

yes	/jes/
youth	/juːθ/

When acting as a vowel, the letter **y** has two main strong pronunciations: a 'short' pronunciation /ɪ/ and a 'long' pronunciation /aɪ/. There are no definite rules for when either of these pronunciations will occur, e.g.:

myth	/mɪθ/
cycle	/ˈsaɪ.kl̩/

At the end of a word, in adjectives and adverbs ending with a letter **y**, a short /i/ is usually used. However, for other types of word, either /i/ or /aɪ/ may occur, e.g.:

happy	/ˈhæp.i/
happily	/ˈhæp.ɪ.li/
study	/ˈstʌd.i/
apply	/əˈplaɪ/

When **y** is followed by **r**, the strong pronunciation is one of four possibilities: /aɪə US aɪɚ/, /aɪə.r US aɪ.r/ or /ɪ/ when followed by a single consonant and then a vowel, otherwise /ɜː, US ɝː/, e.g.:

tyre	/taɪəʳ/	US /taɪɚ/
gyrate (v.)	/dʒaɪəˈreɪt/	US /ˈdʒaɪ.reɪt/
lyric	/ˈlɪr.ɪk/	
myrrh	/mɜːʳ/	US /mɝː/

In addition

When acting as a vowel, **y** can also be realised as /iː/ or /ɪ/ in a small number of words, usually proper nouns, e.g.:

Yves	/iːv/

In weak syllables

When acting as a vowel, the letter **y** is realised with the vowels /ɪ/ and, occasionally, /ə/ and /i/ in word-medial weak syllables, e.g.:

oxygen	/ˈɒk.sɪ.dʒən, -sə-/	US /ˈɑːk.sɪ-/
anybody	/ˈen.iˌbɒd.i/	US /-ˌbɑː.di/

y **(Y)** waɪ **-'s** -z
yacht jɒt US jɑːt **-s** -s **-ing** -ɪŋ US ˈjɑː.t̬ɪŋ **-ed** -ɪd US ˈjɑː.t̬ɪd
yachts|man ˈjɒts|.mən US ˈjɑːts- **-men** -mən **-woman** -ˌwʊm.ən **-women** -ˌwɪm.ɪn
yack jæk **-s** -s **-ing** -ɪŋ **-ed** -t
yah jɑː
yahoo (Y) *(interj.)* jəˈhuː, jɑː- **-s** -z *(n.)* ˈjɑː.huː US ˈjɑː-, ˈjeɪ-
Yahveh ˈjɑː.veɪ, -və, jɑːˈveɪ US ˈjɑː.veɪ
Yahweh ˈjɑː.weɪ
yak jæk **-s** -s
yakka ˈjæk.ə
Yakutsk jækˈʊtsk, jɑːˈkʊtsk, jə- US jɑː-
yakuza ˈjæk.ʊ.zɑː US ˈjɑː.kʊ- **-s** -z
Yalding *surname:* ˈjæl.dɪŋ *place name:* ˈjɔːl.dɪŋ US ˈjɑːl-, ˈjɔːl-
Yale jeɪl
y'all jɔːl
Yalta ˈjæl.tə, ˈjɔːl-, ˈjɒl- US ˈjɑːl.t̬ə, ˈjɔːl-, -tə
yam jæm **-s** -z
Yamaha ˈjæm.ə.hɑː, -hə US ˈjɑː.mə-
Yamamoto ˌjæm.əˈməʊ.təʊ US ˌjɑː.məˈmoʊ.t̬oʊ, -toʊ
yamm|er ˈjæm|.əʳ US -ɚ **-ers** -əz US -ɚz **-ering** -ᵊr.ɪŋ **-ed** -əd US -ɚd
yang jæŋ US jæŋ, jɑːŋ
Yangtze, Yangtse, Yangzi ˈjæŋ*k*t.si US ˈjæŋ*k*t-, ˈjɑːŋ*k*t-
yank (Y) jæŋk **-s** -s **-ing** -ɪŋ **-ed** -t
Yankee ˈjæŋ.ki **-s** -z
Yaoundé jɑːˈʊn.deɪ, -ˈuːn- US ˌjɑː.ʊnˈdeɪ
yap jæp **-s** -s **-ping** -ɪŋ **-ped** -t
Yap jæp US jɑːp, jæp
yard jɑːd US jɑːrd **-s** -z ˈ**yard** ˌ**sale**
yardage ˈjɑː.dɪdʒ US ˈjɑːr- **-s** -ɪz
yardarm ˈjɑːd.ɑːm US ˈjɑːrd.ɑːrm **-s** -z
yardbird ˈjɑːd.bɜːd US ˈjɑːrd.bɝːd **-s** -z
Yardie ˈjɑː.di US ˈjɑːr- **-s** -z
Yardley ˈjɑːd.li US ˈjɑːrd-
yardstick ˈjɑːd.stɪk US ˈjɑːrd- **-s** -s
Yare *in Norfolk:* jeəʳ US jer *in the Isle of Wight:* jɑːʳ US jɑːr
Yarm jɑːm US jɑːrm
yarmelke ˈjʌm.ʊl.kə, ˈjɑː.mʊl-, -mᵊl- US ˈjɑːr.məl-, ˈjɑː- **-s** -z
Yarmouth ˈjɑː.məθ US ˈjɑːr-
yarmulke, yarmulka ˈjʌm.ʊl.kə, ˈjɑː.mʊl-, -mᵊl- US ˈjɑːr.məl-, ˈjɑː- **-s** -z
yarn jɑːn US jɑːrn **-s** -z **-ing** -ɪŋ **-ed** -d
Yaroslavl ˌjær.əʊˈslɑː.vᵊl US ˌjɑːr.oʊˈslɑː.vᵊl, -əˈ-
yarrow (Y) ˈjær.əʊ US ˈjer.oʊ, ˈjær-
yashmak ˈjæʃ.mæk US ˈjɑːʃ.mɑːk, ˈjæʃ.mæk **-s** -s
Yasmin ˈjæz.mɪn
Yasser ˈjæs.əʳ US -ɚ, ˈjɑː.sɚ
yataghan ˈjæt.ə.gən US -gæn, -gən **-s** -z
Yate jeɪt **-s** -s
Yately ˈjeɪt.li
Yatman ˈjæt.mən
Yatton ˈjæt.ᵊn
yaw jɔː US jɑː, jɔː **-s** -z **-ing** -ɪŋ **-ed** -d
Yaweh ˈjɑː.weɪ
yawl jɔːl US jɑːl, jɔːl **-s** -z
yawn jɔːn US jɑːn, jɔːn **-s** -z **-ing/ly** -ɪŋ/li **-ed** -d
yaws jɔːz US jɑːz, jɔːz
Yaxley ˈjæk.sli
yclept ɪˈklept US i-
yd *(abbrev. for* **yard**) *singular:* jɑːd US jɑːrd *plural:* jɑːdz US jɑːrdz
ye *you. Normal form:* jiː *occasional weak form:* ji
Note: The weak form is rarely used, and only in imitation of archaic or dialect sayings such as 'Sit ye down' /ˌsɪt.jiˈdaʊn/.
ye *the:* jiː
Note: As a pronunciation of the definite article, this is rarely used except in joking. It is a mistake resulting from reading the Old English letter "thorn" (which represented 'th' sounds) as a 'y', which it resembles.
yea jeɪ
Yeading ˈjed.ɪŋ
Yeadon ˈjiː.dᵊn
yeah jeə US jeə, jæə
Note: Aside from the examples given for American English, there are many possibilities here, another being /jɑː/.
Yeames jiːmz

yean jiːn **-s** -z **-ing** -ɪŋ **-ed** -d
year jɪəʳ, jɜːʳ (US) jɪr **-s** -z **-ly** -li ˌ**year in (and)** ˌ**year 'out**
yearbook 'jɪə.bʊk, 'jɜː- (US) 'jɪr- **-s** -s
yearling 'jɪə.lɪŋ, 'jɜː- (US) 'jɪr- **-s** -z
yearlong ˌjɪə'lɒŋ, ˌjɜː- (US) 'jɪr.lɑːŋ, -lɔːŋ, ˌ-'- *stress shift, British only:* ˌyearlong 'truce
yearn jɜːn (US) jɝːn **-s** -z **-ing/s** -ɪŋ/z **-ed** -d
yeast jiːst **-y** -i **-iness** -ɪ.nəs, -ɪ.nɪs
Yeates jeɪts
Yeatman 'jiːt.mən, 'jeɪt-, 'jet-
Yeats jeɪts
Yeddo 'jed.əʊ (US) -oʊ
Yehudi je'huː.di, jɪ-, jə-
yell (Y) jel **-s** -z **-ing** -ɪŋ **-ed** -d
Yelland 'jel.ənd
yellow 'jel.əʊ (US) -oʊ **-s** -z **-ing** -ɪŋ **-ed** -d **-y** -i ˌ**yellow 'fever**; ˌ**yellow 'line**; ˌ**Yellow 'Pages** (US) '**Yellow** ˌ**Pages**; ˌ**yellow 'peril**; ˌ**yellow** ˌ**brick 'road**
yellowhammer 'jel.əʊˌhæm.əʳ (US) -oʊˌhæm.ɚ **-s** -z
yellowish 'jel.əʊ.ɪʃ (US) -oʊ- **-ness** -nəs, -nɪs
yellowjacket 'jel.əʊˌdʒæk.ɪt (US) -oʊ- **-s** -s
Yellowknife 'jel.əʊ.naɪf (US) -oʊ-
yellowness 'jel.əʊ.nəs, -nɪs (US) -oʊ-
Yellowstone 'jel.əʊ.stəʊn, -stən (US) -oʊ.stoʊn
yelp jelp **-s** -s **-ing** -ɪŋ **-ed** -t
Yeltsin 'jelt.sɪn
Yemen 'jem.ən, -en (US) -ən, 'jeɪ.mən **-i** -i **-is** -iz
Yemenite 'jem.ən.aɪt (US) 'jem-, 'jeɪ.mən- **-s** -s
yen jen **-s** -z
Yentob 'jen.tɒb (US) -tɑːb
Yeo jəʊ (US) joʊ
Yeoburgh 'jɑː.bᵊr.ə
yeo|man 'jəʊ|.mən (US) 'joʊ- **-men** -mən **-manly** -mən.li
yeomanry 'jəʊ.mən.ri (US) 'joʊ-
Yeomans 'jəʊ.mənz (US) 'joʊ-
Yeovil 'jəʊ.vɪl (US) 'joʊ-
yep jep
yer jeə, jɜː (US) je
Note: This is a written or spoken informal form of **yes** in British English. The **r** in the spelling is not pronounced in American English forms and is not linking in British English.
Yerby 'jɜː.bi (US) 'jɝː-
Yerevan ˌjer.ə'vɑːn
Yerkes 'jɜː.kiːz (US) 'jɝː-
yes jes
yes|-man 'jes|.mæn **-men** -men
yesterday 'jes.tə.deɪ, ˌ--'-, -di (US) -tɚ-
yesteryear 'jes.tə.jɪəʳ, ˌ--'- (US) -tɚ.jɪr
yet jet
Yetholm 'jet.əm (US) 'jeţ-
yeti 'jet.i (US) 'jeţ- **-s** -z
Yevtushenko ˌjev.tʊ'ʃeŋ.kəʊ, -tuː'- (US) -koʊ
yew juː **-s** -z
Y-Front® 'waɪ.frʌnt **-s** -s
Yg(g)drasil 'ɪg.drə.sɪl, ɪg'dræs.ᵊl (US) 'ɪg.drə.sɪl
yid jɪd
Yiddish 'jɪd.ɪʃ
yield jiːld **-s** -z **-ing/ly** -ɪŋ/li **-ed** -ɪd
yin jɪn
yippee jɪ'piː (US) 'jɪp.iː
Yitzhak 'jɪt.sɑːk, -sæk
ylang-ylang ˌiː.læŋ.iː'læŋ (US) -lɑːŋ'iː.lɑːŋ
YMCA ˌwaɪ.em.siː'eɪ
Ynys Mon ˌʌn.ɪs'mɔːn
yo jəʊ (US) joʊ
yob jɒb (US) jɑːb **-s** -z
yobbish 'jɒb.ɪʃ (US) 'jɑː.bɪʃ **-ly** -li **-ness** -nəs, -nɪs
yobbo 'jɒb.əʊ (US) 'jɑː.boʊ **-s** -z
yod jɒd (US) jɑːd **-s** -z
yodel 'jəʊ.dᵊl (US) 'joʊ- **-s** -z **-(l)ing** -ɪŋ, 'jəʊd.lɪŋ (US) 'joʊd- **-(l)ed** -d **-ler/s** -əʳ/z (US) -ɚ/z
yog|a 'jəʊ.g|ə (US) 'joʊ- **-ic** -ɪk
yogh(o)urt 'jɒg.ət, 'jəʊ.gət, -gɜːt (US) 'joʊ.gɚt **-s** -s
yog|i 'jəʊ.g|i (US) 'joʊ- **-is** -iz **-ism** -ɪ.zᵊm ˌ**Yogi 'Bear**, '**Yogi** ˌ**Bear**
yogic 'jəʊ.gɪk (US) 'joʊ-
yogurt 'jɒg.ət, 'jəʊ.gət, -gɜːt (US) 'joʊ.gɚt **-s** -s
Yohji 'jəʊ.dʒi, 'jɒdʒ.i (US) 'joʊ.dʒi
yoicks jɔɪks
yok|e jəʊk (US) joʊk **-es** -s **-ing** -ɪŋ **-ed** -t
yokel 'jəʊ.kᵊl (US) 'joʊ- **-s** -z
Yokohama ˌjəʊ.kəʊ'hɑː.mə (US) ˌjoʊ.kə'-
Yolanda, Yolande jəʊ'læn.də (US) joʊ'lɑːn-, -'læn-
yolk jəʊk (US) joʊk **-s** -s **-y** -i
Yom Kippur ˌjɒm.kɪ'pʊəʳ; -'kɪp.əʳ (US) ˌjɑːm'kɪp.ɚ, ˌjɔːm-; -kɪ'pʊr
yomp jɒmp (US) jɑːmp **-s** -s **-ing** -ɪŋ **-ed** -t **-er/s** -əʳ/z (US) -ɚ/z
yon jɒn (US) jɑːn
yond jɒnd (US) jɑːnd
yonder 'jɒn.dəʳ (US) 'jɑːn.dɚ
Yonge jʌŋ
Yonkers 'jɒŋ.kəz (US) 'jɑːŋ.kɚz, 'jɔːŋ-
yonks jɒŋks (US) jɑːŋks, jɔːŋks
yoof juːf
Yorba Linda ˌjɔː.bə'lɪn.də (US) ˌjɔːr-
yore jɔːʳ (US) jɔːr
Yorick 'jɒr.ɪk (US) 'jɔːr-
York jɔːk (US) jɔːrk
Yorke jɔːk (US) jɔːrk
yorker 'jɔː.kəʳ (US) 'jɔːr.kɚ **-s** -z
Yorkist 'jɔː.kɪst (US) 'jɔːr- **-s** -s
Yorks. *(abbrev. for* **Yorkshire***)* jɔːks (US) jɔːrks
Yorkshire 'jɔːk.ʃəʳ, -ˌʃɪəʳ (US) 'jɔːrk.ʃɚ, -ˌʃɪr ˌ**Yorkshire 'pudding**; ˌ**Yorkshire 'terrier**
Yorkshire|man 'jɔːk.ʃə.|mən (US) 'jɔːrk.ʃɚ- **-men** -mən, -men **-woman** -ˌwʊm.ən **-women** -ˌwɪm.ɪn
Yorktown 'jɔːk.taʊn (US) 'jɔːrk-
Yoruba 'jɒr.ʊ.bə, 'jəʊ.rʊ- (US) 'jɔːr.ə.bə, 'joʊ.rə-, -ruː-, -bɑː
Yosemite jəʊ'sem.ɪ.ti (US) joʊ'sem.ə.ţi **Yo**ˌ**semite** ˌ**National 'Park**; **Yo**ˌ**semite 'Sam**
Yossarian jɒs'eə.ri.ən (US) joʊ'ser.i-, -'sɑːr-
Yost jəʊst (US) joʊst **-s** -s
you *strong form:* juː *weak forms:* ju, jə
Note: Weak form word. The strong form is used contrastively (e.g. 'Will it be you, or me?') or emphatically (e.g. 'It was **you** that broke it'). Elsewhere the weak forms are used: in British English, /ju/ is the form found before vowels and in final position (e.g. 'You ought' /ju'ɔːt (US) -ɑːt/; 'Thank you' /'θæŋk.ju/), while /jə/ is only used before consonants (e.g. 'if you can' /ɪf.jə'kæn/); in American English, /jə/ predominates in both environments. The strong form is also found in unstressed syllables. Sometimes when 'you' is weakly stressed and is preceded by a word normally ending in /d/, the two words are joined closely together as if they formed a single word with the affricate sound /dʒ/ linking the two parts. Thus 'did you' is often pronounced /'dɪdʒ.u/, and 'behind you' /bɪ'haɪn.dʒu/. Similarly when the preceding word normally ends in /t/ (e.g. 'hurt you') it is sometimes pronounced /'hɜː.tʃu (US) 'hɝːr-/ and 'don't you know' as /ˌdəʊn.tʃə'nəʊ (US) ˌdoʊn.tʃə'noʊ/.
you-all juː'ɔːl (US) ju'ɔːl, jɔːl, jɑːl
Youens 'juː.ɪnz
Youghal *near Cork:* jɔːl *on Lake Derg:* 'jɒk.ᵊl, 'jɒx- (US) 'jɑː.kᵊl
Youmans 'juː.mənz
young (Y) jʌŋ **-er** -gəʳ (US) -gɚ **-est** -gɪst, -gəst
Younger 'jʌŋ.əʳ, -gəʳ (US) -gɚ, -ɚ
Younghusband 'jʌŋˌhʌz.bənd
youngish 'jʌŋ.ɪʃ, -gɪʃ
Youngman 'jʌŋ.mən
youngster 'jʌŋk.stəʳ (US) -stɚ **-s** -z
younker 'jʌŋ.kəʳ (US) -kɚ **-s** -z

your *normal forms:* jɔːʳ, jʊəʳ ⓤⓢ jʊr, jɔːr *occasional weak forms:* jəʳ ⓤⓢ jɚ
Note: Weak form word. The strong form /jʊə ⓤⓢ jʊr/ or /jɔː ⓤⓢ jɔːr/ is usually used for emphasis (e.g. 'It's **your** fault') or contrast (e.g. 'with **your** looks and **my** brains'). This pronunciation is quite common also in weakly stressed positions in careful speech. In British English, the weak form is /jə/ before consonants (e.g. 'take your time' /ˌteɪk.jə'taɪm/) and /jər/ before vowels (e.g. 'on your own' /ɒn.jər'əʊn/); in American English, /jɚ/ is used in both cases.
you're *(=* **you are***) strong forms:* jɔːʳ, jʊəʳ ⓤⓢ jʊr, jɔːr *occasional weak forms:* jəʳ ⓤⓢ jɚ
Note: The use of strong and weak forms follows that of **your**.
yours jɔːz, jʊəz ⓤⓢ jʊrz, jɔːrz
yoursel|f jɔː'sel|f, jʊə-, jə- ⓤⓢ jʊr-, jɔːr-, jɚ- **-ves** -vz
you|th juː|θ **-ths** -ðz **'youth ˌclub; 'youth ˌhostel; ˌyouth 'training ˌscheme**
youthful 'juːθ.fəl, -fʊl **-ly** -i **-ness** -nəs, -nɪs
you've *(=* **you have***) normal form:* juːv *occasional weak forms:* jʊv, jəv
yowl jaʊl **-s** -z **-ing** -ɪŋ **-ed** -d
yo-yo 'jəʊ.jəʊ ⓤⓢ 'joʊ.joʊ **-s** -z **-ing** -ɪŋ **-ed** -d
Ypres *in Belgium:* 'iː.prə, 'iː.pəz *sometimes facetiously:* 'aɪ.pəz, 'waɪ.pəz ⓤⓢ 'iː.prə
Ypres *tower at Rye:* 'iː.prə, 'iː.preɪ, 'waɪ.pəz ⓤⓢ 'iː.prə
Note: The 'Ypres Castle', a public house near by, is called locally the /'waɪ.pəz/.
Yser 'iː.zəʳ ⓤⓢ -zɚ, -zer
Ysolde ɪ'zɒl.də ⓤⓢ -'zoʊl-
Ystradgynlais ˌʌs.træd'gʌn.laɪs, -trəd'-
Ystwyth 'ʌs.twɪθ
Ythan 'aɪ.θən
YTS ˌwaɪ.tiː'es
ytterbium ɪ'tɜː.bi.əm ⓤⓢ -'tɝː-
yttrium 'ɪt.ri.əm
Yucatan ˌjuː.kə'tɑːn, ˌjʊk.ə'-, -'tæn ⓤⓢ ˌjuː.kə'tæn, -'tɑːn
yucca 'jʌk.ə **-s** -z
yuck jʌk **-y** -i **-ier** -i.əʳ ⓤⓢ -i.ɚ **-iest** -i.ɪst, -i.əst
Yugoslav 'juː.gəʊ.slɑːv, ˌ--'- ⓤⓢ 'juː.goʊ.slɑːv, -gə- **-s** -z
Yugoslavi|a ˌjuː.gəʊ'slɑː.vi|.ə ⓤⓢ -goʊ'- **-an** -ən
Yuill 'juː.ɪl
yuk jʌk **-ky** -i
Yukon 'juː.kɒn ⓤⓢ -kɑːn
yule (Y) juːl **'yule ˌlog**
yuletide (Y) 'juːl.taɪd
yumm|y 'jʌm|.i **-ier** -i.əʳ ⓤⓢ -i.ɚ **-iest** -i.ɪst, -i.əst
Yum-Yum ˌjʌm'jʌm
Yunnan jʊ'næn
yuppie 'jʌp.i **-s** -z
yuppif|y 'jʌp.ɪ.f|aɪ **-ies** -aɪz **-ying** -aɪ.ɪŋ **-ied** -aɪd
yupp|y, yupp|ie 'jʌp|.i **-ies** -iz
yurt jɜːt, jʊət ⓤⓢ jʊrt, jɝːt **-s** -s
Yussuf 'jʊs.ʊf, -əf
Yves iːv
Yvette ɪ'vet, iː'- ⓤⓢ iː-
Yvonne ɪ'vɒn, iː'- ⓤⓢ iː'vɑːn
Ywain ɪ'weɪn, iː'-
YWCA ˌwaɪˌdʌb.l̩.juː.siː'eɪ, -ju- ⓤⓢ -juː-, -jə-

Pronouncing the letter Z

The consonant letter **z** is most often realised as /z/, e.g.:

zest /zest/
gaze /geɪz/

It can also be pronounced /ʒ/ in words where it is followed by the letter **u**, e.g.:

seizure /ˈsiː.ʒəʳ/ US /-ʒɚ/

In addition

In the word rendezvous, **z** is silent, e.g.:

rendezvous /ˈrɒn.dɪ.vuː/ US /ˈrɑːn.deɪ-/

This is an exceptional case; the word is a borrowing from French.

z (Z) zed US ziː **-'s** -z
zabaglione ˌzæb.ᵊlˈjəʊ.ni, -neɪ, -ælˈ- US ˌzɑː.bᵊlˈjoʊ-, -bɑːlˈ-, -neɪ
Zacchaeus zækˈiː.əs, zəˈkiː-
Zachariah ˌzæk.ᵊrˈaɪ.ə US -əˈraɪ-
Zacharias ˌzæk.ᵊrˈaɪ.əs, -æs US -əˈraɪ-
Zachary ˈzæk.ᵊr.i
Zadar ˈzæd.ɑːʳ US ˈzɑː.dɑːr
Zadok ˈzeɪ.dɒk US -dɑːk
Zagreb ˈzɑː.greb, ˈzæg.reb; zɑːˈgreb US ˈzɑː.greb
zaire zaɪˈɪəʳ, zɑː- US -ˈɪr
Zaïr|e, Zair|e zaɪˈɪəʳ, zɑː- US -ˈɪr **-ean** -i.ən
Zambezi, Zambesi zæmˈbiː.zi
Zambi|a ˈzæm.bi|.ə **-an** -ən
Zamboni® zæmˈbəʊ.ni US -ˈboʊ-
Zamenhof ˈzɑː.mᵊn.hɒf US -hɑːf
Zangwill ˈzæŋ.gwɪl US -gwɪl, -wɪl
Zanu ˈzæn.uː, ˈzɑː.nuː
zan|y ˈzeɪ.n|i **-ies** -iz **-ier** -i.əʳ US -i.ɚ **-iest** -i.ɪst, -i.əst
Zanzibar ˈzæn.zɪ.bɑːʳ, ˌ--ˈ- US -zə.bɑːr
zap zæp **-s** -s **-ping** -ɪŋ **-ped** -t **-per/s** -əʳ/z US -ɚ/z
Zapata zəˈpɑː.tə, zæpˈɑː- US -t̬ə
Zapatista ˌzæp.əˈtɪs.tə **-s** -z
Zaporozhye ˌzæp.əˈrəʊ.ʒeɪ, -ɔːˈ- US ˌzɑː.pəˈroʊ.ʒə
Zapotek ˈzæp.ə.tek, ˈzɑː.pə-, ˌ--ˈ- US ˈzɑː.pə.tek, ˈsɑː- **-s** -s
Zappa ˈzæp.ə
zapp|y ˈzæp|.i **-ier** -i.əʳ US -i.ɚ **-iest** -i.ɪst, -əst
Zaragoza ˌsær.əˈgɒs.ə *as if Spanish:* ˌθær.əˈgɒθ.ə US ˌzær.əˈgoʊ.zə, ˌzer-
Zarathustra ˌzær.əˈθuː.strə, ˌzɑː.rəˈ- US ˌzer.əˈ-, ˌzær-
zareba zəˈriː.bə **-s** -z
Zaria ˈzɑː.rɪ.ə US ˈzɑːr.i-
Zarqa ˈzɑː.kə US ˈzɑːr-
Zatopek ˈzæt.ə.pek US ˈzæt̬-
zeal ziːl
Zealand ˈziː.lənd **-er/s** -əʳ/z US -ɚ/z
zealot ˈzel.ət **-s** -s **-ry** -ri
zealous ˈzel.əs **-ly** -li **-ness** -nəs, -nɪs
Zebedee ˈzeb.ɪ.diː, ˈ-ə- US ˈ-ə-
zebra ˈzeb.rə, ˈziː.brə US ˈziː.brə **-s** -z **ˌzebra ˈcrossing**
zebu ˈziː.buː, -bjuː US -bjuː, -buː **-s** -z
Zebulon, Zebulun ˈzeb.jʊ.lən; zebˈjuː-, zəˈbjuː- US ˈzeb.jʊ-, -lɑːn
Zechariah ˌzek.əˈraɪ.ə
zed zed **-s** -z
Zedekiah ˌzed.ɪˈkaɪ.ə, -əˈ- US -əˈ-
Zeebrugge ziːˈbrʊg.ə, zeɪ-, ˈ--- US ˈziː.brʊg-
Zeeland ˈziː.lənd, ˈzeɪ- US ˈziː-
Zeffirelli ˌzef.əˈrel.i, -ɪˈ-
Zeiss zaɪs *as German:* tsaɪs **-es** -ɪz
zeitgeist ˈtsaɪt.gaɪst, ˈzaɪt-
Zelazny zelˈæz.ni US zəˈlɑːz.ni
Zelda ˈzel.də
Zeller ˈzel.əʳ US -ɚ
Zellweger ˈzelˌweg.əʳ US -ɚ
Zelotes ziːˈləʊ.tiːz, zɪ-, zə- US -ˈloʊ-
zemindar ˈzem.ɪn.dɑːʳ US -dɑːr; zəˈmiːn- **-s** -z
zemstvo ˈzemst.vəʊ US -voʊ **-s** -z
Zen zen
Zena ˈziː.nə
zenana zenˈɑː.nə, zɪˈnɑː- US zenˈɑː- **-s** -z
Zenawi zenˈɑː.wi
Zend zend
Zenda ˈzen.də
Zeneca® ˈzen.ɪ.kə, -ə-
zenica ˈzen.ɪ.kə, ˈzen.ɪt.sə
zenith ˈzen.ɪθ US ˈziː.nɪθ **-s** -s
Zeno ˈziː.nəʊ US -noʊ
Zenobia zɪˈnəʊ.bi.ə, zenˈəʊ- US zəˈnoʊ-
Zenocrate ˈzen.əʊ.kræt US -oʊ-
Zepa ˈʒep.ə
Zephaniah ˌzef.əˈnaɪ.ə
zephyr (Z) ˈzef.əʳ US -ɚ **-s** -z
Zephyrus ˈzef.ᵊr.əs
zeppelin (Z) ˈzep.ᵊl.ɪn US ˈ-lɪn, ˈzep.ə.lɪn **-s** -z
Zermatt ˈzɜː.mæt US ˈzɝː.mɑːt, -ˈ-
zero ˈzɪə.rəʊ US ˈzɪr.oʊ, ˈziː.roʊ **-(e)s** -z **ˈzero ˌhour**
Zerubbabel zɪˈrʌb.ə.bᵊl, zə-; *in Jewish usage also:* zɪˈruːˌbɑː-, zə- US zəˈrʌb.ə-
zest zest **-ful/ly** fᵊl/i, fʊl/i
zest|y ˈzes.t|i **-ier** -i.əʳ US -i.ɚ **-iest** -i.ɪst, -i.əst
zeta ˈziː.tə US ˈzeɪ.t̬ə, ˈziː- **-s** -z
Zetland ˈzet.lənd
zeugma ˈzjuːg.mə, ˈzuːg- US ˈzuːg- **-s** -z
Zeus zjuːs US zuːs
Zhirinovsky ˌʒɪr.ɪˈnɒf.ski US -ˈnɑːf-
Zhivago ʒɪˈvɑː.gəʊ, ʒə- US -goʊ
Zhou ʒuː US dʒoʊ
ziggurat ˈzɪg.ə.ræt, ˈ-ʊ- **-s** -s
zigzag ˈzɪg.zæg **-s** -z **-ging** -ɪŋ **-ged** -d
zilch zɪltʃ
zillion ˈzɪl.jən, -i.ən US ˈ-jən **-s** -z
Zimbabwe zɪmˈbɑːb.weɪ, -ˈbæb-, -wi US -ˈbɑːb-
Zimbabwean zɪmˈbɑːb.wi.ən, -ˈbæb-, -weɪ- US -ˈbɑːb- **-s** -z
Zimmer® ˈzɪm.əʳ US -ɚ **ˈZimmer ˌframe**
Zimmerman ˈzɪm.ə.mən US ˈ-ɚ-
zinc zɪŋk **-s** -s **-king** -ɪŋ **-ked** -t **-ky** -i
zinco ˈzɪŋ.kəʊ US -koʊ **-s** -z
zincograph ˈzɪŋ.kəʊ.grɑːf, -græf US -koʊ.græf, -kə- **-s** -s
zinfandel (Z) ˈzɪn.fən.del, ˌ--ˈ- US ˈzɪn.fən.del
zing zɪŋ **-s** -z **-ing** -ɪŋ **-ed** -d **-y** -i
zingar|o (Z) ˈzɪŋ.gᵊr|.əʊ US -gə.r|oʊ **-i** -iː
zinnia ˈzɪn.i.ə **-s** -z
Zion ˈzaɪ.ən **-ism** -ɪ.zᵊm **-ist/s** -ɪst/s
zip zɪp **-s** -s **-ping** -ɪŋ **-ped** -t **ˈzip ˌcode; ˌzip ˈfastener**
zipper ˈzɪp.əʳ US -ɚ **-s** -z
Zipporah zɪˈpɔː.rə, ˈzɪp.ᵊr.ə US ˈzɪp.ɚ.ə
zipp|y ˈzɪp|.i **-ier** -i.əʳ US -i.ɚ **-iest** -i.ɪst, -i.əst
zircon ˈzɜː.kɒn US ˈzɝː.kɑːn
zirconia zɜːˈkəʊ.ni.ə, zə- US zɚˈkoʊ-
zirconium zɜːˈkəʊ.ni.əm, zə- US zɚˈkoʊ-
zit zɪt **-s** -s
zither ˈzɪð.əʳ, ˈzɪθ- US ˈzɪθ.ɚ, ˈzɪð- **-s** -z
zloty ˈzlɒt.i *as if Polish:* ˈzwɒt- US ˈzlɔː.t̬i, ˈzlɑː- **-s** -z
Zoar ˈzəʊ.ɑːʳ, zəʊəʳ US ˈzoʊ.ɑːr, zoʊɚ

zodiac 'zəʊ.di.æk (US) 'zoʊ-
zodiacal zəʊ'daɪ.ə.kəl (US) zoʊ-
Zoe, Zoë 'zəʊ.i (US) 'zoʊ-
Zog zɒg (US) zɔːg, zɑːg
-zoic -'zəʊ.ɪk (US) -'zoʊ.ɪk
Zola 'zəʊ.lə (US) 'zoʊ-; zoʊ'lɑː
zollverein 'tsɒl.fər.aɪn, 'zɒl.vər- (US) 'tsɔːl.fə.raɪn **-s** -z
zombie 'zɒm.bi (US) 'zɑːm- **-s** -z
zonal 'zəʊ.nəl (US) 'zoʊ- **-ly** -i
zon|e zəʊn (US) zoʊn **-es** -z **-ing** -ɪŋ **-ed** -d **-eless** -ləs, -lɪs
zonked zɒŋkt (US) zɑːŋkt, zɔːŋkt
zoo- zuː.əʊ-, zəʊ.əʊ-; zu'ɒ,- zəʊ'ɒ- (US) zoʊ.oʊ-, zuː.oʊ-, -ə-; zoʊ'ɑː-, zu'ɑː-
Note: Prefix. Normally either takes primary or secondary stress on the first syllable, e.g. **zoophyte** /'zuː.ə.faɪt (US) 'zoʊ-/, **zoomorphic** /ˌzuː.ə'mɔː.fɪk (US) ˌzoʊ.ə'mɔːr-/, or primary stress on the second syllable, e.g. **zoology** /zu'ɒl.ə.dʒi (US) zoʊ'ɑː.lə-/.
zoo zuː **-s** -z
zoochemi|stry ˌzuː.əʊ'kem.ɪ|.stri (US) ˌzoʊ.ə'- **-cal** -kəl
zoograph|er zuː'ɒg.rə.f|ər (US) zoʊ'ɑː.grə.f|ɚ **-ers** -əz (US) -ɚz **-y** -i
zooks zuːks (US) zuːks, zʊks
zoolite 'zuː.əʊ.laɪt (US) 'zoʊ.oʊ.laɪt, '-ə- **-s** -s
zoologic|al ˌzuː.əʊ'lɒdʒ.ɪ.k|əl, ˌzəʊ.ə'- (US) ˌzoʊ.ə'lɑː.dʒɪ- **-ally** -əl.i, -li **zooˌlogical 'gardens**
zoologist zu'ɒl.ə.dʒ|ɪst, zəʊ- (US) zoʊ'ɑː.lə-, zu- **-s** -s
zoolog|y zu'ɒl.ə.dʒ|i, zəʊ- (US) zoʊ'ɑː.lə-, zu- **-ist/s** -ɪst/s
zoom zuːm **-s** -z **-ing** -ɪŋ **-ed** -d **'zoom ˌlens**
zoomorphic ˌzuː.ə'mɔː.fɪk (US) ˌzoʊ.ə'mɔːr-
-zo|on -'zəʊ|.ɒn (US) -'zoʊ|.ɑːn, -ən **-a** -ə
Note: Suffix. Normally carries primary stress as shown, e.g. **protozoon** /ˌprəʊ.təʊ'zəʊ.ɒn (US) ˌproʊ.t̬oʊ'zoʊ.ɑːn/.
zoophyte 'zuː.ə.faɪt (US) 'zoʊ.ə- **-s** -s
zooplankton ˌzuː.əʊ'plæŋk.tən, -tɒn (US) ˌzoʊ.ə'plæŋk.tən **-s** -z
zoot zuːt **-s** -s **'zoot ˌsuit**
zoril 'zɒr.ɪl (US) 'zɔːr- **-s** -z
Zoroaster ˌzɒr.əʊ'æs.tər, 'zɒr.əʊ.æs- (US) 'zɔːr.oʊ.æs.tɚ
Zoroastrian ˌzɒr.əʊ'æs.tri.ən (US) ˌzɔːr.oʊ'- **-s** -z **-ism** -ɪ.zəm
Zorro 'zɒr.əʊ (US) 'zɔːr.oʊ
zouave (Z) zu'ɑːv; zwɑːv; 'zuː.ɑːv (US) zu'ɑːv, zwɑːv **-s** -z
Zouch(e) zuːʃ
zounds zuːndz, zaʊndz (US) zaʊndz
Zsa Zsa 'ʒɑː.ʒɑː
zucchini zʊ'kiː.ni (US) zuː- **-s** -z
Zugspitze 'zʊg.ʃpɪt.sə *as if German:* 'tsuːk-
Zuider Zee ˌzaɪ.də'ziː, -'zeɪ (US) -dɚ'ziː
Zuleika zuː'leɪ.kə, zʊ-, -'laɪ-
Zulu 'zuː.luː **-s** -z
Zululand 'zuː.luː.lænd
Zuñi, Zuni 'zʊn.ji (US) 'zuː.ni, -nji
zuppa inglese ˌzʊp.ɑː.ɪŋ'gleɪ.zeɪ, -zi (US) ˌzuː.pə.ɪn'gleɪ.zeɪ, ˌtsuː-, -ɪŋ'-
Zürich 'zjʊə.rɪk, 'zʊə- *as if German:* 'tsjʊə- (US) 'zʊr.ɪk
Zutphen 'zʌt.fən
Zwelithini ˌzwel.ɪ'θiː.ni
zwieback 'zwiː.bæk, -bɑːk (US) 'zwaɪ.bæk, 'zwiː-, 'swiː-, 'swaɪ-, -bɑːk **-s** -s
zygoma zaɪ'gəʊ.mə, zɪ- (US) -'goʊ- **-ta** -tə (US) -t̬ə
zygote 'zaɪ.gəʊt, 'zɪg.əʊt (US) 'zaɪ.goʊt, 'zɪg.oʊt **-s** -s
zymosis zaɪ'məʊ.sɪs, zɪ- (US) -'moʊ-
zymotic zaɪ'mɒt.ɪk, zɪ- (US) -'mɑː.t̬ɪk
Zyuganov ʒʊ'gɑː.nɒf
zzz zː
Note: This is rarely pronounced, but is used in comic strips to represent sleeping, or, more specifically, snoring. The suggested pronunciation derives from the spelling.